Rating system

★★★★★ Excellent

★★★★ Very Good

★★★ Good

★★ Fair

Turkey

Also by Mick Martin and Marsha Porter
Published by Ballantine Books:

VIDEO MOVIE GUIDE FOR FAMILY VIEWING

VIDEO MOVIE GUIDE 1995

Mick Martin
and Marsha Porter

Contributing Editor:
Derrick Bang

BALLANTINE BOOKS • NEW YORK

Sale of this book without a front cover may be unauthorized. If this book is coverless, it may have been reported to the publisher as "unsold or destroyed" and neither the author nor the publisher may have received payment for it.

Copyright © 1994 by Mick Martin and Marsha Porter

All rights reserved under International and Pan-American Copyright Conventions. Published in the United States of America by Ballantine Books, a division of Random House, Inc., New York, and simultaneously in Canada by Random House of Canada Limited, Toronto.

Library of Congress Catalog Card Number: 94-94425

ISBN 0-345-39027-X

Photo of Holly Hunter in *The Piano* © The Everett Collection.
Photo of Tom Hanks © M. Gerber/LGI Photo Agency.
Photo of Steven Spielberg © Barry King/Gamma-Liaison.

Manufactured in the United States of America

Revised Edition: October 1994

10 9 8 7 6 5 4 3 2 1

CONTENTS

Foreword vii
To Order Videos ix
Introduction xii
Acknowledgments xv
The Videos by Category:
- Action/Adventure 1
- Children's Viewing/Family 143
- Comedy 211
- Documentary 418
- Drama 440
- Foreign Language 710
- Horror 808
- Musical 906
- Mystery/Suspense 950
- Science-Fiction/Fantasy 1034
- Western 1092

Cast Index 1167
Director Index 1426
List of Academy Award Winners 1500
Alphabetical Listing of Movies (Including Alternate Titles) 1507

CHRIS HUNTER

RESEARCH EDITOR

CHIEF CONTRIBUTORS

HARVEY BURGESS

BILL CRETER

M. FAUST

ROCHELLE O'GORMAN FLYNN

JEAN FOURNIER

PAUL FREEMAN

JACK GARNER

RICH GARRISON

WILLIAM GLINES

MARK HALVERSON

ROBERT HOLMAN

PHIL HOOVER

SCOTT HUNTER

BILL KELLEY

JIM LANE

JOHN LARSEN

RICHARD LEATHERS

BILL McLEOD

BOB POLUNSKY

BOB SHAW

JOHN TIBBETTS

TOM TOLLEY

LORI J. TRIBBLE

ROBERT YOUNG, JR.

FOREWORD

You hold in your hands the most comprehensive critical guide to movies on video available. Where other movie review books contain films that may never be released to video stores, *Video Movie Guide* concentrates only on what you can rent at your local shop or purchase through the mail. Even so, this edition still includes over 15,000 titles.

It is also a book written by people who love movies for people who love movies. We treat this annual publication like some kind of holy quest, searching out obscure titles and oddball distributors in order to pack *VMG* with as many titles as possible. This is why you'll find more B movies, foreign films, cartoon collections, comedy concerts, old-time and spaghetti Westerns, TV movies, direct-to-video releases, silents, Japanese animated science-fiction films, and TV series covered here than in any other movie guide.

As in previous years, we have covered all of the major movie releases now available in stores as well as several months of upcoming titles, which we reviewed while they were in theatrical release. Also, we have gone backward as much as forward, catching up on obscure or previously released titles we may have missed in earlier editions. We honestly believe that you cannot find a more complete critical review of movies on video.

To help you find movies reviewed in this book, we have several features: a complete alphabetical listing of titles at the back of the book, a cast index, and a director index. In the complete titles index, a diamond has been placed next to all the top-rated four- and five-star films, and all new reviews have been boldfaced. Alternate titles have also been listed, so that a film like *The Christmas Tree*, for example, can be found under its video title, *When Wolves Cry*, in the index, and so on. We also have an index of Oscar winners for your reference.

A few readers have expressed dismay because we reevaluate films from edition to edition. We feel this is necessary. A good movie might catch us on a bad day or vice versa and lead to a less-than-objective analysis. Some of the better-known film critics balk at being considered consumer guides, but that is exactly what we strive to be. Not everyone is going to like everything. But if a film has merit, even if we don't particularly care for it, we have tried to call attention to its attributes. We want this book to be, given the capriciousness of opinion, the most accurate and useful critical guide to movies.

This is why we rate genre movie against genre movie. For example, dramas are rated against dramas, westerns against westerns, and so on. There is no way the John Wayne/Johnny Mack Brown B-plus Western, *Hell Town*, could be compared with *Lawrence of Arabia*, for example, so we try to keep things in perspective.

Please do not write us to ask where to buy movies. Instead, see the section entitled To Order Videos for a list of companies that specialize in selling and renting videos.

We welcome comments from our readers, but can only answer those that come with a self-addressed, stamped envelope. Our mailing address is Video Movie Guide, P.O. Box 189674, Sacramento, CA 95818. Until next year, happy viewing!

TO ORDER VIDEOS

Video Movie Guide is meant to function as a viewing guide to what is available in video stores for rent and a buyer's guide to titles available by mail order. As with books, some movies may go "out of print" and become unavailable for purchase. A number of video companies have gone out of business in the last few years. However, many videos that can no longer be purchased are still available for rent in many stores, so we do not delete any titles.

A number of Disney titles are released for a brief period of time and then placed on moratorium, which means you can find them for viewing purposes at a rental store, but cannot currently buy them—although they will be rereleased eventually. More and more video companies are using this approach. Other titles that were available at one time exist in some kind of never-never land now, as rights have been transferred from one company to another.

Still others, like Richard Lester's *Three (*and *Four) Musketeers* and *Topkapi* were pulled by their respective distributors and currently are not available for purchase. But they were available on video at one time so we include them in our book. After all, *Those Magnificent Men in Their Flying Machines* was rereleased, so anything can happen.

We regret any inconvenience a reader might have in attempting to buy a particular title listed in this book. However, as much as we would like to help, we do not have the resources to find movies for readers who want to buy them. But some help is available.

Mike Antonaros has graciously agreed to answer letters from *Video Movie Guide* readers about the availability and price of desired movies. Write to him at Mr. Dickens Books and Video, 5764 Antelope Road, Sacramento, CA 95842, or call him toll free at (800) 228-4246.

Readers interested in buying their favorite movies on video cannot order them directly from the distributor, which is why we do not list video companies in the book. Instead, we have found a number of mail-order houses that sell and rent videos.

We have not dealt personally with any of them, and would welcome comments from readers on whether we should or should not list them in the book.

Most of the following companies carry a line of recent video releases in addition to their specialty:

Classic, foreign, silent and contemporary films for rent and for sale: Facets Multimedia, 1517 Fullerton Avenue, Chicago, IL 60614, (800) 331-6197.

Rental outlets: Home Video Festival, P.O. Box 2032, Scranton, PA 18501-9952, (800) 258-FILM; Video Library, 7157 Germantown Ave., Philadelphia, PA 19149, (800) 669-7157; Eddie Brandt's Saturday Matinee, 6310 Colfax Ave., North Hollywood, CA 91606, (818) 506-4242 or (818) 506-7722.

Various: Columbia House Video Club, 1400 N. Fruitridge Ave., Terra Haute, IN 47812-9621, (800) 544-4431; Critics' Choice Video, P.O. Box 549, Elk Grove Village, IL 60009-0549; Home Video Express, P.O. Box 404, Clarks Summit, PA 18411, (800) 822-8820; Value Video International, P.O. Box 22565, Denver, CO 80222.

Classic and creaky oldies (many of which are in public domain): Discount Video, P.O. Box 7122, Burbank, CA 91510; Video Yesteryear, Box C, Sandy Hook, CT 06482; Blackhawk Films, 15959 Triumph Street, Commerce, CA 90040-1688; Captain Bijou, P.O. Box 87, Toney, AL 35773; Hollywood Attic, 138 Fifth Avenue, Pelham, NY 10803; Foothill Video Inc., P.O. Box 547, Tujanga, CA 91043, (818) 353-8591; Grapevine Video, P.O. Box 46161, Phoenix, AZ 85063, (602) 245-0210; Mike LeBell's Video, 75 Fremont Place, Los Angeles, CA 90005, (213) 938-3333; Video Dimensions, 530 West 23 St., New York, NY 10011, (212) 929-6135.

1950s TV shows: Shokus Video, P.O. Box 3125, Chatsworth, CA 91313.

Horror films: Sinister Cinema, P.O. Box 4369, Medford, OR 97501-0168, (503) 773-6860; Something Weird, P.O. Box 33664, Seattle, WA 98133, (206) 361-3759.

B Westerns: Video West, 1901 Paige Place, NE, Albuquerque, NM 87112.

Serials: Stokey's Serials, P.O. Box 426, Selden, NY 11784.

For Beta tapes: Absolute Beta Movies, P.O. Box 130, Remington, VA 22734, (800) WE-R-BETA.

A number of these companies have 35mm or 16mm copies of old fright flicks or shoot-'em-ups from which they make their copies. Quality can vary greatly depending on the condition of the original print and the integrity of the company itself. We have seen videos that were obviously duplicated from other videos instead of an original print, so let the buyer beware. The listing of mail-order houses in *VMG* is purely a service for our readers and does not constitute an endorsement on the part of the authors or the publisher. Good luck!

INTRODUCTION

In creating *Video Movie Guide* we have attempted to give you the most up-to-the-minute book, with a clear rating system and easy access to the titles covered. Only movies that had been scheduled for release as videos at the time of publication are included in this edition. You will find movies listed in alphabetical order at the end of the book and then discussed in depth in their respective genres:

- Action/Adventure
- Children's Viewing/Family
- Comedy
- Documentary
- Drama
- Foreign Language
- Horror
- Musical
- Mystery/Suspense
- Science-Fiction/Fantasy
- Western

The rating system runs from five stars to a turkey. We feel a five-star film is a must; a four-star rating means it's well worth watching. The desirability of a film with a lesser rating depends on your liking for a particular type of film or movie star. A turkey by any other name is still a bad movie. If a film is particularly offensive, even though it has a big-name star, we want you to know why. Likewise, if a little-known gem has special attributes, we've done our best to call your attention to it.

Certain kinds of movies have been purposely ignored. For example, we do not feel that hard-core sex films have a place in a book of this kind.

We have, however, been more lenient about the inclusion of horror films. Since there is a huge audience for them and they are readily available, we've attempted to include even the lowest of the low to help prevent you from getting stuck with a turkey.

When a film has been rated G, PG, PG-13, R, X, or NC-17 by the Motion Picture Association of America we have noted it. Only theatrically released films distributed after November 1967 were considered by the MPAA ratings board, so we have attempted to indicate the potentially objectionable content in films released before then, as well as in made-for-cable and video-only products. Even the MPAA ratings are confusing at times, so, wherever appropriate, we have explained these as well.

Overall, we feel this is the most practical guide to what's available on video. We hope you agree.

ACKNOWLEDGMENTS

The authors are grateful to a number of wonderful people without whose help *Video Movie Guide* would not be a reality. Health and nutrition expert Cary Nosler planted the seed. Our first two editors, Marilyn Abraham and Joe Blades, helped define the book's form and nurture its growth, and our current editor, Jeff Doctoroff, is a consistent source of support, sage advice, and inspiration.

Derrick Bang, a founding contributor, is the film critic for the *Davis Enterprise* as well as the host/producer/writer of the *Cable Connection* TV series. He continues to play an important role in the yearly creation of *VMG* as consulting editor.

Research editor Chris Hunter, in addition to keeping us up to date on the Japanese animation field, reviews a variety of films and helps our other writers keep their facts straight.

Our chief contributors, a splendid crew of film critics, movie buffs, and historians, have also contributed greatly to this tome. Allow us to introduce them:

Harvey Burgess is a free-lance film critic and author.

Taking advantage of his encyclopedic knowledge of films, Bill Creter has just finished work on the movie trivia book to end all movie trivia books.

M. Faust has contributed to *Video Digest*, *Movies on TV*, and *Video* magazine.

Rochelle O'Gorman Flynn has been writing about film, video, and books for twelve years in such publications as the *Boston Herald* and *Pulse!* magazine.

Jean Fournier, our foreign-film expert, is an independent filmmaker and author of several short stories.

Paul Freeman's writings on movies and movie stars appear frequently in the *San Mateo Times*, the *San Francisco Chronicle*, and *S.F. Weekly*.

Jack Garner is the chief film critic for *Gannett News Service*. Just look at the movie ads, and you'll see his name.

Rich Garrison is a free-lance writer and movie buff.

William Glines is an actor and film buff.

Mark Halverson and Jim Lane share film critic duties at the *Sacramento News and Review*. They have been reviewing films for over twenty years.

Robert Holman is an actor and movie buff whose life has been devoted to the appreciation of the movies.

Phil Hoover is a horror-film buff covering his field of expertise while keeping a critical eye on the contributions of others in that vein.

Scott Hunter worked alongside Mick Martin reviewing films for the *Sacramento Union* until it closed. He is now working in the field of video games.

Bill Kelley, a world-class expert on horror films, is a nationally syndicated movie columnist.

John Larsen has been the film editor of the *Ventura County & Coast Reporter* for seventeen years. He is also a main contributor to *Hollywood Hotline*, and a screenwriter with two projects currently in the works.

Richard Leathers is a free-lance writer from Seattle, one of—if not the—biggest movie towns in the country.

Bill McLeod is a life-long movie buff whose work as a film publicist in San Francisco involves him with stars and filmmakers. He sneaks time to write reviews.

Classic-films expert Bob Polunsky is the film critic for San Antonio's *Express News*, KENS-TV, WOAI-AM and KAJA-FM.

Bob Shaw is the film reviewer for KTVU Channel 2's "10 O'Clock News" in San Francisco and a real witty guy.

Kansas City film critic and historian John Tibbets, former editor-publisher of *American Classic Screen*, has added his insight into the silent film era to our pages.

Motion picture historian and collector Tom Tolley is another founding contributor whose amazing knowledge of movies has been a key factor in shaping the book.

Lori J. Tribble is an independent video producer, assistant media specialist at a Sacramento, CA hospital, and film buff.

Another chief contributor since the beginning, Robert Young Jr. has just published *Roscoe "Fatty" Arbuckle*, a bio-bibliography of the life and career of the silent comedy star. He also wrote *Movie Memo*, a short history of the MGM studios, was ghostwriter of the autobiography of Sessue Hayakawa, and is a contributing editor for *American Classic Screen*.

Joining us this year are spaghetti-Westerns expert Tom Betts and *L.A. Daily News* film critic Bob Strauss.

In addition, Gayna Lamb-Bang, Devin Davis, Lon Goddard, Holly Johnson, David Linck, Simon Macmillan, Boyd Magers, D. R. Martin, Craig Modderno, Don Norris, Bill O'Brien, Linda Rajotte, Mike Reynolds, Vicki and Mark Sazaki, Bill Smith, Lisa Smith-Youngs, Sylvia Thornton, Bill and Sam Beau Webb, and Gary Zilaff also wrote reviews.

Thanks also to our families for their support and patience. Eileen and Chuck Porter, Hada Martin, Matt and Norma Condo and Diane Martin have pitched in to help on numerous occasions. Even Francesca Martin has done her bit.

We'd also like to thank Mike and Betty Antonaros, Norton Buffalo, Keith Burton, Henry Chung, George Davidson, Jim Dixon, Stan Goman, Scott Gray, Caron Harris, Carol Johnson, David Johnson, Bob Kronenberg, Bruce Little, Stacey Mendonca, Gary Quattrin, Marcia Raphael, Helen Rees, Nora Reichard, Russ Solomon, Jon Souza, Jerry & Karen Sterchi, Milos Strehlik, Steven Taveira, Walter von Hauffe, Tami Walker, and Bob Wilkins.

ACTION/ ADVENTURE

ABDUCTED ★★½ This is not as sleazy as the video box art would have you believe. A backwoods jogger (Roberta Weiss) is abducted by a crazed mountain man and taken back to his cabin. Nothing new, but some good chase scenes. Not rated, but has violence, profanity, and adult subject matter. 87m. **DIR:** Boon Collins. **CAST:** Roberta Weiss, Lawrence King Phillip, Dan Haggerty. **1985**

ABOVE AND BEYOND ★★★½ Good account of the secret training led by Paul Tibbets (Robert Taylor) to prepare for the first atomic-bomb attack on Hiroshima. Bogs down some when dealing with his home life, but overall a fine biographical drama. Jim Backus has a cameo as General Curtis E. LeMay. B&W; 122m. **DIR:** Melvin Frank. **CAST:** Robert Taylor, Eleanor Parker, James Whitmore, Larry Keating, Jeff Richards, Jim Backus. **1952**

ABOVE SUSPICION ★★★★ Newlyweds Joan Crawford and Fred MacMurray, while honeymooning on the Continent at the outbreak of World War II, innocently become involved in espionage. Conrad Veidt, who died before the movie was released, steals every scene in which he appears. Unrated, but good family entertainment. B&W; 90m. **DIR:** Richard Thorpe. **CAST:** Joan Crawford, Fred MacMurray, Conrad Veidt, Basil Rathbone, Reginald Owen. **1943**

ABOVE THE LAW ★★★½ Director Andrew Davis, who gave credibility to Chuck Norris in *Code of Silence*, teams up with karate expert Steven Seagal (who cowrote the story and coproduced with Davis) for this tough, action-filled cop thriller. Seagal is a Chicago cop and Vietnam veteran who takes on the CIA. The result is a strong entry for action buffs. Rated R for lots of violence, profanity, and drug use. 97m. **DIR:** Andrew Davis. **CAST:** Steven Seagal, Pam Grier, Sharon Stone, Daniel Faraldo, Henry Silva. **1988**

ACCESS CODE 🦃 Dreadful action film about an Orwellian Big Brother surveillance system that takes over the country's national security complex. Not rated, has profanity. 90m. **DIR:** Mark Sobel. **CAST:** Martin Landau, Michael Ansara, Macdonald Carey. **1984**

ACE DRUMMOND ★★½ An arch villain known as The Dragon has thwarted every effort by an international group attempting to establish a round-the-world airline service. Aviation whiz Ace Drummond jumps from the Sunday funnies to the silver screen. Laughable in many respects, this is still a pretty good serial and the only filming of this character's adventures. B&W; 250m. **DIR:** Ford Beebe, Cliff Smith. **CAST:** John King, Jean Rogers, Noah Beery Jr., Lon Chaney Jr. **1936**

ACE OF ACES ★★★½ Aviation drama set in World War I. Richard Dix, as the hero, raises this tough film above literally dozens of flying ace movies made in the early 1930s. B&W; 70m. **DIR:** J. Walter Ruben. **CAST:** Richard Dix, Elizabeth Allan, Ralph Bellamy. **1933**

ACES: IRON EAGLE III ★★★½ Surprisingly effective and entertaining reworking of *The Magnificent Seven/Seven Samurai* formula bears no resemblance to the other two films in the *Iron Eagle* series. It features Lou Gossett Jr. as the character of Chappy. This time, he must lead a group of World War II veterans on a mission to save a village from drug dealers. Rated R for violence and profanity. 98m. **DIR:** John Glen. **CAST:** Lou Gossett Jr., Rachel McLish, Paul Freeman, Horst Buchholz, Christopher Cazenove, Sonny Chiba, Fred Dalton Thompson, Mitchell Ryan. **1992**

ACROSS 110TH STREET ★★★½ This one is a real sleeper! An action-packed, extremely violent film concerning gang warfare between the Mafia and their black counterparts. Entire cast is very good, as are the action scenes. Rated R for violence and language. 102m. **DIR:** Barry Shear. **CAST:** Anthony Quinn, Yaphet Kotto, Anthony Franciosa, Richard Ward. **1972**

ACROSS THE PACIFIC ★★★★ Prior to going off to war himself, director John Huston reassembled three of the stars from *The Maltese Falcon* for this high-spirited World War II propaganda piece. Humphrey Bogart woos Mary Astor while battling spy Sydney Greenstreet. Hugely enjoyable action film. B&W; 97m. **DIR:** John Huston. **CAST:** Humphrey Bogart, Mary Astor, Sydney Greenstreet, Victor Sen Yung, Keye Luke, Richard Loo. **1942**

ACT OF PIRACY ★★½ When modern-day pirate Ray Sharkey and his gang rip off Gary Busey's state-of-the-art yacht, accidentally kidnapping his children at the same time, our hero embarks on a no-holds-barred mission to get his property back. Ho-hum action movie. Unrated, the film has profanity, violence, nudity, and simulated sex. 101m. **DIR:** John "Bud" Cardos. **CAST:** Gary Busey, Belinda Bauer, Ray Sharkey, Nancy Mulford, Ken Gampu. **1990**

ACTION IN ARABIA ★★½ George Sanders fights against time and Nazi agents as he attempts to inform the Allied authorities about German plans for a pact with the Arabs in this wartime romance-adventure. The love of a woman helps to turn the tide for the western powers in this sandy adventure. B&W; 75m. **DIR:** Leonide Moguy. **CAST:** George Sanders, Virginia Bruce, Gene Lockhart, Robert Armstrong, Michael Ansara. **1944**

ACTION IN THE NORTH ATLANTIC ★★★½ Somewhat stodgy, flag-waving morale-booster features a fine cast in World War II-era tribute to the merchant marine. Officers Humphrey Bogart and Raymond Massey must rally their courage and crew when their convoy is attacked by a German U-boat. B&W; 127m. **DIR:** Lloyd Bacon. **CAST:** Humphrey Bogart, Raymond Massey, Alan Hale Sr., Julie Bishop, Ruth Gordon, Sam Levene, Dane Clark. **1943**

ACTION JACKSON ★★ A maverick cop (Carl Weathers) is on the trail of a corrupt auto tycoon (Craig T. Nelson). Unfortunately, *Action Jackson* is a gabfest punctuated by not-so-hot sex scenes. There are a couple of good stunt scenes, though. Rated R for violence, drug use, simulated sex, nudity, and profanity. 95m. **DIR:** Craig R. Baxley. **CAST:** Carl Weathers, Craig T. Nelson, Vanity, Sharon Stone, Thomas F. Wilson, Bill Duke. **1988**

ADVENTURES IN SPYING ★★½ In this harmless romp, bored Bernie Coulson and Jill Schoelen learn that a recent acquaintance is actually a hired killer presumed dead. Now that he knows that they know his secret, they have to outrun numerous bad guys, ranging from crooked cops to evil chemists. G. Gordon Liddy makes a great villain. Rated PG-13 for violence. 91m. **DIR:** Hil Covington. **CAST:** Bernie Coulson, Jill Schoelen, Seymour Cassel, Michael Emil, G. Gordon Liddy. **1991**

ADVENTURES OF CAPTAIN FABIAN 🦃 A lackluster swashbuckler. 100m. **DIR:** William Marshall. **CAST:** Errol Flynn, Vincent Price, Agnes Moorehead. **1951**

ADVENTURES OF CAPTAIN MARVEL, THE ★★★★ Fawcett Comics' Captain Marvel is splendidly brought to life by Republic Studios in what is generally regarded as the best serial of all time, certainly the best superhero chapterplay ever produced. Sincerely acted by all involved, this serial set the standards for flying stunts for years to come. B&W; 12 chapters. **DIR:** William Witney, John English. **CAST:** Tom Tyler, Frank Coghlan Jr., William Benedict, Louise Currie. **1941**

ADVENTURES OF DON JUAN, THE ★★★★ Despite the obvious use of footage from *The Adventures of Robin Hood* and *The Private Lives of Elizabeth and Essex*, this is a solid swashbuckler. Errol Flynn plays the great lover and swordsman of the title with tongue planted firmly in cheek. The years of drinking were beginning to show on his once boyishly handsome face. Yet this is quite appropriate to his portrayal of the famous libertine, who comes to the aid of a queen (Viveca Lindfors) in his later years. 110m. **DIR:** Vincent Sherman. **CAST:** Errol Flynn, Viveca Lindfors, Robert Douglas, Alan Hale Sr., Romney Brent, Ann Rutherford, Robert Warwick, Jerry Austin, Douglas Kennedy, Una O'Connor. **1949**

ADVENTURES OF FORD FAIRLANE, THE ★★ Foul-mouthed shock comic Andrew Dice Clay stars as rock 'n' roll private dick Ford Fairlane. There's something here to offend everybody, especially women. Rated R for profanity and violence. 101m. **DIR:** Renny Harlin. **CAST:** Andrew Dice Clay, Priscilla Presley, Wayne Newton, Robert Englund, Ed O'Neill. **1990**

ADVENTURES OF ROBIN HOOD, THE ★★★★★ This classic presents Errol Flynn at his swashbuckling best. He is backed up in this color spectacular by a perfect cast of supporting actors. Olivia de Havilland is Maid Marian. Alan Hale Sr. and Eugene Pallette are Little John and Friar Tuck. The bad guys are also at their evil best, as played by Basil Rathbone and Claude Rains. Lavish sets and a stirring musical score help place *Robin Hood* among the very best adventure films. 106m. **DIR:** Michael Curtiz, William Keighley. **CAST:** Errol Flynn, Basil Rathbone, Ian Hunter, Olivia de Havilland, Claude Rains, Alan Hale Sr., Eugene Pallette. **1938**

ADVENTURES OF TARTU ★★½ Robert Donat steals the show as a British spy entrusted with the crippling of a poison gas factory behind enemy lines. He is joined in this blend of comedy and suspense by lovely Valerie Hobson and perky Glynis Johns. Nothing really special about this one, but it's fun. B&W; 103m. **DIR:** Harold S. Bucquet. **CAST:** Robert Donat, Valerie Hobson, Glynis Johns, Walter Rilla, Phyllis Morris. **1943**

ADVENTURES OF TARZAN, THE ★★½ Early action star Elmo Lincoln dons a wig for the third time to portray the Lord of the Jungle in this ambitious chapterplay. Lincoln finds himself fighting unscrupulous Bolsheviks, wild animals, a claimant to his family name, and the hordes of the lost city of Opar. Loosely adapted from two Tarzan novels. Silent. B&W; 15 chapters. **DIR:** Robert Hill. **CAST:** Elmo Lincoln, Louise Lorraine, Percy Pembroke. **1921**

ADVENTURES OF THE FLYING CADETS ★★ A mysterious figure known as the Black Hangman has located a secret deposit of helium in Africa and plans to sell it to the Nazis. The young Flying Cadets have been falsely implicated in a series of murders and set out to clear their names and bring the traitorous agent to justice. Not a great serial, but even an excess of stock footage is offset by a good cast and some thrilling action sequences. B&W; 13 chapters. **DIR:** Ray Taylor, Lewis D. Collins. **CAST:** Johnny Downs, Bobby Jordan, Ward Wood, William Benedict, Eduardo Ciannelli, Robert Armstrong. **1943**

AFRICA—TEXAS STYLE! ★★ The idea of a movie about cowboys rounding up animals in Africa must have sounded good in theory. But in practice, it's pretty dull going. Even the location photography doesn't help. Give us *Hatari!* any day. 106m. **DIR:** Andrew Marton. **CAST:** Hugh O'Brian, John Mills, Tom Nardini. **1966**

AFRICAN RAGE ★★★½ Anthony Quinn is a nurse in an African hospital where a tribal leader is admitted amid heavy security. Quinn's kidnapping of the leader, played with great dignity and warmth by Simon Sabela, takes some very unusual and interesting turns. A surprisingly moving film. Unrated. 105m. **DIR:** Peter Collinson. **CAST:** Anthony Quinn, John Phillip Law, Marius Weyers, Sandra Prinsloo, Ken Gampu, Simon Sabela. **1985**

AGAINST ALL FLAGS ★★★ Though Errol Flynn's energy and attractiveness had seriously ebbed by this time, he still possessed the panache to make this simple swashbuckler fun to watch. He portrays a dashing British soldier who infiltrates a pirate stronghold, pausing only to romance the fiery Maureen O'Hara. 83m. **DIR:** George Sherman. **CAST:** Errol Flynn, Maureen O'Hara, Anthony Quinn, Mildred Natwick. **1952**

AGENT ON ICE ★★★½ This exciting action film features Tom Ormeny as John Pope, a former CIA agent who has become a target for both the CIA and the Mafia. Clifford David plays the corrupt CIA official who has been laundering money for Mafia leader Frank Matera (Louis Pastore). Rated R for violence and obscenities. 96m. **DIR:** Clark Worswick. **CAST:** Tom Ormeny, Clifford David, Louis Pastore, Matt Craven. **1985**

AIR AMERICA ★★★★ The cop/buddy formula takes to the air when veteran pilot Mel Gibson teams up with rookie Robert Downey Jr. to fly top-secret U.S. missions behind enemy lines in the early Vietnam War-era jungles of Laos. Plenty of action and comedy bits make this a fun romp for the action crowd. Rated R for profanity and violence. 100m. **DIR:** Roger Spottiswoode. **CAST:** Mel Gibson, Robert Downey Jr. **1990**

AIR FORCE ★★★★ This is essentially wartime propaganda about a flying fortress and its crew taking on the enemy at Pearl Harbor, Manila, and the Coral Sea. However, the direction by Howard Hawks puts the film head and shoulders above similar motion pictures. B&W; 124m. **DIR:** Howard Hawks. **CAST:** John Garfield, John Ridgely, Gig Young, Charles Drake, Harry Carey, Arthur Kennedy, George Tobias. **1943**

AL CAPONE ★★★½ Rod Steiger is mesmerizing as Al Capone in this perceptive portrait of the legendary Chicago gangster. The film covers Capone's life from his first job for $75 a week to his ultimate fate behind prison walls. Filmed in black and white with a documentary-style narrative, which heightens the quality of this film. The supporting cast—Fay Spain in particular—is just right. B&W; 104m. **DIR:** Richard Wilson. **CAST:** Rod Steiger, Fay Spain, James Gregory, Martin Balsam, Nehemiah Persoff. **1959**

ALI BABA AND THE FORTY THIEVES ★★★ Youthful Ali Baba flees from an evil vizier and is protected and raised by forty thieves, the only hope of his downtrodden people. Sit back and enjoy this lighthearted sword-and-turban adventure. Now what are we to do with the forty jars if the thieves are the good guys? 87m. **DIR:** Arthur Lubin. **CAST:** Jon Hall, Maria Montez, Turhan Bey, Andy Devine, Fortunio Bonanova, Crispin Martin, Kurt Katch, Frank Puglia, Scotty Beckett. **1944**

ALICE TO NOWHERE ★★★★ A bungled jewel heist sets in motion this fast-paced adventure. A nurse assigned to a job in central Australia is unknowingly carrying the stolen jewels. The action never lets up as she is pursued by the robbers to the outback. Made for Australian television and shown on independent stations in the United States. 210m. **DIR:** John Power. **CAST:** John Waters, Steve Jacobs, Rosie Jones, Ruth Cracknell. **1986**

ALIEN FROM L.A. ★★½ When a nerdy valley girl goes in search of her archaeologist father, she embarks on the adventure of her life. Although this is a low-budget film, it has enough action and humor to be appropriate for most family members. Rated PG for light violence. 88m. **DIR:** Albert Pyun. **CAST:** Kathy Ireland, Linda Kerridge, William R. Moses. **1983**

ALL QUIET ON THE WESTERN FRONT (1930) ★★★★★ Despite some dated moments and an "old movie" look, this film still stands as a powerful statement against war and man's inhumanity to man. Lew Ayres and Louis Wolheim star in this story, set during World War I, which follows several young men into battle, examining their disillusionment and eventual deaths. B&W; 130m. **DIR:** Lewis Milestone. **CAST:** Lew Ayres, Louis Wolheim. **1930**

ALL THROUGH THE NIGHT ★★★½ Humphrey Bogart and his gang take on Nazi spies in this star-studded romp. The plot is typical World War II flag-waving. But the dialogue and the cast—oh, my! This one's worth a look if only to see Jackie Gleason and Phil Silvers clowning it up a full decade before they'd become icons of the small screen. B&W; 107m. **DIR:** Vincent Sherman. **CAST:** Humphrey Bogart, Conrad Veidt, Kaaren Verne, Jane Darwell, Frank McHugh, Peter Lorre, Judith Anderson, William Demarest, Jackie Gleason, Phil Silvers, Wallace Ford, Barton MacLane, Edward Brophy, Martin Kosleck. **1942**

ALLAN QUARTERMAIN AND THE LOST CITY OF GOLD As if they weren't bad enough in the original, Richard Chamberlain and Sharon Stone reprise their roles from the tongue-in-beak turkey, *King Solomon's Mines*. Rated PG. 95m. **DIR:** Gary Nelson. **CAST:** Richard Chamberlain, Sharon Stone, James Earl Jones, Henry Silva, Robert Donner, Cassandra Peterson. **1987**

ALMOST HUMAN Italian grade-Z auteur Umberto Lenzi ground out this flat, routine kidnap potboiler during a break between his horror and cannibal epics. Rated R. 92m. **DIR:** Umberto Lenzi. **CAST:** Tomas Milian, Henry Silva. **1974**

ALOHA, BOBBY AND ROSE ★★ B-movie treatment of two kids on the lam for a murder they didn't mean to commit. Paul LeMat's first starring role after *American Graffiti*. He is interesting, but the film is downbeat and uninspired. Rated R. 88m. **DIR:** Floyd Mutrux. **CAST:** Paul LeMat, Dianne Hull, Tim McIntire. **1975**

AMAZING SPIDERMAN, THE ★★ Marvel Comics' popular character makes his live-action debut in this made-for-TV adaptation that involves Spidey's origin. Although fairly well-acted, it's missing many of the wisecracking elements that made the comic-book character popular. The production values and special effects are decent, though, especially the wall-crawling scenes. Not rated, but appropriate for all ages. 93m. **DIR:** E. W. Swackhamer. **CAST:** Nicholas Hammond, David White, Michael Pataki, Hilly Hicks, Lisa Eilbacher. **1977**

AMAZON ★★½ On the lam, Kari Vaananen hightails it into the jungles of the Amazon, where he's befriended by pilot Robert Davi. Politically correct film is only so-so. Rated R for violence and language. 88m. **DIR:** Mika Kaurismaki. **CAST:** Robert Davi, Kari Vaananen, Rae Dawn Chong. **1992**

AMAZONS The ridiculousness of the fight scenes in this film rivals that of the worst kung fu flick. This silly film is rated R for nudity, violence, and sex. 76m. **DIR:** Alex Sessa. **CAST:** Windsor Taylor Randolph, Penelope Reed, Joseph Whipp, Danitza Kingsley, Willie Nelson. **1986**

AMBUSHERS, THE Only hard-core Dean Martin fans will want to bother with this one, the third movie in the Matt Helm secret agent series. 102m. **DIR:** Henry Levin. **CAST:** Dean Martin, Senta Berger, Janice Rule, James Gregory, Albert Salmi, Kurt Kasznar, Beverly Adams. **1968**

AMERICAN EAGLE Rehashed garbage about a CIA hit man who wants out of the game. Rated R for violence and profanity. 92m. **DIR:** Robert J. Smawley. **CAST:** Asher Brauner, Robert F. Lyons. **1989**

AMERICAN JUSTICE ★★½ Small-town cops near the Mexican border become involved in an illegal alien/slavery ring. It's brutal and violent and probably truer than you'd think. A fair attempt by TV's *Simon and Simon* to work together in different roles. Rated R for violence, sex, and language. 79m. **DIR:** Gary Grillo. **CAST:** Gerald McRaney, Jameson Parker, Wilford Brimley. **1986**

AMERICAN KICKBOXER ★★ A former world-champion kick boxer must fight his way back to the top following a jail term for manslaughter. Rated R for profanity. 93m. **DIR:** Frans Nel. **CAST:** John Barrett. **1991**

AMERICAN NINJA An American soldier (Michael Dudikoff) single-handedly takes on an army of martial arts mercenaries in the Philippines. Rated R for profanity and violence. 95m. **DIR:** Sam Firstenberg. **CAST:** Michael Dudikoff, Guich Koock, Judie Aronson, Steve James. **1985**

AMERICAN NINJA II ★★ Michael Dudikoff continues to set new standards for nonacting in this mindless but enjoyable-for-fans martial arts movie. Dudikoff and Steve James, who is as watchable as ever, play army rangers who come to the aid of the Marines and wipe out a passel of heroin dealers. Rated R. 96m. **DIR:** Sam Firstenberg. **CAST:** Michael Dudikoff, Steve James, Larry Poindexter, Gary Conway. **1987**

AMERICAN NINJA III Comic-book movie filled with cartoon characters. Rated R for violence and profanity. 89m. **DIR:** Cedric Sundstrom. **CAST:** Steve James, David Bradley, Marjoe Gortner. **1989**

AMERICAN NINJA IV: THE ANNIHILATION This paint-by-numbers action flick has martial arts experts trying to rescue a group of Americans held captive by a mad Arab. Rated R for violence and profanity; 96m. **DIR:** Cedric Sundstrom. **CAST:** Michael Dudikoff, David Bradley, James Booth, Robin Stille, Ken Gampu. **1991**

AMERICAN ROULETTE ★★ Political thriller about a deposed president (Andy Garcia) of a South American nation living in exile in London. The ex-president's life is constantly in jeopardy from Latin death squads—and the CIA and KGB play a tug of war with his loyalities. Robert Stephens gives a fine performance as a sleazy British agent. Light on action, long on talk, with a sappy ending. Rated R. 102m. **DIR:** Maurice

Hatton. **CAST:** Andy Garcia, Kitty Aldridge, Robert Stephens. **1988**

AMERICAN SHAOLIN: KING OF THE KICKBOXERS II ★★★½ A kick boxer is humiliated during a tournament and decides he will travel to China to become a Shaolin monk. By the end you'll be rooting for him. Rated PG-13 for violence. 103m. **DIR:** Lucas Lowe. **CAST:** Reese Madigan, Daniel Dae Kim, Billy Chang, Cliff Lenderman, Zhang Zhi Yen, Trent Bushey, Kim Chan. **1991**

AMERICAN SUMMER, AN 🦃 A teenage boy is shipped off to live with his aunt, only to become embroiled in sex, drugs, and murder. Rated R for profanity, violence, and nudity. 100m. **DIR:** James Slocum. **CAST:** Michael Landes, Amber Susa, Brian Austin Green, Joanna Kerns. **1991**

AMSTERDAM KILL, THE 🦃 Fresh from his successes in *Farewell My Lovely* and *The Yakuza*, Robert Mitchum dived into this dud about an international drug conspiracy. Rated R. 90m. **DIR:** Robert Clouse. **CAST:** Robert Mitchum, Bradford Dillman, Richard Egan, Leslie Nielsen, Keye Luke. **1977**

AND THEN YOU DIE ★★★★ Canadian version of *The Long Good Friday*. Kenneth Welsh is Eddie Griffin, drug czar for Canada's coke freaks. His kingdom starts unraveling around him after the Mafia don in his area is murdered. Eddie gets caught in a squeeze play between the don's successor, an up-and-coming coke dealer, and the police. The film grabs you right from the opening frame and keeps you guessing right up to the final scene. 115m. **DIR:** Francis Mankiewicz. **CAST:** Kenneth Welsh, R. H. Thompson, Wayne Robson, Tom Harvey, George Bloomfield, Graeme Campbell. **1987**

ANGEL 🦃 Bad, low-budget flick about a 15-year-old who moonlights as a Hollywood Boulevard hooker and is menaced by a psychotic killer. Rated R for nudity, violence, suggested sex, and profanity. 94m. **DIR:** Robert Vincent O'Neil. **CAST:** Cliff Gorman, Susan Tyrrell, Dick Shawn, Donna Wilkes. **1983**

ANGEL FIST ★★ This Roger Corman production combines high kicks with hot babes. In it, a beautiful policewoman goes to Manila to avenge her sister's death. Watchable, but not twice! Rated R for nudity, sex, profanity, and violence. 76m. **DIR:** Cirio H. Santiago. **CAST:** Melissa Moore, Michael Shaner, Denise Buick, Jessica Roberts. **1993**

ANGEL OF DEATH 🦃 Even among the lowly subgenre of Nazi revival movies, this rates near the bottom of the list. Rated R for violence and profanity. 90m. **DIR:** Jess Franco. **CAST:** Susan Andrews, Howard Vernon. **1986**

ANGEL OF H.E.A.T. 🦃 Not enough sex and skin for the hard-core crowd, and not enough plot, good acting, or production values for the spy flick lovers. Rated R. 93m. **DIR:** Myrl A. Schreibman. **CAST:** Marilyn Chambers, Dan Jesse, Mary Woronov, Stephen Johnson. **1982**

ANGEL TOWN 🦃 An olympic kick-boxing trainer goes feet to head with street toughs. This anti-Mexican-American, anti-woman film is wimpy and stupid. Rated R for nudity, profanity, and violence. 102m. **DIR:** Eric Karson. **CAST:** Olivier Gruner, Theresa Saldana, Frank Aragon. **1990**

ANGELS DIE HARD ★★ The bikers turn out to help a community during a mining disaster. Less ridiculous than most of its predecessors and contemporaries. Look for Dan Haggerty in an early role. Violence; adult situations. Rated R. 86m. **DIR:** Richard Compton. **CAST:** William Smith, Tom Baker, R. G. Armstrong, Dan Haggerty. **1970**

ANGELS HARD AS THEY COME ★★½ An above-average biker gang movie. Distinguished mainly by its reasonably authentic look and feel, due largely to the contribution of Jonathan Demme, who cowrote and produced. Rated R for violence and nudity. 86m. **DIR:** Joe Viola. **CAST:** Scott Glenn, Charles Dierkop, Gary Busey. **1972**

ANGELS WITH DIRTY FACES ★★★★½ This is thoroughly enjoyable entertainment. The plot is that old Hollywood standby about two childhood friends, the one who goes bad (James Cagney) and the other who follows the right path (Pat O'Brien, as the priest), and the conflict between them. Yet, as directed by Warner Bros. stalwart Michael Curtiz, it often seems surprisingly fresh. B&W; 97m. **DIR:** Michael Curtiz. **CAST:** James Cagney, Pat O'Brien, Humphrey Bogart, Ann Sheridan, George Bancroft, Bobby Jordan. **1938**

ANGKOR: CAMBODIA EXPRESS 🦃 In this subpar variation on *The Killing Fields*, Robert Walker plays an American journalist who left his girlfriend (Nancy Kwan) behind in Cambodia and returns to bring her out. 86m. **DIR:** Alex King. **CAST:** Robert Walker Jr., Christopher George, Woody Strode, Nancy Kwan. **1985**

ANNIHILATORS, THE 🦃 Another film in which Vietnam veterans reunite, organize a vigilante group, annihilate the sadistic gangs, and return to their normal lives. Rated R for grotesque violence and language. 87m. **DIR:** Charles E. Sellier Jr. **CAST:** Christopher Stone, Andy Wood, Lawrence Hilton-Jacobs, Jim Antonio, Gerrit Graham. **1985**

ANOTHER 48 HRS. ★★★★ Solid sequel to the 1982 box-office smash finds director Walter Hill in top form as Eddie Murphy and Nick Nolte take on a mysterious figure known only as the Iceman. While not quite as good as the first film, *Another 48 Hrs.* nevertheless proves that the original cop/buddy team is still the best. Rated R for violence, profanity, and nudity. 95m. **DIR:** Walter Hill.

CAST: Eddie Murphy, Nick Nolte, Brion James, Kevin Tighe, Ed O'Ross. **1990**

ANOTHER STAKEOUT ★★★½ Richard Dreyfuss and Emilio Estevez are back as Seattle detectives assigned to track down an escaped federal witness. Their job is complicated by a bumbling but well-meaning assistant district attorney (played with panache by Rosie O'Donnell). The three stars work well together, and the film is an enjoyable, though not outstanding, combination of comedy, action, and suspense. Rated PG-13 for profanity and violence. 109m. **DIR:** John Badham. **CAST:** Richard Dreyfuss, Emilio Estevez, Rosie O'Donnell, Madeleine Stowe, Cathy Moriarty, Dennis Farina, Marcia Strassman, John Rubinstein, Miguel Ferrer. **1993**

ANZIO ★★ Would-be blockbuster about the Allied invasion of Italy during World War II doesn't make the grade as either history or spectacle and ultimately wastes the talents of a great cast and an often inspired director. 117m. **DIR:** Edward Dmytryk. **CAST:** Robert Mitchum, Peter Falk, Robert Ryan, Earl Holliman, Arthur Kennedy, Patrick Magee, Mark Damon, Reni Santoni. **1968**

APOCALYPSE NOW ★★★★ An exceptional war film in every sense, this work pulsates with artistic ambition. It reaches for truth, struggles for greatness—and almost succeeds. The central character, Captain Willard (Martin Sheen), tells the story of his danger-filled journey toward a fateful meeting with a man named Kurtz, a highly decorated officer who the army contends has gone mad. Rated R. 153m. **DIR:** Francis Ford Coppola. **CAST:** Marlon Brando, Martin Sheen, Robert Duvall, Harrison Ford. **1979**

APPOINTMENT IN HONDURAS ★★½ Good cast helps this farfetched story of an idealistic American (Glenn Ford) helping local misfits free their country from political tyranny. The actors do their best, but rather silly material gets in their way. Plot and dialogue are somewhat laughable. Ann Sheridan is highly watchable, as usual. 79m. **DIR:** Jacques Tourneur. **CAST:** Glenn Ford, Ann Sheridan, Zachary Scott, Jack Elam. **1953**

APPOINTMENT WITH FEAR 🦃 Cancel this appointment! Not rated, but contains sex, nudity, and profanity. 96m. **DIR:** Alan Smithee. **CAST:** Michelle Little, Michael Wyle, Kerry Remsen, Douglas Rowe, Garrick Dowhen. **1987**

ARABESQUE ★★★½ Fast-paced espionage-adventure about college professor Gregory Peck and his nightmarish involvement with death-dealing secret agents is an entertaining chase film and a conscious effort to capture the 1960s. Beautiful Sophia Loren keeps Peck company. 118m. **DIR:** Stanley Donen. **CAST:** Gregory Peck, Sophia Loren, Kieron Moore, Alan Badel, Carl Duering, George Coulouris. **1966**

ARABIAN NIGHTS (1942) ★★★ Scheherazade (Maria Montez) spends 86 minutes, not a thousand-and-one nights, as the prisoner of an evil caliph until rescued by dashing Jon Hall. No magic carpets or flying horses—but John Qualen as Aladdin and Shemp Howard as Sinbad? 86m. **DIR:** John Rawlins. **CAST:** Jon Hall, Maria Montez, Sabu, Leif Erickson, Billy Gilbert, Edgar Barrier, Richard Lane, Turhan Bey, John Qualen, Shemp Howard. **1942**

ARIZONA HEAT 🦃 Run-of-the-mill cop story about a tough but good policeman (Michael Parks) inheriting a female partner (Denise Crosby) and tracking down a crazed cop killer. Rated R for language, violence, and sex. 91m. **DIR:** John G. Thomas. **CAST:** Michael Parks, Denise Crosby, Hugh Farrington. **1988**

ARK OF THE SUN GOD...TEMPLE OF HELL, THE 🦃 Not only are the title and story a rip-off of *Raiders of the Lost Ark*, we are also subjected to anti-Arabic sentiment and a hero who mutters pseudocool 007-style wisecracks. Not rated; violence. 92m. **DIR:** Anthony M. Dawson. **CAST:** David Warbeck, John Steiner, Susie Sudlow, Alan Collins. **1986**

ARMED RESPONSE ★★ In Los Angeles's Chinatown, a Vietnam vet and his family fight a Japanese mob for possession of a jade statue. *Armed Response* starts out parodying the action-adventure genre, but loses its sense of humor in the middle and bogs down for too long, becoming boring and jingoistic. Rated R. 86m. **DIR:** Fred Olen Ray. **CAST:** David Carradine, Lee Van Cleef, Mako, Lois Hamilton, Ross Hagen, Brent Huff, Laurene Landon. **1986**

ARMORED COMMAND ★★ It's World War II, and the U.S. Tank Corps is fighting its way through the German lines. Sound familiar? Predictable programmer. 99m. **DIR:** Byron Haskin. **CAST:** Howard Keel, Tina Louise, Burt Reynolds, Warner Anderson. **1961**

AROUND THE WORLD UNDER THE SEA ★★ Volcanoes, a giant eel, a submarine, scuba gear, and a quarrel over who's in charge make this lackluster, harmless viewing. Shirley Eaton was in *Goldfinger*, in case you're a James Bond fan. 117m. **DIR:** Andrew Marton. **CAST:** Lloyd Bridges, Shirley Eaton, David McCallum, Brian Kelly, Keenan Wynn, Marshall Thompson. **1966**

ARREST BULLDOG DRUMMOND ★★½ Bulldog Drummond and his cronies pursue a murderer to a tropical island where he has taken refuge. Fifth in the popular series featuring John Howard. Available on a double-bill video with *Bulldog Drummond in Africa*. B&W; 57m. **DIR:** James Hogan. **CAST:** John Howard, Heather Angel, George Zucco, H. B. Warner, E. E. Clive, Reginald Denny, John Sutton. **1938**

ARSON INC. ★★ Robert Lowery is an arson-squad investigator and Anne Gwynne is his romantic interest. They perform capably, but the script is at best predictable, and stock footage of fires is quite evident. B&W; 64m. **DIR:** William Berke. **CAST:** Robert Lowery, Anne Gwynne. **1950**

ASHANTI ★★½ A shopping trip turns into a tale of horror when the black wife (Beverly Johnson) of a white doctor (Michael Caine) in Africa is kidnapped and turned over to a slave trader (Peter Ustinov). Thus begins a fairly exciting chase across various exotic locales. Rated R. 118m. **DIR:** Richard Fleischer. **CAST:** Michael Caine, Peter Ustinov, Beverly Johnson, William Holden, Omar Sharif, Rex Harrison. **1979**

ASSASSINATION 🦃 In this predictable, poorly written action flick, Charles Bronson plays a seasoned secret service agent who is called upon to guard the first lady (Jill Ireland). Rated PG-13 for profanity and violence. 105m. **DIR:** Peter R. Hunt. **CAST:** Charles Bronson, Jill Ireland, Stephen Elliott, Jan Gan Boyd, Randy Brooks, Michael Ansara. **1987**

ASSASSINATION GAME, THE 🦃 Dismal espionage film about a rookie CIA agent teaming up with a retired KGB agent. Rated R for violence, nudity, and profanity. 83m. **DIR:** Jonathan Winfrey. **CAST:** Robert Rusler, Theodore Bikel, Denise Bixler, Doug Wert. **1992**

ASSAULT OF THE REBEL GIRLS 🦃 Errol Flynn's last film is a cheaply made bargain-basement production. B&W; 68m. **DIR:** Barry Mahon. **CAST:** Errol Flynn, Beverly Aadland, John McKay. **1959**

ASSAULT ON A QUEEN ★★★ Implausible, improbable, but sometimes fun story by Rod Serling, has Frank Sinatra and pals bluffing their way onto the *Queen Mary* for a million-dollar haul. Originally released at an overlong 146 minutes. Cuts help to move the story along. Okay family viewing. 105m. **DIR:** Jack Donohue. **CAST:** Frank Sinatra, Virna Lisi, Anthony Franciosa, Richard Conte. **1968**

ASSAULT ON AGATHON 🦃 While investigating a series of robberies of Greek banks, a British and an American Interpol agent uncover a plot by a World War II underground leader to start a new revolution. 96m. **DIR:** Laslo Benedek. **CAST:** Nico Minardos, Nina Van Pallandt, John Woodvine, Marianne Faithfull. **1976**

ASSAULT ON PRECINCT 13 ★★★★½ Here's director John Carpenter's riveting movie about a nearly deserted L.A. police station that finds itself under siege by a youth gang. It's a modern-day version of Howard Hawks' *Rio Bravo*, with exceptional performances by its entire cast. Rated R. 90m. **DIR:** John Carpenter. **CAST:** Austin Stoker, Laurie Zimmer, Tony Burton, Nancy Loomis, Darwin Joston. **1976**

ASSISI UNDERGROUND, THE ★★ Melodrama tracing the activities of a Franciscan monastery as part of the Jewish liberation network in World War II Italy. Ben Cross struggles valiantly to bring some life to this dreary fact-based tale; hard work considering the poor dialogue and unrealistic behavior of the Jews he is trying to help escape from Europe. Rated PG. 115m. **DIR:** Alexander Ramati. **CAST:** Ben Cross, James Mason, Irene Papas, Maximilian Schell, Karl Heinz Hackl, Delia Boccardo, Edmund Purdom. **1985**

AT SWORD'S POINT ★★½ The sons (and a daughter) of the fabled Three Musketeers come to the aid of the queen of France, and thwart the ambitions of a throne-hungry duke. Lighthearted adventure yarn. 81m. **DIR:** Lewis Allen. **CAST:** Cornel Wilde, Maureen O'Hara, Dan O'Herlihy, Alan Hale Jr., Robert Douglas, Blanche Yurka, Gladys Cooper. **1952**

ATLAS ★★ Roger Corman's obligatory entry in the sword-and-sandal genre (shot in Greece) is underpopulated (and, as Atlas, Michael Forest is a tad underfed), but it contains enough in-jokes and gore to keep Corman aficionados mildly amused. 80m. **DIR:** Roger Corman. **CAST:** Michael Forest, Barboura Morris, Frank Wolff. **1961**

ATOM MAN VS. SUPERMAN ★★ The second and final serial based on the adventures of Superman reunites most of the principal cast from the first chapterplay and throws in the Man of Steel's nemesis, Lex Luthor. Competently played by the talented and often-seen Lyle Talbot, Luthor is out to blackmail Metropolis by threatening the city with destruction. B&W; 15 chapters. **DIR:** Spencer Gordon Bennet. **CAST:** Kirk Alyn, Noel Neill, Lyle Talbot, Tommy Bond, Pierre Watkin, Jack Ingram, Don Harvey, Terry Frost. **1950**

ATTACK FORCE Z ★★ Okay Australian film concerning a group of commandos on a secret mission against the Japanese in World War II. Most notable is a young Mel Gibson as the leader of the commandos. Unrated. 84m. **DIR:** Tim Burstall. **CAST:** John Phillip Law, Sam Neill, Mel Gibson, Chris Haywood, John Waters. **1981**

AVALANCHE 🦃 It's movies like this bomb that gave disaster pictures a bad name. Rated PG. 91m. **DIR:** Corey Allen. **CAST:** Rock Hudson, Mia Farrow, Robert Forster, Jeanette Nolan. **1978**

AVENGERS, THE (TV SERIES) ★★★½ Patrick Macnee stars in the finest British secret agent series ever as quintessential agent John Steed. Diana Rigg as the rugged, leather-garbed Emma Peel was followed by Linda Thorson's Tara King for the program's final year. Charming, witty, and absolutely ageless, this program will remain loved for generations to come. Suitable for family viewing. 52m. **DIR:** Don Leaver, Robert Day.

CAST: Patrick Macnee, Diana Rigg, Linda Thorson. **1965–1969**

AVENGING ANGEL 🦃 Remember *Angel*, the high school student who doubled as a Hollywood hooker? Well, she's back. Rated R for nudity, profanity, and violence. 96m. **DIR:** Robert Vincent O'Neil. **CAST:** Betsy Russell, Rory Calhoun, Susan Tyrrell, Ossie Davis. **1985**

AVENGING FORCE ★★★ A better-than-average action-adventure flick about a former secret service agent forced out of retirement when his best friend, a black southern politician, is involved in an assassination attempt in which his son is killed. The acting is admittedly dry, but the action is top-notch, with plenty of opportunity to cheer for the hero. Rated R for violence and profanity. 104m. **DIR:** Sam Firstenberg. **CAST:** Michael Dudikoff, Steve James, James Booth, Bill Wallace, John P. Ryan, Marc Alaimo. **1986**

AWAY ALL BOATS ★★ In this lackluster war drama, Jeff Chandler plays Captain Hanks, commander of an attack transport unit in the South Pacific during World War II. We follow Chandler and his men as they train for combat. 114m. **DIR:** Joseph Pevney. **CAST:** Jeff Chandler, George Nader, Julie Adams, Lex Barker, Keith Andes, Richard Boone, Jock Mahoney, William Reynolds, Charles McGraw, John McIntire. **1956**

BABY ON BOARD 🦃 Only if you absolutely love chase scenes could you enjoy this extended chase between a taxi driver, the mob, a mother, and her baby. Not rated, but contains violence. 95m. **DIR:** Franky Schaeffer. **CAST:** Judge Reinhold, Carol Kane, Geza Kovacs. **1991**

BACK IN THE U.S.S.R. ★★★ Young American Frank Whaley is on a two-week tour of Moscow when he gets embroiled in the theft of a rare book stolen from the Church. First American film shot entirely in Moscow is lovely to look at, engaging in its premise. Rated PG-13 for violence. 88m. **DIR:** Deran Sarafian. **CAST:** Frank Whaley, Natalya Negoda, Andrew Divoff, Dey Young, Roman Polanski. **1992**

BACK TO BACK ★★★ Two brothers clear their father, accused of an armored car robbery that happened years earlier. Good performances, action, and some unforeseen twists. Rated R for violence and language. 95m. **DIR:** John Kincade. **CAST:** Bill Paxton, Ben Johnson, Susan Anspach, Apollonia. **1990**

BACK TO BATAAN ★★★ A fun World War II action film with John Wayne at his two-fisted best. Good script, photography, acting, and battle action. Video quality is quite good. B&W; 95m. **DIR:** Edward Dmytryk. **CAST:** John Wayne, Anthony Quinn, Richard Loo, Beulah Bondi. **1945**

BACKDRAFT ★★★½ Spectacular special effects highlight this melodramatic movie about feuding firemen brothers (well acted by Kurt Russell and William Baldwin) whose lives are endangered by the activities of a clever arsonist. Robert De Niro is typically strong as the chief investigator. Rated R for profanity, violence, and nudity. 136m. **DIR:** Ron Howard. **CAST:** Kurt Russell, William Baldwin, Robert De Niro, Donald Sutherland, Scott Glenn, Jennifer Jason Leigh, Rebecca DeMornay. **1991**

BACKGROUND TO DANGER ★★★★ Lots of action makes this one a WWII classic, with a no-nonsense cynic battling spies and attracting beautiful women right and left. Set in the neutral country of Turkey. B&W; 80m. **DIR:** Raoul Walsh. **CAST:** George Raft, Brenda Marshall, Sydney Greenstreet, Peter Lorre, Turhan Bey, Osa Massen. **1943**

BACKLASH ★★★ Subtle story of two cops (David Argue, Lydia Miller) escorting an accused murderess (Gia Carides) across the Australian desert. Argue turns in a fine performance as an embittered, abrasive policeman. Rated R for language and nudity. 85m. **DIR:** Bill Bennett. **CAST:** David Argue, Gia Carides, Lydia Miller, Brian Syron. **1988**

BACKSTREET JUSTICE ★★★½ Writer-director Chris McIntyre must have been reading a lot of Sue Grafton and Sara Paretsky, because this tough-gal–private-eye thriller borrows liberally from both authors...and is occasionally reminiscent of Paretsky's *Burn Marks*. Linda Kozlowski is the hardened investigator trying to live down her father's reputation as a crooked cop, while investigating a series of murders frightening tenants out of her inner-city apartment building. Rated R for violence, nudity, profanity, and simulated sex. 87m. **DIR:** Chris McIntyre. **CAST:** Linda Kozlowski, Hector Elizondo, John Shea, Paul Sorvino. **1993**

BAD GUYS ★★ A somewhat contrived story about two police officers who are suspended indefinitely, without pay. They decide to become professional wrestlers. Rated PG. 87m. **DIR:** Joel Silberg. **CAST:** Adam Baldwin, Mike Jolly, Michelle Nicastro, Ruth Buzzi, Sgt. Slaughter. **1985**

BADGE 373 ★★ This police drama casts Robert Duvall as a cop out to nab his partner's killer. Pretty routine stuff is thrown together in an even more routine fashion. Rated R. 116m. **DIR:** Howard W. Koch. **CAST:** Robert Duvall, Verna Bloom, Eddie Egan, Henry Darrow. **1973**

BAIL OUT ★★★ A funny, and often outright silly, action comedy about three bounty hunters who must bring the daughter of a millionaire to trial on drug charges. Lots of action and some great one-liners. Rated R. 88m. **DIR:** Max Kleven. **CAST:** Linda Blair, David Hasselhoff, John Vernon. **1988**

BAND OF THE HAND ★★½ A Vietnam vet (Stephen Lang) takes a group of incorrigible Florida teens and turns them into an anti-drug squad. That's right, it's *Mod Squad* for the 1980s and just as silly as it sounds. Rated R for profanity, brief nudity, cocaine use, and violence. 109m. **DIR:** Paul Michael Glaser. **CAST:** Stephen Lang, Michael Carmine, Lauren Holly, John Cameron Mitchell, Daniele Quinn, Leon Robinson, James Remar. **1986**

BARE KNUCKLES ★★★ A fun martial arts thriller about a modern-day bounty hunter on the trail of a vicious killer stalking women on the streets of the city. Rated R for brief nudity, violence, and adult language. 90m. **DIR:** Don Edmunds. **CAST:** Robert Viharo, Sherry Jackson, Michael Heit, Gloria Hendry, John Daniels. **1984**

BAT 21 ★★★★ In a typically effective performance, Gene Hackman is a military mastermind who is shot down during a reconnaissance mission in Vietnam, where he is trapped behind enemy lines. It's up to pilot Danny Glover to keep Hackman safe and sane until he can be rescued. Fine telling of a heroic, true-life story guarantees to keep you on the edge of your seat. Rated R for violence and profanity. 105m. **DIR:** Peter Markle. **CAST:** Gene Hackman, Danny Glover, Jerry Reed, David Marshall Grant. **1988**

BATAAN ★★★★½ One of the best films about World War II chronicles the exploits of an army patrol attempting to stall the Japanese onslaught in the Philippines. B&W; 114m. **DIR:** Tay Garnett. **CAST:** Robert Taylor, George Murphy, Thomas Mitchell, Lloyd Nolan, Robert Walker, Desi Arnaz Sr., Barry Nelson. **1943**

BATMAN (1989) ★★★½ So much of *Batman* is exciting, darkly funny, and awe-inspiring that one cannot help being disappointed when this ambitious production all but collapses under its own weight in the last half hour. Still, there's much to enjoy in Jack Nicholson's bizarre, over-the-top performance as the villainous Joker, Michael Keaton's underplayed but effective dual role as millionaire-playboy Bruce Wayne and Batman, and the spectacular, *Blade Runner*-like sets. Director Tim Burton may not have known when to stop, but no one can say he didn't give it his all. Rated PG-13 for profanity and violence. 130m. **DIR:** Tim Burton. **CAST:** Jack Nicholson, Michael Keaton, Kim Basinger, Pat Hingle, Billy Dee Williams, Jack Palance, Robert Wuhl, Michael Gough. **1989**

BATMAN AND ROBIN ★★½ The Caped Crusader and Boy Wonder swoop onto celluloid for the second time as they answer Police Commissioner Gordon's plea for help and run up against "The Wizard." Not really a great serial, but fun—and it avoids the unfortunate racism that makes the 1943 serial unpleasant. B&W; 15 chapters. **DIR:** Spencer Gordon Bennet. **CAST:** Robert Lowery, John Duncan, Lyle Talbot, Jane Adams, Ralph Graves, Don Harvey, Michael Whalen. **1949**

BATMAN RETURNS ★★★½ Director Tim Burton, still fascinated by grotesques, turns Danny DeVito into a villainous Penguin guaranteed to produce nightmares; Michelle Pfeiffer is seductively sensational as the Catwoman, a "wild card" whose every move is unpredictable. Set designer Bo Welch has a field day with his gloomy, "Machine-Age Teutonic" Gotham City. Although bound to please fans, this sequel is marred by its third major baddie—a goofy, fright-wigged Christopher Walken—and too few appearances by its star. Rated PG-13 for violence. 130m. **DIR:** Tim Burton. **CAST:** Michael Keaton, Danny DeVito, Michelle Pfeiffer, Christopher Walken, Pat Hingle, Michael Gough. **1992**

BATTLE BENEATH THE EARTH ★★½ Stalwart Kerwin Mathews leads the fight against the Chinese hordes who intend to invade the United States via underground tunnels. Pretty good adventure-fantasy in the comic-book/pulp magazine tradition. 91m. **DIR:** Montgomery Tully. **CAST:** Kerwin Mathews, Robert Ayres, Martin Benson, Viviane Ventura, Bessie Love. **1967**

BATTLE CRY ★★★ A platoon of Marines is followed into battle during World War II. The conflicts they face on the islands of the Pacific are contrasted to the emotional conflicts faced by their girlfriends at home. All in all, it is a successful piece of wartime fluff. 149m. **DIR:** Raoul Walsh. **CAST:** Van Heflin, Tab Hunter, Dorothy Malone, Anne Francis. **1955**

BATTLE FORCE ★★ The effect of war on the lives of two families, one American, the other German. Passable World War II adventure. 92m. **DIR:** Humphrey Longon. **CAST:** Henry Fonda, John Huston, Stacy Keach, Helmut Berger, Samantha Eggar. **1976**

BATTLE HELL ★★ More British stiff upper lip in this tale of the H.M.S. *Amethyst* battling the communist Chinese on the Yangtze River. Pretty standard war flick, overly long, but with some good battle footage. Not rated: some violence. 112m. **DIR:** Michael Anderson. **CAST:** Richard Todd, Akim Tamiroff, Keye Luke, William Hartnell, Donald Houston, Robert Urquhart, James Kenney. **1956**

BATTLE OF AUSTERLITZ, THE 🦃 This attempt to re-create the epic battle of the Napoleonic wars is slow, dull, abysmally dubbed, and generally uninspired. 123m. **DIR:** Abel Gance. **CAST:** Claudia Cardinale, Leslie Caron, Vittorio De Sica, Orson Welles. **1960**

BATTLE OF BRITAIN ★★½ It's a shame that a film that has a $12 million budget, a cast of characters straight from the British Who's Who of film and stage, great aerial photography, and a subject matter that deals with a vital period of British history could not have been better than this semiepic. 132m. **DIR:** Guy Hamilton. **CAST:** Michael Caine, Ralph Richardson, Robert Shaw, Trevor Howard, Susannah York, Curt Jurgens, Edward Fox, Kenneth More, Christopher Plummer, Laurence Olivier, Harry Andrews, Nigel Patrick. **1969**

BATTLE OF EL ALAMEIN, THE ★★★ A re-creation of the famous twelve-day 1942 turning point clash between the artillery, tanks, and infantry of the British Eighth Army under General Montgomery and the German army's fabled Afrika Korps commanded by Field Marshal Rommel in the windswept Libyan Desert southwest of Alexandria. We know the outcome, but getting there makes for exciting watching. Rated PG. 96m. **DIR:** Calvin Jackson Padget. **CAST:** Michael Rennie, Robert Hossein, Frederick Stafford, Ettore Manni, George Hilton. **1968**

BATTLE OF THE BULGE ★★ This is a fairly decent war film. It has solid acting and exciting battle sequences but suffers on video for two reasons: the small screen hurts the epic scale and 23 minutes are cut from the original print, with some important footage missing. 140m. **DIR:** Ken Annakin. **CAST:** Henry Fonda, Robert Shaw, Robert Ryan, Dana Andrews, Charles Bronson, Telly Savalas. **1965**

BATTLE OF THE COMMANDOS 🦃 Lots of phony battle scenes, bad acting, and a poor script all add up to a big bomb. 94m. **DIR:** Umberto Lenzi. **CAST:** Jack Palance, Curt Jurgens, Thomas Hunter, Diana Largo, Wolfgang Preiss. **1969**

BEAST, THE ★★ A clichéd war film, unique only for its adversaries: Soviet soldiers and Afghan rebels in the deserts of Afghanistan. Though the Afghans speak subtitled native language, the Soviets speak in slang-laced Americanized English. They sound more like California surfers than Russian soldiers. Rated R, with profanity and violence. 109m. **DIR:** Kevin Reynolds. **CAST:** Steven Bauer, George Dzundza. **1988**

BEAU GESTE ★★★★½ Gary Cooper fulfilled every idealistic boy's dream of honor, sacrifice, and brotherly love in this splendid adaptation of P. C. Wren's adventure classic. Director William Wellman took a handpicked cast to the desert wasteland near Yuma, Arizona, and painstakingly re-created the arid setting of the world's most famous Foreign Legion adventure using the silent-film version as his blueprint. The action is brisk and the characters are unforgettable. B&W; 114m. **DIR:** William Wellman. **CAST:** Gary Cooper, Robert Preston, Ray Milland, Brian Donlevy, J. Carrol Naish, Susan Hayward, Broderick Crawford, Albert Dekker, Donald O'Connor, James Stephenson. **1939**

BEHIND THE RISING SUN ★★½ The versatile J. Carrol Naish plays a Japanese publisher whose political views bring him into conflict with his son, educated in the United States. It all takes place when Japan was fighting China, not long before World War II. B&W; 89m. **DIR:** Edward Dmytryk. **CAST:** Margo, Tom Neal, J. Carrol Naish, Robert Ryan. **1943**

BEN-HUR (1959) ★★★★★ In this film, which won eleven Oscars, a wealthy Jewish nobleman during the time of Christ incurs the hostility of the Roman military governor, who was his childhood friend. He is reduced to manning an oar on a slave galley, and his family is sent to prison. Years later he returns to seek vengeance upon his Roman tormentor. This culminates in a spectacular chariot race. Charlton Heston won an Oscar for his first-rate performance in the title role. 211m. **DIR:** William Wyler. **CAST:** Charlton Heston, Jack Hawkins, Sam Jaffe, Stephen Boyd. **1959**

BENEATH THE 12-MILE REEF ★★★ Here is some good old-fashioned Hollywood entertainment. Film deals with sponge divers off the Florida coast. Light, enjoyable fluff. 102m. **DIR:** Robert D. Webb. **CAST:** Robert Wagner, Gilbert Roland, Terry Moore, Richard Boone. **1953**

BERETTA'S ISLAND 🦃 Former Mr. Universe Franco Columbu gets weighted down in this clumsy, low-budget action effort, playing a former Interpol agent out for revenge. Not rated, but contains violence. 97m. **DIR:** Michael Preece. **CAST:** Franco Columbu, Ken Kercheval, Jo Campa, Arnold Schwarzenegger. **1992**

BERLIN CONSPIRACY, THE 🦃 Separate American and East German investigations into germ warfare and Middle East terrorism are hindered by the fall of the Berlin Wall. Bland performances and bad German accents diminish this low-budget thriller. Rated R for violence and profanity. 83m. **DIR:** Terence H. Winkless. **CAST:** Marc Singer, Mary Crosby, Stephen Davies. **1991**

BERLIN EXPRESS ★★★½ A taut, crisply edited espionage thriller from the director of the original *Cat People*. Filmed in semidocumentary style, *Berlin Express* takes full advantage of post–World War II Germany, incorporating actual footage of bombed-out Frankfurt and Berlin into the drama. Thrown together on a train to Berlin, Robert Ryan as an American nutrition expert, Paul Lukas as a marked German statesman trying to reunite his war-torn country, and Merle Oberon as Lukas's aide all give standout performances. B&W; 86m. **DIR:** Jacques Tourneur. **CAST:** Merle Oberon, Robert Ryan, Charles Korvin, Paul Lukas, Robert Coote. **1948**

BERLIN TUNNEL 21 ★★ Richard Thomas stars as an American soldier in Berlin in 1961. His girlfriend cannot leave the eastern section of Berlin to join him. The solution: sneak her out. Predictable. 141m.

DIR: Richard Michaels. **CAST:** Richard Thomas, Horst Buchholz, José Ferrer, Jacques Breuer, Nicolas Farrell, Ute Christensen. **1981**

BEST KEPT SECRETS ★★★½ When a police officer is not promoted to the Special Information Unit, his wife (Patty Duke) decides to find out why. She discovers a secret file that the police department has been using for blacklisting purposes. This TV movie is guaranteed to keep your interest. 94m. **DIR:** Jerrold Freedman. **CAST:** Patty Duke, Frederic Forrest, Peter Coyote, Meg Foster. **1989**

BEST OF THE BEST ★★ An underdog U.S. national karate team battles for the world title in this martial arts *Rocky*. The numerous training montages, slow-motion fight scenes, and lessons in sportsmanship and courage all lead to a predictable, uplifting ending. Rated PG-13 for violence and language. 95m. **DIR:** Robert Radler. **CAST:** Eric Roberts, Phillip Rhee, Christopher Penn, James Earl Jones, Sally Kirkland, John P. Ryan. **1989**

BEST OF THE BEST 2 🦃 Three martial fu buddies from the original *Best* battle a Schwarzeneggeresque brute in an underworld Las Vegas gladiatorial arena that caters to decadent high rollers. Rated R for violence and language. 110m. **DIR:** Robert Radler. **CAST:** Eric Roberts, Phillip Rhee, Christopher Penn, Wayne Newton, Ralph Moeller, Meg Foster. **1993**

BEST REVENGE ★★½ Granger (John Heard), has come to Spain to team up with Bo (Levon Helm), who has promised him the contacts for a $4 million hashish deal. This fast-moving action-adventure has some good acting, but fails to rise above its pedestrian plot. 92m. **DIR:** John Trent. **CAST:** John Heard, Levon Helm, Alberta Watson, John Rhys-Davies. **1984**

BETRAYAL FROM THE EAST ★★ Fast-talking, wisecracking Lee Tracy takes on imperial Japan in this biased World War II espionage programmer. Peppered with the racial slurs and stereotypes so popular during this period. B&W; 82m. **DIR:** William Berke. **CAST:** Lee Tracy, Nancy Kelly, Regis Toomey, Richard Loo, Abner Biberman, Philip Ahn. **1945**

BETRAYED (1954) ★★½ In German-occupied Holland a secret agent called "The Scarf" terrorizes underground attempts to overthrow the Nazis. A dated movie and an obviously much older Clark Gable don't add up in spite of a good supporting cast and authentic European settings. 108m. **DIR:** Gottfried Reinhardt. **CAST:** Clark Gable, Lana Turner, Victor Mature, O. E. Hasse, Louis Calhern, Wilfrid Hyde-White, Ian Carmichael, Nora Swinburne, Roland Culver, Niall MacGinnis. **1954**

BEVERLY HILLS COP ★★★★ In this highly entertaining cops-and-comedy caper, Eddie Murphy plays a streetwise policeman from Detroit who takes a leave of absence to track down the men who killed his best friend. This quest takes him to the unfamiliar hills of ritzy southern California, where he's greeted as anything but a hero. Rated R for violence and profanity. 105m. **DIR:** Martin Brest. **CAST:** Eddie Murphy, Lisa Eilbacher, Judge Reinhold, John Ashton. **1984**

BEVERLY HILLS COP II ★★½ This sequel to *Beverly Hills Cop* lacks most of the charm and freshness of the first film, choosing instead to unwind as a thunderous, pounding assault on the senses. Eddie Murphy needs all his considerable talent to enliven this confusing mess, and he just manages to pull it off. Rated R for profanity and brief nudity. 102m. **DIR:** Tony Scott. **CAST:** Eddie Murphy, Judge Reinhold, Jurgen Prochnow, Ronny Cox, John Ashton, Brigitte Nielsen, Allen Garfield, Dean Stockwell. **1987**

BEVERLY HILLS COP 3 ★★★½ Detroit cop Axel Foley is back in Los Angeles fighting off thugs the LAPD can't handle. Eddie Murphy is in his element as the wisecracking cop and knows how to milk one-liners for laughs. Set in a California theme park with most of the characters from the first two films back on board. Rated R for language. 100m. **DIR:** John Landis. **CAST:** Eddie Murphy, Theresa Randle, Judge Reinhold, Hector Elizondo, Bronson Pinchot, Timothy Carhart, John Saxon, Alan Young, Stephen McHattie. **1994**

BEYOND ATLANTIS ★★ Unexciting movie about a motley bunch of adventurers looking for a fabulous treasure on an uncharted isle. Rated PG for mild violence. 89m. **DIR:** Eddie Romero. **CAST:** Patrick Wayne, John Ashley, Leigh Christian, Sid Haig. **1973**

BEYOND JUSTICE ★★½ A wealthy American hires mercenaries to rescue her son. Her Arab ex-husband has taken the spoiled brat to Morocco to become the next prince of the desert. Lots of guns, explosions, and bad acting. Rated R for profanity and violence. 113m. **DIR:** Duccio Tessari. **CAST:** Rutger Hauer, Carol Alt, Omar Sharif, Elliott Gould, Kabir Bedi. **1990**

BEYOND THE CALL OF DUTY ★★ Another mindless adventure film, this one set on the Mekong River Delta in Vietnam. In the middle of the war, soldier Jan-Michael Vincent finds himself risking his life to save a female journalist. Pedestrian and implausible, and just a tad too late to make an impact. Rated R for violence and language. 93m. **DIR:** Cirio H. Santiago. **CAST:** Jan-Michael Vincent, Jillian McWhirter. **1992**

BEYOND THE POSEIDON ADVENTURE 🦃 Michael Caine heads one of two salvage crews that race each other and time to probe the upside-down wreck of the *Poseidon*. Rated PG for mild violence and language. 114m. **DIR:** Irwin Allen. **CAST:** Michael Caine, Sally Field, Telly Savalas, Jack Warden, Peter Boyle. **1979**

BHOWANI JUNCTION ★★★½ An exciting, often stirring drama, of the movement of passive resistance started by Mahatma Gandhi in post-World War II India. Ava Gardner stars as an Anglo-Indian being stirred by her ties to the Sikhs and their cause. Unrated, but recommended for family viewing. 110m. **DIR:** George Cukor. **CAST:** Ava Gardner, Stewart Granger, Lionel Jeffries, Bill Travers. **1956**

BIG BAD JOHN ★★ Bayou bad boys take leave of the swamps, setting out on a trail of violence to settle an old score. This macho masher offers a heavyweight country-and-western soundtrack. Filmed in Colorado, Texas, and New Mexico. Rated R for violence. 86m. **DIR:** Burt Kennedy. **CAST:** Jimmy Dean, Jack Elam, Ned Beatty, Romy Windsor, Jeff Osterhage, Bo Hopkins. **1990**

BIG BAD MAMA ★★ Here's an okay film concerning a mother (Angie Dickinson), sort of a second-rate Ma Barker, leading her daughters on a robbery spree during the Depression. It's not a classic by any means, but the action keeps things moving along. Rated R for violence, nudity, and sex. 83m. **DIR:** Steve Carver. **CAST:** Angie Dickinson, Tom Skerritt, William Shatner, Joan Prather. **1974**

BIG BAD MAMA II 🦃 A shabby sequel to a so-so movie. Rated R for violence and nudity. 85m. **DIR:** Jim Wynorski. **CAST:** Angie Dickinson, Robert Culp, Danielle Brisebois, Julie McCullough, Bruce Glover. **1987**

BIG BIRD CAGE, THE ★★ Some of the women-in-prison movies that producer Roger Corman cranked out in the Seventies were worth seeing because some talented filmmakers brought a high level of ability and excitement to them. This, however, is one of the boring ones. Rated R for nudity and violence. 88m. **DIR:** Jack Hill. **CAST:** Pam Grier, Anitra Ford, Sid Haig. **1972**

BIG BLUE, THE 🦃 This underwater adventure drowns largely because Rosanna Arquette attempts to recreate her ditzy *Desperately Seeking Susan* persona. Underwater shots are the only plus. Rated PG for mature themes. 118m. **DIR:** Luc Besson. **CAST:** Rosanna Arquette, Jean-Marc Barr, Jean Reno, Griffin Dunne. **1988**

BIG BRAWL, THE ★★★ Director Robert Clouse again fails to reach the heights attained with his *Enter the Dragon*. Nevertheless, this kung fu comedy has its moments—most provided by star Jackie Chan. 95m. **DIR:** Robert Clouse. **CAST:** Jackie Chan, José Ferrer, Kristine DeBell, Mako. **1980**

BIG BUST OUT, THE 🦃 Four female convicts escape from a prison somewhere in the Middle East when they are sent to do janitorial work at a convent. Idiotic. 75m. **DIR:** Richard Jackson. **CAST:** Vonetta McGee, Karen Carter, Linda Fox, Monica Taylor. **1973**

BIG CAT, THE ★★★ A marauding mountain lion complicates feuding between high country ranchers in this enjoyable adventure film. 75m. **DIR:** Phil Karlson. **CAST:** Lon McCallister, Preston Foster, Forrest Tucker. **1949**

BIG COMBO, THE ★★★ A classic American gangster film done in the *film noir* style. Cornel Wilde has the starring role as a half-crazed policeman who is after gangsters and will do whatever is necessary to get them. Quite violent for its time and very well photographed, with an exciting climax. B&W; 89m. **DIR:** Joseph H. Lewis. **CAST:** Cornel Wilde, Jean Wallace, Richard Conte. **1955**

BIG EASY, THE ★★★★ Everything is easy in the Big Easy (a.k.a. New Orleans) for slick and only slightly sleazy police lieutenant Remy McSwain (Dennis Quaid). That is, until Anne Osbourne (Ellen Barkin), an upright and uptight assistant district attorney, comes along. *The Big Easy* is a wild, southern-style variation on the old-fashioned cop films of the Thirties and Forties. Rated R for violence, profanity, and sensuality. 100m. **DIR:** Jim McBride. **CAST:** Dennis Quaid, Ellen Barkin, Ned Beatty, John Goodman, Lisa Jane Persky, Ebbe Roe Smith, Tom O'Brien, Charles Ludlam. **1987**

BIG HEAT, THE ★★★★ A crackerjack classic of crime *film noir*. Homicide detective Dave Bannion (Glenn Ford) is bent on solving the puzzle of an unexpected suicide of a fellow police officer, even though he is told by his superiors to leave bad enough alone. Exceptional acting, especially by Lee Marvin and Gloria Grahame. B&W; 90m. **DIR:** Fritz Lang. **CAST:** Glenn Ford, Gloria Grahame, Jocelyn Brando, Alexander Scourby, Lee Marvin, Jeanette Nolan, Carolyn Jones. **1953**

BIG RED ONE, THE ★★★★½ This release gave Lee Marvin his best role in years. As a grizzled sergeant leading a platoon of "wetnoses" into the dangers of battle, he's excellent. Based on writer-director Sam Fuller's personal reminiscences of World War II. It's a terrific war movie. Rated PG. 113m. **DIR:** Samuel Fuller. **CAST:** Lee Marvin, Mark Hamill, Robert Carradine, Bobby DiCicco. **1980**

BIG SCORE, THE ★★½ Fred Williamson breaks all the rules in going after drug king Joe Spinell. Williamson, the director, doesn't make the story move fast enough. Rated R for violence and profanity. 85m. **DIR:** Fred Williamson. **CAST:** Fred Williamson, John Saxon, Richard Roundtree, Nancy Wilson, Ed Lauter, Joe Spinell, Michael Dante. **1983**

BIG SLICE, THE ★★ Two writers decide to make their lives exciting. Between phone sex and police raids, the plot expands into one big mess. Rated R for violence and suggested sex. 86m. **DIR:** John Bradshaw. **CAST:** Heather Locklear, Casey Siemaszko, Leslie Hope,

Justin Lewis, Kenneth Welsh, Nicholas Campbell, Henry Ramer. **1990**

BIG STEAL, THE ★★★½ Four sets of desperate and disparate characters chase each other over bumpy roads in the Southwest and Mexico following a robbery. An intriguing film, somewhat difficult to follow but great fun to watch. B&W; 71m. **DIR:** Don Siegel. **CAST:** Robert Mitchum, Jane Greer, William Bendix, Ramon Novarro, Patric Knowles. **1949**

BIG SWEAT, THE 🦃 A born loser finds himself running from the law soon after his prison release. Not rated, but contains profanity and violence. 85m. **DIR:** Ulli Lommel. **CAST:** Steve Molone, Robert Z'dar. **1990**

BIG SWITCH, THE 🦃 When a stylish, jet-setting gambler gets caught up in a one-night stand with a mysterious and beautiful female, he unwittingly becomes the central figure in a story of intrigue. Rated R. 68m. **DIR:** Pete Walker. **CAST:** Sebastian Breaks, Virginia Wetherell. **1969**

BIG TREES, THE ★★½ Lumberman Kirk Douglas wants the redwoods on homesteaders' land in this colorful adventure set in northwest California in 1900. A remake of 1938's *Valley of the Giants*. 89m. **DIR:** Felix Feist. **CAST:** Kirk Douglas, Eve Miller, Patrice Wymore, Edgar Buchanan, John Archer, Alan Hale Jr. **1952**

BIG TROUBLE IN LITTLE CHINA ★★★½ An adventure-fantasy with Kurt Russell as a pig trucker unwittingly swept into a mystical world underneath San Francisco's Chinatown ruled by a sinister 2,000-year-old ghost. The movie is a lighthearted special-effects showcase designed to look a bit silly, in the style of old serials. Rated PG-13. 99m. **DIR:** John Carpenter. **CAST:** Kurt Russell, Kim Cattrall, Dennis Dun, James Hong, Victor Wong, Kate Burton. **1986**

BILLY JACK ★★½ A film that seems to suggest that a good kick in the groin will bring "peace and love," *Billy Jack* was a box-office sensation. The star, Tom Laughlin, produced and directed. Rated PG. 114m. **DIR:** Tom Laughlin. **CAST:** Tom Laughlin, Delores Taylor, Clark Howat, Bert Freed, Julie Webb. **1971**

BIRD OF PARADISE ★★½ Even the reliable Joel McCrea can't save this bit of South Sea island silliness. The seafaring McCrea attempts to woo native princess Dolores Del Rio. This kind of thing looks awfully dumb today. B&W; 80m. **DIR:** King Vidor. **CAST:** Joel McCrea, Dolores Del Rio, John Halliday, Skeets Gallagher, Lon Chaney Jr. **1932**

BIRD ON A WIRE ★★½ Formulaic action-comedy casts Goldie Hawn as a hotshot corporate lawyer and Mel Gibson as a mystery man from her past. A promising plot is eschewed in favor of madcap chases. Rated PG-13 for profanity, violence, and nudity. 106m. **DIR:** John Badham. **CAST:** Mel Gibson, Goldie Hawn, David Carradine, Bill Duke, Joan Severance. **1990**

BIRDS OF PREY ★★★★ Ex–World War II fighter pilot turned peacetime Salt Lake City traffic helicopter jockey (David Janssen) hears the siren song of war anew when he witnesses a bank heist in progress and chases the robbers, who make their getaway in their own 'copter. An aerial battle of wits follows. Terrific flying sequences. 81m. **DIR:** William A. Graham. **CAST:** David Janssen, Ralph Meeker, Elayne Heilveil. **1973**

BLACK ARROW, THE (1948) ★★★½ Hero Louis Hayward is in fine form as he fights the evil George Macready in this highly enjoyable entry into the swashbuckler genre. Some fine action scenes, with a slam-bang finale. B&W; 76m. **DIR:** Gordon Douglas. **CAST:** Louis Hayward, George Macready, Janet Blair, Edgar Buchanan. **1948**

BLACK BELT JONES ★★★ A likable kung fu action film about a self-defense school in Watts combating a "Mafioso"-type group. Not a classic film, but an easy pace and good humor make this a fun action movie. Rated PG for violence. 87m. **DIR:** Robert Clouse. **CAST:** Jim Kelly, Scatman Crothers, Gloria Hendry. **1974**

BLACK CAESAR ★★ In this passable gangster flick, Fred Williamson stars as Tommy Gibbs, bloodthirsty, gun-wielding Godfather of Harlem. The soundtrack by the Godfather of Soul, James Brown, doesn't hurt. Rated R. 92m. **DIR:** Larry Cohen. **CAST:** Fred Williamson, Art Lund, Val Avery, Julius W. Harris, William Wellman Jr., D'Urville Martin, Gloria Hendry. **1973**

BLACK COBRA 3 🦃 The CIA has been sending military aid to insurgent forces in a Third World country ripped by war. Rated R for violence. 89m. **DIR:** Dan Edwards. **CAST:** Fred Williamson, Forry Smith, Debra Ward. **1990**

BLACK EAGLE ★★½ A decent martial arts flick about a CIA agent (Sho Kosugi) sent to recover a top-secret laser-tracking device from a U.S. fighter downed in the Mediterranean. The KGB has also sent a man (Jean-Claude Van Damme), and the two agents do the international tango. Rated R for violence. 93m. **DIR:** Eric Karson. **CAST:** Sho Kosugi, Jean-Claude Van Damme, Vladimir Skomarovsky, Doran Clark. **1988**

BLACK GESTAPO, THE 🦃 Violent blaxploitation movie set in the Watts section of L.A. during 1965, when it was the location of rioting. Rated R. 88m. **DIR:** Lee Frost. **CAST:** Rod Perry, Charles P. Robinson, Phil Hoover. **1975**

BLACK GODFATHER, THE ★★★ Public spirited black gangsters take time out from their more nefarious activities to keep the Mafia from selling heroin in their neighborhood. Unpretentious exploitation drama with plenty of action. Rated R for sexual situations and violence. 96m. **DIR:** John Evans. **CAST:** Rod Perry. **1974**

BLACK ICE ★★ When mystery woman Joanna Pacula drops by for her usual rendezvous with a married politician, things get out of hand and he dies. Low-impact thriller. Rated R for nudity, violence, and language. Unrated version contains more of the same. 90m. **DIR:** Neill L. Fearnley. **CAST:** Michael Ironside, Michael Nouri, Joanna Pacula. **1992**

BLACK JACK ★★★ George Sanders is soldier of fortune Michael Alexander who has a drug-smuggling scheme in Tangiers aboard his yacht, the *Black Jack*. Despite the initial feeling that this is a dated film, the twists in plot will hold viewers' attentions. B&W; 103m. **DIR:** Julien Duvivier. **CAST:** George Sanders, Herbert Marshall, Agnes Moorehead, Patricia Roc, Marcel Dalio. **1949**

BLACK KLANSMAN, THE 🦃 This exploitative melodrama follows the efforts of a light-skinned black musician to avenge the death of his daughter, killed when the Ku Klux Klan bombed a church. Unrated, but includes violence and sexual situations. B&W; 88m. **DIR:** Ted V. Mikels. **CAST:** Richard Gilden, Rima Kutner. **1966**

BLACK MOON RISING ★★ The only redeeming point of this little car theft number is its occasional accent on humor. The cast is top-notch, but the material is mostly pedestrian. Rated R for language, nudity, sex, and some rather gruesome violence. 93m. **DIR:** Harley Cokliss. **CAST:** Tommy Lee Jones, Linda Hamilton, Robert Vaughn, Richard Jaeckel, Lee Ving, Bubba Smith. **1986**

BLACK PIRATE, THE ★★★½ One of superstar Douglas Fairbanks's most popular films, this early color production packs enough thrills for a dozen pictures. Written by Fairbanks, *Pirate* contains a duel to the death with cutlasses on the beach, a daring underwater raid on a pirate ship, and one of the most famous of all movie stunts: Fairbanks's ride down the ship's sail on a knife, cleverly achieved with an apparatus hidden from the camera. Silent. B&W; 122m. **DIR:** Albert Parker. **CAST:** Douglas Fairbanks Sr., Donald Crisp, Billie Dove, Anders Randolph. **1926**

BLACK RAIN (1989) ★★★★ Michael Douglas gives a solid performance in this nonstop action film as a maverick New York cop who is assigned to deliver a Yakuza gangster to the Japanese authorities, only to allow him to escape upon arrival at the airport. Despite protests from the Japanese police, Douglas insists on staying on to help recapture the escaped criminal, and it is up to Ken Takakura (so memorable in *The Yakuza* with Robert Mitchum) to baby-sit the hot-tempered American detective. Rated R for violence and profanity. 110m. **DIR:** Ridley Scott. **CAST:** Michael Douglas, Andy Garcia, Ken Takakura, Kate Capshaw. **1989**

BLACK VEIL FOR LISA, A ★★ Serviceable gangster melodrama with John Mills as the token Anglo star imported to Rome to make the movie marketable outside Italy. Tolerable action flick, if a trifle talky. Not rated. 88m. **DIR:** Massimo Dallamano. **CAST:** John Mills, Luciana Paluzzi, Robert Hoffman. **1968**

BLACKBEARD THE PIRATE ★★★ Entertaining pirate yarn with some good action and fine characterizations. Gorgeous Linda Darnell is the charming damsel in distress. In the title role, Robert Newton is a bit overzealous at times, but puts in a fine performance. Go for it. 99m. **DIR:** Raoul Walsh. **CAST:** Robert Newton, Linda Darnell, William Bendix, Keith Andes. **1952**

BLACKBELT ★★ A martial arts instructor protects a rising pop star from a psychopathic fan. Some good action sequences make this film stand out a little from other fight flicks. Rated R for nudity, profanity, and graphic violence. 90m. **DIR:** Charles Philip Moore. **CAST:** Don "The Dragon" Wilson, Matthias Hues, Richard Beymer. **1992**

BLACKBELT 2: FATAL FORCE ★★ A wanna-be epic martial arts action film. It has Vietnam vets, heroin junkies, heavily armed elite missions forces, gunrunners, karate cops—one black, one white—and a strip club for good measurement. Rated R for violence, profanity, and nudity. 83m. **DIR:** Jim Avellana, Kevin Tent. **CAST:** Blake Bahner, Ronald William Lawrence, Roxanne Baird, Michael Vlastas. **1993**

BLACKOUT (1978) ★★★ At times, this movie, about a New York City apartment building attacked by a gang of escaped criminals during a blackout, reeks of a disaster film. Still, there are good action scenes and enough drama to make you almost forget the shortcomings. Rated R for violence. 86m. **DIR:** Eddy Matalon. **CAST:** Jim Mitchum, Robert Carradine, Belinda Montgomery, June Allyson, Jean-Pierre Aumont, Ray Milland. **1978**

BLADE ★★★ Middle-aged New York detective Blade (John Marley) stalks the psycho who murdered the daughter of a powerful right-wing congressman. Along the way he uncovers a lot of other goings-on in the naked city. The story's not much, but TV addicts can count the faces that later went on hit shows (*Barney Miller*'s Steve Landesberg, *The Love Boat*'s Ted Lange, *McMillan and Wife*'s John Schuck). Rated R for violence. 90m. **DIR:** Ernest Pintoff. **CAST:** John Marley, Jon Cypher, Kathryn Walker, William Prince, Michael McGuire, Joe Santos, John Schuck, Keene Curtis, Ted Lange, Marshall Efron, Steve Landesberg. **1973**

BLADE MASTER, THE 🦃 Muscleman Miles O'Keeffe chops his way across the countryside battling nasty sorcerers and spirits in a quest to conquer evil. Rated PG. 92m. **DIR:** David Hills. **CAST:** Miles O'Keeffe, Lisa Foster. **1984**

BLAKE OF SCOTLAND YARD ★★½ A power-mad count offers a king's ransom to the man who helps him to obtain a death-dealing device, and a mysterious cloaked character called The Scorpion begins a reign of terror in his campaign to secure the weapon. Made by Victory Pictures, a bargain-basement independent producer, this cliffhanger lacks the values that Universal or Republic put into their product, but it's still fun. B&W; 15 chapters. **DIR:** Robert Hill. **CAST:** Ralph Byrd, Lloyd Hughes, Joan Barclay, Herbert Rawlinson, Dickie Jones, Bob Terry, Nick Stuart. **1937**

BLASTFIGHTER 🦃 Michael Sopkiw is a dull ex-convict trying to clean up an immoral populace. Not rated, but contains violence. 93m. **DIR:** John Old Jr. **CAST:** Michael Sopkiw, Valerie Blake, George Eastman, Mike Miller. **1984**

BLIND FURY ★★★ In this outrageously violent, tongue-in-cheek martial arts movie, Rutger Hauer stars as a blind swordsman who comes to the aid of an army buddy (Terry O'Quinn) when the latter is kidnapped by gangsters and forced to make designer drugs. Directed in a completely over-the-top fashion by Phillip Noyce, *Blind Fury* is a real hoot. Rated R for violence and profanity. 86m. **DIR:** Phillip Noyce. **CAST:** Rutger Hauer, Terry O'Quinn, Brandon Call, Lisa Blount, Randall "Tex" Cobb. **1990**

BLIND RAGE 🦃 If you really believe that four blind men could rob a bank during business hours, you deserve this film. Rated R for violence and profanity. 81m. **DIR:** Efren C. Pinion. **CAST:** D'Urville Martin, Leo Fong, Tony Ferrer, Dick Adair, Darnell Garcia, Charlie Davao, Leila Hermosa, Fred Williamson, Jessie Crowder. **1978**

BLIND VENGEANCE ★★★½ Gerald McRaney plays the father of a grown son killed by small-town white supremacist Lane Smith and two goons. Rather than blindly orchestrate a bloodbath, McRaney simply shadows his prey... always watching, masked behind dark sunglasses, and waiting for them to panic. Intelligent made-for-cable melodrama. Rated R for violence and profanity. 93m. **DIR:** Lee Philips. **CAST:** Gerald McRaney, Lane Smith, Marg Helgenberger. **1990**

BLINDSIDE ★★ Only the acting talent of Harvey Keitel distinguishes this would-be suspense film yawner. Keitel stars as a former surveillance expert who discovers a murder plot. Rated R for violence and profanity. 102m. **DIR:** Paul Lynch. **CAST:** Harvey Keitel, Lori Hallier, Allen Fawcett. **1988**

BLINK OF AN EYE ★★ Psychic soldier Michael Paré is called into action to rescue the daughter of a rich American from the grasp of Third World terrorists. Interesting premise gets so-so attention from cast and writer. Rated R for violence and language. 90m. **DIR:** Bob Misiorowski. **CAST:** Michael Paré, Janis Lee. **1992**

BLOOD ALLEY ★★ Humphrey Bogart was originally set to star opposite wife Lauren Bacall in this story of a merchant marine captain helping Chinese refugees make it to Hong Kong, but he dropped out. For die-hard Duke Wayne fans only. 115m. **DIR:** William Wellman. **CAST:** John Wayne, Lauren Bacall, Paul Fix, Mike Mazurki. **1955**

BLOOD AND GUNS 🦃 Orson Welles's screen presence is at a loss in this dull action yarn about three men whose lives intertwine after the Mexican revolution. Rated R for profanity and violence. 90m. **DIR:** Giulio Petroni. **CAST:** Orson Welles, Tomas Milian, John Steiner. **1968**

BLOOD IN THE STREETS ★★ In this French-Italian film, a prison warden (Oliver Reed) is forced to release a prisoner as ransom for his kidnapped wife. There are some exciting chase scenes in this overall so-so film. Rated R for sex, nudity, language, and violence. 111m. **DIR:** Sergio Sollima. **CAST:** Oliver Reed, Fabio Testi, Agostina Belli. **1974**

BLOOD OF HEROES ★★½ Fairly decent hybrid of *Rollerball* and *Road Warrior* about bush-league team of wannabes playing a brutal no-holds-barred combination of hockey, squash, and football. Rutger Hauer stars as a former star of the game who takes the team to the majors. Rated R for violence, nudity, profanity, and simulated sex. 91m. **DIR:** David Peoples. **CAST:** Rutger Hauer, Joan Chen. **1989**

BLOOD ON THE BADGE 🦃 When a cop's partner is killed by terrorists, he goes on an unbelievable one-man campaign of revenge. A truly poor film. Not rated, but contains profanity and violence. 92m. **DIR:** Bret McCormick. **CAST:** Joe Estevez, David Harrod. **1992**

BLOOD ON THE SUN ★★★½ This hard-hitting action-drama finds James Cagney fighting Japanese military and government men in Japan just before World War II. An unusual plot and good pace make this worth watching. B&W; 98m. **DIR:** Frank Lloyd. **CAST:** James Cagney, Robert Armstrong, Wallace Ford, Sylvia Sidney. **1945**

BLOODFIST ★★ Typical martial arts chop-out, peopled by actual World Kickboxing Association champs, karate kings, and a wealth of other unsightly folks who just can't act. Forgettable. Rated R for ketchup. 86m. **DIR:** Terence H. Winkless. **CAST:** Don "The Dragon" Wilson, Bob Kaman. **1989**

BLOODFIST 2 ★★ In this martial arts flick, lightweight kick-boxing champ Don Wilson goes to the Philippines and falls into a trap set by the ruler of an island fortress. A rip-off of the genre-classic *Enter the Dragon.* Rated R for nudity, violence, and profanity. 85m. **DIR:** Andy Blumenthal. **CAST:** Don "The Dragon" Wilson. **1989**

BLOODFIST III: FORCED TO FIGHT ★★ This sequel finds star Don "The Dragon" Wilson as a new convict forced into being a target for various prison gangs. Rated R for violence and profanity. 90m. **DIR:** Oley Sassone. **CAST:** Don "The Dragon" Wilson, Richard Roundtree, Richard Paul. **1991**

BLOODFIST IV—DIE TRYING ★★ Repo man Don "The Dragon" Wilson finds himself up against the CIA, FBI, and international terrorists. Plenty of martial arts action. Rated R for violence and profanity. 86m. **DIR:** Paul Ziller. **CAST:** Don "The Dragon" Wilson, Cat Sassoon, Amanda Wyss, Kale Brown, Liz Torres, James Tolkan. **1992**

BLOODFIST V: HUMAN TARGET ★★ Serviceable martial arts entry features Don "The Dragon" Wilson as an undercover FBI agent who, while suffering amnesia is pegged as a double agent. He must fight for his life while fighting to regain his memory. Rated R for violence and adult language. 84m. **DIR:** Jeff Yonis. **CAST:** Don "The Dragon" Wilson, Denice Duff, Danny Lopez, Steve James. **1994**

BLOODMATCH 🦃 Senseless vengefest as a man seeks the five people who fixed a kick boxing contest five years earlier. Unrated, but contains excessive violence and profanity as well as a sprinkling of nudity. 87m. **DIR:** Albert Pyun. **CAST:** Benny Urquidez, Thom Mathews. **1991**

BLOODSPORT ★★ Jean-Claude Van Damme plays a martial arts master who arrives in Hong Kong to compete in the *kumite*, a violent championship contest. The fighting sequences are tremendous, but the framing story offers only clichés. Rated R for violence and language. 100m. **DIR:** Newt Arnold. **CAST:** Jean-Claude Van Damme, Donald Gibb, Leah Ayres, Normann Burton, Forest Whitaker, Bolo Yeung. **1987**

BLOODSTONE ★★ An adventure film in the tradition of *Raiders of the Lost Ark,* this falls short of the mark. The story involves newlyweds who become involved in a jewel heist in the Middle East. Loaded with humor and lots of action, but marred by poor performances. Rated PG-13 for violence. 90m. **DIR:** Dwight H. Little. **CAST:** Brett Stimely. **1988**

BLOODY MAMA ★★½ Shelley Winters plays Ma Barker in this gangster flick. Her four sons share her notoriety as Depression-era bandits. Rated R. 90m. **DIR:** Roger Corman. **CAST:** Shelley Winters, Don Stroud, Pat Hingle, Robert Walden, Bruce Dern, Robert De Niro. **1970**

BLOWING WILD 🦃 Wildcat Barbara Stanwyck lusts almost in vain for Gary Cooper in this foul tale of bandits in the Mexican oil fields. 90m. **DIR:** Hugo Fregonese. **CAST:** Gary Cooper, Barbara Stanwyck, Anthony Quinn, Ruth Roman, Ward Bond. **1953**

BLOWN AWAY (1994) ★★★½ A grudge fight turns into an explosive situation as a bomb-squad expert must deal with a mad bomber he once put away. Tommy Lee Jones holds this good, but not great film together with another strong villainous performance. Rated R for language and violence. 120m. **DIR:** Stephen Hopkins. **CAST:** Jeff Bridges, Tommy Lee Jones, Lloyd Bridges, Suzy Amis, Forest Whitaker. **1994**

BLUE LIGHTING, THE ★★ Lightweight action movie starring Sam Elliott as a hired gun sent to Australia to retrieve a precious gem from IRA renegade Robert Culp. Culp knows Elliott's coming and sets a series of traps for him. A passable time waster. Rated PG. 95m. **DIR:** Lee Philips. **CAST:** Sam Elliott, Robert Culp, Rebecca Gilling. **1986**

BLUE MAX, THE ★★★ For those with a yen for excellent aerial-combat gymnastics, superb photography, and a fine Jerry Goldsmith music score, this is the film. The story line is quite a different matter. Seen from the eyes of Kaiser Wilhelm II, air aces, and their superior officers, the plot is very standard material. The cast is fine but somewhat restrained. See it for the marvelous dogfights. You can tolerate the story. 156m. **DIR:** John Guillermin. **CAST:** George Peppard, James Mason, Ursula Andress, Jeremy Kemp. **1966**

BLUE STEEL (1990) ★★ Female rookie cop gets involved with a Wall Street broker who turns out to be a serial killer in this lurid, visually stunning thriller. The film's high-gloss photography, however, doesn't fully compensate for the often ridiculous story line. Rated R. 102m. **DIR:** Kathryn Bigelow. **CAST:** Jamie Lee Curtis, Ron Silver, Clancy Brown, Elizabeth Peña, Louise Fletcher. **1990**

BLUE THUNDER ★★★★½ A state-of-the-art helicopter is the centerpiece of this action-paced police melodrama. Piloted by Roy Scheider, the craft—a.k.a. "Blue Thunder"—battles a second rogue helicopter commanded by villain Malcolm McDowell high above the crowded streets of downtown Los Angeles. The result is a gripping and immensely entertaining—if somewhat implausible—adventure-thriller. Rated R for violence, nudity, and profanity. 109m. **DIR:** John Badham. **CAST:** Roy Scheider, Malcolm McDowell, Candy Clark, Warren Oates. **1983**

BLUE TORNADO ★★ *Blue Tornado* starts out wanting to be *Top Gun* and ends trying to be *E.T., The Extra-Terrestrial.* It fails on both levels. Some impressive aerial shots save the film. Rated PG-13. 96m. **DIR:** Tony Dobb. **CAST:** Dirk Benedict, Ted McGinley, Patsy Kensit. **1990**

BMX BANDITS ★★★ An exciting story of young Australian kids and their BMX bikes. Features great stunts, funny East End of London villains, and a satisfying ending. Not Rated. 92m. **DIR:** Brian Trenchard-Smith. **CAST:** David Argue, John Ley, Nicole Kidman. **1983**

BOBBIE JO AND THE OUTLAW ★½ Lynda Carter, hungry for excitement, tags along with Marjoe Gortner and his gang. An orgy of murders and robberies ensues. Lots of violence, little credibility. Rated R for nudity, violence, and profanity. 89m. **DIR:** Mark L. Lester. **CAST:** Marjoe Gortner, Lynda Carter, Jesse Vint, Merrie Lynn Ross, Belinda Balaski, Gerrit Graham. **1976**

BODY SLAM ★★ A down-and-out rock 'n' roll promotional manager signs up a couple of renegade professional wrestlers to go on a barnstorming tour. Although this film is silly, it has a lot of heart. Rated PG for mild violence. 92m. **DIR:** Hal Needham. **CAST:** Dirk Benedict, Tanya Roberts, Roddy Piper, Lou Albano, Barry Gordon. **1987**

BOILING POINT ★★★ Cop Wesley Snipes attempts to snare the crook (Dennis Hopper) who masterminded the drug-rip-off-related killing of another officer. Action buffs will be pleased by the high-octane storytelling style of filmmaker James B. Harris, who relies a bit too much on contrivance. Rated R for profanity, violence, and suggested sex. 92m. **DIR:** James B. Harris. **CAST:** Wesley Snipes, Dennis Hopper, Lolita Davidovich, Dan Hedaya, Viggo Mortensen, Seymour Cassel, Jonathan Banks, Christine Elise, Tony Lo Bianco, Valerie Perrine, James Tolkan. **1993**

BOMBARDIER ★★★½ This is a solid action film dealing with the training of flyers during World War II. There is nothing new in the familiar formula of this film, but a good cast and fast pace make it enjoyable. B&W; 99m. **DIR:** Richard Wallace. **CAST:** Pat O'Brien, Randolph Scott, Eddie Albert, Robert Ryan, Anne Shirley, Barton MacLane. **1943**

BONNIE AND CLYDE ★★★★★ This still fresh and innovative gangster film was one of the first to depict graphic violence, turning the genre inside out, combining comedy, bloodshed, pathos, and social commentary with fascinating results. 111m. **DIR:** Arthur Penn. **CAST:** Warren Beatty, Faye Dunaway, Gene Hackman, Estelle Parsons, Michael J. Pollard, Gene Wilder. **1967**

BONNIE'S KIDS ★★½ Two amoral girls molested by their stepfather kill him and move in with their criminal uncle. Lots of action, but all rather pointless. Rated R for simulated sex, nudity, adult themes, and violence. 105m. **DIR:** Arthur Marks. **CAST:** Tiffany Bolling, Steve Sandor, Robin Mattson, Scott Brady. **1982**

BORDER, THE ★★★½ Jack Nicholson is first-rate in this often effective drama about a border patrol officer who rebels against the corruption in his department and the rampant greed of his wife, Valerie Perrine. Rated R. 107m. **DIR:** Tony Richardson. **CAST:** Jack Nicholson, Harvey Keitel, Valerie Perrine, Warren Oates, Elpidia Carrillo. **1982**

BORDER HEAT 🦃 This action flick, set in Texas, has all the excitement of a siesta. Rated R for violence. 93m. **DIR:** Tony Gaudioz. **CAST:** Darlanne Fluegel, John Vernon. **1988**

BORDERLINE ★★★½ Charles Bronson gives one of his better portrayals in this release, which got the jump on the similar *The Border*, with Jack Nicholson, by nearly two years. As in the later film, the central character—a border guard—becomes involved with the problems of an illegal alien and her child. The result is a watchable action film. Rated R. 105m. **DIR:** Jerrold Freedman. **CAST:** Charles Bronson, Bruno Kirby, Bert Remsen, Ed Harris, Wilford Brimley. **1980**

BORN AMERICAN 🦃 Three high school buddies cross the Russian border while on summer vacation in Lapland. Rated R for sex and violence. 103m. **DIR:** Renny Harlin. **CAST:** Mike Norris, Steve Durham, David Coburn, Albert Salmi, Thalmus Rasulala. **1986**

BORN KILLER 🦃 Teenagers on an outing cross paths with two vicious convicts who torture them and leave them for dead. They're the lucky ones: they don't have to sit through this mess. 90m. **DIR:** Kimberley Casey. **CAST:** Ted Prior, Ty Hardin. **1990**

BORN LOSERS ★★★ This biker exploitation movie is better than the celebrated *Billy Jack*, which also starred Tom Laughlin. Granted, we still have to sit through scenes with terrible amateur actors, but at least there is no girl singing off-key about her brother being dead. 112m. **DIR:** T. C. Frank. **CAST:** Tom Laughlin, Elizabeth James, Jeremy Slate, William Wellman Jr., Robert Tessier. **1967**

BORN TO RACE 🦃 This clunker of a film couldn't get off the starting line. Rated R for nudity, simulated sex, violence, and profanity. 95m. **DIR:** James Fargo. **CAST:** Joseph Bottoms, Robert Logan, Marc Singer, George Kennedy. **1988**

BORN TO RIDE ★★★½ A smirking, rebellious, yet likable John Stamos stars as a 1930s motorcycle pioneer with this choice: a year behind bars or an army assignment training the cavalry for a motorcycle mission in Spain. Rated PG for violence and profanity. 90m. **DIR:** Graham Baker. **CAST:** John Stamos, John Stockwell, Teri Polo, Sandy McPeak. **1991**

BORN TO RUN ★★ Acceptable made-for-TV take on teen angst is a good showcase for star Richard Grieco but little else. He's a street racer who must put everything on the line when his brother gets involved with the mob. Pretty predictable. 97m. **DIR:** Albert Magnoli. **CAST:** Richard Grieco, Joe Cortese, Jay Acovone, Shelli Lether. **1993**

BORSALINO ★★★½ Style over substance—and when the result is *this* stylish, that's a major triumph. Jean-Paul Belmondo and Alain Delon are friendly rival gangsters in 1930s Marseilles. Everything is geared to make this an eye-filling, fast-paced romp. The only liability: English dubbing of the French dialogue. Rated PG. 125m. **DIR:** Jacques Deray. **CAST:** Jean-Paul Belmondo, Alain Delon, Michel Bouquet, Catherine Rouvel. **1970**

BOTANY BAY ★★½ Alan Ladd stars as an unjustly accused criminal aboard a ship about to establish a penal colony in British-occupied Australia. He finds himself confronting a cruel captain (James Mason) and romancing a beautiful young actress (Patricia Medina). Atmospheric costume drama. 94m. **DIR:** John Farrow. **CAST:** Alan Ladd, James Mason, Patricia Medina. **1953**

BOUND AND GAGGED: A LOVE STORY ★★½ Ginger Lynn Allen is kidnapped by her friends, Elizabeth Saltarrelli and Chris Denton, and taken on a wild ride through backwoods Minnesota, terrorizing locals and gangsters alike. Complications really set in when Saltarrelli declares her love for Allen. Fun road trip has some potholes, but steers the course. Rated R for language, adult situations, and violence. 96m. **DIR:** Daniel Appleby. **CAST:** Ginger Lynn Allen, Elizabeth Saltarrelli, Chris Mulkey, Karen Black, Chris Denton. **1993**

BOUNTY, THE ★★★★ Mel Gibson is Fletcher Christian, and Anthony Hopkins is Captain William Bligh in this, the fourth and most satisfying screen version of *The Mutiny on the Bounty.* This sweeping seafaring epic from the director of *Smash Palace* is the first movie to present the historic events accurately—and to do so fascinatingly. Rated PG for nudity and violence. 132m. **DIR:** Roger Donaldson. **CAST:** Mel Gibson, Anthony Hopkins, Laurence Olivier, Edward Fox. **1984**

BOUNTY HUNTER ★★ Star-director Robert Ginty plays a federal bounty hunter investigating the murder of an Indian buddy. This pits him against a corrupt sheriff (Bo Hopkins). Unrated, the film has violence and profanity. 91m. **DIR:** Robert Ginty. **CAST:** Robert Ginty, Bo Hopkins. **1989**

BOUNTY TRACKER ★★½ A by-the-numbers kill-or-be-killed saga, with Lorenzo Lamas reasonably adept as a licensed bounty hunter who swears vengeance on the scum who killed his brother. Good for viewers with minimal expectations. Rated R for profanity and violence. 92m. **DIR:** Kurt Anderson. **CAST:** Lorenzo Lamas, Matthias Hues, Cyndi Pass, Paul Regina. **1993**

BOXCAR BERTHA ★★½ Small-town girl (Barbara Hershey) hooks up with a gang of train robbers (led by David Carradine) in this *Bonnie and Clyde* coattailer. Martin Scorsese buffs will be disappointed. Rated R. 97m. **DIR:** Martin Scorsese. **CAST:** David Carradine, Barbara Hershey, Barry Primus, Bernie Casey, John Carradine. **1972**

BOYS IN COMPANY C, THE ★★★ The film opens with the arrival of various draftees in the Marine Corps induction center and comes close, at times, to being the powerful film the subject of the Vietnam war suggests. The combat scenes are particularly effective, and the deaths of soldiers are gory without being overdone. Rated R for violence. 127m. **DIR:** Sidney J. Furie. **CAST:** Stan Shaw, Andrew Stevens, James Canning, James Whitmore Jr. **1978**

BOYS OF THE CITY ★★ Somewhere between their incarnations as the Dead End Kids and the Bowery Boys, the Forties version of the Brat Pack turned up as the East Side Kids in low-budget movies. In this one, the gang takes a trip to the mountains, where they solve the murder of a judge by gangsters. B&W; 68m. **DIR:** Joseph H. Lewis. **CAST:** Bobby Jordan, Leo Gorcey, Dave O'Brien, Donald Haines. **1940**

BRADDOCK: MISSING IN ACTION III ★★ After the war has ended, Colonel Braddock (Chuck Norris) returns to Vietnam to rescue a group of Amerasian children in a POW camp. A dark, grainy, low-budget film cowritten by Norris. If you liked the first two films, you'll probably enjoy this one, too. Rated R for violence. 90m. **DIR:** Aaron Norris. **CAST:** Chuck Norris, Aki Aleong. **1987**

BRADY'S ESCAPE ★★★ A minor HBO-produced film concerning an American attempting to escape the Nazis in Europe during World War II. Nothing original is added to the familiar plot. 96m. **DIR:** Pal Gabor. **CAST:** John Savage, Kelly Reno. **1984**

BRAIN SMASHER...A LOVE STORY ★★★ Andrew Dice Clay is the brain smasher, a notorious professional bouncer who takes pride in his work. Teri Hatcher is an international model who recruits Clay to protect her and her sister from killer Chinese monks. Honest! Veteran character actors help levitate this one above mediocrity. Rated PG-13 for violence and profanity. **DIR:** Albert Pyun. **CAST:** Andrew Dice Clay, Teri Hatcher, Brion James, Tim Thomerson, Charles Rocket, Nicholas Guest, Deborah Van Valkenburgh. **1993**

BRANNIGAN ★★★½ John Wayne travels to London to bring back a fugitive in this enjoyable cops-and-robbers chase film. It's fun to see the Duke in jolly old England and the cast is outstanding. Rated PG. 111m. **DIR:** Douglas Hickox. **CAST:** John Wayne, Richard Attenborough, Judy Geeson, Mel Ferrer, Ralph Meeker, John Vernon. **1975**

BRASS TARGET ★★ Pure Hollywood hokum at its most ridiculous would ask us to believe that Gen. George Patton (George Kennedy) was murdered after World War II because of a large gold robbery committed by his staff. Not much to recommend this boring film. Rated PG for moderate language and violence. 111m. **DIR:** John Hough. **CAST:** Sophia Loren, George Kennedy, John Cassavetes, Robert Vaughn, Max von Sydow, Bruce Davison. **1978**

BREAKER! BREAKER! 🦃 A quickie thrown together to cash in on the CB craze. Rated PG. 86m. **DIR:** Don Hulette. **CAST:** Chuck Norris, George Murdock, Terry O'Connor, Don Gentry. **1977**

BREAKER MORANT ★★★★★ This is one Australian import you won't want to miss. Imagine the high adventure of the original *Gunga Din*, the wisecracking humor of *To Have and Have Not*, and the character drama of *The Caine Mutiny* all rolled into one supermovie. Rated PG. 107m. **DIR:** Bruce Beresford. **CAST:** Edward Woodward, Jack Thompson, John Waters, Bryan Brown, Charles Tingwell. **1979**

BREAKOUT ★★★ While not exactly Charles Bronson at his best, this action-adventure film does have its moments as the star, playing a devil-may-care helicopter pilot, rescues Robert Duvall, an American businessman framed for murder and held captive in a Mexican jail. Rated PG. 96m. **DIR:** Tom Gries. **CAST:** Charles Bronson, Robert Duvall, Jill Ireland, John Huston, Sheree North, Randy Quaid. **1975**

BREAKTHROUGH 🦃 Richard Burton as a heroic German officer who saves the life of an American colonel (Robert Mitchum) after the Nazis thwart an attempt on Hitler's life. Rated PG. 115m. **DIR:** Andrew V. McLaglen. **CAST:** Richard Burton, Robert Mitchum, Rod Steiger, Curt Jurgens. **1978**

BREATHING FIRE ★★½ Better-than-average kick-boxing effort teams brothers Jonathan Ke Quan and Jerry Trimble against their father, the mastermind behind a bank robbery. Good action and decent performances. Rated R for violence. 92m. **DIR:** Lou Kennedy. **CAST:** Jonathan Ke Quan, Jerry Trimble. **1991**

BREED APART, A ★★★½ When a billionaire collector hires an adventurous mountain climber to steal the eggs of an endangered pair of nesting eagles, the result is a nicely paced film that manages to combine drama, suspense, romance, and even a touch of post-Vietnam commentary. Rutger Hauer plays the strange recluse who lives in a tent-palace in the loneliest reaches of the Blue Ridge Mountains. Rated R for sex, nudity, and violence. 95m. **DIR:** Philippe Mora. **CAST:** Rutger Hauer, Kathleen Turner, Powers Boothe, Donald Pleasence. **1984**

BRENDA STARR 🦃 Spoof of long-running comic-strip character features an unconvincing Brooke Shields. This was completed in 1987 but not released until 1992. Rated PG for profanity. 94m. **DIR:** Robert Ellis Miller. **CAST:** Brooke Shields, Timothy Dalton, Tony Peck, Diana Scarwid. **1992**

BRIDE AND THE BEAST, THE 🦃 Stock jungle footage is used to pad out this tale of the new bride of a big-game hunter who, under hypnosis, discovers that she lived a past life as a gorilla. 78m. **DIR:** Adrian Weiss. **CAST:** Charlotte Austin, Lance Fuller, Johnny Roth, Steve Calvert, William Justine. **1958**

BRIDGE ON THE RIVER KWAI, THE ★★★★★ Considered by many to be David Lean's greatest work, this war epic brought the British director his first Oscar. The powerful, dramatic story centers around the construction of a bridge by British and American prisoners of war under the command of Japanese colonel Sessue Hayakawa. Alec Guinness, a Lean semiregular since *Great Expectations*, is the stiff-upper-lipped British commander who uses the task as a way of proving British superiority. 161m. **DIR:** David Lean. **CAST:** William Holden, Alec Guinness, Jack Hawkins, Sessue Hayakawa, James Donald. **1957**

BRIDGE TO HELL ★½ After a group of World War II POWs escape, a bridge is their last obstacle and they decide to take it out after crossing. (Sound familiar?) Lots of shooting and explosions. Unfortunately, not much of a plot. Not rated, but contains violence and profanity. 94m. **DIR:** Umberto Lenzi. **CAST:** Andy J. Forest. **1989**

BRIDGE TOO FAR, A ★★★½ Here's another story of a famous battle with the traditional all-star cast. In this case it's World War II's "Operation Market Garden," a disastrous Allied push to get troops behind German lines and capture an early bridgehead on the Rhine. Rated PG. 175m. **DIR:** Richard Attenborough. **CAST:** Dirk Bogarde, James Caan, Michael Caine, Sean Connery, Laurence Olivier, Robert Redford. **1977**

BRIDGES AT TOKO-RI, THE ★★★★½ With this picture, screenwriter Valentine Davies and director Mark Robson created one of the cinema's most authentic depictions of war. It is certainly the best motion picture about the Korean War. James Michener's novel, as adapted here, centers on a bomber pilot and his crew, part of an aircraft-carrier force assigned to destroy vital North Korean bridges. 103m. **DIR:** Mark Robson. **CAST:** William Holden, Fredric March, Grace Kelly, Mickey Rooney, Earl Holliman, Charles

McGraw, Robert Strauss, Willis Bouchey, Gene Reynolds. **1954**

BRING ME THE HEAD OF ALFREDO GARCIA ★★½ Warren Oates gives an outstanding performance as a piano player in Mexico who becomes mixed-up with vicious bounty hunters. Hard-core Sam Peckinpah fans will appreciate this one more than the casual viewer. Rated R. 112m. **DIR:** Sam Peckinpah. **CAST:** Warren Oates, Isela Vega, Gig Young, Robert Webber, Emilio Fernandez, Kris Kristofferson, Helmut Dantine. **1974**

BROKEN CHAIN, THE ★★★ Solid action film looks at the quandary the Indian Nations faced during the American Revolution. With all sides vying for their help, the Nation is placed in a no-win situation eventually pitting tribe against tribe. Made for TV. 94m. **DIR:** Lamont Johnson. **CAST:** Eric Schweig, Wes Studi, Buffy Sainte-Marie, Pierce Brosnan, J. C. White Shirt, Graham Greene. **1993**

BRONX WAR, THE ★★★ Two drug-dealing factions—one black, one Hispanic—declare war and a nonstop bloodfest ensues. A capable actor (who is credited only as Joseph) leads the Hispanics. Unrated, but equivalent to an R for violence, profanity, and nudity. 91m. **DIR:** Joseph B. Vasquez. **CAST:** Fabio Urena, Charmain Cruz, Andre Brown. **1989**

BROTHER ORCHID ★★★ Comedy, action, sentimentality, and social comment are intertwined in this generally enjoyable gangster movie about a good-natured hood (Edward G. Robinson) who goes broke in Europe trying to get a little class. Old-fashioned fun. B&W; 91m. **DIR:** Lloyd Bacon. **CAST:** Edward G. Robinson, Humphrey Bogart, Ann Sothern, Donald Crisp, Ralph Bellamy, Allen Jenkins, Cecil Kellaway, Morgan Conway, Paul Guilfoyle, Tom Tyler. **1940**

BROTHERHOOD OF DEATH 🦃 Satanic Ku Klux Klansmen battle gun-toting black Vietnam veterans in the pre–civil rights movement South. Rated R for violence and language. 85m. **DIR:** Bill Berry. **CAST:** Roy Jefferson, Le Tari, Haskell V. Anderson. **1976**

BROTHERHOOD OF THE ROSE ★★½ Lifelong friends Peter Strauss and David Morse become CIA operatives, with Morse betraying his friend. Originally a made-for-television miniseries, this film works better in its abbreviated version. Rated PG-13. 103m. **DIR:** Marvin J. Chomsky. **CAST:** Robert Mitchum, Peter Strauss, Connie Sellecca, David Morse. **1989**

BUCCANEER, THE ★★ Studio-bound remake of C. B. De Mille's 1938 romance of pirate Jean Lafitte. A cast capable of hamming *and* acting, but that's not enough to make this stiff color creaker come alive. 121m. **DIR:** Anthony Quinn. **CAST:** Yul Brynner, Charlton Heston, Claire Bloom, Charles Boyer, Douglass Dumbrille, Lorne Greene, Ted de Corsia. **1958**

BUCKTOWN 🦃 This mindless blaxploitation flick finds Fred Williamson journeying to a southern town to bury his brother, who has been killed by corrupt cops. Rated R. 95m. **DIR:** Arthur Marks. **CAST:** Fred Williamson, Pam Grier, Thalmus Rasulala, Tony King, Bernie Hamilton, Art Lund. **1975**

BULLDOG DRUMMOND ★★★ Ronald Colman smoothly segued from silent to sound films playing the title's ex–British army officer adventurer in this exciting, witty, definitive first stanza of what became a popular series. B&W; 89m. **DIR:** F. Richard Jones. **CAST:** Ronald Colman, Joan Bennett, Lilyan Tashman. **1929**

BULLDOG DRUMMOND COMES BACK ★★★ The first of seven films starring John Howard as the adventurer-sleuth is an atmospheric tale of revenge. The crazed widow of one of Bulldog Drummond's former enemies makes off with our hero's girl, Phyllis. A gem available on tape with *Bulldog Drummond Escapes*. B&W; 59m. **DIR:** Louis King. **CAST:** John Howard, John Barrymore, Louise Campbell, E. E. Clive, Reginald Denny, J. Carrol Naish. **1937**

BULLDOG DRUMMOND ESCAPES ★★ Famed ex–British army officer Bulldog Drummond comes to the aid of his ladylove when she becomes embroiled in an international espionage ring. Young Ray Milland stars in his only outing as the World War I hero in this okay series entry. Paired on tape with *Bulldog Drummond Comes Back*. B&W; 65m. **DIR:** James Hogan. **CAST:** Ray Milland, Guy Standing, Heather Angel, Porter Hall, Reginald Denny, E. E. Clive, Fay Holden. **1937**

BULLDOG DRUMMOND IN AFRICA ★★½ An international spy ring has struck again. This time they've kidnapped Colonel Neilson and hidden him somewhere in North Africa, and Hugh "Bulldog" Drummond isn't going to stand for it. Good fun. Double-billed with *Arrest Bulldog Drummond* on tape. B&W; 58m. **DIR:** Louis King. **CAST:** John Howard, Heather Angel, J. Carrol Naish, H. B. Warner, Anthony Quinn. **1938**

BULLDOG DRUMMOND'S BRIDE ★★½ The last of Paramount's Bulldog Drummond series. A crack bank robber uses Drummond's honeymoon flat as a hideout for himself and his explosives. Not the best of the series, but it's still a rousing adventure. On tape with *Bulldog Drummond's Secret Police*. B&W; 56m. **DIR:** James Hogan. **CAST:** John Howard, Heather Angel, Reginald Denny, H. B. Warner, Eduardo Ciannelli. **1939**

BULLDOG DRUMMOND'S PERIL ★★★ Bulldog Drummond has a personal stake in a chase that takes him from London to Switzerland—the synthetic diamond that was stolen is a wedding gift intended for our hero and his patient fiancée, Phyllis. Full of close calls, witty dialogue, and an injection of controlled lunacy by the great John Barrymore. On tape with *Bulldog Drummond's Revenge*. B&W; 66m. **DIR:** James Hogan. **CAST:** John Howard, John Barrymore, Louise Campbell, H. B. Warner, Reginald Denny. **1938**

BULLDOG DRUMMOND'S REVENGE ★★★ The second film in Paramount's Drummond series featuring John Howard, this entry focuses on the hero's attempts to recover a powerful explosive. Aided by the colorful Colonel Neilson (John Barrymore at his most enjoyable), Drummond fights evildoers at every turn. Released on a double bill with *Bulldog Drummond's Peril*. B&W; 55m. **DIR:** Louis King. **CAST:** John Howard, John Barrymore, Louise Campbell, Reginald Denny, E. E. Clive. **1937**

BULLDOG DRUMMOND'S SECRET POLICE ★★½ Stylish entry in the long-running series finds gentleman adventurer Bulldog Drummond searching a forbidding castle for hidden treasure while matching wits with a crazed murderer. Double billed with *Bulldog Drummond's Bride* on videotape. B&W; 54m. **DIR:** James Hogan. **CAST:** John Howard, Heather Angel, Reginald Denny, Leo G. Carroll, H. B. Warner. **1939**

BULLETPROOF ★★½ Gary Busey plays a one-man army named Frank "Bulletproof" McBain, an ex-CIA agent who single-handedly takes on a band of multinational terrorists. It's silly, but fun—thanks to Busey and a strong cast of character actors. Rated R for profanity, nudity, and violence. 95m. **DIR:** Steve Carver. **CAST:** Gary Busey, Darlanne Fluegel, Henry Silva, Thalmus Rasulala, L. Q. Jones, Rene Enriquez, R. G. Armstrong, Luke Askew. **1988**

BULLETS OR BALLOTS ★★★½ A hard-nosed cop (Edward G. Robinson), after being unceremoniously fired from the police force, joins up with the big-time crime boss (Barton MacLane) who has long been his friendly enemy. William Keighley's high-spirited direction helps put over this action-packed but melodramatic gangster movie. B&W; 81m. **DIR:** William Keighley. **CAST:** Edward G. Robinson, Joan Blondell, Barton MacLane, Humphrey Bogart, Frank McHugh. **1936**

BULLFIGHTER AND THE LADY, THE ★★★★ Many of the themes explored in the superb series of low-budget Westerns director Budd Boetticher later made with Randolph Scott (*Decision at Sundown*; *The Tall T*) are evident in this first-rate drama. A skeet-shooting champ (Robert Stack) decides to become a bullfighter. B&W; 123m. **DIR:** Budd Boetticher. **CAST:** Robert Stack, Joy Page, Gilbert Roland, Katy Jurado. **1951**

BULLITT ★★★★ Although a bit dated now, this police drama directed by Peter Yates still features one of star Steve McQueen's best screen performances. The San Francisco car-chase sequence is still a corker. 113m. **DIR:** Peter Yates. **CAST:** Steve McQueen, Robert Vaughn, Jacqueline Bisset, Norman Fell, Don Gordon, Suzanne Somers. **1968**

BUNCO ★★½ Passable made-for-television crime thriller has Robert Urich and Tom Selleck as a pair of police detectives out to bust a confidence ring. Typical TV fare. 90m. **DIR:** Alexander Singer. **CAST:** Robert Urich, Tom Selleck, Donna Mills, Michael Sacks, Will Geer, Arte Johnson, James Hampton, Bobby Van. **1976**

BUSHIDO BLADE 🦃 Richard Boone gives an outrageously hammy performance as Commander Matthew Perry, whose mission is to find a valuable sword. Rated R for violence. 104m. **DIR:** Tom Kotani. **CAST:** Richard Boone, Frank Converse, James Earl Jones, Toshiro Mifune, Mako. **1979**

BUYING TIME ★★½ A young man goes undercover to procure evidence that will convict a drug-dealing killer, but he finds his own life in jeopardy. Rated R for nudity, profanity, violence, and animal abuse. 97m. **DIR:** Mitchell Gabourie. **CAST:** Jeff Schultz, Laura Cruickshank, Page Fletcher, Dean Stockwell. **1989**

C.C. & COMPANY ★★½ Basically idiotic action film has Broadway Joe Namath (in his first feature) cast as C.C. Ryder, misfit member of a rowdy biker gang, attempting to "split" when he falls for top fashion photographer Ann-Margret. Rated R for mild language and nudity. 90m. **DIR:** Seymour Robbie. **CAST:** Joe Namath, Ann-Margret, William Smith, Sid Haig, Jennifer Billingsley, Greg Mullavey. **1970**

CABO BLANCO 🦃 A miserable suspense-thriller remake of *Casablanca*. As good as he can be when he wants to, Charles Bronson is no Humphrey Bogart. Rated R. 87m. **DIR:** J. Lee Thompson. **CAST:** Charles Bronson, Dominique Sanda, Jason Robards Jr. **1982**

CAGE ★★★ Fine actioner features Lou Ferrigno as a brain-damaged Vietnam vet drawn into an underworld gambling arena. Although the dialogue is uninspired, Ferrigno shines. Rated R for violence and profanity. 101m. **DIR:** Lang Elliott. **CAST:** Lou Ferrigno, Reb Brown, Michael Dante. **1988**

CAGED FEAR 🦃 Innocent woman gets thrown behind bars. Not even good trash. Rated R for nudity, violence, language. 93m. **DIR:** Bobby Houston. **CAST:** David Keith, Ray Sharkey, Deborah May, Karen Black. **1991**

CAGED FURY 🦃 Sleazoid trash features an incredibly stupid girl (Roxanna Michaels) being trapped in a female prison that actually fronts for a slave-trade operation. Unrated, contains violence, nudity, and profanity. 95m. **DIR:** Bill Milling. **CAST:** Erik Estrada, Richie Barathy, Roxanna Michaels, Paul Smith. **1989**

CAGED HEAT ★★ A typical R-rated women's prison-break picture from Roger Corman's New World Pictures. For a change, this one is set in the United States. Otherwise its distinctions are marginal, despite direction by Jonathan Demme. 84m. **DIR:** Jonathan Demme. **CAST:** Juanita Brown, Erica Gavin, Barbara Steele. **1974**

CAGED WOMEN Sexploitation flick about a female journalist who poses as a prostitute to get thrown into jail. Not rated, but contains nudity, violence, and profanity. 97m. **DIR:** Vincent Dawn. **CAST:** Laura Gemser, Gabriele Tinti. **1984**

CALL OF THE WILD (1972) ★★★½ Charlton Heston stars in this adaptation of Jack London's famous novel. A domesticated dog is stolen and forced to pull a snow sled in Alaska as John (Charlton Heston) searches for gold. Some profanity and violence. Rated PG. 100m. **DIR:** Ken Annakin. **CAST:** Charlton Heston, Michele Mercier, Maria Rohm, Rik Battaglia. **1972**

CAME A HOT FRIDAY ★★ Mildly amusing film set in 1949 New Zealand, where two con men make their fortune cheating bookmakers all across the country. Rated PG for language and adult situations. 101m. **DIR:** Ian Mune. **CAST:** Peter Bland, Philip Gordon, Billy T. James, Michael Lawrence. **1985**

CANNIBAL ATTACK Arthritic programmer about a gang of thieves who roam around the soundstages wearing crocodile skins. B&W; 69m. **DIR:** Lee Sholem. **CAST:** Johnny Weissmuller, Judy Walsh, David Bruce. **1954**

CANNIBAL WOMEN IN THE AVOCADO JUNGLE OF DEATH ★★½ *Playboy* playmate Shannon Tweed stars in this comedic adventure about a feminist anthropologist in search of the infamous cannibal women, a group of ultraleft feminists who eat their mates. Some great sight gags, with most of the funny bits belonging to semimacho guide Bill Maher. Rated PG-13 for nudity. 90m. **DIR:** J. D. Athens. **CAST:** Shannon Tweed, Adrienne Barbeau, Bill Maher, Barry Primus. **1988**

CANNONBALL ★★ David Carradine plays an unpleasant antihero out to beat the rest of the cast in an exotic race. Rated R for violence. 93m. **DIR:** Paul Bartel. **CAST:** David Carradine, Veronica Hamel, Gerrit Graham, Sylvester Stallone, Robert Carradine, Carl Gottlieb, Belinda Balaski. **1976**

CAPER OF THE GOLDEN BULLS, THE Stephen Boyd plays a wealthy American who is blackmailed into robbing the Royal Bank of Spain. Not rated, has some violence. 106m. **DIR:** Russell Rouse. **CAST:** Stephen Boyd, Yvette Mimieux, Giovanna Ralli, Vito Scotti, J. G. Devlin, Arnold Moss, Walter Slezak. **1966**

CAPONE ★★ Made-for-TV gangster effort brings nothing new to the formula. Behind bars for tax evasion, notorious mobster Al Capone still manages to run Chicago. It's up to FBI agent Keith Carradine to put an end to Capone's reign of terror. Additional footage added for video. Rated R for violence and nudity. 97m. **DIR:** Michael Pressman. **CAST:** Keith Carradine, Ray Sharkey, Debrah Farentino, Charles Haid. **1989**

CAPTAIN AMERICA (1944) ★★★ Joe Simon and Jack Kirby's comic-book character is brought to movie life to tangle with the fiendishly refined Lionel Atwill, who has not only a destructive ray machine but a machine capable of bringing dead animals back to life! Two-fisted District Attorney Dick Purcell manfully pursues Atwill. B&W; 15 chapters. **DIR:** John English, Elmer Clifton. **CAST:** Dick Purcell, Lorna Gray, Lionel Atwill, Charles Trowbridge, Russell Hicks, John Davidson, Frank Reicher, Hugh Sothern. **1944**

CAPTAIN AMERICA (1979) ★★ A criminal genius plots to extort millions from the government with a stolen nuclear device. Of course the only man who can stop him is the star-spangled avenger. This is average TV fare with a disappointingly simple plot. Not rated, but suitable for all viewers. 90m. **DIR:** Rod Holcomb. **CAST:** Reb Brown, Len Birman, Heather Menzies, Steve Forrest. **1979**

CAPTAIN AMERICA (1990) The golden-age comic-book character tries to make the leap to the big screen with disastrous results. In 1941, America's supersoldier is defeated by the Red Skull, and accidentally thrown into suspended animation. Fifty years later, he awakens in time to foil a scheme by his old enemy. Rated PG-13 for violence and profanity. 104m. **DIR:** Albert Pyun. **CAST:** Matt Salinger, Ronny Cox, Ned Beatty, Darren McGavin, Melinda Dillon, Scott Paulin. **1990**

CAPTAIN AMERICA II: DEATH TOO SOON Ridiculous made-for-television adventure of the comic-book hero. Plodding. 100m. **DIR:** Ivan Nagy. **CAST:** Reb Brown, Christopher Lee, Connie Sellecca, Len Birman. **1979**

CAPTAIN BLOOD ★★★★½ Errol Flynn's youthful enthusiasm, great character actors, realistic miniature work, and Erich Wolfgang Korngold's score all meld together under Michael Curtiz's direction and provide audiences with perhaps the best pirate film of all time. B&W; 95m. **DIR:** Michael Curtiz. **CAST:** Errol Flynn, Olivia de Havilland, Basil Rathbone, Lionel Atwill, Ross Alexander, Guy Kibbee, Henry Stephenson. **1935**

CAPTAIN CAUTION ★★½ In command of a ship during the War of 1812 with England, Victor Mature, in the title role, is taken for a coward when he urges prudence. Richard Wallace's fast-paced, cannon-bellowing direction quells all restlessness, however. B&W; 85m. **DIR:** Richard Wallace. **CAST:** Victor Mature, Louise Platt, Bruce Cabot, Leo Carrillo, Vivienne Osborne, El Brendel, Robert Barrat, Miles Mander, Roscoe Ates. **1940**

CAPTAIN GALLANT—FOREIGN LEGION ★★½ Baby boomers should remember this Saturday-morning television series involving the adventures and escapades of Captain Gallant of the French foreign legion who rode the North African deserts outwitting black-turbaned villains. This video release is a compilation of two of the best episodes. Nostalgic fun. B&W; 60m. **DIR:** Sam Newfield. **CAST:** Buster Crabbe, Fuzzy Knight, Cullen "Cuffy" Crabbe. **1956**

CAPTAIN HORATIO HORNBLOWER ★★★★ An enjoyable adventure film that is faithful to the C. S. Forester novels and to the reputation of the rugged British seacoast where it was filmed. Gregory Peck's wooden acting style serves the character well, and he warms up when Virginia Mayo's Lady Wellesley becomes an unwanted passenger aboard his ship. 117m. **DIR:** Raoul Walsh. **CAST:** Gregory Peck, Virginia Mayo, Dennis O'Dea, James Robertson Justice, Robert Beatty. **1951**

CAPTAIN KIDD ★★ Not even Charles Laughton's mugging and posturing can redeem this swashbuckling yarn about the pirate whose treasure is still being sought. 89m. **DIR:** Rowland V. Lee. **CAST:** Charles Laughton, Randolph Scott, Reginald Owen, John Carradine, Sheldon Leonard, Barbara Britton, Gilbert Roland. **1945**

CAPTAIN SCARLETT ★★½ A dashing hero thought to be dead returns to France after the Napoleonic Wars to discover his estate has been confiscated by a nasty nobleman. Saving ladies in distress and righting wrongs becomes his life. Simple, predictable, and good clean fun. 75m. **DIR:** Thomas Carr. **CAST:** Richard Greene, Leonora Amar, Nedrick Young. **1953**

CAPTAINS OF THE CLOUDS ★★★ Set in Canada in 1940, this enjoyable film stars a typically robust James Cagney as a bush pilot who joins the Royal Canadian Air Force. Lots of romance and humor add to the fun. Good color photography, too, but not much action. 113m. **DIR:** Michael Curtiz. **CAST:** James Cagney, Dennis Morgan, Alan Hale Sr., Brenda Marshall, George Tobias. **1942**

CAPTIVE RAGE (turkey) A plane carrying American citizens is hijacked. Rated R for violence, profanity, and nudity. 99m. **DIR:** Cedric Sundstrom. **CAST:** Oliver Reed, Robert Vaughn. **1988**

CARAVAN TO VACCARES (turkey) If this cliché-ridden film had followed the plot of Alistair MacLean's novel, it might have been exciting. Read the book instead. Rated PG. 98m. **DIR:** Geoffrey Reeve. **CAST:** David Birney, Charlotte Rampling, Michel Lonsdale, Marcel Bozzuffi. **1974**

CARIBE ★★ In this bland spy thriller, CIA agent Kara Glover and her partner arrange a weapons sale for their own personal gain. But the contact, Stephen McHattie, has no intention of fulfilling his part of the bargain. He kills Glover's partner and confiscates the weapons. Beautiful photography of the Belize jungles and mountains rescues this tired spy thriller. 90m. **DIR:** Michael Kennedy. **CAST:** John Savage, Kara Glover, Stephen McHattie. **1987**

CARLITO'S WAY ★★★★ Al Pacino is terrific as a former drug dealer trying to go straight in this unofficial sequel to director Brian De Palma's *Scarface*. Like his aging Michael Corleone in *The Godfather, Part III*, Pacino finds himself being pulled back into the criminal underworld when his best friend and attorney (a nicely sleazy Sean Penn) asks for his help. It's trash, but great trash—as Pacino and De Palma expertly deliver thrills, chills, suspense, and even romance. Rated R for nudity, profanity, violence, simulated sex, and drug use. 141m. **DIR:** Brian De Palma. **CAST:** Al Pacino, Sean Penn, Penelope Ann Miller, John Leguizamo, Ingrid Rogers, Luis Guzman, James Rebhorn, Viggo Mortensen, Richard Foronjy, Adrian Pasdar. **1993**

CARTEL (turkey) Atrocious, mean-spirited exploitation film features Miles O'Keeffe as a pilot framed for drug smuggling. Rated R for violence, profanity, and nudity. 88m. **DIR:** John Stewart. **CAST:** Miles O'Keeffe, Don Stroud, Crystal Carson, William Smith. **1989**

CASINO ROYALE (1954) ★★★★ 007 fans who believe Sean Connery to have been the first screen incarnation of their favorite secret agent will be surprised and thrilled by this Bonded treasure, originally aired live on an American television anthology series. Barry Nelson stars as an Americanized "Jimmy" Bond who faces the menacing Le Chiffre (Peter Lorre, in a deliciously evil role) across a gambling table. From the Ian Fleming novel, this remains a surprisingly faithful adaptation of its source material. B&W; 55m. **DIR:** William H. Brown. **CAST:** Barry Nelson, Peter Lorre, Linda Christian. **1954**

CAST A GIANT SHADOW ★★ The early history of Israel is told through the fictionalized biography of American Col. Mickie Marcus (Kirk Douglas). Marcus, an expatriate army officer, is cajoled into aiding Israel in its impending war to wrest independence from its hostile Arab neighbors. Highly romanticized piece of historical fluff. 142m.

DIR: Melville Shavelson. **CAST:** Kirk Douglas, Senta Berger, Angie Dickinson. **1966**

CASTLE OF CAGLIOSTRO, THE ★★★★ Japanese animation with wider appeal than most Japanese animated features. International thief Wolf and his partners in crime attempt to rescue a young princess from a marriage to the wicked Count Cagliostro. Memorable animation, story, and characters. 100m. **DIR:** Hayao Miyazaki. **1980**

CAT CHASER ★★ Peter Weller gives a stiff performance as an ex-Marine who gets mixed up in love, revenge, and murder. Rated R for violence, language, nudity, simulated sex, and rape. 97m. **DIR:** Abel Ferrara. **CAST:** Peter Weller, Kelly McGillis, Charles Durning, Frederic Forrest, Tomas Milian. **1988**

CATCH ME IF YOU CAN ★★★ When financially troubled Cathedral High is threatened with closure, the student council resorts to gambling on illegal car races. Above average teen action flick. Rated PG. 105m. **DIR:** Stephen Sommers. **CAST:** Matt Lattanzi, M. Emmet Walsh, Geoffrey Lewis. **1989**

CATCH THE HEAT ★★ Tiana Alexander is a narcotics cop in San Francisco sent undercover to South America to bust Rod Steiger. Even Alexander's kung fu prowess is routine with these cardboard characters. Rated R. 88m. **DIR:** Joel Silberg. **CAST:** David Dukes, Tiana Alexander, Rod Steiger, Brian Thompson, Jorge Martinez, John Hancock. **1987**

CAUSE OF DEATH ★★ A college student and his girlfriend become entangled in a drug lord's attempt to retrieve an illicit fortune. A cut-rate remake (rip-off?) of *Marathon Man*. Rated R for violence and nudity. 86m. **DIR:** Philip J. Jones. **CAST:** Michael Barak, Sydney Coale Phillips, Daniel Martine. **1991**

CEILING ZERO ★★★★ Once again, director Howard Hawks focuses on a group of professionals: pilots battling thick fog and crude ground-to-air communications to get the mail through. Cocky flier James Cagney joins old friend Pat O'Brien's crew only to neglect his duties in favor of seducing a fellow flier June Travis. Fast-paced and riveting; one of the finest of the Cagney-O'Brien teamings. B&W; 95m. **DIR:** Howard Hawks. **CAST:** James Cagney, Pat O'Brien, June Travis, Stu Erwin, Barton MacLane, Isabel Jewell. **1935**

CERTAIN FURY 🦃 Tatum O'Neal is Scarlet ("Scar")—a dumb white street woman; Irene Cara is Tracy—a dumb pampered black woman. They're thrown together and run for their lives from police and drug dealers. Rated R for violence. 87m. **DIR:** Stephen Gyllenhaal. **CAST:** Tatum O'Neal, Irene Cara, Nicholas Campbell, George Murdock, Moses Gunn, Peter Fonda. **1985**

CHAIN REACTION ★★★ Engrossing drama following a nuclear power plant employee (Ross Thompson) accidentally exposed to a lethal dose of radiation during a near meltdown. Rated R for some explicit sex, nudity, and violence. 87m. **DIR:** Ian Barry, George Miller. **CAST:** Steve Bisley, Anna-Maria Winchester. **1980**

CHAINED HEAT 🦃 The story of women in prison, this cheapo offers few surprises. Rated R. 95m. **DIR:** Paul Nicholas. **CAST:** Linda Blair, John Vernon, Nita Talbot, Stella Stevens, Sybil Danning, Tamara Dobson. **1983**

CHAINS 🦃 Schmaltzy clone of the cult favorite *The Warriors*. Violence and seminudity. 93m. **DIR:** Roger J. Barski. **CAST:** Jimi Jourdan. **1990**

CHALLENGE, THE ★★★½ An American (Scott Glenn) gets caught in the middle of a decades-old private war between two brothers in modern-day Japan. This movie has ample rewards for both samurai film aficionados and regular moviegoers. Rated R for profanity and violence. 112m. **DIR:** John Frankenheimer. **CAST:** Scott Glenn, Toshiro Mifune, Calvin Young. **1982**

CHALLENGE TO WHITE FANG 🦃 White Fang is a German shepherd running loose in the Yukon trying to stop crooks from cheating an old man out of his gold mine. Unrated. 89m. **DIR:** Lucio Fulci. **CAST:** Franco Nero, Virna Lisi, Harry Carey Jr. **1986**

CHANDU THE MAGICIAN ★★½ Stylishly produced and full of exotic sets, sleight of hand, and special effects, this imaginative fantasy suffers from a stolid performance by Edmund Lowe. Bela Lugosi, however, is in rare form as the gleefully maniacal Roxor, master of the black arts. An enjoyable curiosity. B&W; 70m. **DIR:** William Cameron Menzies, Marcel Varnel. **CAST:** Edmund Lowe, Bela Lugosi, Irene Ware, Henry B. Walthall. **1932**

CHANG ★★★★ "Chang" means elephant, and in this remarkable pseudo-documentary by the explorer-filmmakers who later teamed to make *King Kong*, the threat of a rampaging herd of the beasts looms over daily life among villagers in primitive Thailand. This is a restored version, from first-rate source prints, of one of the most vivid location adventures of its day. B&W; 67m. **DIR:** Merian C. Cooper, Ernest B. Schoedsack. **1927**

CHARGE OF THE LIGHT BRIGADE, THE (1936) ★★★★ October 25, 1854: Balaclava, the Crimea; military minds blunder, and six hundred gallant Britishers, sabers flashing, ride to their deaths. The film, which climaxes with one of the most dramatic cavalry charges in history, is based on Tennyson's famous poem. B&W; 116m. **DIR:** Michael Curtiz. **CAST:** Errol Flynn, Olivia de Havilland, Patric Knowles, Donald Crisp, David Niven, Henry Stephenson. **1936**

CHARGE OF THE LIGHT BRIGADE, THE (1968) ★★★½ Good depiction of the events leading up to the ill-fated 1854 Crimea engagement of the famed British unit that was controlled and directed by a glory-seeking and incompetent gentry. The climactic charge is moviemaking at its best. Rated PG-13 for violence. 128m. **DIR:** Tony Richardson. **CAST:** Trevor Howard, John Gielgud, Vanessa Redgrave, Harry Andrews, Jill Bennett, David Hemmings. **1968**

CHARLEY VARRICK ★★★★ A bank robber (Walter Matthau) accidentally steals money from the mob (he hits a bank where its ill-gotten gains are laundered). Matthau is superb as Varrick, the "last of the independents," and Joe Don Baker sends chills up the spine as the hit man relentlessly pursuing him. Rated PG. 111m. **DIR:** Don Siegel. **CAST:** Walter Matthau, Joe Don Baker, Felicia Farr, Andrew Robinson, John Vernon. **1973**

CHASE, THE (1994) ★★ Avoid this frivolous action-comedy unless you want to spend nearly 90 minutes in the front seat of a red BMW. Charlie Sheen plays a wrongly convicted prison escapee who takes the daughter of California's richest man hostage. They feud for several miles and then fall in love with the cops in hot pursuit. Wild action scenes include front-seat sex and cadavers bouncing down the freeway. A predictable yarn. Rated R for nudity, sex, and language. 88m. **DIR:** Adam Rifkin. **CAST:** Charlie Sheen, Kristy Swanson, Ray Wise, Cary Elwes, Henry Rollins. **1994**

CHESTY ANDERSON, U.S. NAVY (A.K.A. ANDERSON'S ANGELS) 🦃 This dated, low-budget, tasteless crime thriller features Shari Eubank as the title character. Rated R for nudity, obscenities, and violence. 83m. **DIR:** Ed Forsyth. **CAST:** Shari Eubank, Scatman Crothers, Fred Willard, Frank Campanella. **1975**

CHINA GIRL 🦃 Romeo and Juliet on Friday the 13th. Rated R for violence and profanity. 90m. **DIR:** Abel Ferrara. **CAST:** James Russo, David Caruso, Richard Panebianco, Sari Chang, Russell Wong, Joey Chin, James Hong. **1987**

CHINA O'BRIEN ★★ A former cop returns home to avenge her father's murder, using kung fu on the drug-dealing perpetrators. Rated R for violence and profanity. 90m. **DIR:** Robert Clouse. **CAST:** Cynthia Rothrock. **1990**

CHINA O'BRIEN 2 ★★ When a vengeful kingpin is sprung from jail, the streets aren't safe in a lady sheriff's town. Rated R for profanity. 85m. **DIR:** Robert Clouse. **CAST:** Cynthia Rothrock, Richard Norton. **1985**

CHINA SEAS ★★★½ Clark Gable is the captain of a Chinese river steamer in pirate-infested waters. Jean Harlow is once again the lady with a spotted past, who we all know is the perfect mate for Gable if he'd only realize it himself. An enjoyable screen romp. B&W; 90m. **DIR:** Tay Garnett. **CAST:** Clark Gable, Jean Harlow, Wallace Beery, Lewis Stone. **1935**

CHINA SKY ★★ Heroic doctor Randolph Scott puts down his stethoscope long enough to pick up a carbine and help Chinese guerrillas knock off hundreds of Japanese soldiers in this potboiler based on a Pearl Buck story. B&W; 78m. **DIR:** Ray Enright. **CAST:** Randolph Scott, Ruth Warrick, Anthony Quinn, Ellen Drew, Richard Loo. **1945**

CHINA WHITE ★★ Shoot-'em-up takes place in Amsterdam's Chinatown when two Chinese drug lords threaten the Italian Mafia's profit margin. Add a romantic liaison and you have a just-watchable actioner. Rated R for violence and profanity. 99m. **DIR:** Ronny Yu. **CAST:** Russell Wong, Steven Vincent Leigh, Lisa Schrage, Billy Drago. **1990**

CHINATOWN MURDERS, THE: MAN AGAINST THE MOB ★★★ L.A. cop George Peppard and his partners battle a prostitution ring operating out of Chinatown. Made-for-TV movie is most effective at recreating the sights and sounds of the 1940s, though the story is average TV fodder. 102m. **DIR:** Michael Pressman. **CAST:** George Peppard, Richard Bradford, Charles Haid, Julia Nickson, Ursula Andress. **1989**

CHINESE CONNECTION, THE ★★★ This action-packed import, in which Bruce Lee plays a martial arts expert out to avenge the death of his mentor, is good, watchable fare. But be forewarned: It's dubbed, and not all that expertly. Rated R. 107m. **DIR:** Lo Wei. **CAST:** Bruce Lee, Miao Ker Hsio. **1979**

CHINESE WEB, THE 🦃 Peter Parker (alias Spiderman) wards off a corrupt businessman. 95m. **DIR:** Don McDougall. **CAST:** Nicholas Hammond, Robert F. Simon, Benson Fong, John Milford, Ted Danson. **1978**

CHOKE CANYON 🦃 A two-fisted physicist takes on an evil industrialist in this absurd action-adventure movie. Rated PG. 96m. **DIR:** Chuck Bail. **CAST:** Stephen Collins, Janet Julian, Lance Henriksen, Bo Svenson. **1986**

CHRISTINA ★★ Contrived mystery film about a wealthy foreigner (Barbara Parkins) who pays an unemployed aircraft engineer (Peter Haskell) twenty-five thousand dollars to marry her so she can acquire a U.S. passport... or so we think. 95m. **DIR:** Paul Krasny. **CAST:** Barbara Parkins, Peter Haskell, James McEachin, Marlyn Mason. **1974**

CHRISTOPHER COLUMBUS (1985) 🦃 Stinkeroo travelogue-as-history, edited down from a lethally boring and misbegotten miniseries. 128m. **DIR:** Alberto Lattuada. **CAST:** Gabriel Byrne, Faye Dunaway, Oliver Reed, Max von Sydow, Eli Wallach, Nicol Williamson, José Ferrer, Virna Lisi, Raf Vallone. **1985**

CHRISTOPHER COLUMBUS: THE DISCOVERY 🦃 For all we care, this lamebrained movie about the famous Italian explorer can remain undiscovered. Tom Selleck as King Ferdinand is the worst casting since John Wayne as Genghis Khan. Rated PG-13 for violence and nudity. 120m. **DIR:** John Glen. **CAST:** Marlon Brando, Tom Selleck, George Corraface, Rachel Ward, Robert Davi. **1992**

CHROME SOLDIERS ★★★ Gary Busey returns home from Desert Storm to find his brother dead. Busey and four other Vietnam veterans take on a corrupt sheriff in this surprisingly good made-for-cable movie. 91m. **DIR:** Thomas Wright. **CAST:** Gary Busey, Ray Sharkey, William Atherton, Nicholas Guest, Yaphet Kotto. **1992**

CIA CODENAME ALEXA 🦃 An intelligence agent and a gungho cop reprogram a terrorist to turn against her boss. Ridiculous. Rated R for violence and profanity. 90m. **DIR:** Joseph Merhi. **CAST:** Lorenzo Lamas, O. J. Simpson, Kathleen Kinmont, Alex Cord. **1992**

CINCINNATI KID, THE ★★★★ Steve McQueen had one of his earliest acting challenges in this study of a determined young poker player on his way to the big time. He lets nothing stand in his way, especially not the reigning king of the card tables, Edward G. Robinson. 113m. **DIR:** Norman Jewison. **CAST:** Steve McQueen, Ann-Margret, Edward G. Robinson, Karl Malden, Tuesday Weld. **1965**

CIRCLE OF FEAR ★★½ Disgruntled Vietnam vet personally biffs almost every Filipino in Manila, searching for the nasties who kidnapped his daughter and sold her into sex slavery. Passable macho-actioner. Patrick Dollaghan does a shameless Michael Douglas impression. Rated R. 87m. **DIR:** Clark Henderson. **CAST:** Patrick Dollaghan, Wesley Penning, Joey Aresco, Vernon Wells. **1989**

CIRCLE OF IRON ★★★ Bruce Lee was preparing the screenplay for this martial arts fantasy shortly before he died. Ironically, the lead role fell to David Carradine, who had also been chosen over Lee for the lead in the television series *Kung Fu*. Fans of the genre will love it. Rated R for violence. 102m. **DIR:** Richard Moore. **CAST:** David Carradine, Jeff Cooper, Christopher Lee, Roddy McDowall, Eli Wallach, Erica Creer. **1979**

CITY OF SHADOWS ★★ It's the old story of Cain and Abel, set in the not-so-distant future. The first brother is a cop who lives by his own rules and deals out justice in like fashion, and the other is a maniac outlaw who kidnaps little boys and kills them. Some good action sequences along with satisfactory acting make this a passable film. 92m. **DIR:** David Mitchell. **CAST:** John P. Ryan, Paul Coufos, Tony Rosato. **1986**

CLAY PIGEON, THE ★★★ It is just after World War II. Sailor Bill Williams comes out of a coma to find he is going to be court-martialed for treason. When he is also accused of murder, he gets on the trail of the real killer. Tight plot and taut direction make this a seat-edge thriller. B&W; 63m. **DIR:** Richard Fleischer. **CAST:** Bill Williams, Barbara Hale, Richard Quine, Richard Loo, Frank Fenton, Frank Wilcox, Martha Hyer. **1949**

CLEARCUT ★★★ Native American Graham Greene finds the destruction of Indian land by a Canadian paper mill an injustice, and to make his point, kidnaps the mill manager. Interesting message complemented by above-average acting and some gorgeous photography. Rated R for language and violence. 98m. **DIR:** Richard Bugajski. **CAST:** Graham Greene, Floyd Red Crow Westerman, Raul Trujillo, Michael Hogan. **1992**

CLEOPATRA JONES 🦃 Secret agent Cleopatra Jones returns from an overseas assignment to save her old neighborhood. Rated PG for violence. 80m. **DIR:** Jack Starrett. **CAST:** Tamara Dobson, Shelley Winters, Bernie Casey, Brenda Sikes. **1973**

CLEOPATRA JONES AND THE CASINO OF GOLD ★★ Tamara Dobson stars as a U.S. agent out to shut down a drug empire run by the Dragon Lady (Stella Stevens). A big budget saves this yawner from turkeydom. Rated R for violence, profanity, and nudity. 96m. **DIR:** Chuck Bail. **CAST:** Tamara Dobson, Stella Stevens, Norman Fell. **1975**

CLIFFHANGER ★★ Expert mountain climber Sylvester Stallone attempts to rescue his girlfriend from the clutches of criminal John Lithgow, who is holding her hostage in the Rockies. Action fans may enjoy this one, but its preponderance of clichés will turn off more discriminating viewers. Rated R for violence and profanity. 115m. **DIR:** Renny Harlin. **CAST:** Sylvester Stallone, John Lithgow, Michael Rooker, Janine Turner. **1993**

CLIMB, THE ★★★ Straightforward account of the 1953 German assault on Nanga Parbat, the world's fifth highest peak. Bruce Greenwood is Herman Buhl, the arrogant climber who reached the summit alone. Rated PG, but suitable for the whole family. 86m. **DIR:** Donald Shebib. **CAST:** Bruce Greenwood, James Hurdle, Kenneth Walsh, Ken Pogue, Thomas Hauff. **1988**

CLINTON AND NADINE ★★★ Andy Garcia and Ellen Barkin enliven this otherwise routine cable-TV revenge thriller. He's determined to learn who killed his brother, and she's a sympathetic call girl in the right place at the right time. Violence and brief nudity. 108m. **DIR:** Jerry Schatzberg. **CAST:** Andy Garcia, Ellen Barkin, Morgan Freeman, Michael Lombard. **1987**

CLOAK AND DAGGER (1984) ★★★ A highly imaginative boy (Henry Thomas, of *E.T.*) who often plays pretend games of espionage with his fantasy friend, Jack Flack (Dabney Coleman), finds himself involved in a real life-and-death situation when he stumbles on to the evil doings of a group of spies (led by Michael Murphy). It's suspenseful and fast-paced but not so scary and violent as to upset the kiddies. Rated PG. 101m. **DIR:** Richard Franklin. **CAST:** Henry Thomas, Dabney Coleman, Michael Murphy, John McIntire, Shelby Leverington. **1984**

CLOUD DANCER ★★★½ This film features one of David Carradine's best performances. As the king of daredevil pilots, he struggles to keep ahead of his ambitious protégé (Joseph Bottoms) as well as fighting his love for Jennifer O'Neill. Rated PG. 108m. **DIR:** Barry Brown. **CAST:** David Carradine, Jennifer O'Neill, Joseph Bottoms, Colleen Camp. **1980**

CLUB LIFE ★★ Neon lovers! May we have your attention please. This is just the film for you. The neon used in the disco surpasses anything you've ever seen. Rated R. 93m. **DIR:** Norman Thaddeus Vane. **CAST:** Tony Curtis, Dee Wallace, Michael Parks, Yana Nirvana. **1987**

CLUTCHING HAND, THE ★★½ This independent chapterplay pits Craig Kennedy, the Scientific Detective, against a shadowy figure known only as the Clutching Hand. A veritable Who's Who of former silent-film heroes and heroines appears here. The plot is standard but the stunts and circumstances make this a fun serial to watch. B&W; 15 chapters. **DIR:** Albert Herman. **CAST:** Jack Mulhall, Marion Shilling, Yakima Canutt, Reed Howes, Ruth Mix, William Farnum, Rex Lease, Mae Busch, Bryant Washburn, Robert Frazer, Franklyn Farnum, Snub Pollard. **1936**

COAST PATROL, THE ★★ Set on the Maine coast and shot on the Pacific off Long Beach, this lively melodrama of smugglers and speedboat chases is Fay Wray's first film of record. If you're a fan, enjoy. Silent with musical score. B&W; 76m. **DIR:** Bud Barsky. **CAST:** Fay Wray, Kenneth McDonald. **1925**

COBRA (1986) ★★ Sylvester Stallone comes back for more *Rambo*-like action as a tough city cop on the trail of a serial killer in this unrelentingly grim and gruesome thriller. It is packed with action and violence. Rated R for violence, gore, and profanity. 95m. **DIR:** George Pan Cosmatos. **CAST:** Sylvester Stallone, Brigitte Nielsen, Reni Santoni, Andrew Robinson. **1986**

COBRA, THE (1967) 🦃 Dana Andrews battles communist drug smugglers in this stultifying spy stinker. Not rated. 97m. **DIR:** Mario Sequi. **CAST:** Dana Andrews, Anita Ekberg, Peter Martell. **1967**

COCAINE COWBOYS 🦃 This inept thriller concerns a struggling rock band whose members resort to drug smuggling in order to finance their music career. Rated R for nudity and graphic violence. 86m. **DIR:** Ulli Lommel. **CAST:** Jack Palance, Tom Sullivan, Andy Warhol, Suzanna Love. **1979**

COCAINE WARS 🦃 John Schneider plays an undercover agent in a South American country who takes on a drug lord's empire. Rated R for violence, profanity, and nudity. 82m. **DIR:** Hector Olivera. **CAST:** John Schneider, Kathryn Witt, Federico Luppi, Royal Dano. **1986**

COCKFIGHTER ★★ Title says it all. Warren Oates and Harry Dean Stanton can't breathe life into this simplistic look at the illegal sport of cockfighting. For Oates fans only. Rated R. 83m. **DIR:** Monte Hellman. **CAST:** Warren Oates, Harry Dean Stanton, Richard B. Shull, Troy Donahue, Millie Perkins. **1974**

CODE NAME: DANCER ★★★ Kate Capshaw plays a former CIA agent living a quiet married life in L.A., when she's called back to Cuba to settle an old score. TV movie originally titled *Her Secret Life*. 93m. **DIR:** Buzz Kulik. **CAST:** Kate Capshaw, Jeroen Krabbé, Gregory Sierra, Cliff De Young. **1987**

CODE NAME: EMERALD ★★★½ Better-than-average World War II espionage film about a double agent (Ed Harris) who attempts to rescue a U.S. Army officer (Eric Stoltz) held for interrogation in a French prison. The plot moves along at a good clip despite the lack of action. Rated PG for violence and sex. 95m. **DIR:** Jonathan Sanger. **CAST:** Ed Harris, Max von Sydow, Horst Buchholz, Helmut Berger, Cyrielle Claire, Eric Stoltz. **1985**

CODE NAME: WILD GEESE ★★ Marginal action-adventure is set in the Golden Triangle of Asia. A group of mercenaries hire out as a task force to destroy the opium trade for the Drug Enforcement Administration. Rated R. 101m. **DIR:** Anthony M. Dawson. **CAST:** Lewis Collins, Lee Van Cleef, Ernest Borgnine, Mimsy Farmer, Klaus Kinski. **1984**

CODE OF SILENCE ★★★★ With this film, Chuck Norris proved himself the heir to Charles Bronson as the king of the nonsense action movie. In *Code of Silence*, the star gives a right-on-target performance as tough cop Sgt. Eddie Cusack, who takes on warring mob families and corrupt police officers. Rated R for violence and profanity. 102m. **DIR:** Andrew Davis. **CAST:** Chuck Norris, Henry Silva, Bert Remsen, Dennis Farina, Mike Genovese, Ralph Foody, Nathan Davis. **1985**

COFFY 🦃 Pam Grier is wasted in this feeble blaxploitation action flick. Rated R. 91m. **DIR:** Jack Hill. **CAST:** Pam Grier, Booker Bradshaw, Sid Haig, Allan Arbus, Robert DoQui. **1973**

COLD HEAT 🦃 This farfetched film is basically about abuse—how two selfish parents abuse their son. Not rated, though there is some profanity and violence. 85m. **DIR:** Ulli Lommel. **CAST:** John Phillip Law, Britt Ekland, Robert Sacchi. **1990**

COLD JUSTICE ★★½ There's plenty of bare-fisted action in this tale of a priest who is actually a con man with an unsaintly agenda. Rated R for violence. 106m. **DIR:** Terry Green. **CAST:** Dennis Waterman, Roger Daltrey, Ron Dean, Penelope Milford. **1989**

COLD STEEL 🦃 Brainless rehash about a cop out for revenge for the murder of his father. Rated R for violence, nudity, and profanity. 91m. **DIR:** Dorothy Ann Puzo. **CAST:** Brad Davis, Adam Ant, Sharon Stone, Jonathan Banks. **1988**

COLD SWEAT (1970) 🦃 Dated, offensively sexist piece of machismo. Rated R. 94m. **DIR:** Terence Young. **CAST:** Charles Bronson, Liv Ullmann, Jill Ireland, James Mason, Gabriele Ferzetti, Michael Constantine. **1970**

COLD SWEAT (1993) ★★ A hit man (Ben Cross) decides to quit the business after he kills an innocent bystander. Persuaded to do one more job, he goes after the ambitious, double-crossing partner of a ruthless businessman, whose wife is cheating on him with his partner and Cross's contact. A good idea overcome by the film's sexual content. Rated R for simulated sex, nudity, violence, and profanity. 93m. **DIR:** Gail Harvey. **CAST:** Ben Cross, Adam Baldwin, Shannon Tweed, Dave Thomas. **1993**

COMBAT KILLERS ★★ The captain of an American platoon in the Philippines during the closing days of World War II puts his men through unnecessary dangers in fighting Japanese forces. Straightforward adventure will please war fans, though others may find it routine. The movie is unrated and contains some violence and profanity. 96m. **DIR:** Ken Loring. **CAST:** Paul Edwards, Marlene Dauden. **1980**

COME AND GET IT ★★★½ Based on Edna Ferber's novel, this involving film depicts life in Wisconsin's lumber country. It captures the robust, resilient nature of the denizens. Edward Arnold is perfectly cast as the grasping capitalist who needs to have his eyes opened. Walter Brennan's performance earned an Oscar for best supporting actor. B&W; 105m. **DIR:** Howard Hawks, William Wyler. **CAST:** Edward Arnold, Joel McCrea, Frances Farmer, Walter Brennan. **1936**

COMMANDO ★★★½ "Commando" John Matrix makes Rambo look like a wimp. As played by big, beefy Arnold Schwarzenegger, he "eats Green Berets for breakfast." He soon goes on the warpath when his 11-year-old daughter is kidnapped by a South American dictator (Dan Hedaya) he once helped depose. Rated R for violence and profanity. 90m. **DIR:** Mark L. Lester. **CAST:** Arnold Schwarzenegger, Rae Dawn Chong, Dan Hedaya, James Olson, Alyssa Milano. **1986**

COMMANDO SQUAD ★★ Lots of action but no substance in this standard tale of American drug agents operating undercover in Mexico. Kathy Shower is a tough female agent who tries to rescue her lover/coagent (Brian Thompson). Rated R for strong language and violence. 90m. **DIR:** Fred Olen Ray. **CAST:** Brian Thompson, Kathy Shower, William Smith, Sid Haig, Robert Quarry, Ross Hagen, Mel Welles. **1987**

COMMANDOS 🦃 Italian World War II film with dubbed English and not enough action. Rated PG for violence. 89m. **DIR:** Armando Crispino. **CAST:** Lee Van Cleef, Jack Kelly, Marino Masé. **1968**

COMMANDOS STRIKE AT DAWN ★★½ Okay WWII tale of underground fighter Paul Muni, who goes up against the Nazis after they invade his Norwegian homeland. The great cast deserved a better script than this, though it is nice to watch Muni and Lillian Gish practice their art. Some good action sequences keep things moving. B&W; 96m. **DIR:** John Farrow. **CAST:** Paul Muni, Lillian Gish, Cedric Hardwicke, Anna Lee, Alexander Knox, Ray Collins. **1942**

COMPANY BUSINESS ★★★ In what may be the first post-Cold War spy thriller, Gene Hackman plays an ex-CIA agent who is enlisted to escort an imprisoned KGB agent (Mikhail Baryshnikov) back to Russia. The two spies must band together to escape double-crossers on both sides of the parting Iron Curtain. Rated PG-13 for violence and profanity. 96m. **DIR:** Nicholas Meyer. **CAST:** Gene Hackman, Mikhail Baryshnikov, Kurtwood Smith, Terry O'Quinn. **1991**

COMRADES IN ARMS 🦃 Extremely bad dialogue kills this film in which a Russian and an American join forces to combat an international drug cartel. Rated R for violence and profanity. 91m. **DIR:** J. Christian Ingvordsen. **CAST:** Lyle Alzado, Lance Henriksen, Rick Washburne. **1991**

CONCRETE JUNGLE, THE (1982) ★★ This women's-prison melodrama has it all: an innocent girl who learns the ropes the hard way, an evil matron in collusion with the head bad girl, gratuitous shower and mud-wrestling scenes, and plentiful overacting. In short, a trash classic. Rated R for violence, nudity, and profanity. 99m. **DIR:** Tom DeSimone. **CAST:** Tracy Bregman, Jill St. John, Barbara Luna, Peter Brown, Nita Talbot. **1982**

CONFIDENTIAL ★★ A film that starts off well but quickly strangles on its own *film noir* style. A newspaper reporter investigating an old murder in 1949 Los Angeles is slain, and a hard-bitten detective tries to find the reasons why. Rated R for nudity, language, and violence. 95m. **DIR:** Bruce Pittman. **CAST:** August Schellenberg, Chapelle Jaffe, Neil Munro. **1988**

CONFLICT OF INTEREST 🦃 Gratuitously sleazy cop thriller. Noteworthy only to watch Judd Nelson put another nail in the coffin of his once-promising career. Rated R for violence, nudity, and profanity. 87m. **DIR:** Gary Davis. **CAST:** Christopher McDonald, Alyssa Milano, Dey Young, Judd Nelson. **1993**

CONQUEROR, THE 🦃 John Wayne plays Genghis Khan, and the results are unintentionally hilarious. 111m. **DIR:** Dick Powell. **CAST:** John Wayne, Susan Hayward, Pedro Armendariz, Agnes Moorehead. **1956**

CONVOY (1978) ★★ Truckers, led by Kris Kristofferson, go on a tri-state protest over police brutality, high gas prices, and other complaints. An uneven script and just fair acting mar this picture. Rated PG. 110m. **DIR:** Sam Peckinpah. **CAST:** Kris Kristofferson, Ali MacGraw, Ernest Borgnine, Madge Sinclair, Burt Young. **1978**

COOGAN'S BLUFF ★★★★ Clint Eastwood and director Don Siegel in their first collaboration. The squinty-eyed star hunts down a murderous fugitive (Don Stroud) in the asphalt jungle. Rated PG. 100m. **DIR:** Don Siegel. **CAST:** Clint Eastwood, Lee J. Cobb, Susan Clark, Tisha Sterling, Don Stroud, Betty Field, Tom Tully. **1968**

COOL HAND LUKE ★★★★★ One of Paul Newman's greatest creations is the irrepressible Luke. Luke is a prisoner on a southern chain gang and not even the deprivations of these subhuman conditions will break his spirit. George Kennedy's performance is equally memorable and won him a supporting Oscar. 126m. **DIR:** Stuart Rosenberg. **CAST:** Paul Newman, George Kennedy, J. D. Cannon, Lou Antonio, Robert Drivas, Strother Martin. **1967**

COP ★★ A supercharged performance by James Woods is not enough to make this crime thriller succeed. The film all too quickly goes from being a fascinating character study to just another sleazy and mindless slasher flick. Rated R for violence, gore, simulated sex, nudity, and profanity. 110m. **DIR:** James B. Harris. **CAST:** James Woods, Lesley Ann Warren, Charles Durning, Charles Haid, Raymond J. Barry, Randi Brooks. **1988**

COP IN BLUE JEANS, THE 🦃 An undercover cop (Thomas Milian) tries to take out an underworld boss (Jack Palance). Not rated; contains violence. 92m. **DIR:** Bruno Corbucci. **CAST:** Tomas Milian, Jack Palance, Maria Rosaria Omaggio, Guido Mannari. **1978**

COPS AND ROBBERS ★★ This mediocre cops-on-the-take caper features two burned-out New York cops who decide to use all they've learned to pull off the perfect crime. Rated PG for violence. 89m. **DIR:** Aram Avakian. **CAST:** Joseph Bologna, Cliff Gorman. **1973**

CORLEONE ★★ Dull Italian drama about two childhood friends in Sicily who decide to fight the powerful landowners who control their homeland. Aside from the title, which is the name of the Sicilian town where they live, this has no connection to the *Godfather* movies. Rated R for profanity, violence. 115m. **DIR:** Pasquale Squiteri. **CAST:** Giuliano Gemma, Claudia Cardinale, Francisco Rabal. **1985**

CORNERED ★★★ Fresh from his success as hardboiled sleuth Philip Marlowe in *Murder, My Sweet*, former song-and-dance man Dick Powell continued to score as a dramatic actor in this thriller about a discharged Canadian airman on the trail of Nazi collaborators who murdered his French wife. The hunt takes him from France to Switzerland to Argentina. B&W; 102m. **DIR:** Edward Dmytryk. **CAST:** Dick Powell, Walter Slezak, Micheline Cheirel, Luther Adler, Morris Carnovsky. **1946**

CORRUPT ONES, THE ★★★ Robert Stack plays a photographer who receives the key to a Chinese treasure. Not surprisingly, he soon finds that he's not alone in his search for the goodies. This is a good—but not great—adventure film. 92m. **DIR:** James Hill. **CAST:** Robert Stack, Nancy Kwan, Elke Sommer, Werner Peters. **1966**

CORSICAN BROTHERS, THE (1941) ★★★½ Alexandre Dumas's classic story of twins who remain spiritually tied, though separated, crackles in this lavish old Hollywood production. Intrigue and swordplay abound. Douglas Fairbanks Jr. is fine, backed by two of the best supporting players ever: J. Carrol Naish and Akim Tamiroff. B&W; 112m. **DIR:** Gregory Ratoff. **CAST:** Douglas Fairbanks Jr., Ruth Warrick, J. Carrol Naish, Akim Tamiroff, H. B. Warner, Henry Wilcoxon. **1941**

CORVETTE SUMMER 🦃 This mindless car-chase film finds Mark Hamill in Las Vegas hunting car thieves who have ripped off his Corvette. Rated PG. 105m. **DIR:** Matthew Robbins. **CAST:** Mark Hamill, Kim Melford, Annie Potts. **1978**

COTTON CLUB, THE ★★★★ Despite all the scandal, an inflated budget of more than $50 million, and some ragged last-minute trimming, *The Cotton Club* is a winner. The story about two pairs of brothers, one black and one white, is set at Harlem's most famous nightclub. Cornet player Gere and moll Diane Lane make love while Gregory Hines dances his way into the heart of songbird Lonette McKee in this flawed but brilliant film. Rated R for violence, nudity, profanity, and suggested sex. 128m. **DIR:** Francis Ford Coppola. **CAST:** Richard Gere, Diane Lane,

James Remar, Gregory Hines, Lonette McKee. **1984**

COUNT OF MONTE CRISTO, THE (1934) ★★★★ In the title role, Robert Donat heads a superb, fine-tuned cast in this now-classic film of Dumas's great story. Innocent sailor Edmond Dantes, falsely accused of aiding the exiled Napoleon and infamously imprisoned for fifteen years, escapes to levy revenge on those who framed him. A secret cache of treasure makes it all very sweet. B&W; 119m. **DIR:** Rowland V. Lee. **CAST:** Robert Donat, Elissa Landi, Irene Hervey, Louis Calhern, Sidney Blackmer, Raymond Walburn, O. P. Heggie. **1934**

COUNT OF MONTE CRISTO, THE (1975) ★★★½ Solid TV adaptation of the Alexandre Dumas classic. Richard Chamberlain cuts a dashing figure as the persecuted Edmond Dantes. The casting of Tony Curtis as the evil Mondego works surprisingly well. 100m. **DIR:** David Greene. **CAST:** Richard Chamberlain, Tony Curtis, Louis Jourdan, Donald Pleasence, Taryn Power. **1975**

COUNTERFEIT TRAITOR, THE ★★★★ A spy story based on a real-life character. William Holden is exceptionally good as the Swedish-American businessman who poses as a Nazi sympathizer. Authentic location work and good production values give this one an edge. 141m. **DIR:** George Seaton. **CAST:** William Holden, Lilli Palmer, Klaus Kinski, Hugh Griffith, Eva Dahlbeck. **1962**

COUNTERFORCE [turkey] An elite special missions force is hired to protect an exiled Middle East democratic leader. A bore. Rated R. 98m. **DIR:** J. Anthony Loma. **CAST:** George Kennedy, Jorge Rivero, Andrew Stevens, Isaac Hayes, Louis Jourdan, Robert Forster. **1987**

COVER-UP (1990) ★★ Reporters flock to Israel after an American military base is bombed. Violence begets violence in this confusing espionage thriller. Unrated, but contains violence, profanity, and nudity. 89m. **DIR:** Manny Coto. **CAST:** Dolph Lundgren, Lou Gossett Jr., John Finn. **1990**

CRACK HOUSE ★★ Okay exploitation film about the tragic world of crack cocaine. Two young lovers from the barrio are swept into the nightmare when the boyfriend avenges the murder of his cousin by a rival gang. Rated R for nudity, violence, and profanity. 97m. **DIR:** Michael Fischa. **CAST:** Richard Roundtree, Jim Brown, Anthony Geary. **1990**

CRASH DIVE ★★★ A stern sub commander and his brash aide clash at sea and over a girl back home. Familiar, but some suspense and fine special effects. Aging sailor James Gleason steals the movie. 105m. **DIR:** Archie Mayo. **CAST:** Tyrone Power, Dana Andrews, Anne Baxter, James Gleason, May Whitty. **1943**

CRASHOUT ★★½ Okay story about the odyssey of six convicts who crash out of prison. Unfortunately, the fine character development is hurt by a sometimes static plot and disappointing climax. William Bendix, however, is wonderfully unsympathetic as the self-serving ringleader. B&W; 82m. **DIR:** Lewis R. Foster. **CAST:** William Bendix, Arthur Kennedy, Luther Adler, William Talman, Marshall Thompson. **1955**

CRAZY MAMA ★★★ Vibrant film blends crime, comedy, and finely drawn characterizations in this story of three women on a crime spree from California to Arkansas and their experiences with the various men they pick up along the way. Successful mixture of music and atmosphere of the 1950s, coupled with a 1970s attitude, makes this an enjoyable film. Rated PG. 82m. **DIR:** Jonathan Demme. **CAST:** Stuart Whitman, Cloris Leachman, Ann Sothern, Jim Backus. **1975**

CRIME KILLER, THE [turkey] A confusing plot has a no-nonsense cop getting suspended, teaming up with two of his ex–Vietnam buddies, and smashing a guns-and-airplane deal with an Arab connection. Insipid. Unrated. 90m. **DIR:** George Pan-Andreas. **CAST:** George Pan-Andreas, Leo Morrell, Athan Karras. **1985**

CRIME LORDS ★★ Wayne Crawford directs and stars in this cop-buddy drama that originates in Los Angeles and ends on the streets of Hong Kong. Both story and stars are predictable. Rated R for violence. 96m. **DIR:** Wayne Crawford. **CAST:** Wayne Crawford, Martin Hewitt. **1990**

CRIME STORY ★★★½ Former Chicago cop Dennis Farina makes a believable and charismatic hero in this pilot for the Michael Mann–produced TV series. As Mike Torello, Farina attempts to stop the rise of ambitious hood Lucca (Anthony Denison) in the Mafia hierarchy. Strong character performances by an offbeat supporting cast make this an exceptional film of its kind. Made for TV. 96m. **DIR:** Abel Ferrara. **CAST:** Dennis Farina, Anthony Denison, Stephen Lang, Darlanne Fluegel, Bill Smitrovich, John Santucci, Steve Ryan, Bill Campbell, Paul Butler. **1986**

CRIMSON GHOST, THE ★★½ Yet another death-dealing device falls into the wrong hands when a physicist loses his counteratomic Cyclotrode to henchmen of the mysterious Crimson Ghost. Criminologist Duncan Richards (Charles Quigley) comes to the rescue. B&W; 12 chapters. **DIR:** William Witney, Fred Brannon. **CAST:** Charles Quigley, Linda Stirling, Clayton Moore, Kenne Duncan, I. Stanford Jolley, Tom Steele, Dale Van Sickel. **1946**

CRIMSON PIRATE, THE ★★★★½ One of the all-time great swashbucklers, this follow-up to *The Flame and the Arrow* features the incredibly agile Burt Lancaster besting villains and winning fair maids in high style.

Lancaster's partner from his circus days, Nick Cravat, joins in for some rousing action scenes. It's part adventure story, part spoof, and always entertaining. 104m. **DIR:** Robert Siodmak. **CAST:** Burt Lancaster, Nick Cravat, Eva Bartok, Torin Thatcher, Christopher Lee. **1952**

CROSS MISSION ★★ There's lots of shooting, some martial arts, even a little voodoo in this predictable tale about a pretty photographer and a handsome soldier of fortune in a banana republic. They are taken prisoner by the rebels, then converted to the cause. Rated R. 90m. **DIR:** Al Bradley. **CAST:** Richard Randall. **1989**

CROSS OF IRON ★★★½ With this action-packed war film, director Sam Peckinpah proved that he hadn't lost the touch that made *Ride the High Country* and *The Wild Bunch* such memorable movies. Still, *Cross of Iron* did not receive much acclaim when released. Perhaps it was the theme: the heroics of weary German soldiers in World War II. A precursor of *Das Boot*, this film is an interesting work by one of Hollywood's more original directors. Rated R. 119m. **DIR:** Sam Peckinpah. **CAST:** James Coburn, Maximilian Schell, James Mason, David Warner. **1977**

CRUSOE ★★½ This film by noted cinematographer-turned-director Caleb Deschanel is an attractive but incomplete examination of *Robinson Crusoe* updated to the early nineteenth century. Crusoe is now a young slave trader in Virginia. Aidan Quinn makes an appealing title character. Rated PG-13. 97m. **DIR:** Caleb Deschanel. **CAST:** Aidan Quinn, Ade Sapara. **1989**

CRY IN THE WILD, A ★★★½ En route to visit his father, an embittered teenager must crash-land a small plane over the Canadian forest when the pilot suddenly dies. Poignant boy-against-nature film. Rated PG for profanity and violence. 81m. **DIR:** Mark Griffiths. **CAST:** Jared Rushton, Ned Beatty, Pamela Sue Martin. **1990**

CRY OF BATTLE ★★ The son (James MacArthur) of a wealthy businessman gets caught in the Philippines during the Japanese occupation and has to resort to guerrilla warfare. Poorly directed, but does address the ethical questions of racism and the conduct of war. Not rated; with violence. B&W; 99m. **DIR:** Irving Lerner. **CAST:** James MacArthur, Van Heflin, Rita Moreno, Leopoldo Salcedo, Sidney Clute. **1957**

CUBA ★★★ A thinly veiled remake of *Casablanca*, this Richard Lester film is nonetheless far superior to J. Lee Thompson's similar *Cabo Blanco* (which starred Charles Bronson). Sean Connery and Brooke Adams play one-time lovers renewing their passion during the fall of Batista in 1959. As usual, Lester invests his tale with memorable bits. Rated R. 121m. **DIR:** Richard Lester. **CAST:** Sean Connery, Brooke Adams, Jack Weston, Hector Elizondo, Denholm Elliott, Chris Sarandon, Lonette McKee. **1979**

CURSE OF THE CRYSTAL EYE ★★★½ Better-than-average update of the Saturday-morning serial obviously owes a debt to *Raiders of the Lost Ark*. Jameson Parker and Cynthia Rhodes attempt to retrieve the infamous Crystal Eye from a hidden desert fortress while fighting off friends and foes alike. Impressive action sequences and a rousing sense of adventure elevate this one above the many low-budget affairs that followed *Raiders*. Rated R for violence. 82m. **DIR:** Joe Tornatore. **CAST:** Jameson Parker, Cynthia Rhodes, Mike Lane, David Sherwood, André Jacobs. **1993**

CUSTODIAN, THE ★★★½ An Australian cop decides he's had it with corruption in the police force, so he tackles the problem in a very unconventional way. He's also dealing with his own problems, including being thrown out of his house by his alcoholic wife. Very well-acted, with an intriguing plot. Not rated, but contains nudity, violence, and profanity. 96m. **DIR:** John Dingwall. **CAST:** Anthony LaPaglia, Hugo Weaving, Barry Otto, Kelly Dingwall, Bill Hunter, Gosia Dobrowolska. **1993**

CYCLONE 🦃 Stupid action flick about a top-secret military experiment. Rated R for violence and profanity. 89m. **DIR:** Fred Olen Ray. **CAST:** Heather Thomas, Martin Landau, Jeffrey Combs, Troy Donahue, Martine Beswick, Robert Quarry, Huntz Hall. **1986**

DADDY-O 🦃 Laughs alternate with yawns in this cheapjack J. D. crime potboiler. Makes *High School Confidential!* look like *The Asphalt Jungle*. B&W; 74m. **DIR:** Lou Place. **CAST:** Dick Contino, Sandra Giles, Bruno Ve Sota, Gloria Victor. **1959**

DADDY'S BOYS ★★ Depression-era crime-drama about an ex-farmer turned bank robber. Typical Roger Corman production has a few surprises but is basically familiar stuff. Rated R for violence and sexual situations. 84m. **DIR:** Joe Minion. **CAST:** Daryl Haney, Laura Burkett. **1988**

DAM BUSTERS, THE ★★★★½ Richard Todd and Michael Redgrave star in this British film about the development and use of a specially designed bomb to destroy a dam in Germany during World War II. An outstanding cast and great script. 205m. **DIR:** Michael Anderson. **CAST:** Richard Todd, Michael Redgrave, Ursula Jeans, Basil Sydney. **1954**

DAMN THE DEFIANT! ★★★★ Authenticity is the hallmark of this sea saga of the Napoleonic period. This British production pits the commanding officer of a British warship against a hated second officer. The performances are superb. 101m. **DIR:** Lewis Gilbert. **CAST:** Alec Guinness, Dirk Bogarde, Maurice Denham, Anthony Quayle. **1962**

DAMNED RIVER ★★★ Four Americans take a rafting adventure vacation down the Zambezi River in Zimbabwe. Things get out of hand when their guide turns out to be a pyschopath and a *Deliverance* game of survival is played out. Rated R for violence. 96m. **DIR:** Michael Schroeder. **CAST:** Stephen Shellen, John Terlesky. **1989**

DAN CANDY'S LAW ★★ The Royal Canadian Mounted Police always get their man. So where's the suspense? Not in this movie, that's for sure. The most appealing element is the glorious Canadian scenery. Originally titled *Alien Thunder*. Rated PG. 90m. **DIR:** Claude Fournier. **CAST:** Donald Sutherland, Kevin McCarthy, Chief Dan George, Francine Racette. **1973**

DANCE OR DIE ★★ Another listless made-for-video thriller. This one pits a drug-addicted Las Vegas choreographer against mob drug dealers and federal drug agents. 81m. **DIR:** Richard W. Munchkin. **CAST:** Ray Kieffer, Rebecca Barrington. **1988**

DANGER MAN (TELEVISION SERIES) ★★★½ CBS-TV imported this British-produced thriller, the first of three spy-flavored dramas to star Patrick McGoohan (see additional entries under *Secret Agent* and *The Prisoner*). The series debuted in May, 1961, and quietly went off the air after an undistinguished run of 24 episodes. (About twice that many were produced.) McGoohan starred as the "Danger Man," a free-lancer named John Drake, who worked as a security investigator in affiliation with NATO. A bit violent, but suitable for family viewing. B&W; 55m. **DIR:** Various. **CAST:** Patrick McGoohan. **1961**

DANGER ZONE, THE 🦃 Contrived low-budget flick about a psychopathic murderer on the loose. Rated R for language, nudity, and violence. 90m. **DIR:** Henry Vernon. **CAST:** Michael Wayne, Jason Williams, Suzanne Tara, Robert Canada, Juanita Ranney. **1986**

DANGEROUS CHARTER 🦃 Three fishermen find an abandoned yacht with a corpse on board. B&W; 74m. **DIR:** Robert Gottschalk. **CAST:** Chris Warfield, Sally Fraser, Chick Chandler. **1962**

DANGEROUS LOVE 🦃 A maniac killer with a camera begins murdering his dates and taping their deaths. Rated R for nudity, profanity, and violence. 96m. **DIR:** Marty Ollstein. **CAST:** Elliott Gould, Lawrence Monoson, Anthony Geary. **1988**

DANGEROUS MOONLIGHT (A.K.A. SUICIDE SQUADRON) ★★★ Polish pianist Anton Walbrook stops tickling the ivories and starts squeezing the trigger as he climbs into the cockpit as a bomber pilot for the RAF during World War II. Excellent aerial sequences. B&W; 83m. **DIR:** Brian Desmond Hurst. **CAST:** Anton Walbrook, Sally Gray, Derrek de Marney. **1941**

DANGEROUS PASSAGE ★★ Routine adventure-drama finds Robert Lowery in Central America, where he discovers that an inheritance awaits him back in the States. Phyllis Brooks provides the love interest. Mysterious shadows and attempts on Lowery's life provide the tension. B&W; 61m. **DIR:** William Burke. **CAST:** Robert Lowery, Phyllis Brooks, Jack LaRue, Victor Kilian. **1944**

DAREDEVILS OF THE RED CIRCLE ★★★ One of the most action-packed serials of all time pits three college athletes (including former Tarzan Bruce Bennett and ace stunt man David Sharpe) against the evil #39013, a former convict who disguises himself in order to gain power and exact vengeance on the society that imprisoned him. Fast-paced and well-acted. B&W; 12 chapters. **DIR:** William Witney, John English. **CAST:** Charles Quigley, Bruce Bennett, David Sharpe, Carole Landis. **1939**

DARING DOBERMANS, THE ★★½ Fun sequel to *The Doberman Gang* is a little more kiddy-oriented, but it's still okay, featuring another well-planned caper for the canine stars. Rated PG for very light violence and language. 90m. **DIR:** Byron Chudnow. **CAST:** Charles Knox Robinson, Tim Considine, David Moses, Joan Caulfield. **1973**

DARING GAME ★★½ Ivan Tors, producer of TV's *Sea Hunt* and *Flipper*, heads back into the water for this unsuccessful series pilot. It's about a team of commandos nicknamed The Flying Fish who are proficient on land, air, and sea. No better or worse than a lot of stuff that *did* make it to TV. 101m. **DIR:** Laslo Benedek, Ricou Browning. **CAST:** Lloyd Bridges, Nico Minardos, Michael Ansara, Joan Blackman, Shepperd Strudwick. **1968**

DARK AGE ★★½ What begins as a blatant *Jaws* rip-off becomes an entertaining thriller about a giant killer crocodile. A bit tough to follow due to Australian accents, but this flick offers a tolerable way to kill an hour and a half. Rated R for violence. 90m. **DIR:** Arch Nicholson. **CAST:** John Jarratt, Nikki Coghill, Max Phipps. **1987**

DARK JUSTICE 🦃 From the TV series, this miserable movie is a combination of two episodes spliced together about a criminal court judge who becomes a vigilante after his wife and child are murdered. He recruits the usual oddball characters to go after the bad guys. 99m. **DIR:** Jeff Freilich. **CAST:** Ramy Zada, Clayton Prince, Begona Plaza, Dick O'Neill. **1991**

DARK OF THE SUN ★★★★ Tough-as-nails mercenary Rod Taylor and his friend Jim Brown lead troops-for-hire deep into hostile guerrilla territory to retrieve a fortune in diamonds, and to rescue (if possible) the inhabitants of a remote European settlement in the Congo. Not rated, but violent and unsettling. 101m. **DIR:** Jack Cardiff. **CAST:** Rod Taylor, Yvette Mimieux, Jim Brown, Peter Carsten, Kenneth More, Andre Morell, Calvin Lockhart. **1968**

DARK RIDER 🦃 A corny chase film about a guy on a bike who saves a desert town from small-time gangsters. Not rated, but contains violence and profanity. 94m. **DIR:** Bob Ivy. **CAST:** Joe Estevez, Doug Shanklin. **1991**

DARKEST AFRICA ★★½ Clyde Beatty comes to the aid of a wild boy and his ape companion, and joins in their attempts to rescue the princess of the lost city of Joba. Plenty of action highlights this landmark serial, the first released by the recently organized Republic Pictures Corporation. B&W; 15 chapters. **DIR:** B. Reeves "Breezy" Eason, Joseph Kane. **CAST:** Clyde Beatty, Manuel King, Elaine Shepard, Lucien Prival, Wheeler Oakman. **1936**

DARKSIDE, THE ★★ A rookie cab driver picks up a porn star who is being pursued by thugs. There's some good suspense here, but melodramatic acting holds it back. Rated R for nudity, violence, and profanity. 95m. **DIR:** Constantino Magnatta. **CAST:** Tony Galati, Cyndy Preston. **1987**

DAVINCI'S WAR ★★ Ex–Special Services agent recruits a hit man to help rout the CIA-sponsored drug smuggling ring responsible for the death of his sister. Standard shoot-'em-up with a bit of a message. Rated R for violence, sex, and profanity. 94m. **DIR:** Raymond Martino. **CAST:** Joey Travolta, Michael Nouri, Vanity, James Russo, Sam Jones. **1993**

DAWN PATROL, THE ★★★★ Basil Rathbone is excellent as a commanding officer of a frontline British squadron during World War I who has no choice but to order raw replacements into the air against veteran Germans. Errol Flynn and David Niven shine as gentlemen at war. A fine film. B&W; 103m. **DIR:** Edmund Goulding. **CAST:** Errol Flynn, Basil Rathbone, David Niven, Melville Cooper, Barry Fitzgerald, Donald Crisp. **1938**

DAWSON PATROL, THE 🦃 A Royal Canadian Mounted Police dogsled expedition turns tragic in this feeble docudrama set at the turn of the century. Not rated, but contains violence. 75m. **DIR:** Peter Kelly. **CAST:** George R. Robertson, Tim Henry, Neil Dainaro, James B. Douglas. **1985**

DAY OF ATONEMENT ★★ A complicated plot, derivative situations, and cardboard characters do little to distinguish this weak mobster effort about warring factions in Miami. Even the high-caliber cast can't save it, despite a noble effort from Christopher Walken as a vicious drug lord. Rated R for violence and language. 119m. **DIR:** Alexandre Arcady. **CAST:** Christopher Walken, Jennifer Beals, Jill Clayburgh, Richard Berry, Roger Hanin. **1993**

DAY OF THE ASSASSIN 🦃 Chuck Connors plays a James Bond–type hero in this dull action film. Not rated; contains violence and profanity. 94m. **DIR:** Brian Trenchard-Smith, Carlos Vasallo. **CAST:** Chuck Connors, Glenn Ford, Richard Roundtree, Jorge Rivero, Henry Silva, Andres Garcia. **1979**

DAYS OF GLORY ★★ A young Gregory Peck (in his first film) and a cast of practically unknown European actors try their darndest to make this story of guerrilla warfare on the Russian front work, but the end result is limp and unconvincing. B&W; 86m. **DIR:** Jacques Tourneur. **CAST:** Gregory Peck, Tamara Toumanova, Alan Reed, Maria Palmer. **1944**

DAYS OF HELL 🦃 Good luck staying awake through this yawner about a group of mercenaries sent into Afghanistan to rescue a scientist. Unrated. 88m. **DIR:** Anthony Richmond. **CAST:** Conrad Nichols, Kiwako Harada. **1984**

DAYS OF THUNDER ★★★★ Star Tom Cruise and director Tony Scott take their *Top Gun* tactics to the racetrack in this fast-car fantasy set during the Daytona 500, and the result is remarkably satisfying. Screenwriter Robert Towne takes the standard story and infuses it with a richness that recalls the golden age of Hollywood. Rated PG-13 for profanity and violence. 108m. **DIR:** Tony Scott. **CAST:** Tom Cruise, Robert Duvall, Nicole Kidman, Randy Quaid, Michael Rooker, Cary Elwes. **1990**

DAYTON'S DEVILS ★★ Leslie Nielsen leads a group of has-beens and ex-cons—or, as the video box says, "a melting pot of losers"—in a robbery of an air force base bank. 107m. **DIR:** Jack Shea. **CAST:** Leslie Nielsen, Rory Calhoun, Lainie Kazan, Barry Sadler, Georg Stanford Brown. **1968**

DEAD AIM (1987) 🦃 Renegade Soviet agents flood the streets of New York with drugs. Rated R for violence and profanity. 91m. **DIR:** William VanDerKloot. **CAST:** Ed Marinaro, Corbin Bernsen, Isaac Hayes. **1987**

DEAD-BANG ★★★½ Don Johnson stars as real-life L.A. detective Jerry Buck, whose investigation into the murder of a police officer leads to the discovery of a chilling conspiracy. Johnson's strong performance is supported by an excellent cast. John Frankenheimer directs with authority and adds texture to the familiar plot. Rated R for violence, profanity, nudity, and simulated sex. 109m. **DIR:** John Frankenheimer. **CAST:** Don Johnson, Penelope Ann Miller, William Forsythe, Bob Balaban, Tim Reid. **1988**

DEAD POOL, THE ★★★★ Clint Eastwood's fifth Dirty Harry adventure is a surprisingly strong entry in the long-running series. Action and chuckles are in abundance as our hero tracks down a weirdo who is murdering celebrities on a list that also carries Harry's name. It's good fun for fans. Rated R for violence and profanity. 92m. **DIR:** Buddy Van Horn. **CAST:** Clint Eastwood, Patricia Clarkson, Liam Neeson, Evan Kim. **1988**

DEAD RECKONING (1947) ★★★ World War II veteran Humphrey Bogart is caught in a web of circumstance when he seeks the solution to an old army buddy's disappearance. Lizabeth Scott and Morris Carnovsky tell too many lies trying to cover it all up. A brutal yet sensitive example of *film noir*. Bogart is excellent. B&W; 100m. **DIR:** John Cromwell. **CAST:** Humphrey Bogart, Lizabeth Scott, Morris Carnovsky, Charles Cane, Marvin Miller, Wallace Ford, George Chandler. **1947**

DEADLINE (1988) ★★★ John Hurt gives a moving performance as an alcoholic British journalist who becomes involved in a doomed love affair with a beautiful noblewoman (Imogen Stubbs). Together they weather a revolution on an island estate in the Persian Gulf. Rated R for nudity, profanity, and graphic violence. 110m. **DIR:** Richard Stroud. **CAST:** John Hurt, Imogen Stubbs, Robert McBain, Greg Hicks. **1988**

DEADLINE AT DAWN ★★ Penned by Clifford Odets, this film is predictable and anticlimactic. While on liberty, sailor Bill Williams is slipped a mickey by Lola Lane and, upon awakening, he finds her dead. With the help of a dancer (Susan Hayward) and a cabbie (played flatly by Paul Lukas), he sets out to clear himself. B&W; 83m. **DIR:** Harold Clurman. **CAST:** Susan Hayward, Paul Lukas, Lola Lane, Bill Williams, Jerome Cowan. **1946**

DEADLY BET ★★½ A compulsive gambler and alcoholic almost loses everything, including his girlfriend, to a ruthless kick boxer. Watchable if unmemorable little film. Rated R for profanity and seemingly endless violence. 93m. **DIR:** Richard W. Munchkin. **CAST:** Jeff Wincott, Charlene Tilton, Steven Vincent Leigh. **1992**

DEADLY CURRENTS ★★★ Exiled CIA agent William L. Petersen finds himself in a political hotbed when he befriends stranger George C. Scott on the small island of Curaçao. Things heat up when several factions arrive on the island to settle an old score with Scott. Exotic locales and double and triple crosses add color and suspense to this thriller, made for cable under the title *Curaçao*. Rated R for language and violence. 93m. **DIR:** Carl Schultz. **CAST:** William L. Petersen, George C. Scott, Julie Carmen, Trish Van Devere, Philip Anglim. **1993**

DEADLY EMBRACE 🦃 Sexual decadence ends in murder. Soft-core porn dud. 82m. **DIR:** Ellen Cabot. **CAST:** Jan-Michael Vincent, Jack Carter, Ken Abraham. **1988**

DEADLY ENCOUNTER (1972) ★★★½ Hounded by mobsters, Susan Anspach enlists the aid of her old lover Larry Hagman, an ex-combat helicopter pilot. Great aerial stunts are a treat and help keep the action moving right along. Pretty good for television. 100m. **DIR:** William A. Graham. **CAST:** Larry Hagman, Susan Anspach, James Gammon, Michael C. Gwynne. **1972**

DEADLY FORCE ★★★ Wings Hauser (*Vice Squad*) plays "Stony" Jackson Cooper, an ex-cop who returns to his old Los Angeles stomping grounds to stomp people until he finds the maniac who stomped a buddy's daughter to death. Rated R for violence, nudity, and profanity. 95m. **DIR:** Paul Aaron. **CAST:** Wings Hauser, Joyce Ingalls, Paul Shenar. **1983**

DEADLY GAME ★★½ What hath Richard Connell wrought? Scripter Wes Claridge is merely the latest to borrow liberally from "The Most Dangerous Game," this time pitting seven virtual strangers against a masked (and well-armed) maniac. Made for cable TV. Rated R for profanity and violence. 93m. **DIR:** Thomas Wright. **CAST:** Michael Beck, Jenny Seagrove, Roddy McDowall, Mitchell Ryan, Marc Singer. **1991**

DEADLY HERO ★★★½ Strange yet engaging bad-cop film with Don Murray as a New York police officer struggling to stay on the force after an incident's repercussions threaten his upcoming pension. The film is dated by the trendy mid-Seventies fashions and popular art, yet that is ironically one of its more interesting qualities. Rated PG for violence and profanity. 102m. **DIR:** Ivan Nagy. **CAST:** Don Murray, Diahn Williams, Lilia Skala, George S. Irving, Conchata Ferrell, Ron Weyand, James Earl Jones, Treat Williams. **1975**

DEADLY IMPACT ★★ Fred Williamson and Bo Svenson work well together in this otherwise contrived, Italian-made action film about an attempt to rip off Las Vegas gambling houses. Rated R. 90m. **DIR:** Larry Ludman. **CAST:** Fred Williamson, Bo Svenson. **1985**

DEADLY INTENT ★★ A murderous archaeologist returns from an expedition with a priceless jewel and blood on his hands. He's soon murdered and everybody who knew him is after the jewel. Although the cast is talented, the film is flawed by poor pacing and bad logic. Rated R for violence and language. 83m. **DIR:** Nigel Dick. **CAST:** Lisa Eilbacher, Steve Railsback, Maud Adams, Lance Henriksen, Fred Williamson. **1988**

DEADLY PREY 🦃 Absolutely wretched piece of celluloid about a secret mercenary boot camp. Rated R for violence and profanity. 87m. **DIR:** David A. Prior. **CAST:** Cameron Mitchell, Troy Donahue. **1987**

DEADLY REVENGE 🦃 Talky crime drama (dubbed in English) about a mild-mannered writer who agrees to take over a nightclub. Rated R for profanity, violence, nudity, and sexual situations. 90m. **DIR:** Juan Carlos Sesanzo. **CAST:** Rodolfo Ranni, Julio de Grazia. **1984**

DEADLY RIVALS 🦃 Emerald smuggling and corporate espionage in this confusing thriller. Rated R for nudity, profanity, and violence. 93m. **DIR:** James Dodson. **CAST:** Andrew Stevens, Cela Wise, Margaux Hemingway, Joseph Bologna, Richard Roundtree. **1992**

DEADLY SPYGAMES ★★½ A government agent and his ex-lover are sent to destroy a Cuban radar station and prevent World War III. James Bond fans may enjoy this spy spoof, but it could be too silly for others. Not rated; contains mild sexual situations. 86m. **DIR:** Jack M. Sell. **CAST:** Jack M. Sell, Adrianne Richmond, Troy Donahue, Tippi Hedren. **1989**

DEADLY STRANGER ★½ A drifter (Michael J. Moore) takes a job on a plantation where the owner and a local union leader are conspiring to exploit migrant workers. Clichéd movie wastes the talents of Fluegel and the time of the viewer. Unrated; nudity. 93m. **DIR:** Max Kleven. **CAST:** Darlanne Fluegel, Michael J. Moore, John Vernon. **1988**

DEADLY SURVEILLANCE ★★★★ An unexpected treat. What could have been another tired and gory struggle between good cops and nasty drug lords emerges as fresh, witty, and engaging, thanks to a deft script from Hal Salwen and director Paul Ziller. Michael Ironside plays against type as a dedicated cop. Rated R for nudity, violence, and profanity. 92m. **DIR:** Paul Ziller. **CAST:** Michael Ironside, Christopher Bondy, Susan Almgren, David Carradine. **1991**

DEADLY TWINS 🦃 A typical revenge flick about twin sisters who are gang raped. Not rated, but contains adult themes. 87m. **DIR:** Joe Oaks. **CAST:** Judy Landers, Audrey Landers. **1985**

DEADLY VENGEANCE 🦃 The poor acting, editing, and lighting in this insipid film make one wonder if it was planned by a couple of beginning film students over a keg of beer. Contains obscenities, simulated sex scenes, and violence. 84m. **DIR:** A. C. Qamar. **CAST:** Arthur Roberts, Alan Marlowe, Bob Holden. **1985**

DEATH BEFORE DISHONOR 🦃 Grade Z war film. Rated R for violence and profanity. 112m. **DIR:** Terry Leonard. **CAST:** Fred Dryer, Brian Keith, Joanna Pacula, Paul Winfield. **1986**

DEATH CHASE ★★ An innocent jogger is caught up in a shoot-out, given a gun by a dying man, and suddenly finds himself in the midst of an elaborate chase. The premise is intriguing, but the execution is uninspired in this shoddily made thriller. 88m. **DIR:** David A. Prior. **CAST:** William Zipp, Paul Smith, Jack Starrett, Bainbridge Scott. **1988**

DEATH HOUSE 🦃 Framed for murder by the mob, Dennis Cole discovers that prisoners are being used for dangerous scientific experiments with nasty side effects. Give this one life without parole. Not rated, but contains nudity, violence, and profanity. 92m. **DIR:** John Saxon. **CAST:** Dennis Cole, John Saxon, Anthony Franciosa. **1992**

DEATH HUNT ★★★½ Based on the true story of a hazardous manhunt in the Canadian Rockies, *Death Hunt* pits trapper Charles Bronson against Mountie Lee Marvin. This gritty adventure film, directed by Peter Hunt, also features vicious dogfights and bloody shoot-outs set against the spectacular scenery of the Yukon Territory. Rated R. 97m. **DIR:** Peter R. Hunt. **CAST:** Charles Bronson, Lee Marvin, Andrew Stevens, Angie Dickinson, Carl Weathers, Ed Lauter. **1981**

DEATH RING 🦃 A cast of star relatives do nothing to freshen this umpteenth update of "The Most Dangerous Game." Rated R for violence, sexual situations, and profanity. 91m. **DIR:** R. J. Kizer. **CAST:** Mike Norris, Billy Drago, Chad McQueen, Don Swayze. **1992**

DEATH SQUAD, THE ★★ A self-appointed coterie of cops is rubbing out criminals beating the rap on legal technicalities. A former officer is given the job of finding out who's doing it and cleaning house. Clint Eastwood did it all infinitely better in *Magnum Force*. Made for television. 78m. **DIR:** Harry Falk. **CAST:** Robert Forster, Michelle Phillips, Claude Akins, Melvyn Douglas. **1974**

DEATH TARGET ★★ Three soldiers for hire reunite in one last bid for fortune. But when one of the guys falls for a drug-addict hooker, her loony pimp gets into the act, putting a wrench in the works for everyone. Macho. No rating. 72m. **DIR:** Peter Hyams. **CAST:** Jorge Montesi, Elaine Lakeman. **1983**

DEATH WARRANT ★★ Action-fu star Jean-Claude Van Damme has plenty to kick about as he plays an undercover cop sent into the slammer to investigate a series of inmate deaths. Before the final showdown, there are beatings and big-house clichés galore. Rated R for language and violence. 89m. **DIR:** Deran Sarafian. **CAST:** Jean-Claude Van Damme, Robert Guillaume, Cynthia Gibb, George Dickerson. **1990**

DEATH WISH ★★★★ Charles Bronson gives an excellent performance as Paul Kersey, a mild-mannered New Yorker moved to violence when his daughter is raped and his wife killed by sleazy muggers. It's a gripping story of one man's revenge. Rated R because of nudity and violence (includes a graphic rape scene). 93m. **DIR:** Michael Winner. **CAST:** Charles Bronson, Hope Lange, Vincent Gardenia, Jeff Goldblum. **1974**

DEATH WISH II 🦃 This carbon-copy sequel to the successful *Death Wish* is a revolting, violent crime chiller. Rated R because of nudity and violence. 93m. **DIR:** Michael Winner. **CAST:** Charles Bronson, Jill Ireland, Vincent Gardenia, J. D. Cannon, Anthony Franciosa. **1982**

DEATH WISH III 🦃 Paul Kersey (Charles Bronson) loses a loved one and then goes on another rampage. Rated R for violence, profanity, drug use, nudity, and sex. 99m. **DIR:** Michael Winner. **CAST:** Charles Bronson, Deborah Raffin, Ed Lauter, Martin Balsam. **1985**

DEATH WISH IV: THE CRACKDOWN 🦃 Charles Bronson is back as the vigilante, but this time he's hired to destroy two drug families operating in Los Angeles. Rated R for violence and language. 98m. **DIR:** J. Lee Thompson. **CAST:** Charles Bronson, Kay Lenz, John P. Ryan, Perry Lopez, Soon-Teck Oh, George Dickerson, Dana Barron. **1987**

DEATH WISH V: THE FACE OF DEATH ★★★½ Vigilante Charles Bronson returns to hunt a ruthless mobster who just happens to be his fiancée's ex-husband. The story is quite captivating, and the film doesn't contain too much gore or violence. Rated R for nudity, profanity, and violence. 95m. **DIR:** Allan A. Goldstein. **CAST:** Charles Bronson, Lesley-Anne Down, Robert Joy, Michael Parks, Chuck Shamata, Kenneth Welsh. **1993**

DEATHFIGHT ★★ Brother battles brother in this decent martial arts flick that features the art of shoot boxing. When the patriarch of the family selects his adopted son to run the family smuggling business, the natural son frames his brother for murder. Rated R for nudity, violence, and profanity. 92m. **DIR:** Anthony Maharaj. **CAST:** Richard Norton, Karen Moncrieff, Chuck Jeffreys, Ron Vreeken, Franco Guerrero, Jose Mari Avellano, Tetchie Agbayani. **1992**

DEATHMASK ★★ This talky, confusing screenplay is interesting in concept but is never sure where it's going. The plot involves a medical investigator who, after his daughter drowns, pours all his energy into investigating the death of a young boy. Not rated. 103m. **DIR:** Richard Friedman. **CAST:** Farley Granger, Lee Bryant, Arch Johnson. **1984**

DEATHSHOT 🦃 Two Illinois detectives will stop at nothing to break up a drug ring. 90m. **DIR:** Mitch Brown. **CAST:** Richard C. Watt, Frank Himes. **1973**

DECEIVERS, THE ★★½ Melodramatic yarn set in 1820s India and based on the true story of the murderous Thuggee cult. Pierce Brosnan goes undercover and joins the cult. This slow-going film has its moments. Rated PG-13. 103m. **DIR:** Nicholas Meyer. **CAST:** Pierce Brosnan, Shashi Kapoor, Saeed Jaffrey. **1988**

DEEP, THE ★★ The success of *Jaws* prompted this screen adaptation of another Benchley novel, but the results weren't nearly as satisfying. A good cast founders in this waterlogged tale of treasure hunting. Rated PG. 123m. **DIR:** Peter Yates. **CAST:** Robert Shaw, Jacqueline Bisset, Nick Nolte, Lou Gossett Jr., Eli Wallach, Robert Tessier. **1977**

DEEP COVER (1992) ★★★★ With this no-nonsense action film about a strait laced cop (brilliantly played by Larry Fishburne) who goes undercover for the DEA, Bill Duke hits his stride as a director. Duke tells his story of Fishburne's descent into decadence, danger, and disillusionment in a compelling, in-your-face fashion. Rated R for violence, profanity, and nudity. 112m. **DIR:** Bill Duke. **CAST:** Larry Fishburne, Jeff Goldblum, Victoria Dillard, Charles Martin Smith, Sidney Lassick, Clarence Williams III, Gregory Sierra. **1992**

DEFENSE PLAY 🦃 Substandard spy story about a group of newly graduated high school geniuses. Not rated; contains profane language, violence, and nudity. 95m. **DIR:** Monte Markham. **CAST:** David Oliver, Monte Markham. **1988**

DEFIANCE ★★★ Potent story depicts savage New York street gang terrorizing helpless neighborhood. Outsider Jan-Michael Vincent reluctantly gets involved. This well-directed film packs quite a wallop. Rated R for violence and profanity. 102m. **DIR:** John Flynn. **CAST:** Jan-Michael Vincent, Art Carney, Theresa Saldana, Danny Aiello, Fernando Lopez. **1980**

DELIVERANCE ★★★★★ Jon Voight, Burt Reynolds, and Ned Beatty are superb in this first-rate film about a canoe trip down a dangerous river that begins as a holiday but soon turns into a weekend of sheer horror. Based on the novel by James Dickey. Rated R for profanity, sex, and violence. 109m. **DIR:** John Boorman. **CAST:** Jon Voight, Burt Reynolds, Ned Beatty, Ronny Cox, James Dickey. **1972**

DELOS ADVENTURE, THE 🦃 Scientists stumble on a secret Soviet military operation. Rated R for gratuitous nudity and excessive violence and gore. 98m. **DIR:** Joseph Purcell. **CAST:** Roger Kern, Jenny Neuman, Kurtwood Smith, Kevin Brophy. **1987**

DELTA FORCE, THE ★★ In this disappointing action film, which is perhaps best described as "The Dirty Dozen at the Airport," Chuck Norris and Lee Marvin are leaders of an antiterrorist group charged with saving the passengers on a hijacked airliner. Rated R for profanity and violence. 126m. **DIR:** Menahem Golan. **CAST:** Chuck Norris, Lee Marvin, Martin Balsam, Joey Bishop, Robert Forster, Lainie Kazan, George Kennedy, Hanna Schygulla, Susan Strasberg, Bo Svenson, Robert Vaughn, Shelley Winters. **1986**

DELTA FORCE 2 ★★ An outrageously exciting skydiving sequence highlights this otherwise routine and overly cold-blooded action-adventure about a commando leader (Chuck Norris) who goes after a Colombian drug lord (Billy Drago). Rated R for language and violence. 115m. **DIR:** Aaron Norris. **CAST:** Chuck Norris, Billy Drago, John P. Ryan, Richard Jaeckel. **1990**

DELTA FORCE 3 ★★½ Platoon of second-generation stars fill in for Chuck Norris in this adequate third entry for the action-seeking Delta Force. Rated R for violence and profanity. 97m. **DIR:** Sam Firstenberg. **CAST:** Nick Cassavetes, Eric Douglas, Mike Norris, Matthew Penn, John P. Ryan. **1990**

DELTA FORCE, COMMANDO TWO 🦃 An enemy government tricks a military official in order to steal nuclear weapons, and impending global disaster has to be halted by the Delta Force. A complete mess throughout. Rated R for violence. 100m. **DIR:** Frank Valenti. **CAST:** Richard Hatch, Fred Williamson, Van Johnson. **1991**

DELTA FOX 🦃 A hired assassin finds that he himself has been set up to be killed. Rated R. 92m. **DIR:** Ferd Sebastian, Beverly Sebastian. **CAST:** Priscilla Barnes, Richard Lynch, Stuart Whitman, John Ireland, Richard Jaeckel. **1977**

DELTA HEAT ★★★ An LAPD police officer teams up with a New Orleans ex-cop-turned-swamp-rat to track down a killer drug dealer. At first this looks like a boring movie, but keep watching; it actually gets better. Rated R for violence and profanity. 91m. **DIR:** Michael Fischa. **CAST:** Anthony Edwards, Lance Henriksen, Betsy Russell, Linda Dona, Rod Masterson. **1992**

DESERT FOX, THE ★★★★ A tour-de-force performance by James Mason marks this film biography of German Field Marshal Rommel. His military exploits are glossed over in favor of the human story of the disillusionment and eventual involvement in the plot to assassinate Hitler. B&W; 88m. **DIR:** Henry Hathaway. **CAST:** James Mason, Jessica Tandy, Cedric Hardwicke, Luther Adler, Desmond Young. **1951**

DESERT KICKBOXER ★★ More kickboxing action, with John Haymes Newton as a border guard who takes on a ruthless drug dealer and his drug empire. You've seen it all before. Rated R for violence. 86m. **DIR:** Isaac Florentine. **CAST:** John Haymes Newton, Paul Smith, Judie Aronson. **1992**

DESPERATE CRIMES 🦃 Aptly titled, this movie *is* a crime as it desperately attempts to tell the tale of a man searching for the murderers of his girlfriend. Rated R for nudity, simulated sex, violence, and profanity. 92m. **DIR:** Andreas Marfori. **CAST:** Denise Crosby, Van Quattro, Rena Niehaus, Franco Columbu, Nicoletta Boris, Elizabeth Kaitan, Randi Ingerman, Traci Lords. **1993**

DESPERATE HOURS (1990) ★★½ Desperate remake of William Wyler's 1955 suspense classic, with Mickey Rourke taking over the Humphrey Bogart role. Rourke's pointless posturing and director Michael Cimino's tendency toward overkill make it more campy than chilling. Rated R for violence and profanity. 106m. **DIR:** Michael Cimino. **CAST:** Mickey Rourke, Anthony Hopkins, Mimi Rogers, Lindsay Crouse, Kelly Lynch, Elias Koteas, David Morse, Shawnee Smith. **1990**

DESTINATION TOKYO ★★★★ Superior World War II adventure focuses on a submarine crew as they attempt to penetrate Tokyo Bay and destroy Japanese vessels. Cary Grant's fine performance as the commander is complemented by a crackling script and assured direction by Delmer Daves. B&W; 135m. **DIR:** Delmer Daves. **CAST:** Cary Grant, John Garfield, Alan Hale Sr., Dane Clark, Warner Anderson. **1943**

DETECTIVE SADIE AND SON ★★★ Debbie Reynolds plays a rough-and-ready street cop forced into early retirement by her yuppie boss. She becomes a neighborhood vigilante, and her heroic deeds land her back on the force—training her less-than-dedicated son. A few funny moments are found among the encounters with numerous assailants and muggers. Made for TV, this contains considerable violence. 94m. **DIR:** John Llewellyn Moxey. **CAST:** Debbie Reynolds, Brian McNamara, Sam Wanamaker. **1988**

DETROIT 9000 (DETROIT HEAT) ★★½ Two Detroit cops, one black and one white, look for the vicious hoods who robbed a political rally. Tamer than usual blaxploitation thriller. Rated R for violence, profanity, and brief nudity. 106m. **DIR:** Arthur Marks. **CAST:** Alex Rocco, Hari Rhodes, Vonetta McGee, Scatman Crothers. **1973**

DEVASTATOR, THE 🦃 Lousy acting and writing ravage this movie about an evil marijuana plantation owner. Rated R for violence and language. 89m. **DIR:** Cirio H. Santiago. **CAST:** Richard Hill, Katt Shea, Crofton Hardester, Kaz Garas, Terence O'Hara, Bill McLaughlin. **1985**

DEVIL DOGS OF THE AIR ★★★ James Cagney is a hotshot barnstormer who joins the Marine Air Corps and refuses to conform to tradition and the authority of Pat O'Brien. Familiar roles for the stars but they play them so well. Great aerial stunt work is a plus. B&W; 86m. **DIR:** Lloyd Bacon. **CAST:** James Cagney, Pat O'Brien, Margaret Lindsay, Frank McHugh, Russell Hicks, Ward Bond. **1935**

DEVIL RIDER! 🦃 No-budget biker movie. Not rated, but contains R-level profanity, violence, and brief nudity. 68m. **DIR:** Brad F. Grinter. **CAST:** Sharon Mahon. **1970**

DEVIL'S BRIGADE, THE ★★½ During World War II, a disciplined Canadian troop is sent to Utah to train with a ragtag gang of American army misfits for a planned joint operation. Unrated, but has graphic battle scenes. 130m. **DIR:** Andrew V. McLaglen. **CAST:** William Holden, Cliff Robertson, Vince Edwards, Michael Rennie, Dana Andrews, Claude Akins, Carroll O'Connor, Richard Jaeckel. **1968**

DIAMONDS ★★★ Well-planned plot and good chemistry between Robert Shaw and Richard Roundtree make this an enjoyable film of action and intrigue. When a British entrepreneur hires an ex-con and his girlfriend to assist him in a $100 million diamond heist the stage is set for an amazing number of plot twists. 108m. **DIR:** Menahem Golan. **CAST:** Robert Shaw, Richard Roundtree, Barbara Hershey, Shelley Winters. **1975**

DIAMONDS ARE FOREVER ★★★★ This release was supposed to be Sean Connery's last appearance as James Bond before he decided to *Never Say Never Again*. It's good fun for 007 fans and far superior to most of the Roger Moore films that followed it. Rated PG. 119m. **DIR:** Guy Hamilton. **CAST:** Sean Connery, Jill St. John, Charles Gray, Bruce Cabot. **1971**

DICK TRACY (1937) ★★★ Chester Gould's comic-strip detective Dick Tracy (Ralph Byrd) chases a mysterious criminal known as *The Spider* who has kidnapped his brother and turned him into a slave. Great stunts and plenty of action in this one. B&W; 15 chapters. **DIR:** Ray Taylor, Alan James. **CAST:** Ralph Byrd, Kay Hughes, Smiley Burnette, Lee Van Atta, Francis X. Bushman. **1937**

DICK TRACY (1990) ★★★★ Chester Gould's comic-strip detective Dick Tracy (Warren Beatty) takes on a bevy of baddies while fending off the affections of the sultry Breathless (Madonna) in this stylish, old-fashioned piece of screen entertainment. Al Pacino has a field day as the main heavy, Big Boy Caprice, while other big-name stars and character actors do cameo bits. Rated PG for violence. 120m. **DIR:** Warren Beatty. **CAST:** Warren Beatty, Madonna, Glenne Headly, Al Pacino, Dustin Hoffman, James Caan, Mandy Patinkin, Paul Sorvino, Charles Durning, Dick Van Dyke, R. G. Armstrong, William Forsythe. **1990**

DICK TRACY, DETECTIVE ★★ Standard second-feature fare with Dick Tracy tangling with the denizens of the underworld. B&W; 62m. **DIR:** William Berke. **CAST:** Morgan Conway, Anne Jeffreys, Mike Mazurki, Jane Greer. **1945**

DICK TRACY MEETS GRUESOME ★★½ Everybody's favorite Dick Tracy, Ralph Byrd, returns to the role he originated in serials for Republic Studios just in time to do battle with Gruesome, played with style by the great Boris Karloff. B&W; 65m. **DIR:** John Rawlins. **CAST:** Ralph Byrd, Boris Karloff, Anne Gwynne, Edward Ashley, June Clayworth. **1947**

DICK TRACY RETURNS ★★★ Ralph Byrd's second outing as comic-strip detective Dick Tracy finds the unbeatable G-man hot on the trail of the murderous Stark gang, an evil family that has killed one of Tracy's men. B&W; 15 chapters. **DIR:** William Witney, John English. **CAST:** Ralph Byrd, Lynne Roberts (Mary Hart), Charles Middleton, David Sharpe, Jerry Tucker, Ned Glass. **1938**

DICK TRACY VS. CRIME INC. ★★★ Dick Tracy is called in to help stop the mysterious "Ghost," a ruthless member of the Council of Eight, a group of influential citizens attempting to rid the city of crime. B&W; 15 chapters. **DIR:** William Witney, John English. **CAST:** Ralph Byrd, Michael Owen, Jan Wiley, John Davidson, Ralph Morgan. **1941**

DICK TRACY VERSUS CUEBALL ★★ Dick Tracy chases a bald strangler who made off with a fortune in jewelry in this low-budget feature film. Morgan Conway's anemic Dick Tracy holds this one back, but Dick Wessel as Cueball peps up this modest programmer. B&W; 62m. **DIR:** Gordon Douglas. **CAST:** Morgan Conway, Anne Jeffreys, Lyle Latell, Rita Corday, Dick Wessel. **1946**

DICK TRACY'S DILEMMA ★★½ Two-fisted detective Dick Tracy (Ralph Byrd) finds himself up against a maniacal killer with an iron hook. B&W; 60m. **DIR:** John Rawlins. **CAST:** Ralph Byrd, Lyle Latell, Kay Christopher, Jack Lambert, Ian Keith. **1947**

DICK TRACY'S G-MEN ★★★ FBI agent Dick Tracy is forced to pursue the evil Zarnoff, the head of an international spy ring, after already capturing him and witnessing his execution. The ruthless spy lord is revived by drugs and redoubles his efforts at sabotage, putting Tracy and his men in one tight spot after another. B&W; 15 chapters. **DIR:** William Witney, John English. **CAST:** Ralph Byrd, Irving Pichel, Ted Pearson, Jennifer Jones, Walter Miller. **1939**

DICK TURPIN ★★ Tom Mix exchanges chaps and six-guns for cape and sword in this rather stolid portrayal of the legendary English highwayman. Good production values and crisp photography, but this one's no match for Mix's more traditional Western adventures. Silent. B&W; 70m. **DIR:** John G. Blystone. **CAST:** Tom Mix, Kathleen Myers. **1925**

DIE HARD ★★★★½ If this rip-roaring action picture doesn't recharge your batteries, you're probably dead. Alan Rickman and Alexander Godunov play terrorists who invade an L.A. high-rise. The direction of John McTiernan packs a wallop. Bruce Willis is more human, not to mention chattier, than most action heroes. Rated R for violence, nudity, profanity, and drug use. 131m. **DIR:** John McTiernan. **CAST:** Bruce Willis, Alan Rickman, Bonnie Bedelia, Alexander Godunov, Paul Gleason, William Atherton, Hart Bochner, James Shigeta, Reginald Vel Johnson. **1988**

DIE HARD 2: DIE HARDER ★★★★ In this solid sequel, maverick cop Bruce Willis takes on terrorists in a Washington D.C. airport, while his wife (Bonnie Bedelia) circles overhead in a plane which is running out of fuel. Willis does a fine job of reprising his wise cracking hero. Rated R for violence and profanity. 124m. **DIR:** Renny Harlin. **CAST:** Bruce Willis, Bonnie Bedelia, William Atherton, Reginald Vel Johnson, Franco Nero, John Amos, Dennis Franz, Art Evans, Fred Dalton Thompson. **1990**

DILLINGER (1945) ★★★ This look at the life and style of archetypal American gangster-antihero John Dillinger bids fair to be rated a *film noir*. Tough guy off-screen Lawrence Tierney is perfect in the title role. B&W; 89m. **DIR:** Max Nosseck. **CAST:** Edmund Lowe, Anne Jeffreys, Lawrence Tierney, Eduardo Ciannelli, Marc Lawrence, Elisha Cook Jr. **1945**

DILLINGER (1973) ★★★★ John Milius made an explosive directorial debut with this rip-roaring gangster film featuring Warren Oates in his best starring role. As a jaunty John Dillinger, he has all the charisma of a Cagney or a Bogart. Rated R for profanity and violence. 96m. **DIR:** John Milius. **CAST:** Warren Oates, Ben Johnson, Cloris Leachman, Michelle Phillips, Richard Dreyfuss, Harry Dean Stanton, Geoffrey Lewis, Steve Kanaly, Frank McRae. **1973**

DINNER AT THE RITZ ★★½ Good cast makes British whodunit about Annabella seeking her father's murderer an enjoyable diversion. Well-produced, with just a light enough touch to balance out all the familiar elements of crime melodrama. Early David Niven effort displays his unique qualities at comedy and light drama. B&W; 77m. **DIR:** Harold Schuster. **CAST:** David Niven, Paul Lukas, Annabella, Romney Brent. **1937**

DIPLOMATIC IMMUNITY ★★ A slipshod actioner about a marine (Bruce Boxleitner) who pursues his daughter's killer to Paraguay. Rated R for violence, profanity, and nudity. 95m. **DIR:** Peter Maris. **CAST:** Bruce Boxleitner, Billy Drago, Tom Breznahan, Christopher Neame, Robert Forster, Meg Foster. **1991**

DIRTY DOZEN, THE ★★★★½ Lee Marvin is assigned to take a group of military prisoners behind German lines and strike a blow for the Allies. It's a terrific entertainment—funny, star-studded, suspenseful, and even touching. 145m. **DIR:** Robert Aldrich. **CAST:** Lee Marvin, Ernest Borgnine, Charles Bronson, Jim Brown, John Cassavetes, Donald Sutherland, Clint Walker. **1967**

DIRTY DOZEN, THE: THE NEXT MISSION ★★ This disappointing made-for-TV sequel brings back Lee Marvin as the hard-as-nails Major Reisman; Ernest Borgnine and Richard Jaeckel also reprise their roles. This time the Dozen are sent to assassinate a German general who is plotting to kill Hitler. Not rated. 99m. **DIR:** Andrew V. McLaglen. **CAST:** Lee Marvin, Ernest Borgnine, Richard Jaeckel, Ken Wahl, Larry Wilcox. **1985**

DIRTY DOZEN, THE: THE DEADLY MISSION ★★ Second TV sequel to the 1967 classic has none of the style or suspense of the original, although some situations were lifted directly from it. The battle scenes are well staged. Telly Savalas, whose character died in the original, is now the commander of twelve new misfits. 100m. **DIR:** Lee H. Katzin. **CAST:** Telly Savalas, Ernest Borgnine, Randall "Tex" Cobb, Vince Edwards, Gary Graham, Wolf Kahler. **1987**

DIRTY DOZEN, THE: THE FATAL MISSION ★★ Telly Savalas again leads a reluctant ragtag gang in this third TV sequel to the 1967 hit. Welcome plot twists include both a Nazi agent and a woman officer among the Dozen. Okay battle scenes. 100m. **DIR:** Lee H. Katzin. **CAST:** Telly Savalas, Ernest Borgnine, Jeff Conaway, Alex Cord, Erik Estrada, Ernie Hudson, James Carroll Jordan, Ray "Boom Boom" Mancini, John Matuszak, Natalija Nogulich, Heather Thomas, Anthony Valentine, Richard Yniguez. **1988**

DIRTY HARRY ★★★★½ This is the original and still the best screen adventure of Clint Eastwood's maverick San Francisco detective. Outfoxed by a maniacal killer (Andy Robinson), "Dirty Harry" Callahan finally decides to deal out justice in his own inimitable and controversial fashion for an exciting, edge-of-your-seat climax. Rated R. 102m. **DIR:** Don Siegel. **CAST:** Clint Eastwood, Harry Guardino, John Mitchum, Reni Santoni, Andrew Robinson, John Vernon. **1971**

DIRTY MARY, CRAZY LARRY ★★★ Race-car driver Peter Fonda and his two accomplices lead Vic Morrow and a small army of law enforcement officers on a frantic, nonstop chase in this satisfying low-budget action film. Rated R for language and violence. 93m. **DIR:** John Hough. **CAST:** Peter Fonda, Susan George, Vic Morrow, Adam Roarke, Roddy McDowall. **1974**

DISAPPEARANCE, THE ★★★★ This exciting film has Donald Sutherland portraying a professional hit man who can't do his job properly after his wife disappears. He pursues a top man in the organization (Christopher Plummer) because he believes that he is responsible for his wife's disappearance. Rated R for sex and violence. 80m. **DIR:** Stuart Cooper. **CAST:** Donald Sutherland, Francine Racette, David Hemmings, John Hurt, Christopher Plummer. **1977**

DISHONORED LADY 🦃 Beautiful magazine executive is accused of killing her former boyfriend. Ponderous adaptation of a successful Broadway drama. B&W; 85m. **DIR:** Robert Stevenson. **CAST:** Hedy Lamarr, Dennis O'Keefe, John Loder, William Lundigan. **1947**

DISORGANIZED CRIME ★★ Misadventures of five ex-cons trying to pull a bank heist in a small Montana town. Some fine performances are wasted in this disorganized mess that can't decide whether it's a comedy or an action-drama. Rated R for violence and profanity. 98m. **DIR:** Jim Kouf. **CAST:** Hoyt Axton, Corbin Bernsen, Rubén Blades, Fred Gwynne, Ed O'Neill, Lou Diamond Phillips, Daniel Roebuck, William Russ. **1989**

DISTANT DRUMS ★★ Good old laconic Gary Cooper tracks down gun smugglers who are selling fire sticks to renegade Seminole Indians in the Everglades. A tired story and screenplay manage to get by on Cooper, good photography, and music. 101m. **DIR:** Raoul Walsh. **CAST:** Gary Cooper, Mari Aldon, Richard Webb, Ray Teal, Arthur Hunnicutt, Robert Barrat, Clancy Cooper. **1951**

DIVE, THE ★★★★ This Norwegian-British production tells of two veteran divers who are asked to return for an emergency dive to fix a broken oil pipeline. Outstanding performances and photography. Unrated but suitable for family viewing. 97m. **DIR:** Tristan DeVere Cole. **CAST:** Bjorn Sundquist, Frank Grimes. **1990**

DIVINE ENFORCER ★★ Kick-boxing psychic priest battles a vampire serial killer who preys on exotic dancers. The weird plot alone is going to attract some viewers, but take our word for it—it's not that great. Rated R for violence and nudity. 89m. **DIR:** Robert Rundle. **CAST:** Michael Foley, Carrie Chambers, Don Stroud, Erik Estrada, Jan-Michael Vincent, Jim Brown, Robert Z'dar. **1991**

DIXIE DYNAMITE 🦃 Imagine one of those cheesy Burt Reynolds good-ol'-boys movies, where he and some buddies raise heck in revenge for mistreatment from the local deputy. Now imagine it without Burt Reynolds. The ever-watchable Warren Oates isn't enough. Rated PG. 89m. **DIR:** Lee Frost. **CAST:** Warren Oates, Christopher George, Jane Anne Johnstone, R. G. Armstrong. **1976**

DO OR DIE 🦃 Fleshfest stars *Playboy* centerfolds Dona Speir and Roberta Vasquez as government agents on the run from a maniacal crime lord (Pat Morita). Nothing makes sense—particularly the fact that Morita is tracking the girls, yet his assassins frequently beat them to their secret destinations. Rated R for nudity and violence. 97m. **DIR:** Andy Sidaris. **CAST:** Erik Estrada, Noriyuki "Pat" Morita, Dona Speir, Roberta Vasquez. **1991**

DOBERMAN GANG, THE ★★½ A vicious pack of Doberman pinschers are trained as bank robbers in this implausible but well-made action tale. Rated PG for language, mild violence. 87m. **DIR:** Byron Chudnow. **CAST:** Byron Mabe, Julie Parrish, Simmy Bow, Hal Reed. **1972**

DR. KILDARE'S STRANGE CASE ★★★ Friendly old Dr. Gillespie and his medical whiz junior, Dr. Kildare, are featured in this tale of the deranged. Lew Ayres deals with a cuckoo. Nurse Laraine Day provides love interest; Lionel Barrymore is at the ready to counsel as Dr. Gillespie. This is one of the best of the Kildare series. B&W; 76m. **DIR:** Harold S. Bucquet. **CAST:** Lew Ayres, Lionel Barrymore, Laraine Day, Nat Pendleton, Samuel S. Hinds, Emma Dunn. **1940**

DR. NO ★★★★ The first of the James Bond movie sensations, it was in this film that Sean Connery began his ascent to stardom as the indomitable British secret agent 007. Bond is sent to Jamaica to confront the evil Dr. No, a villain bent on world domination. Ursula Andress was the first of the (now traditional) sensual Bond heroines. As with most of the series' films, there is a blend of nonstop action and tongue-in-cheek humor. 111m. **DIR:** Terence Young. **CAST:** Sean Connery, Ursula Andress, Jack Lord, Bernard Lee, Joseph Wiseman. **1962**

DR. SYN ★★½ Master character actor George Arliss's final film has him playing a traditional English vicar who blossoms into a pirate when the sun goes down. Nothing earthshaking here, but direction and rich atmosphere make it all palatable. B&W; 80m. **DIR:** Roy William Neill. **CAST:** George Arliss, Margaret Lockwood, John Loder, Roy Emerton, Graham Moffatt. **1937**

DOG DAY 🦃 Lee Marvin is an American fugitive on the run in this maudlin and often offensive tale of intrigue set in France. Sex, profanity, and violence. 101m. **DIR:** Yves Boisset. **CAST:** Lee Marvin, Jean Carmet, Victor Lanoux, Miou-Miou, Tina Louise. **1985**

DOG EAT DOG ★★ Moll Jayne Mansfield and sundry gangsters, hiding out on a Greek island, fight over $1 million in cash. It's a dog all right, though the dialogue is good for some cheap laughs. B&W; 86m. **DIR:** Ray Nazarro. **CAST:** Cameron Mitchell, Jayne Mansfield, Isa Miranda. **1963**

DOGS OF WAR, THE ★★ A graphic account of the coup d'etat of a West African dictatorship (starring Christopher Walken as the leader of a band of mercenaries). Unfortunately, this movie doesn't quite hold together. Rated R for violence. 102m. **DIR:** John Irvin. **CAST:** Christopher Walken, Tom Berenger, Colin Blakely, Hugh Millais. **1980**

DON IS DEAD, THE ★★★½ Director Richard Fleischer gives us yet another story of a Mafia family struggling for control of Las Vegas interests (à la *The Godfather*). Well-acted performances make for better-than-average viewing. Rated R for violence. 115m. **DIR:** Richard Fleischer. **CAST:** Anthony Quinn, Frederic Forrest, Robert Forster, Al Lettieri, Angel Tompkins, Charles Cioffi. **1973**

DON Q, SON OF ZORRO ★★★½ Derring-do in old California as the inimitable Douglas Fairbanks fights evildoers and greedy oppressors while saving ladylove Mary Astor from a fate worse than death. Well-mounted, inventive, and fast-paced. Silent. B&W; 111m. **DIR:** Donald Crisp. **CAST:** Douglas Fairbanks Sr., Mary Astor, Jack McDonald, Donald Crisp. **1925**

DON WINSLOW OF THE COAST GUARD ★★ Popular comic-strip hero Don Winslow returns to the screen to guard America's coastline from saboteurs and fifth columnists. Pretty standard serial stuff with a lot of stock footage and narrow escapes aplenty. B&W; 13 chapters. **DIR:** Ford Beebe, Ray Taylor. **CAST:** Don Terry, Elyse Knox. **1943**

DON WINSLOW OF THE NAVY ★★★ This slam-bang serial, glorifying the U.S. Navy, pits ace Commander Don Winslow against a criminal named Scorpion. Espionage, sabotage, and mayhem abound. Fun stuff. B&W; 234m. **DIR:** Ford Beebe, Ray Taylor. **CAST:** Don Terry, Walter Sande, John Litel, Anne Nagel. **1942**

DOOMED TO DIE ★★ Monogram's popular series about the aged Chinese detective, Mr. Wong, was running out of steam by the time this film, the fourth in the series, was released. Wong (Boris Karloff) is called in by hardboiled homicide captain Grant Withers after a millionaire is murdered and his ship is sunk. B&W; 68m. **DIR:** William Nigh. **CAST:** Boris Karloff, Grant Withers, Marjorie Reynolds, Melvin Lang, Guy Usher. **1940**

DOUBLE BLAST ★★½ Action-packed kick-boxing film finds 10-year-old Lorne Berfield and his 13-year-old sister (Crystal Summer) tracking down the kidnappers of a noted scientist (Linda Blair). Kung fu action mixed with *Indiana Jones*-like adventure makes this a pleasant diversion. Things really kick in when their father, kick-boxing champion Dale "Apollo" Cook, gets involved. Rated PG for violence. 89m. **DIR:** Tim Spring. **CAST:** Linda Blair, Dale "Apollo" Cook, Joe Estevez, Lorne Berfield, Crystal Summer. **1993**

DOUBLE DEAL Casual direction and a poor adaptation of a story that wasn't very good in the first place resulted in this dull programmer from RKO. B&W; 83m. **DIR:** Abby Berlin. **CAST:** Richard Denning, Marie Windsor, Carleton Young, Fay Baker, Taylor Holmes, Paul E. Burns, James Griffith. **1950**

DOUBLE IMPACT ★★★ Jean-Claude Van Damme gets a chance to strut his acting stuff in the dual role of twin brothers—one a Beverly Hills aerobic instructor, the other a Hong Kong smuggler—who join forces to avenge their parents' murder. Enough action for Van Damme fans, coupled with a surprising amount of comedy. Rated R for violence, profanity, and simulated sex. 118m. **DIR:** Sheldon Lettich. **CAST:** Jean-Claude Van Damme, Geoffrey Lewis, Alan Scarfe. **1991**

DOUBLE-O KID, THE ★★ During a summer internship for the CIA, an obnoxious teenager stumbles across a terrorist who plans to make a plane full of scientists disappear into the Bermuda Triangle. Too many chase scenes and unbelievable getaways ruin this film. Rated PG-13 for violence and profanity. 95m. **DIR:** Duncan McLachlan. **CAST:** Corey Haim, Brigitte Nielsen, Wallace Shawn, Nicole Eggert, Basil Hoffman, John Rhys-Davies, Karen Black, Anne Francis. **1992**

DOWN THE DRAIN ★★ A criminal lawyer sets up a big heist. Standard cross, no-honor-among-thieves story. Rated R for nudity, language, and violence. 105m. **DIR:** Robert C. Hughes. **CAST:** Andrew Stevens, Teri Copley, John Matuszak, Joseph Campanella, Don Stroud. **1990**

DOWN TWISTED ★★ Stylish *Romancing the Stone*–type thriller about an innocent waitress who agrees to help her roommate out of a jam. Before she knows it, she's stuck in Central America with a disreputable soldier of fortune and people shooting at her. The convoluted plot gets better as it goes along, though you may not find it worth the effort. Rated PG-13. 88m. **DIR:** Albert Pyun. **CAST:** Carey Lowell, Charles Rocket, Thom Mathews, Linda Kerridge. **1987**

DOWN UNDER Patrick Macnee narrates this crudely shot tale of two southern California surfers in Australia. Stale and pointless. 90m. **DIR:** Not Credited. **CAST:** Don Atkinson, Donn Dunlop, Patrick Macnee. **1984**

DOWNTOWN ★★ Anthony Edwards plays a rookie cop who is transferred to a hard-core inner-city neighborhood. An uneven attempt to balance comedy and violent action. The excellent cast outstrips the project. Rated R. 96m. **DIR:** Richard Benjamin. **CAST:** Anthony Edwards, Forest Whitaker, Penelope Ann Miller, Joe Pantoliano. **1990**

DRAGNET (1947) ★★½ This low-budget feature focuses on international jewelry thievery, with Henry Wilcoxon of Scotland Yard tracking crooks from London to New York, aided by airline hostess Mary Brian. Chock-full of action and skulduggery. B&W; 71m. **DIR:** Leslie Goodwins. **CAST:** Henry Wilcoxon, Mary Brian, Douglass Dumbrille, Virginia Dale. **1947**

DRAGNET (1954) ★★★★ *Dragnet* is the feature-length (color!) version of the popular detective series with director-star Jack Webb as the no-nonsense Sgt. Joe Friday, and Ben Alexander as his original partner, Frank Smith. In the story, based as always on a true case, Friday and Smith are assigned to solve the murder of a mobster. All clues seem to lead to his former associates. 89m. **DIR:** Jack

Webb. **CAST:** Jack Webb, Ben Alexander, Richard Boone, Ann Robinson, Dennis Weaver. **1954**

DRAGON FIGHT 🦃 Completely forgettable characters fill this nonsense set in a future where evil corporations resolve conflicts by combat between champions. Rated R for violence. 84m. **DIR:** Warren Stevens. **CAST:** Paul Coufos, Robert Z'dar, Michael Paré. **1990**

DRAGON: THE BRUCE LEE STORY ★★★★ The life of martial arts superstar Bruce Lee is given first-class treatment, in this mixture of fact and fantasy. The fight scenes are spectacular, and the acting of Jason Scott Lee and Lauren Holly is excellent. Look for Van Williams, Lee's costar in the *Green Hornet* series, in a brief bit as the director of that TV show. Rated PG-13 for violence, profanity, nudity, and simulated sex. 120m. **DIR:** Rob Cohen. **CAST:** Jason Scott Lee, Lauren Holly, Michael Learned, Nancy Kwan, Robert Wagner. **1993**

DRAGSTRIP GIRL ★★ American International's bad-teen drive-in opuses were great campy fun when they popped up on TV in the mid-Sixties, and now are funnier than ever on home video. This one's the standard romantic triangle-morality fable, with an overage cast and a brief running time so the film doesn't outstay its welcome. B&W; 69m. **DIR:** Edward L. Cahn. **CAST:** Fay Spain, Steve Terrell, John Ashley, Frank Gorshin. **1957**

DRIVE LIKE LIGHTNING ★★★ A guilt-ridden ex-daredevil is hired to drive a stunt car to Los Angeles. At first this looks like just another bad cross-country truck driving movie, but don't let first impressions fool you. A nice surprise. Unrated; made for cable. 96m. **DIR:** Bradford May. **CAST:** Steven Bauer, Cynthia Gibb, William Russ, Paul Koslo. **1991**

DRIVER, THE ★★★★ High-energy crime drama focuses on a professional getaway driver (Ryan O'Neal) and his police pursuer (Bruce Dern). Walter Hill's breakneck pacing and spectacular chase scenes make up for the lack of plot or character development. It's an action movie pure and simple. Rated PG for violence and profanity. 90m. **DIR:** Walter Hill. **CAST:** Ryan O'Neal, Bruce Dern, Isabelle Adjani, Ronee Blakley, Matt Clark. **1978**

DRUMS ★★★½ Stiff-upper-lip British Empire epic starts slow but builds to an exciting climax as soldiers of the queen aid young Prince Sabu in his struggle against usurping uncle Raymond Massey. 99m. **DIR:** Zoltán Korda. **CAST:** Sabu, Raymond Massey, Valerie Hobson, Roger Livesey, David Tree. **1938**

DRUMS ALONG THE MOHAWK ★★★★ Claudette Colbert and Henry Fonda are among a group of sturdy settlers of upstate New York during the Revolutionary War. Despite the episodic nature of its story, *Drums Along the Mohawk* emerges as another richly detailed film from director John Ford. Beautifully photographed in color, this work benefits from vibrant supporting performances by Edna May Oliver, Jessie Ralph, John Carradine, and Ward Bond. 103m. **DIR:** John Ford. **CAST:** Claudette Colbert, Henry Fonda, Edna May Oliver, John Carradine, Jessie Ralph, Robert Lowery, Ward Bond. **1939**

DRUMS OF FU MANCHU ★★★½ This exciting serial presents the definitive Fu Manchu with smooth, sinister Henry Brandon splendidly cast as the greatest of all Far Eastern menaces. Sir Dennis Nayland Smith and his associates tackle the deadly doctor to keep him from finding the scepter of the great Genghis Khan. B&W; 15 chapters. **DIR:** William Witney, John English. **CAST:** Henry Brandon, Robert Kellard, Gloria Franklin, Olaf Hytten, Tom Chatterton, Luana Walters, George Cleveland, Dwight Frye. **1940**

DUEL OF CHAMPIONS 🦃 Alan Ladd is a weary centurion leader in ancient Rome fighting for the glory that once was. Forgettable. 105m. **DIR:** Ferdinando Baldi. **CAST:** Alan Ladd, Robert Keith, Franco Fabrizi. **1961**

DUELLISTS, THE ★★★★ *The Duellists* traces a long and seemingly meaningless feud between two soldiers in the Napoleonic Wars. This fascinating study of honor among men is full of irony and heroism. Rated R. 101m. **DIR:** Ridley Scott. **CAST:** Keith Carradine, Harvey Keitel, Albert Finney, Edward Fox, Cristina Raines, Robert Stephens, Tom Conti. **1977**

DUNE WARRIORS ★★ Rip-off of *The Magnificent Seven* set in an apocalyptic future stars David Carradine as the head honcho of a band of mercenaries. Plenty of action to cover up the familiar plot. Rated R for violence, profanity, and nudity. 77m. **DIR:** Cirio H. Santiago. **CAST:** David Carradine, Rick Hill, Luke Askew, Jillian McWhirter. **1991**

DYNAMO 🦃 Miserable rip-off of the Bruce Lee legend. Rated R for violence, nudity, and simulated sex. 93m. **DIR:** Hwa I. Hong. **CAST:** Bruce Li, Mary Han, James Griffith, Steve Sandor. **1978**

EACH DAWN I DIE ★★★★ Energetic Warner Bros. film occasionally slips the bounds of believability but never fails to be entertaining. James Cagney is terrific as the youthful reporter who is framed for murder after exposing a crooked district attorney. B&W; 92m. **DIR:** William Keighley. **CAST:** James Cagney, George Raft, George Bancroft, Jane Bryan, Maxie Rosenbloom. **1939**

EAGLE HAS LANDED, THE ★★★ Michael Caine is a Nazi agent who is given orders to plan and carry out the kidnapping or murder of Prime Minister Churchill. This movie gets started on a promising note, but it is sabotaged by a weak, contrived ending. Rated PG. 123m. **DIR:** John Sturges. **CAST:** Michael Caine, Donald Sutherland, Robert Duvall. **1977**

EARTHQUAKE ★★ Once you get past the special-effects mastery of seeing Los Angeles destroyed, you've got a pretty weak film on your hands. The classic *San Francisco* did it better. Rated PG. 129m. **DIR:** Mark Robson. **CAST:** Charlton Heston, Genevieve Bujold, Lorne Greene, Ava Gardner, Walter Matthau, George Kennedy. **1974**

EAST OF BORNEO ★★★ Intrepid and tenacious Rose Hobart searches the teeming Borneo jungle for her supposedly lost doctor husband Charles Bickford, who isn't lost at all but living it up as personal physician to native prince Georges Renavent. Filled with wildlife, this jungle adventure is lots of fun and ends with a bang. B&W; 77m. **DIR:** George Melford. **CAST:** Rose Hobart, Charles Bickford, Georges Renavent, Noble Johnson. **1931**

EAST OF KILIMANJARO ★★ A deadly virus has affected the cattle of the area in Africa east of Kilimanjaro. A daring photographer throws his weight into the fight against the microbe. Routine adventure. 75m. **DIR:** Arnold Belgard. **CAST:** Marshall Thompson, Gaby André. **1957**

EAT MY DUST ★★ A low-budget 1976 race yarn notable only for the fact that it gave Ron Howard the power to direct his next starring vehicle, *Grand Theft Auto*, which, in turn, led to such treats as *Night Shift* and *Splash*. Rated PG. 90m. **DIR:** Charles B. Griffith. **CAST:** Ron Howard, Christopher Norris, Dave Madden, Warren Kemmerling. **1976**

EDDIE MACON'S RUN ★★½ John Schneider is a prison escapee who manages to stay one step ahead of the law. Kirk Douglas costars as the hard-nosed policeman on his trail. It's a predictable, lightweight movie. Rated PG for vulgar language and violence. 95m. **DIR:** Jeff Kanew. **CAST:** John Schneider, Kirk Douglas, Lee Purcell, Leah Ayres. **1983**

EDGE OF DARKNESS (1943) ★★★★½ Powerful acting by a stage-trained cast make this a better-than-average war picture. The plot focuses on efforts of the Norwegian underground to run off the Nazis during World War II. B&W; 120m. **DIR:** Lewis Milestone. **CAST:** Errol Flynn, Ann Sheridan, Walter Huston, Judith Anderson, Helmut Dantine, Nancy Coleman, Morris Carnovsky, John Beal. **1943**

EDGE OF HONOR ★★★ Group of Explorer Scouts on an expedition come across a cache of high-tech weapons belonging to a group of smugglers. This one gets a merit badge for exciting action and ingenuity. Rated R for language and violence. 92m. **DIR:** Michael Spence. **CAST:** Corey Feldman, Meredith Salenger, Scott Reeves, Ken Jenkins, Don Swayze, Christopher Neame. **1991**

EIGER SANCTION, THE ★★½ Laughable but entertaining adaptation of Trevanian's equally laughable but entertaining novel. Clint Eastwood is a college professor by day and supersecret agent by night. Outrageously overblown characters and plenty of opportunities for Eastwood to strut his macho stuff. Rated R for violence and sex. 128m. **DIR:** Clint Eastwood. **CAST:** Clint Eastwood, George Kennedy, Jack Cassidy, Thayer David, Vonetta McGee. **1975**

8 SECONDS ★★½ This sanitized story of real-life bull rider Lane Frost—the youngest cowboy ever inducted into the Rodeo Hall of Fame—needs more grit. Lane's meteoric rise to superstardom, his showdown with the notorious bull, Red Rock, and the toll of the circuit on his marriage to a championship barrel racer is promising material, but the story—in rodeo lingo—doesn't quite cowboy up. Rated PG-13 for language. 97m. **DIR:** John G. Avildsen. **CAST:** Luke Perry, Cynthia Geary, Stephen Baldwin, Red Mitchell, Carrie Snodgress. **1994**

84 CHARLIE MOPIC ★★★½ Powerfully realistic tour of Vietnam, circa 1969. A reconnaissance patrol sets out "in country" with an army motion picture (MOPIC) cameraman recording everything he can. What begins as a routine mission soon turns into a nightmare of terror and survival. A compelling and engrossing experience. Rated R for violence and profanity. 95m. **DIR:** Patrick Duncan. **CAST:** Richard Brooks, Christopher Borgard. **1989**

800 LEAGUES DOWN THE AMAZON ★★ Exotic locations and capable stars can't save this Jules Verne story from sinking twenty thousand leagues under the sea. Barry Bostwick floats through this tiresome yawner about a falsely accused man who risks capture and execution when he attempts to return home for his daughter's wedding. Adventuresome trip down the Amazon is the only high point. Rated PG-13 for violence. 85m. **DIR:** Luis Llosa. **CAST:** Barry Bostwick, Adam Baldwin, Daphne Zuniga, Tom Verica, E. E. Bell. **1993**

EL CID ★★★ Some of the best battle action scenes ever filmed are included in this 1961 spectacle about the medieval Spanish hero El Cid. Unfortunately, on smaller home screens much of the splendor will be lost. You will be left with the wooden Charlton Heston and the beautiful Sophia Loren in a love story that was underdeveloped due to the movie's emphasis on spectacle. 184m. **DIR:** Anthony Mann. **CAST:** Charlton Heston, Sophia Loren, Raf Vallone, Hurd Hatfield. **1961**

ELECTRA GLIDE IN BLUE ★★★★ Robert Blake plays an Arizona cop with aspirations of being a detective. This extremely violent melodrama features good performances by the entire cast with several twists and turns to keep the viewer guessing. Rated R. 106m. **DIR:** James William Guercio. **CAST:** Robert Blake, Billy Green Bush, Mitchell Ryan, Elisha Cook Jr., Jeannine Riley, Royal Dano. **1973**

ELEPHANT BOY ★★★ Sabu made his film debut and became a star in this drama about a boy who claims to know where elephants go to die. Robert Flaherty's codirection gives the film a travelogue quality, but it interests and delights just the same. B&W; 80m. **DIR:** Robert Flaherty, Zoltán Korda. **CAST:** Sabu, W. E. Holloway, Walter Hudd, Bruce Gordon. **1937**

EMERALD FOREST, THE ★★★★ In this riveting adventure film based on a true story, Powers Boothe stars as Bill Markham, an American engineer who, with his family, goes to the Amazon jungle to build a dam. There, his 5-year-old son is stolen by a native tribe known as the Invisible People. Markham spends the next ten years trying to find his son. Rated R for nudity, suggested sex, profanity, and violence. 110m. **DIR:** John Boorman. **CAST:** Powers Boothe, Meg Foster, Charley Boorman. **1985**

EMPIRE STATE 🦃 Powerful real estate magnate becomes involved with some shady dealings in London. Rated R for nudity and violence. 104m. **DIR:** Ron Peck. **CAST:** Martin Landau, Ray McAnally, Catherine Harrison. **1987**

ENCHANTED ISLAND 🦃 Dull adaptation of Herman Melville's *Typee*. 95m. **DIR:** Allan Dwan. **CAST:** Dana Andrews, Jane Powell, Arthur Shields, Don Dubbins. **1958**

ENDLESS SUMMER, THE ★★★★ The only surfing documentary ever to gain an audience outside the Beach Boy set, this is an imaginatively photographed travelogue that captures the joy, danger, and humor of searching for the perfect wave. Much of the success is attributable to the whimsical narration. 95m. **DIR:** Bruce Brown. **CAST:** Mike Hynson, Robert August. **1966**

ENEMY BELOW, THE ★★★½ Robert Mitchum as the captain of a U.S. Navy destroyer and Curt Jurgens as the commander of a German submarine play a deadly game of chess as they pursue each other across the South Atlantic during World War II. This little-seen aquatic duel is well worth viewing. 98m. **DIR:** Dick Powell. **CAST:** Robert Mitchum, Curt Jurgens, David Hedison, Theodore Bikel, Russell Collins, Kurt Kreuger, Frank Albertson, Doug McClure. **1957**

ENEMY TERRITORY ★★ This film features a good premise but suffers from poor acting, writing, and production values. Gary Frank is an insurance salesman trapped inside a ghetto apartment building and battling a vicious gang. Rated R for language, extreme violence, and brief nudity. 89m. **DIR:** Peter Manoogian. **CAST:** Gary Frank, Ray Parker Jr., Jan-Michael Vincent, Frances Foster. **1987**

ENEMY UNSEEN ★★½ Mercenary tracks down the kidnapped daughter of a wealthy industrialist through the darkest regions of Africa, where she is about to be sacrificed in a ritual to the crocodile spirits. Rated R for violence. 90m. **DIR:** Elmo De Witt. **CAST:** Vernon Wells, Stack Pierce. **1991**

ENFORCER, THE (1951) ★★★½ A big-city district attorney, Humphrey Bogart, attempts to break up the mob in this effective crime drama. At under 90 minutes, it moves like lightning and is refreshingly devoid of most of the clichés of the genre. B&W; 87m. **DIR:** Bretaigne Windust. **CAST:** Humphrey Bogart, Zero Mostel, Everett Sloane, Ted de Corsia, Roy Roberts. **1951**

ENFORCER, THE (1976) ★★★★ A step up from the muddled *Magnum Force* and a nice companion piece to *Dirty Harry*, this third entry in the popular series has detective Harry Callahan grudgingly team with a female cop (Tyne Daly) during his pursuit of a band of terrorists. John Mitchum gives a standout performance in his final series bow as tough cop Frank DiGeorgio. It'll make your day. Rated R. 96m. **DIR:** James Fargo. **CAST:** Clint Eastwood, Tyne Daly, Harry Guardino, Bradford Dillman, John Mitchum. **1976**

ENIGMA ★★ Espionage yarn succumbs to lethargy. The KGB sics an elite group of assassins on five Soviet dissidents. A CIA agent (Martin Sheen) attempts to thwart the insidious scheme by entangling his former lover with the top Russian agent. Rated PG. 101m. **DIR:** Jeannot Szwarc. **CAST:** Martin Sheen, Brigitte Fossey, Sam Neill, Derek Jacobi, Michel Lonsdale, Frank Finlay. **1982**

ENTER THE DRAGON ★★★★ Bruce Lee soared to international superstardom with this fast-paced, tongue-in-cheek kung fu film. A big-budget American version of the popular Chinese genre, it has a good plot and strong performances—from Lee, John Saxon, and Jim Kelly. Rated R, due to violence. 97m. **DIR:** Robert Clouse. **CAST:** Bruce Lee, John Saxon, Jim Kelly, Ahna Capri, Yang Tse, Angela Mao. **1973**

ENTER THE NINJA ★★ A passable martial arts adventure about practitioners of an ancient Oriental art of killing. Rated R. 94m. **DIR:** Menahem Golan. **CAST:** Franco Nero, Susan George, Sho Kosugi, Alex Courtney. **1981**

EQUALIZER, THE: "MEMORIES OF MANON" ★★★ Edward Woodward's commanding performance as *The Equalizer* gives weight to this made-for-TV release about a New York avenger and his discovery of danger stalking the daughter (Melissa Anderson) he didn't know he had. Fans of Woodward will enjoy a second look. 96m. **DIR:** Tony Wharmby. **CAST:** Edward Woodward, Melissa Sue Anderson, Anthony Zerbe, Robert Lansing, Jon Polito, Keith Szarabajka. **1988**

ESCAPE FROM ALCATRAZ ★★★★ Any movie that combines the talents of star Clint Eastwood and director Don Siegel is more than watchable. This is a gripping and believable film about the 1962 breakout from the supposedly perfect prison. Patrick McGoohan is also excellent as the neurotic warden. Rated PG. 112m. **DIR:** Don Siegel. **CAST:** Clint Eastwood, Patrick McGoohan, Roberts Blossom, Jack Thibeau. **1979**

ESCAPE FROM NEW YORK ★★★½ The year is 1997. *Air Force One*—with the president (Donald Pleasence) on board—is hijacked by a group of revolutionaries and sent crashing into the middle of Manhattan, which has been turned into a top-security prison. It's up to Snake Plissken (Kurt Russell), a former war hero gone renegade, to get him out in twenty-four hours. It's fun, surprise-filled entertainment. Rated R. 99m. **DIR:** John Carpenter. **CAST:** Kurt Russell, Lee Van Cleef, Ernest Borgnine, Donald Pleasence, Adrienne Barbeau. **1981**

ESCAPE FROM SOBIBOR ★★★★ Inspiring true-life tale of the largest prisoner escape from a Nazi death camp, with a superior cast led by Alan Arkin. Harrowing prison camp scenes elevate the suspense as the prisoners plan and then execute their daring escape. Edited for video, this made-for-television entry rises to the occasion with a tight script by Reginald Rose. 120m. **DIR:** Jack Gold. **CAST:** Rutger Hauer, Alan Arkin, Joanna Pacula. **1987**

ESCAPE FROM SURVIVAL ZONE ★★ On the eve of World War III, a trio of television journalists take a course in survival training, only to face a whacked-out former Marine commander. Predictable melodrama. Not rated, but contains violence and profanity. 85m. **DIR:** Chris Jones. **CAST:** Terrence Ford, Paris Jefferson, Raymond Johnson. **1991**

ESCAPE FROM THE KGB 🦃 A jet-setting CIA agent is sent to infiltrate a Siberian spaceport. Insipid. Not rated. 99m. **DIR:** Harald Phillipe. **CAST:** Thomas Hunter, Marie Versini, Ivan Desny, Walter Barnes. **1987**

ESCAPE TO ATHENA ★★★ Roger Moore as a Nazi officer? Sonny Bono as a member of the Italian Resistance? Elliott Gould as a hippie in a World War II concentration camp? Sound ridiculous? It is. It's a *Hogan's Heroes* for the big screen but, in a dumb sort of way, entertaining. Rated PG. 101m. **DIR:** George Pan Cosmatos. **CAST:** Roger Moore, Telly Savalas, David Niven, Claudia Cardinale, Stefanie Powers, Richard Roundtree, Elliott Gould, Sonny Bono. **1979**

EVEL KNIEVEL ★★½ Autobiography of motorcycle stuntman Evel Knievel. George Hamilton is surprisingly good as Knievel. Some nice stunts. Rated PG. 90m. **DIR:** Marvin J. Chomsky. **CAST:** George Hamilton, Sue Lyon, Rod Cameron. **1972**

EVIL THAT MEN DO, THE ★★½ Believe it or not, Charles Bronson has made a watchable film for a change. He plays a professional killer who comes out of retirement to avenge the brutal murder of an old friend. Rated R for violence and profanity. 90m. **DIR:** J. Lee Thompson. **CAST:** Charles Bronson, Theresa Saldana, José Ferrer, Joseph Maher. **1984**

EXCESSIVE FORCE ★★★ Good casting and an unexpected, eleventh-hour snap of the tail enliven this otherwise standard kill-or-be-killed actionfest. Van Damme wannabe Thomas Ian Griffith scripts himself a heroic role as a cop determined to nail syndicate boss Burt Young. Plenty o' kicks and licks and enough intelligent plotting to furrow a few brows. Rated R for profanity, nudity, simulated sex, and excessive violence. 87m. **DIR:** Jon Hess. **CAST:** Thomas Ian Griffith, Lance Henriksen, Tom Hodges, James Earl Jones, Charlotte Lewis, Burt Young. **1993**

EXILED IN AMERICA 🦃 Extremely bad acting and a poor script kill this film, in which a revolutionary hero is hunted by Central American terrorists. Not rated, but contains violence. 85m. **DIR:** Paul Leder. **CAST:** Maxwell Caulfield, Edward Albert, Wings Hauser, Viveca Lindfors, Stella Stevens. **1990**

EXPOSURE 🦃 Passive photojournalist (Peter Coyote) working in Brazil learns a gruesome art form of knife fighting in this exotic and senseless thriller. Rated R for profanity, nudity, and violence. 106m. **DIR:** Walter Salles Jr. **CAST:** Peter Coyote, Tcheky Karyo, Amanda Pays. **1992**

EXTERMINATOR, THE ★★ A vigilante who takes the law into his own hands when the law refuses to punish the gang members who made a cripple of his best friend. Rated R. 101m. **DIR:** James Glickenhaus. **CAST:** Christopher George, Samantha Eggar, Robert Ginty, Steve James, Tony DiBenedetto. **1980**

EXTERMINATOR 2, THE 🦃 In this disgusting cheapo, Robert Ginty returns as the one-man vigilante force. 104m. **DIR:** Mark Buntzman. **CAST:** Robert Ginty, Deborah Geffner, Frankie Faison, Mario Van Peebles. **1984**

EXTREME PREJUDICE ★★★★ Nick Nolte is in peak form in this modern-day Western as a two-fisted Texas Ranger whose boyhood friend, Powers Boothe, has become a drug kingpin across the border in Mexico. The federal government sends six high-tech agents to nail Boothe with "extreme prejudice." Rated R for profanity, drug use, nudity, and violence. 96m. **DIR:** Walter Hill. **CAST:** Nick Nolte, Powers Boothe, Maria Conchita Alonso,

Michael Ironside, Rip Torn, Clancy Brown, William Forsythe. **1987**

EYE FOR AN EYE ★★½ This surprisingly entertaining kung fu movie features Chuck Norris as Shawn Kane, an ex-cop trying to crack a narcotics-smuggling ring. With the help of a lovely news editor (Maggie Cooper) and a martial arts master (Mako) who doubles as a walking fortune cookie, Kane confronts a sinister Christopher Lee and, finally, a human tank called The Professor. Rated R. 106m. **DIR:** Steve Carver. **CAST:** Chuck Norris, Christopher Lee, Richard Roundtree, Mako, Maggie Cooper. **1981**

EYE OF THE EAGLE 🦃 Cheap shoot-'em-up focuses on three do-gooders who combat a renegade band of U.S. soldiers. 84m. **DIR:** Cirio H. Santiago. **CAST:** Brett Clark, Robert Patrick, Ed Crick, William Steis. **1987**

EYE OF THE EAGLE 2 🦃 This lousy sequel features a corrupt army major plotting against an honest private. Rated R for nudity and profanity. 79m. **DIR:** Carl Franklin. **CAST:** Todd Field, Andy Wood. **1986**

EYE OF THE EAGLE 3 🦃 A maverick squadron of soldiers takes a stand against enemy Vietnamese troops. More or less the A-team before they went to work in the public sector. Rated R for profanity and nudity. 90m. **DIR:** Cirio H. Santiago. **CAST:** Steve Kanaly, Ken Wright, Peter Nelson, Carl Franklin. **1991**

EYE OF THE TIGER ★★★ Buck Mathews (Gary Busey) stands up against a motorcycle gang and the corrupt law enforcement that have plagued a small town in Texas. Busey and Yaphet Kotto give quality performances that save this formula vengeance film. Rated R for violence and language. 90m. **DIR:** Richard C. Sarafian. **CAST:** Gary Busey, Yaphet Kotto, Seymour Cassel. **1986**

EYEWITNESS TO MURDER 🦃 Detectives try to protect a female artist—blinded after witnessing a murder—from hit men and a corrupt police captain. Rated R for nudity, violence, and profanity. 75m. **DIR:** Jag Mundhra. **CAST:** Andrew Stevens, Adrian Zmed, Sherilyn Wolter. **1992**

FAMILY, THE (1970) ★★★ Charles Bronson is mad. Some creep framed him and, what's worse, stole his girl! Bronson is out for revenge. This film has plenty of action, but nothing new to offer. Rated R. 100m. **DIR:** Sergio Sollima. **CAST:** Charles Bronson, Jill Ireland, Telly Savalas, Michael Constantine, George Savalas. **1970**

FAREWELL TO THE KING ★★★½ In this old-fashioned, boy's-eye-view adventure epic from writer-director John Milius, Nick Nolte plays a World War II soldier who deserts following Gen. Douglas MacArthur's retreat from Corregidor. Nolte ends up in the jungles of Borneo, where he becomes a king. Nigel Havers is excellent as the British officer who incites the natives to battle. *Farewell to the King* is in the style of Edgar Rice Burroughs's *Tarzan* stories, with a touch of *Gunga Din* thrown in. Rated PG-13 for profanity and violence. 114m. **DIR:** John Milius. **CAST:** Nick Nolte, Nigel Havers, Frank McRae, James Fox. **1989**

FAST LANE FEVER ★★½ A street gang with souped-up streetcars bullies others into racing for money. An underdog good guy loses to the bad guys, then comes back against all odds. Interesting cars and a fascinating look at Australia through the camera lens. Rated R for profanity, sex, and violence. 94m. **DIR:** John Clark. **CAST:** Terry Serio, Deborah Conway, Max Cullen, Graham Bond. **1982**

FAST MONEY 🦃 This low-quality bore introduces a group of young men who are getting high and smuggling drugs from Mexico. Rated R for obscenities, drug use, and lawlessness. 92m. **DIR:** Douglas Holloway. **CAST:** Sammy Allred, Sonny Carl Davis, Lou Perry, Marshall Ford, Doris Hargrave. **1985**

FASTER PUSSYCAT! KILL! KILL! ★★★½ This movie has everything you could want from a Russ Meyer film. Beautiful girls, fast-paced action, and lots of wild and wacky humor. In its day it was considered fairly hardcore, yet today it could even be shown on late-night television. B&W; 83m. **DIR:** Russ Meyer. **CAST:** Tura Satana, Haji, Jori Williams, Juan Bernard. **1962**

FATAL BEAUTY 🦃 Whoopi Goldberg stars as an improbably resourceful cop pursuing several smarmy drug pushers. Rated R for language and excessive violence. 104m. **DIR:** Tom Holland. **CAST:** Whoopi Goldberg, Sam Elliott, Rubén Blades, Harris Yulin, John P. Ryan, Jennifer Warren, Brad Dourif. **1987**

FATAL EXPOSURE ★★½ Mare Winningham partially salvages this routine made-for-cable thriller—as a resourceful single parent whose photo order gets mixed up by the processing lab...which sends her home with pictures originally intended for a hired killer. Nick Mancuso is engaging as a neighbor with a mysterious past. Rated PG-13. 89m. **DIR:** Alan Metzger. **CAST:** Mare Winningham, Nick Mancuso, Christopher McDonald, Geoffrey Blake. **1991**

FATAL HOUR, THE ★★½ Boris Karloff is cast as homicide detective Mr. Wong in this suspenseful thriller about murder and jewel smuggling. Grant Withers is solid as Police Captain Street. B&W; 68m. **DIR:** William Nigh. **CAST:** Boris Karloff, Grant Withers, Marjorie Reynolds, Charles Trowbridge. **1940**

FATAL MISSION ★★ It took five screenwriters, including Peter Fonda, to bring this formulaic jungle-action film to the screen. Fonda portrays a Special Forces agent during the Vietnam War. Rated R for violence.

84m. **DIR:** George Rowe. **CAST:** Peter Fonda, Mako, Jim Mitchum, Tia Carrere. **1990**

FATHER HOOD ★★½ A con man finds his latest big score sabotaged by the unexpected arrival of his runaway daughter, who wants him to save his son from the same institution that brutalized her. Not all of the movie works—especially the violent prologue in which the otherwise easygoing title character mistakenly kills an undercover cop while ripping off drug dealers—but Patrick Swayze is funny and believable in a role that seems to have been fashioned out of cardboard. Rated PG-13 for brief profanity and violence. 95m. **DIR:** Darrell Roodt. **CAST:** Patrick Swayze, Halle Berry, Sabrina Lloyd, Brian Bonsall, Michael Ironside, Diane Ladd, Bob Gunton, Adrienne Barbeau. **1993**

FBI MURDERS, THE ★★★★½ Superior made-for-TV drama focuses on the manhunt for two thrill killers, played with penetrating menace by Michael Gross and David Soul. When these two family men go on a robbing rampage, the FBI gets involved. Intelligent screenplay and inspired casting make this a must-see. 95m. **DIR:** Dick Lowry. **CAST:** Ronny Cox, Bruce Greenwood, Michael Gross, Doug Sheehan, David Soul. **1988**

FEAR CITY ★★ After a promising directorial debut with *Ms. 45*, Abel Ferrara backslid with this all-too-familiar tale about a psychopath killing prostitutes in New York City. Some good performances and action sequences still can't save this one. Rated R for violence, nudity, and profanity. 93m. **DIR:** Abel Ferrara. **CAST:** Tom Berenger, Billy Dee Williams, Rae Dawn Chong, Melanie Griffith, Rossano Brazzi, Jack Scalia. **1985**

FEARLESS TIGER 🦃 When his brother dies from a drug overdose, a wealthy man goes to Hong Kong and learns martial arts to avenge him. Toothless nonsense. Rated R for violence and profanity. 88m. **DIR:** Ron Hulme. **CAST:** Jalal Mehri, Jamie Farr, Monika Schnarre, Bolo Yeung. **1993**

FEVER ★★½ Ex-con Armand Assante wants only to go straight and reunite with former girlfriend Marcia Gay Harden, who has set up housekeeping with compassionate lawyer Sam Neill. Macho sparring between the two men is interrupted when Harden is kidnapped by one of Assante's enemies. Lurid and violent made-for-cable fodder. Rated R for violence and language. 99m. **DIR:** Larry Elikann. **CAST:** Sam Neill, Armand Assante, Marcia Gay Harden, Joe Spano. **1991**

FFOLKES ★★★ Of course, no movie with Roger Moore is a classic, but this tongue-in-cheek spy thriller with the actor playing against his James Bond stereotype provides some good, campy entertainment. This film features Moore as a woman-hating, but cat-loving, gun for hire who takes on a band of terrorists. Rated PG. 99m. **DIR:** Andrew V. McLaglen. **CAST:** Roger Moore, James Mason, Anthony Perkins, Michael Parks, David Hedison. **1980**

FIELD OF FIRE 🦃 Battling behind enemy lines in Cambodia, a special combat squad attempts to retrieve a downed military expert. Hokey heroics. Rated R for profanity and nudity. 100m. **DIR:** Cirio H. Santiago. **CAST:** David Carradine. **1992**

FIELD OF HONOR (1986) ★★ Tale of a Dutch infantryman in the Korean War left for dead after a surprise attack by the Chinese. Everett McGill is the survivor who hides out with two shell-shocked kids. Rated R for violence, profanity, and nudity. 93m. **DIR:** Hans Scheepmaker. **CAST:** Everett McGill, Ron Brandsteder, Hey Young Lee. **1986**

FIFTH MUSKETEER, THE ★★ An uninspired retelling of *The Man in the Iron Mask*. Beau Bridges is watchable enough as King Louis XIV and his twin brother, Philipe, who was raised as a peasant by D'Artagnan (Cornel Wilde) and the Three Musketeers (Lloyd Bridges, José Ferrer, and Alan Hale Jr.). The film never springs to life. Rated PG. 103m. **DIR:** Ken Annakin. **CAST:** Beau Bridges, Sylvia Kristel, Ursula Andress, Cornel Wilde, Olivia de Havilland, José Ferrer, Rex Harrison, Lloyd Bridges, Alan Hale Jr. **1979**

FIFTY/FIFTY ★★★ Peter Weller and Robert Hays star as former CIA operatives, now mercenaries on opposite sides of a bloody civil war. Treachery and betrayal soon force them to trust only each other, especially when the CIA sends troubleshooter Charles Martin Smith to get them to organize a rebellion. Rated R for nudity, violence, and profanity. 101m. **DIR:** Charles Martin Smith. **CAST:** Peter Weller, Robert Hays, Charles Martin Smith. **1993**

FIGHT FOR US ★★ After the fall of the Marcos regime in the Philippines, right-wing death squads terrorize the countryside. Poor production values, amateur-night actors, and pedestrian direction take the fight out of this one. Rated R for violence, profanity, and simulated sex. 92m. **DIR:** Lino Brocka. **CAST:** Phillip Salvador. **1990**

FIGHTER ATTACK ★★ An American pilot (Sterling Hayden) shot down in Italy joins up with an Italian terrorist group to block off a Nazi supply tunnel. Familiar World War II melodrama. 80m. **DIR:** Lesley Selander. **CAST:** Sterling Hayden, Joy Page, J. Carrol Naish. **1953**

FIGHTING BACK ★★★ A deli owner decides to organize a neighborhood committee against crime after his wife and mother are victims of violence. You can't help but cheer him on. A rapid succession of violent acts, profanity, and occasional nudity make this R-rated film questionable for young audiences. 98m. **DIR:** Lewis Teague. **CAST:** Tom Skerritt,

Patti LuPone, Michael Sarrazin, Yaphet Kotto, David Rasche, Ted Ross. 1982

FIGHTING DEVIL DOGS, THE ★★ A somewhat listless tale of two Marine lieutenants out to stop the Lightning, a masked madman with a thunderbolt missile. Republic Pictures cut corners by lifting scenes of the Flying Wing, the Zepplin/aircraft hookups, and some cliff-hanging endings directly from their 1937 serial, *Dick Tracy*. B&W; 12 chapters. **DIR:** William Witney, John English. **CAST:** Lee Powell, Bruce Bennett, Eleanor Stewart, Montagu Love. 1938

FIGHTING MARINES, THE ★★ U.S. Marines run up against a modern-day pirate. The plot's thin, the acting forced, but the special effects are remarkable. Pieced together from twelve serial chapters. B&W; 69m. **DIR:** Joseph Kane, B. Reeves "Breezy" Eason. **CAST:** Grant Withers, Adrian Morris, Ann Rutherford, Jason Robards Sr., Pat O'Malley. 1936

FIGHTING SEABEES, THE ★★★ John Wayne and Dennis O'Keefe are construction workers fighting the Japanese in their own way while each attempts to woo Susan Hayward away from the other. This 1944 war film, which costars William Frawley, is actually better than it sounds. B&W; 100m. **DIR:** Edward Ludwig. **CAST:** John Wayne, Dennis O'Keefe, Susan Hayward, William Frawley, Duncan Renaldo. 1944

FIGHTING 69TH, THE ★★★ Tough-guy James Cagney does a good job as a loner who buckles under fire and causes the death of some of his comrades in this all-male World War I story. Based partly on fact, this virile Warner Brothers blockbuster boasts good cinematography and great battle scenes. B&W; 89m. **DIR:** William Keighley. **CAST:** James Cagney, Pat O'Brien, George Brent, Jeffrey Lynn, Alan Hale Sr., Frank McHugh, Dennis Morgan, Dick Foran, William Lundigan. 1940

FINAL ALLIANCE 🦃 Will Colton (David Hasselhoff) returns to a hometown that has been overrun by gangs. Rated R for violence and language. 93m. **DIR:** Mario Di Leo. **CAST:** David Hasselhoff, Bo Hopkins, John Saxon. 1990

FINAL CHAPTER—WALKING TALL 🦃 Garbage. Rated R for violence. 112m. **DIR:** Jack Starrett. **CAST:** Bo Svenson, Margaret Blye, Forrest Tucker, Lurene Tuttle, Morgan Woodward, Libby Boone. 1977

FINAL COMBAT, THE ★★★★ In a post-apocalypse world, a lonely man makes an attempt to break away and find a kind of happiness. He soon discovers that he must fight for what he desires rather than try to run away. This may sound like any one of the *Mad Max* films, but this is a much more sensitive and cerebral story. The performances are good and the story is compelling, and all this is accentuated by the fact that there is no dialogue in the movie. Rated R for violence. B&W; 93m. **DIR:** Luc Besson. **CAST:** Pierre Jolivet, Fritz Wepper, Jean Bouise, Jean Reno. 1984

FINAL COMEDOWN, THE 🦃 Dated, heavy-handed film about a black man who becomes involved with a group of militants. Rated R for violence, profanity, and nudity. 84m. **DIR:** Oscar Williams. **CAST:** Billy Dee Williams, D'Urville Martin, Celia Kaye, Raymond St. Jacques. 1972

FINAL IMPACT ★★ Ex-world kick-boxing champ (Lorenzo Lamas) trains an innocent kid (Mike Worth) for the finals in an effort to avenge his own defeat. Reasonably watchable. Rated R for violence and profanity. 97m. **DIR:** Joseph Merhi, Stephen Smoke. **CAST:** Lorenzo Lamas, Mike Worth, Jeff Langton, Kathleen Kinmont. 1991

FINAL JUSTICE 🦃 Joe Don Baker plays a rural sheriff who travels to Italy to take on the Mafia and halt criminal activities. Rated R for nudity, violence, and language. 90m. **DIR:** Greydon Clark. **CAST:** Joe Don Baker, Venantino Venantini, Helena Abella, Bill McKinney. 1984

FINAL MISSION 🦃 *First Blood* rip-off. Not rated, but with profanity, violence, and nudity. 101m. **DIR:** Cirio H. Santiago. **CAST:** Richard Young, John Dresden, Kaz Garas, Christine Tudor. 1984

FINAL ROUND ★★ Undiscriminating action fans may tolerate this low-rent translation of Richard Connell's "The Most Dangerous Game," but there's little appeal for mainstream viewers. Thanks to poor lighting, Lorenzo Lamas's fight scenes are barely visible...no doubt to hide the $1.98 sets. Rated R for violence, profanity, and nudity. 90m. **DIR:** George Erschbamer. **CAST:** Lorenzo Lamas, Anthony De Longis, Kathleen Kinmont. 1993

FINEST HOUR, THE ★★½ Two new navy SEAL recruits form an alliance after trying to outdo one another. After being separated for a couple of years, they team up again during the Persian Gulf War. Very dull plot that could have been shorter. Rated R for profanity, violence, and nudity. 105m. **DIR:** Shimon Dotan. **CAST:** Rob Lowe, Gale Hansen, Tracy Griffith, Eb Lottimer. 1991

FINGER MAN (1955) ★★ Captured crook saves his hide by helping the Internal Revenue Bureau get the goods on crime kingpin Forrest Tucker. Frank Lovejoy as the reluctant informer does a credible job, but crazy Timothy Carey as Tucker's top enforcer steals the show. B&W; 81m. **DIR:** Harold Schuster. **CAST:** Frank Lovejoy, Forrest Tucker, Peggie Castle, Timothy Carey. 1955

FIRE! ★★ Another of producer Irwin Allen's suspense spectaculars involving an all-star cast caught in a major calamity. This one concerns a mountain town in the path of a forest fire set by an escaped convict. Worth watching once. 100m. **DIR:** Earl Bellamy. **CAST:** Ernest Borgnine, Vera Miles, Alex Cord, Donna Mills, Lloyd Nolan, Ty Hardin, Neville Brand, Gene Evans, Erik Estrada. **1977**

FIRE AND ICE (1987) 🦃 When the musical theme of a film offers only the words of the title sung over and over again, you know you're in for an ordeal. No rating. 80m. **DIR:** Willy Bogner. **CAST:** John Eaves, Suzy Chaffee. **1987**

FIRE BIRDS 🦃 Lame revision of *Top Gun.* Rated PG-13 for violence and language. 89m. **DIR:** David Greene. **CAST:** Nicolas Cage, Sean Young, Tommy Lee Jones. **1990**

FIRE, ICE & DYNAMITE 🦃 Stunt director Willy Bogner oversees ex-James Bond star Roger Moore in this stunt-filled yet ultimately boring crime caper. Rated PG for violence. 105m. **DIR:** Willy Bogner. **CAST:** Roger Moore, Shari Belafonte-Harper. **1990**

FIRE OVER ENGLAND ★★★ A swashbuckling adventure of Elizabethan England's stand against the Spanish Armada. Made in the 1930s, it wasn't released in this country until 1941, in order to evoke American support and sympathy for Britain's plight against the Nazi juggernaut during its darkest days. This is only one of the three films that united husband and wife Laurence Olivier and Vivien Leigh. B&W; 92m. **DIR:** Alexander Korda. **CAST:** Laurence Olivier, Vivien Leigh, Flora Robson. **1936**

FIREFOX ★★★½ Clint Eastwood doffs his contemporary cowboy garb to direct, produce, and star in this action-adventure film about an American fighter pilot assigned to steal a sophisticated Russian aircraft. The film takes a while to take off, but when it does, it's good, action-packed fun. Rated PG for violence. 124m. **DIR:** Clint Eastwood. **CAST:** Clint Eastwood, Freddie Jones, David Huffman, Warren Clarke, Ronald Lacey, Stefan Schnabel. **1982**

FIREHAWK ★★ Walk through the park as survivors of a downed American helicopter platoon must contend with the oncoming Vietcong, plus the traitor among them with his own agenda. Plenty of action keeps this from being a total disaster. Rated R for violence and adult language. 92m. **DIR:** Cirio H. Santiago. **CAST:** Martin Kove, Vic Trevino, Matt Salinger, Terrence "T. C." Carson. **1992**

FIREHEAD 🦃 A dopey Russian/CIA plot that sags even in the middle of low-budget telekinetic special effects. Rated R for language. 88m. **DIR:** Peter Yuval. **CAST:** Brett Porter, Gretchen Becker, Martin Landau, Christopher Plummer, Chris Lemmon. **1990**

FIREHOUSE (1972) ★★ Rookie flame fighter Richard Roundtree saves face and his marriage amid the hostile big-city firehouse environment of racism. 80m. **DIR:** Alex March. **CAST:** Richard Roundtree, Andrew Duggan, Richard Jaeckel, Val Avery, Paul LeMat, Vince Edwards, Sheila Frazier. **1972**

FIREPOWER ★★ *Firepower* is a muddled, mindless mess. A research chemist is blown up by a letter bomb while his wife, Sophia Loren, watches helplessly. The chemist was about to prove that a company owned by the third-richest man in the world, Carl Stegner (George Touliatos), has been distributing drugs responsible for causing the cancerous deaths of many people. The widow joins Justice Department agent James Coburn in trying to bring Stegner out of seclusion. Rated R. 104m. **DIR:** Michael Winner. **CAST:** Sophia Loren, James Coburn, O. J. Simpson, Eli Wallach, Vincent Gardenia, Anthony Franciosa, George Touliatos. **1979**

FIREWALKER 🦃 Two soldiers of fortune search for hidden treasure and end up in a Mayan temple of doom. Rated PG. 96m. **DIR:** J. Lee Thompson. **CAST:** Chuck Norris, Lou Gossett Jr., Melody Anderson, John Rhys-Davies. **1986**

FIRING LINE, THE ★★ Amateurish effort from writer-director John Gale about a rebel uprising in a South American country. Rated R for violence. 93m. **DIR:** John Gale. **CAST:** Reb Brown, Shannon Tweed, Carl Terry. **1991**

FIRST BLOOD ★★★½ Sylvester Stallone is top-notch as a former Green Beret who is forced to defend himself from a redneck cop (Brian Dennehy) in the Oregon mountains. The action never lets up. A winner for fans. Rated R for violence and profanity. 97m. **DIR:** Ted Kotcheff. **CAST:** Sylvester Stallone, Richard Crenna, Brian Dennehy, David Caruso, Jack Starrett. **1982**

FIRST YANK INTO TOKYO 🦃 Tom Neal has plastic surgery so he can pose as a Japanese soldier and help an American POW escape. B&W; 82m. **DIR:** Gordon Douglas. **CAST:** Tom Neal, Barbara Hale, Richard Loo, Keye Luke, Benson Fong. **1945**

FIST FIGHTER ★★ A drifter (Jorge Rivero) heads to Central America to avenge a friend's murder. For fans of two-fisted action-oriented movies. Rated R for violence. 99m. **DIR:** Frank Zuniga. **CAST:** Jorge Rivero, Mike Connors, Edward Albert. **1988**

FISTS OF FURY ★★★ Bruce Lee's first chop-socky movie (made in Hong Kong) is corny, action-filled, and violent. It's no *Enter the Dragon*, but his fans—who have so few films to choose from—undoubtedly will want to see it again. Rated R. 102m. **DIR:** Lo Wei. **CAST:** Bruce Lee, Maria Yi, James Tien, Nora Miao. **1972**

FIT TO KILL 🦃 Filmmaker Andy Sidaris continues his series of female spy movies, which usually serve as just an excuse to get women out of their clothes. This one has less flesh than usual, so there's nothing to watch at all. Rated R for nudity, violence, and adult situations. 94m. **DIR:** Andy Sidaris. **CAST:** Dona Speir, Roberta Vasquez, Julie Strain, Cynthia Brimhall. **1993**

FIVE FOR HELL 🦃 Italian-made World War II bomb. Not rated; has sex and violence. 88m. **DIR:** Frank Kramer. **CAST:** Klaus Kinski, John Garko, Margaret Lee, Nick Jordan, Luciano Rosi, Sam Burke. **1985**

FIVE GOLDEN DRAGONS 🦃 An innocent man runs into an international crime ring in Hong Kong. Boring, poorly made adventure. 93m. **DIR:** Jeremy Summers. **CAST:** Robert Cummings, Rupert Davies, Margaret Lee, Brian Donlevy, Christopher Lee, George Raft, Dan Duryea. **1967**

FIVE WEEKS IN A BALLOON ★★★ Up, up, and away on a balloon expedition to Africa, or, Kenya here we come! Author Jules Verne wrote the story. Nothing heavy here, just good, clean fun and adventure in the mold of *Around the World in Eighty Days*. 101m. **DIR:** Irwin Allen. **CAST:** Red Buttons, Barbara Eden, Fabian, Cedric Hardwicke, Peter Lorre, Herbert Marshall, Billy Gilbert, Reginald Owen, Henry Daniell, Barbara Luna, Richard Haydn. **1962**

FIX, THE 🦃 Tedious film about drug dealers. Not rated, has violence. 95m. **DIR:** Will Zens. **CAST:** Vince Edwards, Tony Dale, Richard Jaeckel, Julie Hill, Byron Cherry, Charles Dierkop, Don Dubbins, Leslie Leah, Robert Tessier. **1984**

FLAME AND THE ARROW, THE ★★★★ Burt Lancaster is at his acrobatic, tongue-in-cheek best in this film as a Robin Hood-like hero in Italy leading his oppressed countrymen to victory. It's a rousing swashbuckler. 88m. **DIR:** Jacques Tourneur. **CAST:** Burt Lancaster, Virginia Mayo, Nick Cravat. **1950**

FLAME OF THE BARBARY COAST ★★½ John Wayne plays a Montana rancher who fights with a saloon owner (Joseph Schildkraut) over the affections of a dance hall girl (Ann Dvorak). It's watchable, nothing more. B&W; 91m. **DIR:** Joseph Kane. **CAST:** John Wayne, Ann Dvorak, William Frawley, Joseph Schildkraut. **1945**

FLAME OVER INDIA ★★★★½ Rip-snorting adventure film has British officer Kenneth More and American governess Lauren Bacall escorting a young Hindu prince to safety during a political and religious uprising. J. Lee Thompson's flawless direction, a fine script, and terrific performances make this little-known film a classic. 130m. **DIR:** J. Lee Thompson. **CAST:** Lauren Bacall, Kenneth More, Herbert Lom, Wilfrid Hyde-White, I. S. Johar, Ian Hunter. **1959**

FLAME TO THE PHOENIX, A ★★ On the eve of Hitler's invasion of Poland, British diplomats plan their strategy while the Polish underground prepares for a long, bloody struggle. This talky drama is hard to follow, with characters of various nationalities all speaking with British accents. Unrated, the movie contains brief nudity and sexual situations. 80m. **DIR:** William Brayne. **CAST:** Frederick Treves, Ann Firbank. **1983**

FLASH AND THE FIRECAT 🦃 Flash (Roger Davis) and Firecat (Tricia Sembera) blaze across the California beaches, stealing cars and robbing banks. 94m. **DIR:** Ferd Sebastian, Beverly Sebastian. **CAST:** Richard Kiel, Roger Davis, Tricia Sembera. **1975**

FLASHBACK ★★ Straitlaced FBI agent Kiefer Sutherland is assigned to take hippie prankster Dennis Hopper to Oregon, where he is to stand trial. On the way Hopper switches places with Sutherland, and the chase is on. Clichés abound in this mushy mishmash. Rated R for profanity and violence. 106m. **DIR:** Franco Amurri. **CAST:** Dennis Hopper, Kiefer Sutherland, Carol Kane, Cliff De Young, Paul Dooley, Richard Masur, Michael McKean. **1990**

FLAT TOP ★★ A mediocre World War II action film following the exploits of an aircraft carrier battling the Japanese forces in the Pacific. Most of the battle scenes are taken from actual combat footage. B&W; 83m. **DIR:** Lesley Selander. **CAST:** Richard Carlson, Sterling Hayden, Keith Larsen, Bill Phillips. **1952**

FLATBED ANNIE AND SWEETIE PIE: LADY TRUCKERS ★★½ Annie Potts is Flatbed Annie, a veteran trucker who trains a novice named Sweetie Pie (Kim Darby). The two team up in an effort to support their costly rig. Mildly entertaining diversion. Made for TV. 104m. **DIR:** Robert Greenwald. **CAST:** Annie Potts, Kim Darby, Harry Dean Stanton, Arthur Godfrey, Rory Calhoun. **1979**

FLESH AND BLOOD ★★★½ Set in medieval Europe, *Flesh and Blood* follows the lives of two men—mercenary soldier Rutger Hauer and the son of a feudal lord (Tom Burlinson)—and their love for the same woman (Jennifer Jason Leigh). The cast is stellar, the sets are lavish, and the plot turns will keep the viewer guessing, but not in the dark. Rated R for violence, sex, nudity, profanity. 126m. **DIR:** Paul Verhoeven. **CAST:** Rutger Hauer, Jennifer Jason Leigh, Tom Burlinson, Susan Tyrrell, Ronald Lacey, Jack Thompson. **1985**

FLIGHT OF THE INTRUDER, THE ★★ Spectacular aerial-action sequences almost salvage this jingoistic, one-dimensional war film in which navy fliers Brad Johnson and Willem Dafoe ignore orders and bomb a restricted area in Hanoi. Based on the novel by Stephen Coonts. Rated PG-13 for profanity and violence. 115m. **DIR:** John Milius. **CAST:**

Danny Glover, Willem Dafoe, Brad Johnson, Rosanna Arquette. **1991**

FLIGHT OF THE PHOENIX, THE ★★★★ An all-star international cast shines in this gripping adventure about the desert crash of a small plane and the grueling efforts of the meager band of passengers to rebuild and repair it against impossible odds, not the least of which are starvation and/or heat prostration. 143m. **DIR:** Robert Aldrich. **CAST:** James Stewart, Richard Attenborough, Peter Finch, Ernest Borgnine, Hardy Krüger, Ronald Fraser, Christian Marquand, Ian Bannen, George Kennedy, Dan Duryea. **1966**

FLIGHT TO FURY ★★½ Jack Nicholson wrote the screenplay for this clever low-budget thriller. Nicholson plays a member of a group of conniving thieves smuggling diamonds out of the Philippines. B&W; 73m. **DIR:** Monte Hellman. **CAST:** Dewey Martin, Fay Spain, Jack Nicholson. **1964**

FLOOD! ★★★ Bureaucratic peevishness is responsible for a small town being caught short when a dam bursts. Slick and predictable, but interesting just the same. If you like this, you'll like its sister film, *Fire!* 100m. **DIR:** Earl Bellamy. **CAST:** Robert Culp, Martin Milner, Barbara Hershey, Richard Basehart, Carol Lynley, Roddy McDowall, Cameron Mitchell, Teresa Wright. **1976**

FLORIDA STRAITS ★★½ Raul Julia is a Cuban refugee who enlists the aid of charter boaters Fred Ward and Daniel Jenkins to help him get back to Cuba and rescue the woman he loves. Although a bit contrived in spots, this is watchable. An unrated HBO production that contains some violence and rough language. 98m. **DIR:** Mike Hodges. **CAST:** Raul Julia, Fred Ward, Daniel H. Jenkins, Jaime Sanchez, Victor Argo, Ilka Tanya Payan, Antonio Fargas. **1986**

FLYING BLIND ★★★ This is the third release of upscale B pictures from the William H. Pine–William C. Thomas production unit that operated at Paramount Pictures from 1941 through 1945. The previous films were *Power Dive* and *Forced Landing*, and all three share the same topic: aviation. The script here is by Maxwell Shane and deals with heroes versus evil foreign agents in the United States. B&W; 70m. **DIR:** Frank McDonald. **CAST:** Richard Arlen, Jean Parker. **1941**

FLYING FOOL, THE ★★½ The story about the protective older brother and his kid brother falling for the same girl was old when this vintage talkie was released, but top-notch dialogue and good aviation sequences make this breezy programmer good entertainment. B&W; 73m. **DIR:** Tay Garnett. **CAST:** William Boyd, Marie Prevost, Russell Gleason, James Gleason. **1929**

FLYING LEATHERNECKS ★★★½ John Wayne is the apparently heartless commander of an airborne fighting squad, and Robert Ryan is the caring officer who questions his decisions in this well-acted war film. The stars play off each other surprisingly well, and it's a shame they didn't do more films together. 102m. **DIR:** Nicholas Ray. **CAST:** John Wayne, Robert Ryan, Jay C. Flippen. **1951**

FLYING TIGERS, THE ★★½ Exciting dogfight action scenes make this low-budget John Wayne World War II vehicle watchable, but the story sags a bit. B&W; 102m. **DIR:** David Miller. **CAST:** John Wayne, John Carroll, Mae Clarke, Gordon Jones. **1942**

FOLLOW THAT CAR [turkey] Typical good-ol'-boy action-adventure. Rated PG for language and violence. 96m. **DIR:** Daniel Haller. **CAST:** Dirk Benedict, Tanya Tucker, Teri Nunn. **1980**

FOR YOUR EYES ONLY ★★★½ For the first time since Roger Moore took over the role of 007 from Sean Connery, we have a film in the style that made the best Bond films—*From Russia with Love* and *Goldfinger*—so enjoyable. *For Your Eyes Only* is genuine spy adventure, closer in spirit to the novels by Ian Fleming. Rated PG. 127m. **DIR:** John Glen. **CAST:** Roger Moore, Carole Bouquet, Lynn-Holly Johnson, Topol. **1981**

FORCE FIVE ★★ In this action-packed but predictable martial arts film, a soldier of fortune and his four buddies rescue a woman held on a remote island. Rated R for violence, nudity, and profanity. 78m. **DIR:** Robert Clouse. **CAST:** Gerald Gordon, Nick Pryor, Bradford Dillman, Tom Villard. **1981**

FORCE OF ONE ★★★ This is the follow-up to *Good Guys Wear Black*. In this karate film, Chuck Norris cleans up a California town that has drug problems. As always, it only takes one good guy (Norris) to kick and/or punch some sense into the bad guys. Rated PG. 90m. **DIR:** Paul Aaron. **CAST:** Chuck Norris, Jennifer O'Neill, James Whitmore, Pepe Serna. **1979**

FORCE TEN FROM NAVARONE [turkey] Poor sequel to the classic *Guns of Navarone*. 118m. **DIR:** Guy Hamilton. **CAST:** Robert Shaw, Harrison Ford, Edward Fox, Franco Nero, Barbara Bach, Carl Weathers, Richard Kiel. **1978**

FORCED VENGEANCE ★★½ Even pacing and a somewhat suspenseful plot are not enough to make this film a must-see—unless you're a die-hard Chuck Norris fan, that is. This time, our martial arts master plays a casino security chief living in the Far East. Rated R for violence, nudity, and profanity. 90m. **DIR:** James Fargo. **CAST:** Chuck Norris, Mary Louise Weller, Camilla Griggs, Michael Cavanaugh, David Opatoshu, Seiji Sakaguchi. **1982**

FORTRESS OF AMERIKKKA ★★ Murderous mercenaries battle the residents of a small California town. Campy Troma nonsense with plenty of gratuitous nudity and bad acting, as promised. Rated R. 97m. **DIR:** Eric Louzil. **CAST:** Gene Le Brock. **1989**

FORTUNE DANE ★★½ Originally a pilot for a TV series, this fair action film features Carl Weathers as a cop out to find who corrupted his banker father. Rated PG for violence. 83m. **DIR:** Nicholas Sgarro, Charles Correll. **CAST:** Carl Weathers, Adolph Caesar. **1986**

FOUR DEUCES, THE ★★ Jack Palance is a gang leader during Prohibition times in this high-camp action film about gangsters. The movie is poorly conceived, with an odd mixture of blood and spoof. *The Four Deuces* does not have an MPAA rating, but it contains sex, nudity, violence, and profanity. 87m. **DIR:** William H. Bushnell Jr. **CAST:** Jack Palance, Carol Lynley, Warren Berlinger, Adam Roarke, Gianni Russo, H. B. Haggerty, John Haymer, Martin Kove, E. J. Peaker. **1975**

FOUR FEATHERS, THE (1939) ★★★★ A young man (John Clements) from a military background is branded a coward when he forsakes military duty for a home and family during time of war. Rejected by his family, friends, and fiancée, he sets out to prove his manhood. This motion picture was one of the few English productions of its era to gain wide acceptance. It still holds up well today. 115m. **DIR:** Zoltán Korda. **CAST:** Ralph Richardson, John Clements, June Duprez, C. Aubrey Smith. **1939**

FOUR FEATHERS, THE (1978) ★★★ Solid television retelling of the A. E. W. Mason story, with plenty of action and derring-do. Beau Bridges portrays the Britisher fighting against Sudanese tribesmen in nineteenth-century Africa. Although the transition of the story from British to American ideals is shaky, the story itself is powerful. 110m. **DIR:** Don Sharp. **CAST:** Beau Bridges, Robert Powell, Simon Ward, Jane Seymour, Harry Andrews. **1978**

FOUR HORSEMEN OF THE APOCALYPSE ★★ The 1921 silent version of this complex anti-war tale of two brothers who fight on opposite sides during World War I is still the best. When Rudolph Valentino played Julio, you cared. This one, updated to World War II, falls flat, despite a fine cast. 153m. **DIR:** Vincente Minnelli. **CAST:** Glenn Ford, Ingrid Thulin, Charles Boyer, Lee J. Cobb, Paul Henreid, Paul Lukas. **1961**

FOUR MUSKETEERS, THE ★★★★★ In this superb sequel to Richard Lester's *The Three Musketeers*, the all-star cast is remarkably good, and the director is at the peak of his form. The final duel between Michael York and Christopher Lee is a stunner. Rated PG. 108m. **DIR:** Richard Lester. **CAST:** Oliver Reed, Raquel Welch, Richard Chamberlain, Frank Finlay, Michael York, Christopher Lee, Faye Dunaway, Charlton Heston. **1975**

1492: THE CONQUEST OF PARADISE ★★ Gérard Depardieu, so effective in character studies, is miscast as Christopher Columbus in this bloated epic. Beautifully filmed by director Ridley Scott and well acted by a strong cast. Rated PG-13 for violence and nudity. 152m. **DIR:** Ridley Scott. **CAST:** Gérard Depardieu, Armand Assante, Sigourney Weaver, Angela Molina, Fernando Rey, Tcheky Karyo, Frank Langella, Michael Wincott, Loren Dean, Kevin Dunn. **1992**

FOURTH WAR, THE ★★ Old war-horse Roy Scheider can't adjust to a peaceful, politicized new army—especially when he confronts a Soviet colonel (Jurgen Prochnow) of similiar persuasions. Fine performances by Scheider and Prochnow are wasted in this mediocre thriller. Rated R for violence and profanity. 95m. **DIR:** John Frankenheimer. **CAST:** Roy Scheider, Jurgen Prochnow, Harry Dean Stanton, Tim Reid. **1990**

FOXTRAP 🦃 Fred Williamson plays a bodyguard sent to Europe to find a missing heiress. Rated R for violence, drug use, and sexual situations. 88m. **DIR:** Fred Williamson. **CAST:** Fred Williamson, Christopher Connelly, Arlene Golonka. **1986**

FOXY BROWN ★★ Pam Grier takes on the mobsters who butchered her boyfriend. Grier and Jack Hill—the man who directed her in several Filipino sexploitation prison flicks—are reteamed for this wildly sadistic urban-crime melodrama. A richly deserved R rating. 94m. **DIR:** Jack Hill. **CAST:** Pam Grier, Peter Brown, Terry Carter. **1974**

FRAME UP ★★ A watchable mishmash about a sheriff's investigation of a boy's murder. Rated R for rape scenes and language. 90m. **DIR:** Paul Leder. **CAST:** Wings Hauser, Bobby DiCicco, Frances Fisher. **1990**

FRAMED (1975) 🦃 Thoroughly nauseating and graphically violent story of a man framed for a crime he did not commit. Rated R for gory violence and language. 106m. **DIR:** Phil Karlson. **CAST:** Joe Don Baker, Conny Van Dyke, Gabriel Dell, Brock Peters, John Marley. **1975**

FREEFALL ★★★½ Although this thriller eventually becomes too tricky for its own good, John Irvin's slick direction doesn't let you ponder apparent plot inconsistencies. Wildlife photographer Pamela Gidley goes to Africa to shoot a rare bird, and winds up involved with assassins and Interpol agents who seem convinced she has something they desire. Plot twists abound, and most of them work. Rated R for violence, nudity, and suggested sex. 96m. **DIR:** John Irvin. **CAST:** Eric Roberts, Pamela Gidley, Jeff Fahey. **1994**

FREEWAY ★★★ A fad film mirroring the real-life series of freeway killings in the Los Angeles area. A nurse (Darlanne Fluegel), dissatisfied with the police investigation of the murder of her boyfriend by a freeway sniper, pursues the killer on her own. Good acting, exciting direction, and some great action sequences make up for the threadbare plot. Rated R for violence, profanity, and nudity. 95m. **DIR:** Francis Delia. **CAST:** Darlanne Fluegel, James Russo, Richard Belzer, Michael Callan. **1988**

FRENCH CONNECTION, THE ★★★★★ Gene Hackman is an unorthodox New York narcotics cop in this Oscar-winning performance. He and his partner (Roy Scheider) are investigating the flow of heroin coming into the city from France. The climactic chase is the best in movie history. Rated R. 104m. **DIR:** William Friedkin. **CAST:** Gene Hackman, Fernando Rey, Roy Scheider, Eddie Egan, Sonny Gross. **1971**

FRENCH CONNECTION II, THE ★★ Disappointing sequel to the 1971 winner for best picture has none of the thrills, chills, and action of the original. Instead, New York detective Popeye Doyle (Gene Hackman), who has journeyed to Paris to track the drug trafficker who eluded him in the States, finds himself addicted to heroin and suffering withdrawal. He isn't the only one who suffers. . . . There's the viewer, too. Rated R. 119m. **DIR:** John Frankenheimer. **CAST:** Gene Hackman, Fernando Rey, Bernard Fresson, Jean-Pierre Castaldi, Charles Milot. **1975**

FRESH KILL 🦃 A would-be actor becomes involved with a not-so-innocent woman. Made-for-video junk marked by some truly repulsive violence. 90m. **DIR:** Joseph Merhi. **CAST:** Flint Keller, Tricia Parks. **1987**

FRIDAY FOSTER ★★½ In this blaxploitation effort, Pam Grier plays the title character, a fashion photographer who doubles as a two-fisted avenger—this time taking on antiblack terrorists. A strong supporting cast helps. Rated R. 90m. **DIR:** Arthur Marks. **CAST:** Pam Grier, Julius W. Harris, Thalmus Rasulala, Carl Weathers, Eartha Kitt, Godfrey Cambridge, Yaphet Kotto. **1975**

FROM HELL TO BORNEO ★★ George Montgomery owns an island. Crooks and smugglers want it. He defends it. Sweat and jungle. 96m. **DIR:** George Montgomery. **CAST:** George Montgomery, Torin Thatcher, Julie Gregg, Lisa Moreno. **1964**

FROM HELL TO VICTORY 🦃 This hokey story of a bunch of strangely allied friends during World War II has nothing to offer. Rated PG. 100m. **DIR:** Hank Milestone. **CAST:** George Peppard, George Hamilton, Capucine, Horst Buchholz, Sam Wanamaker. **1979**

FROM RUSSIA WITH LOVE ★★★★½ The definitive James Bond movie. Sean Connery's second portrayal of Agent 007 is right on target. Lots of action, beautiful women, and great villains. Connery's fight aboard a passenger train with baddy Robert Shaw is as good as they come. 118m. **DIR:** Terence Young. **CAST:** Sean Connery, Lotte Lenya, Robert Shaw, Daniela Bianchi. **1963**

FUGITIVE, THE (1993) ★★★★★ Following in the footsteps of David Janssen's 1960s television character, Harrison Ford keeps viewers on the edges of their seats with his performance as Dr. Richard Kimble, an innocent man accused of murdering his wife. Tracked by the relentless U.S. Marshal Sam Girard (Tommy Lee Jones), an escaped Kimble tries to prove his innocence by finding the one-armed man he believes committed the crime. Action specialist Andrew Davis molds it all into a top-flight thriller. Rated PG-13 for profanity and violence. 133m. **DIR:** Andrew Davis. **CAST:** Harrison Ford, Tommy Lee Jones, Sela Ward, Joe Pantoliano, Jeroen Krabbé, Andreas Katsulas, Daniel Roebuck. **1993**

FUGITIVE, THE: THE LAST EPISODE (TV SERIES) ★★★½ Dr. Richard Kimble (David Janssen) is sentenced to death for the murder of his wife. He escapes from Indiana police lieutenant Philip Gerard (Barry Morse) and goes in search of the one-armed man he believes was the real culprit. After four outstanding seasons, the series ends in run-of-the-mill fashion. Kimble, still pursued by the obsessive Gerard, finally encounters the one-armed man. Though somewhat disappointing, this two-part episode is a must for fans. 120m. **DIR:** Don Medford. **CAST:** David Janssen, Barry Morse, Bill Raisch, Diane Brewster. **1967**

FUGITIVE GIRLS 🦃 Here's a video treasure for camp buffs—a women's prison movie written by Ed *(Plan 9 from Outer Space)* Wood! Rated R for nudity and sexual situations. 90m. **DIR:** A. C. Stephen. **CAST:** Jabee Abercrombie, Rene Bond, Edward D. Wood Jr. **1975**

FULL CONTACT 🦃 Watch this movie if you want to see 90 minutes of kick-boxing, bad acting, and no plot. Rated R for profanity, violence, and nudity. 96m. **DIR:** Rick Jacobson. **CAST:** Jerry Trimble, Gerry Blanck, Denise Buick, Marcus Aurelius, Raymond Storti. **1992**

FULL FATHOM FIVE ★★½ Adequate actioner focuses on Panamanian countermeasures to an American invasion. Michael Moriarty is the captain of an American submarine ordered to destroy a Soviet nuclear sub. Rated PG for violence. 82m. **DIR:** Carl Franklin. **CAST:** Michael Moriarty, Maria Rangel, Michael Cavanaugh. **1990**

FURTHER ADVENTURES OF TENNESSEE BUCK, THE ★★ Yet another cheap imitation of Indiana Jones, with David Keith playing an incorrigible jungle adventurer hired as a guide by a young couple. Kathy Shower, a 1987 *Playboy* playmate, is the female side of the couple; she can't act worth a lick. Rated R for violence, language, nudity, and simulated sex. 90m. **DIR:** David Keith. **CAST:** David Keith, Kathy Shower, Sidney Lassick. **1988**

FURY OF HERCULES, THE ★★ Some Yugoslavian exteriors and the presence of Brad Harris, one of the more formidable post-Steve Reeves sword-and-sandal stars, boost this battle-filled saga about a corrupt kingdom. And, for once, the English dubbing is decent. 97m. **DIR:** Gianfranco Parolini. **CAST:** Brad Harris, Bridgette Corey. **1962**

FURY OF THE CONGO 🦃 There's no fury and precious little Congo in this dull jungle filler. B&W; 69m. **DIR:** William Berke. **CAST:** Johnny Weissmuller, Sherry Moreland, William Henry, Lyle Talbot. **1951**

FUTURE ZONE 🦃 David Carradine stars as a modern-day cop whose son time travels into the past to rescue him from death. Rated R for violence and profanity. 90m. **DIR:** David A. Prior. **CAST:** David Carradine, Ted Prior, Charles Napier. **1990**

G-MEN ★★★★ A huge name cast and personal-best direction by William Keighley support James Cagney in his switch from gangster to good guy in this classic. The film follows the adventures of a young lawyer (Cagney) whose education was paid for by a good-hearted crime boss. B&W; 85m. **DIR:** William Keighley. **CAST:** James Cagney, Ann Dvorak, Margaret Lindsay, Robert Armstrong, Barton MacLane, Lloyd Nolan, Russell Hopton, Noel Madison, Regis Toomey, Addison Richards, Harold Huber, Raymond Hatton. **1935**

G-MEN NEVER FORGET ★★★ Former stuntman and future Lone Ranger Clayton Moore leads his G-Men in a violent battle against master heavy Roy Barcroft. An action-packed serial adventure; master stuntman and legendary second-unit director Yakima Canutt codirected. B&W; 12 chapters. **DIR:** Fred Brannon, Yakima Canutt. **CAST:** Clayton Moore, Roy Barcroft, Ramsay Ames, Tom Steele, Eddie Acuff. **1948**

G-MEN VS. THE BLACK DRAGON ★★½ The British, Chinese, and American secret service team up to fight the deadly Black Dragon Society of Japan. The action and stunts are top-notch in this serial. B&W; 15 chapters. **DIR:** William Witney. **CAST:** Rod Cameron, Constance Worth, George J. Lewis. **1943**

GALLAGHER'S TRAVELS ★★ An English reporter teams up with an Australian photographer to track down an animal-smuggling ring. There's not much adventure. 94m. **DIR:** Michael Caulfield. **CAST:** Ivar Kants, Joanne Samuel, Stuart Campbell, Jennifer Hagan. **1987**

GALLOPING GHOST, THE ★★ College football melodrama starring real-life football legend Red Grange. Antiquated. B&W; 12 chapters. **DIR:** B. Reeves "Breezy" Eason. **CAST:** Harold "Red" Grange, Dorothy Gulliver. **1931**

GAMBLE, THE 🦃 Matthew Modine plays an impoverished nobleman who loses in a bet. Rated R for nudity and violence. 108m. **DIR:** Carlo Vanzina. **CAST:** Matthew Modine, Faye Dunaway, Jennifer Beals. **1988**

GAME, THE ★★½ *The Game* is what the rich and powerful play once a year, a high-tech hunting party in which humans are the prey. Joseph Campanella infiltrates the group to seek revenge on the men who killed his family, while soldier of fortune Craig Alan gives them a run for their money on the battlefield. Unrated, but contains violence. 96m. **DIR:** Cole McKay. **CAST:** Joseph Campanella, Craig Alan. **1988**

GAME FOR VULTURES ★★ A long, dusty, and violent trek through the agonies of South Africa's ongoing conflict. Strong cast, strong theme, weak movie. Rated R for lots of machine-gun violence. 113m. **DIR:** James Fargo. **CAST:** Joan Collins, Richard Harris, Richard Roundtree, Ray Milland. **1986**

GAME OF DEATH 🦃 The climactic twenty minutes of Bruce Lee in action fighting Kareem Abdul-Jabbar and Danny Inosanto are thrilling. The rest of the film is not. Rated R. 102m. **DIR:** Robert Clouse. **CAST:** Bruce Lee, Kareem Abdul-Jabbar, Danny Inosanto, Gig Young, Hugh O'Brian, Colleen Camp, Dean Jagger, Chuck Norris. **1979**

GANG BUSTERS 🦃 As a film about prison life and various attempts at breakout, this picture simply doesn't measure up. B&W; 78m. **DIR:** Bill Karan. **CAST:** Myron Healey, Sam Edwards, Don Harvey, Frank Gerstle. **1955**

GANGS, INC. ★★ Low-budget crime drama about an anguished woman with an unhappy past who seeks justification in a life of crime. Also titled *Paper Bullets*. B&W; 72m. **DIR:** Phil Rosen. **CAST:** Joan Woodbury, Jack LaRue, Alan Ladd, John Archer, Vince Barnett. **1941**

GANGSTER WARS ★★½ This movie traces the lives of mobsters "Lucky" Luciano, "Bugsy" Siegel, and Meyer Lansky from their childhood friendship to becoming the most powerful leaders in organized crime during the 1920s. This is an action-packed gangster movie, which at times is difficult to follow and tends to lead the viewer down some dead ends. Rated PG for violence. 121m. **DIR:** Richard C. Sarafian. **CAST:** Michael Nouri, Brian Benben, Joe Penny. **1981**

GATOR ★★ Burt Reynolds directed this mildly entertaining sequel to *White Lightning*. In it, Burt plays an ex-con out to get revenge—with the help of undercover agent Jack Weston—on some nasty southern politicians. Rated PG. 116m. **DIR:** Burt Reynolds. **CAST:** Burt Reynolds, Jack Weston, Lauren Hutton, Jerry Reed, Alice Ghostley, Mike Douglas, Dub Taylor. **1976**

GATOR BAIT 💔 Claudia Jennings plays a Cajun alligator poacher. Rated R for violence, profanity, and nudity. 91m. **DIR:** Ferd Sebastian, Beverly Sebastian. **CAST:** Claudia Jennings, Sam Gilman, Clyde Ventura. **1973**

GATOR BAIT II—CAJUN JUSTICE ★★ A revenge flick with a twist: a happy ending. Cajun newlyweds are ravaged by a group of bayou inbreds. The low-budget look and poor acting rate only two stars, but this is a decent entry in the revenge category. Rated R for violence. 95m. **DIR:** Ferd Sebastian, Beverly Sebastian. **CAST:** Jan MacKenzie. **1988**

GAUNTLET, THE ★★ One of actor-director Clint Eastwood's few failures, this release features the squinty-eyed star as an alcoholic, barely capable cop assigned to bring a prostitute (Sondra Locke) to trial. Rated R. 109m. **DIR:** Clint Eastwood. **CAST:** Clint Eastwood, Sondra Locke, Pat Hingle, William Prince. **1977**

GENERAL DIED AT DAWN, THE ★★★ Nicely turned story of adventurer Gary Cooper battling Chinese warlord Akim Tamiroff. Film is a bit short on action but draws some fine character studies. Madeleine Carroll is good as Cooper's love interest, but it is Tamiroff who steals the show. B&W; 97m. **DIR:** Lewis Milestone. **CAST:** Gary Cooper, Akim Tamiroff, Madeleine Carroll, Porter Hall, Dudley Digges. **1936**

GET CHRISTIE LOVE! ★★ A television entry in the blaxploitation genre, this adventure centers on a female police detective (Teresa Graves) who tracks drug dealers on the streets of Los Angeles in the 1970s. Fairly tame when compared to others in its genre. 75m. **DIR:** William A. Graham. **CAST:** Teresa Graves, Harry Guardino, Louise Sorel, Paul Stevens. **1974**

GETAWAY, THE (1972) ★★★★ Top-notch adventure and excitement occur when convict Steve McQueen has his wife seduce the Texas Parole Board chairman (Ben Johnson) in exchange for his early freedom. McQueen becomes jealous and resentful after the deal is consummated and kills the chairman, setting off a shotgun-charged chase. Rated PG. 122m. **DIR:** Sam Peckinpah. **CAST:** Steve McQueen, Ali MacGraw, Ben Johnson, Sally Struthers. **1972**

GETAWAY, THE (1994) ★★★½ Surprisingly effective scene-for-scene remake of director Sam Peckinpah's flawed but sometimes brilliant action film. Alec Baldwin is nowhere near as charismatic as Steve McQueen was in the lead role of a convict who secures his release from prison with the help of his wife, but Kim Basinger outdoes Ali MacGraw as the other half of this modern-day outlaw couple. Rated R for violence, profanity, nudity and simulated sex. 115m. **DIR:** Roger Donaldson. **CAST:** Alec Baldwin, Kim Basinger, James Woods, Michael Madsen, David Morse, Jennifer Tilly, James Stephens, Burton Gilliam, Richard Farnsworth. **1994**

GETTING EVEN ★★ This is a fast-paced but unspectacular action-adventure film. The hero is a wealthy industrialist with a passion for danger. Rated R for violence and nudity. 89m. **DIR:** Dwight H. Little. **CAST:** Edward Albert, Audrey Landers, Joe Don Baker. **1986**

GHOST PATROL ★★ Colonel Tim McCoy takes a commanding lead in this low-budget film about a government agent investigating the strange crashes of airplanes carrying top-secret information. An effort to cash in on the unexpected success of Gene Autry's *Phantom Empire* and Tom Mix's *Miracle Rider*. B&W; 57m. **DIR:** Sam Newfield. **CAST:** Tim McCoy, Claudia Dell, Walter Miller, Wheeler Oakman, Slim Whitaker. **1936**

GHOST WARRIOR ★★½ In Japan, two skiers exploring a cave find a 400-year-old samurai warrior entombed in ice. He is taken to the United States in a hush-hush operation and revived. Although slow at times, this film is an entertaining, though violent, diversion. Rated R for violence. 86m. **DIR:** Larry Carbol. **CAST:** Hiroshi Fujioka, John Calvin, Janet Julian, Andy Wood. **1984**

GIRL ON A CHAIN GANG 💔 Grade-C rural exploitation. Not rated; contains violence and coarse language. B&W; 93m. **DIR:** Jerry Gross. **CAST:** William Watson, Julie Ange. **1965**

GIRLS TOWN ★★ It overstays its welcome by about 15 minutes, but this trash opus about a bad girl (Mamie Van Doren) sent to a prison farm is otherwise a laugh riot. And what a cast! The Platters supply some musical numbers. B&W; 92m. **DIR:** Charles Haas. **CAST:** Mamie Van Doren, Mel Torme, Paul Anka, Ray Anthony, Maggie Hayes, Cathy Crosby, Gigi Perreau, Gloria Talbott, Jim Mitchum, Elinor Donahue, Sheilah Graham. **1959**

GLADIATOR, THE ★★ Competent but attenuated TV film about a mechanic (Ken Wahl) who goes on the vengeance trail after his younger brother is killed by a deranged DUI. Some of the drama works, but often the narrative becomes repetitious. 94m. **DIR:** Abel Ferrara. **CAST:** Ken Wahl, Nancy Allen, Robert Culp, Stan Shaw, Rosemary Forsyth, Bart Braverman. **1986**

GLEAMING THE CUBE ★★★ Better-than-average murder-mystery aimed at the teenage crowd. Christian Slater stars as a skateboard ace who kick starts a murder investigation when his adopted Vietnamese brother is found hanged in a motel. Spectacular, exciting skateboard stunts and an appealing performance by Slater help glide over the holes in the plot. Rated PG-13. 104m. **DIR:** Graeme Clifford. **CAST:** Christian Slater, Steven Bauer, Richard Herd, Ed Lauter. **1989**

GLORIA ★★★½ After his family is executed by the Mafia, a little boy hides out with a female neighbor. Together they must flee or be killed. Gena Rowlands is very good in the title role as the streetwise Gloria, whose savvy and brains keep the two alive. Rated R—language, violence. 121m. **DIR:** John Cassavetes. **CAST:** Gena Rowlands, Buck Henry, John Adames, Julie Carmen, Lupe Guarnica. **1980**

GLORY AT SEA ★★ Typical British salute to those who fought in World War II—Trevor Howard, the captain of a decrepit battleship, wins the respect of his men while under fire. B&W; 90m. **DIR:** Compton Bennett. **CAST:** Trevor Howard, Richard Attenborough, Sonny Tufts, James Donald. **1952**

GLORY BOYS, THE ★★½ A many-sided Middle Eastern, terrorist/counterterrorist plot and counterplot. Solid production values, but the overfamiliar scenario is a waste. No rating but contains violence and profanity. 130m. **DIR:** Michael Ferguson. **CAST:** Rod Steiger, Anthony Perkins, Alfred Burke, Joanna Lumley. **1984**

GLORY STOMPERS, THE 🦃 Silly cycle movie, about rival biker clubs. Not rated, some violence. 81m. **DIR:** Anthony M. Lanza. **CAST:** Dennis Hopper, Jody McCrea, Chris Noel, Jock Mahoney, Casey Kasem. **1967**

GO TELL THE SPARTANS ★★★★ In one of the best Vietnam war films, Burt Lancaster is a commander who begins to wonder "what we're doing over there." It's a very honest portrayal of America's early days in Vietnam, with Lancaster giving an excellent performance. Rated R. 114m. **DIR:** Ted Post. **CAST:** Burt Lancaster, Craig Wasson, Marc Singer. **1978**

GOLDEN CHILD, THE ★★ Eddie Murphy stars as a Los Angeles social worker who is stunned when members of a religious sect call him "The Chosen One" and expect him to save a magical child from the forces of evil. You'll be even more stunned when you watch this cheesy comedy-adventure and realize it was one of the biggest hits of its year. Rated PG-13 for violence and profanity. 96m. **DIR:** Michael Ritchie. **CAST:** Eddie Murphy, Charlotte Lewis, Charles Dance, Randall "Tex" Cobb, Victor Wong, James Hong. **1986**

GOLDEN EARRINGS ★★★★ An enjoyable romantic romp that wouldn't have worked with a different cast. Marlene Dietrich plays a gypsy who becomes a spy to help British officer Ray Milland escape the Nazis in Germany's Black Forest. The story sounds silly and contrived, but Dietrich's performance makes it compelling. B&W; 95m. **DIR:** Mitchell Leisen. **CAST:** Marlene Dietrich, Ray Milland, Murvyn Vye, Quentin Reynolds, Reinhold Schunzel, Bruce Lester, Dennis Hoey, John Dehner. **1947**

GOLDFINGER ★★★★ *Goldfinger* is so enjoyable to watch that it's easy to forget the influence of the film on the spy-adventure genre. From the precredits sequence (cut out of most TV versions) to the final spectacular fight with Goldfinger's superhuman henchman, Oddjob (Harold Sakata), the film firmly establishes characters and situations that measured not only future Bond films but all spy films to follow. Sean Connery is the ultimate 007, John Barry's music is unforgettable, and Oddjob made bowler hats fashionable for heavies. 108m. **DIR:** Guy Hamilton. **CAST:** Sean Connery, Gert Fröbe, Honor Blackman, Harold Sakata. **1964**

GOLIATH AND THE BARBARIANS ★★ Steve Reeves plays Goliath in this so-so Italian action film. In this episode, he saves Italy from invading barbaric tribes. As in many of Reeves's films, the only object of interest is the flexing of his muscles. 86m. **DIR:** Carlo Campogalliani. **CAST:** Steve Reeves, Bruce Cabot, Giulia Rubini, Chelo Alonso. **1960**

GOLIATH AND THE DRAGON ★★ The original, Italian version of this film had Maciste (Italy's mythological hero, renamed Goliath by U.S. distributors) fighting a three-headed, fire-breathing dog and other horrors—but *not* a dragon. So the Americans had a life-size dragon's head built for Mark Forest to swing his sword at, and hired Jim Danforth to animate a miniature dragon thrashing about for the long shots—and spliced the whole thing, lasting a couple of minutes, into the existing film. 87m. **DIR:** Vittorio Cottafari. **CAST:** Mark Forest, Broderick Crawford, Gaby André. **1960**

GOLIATH AWAITS ★★½ This undersea adventure is about the discovery of a sunken ocean liner, many of whose original passengers are still alive after years on the bottom. It was much better as a two-part (200-minute) miniseries on TV. 95m. **DIR:** Kevin Connor. **CAST:** Mark Harmon, Robert Forster, Eddie Albert, Emma Samms, Christopher Lee, John Carradine, Frank Gorshin, Jean Marsh. **1981**

GONE IN 60 SECONDS 🦃 Stuntman-turned-film-auteur H. B. Halicki wrecks a bunch of cars faster than you can say Hal Needham. Rated PG for violence. 97m. **DIR:** H. B. Halicki. **CAST:** H. B. Halicki, Marion Busia, George Cole, James McIntire, Jerry Daugirda. **1974**

GOOD GUYS WEAR BLACK ★★ This Chuck Norris action film starts out well but quickly dissolves into a routine political action-thriller that really goes nowhere. Lightweight entertainment. Rated PG. 96m. **DIR:** Ted Post. **CAST:** Chuck Norris, Anne Archer, James Franciscus, Lloyd Haynes, Jim Backus, Dana Andrews. **1979**

GOONIES, THE ★★★ This "Steven Spielberg production" is a mess. But it's sometimes an entertaining mess. The screenplay, taken from a story by Spielberg, concerns a feisty group of underprivileged kids—whose housing project is about to be destroyed—who find a treasure map, which could be the solution to all their problems. Rated PG for profanity. 111m. **DIR:** Richard Donner. **CAST:** Sean Astin, Josh Brolin, Jeff Cohen, Corey Feldman, Kerri Green, Martha Plimpton, Ke Huy-Quan. **1985**

GORDON'S WAR ★★½ Competent but uninspiring variation on *Death Wish* with an all-black cast. Paul Winfield is a Vietnam vet who avenges his wife's drug death. Rated R for violence, language, graphic drug use, and nudity. 90m. **DIR:** Ossie Davis. **CAST:** Paul Winfield, Carl Lee, David Downing, Tony King, Gilbert Lewis. **1978**

GOVERNMENT AGENTS VS. PHANTOM LEGION 🦃 A hijacking gang run by the mysterious "Voice" has been preying on truckers. The government sends in an operative to straighten things up in this ho-hum highway-bound serial. B&W; 12 chapters. **DIR:** Fred Brannon. **CAST:** Walter Reed, Mary Ellen Kay, Dick Curtis. **1951**

GRAND THEFT AUTO ★★½ The basic plot of *It's a Mad Mad Mad Mad World* is given a retread by first-time director—and star—Ron Howard in this frantic 1977 car-chase comedy. Sadly, little of the style that made *Night Shift* and *Splash* such treats is evident here. Rated PG. 89m. **DIR:** Ron Howard. **CAST:** Ron Howard, Nancy Morgan. **1977**

GRAY LADY DOWN ★★★½ This adventure film starring Charlton Heston is action-packed and well-acted. The story concerns a two-man rescue operation of a sunken nuclear sub that has collided with a freighter. Beautiful photography and special effects. 111m. **DIR:** David Greene. **CAST:** Charlton Heston, David Carradine, Stacy Keach, Ned Beatty, Ronny Cox, Rosemary Forsyth. **1977**

GREASED LIGHTNING ★★★ *Greased Lightning* is a funny and exciting film. Richard Pryor is a knockout in the lead role, and the film is a real audience pleaser. Because the story is true, it carries a punch even *Rocky* couldn't match. Wendell Scott's story is more dramatic. Scott was the first black man to win a NASCAR Grand National stock car race. Rated PG. 96m. **DIR:** Michael Schultz. **CAST:** Richard Pryor, Pam Grier, Beau Bridges, Cleavon Little, Richie Havens. **1977**

GREAT CHASE, THE ★★★★ Silent-film chases from several classics comprise the bulk of this compilation, including the running acrobatics of Douglas Fairbanks Sr. in *The Mark of Zorro*, the escape of Lillian Gish over the ice floes in *Way Down East*, and car chases and stunts of all descriptions from silent comedies. A large part of the film is devoted to Buster Keaton's locomotive chase from *The General*. B&W; 79m. **DIR:** Frank Gallop. **CAST:** Buster Keaton, Douglas Fairbanks Sr., Lillian Gish, Pearl White. **1963**

GREAT ESCAPE, THE ★★★★★ If ever there was a movie that could be called pure cheer-the-heroes entertainment, it's *The Great Escape*. The plot centers around a German prison camp in World War II. The commandant has received the assignment of housing all the escape-minded Allied prisoners, or, as he puts it, "putting all the rotten eggs in one basket." The Germans are obviously playing with fire with this all-star group, and, sure enough, all hell breaks loose with excitement galore. 168m. **DIR:** John Sturges. **CAST:** Steve McQueen, James Garner, Charles Bronson, Richard Attenborough, James Coburn. **1963**

GREAT ESCAPE II, THE ★★ In World War II, seventy-five American and British soldiers tunnel themselves out of prison. This star-studded, made-for-television two-parter has been shortened considerably for video, but still plays well. 93m. **DIR:** Paul Wendkos, Jud Taylor. **CAST:** Christopher Reeve, Judd Hirsch, Donald Pleasence, Charles Haid. **1988**

GREAT SMOKEY ROADBLOCK, THE ★★½ Entertaining if somewhat hokey comedy-drama casts Henry Fonda as a trucker on the verge of losing his rig, when along comes a homeless entourage of prostitutes (led by Eileen Brennan), who persuade Henry to take them for a ride. Rated PG for language. 84m. **DIR:** John Leone. **CAST:** Henry Fonda, Eileen Brennan, John Byner, Dub Taylor, Susan Sarandon, Austin Pendleton. **1976**

GREAT TEXAS DYNAMITE CHASE, THE ★★ Bullets and bodies fly in this low-budget cult film about two female bank robbers who blast their way across the countryside. Look for Johnny Crawford, of *The Rifleman* fame, in a featured role. Violence and some nudity. Rated R. 90m. **DIR:** Michael Pressman. **CAST:** Claudia Jennings, Jocelyn Jones, Johnny Crawford, Chris Pennock. **1977**

GREAT WALDO PEPPER, THE ★★★ The daredevil barnstorming pilots of the era between the world wars are sent a pleasant valentine by director George Roy Hill in this flying film. Robert Redford, in a satisfying low-key performance, is Waldo Pepper, a barnstormer who yearns for the action of the World War I dogfights. Rated PG. 108m. **DIR:** George Roy Hill. **CAST:** Robert Redford, Bo Svenson, Susan Sarandon, Bo Boundin. **1975**

GREEN BERETS, THE ★★★ John Wayne's Vietnam war movie is better than its reputation would suggest. We were fully prepared to hate the film after having avoided it when originally released. However, it turned out to be an exciting and enjoyable (albeit typical) Wayne vehicle. Rated G. 141m. **DIR:** John Wayne, Ray Kellogg. **CAST:** John Wayne, David Janssen, Jim Hutton, Aldo Ray, Raymond St.

Jacques, Bruce Cabot, Jack Soo, George Takei, Patrick Wayne. **1968**

GREEN HORNET, THE (TV SERIES) ★★★ Based on the 1930s radio series created by George W. Trendle, this TV show was an attempt to cash in on the *Batman* phenomenon. *The Green Hornet* was more compelling, less campy than the Caped Crusader's adventures. Van Williams ably portrayed the heroic Britt Reid, crime fighter extraordinaire. Today, however, this short-lived series is primarily of interest because it showcased the martial arts wizardry and unique charisma of Bruce Lee, who played Reid's trusty sidekick, Kato. Two episodes are included per tape. All 26 episodes of the series are available. 60m. each tape. **DIR:** Various. **CAST:** Van Williams, Bruce Lee, Wende Wagner, Lloyd Gough, Walter Brooke. **1966–1967**

GREYSTOKE: THE LEGEND OF TARZAN, LORD OF THE APES ★★★½ Director Hugh Hudson made one of the few Tarzan movies to remain faithful to the books and original character created by Edgar Rice Burroughs. Tarzan in one dramatic leap, goes from the dank, dangerous rain forests of West Africa to claim his rightful heritage—a baronial mansion in Scotland and a title as the seventh Earl of Greystoke. Rated PG for nudity and violence. 129m. **DIR:** Hugh Hudson. **CAST:** Christopher Lambert, Andie MacDowell, Ian Holm, Ralph Richardson, James Fox, Cheryl Campbell. **1984**

GUADALCANAL DIARY ★★★★ Timely story of the U.S. Marine Corp's deadly struggle for this South Pacific island is one of the best wartime adventure films. B&W; 93m. **DIR:** Lewis Seiler. **CAST:** Preston Foster, Lloyd Nolan, William Bendix, Richard Conte, Anthony Quinn, Richard Jaeckel. **1943**

GUMBALL RALLY, THE ★★½ First film based on an anything-goes cross-country road race. Featuring some excellent stunt driving, with occasional laughs, it's much better than *Cannonball Run*. Rated PG for language. 107m. **DIR:** Chuck Bail. **CAST:** Michael Sarrazin, Gary Busey, Tim McIntire, Raul Julia, Normann Burton. **1976**

GUNG HO! (1943) ★★½ Although not meant to be funny, this ultrapatriotic war film has its truly outrageous moments. It must have been a real booster for wartime filmgoers in America. Today it's almost embarrassing—particularly during the scene in which a recruit is accepted into a special team of commandos simply because he "hates Japs." B&W; 88m. **DIR:** Ray Enright. **CAST:** Randolph Scott, Grace McDonald, Alan Curtis, Noah Beery Jr., J. Carrol Naish, David Bruce, Robert Mitchum, Sam Levene. **1943**

GUNGA DIN ★★★★★ An acknowledged classic, this release has it all: laughs, thrills, and chills. Howard Hawks was originally set to direct it and played a large part in its creation. Plot: Three soldiers in nineteenth-century India put down a native uprising with the help of an Indian water carrier. B&W; 117m. **DIR:** George Stevens. **CAST:** Cary Grant, Victor McLaglen, Douglas Fairbanks Jr., Joan Fontaine, Sam Jaffe, Eduardo Ciannelli. **1939**

GUNMEN ★★★ Action-packed movie stars Mario Van Peebles as a New York detective who turns bounty hunter to bring down South American drug lord Patrick Stewart. Top-billed Christopher Lambert is the wacko brother of a drug runner, whose whereabouts may be the key to the mission. An oddball cop/buddy movie with touches of the spaghetti Western, it's weird and uneven, but entertaining. Rated R for violence, profanity, nudity, and simulated sex. 97m. **DIR:** Deran Sarafian. **CAST:** Christopher Lambert, Mario Van Peebles, Denis Leary, Patrick Stewart, Sally Kirkland, Kadeem Hardison, Richard Sarafian. **1994**

GUNRUNNER, THE ★★ Kevin Costner plans to make a fortune bootlegging liquor in order to buy guns for China's downtrodden masses. Poor editing destroys the continuity of what might have been an intriguing film. Rated R for violence and a hint of sex. 92m. **DIR:** Nardo Castillo. **CAST:** Kevin Costner, Sara Botsford. **1989**

GUNS 🦃 Erik Estrada, as a sneering gunrunner. Rated R for violence, nudity, and profanity. 96m. **DIR:** Andy Sidaris. **CAST:** Erik Estrada, Dona Speir, Phyllis Davis, Chuck McCann. **1990**

GUNS OF NAVARONE, THE ★★★★ Along with *The Great Escape*, this film is one of the best World War II adventure yarns. Gregory Peck, David Niven, and Anthony Quinn are part of a multinational task force that is sent to Greece with a mission to destroy two huge German batteries that threaten a fleet of Allied troop transports. 145m. **DIR:** J. Lee Thompson. **CAST:** Gregory Peck, David Niven, Anthony Quinn, Stanley Baker, Anthony Quayle, James Darren, Irene Papas. **1961**

GYMKATA 🦃 Disappointing fist-and-foot actioner. Rated R for violence. 90m. **DIR:** Robert Clouse. **CAST:** Kurt Thomas, Tetchie Agbayani, Richard Norton. **1985**

GYPSY WARRIORS, THE ★★ James Whitmore Jr. and Tom Selleck are two American soldiers in World War II who go behind enemy lines to capture a formula for germ warfare. The humor is bland and the action is déjà vu. Not rated. Has violence. 77m. **DIR:** Lou Antonio. **CAST:** James Whitmore Jr., Tom Selleck, Joseph Ruskin, Lina Raymond, Michael Lane, Ted Gehring, Albert Paulsen, Kenneth Tiger. **1978**

H-BOMB 🦃 Stupid martial arts film about two missing U.S. nuclear missiles. Not rated, but there are scenes with violence, profanity, and nudity. 98m. **DIR:** P. Chalong. **CAST:** Chris Mitchum, Olivia Hussey, Krung Srmlai. **1971**

HALLS OF MONTEZUMA ★★★½ There's a minimum of romance and lots of action in this oft-told story of American Marines at war in the South Pacific during World War II. Realistic adventure yarn. 113m. **DIR:** Lewis Milestone. **CAST:** Richard Widmark, Jack Palance, Jack Webb, Robert Wagner, Karl Malden, Reginald Gardiner, Philip Ahn. **1950**

HANGMEN ★★ Extremely violent, poorly acted, and poorly written time killer. An ex–CIA operative (Rick Washburne) is hunted by another agency man (Jake La Motta) who has gone bad. Washburne's family is dragged into the mess. Rated R for violence and language. 88m. **DIR:** J. Christian Ingvordsen. **CAST:** Rick Washburne, Jake La Motta, Doug Thomas. **1987**

HARD TARGET ★★★½ For his first American film, Hong Kong film legend John Woo delivers an action movie that will please both fans of the genre and serious film buffs. Vietnam veteran Jean-Claude Van Damme comes up against bloodthirsty millionaires whose ultimate thrill is to hunt human game. Reminiscent of Walter Hill's earlier films—*The Driver*, for example—this thriller is somewhat short on character development, but for nonstop excitement it has few peers. Rated R for extreme violence and profanity. 92m. **DIR:** John Woo. **CAST:** Jean-Claude Van Damme, Lance Henriksen, Yancy Butler, Wilford Brimley, Arnold Vosloo, Kasi Lemmons. **1993**

HARD TICKET TO HAWAII 🦃 Drug enforcement in Hawaii. Rated R for plentiful nudity and sexual situations. 96m. **DIR:** Andy Sidaris. **CAST:** Dona Speir, Hope Marie Carlton, Ronn Moss. **1987**

HARD TIMES ★★★★½ This release is far and away one of Charles Bronson's best starring vehicles. In it he plays a bare-knuckles fighter who teams up with a couple of hustlers, James Coburn and Strother Martin, to "sting" some local hoods. Bronson's wife, Jill Ireland, is surprisingly good as the love interest. Rated PG. 97m. **DIR:** Walter Hill. **CAST:** Charles Bronson, James Coburn, Jill Ireland, Strother Martin. **1975**

HARD TO KILL ★★★½ Solid action film stars martial arts expert Steve Seagal as an honest cop who falls prey to corruption. Crisply directed by Bruce Malmuth, this is a definite cut above most movies in its genre. Rated R for violence, profanity, and nudity. 95m. **DIR:** Bruce Malmuth. **CAST:** Steven Seagal, Kelly LeBrock. **1990**

HARD WAY, THE (1979) ★★ Patrick McGoohan is an international terrorist who wants out of the business. Unfortunately for him, a former associate (Lee Van Cleef) wants him to do one more job and will have him killed if he doesn't. 88m. **DIR:** Michael Dryhurst. **CAST:** Patrick McGoohan, Lee Van Cleef, Donal McCann, Edna O'Brien. **1979**

HARLEM NIGHTS ★★★ This gangster movie has taken a tremendous critical bashing, but we found it enjoyable. Not only has writer-producer-director-star Eddie Murphy created an old-fashioned melodrama that, save for the continuous profanity, could just as easily have starred Humphrey Bogart or James Cagney but he has given fine roles to some of the industry's finest black performers. Rated R for profanity, violence, and suggested sex. 119m. **DIR:** Eddie Murphy. **CAST:** Eddie Murphy, Richard Pryor, Redd Foxx, Danny Aiello, Michael Lerner, Della Reese, Stan Shaw, Arsenio Hall. **1989**

HARLEY DAVIDSON AND THE MARLBORO MAN ★★ Mickey Rourke is the hog-riding hero, Don Johnson the cowboy in 1996, when a drug called Crystal Dream is killing addicts by the thousands. So our heroes go to war with the pushers. It's hard to believe that the director who helmed the exquisite *Lonesome Dove* was responsible for this post-apocalyptic hogwash. Rated R for violence, profanity, and nudity. 98m. **DIR:** Simon Wincer. **CAST:** Mickey Rourke, Don Johnson, Chelsea Field, Giancarlo Esposito, Vanessa Williams, Julius W. Harris, Robert Ginty. **1991**

HATARI! ★★★ If only Howard Hawks had been able to do as he wanted and cast Clark Gable along with John Wayne in this story of zoo-supplying animal hunters in Africa, this could have been a great film. As it is, it's still enjoyable, with a fine blend of action, romance, and comedy. 159m. **DIR:** Howard Hawks. **CAST:** John Wayne, Elsa Martinelli, Red Buttons, Hardy Krüger. **1962**

HAWK THE SLAYER ★★ In this sword-and-sorcery adventure, John Terry plays the good Hawk, who, with his band of warriors—a dwarf and an elf among them—fights Jack Palance, his evil older brother. Palance's performance saves the film from mediocrity. Not rated; has violence. 90m. **DIR:** Terry Marcel. **CAST:** Jack Palance, John Terry. **1980**

HEARTBREAK RIDGE ★★★ Whoever thought Grenada would be the subject of cinematic war heroics? Though the film could use some trimming, the story of a hard-nosed Marine sergeant whipping a hopeless-looking unit into a crack fighting team is still compelling. Rated R. 126m. **DIR:** Clint Eastwood. **CAST:** Clint Eastwood, Marsha Mason, Everett McGill, Bo Svenson, Mario Van Peebles, Moses Gunn, Tom Villard. **1986**

HEARTS AND ARMOUR ★★½ Warrior Orlando (Rick Edwards) seeks victory over the Moors and the rescue of his love (Tanya Roberts), while his female comrade-in-arms, Bradamante (Barbara de Rossi), falls in love with Ruggero (Ron Moss), the Moor whom Orlando is fated to kill. Unfortunately, the script is not strong enough to do justice to the complex plot. Not rated; has violence and nudity. 101m. **DIR:** Giacomo Battiato. **CAST:** Zenda Araya, Barbara de Rossi, Rick Edwards, Ronn Moss, Tanya Roberts. **1983**

HEAT (1987) ★★½ A good try at an action thriller that doesn't succeed because of awkward pacing, uneven direction, and a mood that swings wildly from raw violence to good-buddy playfulness. Burt Reynolds is a Las Vegas–based troubleshooter with two problems: an old girlfriend who craves revenge and a mousy young executive (Peter MacNicol, stealing every scene he shared with Reynolds) who craves the ability to protect himself. Rated R for language and violence. 101m. **DIR:** Dick Richards. **CAST:** Burt Reynolds, Karen Young, Peter MacNicol, Howard Hesseman, Neill Barry, Diana Scarwid. **1987**

HEATED VENGEANCE ★★ A U.S. serviceman (Richard Hatch) returns to Southeast Asia years after the Vietnam War to bring back his old flame (Jolina Mitchell-Collins). Former enemies abduct him and bring him back to their camp, where he finds that they are dealing with drugs. Unrated, has violence, profanity, sex, and nudity. 91m. **DIR:** Edward Murphy. **CAST:** Richard Hatch, Michael J. Pollard, Dennis Patrick, Mills Watson, Cameron Dye, Robert Walker Jr. **1987**

HELL IN THE PACIFIC ★★★½ John Boorman directed this moody, somewhat trying drama about an American and a Japanese conducting their own private war on a deserted island at the end of World War II. Well acted. 103m. **DIR:** John Boorman. **CAST:** Lee Marvin, Toshiro Mifune. **1968**

HELL IS FOR HEROES ★★★★ This tense, gritty World War II drama is heaven for action fans. Director Don Siegel is at his riveting best, drawing the viewer into the claustrophobic, nightmarish atmosphere. B&W; 90m. **DIR:** Don Siegel. **CAST:** Steve McQueen, Bobby Darin, Fess Parker, James Coburn, Harry Guardino, Mike Kellin, Nick Adams, Bob Newhart. **1962**

HELL ON FRISCO BAY ★★★ A 1930s-type hardboiled crime story of a framed cop who does his time, is released from prison, and goes after the bigwig gangster who set him up. Lots of action on San Francisco's streets and its famous bay. 98m. **DIR:** Frank Tuttle. **CAST:** Alan Ladd, Joanne Dru, Edward G. Robinson, William Demarest, Fay Wray. **1955**

HELL SHIP MUTINY ★★ South Seas programmer with captain Jon Hall battling smugglers who are exploiting island natives. Watchable only for the cast. B&W; 66m. **DIR:** Lee Sholem, Elmo Williams. **CAST:** Jon Hall, John Carradine, Peter Lorre, Roberta Haynes, Mike Mazurki. **1957**

HELL SQUAD (1958) 🦃 Bleak, zero-budget WWII programmer of absolutely no distinction. B&W; 64m. **DIR:** Burt Topper. **CAST:** Wally Campo, Brandon Carrol. **1958**

HELL SQUAD (1985) 🦃 Las Vegas show girls are recruited by the CIA. Rated R for nudity and gore. 88m. **DIR:** Kenneth Hartford. **CAST:** Bainbridge Scott, Glen Hartford, William Bryant, Marvin Miller. **1985**

HELL UP IN HARLEM 🦃 Violent, cheaply made sequel to *Black Caesar*. Rated R. 98m. **DIR:** Larry Cohen. **CAST:** Fred Williamson, Julius W. Harris, Gloria Hendry, Margaret Avery, D'Urville Martin. **1973**

HELLCATS, THE 🦃 Even within the lowly subgenre of biker movies, this one is the pits. Unrated, it features violence. 90m. **DIR:** Robert F. Slatzer. **CAST:** Ross Hagen, Dee Duffy. **1967**

HELLCATS OF THE NAVY ★★★ This none-too-exciting drama has one thing to attract viewers: President Ronald Reagan and First Lady Nancy co-star. B&W; 82m. **DIR:** Nathan Juran. **CAST:** Ronald Reagan, Nancy Davis, Arthur Franz, Harry Lauter. **1957**

HELLDORADO (1934) ★★ A penniless hitchhiker discovers a ghost town with a gold mine. The picture boasts an acclaimed director and a highly professional cast, but it is unpersuasively produced. B&W; 75m. **DIR:** James Cruze. **CAST:** Richard Arlen, Madge Evans, Henry B. Walthall, Ralph Bellamy, James Gleason, Helen Jerome Eddy. **1934**

HELLFIGHTERS ★★ Once again the talents of John Wayne have been squandered. The Duke is cast as a high-priced fireman sent around the world to put out dangerous oil rig fires. Even hard-core Wayne fans may wince at this one. Rated PG. 121m. **DIR:** Andrew V. McLaglen. **CAST:** John Wayne, Katharine Ross, Vera Miles, Jim Hutton, Bruce Cabot. **1969**

HELLFIRE CLUB, THE ★★ Tepid historical swashbuckler, made in England, about a dashing swordsman who is the grown-up son of one of the founders of royalty's legendary sex-and-sin fellowship. Doesn't devote enough screen time to the title organization's nefarious activities. 88m. **DIR:** Robert S. Baker, Monty Berman. **CAST:** Keith Michell, Adrienne Corri, Peter Cushing. **1960**

HELL'S ANGELS ON WHEELS ★★½ This is one of the better 1960s biker films, most notably because Jack Nicholson has a big role in it. Not a great work by any means, but if you like biker movies... 95m. **DIR:** Richard Rush. **CAST:** Adam Roarke, Jack Nicholson, Sabrina Scharf, John Garwood, Jana Taylor. **1967**

HELL'S ANGELS '69 ★★ Two rich kids devise a plan to rob a gambling casino by infiltrating the Hell's Angels and then using the gang to create a diversion. The plan works until the bikers retaliate. Mediocre. 97m. **DIR:** Lee Madden. **CAST:** Tom Stern, Jeremy Slate, Conny Van Dyke, Sonny Barger, Terry the Tramp. **1969**

HELL'S BRIGADE 🦃 Rotten film concerning a commando raid on Hitler's Germany during World War II. 99m. **DIR:** Henry Mankiewirk. **CAST:** Jack Palance, John Douglas. **1980**

HELL'S HOUSE ★★ Gangster and prison films in the 1930s had their junior counterparts. In this barely so-so example, an innocent boy does time in a harsh reformatory because he won't rat on an adult crook friend. Junior Durkin is the poor kid, Pat O'Brien is the crook—a bootlegger—and Bette Davis is his girl. B&W; 72m. **DIR:** Howard Higgin. **CAST:** Junior Durkin, Bette Davis, Pat O'Brien, Frank Coghlan Jr., Charley Grapewin, Emma Dunn. **1932**

HELLTRAIN 🦃 Generic Nazi gorefest about a brothel on rails, with the expected sex and sadism. Rated R. 90m. **DIR:** Alain Payet. **1980**

HERCULES IN THE HAUNTED WORLD ★★★ Easily the best of the many *Hercules* sequels, because it was designed and directed by famed Italian genre master Mario Bava (*Black Sabbath*). Ignore the brief, dopey comic relief and enjoy the escapist, action-filled plot, which sends Hercules on a journey through Hades. Breathtaking visuals. 83m. **DIR:** Mario Bava. **CAST:** Reg Park, Christopher Lee. **1961**

HERCULES, PRISONER OF EVIL ★★ Not bad for its type, this sword-and-sandal action spectacle is really part of the *Ursus* subgenre of Italian muscle-man movies; the Hercules moniker was slapped on when it was dubbed and released straight to U.S. TV. 90m. **DIR:** Anthony M. Dawson. **CAST:** Reg Park, Ettore Manni. **1964**

HERO AND THE TERROR ★★½ Chuck Norris gives a good performance in this otherwise disappointing thriller. He's a police officer suffering from deep trauma after confronting a brutal, demented killer called the Terror (Jack O'Halloran). When the Terror escapes from a mental ward, our hero must battle the monster again. Rated R for violence and profanity. 90m. **DIR:** William Tannen. **CAST:** Chuck Norris, Jack O'Halloran, Brynn Thayer, Jeffrey Kramer, Steve James. **1988**

HEROES DIE YOUNG 🦃 A suicide squad goes behind enemy lines to knock out an oil field in German-occupied Romania. Not rated. B&W; 76m. **DIR:** Gerald S. Shepard. **CAST:** Erika Peters, Scott Borland. **1960**

HEROES IN HELL 🦃 Lame World War II battle picture. Unrated. 90m. **DIR:** Michael Wotruba. **CAST:** Klaus Kinski, Stan Simon, Lars Block, George Manes, Carlos Ewing, Luis Joyce, Rosemary Lindt. **1974**

HEROES OF DESERT STORM ★★½ Flag-waving, made-for-TV movie looks at the men (and women) who fought in Desert Storm. Pedestrian effort shows how quick it was made to cash in on patriotism. 93m. **DIR:** Don Ohlmeyer. **CAST:** Daniel Baldwin, Angela Bassett, Marshall Bell, Kris Kamm, Tim Russ. **1992**

HEROES STAND ALONE ★★★ A plane on a secret mission is shot down behind enemy lines. The not so distant future is the setting for this Vietnam-style war movie. Not rated but contains violence and nudity. 83m. **DIR:** Mark Griffiths. **CAST:** Chad Everett, Bradford Dillman. **1990**

HIDING OUT ★★ Jon Cryer does some top-notch acting in this comedy-drama, and screenwriters Joe Menosky and Jeff Rothberg avoid the obvious clichés in their story of a Boston stockbroker (Cryer) hiding from the mob in a suburban Delaware high school. The result, however, is a collection of bits and pieces rather than a cohesive whole. Rated PG-13 for profanity and violence. 98m. **DIR:** Bob Giraldi. **CAST:** Jon Cryer, Keith Coogan, Annabeth Gish, Oliver Cotton, Claude Brooks, Ned Eisenberg. **1987**

HIGH-BALLIN' ★★ Peter Fonda and Jerry Reed are good old boys squaring off against the bad boss of a rival trucking company. The film has enough action and humor to make it a passable entertainment. Helen Shaver is its most provocative element. Rated PG. 100m. **DIR:** Peter Carter. **CAST:** Peter Fonda, Jerry Reed, Helen Shaver, Chris Wiggins, David Ferry. **1978**

HIGH COMMAND, THE ★★★ Rebellion, a new murder, and a 16-year-old killing absorb the interest of officers and men at an isolated British outpost on an island off the coast of Africa during the fading days of the British empire. B&W; 84m. **DIR:** Thorold Dickinson. **CAST:** Lionel Atwill, Lucie Mannheim, James Mason. **1937**

HIGH COUNTRY, THE ★★ So-so production values drag down this tale of an escaping convict (Timothy Bottoms) and a wide-eyed girl (Linda Purl) in the Canadian Rockies. It's a clichéd story, although Bottoms turns in his usual accomplished performance. Not rated, but has violence and brief nudity. 99m. **DIR:** Harvey Hart. **CAST:** Timothy Bottoms, Linda Purl, George Sims, Jim Lawrence, Bill Berry, Walter Mills. **1980**

HIGH CRIME ★★ Narcotics cop vs. Mafia kingpin in the picturesque Italian seaport of Genoa. Full of action, but no surprises. Rated PG. 100m. **DIR:** Enzo G. Castellari. **CAST:** Franco Nero, James Whitmore, Fernando Rey. **1973**

HIGH RISK ★★½ While snatching $5 million from a South American drug smuggler (James Coburn), four amateur conspirators (James Brolin, Cleavon Little, Bruce Davison, and Chick Vennera) cross paths with a sleazy bandit leader (Anthony Quinn), hordes of Colombian soldiers, and plenty of riotous trouble. This preposterous adventure offers diversion, but a lot of it is just plain awful. Rated R. 94m. **DIR:** Stewart Raffill. **CAST:** James Brolin, Cleavon Little, Bruce Davison, Chick Vennera, Anthony Quinn, James Coburn, Ernest Borgnine, Lindsay Wagner. **1981**

HIGH ROAD TO CHINA ★★★ Tom Selleck stars as a World War I flying ace who, with the aid of his sidekick/mechanic, Jack Weston, helps a spoiled heiress (Bess Armstrong) track down her missing father (Wilford Brimley). It's just like the B movies of yesteryear: predictable, silly, and fun. Rated PG for violence. 120m. **DIR:** Brian G. Hutton. **CAST:** Tom Selleck, Bess Armstrong, Jack Weston, Wilford Brimley, Robert Morley, Brian Blessed. **1983**

HIGH ROLLING 🦃 Two out-of-work carnival workers hitchhike through Australia until they are picked up by a drug runner. Rated PG for profanity and brief nudity. 88m. **DIR:** Igor Auzins. **CAST:** Joseph Bottoms, Grigor Taylor, Sandy Hughs, Judy Davis, John Clayton. **1977**

HIGH SCHOOL CAESAR ★½ A rich high school kid (John Ashley) is ignored by the father he idolizes, so he spends his time running a protection racket, selling exams, and rigging school elections. Neither good nor bad enough to be memorable. B&W; 72m. **DIR:** O'Dale Ireland. **CAST:** John Ashley, Gary Vinson, Lowell Brown. **1960**

HIGH SIERRA ★★★★½ Humphrey Bogart is at his best as a bad guy with a heart of gold in this 1941 gangster film. Bogart pays for the operation that corrects pretty Joan Leslie's crippled foot, but he finds his love is misplaced. One of the finest of the Warner Bros. genre entries. B&W; 100m. **DIR:** Raoul Walsh. **CAST:** Humphrey Bogart, Ida Lupino, Alan Curtis, Arthur Kennedy, Joan Leslie, Henry Hull. **1941**

HIGH STAKES (1989) ★★★ Sally Kirkland turns in a convincing portrayal as a burned-out hooker who meets a financial whiz dealing with his own personal crises. His fascination with Kirkland sweeps him into her sleazy world. Rated R for violence and profanity. 86m. **DIR:** Amos Kollek. **CAST:** Sally Kirkland, Robert LuPone, Richard Lynch. **1989**

HIGH VELOCITY ★★ Run-of-the-mill feature made in Manila about two ex-Vietnam buddies hired to rescue the head of a big corporation from Asian terrorists. Rated PG. 106m. **DIR:** Remi Kramer. **CAST:** Ben Gazzara, Britt Ekland, Paul Winfield, Keenan Wynn, Alejandro Rey, Victoria Racimo. **1977**

HIGH VOLTAGE ★★½ Elements of *Stagecoach* are evident in this early Pathé sound film (made ten years before John Ford's classic) that teams a pre-Hopalong Cassidy William Boyd and a lovely, young Carole Lombard as a world-wise couple who fall for each other while snowbound during a bus trip in California's Sierra Nevada Mountains. Worth watching for Lombard's fine performance. B&W; 57m. **DIR:** Howard Higgin. **CAST:** William Boyd, Carole Lombard, Owen Moore, Diane Ellis, Billy Bevan. **1929**

HIGHEST HONOR, THE ★★★★★ A World War II story of a unique friendship between two enemies: Captain Robert Page, an Australian army officer, and Winoyu Tamiya, a security officer in the Japanese army. This great war film, packed with high adventure and warm human drama, is also a true story. Rated R. 99m. **DIR:** Peter Maxwell. **CAST:** John Howard, Atsuo Nakamura, Stuart Wilson. **1984**

HIGHPOINT 🦃 Confusing comedy-thriller about an accountant who becomes mixed up in a CIA plot. Rated R; contains profanity and violence. 88m. **DIR:** Peter Carter. **CAST:** Richard Harris, Christopher Plummer, Beverly D'Angelo, Kate Reid, Peter Donat, Saul Rubinek. **1980**

HIRED TO KILL ★★ Aimless violence permeates this action film concerning a soldier of fortune and his efforts to infiltrate a Third World island and free a prisoner. Trite and just plain silly. Rated R for violence, nudity, and adult language. 91m. **DIR:** Nico Mastorakis, Peter Rader. **CAST:** Brian Thompson, Oliver Reed, George Kennedy, José Ferrer. **1990**

HIS KIND OF WOMAN ★★★½ Entertaining chase film as two-fisted gambler Robert Mitchum breezes down to South America to pick up $50 thousand only to find out he's being set up for the kill. Jane Russell is in fine shape as the worldly gal with a good heart, and Vincent Price steals the show as a hammy Hollywood actor. B&W; 120m. **DIR:** John Farrow. **CAST:** Robert Mitchum, Jane Russell, Vincent Price, Tim Holt, Charles McGraw, Raymond Burr, Jim Backus, Marjorie Reynolds. **1951**

HIS MAJESTY O'KEEFE ★★★½ A rip-snortin' adventure movie with Burt Lancaster furnishing all the energy as the nineteenth century American businessman who sails to the South Seas and finds a fortune in copra waiting for him. He also teaches the natives how to use gunpowder, and the result is both exciting and hilarious. 92m. **DIR:** Byron Haskin. **CAST:** Burt Lancaster, Joan Rice, Abraham Sofaer, Philip Ahn. **1954**

HIT! ★★½ This is a praiseworthy attempt to bring some legitimacy to the blaxploitation genre. Billy Dee Williams plays an American police detective who tracks drug dealers to Marseilles. Rated R for nudity, violence, and profanity. 134m. **DIR:** Sidney J. Furie. **CAST:** Billy Dee Williams, Paul Hampton, Richard Pryor, Gwen Welles. **1973**

HIT, THE ★★★★ The British seem to have latched on to the gangster film with a vengeance. First, they made the superb film *The Long Good Friday*, and now they've scored again with this gripping character study. John Hurt gives an unusually restrained (and highly effective) performance as a hit man assigned to take care of a squealer (Terence Stamp) who has been hiding in Spain after testifying against the mob. Rated R for violence. 97m. **DIR:** Stephen Frears. **CAST:** John Hurt, Terence Stamp, Tim Roth, Fernando Rey, Laura Del Sol, Bill Hunter. **1984**

HIT AND RUN ★★½ A New York cabdriver, obsessed with the death of his wife in a hit-and-run accident, becomes a pawn in a murder plot. Mystery fans will appreciate the nighttime atmosphere and carefully (if slowly) developed plot. Rated PG. 96m. **DIR:** Charles Braverman. **CAST:** Paul Perri, Claudia Cron, Bart Braverman. **1982**

HIT LADY ★★½ Entertaining twist on an old story has Yvette Mimieux as a hit lady who tries to retire, only to be blackmailed into taking on just one more job. Televison movie; contains some cleaned-up violence. 74m. **DIR:** Tracy Keenan Wynn. **CAST:** Yvette Mimieux, Dack Rambo, Clu Gulager, Joseph Campanella, Keenan Wynn. **1974**

HIT THE DUTCHMAN ★★½ A Jewish exconvict wants to become involved with gangster Legs Diamond, but must first change his name. This run-of-the-mill gangster film drags on way too long. Rated R for profanity, violence, and nudity. 116m. **DIR:** Menahem Golan. **CAST:** Bruce Nozick, Will Kempe, Sally Kirkland. **1992**

HIT WOMAN: THE DOUBLE EDGE ★★½ Soap star Susan Lucci plays dual roles as an assassin and the FBI agent out to find her. The story is quite dull, but Lucci does a fine job portraying two radically different people. Rated R for violence. 94m. **DIR:** Stephen Stafford. **CAST:** Susan Lucci, Robert Urich, Michael Woods, Kevin Dunn, Paul Freeman, Kari Lizer, Robert Prosky. **1992**

HITLER'S CHILDREN ★★★★ A great love story is created with the horror of Nazi Germany as a background. This film shows a young German boy who falls in love with an American girl. The boy gets caught up in Hitler's enticing web of propaganda, while his girlfriend resists all of Hitler's ideas. B&W; 83m. **DIR:** Edward Dmytryk, Irving Reis. **CAST:** Tim Holt, Bonita Granville, Kent Smith, Otto Kruger. **1942**

HITMAN, THE ★★★½ A police officer goes underground after being betrayed and shot by his crooked partner. Officially listed as dead, he becomes the "hit man" for a Seattle crime boss in order to bring down a sophisticated drug operation. Rated R for violence and profanity. 96m. **DIR:** Aaron Norris. **CAST:** Chuck Norris, Michael Parks, Al Waxman, Alberta Watson. **1991**

HITZ ★★ Melodramatic dramatization of kids killing kids among L.A. gangs loses credibility in the courtroom, with judges taking their work too personally. Muddled message film. Rated R for nudity, violence, and profanity. 90m. **DIR:** William Sachs. **CAST:** Emilia Crow, Richard Coca, Elliott Gould. **1992**

HOLLYWOOD COP 🦃 Undercover cop battles the mob. Rated R for nudity and violence. B&W; 100m. **DIR:** Amir Shervan. **CAST:** David Goss, Jim Mitchum, Cameron Mitchell, Troy Donahue, Aldo Ray, Lincoln Kilpatrick. **1987**

HOLLYWOOD VICE SQUAD 🦃 A tepid affair about a runaway in the sleazoid areas of Hollywood. Rated R for nudity, profanity, and violence. 93m. **DIR:** Penelope Spheeris. **CAST:** Ronny Cox, Frank Gorshin, Leon Isaac Kennedy, Trish Van Devere, Carrie Fisher. **1986**

HOLT OF THE SECRET SERVICE ★★ Iron-jawed Jack Holt had become such an institution after almost thirty years as a matinee and action star that Columbia decided to bill him as a secret service agent under his own name. The result is a middling serial with a formula plot. Just agent Holt and his pretty partner Evelyn Brent against a gang of counterfeiters. B&W; 15 chapters. **DIR:** James W. Horne. **CAST:** Jack Holt, Evelyn Brent, C. Montague Shaw, Tristram Coffin, John Ward, Ted Adams, Joe McGuinn, Ray Parsons. **1941**

HOMEBOYS II: CRACK CITY ★★ A good kid falls in with a bad crowd when he moves to Harlem from the suburbs. Well-intentioned message movie is weighed down by too many ridiculous plot elements. It has nothing to do with *Homeboys*. Not rated, but an R equivalent for violence and nudity. 90m. **DIR:** Daniel Matmor. **CAST:** Brian Paul Stewart, Delia Sheppard. **1989**

HONEYBOY ★★ Erik Estrada is the boy, Morgan Fairchild the honey, in this watered-down compilation of every boxing cliché ever employed in the poor-boy-makes-good genre. Unrated and suitable for viewing by families with relatively strong stomachs. 100m. **DIR:** John Berry. **CAST:** Erik Estrada, Morgan Fairchild, Hector Elizondo, James McEachin, Phillip R. Allen. **1982**

HONOR AMONG THIEVES ★★½ Charles Bronson plays a mercenary who is locked in a French bank over the weekend with Alain Delon, a doctor. Bronson is there to rob the bank of its 200 million francs, while Delon is there to replace some misappropriated securities. This is a little different type of picture for Bronson—a bit more subtle, a little slower-paced, and with more dialogue than action. Rated R. 93m. **DIR:** Jean Herman. **CAST:** Charles Bronson, Alain Delon, Brigitte Fossey. **1983**

HONOR AND GLORY 🦃 Below-average actioner features kung fu expert Cynthia Rothrock as an FBI agent out to protect a nuclear arsenal from an evil banker. It turns into a family affair...yawn: *zzzz*. Unrated; contains profanity and violence. 87m. **DIR:** Godfrey Hall. **CAST:** Cynthia Rothrock, Donna Jason, Chuck Jeffreys, Gerald Klein. **1992**

HOODLUM EMPIRE ★★ A racketeer's nephew decides to go straight after a tour of duty in World War II but runs into problems from both sides of the law. A very thinly disguised filmic depiction of the famous Estes Kefauver investigation into Frank Costello and his ties with organized crime, this docudrama is long on talent but short on style. B&W; 98m. **DIR:** Joseph Kane. **CAST:** Brian Donlevy, Claire Trevor, Forrest Tucker, Vera Hruba Ralston, Luther Adler, John Russell, Gene Lockhart, Grant Withers, Taylor Holmes, Richard Jaeckel. **1952**

HORNET'S NEST ★★ Commando Rock Hudson leads a group of orphaned Italian boys in a raid on a Nazi-held dam. Some fair action scenes but pretty farfetched. Rated PG. 110m. **DIR:** Phil Karlson. **CAST:** Rock Hudson, Sylva Koscina. **1970**

HORSEMEN, THE 🦃 In this dull action film, Omar Sharif, as an Afghan tribesman, attempts to outride his father. Rated PG. 109m. **DIR:** John Frankenheimer. **CAST:** Omar Sharif, Jack Palance, Leigh Taylor-Young, Peter Jeffrey, Eric Pohlmann. **1970**

HOSTAGE (1987) 🦃 Idiotic story of a South African farmer who must rescue his wife and child from evil Arabs. Rated R for language and violence. 94m. **DIR:** Hanro Möhr. **CAST:** Wings Hauser, Karen Black, Kevin McCarthy, Nancy Locke. **1987**

HOSTAGE (1992) ★★ Sam Neill stars as a James Bondish secret agent who finds retirement a rather harrowing option. Shooting and bombings pervade. Rated R for sex and violence. 100m. **DIR:** Robert Young. **CAST:** Sam Neill, Talisa Soto, James Fox. **1992**

HOSTAGE TOWER, THE ★★½ A successful international criminal sought by major police organizations puts together a special team of experts for his next spectacular crime, broadly hinted at in the title. Intrigue and private purposes abound in this action film, wherein the cast successfully outweighs the movie. Rated PG for violence. 97m. **DIR:** Claudio Guzman. **CAST:** Peter Fonda, Maud Adams, Billy Dee Williams, Rachel Roberts, Douglas Fairbanks Jr. **1980**

HOT BOX, THE ★★ Low-budget Filipino-shot women's-prison film was cowritten and produced by Jonathan Demme. Rated R; contains nudity, profanity, and violence. 85m. **DIR:** Joe Viola. **CAST:** Margaret Markov, Andrea Cagen, Charles Dierkop. **1972**

HOT CHILD IN THE CITY 🦃 This small-cast whodunit has an insufficient number of suspects. Not rated, has violence, profanity, and nudity. 85m. **DIR:** John Florea. **CAST:** Leah Ayres, Shari Shattuck, Antony Alda, Ronn Moss. **1987**

HOT TARGET 🦃 The bored wife of a British business tycoon finds herself being extorted. Explicit nudity. Rated R. 93m. **DIR:** Denis Lewiston. **CAST:** Simone Griffeth, Bryan Marshall, Steve Marachuk. **1984**

HOTEL COLONIAL 🦃 In this uncredited adaptation of Joseph Conrad's *Heart of Darkness*, John Savage searches the jungles of Colombia for his brother. Rated R for nudity and violence. 107m. **DIR:** Cinzia Torrini. **CAST:** John Savage, Robert Duvall, Rachel Ward, Massimo Troisi. **1987**

HOUR OF THE ASSASSIN ★½ Action thriller set in the fictional South American country of San Pedro where Erik Estrada has been hired by the military forces to kill the president. Robert Vaughn plays the CIA agent who has to stop him. Although this film has its share of car crashes, gunfire, and explosions, it lacks any real suspense. Rated R. 96m. **DIR:** Luis Llosa. **CAST:** Erik Estrada, Robert Vaughn. **1986**

HOUSE OF 1,000 DOLLS ★★ Sexploitation potboiler, a British/Spanish coproduction starring Vincent Price as an illusionist who runs a white slavery racket on the side. Variously campy, sleazy, and boring. 83m. **DIR:** Jeremy Summers. **CAST:** Vincent Price, Martha Hyer, George Nader. **1967**

HOUSE OF THE RISING SUN ★★ Technically sound but artistically soulless film that attempts to give an Eighties look to a Thirties murder mystery. Jamie Barrett is an aspiring reporter, willing to do anything to get the lowdown on pimp Frank Annese. Not rated, but contains adult situations. 86m. **DIR:** Greg Gold. **CAST:** Frank Annese, Jamie Barrett, Tawny Moyer, Deborah Wakeham, James Daughton, John J. York. **1987**

HUDSON HAWK ★★★ Fans of Bruce Willis's wisecracking comedy style will enjoy this critically lambasted spoof of spy thrillers filled with slapstick comedy, unexpected musical numbers, and goofy supporting characters. Willis plays a cat burglar who is forced back into the biz. Rated R for profanity and violence. 95m. **DIR:** Michael Lehmann. **CAST:** Bruce Willis, Danny Aiello, Andie MacDowell, James Coburn, Richard E. Grant, Sandra Bernhard. **1991**

HUMAN EXPERIMENTS 🦃 Cheap, ugly, and viciously sexploitative prison potboiler. Rated R. 85m. **DIR:** Gregory Goodell. **CAST:** Linda Haynes, Geoffrey Lewis, Ellen Travolta. **1980**

HUMAN SHIELD, THE 🦃 This boring, violent story revolves around an Iraqi general who tortures an American. Bad plot, bad acting. Rated R for violence. 92m. **DIR:** Ted Post. **CAST:** Michael Dudikoff, Tommy Hinkley, Steve Inwood. **1991**

HUNTER (1971) ★★½ A brainwashed agent is programmed to release a deadly virus. The scheme is discovered, and a good guy takes his place to catch the bad guys. Made for television. 73m. **DIR:** Leonard Horn. **CAST:** John Vernon, Steve Ihnat, Fritz Weaver, Edward Binns. **1971**

HUNTER, THE (1980) ★★ *The Hunter*, an uneven action film, focuses on a modern-day bounty hunter. Steve McQueen plays real-life troubleshooter Ralph "Papa" Thorson. Though old and a bit awkward, Thorson leads—at least on screen—a dangerous, action-filled life. Rated PG. 97m. **DIR:** Buzz Kulik. **CAST:** Steve McQueen, Eli Wallach, LeVar Burton, Ben Johnson, Kathryn Harrold. **1980**

HURRICANE (1979) 🦃 Another Dino de Laurentiis misfire, an awful remake of the John Ford classic. Rated PG. 119m. **DIR:** Jan Troell. **CAST:** Jason Robards Jr., Mia Farrow, Dayton Ka'ne, Max von Sydow, Trevor Howard. **1979**

HURRICANE EXPRESS ★★ Big John Wayne stars in his second serial for Mascot Pictures and plays an aviator on the trail of the mysterious "Wrecker." This feature, edited down from a twelve-chapter serial, displays a high level of energy and excitement, a great deal of it as a direct result of young Wayne's whole-hearted involvement in this basically simple chase film. B&W; 80m. **DIR:** Armand Schaefer, J. P. McGowan. **CAST:** John Wayne, Tully Marshall, Conway Tearle, Shirley Grey. **1932**

HURRICANE SMITH ★★½ Texas tough Carl Weathers blows into Australia like a hurricane when his sister is killed by drug lord Jurgen Prochnow. Watch Carl weather plenty of evil mates, teaching them a *Rocky* lesson in manners. Rated R for violence and nudity. 87m. **DIR:** Colin Budd. **CAST:** Carl Weathers, Jurgen Prochnow, Tony Bonner. **1991**

HUSTLE ★★½ *Hustle* reteams director Robert Aldrich and actor Burt Reynolds after their box-office success with *The Longest Yard*. Fine character performances from Eddie Albert, Ernest Borgnine, and Jack Carter help to elevate the macho/action yarn, but it is Academy Award–winner Ben Johnson who provides the real show. Rated R. 120m. **DIR:** Robert Aldrich. **CAST:** Burt Reynolds, Catherine Deneuve, Eddie Albert, Ernest Borgnine, Jack Carter, Ben Johnson. **1975**

I COVER THE WATERFRONT ★★★ One, and one of the better, of a spate of newspaper stories that vied with gangster films on 1930s screens. In this one, a ruthless fisherman who smuggles Chinese into the United States doesn't think twice about pushing them overboard when approached by the Coast Guard. Claudette Colbert is his innocent daughter. Ace reporter Ben Lyon courts her in an effort to get at the truth. B&W; 70m. **DIR:** James Cruze. **CAST:** Claudette Colbert, Ernest Torrence, Ben Lyon, Wilfred Lucas, George Humbert. **1933**

I DIED A THOUSAND TIMES ★★½ Color remake of Raoul Walsh's *High Sierra* features Jack Palance as Mad Dog Earle, whose criminal tendencies are softened by a young woman (Lori Nelson) who needs surgery in order to lead a normal life. 110m. **DIR:** Stuart Heisler. **CAST:** Jack Palance, Shelley Winters, Lee Marvin, Lori Nelson, Earl Holliman, Lon Chaney Jr. **1955**

I, MOBSTER ★★★½ Fast-moving gangster story recounted by mob boss Steve Cochran, looking back on his career while he testifies before the Senate Rackets Committee. Familiar stuff, but well-made. B&W; 81m. **DIR:** Roger Corman. **CAST:** Steve Cochran, Lita Milan, Robert Strauss, Celia Lovsky, Lili St. Cyr, Yvette Vickers, Robert Shayne. **1958**

I SEE A DARK STRANGER ★★★½ Known in Great Britain as *The Adventuress*, this delightful picture tells of a high-strung yet charming Irish girl who, hating the British, helps a Nazi spy during World War II. Wry humor serves as counterpoint to the suspense. A class act. B&W; 98m. **DIR:** Frank Launder. **CAST:** Deborah Kerr, Trevor Howard, Raymond Huntley, Liam Redmond. **1947**

I SPY (TV SERIES) ★★★★ Remember Bill Cosby before terminal cuteness and a bank account the size of Guam overwhelmed him? This classic TV series will remind you of his charm and ability. It also focuses much-deserved attention on the colossally cool and clever Robert Culp. There's plenty of fun and suspense as spies Kelly Robinson and Alexander Scott, under the guise of tennis pro and trainer, do battle against the international forces of evil. each episode. 60m. **DIR:** Richard C. Sarafian, Paul Wendkos. **CAST:** Robert Culp, Bill Cosby. **1965–1968**

ICE RUNNER ★★★ CIA agent (Edward Albert) is sentenced to a Russian gulag in Siberia for espionage. During transit by rail, he switches identities with a dead prisoner. When he runs afoul of the camp commandant, a war of wits and nerves begins. Strange mix of political intrigue and mysticism skates around the thin ice in the plot. Rated R for nudity, profanity, and violence. 114m. **DIR:** Barry Samson. **CAST:** Edward Albert, Victor Wong, Olga Kabo, Eugene Lazarev, Alexander Kurnitzov, Basil Hoffman. **1993**

ICE STATION ZEBRA ★★★ This long cold war cliff-hanger about a submarine skipper awaiting orders while cruising to the North Pole under the ice was eccentric billionaire Howard Hughes's favorite film. The suspense comes with a British agent's hunt for the usual Russian spy. Rated G. 148m. **DIR:** John Sturges. **CAST:** Rock Hudson, Ernest Borgnine, Patrick McGoohan, Jim Brown, Tony Bill, Lloyd Nolan. **1968**

IF LOOKS COULD KILL (1991) ★★★ Richard Grieco is a high school student mistaken for an undercover secret agent. As such, he enjoys all the frills (car, clothes, women) that go with the job. Unfortunately, he must also contend with bad guys. A wonderful, action-packed conclusion. Rated PG-13 for profanity and violence. 90m. **DIR:** William Dear. **CAST:** Richard Grieco, Linda Hunt, Roger Rees, Robin Bartlett, Roger Daltrey. **1991**

ILLEGAL ENTRY 🦃 Daughter of murdered scientists looks for their killers while guarding a secret formula. Not a formula for success. Rated R for violence, language, and nudity. 88m. **DIR:** Henri Charr. **CAST:** Barbara Lee Alexander, Gregory Vignolle, Arthur Roberts, Sabyn Gene't. **1993**

IN GOLD WE TRUST 🦃 Renegade MIAs in Southeast Asia murder their own rescue party to steal the ransom money. Insipid. Unrated, contains profanity and violence. 89m. **DIR:** P. Chalong. **CAST:** Jan-Michael Vincent, Sam Jones, James Phillips, Michi McGee, Sherri Rose. **1990**

IN HARM'S WAY ★★ John Wayne leads the United States Navy into a monumental struggle against the Japanese. Kirk Douglas is the antihero who stirs up a fuss. The ships are models and the battles are conducted in a bathtub. It's too big and too long. B&W; 167m. **DIR:** Otto Preminger. **CAST:** John Wayne, Kirk Douglas, Patricia Neal, Tom Tryon, Paula Prentiss, Brandon de Wilde, Stanley Holloway, Jill Haworth, Burgess Meredith, Henry Fonda, Dana Andrews, Franchot Tone, Patrick O'Neal. **1965**

IN LIKE FLINT ★★★ James Coburn's smooth portrayal of super-secret agent Derek Flint is ample reason to catch this spy spoof, the sequel to *Our Man Flint*. An evil organization is substituting duplicates for all the world's leaders. Jerry Goldsmith contributes another droll jazz score. Unrated; suitable for family viewing. 114m. **DIR:** Gordon Douglas. **CAST:** James Coburn, Lee J. Cobb, Jean Hale, Andrew Duggan. **1967**

IN SEARCH OF THE SERPENT OF DEATH 🦃 A *Raiders of the Lost Ark* rip-off. Rated R for violence. 97m. **DIR:** Anwar Kawadri. **CAST:** Jeff Fahey, Camilla More. **1989**

IN THE LINE OF DUTY: AMBUSH IN WACO ★★★½ Riveting, up-to-the-minute TV drama about self-proclaimed evangelical leader David Koresh, and his magnetic hold on his followers. Events depict Koresh's battle with the government, when he held the Bureau of Alcohol, Tobacco and Firearms at bay until a deadly showdown lit the skies of Waco, Texas. Powerful performances from Tim Daly as Koresh, and Dan Lauria as the bureau captain who takes control of the siege. Rated R for violence. 93m. **DIR:** Dick Lowry. **CAST:** Timothy Daly, Dan Lauria, William O'Leary. **1993**

IN THE LINE OF FIRE ★★★★½ Put simply, this is the ultimate *Dirty Harry* movie. Even though Clint Eastwood plays Secret Service agent Frank Horrigan (instead of Harry Callahan), this film is to his cop movies what *Unforgiven* is to his Westerns. Fans of the detective series will recognize familiar plot elements as Eastwood attempts to prevent psycho John Malkovich from assassinating the president, but director Wolfgang Petersen keeps it fresh and involving throughout. Rated R for violence and profanity. 135m. **DIR:** Wolfgang Petersen. **CAST:** Clint Eastwood, John Malkovich, René Russo, Dylan McDermott, Gary Cole, Fred Dalton Thompson, John Mahoney. **1993**

INDIGO ★★ Francesco Quinn stars as a half-breed Marine Corps officer who returns to his native land in the Amazon to find that developers have ravaged the countryside and his people. As a former U.S. army colonel, Brian Dennehy brings a little class to an otherwise routine *Rambo* rip-off. Rated R for violence and profanity. 94m. **DIR:** Anthony M. Dawson. **CAST:** Francesco Quinn, Brian Dennehy. **1989**

INDIGO 2: THE REVOLT 🦃 Marvelous Marvin Hagler isn't so marvelous as Sergeant Iron, a U.S. Marine leading Amazonian tribes against greedy developers. Not rated, but contains violence. 104m. **DIR:** Anthony M. Dawson. **CAST:** Marvin Hagler, Charles Napier, Frank Cuervo. **1990**

INNOCENT MAN, AN ★★★★ Jimmie Rainwood (Tom Selleck) is a decent guy; an airplane mechanic who likes his job and loves his wife. But a mistake by two overzealous undercover detectives changes his simple life into a nightmare. Well directed by Peter Yates, *An Innocent Man* has a solid dramatic story line, and fine performances. Rated R for violence and profanity. 113m. **DIR:** Peter Yates. **CAST:** Tom Selleck, F. Murray Abraham, Laila Robins, David Rasche. **1989**

INSIDE MAN, THE ★★★½ Inspired by a 1981 incident in which a Soviet submarine ran aground in Sweden, this exciting adventure film really moves. A CIA agent (Dennis Hopper) sets up a young ex-Marine (Gosta Ekman) as the inside man who must investigate the theft of a laser-submarine search device. Check this one out. It's unrated, but contains some strong language. 90m. **DIR:** Tom Clegg. **CAST:** Dennis Hopper, Hardy Krüger, Gosta Ekman, Celia Gregory. **1984**

INSIDE OUT (1975) ★★★ An unlikely trio (Telly Savalas, Robert Culp, and James Mason) band together to recover $6 million in gold that Hitler had hidden. The action and suspense in this film should hold most viewers' attention. Rated PG. 98m. **DIR:** Peter Duffell. **CAST:** Telly Savalas, Robert Culp, James Mason, Aldo Ray. **1975**

INSTANT JUSTICE 🦃 Michael Paré plays Marine Sergeant Youngblood, who has a penchant for head-butting. Rated R. 101m. **DIR:** Craig T. Rumar. **CAST:** Michael Paré, Tawny Kitaen, Charles Napier. **1986**

INTERCEPTOR ★★★½ High marks to this spiffy airborne thriller, which finds a pilot as the sole "wild card" able to prevent a terrorist hijacking. Crisp direction and a good, high-tech script from John Brancato and Michael Ferris. Rated PG-13 for profanity and violence. 88m. **DIR:** Michael Cohn. **CAST:** Andrew Divoff, Elizabeth Morehead, Jurgen Prochnow. **1992**

INTERNAL AFFAIRS ★★★ Brutal, sexually charged thriller about an Internal Affairs investigator (Andy Garcia) who is obsessed with busting a degenerate street cop (Richard Gere). The unrelenting tension mounts as the pursuit of justice becomes a very personal vendetta. Gere is at his best here as a creep you'll just love to hate. Rated R for sex, violence, and profanity. 115m. **DIR:** Mike Figgis. **CAST:** Richard Gere, Andy Garcia, Nancy Travis, Laurie Metcalf, William Baldwin. **1990**

INTO THE FIRE 🦃 A young drifter finds himself in the middle of deceit and treachery when he stops at a roadside diner. Rated R for nudity and violence. 88m. **DIR:** Graeme Campbell. **CAST:** Art Hindle, Olivia D'Abo, Lee Montgomery, Susan Anspach. **1988**

INTO THE HOMELAND ★★★ This HBO release is a topical but predictable story starring Powers Boothe as an ex-cop who endeavors to rescue his kidnapped daughter from a white supremacist organization headed by Paul LeMat. The shockingly real portrayal of the supremacists' ethics make this movie worth viewing. Unrated, but contains violence and strong language. 120m. **DIR:** Lesli Linka Glatter. **CAST:** Powers Boothe, C. Thomas Howell, Paul LeMat, Cindy Pickett. **1987**

INTO THE SUN ★★★★ To research a role, an obnoxious movie star rides shotgun with a crack pilot in the Middle East. Some movies, by sheer force of the talent involved, turn out to be much better than anyone had a right to expect. Director Fritz Kiersch and his cast (including a hilarious Terry Kiser) make this one seem fresh and even innovative. Rated R for profanity and violence. 100m. **DIR:** Fritz Kiersch. **CAST:** Anthony Michael Hall, Michael Paré, Terry Kiser. **1992**

INVASION U.S.A. ★★★ Chuck Norris plays a one-man army (as always) who comes to the rescue of the good ol' U. S. A. and pummels the minions of psychotic spy Richard Lynch. Rated R for violence, gore, and profanity. 107m. **DIR:** Joseph Zito. **CAST:** Chuck Norris, Richard Lynch, Melissa Prophet. **1985**

INVINCIBLE SWORD, THE 🦃 A band of traveling acrobats takes on an evil tyrant. Not rated, but contains violence and profanity. 93m. **DIR:** Hsu Tseng Hung. **CAST:** Wang Yu. **1978**

IRON EAGLE ★★ A better name for this modern war movie might have been *Ramboy*, so shamelessly does it attempt to be a *Rambo* for the teen-age set. Jason Gedrick stars as an 18-year-old would-be pilot who steals an F-16 fighter plane to rescue his father (Tim Thomerson), a prisoner of war in the Middle East. A terminally dull fantasy of blood lust. Rated PG-13 for violence and profanity. 115m. **DIR:** Sidney J. Furie. **CAST:** Lou Gossett Jr., Jason Gedrick, Tim Thomerson, David Suchet. **1986**

IRON EAGLE II 🦃 Ridiculous sequel to the preposterous original. Rated PG for violence and profanity. 105m. **DIR:** Sidney J. Furie. **CAST:** Lou Gossett Jr., Mark Humphrey, Stuart Margolin, Alan Scarfe. **1988**

IRON MASK, THE ★★★½ The last of Douglas Fairbanks's truly memorable series of historical adventures is a rousing version of the Dumas story of the later adventures of D'Artagnan and his efforts to restore the rightful king to the throne of France. Well-budgeted and full of good stunts and deadly encounters, this film was released with sound effects and a synchronized score. B&W; 87m. **DIR:** Allan Dwan. **CAST:** Douglas Fairbanks Sr., Nigel de Brulier, Marguerite de la Motte. **1929**

IRON WILL ★★★ Dakota teen enters the world's most grueling dogsled marathon to save the family farm and earn his college tuition in this gloriously old-fashioned adventure. Some events don't gel—the death of the kid's dad seems avoidable, the trek's final short cut isn't really *that* treacherous—but the action cracks along sharply, the bad guys are easy to hate, and a wry subtext about journalists working feverishly to define a race and man-child in legendary terms is entertaining. Rated PG. 97m. **DIR:** Charles Haid. **CAST:** Mackenzie Astin, Kevin Spacey, David Ogden Stiers, August Schellenberg, Brian Cox, Penelope Windust. **1993**

IRONHEART 🦃 Tired vengeance scenario about a cop tracking the white slaver who killed his partner. Rated R for violence and sex. 83m. **DIR:** Robert Clouse. **CAST:** Britton Lee, Bolo Yeung, Richard Norton. **1993**

ISLAND TRADER ★★ A young boy on an island finds a wrecked airplane laden with gold bullion. He is then pursued by a dangerous criminal and a tugboat skipper, both of whom want the treasure. This potentially exciting adventure film is marred by amateurish direction, a low budget, and uninspired acting. 95m. **DIR:** Howard Rubie. **CAST:** John Ewart, Ruth Cracknell, Eric Oldfield. **1970**

IT TAKES A THIEF (TV SERIES) ★★★★ Suave and debonair Robert Wagner secured the television role of his career in this late-Sixties series, very loosely adapted from Alfred Hitchcock's *To Catch a Thief* (1955). Burglar Alexander Mundy put his talents to work for a supersecret government agency (the SIA). Actual European locales added to the show's luxurious tone, as did the occasional appearance of Fred Astaire (as Alexander's father, Alister, a retired thief). Delightful fun. 52m. **DIR:** Various. **CAST:** Robert Wagner, Malachi Throne, Fred Astaire. **1968–70**

IVANHOE (1952) ★★★★ Robert Taylor stars as Sir Walter Scott's dashing knight Ivanhoe. His mission is to secure the ransom for King Richard the Lionhearted, who has been captured while returning from the Crusades. Action and swordplay abound as Ivanhoe strives for Richard's release and protects two very fair maidens (Elizabeth Taylor and Joan Fontaine) from the lecherous grasp of archvillain George Sanders. 106m. **DIR:** Richard Thorpe. **CAST:** Robert Taylor, Elizabeth Taylor, Joan Fontaine, George Sanders, Sebastian Cabot. **1952**

IVANHOE (1982) ★★★★ Lavish remake of the 1952 version of Sir Walter Scott's novel of chivalry and derring-do. This time, Anthony Andrews is the disinherited knight who joins ranks with Robin Hood to recapture King Richard's throne from the sniveling Prince John. Brilliant costuming and pageantry. Originally a TV mini-series. 180m. **DIR:** Douglas Camfield. **CAST:** Anthony Andrews, James Mason, Sam Neill, Olivia Hussey. **1982**

JACKSON COUNTY JAIL ★★★½ This chase film is pretty good. Yvette Mimieux escapes from jail with fellow inmate Tommy Lee Jones. Audiences can't help but sympathize with Mimieux, because she was unfairly arrested and then raped by her jailer. Rated R. 89m. **DIR:** Michael Miller. **CAST:** Yvette Mimieux, Tommy Lee Jones, Robert Carradine. **1976**

JAIL BAIT (1954) ★★ Delightfully awful crime melodrama from everyone's favorite bad auteur, Ed *(Plan 9 From Outer Space)* Wood. Hardboiled punk Tim Farrell, whose face must hurt from sneering so much, involves the son of a famous plastic surgeon in a robbery, then forces the doctor to help him escape from the police. There's lots of ridiculous dialogue, cheap sets, and a final plot twist you'll spot a mile away. Also includes one of the most god awful droning musical scores you'll ever hear. A must-see for camp aficionados. B&W; 70m. **DIR:** Edward D. Wood Jr. **CAST:** Timothy Farrell, Dolores Fuller, Lyle Talbot, Herbert Rawlinson, Steve Reeves. **1954**

JAILBAIT (1992) ★★ C. Thomas Howell is the burnt-out cop who gets involved with a teenage runaway who witnessed a murder. Pretty seedy affair corrals all of the clichés. Unrated and R-rated versions available. Rated R for nudity, violence, and language; unrated version has more nudity. 100m./103m. **DIR:** Rafal Zielinski. **CAST:** C. Thomas Howell, Renee Humphrey. **1992**

JAKE SPANNER PRIVATE EYE ★★ Robert Mitchum plays Jake Spanner, a retired private detective in this mediocre made-for-cable movie. A group of senior citizens decide to help Jake find the double-crossing Ernest Borgnine before an evil drug queen does. 95m. **DIR:** Lee H. Katzin. **CAST:** Robert Mitchum, Ernest Borgnine, John Mitchum, Richard Yniguez, Jim Mitchum, Dick Van Patten, Stella Stevens, Kareem Abdul-Jabbar, Edie Adams. **1989**

JAKE SPEED ★★★½ Quirky little adventure thriller, from the folks involved with the equally deft *Night of the Comet.* When Karen Kopins's younger sister is kidnapped and threatened with white slavery by John Hurt's delightfully oily villain, Speed (Wayne Crawford) and his associate Remo (Dennis Christopher) materialize and offer to help. Rated PG for mild violence. 100m. **DIR:** Andrew Lane. **CAST:** Wayne Crawford, Dennis Christopher, Karen Kopins, John Hurt, Leon Ames, Donna Pescow, Barry Primus, Monte Markham. **1986**

JENNY'S WAR ★★½ When her son, an RAF pilot, is shot down over Germany during World War II, Jenny Baines (Dyan Cannon) disguises herself as a man and heads to Germany to find him. It may have been based on a real story, but this lengthy made-for-TV movie is utterly preposterous. Not rated; contains no objectionable material. 192m. **DIR:** Steven Gethers. **CAST:** Dyan Cannon, Elke Sommer, Robert Hardy, Christopher Cazenove, Hugh Grant. **1985**

JERICHO FEVER ★★★ In this made-for-cable original, two doctors must battle an unknown disease that was accidentally brought into the United States by terrorists. Now the terrorists must be captured to obtain the cure. A solid plot and good acting make this enjoyable. Not rated, but contains violence. 95m. **DIR:** Sandor Stern. **CAST:** Stephanie Zimbalist, Perry King, Branscombe Richmond, Alan Scarfe, Ari Barak, Elyssa Davalos, Kario Salem. **1993**

JET ATTACK 🦃 John Agar tries to rescue an American scientist captured by the North Koreans. B&W; 68m. **DIR:** Edward L. Cahn. **CAST:** John Agar, Audrey Totter, Gregory Walcott. **1958**

JEWEL OF THE NILE, THE ★★★½ This generally enjoyable sequel to *Romancing the Stone* details the further adventures of novelist Joan Wilder (Kathleen Turner) and soldier of fortune Jack Colton (Michael Douglas) in the deserts of North Africa. Danny DeVito supplies the laughs. Rated PG. 106m. **DIR:** Lewis Teague. **CAST:** Michael Douglas, Kathleen Turner, Danny DeVito, Avner Eisenberg. **1985**

JOHNNY ANGEL ★★★ Above-average gangster film provides some nice moments. George Raft seeks the killer of his father while busting up the mob. Nothing special, but fun to watch. B&W; 79m. **DIR:** Edwin L. Marin. **CAST:** George Raft, Claire Trevor, Signe Hasso, Hoagy Carmichael. **1945**

JOHNNY HANDSOME ★★★½ Mickey Rourke plays a badly disfigured criminal double-crossed during a robbery and sent to prison, where plastic surgery is performed on his face as part of a new rehabilitation program. Once released, he plots revenge on those responsible for his capture. Be warned: the violence is extreme. Rated R for violence, language, and nudity. 93m. **DIR:** Walter Hill. **CAST:** Mickey Rourke, Elizabeth McGovern, Ellen Barkin, Lance Henriksen, Morgan Freeman, Forest Whitaker. **1989**

JOSH AND S.A.M. ★★½ Teenager Josh convinces his younger brother, Sam, that he is "S.A.M.," a Strategically Altered Mutant who has been sold to the government by their estranged parents and turned into a robotic child warrior. During one shuffle between Mom and Dad, the troubled youths run away to Canada on an adventure of self-discovery. Part road movie and part domestic drama, this uneven story of adolescent angst has an engaging, offbeat charm. Rated PG-13 for language and violence. 97m. **DIR:** Billy Weber. **CAST:** Jacob Tierney, Noah Fleiss, Martha Plimpton, Stephen Tobolowsky, Joan Allen, Christopher Penn. **1993**

JOURNEY OF HONOR ★★ Historic tale of feuding Japanese warlords in 1602 has epic written all over it, but comes across trite and clichéd. Visuals are the only saving grace. Rated PG-13 for violence. 107m. **DIR:** Gordon Hessler. **CAST:** Sho Kosugi, Christopher Lee, Norman Lloyd, John Rhys-Davies, Toshiro Mifune. **1991**

JUDGMENT NIGHT ★★★ Four buddies get lost in Chicago on the way to a boxing match and end up being chased by a vicious gang in this far from exceptional urban thriller. However, when compared with most action flicks produced these days, it's well above average in the acting, directing, and writing categories. Certainly, high-voltage villain Denis Leary is the main attraction. Rated R for profanity and violence. 109m. **DIR:** Stephen Hopkins. **CAST:** Emilio Estevez, Cuba Gooding Jr., Denis Leary, Stephen Dorff, Jeremy Piven, Peter Greene, Michael DeLorenzo, Michael Wiseman. **1993**

JUNGLE HEAT ★★ Dr. Evelyn Howard (Deborah Raffin), an anthropologist from L.A., hires an alcoholic ex-Vietnam vet (Peter Fonda) to fly her into the jungles of South America. There she looks for an ancient tribe of pygmies but finds instead monsters that greatly resemble the Creature from the Black Lagoon. Rated PG for language and gore. 93m. **DIR:** Gus Trikonis. **CAST:** Peter Fonda, Deborah Raffin, John Amos. **1984**

JUNGLE JIM ★★★ The first entry in Columbia's long-running series starring Johnny Weissmuller finds Alex Raymond's comic-strip hero helping a female scientist search for a rare drug that can help cure polio. Future Superman George Reeves plays the heavy. B&W; 73m. **DIR:** William Berke. **CAST:** Johnny Weissmuller, Virginia Grey, George Reeves, Lita Baron, Rick Vallin. **1948**

JUNGLE MASTER, THE 🦃 An expedition journeys to Africa in search of the legendary ape-man, Karzan, no, not Tarzan—Karzan. 90m. **DIR:** Miles Deem. **CAST:** Johnny Kissmuller, Simone Blondell, Edward Mann. **1985**

JUNGLE PATROL ★★ This is a routine World War II story about a squadron of fliers commanded by a young officer who has been ordered to hold an airfield against the Japanese. The subplot is a silly romance between the officer and a USO performer. Best ingredient: the music score by Emil Newman and Arthur Lange. B&W; 72m. **DIR:** Joseph M. Newman. **CAST:** Kristine Miller, Arthur Franz, Ross Ford, Tommy Noonan, Gene Reynolds, Richard Jaeckel, Harry Lauter. **1948**

JUNGLE RAIDERS ★★ Christopher Connelly plays an adventurer–con man hired to find the Ruby of Gloom in Malaysia. This *Raiders of the Lost Ark* rip-off is too plodding for most viewers. It includes a few fun, action-filled moments but stick to the Lucas-Spielberg classic. Rated PG for violence and profanity. 102m. **DIR:** Anthony M. Dawson. **CAST:** Christopher Connelly, Marina Costa, Lee Van Cleef. **1985**

JUNGLE WARRIORS ★★½ The idea of a group of female models in Peru for a shoot in the jungle is quite absurd. If you can overlook the premise, though, this action film is modestly satisfying. It's rather like an episode of *Miami Vice* but with scantily dressed women packing machine guns. Rated R for violence, profanity, and nudity. 96m. **DIR:** Ernst R. von Theumer. **CAST:** Sybil Danning, Marjoe Gortner, Nina Van Pallandt, Paul Smith, John Vernon, Alex Cord, Woody Strode, Kai Wulfe, Dana Elcar. **1983**

JUNIOR G-MEN ★★ Politely dropped from the Warner Brothers stable after a few years of service, the Dead End Kids split forces and inflicted their obnoxious personae on a wider audience than ever. Do-gooder G-Man Jim Bradford and his insufferable Junior G-Man companion Harry Trent do their best to reform the hardboiled gang and involve them in the search for leader Bill

Barton's father, a famous inventor who has been kidnapped by greedy traitors. B&W; 12 chapters. **DIR:** Ford Beebe, John Rawlins. **CAST:** Billy Halop, Huntz Hall, Gabriel Dell, Bernard Punsley, Philip Terry, Russell Hicks, Cy Kendall, Kenneth Howell. **1940**

JUNKMAN, THE 🦃 From the makers of *Gone in 60 Seconds*, this sequel is tagged as the "chase film for the '80s." Rated PG. 99m. **DIR:** H. B. Halicki. **CAST:** Christopher Stone, Susan Shaw, Lang Jeffries, Lynda Day George. **1982**

K2 ★★ This disappointing adventure, adapted from Patrick Meyers's successful stage play, rehashes every mountain-climbing movie cliché. An obnoxious attorney (Michael Biehn) and his physicist pal (Matt Craven) join a team that climbs the second highest and most treacherous mountain in the world. Rated R for violence and profanity. 104m. **DIR:** Franc Roddam. **CAST:** Michael Biehn, Matt Craven, Raymond J. Barry, Patricia Charbonneau, Hiroshi Fujioka, Luca Bercovici. **1992**

KANSAS CITY MASSACRE, THE ★★★ Dale Robertson reprises his role of the outlandish Melvin Purvis that he originated in 1974's *Melvin Purvis, G-Man*. Practically every notorious gangster who ever lived meets the unstoppable G-Man in this made-for-TV film. Watch for the acting debut of the notorious ex-governor of Georgia, Lester Maddox. Here he's governor of Oklahoma. 120m. **DIR:** Dan Curtis. **CAST:** Dale Robertson, Bo Hopkins, Robert Walden, Mills Watson, Scott Brady, Harris Yulin. **1975**

KARATE COP 🦃 Futuristic chop-socky about the last cop on Earth and a beautiful scientist who team up to find a precious stone. Rated R for violence and language. 91m. **DIR:** Alan Roberts. **CAST:** Ron Marchini, Carrie Chambers, David Carradine, Michael Bristow. **1992**

KASHMIRI RUN, THE 🦃 American adventurer in the Far East is commissioned to take two scientists to India and bring back a load of yak skins. 93m. **DIR:** John Peyser. **CAST:** Pernell Roberts, Alexandra Bastedo, Julian Mateos, Gloria Camara. **1969**

KEATON'S COP ★★ Former mobster Abe Vigoda is on a hit list and requires police protection. Lee Majors becomes his macho bodyguard in this shoot-'em-up that can't decide whether it's a comedy or actioner. Rated R for profanity and violence. 95m. **DIR:** Robert Burge. **CAST:** Lee Majors, Abe Vigoda, Don Rickles. **1990**

KEEPING TRACK ★★★½ Superior action thriller follows Michael Sarrazin and Margot Kidder as two innocent bystanders who witness a murder and a robbery. Once they find the $5 million, they must learn to trust one another because everyone is after them, including the CIA and Russian spies. This one will keep you guessing. Rated R. 102m. **DIR:** Robin Spry. **CAST:** Michael Sarrazin, Margot Kidder, Alan Scarfe, Ken Pogue. **1985**

KELLY'S HEROES ★★★ An amiable rip-off of *The Dirty Dozen*, this 1970 war comedy was funnier at the time of its original release. Stoic Clint Eastwood is stuck with a bunch of goof-offs (Telly Savalas, Donald Sutherland, Don Rickles, and Gavin McLeod) as he searches for Nazi treasure. Sutherland's World War II hippie ("Give me those positive waves, man") is a little tough to take these days, but this caper picture still has its moments. Rated PG. 145m. **DIR:** Brian G. Hutton. **CAST:** Clint Eastwood, Telly Savalas, Donald Sutherland, Don Rickles, Gavin MacLeod, Carroll O'Connor. **1970**

KEY TO REBECCA, THE ★★½ Ken Follett's bestselling World War II-set novel becomes a rather stodgy TV movie, with David Soul as a Nazi spy involved in a battle of wits with British officer Cliff Robertson. It all looks pretty fake, though at least Follett's story holds your attention. 192m. **DIR:** David Hemmings. **CAST:** Cliff Robertson, David Soul, Season Hubley, Anthony Quayle, David Hemmings, Robert Culp. **1985**

KHARTOUM ★★★★ Underrated historical adventure-drama recalls the British defeat in northern Africa by Arab tribesmen circa 1833. Location filming, exciting battle scenes, and fine acting raise this spectacle to the level of superior entertainment. 134m. **DIR:** Basil Dearden. **CAST:** Laurence Olivier, Charlton Heston, Ralph Richardson, Richard Johnson, Alexander Knox. **1966**

KICK FIGHTER 🦃 A martial arts expert kicks his way out of the gutters of Bangkok, only to be held back by crime lords who want him to throw his shot at the championship. Gobble-gobble. 92m. **DIR:** Anthony Maharaj. **CAST:** Richard Norton, Benny Urquidez. **1991**

KICK OR DIE ★★ Predictable campus psycho film has coeds on the run from a sadistic rapist. Enter Kevin Bernhardt as a former kick-boxing champ. Rated R for profanity, violence, and nudity. 87m. **DIR:** Charles Norton. **CAST:** Kevin Bernhardt. **1987**

KICKBOXER ★★½ This flick looks a little like *Rocky* and a lot like *The Karate Kid*, but it is a step up for Jean-Claude Van Damme in the acting department. Good action scenes and a fun plot. Rated R for violence and language. 97m. **DIR:** Mark DiSalle, David Worth. **CAST:** Jean-Claude Van Damme, Dennis Alexio, Dennis Chan. **1989**

KICKBOXER 2: THE ROAD BACK 🦃 With more kick-you-in-the-face action, this sequel, sans original star Jean-Claude Van Damme, is weak in the joints. Rated R for violence.

90m. **DIR:** Albert Pyun. **CAST:** Sasha Mitchell, Peter Boyle, Dennis Chan, John Diehl. **1990**

KICKBOXER THREE—ART OF WAR ★★ While in Rio de Janeiro for a kick-boxing exhibition, America's champion Sasha Mitchell rescues a kidnapped girl. Standard martial arts flick. Rated R for strong violence and profanity. 92m. **DIR:** Rick King. **CAST:** Sasha Mitchell, Dennis Chan. **1992**

KID ★★★½ Exciting thriller about a mysterious stranger (C. Thomas Howell) who wants revenge for his parents' deaths. Great editing and terrific sound effects help make this film quite entertaining. Rated R for violence and profanity. 94m. **DIR:** John Mark Robinson. **CAST:** C. Thomas Howell, Sarah Trigger, Brian Austin Green, R. Lee Ermey. **1990**

KIDNAPPED (1988) 🦃 A woman goes after the kidnappers of her 16-year-old sister. Rated R for language, nudity, and violence. 90m. **DIR:** Howard Avedis. **CAST:** David Naughton, Barbara Crampton, Kim Evenson, Lance LeGault, Chick Vennera, Charles Napier, Kin Shriner, Jimmie Walker. **1988**

KILL AND KILL AGAIN ★★ Kung fu champ James Ryan repeats his starring role from *Kill or Be Killed.* This time, martial arts master Steve Chase (Ryan) has been hired to rescue a Nobel Prize–winning chemist from the clutches of a demented billionaire. Rated R. 100m. **DIR:** Ivan Hall. **CAST:** James Ryan, Anneline Kriel. **1981**

KILL CASTRO 🦃 Implausible adventure yarn. Rated R. 90m. **DIR:** Peter Barton. **CAST:** Stuart Whitman, Caren Kaye, Robert Vaughn, Woody Strode, Albert Salmi, Michael Gazzo, Sybil Danning, Raymond St. Jacques. **1978**

KILL OR BE KILLED ★★ A former Nazi pits himself against the Japanese master who defeated him in an important tournament during World War II. Run-of-the-mill martial arts nonsense. James Ryan shows a glimmer of personality to go with his physical prowess. Rated PG. 90m. **DIR:** Ivan Hall. **CAST:** James Ryan, Norman Combes, Charlotte Michelle. **1980**

KILL POINT 🦃 Gang warfare, revenge, and justice in L.A. Rated R for violence and language. 89m. **DIR:** Frank Harris. **CAST:** Leo Fong, Richard Roundtree, Cameron Mitchell, Stack Pierce, Hope Holiday. **1984**

KILL ZONE 🦃 Totally derivative war film has wigged-out Colonel Wiggins, played by David Carradine, pushing his platoon one mission too far. Director Cirio Santiago pushed this genre one film too far. Rated R for language and violence. 95m. **DIR:** Cirio H. Santiago. **CAST:** David Carradine, Tony Dorsett, Rob Youngblood, Vic Trevino. **1993**

KILLER ELITE, THE ★★½ Secret service agent James Caan is double-crossed by his partner (Robert Duvall) while guarding a witness. Disabled by a bullet wound, he has to begin a long process of recovery. He wants revenge. There are some good action scenes. However, considering all the top-flight talent involved, it is a major disappointment. Rated PG. 120m. **DIR:** Sam Peckinpah. **CAST:** James Caan, Robert Duvall, Arthur Hill, Bo Hopkins, Mako, Burt Young, Gig Young. **1975**

KILLER FISH 🦃 Bad acting and lousy Spanish accents help to make this a total bust. Rated PG, but contains violence and some nudity. 101m. **DIR:** Anthony M. Dawson. **CAST:** Lee Majors, Karen Black, Margaux Hemingway, Marisa Berenson, James Franciscus. **1978**

KILLER FORCE ★★ Diamond security officer fakes a theft to secure the confidence of a ruthless smuggling ring. Predictable heist film. 100m. **DIR:** Val Guest. **CAST:** Telly Savalas, Peter Fonda, Hugh O'Brian, O. J. Simpson, Maud Adams, Christopher Lee. **1983**

KILLER INSTINCT ★★★ Two brothers toughing it out during the 1920s Prohibition become gangsters and take on the mob. Handsome production values and some close-to-the-cuff performances, but this story has been told before, and better. Rated R for violence, language, and nudity. 101m. **DIR:** Greydon Clark, Ken Stein. **CAST:** Ken Stein, Chris Bradley, Rachel York, Bruce Nozick. **1992**

KILLERS, THE ★★★ Two hit men piece together a story on the man they've just killed. A tense thriller loosely based on a short story by Ernest Hemingway. This remake of the 1946 classic emphasizes violence rather than storytelling. Ronald Reagan is excellent as an unscrupulous business tycoon. Rated PG; contains graphic violence. 95m. **DIR:** Don Siegel. **CAST:** Lee Marvin, John Cassavetes, Angie Dickinson, Ronald Reagan. **1964**

KILLER'S KISS ★★ A boxer rescues a singer from the lecherous clutches of her boss. This ultra-low-budget melodrama is a curiosity piece primarily because Stanley Kubrick wrote, photographed, directed, and edited it. 67m. **DIR:** Stanley Kubrick. **CAST:** Jamie Smith, Irene Kane, Frank Silvera. **1955**

KILLING AT HELL'S GATE ★★★ Made-for-TV action film about a group of people, including a controversial U.S. senator, who take a raft trip only to find that the bullets are harder to dodge than the jagged rocks. This ain't no *Deliverance*, but it's watchable. 96m. **DIR:** Jerry Jameson. **CAST:** Robert Urich, Deborah Raffin, Lee Purcell, Joel Higgins, George DiCenzo, Paul Burke, Brion James, John Randolph. **1981**

KILLING GAME, THE 🦃 Made-for-video movie tries to evoke a cynical, hardboiled style but lacks the talent behind (and in front of) the camera. Unrated, but featuring nudity and substantial violence. 83m. **DIR:** Joseph

Merhi. **CAST:** Chad Hayward, Cynthia Killion. **1988**

KILLING STREETS ★★ Michael Paré takes on the dual roles of a government operative kidnapped in Lebanon and his twin brother who leads an attempt to rescue him in this sometimes exciting, but ultimately mediocre, shoot-'em-up. Not rated, but contains violence and profanity. 106m. **DIR:** Stephen Cornwell. **CAST:** Michael Paré, Lorenzo Lamas, Jennifer Runyon. **1991**

KILLING TIME, THE ★★★★ Kiefer Sutherland is a killer posing as a new deputy sheriff in a small resort town. Beau Bridges is to be the new sheriff upon the retirement of Joe Don Baker. But there is much more to be discovered in this tense drama of murder, deception, and suspicion. Rated R for violence and profanity. 94m. **DIR:** Rick King. **CAST:** Beau Bridges, Kiefer Sutherland, Wayne Rogers, Joe Don Baker. **1987**

KILLING ZONE, THE ★★ Daron McBee of television's *American Gladiators* stars in this actioner as the convict nephew of an ex-DEA agent. Not rated, but contains violence and profanity. 90m. **DIR:** Addison Randall. **CAST:** Deron Michael McBee. **1990**

KIM ★★★½ Rudyard Kipling's India comes to life in this colorful story of the young son of a soldier and his adventures with a dashing secret operative in defense of queen and country. Dean Stockwell is one of the finest and most believable of child stars, and the great Errol Flynn is still capable of personifying the spirit of adventure and romance in this one-dimensional but entertaining story. 113m. **DIR:** Victor Saville. **CAST:** Errol Flynn, Dean Stockwell, Paul Lukas, Thomas Gomez, Cecil Kellaway. **1951**

KING ARTHUR, THE YOUNG WARLORD ★★ *King Arthur, the Young Warlord* follows the English legend in his early years through subplots that lead nowhere. It must be noted that the violence displayed may not be some people's idea of good ol' G-rated fun despite the MPAA approval. 96m. **DIR:** Sidney Hayers, Pat Jackson, Peter Sasdy. **CAST:** Oliver Tobias, Michael Gothard, Jack Watson, Brian Blessed, Peter Firth. **1975**

KING OF NEW YORK ★★★½ Overlooked gangster film follows a New York drug kingpin's attempts to reclaim territory, lost during his stay in prison. Cult director Abel Ferrara pulls out all the stops in this violent, fast-paced crime-drama. Rated R for violence, language, drug use, and nudity. 103m. **DIR:** Abel Ferrara. **CAST:** Christopher Walken, Larry Fishburne, David Caruso, Victor Argo, Wesley Snipes, Janet Julian. **1990**

KING OF THE CONGO ★★ Complicated serial has more twists than a maze but basically centers around a U.S. Air Force captain and his quest for missing microfilm. This was Buster Crabbe's last cliffhanger after a career that spanned nearly twenty years. B&W; 15 chapters. **DIR:** Spencer Gordon Bennet, Wallace Grissell. **CAST:** Buster Crabbe, Gloria Dee. **1952**

KING OF THE FOREST RANGERS 🦃 Silly serial about prehistoric towers and ancient tribes—an elongated shoot-'em-up plot about land-hungry villains, archaeologists, bound women, and stalwart heroes. B&W; 12 chapters. **DIR:** Spencer Gordon Bennet, Fred Brannon. **CAST:** Larry Thompson, Helen Talbot, Stuart Hamblen, Anthony Warde, Tom London, Harry Strang. **1946**

KING OF THE KICKBOXERS, THE 🦃 A kung fu cop travels to Thailand to break up a snuff film ring and avenge his brother's murder. An embarrassment. Rated R for violence, nudity, and profanity. 97m. **DIR:** Lucas Lowe. **CAST:** Loren A. Verdon, Richard Jaeckel, Don Stroud. **1991**

KING OF THE KONGO ★★ Historically important as the first serial released in both silent and sound versions, this early Mascot serial features veteran chapterplay hero Walter Miller as a secret service agent searching both for his brother and for the secret of a temple's treasure. Boris Karloff is a standout as the heavy. B&W; 10 chapters. **DIR:** Richard Thorpe. **CAST:** Walter Miller, Jacqueline Logan, Richard Tucker, Boris Karloff. **1929**

KING OF THE ROCKETMEN ★★★ This chapterplay precursor to the *Commando Cody* television series has longtime baddie Tristram Coffin joining the good guys for a change. Strapping on his flying suit, he does battle with evil conspirators. Good fun for serial fans, with highly implausible last-minute escapes. B&W; 12 chapters. **DIR:** Fred Brannon. **CAST:** Tristram Coffin, Mae Clarke, Dale Van Sickel, Tom Steele. **1949**

KING SOLOMON'S MINES (1937) ★★★½ H. Rider Haggard's splendid adventure story received its first sound-film treatment here. This version is superior in many respects to the more famous 1959 color remake. Cedric Hardwicke lacks the flair of a matinee-idol lead but makes a very realistic Allan Quatermain, while Paul Robeson gives perhaps the best performance of his screen career as King Umbopa. The action and battle sequences (many shot on location with real tribesmen) rival the best early MGM Tarzan films for costumes and feel. B&W; 79m. **DIR:** Robert Stevenson. **CAST:** Cedric Hardwicke, Paul Robeson, Roland Young, John Loder, Anna Lee. **1937**

KING SOLOMON'S MINES (1950) ★★★★★ The "great white hunter" genre of adventure films has been a movie staple for ages, yet only this one rates as a cinema classic. Stewart Granger guides a party through darkest Africa in search of a lady's husband. On the way, the hunter and the lady (Deborah Kerr) become fast friends. 102m. **DIR:** Compton Bennett, Andrew Marton. **CAST:** Stewart Granger, Deborah Kerr, Hugo Haas. **1950**

KING SOLOMON'S MINES (1985) 🦃 A crime against H. Rider Haggard's classic adventure novel—a compendium of cornball clichés and stupid slapstick. Rated PG-13 for violence and profanity. 100m. **DIR:** J. Lee Thompson. **CAST:** Richard Chamberlain, Sharon Stone, John Rhys-Davies, Herbert Lom, Ken Gampu. **1985**

KING SOLOMON'S TREASURE 🦃 This mindless adventure features a stuttering David McCallum pursuing treasure in Africa's Forbidden City. 90m. **DIR:** Alvin Rakoff. **CAST:** David McCallum, Britt Ekland, Patrick Macnee, John Colicos. **1976**

KINGS AND DESPERATE MEN: A HOSTAGE INCIDENT ★★★ Improbable but engrossing account of terrorists taking over a radio talk show to present their case to the public. Patrick McGoohan lends his commanding presence as the abrasive, cynical talk-show host. A strange, almost cinema vérité portrayal, the title comes from a John Donne poem that's quoted by McGoohan. Rated PG-13 for language and violence. 117m. **DIR:** Alexis Kanner. **CAST:** Patrick McGoohan, Alexis Kanner, Andrea Marcovicci, Margaret Trudeau. **1989**

KINJITE (FORBIDDEN SUBJECTS) 🦃 Again Charles Bronson plays a vigilante who deals out his own brand of justice. Rated R for nudity, profanity, and violence. 96m. **DIR:** J. Lee Thompson. **CAST:** Charles Bronson, Perry Lopez, Peggy Lipton. **1989**

KISS TOMORROW GOODBYE ★★★ Violent, fast-paced gangster film brings back the days of the B movie. James Cagney is cast once again as a ruthless gangster who knows no limits. A rogue's gallery of character actors lends good support to this overlooked entry into the genre. 102m. **DIR:** Gordon Douglas. **CAST:** James Cagney, Luther Adler, Ward Bond, Barbara Payton, Barton MacLane, Neville Brand, Kenneth Tobey, Steve Brodie. **1950**

KITTY AND THE BAGMAN ★★½ Overambitious period piece about two Australian crime queens battling for control. The Roaring Twenties sets and the constant shifts back and forth from broad comedy to drama to shoot-'em-up action should entertain some viewers. Unrated. 95m. **DIR:** Donald Crombie. **CAST:** John Stanton, Liddy Clark. **1982**

KNIGHTRIDERS ★★★ What was supposed to be a modern-day look at the lost Code of Honor comes across on screen as a bunch of weirdos dressed in armor riding motorcycles in a traveling circus. At a length of almost two-and-a-half hours, there isn't enough to hold the viewer's interest. Rated PG. 145m. **DIR:** George A. Romero. **CAST:** Ed Harris, Tom Savini, Amy Ingersoll. **1981**

KNIGHTS OF THE ROUND TABLE ★★½ Colorful wide-screen epic of King Arthur's court is long on pageantry but lacks the spirit required to make this type of film work well. 115m. **DIR:** Richard Thorpe. **CAST:** Robert Taylor, Ava Gardner, Mel Ferrer, Stanley Baker, Felix Aylmer, Robert Urquhart. **1953**

KOROSHI ★★½ Patrick McGoohan's popular *Secret Agent* television series is poorly represented by this attempt to string two episodes into a full-length feature. The color photography—the series was B&W—is the only legitimate appeal; the episodes themselves are rather weak. For serious fans only. Unrated; suitable for family viewing. 100m. **DIR:** Michael Truman, Peter Yates. **CAST:** Patrick McGoohan, Kenneth Griffith, Amanda Barrie, Ronald Howard. **1966**

KUFFS ★★★½ When police officer Bruce Boxleitner is killed, his ne'er-do-well brother, Christian Slater, takes over the family-owned, patrol-special business in hopes of finding the killer. Director Bruce A. Evans uses a crisp, tongue-in-cheek storytelling style, mixing action, romance, and comedy. Rated PG-13 for profanity and violence. 106m. **DIR:** Bruce A. Evans. **CAST:** Christian Slater, Tony Goldwyn, Milla Jovovich, Bruce Boxleitner. **1992**

KUNG FU ★★★ The pilot of the 1970s television series starring David Carradine has its moments for those who fondly remember the show. Carradine plays a Buddhist monk roaming the Old West. When his wisdom fails to mollify the bad guys, he is forced to use martial arts to see justice done. 75m. **DIR:** Jerry Thorpe. **CAST:** David Carradine, Keye Luke, Philip Ahn, Keith Carradine, Barry Sullivan. **1971**

KUNG FU—THE MOVIE ★★ David Carradine returns to his decade-old hit TV series, as Kwai Chang Caine, a fugitive Buddhist monk. Caine is still on the run from Chinese assassins. Brandon Lee also stars as his son under the spell of an evil sorcerer to kill his father. (Carradine's role as Caine in the TV series was originally offered to Bruce Lee, Brandon Lee's father.) 92m. **DIR:** Richard Lang. **CAST:** David Carradine, Brandon Lee, Kerrie Keane, Mako, Bill Lucking, Luke Askew, Keye Luke, Benson Fong. **1986**

L.A. BOUNTY ★★ Wings Hauser was born to play wigged-out pyschos, and he's a standout in this otherwise pedestrian cop thriller. Rated R for violence and profanity. 85m. **DIR:** Worth Keller. **CAST:** Wings Hauser, Sybil Danning, Henry Darrow. **1989**

L.A. CRACKDOWN ★★ An undercover cop (Pamela Dixon) battles crack dealers and blows away bad guys by the dozen. Made-for-video cheapie that is more concerned with showing sexy women than their problems. The sequel followed so fast, it was probably made at the same time. Unrated; nudity, violence. 84m. **DIR:** Joseph Merhi. **CAST:** Pamela Dixon, Tricia Parks. **1988**

L.A. CRACKDOWN II ★★ More of the same, with Pamela Dixon and her new partner stalking a serial killer with a penchant for bar girls. Unrated; nudity, strong violence. 87m. **DIR:** Joseph Merhi. **CAST:** Pamela Dixon, Anthony Gates. **1988**

L.A. VICE ★★ Detective Jon Chance quits the L.A.P.D. when an old friend is killed, but comes back to solve the case. Sequel to *L.A. Heat* is an improvement, but still not particularly memorable. Unrated, but an R equivalent for violence, profanity, and sexual situations. 83m. **DIR:** Joseph Merhi. **CAST:** Lawrence Hilton-Jacobs, William Smith, Jean Levine, Jastereo Covaire, R. W. Munchkin. **1989**

LADIES CLUB ★★ A policewoman and a female doctor organize a support group to help rape victims deal with their feelings of rage and disgust. The club of the title soon turns into a vigilante group with the women punishing repeat offenders. Rated R for violence and gore. 86m. **DIR:** A. K. Allen. **CAST:** Karen Austin, Diana Scarwid, Christine Belford, Beverly Todd. **1987**

LADY AVENGER ★★ Tough Peggie Sanders busts out of prison to get even with her brother's murderers. Forgettable made-for-video cheap thrills. Rated R for sexual situations, profanity, and violence. 82m. **DIR:** David DeCoteau. **CAST:** Peggie Sanders, Tony Josephs, Jacolyn Leeman, Michelle Bauer, Daniel Hirsch. **1989**

LADY DRAGON ★★ Weak kickboxing effort succeeds only due to presence of star Cynthia Rothrock. She's a bundle of dynamite playing a former government agent, who is ambushed and left for dead while trying to avenge her husband's death. She's saved by a martial-arts expert who nurses her back to health and then retrains her to finish the job. Rated R for violence, nudity, and strong language. 90m. **DIR:** David Worth. **CAST:** Cynthia Rothrock, Richard Norton. **1992**

LADY DRAGON 2 ★★ The stakes are higher, but it's still pretty much the same old thing. This time kickboxing champ Cynthia Rothrock sets out to recover $25 million in diamonds from bad guy Billy Drago. Fans will get a kick out of this workable sequel. Rated R for violence, strong language, and adult situations. 95m. **DIR:** David Worth. **CAST:** Cynthia Rothrock, Billy Drago, Sam Jones. **1993**

LADY IN RED ★★★½ A splendid screenplay by John Sayles energizes this telling of the Dillinger story from the distaff side, with Pamela Sue Martin as the gangster's moll enduring the results of a life of crime. Director Lewis Teague keeps things moving right along. Rated R for profanity, nudity, and violence. 93m. **DIR:** Lewis Teague. **CAST:** Pamela Sue Martin, Robert Conrad, Robert Forster, Louise Fletcher, Robert Hogan. **1979**

LADY KILLER ★★★½ The stars of the smash-hit *Public Enemy*, James Cagney and Mae Clarke, were reunited for this less-popular gangster film. Watching Cagney go from theatre usher to hotshot hood to movie star is a real hoot. B&W; 74m. **DIR:** Roy Del Ruth. **CAST:** James Cagney, Mae Clarke, Margaret Lindsay, Henry O'Neill, Raymond Hatton, Russell Hopton, Douglass Dumbrille. **1933**

LADY MOBSTER 🦃 Susan Lucci wallows in excess as a woman hell bent on revenge when her parents are murdered by the mob, in this made-for-cable film. 94m. **DIR:** John Llewellyn Moxey. **CAST:** Susan Lucci, Michael Nader, Roscoe Born, Thomas Bray. **1988**

LADY OF BURLESQUE ★★★ Slick and amusing adaptation of Gypsy Rose Lee's clever mystery novel of top bananas, blackouts, and strippers, *The G-String Murder*. Interesting look into an aspect of show business that now exists only in fading memories. B&W; 91m. **DIR:** William Wellman. **CAST:** Barbara Stanwyck, Michael O'Shea, J. Edward Bromberg, Iris Adrian, Pinky Lee. **1943**

LADY SCARFACE ★★½ Role reversal is the order of the day for this story of a hardened dame who spits lead and asks questions later, ruling her gang with a velvet glove and leading the police and authorities on a grim chase. Atmospheric but pretentious, this isn't as good as it could have been despite the presence of classy Judith Anderson. B&W; 66m. **DIR:** Frank Woodruff. **CAST:** Judith Anderson, Dennis O'Keefe, Frances Neal, Eric Blore, Marc Lawrence. **1941**

LADY TERMINATOR ★★ Enjoyably bad blood 'n' sex saga. An American anthropology student in the South Seas is possessed by the vengeful spirit of a long-dead queen. Rated R for strong violence and nudity. 83m. **DIR:** Jalil Jackson. **CAST:** Barbara Anne Constable, Christopher J. Hart. **1989**

LADYHAWKE ★★★½ In this 700-year-old legend of love and honor, Rutger Hauer and Michelle Pfeiffer are lovers separated by an evil curse. Hauer, a valiant knight, is aided by a wisecracking thief, Matthew Broderick, in his quest to break the spell by destroying its creator. This is a lush and lavish fantasy that will please the young and the young at heart. Rated PG-13 for violence. 124m. **DIR:** Richard Donner. **CAST:** Matthew Broderick, Rutger Hauer, Michelle Pfeiffer, Leo McKern, John Wood. **1985**

LAS VEGAS LADY 🦃 Lame plot about a big money heist. 87m. **DIR:** Noel Nosseck. **CAST:** Stella Stevens, Stuart Whitman, George DiCenzo, Lynne Moody, Linda Scruggs. **1976**

LASER MISSION ★★ The largest and most precious diamond in the world has been stolen. Ernest Borgnine is a professor with the know-how to turn that power into a destructive laser. Enter Bruce Lee's son Brandon, who saves the world from total destruction without once breaking into sweat. Rated R for violence. 90m. **DIR:** Beau Davis. **CAST:** Brandon Lee, Ernest Borgnine. **1990**

LASSITER ★★★ Tom Selleck stars as yet another jewel thief in the 1930s who attempts to steal a cache of uncut diamonds from the Nazis. Good-but-not-great entertainment. Rated R for nudity, suggested sex, violence, and profanity. 100m. **DIR:** Roger Young. **CAST:** Tom Selleck, Jane Seymour, Lauren Hutton, Bob Hoskins. **1984**

LAST AMERICAN HERO, THE ★★★★ An entertaining action film about the famous whiskey runner from North Carolina who becomes a legend when he proves himself a great stock-car driver. Jeff Bridges's portrait of the rebel Johnson is engaging, but Art Lund steals the show as Johnson's bootlegger father. Rated PG for profanity and sex. 95m. **DIR:** Lamont Johnson. **CAST:** Jeff Bridges, Valerie Perrine, Geraldine Fitzgerald, Ned Beatty, Gary Busey, Art Lund, Ed Lauter, William Smith. **1973**

LAST BOY SCOUT, THE ★★★★ A private detective must team up with an ex-football star to catch the killer of a topless dancer. Bruce Willis bounced back nicely from the *Hudson Hawk* debacle with this rip-roaring action movie in the style of the *Die Hard* films. Rated R for violence, profanity, nudity, and suggested sex. 105m. **DIR:** Tony Scott. **CAST:** Bruce Willis, Damon Wayans, Chelsea Field, Noble Willingham, Taylor Negron, Bruce McGill. **1991**

LAST CONTRACT, THE ★★ In this violent film, Jack Palance stars as an artist and a hit man who is hired to kill his best friend. Unable to do it, he is ordered to assassinate a rival crime lord. When he kills the wrong man, the deadly game of hit and counterhit gets out of hand. Rated R. 85m. **DIR:** Allan A. Buckhantz. **CAST:** Jack Palance, Rod Steiger, Bo Svenson, Richard Roundtree, Ann Turkel. **1986**

LAST DAYS OF POMPEII (1960) ★★ A different scenario than the 1935 original. Steve Reeves plays a hero in the Roman army stationed in Greece who tries to save a group of Christians that has been jailed and condemned to death. The story is interesting, but the action scenes are rather dumb. 93m. **DIR:** Mario Bonnard. **CAST:** Steve Reeves, Fernando Rey, Christine Kaufmann, Barbara Carroll, Angel Aranda. **1960**

LAST DRAGON, THE ★★★½ Produced by Motown Records man Berry Gordy, this is lively, unpretentious nonsense about a shy karate champ (Taimak) fending off villains threatening a disc jockey (Vanity). Good, silly fun. Rated PG-13 for violence. 109m. **DIR:** Michael Schultz. **CAST:** Taimak, Vanity, Christopher Murney. **1985**

LAST FLIGHT TO HELL 🦃 Mundane chase flick has hunky Reb Brown tracking down a group of terrorists who have kidnapped a South American drug lord. Why? 84m. **DIR:** Paul D. Robinson. **CAST:** Reb Brown, Chuck Connors. **1991**

LAST HOUR, THE ★★ A cop tries to rescue his ex-wife from mobsters. Low-budget rip-off of *Die Hard*. Rated R for violence, profanity, nudity, and simulated sex. 85m. **DIR:** William Sachs. **CAST:** Michael Paré, Shannon Tweed, Bobby DiCicco. **1991**

LAST OF THE FINEST, THE ★★ Four Los Angeles undercover cops (led by burly Brian Dennehy) are temporarily suspended. When one member of this elite squad gets murdered, the other three seek revenge. This standard shoot-'em-up is rated R for language and violence. 106m. **DIR:** John Mackenzie. **CAST:** Brian Dennehy, Joe Pantoliano, Jeff Fahey, Bill Paxton, Michael C. Gwynne, Henry Darrow. **1990**

LAST OF THE MOHICANS, THE (1920) ★★★½ The most faithful version of James Fenimore Cooper's story with some surprisingly strong dramatic moments. Almost none of this was shot in a studio, and the location filming is still impressive, now that the film has been restored by the Eastman House. Silent. B&W; 72m. **DIR:** Clarence Brown, Maurice Tourneur. **CAST:** Wallace Beery, Barbara Bedford, Albert Roscoe. **1920**

LAST PLANE OUT 🦃 Poor rip-off of *Under Fire*. 98m. **DIR:** David Nelson. **CAST:** Jan-Michael Vincent, Lloyd Batista, Julie Carmen. **1983**

LAST RIDERS, THE 🦃 The Slavers motorcycle club rides after one of its own in this ridiculous vehicle. Rated R for profanity and violence. 89m. **DIR:** Joseph Merhi. **CAST:** Erik Estrada, William Smith. **1990**

LAST RITES ★★ A young Italian priest (Tom Berenger) runs afoul of the Mafia when he grants sanctuary to a woman (Daphne Zuniga) who has witnessed a murder. Interesting but the story turns silly when priest and witness fall in love. Rated R for violence, nudity, and profanity. 103m. **DIR:** Donald P. Bellisario. **CAST:** Tom Berenger, Daphne Zuniga, Paul Dooley. **1988**

LAST SEASON, THE 🦃 A bunch of redneck hunters invades a peaceful forest. Not rated; contains nudity and violence. 90m. **DIR:** Raja Zahr. **CAST:** Christopher Gosch, Louise Dorsey, David Cox. **1987**

LAST VALLEY, THE ★★★ Impressive and thought-provoking adventure epic about a warrior (Michael Caine) who brings his soldiers to a peaceful valley that, in the seventeenth century, has remained untouched by the Thirty Years War. Rated R. 128m. **DIR:** James Clavell. **CAST:** Michael Caine, Omar Sharif. **1971**

LAST VOYAGE, THE ★★★★ Director Andrew L. Stone has taken a fairly suspenseful disaster-at-sea tale, making it a completely absorbing and fascinating movie. Filmed aboard the famous luxury liner, *Ile de France*, before it was scrapped. 91m. **DIR:** Andrew L. Stone. **CAST:** Robert Stack, Dorothy Malone, George Sanders, Edmond O'Brien, Woody Strode. **1960**

LAST WARRIOR, THE ★★★★ Two Marines, one American, the other Japanese, are left on an island in the closing days of World War II. What ensues is a tightly directed, action-packed fight to the death. Rated R for violence and brief nudity. 94m. **DIR:** Martin Wragge. **CAST:** Gary Graham. **1989**

LAWRENCE OF ARABIA ★★★★★ Director David Lean brings us an expansive screen biography of T. E. Lawrence, the complex English leader of the Arab revolt against Turkey in World War I. This is a tremendous accomplishment in every respect. Peter O'Toole is stunning in his first major film role as Lawrence. A definite thinking person's spectacle. 222m. **DIR:** David Lean. **CAST:** Peter O'Toole, Alec Guinness, Anthony Quinn, Arthur Kennedy, Omar Sharif. **1962**

LAWS OF GRAVITY 🦃 With no redeeming social value, this silly, violence-packed film focuses on two ruthless thieves and their low-life friends. Belongs in filmdom's hall of shame. Rated R for violence and profanity. 93m. **DIR:** Nick Gomez. **CAST:** Adam Trese, Peter Greene, Edie Falco, Arabella Field. **1992**

LEATHER JACKETS ★★ A one-dimensional blue-collar vehicle for leading man Cary Elwes. Rated R for violence, profanity, nudity, and some strongly suggestive sex scenes involving former porn queen Ginger Lynn Allen. 90m. **DIR:** Lee Drysdale. **CAST:** Bridget Fonda, Cary Elwes, D. B. Sweeney, Ginger Lynn Allen. **1992**

LEFT HAND OF GOD, THE ★★★½ Humphrey Bogart is an American forced to pose as a priest while on the run from a renegade Chinese warlord (Lee J. Cobb). It's not the fastest-moving adventure story, but Bogart and Cobb are quite good, and Gene Tierney is an effective heroine. The result is worthy entertainment. 87m. **DIR:** Edward Dmytryk. **CAST:** Humphrey Bogart, Lee J. Cobb, Gene Tierney, Agnes Moorehead. **1955**

LEGAL TENDER ★★ A former cop helps a barmaid discover why people close to her are being eliminated. Even fans of action pictures may wince at the familiar plot devices. Rated R for considerable nudity and profanity. 93m. **DIR:** Jag Mundhra. **CAST:** Robert Davi, Tanya Roberts, Morton Downey Jr. **1990**

LEGEND OF BILLIE JEAN, THE 🦃 A girl from Texas (Helen Slater) becomes an outlaw. Rated PG-13 for language and violence. 92m. **DIR:** Matthew Robbins. **CAST:** Helen Slater, Keith Gordon, Christian Slater, Peter Coyote. **1985**

LEGEND OF THE WHITE HORSE 🦃 The two directors make it obvious: there seems to be two separate films on one tape. Part focuses on a witch and a transforming horse while the rest makes an environmental statement about an exploitative company. Unrated Polish film contains violence. 91m. **DIR:** Jerzy Domaradzki, Janusz Morgenstern. **CAST:** Dee Wallace, Christopher Lloyd, Christopher Stone, Soon-Teck Oh, Luke Askew. **1985**

LEPKE ★★★ Tony Curtis gives an effective performance in the lead role of this gangster drama. He's the head of Murder Inc. The story sticks close to the facts. It's no classic, but watchable. Rated R. 110m. **DIR:** Menahem Golan. **CAST:** Tony Curtis, Anjanette Comer, Michael Callan, Warren Berlinger, Milton Berle, Vic Tayback. **1975**

LETHAL GAMES 🦃 Citizens of a small town band together to fight off the mob. They turn to ex-Vietnam vet Frank Stallone for assistance. Yeah, right! 83m. **DIR:** John Bowen. **CAST:** Frank Stallone, Brenda Vaccaro. **1991**

LETHAL NINJA ★★ Ex-CIA agent journeys to Africa to rescue his wife from evil Ninjas in the employ of a Nostradamus-inspired fanatic out to poison the world's water supply. (Yes, *that* old story again!) For kickboxing fans only. Rated R for strong violence. 83m. **DIR:** Yossi Wein. **CAST:** Ross Kettle, Karyn Hill, Frank Notaro. **1993**

LETHAL OBSESSION 🦃 Contrived suspense yarn about drugs and murder. Rated R; contains nudity, profanity, and violence. 100m. **DIR:** Peter Patzack. **CAST:** Tahnee Welch, Elliott Gould, Michael York, Peter Maffay. **1987**

LETHAL WEAPON ★★★★ This fast, frantic, and wholly improbable police thriller owes its success to the chemistry between the two leads. Mel Gibson is fine as the cop on the edge (the weapon of the title). Danny Glover is equally good as his laid-back, methodical partner. Rated R for violence. 105m. **DIR:** Richard Donner. **CAST:** Mel Gibson, Danny Glover, Gary Busey, Mitchell Ryan, Tom Atkins, Darlene Love. **1987**

LETHAL WEAPON 2 ★★★½ Mel Gibson and Danny Glover return as odd-couple police officers Riggs and Murtaugh in this enjoyable action sequel. This time, our mismatched heroes are up against some bad guys from South Africa. Predictable but fun. Rated R for violence, profanity, nudity, and simulated sex. 110m. **DIR:** Richard Donner. **CAST:** Mel Gibson, Danny Glover, Joe Pesci, Joss Ackland, Patsy Kensit. **1989**

LETHAL WEAPON 3 ★★★½ More madness and mayhem from the lethal team of Mel Gibson and Danny Glover as they, with the help of comic relief Joe Pesci, go after a renegade cop who is selling formerly confiscated weapons to L.A. street gangs. It's almost too much of a good thing, as director Richard Donner and his collaborators pack the movie with every gag, shoot-out, and chase they can come up with. Rated R for violence and profanity. 117m. **DIR:** Richard Donner. **CAST:** Mel Gibson, Danny Glover, Joe Pesci, René Russo, Stuart Wilson, Darlene Love. **1992**

LETHAL WOMAN ★★ A rape victim takes revenge by luring all involved to her island and killing them. Unrated but contains nudity, violence, and gore. 96m. **DIR:** Christian Marnham. **CAST:** Robert Lipton, Merete VanKamp, Shannon Tweed. **1989**

LIBERTY AND BASH ★★ *Tarzan*-star Miles O'Keeffe and *Hercules/Hulk* Lou Ferrigno are featured in this typically on-par action flick about two war buddies out to stop murderous Miami drug runners. Rated R for language. 92m. **DIR:** Myrl A. Schreibman. **CAST:** Miles O'Keeffe, Lou Ferrigno. **1989**

LICENSE TO KILL ★★★★ Timothy Dalton, in his second outing as James Bond, seeks revenge when his pal, former CIA-agent-turned-DEA-man Felix Leiter, is maimed and Leiter's bride is murdered. Uncommonly serious tone is a boost to the once-formulaic series, and Dalton comes into his own as the modern 007. Rated PG-13. 135m. **DIR:** John Glen. **CAST:** Timothy Dalton, Robert Davi, Carey Lowell. **1989**

LIFETAKER, THE 🦃 A boring sex thriller about a housewife who entices a young man into her home. Not rated, but contains violence and sexual scenes. 97m. **DIR:** Michael Papas. **CAST:** Terence Morgan. **1989**

LIGHT AT THE END OF THE WORLD, THE 🦃 Kirk Douglas is a lighthouse keeper whose isolated island is invaded by ruthless pirates. Tedious. Not rated, contains violence and sexual suggestions. 126m. **DIR:** Kevin Billington. **CAST:** Kirk Douglas, Yul Brynner, Samantha Eggar, Jean-Claude Druout, Fernando Rey. **1971**

LIGHTHORSEMEN, THE ★★★½ Vivid dramatization of the encounter between the Australian and Turkish forces at Beersheba in the North African desert during World War I. Film's main focus is on a young recruit who cannot bring himself to kill in battle. Beautiful cinematography and fine performances by the entire cast make this one a winner. Rated PG. 110m. **DIR:** Simon Wincer. **CAST:** Jon Blake, Peter Phelps, Tony Bonner, Bill Kerr, John Walton, Sigrid Thornton. **1988**

LION AND THE HAWK, THE ★★★ Turkey in 1923 is the backdrop for this film about a young rebel (Simon Dutton) who runs off with a woman betrothed to a powerful regional governor's nephew. Not rated; has sex, nudity, and violence. 105m. **DIR:** Peter Ustinov. **CAST:** Peter Ustinov, Herbert Lom, Simon Dutton, Leonie Mellinger, Denis Quilley, Michael Elphick. **1983**

LION OF AFRICA, THE ★★ This HBO action film is long-winded and a tad too derivative of *Romancing the Stone*. Odd couple Brian Dennehy and Brooke Adams race across Africa with a hot rock that attracts a host of bad guys. Not rated, has violence and profanity. 110m. **DIR:** Kevin Connor. **CAST:** Brian Dennehy, Brooke Adams, Don Warrington, Carl Andrews, Katharine Schofield. **1987**

LION OF THE DESERT ★★★½ This epic motion picture gives an absorbing portrait of the 1929–31 war in the North African deserts of Libya when Bedouin troops on horseback faced the tanks and mechanized armies of Mussolini. Anthony Quinn is Omar Mukhtar, the desert lion who became a nationalist and a warrior at the age of 52 and fought the Italians until they captured and hanged him twenty years later. Rated PG. 162m. **DIR:** Moustapha Akkad. **CAST:** Anthony Quinn, Oliver Reed, Rod Steiger. **1981**

LISBON ★★ Maureen O'Hara's husband is in a communist prison. International gentleman thief Claude Rains hires Ray Milland to rescue him. Not James Bond caliber. Not *To Catch a Thief* classy. Not really worth much. 90m. **DIR:** Ray Milland. **CAST:** Ray Milland, Claude Rains, Maureen O'Hara, Francis Lederer, Percy Marmont. **1956**

LITTLE CAESAR ★★★ Historically, this is an important film. Made in 1930, it started the whole genre of gangster films. As entertainment, this veiled biography of Al Capone is terribly dated. Edward G. Robinson's performance is like a Warner Bros. cartoon in places, but one has to remember this is the original. B&W; 80m. **DIR:** Mervyn LeRoy. **CAST:** Edward G. Robinson, Douglas Fairbanks Jr. **1930**

LITTLE LAURA AND BIG JOHN 🦃 *Little Laura and Big John* is about the Ashley Gang, a bunch of losers who can put you to sleep by just saying "Stick 'em up." Rated R for violence, nudity, and profanity. 82m. **DIR:** Luke Moberly, Bob Woodburn. **CAST:** Karen Black, Fabian, Ivy Thayer, Ken Miller. **1972**

LITTLE TREASURE ★★★ While the synopsis on the back of the box may give one the impression this release is a rip-off of *Romancing the Stone*, only the rough outline of the story is lifted from the 1984 hit. The Margot Kidder/Ted Danson team is not a copy of the Kathleen Turner/Michael Douglas couple; these characters are more down-home. And the concentration on domestic drama almost fills the gap left by the absence of action. Rated R for nudity and language.

95m. **DIR:** Alan Sharp. **CAST:** Margot Kidder, Ted Danson, Burt Lancaster. **1985**

LIVE AND LET DIE ★★ The first Roger Moore (as James Bond) adventure is a hodgepodge of the surrealistic and the slick that doesn't quite live up to its Connery-powered predecessors. The chase-and-suspense formula wears thin. Rated PG. 121m. **DIR:** Guy Hamilton. **CAST:** Roger Moore, Jane Seymour, Yaphet Kotto, Geoffrey Holder. **1973**

LIVE BY THE FIST 🦃 Boring choreography and an annoying, trite script drop-kick this martial-arts fistfest right into the turkey pile. Rated R for violence. 77m. **DIR:** Cirio H. Santiago. **CAST:** Jerry Trimble, George Takei. **1993**

LIVE WIRE ★★★ A bomb kills a senator, but no traces of an explosive can be found. An FBI agent (Pierce Brosnan) must find the cause of the explosion while fighting his own inner battles. Very good acting by Brosnan and Ron Silver, who plays a corrupt senator, but the plot is predictable. Rated R for violence, profanity, and nudity. 85m. **DIR:** Christian Duguay. **CAST:** Pierce Brosnan, Ron Silver, Ben Cross, Lisa Eilbacher, Brent Jennings, Tony Plana, Al Waxman. **1992**

LIVES OF A BENGAL LANCER, THE ★★★★½ One of the great adventure films, this action-packed epic stars Gary Cooper and Franchot Tone as fearless friends in the famed British regiment. Their lives become complicated when they take the commander's son (Richard Cromwell) under their wings and he turns out to be less than a model soldier. B&W; 109m. **DIR:** Henry Hathaway. **CAST:** Gary Cooper, Franchot Tone, Richard Cromwell, Guy Standing, C. Aubrey Smith, Monte Blue, Kathleen Burke. **1935**

LIVING DAYLIGHTS, THE ★★★½ Timothy Dalton adds a dimension of humanity to Ian Fleming's famous creation in his screen bow as the ultimate spy hero. The silly set pieces and gimmicks that marred even the best Roger Moore entries in the series are gone. Instead, the filmmakers have opted for a strong plot about a phony KGB defector (Jeroen Krabbé) and a renegade arms dealer (Joe Don Baker). Rated PG. 130m. **DIR:** John Glen. **CAST:** Timothy Dalton, Maryam D'Abo, Jeroen Krabbé, Joe Don Baker, John Rhys-Davies, Art Malik, Desmond Llewellyn. **1987**

LOADED GUNS 🦃 Thoroughly stupid espionage flick from Italy. Not rated. 90m. **DIR:** Fernando Di Leo. **CAST:** Ursula Andress, Woody Strode, Isabella Biagin. **1975**

LOCK UP ★★★½ Sylvester Stallone gives one of his best performances in this melodramatic prison drama, which is reminiscent of similarly themed Warner Bros. movies of the Thirties and Forties. Stallone is a model prisoner who, just before he is about to be released, finds himself transferred to a high-security facility run by an old enemy (Donald Sutherland) who wants to see him dead. Rated R for profanity, violence, and suggested sex. 106m. **DIR:** John Flynn. **CAST:** Sylvester Stallone, Donald Sutherland, John Amos, Darlanne Fluegel. **1989**

LONE DEFENDER, THE ★★ Two prospectors are ambushed and one of them, Rin Tin Tin's master, is murdered. For the next twelve installments of this early sound serial, Rinty chases and is chased by the Cactus Kid and his low-down thievin' gang. B&W; 12 chapters. **DIR:** Richard Thorpe. **CAST:** Rin Tin Tin, Walter Miller. **1930**

LONE RUNNER 🦃 Our hero runs around a desert with a Rambo crossbow (complete with exploding arrows). Rated PG for violence and profanity. 84m. **DIR:** Ruggero Deodato. **CAST:** Miles O'Keeffe, Savina Gersak, Donal Hodson, Ronald Lacey. **1986**

LONE WOLF MCQUADE ★★★½ Chuck Norris plays a Texas Ranger who forgets the rules in his zeal to punish the bad guys. Norris meets his match in David Carradine, the leader of a gun-smuggling ring. The worth-waiting-for climax is a martial arts battle between the two. Rated PG for violence and profanity. 107m. **DIR:** Steve Carver. **CAST:** Chuck Norris, L. Q. Jones, R. G. Armstrong, David Carradine, Barbara Carrera. **1983**

LONG GOOD FRIDAY, THE ★★★★★ This superb British film depicts the struggle of an underworld boss (Bob Hoskins, in a brilliant performance) to hold on to his territory. It's a classic in the genre on a par with *The Godfather*, *The Public Enemy*, and *High Sierra*. Rated R for nudity, profanity, and violence. 114m. **DIR:** John Mackenzie. **CAST:** Bob Hoskins, Helen Mirren, Pierce Brosnan. **1980**

LONG JOHN SILVER ★★★ Avast me hearties, Robert Newton is at his scene-chewing best in this otherwise unexceptional (and unofficial) sequel to Disney's *Treasure Island*. 109m. **DIR:** Byron Haskin. **CAST:** Robert Newton, Connie Gilchrist, Kit Taylor, Grant Taylor. **1954**

LONGEST DAY, THE ★★★★★ A magnificent re-creation of the Allied invasion of Normandy in June of 1944 with an all-star cast, this epic war film succeeds where others may fail—*Midway* and *Tora! Tora! Tora!*, for example. A big-budget film that shows you where the money was spent, it's first-rate in all respects. B&W; 180m. **DIR:** Ken Annakin, Andrew Marton, Bernhard Wicki. **CAST:** John Wayne, Robert Mitchum, Henry Fonda, Richard Burton, Rod Steiger, Sean Connery, Robert Wagner. **1963**

LONGEST YARD, THE ★★★★ An ex-professional football quarterback (Burt Reynolds) is sent to a Florida prison for stealing his girlfriend's car. The warden (Eddie Albert) forces Reynolds to put together a prisoner team to play his semipro team made up of guards. Great audience participation film with the last third dedicated to the game. Rated R for language and violence. 123m. **DIR:** Robert Aldrich. **CAST:** Burt Reynolds, Eddie Albert, Michael Conrad, Bernadette Peters, Ed Lauter. **1974**

LORD JIM ★★★★ Joseph Conrad's complex novel of human weakness has been simplified for easier appreciation and brought to the screen in a lavish visual style. Peter O'Toole is Jim, a sailor in Southeast Asia who is adopted by a suppressed village as its leader in spite of a past clouded by allegations of cowardice. The belief shown in him by the native villagers is put to the test by a group of European thugs. 154m. **DIR:** Richard Brooks. **CAST:** Peter O'Toole, James Mason, Eli Wallach. **1965**

LOSERS, THE 🦃 Imagine *Rambo* made as a biker film and you'll have *The Losers*. Rated R for violence and nudity. 95m. **DIR:** Jack Starrett. **CAST:** William Smith, Bernie Hamilton, Adam Roarke. **1970**

LOST CITY OF THE JUNGLE ★★ Sir Eric Hazarias (Lionel Atwill) wants to rule the world and he thinks he's discovered the way with Meteorium 245, the only defense against the atomic bomb. The only outstanding thing about this minor chapterplay is the presence of Atwill in his last screen role. B&W; 13 chapters. **DIR:** Ray Taylor, Lewis D. Collins. **CAST:** Russell Hayden, Lionel Atwill, Jane Adams, Keye Luke, Helen Bennett, Ted Hecht, John Eldredge, John Miljan, Ralph Lewis. **1946**

LOST COMMAND ★★★ A good international cast and fine direction bring to vivid life this story of French-Algerian guerrilla warfare in North Africa following World War II. Anthony Quinn is especially effective. Great action scenes. 130m. **DIR:** Mark Robson. **CAST:** Anthony Quinn, Alain Delon, George Segal, Michele Morgan, Claudia Cardinale. **1966**

LOST EMPIRE, THE 🦃 Inept, hokey film about the island stronghold of a mysterious ruler. Rated R for some nudity and violence. 86m. **DIR:** Jim Wynorski. **CAST:** Melanie Vincz, Raven De La Croix, Angela Aames, Paul Coufos, Robert Tessier. **1983**

LOST JUNGLE, THE ★★ Clyde Beatty's first serial for Mascot Studios. Our hero's girlfriend and her father are lost on an uncharted jungle island during an expedition and Beatty joins the rescue team. This would be pretty standard fare except for some spectacular animal stunts performed by the inimitable Beatty, one of the finest daredevil peformers of all time. B&W; 12 chapters. **DIR:** Armand Schaefer, David Howard. **CAST:** Clyde Beatty, Cecilia Parker, Syd Saylor, Warner Richmond, Wheeler Oakman, Mickey Rooney. **1934**

LOST PATROL, THE ★★★★ An intrepid band of British cavalrymen lost in the Mesopotamian desert are picked off by the Arabs, one by one. Brisk direction and top-notch characterizations make this a winner—though it is grim. B&W; 65m. **DIR:** John Ford. **CAST:** Victor McLaglen, Boris Karloff, Wallace Ford, Reginald Denny, Alan Hale Sr., J. M. Kerrigan, Billy Bevan. **1934**

LOST SQUADRON ★★★ Mystery-adventure about the "accidental" deaths of former World War I pilots engaged as stunt fliers for the movies. Full of industry "in-jokes," breezy dialogue, and good stunts, this is a fun film—especially for anyone with an interest in stunt flying or aviation in general. B&W; 79m. **DIR:** George Archainbaud. **CAST:** Richard Dix, Mary Astor, Erich Von Stroheim, Joel McCrea, Dorothy Jordan, Robert Armstrong. **1932**

LOST WORLD, THE (1992) ★★ Lackluster adaptation of Sir Arthur Conan Doyle's fanciful tale of a lost land where dinosaurs still roam. The film's low budget betrays its aspirations, making this period piece seem cheap and undermined. A group led by Professor Challenger (John Rhys-Davies) and zoological expert David Warner encounters cave men, the elements, and unconvincing dinosaurs. Not rated, but contains some violence. 99m. **DIR:** Timothy Bond. **CAST:** David Warner, John Rhys-Davies, Eric McCormack, Tamara Gorski. **1992**

LOVE AND BULLETS 🦃 Bronson is hired to snatch Jill Ireland from crime lord Rod Steiger. Rated PG for violence. 103m. **DIR:** Stuart Rosenberg. **CAST:** Charles Bronson, Rod Steiger, Strother Martin, Bradford Dillman, Henry Silva, Jill Ireland. **1979**

LOVE SPELL 🦃 A dud based on the legend of Tristan and Isolde and their doomed love. 90m. **DIR:** Tom Donavan. **CAST:** Richard Burton, Kate Mulgrew, Nicholas Clay, Cyril Cusack. **1979**

LOW BLOW 🦃 A private investigator tries to rescue a millionaire's daughter from a religious cult. Rated R for violence and profanity. 85m. **DIR:** Frank Harris. **CAST:** Leo Fong, Cameron Mitchell, Troy Donahue, Akosua Busia, Stack Pierce. **1986**

LUCKY LUCIANO ★★ The last years of one of crime land's most "influential" bosses. The film started out to be an important one for Francesco Rosi, but the distributors of the English edition went in for the sensationalism with too graphic subtitles and/or dubbing, depending on the version. Not a bad film if you know Italian. If you don't, stick with *The Godfather*. Rated R for profanity and violence. 110m. **DIR:** Francesco Rosi. **CAST:** Gian Maria Volonté, Rod Steiger, Edmond O'Brien, Vincent Gardenia, Charles Cioffi. **1974**

LUST FOR FREEDOM 🦃 Woman unjustly sentenced for a crime she didn't commit finds herself fighting for her life and loins in a brutal prison. Unrated, but contains graphic violence and nudity. 92m. **DIR:** Eric Louzil. **CAST:** Melanie Coll. **1991**

MA BARKER'S KILLER BROOD ★★ Sweet, grandmotherly Lurene Tuttle, delivering an absolutely ferocious, chop-licking portrayal of Ma Barker, lends fleeting interest to this otherwise overlong gangster cheapie. B&W; 82m. **DIR:** Bill Karn. **CAST:** Lurene Tuttle, Tristram Coffin, Paul Dubov. **1960**

MACAO ★★ Jane Russell is a singer in the fabled Oriental port and gambling heaven of Macao, across the bay from Hong Kong. She's in love with Robert Mitchum, a good guy caught in a web of circumstance. Russell is the only thing about this film that isn't flat. B&W; 80m. **DIR:** Josef von Sternberg. **CAST:** Jane Russell, Robert Mitchum, William Bendix, Gloria Grahame, Thomas Gomez. **1952**

MACHINE-GUN KELLY ★★½ Grade-B bio-pic about the famed Depression-era hoodlum, with an excellent performance by Charles Bronson in the title role and an intelligent script by R. Wright Campbell. One of Roger Corman's best early features. B&W; 84m. **DIR:** Roger Corman. **CAST:** Charles Bronson, Susan Cabot, Morey Amsterdam. **1958**

MACON COUNTY LINE ★★★ A very effective little thriller based on a true incident. Set in Georgia in the 1950s, the story concerns three youths hunted by the law for a murder they did not commit. Producer Max Baer Jr. has a good eye for detail and the flavor of the times. Rated R. 89m. **DIR:** Richard Compton. **CAST:** Alan Vint, Max Baer Jr., Geoffrey Lewis. **1974**

MAD DOG MORGAN ★★½ Dennis Hopper plays an Australian bush ranger in this familiar tale of a man forced into a life of crime. Good support from aborigine David Gulpilil and Australian actor Jack Thompson help this visually stimulating film, but Hopper's excesses and a muddled ending weigh against it. Early prison sequences and scattered scenes are brutal. Rated R. 102m. **DIR:** Philippe Mora. **CAST:** Dennis Hopper, Jack Thompson, David Gulpilil, Michael Pate. **1976**

MADAME SIN ★★★ Undistinguished film in which Bette Davis plays a female Fu Manchu opposite Robert Wagner's sophisticated hero. Written expressly for the actress, it was the most expensive made-for-TV movie of its time and won high ratings. 73m. **DIR:** David Greene. **CAST:** Robert Wagner, Bette Davis, Roy Kinnear, Paul Maxwell, Denholm Elliott, Gordon Jackson. **1971**

MADIGAN ★★★½ Well-acted, atmospheric police adventure-drama pits tough Brooklyn cop Richard Widmark and New York's finest against a crazed escaped murderer. Realistic and exciting, this is still one of the best of the "behind-the-scenes" police films. 101m. **DIR:** Don Siegel. **CAST:** Richard Widmark, Henry Fonda, Harry Guardino, James Whitmore, Inger Stevens, Michael Dunn, Steve Ihnat, Sheree North. **1968**

MAGNUM FORCE ★★★ This is the second and least enjoyable of the five Dirty Harry films. Harry (Clint Eastwood) must deal with vigilante cops as well as the usual big-city scum. Clint is iron-jawed and athletic, but the film still lacks something. Rated R for language, violence, nudity, and gore. 124m. **DIR:** Ted Post. **CAST:** Clint Eastwood, Hal Holbrook, David Soul, Tim Matheson, Robert Urich, Suzanne Somers. **1973**

MALONE ★★★½ In this modern-day Western, Burt Reynolds is in top form as Malone, an ex-CIA hit man on the run. Underneath all the car chases, big-bang explosions, and the blitz fire of automatic weapons is the simplest of all B-Western plots—in which a former gunfighter is forced out of retirement by the plight of settlers forced off their land by black-hatted villains. Rated R for profanity, violence, and suggested sex. 92m. **DIR:** Harley Cokliss. **CAST:** Burt Reynolds, Cliff Robertson, Kenneth McMillan, Scott Wilson, Lauren Hutton, Cynthia Gibb. **1987**

MAN CALLED TIGER, A 🦃 Fist-and-foot nonsense about the Chinese Mafia. Rated R for violence and nudity. 70m. **DIR:** Lo Wei. **CAST:** Wang Yu. **1973**

MAN FROM DEEP RIVER 🦃 This shot-on-location Italian exploitation movie ushered in the profitable—and controversial—subgenre of ultraviolent cannibal movies. Sickening. Rated R. 93m. **DIR:** Umberto Lenzi. **CAST:** Ivan Rassimov. **1973**

MAN FROM U.N.C.L.E., THE (TV SERIES) ★★★½ This tongue-in-cheek spy series, one of the mid-Sixties' hottest cult phenomenons, owed more than its tone to the then-fledgling big-screen exploits of James Bond; 007's author, Ian Fleming is credited with naming the central character: Napoleon Solo, suavely rendered by Robert Vaughn. Solo was assisted by Illya Kuryakin (blond-mopped David McCallum, who became a popular teen icon), and both answered to Leo G. Carroll's paternalistic Alexander Waverly, who dispatched his agents on their global, peacekeeping missions. The episodes taken from the show's superior debut season—before light comedic touches gave way to often ludicrous plots—are by far the best. *Star Trek* fans should take note of "The Project Strigas Affair," which includes William Shatner as a down-on-his-luck civilian who helps discredit a Balkan spy and his ham-handed assistant...the latter played by Leonard Nimoy. Each tape contains two hour-length episodes. each. 104m. **DIR:** John

Brahm, Alf Kjellin, Joseph Sargent. **CAST:** Robert Vaughn, David McCallum, Leo G. Carroll. **1964–68**

MAN IN THE IRON MASK, THE (1939) ★★★ Louis Hayward plays twin brothers—a fop and a swashbuckler—in this first sound version of Dumas's classic novel of malice, mayhem, intrigue, and ironic revenge in eighteenth-century France. Separated at birth, one brother becomes the king of France, the other a sword-wielding cohort of the Three Musketeers. Their clash makes for great romantic adventure. B&W; 110m. **DIR:** James Whale. **CAST:** Louis Hayward, Joan Bennett, Warren William, Alan Hale Sr., Joseph Schildkraut. **1939**

MAN IN THE IRON MASK, THE (1977) ★★★ This is the Alexandre Dumas tale of twin brothers, separated at birth. One becomes the wicked king of France, the other, a heroic peasant. The story receives a top-drawer treatment in this classy TV movie. Richard Chamberlain proves he's the most appealing swashbuckler since Errol Flynn retired his sword. 100m. **DIR:** Mike Newell. **CAST:** Richard Chamberlain, Patrick McGoohan, Louis Jourdan, Jenny Agutter, Ralph Richardson. **1977**

MAN INSIDE, THE (1984) ★★½ In this so-so film, James Franciscus is a Canadian vice squad agent who works his way into the organization of a major heroin dealer. In the course of his assignment he has the opportunity to split with $2 million, and is tempted to do so. This Canadian film is unrated. 96m. **DIR:** Gerald Mayer. **CAST:** James Franciscus, Stefanie Powers, Jacques Godin, Len Birman, Donald Davis, Allan Royale. **1984**

MAN ON A STRING ★★½ An undercover government agent tries to break up two mob factions by setting them against each other. Predictable made-for-TV movie. Not rated; contains no objectionable material. 74m. **DIR:** Joseph Sargent. **CAST:** Christopher George, William Schallert, Joel Grey, Keith Carradine, Kitty Winn, Jack Warden, James B. Sikking. **1972**

MAN ON FIRE 🦃 Scott Glenn plays an ex-CIA agent hired to protect the daughter of a wealthy American couple. Glenn is the film's only redemption. Rated R for language and graphic violence. 92m. **DIR:** Elie Chouraqui. **CAST:** Scott Glenn, Brooke Adams, Danny Aiello, Joe Pesci, Jonathan Pryce. **1987**

MAN WHO NEVER WAS, THE ★★★½ British intelligence pulls the wool over Nazi eyes in this intriguing true tale of World War II espionage involving fake invasion plans planted on a corpse dressed as a British officer. 102m. **DIR:** Ronald Neame. **CAST:** Clifton Webb, Gloria Grahame, Robert Flemyng, Stephen Boyd, Laurence Naismith, Michael Hordern. **1955**

MAN WHO WOULD BE KING, THE ★★★★½ A superb screen adventure, this is loosely based on Rudyard Kipling's story and was made at the same time Sean Connery and John Huston starred in the other sand-and-camel flick, the excellent *The Wind and the Lion.* Both are classics in the adventure genre. Rated PG. 129m. **DIR:** John Huston. **CAST:** Sean Connery, Michael Caine, Christopher Plummer. **1975**

MAN WITH THE GOLDEN GUN, THE ★★ In spite of the potentially sinister presence of Christopher Lee as the head baddie, this is the most poorly constructed of all the Bond films. Roger Moore sleepwalks through the entire picture, and the plot tosses in every cliché. Rated PG—some violence. 125m. **DIR:** Guy Hamilton. **CAST:** Roger Moore, Christopher Lee, Britt Ekland, Maud Adams, Herve Villechaize, Bernard Lee, Lois Maxwell. **1974**

MANHATTAN MELODRAMA ★★★★ In MGM's best version of an oft-told story, two boyhood pals (Clark Gable, William Powell) end up on opposite sides of the law as adults but maintain their friendship and friendly competition for the affections of Myrna Loy. The wonderful cast makes it delicious, old-fashioned movie fun. Historical note: this is the movie John Dillinger was watching before he was shot down by the FBI outside the Biograph Theatre in Chicago. B&W; 93m. **DIR:** W. S. Van Dyke. **CAST:** Clark Gable, William Powell, Myrna Loy, Mickey Rooney, Leo Carrillo, Isabel Jewell, Nat Pendleton. **1934**

MANHUNT (1973) ★★ Unbeknownst to him, a small-time Milano crook is framed as a big-time drug dealer, which results in the murder of his wife. He sets out in search of an explanation and revenge. Mediocre action picture was retitled *The Italian Connection* to cash in on the success of *The French Connection.* Dubbed in English. Rated R. 93m. **DIR:** Fernando Di Leo. **CAST:** Mario Adorf, Henry Silva, Woody Strode, Adolfo Celi, Luciana Paluzzi, Sylva Koscina, Cyril Cusack. **1973**

MANHUNT FOR CLAUDE DALLAS ★★½ True-life made-for-television adventure traces the exploits of mountain man Claude Dallas, whose murder spree and eventual capture made headlines. Fascinating look at law enforcement. 100m. **DIR:** Jerry London. **CAST:** Matt Salinger, Claude Akins, Lois Nettleton, Rip Torn. **1986**

MANHUNT IN THE AFRICAN JUNGLE (SECRET SERVICE IN DARKEST AFRICA) ★★ American undercover agent Rod Cameron, posing as a Nazi, joins forces with United Nations agent Joan Marsh, posing as a journalist, to defeat the Axis in North Africa. Not the most thrill-laden of serials. B&W; 15 chapters. **DIR:** Spencer Gordon Bennet. **CAST:** Rod Cameron, Joan Marsh, Duncan Renaldo, Lionel Royce. **1943**

MANHUNT OF MYSTERY ISLAND ★★★ It took three directors to keep up with the nonstop action demands in this slightly above-average Republic serial. The studio's greatest villain, Roy Barcroft, chews the scenery as a reincarnated pirate seeking valuable ore deposits. B&W; 15 chapters. **DIR:** Spencer Gordon Bennet, Wallace Grissell, Yakima Canutt. **CAST:** Richard Bailey, Linda Stirling, Roy Barcroft. **1945**

MANKILLERS 🦃 The FBI hires a band of twelve ruthless female prisoners to dispose of an ex-agent turned renegade. Unrated. 90m. **DIR:** David A. Prior. **CAST:** Edd Byrnes, Gail Fisher, Edy Williams. **1987**

MARATHON MAN ★★★★ A young student (Dustin Hoffman) unwittingly becomes involved in the pursuit of an ex–Nazi War criminal (Laurence Olivier) in this chase thriller. The action holds your interest throughout. Rated R. 125m. **DIR:** John Schlesinger. **CAST:** Dustin Hoffman, Laurence Olivier, Roy Scheider, William Devane, Marthe Keller. **1976**

MARCH OR DIE ★★½ Old-fashioned epic adventure that reminds us of *Beau Geste* and *The Charge of the Light Brigade*, but lacks credibility and style. Gene Hackman stars as an iron-willed major in the French foreign legion, who defends a desert outpost in Africa from marauding Arabs. Catherine Deneuve provides the romance. Not rated, but equivalent to an R for violence and mature situations. 104m. **DIR:** Dick Richards. **CAST:** Gene Hackman, Terence Hill, Max von Sydow, Catherine Deneuve. **1977**

MARINE RAIDERS ★★½ Tough but fair-minded Marine commanding officer tries to steer his favorite captain away from the rocky reefs of romance but finally relents and lets love lead the lucky couple to the altar. B&W; 90m. **DIR:** Harold Schuster. **CAST:** Pat O'Brien, Robert Ryan, Ruth Hussey, Frank McHugh, Barton MacLane, Richard Martin. **1944**

MARK OF ZORRO, THE (1920) ★★★½ Douglas Fairbanks took a chance in 1920 and jumped from comedy-adventures to *costumed* comedy-adventures; with this classic film, he never turned back. Fairbanks made the character of Zorro his own and quickly established himself as an American legend. Silent. B&W; 90m. **DIR:** Fred Niblo. **CAST:** Douglas Fairbanks Sr., Marguerite de la Motte, Noah Beery Sr., Robert McKim. **1920**

MARK OF ZORRO, THE (1940) ★★★★½ Glossy MGM swashbuckler is stylishly directed by Rouben Mamoulian, with Tyrone Power well cast as the foppish aristocrat who lives a secret life as the masked avenger, Zorro, in old California. The inspired casting of Basil Rathbone, Eugene Pallette, and Montagu Love in supporting roles recalls the Errol Flynn classic, *The Adventures of Robin Hood*, while Power's duel with Rathbone almost outdoes it. B&W; 93m. **DIR:** Rouben Mamoulian. **CAST:** Tyrone Power, Basil Rathbone, J. Edward Bromberg, Linda Darnell, Gale Sondergaard, Eugene Pallette, Montagu Love, Robert Lowery. **1940**

MARKED FOR DEATH ★★½ Suburbia is infested with Jamaican drug pushers led by the fearsome, dreadlocked Screwface (Basil Wallace) until a no-nonsense, retired DEA agent (Steve Seagal) decides to clean up the neighborhood. Bone-cruncher Seagal makes a great action-fu star. But this isn't one of his best. Rated R for language and violence. 93m. **DIR:** Dwight H. Little. **CAST:** Steven Seagal, Keith David, Basil Wallace, Joanna Pacula. **1990**

MARKED WOMAN ★★★ Iron-hided district attorney Humphrey Bogart, in one of his early good-guy roles, convinces Bette Davis and other ladies of the evening to squeal on their boss, crime kingpin Eduardo Ciannelli. B&W; 99m. **DIR:** Lloyd Bacon. **CAST:** Bette Davis, Humphrey Bogart, Eduardo Ciannelli, Lola Lane, Isabel Jewell, Allen Jenkins. **1937**

MAROC 7 ★★½ Generic, British-made robbery tale with Gene Barry as a secret agent hot on the trail of a shrewd thief. Efficient, but routine. 91m. **DIR:** Gerry O'Hara. **CAST:** Gene Barry, Elsa Martinelli, Cyd Charisse. **1967**

MARTIAL LAW ★★ Two policemen use hands and feet to fight crime. A film geared entirely to the martial arts viewing public. Rated R for violence. 90m. **DIR:** S. E. Cohen. **CAST:** Chad McQueen, Cynthia Rothrock, David Carradine. **1990**

MARTIAL LAW TWO—UNDERCOVER 🦃 Martial arts expert Cynthia Rothrock goes undercover to catch a cop killer. Nothing revealing here. Rated R for nudity, violence, and profanity. 92m. **DIR:** Kurt Anderson. **CAST:** Jeff Wincott, Cynthia Rothrock, Billy Drago. **1991**

MARTIAL OUTLAW ★★ Brothers Jeff Wincott and Gary Hudson find themselves on opposite sides of the law. Wincott's a DEA agent assigned to infiltrate a $20 million drug deal; Hudson is a crooked cop with a piece of the action. The two stars show off their martial-arts skills, but the story stinks. Rated R for violence. 89m. **DIR:** Kurt Anderson. **CAST:** Jeff Wincott, Gary Hudson, Richard Jaeckel. **1993**

MASCARA 🦃 Luridly exploitative film about a sister and brother with a very kinky relationship. Rated R for nudity, profanity, and violence. 99m. **DIR:** Patrick Conrad. **CAST:** Charlotte Rampling, Michael Sarrazin, Derek de Lint. **1987**

MASK OF FU MANCHU, THE ★★★½ The best of all the movies adapted from Sax Rohmer's novels about an evil mastermind intent on taking over the world features

Boris Karloff as the title character and Lewis Stone as his Sherlock Holmes–style nemesis, Nayland Smith. If one can overlook the unfortunate racial stereotypes (Rohmer often referred to Fu Manchu as "The Yellow Peril"), this film makes for fun viewing. B&W; 72m. **DIR:** Charles Babin. **CAST:** Boris Karloff, Lewis Stone, Karen Morley, Myrna Loy, Charles Starrett, Jean Hersholt. **1932**

MASKED MARVEL, THE ★★½ The mysterious Masked Marvel comes to the aid of the World-Wide Insurance Company to battle the evil Sakima, a former Japanese envoy, and his gang of saboteurs, who are threatening the security of America. Practically nonstop action and top stunt work highlight this wartime Republic serial, which is about as patriotic as a serial can be. B&W; 12 chapters. **DIR:** Spencer Gordon Bennet. **CAST:** William Forrest, Louise Currie, Johnny Arthur. **1943**

MASKS OF DEATH ★★★ Twenty-seven years after playing Sherlock Holmes in the Hammer Films version of *The Hound of the Baskervilles,* Peter Cushing returned to the role for this enjoyable thriller. This time, the Great Detective and Dr. Watson (John Mills) investigate a series of bizarre murders, which leave their victims' faces frozen in expressions of terror. 80m. **DIR:** Roy Ward Baker. **CAST:** Peter Cushing, John Mills, Anne Baxter, Ray Milland. **1986**

MASSIVE RETALIATION 🦃 A group of friends gathers at their own civil-defense fort during a national emergency. Not rated; has profanity and violence. 90m. **DIR:** Thomas A. Cohen. **CAST:** Tom Boyer, Karlene Crockett, Peter Donat, Marilyn Hassett, Jason Gedrick. **1984**

MASTER BLASTER 🦃 A survival-game competition gets out of hand. Rated R for violence, profanity, and nudity. 94m. **DIR:** Glenn Wilder. **CAST:** Jeff Moldovan, Donna Rosae, Joe Hess, Peter Lunblad. **1985**

MASTER OF BALLANTRAE, THE ★★ Errol Flynn's disappointing swan song as a swashbuckler is about two brothers who take different sides in squabbles over the British throne. 89m. **DIR:** William Keighley. **CAST:** Errol Flynn, Anthony Steel, Roger Livesey, Beatrice Campbell, Yvonne Furneaux. **1953**

MATA HARI (1985) ★★ Liberally sprinkled with action, erotica, and existentialism, *Mata Hari* is one of Sylvia (*Emmanuelle*) Kristel's better works. This story traces the erotic dancer from Indonesia as she unwittingly becomes the tool of the German government during World War II. Rated R for sex and nudity. 103m. **DIR:** Curtis Harrington. **CAST:** Sylvia Kristel, Christopher Cazenove, Oliver Tobias. **1985**

MAXIMUM BREAKOUT 🦃 Ridiculous flick about a baby farm features muscle-bound misfits seeking to rescue their leader's girlfriend. Unrated, contains profanity, violence, and sexual situations. 93m. **DIR:** Tracy Lynch Britton. **CAST:** Bobby Johnston. **1991**

MAXIMUM FORCE ★★ Three crackerjack cops go undercover to infiltrate a crime lord and destroy him. The only thing maximum about this action-adventure is the title. Rated R for profanity, nudity, and violence. 90m. **DIR:** Joseph Merhi. **CAST:** John Saxon, Mickey Rooney, Sam Jones, Jason Lively, Richard Lynch, Sherri Rose. **1992**

MCBAIN 🦃 It's hard to keep track of what's going on in this lamebrained action-adventure flick involving a mercenary team out to dethrone a Central American dictator. Rated R for profanity and violence. 104m. **DIR:** James Glickenhaus. **CAST:** Christopher Walken, Maria Conchita Alonso, Michael Ironside. **1991**

MCQ ★★★½ The success of *Dirty Harry* and the slow death of the Western prompted John Wayne to shed his Stetson and six-guns for cop clothes. While this John Sturges film doesn't quite match the Clint Eastwood–Don Siegel production that inspired it, there are some good scenes and suspense. Rated PG. 116m. **DIR:** John Sturges. **CAST:** John Wayne, Al Lettieri, Eddie Albert, Diana Muldaur, Clu Gulager, Colleen Dewhurst. **1974**

ME AND THE KID ★★ Two burglars attempt to rob a mansion, but all they find is an empty safe and a neglected rich kid, whom they decide to kidnap. When one of the burglars attempts to return the victim, the boy doesn't want to go home. Unfortunately, the story drags a bit. Not rated, but contains violence and profanity. 95m. **DIR:** Dan Curtis. **CAST:** Danny Aiello, Joe Pantoliano, Cathy Moriarty, Alex Zuckerman, David Dukes, Anita Morris, Rick Aiello. **1993**

MEAN JOHNNY BARROWS 🦃 Fred Williamson plays a Vietnam war hero, dishonorably discharged for striking an officer. Rated R. 80m. **DIR:** Fred Williamson. **CAST:** Fred Williamson, Roddy McDowall, Stuart Whitman, Elliott Gould. **1976**

MECHANIC, THE ★★½ A professional hit man (Charles Bronson) teaches his craft to a young student (Jan-Michael Vincent). Slow-moving for the most part, with a few good action scenes. Rated R for violence and language. 100m. **DIR:** Michael Winner. **CAST:** Charles Bronson, Jan-Michael Vincent, Jill Ireland, Keenan Wynn. **1972**

MELVIN PURVIS: G-MAN ★★★ In the tradition of the Warner Bros. gangster films of the Thirties, Melvin Purvis (Dale Robertson) holds nothing back in this fictionalized account of the all-consuming search for Machine Gun Kelly. Wild and fast-paced, this made-for-TV film is exciting and entertaining. 78m. **DIR:** Dan Curtis. **CAST:** Dale Robertson, Harris Yulin, Margaret Blye, Dick Sargent. **1974**

MEN IN WAR ★★★★ This outstanding Korean War action film with Robert Ryan and Aldo Ray fighting the Chinese and each other is one of the very best "war is hell" films. B&W; 104m. **DIR:** Anthony Mann. **CAST:** Robert Ryan, Aldo Ray, Vic Morrow. **1957**

MEN OF SHERWOOD FOREST ★★ The inspirational saga of nobleman-turned-outlaw receives scant embellishment in this hohum addition to the Robin Hood canon. Produced by fledgling Hammer Studios hard on the heels of the popular Walt Disney feature and the syndicated Richard Greene television show. 77m. **DIR:** Val Guest. **CAST:** Don Taylor, Reginald Beckwith. **1954**

MEN OF THE FIGHTING LADY ★★★½ Based on two separate factual articles for the *Saturday Evening Post* by James Michener and Navy Commander Harry A. Burns, this story of a jet fighter squadron off the coast of Korea was fashioned to fit Van Johnson. Exciting battle scenes. Unrated. 80m. **DIR:** Andrew Marton. **CAST:** Van Johnson, Walter Pidgeon, Louis Calhern, Dewey Martin, Keenan Wynn, Frank Lovejoy, Robert Horton. **1954**

MERCENARY FIGHTERS ★★ U.S. mercenaries (Peter Fonda and company) are hired to get rid of tribesmen who are blocking the building of a new dam. When they discover the dam would force the tribe off its homeland, the mercenaries begin to fight among themselves. The actors took some heat for participating in this film, which was made in South Africa and the results are certainly nothing you'd want to put your career on the line for. 91m. **DIR:** Riki Shelach. **CAST:** Peter Fonda, Reb Brown, Ron O'Neal, Jim Mitchum, Robert DoQui. **1986**

MESSENGER OF DEATH ★★½ Middling Charles Bronson vehicle features the star in a convincing portrayal of a newspaper reporter investigating the bizarre murder of a Mormon family. A strong, suspenseful opening degenerates into a routine thriller. However, J. Lee Thompson does elicit believable performances from the cast. Rated R for violence and profanity. 98m. **DIR:** J. Lee Thompson. **CAST:** Charles Bronson, Trish Van Devere, John Ireland, Jeff Corey, Laurence Luckinbill, Marilyn Hassett. **1988**

MIAMI BLUES ★★½ A sociopath (Alec Baldwin) goes on a crime spree in Miami, hooks up with a trusting hooker (Jennifer Jason Leigh) and eludes a slow-witted cop (Fred Ward). Director George Armitage was trying for something stylishly offbeat and ended up with something that was mostly off. Rated R for violence, nudity, and profanity. 96m. **DIR:** George Armitage. **CAST:** Fred Ward, Alec Baldwin, Jennifer Jason Leigh, Nora Dunn, Charles Napier. **1990**

MIAMI COPS 🦃 This boring Italian film features a seasoned cop attempting to break up an international drug-smuggling ring. B&W; 103m. **DIR:** Al Bradley. **CAST:** Richard Roundtree. **1989**

MIAMI VICE ★★★★ This pilot for the popular NBC series is slam-bang entertainment. A New York City cop (Philip Michael Thomas) on the trail of the powerful drug kingpin who killed his brother traces him to Miami, running into a vice cop (Don Johnson) who's after the same guy. All the trademarks of the series are here: great music, rapid-fire editing, gritty low-key performances, and bursts of sporadic violence. The only real flaw in this tape is the sound quality, which, even in hi-fi stereo, is muffled. 97m. **DIR:** Thomas Carter. **CAST:** Don Johnson, Philip Michael Thomas, Saundra Santiago, Michael Talbott, John Diehl, Gregory Sierra, Bill Smitrovich, Belinda Montgomery, Martin Ferrero, Mykel T. Williamson, Olivia Brown, Miguel Pinero. **1984**

MIAMI VICE: "THE PRODIGAL SON" ★★★ The pastel duo, Crockett (Don Johnson) and Tubbs (Philip Michael Thomas), trek up to New York in search of the bad guys in this watchable second-season opener. 99m. **DIR:** Paul Michael Glaser. **CAST:** Don Johnson, Philip Michael Thomas, Edward James Olmos, Olivia Brown, Penn Jillette, Pam Grier. **1985**

MIDNIGHT CROSSING 🦃 Poorly written and realized film about four people on a treasure hunt into Cuba. Rated R for language, violence, and nudity. 104m. **DIR:** Roger Holzberg. **CAST:** Faye Dunaway, Daniel J. Travanti, Kim Cattrall, John Laughlin, Ned Beatty. **1988**

MIDNIGHT LACE ★★★ A fine mystery with a cast that makes the most of it. Doris Day is an American living in London and married to successful businessman Rex Harrison. She soon finds her life in danger. Some viewers may find it less sophisticated than present-day thrillers, but there's plenty of suspense and plot twists to recommend it. 100m. **DIR:** David Miller. **CAST:** Doris Day, Rex Harrison, John Gavin, Myrna Loy, Roddy McDowall, Herbert Marshall, Natasha Perry. **1960**

MIDNIGHT RUN ★★★★ Robert De Niro is wonderfully funny as a bounty hunter charged with bringing in fugitive Charles Grodin. The latter is hiding out after stealing $15 million from a crime boss and giving it to charity. Mixing laughs, surprises, and oodles of action, Martin Brest has come up with the perfect follow-up to his megahit, *Beverly Hills Cop*. Rated R for profanity and violence. 125m. **DIR:** Martin Brest. **CAST:** Robert De Niro, Charles Grodin, Yaphet Kotto, John Ashton, Dennis Farina. **1988**

MIDWAY ★★★ An all-star cast was assembled to bring to the screen this famous sea battle of World War II. Midway became famous as the site of the overwhelming victory of American carrier forces, which shifted the balance of power in the Pacific. As a historical drama, this film is accurate and maintains interest. However, a romance subplot is totally out of place. Rated PG. 132m. **DIR:** Jack Smight. **CAST:** Henry Fonda, Charlton Heston, Robert Mitchum, Hal Holbrook, Edward Albert, Cliff Robertson. **1976**

MIGHTY QUINN, THE ★★★ A quirky, entertaining mystery story, set in the reggae world of a Caribbean island. Denzel Washington plays the local police chief—"The Mighty Quinn"—who is on the trail of a murderer. Director Carl Schenkel contributes an inventive visual style and makes ample use of a wonderful reggae score. Rated R, with profanity, violence, and mild sexual situations. 95m. **DIR:** Carl Schenkel. **CAST:** Denzel Washington, Robert Townsend, James Fox, Sheryl Lee Ralph, Mimi Rogers. **1989**

MIND FIELD ★★½ When cop Michael Ironside starts hallucinating, he traces the cause of his delusions to a secret CIA experiment involving LSD. Rated R for violence. 92m. **DIR:** Jean-Claude Lord. **CAST:** Michael Ironside, Sean McCann, Christopher Plummer, Lisa Langlois. **1990**

MINES OF KILIMANJARO ★★ *Raiders of the Lost Ark* imitation with an American college student in Africa searching for the lost diamond mines of Kilimanjaro. Trying to stop him are the Nazis, Chinese gangsters, and native tribesmen. The action footage is badly choreographed, the music is strident, and the historical accuracy is a laugh. Not rated, but contains violence. 88m. **DIR:** Mino Guerrini. **CAST:** Tobias Hoesl, Elena Pompei, Christopher Connelly. **1987**

MINISTRY OF VENGEANCE 🦃 Loathsome in every respect—a minister reverts to his military training to seek revenge on terrorists. Rated R for violence. 93m. **DIR:** Peter Maris. **CAST:** John Schneider, Ned Beatty, James Tolkan, Apollonia Kotero, Robert Miano, Yaphet Kotto, George Kennedy. **1989**

MISFIT BRIGADE, THE ★★★ Oliver Reed and David Carradine have cameo roles in this takeoff on *The Dirty Dozen*. Bruce Davison, David Patrick Kelly, and their buddies are assorted criminals from a Nazi penal brigade. The cast has a lot of fun with the tongue-in-cheek action. Rated R. 99m. **DIR:** Gordon Hessler. **CAST:** Bruce Davison, David Patrick Kelly, D. W. Moffett, Oliver Reed, David Carradine, Jay O. Sanders. **1987**

MISSING IN ACTION ★★★½ Chuck Norris is a one-man army in this Vietnam-based action film. Anyone else might be laughable in such a role. But the former karate star makes it work. The story focuses on an attempt by Col. James Braddock (Norris), a former Vietnam prisoner of war, to free the other Americans he believes are still there. Rated R for profanity, violence, and brief nudity. 101m. **DIR:** Joseph Zito. **CAST:** Chuck Norris, M. Emmet Walsh, Lenore Kasdorf, James Hong. **1984**

MISSING IN ACTION 2: THE BEGINNING ★★½ Following on the heels of the previous year's surprise hit, this "prequel" is really the same movie, only it tells the story of how Colonel Braddock (Chuck Norris) and his men escaped their Vietnam prison camp after ten years of torture. The acting is nonexistent, the action predictable and violent. Rated R for violence. 95m. **DIR:** Lance Hool. **CAST:** Chuck Norris, Cosie Costa, Soon-Teck Oh, Steven Williams. **1985**

MISSING LINK ★★★½ A beautifully photographed story of a man-ape's journey across the desolate African plain after his people are killed by the encroachment of man. A pseudo-documentary style offers a breathtaking view of some of Earth's strangest creatures. First-rate man-ape makeup by Academy Award–winner Rick Baker. Rated PG. 92m. **DIR:** David Hughes, Carol Hughes. **CAST:** Peter Elliott, Michael Gambon. **1988**

MISSION IN MOROCCO ★★ Lex Barker stars as an American oil executive whose murdered partner possessed a microfilm that shows the location of oil in Morocco. Tired adventure yawner shot on location in Morocco. B&W; 79m. **DIR:** Anthony Squire. **CAST:** Lex Barker, Juli Redding. **1959**

MISSION OF JUSTICE ★★★ A large city is plagued with crime, but the woman who is running for mayor has a new solution: the Peacemakers—a group of disadvantaged youths who roam the streets and prevent crime. At first glance, this film looks pretty bad, but you'll keep watching. Rated R for violence and profanity. 95m. **DIR:** Steve Barnett. **CAST:** Jeff Wincott, Brigitte Nielsen, Luca Bercovici, Matthias Hues. **1992**

MR. ACE ★★ Potboiler about a spoiled society woman (Sylvia Sidney) who uses a gangster (George Raft) to win a congressional election goes through the motions but very little else. B&W; 84m. **DIR:** Edwin L. Marin. **CAST:** George Raft, Sylvia Sidney, Stanley Ridges, Sara Haden, Jerome Cowan. **1946**

MR. BILLION ★★½ Sappy but seductive story about a humble Italian mechanic (Terence Hill) who will inherit a financial empire if he can get to the signing over of his uncle's will before a gang of kidnappers or the corporation's chairman (Jackie Gleason) gets to him first. Rated PG for violence and sex. 89m. **DIR:** Jonathan Kaplan. **CAST:** Terence Hill, Valerie Perrine, Jackie Gleason, Slim Pickens, William Redfield, Chill Wills, Dick Miller. **1977**

MR. INSIDE/MR. OUTSIDE ★★ Hal Linden and Tony LoBianco are fine in this made-for-television cop thriller as two New York City detectives attempting to foil a smuggling ring. Director William Graham's pacing makes you forget how much this movie is like so many other works created for TV. 74m. **DIR:** William A. Graham. **CAST:** Hal Linden, Tony Lo Bianco, Phil Bruns, Paul Benjamin, Stefan Schnabèl. **1973**

MR. LUCKY ★★★ Cary Grant is a gambler attempting to bilk money from a charity relief program. He changes his tune when he falls for a wealthy society girl, Laraine Day. This is a slick piece of wartime fluff. The plot has nothing you haven't seen before, but the charm of Grant makes it watchable. B&W; 100m. **DIR:** H. C. Potter. **CAST:** Cary Grant, Laraine Day. **1943**

MR. MAJESTYK ★★★½ In this better-than-average Charles Bronson vehicle, he's a watermelon grower (!) coming up against gangster Al Lettieri (in a first-rate performance). Rated R. 103m. **DIR:** Richard Fleischer. **CAST:** Charles Bronson, Al Lettieri, Linda Cristal, Lee Purcell, Paul Koslo. **1974**

MR. ROBINSON CRUSOE ★★★ Dashing Douglas Fairbanks Sr. bets he can survive like Crusoe on a South Sea island. Just how he does it makes for great fun. Fairbanks was just short of 50 when he made this film; but he was still the agile, athletic swashbuckler whose wholesome charm made him the idol of millions. B&W; 76m. **DIR:** A. Edward Sutherland. **CAST:** Douglas Fairbanks Sr., William Farnum, Maria Alba. **1932**

MIXED BLOOD ★★½ Paul Morrissey, the man who brought you Andy Warhol's versions of *Frankenstein* and *Dracula*, has made a serious film about the Alphabet City drug subculture and its inherent violent nature. Here the surroundings are brutal and unforgiving, and the cheap film stock gives the movie a newsreel feeling. Not rated, but contains violence and profanity. 98m. **DIR:** Paul Morrissey. **CAST:** Marilia Pera, Richard Ulacia, Linda Kerridge, Geraldine Smith, Angel David, Rodney Harvey. **1985**

MOB WAR 🦃 Bargain-basement flick about a young mob turk. Rated R for violence and profanity. 96m. **DIR:** J. Christian Ingvordsen. **CAST:** Johnny Stumper, Jake La Motta. **1988**

MOBSTERS ★★ In what might be called *Young Guns in the Roaring Twenties*, Christian Slater plays Lucky Luciano and Patrick Dempsey is Meyer Lansky in yet another gangster movie. It's no *GoodFellas*, but there's plenty of action, with F. Murray Abraham and Anthony Quinn adding class. Rated R for violence and profanity. 110m. **DIR:** Michael Karbelnikoff. **CAST:** Christian Slater, Patrick Dempsey, Richard Grieco, F. Murray Abraham, Anthony Quinn. **1991**

MOBY DICK ★★★★½ Director John Huston's brilliant adaptation of Herman Melville's classic novel features Gregory Peck in one of his best performances as the driven Captain Ahab. 116m. **DIR:** John Huston. **CAST:** Gregory Peck, Richard Basehart, Leo Genn, Orson Welles. **1956**

MOD SQUAD, THE (TV SERIES) ★★★½ Three youths—one white, one black, one blonde, as the promo spots trumpeted—are busted for minor crimes. They are recruited to go undercover. Pete is a brooding, poor little rich boy who's rebelling against his Beverly Hills parents. Linc is a ghetto black who seethes beneath a stoic exterior. Julie, the sensitive blonde, is the daughter of a prostitute. Based on the real-life exploits of the show's creator, Bud Ruskin, a former cop, the series effectively combined action, positive messages, and a mildly antiestablishment bent. 60m. **DIR:** Various. **CAST:** Michael Cole, Clarence Williams III, Peggy Lipton, Tige Andrews. **1968–1973**

MODEL BY DAY ★★½ After her roommate is attacked, a model decides to do her part to rid the city of crime. The film has some good comedic moments, but the plot is unbelievable. Rated R for nudity and violence. 89m. **DIR:** Christian Duguay. **CAST:** Famke Janssen, Stephen Shellen, Shannon Tweed, Sean Young, Clark Johnson, Traci Lind, Kim Coates. **1993**

MOGAMBO ★★★ This remake of the film classic *Red Dust* stars Clark Gable as the great white hunter who dallies with a sophisticated married woman (Grace Kelly), only to return to the arms of a jaded lady (Ava Gardner, who is quite good in the role of the woman with a past). It's not great John Ford, but it'll do. 115m. **DIR:** John Ford. **CAST:** Clark Gable, Grace Kelly, Ava Gardner. **1953**

MONSTER OF THE ISLAND, THE 🦃 The "Monster" in this cheap, misleadingly titled Italian crime-drama is the ruthless head of a drug-smuggling ring. B&W; 87m. **DIR:** Roberto Montero, Alberto Vecchietti. **CAST:** Boris Karloff. **1953**

MOONRAKER 🦃 The James Bond series hit absolute rock bottom in 1979 with this outer-space adventure. Rated PG. 126m. **DIR:** Lewis Gilbert. **CAST:** Roger Moore, Lois Chiles, Michel Lonsdale. **1979**

MOONSHINE COUNTY EXPRESS ★★ In this bogus action flick, William Conrad has his hands full with the three vengeful daughters of a man he just murdered. Rated PG for mild language and violence. 95m. **DIR:** Gus Trikonis. **CAST:** John Saxon, Susan Howard, William Conrad, Dub Taylor. **1977**

MORGAN THE PIRATE ★★★ This fictionalized account of the adventures of the historical Henry Morgan (with muscle man Steve Reeves in the title role) is perhaps the most entertaining of that actor's many Italian-made features. Even by current standards, there is plenty of action and romance. 93m. **DIR:** André de Toth, Primo Zeglio. **CAST:**

Steve Reeves, Valerie Lagrange, Ivo Garbani. 1961

MORITURI ★★½ Marlon Brando portrays a spy working for the British who, through a series of moral equations involving anti-Nazism versus Nazism, convinces the captain of a German freighter on a voyage from Japan to Germany to side with the Allies. The concept is good, but the script gets weaker and weaker as the film progresses. B&W; 128m. **DIR:** Bernhard Wicki. **CAST:** Marlon Brando, Yul Brynner, Janet Margolin, Trevor Howard, Wally Cox, William Redfield. 1965

MOTHER LODE ★★ Although this modern-day adventure yarn about a search for gold boasts a feasible plot and fine acting by Charlton Heston (who also directed) and John Marley, its liabilities far outweigh its assets. Rated PG, the film contains occasional obscenities and violence. 101m. **DIR:** Charlton Heston. **CAST:** Charlton Heston, John Marley, Nick Mancuso, Kim Basinger. 1982

MOTOR PSYCHO ★★ A woman and a man whose spouses were attacked by a vicious gang of desert bikers team up for revenge. Russ Meyer made this as a second feature for his cult classic *Faster, Pussycat! Kill! Kill!* Meyer aficionados will find it pretty tame. Unrated, the movie contains comparatively mild violence. B&W; 73m. **DIR:** Russ Meyer. **CAST:** Haji, Alex Rocco, Steven Oliver. 1965

MOTORCYCLE GANG ★★ Cut-rate variation on *The Wild One* (and every other teen-J. D. movie cliché they could cram in) runs on too long, but is still lurid fun. Yes, Carl Switzer is indeed "Alfalfa," captured here shortly before his violent offscreen death. B&W; 78m. **DIR:** Edward L. Cahn. **CAST:** Anne Neyland, Steve Terrell, John Ashley, Carl "Alfalfa" Switzer. 1957

MOUNTAINS OF THE MOON ★★★★½ Bob Rafelson's robust African adventure about the search for the source of the Nile is also an engrossing and intelligent portrait of the charismatic explorer Sir Richard Burton. A film of epic scope and exotic textures, a superbly entertaining recreation of the Victorian Age of exploration, and the story of a most complex and colorful explorer. Rated R, with violence, as well as a brief reminder that Burton was also obsessed with erotica. 130m. **DIR:** Bob Rafelson. **CAST:** Patrick Bergin, Iain Glen, Roger Rees, Fiona Shaw. 1990

MOVING TARGET 🦃 Linda Blair plays a woman on the run who has witnessed the murder of her boyfriend. Pathetic. Rated R for violence and language. 85m. **DIR:** Marius Mattei. **CAST:** Ernest Borgnine, Linda Blair. 1990

MOVING VIOLATION ★★½ Another southern car-chase movie from the Roger Corman factory, this one features some pretty good high-speed pyrotechnics. (Those scenes were done by second-unit director Barbara Peeters.) The plot, which is merely an excuse for the chases, has an innocent couple being pursued by a corrupt sheriff. Rated PG. 91m. **DIR:** Charles S. Dubin. **CAST:** Stephen McHattie, Kay Lenz, Eddie Albert, Lonny Chapman, Will Geer, Dick Miller. 1976

MS. .45 ★★★★ An attractive mute woman is raped and beaten twice in the same evening. She slips into madness and seeks revenge with a .45 pistol. A female version of *Death Wish* with an ending at a Halloween costume party that will knock your socks off. Not for all tastes. Rated R for violence, nudity, rape, language, and gore. 90m. **DIR:** Abel Ferrara. **CAST:** Zoe Tamerlis. 1981

MURDER ON FLIGHT 502 ★★ A mad bomber threatens to blow an international airliner to pieces. He is thwarted by Robert Stack and other reluctant heroes. Reminiscent of *Airport* and a half-dozen sequels. The cast alone keeps this made-for-TV potboiler from falling flat on its baggage carousel. 120m. **DIR:** George McCowan. **CAST:** Ralph Bellamy, Polly Bergen, Robert Stack, Theodore Bikel, Sonny Bono, Dane Clark, Laraine Day, Fernando Lamas, George Maharis, Farrah Fawcett, Hugh O'Brian, Brooke Adams, Walter Pidgeon, Molly Picon. 1975

MURDER ONE 🦃 An odyssey of madness, mayhem, and murder. Rated R for nudity, profanity, and violence. 82m. **DIR:** Graeme Campbell. **CAST:** Henry Thomas, James Wilder, Stephen Shellen. 1988

MURDERERS' ROW ★★½ This entry into the Matt Helm secret agent series is pretty dismal. Dean Martin has been much better in other films. The Matt Helm series was an attempt to grab the Bond and Flint audience, but Martin just couldn't cut it as a superspy. 108m. **DIR:** Henry Levin. **CAST:** Dean Martin, Ann-Margret, Karl Malden, James Gregory. 1966

MURPH THE SURF ★★½ In this based-on-real-life thriller, two Florida beachniks connive to do the impossible: steal the fabled 564-carat Star of India sapphire out of New York's American Museum of Natural History. Re-creation of the 1964 crime induces sweat, along with a good speedboat chase, but the picture never really catches a wave. 101m. **DIR:** Marvin J. Chomsky. **CAST:** Robert Conrad, Don Stroud, Donna Mills, Luther Adler. 1975

MURPHY'S LAW 🦃 Charles Bronson is a cop framed for the murder of his ex-wife. Rated R. 101m. **DIR:** J. Lee Thompson. **CAST:** Charles Bronson, Carrie Snodgress, Kathleen Wilhoite. 1986

MURPHY'S WAR ★★★ World War II sea drama follows a British seaman, sole survivor of a brutal massacre of his ship's crew by a German U-boat, as he seeks revenge. Peter O'Toole gives a hard-hitting, no-holds-barred performance as the outraged, bloodthirsty Murphy. Rated PG. 108m. **DIR:** Peter Yates. **CAST:** Peter O'Toole, Sian Phillips, Horst Janson, Philippe Noiret, John Hallam. **1971**

MUTINY ON THE BOUNTY (1935) ★★★★ The first and best known of three versions of the now-classic account of mutiny against the tyranny of Captain William Bligh during a worldwide British naval expedition in 1789. Charles Laughton is superb as the merciless Bligh, Clark Gable unquestionably fine as the leader of the mutiny, Fletcher Christian. The film won an Oscar for best picture and still entertains today. B&W; 132m. **DIR:** Frank Lloyd. **CAST:** Charles Laughton, Clark Gable, Franchot Tone, Dudley Digges, Eddie Quillan, Donald Crisp, Henry Stephenson. **1935**

MUTINY ON THE BOUNTY (1962) ★★ This years-later remake hits the South Seas with a gigantic belly flop. Trevor Howard is commanding as the tyrannical Captain Bligh, but Marlon Brando as mutiny leader Fletcher Christian? Yucko! 179m. **DIR:** Lewis Milestone. **CAST:** Marlon Brando, Trevor Howard, Richard Harris, Hugh Griffith, Richard Haydn, Gordon Jackson. **1962**

MY SAMURAI ★★ A reluctant martial arts student learns the value of his lessons when his master takes on gang members. As martial arts flicks go, this is watchable with some very impressive fight scenes. Unrated; contains plenty of violence. 87m. **DIR:** Fred Dresch. **CAST:** Julian Lee, Mako, Bubba Smith, Terry O'Quinn, Jim Turner, John Kallo. **1992**

MYSTERIOUS DR. SATAN ★★★ Eduardo Cianelli unleashes his death-dealing robot upon a helpless public. Chockful of great stunts, last-minute escapes, and logic that defies description, this prime chapterplay from Republic's thrill factory had just about everything a juvenile audience could ask for and then some. B&W; 15 chapters. **DIR:** William Witney, John English. **CAST:** Eduardo Ciannelli, Robert Wilcox, William Newell, C. Montague Shaw, Dorothy Herbert, Ella Neal, Jack Mulhall, Edwin Stanley. **1940**

MYSTERIOUS MR. WONG, THE ★★ Not to be confused with the Mr. Wong detective series that starred Boris Karloff, this low-budget mystery has Bela Lugosi in the title role, portraying a fiendish criminal bent on possessing twelve coins connected with Confucius. B&W; 68m. **DIR:** William Nigh. **CAST:** Bela Lugosi, Wallace Ford, Arline Judge. **1935**

MYSTERY SQUADRON ★★½ Mascot Studios continued its effort to be the best producer of serials with this fast-moving story of the sinister Mystery Squadron and its fanatical leader, the Black Ace. Bob Steele and "Big Boy" Williams trade in their chaps and horses for parachutes and planes as they do their utmost to apprehend the Black Ace, a deadly saboteur. B&W; 12 chapters. **DIR:** Colbert Clark, David Howard. **CAST:** Bob Steele, Guinn Williams, Lucille Brown, Jack Mulhall, Purnell Pratt. **1933**

NADIA, VOLS. 1–36 ★★★ Japanese animation. Good animation and appealing characters blend in this series about a young girl and her many adventures. Set in the turn-of-the-century past (unusual for this genre), the *Nadia* tales can be enjoyed by all age-groups (also unusual). Unrated. 25m. each **DIR:** Hideaki Anno. **1989**

NAILS ★★ Bad boy Dennis Hopper's *way*-over-the-top performance as a brutal cop barely saves Larry Ferguson's humdrum script from turkeydom. Rated R for nudity, profanity, and considerable violence. 96m. **DIR:** John Flynn. **CAST:** Dennis Hopper, Anne Archer, Tomas Milian, Keith David, Cliff De Young. **1992**

NAKED AND THE DEAD, THE ★★★ This action-packed World War II film is based on Norman Mailer's famous book. Not nearly as good as the book, nevertheless the film is still quite powerful and exciting. Worth a watch. 131m. **DIR:** Raoul Walsh. **CAST:** Aldo Ray, Joey Bishop, Cliff Robertson, Raymond Massey. **1958**

NAKED CAGE, THE 🦃 An innocent young girl finds herself mistakenly arrested for bank robbery. Rated R for violence and loads of nudity. 97m. **DIR:** Paul Nicholas. **CAST:** Shari Shattuck, Angel Tompkins, Lucinda Crosby. **1982**

NAKED JUNGLE, THE ★★ In this studio soap opera made from the short story *Leininnen Versus the Ants*, Charlton Heston is slightly out of place but still powerful as the South American plantation owner. Eleanor Parker is ridiculous as his new wife, and a young, thin William Conrad is along for the ride. Not rated, contains slight violence. 95m. **DIR:** Byron Haskin. **CAST:** Charlton Heston, Eleanor Parker, Abraham Sofaer, William Conrad, Romo Vincent, Douglas Fowley. **1953**

NAKED PREY, THE ★★★★ An African safari takes a disastrous turn and Cornel Wilde winds up running naked and unarmed through the searing jungle as a large band of native warriors keeps on his heels, determined to finish him off. This is an amazingly intense adventure of man versus man and man versus nature. Wilde does a remarkable job, both as star and director. 94m. **DIR:** Cornel Wilde. **CAST:** Cornel Wilde, Gert Van Den Bergh, Ken Gampu. **1966**

NAKED VENGEANCE 🦃 Unpleasant exploitation flick about a woman who seeks vengeance after she is raped and her parents murdered. Available in both R and unrated versions; we'd suggest that you avoid both. 97m. **DIR:** Cirio H. Santiago. **CAST:** Deborah Tranelli, Kaz Garas, Bill McLaughlin, Nick Nicholson. **1986**

NAKED YOUTH ★★ A good kid gets involved with a bad apple and together they wind up in prison—and then break out. It's hardly the camp classic the distributors would have you believe. B&W; 80m. **DIR:** John Schreyer. **CAST:** Robert Hutton, John Goddard, Carol Ohmart. **1961**

NAME OF THE ROSE, THE ★★★ In this passable screen adaptation of Umberto Eco's bestseller, Sean Connery stars as a monkish Sherlock Holmes trying to solve a series of murders in a fourteenth-century monastery. Connery is fun to watch, but the plot is rather feeble. Rated R for nudity, simulated sex, and violence. 118m. **DIR:** Jean-Jacques Annaud. **CAST:** Sean Connery, F. Murray Abraham, Christian Slater, Elya Baskin, Feodor Chaliapin, William Hickey, Michel Lonsdale, Ron Perlman. **1986**

NARROW MARGIN, THE (1952) ★★★½ Tight crime entry has tough cop Charles McGraw assigned to transport the widow of a gangster to trial despite threats of hit men. Action takes place on a speeding train as McGraw and the hit men play a deadly cat-and-mouse game. Unrelenting suspense makes this one of the better films made in the Fifties. B&W; 70m. **DIR:** Richard Fleischer. **CAST:** Charles McGraw, Marie Windsor, Jacqueline White, Queenie Leonard. **1952**

NARROW MARGIN (1990) ★★★ An update of the 1952 thriller, this absorbing drama's lapses in logic are compensated for by two gripping performances by Gene Hackman and Anne Archer. She's a frightened murder witness hiding out in the wilderness; he's the Los Angeles deputy district attorney determined to bring her back. Great fun, until its rather abrupt conclusion. Rated R for language and violence. 97m. **DIR:** Peter Hyams. **CAST:** Gene Hackman, Anne Archer, James B. Sikking, M. Emmet Walsh. **1990**

NASTY HERO ★★ An ex-con comes to Miami to get revenge on the hoods who sent him to prison. Car chases substitute for solid storytelling, but some of the actors are quite good. Rated PG-13. 79m. **DIR:** Nick Barwood. **CAST:** Scott Feraco, Robert Sedgwick, Raymond Serra. **1987**

NATE AND HAYES ★★★ Tommy Lee Jones as a good pirate, Michael O'Keefe as his missionary accomplice, and Max Phipps as their cutthroat nemesis make this a jolly movie. Set in the South Seas of the late nineteenth century, it's unpretentious, old-fashioned movie fun. Rated PG for violence. 100m. **DIR:** Ferdinand Fairfax. **CAST:** Tommy Lee Jones, Michael O'Keefe, Max Phipps. **1983**

NAVY SEALS ★★ When Middle Eastern terrorists acquire some American stinger missiles, it's up to the rough-and-ready Navy SEALS (Sea, Air and Land) to blow them up. Director Lewis Teague cannot overcome the tedium of the predictable screenplay, although the action scenes are robust. Rated R for violence and profanity. 118m. **DIR:** Lewis Teague. **CAST:** Charlie Sheen, Michael Biehn, Joanne Whalley, Rick Rossovich. **1990**

NEON EMPIRE, THE ★★ This tedious, cut-down version of a four-hour made-for-cable gangster flick merely wastes the talents of performers who sleepwalk through their parts. Pete Hamill's pedestrian screenplay should have been the stuff of intrigue and crackling suspense. Unrated but contains profanity and considerable violence. 120m. **DIR:** Larry Peerce. **CAST:** Ray Sharkey, Gary Busey, Linda Fiorentino, Martin Landau, Dylan McDermott, Julie Carmen, Harry Guardino. **1989**

NEVER CRY WOLF ★★★★★ Carroll Ballard made this breathtakingly beautiful, richly rewarding Disney feature about a lone biologist (Charles Martin Smith) learning firsthand about the white wolves of the Yukon by living with them. It's an extraordinary motion picture in every sense of the word. Rated PG for brief nudity. 105m. **DIR:** Carroll Ballard. **CAST:** Charles Martin Smith, Brian Dennehy. **1983**

NEVER LET ME GO ★★★ Clark Gable, a correspondent in post–World War II Russia, marries ballerina Gene Tierney just before he is expelled from the country. When authorities detain her, he sets about to help her escape. B&W; 94m. **DIR:** Delmer Daves. **CAST:** Clark Gable, Gene Tierney, Bernard Miles, Richard Haydn, Belita, Kenneth More, Theodore Bikel. **1953**

NEVER SAY NEVER AGAIN ★★★★½ Sean Connery makes a triumphant return to the role of James Bond in this high-style, tongue-in-cheek remake of *Thunderball.* Once again, agent 007 goes up against the evil Largo (exquisitely played by Klaus Maria Brandauer), the sexy and deadly Fatima (Barbara Carrera), and the ever-present head of SPECTRE, Blofeld (Max von Sydow). Action-packed and peppered with laughs, *Never Say Never Again* falters a bit during the climax, but nevertheless emerges as a solid entry in the Bond film canon. Rated PG for violence and nudity. 137m. **DIR:** Irvin Kershner. **CAST:** Sean Connery, Klaus Maria Brandauer, Max von Sydow, Barbara Carrera, Kim Basinger, Edward Fox, Bernie Casey, Alec McCowen. **1983**

NEVER SO FEW ★★★ Adroitly led by a group of American officers, a band of Burmese guerrillas fight a series of vicious battles against invading Japanese troops in this World War II action picture. The battle scenes are quite good, but the film is marred at times by the philosophizing of U.S. Army officer Frank Sinatra. It's good, but talky. 124m. **DIR:** John Sturges. **CAST:** Frank Sinatra, Gina Lollobrigida, Peter Lawford, Steve

McQueen, Paul Henreid, Charles Bronson, Richard Johnson, Brian Donlevy, Dean Jones. **1959**

NEVER TOO YOUNG TO DIE 🦃 A really rotten film that steals everything it can from the James Bond and *Road Warrior* series. Rated R for violence. 90m. **DIR:** Gil Bettman. **CAST:** John Stamos, Vanity, Gene Simmons, George Lazenby. **1986**

NEW ADVENTURES OF TARZAN ★★½ For the first time on film, Edgar Rice Burroughs's immortal jungle lord spoke and behaved the way he had been created. This sometimes slow, but basically enjoyable twelve-episode chapterplay wove a complex story about a search for Tarzan's missing friend and a treacherous agent intent on stealing an ancient Mayan stone. B&W; 12 chapters. **DIR:** Edward Kull, W. F. McGaugh. **CAST:** Bruce Bennett, Ula Holt, Frank Baker, Dale Walsh, Harry Ernest. **1935**

NEW JACK CITY ★★★★ Wesley Snipes gives an explosive performance as a powerful Harlem drug lord who is targeted to be brought down by two undercover cops (rap singer Ice T and Judd Nelson). Director Mario Van Peebles delivers all the thrills, chills, and suspense the action crowd craves while still creating an effective anti-drug movie. Rated R for profanity, violence, and nudity. 97m. **DIR:** Mario Van Peebles. **CAST:** Wesley Snipes, Ice-T, Chris Rock, Mario Van Peebles, Judd Nelson. **1991**

NEWMAN'S LAW 🦃 George Peppard plays a good cop accused of corruption and suspended from the force. Rated PG for violence. 98m. **DIR:** Richard T. Heffron. **CAST:** George Peppard, Roger Robinson, Abe Vigoda, Eugene Roche. **1974**

NEXT OF KIN (1989) ★★ When his younger brother (Bill Paxton) is killed by a local mobster (Adam Baldwin), Patrick Swayze, as a Chicago cop from the "hollers" of Kentucky, takes justice in his own hands. Formula flick with a preposterous ending. Rated R for profanity and violence. 111m. **DIR:** John Irvin. **CAST:** Patrick Swayze, Liam Neeson, Adam Baldwin, Helen Hunt, Bill Paxton. **1989**

NIGHT AMBUSH ★★★½ Suspenseful World War II drama set in Crete, about a group of British soldiers who kidnap a German general right under the noses of his fellow officers. Solid performances. B&W; 93m. **DIR:** Michael Powell. **CAST:** Dirk Bogarde, Marius Goring, David Oxley, Cyril Cusack. **1957**

NIGHT CROSSING ★★★½ This Disney film is about a real-life escape from East Germany by two families in a gas-filled balloon. Unfortunately, minor flaws, such as mismatched accents and Americanized situations, prevent it from being a total success. Rated PG for violence. 106m. **DIR:** Delbert Mann. **CAST:** John Hurt, Jane Alexander, Beau Bridges, Ian Bannen. **1981**

NIGHT FLIGHT FROM MOSCOW ★★★ A decent, if overly talky, espionage film with a strong cast. Yul Brynner is a Russian diplomat who engages in a complicated plan to defect to the West. Rated PG. 113m. **DIR:** Henri Verneuil. **CAST:** Henry Fonda, Yul Brynner, Farley Granger, Dirk Bogarde, Virna Lisi, Philippe Noiret. **1973**

NIGHT FRIEND 🦃 A crusading priest becomes involved in organized crime. Rated R for profanity, nudity, and violence. 94m. **DIR:** Peter Gerretsen. **CAST:** Art Carney, Chuck Shamata. **1987**

NIGHT OF THE FOX ★★ Preposterous adaptation of Jack Higgins's WWII-set thriller about an undercover mission to rescue an American officer from German-occupied territory. Choppily edited from a six-hour miniseries, leaving nothing but the clichés. 95m. **DIR:** Charles Jarrott. **CAST:** George Peppard, Deborah Raffin, Michael York, David Birney, John Mills. **1990**

NIGHT OF THE GENERALS 🦃 Lurid WWII murder mystery, revolving around a group of Nazi generals. 148m. **DIR:** Anatole Litvak. **CAST:** Peter O'Toole, Omar Sharif, Tom Courtenay, Donald Pleasence, Joanna Pettet, Christopher Plummer. **1967**

NIGHT OF THE JUGGLER ★★ Psychopath kidnaps little girl for ransom. It's the wrong little girl. Her daddy's an ex-cop with no money and lots of rage. The movie, buoyed by James Brolin's potent performance, initially grabs viewers' attention. Eventually, it wheezes to a predictable conclusion. Rated R. 101m. **DIR:** Robert Butler. **CAST:** James Brolin, Cliff Gorman, Richard Castellano, Abby Bluestone, Linda G. Miller, Mandy Patinkin. **1980**

NIGHT OF THE KICKFIGHTERS 🦃 Half of this actioner is wasted on picking a team of good guys to destroy terrorists willing to sell global destructors to the highest bidder. Confrontation between the two groups is saved for the final moments and is not worth the wait. Unrated, but contains violence. 87m. **DIR:** Buddy Reyes. **CAST:** Andy Bauman, Marcia Karr, Adam West. **1990**

NIGHT OF THE SHARKS ★★½ Blackmail and intrigue, washed prettily in the lustrous clear water of Cancun, Mexico, compensate somewhat for the predictable post-*Jaws* approach, in which a one-eyed monster shark makes tropical snorkeling sticky. Rated R. 87m. **DIR:** Anthony Richmond. **CAST:** Treat Williams, Antonio Fargas, Christopher Connelly. **1989**

NIGHT OF THE WARRIOR ★★ Lorenzo Lamas plays the photographer-nightclub proprietor-kick boxer extraordinaire who's been making a fortune for fight promoter

Anthony Geary. When Lamas wants to quit fighting, Geary frames him for murder. Rated R for nudity, profanity, and violence. 96m. **DIR:** Rafal Zielinski. **CAST:** Lorenzo Lamas, Anthony Geary, Kathleen Kinmont, Arlene Dahl. **1990**

NIGHT TRAIN TO MUNICH ★★★★½ Based on Gordon Wellesley's novel *Report on a Fugitive*, this taut thriller concerns a British agent (Rex Harrison) trying to rescue a Czech scientist who has escaped from the Gestapo. Along with a fine cast and superb script and direction, this film is blessed with the moody and wonderful photography of Otto Kanturek. Also known under the title *Night Train*. B&W; 93m. **DIR:** Carol Reed. **CAST:** Rex Harrison, Margaret Lockwood, Paul Henreid, Basil Radford, Naunton Wayne. **1940**

NIGHTFORCE ★★ Linda Blair as a commando. A group of kids venture to Central America to free the kidnapped daughter of a prominent American politician. Rated R for violence. 82m. **DIR:** Lawrence D. Foldes. **CAST:** Linda Blair, Claudia Udy, James Van Patten, Richard Lynch, Chad McQueen, Cameron Mitchell. **1987**

NIGHTHAWKS ★★★★½ From its explosive first scene to the breathtakingly suspenseful denouement, *Nighthawks*, about a police detective hunting a wily terrorist, is a thoroughly enjoyable, supercharged action film. Rated R for violence, nudity, and profanity. 99m. **DIR:** Bruce Malmuth. **CAST:** Sylvester Stallone, Billy Dee Williams, Rutger Hauer, Lindsay Wagner. **1981**

NIGHTSTICK ★★★ A fast-paced thriller with Bruce Fairbairn as an unorthodox cop who is hunting down two ex-convict brothers. The deadly duo are placing bombs in banks and threatening to blow them up unless a ransom is met. A good cast and above-average script make this one worth renting. Equivalent to an R, violent! 94m. **DIR:** Joseph L. Scanlan. **CAST:** Bruce Fairbairn, Robert Vaughn, Kerrie Keane, John Vernon, Leslie Nielsen. **1987**

NINE DEATHS OF THE NINJA 🦃 Another grunt-and-groan, low-budget martial arts mess. Rated R. 94m. **DIR:** Emmett Alston. **CAST:** Sho Kosugi, Brent Huff, Emilia Lesniak, Blackie Dammett. **1985**

99 AND 44/100 PERCENT DEAD 🦃 A hit man is hired to rub out a gangland boss. Rated PG for violence. 98m. **DIR:** John Frankenheimer. **CAST:** Richard Harris, Chuck Connors, Edmond O'Brien, Bradford Dillman, Ann Turkel. **1974**

99 WOMEN 🦃 Eurojunk set in a women's prison with all the usual stereotypes. Rated R. 90m. **DIR:** Jess (Jesus) Franco. **CAST:** Maria Schell, Mercedes McCambridge, Herbert Lom, Luciana Paluzzi. **1969**

NINJA III: THE DOMINATION 🦃 *The Exorcist* meets *Enter the Dragon*. Rated R for violence and profanity. 95m. **DIR:** Sam Firstenberg. **CAST:** Lucinda Dickey, Sho Kosugi. **1984**

NITTI: THE ENFORCER ★★½ Made-for-TV portrait of Frank Nitti (played with conviction by Anthony LaPaglia), who became Al Capone's right-hand man and enforcer in Chicago. Stunning period piece looks great, and supporting cast all do their best. 100m. **DIR:** Michael Switzer. **CAST:** Anthony LaPaglia, Trini Alvarado, Bruno Kirby, Michael Moriarty, Michael Russo. **1988**

NO DEAD HEROES 🦃 Another post–Vietnam War film where our heroes go in and kick some commie tail. Not rated. 86m. **DIR:** J. C. Miller. **CAST:** John Dresden, Max Thayer, Dave Anderson, Nick Nicholson, Mike Monte, Toni Nero. **1986**

NO ESCAPE, NO RETURN ★★ Recognizable faces flesh out this typical actioner. Three rogue cops are sent undercover to bring down a vicious drug lord. Pedestrian effort adds nothing new to the genre. Rated R for violence, language, and sexual situations. 96m. **DIR:** Charles Kanganis. **CAST:** Michael Nouri, John Saxon, Maxwell Caulfield, Denise Loveday, Kevin Benton. **1993**

NO HOLDS BARRED ★★ Muscle-bound rip-off of *Rocky III*. Rated PG-13 for violence and profanity. 92m. **DIR:** Thomas Wright. **CAST:** Hulk Hogan, Joan Severnson, Tiny Lester. **1989**

NO JUSTICE ★★ Rival factions battle for power in a small Southern town. Everything you'd expect from a movie apparently made for the drive-in market. Rated R for violence. 91m. **DIR:** Richard Wayne Martin. **CAST:** Bob Orwig, Cameron Mitchell, Steve Murphy, Phillip Newman, Donald Farmer. **1989**

NO MAN'S LAND ★★½ Predictable police melodrama, with D. B. Sweeney as a young undercover cop tracking a Porsche theft ring in Los Angeles, headed by smoothie Charlie Sheen. The dialogue is sometimes childish, but the film has pace and economy. Rated R for language and violence. 107m. **DIR:** Peter Werner. **CAST:** Charlie Sheen, D. B. Sweeney, Randy Quaid, Lara Harris, Bill Duke, Arlen Dean Snyder. **1987**

NO MERCY ★★ *No Mercy* is a rapid-paced thriller about a Chicago cop (Richard Gere) who travels to New Orleans to avenge the murder of his partner. Kim Basinger is the Cajun woman who is Gere's link to the villain. Rated R for violence, language, and sexual situations. 107m. **DIR:** Richard Pearce. **CAST:** Richard Gere, Kim Basinger, Jeroen Krabbé, George Dzundza, William Atherton, Terry Kinney, Bruce McGill, Ray Sharkey, Gary Basaraba. **1986**

NO PLACE TO HIDE ★★★ Taut thriller finds hard-edged cop Kris Kristofferson attempting to protect Drew Barrymore, who has been targeted for death by the man who killed her sister. The unlikely pair find themselves on the run, trying to stay alive while Kristofferson tracks down the killer. Good performances including Martin Landau as a police chief with an attitude, and fine writing and direction distinguish this entry. Rated R for violence, language, and adult situations. 95m. **DIR:** Richard Danus. **CAST:** Kris Kristofferson, Drew Barrymore, Martin Landau, O. J. Simpson, Dey Young, Bruce Weitz. **1993**

NO RETREAT, NO SURRENDER 🦃 An uninspired cross between *The Karate Kid* and *Rocky IV*. 85m. **DIR:** Corey Yuen. **CAST:** Kurt McKinney, J. W. Fails, Ron Pohnel, Jean-Claude Van Damme. **1985**

NO RETREAT, NO SURRENDER II ★★½ An American attempts to rescue his abducted Thai fiancée, who is being held by Russian and Vietnamese troops in the jungles of Southeast Asia. This is a cross between the *Rambo* movies and *Star Wars*, with the addition of whirling legs, kicking feet, and fists flying fast and furious. Rated R for violence. 92m. **DIR:** Corey Yuen. **CAST:** Loreen Avedon, Max Thayer. **1987**

NO RETREAT, NO SURRENDER 3: BLOOD BROTHERS ★★★ In this largely enjoyable martial arts action film, two rival siblings must avenge their father's murder. Well-choreographed fight scenes, which are a thrill a minute. Rated R for profanity and violence. 97m. **DIR:** Lucas Lo. **CAST:** Loreen Avedon, Keith Vitali, Joseph Campanella. **1990**

NO SAFE HAVEN 🦃 Wings Hauser plays a CIA agent whose family is killed by Bolivian drug smugglers. Rated R for violence, nudity, and suggested sex. 92m. **DIR:** Ronnie Rondell. **CAST:** Wings Hauser, Robert Tessier. **1987**

NONE BUT THE BRAVE ★★½ Story about American and Japanese soldiers stranded on an island during World War II is an interesting premise, but does not make compelling film fare. Frank Sinatra, fine in a small role as a doctor, made his directing debut in this film, the first joint American-Japanese production. 105m. **DIR:** Frank Sinatra. **CAST:** Frank Sinatra, Clint Walker, Tommy Sands, Brad Dexter, Tony Bill. **1965**

NORSEMAN, THE 🦃 This low-budget story of the Vikings is full of stupid historical errors. Rated PG. 90m. **DIR:** Charles B. Pierce. **CAST:** Lee Majors, Charles B. Pierce Jr., Cornel Wilde, Mel Ferrer. **1978**

NORTH STAR, THE ★★★★ This is a well-done World War II film about Russian peasants battling Nazi invaders during the early days of the German invasion of Russia in 1941. It's a bit corny and sentimental in places, but the battle scenes have the usual Milestone high-quality excitement. B&W; 105m. **DIR:** Lewis Milestone. **CAST:** Ruth Gordon, Walter Huston, Anne Baxter, Dana Andrews. **1943**

NORTHEAST OF SEOUL ★★ Three unlikely down-and-outers join forces and end up double-crossing each other in their pursuit of an ancient mystical sword. Very routine. Rated PG for violence. 84m. **DIR:** David Lowell Rich. **CAST:** Anita Ekberg, John Ireland, Victor Buono. **1972**

NORTHERN PURSUIT ★★★ Despite Raoul Walsh's capable direction, this film, about a German heritage Canadian Mountie (Errol Flynn) who feigns defection and guides a party of Nazi saboteurs is pure claptrap. It marked the beginning of Flynn's slow descent into obscurity and, eventually, illness. B&W; 94m. **DIR:** Raoul Walsh. **CAST:** Errol Flynn, Julie Bishop, Tom Tully. **1943**

NORTHVILLE CEMETERY MASSACRE, THE 🦃 A motorcycle gang clashes with the residents of a small town. Rated R. 81m. **DIR:** William Dear. **CAST:** David Hyry, Carson Jackson. **1976**

NORTHWEST PASSAGE ★★★½ Spencer Tracy is the hard-driving, intrepid leader of Roger's Rangers, slogging through swamps and over mountains to open new territory in colonial America. Greenhorns Robert Young and Walter Brennan endure his wrath along the way. Adventure abounds. 125m. **DIR:** King Vidor. **CAST:** Spencer Tracy, Robert Young, Walter Brennan, Ruth Hussey, Nat Pendleton. **1940**

NOWHERE TO HIDE ★★★★ Amy Madigan stars in this exciting adventure of relentless pursuit. Her husband, a marine officer, has uncovered a defective part that is causing accidents in his helicopter squadron. Before he can go public, he is killed. The assassins believe Madigan has the damaging evidence, and the chase is on. An exhilarating climax. Not rated. 100m. **DIR:** Mario Azzopardi. **CAST:** Amy Madigan, Michael Ironside, John Colicos, Daniel Hugh-Kelly. **1987**

NOWHERE TO RUN (1993) ★★½ Jean-Claude Van Damme flexes his biceps and slowly progressing acting ability as an escaped convict who helps a widow save her ranch. Some witty dialogue here and there. Rated R for violence, profanity, and nudity. 90m. **DIR:** Robert Harmon. **CAST:** Jean-Claude Van Damme, Rosanna Arquette, Kiernan Culkin, Ted Levine, Joss Ackland. **1993**

NUMBER ONE WITH A BULLET ★★ Uninspired police thriller-buddy movie suffers from a contrived script. Rated R for violence, profanity, and nudity. 103m. **DIR:** Jack Smight. **CAST:** Robert Carradine, Billy Dee Williams, Valerie Bertinelli, Peter Graves, Doris Roberts. **1987**

NYOKA AND THE TIGER MEN (PERILS OF NYOKA) ★★½ Nyoka, the Jungle Girl, aids archaeologist Clayton Moore in saving and deciphering the long-lost Tablets of Hippocrates, which contain the medical knowledge of the ancient Greeks. The evil Vultura does everything possible to obtain them and do away with her competitors. Plenty of stunts make this an enjoyable afternoon diversion. B&W; 15 chapters. **DIR:** William Witney. **CAST:** Kay Aldrige, Clayton Moore, William Benedict, Lorna Gray. **1942**

OBJECTIVE, BURMA! ★★½ During World War II a tough bunch of paratroopers are dropped into Burma to destroy a radar station and kill Japanese—but even with Errol Flynn in charge, they run into trouble. Overlong action film. B&W; 142m. **DIR:** Raoul Walsh. **CAST:** Errol Flynn, William Prince, James Brown, George Tobias, Henry Hull, Warner Anderson, Richard Erdman, Anthony Caruso, Hugh Beaumont. **1945**

OBSESSION: A TASTE FOR FEAR Tacky, tasteless, disgusting Italian film about the brutal murders of women starring in bondage-type porno films. 90m. **DIR:** Piccio Raffanini. **CAST:** Virginia Hey, Gerard Darmon. **1989**

OCCULTIST, THE Pseudocampy adventure about a private eye hired to protect a visiting Caribbean leader from voodoo and assassins. Unrated, it has mild violence and suggestiveness. 80m. **DIR:** Tim Kincaid. **CAST:** Rick Gianasi, Joe Derrig, Jennifer Kanter, Matt Mitler. **1987**

OCEAN'S ELEVEN ★★★ A twist ending, several stars, and good production values save this tale of an attempted robbery in Las Vegas. Frank Sinatra is the leader of the gang, and his now-famous "rat pack" are the gang members. Lightweight but pleasant. 127m. **DIR:** Lewis Milestone. **CAST:** Frank Sinatra, Dean Martin, Sammy Davis Jr., Peter Lawford, Angie Dickinson, Cesar Romero. **1960**

OCEANS OF FIRE ★★ Predictable formula adventure-saga about five ex-cons and head honcho, Gregory Harrison, putting up an oil rig off the South American coast. Only a star-studded cast saves this one from the depths of mediocrity. Rated PG. 93m. **DIR:** Steve Carver. **CAST:** Gregory Harrison, Billy Dee Williams, Lyle Alzado, Tony Burton, Ray "Boom Boom" Mancini, Ken Norton, Lee Ving, Cynthia Sikes, David Carradine. **1987**

OCTAGON, THE ★★ This "kung fu" flick stars Chuck Norris as a bodyguard for Karen Carlson. Norris naturally takes on multiple opponents and beats them easily. Rated R. 103m. **DIR:** Eric Karson. **CAST:** Chuck Norris, Karen Carlson, Lee Van Cleef, Jack Carter. **1980**

OCTOPUSSY ★★★½ Roger Moore returns as James Bond in the thirteenth screen adventure of Ian Fleming's superspy. It's like an adult-oriented *Raiders of the Lost Ark*: light, fast-paced, funny, and almost over before you know it—almost, because the film tends to overstay its welcome just a bit. Rated PG for violence and suggested sex. 130m. **DIR:** John Glen. **CAST:** Roger Moore, Maud Adams, Louis Jourdan. **1983**

OFF LIMITS (1988) ★★★ Saigon, 1968, makes a noisy and violent background for this murder mystery. Willem Dafoe and Gregory Hines are a pair of military investigators assigned to find the high-ranking killer of local prostitutes. The two leads have good chemistry, Amanda Pays is credible as a sympathetic nun, and Scott Glenn is superb as a warped, messianic infantry colonel. Don't expect the plot to make much sense. Rated R for extreme language, violence, and brief nudity. 102m. **DIR:** Christopher Crowe. **CAST:** Willem Dafoe, Gregory Hines, Fred Ward, Amanda Pays, Scott Glenn. **1988**

OKEFENOKEE ★★ The Florida swamplands are the setting for this forgettable story about smugglers who use the Seminole Indians to help bring drugs into the country. When the Indians are pushed too far, they strike back. What swamp did they dig this one out of? 78m. **DIR:** Roul Haig. **CAST:** Peter Coe, Henry Brandon. **1960**

OLD IRONSIDES ★★ This big-budget, action-packed yarn of wooden ships and iron men besting pirates in the Mediterranean has a big director, big stars, big scenes, and was ballyhooed at its premiere, but it was scuttled by a lackluster script. Silent. B&W; 88m. **DIR:** James Cruze. **CAST:** Charles Farrell, Esther Ralston, Wallace Beery, George Bancroft, Fred Kohler Sr., Boris Karloff. **1926**

OMAR KHAYYAM ★★ Big-budget costume epic with Cornel Wilde as the Persian hero. Unfortunately, the producers skimped on the Saturday-matinee script, which is very weak. 100m. **DIR:** William Dieterle. **CAST:** Cornel Wilde, Debra Paget, John Derek, Raymond Massey, Yma Sumac, Michael Rennie, Sebastian Cabot. **1957**

OMEGA COP Futuristic story of a cop struggling to get three women back to the safety of police headquarters. Rated R for violence. 89m. **DIR:** Paul Kyriazi. **CAST:** Ron Marchini, Adam West, Meg Thayer, Stuart Whitman, Troy Donahue. **1990**

OMEGA SYNDROME ★★ Ken Wahl is a single parent who teams up with his old Vietnam war buddy (George DiCenzo) to track down his daughter's abductors. A very manipulative screenplay makes the film hard to take seriously. Rated R for violence and profanity. 90m. **DIR:** Joseph Manduke. **CAST:** Ken Wahl, George DiCenzo, Doug McClure, Ron Kuhlman, Patti Tippo. **1986**

ON DEADLY GROUND ★★½ Director-star Steven Seagal has come up with a martial arts movie with an environmental message. As you might guess, it's an uneasy combination, although action fans will find Seagal in top form as a one-man army out to stop oil tycoon Michael Caine (in a delightfully over-the-top role) from turning Alaska into one big ecological disaster. Rated R for violence and profanity. 98m. **DIR:** Steven Seagal. **CAST:** Steven Seagal, Michael Caine, Joan Chen, John C. McGinley, R. Lee Ermey, Irvin Brink, Richard Hamilton. **1994**

ON HER MAJESTY'S SECRET SERVICE ★★★★ With Sean Connery temporarily out of the James Bond series, Australian actor George Lazenby stepped into the 007 part for this entry—and did remarkably well. Director Peter Hunt keeps this moving at an incredibly fast pace, and this story about everyone's favorite superspy falling in love with an heiress (Diana Rigg) is one of author Ian Fleming's best. Rated PG. 140m. **DIR:** Peter R. Hunt. **CAST:** George Lazenby, Diana Rigg, Telly Savalas. **1969**

ON THE LINE ★★½ David Carradine smuggles aliens across the Mexican border. Scott Wilson pledges to nail Carradine and his operation. This mediocre adventure is not rated. 103m. **DIR:** José Luis Borau. **CAST:** David Carradine, Scott Wilson, Victoria Abril, Jeff Delger, Paul Richardson, Jesse Vint, Sam Jaffe. **1987**

ON THE YARD ★★ Subpar prison melodrama pits John Heard against a prison-yard boss. Some good peformances help, but this never gets going, nor does it ring true. Rated R. 102m. **DIR:** Raphael D. Silver. **CAST:** John Heard, Mike Kellin, Richard Bright, Thomas Waites, Joe Grifasi. **1979**

ON WINGS OF EAGLES ★★★ Well-acted, long-form TV production about what happens when two business executives are imprisoned in Tehran just before the fall of the shah of Iran. Burt Lancaster is top-notch as the grizzled ex-military man who trains the company's other executives for a raid on the prison. Richard Crenna's take-charge tycoon in this fact-based film was modeled on Ross Perot. 221m. **DIR:** Andrew V. McLaglen. **CAST:** Burt Lancaster, Richard Crenna, Paul LeMat, Jim Metzler, Esai Morales, Constance Towers. **1986**

ONCE A HERO ★★ Yesteryear's comic-book superhero, Captain Justice, is slowly fading away. His fans are deserting him, so he decides to cross from his world of fantasy to our world of today with predictable but occasionally amusing results. Not rated. 74m. **DIR:** Claudia Weill. **CAST:** Jeff Lester, Robert Forster, Milo O'Shea. **1988**

ONCE UPON A TIME IN AMERICA (LONG VERSION) ★★★★ Italian director Sergio Leone's richly rewarding gangster epic; a $30 million production starring Robert DeNiro in a forty-five-year saga of Jewish gangsters in New York City. Leone is best-known for his spaghetti westerns *A Fistful of Dollars, The Good, the Bad and the Ugly,* and *Once Upon a Time in the West.* This release culminates ten years of planning and false starts by the filmmaker. It was well worth the wait. Rated R for profanity, nudity, suggested sex, and violence. 225m. **DIR:** Sergio Leone. **CAST:** Robert De Niro, James Woods, Elizabeth McGovern, Tuesday Weld, Treat Williams, Burt Young. **1984**

ONE DOWN, TWO TO GO ★★ Kung fu fighter (Jim Kelly) suspects a tournament is fixed and calls on his buddies (Jim Brown and director Fred Williamson) for help in this low-budget, theatrically unreleased sequel to *Three the Hard Way.* Some actors are hopelessly amateurish, and the story is a mere sketch. Unrated, the film has violence. 84m. **DIR:** Fred Williamson. **CAST:** Fred Williamson, Jim Brown, Jim Kelly, Richard Roundtree. **1983**

ONE FALSE MOVE ★★★½ Terrific crime drama chronicles the exploits of three criminals, two men and a woman, from their initial cocaine rip-off in Los Angeles to a slam bang finale in a small Arkansas town. Entire cast is excellent under first-time director Carl Franklin's sure hand. Rated R for violence and language. 104m. **DIR:** Carl Franklin. **CAST:** Bill Paxton, Cynda Williams, Michael Beach, Jim Metzler. **1992**

ONE MAN ARMY 🦃 Low-rent kick-boxing effort pits champ Jerry Trimble against the crooked small-town officials who killed his grandfather, but doesn't bring anything new to the arena. Rated R for violence and strong language. 90m. **DIR:** Cirio H. Santiago. **CAST:** Jerry Trimble, Melissa Moore, Dennis Hayden, Yvonne Michelle, Rick Dean. **1994**

ONE-MAN FORCE ★★★ John Matuszak plays an L.A. cop seeking to avenge his partner's murder. Good action drama. Rated R for violence and profanity. 90m. **DIR:** Dale Trevillion. **CAST:** John Matuszak, Ronny Cox, Charles Napier. **1989**

ONE MINUTE TO ZERO ★★ Sluggish film about the Korean War benefits from some good acting by the male leads. The romantic subplot doesn't help much, but then not much could help this barely serviceable story about servicemen. B&W; 105m. **DIR:** Tay Garnett. **CAST:** Robert Mitchum, Ann Blyth, William Talman, Charles McGraw, Richard Egan. **1952**

ONE OF OUR AIRCRAFT IS MISSING ★★★★ This British production is similar to *Desperate Journey* (1942) with Errol Flynn and Ronald Reagan. The story concerns an RAF crew who are shot down over Holland during World War II and who try to escape to England. High-caliber suspense. B&W; 106m. **DIR:** Michael Powell, Emeric Pressburger. **CAST:** Godfrey Tearle, Eric Portman, Pamela

Brown, Hugh Williams, Googie Withers, Peter Ustinov. **1941**

ONE RIOT, ONE RANGER ★★★ Decent pilot for Chuck Norris's TV series *Walker, Texas Ranger* features the martial artist taking on a ruthless gang of bank robbers. His new partner (Clarence Gilyard Jr.) steals a number of scenes, but fights between lesser characters are poorly staged. Rated PG-13 for violence. 95m. **DIR:** Virgil Vogel. **CAST:** Chuck Norris, Clarence Gilyard Jr., Sheree Wilson, Gailard Sartain, Floyd Red Crow Westerman. **1993**

ONE STEP TO HELL ★★ On their way to a South African jail, a trio of killers escape and head for the jungle in search of a hidden gold mine, with police officer Ty Hardin hot on their trail. Not bad, but you wouldn't want to expend a lot of effort looking for it. 94m. **DIR:** Sandy Howard. **CAST:** Ty Hardin, Pier Angeli, Rossano Brazzi, George Sanders. **1968**

ONE THAT GOT AWAY, THE ★★★★ Excellent adaptation of the book by Kendal Burt and James Leasor about a captured German aviator who keeps escaping from a multitude of British prisoner-of-war camps. Based on a true story and especially well directed and performed, this adventure is highly recommended. B&W; 106m. **DIR:** Roy Ward Baker. **CAST:** Hardy Krüger, Colin Gordon, Michael Goodliffe. **1958**

ONLY ANGELS HAVE WINGS ★★★★ Director Howard Hawks at his best tells yet another tale of professionals: pilots who fly the mail through treacherous weather and terrain in South America. Snappy dialogue and no-nonsense characters are handled deftly by the entire cast. It's great stuff, with Rita Hayworth getting a career-starting, glamorous role. B&W; 121m. **DIR:** Howard Hawks. **CAST:** Cary Grant, Jean Arthur, Richard Barthelmess, Rita Hayworth, Thomas Mitchell, John Carroll, Sig Ruman, Allyn Joslyn, Noah Beery Jr. **1939**

ONLY THE STRONG ★★★ A world-class, martial-arts champion pits his strength and know-how against juvenile gangs and teaches them self-respect. The martial-arts sequences using the Brazilian Capoeira techniques are exciting to watch, and the story, though predictable, is well staged and well acted. Rated R for violence and profanity. 112m. **DIR:** Sheldon Lettich. **CAST:** Mark Dascascos, Stacey Travis, Paco Prieto, Tod Susman, Richard Coca, Geoffrey Lewis. **1993**

OPERATION AMSTERDAM ★★★ It's 1940 and Allied spies penetrate Holland to prevent the invading Nazis from getting their hands on Amsterdam's rich cache of diamonds. Filmed in a semidocumentary style, this movie is standard but well acted and produced. B&W; 105m. **DIR:** Michael McCarthy. **CAST:** Peter Finch, Eva Bartok, Tony Britton, Alexander Knox. **1960**

OPERATION C.I.A. ★★½ Political intrigue in Vietnam before the United States's full involvement finds a youthful Burt Reynolds as an agent assigned to derail an assassination attempt. Good location photography and Reynolds's enthusiasm and believability mark this film as one of the best chase films of the mid-1960s. B&W; 90m. **DIR:** Christian Nyby. **CAST:** Burt Reynolds, Kieu Chinh, Danielle Aubry, John Hoyt. **1965**

OPERATION CROSSBOW ★★★★ A trio of specially trained commandos are sent to head off Hitler's rapidly developing rocket program. Suspenseful and exciting, with a top-notch international cast, fine special effects. 116m. **DIR:** Michael Anderson. **CAST:** George Peppard, Sophia Loren, Trevor Howard, John Mills, Richard Johnson, Tom Courtenay, Lilli Palmer, Jeremy Kemp, Paul Henreid, Helmut Dantine, Richard Todd, Sylvia Syms. **1965**

OPERATION 'NAM ★★ Run-of-the-mill tale about a group of bored Vietnam vets going back to Vietnam to rescue their leader, still held in a POW camp. Notable only for the appearance of Ethan Wayne, one of John's sons. Not rated, but contains violence, language, and nudity. 85m. **DIR:** Larry Ludman. **CAST:** Oliver Tobias, Christopher Connelly, Manfred Lehman, John Steiner, Ethan Wayne, Donald Pleasence. **1985**

OPERATION THUNDERBOLT ★★ Another film, like *The Raid on Entebbe*, dealing with the Israeli commando raid in Uganda in 1976 to free 104 hijacked airline passengers. Overly sentimental, with routine action sequences. No MPAA rating. 125m. **DIR:** Menahem Golan. **CAST:** Yehoram Gaon, Klaus Kinski, Assaf Dayan. **1977**

OPERATION WAR ZONE 🦃 Courier lost in Vietnam possesses a document that could affect the outcome of the war. Too bad it wasn't the script for this film. 89m. **DIR:** David A. Prior. **CAST:** David Marriott, Joe Spinell. **1989**

OPPONENT, THE ★★½ A boxer rescues a mob boss's daughter, only to be swept up in her father's corrupt world. Now he's fighting for his life in a film that plays like a low-budget *Rocky*. Rated R for violence. 102m. **DIR:** Sergio Martino. **CAST:** Daniel Greene, Ernest Borgnine, Mary Stavin. **1990**

OPPOSING FORCE ★★½ In this average action-adventure movie, a group of soldiers undergo simulated prisoner-of-war training. When the commanding officer (Anthony Zerbe) goes insane, he rapes the sole female soldier (Lisa Eichhorn) and sets into motion a chain of violent events. Rated R for profanity and violence. 97m. **DIR:** Eric Karson. **CAST:** Tom Skerritt, Lisa Eichhorn, Anthony Zerbe, Richard Roundtree, John Considine. **1986**

ORDER OF THE BLACK EAGLE ★★ Ian Hunter is the James Bondish main character, Duncan Jax, abetted in destroying a neo-Nazi group by his sidekick, a baboon, and a band of misfits. Rated R for violence and language. 93m. **DIR:** Worth Keeter. **CAST:** Ian Hunter, Charles K. Bibby, William T. Hicks, Jill Donnellan, Anna Rappagna, Flo Hyman. **1987**

ORDER OF THE EAGLE ★★★ On a camping trip in the woods, a boy scout discovers computer discs in a plane wreck. They contain secret military plans that bad guy Frank Stallone wants back. Well-written thriller. Unrated; contains mild violence. 82m. **DIR:** Thomas Baldwin. **CAST:** Frank Stallone, William Zipp, Casey Hirsch. **1989**

ORGANIZATION, THE ★★★ This is the third and last installment of the Virgil Tibbs series based on the character Sidney Poitier originated in *In the Heat of the Night*. Tibbs is out to break up a ring of dope smugglers. A pretty good cop film, with some exciting action scenes. Rated PG; some strong stuff for the kids. 107m. **DIR:** Don Medford. **CAST:** Sidney Poitier, Barbara McNair, Raul Julia, Sheree North. **1971**

OSTERMAN WEEKEND, THE ★★ Sam Peckinpah's last is a confusing action movie with scarce viewing rewards for the filmmaker's fans. Based on Robert Ludlum's novel, it tells a complicated and convoluted story of espionage, revenge, and duplicity. Rated R for profanity, nudity, sex, and violence. 102m. **DIR:** Sam Peckinpah. **CAST:** Rutger Hauer, John Hurt, Burt Lancaster, Dennis Hopper, Chris Sarandon, Meg Foster. **1983**

OUR MAN FLINT ★★★½ Of the numerous imitators who followed James Bond's footsteps in the spy-crazed 1960s, Derek Flint of ZOWIE was by far the best. Ultracool and suavely sophisticated, James Coburn puts his earsplitting grin to good use as a renegade secret agent. One sequel followed: *In Like Flint*. Unrated; suitable for family viewing. 107m. **DIR:** Daniel Mann. **CAST:** James Coburn, Lee J. Cobb, Gila Golan, Edward Mulhare. **1966**

OUT ★★ You may want out before the final countdown of this offbeat, surrealistic action film. Peter Coyote is an urban guerrilla who starts out in Greenwich Village and goes cross-country on assignments from a mysterious commander. This comedy-action pastiche tries very hard to be artsy. Rated PG. 88m. **DIR:** Eli Hollander. **CAST:** Peter Coyote, Danny Glover, O-Lan Shephard, Gail Dartez, Jim Haynie, Scott Beach. **1983**

OUT FOR JUSTICE ★★★★½ Steven Seagal is top-notch as a maverick police detective out to avenge the death of his partner. The best fist-and-foot-style action film to date, this release has pure adrenaline-pumping, jaw-dropping thrills and chills from beginning to end. Rated R for violence, drug use, profanity, and nudity. 90m. **DIR:** John Flynn. **CAST:** Steven Seagal, William Forsythe, Jerry Orbach. **1991**

OUT OF BOUNDS 🦃 A naïve Iowa boy journeys to Los Angeles and accidentally switches luggage with a nasty heroin smuggler. Rated R for extreme violence. 93m. **DIR:** Richard Tuggle. **CAST:** Anthony Michael Hall, Jenny Wright, Jeff Kober, Glynn Turman, Raymond J. Barry. **1986**

OUT ON BAIL ★★½ Sort of a redneck version of *A Fistful of Dollars*. Drifter Robert Ginty turns the tables on small-town bad guys who try to force him to do their dirty work. Too bad it doesn't go all the way into spaghetti territory. Rated R for sexual situations and violence. 102m. **DIR:** Gordon Hessler. **CAST:** Robert Ginty, Kathy Shower, Tom Badal, Sidney Lassick, Leo Sparrowhawk. **1989**

OUTFIT, THE 🦃 Boring mishmash about Dutch Schultz, Legs Diamond, and Lucky Luciano creaks under the weight of macho posturing and a script shot full of holes. Rated R for violence, nudity, and profanity. 92m. **DIR:** J. Christian Ingvordsen. **CAST:** Lance Henriksen, Billy Drago, Martin Kove. **1993**

OUTLAW FORCE ★★ It had to happen. Somebody crossed *Rambo* with *Urban Cowboy*. A gang run out of town by a handsome country singer (David Heavener) gets revenge when they rape and kill his wife, then kidnap his daughter and return to (where else?) Hollywood. Heavener, a Vietnam vet, takes justice into his own hands. Rated R for violence. 95m. **DIR:** David Heavener. **CAST:** David Heavener, Paul Smith, Frank Stallone, Warren Berlinger. **1987**

OUTPOST IN MOROCCO ★★ George Raft is out of his element as a French legionnaire assigned to stop the activities of desert rebels only to find himself falling in love with the daughter (Marie Windsor) of their leader (Akim Tamiroff). Pure hokum and slow moving, too. B&W; 92m. **DIR:** Robert Florey. **CAST:** George Raft, Marie Windsor, Akim Tamiroff. **1949**

OVERKILL 🦃 Racist, violent *Miami Vice*-type of crime story. Rated R for extreme violence and nudity. 81m. **DIR:** Ulli Lommel. **CAST:** Steve Rally, John Nishio, Laura Burkett, Allen Wisch, Roy Summersett, Antonio Caprio. **1986**

P.O.W.: THE ESCAPE ★★½ David Carradine's considerable acting talents are wasted once again in this *Rambo* rip-off that is missing everything but action. Rated R for profanity and violence. 90m. **DIR:** Gideon Amir. **CAST:** David Carradine, Mako, Charles R. Floyd, Steve James. **1986**

PACIFIC INFERNO ★★½ This war adventure film is set in the Philippines during the final fall and capture of U.S. and Filipino soldiers. Jim Brown and Richard Jaeckel are American navy prisoners. Good, steady action follows. Unrated. 90m. **DIR:** Rolf Bayer.

CAST: Jim Brown, Richard Jaeckel, Tim Brown, Tad Horino, Wilma Redding, Vic Diaz. **1985**

PAINT IT BLACK ★★★½ Talented young sculptor (Rick Rossovich) is under bondage to an unscrupulous gallery owner (Sally Kirkland). He meets a slightly off-center art collector (Doug Savant) who complicates his life with favors. Impressive little thriller. Rated R for violence, nudity, and adult situations. 101m. **DIR:** Tim Hunter. **CAST:** Rick Rossovich, Sally Kirkland, Martin Landau, Julie Carmen, Doug Savant. **1989**

PALAIS ROYALE ★★ The Hollywood gangster is viewed through a peculiarly Canadian prism in this Toronto-made *film noir.* Matt Craven plays an ambitious advertising executive, circa 1959, who stumbles into a world of gangsters and goons. Slovenly. 100m. **DIR:** Martin Lavut. **CAST:** Dean Stockwell, Kim Cattrall, Matt Craven. **1988**

PANTHER GIRL OF THE CONGO 🦃 Republic Studio's last cliffhanger about a chemist who creates giant crayfish to guard his diamond hoard was a definite contributor to the genre's demise. B&W; 12 chapters. **DIR:** Franklin Adreon. **CAST:** Phyllis Coates, Myron Healey, Arthur Space. **1955**

PAPER TIGER ★★ Stiffly British David Niven is tutor to the son (Ando) of a Japanese ambassador (Toshiro Mifune). He and his young charge are kidnapped by terrorists for political reasons. Derring-do follows, but it's all lukewarm and paplike. Rated PG. 99m. **DIR:** Ken Annakin. **CAST:** David Niven, Toshiro Mifune, Ando, Hardy Krüger. **1976**

PAPILLON ★★★★½ Unfairly criticized, this is a truly exceptional film biography of the man who escaped from Devil's Island. Steve McQueen gives an excellent performance, and Dustin Hoffman is once again a chameleon. Director Frank Schaffner invests the same gusto here that he did in *Patton.* Rated PG. 150m. **DIR:** Franklin J. Schaffner. **CAST:** Steve McQueen, Dustin Hoffman, Victor Jory, Don Gordon. **1973**

PARADISE (1982) ★★ Willie Aames and Phoebe Cates star as two teenagers who, as members of a caravan traveling from Baghdad to Damascus in the nineteenth century, escape a surprise attack by a sheikh intent on adding Cates to his harem. Rated R for frontal male and female nudity. 100m. **DIR:** Stuart Gillard. **CAST:** Willie Aames, Phoebe Cates, Tuvia Tavi. **1982**

PARATROOP COMMAND ★★½ World War II drama set in North Africa, where a paratrooper tries to make amends after he accidentally shoots a member of his own squadron. Effective action direction lifts this above the pedestrian. B&W; 71m. **DIR:** William Witney. **CAST:** Dick Bakalyan. **1959**

PARIS EXPRESS, THE ★★½ Based on acclaimed mystery writer Georges Simenon's novel, this film details the exploits of a finance clerk (Claude Rains) who turns embezzler. Hoping to travel the world with his ill-gotten gains, he runs into more trouble and adventure than he can handle. 80m. **DIR:** Harold French. **CAST:** Claude Rains, Marta Toren, Anouk Aimée, Marius Goring, Herbert Lom. **1953**

PARTY LINE 🦃 Disconnected nonsense about telephone party-line callers who turn up dead. Rated R for violence, profanity, and nudity. 91m. **DIR:** William Webb. **CAST:** Richard Hatch, Leif Garrett, Richard Roundtree. **1988**

PASSAGE TO MARSEILLES ★★★ The performances of Humphrey Bogart, Claude Rains, Sydney Greenstreet, and Peter Lorre are all that's good about this muddled film about an escape from Devil's Island during World War II. Directed by Michael Curtiz, its flashback-within-flashback scenes all but totally confuse the viewer. B&W; 110m. **DIR:** Michael Curtiz. **CAST:** Humphrey Bogart, Claude Rains, Sydney Greenstreet, Peter Lorre. **1944**

PASSENGER 57 ★★★★½ Slam-bang action film is an airborne variation on *Die Hard.* This time, the hero is an airline security expert who is caught on a plane skyjacked by terrorists. Featuring a strong lead performance by Wesley Snipes, this little gem is so exciting, funny, suspenseful, and packed with great bits that you don't dare take your eyes off the screen for a second. Rated R for violence and profanity. 85m. **DIR:** Kevin Hooks. **CAST:** Wesley Snipes, Bruce Payne, Tom Sizemore, Bruce Greenwood, Robert Hooks, Michael Horse. **1992**

PASSION (1954) ★★ Colorful hokum about a hot-blooded adventurer (Cornel Wilde) and his quest for vengeance in old California. Directed by veteran filmmaker Allan Dwan, this okay adventure boasts a nice cast of character actors. 84m. **DIR:** Allan Dwan. **CAST:** Cornel Wilde, Yvonne De Carlo, Raymond Burr, Lon Chaney Jr., John Qualen. **1954**

PATRIOT 🦃 Underwater commandos fight terrorists. Rated R for nudity and violence. 90m. **DIR:** Frank Harris. **CAST:** Gregg Henry, Simone Griffeth, Michael J. Pollard, Jeff Conaway, Stack Pierce, Leslie Nielsen. **1986**

PATRIOT GAMES ★★★★½ First-rate suspense-thriller has Harrison Ford taking over the role of novelist Tom Clancy's CIA analyst Jack Ryan from Alec Baldwin, who played the character in *The Hunt for Red October.* This time Ryan must save his wife and daughter from renegade Irish terrorists. Taut and exciting, especially during the nail-biting climax. Rated R for profanity and violence. 118m. **DIR:** Phillip Noyce. **CAST:** Harrison Ford, Anne Archer, Patrick Bergin, Sean Bean, James Earl Jones, Richard Harris, James Fox. **1992**

PAYBACK ★★★½ Prison detail escapee falls in love with a small-town sheriff's daughter. Rated R for language and delicate seduction scenes. 94m. **DIR:** Russell Solberg. **CAST:** Corey Michael Eubanks, Michael Ironside, Don Swayze, Teresa Blake, Bert Remsen. **1990**

PAYOFF ★★★½ Keith Carradine is sympathetic as an affable fellow forever haunted by the memory of—while a child—having unknowingly delivered a bomb that killed his parents. Earnest performances and slick pacing hide the plot flaws in this engaging little thriller. Made for cable, with violence and brief nudity. 111m. **DIR:** Stuart Cooper. **CAST:** Keith Carradine, Kim Greist, Harry Dean Stanton, John Saxon, Robert Harper. **1991**

PENITENTIARY ★★ Leon Isaac Kennedy dons boxing gloves as the black Rocky to triumph over pure evil in this lurid, but entertaining, movie. 94m. **DIR:** Jamaa Fanaka. **CAST:** Leon Isaac Kennedy, Thommy Pollard. **1979**

PENITENTIARY II 🦃 A retread. Rated R for violence and profanity. 108m. **DIR:** Jamaa Fanaka. **CAST:** Leon Isaac Kennedy, Glynn Turman, Ernie Hudson, Mr. T. **1982**

PENITENTIARY III 🦃 Lock this one up in solitary confinement. 91m. **DIR:** Jamaa Fanaka. **CAST:** Leon Isaac Kennedy, Anthony Geary, Steve Antin, Ric Mancini, Jim Bailey. **1987**

PERFECT WEAPON ★★½ Standard martial arts action, as our strong, silent hero (Jeff Speakman) goes after the killers of an old family friend. Fans of the genre will like this one; the fight scenes are quite well staged. Rated R for violence. 90m. **DIR:** Mark DiSalle. **CAST:** Jeff Speakman, Mako. **1991**

PERILS OF GWENDOLINE, THE 🦃 Poorly acted escapade. Rated R for violence, profanity, and sexual content. 96m. **DIR:** Just Jaeckin. **CAST:** Tawny Kitaen, Brent Huff. **1985**

PERILS OF PAULINE, THE (1933) ★★ Sound serial version of the famous Pearl White cliff-hanger retains only the original title. The daughter of a prominent scientist and her companion struggle to keep the formula for a deadly gas out of the hands of evil Dr. Bashan and his slimy assistant Fang. This serial lacks the charisma of later efforts from Universal Studios. B&W; 12 chapters. **DIR:** Ray Taylor. **CAST:** Evalyn Knapp, Robert Allen, James Durkin, John Davidson, Sonny Ray. **1933**

PERILS OF THE DARKEST JUNGLE ★★½ This is a pretty good Republic serial due largely to fast pacing (by serial veteran director Spencer Bennet), a fetching heroine (former model Stirling, here ably portraying a Nyoka-type white African queen), some breathtaking matte paintings, and surprisingly graphic violence, particularly in the opening chapter. Six writers concocted the 12-episode affair. Original title: *Tiger Woman.* B&W; 12 chapters. **DIR:** Spencer Gordon Bennet, Wallace Grissell. **CAST:** Allan "Rocky" Lane, Linda Stirling, Duncan Renaldo. **1944**

PERMISSION TO KILL ★★ An exiled politician (Bekim Fehmiu) from an Eastern bloc nation living in Austria decides to return to his native country. A Western intelligence agent (Dirk Bogarde) must stop him. Rated PG for violence, profanity, and nudity. 96m. **DIR:** Cyril Frankel. **CAST:** Dirk Bogarde, Ava Gardner, Bekim Fehmiu, Timothy Dalton, Nicole Calfan, Frederic Forrest. **1975**

PERSUADERS, THE (TV SERIES) ★★★ This tongue-in-cheek adventure series lasted just one season on ABC, but it offers a fair bit of action, humor, and style. Set in the glamour spots of Europe, the show follows two dashing playboys: Brett Sinclair (Roger Moore), a British lord, and Daniel Wilde (Tony Curtis), a self-made millionaire from the Bronx. Moore and Curtis are fun to watch in these tailor-made roles, smoothly handling the roughhousing, rivalry, and romance. The first two episodes to be released on tape are "Overture," guest starring Imogen Hassal, and "Five Miles to Midnight," with Joan Collins. 60m. **DIR:** Basil Dearden, Val Guest. **CAST:** Roger Moore, Tony Curtis, Laurence Naismith. **1972**

PETER GUNN (TV SERIES) ★★★½ Long before *The Pink Panther* and superstardom, writer-director Blake Edwards earned his Hollywood reputation with this stylish television detective series. Star Craig Stevens established an image that was to be endlessly imitated: suave, urbane, and self-mocking in the face of certain peril. Despite the temptation of silkily lethal ladies, Gunn always remained true to his steady girl, Edie (Lola Albright), who worked as a singer in a waterfront nightclub dubbed Mother's (with Mother herself played by Hope Emerson). The most fun resulted from Gunn's contacts: a truly outrageous assortment of snitches and stoolies, all willing to sing for a discreetly tendered sawbuck (a concept lampooned deliciously in *Police Squad*). Composer Henry Mancini also began a trend with his smooth, jazzy themes. Each volume includes two episodes; the best are the explosive "Death House Testament" and the deftly scripted "The Comic" (which earned Edwards an award from the Mystery Writers of America). B&W; each 55m. **DIR:** Blake Edwards, Boris Sagal. **CAST:** Craig Stevens, Lola Albright, Herschel Bernardi, Hope Emerson. **1958–1961**

PHANTOM EMPIRE (1935) ★★★ Gene Autry, with the aid of Frankie Darro, champion rider Betsy King Ross, and the Junior Thunder Riders, overcomes threats from greedy crooks and the deadly threat of Murania, the futuristic city twenty thousand feet beneath the ground. Plenty of action, the wonders of the "city of the future," and good special effects (including a death ray) make this one of Mascot Films's best serials. B&W; 12 chapters. **DIR:** Otto Brewer, B. Reeves "Breezy" Eason. **CAST:** Gene Autry, Frankie Darro, Betsy King Ross, Smiley Burnette. **1935**

PHANTOM EMPIRE, THE (1986) ★★★ Fans of old serials and Fifties sci-fi adventures will want to check out this good-natured parody. The plot, about a group of adventurers trying to salvage a cache of diamonds from a mutant-infested cavern, is a thin frame for lots of tongue-in-cheek dialogue and in-jokes. Rated R for nudity. 83m. **DIR:** Fred Olen Ray. **CAST:** Ross Hagen, Jeffrey Combs, Russ Tamblyn, Sybil Danning. **1986**

PHANTOM EXPRESS ★★ J. Farrell MacDonald loses his job and his pension with the railroad after his own engine is ruined in a wreck with a mysterious train. Shunned by his friends and co-workers, the salty old engineer decides to bring the villains to justice himself and does so with the help of young Sally Blane. Nothing new here, but the vintage trains are a treat to look at. B&W; 65m. **DIR:** Emory Johnson. **CAST:** J. Farrell MacDonald, Sally Blane, William Collier Jr., Hobart Bosworth. **1932**

PIMPERNEL SMITH ★★★ Star Leslie Howard, who also produced, brought his 1934 role in *The Scarlet Pimpernel* up to modern times in this anti-Nazi thriller involving a daring rescue of important scientists from prison. B&W; 122m. **DIR:** Leslie Howard. **CAST:** Leslie Howard, David Tomlinson, Philip Friend, Hugh McDermott, Mary Morris. **1942**

PINK CADILLAC ★★ Clint Eastwood returns to the *Every Which Way But Loose*–style action-comedy with this mediocre effort, in which he plays a skip tracer out to nab the bail-jumping Bernadette Peters. There are some good lines in this formula film, but it is predictable, overdone, and ultimately boring. Rated PG-13 for violence, profanity, and suggested sex. 122m. **DIR:** Buddy Van Horn. **CAST:** Clint Eastwood, Bernadette Peters, John Dennis Johnston, William Hickey, Geoffrey Lewis, Bill McKinney. **1989**

PIRATES OF THE HIGH SEAS ★★ Buster Crabbe plays a rugged adventurer who sails to the aid of an old friend whose freight line is being sabotaged. This serial is pretty long in the tooth and if it weren't for the welcome presence of the heroic Crabbe, it would barely be worth watching. B&W; 15 chapters. **DIR:** Spencer Gordon Bennet, Thomas Carr. **CAST:** Buster Crabbe, Lois Hall, Tommy Farrell, Gene Roth, Tristram Coffin. **1950**

PLATOON LEADER 🦃 Leaden bore. Rated R for violence. 93m. **DIR:** Aaron Norris. **CAST:** Michael Dudikoff, Robert F. Lyons, Rick Fitts, William Smith. **1988**

PLUNDER ROAD ★★ This ingenious update to *The Great Train Robbery* leaves five men on the run with $10 million in gold. The crime-does-not-pay theme prevails. The acting is not the greatest. B&W; 76m. **DIR:** Hubert Cornfield. **CAST:** Gene Raymond, Wayne Morris, Jeanne Cooper. **1957**

POINT BREAK ★★★½ For most of its running time, this release, about two FBI agents (Keanu Reeves, Gary Busey) attempting to catch the perpetrators (who may be led by surfer/guru Patrick Swayze) behind a series of bank robberies, is a terrific action movie. But *Point Break* tends to overstay its welcome with more false endings than we've ever seen. Rated R for violence and profanity. 125m. **DIR:** Kathryn Bigelow. **CAST:** Patrick Swayze, Keanu Reeves, Gary Busey, Lori Petty, John C. McGinley. **1991**

POINT OF IMPACT ★★½ A talented cast is wasted in this humdrum cop thriller where plot exists only to fill the spaces between the energetic coupling by Michael Paré and Barbara Carrera. He's a former U.S. Customs agent, she's a crime lord's wife needing protection from parties never adequately specified. Available in both R and unrated versions, each with considerable profanity, violence, nudity, and simulated sex. 96m. **DIR:** Bob Misiorowski. **CAST:** Michael Paré, Barbara Carrera, Michael Ironside, Lehua Reid. **1993**

POINT OF NO RETURN ★★★ American, scene-for-scene remake of French director Luc Besson's *La Femme Nikita* lacks the subtlety and poignance of the original. Instead, director John Badham puts the emphasis on violence, with street punk Bridget Fonda drafted as an assassin by a supersecret, government organization. Fonda's committed performance is the only high-quality element in this no-excuses action romp. Rated R for violence, profanity, nudity, and simulated sex. 108m. **DIR:** John Badham. **CAST:** Bridget Fonda, Gabriel Byrne, Dermot Mulroney, Anne Bancroft, Harvey Keitel, Miguel Ferrer, Olivia D'Abo, Richard Romanus, Geoffrey Lewis. **1993**

POPPY IS ALSO A FLOWER, THE ★★ James Bond creator Ian Fleming wrote the original story for this movie about efforts to put an end to an international drug ring. Many in the huge cast worked for scale as a protest against drug abuse, but it backfired. There are so many stars popping up in small roles that they overwhelm the plot. Originally made for television, later released theatrically with added footage. Unrated, the film contains violence. 105m. **DIR:** Terence Young. **CAST:** E. G. Marshall, Trevor Howard, Gilbert Roland, Rita Hayworth, Anthony Quayle, Angie Dickinson, Yul Brynner, Eli Wallach, Marcello Mastroianni, Omar Sharif, Grace Kelly. **1966**

POSEIDON ADVENTURE, THE ★★★ It's New Year's Eve on the passenger liner *Poseidon*. A tidal wave overturns the ship, and from here on out the all-star cast, special effects, and imaginative sets take over. It's a fairly watchable disaster flick, nothing more. Rated PG. 117m. **DIR:** Ronald Neame. **CAST:** Gene Hackman, Ernest Borgnine, Shelley Winters, Roddy McDowall, Red Buttons, Stella Stevens. **1972**

PRAY FOR THE WILDCATS 🦃 Three businessmen on a macho motorcycle trip in the desert. Made for TV. 100m. **DIR:** Robert Michael Lewis. **CAST:** Andy Griffith, William Shatner, Angie Dickinson, Janet Margolin, Robert Reed, Marjoe Gortner, Lorraine Gary. **1974**

PRAYER OF THE ROLLERBOYS ★★½ The Rollerboys are a gang of fascistic, drug-running teens who terrorize Los Angeles of the near future, zipping around on roller blades. Good stunt work and a *Blade Runner*-like look at the future make up for a too-familiar plot. Rated R for violence. 94m. **DIR:** Rick King. **CAST:** Corey Haim, Patricia Arquette, Christopher Collet, J. C. Quinn. **1991**

PREHISTORIC WOMEN (1967) 🦃 A dreadful film about a tribe of phallus-worshipping women. 91m. **DIR:** Michael Carreras. **CAST:** Martine Beswick. **1967**

PRESIDENT'S TARGET 🦃 Badly acted, choppy story about two CIA operatives and a powerful South American drug cartel. Rated R for violence and profanity. 82m. **DIR:** Yvan Chiffre. **CAST:** John Coleman, Martin Kove, Bo Hopkins, Brigitte Audrey. **1993**

PRESIDIO, THE ★★★ An old-fashioned star vehicle, this murder mystery features Sean Connery as a military provost marshal at San Francisco's Presidio. Police detective Mark Harmon, who once served under Connery and still bears a grudge, is assigned to work with his former commanding officer. Forget the plot and enjoy seeing Connery excel in a tailor-made role. Rated R for violence and profanity. 97m. **DIR:** Peter Hyams. **CAST:** Sean Connery, Mark Harmon, Meg Ryan, Jack Warden, Dana Gladstone, Mark Blum. **1988**

PREY FOR THE HUNTER 🦃 A lame reworking of *The Most Dangerous Game*, as businessmen hunt down a photographer deep in the African jungle. Dull presentation of an overused plot. Rated R for violence and profanity. 90m. **DIR:** John H. Parr. **CAST:** Todd Jensen, André Jacobs. **1992**

PRIME CUT ★★ Sissy Spacek made her film debut in this sleazy but energetic crime thriller about big-time gangsters and the slaughterhouse they use to convert their enemies into sausage. The talents of Lee Marvin and Gene Hackman elevate this essentially tasteless offering. Rated R for nudity, gore, and violence. 86m. **DIR:** Michael Ritchie. **CAST:** Lee Marvin, Gene Hackman, Angel Tompkins, Gregory Walcott, Sissy Spacek. **1972**

PRIME RISK ★★★½ Two frustrated young people (Lee Montgomery and Samuel Bottoms) devise a scheme to rip off automatic-teller machines. Trouble arises when they stumble on to a greater conspiracy involving foreign agents. Nonstop action with Keenan Wynn as a suitable villain. Rated PG-13 for mature situations and language. 98m. **DIR:** Michael Frakas. **CAST:** Lee Montgomery, Sam Bottoms, Toni Hudson, Keenan Wynn, Clu Gulager. **1984**

PRIME TARGET 🦃 While a courier for the FBI, a hick lawman discovers that he and the handcuffed crime boss he's transporting are moving targets. A third-rate version of *Midnight Run*. Rated R for nudity, violence, and profanity. 87m. **DIR:** David Heavener. **CAST:** David Heavener, Isaac Hayes, Robert Reed, Andrew Robinson, Jenilee Harrison, Don Stroud, Tony Curtis. **1991**

PRIME TIME MURDER ★★½ Sleazy TV reporter hooks up with homeless ex-cop to stalk a slasher who only attacks defenseless street people. Tim Thomerson is intriguing as the eccentric former cop, but the script is much too typical. Rated R for violence and profanity. 95m. **DIR:** Gary Skeen Hall. **CAST:** Tim Thomerson, Anthony Finetti, Laura Reed, Sally Kirkland. **1992**

PRINCE VALIANT ★★★½ Harold Foster's splendid saga of a young Scandinavian prince who enters the court of King Arthur and returns his family to their throne and restores his birthright. High adventure and great to look at. Fun for the whole family. 100m. **DIR:** Henry Hathaway. **CAST:** Robert Wagner, James Mason, Janet Leigh, Debra Paget, Sterling Hayden, Victor McLaglen, Donald Crisp, Brian Aherne, Tom Conway, Neville Brand. **1954**

PRISONER OF ZENDA, THE (1937) ★★★½ An outstanding cast, lavish costuming and sets, and a wholesome derring-do plot combine to make this a highly entertaining film. Commoner Ronald Colman is forced to stand in for a "twin" cousin in a political plot to gain control of a small European kingdom. Of the five screen versions of Anthony Hope's famous 1894 novel, this is absolutely the best. B&W; 101m. **DIR:** John Cromwell. **CAST:** Ronald Colman, Madeleine Carroll, Mary Astor, Douglas Fairbanks Jr., C. Aubrey Smith, Raymond Massey, David Niven. **1937**

PRISONER OF ZENDA, THE (1952) ★★★ An innocent traveler in a small European country is the exact double of its king and gets involved in a murder plot. This is a flashy Technicolor remake of the famous 1937 Ronald Colman version. 101m. **DIR:** Richard Thorpe. **CAST:** Stewart Granger, Deborah Kerr, Jane Greer, Louis Calhern, James Mason, Lewis Stone. **1952**

PRIVATE FILES OF J. EDGAR HOOVER, THE ★★½ A soap-opera-style account of the life and times of J. Edgar Hoover, concentrating on the seamier side of the FBI man's investigations. James Wainwright plays the young protagonist with low-key (some would say boring) intensity, while Broderick Crawford growls his way through Hoover's elder years. Rated PG for language and gangster violence. 111m. **DIR:** Larry Cohen. **CAST:** Broderick Crawford, Michael Parks, José Ferrer, Celeste Holm, Rip Torn, Ronee Blakley, James Wainwright, Dan Dailey, Lloyd Nolan. **1977**

PRIVATE INVESTIGATIONS 🦃 Los Angeles architect is chased around town by bad guys who think he knows something that could expose their schemes. Rated R for language and violence. 91m. **DIR:** Nigel Dick. **CAST:** Clayton Rohner, Ray Sharkey, Paul LeMat, Talia Balsam, Anthony Zerbe. **1987**

PROBE ★★½ Pilot film for the TV series *Probe*. Hugh O'Brian stars as an agent with an electronic transmitter implanted in him, which allows him to relay and receive information from headquarters. 97m. **DIR:** Russ Mayberry. **CAST:** Hugh O'Brian, Elke Sommer, Lilia Skala, Burgess Meredith. **1972**

PROFESSIONALS, THE ★★★★½ A rip-snorting adventure film with Lee Marvin, Burt Lancaster, Robert Ryan, and Woody Strode as the title characters out to rescue the wife (Claudia Cardinale) of a wealthy industrialist (Ralph Bellamy) from the clutches of a Mexican bandit (Jack Palance) who allegedly kidnapped her. Directed with a fine eye for character and action by Richard Brooks. 117m. **DIR:** Richard Brooks. **CAST:** Lee Marvin, Burt Lancaster, Robert Ryan, Woody Strode, Claudia Cardinale, Ralph Bellamy. **1966**

PROJECT: ELIMINATOR 🦃 Government agents track down terrorists who have kidnapped a special weapons specialist. A trying and tired film. Even David Carradine is powerless to add a little kick to the proceedings. Rated R for violence. 89m. **DIR:** H. Kaye Dyal. **CAST:** David Carradine, Frank Zagarino, Drew Snyder. **1989**

PROJECT: SHADOWCHASER ★★ This half-baked *Die Hard* rip-off with *Terminator* overtones has Martin Kove trapped in a high-rise hospital that has been overtaken by terrorists. Plenty of action, along with quips from Kove, make this shoot-'em-up at least somewhat palatable. Rated R for violence and profanity. 97m. **DIR:** John Eyres. **CAST:** Martin Kove, Meg Foster, Frank Zagarino, Paul Koslo, Joss Ackland. **1992**

PROTECTOR, THE ★★½ Standard kung fu film distinguished by nicely photographed action sequences and a sense of humor. Story has Jackie Chan as an undercover New York cop traveling to Hong Kong to break up a big heroin ring. Rated R for violence, nudity, and language. 94m. **DIR:** James Glickenhaus. **CAST:** Jackie Chan, Danny Aiello, Roy Chiao. **1985**

PUBLIC ENEMY ★★★★½ *Public Enemy*, with a snarling, unredeemable James Cagney in the title role, is still a highly watchable gangster film. William Wellman expertly directed this fast-paced and unpretentious portrait of the rise and fall of a vicious hoodlum. B&W; 84m. **DIR:** William Wellman. **CAST:** James Cagney, Jean Harlow, Mae Clarke, Edward Woods, Beryl Mercer. **1931**

PUNCH THE CLOCK 🦃 A professional car thief and the law school grad who has the hots for her. A movie this bad is a crime. Rated R for violence. 88m. **DIR:** Eric L. Schlagman. **CAST:** Mike Rogen. **1990**

PUNISHER, THE ★★★ Lean and mean adaptation of the Marvel Comics publication has Dolph Lundgren (looking like a cross between Elvis Presley and Clint Walker in his *Cheyenne* days) as the Punisher, a police-officer-turned-vigilante. Solid entertainment in a comic-book vein. Rated R for violence and profanity. 92m. **DIR:** Mark Goldblatt. **CAST:** Dolph Lundgren, Lou Gossett Jr., Jeroen Krabbé, Kim Miyori. **1990**

PUPPET ON A CHAIN ★★½ American agent battles a Dutch heroin ring in this lackluster Alistair MacLean thriller. There's an exciting speedboat chase through the canals of Amsterdam, but the rest of the film is a snoozer. Rated PG. 97m. **DIR:** Geoffrey Reeve. **CAST:** Sven-Bertil Taube, Barbara Parkins, Alexander Knox. **1972**

PURPLE MONSTER STRIKES, THE ★★★ The Purple Monster lands near Dr. Cyrus Layton's observatory and tricks him into revealing the plans for a new spaceship. Although the science is ridiculous and the effects unsophisticated by today's standards, this is one of Republic Studios' best-remembered serials of the mid-1940s and features master heavy Roy Barcroft in one of his finest roles. B&W; 15 chapters. **DIR:** Spencer Gordon Bennet, Fred Brannon. **CAST:** Dennis Moore, Linda Stirling, Roy Barcroft. **1945**

PURSUIT ★★ So-so mercenary flick pits a purist against greedy cohorts in an attempt to recover the gold meant to stabilize an African nation's economy. Rated R for nudity, violence, and profanity. 94m. **DIR:** John H. Parr. **CAST:** James Ryan. **1990**

PURSUIT OF THE GRAF SPEE ★★★½ Highly enjoyable account of the World War II sea chase and eventual battle involving British naval forces and the German's super warship, the *Graf Spee*. Featuring a solid cast, the film benefits from attention to detail and a realistic building of tension. 106m. **DIR:** Michael Powell, Emeric Pressburger. **CAST:** John Gregson, Anthony Quayle, Peter Finch, Bernard Lee, Ian Hunter, Patrick Macnee, Christopher Lee. **1957**

PUSHED TO THE LIMIT ★★ Vengefest features a young woman taking on a ruthless

Asian drug dealer who has killed her brother. Unrated; contains seemingly endless violence. 96m. **DIR:** Michael Mileham. **CAST:** Mimi Lesseos, Henry Hayshi. **1992**

QUICK ★★★½ Scripter Frederick Bailey's apparently routine crime thriller takes an intriguing turn when hit lady Teri Polo spares her latest target—a nerdish accountant, superbly played by Martin Donovan—and employs him as a bargaining chip to save her own skin. Their blossoming relationship sparkles in this low-budget saga. Rated R for nudity, simulated sex, profanity, and violence. 99m. **DIR:** Rick King. **CAST:** Jeff Fahey, Teri Polo, Robert Davi, Martin Donovan, Tia Carrere. **1993**

QUICKER THAN THE EYE ★★ Magic is the gimmick in this story of a group of terrorists who plan to assassinate a foreign diplomat. Poorly dubbed Swiss-produced film. Rated PG for language and violence. 94m. **DIR:** Nicolas Gessner. **CAST:** Ben Gazzara, Mary Crosby. **1989**

QUIET COOL 🦃 New York cop journeys to the Pacific Northwest to take on maniacal marijuana growers. Rated R. 80m. **DIR:** Clay Borris. **CAST:** James Remar, Adam Coleman Howard, Daphne Ashbrook, Jared Martin, Nick Cassavetes. **1986**

QUIET FIRE ★★ Passable low-budget shoot-'em-up features Lawrence-Hilton Jacobs running for his life when a corrupt senate candidate decides to eliminate anyone capable of exposing his past. Rated R for nudity, profanity, and violence. 90m. **DIR:** Lawrence Hilton-Jacobs. **CAST:** Lawrence Hilton-Jacobs, Robert Z'Dar, Karen Black. **1991**

QUIET THUNDER 🦃 Inane cross between *Raiders of the Lost Ark* and *Crocodile Dundee*. No rating, but contains violence and brief nudity. 94m. **DIR:** David Rice. **CAST:** Wayne Crawford, June Chadwick. **1988**

QUILLER MEMORANDUM, THE ★★★½ First-rate espionage film abandons the gadgets and gimmickry that marked most of the spy movies of the 1960s and concentrates on Harold Pinter's intelligent script. An American secret agent (George Segal) goes undercover to shatter a neo-Nazi hate organization that is gaining strength in Berlin. 105m. **DIR:** Michael Anderson. **CAST:** George Segal, Alec Guinness, Max von Sydow, George Sanders, Senta Berger, Robert Helpmann. **1966**

RACE FOR GLORY ★★ In his quest to be a "legend in my own time," a talented, young motorcyclist (Alex McArthur) abandons his friends for a chance to compete on the international racing circuit. This unrated mediocrity has profanity and violence. 105m. **DIR:** Rocky Lang. **CAST:** Alex McArthur, Peter Berg, Lane Smith. **1989**

RACKETEER ★★½ This early sound gangster film finds gang leader Robert Armstrong involved in the familiar eternal triangle as he falls for Carole Lombard. She, in turn, pines for ailing concert violinist Roland Drew. Though the story has been done with some variations dozens of times, this primitive talkie has some snappy dialogue and features lively performances. B&W; 68m. **DIR:** Howard Higgin. **CAST:** Robert Armstrong, Carole Lombard, John Loder, Paul Hurst, Hedda Hopper. **1930**

RAD ★★½ Staunch character players Talia Shire, Ray Walston, and Jack Weston support this film about a daredevil bicyclist (Bill Allen) who competes to win a thousand dollars. *Rad* turns out to be fairly entertaining, thanks to the exciting race sequences. Rated PG. 95m. **DIR:** Hal Needham. **CAST:** Bill Allen, Lori Loughlin, Talia Shire, Ray Walston, Jack Weston. **1986**

RADAR MEN FROM THE MOON ★★ Commando Cody, Sky Marshal of the Universe and inventor of a flying suit and a rocket ship, uses all the means at his disposal to aid America in combating Retik, the ruler of the moon, who is bent on (what else?) invading the Earth. The bullet-headed hero chases villains on land, in the air, and all the way to the moon and back and gets his fair share of abuse along the way. Lots of fisticuffs and stock footage. B&W; 12 chapters. **DIR:** Fred Brannon. **CAST:** George Wallace, Aline Towne, Roy Barcroft. **1952**

RADIO PATROL ★★ This testimonial to the police radio cop is okay for the kids who are bound to fall in love with young Pinky Adams and his canine helper Irish (played by Mickey Rentschler and Silver Wolf, respectively). There's not much here plot-wise. B&W; 12 chapters. **DIR:** Ford Beebe, Cliff Smith. **CAST:** Grant Withers, Catherine Hughes, Mickey Rentschler, Adrian Morris, Monte Montague, Silver Wolf. **1937**

RAGE AND HONOR ★★ Martial-arts greats Cynthia Rothrock and Richard Norton team up to expose drug-dealing cops. She tries to protect her video camera-wielding student while Norton attempts to clear his name after being framed for murder. If the gratuitous sleaze had been left out, this could have been an above-average kickfest. Rated R for profanity and violence. 93m. **DIR:** Terence H. Winkless. **CAST:** Cynthia Rothrock, Richard Norton, Terri Treas, Brian Thompson, Catherine Bach. **1992**

RAGE AND HONOR II: HOSTILE TAKEOVER ★★ Predictable martial-arts sequel finds CIA operative Cynthia Rothrock battling bad guys in Jakarta. Richard Norton, her former partner, helps her resolve a dispute between her employer and his greedy son. High kicks and little else. Rated R for violence and language. 98m. **DIR:** Guy Norris. **CAST:** Cynthia Rothrock, Richard Norton, Patrick Muldoon, Frans Tumnaum. **1992**

RAGE IN HARLEM, A ★★★ Adapted from the novel by Chester Himes, this movie can't make up its mind whether to be a comedy à la *The Sting* or a violent action film like *New Jack City*. Still, it's quite a roller-coaster ride as southern con-woman Robin Givens makes her way to Harlem with a load of stolen gold, seduces sweet-natured accountant Forest Whitaker, and tries to deal with gangster Danny Glover. Rated R for violence, nudity, and profanity. 115m. **DIR:** Bill Duke. **CAST:** Forest Whitaker, Gregory Hines, Danny Glover, Zakes Mokae, John Toles-Bay, Robin Givens. **1991**

RAGE OF HONOR 🦃 Sho Kosugi is an able martial artist, but he speaks English with such a thick accent that he's completely incomprehensible. Rated R for strong violence. 91m. **DIR:** Gordon Hessler. **CAST:** Sho Kosugi, Robin Evans. **1987**

RAID ON ROMMEL 🦃 Substandard war film. Rated PG for violence. 98m. **DIR:** Henry Hathaway. **CAST:** Richard Burton, John Colicos, Clinton Greyn, Wolfgang Preiss. **1971**

RAIDERS OF THE SUN ★★ Roger Corman produced this trite postnuclear-holocaust shoot-'em-up. Rated R for nudity, violence, and profanity. 80m. **DIR:** Cirio H. Santiago. **CAST:** Richard Norton. **1991**

RAINBOW DRIVE ★★½ Roderick Thorpe's suspense novel is not well served by this turgid made-for-cable police melodrama, which features Peter Weller as an honest cop embroiled in a cover-up. The cast tries to rise above the material. Unrated, but with violence and brief nudity. 96m. **DIR:** Bobby Roth. **CAST:** Peter Weller, Sela Ward, David Caruso, Bruce Weitz, Kathryn Harrold. **1990**

RAISE THE TITANIC 🦃 Disastrously dull disaster flick. Rated PG. 112m. **DIR:** Jerry Jameson. **CAST:** Jason Robards Jr., David Selby, Richard Jordan, Anne Archer, Alec Guinness, J. D. Cannon. **1980**

RAMBO: FIRST BLOOD II ★★★ This sequel to *First Blood* is an old-fashioned war movie. Its hero is larger than life, and the villains are pure mule-mean. In other words, it's an action fan's delight. Sylvester Stallone goes back to Vietnam to rescue American prisoners of war. Rated R. 94m. **DIR:** George Pan Cosmatos. **CAST:** Sylvester Stallone, Richard Crenna, Charles Napier, Steven Berkoff, Julia Nickson, Martin Kove. **1985**

RAMBO III ★★ Sylvester Stallone's hammer-handed tendencies operate at overdrive in this second sequel to *First Blood*. As co-writer, Stallone is responsible for the jingoistic story that makes child-killing sadists of the Russians (led by Marc de Jonge's near-hysterical Soviet colonel) who control a particular sector of Afghanistan. This is button-pushing, lowest-common-denominator filmmaking all the way. Rated R for extreme violence. 101m. **DIR:** Peter MacDonald. **CAST:** Sylvester Stallone, Richard Crenna, Marc de Jonge, Kurtwood Smith. **1988**

RAPE OF THE SABINES 🦃 Roger Moore plays Romulus, founder of Rome, in this cheesy Italian-French coproduction. 100m. **DIR:** Richard Pottier. **CAST:** Mylene Demongeot, Roger Moore. **1961**

RAPID FIRE ★★★½ Compact action film casts Brandon Lee as a college student who runs afoul of the mob. Lee shows his father Bruce's talent for incorporating comedy into the fist-and-foot action. This is definitely better than the average kung fu flick. Rated R for violence, simulated sex, and profanity. 95m. **DIR:** Dwight H. Little. **CAST:** Brandon Lee, Powers Boothe, Nick Mancuso, Raymond J. Barry. **1992**

RAW COURAGE ★★★★ Three cross-country runners must fend for themselves when they run into a group of weekend warriors in the Colorado desert lands. Ronny Cox is excellent as one of the runners. However, Cox, who wrote the screenplay, has taken a few too many pages from James Dickey's *Deliverance*. Still, *Raw Courage* has enough white-knuckle moments to make you forget about the lack of originality. Rated R for violence and profanity. 90m. **DIR:** Robert L. Rosen. **CAST:** Ronny Cox, Tim Maier, Art Hindle, M. Emmet Walsh, William Russ, Lisa Sutton, Lois Chiles. **1983**

RAW DEAL ★★★½ Big Arnold Schwarzenegger stars in this fast-paced action film as a former FBI agent who is recruited by his former boss (Darren McGavin) to infiltrate the Chicago mob as an act of revenge. It's predictable, even formula. But the formula works. Rated R for profanity and violence. 107m. **DIR:** John Irvin. **CAST:** Arnold Schwarzenegger, Kathryn Harrold, Darren McGavin, Sam Wanamaker, Paul Shenar, Steven Hill, Joe Regalbuto, Ed Lauter, Robert Davi. **1986**

RAW NERVE ★★½ A race car driver suddenly finds himself psychically connected with a killer. Better-than-average thriller utilizes best elements of the exploitation genre to its advantage. Rated R for violence and nudity. 91m. **DIR:** David A. Prior. **CAST:** Glenn Ford, Traci Lords, Ted Prior, Sandahl Bergman, Jan-Michael Vincent. **1991**

REAL GLORY, THE ★★★★ After the American army pulls out of the Philippines in 1910, it's left to a small band of professional soldiers to equip and train the natives to fight off a pirate-like tribe of cutthroats. This lesser-known adventure film ranks alongside *Beau Geste* and *The Lives of a Bengal Lancer* as one of Gary Cooper's best in the genre. B&W; 109m. **DIR:** Henry Hathaway. **CAST:** Gary Cooper, Andrea Leeds, David Niven, Reginald Owen, Broderick Crawford. **1939**

REAP THE WILD WIND ★★★½ Bawdy tale of the shipping and salvage business off the coast of Georgia during the early nineteenth century. John Wayne is a robust sea captain and Ray Milland is a well-to-do owner of a shipping company. Plenty of old-fashioned action and humor with the typical Cecil B. DeMille touches. Entire cast is first-rate, especially the villainous Raymond Massey. The final underwater action scenes are classics. 124m. **DIR:** Cecil B. DeMille. **CAST:** John Wayne, Ray Milland, Raymond Massey, Paulette Goddard, Robert Preston, Charles Bickford, Susan Hayward. **1942**

REBEL (1973) ★★ This early Sylvester Stallone movie casts him as a student radical who begins to ponder his future. This low-budget production only proves that Stallone started out mumbling. It is unrated. 80m. **DIR:** Robert Schnitzer. **CAST:** Sylvester Stallone, Anthony Page, Henry G. Sanders. **1973**

REBEL ROUSERS ★★ This drive-in biker film from the late 1960s would barely rate a second look if it weren't for a crop of future big-name stars and character performers who inhabit it. The ill-mannered-youth-on-motorcycles-versus-uptight-establishment-straights story takes a backseat to flamboyant characterizations in this one. 78m. **DIR:** Martin B. Cohen. **CAST:** Cameron Mitchell, Jack Nicholson, Bruce Dern, Diane Ladd, Harry Dean Stanton. **1967**

RED ALERT ★★★½ This 1977 made-for-TV film about a nuclear power plant is just as timely today as when it first aired. An incident at the plant has killed fourteen workers. Was it an accident, sabotage, or computer fault? A fine cast lends an air of reality and immediacy to this gripping mystery. 95m. **DIR:** William Hale. **CAST:** William Devane, Michael Brandon, Ralph Waite, Adrienne Barbeau, David Hayward, M. Emmet Walsh, Don Wiseman. **1977**

RED BARRY ★★½ Serial superstar Buster Crabbe plays comic-strip sleuth Red Barry in this decent chapterplay. It seems some scurrilous spies have stolen $2 million in negotiable bonds from a friendly ally, and the fate of the world hangs in the balance. B&W; 13 chapters. **DIR:** Ford Beebe, Alan James. **CAST:** Buster Crabbe, Frances Robinson, Edna Sedgewick. **1938**

RED DAWN ★★★½ Some viewers undoubtedly will feel that right-wing writer-director John Milius (*The Wind and the Lion* and *Conan the Barbarian*) has gone too far with this tale of the Russians invading a small American town. But we took this film as a simple "what if?" entertainment and really enjoyed it. Rated PG-13 for violence and profanity. 114m. **DIR:** John Milius. **CAST:** Patrick Swayze, C. Thomas Howell, Ron O'Neal, Lea Thompson, Ben Johnson, Harry Dean Stanton, William Smith, Powers Boothe, Charlie Sheen. **1984**

RED FLAG: THE ULTIMATE GAME ★★½ The air force has a jet-fighter combat course located near Las Vegas that over the years has fine-tuned thousands of the best pilots in the air force. The combat game is called Red Flag. It's an older and weaker version of *Top Gun* and suffers by comparison. 90m. **DIR:** Don Taylor. **CAST:** Barry Bostwick, Joan Van Ark, Fred McCarren, George Coe. **1981**

RED HEAT (1988) ★★★★ Director Walter Hill has taken his biggest hit, *48 Hrs.*, and reworked it as a vehicle for Arnold Schwarzenegger and James Belushi. Big Arnold plays a Soviet police officer forced to team up with a wisecracking Chicago cop (Belushi) to track down a Russian drug dealer (Ed O'Ross). It's fast and exciting; a best bet for action buffs. Rated R for violence, profanity, and nudity. 107m. **DIR:** Walter Hill. **CAST:** Arnold Schwarzenegger, James Belushi, Peter Boyle, Ed O'Ross, Larry Fishburne, Gina Gershon, Richard Bright. **1988**

RED LINE 7000 ★★½ Car-race melodrama about three drivers and the women in their lives bogs down when the story leaves the track. Veteran director Howard Hawks would make only two more films after this tired actioner. 110m. **DIR:** Howard Hawks. **CAST:** James Caan, Laura Devon, Charlene Holt, Marianna Hill, James Ward, Norman Alden, George Takei. **1965**

RED SCORPION A Soviet agent is sent to infiltrate and kill the leader of a band of African rebels. Rated R for violence. 100m. **DIR:** Joseph Zito. **CAST:** Dolph Lundgren, M. Emmet Walsh. **1989**

RED SONJA Dreadful sword-and-sorcery film. Rated PG-13 for violence. 89m. **DIR:** Richard Fleischer. **CAST:** Arnold Schwarzenegger, Brigitte Nielsen, Sandahl Bergman, Paul Smith, Ernie Reyes Jr. **1985**

RED SURF ★★½ Two drug-dealing surf bums try for one last big score. Things begin falling apart when one of their friends turns informer. Rated R for violence, profanity, and nudity. 104m. **DIR:** H. Gordon Boos. **CAST:** George Clooney, Doug Savant, Dedee Pfeiffer, Gene Simmons, Philip McKeon. **1990**

REDNECK Vile crime story about two criminals who take a young boy hostage. Unrated. 89m. **DIR:** Silvio Narizzano. **CAST:** Telly Savalas, Franco Nero, Mark Lester. **1972**

REFORM SCHOOL GIRL ★★ Gloria Castillo, a long way from her supporting role in *Night of the Hunter*, is the innocent teen packed off to reform school. Standard late-Fifties American-International programmer. B&W; 71m. **DIR:** Edward L. Bernds. **CAST:** Gloria Castillo, Ross Ford, Edd Byrnes, Ralph Reed, Sally Kellerman. **1957**

REFORM SCHOOL GIRLS ★★ "So young. So bad. So what?" That was the promo line for this spoof of the women-in-prison genre. Writer-director Tom DeSimone manages to get in the usual exploitative ingredients—women taking showers, etc.—while simultaneously making fun of them. Rated R for violence, profanity, nudity, and simulated sex. 94m. **DIR:** Tom DeSimone. **CAST:** Wendy O. Williams, Sybil Danning, Pat Ast, Linda Carol. **1986**

REMO WILLIAMS: THE ADVENTURE BEGINS ★★★ This adaptation of the *Destroyer* novels is like a second-rate James Bond adventure. Fred Ward is fine as the hero of the title and Joel Grey is a kick as his Asian martial arts mentor, but the film takes too much time establishing the characters and too little giving us the adventure promised in the title. Rated PG-13 for violence and profanity. 121m. **DIR:** Guy Hamilton. **CAST:** Fred Ward, Joel Grey, Wilford Brimley, J. A. Preston, George Coe, Charles Cioffi, Kate Mulgrew. **1985**

RENEGADES 🦃 Disappointing, lackluster thriller from the director of *The Hidden*. Rated R for profanity and violence. 110m. **DIR:** Jack Sholder. **CAST:** Kiefer Sutherland, Lou Diamond Phillips, Jami Gertz. **1989**

RENT-A-COP 🦃 When a drug bust goes awry and both cops and crooks are killed, a police detective is accused of masterminding the hit. Rated R for violence and profanity. 95m. **DIR:** Jerry London. **CAST:** Burt Reynolds, Liza Minnelli, James Remar, Richard Masur, Bernie Casey, Robby Benson, John P. Ryan. **1988**

RESCUE, THE ★★ Another dopey movie about a group of teens who set out to rescue their dads from a prisoner-of-war camp. Ferdinand Fairfax achieves some genuine excitement and suspense along the way, but the basic premise is preposterous. Rated PG for profanity and violence. 99m. **DIR:** Ferdinand Fairfax. **CAST:** Kevin Dillon, Kristina Harnos, Marc Price, Charles Haid, Edward Albert. **1988**

RESCUE FORCE ★★ The female CIA agents in this rescue force have names like Candy and Angel and run around half-dressed. You get the picture. Rated R for violence and nudity. 92m. **DIR:** Charles Nizet. **CAST:** Richard Harrison. **1980**

RESCUE ME 🦃 High-school loser bribes a Vietnam-vet drifter to rescue a cheerleader after she is kidnapped by two dim-witted hoods. Rated PG. 90m. **DIR:** Arthur Allan Seidelman. **CAST:** Stephen Dorff, Ami Dolenz, Michael Dudikoff, Peter DeLuise. **1993**

RESERVOIR DOGS ★★★★½ Writer-director Quentin Tarantino makes a startling debut with this story of a diamond heist gone awry. Strong ensemble acting from a terrific cast and a brain-twisting array of unexpected plot turns make this one of the best crime-thrillers ever made. The brutal and unsettling violence may be too much for some viewers, but it is never glorified in this one-of-a-kind winner. Rated R for violence and profanity. 99m. **DIR:** Quentin Tarantino. **CAST:** Harvey Keitel, Tim Roth, Michael Madsen, Christopher Penn, Steve Buscemi, Lawrence Tierney, Randy Brooks, Quentin Tarantino. **1992**

RETREAT HELL ★★½ In this predictable war film, an untested Marine Corps combat unit battles it out behind enemy lines near the Chosin Reservoir in North Korea. All the tried-and-true ingredients are here, including a wet-behind-the-ears private and a tough-talking platoon sergeant. B&W; 95m. **DIR:** Joseph H. Lewis. **CAST:** Frank Lovejoy, Richard Carlson, Russ Tamblyn. **1954**

RETURN FIRE: JUNGLE WOLF II 🦃 Martial artist Ron Marchini resorts to grenades, dynamite, and automatic weapons as he takes on both good and bad guys. Ridiculous film cuts in flashes of two previous Marchini films. Rated R for endless violence and profanity. 97m. **DIR:** Neil Callaghan. **CAST:** Ron Marchini, Adam West. **1988**

RETURN OF CHANDU (THE MAGICIAN) ★★½ Crackerjack fantasy-adventure serial has enough action, trickery, and plot twists for two chapterplays as Bela Lugosi plays Chandu, Master of White Magic, hot on the trail of evil Lemurians who have stolen his beloved Princess Nadji. Hokey but fun family fare. B&W; 12 chapters. **DIR:** Ray Taylor. **CAST:** Bela Lugosi, Maria Alba, Clara Kimball Young, Lucien Prival, Bryant Washburn. **1934**

RETURN OF SUPERFLY, THE ★★ Priest (Nathan Purdee) returns to the United States, only to be hunted by both the law and drug lords. The shaky plot and acting are marginally redeemed by the anti-drug message. Rated R for nudity, profanity, and violence. 94m. **DIR:** Sig Shore. **CAST:** Nathan Purdee, Margaret Avery, Christopher Curry, David Groh. **1990**

RETURN OF THE DRAGON ★★★½ After seeing *Return of the Dragon*, we have no doubt that Bruce Lee, not Robert Clouse, directed *Enter the Dragon*. Lee was credited with staging the fight scenes, but our guess is that he was well aware of the latter film's possible impact and exercised control over the creative nonacting facets of the film whenever he could. *Return of the Dragon* was made before *Enter*, and it shows Lee's considerable directorial talent. A delightful film, brimful of comedy, action, and acrobatics. Rated R. 91m. **DIR:** Bruce Lee. **CAST:** Bruce Lee, Chuck Norris, Nora Miao. **1973**

RETURN OF THE MAN FROM U.N.C.L.E., THE ★★★ Secret agents Napoleon Solo (Robert Vaughn) and Illya Kuryakin (David McCallum) are called out of a fifteen-year retirement. Fans of the original series will find this lighthearted spy adventure especially entertaining. 109m. **DIR:** Ray Austin. **CAST:** Robert Vaughn, David McCallum, Patrick Macnee, Tom Mason, Gayle Hunnicutt, Geoffrey Lewis, Anthony Zerbe, Keenan Wynn, George Lazenby. **1983**

RETURN OF THE MUSKETEERS ★★★★ Filled with wonderful moments of humor and plenty of swashbuckling high adventure, this adaptation of Alexandre Dumas's *Twenty Years After* finds D'Artagnan (Michael York) and Porthos (Frank Finlay) pitted against Athos (Oliver Reed) and Aramis (Richard Chamberlain) when they mistakenly ally themselves with the queen (Geraldine Chaplin) and her power-crazed lover/cardinal (Philippe Noiret). Dedicated to the memory of the marvelous character-actor/comedian Roy Kinnear, who died as the result of an accident during the filming. 100m. **DIR:** Richard Lester. **CAST:** Michael York, Oliver Reed, Richard Chamberlain, Frank Finlay, C. Thomas Howell, Kim Cattrall, Geraldine Chaplin, Christopher Lee, Philippe Noiret, Roy Kinnear, Jean-Pierre Cassel, Alan Howard, Bill Paterson. **1989**

RETURN TO MACON COUNTY 🦃 Two fun-loving boneheads run afoul of the law in the rural South. Rated PG. 104m. **DIR:** Richard Compton. **CAST:** Don Johnson, Nick Nolte, Robin Mattson. **1975**

RETURN TO PARADISE ★★½ An American arrives on a remote South Seas island and locks horns with a religious fanatic who dominates the natives. *Very* loosely based on part of James Michener's *Tales of the South Pacific*. 88m. **DIR:** Mark Robson. **CAST:** Gary Cooper, Barry Jones, Roberta Haynes. **1953**

REVENGE (1990) ★★ Pilot Kevin Costner falls in love with the beautiful young wife (Madeleine Stowe) of a powerful Mexican gangster (Anthony Quinn), whose life Costner once saved. Poorly paced melodrama, rated R for nudity, profanity, simulated sex, and violence. 120m. **DIR:** Tony Scott. **CAST:** Kevin Costner, Anthony Quinn, Madeleine Stowe, Sally Kirkland. **1990**

REVENGE OF THE KICKFIGHTER 🦃 Marines discover gold in a Vietnamese village and plan to return for it after the war. Unfortunately they're being systematically bumped off. Thin, unbelievable plot and inferior acting mar otherwise average actioner. Unrated, but contains profanity, simulated sex, and violence. 89m. **DIR:** Anthony Maharaj. **CAST:** Richard Norton. **1991**

REVENGE OF THE NINJA 🦃 Japanese karate experts take on the mob in this kung fu flick. Rated R for violence and nudity. 88m. **DIR:** Sam Firstenberg. **CAST:** Sho Kosugi, Keith Vitali, Arthur Roberts, Mario Gallo. **1983**

REVOLVER ★★½ Robert Urich is fine as a secret service agent who's felled by a bullet, paralyzed and must come to accept his new life in a wheelchair if he is to track down the gangster who put him there. Made-for-TV action entry is most involving during Urich's struggles to adapt. 93m. **DIR:** Gary Nelson. **CAST:** Robert Urich, Dakin Matthews, Steven Williams. **1992**

RICOCHET ★★★½ A rookie cop rises to the position of deputy district attorney after capturing a heartless killer. This is a taut, action-packed crime-drama that is elevated above others in its genre by the acting. Rated R for violence, profanity, and nudity. 105m. **DIR:** Russell Mulcahy. **CAST:** Denzel Washington, John Lithgow, Ice-T, Kevin Pollak, Lindsay Wagner, Josh Evans. **1991**

RIDDLE OF THE SANDS ★★★★ Based on the spy novel by Erskine Childers, this is the story of two young Englishmen (Michael York, Simon MacCorkindale) who set sail on a holiday just prior to World War I and stumble upon political intrigue and adventure in the North Sea. The result is an absorbing adventure film. Rated PG for slight violence and profanity. 102m. **DIR:** Tony Maylam. **CAST:** Michael York, Jenny Agutter, Simon MacCorkindale. **1984**

RIDING THE EDGE ★★ Formulaic adventure flick set in the Middle East—a ground attempt at *Iron Eagle*. A man has been captured by terrorists, so who do you send in? A trained professional? Nonsense. Send in his teenage son. Rated PG-13. 100m. **DIR:** James Fargo. **CAST:** Peter Haskell, Raphael Sbarge, Catherine Mary Stewart. **1990**

RIFFRAFF (1947) ★★½ Two-fisted private eye Pat O'Brien is hired as a bodyguard by a man with a chart to some rich South American oil fields, but when O'Brien signs on, he doesn't know that his employer is a killer and some heavy competition is gunning for them. This race-for-riches programmer quickly bogs down and runs out of pep. B&W; 80m. **DIR:** Ted Tetzlaff. **CAST:** Pat O'Brien, Walter Slezak, Anne Jeffreys, Percy Kilbride, Jerome Cowan. **1947**

RING OF STEEL ★★★ An Olympic fencer accidently kills a man during a regional tournament. Expelled from the sport, he is hired by an illicit nightclub that stages duels for money. He soon learns that he either fights to the death or he and his girlfriend will be killed. Good swashbuckling action, fast-paced direction, humor, and style make for an entertaining film. Rated R for simulated sex, nudity, violence, and profanity. 94m. **DIR:** David Frost. **CAST:** Joe Don Baker, Carol Alt, Richard Chapin, Gary Kasper, Darlene Vogel. **1994**

RIOT ★★½ Familiar story of tough cons turning the tables on tough guards, taking over part of a prison in an escape attempt. Violence for violence sake. Filmed at the Arizona State Prison. Rated R. 97m. **DIR:** Buzz Kulik. **CAST:** Jim Brown, Gene Hackman, Mike Kellin, Gerald S. O'Loughlin. **1969**

RIOT IN CELL BLOCK ELEVEN ★★★½ This taut prison drama with a message depicts an aborted prison escape that ends with the convicts barricaded and demanding to be heard. Made at the height of the "exposé" and true-crime wave in the mid-Fifties, this film avoids the sensational and documentary style of its contemporaries and focuses on the action and the characterizations of the convicts, the prison staff, and the media. B&W; 80m. **DIR:** Don Siegel. **CAST:** Neville Brand, Leo Gordon, Emile Meyer, Frank Faylen. **1954**

RISE AND FALL OF LEGS DIAMOND, THE ★★★½ One of the best gangster films, punchily directed and heartily acted by Ray Danton as the self-centered, manipulative lowlife who became a Prohibition-era bigshot. Dyan Cannon's debut. 101m. **DIR:** Budd Boetticher. **CAST:** Ray Danton, Karen Steele, Elaine Stewart, Jesse White, Warren Oates, Dyan Cannon. **1960**

RIVER OF DEATH 🦃 An adventurer wades his way through hostile Indians, cannibals, river pirates, and Nazis to rescue an archaeologist's daughter. Rated R for violence and profanity. 103m. **DIR:** Steve Carver. **CAST:** Michael Dudikoff, Robert Vaughn, Donald Pleasence, Herbert Lom, L. Q. Jones. **1990**

RIVER OF DIAMONDS 🦃 An adventurer braves villains to seek his fortune on a mysterious island. Rated PG-13 for violence and profanity. 88m. **DIR:** Robert J. Smawley. **CAST:** Dack Rambo, Angela O'Neill, Ferdinand Mayne. **1990**

ROAD HOUSE (1989) ★★ Hot on the heels of *Dirty Dancing,* Patrick Swayze turns to a rowdy, rough-house movie about a bar bouncer who cleans out a Missouri saloon. A male action film with lots of fistfights, a high body count, and a disappointing level of sexist humor. Rated R. 108m. **DIR:** Rowdy Herrington. **CAST:** Patrick Swayze, Ben Gazzara, Sam Elliott. **1989**

ROADHOUSE 66 ★★★½ As teen exploitation films go, this one is pretty good. Judge Reinhold plays a yuppie stuck in a small New Mexico town with car trouble. Willem Dafoe is an ex-rock-and-roller and all-around tough guy. The film drags a bit and Dafoe overplays his role, but there are some good moments to be had. Rated R for sex, nudity, violence, and profanity. 94m. **DIR:** John Mark Robinson. **CAST:** Willem Dafoe, Judge Reinhold, Kaaren Lee, Kate Vernon, Stephen Elliott, Alan Autry. **1984**

ROARING TWENTIES, THE ★★★★½ James Cagney and Humphrey Bogart star in this superb Warner Bros. gangster entry. Produced by Mark Hellinger and directed by Raoul Walsh (*White Heat*), it's one of the best of its kind, with Cagney featured as a World War I veteran who comes back to no job and no future after fighting for his country. Embittered by all this, he turns to crime. B&W; 104m. **DIR:** Raoul Walsh. **CAST:** James Cagney, Humphrey Bogart, Priscilla Lane, Gladys George, Jeffrey Lynn, Frank McHugh, Joe Sawyer. **1939**

ROBBERS OF THE SACRED MOUNTAIN ★★ This action-adventure film could have been another *Raiders of the Lost Ark*. Unfortunately, poor acting and choppy editing leave it in the mediocre range. Rated R for sex, nudity, and violence. 90m. **DIR:** Bob Schulz. **CAST:** John Marley, Simon MacCorkindale, Louise Vallance, George Touliatos. **1982**

ROBIN AND MARIAN ★★★★½ Take the best director of swashbucklers, Richard Lester; add the foremost adventure film actor, Sean Connery; mix well with a fine actress with haunting presence, Audrey Hepburn; and finish off with some of the choicest character actors. You get *Robin and Marian*, a triumph for everyone involved. Rated PG. 112m. **DIR:** Richard Lester. **CAST:** Sean Connery, Audrey Hepburn, Richard Harris, Ian Holm, Robert Shaw, Nicol Williamson, Denholm Elliott, Kenneth Haigh. **1976**

ROBIN HOOD (1923) ★★★★ A rousing, fast-moving silent movie that established the character as a devil-may-care adventurer with a passion for justice and the wistful Maid Marian—in that order. Fairbanks wrote the screenplay and financed the then astronomical $1.5 million film. B&W; 118m. **DIR:** Allan Dwan. **CAST:** Douglas Fairbanks Sr., Enid Bennett, Wallace Beery, Alan Hale Sr. **1923**

ROBIN HOOD (1991) ★★★ In an adventure film whose style of storytelling and atmosphere are reminiscent of John Boorman's *Excalibur*, the legend of Robin Hood is played out with most of the well-known events staged with conviction and an occasional twist. This made-for-television production doesn't have the high spirits of Errol Flynn's *The Adventures of Robin Hood* or the spectacle of Kevin Costner's *Robin Hood: Prince of Thieves*, but it's enjoyable nonetheless. 116m. **DIR:** John Irvin. **CAST:** Patrick Bergin, Uma Thurman, Jurgen Prochnow, Edward Fox, Jeroen Krabbé. **1991**

ROBIN HOOD AND THE SORCERER ★★★★ While the telling of the Robin Hood legend in this film may be less straightforward than most, the added element of the mysticism enhances the all-too-familiar story and gives the dusty old characters new life. Michael Praed plays the legendary English outlaw with conviction. 115m. **DIR:** Ian Sharp. **CAST:** Michael Praed, Anthony Valentine, Nickolas Grace, Clive Mantle, Peter Williams. **1983**

ROBIN HOOD: HERNE'S SON ★★★ The third in this series from the BBC begins with the death of Robin of Locksley and the choosing of Robert of Hunnington (Jason Connery) as his successor by Herne the Hunter. The refusal of the new Robin to serve leads to the breakup of the band, followed by the abduction of Maid Marion. The new Robin must then unite his followers and save his love. 101m. **DIR:** Robert Young. **CAST:** Jason Connery, Oliver Cotton, George Baker, Michael Craig, Nickolas Grace. **1986**

ROBIN HOOD: PRINCE OF THIEVES ★★★★ The Robin Hood legend gets a fresh, innovative telling in this action-packed, funny, and suspenseful adult-oriented adventure, which presents Kevin Costner in fine fettle as the title hero. The film builds in tension and excitement toward the surprise-filled ending. Alan Rickman is delightfully sinister—and often hilarious—as the evil Sheriff of Nottingham, and Morgan Freeman has a tradition-breaking role as a Moorish warrior who aids Robin in his robbing of the rich to give to the poor. Rated PG-13 for violence and profanity. 138m. **DIR:** Kevin Reynolds. **CAST:** Kevin Costner, Morgan Freeman, Mary Elizabeth Mastrantonio, Alan Rickman, Christian Slater, Sean Connery, Brian Blessed. **1991**

ROBIN HOOD: THE SWORDS OF WAYLAND ★★★★ The second of the *Robin Hood* series from the BBC is as good as the first, if not better. This adventure pits Robin against the forces of darkness represented by the sorceress Morgwyn of Ravenscar (Rula Lenska). The story twists and turns as the sorceress gathers the seven swords of Wayland, one of which is in Robin's hands. 105m. **DIR:** Robert Young. **CAST:** Michael Praed, Rula Lenska, Nickolas Grace. **1986**

ROBINSON CRUSOE OF CLIPPER ISLAND ★★ Special agent Mala of the FBI teams up with his dog Buck and Rex the Wonder Horse to break a team of spies and saboteurs responsible for the crash of a dirigible. Exploding volcanoes, stock footage, a lovely princess—this one has all of 'em. B&W; 14 chapters. **DIR:** Mack V. Wright, Ray Taylor. **CAST:** Mala, Mamo Clark. **1937**

ROCK 'N' ROLL WRESTLING WOMEN VS. THE AZTEC APE ★★ As if your usual lady-wrestlers-battling-evil-monsters movie wasn't funny enough, this one features rockabilly songs newly dubbed in over the wrestling scenes! Sort of like *Wrestlemania* without Vince McMahon. B&W; 77m. **DIR:** René Cardona Sr. **CAST:** Elizabeth Campbell. **1962**

ROCK HOUSE 🦃 When narcotics agent Joseph Jennings loses his wife to vicious drug dealers, he takes the law into his own hands. If this guy were a football player, he would have fumbled the ball. Not rated, but contains violence. 98m. **DIR:** Jack Vacek. **CAST:** Joseph Jennings. **1988**

ROCKETEER, THE ★★★★½ Bill Campbell stars as a young pilot who is transformed into a jet-propelled hero when Nazi agents attempt to steal a top-secret invention and it lands in his lap. This is Commando Cody done right; a glorious adventure for the young and the young at heart. Rated PG for violence. 110m. **DIR:** Joe Johnston. **CAST:** Bill Campbell, Alan Arkin, Jennifer Connelly, Timothy Dalton, Paul Sorvino, Terry O'Quinn, Ed Lauter. **1991**

ROCKFORD FILES, THE (TV SERIES) ★★★★ In Jim Rockford, an ex-con turned private eye, James Garner found the perfect character to finally break his typecasting as *Maverick*. In the pilot episode for this uniformly fine series, Lindsay Wagner comes to Rockford's beachside trailer with a question: was her father killed or did he commit suicide? Robert Donley was replaced in the role of Rockford's father by Noah Beery Jr. when the show began its run on NBC. Made for TV. 90m. **DIR:** Richard T. Heffron. **CAST:** James Garner, Lindsay Wagner, William Smith, Nita Talbot, Joe Santos, Robert Donley. **1974**

ROLLING THUNDER ★★★★ William Devane delivers a fine performance as a Vietnam POW returned home to Texas. For his courage and endurance under torture, he is honored with two thousand silver dollars by the local merchants. (A dollar for every day served as a POW.) A gang of vicious killers attempts to rob him, but he will not tell them where the silver is, even when they begin to torture him. After some hospitalization, Devane recruits his Vietnam buddy (played superbly by Tommy Lee Jones) and the hunt is violently and realistically played out. Rated R. 99m. **DIR:** John Flynn. **CAST:** William Devane, Tommy Lee Jones, Linda Haynes, James Best, Dabney Coleman, Lisa Richards, Luke Askew. **1977**

ROLLING VENGEANCE ★★½ A young trucker avenges the murder of his family and the rape of his girlfriend. A cross between a trucker movie and *Rambo*. Rated R for violence and language. 92m. **DIR:** Steven H. Stern. **CAST:** Don Michael Paul, Lawrence Dane, Ned Beatty, Lisa Howard. **1987**

ROMANCING THE STONE ★★★★½ A rip-snorting adventure film that combines action, a love story, suspense, and plenty of laughs, this movie stars Kathleen Turner as a timid romance novelist who becomes involved in a situation more dangerous, exciting, and romantic than anything she could ever dream up. Michael Douglas plays the shotgun-wielding soldier of fortune who comes to her aid while Danny DeVito, Alfonso Arau, and Zack Norman add delightful bits of comedy. Rated PG for violence, nudity, and profanity. 105m. **DIR:** Robert Zemeckis. **CAST:** Kathleen Turner, Michael Douglas, Danny DeVito, Alfonso Arau, Zack Norman. **1984**

ROMEO IS BLEEDING ★★★★ In this bizarre, over-the-top thriller, crooked cop Gary Oldman's avaricious plans come a cropper when he runs into maniacal hit woman Lena Olin (in an unforgettable, eye-poppingly weird performance). Some viewers are likely to be offended by the outrageous sex and violence in this movie, which seems more like a send-up of *film noir* than a straightforward entry in the genre. That said, folks who enjoyed *Reservoir Dogs*, *True Romance*, and *Bad Lieutenant* will find this nightmarish flick to be right up their dark alley. Rated R for violence, profanity, nudity, and simulated sex. 97m. **DIR:** Peter Medak. **CAST:** Gary Oldman, Lena Olin, Annabella Sciorra, Juliette Lewis, David Proval, Will Patton, Ron Perlman, Dennis Farina. **1994**

ROMPER STOMPER ★★★ A group of skinheads terrorizes the Asian community in Melbourne, Australia, and a bizarre love story is mixed between countless acts of violence. At first this movie may disgust the viewer, but keep watching—you could end up enjoying it. Available in R-rated and unrated versions; contains violence, profanity, nudity, and graphic sex. 83m. **DIR:** Geoffrey Wright. **CAST:** Russell Crowe, Daniel Pollock, Jacqueline McKenzie, Alex Scott. **1992**

ROOKIE, THE ★★½ Clint Eastwood is a maverick detective who is saddled with the rookie (Charlie Sheen) of the title while attempting to get the goods on a German criminal. Although it delivers the goods for the action crowd, this is an otherwise disappointing effort from star-director Eastwood. Rated R for violence and profanity. 121m. **DIR:** Clint Eastwood. **CAST:** Clint Eastwood, Charlie Sheen, Raul Julia, Sonia Braga, Tom Skerritt, Pepe Serna, Tony Plana. **1990**

ROOTS OF EVIL Soft-porn, erotic thriller concerning two police detectives stalking a serial killer with a penchant for killing prostitutes. Badly acted and horrendously stereotypical. Unrated, but contains violence and simulated sex. 95m. **DIR:** Gary Graver. **CAST:** Alex Cord, Delia Sheppard, Charles Dierkop. **1991**

ROUGHNECKS ★★ This TV miniseries centers around a bunch of good old boys trying to drill a geothermal well in Texas. The old-timers resent the land being disrupted. Protracted would-be-actioner. 180m. **DIR:** Bernard McEveety. **CAST:** Sam Melville, Cathy Lee Crosby, Vera Miles, Harry Morgan, Steve Forrest. **1980**

ROUSTERS, THE ★★★ TV pilot actioner features Chad Everett as a carnival bouncer named Wyatt Earp III. He cleverly deals with insurance fraud, domestic abuse, and an armed robbery. Fun blend of violence, humor, and crime resolution. Rated PG for violence. 72m. **DIR:** E. W. Swackhamer. **CAST:** Chad Everett, Jim Varney, Mimi Rogers. **1983**

ROYCE ★★★ Amiable spy foolishness, with James Belushi as a wisecracking agent operating for a covert U.S. organization—the Black Hand. Our hero goes into action after cutbacks disband the unit, and disgruntled members steal some nuclear warheads. Rated R for violence, profanity, and nudity. 100m. **DIR:** Rod Holcomb. **CAST:** James Belushi, Chelsea Field, Miguel Ferrer, Peter Boyle. **1994**

RUCKUS ★★★½ This lighthearted adventure film is like *Rambo* without the killing. That's one of the appealing things about this tale of a Vietnam soldier, Dirk Benedict, who escapes from an army psycho ward in Mobile and ends up in a little southern town where he is harassed by the locals—but not for long. PG for violence and language. 91m. **DIR:** Max Kleven. **CAST:** Dirk Benedict, Linda Blair, Ben Johnson, Richard Farnsworth, Matt Clark. **1984**

RUMOR OF WAR, A ★★★ A well-made television movie about a Marine combat unit in Vietnam. Brad Davis plays a young officer who bravely leads his men into combat. He eventually gets charged with murder. The video version is about an hour and a half shorter than the original television print. Too bad. 105m. **DIR:** Richard T. Heffron. **CAST:** Brad Davis, Keith Carradine, Stacy Keach, Michael O'Keefe. **1980**

RUN ★★★ Patrick Dempsey is a young law student who is wrongly accused of murdering the son of a mob boss, and must now avoid the vengeful father and the corrupt local police force. The action is nonstop and Dempsey's one-liners are always perfectly timed. Rated R for violence and profanity. 89m. **DIR:** Geoff Burrowes. **CAST:** Patrick Dempsey, Kelly Preston, Ken Pogue, Christopher Lawford. **1991**

RUN FOR THE SUN ★★★½ There have been many adaptations of Richard Connell's masterful suspense tale, *The Most Dangerous Game*—some authorized, most ersatz—and this crackling remake is the first one in color. Plane crash survivors Richard Widmark and Jane Greer are the quarry of fugitive Nazi Peter Van Eyck in the South American jungle. Ferocious, imaginative, and exciting, with a script coauthored by the great Dudley Nichols. Filmed in Mexico. 99m. **DIR:** Roy Boulting. **CAST:** Richard Widmark, Jane Greer, Trevor Howard, Peter Van Eyck. **1956**

RUN SILENT, RUN DEEP ★★★★ Clark Gable becomes the captain of a submarine that Burt Lancaster was to command. Although he resents his new boss, Lancaster stays on. Tensions rise among Lancaster, Gable, and the crew as they set out from Pearl Harbor to destroy a Japanese cruiser. This film is noted as one of the finest World War II submarine movies. B&W; 93m. **DIR:** Robert Wise. **CAST:** Clark Gable, Burt Lancaster, Jack Warden, Don Rickles. **1958**

RUNAWAY NIGHTMARE Two Nevada worm ranchers are kidnapped by a gang of beautiful women. 104m. **DIR:** Michael Cartel. **CAST:** Michael Cartel, Al Valletta. **1984**

RUNAWAY TRAIN ★★★★ In this riveting, pulse-pounding adventure movie, two convicts escape from prison and, accompanied by a hostage (Rebecca DeMornay), make the mistake of hopping a train speeding straight for disaster. While the story gets a bit too allegorical and philosophical on occasion, the unrelenting intensity more than makes up for it. Rated R for violence, gore, and profanity. 112m. **DIR:** Andrei Konchalovsky. **CAST:** Jon Voight, Eric Roberts, Rebecca DeMornay, John P. Ryan, Kenneth McMillan, Kyle T. Heffner, T. K. Carter. **1986**

RUNNING COOL ★★★ Surprisingly decent biker story stars Andrew Divoff as a gallant cycle cowboy helping an old friend save wetlands from developers. Sexism mars the eco-friendly spirit, but it's fun to watch "outlaw" bikers save the day. Rated R for language and sexuality. 106m. **DIR:** Ferd Sebastian, Beverly Sebastian. **CAST:** Andrew Divoff, Dedee Pfeiffer, James Gammon, Paul Gleason. **1993**

RUNNING DELILAH ★★ Kim Cattrall stars as an undercover agent who is ambushed by a notorious international arms dealer. Her partner (Billy Zane) races her body to a secret government laboratory where they turn her into a cyborg. Lifeless rip-off of TV's *The Bionic Woman*. Rated PG-13 for violence. 85m. **DIR:** Richard Franklin. **CAST:** Kim Cattrall, Billy Zane, Francois Guetary, Yorgo Voyagis, Diana Rigg. **1993**

RUNNING SCARED (1980) ★★★ Ken Wahl and Judge Reinhold are servicemen returning home after two years in the Panama Canal Zone. Reinhold unknowingly filmed a secret base that is to be used in the Bay of Pigs operation. When their plane lands, authorities find negatives and the chase is on. Unrated. 82m. **DIR:** Paul Glicker. **CAST:** Ken Wahl, Judge Reinhold, Bradford Dillman, Pat Hingle, Lonny Chapman, John Saxon. **1980**

RUNNING SCARED (1986) ★★★★ Fast, funny, and exciting, this *Beverly Hills Cop*–style comedy–cop thriller features inspired on-screen teamwork from Gregory Hines and Billy Crystal as a pair of wisecracking detectives on the trail of a devious drug dealer. Rated R for violence, nudity, and profanity. 107m. **DIR:** Peter Hyams. **CAST:** Gregory Hines, Billy Crystal, Steven Bauer, Darlanne Fluegel, Joe Pantoliano, Dan Hedaya, Jimmy Smits, Jonathan Gries, Tracy Reed. **1986**

RUSSIAN ROULETTE ★★ George Segal plays a Royal Canadian Mountie sucked into a secret service plot to kidnap a Russian dissident prior to a visit from the Soviet premier. Good premise, but no action or thrills. Rated PG. 100m. **DIR:** Lou Lombardo. **CAST:** George Segal, Cristina Raines, Bo Brudin, Denholm Elliott, Richard Romanus, Gordon Jackson, Peter Donat, Nigel Stock, Louise Fletcher. **1975**

RUTHERFORD COUNTY LINE ★★ Wooden acting dampens an otherwise decent script about real-life Rutherford County, North Carolina, Sheriff Damon Husky (Earl Owensby) and his efforts to police the rural Blue Ridge community. The actors appear to read their lines from cue cards. Not rated; the film contains episodes of profanity and graphic violence. 98m. **DIR:** Thom McIntyre. **CAST:** Earl Owensby, Terry Loughlin. **1985**

S.H.E. ★★★ This average made-for-TV spy-action thriller has one twist...a female James Bond. Beautiful Cornelia Sharpe is S.H.E. (Security Hazards Expert). She pursues Robert Lansing, the U.S. syndicate boss, throughout Europe. Omar Sharif makes an appearance as a wine baron. 105m. **DIR:** Robert Lewis. **CAST:** Omar Sharif, Cornelia Sharpe, Robert Lansing, Anita Ekberg. **1979**

SAGA OF THE VIKING WOMEN AND THEIR VOYAGE TO THE WATERS OF THE GREAT SEA SERPENT, THE 🦃 Even director Roger Corman called this Nordic snoozer, "One of the biggest mistakes of my life." B&W; 66m. **DIR:** Roger Corman. **CAST:** Abby Dalton, Susan Cabot. **1957**

SAHARA (1943) ★★★½ One of the better war films, this production contains plenty of action, suspense, and characterization. Humphrey Bogart plays the head of a British-American unit stranded in the desert. The soldiers must keep the ever-present Nazi forces at bay while searching for the precious water they need to stay alive. It's a down-to-the-bone, exciting World War II drama. B&W; 97m. **DIR:** Zoltán Korda. **CAST:** Humphrey Bogart, Bruce Bennett, Lloyd Bridges, Dan Duryea, J. Carrol Naish. **1943**

SAHARA (1984) 🦃 A young heiress enters "the world's most treacherous auto race" (across the Sahara Desert). Rated PG for violence and profanity. 104m. **DIR:** Andrew V. McLaglen. **CAST:** Brooke Shields, Lambert Wilson, Horst Buchholz, John Rhys-Davies, John Mills. **1984**

SAIGON COMMANDOS ★★½ In Vietnam, U.S. military cop Richard Young investigates the murders of local drug dealers. Okay action drama, with more than a passing resemblance to *Off Limits* (though this was made earlier). Rated R for strong violence and profanity. 91m. **DIR:** Clark Henderson. **CAST:** Richard Young, P. J. Soles, John Allen Nelson. **1987**

ST. IVES ★★★½ This is a good Charles Bronson film about a former police reporter who becomes involved in a murder. Director J. Lee Thompson pulls an understated and believable performance out of the star. Rated PG. 93m. **DIR:** J. Lee Thompson. **CAST:** Charles Bronson, Jacqueline Bisset, John Houseman, Maximilian Schell, Harry Guardino, Dana Elcar, Dick O'Neill, Elisha Cook Jr. **1976**

ST. VALENTINE'S DAY MASSACRE, THE ★★ Watching the leads ham it up provides sporadic fun, but this gaudy gangster picture is long on violence and short on dramatic impact. Where's Eliot Ness when you need him? 100m. **DIR:** Roger Corman. **CAST:** Jason Robards Jr., George Segal, Ralph Meeker, Jean Hale, Frank Silvera, Joseph Campanella, Bruce Dern. **1967**

SALAMANDER, THE 🦃 Abysmal political action-thriller. Rated R; contains violence and profanity. 101m. **DIR:** Peter Zinner. **CAST:** Franco Nero, Anthony Quinn, Martin Balsam, Sybil Danning, Christopher Lee, Cleavon Little, Paul Smith, Claudia Cardinale, Eli Wallach. **1981**

SALZBURG CONNECTION, THE ★★ This incredibly bad spy film set in Europe has Barry Newman playing an American lawyer on vacation who gets mixed up with Nazi spies. Rated PG for violence and language. 93m. **DIR:** Lee H. Katzin. **CAST:** Barry Newman, Anna Karina, Joe Maross, Wolfgang Preiss, Helmut Schmid, Udo Kier, Klaus Maria Brandauer. **1972**

SAND PEBBLES, THE ★★★½ Steve McQueen gives his most compelling performance as Hollman, an ordinary seaman on an American warship stationed off China in 1925. He prefers to remain below deck with his only love, the ship's engines. That way he avoids involvement or decisions. Hollman is forced by changes in China to become involved with the world outside his engine room. The result is an enjoyable, sweeping epic with unforgettable characters. 179m. **DIR:** Robert Wise. **CAST:** Steve McQueen, Richard Crenna, Richard Attenborough, Candice Bergen, Mako, Simon Oakland, Gavin MacLeod. **1966**

SANDERS OF THE RIVER ★★½ "Sandy the lawgiver" is the heavy right hand of the British Empire in this action-drama of colonialism in darkest Africa. Paul Robeson rises above demeaning circumstances and fills the screen with his commanding presence. Great footage of the people and terrain of Africa add to the mood of this adventure and give it an aura lacking in many jungle films. B&W; 98m. **DIR:** Zoltán Korda. **CAST:** Paul Robeson, Leslie Banks, Nina Mae McKinney, Robert Cochran. **1935**

SANDS OF IWO JIMA ★★★★½ Superb war film. The Duke was never better than as the haunted Sergeant Stryker, a man hated by his men (with a few exceptions) for his unyielding toughness, but it is by that attitude that he hopes to keep them alive in combat. Watch it and see how good the Duke really was. B&W; 110m. **DIR:** Allan Dwan. **CAST:** John Wayne, John Agar, Forrest Tucker, Richard Jaeckel, Arthur Franz. **1949**

SATAN'S SATELLITES ★★ Heroic Judd Holdren of the Inter-Planetary Patrol, aided by his two assistants and his flying suit, battles otherworldly villains Lane Bradford and Leonard Nimoy, who want to blow the Earth out of its orbit. Originally released by Republic Studios as a twelve-episode serial entitled *Zombies of the Stratosphere*, this sequel to *Radar Men from the Moon* is a cheaply done paste-up job. B&W; 70m. **DIR:** Fred Brannon. **CAST:** Judd Holdren, Aline Towne, Wilson Wood, Lane Bradford, John Crawford, Leonard Nimoy. **1958**

SATURDAY NIGHT SPECIAL 🦃 This plotless film is just a 90-minute music video with some sex and violence thrown in. A handsome musician arrives in a small town and trouble starts. Available in R and unrated versions; contains violence, nudity, graphic sex, and profanity. 97m. **DIR:** Dan Golden. **CAST:** Billy Burnette, Maria Ford, Rick Dean, Robert Van Luik, Duane Whitaker. **1994**

SAVAGE BEACH 🦃 In this sequel to *Picasso Trigger*, two female agents with the Drug Enforcement Division uncover a plot to retrieve gold lost during World War II. Rated R. 95m. **DIR:** Andy Sidaris. **CAST:** Dona Speir, Hope Marie Carlton, Bruce Penhall, John Aprea. **1990**

SAVAGE DAWN 🦃 A motorcycle gang takes over a small town in the desert. Rated R for violence, nudity, and profanity. 102m. **DIR:** Simon Nuchtern. **CAST:** George Kennedy, Richard Lynch, Lance Henriksen, Karen Black, William Forsythe. **1984**

SAVAGE INSTINCT 🦃 When Debra Sweaney accidentally walks into the dark and seedy world of a drug dealer, she is beaten and left for dead. She survives and comes back with a vengeance. Charles Bronson did it with more conviction. Unrated, but contains graphic violence. 88m. **DIR:** Patrick G. Donahue. **CAST:** Debra Sweaney. **1991**

SAVAGE JUSTICE 🦃 The daughter of an American ambassador is caught up in a revolution in a foreign country. Unrated, the film has nudity and violence. 90m. **DIR:** Joey Romero. **CAST:** Julie Montgomery, Steve Memel. **1988**

SAVAGE STREETS 🦃 Linda Blair is the tough leader of a street gang. Rated R for everything imaginable. 90m. **DIR:** Danny Steinmann. **CAST:** Linda Blair, Robert Dryer, Sal Landi, John Vernon. **1985**

SCALAWAG BUNCH, THE ★★ Italian-made adaptation of the Robin Hood story is cheaply made and poorly dubbed into English. But the story is still entertaining. Unrated. 103m. **DIR:** Giorgio Ferroni. **CAST:** Mark Damon. **1975**

SCARAMOUCHE ★★★★ This big-screen adaptation of the Rafael Sabatini story is first-class entertainment for the whole family. Stewart Granger is perfectly cast as the swashbuckling Scaramouche, who sets out to avenge his brother's murder by a villainous master swordsman (Mel Ferrer). A wonderfully witty script, splendid cinematography, fine performances, and outstanding action scenes. 118m. **DIR:** George Sidney. **CAST:** Stewart Granger, Eleanor Parker, Mel Ferrer, Janet Leigh. **1952**

SCARFACE (1932) ★★★★½ Subtitled "Shame of the Nation" when released in the 1930s, this thinly veiled account of the rise and fall (the latter being fictional) of Al Capone easily ranks as one of the very best films in the gangster genre—right up there with *The Public Enemy, The Roaring Twenties, High Sierra,* and *White Heat*. Paul Muni is first-rate as the Chicago gangster and receives excellent support from Ann Dvorak, George Raft, and, outstanding as a rival gangster, Boris Karloff. See it. B&W; 93m. **DIR:** Howard Hawks. **CAST:** Paul Muni, Ann Dvorak, George Raft, Boris Karloff, Osgood Perkins. **1932**

SCARFACE (1983) ★★★★½ Onetime "Godfather" Al Pacino returns to his screen beginnings with a bravura performance in the title role of this updating of Howard Hawks's 1932 gangster classic. Rather than bootleg gin as Paul Muni did in the original, Pacino imports and sells cocaine. Directed by Brian De Palma, it's the most violent, thrilling, revolting, surprising, and gruesome gangster movie ever made. Rated R for nudity, violence, sex, and profanity. 170m. **DIR:** Brian De Palma. **CAST:** Al Pacino, Steven Bauer, Robert Loggia, Paul Shenar. **1983**

SCARLET AND THE BLACK, THE ★★½ The action in this film is centered around the Vatican during the time of the German occupation of Rome in 1943. Based on "The Scarlet Pimpernel of the Vatican," it chronicles the adventures of an Irish priest who manages to elude the German captors in true Pimpernel fashion. Moderately entertaining. 143m. **DIR:** Jerry London. **CAST:** Gregory Peck, Christopher Plummer, John Gielgud. **1983**

SCARLET PIMPERNEL, THE (1934) ★★★ Leslie Howard plays Sir Percy, an English aristocrat engaged in the underground effort to snatch out from under the blade of the guillotine Frenchmen caught in the Reign of Terror. His ruse may throw off the French authorities, as ably represented by a sinister Raymond Massey, but he is also turning off his beautiful wife, Merle Oberon. B&W; 95m. **DIR:** Harold Young. **CAST:** Leslie Howard, Raymond Massey, Merle Oberon, Nigel Bruce. **1934**

SCARLET PIMPERNEL, THE (1982) ★★★½ This is the made-for-TV version of the much-filmed (seven times) adventure classic. Anthony Andrews makes a dashing hero leading a double life aiding French revolutionaries while posing as a foppish member of British society. Jane Seymour is breathtakingly beautiful as his ladylove. This lavish production proves that remakes, even for television, can be worthwhile. 150m. **DIR:** Clive Donner. **CAST:** Anthony Andrews, Jane Seymour, Ian McKellen, James Villiers, Eleanor David. **1982**

SCARLET SPEAR, THE 🦃 The son of an African chief undertakes a series of ritual tasks to prove his manhood. 78m. **DIR:** George Breakston, Ray Stahl. **CAST:** Ray Bentley, Martha Hyer. **1954**

SCENES FROM A MURDER 🦃 Inept thriller about a killer who stalks an actress. Filmed in Italy. 90m. **DIR:** Alberto De Martino. **CAST:** Telly Savalas, Anne Heywood. **1972**

SCORCHY 🦃 Connie Stevens is an undercover cop trying to bust a major drug ring. Rated R. 99m. **DIR:** Howard Avedis. **CAST:** Connie Stevens, Cesare Danova, William Smith, Marlene Schmidt, Normann Burton, Joyce Jameson. **1976**

SCORPION 🦃 Dim-witted martial arts film stars nonactor Tonny Tulleners, who takes on a band of terrorists. Grade Z gobbler. Rated R. 98m. **DIR:** William Riead. **CAST:** Tonny Tulleners, Don Murray. **1987**

SEA CHASE, THE ★★ Weak and generally uninvolving World War II story finds German sea captain John Wayne attempting to elude capture by British naval forces. Film moves at a snail's pace. 117m. **DIR:** John Parrow. **CAST:** John Wayne, Lana Turner, James Arness, Tab Hunter, Lyle Bettger, Claude Akins, David Farrar. **1955**

SEA DEVILS ★★ Victor McLaglen and Ida Lupino play father and daughter in this soggy tale of Coast Guard trial and tribulation. McLaglen and Preston Foster are service rivals given to settling problems with their fists. Unfortunately, the audience can't fight back. B&W; 88m. **DIR:** Ben Stoloff. **CAST:** Victor McLaglen, Preston Foster, Ida Lupino, Donald Woods. **1937**

SEA HAWK, THE ★★★★ Errol Flynn was the best of the screen's costumed adventurers. *The Sea Hawk* shows him at his swashbuckling peak. He plays a buccaneer sea captain who is given tacit approval by Queen Elizabeth I (Flora Robson) to wreak havoc on the Spanish fleet and their cities in the New World. B&W; 109m. **DIR:** Michael Curtiz. **CAST:** Errol Flynn, Flora Robson, Claude Rains, Donald Crisp, Alan Hale Sr., Henry Daniell, Gilbert Roland. **1940**

SEA HOUND, THE ★★ Modern-day pirates searching for a buried Spanish treasure on an uncharted island find that they've bitten off more than they can chew when veteran action star Buster Crabbe shows up to spoil their plans. Every generation deserves its own pirate adventures, and with good-natured, dedicated Crabbe along, it's always an enjoyable ride. B&W; 15 episodes. **DIR:** Walter B. Eason, Mack V. Wright. **CAST:** Buster Crabbe, Jimmy Lloyd, Pamela Blake, Ralph Hodges, Robert Barron, Hugh Prosser, Rick

Vallin, Jack Ingram, Spencer Chan, Pierce Lyden. 1947

SEA SHALL NOT HAVE THEM, THE ★★★ Nicely done World War II film about British air rescue operations. Main story follows an RAF bomber crew shot down over the North Sea and their rescue from the ocean. B&W; 92m. **DIR:** Lewis Gilbert. **CAST:** Michael Redgrave, Dirk Bogarde, John Mitchell. 1955

SEA WOLF, THE (1941) ★★★★½ Rousing version of Jack London's dark seafaring adventure features a splendidly complex portrayal by Edward G. Robinson as the evil ship captain of the title. One of director Michael Curtiz's best films. B&W; 90m. **DIR:** Michael Curtiz. **CAST:** Edward G. Robinson, John Garfield, Ida Lupino, Alexander Knox, Gene Lockhart, Barry Fitzgerald, Stanley Ridges, David Bruce, Howard DaSilva. 1941

SEA WOLF, THE (1993) 🦃 Boredom washes over the deck in waves in this painful-to-watch remake of the oft-filmed Jack London novel. A flat script and poor performances combine to sink this unworthy effort. Made for TV. 96m. **DIR:** Michael Anderson. **CAST:** Charles Bronson, Christopher Reeve, Catherine Mary Stewart, Marc Singer. 1993

SEA WOLVES, THE ★★★ A World War II version of *The Over the Hill Gang*. Gregory Peck and Roger Moore play British officers who recruit a bunch of Boer War veterans now in their autumn years to do some espionage along the coast of India. While the film relies too heavily on comedy that doesn't work, the last twenty minutes have enough spirit to redeem it. The film is based on a true story. Rated PG for violence and sex. 120m. **DIR:** Andrew V. McLaglen. **CAST:** Gregory Peck, Roger Moore, David Niven, Trevor Howard, Barbara Kellerman, Patrick Macnee. 1980

SEARCH AND DESTROY (1981) 🦃 Vietnam veteran is chased by a Vietnamese villain. Not rated, the film has violence and profanity. 93m. **DIR:** William Fruet. **CAST:** Perry King, Don Stroud, Tisa Farrow, George Kennedy, Park Jong Soo. 1981

SECOND CHANCE ★★½ Robert Mitchum plays protector to a former gangster's girlfriend (Linda Darnell) as they are pursued through South America by hit man Jack Palance. This passable chase melodrama was Howard Hughes's first excursion into wide screen, and the often-imitated climax aboard the gondola cars suspended above a deep chasm is the centerpiece of the film. 82m. **DIR:** Rudolph Maté. **CAST:** Robert Mitchum, Linda Darnell, Jack Palance, Reginald Sheffield, Roy Roberts. 1953

SECRET AGENT (TV SERIES) ★★★½ The suave and resourceful John Drake (Patrick McGoohan) turned out to have more than one life; after the limited success of his 1961 series, *Danger Man*, he returned in 19[illegible] with the far more flamboyant—and pop[illegible]lar—*Secret Agent*. The new show disappeared after forty-five episodes had been aired. (But Drake would appear again—in a sense—as *The Prisoner*.) Creator and executive producer Ralph Smart, who wore the same hats during *Danger Man*, changed the format a bit for this outing; now Drake worked for the specifically British agency known as M.I.9 and took orders from an "M"-like figure named Hobbs (Peter Madden). The hour-length dramas were far grittier and more realistic than their American counterparts. B&W; each 53m. **DIR:** Don Chaffey, Peter Maxwell, Michael Truman. **CAST:** Patrick McGoohan, Peter Madden. 1965–1966

SECRET WEAPONS 🦃 Sleazy made-for-TV potboiler about a Russian espionage training camp. 96m. **DIR:** Don Taylor. **CAST:** James Franciscus, Sally Kellerman, Linda Hamilton, Geena Davis. 1985

SELL-OUT, THE ★★½ Double agent Oliver Reed screws up and finds that both the Soviets and the Americans have put out contracts on him. Okay spy stuff, though a bit heavy on the shoot-outs and car chases toward the end. Filmed in Israel. Rated PG. 88m. **DIR:** Peter Collinson. **CAST:** Richard Widmark, Oliver Reed, Gayle Hunnicutt, Sam Wanamaker. 1976

SERGEANT YORK ★★★ A World War II morale booster that is still good entertainment today. Gary Cooper got an Academy Award as the deeply religious young farmer from backwoods Tennessee who tries to avoid service in World War I because of his religious convictions only to become the war's most decorated American hero! B&W; 134m. **DIR:** Howard Hawks. **CAST:** Gary Cooper, Walter Brennan, George Tobias, Ward Bond, Noah Beery Jr., June Lockhart, Joan Leslie. 1941

SEVEN HOURS TO JUDGMENT ★★ An action-thriller that loses much of its thrill due to its baby-faced star (and his jumpy direction). Bridges is a judge who, after letting a gang of thugs off on a technicality, must run a gauntlet through their territory. Ron Leibman steals the film as the distraught (and psychotic) husband of the gang's victim. Rated R for violence and profanity. 89m. **DIR:** Beau Bridges. **CAST:** Beau Bridges, Ron Leibman, Julianne Phillips, Reginald Vel Johnson, Al Freeman Jr. 1988

SEVEN MAGNIFICENT GLADIATORS, THE 🦃 Seven gladiators defend the people of a small village. Rated PG. 86m. **DIR:** Bruno Mattei. **CAST:** Lou Ferrigno, Sybil Danning, Brad Harris, Dan Vadis, Mandy Rice-Davies. 1983

SEVEN SINNERS ★★★ A brawling story of saloon life in the steamy tropics, as John Wayne and Albert Dekker vie for sultry Marlene Dietrich, who walks through this slight story with good humor as a heartbreaking "entertainer." A serviceable action tale. B&W; 87m. **DIR:** Tay Garnett. **CAST:** John Wayne, Marlene Dietrich, Albert Dekker, Broderick Crawford, Mischa Auer, Anna Lee. 1940

SEVEN-UPS, THE ★★ Hoping to cash in on the popularity of *The French Connection*, the producer of that film directs this slam-bang action flick in an intellectual vacuum. All that's missing are William Friedkin, Gene Hackman, and an intelligent story...but what the hey, we've got a better car chase! Roy Scheider is, as always, quite appealing, but he can't make something out of this nothing. Rated PG for violence. 103m. **DIR:** Philip D'Antoni. **CAST:** Roy Scheider, Tony Lo Bianco, Richard Lynch. 1973

SEX CRIMES ★★ After a female judge is raped, she collects the names of all known sex offenders and systematically kills them. Incredibly bad acting wrecks this revenge drama. Not rated, but contains violence, profanity, and nudity. 90m. **DIR:** David Garcia. **CAST:** Jeff Osterhage, Maria Richwine. 1991

SGT. KABUKIMAN N.Y.P.D. ★★★ Wacky cop movie with a sci-fi twist from the guys at Troma. A New York detective inherits the superhuman powers of the Kabuki and changes into a colorfully dressed, if not totally competent, crime fighter. Some bad acting and a certain tongue-in-cheek attitude, make this a fun one to watch with a group of friends. Rated PG-13 for violence, profanity, and simulated sex. 99m. **DIR:** Lloyd Kaufman, Michael Herz. **CAST:** Rick Gianasi, Susan Byun, Bill Weeden, Thomas Crnkovich, Noble Lee Lester, Brick Bronsky, Larry Robinson, Pamela Alster, Shaler McClure, Fumio Furuya. 1991

SHADOW OF THE EAGLE ★★½ John Wayne's second serial for Mascot Pictures is another one of those stolen inventions–kidnapped scientist affairs, this time masterminded by a mysterious criminal known as The Eagle, who likes to write his threats in the sky with an airplane. Although a bit creaky, this is fun to watch. B&W; 12 chapters. **DIR:** Ford Beebe. **CAST:** John Wayne, Dorothy Gulliver, Walter Miller, Kenneth Harlan, Yakima Canutt. 1932

SHADOW OF THE WOLF ★★½ This gorgeously filmed Arctic adventure-soap about the encroachment of white men on Eskimo land and culture during the 1930s is also part mediocre crime-drama. Lou Diamond Phillips is physically convincing as an outcast Inuit hunter in a mediocre story heightened by enthralling anthropological detail and scenery. Rated PG-13 for violence and language. 108m. **DIR:** Jacques Dorfmann. **CAST:** Lou Diamond Phillips, Toshiro Mifune, Jennifer Tilly, Donald Sutherland. 1993

SHAFT ★★★ One of the best black films from the late 1960s and early 1970s. There is plenty of action and raw energy as private eye Shaft (Richard Roundtree) battles the bad guys in order to rescue a kidnapped woman. Great musical score by Isaac Hayes. Rated PG for violence. 100m. **DIR:** Gordon Parks Jr. **CAST:** Richard Roundtree, Charles Cioffi, Moses Gunn. 1971

SHAFT'S BIG SCORE! ★★★ Obligatory first sequel to the original *Shaft* is one of the best blaxploitation action films of the Seventies. Topflight violence competes for screen time with pungent dialogue by *French Connection* scriptwriter Ernest Tidyman. Ball-of-twine plot has Shaft take on the mob. Rated R for profanity and mayhem. 104m. **DIR:** Gordon Parks Jr. **CAST:** Richard Roundtree, Moses Gunn, Joseph Mascolo. 1972

SHAKE HANDS WITH THE DEVIL ★★★★ In 1921 Dublin, an Irish-American student (Don Murray) innocently becomes involved in rebel activities and finds himself a fugitive. He joins an IRA cell led by James Cagney, whom he at first admires, but soon comes to realize is a murderous fanatic. Another spellbinding performance by the magnificent Cagney in this hard-hitting, action-filled drama. B&W; 110m. **DIR:** Michael Anderson. **CAST:** James Cagney, Don Murray, Dana Wynter, Glynis Johns, Cyril Cusack, Michael Redgrave, Sybil Thorndike, Richard Harris. 1959

SHAKEDOWN 💔 Loud, sleazy action-thriller. Rated R for violence, nudity, and profanity. 112m. **DIR:** James Glickenhaus. **CAST:** Peter Weller, Sam Elliott, Patricia Charbonneau, Antonio Fargas, Blanche Baker. 1988

SHAKER RUN ★★ A New Zealand laboratory accidentally creates a deadly virus. Not rated, but the equivalent of a PG for violence and profanity. 91m. **DIR:** Bruce Morrison. **CAST:** Cliff Robertson, Leif Garrett, Lisa Harrow, Shane Briant. 1985

SHALLOW GRAVE 💔 Four college girls witness a killing. Not rated, but contains violence and nudity. 90m. **DIR:** Richard Styles. **CAST:** Tony March, Lisa Stahl, Tom Law. 1987

SHAME (1987) ★★★★ While on a motorcycling vacation, a lawyer (Deborra-Lee Furness) ends up in an out-of-the-way Australian town where young women are terrorized and ritually raped by a gang of young toughs. So the two-fisted Furness decides to make them pay for their crimes. It sounds corny, but *Shame* is really quite effective. Rated R for violence and profanity. 90m. **DIR:** Steve Jodrell. **CAST:** Deborra-Lee Furness, Tony Barry, Simone Buchanan. 1987

SHARK! (A.K.A. MANEATERS!) 💔 Waterlogged undersea adventure. Rated PG. 92m. **DIR:** Samuel Fuller. **CAST:** Burt Reynolds, Barry Sullivan, Arthur Kennedy, Silvia Pinal, Enrique Lucero. 1969

SHARK HUNTER, THE 💔 A Caribbean island recluse beats up sharks and searches for buried treasure. Not rated, but the equivalent of a PG for violence and brief nudity. 92m. **DIR:** Enzo G. Castellari. **CAST:** Franco Nero, Jorge Luke, Mike Forrest. **1984**

SHARK'S TREASURE 🦃 Good guys and bad guys search for sunken treasure. Rated PG for violence. 95m. **DIR:** Cornel Wilde. **CAST:** Cornel Wilde, Yaphet Kotto, John Neilson, Cliff Osmond. **1975**

SHARKY'S MACHINE ★★★★½ This is one of the best cop thrillers ever made. It's exciting, suspenseful, funny, and intelligent, so good it joins *48 Hrs.*, *Dirty Harry*, and *Tightrope* as the best of the genre. Burt Reynolds stars under his own direction as an undercover cop who has a compulsion to crack down on a new wave of crime in his city. Rated R because of violence and profanity. 119m. **DIR:** Burt Reynolds. **CAST:** Burt Reynolds, Rachel Ward, Brian Keith, Bernie Casey, Vittorio Gassman, Charles Durning. **1981**

SHE-DEVILS ON WHEELS 🦃 Atrocious Florida biker flick. Unrated. 83m. **DIR:** Herschell Gordon Lewis. **CAST:** Cristie Wagner. **1968**

SHEBA BABY ★★ One of Pam Grier's last blaxploitation opuses. This time, she's a private eye struggling to save the family business. Less raunchy than some entries in the series, but still mostly routine. Rated R. 90m. **DIR:** William Girdler. **CAST:** Pam Grier, Austin Stoker, D'Urville Martin. **1975**

SHEENA 🦃 Tanya Roberts as the Queen of the Jungle. Rated PG. 117m. **DIR:** John Guillermin. **CAST:** Tanya Roberts, Ted Wass, Donovan Scott. **1984**

SHIPS WITH WINGS ★★½ Typical patriotic British war movie, this one is set on an aircraft carrier preparing for battle. Some good character bits, but on the whole rather perfunctory. B&W; 103m. **DIR:** Sergei Nolbandov. **CAST:** John Clements, Ann Todd, Leslie Banks, Hugh Williams, Michael Wilding, Michael Rennie, Cecil Parker. **1941**

SHOGUN (FULL-LENGTH VERSION) ★★★★ Forget about the shortened version that is also out on video; this ten-hour original is the only one that does justice to James Clavell's sweeping novel. Richard Chamberlain began his reign as king of the miniseries with his portrayal of Blackthorne, the English sailor shipwrecked among the feudal Japanese. Rarely has television been the original home for a program of this epic scope, and it all works, from the breathtaking cinematography to the superb acting. 600m. **DIR:** Jerry London. **CAST:** Richard Chamberlain, Toshiro Mifune, Yoko Shimada, Damien Thomas. **1980**

SHOOT (1976) ★★★½ A group of buddies spending a weekend hunting are attacked by another group of hunters who are after game more interesting than deer. When one of their party is wounded, the attacked hunters, led by Cliff Robertson and Ernest Borgnine, want revenge and mount a military-style campaign to get it. Rated R for violence and profanity. 98m. **DIR:** Harvey Hart. **CAST:** Cliff Robertson, Ernest Borgnine, Henry Silva. **1976**

SHOOT TO KILL ★★★½ Sidney Poitier returns to the screen after a ten-year absence to portray a streetwise FBI agent determined to track down a ruthless killer. The chase leads to the mountains of the Pacific Northwest, where Poitier teams with tracker Tom Berenger. A solid thriller. Rated R for language and violence. 110m. **DIR:** Roger Spottiswoode. **CAST:** Sidney Poitier, Tom Berenger, Kirstie Alley, Clancy Brown, Richard Masur, Andrew Robinson. **1988**

SHOOTFIGHTER ★★★ Two friends in the deadly world of shootfighting—a brutal, sometimes lethal sport—team up to stay alive. A workable cast, combined with some extremely brutal fight sequences, blend together for an action film that rises above the genre. Two versions available: one rated R for violence, and one unrated with more of the same. Unrated 96m.; Rated R 94m. **DIR:** Pat Alan. **CAST:** Bolo Yeung, Maryam D'Abo, William Zabka, Martin Kove, Edward Albert. **1993**

SHORT FUSE 🦃 Racial tensions between the black community and the police. Rated R for violence and profanity. 91m. **DIR:** Blaine Novak. **CAST:** Art Garfunkel, Harris Yulin. **1989**

SHOUT AT THE DEVIL ★★ Good action scenes elevate this otherwise distasteful and overly complicated film about a hard-drinking American adventurer (Lee Marvin) and an upper-crust Englishman (Roger Moore) who join forces to blow up a German battleship before the breakout of World War I. Rated PG. 119m. **DIR:** Peter R. Hunt. **CAST:** Lee Marvin, Roger Moore, Barbara Parkins, Ian Holm. **1976**

SHOWDOWN IN LITTLE TOKYO ★★ As martial arts films go, this one is only fair. Its appeal lies in the action sequences and with the stars Dolph Lundgren and Brandon Lee. Rated R for violence, profanity, and nudity. 77m. **DIR:** Mark L. Lester. **CAST:** Dolph Lundgren, Brandon Lee, Tia Carrere. **1991**

SICILIAN, THE 🦃 This adaptation of Mario Puzo's novel becomes a tedious bore thanks to heavy-handed and pretentious direction. Rated R for violence and profanity. 105m. **DIR:** Michael Cimino. **CAST:** Christopher Lambert, Terence Stamp, Joss Ackland, John Turturro, Richard Bauer, Barbara Sukowa, Giula Boschi, Barry Miller, Andreas Katsulas, Ramon Bieri. **1987**

SIDEWINDER 1 ★★ Michael Parks is a quiet, reclusive motocross racer who becomes a partner in developing a new dirt bike. *Sidewinder 1* has good racing scenes—motocross fans will love them—but the story is studded with sexist remarks and attitudes. Rated PG. 97m. **DIR:** Earl Bellamy. **CAST:** Marjoe Gortner, Michael Parks, Susan Howard, Alex Cord. **1977**

SIEGE OF FIREBASE GLORIA, THE ★★★ Outnumbered five to one, our Marines defended the hilltop outpost called Firebase Gloria during the Tet offensive in 1968. This is the dramatization of their seemingly hopeless struggle. Grisly scenes of death and destruction bring the Vietnam War close to home. Rated R. 95m. **DIR:** Brian Trenchard-Smith. **CAST:** Wings Hauser, R. Lee Ermey. **1988**

SILENCER, THE ★★½ Newcomer Lynette Walden reaches the point of no return as a hit woman for a top-secret government agency. After she takes out the garbage, she drags in the trash, fulfilling her sexual desires by bedding down strangers off the street. She begins to suspect that she's on someone else's hit list. Decent action entry. Rated R for nudity, violence, and language. 85m. **DIR:** Amy Goldstein. **CAST:** Lynette Walden, Chris Mulkey, Paul Ganus, Jamie Gomez. **1992**

SILENT ASSASSINS 🦃 Stupid action flick about a CIA biggie gone bad. Not rated, but has violence and profanity. 91m. **DIR:** Lee Doo Young, Scott Thomas. **CAST:** Sam Jones, Linda Blair, Jun Chong, Phillip Rhee, Bill Erwin, Mako. **1987**

SILENT ENEMY, THE ★★½ World War II adventure has frogmen fighting it out in Gibraltar Harbor. Highlight: the underwater photography. B&W; 91m. **DIR:** William Fairchild. **CAST:** Laurence Harvey, Dawn Addams, John Clements. **1958**

SILENT RAGE 🦃 A Texas sheriff is pitted against a psychotic killer. Rated R for nudity, profanity, and violence. 105m. **DIR:** Michael Miller. **CAST:** Chuck Norris, Ron Silver, Stephen Furst. **1982**

SILK 2 🦃 Former Playmate of the Year Monique Gabrielle plays a hard-core policewoman who will do anything to help her partner who's been kidnapped. Rated R. 76m. **DIR:** Cirio H. Santiago. **CAST:** Monique Gabrielle, Peter Nelson, Jan Merlin. **1989**

SINBAD OF THE SEVEN SEAS ★★ Lou Ferrigno stars in this mediocre Italian adaptation of the familiar fairy tale. Ferrigno, as Sinbad, must take on an evil wizard and return his Kingdom to its former bliss. Rated PG-13 for violence. 95m. **DIR:** Enzo G. Castellari. **CAST:** Lou Ferrigno, John Steiner. **1989**

SINBAD THE SAILOR ★★★ Aping his father, Douglas Fairbanks Jr., as Sinbad, sails forth in search of Alexander the Great's fabled treasure and hits a variety of reefs. Unfortunately, the plot not only thickens but gets murky, to boot. Some say it's all tongue-in-cheek, but it's really more foot-in-mouth. Nonetheless, it is fun. 117m. **DIR:** Richard Wallace. **CAST:** Douglas Fairbanks Jr., Walter Slezak, Maureen O'Hara, Jane Greer, Anthony Quinn, Sheldon Leonard. **1947**

SINISTER URGE, THE ★★ Ed *(Plan 9 From Outer Space)* Wood's last film as a writer-director is one his fans won't want to miss. The police battle a ring of pornographers and a killer who gets so worked up by looking at these "dirty pictures" that he then goes to the park to kill innocent young women. In the best early-Sixties fashion, Wood got away with flashes of nudity by claiming social significance. Look for him in a brief appearance as a participant in a fistfight. B&W; 75m. **DIR:** Edward D. Wood Jr. **CAST:** Kenne Duncan, James Moore, Jean Fontaine. **1961**

SINK THE BISMARCK ★★★★ True story of the British Navy's relentless search for the German "super" battleship *Bismarck* is topflight war adventure. A standout production admired by both action fans and military historians. B&W; 97m. **DIR:** Lewis Gilbert. **CAST:** Kenneth More, Dana Wynter, Carl Mohner, Laurence Naismith, Geoffrey Keen, Karel Stepanek, Michael Hordern. **1960**

SIROCCO ★★★ Humphrey Bogart plays a successful crook operating in postwar Syria. He is forced to intercede in a terrorist-police situation and gets himself in trouble with both factions. One of Bogart's best later works and a representative sample of the darker side of romance and intrigue, poles apart from, but structurally related to, films like *Casablanca* and *Beat the Devil*. Give it a try. B&W; 98m. **DIR:** Curtis Bernhardt. **CAST:** Humphrey Bogart, Marta Toren, Lee J. Cobb, Everett Sloane, Zero Mostel. **1951**

633 SQUADRON ★★★ A British squadron of bomber pilots prepare for a difficult but important mission against a Nazi rocket fuel factory in Norway. Unrated, but there is graphic action. 95m. **DIR:** Walter Grauman. **CAST:** Cliff Robertson, George Chakiris, Harry Andrews, Donald Houston. **1963**

16 FATHOMS DEEP ★★ Sponge fisherman Creighton Chaney (Lon Chaney Jr.) borrows money to buy a boat so he and his girl can get married, but his efforts are sabotaged. Low-rent offering from Monogram uses a lot of stock underwater shots and original footage taken on Catalina Island. B&W; 59m. **DIR:** Armand Schaefer. **CAST:** Sally O'Neil, Lon Chaney Jr. **1934**

SKINHEADS 🦃 Three college friends and two female backpackers encounter a gang of skinheads. Rated R for violence and partial nudity. 93m. **DIR:** Greydon Clark. **CAST:** Chuck Connors, Barbara Bain, Brian Brophy, Jason Culp. **1988**

SKY BANDITS 🦃 An uninspired mixing of *Butch Cassidy and the Sundance Kid* and *The Blue Max*. Rated PG for violence. 95m. **DIR:**

Zoran Perisic. **CAST:** Scott McGinnis, Jeff Osterhage, Ronald Lacey. **1986**

SKY HEIST ★★ Frank Gorshin and Stefanie Powers hijack a police helicopter to help steal a fortune in gold bullion. Lots of familiar faces in this otherwise unmemorable TV movie. Not rated; contains no objectionable material. 96m. **DIR:** Lee H. Katzin. **CAST:** Don Meredith, Joseph Campanella, Larry Wilcox, Ken Swofford, Stefanie Powers, Frank Gorshin, Shelley Fabares, Steve Franken, Suzanne Somers, Richard Jordan. **1975**

SKY PIRATES 🦃 Terrible acting, a stupid plot, and poorly executed stunts. Rated PG-13 for violence. 89m. **DIR:** Colin Eggleston. **CAST:** John Hargreaves, Meredith Phillips, Max Phipps. **1986**

SLAUGHTER ★★½ The first, and tightest (thanks to the direction of underrated action specialist Jack Starrett) of two blaxploitation sagas in which Jim Brown portrays a heroic Vietnam vet who returns home to avenge his family's murder. Augmented by a cast of upscale character actors, slumming in roles far beneath them. 92m. **DIR:** Jack Starrett. **CAST:** Jim Brown, Stella Stevens, Rip Torn, Don Gordon. **1972**

SLAUGHTER IN SAN FRANCISCO 🦃 Another abysmal martial arts chop-socky fest. Rated R for violence and profanity. 87m. **DIR:** William Lowe. **CAST:** Chuck Norris, Robert Jones, Daniel Ivan. **1974**

SLAUGHTER'S BIG RIP-OFF ★★ The second, and less interesting, of Jim Brown's popular blaxploitation pair in which our indestructible one-man army takes on assorted sadistic criminals. Tepid entry in a waning action cycle. 93m. **DIR:** Gordon Douglas. **CAST:** Jim Brown, Ed McMahon, Brock Peters, Don Stroud. **1973**

SLAVE OF THE CANNIBAL GOD 🦃 A woman encounters a cult of flesh-eaters while attempting to find her missing husband in New Guinea. Rated R for violence and nudity. 87m. **DIR:** Sergio Martino. **CAST:** Stacy Keach, Ursula Andress. **1979**

SLAVERS ★★ Ray Milland plays an Arab slave trader in nineteenth-century Africa who treats his charges like cattle. Rated R for violence, nudity, and sexual situations. 102m. **DIR:** Jurgen Goslar. **CAST:** Trevor Howard, Ron Ely, Britt Ekland, Ray Milland, Cameron Mitchell. **1977**

SLEEPING DOGS ★★½ Here's a "what if?" film set in New Zealand during a time of economic crisis. Sam Neill discovers his wife is having an affair, so he goes off to live by himself for a while. Meanwhile, a group of government agents kill innocent bystanders during demonstrations and make it look like the work of the protesters. No MPAA rating. 107m. **DIR:** Roger Donaldson. **CAST:** Sam Neill, Warren Oates, Nevan Rowe, Ian Mune. **1977**

SLIPPING INTO DARKNESS ★★ An ex-motorcycle gang member's brother is murdered. So the biker gets his former buddies together to find out whodunit. Rated R for violence, nudity, and profanity. 87m. **DIR:** Eleanor Gawer. **CAST:** Michelle Johnson, Neill Barry. **1988**

SLOANE 🦃 Organized crime in Manila. Not rated, but has plenty of violence and profanity. 95m. **DIR:** Dan Rosenthal. **CAST:** Robert Resnik, Debra Blee, Raul Aragon. **1984**

SMALL TOWN IN TEXAS, A ★★ Fairly effective B picture pits a revenge-lusting Timothy Bottoms against the crooked sheriff (Bo Hopkins) who framed him in a drug bust and stole his wife (Susan George). Car crashes, fights, and even a little suspense. Rated R. 95m. **DIR:** Jack Starrett. **CAST:** Timothy Bottoms, Susan George, Bo Hopkins, Art Hindle, Morgan Woodward. **1976**

SNAKE EATER 🦃 Lorenzo Lamas is a lone wolf cop in pursuit of the hillbillies who killed his parents. This hybrid of *Rambo* and *The Hills Have Eyes* had us laughing at all the wrong moments. Rated R for profanity, violence, and nudity. 89m. **DIR:** George Erschbamer. **CAST:** Lorenzo Lamas. **1989**

SNAKE EATER 2, THE DRUG BUSTER ★★ Mel Gibson's marketable character from the *Lethal Weapon* movies finds new merchandising life in this rip-off action flick. Lorenzo Lamas portrays Soldier, an unorthodox cop turned vigilante. Rated R for violence and profanity. 93m. **DIR:** George Erschbamer. **CAST:** Lorenzo Lamas, Michele Scarabelli, Larry B. Scott, Vittorio Rossi. **1989**

SNAKE EATER III: HIS LAW ★★½ Renegade cop Lorenzo Lamas returns. This outing, he helps a family whose daughter was brutalized by a gang of bikers called Hell's Furies. Rated R for violence, simulated sex, and profanity. 109m. **DIR:** George Erschbamer. **CAST:** Lorenzo Lamas, Minor Mustain. **1992**

SNATCHED ★★½ In this mediocre made-for-television film, the wives of three rich men are kidnapped and held for ransom. The crime is complicated when one of the husbands refuses to pay his share of the ransom. 73m. **DIR:** Sutton Roley. **CAST:** Howard Duff, Leslie Nielsen, Sheree North, Barbara Parkins, Robert Reed, John Saxon, Tisha Sterling, Anthony Zerbe, Richard Davalos. **1973**

SNIPER ★★½ Male posturing reaches ludicrous heights in this tedious jungle drama, which finds Marine sniper Tom Berenger sent into the wilds of Panama to assassinate a Colombian drug baron. Rated R for violence and profanity. 98m. **DIR:** Luis Llosa. **CAST:** Tom Berenger, Billy Zane, J. T. Walsh. **1993**

SNO-LINE 🦃 A Texas cocaine operation is threatened by the mob. Rated R for violence and language. 89m. **DIR:** Douglas F. O'Neans.

CAST: Vince Edwards, Paul Smith, June Wilkinson. **1984**

SNOW KILL ★★★½ An executive's plan for a weekend survival trip on a mountain turns into trouble when three escaped convicts try to recover their cocaine stash. Good action with David Dukes shining as the villain. Unrated, but has violence. 94m. **DIR:** Thomas Wright. **CAST:** Terence Knox, Patti D'Arbanville, David Dukes. **1990**

SNOWS OF KILIMANJARO, THE ★★★★ A broad and colorful canvas of foreign adventure with author-hero (Gregory Peck) lying injured on the slope of Africa's famous mountain reflecting on his life. From Africa to Spain to the Riviera and back again. One of the better renderings of a Hemingway novel. 117m. **DIR:** Henry King. **CAST:** Gregory Peck, Susan Hayward, Ava Gardner, Leo G. Carroll, Hildegarde Neff, Torin Thatcher. **1952**

SOLDIER, THE 🦃 Russian agents steal enough plutonium for a large nuclear explosion. Rated R for violence and profanity. 96m. **DIR:** James Glickenhaus. **CAST:** Ken Wahl, Klaus Kinski, William Prince. **1982**

SOLDIER OF FORTUNE ★★½ Clark Gable helps Susan Hayward search for her husband, lost in Red China. Exotic Asian locations are the main reason to see this standard adventure-drama. Gable is virile, Hayward makes a good match for him, and Hong Kong never looked better. 96m. **DIR:** Edward Dmytryk. **CAST:** Clark Gable, Susan Hayward, Michael Rennie, Gene Barry, Tom Tully, Alex D'Arcy, Anna Sten. **1955**

SOLDIER'S FORTUNE ★★½ When ex-Green Beret turned mercenary Gil Gerard finds out that his daughter has been kidnapped, he pulls together an elite fighting team in order to bring her back alive. Likable cast helps move things along. Rated R for violence. 92m. **DIR:** Arthur N. Mele. **CAST:** Gil Gerard, Charles Napier, Dan Haggerty. **1990**

SOMETHING OF VALUE ★★★ White settlers in Kenya are preyed upon by bloodthirsty Mau Mau tribesmen sick of oppression in this often too-graphic drama, which opens with a specially filmed foreword from Winston Churchill. B&W; 113m. **DIR:** Richard Brooks. **CAST:** Rock Hudson, Dana Wynter, Sidney Poitier, Wendy Hiller, Frederick O'Neal, Juano Hernandez, William Marshall, Michael Pate. **1957**

SON OF ALI BABA ★★½ Aged Ali Baba is kidnapped by an evil caliph. His son comes to the rescue and wins a beautiful princess to boot. Juvenile, but fun. Victor Jory again plays a great villain. 85m. **DIR:** Kurt Neumann. **CAST:** Tony Curtis, Piper Laurie, Susan Cabot, William Reynolds, Hugh O'Brian, Victor Jory, Gerald Mohr. **1952**

SON OF CAPTAIN BLOOD 🦃 Poorly produced, amateurishly acted pirate programmer. 88m. **DIR:** Tulio Demichell. **CAST:** Sean Flynn, Alessandra Panaro, Jose Nieto, Ann Todd. **1962**

SON OF MONTE CRISTO, THE ★★★ True to established swashbuckler form, masked avenging hero Louis Hayward crosses wits, then swords, with would-be dictator George Sanders. Honoring tradition, he then frees imprisoned fair lady Joan Bennett from the villain's clutches. B&W; 102m. **DIR:** Rowland V. Lee. **CAST:** Louis Hayward, Joan Bennett, George Sanders, Florence Bates, Montagu Love, Ian Wolfe, Clayton Moore, Ralph Byrd. **1941**

SON OF THE SHEIK ★★½ This sequel to the 1921 adventure, *The Sheik*, proved to be bedroom-eyed, ex-gardener Rudolph Valentino's final film. It was released to coincide with his funeral and was an immediate hit. In the title role, the legendary Valentino acquitted himself with confidence and flair, foiling his enemies and winning the heart of nomadic dancer Vilma Banky. Silent. B&W; 62m. **DIR:** George Fitzmaurice. **CAST:** Rudolph Valentino, Vilma Banky, Bull Montana, Montagu Love, George Fawcett, Karl Dane. **1926**

SON OF ZORRO ★★ A Civil War veteran returns home to find nothing but corruption and graft. He enlists the aid of the local postmistress to assume the role of distant relative Zorro and set things straight. Republic's excellent action standards can't save this stale formula from the anonymity it deserves. B&W; 13 chapters. **DIR:** Spencer Gordon Bennet, Fred Brannon. **CAST:** George Turner, Peggy Stewart, Roy Barcroft. **1947**

SORORITY GIRL ★★ Susan Cabot is the bad girl who makes life difficult for new sorority pledge Barboura Morris. The ads promised spankings and even a hint of lesbianism, but the movie itself is tame enough for 1950s TV. B&W; 60m. **DIR:** Roger Corman. **CAST:** Susan Cabot, Dick Miller, Barboura Morris, June Kenney. **1957**

SOS COAST GUARD ★★½ All-American Coast Guard stalwart Terry Kent (Ralph Byrd) has his hands full as he battles crazed inventor Boroff (Bela Lugosi). There's so much going on in this serial that it's best just to forget about the story line and sit back and enjoy the action. B&W; 12 chapters. **DIR:** William Witney, Alan James. **CAST:** Ralph Byrd, Bela Lugosi. **1937**

SOUL HUSTLER 🦃 A drug-using wanderer swindles gullible hicks. Execrable. Rated PG for strong language. 81m. **DIR:** Burt Topper. **CAST:** Fabian, Nai Bonet, Tony Russell. **1986**

SOUL VENGEANCE ★★★ Wildly over-the-top blaxploitation film, originally released as *Welcome Home Brother Charles*, about an ex-con seeking revenge on the men who sent him to prison. A must-see for sheer weirdness, including a strangulation scene we can't describe here. Rated R for nudity, sex, profanity, and strong violence. 91m. **DIR:** Jamaa Fanaka. **CAST:** Mario Monte, Reatha Grey. **1975**

SOUTH OF PAGO PAGO ★★ A good title is wasted on this so-so action tale of pirates heisting native-harvested pearls and being pursued and engaged by the locals. Typical South Sea fare. B&W; 98m. **DIR:** Alfred E. Green. **CAST:** Victor McLaglen, Jon Hall, Frances Farmer, Olympe Bradna, Gene Lockhart. **1940**

SOUTHERN COMFORT ★★★★ Director Walter Hill's 1981 "war" film focuses on the plight of a National Guard unit lost in Cajun country while on routine training maneuvers. Armed only with M-16 rifles loaded with blanks, the soldiers (who include Keith Carradine and Powers Boothe) find themselves ill-equipped to deal with the hostile locals—and an edge-of-your-seat entertainment is the result. Rated R for violence. 106m. **DIR:** Walter Hill. **CAST:** Keith Carradine, Powers Boothe, Fred Ward, Brion James. **1981**

SPARTACUS ★★★★½ One of the more rewarding big-budget epics that marked the late 1950s and 1960s. Even though this fictional story of an actual slave revolt against the Roman Empire is large-scale in every detail, it never lets the human drama get lost in favor of spectacle. 196m. **DIR:** Stanley Kubrick. **CAST:** Kirk Douglas, Jean Simmons, Laurence Olivier, Peter Ustinov, Charles Laughton, Tony Curtis. **1960**

SPEED ZONE 🦃 Another yawner about the *Cannonball Run* cross-country road race. Rated PG. 87m. **DIR:** Jim Drake. **CAST:** John Candy, Donna Dixon, Joe Flaherty, Eugene Levy, Tom Smothers, Tim Matheson, Jamie Farr, Peter Boyle, Brooke Shields. **1989**

SPIDERS, THE ★★★ Long considered a lost film, *The Spiders* (written and directed by Fritz Lang) is an adventure story about a gang of organized criminals. Although planned as a serial, only the first two parts were completed. Fritz Lang used exotic locations, combining a labyrinth of plots. The film had its first American showing in 1979. Tinted B&W; 137m. **DIR:** Fritz Lang. **CAST:** Carl de Vogy, Ressel Orla, Lil Dagover. **1919**

SPIRIT OF THE EAGLE ★★ A widowed father takes his son into the wilderness to begin a new life, only to see the child kidnapped. This slow-moving adventure film may be rousing to youngsters, but most adults will probably nod off quickly. Not rated. 93m. **DIR:** Boon Collins. **CAST:** Dan Haggerty, William Smith. **1990**

SPY SMASHER ★★★ The costumed radio hero (Kane Richmond) takes on the Nazis in this fun-for-fans cliff-hanger serial. B&W; 12 chapters. **DIR:** William Witney. **CAST:** Kane Richmond, Sam Flint, Marguerite Chapman, Hans Schumm, Tristram Coffin. **1942**

SPY WHO LOVED ME, THE ★★★★ This, the tenth James Bond epic, is Roger Moore's third, and he finally hits his stride. Directed with a blend of excitement and tongue-in-cheek humor, the film teams Bond with Russian agent XXX (Barbara Bach) in an effort to stop an industrialist (Curt Jurgens) from destroying the surface world so he can rule an undersea kingdom. Rated PG for violence and sexual situations. 125m. **DIR:** Lewis Gilbert. **CAST:** Roger Moore, Barbara Bach, Curt Jurgens, Richard Kiel, Bernard Lee, Lois Maxwell, Desmond Llewellyn, Caroline Munro. **1977**

SPYMAKER: THE SECRET LIFE OF IAN FLEMING ★★★ Enjoyable fluff concentrates on writer Ian Fleming's exploits during World War II and his work with British intelligence. Jason Connery, Sean's son, is quite good as Fleming, bringing the right amounts of humor and derring-do to the character. Made for TV. 77m. **DIR:** Ferdinand Fairfax. **CAST:** Jason Connery, Kristin Scott Thomas, Joss Ackland, Patricia Hodge, David Warner, Richard Johnson, Colin Welland. **1990**

SQUIZZY TAYLOR ★★½ Fairly interesting film about the notorious Australian gangster of the 1920s. David Atkins gives a convincing performance. But the story begins to lose its edge after a while. Not rated. Has sex, nudity, and violence. 103m. **DIR:** Kevin Dobson. **CAST:** David Atkins, Jacki Weaver, Alan Cassell, Michael Long. **1983**

STAKEOUT ★★★★½ The fastest and funniest cop thriller since the original *Beverly Hills Cop*. A pair of detectives (Richard Dreyfuss and Emilio Estevez) strive to apprehend psychotic killer Aidan Quinn, who has escaped from prison. Rated R for profanity, nudity, and suggested sex, and violence. 116m. **DIR:** John Badham. **CAST:** Richard Dreyfuss, Emilio Estevez, Madeleine Stowe, Aidan Quinn, Dan Lauria, Forest Whitaker. **1987**

STALAG 17 ★★★★★ Many critics felt William Holden's Academy Award for *Stalag 17* was a gift for failing to give him proper recognition in *Sunset Boulevard*. Those critics should view this prison camp comedy-drama again. This film still holds up brilliantly today. Billy Wilder successfully alternated between suspense and comedy in this story of a World War II prison camp. Holden plays an opportunistic and cynical sergeant whose actions make him a natural suspect as the spy in the POWs' midst. B&W; 120m. **DIR:** Billy Wilder. **CAST:** William Holden, Robert Strauss, Peter Graves, Otto Preminger. **1953**

STARK ★★★½ Above-average TV movie about a Kansas cop butting heads against corrupt Las Vegas politicians and mobsters as he searches for the killers of his sister. Nicolas Surovy's sure performance and Ernest

Tidyman's script make this a must for private eye buffs. 95m. **DIR:** Rod Holcomb. **CAST:** Nicolas Surovy, Marilu Henner, Dennis Hopper. 1985

STEEL ★★★ Plenty of action and stunts keep this minor film popping along surprisingly well. Lee Majors stars as the head of a construction crew struggling to complete a skyscraper on schedule. Majors is almost convincing, and a strong cast of character actors are great fun to watch. Rated R. 99m. **DIR:** Steve Carver. **CAST:** Lee Majors, Jennifer O'Neill, Art Carney, George Kennedy, Harris Yulin, Terry Kiser, Richard Lynch, Roger E. Mosley, Albert Salmi, R. G. Armstrong. 1980

STEEL HELMET, THE ★★★½ Director-writer Samuel Fuller's war movies actually improve with age. This one, shot (as usual) on a low budget and set in the Korean War, is packed with irony, lightning pace and vivid action. A war movie made with style and authority. B&W; 84m. **DIR:** Samuel Fuller. **CAST:** Gene Evans, Robert Hutton, Steve Brodie, James Edwards. 1951

STEELE JUSTICE 🦃 One-man-army Martin Kove is hired to wipe out the Vietnamese Mafia in Los Angeles. Rated R for profanity and violence. 94m. **DIR:** Robert Boris. **CAST:** Martin Kove, Sela Ward, Ronny Cox, Bernie Casey, Joseph Campanella, Sarah Douglas, Soon-Teck Oh. 1987

STEELE'S LAW ★★ Fred Williamson is Chicago's answer to *Dirty Harry* as he goes undercover in Texas. Williamson wears all hats—as director, producer, story-idea creator, and star—in this barely watchable actioner. Unrated, contains nudity, profanity, and violence. 90m. **DIR:** Fred Williamson. **CAST:** Fred Williamson, Bo Svenson. 1991

STICK ★★★ *Stick* is an odd mixture of comedy and violence that more than once strains the viewer's suspension of disbelief. Fans of the original novel, by Elmore Leonard, will be shocked at how far Reynolds's film strays from its source. What should have been a tough, lean, and mean movie contains a surprising amount of clowning by its stars. Despite all this, it has enough action and genuine laughs to please Reynolds's fans. Rated R for profanity and violence. 109m. **DIR:** Burt Reynolds. **CAST:** Burt Reynolds, Charles Durning, George Segal, Candice Bergen. 1985

STILETTO 🦃 A rich jet-setter also happens to be a professional killer. Rated R. 98m. **DIR:** Bernard Kowalski. **CAST:** Alex Cord, Britt Ekland, Patrick O'Neal, Barbara McNair. 1969

STING, THE ★★★★½ Those *Butch Cassidy and the Sundance Kid* stars, Paul Newman and Robert Redford, were reunited for this fast-paced entertainment as two con men who outcon a con. Winner of seven Academy Awards—including best picture—this film, directed by George Roy Hill (*A Little Romance* and *Butch Cassidy*) revived Scott Joplin's music. For that, and the more obvious reasons, it is not to be missed. Rated PG. 129m. **DIR:** George Roy Hill. **CAST:** Paul Newman, Robert Redford, Robert Shaw, Charles Durning, Ray Walston, Eileen Brennan, Harold Gould, Dana Elcar. 1973

STING II, THE ★★ You could hardly expect a sequel to such a joyously entertaining film as *The Sting* to measure up. True to those expectations, this film, starring Jackie Gleason, Mac Davis, Teri Garr, and Karl Malden, doesn't come close. Rated PG for violence. 102m. **DIR:** Jeremy Paul Kagan. **CAST:** Jackie Gleason, Mac Davis, Teri Garr, Karl Malden, Oliver Reed, Bert Remsen. 1983

STINGRAY 🦃 Two young men buy a Stingray, unaware that it's filled with stolen cash and drugs. Rated R for violence and profanity. 100m. **DIR:** Richard Taylor. **CAST:** Chris Mitchum, Sherry Jackson, Bill Watson. 1978

STONE COLD ★★★ Ex-football player Brian Bosworth's motion picture debut is better than might be expected. "The Boz" plays an undercover cop who infiltrates a sleazy group of motorcycle outlaws. Rated R for violence, nudity, and profanity. 90m. **DIR:** Craig R. Baxley. **CAST:** Brian Bosworth, Lance Henriksen, William Forsythe, Sam McMurray. 1991

STONE KILLER, THE ★★★½ A *Dirty Harry*-style cop thriller, this casts Charles Bronson as a no-nonsense New York cop who gets transferred to Los Angeles because of his direct way of dealing with gun-toting criminals...he shoots them. It packs a wallop. Rated R. 95m. **DIR:** Michael Winner. **CAST:** Charles Bronson, Martin Balsam, David Sheiner, Norman Fell, Ralph Waite. 1973

STOPOVER TOKYO ★★ Based on a story by John P. Marquand, this ho-hum espionage tale has an American spy (Robert Wagner) chasing a communist undercover agent all over Tokyo. Wagner is earnest, as usual, but even the cast's enthusiasm can't put life into this one. Joan Collins is worth watching, as always. 100m. **DIR:** Richard L. Breen. **CAST:** Robert Wagner, Edmond O'Brien, Joan Collins, Ken Scott. 1957

STORM AND SORROW ★★½ Lori Singer is the "Rocky Mountain Spider Woman" who joins a 1974 expedition to climb one of Russia's highest mountains. Gorgeous scenery, but s-l-o-w going as people trudge through snow, pant, rest, then trudge some more. Made for TV. 96m. **DIR:** Richard A. Colla. **CAST:** Lori Singer, Todd Allen. 1990

STRAIGHT LINE ★★½ Laughable action film stars Mr. T as a private eye who gets the job of a lifetime: track down the man brainwashing kids into enforcing white supremacy by killing. Hokey, unbelievable, and quite entertaining in a goofy sort of way. 95m. **DIR:** George Mihalka. **CAST:** Mr. T, Kenneth Welsh. **1988**

STRANGE SHADOWS IN AN EMPTY ROOM 🦃 A cop investigates his sister's mysterious death. Not rated, but contains violence. 97m. **DIR:** Martin Herbert. **CAST:** Stuart Whitman, John Saxon, Martin Landau, Tisa Farrow. **1976**

STREET ASYLUM 🦃 A Los Angeles street cop gets recruited into a special strike force. Rated R for language, violence, and nudity. 90m. **DIR:** Gregory Brown. **CAST:** Wings Hauser, G. Gordon Liddy, Alex Cord, Brion James. **1990**

STREET CRIMES ★★½ Dennis Farina adds integrity to this tale of a police officer who creates a youth center so that gang kids can settle their differences with fists and feet in the ring. A drug lord takes exception and soon both cops and kids find themselves to be targets. It's *Rocky* with a not-so-new twist. Rated R for profanity and violence. 93m. **DIR:** Stephen Smoke. **CAST:** Dennis Farina, Max Gail, Mike Worth. **1992**

STREET FIGHTER ★★ Sonny Chiba first caught the attention of American audiences in this martial arts hit. But the extreme violence (so strong that the film was originally rated X) is missing from this video version: shorn of 10 minutes, what's left is often hard to follow. Rated R. 75m. **DIR:** S. Ozawa. **CAST:** Sonny Chiba. **1975**

STREET HITZ 🦃 Low-budget drama about two brothers caught up in the violent world of street gangs in South Bronx. Pretty cheesy. Not rated, but contains violence. Originally titled *Street Story*. 90m. **DIR:** Joseph B. Vasquez. **CAST:** Angelo Lopez, Cookie, Lydia Ramirez, Melvin Muza. **1991**

STREET HUNTER 🦃 Drugs and gang wars. Rated R for violence. 96m. **DIR:** John Gallagher. **CAST:** Steve Harris, Reb Brown. **1990**

STREET JUSTICE ★★ Ex-CIA agent returns home after thirteen years of captivity to find his wife has remarried a political reformer involved in a power struggle with a corrupt political machine. Rated R for violence and profanity. 93m. **DIR:** Richard C. Sarafian. **CAST:** Michael Ontkean, Joanna Kerns, Catherine Bach. **1987**

STREET KNIGHT ★★★ *Perfect Weapon*'s Jeff Speakman returns to clean up the streets of Los Angeles in this satisfying action thriller. He's a retired cop forced back into action when a mysterious group attempts to incite rival gangs into war. There's more plot than usual, so martial-artist Speakman has more to do than beat up the bad guys, led by Christopher Neame. Rated R for violence, language, and nudity. 91m. **DIR:** Albert Magnoli. **CAST:** Jeff Speakman, Christopher Neame. **1993**

STREET PEOPLE 🦃 Roger Moore and Stacy Keach travel from Italy to San Francisco to rub out a mobster. Rated R for violence. 92m. **DIR:** Maurizio Lucidi. **CAST:** Roger Moore, Stacy Keach. **1976**

STREET SOLDIERS ★★½ Better-than-average revenge flick has a group of high school students banding together to take out the hoodlums who killed one of their ranks. Slick production values and fast-paced action sequences add up to a rousing tale. Rated R for violence and language. 99m. **DIR:** Lee Harry. **CAST:** Jun Chong, Jeff Rector. **1990**

STREETHAWK ★★ Only kiddies—and fans of the short-lived television series, if there are any—will find much to enjoy in this story of a police officer (Rex Smith) left for dead by drug dealers. 60m. **DIR:** Virgil Vogel. **CAST:** Rex Smith, Jayne Modean, Christopher Lloyd, Joe Regalbuto, Lawrence Pressman, Robert Beltran. **1986**

STREETS 🦃 A prostitute is pursued by a psychotic cop. Rated R for violence, nudity, and depiction of drug use. 86m. **DIR:** Katt Shea Ruben. **CAST:** Christina Applegate, David Mendenhall. **1989**

STREETS OF FIRE ★★★ This comic book–style movie is a diverting compendium of nonstop action set to a rocking backbeat. In it a famous rock singer (Diane Lane) is captured by a motorcycle gang in Walter Hill's mythic world, which combines 1950s attitudes and styles with a futuristic feel. It's up to her two-fisted former boyfriend, Tom Cody (Michael Paré) to save her. Rated R for profanity and violence. 93m. **DIR:** Walter Hill. **CAST:** Diane Lane, Michael Paré, Rick Moranis, Amy Madigan, Willem Dafoe. **1984**

STRIKE COMMANDO 🦃 A Vietnam vet goes behind enemy lines. Rated R for Refuse. 92m. **DIR:** Vincent Dawn. **CAST:** Reb Brown, Christopher Connelly. **1987**

STRIKE FORCE ★★ A *French Connection* rehash, this made-for-television movie stars Richard Gere as a cop out to make a big drug bust. Lots of action, not much story. 74m. **DIR:** Barry Shear. **CAST:** Richard Gere, Cliff Gorman, Donald Blakely, Edward Grover, Joe Spinell. **1975**

STRIKER'S MOUNTAIN ★★ Predictable plot with suspenseless conflicts. A small-time resort owner alternately courts and repels the big corporate backing that Leslie Nielsen, as a ruthless millionaire, controls. The ski scenes are the best part of the film. Unrated. 99m. **DIR:** Allen Simmonds. **CAST:** Leslie Nielsen, August Schellenberg, Mimi Kuzyk, Bruce Greenwood. **1987**

STRIKING DISTANCE ★★★½ Bruce Willis enters Charles Bronson territory as an honest cop who finds himself on river patrol after testifying against his cousin, another police officer who brutally beat a suspect to death. Willis is saved from guilt and alcohol when he picks up the trail of a serial killer. While not up to the high standards of the star's *Die Hard* movies, this is still enjoyable action fare. Rated R for profanity, violence, and simulated sex. 97m. **DIR:** Rowdy Harrington. **CAST:** Bruce Willis, Sarah Jessica Parker, Dennis Farina, Tom Sizemore, Robert Pastorelli, Timothy Busfield, John Mahoney, Andre Braugher, Tom Atkins. **1993**

STRIPPED TO KILL ★★★ This generally impressive terror film wastes thirty minutes on striptease acts. Two undercover cops (Kay Lenz and Greg Evigan) investigate the murder of a young stripper. Norman Fell plays the jaded strip-joint owner. Rated R for excessive nudity, erotic dancing, and violence. 83m. **DIR:** Katt Shea Ruben. **CAST:** Kay Lenz, Greg Evigan, Norman Fell. **1987**

SUDDEN DEATH 🦃 Cheaply made rehash of *Death Wish* and *Ms. .45*. Rated R. 93m. **DIR:** Sig Shore. **CAST:** Denise Coward, Frank Runyeon, Jaime Tinelli. **1986**

SUDDEN IMPACT ★★★★ "Dirty Harry" Callahan (Clint Eastwood) is back, and he's meaner, nastier, and—surprise!—funnier than ever in this, his fourth screen adventure. In the story, a killer (Sondra Locke, in a rare, effective performance) is methodically extracting bloody revenge on the sickos who raped her and a younger sister. It becomes Harry's job to track her down, but not until he's done away with a half-dozen villains and delivered twice as many quips including, "Go ahead, make my day." Rated R for violence and profanity. 117m. **DIR:** Clint Eastwood. **CAST:** Clint Eastwood, Sondra Locke, Pat Hingle, Bradford Dillman. **1983**

SUDDEN THUNDER 🦃 Umpteenth take on the female cop avenging her father's death by taking on the mob. The only thunder is this bomb going off. Not rated, but contains violence. 90m. **DIR:** David Hunt. **CAST:** Andrea Lamatsch, Corwyn Sperry, James Paoleilei, Ernie Santana. **1990**

SUGAR HILL ★★½ Despite fine performances by Wesley Snipes and Michael Wright, this story of two brothers involved in the Harlem drug trade does not have the punch of *New Jack City*. Director Leon Ichaso has a great eye for detail and settings, but he is unable to add excitement to the all-too-familiar story line that has Snipes attempting to leave his gangster ways behind. Rated R for violence, profanity, and nudity. 123m. **DIR:** Leon Ichaso. **CAST:** Wesley Snipes, Michael Wright, Theresa Randle, Clarence Williams III, Abe Vigoda, Larry Joshua, Ernie Hudson, Leslie Uggams. **1994**

SUICIDE BATTALION 🦃 The newsreel stock footage is more exciting than the movie itself in this stage-bound WWII programmer set at Pearl Harbor. B&W; 79m. **DIR:** Edward L. Cahn. **CAST:** Mike Connors, John Ashley, Russ Bender. **1958**

SUMMER CITY ★★ Mel Gibson stars in this Australian teen rebel flick that lacks a fresh approach to one of the oldest stories in film: four teens go on a surfing weekend at a sleepy little seaside community only to find trouble when one of the delinquents messes around with a local's daughter. A few intense moments, and the acting is not bad, but some of the dialogue is indistinguishable in the muddy audio. Not rated, but the equivalent of PG for some sex, partial nudity, and violence. 83m. **DIR:** Christopher Fraser. **CAST:** Mel Gibson, Phil Avalon, Steve Bisley. **1976**

SUMMERTIME KILLER, THE ★★½ A 6-year-old boy witnesses the beating and drowning of his father by a gang of hoods. Twenty years pass, and we follow the grownup son (Chris Mitchum) as he systematically pursues and kills these men in New York, Rome, and Portugal. While a police detective (Karl Malden) is investigating one of the murders, a Mafia boss hires him to privately track down the killer. There are some exciting motorcycle pursuits along the way before the ending takes a slight twist. Rated R for violence and language. 100m. **DIR:** Antonio Isasi. **CAST:** Chris Mitchum, Karl Malden, Olivia Hussey, Raf Vallone, Claudine Auger, Gerard Tichy. **1972**

SUNSET HEAT ★★½ Photojournalist Michael Paré finds his former life as a drug dealer intruding on his new career when he returns to Los Angeles. A reunion with his old buddy Adam Ant results in Paré being hunted by drug lord Dennis Hopper, his former partner. Sleazy, but well acted. Rated R for profanity, nudity, and violence. 94m. **DIR:** John Nicolella. **CAST:** Michael Paré, Dennis Hopper, Adam Ant, Little Richard, Charlie Schlatter, Daphne Ashbrook. **1992**

SUPERCARRIER ★★★ This is the TV-movie premiere of the short-lived series of the same name. The action takes Top Gun graduates on a mission aboard a supercarrier. The Russians have a plane in U.S. air space and two pilots are assigned to escort it out. The flight and action scenes are engrossing, but on the ground *Supercarrier* is pretty routine. 90m. **DIR:** William A. Graham. **CAST:** Robert Hooks, Paul Gleason, Ken Olandt, Richard Jaeckel. **1988**

SUPERFLY ★★★ This exciting film follows a Harlem drug dealer's last big sale before he attempts to leave the drug world for a normal life. Rated R. 96m. **DIR:** Gordon Parks Jr. **CAST:** Ron O'Neal, Carl Lee, Sheila Frazier, Julius W. Harris. **1972**

SUPERFLY T.N.T. 🦃 The first mistake connected with this sequel to *Superfly* was allowing its star, Ron O'Neal, to direct it. The second mistake was removing the title character from the tense, urban setting of the first movie. Here, the ex-drug dealer is living in exile in Europe when he decides to become involved in the plight of an African nationalist. 87m. **DIR:** Ron O'Neal. **CAST:** Ron O'Neal, Roscoe Lee Browne, Sheila Frazier, Robert Guillaume. **1973**

SUPERVIXENS ★★½ If you've never seen a Russ Meyer movie, this isn't the one to start with. This frenzied, campy tale of sex and violence is meant to be taken in the spirit of a Road Runner cartoon, but the brutality is extremely strong. That aside, the movie features plenty of the usual Meyer Amazons and a suitably sneering performance by Charles Napier as an evil southwestern sheriff. Unrated, but for adults *only!* 105m. **DIR:** Russ Meyer. **CAST:** Shari Eubank, Charles Napier. **1975**

SURF NAZIS MUST DIE ★★½ The Surf Nazis are a gang of weirdos who rule the Los Angeles beaches. Vile, stupid, and pointless, but there's something about this film... Rated R for violence, language, sex, and nudity. 83m. **DIR:** Peter George. **CAST:** Barry Brenner, Gail Neely, Dawn Wildsmith. **1987**

SURFACING 🦃 *Deliverance* stirred with pyschological mumbo jumbo and kinky sex. Rated R. 90m. **DIR:** Claude Jutra. **CAST:** Joseph Bottoms, Kathleen Beller, R. H. Thompson. **1984**

SURVIVAL GAME 🦃 Mike Norris, Chuck's son, fails to fill his father's boots. R rating for mild profanity. 89m. **DIR:** Herb Freed. **CAST:** Mike Norris, Deborah Goodrich, Seymour Cassel, Arlene Golonka. **1987**

SURVIVAL QUEST ★★★½ Survival course students encounter a paramilitary group on maneuvers. Their adventure then turns into a genuine and compelling fight for survival. Rated R for violence. 91m. **DIR:** Don Coscarelli. **CAST:** Lance Henriksen, Dermot Mulroney. **1989**

SURVIVALIST, THE 🦃 A tepid action-thriller that purports to dramatize the confusion that mounts before the bombs are dropped. The real bomb is this hokey doomsday entry that literally goes up in smoke. Rated R for violence and profanity. 96m. **DIR:** Sig Shore. **CAST:** Steve Railsback, Susan Blakely, Cliff De Young, Marjoe Gortner, David Wayne. **1987**

SURVIVING THE GAME 🦃 Homeless African-American is hunted for perverse sport by a group of men in the Pacific Northwest wilderness. Rated R for language and violence. 93m. **DIR:** Ernest R. Dickerson. **CAST:** Ice-T, Rutger Hauer, Charles S. Dutton, John C. McGinley, Gary Busey, William McNamara, F. Murray Abraham. **1994**

SWASHBUCKLER (1976) ★★ Only a strong cast saves this pirate movie from being a total swashbungler. Even so, it's a stylistic nightmare as a sword-wielding hero (Robert Shaw) who comes to the aid of a damsel (Genevieve Bujold) in distress. Rated PG for violence and nudity. 101m. **DIR:** James Goldstone. **CAST:** Robert Shaw, James Earl Jones, Peter Boyle, Genevieve Bujold, Beau Bridges, Geoffrey Holder, Avery Schreiber, Anjelica Huston. **1976**

SWASHBUCKLER, THE (1984) 🦃 Stupid story about a naturalized American who gets caught up in the French Revolution while delivering grain and seeking a divorce from his wife. 100m. **DIR:** Jean-Paul Rappeneau. **CAST:** Jean-Paul Belmondo, Marlene Jobert, Laura Antonelli, Michel Auclair, Julien Guiomar. **1984**

SWEET JUSTICE ★★ Women vigilantes battle small-town gangsters. Not to be taken seriously—the cast certainly didn't. Rated R for violence and nudity. 92m. **DIR:** Allen Plone. **CAST:** Finn Carter, Kathleen Kinmont, Marc Singer, Frank Gorshin, Mickey Rooney. **1991**

SWEET POISON ★★ This psychological thriller, which explores how far a decent man can be pushed, might play better if the dialogue weren't so weak and the performances so overblown. Rated R for language, sexual situations, and violence. 101m. **DIR:** Brian Grant. **CAST:** Steven Bauer, Edward Herrmann, Patricia Healy, Noble Willingham. **1991**

SWEET REVENGE (1987) ★★ Nancy Allen plays a Los Angeles newswoman investigating the disappearance of several young women. She gets her story the hard way when she is kidnapped and taken to a slave market in Southeast Asia. Average action tale is marred by a disappointing ending and the miscasting of Allen. Rated R for violence, nudity, and sexual situations. 99m. **DIR:** Mark Sobel. **CAST:** Nancy Allen, Ted Shackelford, Martin Landau. **1987**

SWEET SIXTEEN ★★ In this static mystery, a young woman (Aliesa Shirley) from the big city reluctantly spends her summer—and her sixteenth birthday—in a small Texas town and becomes the chief suspect in a series of murders. Rated R for profanity and partial nudity. 96m. **DIR:** Jim Sotos. **CAST:** Aliesa Shirley, Bo Hopkins, Patrick Macnee, Susan Strasberg, Don Stroud. **1984**

SWEET SWEETBACK'S BAADASSSSS SONG ★★★½ Minor cult black film about a man running from racist white police forces. Melvin Van Peebles plays the title character, who will do anything to stay free. Very controversial when released in 1971. Lots of sex and violence gave this an X rating at the time. Probably the best of the black-produced and -directed films of the early 1970s. Rated R. 97m. **DIR:** Melvin Van Peebles. **CAST:** Melvin Van Peebles, Rhetta Hughes, Simon Chuckster, John Amos. **1971**

SWORD OF GIDEON ★★★½ To avenge the 1972 murders of Israeli Olympic-team members in Munich, five commandos are sent on a globe-hopping mission to destroy selected leaders of the terrorist Black September movement. Location filming is a plus in this suspenseful and action-packed TV movie. Colleen Dewhurst has a touching cameo as Prime Minister Golda Meir. 150m. **DIR:** Michael Anderson. **CAST:** Steven Bauer, Michael York, Rod Steiger, Robert Joy, Leslie Hope, Laurent Malet, Linda Griffiths, Lino Ventura, Cyrielle Claire, Colleen Dewhurst. **1986**

SWORD OF LANCELOT ★★★ Colorful production and location photography highlight this pre-*Camelot* version of life at the court of King Arthur and the forbidden love between Lancelot and Queen Guinevere (Mr. and Mrs. Cornel Wilde in real life). Long on pageantry, action, and chivalrous acts of derring-do, this is a "fun" film in the same vein as *Ivanhoe* and *The Vikings*. 116m. **DIR:** Cornel Wilde. **CAST:** Cornel Wilde, Jean Wallace, Brian Aherne, George Baker. **1963**

SWORDSMAN, THE 🦃 A psychic police detective sword-battles his way through a case involving stolen antiquities and mass murder, eventually discovering that he is the reincarnation of Alexander the Great. Rated R for violence and profanity. 98m. **DIR:** Michael Kennedy. **CAST:** Lorenzo Lamas, Claire Stansfield, Michael Champion. **1992**

TAFFIN ★★★ The ever-watchable Pierce Brosnan plays a surprisingly tough "collector" in this fun-to-watch Irish film. The city folks approach Brosnan to get rough with the chemical plant thugs who are bulldozing their fair countryside. Rated R for violence, profanity, and nudity. 96m. **DIR:** Francis Megahy. **CAST:** Pierce Brosnan, Ray McAnally, Alison Doody. **1987**

TAG—THE ASSASSINATION GAME ★★★½ The short-lived fad for campus war games, in which students stalked each other with rubber darts, is the basis for this comic thriller. Student reporter Robert Carradine, smitten with star player Linda Hamilton, follows her on her hunt. Neither realizes that one player has started using a real gun. Rated PG. 92m. **DIR:** Nick Castle. **CAST:** Robert Carradine, Linda Hamilton, Bruce Abbott, Michael Winslow. **1982**

TAGGET ★★★½ A smooth and sympathetic lead performance from Daniel J. Travanti highlights this intriguing tale of a disabled Vietnam veteran plagued by disturbing flashbacks. His efforts to decipher the dreams reveal traces of a decade-old CIA dirty tricks cover-up. Slick, violent made-for-cable thriller. 89m. **DIR:** Richard T. Heffron. **CAST:** Daniel J. Travanti, Roxanne Hart, Peter Michael Goetz, Bill Sadler. **1991**

TAI-PAN ★★ Pretentious, overblown adaptation of James Clavell's bestseller, this disjointed mess plays like a television miniseries chopped from eight hours to two. Bryan Brown is properly stoic as the "Tai-Pan," chief trader, who dreams of establishing a colony to be named Hong Kong. Joan Chen is ludicrous as his concubine. Rated R for brief nudity and violence. 127m. **DIR:** Daryl Duke. **CAST:** Bryan Brown, John Stanton, Joan Chen, Tim Guinee. **1986**

TAKE, THE ★★ This lurid, by-the-numbers cop thriller features Ray Sharkey as a Miami police officer who does jail time for attempting to cut himself into a drug deal, and then—surprise, surprise—faces exactly the same temptation after being released. Unrated, but with considerable violence. 95m. **DIR:** Leon Ichaso. **CAST:** Ray Sharkey, R. Lee Ermey, Larry Manetti, Lisa Hartman. **1990**

TAKING OF BEVERLY HILLS, THE ★★★ Fans of nonstop action will cheer this *Die Hard*-esque movie about a quarterback who teams up with a crooked cop to stop the looting of Beverly Hills by a clever crime boss. Rated R for violence and profanity. 102m. **DIR:** Sidney J. Furie. **CAST:** Ken Wahl, Matt Frewer, Harley Jane Kozak, Robert Davis, Lee Ving, Lyman Ward, Michael Bowen, William Prince. **1991**

TALONS OF THE EAGLE ★★ Nothing special. Two DEA agents go undercover to bust a notorious crime lord. Once they gain his trust, they take him down in one of those extended martial-arts sequences that cap such affairs. Rated R for violence, language, and adult situations. 96m. **DIR:** Michael Kennedy. **CAST:** Billy Blanks, Jalal Merhi, James Hong, Priscilla Barnes. **1992**

TAMARIND SEED, THE ★★★ A sudsy melodrama in the old tradition, but still a lot of fun. Julie Andrews falls in love with a foreign emissary played by Omar Sharif, only to be told (by her own State Department) to stay away from him. The cold war intrigue seems pretty absurd these days, but Andrews and Sharif generate a playful chemistry that overlooks many sins. Rated PG. 123m. **DIR:** Blake Edwards. **CAST:** Omar Sharif, Julie Andrews, Anthony Quayle. **1974**

TANGO AND CASH ★★ Sylvester Stallone and Kurt Russell play rival L.A. detectives who find themselves framed by a powerful drug lord (Jack Palance) and must join forces to clear their names. *Tango and Cash* starts off well, with plenty of action and great comic quips, and then descends into a near parody of itself. Rated R for profanity, nudity, and violence. 98m. **DIR:** Andrei Konchalovsky. **CAST:** Sylvester Stallone, Kurt Russell, Jack Palance, Michael J. Pollard, Brion James, James Hong, Geoffrey Lewis. **1989**

TANK ★★½ The always likable James Garner plays Sgt. Maj. Zack Carey, an army career soldier who has to use his privately owned Sherman tank to rescue his family (Shirley Jones and C. Thomas Howell) from the clutches of a mean country sheriff (G. D. Spradlin). It's all a bunch of hokum, but a sure audience pleaser. Rated PG. 113m. **DIR:**

Marvin J. Chomsky. **CAST:** James Garner, Shirley Jones, C. Thomas Howell, G. D. Spradlin. **1984**

TARAS BULBA ★★★ Tony Curtis and Yul Brynner give top-notch performances in this action-packed adventure centering on Cossack life during the sixteenth century in the Ukraine. Great location photography in Argentina by Joe MacDonald, and a fine musical score by Franz Waxman. Solid entertainment. 122m. **DIR:** J. Lee Thompson. **CAST:** Tony Curtis, Yul Brynner. **1962**

TARGET ★★★ In this fast-paced, entertaining suspense-thriller directed by Arthur Penn (*Bonnie and Clyde*), a father (Gene Hackman) and son (Matt Dillon) put aside their differences when they become the targets of an international spy ring. *Target* is a tad predictable, but it is the kind of predictability that adds to the viewer's enjoyment. Rated R for violence, profanity, and nudity. 117m. **DIR:** Arthur Penn. **CAST:** Gene Hackman, Matt Dillon, Gayle Hunnicutt, Josef Sommer, Victoria Fyodora, Herbert Berghof. **1985**

TARGET EAGLE 🦃 A mercenary is hired by a Spanish police department to infiltrate a drug-smuggling ring. Not rated, has violence. 101m. **DIR:** J. Anthony Loma. **CAST:** Jorge Rivero, Maud Adams, George Peppard, Max von Sydow, Chuck Connors. **1982**

TARZAN AND HIS MATE ★★★★★ Tarzan against ivory hunters. The best MGM Tarzan movie is a bona fide film classic, one of the few sequels to surpass the original. A marvelously entertaining motion picture. B&W; 105m. **DIR:** Cedric Gibbons. **CAST:** Johnny Weissmuller, Maureen O'Sullivan, Neil Hamilton, Paul Cavanagh. **1934**

TARZAN AND THE GREEN GODDESS ★★ Olympic champion Herman Brix (a.k.a. Bruce Bennett) makes one of the best-looking of all movie Tarzans as he journeys to South America to help secure a priceless stone image known as the "Green Goddess." Edited down from the serial *New Adventures of Tarzan* (released in 1935), this disjointed film and its companion, *Tarzan's New Adventures*, did all right at the box office despite competition from MGM's Johnny Weissmuller films. However, primitive filming conditions and a horrible sound track hinder the jungle nonsense. B&W; 72m. **DIR:** Edward Kull. **CAST:** Bruce Bennett, Ula Holt, Frank Baker. **1938**

TARZAN AND THE TRAPPERS ★★ This oddity is actually three television pilots that producer Sol Lesser was unable to sell to networks back in 1958. This is pretty ordinary, uninspired stuff, but it's a one-of-a-kind Tarzan film, unavailable for years. B&W; 74m. **DIR:** H. Bruce Humberstone. **CAST:** Gordon Scott, Evelyn Brent, Rickie Sorenson, Maurice Marsac. **1958**

TARZAN ESCAPES ★★★ Once again greed spurs an expedition to scale the Mutia escarpment, but instead of ivory, Tarzan, the white ape, is the prize. This troubled production took two years and three directors before it reached the screen due to negative audience reaction to the grim nature of many scenes (including man-eating bats that snatched the unfortunate and flew them screaming to their fate) as well as the inevitable pressure brought on all productions by the Breen Office and the Legion of Decency. B&W; 95m. **DIR:** Richard Thorpe. **CAST:** Johnny Weissmuller, Maureen O'Sullivan, Benita Hume, William Henry, E. E. Clive. **1936**

TARZAN FINDS A SON ★★★½ Tarzan and Jane find an infant, the only survivor of a plane crash, and raise him as their "Boy." Five years later, relatives of his rich parents arrive and attempt to return him to civilization. Plenty of jungle action. B&W; 82m. **DIR:** Richard Thorpe. **CAST:** Johnny Weissmuller, Maureen O'Sullivan, Johnny Sheffield, Ian Hunter, Henry Stephenson, Frieda Inescort, Henry Wilcoxon, Laraine Day. **1939**

TARZAN OF THE APES ★★★½ The first filmed version of Edgar Rice Burroughs's classic tells the story of Lord and Lady Greystoke, their shipwreck and abandonment on the African coast, and the fate of their boy child, John. Raised by Kala the she-ape, infant John becomes Tarzan of the Apes. Barrel-chested Elmo Lincoln portrayed Tarzan as an adult and actually killed the lion he fights in one of the film's more exciting moments. Enhanced with a synchronized musical score, this silent extravaganza is well worth the watch. Silent. B&W; 130m. **DIR:** Scott Sidney. **CAST:** Elmo Lincoln, Enid Markey, George French. **1918**

TARZAN THE APE MAN (1932) ★★★½ *Tarzan the Ape Man* is the film that made Johnny Weissmuller a star and Tarzan an idiot. That classic "Me Tarzan, you Jane" blasphemy is here in its original splendor. Maureen O'Sullivan seduces the dumb beast, and it's all great fun. Hollywood at its peak...but no relation to Edgar Rice Burroughs's hero. B&W; 99m. **DIR:** W. S. Van Dyke. **CAST:** Johnny Weissmuller, Maureen O'Sullivan, Neil Hamilton. **1932**

TARZAN THE APE MAN (1981) 🦃 Even counting the lowest of the Tarzan flicks, this remake is the absolute worst. Rated R for profanity and nudity. 112m. **DIR:** John Derek. **CAST:** Bo Derek, Richard Harris, Miles O'Keeffe, John Phillip Law. **1981**

TARZAN THE FEARLESS 🦃 Leave this one on the vine. B&W; 85m. **DIR:** Robert Hill. **CAST:** Buster Crabbe, Jacqueline Wells, E. Alyn Warren, Edward Woods. **1933**

TARZAN THE MIGHTY ★★½ Tarzan number five Frank Merrill once earned the title of "World's Most Perfect Man" and his jungle heroics made this Universal serial the hit of 1928. It was expanded from twelve to fifteen episodes by astute executives who correctly gauged a receptive audience. Merrill pioneered many of the stunts associated with the series, especially the vine swinging and aerial acrobatics. Silent. B&W; 15 chapters. **DIR:** Jack Nelson. **CAST:** Frank Merrill, Natalie Kingston, Al Ferguson. **1928**

TARZAN THE TIGER ★★ Based loosely on Edgar Rice Burroughs's *Tarzan and the Jewels of Opar*, this serial was shot as a silent but released with sychronized musical score and sound effects. Frank Merrill as Tarzan inaugurated the popular vine swing used by later ape-men and was the first to give his rendition of the famous cry of the bull ape—sans mixer and dubbers. This sequel to *Tarzan the Mighty* was long considered a lost film. B&W; 15 chapters. **DIR:** Henry McRae. **CAST:** Frank Merrill, Natalie Kingston, Lillian Worth, Al Ferguson. **1929**

TARZAN'S NEW YORK ADVENTURE ★★★½ Boy is kidnapped by a circus owner and taken to New York to be put on display. Tarzan and Jane follow. Lots of fun with the jungle man out of his element, then scaling skyscrapers, swinging on flagpole lines until chased atop the Brooklyn Bridge. Maureen O'Sullivan's sixth and last appearance as Jane. B&W; 72m. **DIR:** Richard Thorpe. **CAST:** Johnny Weissmuller, Maureen O'Sullivan, Johnny Sheffield, Virginia Grey, Charles Bickford, Paul Kelly, Chill Wills. **1942**

TARZAN'S REVENGE 🦃 Back-lot nonsense. B&W; 70m. **DIR:** D. Ross Lederman. **CAST:** Glenn Morris, Eleanor Holm, George Barbier, C. Henry Gordon, Hedda Hopper, George Meeker. **1938**

TARZAN'S SECRET TREASURE ★★★ Members of a scientific expedition are corrupted by gold found in Tarzan's paradise. By this fifth teaming of Johnny Weissmuller and Maureen O'Sullivan as Tarzan and Jane, the situations were becoming predictable. Yet, there is lots of terrific action. B&W; 81m. **DIR:** Richard Thorpe. **CAST:** Johnny Weissmuller, Maureen O'Sullivan, Johnny Sheffield, Barry Fitzgerald, Reginald Owen, Tom Conway, Philip Dorn. **1941**

TASTE FOR KILLING, A ★★½ Two rich boys spend their summer vacation on an offshore oil rig only to become involved in a murder. Of course it looks like they did the killing. A boring premise, but nicely acted made-for-cable thriller. 96m. **DIR:** Lou Antonio. **CAST:** Michael Biehn, Jason Bateman, Henry Thomas, Helen Cates, Blue Deckert. **1992**

TATTOO CONNECTION 🦃 Typical chop-phooey fare. Rated R for violence, profanity, and nudity. 95m. **DIR:** Lee Tso-Nan. **CAST:** Jim Kelly. **1978**

TEENAGE BONNIE AND KLEPTO CLYDE ★★½ Minor hoods Scott Wolf and Maureen Flannigan chuck their comfortable lives for a little excitement. What starts off as teen rebellion quickly turns deadly as the pair rob and kill their way to mythic status. Rated R for violence, nudity, language, and adult situations. 90m. **DIR:** John Shepphird. **CAST:** Scott Wolf, Maureen Flannigan, Bentley Mitchum, Don Novello. **1993**

TEN TO MIDNIGHT 🦃 Old "Death Wish" himself goes up against a *Friday the 13th*–type killer. Rated R for nudity, profanity, and violence. 101m. **DIR:** J. Lee Thompson. **CAST:** Charles Bronson, Andrew Stevens, Lisa Eilbacher, Cosie Costa. **1983**

10 VIOLENT WOMEN 🦃 Female coal miners land in jail after a jewel robbery and a cocaine deal go bad. Rated R for violence and a little nudity. 95m. **DIR:** Ted V. Mikels. **CAST:** Sherri Vernon, Dixie Lauren, Georgia Morgan. **1982**

TENNESSEE STALLION ★★★ Interesting background, beautiful photography, and more than competent acting save this otherwise ordinary action-adventure film set in the world of the Tennessee walking-horse show circuit. Jimmy Van Patten is excellent as a man who makes it to the big time with his outstanding horse and the help of the woman who loves him. 87m. **DIR:** Don Hulette. **CAST:** Audrey Landers, Judy Landers, James Van Patten. **1978**

TEQUILA SUNRISE ★★★★½ In his second film as a director, legendary screenwriter Robert Towne *(Chinatown, The Last Detail)* takes an oft-used plot and makes it new. Mel Gibson and Kurt Russell play two childhood friends who end up on opposite sides of the law. Michelle Pfeiffer is the beautiful object of their affections. Because Towne makes his characters seem real and the situations believably low-key, *Tequila Sunrise* emerges as a fascinating and often surprising movie. Rated R for profanity, violence, suggested sex, and drug use. 116m. **DIR:** Robert Towne. **CAST:** Mel Gibson, Kurt Russell, Michelle Pfeiffer, Raul Julia. **1988**

TERMINAL ISLAND 🦃 Trite piece of exploitation. Rated R. 88m. **DIR:** Stephanie Rothman. **CAST:** Phyllis Davis, Tom Selleck, Don Marshall, Marta Kristen. **1977**

TERROR IN PARADISE 🦃 Grade-Z thriller finds an American couple battling terrorists on a small island getaway. Paradise lost! Rated R for nudity and violence. 81m. **DIR:** Peer J. Oppenheimer. **CAST:** Gary Lockwood, Joanna Pettet, David Anthony Smith, Leslie Ryan, David McKnight. **1992**

TERROR OF THE TONGS, THE ★★★ In 1910 Hong Kong, sea captain Geoffrey Toone's daughter is killed by Christopher Lee's Red Dragon Tong. Competent, atmospheric revenge adventure. Unrated, but contains violence. 80m. **DIR:** Anthony Bushell. **CAST:** Christopher Lee, Geoffrey Toone, Yvonne Monlaur, Marne Maitland. **1961**

TERROR SQUAD ★★★ Better-than-average action movie about small-town Indiana police chief Chuck Connors battling Libyan terrorists. This offers some thrills and style despite the obvious low budget. Unrated. 92m. **DIR:** Peter Maris. **CAST:** Chuck Connors, Kerry Brennan. **1987**

THARUS, SON OF ATTILA 🦃 Poorly staged battles and stupid (and badly dubbed) dialogue. Not rated. 89m. **DIR:** Roberto Montero. **CAST:** Jerome Courtland, Lisa Gastoni, Rik Von Nutter. **1987**

THAT'S ACTION ★★ A surprisingly lukewarm collection of movie stunts and action sequences. Not rated. 78m. **DIR:** Uncredited. **CAST:** Robert Culp, David Carradine, Oliver Reed, Robert Ginty, Reb Brown. **1990**

THELMA & LOUISE ★★★★ Director Ridley Scott and screenwriter Callie Khouri skillfully interweave suspense and comedy in this distaff *Easy Rider*, in which two buddies set off on a vacation and end up running from the law after one of them shoots a would-be rapist. Entertaining action-movie/road-picture. Rated R for violence, profanity, and suggested sex. 128m. **DIR:** Ridley Scott. **CAST:** Susan Sarandon, Geena Davis, Harvey Keitel, Michael Madsen, Christopher McDonald. **1991**

THEY CALL ME MISTER TIBBS ★★★ An inferior follow-up, this contains the further adventures of the character Sidney Poitier created for the film *In the Heat of the Night*. Detective Virgil Tibbs is again investigating a murder and trying to clear his friend, as well. Rated PG—contains strong language and some violence. 108m. **DIR:** Gordon Douglas. **CAST:** Sidney Poitier, Barbara McNair, Martin Landau. **1970**

THEY DRIVE BY NIGHT ★★★★ Here's a Warner Bros. gem! George Raft and Humphrey Bogart star as truck-driving brothers who cope with crooked bosses while wooing Ann Sheridan and Ida Lupino. The dialogue is terrific, and the direction by Raoul Walsh is crisp. B&W; 93m. **DIR:** Raoul Walsh. **CAST:** George Raft, Humphrey Bogart, Ann Sheridan, Ida Lupino. **1940**

THEY MET IN BOMBAY ★★★ Clark Gable and Rosalind Russell are jewel thieves pursued from Bombay to Hong Kong. He is mistaken for a British officer and becomes a reluctant war hero in this odd mixture of light comedy and action-drama. The stars are fun to watch. B&W; 93m. **DIR:** Clarence Brown. **CAST:** Clark Gable, Rosalind Russell, Peter Lorre, Jessie Ralph, Reginald Owen, Eduardo Ciannelli. **1941**

THEY WERE EXPENDABLE ★★★★½ First-rate action-drama about American PT boat crews fighting a losing battle against advancing Japanese forces in the Philippines. Director John Ford based this film, his most personal, on his war experiences and the people he knew in the conflict. No phony heroics or glory here, but a realistic, bleak, and ultimately inspiring picture of men in war. B&W; 136m. **DIR:** John Ford. **CAST:** John Wayne, Robert Montgomery, Donna Reed, Jack Holt, Ward Bond, Marshall Thompson, Louis Jean Heydt. **1945**

THIEF (1981) ★★★★ James Caan stars in this superb study of a jewel thief. Caan's character tries desperately to create the life he visualized while in prison—one complete with a car, money, house, wife, and kids. But as soon as he manages to acquire these things, they start slipping away. It's an interesting plot, and Michael Mann's direction gives it a sense of realism. Visually stunning, with a great score by Tangerine Dream. Rated R for violence, language, and brief nudity. 122m. **DIR:** Michael Mann. **CAST:** James Caan, Tuesday Weld, James Belushi, Willie Nelson. **1981**

THIEF OF BAGHDAD (1978) ★★ A passable television version of the Arabian Nights fable made bland by low-budget special effects but offset, if marginally, by an excellent cast. Unrated, it's certainly suitable for family viewing. 100m. **DIR:** Clive Donner. **CAST:** Peter Ustinov, Terence Stamp, Roddy McDowall, Ian Holm, Pavla Ustinov. **1978**

THIEVES OF FORTUNE ★★½ Shawn Weatherly attempts to win a $28 million bet that involves outrageous cliff-hanging stunts. Rated R for language and violence. 100m. **DIR:** Michael McCarthy. **CAST:** Michael Nouri, Shawn Weatherly, Lee Van Cleef, Liz Torres. **1989**

13 RUE MADELEINE ★★★ Espionage thriller, inspired by the *March of Time* series, shot in semidocumentary style. James Cagney is an OSS chief who goes to France to complete a mission when one of his men is killed. B&W; 95m. **DIR:** Henry Hathaway. **CAST:** James Cagney, Annabella, Walter Abel, Frank Latimore, Melville Cooper, E. G. Marshall, Karl Malden, Sam Jaffe, Richard Conte. **1946**

THIRTY SECONDS OVER TOKYO ★★★★ Spencer Tracy is in top form as General Doolittle, who led the first bombing attack on Tokyo during World War II. Robert Mitchum and Van Johnson give effective supporting performances as air crew chiefs. We follow Doolittle and his men as they train for the big mission, bomb Tokyo, and make their way home on foot through China. A true-life adventure that, despite its length, never bogs down. B&W; 138m. **DIR:** Mervyn LeRoy. **CAST:** Spencer Tracy, Van Johnson,

Robert Walker, Phyllis Thaxter, Scott McKay, Robert Mitchum, Stephen McNally. **1944**

THIS GUN FOR HIRE (1942) ★★★★ Alan Ladd made his first big impression in this 1942 gangster film as a bad guy who turns good guy in the end. Robert Preston and Veronica Lake costar in this still enjoyable revenge film. B&W; 80m. **DIR:** Frank Tuttle. **CAST:** Alan Ladd, Robert Preston, Veronica Lake. **1942**

THIS GUN FOR HIRE (1991) ★★★ Graham Greene's moody thriller gets another go-around, this time with Robert Wagner reprising the role that made Alan Ladd a star. Wagner's an implacable hired gunman who finds his soul at the wrong moment. Greene's cynical view of humanity remains seductive. Made for cable TV. Rated R for violence and sexual themes. 89m. **DIR:** Lou Antonio. **CAST:** Robert Wagner, Nancy Everhard, Frederic Lehne, John Harkins. **1991**

THOMAS CROWN AFFAIR, THE ★★★★ Combine an engrossing bank-heist caper with an offbeat romance and you have the ingredients for a fun-filled movie. Steve McQueen and Faye Dunaway are at their best as the sophisticated bank robber and unscrupulous insurance investigator. The emotional tricks and verbal sparring between these two are a joy. This is one of the few films where the split-screen technique really moves the story along. 102m. **DIR:** Norman Jewison. **CAST:** Steve McQueen, Faye Dunaway, Paul Burke. **1968**

THOMPSON'S LAST RUN ★★★½ Robert Mitchum plays a criminal who is being transferred to a new prison by a school friend who chose the right side of the law and is ready to retire. Bittersweet story with solid performances by all. 95m. **DIR:** Jerrold Freedman. **CAST:** Robert Mitchum, Wilford Brimley, Kathleen York. **1986**

THRASHIN' 🦃 Hotshot skateboarder comes to L.A. and gets on the bad side of a gang of street skaters. Rated PG-13 for sexual situations. 92m. **DIR:** David Winters. **CAST:** Josh Brolin, Robert Rusler, Chuck McCann. **1986**

THREE DAYS TO A KILL ★★ Serviceable macho heroics from some old (and we do mean old) familiar faces. Seasoned mercenaries Fred Williamson and Bo Svenson rescue a U.S. diplomat from sneering drug lord Henry Silva. Rated R for violence. 90m. **DIR:** Fred Williamson. **CAST:** Fred Williamson, Bo Svenson, Henry Silva, Chuck Connors, Van Johnson, Sonny Landham. **1991**

3:15—THE MOMENT OF TRUTH ★★½ *High Noon* in high school, as Adam Baldwin prepares for a showdown. Director Larry Gross, a Walter Hill protégé, doesn't have Hill's ability to rise above the too-plentiful action clichés. Rated R for violence. 85m. **DIR:** Larry Gross. **CAST:** Adam Baldwin, Deborah Foreman, René Auberjonois, Ed Lauter, Mario Van Peebles, Wings Hauser. **1985**

THREE KINDS OF HEAT 🦃 Low-budget spy adventure cheapie. Rated R for language. 87m. **DIR:** Leslie Stevens. **CAST:** Robert Ginty, Victoria Barrett, Shakti, Sylvester McCoy, Barry Foster. **1987**

THREE MUSKETEERS, THE (1933) ★★ The weakest and least-seen of John Wayne's three serials for Mascot Studios. This desert-bound story presents four friends who fight against a harsh environment and the evil Devil of the Desert. Standard Foreign Legion stuff. B&W; 12 chapters. **DIR:** Armand Schaefer, Colbert Clark. **CAST:** John Wayne, Ruth Hall, Jack Mulhall, Raymond Hatton, Francis X. Bushman, Noah Beery Jr., Lon Chaney Jr. **1933**

THREE MUSKETEERS, THE (1935) ★★★ With middle-aged actors in the swashbuckling roles, this is the most sedate of the many versions of the story. They don't swash as many buckles as those who followed, but they do tell a good story and keep it on a very serious level. John Ford was scheduled to direct but wasn't available when the studio was. The cast members don't have the vibrant personalities we've come to expect, but author Alexandre Dumas would be pleased with the attention paid to the details of his story. B&W; 90m. **DIR:** Rowland V. Lee. **CAST:** Walter Abel, Paul Lukas, Morni Olsen, Onslow Stevens, Heather Angel, Margot Grahame, Ian Keith, Ralph Forbes, Rosamond Pinchot, John Qualen, Nigel de Brulier. **1935**

THREE MUSKETEERS, THE (1948) ★★ MGM's all-star version of the classic swashbuckler by Alexandre Dumas gets its swords crossed up, primarily due to some blatant miscasting. Gene Kelly as D'Artagnan and June Allyson playing the queen's seamstress are never convincing as French citizens during the reign of Louis XIII. Fans of Lana Turner may find the movie worthwhile, because hidden in this fluff is one of her finest performances as the villainous Lady DeWinter. B&W; 128m. **DIR:** George Sidney. **CAST:** Gene Kelly, Lana Turner, June Allyson, Van Heflin, Vincent Price, Gig Young, Angela Lansbury, Keenan Wynn. **1948**

THREE MUSKETEERS, THE (1973) ★★★★★ Alexandre Dumas's oft-filmed swashbuckler classic—there may have been as many as ten previous versions—finally came to full life with this 1973 release. It is a superb adventure romp with scrumptious moments of comedy, character, and action. Throughout, director Richard Lester injects throwaway bits of slapstick and wordplay—you have to pay careful attention to catch them, and it's well worth it. Rated PG. 105m. **DIR:** Richard Lester. **CAST:** Michael York, Oliver Reed, Raquel Welch, Richard Chamberlain, Faye Dunaway, Charlton Heston. **1973**

THREE MUSKETEERS, THE (1993) ★★★½ The Brat Pack tackles Alexandre Dumas's swashbuckling classic with generally pleasing results. Comedic Oliver Platt easily steals every scene, but Kiefer Sutherland and Rebecca DeMornay also impress with their dramatic encounters. We still prefer the Richard Lester triptych, but every generation needs a cast of its own to proclaim, "All for one, one for all." Rated PG for light violence. 105m. **DIR:** Stephen Herek. **CAST:** Charlie Sheen, Kiefer Sutherland, Chris O'Donnell, Oliver Platt, Tim Curry, Rebecca DeMornay, Gabrielle Anwar, Paul McGann, Julie Delpy, Hugh O'Connor. **1993**

THREE THE HARD WAY ★★★ A white supremacist (Jay Robinson) attempts to wipe out the black race by putting a deadly serum in the country's water supply. Fred Williamson, Jim Brown and Jim Kelly team up to stop him in this action-packed movie. Rated PG for violence. 93m. **DIR:** Gordon Parks Jr. **CAST:** Fred Williamson, Jim Brown, Jim Kelly, Sheila Frazier, Jay Robinson. **1974**

THROUGH NAKED EYES ★★★ A pretty good made-for-TV mystery thriller with voyeurism in high-rise apartments as the pivotal plot line. David Soul is watching Pam Dawber across the way, but she's also been watching him. When a series of murders occurs in their buildings, it appears someone else is watching, too. Unrated. 91m. **DIR:** John Llewellyn Moxey. **CAST:** David Soul, Pam Dawber, Rod McCary. **1983**

THUNDER AND LIGHTNING ★★ Weak "action film" about moonshiners. Stars David Carradine and Kate Jackson are watchable enough, but a few touches of originality wouldn't have hurt. Rated PG for profanity and violence. 95m. **DIR:** Corey Allen. **CAST:** David Carradine, Kate Jackson, Roger C. Carmel, Sterling Holloway. **1977**

THUNDER BAY ★★★½ James Stewart plays an oil driller forced to take on a nasty group of Louisiana shrimp fishermen. The story is full of action and fine characterizations from a talented cast. 102m. **DIR:** Anthony Mann. **CAST:** James Stewart, Dan Duryea, Joanne Dru, Jay C. Flippen, Gilbert Roland. **1953**

THUNDER IN PARADISE ★★★ A hotel owner must marry within two days or she will lose her hotel to her greedy uncle. A nice mix of kidnapping and treasure hunting, plus an amazing high-speed boat race make for an enjoyable film. Even Hulk Hogan manages to perform well in a likable role. Rated PG. 104m. **DIR:** Douglas Schwartz. **CAST:** Hulk Hogan, Felicity Waterman, Carol Alt, Robin Weisman, Chris Lemmon, Patrick Macnee, Sam Jones, Charlotte Rae. **1993**

THUNDER ROAD ★★★★ Robert Mitchum wrote the original story and hit theme song for this fast-paced, colorful tale of a bootlegger (Mitchum) who attempts to outwit revenuer Gene Barry. It's one of Mitchum's few all-around, big-screen successes and a tribute to his talents in front of and behind the camera. The star's son, Jim Mitchum, made his film debut as Robert's younger brother. B&W; 92m. **DIR:** Arthur Ripley. **CAST:** Robert Mitchum, Gene Barry, Keely Smith, Jim Mitchum. **1958**

THUNDER RUN 🦃 Grade Z action flick. Rated R for nudity, profanity, suggested sex, and violence. 89m. **DIR:** Gary Hudson. **CAST:** Forrest Tucker, John Ireland, John Shepherd, Jill Whitlow, Cheryl M. Lynn. **1986**

THUNDER WARRIOR 🦃 In this shameless rip-off of the action scenes in *First Blood*, a tough Indian goes on a one-man rampage. Rated R for profanity, violence, and nudity. 84m. **DIR:** Larry Ludman. **CAST:** Mark Gregory, Bo Svenson. **1983**

THUNDER WARRIOR II 🦃 Sleazy, Italian-made action flick. Rated R. 84m. **DIR:** Larry Ludman. **CAST:** Mark Gregory, Bo Svenson. **1985**

THUNDERBALL ★★★ When originally released in 1965, this fourth entry in the James Bond series suffered from comparison to its two admittedly superior predecessors, *From Russia with Love* and *Goldfinger*. However, time has proved it to be one of the more watchable movies based on the books by Ian Fleming, with Sean Connery in top form as 007 and assured direction by Terence Young. 129m. **DIR:** Terence Young. **CAST:** Sean Connery, Claudine Auger, Adolfo Celi. **1965**

THUNDERBOLT AND LIGHTFOOT ★★★★ Clint Eastwood's right-on-target performance is equaled by those of costars Jeff Bridges, George Kennedy, and Geoffrey Lewis in this decidedly offbeat caper picture. The stoic top-lined actor plays an ex-con who hooks up with petty thief Bridges to hunt down the hidden spoils of a heist committed years before. The only problem is that his ex-partners in the crime, Kennedy and Lewis, have the same idea. *Thunderbolt and Lightfoot* is a little-known action gem that proved a little too offbeat when originally released in 1974. However, movie buffs have since proclaimed it a cinematic gem, a reputation it deserves. Rated R. 114m. **DIR:** Michael Cimino. **CAST:** Clint Eastwood, Jeff Bridges, George Kennedy, Geoffrey Lewis, Gary Busey. **1974**

TICK ... TICK ... TICK ... ★★★ Newly elected sheriff Jim Brown struggles against racism, ignorance, and some good-ole-boys to keep a rural southern community from exploding. Dated but still entertaining. Rated PG for violence. 100m. **DIR:** Ralph Nelson. **CAST:** Jim Brown, George Kennedy, Fredric March, Don Stroud, Clifton James, Lynn Carlin, Janet MacLachlan. **1970**

TIGRESS, THE ★★ Tired blood makes this kitty roll over and play dead. Sultry Valentina Vargas gets involved with con man James Remar. Available in two versions: unrated for less-than-titillating sex scenes, and rated R for less of the same. Unrated 89m.; Rated R 87m. **DIR:** Karin Howard. **CAST:** James Remar, Valentina Vargas, George Peppard, Hannes Jaenicke. **1992**

TIME TO DIE, A (1983) ★★ Despite the name actors and source material by Mario Puzo, this vengeance flick has a story as dog-eared as they come. An American spy returns to Europe after World War II to hunt the Nazis who killed his French wife. The twists unravel too easily to make for a thrilling affair. Rated R for nudity and violence. 89m. **DIR:** Matt Cimber. **CAST:** Rex Harrison, Rod Taylor, Edward Albert, Raf Vallone. **1983**

TIMERIDER 🦃 A motorcycle rider and his motorcycle break the time barrier and end up being chased by cowboys in the Old West. Rated PG. 94m. **DIR:** William Dear. **CAST:** Fred Ward, Belinda Bauer, Peter Coyote, L. Q. Jones, Ed Lauter. **1983**

TNT JACKSON 🦃 A sexy kung fu expert who comes to Hong Kong to exact revenge on her brother's killer. Rated R for nudity, profanity, and violence. 73m. **DIR:** Cirio H. Santiago. **CAST:** Jeanne Bell, Stan Shaw, Pat Anderson. **1975**

TO DIE STANDING ★★★ Easily irritated FBI agent Cliff De Young goes to Peru to extradite a drug boss. Thrilling, intertwined tale of love and power. Rated R for violence and profanity. 87m. **DIR:** Louis Morneau. **CAST:** Cliff De Young, Robert Beltran, Jamie Rose, Gerald Anthony. **1990**

TO HAVE AND HAVE NOT ★★★★½ Director Howard Hawks once bet Ernest Hemingway he could make a good film from one of the author's worst books. Needless to say, he won the bet with this exquisite entertainment, which teamed Humphrey Bogart and Lauren Bacall for the first time. B&W; 100m. **DIR:** Howard Hawks. **CAST:** Humphrey Bogart, Lauren Bacall, Walter Brennan. **1944**

TO HELL AND BACK ★★½ Real-life war hero Audie Murphy plays himself in this sprawling World War II action film. We follow Audie Murphy and his buddies (Marshall Thompson, Jack Kelly, and David Janssen) from North Africa to Berlin. Murphy received twenty-four medals, including the Congressional Medal of Honor, which made him the most decorated soldier in World War II. Good performances and true-life drama make up for a static script. 106m. **DIR:** Jesse Hibbs. **CAST:** Audie Murphy, Marshall Thompson, Charles Drake, Gregg Palmer, Jack Kelly, Paul Picerni, Susan Kohner, David Janssen. **1955**

TO LIVE AND DIE IN L.A. 🦃 Overly violent account of lone wolf William L. Petersen's attempt to shut down counterfeiter Willem Dafoe. Rated R for nudity and excessive violence. 114m. **DIR:** William Friedkin. **CAST:** William L. Petersen, Willem Dafoe, John Pankow, Dean Stockwell, Debra Feuer, John Turturro, Darlanne Fluegel. **1985**

TO PLEASE A LADY ★★★ Racing film designed to sustain Clark Gable's macho image didn't win at the box office but looks pretty good today. The star-powered love/hate relationship between Gable's devil-may-care driver and Barbara Stanwyck's tough newspaper columnist is more exciting than the speedway scenes. B&W; 91m. **DIR:** Clarence Brown. **CAST:** Clark Gable, Barbara Stanwyck, Adolphe Menjou, Will Geer, Roland Winters. **1950**

TO PROTECT AND SERVE ★★★ C. Thomas Howell is quite effective in this hard-hitting, gritty thriller about a renegade group of killer cops who are being picked off themselves by someone who's in on their scheme. The cast is both attractive and believable. Rated R for nudity, violence, and language. 93m. **DIR:** Eric Weston. **CAST:** C. Thomas Howell, Lezlie Deane, Richard Romanus, Joe Cortese. **1992**

TO THE SHORES OF TRIPOLI ★★★ This wartime tribute to the Marines has smart-aleck recruit John Payne earning the love of navy nurse Maureen O'Hara after learning some humility and respect for the Corps. 87m. **DIR:** H. Bruce Humberstone. **CAST:** Maureen O'Hara, John Payne, Randolph Scott, Nancy Kelly, Maxie Rosenbloom, Alan Hale Jr. **1942**

TOBRUK ★★★ Rock Hudson, Nigel Green, and George Peppard lead a ragtag group of British soldiers and homeless Jews against the Nazi and Italian armies in the North African desert during World War II. An exciting climax, beautiful photography, and good performances help offset a far-fetched script. 110m. **DIR:** Arthur Hiller. **CAST:** Rock Hudson, George Peppard, Guy Stockwell, Nigel Green. **1966**

TOKYO JOE ★★ Sinister intrigue in post-war Japan has Humphrey Bogart dealing with a blackmailing Sessue Hayakawa. Definitely not vintage Bogie. B&W; 88m. **DIR:** Stuart Heisler. **CAST:** Humphrey Bogart, Alexander Knox, Sessue Hayakawa. **1949**

TOMBOY 🦃 Mindless nonsense (with plenty of skin) about a female race car driver. Rated R. 91m. **DIR:** Herb Freed. **CAST:** Betsy Russell, Kristi Somers, Jerry Dinome. **1985**

TOO HOT TO HANDLE ★★★ Daredevil newsreel photographer Clark Gable and spunky pilot Myrna Loy team up in this fast-paced comedy-adventure that bounces from China to Borneo. Gable and Loy, the "king and queen" of Hollywood that year, make this screwy adventure click. B&W; 105m. **DIR:** Jack Conway. **CAST:** Clark Gable, Myrna Loy, Walter Pidgeon, Leo Carrillo, Virginia Weidler, Marjorie Main. **1938**

TOO LATE THE HERO ★★★½ Great World War II action-drama about two reluctant soldiers who are sent on a suicide mission to an island in the Pacific Ocean. Shown on network TV as *Suicide Run*. Rated PG. 133m. **DIR:** Robert Aldrich. **CAST:** Michael Caine, Cliff Robertson, Henry Fonda. **1970**

TOP GUN ★★★½ Tom Cruise stars as a student at the navy's Fighter Weapons School, where fliers are turned into crack fighter pilots. While competing for the title of Top Gun there, he falls in love with an instructor (Kelly McGillis of *Witness*). Rated PG for light profanity, suggested sex, and violence. 110m. **DIR:** Tony Scott. **CAST:** Tom Cruise, Kelly McGillis, Val Kilmer, Anthony Edwards, Tom Skerritt, Michael Ironside, John Stockwell, Rick Rossovich, Barry Tubb, Whip Hubley. **1986**

TORA! TORA! TORA! ★★★★ An American-Japanese cooperative venture reenacts the events up to and including the December 7 attack on Pearl Harbor. Although many well-known actors contribute their skills, they are overshadowed by the technical brilliance of the realistic re-creation of the climactic attack. Rated G. 143m. **DIR:** Richard Fleischer, Toshio Masuda, Kinji Fakasaku. **CAST:** Jason Robards Jr., Martin Balsam, James Whitmore, Joseph Cotten. **1970**

TORPEDO ALLEY ★★ World War II pilot Bob Bingham (Mark Stevens) is haunted by guilt after the deaths of his flight crew. He gets a second chance to prove himself when he applies for submarine duty during the Korean War. B&W; 84m. **DIR:** Lew Landers. **CAST:** Mark Stevens, Dorothy Malone, Charles Winninger, Bill Williams. **1953**

TORPEDO RUN ★★★½ A driving pace marks this tautly exciting World War II mouse-chases-cat story about a navy submarine tracking, catching, and destroying a Japanese aircraft carrier in Tokyo Bay. 98m. **DIR:** Joseph Pevney. **CAST:** Glenn Ford, Ernest Borgnine, Dean Jones, Diane Brewster. **1958**

TOUGH ENOUGH ★★½ Dennis Quaid plays the "Country-and-Western Warrior," a singer-fighter who slugs his way through taxing "Toughman" contests from Fort Worth to Detroit in a quest for fame and fortune. It's *Rocky* meets *Honeysuckle Rose*, yet still mildly enjoyable. Rated PG for profanity and violence. 106m. **DIR:** Richard Fleischer. **CAST:** Dennis Quaid, Warren Oates, Stan Shaw, Pam Grier, Wilford Brimley. **1983**

TOUGHER THAN LEATHER 🦃 Low-budget quickie about murder and revenge in the music industry. Rated R for violence, profanity, and nudity. 92m. **DIR:** Rick Rubin. **CAST:** Run-DMC, The Beastie Boys. **1988**

TOUR OF DUTY ★★★ Pilot for the TV series of the same name, *Tour of Duty* is like a 90-minute course in Vietnam War history with prime-time cleanliness. And while the cleanliness hinders the film's credibility, the action scenes make it worth watching. Not rated, has violence. 93m. **DIR:** B.W.L. Norton. **CAST:** Terence Knox, Stephen Caffrey, Joshua Maurer, Kevin Conroy. **1987**

TOWERING INFERNO, THE ★★★★ This is the undisputed king of the disaster movies of the 1970s. An all-star cast came together for this big-budget thriller about a newly constructed San Francisco high-rise hotel and office building that is set ablaze due to substandard materials. Rated PG. 165m. **DIR:** John Guillermin, Irwin Allen. **CAST:** Steve McQueen, Paul Newman, William Holden, Faye Dunaway, Fred Astaire, Richard Chamberlain. **1974**

TOWN CALLED HELL, A 🦃 Confusing action yarn about a manhunt for a Mexican revolutionary. Rated R. 95m. **DIR:** Robert Parrish. **CAST:** Robert Shaw, Telly Savalas, Stella Stevens. **1971**

TOY SOLDIERS (1983) 🦃 Inept film about a group of vacationing college students in Latin America. Rated R. 85m. **DIR:** David Fisher. **CAST:** Jason Miller, Cleavon Little, Rodolfo DeAnda. **1983**

TOY SOLDIERS (1991) ★★★½ In what might be called *The Godfather Meets Taps*, a group of rich-kid rejects take on a band of terrorists who are holding them hostage to force the release of a South American drug lord. The preposterous story line benefits from assured performances by Denholm Elliott and young leads Sean Astin, Keith Coogan, Wil Wheaton, and George Perez. Rated R for violence and profanity. 112m. **DIR:** Daniel Petrie Jr. **CAST:** Sean Astin, Wil Wheaton, Keith Coogan, Lou Gossett Jr., Denholm Elliott, R. Lee Ermey, Jerry Orbach, George Perez. **1991**

TRADER TOM OF THE CHINA SEAS 🦃 Hodgepodge adventure about the United Nations, spies, and revolution makes the most of stock highlights from previous Republic serials, but leaves a fine cast to patch the story together any way they can. B&W; 12 chapters. **DIR:** Franklin Adreon. **CAST:** Harry Lauter, Aline Towne, Lyle Talbot, Robert Shayne, Victor Sen Yung. **1954**

TRAIN, THE ★★★★ A suspenseful World War II adventure about the French Resistance's attempt to stop a train loaded with fine art, seized from French museums, from reaching its destination in Nazi Germany. Burt Lancaster is fine as the head of the French railway system, but he is far outclassed by the performance of Paul Scofield as the unrelenting German commander. B&W; 133m. **DIR:** John Frankenheimer. **CAST:** Burt Lancaster, Paul Scofield, Michel Simon, Jeanne Moreau. 1965

TRAINED TO FIGHT ★★ Average martial arts actioner features a college freshman pursuing his interest in kung fu. He must win the $25,000 tournament money to help underprivileged kids. His master tries to explain why his moves are meant to promote nonviolence, but that's stretching it. Unrated; contains violence. 95m. **DIR:** Eric Sherman. **CAST:** Ken McLeod, Tang Tak Wing, Matthew Roy Cohen, Mark Williams. 1991

TRAPPER COUNTY WAR ★★ Two city boys trigger a blood feud when one of them falls for a country girl who's already spoken for. An oft-told tale of backwoods romance and revenge. Rated R for violence and profanity. 98m. **DIR:** Worth Keeter. **CAST:** Rob Estes, Betsy Russell, Bo Hopkins, Ernie Hudson. 1989

TRAXX ★★★ Wacky, often funny tale about a mercenary turned cookie maker who cleans the criminal element out of Hadleyville, Texas. Shadoe Stevens is Traxx, a man who derives simple pleasure from shooting people, causing mayhem—and baking the oddest-flavored cookies he can imagine. Rated R for cartoon violence and slight nudity. 85m. **DIR:** Jerome Gray. **CAST:** Shadoe Stevens, Priscilla Barnes, Robert Davi, John Hancock. 1988

TREASURE OF THE AMAZON 🦃 Mexican-made action flick about a fortune in diamonds. Unrated, the film contains some violence. 105m. **DIR:** René Cardona Jr. **CAST:** Stuart Whitman, Bradford Dillman, Donald Pleasence, John Ireland. 1983

TREASURE OF THE FOUR CROWNS 🦃 Adventurers attempt to steal invaluable Visigoth treasures from a crazed cult leader. Rated PG for violence and gore. 97m. **DIR:** Ferdinando Baldi. **CAST:** Tony Anthony, Ana Obregon, Gene Quintano. 1983

TREASURE OF THE SIERRA MADRE ★★★★★ Humphrey Bogart gives a brilliant performance in this study of greed. The setting is rugged mountains in Mexico where Bogart, with Tim Holt and a grizzled prospector, played marvelously by Walter Huston, set out to make a fortune in gold prospecting. They do, with their troubles getting worse. Seamless script and magnificent performances add up to a classic. B&W; 126m. **DIR:** John Huston. **CAST:** Humphrey Bogart, Tim Holt, Walter Huston, Bruce Bennett. 1948

TREASURE OF THE YANKEE ZEPHYR ★★½ When an old trapper (Donald Pleasence) discovers a sunken treasure of military medals and liquor, he enlists the aid of his partner (Ken Wahl) and his daughter (Lesley Ann Warren) to bring in the haul. A ruthless claim jumper (George Peppard) and his henchmen follow. Rated PG for violence. 97m. **DIR:** David Hemmings. **CAST:** Ken Wahl, Lesley Ann Warren, Donald Pleasence, George Peppard, Bruno Lawrence. 1981

TRESPASS ★★★★ Nobody directs action better than Walter Hill, and, by working from a tight script by Bob Gale and Robert Zemeckis, this rough-and-tumble, modern-day shoot-'em-up ranks as one of his best films. Two Arkansas firemen's search for lost treasure leads them to a taut battle of wits, fists, and flying bullets that will have fans of the genre cheering. Rated R for profanity and violence. 101m. **DIR:** Walter Hill. **CAST:** Bill Paxton, Ice T, Bill Sadler, Ice Cube, Art Evans. 1992

TRIPLE IMPACT 🦃 Tedious entry in kick-fighting series has three world champions battling the usual array of bad guys. Even three stars can't kick start this mess. Not rated, but contains violence. 97m. **DIR:** David Hunt. **CAST:** Ron Hall, Dale "Apollo" Cook, Bridget "Baby Doll" Riley, Robert Marius. 1992

TRIPWIRE ★★★ During a gun exchange, a terrorist leader's son is killed by a special agent. Fast-paced and well-acted adventure that allows for character development as well. Rated R for violence. 92m. **DIR:** James Lemmo. **CAST:** Terence Knox, David Warner, Isabella Hoffman, Yaphet Kotto. 1989

TROMA'S WAR ★★½ A shoot-'em-up about a group of air-crash survivors stranded on a deserted island. This ragtag bunch soon find themselves fighting terrorists bent on taking over the United States with the AIDS virus. Made by the people responsible for *The Toxic Avenger*, this frequently tasteless flick combines violent action with totally deadpan comedy. Unrated. 105m. **DIR:** Michael Herz, Samuel Weil. **CAST:** Carolyn Beauchamp, Sean Bowen. 1988

TROPICAL SNOW ★★★★ Realistic story about two lovers from South America whose dream is to get to America and make enough money to support their families. Suspenseful and harrowing. Rated R for nudity. 87m. **DIR:** Ciro Duran. **CAST:** Nick Corri, Madeline Stone, David Carradine. 1988

TRUCK TURNER ★★ Singer Isaac Hayes traded in his gold chains for guns in this disappointing action-thriller. He and Alan Weeks play bounty hunters on the run from vengeful gangster Yaphet Kotto. Rated R for violence, profanity, and sexual situations. 91m. **DIR:** Jonathan Kaplan. **CAST:** Isaac Hayes, Yaphet Kotto, Alan Weeks, Scatman Crothers, Stan Shaw. 1974

TRUCKSTOP WOMEN 🦃 A truck-stop prostitution racket. Rated R. 82m. **DIR:** Mark L. Lester. **CAST:** Claudia Jennings, Lieux Dressler, John Martino. 1974

TRUE ROMANCE ★★★★ Quentin Tarantino, the director of *Reservoir Dogs*, supplied the screenplay for this outrageously violent black comedy about a modern-day Bonnie and Clyde (albeit of the naive and innocent variety) who inadvertently rip off a cocaine dealer and get chased across the United States by the police and the mob. It's not for all tastes, but the wild performances by an all-star cast are certainly something to see and the story constantly surprises. Rated R for violence, profanity, simulated sex, and drug use. 120m. **DIR:** Tony Scott. **CAST:** Christian Slater, Patricia Arquette, Dennis Hopper, Christopher Walken, Val Kilmer, Gary Oldman, Brad Pitt, Bronson Pinchot, Conchata Ferrell, Saul Rubinek, Samuel L. Jackson, Michael Rapaport, Tom Sizemore, Christopher Penn. **1993**

TRY AND GET ME ★★★½ A desperate, unemployed husband and father (Frank Lovejoy) teams up with a ruthless thief and murderer (Lloyd Bridges) but can't live with his guilt after their crime spree. Interesting analysis of criminality, yellow journalism, and mob rule. Unrated, but contains violence. 91m. **DIR:** Cy Endfield. **CAST:** Frank Lovejoy, Lloyd Bridges, Kathleen Ryan, Richard Carlson. **1950**

TUSKS ★★½ Shot in the African wilderness, this tale of a conservationist kidnapped by a poacher to act as bait for the game warden is sometimes bogged down by bad writing and uneven pacing. When it is in stride, though, it is a tense and vicious look at man against animal. Rated R for nudity and profanity. 99m. **DIR:** Tara Moore. **CAST:** Lucy Gutteridge, Andrew Stevens, John Rhys-Davies, Julian Glover. **1990**

TUXEDO WARRIOR ★★ Trite story about a bar owner/soldier of fortune (John Wyman) who becomes embroiled with diamond thieves in South Africa. Two stars for the British accents and some decent action. Not rated, but contains violence and profanity. 93m. **DIR:** Andrew Sinclair. **CAST:** John Wyman, Carol Royle, Holly Palance, James Coburn Jr. **1982**

TV CLASSICS: ADVENTURES OF ROBIN HOOD, THE—TV SERIES ★★★ Part of a series of tapes of Fifties TV classics, this episode centers on the young nephew of Maid Marion who wants to prove he is a man by turning Robin Hood and his Merry Men over to the Sheriff of Nottingham. 30m. **DIR:** Robert Day. **CAST:** Richard Greene, Patricia Driscoll, Archie Duncan. **1955**

TWELVE O'CLOCK HIGH ★★★★ Gregory Peck is the flight commander who takes over an England-based bomber squadron during World War II. He begins to feel the strain of leadership and becomes too involved with the men in his command. This is a well-produced and well-acted film. Dean Jagger won an Oscar for supporting actor for his fine performance. B&W; 132m. **DIR:** Henry King. **CAST:** Gregory Peck, Dean Jagger, Gary Merrill, Hugh Marlowe. **1950**

20,000 LEAGUES UNDER THE SEA (1954) ★★★★ In this Disney version of the famous Jules Verne adventure-fantasy, a sailor (Kirk Douglas) and a scientist (Paul Lukas) get thoroughly involved with Captain Nemo, played by James Mason, and his fascinating submarine of the future. The cast is great, the action sequences ditto. 127m. **DIR:** Richard Fleischer. **CAST:** Kirk Douglas, James Mason, Paul Lukas, Peter Lorre. **1954**

TWILIGHT'S LAST GLEAMING ★★★ Although this is another maniac-at-the-button doomsday chronicle, it is so convincing that it makes the well-worn premise seem new. From the moment a group of ex-cons (Burt Lancaster, Paul Winfield, Burt Young, and William Smith) seize control of an air force pickup truck, it becomes obvious the audience is in the front seat of a nonstop roller coaster. Rated R for violence and profanity. 146m. **DIR:** Robert Aldrich. **CAST:** Burt Lancaster, Paul Winfield, Burt Young, William Smith, Charles Durning, Richard Widmark, Melvyn Douglas, Joseph Cotten. **1977**

TWO LOST WORLDS 🦃 Pointless story involving pirates and kidnapping. B&W; 61m. **DIR:** Norman Dawn. **CAST:** James Arness, Laura Elliot, Bill Kennedy, Gloria Petroff, Tom Hubbard, Pierre Watkin, James Guilfoyle. **1950**

TWO TO TANGO ★★½ Satisfying little thriller starring Don Stroud as a burned-out hit man for an ominous organization called the Company. He's terminated one too many targets and bargains with his superior to do one last hit in Buenos Aires, Argentina; then he'll retire to Nepal. Rated R for violence and nudity. 87m. **DIR:** Hector Olivera. **CAST:** Don Stroud, Adrienne Sachs, Michael Cavanaugh, Dulio Marzio. **1988**

TYCOON 🦃 A would-be epic about the building of a railroad through the Andes. 128m. **DIR:** Richard Wallace. **CAST:** John Wayne, Laraine Day, Cedric Hardwicke, Judith Anderson, Anthony Quinn, James Gleason. **1947**

ULTERIOR MOTIVES ★★ A reporter pursuing a story about a research scientist stumbles onto a complex espionage plot involving the Japanese and the *yakuza*. Rated R for nudity, violence, and profanity. 95m. **DIR:** James Beckett. **CAST:** Thomas Ian Griffith, Mary Page Keller, Joe Yamanaka, Ellen Crawford, M. C. Gainey, Ken Howard. **1992**

ULTRAVIOLET ★★ A reconciling couple is forcibly separated by a sadistic madman in the vast expanse of Death Valley. A *Dead Calm* variation. Rated R for nudity and profanity. 80m. **DIR:** Mark Griffiths. **CAST:** Esai Morales, Patricia Healy, Stephen Meadows. **1992**

ULYSSES ★★ One of Kirk Douglas's least successful independent productions, this heavily dubbed Italian epic emphasizes dialogue over thrills. Kirk Douglas does his best, but he gets mired down in this slow retelling of Ulysses's long voyage home after the Trojan War. 104m. **DIR:** Mario Camerini. **CAST:** Kirk Douglas, Silvana Mangano, Anthony Quinn, Rossana Podesta, Sylvie. **1955**

UNCOMMON VALOR ★★★★ In this action-packed adventure film, retired Marine Gene Hackman learns that his son may still be alive in a Vietnamese prison camp ten years after being listed as missing in action. He decides to go in after him. Rated R for profanity and violence. 105m. **DIR:** Ted Kotcheff. **CAST:** Gene Hackman, Fred Ward, Reb Brown, Randall "Tex" Cobb, Harold Sylvester, Robert Stack. **1983**

UNDEFEATABLE 🦃 Kung fu queen Cynthia Rothrock is at it again. She's out to avenge the murder of her sister by a serial killer, who's also a martial arts expert. Rated R for nudity, violence, and profanity. 95m. **DIR:** Godfrey Hall. **CAST:** Cynthia Rothrock, Don Niam, John Miller, Donna Jason, Emilie Davazac, Hang Yip Kim, Gerald Klein. **1993**

UNDER FIRE ★★½ Nick Nolte, Gene Hackman, and Joanna Cassidy are journalists covering political upheaval in Central America circa 1979. While *Under Fire* has its moments (found primarily in the superb supporting performances of Ed Harris and French actor Jean-Louis Trintignant), you have to wade through a bit of sludge to get to them. Rated R for profanity, violence, and gore. 128m. **DIR:** Roger Spottiswoode. **CAST:** Nick Nolte, Gene Hackman, Joanna Cassidy, Ed Harris, Jean-Louis Trintignant. **1983**

UNDER SIEGE ★★★★½ Reuniting with director Andrew Davis, Steven Seagal comes up with another winner. A gang of terrorists take over a naval ship with nuclear capabilities only to discover that one-man-army Seagal is on board to give 'em hell. Rip-roaring entertainment. Rated R for profanity, nudity, and violence. 103m. **DIR:** Andrew Davis. **CAST:** Steven Seagal, Tommy Lee Jones, Gary Busey, Nick Mancuso, Erika Eleniac, Patrick O'Neal, Colm Meaney. **1992**

UNDERCOVER ★★ Cliché-ridden cop story. David Neidorf is a policeman who goes undercover in a South Carolina high school. Rated R for language and nudity. 92m. **DIR:** John Stockwell. **CAST:** David Neidorf, Jennifer Jason Leigh, Barry Corbin, David Harris, Kathleen Wilhoite. **1987**

UNDERWATER! ★★ The best stories about this sopping-wet adventure center around the elaborate publicity launched by reclusive millionaire Howard Hughes to sell it to the public. Hughes's original idea of supplying the press with Aqua-lungs and screening the film in an underwater theater didn't help the reviews and only made this costly, overblown story of sea scavengers more of a hoot than it already was. 99m. **DIR:** John Sturges. **CAST:** Jane Russell, Gilbert Roland, Richard Egan, Jayne Mansfield, Lori Nelson. **1955**

UNIVERSAL SOLDIER ★★½ Jean-Claude Van Damme and Dolph Lundgren are part of a top-secret, scientific project to create perfect human fighting machines from dead soldiers. The program goes awry when Van Damme begins remembering his past, and a personal war develops between him and Lundgren. Average. Rated R for violence and profanity. 98m. **DIR:** Roland Emmerich. **CAST:** Jean-Claude Van Damme, Dolph Lundgren, Ally Walker, Ed O'Ross, Jerry Orbach. **1992**

UNTOUCHABLES, THE ★★★★½ An absolutely superb retelling of the beloved television series, with director Brian De Palma working his stylish magic in tandem with a deft script from Pulitzer-winning playwright David Mamet. Prohibition-era Chicago has been beautifully re-created to emphasize big-city decadence. Al Capone (a grand seriocomic performance by Robert De Niro) was the populist hero for providing alcohol for the masses; Eliot Ness was the arrow-straight federal agent who rose to the challenge. Kevin Costner plays Ness as the ultimate *naif* who fails miserably until taken under the protective wing of an honest beat cop (Sean Connery, in the performance of his career). Rated R for language and extreme violence. 119m. **DIR:** Brian De Palma. **CAST:** Kevin Costner, Sean Connery, Robert De Niro, Charles Martin Smith, Andy Garcia, Billy Drago, Richard Bradford. **1987**

UNTOUCHABLES, THE: SCARFACE MOB (TV) ★★★ This violence-ridden film was released theatrically in 1962 but was actually the original two-part pilot for this popular series, first telecast in 1959. Steely-eyed Robert Stack as Eliot Ness gets the government's go-ahead to form his own special team of uncorruptible agents and leads them in forays against the bootleggers, racketeers, and especially the minions of kingpin Al "Scarface" Capone. B&W; 90m. **DIR:** Phil Karlson. **CAST:** Robert Stack, Keenan Wynn, Barbara Nichols, Pat Crowley, Neville Brand, Bruce Gordon, Anthony George, Abel Fernandez, Nick Giorgiade. **1962**

UP PERISCOPE ★★½ Edmond O'Brien is a by-the-book sub commander who risks his command and men on a dangerous mission. Well-done, but too familiar. 111m. **DIR:** Gordon Douglas. **CAST:** James Garner, Edmond O'Brien, Alan Hale Sr., Carleton Carpenter. **1959**

URBAN WARRIORS 🦃 A group of scientists survive a nuclear holocaust. Rated R for violence. 90m. **DIR:** Joseph Warren. **CAST:** Karl Landgren. **1989**

UTU ★★★★★ This stunner from New Zealand contains all the action of the great American Westerns, but with a moral message that leaves most of that genre's best in the dust. Anzac Wallace plays Te Wheke, a Maori corporal in the nineteenth-century British army who finds his family slaughtered by his own army. It is there at his burning village that he vows "utu" (Maori for revenge) and goes on a march with fellow Maori rebels to rid his land of white people. Rated R for violence. 100m. **DIR:** Geoff Murphy. **CAST:** Anzac Wallace, Bruno Lawrence, Kelly Johnson, Tim Elliot. **1985**

VANISHING POINT ★★½ Interesting story of a marathon car chase through Colorado and California. Cleavon Little gives a standout performance as the disc jockey who helps a driver (Barry Newman) elude the police. Richard Sarafian's direction is competent, but the story eventually runs out of gas before the film ends. Rated PG. 107m. **DIR:** Richard C. Sarafian. **CAST:** Cleavon Little, Barry Newman, Dean Jagger. **1971**

VEGA$ ★★½ A few days in the life of a high-flying, T-Bird-driving private eye whose beat is highways, byways, and gambling casinos of Las Vegas. Robert Urich, an ex-cop, is hired to find a runaway teenage girl who's gotten in too deep with the sleazy side of Fortune Town. 104m. **DIR:** Richard Lang. **CAST:** Robert Urich, Judy Landers, Tony Curtis, Will Sampson, Greg Morris. **1978**

VENDETTA A laughably bad women's prison flick. Rated R. 89m. **DIR:** Bruce Logan. **CAST:** Karen Chase, Sandy Martin, Roberta Collins, Kin Shriner. **1985**

VENGEANCE Dull account of an escape from a Latin American prison camp. Unrated, the film has graphic violence and sex. 114m. **DIR:** Antonio Isasi. **CAST:** Jason Miller, Lea Massari, Marisa Peredes. **1987**

VENGEANCE IS MINE (1976) ★★ A stark and brutal story of backcountry justice. Murderous bank robbers run into Ernest Borgnine, who matches brutality with brutality. A bleak and stilted movie. Not rated; contains violence and profanity. 90m. **DIR:** John Trent. **CAST:** Ernest Borgnine, Michael J. Pollard, Hollis McLaren. **1976**

VENUS IN FURS Poor mystery involving a musician and a mutilated woman who washes ashore. Rated R. 86m. **DIR:** Jess (Jesus) Franco. **CAST:** James Darren, Barbara McNair, Klaus Kinski, Dennis Price. **1970**

VERNE MILLER ★★ Scott Glenn stars as the infamous gunman who masterminded and executed the violent Kansas City massacre at the insistence of crime czar Al Capone. Too many dull gunfights and too little story line or character development. Rated R for nudity and violence. 95m. **DIR:** Rod Hewitt. **CAST:** Scott Glenn, Barbara Stock, Thomas Waites, Lucinda Jenney, Sonny Carl Davis, Andrew Robinson. **1988**

VICE SQUAD ★★★½ Slick, fast-paced thriller set in the seamy world of pimps and prostitutes. Season Hubley is an adorable mom by day and a smart-mouthed hooker by night forced to help cop Gary Swanson capture a sicko killer, played with frightening intensity by Wings Hauser. A total fairy tale, but it moves quickly enough to mask improbabilities. Not for the squeamish. Rated R. 97m. **DIR:** Gary A. Sherman. **CAST:** Season Hubley, Wings Hauser, Gary Swanson, Beverly Todd. **1982**

VICIOUS ★★ In this bland Australian film a young man is unwittingly the provocateur of a sadistic attack on his wealthy girlfriend and her parents by a trio of thugs. The ensuing revenge is predictable. Rated R for graphic violence. 90m. **DIR:** Karl Zwicky. **CAST:** Tamblyn Lord, Craig Pearce. **1988**

VICTORY ★★★ Sylvester Stallone and Michael Caine star in this entertaining but predictable World War II drama about a soccer game between Allied prisoners of war and the Nazis. With a title like *Victory*, guess who wins. Rated PG. 110m. **DIR:** John Huston. **CAST:** Sylvester Stallone, Michael Caine, Pelé, Max von Sydow. **1981**

VIETNAM, TEXAS ★★½ A Texas priest, haunted by guilt over the pregnant woman he abandoned when he was a soldier in Vietnam, tracks her down in Houston. He determines to save her from the drug-running mobster she has married. Shoot-'em-up with a social conscience. Rated R for violence. 92m. **DIR:** Robert Ginty. **CAST:** Robert Ginty, Haing S. Noir, Tim Thomerson. **1990**

VIEW TO A KILL, A ★★★ Despite a spectacular opening sequence, the James Bond series is starting to look a little old and tired—just like Roger Moore. Christopher Walken costars as the maniacal villain who plans to corner the world's microchip market by flooding the San Andreas Fault. For fans only. Rated PG for violence and suggested sex. 131m. **DIR:** John Glen. **CAST:** Roger Moore, Tanya Roberts, Christopher Walken, Grace Jones. **1985**

VIKINGS, THE ★★★½ Well-done action film following the exploits of a group of Vikings (led by Tony Curtis and Kirk Douglas). Many good battle scenes and beautiful photography and locations make the picture a standout. Ernest Borgnine gives a great performance. Don't miss it. 114m. **DIR:** Richard Fleischer. **CAST:** Kirk Douglas, Tony Curtis, Ernest Borgnine, Janet Leigh. **1958**

VILLAIN STILL PURSUED HER, THE Dull, old-fashioned melodrama. B&W; 66m. **DIR:** Eddie Cline. **CAST:** Anita Louise, Richard Cromwell, Hugh Herbert, Alan Mowbray, Buster Keaton, Billy Gilbert, Margaret Hamilton. **1940**

VIOLATED 💔 Soap-opera starlets are invited to Mafia parties, where they are brutally raped. Rated R for violence and nudity. 90m. **DIR:** Richard Cannistraro. **CAST:** J. C. Quinn, John Heard. **1984**

VIOLENT BREED, THE 💔 The CIA goes into Vietnam to stop a guerrilla gang. Gratuitous nudity and violence galore. 91m. **DIR:** Fernando Di Leo. **CAST:** Henry Silva, Harrison Muller, Woody Strode, Carole André. **1983**

VIOLENT YEARS, THE ★★ The screenwriter of this camp classic was Edward D. Wood Jr., and it bears his unmistakable touch. A gang of rich girls don men's clothing and rob gas stations. In their spare time, they pet heavily at a combination pajama-cocktail party, rape a lover's-lane Lothario, and even get involved in an international communist conspiracy! Their response to every query is a sneered "So what?" A must-see for buffs of bad movies! 65m. **DIR:** Franz Eichorn. **CAST:** Jean Moorehead, Barbara Weeks, Glenn Corbett, I. Stanford Jolley. **1956**

VIPER 💔 A CIA operation breaks into a university and kills the members of the administration. Rated R for language and violence. 96m. **DIR:** Peter Maris. **CAST:** Linda Purl, James Tolkan, Jeff Kober, Chris Robinson. **1988**

VIVA KNIEVEL 💔 Evel Knievel (playing himself) is duped by a former buddy into doing a stunt tour of Mexico. Rated PG. 106m. **DIR:** Gordon Douglas. **CAST:** Evel Knievel, Marjoe Gortner, Leslie Nielsen, Gene Kelly, Lauren Hutton. **1977**

VON RYAN'S EXPRESS ★★★★ This is a first-rate World War II tale of escape from a prisoner-of-war camp aboard a German train to neutral Switzerland. Trevor Howard is the officer in charge until a feisty Frank Sinatra takes over the escape plan. This is a great action story, with Sinatra playing the hero's role perfectly. 117m. **DIR:** Mark Robson. **CAST:** Frank Sinatra, Trevor Howard, Edward Mulhare, James Brolin, Luther Adler. **1965**

WAKE ISLAND ★★★★ Hard-hitting tale of a small gallant detachment of U.S. Marines holding out against attack after attack by the Japanese army, navy, and air force. A true story from the early dark days of World War II. Brian Donlevy commands the troops, and William Bendix and Robert Preston fight each other as much as the Japanese. *Wake Island* received four Academy Award nominations and was the first realistic American film made about World War II. B&W; 88m. **DIR:** John Farrow. **CAST:** Brian Donlevy, Macdonald Carey, Robert Preston, Albert Dekker, William Bendix, Walter Abel. **1942**

WAKE OF THE RED WITCH ★★★★ Good, seafaring adventure tale with John Wayne outstanding as a wronged ship's captain seeking justice and battling an octopus for sunken treasure. B&W; 106m. **DIR:** Edward Ludwig. **CAST:** John Wayne, Gail Russell, Gig Young, Luther Adler. **1948**

WALK IN THE SUN, A ★★★★½ Based on Harry Brown's novel, this picture really gets to the heart of the human reaction to war. The story of an American army unit's attack on a German stronghold in World War II Italy is a first-rate character study. B&W; 117m. **DIR:** Lewis Milestone. **CAST:** Dana Andrews, Richard Conte, Sterling Holloway, John Ireland. **1945**

WALK INTO HELL ★★★ Popular Australian star Chips Rafferty is something of a precursor to "Crocodile" Dundee in this outback adventure. He plays a bush explorer who helps a businessman find oil in New Guinea. Of course, the aborigines aren't all too happy about this. Plenty of *National Geographic*-type footage pads out this okay adventure. 93m. **DIR:** Les Robinson. **CAST:** Chips Rafferty, Françoise Christophe, Reg Lye. **1957**

WALKING TALL ★★½ Poor Joe Don Baker never outran his one-note performance as Buford Pusser, the baseball bat–toting southern sheriff who decided to take the law into his own hands in his fight against the cancerous scum of society. Unpleasantly brutal and difficult to enjoy for any reason. Talented Elizabeth Hartman is completely wasted. Not a family picture. Rated R. 125m. **DIR:** Phil Karlson. **CAST:** Joe Don Baker, Elizabeth Hartman, Noah Beery Jr., Rosemary Murphy. **1973**

WALKING TALL PART II ★★ This follow-up to the successful *Walking Tall* proves that sequels are better off not being made at all. This story line gives Svenson a chance to look mean, but that's about it. Rated R for violence and language. 109m. **DIR:** Earl Bellamy. **CAST:** Bo Svenson, Luke Askew, Richard Jaeckel, Noah Beery Jr. **1975**

WANDA NEVADA ★★½ Interesting little film with Peter Fonda as a shifty, amoral gambler who wins Brooke Shields in a poker game. They come into the possession of a map that marks a gold strike. If you watch carefully, you'll see Henry Fonda as a gold prospector. It's the only film that father and son ever did together. Rated PG for violence and mature situations. 105m. **DIR:** Peter Fonda. **CAST:** Peter Fonda, Brooke Shields, Fiona Lewis. **1979**

WANTED: DEAD OR ALIVE ★★★ In this lean action thriller, Rutger Hauer stars as Nick Randall, the great-grandson of Old West bounty hunter Josh Randall (played by Steve McQueen in the *Wanted: Dead or Alive* television series). Nick is a former CIA agent who is brought out of retirement when an international terrorist (Gene Simmons) begins leaving a bloody trail across Los Angeles. Rated R for profanity and violence. 104m. **DIR:** Gary A. Sherman. **CAST:** Rutger Hauer, Gene

Simmons, Robert Guillaume, Mel Harris, William Russ. 1987

WAR BOY, THE ★★★½ A 12-year-old boy (Jason Hopely) living in World War II Germany suffers the experiences of growing up amid the brutalities of conflict. Hopely's performance is terrific. The story and production are nowhere near as ambitious as *Hope and Glory* or *Empire of the Sun*, but *The War Boy* is a good film in its own right. Rated PG for violence and some sex. 96m. DIR: Allan Eastman. CAST: Helen Shaver, Kenneth Welsh, Jason Hopely. 1985

WAR LORD, THE ★★★½ In the eleventh century, the warlord (Charlton Heston) of the Duke of Normandy moves to secure the coastline against invaders and to claim a maiden. The battle scenes are great and Richard Boone, as the title character's right hand, turns in a fine performance. 120m. DIR: Franklin S. Schaffner. CAST: Charlton Heston, Richard Boone, Rosemary Forsyth, Maurice Evans, Guy Stockwell, Henry Wilcoxon, James Farentino. 1965

WAR PARTY ★★ An interesting idea, but not suitably developed, this film details what happens when a group of disgruntled, modern-day native Americans go on the warpath. They disrupt a summer festival by taking the cowboy-and-Indian war games seriously—and use real ammunition. Rated R, with strong violence. 100m. DIR: Franc Roddam. CAST: Kevin Dillon, Billy Wirth, Tim Sampson, M. Emmet Walsh. 1988

WARBIRDS 🦃 Inept action flick concerns American intervention in a Middle Eastern revolution. Rated R for violence and profanity. 88m. DIR: Ulli Lommel. CAST: Jim Eldbert. 1988

WARBUS ★★ A Vietnam adventure about a motley crew fleeing a mission in a school bus, heading south during the closing days of the war. Hardly realistic, but the characters are likable and the action is tightly paced. Rated R for violence and profanity. 90m. DIR: Ted Kaplan. CAST: Daniel Stephen, Rom Kristoff, Urs Althaus, Gwendoline Cook, Ernie Zarte, Don Gordon. 1985

WARLORDS OF HELL 🦃 Two dirt bike–riding brothers wander into a marijuana plantation south of the border. Rated R for nudity, violence, and profanity. 76m. DIR: Clark Henderson. CAST: Brad Henson, Jeffrey D. Rice. 1987

WARNING, THE 🦃 Convoluted dirty-cop flick from Italy. Not rated, but probably equal to an R for violence, profanity, and nudity. 101m. DIR: Damiano Damiani. CAST: Martin Balsam, Giuliano Gemma, Giancarlo Zanetti. 1985

WARRIOR QUEEN 🦃 This stinker robs footage from an Italian epic about the eruption of Mount Vesuvius and pads it out with a nonstory about an emissary from Rome inspecting the city of Pompeii. There are two different versions, an R-rated one with nudity and violence and an unrated one with more nudity. 69/79m. DIR: Chuck Vincent. CAST: Sybil Danning, Donald Pleasence, Richard Hill, Josephine Jacqueline Jones. 1987

WARRIORS, THE (1955) ★★★ In this, his last swashbuckling role, Errol Flynn looks older than his 46 years. Cast as a British prince, he seems more qualified to battle the bulge and the bottle than the murderous hordes of nasty Peter Finch. Nevertheless, even in his decline, Flynn was more adept with a sword and a leer than anyone else in Hollywood. Though the movie is predictable, it's also quite entertaining. 85m. DIR: Henry Levin. CAST: Errol Flynn, Joanne Dru, Peter Finch, Yvonne Furneaux, Michael Hordern. 1955

WARRIORS, THE (1979) ★★★★ Comic book–style violence and sensibilities made this Walter Hill film an unworthy target for those worried about its prompting real-life gang wars. It's just meant for fun, and mostly it is, as a group of kids try to make their way home through the territories of other, less understanding gangs in a surrealistic New York. Rated R. 94m. DIR: Walter Hill. CAST: Michael Beck, James Remar, Thomas Waites, Deborah Van Valkenburgh. 1979

WARRIORS FROM HELL 🦃 When ruthless rebels take over a small African country, a ragtag group of commandos save the day. War truly is hell. Rated R for violence and language. 90m. DIR: Ronnie Isaacs. CAST: Deon Stewardson, Glen Gabela, Shayne Leith, Adrian Pearce. 1990

WATCHED! 🦃 A former U.S. attorney suffers a drug-related mental breakdown and kills a narcotics agent. Unrated. 95m. DIR: John Parsons. CAST: Stacy Keach, Harris Yulin, Brigid Polk, Tony Serra. 1973

WE DIVE AT DAWN ★★★½ Tense story about a British submarine's duel with a German battleship during World War II is top-notch entertainment with a documentary feel. A fine cast and sensitive direction by Anthony Asquith lend this film dignity. B&W; 93m. DIR: Anthony Asquith. CAST: John Mills, Eric Portman. 1943

WE OF THE NEVER NEVER ★★★★½ The compelling story of a woman's year in the Australian outback, where she learns about aborigines and they learn about her, is based on a true-life account written by Jeannie Gunn and published in 1908. Rated G. 132m. DIR: Igor Auzins. CAST: Angela Punch McGregor, Arthur Dignam, Tony Barry. 1983

WE'RE IN THE LEGION NOW 🦃 Gangsters on the lam and fellow racketeers head to Europe and join the foreign legion when their enemies find them in Paris. 58m. DIR:

Crane Wilbur. **CAST:** Reginald Denny, Esther Ralston, Vince Barnett. 1937

WET GOLD 🦃 A waitress who follows an old alcoholic's lead to sunken gold. Substandard made-for-TV film. 95m. **DIR:** Dick Lowry. **CAST:** Brooke Shields, Burgess Meredith, Tom Byrd, Brian Kerwin. 1984

WHEELS OF FIRE 🦃 Shameless rip-off of *The Road Warrior.* Rated R for nudity, violence, and profanity. 81m. **DIR:** Cirio H. Santiago. **CAST:** Gary Watkins, Laura Banks, Lynda Wiesmeiser, Linda Grovenor. 1984

WHEELS OF TERROR 🦃 Interminable trash that pits spunky school-bus driver Joanna Cassidy against an unseen child molester who uses his dirty black sedan as a weapon, clearly having seen Steven Spielberg's *Duel* a few too many times. Unwatchable made-for-cable junk. 85m. **DIR:** Christopher Cain. **CAST:** Joanna Cassidy, Marcie Leeds, Arlen Dean Snyder. 1990

WHEN GANGLAND STRIKES ★★ Stale story of a lawman who has to knuckle under to hoodlums who have some dirt on him is adequate but nothing dynamic. B&W; 70m. **DIR:** R. G. Springsteen. **CAST:** Raymond Greenleaf, Marjie Millar, John Hudson, Anthony Caruso. 1956

WHEN LIGHTNING STRIKES 🦃 That's Lightning as in Lightning, the Wonder Dog, star of this ridiculous Rin Tin Tin rip-off. B&W; 51m. **DIR:** Burton King. **CAST:** Francis X. Bushman. 1934

WHERE EAGLES DARE ★★★ Clint Eastwood and Richard Burton portray Allied commandos in this World War II adventure film which is short on realism. Instead we have farfetched but exciting shoot-outs, explosions, and mass slaughter. Our heroes must break out an American general being held captive in a heavily fortified German castle. 158m. **DIR:** Brian G. Hutton. **CAST:** Richard Burton, Clint Eastwood, Mary Ure, Michael Hordern, Patrick Wymark, Anton Diffring, Robert Beatty, Donald Houston, Ingrid Pitt. 1969

WHERE EAST IS EAST ★★★ Despite the presence of director Tod Browning and silent star Lon Chaney, this isn't a horror movie. It's an Oriental revenge melodrama, set in Indochina. Full of kinky sexual peccadilloes that would have had a rough time getting by the censors had it been made a decade later. B&W; 68m. **DIR:** Tod Browning. **CAST:** Lon Chaney Sr., Lupe Velez, Lloyd Hughes. 1925

WHICH WAY HOME ★★½ In 1979, a Red Cross nurse flees to Thailand and Australia with a small group of Cambodian and Vietnamese orphans. Often implausible, overlong cable-TV production. 141m. **DIR:** Carl Schultz. **CAST:** Cybill Shepherd, John Waters. 1991

WHILE THE CITY SLEEPS ★★½ An impressive cast and the talents of director Fritz Lang can't transform this standard newspaper-crime story into a great film, although so many of the necessary elements seem to be present. Rival newspaper executives compete with each other and the police in an effort to come up with the identity of a mad killer who has been stalking the city, but this convoluted gabfest quickly bogs down and wastes the considerable acting talents involved. B&W; 100m. **DIR:** Fritz Lang. **CAST:** Dana Andrews, Ida Lupino, Rhonda Fleming, George Sanders, Vincent Price, John Drew Barrymore, Thomas Mitchell, Howard Duff, Mae Marsh. 1956

WHISPERING SHADOW, THE ★★★ In this early Mascot serial Bela Lugosi is the sinister Professor Strang, maker of wax figures that move and speak like humans. The Whispering Shadow is an unseen leader of henchmen who attack each time a figure is trucked to a warehouse. B&W; 12 chapters. **DIR:** Albert Herman, Colbert Clark. **CAST:** Bela Lugosi, Henry B. Walthall. 1933

WHISTLE STOP 🦃 Small-town girl returns from the big city. Tripe. B&W; 85m. **DIR:** Leonide Moguy. **CAST:** George Raft, Ava Gardner, Tom Conway, Victor McLaglen, Charles Drake, Jimmy Conlin. 1946

WHITE DAWN, THE ★★★★ This is a gripping and thought-provoking adventure film. Three whalers (Warren Oates, Lou Gossett Jr., and Timothy Bottoms) get lost in the Arctic and are rescued by Eskimos, whom they end up exploiting. Rated PG. 109m. **DIR:** Phil Kaufman. **CAST:** Warren Oates, Lou Gossett Jr., Timothy Bottoms. 1974

WHITE GHOST 🦃 William Katt does an embarrassing Rambo imitation in this miserable rip-off. Rated R for violence and profanity. 93m. **DIR:** B. J. Davis. **CAST:** William Katt, Rosalind Chao, Martin Hewitt, Wayne Crawford, Reb Brown. 1988

WHITE HEAT ★★★★½ James Cagney gives one of his greatest screen performances as a totally insane mama's boy and gangster, Cody Jarrett, in this film. Margaret Wycherly is chillingly effective as the evil mom, and Virginia Mayo is uncommonly outstanding as the badman's moll. But it is Cagney's picture pure and simple as he ironically makes it to "the top of the world, Ma!" B&W; 114m. **DIR:** Raoul Walsh. **CAST:** James Cagney, Margaret Wycherly, Virginia Mayo, Edmond O'Brien, Steve Cochran. 1949

WHITE HOT ★★½ A quick-paced drama about a yuppie couple's fall from grace. Robby Benson (in his directorial debut) and Tawny Kitaen take over a drug lord's trade and become hopelessly immersed in the high life. Rated R for violence and drug use. 95m. **DIR:** Robby Benson. **CAST:** Robby Benson, Tawny Kitaen, Danny Aiello. 1989

WHITE LIGHTNING ★★ Good old boy Burt Reynolds as a speed-loving moonshiner fights the inevitable mean and inept cops and revenue agents in this comic-book chase and retribution film. A good cast of character actors makes this stock drive-in movie entertaining, although it is just like the majority of Burt Reynolds's car films—gimmicky and predictable. Rated PG. 101m. **DIR:** Joseph Sargent. **CAST:** Burt Reynolds, Jennifer Billingsley, Ned Beatty, Bo Hopkins, Matt Clark, Louise Latham, Diane Ladd. **1973**

WHITE LINE FEVER ★★★ Jan-Michael Vincent plays an incorruptible young trucker in this film. He is angered when forced to smuggle goods in his truck. He fights back after he and his pregnant wife (Kay Lenz) are attacked. Rated PG. 92m. **DIR:** Jonathan Kaplan. **CAST:** Jan-Michael Vincent, Kay Lenz, Slim Pickens, L. Q. Jones, Leigh French, Don Porter. **1975**

WHITE PHANTOM ★★ A Ninja gang attempts to deliver a plutonium weapon to terrorists. Bo Svenson is out to break up the plan and blackmails a dancer into infiltrating the gang. Unrated, but with the usual genre violence. 89m. **DIR:** Dusty Nelson. **CAST:** Jay Roberts Jr., Page Leong, Bo Svenson. **1987**

WHITE WATER SUMMER ★★★ Kevin Bacon plays a ruthless wilderness guide who intends to transform four boys into men. Sean Astin is the boy most abused by Bacon and he must decide what to do when Bacon is seriously injured. Interesting coming-of-age adventure. Rated PG for profanity. 87m. **DIR:** Jeff Bleckner. **CAST:** Kevin Bacon, Sean Astin, Jonathan Ward, Matt Adler. **1987**

WHITE WOLVES: A CRY IN THE WILD II ★★½ During a camping trip a teacher falls over a cliff and his students must find and save him. Very predictable film about teenagers learning to understand and like each other. The young cast needs acting lessons. Rated PG. 74m. **DIR:** Catherine Cyran. **CAST:** Ami Dolenz, Mark Paul, David Moscow, Amy O'Neill, Marc Riffon, Matt McCoy. **1993**

WHO'LL STOP THE RAIN ★★★★½ In this brilliant film, Nick Nolte gives one of his finest performances as a hardened vet who agrees to smuggle drugs for a buddy (the always effective Michael Moriarty). What neither of them knows is that it's a setup, so Nolte and Moriarty's neurotic wife, played to perfection by Tuesday Weld, have to hide out from the baddies (Anthony Zerbe, Richard Masur, and Ray Sharkey). Rated R. 126m. **DIR:** Karel Reisz. **CAST:** Nick Nolte, Michael Moriarty, Tuesday Weld, Anthony Zerbe, Richard Masur, Ray Sharkey, David Opatoshu, Gail Strickland. **1978**

WHY ME? 🦃 Two career burglars steal a cursed ruby. Badly acted, poorly written adventure. Rated R for profanity. 87m. **DIR:** Gene Quintano. **CAST:** Christopher Lambert, Kim Greist, Christopher Lloyd. **1989**

WICKED LADY, THE (1983) 🦃 An absolutely awful swashbuckler. Rated R. 98m. **DIR:** Michael Winner. **CAST:** Faye Dunaway, Alan Bates, John Gielgud, Denholm Elliott, Prunella Scales, Oliver Tobias, Glynis Barber. **1983**

WILD ANGELS, THE ★★ It's 1960s hip, low-budget Hollywood style. If they gave Oscars for cool, Peter Fonda—in shades, three-day growth of beard, and leather—would win for sure. This cool motorcycle gang leader needs a hot mama. Unfortunately, he has to make do with Nancy ("These Boots Are Made for Walkin'") Sinatra. But the movie's greatest asset is "Blue's Theme," which revs up the proceedings with wonderfully tacky fuzz-tone guitar. 93m. **DIR:** Roger Corman. **CAST:** Peter Fonda, Nancy Sinatra, Bruce Dern, Michael J. Pollard, Diane Ladd, Gayle Hunnicutt. **1966**

WILD CACTUS ★★ Desert-bound thriller features many erotic encounters in a sordid plot line about a young wife held hostage by a murderous ex-con and his girlfriend. Available in R and unrated versions; both feature sex, violence, and profanity. 92m./96m. **DIR:** Jag Mundhra. **CAST:** David Naughton, India Allen, Gary Hudson, Michelle Moffett, Kathy Shower, Robert Z'dar. **1993**

WILD GEESE, THE ★★★ *The Wild Geese* features the unlikely combination of Richard Burton, Roger Moore, and Richard Harris as three mercenaries hired by a rich British industrialist (Stewart Granger) to go into Rhodesia and free a captured humanist leader. Better than you would expect. Rated R. 134m. **DIR:** Andrew V. McLaglen. **CAST:** Richard Burton, Roger Moore, Richard Harris, Stewart Granger, Hardy Krüger, Jack Watson, Frank Finlay. **1978**

WILD GEESE II 🦃 A new group of mercenaries attempts to break into a Berlin prison to free Nazi war criminal Rudolf Hess. Rated R for violence and language. 118m. **DIR:** Peter R. Hunt. **CAST:** Scott Glenn, Barbara Carrera, Edward Fox, Laurence Olivier, Stratford Johns. **1985**

WILD MAN 🦃 An ex-CIA agent Eric Wild who is pressured to take on one more assignment. Rated R for nudity, profanity, and violence. 105m. **DIR:** F. J. Lincoln. **CAST:** Don Scribner. **1989**

WILD ONE, THE ★★★½ This classic film (based loosely on a real event in Hollister, California) about rival motorcycle gangs taking over a small town is pretty tame stuff these days and provides more laughs than thrills. Marlon Brando and his brooding Johnny are at the heart of this film's popularity; that coupled with the theme of motorcycle nomads have assured the film a cult following. B&W; 79m. **DIR:** Laslo Benedek. **CAST:**

Marlon Brando, Mary Murphy, Robert Keith, Lee Marvin, Jay C. Flippen, Jerry Paris, Alvy Moore. 1953

WILD PAIR, THE ★★ Beau Bridges, a yuppie FBI agent, and Bubba Smith, a streetwise city cop, are assigned to investigate a drug-related murder. The two clash as they find surprises around each corner. Bridges's acting, even as Smith's, is fine, but his directing is wanting. Rated R for profanity, violence, and nudity. 89m. **DIR:** Beau Bridges. **CAST:** Beau Bridges, Bubba Smith, Lloyd Bridges, Raymond St. Jacques, Gary Lockwood, Danny De La Paz. 1987

WILDING, THE CHILDREN OF VIOLENCE 🦃 Taking its name from the highly publicized rape in New York City's Central Park, this film trivializes the case. By associating itself with that factual incident with its opening scene, the film hints at condemning that crime while depicting an unrelated series of fictional beatings by a band of suburbanite youths on a rampage against L.A.'s police and residents. Not rated, though there is partial nudity, violence, and profanity. 92m. **DIR:** Eric Louzil. **CAST:** Wings Hauser, Joey Travolta. 1990

WIND (1992) ★★★ This gorgeously photographed and highly romanticized *Rocky* of the seven seas stars Matthew Modine as a sailing enthusiast who pursues the America's Cup and an ex-girlfriend. The story has the feel of an ancient John Wayne action-comedy, but manages to stay rather dreamily afloat. Rated PG-13 for language. 123m. **DIR:** Carroll Ballard. **CAST:** Matthew Modine, Stellan Skarsgard, Rebecca Miller, Cliff Robertson, Jack Thompson, Jennifer Grey. 1992

WIND AND THE LION, THE ★★★★ In the 1970s, Sean Connery made a trio of memorable adventure movies, one being this release, impressively directed by John Milius. As in the other two films—*The Man Who Would Be King* and *Robin and Marian*—*The Wind and the Lion*, in which Connery plays a dashing Arab chieftain, is a thoroughly satisfying motion picture. Rated PG. 119m. **DIR:** John Milius. **CAST:** Sean Connery, Brian Keith, Candice Bergen, John Huston, Geoffrey Lewis, Steve Kanaly, Vladek Sheybal. 1975

WINDJAMMER ★★★½ Western hero George O'Brien trades the wide open spaces of the range for vast wastes of the Pacific Ocean in this story of high-seas smuggling. Solid adventure. B&W; 58m. **DIR:** Ewing Scott. **CAST:** George O'Brien, Constance Worth. 1937

WINDRIDER 🦃 A self-centered windsurfer becomes obsessed with his quest to perform a 360-degree flip on his sailboard. Rated R for profanity and simulated sex. 83m. **DIR:** Vincent Morton. **CAST:** Tom Burlinson. 1986

WING AND A PRAYER, A ★★★★ An all-male cast in an excellent film about the war in the South Pacific. A combination of actual wartime action photography and soundstage settings give the film an unusual look. One of the most successful propaganda films to be released during World War II. B&W; 98m. **DIR:** Henry Hathaway. **CAST:** Don Ameche, William Eythe, Dana Andrews, Charles Bickford, Cedric Hardwicke, Richard Jaeckel, Harry Morgan, Glenn Langan, Richard Crane. 1944

WINGS ★★★★ The first recipient of the Academy Award for best picture, this is a silent film with organ music in the background. The story concerns two buddies who join the Air Corps in World War I and go to France to battle the Germans. War scenes are excellent, even by today's standards. Antiwar message is well-done, although the love story tends to bog the film down a bit. Look for a young Gary Cooper. Much of the story rings true. B&W; 139m. **DIR:** William Wellman. **CAST:** Clara Bow, Charles "Buddy" Rogers, Richard Arlen, Jobyna Ralston, Gary Cooper, Arlette Marchal, El Brendel. 1927

WINNERS TAKE ALL ★★½ A California teen decides to compete in a Texas regional motocross competition. All of the usual sports-movie clichés are present and accounted for, though the final grudge race is full of high-spirited stunts that even nonracing fans should enjoy. Rated PG-13. 103m. **DIR:** Fritz Kiersch. **CAST:** Don Michael Paul, Kathleen York, Robert Krantz. 1986

WINNING ★★★½ Paul Newman is very good as a race car driver who puts winning above all else, including his family. Some very good racing sequences and fine support from Joanne Woodward and Richard Thomas. Rated PG. 123m. **DIR:** James Goldstone. **CAST:** Paul Newman, Joanne Woodward, Robert Wagner, Richard Thomas. 1969

WISDOM 🦃 Writer-director Emilio Estevez plays a modern-day Robin Hood who comes to the aid of farmers. Rated R for violence. 109m. **DIR:** Emilio Estevez. **CAST:** Emilio Estevez, Demi Moore, Tom Skerritt, Veronica Cartwright, William Allen Young. 1986

WOMAN HUNT, THE 🦃 Every couple of years, someone decides that the world needs a remake of *The Most Dangerous Game*, the classic about a madman who hunts human beings for sport. They're almost always lousy, and this one, made in the Philippines, is no exception. Rated R for nudity and violence. 80m. **DIR:** Eddie Romero. **CAST:** John Ashley, Patricia Woodell, Sid Haig. 1975

WOMEN IN CELL BLOCK 9 🦃 Sleazy women's prison melodrama. Filmed in Spain; poorly dubbed into English. No rating, but packed with nudity and gore. 78m. **DIR:** Jess (Jesus) Franco. **CAST:** Susan Hemingway, Howard Vernon. 1977

WORLD WAR III ★★★½ In this made-for-TV thriller, Rock Hudson, as a U.S. president, must send a crack military unit to Alaska to stop the Russians from capturing the Alaska pipeline. The battle scenes are tense and effective, and Brian Keith, as the Russian secretary-general, is terrific. It's long but certainly worth a view. 200m. **DIR:** David Greene. **CAST:** Rock Hudson, David Soul, Brian Keith, Cathy Lee Crosby, Katherine Helmond, Jeroen Krabbé. **1982**

WRANGLER ★★½ Set in the Aussie outback, B-movie hunkster Jeff Fahey is the dashing businessman out to save Tushka Bergen from an evil rancher and a dangerous drover. The plot could have been lifted from a dime novel, but very pretty fluff. 93m. **DIR:** Ian Barry. **CAST:** Jeff Fahey, Tushka Bergen, Steven Vidler. **1993**

WRECK OF THE MARY DEARE, THE ★★★ Sea captain Gary Cooper, in attempting to prove the crew and owners of his ship were involved in an insurance scam, is himself accused of dereliction. After a suspenseful start, this bogs down and becomes predictable. 100m. **DIR:** Michael Anderson. **CAST:** Gary Cooper, Charlton Heston, Michael Redgrave, Emlyn Williams, Cecil Parker, Alexander Knox, Virginia McKenna, Richard Harris. **1959**

YAKUZA, THE ★★★★★ In this superb blending of the American gangster and Japanese samurai genres, Robert Mitchum plays Harry Kilmer, an ex-G.I. who returns to Japan to do a dangerous favor for a friend, George Tanner (Brian Keith). The latter's daughter has been kidnapped by a Japanese gangster—a Yakuza—who is holding her for ransom. This forces Kilmer to call on Tanaka (Ken Takakura), a onetime enemy who owes him a debt. Thus begins a clash of cultures and a web of intrigue that keep the viewers on the edge of their seats. Rated R. 112m. **DIR:** Sydney Pollack. **CAST:** Robert Mitchum, Brian Keith, Ken Takakura, Herb Edelman, Richard Jordan. **1975**

YANKEE CLIPPER ★★½ Future Hopalong Cassidy William Boyd plays a tough seadog determined to win a race against a British ship as they sail from China to Boston. Plenty of good sea footage is interspersed with a sticky love story between Boyd and an English girl, Elinor Fair, but a near mutiny and Walter Long as the villainous Iron-Head Joe help offset the mush. Silent, with sound track. B&W; 51m. **DIR:** Rupert Julian. **CAST:** William Boyd, Elinor Fair, Frank Coghlan Jr., John Miljan, Walter Long. **1927**

YEAR OF LIVING DANGEROUSLY, THE ★★★★½ *The Year of Living Dangerously* is set in 1965 Indonesia when the Sukarno regime was toppling from pressures left and right. Mel Gibson and Sigourney Weaver star as an Australian journalist and a British diplomatic attaché, respectively. The film, however, belongs to Linda Hunt, in her Academy Award–winning role as free-lance photographer Billy Kwan. Rated R for profanity, nudity, and violence. 115m. **DIR:** Peter Weir. **CAST:** Mel Gibson, Sigourney Weaver, Linda Hunt, Michael Murphy, Bill Kerr, Noel Ferrier. **1983**

YEAR OF THE DRAGON 🦃 Youth gangs in New York's Chinatown. Rated R for violence, profanity, gore, simulated sex, and nudity. 136m. **DIR:** Michael Cimino. **CAST:** Mickey Rourke, John Lone, Ariane, Leonard Termo. **1985**

YOU ONLY LIVE TWICE ★★★ Sean Connery as James Bond—who could expect more? Well, a better plot and more believable cliff-hanger situations come to mind. Still, this entry isn't a bad 007, and it does star the best Bond. 116m. **DIR:** Lewis Gilbert. **CAST:** Sean Connery, Akiko Wakabayashi, Tetsuro Tamba, Mie Hama, Karin Dor, Bernard Lee, Lois Maxwell, Desmond Llewellyn, Donald Pleasence. **1967**

YOU TALKIN' TO ME ★★★ A struggling young New York actor whose idol is Robert De Niro (particularly De Niro's performance in *Taxi Driver*) moves to Los Angeles seeking his big break. Quirky offbeat film that eventually succeeds despite weak direction and clumsy dialogue. Rated R for violence and profanity. 97m. **DIR:** Charles Winkler. **CAST:** Jim Youngs, Faith Ford, Mykel T. Williamson, James Noble. **1987**

YOUNG SHERLOCK HOLMES ★★½ This disappointingly derivative Steven Spielberg production speculates on what might have happened if Sherlock Holmes (Nicholas Rowe) and Dr. John H. Watson (Alan Cox) had met during their student days in 1870 England. A better name for it might be *Sherlock Holmes and the Temple of Doom*. While youngsters are likely to enjoy it, most adults are cautioned to avoid it. Rated PG-13 for violence and scary stuff. 115m. **DIR:** Barry Levinson. **CAST:** Nicholas Rowe, Alan Cox, Sophie Ward, Anthony Higgins, Freddie Jones. **1985**

YOUNG WARRIORS, THE ★★ Revenge exploitation with James Van Patten leading his college-frat brothers on a hunt for the psychos who raped and killed his sister. Rated R for violence. 105m. **DIR:** Lawrence D. Foldes. **CAST:** Ernest Borgnine, Richard Roundtree, Lynda Day George, James Van Patten, Anne Lockhart, Mike Norris, Dick Shawn, Linnea Quigley. **1983**

ZOMBIES OF THE STRATOSPHERE (SATAN'S SATELLITES) ★★ Judd Holdren, representing the Inter-Planetary Patrol, dons a flying suit and tracks down part-human zombies who have enlisted the aid of a renegade scientist to construct a hydrogen bomb that will blow Earth off its orbit and enable them to conquer what's left of the world. Balsa wood rocket ships and stock footage from the other "Rocket Man" serials make this one of the more ludicrous entries from Republic Studios in the last years of the movie serial. Enjoy the stunts in this one and skip the story. B&W; 12 chapters. **DIR:** Fred Brannon. **CAST:** Judd Holdren, Aline Towne, Wilson Wood, Lane Bradford. **1952**

ZORRO ★★★ The dashing swordsman with the black mask and the flashing rapier rides against injustice, though in this version he rides in South America instead of California. Suitably swashbuckling, if a notch below the 1940 *Mark of Zorro*. Rated G. 88m. **DIR:** Duccio Tessari. **CAST:** Alain Delon, Stanley Baker, Enzo Cerusico, Ottavia Piccolo, Adriana Asti. **1975**

ZULU ★★★★½ Several films have been made about the British army and its exploits in Africa during the nineteenth century. *Zulu* ranks with the finest. A stellar cast headed by Stanley Baker and Michael Caine who charge through this story of an outmanned British garrison laid to siege by several thousand Zulu warriors. Based on fact, this one delivers the goods for action and tension. 138m. **DIR:** Cy Endfield. **CAST:** Stanley Baker, Michael Caine, Jack Hawkins, Nigel Green. **1964**

ZULU DAWN ★★★ This prequel to the film *Zulu*, which was made fifteen years earlier, seems quite pale when compared with the first. Based on the crushing defeat of the British army at the hands of the Zulu warriors, *Zulu Dawn* depicts the events leading up to the confrontation portrayed in *Zulu*. Considering all involved, this is a disappointment. Rated PG for violence. 121m. **DIR:** Douglas Hickox. **CAST:** Burt Lancaster, Peter O'Toole, Simon Ward, John Mills, Nigel Davenport. **1979**

CHILDREN'S VIEWING/ FAMILY

ABSENT-MINDED PROFESSOR, THE ★★★★ One of Disney's best live-action comedies, this stars Fred MacMurray in the title role of a scientist who discovers "flubber" (flying rubber). Only trouble is, no one will believe him—except Keenan Wynn, who tries to steal his invention. B&W; 104m. **DIR:** Robert Stevenson. **CAST:** Fred MacMurray, Nancy Olson, Tommy Kirk, Ed Wynn, Keenan Wynn. **1961**

ACROSS THE GREAT DIVIDE ★★ *Across the Great Divide* is family entertainment at its most unchallenging. Two kids (Heather Rattray and Mark Hall) meet up with a shifty gambler (Robert Logan), and the three eventually unite for safety on their monotonous trek through valleys, mountains, and rivers. Rated G. 89m. **DIR:** Stewart Raffill. **CAST:** Robert Logan, George (Buck) Flower, Heather Rattray, Mark Edward Hall. **1976**

ADVENTURES IN DINOSAUR CITY ★★ Three teens enter a dimension in which cartoon characters—dinosaurs—become real. Muppet-like creatures are very well done but can't make up for the flimsy plot and silly dialogue. Rated PG for comical violence. 88m. **DIR:** Brett Thompson. **CAST:** Omri Katz, Shawn Hoffman. **1991**

ADVENTURES IN WONDERLAND ★★★ Live-action series blending songs and lessons for older kids and preteens in continuing adventures of the magical Wonderland characters. Good-natured silliness with the usual Disney attention to production and learning. Two episodes per tape. 50m. each. **DIR:** Gary Halvorson. **CAST:** Robert Barry Fleming, Elisabeth Harnois, John Robert Hoffman, Reece Holland, Richard Kuhlman, John Lovelady, Wesley Mann, Amelia M. Queen, Harry Waters Jr. **1993**

ADVENTURES OF AN AMERICAN RABBIT, THE ★★★ In this enjoyable-for-kids feature-length cartoon, mild-mannered and sweet-natured Rob Rabbit becomes the heir to the Legacy, which magically transforms him into the star-spangled protector of all animalkind, the American Rabbit. Rated G. 85m. **DIR:** Steward Moskowitz. **1986**

ADVENTURES OF BULLWHIP GRIFFIN, THE ★★ Typical, flyweight Disney comedy, this rip-off of *Ruggles of Red Gap* is textured with unique character performers, such as Richard Haydn and Karl Malden, but fails to offer anything original. Roddy McDowall plays a proper English butler who finds himself smack-dab in the wilds of California during the Gold Rush. Okay for the kids but not much to recommend for a discriminating audience. 110m. **DIR:** James Neilson. **CAST:** Roddy McDowall, Suzanne Pleshette, Karl Malden, Harry Guardino, Richard Haydn, Hermione Baddeley, Cecil Kellaway, Bryan Russell. **1966**

ADVENTURES OF DROOPY ★★★½ Next to Tom and Jerry, Tex Avery's Droopy was MGM's most famous cartoon character. The slow-talking, sad-eyed pooch is represented here in a half-dozen animated shorts, including "Dumb-Hounded," "Wags to Riches," "The Shooting of Dan McGoo," "Droopy's Good Deed," "Dragalong Droopy," and "Deputy Droopy." The stories and gags are sometimes repetitive, but a few bits are priceless. 53m. **DIR:** Tex Avery. **1985**

ADVENTURES OF FELIX THE CAT, THE 🦃 Made for television by Paramount Pictures, these cheesy and cheap works of unimagination can't hold a candle to Pat Sullivan's original cartoons from the Twenties. 54m. **DIR:** Joseph Oriolo. **1960**

ADVENTURES OF HUCK FINN, THE (1993) ★★★★ In this high-gloss family film from Walt Disney Pictures that recalls Hollywood's golden age, adaptor-director Stephen Sommers lovingly captures Mark Twain's witty, wink-of-the-eye style. Elijah Wood is delightful as the barefoot boy who learns some important life lessons while traveling. Rated PG for brief violence. 108m. **DIR:** Stephen Sommers. **CAST:** Elijah Wood, Courtney B. Vance, Robbie Coltrane, Jason Robards Jr., Ron Perlman, Dana Ivey, Anne Heche, James Gammon, Curtis Armstrong. **1993**

ADVENTURES OF HUCKLEBERRY FINN, THE (1939) ★★★★ Fun-filled telling of the misadventures of Mark Twain's "other hero," as he outdoes the evil thieves, "King" and "Duke," becomes smitten over Mary Jane, and develops a conscience concerning the treatment of blacks. Mickey Rooney is fine in a subdued performance, and Rex Ingram is impressive as the slave, Jim. Originally released as *Huckleberry Finn*. B&W; 90m. **DIR:** Richard Thorpe. **CAST:** Mickey

Rooney, Walter Connolly, William Frawley, Rex Ingram, Minor Watson, Lynn Carver. **1939**

ADVENTURES OF HUCKLEBERRY FINN, THE (1960) ★★★★ A delightful version of the Mark Twain classic produced to commemorate the seventy-fifth anniversary of its publication. A host of colorful character players bring the famous characters to life, and Burton Lane wrote four songs that are integrated into the story. 107m. **DIR:** Michael Curtiz. **CAST:** Eddie Hodges, Archie Moore, Buster Keaton, Tony Randall, Andy Devine, Patty McCormack, Judy Canova, John Carradine, Mickey Shaughnessy, Sterling Holloway, Neville Brand, Royal Dano, Josephine Hutchinson. **1960**

ADVENTURES OF HUCKLEBERRY FINN, THE (1978) ★★ This drawn-out version of Mark Twain's classic has its moments but lacks continuous action. In it, young Huck fakes his own drowning to avoid attendance at a proper eastern school for boys. When his friend, Jim (Brock Peters), is accused of his murder, he must devise a plan to free him. 97m. **DIR:** Jack B. Hively. **CAST:** Forrest Tucker, Larry Storch, Brock Peters. **1978**

ADVENTURES OF MARK TWAIN, THE (1985) ★★★★ A superior work of Claymation provides insights into the creative genius of Samuel Clemens. Includes vignettes of Twain's "The Diary of Adam and Eve" and "The Mysterious Stranger" in which the character of Satan spouts an existential perspective on life and death. 86m. **DIR:** Will Vinton. **1985**

ADVENTURES OF MILO AND OTIS, THE ★★★★ Japanese director Masanori Hata spent four years making this splendid family film, in which a dog named Otis sets out to rescue his lifelong friend, a kitten named Milo, when the feline is carried away by a rushing river. Adults will enjoy this one as much as their children. Rated G. 76m. **DIR:** Masanori Hata. **CAST:** Dudley Moore. **1989**

ADVENTURES OF MILO IN THE PHANTOM TOLLBOOTH, THE ★★★ An assortment of cartoon talents, including director Chuck Jones and voice greats like Mel Blanc, Hans Conried, Daws Butler, and June Foray, make this unusual but entertaining film coalesce. Live-action footage combines with animation to tell the story of a young boy who enters a booth that takes him into the Land of Wisdom. Rated G. 89m. **DIR:** Chuck Jones, Abe Levitow, Dave Monahan. **CAST:** Butch Patrick. **1969**

ADVENTURES OF ROCKY AND BULLWINKLE, THE ★★★★★ Rocky the Flying Squirrel and his pal, Bullwinkle the Moose, are still as funny as ever in these witty, limited-animation cartoons from Jay Ward and company. Only in Ward's hands could limited animation be an attribute. Nicely packaged with a complete Rocky & Bullwinkle cliffhanger serial per tape, the series also features "Fractured Fairy Tales," "Aesop and Son," "Mr. Peabody," "Dudley Do-right," and other winning Ward creations. per tape (approx.) 50m. **DIR:** Jay Ward, Bill Scott. **1961**

ADVENTURES OF SINBAD, THE ★★ Slow re-telling of a tale from *The Thousand and One Nights.* Sinbad the sailor sets out to retrieve the proverbial magic lamp when it is stolen by the Old Man of the Sea. 48m. **DIR:** Richard Slapczynski. **1979**

ADVENTURES OF THE GREAT MOUSE DETECTIVE, THE ★★★★ Before going on to even more spectacular success with *The Little Mermaid,* directors John Musker and Ron Clements collaborated on this charming adaptation of Eve Titus's *Basil of Baker Street,* a children's book inspired by the stories of Conan Doyle. Featuring the voice of Vincent Price as the villain, Rattigan, and a delightful, suspenseful story, this film gave the first indication that the Walt Disney animation department had at last awoken from its long slumber. Rated G. 90m. **DIR:** John Musker, Ron Clements, Dave Michener, Bunny Mattison. **1986**

ADVENTURES OF THE WILDERNESS FAMILY ★★★½ This is a variation on the Swiss Family Robinson story. A family (oddly enough named Robinson) moves to the Rocky Mountains to escape the frustrations and congestion of life in Los Angeles. They're sick of smog, hassles, and crime. They build a cabin and brave the dangers of the wild. Rated G. 100m. **DIR:** Stewart Raffill. **CAST:** Robert Logan, Susan D. Shaw, Ham Larsen, Heather Rattray, George (Buck) Flower, Hollye Holmes. **1975**

ADVENTURES OF TOM SAWYER, THE ★★★★ One of the better screen adaptations of Mark Twain's works. Tommy Kelly is a perfect Tom Sawyer, but it's Victor Jory as the villainous Indian Joe who steals the show. Good sets and beautiful cinematography make this one work. Fine family entertainment for young and old. B&W; 93m. **DIR:** Norman Taurog. **CAST:** Tommy Kelly, Jackie Moran, Victor Jory, May Robson, Walter Brennan, Ann Gillis. **1938**

ALADDIN (1987) ★★ Update of the Aladdin tale, with Bud Spencer as the genie from the lamp, discovered this time by a boy in a junk shop in a modern city. A little too cute at times, and the humor is forced. Not rated; contains some violence. 95m. **DIR:** Bruno Corbucci. **CAST:** Bud Spencer, Luca Venantini, Janet Agren. **1987**

ALADDIN (1992) ★★★★★ The over-the-edge, manic voice work of an unleashed Robin Williams, as the genie of the lamp, supplies the laughs in this exquisite magic-carpet ride from Walt Disney Pictures. A worthy successor to *The Little Mermaid* and *Beauty and the Beast, Aladdin* is a classic feature-length cartoon blessed with excellent songs and a story that will fascinate all ages. The crowning touch is the deft illustration by Disney's animators. Rated G. 83m. **DIR:** John Musker, Ron Clements. **1992**

ALADDIN AND HIS MAGIC LAMP ★★★ Artful animation helps to make this an engrossing version of the classic story. Young Aladdin finds the magic lamp and rescues the genie, but things go amiss when a black-hearted sorcerer puts the genie's power to evil use. 70m. **DIR:** Jean Image. **1985**

ALADDIN AND HIS WONDERFUL LAMP ★★★½ This *Faerie Tale Theatre* interpretation of the classic Arabian Nights tale adds a few twists. One is the offer of the genie (James Earl Jones) to rearrange Aladdin's (Robert Carradine) face when Aladdin makes demands on him. The second surprise is the TV the genie produces to satisfy the sultan and win the princess (Valerie Bertinelli) for Aladdin. The whole family can enjoy this one. 60m. **DIR:** Tim Burton. **CAST:** Valerie Bertinelli, Robert Carradine, James Earl Jones, Leonard Nimoy. **1985**

ALADDIN AND THE MAGIC LAMP ★★★ Although pleasant on the eyes, this Rabbit Ears animated production seems tame compared to other versions of the classic Arabian Nights tale. John Hurt smoothly narrates the saga of a shiftless tailor's son who uses a magic lamp to woo and win the sultan's daughter. 30m. **DIR:** C. W. Rogers. **1994**

ALAKAZAM THE GREAT ★★½ Musical morality play for kids about the evils of pride and the abuse of power. When naïve little Alakazam the monkey is made king of the animals, he quickly develops an abusive personality that can only be set to rights through an arduous pilgrimage. Somewhat muddled, but watchable. 84m. **DIR:** James H. Nicholson, Samuel Z. Arkoff. **1961**

ALICE IN WONDERLAND (1951) ★★★½ The magic of the Walt Disney Studio animators is applied to Lewis Carroll's classic in this feature-length cartoon with mostly entertaining results. As with the book, the film is episodic and lacking the customary Disney warmth. But a few wonderful sequences—like the Mad Hatter's tea party and the appearances of the Cheshire cat—make it worth seeing. Rated G. 75m. **DIR:** Clyde Geronimi, Hamilton Luske, Wilfred Jackson. **1951**

ALICE IN WONDERLAND (1985) ★★★½ Natalie Gregory makes an endearing Alice in this charming live-action TV adaptation of the Lewis Carroll classic. Adults will enjoy some of their favorite stars as the zany characters she meets on her dreamlike journey. Steve Allen wrote the witty original songs. Followed by a continuation, 1985's *Alice through the Looking Glass*. 94m. **DIR:** Harry Harris. **CAST:** Natalie Gregory, Sheila Allen, Scott Baio, Red Buttons, Sid Caesar, Imogene Coca, Sammy Davis Jr., Sherman Hemsley, Arte Johnson, Roddy McDowall, Jayne Meadows, Robert Morley, Anthony Newley, Donald O'Connor, Martha Raye, Telly Savalas, Ringo Starr, Shelley Winters. **1985**

ALICE THROUGH THE LOOKING GLASS (1985) ★★★½ A continuation of 1985's *Alice in Wonderland* with Natalie Gregory returning to the mystical land in search of her missing parents. Again adults will enjoy many of their favorite stars as characters from the treasured fairy tale of their youth. A special nod to Lloyd Bridges as the gallant, albeit bald, White Knight. The chase scenes with the monster Jabberwocky may be too scary for very young viewers. Made for TV. 93m. **DIR:** Harry Harris. **CAST:** Natalie Gregory, Sheila Allen, Steve Allen, Ernest Borgnine, Beau Bridges, Lloyd Bridges, Red Buttons, Carol Channing, Patrick Duffy, George Gobel, Eydie Gorme, Merv Griffin, Ann Jillian, Arte Johnson, Harvey Korman, Steve Lawrence, Karl Malden, Roddy McDowall, Jayne Meadows, Donna Mills, Noriyuki "Pat" Morita, Robert Morley, Anthony Newley, Louis Nye, John Stamos, Sally Struthers, Jack Warden, Jonathan Winters. **1985**

ALICE'S ADVENTURES IN WONDERLAND ★★ This British live-action version of Lewis Carroll's classic tale is too long and boring. It is a musical that employs an endless array of silly songs, dances, and riddles. Although it sticks closely to the book, it's not as entertaining as Disney's fast-paced animated version of 1951. Rated G. 97m. **DIR:** William Sterling. **CAST:** Fiona Fullerton, Dudley Moore, Peter Sellers, Ralph Richardson, Spike Milligan. **1973**

ALL CREATURES GREAT AND SMALL ★★★½ This feature-length film picks up where the popular British television series left off, with veterinarian James Herriot (Christopher Timothy) returning to his home and practice after having served in World War II. Although he has been away for years, things quickly settle into a comfortable routine. The animal stories are lifted from Dr. Herriot's poignant, bittersweet books, with a few moments likely to require a hanky or two. 94m. **DIR:** Terence Dudley. **CAST:** Christopher Timothy, Robert Hardy, Peter Davison. **1986**

ALL DOGS GO TO HEAVEN ★★½ Somewhat disappointing feature-length cartoon from Disney defector Don Bluth. The convoluted story, about a con-artist dog who gets a glimpse of the afterlife, is more crude than charming. Burt Reynolds, Dom DeLuise, Loni Anderson, and Vic Tayback are among those who supply the voices. Rated G. 80m. **DIR:** Don Bluth. **1989**

ALL I WANT FOR CHRISTMAS ★★★ All 7-year-old Thora Birch wants for Christmas is to see her divorced mother and father get back together, so she enlists the aid of a department-store Santa. It's a charming little movie, but be forewarned: children of divorced parents could get the wrong idea and be quite disturbed by the story. Rated G. 89m. **DIR:** Robert Lieberman. **CAST:** Harley Jane Kozak, Jamey Sheridan, Lauren Bacall, Leslie Nielsen, Kevin Nealon, Thora Birch. **1991**

ALMOST ANGELS ★★½ Schmaltzy film focusing on the Vienna Boys' Choir and the problems one boy encounters when his voice changes and he can no longer sing in the choir. Rated G. 93m. **DIR:** Steve Previn. **CAST:** Peter Weck, Hans Holt, Fritz Eckhardt, Bruni Lobel, Sean Scully. **1962**

ALPHABET CONSPIRACY, THE ★★★½ This is a great Bell science film for introducing youngsters to language through live action and animation—as the Mad Hatter (Hans Conried) plots to do away with the alphabet. Animation by the great Friz Freleng. 56m. **DIR:** Robert Sinclair. **CAST:** Dr. Frank Baxter, Hans Conried. **1959**

ALVIN AND THE CHIPMUNKS: SING-ALONGS ★★★★ Alvin, Simon, and Theodore the famous singing chipmunks are back with their harried manager Dave in a new series of appealing sing-along songs easily followed by youngsters. Lots of fun. 30m. each. **DIR:** Ross Bagdasarian Jr. **1993**

AMAZING DOBERMANS ★★ Third in a series of films about do-gooder dogs pits a treasury agent (James Franciscus) against inept crooks who can't compete with the dogged determination of the Dobermans. Harmless, but hardly inspired. Rated G. 94m. **DIR:** David Chudnow, Byron Chudnow. **CAST:** James Franciscus, Barbara Eden, Fred Astaire, Jack Carter. **1976**

AMAZING MR. BLUNDEN, THE ★★★ Neat little ghost story about children from the twentieth century (Lynne Frederick, Garry Miller) helping right a wrong done 100 years previously. Laurence Naismith is the mysterious (and amazing) Mr. Blunden, a nineteenth-century lawyer who is at home in the twentieth century. The children seem a little old, but on the whole the story is delightful. Rated PG. 100m. **DIR:** Lionel Jeffries. **CAST:** Laurence Naismith, Lynne Frederick, Garry Miller, Dorothy Alison, Diana Dors. **1972**

AMERICAN CHRISTMAS CAROL, AN ★★ Lackluster made-for-television rendering of Charles Dickens's Christmas favorite, set in 1930s New England. Scrooge is played by Henry Winkler with some panache. 100m. **DIR:** Eric Till. **CAST:** Henry Winkler, David Wayne, Dorian Harewood, Chris Wiggins. **1979**

AMERICAN TAIL, AN ★★★ An immigrant mouse becomes separated from his family while voyaging to the United States. The execution and lavish animation make up for the trite and predictable story. Film picks up steam with the introduction of Dom DeLuise, as a vegetarian cat. Rated G. 82m. **DIR:** Don Bluth. **CAST:** Dom DeLuise, Phillip Glasser, Madeline Kahn, Nehemiah Persoff, Christopher Plummer (voices). **1986**

AMERICAN TAIL, AN: FIEVEL GOES WEST ★★★½ Fievel Mousekewitz and his family leave behind the crowded city at the urgings of a conniving cat, Cat R. Waul (voiced by John Cleese). An improvement on the first film, this sequel is a straight-ahead, comedy-propelled ode to the Old West. James Stewart is wonderful as the voice of an over-the-hill law dog, and Dom DeLuise returns for more laughs as the wild and crazy Tiger. Rated G. 85m. **DIR:** Phil Nibbelink, Simon Wells. **1991**

AMY ★★★½ Disney warmth runs though this sensitive story. Jenny Agutter is Amy, a young woman who leaves her domineering husband after the death of their deaf son. She decides to teach at a school for the deaf. A film for the whole family. Rated G. 100m. **DIR:** Vincent McEveety. **CAST:** Jenny Agutter, Barry Newman, Kathleen Nolan, Chris Robinson, Margaret O'Brien, Nanette Fabray. **1981**

ANIMALYMPICS ★★★ Featuring the voices of Billy Crystal, Gilda Radner, and Harry Shearer, this feature brings the Olympics to life with animals from around the world. Though the production seems somewhat overlong, there are bright spots: a news commentator called Ba Ba Wawa and a pole-vaulting hippo. 78m. **DIR:** Steven Lisberger. **1980**

ANIMATION LEGEND WINDSOR MCKAY ★★★★★ Windsor McKay didn't invent movie cartoons, but he was the first with the patience to make them for a general audience. All of his surviving works are collected on this tape, and they are amazingly clever and funny. Best of all is Gertie the dinosaur, an utterly beguiling character even though only a few minutes of her still exist. Silent. B&W/color; 100m. **DIR:** Windsor McKay. **1911–1921**

ANNE OF GREEN GABLES (1934) ★★★ L. M. Montgomery's popular juvenile book about a spunky young orphan's influence on a conservative household receives its first sound treatment in this sentimental but entertaining picture. A good version of the classic and fine family entertainment. B&W; 80m. **DIR:** George Nicholls Jr. **CAST:** Anne Shirley, Tom Brown, O. P. Heggie, Helen Westley, Sara Haden, Charley Grapewin. **1934**

ANNIE OAKLEY (1985) ★★★ This first episode of Shelley Duvall's new series, *Tall Tales and Legends*, deals with true-life character Annie Oakley. Jamie Lee Curtis convincingly plays the sharp-shooting Annie with Brian Dennehy as her Wild West show boss, Buffalo Bill. 52m. **DIR:** Michael Lindsay-Hogg.

CAST: Jamie Lee Curtis, Brian Dennehy, Cliff De Young, Nick Ramus, Joyce Van Patten. **1985**

ANNIE OAKLEY (1992) ★★★ Part of the *American Heroes and Legends* collection, *Annie Oakley* utilizes limited animation and illustrations by Fred Warter, and rousing narration by Keith Carradine, to tell the story of the young woman who became a star in Buffalo Bill's Wild West Show. There's a great musical score by Los Lobos. Not rated. 30m. **DIR:** John McCally. **CAST:** Keith Carradine. **1992**

ANT AND THE AARDVARK, THE ★★★ Relying on dialogue and characterizations that are obviously aimed at adults, this laugh-filled cartoon series is strongly reminiscent of the Warner Bros. Road Runner cartoons. Here, a hungry aardvark is continually confounded by an inventive red ant. Five episodes are offered on this tape. 32m. **DIR:** Friz Freleng, George Gordon, Gerry Chiniqy. **1969**

ANY FRIEND OF NICHOLAS NICKLEBY IS A FRIEND OF MINE ★★★½ A charming period piece by author Ray Bradbury. Fred Gwynne shines as a mysterious stranger who comes to a small Illinois town where he takes an imaginative schoolboy under his wing. This is a poignant and humorous drama comparable to PBS's award-winning *Anne of Green Gables*. 55m. **DIR:** Ralph Rosenblum. **CAST:** Fred Gwynne. **1981**

APPLE DUMPLING GANG, THE ★★ A gambler (Bill Bixby) inherits three children who find a huge gold nugget in 1870. Tim Conway and Don Knotts trip and foul up as left-footed bad guys. Good, clean, unoriginal, predictable fare from Disney. The kids will love it. Rated G. 100m. **DIR:** Norman Tokar. **CAST:** Bill Bixby, Tim Conway, Don Knotts, Susan Clark, David Wayne, Slim Pickens, Harry Morgan. **1975**

APPLE DUMPLING GANG RIDES AGAIN, THE ★★ In this sequel to the 1975 original, Tim Conway and Don Knotts again play bumbling, inept outlaws in the Old West. Rated G. 88m. **DIR:** Vincent McEveety. **CAST:** Tim Conway, Don Knotts, Harry Morgan, Jack Elam, Kenneth Mars, Ruth Buzzi, Robert Pine. **1979**

ARCHER'S ADVENTURE ★★★ The two-hour running time may be a bit long for young children, but otherwise this adventure makes for good family viewing. In nineteenth-century Australia, a young man crosses the country with an untried horse that he wants to enter in a race. *Archer's Adventure* has plenty of engaging characters and incidents. Unrated. 120m. **DIR:** Denny Lawrence. **CAST:** Brett Climo, Robert Coleby, Tony Barry. **1985**

AROUND THE WORLD IN 80 DAYS (1974) ★★★ A turn-of-the-century English gentleman, Phileas Fogg, undertakes a wager to go around the globe in eighty days despite endless obstacles. This is well paced for youngsters, but includes dialogue that even adults will find amusing. Made for television. 60m. **DIR:** Arthur Rankin Jr., Jules Bass. **1974**

ASTERIX: THE GAUL (SERIES) ★★★ Walt Disney Productions picked up this series of history-spoofing cartoons from a talented French cartoon maker for release on videocassette. Asterix, a mysteriously powerful Gallic warrior, tromps through a variety of notable periods in history, telling the tales from a whimsical, action-filled perspective. 67m. **DIR:** René Goscinny. **1967**

BABAR: THE MOVIE ★★ This adaptation of the beloved *Babar* books by Jean and Laurent de Brunhoff is hampered by a formulaic story and uninspired animation. Produced by Nelvana Studios, which also makes the Care Bears movies, it is passable kiddie fare. Rated G. 75m. **DIR:** Alan Bunce. **1989**

BABES IN TOYLAND (1961) ★★ A disappointing Disney version of the Victor Herbert operetta. In Mother Goose Land, Barnaby (Ray Bolger) kidnaps Tom the Piper's Son (Tommy Sands) in order to marry Mary (Annette Funicello). The Toymaker (Ed Wynn) and his assistant (Tommy Kirk) eventually provide the means for Tom to save the day. Despite a good Disney cast, this film never gels. Rated G. 105m. **DIR:** Jack Donohue. **CAST:** Ray Bolger, Tommy Sands, Ed Wynn, Annette Funicello, Tommy Kirk. **1961**

BABES IN TOYLAND (1986) ★★ Disappointing film about an adultlike child who must save the mythical town of Toyland by believing in the magic of toys. Richard Mulligan creates a wonderful evil Barnaby Barnacle. Rated G. 96m. **DIR:** Clive Donner. **CAST:** Drew Barrymore, Noriyuki "Pat" Morita, Richard Mulligan, Eileen Brennan, Keanu Reeves, Jill Schoelen. **1986**

BABY TAKE A BOW ★★½ In Shirley Temple's first starring vehicle, she helps her dad, who's accused of stealing a valuable necklace. Shirley must outthink the investigators in order to clear Dad's name. She pouts a lot but makes up for it with her charming rendition of "On Accounta' I Love You." B&W; 76m. **DIR:** Harry Lachman. **CAST:** Shirley Temple, James Dunn, Claire Trevor. **1934**

BACH AND BROCCOLI ★★ Slow-moving family-fare film made in Quebec. A 12-year-old girl is forced to live with her bachelor uncle. The two establish an uneasy relationship. Not rated, but equivalent to G. 96m. **DIR:** André Melançon. **CAST:** Andrée Pelletier. **1986**

BACK HOME ★★★½ After spending the war years in the safety of the United States, an English girl returns to her family in 1945. Unfortunately, she has become too Americanized and can't fit in. Hayley Mills plays her mother, a woman too preoccupied with her husband's homecoming to notice her daughter's heartache. A Disney Channel film, this has high production values. Unrated; contains mature themes. 103m. **DIR:** Piers Haggard. **CAST:** Hayley Mills, Hayley Carr, Jean Anderson, Rupert Frazer, Brenda Bruce. **1989**

BACK TO THE FOREST ★★ Peter (a fairy) and his animal friends must save their home, Placid Forest, when greedy local villagers decide to level the forest for financial gain. This Japanese rendition of Scandinavian author Boy Lornsen's *Jakobus Nimmersatt* has lost something in the translation. 75m. **DIR:** Yoshio Koruda. **1989**

BAKER'S HAWK ★★★★ No-nonsense Westerner Clint Walker helps the local law get a group of vigilantes under control, while his son embarks on an adventure of his own involving a hawk and a mysterious hermit. An exceptional family film. Rated G. 98m. **DIR:** Lyman Dayton. **CAST:** Clint Walker, Burl Ives, Diane Baker, Lee Montgomery, Alan Young. **1976**

BALLAD OF PAUL BUNYAN, THE ★★ Typical Rankin-Bass fare, featuring the legendary American giant. Our good-humored hero is pitted against a behemoth lumbercamp boss who picks on the "little guys." 30m. **DIR:** Arthur Rankin Jr., Jules Bass. **1972**

BAMBI ★★★★★ This lush adaptation of Felix Salten's beloved story represents the crowning achievement of Walt Disney's animation studio. Never again would backgrounds be delineated with such realistic detail, with animation so precise that it resembled live photography. The screenplay, too, has a bit more bite than the average Disney yarn, with equal helpings of comedy and tragedy fueling a confrontation between forest animals and that most horrific of two-legged interlopers: man. 69m. **DIR:** David Hand. **1942**

BAMBI VS. GODZILLA ★★½ Unusual compilation of animated shorts featuring Betty Boop in "Crazy Town" and "You Auto Lay an Egg," and the remarkable "Frogland" by Starewitch, made in the early 1920s. You'll also like the Fleischer brothers' cartoon classics, "Cobweb Hotel" and "Small Fry," as well as Marv Newland's cult classic "Bambi vs. Godzilla." Not rated. B&W; 40m. **DIR:** Max Fleischer, Dave Fleischer, Starewitch, Marv Newland. **1989**

BAREFOOT EXECUTIVE, THE ★★ Mild Disney comedy about an individual (Kurt Russell) who finds a chimpanzee that can select top television shows. Rated G. 92m. **DIR:** Robert Butler. **CAST:** Kurt Russell, Joe Flynn, Harry Morgan, Wally Cox, Heather North, Alan Hewitt, John Ritter. **1971**

BARNEY BEAR CARTOON FESTIVAL ★★½ This collection of Barney Bear cartoons is interesting because the main character is different in three of the four features. Nevertheless, he never fails to come out a loser. These cartoons find him coping with everything from a leaky roof to the pursuit of a wild Mexican jumping bean. 32m. **DIR:** Rudolf Ising, Michael Lah, Preston Blair, Hugh Harman. **1939–1948**

BARON MUNCHAUSEN ★★★ The adventures of the German folk hero, noted for the tallest tales ever told, are recounted here in a blend of live-action and inventive animation. Unfortunately, the story itself is rather boring, so kids are likely to get antsy. Also known as *The Fabulous Baron Munchausen*. In German with English subtitles. 110m. **DIR:** Karel Zeman. **CAST:** Milos Kopecky, Hana Brejchova. **1961**

BATMAN (1966) ★★★ Holy success story! The caped crusader and his youthful sidekick jump from their popular mid-1960s television series into a full-length feature film. Adam West and Burt Ward keep quip in cheek as they battle the Fearsome Foursome: the Riddler (Frank Gorshin), the Penguin (Burgess Meredith), the Catwoman (Lee Meriwether), and the Joker (Cesar Romero). A lot of fun. 105m. **DIR:** Leslie Martinson. **CAST:** Adam West, Burt Ward, Frank Gorshin, Burgess Meredith, Lee Meriwether, Cesar Romero. **1966**

BATMAN: MASK OF THE PHANTASM ★★★½ The caped crusader's slick animated series made an engaging feature-length debut with all of its *film noir* sensibilities intact. Definitely too story heavy for youngsters, this moody thriller—based strongly on Frank Miller's Dark Knight comics—finds Batman forced to defend a reputation tarnished by both the Joker (wonderfully voiced by Mark Hamill) and the title villain. Rated PG. 76m. **DIR:** Eric Radomski, Bruce W. Timm. **1993**

BATTERIES NOT INCLUDED ★★★ Pleasant fantasy feature about tenement dwellers who are terrorized by thugs hired by a land developer. All seems lost until a group of tiny aliens comes to their aid. Often the movie is simply too derivative and predictable. That said, the younger set will love it. Rated PG. 106m. **DIR:** Matthew Robbins. **CAST:** Hume Cronyn, Jessica Tandy, Frank McRae, Elizabeth Peña. **1987**

BE MY VALENTINE, CHARLIE BROWN ★★★ Writer Charles Schulz goes overboard with his cruelty toward Charlie Brown in this holiday saga, which finds our hero dragging a suitcase to school in anticipation of all the cards he'll receive during a classwide valentine exchange. Linus, meanwhile, empties his piggy bank to purchase an elaborate chocolate heart for his favorite teacher, Miss Othmar. 25m. **DIR:** Phil Roman. **1975**

BEANY AND CECIL ★★★★ Baby boomers will love the references to 1960s television shows and events in this classic series of cartoons on tape, though today's kids may find it somewhat confusing. Nevertheless, the adventures of Beany and Cecil offer enough fun-filled entertainment for viewers of all ages to enjoy. Each of the ten volumes in this series offers six pun-filled adventures. 60m. **DIR:** Bob Clampett. **1984**

BEAR, THE ★★★★★ *The Bear* is a wildlife adventure film that transcends its genre. It's the *Gone with the Wind* of animal movies. Some scenes might be a little frightening for the younger set. Rated PG for violence. 93m. **DIR:** Jean-Jacques Annaud. **CAST:** Jack Wallace, Tcheky Karyo. **1989**

BEAR WHO SLEPT THROUGH CHRISTMAS, THE ★★½ Tommy Smothers is the voice of Ted E. Bear, who, defying the mandate of his employer at the honey factory, skips winter hibernation to find out what all the hubbub behind Christmas is. Other voices you'll recognize include those of Barbara Feldon and Arte Johnson. 60m. **DIR:** Hawley Pratt, Gerry Chiniqy. **1983**

BEAUTY AND THE BEAST (1983) ★★★★ A merchant's daughter takes her father's place as the prisoner of a melancholy beast and finds that love can change all things. Klaus Kinski is marvelous as the Beast and Susan Sarandon a fine Beauty in this *Faerie Tale Theatre* production. 52m. **DIR:** Roger Vadim. **CAST:** Klaus Kinski, Susan Sarandon. **1983**

BEAUTY AND THE BEAST (1991) ★★★★★ A classic feature-length cartoon from Walt Disney Pictures, this adaptation of the classic fairy tale is the animated equivalent of the stage production of *Les Miserables*; a spectacular piece of musical theater complete with heartwarming moments, uproarious comedy, even suspense. Oscars went to Alan Menken for his score and to Menken and Howard Ashman for the title song. Rated G. 85m. **DIR:** Gary Trousdale, Kirk Wise. **1991**

BEDKNOBS AND BROOMSTICKS ★★★½ Angela Lansbury is a witch who uses her powers to aid the Allies against the Nazis during World War II. She transports two children to faraway and strange locales during which they meet and play soccer with talking animals, among other things. This Disney film is an effective combination of special effects, animation, and live action. Rated G. 117m. **DIR:** Robert Stevenson. **CAST:** Angela Lansbury, David Tomlinson, Roddy McDowall. **1971**

BEETHOVEN (1992) ★★★ When an adopted puppy grows up to be a 185-pound Saint Bernard, businessman Charles Grodin wishes he'd never allowed his family to take the dog in. Good family fun. Rated PG for doggy messes. 87m. **DIR:** Brian Levant. **CAST:** Charles Grodin, Bonnie Hunt, Dean Jones, Stanley Tucci, David Duchovny. **1992**

BEETHOVEN LIVES UPSTAIRS ★★½ For kids, this film is a fair introduction to the composer and his music. Unfortunately, they meet the temperamental man through the eyes of a young boy. Though the famous musician has a tender relationship with the boy, we see that Beethoven is prone to frequent tantrums. The message younger viewers may get is that violent behavior can be tolerated and even admired. 52m. **DIR:** David Devine. **CAST:** Neil Munro, Illya Woloshyn, Fiona Reid, Paul Soles. **1992**

BEETHOVEN'S 2ND ★★★ Beethoven—a massive Saint Bernard—starts a family of his own in this lightweight sequel with more charm and less slobber than the original. Beethoven's mate is owned by a modern Cruella de Vil who is holding the canine as a trump card in her divorce case—and do she and her new boyfriend ever hate dogs! Charles Grodin also returns as an air-freshener marketer who is up to his armpits in financial and domestic problems. Rated PG. 86m. **DIR:** Rod Daniel. **CAST:** Charles Grodin, Bonnie Hunt, Nicole Tom, Christopher Castille, Sarah Rose Carr, Debi Mazar, Christopher Penn, Kevin Dunn. **1993**

BELSTONE FOX, THE ★★ An orphaned fox cub is raised in captivity and cleverly eludes both hounds and hunters. The film is worth watching for the animal photography. Unrated, but contains some violence to animals. 103m. **DIR:** James Hill. **CAST:** Eric Porter, Jeremy Kemp, Bill Travers, Rachel Roberts. **1973**

BEN AND ME ★★★★ Walt Disney's entire animation team contributed to the luxurious look of this short, which follows the adventures of Amos the Mouse (voiced by Sterling Holloway), companion and unknown confidant to Benjamin Franklin. Apparently Amos helped ol' Ben come up with his most famous ideas! 25m. **DIR:** Hamilton Luske. **1954**

BENIKER GANG, THE ★★½ Pleasant family film has Andrew McCarthy as Arthur Beniker, 18-year-old orphanage inmate who leads an "orphanage break" of four other incorrigibles. Not too cutesy, and the story even makes some sense. Rated G; suitable for the entire family. 87m. **DIR:** Ken Kwapis. **CAST:** Andrew McCarthy, Jennie Dundas, Charles Fields, Jeff Alan-Lee, Danny Pintauro. **1985**

BENJI ★★★★ *Benji* parallels *Lassie* and *Rin Tin Tin* by intuitively doing the right thing at the right time. In this film, a dog saves two children who get kidnapped. Unlike Lassie or Rin Tin Tin, Benji is a small, unassuming mutt, which makes him all the more endearing. Rated G. 86m. **DIR:** Joe Camp. **CAST:** Peter Breck, Deborah Walley, Edgar Buchanan, Frances Bavier, Patsy Garrett. **1974**

BENJI THE HUNTED ★★★ Most kids will love this adventure featuring everyone's favorite sweet-faced mutt slogging his poor little lost way through the wilderness of the Pacific Northwest to civilization. Rated G. 90m. **DIR:** Joe Camp. **CAST:** Benji. **1987**

BEST CHRISTMAS PAGEANT EVER, THE ★★★ An engaging television movie about a group of grade-school misfits who come of age during preparation for a school Christmas play. Well-acted but already dated. 80m. **DIR:** George Schaefer. **CAST:** Dennis Weaver, Loretta Swit, Karen Grassle. **1986**

BEST OF BUGS BUNNY AND FRIENDS, THE ★★★★ Some of the best pre-1947 Warner Bros. cartoons have been collected for this long overdue package. Highlights include Bob Clampett's "What's Cookin' Doc?" (in which Bugs Bunny campaigns shamelessly for an Oscar) and Friz Freleng's Oscar-winning "Tweetie Pie," as well as Chuck Jones's touching and clever "Bedtime for Sniffles." A treasure for fans of classic cartoons. For all ages. 53m. **DIR:** Tex Avery, Bob Clampett, Arthur Davis, Friz Freleng, Chuck Jones. **1986**

BEST OF LITTLE LULU ★★★ This is a fine collection of six of the original Famous Studios Lulu cartoons. Particularly delightful is "Lulu Gets the Birdie," in which our heroine drives a photographer nuts as she tries to get her picture taken. 55m. **DIR:** Seymour Kneitel, Isadore Sparber. **1943**

BEST OF WARNER BROTHERS, VOL. 1 ★★★★ A selection of eight exceptional late 1930s/early 1940s Warner Brothers cartoons from the gang that gave us Bugs Bunny and Daffy Duck. Included are Bugs in "Fresh Hare," Daffy and Elmer Fudd in "To Duck Or Not To Duck," and "An Itch in Time," the memorable classic featuring flea versus dog to the tune of "Food Around the Corner." B&W/color; 60m. **DIR:** Bob Clampett, Friz Freleng, Norman McCabe, Tex Avery, Chuck Jones. **1937–1943**

BEST OF WARNER BROTHERS, VOL. 2 ★★★★ Headed by Chuck Jones's trail-breaking send-up of mustache-villained melodramas, "The Dover Boys," this carefully selected Warner Brothers cartoon collection is a delight that all ages will enjoy. Included in the lineup are "The Haunted Mouse," "Daffy and the Dinosaur," "Bars and Stripes Forever," "Yankee Doodle Daffy," and "Hamateur Night." B&W/color; 55m. **DIR:** Chuck Jones, Tex Avery, Ben Hardaway, Cal Dalton, Friz Freleng. **1939–1943**

BETTY BOOP—A SPECIAL COLLECTOR'S EDITION ★★★★ The zany, often bizarre Boop cartoons of the 1930s, with lecherous villains drooling over wide-eyed, luscious-legged, skimpily clad Betty, are best suited for older children or adults. The special collector's edition offers a winning array of the best adventures featuring the "oop poop a doop" girl, including "Betty Boop's Rise to Fame" with special live action provided by "Uncle" Max Fleischer. Other segments include the talents of Cab Calloway and Louis Armstrong. 90m. **DIR:** Dave Fleischer. **1930**

BIG RED ★★★ This pleasant family film drawn from the beloved children's book of the same title features Walter Pidgeon as the owner of a sleek Irish setter named Big Red, which spends its formative years with young Gilles Payant. 89m. **DIR:** Norman Tokar. **CAST:** Walter Pidgeon, Gilles Payant, Emile Genest, Janette Bertrand. **1962**

BILL AND COO ★★★½ Cute film acted entirely by a wide variety of trained birds. The gimmick works much better than it sounds, and even adults will enjoy watching these feathered thespians go through their paces. 61m. **DIR:** Dean Riesner. **1947**

BILLIE ★★½ Tomboyish Patty Duke upsets everyone when she joins a boys' track team. Lightweight story with a good turn by Billy DeWolfe as the town mayor. Unrated. 87m. **DIR:** Don Weis. **CAST:** Patty Duke, Jim Backus, Warren Berlinger, Jane Greer, Billy DeWolfe, Dick Sargent, Ted Bessell. **1965**

BILLION DOLLAR HOBO, THE ★★ This film has Tim Conway playing his familiar down-and-out bumpkin role, but the rest of the cast is wasted. The slow pace is a further drawback. Rated G for family viewing. 96m. **DIR:** Stuart E. McGowan. **CAST:** Tim Conway, Will Geer. **1978**

BIRCH INTERVAL, THE ★★★ Engaging, poignant 11-year-old Susan McClung learns lessons of life and love while living with relatives in Amish Pennsylvania. An excellent cast makes this sadly neglected film a memorable viewing experience. 104m. **DIR:** Delbert Mann. **CAST:** Eddie Albert, Rip Torn, Susan McClung, Ann Wedgeworth, Anne Revere. **1976**

BLACK ARROW (1984) ★★★½ In this enjoyable Disney adventure film, Sir Daniel Brackley (Oliver Reed), a corrupt and wealthy landowner, is robbed by the Black Arrow, an outlaw. He then conceives of a plan to marry his ward, Joanna (Georgia Slowe), and send his nephew (Benedict Taylor) to his death. The tide turns when his nephew and the Black Arrow combine forces to rescue Joanna. 93m. **DIR:** John Hough. **CAST:** Oliver Reed, Georgia Slowe, Benedict Taylor, Fernando Rey, Donald Pleasence. **1984**

BLACK BEAUTY (1946) ★★★ Based on Anna Sewell's novel that is about a little girl's determined effort to find her missing black colt. Though pedestrian at times, the treatment is still effective enough to hold interest and bring a tear or two. B&W; 74m. **DIR:** Max Nosseck. **CAST:** Mona Freeman, Richard Denning, Evelyn Ankers, J. M. Kerrigan, Terry Kilburn. **1946**

BLACK BEAUTY (1971) ★★ One of the world's most-loved children's books, *Black Beauty* has never been translated adequately to the screen. This version is passable at best. Kids who've read the book may want to see the movie, though this movie won't make anyone want to read the book. Great Britain/Germany/Spain. 106m. **DIR:** James Hill. **CAST:** Mark Lester, Walter Slezak, Patrick Mower. **1971**

BLACK PLANET, THE 🦃 Two warring factions of the mythical planet Terra Verte consider destroying each other with doomsday weapons. 78m. **DIR:** Paul Williams. **1984**

BLACK STALLION, THE ★★★★★ Before taking our breath away with the superb *Never Cry Wolf*, director Carroll Ballard made an impressive directorial debut with this gorgeous screen version of the well-known children's story. Kelly Reno plays the young boy stranded on a deserted island with "The Black," a wild, but very intelligent, horse who comes to be his best friend. It's a treat the whole family can enjoy. Rated G. 118m. **DIR:** Carroll Ballard. **CAST:** Kelly Reno, Mickey Rooney, Teri Garr, Hoyt Axton, Clarence Muse. **1979**

BLACK STALLION RETURNS, THE ★★★★ A sequel to the 1979 film *The Black Stallion*, this is first-rate fare for the young and the young at heart. The story, based on the novel by Walter Farley, picks up where the first film left off. Alec Ramsey (Kelly Reno) is a little older and a little taller, but he still loves his horse, "The Black." And this time, Alec must journey halfway around the world to find the stallion, which has been stolen by an Arab chieftain. Rated PG for slight violence. 93m. **DIR:** Robert Dalva. **CAST:** Kelly Reno, Vincent Spano, Teri Garr, Allen Garfield, Woody Strode. **1983**

BLACKBEARD'S GHOST ★★★ This fun Disney comedy has Peter Ustinov playing a ghost who must prevent his ancestors' home from becoming a gambling casino. 107m. **DIR:** Robert Stevenson. **CAST:** Peter Ustinov, Dean Jones, Suzanne Pleshette, Elsa Lanchester. **1968**

BLANK CHECK ★★★½ When 11-year-old Brian Bonsall's bike is run over by mobster Miguel Ferrer, the boy ends up with the little item of the title. Our young hero uses it for $1 million worth of fun, only to find that money can't buy happiness. Not a great flick, but kids will definitely enjoy Bonsall's adventures and the state-of-the-art toys. Rated PG for light violence. 93m. **DIR:** Rupert Wainwright. **CAST:** Brian Bonsall, Karen Duffy, James Rebhorn, Jayne Atkinson, Michael Faustino, Chris Demetral, Miguel Ferrer, Rick Ducommun, Tone Loc, Michael Lerner, Debbie Allen, Lu Leonard. **1994**

BLUE BIRD, THE ★★½ Following on the success of *The Wizard of Oz*, this extravagant fantasy features Shirley Temple as a spoiled brat who seeks true happiness by leaving her loving parents' home. Film is remarkable for the star's characterization of a spiteful little crab, which contrasts markedly with her usual sunny roles. 88m. **DIR:** Walter Lang. **CAST:** Shirley Temple, Spring Byington, Nigel Bruce. **1940**

BLUE FIN ★★ The son of a commercial fisherman finds that growing up is hard to do, especially when he has to do so before he's ready. On a fishing trip with his father, the boy is caught in a storm, and must act responsibly for the first time in his life. 93m. **DIR:** Carl Schultz. **CAST:** Hardy Krüger, Greg Rowe, Liddy Clark, Hugh Keays-Byrne. **1977**

BLUE FIRE LADY ★★½ The story of racetracks and horse racing, the trust and love between an animal and a person are well handled in this family film. It chronicles the story of Jenny (Cathryn Harrison) and her love for horses, which endures despite her father's disapproval. 96m. **DIR:** Ross Dimsey. **CAST:** Catherine Harrison, Mark Holden, Peter Cummins. **1983**

BLUE YONDER, THE ★★★½ Heartfelt tale of a boy (Huckleberry Fox) who goes back in time via a time machine to warn his late grandfather (Peter Coyote) of his unsuccessful attempt at a nonstop transatlantic flight. Good performances keep the creaky plot airborne. 89m. **DIR:** Mark Rosman. **CAST:** Peter Coyote, Huckleberry Fox, Art Carney, Dennis Lipscomb, Joe Flood, Mittie Smith, Frank Simons. **1985**

BOATNIKS, THE ★★½ Disney comedy in which Robert Morse plays a heroic Coast Guard officer who manages a romantic relationship with Stephanie Powers while pursuing bumbling thieves (Phil Silvers, Norman Fell, and Mickey Shaughnessy). Rated G. 99m. **DIR:** Norman Tokar. **CAST:** Stefanie Powers, Phil Silvers, Norman Fell, Robert Morse, Mickey Shaughnessy. **1970**

BOB THE QUAIL ★★ This collection of three episodes featuring Bob the Quail and his woodland friends offers some lessons on the lives of wild creatures. Storytelling goes in-depth here to explain the way these birds mate, raise their young, and relate to other animals in the food chain. A subsequent video, *Chatterer the Squirrel*, provides the same information from a squirrel's perspective. 60m. **DIR:** Not Credited. **1978**

BON VOYAGE! ★★★½ One of Walt Disney's few adult-oriented comedies, this film combines elements of sophisticated comedy with dialogue and props from old-fashioned slapstick yarns. All the problems that could possibly befall this family on an overseas vacation is captured in pie-in-the-face detail. 130m. **DIR:** James Neilson. **CAST:** Fred MacMurray, Jane Wyman, Michael Callan, Tommy Kirk, Kevin Corcoran, Deborah Walley. **1962**

BON VOYAGE, CHARLIE BROWN ★★★ An animated film starring the "Peanuts" gang, this is well suited for viewing by the younger generation. It's basically a "Peanuts" guide to world travel. Rated G. 75m. **DIR:** Bill Melendez. **1980**

BONGO ★★ Originally part of a Disney feature-length blend of live action and animation called *Fun and Fancy Free,* this cartoon short follows a little circus bear who flees the big top for the wonders of the open woods. The flimsy story is marred by pathetic songs and endless countryside vistas, but note an early appearance by the chipmunks who would shortly become Chip 'n' Dale. 36m. **DIR:** Jack Kinney, Bill Roberts, Hamilton Luske. **1947**

BORN FREE ★★★★★ An established family classic, this is the tale of Elsa the lioness and her relationship with an African game warden and his wife. 96m. **DIR:** James Hill. **CAST:** Virginia McKenna, Bill Travers, Geoffrey Keen, Peter Lukoye. **1966**

BORROWERS, THE ★★★ Quaint BBC miniseries sticks to Mary Norton's books, but lacks the visual flair necessary to suspend disbelief. The title characters are a little family who live under the floorboards of an English home and borrow items to make their living space more comfortable. When they're discovered, they flee outdoors where every step is a new adventure. The cast rises to the occasion, but poor special effects help expose the illusion. Not rated. 199m. **DIR:** John Henderson. **CAST:** Ian Holm, Penelope Wilton, Rebecca Callard, Sian Phillips. **1993**

BOY GOD, THE 🦃 Rocco, the boy god and his fights against the forces of the netherworld. Poorly dubbed and not rated, but contains some violence. 100m. **DIR:** J. Erastheo Navda. **CAST:** Niño Muhlach. **1986**

BOY NAMED CHARLIE BROWN, A ★★★★ Charles Schulz's "Peanuts" gang jumps to the big screen in this delightful, wistful tale of Charlie Brown's shot at fame in a national spelling bee. Rated G. 85m. **DIR:** Bill Melendez. **1969**

BOY TAKES GIRL ★★ A young girl learns to adapt when her parents leave her at a farming cooperative one summer. Some adult themes and more romance than may be acceptable for younger viewers, but this comedy-drama is passable for older kids. 93m. **DIR:** Michal Bat-Adam. **CAST:** Gabi Eldor, Hillel Neeman, Dina Limon. **1983**

BOY WHO LEFT HOME TO FIND OUT ABOUT THE SHIVERS, THE ★★★½ In this *Faerie Tale Theatre* production narrated by Vincent Price, a boy (Peter MacNicol) goes off to a Transylvanian castle (operated by Christopher Lee, no less) to find out about fear. Good moments overcome a rather protracted midsection. Not for young children. 54m. **DIR:** Graeme Clifford. **CAST:** Peter MacNicol, Dana Hill, Christopher Lee, David Warner, Frank Zappa, Jeff Corey. **1985**

BRAVE LITTLE TOASTER, THE ★★★★ This delightful animated feature, based on a charming children's story by sci-fi author Thomas M. Disch, concerns a quintet of electrical appliances that journey to the big city in the hopes of finding the human master who abandoned them in a country summer cottage. Suitable for family viewing. 92m. **DIR:** Jerry Rees. **1987**

BRAVE ONE, THE ★★★★ Above-average family film about a Mexican boy whose pet bull is sold. Knowing that its fate is to die in the bullfighting ring, the boy tracks his pet to Mexico City, where he does everything he can to save it. Winner of an Academy Award for best original story, which went unclaimed for almost twenty years because screenwriter "Robert Rich" was really the blacklisted Dalton Trumbo. 102m. **DIR:** Irving Rapper. **CAST:** Michel Ray, Rodolfo Hoyos, Elsa Cardenas, Joi Lansing. **1956**

BRER RABBIT AND THE WONDERFUL TAR BABY ★★★ Taj Mahal's background score and Danny Glover's energetic narration partially save this Rabbit Ears animated production, but they cannot overcome Henrik Drescher's uninspired artwork. The familiar Uncle Remus tale received far better service years ago in Disney's *Song of the South*. 30m. **DIR:** Tim Raglin. **1990**

BRIGHT EYES ★★★½ Delicious melodrama finds Shirley Temple living in a fine mansion as the maid's daughter. After her mom's untimely death, three people vie for her adoption rights. Curly Shirley is irresistible as the ever-cheerful little Bright Eyes. 83m. **DIR:** David Butler. **CAST:** Shirley Temple, James Dunn, Jane Withers, Judith Allen. **1934**

BRIGHTY OF THE GRAND CANYON ★★ Acceptable little film for the family. Brighty is a desert mule who teams up with Dick Foran, a prospector who has discovered a large vein of gold in the Grand Canyon. The photography is quite good. 89m. **DIR:** Norman Foster. **CAST:** Joseph Cotten, Dick Foran, Karl Swensen, Pat Conway. **1967**

BROTHERS LIONHEART, THE ★★½ This slow-moving children's fantasy filmed in Sweden, Denmark, and Finland features two brothers who are reunited after death in a medieval world where they fight dragons and villains in an attempt to free their war leader, Ulva, who will rid the country of tyrants. If you don't fall asleep within the first forty-five minutes, you will be rewarded with a fine fairy tale. Rated G. 108m. **DIR:** Olle Hellbron. **CAST:** Staffan Gotestam, Lars Soderdahl, Allan Edwall. **1977**

BUGS AND DAFFY: THE WARTIME CARTOONS ★★★★★ This is a tape you'll want to own. Due to their war-theme content and blatant propaganda, most of these eleven cartoons haven't been seen in decades. The classic standouts include Chuck Jones's "Super Rabbit" and Bob Clampett's "Drafty Daffy" (with our daft hero attempting to escape the draft board) and "Falling Hare" (featuring Bugs's frantic battle with an airplane gremlin). Chaotic pacing and inspired animation make these must-see cartoons. And you truly haven't lived until you've seen how a certain Herr Hitler fares in these shorts.... 120m. **DIR:** Bob Clampett, Friz Freleng, Chuck Jones, Frank Tashlin. **1943–1945**

BUGS AND DAFFY'S CARNIVAL OF THE ANIMALS ★★★ The Saint-Saëns is given an animated twist by director Chuck Jones, who uses Bugs Bunny and Daffy Duck to introduce each of the individual themes. For once, the limited animation found in these late-entry specials is appropriate; the simpler style blends nicely with the music and generates fond memories of Disney's *Fantasia*. 26m. **DIR:** Chuck Jones. **1976**

BUGS BUNNY: ALL AMERICAN HERO ★★★½ Everybody's favorite varmint takes a rabbit's-eye view of American history in this expanded rendition of Friz Freleng's "Yankee Doodle Bugs" (1954), which includes clips from "Southern Fried Rabbit" (1953) and "Ballot Box Bunny" (1951). The funniest conflict, however, is the Revolutionary War's Battle of Bagel Heights in "Bunker Hill Bunny," from 1950. 24m. **DIR:** Friz Freleng, David Detiege. **1981**

BUGS BUNNY AND ELMER FUDD CARTOON FESTIVAL FEATURING "WABBIT TWOUBLE" ★★★★ Another winning collection of vintage Warner Bros. cartoons, this tape features some real classics. For example, Bob Clampett's "The Big Snooze" has Elmer Fudd quitting the studio because of a contract dispute. It's a riot. So is Friz Freleng's "Slick Hare," in which tough-guy Humphrey Bogart demands a rabbit dinner from restauranteur Elmer. 54m. **DIR:** Tex Avery, Bob Clampett, Friz Freleng. **1940–1946**

BUGS BUNNY CARTOON FESTIVAL FEATURING "HOLD THE LION PLEASE" ★★★ Two of the cartoons in this collection—Friz Freleng's "Racketeer Rabbit" and Chuck Jones's "Super Rabbit"—are recognized classics in the wascally wabbit's career; the former, in particular, is a showcase for Bugs's impressive abilities at chaotic improvisation. (It also includes an early appearance by the Edward G. Robinson–type baddie who later evolved into the semiregular dubbed Rocky.) The others, Jones's "Hold the Lion Please" and Bob Clampett's "Buckaroo Bugs," are worth a chuckle or two. 34m. **DIR:** Bob Clampett, Friz Freleng, Chuck Jones. **1942–1946**

BUGS BUNNY CLASSICS ★★★★★ Absolutely the finest collection of Bugs Bunny cartoons currently available. Beginning with a fast-paced early entry—Tex Avery's "Heckling Hare"—this tape moves up to Marvin the Martian's first appearance, in Chuck Jones's "Haredevil Hare." Friz Freleng also contributes a related pair, with "Hare Trigger" (Yosemite Sam's debut) and "Bugs Bunny Rides Again" (Sam's third appearance). Throw in Robert McKimson's "Acrobatty Bunny" and one more each from Freleng and Jones, and you've got a great hour's entertainment. 60m. **DIR:** Tex Avery, Friz Freleng, Chuck Jones, Robert McKimson. **1941–1948**

BUGS BUNNY IN KING ARTHUR'S COURT ★★★ Improper travel advice ". . . from Ray Bradbury" sends Bugs Bunny on a decidedly wrong turn in this special, originally made for network television. Although King Arthur's territory has been mined by earlier and better Warner Brothers cartoons, writer-director Chuck Jones manages to produce a few genuine chuckles. 25m. **DIR:** Chuck Jones. **1977**

BUGS BUNNY MOTHER'S DAY SPECIAL, THE ★★★ Motherhood and mis-delivered bundles of joy are the running themes in this compilation bound together by a new framing story. Although the cut-and-paste is a bit better than average, it's still frustrating to see only bits of classic entries such as Friz Freleng's "Stork Naked" (1955) and "Apes of Wrath" (1959). 23m. **DIR:** Jim Davis. **1979**

BUGS BUNNY MYSTERY SPECIAL, THE ★★★½ Porky Pig's impersonation of Alfred Hitchcock is worth the price of admission, but only one cartoon—Friz Freleng's "Big House Bunny" (1950)—appears in its entirety. The rest of the tape includes only highlights from varied crime-themed efforts like "Catty Cornered" and "Bugs and Thugs." 24m. **DIR:** Gerry Chiniqy. **1980**

BUGS BUNNY/ROAD RUNNER MOVIE, THE ★★★★ Classic cartoons made by Chuck Jones for Warner Bros. are interwoven into this laughfest; the first and best of the 1970s and '80s feature-length compilations. Includes such winners as "Duck Amuck" and "What's Opera, Doc?" Rated G. 92m. **DIR:** Chuck Jones, Phil Monroe. **1979**

BUGS BUNNY, SUPERSTAR ★★★★ A delightful collection of nine classic Warner Bros. cartoons from the Thirties and Forties. Produced mainly as a tribute to director Bob Clampett, this tape is a must-see if only for the hilarious *Fantasia* parody "Corny Concerto." Rated G. 90m. **DIR:** Larry Jackson. **1975**

BUGS BUNNY: TRUTH OR HARE ★★★ This largely unremarkable quintet of cartoons is highlighted by a couple of Chuck Jones efforts: a somewhat surrealistic

"Water, Water Every Hare" (1952) and "Hare-Way to the Stars" (1958), which features the return of Marvin the Martian. The other entries include "Wideo Wabbit," "The Fair-Haired Hare," and "Dr. Devil and Mr. Hare" (noteworthy as the last theatrical cartoon guest starring the Tasmanian Devil). 36m. **DIR:** Friz Freleng, Chuck Jones, Robert McKimson. **1951–64**

BUGS BUNNY'S BUSTIN' OUT ALL OVER ★★★★½ Veteran Warner Brothers animator Chuck Jones's final three original cartoons make this release a buried treasure of classic material. Unlike most of the Bugs Bunny television specials, this is not pasted together from older cartoons; it's all new stuff. A youthful Bugs and Elmer study gravity in "Portrait of the Artist as a Young Bunny," while the adult Bugs crosses swords with Marvin the Martian in "Spaced-Out Bunny." The highlight, however, is "Soup or Sonic," Jones's last Road Runner epic. 24m. **DIR:** Chuck Jones. **1980**

BUGS BUNNY'S CUPID CAPERS ★★★ Yet another holiday-themed television special comprised mostly of disjointed moments from numerous cartoons. Fortunately, the funniest entry—Friz Freleng's "Hare Trimmed" (1953)—appears intact, so you can savor every hysterical moment of the frenetic courtship duel between Bugs and Yosemite Sam for Granny's hand. (Drag jokes abound.) 24m. **DIR:** Hal Geer. **1979**

BUGS BUNNY'S EASTER FUNNIES ★★★★★ This early television compilation is far superior to most of its successors because it contains several intact cartoons rather than just a hodgepodge of clips. The tape includes three Academy Award winners: Friz Freleng's "Birds Anonymous" (1957) and "Knighty-Knight Bugs" (1958), as well as Chuck Jones's "For Scent-imental Reasons" (1949). Freleng's "Sahara Hare" (1955) and Jones's "Robin Hood Daffy" are also amusing, as is the new material, which shows Bugs's attempts to help an ailing Easter Rabbit. 48m. **DIR:** Hal Geer, Friz Freleng, Chuck Jones, Robert McKimson, Gerry Chiniqy. **1977**

BUGS BUNNY'S HARE-RAISING TALES ★★★ Bugs Bunny tackles the classics in this amusing collection, from the three little pigs and the big, bad wolf (Robert McKimson's "The Wind-Blown Hare") to William Shakespeare (Abe Levitow's "A Witch's Tangled Hare"). The two standouts are Friz Freleng's "Rabbitson Crusoe," costarring a shipwrecked Yosemite Sam, and Chuck Jones's "Rabbit Hood," which features a last-minute appearance by a most unexpected Robin Hood. 45m. **DIR:** Friz Freleng, Chuck Jones, Abe Levitow, Robert McKimson. **1948–1959**

BUGS BUNNY'S HOWL-OWEEN SPECIAL ★★ Even small children are apt to notice the jarring mix of styles present in this aggravating cut-and-paste sandwich of Warner Brothers cartoons, all bound by a unifying Halloween theme. 25m. **DIR:** David Detiege. **1978**

BUGS BUNNY'S LOONEY CHRISTMAS TALES ★★★ "Freeze Frame," a brand-new Coyote/Road Runner cartoon from Chuck Jones—perhaps his last—is the primary highlight of this holiday assemblage. Bugs and the Tasmanian Devil enjoy a "Fright Before Christmas," and the entire gang torments Yosemite Sam's Scrooge in "Bugs Bunny's Christmas Carol." 25m. **DIR:** Friz Freleng, Chuck Jones. **1979**

BUGS BUNNY'S LUNAR TUNES ★★★★ Fans of Marvin the Martian will particularly enjoy this superior compilation, which includes three of his best appearances: "The Hasty Hare" (1952), "Hare-Way to the Stars" (1958), and "Mad as a Mars Hare" (1963), all directed for maximum giggles by Chuck Jones. Sadly, we get only clips of his equally amusing "Duck Dodgers in the 24½ Century." 24m. **DIR:** Chuck Jones. **1977**

BUGS BUNNY'S MAD WORLD OF TELEVISION ★★★ Mass media gets roasted in this compilation show, which includes only one uncut cartoon: Friz Freleng's "This Is a Life?" (1955). The rest of the wascally wabbit's shenanigans at the QTTV Network involve disconnected clips from such efforts as "Ducksters" (1950) and "Wideo Wabbit" (1956). 24m. **DIR:** David Detiege. **1982**

BUGS BUNNY'S WACKY ADVENTURES ★★★★ Warner Home Video pulled out all the stops on its Golden Jubilee 14-Karat Collection. Included are such Chuck Jones–directed classics as "Duck! Rabbit! Duck!," "Ali Baba Bunny," "Bunny Hugged," and "Long-Haired Hare." This is cartoon fun for all ages. 59m. **DIR:** Friz Freleng, Chuck Jones. **1985**

BUGS BUNNY'S WILD WORLD OF SPORTS ★★ Needless—and rather boring—filler mars this compilation of sports-themed Warner Brothers cartoons, which includes only tantalizing excerpts from Chuck Jones 1940s and 1950s classics such as "Bunny Hugged" (wrestling), "My Bunny Lies Over the Sea" (golf), and "To Duck or Not to Duck" (boxing). 24m. **DIR:** Greg Ford, Terry Lennon. **1989**

BUGS VS. DAFFY: BATTLE OF THE MUSIC VIDEO STARS ★★ A *very* weak excuse for Warner Brothers clips, with rival video jocks Bugs and Daffy showcasing musical numbers from extremely old cartoons...most of which—deservedly—have not seen the light of day in decades. 24m. **DIR:** Greg Ford, Terry Lennon. **1988**

BUGS VS. ELMER ★★★½ All but two of the cartoons in this collection duplicate material from *Bugs and Elmer Cartoon Festival Featuring "Wabbit Twouble,"* but one of those new entries is a corker: Frank Tashlin's "Hare Remover," with Elmer the chemist conducting experiments on an unwilling bunny. 60m. **DIR:** Bob Clampett, Friz Freleng, Frank Tashlin. **1941–1947**

BUGSY MALONE ★★★½ The 1920s gangsters weren't really as cute as these children, who run around shooting whipping cream out of their pistols. But if you can forget that, this British musical provides light diversion. Rated G. 93m. **DIR:** Alan Parker. **CAST:** Scott Baio, Florrie Augger, Jodie Foster, John Cassisi, Martin Lev, Patrick Dempsey. **1976**

C.H.O.M.P.S. ★★ A small-town enterprise is saved from bankruptcy when a young engineer (Wesley Eure) designs a computer-controlled watchdog. *C.H.O.M.P.S.* has a lot of the absurdity of a cartoon. Kids under twelve may enjoy it, but the profanity thrown in for the PG rating is purely gratuitous. 90m. **DIR:** Don Chaffey. **CAST:** Wesley Eure, Valerie Bertinelli, Conrad Bain, Chuck McCann, Red Buttons, Jim Backus. **1979**

CAMERAMAN'S REVENGE AND OTHER FANTASTIC TALES, THE: THE AMAZING PUPPET ANIMATION OF LADISLAW STAREWICZ ★★★★★ These absolutely wonderful stop-action shorts by Polish-born animator Ladislaw Starewicz are an obvious inspiration for *The Nightmare before Christmas.* Though he used dolls and insect characters, Starewicz did not simply make children's films, although the adult implications will go safely over the heads of young viewers. B&W/color; 80m. **DIR:** Ladislaw Starewicz. **1912–1958**

CANDLESHOE ★★½ Confused Disney comedy about a street kid (Jodie Foster) duped by shady Leo McKern into posing as an heir to Helen Hayes. Marred by typically excessive Disney physical "humor" (read: slapstick). Rated G. 101m. **DIR:** Norman Tokar. **CAST:** David Niven, Helen Hayes, Jodie Foster, Leo McKern, Vivian Pickles. **1977**

CANINE COMMANDO ★★★★½ Pluto goes to war in this impeccable trio of cartoons drawn from Disney's World War II years, serving hitches in the army ("The Army Mascot"), the navy ("Dog Watch"), and the Coast Guard ("Canine Patrol"). The first is the funniest, with Pluto's attempt to chew tobacco; the last is the cutest, with an early appearance by the little turtle with the spring in its step. 23m. **DIR:** Walt Disney. **1942–1945**

CANNON MOVIE TALES: RED RIDING HOOD ★★ Ho-hum version of "Little Red Riding Hood" presents some major changes in the familiar story. Our heroine must deal with an absent father, a sleazy wolf-man, and a grandmother who turns out to be a witch. Rated G. 84m. **DIR:** Adam Brooks. **CAST:** Craig T. Nelson, Isabella Rossellini. **1989**

CANNON MOVIE TALES: SLEEPING BEAUTY ★★★ Impressive but overly long retelling of the classic fairy tale. Morgan Fairchild is the queen; Tahnee Welch is her beautiful daughter who falls under the evil spell. Rated G. 90m. **DIR:** David Irving. **CAST:** Morgan Fairchild, Tahnee Welch, Nicholas Clay, Sylvia Miles, Kenny Baker, David Holliday. **1989**

CANNON MOVIE TALES: SNOW WHITE ★★★½ Diana Rigg is outstanding as the evil queen–wicked stepmother in this enjoyable live-action version of the Brothers Grimm fairy tale. Rigg plots to do away with Snow White, but a septet of dwarfs and a handsome prince thwart her plans. 85m. **DIR:** Michael Berz. **CAST:** Diana Rigg, Sarah Peterson, Billy Barty. **1989**

CANNON MOVIE TALES: THE EMPEROR'S NEW CLOTHES ★★★ Excellent big-budget version of Hans Christian Andersen's classic. Sid Caesar lends his broad comedic presence as the Emperor, and Robert Morse hams it up as the con man–tailor. Not rated, but suitable for the family. 85m. **DIR:** David Irving. **CAST:** Sid Caesar, Robert Morse, Clive Revill. **1989**

CANTERVILLE GHOST, THE (1944) ★★★ It's a battle of two of filmdom's most notorious scene stealers: Charles Laughton as a 300-year-old ghost and oh-so-cute pigtailed little Margaret O'Brien. The fantasy tale of American soldiers in a haunted English castle during World War II takes second place to these two scenery munchers. B&W; 92m. **DIR:** Jules Dassin. **CAST:** Charles Laughton, Robert Young, Margaret O'Brien, William Gargan, Reginald Owen. **1944**

CANTERVILLE GHOST, THE (1986) ★★★ Modern retelling of the classic Oscar Wilde short story, with John Gielgud as the blowhard ghost who tries to terrorize a spunky American family. Gielgud is excellent as the ghost, but Ted Wass is highly unsatisfactory as the father, and the ghostly shenanigans have a dangerous quality about them that was not present in the original. Unrated; suitable for older children. 96m. **DIR:** Paul Bogart. **CAST:** John Gielgud, Ted Wass, Andrea Marcovicci, Alyssa Milano, Harold Innocent, Lila Kaye. **1986**

CAPTAIN JANUARY ★★★ Orphan Shirley Temple is taken in by a lonely lighthouse keeper (Guy Kibbee). The incredible dance number featuring Shirley and a local fisherman (Buddy Ebsen) is worth the price of the rental. B&W; 75m. **DIR:** David Butler. **CAST:** Shirley Temple, Guy Kibbee, Buddy Ebsen, Jane Darwell. **1936**

CAPTAIN MIDNIGHT—VOLS. 1–2 ★★★½ Two separate TV episodes, including commercials, are featured in this fun romp. Captain Midnight (a.k.a. Jet Jackson) enlists the help of his secret squad against, first, diamond smugglers, and then kidnappers. While rather silly by today's standards, kids will love it, and parents will enjoy a blast from the past. Not rated. B&W; 60m. **DIR:** D. Ross Lederman. **CAST:** Richard Webb, Sid Melton, Olan Soule, Gary Gray, John Hamilton. **1955**

CAPTAIN SCARLET VS. THE MYSTERONS ★★★½ Captain Scarlet, along with the Spectrum organization, must fight back when Martian invaders, the Mysterons, attack the planet Earth. Instead of standard animation, the film uses sophisticated puppets and technique called Supermarionation, which should fascinate young viewers. Rated G. 90m. **DIR:** David Lane, Alan Perry, Desmond Saunders, Ken Turner. **1967**

CAPTAIN SINBAD ★★½ This whimsical fantasy pits Sinbad against the evil El Kerim. There's plenty of color and magic to enthrall younger audiences. 85m. **DIR:** Byron Haskin. **CAST:** Guy Williams, Heidi Bruhl, Pedro Armendariz, Abraham Sofaer, Henry Brandon, Geoffrey Toone. **1963**

CAPTURE OF GRIZZLY ADAMS, THE ★★½ Like an 1850s version of *The Fugitive*'s Richard Kimble, Grizzly Adams hides in the woods with his animal friends to avoid punishment for a murder he didn't commit. In this TV movie, a sequel to the popular series, he risks capture to visit his orphanage-bound daughter. Unrated; contains no objectionable material. 96m. **DIR:** Don Keeslar. **CAST:** Dan Haggerty, Kim Darby, Noah Beery Jr., Keenan Wynn, June Lockhart, Chuck Connors, G. W. Bailey. **1982**

CARE BEARS MOVIE, THE ★★★ Poor animation mars this children's movie about bears who cheer up a pair of kids. Rated G, no objectionable material. 80m. **DIR:** Aran Selznick. **CAST:** Mickey Rooney, Georgia Engel. **1985**

CARTOON MOVIESTARS: BUGS! ★★★½ Bugs Bunny performs without his regular costars in this collection, which includes first appearances by lesser lights in the Warners animated rogues' gallery: the Three Bears (in Chuck Jones's wonderful "Bugs Bunny and the Three Bears") and Beaky Buzzard (in Bob Clampett's superb "Bugs Bunny Gets the Boid"). Of the others, Robert McKimson's "Gorilla My Dreams" has become a minor classic, with its use of hilarious gags. A good collection. 60m. **DIR:** Bob Clampett, Friz Freleng, Chuck Jones, Robert McKimson. **1942–1948**

CARTOON MOVIESTARS: DAFFY! ★★★★ Bob Clampett's classic "The Great Piggybank Robbery" is the showpiece in this octet of Daffy Duck cartoons, and it's a chaotic blend of *film noir* and Dali-esque art that could only have come from Clampett's fevered imagination. Other high points include Clampett's "Book Revue" and a rare World War II–era entry, Friz Freleng's "Yankee Doodle Daffy." Historians will also appreciate Tex Avery's "Daffy Duck and Egghead," featuring an early appearance of the character who would mature into Elmer Fudd. 60m. **DIR:** Tex Avery, Bob Clampett, Arthur Davis, Friz Freleng, Robert McKimson. **1938–1946**

CARTOON MOVIESTARS: ELMER! ★★★★ Historians eager to follow the progress of Elmer Fudd will be delighted by this collection. A high point is Friz Freleng's "The Hare-Brained Hypnotist," in which Elmer and Bugs Bunny swap minds and bodies, and Mr. Fudd gets to torment his old foe in a new form. Also included are two later entries with Daffy Duck: Arthur Davis's "What Makes Daffy Duck?" and Chuck Jones's "A Pest in the House." Both are hysterical. 60m. **DIR:** Arthur Davis, Friz Freleng, Chuck Jones. **1940–1948**

CARTOON MOVIESTARS: PORKY! ★★★½ Travel with us all the way back to 1935 and the birth of the Warners animation studio's first "modern" star: Porky Pig, in Friz Freleng's "I Haven't Got a Hat." Most of the other cartoons in this collection showcase Porky's excellent ability as a supporting player, including three wonderful team-ups with Daffy Duck: Chuck Jones's "My Favorite Duck," Bob Clampett's "Baby Bottleneck," and Robert McKimson's "Daffy Doodles." The best, however, is Jones's "Little Orphan Airedale." 60m. **DIR:** Tex Avery, Bob Clampett, Friz Freleng, Chuck Jones, Robert McKimson, Frank Tashlin. **1935–1947**

CARTOON MOVIESTARS: STARRING BUGS BUNNY ★★★★ Bugs Bunny's second team-up with Yosemite Sam—Friz Freleng's "Buccaneer Bunny"—is the high point of this seven-cartoon collection, which also features a rare World War II–era title: Freleng's "Hare Force" (costarring an early rendition of Tweety Pie's owner, Granny). Of the three by Chuck Jones, "Hare Tonic" is easily the funniest. 54m. **DIR:** Friz Freleng, Chuck Jones, Robert McKimson. **1944–1948**

CARTOONS FOR BIG KIDS ★★★ Aside from Tex Avery's deliciously manic "Red-Hot Riding Hood," this collection of the more mature World War II–era animated shorts treads fairly routine and comfortable territory. Host Leonard Maltin clearly adores the animated genre and speaks with an enthusiasm that is certainly infectious. 44m. **DIR:** Mark Lamberti. **1989**

CASEY AT THE BAT ★★½ One of Shelley Duvall's *Tall Tales and Legends*. Howard Cosell narrates this embellishment of the Casey legend, with Elliott Gould's Casey as the father of baseball. Fairly imaginative. 52m. **DIR:** David Steinberg. **CAST:** Elliott Gould,

Bill Macy, Hamilton Camp, Carol Kane, Howard Cosell. 1986

CASEY'S SHADOW ★★½ Only the droll playing of star Walter Matthau makes this family film watchable. Matthau is a horse trainer deserted by his wife and left to raise three sons. Only the star's fans will want to ride it out. Rated PG. 116m. **DIR:** Martin Ritt. **CAST:** Walter Matthau, Alexis Smith, Robert Webber, Murray Hamilton. 1978

CASPER'S FIRST CHRISTMAS 🦃 Cheap production values make this a chore to watch. 28m. **DIR:** Carl Urbano. 1987

CASTAWAY COWBOY, THE ★★★½ James Garner plays a Texas cowboy in Hawaii during the 1850s. There he helps a lovely widow (Vera Miles) start a cattle ranch despite problems created by a land-grabbing enemy (played by Robert Culp). Good family entertainment. Rated G. 91m. **DIR:** Vincent McEveety. **CAST:** James Garner, Vera Miles, Robert Culp, Eric Shea. 1974

CAT, THE 🦃 Poor story of a lost boy who is rescued by a wildcat. 87m. **DIR:** Ellis Kadison. **CAST:** Peggy Ann Garner, Barry Coe, Roger Perry, Dwayne Rekin. 1966

CAT FROM OUTER SPACE, THE ★★½ Disney comedy-sci-fi about a cat from outer space with a magical collar. The cat needs the United States to help it return to its planet. Rated G. 103m. **DIR:** Norman Tokar. **CAST:** Ken Berry, Sandy Duncan, Harry Morgan, Roddy McDowall. 1978

CHALLENGE TO BE FREE ★★ This forgettable film features a fur trapper being chased across one thousand miles of frozen Arctic wasteland by twelve men and one hundred dogs. Rated G. 88m. **DIR:** Tay Garnett, Ford Beebe. **CAST:** Mike Mazurki, Vic Christy, Jimmy Kane. 1974

CHALLENGE TO LASSIE ★★ A Disney-type fable rewritten to suit Lassie at the height of her fame. The Disney remake (*Greyfriar's Bobby*) is more believable and better suited to family tastes. This one is strictly for Lassie buffs. 76m. **DIR:** Richard Thorpe. **CAST:** Edmund Gwenn, Donald Crisp, Alan Webb, Alan Napier, Henry Stephenson, Sara Allgood, Geraldine Brooks, Reginald Owen. 1949

CHARLEY AND THE ANGEL ★★ Time-worn plot about a guardian angel who teaches an exacting man (Fred MacMurray) a few lessons in kindness and humility. The kids won't mind, but chances are you've seen a better version already. 93m. **DIR:** Vincent McEveety. **CAST:** Fred MacMurray, Cloris Leachman, Harry Morgan, Kurt Russell, Vincent Van Patten. 1973

CHARLIE BROWN AND SNOOPY SHOW, THE (VOLUME I) ★★★ These eight vignettes, all taken from the Saturday-morning series of the same name, are marred by some weak material. The better episodes include Snoopy's Foot, in which the wounded beagle is traded for Marcie in a baseball exchange; "Vulture," a quickie with Snoopy's imitation of that bird of prey; and "Peppermint Patty," during which she finally learns that Snoopy *isn't* the "funny-looking kid with the big nose." 45m. **DIR:** Bill Melendez, Sam Jaimes. 1983–1985

CHARLIE BROWN AND SNOOPY SHOW, THE (VOLUME II) ★★★★ This collection of seven vignettes features some of the funnier tales drawn from Charles Schulz's newspaper strip. Peppermint Patty goes undercover to find the "Gold Stars" misplaced by her teacher; Lucy throws Schroeder's "Piano" into the dreaded kite-eating tree; and Charlie Brown's misthrown bowling ball proves a surprise to Linus and Sally while they await the "Great Pumpkin." 45m. **DIR:** Bill Melendez, Sam Jaimes. 1983–1985

CHARLIE BROWN CELEBRATION, A ★★★★½ Charles Schulz introduces this potpourri of tales lifted directly from his newspaper strip (a format later used on Saturday morning's *The Charlie Brown and Snoopy Show*). Peppermint Patty enrolls in the Ace (Dog) Obedience School in the belief that a diploma there will eliminate her need for conventional education; Lucy throws Schroeder's piano down a sewer; and Charlie Brown checks himself into a hospital after "feeling woozy." 50m. **DIR:** Bill Melendez. 1981

CHARLIE BROWN CHRISTMAS, A ★★★★★ The Peanuts cast made its animated debut in this adorable seasonal special, which should be required viewing for anybody concerned about losing the Christmas spirit. Charlie Brown searches through aluminum monstrosities and finds a forlorn wooden tree that needs "a little love," and Snoopy jumps on the commercial bandwagon by entering an outdoor decoration contest. Vince Guaraldi's jazz themes, which immediately became a series trademark, are a highlight. 25m. **DIR:** Bill Melendez. 1965

CHARLIE BROWN THANKSGIVING, A ★★★★ Marcie and Woodstock make their animated debuts in this holiday fable that allows Linus (ever the sage) to explain the true meaning of Thanksgiving. Peppermint Patty invites herself and several friends to Charlie Brown's house for what she imagines to be a feast, but chef Snoopy has other ideas: buttered toast, popcorn, pretzels, and jelly beans. Vince Guaraldi's jazz background is particularly splendid. 25m. **DIR:** Bill Melendez, Phil Roman. 1973

CHARLIE BROWN'S ALL-STARS ★★★★★ After a previous season with 999 losses and an opening game with a score of 123–0, Charlie Brown's baseball team decides to quit, in this second animated Peanuts outing. Chuck wins them back by promising team uniforms but then learns the sponsor won't endorse a team with (shudder) several girls and a dog. What will poor Charlie Brown do? As always, Vince Guaraldi's music is dazzling. 26m. **DIR:** Bill Melendez. **1966**

CHARLIE, THE LONESOME COUGAR ★★★ A misunderstood cougar comes into a lumber camp in search of food and companionship. After adopting the animal, the men are not certain whether it will adapt back to its wild habitat, or even if they want it to. More believable than the story line would suggest. Rated G. 75m. **DIR:** Not Credited. **CAST:** Ron Brown, Bryan Russell, Linda Wallace, Jim Wilson, Rex Allen (narrator). **1968**

CHARLOTTE'S WEB ★★ Disappointing adaptation of E. B. White's beloved children's book. Charlotte the spider, Wilbur the pig, and Templeton the rat lose all their charm and turn into simpering participants in a vacuous musical. For kids only. Rated G. 85m. **DIR:** Charles A. Nichols, Iwao Takamoto. **1973**

CHEETAH ★★★ Two L.A. teens journey to Kenya to spend six months with their parents. A chance encounter with a cheetah cub sets the stage for a well-handled version of the old-fashioned Disney adventure movies for kids. Rated G. 83m. **DIR:** Jeff Blyth. **CAST:** Keith Coogan, Lucy Deakins. **1989**

CHILD OF GLASS ★★ When a boy's parents buy an old New Orleans mansion, he discovers that it is haunted. Inoffensive Disney made-for-TV movie with a hammy performance by Olivia Barash as the ghost. 93m. **DIR:** John Erman. **CAST:** Steve Shaw, Katy Kurtzman, Barbara Barrie, Biff McGuire, Nina Foch, Anthony Zerbe, Olivia Barash. **1978**

CHILDREN'S SONGS AND STORIES WITH THE MUPPETS ★★★★½ A fun-filled collection of excerpts from the popular children's television series. One to watch for: an adorable all-baby band does "Tuxedo Junction." Closed captioned. 56m. **DIR:** Peter Harris, Philip Casson. **1984**

CHILD'S CHRISTMAS IN WALES, A ★★ Dylan Thomas's holiday classic gets a tasteful but disappointingly clumsy treatment in this made-for-public-television special. Director Don McBrearty's images do not complement Thomas's brilliantly evocative words, and often actually contradict them. More like Walton Mountain than Thomas's mythical Welsh town of Llareggub. Not rated. 55m. **DIR:** Don McBrearty. **CAST:** Denholm Elliott, Mathonwy Reeves. **1987**

CHIP 'N' DALE AND DONALD DUCK ★★★★ The scruffier, less refined chipmunks of "Chip 'n' Dale" (1947) are the high point of this collection. There's a freshness to the cartoon that is absent in the later, more formulaic clashes between Donald Duck and the chipmunks. Still, "Out of Scale" is quite clever, as Chip 'n' Dale invade Donald's backyard train layout; and the creative use of tar in "Out on a Limb" is quite funny. 48m. **DIR:** Walt Disney. **1947–1955**

CHIP 'N' DALE: RESCUE RANGERS ★★★ Disney's rascally chipmunks, Chip 'n' Dale, are joined by three new friends—Zipper, the housefly; Monterey Jack, an Australian mouse; and the resourceful Gadget (a refreshingly positive female role model)—to form the Rescue Rangers. Simplistic animation, static backgrounds, and formulaic music limit the quality of these animated cartoons, collected from the syndicated television series. Each tape contains two stories. each. 44m. **DIR:** John Kimball, Bob Zamboni. **1989**

CHIPMUNK ADVENTURE, THE ★★ Alvin, Simon, and Theodore go on a round-the-world adventure in this uninspired feature-length cartoon. What made the original, scruffy chipmunks so appealing is missing here, replaced by a sort of ersatz Disney plot about jewel-smuggling villains. The kids may get a kick out of this, but anyone over the age of nine is advised to find something else to do. Rated G. 76m. **DIR:** Janice Karman. **1987**

CHIPS, THE WAR DOG ★★★½ This heart-wrenching account of the Dogs for Defense program formed during World War II focuses on the incredible bond formed between a lonely private and a heroic German shepherd. William Devane plays the military leader determined to train donated family pets to accompany soldiers on dangerous missions. Made for the Disney Channel, the only objectionable scenes take place on the battlefield. 95m. **DIR:** Ed Kaplan. **CAST:** Brandon Douglas, William Devane, Ned Vaughn, Paxton Whitehead, Ellie Cornell, Robert Miranda. **1989**

CHITTY CHITTY BANG BANG ★★½ This musical extravaganza, based on a book by Ian Fleming, is aimed at a children's audience. In it, a car flies, but the flat jokes and songs leave adult viewers a bit seasick as they hope for a quick finale. However, the kiddies will like it. Rated G. 142m. **DIR:** Ken Hughes. **CAST:** Dick Van Dyke, Sally Ann Howes, Anna Quayle, Lionel Jeffries, Benny Hill. **1968**

CHRISTIAN THE LION ★★½ A lion born in a London zoo is returned to the wilds in Kenya. This pleasant film is also interesting for the real-life drama. Bill Travers portrayed George Adamson, the wildlife expert, in *Born Free*. Now, Adamson is seen helping Christian adapt to his natural habitat. Rated G for family viewing. 89m. **DIR:** Bill Travers, James Hill. **CAST:** Bill Travers, Virginia McKenna, George Adamson. **1976**

CHRISTMAS CAROL, A (1938) ★★★½ This film version of Charles Dickens's

Christmas classic is a better-than-average retelling of Ebenezer Scrooge's transformation from a greedy malcontent to a generous, compassionate businessman. Reginald Owen is fine as Scrooge, and so is the rest of the cast. B&W; 69m. **DIR:** Edwin L. Marin. **CAST:** Reginald Owen, Gene Lockhart, Kathleen Lockhart, Leo G. Carroll, Terry Kilburn. **1938**

CHRISTMAS CAROL, A (1951) ★★★★★ Starring Alastair Sim as Ebenezer Scrooge, the meanest miser in all of London, this is a wondrously uplifting story—as only Charles Dickens could craft one. Recommended for the whole family, *A Christmas Carol* is sure to bring a tear to your eye and joy to your heart. B&W; 86m. **DIR:** Brian Desmond Hurst. **CAST:** Alastair Sim, Kathleen Harrison, Jack Warner, Michael Hordern. **1951**

CHRISTMAS COAL MINE MIRACLE, THE ★★★ In this made-for-television film a crew of striking coal miners, threatened by their union-busting bosses, enter a mine and are trapped by an explosion. The action is good, but the tone is too sweet. Also known as *Christmas Miracle in Caulfield, U.S.A.* 100m. **DIR:** Jud Taylor. **CAST:** Mitchell Ryan, Kurt Russell, Andrew Prine, John Carradine, Barbara Babcock, Melissa Gilbert, Don Porter, Shelby Leverington. **1977**

CHRISTMAS LILIES OF THE FIELD ★★★ A handyman (Billy Dee Williams) returns to help nuns and orphans once again, in this sequel to the award-winning 1963 film. A solid, well-intentioned movie, yet not quite achieving the charm of the original. Not rated, but suitable for all ages. 98m. **DIR:** Ralph Nelson. **CAST:** Billy Dee Williams, Maria Schell, Fay Hauser. **1984**

CHRISTMAS STORY, A ★★★★ Both heartwarming and hilarious, this is humorist Jean Shepherd's recollections of being a kid in the 1940s and the monumental Christmas that brought the ultimate longing—for a regulation Red Ryder air rifle. Problem is, his parents don't think it's such a good idea. Peter Billingsley is marvelous as the kid. Melinda Dillon and Darren McGavin also shine as the put-upon parents. A delight for young and old. Rated PG. 98m. **DIR:** Bob Clark. **CAST:** Peter Billingsley, Darren McGavin, Melinda Dillon, Ian Petrella. **1983**

CINDERELLA (1950) ★★★★ In this underappreciated Disney delight, a pretty youngster, who is continually berated and abused by her stepmother and stepsisters, is given one night to fulfill her dreams by a fairy godmother. The mice characters are among the studio's best, and the story moves along at a good clip. Almost in the league of *Snow White and the Seven Dwarfs* and *Pinocchio*, this animated triumph is sure to please the young and the young-at-heart. Rated G. 75m. **DIR:** Wilfred Jackson, Hamilton Luske, Clyde Geronimi. **1950**

CINDERELLA (1985) ★★★★ This is one of the most entertaining of producer Shelley Duvall's *Faerie Tale Theatre* entries. Jennifer Beals is a shy, considerate, and absolutely gorgeous Cinderella; Matthew Broderick does his aw-shucks best as the smitten Prince Henry. Sweetly romantic, a treat for all. Unrated—family fare. 60m. **DIR:** Mark Cullingham. **CAST:** Jennifer Beals, Matthew Broderick, Jean Stapleton, Eve Arden, Edie McClurg. **1985**

CLARENCE, THE CROSS-EYED LION ★★ A family comedy that plays like a TV sitcom because that's basically what it is. Writer-star Marshall Thompson wrote this story about an adult lion with a focus problem and an American family in Africa with soft hearts. The story and characters were immortalized on TV in *Daktari*. 98m. **DIR:** Andrew Marton. **CAST:** Marshall Thompson, Betsy Drake, Richard Haydn, Cheryl Miller. **1965**

COLD RIVER ★★★★ In the autumn of 1932, an experienced guide takes his 14-year-old daughter and his 12-year-old stepson on an extended camping trip. Far out in the wilderness, the father dies of a heart attack, and the children must survive a blizzard, starvation, and an encounter with a wild mountain man. A fine family movie. Rated PG. 94m. **DIR:** Fred G. Sullivan. **CAST:** Suzanna Weber, Pete Teterson, Richard Jaeckel. **1981**

COLUMBIA PICTURES CARTOON CLASSICS ★★★★½ Superb collection of cartoons produced by the UPA Studios for Columbia Pictures is highlighted by a sensational version of Edgar Allan Poe's chilling "The Tell-Tale Heart," which is read by James Mason. Other classics include "Gerald McBoing-Boing" (from the story by Dr. Seuss), "Ragtime Bear" (the first Mr. Magoo cartoon), James Thurber's wryly funny "A Unicorn in the Garden," and "Robin Hoodlum," a selection from the seldom seen Fox and Crow series. For all ages. 56m. **DIR:** John Hubley, Robert Cannon, Pete Burness. **1948–1956**

COMPUTER WORE TENNIS SHOES, THE ★★ A student becomes a genius after being short-circuited with a computer. The movie is weak, with the "excitement" provided by mobsters and gamblers. 87m. **DIR:** Robert Butler. **CAST:** Kurt Russell, Cesar Romero, Joe Flynn, William Schallert. **1969**

CONDORMAN ★★ This Disney film has everything you've ever seen in a spy film—but it was better the first time. A comic-book writer (Michael Crawford) gets his chance to become a spy when he goes after a beautiful Russian defector (Barbara Carrera). Rated PG. 90m. **DIR:** Charles Jarrott. **CAST:** Michael Crawford, Oliver Reed, James Hampton, Barbara Carrera. **1981**

CONNECTICUT YANKEE IN KING ARTHUR'S COURT, A (1970) 🦃 Bland retelling of the

Mark Twain time-travel yarn is further destroyed by even blander animation. 74m. **DIR:** Zoran Janjic. **1970**

CONTINUING ADVENTURES OF CHIP 'N' DALE, THE ★★★½ Contrary to this collection's theme, its best cartoon doesn't feature the chipmunks at all, but is instead a solo performance by Donald Duck: "Modern Inventions," full of gorgeously rendered labor-saving devices. Chip 'n' Dale make their best appearance in a rare team-up with Pluto, "Food for Feudin'." 50m. **DIR:** Walt Disney. **1937–1951**

COP AND A HALF ★★★½ When youngster Norman D. Golden witnesses a gang-style murder, he uses his knowledge to coerce the authorities into making him a police officer. Burt Reynolds is in his element as the gruff detective assigned to take care of the boy. A predictable but fun romp. Rated PG for brief profanity and violence. 93m. **DIR:** Henry Winkler. **CAST:** Burt Reynolds, Ray Sharkey, Ruby Dee, Holland Taylor, Frank Silvera, Norman D. Golden II. **1993**

COURAGE MOUNTAIN ★★★★ Ignore all those highfalutin critics who gave this well-made family film a thumbs-down. Director Christopher Leitch has done a marvelous job in turning this quasi-sequel to *Heidi* into compelling entertainment. Plenty of suspense, strong characterizations, and an edge-of-your-seat ending. Rated PG for brief violence. 120m. **DIR:** Christopher Leitch. **CAST:** Juliette Caton, Charlie Sheen, Leslie Caron. **1990**

COURAGE OF LASSIE ★★½ Everybody's favorite collie is called Bill and suffers postwar trauma in this unusual entry into the popular series. Bill leaves his wilderness home to become Elizabeth Taylor's dog, but is injured and somehow ends up in the canine corps. 92m. **DIR:** Fred M. Wilcox. **CAST:** Elizabeth Taylor, Frank Morgan, Tom Drake, Selena Royle, Harry Davenport, George Cleveland. **1946**

CRICKET IN TIMES SQUARE, A ★★★½ This Chuck Jones production is the delightful tale of a country cricket named Chester who finds himself in the relatively unfriendly city of New York. A Parent's Choice award winner, recommended for all ages. 30m. **DIR:** Chuck Jones. **1973**

CRY FROM THE MOUNTAIN ★★½ A man takes his preteen son on a camping trip, during which he plans to reveal that he and the boy's mother are getting divorced. Created by the Billy Graham Ministry, this film features attractive Alaskan scenery but is extremely preachy. Rated PG; no objectionable material. 88m. **DIR:** James F. Collier. **CAST:** Chris Kidd, Wes Parker, Rita Walter. **1985**

CRYSTALSTONE ★★½ Although it has a magical undercurrent, *Crystalstone* is more about the very down-to-earth adventures of two children escaping from a wicked guardian than about the fantastical Crystalstone. A good film for older children, with just enough action and ghoulishness to amuse them. Rated PG. 103m. **DIR:** Antonio Pelaez. **CAST:** Frank Grimes, Kamlesh Gupia. **1987**

D2: THE MIGHTY DUCKS ★★★ Just a notch below the original. Coach Emilio Estevez and his youthful team of hockey players and misfits represent America in an international competition. Sure it's contrived, but kids won't care. Rated PG. 107m. **DIR:** Sam Weisman. **CAST:** Emilio Estevez, Michael Tucker, Jan Rubes, Kathryn Erbe, Cartsen Norgaard. **1994**

DAFFY DUCK AND COMPANY ★★★ Numerous familiar faces populate Daffy's starring vehicles here, with Peter Lorre doing his heavy breathing as a mad scientist in Robert McKimson's "Birth of a Notion," and Jack Benny turning prehistoric caveman in Chuck Jones's "Daffy Duck and the Dinosaur." The funniest entry doesn't feature the duck at all: Jones's "House-Hunting Mice," with the wisecracking Hubie and Bertie. 60m. **DIR:** Bob Clampett, Chuck Jones, Robert McKimson. **1939–1948**

DAFFY DUCK CARTOON FESTIVAL: AIN'T THAT DUCKY ★★★★ Fans must not miss this collection's prize—Bob Clampett's "The Wise Quacking Duck"—because it represents one of the most hilarious team-ups between Warners Studio's most frenetic talent (Daffy) and its most manic animator (Clampett). Robert McKimson's "Daffy Duck Slept Here" is another standout, as it signifies one of the first partnerships with the mature, post–World War II Porky Pig. 35m. **DIR:** Bob Clampett, Friz Freleng, Chuck Jones, Robert McKimson. **1942–1948**

DAFFY DUCK: TALES FROM THE DUCKSIDE ★★★½ Daffy Duck's crazed origins are nicely exploited by several of these early Warner Bros. cartoons, notably "Porky and Daffy" (1938), which milks every conceivable boxing-ring gag, and "Porky's Pig Feat" (1943), featuring a last-minute cameo by Bugs Bunny. By comparison, "The Impatient Patient" (1942) and "Stork Naked" (1955) are practically sedate. Be wary of "Wise Quackers" (1948); the humor milked from its slavery theme has become quite awkward. 35m. **DIR:** Bob Clampett, Friz Freleng, Norman McCabe, Frank Tashlin. **1938–55**

DAFFY DUCK: THE NUTTINESS CONTINUES ★★★★½ Chuck Jones's superb "Duck Amuck," in which the vain and selfish Daffy Duck gets more than his just deserts from an animated witch is but one of many treats in this absolutely first-rate cartoon collection. 59m. **DIR:** Tex Avery, Bob Clampett, Chuck Jones. **1985**

DAFFY DUCK'S EASTER EGG-CITEMENT ★★½ Three new Friz Freleng Daffy Duck cartoons suffer from the limited animation and poor pacing that marred most late-entry Warner Brothers shorts. "Chocolate Chase" is perhaps noteworthy as Speedy Gonzales's final appearance, but Warners fans will immediately recognize that the framing device is a rip-off of Chuck Jones's classic "Duck Amuck." 25m. **DIR:** Friz Freleng. **1980**

DAFFY DUCK'S MADCAP MANIA ★★★ These late-period entries in Daffy Duck's canon feature numerous supporting faces, but the cartoons themselves are only average. Friz Freleng's "A Star Is Bored" is the best, with Daffy taking a new job as Bugs Bunny's stand-in. Chuck Jones's "You Were Never Duckier" is intriguing, as it also features Henry Hawk, usually associated with Foghorn Leghorn. The only other noteworthy selection is Freleng's "Golden Yeggs," with guest appearances by gangsters Rocky and Mugsy. 45m. **DIR:** Friz Freleng, Chuck Jones, Robert McKimson. **1948–1956**

DAFFY DUCK'S MOVIE: FANTASTIC ISLAND ★★ This pedestrian compilation is for Warner Bros. cartoon fanatics and toddlers only. Chunks of fairly funny shorts are strung together with a weak, dated parody of TV's *Fantasy Island*. Daffy deserved better. Rated G. 78m. **DIR:** Friz Freleng. **1983**

DAFFY DUCK'S QUACKBUSTERS ★★★★★ The best feature-length compilation of Warner Brothers cartoons since Chuck Jones's *The Bugs Bunny/Road Runner Movie*, this release features two new cartoons—"Quackbusters" and "Night of the Living Duck"—as well as classics from Jones ("Claws for Alarm," "Transylvania 6-5000," and "The Abominable Snow Rabbit") and Friz Freleng ("Hyde and Go Tweet"). The wraparound story is animated with as much care as the original cartoons, and the result is a delight for young and old. 80m. **DIR:** Greg Ford, Terry Lennon. **1988**

DAISY (LIMITED GOLD EDITION 1) ★★★½ Daisy Duck, never one of Disney's better stars, plays only a marginal role in these seven cartoons, most of which are nearly solo vehicles for Donald Duck. The animation is superb in "Mr. Duck Steps Out," which follows Donald and his nephews as they get ready for a date with Daisy. Of the remaining entries—marred by the noticeably weaker post–World War II art—"Sleepytime Donald" and "Donald's Dilemma" are the funniest. 48m. **DIR:** Walt Disney. **1940–1950**

DANCING PRINCESSES, THE ★★★★ This enchanting *Faerie Tale Theatre* production features Roy Dotrice as an overprotective king who locks his daughters in their room each night. When the shoe cobbler insists the princesses are wearing out a pair of dancing slippers each day, the king offers one of his daughters to any man who can discover where the girls go each night. A charming tale which is suitable for the entire family. 50m. **DIR:** Peter Medak. **CAST:** Lesley Ann Warren, Peter Weller, Roy Dotrice. **1984**

DANNY ★★★ A warm, touching, predictable story of an unhappy little girl who obtains a horse that has been injured and then sold off by the spoiled daughter of the wealthy stable owners. A fine family film. Rated G. 90m. **DIR:** Gene Feldman. **CAST:** Rebecca Page, Janet Zarish. **1977**

DARBY O'GILL AND THE LITTLE PEOPLE ★★★½ Darby O'Gill is an Irish storyteller who becomes involved with some of the very things he talks about, namely leprechauns, the banshee, and other Irish folk characters. This wonderful tale is one of Disney's best films and a delightful fantasy film in its own right. It features a young and relatively unknown Sean Connery as Darby's future son-in-law. 93m. **DIR:** Robert Stevenson. **CAST:** Albert Sharpe, Janet Munro, Sean Connery, Jimmy O'Dea. **1959**

DARK HORSE ★★★½ Inspirational tale of a lonely teenage girl who gets into trouble and is sentenced to ten weekends of community service at a horse ranch. Great family entertainment, played out in heart-tugging, sentimental fashion. Not rated. 98m. **DIR:** David Hemmings. **CAST:** Ed Begley Jr., Mimi Rogers, Ari Meyers, Donovan Leitch, Samantha Eggar, Tab Hunter. **1992**

DAVY CROCKETT AND THE RIVER PIRATES ★★★ Fess Parker, as idealized Davy Crockett, takes on Big Mike Fink (Jeff York) in a keelboat race and tangles with Indians in the second Walt Disney–produced Davy Crockett feature composed of two television episodes. Thoroughly enjoyable and full of the kind of boyhood images that Disney productions evoked so successfully in the late 1940s and '50s. Fun for the whole family. 81m. **DIR:** Norman Foster. **CAST:** Fess Parker, Buddy Ebsen, Kenneth Tobey, Jeff York. **1956**

DAVY CROCKETT, KING OF THE WILD FRONTIER ★★★½ Finely played by all involved, this is actually a compilation of three episodes that appeared originally on television and were then released theatrically. 88m. **DIR:** Norman Foster. **CAST:** Fess Parker, Buddy Ebsen, Hans Conried, Kenneth Tobey. **1955**

DAYDREAMER, THE ★★★ This *Children's Treasures* presentation combines live action with puppetry to bring a young Hans Christian Andersen and his tales to life. 80m. **DIR:** Jules Bass. **CAST:** Paul O'Keefe, Burl Ives, Tallulah Bankhead, Terry-Thomas, Victor Borge, Ed Wynn, Patty Duke, Boris Karloff, Ray Bolger, Hayley Mills, Jack Gilford, Margaret Hamilton. **1966**

DENNIS THE MENACE ★★★★ The first movie to be made from the famous comic strip has the advantage of a John Hughes script to give it wit and style. The story centers on the relationship between 6-year-old Dennis Mitchell and his grouchy neighbor, Mr. Wilson. An affable mixture of talents in a classy family-oriented movie. Rated PG. 101m. **DIR:** Nick Castle. **CAST:** Walter Matthau, Christopher Lloyd, Joan Plowright, Lea Thompson, Mason Gamble, Robert Stanton. **1993**

DENNIS THE MENACE: DINOSAUR HUNTER ★★½ Dennis unearths a dinosaur bone in the front yard. A friend of his father's, who majored in paleontology, comes to live with the family and causes chaos for the entire neighborhood. The story is predictable and viewers will wish the father would just get a backbone. Rated G. 95m. **DIR:** Doug Rogers. **CAST:** William Windom, James W. Jansen, Patricia Estrinn, Patsy Garrett, Victor DiMattia, Barton Tinapp. **1987**

DIAMOND'S EDGE ★★★½ When his detective older brother is thrown in jail, a young teen takes over his current case. Though it was made for younger viewers, adults will enjoy this private eye spoof's clever homages to classic mystery films. Rated PG. 83m. **DIR:** Stephen Bayly. **CAST:** Dursley McLinden, Colin Dale, Susannah York, Patricia Hodge, Roy Kinnear, Bill Paterson, Jimmy Nail, Saeed Jaffrey. **1988**

DIAMONDS ON WHEELS ★★ Subpar Disney adventure pits a group of teenage auto-racing enthusiasts against a mob of jewel thieves. Strictly formula; even toddlers will realize they've seen it before. Rated G. 87m. **DIR:** Jerome Courtland. **CAST:** Peter Firth, Patrick Allen. **1973**

DICK TRACY CARTOONS ★★★ "Okay, Chief, I'll get on it right away," says Dick Tracy at the beginning of each of the cartoons in this multivolume collection, but instead of ol' hook nose being on the case, he assigns one of several detectives—Hemlock Holmes, Joe Jitsu, Go Go Gomez—to track down Pruneface, Itchy, Mumbles, Flattop, and so on. These are okay action cartoons for kids, although some parents might be upset by the racial stereotypes. per tape. approx. 60m. **DIR:** Abe Levitow. **1960s**

DIRT BIKE KID, THE 🦃 A boy buys an old dirt bike that turns out to have a life of its own. Rated PG for vulgarity. 91m. **DIR:** Hoite C. Caston. **CAST:** Peter Billingsley, Stuart Pankin, Anne Bloom, Patrick Collins. **1985**

DISNEY CHRISTMAS GIFT, A ★★★★ A collection of memorable scenes from Disney's animated classics, including *Peter Pan*, *Cinderella*, and *Bambi*, in addition to a variety of yuletide short subjects. Made for cable TV. 47m. **DIR:** William Robert Yates. **1982**

DISNEY'S BEST: 1931–1948 ★★★★ Two of the finest cartoons Disney ever produced highlight this collection, but the other four entries fall far short of that mark. The standout is the Oscar-winning "Ugly Duckling" (1939), luxuriously rendered with Dick Lundy's animation of the central character; this one'll draw tears from granite. The other classic is "Truant Officer Donald," wherein the badge-toting duck attempts to drag his free-spirited nephews back to school. 48m. **DIR:** Walt Disney. **1931–1948**

DISNEY'S DREAM FACTORY: 1933–1938 (LIMITED GOLD EDITION 2) ★★★ Although most of these song-laden fairy tales are aimed at the small fry, adults will be impressed by the sumptuous animation of "Wynken, Blynken, and Nod" (1938). The Disney studios never made a more luxurious short cartoon. Albert Hurter's design work on the Shakespeare-themed "Music Land" is also quite lush. 50m. **DIR:** Walt Disney. **1933–1938**

DISNEY'S HALLOWEEN TREAT ★★★ Little of this cable-TV production has to do with Halloween, although it does have its moments. Highlights include the complete *Legend of Sleepy Hollow* and a portion of *Fantasia*. Enthusiasts of Disney animation will enjoy this regardless of its somewhat misleading title. 47m. **DIR:** William Robert Yates. **1982**

DISNEY'S TALL TALES ★★½ Lesser American folk legends take the spotlight in this weak collection of Disney cartoons, which is highlighted only by a spirited rendition of "Casey at the Bat" (extracted from the 1946 feature, *Make Mine Music*). The rest of these tales are only average. 50m. **DIR:** Walt Disney. **1934–1961**

DOCTOR DOLITTLE ★★½ Rex Harrison plays the title role in this children's tale, about a man who finds more satisfaction being around animals than people. Children may find this film amusing, but for the most part, the acting is weak, and any real script is nonexistent. 152m. **DIR:** Richard Fleischer. **CAST:** Rex Harrison, Samantha Eggar, Anthony Newley, Richard Attenborough. **1967**

DR. SEUSS: HORTON HEARS A WHO/THE GRINCH WHO STOLE CHRISTMAS ★★★★ Veteran cartoon director Chuck Jones brings his talent to the telling of these made-for-television Dr. Seuss tales. Children will be engrossed in the story of Horton the elephant who must save the tiny society living on a speck of dust, while all those around him balk at his absurd notions. *The Grinch Who Stole Christmas* follows with a warm tale made especially for holiday viewing. 51m. **DIR:** Chuck Jones. **1974**

DR. SEUSS: THE CAT IN THE HAT/DR. SEUSS ON THE LOOSE ★★★★ Parents and children familiar with Dr. Seuss's *Cat in the Hat* book will notice some changes in this story, which still has two kids stuck in a house on a rainy day. The Cat in the Hat shows up and turns their home upside down. Even better are the shorts in *Dr. Seuss on the Loose*, which include "The Sneetches," "The Zax," and the delightful "Green Eggs and Ham." 51m. **DIR:** Hawley Pratt, Alan Zaslove. **1974**

DR. SEUSS: THE GRINCH GRINCHES THE CAT IN THE HAT/PONTOFFEL POCK ★★★★ Two of Dr. Seuss's most famous characters go head-to-head in part one of this delightful children's tape, in which the Cat teaches the grouchy Grinch a few lessons in manners. *Pontoffel Pock* features a lonely boy who gets a magical piano. 49m. **DIR:** Joe Baldwin. **1982**

DR. SEUSS: THE LORAX/THE HOOBER BLOOB HIGHWAY ★★★★ The enticingly bizarre world of Dr. Seuss is colorfully brought to the screen in this collection of two made-for-TV specials. *The Lorax* relates the importance of our environment, while *The Hoober Bloob Highway* brims with sound principles about self-worth. This makes for good family-time viewing. 48m. **DIR:** Hawley Pratt, Alan Zaslove. **1974**

DR. SYN, ALIAS THE SCARECROW ★★½ Showcased in America as a three-part television program in 1964, colorful tale of a man who poses as a minister by day and a champion of the oppressed by night. Patrick McGoohan brings style and substance to the legendary Dr. Syn. 129m. **DIR:** James Neilson. **CAST:** Patrick McGoohan, George Cole, Tony Britton, Geoffrey Keen, Kay Walsh. **1962**

DOG OF FLANDERS, A ★★★★ Ouida's world-famous 1872 tear jerking novel about a boy and his dog and their devotion to each other tastefully filmed in its European locale. Nello (David Ladd) delivers milk from a cart pulled by the dog Patrasche. Donald Crisp and Theodore Bikel shine in character roles, but the picture belongs to Ladd and the scene-stealing mutt fans will recall from *Old Yeller*. Have Kleenex handy. 96m. **DIR:** James B. Clark. **CAST:** David Ladd, Donald Crisp, Theodore Bikel. **1960**

DONALD (LIMITED GOLD EDITION 1) ★★★★ These early adventures of Donald Duck are noteworthy for the richer animation of Disney's World War II years, and all are solo vehicles for Disney's famous duck. "Autograph Hound" is the most ambitious, with Donald trying to crash a movie studio to collect signatures. Donald seeks gainful employment in "The Riveter" and then enjoys himself in an arcade in "Good Time for a Dime." Amid these gems, the poor quality of "The New Neighbor" makes its inclusion something of a mystery. 51m. **DIR:** Walt Disney. **1939–1953**

DONALD DUCK IN MATHEMAGIC LAND ★★★★ This clever instructional feature marks one of Donald Duck's final appearances in a theatrical animated short. Donald serves as a guide through a mystical land filled with numbers and inventive explanations of simple mathematical principles. In pre–*Sesame Street* times, this was the closest children got to creative teaching, and the tape remains engaging to this day. 27m. **DIR:** Walt Disney. **1959**

DONALD DUCK: THE FIRST 50 YEARS ★★★½ The need to feature highlights from Donald Duck's career makes this an uneven collection. "The Wise Little Hen" is noteworthy only for Donald's debut, complete with trademark sailor suit. Daisy Duck is introduced in "Don Donald," and Huey, Dewie, and Louie in "Donald's Nephews," but both cartoons are shrill and obnoxious. The highlight is the Oscar-nominated "Rugged Bear" (1953), with Humphrey absolutely hilarious as a bear who masquerades as a rug to escape hunters. 45m. **DIR:** Walt Disney. **1934–1953**

DONALD'S BEE PICTURES (LIMITED GOLD EDITION 2) ★★★½ This collection wears thin pretty quickly, since all seven cartoons feature Donald Duck's battles with a remarkably persistent honeybee. Most also employ the noticeably limited animation of Disney's later period; the one exception is the bee's debut in "Window Cleaners" (1940), which showcases stunning artwork to tell its story of Donald and Pluto as inept high-rise window cleaners. 50m. **DIR:** Walt Disney. **1940–1952**

DOT AND THE BUNNY ★★★ A little girl falls asleep, dreaming of her adventures with a lop-eared rabbit as they search for a missing baby kangaroo. Real-life backgrounds make this a unique production that involves animated characters parading about the Australian jungle. 79m. **DIR:** Yoram Gross. **1982**

DOUBLE MCGUFFIN, THE ★★★½ Here's another family (as opposed to children's) movie. It's full of Hitchcock references in a story about some smart kids who uncover a plot to kill the leader of a Middle Eastern country. The three nominal stars only have supporting parts; they get top billing just for marquee value. From Joe Camp, the one-man movie factory who created the *Benji* films. Rated PG. 101m. **DIR:** Joe Camp. **CAST:** Ernest Borgnine, George Kennedy, Elke Sommer, Rod Browning, Lisa Whelchel, Vincent Spano, Lyle Alzado. **1979**

DREAM FOR CHRISTMAS, A ★★ Overwhelmed by a sound track far too dramatic for its simple settings, this tale of a black pastor and his family who move to California to start a congregation is full-fledged Americana. A very basic production that parallels the television hit, *The Waltons*. And it came from the very same creator: Earl Hamner. 100m. **DIR:** Ralph Senensky. **CAST:** George Spell, Hari Rhodes, Beah Richards. **1973**

DROOPY AND COMPANY ★★ This collection scrapes the bottom of the barrel, with a quartet of late-entry Droopy cartoons marred by stagnant animation, lousy (and sexist) writing, and Michael Lah's ham-handed direction. The remaining two—"The Hungry Wolf" and "Officer Pooch"—employ equally weak story lines, but their classic animation saves the whole tape from turkeydom. 44m. **DIR:** Michael Lah, William Hanna, Joseph Barbera. **1942–1957**

DUCKTALES (TV SERIES) ★★★½ The entire family will enjoy this colorful and witty Walt Disney animated series, which concerns the often amusing—and always action-packed—adventures of Scrooge McDuck, his niece Webigail, and nephews Huey, Dewey, and Louie. "Unca" Scrooge's insatiable greed leads the ducks to some very unusual locations, such as the Lost City of Troy (in "Raiders of the Lost Harp"). Each tape 44m. **DIR:** David Block, Steve Clark, Alan Zaslove. **1987**

DUCKTALES: THE MOVIE—TREASURE OF THE LOST LAMP ★★★ Adapted from a Disney cartoon series for television, this is a *Raiders of the Lost Ark*–style animated adventure in which Uncle Scrooge McDuck and his three great-nephews set out after lost treasure. In the style of the classic Donald Duck comic books by Carl Barks. Rated G. 106m. **DIR:** Bob Hathcock. **1990**

DUMBO ★★★★ Disney's cartoon favorite about the outcast circus elephant with the big ears is a family classic. It has everything: personable animals, a poignant story, and a happy ending. It is good fun and can still invoke a tear or two in the right places. 64m. **DIR:** Ben Sharpstein. **1941**

DUSTY ★★★ An emotional story of a retired, lonely shepherd in Australia who is adopted by Dusty, a stray sheepdog. 89m. **DIR:** John Richardson. **CAST:** Bill Kerr, Noel Trevarthen, Carol Burns, Nicholas Holland, John Stanton. **1985**

EARTHLING, THE ★★★½ A dying man (William Holden) and an orphaned boy (Rick Schroder) meet in the Australian wilderness in this surprisingly absorbing family film. A warning to parents: There is a minor amount of profanity, and a scene in which the boy's mother and father are killed may be too shocking for small children. Rated PG. 102m. **DIR:** Peter Collinson. **CAST:** William Holden, Rick Schroder, Jack Thompson, Olivia Hamnett, Alwyn Kurts. **1980**

ELEPHANT'S CHILD, THE ★★★★ Once upon a time, narrator Jack Nicholson informs us, the elephant had only a "blackish, bulgy nose as big as a boot, that he could wriggle from side to side." This changes only after the overly inquisitive Elephant's Child encounters a particularly hungry crocodile, producing a result which only could have come from Rudyard Kipling's "Just So" stories. Quite droll. 30m. **DIR:** Mark Sottnick. **1986**

ELMER FUDD CARTOON FESTIVAL: AN ITCH IN TIME ★★★½ Elmer Fudd sheds his image as a hunter in this lively quartet of cartoons, which includes two recognized classics: Bob Clampett's "An Itch in Time," and Friz Freleng's "Back Alley Oproar." In both cases, poor Elmer is befuddled by obnoxious house pets. One of the other cartoons—Chuck Jones's "Elmer's Pet Rabbit"—is a golden oldie: the second team-up between Mr. Fudd and an early Bugs Bunny. 33m. **DIR:** Bob Clampett, Friz Freleng, Chuck Jones. **1940–1948**

ELMER FUDD'S COMEDY CAPERS ★★★★ An outstanding collection of Warner Bros. cartoons, this set is highlighted by a quartet of Chuck Jones gems: "The Rabbit of Seville," "Bugs' Bonnets," "What's Opera, Doc?," and "Rabbit Seasoning." 57m. **DIR:** Friz Freleng, Chuck Jones, Robert McKimson. **1950–1957**

EMIL AND THE DETECTIVES ★★★½ One of the better live-action adventures made by the Disney Studios in the early 1960s, this grand little tale follows the escapades of a young boy who hires a gang of young, amateur sleuths after he's been robbed. Wholly improbable, but neatly constructed from the classic children's novel by Erich Kastner. 99m. **DIR:** Peter Tewksbury. **CAST:** Roger Mobley, Walter Slezak, Bryan Russell, Heinz Schubert. **1964**

EMPEROR AND THE NIGHTINGALE, THE ★★★ Glenn Close narrates the Hans Christian Andersen tale with superb attention to the different voices, but the pace is a bit too languid. Robert Van Nutt's paintings might be too stylized for Western audiences, and Mark Isham's music—although perfectly suited to the story—might be too exotic for younger viewers. 40m. **DIR:** Mark Sottnick. **1987**

EMPEROR'S NEW CLOTHES, THE (1984) ★★ This *Faerie Tale Theatre* production presents a narcissistic king (Dick Shawn) whose vanity eventually makes him the laughingstock of his country. Alan Arkin and Art Carney have to deliver some painfully banal lines—in modern argot and out of sync with the story's time and setting. 54m. **DIR:** Peter Medak. **CAST:** Alan Arkin, Art Carney, Dick Shawn, Timothy Dalton (narrator). **1984**

EMPEROR'S NEW CLOTHES, THE (1990) ★★★½ Robert Van Nutt's gorgeous paintings highlight this Rabbit Ears animated production, which is given a properly refined tone by John Gielgud's narration. Sadly, the pacing is interminably slow, and the story has not been fleshed out sufficiently to cover several dead-air sequences. 30m. **DIR:** Robert Van Nutt. **1990**

ENCHANTED FOREST, THE ★★★ Pleasant fantasy about an old hermit who teaches a young boy to love the forest and its creatures lacks a big-studio budget but is fine family fare. 77m. **DIR:** Lew Landers. **CAST:** Edmund Lowe, Harry Davenport, Brenda Joyce, Billy Severn, John Litel. **1945**

ERNEST GREEN STORY, THE ★★★★½ Powerful Disney production shows racism at its ugliest and determination at its most magnificent. This is the true story of the first black graduate of Little Rock, Arkansas's Central High School in 1958. Ernest Green, along with eight other brave black students, withstood taunts, threats, and attacks to enforce the 1954 Supreme Court decision opposing segregated schools. Superb acting and an outstanding musical score. Unrated; contains violence and racial slurs. 101m. **DIR:** Eric Laneville. **CAST:** Morris Chestnut, C.C.H. Pounder, Gary Grubbs, Tina Lifford, Avery Brooks, Ruby Dee. **1992**

ERNEST SAVES CHRISTMAS ★★★ In this family movie, a vast improvement over *Ernest Goes to Camp*, TV pitchman Jim Varney returns as Ernest P. Worrell. This time the obnoxious but well-meaning Ernest attempts to help Santa Claus (Douglas Seale) find a successor. The script is funny without being moronic, and sentimental without being maudlin. Rated PG. 95m. **DIR:** John R. Cherry III. **CAST:** Jim Varney, Douglas Seale, Oliver Clark, Billie Bird. **1988**

ESCAPADE IN FLORENCE 🦃 Uninspired story about two young men and their misadventures in picturesque Italy. 80m. **DIR:** Steve Previn. **CAST:** Ivan Desny, Tommy Kirk, Annette Alliotto, Nino Castelnuovo. **1962**

ESCAPADE IN JAPAN ★★★½ Little Jon Provost, his friend Roger Nakagawa, and Japan itself are the stars of this charming film about a young boy who survives an airplane crash in Japan and is taken in by a family of isolated fishers. This is one of the all-time best kids-on-the-run films. 93m. **DIR:** Arthur Lubin. **CAST:** Jon Provost, Roger Nakagawa, Cameron Mitchell, Teresa Wright. **1957**

ESCAPE ARTIST, THE ★★ Confusing, rambling account of a boy (Griffin O'Neal, who might be appealing with better material) who uses a love of magic and escape artistry to frame the city politicos responsible for killing his father. Rated PG—mild violence and profanity. 96m. **DIR:** Caleb Deschanel. **CAST:** Griffin O'Neal, Raul Julia, Teri Garr, Joan Hackett, Desi Arnaz Sr. **1982**

ESCAPE TO WITCH MOUNTAIN ★★★½ In this engaging Disney mystery-fantasy, two children with strange powers are pursued by men who want to use them for evil purposes. It's good! Rated G. 97m. **DIR:** John Hough. **CAST:** Eddie Albert, Ray Milland, Kim Richards, Ike Eisenmann. **1975**

EWOK ADVENTURE, THE ★★ Two children use the help of the friendly Ewok people to find their kidnapped parents in this dull entry in the *Star Wars* family of films. Subpar special effects. Not rated, but would probably rank a PG for mild violence. 96m. **DIR:** John Korty. **CAST:** Eric Walker, Warwick Davis, Fionnula Flanagan, Guy Boyd. **1984**

EWOKS: THE BATTLE FOR ENDOR ★★ Those almost too lovable, diminutive rascals from *Return Of The Jedi* appear in their own adventure as they try to help two orphans stop an evil entity from destroying them all. Hokey and a bit cutesy. Contains some scenes that may be too intense for children. 98m. **DIR:** Jim Wheat, Ken Wheat. **CAST:** Wilford Brimley, Warwick Davis, Paul Gleason. **1986**

EYES OF THE AMARYLLIS ★★½ A young girl goes to Nantucket to care for her grandmother, an invalid awaiting the return of her long-dead husband. This well-intended low-budget film is likely to bore kids, though it may interest adults who recall the Natalie Babbitt novel on which it was based. Unrated; contains no objectionable material. 84m. **DIR:** Frederick King Keller. **CAST:** Ruth Ford, Martha Byrne. **1982**

FABULOUS FIFTIES (LIMITED GOLD EDITION–1), THE ★★★★½ This eclectic quartet represents some of the finest experimental animation produced by the Disney studio, and every short included here captured at least an Oscar nomination. The stop-motion stick figures of "Noah's Ark" are a technical standout, but older viewers will no doubt prefer Ward Kimball's Oscar-winning history of music: "Toot, Whistle, Plunk, and Boom," Disney's first Cinemascope cartoon. Rounding out the package are the traditionally cute "Lambert, the Sheepish Lion" and the wacky "Pigs Is Pigs." 49m. **DIR:** Walt Disney. **1951–1959**

FABULOUS FLEISCHER FOLIO, THE (VOLUME ONE) ★★★ Max and Dave Fleischer ran neck and neck with Disney in terms of animation quality in the 1930s. Some of their more adorable efforts are on view here. "Small Fry" is a bubbly cartoon about a young catfish playing hooky. In "Hunk and Spunky," our heroes are a pair of donkeys. Also included are "The Golden State," "Play Safe," "Ants in the Plants," and the lovely "Song of the Birds." 50m. **DIR:** Max Fleischer, Dave Fleischer. **1930**

FABULOUS FLEISCHER FOLIO, THE (VOLUME TWO) ★★★ This is a nicely balanced package that should please all ages. "Snubbed by a Snob" features Hunk and Spunky. There's an entertaining version of the children's rhyme in "Greedy Humpty Dumpty." Other enchanti🦃 features include "The Hawaiian Birds" and "Somewhere in Dreamland." 50m. **DIR:** Dave Fleischer. **1930**

FABULOUS FLEISCHER FOLIO, THE (VOLUME THREE) ★★★ There's everything from supercuteness to black comedy on this tape. "Cobweb Hotel" is the frighteningly funny tale of a cunning spider running a hotel for flies (yum-yum). "Fresh Vegetable Mystery" is a winner that features cuddly veggies. "The Stork Market" takes viewers to a baby factory and lets us sing along to "Pretty Baby." Also on this tape are "Farm Foolery," "The Little Stranger," and "A Kick in Time." 50m. **DIR:** Dave Fleischer. **1930**

FABULOUS FLEISCHER FOLIO, THE (VOLUME FOUR) ★★½ More cartoons crafted by Max and Dave Fleischer in the Thirties and Forties are featured in this edition. Among the highlights are "Toys Will Be Toys," an old-fashioned sing-along featuring "Oh! You Beautiful Doll," and a Mother Goose takeoff, "The Kids in the Shoe." Other titles include: "To Spring," "Funshine State," "Musical Memories," and "An Elephant Never Forgets." 43m. **DIR:** Dave Fleischer. **1934–1949**

FABULOUS FLEISCHER FOLIO, THE (VOLUME FIVE) ★★ The Christmas cartoons of Max and Dave Fleischer are featured in this Disney video release, which is for animation buffs and youngsters only. Included are: "Rudolph the Red-Nosed Reindeer," "The Ski's the Limit," "Peeping Penguins," "Bunny Mooning," "Snow Fooling," and "Christmas Comes But Once a Year." 43m. **DIR:** Dave Fleischer. **1937–1949**

FAMILY CIRCUS CHRISTMAS, A ★★½ Lighthearted holiday fare involving the characters of the popular comic strip. One of the children wishes for Santa to bring their dead grandfather home for Christmas. Of course, Santa comes through. Made for television. 60m. **DIR:** Al Kouzel. **1986**

FAMILY DOG ★★★ As an isolated 1986 episode of television's *Amazing Stories*, the premiere of this acerbic animated series was a howl. But before executive producers Steven Spielberg and Tim Burton got their act together *The Simpsons* redefined television animation. As a result, this six-episode series was barely noticed...a fate it did not deserve. While not as piquant as *The Simpsons*, *Family Dog* will make pet owners howl with laughter. Each tape contains two episodes. 47m. **DIR:** Chris Buck. **1993**

FAMOUS FIVE GET INTO TROUBLE, THE 🦃 Four kids go on an unchaperoned camping trip. 90m. **DIR:** Trine Hedman. **CAST:** Astrid Villaume, Ova Sprogoe, Lily Broberg. **1987**

FANTASIA ★★★★★ Originally intended as the first in a continuing series of projects blending animation with classical music, *Fantasia* proved disappointing for Walt Disney (although its box-office take was still strong enough to make it the year's second most popular picture...lagging behind another Disney release, *Pinocchio*). Plans for a sequel were abandoned, but the original grew steadily more popular during subsequent rereleases...particularly with the counterculture crowd, which embraced the new 70mm prints and Dolby sound of its 1970s reissue. *Fantasia* was first conceived as a feature-length vehicle for Mickey Mouse, but his comedic segment—set to Dukas's "The Sorcerer's Apprentice"—is far from the film's most popular sequence. Fans generally cite the delicacy of various movements from Tchaikovsky's "The Nutcracker Suite," or the genuine terror inflicted by the dark figure of evil in Mussorgsky's "Night on Bald Mountain." 120m. **DIR:** Walt Disney. **1940**

FAR OFF PLACE, A ★★★½ Disney adventure film is an awkward blend of *The Gods Must Be Crazy* and *The Rescuers Down Under*. In order to escape the ivory poachers who killed their parents, two teenagers must cross the treacherous Kalahari Desert with the aid of a young Bushman. Two scenes of extreme violence make this film a bit too strong for children under 10. Rated PG for violence and brief profanity. 107m. **DIR:** Mikael Salomon. **CAST:** Reese Witherspoon, Ethan Randall, Jack Thompson, Sarel Bok, Maximilian Schell. **1993**

FAST TALKING ★★ This Australian comedy stars Rod Zuanic as a little punk that you'd love to shake and put on the straight and narrow. The fact that he has a miserable home life that doesn't hold much of a future for him doesn't make this fast talker any more endearing. 93m. **DIR:** Ken Cameron. **CAST:** Rod Zuanic, Steve Bisley, Tracy Mann, Dennis Moore, Toni Allaylis, Chris Truswell. **1986**

FATTY FINN ★★★ This film seems to borrow from the Little Rascals comedy series. In it, young Fatty Finn is desperately trying to earn money to buy a radio. But the neighborhood bully and his gang sabotage Fatty's efforts. The happy ending makes up for all the hardships 10-year-old Fatty has endured. 91m. **DIR:** Maurice Murphy. **CAST:** Ben Oxenbould, Bert Newton. **1984**

FELIX'S MAGIC BAG OF TRICKS 🦃 Though this little guy provided plenty of entertainment for his audience in the 1920s, he seems to have completely lost his charm in the transition to the modern age. 60m. **DIR:** Joseph Oriolo. **1960**

FERNGULLY—THE LAST RAINFOREST ★★★ A fairy discovers the ugly truth about the human race, which once worked alongside her magical peoples in nurturing the rain forest but is now destroying it. Robin Williams's inspired voice work (as Batty) elevates this environmental plea aimed at children. Other voices are provided by Tim Curry, Samantha Mathis, Christian Slater, Grace Zabriskie, Richard "Cheech" Marin, and Tommy Chong. Rated G. 76m. **DIR:** Bill Kroyer. 1992

FIGHTING PRINCE OF DONEGAL, THE ★★★½ A rousing adventure-action film set in sixteenth-century Ireland. When Peter McEnery succeeds to the title of Prince of Donegal, the Irish clans are ready to fight English troops to make Ireland free. This is a Disney British endeavor that is definitely worth watching. 110m. **DIR:** Michael O'Herlihy. **CAST:** Peter McEnery, Susan Hampshire, Tom Adams, Gordon Jackson. 1966

FISHER PRICE SOMEDAY ME SERIES VOL. I: IT'S A DOG'S LIFE ★★★ A mischievous brother and sister experience a variety of adventures in this animated musical series. *It's a Dog's Life* is an entertaining look at what sort of jobs kids may aspire to later in life. Subsequent volumes cover parenting and transportation. For tots. 30m. **DIR:** David High. 1988

FISHER PRICE VIDEO: GRIMMS' FAIRY TALES: HANSEL AND GRETEL/KING GRIZZLE BEARD ★★★ Well-produced and fast-paced, this animated feature holds pretty much true to the original tale, including the wicked stepmother who doesn't mind leaving the kids out alone in the elements. Too slow for kids over five. 31m. **DIR:** Tom Wyner, Kerrigan Mahan. 1988

FIVE THOUSAND FINGERS OF DR. T, THE ★★★★ A delightful fantasy about children. Tommy Rettig would rather play baseball than practice the piano. Hans Conried plays Dr. Terwilliker, the piano teacher who gives the kid nightmares. Dr. Seuss cowrote the script. 89m. **DIR:** Roy Rowland. **CAST:** Hans Conried, Mary Healy, Peter Lind Hayes, Henry Kulky, Tommy Rettig. 1952

FLIGHT OF DRAGONS, THE ★★★★ Stop-motion animation and the voices of John Ritter, James Earl Jones, Harry Morgan, and James Gregory bring this fantasy to life. Good wizards select a man to stop the evil reign of the Red Wizards. Grade-schoolers will be fascinated by this tale. 98m. **DIR:** Arthur Rankin Jr., Jules Bass. 1982

FLINTSTONES, THE ★★★ Yuppie nostalgia and the amazing efforts of Jim Henson's Creature Shop are this film's major attractions, but the appeal wears thin pretty quickly. In spite of—or because of—the efforts of a rumored thirty-five writers, this live-action re-creation of the 1960s animated series lurches awkwardly from one scene to the next. Very small children will love it, but they won't understand the topical references or the occasionally risqué humor. Rated PG for cartoonish violence and mild sexuality. 105m. **DIR:** Brian Levant. **CAST:** John Goodman, Elizabeth Perkins, Rick Moranis, Rosie O'Donnell, Elizabeth Taylor, Kyle MacLachlan, Halle Berry. 1994

FLIPPER ★★★ America's love of dolphins took root in this gentle adventure. After Luke Halpin saves a wounded dolphin, he must convince his fisherman father (Chuck Connors) that dolphins help man and should not be destroyed. Filmed in the Florida Keys. 85m. **DIR:** James B. Clark. **CAST:** Chuck Connors, Luke Halpin. 1963

FLIPPER'S NEW ADVENTURE ★★★ One of the better sequels shows the affection and teamwork enjoyed by a young boy and his pet dolphin when they outwit blackmailers. Filmed in the Bahamas and released less than a year after, Flipper made a sensational movie debut. The sequel led to a TV series. 103m. **DIR:** Leon Benson. **CAST:** Luke Halpin, Brian Kelly, Pamela Franklin, Francesca Annis, Tom Helmore. 1964

FLIPPER'S ODYSSEY ★★½ Rin Tin Tin with fins heroically saves a photographer, a lonely fisherman's dog, and his own young master. Flipper outacts the rest of the cast. Underwater shots are the highlight. 77m. **DIR:** Paul Landres. **CAST:** Brian Kelly, Luke Halpin, Tommy Norden. 1965

FOGHORN LEGHORN'S FRACTURED FUNNIES ★★★½ Robert McKimson made some hilarious Bugs Bunny, Daffy Duck, and Porky Pig cartoons, but his best work was to be found in this series about a cantankerous country rooster and a young chicken hawk. 58m. **DIR:** Robert McKimson. 1948–1955

FOLLOW ME, BOYS! ★★★½ Heartwarming Disney film in which Fred MacMurray plays the new Boy Scout leader in a small 1930s town. 131m. **DIR:** Norman Tokar. **CAST:** Vera Miles, Fred MacMurray, Lillian Gish, Kurt Russell. 1966

FOOL AND THE FLYING SHIP, THE ★★★½ Robin Williams has a lot of fun narrating this Russian folktale, which contains recognizable elements from the Baron Münchhausen legends. Unlike most Rabbit Ears productions, the animation—credited to Henrik Drescher—eschews lush watercolors for a scratchier look reminiscent of *Rugrats*. While not as visually appealing, the story benefits from Williams's ad-libs and the Klezmer Conservatory Band's spirited music. 30m. **DIR:** C. W. Rogers. 1991

FOR BETTER OR FOR WORSE: THE BESTEST PRESENT ★★★★ Lynn Johnston, winner of several awards for cartooning and comic strips, brings her comic-strip family to animated life in this Christmas tale. The family, which is modeled after Johnston's own, faces a crisis when little Elizabeth loses her beloved stuffed bunny. Surprisingly effective and affecting. 23m. **DIR:** Lynn Johnston. 1985

FOR THE LOVE OF BENJI ★★★½ The adorable mutt cleverly saves the day again when he takes on a spy ring in Athens. The whole family can enjoy this one together.

Rated G. 85m. **DIR:** Joe Camp. **CAST:** Benji, Patsy Garrett, Cynthia Smith, Allen Fuizat, Ed Nelson. **1977**

FOX AND THE HOUND ★★★½ Gorgeous animation in the classic Disney style elevates this not-so-classic children's film in which a little fox and a puppy become friends. Later, when they've grown up, their bond clashes with their natural instincts. The younger set will enjoy this lightweight film, but it falls squarely in the void between the studio's two great eras of feature-length cartoons. Rated G. 83m. **DIR:** Art Stevens, Ted Berman, Richard Rich. **1981**

FRASIER THE LOVABLE LION (FRASIER THE SENSUOUS LION) ★★½ Cute film about a zoology professor who discovers he can talk with Frasier, the oversexed lion at the Lion Country Safari Theme Park in Irvine, California. It is a children's film, even though the subject matter does border on being adult. 97m. **DIR:** Pat Shields. **CAST:** Michael Callan, Katherine Justice. **1973**

FREAKY FRIDAY ★★★½ One of Disney's better comedies from the 1970s, this perceptive fantasy allows mom Barbara Harris and daughter Jodie Foster to share a role-reversing out-of-body experience. Adapted with wit by Mary Rodgers from her own book. Rated G. 95m. **DIR:** Gary Nelson. **CAST:** Jodie Foster, Barbara Harris, John Astin, Ruth Buzzi, Kaye Ballard. **1977**

FREDDIE AS F.R.O.7 ★★½ The British fascination with secret agents and magical kingdoms has been fused somewhat awkwardly in this kiddies-only animated film. The cast supplying voices is impressive, however, with Ben Kingsley, Billie Whitelaw, Michael Hordern, and Jonathan Pryce among the participants. Rated G. 90m. **DIR:** Jon Acevski. **1992**

FREE WILLY ★★★★ This family entertainment about a friendship between a troubled boy and an endangered killer whale has a true dramatic edge. Director Simon Wincer is not one for making pap, and, true to form, he brings substance and intelligence to this "boy-and-his-dog" adventure. Strong character development and a staunch avoidance of clichés make this a treat for the entire family. Rated PG for brief profanity. **DIR:** Simon Wincer. **CAST:** Jason James Richter, Lori Petty, Jayne Atkinson, August Schellenberg, Michael Madsen, Michael Ironside, Richard Riehle. **1993**

FREEZE FRAME ★★½ This totally unbelievable tale of how a team of would-be high school reporters expose corporate corruption is just the right confection for younger, after-school viewers. The idea comes across loud and clear: it's okay to be a smart young woman. Unrated, but with mild violence. 78m. **DIR:** William Bindley. **CAST:** Shannen Doherty, Charles Haid, Robyn Douglass, Seth Michaels. **1992**

FROG ★★★½ A nerdish teenager (Scott Grimes) who prefers reptiles to girls discovers a prince who just happens to be in the shape of a frog. Now he's agreed to find a beautiful girl to release him from a witch's evil spell. Lots of laughs for the whole family. 58m. **DIR:** David Grossman. **CAST:** Scott Grimes, Shelley Duvall, Elliott Gould, Paul Williams. **1988**

FROM PLUTO WITH LOVE (LIMITED GOLD EDITION 2) ★★★★ Seen here without his regular costars, Pluto proves quite capable on his own. "T-Bone for Two," in which he tries to snatch a bone from a nasty bulldog, remains one of Disney's funniest cartoons. A frisky little seal turns up in "Pluto's Playmate" (with gorgeous animation by Grant Simmons), and a little turtle comes COD in "Pluto's Surprise Package." The collection is slightly marred by two late-period entries—"Cold Turkey" and "Plutopia"—but all the others are enchanting. 50m. **DIR:** Walt Disney. **1941–1951**

FUN AND FANCY FREE ★★★½ The first segment of this Disney feature is the story of Bongo, a circus bear who runs away and falls for a female bear. It's a moderately entertaining tale. When Edgar Bergen narrates the clever version of "Jack and the Beanstalk," pitting Mickey, Donald, and Goofy against Willie the Giant, things pick up considerably. 96m. **DIR:** Walt Disney. **CAST:** Edgar Bergen, Luana Patten, Dinah Shore. **1947**

G.I. JOE: THE MOVIE ★★ The famous action figure takes on his evil rival COBRA in this feature-length cartoon. The animation is as economical as in the Saturday-morning series and the violence might be objectionable to some parents. Not rated. 93m. **DIR:** Don Jurwich. **1987**

GALAXY EXPRESS, THE 🦃 This Japanese production seems too chilling for youngsters. An actual locomotive moves through the solar system carrying its passengers in search of their dreams. Rated PG. 94m. **DIR:** Taro Rin. **1980**

GARBAGE PAIL KIDS MOVIE, THE 🦃 Disgusting would-be comedy. Rated PG-13. 100m. **DIR:** Rod Amateau. **CAST:** Anthony Newley, Mackenzie Astin, Katie Barberi. **1987**

GATEWAY TO THE MIND ★★★★ Age has not diminished the entertainment value of this Bell science series. Through live action and Chuck Jones's animation, this episode explains the five senses. 58m. **DIR:** Owen Crump. **CAST:** Dr. Frank Baxter. **1958**

GAY PURR-EE ★★★ Feature-length cartoon about the adventures of three country cats in the big city of Paris. Okay for kids, though it's really meant for adults who enjoy musicals, with some good Harold Arlen songs. Unrated. 86m. **DIR:** Abe Levitow. **CAST:** Judy Garland, Robert Goulet, Red Buttons, Morey Amsterdam, Hermione Gingold, Mel Blanc. **1962**

GENERAL SPANKY ★★ A feature-length version of the *Our Gang* series, later popular on TV as *The Little Rascals*. A good attempt to give new life to the characters, but it just proved that audiences can sit still just so long while kids get mischief out of their systems. B&W; 71m. **DIR:** Fred Newmeyer, Gordon Douglas. **CAST:** Spanky McFarland, Buckwheat Thomas, Carl "Alfalfa" Switzer, Phillips Holmes, Rosina Lawrence, Louise Beavers, Hobart Bosworth, Ralph Morgan, Irving Pichel. **1936**

GENTLE GIANT ★★★ A touching, Disneyesque story of a lonely boy and an orphaned black bear cub. Mildly awkward acting and editing, but the film's heart is pure and the animal scenes are very good. Unrated, with only minimal violence. 93m. **DIR:** James Neilson. **CAST:** Dennis Weaver, Vera Miles, Clint Howard, Ralph Meeker. **1967**

GEORGE AND THE CHRISTMAS STAR ★★½ George lives out in space on a desolate planetoid. While decorating his Christmas tree, he dreams of capturing a real star to adorn the topmost branches. He sets off in a self-made spaceship to get the star. Songs written and performed by Paul Anka. 25m. **DIR:** Gerald Potterton. **1985**

GEORGE OF THE JUNGLE ★★★★★ Three cheers for Jay Ward, the late great animator who breathed life into "George, George, George of the Jungle!" Like Ward's other creations, *Rocky and Bullwinkle*, our superhero shares space with other characters in each 34-minute adventure, though Super Chicken and Tom Slick take a backseat to George's jungle (mis)adventures. All seventeen episodes provide a trip down memory lane. Rated G. 578m. **DIR:** Jay Ward. **1967**

GEORGE'S ISLAND ★★★½ Adventure looms for 10-year-old orphan George when he's taken away from his grandfather and placed in a foster home. Escaping in a boat, he comes across an island that's a virtual playground, if it weren't for the ghosts of swashbuckling pirates guarding a treasure. Rated PG for some pirate violence that might scare younger children. 89m. **DIR:** Paul Donovan. **CAST:** Ian Bannen, Sheila McCarthy, Maury Chaykin. **1991**

GERALD MCBOING-BOING (COLUMBIA PICTURES CARTOONS VOLUME THREE) ★★★ This little guy helped to establish his studio of origin, UPA, as a predominant force in the cartoon business of the 1950s. Gerald, created by Dr. Seuss, is an unusual character who communicates only with a series of noises, which is acceptable, since he is only a toddler. First-time viewers will enjoy the opening episode but will notice, as audiences did at the time of his popularity, that his adventures become somewhat repetitive. 30m. **DIR:** Robert Cannon. **1950–1954**

GIGANTOR—VOLS. 1–3 ★★ Early adventure-oriented Japanese animated television series with Inspector Blooper, Jimmy, and his huge, remote-controlled robot superhero, Gigantor. Hilarious corny dialogue. B&W; 75m. each. **DIR:** Fred Ladd. **1964**

GIRL WHO SPELLED FREEDOM, THE ★★★★½ Disney does an excellent job of adapting the Yann family's true story, dramatizing their flight from Cambodia to find refuge with a Tennessee family. Made for TV, this fine film is unrated. 90m. **DIR:** Simon Wincer. **CAST:** Wayne Rogers, Mary Kay Place, Jade Chinn, Kathleen Sisk. **1985**

GNOME-MOBILE, THE ★★½ This one is kid city. From Disney, of course. Walter Brennan doubles as a wealthy businessman and a gnome who must find a wife for his grandson-gnome. The Gnome-Mobile is one fancy Rolls-Royce. 104m. **DIR:** Robert Stevenson. **CAST:** Walter Brennan, Ed Wynn, Matthew Garber, Karen Dotrice. **1967**

GOING BANANAS 💔 Idiotic safari film. Rated PG. 95m. **DIR:** Boaz Davidson. **CAST:** Dom DeLuise, Jimmie Walker, David Mendenhall, Herbert Lom. **1988**

GOLDEN AGE OF LOONEY TOONS, THE: BOB CLAMPETT ★★★★ Before he jumped ship to create Beany & Cecil on his own, Bob Clampett directed some positively manic Warner Bros. cartoons. This collection, which includes most of his best—and his last, "The Big Snooze" (1946)—is highlighted by two undeniable classics: "A Corny Concerto" (1943), a superb lampoon of Disney's *Fantasia*, and "The Great Piggy Bank Robbery" (1946), an existentialist tour-de-force that gave Daffy Duck one of his best starring vehicles. Another surprise is "Horton Hatches an Egg" (1942), an unexpectedly poignant rendition of the Dr. Seuss tale. 54m. **DIR:** Bob Clampett. **1941–46**

GOLDEN AGE OF LOONEY TOONS, THE: BUGS BUNNY BY EACH DIRECTOR ★★★½ Although this represents a great opportunity to compare differing directorial interpretations of the same character, it's a shame some of the examples weren't a bit stronger. Bob Clampett's "Hare Ribbin'" repeats many of the same gags found in other earlier cartoons on this tape, and Friz Freleng's WWII-era "Bugs Bunny Nips the Nips" will dismay mainstream viewers unprepared for its unflattering racial stereotypes. Fred Avery's "The Heckling Hare" is worth historical note, since a dispute over its conclusion eventually cost Avery his job at Warner Bros. The funniest entries, though, are Frank Tashlin's "The Unruly Hare" and Chuck Jones's "Hare Tonic." 55m. **DIR:** Fred Avery, Bob Clampett, Friz Freleng, Chuck Jones, Robert McKimson, Frank Tashlin. **1941–48**

GOLDEN AGE OF LOONEY TOONS, THE: CHUCK JONES ★★★ Chuck Jones was a slow starter. As a result, the seven cartoons on this tape are interesting mostly from an historical standpoint; only a few demonstrate the impeccable timing and sly facial expressions soon to become his trademark. "Porky and Daffy" (1942), definitely the funniest, foreshadows encounters between Bugs, Daffy, Elmer Fudd, and a variety of hand-held signs. The other noteworthy addition is "Inki at the Circus" (1947), a rare appearance for a character that relied overmuch on racial stereotypes. 55m. **DIR:** Chuck Jones. **1938–47**

GOLDEN AGE OF LOONEY TOONS, THE: FIRSTS ★★★★ What a *great* idea for a collection! These seven cartoons represent the debut performances of Warner Bros. most famous animated stars, from Porky Pig (in Friz Freleng's "I Haven't Got a Hat," the weakest entry) to Foghorn Leghorn (in Robert McKimson's "Walky Talky Hawky"). High points include the rather anemic Tweety Bird, who bedevils comedic felines Babbit and Castello in Bob Clampett's "A Tale of Two Kitties" (Sylvester wouldn't come along for another three years), and Chuck Jones's "Odor-able Kitty," marking the first appearance of skunk Pepe Le Pew....here lusting after a disguised *male* cat! 51m. **DIR:** Tex Avery, Bob Clampett, Friz Freleng, Chuck Jones, Robert McKimson. **1935–46**

GOLDEN AGE OF LOONEY TOONS, THE: FRIZ FRELENG ★★★★½ Although sometimes unfairly pilloried as the Warner Bros. animator who assembly lined the dreadful final appearances of Bugs Bunny and crew during the cost-cutting mid-Sixties, Friz Freleng's early years were marked by lush composition and genuinely amusing story lines. This collection has a great mix, including two Oscar nominees ("Rhapsody in Rivets" and "Pigs in a Polka," both gentle spoofs of Disney's *Fantasia*) and one Oscar winner: "Tweetie Pie" (1947), wherein the scrawny bird first teamed with nemesis Sylvester the Cat. "Little Red Riding Rabbit" (1944), which remakes Red as an obnoxious teenaged bobby-soxer, is also a howl. 52m. **DIR:** Friz Freleng. **1941–48**

GOLDEN AGE OF LOONEY TOONS, THE: HURRY FOR HOLLYWOOD ★★★ This collection will probably appeal to animation historians and old-cinema buffs, who will delight at the many caricatures of Hollywood luminaries in the 1930s and 1940s. Friz Freleng's "Hollywood Daffy" and "Slick Hare" are the funniest entries, although Bob Clampett's "What's Cookin', Doc?" (featuring Bugs Bunny's frantic campaign for an Oscar) is also pretty warped. The remaining four cartoons, while slow, undoubtedly will send curious viewers to their old issues of *Life* magazine. 53m. **DIR:** Fred Avery, Bob Clampett, Friz Freleng, Frank Tashlin. **1936–47**

GOLDEN AGE OF LOONEY TOONS, THE: 1930S MUSICALS ★★ Only completists and animation historians should bother with this collection, which features seven *very* early Warner Bros. cartoon-musicals (a subgenre even Disney couldn't always pull off). The most watchable entry is Chuck Jones's "I Love to Singa." 51m. **DIR:** Tex Avery, Friz Freleng, Ben Hardaway, Chuck Jones, Frank Tashlin. **1931–38**

GOLDEN AGE OF LOONEY TOONS, THE: 1940S ZANIES ★★★★ This collection is highlighted by three of Bob Clampett's most deranged Warner Bros. cartoons, the funniest of which is "Baby Bottleneck" (1946), which mixes Porky Pig, Daffy Duck, and a chaotic automated baby-delivery machine (the poor, post–WWII stork having collapsed from overwork). Chuck Jones hits two high points: "Hair-Raising Hare" (1946), with a Peter Lorre-esque mad scientist and his huge, orange, tennis-shod monster; and "Little Orphan Airdale" (1947), featuring the first meeting between Porky Pig and obnoxious Charlie Dog. 50m. **DIR:** Bob Clampett, Chuck Jones, Robert McKimson, Frank Tashlin. **1945–47**

GOLDEN AGE OF LOONEY TOONS, THE: TEX AVERY ★★ Screwball classics, these ain't. These early-entry Warner Bros. cartoons demonstrate only a glimmer of the manic fury for which Tex Avery would become famous, once he switched to MGM Studios. The entries in this package rely too heavily on sight gags lampooning long-forgotten B movies; only "The Bear's Tale" (1940), with its mix of Goldilocks and Little Red Riding Hood, foreshadows the glee with which Avery soon would skewer fairy tales. 58m. **DIR:** Tex Avery. **1938–41**

GOLDEN AGE OF LOONEY TOONS, THE: THE ART OF BUGS ★★★★ Different directors tackle duplicate themes in this intriguing collection, which opens with three different renditions of Bugs Bunny's race with Cecil Turtle: Fred Avery's "Tortoise Beats Hare," Bob Clampett's "Tortoise Wins by a Hare," and Friz Freleng's "Rabbit Transit." Clampett's "The Old Grey Hare" is an undeniable classic, with its look at a youthful Bugs and Elmer Fudd; the best entry, however, is Chuck Jones's "Haredevil Hare," which features the debut of Marvin the Martian. 54m. **DIR:** Fred Avery, Bob Clampett, Friz Freleng, Chuck Jones. **1941–48**

GOLDEN SEAL, THE ★★★½ A young boy (Torquil Campbell) living with his parents (Steven Railsback and Penelope Milford) on the Aleutian Islands makes friends with a rare golden seal and her pup. It's a good story, predictably told. Rated PG. 95m.

DIR: Frank Zuniga. **CAST:** Torquil Campbell, Steve Railsback, Penelope Milford. **1983**

GOLDILOCKS AND THE THREE BEARS ♥ This *Faerie Tale Theatre* production is a lifeless adaptation of the story about a little girl who trespasses into the home of three bears and creates havoc. 51m. **DIR:** Gilbert Cates. **CAST:** Tatum O'Neal, Hoyt Axton, Alex Karras, John Lithgow, Donovan Scott. **1982**

GOLDY, THE LAST OF THE GOLDEN BEARS ♥ Low production values, inane dialogue, and inconsistent time jumps make a mess of this let's-save-a-bear programmer. 91m. **DIR:** Trevor Black. **CAST:** Jeff Richards. **1984**

GOOD GRIEF, CHARLIE BROWN ★★★★ Linus and his blanket are the subject of these five tales, all drawn from *The Charlie Brown and Snoopy Show.* Poor Linus can't get much respect; Lucy locks the blanket in a closet for two weeks, Sally ransoms it for a marriage proposal, and it winds up in the claws of the neighborhood cat. 30m. **DIR:** Bill Melendez, Sam Jaimes, Phil Roman. **1983–1985**

GOOD, THE BAD, AND HUCKLEBERRY HOUND, THE ★★½ Every Western cliché in the book gets spoofed when a "mysterious, steely-eyed, and silent-type stranger" (Huckleberry Hound) rides into the town of Two-Bit, California, to battle the socially inept Dalton Gang. Like most full-length Hanna-Barbera productions, this one runs on a bit, but the script is better than average. 94m. **DIR:** Ray Patterson. **1988**

GOODBYE BIRD, THE ★★ A teenaged boy having a difficult time coping with his parents' divorce gets in trouble at school and is assigned to a work program at the local pound. He decides to rescue the unwanted creatures therein by setting up an animal shelter in a deserted barn. Sentimental, far-fetched story may still please youngsters. Rated G. 91m. **DIR:** William Clark. **CAST:** Christopher Pitt, Cindy Pickett, Wayne Rogers. **1992**

GOODBYE, MISS 4TH OF JULY ★★★½ Inspirational true story of a young Greek immigrant who refuses to let her American dream be tarnished by bigotry in 1917 West Virginia. Roxana Zal plays spunky Niki Janus, who befriends Big John Creed (Lou Gossett Jr.) and thus attracts the wrath of the Ku Klux Klan. Made for the Disney Channel, this has high production values. Unrated; contains frightening scenes of night riders in action. 89m. **DIR:** George Miller. **CAST:** Roxana Zal, Lou Gossett Jr., Chris Sarandon, Chantal Contouri, Chynna Phillips, Mitchell Anderson. **1988**

GOODBYE, MY LADY ★★★ A young boy in the bayou country finds a lost dog and takes it to his heart, knowing that it probably belongs to someone else and that he might have to give it up. Director William Wellman transforms James Street's novel into a warm, enduring film. This uncluttered little gem features standout performances by Brandon de Wilde and Walter Brennan as the youngster and his uncle. B&W; 94m. **DIR:** William Wellman. **CAST:** Walter Brennan, Phil Harris, Brandon de Wilde, Sidney Poitier, William Hopper, Louise Beavers. **1956**

GOOF TROOP ★★★ The world's most uncoordinated animated animal, Goofy, is joined by his son Max and conniving neighbor Pete in this series of mishaps and adventures from the Disney Studios. The animators strive to keep the timing and pratfalls of the classic Goofy features and succeed more often than not. 50m. **DIR:** Glen Kennedy. **1993**

GREAT EXPECTATIONS (1983) ★★ Spotty though interesting-enough animated adaptation of Charles Dickens's classic tale about a young man's lessons in maturity. There's a lot of tragedy here (as expected), which may catch the attention of older children, but small youngsters will no doubt find this too low-key. 72m. **DIR:** Jean Tych. **1983**

GREAT EXPECTATIONS (1989) ★★★★½ First-rate, British-made miniseries of the Charles Dickens classic features outstanding performances, especially by Anthony Hopkins as Magwitch and Jean Simmons (Estella in director David Lean's 1946 version) as the mysterious and poignant Miss Haversham. Recommended for the whole family. 310m. **DIR:** Kevin O'Connor. **CAST:** Anthony Hopkins, Jean Simmons, John Rhys-Davies, Ray McAnally, Kim Thomson. **1989**

GREAT LAND OF SMALL, THE ★★ Beautifully photographed but slightly disjointed tale of a magical dwarf who can only be seen by children. Rated G; should appeal to children, but nothing in it for adults. 94m. **DIR:** Vojta Jasny. **CAST:** Karen Elkin, Michael Blouin, Michael J. Anderson, Ken Roberts. **1987**

GREAT LOCOMOTIVE CHASE, THE ★★★½ Fess Parker and his band of spies infiltrate the South and abscond with a railroad train. Jeffrey Hunter is the conductor who chases them to regain possession of the train. This is a straightforward telling of actual events, emphasizing action and suspense. 85m. **DIR:** Francis D. Lyon. **CAST:** Fess Parker, Jeffrey Hunter, Jeff York, John Lupton. **1956**

GREAT MUPPET CAPER, THE ★★★★ Miss Piggy, Kermit the Frog, Fozzie Bear, and the Great Gonzo attempt to solve the mysterious theft of the fabulous Baseball Diamond in this, the second feature-length motion picture Muppet outing. Rated G. 95m. **DIR:** Jim Henson. **CAST:** Muppets, Diana Rigg, Charles Grodin, Peter Falk, Peter Ustinov, Jack Warden, Robert Morley. **1981**

GREAT SPACE CHASE ★★ In this feature-length cartoon, Mighty Mouse must battle the evil Harry the Heartless when he tries to steal the Dreaded Doomsday Machine. So-so Terrytoons animation and feeble plotting. 88m. **DIR:** Marsh Lamore, Ed Friedman, Lou Zukor, Gwen Wetzler. **1983**

GREENSTONE, THE ★★★ A young boy and his family live on the edge of an enchanted forest. But the forest and the Greenstone inside call to the young boy. He goes into the forest and finds the stone, which transports him to a magical fantasy world. A good family film for all ages. Rated G. 48m. **DIR:** Kevin Irvine. **CAST:** Joseph Corey, John Riley, Kathleen Irvine, Jack Mauck. **1985**

GRENDEL, GRENDEL, GRENDEL ★★★ Charming animated feature that recasts the legend of Beowulf from the point of view of the monster, depicted sympathetically as a peaceable sort with the bad habit of munching on the occasional villager. Adapted from John Gardner's novel, this is fine for kids and grownups. Unrated. 88m. **DIR:** Alexander Stitt. **CAST:** Peter Ustinov, Keith Michell. **1979**

GREYFRIARS BOBBY ★★★ Somewhat lethargic tale of a dog that is befriended by an entire town after his owner dies. The plot drags, but the cast and the atmosphere of the settings make it worth watching. 91m. **DIR:** Don Chaffey. **CAST:** Donald Crisp, Laurence Naismith, Alex Mackenzie, Kay Walsh. **1961**

GULLIVER'S TRAVELS (1939) ★★½ Made and issued as an answer to Disney's *Snow White and the Seven Dwarfs*, this full-length cartoon of the famous Jonathan Swift satire about an English sailor who falls among tiny people in a land called Lilliput is just so-so. 74m. **DIR:** Dave Fleischer. **CAST:** Lanny Ross, Jessica Dragonette (voices). **1939**

GULLIVER'S TRAVELS (1977) ★★ Richard Harris seems lost in this meager re-telling of the Jonathan Swift satire. The combination of live action and animation further detracts from the story. Rated G. 80m. **DIR:** Peter R. Hunt. **CAST:** Richard Harris, Catherine Schell. **1977**

GUMBY AND THE WILD WEST (VOLUME FOUR) ★★ While there are a few out West selections in this volume, the title is somewhat misleading because Gumby and Pokey find more to do here than spend time with cowboys and Indians. Shorts included: "The Glob," "The Kachinas," "School for Squares," and "The Golden Iguana." 60m. **DIR:** Art Clokey. **1956**

GUMBY CELEBRATION, A (VOLUME TEN) 🦃 Most certainly a collection of Gumby adventures that would have even our little clay hero crimson with embarrassment. 60m. **DIR:** Art Clokey. **1956**

GUMBY FOR PRESIDENT (VOLUME NINE) ★★ Long-term Gumby constituents will be disappointed in viewing this assortment, which includes: "Candidate for President," "Little Lost Pony," "Toy Joy," "Yard Work Made Easy," "Point of Honor," "Mysterious Fires," "Do-It-Yourself Gumby," "Siege of Boonesboro," "Gold Rush Gumby," and "Wishful Thinking." 60m. **DIR:** Art Clokey. **1956**

GUMBY MAGIC (VOLUME TWO) ★★ A tape for true Gumby purists, including the first three (Gumby in his primitive period) Gumby adventures, which find Old Pointy Head on a "Moon Trip," "Trapped on the Moon," and just plain old "Gumby on the Moon" (Is there something we don't know?) Six other adventures, including the somewhat unsettling "Robot Rumpus," round out the menu. 60m. **DIR:** Art Clokey. **1956**

GUMBY RIDES AGAIN (VOLUME FIVE) ★★ Run-of-the-mill Gumby fare here in ten different features, including "How Not to Trap Lions," "Odd Ball," "Toy Capers," and "The Ferris Wheel Mystery." May be too tame for older youngsters, and most adults will tire of this one quickly. 60m. **DIR:** Art Clokey. **1956**

GUMBY SUMMER, A (VOLUME EIGHT) ★★ Though hardier Gumby fans may be able to recall one or two offerings in this collection of adventures, most of this is bottom-of-the-clay barrel. This volume includes "The Blue Goo," "Gumby League," "The Missile Bird" (mildly entertaining), "Shady Lemonade," "Motor Mania," "Making Squares," "Pokey Express," and three additional adventures. 60m. **DIR:** Art Clokey. **1956**

GUMBY'S FUN FLING (VOLUME ELEVEN) 🦃 More scrapings from the bottom of the Gumby archives. 30m. **DIR:** Art Clokey. **1956**

GUMBY'S HOLIDAY SPECIAL (VOLUME SEVEN) ★★★ A collection of Gumby adventures with holiday themes, such as "Son of Liberty," "Santa Witch," "The Golden Gosling," "Gumby Crosses the Delaware," "Scrooge Loose," and "Pilgrims on the Rocks," in addition to two other featurettes. 60m. **DIR:** Art Clokey. **1956**

GUMBY'S INCREDIBLE JOURNEY (VOLUME SIX) ★★ Here's an easy-to-pass-up collection. Titles include: "Fantastic Farmer," "Too Loo," "The Racing Game," "Treasure for Henry," "Who's What?," and by far the most interesting adventure, "The Small Planets," in which Gumby and his pal run away from home in a spaceship. 60m. **DIR:** Art Clokey. **1956**

GUS ★★★½ This Disney comedy has a mule named Gus delivering the winning kicks for a losing football team. Naturally, the rival team kidnaps the mule before the big game, and the search is on. Lots of slapstick comedy for the kids to enjoy in this one. Rated G. 96m. **DIR:** Vincent McEveety. **CAST:** Edward Asner, Don Knotts, Gary Grimes, Dick Van Patten. **1976**

GYPSY COLT ★★★ A good Americanized updating of *Lassie Come Home* with a girl and her horse. The exciting and well-filmed scenes of the horse, Gypsy, alone and in peril will hold the interest of children and adults. Fine Western scenery is a plus. 72m. **DIR:** Andrew Marton. **CAST:** Donna Corcoran, Ward Bond, Frances Dee, Larry Keating, Lee Van Cleef. **1954**

HADLEY'S REBELLION ★★★ Low-key drama of the growing pains encountered by a country boy as he tries to adjust to a new life in California. Well-intentioned script lacks impact, and Griffin O'Neal makes for a bland hero. Rated PG. 96m. **DIR:** Fred Walton. **CAST:** Griffin O'Neal, William Devane, Charles Durning, Adam Baldwin. **1984**

HANS BRINKER ★★★ This is the well-known tale of Hans Brinker and his silver skates. Made this time as a musical, it stars Robin Askwith as Hans with Eleanor Parker and Richard Basehart as his mother and invalid father, and there are some pleasant skating sequences. This film would make particularly good family viewing for the holidays. It is not rated, but would be considered a G. 103m. **DIR:** Robert Scheerer. **CAST:** Robin Askwith, Eleanor Parker, Richard Basehart, Roberta Torey, John Gregson, Cyril Ritchard. **1979**

HANS CHRISTIAN ANDERSEN'S THUMBELINA ★★★ Perhaps we've been spoiled by recent Disney works like *The Little Mermaid, Beauty and the Beast,* and *Aladdin,* but this telling of the famous children's tale seems awfully slight in the story and song departments. The animation is fine, although not up to Don Bluth's highest standards, but the adventures of its tiny heroine are a bit on the ho-hum side. That said, little girls will adore it. Rated G. 83m. **DIR:** Don Bluth, Gary Goldman. **1994**

HANSEL AND GRETEL ★★★ Joan Collins is a perfectly wicked stepmother-cum-witch in this *Faerie Tale Theatre* production of the classic tale of two children who learn a valuable lesson when they take candy from a stranger. 51m. **DIR:** James Frawley. **CAST:** Joan Collins, Rick Schroder, Paul Dooley, Bridgette Anderson. **1982**

HAPPIEST MILLIONAIRE, THE ★★★ The Disney version of a factual memoir of life in the Philadelphia household of eccentric millionaire Anthony J. Drexel Biddle. Lively light entertainment that hops along between musical numbers. 118m. **DIR:** Norman Tokar. **CAST:** Fred MacMurray, Tommy Steele, Greer Garson, Geraldine Page, Gladys Cooper, John Davidson. **1967**

HAPPY BIRTHDAY BUGS: 50 LOONEY YEARS ★★★★★ Tributes just don't get better! Director Gary Smith uses rabbit-fire pacing to blend an animated history with genuinely amusing commendations from various stars. The best is saved for last: "50 Years of Bugs in 3½ minutes," a frenetic collection of clips assembled by Chuck Workman (an Oscar winner for his short, *Precious Images*). Don't miss this one. 48m. **DIR:** Gary Smith. **CAST:** Harry Anderson, Milton Berle, Bill Cosby, Little Richard, Pierce Brosnan. **1990**

HAPPY NEW YEAR, CHARLIE BROWN ★★★ Charlie Brown's hopes of a carefree Christmas vacation are dashed when he is assigned the task of turning *War and Peace* into a book report. His resolve weakens when Peppermint Patty hosts a New Year's Eve party that includes Heather (the little red-haired girl). Desiree Goyette and Ed Bogas bring events to a crashing halt with their banal music and lyrics. 25m. **DIR:** Bill Melendez, Sam Jaimes. **1985**

HAVE PICNIC BASKET, WILL TRAVEL ★★ This "feature" is a collection of cartoon shorts—and not very good ones, at that—loosely grouped around the common theme of picnics and vacations. A full-length Flintstones drama and two Huckleberry Hound shorts are the best of a mediocre lot. 90m. **DIR:** William Hanna, Joseph Barbera. **CAST:** Animated. **1958–1965**

HE-MAN AND THE MASTERS OF THE UNIVERSE (SERIES) 🦃 A poorly produced cartoon series about the heroic exploits of Prince Adam of the planet Eternia. 45m. **DIR:** Hal Sutherland. **1983**

HEARTBEEPS ★★★ Andy Kaufman and Bernadette Peters play robots who fall in love and decide to explore the world around them. It's a good family film, and the kids will probably love it. Rated PG. 79m. **DIR:** Allan Arkush. **CAST:** Andy Kaufman, Bernadette Peters, Randy Quaid. **1981**

HEATHCLIFF—THE MOVIE 🦃 An example of everything that is wrong with cartoons today, this release is sloppily drawn, poorly scripted, and generally pointless. Rated G. 89m. **DIR:** Bruno Bianchi. **1986**

HEIDI (1937) ★★★★ This classic stars a spunky Shirley Temple as the girl who is taken away from her kind and loving grandfather's home in the Swiss Alps and forced to live with her cruel aunt. B&W; 88m. **DIR:** Allan Dwan. **CAST:** Shirley Temple, Jean Hersholt, Arthur Treacher. **1937**

HEIDI (1965) ★★★★ Shirley Temple fans will disagree, but we think that the beautiful location scenes filmed in the Swiss Alps and the generally high level of production and performances make this the best version on video of the classic children's tale. It's been updated to the present day, but otherwise it is faithful to Johanna Spyri's book. Dubbed in English. 95m. **DIR:** Werner Jacobs. **CAST:** Eva Maria Singhammer. **1965**

HEIDI'S SONG ★★ Only those 5 years old and younger will enjoy this feature-length cartoon adaptation of Johanna Spyri's classic children's tale. Rated G. 94m. **DIR:** Robert Taylor. **1982**

HERBIE GOES BANANAS ★★½ This is the corniest and least funny of Disney's "Love Bug" series. This time Herbie is headed for Brazil to compete in the Grand Primio. Rated G. 93m. **DIR:** Vincent McEveety. **CAST:** Cloris Leachman, Charles Martin Smith, John Vernon, Stephan W. Burns, Harvey Korman. **1980**

HERBIE GOES TO MONTE CARLO ★★★½ Herbie the VW falls in love with a sports car as they compete in a race from Paris to Monte Carlo. There are lots of laughs in this one. Rated G. 104m. **DIR:** Vincent McEveety. **CAST:** Dean Jones, Don Knotts, Julie Sommars, Eric Braeden, Roy Kinnear, Jacque Marin. **1977**

HERBIE RIDES AGAIN ★★★½ This Disney comedy-adventure is a sequel to *The Love Bug*. This time, Helen Hayes, Ken Berry, and Stephanie Powers depend on Herbie, the magical Volkswagen, to save them from an evil Keenan Wynn. Rated G. 88m. **DIR:** Robert Stevenson. **CAST:** Helen Hayes, Ken Berry, Stefanie Powers, Keenan Wynn. **1974**

HERE COMES DROOPY ★★★ Cartoonist Tex Avery's diminutive mutt, conceived in 1943 as a tribute to Bill Thompson's "Mr. Wimple" on the radio series *Fibber McGee & Molly* (and Thompson did Droopy's voice, as well), absolutely never lost his cool. Alas, this collection includes only latter-day adventures, after limited-animation had transformed Droopy from his original pudgy self to just another two-dimensional straight man. 44m. **DIR:** Tex Avery, Michael Lah. **1951–57**

HERE COMES SANTA CLAUS 🦃 Two kids visit Santa at the North Pole to make a personal plea for the return of the boy's parents on Christmas. 78m. **DIR:** Christian Gion. **CAST:** Karen Cheryl, Armand Meffre. **1984**

HERE'S DONALD ★★★★ The avian star of the luxuriously rendered "Donald's Ostrich" is clearly an ancestor of the stars used in the "Dance of the Hours" sequence in *Fantasia;* aside from that historical reference, the cartoon itself is marvelous, as poor Donald tries to prevent the waddling bird from swallowing everything that isn't nailed down. Donald and Goofy also go "Crazy With the Heat" during a desert trek for gasoline. 22m. **DIR:** Walt Disney. **1937–1947**

HERE'S GOOFY ★★★½ The rubberized Goofy is best represented in this trio of cartoons by "Knight for a Day," which proves that underdogs can sometimes beat the best. "For Whom the Bull Toils" is the better of the remaining two entries, both of which employ the more limited post–World War II artwork. 22m. **DIR:** Walt Disney. **1945–1953**

HERE'S MICKEY ★★★½ Donald Duck's frantic attempts to complete a nursery rhyme in "Orphan's Benefit" are the best part of the finest cartoon in this trio; Dick Lundy's rendering of the mumbling mallard is simply priceless. A surrealistic touch is employed for "Mickey's Garden," which finds the famous mouse battling house-size insects. By contrast, "Mickey's Birthday Party" is lethargic and boring. 27m. **DIR:** Walt Disney. **1935–1941**

HERE'S PLUTO ★★★ The needlessly infantile "Springtime for Pluto," complete with mawkish songs, mars this trilogy; fortunately, the luxurious artwork of "Pantry Pirate" (as Pluto tries for a roast ham) is compensation of sorts. "Mail Dog," with supporting lunacy by a snowshoe hare, is moderately amusing. 23m. **DIR:** Walt Disney. **1941–1947**

HE'S YOUR DOG, CHARLIE BROWN ★★★★½ Snoopy misbehaves and is ordered back to the Daisy Hill Puppy Farm in this delightful entry, the last to employ the original character voices first heard in *A Charlie Brown Christmas*. Our hero postpones his fate by hiding out with Peppermint Patty, who still—at this point—thinks of him as the "funny-looking kid with the big nose." 25m. **DIR:** Bill Melendez. **1968**

HEY CINDERELLA! ★★★½ A completely Muppetized, musical retelling of the classic fairy tale, complete with a coach driven by Kermit and pulled by a purple beastie named Splurge. Charming and fun for parents as well as children. 54m. **DIR:** Jim Henson. **1970**

HEY THERE, IT'S YOGI BEAR ★★★ With this movie, Hanna-Barbera Studios made the jump from TV to feature-length cartoon. The result is consistently pleasant. Rated G. 89m. **DIR:** William Hanna, Joseph Barbera. **CAST:** Mel Blanc, J. Pat O'Malley, Julie Bennett, Daws Butler, Don Messick. **1964**

HIDEAWAYS, THE ★★★ Two bored suburban kids spend a week hiding out in the Metropolitan Museum of Art. Interested in one of the statues, the duo tracks down its donor, an eccentric rich woman (Ingrid Bergman) who lives in a mansion in New Jersey. Fanciful tale won't appeal to all children, but it has a legion of admirers. Originally titled *From the Mixed-Up Files of Mrs. Basil E. Frankweiler.* Rated G. 105m. **DIR:** Fielder Cook. **CAST:** Ingrid Bergman, Sally Prager, Johnny Doran, George Rose, Richard Mulligan, Madeline Kahn. **1973**

HILLS OF HOME ★★★★ Effective family fare about an aging doctor and his devoted collie, Lassie. While tending to the townspeople, the kindly physician attempts to cure his dog's fear of water only to need help himself. A satisfying tearjerker in the mold of *All Creatures Great and Small*. 97m. **DIR:** Fred M. Wilcox. **CAST:** Edmund Gwenn, Tom Drake, Janet Leigh, Donald Crisp, Rhys Williams, Reginald Owen, Alan Napier, Eileen Erskine. **1948**

HOBBIT, THE ★★ Disappointing cartoon version of the classic J. R. R. Tolkien fantasy. Orson Bean provides the voice of the dwarflike Hobbit, Bilbo Baggins, and John Huston, at his stentorian best, is the wizard Gandalf. Unfortunately, all the creatures have a cutesy look, which doesn't gel with the story. An unrated TV movie. 78m. **DIR:** Arthur Rankin Jr., Jules Bass. **1978**

HOBSON'S CHOICE (1983) ★★★½ Sharon Gless is the main attraction in this quaint period drama, set in 1914 New Orleans. She's the spirited and capable eldest daughter of the irascible Henry Horatio Hobson (Jack Warden), seller of shoes and self-proclaimed "pillar of the community." Gless methodically arranges a marriage with his finest shoemaker (Richard Thomas). Unrated; suitable for family viewing. 100m. **DIR:** Gilbert Cates. **CAST:** Sharon Gless, Jack Warden, Richard Thomas, Bert Remsen, Robert Englund, Lillian Gish. **1983**

HOCUS POCUS ★★★½ While not much of a box-office hit, this cauldron's brew of thrills and laughs will delight children. Three witches, revived after 300 years, wreak havoc in modern-day Salem, Massachusetts. The movie is scary enough to involve youngsters but not so frightening as to give them nightmares. We also enjoyed the over-the-top performances by Bette Midler, Sarah Jessica Parker, and Kathy Najimy as the broom-riding trio. Rated PG for brief vulgarity and scary stuff. **DIR:** Kenny Ortega. **CAST:** Bette Midler, Sarah Jessica Parker, Kathy Najimy, Omri Katz, Thora Birch, Vinessa Shaw, Amanda Shepherd. **1993**

HOME ALONE 2: LOST IN NEW YORK ★★★★ Essentially a bigger-budgeted remake of the first film, this sequel is filled with belly laughs. Writer-producer John Hughes does tend to get a bit maudlin, but Macaulay Culkin's misadventures in the Big Apple, after being more believably separated from his parents this time, are more consistently entertaining than his first time *Home Alone.* Rated PG for profanity and slapstick violence. 113m. **DIR:** Chris Columbus. **CAST:** Macaulay Culkin, Joe Pesci, Daniel Stern, Catherine O'Hara, John Heard, Tim Curry, Brenda Fricker, Eddie Bracken. **1992**

HOMEWARD BOUND: THE INCREDIBLE JOURNEY ★★★★½ The folks at Walt Disney Pictures take the animal adventure to artistic heights. A remake of Disney's *The Incredible Journey,* this highly entertaining movie gives voices (supplied by Sally Field, Michael J. Fox, and Don Ameche) and hilarious dialogue to two dogs and a cat, who attempt to make their way home through the untamed wilderness of a national forest. A delight for all ages. Rated G. 84m. **DIR:** Duwayne Dunham. **CAST:** Robert Hays, Kim Greist, Jean Smart, Veronica Lauren, Kevin Chevalia, Benj Thall. **1993**

HONEY, I BLEW UP THE KID ★★★★ This is a delightful sequel to *Honey, I Shrunk The Kids.* The new adventure once again finds scientist Rick Moranis working on an experiment, only this time it's an enlargement ray that blows up his kid to 112 feet tall! The special effects are remarkable. Rated PG. 89m. **DIR:** Randal Kleiser. **CAST:** Rick Moranis, Marcia Strassman, Lloyd Bridges, Robert Oliveri, John Shea. **1992**

HONEY, I SHRUNK THE KIDS ★★★½ Old-fashioned Disney fun in the *Absent-Minded Professor* tradition gets contemporary special effects and solid bits of comedy. Rick Moranis is the scientist who invents a machine that, when accidentally triggered, shrinks his and the neighbors' kids to ant-size. Rated PG for slight profanity. 100m. **DIR:** Joe Johnston. **CAST:** Rick Moranis, Jared Rushton, Matt Frewer. **1989**

HOOK ★★★½ For all its minor flaws, director Steven Spielberg's heartfelt continuation of James M. Barrie's *Peter Pan* is fine family entertainment. There are some dull spots, but it's doubtful they'll be as glaring on the small screen. Look for Glenn Close and singer David Crosby in brief bits as pirates on Hook's ship. Rated PG for vulgar language. 137m. **DIR:** Steven Spielberg. **CAST:** Robin Williams, Dustin Hoffman, Julia Roberts, Bob Hoskins, Maggie Smith, Charlie Korsmo, Phil Collins, Glenn Close, David Crosby. **1991**

HOPPITY GOES TO TOWN ★★★ Max and Dave Fleischer, of Betty Boop and Popeye fame, brought their distinctive style of animation to this feature about the insect residents of Bugtown. The Fleischers were better at making short cartoons—there's not enough plot or characterization here to justify a feature—but their style is always delightful. Adults may enjoy it more than kids. 77m. **DIR:** Dave Fleischer. **CAST:** Kenny Gardner, Gwen Williams, Jack Mercer, Ted Pierce. **1941**

HORSE IN THE GRAY FLANNEL SUIT, THE ★★ This Disney film takes you back to America's early awareness of Madison Avenue and the many games and gimmicks it devises to get the almighty dollar. Dean Jones is an ad executive who develops an ad campaign around his daughter's devotion to horses. 113m. **DIR:** Norman Tokar. **CAST:** Dean Jones, Diane Baker, Lloyd Bochner, Fred Clark, Kurt Russell. **1968**

HORSE WITHOUT A HEAD, THE ★★★ Good old Disney fun as a group of boys give more trouble to a band of thieves than they can handle. An excellent cast headed by Leo McKern as a devious no-gooder. The whole family will enjoy this unrated film. 89m. **DIR:** Don Chaffey. **CAST:** Leo McKern, Jean-Pierre Aumont, Herbert Lom, Pamela Franklin, Vincent Winter. 1963

HORSEMASTERS ★★ Annette and Tommy team up once again in this average story about young Americans pursuing their careers in horse training among the great riding academies of Europe. 77m. **DIR:** Bill Fairchild. **CAST:** Annette Funicello, Janet Munro, Tommy Kirk, Donald Pleasence, Tony Britton. 1961

HOT LEAD AND COLD FEET ★★ This predictable, occasionally funny Western stars Jim Dale as twin brothers; one is a drunk who terrorizes the town and the other a missionary. Rated G. 89m. **DIR:** Robert Butler. **CAST:** Jim Dale, Karen Valentine, Don Knotts, Jack Elam, Darren McGavin. 1978

HOW BUGS BUNNY WON THE WEST ★★★ Something of an oddity with actor Denver Pyle recounting the wascally wabbit's exploits in the Old West. Regrettably, no complete cartoons are included, but we do get choice moments from Chuck Jones's "Drip-Along Daffy" (1951) and "Barbary Coast Bunny" (1956), Friz Freleng's "Wild and Woolly Hare" (1959), and several others. 24m. **DIR:** Hal Geer. 1978

HOW THE BEST WAS WON (LIMITED GOLD EDITION 2) ★★★ Look for Ward Kimball's caricatures of Disney-studio animators (as picadors) in the Oscar-winning "Ferdinand the Bull" (1938), but don't expect much from the four other cartoons. This collection will appeal mostly to the very young. "Three Orphan Kittens" and "Funny Little Bunnies" are overbearingly cute, and the one Mickey Mouse entry—"Building a Building"—is a routine black-and-white adventure. 48m. **DIR:** Walt Disney. 1933–1960

HOW THE LEOPARD GOT HIS SPOTS ★★★½ Rudyard Kipling's "Just So Stories" receive another reworking by the Windham Hill/Rabbit Ears team, and the result is another little gem. Narrator Danny Glover lacks the wry verbal parody of Jack Nicholson (who handles the other Kipling adaptations), but Lori Lohstoeter's illustrations provide ample humor of their own. 30m. **DIR:** Tim Raglin. 1989

HOW THE RHINOCEROS GOT HIS SKIN AND HOW THE CAMEL GOT HIS HUMP ★★★★½ Jack Nicholson's soft-spoken wryness adds considerable depth to a pair of entries from Rudyard Kipling's "Just So Stories." The first tale explains how the rhinoceros went from a creature of "no manners" to one of a "very bad temper," while the second shows the fate that befalls a snooty camel. 30m. **DIR:** Mark Sottnick. 1987

HUCKLEBERRY FINN (1974) ★★ The weakest version of the popular story, mainly because forgettable songs take the place of personality. The basic plot of a young boy learning about life from a runaway slave is there, but the players look and act bored. Rated G. 117m. **DIR:** J. Lee Thompson. **CAST:** Jeff East, Paul Winfield, David Wayne, Harvey Korman, Arthur O'Connell, Gary Merrill, Kim O'Brien. 1974

HUCKLEBERRY FINN (1975) ★★★★ Ron Howard does a fine job as Mark Twain's mischievous misfit. This made-for-TV film is well worth watching. The supporting actors are fun to watch, too. 74m. **DIR:** Robert Totten. **CAST:** Ron Howard, Donny Most, Antonio Fargas, Merle Haggard, Jack Elam, Royal Dano, Sarah Selby. 1975

HUMAN RACE CLUB, THE ★★ Good intentions cannot compensate for the heavy-handed sermonizing found in these morality tales for 8-to-12-year-olds. Each of the three tapes in this series contains two 30-minute "value lessons" presented in limited animation. Each tale ends with an epilogue by creator Joy Berry (author of numerous children's self-help books) and an insipid song. 60m. **DIR:** Steve Sheldon. 1987

HURRAY FOR BETTY BOOP 💔 Snippets of classic cartoons (in their artificially recolored state) are clumsily strung together with all new narration. 81m. **DIR:** Max Fleischer, Dave Fleischer. 1980

IMPORTANCE OF BEING DONALD, THE ★★★★½ The evils of smoking are illustrated by "Donald's Better Self," a luxuriously animated, early starring vehicle capturing Don in his childhood phase. The equally gorgeous "Timber!" concludes with a great chase between Donald and the evil Black Pete. The final feature, "Polar Trappers," teams Donald with Goofy. Don't miss this top-notch collection. 26m. **DIR:** Walt Disney. 1938–1941

IN SEARCH OF THE CASTAWAYS ★★★★ Young Hayley Mills enlists the aid of financial backers Maurice Chevalier and Wilfrid Hyde-White in search for her missing father, a ship captain. Superb special effects depict the many obstacles and natural disasters the searchers must overcome. 100m. **DIR:** Robert Stevenson. **CAST:** Hayley Mills, Maurice Chevalier, George Sanders, Wilfrid Hyde-White, Michael Anderson Jr. 1962

IN SEARCH OF THE WOW WOW WIBBLE WOGGLE WAZZLE WOODLE WOO! ★★★★ An infectiously scored, engagingly staged musical, featuring Tim Noah in what is virtually a one-man show. The talented Noah is assisted by a company of Muppet-like soft-sculpture creatures, such as Musty Moldy Melvin and Greasy Grimy Gerty. A celebration of the imagination, this film will appeal to the child in everyone. Rated G. 55m. **DIR:** Barry Caillier. **CAST:** Tim Noah. 1985

INCREDIBLE JOURNEY, THE ★★★★½ This live-action Walt Disney film is the story of two dogs and a cat that make a treacherous journey across Canada to find their home and family. It's impossible to dislike this heartwarming tale. 80m. **DIR:** Fletcher Markle. **CAST:** Emile Genest, John Drainie. **1963**

INSPECTOR GADGET (SERIES) ★★★ Don Adams supplies the voice for the title hero, whom adults will find strikingly reminiscent of Adams's Maxwell Smart character. Children seem to have a particular fondness for the inspector's "gadgets," which he always has on hand to get him out of a fix. Animated in Japan, tapes provide an hour and a half of entertainment (3–4 episodes) with a likable hero. 90m. **DIR:** Jean Chalopin, Bruno Bianchi. **1983**

INTERNATIONAL VELVET ★★ A disappointing sequel to *National Velvet* (1944), with Tatum O'Neal only passable as the young horsewoman who rides to victory. Rated PG. 127m. **DIR:** Bryan Forbes. **CAST:** Tatum O'Neal, Christopher Plummer, Anthony Hopkins. **1978**

INTO THE WEST ★★★★ Here's a wonderful family film that kids will adore and adults will find fascinating. Two Irish boys find themselves off on an exciting journey after they are "adopted" by a magical horse. The lads are part of a little-known Irish subculture: the Travelers, a gyspylike clan descended from an ancient Celtic tribe. Rated PG for very brief profanity. 91m. **DIR:** Mike Newell. **CAST:** Gabriel Byrne, Ellen Barkin, Colm Meaney, Ciaran Fitzgerald, Rory Conroy, David Kelly, Johnny Murphy. **1993**

IS THIS GOODBYE, CHARLIE BROWN? ★★★ Snoopy takes over the psychiatric booth and inherits the blanket when Linus and Lucy are forced to move, victims of a father with changing jobs. The kids' world is inappropriately invaded by adults (a rare miscalculation in this series). 25m. **DIR:** Phil Roman. **1983**

IT CAME UPON A MIDNIGHT CLEAR ★★ Cornball story about a New York cop (Mickey Rooney) who dies from a heart attack but arranges with heavenly higher-ups to spend one last Christmas with his grandson (Scott Grimes). *It's a Wonderful Life* this is not. Made for television. 99m. **DIR:** Peter H. Hunt. **CAST:** Mickey Rooney, Scott Grimes, Barrie Youngfellow, George Gaynes, Hamilton Camp. **1984**

IT WAS A SHORT SUMMER, CHARLIE BROWN ★★★★ Lucy signs everybody up for summer camp, where the girls easily beat the boys at every sporting event—until a climactic wrist-wrestling challenge from the mysterious Masked Marvel. The flashback framing device (a school assignment) is quite clever. 26m. **DIR:** Bill Melendez. **1969**

IT'S A DOG'S LIFE ★★ A scrappy bullterrier from the waterfront becomes the Bowery's paws-down champ under Jeff Richards's patronage, but cleans up his act when he comes under the influence of kindly Edmund Gwenn and his loving daughter Sally Fraser. Should warm the hearts of dog lovers everywhere. 88m. **DIR:** Herman Hoffman. **CAST:** Jeff Richards, Jarma Lewis, Edmund Gwenn, Dean Jagger, Sally Fraser, Richard Anderson. **1955**

IT'S A MYSTERY, CHARLIE BROWN ★★★½ When Woodstock's nest mysteriously disappears, Sherlock Snoopy—complete with dripping bubble-pipe—interrogates the Peanuts gang. To the amazement of everybody, it turns up at a school science exhibit. Vince Guaraldi contributes appropriately eerie music. 26m. **DIR:** Phil Roman. **1974**

IT'S AN ADVENTURE, CHARLIE BROWN ★★★★ Charlie Brown gets to shine in this compilation of tales lifted from Charles Schulz's newspaper strip. When the EPA threatens action after he bites the kite-eating tree, Charlie Brown flees to another neighborhood and becomes a hero to a gaggle of peewee baseball players. Schulz appears in a brief introduction. 50m. **DIR:** Bill Melendez. **1983**

IT'S ARBOR DAY, CHARLIE BROWN ★★★½ Charles Schulz turns conservationist in this timely tale, which also marks the animated debut of Re-run Van Pelt (Linus and Lucy's younger brother). Lucy plants a tree on the pitcher's mound while the other kids fill the area with other assorted shrubs and vines; the chaotic greenery then gives them an edge when Peppermint Patty's team shows up for the first baseball game of the season. This was jazz composer Vince Guaraldi's final bow in the series. 25m. **DIR:** Phil Roman. **1976**

IT'S CHRISTMASTIME AGAIN, CHARLIE BROWN ★★★½ Although not up to the standards of the first Peanuts Christmas outing, this episodic holiday entry has plenty of appeal, starting with David Benoit's new interpretations of Vince Guaraldi's classic Peanuts jazz themes. Sally struggles to remember her sole line in the school Christmas play, while Charlie Brown sells off his comic books to get money for a gift. 30m. **DIR:** Bill Melendez. **1992**

IT'S FLASHBEAGLE, CHARLIE BROWN ★★ Blame *Flashdance* for this animated aberration that inappropriately crams the Peanuts gang into an exercise video (led by Lucy, no less). Blame Ed Bogas and Desiree Goyette for the abysmal music with inane lyrics. Mostly, though, blame Charles Schulz for approving this ill-advised travesty, definitely the series' lowest point. 25m. **DIR:** Bill Melendez. **1984**

IT'S MAGIC, CHARLIE BROWN ★★★★ The "Great Houndini" (a.k.a. Snoopy) performs a magic show with lamentable results; every trick misfires except one—which makes Charlie Brown invisible. While Snoopy cracks the books to solve this dilemma, Chuck recognizes his golden opportunity: Lucy won't know when to pull the football away if she *can't see him kick it!* 25m. **DIR:** Phil Roman. **1981**

IT'S THE EASTER BEAGLE, CHARLIE BROWN ★★★★ A running gag involving Peppermint Patty's attempts to explain egg coloring to Marcie is merely one of this holiday tale's treats; others involve Snoopy's construction of a birdhouse for Woodstock and a wicked jab from writer Charles Schulz at the avarice of stores with pre-pre-pre-Christmas sales. 25m. **DIR:** Phil Roman. **1974**

IT'S THE GREAT PUMPKIN, CHARLIE BROWN ★★★★★ In this third animated Peanuts outing, Linus persuades Sally to forgo trick-or-treating by joining him in a "sincere" pumpkin patch wait for the Great Pumpkin. Great in all respects. 26m. **DIR:** Bill Melendez. **1966**

IT'S THREE STRIKES, CHARLIE BROWN ★★★★ Eight vignettes lifted from Charles Schulz's newspaper strip—all with a baseball theme. By far the best story finds Re-Run joining Charlie Brown's team, which then wins a game...under clouded circumstances. Another tale finds Snoopy quitting his playing position in disgust and then returning as the team manager. 41m. **DIR:** Bill Melendez, Robert E. Balzer, Sam Nicholson, Phil Roman. **1983–1985**

IT'S YOUR FIRST KISS, CHARLIE BROWN ★★★ This weak entry will be remembered as the story that gave the little red-haired girl a name: Heather. After suffering through a football game, Charlie Brown is selected to escort the homecoming queen, a responsibility that culminates with a task he approaches with mixed feelings: a kiss on her cheek. 25m. **DIR:** Phil Roman. **1977**

JACK AND THE BEANSTALK ★★★ This *Faerie Tale Theatre* production sticks more to the original story than most. Katherine Helmond plays Jack's complaining mom. Jean Stapleton plays a kind giantess, while Elliott Gould is a very dumb giant. 60m. **DIR:** Lamont Johnson. **CAST:** Dennis Christopher, Elliott Gould, Jean Stapleton, Mark Blankfield, Katherine Helmond. **1982**

JACK THE GIANT KILLER ★★★½ A delightful reworking of "Jack and the Beanstalk," with many innovative special effects to give it adult appeal. Kerwin Mathews of Ray Harryhausen's *Sinbad* movies fights giants and monsters molded by Harryhausen's disciple, Jim Danforth. Lots of fun. 94m. **DIR:** Nathan Juran. **CAST:** Kerwin Mathews, Torin Thatcher, Judi Meredith. **1962**

JACOB TWO-TWO MEETS THE HOODED FANG ★★★½ Delightful tale of a boy nicknamed Jacob Two-Two because he has to say everything twice when talking to grownups. (They never listen to him the first time.) Fed up with adults, he dreams that he is sentenced to Slimer's Island, a children's prison where his guard is the Hooded Fang (a funny performance by Alex Karras). The low budget shows, but most of the humor of Mordecai Richler's book is retained. Rated G. 80m. **DIR:** Theodore J. Flicker. **CAST:** Stephen Rosenberg, Alex Karras. **1979**

JETSON'S CHRISTMAS CAROL, A ★★ The Jetsons' Christmas Eve plans seem doomed when poor George's Scrooge-like boss, Mr. Spacely, forces him to work overtime. While waiting for George, the rest of the family—wife Jane, daughter Judy, "his boy" Elroy, and Astro the dog—deal with problems at home. Simplistic animation and lack of story originality make for a disappointment. 25m. **DIR:** Ray Patterson. **1985**

JETSONS MEET THE FLINTSTONES, THE ★★★ There are a surprising number of laughs when the family from the future travels back to Bedrock in a time machine. Comic complications develop when the Flintstones and the Rubbles jet to the twenty-fifth century. Predictable fare perhaps, but fun for the whole family nonetheless. Rated G. 100m. **DIR:** Ray Patterson. **1988**

JETSONS: THE MOVIE ★★ Those futuristic Flintstones—George, Jane, Judy, and Elroy Jetson—get the big-screen treatment with a movie that suffers from too many commercial tie-ins and songs by Tiffany (who voices Judy Jetson). Still there are some funny moments in the story, which has Mr. Spacely (a last bow by the late Mel Blanc) transferring George and family to an outpost in outer space. Rated G. 87m. **DIR:** William Hanna, Joseph Barbera. **1990**

JIMINY CRICKET'S CHRISTMAS ★★★½ Most of this compilation program, which includes highlights from numerous Disney full-length animated features, is lifted directly from the 1958 Christmas episode of Walt Disney's television series. As a result, the narration is a bit dated, but the sequences—from *Fantasia, Peter Pan, Snow White*, and others—are well chosen. The package is rounded out by some cartoons: "The Art of Skiing" (1941), one of Goofy's funniest sports how-to's, and, from 1932, "Mickey's Good Deed" (a rare black-and-white entry). 47m. **DIR:** Walt Disney. **1986**

JIMMY THE KID ★★ Paul LeMat leads a band of bungling criminals in an attempt to kidnap the precocious son (Gary Coleman) of extremely wealthy singers (Cleavon Little and Fay Hauser). To everyone's surprise, Jimmy doesn't mind being kidnapped. Yawn. Rated PG. 85m. **DIR:** Gary Nelson. **CAST:** Paul

LeMat, Gary Coleman, Cleavon Little, Fay Hauser, Dee Wallace. **1983**

JOHNNY APPLESEED/PAUL BUNYAN ★★ One in the series of the Rankin/Bass Festival of Family Classics—you may have seen the American Legend Series on television. If so, neither you nor older children will enjoy it again. With less than poor animation and plot development, only small children will find this duo entertaining. Undated; 60m. **DIR:** Arthur Rankin Jr., Jules Bass.

JOHNNY SHILOH ★★★½ After his parents are killed during the Civil War, young Johnny Shiloh joins up with a group of soldiers led by the crusty Brian Keith. The performances are good and it's pure Walt Disney adventure. 90m. **DIR:** James Neilson. **CAST:** Brian Keith, Kevin Corcoran, Darryl Hickman, Skip Homeier. **1963**

JOHNNY TREMAIN ★★★½ Colorful Walt Disney Revolutionary War entry is a perfect blend of schoolboy heroics and Hollywood history, with young Johnny Tremain an apprentice silversmith caught up in the brewing American Revolution. Heavy on the patriotism, with picture-book tableaus of the Boston Tea Party, Paul Revere's ride, and the battles at Concord. Infectious score throughout. 80m. **DIR:** Robert Stevenson. **CAST:** Hal Stalmaster, Luana Patten, Sebastian Cabot, Richard Beymer. **1957**

JOURNEY BACK TO OZ ★★½ This cartoon version sequel to *The Wizard of Oz* leaves the Wizard out. The voices of famous stars help maintain adult interest. Rated G. 90m. **DIR:** Hal Sutherland. **1974**

JOURNEY OF NATTY GANN, THE ★★★★★ With this superb film, the Disney Studios returned triumphantly to the genre of family films. Meredith Salenger stars as Natty, a 14-year-old street urchin who must ride the rails from Chicago to Seattle during the Depression to find her father (Ray Wise). Rated PG for light violence. 101m. **DIR:** Jeremy Paul Kagan. **CAST:** Meredith Salenger, Ray Wise, John Cusack, Lainie Kazan, Scatman Crothers. **1985**

JOURNEY TO SPIRIT ISLAND ★★★½ A teenage Native American girl takes up her grandmother's quest to save a sacred island, used to bury their ancestors, from unscrupulous developers. Above-average family adventure, beautifully photographed in the Pacific Northwest by Vilmos Zsigmond. Rated PG. 93m. **DIR:** Laszlo Pal. **CAST:** Bettina, Maria Antoinette Rodgers, Brandon Douglas. **1988**

JUNGLE BOOK (1942) ★★★★ This one's for fantasy fans of all ages. Sabu stars in Rudyard Kipling's tale of a boy raised by wolves in the jungle of India. Beautiful color presentation holds the viewer from start to finish. Rated G. 109m. **DIR:** Zoltán Korda. **CAST:** Sabu, Joseph Calleia, John Qualen. **1942**

JUNGLE BOOK, THE (1967) ★★★★ Phil Harris's Baloo the Bear steals the show in this rendition of Rudyard Kipling's *Mowgli* stories, the last full-length animated film that reflected Walt Disney's personal participation. Although not as lavishly illustrated as earlier Disney efforts, *The Jungle Book* benefits from its clever songs ("The Bare Necessities," among others) and inspired vocal casting. 78m. **DIR:** Wolfgang Reitherman. **1967**

JUNGLE BOOK, THE—A DEVIL IN MIND ★★★ This Rudyard Kipling tale focuses on trust. The Japanese animation lacks sophistication, but younger audiences may still be entertained. 30m. **DIR:** Fumio Kurolawa. **1990**

JUNGLE BOOK, THE—A TRIP OF ADVENTURE ★★½ This Rudyard Kipling tale deals with accepting responsibility. Even at its best, Japanese animation is not up to Disney standards, but the characters in this series are appealing and whimsical. 30m. **DIR:** Fumio Kurolawa. **1990**

JUNGLE CAT ★★★★ This Disney True Life Adventure won the best feature documentary award at the Berlin International Film Festival in 1960. It follows the life of a spotted female jaguar in a South American jungle. Fascinating and educational. 69m. **DIR:** James Algar. **1960**

JUST PLAIN DAFFY ★★★½ Most of the cartoons on this tape have been released in previous MGM/UA collections, so it doesn't win points for originality. The new material includes two World War II–era entries: Frank Tashlin's "Nasty Quacks" and Friz Freleng's "Duck Soup to Nuts," the latter once more teaming Daffy and Porky. 60m. **DIR:** Bob Clampett, Friz Freleng, Robert McKimson, Frank Tashlin. **1943–1948**

JUST WILLIAM'S LUCK ★★ Based on a series of children's books that were popular in Great Britain, this isn't likely to do as well with American kids. William and his pals are mischief-makers who spend most of the film getting into various sorts of trouble. 87m. **DIR:** Val Guest. **CAST:** William Graham, Garry Marsh. **1947**

JUSTIN MORGAN HAD A HORSE ★★★ Agreeable Disney film focuses on the ingenuity and foresight of a poor Vermont schoolteacher following the Revolutionary War. He trained and bred the first Morgan horse, which was noted for its speed, strength, and stamina. 91m. **DIR:** Hollingsworth Morse. **CAST:** Don Murray, Lana Wood, Gary Crosby. **1972**

KAVIK THE WOLF DOG ★★★ This average made-for-TV movie is the story of Kavik, a brave sled dog who journeys back to the boy he loves when a ruthless, wealthy man transports him from Alaska to Seattle. 104m. **DIR:** Peter Carter. **CAST:** Ronny Cox, John Ireland, Linda Sorenson, Andrew Ian McMillan, Chris Wiggins. 1980

KID FROM LEFT FIELD, THE ★★★ Gary Coleman plays a batboy who leads the San Diego Padres to victory through the advice of his father (a former baseball great). Ed McMahon costars in this remake of the 1953 Dan Dailey version. Made for TV. 100m. **DIR:** Adell Aldrich. **CAST:** Gary Coleman, Tab Hunter, Gary Collins, Ed McMahon. 1979

KID WHO LOVED CHRISTMAS, THE ★★★★ Heartwarming Christmas tale about an orphan who will do anything to be with his adopted father for the holidays. With an all-star cast and a wonderful message, this made-for-TV drama is pure magic. 100m. **DIR:** Arthur Allan Seidelman. **CAST:** Trent Cameron, Cicely Tyson, Mike Warren, Sammy Davis Jr., Gilbert Lewis, Della Reese. 1990

KID WITH THE 200 I.Q., THE ★★ In this predictable TV movie, Gary Coleman plays a 13-year-old genius who enters college. Mildly amusing at best. 96m. **DIR:** Leslie Martinson. **CAST:** Gary Coleman, Robert Guillaume, Dean Butler, Kari Michaelson, Harriet Nelson. 1983

KIDNAPPED (1960) ★★★ Walt Disney takes a shot at this Robert Louis Stevenson eighteenth-century adventure. A young man (James MacArthur) is spirited away to sea just as he is about to inherit his family's estate. Plenty of swashbuckling for children of all ages. 94m. **DIR:** Robert Stevenson. **CAST:** James MacArthur, Peter Finch. 1960

KIDS IS KIDS ★★★½ The Oscar-nominated "Good Scouts," from 1938, with Donald Duck and his nephews battling a bear in Yellowstone Park, stands far above the other four cartoons in this collection. The rest pit Donald against the boys (who grow into spoiled teens with cars in "Lucky Number") in a variety of nasty revenge schemes that show all four ducks in a rather unflattering light. 50m. **DIR:** Walt Disney. 1938–1953

KING OF THE GRIZZLIES ★★½ Wahb, a grizzly cub, loses his mother and sister to cattlemen protecting their herd. He quickly gets into trouble but is rescued by John Yesno, a Cree Indian. Average animal adventure film in the Disney mold. Rated G. 93m. **DIR:** Ron Kelly. **CAST:** John Yesno, Chris Wiggins, Hugh Webster. 1969

KING OF THE WIND ★★★½ Rousing family entertainment based on the popular novel by Marguerite Henry. Teenager Navin Chowdhry tames a wild Arabian horse. The horse is sent from Northern Africa to the King of France, and Chowdhry follows. When he discovers that the magnificent creature will be sent to war, he attempts to steal it. The youth lands in jail, and his only way out is to ride the horse in a special race. Exciting and enthralling every hoof step of the way. Not rated. 101m. **DIR:** Peter Duffell. **CAST:** Richard Harris, Glenda Jackson, Jenny Agutter, Navin Chowdhry. 1993

LADY AND THE TRAMP ★★★★ One of the sweetest animated tales from the Disney canon, this fantasy concerns a high-bred cocker spaniel (Lady) and the adventures she has with a raffish mongrel stray (The Tramp). Since Disney originally had the film released in CinemaScope, more attention has been given to the lush backgrounds. Unrated; suitable for family viewing. 75m. **DIR:** Hamilton Luske, Clyde Geronimi, Wilfred Jackson. 1955

LAND BEFORE TIME, THE ★★★★ This terrific animated film from director Don Bluth follows the journey of five young dinosaurs as they struggle to reach the Great Valley, the only place on Earth as yet untouched by a plague that has ravaged the world. On the way, they have several funny, suspenseful, and life-threatening adventures. The result is a wonderful film for the younger set. Rated G. 66m. **DIR:** Don Bluth. 1988

LAND OF FARAWAY, THE ★★ An orphaned 11-year-old boy is rescued from his dreary, dismal existence and spirited away to *The Land of Faraway.* The boy's father turns out to be the king of Faraway, and he finds the joy in life that he's been missing. But he has to earn his new inheritance by destroying the evil knight, Kato. Poor production values and sloppy direction spoil an otherwise good fairy tale. Rated PG. 95m. **DIR:** Vladimir Grammatikor. **CAST:** Timothy Bottoms, Susannah York, Christopher Lee. 1987

LANTERN HILL ★★★★ A brilliant new *Wonderworks* production partially filmed on Prince Edward Island in Canada. Marion Bennett is Jane Stewart, a young girl whose powers are revealed in uniting her estranged parents in the mysterious Maritime Islands. A classic tale of family love. Made for television. 120m. **DIR:** Kevin Sullivan. **CAST:** Zoe Caldwell, Sam Waterston, Colleen Dewhurst, Marion Bennett, Sarah Polley. 1991

LASSIE COME HOME ★★★★ Heart-tugging story of a boy forced to give up the pet he loves is family drama at its best. An impeccable cast, beautiful photography, and intelligent scripting of Eric Knight's timeless novel highlight this wonderful tale of unsurmountable obstacles overcome by kindness and fidelity. 88m. **DIR:** Fred M. Wilcox. **CAST:** Roddy McDowall, Donald Crisp, Elizabeth Taylor, Nigel Bruce, Elsa Lanchester, May Whitty, Edmund Gwenn. 1943

LAST FLIGHT OF NOAH'S ARK ★★★ This is the story of an unemployed pilot (Elliott Gould) who, against his better judgment, agrees to fly a plane full of farm animals to a Pacific island for a young missionary (Genevieve Bujold). This film, while not one of Disney's best, does offer clean, wholesome fun for the younger (and young-at-heart) audience. Rated G. 97m. **DIR:** Charles Jarrott. **CAST:** Elliott Gould, Genevieve Bujold, Rick Schroder, Vincent Gardenia. **1980**

LAST TRAIN HOME ★★★ When a Canadian family is broken up by their father's participation in a barroom brawl, the teenage son treks cross-country seeking his fleeing dad. The family dog, an adorable Benji look-alike, steals every scene. Made for the Family Channel. 92m. **DIR:** Randy Bradshaw. **CAST:** Noam Zylberman, Ron White, Nick Mancuso, Ned Beatty. **1990**

LAST UNICORN, THE ★★★½ Well-written and nicely animated feature about a magical unicorn who goes on a quest to find the rest of her kind. Strong characters and a sprightly pace make this a gem, which features the voices of Alan Arkin, Jeff Bridges, Mia Farrow, Tammy Grimes, Robert Klein, Angela Lansbury, Christopher Lee, and Keenan Wynn. It's a class act. Rated G. 85m. **DIR:** Arthur Rankin Jr., Jules Bass. **1982**

LEGEND OF HILLBILLY JOHN, THE ★★ When a young man's grandfather challenges the devil and loses, he decides to take on the master of Hell himself, armed with only his guitar. Flawed low-budget production with intermittent charms. 86m. **DIR:** John Newland. **CAST:** Hedge Capers, Severn Darden, Denver Pyle. **1973**

LEGEND OF SLEEPY HOLLOW, THE (1949) ★★★★ One of the finest of the Disney "novelette" cartoons, this adaptation is given a properly sepulchral tone by narrator Bing Crosby. Reasonably scary, particularly for small fry, who might get pretty nervous during poor Ichabod Crane's final, fateful ride. 49m. **DIR:** Jack Kinney, Clyde Geronimi, James Algar. **1949**

LEGEND OF SLEEPY HOLLOW, THE (1988) ★★★★ Glenn Close narrates Washington Irving's spooky tale of schoolmaster Ichabod Crane. Composer Tim Story contributes grand background themes that perfectly complement Close's lively reading. Directed by illustrator Robert Van Nutt. 30m. **DIR:** Robert Van Nutt. **1988**

LT. ROBIN CRUSOE, U.S.N. 🦃 Modern-day story of Robinson Crusoe, poorly done and with few laughs. Rated G. 113m. **DIR:** Byron Paul. **CAST:** Dick Van Dyke, Nancy Kwan, Akim Tamiroff. **1966**

LIFE AND TIMES OF GRIZZLY ADAMS, THE ★★ Fur trapper Dan Haggerty heads for the hills when he's unjustly accused of a crime. There he befriends an oversized bear and they live happily ever after. Rated G. 93m. **DIR:** Dick Friedenberg. **CAST:** Dan Haggerty, Don Shanks, Lisa Jones, Marjory Harper, Bozo. **1976**

LIFE IS A CIRCUS, CHARLIE BROWN ★★½ Snoopy runs off and joins Miss Molly and her trained poodles in this lightweight entry, notable only for Charlie Brown's recollection of how he first met his faithful (?) beagle. Charles Schulz's script is unusually thin. 25m. **DIR:** Phil Roman. **1980**

LIFE WITH MICKEY (LIMITED GOLD EDITION 2) ★★★★½ Three 1936 cartoons are the treasures of this collection. "Alpine Climbers" teams Mickey Mouse with Donald Duck and Pluto. Artist Art Babbitt contributes great caricatures of Hollywood luminaries in "Mickey's Polo Team," and Donald Duck has a great time with trained seals in "Mickey's Circus." The tape also includes "Shanghaied," an early black-and-white adventure with Minnie Mouse. 51m. **DIR:** Walt Disney. **1934–1951**

LIGHT IN THE FOREST, THE ★★½ James MacArthur stars as a young man who had been captured and raised by the Delaware Indians and is later returned to his white family. Generally a good story with adequate acting, the ending is much too contrived and trite. 92m. **DIR:** Herschel Daugherty. **CAST:** James MacArthur, Fess Parker, Wendell Corey, Joanne Dru, Carol Lynley. **1958**

LIGHTNING, THE WHITE STALLION 🦃 In this disappointing family film, Mickey Rooney plays a down-on-his-luck gambler who owns a champion jumper. Rated PG. 93m. **DIR:** William A. Levey. **CAST:** Mickey Rooney, Susan George. **1986**

LION, THE WITCH AND THE WARDROBE, THE ★★★½ Four children pass through a wardrobe into a wondrous land of mythical creatures where an evil Ice Queen has been terrorizing her subjects. This enjoyable made-for-television cartoon was based on C. S. Lewis's *Chronicles of Narnia*. 95m. **DIR:** Bill Melendez. **1979**

LIONHEART ★★★ On his way to join King Richard's crusade in France, a young knight is joined by a ragtag band of kids on the run from the evil Black Prince. It's enjoyable and suitable for children. It's also captioned for the hearing impaired. Rated PG. 105m. **DIR:** Franklin J. Schaffner. **CAST:** Eric Stoltz, Gabriel Byrne, Nicola Cowper, Dexter Fletcher. **1986**

LITTLE HEROES ★★½ Adorable tale of a little girl and her trusty mutt, who prove to a small town that miracles can still come true. There's a lot of heart and some great messages in this family film. 78m. **DIR:** Craig Clyde. **CAST:** Raeanin Simpson. **1991**

LITTLE HOUSE ON THE PRAIRIE (TV SERIES) ★★★ The long-running series was based on Laura Ingalls Wilder's novels about her family's adventures on the Kansas frontier. Michael Landon, who had creative control over the show, made people forget

Little Joe Cartwright with his strong portrayal of Charles Ingalls, the idealistic, sensitive husband and father. Episodes tend to be genuinely heartwarming, rather than sappy. Each episode 60m. (Special TV-movies are 100 minutes.) **DIR:** Michael Landon. **CAST:** Michael Landon, Karen Grassle, Melissa Gilbert, Melissa Sue Anderson, Lindsay and Sidney Greenbush, Victor French, Dean Butler, Matthew Laborteaux. **1974–1984**

LITTLE LORD FAUNTLEROY (1980) ★★★★ This is the made-for-television version of the heartwarming classic about a poor young boy (Rick Schroder) whose life is dramatically changed when his wealthy grandfather (Alec Guinness) takes him in. Well-done. 120m. **DIR:** Jack Gold. **CAST:** Rick Schroder, Alec Guinness, Eric Porter, Colin Blakely, Connie Booth. **1980**

LITTLE MAN TATE ★★★★ For her directorial debut, actress Jodie Foster joins forces with screenwriter Scott Frank to dramatize the struggle between a working-class mother and a wealthy educator for custody of a gifted child. It isn't often that a family film is both heartwarming and thought-provoking, but this little gem is one of the exceptions. Rated PG for brief profanity. 106m. **DIR:** Jodie Foster. **CAST:** Jodie Foster, Dianne Wiest, Adam Hann-Byrd, Harry Connick Jr., David Pierce, Josh Mostel. **1991**

LITTLE MATCH GIRL, THE (1983) ★★ This *Children's Treasures* production was originally a stage play. Unfortunately, the pageantry and emotion of the live-action production are lost in the video translation. A poor girl's grandmother reveals a magic in the matches that they sell. After the grandmother's death, the girl (Monica McSwain) gets so caught up in the magic that she neglects to sell her wares. *Not* advised for children under 10. 54m. **DIR:** Mark Hoeger, Wally Broodbent. **CAST:** Monica McSwain, Nancy Duncan, Matt McKim, Dan Hays. **1983**

LITTLE MATCH GIRL, THE (1990) ★★★ F. Murray Abraham narrates this animated version of the Hans Christian Andersen classic. It is set in the year 1999 and subtly refers to compassion for the homeless. 30m. **DIR:** Michael Sporn. **1990**

LITTLE MEN (1935) ★★ A sentimental tale about a boys' school, and the wayward youths who live there is told with honesty and sincerity but not much personality. This is a poor man's *Boys Town* and needs the likes of a Mickey Rooney or Spencer Tracy to make it come alive. B&W; 56m. **DIR:** Phil Rosen. **CAST:** Frankie Darro, Erin O'Brien-Moore, Ralph Morgan, Junior Durkin, Dickie Moore, Richard Quine. **1935**

LITTLE MERMAID, THE (1978) ★★ Not to be confused with the Disney classic, this is a passably animated version of the Hans Christian Andersen story, and it hews closer to the original tale. Children may be disappointed by the downbeat ending. Rated G. 71m. **DIR:** Tim Reid. **1978**

LITTLE MERMAID, THE (1984) ★★★½ In this segment of Shelley Duvall's *Faerie Tale Theatre*, Pam Dawber plays Pearl, a mermaid daughter of King Neptune. She falls hopelessly in love with a human and sacrifices all to win his love. Although this is a low-budget production, it still manages to keep its viewers entertained. 50m. **DIR:** Robert Iscove. **CAST:** Pam Dawber, Karen Black, Treat Williams, Brian Dennehy, Helen Mirren. **1984**

LITTLE MERMAID, THE (1989) ★★★★★ This adaptation of the Hans Christian Andersen story is, in our opinion, even better than the celebrated movies produced during Walt Disney's heyday. Writer-directors John Musker and Ron Clements, with invaluable assistance from producer Howard Ashman and his songwriting partner Alan Menken, have created the best screen fairy tale of them all. Even the songs are integral to the story, which has some of the most memorable characters to grace an animated film. Rated G. 76m. **DIR:** John Musker, Ron Clements. **1989**

LITTLE MERMAID, THE: ARIEL'S UNDERSEA ADVENTURES ★★★ Two episodes of the TV series derived from Disney's *The Little Mermaid* make up these tapes for the younger set. In each adventure, Ariel the mermaid, Sebastian the crab, and Flounder the fish encounter a situation that entertains children while delivering an educational message. 44m. each. **DIR:** Various. **1993**

LITTLE MISS MARKER (1934) ★★★★ Delightful Shirley Temple vehicle has our heroine left as an I.O.U. on a gambling debt and charming hard-hearted racetrack denizens into becoming better people. The best of the screen adaptations of Damon Runyon's story. B&W; 88m. **DIR:** Alexander Hall. **CAST:** Adolphe Menjou, Shirley Temple, Dorothy Dell, Charles Bickford, Lynne Overman. **1934**

LITTLE MISS MARKER (1980) 🦃 Turgid remake. Rated PG. 103m. **DIR:** Walter Bernstein. **CAST:** Walter Matthau, Julie Andrews, Tony Curtis, Bob Newhart, Sara Stimson, Lee Grant. **1980**

LITTLE MISS MILLIONS ★★ Winsome comedy finds poor-little-rich-girl Love Hewitt looking for her real mother, while greedy stepmother Anita Morris hires private eye Howard Hesseman to find her. He does, but then Morris claims he kidnapped the girl. The two hit the road to clear their names and find Hewitt's real mom. Congenial fun. Rated PG. 90m. **DIR:** Jim Wynorski. **CAST:** Howard Hesseman, Love Hewitt, Anita Morris, Steve Landesberg. **1993**

LITTLE MISS TROUBLE AND FRIENDS ★★ With an animation style reminiscent of Terrytoon's "Tom Terrific," this collection of episodes offers youngsters an education in proper social behavior. However, Miss Trouble and her friends, who are named after various aspects of their own personalities (Mr. Small, etc.), spend a lot of time displaying poor ethics before learning their lessons. Unimaginative, though based on bestselling children's fiction. 43m. **DIR:** Trevor Bond, Terry Ward. **1983**

LITTLE NEMO: ADVENTURES IN SLUMBERLAND ★★★. In this fairly entertaining animated movie, Little Nemo is a youngster whose dreams lead him into Slumberland, where the Dream King has plans for the boy to be his successor. Meanwhile, the mischievous Flip (voiced by Mickey Rooney) leads our hero to unintentionally unleash the Nightmare King. Rated G. 83m. **DIR:** Masanori Hata, William Hurtz. **1992**

LITTLE NINJAS ★★½ Slight, derivative kiddy romp about three karate-chopping youngsters who come into possession of a treasure map while on vacation. When they return home to Los Angeles, they must join forces to fight off the bad guys who have come for the map. Kids will enjoy this mindless exercise. Rated PG. 85m. **DIR:** Emmett Alston. **CAST:** Jon Anzaldo, Steven Nelson. **1993**

LITTLE ORPHAN ANNIE ★★½ The first sound version featuring the adventures of Harold Gray's pupilless, precocious adolescent. A good cast and engaging score by Max Steiner add to the charm of this undeservedly neglected comic-strip adaptation. B&W; 60m. **DIR:** John S. Robertson. **CAST:** Mitzi Green, Edgar Kennedy, Buster Phelps, May Robson. **1932**

LITTLE PRINCE, THE (SERIES) ★★½ Recommended by the National Educational Association, this takeoff of the Antoine de Saint-Exupéry story will bore older kids to tears. Little viewers may be fascinated by the adventures of the little humanoid hero who lives on the faraway planet of B-612. Five volumes compose this series. 60m. **DIR:** Jameson Brewer. **1986**

LITTLE PRINCESS, A ★★½ Melodramatic tale of an indulged girl who, having lived in India with her lively, free-spending father, is enrolled in a prissy English boarding school. The girl's constant sermonizing about her plight is most annoying. A lesser WonderWorks production. 174m. **DIR:** Carol Wiseman. **CAST:** Amelia Shankley, Nigel Havers, Maureen Lipman. **1986**

LITTLE PRINCESS, THE ★★★½ The 1930s supertyke Shirley Temple had one of her very best vehicles in this Victorian era tearjerker. In it, she's a sweet-natured child who is mistreated at a strict boarding school when her father disappears during the Boer War. Get out your handkerchiefs. B&W; 93m. **DIR:** Walter Lang. **CAST:** Shirley Temple, Richard Greene, Anita Louise, Ian Hunter, Cesar Romero, Arthur Treacher. **1939**

LITTLE RASCALS, THE ★★★★★ There are thirty-eight different compilations of Little Rascals shorts on video. The tapes range from two to four shorts each, and most of the featurettes run approximately 10 minutes. Almost half of the 221 Our Gang featurettes are represented in selections that star 3-year-old Spanky McFarland, 5-year-old Jackie Cooper, and a very thin 25-year-old Oliver Hardy. There isn't a loser in the lot, and some of the eighty-two featurettes are available in more than one collection. Even the most contrived plots are made entertaining by the earnestness of youngsters who developed international reputations just by being themselves. The Oscar-winning short, "Bored of Education" (1936) is paired with "Arbor Day" (1936) in two different 30-minute collections. The oldest featurette on video is "The Pickaninny" (1921). **DIR:** Hal Roach. **CAST:** Jackie Cooper, Spanky McFarland, Oliver Hardy, Sammy Morrison, Carl "Alfalfa" Switzer, Buckwheat Thomas, Darla Hood, Porky Lee, Dickie Moore.

LITTLE RASCALS CHRISTMAS SPECIAL, THE ★★ An animated cast resembling the original Little Rascals cooks up a scheme to buy Spanky's mom a new winter coat. This longer tale is complemented by a collection of vintage holiday cartoons from Ub Iwerks and the Fleischer brothers. 60m. **DIR:** Fred Wolf, Charles Swenson. **1979**

LITTLE RED RIDING HOOD ★★★★ Malcolm McDowell plays a brazenly wicked wolf to a perky Red Riding Hood (Mary Steenburgen). Frances Bay makes for a rather zany grandmother. Although highly entertaining, don't expect it to stick to the tale as most would remember it. 51m. **DIR:** Graeme Clifford. **CAST:** Mary Steenburgen, Malcolm McDowell, Darrell Larson. **1983**

LITTLE TWEETIE AND LITTLE INKI CARTOON FESTIVAL ★★★½ Tweetie Pie remains one of animator Bob Clampett's greatest creations. This collection begins with Tweetie's second appearance (although the first in which he was so named): Clampett's "Birdy and the Beast." Fans will also appreciate Friz Freleng's "I Taw a Putty Tat." Animator Chuck Jones is barely remembered today, in light of his later achievements, for the creation of Inki, a youthful African warrior whose great courage comes packed in a small body. Inki's first appearance—in "Little Lion Hunter"—is one of three cartoons rounding out this package. 50m. **DIR:** Bob Clampett, Friz Freleng, Chuck Jones. **1939–1948**

LITTLE WOMEN (1981) ★★ Parents may be fooled by the packaging of this video, which presents only a small portion of

Louisa May Alcott's famous book. Run-of-the-mill Japanese animation belies the fact that this production was simplified for a young audience and further simplified for translation to a foreign culture. 23m. **DIR:** John Matsuura, Kazuya Miyazaki. **1981**

LITTLEST ANGEL, THE ★★ This made-for-TV musical fantasy loses something in its video translation. A young shepherd finds his transition into heaven difficult to accept. 77m. **DIR:** Joe Layton. **CAST:** Johnny Whitaker, Fred Gwynne, Connie Stevens, James Coco, E. G. Marshall, Tony Randall. **1969**

LITTLEST HORSE THIEVES, THE ★★★ At the turn of the century, some children become alarmed that the ponies working in the coal mines are to be destroyed. The children decide to steal the ponies. Rather predictable but with good characterizations and a solid period atmosphere. Rated G. 104m. **DIR:** Charles Jarrott. **CAST:** Alastair Sim, Peter Barkworth, Maurice Colbourne, Susan Tebbs, Andrew Harrison, Chloe Franks. **1976**

LITTLEST OUTLAW, THE ★★★ This Walt Disney import from Mexico tells a familiar but pleasant story of a young boy who befriends a renegade horse and saves him from destruction. The kids should like it, and this one will appeal to the adults as well. 73m. **DIR:** Roberto Gavaldon. **CAST:** Pedro Armendariz, Joseph Calleia, Rodolfo Acosta, Andres Velasquez. **1954**

LIVING FREE ★★ Disappointing sequel to *Born Free*, with Elsa the lioness now in the wilderness and raising three cubs. The chemistry just isn't here in this film. 91m. **DIR:** Jack Couffer. **CAST:** Susan Hampshire, Nigel Davenport, Geoffrey Keen. **1972**

LOONEY, LOONEY, LOONEY BUGS BUNNY MOVIE ★★★½ This follow-up to the *Bugs Bunny/Road Runner Movie* lacks the earlier film's inventiveness, but then Chuck Jones was always the most cerebral of the Warner Bros. cartoon directors. Friz Freleng, on the other hand, only tried to make people laugh. This collection of his cartoons—which feature Daffy Duck, Porky Pig, Tweety Pie, and Yosemite Sam, among others, in addition to Bugs—does just that with general efficiency. Rated G. 79m. **DIR:** Friz Freleng. **1981**

LOONEY TUNES VIDEO SHOW, THE (VOLUME 1) ★★★½ By far the best in this series, this collection is highlighted by Chuck Jones's "The Ducksters," a frenetic masterpiece that stands as one of the best Daffy Duck–Porky Pig teamings. Robert McKimson's "Devil May Hare" introduces Bugs Bunny to the Tasmanian Devil, and Friz Freleng's "Mexican Shmoes" (a Speedy Gonzales vehicle) is noteworthy, too. Finally, Jones's "Zipping Along" is one of his earlier Road Runner shorts. 49m. **DIR:** Friz Freleng, Chuck Jones, Robert McKimson. **1950–1961**

LOONEY TUNES VIDEO SHOW, THE (VOLUME 2) ★★ It's filler time. Post-1960 entries mar this collection, which contains only one decent cartoon: Chuck Jones's Pepe Le Pew romp titled "Two Scents Worth." Although most of the regular stars are represented, the selections leave much to be desired. 48m. **DIR:** Friz Freleng, Chuck Jones, Robert McKimson. **1950–1965**

LOONEY TUNES VIDEO SHOW, THE (VOLUME 3) ★★★ A mixed bag of the reasonably good and the extremely bad. The former is represented by one of the better Foghorn Leghorn shorts, Robert McKimson's "Fractured Leghorn"; the latter is covered by Rudy Larriva's wretched "Quacker Tracker," one of Daffy Duck's post-1960 limited-animation duels with Speedy Gonzales. 48m. **DIR:** Chuck Jones, Rudy Larriva, Robert McKimson. **1950–1967**

LOVE BUG, THE ★★★½ This is a delightful Disney comedy. A family film about a Volkswagen with a mind of its own and some special talents as well, it was the first of the four "Herbie" films. Rated G. 107m. **DIR:** Robert Stevenson. **CAST:** Michele Lee, Dean Jones, Buddy Hackett, Joe Flynn. **1969**

LUCKY LUKE: THE BALLAD OF THE DALTONS ★★ Overlong yarn of the Old West starring an all-American cowboy (complete with immovable cigarette on the lower lip): Lucky Luke. References to killing are taken in stride, but for the most part this is harmless cartoon fare. Not rated. 82m. **DIR:** René Goscinny. **1978**

MAD, MAD MONSTERS, THE 🦃 A gruesome conglomeration of ghoulies gathers for the wedding celebration of Frankenstein's monster. 60m. **DIR:** Arthur Rankin Jr., Jules Bass. **1972**

MAD MONSTER PARTY ★★½ An amusing little puppet film; a lot more fun for genre buffs who will understand all the references made to classic horror films. Worth seeing once, as a novelty. 94m. **DIR:** Jules Bass. **CAST:** Boris Karloff, Phyllis Diller, Ethel Ennis, Gale Garnett. **1967**

MADELINE ★★★½ French author Ludwig Bemelmans's classic tale of mischievous little Madeline and her boarding school friends has been turned into a delightful animated short. The story, charmingly narrated in verse by Christopher Plummer, follows Miss Clavel (a nun at the school) and her dozen charges through various escapades: walks at the zoo, strolls through the city, and bedtime fun. 30m. **DIR:** Stephan Martinere. **1988**

MAGIC CHRISTMAS TREE, THE 🦃 A laughable effort, with only the most tenuous connection to Christmas. Not rated. 70m. **DIR:** Richard C. Parish. **CAST:** Chris Kroegen,

Valerie Hobbs, Robert Maffei, Dick Parish, Terry Bradshaw. 1966

MAGIC OF DR. SNUGGLES, THE ★★★ Three separate episodes of the award-winning cartoon series feature the adventures of Dr. Snuggles and his animal friends. This series is particularly attractive in that characters are motivated by compassion without relying on villains or violence. 60m. **DIR:** Jim Terry. 1985

MAGIC OF LASSIE, THE ★★½ Like the Disney live-action films of yore, *The Magic of Lassie* tries to incorporate a little of everything: heartwarming drama, suspense, comedy, and even music. But here the formula is bland. The story is okay, but it is all too long. Rated G. 100m. **DIR:** Don Chaffey. **CAST:** James Stewart, Mickey Rooney, Pernell Roberts, Stephanie Zimbalist, Michael Sharrett, Alice Faye, Gene Evans, Lane Davies, Mike Mazurki, Lassie. 1978

MAGIC SWORD, THE ★★ Young Gary Lockwood is on a quest to free an imprisoned princess and fights his way through an ogre, dragon, and other uninspired monsters with the help of the witch in the family, Estelle Winwood. Basil Rathbone makes a fine old evil sorcerer, relishing his foul deeds and eagerly planning new transgressions. The kids might like it, but it's laughable. 80m. **DIR:** Bert I. Gordon. **CAST:** Gary Lockwood, Anne Helm, Basil Rathbone, Estelle Winwood, Liam Sullivan. 1962

MAGIC VOYAGE, THE ★★ This mediocre animated film is meant to be a history lesson about Christopher Columbus's voyage to America, but it's actually just a love story between a wood worm and a firefly. Rated G. 80m. **DIR:** Michael Schoemann. 1994

MAN CALLED FLINTSTONE, A ★★★½ The Ralph Kramden and Ed Norton of the kiddie-set, Fred Flintstone and Barney Rubble are featured in this full-length animated cartoon. Fred takes over for lookalike secret agent, Rack Slag, and goes after the "Green Goose" and his henchmen, SMIRK agents. Great fun for the kids. 87m. **DIR:** William Hanna, Joseph Barbera. 1966

MAN IN THE SANTA CLAUS SUIT, THE ★★★ In one of his last performances, Fred Astaire plays seven characters who enrich the lives of everybody in a small community. This made-for-TV production is a delightful Christmastime picture. 100m. **DIR:** Corey Allen. **CAST:** Fred Astaire, John Byner, Nanette Fabray, Gary Burghoff, Bert Convy, Harold Gould. 1978

MANNY'S ORPHANS 🦃 Another *Bad News Bears* movie, but of course not within striking distance of the original.(First released as *Here Come the Tigers.*) 90m. **DIR:** Sean S. Cunningham. **CAST:** Richard Lincoln. 1978

MAN'S BEST FRIEND (1985) ★★★½ The creations of Walter Lantz, including Woody Woodpecker, Andy Panda, and Chilly Willy, cavort with canines in this loose-knit collection. But the best in this group has nothing to do with his more famous characters. Instead Tex Avery's wild and crazy "Dig That Dog" takes the prize. It's an old bit where the man thinks he's a dog and vice versa, but watch what Avery does with it. 51m. **DIR:** Walter Lantz, Tex Avery. 1985

MARCO POLO JR. ★★ An ancient prophecy sends a young man on a musical mission to the fabled kingdom of Xanadu. The sound track is reminiscent of those moldy Bobby Vinton albums hidden away in your attic. 82m. **DIR:** Eric Porter. 1972

MARK TWAIN'S CONNECTICUT YANKEE IN KING ARTHUR'S COURT ★★ A pedestrian adaptation of Mark Twain's story in which a Connecticut blacksmith dreams that he has been transported to the England of King Arthur. Made for television. 60m. **DIR:** David Tapper. **CAST:** Richard Basehart, Roscoe Lee Browne, Paul Rudd. 1978

MARTIN'S DAY ★★½ Richard Harris plays an escaped convict who kidnaps young Justin Henry but ends up being his friend in this Canadian production. A good idea with a pedestrian resolution. Rated PG. 98m. **DIR:** Alan Gibson. **CAST:** Richard Harris, Lindsay Wagner, John Ireland, James Coburn, Justin Henry, Karen Black. 1984

MARVEL COMICS VIDEO LIBRARY ★★½ It's hard for us to say whether comic-book fans will enjoy these uninspired cartoons featuring the superheroes from the Marvel line of comics. The animation is generally poor, and all of the cartoons look insipid next to Max and Dave Fleischer's Superman cartoons of the 1940s. That said, some of Ralph Bakshi's Spiderman cartoons are okay, and the Captain America series gets around the problems of limited animation by using what look like comic-book panels combined with slight animation. each tape. 60m. **DIR:** Various. 1985–1986

MARVELOUS LAND OF OZ, THE ★★★ This teleplay, based on the works of L. Frank Baum, is an excellent means of introducing children to the experience of live theatre. It boasts marvelous costuming and presentation by the Minneapolis Children's Theatre Company and School. 101m. **DIR:** John Driver, John Clark Donohue. **CAST:** Wendy Lehr, Christopher Passi. 1981

MARY POPPINS ★★★★★ Here's Julie Andrews in her screen debut. She plays a nanny who believes that "a spoonful of sugar makes the medicine go down." Andrews is great in the role and sings ever so sweetly. The song and dance numbers are attractively laid on, with Dick Van Dyke, as Mary's Cockney beau, giving an amusing performance. Rated G. 140m. **DIR:** Robert Stevenson. **CAST:** Julie Andrews, Dick Van Dyke, David Tomlinson, Glynis Johns, Karen Dotrice, Matthew Garber, Jane Darwell, Ed Wynn, Arthur Treacher, Hermione Baddeley. **1964**

MARZIPAN PIG, THE ★★★ Tim Curry narrates this animated food chain fable about the effect of a candy pig on the mouse who ate him and the owl who ate the mouse. Seems a harsh metaphor for the 5- to 8-year-olds it's aimed at, but ends on a light, upbeat note. 30m. **DIR:** Michael Sporn. **1990**

MASTERMIND (TV SERIES) ★★★½ This British TV adventure series features Sam Waterston as Professor Quentin E. Deverill, an American inventor and scientist in 1912, London. The "Target London" episode has Deverill solving a kidnapping case. In "The Great Motor Race" archvillain Kilkiss (Julian Glover) tries to create a global empire. "The Infernal Devise" episode is about a remote-control system Deverill has invented to better mankind. It's a little like Saturday-matinee material, but the acting, set decoration, costumes, and gadgetry make it a lot of fun. 50m. **DIR:** Don Sharp. **CAST:** Sam Waterston, Julian Glover, Barrie Houghton. **1981–1982**

MASTERS OF THE UNIVERSE ★★½ Those toy and cartoon characters come to life on the silver screen, and all things considered, the translation is fairly successful. He-Man and friends are exiled to Earth, where they befriend a teenage couple and battle Skeletor's evil minions. A small amount of foul language and one scene of graphic violence may be deemed unsuitable for young children by some parents. Rated PG. 106m. **DIR:** Gary Goddard. **CAST:** Dolph Lundgren, Frank Langella, Courteney Cox, James Tolkan, Meg Foster. **1987**

MATT THE GOOSEBOY ★★★½ Beautifully detailed animation garnishes this presentation of a classic Hungarian folktale, wherein a young peasant boy must act to end the oppression of his people and country. 77m. **DIR:** Attila Durgay, Luis Elman. **1978**

MAYA ★★★ A boy living with his hunter father in India feels neglected and takes off with a native boy to deliver a sacred white elephant to a remote holy city. Preteens will enjoy this; location filming is a plus. 91m. **DIR:** John Berry. **CAST:** Clint Walker, Jay North, I. S. Johar. **1966**

MEDICINE HAT STALLION, THE ★★ Decent TV movie about a young lad (Leif Garrett) who, with the help of Indian Chief Red Cloud (Ned Romero), runs off to join the Pony Express. Well acted, but overlong, and the commercial breaks are jarring and obvious. 85m. **DIR:** Michael O'Herlihy. **CAST:** Leif Garrett, Mitchell Ryan, Bibi Besch, John Anderson, Charles Tyner, John Quade, Milo O'Shea, Ned Romero. **1977**

MEET THE RAISINS ★★★½ This surprisingly entertaining "documentary" on the phenomenal rise of the California Raisins is good fun for the whole family. The video cleverly spoofs everything from the Beatles to educational programming to television commercials. The witty send-ups almost make you forget that the Raisins themselves are just the end product of an ad campaign. 28m. **DIR:** Will Vinton. **1988**

MEET THE WOMBLES ★★½ Stop-animation of hairy little figures resembling shrews teach viewers to appreciate the environment. The Wombles spend their days making use of humans' garbage. Unfortunately this program will be unbearably slow for most tykes. 60m. **DIR:** Ivor Wood. **1983**

MEET YOUR ANIMAL FRIENDS ★★★ A video primer to familiarize youngsters with the animal kingdom. Narrated by Lynn Redgrave, twenty-three separate segments cover everything from Aardvarks to Zebras. 52m. **DIR:** David N. Gottlieb. **1985**

MELODY ★★ A cute story, completely destroyed by montage after montage set to a musical score by the Bee Gees. Not enough dialogue here to carry this innocent tale about two 10-year-olds who fall in love and decide to get married. Slow. 130m. **DIR:** Waris Hussein. **CAST:** Jack Wild, Mark Lester, Tracy Hyde, Roy Kinnear, Kate Williams, Ken Jones. **1972**

METEOR MAN ★★★ A timid schoolteacher in a crime-ridden inner-city neighborhood acquires superpowers. There are some very funny moments in this uneven, family-oriented comedy, especially as our hero learns about his new abilities. Good cast, too. Rated PG for light violence. 100m. **DIR:** Robert Townsend. **CAST:** Robert Townsend, Marla Gibbs, Robert Guillaume, James Earl Jones, Bill Cosby, Eddie Griffin, Sinbad, Frank Gorshin, Nancy Wilson. **1993**

MGM CARTOON MAGIC ★★★½ Droopy and Tom & Jerry weren't the only cartoon characters at MGM in the Forties and Fifties, as demonstrated by this enjoyable collection. Barney Bear is represented here by "Unwelcome Guest." The Captain and Kids put on "The Captain's Christmas," while Director Tex Avery brings this collection's greatest chuckles in "Screwball Squirrel," "Little Rural Riding Hood" (which is almost for adults only), and "King Size Canary." For all ages. 53m. **DIR:** Tex Avery, George Gordon. **1983**

MICKEY (LIMITED GOLD EDITION 1) ★★★★½ Mickey Mouse's first appearance, in "Steamboat Willie" (1928), is reason enough to view this tape; the impressively inventive animation, entirely the work of Ub Iwerks, remains enchanting to this day. Of the remaining entries, most from Disney's classic period, "Symphony Hour" is the standout. 51m. **DIR:** Walt Disney. **1928–1953**

MICKEY AND THE BEANSTALK ★★★★½ This gorgeous rendition of the classic fairy tale is a must-see for all Disney animation fans. It's the most ambitious adventure created for the Terrific Trio—Mickey Mouse, Donald Duck, and Goofy—as they struggle to free the Magic Harp from the shape-changing clutches of Willie the Giant. 29m. **DIR:** Walt Disney. **1947**

MICKEY AND THE GANG ★★★★½ This trio of cartoons is highlighted by 1938's "Boat Builders," which teams Mickey Mouse, Donald Duck, and Goofy in an effort to assemble a boat from a rather complex kit. The threesome also gets together for "Moose Hunters," and Pluto battles a gopher while working as Mickey's "Canine Caddy." 25m. **DIR:** Walt Disney. **1937–1941**

MICKEY KNOWS BEST ★★★★★ Fred Spencer's animation of Donald Duck, as he attempts to extricate himself from a plumber's helper, is just one of the high points in "Moving Day." Donald also generates plenty of laughs trying to recite "Twinkle, Twinkle, Little Star" in "Mickey's Amateurs," and Pluto takes an immediate dislike to a most endearing pachyderm in "Mickey's Elephant." 26m. **DIR:** Walt Disney. **1936–1937**

MICKEY'S CHRISTMAS CAROL ★★★★ Mickey Mouse plays Bob Cratchit in this pleasant adaptation of the Dickens classic. Rated G. 26m. **DIR:** Burney Matinson. **1984**

MICKEY'S CRAZY CAREERS ★★★★½ Forget this collection's one weak black-and-white entry ("The Mail Pilot") and concentrate on the other five cartoons, every one a classic. "The Band Concert," Disney's first Technicolor Mickey Mouse vehicle, is hilarious as a young Donald Duck ruins a performance of "The William Tell Overture." The famous trio—Mickey, Donald, and Goofy—are put to work in "Clock Cleaners," "Tugboat Mickey," "Magician Mickey," and "Mickey's Fire Brigade." 48m. **DIR:** Walt Disney. **1933–1940**

MICKEY'S MAGICAL WORLD ★★ The Disney studio has turned into the serpent devouring its own tail, by releasing this collection of *excerpts* from classic Mickey Mouse cartoons. These adventures, introduced by a badly overdubbed Jiminy Cricket, include glimpses of 1936's "Thru the Mirror," 1934's "Gulliver Mickey," and several other shorts from Disney's golden age; most are available, intact, in other collections. 27m. **DIR:** Walt Disney. **1934–1940**

MIGHTY DUCKS, THE ★★★½ Fast-living lawyer Emilio Estevez is assigned 500 hours of community service after being convicted on a drunk-driving arrest, and he finds himself coaching a hockey team made up of league misfits. *The Bad News Bears* on ice. Rated PG for brief vulgarity. 93m. **DIR:** Stephen Herek. **CAST:** Emilio Estevez, Joss Ackland, Lane Smith, Heidi Kling. **1992**

MILLION DOLLAR DUCK, THE ★★ A duck is accidentally given a dose of radiation that makes it produce eggs with solid gold yolks. Dean Jones and Sandy Duncan, as the owners of the duck, use the yolks to pay off bills until the Treasury Department gets wise. Mildly entertaining comedy in the Disney tradition. Rated G. 92m. **DIR:** Vincent McEveety. **CAST:** Dean Jones, Sandy Duncan, Joe Flynn, Tony Roberts. **1971**

MINNIE (LIMITED GOLD EDITION 1) ★★★½ The phenomenal perspective animation of Ub Iwerks in the black-and-white "Plane Crazy" makes it this collection's most visually impressive entry. "Mickey's Rival" features the only appearance of Mortimer Mouse, who also desires Minnie Mouse's love. Most of the others employ Minnie as a lesser supporting character. 52m. **DIR:** Walt Disney. **1928–1947**

MINOR MIRACLE, A ★★½ A heartwarming story about a group of orphaned children and their devoted guardian (John Huston), who band together to save the St. Francis School for Boys. If you liked *Going My Way* and *Oh God!* you'll like this G-rated movie. 100m. **DIR:** Raoul Lomas. **CAST:** John Huston, Pelé, Peter Fox. **1983**

MIRACLE DOWN UNDER ★★★½ This moving drama is actually *A Christmas Carol* Australian style. Only a small boy's kindness can rekindle an evil miser's Christmas spirit. This fine family film contains no objectionable material. 106m. **DIR:** George Miller. **CAST:** Dee Wallace, John Waters, Charles Tingwell, Bill Kerr, Andrew Ferguson. **1987**

MIRACLE OF THE WHITE STALLIONS ★★ True story of the evacuation of the famed Lipizzan stallions from war-torn Vienna doesn't pack much of a wallop, kids and horse fans should enjoy it. 92m. **DIR:** Arthur Hiller. **CAST:** Robert Taylor, Lilli Palmer, Curt Jurgens, Eddie Albert, James Franciscus, John Larch. **1963**

MIRACLE ON 34TH STREET ★★★★★ In this, one of Hollywood's most delightful fantasies, the spirit of Christmas is rekindled in a young girl (Natalie Wood) by a department store Santa. Edmund Gwenn is perfect as the endearing Macy's employee who causes a furor when he claims to be the real Kris Kringle. Is he or isn't he? That is for you to decide in this heartwarming family classic. B&W; 96m. **DIR:** George Seaton. **CAST:** Natalie Wood, Edmund Gwenn, Maureen O'Hara. **1947**

MISADVENTURES OF GUMBY, THE (VOLUME THREE) ★★★ Better-than-average Gumby tales highlight this package, which includes "Baker's Tour," "Gumby Concerto," "The Black Knight" (an example of the more unpleasant side of Gumby stories), and six other misadventures. 60m. **DIR:** Art Clokey. **1956**

MISADVENTURES OF MERLIN JONES, THE ★★½ Tommy Kirk stars as a boy genius whose talents for mind reading and hypnotism land him in all sorts of trouble. Entertaining for the young or indiscriminate; pretty bland for everybody else. 88m. **DIR:** Robert Stevenson. **CAST:** Tommy Kirk, Annette Funicello, Leon Ames, Stu Erwin, Alan Hewitt. **1964**

MISS ANNIE ROONEY ★★ The highlight of this film comes when Dickie Moore gives Shirley Temple her first screen kiss. The rest of this average picture involves a poor girl who falls in love with a rich dandy. No sparks here. 84m. **DIR:** Edwin L. Marin. **CAST:** Shirley Temple, William Gargan, Guy Kibbee, Dickie Moore, Peggy Ryan, Gloria Holden. **1942**

MISS PEACH OF THE KELLY SCHOOL ★★ Muppet-like characters play the kids in this school (based on a comic strip), where simple problems are blown completely out of proportion. Made for TV. 115m. **DIR:** Sheldon Larry, Peter Rosemond. **1982**

MR. MAGOO IN SHERWOOD FOREST ★★★½ Mr. Magoo, as the jolly Friar Tuck, joins Robin Hood and his merry men to thwart the evil designs of King John and the sheriff of Nottingham. Appealing. 85m. **DIR:** Abe Levitow. **1964**

MR. MAGOO IN THE KING'S SERVICE ★★½ A trio of tales featuring Mr. Magoo as D'Artagnan, Cyrano de Bergerac, and Merlin the magician. An average installment in the long-running series. 97m. **DIR:** Abe Levitow. **1964**

MR. MAGOO, MAN OF MYSTERY ★★★ Mr. Magoo, as Dr. Watson, aids supersleuth Sherlock Holmes. As Dr. Frankenstein, he creates a man from the parts of dead bodies and must suffer the consequences. As the Count of Monte Cristo, Magoo exacts revenge against his enemies. And finally, as Dick Tracy, he fights a bevy of bizarre baddies. 96m. **DIR:** Abe Levitow. **1964**

MR. MAGOO'S CHRISTMAS CAROL ★★★★★ Mr. Magoo is Ebenezer Scrooge in this first-rate animated musical of Charles Dickens's holiday classic, which remains the best animated adaptation to date. The songs by Jule Styne and Bob Merrill are magnificent. 53m. **DIR:** Abe Levitow. **1962**

MR. MAGOO'S STORYBOOK ★★★★ Magoo is all seven dwarfs in "Snow White"; portrays the idealistic knight, Don Quixote of La Mancha; and plays Puck in William Shakespeare's *A Midsummer Night's Dream.* 117m. **DIR:** Abe Levitow. **1964**

MR. NANNY ★★ A retired professional wrestler (Hulk Hogan) wants work as a bodyguard but winds up baby-sitting two neglected kids. Hogan is no Anthony Hopkins, but he is likable on screen; too bad the film, with a labored plot and unfunny gags, doesn't give him the support he needs. Rated PG. 83m. **DIR:** Michael Gottlieb. **CAST:** Hulk Hogan, Austin Pendleton, Sherman Hemsley, David Johansen. **1993**

MR. SUPERINVISIBLE ★★ Disney-like comedy with Dean Jones as the scientist who stumbles upon a virus that causes invisibility. Cute in spots; kids should like it. 90m. **DIR:** Anthony M. Dawson. **CAST:** Dean Jones, Gastone Moschin, Ingeborg Schoener, Rafael Alonso, Peter Carsten. **1973**

MISTY ★★★ A thoroughly enjoyable family film about two youngsters who teach a young horse new tricks. Film version of Marguerite Henry's bestseller *Misty of Chincoteague.* Filmed on an island off the Virginia coast, so the scenery is a selling point. 92m. **DIR:** James B. Clark. **CAST:** David Ladd, Arthur O'Connell, Jane Seymour, Pam Smith. **1961**

MOM AND DAD SAVE THE WORLD ★★★½ Kids will get plenty of howls out of this goofy comedy, in which an American family is whisked away to the planet Spengo—in the station wagon. The result is a latter-day version of those so-bad-they're-funny sci-fi flicks of the 1950s. Rated PG for silly violence. 87m. **DIR:** Greg Beeman. **CAST:** Teri Garr, Jeffrey Jones, Jon Lovitz, Eric Idle, Wallace Shawn, Thalmus Rasulala. **1992**

MONKEY TROUBLE ★★★★ Delightful film about a youngster (Thora Birch) who finds a capuchin monkey, whom she calls Dodger. Soon both of them are dodging cops, criminals, and befuddled parents because the cute little monkey is actually a well-trained jewel thief. His original master (Harvey Keitel) needs him back to make good on a promise to a powerful and ruthless mobster. Rated PG for brief profanity and light violence. 95m. **DIR:** Franco Amurri. **CAST:** Thora Birch, Harvey Keitel, Mimi Rogers, Christopher McDonald, Kevin Scannell, Alison Elliott, Robert Miranda, Victor Argo. **1994**

MONKEYS GO HOME 🦃 Stupid monkeyshines. Rated G. 89m. **DIR:** Andrew V. McLaglen. **CAST:** Maurice Chevalier, Dean Jones, Yvette Mimieux. **1966**

MONKEY'S UNCLE, THE ★★ This sequel to *The Misadventures of Merlin Jones* finds whiz kid Tommy Kirk up to no good with a flying machine and a sleep-learning technique employed on a monkey. More of the same from Disney, really: mild slapstick, and G-rated romance with Annette Funicello. For young minds only. 87m. **DIR:** Robert Stevenson. **CAST:** Tommy Kirk, Annette Funicello, Leon Ames, Arthur O'Connell, Frank Faylen. **1965**

MOON PILOT ★★★½ Tom Tryon gets volunteered to become the first astronaut to circle the moon. Good script, with satire and laughs in ample quantities. Rated G. 98m. **DIR:** James Neilson. **CAST:** Tom Tryon, Brian Keith, Edmond O'Brien, Dany Saval. **1962**

MOONCUSSERS ★★½ Kevin Corcoran stars as a boy who discovers the secrets of the Mooncussers—pirates who work on moonless nights to draw ships to their doom by means of false signal lamps on shore. 85m. **DIR:** James Neilson. **CAST:** Oscar Homolka, Kevin Corcoran, Robert Emhardt, Joan Freeman. **1962**

MOONSPINNERS, THE ★★★ A young girl (Hayley Mills) becomes involved in a jewel theft in Crete. The best features of this film are the appearance of a "grownup" Hayley Mills and the return to the screen of Pola Negri. The film is essentially a lightweight melodrama in the Hitchcock mold. 118m. **DIR:** James Neilson. **CAST:** Hayley Mills, Eli Wallach, Pola Negri, Peter McEnery, Joan Greenwood, Irene Papas. **1964**

MORE OF DISNEY'S BEST: 1932–1946 ★★★★★ This sextet, which is vastly superior to its companion collection, includes three "Silly Symphonies" and three cartoons with the better-known stars. "The Brave Little Tailor" is one of Mickey Mouse's best solo vehicles. The Oscar-winning "The Old Mill" (1937) draws considerable drama from the plight of forest creatures trying to ride out a fierce storm, and 1933's "Three Little Pigs" (also an Oscar winner) proves just who's "…afraid of the Big, Bad Wolf." 50m. **DIR:** Walt Disney. **1932–1946**

MOTHER GOOSE ROCK N' ROLL RHYME ★★★ Fanciful musical follows Mother Goose's son Dan Gilroy on an expedition through Rhymeland looking for his mother. Accompanied by Little Bo Peep, played by Shelley Duvall, they encounter the residents of Rhymeland, all played by celebrities. Rated G. 97m. **DIR:** Jeff Stein. **CAST:** Harry Anderson, Jean Stapleton, Shelley Duvall, Bobby Brown, Art Garfunkel, Teri Garr, Dan Gilroy. **1990**

MOTHER GOOSE VIDEO TREASURY VOL. I–IV ★★½ Actors and "advanced puppetronics" are combined to bring a number of nostalgic nursery rhymes to life. This is cute but somehow can't avoid looking like a lackluster version of *The Muppet Show*. 30m. **DIR:** Caroline Hay. **CAST:** Cheryl Rhoads, Joe Giambalva. **1987**

MOUNTAIN FAMILY ROBINSON ★★½ *Mountain Family Robinson* delivers exactly what it sets out to achieve. Predictable and a bit corny. The cast displays an affability that should charm the children and make this film a relaxing, easy time passer for parents as well. Rated G. 100m. **DIR:** John Cotter. **CAST:** Robert Logan, Susan D. Shaw, Heather Rattray, Ham Larsen. **1979**

MOUSE AND HIS CHILD, THE ★★ Muddled cartoon feature about a pair of windup toys who attempt to escape from the tyranny of an evil rat. It's an uneasy combination of a simple children's story with a heavy-handed metaphor. The voices are provided by Peter Ustinov, Cloris Leachman, Andy Devine, and Sally Kellerman. Rated G. 82m. **DIR:** Fred Wolf, Charles Swenson. **1977**

MOUSE AND THE MOTORCYCLE, THE ★★★½ A lonely boy meets a talkative mouse who takes a liking to the boy's toy motorcycle. This adaptation of the Beverly Cleary novel is a joy, combining live-action and the stop-motion animation of John Matthews. 42m. **DIR:** Ron Underwood. **CAST:** Ray Walston, John Byner, Phillip Waller. **1991**

MOWGLI'S BROTHERS ★★★★ The classic tale by Rudyard Kipling is brought to life by animator Chuck Jones and the voices of Roddy McDowall and June Foray. Though the animation here is far simpler than Jones's earlier "Rikki Tikki Tavi," this story of a foundling who is raised by a pack of wolves will be a delight to viewers of all ages. 30m. **DIR:** Chuck Jones. **1977**

MUPPET CHRISTMAS CAROL, THE ★★★½ Kermit the Frog as Bob Crachit? Director Brian Henson somehow makes it work in this family-oriented telling of the classic Charles Dickens tale. It's no match for the acclaimed 1951 version starring Alastair Sim, but Michael Caine makes a fine Scrooge. Rated G. 86m. **DIR:** Brian Henson. **CAST:** Michael Caine. **1992**

MUPPET MOVIE, THE ★★★½ Though there is a huge all-star guest cast, the Muppets are the real stars of this superior family film in which the characters trek to Hollywood in search of stardom. Rated G. 94m. **DIR:** James Frawley. **CAST:** Muppets, Edgar Bergen, Milton Berle, Mel Brooks, James Coburn, Dom DeLuise, Elliott Gould, Bob Hope, Madeline Kahn, Carol Kane, Cloris Leachman, Steve Martin, Richard Pryor, Telly Savalas, Orson Welles, Paul Williams. **1979**

MUPPET SING-ALONGS ★★★ Some of the songs may be a bit too complex for the youngest viewers to follow, but the variety of Muppets are entertaining enough for all ages. Kermit the Frog takes the role of host in these delightful songfests. 30m. **DIR:** David Gumpel. **1993**

MUPPETS TAKE MANHATTAN, THE ★★★ Jim Henson's popular puppets take a bite of the Big Apple in their third and least effective screen romp. Playwright Kermit and his pals try to get their musical on the Broadway stage. Rated G. 94m. **DIR:** Frank Oz. **CAST:** Muppets, Art Carney, Dabney Coleman, Joan Rivers, Elliott Gould, Liza Minnelli, Brooke Shields. **1984**

MY FRIEND FLICKA ★★★½ A young boy raises and nourishes a sickly colt despite his father's warning that the horse came from wild stock and could be unstable. Fine rendition of Mary O'Hara's timeless novel and one of the best of a genre that flourished in the 1940s before Disney cornered the market a few years later. 89m. **DIR:** Harold Schuster. **CAST:** Roddy McDowall, Preston Foster, Rita Johnson, James Bell, Jeff Corey, Diana Hale, Arthur Loft. **1943**

MY FRIEND LIBERTY ★★★½ An entertaining and enlightening look at the history of America's most famous statue in a claymation perspective by Academy Award–winner Jimmy Picker. Viewers of all ages will find this an enjoyable lesson about who we are and where we came from. 30m. **DIR:** Jimmy Picker. **1986**

MY GIRL ★★★★ A genuinely touching, frequently hilarious and heartfelt film about the difficult adjustments forced on an 11-year-old girl who secretly fears that she was responsible for her mother's death. Lovable characters and the essence of truth make this a good film for families to watch and discuss afterward. Rated PG for brief vulgarity. 90m. **DIR:** Howard Zieff. **CAST:** Dan Aykroyd, Jamie Lee Curtis, Macaulay Culkin, Anna Chlumsky, Richard Masur, Griffin Dunne. **1991**

MY GIRL 2 Vada Sultenfuss, the hypochondriac daughter of a widowed mortician, hits her teens in this terminally dull sequel as she researches the life of the mother she never knew. Rated PG. 99m. **DIR:** Howard Zieff. **CAST:** Anna Chlumsky, Austin O'Brien, Dan Aykroyd, Jamie Lee Curtis, Richard Masur. **1994**

MY LITTLE PONY: THE MOVIE ★★★ Darling ponies are threatened by the evil witch family (Cloris Leachman, Madeline Kahn, and Rhea Perlman). Children under 7 should enjoy this, but older children and adults may feel it's too long. Rated G. 85m. **DIR:** Michael Joens. **CAST:** Danny DeVito, Madeline Kahn, Cloris Leachman, Rhea Perlman, Tony Randall (voices). **1986**

MY SIDE OF THE MOUNTAIN ★★★★ File this in that all-too-small category of films that both you and your kids can enjoy. A 13-year-old Toronto boy decides to prove his self-worth by living in a Quebec forest for one year with no resources other than his own wits. Gus the Raccoon steals the show, but you'll be charmed and entertained by the rest of the movie as well. Rated G. 100m. **DIR:** James B. Clark. **CAST:** Teddy Eccles, Theodore Bikel. **1969**

MYSTERIOUS STRANGER, THE ★★★★ A wonderful adaptation of a Mark Twain story about a printer's apprentice who daydreams he is back in the sixteenth century. Add to this a magical stranger and a not so magical alchemist, and you have fun for the whole family. Not rated. 89m. **DIR:** Peter H. Hunt. **CAST:** Chris Makepeace, Lance Kerwin, Fred Gwynne, Bernhard Wicki. **1982**

MYSTERY ISLAND ★★★ When four children whose boat has run out of gas discover what appears to be a deserted island, they promptly name it Mystery Island. The children find a case of counterfeit money which belongs to villains, who later return to the island for it. The best part about this children's film is the beautiful underwater photography. 75m. **DIR:** Gene Scott. **CAST:** Jayson Duncan, Niklas Juhlin. **1981**

MYSTERY MANSION A girl with strange but true dreams, two escaped convicts, and hidden treasure—all involved with an old Victorian mystery house. Rated G. 95m. **DIR:** David F. Jackson. **CAST:** Dallas McKennon, Greg Wynne, Jane Ferguson. **1986**

NAMU, THE KILLER WHALE ★★★½ A well-made family film that isn't as sinister as its title. It's based on the true story of a whale in a public aquarium. Namu was so friendly and intelligent it was set free. The 1993 movie, *Free Willy*, was inspired by this film. 86m. **DIR:** Laslo Benedek. **CAST:** Robert Lansing, Lee Meriwether, John Anderson, Richard Erdman, Robin Mattson. **1966**

NAPOLEON AND SAMANTHA ★★★½ This Disney film features Johnny Whitaker as Napoleon, an orphan who decides to hide his grandpa's body when the old man dies and care for their pet lion, Major. When a college student/goat herder named Danny (Michael Douglas) helps bury Grandpa, Napoleon decides to follow him to his flock. Samantha (Jodie Foster) joins him and the lion as they face the dangers of a fierce mountain lion and a bear. Rated G. 91m. **DIR:** Bernard McEveety. **CAST:** Johnny Whitaker, Jodie Foster, Michael Douglas, Will Geer, Arch Johnson, Henry Jones. **1972**

NATIONAL VELVET ★★★★ This heartwarming tale of two youngsters determined to train a beloved horse to win the famed Grand National Race is good for the whole family, especially little girls who love horses and sentimentalists who fondly recall Elizabeth Taylor when she was young, innocent, and adorable. Have Kleenex on hand. 125m. **DIR:** Clarence Brown. **CAST:** Mickey Rooney, Elizabeth Taylor, Donald Crisp, Anne Revere, Angela Lansbury, Reginald Owen. **1944**

NELVANAMATION (VOLUME ONE) ★★★ Four made-for-television cartoons. In "A Cosmic Christmas," a kindhearted boy attempts to explain the celebration to some friendly aliens. "The Devil and Daniel Mouse" is an outstanding short about a folk singing rodent (music by John Sebastian). A robotic version of the Shakespearean love story is brought to life in "Romie-0 and Julie-8." The last episode, "Please Don't Eat the Planet," is subtitled "An Intergalactic Thanksgiving." 100m. **DIR:** Clive Smith. **1980**

NELVANAMATION (VOLUME TWO) ★★½ More enjoyable cartooning from Canada's Nelvana Studios. This well-written collection includes "Take Me Out to the Ball Game," a sci-fi baseball story with music by Rick Danko of The Band, and "The Jack Rabbit Story," with music by John Sebastian. 100m. **DIR:** Ken Stephenson, Gian Celestri, Greg Duffell. **1980**

NEVER A DULL MOMENT 🦃 Dick Van Dyke doing his sophisticated version of Jerry Lewis at his worst. Rated G. 100m. **DIR:** Jerry Paris. **CAST:** Dick Van Dyke, Edward G. Robinson, Dorothy Provine, Henry Silva. **1968**

NEW ADVENTURES OF PIPPI LONGSTOCKING, THE ★★ Something has been lost in the film adaptation of Astrid Lindgren's tale. This time spunky but lovable Pippi is a brat who manages to give adult viewers a headache and children ideas about driving adults over the edge. A few catchy tunes but nothing else to recommend this. Rated G. 100m. **DIR:** Ken Annakin. **CAST:** Tami Erin, Eileen Brennan, Dennis Dugan, Dianne Hull. **1988**

NEW ADVENTURES OF WINNIE THE POOH, THE ★★ *New*, indeed. This series of Disney animated shorts, loosely (at times *very* loosely) taken from A. A. Milne's stories, hardly compares to the original adaptations. The animation is strictly low-budget, with simplistic backgrounds and limited movement. The music is tinny and jolting, a far cry from the flowing orchestral themes and witty songs of those earlier installments. each. 44m. **DIR:** Karl Geurs. **1988**

NIGHT THEY SAVED CHRISTMAS, THE ★★★★ In this excellent made-for-television film, three kids strive to protect Santa's toy factory from being destroyed by an oil company. Art Carney is delightful as Saint Nick. 100m. **DIR:** Jackie Cooper. **CAST:** Jaclyn Smith, Art Carney, Paul LeMat, Mason Adams, June Lockhart, Paul Williams. **1984**

NIGHTINGALE, THE ★★★½ An emperor (Mick Jagger) survives court intrigue to discover true friendship from a lowly maid (Barbara Hershey) with the help of a nightingale in this enjoyable *Faerie Tale Theatre* production. 51m. **DIR:** Ivan Passer. **CAST:** Mick Jagger, Bud Cort, Barbara Hershey, Edward James Olmos. **1983**

NIKKI, WILD DOG OF THE NORTH ★★★ The rugged wilderness of northern Canada provides the backdrop to this story of a dog that is separated from his owner. 73m. **DIR:** Jack Couffer. **CAST:** Don Haldane, Jean Coutu, Emile Genest. **1961**

NO DEPOSIT, NO RETURN ★★ Two kids decide to escape from their multimillionaire grandfather (David Niven) and visit their mother in Hong Kong. On their way to the airport, they end up in a getaway car with two incompetent safecrackers. It is unrealistic and not very believable, with occasional bits of real entertainment. Rated G. 115m. **DIR:** Norman Tokar. **CAST:** David Niven, Don Knotts, Darren McGavin, Herschel Bernardi, Barbara Feldon. **1976**

NO GREATER GIFT ★★★ A disadvantaged boy with a malignant tumor learns trust and compassion from his hospital roommate who needs a kidney. This is a simple and sensitive story, useful in familiarizing youngsters with the organ-donor program. 45m. **DIR:** Anson Williams. **CAST:** Betty Thomas, Reni Santoni. **1985**

NOBODY'S BOY ★★ Blandly animated run-of-the-mill video fare about an orphan's search for his mother. Along the way he's befriended by a St. Bernard, a chimp, and a parrot. Featuring the voice of Jim Backus. 80m. **DIR:** Jim Flocker. **1985**

NORTH AVENUE IRREGULARS, THE ★★½ Average Disney film about a young priest (Edward Herrmann) who wants to do something about crime. He enlists a group of churchgoing, do-good women to work with him. Quality cast is wasted on marginal script. Rated G. 100m. **DIR:** Bruce Bilson. **CAST:** Edward Herrmann, Barbara Harris, Cloris Leachman, Susan Clark, Karen Valentine, Michael Constantine, Patsy Kelly, Virginia Capers. **1979**

NOW YOU SEE HIM, NOW YOU DON'T ★★ Kurt Russell discovers a formula that will make a person or item invisible. Bad guy Cesar Romero attempts to hijack the discovery for nefarious purposes, which leads to disastrous results. Rated G. 85m. **DIR:** Robert Butler. **CAST:** Kurt Russell, Joe Flynn, Jim Backus, Cesar Romero, William Windom. **1972**

NUKIE 🦃 Even children will be bored by this tale of two alien brothers who get lost on Earth and must find each other. Rated G. 99m. **DIR:** Sias Odendal. **CAST:** Glynis Johns, Steve Railsback. **1993**

NUTCRACKER PRINCE, THE ★★½ Animated version of E.T.A. Hoffman's book *The Nutcracker and the Mouse King* benefits greatly from the voice talents of Kiefer Sutherland, Megan Follows, Peter O'Toole, Mike McDonald, and Phyllis Diller, who bring life to this fanciful tale of a young girl who joins the Nutcracker in his battle against the evil Mouse King. Rated G. 75m. **DIR:** Paul Schibli. **1990**

NUTS ABOUT CHIP 'N' DALE ★★★ Pluto's attempts to bury a bone cause problems with the two chipmunks in "Food for Feudin'," easily the best cartoon of this collection. In "Two Chips and a Miss" both chipmunks fall in love with Clarice (in her only appearance). The noisy and somewhat cruel struggles with Donald Duck in "Trailer

Horn" end things on an unfortunate note. 22m. **DIR:** Walt Disney. 1950–1952

OFF ON A COMET ★★ A re-creation of the Jules Verne fantasy. A French captain must solve the riddle of what's happened to the world when it collides with a comet. The characters' accents are somewhat bothersome and may get in the way of understanding for younger viewers. 52m. **DIR:** Richard Slapczynski. 1979

OFFICER AND A DUCK, AN (LIMITED GOLD EDITION 2) ★★★★½ Six exceptional animated treats. Donald Duck turns unwilling soldier in these rarely seen entries, from his first days of "Donald Gets Drafted" to his ambitious scheme to go AWOL in "The Old Army Game," a plan that backfires with hilarious results. 50m. **DIR:** Walt Disney. 1942–1943

OH, HEAVENLY DOG! ★★ Chevy Chase should have known better. This movie is an overly silly cutesy about a private eye (Chase) who is murdered and then comes back as a dog (Benji) to trap his killers. Kids, however, should enjoy it. Rated PG. 103m. **DIR:** Joe Camp. **CAST:** Benji, Chevy Chase, Jane Seymour, Omar Sharif, Robert Morley. 1980

OLD EXPLORERS ★★½ Family adventure about two senior citizens who refuse to let old age stand in their way of having a full, exciting life. Using their imaginations, they span the globe, taking in such sights as the Sahara and the jungles of South America. Rated PG. 91m. **DIR:** William Pohlad. **CAST:** José Ferrer, James Whitmore. 1990

OLD YELLER ★★★★ Here's a live-action Walt Disney favorite. A big yellow mongrel is taken in by a southwestern family. The warm attachment and numerous adventures of the dog and the two boys of the family are sure to endear this old mutt to your heart. A few tears are guaranteed to fall at the conclusion, so you'd best have a hankie. 83m. **DIR:** Robert Stevenson. **CAST:** Dorothy McGuire, Fess Parker, Tommy Kirk, Chuck Connors. 1957

OLLIE HOPNOODLE'S HAVEN OF BLISS ★★★★ Fans of Jean Shepherd's autobiographical *A Christmas Story* will be equally delighted by this sequel, in which the author's childhood alter ego has grown (but not matured) into a teenager. Various events conspire against the family's annual cabin outing, including a runaway dog and our young hero's first experience with a real summer job. As always, Shepherd's witty narration evokes both whimsy and nostalgia. Made-for-cable; family fare. 90m. **DIR:** Richard Bartlett. **CAST:** Jerry O'Connell, James B. Sikking, Dorothy Lyman, Jason Adams, Jean Shepherd. 1988

ON THE RIGHT TRACK ★★ Gary Coleman (of television's "Diff'rent Strokes") plays a tyke with a talent for picking the winners in horse races. Without Coleman, this would be an awful movie. Even with him, it is nothing to shout about. Rated PG. 98m. **DIR:** Lee Philips. **CAST:** Gary Coleman, Maureen Stapleton, Michael Lembeck, Norman Fell. 1981

ONCE UPON A FOREST ★★½ Only Robin Williams's humorous antics as the voice of klutzy Batty make this animated environmental fable worth watching. An idealistic fairy discovers to her horror that humankind is ravaging her rain-forest home. It's a bit too preachy for adults, but kids will enjoy it. Rated G. 71m. **DIR:** Charles Grosvenor. 1993

ONCE UPON A MIDNIGHT SCARY ★★½ Interesting television production of a trilogy of children's classic ghost stories, hosted by Vincent Price. *The Ghost Belongs to Me*, *The Legend of Sleepy Hollow*, and *The House with a Clock in its Walls* are presented in that order, with the first two stories the standouts. All are given a preteen treatment, which means no gore and no bad language, just some old-fashioned scares. 50m. **DIR:** Neil Cox. **CAST:** Vincent Price, René Auberjonois, Severn Darden. 1979

ONCE UPON A TIME AND THE EARTH WAS CREATED... ★★½ A basic trek through the evolution theory, reminiscent of those physical science films you may remember from fifth grade. There's a disquieting air of indifference when it comes to the elimination of characters through "natural selection," as well as some violent confrontations between neighboring tribes and hungry dinosaurs. Otherwise pretty harmless. 77m. **DIR:** Albert Barillé. 1985

ONE AND ONLY, GENUINE, ORIGINAL FAMILY BAND, THE ★★½ This period comedy, set in the Dakota territories, features Walter Brennan—who struggles to keep his family's band together in order to get invited to the Democratic convention in St. Louis. This is a lightweight movie but is, nonetheless, moderately enjoyable for the whole family. Rated G. 110m. **DIR:** Michael O'Herlihy. **CAST:** Walter Brennan, Buddy Ebsen, Lesley Ann Warren, John Davidson, Goldie Hawn. 1967

ONE HUNDRED AND ONE DALMATIANS ★★★★ Walt Disney animated charmer, concerning a family of Dalmations—far fewer than 101, at least initially—which runs afoul of the deliciously evil Cruella de Vil. In keeping with the jazzier sound track, the animation has rougher edges and more vibrant colors, rather than the pastels that marked the studio's earlier efforts. 79m. **DIR:** Wolfgang Reitherman, Hamilton Luske, Clyde Geronimi. 1961

ONE OF OUR DINOSAURS IS MISSING ★★½ In this moderately entertaining comedy-spy film, Peter Ustinov plays a Chinese intelligence agent attempting to recover some stolen microfilm. Helen Hayes plays a nanny who becomes involved in trying to get the film to the British authorities. Rated G. 101m. **DIR:** Robert Stevenson. **CAST:** Peter Ustinov, Helen Hayes, Derek Nimmo, Clive Revill. **1975**

1001 RABBIT TALES ★★★★ Fourteen classic cartoons are interwoven with new footage to make another feature-length film out of the well-known Warner Bros. characters. This time the theme is fairy tales. Bugs and the gang spoof "Goldilocks and the Three Bears," "Jack and the Bean Stalk," and "Little Red Riding Hood," among others. This one also contains Chuck Jones's "One Froggy Evening," one of the greatest cartoons ever! Rated G. 76m. **DIR:** Friz Freleng, Chuck Jones. **1982**

OPUS 'N' BILL IN A WISH FOR WINGS THAT WORK ★★★★★ You couldn't ask for a better animated adaptation of Bloom County's avian superstar, Opus the Penguin. Michael Bell's somewhat nasal voice is just right for the big-nosed birdbrain, who begs Santa Claus for full-sized wings, which would enable an overweight, herring-loving penguin to fly. Bill the Cat is also on hand in this glossy Amblin Entertainment rendition of Berke Breathed's picture book, which suggests we be content with our own, uniquely individual attributes. 30m. **DIR:** Skip Jones. **1991**

OUR LITTLE GIRL ★★★ Curly-top Shirley's physician father (Joel McCrea) is away so much that his lovely wife (Rosemary Ames) seeks solace from neighbor Lyle Talbot. Shirley is so distressed by this turn of events that she runs away, forcing her parents to reunite in their search for her. Fine melodrama. B&W; 63m. **DIR:** John S. Robertson. **CAST:** Shirley Temple, Rosemary Ames, Joel McCrea, Lyle Talbot. **1935**

OUR MR. SUN ★★★★ Written and directed by Frank Capra, this Bell Science educational film explores the mysteries of the sun. Animation (with the voice of Lionel Barrymore as Father Time) and live footage of the sun's surface enhance this excellent production. 59m. **DIR:** Frank Capra. **CAST:** Dr. Frank Baxter, Eddie Albert. **1958**

OUR VINES HAVE TENDER GRAPES ★★★★★ A shining example of a sentimental movie that doesn't go overboard, this film is set in Wisconsin among Scandinavian immigrants. The focus is on the relationship between two youngsters and their very wise father with lots of witty dialogue and plenty of humorous situations. B&W; 105m. **DIR:** Roy Rowland. **CAST:** Edward G. Robinson, Margaret O'Brien, "Butch" Jenkins, Agnes Moorehead, James Craig, Frances Gifford, Sara Haden. **1945**

OUTSIDE CHANCE OF MAXIMILIAN GLICK, THE ★★★★ Delightfully engaging character study of a young Jewish boy's introduction to real life. He wants to enter a dual piano competition with a pretty gentile girl. But his parents disapprove of this relationship, and try to keep him from seeing her. Rated G. 95m. **DIR:** Allan A. Goldstein. **CAST:** Saul Rubinek, Jan Rubes, Fairuza Balk. **1989**

PACKIN' IT IN ★★★½ When Gary and Dianna Webber (Richard Benjamin and Paula Prentiss) flee from the pollution and crime of Los Angeles, they find themselves living among survivalists in Woodcrest, Oregon. The laughs begin as these city folks, including their punked-out daughter (played by Molly Ringwald), try to adjust to life in the wilderness. 92m. **DIR:** Jud Taylor. **CAST:** Richard Benjamin, Paula Prentiss, Molly Ringwald, Tony Roberts, Andrea Marcovicci. **1982**

PADDINGTON BEAR (SERIES) ★★★ This British production successfully uses a charming stuffed bear and stop-action along with flat, cutout human figures. Paddington is a darling bear who came to England from Peru. He manages to get into many scrapes (each volume in the series of tapes has eleven featurettes) and somehow comes out on top by virtue of his wit and imagination. Children under seven will find this entertaining. 50m. **DIR:** Michael Bond. **1983**

PAINTED HILLS, THE ★★★½ A sentimental tale with Lassie starring as an intelligent canine who doesn't let human beings get away with anything. Set in the 1870s with greedy gold miners killing partners and rivals. But Lassie knows who the real good guys are! Well-photographed and nicely choreographed with a beautifully edited performance by Lassie that will make an animal lover out of just about anybody. 65m. **DIR:** Harold F. Kress. **CAST:** Gary Gray, Paul Kelly, Bruce Cowling, Ann Doran, Chief Yowlachie, Andrea Virginia Lester. **1951**

PANDA AND THE MAGIC SERPENT ★★★ A young man is reunited with his true love by his animal friends in this fancifully animated production of an ancient Chinese legend. 78m. **DIR:** Robert Tafur. **1969**

PANDA'S ADVENTURES ★★½ Panda, a young prince of the animal kingdom, must face a series of challenges in order to learn the meaning of courage. 55m. **DIR:** Yugo Serikawa. **1984**

PARENT TRAP, THE ★★★★ Walt Disney doubled the fun in this comedy when he had Hayley Mills play twins. Mills plays sisters who meet for the first time at camp and decide to reunite their divorced parents (Brian Keith and Maureen O'Hara). 124m. **DIR:** David Swift. **CAST:** Hayley Mills, Brian Keith, Maureen O'Hara, Joanna Barnes. **1961**

PATCHWORK GIRL OF OZ, THE ★★★ One of the many sequels to L. Frank Baum's now-classic fantasy story, this film version tells the story of a poor Munchkin boy's adventures en route to Oz's Emerald City. The Patchwork Girl is just one of many strange and wonderful characters encountered. Silent, with musical score. B&W; 81m. **DIR:** J. Farrell McDonald. **1914**

PAUL BUNYAN ★★★★ This Rabbit Ears rendition of the famed American folktale is a success on all counts, from Leo Kottke's lively music to Rick Meyerowitz's intricate, *Mad Magazine*–style animation. It's held together brilliantly by Jonathan Winters, whose seriocomic narration makes this story a treat for all ages. 30m. **DIR:** Tim Raglin. **1990**

PEACHBOY ★★★ An old Japanese legend is the basis for this passable Rabbit Ears production, which uses Ryuichi Sakamoto's music and Jeffrey Smith's soft watercolor artwork to tell the story of a great warrior who bands with a dog, an ape, and a pheasant to battle nasty ogres on the Isle of the Dead. Sigourney Weaver provides the narration. 30m. **DIR:** C. W. Rogers. **1991**

PEANUT BUTTER SOLUTION, THE ★★½ Remember sitting around a campfire when you were a kid and creating a story that just went on and on? This is a campfire movie. Part of the *Tales for All* series, it combines old houses, ghosts, an evil madman, enforced child labor, and a main character with a real hairy problem, all mixed together in sort of a story. 96m. **DIR:** Michael Rubbo. **CAST:** Mathew Mackay, Siluk Saysanasy, Helen Hughes. **1985**

PECK'S BAD BOY ★★★ Jackie Coogan shines as the mischievous scamp who commits all manner of mayhem, yet miraculously escapes the lethal designs his victims must harbor. Silent. B&W; 54m. **DIR:** Sam Wood. **CAST:** Jackie Coogan, Wheeler Oakman, Doris May, Raymond Hatton, Lillian Leighton. **1921**

PECK'S BAD BOY WITH THE CIRCUS ★★ Tommy Kelly, the mischievous Peck's Bad Boy, and his ragamuffin gang of troublemakers (including an aging Spanky MacFarland) wreak havoc around the circus. Comedy greats Edgar Kennedy and Billy Gilbert are the best part of this kids' film. B&W; 78m. **DIR:** Eddie Cline. **CAST:** Tommy Kelly, Ann Gillis, Edgar Kennedy, Billy Gilbert, Benita Hume, Spanky McFarland, Grant Mitchell. **1938**

PECOS BILL ★★★★★ This may well be the finest and funniest half hour you *ever* experience. Robin Williams enthusiastically narrates Brian Gleeson's wildly amusing interpretation of Pecos Bill, that great American folk legend who rode a cougar, taught cowboys about cattle drives, and lassoed a tornado. Tim Raglin's antic illustrations perfectly counterpoint Williams's vocal performance, as does Ry Cooder's suitably Wild Westish music. 30m. **DIR:** Mark Sottnick, Tim Raglin. **1988**

PECOS BILL, KING OF THE COWBOYS ★★★½ This episode from Shelley Duvall's *Tales and Legends* is fun for the whole family. Steve Guttenberg is irresistible as Bill. Truly entertaining! 60m. **DIR:** Howard Storm. **CAST:** Steve Guttenberg, Martin Mull, Dick Schaal, Rebecca DeMornay, Claude Akins. **1986**

PEE-WEE'S PLAYHOUSE CHRISTMAS SPECIAL ★★★½ In this TV special, Pee-Wee plans a Christmas celebration for his friends. Pee-Wee is zany, offbeat, very funny, and a nice break from traditional holiday fare. Not rated. 49m. **DIR:** Wayne Orr, Paul Reubens. **CAST:** Pee-Wee Herman, Frankie Avalon, Annette Funicello, Grace Jones, Little Richard, Dinah Shore, Whoopi Goldberg, Oprah Winfrey, Zsa Zsa Gabor. **1988**

PEPE LE PEW'S SKUNK TALES ★★★ Once again, Warner Bros. director Chuck Jones takes top honors in a Warner Bros. cartoon release. His 1949 Oscar-winning "For Scent-imental Reasons" features the amorous skunk, Pepe Le Pew, at his cat-wooing best. 56m. **DIR:** Chuck Jones, Arthur Davis, Abe Levitow. **1948–1960**

PERFECT HARMONY ★★★★ Heartwarming film about enlightenment in a sleepy South Carolina town and its exclusive boys' prep school in 1959. A Yankee schoolteacher (Peter Scolari) exposes the boys to non-Southern views of the Civil War, equality, etc. Amidst this awakening, a friendship blossoms between the caretaker's grandson and one of the privileged students. David Faustino convincingly plays the ultimate bigoted bully. Unrated, this Disney-channel film uses a minimum of violence and racial slurs to prove its point. 93m. **DIR:** Will Mackenzie. **CAST:** Peter Scolari, Darren McGavin, Moses Gunn, Justin Whalin, David Faustino. **1990**

PETER AND THE WOLF ★★★★★ Originally intended as the centerpiece for Walt Disney's planned sequel to *Fantasia*, this luxuriously animated rendition of Prokofiev's musical fable was instead repackaged as part of 1946's *Make Mine Music*. Sterling Holloway's narration adds a bit of contemporary humor to the gentle fable of a small Russian boy who goes wolf hunting. 30m. **DIR:** Walt Disney. **1946**

PETER PAN (1953) ★★★½ While this 1953 Disney release doesn't qualify as one of the studio's animated classics, it is nonetheless an entertaining version of James M. Barrie's children's play about Never-Never-Land, and the three Darling children taken there by Peter Pan and his fairy companion, Tinker Bell. Rated G. 77m. **DIR:** Hamilton Luske, Clyde Geronimi, Wilfred Jackson. **1953**

PETER PAN (1960) ★★★★ The magic is still there, remarkably, in this 1960 NBC Television production of the musical based on the book by James M. Barrie. Mary Martin stars in her most beloved role. Unusually high-quality release from GoodTimes Video, which has added four minutes of footage not seen in twenty years. 100m. **DIR:** Vincent J. Donehue. **CAST:** Mary Martin, Cyril Ritchard, Sondra Lee, Margalo Gilmore. **1960**

PETE'S DRAGON ★★½ Only the kiddies will get a kick out of this Disney feature, which combines live action with animation. In Maine, circa 1908, a 9-year-old boy (Sean Marshall) escapes his overbearing foster parents with the aid of the pet dragon that only he can see. Sort of a children's version of *Harvey*, it's generally lackluster and uninspired. Rated G. 134m. **DIR:** Don Chaffey. **CAST:** Mickey Rooney, Jim Dale, Helen Reddy, Red Buttons, Jim Backus, Sean Marshall. **1977**

PETRONELLA ★★★★ This live-action production of *Enchanted Musical Playhouse* stars the lovely country-pop singer Sylvia as a liberated princess who sets out to rescue an imprisoned prince. The whole family can enjoy its cheerful songs and humorous moments. 30m. **DIR:** Rick Locke. **CAST:** Sylvie, Mayf Nutter, James Arrington, Jerry Maren, David Jensen, David E. Morgan. **1985**

PIED PIPER OF HAMELIN, THE ★★★★★ Nicholas Meyer, who also directed *The Day After* and *Star Trek II*, does a terrific job of adapting Robert Browning's eerie poem for this *Faerie Tale Theatre* episode. 60m. **DIR:** Nicholas Meyer. **CAST:** Eric Idle, Tony Van Bridge, Keram Malicki-Sanchez, Peter Blaise. **1985**

PINK AT FIRST SIGHT ★★★★ This was a Valentine's Day TV special in which the Pink Panther, Blake Edwards's lovable and zany cartoon character, longs to have a lady panther and enough money to buy her a special present. To this end, he attempts to make some money as a singing messenger. Also included on this tape are four shorter features. 49m. **DIR:** Friz Freleng, David H. DePatie. **1964–1981**

PINK PANTHER CARTOON FESTIVAL, THE: A FLY IN THE PINK ★★★½ The featured short on this nine-cartoon tape has the Pink Panther pursuing a fruit fly. Among the other installments: "Pink-a-Rella," in which our hero finds a magic wand, and "Pink Plasma," depicting a less than enjoyable stay in Transylvania. 57m. **DIR:** Friz Freleng, David H. DePatie. **1968–1975**

PINK PANTHER CARTOON FESTIVAL, THE: PINK-A-BOO ★★★ The featured short on this tape has the Pink Panther desperately trying to rid his house of a pesky mouse that constantly outwits him. Also offered are "Slink Pink," "Pink Aye," "In the Pink of the Night," and four other titles. 56m. **DIR:** Friz Freleng, David H. DePatie. **1964–1979**

PINOCCHIO (1940) ★★★★★ In this timeless Walt Disney animated classic, a puppet made by a lonely old man gets the chance to become a real boy. *Pinocchio* is one of those rare motion pictures that can be enjoyed over and over again by adults as well as children. If you remember it as a "kid's show," watch it again. You'll be surprised at how wonderfully entertaining it is. Rated G. 87m. **DIR:** Walt Disney. **1940**

PINOCCHIO (1983) ★★★★ An excellent adaptation of the classic tale about a wooden puppet who turns into a real boy. This *Faerie Tale Theatre* production, as with most of the others, will be best appreciated—and understood—by adults. It's blessed with just the right touch of humor, and Lainie Kazan is wonderful as the "Italian" fairy godmother. 51m. **DIR:** Peter Medak. **CAST:** James Coburn, Carl Reiner, Pee-Wee Herman, James Belushi, Lainie Kazan, Don Novello. **1983**

PINOCCHIO AND THE EMPEROR OF THE NIGHT ★★ This scary continuation of the classic tale features an incorrigible Pinocchio who manages to lose his father's prized jewel box as well as his own right to be a real boy. Animation is okay, but somehow you feel as though you're watching an overlong Saturday-morning cartoon. Rated G. 91m. **DIR:** Hal Sutherland. **CAST:** Edward Asner, Tom Bosley, James Earl Jones, Don Knotts, William Windom. **1987**

PIPPI LONGSTOCKING, PIPPI IN THE SOUTH SEAS, PIPPI GOES ON BOARD, PIPPI ON THE RUN ★★ These four movies about the little Swedish girl with the red pigtails and the magical powers were all made at the same time but released in this country over several years. Each has Pippi and her friends annoying grownups and having adventures in faraway lands. Young kids seem to like the movies, even though adults will be appalled at how poorly made and atrociously dubbed they are. Be warned, though, that active children emulating Pippi are even worse than kids shouting Pee-Wee Herman's "secret word" all day. Rated G. 99m. **DIR:** Olle Hellbron. **CAST:** Inger Nilsson. **1969**

PIRATES OF DARK WATERS, THE: THE SAGA BEGINS ★★★ Animated high seas adventure about a young prince who must restore his kingdom by discovering the secrets of thirteen hidden treasures. Voices by Dick Gautier, Hector Elizondo, Brock Peters, Tim Curry, Darleen Carr, and Roscoe Lee Browne. Unrated, but contains violence. 90m. **DIR:** Don Lusk. **1991**

PISTOL, THE: THE BIRTH OF A LEGEND ★★★★ Writer Darrel Campbell did a fantastic job of transforming the life of basketball great Pistol Peter Maravich into a delightful film. Adam Guier does a great job as the young Pistol and has the viewer rooting for him the entire time. Rated G. 104m. **DIR:** Frank C. Schroeder. **CAST:** Millie Perkins, Nick Benedict, Adam Guier. **1990**

PLUTO ★★★★ "The Pointer" is the treasure of this uneven collection. "Bone Trouble" and "Private Pluto" (featuring early appearances by the as-yet-unnamed Chip 'n' Dale) are the other highlights. 52m. **DIR:** Walt Disney. **1939–1950**

PLUTO (LIMITED GOLD EDITION 1) ★★★★ Dinah the dachshund plays the romantic lead, with Butch the bulldog a constant threat, in many of these delightful Pluto cartoons. Still, his best adventures are a pair of richly animated World War II–era cartoons: "Pluto at the Zoo" and "Pluto Junior" (which proves the dangers of fathering a child who resembles the parent *too* much). All seven of these entries are quite enjoyable. 47m. **DIR:** Walt Disney. **1942–1950**

POGO'S SPECIAL BIRTHDAY SPECIAL, THE ★★★ Walt Kelly's beloved characters from the popular comic strip come to life here in the expected nonsensical fashion. Catch the masterful Kelly adaptation of Cajun dialects, as director Chuck Jones takes a sideways look at American holidays and their origins. 26m. **DIR:** Chuck Jones. **1986**

POINT, THE ★★★★½ The cartoon adventures of Oblio, a little boy who is banished from his homeland because (unlike everyone else there) his head doesn't come to a point. Completely irresistible for kids and grownups, with narration by Ringo Starr and songs by Harry Nilsson (including "Me and My Arrow"). Made for TV. 74m. **DIR:** Fred Wolf. **1971**

POLLYANNA (1920) ★★★½ Mary Pickford (at age 27 in 1920) portrays 12-year-old Pollyana, and she melts the hearts of everyone. If you admire silent films or Pickford, or both, you should see this one. B&W; 78m. **DIR:** Paul Powell. **CAST:** Mary Pickford, Katharine Griffith, Howard Ralston. **1920**

POLLYANNA (1960) ★★★½ Walt Disney's version of this classic childhood book is good entertainment for the whole family. Hayley Mills is the energetic and optimistic young girl who improves the lives of everyone she meets. Jane Wyman, Agnes Moorehead, and Adolphe Menjou head an exceptional supporting cast for this film. 134m. **DIR:** David Swift. **CAST:** Hayley Mills, Jane Wyman, Agnes Moorehead, Adolphe Menjou, Karl Malden, Nancy Olson. **1960**

PONCE DE LEON AND THE FOUNTAIN OF YOUTH 🦃 This production of *Tall Tales and Legends* wastes the talents of Michael York by reducing him to an unbelievably vain Ponce de Leon. 50m. **DIR:** Sheldon Larry. **CAST:** Michael York, Sally Kellerman, Paul Rodriguez, Dr. Ruth Westheimer. **1986**

POPEYE ★★★ This adaptation of the famous comic strip by director Robert Altman is the cinematic equivalent of the old "good news, bad news" routine. The good news is that Robin Williams makes a terrific Popeye, and Shelley Duvall was born to play Olive Oyl. The bad news is that it's often boring. Still, it's hard to really dislike *Popeye*—it's so wonderfully weird to look at and so much fun at times. Rated PG. 114m. **DIR:** Robert Altman. **CAST:** Robin Williams, Shelley Duvall, Ray Walston, Paul Smith, Paul Dooley, Richard Libertini, Wesley Ivan Hurt. **1980**

POPEYE CARTOONS ★★★★ Popeye the Sailor Man gets his finest treatment in this trio of classic big-screen cartoons from Max and Dave Fleischer: "Popeye Meets Sinbad," "Aladdin and His Wonderful Lamp," and "Popeye Meets Ali Baba." 56m. **DIR:** Dave Fleischer. **1930–1940**

PORKY PIG AND COMPANY ★★★★ The "company" is the most fun in this octet of Warner Brothers cartoons, which boasts three entries starring Hubie and Bertie, the smarty-pants mice who so devilishly torture hapless cats. The collection includes their first appearance (with Porky) in Chuck Jones's "The Aristo-Cat." 60m. **DIR:** Bob Clampett, Arthur Davis, Chuck Jones. **1939–1947**

PORKY PIG AND DAFFY DUCK CARTOON FESTIVAL FEATURING "TICK TOCK TUCKERED" ★★★★ Bob Clampett takes the top prizes for the sheer hilarity of his contributions: "Baby Bottleneck," in which Porky and Daffy go boom in the baby boom; "Wagon Heels"; and "Tick Tock Tuckered," in which our guys play Beat the Clock. It's a cartoonaholic's dream come true. 57m. **DIR:** Bob Clampett, Chuck Jones, Robert McKimson. **1943–1947**

PORKY PIG CARTOON FESTIVAL FEATURING "NOTHING BUT THE TOOTH" ★★½ Porky Pig's star vehicle "The Swooner Crooner" is the only noteworthy entry in this otherwise unremarkable collection. "Crooner" is a World War II–era short, in which farmer Porky employs roosters resembling Bing Crosby and Frank Sinatra to move a group of hens to complete eggshaustion. Bob Clampett's "Kitty Kornered" features a team-up with Sylvester the cat. 36m. **DIR:** Bob Clampett, Arthur Davis, Chuck Jones, Frank Tashlin. **1944–1948**

PORKY PIG: DAYS OF SWINE AND ROSES ★★½ This disappointing collection wastes too much time with Porky Pig's very early escapades, before he had matured into a full-fledged Warner Bros. star. Only one cartoon—Arthur Davis's "Bye, Bye Bluebeard"—has any real merit, although Robert McKimson's "Thumb Fun" has moments. 36m. **DIR:** Bob Clampett, Arthur Davis, Robert McKimson. **1937–52**

PORKY PIG TALES ★★★★ Animator Chuck Jones is well represented by this late-period sextet of Porky Pig cartoons, the best being "Jumpin' Jupiter," in which campers Porky and Sylvester the cat are "space-napped" by a rather exotic alien. The collection concludes with one of Porky's last appearances: with Daffy Duck in Robert McKimson's "China Jones," originally released in 1959. 44m. **DIR:** Arthur Davis, Chuck Jones, Robert McKimson. **1948–1959**

PORKY PIG'S SCREWBALL COMEDIES ★★★ A fun collection with two delightful Friz Freleng–directed cartoons, the standouts: "You Ought to Be in Pictures," in which Porky lets Daffy Duck talk him into quitting cartoons for feature films; and the "Dough for Do-Do," in which Porky goes after the priceless dodo in Africa amidst surreal backgrounds. 59m. **DIR:** Friz Freleng, Chuck Jones, Robert McKimson. **1985**

PRANCER ★★★ With some movies you have to hang in there. So it is with this film about a troubled girl who finds an injured reindeer just before Christmas. It takes nearly an hour for the story to engage the viewer fully, but from then on *Prancer* is very satisfying. Rated G. 100m. **DIR:** John Hancock. **CAST:** Sam Elliott, Cloris Leachman, Abe Vigoda, Michael Constantine. **1989**

PREHYSTERIA ★★★★ The plot may be derivative, but this solid slice of kiddie entertainment has surprisingly imaginative dialogue. A comic-book bad guy tries to strong-arm a farming family into handing over five dino eggs they accidentally acquired. A lot of fun for the kids, especially the pygmy dinos. Rated PG for mild profanity. 86m. **DIR:** Charles Band, Albert Band. **CAST:** Austin O'Brien, Brett Cullen, Samantha Mills. **1993**

PRIMO BABY ★★★½ A ward of the state is forced to live with a widowed rancher who has a mean-spirited, wheelchair-bound son. Though a rip-off of *The Secret Garden*, this film is still fun to watch. Not rated. 97m. **DIR:** Eda Lever Lishman. **CAST:** Duncan Regehr, Janet Laine Green. **1988**

PRINCE AND THE PAUPER, THE (1937) ★★★½ Enjoyable story of the young Prince of England trading places with his identical look-alike, a street beggar. One of Errol Flynn's lesser-known films. Erich Wolfgang Korngold wrote the music. B&W; 120m. **DIR:** William Keighley. **CAST:** Errol Flynn, Claude Rains, Barton MacLane, Alan Hale Sr., Billy Mauch, Bobby Mauch. **1937**

PRINCE AND THE PAUPER, THE (1978) ★★★½ An all-star cast brings Mark Twain's novel of mistaken identity in not-so-jolly old England to life. Edward, the only son of King Henry VIII (Charlton Heston), trades places with his double, a child from the London slums. The young prince has trouble even with the aid of a swashbuckling soldier-of-fortune (Oliver Reed). Nothing pretentious here, just a costumed adventure that should satisfy young and old. Rated PG. 113m. **DIR:** Richard Fleischer. **CAST:** Charlton Heston, Oliver Reed, George C. Scott, Rex Harrison, Mark Lester. **1978**

PRINCE AND THE PAUPER, THE (1990) ★★★★ Mickey Mouse, Donald Duck, Goofy, and Minnie Mouse are featured in this spin on Mark Twain's timeless tale of a peasant boy and a young prince who switch places. Director George Scribner and his animators went back to the Disney cartoons of the Thirties and Forties, such as "The Little Tailor," for the vintage look of this short, and the result is a delight for the whole family. Rated G. 23m. **DIR:** George Scribner. **1990**

PRINCE OF CENTRAL PARK, THE ★★ Ruth Gordon is, as usual, a bright spot in this made-for-TV children's film about an orphaned brother and sister who flee their foster home for a tree house in Central Park. The script is a bit cynical for a story aimed at children, but Gordon's charm serves to turn that around to her benefit. 76m. **DIR:** Harvey Hart. **CAST:** T. J. Hargrave, Lisa Richards, Ruth Gordon, Marc Vahanian. **1976**

PRINCESS AND THE PEA, THE ★★★½ One of the most interesting *Faerie Tale Theatre* productions, this film features fine performances from Liza Minnelli and Tom Conti. In a way, it's sort of a takeoff on *Arthur*, in which Minnelli starred with Dudley Moore. The actress plays a princess tested for her royal qualities, which include a special kind of sensitivity. 53m. **DIR:** Tony Bill. **CAST:** Liza Minnelli, Tom Conti, Beatrice Straight, Tim Kazurinsky. **1983**

PRINCESS WHO HAD NEVER LAUGHED, THE ★★★★ In this funny Grimm's fairy tale, laughter does prove to be the best medicine for the forlorn princess (Ellen Barkin). When she locks herself in her room, her father decrees a Royal Laugh-off to make his daughter happy. 51m. **DIR:** Mark Cullingham. **CAST:** Howie Mandel, Ellen Barkin, Howard Hesseman. **1984**

PRIZEFIGHTER, THE ★★½ In addition to starring in this goofy comedy, Tim Conway wrote the story. In it, we get a glimpse of 1930s boxing, with Conway playing a stupid boxer who has Don Knotts for his manager. Children may find the corny gags amusing, but most adults will be disappointed. Rated PG. 99m. **DIR:** Michael Preece. **CAST:** Tim Conway, Don Knotts, David Wayne. **1979**

PUPPETOON MOVIE, THE ★★★★ Pioneering fantasy director-producer George Pal established his initial Hollywood credentials with a series of so-called "Puppetoon" shorts, all made with a rarely used technique known as replacement animation. Pal and staff constructed up to five *thousand* wooden figures for each cartoon; minor distinctions from one figure to the next, when filmed one frame at a time, thus conveyed the illusion of movement. This collection of shorts gathers the best of Pal's work. 80m. **DIR:** Arnold Leibovit. 1987

PURPLE PEOPLE EATER ★★½ A sappy family flick about an alien (the title character) who comes to Earth to join a rock 'n' roll band. The fine cast, headed by Ned Beatty, is overshadowed by a sickeningly sweet alien puppet. Rated PG. 91m. **DIR:** Linda Shayne. **CAST:** Ned Beatty, Shelley Winters, Neil Patrick Harris, Peggy Lipton. 1988

PUSS IN BOOTS ★★★★ To ensure himself an easy life, a wily feline carries out a plan to turn his impoverished master into a rich marquis by winning him the hand of the king's daughter. Ben Vereen is purringly convincing as the cat and Brock Peters a standout as the ogre in this *Faerie Tale Theatre* production. 53m. **DIR:** Robert Iscove. **CAST:** Ben Vereen, Gregory Hines, George Kirby, Brock Peters, Alfre Woodard. 1984

RACE FOR YOUR LIFE, CHARLIE BROWN ★★★ Third entry in the "Peanuts" film series has moved further away from the poignant sophistication of *A Boy Named Charlie Brown* and closer to the mindless pap of Saturday-morning cartoon fare. Rated G. 75m. **DIR:** Bill Melendez. 1977

RAFFI AND THE SUNSHINE BAND ★★★★½ This delightfully tuneful follow-up to *A Young Children's Concert with Raffi* is guaranteed to keep the young ones happy. This time, the Canadian folk singer is accompanied by a four-piece band on old favorites and new songs, including "Day-O," "Time to Sing," "Rise and Shine," and "Five Little Ducks." 60m. **DIR:** David Devine. **CAST:** Raffi. 1988

RAILWAY CHILDREN, THE ★★★★½ Wonderful family fare from Great Britain. Set in 1905, this tale focuses on a family whose idyllic life is shattered. Director Lionel Jeffries, a popular British comic actor, also wrote the screenplay based on the novel by E. Nesbit. Warmth, comedy, and adventure—a must-see. 104m. **DIR:** Lionel Jeffries. **CAST:** Dinah Sheridan, Bernard Cribbins, William Mervyn, Ian Cuthbertson, Jenny Agutter, Sally Thomsett, Gary Warren. 1972

RAINBOW BRITE AND THE STAR STEALER ★★★ When the Dark Princess tries to steal Spectra (the world's light source), Rainbow Brite teams up with a chauvinistic, but admittedly brave, little boy named Krys to prevent the theft. This should continue to thrill the little girls who tend to be her most avid fans. 85m. **DIR:** Bernard Deyries, Kimio Yabuki. 1985

RAMONA (SERIES) ★★★★ Author Beverly Cleary's beloved young scamp makes the transition to video with considerable charm and energy in this fifteen-volume series. Perky Sarah Polley is perfectly cast as the wonky, 8-year-old Ramona, and the rest of her family is rendered with equal faithfulness and accuracy. With their credible and heartwarming portrait of growing up in Middle America, these tales are entertaining for the entire family. each. 28m. **DIR:** Randy Bradshaw. **CAST:** Sarah Polley. 1987

RAPUNZEL ★★★½ A pregnant woman's desire for radishes results in her having to give her baby daughter to the witch who owns the radish garden. Shelley Duvall is amusing as both the mother and a grown Rapunzel. Jeff Bridges makes a fine put-upon husband and a handsome prince who must rescue Rapunzel from the man-hating witch, delightfully played by Gena Rowlands. Another *Faerie Tale Theatre* production. 51m. **DIR:** Gilbert Cates. **CAST:** Jeff Bridges, Shelley Duvall, Gena Rowlands. 1982

RARE BREED, A (1981) 🦃 Story of the abduction of an Italian racehorse. 94m. **DIR:** David Nelson. **CAST:** George Kennedy, Forrest Tucker, Tracy Vaccaro, Don DeFore, Tom Hallick. 1981

RED BALLOON, THE ★★★★★ This fanciful, endearing tale of a giant balloon that befriends a small boy in Paris is a delight for children and adults alike. Outside of a catchable word or two here and there, the film is without dialogue. The story is crystal clear in the visual telling, punctuated by an engaging musical score. 34m. **DIR:** Albert Lamorisse. **CAST:** Pascal Lamorisse, Georges Sellier. 1956

RED PONY, THE ★★ It is very hard to make a dull movie from a John Steinbeck novel. This rendition manages to. Myrna Loy and Robert Mitchum are wasted in this story of a young northern California boy who is given a colt, which runs away. 89m. **DIR:** Lewis Milestone. **CAST:** Myrna Loy, Robert Mitchum, Peter Miles, Louis Calhern, Shepperd Strudwick, Margaret Hamilton. 1948

RED RIDING HOOD/GOLDILOCKS ★★★★ Meg Ryan's lively narration is the main attraction in this Rabbit Ears animated production that also deftly blends Laszlo Kubinyi's lush watercolor artwork with Art Lande's spirited piano music. The first tale comes complete with its authentically gruesome conclusion—parents be advised—and the second is given a droll contemporary spin. 30m. **DIR:** C. W. Rogers. 1990

RELUCTANT DRAGON, THE ★★★★½ This delightful, though somewhat unorthodox, medieval dragon tale is a must-see for anyone! Director Charles Nichols orchestrates a fast-paced, hilarious romp—a droll encounter between a bard and a dragon. This is truly a Disney gem. Not rated. Suitable for the entire family. 28m. **DIR:** Charles A. Nichols. 1957

REMOTE ★★★ This *Home Alone* wannabe stars Chris Carrara as a 13-year-old whiz kid trapped in a model home with three bungling burglars. Draggy in parts but kids may find it diverting. Rated PG for cartoonish violence. 80m. **DIR:** Ted Nicolaou. **CAST:** Chris Carrara, Jessica Bowman, John Diehl, Derya Ruggles, Tony Longo, Stuart Fratkin. **1993**

RESCUERS, THE ★★★★ The first adventure of Mouse Rescue Aid Society operatives Bernard (voiced by Bob Newhart) and Bianca (Eva Gabor) is a little gem that signaled the awakening of the Disney animation giant after a long slumber of mediocrity. Don Bluth was partly responsible for the studio's return to quality in this story, based on the writings of Margery Sharp. Rated G. 77m. **DIR:** Wolfgang Reitherman, John Lounsbery, Art Stevens. **1977**

RESCUERS DOWN UNDER ★★★ Disney's first sequel to an animated film doesn't match the charm of the original. Nevertheless, children will enjoy this feature about an Australian boy who takes on a ruthless trapper with the help of mouse heroes. Fine voice work by Bob Newhart, Eva Gabor, George C. Scott, and John Candy. Rated G. 74m. **DIR:** Hendel Butoy, Mike Gabriel. **1990**

RETURN FROM WITCH MOUNTAIN ★★ Christopher Lee and Bette Davis capture Ike Eisenmann to use his supernatural powers to accomplish their own purposes. Sequel to *Escape to Witch Mountain*, in which Eisenmann and Kim Richards discover their powers and the effect they can have on humans. A good children's film, but weak Disney. Rated G. 93m. **DIR:** John Hough. **CAST:** Bette Davis, Christopher Lee, Kim Richards, Ike Eisenmann. **1978**

RETURN OF GUMBY, THE (VOLUME ONE) ★★★½ Though Gumby will always in some respects represent a certain aspect of Americana, he seems to have lost some of his initial charm in the transfer to videocassette. This tape, however, offers the best collection of Gumby's through-the-storybook episodes, such as "King for a Day" and "Hot Rod Granny." 60m. **DIR:** Art Clokey. **1956**

RETURN TO OZ ★★★★ In this semisequel to *The Wizard of Oz*, viewers will hear no songs nor see any Munchkins. It is a very different, but equally enjoyable, trip down the Yellow Brick Road, with young star Fairuza Balk outstanding as Dorothy. It gets pretty scary at times and isn't all fluff and wonder like the Oz of yore. This is nevertheless a magical film for the child in everyone. Rated PG for scary stuff. 110m. **DIR:** Walter Murch. **CAST:** Fairuza Balk, Nicol Williamson, Jean Marsh, Piper Laurie, Matt Clark. **1985**

RETURN TO TREASURE ISLAND ★★★½ This five-tape series was produced for the Disney Channel. It is a sequel to Disney's 1950 film *Treasure Island*, based on Robert Louis Stevenson's classic novel. The action here takes place ten years later with young Jim Hawkins (Christopher Guard) now an educated young man being reunited with the scheming Long John (Brian Blessed). 101m. **DIR:** Piers Haggard. **CAST:** Brian Blessed, Christopher Guard, Kenneth Colley. **1985**

RIDE A WILD PONY ★★★ This entertaining Disney film is the tale of a horse and the two children who want to own him. A poor boy and a rich girl with polio. The setting is Australia. Rated G. 86m. **DIR:** Don Chaffey. **CAST:** Michael Craig, John Meillon. **1976**

RIDE 'EM DENVER ★★ Denver, who looks like a cuddly dragon, is the hero preserving a settlement for wild mustangs and saving children on a broken roller coaster. Poor animation mars this entry. 45m. **DIR:** Tom Burton. **1989**

RIKKI-TIKKI-TAVI ★★★★ An outstanding feature from landmark cartoonist Chuck Jones detailing the adventures of a brave mongoose. This is a first-rate adaptation of the story by Rudyard Kipling. 30m. **DIR:** Chuck Jones. **1975**

RING OF BRIGHT WATER ★★★★ The stars of *Born Free* return for this delightful story of a secluded writer and his pet otter. The story has some odd quirks that adults will appreciate, but this underrated film also has terrific production values and an utterly irresistible animal star. Unrated. 107m. **DIR:** Jack Couffer. **CAST:** Bill Travers, Virginia McKenna. **1969**

RIP VAN WINKLE ★★½ This episode of *Faerie Tale Theatre* will probably not grab most viewers. Francis Ford Coppola does not seem suited to directing fantasies. The story remains basically unchanged as Rip falls asleep for twenty years in the Catskill Mountains only to awaken as an old man. 60m. **DIR:** Francis Ford Coppola. **CAST:** Harry Dean Stanton, Talia Shire, Ed Begley Jr., Mark Blankfield, Tim Conway, Hunter Carson. **1985**

ROAD RUNNER AND WILE E. COYOTE, THE: THE SCRAPES OF WRATH ★★★★ Great sight gags abound in this impressive quintet of Road Runner-Coyote battles, with high points including "Stop! Look! and Hasten!" (1954) and "Guided Muscle" (1955). To vary the mix a bit, we also get one of the rare Coyote-Bugs Bunny contests "Rabbit's Feat" (although the Coyote loses some of his charm when he talks). Don't watch these in one sitting, lest you die laughing. 36m. **DIR:** Chuck Jones. **1954–60**

ROAD RUNNER VS. WILE E. COYOTE: THE CLASSIC CHASE ★★★★ Although Chuck Jones deserves credit for some of the funniest Bugs Bunny/Daffy Duck cartoons and for creating Pepe Le Pew, for many, the cliff-hanging (and falling) attempts of Wile E. Coyote to catch the uncatchable Road Runner stand as his greatest achievements.

This first-rate collection includes several of his best shorts. 54m. **DIR:** Chuck Jones. **1985**

ROB ROY, THE HIGHLAND ROGUE ★★ Slow-moving historical saga is not up to the usual Walt Disney adventure film and is perhaps the weakest of the three films made in England with sturdy Richard Todd as the heroic lead. The few battle scenes are enjoyable enough and the scenery is lovely, but the pace is erratic and there is just too much dead time. 85m. **DIR:** Harold French. **CAST:** Richard Todd, Glynis Johns, James Robertson Justice, Michael Gough, Finlay Currie. **1954**

ROBIN HOOD (1973) ★★★ A feature-length cartoon featuring Robin Hood and his gang, this is one of the lesser animated works from the Walt Disney Studios, but still good for the kiddies. Rated G. 83m. **DIR:** Wolfgang Reitherman. **1973**

ROBOT IN THE FAMILY 🦃 This cheap, sophomoric comedy about an ambulatory robot is one of the worst films we've ever seen; the producers apparently felt they could get away with a $1.98 budget and that kids wouldn't know the difference. (Ours did.) Rated G. 85m. **DIR:** Jack Shaoul, Mark Richardson. **CAST:** Joe Pantoliano, Amy Wright, Peter Maloney, Danny Gerard, John Rhys-Davies. **1991**

ROCK-A-DOODLE ★★★★ Former Disney animation director Don Bluth recovers nicely from the debacle of *All Dogs Go to Heaven* with this delightfully tuneful tale of a barnyard rooster who leaves his home for the big city. It's Elvis Presley as myth, with fine voice work by Glen Campbell, Christopher Plummer, Phil Harris, Sandy Duncan, Eddie Deezen, Charles Nelson Reilly, and Ellen Greene. Rated G. 74m. **DIR:** Don Bluth. **1992**

ROGER RAMJET ★★★ The manic Ken Snyder (later to work on television's *Sesame Street*) invented the All-American Roger Ramjet, who swallows his proton energy pill and gains the strength of twenty atom bombs for twenty seconds. The *very* limited animation may prove dull for contemporary youngsters, but the clever wordplay will have adults in stitches. Each half-hour volume contains six cartoons. 30m. **DIR:** Fred Crippen. **1985**

ROOKIE OF THE YEAR ★★★★ Sweet-natured family comedy is sure to be a hit with all ages. A 12-year-old boy achieves the ultimate fantasy: his broken arm heals oddly, leaving Thomas Ian Nicholas with a powerful pitching arm that he uses to lead the Chicago Cubs to victory. Terrific supporting cast and deft comedy bits make Daniel Stern's directorial debut memorable. Rated PG for brief profanity. 103m. **DIR:** Daniel Stern. **CAST:** Thomas Ian Nicholson, Gary Busey, Albert Hall, Amy Morton, Dan Hedaya, Bruce Altman, Eddie Bracken, Daniel Stern. **1993**

ROVER DANGERFIELD ★★★ Rodney Dangerfield takes the plunge as an animated character in this feature-length cartoon about a city dog who ends up on a farm. Some harder-edged elements—suggestions of violence and songs about dogs "doing their business" on a Christmas tree—may offend some parents. Otherwise, it's generally enjoyable. Rated G. 71m. **DIR:** Jim George, Bob Seely. **1991**

RUDOLPH THE RED-NOSED REINDEER (AND OTHER WONDERFUL CHRISTMAS STORIES) ★★★ The title episode on this tape will be a real treat for those who enjoy vintage animation. It's a 1944 effort by Max Fleischer. Two black-and-white live-action shorts accompany the cartoon portions of this offering, which also includes a story called "Madeline's Christmas," a French holiday classic that is marred by continual dropouts in the picture. 30m. **DIR:** Max Fleischer, Rene Bras. **1944**

RUDY ★★★★½ Based on the life of Daniel E. (Rudy) Ruettiger, this is an excellent family film about a young man who sets a goal for himself and pursues it with dogged determination. From the people who made the equally impressive *Hoosiers* it's a down-to-earth story with spirit-lifting rewards. Like young Rudy, played with engaging sincerity by Sean Astin, the filmmakers have us cheering them all the way. Rated PG for brief profanity. 112m. **DIR:** David Anspaugh. **CAST:** Sean Astin, Ned Beatty, Charles S. Dutton, Robert Prosky, Jason Miller, Lili Taylor, Greta Lind, Chelcie Ross. **1993**

RUMPELSTILTSKIN (1980) ★★★½ In this *Faerie Tale Theatre* production, a poor miller's daughter (Shelley Duvall, the series' executive producer) becomes a queen by outwitting a dwarf (Herve Villechaize) and fulfilling her boastful father's promise that she can spin straw into gold. Villechaize is great as a rather unsavory Rumpelstiltskin, and Ned Beatty is convincing as the selfish king. The sets are especially beautiful. 53m. **DIR:** Emile Ardolino. **CAST:** Herve Villechaize, Shelley Duvall, Ned Beatty, Jack Fletcher, Bud Cort. **1982**

RUMPELSTILTSKIN (1986) ★★½ Run-of-the-mill cartoon adaptation of the classic fairy tale about a pesky little man who aids a lovely young maiden in her attempt to spin straw into gold in order to serve his own selfish ends. Animation style here is comparable to the taste of fast food. 30m. **DIR:** Pino Van-Lamsweerde. **1986**

RUMPELSTILTSKIN (1987) ★★★½ This musical, based on the Brothers Grimm fairy tale, will delight most viewers under the age of 12. In it, Amy Irving plays a poor daydreamer who is summoned by the greedy king (Clive Revill) to spin straw into gold. Rumpelstiltskin (Billy Barty) rescues her from this impossible task but expects her to repay him with her firstborn child. Rated G. 85m. **DIR:** David Irving. **CAST:** Amy Irving, Billy Barty, Clive Revill, Priscilla Pointer, John Moulder-Brown. **1987**

RUN FOR THE ROSES ★★½ Originally titled *Thoroughbred*, this is a *Rocky*-ish saga about a horse that eventually competes in the Kentucky Derby. A Puerto Rican boy, devotes himself to making the nearly lame horse a winner. Rated PG. 93m. **DIR:** Henry Levin. **CAST:** Vera Miles, Stuart Whitman, Sam Groom, Panchito Gomez. **1978**

RUN, REBECCA, RUN ★★★★ This action-filled adventure finds a brave young girl captured by an illegal alien on an Australian island. Her fear of him soon dissolves as she helps him face the Australian authorities in order to be legally admitted to their country. 81m. **DIR:** Peter Maxwell. **CAST:** Henri Szeps, Simone Buchanan, John Stanton. **1983**

RUNAWAY RALPH ★★★½ Delightfully silly *ABC Kidtime* special is based on Beverly Cleary's novel about a hip mouse named Ralph. Hopping on his motorcycle, he hits the highway and ends up at a summer camp. (Ralph's voice is provided by John Matthews.) Fun for all ages! 42m. **DIR:** Ron Underwood. **CAST:** Fred Savage, Ray Walston, Summer Phoenix, Conchata Ferrell, Sara Gilbert. **1988**

SALUTE TO CHUCK JONES, A ★★★★½ This terrific package includes "One Froggy Evening" (perhaps the best cartoon of all time), along with "Duck Dodgers in the 25½ Century," "What's Opera, Doc?" (a superb Wagnerian takeoff) and the Oscar-winning "For Scent-imental Reasons," among others. 56m. **DIR:** Chuck Jones. **1985**

SALUTE TO FRIZ FRELENG, A ★★★½ Three Academy Award–winning shorts—"Knighty Knight Bugs," "Speedy Gonzales," and "Birds Anonymous" (with Sylvester and Tweety Pie)—highlight this tribute to Friz Freleng. 57m. **DIR:** Friz Freleng. **1985**

SALUTE TO MEL BLANC, A ★★★★ The main voice behind the Warner Bros. cartoons gets a fitting tribute in this superb collection of animated shorts, particularly "The Rabbit of Seville." 58m. **DIR:** Friz Freleng, Chuck Jones, Robert McKimson. **1985**

SAMMY, THE WAY-OUT SEAL ★★½ Better than the title would imply. This series of misadventures involves two young brothers and the seal they attempt to keep as a pet. The film moves along briskly and features larger-than-life comic Jack Carson in one of his last performances. 89m. **DIR:** Norman Tokar. **CAST:** Jack Carson, Robert Culp, Patricia Barry, Billy Mumy, Ann Jillian, Michael McGreevey, Elisabeth Fraser. **1962**

SANDLOT, THE ★★★½ Youngsters will get a big kick out of this kids'-eye-view story of what happens when a shy boy moves to a new neighborhood and becomes involved with a ragtag baseball team. Wonderfully funny moments mix with a few ineffective ones for a show that will even keep Mom and Dad entertained. Rated PG for scary stuff. 100m. **DIR:** David Mickey Evans. **CAST:** Karen Allen, Denis Leary, James Earl Jones, Arliss Howard, Tom Guiry. **1993**

SANTA AND THE THREE BEARS ★★ Bland holiday cartoon fare puts a park ranger in the role of St. Nicholas to teach a mother bear and her cubs the meaning of Christmas. The bears miss their winter nap, but learn a valuable lesson of love. 60m. **DIR:** Tony Benedict. **1969**

SANTA CLAUS—THE MOVIE ★★★ In this enjoyable family film, one of Santa's helpers (Dudley Moore), visits Earth and innocently joins forces with an evil toy manufacturer (delightfully played by John Lithgow). It is up to Santa (David Huddleston) to save him—and the spirit of Christmas. Rated PG for light profanity and adult themes. 105m. **DIR:** Jeannot Szwarc. **CAST:** Dudley Moore, John Lithgow, David Huddleston, Burgess Meredith, Judy Cornwell. **1985**

SANTABEAR'S FIRST CHRISTMAS ★★★★½ A polar bear cub makes new friends and meets Saint Nick. Kelly McGillis handles Barbara Read's tale with enthusiasm and musician Michael Hedges contributes a cheerfully seasonal background sound track. 30m. **DIR:** Mark Sottnick. **1986**

SAVAGE SAM ★★½ Officially a sequel to *Old Yeller*, the film has little in common with its predecessor, except for some of the character names. Captured by Indians, the only hope of rescue for three children lies with Savage Sam, Old Yeller's son. An entertaining action film, without the depth of its predecessor. 103m. **DIR:** Norman Tokar. **CAST:** Brian Keith, Tommy Kirk, Kevin Corcoran, Dewey Martin, Jeff York, Marta Kristen. **1963**

SAVANNAH SMILES ★★★½ In this surprisingly good, independently made family film, a 6-year-old runaway named Savannah (Bridgette Anderson) accidentally hides in the backseat of a car operated by two small-time crooks, Alvie (Mark Miller) and Boots (Donovan Scott). It's love at first sight for the trio, who decide to try to be a real family. The authorities, however, have other ideas. Rated G. 107m. **DIR:** Pierre DeMoro. **CAST:** Bridgette Anderson, Mark Miller, Donovan Scott, Peter Graves, Chris Robinson, Michael Parks. **1982**

SAVE THE LADY ★★★ Four kids set out to fight City Hall after a bureaucrat orders the historic *Lady Hope* steam ferry to be destroyed. The kids rescue *Lady Hope*'s former skipper from a retirement home. Together with an expert engineer, the team valiantly repairs and repaints the boat. 76m. **DIR:** Leon

Thau. **CAST:** Matthew Excell, Robert Clarkson, Miranda Cartledge, Kim Clifford. **1981**

SCANDALOUS JOHN ★★★ Brian Keith stars as an eccentric ranch owner fighting to maintain his way of life. In his world, a cattle drive consists of one steer, and gunfights are practiced in the house with live ammunition. He must battle with the law, the world in general, and reality to keep his ranch and the life he loves. Laughs and poignancy are combined in this movie. Rated G. 113m. **DIR:** Robert Butler. **CAST:** Brian Keith, Alfonso Arau, Michele Carey, Rick Lenz, Harry Morgan, Simon Oakland. **1971**

SCARY TALES ★★★½ This collection contains two superb Donald Duck vehicles: "Donald's Lucky Day" (with its affectionate black cat) and "Duck Pimples" (an unusually chaotic cartoon for Disney, quite reminiscent of a Bob Clampett Daffy Duck cartoon). The balance of the tape includes two early black-and-white shorts, both sadly dated: "Skeleton Dance" and "Haunted House." 43m. **DIR:** Walt Disney. **1928–1945**

SEA GYPSIES, THE ★★★ Director Stewart Raffill wrote this adventure movie which tells of five castaways in the Pacific who end up on a remote Aleutian island. This Disney-style tale is climaxed by a race against the approaching Alaskan winter to build a makeshift escape craft. 102m. **DIR:** Stewart Raffill. **CAST:** Robert Logan, Mikki Jamison-Olsen, Heather Rattray. **1978**

SEABERT: THE ADVENTURE BEGINS ★★½ This feature provides a mild ecological message when a baby seal is saved from destruction by a young Eskimo girl and her American companion. Seabert and his new pals set off on a series of adventures that lead them all over the Arctic. Youngsters will find this as entertaining as Saturday-morning television, but not much more. 90m. **DIR:** John Armstrong, Al Lowenheim. **1987**

SEARCHING FOR BOBBY FISCHER ★★★★½ This remarkable film is based on the true story of prodigy Josh Waitzkin, a 7-year-old boy whose seemingly innate understanding of chess puts him in the running to be "the next Bobby Fischer." This bit of praise could just as easily be a curse—Fischer devoted his life to the game and then became a recluse after becoming the world champion. Based on the book by Josh's father, Fred Waitzkin, this thought-provoking commentary explores how success in America is all too often emphasized over decency. Rated PG for brief profanity. 107m. **DIR:** Steven Zaillian. **CAST:** Joe Mantegna, Ben Kingsley, Larry Fishburne, Joan Allen, Max Pomeranc, Robert Stephens, David Paymer, William H. Macy, Dan Hedaya. **1993**

SECRET GARDEN, THE (1949) ★★★★ A captivating adaptation of Frances Hodgson Burnett's classic. Margaret O'Brien dominates the story as the youngster who finds a beautiful garden in the midst of adult confusion in Victorian England. Dean Stockwell considers this his best child star movie, and the story itself was popular enough to inspire a made-for-TV movie in 1987 and a grandiose Broadway musical in 1991. The final sequence is in Technicolor. B&W; 92m. **DIR:** Fred M. Wilcox. **CAST:** Margaret O'Brien, Dean Stockwell, Herbert Marshall, Gladys Cooper, Elsa Lanchester. **1949**

SECRET GARDEN, THE (1984) ★★½ Slow BBC production about a little girl uprooted from India and placed in the care of her cold, stern uncle in his manor house in England. Of course the girl thaws her uncle because of her resemblance to his dear, late wife. Pretty standard stuff, although it's well acted at least. Not rated; suitable for all. 107m. **DIR:** Katrina Murray. **CAST:** Sarah Hollis Andrews, David Patterson. **1984**

SECRET GARDEN, THE (1987) ★★★★ *Hallmark Hall of Fame*'s adaptation of the classic children's story. Gennie James is fantastic as Mary Lennox, the spoiled girl who must live with her mean-spirited uncle after her parents die of cholera. Good acting from the entire cast, a wonderful plot, and beautiful sets make this an enjoyable film for the whole family. 100m. **DIR:** Alan Grint. **CAST:** Gennie James, Barret Oliver, Michael Hordern, Billie Whitelaw, Derek Jacobi. **1987**

SECRET GARDEN, THE (1993) ★★★★ Director Agnieszka Holland creates a truly gorgeous, remarkably subtle and stately version of the children's classic. After her self-indulgent, unloving parents are killed during an earthquake in India, a spoiled, headstrong little girl is sent to live with her uncle in a house full of mysterious secrets. Magical. Rated G. 106m. **DIR:** Agnieszka Holland. **CAST:** Kate Maberly, Heydon Prowse, Andrew Knott, Maggie Smith, Laura Crossley, John Lynch. **1993**

SECRET OF NIMH, THE ★★★★★ Lovers of classic screen animation, rejoice! Don Bluth's *The Secret of Nimh* is the best feature-length cartoon to be released since the golden age of Walt Disney. This movie, about the adventures of a widow mouse, is more than just a children's tale. Adults will enjoy it, too. Rated G. 82m. **DIR:** Don Bluth. **CAST:** Dom DeLuise, Peter Strauss, John Carradine (voices). **1982**

SECRET OF THE SWORD, THE 🦃 Characters from the television series *He-Man and the Masters of the Universe* are featured in this poorly animated, ineptly written feature-length cartoon. Rated G. 90m. **DIR:** Bill Reed, Gwen Wetzler, Ed Friedman, Lou Kachivas, Marsh Lamore. **1985**

SERENDIPITY, THE PINK DRAGON ★★½ "The fates had been kind," intones the narrator with unintended irony, as a shipwrecked young boy floats to the safety of Paradise Island. That's pretty glib, considering the poor lad moments earlier had lost both his parents. Once past this questionable introduction, we settle into the pleasant little tale of the boy, his massive pink friend, and their attempts to save Paradise Island from the greedy Captain Smudge. 90m. **DIR:** Yoshikuni Nishi, Toyo Ebishima. **1989**

SESAME STREET PRESENTS FOLLOW THAT BIRD ★★★★ Although this kiddie film has an impressive "guest cast," the real stars are *Sesame Street* TV show regulars Big Bird, the Cookie Monster, Oscar the Grouch, Count von Count, the Telly Monster, etc. Children will love this story about Big Bird being evicted from Sesame Street. Rated G. 88m. **DIR:** Ken Kwapis. **CAST:** Sandra Bernhard, Chevy Chase, John Candy, Dave Thomas, Joe Flaherty, Waylon Jennings. **1985**

SEVENTH COIN, THE ★★★½ Were it not for some brutality and a wholly pointless scene in a Turkish-style bath, this lively adventure would be acceptable for all ages. American Alexandra Powers and Arabian Navin Chowdhry flee through modern Jerusalem with the implacably villainous Peter O'Toole hot on their heels, all because of a rare coin. The film has strong echoes of Hayley Mills's teen years with Disney, notably *The Moonspinners*. Rated PG-13 for violence, profanity, and brief nudity. 95m. **DIR:** Dror Soref. **CAST:** Alexandra Powers, Navin Chowdhry, Peter O'Toole, John Rhys-Davies, Ally Walker. **1993**

SHAGGY D.A., THE ★★ So-so sequel to Disney's far superior *The Shaggy Dog*, this retread stars Dean Jones as the victim of an ancient curse that turns him into a canine at the worst of moments. Rated G. 91m. **DIR:** Robert Stevenson. **CAST:** Dean Jones, Tim Conway, Suzanne Pleshette. **1976**

SHAGGY DOG, THE ★★★½ An ancient spell turns a boy into a sheepdog, and the fur flies in this slapstick Disney fantasy. Many of the gags are good, but the film sometimes drags. 104m. **DIR:** Charles Barton. **CAST:** Fred MacMurray, Jean Hagen, Tommy Kirk, Annette Funicello. **1959**

SHE LIKES YOU, CHARLIE BROWN ★★★½ Puppy love is the theme of these ten stories, all taken from *The Charlie Brown and Snoopy Show*. Many are brief blackout sketches; the longer pieces include a wry date involving Peppermint Patty and Snoopy. 41m. **DIR:** Bill Melendez, Sam Jaimes, Sam Nicholson, Phil Roman. **1983–1985**

SHE-RA, PRINCESS OF POWER (VOLUME ONE) 🦃 Only a modicum of imagination went into this companion series to *He-Man*. Here, his twin sister, Adora, also has a magic sword. 45m. **DIR:** Hal Sutherland. **1985**

SHELLEY DUVALL'S BEDTIME STORIES (SERIES) ★★★ Shelley Duvall's gift to grandparents and sitters of children of an age to delay bedtime with "Tell me a story." Each cassette contains two short animated tales based on currently popular children's picture books (*Choo Choo*, *Elizabeth and Larry*, *Bill and Pete*, etc.). The animation is simple, keeping faith with the drawings from the books. Narrators include Bette Midler, Dudley Moore, Rick Moranis, Bonnie Raitt, Jean Stapleton, and Ringo Starr. 25m. each. **DIR:** Arthur Leonardi, Jeff Stein. **1992**

SHERLOCK HOLMES AND THE BASKERVILLE CURSE ★★ We weren't very impressed by this feature-length cartoon version of Sir Arthur Conan Doyle's oft-filmed "The Hound of the Baskervilles." The animation is way below par, and the story trifled with a bit too much for our tastes. It may be an effective introduction for youngsters to the joys of the canon. Rated G. 60m. **DIR:** Eddy Graham. **1984**

SHERLOCK HOLMES AND THE VALLEY OF FEAR ★★ Second in a series of mystery stories for kids, based on Sir Arthur Conan Doyle's legendary sleuth. Children mature enough to sit through this dry production shouldn't be disturbed by its talk of secret societies and their bloody rites. 49m. **DIR:** Warwick Gilbert. **1984**

SHE'S A GOOD SKATE, CHARLIE BROWN ★★★½ Snoopy trains Peppermint Patty for a skating competition, and Marcie gets in over her head while sewing a skating dress for her friend. Woodstock's involvement in the climactic sequence is particularly touching. Faithful fans will also object to adults who actually speak (rather than *blat* like a muted trumpet). 25m. **DIR:** Phil Roman. **1980**

SHIPWRECKED ★★★★ A sort of *Home Alone* meets *Treasure Island*, this is a rousing adventure film based on the classic Norwegian novel, *Haakon Haakonsen* by O.V. Falck-Ytter. About a young lad who goes to sea to help get his parents out of debt, and finds himself battling a bloodthirsty pirate (Gabriel Byrne) for buried treasure. This Disney release has plenty of action, thrills, and suspense. Rated PG for light violence. 93m. **DIR:** Nils Gaup. **CAST:** Stian Smestad, Gabriel Byrne, Bjorn Sundquist. **1991**

SIDE BY SIDE: THE TRUE STORY OF THE OSMOND FAMILY ★★ If the title alone hasn't scared you away, you'll probably enjoy this schmaltzy TV movie featuring Marie Osmond as her own mother, raising nine children. It was produced by the Osmond family's own company, and it's every bit as squeaky-clean as that would indicate. 98m. **DIR:** Russ Mayberry. **CAST:** Marie Osmond, Joseph Bottoms. **1982**

SIDEKICKS ★★★½ One of the best underdog fairy tales to emerge in years.

Jonathan Brandis stars as an asthmatic high school kid who daydreams himself into elaborate, Walter Mitty–esque fantasies at the side of longtime hero Chuck Norris (who plays himself, and superbly spoofs many of his macho action hits). The supporting cast is excellent. Rated PG for fantasy-level violence. 100m. **DIR:** Aaron Norris. **CAST:** Beau Bridges, Mako, Jonathan Brandis, Chuck Norris, Julia Nickson, Richard Moll, Joe Piscopo. **1993**

SIGN OF ZORRO, THE ★★½ Baby boomers, beware. If you have fond memories of this swashbuckling Disney television series about the Z-slashing Robin Hood of Old Mexico, skip this uneven feature compilation of original episodes. It's still fine for the kiddies, however. B&W; 91m. **DIR:** Norman Foster, Lewis R. Foster. **CAST:** Guy Williams, Henry Calvin, Gene Sheldon, Britt Lomond, George J. Lewis, Lisa Gaye. **1960**

SILENT MOUSE ★★★★ A mouse rescued by a young village boy determines to repay his kindness by becoming the church mouse. Filmed in the magic mountains of Austria and Czechoslovakia and featuring many of Europe's most famous ensembles, choirs, and orchestras, this playful made-for-TV story will delight viewers of all ages. 50m. **DIR:** Robin Crichton. **CAST:** Lynn Redgrave, Gregor Fisher, Jack McKenzie. **1990**

SILLY SYMPHONIES ★★★ Ward Kimball's animation for "Toby Tortoise Returns" makes this entry the high point of the trio; the tortoise and the hare get together for one more round—this time in a boxing ring. Animator Fred Moore brings some energy to another variation on an old theme with "Three Little Wolves." "Water Babies," by contrast, is an attractive, but pointless, piece of fluff. 25m. **DIR:** Walt Disney. **1935–1936**

SILLY SYMPHONIES (LIMITED GOLD EDITION 1) ★★½ Only the very young will sit still for these syrupy and badly dated fairy tales. The one exception is "The Flying Mouse," with its emphasis on character and personality rather than stock gags and silliness. 54m. **DIR:** Walt Disney. **1933–1938**

SILLY SYMPHONIES: ANIMAL TALES ★★½ Although this collection is highlighted by "Elmer Elephant," most of the other cartoons are lamentably uninvolving. "Cock o' the Walk" and "More Kittens" are the best of what remains. 50m. **DIR:** Walt Disney. **1930–1936**

SILLY SYMPHONIES: ANIMALS TWO BY TWO ★★★½ "The Tortoise and the Hare," a 1935 Oscar winner, is the classic in this trio of early Disney cartoons; the luxurious animation is blended with a strong story that manages to be exciting in spite of its (by now) foregone conclusion. By comparison, "Father Noah's Ark" and "Peculiar Penguins" are pretty, but uninvolving. 26m. **DIR:** Walt Disney. **1933–1935**

SILLY SYMPHONIES: FANCIFUL FABLES ★★ Only historians will find this tape appealing, since several of its six cartoons go all the way back to the primitive black-and-white days of the late 1920s. Even youngsters will yawn through most of the simplistic scripts. 50m. **DIR:** Walt Disney. **1928–1937**

SIMPLY MAD ABOUT THE MOUSE ★★★★ The clever concept behind this video is irresistible: updated, up-tempo renditions of classic Disney songs, backed by live-action and animated rock video montages. Highlights include L. L. Cool J's whimsical "Who's Afraid of the Big, Bad Wolf?" and Harry Connick Jr.'s swinging version of "The Bare Necessities." There's only one glaring disappointment: Michael Bolton's overwrought "A Dream Is a Wish Your Heart Makes." 35m. **DIR:** Scott Garen. **CAST:** Billy Joel, L. L. Cool J, Rick Ocasek, Bobby McFerrin, Michael Bolton, Harry Connick Jr. **1991**

SIMPSON'S CHRISTMAS SPECIAL, THE ★★★★ After years of the brief blackout sketches between acts of *The Tracy Ullman Show*, Matt Groening's family of misfits made its full-length network debut with this bittersweet holiday tale. When the carefully saved Christmas money goes to surgically remove a tattoo on Bart's arm, poor Homer takes a job as a mall Santa to raise gift money. Groening's acerbic wit and sly social commentary are in full view; shortly after this appearance, the Simpsons became a national phenomenon. 23m. **DIR:** David Silverman. **1990**

SING-ALONG SONGS ★★★ Aside from their lavish animation, Disney features also boasted many poignant, memorable, and just plain silly tunes (many of which were nominated for or received Academy Awards). This multiple-volume series extracts the best—from animated films, live-action features, and even Disneyland attractions—and presents them in an easily learned, follow-the-bouncing-mouse-ears format. each. 26–28m. **DIR:** Walt Disney. **1986–1989**

SINGING NUN, THE ★★ Unbearably cheerful little bio-pic about the Dominican nun who sang on Ed Sullivan's TV show and supposedly captured the hearts of the nation. Just as slim as you'd expect. 98m. **DIR:** Henry Koster. **CAST:** Debbie Reynolds, Ricardo Montalban, Greer Garson, Agnes Moorehead, Chad Everett, Katharine Ross, Ed Sullivan. **1966**

SLEEPING BEAUTY (1959) ★★★★½ This Disney adaptation of Charles Perrault's seventeenth-century version of the famous fairy tale features storybook-style animation that may surprise those accustomed to the softer style of the studio's other feature-length cartoons. Nevertheless, it is the last genre classic to be supervised by Walt Disney himself and belongs in any list of the best children's films (while having the added asset of being enjoyable for adults, as well). Rated G. 75m. **DIR:** Clyde Geronimi. **1959**

SLEEPING BEAUTY (1983) ★★★★ This is one of the funniest *Faerie Tale Theatre* episodes. Christopher Reeve is excellent as the handsome prince, and Bernadette Peters makes a sweet and pretty princess. Sally Kellerman is wonderful as the queen. 60m. **DIR:** Jeremy Paul Kagan. **CAST:** Beverly D'Angelo, Bernadette Peters, Christopher Reeve, Sally Kellerman. **1983**

SMOKE ★★★ Distraught over his father's death and his mother's remarriage, a farm boy gives his affection to an injured German shepherd instead. Well-acted, satisfying family drama from the Disney studios. 90m. **DIR:** Vincent McEveety. **CAST:** Ron Howard, Earl Holliman, Andy Devine. **1970**

SMOKY MOUNTAIN CHRISTMAS ★★★ Typical made-for-TV seasonal heartwarmer, this features Dolly Parton as a burned-out singer-actress who takes to the hills of Tennessee for rest and seclusion. There she rediscovers the real meaning of Christmas. Suitable for family viewing. 100m. **DIR:** Henry Winkler. **CAST:** Dolly Parton, Lee Majors, Dan Hedaya, Bo Hopkins, John Ritter. **1986**

SMURFS AND THE MAGIC FLUTE, THE ★★ Those little blue people from the popular television cartoon show are featured in their first movie. The kiddies will probably love it, but parents should read a book. Rated G. 80m. **DIR:** John Rust. **1983**

SNIFFLES THE MOUSE CARTOON FESTIVAL FEATURING "SNIFFLES BELLS THE CAT" ★★★★ The sweet-natured Sniffles the Mouse was created during Warner Bros. cartoon-director Chuck Jones's Disneyesque period. Three of the four cartoons in this package, "Sniffles Bells the Cat," "The Brave Little Mouse," and "Toy Trouble," feature exquisite animation and inventive stories that will particularly charm the younger set. 36m. **DIR:** Chuck Jones. **1940–1944**

SNOOPY, COME HOME ★★★½ Charming second entry in the "Peanuts" film series doesn't contain the childhood *angst* of the first but maintains the irreverent view of life found in the best of Charles Schulz's comic strips. Snoopy decides life at home ain't all it's cracked up to be, so he and Woodstock set off to find America. Needless to say, there's no place like home. Rated G. 70m. **DIR:** Bill Melendez. **1972**

SNOOPY'S GETTING MARRIED, CHARLIE BROWN ★★★½ While guarding Peppermint Patty's house one night, Snoopy meets Genevieve, the poodle of his dreams (both agree that *Citizen Kane* is the best movie ever made), and he decides to get hitched. Snoopy's brother, Spike (in his animated debut), turns up as best beagle, but things don't turn out the way our favorite dog expects. 25m. **DIR:** Bill Melendez. **1985**

SNOW QUEEN ★★ An exceedingly dull *Faerie Tale Theatre* tale, the Snow Queen (played by Lee Remick), teaches an unruly boy a lesson. The sets and special effects are second only to the actors' lines for their banality. 48m. **DIR:** Peter Medak. **CAST:** Melissa Gilbert, Lance Kerwin, Lee Remick, Lauren Hutton, Linda Manz, David Hemmings. **1983**

SNOW WHITE AND THE SEVEN DWARFS (1938) ★★★★★ This first full-length animated film produced by Walt Disney was the culmination of a dream that had taken five years to bring to the big screen. After the phenomenal success of his cartoon shorts, starring Mickey Mouse and many others, Disney yearned to stretch the animated medium. His achievement, *Snow White*, is nothing short of breathtaking. The animation has a richness and clarity that even the Disney studio would shortly cease producing. The fairy tale, adapted from the works of the Brothers Grimm, has arrived with most of its power intact; few will quickly forget the final haglike appearance of the evil queen (with a deliciously evil voice rendered by Lucille La Verne). Disney collected a special Academy Award for this film—one normal-sized statuette and seven little ones. Unrated; suitable for family viewing. 83m. **DIR:** David Hand. **1938**

SNOW WHITE AND THE SEVEN DWARFS (1983) ★★★★ Both Vincent Price and Vanessa Redgrave are wickedly wonderful in this splendid adaptation of the Grimm's tale. Price plays the evil queen's (Redgrave) advising mirror. Lovely Elizabeth McGovern plays a sweet Snow White. 51m. **DIR:** Peter Medak. **CAST:** Elizabeth McGovern, Vanessa Redgrave, Vincent Price, Rex Smith. **1983**

SNOW WHITE AND THE THREE STOOGES 🦃 Sad entry from what was left of the Three Stooges. 107m. **DIR:** Walter Lang. **CAST:** The Three Stooges, Patricia Medina, Carol Heiss, Guy Rolfe, Buddy Baer, Edgar Barrier. **1961**

SNOW WHITE CHRISTMAS, A 🦃 The whole Charming kingdom is thrown into chaos by an evil queen who hates holiday cheer. 60m. **DIR:** Kay Wright. **1979**

SNOWBALL EXPRESS ★★ This formula comedy stars the Disney stable of players from the 1960s and 1970s. Dean Jones inherits a run-down hotel and attempts to turn it into a ski resort. Standard family viewing with a ski chase to help the pace. Rated G. 99m. **DIR:** Norman Tokar. **CAST:** Dean Jones, Nancy Olson, Harry Morgan, Keenan Wynn, Johnny Whitaker. **1972**

SO DEAR TO MY HEART ★★★★ One of the finest of all feature-length Walt Disney films, this loving re-creation of small-town life in the early years of this century is wonderful entertainment. Young Bobby Driscoll (one of the finest of all child actors) has taken a notion to enter his black lamb Danny in the county fair. A singing blacksmith (Burl Ives in his film debut) encourages him in his dreams. This gentle film presents a beautiful evocation of a time that has passed, and is loaded with love, goodwill, and sentiment. 84m. **DIR:** Harold Schuster. **CAST:** Burl Ives, Beulah Bondi, Harry Carey, Luana Patten, Bobby Driscoll, Matt Willis. **1949**

SOMEDAY YOU'LL FIND HER, CHARLIE BROWN ★★½ Lamentable values pervade this tale, when Charlie Brown falls in love with a girl seen briefly during a "honey shot" of a televised ball game. (So much for the little red-haired girl.) 25m. **DIR:** Phil Roman. **1981**

SOMEWHERE, TOMORROW ★★★ *The Ghost and Mrs. Muir* for a teen audience, this film is about a girl, played by Sarah Jessica Parker, who learns how to deal with her father's death by falling in love with the ghost of a teenage boy. The result is good family entertainment. 91m. **DIR:** Robert Wiemer. **CAST:** Sarah Jessica Parker, Nancy Addison, Tom Shea, Rick Weber. **1986**

SON OF FLUBBER ★★★½ This Disney sequel to *The Absent-Minded Professor* once again stars Fred MacMurray as the inventor of Flubber. Two new discoveries are featured: "dry rain" and "flubbergas." While not as good as the original, it does have some moments reminiscent of the original. B&W; 100m. **DIR:** Robert Stevenson. **CAST:** Fred MacMurray, Nancy Olson, Keenan Wynn, Tommy Kirk, William Demarest, Paul Lynde. **1963**

SON OF LASSIE ★★½ Lassie's son, Laddie, follows in his parent's pawprints by smuggling himself aboard master Peter Lawford's bomber on a mission over enemy territory. Mixture of sentiment and war action doesn't really jell. 100m. **DIR:** S. Sylvan Simon. **CAST:** Peter Lawford, Donald Crisp, June Lockhart, Nigel Bruce, Leon Ames, Nils Asther, Donald Curtis. **1945**

SORCERER'S APPRENTICE, THE ★★ The greatest merits of this re-telling of the renowned Brothers Grimm tale are its narration by Vincent Price and its brevity. Stilted, almost scary animation and backdrops make this an awfully dark version of the story about a youngster who becomes the hostage apprentice of a black-hearted sorcerer. 22m. **DIR:** Peter Sander. **1985**

SPACED INVADERS ★★ There are some funny moments in this spoof about inept mini-Martians who mistake a fiftieth anniversary broadcast of Orson Welles's *War of the Worlds* radio show for the real thing. Too many hick jokes drag this one down. Rated PG for vulgarity and violence. 100m. **DIR:** Patrick Johnson. **CAST:** Douglas Barr, Royal Dano. **1990**

SPEED RACER: THE MOVIE ★★ The popular 1960s Japanese animated series returns in this compilation of three episodes. Fans of the series won't be disappointed, but billing this as a full-length movie is stretching things a bit. Tape even includes classic television commercials from the era. Rated G. 80m. **DIR:** Jack Schleh. **1966**

SPEEDY GONZALES' FAST FUNNIES ★★½ Subtle racism always makes this character an uncomfortable experience under the best of conditions, and many of the entries in this collection are far from the best. Speedy's debut is included ("Cat-Tails for Two," an amusing reworking of Steinbeck's *Of Mice and Men*), although he looks nothing like his later dashing self. Also noteworthy are "Tabasco Road" and "Pied Piper of Guadalupe." 54m. **DIR:** Friz Freleng, Robert McKimson. **1953–1961**

SPORT GOOFY ★★★★ Do-it-yourselfers will love this tape, which employs Goofy as a foil to demonstrate everything you *never* wanted to know about various sporting events. "Olympic Champ" and "Hockey Homicide" are the acknowledged classics. 43m. **DIR:** Walt Disney. **1942–1949**

SPORT GOOFY'S VACATION ★★★½ As usual, Goofy's World War II–era adventures are vastly superior to those that followed, and this collection includes only two of the classics: "How to Fish" and "Tiger Trouble." Later entries turn the Goof into a family man, complete with young son, and the results simply aren't as satisfying. 43m. **DIR:** Walt Disney. **1942–1961**

STAND UP AND CHEER ★★★ Depression-plagued Americans need something to bring them out of their slump. Is it jobs, money, a chicken in every pot? No! The president says it's the curly-headed little dynamo he appoints as the Secretary of Amusement. Little Shirley manages to buoy spirits through her songs, dances, and sage advice. B&W; 80m. **DIR:** Hamilton MacFadden. **CAST:** Warner Baxter, Shirley Temple, Madge Evans, James Dunn, Stepin Fetchit. **1934**

STAR FOR JEREMY, A ★★★½ Thoughtful animation and a thought-provoking story line make this a video parents will enjoy sharing with children. Young Jeremy wonders about the origins of the Christmas star and is treated to a wonderful adventure. 22m. **DIR:** Barry Mowat. **1985**

STARBIRDS ★★ Refugees from a destroyed solar system plot to invade Earth in order to survive. The fact that these aliens look suspiciously like angels is somewhat disturbing. Mediocre. 75m. **DIR:** Michael Part, Tadao Nagahama. **1986**

STARRING CHIP 'N' DALE ★★★★½ The clever wordplay of Chip 'n' Dale's best cartoon, "Donald Applecore," makes this the most satisfying of the chipmunk collections. "Working for Peanuts" pits the critters against a nut-loving elephant, and the chipmunks battle the tree-destroying earthmover of "Dragon Around." 22m. **DIR:** Walt Disney. **1951–1954**

STARRING DONALD AND DAISY ★★ This shrill and unpleasant trio of cartoons does little for Donald or Daisy (and two of these shorts can be found in other, better collections). 23m. **DIR:** Walt Disney. **1936–1953**

STARRING MICKEY AND MINNIE ★★★★★ No doubt about it, Walt Disney used his best scripters and animators on the pre–World War II cartoons featuring his trademark star, Mickey Mouse. All three of these shorts are gems. The best is "Hawaiian Holiday," with its interludes between Pluto and a crab. Mickey also makes a stalwart "Brave Little Tailor" and encounters an unusual pest while trying to clean Minnie's yard in "The Little Whirlwind." 25m. **DIR:** Walt Disney. **1937–1941**

STARRING PLUTO AND FIFI ★★★★ Mickey Mouse's faithful dog, Pluto, first meets his occasional sweetie, Fifi, in "Pluto's Quin-puplets," a 1937 short that also demonstrates the phenomenal importance of music in an animated cartoon. The collection is highlighted by "Pluto's Blue Note," an Oscar-nominated feature that transforms Pluto into a crowd-pleasing crooner of the Sinatra variety. 24m. **DIR:** Walt Disney. **1937–1947**

STONE FOX, THE ★★★ A boy and his dog enter a sled race hoping to win enough money to save the family farm. Predictable, made-for-TV story with some memorable race sequences. Not rated; contains no objectionable scenes. 96m. **DIR:** Harvey Hart. **CAST:** Joey Cramer, Buddy Ebsen, Belinda Montgomery, Gordon Tootoosis. **1987**

STORY OF BABAR, THE ★★★★½ This delightfully narrated (featuring the voice characterizations of Peter Ustinov) featurette does well by following closely to the form of the classic children's book by Jean de Brunhoff. Little Babar is left an orphan after a hunter kills his mother in the jungle. He flees to Paris, where he learns the ways of gentility and is made King of the Elephants upon his return to the wild. No rating. 30m. **DIR:** Bill Melendez, Ed Levitt. **1986**

STORY OF DAVID, THE ★★★½ The first half of this two-part TV movie tells the story of young David's defeat of the Philistine champion Goliath. The second half presents David as king, in love with the forbidden Bathsheba. Lavish, respectfully produced biblical epic. Not rated; contains no objectionable material. 192m. **DIR:** Alex Segal, David Lowell Rich. **CAST:** Timothy Bottoms, Anthony Quayle, Norman Rodway, Keith Michell, Jane Seymour, Brian Blessed, Barry Morse. **1976**

STORY OF JACOB AND JOSEPH, THE ★★★½ Handsome adaptation of two Bible stories. First, Jacob battles his brother Esau over their birthright. Later, Jacob's favorite son, Joseph, has his own sibling problems when his jealous brothers sell him into slavery. Not rated; contains no objectionable material. 96m. **DIR:** Michael Cacoyannis. **CAST:** Keith Michell, Tony Lo Bianco, Colleen Dewhurst, Herschel Bernardi, Harry Andrews, Julian Glover. **1974**

STORY OF ROBIN HOOD, THE ★★★ Disney's live-action version of the Robin Hood legend has elements that give the movie its own identity. One nice touch is the use of a wandering minstrel, who draws the story together. Richard Todd is a most appealing Robin Hood, while James Robertson Justice, as Little John, and Peter Finch, as the Sheriff of Nottingham, are first-rate. 83m. **DIR:** Ken Annakin. **CAST:** Richard Todd, Joan Rice, Peter Finch, James Hayter, James Robertson Justice, Michael Hordern. **1952**

STORY OF SEABISCUIT, THE ★★½ A thoroughbred horse recovers from an injury to become a big prizewinner. Based on a true incident, this predictable family programmer gives Barry Fitzgerald as the trainer full throttle to ham and charm his way into the audience's heart. 92m. **DIR:** David Butler. **CAST:** Shirley Temple, Barry Fitzgerald, Lon McCallister, Rosemary DeCamp, Pierre Watkin, Donald MacBride. **1949**

STORYBOOK SERIES, THE (VOLUME ONE) ★★★ Hayley Mills hosts this made-for-television program that features three moralistic stories for kiddies. Entertaining for adults, too! Other volumes are hosted by Michael York, Mickey Rooney, and John Carradine. 30m. **DIR:** Sam Weiss. **1986**

STRANGE CASE OF THE COSMIC RAYS, THE ★★★½ This Bell Science educational film introduces the atom, ultraviolet radiation, and galactic phenomenon. All this is explained by Dr. Frank Baxter with the help of the Bill and Cora Baird puppets and the animation of Shamus Culhane. 59m. **DIR:** Frank Capra. **CAST:** Dr. Frank Baxter. **1957**

STRAWBERRY SHORTCAKE AND PETS ON PARADE (TV SERIES) ★★½ To steal a pet-show prize, the conniving Purple Pieman frames Strawberry Shortcake on a bribery charge. Her fruity friends come to her rescue. A number of Strawberry Shortcake cartoons are available on video. They're wonderful...for the preschool crowd. Older kids might gag on the sweetness. 60m. **DIR:** Fred Wolf. **1982**

SUMMER MAGIC ★★½ Dorothy McGuire is a recent widow who finds out she has no money available. She moves her family to Maine, where they live in a fixer-upper house but are charged no rent by Burl Ives. Deborah Walley, a snobbish cousin, comes to visit and causes trouble. Lightweight and enjoyable. Rated G. 100m. **DIR:** James Neilson. **CAST:** Hayley Mills, Burl Ives, Dorothy McGuire, Deborah Walley, Eddie Hodges, Peter Brown. **1963**

SUN COMES UP, THE ★★★ A script custom designed for Jeanette MacDonald in her later years suits her personality and gives her a chance to sing some sentimental favorites. Her character, Helen Winter, is a bitter war widow who is taken aback when an orphan enters her life and endears himself to her. So does his dog, Lassie, in this tearjerker that probably wouldn't have worked with anyone else in the primary roles. 93m. **DIR:** Richard Thorpe. **CAST:** Jeanette MacDonald, Claude Jarman Jr., Lloyd Nolan, Percy Kilbride, Lewis Stone, Margaret Hamilton. **1949**

SUPER MARIO BROTHERS, THE ★★★ A big-screen version of a popular Nintendo game, this movie is aimed at indiscriminating kids and young adults. Most of the action takes place in Dinohattan where dinosaurs have evolved to near-human form. When the dirty dinos kidnap pretty Princess Daisy, a couple of plumbers from Brooklyn save the day. A fast-moving action/comedy that could have used a bit more sense mixed with the nonsense. Rated PG. 118m. **DIR:** Rocky Morton, Annabel Jankel. **CAST:** Bob Hoskins, John Leguizamo, Dennis Hopper, Samantha Mathis, Fisher Stevens, Fiona Shaw, Richard Edson. **1993**

SUPER POWERS COLLECTION 🦃 These made-for-television cartoons featuring DC Comic heroes Superman, Batman, Aquaman, and Superboy are just pitiful. each. 60m. **DIR:** Various. **1985**

SUPERDAD ★★½ Bob Crane doesn't approve of his daughter's boyfriend (Kurt Russell) or the crowd she runs with. She claims that he just doesn't understand them. He decides to find out about the kids firsthand. Rated G. 94m. **DIR:** Vincent McEveety. **CAST:** Bob Crane, Barbara Rush, Kurt Russell, Joe Flynn. **1973**

SUPERMAN CARTOONS ★★★★ All other superhero cartoons pale in comparison to this collection of excellent "Man of Steel" shorts from the Max Fleischer Studios. Made between 1941 and 1943, these actually constitute the company's finest work, its Popeye cartoons notwithstanding. There are several tapes available with a selection of seven or eight shorts (approximately 75 minutes) made from 16mm prints of varying quality. One company (Video Rarities) offers a 150-minute tape with all seventeen Superman shorts taken from mint-condition 35mm Technicolor prints, and the difference is amazing. 75m. **DIR:** Dave Fleischer, Seymour Kneitel, Isadore Sparber. **1940**

SURF NINJAS ★★★ Ninja nonsense. Two California-surf dudes discover that they're actually heirs to a small South Seas kingdom. That's the good news. The bad news is that evil warlord Leslie Nielsen will stop at nothing to keep them off the throne. This mix of several different genres loses focus, but kids will get a big kick out of it. Rated PG for make-believe violence. 87m. **DIR:** Neal Israel. **CAST:** Ernie Reyes Jr., Rob Schneider, Tone Loc, Leslie Nielsen, Nicolas Cowan. **1993**

SUSANNAH OF THE MOUNTIES ★★★ After her parents are killed in an Indian attack, curly Shirley is raised by a kind Canadian Mountie (Randolph Scott). Not one to hold a grudge, Shirley decides to play peacemaker for the whites and Indians by befriending the chief's son. B&W; 78m. **DIR:** William A. Seiter. **CAST:** Shirley Temple, Randolph Scott, Margaret Lockwood. **1939**

SWISS FAMILY ROBINSON, THE ★★★½ Walt Disney's comedy-adventure film, adapted from the classic children's story by Johann Wyss about a family shipwrecked on a lush South Seas island. 128m. **DIR:** Ken Annakin. **CAST:** John Mills, Dorothy McGuire, James MacArthur, Tommy Kirk, Sessue Hayakawa. **1960**

SWORD AND THE ROSE, THE (1953) ★★½ Romance, intrigue, and heroic acts of derring-do are the order of the day in this colorful Walt Disney adaptation of *When Knighthood Was in Flower.* Richard Todd makes an ideal lead and Michael Gough is a truly malevolent heavy. 93m. **DIR:** Ken Annakin. **CAST:** Richard Todd, Glynis Johns, James Robertson Justice, Michael Gough. **1953**

SWORD IN THE STONE, THE ★★★½ The legend of King Arthur provided the story line for this animated feature film from the Walt Disney studios. Although not up to the film company's highest standards, it still provides fine entertainment for the young and the young at heart. Rated G. 80m. **DIR:** Wolfgang Reitherman. **1963**

SWORD OF THE VALIANT ★★★½ The Old English tale of Sir Gawain and the Green Knight is brought to the screen with an appealing blend of action-adventure and tongue-in-cheek humor. Rated PG. 162m. **DIR:** Stephen Weeks. **CAST:** Miles O'Keeffe, Sean Connery, Trevor Howard. **1984**

SYLVESTER AND TWEETY: THE BEST YEOWS OF OUR LIVES ★★★★ It doesn't matter how many times we hear it, when Tweety-Bird squawks, "I tought I taw a Putty Tat," it puts us on the floor every time. This collection of five classic bird-and-cat chases leads off with the train-bound shenanigans of "All A Bir-r-r-d" and concludes with the equally hysterical "A Bird in a Guilty Cage." The other entries are "Tweet Tweet Tweety," "Home, Tweet Home," and "Tweet and Sour" (with Sylvester trying to *protect* his usual prey from another cat!). 36m. **DIR:** Friz Freleng. **1950–56**

SYLVESTER AND TWEETY'S CRAZY CAPERS ★★★ More Warner Bros. madness with that "bad old puddy tat" and the ready-for-anything little birdy. Sylvester goes solo in "Mouse-Taken Identity," but those cartoons pitting him against Tweety Pie are the best. For all ages. 54m. **DIR:** Friz Freleng, Robert McKimson. **1985**

TAILOR OF GLOUCESTER, THE ★★★★ A spiteful cat nearly spells doom for the poor tailor of this Beatrix Potter fable, lovingly brought to life with David Jorgensen's gentle illustrations. Meryl Streep narrates and provides superb cat and mouse voices. Background music by the Chieftans adds to the poignance. 30m. **DIR:** Mark Sottnick. **1988**

TALE OF MR. JEREMY FISHER AND THE TALE OF PETER RABBIT, THE ★★★★½ Narrator Meryl Streep once again proves adept with accents and voices in these two charming stories from the pen of Beatrix Potter. The first concerns a frog's near-fatal fishing expedition; the second follows bad little Peter Rabbit's visit to Mr. McGregor's garden. 30m. **DIR:** Mark Sottnick. **1987**

TALE OF THE FROG PRINCE ★★★★ Perhaps the best of the *Faerie Tale Theatre* presentations, this story about a slighted fairy godmother who exacts revenge by turning a prince (Robin Williams) into a frog was inventively written and directed by Eric Idle, of Monty Python fame. It's witty and well acted. 51m. **DIR:** Eric Idle. **CAST:** Robin Williams, Teri Garr, René Auberjonois, Candy Clark. **1982**

TALE OF TWO CHIPMUNKS, A ★★ Chip 'n' Dale are badly served by this inferior trio of cartoons, which hits a low point with "The Lone Chipmunks," a rather clumsy attempt to imitate the Road Runner series. Donald Duck costars in the equally weak "Chips Ahoy," which leaves "Chicken in the Rough" (wherein Dale imagines hen's eggs to be larger, tastier acorns) as the only attraction. 24m. **DIR:** Walt Disney. **1951–1956**

TALES FROM AVONLEA (TV SERIES) ★★★★ Based on the works of Lucy Maud Montgomery, this account of a simpler time in a small country town is both refreshing and entertaining for the entire family. Early episodes focus on the trials and tribulations of a pampered city girl (Sarah Polley) suddenly thrust upon her country kin. Made for the Disney channel with the highest production values. Six tapes, each with two episodes and ranging from 93m to 106m. **DIR:** Paul Shapiro, Richard Benner, Don McBrearty. **CAST:** Sarah Polley, Jackie Burroughs, Mag Ruffman, Lally Cadeau, Cedric Smith, Zachary Bennett, Gema Zamprogna. **1990**

TALES OF BEATRIX POTTER ★★★ Produced in a quietly fascinating storybook fashion with little movement on the part of the characters, this production utilizes Potter's original illustrations to tell the stories. Each tale reinforces the folly that occurs when the central characters fail to stay on the straight and narrow. 43m. **DIR:** Brian MacNamara. **1986**

TARO, THE DRAGON BOY ★★★★ Distinctive animation, reminiscent of Japanese silkscreens, provides an engaging forum for introducing young viewers to Japanese mythology and culture. Here, young Taro makes a pilgrimage to a faraway lake to rescue his mother, who has been turned into a dragon. 75m. **DIR:** K. Urayama. **1985**

TEENAGE MUTANT NINJA TURTLES ★★★★ Cowabunga, dude, the movie debut of the *Teenage Mutant Ninja Turtles* is a fun- and action-packed comic book for the screen. Leonardo, Raphael, Michelangelo, and Donatello come to the aid of a female newscaster (Judith Hoag) when her life is threatened by the minions of the evil Shredder. Rated PG for comic-book-style violence and vulgarity. 93m. **DIR:** Steve Barron. **CAST:** Judith Hoag, Elias Koteas. **1990**

TEENAGE MUTANT NINJA TURTLES: THE EPIC BEGINS ★★★½ Those bestselling comic-book heroes in a half shell make their entrance into the video world. The story tells of their origins and of their first battle with their archenemy, Shredder. There's lots of action and suspense and some fair animation. Its only drawback is having been edited down from five half-hour episodes into little over an hour. Still, it holds together pretty well. Not rated, but contains light violence. 72m. **DIR:** Yoshikasu Kasai. **1988**

TEENAGE MUTANT NINJA TURTLES II: THE SECRET OF THE OOZE ★★★½ The lean, green teens return to face their archenemy Shredder, and find the secret to their origins in the sewers of New York. David Warner costars as the professor who developed the toxic green ooze responsible for the Turtles' large size and superpowers. Rated PG for mild violence. 88m. **DIR:** Michael Pressman. **CAST:** Paige Turco, David Warner, Ernie Reyes Jr. **1991**

TEENAGE MUTANT NINJA TURTLES III ★★ This franchise has been taken to the well once too often. Although writer-director Stuart Gillard gets off to a good start by sending our youthful ninjas-on-the-half-shell back in time to feudal Japan, the setting is wasted on wafer-thin foes who don't even prompt our heroes to work up a sweat. Rated PG for comic-book violence. 95m. **DIR:** Stuart

Gillard. **CAST:** Elias Koteas, Paige Turco, Stuart Wilson, Sab Shimono, Vivian Wu. **1993**

TEN WHO DARED 🦃 In 1869, Major John Wesley Powell and nine other explorers set out to explore the wild Colorado River. 92m. **DIR:** William Beaudine. **CAST:** Brian Keith, John Beal, James Drury, David Stollery. **1960**

TEX AVERY'S SCREWBALL CLASSICS ★★★★ Anybody wondering about the origins of the voluptuous Jessica in *Who Framed Roger Rabbit* need look no further than "Swing Shift Cinderella," a 1945 cartoon classic that perfectly captures Tex Avery's chaotic and frantic imagination. Seven entries of this collection are exceptional; the eighth, "A Symphony in Slang," is quite weak—so you're advised to limit viewing to small doses. 59m. **DIR:** Tex Avery. **1943–1954**

TEX AVERY'S SCREWBALL CLASSICS (VOLUME 2) ★★★½ The voluptuous chanteuse from the previous collection's "Swing Shift Cinderella" turns up in three of the entries in this manic octet: "Red Hot Riding Hood," "Big Heel-Watha" (also featuring Screwy Squirrel), and "Wild and Woolfy" (with nasal-voiced Droopy Dog). As usual, director Tex Avery pushes his gags to the edge—and then keeps on going. "Northwest Hounded Police" (another Droopy vehicle) and "Ventriloquist Cat" are by far the funniest. Watch this tape in small doses to avoid getting numbed by Avery's sledgehammer style. 60m. **DIR:** Tex Avery. **1943–1950**

TEX AVERY'S SCREWBALL CLASSICS (VOLUME 4) ★★½ An otherwise pedestrian package is salvaged by 1942's "Blitz Wolf," which unashamedly lampoons Adolf Hitler (by employing a mustachioed wolf who signs a "nonaggression pact" with the first two of the three little pigs). The remaining five entries are pale shadows of Avery's best work. 46m. **DIR:** Tex Avery. **1942–1952**

THANKSGIVING STORY, THE ★★½ Originally a TV holiday special, this features the wholesome Walton family. John-boy (Richard Thomas) tries to impress the girl of his dreams while applying for a college scholarship. An accident causing brain damage threatens his future. A bit slow-paced and overly sweet. 95m. **DIR:** Philip Leacock. **CAST:** Richard Thomas, Ralph Waite, Michael Learned, Ellen Corby, Will Geer. **1973**

THAT DARN CAT ★★½ Trust Disney to take a great book—*Undercover Cat*, by Gordon and Mildred Gordon—and turn it into a moronic slapstick farce. Hayley Mills and Dorothy Provine are owners of a fulsome feline christened "DC" (for Darn Cat). One evening DC returns from his nightly rounds with a watch belonging to a woman taken hostage in a recent bank robbery. Enter Dean Jones as an aelurophobic FBI agent. 116m. **DIR:** Robert Stevenson. **CAST:** Dean Jones, Hayley Mills, Dorothy Provine, Roddy McDowall, Elsa Lanchester, Neville Brand, William Demarest, Ed Wynn, Frank Gorshin. **1965**

THEIR ONLY CHANCE ★★ True-life adventure film about a young man (Steve Hoddy) who has a way with wild animals. Former Tarzan Jock Mahoney has a dual role as a rancher and a mountain man. A nice, quiet wildlife film suitable for the entire family. 84m. **DIR:** David Siddon. **CAST:** Jock Mahoney, Steve Hoddy. **1975**

THERE'S NO TIME FOR LOVE, CHARLIE BROWN ★★★½ This misnamed adventure concerns Charlie Brown's efforts to earn a good grade on a classroom report written about a field trip to an art museum. Alas, he and Peppermint Patty get separated from the others and mistakenly wind up in a supermarket. 25m. **DIR:** Bill Melendez. **1973**

THEY WENT THAT-A-WAY AND THAT-A-WAY ★★ Tim Conway wrote and stars in this comedy. He plays a small-town deputy who follows the governor's orders by being secretly placed in a maximum-security prison as an undercover agent. Fellow deputy (Chuck McCann) is his partner. When the governor suddenly dies, the two must escape from the prison. There are some silly gags, but this film does provide a few laughs and no deep plots. Rated PG. 106m. **DIR:** Edward Montagne, Stuart E. McGowan. **CAST:** Tim Conway, Chuck McCann, Reni Santoni, Richard Kiel, Dub Taylor. **1978**

THIRD MAN ON THE MOUNTAIN ★★★ James MacArthur stars as a young man whose father was killed in a climbing accident. The Citadel (actually the Matterhorn) has never been scaled. Miraculously, he finds the secret passage his father had been seeking. Breathtaking scenery and an excellent script make this an excellent adventure story for the family. Not rated. 106m. **DIR:** Ken Annakin. **CAST:** Michael Rennie, James MacArthur, Janet Munro, Herbert Lom. **1959**

THOMAS THE TANK ENGINE AND FRIENDS ★★ Stuffy three-volume live-action animation feature based on *The Railway Series* by the Rev. W. Awdry. This European series has welcome continuity, often referring to the events of previous episodes, but largely lifeless railroad sets tend to be dull and boring after a while. Storyteller: Ringo Starr. each. 40m. **DIR:** David Mitton. **1989**

THOROUGHBREDS DON'T CRY ★★★ In this first teaming of Mickey Rooney and Judy Garland, he is a discredited jockey (sound familiar?), and they help a young English boy win a big race with his horse, The Pookah. Garland does get to sing, but Sophie Tucker, as her aunt, is wasted in a nonsinging role. B&W; 80m. **DIR:** Alfred E. Green. **CAST:** Judy Garland, Mickey Rooney, Sophie Tucker, C. Aubrey Smith. **1937**

THOSE CALLOWAYS ★★★★ Sensitive, sentimental film about a family in New England. Man battles townspeople and nature to preserve a safe haven for geese. Marvelous scenes of life in a small town and the love between individuals. Rated G. 131m. **DIR:** Norman Tokar. **CAST:** Brian Keith, Vera Miles, Brandon de Wilde, Linda Evans. **1965**

THREE BILLY GOATS GRUFF AND THE THREE LITTLE PIGS, THE ★★★★½ Narrator Holly Hunter does a phenomenal job supplying voices for the various characters—eight in all, between the two stories. Tom Roberts's script has some great one-liners, and composer Art Lande's sound track provides a deliciously jazzy background. One note of warning; those familiar only with Disney's "Three Little Pigs" may be surprised by the brutality of this more faithful adaptation. 30m. **DIR:** David Jorgensen, Mark Sottnick. **1989**

THREE CABALLEROS, THE ★★★ In Walt Disney's first attempt at combining animation and live action, Donald Duck is joined by two Latin feathered friends. Originally designed as a World War II propaganda piece promoting inter-American unity, it still holds up well today and remains a timeless learning experience for the kids. 72m. **DIR:** Walt Disney. **1942**

THREE LITTLE PIGS, THE ★★★★ Billy Crystal plays the industrious little pig who proves that "haste makes waste" when he takes his time building a sturdy house to keep the big, bad wolf away. Jeff Goldblum makes a hilarious, cigar-chomping wolf. 51m. **DIR:** Howard Storm. **CAST:** Billy Crystal, Jeff Goldblum, Valerie Perrine. **1984**

THREE LIVES OF THOMASINA, THE ★★★★ An excellent cast and innovative ways of telling the story highlight this tale of love and caring. A young girl's cat is brought back to life by a woman who also teaches the girl's father to let others into his life. The cat's trip to cat heaven is outstandingly executed. 97m. **DIR:** Don Chaffey. **CAST:** Patrick McGoohan, Susan Hampshire, Karen Dotrice, Vincent Winter. **1964**

THREE NINJAS ★★★½ Kids will love this *Karate Kid* knockoff about youngsters who help their mentor-grandfather take on a criminal and his army of evil ninjas. Rated PG for light violence. 85m. **DIR:** Jon Turteltaub. **CAST:** Victor Wong, Michael Treanor, Max Elliott Slade, Chad Power. **1992**

THREE NINJAS KICK BACK ★★★½ More kid-pleasing entertainment has our three youthful heroes forced to choose between playing in a championship baseball game and accompanying their all-wise grandfather to Japan for a martial arts tournament. It's *The Karate Kid*, *The Three Stooges*, *The Bad News Bears*, and *Indiana Jones* all crammed into one fast-paced movie that works surprisingly well. Rated PG for goofy violence. 99m. **DIR:** Mark Saltzman. **CAST:** Victor Wong, Sab Shimono, Max Elliott Slade, Evan Bonifant, Caroline Junko King, Alan McRae, Margarita Franco. **1994**

THROUGH THE LOOKING GLASS ★★½ A likable adaptation of the adventures of Alice after her trip to Wonderland. This production loses some of its charm due to a more contemporary telling, but voice characterizations by Phyllis Diller, Mr. T, and Jonathan Winters help. No rating. 70m. **DIR:** Andrea Bresciani, Richard Slapczynski. **1987**

THUMBELINA (1983) ★★★★ This is an *Alice in Wonderland*–type tale of a thumb-size girl (Carrie Fisher) and her adventures as she tries to find her way home. The creatures she meets along the way are well characterized. This is one of the more rewarding *Faerie Tale Theatre* productions. 48m. **DIR:** Michael Lindsay-Hogg. **CAST:** Carrie Fisher, William Katt, Burgess Meredith, narration by David Hemmings. **1983**

THUMBELINA (1989) ★★★★ David Johnson's exquisitely delicate illustrations are the primary appeal here. The Hans Christian Andersen tale concerns a little girl—no larger than the tip of one's thumb. Kelly McGillis narrates the story, and background music is provided by Mark Isham. 30m. **DIR:** Tim Raglin. **1989**

TIGER TOWN ★★½ In this passable movie, made for the Disney Channel, Roy Scheider stars as a legendary baseball player whose final year with the Detroit Tigers looks dismal until a young boy (Justin Henry) "wishes" him to success. At least, that's what the boy believes. Both Scheider and Henry give good performances, but the overall effect is not as impressive as it could have been. Rated G. 76m. **DIR:** Alan Shapiro. **CAST:** Roy Scheider, Justin Henry. **1984**

TIGER WALKS, A ★★½ This Disney drama about an escaped circus tiger and the impact his fate has on a small town boasts a good cast of veteran film personalities as well as a jaundiced view of politics and mass hysteria. 88m. **DIR:** Norman Tokar. **CAST:** Brian Keith, Vera Miles, Pamela Franklin, Sabu, Kevin Corcoran, Peter Brown, Una Merkel, Frank McHugh. **1964**

TINY TOON ADVENTURES ★★★★ Downsized classic cartoon characters have not always been successful—*The Flintstone Kids* being a nauseous example—but the pint-sized inhabitants of Warner Bros. Tiny Toons universe are wisecracking strokes of genius. The ACME Acres crew includes blue Bugs Bunny–wannabe Buster Bunny, pink Babs Bunny, maniacal Plucky Duck, and stalwart sidekick Hamton Pig. Elmyra, a shrill little girl who *looooves* her "fuzzy-wuzzy buddies," is a wholly original character clearly shaped by executive producer Steven Spielberg. The brightly colored cartoons are fast-paced and often contain storylines that rely on adult humor, and certain parodies may be too scary for small-fry. Each collection includes a mix of shorter and longer stories. 40m. **DIR:** Various. **1993**

TINY TOONS ADVENTURES: HOW I SPENT MY VACATION ★★★★ The Warner Brothers cartoon legacy lives on, thanks to producer Steven Spielberg's lovingly crafted pint-sized renditions of the classic animated superstars. This made-for-video feature concerns the various members of ACME Acres, as school lets out for summer. Babs and Buster Bunny take a river journey that winds through the deep South; Plucky Duck and Hampton Pig share the family car-trip from hell, en route to HappyWorldLand; holy terror Elmira (who "wuvs kitties") has a close encounter with the big cats of a safari park. 80m. **DIR:** Steven Spielberg. **1992**

TOBY AND THE KOALA BEAR ★★ Adventure tale from Australia in which cartoon characters are placed in real-life settings. Toby is a youngster living in the Australia of yesteryear, in a camp for convicts. After he adopts an adorable pet koala bear, he sets off on a walkabout. 76m. **DIR:** Yoram Gross. **CAST:** Rolf Harris. **1981**

TOBY MCTEAGUE ★★★ Solid children's story about Canadian teenager Toby McTeague, who has to take over the reins of his father's dog-racing team for the big race. Some profane language, but otherwise suitable for almost everyone. 94m. **DIR:** Jean-Claude Lord. **CAST:** Winston Rekert, Yannick Bisson, Timothy Webber. **1987**

TOBY TYLER ★★★½ Disney version of the popular juvenile book about a young runaway and his adventures with the circus is breezy entertainment and a showcase for young Kevin Corcoran (Moochie of many Disney television shows and the *Mickey Mouse Club*). 96m. **DIR:** Charles Barton. **CAST:** Kevin Corcoran, Henry Calvin, Gene Sheldon, Bob Sweeney, James Drury. **1960**

TOM & JERRY: THE MOVIE ★★ This full-length animated feature begins with the manic intensity expected of the dueling cat and mouse, but everything goes awry about ten minutes in when our hitherto mute heroes begin to *talk*. It's bad enough that Tom and Jerry suddenly lose their Buster Keaton–style charm—then they become another tediously smarmy couple of chums determined to reunite a girl with her missing father. Rated G. 84m. **DIR:** Phil Roman. **1993**

TOM AND JERRY CARTOON FESTIVALS (VOLUME ONE) ★★★ The sometimes violent slapstick adventures of Tom the cat and Jerry the mouse won several Oscars for MGM. In this collection, titles include the Academy Award–winning "Cat Concerto," "The Flying Cat," "The Little Orphan," "Jerry's Cousin," "Dr. Jekyll and Mr. Mouse," "The Bodyguard," "Mouse Follies," and "The Cat and the Mermouse." For all ages. 58m. **DIR:** William Hanna, Joseph Barbera. **1940–1960**

TOM AND JERRY CARTOON FESTIVALS (VOLUME TWO) ★★½ This okay collection has "Mouse in Manhattan," "Hic-Up Pup," "The Milky Waif," "Cat Napping," "Mouse Trouble," "Jerry and the Lion," "Saturday Evening Puss," and "Invisible Mouse." 58m. **DIR:** William Hanna, Joseph Barbera. **1940–1960**

TOM AND JERRY CARTOON FESTIVALS (VOLUME THREE) ★★★ Featured in this enjoyable collection are "Million Dollar Cat," "The Night Before Christmas," "Polka Dot Puss," "Two Little Indians," "Trap Happy," "Tom and Jerry at the Hollywood Bowl," "Cue Ball Cat," and "Little Runaway." 59m. **DIR:** William Hanna, Joseph Barbera. **1940–1960**

TOM AND JERRY ON PARADE ★★★ These half-dozen cartoons provide an acceptable entry into the world of Tom and Jerry, although their best stuff appeared in the 1940s. The high point here is "Designs on Jerry" (1953), a delightfully clever yarn concerning Tom's efforts to build a Rube Goldberg–ish mousetrap. Beware of "Push-Button Kitty" (1952), which includes more of the series' infrequent use of awkward racial humor. 41m. **DIR:** William Hanna, Joseph Barbera. **1951–54**

TOM & JERRY'S CARTOON CAVALCADE ★★★½ These half-dozen cartoons are highlighted by impeccably timed and luxuriously drawn "Fine Feathered Friend" (1942), one of the duo's earliest escapades. Other attractions include the Oscar-nominated "Jerry's Cousin," wherein Tom the Cat gets his comeuppance thanks to look-alike Muscles Mouse; and "Jerry and the Lion," which puts a spin on Aesop. Beware of the awkward racial humor present in "Casanova Cat" (1950). 42m. **DIR:** William Hanna, Joseph Barbera. **1942–53**

TOM AND JERRY'S COMIC CAPERS ★★½ Limited animation and weary gags were dominating the series by the time most of these entries came along. Not one of the six cartoons approaches the duo's best, but "Puppy Tale" (1953) and "Fit to be Tied" (1952) are reasonably amusing. The same cannot be said of 1955's "The Flying Sorceress," a poor imitation of Bugs Bunny's encounters with Witch Hazel (right down to June Foray's voice). 42m. **DIR:** William Hanna, Joseph Barbera. **1948–1955**

TOM & JERRY'S FESTIVAL OF FUN ★★★ Don't be put off by this collection's first entry, "Blue Cat Blues" (1956), which ranks among the worst Tom & Jerry outings ever produced. The other five cartoons are far better fare, particularly Oscar-nominated "Touche, Pussycat" (1954), a sequel to "Two Mouseketeers" (1951)—found on another tape. 43m. **DIR:** William Hanna, Joseph Barbera. **1944–56**

TOM & JERRY'S 50TH BIRTHDAY BASH 🦃 This miserable excuse for a tribute mostly features host John Goodman behaving like a blithering idiot. 45m. **DIR:** Jim Coane. **1990**

TOM AND JERRY'S 50TH BIRTHDAY CLASSICS ★★★½ Jerry the mouse first met his nemesis—initially named Jasper—in 1940's Oscar-nominated "Puss Gets the Boot," one of the seven cartoons in this frantic collection. The highlight is 1943's Oscar-winning "Yankee Doodle Mouse" (first in the series to be so honored). Scott Bradley's music is by far the most inventive accompaniment ever to grace a cartoon series. 57m. **DIR:** William Hanna, Joseph Barbera. **1940–1948**

TOM AND JERRY'S 50TH BIRTHDAY CLASSICS II ★★★ 1946's Oscar-winning "The Cat Concerto"—definitely one of the best Tom & Jerry cartoons ever made—highlights this appealing six-cartoon package, which also boasts 1942's superb "Fraidy Cat." A major misstep occurs when the normally mute characters talk in "The Zoot Cat" (1944). 45m. **DIR:** William Hanna, Joseph Barbera. **1942–1951**

TOM AND JERRY'S 50TH BIRTHDAY CLASSICS III ★★★★ Strange but true: this six-cartoon collection is a significant notch above its predecessors. Highlights: two Oscar winners ("Mouse Trouble," from 1944 and "Johann Mouse," from 1952) and one Oscar nominee, "The Night Before Christmas," from 1941. 45m. **DIR:** William Hanna, Joseph Barbera. **1941–1953**

TOM EDISON—THE BOY WHO LIT UP THE WORLD ★★★★ A fine cast makes this film enjoyable. Tom Edison (David Huffman) and Cole Bogardis (Adam Arkin) begin working for the telegraph company at the same time. In Tom's spare time, he works on an assortment of inventions, including a cockroach electrocutor and a direct telegraph machine. 49m. **DIR:** Henning Schellerup. **CAST:** David Huffman, Adam Arkin, Michael Callan, Rosemary DeCamp, James Griffith. **1983**

TOM SAWYER (1973) ★★ Mark Twain's classic story loses its satirical edge in this homogenized made-for-television production about the adventures of Tom Sawyer (Josh Albee) and Huckleberry Finn (Jeff Tyler). The kids may enjoy it, but adults will want to reread the book. Better yet, read the book to your kids. Rated G. 78m. **DIR:** James Nielson. **CAST:** Josh Albee, Jeff Tyler, Jane Wyatt, Buddy Ebsen, Vic Morrow, John McGiver. **1973**

TOM THUMB ★★★½ This underrated George Pal fantasy is a treat for young and old viewers. Good effects, pleasant tunes, and a distinguished cast of veteran British performers combine with Russ Tamblyn's infectious lead to make this a surefire choice for the kids. 98m. **DIR:** George Pal. **CAST:** Russ Tamblyn, June Thorburn, Peter Sellers, Terry-Thomas, Alan Young, Jessie Matthews, Bernard Miles. **1958**

TOMBOY AND THE CHAMP 🦃 The kids will hate this overwrought story of a young Texas tomboy and her pet heifer. But adults who cherish really bad movies are sure to love its inane melodramatics, with tunes from cowboy singer Rex Allen. Unrated. 92m. **DIR:** Francis D. Lyon. **CAST:** Candy Moore, Ben Johnson, Rex Allen, Jesse White. **1961**

TOMI UNGERER LIBRARY, THE ★★★ Delightful collection of children's fables written by Tomi Ungerer in the 1960s and 1970s. Although the animation is not outstanding, the stories are absolutely charming. They include: "The Three Robbers," in which wayward men find purpose in their lives, "The Moon Man," which allows the man on the moon to kick up his heels on earth, and a childish prank brought to life in "The Beast of Monsieur Racine." The common thread is that man is lonely and needs friendship. An added bonus is the interview with Ungerer in which he shares his inspiration. 35m. **DIR:** Gene Deitch. **1993**

TONKA ★★★ Sal Mineo is White Bull, a Sioux Indian who captures and tames a wild stallion and names it Tonka Wakan—The Great One. Tribal law requires him to give the horse to his older Indian cousin, a bully who would mistreat the animal. Rather than do so, Mineo frees the horse. Thus begins an enjoyable adventure story for the family. 97m. **DIR:** Lewis R. Foster. **CAST:** Sal Mineo, Philip Carey, Jerome Courtland. **1958**

TOP CAT AND THE BEVERLY HILLS CATS ★★ Top Cat's "Alley Scouts" learn how the other half lives, when kindhearted Benny saves a little old lady's life and winds up the sole beneficiary of her considerable fortune. This video is marred by a couple of breakfast cereal commercials—which *proves* we're dealing with humdrum Saturday-morning fare. 92m. **DIR:** Ray Patterson. **1988**

TRANSFORMERS, THE MOVIE 🦃 Animated vehicle for violence and destruction. Rated PG for violence and occasional obscenities. 80m. **DIR:** Nelson Shin. **1986**

TREASURE ISLAND (1934) ★★★★ This is an MGM all-star presentation of Robert Louis Stevenson's children's classic of a young boy's adventure with pirates, buried treasure, and that delightful rogue of fiction Long John Silver. It seems all the great character actors of the 1930s put in an appearance, including Wallace Beery, as Silver, and Lionel Barrymore, as Billy Bones. B&W; 105m. **DIR:** Victor Fleming. **CAST:** Wallace Beery, Lionel Barrymore, Jackie Cooper, Lewis Stone. 1934

TREASURE ISLAND (1950) ★★★★ Disney remake of the Robert Louis Stevenson pirate adventure is powered by a memorable Robert Newton as Long John Silver. 87m. **DIR:** Byron Haskin. **CAST:** Robert Newton, Bobby Driscoll, Basil Sydney. 1950

TREASURE ISLAND (1990) ★★★★½ Robert Louis Stevenson's classic adventure yarn receives its best treatment in this rousing made-for-cable adaptation. Christian Bale is thoroughly believable as courageous Jim Hawkins, who finds the map that starts the adventure and consistently risks his life to save his adult companions. The location photography is gorgeous, the sailing ship *Hispaniola* is a beauty, and the pirates look like N. C. Wyeth and Howard Pyle illustrations come to life. A nearly flawless retelling of one of the world's favorite stories. 132m. **DIR:** Fraser Heston. **CAST:** Charlton Heston, Christian Bale, Oliver Reed, Julian Glover, Richard Johnson, Clive Wood, Christopher Lee. 1990

TUCK EVERLASTING ★★★½ Entertaining family film about a 12-year-old girl who discovers a family of immortals living in the woods on her father's property. She becomes involved in their lives and is eventually entrusted with their secret. Rated G. 100m. **DIR:** Frederick King Keller. **CAST:** Margaret Chamberlain, Fred A. Keller, James McGuire, Sonia Raimi. 1980

TUKIKI AND HIS SEARCH FOR A MERRY CHRISTMAS ★★½ Featuring the voices of Sterling Holloway and Adam Rich, this richly animated tale follows an Eskimo boy in his search for a deeper meaning to Christmas. Along the way, viewers are treated to lessons about the cultures of many lands. 30m. **DIR:** Vic Atkinson. 1979

TWEETY AND SYLVESTER ★★★★½ This tape is a joy, beginning with three of Tweety Bird's solo adventures: "A Tale of Two Kitties," "Birdie and the Beast," and "A Gruesome Twosome" (with a Jimmy Durante cat). Sylvester the cat solos in his debut, "Life with Feathers," along with two other cartoons; the two team up in "Tweetie Pie," which won the Warners animation department its first Oscar. 60m. **DIR:** Bob Clampett, Friz Freleng, Robert McKimson. 1942–1948

TWELVE MONTHS ★★½ A good-hearted waif is rewarded for her kindness by the incarnations of each month of the year when she is sent on an impossible errand by her evil stepmother. What might have been an entertaining tale is marred by a dragging pace. 90m. **DIR:** Kimio Yabuki. 1985

TWENTY THOUSAND LEAGUES UNDER THE SEA (1972) ★★ Less than thrilling adaptation of the Jules Verne classic. Here, Captain Nemo and his amazing submarine, the *Nautilus*, are the centerpiece of a number of deep-sea adventures. 60m. **DIR:** Arthur Rankin Jr., Jules Bass. 1972

TWICE UPON A TIME ★★★★ Sardonic wit is laced throughout this wild and wacky animated fairy tale from producer George Lucas. Filmmakers utilize a cut-and-paste animation process called Lumage to present intrepid heroes attempting to stop the evil Murkworks from blanketing the world in nightmares. Rated PG. 75m. **DIR:** John Korty, Charles Swenson. 1983

UB IWERKS CARTOON FESTIVAL VOL. I–V ★★ Ub Iwerks was a Disney animator who left in 1930 to start his own studio. Ten years later, he returned as director of technical research for Disney. In between, he made a series of so-so cartoons, generally derived from fairy tales. 57m.. **DIR:** Ub Iwerks. 1930

UGLY DACHSHUND, THE ★★ In this Disney movie, Dean Jones and Suzanne Pleshette are husband and wife; she loves dachshunds and owns a number of puppies. Charlie Ruggles convinces Jones to take a Great Dane puppy to raise. Since all of its peers are dachshunds, the Great Dane tries to act like them. Somewhat entertaining along the lines of a made-for-TV-movie. Not rated. 93m. **DIR:** Norman Tokar. **CAST:** Dean Jones, Suzanne Pleshette, Charlie Ruggles, Parley Baer, Kelly Thordsen. 1966

UNDERGRADS, THE ★★★½ This made-for-cable Disney film has only sporadic funny moments. Art Carney plays a spunky senior citizen whose son would like to put him into a rest home. Chris Makepeace (Carney's movie grandson) refuses to allow this. Instead, he and his grandfather become college roommates. A good film with some heavy moments. 102m. **DIR:** Steven H. Stern. **CAST:** Art Carney, Chris Makepeace, Jackie Burroughs, Len Birman, Alfie Scopp. 1984

UNICORN, THE ★★★ An innocent boy learns that even the magical powers of the Unicorn's horn can't change the world. Sadly, he learns this by buying a one-horned goat instead of the mythical beast. 29m. **DIR:** Carol Reed. **CAST:** Celia Johnson, Diana Dors, David Kossof. 1983

UNIDENTIFIED FLYING ODDBALL ★★½ Inept astronaut is transported to the court of King Arthur in his spacecraft. Once there, he discovers that Merlin and a knight are plotting against the king and sets out to expose them. Uneven script with situations not fully developed or explored hampers this Disney trifle. Rated G. 92m. **DIR:** Russ Mayberry. **CAST:** Dennis Dugan, Jim Dale, Ron Moody, Kenneth More. 1979

UNSINKABLE DONALD DUCK, THE ★★★½ Donald Duck meets Jaws the shark in the impeccably animated "Sea Scouts," one of the finest examples of Disney's pre–World War II cartoons. By comparison, "Lion Around" (1950) is woefully inadequate. The middle entry, "Donald's Off Day" is average. 24m. **DIR:** Walt Disney. **1939–1950**

VELVETEEN RABBIT, THE ★★★★★ Luxuriously illustrated and poignantly narrated adaptation of Margery Williams's tale of a stuffed rabbit who wishes to become real. George Winston's delicate piano themes superbly counterpoint David Jorgensen's pastel drawings, and Meryl Streep tells the story with intensity. 30m. **DIR:** Mark Sottnick. **1984**

VERY BEST OF BUGS BUNNY: VOLUME 1, THE ★★★★★ This superior collection includes five of the wascally wabbit's best escapades, highlighted by Chuck Jones's "Bugs Bunny and the Three Bears" and Robert Clampett's final Warner Brothers cartoon, "The Big Snooze" (which sends poor Elmer Fudd into the nightmare of dreamland). Bugs meets Humphrey Bogart and Lauren Bacall in "Slick Hare," and Beaky Buzzard in "Bugs Bunny Gets the Boid." The set is rounded out by "Gorilla My Dreams." 38m. **DIR:** Bob Clampett, Friz Freleng, Chuck Jones, Robert McKimson. **1942–48**

VERY BEST OF BUGS BUNNY: VOLUME 2, THE ★★★★½ Poor Tex Avery lost his job as a Warner Brothers animator because of his original conclusion to "The Heckling Hare," where it appeared Bugs Bunny actually perished (although viewers knew better). Bugs gets the better of an obnoxious little girl in Friz Freleng's superior "Little Red Riding Rabbit," and he makes an Oscar bid in Bob Clampett's "What's Cookin', Doc?" The collection is rounded out by two Chuck Jones entries: "Rabbit Punch" and "Wackiki Wabbit." 38m. **DIR:** Tex Avery, Bob Clampett, Friz Freleng, Chuck Jones. **1941–48**

VERY BEST OF BUGS BUNNY: VOLUME 3, THE ★★★★ Bugs gets introduced by name for the first time—although his voice was destined to change—in "Elmer's Pet Rabbit" (1940). Far more notable are Chuck Jones's rarely seen "Super Rabbit" and the World War II–themed "Buckaroo Bugs." The collection is rounded out by "Hold the Lion, Please" and "Jack Wabbit and the Beanstalk." 38m. **DIR:** Bob Clampett, Friz Freleng, Chuck Jones. **1940–44**

VERY BEST OF BUGS BUNNY: VOLUME 4, THE ★★★★ Friz Freleng's "Rhapsody Rabbit"—which finds our hero wrestling with a concert-hall piano solo—is the strongest entry in this collection of five cartoons. Also included: "Baseball Bugs," "Hare Ribbin'," "The Wacky Wabbit," and "The Wabbit Who Came to Supper." 40m. **DIR:** Bob Clampett, Friz Freleng. **1942–46**

VERY BRADY CHRISTMAS, A ★★★★ One of television's most revered families decides to get together for Christmas. All of the kids have grown up, and all but one of the original stars returns to help. A little sappy, a little corny, but part of the American culture. 94m. **DIR:** Peter Baldwin. **CAST:** Robert Reed, Florence Henderson, Ann B. Davis. **1988**

VERY FUNNY, CHARLIE BROWN ★★★½ Snoopy is the star in this baker's dozen of short stories taken from Charles Schulz's newspaper strip. The famed beagle extorts endorsements from the Peanuts gang in his attempt to win the Daisy Hill Puppy Cup. 39m. **DIR:** Bill Melendez, Sam Nicholson, Phil Roman. **1983–1985**

VERY MERRY CRICKET, A ★★★ The sequel to Jones's earlier production, *A Cricket in Times Square.* Here, the talented virtuoso bug is drawn back to the Big Apple by a cat-and-mouse team who serve as his best friends. Fast-paced and entertaining. 26m. **DIR:** Chuck Jones. **1973**

VIDEO WONDERS: HOME FOR A DINOSAUR/THE MONSTER UNDER MY BED ★★★ Animated storybook production is presented in a style that makes reading a fun activity and includes a sing-along portion after each story to reinforce word and letter recognition. Here a dinosaur learns there's no place like home, and a baby bear finds there's nothing to fear from the dark. 16m. **DIR:** Alan J. Shalleck. **1989**

VIDEO WONDERS: MAXWELL MOUSE/THE GREAT BUNNY RACE ★★★ Storybook-style video to familiarize toddlers with words, letters, and vocabulary. A mouse investigates the source of a mysterious sound and a rabbit must learn that winning isn't everything. 16m. **DIR:** Alan J. Shalleck. **1989**

WALKING ON AIR ★★★★ Uplifting Ray Bradbury tale about a paralyzed boy who refuses to submit to the law of gravity. Inspired by his zany science teacher (played to perfection by Lynn Redgrave), he petitions NASA for a chance to float in space. This WonderWorks production is suitable for the entire family. 58m. **DIR:** Ed Kaplan. **CAST:** Lynn Redgrave, Jordan Marder. **1986**

WALT DISNEY CHRISTMAS, A ★★★ Since half the cartoons collected on this tape do not include the famous faces, this package may appeal only to the very small fry. Hamilton Luske's "Once Upon a Wintertime," lifted from *Melody Time* (1948), is a luxurious Hallmark greeting card come to life, but the story is overly quaint; similarly, two Silly Symphonies—"Santa's Workshop" and "The Night Before Christmas"—are pretty minor entries. "Donald's Snow Fight" (1942), however, is a classic. 46m. **DIR:** Walt Disney. **1981**

WALTZ KING, THE ★★★½ The wonderful music of Johann Strauss Jr. is the real star of this Walt Disney biography filmed on location in Vienna. A treat to the eyes and ears, this is a good family film. 94m. **DIR:** Steve Previn. **CAST:** Kerwin Mathews, Brian Aherne, Senta Berger, Peter Kraus, Fritz Eckhardt. **1963**

WALTZ THROUGH THE HILLS ★★★½ Two Australian orphans, fearing separation, set off for a ship to take them to their grandparents in England. They are helped by an outback native (Ernie Dingo) who is both frightening and endearing. A WonderWorks production, this is fine family fare. 116m. **DIR:** Frank Arnold. **CAST:** Tina Kemp, Andre Jansen, Ernie Dingo, Dan O'Herlihy. **1988**

WATER BABIES, THE ★★★ Big fans of *Mary Poppins* should enjoy this. In Victorian England a chimney sweep's apprentice has a series of adventures with animated characters who live underwater. Designed more for kids than for families, though adults can enjoy the cast of fine British character actors. Rated G. 93m. **DIR:** Lionel Jeffries. **CAST:** James Mason, Billie Whitelaw, Bernard Cribbins, Joan Greenwood, David Tomlinson. **1979**

WEE WILLIE WINKIE ★★★★ The best of Shirley Temple's features from her star period is this adaptation of a Rudyard Kipling tale. Temple and her screen mother Constance Collier go to live with her disapproving grandfather C. Aubrey Smith in India. It's a real charmer and a fine adventure film to boot. B&W; 100m. **DIR:** John Ford. **CAST:** Shirley Temple, Victor McLaglen, C. Aubrey Smith, Cesar Romero, Constance Collier. **1937**

WE'RE BACK! A DINOSAUR'S STORY ★★½ Jumbled animated adaptation of the popular book by Hudson Talbott. A quartet of dinosaurs are fed intelligence-increasing Brain Grain by an intergalactic traveler and brought forward in time to fulfill the wishes of modern-day kids. The animation is first-rate, but the screenplay by John Patrick Shanley will confuse even adults. In addition, scenes set in a scary circus may be too frightening for the small fry. Rated G. 72m. **DIR:** Dick Zondag, Ralph Zondag, Phil Nibbelink, Simon Wells. **1993**

WESTWARD HO, THE WAGONS ★★½ Episodic film about a wagon train traveling west. The basic appeal is seeing Fess Parker in another Davy Crockett–type role and four of the Mouseketeers as children in the train. Devoid of a real beginning or end, this movie just rambles along. Not rated. 90m. **DIR:** William Beaudine. **CAST:** Fess Parker, Kathleen Crowley, Jeff York, David Stollery, Sebastian Cabot, George Reeves. **1956**

WHAT A NIGHTMARE, CHARLIE BROWN ★★ Snoopy eats too much pizza and dreams of being an Alaskan sled dog, where his "civilized upbringing" makes him no match for the environment. Boring and repetitious saga. 25m. **DIR:** Phil Roman, Bill Melendez. **1978**

WHAT HAVE WE LEARNED, CHARLIE BROWN? ★★★★ This somber and moving tribute to fallen war heroes acts as a postscript to the Peanuts feature film, *Bon Voyage, Charlie Brown.* While in France, Linus explains the history of the World War II invasion at Omaha Beach and World War I's legend of the white-crossed red poppies. Judy Munsen's haunting background themes contribute greatly to this most unusual Peanuts offering. 24m. **DIR:** Bill Melendez. **1983**

WHAT NEXT, CHARLIE BROWN? ★★★ Poor Charlie Brown has a mighty tough time in these thirteen tales battling kite-eating trees and Lucy's big mouth. Several of the vignettes (all taken from *The Charlie Brown and Snoopy Show*) are rather cruel, and others are quickie blackouts united by common themes such as snow fights and Schroeder's piano. 47m. **DIR:** Bill Melendez, Sam Jaimes, Sam Nicholson, Phil Roman. **1983–1985**

WHAT'S UP DOC?—A SALUTE TO BUGS BUNNY ★★★★★ The ten cartoons in this package represent the wascally wabbit's finest moments, from his first appearance (in 1940's Oscar-nominated "A Wild Hare") to the debut of Yosemite Sam (in 1945's "Hare Trigger") and Bob Clampett's classic "The Big Snooze." But while the cartoons are undeniably wonderful, this fiftieth anniversary tribute is highlighted by rare, behind-the-scenes footage of the antic animators. 95m. **DIR:** Carl Lindahl. **1990**

WHERE THE LILIES BLOOM ★★★½ Heartwarming melodrama about four orphaned children in rural America who pretend their father is still alive in order to keep the authorities from separating them. The settings are beautiful, and the actors are all fine, especially Harry Dean Stanton. Background score by bluegrass legend Earl Scruggs. 96m. **DIR:** William A. Graham. **CAST:** Julie Gholson, Jan Smithers, Harry Dean Stanton, Sudie Bond. **1974**

WHERE THE RED FERN GROWS ★★★★ Fine family fare about a boy's love for two hunting dogs and his coming of age in Oklahoma in the 1930s. Rated G. 90m. **DIR:** Norman Tokar. **CAST:** James Whitmore, Beverly Garland, Jack Ging, Lonny Chapman, Stewart Peterson. **1974**

WHISTLE DOWN THE WIND ★★★½ Bryan Forbes's first film is a thoughtful, allegorical tale about three children who encounter an accused murderer hiding in a barn and take him to be a Christ figure fleeing from his persecutors. Based on Mary Hayley Bell's popular novel, this is one of the best films ever made dealing with the fragile nature of childhood trust and beliefs. B&W; 99m. **DIR:** Bryan Forbes. **CAST:** Hayley Mills, Alan Bates, Bernard Lee, Norman Bird, Elsie Wagstaff. **1961**

WHITE FANG ★★★★ A young man travels to Alaska in search of his father's lost gold mine and meets up with an old miner, an evil dogfight promoter, and a wolf. A wonderful Disney adventure film. Rated PG for violence. 104m. **DIR:** Randal Kleiser. **CAST:** Klaus Maria Brandauer, Ethan Hawke, Seymour Cassel, James Remar, Susan Hogan. **1991**

WHITE FANG 2: MYTH OF THE WHITE WOLF ★★½ This disappointing sequel banishes former star Ethan Hawke to cameo status and replaces him with overly wholesome Scott Bairstow. The insufferably politically correct story finds our hero and his loyal pooch battling greedy miners and helping Alaskan Native Americans. The stupid story line will annoy adults, and kids will be put off by the film's length and lack of action. Rated PG for mild violence. 105m. **DIR:** Ken Olin. **CAST:** Scott Bairstow, Charmaine Craig, Al Harrington, Alfred Molina, Geoffrey Lewis, Ethan Hawke. **1994**

WHITE FANG AND THE HUNTER ★★ A dog, White Fang, and his master, Daniel (Robert Wood), are attacked by wolves. They are taken in by a young widow who is being forced to marry. So Daniel and the dog come to her aid. Poor acting and directing hamper this familiar story. Rated G. 87m. **DIR:** Alfonso Brescia. **CAST:** Robert Wood, Pedro Sanchez. **1985**

WHITE SEAL, THE ★★★ Roddy McDowall narrates the classic Rudyard Kipling tale of a baby white seal who grows up to save his tribe from men. This is not disturbingly graphic so it's fine for the young ones. 30m. **DIR:** Chuck Jones. **1975**

WHITEWATER SAM ★★½ Keith Larsen wrote, directed, coproduced, and stars in this wilderness adventure. He plays the legendary Whitewater Sam, the first white man to survive the harsh Rocky Mountain winters. The real star, however, seems to be his dog, Sybar. The beautiful scenery makes this film more than watchable. Rated PG for violence. 85m. **DIR:** Keith Larsen. **CAST:** Keith Larsen. **1978**

WILBUR AND ORVILLE: THE FIRST TO FLY ★★★★ This entertaining biography of the Wright brothers shows their determination in the face of ridicule and harassment.The moral of this delightful film lies in sticking to something when you know you're right. 47m. **DIR:** Henning Schellerup. **CAST:** James Carroll Jordan, Chris Beaumont, John Randolph, Louise Latham, Edward Andrews. **1973**

WILD AND WOODY ★★ Woody Woodpecker wanders the West in search of feeble laughs in this collection of Walter Lantz "cartunes." Some of the gags work well, but this grouping suffers from repetition, especially due to the lack of any other Lantz characters (such as Andy Panda or Chilly Willy). 51m. **DIR:** Walter Lantz. **1951–1963**

WILD HEARTS CAN'T BE BROKEN ★★★★ A rebellious teenager (Gabrielle Anwar) in the 1920s runs away to join a traveling show, where she learns how to leap on horseback into a water tank from a forty-foot-high platform. Sparkling family film from the folks at Disney. Rated G. 90m. **DIR:** Steve Miner. **CAST:** Gabrielle Anwar, Michael Schoeffling, Cliff Robertson. **1991**

WILD HORSE HANK ★★½ Linda Blair is a horse lover pitted against a family that is stampeding wild horses. Richard Crenna plays her father. This Canadian feature is not rated. 94m. **DIR:** Eric Till. **CAST:** Linda Blair, Richard Crenna, Al Waxman, Michael Wincott. **1978**

WILDERNESS FAMILY, PART 2, THE ★★★ Taken on its own terms, *The Wilderness Family, Part 2* isn't a bad motion picture. Film fans who want thrills and chills or something challenging to the mind should skip it. Rated G. 105m. **DIR:** Frank Zuniga. **CAST:** Robert Logan, Susan D. Shaw, Heather Rattray, Ham Larsen, George (Buck) Flower, Brian Cutler. **1978**

WILLIE MCBEAN AND HIS MAGIC MACHINE ★★ Saddled with a slow story line in which the hero must thwart the efforts of a mad scientist to change history, *Willie* lacks the charm and style of better animated characters and has little to offer compared to more sophisticated contemporary productions. 94m. **DIR:** Arthur Rankin Jr. **1959**

WILLIE, THE OPERATIC WHALE ★★★★ High comedy mixes with tragedy in this tale of a silver-throated whale who dreams of playing Pagliacci at the Met. A self-obsessed opera impresario dubbed Professor Tetti Tatti—vocalized by Nelson Eddy, who also handles the narration and all the other characters—chooses to believe the whale has swallowed an opera singer. 29m. **DIR:** Walt Disney. **1946**

WILLY WONKA AND THE CHOCOLATE FACTORY ★★★ Gene Wilder plays a candy company owner who allows some lucky kids to tour the facility. However, a few of his guests get sticky fingers (pun intended) and suffer the consequences. This essentially entertaining movie has its memorable moments—as well as bad. Rated G. 98m. **DIR:** Mel Stuart. **CAST:** Gene Wilder, Jack Albertson, Peter Ostrum, Roy Kinnear. **1971**

WIND IN THE WILLOWS, THE (1949) ★★★★★ One of Disney's finest. This adaptation of Kenneth Grahame's classic deals with the adventures of J. Thaddeus Toad and his friends Cyril, Mole, Rat, and Mac Badger. Basil Rathbone narrates this classic short. 75m. **DIR:** Wolfgang Reitherman. **1949**

WIND IN THE WILLOWS, THE (1983) ★★★★½ Based on the famous Kenneth Grahame book, this collection of three separate stories is a delight of stop-motion animation. The much-loved characters of Mole, Ratty, and of course, Toad, are brought beautifully to life in miniature Edwardian settings. 60m. **DIR:** Mark Hall. **1983**

WINNIE THE POOH AND A DAY FOR EEYORE ★★½ Corners were being cut when this installment in Disney's Pooh series came out, compared to the earlier three. Sterling Holloway is sorely missed as Pooh's voice, the bear's theme song has been needlessly updated, and the animation is overly garish and simplistic. 25m. **DIR:** Rick Reinert. **1983**

WINNIE THE POOH AND THE BLUSTERY DAY ★★★★★ A. A. Milne's magical charm is truly captured in this Oscar-winning short from the Disney Studios. As with the first entry, Sebastian Cabot once again handles narration, and Pooh is voiced by Sterling Holloway. The episodic tale follows Pooh and his friends in the hundred-acre woods as they have some exciting experiences during a particularly "blustery" day. Animation just doesn't get better than this. 25m. **DIR:** Wolfgang Reitherman. **1968**

WINNIE THE POOH AND THE HONEY TREE ★★★★½ Disney's first animated adaptation of A. A. Milne's classic stories about a stuffed bear and his friends is a delight; the visual style is completely faithful to E. H. Shepard's original illustrations and Sebastian Cabot's narration is lifted from the actual text. Milne's familiar characters—Christopher Robin, Pooh (voiced with beguiling charm by Sterling Holloway), Piglet, and the others—have been supplemented by a decidedly American gopher, but the others remain true to their British origins. 25m. **DIR:** Wolfgang Reitherman. **1966**

WINNIE THE POOH AND TIGGER TOO ★★★★½ Following in the tradition of the two previous Disney animated versions of the classic A.A. Milne stories, this Oscar-nominated animated short will delight children and adults. Pooh, Piglet, and Rabbit try to "get the bounce out of" Tigger, whose corkscrew hopping continually knocks down his friends. Paul Winchell gives droll voice to the manic Tigger, and Pooh is once again handled by Sterling Holloway. 25m. **DIR:** John Lounsbery. **1974**

WIZARD, THE ★★ It's *Rain Man* meets the *Pinball Wizard* as Fred Savage takes his emotionally disturbed half brother (Luke Edwards) to the national video game championship. Little more than a cleverly disguised advertisement for Nintendo games and the Universal Studios Tour. Rated PG for light violence and profanity. 100m. **DIR:** Todd Holland. **CAST:** Fred Savage, Beau Bridges, Christian Slater, Luke Edwards, Jenny Lewis. **1989**

WIZARD OF OZ, THE ★★★★★ Fifty years old and still going strong—on a fresh, bright Technicolor print with special rare footage additions—this all-time classic continues to charm audiences of all ages. In this case, for watching great movies, "there is no place like home." Right, Toto? 119m. **DIR:** Victor Fleming. **CAST:** Judy Garland, Ray Bolger, Bert Lahr, Jack Haley, Frank Morgan, Billie Burke, Margaret Hamilton, Charley Grapewin, Clara Blandick. **1939**

WOODY WOODPECKER AND HIS FRIENDS (VOLUME ONE) ★★★★ The first in a series of classic cartoons. The eight in this collection include the first Woody Woodpecker cartoon, "Knock Knock," plus "Ski for Two" and "The Bandmaster." 80m. **DIR:** Walter Lantz.

WOODY WOODPECKER AND HIS FRIENDS (VOLUME TWO) ★★★ This collection of eight cartoons features "The Poet and the Peasant," "Fish Fry," "The Screwdriver," "Wacky Bye Baby," "Woody Dines Out," "Loose Nut," "S-H-H-H," and "Convict Concerto." 59m. **DIR:** Walter Lantz.

WOODY WOODPECKER AND HIS FRIENDS (VOLUME THREE) ★★★★ The excellent "The Barber of Seville" and "Dog Tax Collector" are among the cartoons in this collection, which features Woody Woodpecker, Andy Panda, Wally Walrus, and Chilly Willy. 55m. **DIR:** Walter Lantz.

WORLD ACCORDING TO GOOFY, THE (LIMITED GOLD EDITION 2) ★★★★ Two classics from the early 1940s highlight this collection. Goofy attempts to deal with a magician's trunk in "Baggage Buster"; "Goofy's Glider" finds the poor guy becoming airborne by every means except that suggested by the cartoon's title. "Home Made Home" can be viewed as the animated answer to "Mr. Blandings Builds His Dream House," and "They're Off" illustrates the folly of track betting. 50m. **DIR:** Walt Disney. **1940–1953**

WORLD OF ANDY PANDA, THE ★★½ The black-and-white Micky Mouse look-alike, Andy Panda, went through a number of changes in appearance, and these cartoons from 1941 to 1946 reflect this. Many of his animated adventures often feature other, less bland critters. That said, "Apple Andy" is a near-classic, and the rest aren't bad. 62m. **DIR:** Walter Lantz.

WORLD'S GREATEST ATHLETE, THE ★★★ John Amos is the athletics instructor at Merrivale College. He and his assistant, Tim Conway, travel to Africa to get away from their toubles and come across Nanu (Jan-Michael Vincent), the greatest natural athlete in the world. One of the better Disney college films. Rated G. 89m. **DIR:** Robert Scheerer. **CAST:** Jan-Michael Vincent, John Amos, Tim Conway, Roscoe Lee Browne. **1973**

WORST WITCH, THE ★★★★ Jill Murphy's charming children's book gets first-cabin treatment in this delightful made-for-cable adaptation that features Fairuza Balk as hapless young Mildred Hubble, the only student at Miss Cackle's International Academy for Witches who cannot properly perform her spells. Screenwriter Mary Pleshette Willis retains the book's whimsical tone, and Diana Rigg is deliciously spooky as the imperious head mistress. 70m. **DIR:** Robert Young. **CAST:** Diana Rigg, Charlotte Rae, Tim Curry, Fairuza Balk, Sabina Franklyn. 1986

YEARLING, THE ★★★★½ A beautiful film version of Marjorie Kinnan Rawlings's sensitive story of a young boy's love for a pet fawn that his father must destroy. Simply told, this emotionally charged drama has been rated one of the finest films ever made. 134m. **DIR:** Clarence Brown. **CAST:** Gregory Peck, Jane Wyman, Claude Jarman Jr., Chill Wills. 1946

YELLOW SUBMARINE ★★★★ Clever cartoon versions of John, Paul, George, and Ringo journey into Pepperland to save it from the Blue Meanies in this delightful blend of psychedelic animation and topflight Beatles music. "All You Need Is Love," "When I'm 64," "Lucy in the Sky with Diamonds," and "Yellow Submarine" provide the background and power the action in a film that epitomized the flower generation. 85m. **DIR:** George Dunning. **CAST:** Animated. 1968

YOGI AND THE MAGICAL FLIGHT OF THE SPRUCE GOOSE ★★ Those planning a trip to Long Beach, California, to visit Howard Hughes's fabled Spruce Goose might be intrigued by the early portions of this interminable full-length cartoon; some newsreel footage explains a bit about this remarkable airplane. Aside from that, we're left with another humdrum adventure with Yogi Bear, Boo-Boo, and the rest of the Hanna-Barbera gang. 96m. **DIR:** Ray Patterson. 1988

YOGI'S FIRST CHRISTMAS ★★ Yogi and Boo-Boo have never experienced Christmas—until grand old Jellystone Lodge is threatened by the construction of a new freeway. The insipid songs that permeate this overlong feature are insufferable, as is Cindy Bear's attempt to corner Yogi under the mistletoe for a kiss. 99m. **DIR:** Ray Patterson. 1980

YOGI'S GREAT ESCAPE ★★ Diabetics, beware; the cutesy antics of three overly adorable bear cub orphans may induce sugar shock. Aside from dealing with these three newcomers, Yogi and Boo-Boo head for parts unknown in a souped-up car when the threatened closure of Jellystone Park mandates the average bear's transfer to a zoo. 96m. **DIR:** Ray Patterson. 1987

YOSEMITE SAM: THE GOOD, THE BAD, AND THE ORNERY ★★★½ Manic animator Friz Freleng and pint-size baddie Yosemite Sam are showcased in this quintet of cartoons, which leads off with its strongest entry: a fast-paced "Mutiny on the Bunny" (1950), wherein Bugs clashes yet again with his second-favorite nemesis—after Elmer Fudd, of course. "Sahara Hare," "Rabbit Every Monday," and "Wild and Wooly Hare"—the final Bugs-Sam Western—are also quite good; sadly, the package is compromised by the extremely lame "Honey's Money." 36m. **DIR:** Friz Freleng. 1950–62

YOU CAN'T WIN, CHARLIE BROWN ★★★½ These ten stories from Charles Schulz's newspaper strip, find the Peanuts gang at school. Sally takes Snoopy to class as a show-and-tell exhibit (and the other kids jeer that he's a chicken or a small moose), and Charlie Brown and Peppermint Patty wind up in a shoving match when forced to share the same desk. 36m. **DIR:** Bill Melendez, Sam Jaimes, Phil Roman. 1983–1985

YOUNG CHILDREN'S CONCERT WITH RAFFI, A ★★★★ Put on this tape and watch the magic happen. Canadian folksinger Raffi has a way with children, and his delightful, lighthearted tunes are easy on adult ears as well. Not only do his songs—which include "Down by the Bay," "Baby Beluga," "Wheels on the Bus," "Bumping Up and Down," and "Shake My Sillies Out"—teach youngsters to rhyme and reason, they also give them things to do while watching. 50m. **DIR:** David Devine. **CAST:** Raffi. 1984

YOUNG MAGICIAN, THE ★★ Trite tale of a young man (Rusty Jedwab) who discovers he has magical powers and has a run-in with society. Special effects are good, but the dubbing in this Polish-Canadian production detracts a lot from the story. Not rated; suitable for the entire family. 99m. **DIR:** Waldemar Dziki. **CAST:** Rusty Jedwab. 1986

YOU'RE A GOOD MAN, CHARLIE BROWN ★★★ The famous Broadway musical is given the animated treatment, with mixed results. Several of Clark Gesner's witty songs are garbled and difficult to understand, and the notion of an animated Snoopy with a voice—after lacking one for twenty years—doesn't quite work. 60m. **DIR:** Sam Jaimes. 1985

YOU'RE A GOOD SPORT, CHARLIE BROWN ★★★½ Anybody tired of seeing poor Charlie Brown constantly winding up with the fuzzy end of the lollipop will *love* this story. Peppermint Patty challenges Chuck to a motocross race—his bike, naturally, is number 13—but both of them must work hard to keep up with the mystery contestant: the Masked Marvel. 26m. **DIR:** Phil Roman. 1975

YOU'RE IN LOVE, CHARLIE BROWN ★★★★★ Charlie Brown first spots the little red-haired girl in this fourth animated

Peanuts short, and he loses his already shaky abilities of coherent thought and rational behavior. Peppermint Patty (in her animated debut) mistakes his interest and sets him up for a late-night rendezvous with Lucy. 26m. **DIR:** Bill Melendez. **1967**

YOU'RE IN THE SUPERBOWL, CHARLIE BROWN ★★ A low point in the Peanuts series, due to dumb, redundant sequences involving Snoopy, Woodstock and the "Animal Football League." Charlie Brown's attempts to win tickets to the "Splendid Bowl" (as Marcie calls it) are somewhat more amusing. 30m. **DIR:** Bill Melendez. **1993**

YOU'RE THE GREATEST, CHARLIE BROWN ★★★ Hoping to bring honor to his school, Charlie Brown trains hard and enters the Junior Olympics Decathlon; his opponents include Marcie, Freddy Fabulous (the previous year's all-city champ), and a mysterious entrant dubbed the Masked Marvel. The thin story doesn't allow much of the gang's personalities to emerge. 25m. **DIR:** Phil Roman. **1979**

ZEBRA IN THE KITCHEN ★★ When a family moves to the city, their tame pet wildcat must go to an overcrowded zoo to comply with local regulations. Feeling a little mischievous, young star Jay North lets the animals loose. One-dimensional. 92m. **DIR:** Ivan Tors. **CAST:** Jay North, Martin Milner, Andy Devine, Joyce Meadows, Jim Davis. **1965**

ZIGGY'S GIFT ★★★½ Tom Wilson's comic-strip character is brought to delightful life. Ziggy naïvely goes to work as a street-corner Santa for a bogus charity. This has a certain contemporary charm that can be enjoyed by young and old alike. 30m. **DIR:** Richard Williams. **1982**

ZILLION—VOLS. 1–5 🦃 A five-part, Japanese animation miniseries chronicling the adventures of the White Knights as they fight alien invaders. This simpleminded, direct-to-video entry features only average animation and a poor story line. Unrated violence. each. 30m. **DIR:** Carl Macek. **1991**

COMEDY

ABBOTT AND COSTELLO IN HOLLYWOOD ★★ Lesser Abbott and Costello effort has Bud and Lou trying to make it big as movie stars. Best scenes occur early in the film, with Lou playing a barber. B&W; 83m. **DIR:** S. Sylvan Simon. **CAST:** Bud Abbott, Lou Costello, Frances Rafferty, Robert Stanton. **1945**

ABBOTT AND COSTELLO MEET CAPTAIN KIDD ★★ One of Abbott and Costello's few color films, this is strictly preschooler fare. The boys get chased around uncharted islands, pirate ships, etc., by the infamous Captain Kidd, as portrayed by Charles Laughton, who makes every effort to retain his dignity. 70m. **DIR:** Charles Lamont. **CAST:** Bud Abbott, Lou Costello, Charles Laughton, Hillary Brooke, Leif Erickson. **1952**

ABBOTT AND COSTELLO MEET DR. JEKYLL AND MR. HYDE ★★★½ Fun mixture of comedy and horror has the team up against the smooth Dr. Jekyll and the maniacal Mr. Hyde. One of the boys' better films of the 1950s. Boris Karloff is in top form in the dual role, and don't miss the hilarious scene in which Lou is turned into a mouse! B&W; 77m. **DIR:** Charles Lamont. **CAST:** Bud Abbott, Lou Costello, Boris Karloff. **1953**

ABBOTT AND COSTELLO MEET FRANKENSTEIN ★★★★ Whenever someone writes about the Universal horror classics, they always cite this film as evidence of how the series fell into decline. Likewise, screen historians call it the beginning of the end for the comedy team. It deserves neither rap. For Bud Abbott and Lou Costello, it meant a resurgence of popularity after a slow fall from favor as the 1940s box-office champs. Yet it never compromises the characters of Dracula (Bela Lugosi), the Wolfman (Lon Chaney), or the Frankenstein monster (Glenn Strange). Director Charles Barton mixes fright and fun without sacrificing either. B&W; 83m. **DIR:** Charles Barton. **CAST:** Bud Abbott, Lou Costello, Lon Chaney Jr., Bela Lugosi, Glenn Strange. **1948**

ABBOTT AND COSTELLO MEET THE INVISIBLE MAN ★★ Bud and Lou are private eyes hired by a prizefighter to clear him of his manager's murder. The fighter injects himself with a serum that renders him invisible and helps Lou kayo his opponents in the ring before the real murderer is exposed. B&W; 82m. **DIR:** Charles Lamont. **CAST:** Bud Abbott, Lou Costello, Arthur Franz, Nancy Guild, Adele Jergens, Sheldon Leonard, William Frawley. **1951**

ABBOTT AND COSTELLO MEET THE KILLER, BORIS KARLOFF ★★★ Second in the duo's *Abbott and Costello Meet ...* series, brought on by the tremendous popularity of their *Frankenstein* send-up the year before. In this enjoyable outing, Bud and Lou match wits with Boris Karloff, in classic form as a sinister swami doing away with his enemies at a posh hotel. B&W; 84m. **DIR:** Charles Barton. **CAST:** Bud Abbott, Lou Costello, Boris Karloff, Lenore Aubert, Gar Moore, James Flavin. **1949**

ABBOTT AND COSTELLO MEET THE MUMMY ★★ Final (and overdue) entry in the seven-year cycle of "horror comedies" pitting Abbott and Costello against Universal Pictures' monster stable. Not without amusing moments, but mostly, the same tired vaudeville routines are dragged out as the boys flee two mummies—one real, one fake—in Egypt. B&W; 79m. **DIR:** Charles Lamont. **CAST:** Bud Abbott, Lou Costello, Marie Windsor, Richard Deacon. **1955**

ABBOTT AND COSTELLO SHOW, THE (TV SERIES) ★★★ Set in Hollywood, this comedy series depicts Bud Abbott's and Lou Costello's efforts to improve their financial situation. Though the comics appear somewhat weary and the humor is often forced, enough of the gags work to make the episodes worth a glance. Many of Abbott and Costello's classic routines are incorporated into the shows, boosting the slim plots. 53m. **DIR:** Various. **CAST:** Bud Abbott, Lou Costello, Sidney Fields, Hillary Brooke, Joe Besser. **1952–1954**

ABDULLA THE GREAT 🦃 An Egyptian nobleman sets out to win the affections of an English girl. 103m. **DIR:** Gregory Ratoff. **CAST:** Gregory Ratoff, Kay Kendall, Sydney Chaplin. **1954**

ACE VENTURA: PET DETECTIVE ★★½ Gangly Jim Carrey of TV's *In Living Color* proves that comedy doesn't have to be pretty to be a scream. Carrey hams it up as a goofy Florida gumshoe who cracks missing-animal cases. This giddy, crude comedy doesn't really have a personality of its own—it's an extension of Carrey's own hyper-nuttiness. Ace must locate the Miami Dolphins' mascot and star quarterback just before the Super Bowl. Rated PG-13 for violence, profanity, and suggested sex. 85m. **DIR:** Tom Shadyac. **CAST:** Jim Carrey, Sean Young, Courteney Cox, Tone Loc, Dan Marino. **1994**

ADAM'S RIB ★★★★½ The screen team of Spencer Tracy and Katharine Hepburn was always watchable, but never more so than in this comedy. As husband-and-wife lawyers on opposing sides of the same case, they remind us of what movie magic is really all about. The supporting performances by Judy Holliday, Tom Ewell, David Wayne, and Jean Hagen greatly add to the fun. B&W; 101m. **DIR:** George Cukor. **CAST:** Spencer Tracy, Katharine Hepburn, Judy Holliday, Tom Ewell, David Wayne. **1949**

ADDAMS FAMILY, THE ★★★½ It's murder and mayhem at the Addams mansion when two sleazy promoters try to force a fake Uncle Fester (Christopher Lloyd) on the unassuming Morticia (Anjelica Huston) and Gomez (Raul Julia). Perfectly cast and filled with touches of macabre humor. This movie actually improves upon the cult television series. Rated PG-13 for brief profanity and goofy violence. 101m. **DIR:** Barry Sonnenfeld. **CAST:** Anjelica Huston, Raul Julia, Christopher Lloyd, Christina Ricci, Jimmy Workman, Judith Malina, Elizabeth Wilson, Dan Hedaya. **1991**

ADDAMS FAMILY, THE (TV SERIES) ★★★ Mid-Sixties television viewers never knew quite what to make of the deliciously bent humor in *The Addams Family,* which stretched Charles Addams' *New Yorker* cartoons into two full seasons of decidedly offbeat entertainment. John Astin played Gomez Addams with maniacal intensity, while his lady-love, Morticia Frump, was brought to somber life by Carolyn Jones. Fans of the 1991 big-screen rendition are encouraged to investigate these humbler—but no less delightful—origins. Each tape contains two half-hour episodes. each 52m. **DIR:** Arthur Hiller, Jerry Hopper, Sidney Lanfield. **CAST:** Carolyn Jones, John Astin, Jackie Coogan, Ted Cassidy. **1964–1966**

ADDAMS FAMILY VALUES ★★★★ Fine performances make this second big-screen romp of the Addams family every bit as entertaining as the first. The zany plot involves the birth of a new family member, the seduction of Uncle Fester by a femme fatale and a trip to camp for Wednesday and Pugsley. Forget sense and enjoy the nonsense. Rated PG-13 for ghoulish goings-on. 88m. **DIR:** Barry Sonnenfeld. **CAST:** Anjelica Huston, Raul Julia, Christopher Lloyd, Joan Cusack, Carol Kane, Christina Ricci, Jimmy Workman, Carel Struycken, David Krumholtz, Christopher Hart, Dana Ivey, Peter MacNicol, Sam McMurray, Nathan Lane, Peter Graves. **1993**

ADMIRAL WAS A LADY, THE ★★½ Romantic comedy about a group of ex-GI's asked to watch over a young woman until she can be reunited with her fiancé. Clichéd and somewhat bland, it's not without a certain amount of charm. B&W; 87m. **DIR:** Albert S. Rogell. **CAST:** Edmond O'Brien, Wanda Hendrix, Rudy Vallee, Johnny Sands. **1948**

ADVENTURES BEYOND BELIEF 🦃 In this incoherent excuse for madcap comedy, an Elvis Presley fan helps a mobster's daughter escape from an all-girls' school. Unrated. 95m. **DIR:** Marcus Tompson. **CAST:** Skyler Cole, Jill Whitlow, Elke Sommer, Stella Stevens, Edie Adams, John Astin, Larry Storch. **1987**

ADVENTURES IN BABYSITTING ★★★½ A sort of *After Hours* for the teen crowd, this is a surprisingly entertaining film about what happens when 17-year-old Chris Parker (Elisabeth Shue) accepts a baby-sitting assignment. There are a number of hilarious moments—our favorite being a sequence in a blues club presided over by superguitarist Albert Collins. Rated PG-13 for profanity and violence. 100m. **DIR:** Chris Columbus. **CAST:** Elisabeth Shue, Keith Coogan, Anthony Rapp, Maia Brewton, Penelope Ann Miller, Vincent D'Onofrio. **1987**

ADVENTURES OF A PRIVATE EYE ★★ Boring British comedy about a detective's assistant who tries his hand at investigating a blackmail case while his boss is on vacation. The film has plenty of nudity and some scenes of rather explicit sex. Not rated. 96m. **DIR:** Stanley Long. **CAST:** Christopher Neil, Suzy Kendall, Harry H. Corbett, Diana Dors, Fred Emney, Liz Fraser, Irene Handl, Ian Lavender, Jon Pertwee, Adrienne Posta. **1987**

ADVENTURES OF OZZIE AND HARRIET, THE (TV SERIES) ★★★★ This is the prototypical family sitcom. Though it's primarily remembered for its all-American wholesomeness, the show was genuinely funny. That remarkable accomplishment must be primarily credited to Ozzie Nelson, who produced, directed, and co-wrote, as well as starred as the earnest father who could create chaos out of the simplest situations. Real-life wife Harriet and sons Ricky and David added warmth and naturalness. B&W; 60m. **DIR:** Ozzie Nelson. **CAST:** Ozzie Nelson, Harriet Nelson, Ricky Nelson, David Nelson, Kris Nelson, June Nelson, Don DeFore, Lyle Talbot. **1952–1966**

ADVENTURES OF PICASSO, THE ★★★ Witty, off-the-wall Swedish comedy about the life of Picasso. The rubber-faced Gosta Eckman looks like Buster Keaton playing Picasso, and Bernard Cribbins is a scream in drag as Gertrude Stein. Some truly funny moments make this semislapstick film shine. In overly simplistic Spanish, French, and English, so no subtitles are needed. Not rated; contains some ribald humor. 94m.

DIR: Tage Danielsson. **CAST:** Gosta Ekman, Hans Alfredson, Margaretha Krook, Bernard Cribbins, Wilfred Brambell. **1988**

ADVENTURES OF SADIE ★★ Three men and a very young Joan Collins shipwrecked on a desert island; you can guess the rest. 88m. **DIR:** Noel Langley. **CAST:** George Cole, Kenneth More, Joan Collins, Hattie Jacques, Hermione Gingold. **1953**

ADVENTURE OF SHERLOCK HOLMES' SMARTER BROTHER, THE ★★½ Even discounting the effrontery of writer-director-star Gene Wilder's creating a smarter sibling, Sigerson Holmes (Gene Wilder), one is still left with a highly uneven romp. Though the principals—who also include Marty Feldman and Dom DeLuise—try hard, the film's soggy structure (and Wilder's poor research into the canon) plunge the whole thing into mediocrity. Rated PG. 91m. **DIR:** Gene Wilder. **CAST:** Gene Wilder, Madeline Kahn, Marty Feldman, Dom DeLuise. **1975**

ADVENTURES OF THE KUNG FU RASCALS, THE ★★ Wacky spoof of the kung fu genre is helped by decent special effects and creature makeup. Three Stooges–like heroes—Lao Ze, Reepo, and Chen Chow Mein—fight to free their land from an evil ruler. Toilet humor is unnecessarily offensive. Rated PG-13 for comic-book violence. 90m. **DIR:** Steve Wang. **CAST:** Steve Wang, Troy Fromin, Johnnie Saiko Espiritu, Les Claypool, Ted Smith, Aaron Sims. **1991**

ADVENTURES OF TOPPER, THE ★★★ This television comedy consistently earned chuckles, if not an abundance of belly laughs as this video compilation attests. Leo G. Carroll is delightful as Cosmo Topper, the henpecked bank vice president who is the only one who can see a trio of ghosts—Marion Kirby (Anne Jeffreys), her husband George (Robert Sterling), "that most sporting spirit," and their booze-swilling Saint Bernard, Neil. 93m. **DIR:** Philip Rapp. **CAST:** Anne Jeffreys, Robert Sterling, Leo G. Carroll, Lee Patrick, Thurston Hall, Kathleen Freeman. **1953–1956**

AFFAIRS OF ANNABEL, THE ★★★★ The pre–*I Love Lucy* Lucille Ball is very funny in this fast-paced comedy as a none-too-bright movie star whose manager (Jack Oakie) is continually dreaming up outrageous publicity stunts for her. The supporting cast of familiar Thirties faces also provides plenty of laughs, especially Fritz Feld as a supercilious foreign director. 73m. **DIR:** Ben Stoloff. **CAST:** Jack Oakie, Lucille Ball, Ruth Donnelly, Fritz Feld, Thurston Hall. **1937**

AFRICA SCREAMS ★★ Bud and Lou are joined by circus great Clyde Beatty and Frank (*Bring 'Em Back Alive*) Buck in this thin but enjoyable comedy, one of their last feature films. Most of the jungle and safari clichés are evident in this fast-paced, oddball film but they work acceptably. Fun for the kids as well as the adults. B&W; 79m. **DIR:** Charles Barton. **CAST:** Bud Abbott, Lou Costello, Hillary Brooke, Shemp Howard, Max Baer, Clyde Beatty, Frank Buck. **1949**

AFTER HOURS ★★★★ *After Hours* is the most brutal and bizarre black comedy we are ever likely to see—a mixture of guffaws and goose pimples. Griffin Dunne stars as a computer operator who unwillingly spends a night in downtown Manhattan. A trio of strange women (played by Rosanna Arquette, Teri Garr, and Linda Fiorentino) mystify, seduce, and horrify our hapless hero, and his life soon becomes a total nightmare. Rated R for profanity, nudity, violence, and general weirdness. 94m. **DIR:** Martin Scorsese. **CAST:** Griffin Dunne, Rosanna Arquette, Teri Garr, John Heard, Linda Fiorentino, Richard "Cheech" Marin, Tommy Chong, Catherine O'Hara, Verna Bloom. **1985**

AFTER THE FOX 🦃 Peter Sellers is at his worst, playing an Italian movie director in this flat farce. 103m. **DIR:** Vittorio De Sica. **CAST:** Peter Sellers, Victor Mature, Britt Ekland, Martin Balsam. **1966**

AGE ISN'T EVERYTHING 🦃 Age-reversal comedy with a twist: young Jonathan Silverman has his body taken over by an old man in a comedy that's as old as the hills and just as dusty. Rated R for language. 91m. **DIR:** Douglas Katz. **CAST:** Jonathan Silverman, Robert Prosky, Rita Moreno, Paul Sorvino. **1991**

AGGIE APPLEBY, MAKER OF MEN ★★ The heroine teaches a wimp to act like a tough guy so he can impersonate her tough boyfriend. A mixed bag that's watchable in spite of itself. But only up to a point. B&W; 73m. **DIR:** Mark Sandrich. **CAST:** Wynne Gibson, William Gargan, Charles Farrell, ZaSu Pitts, Jane Darwell, Betty Furness. **1933**

AH, WILDERNESS ★★★★ An American classic, this story of a family in 1910 mid-America is one of the most tasteful coming-of-age stories ever written. Playwright Eugene O'Neill based his stage play on memories of his youth at the turn of the century. B&W; 101m. **DIR:** Clarence Brown. **CAST:** Wallace Beery, Lionel Barrymore, Aline MacMahon, Cecilia Parker, Mickey Rooney, Eric Linden, Bonita Granville, Frank Albertson. **1935**

AIR RAID WARDENS ★★ The title tells all in this lesser effort from Stan Laurel and Oliver Hardy, which has them messing up on the home front until they capture a nest of saboteurs. Dated and disappointing. B&W; 67m. **DIR:** Edward Sedgwick. **CAST:** Stan Laurel, Oliver Hardy, Edgar Kennedy, Stephen McNally, Donald Meek. **1943**

AIR UP THERE, THE ★★ Aggressive college-basketball coach Kevin Bacon tries to recruit a Kenyan tribesman in a predictable, *Rocky*-type comedy-adventure about global sports imperialism. The white, alleged hero—who has a terminal me-first attitude—ends up leading the Winabi tribe in a hoops game against a rival clan for ancestral lands. Shot on location in South Africa and Kenya. Rated PG. 107m. **DIR:** Paul Michael Glaser. **CAST:** Kevin Bacon, Charles Gitonga Maina. **1994**

AIRBORNE ★★★ California-surf teen moves in with nerdy Cincinnati relatives and becomes a target of local toughs in this pubescent comedy. The landlocked hotdogger embraces a Gandhiesque pacifism when confronted by toughs, dates one bully's sister and—when the Midwest frost thaws—struts some amazing stuff on roller blades in a scorching downhill race finale. The rock-charged soundtrack includes original music by former Police drummer Stewart Copeland. Rated PG. 89m. **DIR:** Rob Bowman. **CAST:** Shane McDermott, Seth Green, Brittney Powell, Chris Conrad, Patrick O'Brien. **1993**

AIRPLANE! ★★★★ This is a hilarious spoof of the *Airport* series—and movies in general. While the jokes don't always work, there are so many of them that this comedy ends up with enough laughs for three movies. Rated PG. 88m. **DIR:** Jim Abrahams, David Zucker, Jerry Zucker. **CAST:** Robert Hays, Julie Hagerty, Leslie Nielsen, Kareem Abdul-Jabbar, Lloyd Bridges, Peter Graves, Robert Stack. **1980**

AIRPLANE II: THE SEQUEL ★★★½ Viewers who laughed uncontrollably through *Airplane!* will find much to like about this sequel. The stars of the original are back, with silly jokes and sight gags galore. However, those who thought the original was more stupid than funny undoubtedly will mutter the same about the sequel. Rated PG for occasional adult content. 85m. **DIR:** Ken Finkleman. **CAST:** Robert Hays, Julie Hagerty, Peter Graves, William Shatner. **1982**

ALEX IN WONDERLAND ★★ A self-conscious look at the film world that misses its mark in spite of good performances and some sharp jabs at the greed that controls Hollywood. Donald Sutherland is appropriately humble as a movie director trying to follow his first film with an even better one. Rated R. 110m. **DIR:** Paul Mazursky. **CAST:** Donald Sutherland, Ellen Burstyn, Paul Mazursky, Jeanne Moreau, Federico Fellini. **1970**

ALFIE ★★★★ Wild and ribald comedy about a Cockney playboy (Michael Caine) who finds "birds" irresistible. Full of sex and delightful charm, this quick-moving film also tells the poignant tragedy of a man uncertain about his life-style. Nominated for five Oscars, including best picture and best actor. 113m. **DIR:** Lewis Gilbert. **CAST:** Michael Caine, Shelley Winters, Millicent Martin, Julia Foster, Shirley Anne Field. **1966**

ALICE (1990) ★★★½ This takeoff on *Alice in Wonderland* is another light and sweet fantasy written and directed by Woody Allen. Supported by an all-star cast, Mia Farrow plays a wealthy New Yorker whose inner self is no longer fulfilled by an immense shopping habit. So she turns to a Chinese doctor (Keye Luke), whose magical herbs bring romance, spirituality, and even invisibility into her life. Rated PG-13 for profanity and sexual frankness. 100m. **DIR:** Woody Allen. **CAST:** Mia Farrow, Alec Baldwin, Blythe Danner, Judy Davis, William Hurt, Julie Kavner, Keye Luke, Joe Mantegna, Bernadette Peters, Cybill Shepherd, James Toback, Gwen Verdon. **1990**

ALL IN A NIGHT'S WORK ★★★ The heir to a publishing empire falls in love with a girl he believes has, at one time, been the mistress of his own uncle. This comedy starts well but lags before the finale. Harmless fun. 94m. **DIR:** Joseph Anthony. **CAST:** Shirley MacLaine, Dean Martin, Charlie Ruggles, Cliff Robertson, Gale Gordon, Jack Weston. **1961**

ALL IN THE FAMILY TWENTIETH ANNIVERSARY SPECIAL ★★★ Show creator Norman Lear hosts this nostalgic look back at one of the most influential television series in history. Includes vignettes from the program as well as interviews with the cast and viewers. Made for TV. 74m. **DIR:** Johnny Speight. **CAST:** Carroll O'Connor, Jean Stapleton, Rob Reiner, Sally Struthers. **1991**

ALL NIGHT LONG ★★★ Praised by some for its offbeat style and story, this comedy, starring the odd couple of Gene Hackman and Barbra Streisand, is only occasionally convincing. Hackman stars as an executive demoted to the position of managing a twenty-four-hour grocery store. There, he meets a daffy housewife (played by a miscast Streisand) and love blooms. 95m. **DIR:** Jean-Claude Tramont. **CAST:** Gene Hackman, Barbra Streisand. **1981**

ALL OF ME ★★★★½ Steve Martin finds himself haunted from within by the soul of a recently deceased Lily Tomlin when an attempt to put her spirit in another woman's body backfires. This delightful comedy gives its two stars the best showcase for their talents to date. Rated PG for suggested sex, violence, and profanity. 93m. **DIR:** Carl Reiner. **CAST:** Steve Martin, Lily Tomlin, Victoria Tennant, Richard Libertini. **1984**

ALL OVER TOWN ★★½ Stage favorites of the 1920s and 1930s, Olsen and Johnson display their zany patter and antics as they try to produce a show in a theater on which a hex has been put. Some funny moments, but most of this low-budget comedy is antiquated. B&W; 62m. **DIR:** James W. Horne. **CAST:** Chic Johnson, Ole Olsen, Franklin Pangborn, Mary Howard, James Finlayson. **1937**

ALL-STAR TOAST TO THE IMPROV, AN ★★★½ Robert Klein hosts this hour of outrageous comedy from the famous Improv club in Los Angeles. On view are some of the most gifted funny men to grace the stand-up spotlight. Originally produced for HBO cable television. Not rated. 60m. **DIR:** Walter C. Miller. **CAST:** Robert Klein, Billy Crystal, Richard Lewis, Martin Mull, Paul Rodriguez, Robin Williams. **1988**

ALL THE MARBLES 🦃 Peter Falk stars as the unscrupulous manager of two female wrestlers. Rated R because of nudity, violence, and profanity. 113m. **DIR:** Robert Aldrich. **CAST:** Peter Falk, Vicki Frederick, Laurene Landon, Burt Young, Tracy Reed. **1981**

ALL TIED UP ★★ C. Thomas Howell promises to give up his wild bachelor days for Teri Hatcher, but her roommates don't believe him. When he wavers, they kidnap him to teach him a lesson. Bondage has never been so mundane. Rated R for language and adult situations. 90m. **DIR:** John Mark Robinson. **CAST:** C. Thomas Howell, Teri Hatcher, Lara Harris, Tracy Griffith, Abel Folk. **1992**

ALLNIGHTER, THE 🦃 Terminally dumb 1980s beach movie. Rated PG-13. 90m. **DIR:** Tamar Simon Hoffs. **CAST:** Susanna Hoffs, John Terlesky, Joan Cusack, Dedee Pfeiffer, James Anthony Shanta, Janelle Brady. **1987**

ALL'S FAIR ★★ Male corporate executives battle their wives and female coworkers in a weekend war game. Good cast and a promising premise are both wasted in a lot of second-rate slapstick. Rated PG-13 for double entendre humor. 89m. **DIR:** Rocky Lane. **CAST:** George Segal, Sally Kellerman, Robert Carradine, Jennifer Edwards, Jane Kaczmarek, Lou Ferrigno. **1989**

...ALMOST ★★★ This Australian comedy is almost—but not quite —hilarious. Uneven timing takes the punch out of many of the sight gags as Rosanna Arquette recreates her bored wife ready-for-adventure role from *Desperately Seeking Susan.* Rated PG. 87m. **DIR:** Michael Pattinson. **CAST:** Rosanna Arquette, Bruce Spence. **1990**

ALMOST AN ANGEL ★★½ Paul Hogan gets his first non–"Crocodile" Dundee role as a professional thief in Los Angeles who becomes a probational angel in heaven. The film falls from there, as Hogan's comedy turns decidedly downbeat. Rated PG for mild profanity. 96m. **DIR:** John Cornell. **CAST:** Paul Hogan, Elias Koteas, Linda Kozlowski. **1990**

ALMOST PERFECT AFFAIR, AN ★★★½ A very human love triangle evolves amidst the frenzy of film politics that surrounds the Cannes Film Festival. This romantic comedy about a young American filmmaker and the worldly but lovable wife of a powerful Italian film mogul is slow to start, but leaves you with a warm feeling. Rated PG with suggested sex and partial nudity. 92m. **DIR:** Michael Ritchie. **CAST:** Keith Carradine, Monica Vitti, Raf Vallone. **1979**

ALMOST PREGNANT ★★½ Bedroom farce features Tanya Roberts as Jeff Conaway's desperate-to-be-pregnant wife. She recruits both a neighbor and an in-law as donors while her husband finds his own diversions. In both an R and an unrated version, each containing nudity and profanity. 93m. **DIR:** Michael DeLuise. **CAST:** Tanya Roberts, Jeff Conaway, Joan Severance, Dom DeLuise. **1991**

ALMOST YOU ★★★★ Brooke Adams and Griffin Dunne give excellent performances as a restless husband and his down-to-earth wife. Dunne perfectly emulates the frustrated over-30 businessman and husband with comic results. Adams plays his wife, who is recovering from a car accident that gives her a new perspective on life. Rated R for language, sex, and nudity. 91m. **DIR:** Adam Brooks. **CAST:** Brooke Adams, Griffin Dunne, Karen Young, Marty Watt. **1985**

ALWAYS (1984) ★★★ Largely autobiographical, *Always* follows Henry Jaglom and Patrice Townsend through their breakup and their reckoning of the relationship. This movie has a bittersweet feeling that is reminiscent of some of Woody Allen's films dealing with romance. Unfortunately, the movie doesn't have the laughs that Allen provides. Rated R for profanity and nudity. 105m. **DIR:** Henry Jaglom. **CAST:** Henry Jaglom, Patrice Townsend, Joanna Frank, Alan Rachins, Melissa Leo. **1984**

AMAZING ADVENTURE ★★★ Feeling guilty after inheriting a fortune, Cary Grant sets out to earn his living in this comedy of stout hearts among the poor-but-honest in England during the Depression. B&W; 70m. **DIR:** Alfred Zeisler. **CAST:** Cary Grant, Mary Brian, Peter Gawthorne, Henry Kendall, Leon M. Lion. **1936**

AMAZON WOMEN ON THE MOON ★★★ This silly scrapbook send-up of Saturday morning, sci-fi, and sitcom TV schlock stitches together star-strewn skits, but many of the plots are threadbare. When on the mark the chuckles come easily. More often, it's like the Not Ready for Prime Time Players on a not-so-prime night. Rated R for nudity. 85m. **DIR:** John Landis, Joe Dante, Carl Gottlieb, Peter Horton, Robert K. Weiss. **CAST:** Rosanna Arquette, Ralph Bellamy, Carrie Fisher, Sybil Danning, Steve Allen, Griffin Dunne, Steve Guttenberg, Ed Begley Jr., Arsenio Hall, Howard Hesseman, Russ Meyer, B. B. King, Henny Youngman. **1987**

AMBASSADOR BILL ★★★ This contrived comedy of pompous protocol versus common sense has amiable inexperienced cowpoke Will Rogers appointed ambassador to a revolution-wracked monarchy somewhere in Europe. Funny dialogue and absurd situations give the star plenty of laugh opportunities. B&W; 68m. **DIR:** Sam Taylor.

CAST: Will Rogers, Marguerite Churchill, Gustav von Seyffertitz, Ray Milland. 1931

AMBASSADOR'S DAUGHTER, THE ★★★ A beautiful Olivia de Havilland and a handsome John Forsythe star in this sophisticated romantic comedy about a congressman (Edward Arnold) attempting to curtail the amorous adventures of GIs in Paris. Winningly performed by all. 102m. **DIR:** Norman Krasna. **CAST:** Olivia de Havilland, John Forsythe, Myrna Loy, Adolphe Menjou, Tommy Noonan, Edward Arnold. 1956

AMERICA 🦃 This mess has a down-and-out cable station trying to get financial support from New York's latest $10 million lottery winner. Rated R. 90m. **DIR:** Robert Downey. **CAST:** Zack Norman, Tammy Grimes, Michael J. Pollard, Richard Belzer, Laura Ashton, Liz Torres. 1986

AMERICAN ARISTOCRACY, AN ★★★★ One of those early Douglas Fairbanks gems when he was more interested in strenuous acrobatics and satiric commentary than ponderous costume adventures. This one deflates the pretensions of Rhode Island society. Silent. B&W; 52m. **DIR:** Lloyd Ingraham. **CAST:** Douglas Fairbanks Sr., Jewel Carmen. 1916

AMERICAN DREAMER ★★★ JoBeth Williams plays Cathy Palmer, a would-be novelist who, in a short story contest, successfully captures the style of adventure stories that feature a superspy named Rebecca Ryan and wins a trip to Paris. But once there, Palmer is hit by a car and wakes up believing she is the fictional character. The picture never quite shines as brightly as one expects. Rated PG for violence. 105m. **DIR:** Rick Rosenthal. **CAST:** JoBeth Williams, Tom Conti, Giancarlo Giannini. 1984

AMERICAN FRIENDS ★★★★½ Michael Palin is an uptight Oxford instructor who learns to loosen up after meeting two American women while hiking in Switzerland. Cowriter Palin based this leisurely, elegant period piece, set in 1861, on one of his upstart ancestors. Witty and wonderful, it is a true romance in every sense of the word. Rated PG for adult themes. 95m. **DIR:** Tristram Powell. **CAST:** Michael Palin, Trini Alvarado, Connie Booth, Alfred Molina. 1993

AMERICAN GRAFFITI ★★★★½ *Star Wars* creator George Lucas discovered his talent for creating lighthearted, likable entertainment with this film about the coming-of-age of a group of high school students in northern California. Blessed with a superb rock 'n' roll score and fine performances, it's the best of its kind and inspired the long-running television series *Happy Days*. Rated PG. 110m. **DIR:** George Lucas. **CAST:** Richard Dreyfuss, Ron Howard, Paul LeMat, Cindy Williams, Candy Clark, Mackenzie Phillips, Harrison Ford, Bo Hopkins, Charles Martin Smith. 1973

AMERICANIZATION OF EMILY, THE ★★★½ Who would think of turning the Normandy invasion into a massive publicity event? According to screenwriter Paddy Chayefsky, the American military brass would drool over the possibilities. James Garner winningly plays the naval officer designated to be the first casualty on the beach. The script, intelligently handled by director Arthur Hiller, bristles with hard-edged humor. B&W; 117m. **DIR:** Arthur Hiller. **CAST:** James Garner, Julie Andrews, Melvyn Douglas, James Coburn, Joyce Grenfell, Keenan Wynn, Judy Carne. 1964

AMERICATHON 🦃 Abysmal comedy about a bankrupt American government staging a telethon to save itself. Rated R for profanity and sleaze. 86m. **DIR:** Neal Israel. **CAST:** John Ritter, Harvey Korman, Nancy Morgan, Peter Riegert, Zane Buzby, Fred Willard, Chief Dan George. 1979

AMOROUS ADVENTURES OF MOLL FLANDERS, THE ★★ Silly sex romp features a naughty Kim Novak sampling Englishmen's wares circa 1700. Howls rather than laughs result from her many sexual escapades. Unrated, this would be equivalent to a PG-13 for endless sexual situations and innuendo. 126m. **DIR:** Terence Young. **CAST:** Kim Novak, Angela Lansbury, Richard Johnson, George Sanders. 1965

AMOS & ANDREW ★★½ Samuel L. Jackson is a famous African-American playwright and activist who is mistaken for a burglar the first night in his new home on an exclusive New England resort island. Local sheriff Dabney Coleman forces jailed misfit Nicolas Cage to pretend to be a criminal who has taken Jackson hostage. Dumb but sometimes funny comedy full of goofy misunderstandings. Rated PG-13 for profanity and violence. 95m. **DIR:** E. Max Frye. **CAST:** Nicolas Cage, Samuel L. Jackson, Dabney Coleman, Michael Lerner, Margaret Colin, Brad Dourif, Chelcie Ross, Giancarlo Esposito. 1993

AMOS AND ANDY (TV SERIES) ★★★ Amos runs a cab company. Andy is his amiable, slow-witted partner. Kingfish is an inept con man who tries to get Andy involved in an endless series of often hilarious get-rich-quick schemes. The first major television show with an all-black cast, *Amos and Andy* features sharp writing, energetic humor, and witty, memorable performances. CBS pulled the show in 1966 amid charges of racism, and rightfully so in that era. Now these surprisingly timeless comedies have been released on video, and they can be enjoyed if taken in the proper context. B&W; 30m. **DIR:** Charles Barton. **CAST:** Tim Moore, Spencer Williams Jr., Alvin Childress, Ernestine Wade, Amanda Randolph. 1951–1953

AND NOW FOR SOMETHING COMPLETELY DIFFERENT ★★★½ Fitfully funny but still a treat for their fans, this was the first screen outing of the Monty Python comedy troupe. It's a collection of the best bits from the team's television series. With delightful ditties, such as "The Lumberjack Song," how can you go wrong? Rated PG. 89m. **DIR:** Ian McNaughton. **CAST:** John Cleese, Eric Idle, Terry Jones, Michael Palin, Graham Chapman, Terry Gilliam. **1972**

AND YOU THOUGHT YOUR PARENTS WERE WEIRD ★★ After the death of their inventor father, two brothers devote their time and energy to following in his footsteps. Celestial intervention instills the spirit of their dad into their latest invention: a robot. Thin family fare. Rated PG. 92m. **DIR:** Tony Goodson. **CAST:** Marcia Strassman, Joshua Miller, Edan Gross, Alan Thicke. **1991**

ANDROCLES AND THE LION ★★½ An incredible cast still can't save this plodding story of a mild-mannered tailor (Alan Young) whose act of kindness toward a lion helps to save a group of Christians. George Bernard Shaw's pointed retelling of an old fable loses its bite in this rambling production. B&W; 105m. **DIR:** Chester Erskine. **CAST:** Alan Young, Jean Simmons, Victor Mature, Robert Newton, Maurice Evans, Elsa Lanchester, Reginald Gardiner, Gene Lockhart, Alan Mowbray, John Hoyt, Jim Backus. **1952**

ANDY GRIFFITH SHOW, THE (TV SERIES) ★★★★ As of this writing, six volumes have been released of one of television's most fondly remembered situation comedies. This series takes place in fictitious Mayberry, North Carolina, a sleepy little town looked after by laid-back sheriff Andy Taylor (Andy Griffith) and his manic deputy, Barney Fife (Don Knotts, winner of numerous Emmy Awards for his portrayal). The volumes now available are *The Best of Barney, The Best of Floyd, The Best of Otis, The Best of Gomer, The Best of Ernest T. Bass,* and *The Vintage Years.* Each volume contains four episodes spotlighting a particular character's most memorable moments. B&W; 100m. **DIR:** Various. **CAST:** Andy Griffith, Don Knotts, Ron Howard, Jim Nabors, Frances Bavier, Howard McNear, George Lindsey, Hal Smith, Howard Morris. **1960–1965**

ANDY HARDY GETS SPRING FEVER ★★★ Another in the long-running series about all-American life in a small town. This installment finds Andy Hardy (Mickey Rooney) saddled with the trials and tribulations of producing his high school play. B&W; 85m. **DIR:** W. S. Van Dyke. **CAST:** Mickey Rooney, Lewis Stone, Fay Holden, Cecilia Parker, Ann Rutherford. **1939**

ANDY HARDY MEETS A DEBUTANTE ★★★ Mickey Rooney again portrays the all-American teenager who dominated the long-running series. Good, wholesome family-film fare. B&W; 86m. **DIR:** George B. Seitz. **CAST:** Mickey Rooney, Lewis Stone, Cecilia Parker, Fay Holden, Judy Garland. **1940**

ANDY HARDY'S DOUBLE LIFE ★★★ Fresh from championship swimming, Esther Williams got her studio start in this warm and sentimental addition to the hit series. B&W; 92m. **DIR:** George B. Seitz. **CAST:** Mickey Rooney, Lewis Stone, Cecilia Parker, Fay Holden, Ann Rutherford, Esther Williams, William Lundigan. **1942**

ANDY HARDY'S PRIVATE SECRETARY ★★★ Kathryn Grayson is the focus in this slice of wholesome Americana from the innocent days just before World War II. Fun for the whole family. B&W; 101m. **DIR:** George B. Seitz. **CAST:** Mickey Rooney, Lewis Stone, Fay Holden, Ian Hunter, Kathryn Grayson, Gene Reynolds, Ann Rutherford. **1940**

ANDY KAUFMAN SPECIAL, THE 🦃 It's not apparent why ABC would give Andy Kaufman any money to come up with this poor excuse for a network special, since Kaufman is about as funny as a hernia. Not rated. 59m. **DIR:** Tom Trbovich. **CAST:** Andy Kaufman, Cindy Williams. **1977**

ANIMAL BEHAVIOR ★★★ This comedy features Karen Allen as a behaviorist testing a chimp named Michael. Armand Assante, as the university's new music professor, falls for Allen. Plenty of misunderstandings add to the fun. Rated PG for no apparent reason. 79m. **DIR:** H. Anne Riley. **CAST:** Armand Assante, Karen Allen, Holly Hunter, Josh Mostel. **1989**

ANIMAL CRACKERS ★★★★ *Animal Crackers* is pure Marx Brothers, a total farce loosely based on a hit play by George S. Kaufman. Highlights include Groucho's African lecture—"One morning I shot an elephant in my pajamas. How he got into my pajamas, I'll never know"—and the card game with Harpo, Chico, and the ever-put-upon Margaret Dumont. B&W; 98m. **DIR:** Victor Heerman. **CAST:** The Marx Brothers, Margaret Dumont, Lillian Roth. **1930**

ANIMAL HOUSE ★★★★½ Although it has spawned a seemingly relentless onslaught of inferior carbon copies, this comedy is still one of the funniest movies ever made. If you're into rock 'n' roll, partying, and general craziness, this picture is for you. We gave it a 95, because it has a good beat and you can dance to it. Rated R. 109m. **DIR:** John Landis. **CAST:** John Belushi, Tim Matheson, Karen Allen, Peter Riegert, John Vernon, Tom Hulce. **1978**

ANNABEL TAKES A TOUR ★★½ A dizzy movie star and her fast-talking press agent concoct a publicity scheme. Harmless and mildly amusing, this brief programmer was the second in a series Lucille Ball and Jack Oakie did for RKO. B&W; 66m. **DIR:** Lew Landers. **CAST:** Lucille Ball, Jack Oakie, Ruth

Donnelly, Frances Mercer, Donald MacBride. 1938

ANNIE HALL ★★★★★ Woody Allen's exquisite romantic comedy won the 1977 Academy Awards for best picture, actress (Diane Keaton), director (Allen), and screenplay (Allen and Marshall Brickman)—and deserved every one of them. This delightful semiautobiographical romp features Allen as Alvy Singer, a more assured version of Alan Felix, from *Play It Again, Sam,* who falls in love (again) with Keaton (in the title role). Rated PG for profanity and bedroom scenes. 94m. **DIR:** Woody Allen. **CAST:** Woody Allen, Diane Keaton, Tony Roberts, Paul Simon, Shelley Duvall, Carol Kane. 1977

ANOTHER CHANCE ★★ An oversexed actor (Bruce Greenwood) is allowed to return to Earth in an attempt to be faithful to one woman. Greenwood's talented large white dog and the decent special effects in Heaven and Hell make this romp watchable. Rated R for nudity and profanity. 99m. **DIR:** Jerry Vint. **CAST:** Bruce Greenwood. 1988

ANOTHER YOU ★★ In their fourth film together, Gene Wilder and Richard Pryor star in a disappointing comedy involving mistaken identities. Wilder is a pathological liar just released from a mental institution, and Pryor is a con man doing community service as his caretaker. Rated R for profanity. 100m. **DIR:** Maurice Phillips. **CAST:** Gene Wilder, Richard Pryor, Mercedes Ruehl, Stephen Lang, Vanessa Williams. 1991

ANTONIA & JANE ★★★★ A perceptive British comedy about an unlikely friendship between two wildly different women. Antonia and Jane are the yin and yang of personalities, and neither has ever appreciated the turmoil in the other's life. Imagine a female and British twist on Woody Allen's comedic style. Unrated; the film has nudity, sex, and profanity. 77m. **DIR:** Beeban Kidron. **CAST:** Imelda Staunton, Saskia Reeves. 1991

ANY WEDNESDAY ★★ The spiciness of the original Broadway script gets lost in this film adaptation. Jason Robards Jr. plays the New York businessman who deducts his paramour's (Jane Fonda) apartment as a business expense. A poor man's *The Apartment.* 109m. **DIR:** Robert Ellis Miller. **CAST:** Jane Fonda, Jason Robards Jr., Dean Jones, Rosemary Murphy, Ann Prentiss. 1966

ANY WHICH WAY YOU CAN 💔 Another comedy clinker from Clint Eastwood and company. Rated PG. 116m. **DIR:** Buddy Van Horn. **CAST:** Clint Eastwood, Sondra Locke, Geoffrey Lewis, William Smith, Ruth Gordon. 1980

APARTMENT, THE ★★★★★ Rarely have comedy and drama been satisfyingly blended into a cohesive whole. Director Billy Wilder does it masterfully in this film. With career advancement in mind, Jack Lemmon permits his boss (Fred MacMurray) to use his apartment for illicit love affairs. Then he gets involved with the boss's emotionally distraught girlfriend (Shirley MacLaine). Lemmon sparkles. MacLaine is irresistible. And MacMurray, playing a heel, is a revelation. B&W; 125m. **DIR:** Billy Wilder. **CAST:** Jack Lemmon, Shirley MacLaine, Fred MacMurray, Ray Walston, Jack Kruschen, Edie Adams. 1960

APRIL FOOLS, THE 💔 A failed attempt at a serious romantic comedy that veers too often into awkward slapstick. Rated PG for adult situations. 95m. **DIR:** Stuart Rosenberg. **CAST:** Jack Lemmon, Catherine Deneuve, Peter Lawford, Sally Kellerman, Myrna Loy, Charles Boyer. 1969

ARE PARENTS PEOPLE? ★★★★ Lita (Betty Bronson) realizes she can get her estranged parents back together by indulging in some scandalous behavior. Nifty satire of 1920s social mores. Silent. B&W; 63m. **DIR:** Malcolm St. Clair. **CAST:** Betty Bronson, Florence Vidor, Adolphe Menjou. 1925

ARMED AND DANGEROUS 💔 Fired cop Frank Dooley (John Candy) and former lawyer Norman Kane (Eugene Levy), become private security guards. Rated PG-13 for language. 89m. **DIR:** Mark L. Lester. **CAST:** John Candy, Eugene Levy, Robert Loggia, Kenneth McMillan, Meg Ryan, Jonathan Banks, Brion James. 1986

ARMY BRATS 💔 This ridiculous comedy centers around the war taking place within the Gisbert family. Foreign, it is dubbed and unrated. The obscene language and nudity make it comparable to an R. 103m. **DIR:** Ruud van Hemert. **CAST:** Frank Schaafsma, Geert DeJong, Akemay, Peter Faber. 1984

AROUND THE WORLD IN 80 DAYS (1956) ★★★ An all-star extravaganza with David Niven, Cantinflas, and Shirley MacLaine in the pivotal roles, this inflated travelogue was a spectacular success when originally released. However, it seems hopelessly dated today and loses all too much on the small screen. Even picking out the dozens of stars in cameo roles doesn't yield as much joy as it could have. It's a curiosity at best. 167m. **DIR:** Michael Anderson. **CAST:** David Niven, Cantinflas, Shirley MacLaine, Marlene Dietrich, Robert Newton. 1956

AROUND THE WORLD IN 80 WAYS ★★ Despite a wonderfully goofy premise, this comedy from Down Under is just not very funny. Philip Quast is a young tour guide who must take his decrepit father on a world tour, but lacks the money so he fakes it, never leaving his neighborhood. Rated R for language and crudity. 90m. **DIR:** Stephen MacLean. **CAST:** Philip Quast. 1988

ARSENIC AND OLD LACE ★★★★½ Two sweet old ladies have found a solution for the loneliness of elderly men with no family or friends—they poison them! Then they give them a proper Christian burial in their basement. Their nephew, Mortimer (Cary Grant), an obvious party pooper, finds out and wants them to stop. This delightful comedy is crammed with sparkling performances. B&W; 118m. **DIR:** Frank Capra. **CAST:** Cary Grant, Priscilla Lane, Jack Carson, James Gleason, Peter Lorre, Raymond Massey, Jean Adair, Josephine Hull. **1944**

ARTHUR ★★★★ Dudley Moore is Arthur, the world's richest (and obviously happiest) alcoholic. But all is not well in his pickled paradise. Arthur will lose access to the family's great wealth if he doesn't marry the uptight debutante picked out for him by his parents. He doesn't love her...in fact, he doesn't even like her. And what's worse, he's in love with a wacky shoplifter (Liza Minnelli). Most of the time, it's hilarious, with John Gielgud as a sharp-tongued butler providing the majority of the laughs. Rated PG because of profanity. 97m. **DIR:** Steve Gordon. **CAST:** Dudley Moore, Liza Minnelli, Stephen Elliott, John Gielgud. **1981**

ARTHUR 2: ON THE ROCKS ★★ Some sequels simply don't take characters in the directions imagined by those who loved the original film, and *Arthur 2* is a case in point. Morose, uncomfortable, and marred by its badly contrived conclusion, call this one a good try. Rated PG for mild profanity. 99m. **DIR:** Bud Yorkin. **CAST:** Dudley Moore, Liza Minnelli, John Gielgud, Cynthia Sikes, Stephen Elliott, Paul Benedict, Geraldine Fitzgerald, Barney Martin. **1988**

ARTISTS AND MODELS ★★★ One of the better Martin and Lewis films features Dino as a cartoonist who gets his ideas from Jerry's dreams. Cowriter and director Frank Tashlin was a former cartoonist, and brought that preposterous visual style to this movie. 109m. **DIR:** Frank Tashlin. **CAST:** Dean Martin, Jerry Lewis, Shirley MacLaine, Eva Gabor, Anita Ekberg, Eddie Mayehoff. **1955**

AS YOU LIKE IT ★★★ Laurence Olivier is commanding as Orlando to beautiful Elisabeth Bergner's stylized Rosalind in this early filming of Shakespeare's delightful comedy. Lovers of the Bard will be pleased. B&W; 96m. **DIR:** Paul Czinner. **CAST:** Elisabeth Bergner, Laurence Olivier, Felix Aylmer, Leon Quartermaine. **1936**

AS YOUNG AS YOU FEEL ★★½ Marilyn Monroe's presence in a bit part, and the fact that Paddy Chayefsky provided the original story, are the main drawing cards today in this broad spoof of big business. B&W; 77m. **DIR:** Harmon Jones. **CAST:** Monty Woolley, Thelma Ritter, David Wayne, Jean Peters, Marilyn Monroe. **1951**

ASK ANY GIRL ★★★ A motivation researcher tries out his theories by helping a husband hunter to snag his playboy brother. The third male lead, lecherous Rod Taylor, steals the movie. 101m. **DIR:** Charles Walters. **CAST:** David Niven, Shirley MacLaine, Gig Young, Rod Taylor, Jim Backus. **1959**

ASSAULT & MATRIMONY ★★★ Likable made-for-television comedy pitting real-life husband-and-wife team Jill Eikenberry and Michael Tucker against each other as warring spouses trying to kill each other. 100m. **DIR:** James Frawley. **CAST:** Jill Eikenberry, Michael Tucker, John Hillerman, Michelle Phillips. **1987**

AT THE CIRCUS ★★★½ The Marx Brothers were running out of steam as a comedy team by this time. Still, any film with Groucho, Harpo, and Chico is worth watching, although you'll probably feel like punching the comedy's "hero" (or is that a zero?), Kenny Baker, when he sings that highly forgettable ditty "Step Up, Take a Bow." B&W; 87m. **DIR:** Edward Buzzell. **CAST:** The Marx Brothers, Margaret Dumont, Kenny Baker, Eve Arden. **1939**

AT WAR WITH THE ARMY ★★★★ Dean Martin and Jerry Lewis were still fresh and funny at the time of this comedy release, but a classic it isn't (though some scenes are gems). B&W; 93m. **DIR:** Hal Walker. **CAST:** Dean Martin, Jerry Lewis, Polly Bergen, Angela Greene, Mike Kellin. **1950**

ATOLL K (UTOPIA) 🦃 The final screen outing of the great comedy team of Stan Laurel and Oliver Hardy is a keen disappointment. B&W; 80m. **DIR:** Léo Joannon. **CAST:** Stan Laurel, Oliver Hardy. **1950**

ATOMIC KID, THE 🦃 Stupid story about prospector Mickey Rooney surviving an atomic bomb blast and attracting spies. B&W; 86m. **DIR:** Leslie Martinson. **CAST:** Mickey Rooney, Robert Strauss, Whit Bissell, Hal March. **1954**

ATTACK OF THE KILLER TOMATOES 🦃 In this campy cult film, the tomatoes are funnier than the actors, most of whom are rank amateurs. Rated PG. 87m. **DIR:** John DeBello. **CAST:** David Miller, Sharon Taylor, George Wilson, Jack Riley. **1980**

AUDIENCE WITH MEL BROOKS, AN ★★★½ This is a reserved, delightfully anecdotal evening with the comic genius. Filmed in England, it features Brooks answering questions from the audience about his career, life, and famous collaborators. 55m. **DIR:** Mel Brooks. **CAST:** Mel Brooks. **1984**

AUNTIE MAME ★★★½ Rosalind Russell, in the title role, plays a free-thinking eccentric woman whose young nephew is placed in her care. Russell created the role on the stage; it was a once-in-a-lifetime showcase that she made uniquely her own. 143m. **DIR:** Morton Da Costa. **CAST:** Rosalind Russell, Forrest Tucker, Coral Browne, Fred Clark. **1958**

AUTHOR! AUTHOR! ★★★ Al Pacino stars as a playwright whose wife (Tuesday Weld) leaves him with five kids (not all his) to raise in this nicely done bittersweet comedy. Dyan Cannon plays the actress with whom he falls in love. Rated PG for brief profanity. 110m. **DIR:** Arthur Hiller. **CAST:** Al Pacino, Dyan Cannon, Alan King, Tuesday Weld. **1982**

AVANTI! ★★★★ A cynical comedy in true Billy Wilder fashion with the antics of Jack Lemmon to make the ridiculous look sublime. Lemmon plays a man who goes to Europe to claim the body of his father and learns that Dad had a mistress, and the mistress had a voluptuous daughter. 144m. **DIR:** Billy Wilder. **CAST:** Jack Lemmon, Juliet Mills, Clive Revill, Edward Andrews. **1972**

AVERY SCHREIBER—LIVE FROM THE SECOND CITY ★★★½ Avery Schreiber hosts this TV special from Second City, the home of skit and improvisational comedy. Great skits and some familiar faces highlight this laughfest. Not rated but suitable for the whole family. 67m. **DIR:** Stan Jacobson. **CAST:** Avery Schreiber, Mary Gross, Tim Kazurinsky, Danny Breen, George Wendt. **1979**

AWFUL TRUTH, THE ★★★★ Irene Dunne and Cary Grant divorce so that they can marry others. Then they do their best to spoil one another's plans. Leo McCarey won an Oscar for directing this prime example of the screwball comedies that made viewing such a delight in the 1930s. Grant—a master of timing—is in top form, as is costar Dunne. It's hilarious all the way. B&W; 92m. **DIR:** Leo McCarey. **CAST:** Irene Dunne, Cary Grant, Ralph Bellamy, Molly Lamont. **1937**

BABY BOOM ★★★½ Yuppie fairy tale about a career woman (Diane Keaton) who finds her eighty-hour-per-week corporate job interrupted by the untimely arrival of a babe-in-arms. The laughs are frequent, but the film doesn't find any warmth until Keaton flees to the country and meets local veterinarian Sam Shepard. Rated PG for language. 103m. **DIR:** Charles Shyer. **CAST:** Diane Keaton, Harold Ramis, Sam Wanamaker, Pat Hingle, Sam Shepard. **1987**

BABY LOVE 🦃 This poorly dubbed Israeli-German teen sex comedy has no redeeming value. Unrated. 81m. **DIR:** Dan Wolman. **CAST:** Yftach Katzur, Zachi Noy, Jonathan Segall. **1983**

BABY OF THE BRIDE 🦃 Fifty-three-year-old bride Rue McClanahan finds herself pregnant at the same time as daughter Kristy McNichol, an unmarried former nun. Just too, too wacky. 93m. **DIR:** Bill Bixby. **CAST:** Rue McClanahan, Ted Shackelford, Kristy McNichol. **1991**

BACHELOR AND THE BOBBY-SOXER, THE ★★½ Lady judge Myrna Loy cleverly sentences playboy Cary Grant to baby-sit Shirley Temple, a panting nubile teenager. Some hilarious moments, but the comedy gets thin as Loy's lesson begins to cloy. Best bit is the play on words about the Man with the Power, Voodoo and Youdo. B&W; 95m. **DIR:** Irving Reis. **CAST:** Cary Grant, Myrna Loy, Shirley Temple, Rudy Vallee. **1947**

BACHELOR APARTMENT ★★½ Loose-living, wisecracking Lothario meets an unyielding stenographer. Oft-used plot gets special treatment from actor-director Lowell Sherman, who sacrifices anything for a great one-liner and makes this pre-Code corker remarkably fresh and fun. B&W; 74m. **DIR:** Lowell Sherman. **CAST:** Lowell Sherman, Irene Dunne, Mae Murray, Norman Kerry. **1931**

BACHELOR IN PARADISE ★★½ Author Bob Hope rents a home to do research on suburban mores and becomes confidant and adviser to the housewives in his neighborhood. Janis Paige and Paula Prentiss steal the movie. 109m. **DIR:** Jack Arnold. **CAST:** Bob Hope, Lana Turner, Janis Paige, Paula Prentiss, Jim Hutton, Agnes Moorehead, Don Porter. **1961**

BACHELOR MOTHER ★★★ The old story about a single woman who finds a baby on a doorstep and is mistaken for its mother has never been funnier than in this witty film by writer-director Garson Kanin. Ginger Rogers as the shop girl who finds her whole life upside down as a result of the confusion shows her considerable skill for comedy. David Niven, in an early starring role, is just great as the store owner's son who attempts to "rehabilitate" the fallen Rogers. B&W; 82m. **DIR:** Garson Kanin. **CAST:** Ginger Rogers, David Niven, Charles Coburn, Frank Albertson, Ernest Truex. **1939**

BACHELOR PARTY ★★ Even Tom Hanks (of *Splash*) can't save this "wild" escapade into degradation when a carefree bus driver who has decided to get married is given an all-out bachelor party by his friends. Rated R for profanity and nudity. 106m. **DIR:** Neal Israel. **CAST:** Tom Hanks, Tawny Kitaen, Adrian Zmed, George Grizzard, Robert Prescott. **1984**

BACK TO SCHOOL ★★★½ A true surprise from the usually acerbic Rodney Dangerfield, who sheds his lewd 'n' crude image in favor of one more sympathetic and controlled. He stars as the self-made owner of a chain of "Tall and Fat" stores who decides to return to college. He selects the college of his son in order to spend more time with the boy (well played by Keith Gordon). Rated PG-13 for occasionally vulgar humor. 96m. **DIR:** Alan Metter. **CAST:** Rodney Dangerfield, Sally Kellerman, Burt Young, Keith Gordon, Robert Downey Jr., Ned Beatty, M. Emmet Walsh, Adrienne Barbeau, William Zabka, Severn Darden. **1986**

BACKFIELD IN MOTION ★★★ Plenty to cheer about in this congenial comedy that makes it easy to rally behind Roseanne Arnold as the new mom-on-the-block, who organizes the local women into a football team to compete against their kids. Made-for-TV comedy, just wants to entertain, which it does. 95m. **DIR:** Richard Michaels. **CAST:** Roseanne Arnold, Tom Arnold, Colleen Camp, Conchata Ferrell. **1991**

BAD BEHAVIOUR ★★★½ There's not much plot in this slice-of-life film about the intertwining lives of several middle-class Londoners. What it lacks in story, though, it makes up for with warmth, humor, and nicely turned character touches. Improvised by the talented cast, the film takes awhile to get rolling, but patience will be rewarded. Rated R for language and mature themes. 103m. **DIR:** Les Blair. **CAST:** Stephen Rea, Sinead Cusack, Philip Jackson, Phil Daniels, Saira Todd. **1993**

BAD GOLF MADE EASIER ★★★ Leslie Nielsen, playing up the image for foolishness he gained as Frank Drebin in *Police Squad!*, removes some of the mystery found within the game "...called golf because all the other four-letter words were taken." While amusing in its own right, this made-for-video piece also takes a badly needed swipe at many of the game's pretentious conventions. 40m. **DIR:** Rick Friedberg. **CAST:** Leslie Nielsen, Robert Donner, Archie Hahn. **1993**

BAD MANNERS ★★ Wickedly selfish Martin Mull and Karen Black adopt a ratty little boy in the hopes of bringing some normalcy into their strange family. The idea probably looked hysterical on paper, but quickly turns into a sophomoric take on life. Rated R. 85m. **DIR:** Bobby Houston. **CAST:** Martin Mull, Karen Black, Anne De Salvo, Murphy Dunne. **1984**

BAD MEDICINE ★★★½ Steve Guttenburg and Julie Hagerty play students attending a "Mickey Mouse" med school in Central America. When they find the health conditions in a nearby village unacceptable, they set up a medical clinic. The all-star cast does not disappoint. Rated PG-13 for profanity, sex, and adult situations. 97m. **DIR:** Harvey Miller. **CAST:** Steve Guttenberg, Julie Hagerty, Alan Arkin, Bill Macy, Curtis Armstrong, Julie Kavner, Joe Grifasi, Robert Romanus, Taylor Negron. **1985**

BAD NEWS BEARS, THE ★★★★★ An utterly hilarious comedy directed by Michael Ritchie, this film focuses on the antics of some foul-mouthed Little Leaguers, their beer-guzzling coach (Walter Matthau), and girl pitcher (Tatum O'Neal). But be forewarned, the sequels, *Breaking Training* and *The Bad News Bears Go to Japan*, are strictly no-hitters. Rated PG. 102m. **DIR:** Michael Ritchie. **CAST:** Walter Matthau, Tatum O'Neal, Vic Morrow, Alfred Lutter, Jackie Earle Haley. **1976**

BAD NEWS BEARS GO TO JAPAN, THE 🦃 Worst of the *Bad News Bears* trio of films, this features Tony Curtis as a small-time promoter with big ideas. Rated PG. 91m. **DIR:** John Berry. **CAST:** Tony Curtis, Jackie Earle Haley, Tomisaburo Wakayama, George Wyner, Lonny Chapman. **1978**

BAD NEWS BEARS IN BREAKING TRAINING, THE ★★ Without Walter Matthau, Tatum O'Neal, and director Michael Ritchie, this sequel to *The Bad News Bears* truly is bad news...and rather idiotic. Jackie Earle Haley returns as the team star, and William Devane has a reasonable part as Haley's footloose father. Don't expect much. Rated PG for mild profanity. 100m. **DIR:** Michael Pressman. **CAST:** William Devane, Jackie Earle Haley, Clifton James. **1977**

BAGDAD CAFÉ ★★★★ This delightfully offbeat comedy-drama concerns a German businesswoman who appears in the minuscule desert town in California called Bagdad. She and the highly strung owner of the town's only diner-hotel have a major culture and personality clash. Jack Palance as a bandanna-wearing artist is so perfectly weird he practically walks off with the film. Rated PG. 91m. **DIR:** Percy Adlon. **CAST:** Marianne Sägebrecht, C.C.H. Pounder, Jack Palance. **1988**

BALL OF FIRE ★★★½ Stuffy linguistics professor Gary Cooper meets hotcha-cha dancer Barbara Stanwyck. He and seven lovable colleagues are putting together an encyclopedia. She's recruited to fill them in on slanguage. She does this, and more! Gangster Dana Andrews and motor-mouthed garbage man Allen Jenkins add to the madcap antics in what has been dubbed the last of the prewar screwball comedies. Good show! B&W; 111m. **DIR:** Howard Hawks. **CAST:** Gary Cooper, Barbara Stanwyck, Dana Andrews, Oscar Homolka, S. Z. Sakall, Richard Haydn, Henry Travers, Tully Marshall, Allen Jenkins. **1941**

BALLOONATIC, THE/ONE WEEK ★★★ The comedic invention and physical stamina of the Great Stone Face, as Buster Keaton was called, are shown to perfect advantage in these early 1920s silent shorts. In *The Balloonatic* Buster is "skyjacked" by a runaway balloon and dropped into the wilderness. In *One Week* he constructs a kit house from fouled-up assembly plans. An ample demonstration of why Keaton was one of the great silent comics. Silent. B&W; 48m. **DIR:** Buster Keaton, Eddie Cline. **CAST:** Buster Keaton, Phyllis Haver, Sybil Seely. **1920–1923**

BALTIMORE BULLET, THE ★★½ In this tale of big-league pool hustling, clever cuesters James Coburn and Bruce Boxleitner carefully build up to scoring big in a nail-biting shoot-out with suave Omar Sharif. Rated PG. 103m. **DIR:** Robert Ellis Miller. **CAST:** James Coburn, Bruce Boxleitner, Omar Sharif, Ronee Blakley. **1980**

BANANAS ★★★★ Before he started making classic comedies, such as *Annie Hall*, *Zelig*, and *Broadway Danny Rose*, writer-director-star Woody Allen made some pretty wild—though generally uneven—wacky movies. This 1971 comedy, with Woody's hapless hero becoming involved in a South American revolution, does have its share of hilarious moments. Rated PG. 82m. **DIR:** Woody Allen. **CAST:** Woody Allen, Louise Lasser, Carlos Montalban, Howard Cosell. **1971**

BANANAS BOAT, THE 🦃 This purported comedy has no plot, no acting, and no laughs. Rated PG for naughty language and nudity. 91m. **DIR:** Sidney Hayers. **CAST:** Doug McClure, Hayley Mills, Lionel Jeffries, Warren Mitchell. **1974**

BANG BANG KID, THE ★★½ Goofy comedy-Western with Tom Bosley as Merriweather Newberry, the inventor of a robot gunfighter (dubbed The Bang Bang Kid). The residents of a mining community hope that they can use it to defeat Bear Bullock (Guy Madison), the town boss. Good for kids; passable for grownups in a silly mood. 90m. **DIR:** Stanley Prager. **CAST:** Guy Madison, Sandra Milo, Tom Bosley, Riccardo Garrone. **1968**

BANK DICK, THE ★★★★★ W. C. Fields is at his best in this laugh-filled comedy. In it, Fields plays a drunkard who becomes a hero. But the story is just an excuse for the moments of hilarity—of which there are many. B&W; 74m. **DIR:** Eddie Cline. **CAST:** W. C. Fields, Cora Witherspoon, Una Merkel, Shemp Howard. **1940**

BANK ROBBER 🦃 Shallow, bungling thief sticks up a downtown bank and spends the rest of the movie hiding out in a seedy, nearby hotel in this offbeat but dumb comedy caper. Rated NC-17 for sex, violence, and language. 95m. **DIR:** Nick Mead. **CAST:** Patrick Dempsey, Lisa Bonet, Olivia D'Abo, Forest Whitaker, Judge Reinhold, Michael Jeter. **1993**

BANK SHOT 🦃 George C. Scott as a lisping mastermind who plots to steal a bank by putting it on wheels. PG for language. 100m. **DIR:** Gower Champion. **CAST:** George C. Scott, Joanna Cassidy, Don Calfa. **1974**

BARE ESSENTIALS ★★ A yuppie guy and gal find themselves reevaluating their relationship after being shipwrecked on a tiny atoll. Plodding. 94m. **DIR:** Martha Coolidge. **CAST:** Mark Linn-Baker, Lisa Hartman, Gregory Harrison, Charlotte Lewis. **1990**

BAREFOOT IN THE PARK ★★★★½ A young Robert Redford and Jane Fonda team up as newlyweds in this adaptation of Neil Simon's Broadway play. The comedy focuses on the adjustments of married life. Mildred Natwick plays the mother-in-law, and Charles Boyer is a daffy, unconventional neighbor. 105m. **DIR:** Gene Saks. **CAST:** Robert Redford, Jane Fonda, Charles Boyer, Mildred Natwick, Herb Edelman. **1967**

BARNABY AND ME ★★★ Sid Caesar's considerable comic talents aren't exactly strained in this Australian feature. Still, this lightweight story of a con man who mends his ways when he meets a young girl and her pet koala is good family viewing—a few laughs, and who can resist a koala bear? Rated G. 90m. **DIR:** Norman Panama. **CAST:** Sid Caesar, Juliet Mills. **1977**

BARRY MCKENZIE HOLDS HIS OWN ★★½ Extremely vulgar comedy based on a popular Australian comic strip about the adventures of beer-swilling Aussie Barry Crocker trying to rescue his auntie (Barry Humphries in drag as "Dame Edna Everage") from vampire Count Plasma (Donald Pleasence). You'll either be appalled or laugh yourself sick, though the impenetrable slang may make you wish the movie was subtitled. Unrated. 93m. **DIR:** Bruce Beresford. **CAST:** Barry Crocker, Barry Humphries, Donald Pleasence. **1974**

BARTON FINK ★★★★ More inspired madness from the Coen Brothers, Joel and Ethan. John Turturro stars as a New York playwright whose success on the stage, with a play celebrating the common man, leads to a lucrative screenwriting assignment. Funny but surreal. Rated R for profanity. 112m. **DIR:** Joel Coen. **CAST:** John Turturro, John Goodman, John Mahoney, Judy Davis, Jon Polito, Michael Lerner, Tony Shaloub. **1991**

BASED ON AN UNTRUE STORY ★★ A good cast and strong script can sometimes pull off a tongue-in-cheek farce. But not this time. This made-for-TV movie—about a perfume maker (Morgan Fairchild) who must find her long-lost siblings in order to save her damaged olfactory nerves—is short on laughs and long on tedium. The only funny bits involve a child trapped in a Gucci-painted trash dumpster in Beverly Hills, but that has nothing to do with the rest of the film. Not rated, but contains suggested sex. 91m. **DIR:** Jim Drake. **CAST:** Morgan Fairchild, Dan Hedaya, Victoria Jackson, Harvey Korman, Robert Goulet, David Byron, Ricki Lake, Dyan Cannon. **1993**

BASIC TRAINING 🦃 A small-town girl ends up at the Pentagon. A vehicle for T&A. Rated R for language. 86m. **DIR:** Andrew Sugerman. **CAST:** Ann Dusenberry, Rhonda Shear, Angela Aames, Walter Gotell. **1984**

BATTLE OF THE BOMBS ★★★ For viewers who aren't rabid bad-movie buffs, this compilation selects the highlights (or should we say lowlights?) of some of the most entertainingly awful movies ever made, including *Eegah! The Terror of Tiny Town*, *Plan 9 From Outer Space*, and *The Creeping Terror*. Unrated, no objectionable material. 60m. **DIR:** Johnny Legend. **1991**

BATTLE OF THE SEXES, THE ★★★½ Peter Sellers is wonderful as an elderly Scottish Highlander bent on murder. Robert Morley, always a favorite, is simply delightful and helps keep this British comedy on a fast and funny track. B&W; 88m. **DIR:** Charles Crichton. **CAST:** Peter Sellers, Robert Morley, Constance Cummings, Jameson Clark. **1960**

BAWDY ADVENTURES OF TOM JONES, THE 🦃 This ridiculous romp features Trevor Howard as the lecherous Squire Western. Young Tom Jones (played by an innocent-looking Nick Henson), is in love with Western's daughter and spends the entire film hoping to win her hand. Rated R for nudity. 89m. **DIR:** Cliff Owen. **CAST:** Nicky Henson, Trevor Howard, Joan Collins, Arthur Lowe, Georgia Brown, Madeleine Smith, Jeremy Lloyd. **1976**

BEACH GIRLS, THE 🦃 Teenage girls throw a big party at their uncle's Malibu beach house. Rated R for nudity. 91m. **DIR:** Pat Townsend. **CAST:** Debra Blee, Val Kline, Jeana Tomasina. **1982**

BEACH HOUSE 🦃 Mirthless comedy about a feud between Italian kids from Brooklyn and snobs from Philadelphia. Rated PG. 75m. **DIR:** John Gallagher. **CAST:** Ileana Seidel, John Cosola. **1982**

BEACHBALLS 🦃 Another sleazy teen tumble. Rated R for nudity and profanity. 79m. **DIR:** Joe Ritter. **CAST:** Phillip Paley, Heidi Helmer. **1988**

BEAT THE DEVIL ★★★★ Because it's all played straight, critics and audiences alike didn't know what to make of this delightful though at times baffling satire of films in the vein of *The Maltese Falcon* and *Key Largo* when it first hit screens. Sadly, some still do not. Nonetheless, this droll comedy, cobbled on location in Italy by John Huston and Truman Capote, is a twenty-four-carat gem. B&W; 93m. **DIR:** John Huston. **CAST:** Humphrey Bogart, Robert Morley, Peter Lorre, Jennifer Jones, Gina Lollobrigida. **1954**

BEAUTIFUL BLONDE FROM BASHFUL BEND, THE ★★½ Sharpshooter-schoolmarm Betty Grable has boyfriend trouble and must deal with a kidnapping and a philandering Cesar Romero in this wacky Western farce. Tolerable family fun, but not a highlight in director Preston Sturges's career. 77m. **DIR:** Preston Sturges. **CAST:** Betty Grable, Cesar Romero, Rudy Vallee, Olga San Juan, Sterling Holloway, Hugh Herbert, Porter Hall, Margaret Hamilton. **1949**

BEAUTY SCHOOL 🦃 *Emmanuelle* star Sylvia Kristel seriously needs a career make over as the owner of a beauty school who's in a desperate race to win a lucrative advertising contract. Just another lame excuse to get women naked. Rated R for nudity and adult situations. 95m. **DIR:** Ernest G. Sauer. **CAST:** Sylvia Kristel, Kevin Bernhardt, Kimberly Taylor, Jane Hamilton. **1992**

BEBE'S KIDS ★★½ The comedy routines of the late, great black comedian Robin Harris were adapted to create this animated comedy. Harris's first date with a beautiful woman becomes a nightmare when he reluctantly agrees to take along her neighbor's troublemaking kids. Part *The Simpsons*, part *Alvin and the Chipmunks*, and part Harris, this was obviously a heartfelt project for all concerned. It just isn't that good. Rated PG-13 for profanity and violence. 93m. **DIR:** Bruce Smith. **1992**

BEDAZZLED ★★★★ A cult favorite, this British comedy stars Dudley Moore as a fry cook tempted by the devil (played by his onetime comedy partner, Peter Cook). Costarring Raquel Welch, it's an often hilarious updating of the Faust legend. 107m. **DIR:** Stanley Donen. **CAST:** Peter Cook, Dudley Moore, Raquel Welch, Eleanor Bron. **1967**

BEDTIME FOR BONZO ★★★ This sweet-natured film is worth watching. Ronald Reagan plays a young college professor who uses a chimpanzee to prove that environment, not heredity, determines a person's moral fiber. He hires a young woman (Diana Lynn) to pose as the chimp's mom while he plays father to it. Not surprisingly, Mom and Dad fall in love. B&W; 83m. **DIR:** Frederick de Cordova. **CAST:** Ronald Reagan, Diana Lynn, Walter Slezak, Jesse White. **1951**

BEDTIME STORY ★★★ A European playboy (David Niven) and a wolfish American GI (Marlon Brando, somewhat miscast), propose to settle their differences with a bet: the first to seduce naive contest winner Shirley Jones becomes King of the Cosmopolitan Hill, and the other must quietly fade away. Although often quite sexist, the result is much funnier than the shallow concept would suggest. Remade as *Dirty Rotten Scoundrels*. Suggestive themes. 99m. **DIR:** Ralph Levy. **CAST:** David Niven, Marlon Brando, Shirley Jones. **1964**

BEER ★★★★ Hilarious comedy that examines the seamy side of the advertising industry. Loretta Swit plays a cold-blooded advertising agent who tries to turn three ordinary guys (David Alan Grier, William Russ, and Saul Stein) into beer-drinking American heroes. Dick Shawn's impression of Phil Donahue must be seen to be believed. Rated R for profanity, sex, and adult subject matter. 83m. **DIR:** Patrick Kelly. **CAST:** Loretta Swit, Rip Torn, Kenneth Mars, David Alan Grier, William Russ, Peter Michael Goetz, Dick Shawn, Saul Stein. **1985**

BEETLEJUICE ★★★ Like a cinematic trip through the Haunted Mansion, this film may require two viewings just to catch all the complex action and visual jokes. Alec Baldwin and Geena Davis play a young couple who accidentally drown and return as novice ghosts. The family that moves into their pretty little Connecticut farmhouse seems intent on destroying it aesthetically, and the ghostly couple are forced to call on the evil Betelguese (Michael Keaton). Rated PG for shock action and language. 93m. **DIR:** Tim Burton. **CAST:** Alec Baldwin, Geena Davis, Michael Keaton, Jeffrey Jones, Catherine O'Hara, Winona Ryder. **1988**

BEING THERE ★★★★½ This sublimely funny and bitingly satiric comedy features Peter Sellers's last great screen performance. His portrayal of a simple-minded gardener—who knows only what he sees on television yet rises to great political heights—is a classic. Shirley MacLaine and Melvyn Douglas are also excellent in this memorable film, directed by Hal Ashby. Rated PG. 130m. **DIR:** Hal Ashby. **CAST:** Peter Sellers, Shirley MacLaine, Melvyn Douglas, Jack Warden. **1979**

BELL, BOOK AND CANDLE ★★★½ A modestly entertaining bit of whimsy about a beautiful witch (Kim Novak) who works her magic on an unsuspecting publisher (James Stewart). Although the performances (including those in support by Jack Lemmon, Ernie Kovacs, and Hermione Gingold) are fine, this comedy is only mildly diverting. 103m. **DIR:** Richard Quine. **CAST:** James Stewart, Kim Novak, Jack Lemmon, Ernie Kovacs. **1958**

BELLBOY, THE ★★ A typical hour-plus of Jerry Lewis mugging and antics so dear to those who find him funny. This time around, Jerry is a bellboy at a swank hotel. Years ago, "Fatty" Arbuckle made a film of the same name that was funny. This, unfortunately, is plotless drivel seasoned with guest appearances by Milton Berle and Walter Winchell. Rated G when rereleased in 1972. B&W; 72m. **DIR:** Jerry Lewis. **CAST:** Jerry Lewis, Alex Gerry, Sonny Sands. **1960**

BELLBOY AND THE PLAYGIRLS, THE ★★ Innocuous sex comedy about a bellboy who practices to be a private eye. This would be long forgotten but for the fact that it's Francis Ford Coppola's first screen credit. He added some color sequences for the U.S. release of this 1958 German movie. Unrated, the film has nudity. 94m. **DIR:** Fritz Umgelter, Francis Ford Coppola. **CAST:** June Wilkinson. **1962**

BELLE OF THE NINETIES ★★★½ A stereotypical Mae West vehicle, but the censors' scissors are obvious. She sings, talks back, and tangles with a boxer who wants to tame her. Some of her most famous witticisms and her better songs are in this film. Like other Mae West films, this one is a series of one-liners between clinches that spoof the battle of the sexes. B&W; 73m. **DIR:** Leo McCarey. **CAST:** Mae West, Johnny Mack Brown, Roger Pryor, John Miljan, Duke Ellington. **1934**

BELLES OF ST. TRINIAN'S, THE ★★★½ Alastair Sim doubles as the dotty headmistress of a bonkers school for girls and her crafty bookie brother, who wants to use the place as a cover for his nefarious operations. Joyce Grenfell adds to the hilarity in this British comedy based on English cartoonist Ronald Searle's schoolgirls with a genius for mischief. B&W; 90m. **DIR:** Frank Launder. **CAST:** Alastair Sim, Joyce Grenfell, Hermione Baddeley, George Cole. **1955**

BENEATH THE VALLEY OF THE ULTRA-VIXENS 🦃 A chaotic sexual odyssey concerning neurotic behavior among the residents of a small southern California community. Explicit nudity and language. 93m. **DIR:** Russ Meyer. **CAST:** Francesca "Kitten" Natividad, Anne Marie, Ken Kerr, June Mack. **1979**

BENNY & JOON ★★★½ Most viewers will enjoy this bittersweet comedy about a mentally ill artist who finds love with a quirky outsider, much to her older brother-guardian's chagrin. Folks coping with mental illness in real life will be offended by yet another film in which the problem is sanitized and trivialized. Rated PG for suggested sex and brief violence. 100m. **DIR:** Jeremiah S. Chechik. **CAST:** Johnny Depp, Mary Stuart Masterson, Aidan Quinn, Julianne Moore, Oliver Platt, C.C.H. Pounder, Dan Hedaya, Joe Grifasi, William H. Macy. **1993**

BERNARD AND THE GENIE ★★★ Pleasantly amusing Christmas movie from BBC-TV stars British comedian Lenny Henry as the genie in the lamp, released by a mild-mannered London art dealer who's having a really bad day. Once the genie is freed, the fun begins. 70m. **DIR:** Paul Welland. **CAST:** Lenny Henry, Rowan Atkinson. **1991**

BERNICE BOBS HER HAIR ★★★★ The perceptions of self-worth and personal integrity form the core of this droll adaptation of F. Scott Fitzgerald's ode to a shy young girl. Bernice (Shelley Duvall) sacrifices her luxuriously long hair for a shot at the inner circle of popularity jealously guarded by her hedonistic Jazz Era friends. Veronica Cartwright is wonderfully malignant as the fickle society girl who plays *Pygmalion* with her shy, unassuming cousin. Introduced by Henry Fonda. 49m. **DIR:** Joan Micklin Silver. **CAST:** Shelley Duvall, Veronica Cartwright, Bud Cort, Dennis Christopher, Gary Springer, Lane Binkley, Polly Holliday. **1976**

BEST DEFENSE ★★★ Any movie that features the talents of Dudley Moore and Eddie Murphy has to be funny. Sometimes, however, laughs aren't enough. It's very easy to get confused in this film featuring Moore as the inept inventor of a malfunctioning piece of defense equipment, and Murphy as the hapless soldier forced to cope with it.

The liberal use of profanity and several sex scenes make this R-rated romp unfit for youngsters. 94m. **DIR:** Willard Huyck. **CAST:** Dudley Moore, Eddie Murphy, Kate Capshaw, George Dzundza, Helen Shaver. 1984

BEST FRIENDS ★★ Burt Reynolds and Goldie Hawn star in this disappointingly tepid romantic comedy as a pair of successful screenwriters who decide to marry—thus destroying their profitable working relationship. A mess. Rated PG for profanity and adult situations. 116m. **DIR:** Norman Jewison. **CAST:** Burt Reynolds, Goldie Hawn, Ron Silver, Jessica Tandy. 1982

BEST LEGS IN THE 8TH GRADE, THE ★★★ Bittersweet made-for-TV comedy focusing on the complexities of modern romance. Tim Matheson is a yuppie lawyer who gets some much-needed advice on the affairs of the heart. Annette O'Toole plays his girlfriend. 48m. **DIR:** Tom Patchett. **CAST:** Tim Matheson, Annette O'Toole, James Belushi, Kathryn Harrold. 1984

BEST OF AMERICA'S FUNNIEST HOME VIDEOS, THE ★★★ A collection of the best clips from the hit TV series in which people send in funny or memorable moments captured on video. 35m. **DIR:** Steve Hirsen. **CAST:** Bob Saget. 1991

BEST OF BENNY HILL, THE ★★★ If lewd and crude don't offend thee, then you'll enjoy this compilation of Benny Hill's antics for British TV. Hill's slapstick flair is best in a skit about Robin Hood. Unrated, but contains sexual innuendos. 120m. **DIR:** Dennis Kirkland. **CAST:** Benny Hill. 1980

BEST OF CANDID CAMERA, THE ★★★½ Classic moments in candid comedy date from the Sixties forward. Woody Allen deadpans as a boss composing a dramatic love letter to his unsuspecting secretary, while Loni Anderson poses as a sexy counselor to some overwhelmed teenage boys. B&W/color; 30m. **DIR:** Allen Funt. **CAST:** Allen Funt. 1985

BEST OF CHEVY CHASE, THE ★★★½ Though he only appeared on *Saturday Night Live* for one year, Chevy Chase was the series' first star and this compilation of skits shows why. Chase never sank deep into character like Dan Aykroyd or John Belushi; rather, he basically played himself. This tape contains some of Chase's most memorable pieces of comedy: Gerald Ford in the Oval Office, the sneaky land shark in a *Jaws* sequel... The "Weekend Update" segments, though, are pulled from several different broadcasts, which throws off their pacing. 60m. **DIR:** Dave Wilson. **CAST:** Chevy Chase, Dan Aykroyd, John Belushi, Jane Curtin, Garrett Morris, Bill Murray, Laraine Newman, Gilda Radner, Candice Bergen, Ron Nessen, Richard Pryor. 1987

BEST OF COMIC RELIEF, THE ★★ A very disappointing concert tape by some of the great names of stand-up comedy, past and present, who banded together on March 29, 1986, in a benefit concert for the homeless of Los Angeles. The original HBO show was three hours long, yet the tape is only two hours. The editor went after the older comedians with a chain saw, thereby desecrating some classic bits, and left some unfunny stuff by the new wave of comics. Unrated, but contains adult situations and profanity. 120m. **DIR:** Walter C. Miller. **CAST:** Robin Williams, Billy Crystal, Whoopi Goldberg, Martin Short, Harold Ramis, George Carlin, Sid Caesar, Carl Reiner, Steve Allen. 1986

BEST OF DAN AYKROYD, THE ★★★★ The title notwithstanding, this is a collaborative effort; some of the best skits of *Saturday Night Live* from 1975 to 1979. As in *The Best of John Belushi*, the namesake is not always the center of attention. Also, some of these pieces ("The Two Wild and Crazy Guys: the Festrunk Brothers" and "The Final Days of the Nixon Presidency") haven't worn well over the last half decade. Even so, the shortcomings don't matter when you are rolling on the floor. 56m. **DIR:** Dave Wilson. **CAST:** Dan Aykroyd, John Belushi, Chevy Chase, Jane Curtin, Garrett Morris, Bill Murray, Laraine Newman, Gilda Radner, Shelley Duvall, Madeline Kahn, Margot Kidder, Steve Martin. 1986

BEST OF DC FOLLIES ★★ A rather unfunny compilation of skits from the TV show of the same name. If you happen to like *DC Follies* (the Krofft puppets are very good), then you would like this series of tapes. Everybody else should leave it on the shelf. Not rated. 45m. **DIR:** Rick Locke. **CAST:** Fred Willard. 1988

BEST OF GILDA RADNER, THE ★★★★ Of all the *Saturday Night Live* stars, none shone brighter than Gilda Radner. Her characterizations—of Baba Wawa, Emily Litella, Roseanne Rosannadanna, and Lisa Loopner—were classics, and are well represented in this package produced by the show's creator, Lorne Michaels. Also included is her brilliant bit with Steve Martin, "Dancing in the Dark," and an homage to *I Love Lucy*. Hilarious and poignant reminder of a great talent. 59m. **DIR:** Dave Wilson. **CAST:** Gilda Radner, John Belushi, Chevy Chase, Dan Aykroyd, Jane Curtin, Bill Murray, Steve Martin, Candice Bergen, Madeline Kahn, Buck Henry. 1989

BEST OF JOHN BELUSHI, THE ★★★½ A collection of skits from *Saturday Night Live* shows between 1975 and 1979. From "Samurai Delicatessen" to his hilarious Joe Cocker impression, this is John Belushi at his best. The tape ends with Tom Schiller's short subject "Don't Look Back in Anger," the now-ironic piece that is set in the future where Belushi visits the graves of his fellow Not Ready for Prime Time Players who he "outlived." 60m. **DIR:** Dave Wilson. **CAST:** John Belushi, Dan Aykroyd, Chevy Chase, Jane Curtin, Garrett Morris, Bill Murray, Laraine Newman, Gilda Radner, Elliott Gould, Buck Henry, Robert Klein, Rob Reiner. **1985**

BEST OF JOHN CANDY, THE ★★★★ No tape running a little over one hour could contain all of the best of John Candy's work from the classic show *SCTV*, but at least this compilation touches on all of his best characters. Johnny LaRue, Yosh Schmenge, and Dr. Tongue (star of the world's cheesiest 3-D movies) share space with hilarious impressions of Divine, Jake LaMotta, Luciano Pavarotti, and Julia Child (as a wrestler!). 62m. **DIR:** John Bell, Milad Bessada, John Blanchard, George Bloomfield, Jim Drake. **CAST:** John Candy, Joe Flaherty, Dave Thomas, Andrea Martin, Rick Moranis, Catherine O'Hara, Eugene Levy, Martin Short. **1992**

BEST OF NOT NECESSARILY THE NEWS, THE ★★★★ A first-rate collection of some of the wittiest and funniest moments from the HBO comedy series, which satirizes network news and its commercials. Bits range from cerebral to pure slapstick as the zany cast covers everything from Reagan to feminine hygiene products. Unrated. 57m. **DIR:** John Moffitt, Hoite C. Caston. **CAST:** Anne Bloom, Danny Breen, Rich Hall, Mitchell Laurance, Stuart Pankin, Lucy Webb. **1988**

BEST OF SPIKE JONES, VOLUMES 1 & 2, THE ★★★ Compilations from Jones's 1954 TV show, these tapes are a nostalgic record of the star's manic comedy style. There are truly funny, if sporadic, moments. Jones's humor derived from destroying a well-known piece of music with outrageous sight and sound gags. He and his band, the City Slickers, had two memorable songs: "Der Fuehrer's Face"(1942) and "Cocktails for Two" (1944). B&W; 51m. **DIR:** Bud Yorkin. **CAST:** Spike Jones & His City Slickers, Earl Bennett, Billy Barty. **1954**

BEST OF THE BIG LAFF OFF, THE ★★★½ Hundreds of hungry comics have competed in the annual Laff Off contests around the country. This collection features more losers than winners, although Paul Rodriguez, Harry Anderson, Sandra Bernhard, and an already shocking, green but confident 19-year-old Eddie Murphy appear. David Steinberg ties the performance clips together with a mixture of warmth and wit. Rated R for language. 60m. **DIR:** Various. **CAST:** Eddie Murphy, Sandra Bernhard, Ronn Lucas, Harry Anderson, Mike Davis, Steve Mittleman, Paul Rodriguez, David Steinberg. **1983**

BEST OF THE FESTIVAL OF CLAYMATION, THE ★★ A visually stunning but unfulfilling and overlong collection of Claymation shorts. Claymation is the word coined by Will Vinton to describe the cartoon animation of sculpted clay (the singing raisins from the TV ad are examples). The framing story is good, lampooning film critics Gene Siskel and Roger Ebert. The film's limited scope, however, inhibits it from becoming more than a simple showcase of effects. Unrated. 53m. **DIR:** Will Vinton. **CAST:** Animated. **1987**

BEST OF THE KIDS IN THE HALL, THE ★★★★ Canada's comedy quintet brings its irreverent humor to home video in this venomous compilation. The humor is of the Monty Python–SCTV variety, with the five talented stars frequently dressing in drag. The Kids are at their best when they push the envelope, which is frequently. Ribald humor proves that Canadian censors are hipper than their American counterparts. Not rated, but contains adult language and situations. 108m. **DIR:** John Blanchard, Jack Budgell. **CAST:** Dave Foley, Bruce McCulloch, Kevin McDonald, Mark McKinney, Scott Thompson. **1993**

BEST OF TIMES, THE ★★★ This comedy starts off well, then continues to lose momentum right up to the *Rocky*-style ending. That said, it is an amiable enough little movie which benefits from likable performances by its lead players. Robin Williams and Kurt Russell star as two former football players who dropped the ball when their moment for glory came. But they get a second chance to win one for Taft (formerly Moron), California. Rated PG-13 for profanity and suggested sex. 100m. **DIR:** Roger Spottiswoode. **CAST:** Robin Williams, Kurt Russell, Pamela Reed, Holly Palance, Donald Moffat, Margaret Whitton, M. Emmet Walsh, R. G. Armstrong, Dub Taylor. **1986**

BEST OF WILLIAM WEGMAN 🦃 A collection of experimental vignettes by video artist William Wegman suffers from subversive self-indulgence. Assembled by Electronic Art Intermix. Not rated. B&W; 20m. **DIR:** William Wegman. **CAST:** William Wegman. **1978**

BETSY'S WEDDING ★★★★ In this warm hearted and often uproarious comedy-drama, writer-director Alan Alda plays a down-on-his-luck dad who tries to raise money to give his daughter (Molly Ringwald) a big wedding. Ally Sheedy and newcomer Anthony LaPaglia are the standouts in a uniformly fine ensemble cast. Rated R for profanity. 106m. **DIR:** Alan Alda. **CAST:** Alan Alda, Molly Ringwald, Madeline Kahn, Joe Pesci, Ally Sheedy, Burt Young, Joey Bishop, Catherine O'Hara, Anthony LaPaglia. **1990**

BETTE MIDLER'S MONDO BEYONDO ★★★★ Bette Midler has created another outrageous and hilarious character: an Italian sexpot who is hostess to a cable variety show. The avant-garde performers who support her are a delight. Trivia note: Midler's husband is one of the Kipper Kids. 60m. **DIR:** Thomas Schlamme. **CAST:** Bette Midler, Bill Irwin. **1988**

BETTER LATE THAN NEVER ★★½ Average made-for-television comedy about nursing home inhabitants who revolt against house rules. The premise is good, the execution so-so. Theft of a train is a nice touch. Rated PG. 100m. **DIR:** Richard Crenna. **CAST:** Harold Gould, Larry Storch, Strother Martin, Tyne Daly, Harry Morgan, Victor Buono, George Gobel, Donald Pleasence, Lou Jacobi. 1979

BETTER OFF DEAD ★★ A mixture of clever ideas and awfully silly ones, this comedy focuses on the plight of teenage Everyman, Lance Meyer (John Cusack), who finds his world shattered when the love of his life, Beth (Amanda Wyss), takes up with a conceited jock. Lance figures he is "better off dead" than Beth-less. The film is at its best when writer-director Savage Steve Holland throws in little sketches that stand out from the familiar plot. Rated PG for profanity. 97m. **DIR:** Savage Steve Holland. **CAST:** John Cusack, David Ogden Stiers, Diane Franklin, Kim Darby, Amanda Wyss. 1985

BETWEEN THE LINES ★★★★ Very good post-Sixties film in the tradition of *Return of the Secaucus 7* and *The Big Chill*. Staff of a once-underground newspaper has to come to terms with the paper's purchase by a large publisher. Superb ensemble acting. Rated R for profanity and nudity. 101m. **DIR:** Joan Micklin Silver. **CAST:** John Heard, Jeff Goldblum, Lindsay Crouse, Stephen Collins, Jill Eikenberry, Bruno Kirby, Gwen Welles, Lewis J. Stadlen, Jon Korkes, Michael J. Pollard, Lane Smith, Joe Morton, Richard Cox, Marilu Henner. 1977

BEVERLY HILLBILLIES, THE ★★★ It's scary how much Cloris Leachman looks and sounds like Irene Ryan's Granny in this big-screen version of the backwoods Clampett family's invasion of Beverly Hills. Featuring good work from Jim Varney, Lily Tomlin, and Dabney Coleman, it's fun for adults who fondly remember the series and kids looking for a silly laugh. Rated PG for brief profanity. 93m. **DIR:** Penelope Spheeris. **CAST:** Jim Varney, Cloris Leachman, Lily Tomlin, Dabney Coleman, Lea Thompson, Diedrich Bader, Erika Eleniak, Rob Schneider, Dolly Parton, Buddy Ebsen, Zsa Zsa Gabor. 1993

BEVERLY HILLBILLIES, THE (TV SERIES) ★★★ Selected episodes from the long-running TV series. Corny but effective. The immensely popular series was finally canceled not because of sagging ratings but because CBS decided to upgrade its network image. 30m. **DIR:** Ralph Levy. **CAST:** Buddy Ebsen, Irene Ryan, Donna Douglas, Max Baer, Raymond Bailey, Nancy Kulp. 1962–1971

BEVERLY HILLBILLIES GO HOLLYWOOD, THE ★★★ Enjoyable compilation of four episodes of the popular television series finds the Clampett clan with a controlling interest in Mammoth Pictures. The studio is turned head-over-heels when the Clampetts decide to take an active interest in making movies. Plenty of the corn-fed humor that made the series so popular. 104m. **DIR:** Joseph DePew. **CAST:** Buddy Ebsen, Irene Ryan, Donna Douglas, Max Baer, Nancy Culp, Raymond Bailey. 1964

BEVERLY HILLS BODYSNATCHERS 🦃 Dark comedy about a mortician and his mad-scientist assistant. R for nudity, profanity, and violence. 85m. **DIR:** Jon Mostow. **CAST:** Vic Tayback, Frank Gorshin, Art Metrano. 1989

BEVERLY HILLS BRATS ★★ The son of a wealthy plastic surgeon convinces a would-be robber to kidnap him. Zany and outrageous situations make this watchable. PG-13 for nudity and profanity. 90m. **DIR:** Dimitri Sotirakis. **CAST:** Peter Billingsley, Burt Young, Martin Sheen, Terry Moore. 1989

BEVERLY HILLS VAMP 🦃 Writer-director Fred Olen Ray labors in vain, trying to make this vampire movie funny. Rated R for nudity, profanity, and simulated sex. 88m. **DIR:** Fred Olen Ray. **CAST:** Eddie Deezen, Tim Conway Jr., Britt Ekland. 1989

BEWARE OF SPOOKS ★★★ Joe E. Brown is hilarious as a cop afraid of his own shadow. He gets mixed up with a pretty girl and some thugs in a haunted house. B&W; 76m. **DIR:** Edward Sedgwick. **CAST:** Joe E. Brown, Mary Carlisle, Clarence Kolb. 1939

BEYOND THERAPY ★★ Robert Altman is a hit-and-miss director and his *Beyond Therapy* (adapted from Christopher Durang's play) qualifies as a miss. The movie, which pokes fun at psychiatrists and their patients, really is a mess filled with unconnected episodes. Most of the performances and much of the dialogue are salvageable and hilarious, however. Most notable are Tom Conti and, as a bizarre psychiatrist, Glenda Jackson. Rated R. 93m. **DIR:** Robert Altman. **CAST:** Julie Hagerty, Jeff Goldblum, Glenda Jackson, Tom Conti, Christopher Guest, Cris Campion. 1987

BIG ★★★★ This endearing fantasy is enlivened by a deft performance from Tom Hanks and an unusually intelligent script from Gary Ross and Anne Spielberg. Hanks stars as the "big person" embodiment of young David Moscow, who wishes for a creaky amusement-park fortune-telling machine to make him "big." Hanks, as the result, performs brilliantly as the 13-year-old in a 35-year-old body; he's ably assisted by spunky Elizabeth Perkins as an associate at the children's toy company (what else?) where he's able to land a job. Forget all the other soul-transference films that sprouted in late 1987 and early 1988; this is the only one that matters. Rated PG for mild sexual themes. 102m. **DIR:** Penny Marshall. **CAST:** Tom Hanks, Elizabeth Perkins, Robert Loggia, John Heard, Jared Rushton, David Moscow. 1988

BIG BET, THE 🦃 Lurid sex comedy that tries to cash in on the high school–film craze. Unrated, contains nudity. 90m. **DIR:** Bert I. Gordon. **CAST:** Lance Sloane, Kim Evenson, Sylvia Kristel, Ron Thomas. **1985**

BIG BUS, THE ★★★ A superluxurious nuclear-powered bus runs into trouble while carrying a group of misfits from New York to Denver. This spoof appeared four years before *Airplane!* It's not as funny, but it does have a silly and sarcastic playfulness. One of those few films that work better on the small screen. Rated PG. 88m. **DIR:** James Frawley. **CAST:** Joseph Bologna, Stockard Channing, John Beck, Lynn Redgrave, José Ferrer, Ruth Gordon, Richard B. Shull, Sally Kellerman, Ned Beatty, Richard Mulligan, Larry Hagman, Howard Hesseman, Harold Gould. **1976**

BIG BUSINESS ★★★½ Bette Midler and Lily Tomlin play two sets of mismatched twins, one raised in a West Virginia country setting and another accustomed to wealth and power in New York City. Despite the unoriginal, one-joke plot, the stars manage some genuinely hysterical moments. Rated PG for light profanity. 95m. **DIR:** Jim Abrahams. **CAST:** Bette Midler, Lily Tomlin, Fred Ward, Edward Herrmann, Michele Placido, Daniel Gerroll, Barry Primus, Michael Gross, Deborah Rush, Nicolas Coster. **1988**

BIG CITY COMEDY ★★ This is a compilation of skits from a 1980 John Candy syndicated TV series. Even with funny guys Billy Crystal, Martin Mull, and Tim Kazurinsky on hand as guests, this is a disappointing tape. Candy can be very funny but, unfortunately, not here. He is quite a sight to behold as Queen Victoria, but you can see that on the cassette box. 56m. **DIR:** Mark Warren. **CAST:** John Candy, Billy Crystal, McLean Stevenson, Martin Mull, Tim Kazurinsky, Fred Willard. **1986**

BIG GAG, THE 🦃 This adult version of *Candid Camera* is an exercise in boredom. PG-13. 87m. **DIR:** Yuda Barkan, Igal Shilon. **CAST:** Danuta, Caroline Langford. **1988**

BIG GIRLS DON'T CRY...THEY GET EVEN ★★★½ Don't let the awful title (it was originally called *Stepkids*) keep you away from this low-key but charming comedy about a young teen who revolts against the revolving-door marriages of her parents that has left her part of a bizarrely extended family. Rated PG-13 for profanity. 96m. **DIR:** Joan Micklin Silver. **CAST:** Hilary Wolf, David Strathairn, Margaret Whitton, Griffin Dunne, Adrienne Shelly. **1992**

BIG HANGOVER, THE ★★½ One-joke movie, with Van Johnson as a veteran who almost drowned in a bombed-out wine cellar, becoming drunk at the slightest odor of alcohol. Becomes preachy when he, as a junior lawyer, turns against his employer for racial discrimination. B&W; 82m. **DIR:** Norman Krasna. **CAST:** Van Johnson, Elizabeth Taylor, Fay Holden, Leon Ames, Edgar Buchanan, Selena Royle, Gene Lockhart, Rosemary DeCamp. **1950**

BIG MAN ON CAMPUS ★★★ This spoofy retelling of *The Hunchback of Notre Dame* story is a surprising bit of good-natured fun. Sincere comic touches by Allan Katz and Corey Parker help make this teen-marketed sexual-oriented fluff seem a little more substantial. Above average. Rated PG-13 for mild profanity. 102m. **DIR:** Jeremy Paul Kagan. **CAST:** Allan Katz, Corey Parker, Tom Skerritt, Cindy Williams. **1989**

BIG MOUTH, THE ★★ The bloom was off the rose by this point in Jerry Lewis's solo career, and this standard gangster comedy is a profound disappointment. Title character Jerry (an apt description in a film where everybody shouts all the time) gets involved in a witless search for stolen diamonds. Lewis's character bits and attempts at disguise are pretty flimsy. For true fans only. 107m. **DIR:** Jerry Lewis. **CAST:** Jerry Lewis, Harold J. Stone. **1967**

BIG NEWS ★★★ Robert Armstrong plays a boozing newspaper reporter who gets framed for the murder of his editor. Armstrong's wife, Carole Lombard, writes a women's column for a rival paper and puts in some time trying to sober up her hubby and clear him of the crime. Snappy comedy-mystery. B&W; 75m. **DIR:** Gregory La Cava. **CAST:** Robert Armstrong, Carole Lombard. **1929**

BIG PICTURE, THE ★★★★ *This Is Spinal Tap* stars and co-creators Christopher Guest and Michael McKean spoof the film industry in this engaging, hip, and sometimes uneven story of a promising young filmmaker (Kevin Bacon) who finds himself thoroughly corrupted by the temptations of Hollywood. Guest (who also directed) and McKean (who plays Bacon's cinematographer buddy) hit most of their targets with skilled assistance from Martin Short as a wacked-out agent. Rated PG-13 for brief profanity and brief nudity. 100m. **DIR:** Christopher Guest. **CAST:** Kevin Bacon, Michael McKean, Martin Short, Jennifer Jason Leigh. **1989**

BIG SHOTS ★★★½ A funny and exciting film about kids, but not just for kids. After the death of his father, an 11-year-old boy from the suburbs strikes up a friendship with a young black boy who teaches him the ways of the street. Rated PG-13. 91m. **DIR:** Robert Mandel. **CAST:** Ricky Busker, Darius McCrary, Robert Joy, Robert Prosky, Paul Winfield, Jerzy Skolimowski. **1988**

BIG STORE, THE ★★ Singer (and nonactor) Tony Martin inherits a department store and calls on the Marx Brothers to save him. The last and weakest of the Marx Brothers' movies for MGM, this misfire is woefully understocked in laughs. Even so, Groucho manages some good bits, often in scenes with his classic foil, Margaret Dumont, and Chico and Harpo team for a delightful piano duet. 103m. **DIR:** Charles F. Riesner. **CAST:** The Marx Brothers, Tony Martin, Virginia Grey, Margaret Dumont, Douglass Dumbrille. **1941**

BIG TOP PEE-WEE ★★ Pee-Wee Herman plays a country bumpkin whose greatest pleasure in life is his pet hog. The circus comes to town, and Pee-Wee invites them to pitch the Big Top on his land. Film contains the longest kiss in screen history. Rated PG for hog and human love rites. 86m. **DIR:** Randal Kleiser. **CAST:** Pee-Wee Herman, Kris Kristofferson, Susan Tyrrell, Valeria Golino. **1988**

BIG TROUBLE ★★ *Big Trouble* has its moments, but alas, they are few and far between. Alan Arkin meets up with a rich married woman (Beverly D'Angelo), and the two plot against her husband (Peter Falk). Crazy plot twists abound, but none of them are all that funny. Rated R for profanity and adult subject matter. 93m. **DIR:** John Cassavetes. **CAST:** Peter Falk, Alan Arkin, Beverly D'Angelo, Charles Durning, Robert Stack, Paul Dooley, Valerie Curtin, Richard Libertini. **1985**

BIKINI CARWASH COMPANY, THE 🦃 When naive Midwesterner Joe Dusic agrees to take over his uncle's California car wash, he revives the failing business by employing some of the beach's best babes. Tedious male fantasy. Two versions available: R-rated for nudity and an unrated version featuring even more of the same. 87m. **DIR:** Ed Hansen. **CAST:** Joe Dusic. **1990**

BIKINI CARWASH COMPANY 2 🦃 After being tricked into selling their beloved carwash chain to a crooked developer, the beautiful entrepreneurs launch a new business: a 24-hour lingerie shopping network. Need we say more? Available in two versions, R-rated and unrated, both with nudity and sexual situations. 94m. **DIR:** Gary Orona. **CAST:** Kristi Ducati, Suzanne Browne, Neriah Napaul, Rikki Brando. **1993**

BILL AND TED'S BOGUS JOURNEY ★★★★ This sequel, which finds our heroes traveling through Heaven and Hell rather than through time, is better than its predecessor. The special effects are first rate, and the comedy has moved up a notch. Rated PG. 90m. **DIR:** Pete Hewitt. **CAST:** Keanu Reeves, Alex Winter, Bill Sadler, Joss Ackland, Pam Grier, George Carlin. **1991**

BILL AND TED'S EXCELLENT ADVENTURE ★★★ A wild romp through time with two total idiots who must find a way to pass history class. Using a time-traveling telephone booth, these two go through history enlisting the help of famous people such as Napoleon and Socrates. A good, clean, excellent way to waste an hour and a half, dude. Rated PG. 90m. **DIR:** Stephen Herek. **CAST:** Keanu Reeves, Alex Winter, George Carlin. **1989**

BILL COSBY: 49 ★★★½ This recorded stage performance is a perfect follow-up to Bill Cosby's hugely entertaining *Bill Cosby—Himself*. It reflects the years that have passed since his earlier video, which dealt with childbirth and child rearing. Now we get Cosby's special insight into the everyday adventures of advancing into middle age. This master funnyman does not disappoint. 67m. **DIR:** David Lewis, Camille Cosby. **CAST:** Bill Cosby. **1987**

BILL COSBY—HIMSELF ★★★★ The wit and wisdom of Bill Cosby on the subjects of childbirth, raising a family (and being raised), going to the dentist, taking drugs and drinking, and life in general provide laughs and food for thought in this excellent comedy video. One can see how the hugely successful television series *The Cosby Show* evolved from his family and observations of their behavior. Rated G. 104m. **DIR:** William H. Cosby Jr. **CAST:** Bill Cosby. **1985**

BILL FIELDS AND WILL ROGERS ★★★ Comedy duet: W. C. Fields, in his film debut, piles his sadistic style of humorous mayhem in "Pool Sharks," while in "The Ropin' Fool," Will Rogers documents his loop prowess by lassoing everything and everybody. Silent with musical score. B&W; 48m. **DIR:** Edwin Middleton, Clarence Badger. **CAST:** W. C. Fields, Bud Ross, Will Rogers, Irene Rich, Guinn Williams. **1915–1921**

BILLION FOR BORIS, A 🦃 Boris discovers that his TV set can view the future. He uses this knowledge to win big at the racetrack. Not rated, but contains some foul language. 94m. **DIR:** Alex Grasshoff. **CAST:** Tim Kazurinsky, Lee Grant. **1990**

BILLY CRYSTAL: A COMIC'S LINE ★★★★ This HBO special released on tape features an innovative and very funny performance by Billy Crystal. Using the premise of a Broadway musical audition, he presents various characters trying out for the part. There is also an amusing yet wonderfully warm sequence with Crystal as a small boy being left at home for the first time. He shows much more than just a flair for comedy and timing. 59m. **DIR:** Bruce Gowers. **CAST:** Billy Crystal. **1984**

BILLY CRYSTAL: DON'T GET ME STARTED ★★★ In the first part of this video, Rob Reiner takes the role of interviewer in a "yockumentary" on the making of a Billy Crystal special. Eugene Levy is manager and promoter, and Crystal shows up as Sammy Davis Jr., Whoopi Goldberg, and himself as they attempt to show us what happens behind the scenes prior to showtime. The second half is the actual live performance. 60m. **DIR:** Paul Flaherty, Billy Crystal. **CAST:** Billy Crystal, Rob Reiner, Christopher Guest, Eugene Levy, Brother Theodore. **1986**

BILLY CRYSTAL: MIDNIGHT TRAIN TO MOSCOW ★★★ Endearing stand-up comedy performance in Moscow by comic Billy Crystal is neatly wrapped in a *Roots* format, as he traces his Russian ancestry forward from great-grandmother Sophie (played by daughter Jennifer). High point: a brief Martin Scorsese imitation. 90m. **DIR:** Paul Flaherty. **CAST:** Billy Crystal. **1989**

BILOXI BLUES ★★★★ As second in Neil Simon's loosely autobiographical trilogy (after *Brighton Beach Memoirs*), this witty glimpse of growing up in a Deep South World War II boot camp stars Matthew Broderick as Simon's observant alter ego. When not clashing with Christopher Walken's sly drill sergeant or learning about the birds and bees from an amused wartime prostitute, Broderick makes perceptive comments about life, the war, and his army buddies. Rated PG-13 for language and sexual themes. 106m. **DIR:** Mike Nichols. **CAST:** Matthew Broderick, Christopher Walken, Matt Mulhern, Casey Siemaszko. **1988**

BINGO 🦃 This mishmash attempt at comedy follows a dog who chases his master cross-country. The cute dog of the title can't save this film from the fleas. Rated PG for brief violence and brief profanity. 87m. **DIR:** Matthew Robbins. **CAST:** Cindy Williams, David Rasche. **1991**

BINGO LONG TRAVELING ALL-STARS AND MOTOR KINGS, THE ★★★ This is a comedy-adventure of a barnstorming group of black baseball players as they tour rural America in the late 1930s. Billy Dee Williams, Richard Pryor, and James Earl Jones are three of the team's players. Only the lack of a cohesive script keeps this from receiving more stars. Rated PG. 110m. **DIR:** John Badham. **CAST:** Billy Dee Williams, James Earl Jones, Richard Pryor, Ted Ross. **1976**

BIRDS AND THE BEES, THE ★★ This poor remake of the 1941 Barbara Stanwyck–Henry Fonda comedy hit, *The Lady Eve*, has military cardsharper David Niven setting daughter Mitzi Gaynor on playboy millionaire George Gobel in hopes of getting rich from the marriage. "Lonesome George" wiggles free, but falls for her anyway. Don't settle for imitations. Insist on the original. 94m. **DIR:** Norman Taurog. **CAST:** George Gobel, Mitzi Gaynor, David Niven. **1956**

BIRTHDAY BOY, THE ★★ A Cinemax Comedy Experiment that proves once again how difficult it is to produce an even moderately funny film. James Belushi (who also wrote the script) is a sporting-goods salesman who journeys cross-country on his birthday in an attempt to sell his old gym coach a load of basketballs. Unrated, but contains adult language. 30m. **DIR:** Claude Conrad. **CAST:** James Belushi, Michelle Riga, Dennis Farina, Ron Dean, Jim Johnson, Ed Blatchford, Fred Kaz. **1986**

BISHOP'S WIFE, THE ★★★ Harmless story of debonair angel (Cary Grant) sent to Earth to aid a bishop (David Niven) in his quest for a new church. The kind of film they just don't make anymore. No rating, but okay for the whole family. B&W; 108m. **DIR:** Henry Koster. **CAST:** Cary Grant, Loretta Young, David Niven, James Gleason. **1947**

BLACK ADDER III (TV SERIES) ★★★★ Third in a trilogy of the *Black Adder* series, this is one of the most wicked, delightfully sardonic send-ups of British costume drama ever made. Rat-faced Rowan Atkinson is a sly former aristocrat and butler to the Prince of Wales, son of mad King George III. He's kept perpetually on his toes by the unpredictable idiocy of his twit of a prince, played with exquisite vacuousness by Hugh Laurie. each tape. 60m. **DIR:** Mandie Fletcher. **CAST:** Rowan Atkinson, Hugh Laurie. **1989**

BLACK BIRD, THE ★★★ Surprisingly enjoyable comedy produced by and starring George Segal as Sam Spade Jr. The visual gags abound, and an air of authenticity is added by the performances of 1940s detective film regulars Lionel Stander, Elisha Cook, and Lee Patrick. The latter two costarred with Humphrey Bogart in *The Maltese Falcon*, on which the film is based. It's funny, with a strong performance from Segal. Rated PG. 98m. **DIR:** David Giler. **CAST:** George Segal, Stéphane Audran, Lionel Stander, Lee Patrick. **1975**

BLACKSMITH, THE/COPS ★★★½ Two shining examples of deadpan silent comedian Buster Keaton at his best. What he does to a white luxury limo in *The Blacksmith* is a hilarious crime. His antics in *Cops* bid fair to prove him Chaplin's master. The chase scene is a classic of timing and invention. Silent. B&W; 38m. **DIR:** Buster Keaton. **CAST:** Buster Keaton, Virginia Fox. **1922**

BLAME IT ON RIO ★★½ A middle-aged male sex fantasy directed by Stanley Donen (*Lucky Lady; Charade*), features Michael Caine as a befuddled fellow who finds himself involved in an affair with the teenage daughter (Michelle Johnson) of his best friend (Joseph Bologna). Although essentially in bad taste, *Blame It on Rio* does have a number of very funny moments. Rated R for nudity, profanity, and suggested sex. 110m. **DIR:** Stanley Donen. **CAST:** Michael Caine, Joseph Bologna, Valerie Harper, Michelle Johnson. **1984**

BLAME IT ON THE BELLBOY ★★★★ An English-mangling Italian bellboy (Bronson Pinchot) manages to mix up the identities of a real estate salesman (Dudley Moore), a hit man (Bryan Brown), and a philandering husband (Richard Griffiths). What could have been hopelessly moronic is deliciously giddy and frequently funny. Rated PG-13 for profanity, brief violence, and silly simulated sex. 78m. **DIR:** Mark Herman. **CAST:** Dudley Moore, Bryan Brown, Richard Griffiths, Andreas Katsulas, Patsy Kensit, Alison Steadman, Penelope Wilton, Bronson Pinchot. **1992**

BLAZE STARR: THE ORIGINAL ★★ The famous stripper plays an actress who finds relief from the stresses of making movies by joining a Florida nudist camp. Campy in the extreme. Original title: *Blaze Starr Goes Nudist*. Unrated, no sexual content, but lotsa nude volleyball games (and nude checkers, too!) 79m. **DIR:** Doris Wishman. **CAST:** Blaze Starr. **1962**

BLAZING SADDLES ★★★½ Mel Brooks directed this sometimes hilarious, mostly crude spoof of Westerns. The jokes come with machine-gun rapidity, and the stars race around like maniacs. If it weren't in such bad taste, it would be perfect for the kiddies. Rated R. 93m. **DIR:** Mel Brooks. **CAST:** Cleavon Little, Gene Wilder, Harvey Korman, Madeline Kahn, Mel Brooks, Slim Pickens. **1974**

BLESSED EVENT ★★★★ Lee Tracy plays a tabloid columnist whose specialty is uncovering celebrity marriages caused by pre-nuptial pregnancies. It's always fun to watch fast-talking Tracy, and here he's perfectly complemented by the delightfully grumpy Ned Sparks. B&W; 84m. **DIR:** Roy Del Ruth. **CAST:** Lee Tracy, Ned Sparks, Mary Brian, Dick Powell. **1932**

BLIND DATE (1987) 🦃 A tasteless exercise in slapstick that sends Bruce Willis on a last-minute blind date with Kim Basinger. Rated PG-13 for adult situations. 93m. **DIR:** Blake Edwards. **CAST:** Bruce Willis, Kim Basinger, John Larroquette, William Daniels, George Coe, Mark Blum, Phil Hartman. **1987**

BLISS ★★★★ In this biting black comedy from Australia, a business executive (Barry Otto) nearly dies from a heart attack. He finds himself in a hellish version of the life he once had. Not everyone will appreciate this nightmarish vision of modern life, but it is one of the most original motion pictures of recent years. Rated R. 93m. **DIR:** Ray Lawrence. **CAST:** Barry Otto, Lynette Curran, Helen Jones, Jeff Truman. **1986**

BLISS OF MRS. BLOSSOM, THE ★★★½ Good farce, as only the British can produce it, with Shirley MacLaine as the discontented wife of brassiere manufacturer Richard Attenborough. Witty, adult story, with fine plot twists. Rated PG. 93m. **DIR:** Joseph McGrath. **CAST:** Shirley MacLaine, Richard Attenborough, James Booth. **1968**

BLOCK-HEADS ★★★★ Twenty years after the end of World War I, Stan Laurel is discovered still guarding a bunker. He returns to a veterans' home, where Oliver Hardy comes to visit and take him to dinner. A well-crafted script provides the perfect setting for the boys' escapades. Their characters have seldom been used as well in feature films. B&W; 55m. **DIR:** John G. Blystone. **CAST:** Stan Laurel, Oliver Hardy, Patricia Ellis, Minna Gombell, Billy Gilbert, James Finlayson. **1938**

BLONDE CRAZY ★★★ An early version of *The Sting*, where small-time con artists James Cagney and Joan Blondell are tricked out of $5 thousand and plot to get it back—with interest. B&W; 79m. **DIR:** Roy Del Ruth. **CAST:** James Cagney, Joan Blondell, Louis Calhern, Guy Kibbee, Ray Milland. **1931**

BLONDIE ★★★½ The first and one of the best in the long-running series, this film establishes the characters by putting them in a stressful situation and letting them get some laughs out of it. Dagwood loses his job on the eve of his fifth wedding anniversary and doesn't want it to spoil the family celebration. B&W; 75m. **DIR:** Frank Strayer. **CAST:** Penny Singleton, Arthur Lake, Larry Simms, Jonathan Hale, Gene Lockhart, Ann Doran, Gordon Oliver, Kathleen Lockhart. **1938**

BLONDIE HAS TROUBLE ★★★ A funny blend of comic-strip characters and haunted-house shenanigans even though the setup is more contrived than usual. Mr. Dithers wants the Bumsteads to move into a haunted house for business reasons. The outcome is predictable but still funny. B&W; 75m. **DIR:** Frank Strayer. **CAST:** Penny Singleton, Arthur Lake, Jonathan Hale, Esther Dale, Larry Simms, Irving Bacon, Fay Helm. **1940**

BLONDIE HITS THE JACKPOT ★★ This weak series entry was the next-to-last feature made in a 12-year period and boredom was setting in. Dagwood loses his job (again) and has to go to work on a construction crew. Blondie helps the family budget by entering a radio quiz show with predictable results. B&W; 75m. **DIR:** Edward L. Bernds. **CAST:** Penny Singleton, Arthur Lake, Larry Simms, Marjorie Kent, Jerome Cowan, Lloyd Corrigan. **1949**

BLONDIE IN SOCIETY ★★★½ A doggone cute comedy, this feature has the Bumsteads competing with a Great Dane for laughs. Dagwood brings the dog home and Blondie promptly enters the animal in a dog show. Then a very important client decides he wants the dog and causes complications. B&W; 75m. **DIR:** Frank Strayer. **CAST:** Penny Singleton, Arthur Lake, Larry Simms, Jonathan Hale, William Frawley, Garry Owen, Robert Mitchell Boys Choir. **1941**

BLONDIE KNOWS BEST ★★★½ One of the funnier entries, chiefly due to Shemp Howard's comedic timing. Dagwood impersonates his boss, Mr. Dithers, and winds up in the care of a couple of psychologists and a half dozen dogs. B&W; 75m. **DIR:** Abby Berlin. **CAST:** Penny Singleton, Arthur Lake, Larry

Simms, Marjorie Kent, Jonathan Hale, Shemp Howard, Jerome Cowan. 1946

BLONDIE TAKES A VACATION ★★★½ Scene-stealing character players almost take the spotlight away from the Bumstead family. Everybody takes more pratfalls than usual in a clever episode as the Bumsteads try to save a mountain lodge from bankruptcy. B&W; 75m. **DIR:** Frank Strayer. **CAST:** Penny Singleton, Arthur Lake, Donald Meek, Donald MacBride, Elizabeth Dunne, Irving Bacon. 1939

BLONDIE'S BLESSED EVENT ★★★ Blondie's daughter, Cookie, makes her first appearance in the series, making the film one of the most anxiously awaited episodes in the series. Because of Cookie, the film has more heart and personality. It also shifts the focus from Blondie and Dagwood to Cookie and Alexander. B&W; 75m. **DIR:** Frank Strayer. **CAST:** Penny Singleton, Arthur Lake, Hans Conried, Mary Wickes, Arthur O'Connell, Norma Jean Wayne. 1942

BLOODBATH AT THE HOUSE OF DEATH ★★ Although advertised as one, this British movie is not all that much of a spoof on horror films. There is realistic gore (especially in the opening scene, where the film lives up to its not-so-ironic title), and near the film's end the camp antics turn serious. In the story, a team of paranormal specialists investigates a house that was the scene of a mysterious massacre. Vincent Price plays a nutty devil worshiper. Not rated, but equivalent to an R for violence, gore, sex, nudity, and profanity. 92m. **DIR:** Ray Cameron. **CAST:** Vincent Price, Kenny Everett, Pamela Stephenson, Gareth Hunt, Don Warrington, John Fortune, Sheila Steafel. 1985

BLOODHOUNDS OF BROADWAY ★★★ This featherweight period comedy was stitched together by writer-director Howard Brookner from four stories by Damon Runyan. While not as hilarious as one might hope, this story has its moments, the best of which are provided by Randy Quaid as a lovesick loser and Madonna as the object of his affections. Rated PG for brief profanity and stylized violence. 90m. **DIR:** Howard Brookner. **CAST:** Matt Dillon, Jennifer Grey, Julie Hagerty, Rutger Hauer, Madonna, Esai Morales, Anita Morris, Randy Quaid. 1989

BLOOPERS FROM STAR TREK AND LAUGH-IN ★★½ Don't try to explain the melding of these two television shows. Just sit back and enjoy the *Star Trek* bloopers and ignore the *Laugh-In* gaffes. It's genuinely funny to see the unemotional Spock (Leonard Nimoy) dissolve into laughter when he walks into one of the sliding *Enterprise* doors that is supposed to open smoothly at his approach. *Rowan and Martin's Laugh-In* will leave people of the Eighties wondering what was so funny about this Sixties telehit. 26m. **DIR:** Various. **CAST:** William Shatner, Leonard Nimoy, DeForest Kelley, Dan Rowan, Dick Martin, Martin Milner, Kent McCord, Sammy Davis Jr., Dean Martin. 1966

BLUE DE VILLE ★★★ Engaging cross-country odyssey in which three diverse types travel together in a classic, mint blue 1959 Cadillac. Interesting characters, outrageous situations, and gorgeous scenery. 100m. **DIR:** Jim Johnston. **CAST:** Jennifer Runyon, Kimberly Pistone, Mark Thomas Miller. 1986

BLUE IGUANA ★★ For his first film, writer-director John Lafia attempted a *Raising Arizona*–style spoof of the hard boiled detective story—and failed. The story concerns a "recovery specialist" (Dylan McDermott) who is coerced by IRS agents Tovah Feldshuh and Dean Stockwell into going after $40 million in contraband money. The supporting actors are allowed to overact to bizarre proportions. Rated R for violence. 90m. **DIR:** John Lafia. **CAST:** Dylan McDermott, Jessica Harper, James Russo, Tovah Feldshuh, Dean Stockwell. 1988

BLUE MONEY ★★★ Larry Gormley (Tim Curry) discovers a suitcase with half a million dollars in his cab. The money turns out to belong to the mob, and they want it back. Not a very original idea, but well written, acted, and directed, this comedy provides plenty of fast-moving fun. Made for British television. 82m. **DIR:** Colin Bucksey. **CAST:** Tim Curry, Debby Bishop, Billy Connolly, Frances Tomelty. 1984

BLUE MOVIES ★★ Poorly directed, cheaply made comedy about two young entrepreneurs and their quest to make a pornographic movie. It has some funny moments. Rated R for profanity and nudity. 92m. **DIR:** Ed Fitzgerald. **CAST:** Steve Levitt, Larry Poindexter, Lucinda Crosby, Darian Mathias, Christopher Stone, Don Calfa, Larry Linville. 1988

BLUES BROTHERS, THE ★★★½ Director John Landis attempted to film an epic comedy and came pretty darn close. In it, the musicians of the title, John Belushi and Dan Aykroyd, attempt to save an orphanage. The movie's excesses—too many car crashes and chases—are offset by Belushi and Aykroyd as the Laurel and Hardy of backbeat; the musical turns of Aretha Franklin, James Brown, and Ray Charles; and Landis's flair for comic timing. Rated R. 132m. **DIR:** John Landis. **CAST:** John Belushi, Dan Aykroyd, John Candy, Carrie Fisher. 1980

BLUES BUSTERS ★★½ One of the best Bowery Boys comedies, with a clever gimmick—a case of tonsillitis gives Sach (Huntz Hall) a crooner's pipes. An all-star B-movie cast keeps the low-budget formula humming like a well-oiled machine. B&W; 67m. **DIR:** William Beaudine. **CAST:** Leo Gorcey, Huntz Hall,

Adele Jergens, Gabriel Dell, Craig Stevens, Phyllis Coates, William Benedict, Bernard Gorcey. 1950

BOARDING SCHOOL ★★★½ A European boarding school for girls, located next to an all-boys' boarding school, creates the setting for sexual high jinks and young love in this sexy comedy. The 1956 theme is enhanced by some Bill Haley music. Rated R for nudity. 100m. **DIR:** André Farwagi. **CAST:** Nastassja Kinski, Gerry Sundquist, Kurt Raab. 1978

BOB & CAROL & TED & ALICE ★★★★½ In this comedy, Natalie Wood and Robert Culp (Carol and Bob) play a modern couple who believe in open marriage, pot smoking, etc. Their friends, conservative Elliott Gould and Dyan Cannon (Ted and Alice), are shocked by Bob and Carol's behavior. Meanwhile, Bob and Carol try to liven up Ted and Alice's marriage by introducing them to their way of life. Lots of funny moments. Rated R. 104m. **DIR:** Paul Mazursky. **CAST:** Natalie Wood, Robert Culp, Elliott Gould, Dyan Cannon. 1969

BOB & RAY, JANE, LARAINE & GILDA ★★★ The low-key humor of Bob & Ray takes center stage in this summer replacement special from the *Saturday Night Live* folks. As far as these two fellows are concerned, you either love 'em or hate 'em. If routines like "House of Toast," in which Bob & Ray introduce a restaurant that specializes in you-know-what, or a deadpan reading of the lyrics of Rod Stewart's "If You Think I'm Sexy" by the middle-aged humorists sound like fun to you, this is the tape you've been waiting for. 75m. **DIR:** Dave Wilson. **CAST:** Bob Elliott, Ray Goulding, Jane Curtin, Laraine Newman, Gilda Radner, Willie Nelson. 1979

BOB ROBERTS ★★★★ The writing-directing debut of star Tim Robbins is a fake documentary about a folk-singing, millionaire crypto-fascist's campaign for a seat in the Senate. Robbins's occasionally pedantic but most often clever satire features numerous cameos and his own hilarious, hate-filled compositions. (Robbins, by the way, refused to release a soundtrack album—lest real right-wing politicians appropriate the songs for their own anthems.) Rated R for profanity and sexual themes. 105m. **DIR:** Tim Robbins. **CAST:** Tim Robbins, Alan Rickman, Giancarlo Esposito, Gore Vidal. 1992

BOBO, THE 🦃 A bumbling matador (Peter Sellers) has to seduce a high-priced courtesan (Britt Ekland) in order to get employment as a singer. 105m. **DIR:** Robert Parrish. **CAST:** Peter Sellers, Britt Ekland, Rossano Brazzi. 1967

BODYWAVES 🦃 Two studs/tanning-lotion salesmen end up teaching three nerds how to "make it" in L.A. All the finesse of a *Three Stooges* beach party. Rated R for nudity and profanity. 80m. **DIR:** P. J. Pesce. **CAST:** Larry Linville, Dick Miller, Bill Calvert. 1992

BOEING, BOEING ★★★ An obviously bored Jerry Lewis plays straight man to Tony Curtis's oversexed American news hound, who keeps a Parisian apartment for dalliances with stewardesses. Although it tries for the manic intensity of a 1940s screwball comedy, this mildly amusing sex farce never rises above kitsch...and is rather dated. 102m. **DIR:** John Rich. **CAST:** Jerry Lewis, Tony Curtis, Dany Saval, Thelma Ritter. 1965

BOHEMIAN GIRL, THE ★★★ Laurel and Hardy portray gypsies in this typical tale of the gypsy band versus the country officials. A variety of misadventures occur, and the film is entertaining, especially with the hilarious scene of Stan attempting to fill wine bottles and becoming more and more inebriated. B&W; 70m. **DIR:** James W. Horne, Charles R. Rogers. **CAST:** Stan Laurel, Oliver Hardy, Thelma Todd, Antonio Moreno. 1936

BOMBSHELL ★★★★ A fast-moving satire on Hollywood types that hasn't lost its bite or its hilarity. One reason is Jean Harlow, as she essentially plays herself in this story of a sex symbol who is used and abused. B&W; 97m. **DIR:** Victor Fleming. **CAST:** Jean Harlow, Lee Tracy, Pat O'Brien, Frank Morgan, Franchot Tone, Una Merkel, C. Aubrey Smith. 1933

BONNIE SCOTLAND ★★★ Stan Laurel and Oliver Hardy venture to Scotland so that Stan can reap a "major" inheritance—which turns out to be merely bagpipes and a snuffbox. By mistake, they join the army and are sent to India, where they help to quell a native uprising. The thin plot offers the boys an opportunity to play off each other's strengths: Ollie's reactions and Stan's fantasy world that keeps becoming reality. B&W; 80m. **DIR:** James W. Horne. **CAST:** Stan Laurel, Oliver Hardy, James Finlayson, June (Vlasek) Lang, William Janney. 1935

BOOB TUBE, THE 🦃 Amateurish soft-core porn and pseudomasochism trying to pass as a spoof of television soap operas, using bad taste instead of humor and wit. Rated R for language, nudity, and simulated sex. 90m. **DIR:** Christopher Odin. **CAST:** John Alderman. 1975

BOOK OF LOVE ★★ *Porky's*-like humor doesn't help the story of a new-kid-in-town who falls for the girlfriend of the guy who plays the front four on the high school football team. Familiar. Rated PG-13 for brief profanity and teenage high jinks. 85m. **DIR:** Robert Shaye. **CAST:** Chris Young, Keith Coogan, Michael McKean. 1991

BOOM IN THE MOON 🦃 Buster Keaton's worst film. It involves his being conned by villains into flying a rocket to the moon. 83m. **DIR:** Jaime Salvador. **CAST:** Buster Keaton. 1946

BOOMERANG ★★½ Dapper advertising executive Eddie Murphy is a real ladies' man who likes to love 'em and lead 'em on—until his sexy, new boss Robin Givens gives him a taste of his own medicine. A few laughs (mostly supplied by Martin Lawrence) and a little bit of heart (courtesy of the gorgeous Halle Berry) help this predictable romantic comedy. Rated R for nudity and profanity. 118m. **DIR:** Reginald Hudlin. **CAST:** Eddie Murphy, Robin Givens, Halle Berry, David Alan Grier, Martin Lawrence, Grace Jones, Geoffrey Holder, Eartha Kitt. **1992**

BORIS AND NATASHA ★★★ Reasonably amusing live-action rendition of animator Jay Ward's most famous no-goodniks, the cold war klutzes from Pottsylvania who bedeviled Rocky and Bullwinkle. Our "heroes" are sent to the United States . . . little knowing their beloved "Fearless Leader" has merely set them up as bait. Unbilled appearances are made by John Candy, John Travolta, and June Foray (Rocky's original cartoon voice). Originally shown on cable. 88m. **DIR:** Charles Martin Smith. **CAST:** Sally Kellerman, Dave Thomas, Paxton Whitehead, Andrea Martin, Alex Rocco, Anthony Newley. **1992**

BORN IN EAST L.A. ★★★½ Cheech, minus Chong, had a surprise box-office hit with this comedy, which started off as a video takeoff of Bruce Springsteen's "Born in the U.S.A." While not a comedy classic, this low-budget film has a number of funny moments. Rated R for profanity. 85m. **DIR:** Richard "Cheech" Marin. **CAST:** Richard "Cheech" Marin, Daniel Stern, Paul Rodriguez, Jan-Michael Vincent. **1987**

BORN YESTERDAY (1950) ★★★★½ Judy Holliday is simply delightful as a dizzy dame who isn't as dizzy as everyone thinks she is, in this comedy directed by George Cukor. William Holden is the professor hired by a junk-dealer-made-good (Broderick Crawford) to give Holliday lessons in how to be "high-toned." The results are highly entertaining—and very funny. B&W; 103m. **DIR:** George Cukor. **CAST:** Judy Holliday, William Holden, Broderick Crawford, Howard St. John. **1950**

BORN YESTERDAY (1993) ★★★★ Updated remake of the classic 1950 George Cukor comedy works well because of the chemistry among stars Melanie Griffith, Don Johnson, and John Goodman. Married in real life, Griffith and Johnson send off almost visible sparks. Goodman adds a deceptive likability to a crooked wheeler-dealer. Rated PG for profanity. 100m. **DIR:** Luis Mandoki. **CAST:** Melanie Griffith, John Goodman, Don Johnson, Edward Herrmann, Max Perlich, Fred Dalton Thompson, Nora Dunn. **1993**

BOSS' WIFE, THE ★★★½ After the first twenty minutes, this comedy starts rolling. Daniel Stern and Melanie Mayron play Joel and Janet, a two-career couple trying to make time for a baby. When Joel's boss (Christopher Plummer) finally notices him, he expects Joel to spend the weekend at the company resort. Laughs abound when Joel is pursued by the boss's nymphomaniac wife (beautiful Arielle Dombasle). Rated R for nudity, obscenities and sexual situations. 83m **DIR:** Ziggy Steinberg. **CAST:** Daniel Stern, Christopher Plummer, Arielle Dombasle, Fisher Stevens, Melanie Mayron, Martin Mull. **1986**

BOWERY BOYS, THE (SERIES) ★★½ When William Wyler brought Sidney Kingsley's play, *Dead End,* to the big screen in 1937, he unknowingly created a phenomenon known over the years as *The Dead End Kids, The Little Tough Guys, The East Side Kids* and, finally, *The Bowery Boys.* While the Dead End Kids enlivened a number of terrific Warner Bros. gangster films (most notably *Angels with Dirty Faces*), the end-of-the-line Bowery Boys were the low-camp clowns of their day. Still, the series has its devoted fans. Leo Gorcey and Huntz Hall were the leaders of a group of (by then) middle-aged men playing teenagers hatching knuckle-headed schemes in a sweet shop run by Gorcey's father, Bernard (as Louie), whom he cast, along with brother David, in the series after seizing creative control in 1946. When Bernard Gorcey died in 1956, Leo left the series, and seven films were made with Stanley Clements teaming up with Hall to lead the "boys" in their final and least interesting adventures. B&W; 60m. **DIR:** William Beaudine, Edward L. Bernds. **CAST:** Leo Gorcey, Huntz Hall, Bobby Jordan, William Benedict, David Gorcey, Gabriel Dell, Bernard Gorcey, Stanley Clements. **1946–1958**

BOY, DID I GET A WRONG NUMBER! 🦃 When you get a wrong number, hang up and dial again. Too bad the cast and director didn't. 99m. **DIR:** George Marshall. **CAST:** Bob Hope, Elke Sommer, Phyllis Diller. **1966**

BOY MEETS GIRL ★★★ An early spoof of Hollywood with James Cagney and Pat O'Brien as wisecracking, irreverent studio contract writers. On the side they help a young widow with her romantic problems. B&W; 86m. **DIR:** Lloyd Bacon. **CAST:** James Cagney, Pat O'Brien, Marie Wilson, Ralph Bellamy, Frank McHugh, Dick Foran, Ronald Reagan, Penny Singleton. **1938**

BOYS' NIGHT OUT ★★★½ Three otherwise staid married men finance an apartment and set out to share a live-in girl on the one night a week they are "allowed" out. They pick Kim Novak unaware she is a sociology student studying the sexual fantasies of suburban males. Good farce, and not the least bit smutty. Well ahead of its time with a wonderful cast. 115m. **DIR:** Michael Gordon. **CAST:** Kim Novak, James Garner, Tony Randall, Howard Duff, Janet Blair, Patti Page, Jessie Royce Landis, Oscar Homolka, Howard Morris,

Anne Jeffreys, Zsa Zsa Gabor, Fred Clark, William Bendix. 1962

BRAIN DONORS ★★★½ Three bumbling misfits—a shyster lawyer, a quick-witted taxi driver, and a dim-witted houseboy—join together to form a ballet company in this often hilarious take on the Marx Brothers's. John Turturro steals the show as he spews out an endless stream of lightning fast jokes à la Groucho. Rated PG for sexual innuendo and nudity. 79m. **DIR:** Dennis Dugan. **CAST:** John Turturro, Bob Nelson, Mel Smith, Nancy Marchand, John Savident, George de La Pena, Spike Alexander. 1992

BRAZIL ★★★★ A savage blend of *1984* and *The Time Bandits* from Monty Python director Terry Gilliam. Jonathan Pryce stars as a bemused paper shuffler in a red tape-choked future society at the brink of collapsing under its own bureaucracy. Definitely not for all tastes, but a treat for those with an appreciation for social satire. Were it not for a chaotic conclusion and slightly overlong running time, this would be a perfect picture. Rated R for language and adult situations. 131m. **DIR:** Terry Gilliam. **CAST:** Jonathan Pryce, Robert De Niro, Katherine Helmond, Ian Holm, Bob Hoskins, Michael Palin, Ian Richardson. 1985

BREAKFAST CLUB, THE ★★★★ A group of assorted high school misfits gets to be friends while serving weekend detention in this terrific comedy, directed by John Hughes, the king of watchable teen films. Rated R. 100m. **DIR:** John Hughes. **CAST:** Emilio Estevez, Molly Ringwald, Paul Gleason, Judd Nelson, Anthony Michael Hall, Ally Sheedy. 1985

BREAKFAST IN HOLLYWOOD ★★ This is a romantic comedy based on the radio series of the same name. The plot is thin, but there are some nice musical moments from Nat King Cole and Spike Jones. B&W; 91m. **DIR:** Harold Schuster. **CAST:** Bonita Granville, Beulah Bondi, Tom Breneman. 1946

BREAKING ALL THE RULES 🦃 Teenagers look for love (translation: lust) and adventure on the last day of summer vacation. 91m. **DIR:** James Orr. **CAST:** Carl Marotte, Thor Bishopric, Carolyn Dunn. 1984

BREAKING AWAY ★★★★★ There comes a time in every young man's life when he must loose the ties of home, family, and friends and test his mettle. Dennis Christopher is the young man who retains an innocence we too often mistake for naïveté; Paul Dooley and Barbara Barrie are the often humorously confused parents who offer subtle, sure guidance. This is a warm portrayal of family life and love, of friendships, of growing up and growing away. Rated PG for brief profanity. 100m. **DIR:** Peter Yates. **CAST:** Dennis Christopher, Dennis Quaid, Daniel Stern, Jackie Earle Haley, Paul Dooley, Barbara Barrie. 1979

BREAKING IN ★★★★ This low-key character comedy comes from director Bill Forsyth and screenwriter John Sayles. Burt Reynolds, in one of his finest screen performances, is a professional thief who becomes the mentor for a crazy housebreaker (Casey Siemaszko). A fascinating slice of life. Rated R for profanity. 95m. **DIR:** Bill Forsyth. **CAST:** Burt Reynolds, Casey Siemaszko, Albert Salmi, Harry Carey Jr. 1989

BREATH OF SCANDAL, A ★★ This intended high-style romantic comedy set in Austria in the gossip-rife court of Franz Joseph has little going for it. The script, taken from the Molnar play that poor John Gilbert adapted for his disastrous first talkie, is uninspired. The casting is uninspired. The directing is uninspired. But the scenery and costumes are nice. 98m. **DIR:** Michael Curtiz. **CAST:** Sophia Loren, John Gavin, Maurice Chevalier, Angela Lansbury. 1960

BREWSTER MCCLOUD ★★★ If you liked Robert Altman's *M*A*S*H* (the movie) and *Harold and Maude*, and your humor lies a few degrees off-center, you'll enjoy this "flight of fantasy" about a boy (Bud Cort) who wants to make like a bird. Rated R. 104m. **DIR:** Robert Altman. **CAST:** Bud Cort, Sally Kellerman. 1970

BREWSTER'S MILLIONS (1945) ★★½ This is the fifth of seven film versions of the 1902 novel and stage success about a young man who will inherit millions if he is able to spend $1 million quickly and quietly within a set period of time. Dennis O'Keefe and company perform this Tinsel Town stalwart in fine fashion, making for a bright, entertaining comic romp. B&W; 79m. **DIR:** Allan Dwan. **CAST:** Dennis O'Keefe, Helen Walker, June Havoc, Mischa Auer, Eddie "Rochester" Anderson, Gail Patrick. 1945

BREWSTER'S MILLIONS (1985) ★★★ It took director Walter Hill to bring Richard Pryor out of his movie slump with this unspectacular, but still entertaining, comedy about a minor-league baseball player who stands to inherit $300 million if he can fulfill the provisions of a rather daffy will. It's no classic, but still much, much better than *The Toy* or *Superman III*. Rated PG for profanity. 97m. **DIR:** Walter Hill. **CAST:** Richard Pryor, John Candy, Lonette McKee, Stephen Collins, Pat Hingle, Tovah Feldshuh, Hume Cronyn. 1985

BRIDE CAME C.O.D., THE ★★★ Bette Davis plays a runaway bride, and James Cagney goes after her on behalf of her rich father. A fun comedy in spite of an overused plot line. B&W; 92m. **DIR:** William Keighley. **CAST:** Bette Davis, James Cagney, Jack Carson, Eugene Pallette, George Tobias. 1941

BRIDE WALKS OUT, THE ★★★ This fast-paced comedy relies more on the dialogue and personalities of the supporting cast than on the stars or the story. Newlyweds Barbara Stanwyck and Gene Raymond can't get along on the amount of money he makes, and her spending estranges them. Lots of fun. B&W; 75m. **DIR:** Leigh Jason. **CAST:** Barbara Stanwyck, Gene Raymond, Robert Young, Ned Sparks, Helen Broderick, Billy Gilbert, Ward Bond, Hattie McDaniel. **1936**

BRIGHTON BEACH MEMOIRS ★★★½ Neil Simon's reminiscences of his adolescence make for genuinely enjoyable viewing. Refreshingly free of Simon's often too-clever dialogue, it aims for the heart and, more often than not, hits its mark. Rated PG-13 for sexual references. 110m. **DIR:** Gene Saks. **CAST:** Jonathan Silverman, Blythe Danner, Bob Dishy, Brian Brillinger, Stacey Glick, Judith Ivey, Lisa Waltz. **1986**

BRINGING UP BABY ★★★★★ A classic screwball comedy, this Howard Hawks picture has lost none of its punch even after fifty years. Katharine Hepburn plays a daffy rich girl who gets an absentminded professor (Cary Grant) into all sorts of trouble. *Bringing Up Baby* is guaranteed to have you falling out of your seat with helpless laughter. B&W; 102m. **DIR:** Howard Hawks. **CAST:** Cary Grant, Katharine Hepburn, Charlie Ruggles, May Robson. **1938**

BRINKS JOB, THE ★★★½ Peter Falk stars in this enjoyable release in which a gang of klutzy crooks pulls off "the crime of the century." It's a breezy caper film reminiscent of George Roy Hill's *Butch Cassidy and the Sundance Kid* and *The Sting*. Rated PG. 103m. **DIR:** William Friedkin. **CAST:** Peter Falk, Peter Boyle, Allen Garfield, Warren Oates, Paul Sorvino, Gena Rowlands. **1978**

BRITANNIA HOSPITAL ★★★ A wildly inadequate hospital serves as a metaphor for a sick society in this okay black comedy by British director Lindsay Anderson (*If; O Lucky Man*). Rated R. 115m. **DIR:** Lindsay Anderson. **CAST:** Leonard Rossiter, Graham Crowden, Malcolm McDowell, Joan Plowright. **1982**

BROADCAST NEWS ★★★★★ Writer-director-producer James L. Brooks tackles the flashy emptiness of contemporary television journalism and takes no hostages. William Hurt stars as the coming trend in news anchors—all enthusiasm and no education—who clashes amiably with Albert Brooks as the reporter's reporter: blessed with insight and a clever turn of phrase, but no camera presence. Both are attracted to dedicated superproducer Holly Hunter, an overachiever who schedules brief nervous breakdowns into her workday. Deft scripting and superb performances are just a few of the attractions in this great film. Not to be missed. Rated R for profanity. 131m. **DIR:** James L. Brooks. **CAST:** William Hurt, Albert Brooks, Holly Hunter, Jack Nicholson, Robert Prosky, Joan Cusack. **1987**

BROADWAY DANNY ROSE ★★★★½ The legendary talent agent Broadway Danny Rose (Woody Allen) takes on an alcoholic crooner (Nick Apollo Forte) and carefully nurtures him to the brink of stardom in this hilarious comedy, also written and directed by Allen. Mia Farrow is delightful as a gangster's moll who inadvertently gets Rose in big trouble. Rated PG for brief violence. B&W; 86m. **DIR:** Woody Allen. **CAST:** Woody Allen, Mia Farrow, Milton Berle, Sandy Baron. **1984**

BRONCO BILLY ★★★ This warm-hearted character study centers around Clint Eastwood as Bronco Billy, the owner of a run-down Wild West show. Sondra Locke is deserted on her honeymoon by her husband (Geoffrey Lewis). Desperate, she agrees to join the show as Eastwood's assistant and that's when the lightweight tale takes a romantic turn. Rated PG. 119m. **DIR:** Clint Eastwood. **CAST:** Clint Eastwood, Sondra Locke, Geoffrey Lewis, Scatman Crothers, Sam Bottoms, Bill McKinney, Dan Vadis. **1980**

BROTHERS IN LAW ★★★★ Callow young lawyer Ian Carmichael learns how the British courts really work when an elder barrister takes him under his wing. A most enjoyable British satire, with Terry-Thomas particularly funny as a perennial defendant. 94m. **DIR:** Roy Boulting. **CAST:** Ian Carmichael, Richard Attenborough, Terry-Thomas, Jill Adams, John Le Mesurier. **1957**

BRUCE CONNERS FILMS 1 ★★ Five short films by one of the leading figures in contemporary American avant-garde cinema. Bruce Conners uses static editing combining bizarre archive footage to create a humorous observation on pop culture and the human condition. This package contains his famous short "Mongoloid," with music by the pop groups Devo and America Is Waiting. B&W; 24m. **DIR:** Bruce Conners. **1989**

BUCK BENNY RIDES AGAIN ★★★ A Western spoof made to capitalize on Jack Benny's popular radio program. Most of his radio colleagues join him as he tries to impersonate a wild and woolly cowboy. Benny's humor hasn't dated nearly as much as some of his contemporaries. B&W; 82m. **DIR:** Mark Sandrich. **CAST:** Jack Benny, Eddie "Rochester" Anderson, Ellen Drew, Phil Harris, Dennis Day, Andy Devine, Virginia Dale. **1940**

BUCK PRIVATES ★★★ Abbott and Costello are at their best in their first starring film, but it's still no classic. On the lam, the two are forced to enlist during World War II. B&W; 82m. **DIR:** Arthur Lubin. **CAST:** Bud Abbott, Lou Costello, Lee Bowman, Alan Curtis, Jane Frazee. **1941**

BUCK PRIVATES COME HOME ★★ Bud Abbott and Lou Costello reprise their roles from their first big hit, this time mustering out of the service and bringing an orphan with them. B&W; 77m. **DIR:** Charles Barton. **CAST:** Bud Abbott, Lou Costello, Beverly Simmons, Nat Pendleton, Tom Brown, Don Beddoe, Donald MacBride. **1947**

BUDDY, BUDDY ★★ Jack Lemmon is a clumsy would-be suicide who decides to end it all in a hotel. Walter Matthau is a hit man who rents the room next door and finds the filling of his contract difficult. The results are less than hilarious but do provoke a few smiles. Rated R because of profanity and brief nudity. 96m. **DIR:** Billy Wilder. **CAST:** Jack Lemmon, Walter Matthau, Paula Prentiss, Klaus Kinski. **1981**

BUFFY, THE VAMPIRE SLAYER ★★★½ A high school cheerleader has to put down her pom-poms and forgo hanging out at the mall when she discovers that she's the latest in a long line of women whose job it is to kill vampires. It's better than it sounds. Rated PG-13 for violence and profanity. 100m. **DIR:** Fran Rubel Kuzui. **CAST:** Kristy Swanson, Donald Sutherland, Rutger Hauer, Luke Perry. **1992**

BUFORD'S BEACH BUNNIES ★★ Harry Buford, owner of the Bunny Hole, offers a large reward to whichever Bunny employee can make his son Cheeter lose his virginity. Extremely bad acting and dialogue. The background action is funnier than the plot. Rated R for nudity, profanity, and graphic sex. 94m. **DIR:** Mark Pirro. **CAST:** Jim Hanks, Rikki Brando, Monique Parent, Amy Page, Barrett Cooper, Ina Rogers, Charley Rossman, David Robinson. **1992**

BULL DURHAM ★★★★ Tim Robbins plays a rookie pitcher for a minor league baseball team. He has a lightning-fast throw, but he's apt to hit the team mascot as often as the strike zone. Kevin Costner is a dispirited catcher brought in to "mature" Robbins. A quirky, intelligent comedy with plenty of surprises, the film contains some of the sharpest jabs at sports since *Slap Shot*. Rated R for profanity and sexual content. 104m. **DIR:** Ron Shelton. **CAST:** Kevin Costner, Susan Sarandon, Tim Robbins, Trey Wilson, Robert Wuhl. **1988**

BULLFIGHTERS, THE ★★★ While not a classic, this latter-day Laurel and Hardy film is surprisingly good—especially when you consider that the boys had lost all control over the making of their pictures by this time. The story has Laurel resembling a famous bullfighter, and, of course, this leads to chaos in the ring. B&W; 61m. **DIR:** Malcolm St. Clair. **CAST:** Stan Laurel, Oliver Hardy, Margo Woode, Richard Lane, Carol Andrews. **1945**

BULLSEYE ★★★ In this surprisingly entertaining—albeit featherweight—caper comedy from director Michael Winner, Michael Caine and Roger Moore essay dual roles as two identical pairs of con men. Sally Kirkland costars as the brains (and body) of the organization. Rated PG-13 for profanity. 95m. **DIR:** Michael Winner. **CAST:** Michael Caine, Roger Moore, Sally Kirkland. **1990**

BULLSHOT ★★½ A movie can be fun for a while, then overstay its welcome. Such is the case with this spoof of Herman Cyril "Scapper" McNiele's *Bulldog Drummond* mystery-spy adventures. Everything is played to the hilt, and the characters become caricatures. Although this is occasionally irritating, the star-screenwriters do create some funny moments. Rated PG for profanity, sex, and violence. 95m. **DIR:** Dick Clement. **CAST:** Alan Shearman, Diz White, Ron House, Frances Tomelty, Michael Aldridge. **1985**

BUNDLE OF JOY ★★★ In this breezy remake of Ginger Rogers's *Bachelor Mother*, Debbie Reynolds portrays a department-store salesgirl who takes custody of an infant. (Eddie Fisher is suspected of being the father.) A scandal ensues. 98m. **DIR:** Norman Taurog. **CAST:** Debbie Reynolds, Eddie Fisher, Adolphe Menjou, Tommy Noonan. **1956**

BUONO SERA, MRS. CAMPBELL ★★★½ Great farce, with Gina Lollobrigida having convinced three World War II soldiers that they fathered her child, collecting support payments from each. Then she learns the ex-GIs are returning to Italy for a twenty-year reunion. 113m. **DIR:** Melvin Frank. **CAST:** Gina Lollobrigida, Peter Lawford, Phil Silvers, Telly Savalas, Shelley Winters, Lee Grant. **1968**

'BURBS, THE ★★ In this weird and ultimately unsatisfying comedy, Tom Hanks plays a suburbanite who becomes more and more concerned about the bizarre family who has moved in next door. Essentially it's *Neighbors* all over again, with Hanks, Carrie Fisher, Rick Ducommun, and Bruce Dern turning in strong performances. Despite some inspired touches from director Joe Dante, it falls flat in the final third. Rated PG for violence and profanity. 102m. **DIR:** Joe Dante. **CAST:** Tom Hanks, Bruce Dern, Carrie Fisher, Rick Ducommun, Corey Feldman, Wendy Schaal, Henry Gibson. **1989**

BURGLAR (1987) ★★★ Whoopi Goldberg stars in this amiable but unspectacular caper comedy as a retired cat burglar forced back into a life of crime by a crooked cop (G. W. Bailey). She ends up the prime suspect in a rather messy murder case. Goldberg does well in a role originally written for Bruce Willis, but one wishes she would find a comedy script tailored specifically for her impressive talents. Rated R for profanity and violence. 91m. **DIR:** Hugh Wilson. **CAST:** Whoopi Goldberg, Bob Goldthwait, G. W. Bailey, Lesley Ann Warren. **1987**

BURLESQUE OF CARMEN ★★ Charles Chaplin portrays Darn Hosiery, a soldier who is seduced by a gypsy girl, Carmen (Edna Purviance). Violence ensues when she leaves him for a toreador. The send-up ending reveals all the murderous shenanigans have been mere hoaxes. By no means a major Chaplin effort. Silent. B&W; 40m. **DIR:** Charles Chaplin. **CAST:** Charlie Chaplin, Edna Purviance. **1916**

BUS STOP ★★★★½ Marilyn Monroe plays a show girl who is endlessly pursued by an oaf of a cowboy named Bo (Don Murray). He even kidnaps her when she refuses to marry him. Lots of laughs as Bo mistreats his newly found "angel." Arthur O'Connell is excellent as Verg, Bo's older and wiser friend who advises Bo on the way to treat women. 96m. **DIR:** Joshua Logan. **CAST:** Marilyn Monroe, Don Murray, Arthur O'Connell, Betty Field, Casey Adams. **1956**

BUSTER KEATON FESTIVAL: VOL. 1 ★★★ The legendary Buster Keaton shines in these three short slapstick comedies first released in the roaring 1920s: *Paleface*, *The Blacksmith*, and *Cops*. The last, in particular, is a gem of silent-film shenanigans contrived around Keaton's pursuit by an entire city police force. B&W; 55m. **DIR:** Buster Keaton, Eddie Cline, Malcolm St. Clair. **CAST:** Buster Keaton, Virginia Fox, Joe Roberts, Eddie Cline. **1921–1922**

BUSTER KEATON FESTIVAL: VOL. 2 ★★★ Conjuring warm silent-comedy memories, Keaton cavorts sublimely in this trio of short features: *The Boat*, *The Frozen North*, and *The Electric House*. The premise of the third film is priceless, the technical execution pure genius. B&W; 55m. **DIR:** Buster Keaton, Eddie Cline. **CAST:** Buster Keaton, Sybil Seely, Eddie Cline, Bonnie Hill, Freeman Wood, Joe Roberts, Virginia Fox, Joseph Keaton, Myra Keaton, Louise Keaton. **1921–1922**

BUSTER KEATON FESTIVAL: VOL. 3 ★★★ Another hilarious collection of Keaton's slapstick comedies: *Daydreams*, *The Balloonatic*, and *The Garage*. Keaton at the mercy of a folding boat in a raging river in *The Balloonatic* is outstanding. Good, clean fun, all around. B&W; 54m. **DIR:** Buster Keaton, Eddie Cline. **CAST:** Buster Keaton, Virginia Fox, Phyllis Haver, Renée Adorée, Joe Roberts. **1921–1922**

BUSTER KEATON SCRAPBOOK, VOL. I ★★★★ *The Paleface*, *Daydreams*, *The Blacksmith*—three silent-comedy gems from the fertile mind of one of film's most inventive and innovative actor-directors. Standout scenes include the paddle-wheel sequence in *Daydreams*, and the magnet and Rolls-Royce destruction in *The Blacksmith*. B&W; 58m. **DIR:** Buster Keaton. **CAST:** Buster Keaton, Eddie Cline. **1921–1922**

BUSTER KEATON: THE GOLDEN YEARS ★★★ The incomparable "Great Stone Face" Buster Keaton and his often imperious and domineering costar Joe Roberts once more create good, clean laughter in three of Keaton's early silents: *The Paleface*, *Daydreams*, and *The Blacksmith*. The viewer is double-dared to keep a straight face. Great, timeless, nostalgic movie memories for everyone. Silent with musical score. B&W; 60m. **DIR:** Buster Keaton, Eddie Cline. **CAST:** Buster Keaton, Joe Roberts, Renée Adorée, Virginia Fox. **1921–1922**

BUSTER KEATON: THE GREAT STONE FACE ★★★½ Narrated by comedian Henry Morgan, this roundup brings together these Keaton classics: *Daydreams*, *Cops*, *The Balloonatic*, *The General*, and *Fatty at Coney Island*. Gags in *Cops* and *The General* alone document the genius of the "Great Stone Face." B&W; 60m. **DIR:** Buster Keaton. **CAST:** Buster Keaton, Roscoe "Fatty" Arbuckle, Mabel Normand, Phyllis Haver, Marion Mack, Joseph Keaton, Al St. John. **1968**

BUSTIN' LOOSE ★★½ Take superbad ex-con Richard Pryor, stick him on a school bus with goody-two-shoes teacher Cicely Tyson and eight ornery schoolchildren, and what have you got? A cross-country, comic odyssey as long as Pryor is up to his madcap antics. But *Bustin' Loose* bogs down in its last half hour. Rated R for profanity and violence. 94m. **DIR:** Oz Scott. **CAST:** Richard Pryor, Cicely Tyson, Robert Christian, Alphonso Alexander, Janet Wong. **1981**

BUTCHER'S WIFE, THE ★★ You don't have to be clairvoyant to know what's going to happen in this comedy about a North Carolina psychic who weds a New York City butcher because she thinks he's the man of her dreams. Apart from isolated moments of inspiration, *The Butcher's Wife* is comparable with a so-so episode of *Bewitched*. Rated PG-13 for profanity. 105m. **DIR:** Terry Hughes. **CAST:** Demi Moore, Jeff Daniels, George Dzundza, Mary Steenburgen, Frances McDormand, Margaret Colin. **1991**

BUY AND CELL 🦃 A Wall Street broker takes the rap for his boss's insider trading. Rated R. 91m. **DIR:** Robert Boris. **CAST:** Robert Carradine, Michael Winslow, Randall "Tex" Cobb, Fred Travalena, Ben Vereen, Malcolm McDowell. **1989**

CABIN BOY 🦃 Pathetic, filthy-rich geek mistakes a grungy fishing trawler for a cruise ship in this lame fantasy-comedy version of *Captains Courageous*. Rated PG-13 for language. 80m. **DIR:** Adam Resnick. **CAST:** Chris Elliott, Ritch Brinkley, Brian Doyle-Murray, James Gammon, Brion James, Melora Walters, Andy Richter. **1994**

CACTUS FLOWER ★★★ Watch this one for Goldie Hawn's performance that earned her an Academy Award as best supporting actress. She's the slightly wonky girlfriend of dentist Walter Matthau, who actually loves his nurse (Ingrid Bergman). Although adapted from a hit Broadway play by Abe Burrows, this film version is pretty short on laughs. Ingrid Bergman is far too serious in her role, and Matthau simply doesn't make a credible dentist. Rated PG for adult situations. 103m. **DIR:** Gene Saks. **CAST:** Walter Matthau, Ingrid Bergman, Goldie Hawn. **1969**

CADDY, THE ★★★ In this lesser comedy from the Martin and Lewis team, the fellas enter the world of golf. Jerry plays a would-be golf pro. Strictly formulaic, but highlighted by several entertaining clashes between the two stars. 95m. **DIR:** Norman Taurog. **CAST:** Dean Martin, Jerry Lewis, Donna Reed, Fred Clark. **1953**

CADDYSHACK ★★ Only Rodney Dangerfield, as an obnoxious refugee from a leisure-suit collectors' convention, offers anything of value in this rip-off of the *Animal House* formula. Chevy Chase and Bill Murray sleepwalk through their poorly written roles, and Ted Knight looks a little weary. Rated R for nudity and sex. 99m. **DIR:** Harold Ramis. **CAST:** Chevy Chase, Rodney Dangerfield, Ted Knight, Michael O'Keefe, Bill Murray. **1980**

CADDYSHACK II 🦃 Deciding to pass on this abysmal sequel may be the smartest career move Rodney Dangerfield ever made. Rated PG for profanity. 103m. **DIR:** Allan Arkush. **CAST:** Jackie Mason, Chevy Chase, Dan Aykroyd, Robert Stack, Dyan Cannon, Randy Quaid, Jonathan Silverman. **1988**

CADILLAC MAN ★★★★ Philandering car salesman Robin Williams embarks on the worst few days of his life when his wife (Pamela Reed) demands more alimony, a gangster wants payment on a $20,000 gambling debt, and his boss demands that he sell a month's worth of cars in one day—then distraught husband Tim Robbins comes roaring into the dealership with an automatic weapon looking for the man who has been bedding his wife. Well acted and often hilarious. Rated R for violence, profanity, and nudity. 95m. **DIR:** Roger Donaldson. **CAST:** Robin Williams, Tim Robbins, Pamela Reed, Fran Drescher, Zack Norman. **1990**

CAFE ROMEO ★★★ Raised with old-world traditions that no longer apply to them, six lifelong friends seek out a niche in the world as they venture from their neighborhood coffeehouse. Second-generation Italian-Americans are the focus of this somewhat uneven romantic comedy. Rated R for profanity. 93m. **DIR:** Rex Bromfield. **CAST:** Catherine Mary Stewart, Jonathan Crombie. **1991**

CALENDAR GIRL ★★ Three teenage Nevada boys head for Hollywood to meet Marilyn Monroe. Clearly intended as both a tribute to Monroe and a warm memoir of adolescence, the film fails on both counts as it swings between dumb slapstick and even dumber sentimentality. Anyone old enough to remember Monroe is too old to fall for this. Rated PG-13 for mild profanity. 90m. **DIR:** John Whitesell. **CAST:** Jason Priestley, Gabriel Olds, Jerry O'Connell. **1993**

CALIFORNIA CASANOVA ★★★ Tyrone Power Jr. is delightful as a bumbling nerd who is transformed by a charming count. Best scenes: when Power receives advice from a number of sources on how to be irresistible. Rated R for nudity and profanity. 94m. **DIR:** Nathaniel Christian. **CAST:** Jerry Orbach, Audrey Landers, Tyrone Power Jr. **1991**

CALIFORNIA SUITE ★★★½ This enjoyable adaptation of the Neil Simon play features multiple stars.The action revolves around the various inhabitants of a Beverly Hills hotel room. We are allowed to enter and observe the private lives of the various guests in the room during the four watchable short stories within this film. Rated PG. 103m. **DIR:** Herbert Ross. **CAST:** Jane Fonda, Alan Alda, Maggie Smith, Richard Pryor, Bill Cosby. **1978**

CALL ME BWANA ★★½ A bogus writer of safari books sent to Africa to locate a downed space capsule encounters Russian agents. Too few one-liners by the past master. 103m. **DIR:** Gordon Douglas. **CAST:** Bob Hope, Anita Ekberg, Edie Adams, Lionel Jeffries. **1963**

CALL OUT THE MARINES ★★½ The prime attraction here is the team of Victor McLaglen and Edmund Lowe in their last comedy together. As always, they play a pair of battling marine buddies, this time engaged in a rivalry over saloon singer Binnie Barnes. Several songs (by Mort Greene and Harry Revel) are no great shakes. 66m. **DIR:** Frank Ryan. **CAST:** Victor McLaglen, Edmund Lowe, Binnie Barnes, Paul Kelly, Robert Smith, Franklin Pangborn. **1942**

CAMERAMAN, THE ★★★★ This silent casts Buster Keaton as a free-lance news cameraman trying desperately to impress a girl and earn his spurs with a scoop. He finally gets in the thick of a Chinese tong war, filming his way to success in a hail of bullets. A superb example of Keaton comedy genius. Silent. B&W; 70m. **DIR:** Edward Sedgwick. **CAST:** Buster Keaton, Marceline Day, Edward Brophy. **1928**

CAMPUS MAN ★★ In this well-intended and generally watchable movie, a college student (John Dye) produces an all-male pinup calendar and strikes it rich. Rated PG. 95m. **DIR:** Ron Casden. **CAST:** John Dye, Kim Delaney, Kathleen Wilhoite, Steve Lyon, Morgan Fairchild, Miles O'Keeffe. **1987**

CAN I DO IT 'TIL I NEED GLASSES? 🦃 A follow-up to *If You Don't Stop, You'll Go Blind.* Rated R for nudity and profanity. 72m. **DIR:** I. Robert Levy. **CAST:** Robin Williams, Roger Behr, Debra Klose, Moose Carlson, Walter Olkewicz. **1980**

CAN IT BE LOVE 🦃 Run-of-the-mill teen sex comedy about two horny guys looking to do something about it. Dreadful. Rated R for nudity and language. 90m. **DIR:** Peter Maris. **CAST:** Charles Klausmeyer, Richard Beaumont. **1992**

CAN SHE BAKE A CHERRY PIE? ★★★ Karen Black plays a woman whose husband leaves her before she has fully awakened one morning. She meets Eli, played by Michael Emil, a balding character actor whose body is slowly sliding into his knees. This is a small film, and its appeal is quiet. It also is an example of what can be right with American movie-making, even when the money isn't there. No rating, but considerable vulgar language, sexual situations. 90m. **DIR:** Henry Jaglom. **CAST:** Karen Black, Michael Emil. **1984**

CANCEL MY RESERVATION ★★ Tired reworking of a Bob Hope formula comedy is slow going despite a pretty good cast and a plot lifted from a Louis L'Amour novel. Hope plays a popular TV show host who heads to Arizona for a rest and gets mixed up with crooks. Highlight of the film is a nightmare sequence with cameos of celebrities including John Wayne and Bing Crosby. 99m. **DIR:** Paul Bogart. **CAST:** Bob Hope, Eva Marie Saint, Ralph Bellamy, Forrest Tucker, Anne Archer, Keenan Wynn, Chief Dan George. **1972**

CANNERY ROW ★★★ It's hard to dislike this film, starring Nick Nolte and Debra Winger. Despite its artificiality, halting pace, and general unevenness, there are so many marvelous moments—most provided by Frank McRae as the lovable simpleton Hazel—that you don't regret having seen it. Rated PG for slight nudity, profanity, and violence. 120m. **DIR:** David S. Ward. **CAST:** Nick Nolte, Debra Winger, Audra Lindley, M. Emmet Walsh, Frank McRae. **1982**

CANNONBALL RUN 🦃 This star-studded bore is the story of an unsanctioned, totally illegal cross-country car race in which there are no rules and few survivors. Rated PG for profanity. 95m. **DIR:** Hal Needham. **CAST:** Burt Reynolds, Roger Moore, Farrah Fawcett, Dom DeLuise, Dean Martin, Sammy Davis Jr. **1981**

CANNONBALL RUN II 🦃 Awful rehash of *Cannonball Run*. Rated PG. 108m. **DIR:** Hal Needham. **CAST:** Burt Reynolds, Dom DeLuise, Shirley MacLaine, Marilu Henner, Telly Savalas, Dean Martin, Sammy Davis Jr., Frank Sinatra. **1984**

CAN'T BUY ME LOVE ★★ The title song is the Beatles' classic tune. Unfortunately, this film is all downhill from there. Patrick Dempsey plays a nerd who learns that popularity isn't all it's cracked up to be. The message is delivered in heavy-handed style. Still, teens will love it. Rated PG-13 for profanity. 94m. **DIR:** Steve Rash. **CAST:** Amanda Peterson, Patrick Dempsey, Courtney Gains, Tina Caspary, Seth Green, Sharon Farrell, Dennis Dugan, Ami Dolenz, Steve Franken. **1987**

CAPTAIN RON ★★★ A lighthearted comedy about a Chicago businessman (Martin Short) who inherits his uncle's yacht and drags his family to the Caribbean. In search of someone to pilot the boat—actually a broken-down hulk—the group finds Captain Ron (Kurt Russell), a less than skilled skipper. Some hilarious bits. Rated PG-13 for profanity. 100m. **DIR:** Thom Eberhardt. **CAST:** Kurt Russell, Martin Short, Mary Kay Place, Paul Anka. **1992**

CAPTAIN'S PARADISE, THE ★★★★ From the opening shot, in which he is "shot," Alec Guinness displays the seemingly artless comedy form that marked him for stardom. He plays the bigamist skipper of a ferry, a wife in each port, flirting with delicious danger. Timing is all, and close shaves—including a chance meeting of the wives—yields edge of seat entertainment. Lotsa fun. B&W; 77m. **DIR:** Anthony Kimmins. **CAST:** Alec Guinness, Celia Johnson, Yvonne De Carlo, Bill Fraser. **1953**

CAPTAIN'S TABLE ★★½ This is a delightful comedy about a skipper of a cargo vessel who is given trial command of a luxury liner. Has some wildly funny moments. Not rated. B&W; 90m. **DIR:** Jack Lee. **CAST:** John Gregson, Peggy Cummins, Donald Sinden, Nadia Gray. **1960**

CAR 54, WHERE ARE YOU? 🦃 David Johansen, as Officer Toody, is hilarious, but this goofy comedy can't hold it together. Lingering too long on numerous sight gags costs them their punch and several musical scenes seem very out of place. The fragile plot about catching a gangster is overshadowed by numerous unimportant subplots. Original TV-series cast members make cameo appearances. Rated PG-13 for comic-book voilence. 85m. **DIR:** Bill Fishman. **CAST:** David Johansen, John C. McGinley, Fran Drescher, Nipsey Russell, Al Lewis, Rosie O'Donnell. **1991**

CAR 54 WHERE ARE YOU? (TV SERIES) ★★★½ Early-60s television series about the comic misadventures of Bronx policemen Gunther Toody and Francis Muldoon. The laugh track is annoyingly loud but the shows are quite funny, with outrageous situations and memorable characters. Each cassette contains two episodes; there were sixty in all. 1961–1963; B&W; 50m. **DIR:** Nat Hiken, Stanley Prager. **CAST:** Joe E. Ross, Fred Gwynne, Paul Reed, Al Lewis, Charlotte Rae.

CAR WASH ★★★½ This is an ensemble film that features memorable bits from Richard Pryor, George Carlin, Franklin Ajaye, Ivan Dixon, and the Pointer Sisters. There are plenty of laughs, music, and even a moral in this fine low-budget production. Rated PG. 97m. **DIR:** Michael Schultz. **CAST:** Richard Pryor, Franklin Ajaye, Sully Boyar, Ivan Dixon. **1976**

CARBON COPY ★★★½ This amiable, lightweight comedy of racial manners stars George Segal as a white corporate executive who suddenly discovers he has a teenage black son just itching to be adopted in lily-white San Marino, California. Rated PG. 92m. **DIR:** Michael Schultz. **CAST:** George Segal, Susan Saint James, Jack Warden, Dick Martin. **1981**

CAREER OPPORTUNITIES ★★ The town liar is locked in a department store overnight with the town beauty and two bumbling burglers in this just passable film written and coproduced by John Hughes. Rated PG-13 for brief profanity and violence. 83m. **DIR:** Bryan Gordon. **CAST:** Frank Whaley, Jennifer Connelly, Barry Corbin, Noble Willingham, William Forsythe, Dermot Mulroney, Kieran Mulroney, John Candy. **1991**

CARLIN AT CARNEGIE ★★★½ This Home Box Office–backed video may not be as consistently funny as other comedy videos, but it has that special quality of having come from the heart—as well as hard-earned experience and deep thought. It's funny and sad at the same time. Carlin has found that you can't always have a nice day and does a very funny, brilliant routine on how being told to have one can be irritating. And, as always, Carlin uses the English language—and our taboos on certain parts of it—against itself in several bits. 60m. **DIR:** Steve Santos. **CAST:** George Carlin. **1983**

CARLIN ON CAMPUS ★★★½ An uproarious show by one of America's funniest men, George Carlin, recorded live for HBO. Carlin has some classic bits on this tape, including "A Place for My Stuff" and observations on driving. The only drawback is the infantile and ribald cartoons that are plugged in at odd moments. Unrated, but contains raw language. 59m. **DIR:** Steve Santos. **CAST:** George Carlin. **1984**

CARLTON-BROWNE OF THE F.O. ★★½ A British foreign-office secretary is assigned to a small island nation, formerly of the empire. For serious buffs this is an interesting, but not classic, bit of movie history. Not rated and only mildly ribald. B&W; 88m. **DIR:** Jeffrey Dell. **CAST:** Terry-Thomas, Peter Sellers, Luciana Paluzzi. **1958**

CAROL BURNETT'S MY PERSONAL BEST ★★★½ Carol Burnett showcases four of the funniest and most memorable skits from her television show. These classic sketches are sure to bring back memories and make you laugh all over again. Not rated. Suitable for the whole family. 60m. **DIR:** Dave Powers. **CAST:** Carol Burnett, Harvey Korman, Vicki Lawrence, Tim Conway, Sammy Davis Jr., Anthony Newley, Bernadette Peters. **1987**

CARRY ON ADMIRAL ★★ His Majesty's navy suffers semi-hilariously at the hands of a madcap crew tangled in ribald high jinks, double identity, and comic cuts. Originally titled *The Ship Was Loaded*. 81m. **DIR:** Val Guest. **CAST:** David Tomlinson, Peggy Cummins, Alfie Bass, Ronald Shiner. **1957**

CARRY ON AT YOUR CONVENIENCE ★★ The British *Carry On* comedy players were still carrying on in 1971, but they were starting to run out of breath. Unrated, but full of innuendoes. 86m. **DIR:** Gerald Thomas. **CAST:** Sidney James, Kenneth Williams, Charles Hawtrey, Joan Sims. **1971**

CARRY ON BEHIND 🦃 Archaeologists and holiday campers stumble over each other while trying to share the same location. Unrated. 90m. **DIR:** Gerald Thomas. **CAST:** Elke Sommer, Kenneth Williams, Sidney James, Joan Sims. **1975**

CARRY ON CLEO ★★★½ It's a matter of personal taste, but we find this to be the funniest of the *Carry On* series. (Of course, you might not find any of them funny.) It's designed as a spoof of the then-current Burton-Taylor *Cleopatra*. *Dr. Who* fans will spot Jon Pertwee in a small role. 92m. **DIR:** Gerald Thomas. **CAST:** Amanda Barrie, Sidney James, Kenneth Williams, Kenneth Connor, Joan Sims, Charles Hawtrey, Jim Dale, Jon Pertwee. **1965**

CARRY ON COWBOY ★★½ Another in a very long, and weakening, line of British farces, many of them spoofs of highly popular films. Replete with the usual double-entendre jokes and sight gags, this one sends up *High Noon*. 91m. **DIR:** Gerald Thomas. **CAST:** Sidney James, Kenneth Williams, Joan Sims, Angela Douglas, Jim Dale. **1966**

CARRY ON CRUISING ★★★ One of the earlier, and therefore better, entries in the long-lived British series. The jokes are more energetic, less forced. In this one, the players try desperately to fill in for the regular crew of a Mediterranean cruise ship. Unrated. B&W; 99m. **DIR:** Gerald Thomas. **CAST:** Sidney James, Kenneth Williams, Kenneth Connor, Liz Fraser. **1962**

CARRY ON DOCTOR ★★★ Adding veteran British comic Frankie Howerd to the cast helped perk up this *Carry On* entry a bit. The usual gang plays the bumbling staff of a hospital, caught up in a battle over a secret weight-loss formula. Unrated. 95m. **DIR:** Gerald Thomas. **CAST:** Frankie Howerd, Sidney James, Kenneth Williams, Charles Hawtrey, Jim Dale, Hattie Jacques, Joan Sims, Peter Butterworth. **1968**

CARRY ON EMMANUELLE 🦃 The last of the *Carry On* series, and not a moment too soon. Unrated. 88m. **DIR:** Gerald Thomas. **CAST:** Suzanne Danielle, Kenneth Williams, Kenneth Connor, Joan Sims, Peter Butterworth, Beryl Reid. **1978**

CARRY ON NURSE ★★★ Daffy struggle between patients and hospital staff. It's one of the most consistently amusing entries in this British comedy series. 90m. **DIR:** Gerald Thomas. **CAST:** Kenneth Connor, Kenneth Williams, Charles Hawtrey, Terence Longden. **1960**

CARTIER AFFAIR, THE 🦃 Less than funny comic romance that involves a male secretary falling in love with his soap-opera-legend boss. 96m. **DIR:** Rod Holcomb. **CAST:** Joan Collins, David Hasselhoff, Telly Savalas, Jay Gerber, Hilly Hicks. **1985**

CASANOVA (1987) ★★ After infamous eighteenth century ladies' man Richard Chamberlain is arrested as an undesirable, the viewer—unfortunately—suffers through his entire life story. A drag. Not rated, but contains nudity and sexual situations. 122m. **DIR:** Simon Langton. **CAST:** Richard Chamberlain, Faye Dunaway, Sylvia Kristel, Ornella Muti, Hanna Schygulla, Sophie Ward. **1987**

CASANOVA BROWN ★★★ Gary Cooper's plans to remarry are complicated when he learns his recently divorced ex-wife (Teresa Wright) is about to have a baby. Mild laughs but good performances. Frank Morgan steals the show. B&W; 94m. **DIR:** Sam Wood. **CAST:** Gary Cooper, Teresa Wright, Frank Morgan, Anita Louise, Jill Esmond. **1944**

CASANOVA'S BIG NIGHT ★★½ The evergreen Bob Hope is a lowly tailor's assistant masquerading as the great lover Casanova in this costume comedy set in plot-and-intrigue-ridden Venice. Old Ski Nose is irrepressible, sets are sumptuous, and costumes lavish, but the script and direction don't measure up. Funny, but not *that* funny. 86m. **DIR:** Norman Z. McLeod. **CAST:** Bob Hope, Joan Fontaine, Basil Rathbone, Audrey Dalton, Frieda Inescort, Hope Emerson, Hugh Marlowe, John Carradine, John Hoyt, Robert Hutton, Raymond Burr, Lon Chaney Jr. **1954**

CASE OF THE MUKKINESE BATTLE HORN, THE ★★★ Two-thirds of the cast of Britain's memorable *Goon Show* reunite for this indescribable free-form comedy short. A must-see for fans of *SCTV* and *Monty Python*. 27m. **DIR:** Uncredited. **CAST:** Peter Sellers, Spike Milligan. **1958**

CASH MCCALL ★★★ James Garner is great as a fast-moving financial wizard who must slow down his plan to take over a plastic factory when he pauses to woo the owner's daughter. Lightweight—but the stars shine. 102m. **DIR:** Joseph Pevney. **CAST:** James Garner, Natalie Wood, Dean Jagger, Nina Foch, Henry Jones, E. G. Marshall. **1959**

CASINO ROYALE (1967) ★★ What do you get when you combine the talents of this all-star ensemble? Not much. This is the black sheep of the James Bond family of films. The rights to *Casino Royale* weren't part of the Ian Fleming package. Not wanting to compete with the Sean Connery vehicles, this film was intended to be a stylish spoof. For the most part, it's an overblown bore. 130m. **DIR:** John Huston, Ken Hughes, Robert Parrish, Joseph McGrath, Val Guest. **CAST:** Peter Sellers, Ursula Andress, David Niven, Orson Welles, Joanna Pettet, Woody Allen, Deborah Kerr, William Holden, Charles Boyer, John Huston, George Raft, Jean-Paul Belmondo. **1967**

CASUAL SEX? ★★★ Oddball, likable comedy about two single girls (Lea Thompson and Victoria Jackson) who go hunting for men at a health resort. Although not providing roll-in-the-aisles laughter, *Casual Sex?* is a real attempt at making some sense of the safe-sex question. Rated R for sexual frankness, language and nudity. 90m. **DIR:** Genevieve Robert. **CAST:** Lea Thompson, Victoria Jackson, Stephen Shellen, Mary Gross. **1988**

CATCH AS CATCH CAN ★★ Vittorio Gassman plays a television-commerical actor who finds the animal kingdom out to get him. The dubbed English makes it worse. Not rated, has sex and nudity. 92m. **DIR:** Franco Indovina. **CAST:** Vittorio Gassman, Martha Hyer, Gila Golan, Claudio Gora, Massimo Serato. **1968**

CATCH-22 ★★★ This release stars Alan Arkin as a soldier in World War II most interested in avoiding the insanity of combat. Its sarcasm alone is enough to sustain interest. Rated R. 121m. **DIR:** Mike Nichols. **CAST:** Alan Arkin, Martin Balsam, Richard Benjamin, Anthony Perkins, Art Garfunkel. **1970**

CAUGHT IN THE DRAFT ★★★½ A gun-shy movie idol attempts to avoid the draft and mistakenly enlists in the army. Some very good gags; even the (then) topical ones stand up. B&W; 82m. **DIR:** David Butler. **CAST:** Bob Hope, Dorothy Lamour, Eddie Bracken, Lynne Overman, Irving Bacon. **1941**

CAVEMAN ★★ Ex-Beatle Ringo Starr plays the prehistoric hero in this spoof of *One Million Years B.C.* Because of the amount of sexual innuendo, it is definitely not recommended for kids. Rated PG. 92m. **DIR:** Carl Gottlieb. **CAST:** Ringo Starr, Barbara Bach, John Matuszak, Shelley Long, Dennis Quaid. **1981**

CB4 ★★ This attempt to parody the rap music industry has some very funny moments, but overall it fails as a satire and becomes a silly sex comedy full of profanity and misogyny. Rated R for violence, profanity, and nudity. 88m. **DIR:** Tamra Davis. **CAST:** Chris Rock, Allen Payne, Deezer D, Phil Hartman, Art Evans, Theresa Randle, Willard E. Pugh, Richard Gant, Charlie Murphy, Chris Elliott. **1993**

CHAMPAGNE FOR CAESAR ★★★★ Satire of early television and the concept of game shows is funnier now than when it was originally released. A treasure trove of trivia and great one-liners, this intelligent spoof features actor Ronald Colman as Beauregarde Bottomley, self-proclaimed genius and scholar who exacts his revenge on soap tycoon Vincent Price by appearing on his quiz show and attempting to bankrupt his company by winning all their assets. B&W; 99m. **DIR:** Richard Whorf. **CAST:** Ronald Colman, Celeste Holm, Vincent Price, Barbara Britton, Art Linkletter. **1950**

CHAN IS MISSING ★★★★ In this delightful independent production, filmed in San Francisco's Chinatown, two cab drivers attempt to track down a friend who disappeared after they gave him $5,000 to purchase a taxi license. Although in form a mystery, this comedy is also a gentle jab at racial stereotypes and a revealing study of problems faced by members of the Asian-American community. Unrated, the film has some profanity. 81m. **DIR:** Wayne Wang. **CAST:** Wood Moy, Marc Hayashi. **1982**

CHANCES ARE ★★★½ In this derivative but generally charming romantic comedy, a surprisingly effective Robert Downey Jr. plays the reincarnated soul of Cybill Shepherd's husband (Christopher McDonald). Downey has retained a dormant memory of his past life. It returns during a visit to Shepherd's home just as he is about to seduce "their" daughter (Mary Stuart Masterson). It's good silly fun from then on—even if you've seen *Here Comes Mr. Jordan* or *Heaven Can Wait*. Rated PG for mild profanity. 108m. **DIR:** Emile Ardolino. **CAST:** Cybill Shepherd, Robert Downey Jr., Ryan O'Neal, Mary Stuart Masterson, Christopher McDonald, Josef Sommer. **1989**

CHANGE OF SEASONS, A 🦃 Poor Shirley MacLaine. The only difference between this and *Loving Couples*, which closely followed it into release, is that Anthony Hopkins and Bo Derek costar as the ultramodern mate swappers. Rated R. 102m. **DIR:** Richard Lang. **CAST:** Shirley MacLaine, Anthony Hopkins, Bo Derek, Michael Brandon. **1980**

CHAPLIN REVUE, THE ★★★★ Assembled and scored by Charlie Chaplin for release in 1959, this revue is composed of three of his longer, more complex and polished films: *A Dog's Life*, which established Chaplin's reputation as a satirist; *Shoulder Arms*, a model for *The Great Dictator*; and *The Pilgrim*, in which escaped convict Chaplin assumes the garb of a minister. B&W; 121m. **DIR:** Charles Chaplin. **CAST:** Charlie Chaplin, Edna Purviance, Tom Wilson, Sydney Chaplin. **1959**

CHARLIE CHAN AND THE CURSE OF THE DRAGON QUEEN ★★ Although there are moments in this tongue-in-cheek send-up of the 1930s Charlie Chan mystery series that recapture the fun of yesteryear, overall it's just not a very good movie. Rated PG. 97m. **DIR:** Clive Donner. **CAST:** Peter Ustinov, Lee Grant, Angie Dickinson, Richard Hatch. **1981**

CHARLIE CHAPLIN CARNIVAL ★★★ One of a number of anthologies made up of two-reel Chaplin films, this one is composed of *The Vagabond*, *The Count*, *Behind the Screen*, and *The Fireman*. Charlie Chaplin, Edna Purviance (forever his leading lady), and the giant Eric Campbell provide most of the hilarious, romantic, touching moments. Bedrock fans will find *The Vagabond* a study for the longer films that followed in the 1920s—*The Kid*, in particular. B&W; 80m. **DIR:** Charles Chaplin. **CAST:** Charlie Chaplin, Edna Purviance, Eric Campbell, Lloyd Bacon. **1916**

CHARLIE CHAPLIN CAVALCADE ★★★ Another in a series of anthologies spliced up out of two- and three-reel Chaplin comedies. This features four of his best: *One A.M.*, *The Pawn-shop*, *The Floorwalker*, *The Rink*. As in most of Chaplin's short comedies, the side-splitting action results mainly from underdog Chaplin clashing with the short-fused giant Eric Campbell. B&W; 81m. **DIR:** Charles Chaplin. **CAST:** Charlie Chaplin, Henry Bergman, Edna Purviance, John Rand, Wesley Ruggles, Frank J. Coleman, Albert Austin, Eric Campbell, Lloyd Bacon, Leo White. **1916**

CHARLIE CHAPLIN FESTIVAL ★★★ The third in a number of Chaplin film anthologies. Featuring *Easy Street*, one of his best-known hits, this group contains *The Cure*, *The Adventurer*, and *The Immigrant*, and gives viewers the full gamut of famous Chaplin emotional expressions. The coin sequence in the latter is sight-gag ingenuity at its best. B&W; 80m. **DIR:** Charles Chaplin. **CAST:** Charlie Chaplin, Eric Campbell, Edna Purviance, Albert Austin, Henry Bergman. **1917**

CHARLIE CHAPLIN...OUR HERO ★★★ Another trio of slapstick comedies starring Charlie Chaplin, who also scripted and directed the first two: "A Night At the Show" and "In the Park." The third, "Hot Finish," was originally titled "Mabel At the Wheel." B&W; 58m. **DIR:** Charles Chaplin, Mabel Normand, Mack Sennett. **CAST:** Charlie Chaplin, Edna Purviance, Lloyd Bacon, Mabel Normand, Chester Conklin, Al St. John. **1914–15**

CHARLIE CHAPLIN—THE EARLY YEARS, VOL. 1 ★★★★★ In this collection of early Charlie Chaplin shorts, we get three outstanding stories. *The Immigrant* finds Charlie, who meets Edna Purviance on the boat to America, in love and broke. *The Count* has Charlie trying to lead the high life with no money. *Easy Street* finds Charlie "saved" by missionary Purviance and out to save everyone else. B&W; 62m. **DIR:** Charles Chaplin. **CAST:** Charlie Chaplin, Edna Purviance, Eric Campbell, Albert Austin. **1917**

CHARLIE CHAPLIN—THE EARLY YEARS, VOL. 2 ★★★★★ Volume Two of the Charlie Chaplin series presents three more classic shorts. The first is *The Pawnbroker*, with Charlie running a pawnshop. The second feature is *The Adventure*, as Charlie plays an escaped con who gets mistaken for a high-society man and finds himself in the middle of wealthy society. And *One A.M.* ends the collection as Charlie tries desperately to get some sleep after a long night of boozing it up. B&W; 61m. **DIR:** Charles Chaplin. **CAST:** Charlie Chaplin, Edna Purviance, Eric Campbell, Albert Austin. **1916**

CHARLIE CHAPLIN—THE EARLY YEARS, VOL. 3 ★★★★★ Volume Three of this great series. First is *The Cure*, where Charlie plays a drunk who goes to a health spa to dry out. Next Charlie shows up as *The Floorwalker* in a large department store. Last Charlie is *The Vagabond*, a wandering violinist who saves a young girl's life and also falls in love with her. B&W; 64m. **DIR:** Charles Chaplin. **CAST:** Charlie Chaplin, Edna Purviance, Eric Campbell, Henry Bergman. **1917**

CHARLIE CHAPLIN—THE EARLY YEARS, VOL. 4 ★★★★★ In Volume Four of the Charlie Chaplin series, we start out with *Behind the Screen*, as Charlie plays a movie studio stagehand who goes crazy from being overworked. The final pie-throwing clash is a classic. Next is *The Fireman*, with Charlie a brave firefighter who must rescue Edna Purviance, his girlfriend, from a fire. The final story is *The Ring*, with Charlie playing a bumbling waiter in a high-class restaurant. B&W; 63m. **DIR:** Charles Chaplin. **CAST:** Charlie Chaplin, Edna Purviance, Eric Campbell, Albert Austin, Lloyd Bacon, Charlotte Mineau, James T. Kelly, Leo White. **1916**

CHASERS ★★½ The misadventures of two Navy Shore Patrol lawmen (Tom Berenger, William McNamara) escorting a female prisoner (Erika Eleniak) to Charleston, SC. The premise is borrowed from *The Last Detail*, but the drawn out story never really gets rolling. Still, the stars are attractive, and the supporting cast is good; it might be worth a look on a slow night. Rated R for profanity, nudity, and sexual scenes. 103m. **DIR:** Dennis Hopper. **CAST:** Tom Berenger, William McNamara, Erika Eleniak, Gary Busey, Crispin Glover, Dean Stockwell, Marilu Henner, Dennis Hopper. **1994**

CHATTANOOGA CHOO CHOO ★★ The story deals with a bet to make a New York–to–Chattanooga train trip within a deadline. George Kennedy plays the comedy villain and owner of a football team of which Joe Namath is the coach. Rated PG for mild profanity. 102m. **DIR:** Bruce Bilson. **CAST:** George Kennedy, Barbara Eden, Joe Namath, Melissa Sue Anderson. **1984**

CHEAP DETECTIVE, THE ★★★ Follow-up to *Murder By Death* from director Robert Moore and writer Neil Simon is an affectionate parody of the Humphrey Bogart classics. Generally enjoyable. Rated PG. 92m. **DIR:** Robert Moore. **CAST:** Peter Falk, Ann-Margret, Eileen Brennan, Sid Caesar, Stockard Channing, James Coco, Dom DeLuise, Louise Fletcher, John Houseman, Madeline Kahn, Fernando Lamas, Marsha Mason, Phil Silvers, Vic Tayback, Abe Vigoda, Paul Williams, Nicol Williamson. **1978**

CHEAP SHOTS ★★ An aging Greek proprietor tries to save his motel from ruin. Urged by a full-time boarder, he makes blue films of a couple staying in one of his cabins. Not rated. The film includes some profanity and nudity. 92m. **DIR:** Jeff Ureles, Jerry Stoeffhaas. **CAST:** Louis Zorich, David Patrick Kelly, Mary Louise Wilson, Patience Moore. **1991**

CHEAPER TO KEEP HER A sexist private detective tracks down ex-husbands who haven't paid their alimony. Rated R. 92m. **DIR:** Ken Annakin. **CAST:** Mac Davis, Tovah Feldshuh, Art Metrano, Ian McShane. **1980**

CHECK AND DOUBLE CHECK This sad comedy starring radio's Amos 'n' Andy in blackface was RKO's biggest hit for the 1930 season and made Freeman Gosden and Charles Correll the top stars for that year—but they never made another film. B&W; 80m. **DIR:** Melville Brown. **CAST:** Freeman Gosden, Charles Correll, Sue Carol, Charles Norton. **1930**

CHECK IS IN THE MAIL, THE Story of a man who is tired of the capitalist system. Rated R for profanity. 83m. **DIR:** Joan Darling. **CAST:** Brian Dennehy, Anne Archer, Hallie Todd, Chris Herbert, Michael Bowen, Dick Shawn, Beau Starr. **1986**

CHECKING OUT A nervous fellow believes his own fatal heart attack is mere hours away. Rated R for language. 95m. **DIR:** David Leland. **CAST:** Jeff Daniels, Melanie Mayron, Michael Tucker, Ann Magnuson. **1989**

CHEECH AND CHONG'S NEXT MOVIE ★★ This is Cheech and Chong's (Richard Marin and Thomas Chong) in-between movie—in between *Up in Smoke*, their first, and *Nice Dreams*, number three. If you liked either of the other two, you'll like *Next Movie*. But if you didn't care for the duo's brand of humor there, you won't in this one either. Rated R for nudity and profanity. 99m. **DIR:** Thomas Chong. **CAST:** Cheech and Chong, Evelyn Guerrero, Betty Kennedy. **1980**

CHEERLEADERS Dated sex farce. Rated X at one time; now equivalent to an R for nudity and profanity. 84m. **DIR:** Paul Glicker. **CAST:** Stephanie Fondue, Denise Dillaway, Jovila Bush, Debbie Lowe. **1972**

CHICKEN CHRONICLES, THE The carnal pursuits of a high school senior. Rated PG. 95m. **DIR:** Francis Simon. **CAST:** Steve Guttenberg, Ed Lauter, Lisa Reeves, Meredith Baer, Phil Silvers. **1977**

CHORUS OF DISAPPROVAL, A ★★★ Film version of the hilarious Alan Ayckbourn play. Jeremy Irons is fun to watch as the protagonist, who stirs up intrigue in a small town when he joins its little theatre company, and Anthony Hopkins is truly bizarre as its domineering director. Rated PG for profanity and suggested sex. 92m. **DIR:** Michael Winner. **CAST:** Jeremy Irons, Anthony Hopkins, Jenny Seagrove. **1989**

CHRISTMAS IN CONNECTICUT (1945) ★★★½ In this spirited comedy, a successful newspaper family-advice columnist (Barbara Stanwyck) arranges a phony family for herself—all for the sake of publicity. The acting is good and the pace is quick, but the script needs polishing. Nonetheless, it's a Christmas favorite. B&W; 101m. **DIR:** Peter Godfrey. **CAST:** Barbara Stanwyck, Dennis Morgan, Sydney Greenstreet, S. Z. Sakall, Reginald Gardiner, Una O'Connor. **1945**

CHRISTMAS IN CONNECTICUT (1992) ★★ A New York cooking show host, Dyan Cannon, actually knows nothing about the culinary arts and a national park ranger, Kris Kristofferson, hailed a hero for his rescue of a little boy during a snowstorm, are brought together and fall in love. This lightweight, syrupy romance farce is strictly by the numbers. Cannon tries hard but Kristofferson is as wooden as ever. Directorial debut of Arnold Schwarzenegger. No rating. 93m. **DIR:** Arnold Schwarzenegger. **CAST:** Dyan Cannon, Kris Kristofferson, Tony Curtis, Richard Roundtree, Kelly Cinnante. **1992**

CHRISTMAS IN JULY ★★★½ Touching, insightful comedy-drama about a young couple's dreams and aspirations. Dick Powell is fine as the young man who mistakenly believes that he has won a contest and finds all doors opening to him—until the error is discovered. This one is a treat for all audiences. Once you've seen it, you'll want to see all of Preston Sturges's films. B&W; 67m. **DIR:** Preston Sturges. **CAST:** Dick Powell, Ellen Drew, Raymond Walburn, William Demarest, Ernest Truex, Franklin Pangborn. **1940**

CHU CHU AND THE PHILLY FLASH ★★ This is another bittersweet comedy about a couple of losers. It's supposed to be funny. It isn't. The stars, Alan Arkin and Carol Burnett, do manage to invest it with a certain wacky charm, but that isn't enough to make up for its shortcomings. Rated PG. 100m. **DIR:** David Lowell Rich. **CAST:** Alan Arkin, Carol Burnett, Jack Warden, Ruth Buzzi. **1981**

CHUMP AT OXFORD, A ★★★ Stan Laurel receives a scholarship to Oxford, and Oliver Hardy accompanies him. They are the butt of pranks and jokes until Stan receives a blow on the head and becomes a reincarnation of a college hero. A fair script, but the Stan and Ollie characters never seem to fit well into it. B&W; 63m. **DIR:** Alf Goulding. **CAST:** Stan Laurel, Oliver Hardy, Wilfred Lucas, Forrester Harvey, James Finlayson, Anita Garvin. **1940**

CIRCUS, THE/A DAY'S PLEASURE ★★★ This double feature admirably showcases Charlie Chaplin's world-famous gifts for comedy and pathos. In the first, vagabond Charlie hooks up with a traveling circus and falls for the bareback rider, who loves a muscle-bound trapeze artist. The film earned Chaplin a special Oscar at the first Academy Awards ceremony for writing, acting, directing, and producing. In the second feature, Charlie and his family try in vain to have Sunday fun. Silent. B&W; 105m. **DIR:** Charles Chaplin. **CAST:** Charlie Chaplin, Allan Garcia, Merna Kennedy, Harry Crocker, Betty Morrisey, George Davis, Henry Bergman. **1928**

CITIZEN'S BAND ★★★★ Delightful character study centers around a group of people who use citizens band radios. Screenwriter Paul Brickman and director Jonathan Demme turn this slight premise into a humorous and heartwarming collection of vignettes with Paul LeMat appealing as the central character and Charles Napier screamingly funny as a philandering truck driver. Rated PG. 98m. **DIR:** Jonathan Demme. **CAST:** Paul LeMat, Candy Clark, Ann Wedgeworth, Marcia Rodd, Charles Napier, Alix Elias, Roberts Blossom, Bruce McGill, Ed Begley Jr. **1977**

CITY HEAT ★★★ Clint Eastwood and Burt Reynolds portray a cop and a private eye, respectively, in this enjoyable action-comedy, directed by Richard Benjamin. It's fun for fans of the stars. Rated PG for violence. 94m. **DIR:** Richard Benjamin. **CAST:** Clint Eastwood, Burt Reynolds, Jane Alexander, Madeline Kahn, Irene Cara, Richard Roundtree, Rip Torn, Tony Lo Bianco. **1984**

CITY LIGHTS ★★★★★ In his finest film, Charlie Chaplin's little tramp befriends a blind flower seller, providing her with every kindness he can afford. Charlie develops a friendship with a drunken millionaire and takes advantage of it to help the girl even more. Taking money from the millionaire so the girl can have an eye operation, he is arrested and sent to jail. His release from jail and the subsequent reunion with the girl may well be the most poignant ending of all his films. B&W; 81m. **DIR:** Charles Chaplin. **CAST:** Charlie Chaplin, Virginia Cherrill, Harry Myers, Hank Mann. **1931**

CITY SLICKERS ★★★★ Three buddies experiencing individual midlife crises decide that going on a cattle drive will be just the thing to cure their collective depression. The result is a comedy guaranteed to cheer anyone up, with great one-liners and hilarious physical comedy. Jack Palance is outstanding as the leathery trail boss who terrifies his city-bred drovers. Rated PG-13 for profanity. 109m. **DIR:** Ron Underwood. **CAST:** Billy Crystal, Bruno Kirby, Daniel Stern, Patricia Wettig, Helen Slater, Jack Palance, Tracey Walter, Josh Mostel. **1991**

CITY SLICKERS II ★★★★ The city slickers look for a lost treasure and trip all over themselves. The often funny screenplay has the same flavor as the first film with a different slant on the personalities—Jon Lovitz replaces Bruno Kirby, but the rest of the cast is the same, with Jack Palance playing his original character's twin brother. Rated PG-13 for language. 110m. **DIR:** Paul Weiland. **CAST:** Billy Crystal, Jack Palance, Daniel Stern, Jon Lovitz, Patricia Wettig, Bill McKinney, Noble Willingham, Josh Mostel, Bob Balabon. **1994**

CLARENCE ★★★ Clarence, the angel who guided Jimmy Stewart through *It's A Wonderful Life*, is back for more fun in this charming (made-for-TV) sequel that finds the guardian angel assisting a young mother headed for tragedy. Not a classic, but filled with the best of intentions. Rated G. 92m. **DIR:** Eric Till. **CAST:** Robert Carradine, Kate Trotter. **1990**

CLARK AND MCCULLOUGH: INSPIRED MADNESS ★★★ Cashing in like many of its contemporaries, the vaudeville team of Clark and McCullough made a number of weird but wonderful short comedies after the silver screen found its voice. This anthology presents three of their best: "The Druggist's Dilemma," "Fits in a Fiddle," and "Alibi Bye Bye." B&W; 53m. **CAST:** Bobby Clark, Paul McCullough, James Finlayson. **1932–1934**

CLASS 🦃 Unfunny comedy about two preppies, one of whom falls in love with the other's alcoholic mother. Rated R for nudity, profanity, sex, and violence. 98m. **DIR:** Lewis John Carlino. **CAST:** Rob Lowe, Jacqueline Bisset, Andrew McCarthy, Stuart Margolin. **1983**

CLASS ACT ★★★ Rap singers Kid 'N Play follow up their *House Party* successes with this ingratiating, lightweight teen comedy. Kid (Christopher Reid, the one with the mile-high hair) plays a brilliant, straight-A student who moves to a new school. Unfortunately, his official record gets switched with those belonging to a nonachieving, streetwise troublemaker (played by Play, Christopher Martin). Rated PG-13, with profanity and sexual references. 98m. **DIR:** Randall Miller. **CAST:** Christopher Reid, Christopher Martin, Lamont Jackson, Doug E. Doug. **1992**

CLEAN SLATE (1994) ★★★½ Private eye Dana Carvey starts each day fresh—with no idea of who he is. This strange form of amnesia means trouble, since he's supposed to testify against a powerful crime boss who commited a murder our hero doesn't remember. Carvey is fun to watch in a movie that is only occasionally funny. The best scenes involve Carvey's comic canine co-star, Barkley. Rated PG-13 for violence and profanity. 107m. **DIR:** Mick Jackson. **CAST:** Dana Carvey, Valeria Golino, James Earl Jones, Kevin Pollak, Michael Murphy, Michael Gambon. **1994**

CLEO/LEO 🦃 This *Goodbye Charlie* rip-off becomes unwatchable due to its many toilet jokes and sex gags. Rated R for nudity. 92m. **DIR:** Chuck Vincent. **CAST:** Jane Hamilton. **1989**

CLIFFORD 🦃 The novelty of seeing the full-grown Martin Short playing a malevolent 10-year-old wears off *very* quickly. Rated PG, but not suitable for small children. 90m. **DIR:** Paul Flaherty. **CAST:** Martin Short, Charles Grodin, Dabney Coleman, Mary Steenburgen. **1994**

CLOCKWISE ★★★½ No one plays a pillar of pomposity better than John Cleese. In *Clockwise*, he gets a perfect role for his patented persona. Brian Stimpson, a headmaster, runs everything by the clock—in the extreme. However, his complete control is soon shattered by a misunderstanding—and hilarity is the result. Rated PG. 96m. **DIR:** Christopher Morahan. **CAST:** John Cleese, Penelope Wilton, Alison Steadman, Stephen Moore, Sharon Maiden, Joan Hickson. **1987**

CLUB FED ★★ Ganster's moll Judy Landers, framed on a murder charge, is sent to a minimum security prison run by a corrupt warden. There are more "guest stars" than laughs in this too-familiar comedy. Rated PG-13 for double entendre humor. 91m. **DIR:** Nathaniel Christian. **CAST:** Judy Landers, Burt Young, Lance Kinsey, Karen Black, Sherman Hemsley, Allen Garfield, Joseph Campanella, Lyle Alzado, Mary Woronov. **1991**

CLUB PARADISE ★★ Robin Williams and Jimmy Cliff start their own little Club Med–style resort. PG-13 for language and drug humor. 104m. **DIR:** Harold Ramis. **CAST:** Robin Williams, Peter O'Toole, Jimmy Cliff, Twiggy, Rick Moranis, Adolph Caesar, Eugene Levy, Joanna Cassidy. **1986**

CLUE ★★½ Inspired by the popular board game, the movie is a pleasant spoof of whodunits. The delightful ensemble establishes a suitably breezy style. Silliness eventually overwhelms the proceedings. As a gimmick, the film was originally shown in theatres with three different endings. All versions are included on the videocassette. Rated PG. 100m. **DIR:** Jonathan Lynn. **CAST:** Eileen Brennan, Tim Curry, Madeline Kahn, Christopher Lloyd, Michael McKean, Martin Mull, Lesley Ann Warren. **1985**

COAST TO COAST ★★ Dyan Cannon stars as a wacko blonde who's been railroaded into a mental hospital by her husband. Cannon escapes by bopping her psychiatrist over the head with a bust of Freud, and the chase is on. A trucker (Robert Blake) gives Cannon a lift, and they romp from Pennsylvania to California. Rated PG for profanity. 95m. **DIR:** Joseph Sargent. **CAST:**

Dyan Cannon, Robert Blake, Quinn Redeker, Michael Lerner, Maxine Stuart, Bill Lucking. 1980

COCA COLA KID, THE ★★★ A nude scene between Eric Roberts and Greta Scacchi in a bed covered with feathers is enough to make anyone's temperature rise, but as a whole this little film doesn't have enough bite to it. Roberts plays a gung-ho troubleshooter from the popular beverage company who comes to Australia to sell the drink to a hard-nosed businessman (Bill Kerr) who has a monopoly on a stretch of land with his own soft drink. Worth a look. Rated R for nudity. 90m. **DIR:** Dusan Makavejev. **CAST:** Eric Roberts, Greta Scacchi, Bill Kerr. 1985

COCKEYED CAVALIERS ★★★ One of the better Wheeler and Woolsey vehicles, a costume comedy set in sixteenth-century Britain with the wacky duo posing as the king's physicians. Funniest bit is a parody of Garbo's *Queen Christina*. B&W; 72m. **DIR:** Mark Sandrich. **CAST:** Bert Wheeler, Robert Woolsey, Thelma Todd, Noah Beery Sr. 1934

COCOANUTS ★★★½ The Marx Brothers' first movie was one of the earliest sound films and suffers as a result. Notice how all the maps and newspapers are sopping wet (so they wouldn't crackle into the supersensitive, primitive microphones). The romantic leads are laughably stiff, and even the songs by Irving Berlin are forgettable. However, the Marxes—all four of them, Groucho, Harpo, Chico, and Zeppo—supply some classic moments, making the picture well worth watching. B&W; 96m. **DIR:** Joseph Santley, Robert Florey. **CAST:** The Marx Brothers, Kay Francis, Margaret Dumont. 1929

CODE NAME: CHAOS ★★ Stellar cast works desperately to save this misguided comedy about former CIA spooks gathering their resources on a tropical island in order to send the rest of the world into chaos. Rated R for profanity. 96m. **DIR:** Antony Thomas. **CAST:** Diane Ladd, Robert Loggia, David Warner, Alice Krige, Brian Kerwin. 1989

COLD FEET (1984) ★★★½ This enjoyable low-key romance features a film writer (Griffin Dunne) who has just left his complaining, childlike wife (Blanche Baker) and vowed to go it alone. Enter an attractive scientist (Marissa Chibas) who has just dumped her overbearing boyfriend. Rated PG for slight profanity. 91m. **DIR:** Bruce Van Dusen. **CAST:** Griffin Dunne, Marissa Chibas, Blanche Baker. 1984

COLD FEET (1989) ★★★½ The scheme is to smuggle emeralds from Mexico into the United States inside a horse that is being imported for stud purposes. Offbeat fun. Rated R for nudity and language. 94m. **DIR:** Robert Dornhelm. **CAST:** Keith Carradine, Sally Kirkland, Tom Waits, Rip Torn. 1989

COLD TURKEY ★★ This comedy, about a small town in Iowa where the whole populace tries to give up smoking at once, sat on the shelf for two years, and understandably—despite the knockout cast and a few funny scenes, the humor is mean-spirited and decidedly unpleasant. Rated PG. 99m. **DIR:** Norman Lear. **CAST:** Dick Van Dyke, Pippa Scott, Tom Poston, Bob Newhart, Edward Everett Horton, Vincent Gardenia, Barnard Hughes. 1971

COLLEGE ★★★½ An anti-athletics bookworm, Buster Keaton, goes to college on a scholarship. His girl falls for a jock, and Keaton decides to succeed in athletics to win her back. He fails hilariously in every attempt, but finally rescues her by unwittingly using every athletic skill. B&W; 65m. **DIR:** James W. Horne. **CAST:** Buster Keaton, Anne Cornwall, Flora Bramley, Grant Winters. 1927

COLLISION COURSE ★★ A tough Detroit cop gets mixed up with a Japanese police officer as they track the smugglers of an experimental car part. Some nice bits of comedy can't save this mishmash of action and Japan bashing. Rated PG for violence and profanity. 99m. **DIR:** Lewis Teague. **CAST:** Noriyuki "Pat" Morita, Jay Leno, Chris Sarandon, Ernie Hudson, John Hancock, Al Waxman, Randall "Tex" Cobb, Tom Noonan. 1989

COLONEL EFFINGHAM'S RAID ★★½ Slight small-town story about Charles Coburn's efforts to preserve a local monument is pleasant enough and has marvelous characters. Not a great film, but harmless fun and at times thought-provoking. B&W; 70m. **DIR:** Irving Pichel. **CAST:** Charles Coburn, Joan Bennett, William Eythe, Allyn Joslyn, Elizabeth Patterson, Donald Meek. 1945

COME ALONG WITH ME ★★★ Rather high-brow amusement is provided by this adaptation of Shirley Jackson's unfinished novel. Estelle Parsons portrays an eccentric widow who sells everything before moving on to a new town. With a new name she begins her career as a dabbler in the supernatural. Unrated, but suitable for all ages. 60m. **DIR:** Joanne Woodward. **CAST:** Estelle Parsons, Barbara Baxley, Sylvia Sidney. 1981

COME BLOW YOUR HORN ★★★½ Frank Sinatra looks very much at home as a bachelor playboy, teaching his younger brother how to live the good life. Based on Neil Simon's hit play, coproduced by director Bud Yorkin and screenwriter Norman Lear. Unrated, with (now) innocent sexual innuendo. 112m. **DIR:** Bud Yorkin. **CAST:** Frank Sinatra, Lee J. Cobb, Molly Picon, Barbara Rush, Jill St. John, Tony Bill, Dan Blocker. 1963

COMEDY TONIGHT 🦃 A lot of bad comedy, sandwiched between some inspired early bits by Gallagher and Robin Williams, makes this HBO special almost worthless. Not rated, but contains adult language. 76m.

DIR: Marty Callner. **CAST:** David Steinberg, Gallagher, Andy Kaufman, Ed Bluestone, Robin Williams, Richard Libertini, MacIntyre Dixon. **1977**

COMFORT AND JOY ★★★★½ Scottish filmmaker Bill Forsyth scores again with this delightful tale of a disc jockey (Bill Paterson) whose life is falling apart. His girlfriend walks out on him, taking nearly everything he owns. Birds seem to like decorating his pride and joy: a red BMW. And what's worse, he gets involved in a gangland war over—are you ready for this?—the control of ice-cream manufacturing and sales. It's one you'll want to see. Rated PG. 90m. **DIR:** Bill Forsyth. **CAST:** Bill Paterson, Eleanor David, C. P. Grogan, Alex Norton. **1984**

COMIC CABBY 💔 Based on Jim Pietsch's book *The New York City Cab Driver's Joke Book*, it's an extended skit that dramatizes a day in the life of a rookie cabby. 60m. **DIR:** Carl Lindahl. **CAST:** Bill McLaughlin, Al Lewis, Frank Guy. **1986**

COMIC RELIEF 2 ★★ Some funny bits, but each comedian is allowed only brief screen time. You'll want more, but it's not there. Not rated, but contains adult language. 120m. **DIR:** Walter C. Miller. **CAST:** Billy Crystal, Whoopi Goldberg, Robin Williams. **1987**

COMING TO AMERICA ★★★½ Eddie Murphy deserves credit for trying to do something different in *Coming to America*. Murphy, who also wrote the story, stars as a pampered African prince who refuses to marry the pretty and pliable queen his father (James Earl Jones) has picked for him, opting instead to journey to New York City to find an intelligent, independent woman to be his lifelong mate. The film is a little slow at times, but the laughs are frequent enough to hold one's interest. Rated R for profanity, nudity, and suggested sex. 116m. **DIR:** John Landis. **CAST:** Eddie Murphy, Arsenio Hall, James Earl Jones, John Amos, Madge Sinclair. **1988**

COMMIES ARE COMING, THE COMMIES ARE COMING, THE ★★ Jack Webb narrates this 1950s anti-communist pseudodocumentary about what would happen if the Russians captured the United States. It's easy to laugh at this silly film. Unrated. B&W; 60m. **DIR:** George Waggner. **CAST:** Jack Kelly, Jean Cooper, Peter Brown, Patricia Woodell, Andrew Duggan, Robert Conrad. **1984**

COMPLEAT "WEIRD AL" YANKOVIC, THE ★★½ This is all that you ever wanted to know about "Weird Al" Yankovic. At 100 minutes, it's probably more. Filmed in documentary fashion, it traces Al's birth on October 23, 1959, through school, early jobs, and finally his entertainment career. Eight of his videos are shown, including *Eat It, I Love Rocky Road, I Lost on Jeopardy*, and *Like a Surgeon*. The two best sequences show Al going to Michael Jackson for permission to do a parody of *Beat It* and a Devo send-up entitled *Dare to Be Stupid*. Weird Al—the man, the myth, the legend? You decide. 100m. **DIR:** Jay Levey, Robert K. Weiss. **CAST:** "Weird Al" Yankovic. **1985**

COMPROMISING POSITIONS ★★ In the first half hour, this is a hilarious and innovative takeoff on murder mysteries and a devastatingly witty send-up of suburban life. However, it soon descends into the clichés of the mystery genre. That's too bad, because the plot, about an overly amorous dentist who is murdered, has great possibilities. Rated R for nudity, profanity, and violence. 98m. **DIR:** Frank Perry. **CAST:** Susan Sarandon, Raul Julia, Edward Herrmann, Judith Ivey, Mary Beth Hurt, Anne De Salvo, Josh Mostel. **1985**

COMRADE X ★★★ American reporter Clark Gable pursues Russian streetcar conductor Hedy Lamarr in this fair reworking of the *Ninotchka* theme. Eve Arden is a standout. B&W; 90m. **DIR:** King Vidor. **CAST:** Clark Gable, Hedy Lamarr, Oscar Homolka, Felix Bressart, Eve Arden, Sig Ruman. **1940**

COMRADES OF SUMMER, THE ★★★½ Sports fans will get a kick out of this amiable made-for-cable fairy tale, which finds washed-up player Joe Mantegna sent to help the Russians field a baseball team for the 1992 Olympics. Although patterned after a slew of similar underdog fantasies, this one works thanks to Mantegna's enthusiasm and Robert Rodat's script. Rated R for profanity and suggested sex. 106m. **DIR:** Tommy Lee Wallace. **CAST:** Joe Mantegna, Natalya Negoda, Mark Rolston, Michael Lerner. **1992**

CONEHEADS ★★★ Critically lambasted comedy based on the old *Saturday Night Live* sketch is bound to be a hit with preteens. Dan Aykroyd and Jane Curtin reprise their roles as Beldar and Prymaat, aliens from the planet Remulac who are forced to masquerade as humans after being stranded on Earth. Rated PG for brief profanity and some gross comedy bits. 87m. **DIR:** Steve Barron. **CAST:** Dan Aykroyd, Jane Curtin, Michelle Burke, Michael McKean, Jason Alexander, Lisa Jane Persky, Laraine Newman, Chris Farley, Dave Thomas, Sinbad, Jan Hooks, Phil Hartman, Jon Lovitz, David Spade, Michael Richards. **1993**

CONNECTICUT YANKEE, A ★★★½ Based on Mark Twain's famous 1889 fantasy of a "modern man" thrust back to King Arthur's Court in a dream caused by a blow to the head. In the title role, Will Rogers happily helps young love in both the story and the story within the story. B&W; 96m. **DIR:** David Butler. **CAST:** Will Rogers, William Farnum, Frank Albertson, Maureen O'Sullivan, Myrna Loy. **1931**

CONNECTICUT YANKEE IN KING ARTHUR'S COURT, A (1948) ★★★ The third film version of Mark Twain's intriguing social satire, this costly but profitable production presents Bing Crosby as the blacksmith who dreams himself back to Camelot and is proclaimed a wizard because of his modern knowledge. It's good, clean, happy fun for all. 107m. **DIR:** Tay Garnett. **CAST:** Bing Crosby, Rhonda Fleming, Cedric Hardwicke, William Bendix, Henry Wilcoxon, Murvyn Vye. **1948**

CONSUMING PASSIONS ★★ Morbid, gross, and sometimes amusing movie about a nerdish junior executive who discovers a "secret ingredient"—human beings—that saves a sagging candy company. Adapted from a play written by Michael Palin and Terry Jones of *Monty Python's Flying Circus* fame, the film suffers from the one-joke premise. Rated R for language, sexual situations, and overall grossness. 95m. **DIR:** Giles Foster. **CAST:** Tyler Butterworth, Jonathan Pryce, Freddie Jones, Sammi Davis, Prunella Scales, Vanessa Redgrave, Thora Hird. **1988**

CONTINENTAL DIVIDE ★★★½ As lighthearted romantic comedies go, this one is tops. John Belushi stars as Ernie Souchak, a Chicago newspaper columnist unexpectedly sent into the Rockies to write a story about an ornithologist (Blair Brown). Just as unexpectedly, they fall in love. Rated PG because of slight amounts of nudity. 103m. **DIR:** Michael Apted. **CAST:** John Belushi, Blair Brown, Allen Garfield, Carlin Glynn. **1981**

COOK, THE THIEF, HIS WIFE & HER LOVER, THE ★★★★ British film about a long-suffering wife who carries on an affair in a restaurant owned by her sadistic, obnoxious husband. Gorgeously crafted yet explicit and sometimes distressingly brutal. A dark, haunting comedy with few bodily functions ignored, but the story is about excessive behavior—so nothing seems gratuitous. Rated NC-17 for nudity, violence, profanity, and simulated sex ... you name it. 123m. **DIR:** Peter Greenaway. **CAST:** Michael Gambon, Helen Mirren, Richard Bohringer, Alan Howard. **1990**

COOKIE ★★★½ In this frothy piece of fluff, Emily Lloyd stars as the rebellious daughter of a gangster (Peter Falk) who cannot figure out how to keep his offspring in line. It's entertaining but forgettable. Rated R for profanity and violence. 93m. **DIR:** Susan Seidelman. **CAST:** Emily Lloyd, Peter Falk, Dianne Wiest, Jerry Lewis, Michael Gazzo, Brenda Vaccaro, Adrian Pasdar. **1989**

COOL RUNNINGS ★★★★ Inspired by the phenomenal popularity of the 1988 Olympics' Jamaican bobsled team, this is a wildly fictionalized *Rocky*-type comedy. Four black tropical sportsmen (a soapbox-derby racer and three sprinters) take the Calgary Winter Olympics by storm while overcoming physical, social, and personal adversity. Their misadventures produce an avalanche of infectious belly laughs. One of John Candy's last films. Rated PG. 95m. **DIR:** Jon Turteltaub. **CAST:** Doug E. Doug, Leon, Malik Yoba, Rawle D. Lewis, John Candy. **1993**

COOLEY HIGH ★★★★ Highly enjoyable comedy-drama set in an inner-city Chicago high school in the early 1960s. This is probably the only *American Graffiti* clone that doesn't suffer by comparison. Featuring a first-rate sound track of vintage Motown tunes. Rated PG for mild profanity and sexual concerns. 107m. **DIR:** Michael Schultz. **CAST:** Glynn Turman, Lawrence Hilton-Jacobs, Garrett Morris, Cynthia Davis. **1975**

COPACABANA 🦃 Not even Groucho Marx can save this slight comedy about the problems caused by a woman applying for two jobs at the same nightclub. B&W; 92m. **DIR:** Alfred E. Green. **CAST:** Groucho Marx, Carmen Miranda, Andy Russell, Steve Cochran, Abel Green. **1947**

COPS AND ROBBERSONS ★★½ Mild-mannered suburban dad Chevy Chase is a wannabe detective who gets a taste of the real thing. Hardboiled cop Jack Palance moves in to set up surveillance on Chase's new neighbor (Robert Davi), a counterfeiter with the nasty habit of murdering his customers. The few chuckles almost make it worthwhile. Rated PG for violence. 95m. **DIR:** Michael Ritchie. **CAST:** Chevy Chase, Jack Palance, Dianne Wiest, Robert Davi, David Barry Gray, Jason James Richter, Fay Masterson, Miko Hughes, M. Emmet Walsh. **1994**

CORPORATE AFFAIRS ★★ Short on laughs, sex comedy focuses on the sexcapades of corporate executives, each clawing his or her way to the top. Rated R for nudity, profanity, and violence. 82m. **DIR:** Terence H. Winkless. **CAST:** Peter Scolari, Mary Crosby, Chris Lemmon, Ken Kercheval. **1990**

CORSICAN BROTHERS, THE (1984) 🦃 Loosely based on the book by Alexandre Dumas, this forgettable film features Tommy Chong and Richard "Cheech" Marin as twins. Rated R. 90m. **DIR:** Thomas Chong. **CAST:** Cheech and Chong, Roy Dotrice. **1984**

COUCH POTATO WORKOUT TAPE 🦃 Larry "Bud" Melman, of *Late Night with David Letterman* fame, is the ultimate couch potato, a tuber who treats inertia as exercise. The gags fall flat. 35m. **DIR:** Brian Cury. **CAST:** Larry "Bud" Melman. **1989**

COUCH TRIP, THE ★★½ Dan Aykroyd and Walter Matthau offer a few moments of mirth in this middling comedy about a computer hacker (Aykroyd) who escapes from a mental institution and becomes a hugely successful media shrink. Charles Grodin is exceptional as the neurotic radio doctor Aykroyd replaces, and Mary Gross has some terrific scenes as Grodin's wacky wife. Rated R for profanity and suggested sex. 95m. **DIR:** Michael Ritchie. **CAST:** Dan Aykroyd, Walter Matthau, Charles Grodin, Donna Dixon, Richard Romanus, Mary Gross, David Clennon, Arye Gross. 1988

COUNTRY GENTLEMEN ★★ Fast-talking confidence men Ole Olsen and Chic Johnson sell shares in a worthless oil field to a group of World War I veterans, then learn thar's oil in them thar hills! Humorous, but what a weary plot! This flick did little for the comic duo, who always fared better on the stage. B&W; 54m. **DIR:** Ralph Staub. **CAST:** Ole Olsen, Chic Johnson, Joyce Compton, Lila Lee. 1936

COUPE DE VILLE ★★★★½ It's 1963, the last glorious months before the fall of Kennedy's Camelot, and three estranged brothers are recruited to bring a 1954 Cadillac from Michigan to Florida as a surprise gift for their mother's fiftieth birthday. Delightful comedy. Rated PG-13 for profanity and brief violence. 110m. **DIR:** Joe Roth. **CAST:** Daniel Stern, Patrick Dempsey, Arye Gross, Alan Arkin. 1990

COURT JESTER, THE ★★★ Romance, court intrigue, a joust, and in the middle of it all the one and only Danny Kaye as a phony court jester full of double-takes and double-talk. This is one funny film of clever and complicated comic situations superbly brought off. 101m. **DIR:** Norman Panama, Melvin Frank. **CAST:** Danny Kaye, Glynis Johns, Basil Rathbone, Angela Lansbury, Mildred Natwick, Robert Middleton. 1956

COURTSHIP OF EDDIE'S FATHER, THE ★★★ A delightful blend of sophisticated romance and family idealism that inspired a successful TV series in the 1960s. Little Ronny Howard is exceptional as the motherless son who gives Dad, Glenn Ford, advice on his love life. 117m. **DIR:** Vincente Minnelli. **CAST:** Glenn Ford, Ron Howard, Stella Stevens, Dina Merrill, Shirley Jones, Jerry Van Dyke, Roberta Sherwood. 1963

COUSINS ★★★★½ *Cousins* is an utter delight; a marvelously acted, written, and directed romance. Ted Danson, Isabella Rossellini, Sean Young, and William Petersen star as star-crossed spouses, cousins, and lovers in this Americanized takeoff on the 1975 French comedy hit, *Cousin, Cousine*. *Cousins* is about love rather than sex, making it a rare modern movie with heart. Rated PG-13 for profanity and suggested sex. 109m. **DIR:** Joel Schumacher. **CAST:** Ted Danson, Isabella Rossellini, Sean Young, William L. Petersen, Lloyd Bridges, Norma Aleandro, Keith Coogan. 1989

COWBOY AND THE LADY, THE ★★ Offbeat casting did not help in this slow comedy about a city girl who falls for a rodeo star. The Oscar-nominated title song is by Lionel Newman and Arthur Quenzer. B&W; 91m. **DIR:** H. C. Potter. **CAST:** Gary Cooper, Merle Oberon, Walter Brennan, Patsy Kelly, Harry Davenport. 1938

CRACKERS 🦃 A bunch of down-and-out San Franciscans decide to turn to crime in order to survive. Rated PG. 92m. **DIR:** Louis Malle. **CAST:** Donald Sutherland, Jack Warden, Sean Penn, Wallace Shawn. 1984

CRACKING UP 🦃 No laughs here. Rated R. 83m. **DIR:** Jerry Lewis. **CAST:** Jerry Lewis, Herb Edelman, Zane Buzby, Dick Butkus, Milton Berle. 1983

CRAZY PEOPLE ★★★½ Dudley Moore is an ad writer who grows weary of lying to people. His "honest" ad campaigns get him confined to a mental institution. Pure formula, but the ads are often hilarious. Rated R for profanity and scatological humor. 91m. **DIR:** Tony Bill. **CAST:** Dudley Moore, Daryl Hannah, Paul Reiser, J. T. Walsh. 1990

CRIME & PASSION ★★ A weak comedy of sex and money that gives us Omar Sharif as a rich businessman who becomes sexually aroused when bad things happen to him. Karen Black provides some moments of zing with her particular brand of oddness. Her seduction of Joseph Bottoms is a classic. Weird and wild. Rated R. 92m. **DIR:** Ivan Passer. **CAST:** Omar Sharif, Karen Black, Joseph Bottoms, Bernhard Wicki. 1975

CRIMES OF THE HEART ★★★★½ In this superb screen adaptation of Beth Henley's Pulitzer Prize–winning play, Diane Keaton, Jessica Lange, and Sissy Spacek star as three eccentric sisters who stick together despite an onslaught of extraordinary problems. It is a film of many joys. Not the least of which are the performances of the stars, fine bits by Sam Shepard and Tess Harper in support, the biting humor, and the overall intelligence. Rated PG-13 for subject matter. 105m. **DIR:** Bruce Beresford. **CAST:** Diane Keaton, Jessica Lange, Sissy Spacek, Sam Shepard, Tess Harper, David Carpenter, Hurd Hatfield. 1986

CRIMEWAVE ★★★ Hired assassins try to silence a housewife in this hyperkinetic slapstick comedy. Too scattered to be satisfying (and too low-budget for its ambition), it nevertheless has many inventive and hilarious moments. Cowritten by Sam Raimi and Joel and Ethan Coen. Rated PG-13 for violence. 83m. **DIR:** Sam Raimi. **CAST:** Louise Lasser, Brion James, Bruce Campbell. 1985

CRITICAL CONDITION ★★½ Mishmash of a comedy has some funny moments but ultimately tests the viewer's patience. Richard Pryor stars as a hustler who must feign insanity to stay out of prison. While under observation in a psychiatric ward of a big hospital, Pryor surprisingly finds himself in charge of the institution. Rated R for profanity, violence, and scatological humor. 105m. **DIR:** Michael Apted. **CAST:** Richard Pryor, Rachel Ticotin, Rubén Blades, Joe Mantegna, Bob Dishy, Joe Dallesandro, Garrett Morris, Randall "Tex" Cobb. 1987

CRITIC'S CHOICE ★★ A disappointment in spite of its cast, the film is a superficial version of Ira Levin's successful Broadway play. The contrivances begin when a theatre critic has to review his wife's new play, then goes to his first wife for advice. Good cast tries to make the best of poor script and uninspired direction. 100m. **DIR:** Don Weis. **CAST:** Bob Hope, Lucille Ball, Rip Torn, Marilyn Maxwell, Jim Backus, Marie Windsor, Jerome Cowan. 1963

"CROCODILE" DUNDEE ★★★★½ Those folks who moan that they don't make movies like they used to will be delighted by this hilarious Australian import. Paul Hogan plays the title character, a hunter who allegedly crawled several miles for help after a king-size crocodile gnawed off a leg. This slight exaggeration is enough to persuade an American newspaper reporter (Linda Kozlowski) to seek him out and persuade him to join her on a trip to New York, where the naive outbacker faces a new set of perils (and deals with them in high comic style). Rated PG-13 for profanity and violence. 98m. **DIR:** Peter Faiman. **CAST:** Paul Hogan, Linda Kozlowski, John Meillon, Mark Blum, David Gulpilil, Michael Lombard. 1986

"CROCODILE" DUNDEE II ★★★½ This follow-up to the wildly successful release from Down Under adds action to the winning formula of laughs, surprises, romance, and adventure. Mick Dundee (Paul Hogan) and Sue Charlton (Linda Kozlowski) are living a relatively quiet life in New York City until some Colombian drug dealers step in. The results should please fans of the first film. Rated PG for violence and light profanity. 110m. **DIR:** John Cornell. **CAST:** Paul Hogan, Linda Kozlowski, John Meillon, Charles S. Dutton, Hector Ubarry, Juan Fernandez. 1988

CROOKLYN ★★★½ As low key as Spike Lee gets, this episodic movie focuses on an African-American family in 1970s Brooklyn. It's filled with shouting matches, but it's also a warm and well-observed character comedy, featuring a tough, natural performance by young Zelda Harris as the only girl in a brood full of rambunctious boys. Though Lee cowrote with his sister, Joie Susannah, and his brother, Cinqué, the director claims the film is *not* autobiographical. Delroy Lindo, impressive as the West Indian gangster in Lee's *Malcolm X*, plays the musician father who could have been inspired by Spike's own dad. Rated PG-13. 132m. **DIR:** Spike Lee. **CAST:** Zelda Harris, Alfre Woodard, Delroy Lindo, David Patrick Kelly, Carlton Williams. 1994

CROOKS AND CORONETS (SOPHIE'S PLACE) ★★ This picture had only a limited release in the United States and for good reason. It wasn't cunning and bold enough for a good crime picture, and certainly not funny enough for a quality comedy. Dame Edith Evans owns a large estate and the other characters are villains trying to steal the valuable property from her. Not rated. 102m. **DIR:** Jim O'Connolly. **CAST:** Edith Evans, Telly Savalas, Cesar Romero, Warren Oates, Harry H. Corbett. 1970

CROSS MY HEART (1987) ★★ Interminable comedy about the disastrous third date of two vulnerable people trying to keep silly secrets from each other. Martin Short and Annette O'Toole are unmemorable as the couple. Rated R for nudity and language. 88m. **DIR:** Armyan Bernstein. **CAST:** Martin Short, Annette O'Toole, Paul Reiser, Joanna Kerns. 1987

CRY UNCLE! ★★ This is a sometimes very funny spoof of private eye yarns. Allen Garfield is good as a detective who gets involved in all sorts of trouble, but the script is next to tasteless. 87m. **DIR:** John G. Avildsen. **CAST:** Allen Garfield. 1971

CURLY SUE ★★ Writer-director John Hughes pours on the syrupy sweetness again with this tale of a homeless father-daughter duo who con their way into the life of a beautiful attorney. A diabetic's nightmare. Rated PG for brief profanity. 98m. **DIR:** John Hughes. **CAST:** James Belushi, Kelly Lynch, Alisan Porter, John Getz, Fred Dalton Thompson. 1991

CURSE OF THE PINK PANTHER, THE ★★★ No, this isn't another trashy compilation of outtakes featuring the late Peter Sellers. Instead, series producer-writer-director Blake Edwards has hired Ted Wass (of TV's *Soap*) to play a bumbling American detective searching for the still-missing Jacques Clouseau, and he's a delight. When Wass is featured, *Curse* is fresh and diverting—and, on a couple of memorable occasions, it's hilarious. Rated PG for nudity, profanity, violence, and scatological humor. 109m. **DIR:** Blake Edwards. **CAST:** Ted Wass, David Niven, Robert Wagner, Harvey Korman, Herbert Lom. 1983

D.C. CAB 🦃 Take the bus. Rated R. 99m. **DIR:** Joel Schumacher. **CAST:** Gary Busey, Mr. T, Adam Baldwin, Max Gail. 1983

DADDY'S DYIN' AND WHO'S GOT THE WILL ★★★½ Mildly enjoyable comedy about a group of southern eccentrics who just may be rich—if they can find the last will and testament of their nearly dearly departed dad. Entertaining, although the feudin' and fussin' does get to be a bit much. Rated PG-13 for profanity. 117m. **DIR:** Jack Fisk. **CAST:** Beau Bridges, Beverly D'Angelo, Tess Harper, Judge Reinhold, Amy Wright, Keith Carradine, Bert Remsen. 1990

DANCE, GIRL, DANCE ★★★½ Lucille Ball doing a striptease! That's just one of the highlights of this RKO comedy-drama about a couple of ambitious chorus girls who struggle to make it big on Broadway. B&W; 89m. **DIR:** Dorothy Arzner. **CAST:** Maureen O'Hara, Louis Hayward, Lucille Ball. **1940**

DANCE 'TIL DAWN 🦃 Typical teen tripe traps vapid rich kids in the same room as geeky teens with their chaperoning, shallow parents. Blech. Rated PG for sexual innuendo. 96m. **DIR:** Paul Schneider. **CAST:** Christina Applegate, Tempestt Bledsoe, Tracey Gold, Kelsey Grammer, Edie McClurg, Alyssa Milano, Alan Thicke. **1988**

DANCING MOTHERS ★★★ Bee-sting-lipped Jazz Age flapper Clara Bow romps through this verge-of-sound silent about flaming youth. Enthusiastic performances offset the simple plot. B&W; 60m. **DIR:** Herbert Brenon. **CAST:** Clara Bow, Alice Joyce, Dorothy Cumming, Norman Trevor. **1926**

DANGEROUS CURVES ★★★½ A college senior gets a chance to earn a position with a corporation if he can deliver a birthday present to the boss's daughter. The present is a bright red Porsche. This zany comedy, aimed at the younger set, actually has a wider appeal. The young leads are appealing, and the support of Robert Klein and Robert Stack add to the enjoyment. Rated PG. 93m. **DIR:** David Lewis. **CAST:** Tate Donovan, Danielle von Zerneck, Robert Stack, Robert Klein, Robert Romanus. **1988**

DARING YOUNG MAN, THE ★★★ Above-average comedy featuring Joe E. Brown as a bumbling serviceman who becomes mixed up with foreign spies and a radio-controlled bowling ball. B&W; 73m. **DIR:** Frank Strayer. **CAST:** Joe E. Brown, Marguerite Chapman, William Wright. **1942**

DARK BACKWARD, THE ★★ A self-professed comedian can't get a laugh from his audience. Eventually, he is given a hand—a third one, growing from an arm in the middle of his back. Likely to become a cult film. Rated R for profanity. 100m. **DIR:** Adam Rifkin. **CAST:** Judd Nelson, Bill Paxton, Wayne Newton, James Caan, Lara Flynn Boyle. **1991**

DATE WITH AN ANGEL 🦃 A beautiful angel loses control of her wings and lands in the arms of a mortal. Rated PG for profanity. 105m. **DIR:** Tom McLoughlin. **CAST:** Michael E. Knight, Phoebe Cates, Emmanuelle Beart, David Dukes. **1987**

DAVE ★★★★ Moments of sheer hilarity elevate this Capra-esque fantasy, in which an actor is hired to impersonate the president. When the chief executive has a heart attack, our hero is coerced into continuing the masquerade—and this allows him to start turning the country around. Kevin Kline is superb in a dual role, with Sigourney Weaver, Frank Langella, Ben Kingsley, and Charles Grodin lending outstanding support. This one will tickle your funny bone and warm your heart. Rated PG for profanity and suggested sex. 100m. **DIR:** Ivan Reitman. **CAST:** Kevin Kline, Sigourney Weaver, Frank Langella, Kevin Dunn, Ving Rhames, Ben Kingsley, Charles Grodin, Arnold Schwarzenegger, Jay Leno, Oliver Stone. **1993**

DAY AT THE RACES, A ★★★½ The Marx Brothers—Groucho, Harpo, and Chico, that is—were still at the peak of their fame in this MGM musical-comedy. Though not as unrelentingly hilarious and outrageous as the films they made at Paramount with Zeppo, it is nonetheless an enjoyable film. The first to follow *A Night at the Opera*, their biggest hit, and use a variation on its formula, it works very well—which, sadly, did not prove to be the case with most of the Marx Brothers movies that followed. B&W; 111m. **DIR:** Sam Wood. **CAST:** The Marx Brothers, Allan Jones, Maureen O'Sullivan, Margaret Dumont. **1937**

DAY IN THE DEATH OF JOE EGG, A ★★★ This competent British production features the wonderful Alan Bates and Janet Suzman as a married couple whose small son, physically and mentally disabled since birth, causes them to consider euthanasia. Doesn't sound too funny, but in a strange way it is. 106m. **DIR:** Peter Medak. **CAST:** Alan Bates, Janet Suzman, Peter Bowles. **1972**

DAYS OF THRILLS AND LAUGHTER ★★★½ An homage to classic silent-film comedians and daredevils, this collection of clips includes, among other winners, Charlie Chaplin's dinner-roll dance from *Gold Rush*. A worthwhile nostalgia film. B&W; 93m. **DIR:** Robert Youngson. **CAST:** Buster Keaton, Stan Laurel, Oliver Hardy, Charlie Chaplin, Harold Lloyd, Douglas Fairbanks Sr., The Keystone Kops. **1961**

DEAD MEN DON'T DIE ★★½ Nosy television newscaster Elliott Gould stumbles across a story most reporters would die for. Unfortunately, Gould does, but is resurrected through a voodoo spell. Now a zombie, he sets out to solve his own murder. Somewhat funny, proves that for television anchors there is life after death. Rated R for violence and language. 94m. **DIR:** Malcolm Marmorstein. **CAST:** Elliott Gould, Melissa Sue Anderson, Mark Moses, Mabel King. **1991**

DEAD MEN DON'T WEAR PLAID ★★★★ In this often hilarious and always entertaining comedy, Steve Martin plays a private eye who confronts the suspicious likes of Humphrey Bogart, Burt Lancaster, Alan Ladd, Bette Davis, and other stars of Hollywood's Golden Age, with the help of tricky editing and writer-director Carl Reiner. Rachel Ward co-stars as Martin's sexy client. Rated PG for adult themes. B&W; 89m. **DIR:** Carl Reiner. **CAST:** Steve Martin, Rachel Ward, Reni Santoni, Carl Reiner, George Gaynes. **1982**

DEAD SILENCE 🦃 When a financially strapped film director is sponsored by a mob leader, he must use the mobster's no-talent son in the lead. What could have been hilarious and clever falls short. Rated R for profanity and violence. 90m. **DIR:** Harrison Ellenshaw. **CAST:** Clete Keith, Doris Anne Soyka, Joseph Scott, Craig Fleming. **1989**

DEAL OF THE CENTURY ★★ A two-bit arms hustler (Chevy Chase) peddles an ultrasophisticated superweapon to a Central American dictator. This black comedy ends up in that nether world of the near misses. Rated PG for violence and profanity. 99m. **DIR:** William Friedkin. **CAST:** Chevy Chase, Sigourney Weaver, Gregory Hines, Vince Edwards. **1983**

DEAR BRIGITTE ★★½ A clever premise gone wrong. Boy genius who handicaps horses won't play unless he gets to go to meet Brigitte Bardot. What could have been charming comes across as contrived pap. 100m. **DIR:** Henry Koster. **CAST:** James Stewart, Fabian, Glynis Johns, Billy Mumy, Cindy Carol, Jesse White, Ed Wynn, Brigitte Bardot. **1965**

DEAR WIFE ★★½ The second of three amusing films involving the same cast of characters, and mostly the same players. This sequel to *Dear Ruth* has fresh-faced younger sister (to Joan Caulfield) Mona Freeman conniving to elect heartthrob William Holden to the state senate seat sought by her politician father Edward Arnold. Billy DeWolfe fills it all out with his peculiar brand of haughty humor. B&W; 88m. **DIR:** Richard Haydn. **CAST:** Joan Caulfield, William Holden, Mona Freeman, Edward Arnold, Billy DeWolfe. **1949**

DEATHROW GAMESHOW 🦃 Incredibly dull comedy about a detestable game show host who's on the run from mobsters. Rated R. 78m. **DIR:** Mark Pirro. **CAST:** Robin Blythe, John McCafferty. **1988**

DECAMERON NIGHTS ★★★ Louis Jourdan is Boccaccio, the poet, storyteller, and humanist best known for *The Decameron*. Three of his tales are told within the overall frame of his trying to win the love of a recent widow (Joan Fontaine). Each story features the cast members as various characters. The sets and costumes add greatly to this period comedy. 75m. **DIR:** Hugo Fregonese. **CAST:** Joan Fontaine, Louis Jourdan, Joan Collins, Binnie Barnes, Marjorie Rhodes, Godfrey Tearle. **1953**

DEFENDING YOUR LIFE ★★★★½ Once again, star-writer-director Albert Brooks has come up with that increasing rarity: an intelligent comedy. Brooks plays an advertising executive who dies in a car accident and finds himself in Judgment City, where he must defend the cowardly, self-involved life he led on Earth. Fine support from Meryl Streep, Rip Torn, Lee Grant and Buck Henry. Rated PG for brief profanity. 100m. **DIR:** Albert Brooks. **CAST:** Albert Brooks, Meryl Streep, Rip Torn, Lee Grant, Buck Henry. **1991**

DELICATE DELINQUENT, THE ★★★ Jerry Lewis stars on his own for the first time in this surprisingly agreeable story about a goofball delinquent who ends up as a policeman. B&W; 100m. **DIR:** Don McGuire. **CAST:** Jerry Lewis, Darren McGavin, Horace McMahon, Martha Hyer. **1957**

DELINQUENT SCHOOL GIRLS 🦃 Ridiculously racist and sexist sleaze-a-thon features three cons on the run. Rated R for profanity, violence, and nudity. 89m. **DIR:** Gregory Corarito. **CAST:** Michael Pataki, Bob Minor, Stephen Stucker. **1974**

DELIRIOUS ★★★½ In this frequently funny, albeit outrageous, fantasy, soap-opera writer John Candy has a car accident and wakes up to find himself in the fictional town of his television show. *Delirious* was not a critical or box-office success, but we found it clever, surprising, and amiably goofy. Rated PG. 94m. **DIR:** Tom Mankiewicz. **CAST:** John Candy, Mariel Hemingway, Raymond Burr, David Rasche, Charles Rocket, Dylan Baker, Jerry Orbach, Renee Baker. **1991**

DELIVERY BOYS ★★½ This average teen comedy features pizza delivery boys who break dance during their time off. They plan to compete in a break dance contest that offers a $10,000 prize but encounter problems in getting there on time. Rated R. 94m. **DIR:** Ken Handler. **CAST:** Jody Olivery, Joss Marcano, Mario Van Peebles. **1984**

DENNIS MILLER: BLACK AND WHITE ★★ Comic virtuoso Dennis Miller is a throwback to the 1980s—a time when many sarcastic cynics graced comedy-club stages. If you're in the right mood, Miller's who-was-who of pop culture is as worthwhile as a game of Trivial Pursuit. His esoteric hyper-referencing may even be misconstrued as clever, however, it's the sort of thing Robin Williams is better suited for. Unrated, but has profanity. B&W; 60m. **DIR:** Jim Yukich. **CAST:** Dennis Miller. **1992**

DESIGNING WOMAN ★★★½ Diverting comedy with sportswriter Gregory Peck and successful dress designer Lauren Bacall marrying after a whirlwind romance. Mickey Shaughnessy, as Peck's bodyguard, steals the show. 118m. **DIR:** Vincente Minnelli. **CAST:** Gregory Peck, Lauren Bacall, Sam Levene, Dolores Gray, Mickey Shaughnessy, Chuck Connors. **1957**

DESK SET ★★★½ Rober Fryer and Lawrence Carr's Broadway play benefits from the chemistry between Tracy and Hepburn. This isn't their best movie, but it's still fun to watch. Hepburn bucks Tracy's attempts to rework the research department of a TV station. Joan Blondell steals her every scene as a wisecracking coworker.

103m. **DIR:** Walter Lang. **CAST:** Spencer Tracy, Katharine Hepburn, Joan Blondell, Dina Merrill, Neva Patterson. **1957**

DESPERATE LIVING ★★ A "monstrous fairy tale," director John Waters calls it. This story is about a murderess (played by Mink Stole) and her escapades through a village of criminals who are ruled by a demented queen (Edith Massey). But various scenes provide enough humor and wit for anyone with a taste for the perverse and a yen for some good old-fashioned misanthropy. Unrated, but the equivalent of an X, due to violence, nudity, and unbridled gore. 95m. **DIR:** John Waters. **CAST:** Mink Stole, Edith Massey, Jean Hill, Liz Renay, Susan Lowe. **1977**

DESPERATE MOVES ★★★ Steve Tracy plays a young nerd from a small Oregon town traveling to California to pursue his dreams. Touching and amusing, if occasionally silly. Good effort by supporting cast. Not rated, but would probably fall near the PG-13 category. 106m. **DIR:** Oliver Hellman. **CAST:** Steve Tracy, Eddie Deezen, Isabel Sanford, Paul Benedict, Christopher Lee. **1986**

DESPERATELY SEEKING SUSAN ★★★★½ A delightfully daffy, smart, and intriguing comedy made from a feminine perspective. Rosanna Arquette stars as a bored housewife who adds spice to her life by following the personal column love adventures of the mysterious Susan (Madonna). One day, our heroine decides to catch a glimpse of her idol and, through a set of unlikely but easy-to-take plot convolutions, ends up switching places with her. Rated PG-13 for violence. 104m. **DIR:** Susan Seidelman. **CAST:** Rosanna Arquette, Madonna, Robert Joy, Mark Blum, Laurie Metcalf, Aidan Quinn. **1985**

DESTINY TO ORDER ★★½ A writer's creations come to life to haunt him in this strange love story. A bit disjointed, this is nonetheless a fun film. Not rated, but contains violence and profanity. 93m. **DIR:** Jim Purdy. **CAST:** Stephen Quimette, Alberta Watson, Michael Ironside. **1990**

DETECTIVE SCHOOL DROPOUTS ★★★★ David Landsberg and Lorin Dreyfuss co-star in this hilarious comedy. (The two wrote the screenplay as well.) Landsberg plays Wilson, whose obsession with detective stories loses him a string of jobs. Finally, he goes to P.I. Miller (Dreyfuss) for lessons in investigation. The two accidentally become involved in an intrigue with star-crossed lovers. Rated PG for obscenities. 92m. **DIR:** Filippo Ottoni. **CAST:** David Landsberg, Lorin Dreyfuss, Christian De Sica, Valeria Golino, George Eastman. **1985**

DEVIL AND MAX DEVLIN, THE ★★ This is visible proof that it takes more than just a few talented people to create quality entertainment. Despite Elliott Gould, Bill Cosby, and Susan Anspach, this Disney production—another takeoff on the Faustian theme of a pact made with the devil—offers little more than mediocre fare. It's basically a waste of fine talent. Rated PG. 96m. **DIR:** Steven H. Stern. **CAST:** Elliott Gould, Bill Cosby, Susan Anspach, Adam Rich. **1981**

DEVIL AND MISS JONES, THE ★★★★ One of those wonderful comedies Hollywood used to make. Witty, sophisticated, poignant, and breezy, this one has millionaire Charles Coburn going undercover as a clerk in his own department store in order to probe employee complaints and unrest. Delightful doings. B&W; 92m. **DIR:** Sam Wood. **CAST:** Jean Arthur, Robert Cummings, Charles Coburn, Spring Byington, S. Z. Sakall, William Demarest. **1941**

DEVIL'S DISCIPLE, THE ★★★½ An amusing romp through the American Revolution, by way of George Bernard Shaw. The movie follows a straitlaced pastor (Burt Lancaster) and an engaging rogue (Kirk Douglas), who suspend their differences long enough to outwit a British garrison. B&W; 82m. **DIR:** Guy Hamilton. **CAST:** Burt Lancaster, Kirk Douglas, Laurence Olivier, Janette Scott, Eva LeGallienne, Harry Andrews, George Rose. **1959**

DIARY OF A YOUNG COMIC ★★½ This watchable low-budget comedy follows the adventures of a young New York comic, Richard Lewis. Along the way we are given vignettes as he finds an apartment, encounters an agent, gets a booking, takes odd jobs, and finally performs at the Improvisation in Los Angeles. 67m. **DIR:** Gary Weis. **CAST:** Richard Lewis, Stacy Keach, Dom DeLuise, Nina Van Pallandt, Bill Macy, George Jessel. **1979**

DICE RULES ★★ This concert film featuring the extremely profane comic Andrew "Dice" Clay is definitely not for everyone. But those who can stand his brand of raunchy, sexist, sarcastic humor will find much cause for laughter. A "fantasy" sequence which opens the flick is a waste of film. Rated NC-17 for over-the-top profanity. 87m. **DIR:** Jay Dubin. **CAST:** Andrew Dice Clay. **1991**

DIE LAUGHING 🦃 Robby Benson stars as Pinsky, a young cabbie with aspirations of becoming a rock recording star. Rated PG. 108m. **DIR:** Jeff Werner. **CAST:** Robby Benson, Linda Grovenor, Charles Durning, Bud Cort. **1980**

DIGGSTOWN ★★★★½ Imagine the best parts of *The Sting* and *Rocky* combined in one terrific movie, and you get a good idea how supremely entertaining *Diggstown* is. James Woods and Lou Gossett work wonderfully together as a pair of con men who attempt to scam crook Bruce Dern, at his slimy best. Rated R for profanity and violence. 97m. **DIR:** Michael Ritchie. **CAST:** James Woods, Lou Gossett Jr., Bruce Dern, Oliver Platt, Heather Graham, Randall "Tex" Cobb. **1992**

DINER ★★★★½ Writer-director Barry Levinson's much-acclaimed bittersweet tale of growing up in the late 1950s, unlike *American Graffiti*, is never cute or idealized. Instead, it combines insight, sensitive drama, and low-key humor. Rated R for profanity and adult themes. 110m. **DIR:** Barry Levinson. **CAST:** Steve Guttenberg, Daniel Stern, Mickey Rourke, Kevin Bacon, Ellen Barkin. **1982**

DINNER AT EIGHT (1933) ★★★★★ A sparkling, sophisticated, and witty comedy of character written by George S. Kaufman and Edna Ferber for the Broadway stage, this motion picture has a terrific all-star cast and lots of laughs. It's an all-time movie classic. B&W; 113m. **DIR:** George Cukor. **CAST:** John Barrymore, Jean Harlow, Marie Dressler, Billie Burke, Wallace Beery. **1933**

DINNER AT EIGHT (1990) ★★★ Commendable television remake of MGM's classic comedy. Socialite Marsha Mason has nothing but problems while planning a dinner party for visiting English dignitaries. The lives of those on her guest list are equally explored as the night of the party arrives. 92m. **DIR:** Ron Lagomarsino. **CAST:** John Mahoney, Marsha Mason, Stacy Edwards, Joel Brooks, Tim Kazurinsky, Harry Hamlin, Ellen Greene, Lauren Bacall, Charles Durning. **1990**

DIRTY LAUNDRY 🦃 Stupid chase film involving a young man and a group of drug-dealing thugs. Rated PG-13 for profanity. 81m. **DIR:** William Webb. **CAST:** Leigh McCloskey, Jeanne O'Brien, Frankie Valli, Sonny Bono. **1987**

DIRTY ROTTEN SCOUNDRELS ★★★★½ Here's one of those rare instances where the remake is far better than the original. In retooling *Bedtime Story,* which starred Marlon Brando and David Niven, director Frank Oz came up with a genuine laugh riot. Michael Caine plays a sophisticated con man whose successful bilking of wealthy female tourists is endangered by upstart Steve Martin. Their battle of wits reaches true comic highs when they duel over the fortune and affections of American heiress Glenne Headly. Rated PG for profanity. 110m. **DIR:** Frank Oz. **CAST:** Steve Martin, Michael Caine, Glenne Headly, Barbara Harris. **1988**

DIRTY TRICKS 🦃 This Canadian-made movie brings the comedy-thriller genre to an all-time low. Rated PG. 91m. **DIR:** Alvin Rakoff. **CAST:** Elliott Gould, Kate Jackson, Rich Little, Arthur Hill, Nicholas Campbell. **1980**

DISORDERLY ORDERLY, THE ★★★ Jerry Lewis is out of control at a nursing home in a good solo effort directed by comedy veteran Frank Tashlin, who reached his peak here. Comic gems abound in this film, which isn't just for fans. In fact, if you've never been one of Jerry's faithful, give this one a try to see if you can't be swayed. You just might be surprised. 90m. **DIR:** Frank Tashlin. **CAST:** Jerry Lewis, Glenda Farrell, Susan Oliver, Everett Sloane, Jack E. Leonard, Kathleen Freeman. **1964**

DISTINGUISHED GENTLEMAN, THE ★★★½ Con man–style takeoff on *Mr. Smith Goes to Washington*. Eddie Murphy is a street hustler who hustles a seat in the House of Representatives. The first two-thirds of the movie, with an accent on comedy, are the best. Rated R for profanity, suggested sex, and nudity. 100m. **DIR:** Jonathan Lynn. **CAST:** Eddie Murphy, James Garner, Sheryl Lee Ralph, Lane Smith, Joe Don Baker, Grant Shaud, Kevin McCarthy, Charles S. Dutton. **1992**

DIVINE 🦃 Filmmaker John Waters's special tribute to the famous transvestite comic features Divine in a rare, early short "The Diane Linkletter Story" and the only existing performance of the famous "The Neon Woman" show. Unless you're a die hard fan of John Waters or Divine, this exercise in cinema of the absurd could be torture. Not rated, but contains profanity and nudity. 110m. **DIR:** John Waters. **CAST:** Divine. **1990**

DIVORCE OF LADY X, THE ★★★★ In this British comedy, Laurence Olivier plays a lawyer who allows Merle Oberon to spend the night at his place. Although nothing actually happened that night, Olivier finds himself branded "the other man" in her divorce. A series of hilarious misunderstandings are the result. 90m. **DIR:** Tim Whelan. **CAST:** Merle Oberon, Laurence Olivier, Binnie Barnes, Ralph Richardson. **1938**

DIXIE CHANGING HABITS ★★★½ Suzanne Pleshette plays Dixie, who runs a highly successful prostitution ring. When she's busted, she must spend time in a convent directed by Cloris Leachman as the Mother Superior. All in all, this made-for-TV comedy is highly entertaining. 96m. **DIR:** George Englund. **CAST:** Suzanne Pleshette, Cloris Leachman, Kenneth McMillan, John Considine. **1982**

DIXIE LANES 🦃 Chaotic comedy revolving around the bad luck of a family named Laid Law. Not rated, but equivalent to a PG-13. 90m. **DIR:** Don Cato. **CAST:** Hoyt Axton, Karen Black, Art Hindle, Tina Louise, Ruth Buzzi, Moses Gunn, John Vernon. **1988**

DOC HOLLYWOOD ★★★ En route to Beverly Hills, Dr. Benjamin Stone (Michael J. Fox) has a car accident in South Carolina, where the local residents are in need of an M.D. Doc Stone persists in his hopes for fame and fortune until he meets the pretty Lou (Julie Warner) and falls in love. Good formula fun. Rated PG-13 for nudity and profanity. 110m. **DIR:** Michael Caton-Jones. **CAST:** Michael J. Fox, Julie Warner, Bridget Fonda, Woody Harrelson, George Hamilton. **1991**

DOCTOR AT LARGE ★★★ Young Dr. Simon Sparrow wants to join the hospital staff, but the grumpy superintendent isn't buying. Comic conniving ensues as Sparrow seeks a place. Third in a series of six films featuring Dr. Sparrow. 98m. **DIR:** Ralph Thomas. **CAST:** Dirk Bogarde, James Robertson Justice, Shirley Eaton. **1957**

DOCTOR AT SEA ★★★ Fed up with the myriad complications of London life and romance, young, handsome Dr. Simon Sparrow seeks a rugged man's world by signing up on a passenger-carrying freighter as ship's doctor. He goes from the frying pan into the fire when he meets Brigitte Bardot on the high seas! Second in the highly successful British comedy series. 92m. **DIR:** Ralph Thomas. **CAST:** Dirk Bogarde, Brigitte Bardot, Brenda de Banzie, James Robertson Justice. **1955**

DOCTOR DETROIT ★★½ Dan Aykroyd stars in this comedy as a soft-spoken English professor who becomes a comic book–style pimp. Aykroyd has some genuinely funny moments, but the movie is uneven overall. Rated R for profanity, nudity, and violence. 89m. **DIR:** Michael Pressman. **CAST:** Dan Aykroyd, Howard Hesseman, Nan Martin, T. K. Carter. **1983**

DOCTOR DUCK'S SUPER SECRET ALL-PURPOSE SAUCE ★★★ Generally funny assortment of sketches and stand-up comedy, mixed with some imaginative music videos by ex-Monkee Michael Nesmith. The highlights are Lois Bromfield impersonating a Fifties B-movie star and a Jay Leno bit about American cars, but there's enough variety to please everyone. Unrated, with no objectionable material. 82m. **DIR:** William Dear, Alan Myerson, Edward Bianchi, Graham Henman. **CAST:** Mike Nesmith, Jimmy Buffett, Dick Cavett, Bob Goldthwait, Jay Leno, Whoopi Goldberg, Roseanne Cash, Ed Begley Jr., Martin Mull, Lois Bromfield. **1986**

DR. HECKYL AND MR. HYPE ★★★½ Oh, no, not another *Dr. Jekyll and Mr. Hyde* parody! But this is quite funny, right up there with Jerry Lewis's *The Nutty Professor.* Oliver Reed is hilarious as both an ugly podiatrist and his alter ego, a handsome stud. Writer-director Charles B. Griffith, who wrote the original *Little Shop of Horrors,* has a field day here. Rated R for nudity. 99m. **DIR:** Charles B. Griffith. **CAST:** Oliver Reed, Sunny Johnson, Mel Welles, Jackie Coogan, Corinne Calvet, Dick Miller. **1980**

DOCTOR IN DISTRESS ★★★ In this high jinks–jammed British comedy of medical student and young physician trials and tribulations, head of hospital Sir Lancelot Spratt reveals he is human when he falls in love. Hero Dr. Simon Sparrow has trouble romancing a beautiful model. It's all fast-pace and very funny. Fourth in a series of six that began with *Doctor in the House.* B&W; 103m. **DIR:** Ralph Thomas. **CAST:** Dirk Bogarde, Samantha Eggar, James Robertson Justice. **1963**

DOCTOR IN THE HOUSE ★★★½ This well-paced farce features a superb British cast. It's about the exploits of a group of medical students intent on studying beautiful women and how to become wealthy physicians. This low-key comedy of manners inspired six other *Doctor* movies and eventually led to a TV series. Not rated. 92m. **DIR:** Ralph Thomas. **CAST:** Dirk Bogarde, Muriel Pavlow, Kenneth More, Donald Sinden, Kay Kendall, James Robertson Justice, Donald Houston. **1954**

DR. OTTO AND THE RIDDLE OF THE GLOOM BEAM ★★★ A fun and wacky journey into the mind of Jim Varney. Dr. Otto has a deranged plan and Lance Sterling is the only person who can stop him. Varney plays both Otto and Sterling in this refreshingly strange comedy. A must for Varney fans. Rated PG. 97m. **DIR:** John R. Cherry III. **CAST:** Jim Varney. **1986**

DR. STRANGELOVE OR HOW I LEARNED TO STOP WORRYING AND LOVE THE BOMB ★★★★★ Stanley Kubrick's black comedy masterpiece about the dropping of the "bomb." Great performances from an all-star cast, including Peter Sellers in three hilarious roles. Don't miss it. B&W; 93m. **DIR:** Stanley Kubrick. **CAST:** Peter Sellers, Sterling Hayden, George C. Scott, Slim Pickens, Keenan Wynn, James Earl Jones. **1964**

DOCTOR TAKES A WIFE, THE ★★★½ This delightful comedy employs an oft-used plot. Through a series of misadventures, Ray Milland is incorrectly identified as Loretta Young's handsome husband. So he takes advantage of the misunderstanding. All ends happily. B&W; 89m. **DIR:** Alexander Hall. **CAST:** Ray Milland, Loretta Young, Reginald Gardiner, Edmund Gwenn, Gail Patrick. **1940**

DOES THIS MEAN WE'RE MARRIED? ★★½ Romantic comedy contains a sprinkling of bittersweet moments as an American comedienne earns her French green card by marrying an irresponsible playboy. Rated PG-13 for profanity, nudity, and violence. 93m. **DIR:** Carol Wiseman. **CAST:** Patsy Kensit, Stephane Freiss. **1990**

DOGPOUND SHUFFLE 🦃 Ron Moody and David Soul as two drifters who rescue a dog from the pound. Rated PG for language. 98m. **DIR:** Jeffrey Bloom. **CAST:** Ron Moody, David Soul, Raymond Sutton, Pamela McMyler, Ray Stricklyn. **1974**

DOIN' TIME 🦃 *Doin' Time* is a bum rap. Rated R for profanity and sex. 84m. **DIR:** George Mendeluk. **CAST:** Jeff Altman, Dey Young, Richard Mulligan, John Vernon, Judy Landers, Colleen Camp, Melanie Chartoff, Graham Jarvis, Pat McCormick, Eddie Velez, Jimmie Walker. **1984**

DOIN' TIME ON PLANET EARTH ★★½ A teenage nerd living in Sunnydale, Arizona ("Prune Capital of the World"), feels so out of place that he wonders if he isn't really from another planet. His unique "adoption fantasy" is fed by the arrival of two weirdos (Adam West and Candace Azzara). First-time director Charles Matthau (son of Walter) makes the most of a meager budget and an uneven cast. Rated PG. 83m. **DIR:** Charles Matthau. **CAST:** Nicholas Strouse, Adam West, Candy Azzara, Martha Scott, Matt Alden, Andrea Thompson. **1988**

DOLEMITE ★★ Nightclub owner tracks down the drug dealers who framed him. Supposedly a parody of blaxploitation movies, you'll be laughing at this rather than with it. Rated R for nudity, sexual situations, violence, and profanity. 89m. **DIR:** D'Urville Martin. **CAST:** Rudy Ray Moore, D'Urville Martin, Jerry Jones. **1975**

DON RICKLES: BUY THIS TAPE YOU HOCKEY PUCK 🦃 With Don Rickles cracking the same tired jokes in a Las Vegas lounge setting, one may ask: Why has he put out this video of his 1975 television special? 51m. **DIR:** Barry Shear. **CAST:** Don Rickles, Jack Klugman, Don Adams, Michele Lee, James Caan, Michael Caine, José Ferrer, Arthur Godfrey, Elliott Gould. **1975**

DONOVAN'S REEF ★★★ Director John Ford's low, knock-about style of comedy prevails in this tale of two old drinking, seafaring buddies—John Wayne and Lee Marvin—forced to aid another pal, Jack Warden, in putting on an air of respectability to impress the latter's visiting daughter (Elizabeth Allen). 109m. **DIR:** John Ford. **CAST:** John Wayne, Lee Marvin, Elizabeth Allen, Jack Warden, Dorothy Lamour. **1963**

DON'S PARTY ★★★½ *Don's Party* is a hilarious, and at times vulgar, adult comedy. Like the characters in *Who's Afraid of Virginia Woolf?*, the eleven revelers at Don's party lose all control, and the evening climaxes in bitter hostilities and humiliating confessions. With no MPAA rating, the film has nudity and profanity. 91m. **DIR:** Bruce Beresford. **CAST:** John Hargreaves, Pat Bishop, Graham Kennedy. **1976**

DON'T DRINK THE WATER ★★★★½ Jackie Gleason plays a caterer on a vacation with his wife (Estelle Parsons) and daughter (Joan Delaney). When the plane taking them to Greece is hijacked behind the Iron Curtain, Gleason is accused of spying and finds asylum in the U.S. embassy. Gleason's cranky *Honeymooners* attitude is perfectly balanced by Parsons's bubbleheaded comments. Based on Woody Allen's wacky play. Rated G. 100m. **DIR:** Howard Morris. **CAST:** Jackie Gleason, Estelle Parsons, Ted Bessell, Joan Delaney, Michael Constantine, Howard St. John, Danny Meehan, Richard Libertini. **1969**

DON'T GO NEAR THE WATER ★★★ World War II navy public-relations personnel try to grab the glory away from the other services. Generally misfires but scene-stealer Fred Clark is in charge and Mickey Shaughnessy is funny as a foul-mouthed enlisted man. His role is one of the greatest jokes ever played on movie censors. Turn up the sound and pay attention—they apparently didn't. 107m. **DIR:** Charles Walters. **CAST:** Glenn Ford, Gia Scala, Earl Holliman, Anne Francis, Keenan Wynn, Fred Clark, Eva Gabor, Russ Tamblyn, Mickey Shaughnessy, Mary Wickes, Jack Albertson. **1957**

DON'T RAISE THE BRIDGE, LOWER THE RIVER 🦃 Weak vehicle for Jerry Lewis concerns his efforts to keep his marriage alive. Rated G. 99m. **DIR:** Jerry Paris. **CAST:** Jerry Lewis, Terry-Thomas, Jacqueline Pearce, Bernard Cribbins. **1968**

DON'T TELL HER IT'S ME ★★★ A syrupy-sweet romantic comedy about a cancer patient (Steve Guttenberg) who can't get back into dating after his recovery has left him with no hair and a bloated face. His sister (Shelley Long) comes to his aid and turns him into the type of man the girl of his dreams (Jami Gertz) would want. Rated PG-13 for mild violence and brief profanity. 103m. **DIR:** Malcolm Mowbray. **CAST:** Steve Guttenberg, Jami Gertz, Shelley Long, Kyle MacLachlan, Madchen Amick. **1991**

DON'T TELL MOM THE BABYSITTER'S DEAD ★★ After their baby-sitter drops dead, four rowdy kids rely on their 17-year-old sister to put food on the table. Unfortunately, the funniest line in this adolescent comedy is the film's title. Rated PG-13 for language. 142m. **DIR:** Stephen Herek. **CAST:** Christina Applegate, Joanna Cassidy, John Getz, Keith Coogan, Josh Charles. **1991**

DOOR TO DOOR ★★★½ An aspiring salesman learns the ropes from a veteran who has a variety of other ways of augmenting his income (very few of them legal). A gentle, offbeat comedy. Rated PG. 85m. **DIR:** Patrick Bailey. **CAST:** Ron Leibman, Arliss Howard, Jane Kaczmarek. **1984**

DORF AND THE FIRST GAMES OF MOUNT OLYMPUS ★★★ Tim Conway reprises his amusing character, Dorkus Dorf, in this follow-up to *Dorf on Golf*. This time, more variety is given as Dorf demonstrates some twelve events in the first Olympian meet. Some are quite innovative; some just silly. 35m. **DIR:** Lang Elliott. **CAST:** Tim Conway. **1988**

DORF GOES AUTO RACING 🦃 This attempt to spoof auto racing is really an extended commercial for Budweiser beer. 70m. **DIR:** Berry Landen. **CAST:** Tim Conway, Eddie Deezen. **1990**

DORF ON GOLF ★★½ Tim Conway has created a humorous character, measuring approximately three feet tall, called Dorkus Dorf. In this video he gives tips on playing and enjoying golf. As with most comedy skits, some of them work and some of them fall short. This spawned a sequel, *Dorf and the First Games of Mount Olympus*, which is more fun. 30m. **DIR:** Roger Beatty. **CAST:** Tim Conway. **1987**

DOUBLE DYNAMITE ★★½ Disappointing comedy about a bank teller (Frank Sinatra) who receives a generous reward for saving a gangster's life completely by accident. Sinatra and Groucho Marx can't rise above the weak script and direction. B&W; 80m. **DIR:** Irving Cummings. **CAST:** Frank Sinatra, Jane Russell, Groucho Marx. **1951**

DOUBLE EXPOSURE (1987) ★★★ Two aspiring Venice Beach photographers divide their time between trying to impress the local bathing beauties and solving a murder that they accidentally photographed (shades of *Blow-up!*). Standard comedy thriller done with a little panache. Rated R for nudity. 100m. **DIR:** Nico Mastorakis. **CAST:** Mark Hennessy, Scott King, John Vernon. **1987**

DOUBLE TROUBLE (1991) ★★ Inane actioner features muscle-bound twins (wrestling duo Peter Paul and David Paul) on either side of the law. They team up to pursue a deadly diamond thief. Rated R for violence and profanity. 87m. **DIR:** John Paragon. **CAST:** Peter Paul, David Paul, Roddy McDowall, Steve Kanaly. **1991**

DOUBLE WEDDING ★★★★ William Powell as a painter and Myrna Loy as a dress designer play Cupid in an effort to get Florence Rice married to John Beal. But the plan backfires. A delightful slapstick comedy. Lots of fun. B&W; 87m. **DIR:** Richard Thorpe. **CAST:** William Powell, Myrna Loy, Florence Rice, Edgar Kennedy, Sidney Toler, Jessie Ralph, Mary Gordon, John Beal. **1937**

DOUBTING THOMAS ★★★ Wealthy manufacturer Will Rogers foils his stagestruck wife's acting ambition in this moderately amusing but outdated comedy. B&W; 78m. **DIR:** David Butler. **CAST:** Will Rogers, Billie Burke, Alison Skipworth, Sterling Holloway, Frank Albertson, John Qualen. **1935**

DOUGH AND DYNAMITE/KNOCKOUT, THE ★★★ Two of the best slapstick two-reelers Mack Sennett's famous Keystone Studios churned out during the heyday of fast-and-furious, rough-and-tumble comedies. *The Knockout*, actually a Fatty Arbuckle film, has Charlie Chaplin playing the referee, the third man in the ring, in a fight sequence between behemoths (to him) Edgar Kennedy and Arbuckle. *Dough and Dynamite* is set in a French restaurant. B&W; 54m. **DIR:** Mack Sennett, Charles Chaplin. **CAST:** Keystone Kops. **1914**

DOUGHBOYS ★★ Buster Keaton mistakenly enlists in the army and in spite of himself becomes a hero. His second sound film, and a letdown from start to finish. B&W; 79m. **DIR:** Edward Sedgwick. **CAST:** Buster Keaton, Sally Eilers, Cliff Edwards, Edward Brophy. **1930**

DOUGHGIRLS, THE ★★ The setting is crowded Washington D.C. during World War II when a hotel room could hardly be had. Not even for honeymooners who find they have to share their suite with an assortment of military men and women. A comedy that relies on the wartime era for its laughs, and the personalities take a backseat to the dated dialogue. B&W; 102m. **DIR:** James V. Kern. **CAST:** Ann Sheridan, Jane Wyman, Eve Arden, Alexis Smith, Jack Carson, Craig Stevens, Charlie Ruggles, Alan Mowbray, Regis Toomey. **1944**

DOWN AMONG THE "Z" MEN 🦃 Before there was a Monty Python there were the Goons, a British comedy team that featured Peter Sellers, among others (see cast). B&W; 82m. **DIR:** Maclean Rogers. **CAST:** Peter Sellers, Harry Secombe, Michael Bentine, Spike Milligan, Carol Carr. **1961**

DOWN AND OUT IN BEVERLY HILLS ★★★½ When a Los Angeles bum (Nick Nolte) loses his dog to a happy home, he decides to commit suicide in a Beverly Hills swimming pool. The pool's owner (Richard Dreyfuss) saves the seedy-looking character's life and thereby sets in motion a chain of events that threatens to destroy his family's rarefied existence. Rated R. 102m. **DIR:** Paul Mazursky. **CAST:** Nick Nolte, Bette Midler, Richard Dreyfuss, Little Richard, Tracy Nelson, Elizabeth Peña, Evan Richards. **1986**

DOWN BY LAW ★★★★½ *Stranger Than Paradise* director Jim Jarmusch improves on his static deadpan style by allowing his *Down by Law* characters a bit more life. In fact, he appears to be leaning more optimistically toward activity. He gives the film an energetic Italian comedian (Roberto Benigni), who looks like a dark-haired Kewpie doll. This lively imp inspires his lethargic companions (John Lurie, Tom Waits) to speak, sing, and generally loosen up a little. Rated R for nudity and profanity. 90m. **DIR:** Jim Jarmusch. **CAST:** John Lurie, Tom Waits, Roberto Benigni, Ellen Barkin. **1986**

DOWN TO EARTH ★★★★ One of the brightest of the early Douglas Fairbanks social comedies. All the "big guns" are here—scenarist Anita Loos; her husband, director John Emerson; and some sparkling camerawork by Victor Fleming (before he turned full-time director). Silent. B&W; 52m. **DIR:** John Emerson. **CAST:** Douglas Fairbanks Sr., Eileen Percy, Gustav von Seyffertitz. **1917**

DRAGNET (1987) ★★½ Dan Aykroyd's deliriously funny impersonation of Jack Webb can only carry this comedy so far.

While Tom Hanks adds some moments of his own, the screenplay about political double-dealing tends to bog down. Rated PG-13 for profanity and violence. 107m. **DIR:** Tom Mankiewicz. **CAST:** Dan Aykroyd, Tom Hanks, Alexandra Paul, Harry Morgan, Christopher Plummer, Dabney Coleman, Elizabeth Ashley, Jack O'Halloran, Kathleen Freeman. **1987**

DREAM A LITTLE DREAM ★★ An obnoxious teen has the hots for Miss Unattainable (Meredith Salenger). When the two get caught up in Jason Robards Jr.'s dream, he gets his chance to be with her. Mediocre. Rated PG-13 for language. 115m. **DIR:** Marc Rocco. **CAST:** Jason Robards Jr., Corey Feldman, Meredith Salenger, Piper Laurie. **1989**

DREAM DATE ★★½ Single father Clifton Davis remembers what he was like when he started dating, and doesn't like it when his daughter is ready for her first date. Made-for-TV farce enlivened by an effective cast. Not rated. 96m. **DIR:** Anson Williams. **CAST:** Clifton Davis, Tempestt Bledsoe, Kadeem Hardison, Anne-Marie Johnson, Richard Moll, Pauly Shore. **1989**

DREAM MACHINE 🦃 Macho male teen fantasy has Corey Haim securing the automobile of his dreams by being in the right place at the right time. This comedy starts to run on empty long before it reaches the finishing line. Rated PG. 85m. **DIR:** Lyman Dayton. **CAST:** Corey Haim, Evan Richards, Susan Seaforth Hayes, Jeremy Slate. **1990**

DREAM TEAM, THE ★★★★½ When a psychiatrist (Dennis Boutsikaris) takes four mental patients on a field trip to Yankee Stadium, he is unexpectedly waylaid and his quartet of lovable loonies is let loose in the Big Apple. This gem of a comedy features terrific ensemble performances. It'll steal your heart—guaranteed. Rated PG for profanity and violence. 113m. **DIR:** Howard Zieff. **CAST:** Michael Keaton, Christopher Lloyd, Peter Boyle, Stephen Furst, Lorraine Bracco, Dennis Boutsikaris. **1989**

DREAMING OUT LOUD ★★½ Chester Lauck and Norris Goff, better known as radio's Lum and Abner, fare well in this first of a film series based on their misadventures at the Jot-em Down Store in Pine Ridge, Arkansas. The cracker-barrel philosophers quietly, and with humor, exert a variety of influences on their fellow citizens. It's corn, but clean corn. B&W; 65m. **DIR:** Harold Young. **CAST:** Chester Lauck, Norris Goff, Frances Langford, Robert Wilcox, Irving Bacon, Frank Craven, Phil Harris. **1940**

DRIVE-IN ★★★ Enjoyable film about a day in the life of a small Texas town. At dusk all the citizens head off for the local drive-in theater. With as many as three plots developing, *Drive-In* is like a Southern *American Graffiti*. Rated PG. 96m. **DIR:** Rod Amateau. **CAST:** Lisa Lemole, Glen Morshower, Gary Cavagnaro, Trey Wilson. **1976**

DRIVING ME CRAZY ★★★½ Charming comedy stars German actor Thomas Gottschalk as the inventor of a car that runs on turnips. He discovers capitalism and Los Angeles with the help of Billy Dee Williams. Predictable, but fun in a low-key way. Rated PG-13. 88m. **DIR:** Jon Turteltaub. **CAST:** Billy Dee Williams, Thomas Gottschalk, Dom DeLuise, Michelle Johnson, George Kennedy. **1991**

DROP DEAD FRED ★★½ A young woman has a childhood imaginary friend who reappears to help her through a crisis. A wild romp with stunning visual effects that some viewers may find offensive. Rated PG-13 for profanity and brief nudity. 98m. **DIR:** Ate De Jong. **CAST:** Phoebe Cates, Rik Mayall, Marsha Mason, Tim Matheson, Carrie Fisher, Ron Eldard. **1991**

DUCK SOUP ★★★★★ Groucho, Harpo, Chico, and Zeppo in their best film: an antiestablishment comedy that failed miserably at the box office at the time of its release. Today, this Leo McCarey–directed romp has achieved its proper reputation as the quintessential Marx Brothers classic. B&W; 70m. **DIR:** Leo McCarey. **CAST:** The Marx Brothers, Margaret Dumont, Louis Calhern, Raquel Torres, Edgar Kennedy. **1933**

DUTCH ★★★ Dutch Dooley (Ed O'Neill) agrees to what seems like a simple task: picking up his girlfriend's son from an Atlanta boarding school and driving him home to Chicago. Written by John Hughes, isn't quite *Planes, Trains and Automobiles*. Rated PG-13 for profanity. 95m. **DIR:** Peter Faiman. **CAST:** Ed O'Neill, JoBeth Williams, Ethan Randall. **1991**

EAGLE, THE ★★★ Produced to boost the legendary Rudolph Valentino's then-sagging popularity, this satirical romance of a Russian Cossack lieutenant who masquerades as a do-gooder bandit to avenge his father's death proved a box-office winner for the star. Valentino is at his romantic, swoon-inducing, self-mocking best in the title role. Silent. B&W; 72m. **DIR:** Clarence Brown. **CAST:** Rudolph Valentino, Vilma Banky, Louise Dresser, Clark Ward, Spottiswoode Aitken. **1925**

EARTHWORM TRACTORS ★★★ Big mouth Joe E. Brown plays braggart salesman Alexander Botts for all the comedy he can squeeze out of tractor jokes. Based on the noted *Saturday Evening Post* stories of the 1930s, this is one of Brown's better efforts. Fun stuff. B&W; 63m. **DIR:** Ray Enright. **CAST:** Joe E. Brown, Gene Lockhart, Guy Kibbee, Dick Foran. **1936**

EASY MONEY ★★ In this fitfully funny comedy, slob Rodney Dangerfield attempts to clean up his act, with the help of pal Joe

Pesci, to qualify for a large inheritance. Rated R for profanity and suggested sex. 95m. **DIR:** James Signorelli. **CAST:** Rodney Dangerfield, Joe Pesci, Geraldine Fitzgerald, Candy Azzara. **1983**

EASY WHEELS ★★★ Life, love, and the pursuit of a better draft beer with the leather-bound unshaven. Dumb fun. Rated R. 94m. **DIR:** David O'Malley. **CAST:** Paul LeMat, Eileen Davidson, Barry Livingston, George Plimpton. **1989**

EAT OR BE EATEN ★★★ This spoof centers around newscasters Haryll Hee and Sharyll Shee as they cover the crisis in Labyrinth County. Between news coverage we see clever commercials that poke fun at those we normally see, as well as takeoffs on TV evangelists and sitcoms. This one has lots of laughs. Unrated, it deals with adult topics and is comparable to a PG. 30m. **DIR:** Phil Austin. **CAST:** Firesign Theatre Players. **1985**

EAT THE PEACH ★★ *Eat the Peach* takes place in an Irish village and tells the story of Vinnie and Arthur, two friends who see the Elvis Presley film *Roustabout* in which a cyclist rides the carnival Wall of Death, and decide to create their own. A slight and subtle movie. You want to like it, but it just never kicks in. Rated PG. 90m. **DIR:** Peter Ormrod. **CAST:** Stephen Brennan, Eamon Morrissey, Catherine Byrne, Niall Toibin. **1987**

EAT THE RICH 🦃 This ludicrous exercise in bad taste uses profanity, violence, and toilet jokes to elicit laughs. Rated R. 92m. **DIR:** Peter Richardson. **CAST:** Lanah Pellay, Ronald Allen, Sandra Dorne. **1987**

EATING RAOUL ★★★★ A hilarious black comedy cowritten and directed by Paul Bartel, this low-budget film presents an inventive but rather bizarre solution to the recession. When Mary Bland (Mary Woronov) is saved by her frying-pan-wielding husband, Paul (Bartel), from a would-be rapist, the happily married couple happily discover that the now-deceased attacker was rolling in dough—so they roll him and hit on a way to end their economic woes. Rated R for nudity, profanity, sexual situations, and violence. 83m. **DIR:** Paul Bartel. **CAST:** Paul Bartel, Mary Woronov, Robert Beltran, Susan Saiger. **1982**

ED & HIS DEAD MOTHER ★★★½ Goofy fun finds mamma's boy Steve Buscemi so desperate to get dear old Mom back that he pays shyster salesman John Glover to bring her back from the dead. Well, *Guess Who's Coming to Dinner*? One problem: Mom now eats bugs and has other undead habits as well. Traditional havoc ensues. Rated PG-13 for language, adult situations, and horror violence. 93m. **DIR:** Jonathan Wacks. **CAST:** Steve Buscemi, Ned Beatty, Miriam Margoyles, John Glover, Sam Jenkins. **1992**

EDDIE MURPHY—DELIRIOUS ★★★ Stand-up comedy performance by the superstar at Constitution Hall, Washington, D.C., runs more hot than cold, as Eddie hurls barbs at gays, Michael Jackson, Ralph Kramden and Ed Norton of *The Honeymooners*, his parents, Mr. T, etc. Most of the gags are obscene and often hilarious, but there are also occasional stretches of boredom as the show progresses. Be forewarned: contains strong language. 70m. **DIR:** Bruce Gowers. **CAST:** Eddie Murphy, The Bus Boys. **1983**

EDDIE MURPHY RAW ★★ Little of Eddie Murphy's talent comes across in this live-performance film. While there are some funny bits, the comedian too often relies on shock and plain bad taste. The show ends on a flat note with a silly routine about his family having to eat toys because they were poor. Rated R for profanity, scatological humor, and sexual descriptions. 91m. **DIR:** Robert Townsend. **CAST:** Eddie Murphy. **1987**

EDUCATING RITA ★★★★½ A boozing, depressed English professor (Michael Caine) takes on a sharp-witted, eager-to-learn hairdresser (Julie Walters) for Open University tutorials and each educates the other, in this delightful romantic comedy based on a London hit play. Rated PG for profanity. 110m. **DIR:** Lewis Gilbert. **CAST:** Michael Caine, Julie Walters, Michael Williams. **1983**

EGG AND I, THE ★★★ Hayseed Fred MacMurray spirits his finishing-school bride Claudette Colbert away from Boston to cope with chicken farming in the rural Pacific Northwest. Everything goes wrong. Marjorie Main and Percy Kilbride as Ma and Pa Kettle made comic marks bright enough to earn them their own film series. Not a laugh riot, but above-average funny. B&W; 108m. **DIR:** Chester Erskine. **CAST:** Claudette Colbert, Fred MacMurray, Louise Allbritton, Marjorie Main, Percy Kilbride, Donald MacBride, Samuel S. Hinds, Fuzzy Knight. **1947**

18 AGAIN 🦃 Yet another unsuccessful attempt to portray the older man magically switching into a young man's body. Rated PG for language and sexual suggestion. 100m. **DIR:** Paul Flaherty. **CAST:** George Burns, Charlie Schlatter, Tony Roberts, Anita Morris, Miriam Flynn, Jennifer Runyon, Red Buttons. **1988**

ELAYNE BOOSLER—BROADWAY BABY ★★★ Comic Elayne Boosler takes her stand-up routine to Broadway. A strong start and a hilarious finish help overshadow the slow middle. Sit back and laugh. Not rated, but contains adult language. 60m. **DIR:** Steve Gerbson. **CAST:** Elayne Boosler. **1987**

ELAYNE BOOSLER: PARTY OF ONE ★★★ Hilarious stand-up routine from Elayne Boosler, who relates events in her life with help from guest stars Bill Cosby, David Letterman, and Larry "Bud" Melman. 60m. **DIR:** Elayne Boosler. **1989**

ELECTRIC DREAMS ★★★ An ingenious blending of the motion picture with the rock music video, this release deals with the complications that arise when an absentminded architect, Miles (Lenny Von Dohlen), buys his first home computer. It isn't long before the computer (the voice is Bud Cort, of *Harold and Maude* fame) begins to develop a rather feisty personality. Rated PG for profanity. 96m. **DIR:** Steve Barron. **CAST:** Lenny Von Dohlen, Virginia Madsen, Bud Cort (voice). **1984**

ELLA CINDERS ★★★ Solid vehicle for comedienne Colleen Moore (then approaching the peak of her screen fame). It's an update on the Cinderella story, locating the fairy tale's events in contemporary Hollywood. The best scenes satirize moviemaking and the big studios of the day. Silent. B&W; 60m. **DIR:** Alfred E. Green. **CAST:** Colleen Moore, Lloyd Hughes. **1926**

ELVIRA, MISTRESS OF THE DARK ★★★½ The late-night TV scream queen of B-film horror makes her debut as a movie star. It was well worth the wait! Elvira descends upon a midwestern town to sell her late aunt's estate. What ensues is a laugh riot, albeit with more breast jokes than you can count. You'll scream when you see Elvira as a baby. Rated PG-13 for profanity. 90m. **DIR:** James Signorelli. **CAST:** Elvira (Cassandra Peterson), Morgan Shepherd, Daniel Greene, Jeff Conaway, Susan Kellerman. **1988**

ELVIS STORIES 🦃 Fans of the King will not appreciate this *Enquirer*-type spoof on Elvis sightings, obsessions, and possessions. 30m. **DIR:** Ben Stiller. **CAST:** Rick "Elvis" Saucedo, John Cusack, Ben Stiller, Joel Murray. **1987**

EMANON 🦃 The Messiah comes to New York City. Rated PG-13 for minor obscenities. 98m. **DIR:** Stuart Paul. **CAST:** Stuart Paul, Cheryl M. Lynn, Jeremy Miller. **1986**

EMO PHILIPS LIVE ★★★★ A high-level comedy concert. Emo Philips has the delivery of a frightened 3-year-old and the body movements of an android. He may act strange, but he possesses a unique, off-center perception that crashes through the boundaries of normal comedy into a netherworld of twisted humor. Not rated; free of profanity. 55m. **DIR:** Cynthia L. Sears. **CAST:** Emo Philips. **1987**

EMPLOYEES' ENTRANCE ★★★½ Warren William is especially sleazy as the manager of a department store who takes advantage of the fact that jobs are scarce due to the Depression. Surprisingly frank comedy-drama made before the Hays Office started to clamp down. B&W; 75m. **DIR:** Roy Del Ruth. **CAST:** Warren William, Loretta Young, Wallace Ford, Allen Jenkins. **1933**

ENCHANTED APRIL ★★★★½ In order to escape their boring lives and demanding husbands, two female friends hatch a plot, with the help of two women they've never met, to rent a luxurious mansion on the Italian Riviera. For all four of them, their little getaway turns out to be full of surprises, delights, and life-changing realizations. A warm-hearted romp that is as magical as its setting. Rated PG. 97m. **DIR:** Mike Newell. **CAST:** Miranda Richardson, Joan Plowright, Josie Lawrence, Polly Walker, Alfred Molina, Michael Kitchen, Jim Broadbent. **1992**

ENCINO MAN ★★★ This teen comedy—about a couple of misfits who find a caveman frozen in their backyard—is surprisingly funny. Sean Astin and Pauly Shore are best friends who defrost the prehistoric man. Rated PG for mild sexual innuendos. 88m. **DIR:** Les Mayfield. **CAST:** Sean Astin, Brendan Fraser, Pauly Shore, Megan Ward, Michael DeLuise, Mariette Hartley, Richard Masur. **1992**

END, THE ★★★½ The blackest of black comedies, this stars Burt Reynolds (who also directed) as an unfortunate fellow who is informed he's dying of a rare disease. Poor Burt can hardly believe it. So he decides to end it all. In the process, he meets a maniac (Dom DeLuise) who is more than willing to lend a hand. It's surprisingly funny. Rated R. 100m. **DIR:** Burt Reynolds. **CAST:** Burt Reynolds, Sally Field, Dom DeLuise, Joanne Woodward, David Steinberg, Pat O'Brien, Myrna Loy, Kristy McNichol, Robby Benson. **1978**

ENDURANCE 🦃 Grown Japanese men subject themselves to all kinds of torture and humiliation in this Japanese game show aimed at American audiences. Not rated, but not for the squeamish. 90m. **DIR:** Edward Simons, Peter McRae. **CAST:** None Credited. **1985**

ENSIGN PULVER ★★★ This sequel to *Mr. Roberts* doesn't quite measure up. The comedy, which takes place aboard a World War II cargo ship, can't stay afloat despite the large and impressive cast. Robert Walker Jr. is no match for Jack Lemmon, who played the original Ensign Pulver in 1955. 104m. **DIR:** Joshua Logan. **CAST:** Robert Walker Jr., Burl Ives, Walter Matthau, Tommy Sands, Millie Perkins, Kay Medford, Larry Hagman, Jack Nicholson. **1964**

ENTER LAUGHING ★★½ Carl Reiner's semiautobiographical comedy, about a young man who shucks his training and ambitions as a pharmacist to become a comedian, is studded with familiar faces and peopled by engaging personalities—but doesn't really leave a lasting memory. 112m. **DIR:** Carl Reiner. **CAST:** Reni Santoni, José Ferrer, Shelley Winters, Elaine May, Jack Gilford, Janet Margolin, Michael J. Pollard, Don Rickles, Rob Reiner, Nancy Kovack. **1967**

ENTERTAINING MR. SLOANE ★★ Joe Orton, the young British playwright whose short life formed the basis of *Prick Up Your Ears,* wrote the play from which this film was made. Neither play nor film has aged well. An amoral young man is taken in at a house where both a grotesque middle-aged woman and her brother, a latent homosexual, have romantic designs on him. Well performed, but no longer shocking enough to be effective. Unrated. 94m. **DIR:** Douglas Hickox. **CAST:** Beryl Reid, Peter McEnery, Harry Andrews, Alan Webb. **1970**

ERIC BOGOSIAN—FUNHOUSE ★★★★ Eric Bogosian is one of the most imaginative and versatile performers currently working in theatre and motion pictures. His sensational one-man show taped in Los Angeles features the actor doing a cross-section of characters including derelicts, street hoods, evangelists, radio announcers, television newsmen, and prison inmates. Hilarious, poignant, terrifying, and thought-provoking. Rated R for strong language and subject matter. 80m. **DIR:** Lewis MacAdams. **CAST:** Eric Bogosian. **1988**

ERNEST FILM FESTIVAL ★★ This appears to be a promo tape used to secure future commercials for Jim Varney's character, Ernest. On it you will see, if you can stand it, 101 commercials and bloopers of the Ernest and Vern variety. He sells everything from cars to eggs using his country-hick lingo. 55m. **DIR:** John R. Cherry III. **CAST:** Jim Varney. **1986**

ERNEST GOES TO CAMP 🦃 Could have been called *Meatballs XI* for all the originality it contains. Rated PG for profanity and scatological humor. 95m. **DIR:** John R. Cherry III. **CAST:** Jim Varney, Victoria Racimo, John Vernon, Iron Eyes Cody, Lyle Alzado. **1987**

ERNEST GOES TO JAIL ★★★★ Comic gem in which the indisputably talented Jim Varney plays not only the well-meaning and dim-witted Ernest P. Worrell but also the crafty villain of the piece. Rated PG for brief violence. 82m. **DIR:** John R. Cherry III. **CAST:** Jim Varney, Gailard Sartain, Randall "Tex" Cobb, Charles Napier. **1990**

ERNEST RIDES AGAIN ★★ *Ernest Rides Again,* and again, and again. The series has almost run out of steam in this weak entry, as Ernest discovers a long-lost Revolutionary War cannon, rumored to hold the real Crown Jewels of England. It's a race to see who can get to the cannon first, but no one crosses the finish line in terms of evoking laughs. Tape contains featurette, *Mr. Bill Goes to Washington.* Rated PG for mild innuendo. 100m. **DIR:** John R. Cherry III. **CAST:** Jim Varney, Ron K. James, Duke Ernsberger, Linda Kash, Jeffrey Pillars. **1993**

ERNEST SCARED STUPID ★★★½ Ernest P. Worrell accidentally reawakens a troll from its 200-year-old tomb and puts the town's children in danger. While those with an aversion to slapstick may not enjoy it, this horror spoof is old-fashioned movie fun. Rated PG for scary stuff. 91m. **DIR:** John R. Cherry III. **CAST:** Jim Varney, Eartha Kitt. **1991**

ERNIE KOVACS: TELEVISION'S ORIGINAL GENIUS ★★★★ This tribute to the late Ernie Kovacs was produced for cable television. It is a series of clips from Kovacs's television career along with comments from friends (Jack Lemmon and Steve Allen) and family (wife Edie Adams and daughter). Narration is provided by John Barbour of *Real People.* Those familiar with Kovacs's work will fondly remember his innovative creations: Percy Dovetonsils, Eugene, and the Nairobi Trio. For others, this serves as an introduction to Kovacs's comic genius. 86m. **DIR:** Keith Burns. **CAST:** Ernie Kovacs, Edie Adams, Jack Lemmon, Steve Allen, Chevy Chase, John Barbour. **1982**

ERRAND BOY, THE ★★★ One of Jerry Lewis's better solo efforts, as he proceeds (in his own inimitable style) to make a shambles of the Hollywood movie studio where he is employed as the local gofer. Very funny. B&W; 92m. **DIR:** Jerry Lewis. **CAST:** Jerry Lewis, Brian Donlevy, Sig Ruman. **1961**

EVEN COWGIRLS GET THE BLUES ★★ Born with unusually large thumbs, Sissy Hankshaw (a miscast Uma Thurman) becomes the world's greatest hitchhiker, a passion she pursues when not hanging out at a health spa with a band of nonconformist cowgirls. Incoherent, undramatic and humorless, this adaptation of Tom Robbins's popular, counterculture novel does justice to neither its source nor the viewer. Rated R for profanity, violence, and suggested sex. 102m. **DIR:** Gus Van Sant. **CAST:** Uma Thurman, John Hurt, Rain Phoenix, Noriyuki "Pat" Morita, Keanu Reeves, Lorraine Bracco, Angie Dickinson, Sean Young, Crispin Glover, Ed Begley Jr., Carol Kane, Roseanne Arnold, Buck Henry, Grace Zabriskie, Udo Kier. **1994**

EVENING WITH BOB GOLDTHWAIT, AN: SHARE THE WARMTH ★★★★ Bob Goldthwait lashes out at Ronald and Nancy Reagan, Bruce Willis, Bob Hope, Lucille Ball, *Rolling Stone* magazine, and the world in general, with a delivery so maniacal, it's downright scary. This is caustic comedy at its funniest. See Goldthwait before someone sues him or locks him away. Not rated, but filled with profanity. 55m. **DIR:** Anthony Eaton. **CAST:** Bob Goldthwait. **1987**

EVENING WITH ROBIN WILLIAMS, AN ★★★★ Here's a remarkably good comedy video with Robin Williams going back to his stand-up comedy roots. He's totally unpredictable when improvising onstage, and this adds to his charm. Filmed at San Francisco's Great American Music Hall, it provides ample proof why Williams was considered one of the finest live comedians of his era before scoring on television (with *Mork and Mindy*) and in the movies. Unrated, it contains profanity. 60m. **DIR:** Don Mischer. **CAST:** Robin Williams. **1983**

EVERY DAY'S A HOLIDAY ★★★½ A heavily censored script weakens the Mae West allure, but she still gives us a fascinating picture of highly suggestive sex. West is the only woman in the movie (which she wrote) about a shady lady who impersonates a French singer to get the cops off her back. Most of the movie is just an excuse for her to sing some of her trademark songs. B&W; 80m. **DIR:** A. Edward Sutherland. **CAST:** Mae West, Edmund Lowe, Charles Winninger, Lloyd Nolan, Walter Catlett, Chester Conklin, Charles Butterworth, Louis Armstrong. **1938**

EVERY GIRL SHOULD BE MARRIED ★★½ A bit of light comic froth balanced mostly on Cary Grant's charm and polish. He plays a baby doctor. Betsy Drake, who later got him offscreen, plays a salesgirl bent on leading him to the altar. The title is irksome, but the picture's diverting, innocent fun. B&W; 85m. **DIR:** Don Hartman. **CAST:** Cary Grant, Betsy Drake, Franchot Tone, Diana Lynn, Alan Mowbray. **1948**

EVERY WHICH WAY BUT LOOSE ★★★ After *Smokey and the Bandit* cleaned up at the box office, Clint Eastwood decided to make his own modern-day cowboy movie. This 1978 release proved to be one of the squinty-eyed star's biggest money-makers. The film is far superior to its sequel, *Any Which Way You Can*. Rated R. 114m. **DIR:** James Fargo. **CAST:** Clint Eastwood, Sondra Locke, Geoffrey Lewis, Clyde (the ape), Ruth Gordon. **1978**

EVERYTHING HAPPENS AT NIGHT ★★★ A Sonja Henie movie with a minimum of ice-skating scenes, this film is largely a vehicle for then newcomers Ray Milland and Robert Cummings. Both fall for Henie, a skater they meet in Europe while trying to uncover the mystery behind a political assassination. It's rather contrived, but it works. B&W; 76m. **DIR:** Irving Cummings. **CAST:** Sonja Henie, Ray Milland, Robert Cummings, Maurice Moscovich, Leonid Kinskey, Alan Dinehart, Fritz Feld, Victor Varconi. **1939**

EVERYTHING YOU ALWAYS WANTED TO KNOW ABOUT SEX BUT WERE AFRAID TO ASK ★★★★ *Everything You Always Wanted to Know about Sex But Were Afraid to Ask* gave Woody Allen, scriptwriter, star, and director, an opportunity to stretch out without having to supply all the talent himself. Several sequences do not feature Woody at all. The film is broken up into vignettes supposedly relating to questions asked. Rated R. 87m. **DIR:** Woody Allen. **CAST:** John Carradine, Woody Allen, Lou Jacobi, Louise Lasser, Anthony Quayle, Lynn Redgrave, Tony Randall, Burt Reynolds, Gene Wilder. **1972**

EVIL TOONS 🦃 Silly slasher spoof features an animated beast possessing the cleaning lady's body. Rated R for nudity, profanity, and violence. 88m. **DIR:** Fred Olen Ray. **CAST:** Madison Stone, David Carradine, Arte Johnson, Dick Miller. **1990**

EXPERIENCE PREFERRED...BUT NOT ESSENTIAL ★★★★★ This delightful British import, which is somewhat reminiscent of Scottish director Bill Forsyth's *Gregory's Girl* and *Local Hero*, follows the awkward and amusing adventures of a young woman during her first summer job at a Welsh coastal resort in 1962. She comes to town insecure and frumpy and leaves at the end of the summer pretty, sexy, and confident. Rated PG for language. 80m. **DIR:** Peter Duffell. **CAST:** Elizabeth Edmonds, Sue Wallace, Geraldine Griffith, Karen Meagher, Ron Bain, Alun Lewis, Robert Blythe. **1983**

EXPERTS, THE ★★ John Travolta and Ayre Gross star as two hip nightclub entrepreneurs from New York City. Charles Martin Smith is a KGB agent who whisks the boys off to a secret American-like community in Russia. Top-notch cast. Rated PG-13 for violence and profanity. 94m. **DIR:** Dave Thomas. **CAST:** John Travolta, Arye Gross, Kelly Preston, Deborah Foreman, James Keach, Charles Martin Smith. **1988**

EXTRA GIRL, THE ★★★ Madcap silent comedienne Mabel Normand's last film—and a winner! Normand plays a naïve, starstruck midwestern girl who fantasizes about fame in films. She wins a beauty contest, goes to Hollywood, and winds up a no-name extra. Silent with music score. B&W; 87m. **DIR:** Dick Jones. **CAST:** Mabel Normand, Ralph Graves. **1923**

FACE THE MUSIC ★★½ Molly Ringwald and Patrick Dempsey are divorced songwriters forced to write one last ditty together. The plot is contrived and Ringwald just can't sing, but this romance is pleasant enough, if predictable. Rated PG-13 for profanity and sexual situations. 93m. **DIR:** Carol Wiseman. **CAST:** Molly Ringwald, Patrick Dempsey, Lysette Anthony. **1992**

FALLING IN LOVE AGAIN ★★½ Elliott Gould stars as a middle-aged dreamer who is obsessed with his younger days in the Bronx. Gould and wife (Susannah York) are on vacation and headed east to recapture the past. The film suffers from countless long flashbacks of his youthful romance with a WASP princess (Michelle Pfeiffer) and is a poor attempt at romantic comedy. Rated R. 103m. **DIR:** Steven Paul. **CAST:** Elliott Gould, Susannah York, Michelle Pfeiffer, Stuart Paul. **1980**

FAMILY JEWELS, THE ★★½ Jerry Lewis tries to outperform Alec Guinness (from *Kind Hearts and Coronets*) in this syrupy tale of a wealthy young heiress (Donna Butterworth) forced to select a guardian from among six uncles. Lewis plays all six, but his seventh—the family chauffeur—is the only one with any credibility. It's a long stretch for thin material. 100m. **DIR:** Jerry Lewis. **CAST:** Jerry Lewis, Donna Butterworth, Sebastian Cabot. **1965**

FANCY PANTS ★★★½ Bob Hope and Lucille Ball in their prime were an unbeatable comic team. Here they specialize in slapstick with Hope posing as a British earl to impress the locals in her New Mexican town. 92m. **DIR:** George Marshall. **CAST:** Bob Hope, Lucille Ball, Bruce Cabot. **1950**

FANDANGO ★★ This is an unfunny comedy about a group of college chums (led by Kevin Costner and Judd Nelson) going on one last romp before being inducted into the army—or running away from the draft—in 1971. *Fandango* seems as if it's going to get better any minute, but it doesn't. Rated PG for profanity. 91m. **DIR:** Kevin Reynolds. **CAST:** Kevin Costner, Judd Nelson, Sam Robards, Chuck Bush, Brian Cesak. **1984**

FAR NORTH ★★★ Actor-playwright Sam Shepard's first film as a director is a surprisingly funny comedy-drama about three generations of a farming family. Yet underlying the humor is a typically Shepardian sense of tragedy as wayward daughter Jessica Lange comes home after her father is hurt in a farming accident. Rated PG-13 for profanity and sexy scenes. 87m. **DIR:** Sam Shepard. **CAST:** Jessica Lange, Charles Durning, Tess Harper, Donald Moffat, Ann Wedgeworth, Patricia Arquette. **1988**

FAR OUT MAN 🦃 A bad script, worse acting, frequent play on gastric distress. Rated R. 85m. **DIR:** Thomas Chong. **CAST:** Tommy Chong, Martin Mull, Rae Dawn Chong, C. Thomas Howell, Judd Nelson, Richard "Cheech" Marin. **1990**

FARMER'S DAUGHTER, THE ★★★ Loretta Young won the best actress Oscar for her delightful performance in this charming comedy about a Swedish woman who clashes with the man she loves over a congressional election. B&W; 97m. **DIR:** H. C. Potter. **CAST:** Loretta Young, Joseph Cotten, Ethel Barrymore, Charles Bickford, Lex Barker, Keith Andes, James Arness. **1947**

FARMER'S OTHER DAUGHTER, THE 🦃 Incredibly lame film about a family trying to save their farm from foreclosure. 84m. **DIR:** John Patrick Hayes. **CAST:** Judy Pennebaker, Bill Michael, Ernest Ashworth. **1965**

FAST BREAK ★★½ As a basketball coach, Gabe Kaplan resurrects some of the laughs he got with his sweathogs on *Welcome Back, Kotter*. Kaplan plays a New York deli worker who quits to coach a college basketball team in Nevada. Kaplan must beat a tough rival team in order to get a contract at the university, so he whips the unpromising team into shape. Rated PG. 107m. **DIR:** Jack Smight. **CAST:** Gabe Kaplan, Harold Sylvester, Mike Warren, Bernard King, Reb Brown. **1979**

FAST FOOD 🦃 Typical inane college sex comedy. Rated PG-13 for sexual situations. 91m. **DIR:** Michael A. Simpson. **CAST:** Jim Varney, Traci Lords. **1989**

FAST GETAWAY 🦃 Spectaular stunts aren't enough to save this mindless tale of a 16-year-old kid who robs banks with his dad. There's not enough here to make a withdrawal. Rated PG-13 for violence. 85m. **DIR:** Spiro Razatos. **CAST:** Corey Haim, Cynthia Rothrock, Leo Rossi, Marcia Strassman. **1990**

FAST TIMES AT RIDGEMONT HIGH ★★½ In 1979, Cameron Crowe went back to high school to discover what today's teens are up to and wrote about his experiences. Youngsters will love it, but adults will probably want to skip the movie and read the book. Rated R for nudity, profanity, and simulated sex. 92m. **DIR:** Amy Heckerling. **CAST:** Sean Penn, Jennifer Jason Leigh, Judge Reinhold, Brian Backer, Phoebe Cates, Ray Walston. **1982**

FATAL GLASS OF BEER, A/POOL SHARKS ★★★ This pairing brings together two distinct examples of the unique comedy of W. C. Fields. The first, produced by Mack Sennett, finds Fields practicing his peculiar art in the frozen North, complete with snow on cue and misplaced Indians. *Pool Sharks*, made eighteen years earlier, is the comedian's first distributed film. In it, he is pitted against Bud Ross in the pool game of all pool games—played for the love of a mutually sought girl. Fields's bizarre brand of humor highlights both. B&W; 60m. **DIR:** Clyde Bruckman, Edwin Middleton. **CAST:** W. C. Fields, George Chandler, Rosemary Theby, Bud Ross. **1933**

FATAL INSTINCT (1993) ★★★ Director Carl Reiner sends up a bevy of thrillers—*Fatal Attraction*, *Body Heat*, *Basic Instinct*, *Double Indemnity*, *The Postman Always Rings Twice*, etc.—in this hit-and-miss spoof. Armand Assante is a dumb-as-dirt detective who gets mixed up with femme fatale Sean Young. This goofy movie does have its share of laughs. Rated PG-13 for light profanity, silly violence, and wacky sex. 89m. **DIR:** Carl Reiner. **CAST:** Armand Assante, Sean Young, Sherilyn Fenn, Kate Nelligan, Christopher McDonald, James Remar, Tony Randall, Clarence Clemmons, Eartha Kitt, Ronnie Schell, Carl Reiner. **1993**

FATE 🦃 The last of the good guys searches for the woman who deserves him in this strange, self-proclaimed romantic comedy. Rated PG-13. 114m. **DIR:** Stuart Paul. **CAST:** Stuart Paul, Cheryl M. Lynn, Kaye Ballard, Susannah York. **1990**

FATHER GOOSE ★★★ A bedraggled, unshaven, and unsophisticated Cary Grant is worth watching even in a mediocre comedy. Grant plays a hard-drinking Australian coast watcher during the height of World War II. His reclusive life-style on a remote Pacific island is interrupted when he is forced to play nursemaid to a group of adolescent schoolgirls and their prudish teacher (Leslie Caron). 115m. **DIR:** Ralph Nelson. **CAST:** Cary Grant, Leslie Caron. **1964**

FATHER GUIDO SARDUCCI GOES TO COLLEGE ★★ Don Novello re-creates his *Saturday Night Live* character of Father Guido Sarducci during a live concert at U.C. Santa Barbara. He touches on birthdays, life insurance, his years at DooDa U., and President Reagan. His priestly character is sometimes lost in his more worldly comments. We guess you had to be there to really enjoy it. 59m. **DIR:** Steve Binder. **CAST:** Don Novello, Billy Vera and The Beaters. **1985**

FATHER OF THE BRIDE (1950) ★★★½ Spencer Tracy's proud and frantic papa is the chief attraction in this droll examination of last-minute preparations prior to daughter Elizabeth Taylor's wedding. Writers Frances Goodrich and Albert Hackett include a few too many scenes of near-slapstick hysteria, but the quieter moments between father and daughter are wonderful (if a bit dated). 93m. **DIR:** Vincente Minnelli. **CAST:** Spencer Tracy, Elizabeth Taylor, Joan Bennett, Leo G. Carroll, Don Taylor, Billie Burke. **1950**

FATHER OF THE BRIDE (1991) ★★★½ Steve Martin is the father who becomes increasingly aghast at the costs and craziness involved in his daughter's marriage. With this remake of the 1950 Spencer Tracy film, director Charles Shyer and the star create a heartwarming comedy the whole family can enjoy. Rated PG for brief profanity. 105m. **DIR:** Charles Shyer. **CAST:** Steve Martin, Diane Keaton, Martin Short, Kimberly Williams, George Newbern, B. D. Wong. **1991**

FATHER'S LITTLE DIVIDEND ★★★ In *Father of the Bride*, the marriage of daughter Elizabeth Taylor to Don Taylor made a wreck out of Spencer Tracy. Now, in the sequel, she's expecting. This play off of a winner doesn't measure up to the original, but it's entertaining fare anyway. Spencer Tracy could bluster and be flustered with the best. 82m. **DIR:** Vincente Minnelli. **CAST:** Spencer Tracy, Elizabeth Taylor, Joan Bennett, Don Taylor, Billie Burke. **1951**

FATSO ★★½ Too many juvenile toilet jokes mar what might have been a humorous study of a man's confrontation with his own obesity. Dom DeLuise stars as the chubby Italian-American who wrestles with a variety of diets. Messages get lost amid the shrill performances. Rated PG for language and questionable humor. 94m. **DIR:** Anne Bancroft. **CAST:** Dom DeLuise, Anne Bancroft, Candy Azzara, Ron Carey. **1980**

FATTY AND HIS FUNNY FRIENDS ★★★ Slapstick action marks this anthology of four short comic excursions: "How Fatty Made Good," "Miss Fatty's Seaside Lovers," "Mike and Meyer," and "Skylarking." Fun for everyone. Silent with musical score. B&W; 53m. **DIR:** Various. **CAST:** Roscoe "Fatty" Arbuckle, Harold Lloyd, Edgar Kennedy. **1913–1923**

FATTY AND MABEL ADRIFT/MABEL, FATTY AND THE LAW ★★★ Solo and as a duet, Fatty Arbuckle and Mabel Normand were near peerless in the halcyon days of silent comedies. These two Mack Sennett features are outstanding examples of why the public held them both in admiration. The kiss-goodnight sequence in *Fatty and Mabel Adrift* is reason enough to see the film. B&W; 40m. **DIR:** Roscoe Arbuckle. **CAST:** Roscoe "Fatty" Arbuckle, Mabel Normand, Frank Hayes, May Wells, Al St. John. **1916**

FATTY ARBUCKLE COMEDY COLLECTION, VOL. 1 ★★★ This new silent series brings together four of "Fatty" Arbuckle's simple premise Keystone comedies: "Fatty Joins the Force," "Fatty's Suitless Day," "Fatty's Spooning Days," and "The Speed Kings"—the latter (for a change) featuring Fatty as a villain, and a wild auto race with Mabel Normand as the prize. Silent. B&W; 46m. **DIR:** Roscoe Arbuckle. **CAST:** Roscoe "Fatty" Arbuckle, Mabel Normand, Minta Durfee, Al St. John. **1913–15**

FATTY'S TIN-TYPE TANGLE/OUR CONGRESSMAN ★★★ This is a curious pairing of a Mack Sennett Keystone comedy and a Hal Roach satire made a decade apart and totally unrelated in subject matter. In the first, Fatty gets Mabel's goat by making goo-goo eyes at the maid. In the second, newly elected Congressman Will Rogers, straight from the sticks, bombs in Washington society. B&W; 44m. **DIR:** Roscoe Arbuckle, Rob Wagner. **CAST:** Roscoe "Fatty" Arbuckle, Mabel Normand, Al St. John, Will Rogers, Mollie Thompson. **1924**

FAVOR, THE ★★★ Although this romantic comedy desperately wants to be a ribald sex farce, it's just not played with the proper tone. Harley Jane Kozak, pining for a long-unseen high-school sweetheart, emerges as an unsympathetic busybody when she persuades best friend Elizabeth McGovern to meet and sleep with the guy. Despite a rather amusing climax, we never really like any of these people. Rated R for profanity and frank sexuality. 97m. **DIR:** Donald Petrie. **CAST:** Harley Jane Kozak, Elizabeth McGovern, Bill Pullman, Brad Pitt, Ken Wahl, Larry Miller. **1994**

FAVOR, THE WATCH AND THE VERY BIG FISH, THE ★★ In this muddled madcap comedy, Bob Hoskins tries hard as a photographer who gets distracted by the mysterious Natasha Richardson while searching for the perfect model to portray Jesus Christ—whom he finally finds in Jeff Goldblum. Annoyingly frantic. Rated R for profanity, nudity, and violence. 89m. **DIR:** Ben Lewin. **CAST:** Bob Hoskins, Jeff Goldblum, Natasha Richardson, Michel Blanc, Jean-Pierre Cassel, Angela Pleasence. **1992**

FAWLTY TOWERS ★★★★ This British television series is a true comedy classic. Written by Monty Python's John Cleese and his ex-wife Connie Booth, the show is a situation comedy about the problems of running a small seaside inn. The characters are typical (harried husband, shrewish wife, incompetent help) and the story lines mundane (guest loses money; fire drill; restaurant critics arrive), but in the hands of Cleese and company, each episode is a near-perfect ballet of escalating frustration. For sheer, double-over belly laughs, this series has never been equaled. 75m. **DIR:** John Cleese, Connie Booth. **CAST:** John Cleese, Prunella Scales, Connie Booth. **1975**

FEAR, ANXIETY AND DEPRESSION ★★ Todd Solondz wrote and directed this Woody Allen-ish vehicle for himself. He plays a nerdish playwright who pursues an outrageously punk performer and his best friend's girl while being relentlessly chased by his female counterpart. Rated R for profanity and violence. 84m. **DIR:** Todd Solondz. **CAST:** Todd Solondz, Jill Wisoff. **1989**

FEDS ★★ A second-string comedy about two women (Mary Gross and Rebecca DeMornay) who work to beat the odds and graduate from the FBI's training academy. Some good laughs, but not enough. Rated PG-13 for mild language. 83m. **DIR:** Dan Goldberg. **CAST:** Mary Gross, Rebecca DeMornay, Ken Marshall. **1988**

FEEL MY PULSE ★★½ Silent screwball comedy boasts a hypochondriac heiress who inherits a sanitarium that is used by bootleggers as a front and a hideout. Bebe Daniels does a fine job as the germ-wary, sheltered young girl who encounters a life she didn't dream existed. Silent. B&W; 86m. **DIR:** Gregory La Cava. **CAST:** Bebe Daniels, Richard Arlen, William Powell. **1928**

FEMALE ★★★ The lady president of an automobile manufacturing company, used to having things her own way, falls in love with a man who won't bend. Amusing romantic comedy with a feminist undercurrent. B&W; 60m. **DIR:** Michael Curtiz. **CAST:** Ruth Chatterton, George Brent, Johnny Mack Brown, Ruth Donnelly, Douglass Dumbrille. **1933**

FEMALE TROUBLE ★★ The story of Dawn Davenport (Divine) from her days as a teenage belligerent through her rise to fame as a criminal and then to her death as a convicted murderer. As in other films by Waters, the theme here is the Jean Genet-like credo "crime equals beauty." Though it is unrated, this film is the equivalent of an X, due to sex, nudity, and violence. 90m. **DIR:** John Waters. **CAST:** Divine, Edith Massey, Cookie Mueller, David Lochary, Mink Stole, Michael Potter. **1973**

FEROCIOUS FEMALE FREEDOM FIGHTERS ★★ A la Woody Allen's *What's Up Tiger Lily?*, this is a junky martial arts movie redubbed by a Los Angeles comedy troupe. The spotty results tend toward the sophomoric, though you'll probably laugh at some of it. Unrated; the film contains violence and crude humor. 74m. **DIR:** Jopi Burnama. **CAST:** Eva Arnez, Barry Prima. **1989**

FERRIS BUELLER'S DAY OFF ★★★★ Writer-director John Hughes strikes again, this time with a charming tale of a high school legend in his own time (Matthew Broderick, playing the title character) who pretends to be ill in order to have a day away from school. The expressive Broderick owns the film, although he receives heavy competition from Jeffrey Jones, whose broadly played dean of students has been trying to nail Ferris Bueller for months. Rated PG-13 for mild profanity. 104m. **DIR:** John Hughes. **CAST:** Matthew Broderick, Alan Ruck, Mia Sara, Jeffrey Jones, Jennifer Grey, Charlie Sheen, Cindy Pickett, Lyman Ward. **1986**

FEUD, THE ★★★ Two families in neighboring small towns are drawn into a feud that neither wants—but which neither will be the first to quit. This film isn't as satirical as the Thomas Berger novel on which it is based, but it's an agreeable farce nonetheless. Rated R. 96m. **DIR:** Bill D'Elia. **CAST:** René Auberjonois, Ron McLarty, Joe Grifasi. **1988**

FIENDISH PLOT OF DR. FU MANCHU, THE 🦃 Peter Sellers plays a dual role of "insidious Oriental villain" Fu Manchu, who is out to rule the world, and his arch-enemy, the Holmes-like Nayland Smith of Scotland Yard. Rated PG. 108m. **DIR:** Piers Haggard. **CAST:** Peter Sellers, Helen Mirren, Sid Caesar, David Tomlinson. **1980**

FIFTH AVENUE GIRL ★★ Limp social comedy features Ginger Rogers as a homeless but levelheaded young lady who is taken in by Walter Connolly, one of those unhappy movie-land millionaires who is just dying to find someone to lavish gifts on. B&W; 83m. **DIR:** Gregory La Cava. **CAST:** Ginger Rogers, Walter Connolly, Verree Teasdale, Tim Holt, James Ellison, Kathryn Adams. **1939**

FILM HOUSE FEVER ★★½ An hour's worth of coming attractions and clips from creaky horror and exploitation movies. Enough are from movies not featured in other such anthologies that buffs will want to check it out, though the dumb comedy skits scattered throughout slow things down. Unrated, includes gore, violence, and nudity. 58m. **DIR:** Domonic Paris. **1986**

FILM MUSICALS ★★ Two experimental film shorts by the New York writer and Hollywood emigré Tina Lhotsky. In "Barbie," a bizarre, surrealist self-portrait, the filmmaker cooks and eats a doll in the nude. "Snakewoman" is a 1930s-style adventure story about a white woman who conquers the wilds of Africa after her plane crashes in the jungle. A campy hodgepodge that may appeal to those who enjoy Kenneth Anger–style moviemaking. Not rated, but contains nudity. B&W; 45m. **DIR:** Tina Lhotsky. **CAST:** Patti Astor, Tina Lhotsky. **1977**

FIND THE LADY ★★★ In this slapstick rendition of a cops-and-robbers spoof, John Candy, as the cop, and Mickey Rooney, as a kidnapper, create lots of laughs on the way to a very funny finish. 90m. **DIR:** John Trent. **CAST:** John Candy, Mickey Rooney, Peter Cook, Lawrence Dane, Alexandra Bastedo. **1986**

FINDERS KEEPERS ★★½ Director Richard Lester went back to his comedy roots with this disappointingly uneven slapstick chase film, which stars Louis Gossett Jr., Michael O'Keefe, and Beverly D'Angelo as a trio of wacky characters. The story deals with a missing $5 million. Rated PG for profanity and violence. 96m. **DIR:** Richard Lester. **CAST:** Lou Gossett Jr., Michael O'Keefe, Beverly D'Angelo. **1983**

FINE MADNESS, A ★★★ Whimsical story of a daffy, radical poet, well portrayed by Sean Connery (proving that, even in the 1960s, he could stretch further than James Bond). Many of the laughs come from his well-developed relationship with wife Joanne Woodward, although the film occasionally lapses into lurid slapstick. Unrated; adult themes. 104m. **DIR:** Irvin Kershner. **CAST:** Sean Connery, Joanne Woodward, Jean Seberg. **1966**

FINE MESS, A 🦃 Supposedly inspired by the Laurel and Hardy classic, *The Music Box*. Gag after gag falls embarrassingly flat. Rated PG. 100m. **DIR:** Blake Edwards. **CAST:** Ted Danson, Howie Mandel, Richard Mulligan, Stuart Margolin, Maria Conchita Alonso, Jennifer Edwards, Paul Sorvino. **1986**

FINE ROMANCE, A ★★★ This is a lovely little romantic comedy with Julie Andrews and Marcello Mastroianni as a couple of discarded lovers whose spouses have left them. Thrust together to contemplate their options, both go through emotional withdrawal and loss, eventually finding happiness with each other. Rated PG-13 for profanity. 83m. **DIR:** Gene Saks. **CAST:** Julie Andrews, Marcello Mastroianni. **1993**

FINNEGAN BEGIN AGAIN ★★★★ In this endearing romance, Robert Preston plays Michael Finnegan, an eccentric retired advice columnist who befriends schoolteacher Elizabeth (Mary Tyler Moore) after learning of her secret affair with a married undertaker (Sam Waterston). Their eventual romance becomes a warm, funny, and tender portrayal of love blossoming in later life. Made for cable. 97m. **DIR:** Joan Micklin Silver. **CAST:** Mary Tyler Moore, Robert Preston, Sam Waterston, Sylvia Sidney. **1985**

FIREHOUSE (1987) 🦃 *Charlie's Angels* clone set in a firehouse. Rated R. 91m. **DIR:** J. Christian Ingvordsen. **CAST:** Barrett Hopkins, Shannon Murphy, Violet Brown, John Anderson, Peter Onorati. **1987**

FIRESIGN THEATRE'S HOT SHORTS ★★ Occasionally amusing collection of old black-and-white serial movies with new dialogue added by the Los Angeles–based troupe. Titles such as "Sperm Bank Holdup," "Mounties with Herpes" and "Nazi Diet Doctors" should give you an idea of the contents. Not rated, but contains adult language and humor. 73m. **DIR:** Richard Patterson. **CAST:** Peter Bergman, Philip Proctor. **1985**

FIRST AND TEN ★★½ A pilot for the Home Box Office series of the same name, this football satire chronicles the hapless exploits of a West Coast team. Its locker room humor may limit it to an adult audience, but there are sufficient laughs. 97m. **DIR:** Donald Kushner. **CAST:** Fran Tarkenton, Geoffrey Scott, Reid Shelton, Ruta Lee, Delta Burke. **1985**

FIRST FAMILY 🦃 Unfunny farce about an inept president, his family, and his aides. Rated R. 104m. **DIR:** Buck Henry. **CAST:** Bob Newhart, Gilda Radner, Madeline Kahn, Richard Benjamin, Harvey Korman, Bob Dishy, Rip Torn. **1980**

FIRST HOWIE MANDEL SPECIAL, THE ★★½ This Howie Mandel concert was filmed live in Toronto, Canada. Mandel is from Canada and his countrymen give him a surprisingly lukewarm reception. They seem to like his comedy, but they are reluctant to participate in the performance. If you like Mandel's screaming, his nervous off-the-wall delivery, and X-rated material meant to shock, you'll enjoy this one. 57m. **DIR:** Maurice Abraham. **CAST:** Howie Mandel. **1983**

FIRST TIME, THE ★★★ With parents pushing poor Charlie into a relationship with a girl—any girl!—he resists. But when he gets into filmmaking, the opposite sex goes mad for him. This campus comedy is rated PG-13 for mature situations and language. 96m. **DIR:** Charlie Loventhal. **CAST:** Tim Choate, Krista Erickson, Wallace Shawn, Wendie Jo Sperber. **1982**

FIRST TURN-ON, THE 🦃 This cheapie features four campers and their counselor trapped in a cave seeking amusement. Unrated, but contains nudity and profanity and sexual situations. 88m. **DIR:** Michael Herz, Samuel Weil. **CAST:** Michael Sanville. **1983**

FISH CALLED WANDA, A ★★★★½ Monty Python veteran John Cleese wrote and starred in this hilarious caper comedy.

Jamie Lee Curtis and Kevin Kline are American crooks who plot to double-cross their British partners in crime (Michael Palin and Tom Georgeson) with the unwitting help of barrister Cleese. Be forewarned: *Wanda* has something in it to offend everyone. Rated R for profanity and violence. 108m. **DIR:** Charles Crichton. **CAST:** John Cleese, Jamie Lee Curtis, Kevin Kline, Michael Palin, Tom Georgeson, Patricia Hayes. **1988**

FISH THAT SAVED PITTSBURGH, THE ★★½ Curious mixture of disco, astrology, and comedy. A failing basketball team turns to a rather eccentric medium for help, and the resulting confusion makes for a few amusing moments. Features a veritable smorgasbord of second-rate actors, from Jonathan Winters to basketball great Julius Irving (Dr. J.). Proceed at your own risk. Rated PG for profanity. 102m. **DIR:** Gilbert Moses. **CAST:** Stockard Channing, Flip Wilson, Jonathan Winters, Julius Erving. **1979**

FIVE GOLDEN HOURS ★★★ Ernie Kovacs is hilarious as a professional mourner who lives off the generosity of grieving widows. Things become complicated when he falls for penniless Italian baroness Cyd Charisse. B&W; 89m. **DIR:** Mario Zampi. **CAST:** Ernie Kovacs, Cyd Charisse, Dennis Price, John Le Mesurier, Kay Hammond, George Sanders. **1961**

FLAMINGO KID, THE ★★★½ A teen comedy-drama with more on its mind than stale sex jokes. Matt Dillon stars as Jeffrey Willis, a Brooklyn kid who discovers how the other half lives when he takes a summer job at a beach resort. A good story which explores the things (and people) that shape our values as we reach adulthood. A genuine pleasure, and you'll be glad you tried it. Rated PG-13 for frank sexual situations. 100m. **DIR:** Garry Marshall. **CAST:** Matt Dillon, Richard Crenna, Jessica Walter, Janet Jones, Hector Elizondo. **1984**

FLASK OF FIELDS, A ★★★★½ *The Golf Specialist*, *A Fatal Glass of Beer*, and *The Dentist*—three short comedy gems—amply display the matchless talents of W. C. Fields. This is an entertaining tribute. Don't be misled by the credits; Fields directed himself. Hilarious. Bawdy is the only word for the tooth-pulling sequence in *The Dentist*. B&W; 61m. **DIR:** Monte Brice, Clyde Bruckman, Leslie Pearce. **CAST:** W. C. Fields, Rosemary Theby, George Chandler. **1930**

FLICKS 🦃 *Flicks* is a structureless string of movie parodies that's long on mediocre satire and short on laughs. Rated R. 79m. **DIR:** Peter Winograd. **CAST:** Pamela Sue Martin, Joan Hackett, Martin Mull, Richard Belzer, Betty Kennedy. **1985**

FLUSTERED COMEDY OF LEON ERROL, THE ★★★ When he wasn't portraying a rubber-legged drunk in features, former vaudeville and burlesque comic Leon Errol scored big in dozens of comedy shorts. This compilation—"Crime Rave," "Man I Cured," and "A Panic in the Parlor"—shows why. B&W; 56m. **DIR:** Hal Yates. **CAST:** Leon Errol, Virginia Vale, Frank Faylen. **1939–1941**

FLYING DEUCES ★★★ Stan Laurel and Oliver Hardy join the foreign legion to help Ollie forget his troubled romantic past. Many laugh-filled situations, although the script has weak areas and the movie occasionally drags. B&W; 65m. **DIR:** A. Edward Sutherland. **CAST:** Stan Laurel, Oliver Hardy, Jean Parker. **1939**

FM ★★★ Before television's *WKRP in Cincinnati* spoofed hip radio, there was this enjoyable comedy, with Martin Mull stealing scenes as a crazed disc jockey. Fans of Seventies rock will enjoy the sound track and live appearances by the era's superstars. Rated PG for profanity. 104m. **DIR:** John A. Alonzo. **CAST:** Michael Brandon, Martin Mull, Eileen Brennan, Cleavon Little, Cassie Yates, Alex Karras, Norman Lloyd, James Keach. **1978**

FOLKS ★★½ Comedy about a stock-exchange whiz who finds his perfect life turned upside down. Depending on your mood, this can be entertaining, or tasteless, and unfunny. Rated PG-13 for violence and profanity. 108m. **DIR:** Ted Kotcheff. **CAST:** Tom Selleck, Don Ameche, Anne Jackson, Christine Ebersole, Wendy Crewson, Michael Murphy. **1992**

FOLLOW THAT CAMEL ★★★½ This British comedy, part of the *Carry On* series, features Phil Silvers as the conniving Sgt. Knockers. Lots of laughs, mostly derived from puns and sexist jokes. Some dialogue is a bit racy for young children. Unrated. 91m. **DIR:** Gerald Thomas. **CAST:** Phil Silvers, Jim Dale, Peter Butterworth, Charles Hawtrey, Anita Harris, Joan Sims, Kenneth Williams. **1967**

FOLLOW THAT DREAM ★★★½ Elvis is almost too sweet as the naive hillbilly who, along with his family, moves to a Florida beach. Some laughs result from their inability to fit in. The story is based on Richard Powell's novel *Pioneer Go Home*. Unrated, but contains no objectionable material. 110m. **DIR:** Gordon Douglas. **CAST:** Elvis Presley, Arthur O'Connell, Joanne Moore, Anne Helm, Jack Kruschen. **1962**

FOOLIN' AROUND ★★★ Gary Busey went from his acclaimed title performance in *The Buddy Holly Story* to starring in this amiable rip-off of *The Graduate* and *The Heartbreak Kid*. Still, Busey, as a working-class boy who falls in love with rich girl Annette O'Toole, is always watchable. He and O'Toole make the movie's lack of originality easier to take. Rated PG. 111m. **DIR:** Richard T. Heffron. **CAST:** Gary Busey, Annette O'Toole, John Calvin, Eddie Albert, Cloris Leachman, Tony Randall. **1980**

FOR BETTER AND FOR WORSE ★★ A mixture of misguided "slapschtick" and unfunny lines sinks this otherwise passable comedy in which the pope is invited to a wedding—and accepts. Rated PG-13 for mild profanity. 94m. **DIR:** Paolo Barzman. **CAST:** Patrick Dempsey, Kelly Lynch, Gerard Rinaldi. **1992**

FOR LOVE OF IVY ★★★★ Sidney Poitier delivers a terrific performance as Jack Parks, trucking company owner by day and gambling operator by night. Ivy (Abbey Lincoln) is a maid for a wealthy family. When she decides to leave their employ, the family's children (Beau Bridges and Lauri Peters) connive to get Parks to take her out and make her happy. Carroll O'Connor and Nan Martin play Ivy's employers. This is a fine comedy-drama with a wonderful ending. 101m. **DIR:** Daniel Mann. **CAST:** Sidney Poitier, Abbey Lincoln, Beau Bridges, Nan Martin, Carroll O'Connor, Lauri Peters. **1968**

FOR LOVE OR MONEY ★★★½ An ambitious, fast-talking hotel concierge is on the way to realizing his ultimate dream until romance conflicts with finance. This movie is the kind of thing Michael J. Fox does best and could have been titled *The Secret of My Success, Part II*. That's not a put-down, either; this entertaining comedy should be popular with Fox's fans. Rated PG for brief profanity and suggested sex. 95m. **DIR:** Barry Sonnenfeld. **CAST:** Michael J. Fox, Gabrielle Anwar, Anthony Higgins, Bob Balaban, Michael Tucker, Udo Kier, Dan Hedaya, Isaac Mizrahi, Patrick Breen, Simon Jones. **1993**

FOR PETE'S SAKE ★★★ Lightweight comedy vehicle tailor-made to fit the talents of Barbra Streisand. In this one she plays the wife of cabdriver Michael Sarrazin, trying to raise money for him while becoming involved with underworld thugs. Strictly for Streisand fans. Rated PG. 90m. **DIR:** Peter Yates. **CAST:** Barbra Streisand, Michael Sarrazin, Estelle Parsons, Molly Picon. **1974**

FOR RICHER, FOR POORER ★★ Self-made millionaire Jack Lemmon despairs when son Jonathan Silverman seems content to do little beyond spending Dad's money. The solution? Give it all away, thus *forcing* the bum to pull his own weight. Lame made-for-cable comedy. Rated PG. 90m. **DIR:** Jay Sandrich. **CAST:** Jack Lemmon, Talia Shire, Jonathan Silverman, Joanna Gleason, Madeline Kahn. **1992**

FOR THE LOVE OF IT ★★½ This would-be wacky comedy is so confusing, you'll find yourself absorbed. Don Rickles wants the Russians' secret plans to take over the Middle East to create a new video game called "Doom's Day," but the CIA and FBI are also interested in them. Some of the chase scenes become so involved that the viewer forgets this is a comedy. Rated PG for violence and adult themes. 98m. **DIR:** Hal Kanter. **CAST:** Don Rickles, Deborah Raffin, Jeff Conaway, Tom Bosley, Henry Gibson, Barbi Benton, Adam West, Norman Fell, Noriyuki "Pat" Morita. **1980**

FOREIGN BODY ★★★ An Indian émigré in London, longing to make a fortune and lose his virginity, makes both wishes come true by posing as a doctor to upper-class hypochondriacs. So-so script benefits from perky performances by a superior British cast. Rated PG-13 for ribald humor. 108m. **DIR:** Ronald Neame. **CAST:** Victor Banerjee, Warren Mitchell, Amanda Donohoe, Trevor Howard. **1986**

FOREVER DARLING ★★½ Lucille Ball's marriage to chemist Desi Arnaz Sr. is in trouble. Her guardian angel (James Mason) tries to put things right. Mild romantic comedy with too few of the *I Love Lucy*–style antics. 96m. **DIR:** Alexander Hall. **CAST:** Lucille Ball, Desi Arnaz Sr., James Mason, Louis Calhern, Marilyn Maxwell. **1956**

FOREVER LULU 🦃 Ridiculous rip-off of *Desperately Seeking Susan*. Rated R for nudity, profanity, and violence. 86m. **DIR:** Amos Kollek. **CAST:** Hanna Schygulla, Deborah Harry, Alec Baldwin, Paul Gleason, Annie Golden, Dr. Ruth Westheimer, Charles Ludlam. **1987**

FORSAKING ALL OTHERS ★★★ Offbeat casting with Clark Gable as the nice guy, for years secretly in love with Joan Crawford, while she allows herself to be manipulated by a cad. The movie is stolen by lovely Billie Burke and droll Charles Butterworth. B&W; 84m. **DIR:** W. S. Van Dyke. **CAST:** Joan Crawford, Clark Gable, Robert Montgomery, Charles Butterworth, Billie Burke, Rosalind Russell. **1934**

FORTUNE COOKIE, THE ★★★★½ Jack Lemmon is accidentally injured by a player while filming a football game from the sidelines. His brother-in-law, Walter Matthau, sees this as an ideal attempt to make some lawsuit money. So starts the first of the usually delightful Lemmon-Matthau comedies. Matthau is at his scene-stealing best in this Oscar-winning role. B&W; 125m. **DIR:** Billy Wilder. **CAST:** Jack Lemmon, Walter Matthau, Ron Rich, Cliff Osmond. **1966**

FORTY CARATS ★★★½ This comedy has Liv Ullmann playing a 40-year-old divorcée being pursued by a rich 22-year-old, Edward Albert. Laughs abound as Ullmann's grown daughter (Deborah Raffin) and ex-husband (Gene Kelly) react to her latest suitor. Rated PG. 110m. **DIR:** Milton Katselas. **CAST:** Liv Ullmann, Edward Albert, Gene Kelly, Nancy Walker, Deborah Raffin. **1973**

48 HRS. ★★★★½ Add *48 Hrs.* to the list of the best cops-and-robbers movies ever made. It's so action-packed, it'll keep you on the edge of your seat. There's more good news: It's funny too. In the story, a cop (Nick Nolte) goes looking for a psychotic prison escapee (James Remar) with the help of a fast-talking con man (Eddie Murphy). There's never a dull moment. Rated R for violence, profanity, and nudity. 96m. **DIR:** Walter Hill. **CAST:** Eddie Murphy, Nick Nolte, Annette O'Toole, Frank McRae, James Remar, David Patrick Kelly. 1982

FOUL PLAY ★★★ Gloria Mundy (Goldie Hawn) accidentally becomes involved in a plot to assassinate the Pope. Detective Tony Carlson (Chevy Chase) tries to protect and seduce her. Hawn is good as the damsel in distress, but Chase is hardly the Cary Grant type. Still it's fun. Rated PG. 116m. **DIR:** Colin Higgins. **CAST:** Goldie Hawn, Chevy Chase, Dudley Moore, Burgess Meredith, Marilyn Sokol. 1978

FOUR WEDDINGS AND A FUNERAL ★★★★ A reserved Englishman (Hugh Grant) meets attractive American Andie MacDowell at a wedding and falls in love with her, but his inability to express his feelings seems to forestall any possibility of a relationship—until they meet again and again. This clever film recalls *When Harry Met Sally* in its own funny, romantic, and original way, with the ensemble cast giving it true charm. Rowan Atkinson is absolutely hilarious as a nervous novice priest. Rated R for profanity, suggested sex, and adult themes. 118m. **DIR:** Mike Newell. **CAST:** Hugh Grant, Andie MacDowell, Kristin Scott Thomas, Simon Callow, James Fleet, John Hannah, Charlotte Coleman, David Bower, Corin Redgrave, Rowan Atkinson, Anna Chancellor. 1994

FRAMED (1990) ★★★ This wry little caper comedy plunges Jeff Goldblum, as a talented art forger, into the realm of bewilderment and uncertainty he occupied so well with *Into the Night*. Gary Rosen's script goes for chuckles rather than belly laughs, but the tricky finale will be enjoyed by those who appreciate the genre. Unrated, with mild profanity and sexual situations. 90m. **DIR:** Dean Parisot. **CAST:** Jeff Goldblum, Kristin Scott-Thomas, Todd Graff, Michael Lerner, James Hong. 1990

FRANCIS GOES TO THE RACES ★★★ Francis the talking mule teaches another mule how to win races so he can help Donald O'Connor cope with some crooks at the track. Enjoyable in spite of a very hokey plot. B&W; 88m. **DIR:** Arthur Lubin. **CAST:** Donald O'Connor, Piper Laurie, Cecil Kellaway, Larry Keating, Jesse White. 1951

FRANCIS IN THE NAVY ★★ Sixth of the seven-picture series starring Francis, the talking mule. (Chill Wills provides his voice.) Silly, but the kids will enjoy it. B&W; 80m. **DIR:** Arthur Lubin. **CAST:** Donald O'Connor, Martha Hyer, Jim Backus, David Janssen, Clint Eastwood, Martin Milner, Paul Burke. 1955

FRANCIS JOINS THE WACS ★★★ Chill Wills appears in person and does the voice of the talking mule. He competes with himself for laughs in a comedy that sends Francis and his human pal to the Wacs by mistake. B&W; 94m. **DIR:** Arthur Lubin. **CAST:** Donald O'Connor, Chill Wills, Mamie Van Doren, ZaSu Pitts, Lynn Bari, Julie Adams, Joan Shawlee. 1954

FRANCIS, THE TALKING MULE ★★★½ First in a series from Universal, this well-known comedy tells the story of how a dim-witted student at West Point (Donald O'Connor) first met up with the famous talking mule of the title. The gags really fly as Francis proceeds to get O'Connor in all sorts of outrageous predicaments, consistently pulling him out just in the nick of time. Some screamingly funny scenes. Followed by six sequels. B&W; 91m. **DIR:** Arthur Lubin. **CAST:** Donald O'Connor, Patricia Medina, ZaSu Pitts, Tony Curtis, Ray Collins, Chill Wills (voice). 1950

FRANKEN AND DAVIS AT STOCKTON STATE ★★★ The weird, cerebral humor of Al Franken and Tom Davis is undoubtedly an acquired taste. Those who enjoyed their occasional stints—with "The Franken and Davis Show"—on the original *Saturday Night Live* will find much to appreciate in this live comedy concert, taped at Stockton College in New Jersey. Others may be a little perplexed by what they see at first. But we suggest you stick it out; there are some gems here. 55m. **DIR:** Randy Cohen. **CAST:** Al Franken, Tom Davis. 1984

FRANKENSTEIN GENERAL HOSPITAL ★★ Horror fans will appreciate some of the in-jokes in this parody, set in a hospital where the original Dr. Frankenstein's great-great-grandson is at work on the usual monster. Mark Blankfield has some funny bits as Bob Frankenstein, but the rest is thin going. Rated R for nudity. 92m. **DIR:** Deborah Roberts. **CAST:** Mark Blankfield. 1988

FRANKENWEENIE ★★★★ Young Barret Oliver brings his dog Sparky back to life. *Batman* director Tim Burton's first live-action short subject, made during his tenure at Walt Disney Studios, reworks the classic Mary Shelley tale of life after death into an affectionate tribute to the style of James Whale. Exquisite! Rated PG. 28m. **DIR:** Tim Burton. **CAST:** Daniel Stern, Shelley Duvall, Joseph Maher, Barret Oliver. 1984

FRATERNITY DEMON 🦃 A college student comes across the incantation that frees Isha, demon of lust and sex, just in time for a big frat house party. Rated R for nudity and sexual situations. 85m. **DIR:** C. B. Rubin. **CAST:** Trixxie Bowie, Charles Laurette, Al Darrough, Deborah Carlin. 1992

FRATERNITY VACATION 🦃 A teen-lust comedy with no laughs, no imagination, and no point. Rated R for profanity and nudity. 95m. **DIR:** James Frawley. **CAST:** Stephen Geoffreys, Sheree Wilson, Cameron Dye, Leigh McCloskey. **1985**

FRAUDS ★★½ Demented insurance-investigator Phil Collins turns a young couple's claim into a deadly game of cat and mouse. Teetering between black comedy and chills, this is an artistic jumble, though its very weirdness gives it a curious appeal. The plot slips past the realm of plausibility in the final act. Rated R for violence and profanity. 94m. **DIR:** Stephan Elliott. **CAST:** Phil Collins, Hugo Weaving, Josephine Byrnes. **1992**

FREAKED ★★★½ Hilariously demented comedy about a sideshow proprietor who uses toxic waste to create custom-made freaks. Like *Gremlins* made by the *Airplane!* team with an MTV-rude attitude: loud, fast, gross, and obnoxious—and we mean that in a good way. Rated R for profanity and general tastelessness. 80m. **DIR:** Alex Winter, Tom Stern. **CAST:** Alex Winter, Randy Quaid, Bill Sadler, Megan Ward, Mr. T, Bob Goldthwait, Brooke Shields. **1993**

FREE AND EASY ★★★ Buster Keaton's first sound movie has him chaperoning a beauty pageant winner to Hollywood, and stumbling into the movies himself. A good transition from silents to talkies for this wonderful clown. B&W; 92m. **DIR:** Edward Sedgwick. **CAST:** Buster Keaton, Anita Page, Robert Montgomery, Dorothy Sebastian. **1930**

FREE RIDE ★★ Disjointed rip-off of *Animal House*, with Gary Herschberger playing a supercool professional student, and Reed Rudy as his bunkie. Fitfully funny. Rated R for language and nudity. 92m. **DIR:** Tom Trbovich. **CAST:** Gary Herschberger, Reed Rudy, Dawn Schneider, Peter DeLuise, Warren Berlinger, Mamie Van Doren, Frank Campanella. **1986**

FREEBIE AND THE BEAN ★★★ Before astounding filmgoers with the outrageous black comedy *The Stunt Man*, director Richard Rush twisted the cop genre around with this watchable (but not spectacular) release. James Caan and Alan Arkin play San Francisco detectives who wreak havoc while on the trail of gangster Jack Kruschen. Rated R. 113m. **DIR:** Richard Rush. **CAST:** Alan Arkin, James Caan, Valerie Harper, Loretta Swit. **1974**

FRENCH LESSONS ★★★½ Romantic comedy about an English teenager who goes to Paris to study French for the summer. She is determined to fall in love and learns more out of the classroom than in. Rated PG. 90m. **DIR:** Brian Gilbert. **CAST:** Jane Snowden, Diana Blackburn, Françoise Brion. **1986**

FRENCH POSTCARDS ★★★½ Written, produced, and directed by the couple who gave us *American Graffiti*, Gloria Katz and Willard Huyck, this film benefits greatly from the skillful supporting performances by two noted French film stars, Marie-France Pisier and Jean Rochefort. The younger set of characters are well played by David Marshall Grant, Miles Chapin, Valerie Quennessen, and Blanche Baker. *French Postcards* is an enjoyable way to spend a couple of hours. Rated PG. 92m. **DIR:** Willard Huyck. **CAST:** David Marshall Grant, Blanche Baker, Miles Chapin, Debra Winger, Marie-France Pisier, Valerie Quennessen, Jean Rochefort. **1979**

FRESHMAN, THE ★★★★ This offbeat comedy stars Matthew Broderick as a film student who gets a job with an Italian-American importer who looks suspiciously like Don Corleone. Marlon Brando gets a wonderful opportunity to parody his Oscar-winning *Godfather* performance. Brando and Broderick are superb. Rated PG. 102m. **DIR:** Andrew Bergman. **CAST:** Marlon Brando, Matthew Broderick, Bruno Kirby, Penelope Ann Miller, Maximilian Schell. **1990**

FRIENDS, LOVERS & LUNATICS ★★ Chaos abounds as six different relationships evolve. Everything comes to a head when the title characters all arrive at a cabin on the same weekend. Listless attempt at screwball comedy. Rated R. 87m. **DIR:** Stephen Withrow. **CAST:** Daniel Stern, Sheila McCarthy, Page Fletcher, Deborah Foreman. **1989**

FRITZ THE CAT ★★★ This is an X-rated rendition of Robert Crumb's revolutionary feline, and it's the most outrageous cartoon ever produced. Fritz the Cat has appeared in Zap Comix and Head Comix, as well as in other underground mags. It's sometimes funny and sometimes gross, but mostly just so-so. 77m. **DIR:** Ralph Bakshi. **1972**

FROM THE HIP ★★★ Thoroughly unrealistic but nonetheless entertaining courtroom comedy that works in spite of director Bob Clark's tendency to forget that he's no longer making *Porky's*. Judd Nelson stars as a brash young attorney. John Hurt delivers a particularly fine, high-powered performance as a ruthless egomaniac who considers himself better than the rest of humanity. Rated PG for language. 111m. **DIR:** Bob Clark. **CAST:** Judd Nelson, Elizabeth Perkins, John Hurt, Ray Walston, Darren McGavin. **1987**

FRONT PAGE, THE (1931) ★★★★ A newspaper editor and his ace reporter do battle with civic corruption and each other in the first version of this oft-filmed hit comedy. The fast-paced, sparkling dialogue and the performances of the Warner Bros. stable of character actors have not aged after more than fifty years. This classic movie retains a great deal of charm. B&W; 99m. **DIR:** Lewis Milestone. **CAST:** Pat O'Brien, Adolphe Menjou, Mary Brian, Edward Everett Horton. **1931**

FRONT PAGE, THE (1974) ★★★½ Third version (of four to date) of the Ben Hecht–Charles MacArthur play is not quite as frantic as its predecessors, but retains some flavor of the era. Rated PG for profanity. 105m. **DIR:** Billy Wilder. **CAST:** Jack Lemmon, Walter

Matthau, Carol Burnett, Charles Durning, Herb Edelman, Vincent Gardenia, Allen Garfield, Harold Gould, Susan Sarandon, David Wayne. 1974

FROZEN ASSETS 💔 About what you'd expect from a comedy about a sperm bank. The plot is even worse than the performances by Shelley Long and Corbin Bernsen. Rated PG-13 for profanity and sexual themes. 92m. **DIR:** George Miller. **CAST:** Corbin Bernsen, Shelley Long. 1992

FULL MOON IN BLUE WATER ★★ Gene Hackman and Teri Garr bring wonderful moments to this offbeat comedy-drama. Otherwise, the film is corny and uneven. Rated R for profanity and light violence. 94m. **DIR:** Peter Masterson. **CAST:** Gene Hackman, Teri Garr, Burgess Meredith, Elias Coteas, Kevin Cooney. 1988

FULLER BRUSH GIRL, THE ★★★ Lucy's in typical form as a dizzy cosmetics salesgirl up to her mascara in murder and hoodlums. Wisecracking dialogue and familiar character faces help this one out. Harmless fun. B&W; 85m. **DIR:** Lloyd Bacon. **CAST:** Lucille Ball, Eddie Albert, Jerome Cowan, Lee Patrick. 1950

FULLER BRUSH MAN, THE ★★★ Red Skelton slapsticks along his route as a door-to-door salesman and gets involved with murder. Sadly unsung master gagster Buster Keaton deserves a lot of credit for the humor he adds to many other Skelton films. B&W; 93m. **DIR:** S. Sylvan Simon. **CAST:** Red Skelton, Janet Blair, Don McGuire, Adele Jergens, Buster Keaton. 1948

FUN WITH DICK AND JANE ★★★★ How does one maintain one's life-style after a sacking from a highly paid aerospace position? George Segal and Jane Fonda have a unique solution. They steal. This comedy caper is well named, because some quality fun is in store for the audience. Rated PG. 95m. **DIR:** Ted Kotcheff. **CAST:** Jane Fonda, George Segal, Ed McMahon. 1977

FUNLAND ★★½ Schizophrenic comedy about a family amusement park taken over by the mob. Although scripted by two *Saturday Night Live* writers, this flick doesn't know whether it wants to be a comedy, a drama, or a thriller. It does offer some weird and funny bits, though. Rated PG-13. 98m. **DIR:** Michael A. Simpson. **CAST:** William Windom, David L. Lander, Bruce Mahler, Jan Hooks, Lane Davies. 1986

FUNNY ABOUT LOVE ★★ We love Gene Wilder, but he's neither lovable nor funny in this misbegotten movie about a cartoonist who feels his "biological clock" ticking and attempts to have a baby with a caterer (Christine Lahti). Rated PG-13 for suggested sex and profanity. 92m. **DIR:** Leonard Nimoy. **CAST:** Gene Wilder, Christine Lahti, Mary Stuart Masterson, Stephen Tobolowsky, Robert Prosky, Susan Ruttan, Anne Jackson. 1990

FUNNY FARM ★★ Chevy Chase and Madolyn Smith star as Andy and Elizabeth Farmer who give up the city life for greener pastures in Vermont. Their idyllic country life goes awry with a series of predictable disasters, laboriously dramatized. Rated PG for adult language and situations. 101m. **DIR:** George Roy Hill. **CAST:** Chevy Chase, Madolyn Smith, Joseph Maher, Brad Sullivan, MacIntyre Dixon. 1988

FUNNY THING HAPPENED ON THE WAY TO THE FORUM, A ★★★★ Ancient Rome is the setting for this fast-paced musical comedy. Zero Mostel is a never-ending source of zany plots to gain his freedom and line his toga with loot as a cunning slave. He is ably assisted by Phil Silvers and Jack Gilford in this bawdy romp through classic times. Look for Buster Keaton in a nice cameo. 99m. **DIR:** Richard Lester. **CAST:** Zero Mostel, Phil Silvers, Jack Gilford, Michael Crawford, Buster Keaton. 1966

FUZZ ★★★ Raquel Welch and Burt Reynolds star as police in this comedy-drama. Yul Brynner plays a bomb-happy villain. It has a few good moments, but you'd have to be a member of the Burt Reynolds fan club to really love it. Rated PG. 92m. **DIR:** Richard A. Colla. **CAST:** Raquel Welch, Burt Reynolds, Yul Brynner, Tom Skerritt. 1972

GABE KAPLAN AS GROUCHO ★★★ Even avid Grouchophiles will enjoy this one-man made-for-cable show about everyone's favorite Marx brother. Gabe Kaplan does a comfortable impersonation, and the script mixes laughs with honest (but never spiteful) biography. 89m. **DIR:** John Bowab. **CAST:** Gabe Kaplan. 1982

GALACTIC GIGOLO ★★ Brainless, relentlessly silly movie about an alien (Carmine Capobianco) who wins a trip to Prospect, Connecticut. Rated R for language and nudity. 80m. **DIR:** Gorman Bechard. **CAST:** Carmine Capobianco, Debi Thibeault, Frank Stewart, Ruth Collins. 1987

GALLAGHER—MELON CRAZY ★★★★ Mr. Smash and Splash considers his favorite fruit in all its various incarnations. Things get as wild as three-piece melon suits, melon blimps, and giant, 30-foot melons. All this is climaxed by a Super-Sledge-o-Matic smashing spree. It's funny stuff. 58m. **DIR:** Joe Hostettler. **CAST:** Gallagher, Bill Kirchenbauer. 1984

GALLAGHER—OVER YOUR HEAD ★★★★ Gallagher performs in the Lone Star state. The Texas audience goes wild when he enters wearing a 20-gallon hat and carrying a pistol with a 10-foot barrel. It gets better from there. He takes sarcastic swipes at politicians, ancient history, and gun control. 58m. **DIR:** Joe Hostettler. **CAST:** Gallagher. **1984**

GALLAGHER—STUCK IN THE 60S ★★★★ If you're a product of the 1960s, and even if you're not, you'll love this hilarious comedy video. It's all playfully honest and enjoyably silly. 58m. **DIR:** Wayne Orr. **CAST:** Gallagher. **1983**

GALLAGHER—THE BOOKKEEPER ★★★★ Gallagher takes a potshot at what seems to matter most in our society: the almighty dollar. In this concert performance, he whimsically attacks the IRS, banking, and what we spend our money on. And, of course, be prepared for the Sledge-o-Matic! 58m. **DIR:** Joe Hostettler. **CAST:** Gallagher. **1985**

GALLAGHER—THE MADDEST ★★★½ Here's more inspired Gallagher-style madness for comedy fans. Bits include the introduction of a mutant sofa, a treatise on hats with and without handles, and, of course, everything ends with the gush of Gallagher's Sledge-o-Matic. Filmed live in concert. 59m. **DIR:** Wayne Orr. **CAST:** Gallagher. **1984**

GAMBIT ★★★½ An engaging caper comedy that teams Michael Caine's inventive but unlucky thief with Shirley MacLaine's mute and mysterious woman of the world... or *is* she? The target is a valuable art treasure, jealously guarded by ruthless owner Herbert Lom, and Caine's plan is—to say the least—unusual. Caine and MacLaine make a grand pair; it's a shame they didn't get together for another film of this sort. Unrated; suitable for family viewing. 108m. **DIR:** Ronald Neame. **CAST:** Michael Caine, Shirley MacLaine, Herbert Lom. **1966**

GARBO TALKS ★★★★ In this often funny and touching contemporary comedy, Anne Bancroft is delightful as an outspoken crusader against the small injustices in the world. But she has her fantasies, too, and enlists the aid of her son (Ron Silver) in finding Greta Garbo, who at age 79 can occasionally be spotted walking around New York. Rated PG for profanity. 103m. **DIR:** Sidney Lumet. **CAST:** Anne Bancroft, Ron Silver, Carrie Fisher, Howard DaSilva, Dorothy Loudon, Hermione Gingold. **1984**

GARRY SHANDLING: ALONE IN VEGAS ★★★★ Nothing seems especially funny about stand-up comic Garry Shandling—not even his material. He's just an average guy, and that's his charm. In a world where every other comedian wants to be cooking like a gourmet chef, Shandling is like mama's recipes—warm and familiar. 60m. **DIR:** William Dear. **CAST:** Garry Shandling. **1984**

GARRY SHANDLING SHOW, THE ★★★ Garry Shandling spoofs late-night talk shows, specifically Johnny Carson's anniversary shows. He looks back over the last twenty-five years of this mock variety show. Zany comedy abounds with guest stars coming out of the walls. 60m. **DIR:** Tom Trbovich. **CAST:** Garry Shandling, Paul Willson, Rose Marie, Doug McClure, Donny Osmond, Johnny Carson. **1985**

GAS 🦃 Tasteless, tedious comedy about an artificial gas crisis in a Midwest city. Rated R. 94m. **DIR:** Les Rose. **CAST:** Sterling Hayden, Peter Aykroyd, Susan Anspach, Donald Sutherland, Howie Mandel, Helen Shaver. **1981**

GAS PUMP GIRLS 🦃 This teen comedy features four beautiful girls who take on a big oil company. Rated PG for nudity. 102m. **DIR:** Joel Bender. **CAST:** Kirsten Baker, Dennis Bowen, Huntz Hall, Rikki Marin, William Smith. **1978**

GAZEBO, THE ★★★★ Hilarious dark comedy about blackmail, murder, and a body that keeps coming back. Many plot twists add to the fun. There is a lot more, but worth renting if only to see Glenn Ford make elaborate preparations to commit a murder. 102m. **DIR:** George Marshall. **CAST:** Glenn Ford, Debbie Reynolds, Carl Reiner, John McGiver, Bert Freed, Martin Landau, Dick Wessel. **1959**

GEEK MAGGOT BINGO 🦃 Stupid horror-movie parody filled with in-jokes about the filmmakers and their friends. Unrated, but filled with gore and violence. 70m. **DIR:** Nick Zedd. **CAST:** Robert Andrews, Richard Hell, Zacherley. **1983**

GENERAL, THE ★★★★★ *The General* is a film based on an incident in the Civil War. Buster Keaton is an engineer determined to recapture his stolen locomotive. Magnificent battle scenes are mere backdrops for Keaton's inspired acrobatics and comedy. Solid scripting, meticulous attention to detail, and ingenious stunt work make this picture excellent. B&W; 74m. **DIR:** Buster Keaton. **CAST:** Buster Keaton, Marion Mack, Glen Cavender, Jim Farley, Joseph Keaton. **1927**

GENERATION ★★★ Remember the generation gap? If not, then you're not likely to enjoy this dated but modestly amusing comedy about a businessman (David Janssen) trying to cope with his pregnant daughter and hippie son-in-law, who want to have their baby at home. Rated PG. 104m. **DIR:** George Schaefer. **CAST:** David Janssen, Kim Darby, Peter Duel, Carl Reiner, Andrew Prine, James Coco, Sam Waterston. **1969**

GENEVIEVE ★★★½ Captivating, low-key comedy about friendly rivals who engage in a race after finishing a sports car rally in England. No pretenses or false claims in this charming film, just great performances, beautiful countryside, and a spirit of fun and camaraderie. This stylish feature gave Kenneth More one of his best roles and showcased the charm and comedy flair of Kay Kendall, one of Britain's top talents. 86m. **DIR:** Henry Cornelius. **CAST:** Kenneth More, Kay

Kendall, Dinah Sheridan, John Gregson, Arthur Wontner. 1954

GENTLEMEN PREFER BLONDES ★★ Howard Hawks gets surprisingly good performances from his stars, Jane Russell and Marilyn Monroe, in this 1953 musical comedy. As usual, Hawks does his best to make good scenes, but this time the silly plot—about two women searching for husbands—thwarts his esteemable talents. 91m. **DIR:** Howard Hawks. **CAST:** Jane Russell, Marilyn Monroe, Charles Coburn, Tommy Noonan, Elliott Reid, George Winslow. 1953

GEORGE BURNS AND GRACIE ALLEN SHOW, THE (TV SERIES) ★★★½ In this classic series, George Burns plays a nearly imperturbable entertainer, married to madcap Gracie Allen. Allen turns everyday life into a nonstop adventure by innocently causing a whirlwind of confusion. She's endlessly endearing. Burns is dryly delightful, puffing on his cigar and looking into the camera, commenting on the developing plot. B&W; 120m. **DIR:** Ralph Levy. **CAST:** George Burns, Gracie Allen, Harry Von Zell, Ronnie Burns, Bea Benaderet, Hal March, Bob Sweeney, Fred Clark, Larry Keating. 1950–1958

GEORGE BURNS—HIS WIT AND WISDOM ★★★ A day in the life of George Burns. Burns's dry-witted charm is the main attraction; the "special appearances," which are trotted out like surprise celebrity guests on a talk show, range from delightful (Carol Channing) to pointless (Emma Samms). Not rated. 45m. **DIR:** Mort Fallick. **CAST:** George Burns. 1989

GEORGE BURNS IN CONCERT ★★★★ George Burns is at his funniest in this live, onstage performance produced for Home Box Office. It's all stand-up jokes and stories that Burns aims at himself. He spends a lot of time talking in a hilarious fashion about his part in the film *Oh, God* and of his extraordinary life-span. A number of delightfully silly songs sound suspiciously like vaudeville. Thoroughly enjoyable. 55m. **DIR:** Jim Shaw. **CAST:** George Burns. 1982

GEORGE CARLIN: DOIN' IT AGAIN ★★★ Taped before a live audience (where he seems most comfortable), this is from Carlin's long line of mostly hilarious made-for-cable specials, complete with the unusual observations that we have come to associate with the man. In this round, Carlin pokes fun at language, dogs, and political correctness. Not rated; contains lots of profanity. 59m. **DIR:** Rocco Urbishi. **CAST:** George Carlin. 1990

GEORGE CARLIN: JAMMIN' IN NEW YORK ★★★★ More irreverent humor from the master of wordplay. Comedian George Carlin disburses hilarious words of wisdom on everything from the Persian Gulf War to airline announcements. Taped at The Paramount in Madison Square Garden, New York City. Not rated, contains adult language. 60m. **DIR:** Rocco Urbishi. **CAST:** George Carlin. 1992

GEORGE CARLIN LIVE! WHAT AM I DOING IN NEW JERSEY? ★★★★ George Carlin is at his hilarious best in this HBO special taped before a live audience in New Jersey. Carlin blasts away at politics, stupid motorists, the FCC, and FM radio. Hysterical insights in this unpredictable hour of caustic, no-holds-barred humor. Not rated; contains some profanity. 60m. **DIR:** Bruce Gowers. **CAST:** George Carlin. 1988

GEORGE CARLIN—PLAYIN' WITH YOUR HEAD ★★ There's little of the classic Carlin character to be seen in this comedy video. The one redeeming factor is a black-and-white short at the beginning—"The Envelope," in which Carlin plays a Sam Spade character named Mike Holder. Vic Tayback co-stars as the ringleader of a bunch of hooligans. No rating, but there's an ample helping of raw language. 58m. **DIR:** Rocco Urbishi. **CAST:** George Carlin, Vic Tayback. 1986

GEORGE WASHINGTON SLEPT HERE ★★★ Some mild laughs when Jack Benny and Ann Sheridan buy a run-down Colonial house and are frustrated at every attempt to make it habitable. Many of the situations were repeated, to better advantage, in *Mr. Blandings Builds His Dream House*. B&W; 91m. **DIR:** William Keighley. **CAST:** Jack Benny, Ann Sheridan, Charles Coburn, Percy Kilbride, Hattie McDaniel. 1942

GEORGY GIRL ★★★½ Generations clash as suave, patient fairy godfather James Mason works to make chubby London mod girl Lynn Redgrave his mistress in this totally engaging British comedy. Charlotte Rampling is a standout as the chubby's tough-bitch roommate. Mason, of course, gives another of his flawless characterizations. B&W; 100m. **DIR:** Silvio Narizzano. **CAST:** Lynn Redgrave, James Mason, Alan Bates, Charlotte Rampling. 1966

GET CRAZY ★★★½ Here's the wildest, weirdest, and most outrageous rock 'n' roll comedy any of us is likely to see. It's a story about a rock concert on New Year's Eve. Malcolm McDowell plays a Mick Jagger–style rock singer, Allen Goorwitz is a Bill Graham–ish promoter, and Daniel Stern is his lovesick stage manager. Rated R for nudity, profanity, violence, and suggested sex. 92m. **DIR:** Allan Arkush. **CAST:** Malcolm McDowell, Allen Garfield, Daniel Stern, Ed Begley Jr., Miles Chapin, Lou Reed, Stacey Nelkin, Bill Henderson, Franklin Ajaye, Bobby Sherman, Fabian. 1983

GET OUT OF MY ROOM 🦃 Cheech and Chong talk about how to make videos and decide that the main thing to do is to hire lots of beautiful girls. 53m. **DIR:** Richard "Cheech" Marin. **CAST:** Cheech and Chong, John

Paragon, Elvira (Cassandra Peterson), Jan-Michael Vincent. 1985

GET SMART AGAIN ★★½ This pleasant trip down memory lane reunites the cast of the TV sitcom for one last go at the creeps of KAOS. Breezy, pleasant, and funnier than you'd expect, in a silly way. Made for TV. 93m. **DIR:** Gary Nelson. **CAST:** Don Adams, Barbara Feldon. 1989

GET TO KNOW YOUR RABBIT ★★★ This cute comedy won't appeal to everyone but will captivate fans of the Smothers Brothers' brand of offbeat humor. Tom Smothers wants to be a magician so he takes lessons from Orson Welles. But it's a lost cause. The satire hurts, but the laughs help. Rated R. 91m. **DIR:** Brian De Palma. **CAST:** Tom Smothers, Orson Welles, John Astin, Katharine Ross, Samantha Jones, Emmet Walsh. 1972

GETTING EVEN WITH DAD ★★★½ An enjoyable, lightweight comedy that serves mainly as a showcase for its big-name Hollywood players. An 11-year-old boy blackmails his con man father into going straight in an effort to bond with him. Rated PG. 110m. **DIR:** Howard Deutch. **CAST:** Ted Danson, Macaulay Culkin, Glenne Headly, Hector Elizondo, Gailard Sartain, Saul Rubinek. 1994

GETTING IT RIGHT ★★★★½ Surrounded by a wonderful cast of endearing eccentrics, Jesse Birdsall sails through his role as a 31-year-old virgin who becomes a sensitive lover (to Lynn Redgrave's madcap neglected socialite). Something of an updated version of the British social comedies of the Sixties (*Georgy Girl, Alfie*). Highly recommended. Rated R for nudity and sexual situations. 102m. **DIR:** Randal Kleiser. **CAST:** Jesse Birdsall, Helena Bonham Carter, Peter Cook, John Gielgud, Jane Horrocks, Lynn Redgrave. 1989

GHOST AND MRS. MUIR, THE ★★★★ Romantic comedy at its best in this heartwarming tale about a young widow who decides to live in the lighthouse home of a long-dead sailor, setting the stage for a perfect love story. 104m. **DIR:** Joseph L. Mankiewicz. **CAST:** Gene Tierney, Rex Harrison, Edna Best, George Sanders, Anna Lee, Natalie Wood. 1947

GHOST BREAKERS ★★★½ Amusing Bob Hope romp finds him investigating the eerie mansion inherited by Paulette Goddard. The laughs mix evenly with the thrills in this hilarious blend of gags and mayhem. Often imitated (film was inspiration for Martin-Lewis vehicle *Scared Stiff*) but never equaled. Great atmosphere. 85m. **DIR:** George Marshall. **CAST:** Bob Hope, Paulette Goddard, Richard Carlson, Anthony Quinn, Paul Lukas. 1940

GHOST DAD ★★★½ This family-oriented, *Topper*-style comedy casts Bill Cosby as a daddy (what else?) who continues to provide for his family—even after he's dead. The story's serious underpinnings give resonance to this comic delight. Rated PG. 95m. **DIR:** Sidney Poitier. **CAST:** Bill Cosby, Denise Nicholas, Kimberly Russell. 1990

GHOST FEVER 🦃 Southern cops investigate strange happenings at Magnolia Mansion. Director Alan Smithee doesn't exist; it's a fake name applied when the real director (in this case, Lee Madden) doesn't want his name on the final product. Rated PG. 86m. **DIR:** Alan Smithee. **CAST:** Sherman Hemsley, Luis Avalos. 1985

GHOST GOES WEST, THE ★★★★ A millionaire buys a Scottish castle and transports it stone by stone to America only to discover that it comes complete with a ghost. Robert Donat gives a memorable performance in this bit of whimsy. B&W; 100m. **DIR:** René Clair. **CAST:** Robert Donat, Jean Parker. 1935

GHOST IN THE NOONDAY SUN 🦃 Too silly pirate parody. Not rated. 90m. **DIR:** Peter Medak. **CAST:** Peter Sellers, Anthony Franciosa, Peter Boyle, Spike Milligan, Clive Revill. 1974

GHOSTBUSTERS ★★★★ Bill Murray, Dan Aykroyd, Sigourney Weaver, and Harold Ramis are terrific in this very funny and often frightening comedy-horror film about a special organization that fights evil spirits. Is it *The Exorcist* meets *Saturday Night Live*? That's pretty close—but it's better. Rated PG for profanity and scary scenes. 107m. **DIR:** Ivan Reitman. **CAST:** Bill Murray, Dan Aykroyd, Sigourney Weaver, Harold Ramis, Annie Potts, Ernie Hudson, William Atherton, Rick Moranis. 1984

GHOSTBUSTERS II ★★½ In this watchable sequel to the 1984 box-office blockbuster, the original cast returns to take on an explosion of evil spirits on a fateful New Year's Eve. The formula now seems fairly tired, despite some funny moments at the outset. Older kids are more likely to enjoy the shenanigans than adults. Rated PG. 110m. **DIR:** Ivan Reitman. **CAST:** Bill Murray, Dan Aykroyd, Sigourney Weaver, Harold Ramis, Rick Moranis, Ernie Hudson, Annie Potts. 1989

GHOSTS CAN'T DO IT ★★ Bo knows breast exposure. Too bad hubby-director John doesn't know anything about making a coherent or even moderately funny movie. Anthony Quinn is Bo's dead husband who appears to her somewhere in the sky, which is a guess because the two only appear on the screen together at the very beginning. Poor ghost effects don't help. Rated R for nudity and profanity. 95m. **DIR:** John Derek. **CAST:** Bo Derek, Anthony Quinn, Don Murray, Julie Newmar, Leo Damien. 1990

GHOSTS OF BERKELEY SQUARE ★★½ After accidentally killing themselves while plotting to murder a superior officer, two British officers are condemned to haunt an old mansion until it is visited by royalty. Routine ghost comedy made palatable by a good cast. B&W; 85m. **DIR:** Vernon Sewell. **CAST:** Robert Morley, Felix Aylmer, Ernest Thesiger, Wilfrid Hyde-White. **1947**

GHOSTS ON THE LOOSE 🦃 Silly movie pits moronic East Side Kids against a bored Bela Lugosi and his German henchmen in this pallid variation on the "old haunted house" theme. B&W; 65m. **DIR:** William Beaudine. **CAST:** The East Side Kids, Bela Lugosi, Ava Gardner, Rick Vallin. **1943**

GIDGET ★★½ The eternal beach bunny, Gidget (Sandra Dee), becomes involved with Cliff Robertson in order to make the man she's infatuated with (James Darren) notice her. This is the first and the best of a subpar surfer series. 95m. **DIR:** Paul Wendkos. **CAST:** Sandra Dee, James Darren, Arthur O'Connell, Cliff Robertson, Doug McClure. **1959**

GIDGET GOES HAWAIIAN ★★ Everyone's favorite "girl-midget" (played here by Deborah Walley, taking over from Sandra Dee) returns to the screen in this inoffensive, brainless sequel to the 1959 box-office hit. 102m. **DIR:** Paul Wendkos. **CAST:** Deborah Walley, James Darren, Michael Callan, Carl Reiner, Peggy Cass, Eddie Foy Jr. **1961**

GIDGET GOES TO ROME ★★ The irrepressible beach bunny presses onward, if not upward, in this below-average sequel to *Gidget*. 101m. **DIR:** Paul Wendkos. **CAST:** Cindy Carol, James Darren, Jeff Donnell, Jessie Royce Landis. **1963**

GIG, THE ★★★ Very nicely done comedy-drama concerning a group of men who get together once a week to play Dixieland jazz. Film admirably avoids the clichés associated with this type of buddy film. Nice ensemble acting, with Cleavon Little and Joe Silver leading the way. Give this one a try. 92m. **DIR:** Frank D. Gilroy. **CAST:** Wayne Rogers, Cleavon Little, Joe Silver, Andrew Duncan, Daniel Nalbach. **1985**

GILDA LIVE ★★ We've always loved Gilda Radner's characters from *Saturday Night Live,* and they're all represented in *Gilda Live*. But something is missing in her live show. The result is very few laughs. Rated R. 96m. **DIR:** Mike Nichols. **CAST:** Gilda Radner, Don Novello, Paul Shaffer. **1980**

GIMME AN "F" 🦃 Blame *Flashdance* for this tawdry little teen-exploitation flick concerned with a cheerleaders' competition. Rated R for nudity and language. 100m. **DIR:** Paul Justman. **CAST:** Stephen Shellen, Mark Keyloun, Jennifer Cooke, John Karlen, Daphne Ashbrook. **1984**

GINGER ALE AFTERNOON 🦃 Tedious would-be comedy about a bickering couple. Rated R for profanity and brief nudity. 88m. **DIR:** Rafal Zielinski. **CAST:** Dana Andersen, John M. Jackson, Yeardley Smith. **1989**

GIRL, A GUY AND A GOB, A ★★★ A silly, predictable comedy that tends to grow on you; it focuses on a working girl, her happy-go-lucky sailor boyfriend, and an upper-crust executive. Dated, of course, but cute and polished. Movie buffs will be interested to note the producer was legendary Harold Lloyd. Not rated, but contains nothing offensive. B&W; 90m. **DIR:** Richard Wallace. **CAST:** Lucille Ball, George Murphy, Edmond O'Brien, Henry Travers. **1941**

GIRL CAN'T HELP IT, THE ★★★ Tom Ewell is given the task of turning squealing Jayne Mansfield into a singer on the clear understanding that he keep his hands to himself, a tough request when faced with the would-be singer's winning ways and obvious charms. Great rock 'n' roll by some of its premier interpreters is the real reason for watching this film. 99m. **DIR:** Frank Tashlin. **CAST:** Tom Ewell, Jayne Mansfield, Edmond O'Brien, Julie London, Henry Jones, Fats Domino, The Platters, The Treniers, Little Richard, Gene Vincent and His Blue Caps, Eddie Cochran, Barry Gordon, Ray Anthony, Nino Tempo, The Chuckles. **1957**

GIRL FROM MISSOURI, THE ★★★★½ A delightful comedy that shows Jean Harlow's comedic style to advantage, this is the movie that gave censors headaches because it boldly and bluntly said that some women will do anything for money. B&W; 74m. **DIR:** Jack Conway. **CAST:** Jean Harlow, Franchot Tone, Patsy Kelly, Lewis Stone, Lionel Barrymore, Alan Mowbray, Nat Pendleton, Clara Blandick. **1934**

GIRL IN EVERY PORT, A ★★ Silly film about sailors involved in horse-racing scheme milks the old hide-the-horse-on-the-ship gag for all that it's worth (which isn't much) and then some. B&W; 86m. **DIR:** Chester Erskine. **CAST:** Groucho Marx, William Bendix, Marie Wilson, Don DeFore, Gene Lockhart. **1952**

GIRL IN THE PICTURE, THE ★★★ *The Girl in the Picture* is a slight but very charming movie from Scotland. John Gordon Sinclair plays a Glasgow photographer who's feeling stagnant in his relationship with his design-student girlfriend. The problems they face are never dealt with, but it doesn't seem to matter because the going is so enjoyable. The lovers are an amusing pair—Gordon Sinclair, with his trademark understated manner, and Irina Brook, with her intelligence and graceful strength. Rated PG. 90m. **DIR:** Cary Parker. **CAST:** Gordon John Sinclair, Irina Brook, David McKay, Gregor Fisher, Paul Young, Rikki Fulton. **1985**

GIRL RUSH ★★½ Mildly amusing comedy about vaudeville performers who attempt to stage a show called *The Frisco Follies* for a group of miners. Their efforts are met with resistance by a menacing gambler played by Robert Mitchum. B&W; 65m. **DIR:**

Gordon Douglas. **CAST:** Robert Mitchum, Frances Langford, Wally Brown. **1944**

GIRLFRIEND FROM HELL ★★★½ A painfully shy girl becomes the life—and death—of the party when she is possessed by the devil. Inventive low-budget comedy. Rated R for sexual situations and profanity. 92m. **DIR:** Daniel M. Paterson. **CAST:** Liane Curtis, Dana Ashbrook, James Daughton. **1989**

GIRLS JUST WANT TO HAVE FUN 🦃 Sarah Jessica Parker stars as a young woman who just *lovvves* to dance. Rated PG for profanity. 90m. **DIR:** Alan Metter. **CAST:** Sarah Jessica Parker, Lee Montgomery, Morgan Woodward, Jonathan Silverman. **1985**

GLASS BOTTOM BOAT, THE ★★★ Doris Day is hired by amorous scientist Rod Taylor as his biographer. Slapstick complications arise when she is suspected of being a Russian spy. 110m. **DIR:** Frank Tashlin. **CAST:** Doris Day, Rod Taylor, Arthur Godfrey, Paul Lynde, Dom DeLuise. **1966**

GLITCH! 🦃 Inane comedy features two bumbling burglars posing as sleazy filmmakers. Rated R for nudity and profanity. 88m. **DIR:** Nico Mastorakis. **CAST:** Julia Nickson, Will Egan, Steve Donmyer, Dick Gautier, Ted Lange. **1988**

GLOBAL AFFAIR, A ★★½ When a child is abandoned at the United Nations, all nation members put in a claim for custody. Nothing much. B&W; 84m. **DIR:** Jack Arnold. **CAST:** Bob Hope, Michele Mercier, Robert Sterling, Lilo Pulver, Elga Andersen, Yvonne De Carlo. **1964**

GLORY! GLORY! ★★★½ Marvelously irreverent spoof of television evangelism features Richard Thomas as the dedicated but boring successor to his father's multi-million-dollar church. Thomas hires delightfully saucy Ellen Greene, a hard-core rock 'n' roll singer, to be Sister Ruth. Made for cable. 152m. **DIR:** Lindsay Anderson. **CAST:** Richard Thomas, Ellen Greene, James Whitmore, Winston Rekert. **1989**

GLORY YEARS ★★ Three old high school buddies on their twenty-year reunion use their alumni fund to gamble in Las Vegas. The whole film reeks of a bad *Big Chill* rip-off. Originally an HBO miniseries. Not rated, has profanity, sex, and nudity. 150m. **DIR:** Arthur Allan Seidelman. **CAST:** George Dzundza, Archie Hahn, Tim Thomerson, Tawny Kitaen, Michael Fairman, Sandy Simpson, Beau Starr, Donna Pescow. **1987**

GO WEST ★★★½ Far from prime-screen Marx Brothers, this is still one of their best MGM movies and a treat for their fans. Good comedy bits combine with a rip-roaring climax (stolen by screenwriter Buster Keaton from *The General*) for a highly watchable star comedy. B&W; 81m. **DIR:** Edward Buzzell. **CAST:** The Marx Brothers, John Carroll, Diana Lewis, Walter Woolf King. **1940**

GO WEST, YOUNG MAN ★★ No Mae West movie is all bad, but this one comes close. West based her screenplay on someone else's story so it doesn't fit very well. The censors snipped her usual one-liners and diluted the humor. She plays a glamorous movie star who falls for a handsome stranger and decides to steal him from his girlfriend with predictable results. B&W; 80m. **DIR:** Henry Hathaway. **CAST:** Mae West, Randolph Scott, Warren William, Alice Brady, Lyle Talbot, Isabel Jewell, Jack LaRue, Margaret Perry. **1936**

GODS MUST BE CRAZY, THE ★★★★★ This work, by South African filmmaker Jamie Uys, is a hilarious, poignant, exciting, thought-provoking, violent, and slapstick concoction that involves three separate stories. One is about a Bushman whose tribe selects him to get rid of an evil thing sent by the gods: a Coke bottle. The second features the awkward love affair of a teacher and a klutzy scientist. The last involves a band of terrorists fleeing for their lives. These all come together for a surprising and satisfying climax. Unrated, the film has violence. 109m. **DIR:** Jamie Uys. **CAST:** Marius Meyers, Sandra Prinsloo. **1980**

GODS MUST BE CRAZY II, THE ★★★★ Those who loved the original *Gods Must Be Crazy* will find more to enjoy in this gentle tale, which has the Bushman hero trying to find his two children after they've been carried away in a poacher's truck. Rated PG for brief profanity and light violence. 97m. **DIR:** Jamie Uys. **CAST:** N!Xau, Lena Farugia, Hans Strydom. **1990**

GOIN' TO TOWN ★★★ A Mae West comedy that poses the idea that there are men who can resist La West. That's far-fetched, even for Hollywood. She plays a cattle queen who inherits an oil field and falls hard for the British engineer who surveys her property. He rebuffs her. She does a Pygmalion twist on herself and becomes a sophisticated lady and even sings opera to impress the guy. Good one-liners and enjoyable songs, but Mae West is the only impressive player. B&W; 74m. **DIR:** Alexander Hall. **CAST:** Mae West, Paul Cavanagh, Ivan Lebedeff, Marjorie Gateson, Monroe Owsley, Grant Withers. **1935**

GOING APE! ★★ Tony Danza plays the heir to a million-dollar fortune-with-a-catch: he has to care for three unpredictable simians. Because the film is padded with familiar material, little fun shines through. Rated PG. 87m. **DIR:** Jeremy Joe Kronsberg. **CAST:** Tony Danza, Jessica Walter, Stacey Nelkin, Danny DeVito, Art Metrano, Joseph Maher. **1981**

GOING BERSERK 🦃 This is an unfunny comedy starring former *SCTV* regulars John

Candy, Joe Flaherty, and Eugene Levy. Rated R. 85m. **DIR:** David Steinberg. **CAST:** John Candy, Joe Flaherty, Eugene Levy, Alley Mills, Pat Hingle, Richard Libertini. **1983**

GOING IN STYLE ★★★★ Three retirees who gather daily on a park bench need to add some spice to their empty existence. So they decide to rob a bank. This crime caper has some unexpected plot twists with a perfect sprinkling of humor. A delight throughout. Rated PG. 96m. **DIR:** Martin Brest. **CAST:** George Burns, Art Carney, Lee Strasberg, Charles Hallahan, Pamela Payton-Wright. **1979**

GOING TO CONGRESS AND DON'T PARK THERE ★★★ Two Will Rogers shorts. Shown at the Republican and Democratic national conventions in 1924, "Going To Congress" dramatizes the selection, nomination, and election of a bumbling dolt. "Don't Park There" zeroes in on the exasperation of the auto age: finding a parking space. B&W; 57m. **DIR:** Rob Wagner, Fred L. Guiol. **CAST:** Will Rogers. **1924**

GOING UNDER ★★ The wacky crew of the sub-*Standard* set sail for *Airplane*-style high jinx on the open sea. The jokes are seaworthy, but the execution is all wet. Rated PG. 81m. **DIR:** Mark W. Travis. **CAST:** Bill Pullman, Wendy Schaal, Ned Beatty, Robert Vaughn, Bud Cort, Michael Winslow. **1991**

GOING UNDERCOVER 🦃 Chris Lemmon plays an airhead gumshoe hired by Jean Simmons to protect her stepdaughter. Rated PG-13 for violence. 89m. **DIR:** James Keneim Clarke. **CAST:** Jean Simmons, Lea Thompson, Chris Lemmon. **1988**

GOLD RUSH, THE ★★★★★ Charlie Chaplin's classic comedy is immortal for the scrumptious supper of a boiled boot, the teetering Klondike cabin, and the dance of the dinner rolls. Some parts are very sentimental, but these give the viewer time to catch his or her breath after laughing so much. B&W; 100m. **DIR:** Charles Chaplin. **CAST:** Charlie Chaplin, Mack Swain, Georgia Hale. **1925**

GOLDEN AGE OF COMEDY, THE ★★★★ First and most popular of Robert Youngson's tributes to silent film comedy, this compilation of highlights introduced new generations of moviegoers to the great years of silent comedy and continues to do so. Many of the shorts with Laurel and Hardy (including the classic "Two Tars") will be familiar to viewers due to their popularity and availability, but the segments with Will Rogers spoofing silent-film greats Douglas Fairbanks and Tom Mix, and the footage with Harry Langdon (who was at one time considered a comedic equal to Charlie Chaplin, Buster Keaton, and Harold Lloyd) are seldom seen and well worth the wait. B&W; 78m. **DIR:** Robert Youngson. **CAST:** Stan Laurel, Oliver Hardy, Will Rogers, Harry Langdon, Ben Turpin, Carole Lombard, Snub Pollard. **1957**

GONE ARE THE DAYS ★★★ After witnessing a shooting, the Daye family is assigned to a witness relocation agent (Harvey Korman), who is creatively unsuccessful in a long-distance game of hide-and-seek. This wacky comedy is pleasantly acted and well photographed. A Disney made-for-cable production. Good fun for the family. 90m. **DIR:** Gabrielle Beaumont. **CAST:** Harvey Korman, Susan Anspach, Robert Hogan. **1984**

GOOD IDEA ★★ Odd characters abound in this anarchic comedy. Anthony Newley tries to win his ex-wife back from her new husband, a crooked architect. John Candy is funny as a daft cop, but it's only a small role, although the video packaging makes him look like the star. Original title: *It Seemed Like a Good Idea at the Time*. Rated PG. 106m. **DIR:** John Trent. **CAST:** Anthony Newley, Stefanie Powers, Isaac Hayes, Lloyd Bochner, Yvonne De Carlo, Lawrence Dane, John Candy. **1975**

GOOD NEIGHBOR SAM ★★★ This comedy is similar to many of the lightweight potboilers given to Jack Lemmon in the 1960s. It is an overlong farce about a married advertising designer who pretends marriage to his foreign neighbor next door so she can secure an inheritance. 130m. **DIR:** David Swift. **CAST:** Jack Lemmon, Romy Schneider, Dorothy Provine, Edward G. Robinson. **1964**

GOOD NIGHT, MICHELANGELO ★★½ In this bizarre but whimsical film, we see the intertwined lives of four Italian families. Confusing but ultimately rewarding. Rated R for profanity. 91m. **DIR:** Carlo Liconti. **CAST:** Lina Sastri, Kim Cattrall, Tony Nardi. **1989**

GOOD SAM ★★ Gary Cooper plays a guy who can't say no in this barely watchable "comedy." He's Mr. Nice-Guy to everyone but his own family. He feels he has to help everyone, so he lends all his money to "friends" and the "needy." B&W; 114m. **DIR:** Leo McCarey. **CAST:** Gary Cooper, Ann Sheridan, Edmund Lowe. **1948**

GOODBYE COLUMBUS ★★★★ This film marked the start of Ali MacGraw's and Richard Benjamin's movie careers. Ali plays a rich, spoiled Jewish-American princess who meets a college dropout (Benjamin) at her country club. They have an affair, and we get to see her flaws through his "average guy" eyes. Rated R. 105m. **DIR:** Larry Peerce. **CAST:** Richard Benjamin, Ali MacGraw, Jack Klugman. **1969**

GOODBYE GIRL, THE ★★★★½ Neil Simon's sparkling screenplay and the acting of Marsha Mason and Richard Dreyfuss combine to produce one of the best pure comedies since Hollywood's golden '30s. Mason and Dreyfuss are a mismatched pair of New Yorkers forced to become roommates. Rated PG. 110m. **DIR:** Herbert Ross. **CAST:** Richard Dreyfuss, Marsha Mason, Quinn Cummings. **1977**

GOODBYE NEW YORK ★★★ In this amusing comedy, an insurance salesperson (Julie Hagerty) becomes fed up with her job and husband and leaves for Paris. After falling asleep on the plane, she wakes up in Israel with no money and no luggage. Rated R for language and very brief nudity. 90m. **DIR:** Amos Kollek. **CAST:** Julie Hagerty, Amos Kollek, David Topaz, Shmuel Shiloh. **1984**

GOOF BALLS 🦃 This lame comedy opens with a bungled robbery performed by a bunch of inept losers. Gangsters, oil sheiks, bikinied girls, and a number of other stupid characters abound. Unrated. 89m. **DIR:** Brad Turner. **CAST:** Ben Gordon. **1987**

GORILLA, THE ★★ This is another one of those horror comedies that takes place in an old mansion and again wastes poor Bela Lugosi's acting talents. The Ritz Brothers were an acquired taste, to be sure. B&W; 66m. **DIR:** Allan Dwan. **CAST:** The Ritz Brothers, Bela Lugosi, Lionel Atwill. **1939**

GORP 🦃 Particularly unfunny summer-camp flick. Rated R for nudity and profanity. 91m. **DIR:** Joseph Ruben. **CAST:** Michael Lembeck, Philip Casnoff, Dennis Quaid, David Huddleston, Rosanna Arquette. **1980**

GOSPEL ACCORDING TO VIC, THE ★★★½ In this delightful comedy from Scotland, a teacher (Tom Conti) at a Glasgow parochial school finds that he can create miracles—even though he doesn't believe in them. Those who have reveled in the subtle, sly humor of *Gregory's Girl*, *Local Hero*, and other Scottish films will find similar joys in this. Rated PG-13 for adult content. 92m. **DIR:** Charles Gormley. **CAST:** Tom Conti, Helen Mirren, David Hayman, Brian Pettifer, Jennifer Black. **1986**

GRACE QUIGLEY ★★½ After witnessing the murder of her landlord, spinster Katharine Hepburn enlists the aid of freelance hit man Nick Nolte. Hepburn wants Nolte to end her life, but not before he puts to rest some of her elderly friends who feel it is time for them to die. Extremely black comedy doesn't have enough humor and warmth to rise above its gruesome subject matter. Rated R. 87m. **DIR:** Anthony Harvey. **CAST:** Katharine Hepburn, Nick Nolte, Elizabeth Wilson, Chip Zien, Christopher Murney. **1985**

GRAND LARCENY ★★ A miscast Marilu Henner brings low this caper comedy about the American-raised daughter of a French thief, whose death results in her having to take over the "family business." Only the presence of debonair Ian McShane saves this from being a complete failure. Made for TV. 95m. **DIR:** Jeannot Szwarc. **CAST:** Marilu Henner, Ian McShane, Louis Jourdan, Omar Sharif. **1988**

GRASS IS ALWAYS GREENER OVER THE SEPTIC TANK, THE ★★★½ Carol Burnett and Charles Grodin shine in this tale of the domestic horrors of suburban life taken from Erma Bombeck's bestseller. The comedy doesn't always work, but when it does it rivals Grodin's *The Heartbreak Kid* and some of the best moments of Burnett's TV show. No rating, but the equivalent of a PG for language. 98m. **DIR:** Robert Day. **CAST:** Carol Burnett, Charles Grodin, Alex Rocco, Linda Gray. **1978**

GRASS IS GREENER, THE ★★★½ Cary Grant and Deborah Kerr star as a married couple experimenting with extramarital affairs in this comedy. Some funny moments, but it's not hilarious. 105m. **DIR:** Stanley Donen. **CAST:** Cary Grant, Deborah Kerr, Jean Simmons, Robert Mitchum. **1960**

GREAT BANK HOAX, THE ★★½ It is doubtful that viewers today will think of Watergate when watching this comedy caper, but it was originally intended as a parable. When the pillars of the community find out that the bank has been embezzled, they decide to rob it. Great characterizations by all-star cast. Rated PG. 89m. **DIR:** Joseph Jacoby. **CAST:** Richard Basehart, Burgess Meredith, Paul Sand, Ned Beatty, Michael Murphy, Arthur Godfrey. **1977**

GREAT DICTATOR, THE ★★★★★ Charlie Chaplin stars in and directs this devastating lampoon of the Third Reich. The celebrated clown's first all-talking picture, it casts him in two roles—as his famous Little Tramp and as Adenoid Hynkel, the Hitler-like ruler of Tomania. As with the similarly themed *Duck Soup*, starring the Marx Brothers, the comedy was a little too whimsical for wartime audiences. But it has to be regarded as a classic. B&W; 128m. **DIR:** Charles Chaplin. **CAST:** Charlie Chaplin, Jack Oakie, Paulette Goddard. **1940**

GREAT GUNS ★★ Although it's a cut below their classics, Sons of the Desert will love it, and so will most—especially the young. Stan and Ollie have jobs guarding a rich man's playboy son, Dick Nelson. He gets drafted; the fellows join up to continue their work. The playboy gets along just fine in khaki. The boys get up to their ears in trouble with an archetypical sergeant. B&W; 74m. **DIR:** Monty Banks. **CAST:** Stan Laurel, Oliver Hardy, Sheila Ryan. **1941**

GREAT LOVER, THE ★★★★ This is top-notch Bob Hope. The story, as usual, is simple. While on a transatlantic steamship, a timid Boy Scout leader romances lovely Rhonda Fleming and tracks down a strangler. Comedic suspense is well played. B&W; 80m. **DIR:** Alexander Hall. **CAST:** Bob Hope, Rhonda Fleming, Roland Young, Jim Backus, Roland Culver, George Reeves. **1949**

GREAT MAN VOTES, THE ★★★½ Drunken widower raises his two spunky kids in a rather unorthodox home. They are constantly harassed by the children of the more successful fathers until the party relies on Barrymore's vote to set the tone for other precincts. B&W; 72m. **DIR:** Garson Kanin. **CAST:** John Barrymore, Peter Holden, Virginia Weidler, Katharine Alexander. **1939**

GREAT MCGINTY, THE ★★★½ The ups and downs of hobo Brian Donlevy and his crooked cohort Akim Tamiroff make for very funny satire in this refreshing gem from the inventive Preston Sturges. The action is secondary to the great dialogue. The leads are fine and the rapport they share on screen is truly engaging. B&W; 83m. **DIR:** Preston Sturges. **CAST:** Brian Donlevy, Akim Tamiroff, Muriel Angelus, Louis Jean Heydt, Arthur Hoyt. **1940**

GREAT MOMENT, THE ★★ A nineteenth-century dentist promotes the use of ether as an anesthetic. Confusing blend of comedy and drama makes this bio-pic very uneven. B&W; 83m. **DIR:** Preston Sturges. **CAST:** Joel McCrea, Betty Field, William Demarest, Harry Carey, Grady Sutton, Franklin Pangborn, Jimmy Conlin, Louis Jean Heydt, Thurston Hall, Porter Hall. **1944**

GREAT OUTDOORS, THE ★★½ Another screwball comedy featuring former members of *Saturday Night Live* and *SCTV*, this stars Dan Aykroyd and John Candy as brothers-in-law battling to take charge of a family vacation in the country, where almost everything goes wrong. Aside from Aykroyd, all the characters are shallow. Rated PG for profanity. 90m. **DIR:** Howard Deutch. **CAST:** Dan Aykroyd, John Candy, Stephanie Faracy. **1988**

GREAT RACE, THE ★★★½ Set in the early 1900s, this film comically traces the daily events of the first New York–to–Paris car race. Unfortunately, two-and-a-half hours of silly spoofs will have even the most avid film fan yawning. 147m. **DIR:** Blake Edwards. **CAST:** Tony Curtis, Natalie Wood, Jack Lemmon, Peter Falk, Keenan Wynn, Larry Storch, Arthur O'Connell, Vivian Vance. **1965**

GREAT ST. TRINIAN'S TRAIN ROBBERY, THE ★★★ The last in the series of British comedies based on Ronald Searle's cartoons depicting a girls' school populated by monstrously awful brats. In this one, the students prove more than a match for thieves who have hidden loot on the school premises. Not the best of the series, but fun nonetheless. 94m. **DIR:** Frank Launder, Sidney Gilliat. **CAST:** Frankie Howerd, Reg Varney, Dora Bryan. **1966**

GREAT WALL, A ★★★½ *A Great Wall* is not a documentary about the 1,500-mile structure that rolls wavelike through northern China. Instead, it is a warm comedy about the clash of cultures that results when a Chinese-American family returns to its homeland. It is also the first American movie to be made in the People's Republic of China. As such, it gives some fascinating insights into Chinese culture and often does so in a marvelously entertaining way. Rated PG. 100m. **DIR:** Peter Wang. **CAST:** Peter Wang, Sharon Iwai, Kelvin Han Yee. **1986**

GREATEST MAN IN THE WORLD, THE ★★★★ A droll adaptation of James Thurber's tale. Brad Davis is an uncouth amateur barnstormer who outperforms Charles Lindbergh by flying nonstop around the *world*... aided by a brilliant method of fuel conservation, and fortified—during the four-day trip—by a hunk of salami and a gallon of gin. Introduced by Henry Fonda; suitable for family viewing. 51m. **DIR:** Ralph Rosenblum. **CAST:** Brad Davis, Reed Birney, John McMartin, Howard DaSilva, Carol Kane, William Prince, Sudie Bond. **1980**

GREEDY ★★★½ An aging Kirk Douglas is typically robust in this aptly named comedy. A group of scheming relatives recruit Douglas's favorite nephew, Michael J. Fox, to keep the rich old coot from throwing his millions away on a young mistress. It's only occasionally funny, but never boring. Phil Hartman is terrific as the nastiest family member. Rated PG-13 for profanity and suggested sex. 113m. **DIR:** Jonathan Lynn. **CAST:** Michael J. Fox, Kirk Douglas, Olivia d'Abo, Phil Hartman, Ed Begley Jr., Jere Burns, Colleen Camp, Bob Balaban, Joyce Hyser, Mary Ellen Trainor, Kevin McCarthy. **1994**

GREEN CARD ★★★★ Delightful old-fashioned comedy-romance from Australian writer-director Peter Weir. Gérard Depardieu plays a French immigrant-songwriter who attempts to stay in America by marrying Andie MacDowell, who needs a husband to land a choice apartment in Manhattan. Hilarious and heartwarming. Rated PG-13 for brief profanity. 108m. **DIR:** Peter Weir. **CAST:** Gérard Depardieu, Andie MacDowell, Bebe Neuwirth. **1990**

GREETINGS ★★★ Robert De Niro shines in his starring debut, an offbeat comedy about a young man's sexual odyssey through New York City. Director Brian De Palma takes a satirical overview on free love, the JFK assassination, and Vietnam. Made on a shoestring budget. Rated R for nudity and profanity. 85m. **DIR:** Brian De Palma. **CAST:** Robert De Niro, Jonathan Warden, Gerrit Graham, Allen Garfield. **1968**

GREGORY'S GIRL ★★★★½ In this utterly delightful movie from Scotland, a gangly, good-natured kid named Gregory—who has just gone through a five-inch growth spurt that has left him with the physical grace of a drunken stilt walker and made him a problem player on the school's winless soccer team—falls in love with the team's newest and best player: a girl named Dorothy. Unrated, the film has no objectionable content. 91m. **DIR:** Bill Forsyth. **CAST:**

Gordon John Sinclair, Dee Hepburn, Chic Murray, Jake D'Arcy, Alex Norton, John Bett, Clare Grogan. 1981

GROOVE TUBE, THE ★★½ A sometimes funny and most times just silly—or gross—1974 takeoff on television by writer-director Ken Shapiro. The V.D. commercial is a classic, however. Look for Chevy Chase in his first, brief screen appearance. Rated R. 75m. **DIR:** Ken Shapiro. **CAST:** Ken Shapiro, Lane Sarasohn, Chevy Chase, Richard Belzer. 1974

GROSS JOKES ★★ A group of comedians tell off-color and somewhat gross jokes culled from the book by Julius Alvin. Moderately funny. Not rated, but contains adult language and humor. 53m. **DIR:** Bob Williams. **CAST:** George Wallace, Tommy Sledge, Sheryl Bernstein, Tim Jones, Barry Diamond, Joe Alaskey, Budd Friedman. 1985

GROUNDHOG DAY ★★★½ Arrogantly self-centered TV weatherman Phil Connors (Bill Murray), practically convinced he *creates* the weather, stumbles into a time warp and winds up repeating the most insipid day of his life: twenty-four hours in Punxsutawney, Pennsylvania, during its annual Groundhog Day festivities. The film actually displays some heart in its last act. Rated PG for profanity. 103m. **DIR:** Harold Ramis. **CAST:** Bill Murray, Andie MacDowell, Chris Elliott, Stephen Tobolowsky. 1993

GRUMPY OLD MEN ★★★★ A howlingly funny tale of two longtime rivals (Walter Matthau and Jack Lemmon) fighting over the affections of sexy new neighbor Ann-Margret. Lemmon and Matthau are in top form, but 84-year-old Burgess Meredith, as Lemmon's irascible father, has the film's funniest lines. Be sure to catch the outtakes shown during the closing credits for a laugh-filled capper to this comic gem. Rated PG-13 for sexual references. 105m. **DIR:** Donald Petrie. **CAST:** Jack Lemmon, Walter Matthau, Ann-Margret, Daryl Hannah, Burgess Meredith, Kevin Pollak, Ossie Davis, Buck Henry. 1993

GUARDING TESS ★★★★ Secret service agent Nicolas Cage wants out of his current assignment—looking after feisty former first lady Shirley MacLaine—but she has other ideas in this highly entertaining comedy-drama. MacLaine and Cage do not immediately spring to mind as a perfect pairing, but they work extremely well together. Intriguing characters, some genuine laughs, a few tears, and even a sprinkle of suspense. Rated PG-13 for profanity and light violence. 98m. **DIR:** Hugh Wilson. **CAST:** Shirley MacLaine, Nicolas Cage, Austin Pendleton, Edward Albert, James Rebhorn, Richard Griffiths, Harry J. Lennix. 1994

GUARDSMAN, THE ★★★★ A movie landmark since it is the only film to costar Broadway's Alfred Lunt and Lynn Fontanne. This film also recorded their most successful roles for posterity. Ferenc Molnar wrote the original play about a man who tests his wife's faithfulness by posing as a macho, romantic Russian guardsman. B&W; 83m. **DIR:** Sidney Franklin. **CAST:** Alfred Lunt, Lynn Fontanne, Roland Young, ZaSu Pitts, Maude Eburne, Herman Bing. 1931

GUEST WIFE ★★½ Claudette Colbert poses as foreign correspondent Don Ameche's wife to fool the boss, who thinks he's married. Funny and cute but not that funny and cute. B&W; 90m. **DIR:** Sam Wood. **CAST:** Claudette Colbert, Don Ameche, Dick Foran, Charles Dingle, Grant Mitchell, Irving Bacon. 1945

GUIDE FOR THE MARRIED MAN, A ★★★½ Worldly Robert Morse tries to teach reluctant Walter Matthau the fundamentals of adultery. His lessons are acted out by a dazzling roster of top comedy stars. This episodic film provides a steady stream of laughs. The bit in which Joey Bishop is caught red-handed and practices the "deny, deny, deny" technique is a classic. 89m. **DIR:** Gene Kelly. **CAST:** Walter Matthau, Inger Stevens, Robert Morse, Sue Ane Langdon, Lucille Ball, Jack Benny, Joey Bishop, Art Carney, Jayne Mansfield, Carl Reiner, Sid Caesar, Phil Silvers, Jeffrey Hunter, Sam Jaffe. 1967

GUIDE FOR THE MARRIED WOMAN, A ★★½ In this made-for-television movie, Cybill Shepherd plays a frustrated housewife who decides that life must hold more excitement than her current predictable situation. Though the cast includes many big names, this film never really takes off and is no match for the earlier *Guide for the Married Man.* 100m. **DIR:** Hy Averback. **CAST:** Cybill Shepherd, Charles Frank, John Hillerman, Elaine Joyce, Peter Marshall, Eve Arden. 1978

GUILTY AS CHARGED 🦃 Black comedy fans are in for a shock with this unfunny tale of a vigilante who tracks down criminals and gives them the hot seat in his homemade electric chair. Pull the plug on this puppy before it short-circuits. Rated R for violence. 93m. **DIR:** Sam Irvin. **CAST:** Rod Steiger, Lauren Hutton, Isaac Hayes, Heather Graham. 1991

GULLIVER IN LILLIPUT ★★ This British TV movie stays fairly close to the Jonathan Swift classic satire of small-minded people. Probably too close because it's not long before these bickering people stop being funny and start getting on your nerves. Not rated, but contains no objectionable material. 107m. **DIR:** Barry Letts. **CAST:** Andrew Burt, Elizabeth Sladen. 1982

GUMSHOE ★★★½ Every hard-bitten private-eye film and *film noir* is saluted in this crime-edged comedy. Liverpool bingo caller Albert Finney finds himself in deep, murky water when he tries to live his fantasy of being a Humphrey Bogart–type shamus. Raymond Chandler and Dashiell Hammett fans will love every frame. Rated PG. 88m. **DIR:** Stephen Frears. **CAST:** Albert Finney, Billie Whitelaw, Frank Finlay, Janice Rule, Caroline Seymour. **1972**

GUMSHOE KID, THE ★★½ Wannabe gumshoe Jay Underwood quits school to join the family private eye business. Rated R for nudity and violence. 98m. **DIR:** Joseph Manduke. **CAST:** Jay Underwood, Tracy Scoggins, Vince Edwards. **1990**

GUN IN BETTY LOU'S HANDBAG, THE ★★½ In order to get into the spirit of this generally predictable screwball comedy, one has to accept screenwriter Grace Cary Bickley's premise that a neglected wife would claim to be a murderer to get her police-detective husband's attention. Breathlessly sincere performances by Penelope Ann Miller and Eric Thal make it as entertaining as it is dumb. Rated PG-13 for profanity and violence. 90m. **DIR:** Alan Moyle. **CAST:** Penelope Ann Miller, Eric Thal, Alfre Woodard, William Forsythe, Cathy Moriarty. **1992**

GUNG HO (1985) ★★★★ Another winner from director Ron Howard and writers Lowell Ganz and Babaloo Mandel, who previously teamed on *Night Shift* and *Splash*. This is a pointed study of the cultural chaos that occurs when small-town Hadleyville's automobile plant is rescued by imported Japanese management. Rated PG-13 for language. 111m. **DIR:** Ron Howard. **CAST:** Michael Keaton, Gedde Watanabe, George Wendt, Mimi Rogers, John Turturro, Clint Howard. **1985**

H.O.T.S. ★★ Drive-in special about two feuding sororities whose battles culminate in a topless football game. Cheerfully raunchy trash for those times when you're not quite up to Ingmar Bergman. Rated R for plentiful nudity. 95m. **DIR:** Gerald Sindell. **CAST:** Susan Kiger, Lisa London, Danny Bonaduce. **1979**

HAIL CAESAR 🦃 Director-star Anthony Michael Hall tries to prove his worth to his girlfriend's father so that he may pursue his first love: rock and roll. This *Caesar* takes a stab at comedy and misses. Rated PG for language and adult situations. 93m. **DIR:** Anthony Michael Hall. **CAST:** Anthony Michael Hall, Robert Downey Jr., Judd Nelson, Samuel L. Jackson, Frank Gorshin. **1994**

HAIL THE CONQUERING HERO ★★★★½ Defense plant worker Eddie Bracken is passed off by Marine buddies as the hero of Guadalcanal and his hometown goes overboard in adulation and tribute. Another winning satire from writer-director Preston Sturges. Fine family viewing. B&W; 101m. **DIR:** Preston Sturges. **CAST:** Eddie Bracken, Ella Raines, William Demarest, Raymond Walburn, Franklin Pangborn. **1944**

HAIRSPRAY ★★★ Writer-director John Waters's ode to the dance craze of the Sixties features some outrageously campy performances. The story revolves around the desire of a pudgy teen (Ricki Lake) to be one of the featured stars on a Baltimore TV show in 1963. Rated PG. 87m. **DIR:** John Waters. **CAST:** Sonny Bono, Divine, Colleen Fitzpatrick, Deborah Harry, Ricki Lake, Leslie Ann Powers, Clayton Prince, Jerry Stiller, Mink Stole, Shawn Thompson, Pia Zadora. **1988**

HALF-SHOT AT SUNRISE 🦃 This dated story of World War I doughboys trying to score with the gals was stale even when it was released. B&W; 78m. **DIR:** Paul Sloane. **CAST:** Bert Wheeler, Robert Woolsey, Dorothy Lee, Edna May Oliver. **1930**

HAMBURGER—THE MOTION PICTURE 🦃 A very funny comedy could be made about the fast-food industry, but this isn't it. Rated R for profanity, nudity, suggested sex, and violence. 90m. **DIR:** Mike Marvin. **CAST:** Leigh McCloskey, Sandy Hackett, Randi Brooks, Charles Tyner, Chuck McCann, Dick Butkus. **1986**

HAMMERED: THE BEST OF SLEDGE ★★ Well-intentioned but flat takeoff of tough cop movies and TV shows, *Hammered* stars David Rasche as Detective Sledge Hammer, a man who talks to his gun and loves extreme and senseless violence. This is a compilation of four *Sledge Hammer* TV shows. 104m. **DIR:** Jackie Cooper, Gary Walkow, Martha Coolidge. **CAST:** David Rasche, Anne-Marie Martin, Harrison Page, John Vernon. **1986**

HAMMERSMITH IS OUT ★★★½ In this black comedy an insane criminal is sprung from an asylum by an ambitious attendant. Gaining strength and polish as the plot unfolds, the film promises a bit more than it actually offers. Rated R for profanity, sexual situations, and mild violence. 108m. **DIR:** Peter Ustinov. **CAST:** Elizabeth Taylor, Richard Burton, Peter Ustinov, Beau Bridges, George Raft, John Schuck. **1971**

HANDS UP! ★★★★ A rare opportunity to see the amazing, dapper Raymond Griffith, one of the neglected comic stylists of the 1920s. He's a Confederate spy during the Civil War. A major find. Silent. B&W; 58m. **DIR:** Clarence Badger. **CAST:** Raymond Griffith, Marion Nixon, Mack Swain. **1926**

HANGIN' WITH THE HOMEBOYS ★★★★ A multicultural *Wayne's World*, this features four young men—two black, two Puerto Rican—on the brink of nowhere. All unsuccessful, they gather for a boys' night out. Bittersweet, with both hilarious and tragic scenes. A low-budget gem. Rated R for nudity, violence, and profanity. 89m. **DIR:** Joseph B. Vasquez. **CAST:** Doug E. Doug, Mario Joyner, John Leguizamo. **1991**

HANKY PANKY ★★ In an obvious takeoff on the Hitchcock suspense formula, this seldom funny comedy features Gene Wilder as an innocent man caught up in international intrigue and murder. Rated PG for violence and gore. 110m. **DIR:** Sidney Poitier. **CAST:** Gene Wilder, Gilda Radner, Richard Widmark, Kathleen Quinlan, Robert Prosky. **1982**

HANNAH AND HER SISTERS ★★★★★ One of Woody Allen's very best, a two-year study of a family held together by housemother Mia Farrow. Hannah is best friend, trusted confidante, and sympathetic peacemaker for sisters Barbara Hershey and Dianne Wiest, husband Michael Caine, and parents Maureen O'Sullivan and Lloyd Nolan. Woody's along for a glib part as a hypochondriac who may get his fondest wish: a fatal disease. Rated PG-13 for sexual situations. 106m. **DIR:** Woody Allen. **CAST:** Woody Allen, Michael Caine, Mia Farrow, Carrie Fisher, Barbara Hershey, Maureen O'Sullivan, Dianne Wiest, Max von Sydow, Daniel Stern, Lloyd Nolan, Sam Waterston. **1986**

HAPPY BIRTHDAY, GEMINI ★★ A strong play about a sexual-identity crisis becomes a weak movie when the sexuality is toned down too much. The movie doesn't need graphic sex scenes, just some intelligent dialogue so the characters can communicate with each other. The story is about a newly graduated Harvard man who thinks he may be gay. The sparkling supporting cast keeps the movie moving. Rated R. 107m. **DIR:** Richard Benner. **CAST:** Madeline Kahn, Rita Moreno, David Marshall Grant, Robert Viharo. **1980**

HAPPY HOOKER, THE ★★★ After Xaviera Hollander's novel became a bestseller, Lynn Redgrave was cast as Hollander in this offbeat comedy. Redgrave recounts Hollander's rise from free-lance prostitute to one of New York's most infamous madams. Viewers get a peek at the kinky scenes when they play the sex-for-hire game. Rated R for nudity and sex. 96m. **DIR:** Nicholas Sgarro. **CAST:** Lynn Redgrave, Jean-Pierre Aumont, Elizabeth Wilson, Tom Poston, Lovelady Powell, Nicholas Pryor. **1975**

HAPPY HOOKER GOES HOLLYWOOD, THE ★★ If you've ever wanted to see Adam (*Batman*) West in drag, here's your chance. Lots of other people embarrass themselves as well in this comedy that certainly tries hard for laughs (though it gets very few). Rated R, but it's all talk and no action. 85m. **DIR:** Alan Roberts. **CAST:** Martine Beswick, Chris Lemmon, Adam West, Phil Silvers, Richard Deacon, Edie Adams, Dick Miller. **1980**

HAPPY HOOKER GOES TO WASHINGTON, THE 🦃 Xaviera Hollander (Joey Heatherton) is called to Washington. Rated R. 89m. **DIR:** William A. Levey. **CAST:** Joey Heatherton, George Hamilton, Ray Walston, Jack Carter. **1977**

HAPPY HOUR ★★ Blah comedy about a chemist's discovery of a secret ingredient that makes beer irresistible. A lot of T&A, and a good peformance by Rich Little as a superspy, but the premise keeps the film's comedic stock low. Not rated, coarse language. 88m. **DIR:** John DeBello. **CAST:** Richard Gilliland, Jamie Farr, Tawny Kitaen, Rich Little. **1986**

HAPPY NEW YEAR ★★★½ Another film that was the victim of the studio system; it received only a marginal theatrical release. Peter Falk deserves to be seen in his multirole performance. He and Charles Durning are a couple of con men planning a jewel heist in Florida. (Based on Claude Lelouch's 1973 French film of the same name.) Rated PG. 86m. **DIR:** John G. Avildsen. **CAST:** Peter Falk, Charles Durning, Tom Courtenay, Wendy Hughes. **1987**

HAPPY TOGETHER ★★½ This college romance is basically a 1990s retread of *The Sterile Cuckoo,* with Helen Slater taking a spirited whirl at the Liza Minnelli role. Slater is a charming, underrated actress, but she tries too hard—as does the film as a whole. Rated PG-13. 102m. **DIR:** Mel Damski. **CAST:** Patrick Dempsey, Helen Slater. **1990**

HARD COUNTRY ★★★½ Though it tries to make a statement about the contemporary cowboy lost in the modern world and feminism in the boondocks, this is really just lighthearted entertainment. A rockabilly love story of the macho man (Jan-Michael Vincent) versus the liberated woman (Kim Basinger). Rated PG. 104m. **DIR:** David Greene. **CAST:** Jan-Michael Vincent, Michael Parks, Kim Basinger, Tanya Tucker, Ted Neeley, Daryl Hannah. **1981**

HARD WAY, THE (1991) ★★★½ Formulaic buddy movie about a movie star attempting to research a cop role by hanging out with the real thing. Engaging performances by Michael J. Fox and James Woods. Rated R for profanity and violence. 95m. **DIR:** John Badham. **CAST:** Michael J. Fox, James Woods, Penny Marshall, Stephen Lang, Annabella Sciorra. **1991**

HARDBODIES 🦃 Three middle-aged men rent a summer beach house in hopes of seducing teenage girls. Rated R for nudity, simulated sex, and profanity. 90m. **DIR:** Mark Griffiths. **CAST:** Grant Cramer, Teal Roberts, Gary Wood, Michael Rappaport, Roberta Collins. **1984**

HARDBODIES 2 🦃 Sexual antics of a group of students on an academic cruise. Rated R for nudity and profanity. 89m. **DIR:** Mark Griffiths. **CAST:** Brad Zutaut, James Karen. **1986**

HARDLY WORKING ★★ Jerry Lewis's 1980s screen comeback is passable family fare. As a middle-aged, out-of-work clown, he tries his hand at a number of jobs and flubs them all. His fans will love it; others need not apply. Rated PG. 91m. **DIR:** Jerry Lewis. **CAST:** Jerry Lewis, Susan Oliver, Roger C. Carmel, Deanna Lund, Harold J. Stone, Steve Franken. **1981**

HAROLD AND MAUDE ★★★★★ Hal Ashby directed this delightful black comedy about an odd young man named Harold (Bud Cort) who devises some rather elaborate fake deaths to jar his snooty, manipulative mother (Vivian Pickles). Soon his attention turns to an octogenarian named Maude (Ruth Gordon), with whom he falls in love. Featuring a superb sound track of songs by Cat Stevens, this is one of the original cult classics—and deservedly so. Rated PG. 90m. **DIR:** Hal Ashby. **CAST:** Bud Cort, Vivian Pickles, Ruth Gordon, Cyril Cusack, Charles Tyner, Ellen Geer. **1972**

HAROLD LLOYD'S COMEDY CLASSICS ★★★ This nostalgic retrospective combines four of Harold Lloyd's prestardom shorts: *The Chef, The Cinema Director, Two Gun Gussie,* and *I'm On My Way.* Silent with musical score. Compiled after Lloyd's death. B&W; 47m. **DIR:** Harold Lloyd. **CAST:** Harold Lloyd, Bebe Daniels, Snub Pollard. **1919**

HARPER VALLEY P.T.A. ★★ Based on the popular country song, this silly piece of fluff features Barbara Eden as the sexy woman who gives her gossiping neighbors their proper comeuppance. Rated PG. 102m. **DIR:** Richard Bennett. **CAST:** Barbara Eden, Ronny Cox, Nanette Fabray, Susan Swift, Ron Masak. **1978**

HARRY AND WALTER GO TO NEW YORK ★★½ James Caan and Elliott Gould appear to be having the time of their lives portraying two inept con men. Michael Caine and Diane Keaton are, as always, excellent. *Harry and Walter* is sort of like Chinese food—an hour later, you feel as if you haven't had anything. Rated PG. 123m. **DIR:** Mark Rydell. **CAST:** James Caan, Elliott Gould, Michael Caine, Diane Keaton, Charles Durning. **1976**

HARRY'S WAR ★★ In this cornball comedy, Harry Johnson (Edward Herrmann) takes on the Internal Revenue Service, which made a mistake on his return. Rated PG. 98m. **DIR:** Kieth Merrill. **CAST:** Edward Herrmann, Geraldine Page, Karen Grassle, David Ogden Stiers, Salome Jens, Elisha Cook Jr. **1981**

HARVEY ★★★★½ James Stewart has one of his best screen roles as Elwood P. Dowd, a delightful drunk whose companion is a six-foot rabbit named Harvey. Josephine Hull is the concerned relative who wants Elwood committed to a mental institution, and Cecil Kellaway is the psychiatrist who discovers there's more magic than madness to our hero's illusion. B&W; 104m. **DIR:** Henry Koster. **CAST:** James Stewart, Josephine Hull, Peggy Dow, Charles Drake, Cecil Kellaway. **1950**

HAUNTED HONEYMOON 🦃 Limp chiller spoof. Rated PG. 90m. **DIR:** Gene Wilder. **CAST:** Gene Wilder, Gilda Radner, Dom DeLuise, Jonathan Pryce, Paul Smith, Peter Vaughan. **1986**

HAVING A WONDERFUL CRIME ★★★ Pat O'Brien plays a lawyer who gets together with amateur sleuths Carole Landis and George Murphy to find out why a magician mysteriously disappeared. A murder mystery played for laughs with a cast who can put it across. B&W; 71m. **DIR:** A. Edward Sutherland. **CAST:** Pat O'Brien, Carole Landis, George Murphy, Gloria Holden, George Zucco. **1945**

HAVING A WONDERFUL TIME 🦃 Based on a Broadway stage hit, this was *supposed* to be romance and comedy at a famed Catskills resort hotel. B&W; 71m. **DIR:** Alfred Santell. **CAST:** Ginger Rogers, Douglas Fairbanks Jr., Red Skelton, Lucille Ball, Eve Arden, Lee Bowman, Jack Carson. **1938**

HAVING IT ALL ★★★ Dyan Cannon makes up for any script deficiencies with sheer exuberance. In this remake of *The Captain's Paradise,* the roles are reversed, and Cannon plays the bigamist. As a fashion designer, she is constantly traveling between New York and Los Angeles. She has a home and husband in each and manages to juggle the two. Made for TV, this is unrated. 100m. **DIR:** Edward Zwick. **CAST:** Dyan Cannon, Hart Bochner, Barry Newman, Sylvia Sidney, Melanie Chartoff. **1982**

HAWMPS! 🦃 Old West cavalry unit uses camels instead of horses. Rated G. 120m. **DIR:** Joe Camp. **CAST:** James Hampton, Christopher Connelly, Slim Pickens, Denver Pyle, Jack Elam. **1976**

HE SAID, SHE SAID ★★★½ When telling friends how they got together, married directors Ken Kwapis and Marisa Silver were surprised to hear how much their stories differed. So they decided to make a movie about a courting couple (Kevin Bacon, Elizabeth Perkins) and the male/female opposing views of the romance. Slight, but charming. Rated PG-13 for profanity. 115m. **DIR:** Ken Kwapis, Marisa Silver. **CAST:** Kevin Bacon, Elizabeth Perkins, Sharon Stone, Nathan Lane, Anthony LaPaglia. **1990**

HEAD OFFICE ★★ A sometimes funny comedy about the son of an influential politician who upon graduating from college gets a high-paying job with a major corporation. Rated PG-13. 90m. **DIR:** Ken Finkleman. **CAST:** Judge Reinhold, Lori-Nan Engler, Eddie Albert, Merritt Butrick, Ron Frazier, Richard Masur, Rick Moranis, Jane Seymour, Danny DeVito. **1985**

HEADS ★★★ Talk about disappointments! This darkly satirical slice of small-town somnambulism opens brilliantly, but fails to fulfill its potential. Jon Cryer is perfect as a rookie reporter for the moribund *Dry Falls Daily Document,* the newspaper for a community brought to life when decapitated townsfolk start popping up. Sadly, events quickly collapse into a conventional (and boring) murder mystery. Rated R for gore, profanity, and simulated sex. 102m. **DIR:** Paul Shapiro. **CAST:** Jon Cryer, Edward Asner, Jennifer Tilly, Shawn Thompson, Roddy McDowall. **1994**

HEAR MY SONG ★★★★ A gentle satire in the style of *Local Hero* and *Gregory's Girl*, this English import tells the sly story of a promoter (Adrian Dunbar, who cowrote the screenplay) who attempts to fool the public one time too many. It's charming, heartwarming, and funny. Rated R for profanity, nudity, and brief violence. 104m. **DIR:** Peter Chelsom. **CAST:** Ned Beatty, Adrian Dunbar, Shirley Anne Field, Tara Fitzgerald, William Hootkins. **1991**

HEART CONDITION ★★★ By sheer force of talent, Bob Hoskins and Denzel Washington turn this formulaic movie into something worth watching. Hoskins is a racist cop who has a heart attack and is given recently deceased Washington's heart in a transplant operation. Rent this one on discount night, and it just may put a smile on your face. Rated R for profanity, sexual situations, and violence. 90m. **DIR:** James D. Parriott. **CAST:** Bob Hoskins, Denzel Washington, Chloe Webb, Roger E. Mosley. **1990**

HEARTBREAK HOUSE ★★★½ Rex Harrison is ideally cast as George Bernard Shaw's Captain Shotover. At Shotover's house the guests include his two daughters and a visiting young woman, each in the grip of romantic trauma. What is presented is essentially an ongoing collision of philosophies, but the able cast keeps the debate lively. Unrated, but with no objectionable material. 122m. **DIR:** Anthony Page. **CAST:** Rex Harrison, Amy Irving, Rosemary Harris. **1985**

HEARTBREAK KID, THE ★★★★ The lack of care or commitment in the modern marriage is satirized in this comedy. Charles Grodin plays a young man who's grown tired of his wife while driving to their honeymoon in Florida. By the time he sees beautiful Cybill Shepherd on the beach, his marriage has totally disintegrated. Jeannie Berlin, director Elaine May's daughter, is the big scene stealer as Grodin's whining bride. Rated PG. 104m. **DIR:** Elaine May. **CAST:** Charles Grodin, Cybill Shepherd, Jeannie Berlin, Eddie Albert, Audra Lindley. **1972**

HEARTBURN ★★★½ Uneven adaptation of Nora Ephron's novel (she also wrote the screenplay) and a thinly disguised account of her own separation from Watergate journalist Carl Bernstein. Jack Nicholson and Meryl Streep fall in love, get married, and drift apart. Its strength comes from the superb performances by the stars and an incredible supporting cast. Needlessly rated R for language. 108m. **DIR:** Mike Nichols. **CAST:** Meryl Streep, Jack Nicholson, Jeff Daniels, Maureen Stapleton, Stockard Channing, Richard Masur, Catherine O'Hara, Milos Forman. **1986**

HEARTS OF THE WEST ★★★ Pleasant little comedy-drama about an aspiring writer from Iowa (Jeff Bridges) who, determined to pen masterful Westerns, winds up in Hollywood as a most reluctant cowboy. The setting is the early 1920s, and the story playfully explores many classic Western myths. Rated PG. 103m. **DIR:** Howard Zieff. **CAST:** Jeff Bridges, Alan Arkin, Blythe Danner, Andy Griffith. **1975**

HEATHERS ★★★★ A *Dr. Strangelove* or *Blue Velvet* of the teen set, this brash black comedy tackles such typically adolescent issues as peer pressure, high school cliques, heterosexuality, and homosexuality—and even teen suicide—in ways that are inventive, irreverent, startling, and occasionally offensive. Rated R; with violence and profanity. 110m. **DIR:** Michael Lehmann. **CAST:** Winona Ryder, Christian Slater, Kim Walker. **1989**

HEAT'S ON, THE ★★½ After a three-year absence Mae West returned to the screen as a Broadway star caught between two rival producers. She shouldn't have bothered, since the firmly entrenched Hays Office knocked out the double entendres for which she was noted. Her last film until 1970's dismal *Myra Breckenridge*. B&W; 80m. **DIR:** Gregory Ratoff. **CAST:** Mae West, Victor Moore, William Gaxton, Lloyd Bridges, Lina Romay, Xavier Cugat, Hazel Scott. **1943**

HEAVEN CAN WAIT (1943) ★★★★★ Newly deceased Don Ameche meets "Your Excellency" (the devil) and reviews his roguish life. If ever you wondered what was meant by "the Lubitsch touch," *Heaven Can Wait* explains it. Quite simply this is the most joyful fantasy-love story ever filmed. 112m. **DIR:** Ernst Lubitsch. **CAST:** Don Ameche, Gene Tierney, Charles Coburn, Laird Cregar, Spring Byington, Eugene Pallette, Marjorie Main, Louis Calhern, Signe Hasso, Allyn Joslyn, Florence Bates. **1943**

HEAVEN CAN WAIT (1978) ★★★★½ In this charming, thoroughly entertaining remake of *Here Comes Mr. Jordan* (1941), Warren Beatty stars as quarterback Joe Pendleton, who meets a premature demise when an overzealous angel (Buck Henry) takes the athlete's spirit out of his body after an accident. As it turns out, it wasn't Joe's time to die. However, in the interim, his body is cremated. Thus begins a quest by Joe, the angel, and his superior (James Mason) to find a proper earthly replacement. Rated PG. 100m. **DIR:** Warren Beatty, Buck Henry. **CAST:** Warren Beatty, Julie Christie, Jack Warden, Dyan Cannon, Charles Grodin, James Mason, Buck Henry, Vincent Gardenia. **1978**

HEAVEN HELP US ★★ Donald Sutherland, John Heard, Wallace Shawn, and Kate Reid support the youthful cast of this comedy about a group of schoolboys (played by Andrew McCarthy, Kevin Dillon, Malcolm Dunarie, and Stephen Geoffreys) discovering the opposite sex and other adolescent pursuits. Rated R. 90m. **DIR:** Michael Dinner. **CAST:** Andrew McCarthy, Kevin Dillon, Malcolm Dunarie, Stephen Geoffreys, Donald Sutherland, John Heard, Wallace Shawn, Kate Reid. **1985**

HEAVENLY BODIES 🦃 More sweaty dancing bodies à la *Flashdance*. Rated R for nudity, profanity, and sexual innuendo. 90m. **DIR:** Lawrence Dane. **CAST:** Cynthia Dale, Richard Rebiere, Laura Henry. **1985**

HEAVENLY KID, THE ★★ *The Heavenly Kid* is earthbound. Cocky Bobby Fontana (Lewis Smith) bit the big one in a chicken race seventeen years ago: which would make it 1968, but the sound track and the wardrobe are definitely 1955—a basic problem rendering this otherwise simply stupid film completely unintelligible. Rated PG-13 for language, situations, and bare body parts. 90m. **DIR:** Cary Medoway. **CAST:** Lewis Smith, Jason Gedrick, Jane Kaczmarek, Richard Mulligan. **1985**

HEAVENS ABOVE ★★★½ Another low-key gem from the late Peter Sellers, this irreverent story of a clergyman with the common touch spoofs just about everything within reach, some of it brilliantly. Sellers shows his congregation the error of their selfish ways and engages them in some odd charities, often with hilarious results. B&W; 105m. **DIR:** John Boulting, Roy Boulting. **CAST:** Peter Sellers, Cecil Parker, Isabel Jeans, Eric Sykes. **1963**

HELLO AGAIN ★★½ Suburban housewife Shelley Long chokes to death on a Korean meatball only to find herself brought back to life via a magic spell cast by her wacky sister (Judith Ivey). Screenplay by Susan Isaacs. Rated PG for profanity. 95m. **DIR:** Frank Perry. **CAST:** Shelley Long, Judith Ivey, Gabriel Byrne, Corbin Bernsen, Sela Ward, Austin Pendleton. **1987**

HER ALIBI ★★★ This clever comedy-mystery presents Tom Selleck as a suspense writer who provides an alibi for a beautiful murder suspect (Paulina Porizkova). Fans of director Bruce Beresford may think this ditty is beneath him, but only a curmudgeon can resist its daffy charms. Rated PG for profanity and comic violence. 110m. **DIR:** Bruce Beresford. **CAST:** Tom Selleck, Paulina Porizkova, William Daniels, Tess Harper, Patrick Wayne, Hurd Hatfield. **1989**

HERCULES GOES BANANAS 🦃 Ridiculous piece of celluloid starring a very young Arnold Schwarzenegger as Hercules. 73m. **DIR:** Arthur Allan Seidelman. **CAST:** Arnold Schwarzenegger, Arnold Stang. **1972**

HERE COME THE CO-EDS ★★½ Standard-issue Abbott and Costello romp of the mid-1940s, with our heroes cast as custodians of a prim girls' academy. High energy, low IQ comedy. B&W; 87m. **DIR:** Jean Yarbrough. **CAST:** Bud Abbott, Lou Costello, Peggy Ryan, Martha O'Driscoll, Lon Chaney Jr. **1945**

HERE COMES MR. JORDAN ★★★★★ We all know that bureaucracy can botch up almost anything. Well, the bureaucrats of heaven can really throw a lulu at boxer Joe Pendleton (Robert Montgomery). The heavenly administrators have called Joe up before his time, and they've got to set things straight. That's the basis for the delightful fantasy *Here Comes Mr. Jordan*. B&W; 93m. **DIR:** Alexander Hall. **CAST:** Robert Montgomery, Evelyn Keyes, Claude Rains, Rita Johnson, Edward Everett Horton, James Gleason. **1941**

HERE COMES TROUBLE ★★★ Jewel thief Mona Barrie mistakenly involves Paul Kelly in a crime when she gives him a cigarette case containing some loot. A mixture of comedy and crime—a perfect hour-long time filler. B&W; 62m. **DIR:** Lewis Seiler. **CAST:** Paul Kelly, Arline Judge, Mona Barrie, Gregory Ratoff. **1936**

HERO ★★★★½ This saucy spin on Frank Capra's *Meet John Doe* is an acerbic—and often tremendously funny—indictment of American hero-worship. Andy Garcia is revered for having rescued passengers from a stricken airplane; unfortunately, he's taking credit for an act actually performed by small-potatoes criminal Dustin Hoffman (who, looking more ferret-like than ever, is simply priceless). Rated PG-13 for profanity. 116m. **DIR:** Stephen Frears. **CAST:** Dustin Hoffman, Geena Davis, Andy Garcia, Joan Cusack, Chevy Chase, Tom Arnold. **1992**

HERO AT LARGE ★★★½ In this enjoyably lightweight film, John Ritter plays Steve Nichols, an out-of-work actor who takes a part-time job to promote a movie about a crusading superhero, *Captain Avenger*. Rated PG. 98m. **DIR:** Martin Davidson. **CAST:** John Ritter, Anne Archer, Bert Convy, Kevin McCarthy. **1980**

HE'S MY GIRL 🦃 Two musicians win a chance at a recording contract. Rated PG-13 for profanity. 104m. **DIR:** Gabrielle Beaumont. **CAST:** T. K. Carter, David Hallyday. **1987**

HEXED ★★ A hotel desk clerk with pathological liar tendencies gets mixed up in a bizarre twist of mistaken identity. This wannabe curiosity comedy from the creator of the TV series *Sledge Hammer* doesn't quite know the difference between being outrageous and being absolutely tasteless. Rated R for violence, simulated sex, and language. 100m. **DIR:** Alan Spencer. **CAST:** Arye Gross, Claudia Christian, Adrienne Shelly, Norman Fell, Michael E. Knight, Ray Baker. **1993**

HEY ABBOTT! ★★★★ This is a hilarious anthology of high points from Abbott and

Costello television programs. Narrated by Milton Berle, the distillation includes the now-legendary duo's classic routines: "Who's on First?," "Oyster Stew," "Floogle Street," and "The Birthday Party." B&W; 76m. **DIR:** Jim Gates. **CAST:** Bud Abbott, Lou Costello, Joe Besser, Phil Silvers, Steve Allen. **1978**

HI MOM ★★★ Robert De Niro reprises his role as a Vietnam vet in this award-winning comedy under the direction of a young Brian De Palma. In this semi-sequel to *Greetings*, De Niro continues his adventures as an amateur filmmaker in Greenwich Village. Rated R for nudity and profanity. 87m. **DIR:** Brian De Palma. **CAST:** Robert De Niro, Jennifer Salt, Allen Garfield. **1970**

HIGH ANXIETY ★★ Mel Brooks successfully spoofed the horror film with *Young Frankenstein* and the Western with *Blazing Saddles*. However, this takeoff of the Alfred Hitchcock suspense movies falls miserably flat. Rated PG. 94m. **DIR:** Mel Brooks. **CAST:** Mel Brooks, Madeline Kahn, Cloris Leachman, Harvey Korman, Dick Van Patten, Ron Carey. **1977**

HIGH HOPES ★★★★★ A biting satire of Margaret Thatcher's England, as viewed by three distinct, combative couples in modern London. Ruth Sheen and Philip Davis are memorable as two latter-day hippie leftists who name their cactus Thatcher because it's a pain in the you-know-where. 100m. **DIR:** Mike Leigh. **CAST:** Ruth Sheen, Philip Davis. **1989**

HIGH SCHOOL, USA ★★ The fact that the dancing robot is the best actor in this film should tell you something. This made-for-TV feature is your typical teen flick, which is exceptional only because it doesn't rely on nudity and foul language to hold its audience's attention. 96m. **DIR:** Rod Amateau. **CAST:** Michael J. Fox, Dwayne Hickman, Angela Cartwright. **1983**

HIGH SEASON ★★★★ This delightfully pixilated comedy-mystery presents a group of people feuding, faking, laughing, and loving on a breathtaking Greek isle. Cowritten and directed by Clare Peploe, the wife of Bernardo Bertolucci, *High Season* offers Jacqueline Bisset as a photographer and James Fox as her sculptor husband. Rated R for brief nudity and adult themes. 104m. **DIR:** Clare Peploe. **CAST:** Jacqueline Bisset, Irene Papas, James Fox, Kenneth Branagh, Sebastian Shaw, Robert Stephens. **1988**

HIGH SPIRITS 🦃 Peter O'Toole tries to generate revenue for the ancient family castle by proclaiming it a haunted tourist trap. Rated PG-13 for language and mild sexual themes. 97m. **DIR:** Neil Jordan. **CAST:** Peter O'Toole, Steve Guttenberg, Daryl Hannah, Beverly D'Angelo, Jennifer Tilly, Liam Neeson. **1988**

HIGH STAKES (1986) ★★ Hoping to become a star reporter, a young daydreamer gets his chance when he uncovers a criminal plot to unearth a hidden Nazi treasure. His Walter Mitty–ish fantasies are the least appealing part of the movie, but some funny supporting characters and one-liners compensate. Unrated. 82m. **DIR:** Larry Kent. **CAST:** David Foley, Roberta Weiss, Winston Rekert. **1986**

HIGHWAY 61 ★★★ A wacky, somewhat surreal road comedy about a small-town Canadian barber whose claim to fame is finding a dead body. When the corpse's sister—a refugee from a rock 'n' roll crew—appears, they go on a journey down one of North America's most famous highways. Rated R for profanity, simulated sex, and nudity. 105m. **DIR:** Bruce McDonald. **CAST:** Valerie Buhagiar, Don McKellar, Earl Pastko. **1992**

HILLBILLYS IN A HAUNTED HOUSE 🦃 Unbelievably bad mishmash of country corn and horror humor. 88m. **DIR:** Jean Yarbrough. **CAST:** Ferlin Husky, Joi Lansing, Don Bowman, John Carradine, Lon Chaney Jr., Basil Rathbone, Molly Bee, Merle Haggard, Sonny James. **1967**

HIPS, HIPS, HOORAY ★★★ Clowns Bert Wheeler and Robert Woolsey liven up this early, somewhat blue, comedy-musical. The pair play havoc as they invade Thelma Todd's ailing cosmetic business. B&W; 68m. **DIR:** Mark Sandrich. **CAST:** Bert Wheeler, Robert Woolsey, Thelma Todd, Ruth Etting, George Meeker, Dorothy Lee. **1934**

HIS DOUBLE LIFE ★★★ Edwardian novelist Arnold Bennett's comedy about a wealthy recluse who finds a better life by becoming a valet when his valet dies and is buried under his name. Remade with Monty Woolley and Gracie Fields as *Holy Matrimony* in 1943. B&W; 67m. **DIR:** Arthur Hopkins, William C. de Mille. **CAST:** Lillian Gish, Roland Young. **1933**

HIS GIRL FRIDAY ★★★★★ Based on Ben Hecht and Charles MacArthur's *The Front Page*, which was filmed on three other occasions, this is undoubtedly the best of Howard Hawks's comedies. Originally with two male leads, Hawks converted this gentle spoof of newspapers and reporters into a hilarious battle of the sexes. Rosalind Russell is the reporter bent on retirement, and Cary Grant is the editor bent on maneuvering her out of it—and winning her heart in the process. B&W; 92m. **DIR:** Howard Hawks. **CAST:** Cary Grant, Rosalind Russell, Ralph Bellamy, Gene Lockhart, Helen Mack, Ernest Truex. **1940**

HIS PICTURE IN THE PAPERS ★★★½ This clever film has Douglas Fairbanks performing a variety of Herculean feats—all aimed at getting his picture on the front pages of the New York papers. This comedy helped to define Fairbanks's motion-picture persona as the boisterous, buoyant, devil-may-care, ultra-athletic young go-getter. Silent. B&W; 68m. **DIR:** John Emerson. **CAST:** Douglas Fairbanks Sr. **1916**

HIS ROYAL SLYNESS/HAUNTED SPOOKS ★★★½ Silent comedy star Harold Lloyd spreads his considerable talent in this pair of bellybusters from Hal Roach's fun factory. In the first, Lloyd impersonates the king of a small monarchy; in the second, he is maneuvered into living in a haunted mansion. Sight gags and double takes highlight both these shorts. Silent, with music. B&W; 52m. **DIR:** Hal Roach, Alf Goulding. **CAST:** Harold Lloyd, Mildred Davis, Harry Pollard, Wallace Howe, Gaylord Lloyd. **1920**

HISTORY OF THE WORLD, PART ONE, THE 🦃 Mel Brooks is lost in this collection of bits that emerge like unused footage from *Monty Python's The Meaning of Life*. Rated R for crude language. 86m. **DIR:** Mel Brooks. **CAST:** Mel Brooks, Dom DeLuise, Madeline Kahn, Harvey Korman, Gregory Hines, Cloris Leachman. **1981**

HISTORY OF WHITE PEOPLE IN AMERICA, THE ★★★½ Martin Mull narrates this hilarious spoof documentary on white heritage, current hobbies, and food preferences. He takes us to the Institute for White Studies and into the home of a very white family. Made for cable TV, this is unrated, but it contains obscenities and sexual topics. 48m. **DIR:** Harry Shearer. **CAST:** Martin Mull, Mary Kay Place, Fred Willard, Steve Martin. **1985**

HISTORY OF WHITE PEOPLE IN AMERICA, THE (VOLUME II) ★★★½ Martin Mull returns in four hilarious new episodes with the very white Harrison family. In "White Religion," Mr. and Mrs. Harrison (Fred Willard and Mary Kay Place) must deal with their daughter's teen pregnancy. "White Stress" features Mr. Harrison coming unglued, seeing a psychiatrist, and trying to relax. In "White Politics," Mr. Harrison runs for water commissioner because their water is polluted. The last episode, "White Crime," finds Mr. Harrison, his son, and Martin Mull in court with Eileen Brennan as the judge. Unrated, this does contain obscenities. 100m. **DIR:** Harry Shearer. **CAST:** Fred Willard, Mary Kay Place, Martin Mull, Michael McKean, Amy Lynn, George Gobel, Christian Jacobs, Eileen Brennan, Stella Stevens. **1986**

HIT THE ICE ★★★ Abbott and Costello play a pair of photographers in this outing, eluding assorted crooks. Gags abound, but so do musical numbers, which always seem to grind these films to a halt. On a par with most of their other efforts, it guarantees a great time for A&C fans. B&W; 82m. **DIR:** Charles Lamont. **CAST:** Bud Abbott, Lou Costello, Patric Knowles, Elyse Knox. **1943**

HOBSON'S CHOICE (1954) ★★★★★ Charles Laughton gives one of his most brilliant performances as a turn-of-the-century London shoemaker whose love for the status quo and his whiskey is shattered by the determination of his daughter to wed. This is the original 1954 movie version of the British comedy. Laughton is expertly supported by John Mills and Brenda de Banzie as the two who wish to marry. B&W; 107m. **DIR:** David Lean. **CAST:** Charles Laughton, John Mills, Brenda de Banzie, Daphne Anderson. **1954**

HOLD 'EM JAIL ★★★ Fast-moving Wheeler and Woolsey burlesque puts them in prison with a warden (slow burning Edgar Kennedy) whose passion is football. To get on his good side, they put together a prison football team and challenge a rival prison to a gridiron battle. B&W; 74m. **DIR:** Norman Taurog. **CAST:** Bert Wheeler, Robert Woolsey, Betty Grable, Robert Armstrong, Edgar Kennedy. **1932**

HOLD ME, THRILL ME, KISS ME ★★★½ Offbeat, slightly sleazy comedy about a drifter who hooks up with a sex-obsessed stripper and her sweet-natured sister only to find violence, depravity, and danger. Writer-director Joel Hershman set out to, in his words, "make a movie just as tasteless, vulgar and tacky as Hollywood for a lot less money." He's succeeded. Unrated, the film has profanity, nudity, simulated sex, and violence. 97m. **DIR:** Joel Hershman. **CAST:** Adrienne Shelly, Max Parrish, Sean Young, Diane Ladd, Andrea Naschak, Bela Lehoczky, Timothy Leary. **1993**

HOLD THAT GHOST ★★★½ Abbott and Costello score in this super comedy about two goofs (guess who) inheriting a haunted house where all kinds of bizarre events occur. You may have to watch this one a few times to catch all the gags. B&W; 86m. **DIR:** Arthur Lubin. **CAST:** Bud Abbott, Lou Costello, Richard Carlson, Joan Davis. **1941**

HOLE IN THE HEAD, A ★★★ Frank Sinatra plays a Florida motel owner who never quite manages to get his life together, torn between his adoring son (Eddie Hodges) and his nagging brother (Edward G. Robinson). The veteran cast keeps this wispy comedy afloat, and its virtues include the Oscar-winning song "High Hopes." Not rated; suitable for the whole family. 120m. **DIR:** Frank Capra. **CAST:** Frank Sinatra, Edward G. Robinson, Eleanor Parker, Eddie Hodges, Carolyn Jones, Thelma Ritter, Keenan Wynn, Joi Lansing. **1959**

HOLIDAY ★★★★½ This delightful film was adapted from the Broadway play by Phillip Barry and features Cary Grant as a nonconformist, who, for love's sake, must confront New York City's upper-class society. Indeed, he must make the ultimate sacrifice to please his fiancée (Doris Nolan) and join her father's banking firm. Only her sister (Katharine Hepburn) seems to understand Grant's need to live a different kind of life.

B&W; 93m. **DIR:** George Cukor. **CAST:** Katharine Hepburn, Cary Grant, Doris Nolan, Lew Ayres, Edward Everett Horton, Binnie Barnes, Henry Daniell. **1938**

HOLLYWOOD BOULEVARD ★★★ A would-be actress goes to work for inept moviemakers in this comedy. This is the first film that Joe Dante (*Gremlins*) directed. Rated R. 83m. **DIR:** Joe Dante, Allan Arkush. **CAST:** Candice Rialson, Mary Woronov, Rita George, Jeffrey Kramer, Dick Miller, Paul Bartel. **1976**

HOLLYWOOD HARRY ★★★½ Robert Forster stars in this comedy about a down-and-out detective who is forced to take his runaway niece on his investigations. Rated PG-13 for profanity. 99m. **DIR:** Robert Forster. **CAST:** Robert Forster, Joe Spinell, Shannon Wilcox, Kathrine Forster, Marji Martin, Mallie Jackson, Read Morgan. **1985**

HOLLYWOOD HIGH 🦃 Four girls in their quest for a place to "get it on." Rated R for profanity and nudity. 81m. **DIR:** Patrick Wright. **CAST:** Marcy Albrecht, Sherry Hardin. **1976**

HOLLYWOOD HIGH, PART II 🦃 Teen sexploitation at its worst. Rated R for profanity and nudity. 86m. **DIR:** Caruth C. Byrd, Lee Thomburg. **CAST:** April May, Donna Lynn, Camille Warner, Drew Davis, Bruce Dobos. **1981**

HOLLYWOOD HOT TUBS 🦃 A young man wangles a job at a local hot tub firm in L.A. Rated R for nudity. 103m. **DIR:** Chuck Vincent. **CAST:** Paul Gunning, Donna McDaniel. **1984**

HOLLYWOOD ON PARADE ★★ The most interesting aspects of this collection of short films from Paramount are the brief glimpses of some of Hollywood's best-known stars of the period. The practically nonexistent plot is tepid. Watch for the stars and forget the rest. B&W; 59m. **DIR:** Louis Lewyn. **CAST:** Fredric March, Ginger Rogers, Jean Harlow, Jeanette MacDonald, Maurice Chevalier, Mary Pickford, Jackie Cooper. **1934**

HOLLYWOOD OR BUST ★★½ One of Dean Martin and Jerry Lewis's lesser efforts concerns the boys' misadventures on a trip to Hollywood where movie nut Jerry hopes to meet his dream girl, Anita Ekberg (who plays herself). Starts off well, but stalls as soon as the musical interludes begin. The final teaming of Martin and Lewis. 95m. **DIR:** Frank Tashlin. **CAST:** Jerry Lewis, Dean Martin, Pat Crowley, Anita Ekberg. **1956**

HOLLYWOOD OUTTAKES ★★½ This is a sometimes terrific, most times passable, collection of blooper and newsreel footage from the 1930s, 1940s, and 1950s. No MPAA rating. 90m. **DIR:** Bruce Goldstein. **CAST:** Humphrey Bogart, Bette Davis, Errol Flynn, George Raft, James Cagney, Judy Garland, Mickey Rooney. **1984**

HOLLYWOOD PARTY ★★★ Jimmy Durante's jungle series as "Schnarzan, the Conqueror" are box-office failures, so he hosts a large party to generate interest in them. That's it, but it opens the door for some lavish musical numbers and cameo appearances by Stan Laurel, Oliver Hardy, the Three Stooges, Jack Pearl (as Baron Muenchhausen), and Mickey Mouse. A Walt Disney cartoon short is in color. B&W/Color; 69m. **DIR:** Allan Dwan, Roy Rowland. **CAST:** Jimmy Durante, Stan Laurel, Oliver Hardy, Lupe Velez. **1934**

HOLLYWOOD SHUFFLE ★★★½ In the style of *Kentucky Fried Movie*, writer-director-star Robert Townsend lampoons Hollywood's perception of blacks—and racial stereotypes in general. It's not always funny, but some scenes are hilarious. A private-eye spoof called "Death of a Break Dancer," and something entitled "Black Acting School" are the standouts. Rated R for profanity and adult content. 82m. **DIR:** Robert Townsend. **CAST:** Robert Townsend, Anne-Marie Johnson, Starletta Dupois. **1987**

HOLLYWOOD ZAP 🦃 A country bumpkin goes off to Los Angeles to find his long-lost father. Rated R. 85m. **DIR:** David Cohen. **CAST:** Ivan E. Roth, Ben Frank. **1986**

HOLY MATRIMONY ★★½ Well-intentioned comedy has a moral and some good performances, but a formulaic chase story keeps it mired in mediocrity. Patricia Arquette dreams of becoming a star in Hollywood, so she helps her ne'er-do-well boyfriend rob a carnival owner only to find herself hiding out in a strict, religious Hutterite settlement. This leads to all sorts of rarely hilarious complications. Rated PG-13 for profanity, violence, and suggested nudity. 93m. **DIR:** Leonard Nimoy. **CAST:** Patricia Arquette, Armin Mueller-Stahl, Joseph Gordon-Levitt, Tate Donovan, John Schuck. **1994**

HOME ALONE ★★★★ A child's eye view of *It's a Wonderful Life* in which youngsters are reminded of the importance of family and real values. It all begins when 8-year-old Kevin McAllister (Macaulay Culkin) wishes his family would just go away, and they, unbeknownst to him, accidentally go on vacation without him. From there on it's a roller-coaster ride of chuckles and chills. Rated PG for brief vulgarity and silly violence. 100m. **DIR:** Chris Columbus. **CAST:** Macaulay Culkin, Joe Pesci, Daniel Stern, John Heard, Catherine O'Hara, Roberts Blossom, John Candy. **1990**

HOME IS WHERE THE HART IS 🦃 Lethargic, unfunny attempt at a black comedy. Rated PG-13. 85m. **DIR:** Rex Bromfield. **CAST:** Valri Bromfield, Stephen E. Miller, Eric Christmas, Leslie Nielsen, Martin Mull. **1987**

HOME MOVIES ★★ A little film produced with the help of Brian De Palma's filmmaking students at Sarah Lawrence College. A director, played by Kirk Douglas, gives "star therapy" to a young man who feels he is a mere extra in his own life. The film is quirky and fun at times, but as entertainment, it's quite tedious. Rated PG. 90m. **DIR:** Brian De Palma. **CAST:** Nancy Allen, Keith Gordon, Kirk Douglas, Gerrit Graham, Vincent Gardenia. **1980**

HOME REMEDY ★★★ A young New Jersey man retreats into his suburban house, where the noisy woman next door is his only obstacle to complete and blissful inertia. Odd, talky black comedy. Unrated, mild sexual situations. 92m. **DIR:** Maggie Greenwald. **CAST:** Seth Barrish, Maxine Albert. **1988**

HOMETOWN BOY MAKES GOOD ★★★ Waiter Anthony Edwards returns home to Minnesota for a visit and finds out that the little white lie he told his mother has spread. It seems the whole town thinks he's a famous psychiatrist, and pretty soon he's Doc Minnesota. Half the fun is watching Edwards cover his bases while continuing the sham. Good supporting cast pitches in to make this a fun outing. Not rated, but contains adult language. 88m. **DIR:** David Burton Morris. **CAST:** Anthony Edwards, Grace Zabriskie, Chris Mulkey. **1993**

HONEY POT, THE ★★ Rex Harrison summons three of his former loves to his deathbed for the reading of his will. This bloated, star-studded extravaganza could lose thirty minutes from its first half and become an entertaining little whodunit. 131m. **DIR:** Joseph L. Mankiewicz. **CAST:** Rex Harrison, Susan Hayward, Cliff Robertson, Maggie Smith, Capucine, Edie Adams. **1967**

HONEYMOON ACADEMY ★★ A secret agent (Kim Cattrall) marries unsuspecting Robert Hays. Reliance on sight gags and slapstick for laughs doesn't pan out. Rated PG-13 for violence. 94m. **DIR:** Gene Quintano. **CAST:** Robert Hays, Kim Cattrall, Leigh Taylor-Young, Jonathan Banks. **1990**

HONEYMOON IN VEGAS ★★★★ Private detective Nicolas Cage finally overcomes his fear of commitment and agrees to marry longtime love Sarah Jessica Parker. On their honeymoon, they go to Las Vegas where everything begins going wrong, and they end up in the clutches of gangster James Caan. More inspired madcap madness from writer-director Andrew Bergman. Rated PG-13. 100m. **DIR:** Andrew Bergman. **CAST:** James Caan, Nicolas Cage, Sarah Jessica Parker, Anne Bancroft, Peter Boyle, Noriyuki "Pat" Morita. **1992**

HONEYMOON MACHINE, THE ★★½ Three sailors use the master computer of their cruiser in an attempt to beat the roulette at a casino in Venice. Dean Jagger is fun as a bellowing admiral. 87m. **DIR:** Richard Thorpe. **CAST:** Steve McQueen, Brigid Bazlen, Jim Hutton, Paula Prentiss, Dean Jagger, Jack Weston, Jack Mullaney. **1961**

HONEYMOONERS, THE (TV SERIES) ★★★★★ A tacky apartment in Bensonhurst, Brooklyn, is the setting for the misadventures of bus driver Ralph Kramden, his wife Alice, and their best friends, Ed and Trixie Norton. When pragmatic Alice derides Ralph's get-rich-quick schemes, he's apt to bellow, "One of these days—Pow! Right in the kisser!" But, Gleason tempers the bluster with childlike appeal and, by the end of the episode, contrite Ralph will embrace Alice and earnestly proclaim, "Baby, you're the greatest!" This is the sitcom form at its zenith. Brilliantly written and performed, each of the thirty-nine filmed episodes is a comic gem. Two episodes per tape. B&W; 50m. each tape. **DIR:** Frank Satenstein. **CAST:** Jackie Gleason, Art Carney, Audrey Meadows, Joyce Randolph. **1955–1956**

HONEYMOONERS, THE: LOST EPISODES (TV SERIES) ★★★★½ For years, the thirty-nine filmed episodes of *The Honeymooners*, all created during the 1955–1956 season, were the only ones the public could view. Then, with a dramatic flourish, Jackie Gleason announced that he had uncovered dozens of other episodes, preserved on kinescope. Fans of the series thought they had died and gone to heaven. The skits, performed live on Gleason's variety show, often matched the classic thirty-nine in the categories of heart and hilarity. At their worst, these sketches surpass ninety-nine percent of what passes for comedy on television today. Twenty-two volumes; two or three episodes per tape. B&W; 47–55m. each tape. **DIR:** Frank Satenstein. **CAST:** Jackie Gleason, Art Carney, Audrey Meadows, Joyce Randolph. **1952–1957**

HONKY TONK FREEWAY ★★★ Director John Schlesinger captures the comedy of modern American life in a small Florida town. The stars keep you laughing. Rated R. 107m. **DIR:** John Schlesinger. **CAST:** William Devane, Beverly D'Angelo, Beau Bridges, Geraldine Page, Teri Garr. **1981**

HOOK, LINE AND SINKER ★★ Silly story of two nitwits who woo a mother and daughter. The popular comedy team of Wheeler and Woolsey did better work than this sort of a watered-down version of The Marx Brothers'. B&W; 71m. **DIR:** Eddie Cline. **CAST:** Bert Wheeler, Robert Woolsey, Dorothy Lee, Hugh Herbert, Natalie Moorhead. **1930**

HOOPER ★★★★ Fresh from their success with *Smokey and the Bandit*, director Hal Needham and stars Burt Reynolds and Sally Field are reunited for this humorous, knockabout comedy about Hollywood stuntmen. Jan-Michael Vincent adds to the film's impact as an up-and-coming fall guy out to best top-of-the-heap Reynolds. Good fun. Rated

PG. 99m. **DIR:** Hal Needham. **CAST:** Burt Reynolds, Sally Field, Jan-Michael Vincent, Brian Keith. **1978**

HORIZONTAL LIEUTENANT, THE ★★★ A bumbling World War II junior officer is assigned to catch an elusive supplies thief at a Pacific island storage base. Mild service comedy with likable stars. 90m. **DIR:** Richard Thorpe. **CAST:** Jim Hutton, Paula Prentiss, Jack Carter, Jim Backus, Charles McGraw, Miyoshi Umeki, Marty Ingels. **1962**

HORN BLOWS AT MIDNIGHT, THE ★★★ A comedy classic that has improved with age. Jack Benny ridiculed it because it flopped when first released. But his kidding elevated it to a cult status, and it is delightful to watch today. The plot about an angel sent to Earth to blow his trumpet and end the world may be a cliché, but Benny gives it style. B&W; 78m. **DIR:** Raoul Walsh. **CAST:** Jack Benny, Alexis Smith, Dolores Moran, John Alexander, Reginald Gardiner, Allyn Joslyn, Margaret Dumont, Guy Kibbee, Franklin Pangborn. **1945**

HORSE FEATHERS ★★★★★ The funniest of the films starring the four Marx Brothers, this features Groucho as the president of Huxley College, which desperately needs a winning football team. So Groucho hires Chico and Harpo to help him fix the season. Meanwhile, Groucho is competing for the attentions of the sexy college widow, Thelma Todd. The team's most outrageous and hilarious gagfest. B&W; 69m. **DIR:** Norman Z. McLeod. **CAST:** The Marx Brothers, Thelma Todd, David Landau. **1932**

HORSE'S MOUTH, THE ★★★½ Star Alec Guinness, who also penned the script, romps in high comic style through this film version of Joyce Cary's mocking novel about an eccentric painter. 93m. **DIR:** Ronald Neame. **CAST:** Alec Guinness, Kay Walsh, Renee Houston, Michael Gough. **1958**

HOSPITAL, THE ★★★★½ You definitely don't want to check in. But if you like to laugh, you'll want to check it out. This 1971 black comedy did for the medical profession what *...And Justice for All* did for our court system and *Network* did for television. Paddy Cheyefsky's Oscar-winning screenplay casts George C. Scott as an embittered doctor battling against the outrageous goings-on at the institution of the title. Rated PG. 103m. **DIR:** Arthur Hiller. **CAST:** George C. Scott, Diana Rigg, Barnard Hughes. **1971**

HOT CHOCOLATE ★★½ A French chocolate factory is going broke and a millionaire Texas cowgirl (Bo Derek) wants to buy it. Low-expectation fun. Rated PG-13 for violence. 93m. **DIR:** Josee Dayan. **CAST:** Robert Hays, Bo Derek, Francois Mathouret, Howard Hesseman. **1992**

HOT DOG...THE MOVIE ★★ David Naughton costars with onetime Playboy Playmate of the Year Shannon Tweed in this comedy about high jinks on the ski slopes. Rated R for nudity, profanity, and suggested sex. 96m. **DIR:** Peter Markle. **CAST:** David Naughton, Patrick Houser, Shannon Tweed. **1984**

HOT MILLIONS ★★★★ A wry comedy with a skillful cast that pokes fun at the computer age. A con man poses as a computer genius and gets a job with a million dollar corporation. He then transfers the company's funds into his own account. When he gets caught, he uses his wits to stay one step ahead. Rated G. 106m. **DIR:** Eric Till. **CAST:** Peter Ustinov, Bob Newhart, Maggie Smith, Karl Malden, Robert Morley, Cesar Romero, Julie May, Melinda May. **1968**

HOT MOVES 🦃 Here's another teen lust comedy. Rated R. 80m. **DIR:** Jim Sotos. **CAST:** Michael Zorek, Adam Silbar, Jeff Fishman, Johnny Timko. **1985**

HOT PURSUIT ★★ In this comedy, a college student (John Cusack) misses the plane on which he was to join his girlfriend (Wendy Gazelle) and her wealthy parents on a vacation cruise. He then finds himself embarking on a series of wildly improbable misadventures as he attempts to catch up with them. Rated PG-13 for profanity and violence. 90m. **DIR:** Steven Lisberger. **CAST:** John Cusack, Robert Loggia, Wendy Gazelle, Jerry Stiller, Monte Markham. **1987**

HOT RESORT 🦃 *Airplane*-style takeoff on the resort industry. Rated R for nudity, profanity, and simulated sex. 92m. **DIR:** John Robins. **CAST:** Tom Parsekian, Michael Berz, Bronson Pinchot, Marcy Walker, Frank Gorshin. **1984**

HOT SHOTS ★★★★ This hilarious parody of *Top Gun*–style films stars Charlie Sheen as a renegade navy pilot who must live with the stigma of his father's past. Look for scenes poking fun at movies as diverse as *The Fabulous Baker Boys, Gone With the Wind, Dances With Wolves,* and—in the film's funniest scene—*9 1/2 Weeks*. Rated PG-13 for brief profanity. 85m. **DIR:** Jim Abrahams. **CAST:** Charlie Sheen, Cary Elwes, Valeria Golino, Lloyd Bridges, Kevin Dunn, Jon Cryer, William O'Leary, Efrem Zimbalist Jr. **1991**

HOT SHOTS PART DEUX ★★★½ *Airplane* codirector Jim Abrahams is at it again with this slapstick sequel that blasts *Rambo*esque action flicks. Charlie Sheen leads the assault with fellow *Hot Shot*-ers Valeria Golino and Lloyd Bridges. Rated PG-13 for profanity and violence. 90m. **DIR:** Jim Abrahams. **CAST:** Charlie Sheen, Lloyd Bridges, Valeria Golino, Richard Crenna, Brenda Bakke. **1993**

HOT STUFF ★★★½ An entertaining, old-fashioned comedy that whips right along. Director-star Dom DeLuise makes the most of his dual role. The story concerns a government fencing operation for capturing crooks and the results are humorous. Rated PG. 87m. **DIR:** Dom DeLuise. **CAST:** Dom DeLuise, Jerry Reed, Suzanne Pleshette, Ossie Davis. **1979**

HOT TO TROT ★★½ Cute update on the Francis the Talking Mule comedies of the Fifties. This time we have a witty horse. What gets tiresome is the horse's dumb friend Fred (Bob Goldthwait). The best lines go to John Candy as the horse's voice. Rated PG for profanity. 83m. **DIR:** Michael Dinner. **CAST:** Bob Goldthwait, Dabney Coleman, Virginia Madsen, Cindy Pickett, Mary Gross. **1988**

HOT UNDER THE COLLAR ★★½ Poor Richard Gabai. He's so in love with Angela Visser that he'll follow her anywhere, even when she checks into the local convent. Desperate, Gabai disguises himself as a priest, and then a nun, and then must really go undercover when the convent is infiltrated by a gangster in search of hidden loot. Congenial comedy. Rated R. 87m. **DIR:** Richard Gabai. **CAST:** Angela Visser, Richard Gabai. **1991**

HOTEL PARADISO ★★★ Mild sex farce. Alec Guinness attempts a tryst with his neighbor's wife, but everything and everyone blocks his way. 96m. **DIR:** Peter Glenville. **CAST:** Alec Guinness, Gina Lollobrigida, Robert Morley, Akim Tamiroff. **1966**

HOUND OF THE BASKERVILLES, THE (1977) 🦃 Truly abysmal send-up of the novel by Conan Doyle. 84m. **DIR:** Paul Morrissey. **CAST:** Dudley Moore, Peter Cook, Denholm Elliott, Joan Greenwood, Hugh Griffith, Terry-Thomas, Roy Kinnear. **1977**

HOUSE CALLS ★★★★½ Here's a romantic comedy reminiscent of films Spencer Tracy and Katharine Hepburn made together mostly because of the teaming of Walter Matthau and Glenda Jackson. A recently widowed doctor (Matthau) finds his bachelor spree cut short by a romantic encounter with a nurse (Jackson) who refuses to be just another conquest. A delightful battle of the sexes with two equally matched opponents. Rated PG. 96m. **DIR:** Howard Zieff. **CAST:** Walter Matthau, Glenda Jackson, Richard Benjamin, Art Carney. **1978**

HOUSEBOAT ★★★ A minor entry in Cary Grant's *oeuvre* of romantic fluff, largely unremarkable because of its ho-hum script. With this sort of insubstantial material coming his way, it's little wonder Grant chose to retire eight years later. He lives on a houseboat *sans* wife; Sophia Loren is the housekeeper-maid with whom he falls in love. Unrated; suitable for family viewing. 110m. **DIR:** Melville Shavelson. **CAST:** Cary Grant, Sophia Loren, Martha Hyer, Harry Guardino. **1958**

HOUSESITTER ★★★½ Architect Newton Davis (Steve Martin) is rebuffed in love, then finds a relative stranger (Goldie Hawn) posing as his wife. Hawn, Martin, and director Frank Oz manage to hit the funnybone consistently enough for this to be a fun romp. Rated PG. 102m. **DIR:** Frank Oz. **CAST:** Steve Martin, Goldie Hawn, Dana Delany, Julie Harris, Donald Moffat, Peter MacNicol. **1992**

HOW I GOT INTO COLLEGE 🦃 Uninspired and dull adolescent comedy. Rated PG-13. 98m. **DIR:** Savage Steve Holland. **CAST:** Anthony Edwards, Corey Parker. **1989**

HOW I WON THE WAR ★★★½ John Lennon had his only solo screen turn (away from the Beatles) in this often hilarious war spoof. Directed by Richard Lester, it features Michael Crawford as a military man who has a wacky way of distorting the truth as he reminisces about his adventures in battle. 109m. **DIR:** Richard Lester. **CAST:** Michael Crawford, John Lennon, Michael Hordern, Jack MacGowran. **1967**

HOW TO BEAT THE HIGH CO$T OF LIVING ★★ A great cast all dressed up with no place to go...except Jane Curtin, whose shopping-mall striptease is a marginal high point in a caper comedy not even up to the substandards of an average made-for-television movie. Tiresome and taxing. Rated PG. 110m. **DIR:** Robert Scheerer. **CAST:** Jessica Lange, Susan Saint James, Jane Curtin, Richard Benjamin, Fred Willard, Dabney Coleman. **1980**

HOW TO BREAK UP A HAPPY DIVORCE ★★★ Ex-wife Barbara Eden wants ex-husband Hal Linden back. To make him jealous, she dates a well-known playboy. Comic mayhem follows. Lots of sight gags. This is an unrated TV movie. 78m. **DIR:** Jerry Paris. **CAST:** Hal Linden, Barbara Eden, Harold Gould. **1976**

HOW TO GET AHEAD IN ADVERTISING ★★ During an ad campaign for a new pimple cream, a British advertising executive goes completely berserk when a boil erupts on his neck, grows into a human head, and spews forth abrasive slogans ad nauseam. This heavy-handed assault on the marketing of useless and even harmful commodities is ultimately more abrasive than fun. Rated PG-13. 94m. **DIR:** Bruce Robinson. **CAST:** Richard E. Grant, Rachel Ward, Jacqueline Tong, Susan Wooldridge. **1989**

HOW TO IRRITATE PEOPLE ★★★★★ Even before *Monty Python*, John Cleese's sense of aggressive humor was fully developed, as can be seen in this hilarious collection of skits. As in all of his best work, Cleese (who wrote this BBC special along with future *Python* mate Graham Chapman) mines humor from the disparity between the surface politeness of the English and the frustrated rage underneath. Not rated. 65m. **DIR:** Ian Fordyce. **CAST:** John Cleese, Graham Chapman, Michael Palin, Connie Booth, Tim Brooke-Taylor. 1968

HOW TO MARRY A MILLIONAIRE ★★★ The stars, Marilyn Monroe, Lauren Bacall, and Betty Grable, are fun to watch in this comedy. However, director Jean Negulesco doesn't do much to keep our interest. The story in this slight romp is all in the title—with William Powell giving the girls a run for his money. 96m. **DIR:** Jean Negulesco. **CAST:** Lauren Bacall, Marilyn Monroe, Betty Grable, William Powell, Cameron Mitchell, David Wayne, Rory Calhoun. 1953

HOW TO MURDER YOUR WIFE ★★½ Jack Lemmon plays a comic-strip artist whose well-structured life is disrupted when he discovers he has married a beautiful woman after a night of drunken partying. Finding the situation intolerable, Lemmon contrives to take out his frustration by murdering his new bride in the comic strip. Some clever bits, but the premise and attitudes are unbelievably sexist. 118m. **DIR:** Richard Quine. **CAST:** Jack Lemmon, Virna Lisi, Terry-Thomas, Eddie Mayehoff, Claire Trevor, Sidney Blackmer, Jack Albertson, Mary Wickes. 1965

HOW U LIKE ME NOW ★★★ Extremely low-budget account of the struggles of a group of African-American friends on Chicago's South Side. The acting is uneven, but writer/director/producer Darryl Roberts turned out a gritty, honest, and funny script with enough warmth and humor to help you over the rough patches. Rated R for profanity and sexual situations. 109m. **DIR:** Darryl Roberts. **CAST:** Darnell Williams, Salli Richardson, Daniel Gardner, Raymond Whitfield, Darryl Roberts. 1992

HOWIE FROM MAUI 🦃 Howie Mandel's self-centered style of comedy is funny for a mere five minutes. Rated R for profanity. 60m. **DIR:** Walter C. Miller. **CAST:** Howie Mandel. 1987

HOWIE MANDEL'S NORTH AMERICAN WATUSI TOUR ★★★½ This Howie Mandel concert was filmed in Chicago and shows how much he has improved in his timing and delivery since his first special in 1983. His screaming and sight-gag props are still here, but his improvisation and interplay with the audience are now the highlights of his act. This group of fans really gets into the performance and you will, too. 52m. **DIR:** Jerry Kramer. **CAST:** Howie Mandel. 1986

HUDSUCKER PROXY, THE ★★★½ Filmmaking brothers Joel and Ethan Coen fall a little short with this typically (for them) twisted send-up of Frank Capra's populist dramas of the 1930s and 1940s. Tim Robbins is a schnook who is promoted from the mailroom to the presidency of a corporation after his predecessor leaps to his death (presumably out of boredom). Paul Newman steals the movie as the main manipulator, while Jennifer Jason Leigh goes a little overboard as a tough gal reporter. Rated PG. 111m. **DIR:** Joel Coen. **CAST:** Tim Robbins, Paul Newman, Jennifer Jason Leigh, Charles Durning, John Mahoney, Jim True, Bill Cobbs, Bruce Campbell. 1994

HULLABALOO OVER GEORGE AND BONNIE'S PICTURES ★★½ British and American art dealers compete to gain access to a valuable art collection belonging to an Indian prince. A lesser effort from the team behind *A Room with a View*; gently funny in spots, but it never really goes anywhere. Unrated, but nothing objectionable. 85m. **DIR:** James Ivory. **CAST:** Peggy Ashcroft, Victor Banerjee, Saeed Jaffrey. 1976

HUNGRY I REUNION ★★★½ Wonderful documentary highlighting some of the talents that came out of San Francisco's hungry i nightclub. Interviews and performances are included in this insightful look at one of America's first comedy and folk music clubs. Not rated, but contains adult language. 90m. **DIR:** Thomas A. Cohen. **CAST:** Enrico Banducci, Mort Sahl, Jonathan Winters, Professor Irwin Corey, Ronnie Schell, Jackie Vernon, The Kingston Trio, The Limeliters. 1980

HUNK 🦃 A social outcast makes a deal with the devil. Rated PG. 90m. **DIR:** Lawrence Bassoff. **CAST:** John Allen Nelson, Steve Levitt, Rebeccah Bush, Robert Morse, James Coco, Avery Schreiber, Deborah Shelton. 1987

HURRY UP OR I'LL BE 30 ★★★ Aimless comedy-drama will appeal to those with a fondness for slice-of-life movies. Set in Brooklyn, the movie follows an almost-thirty single guy (John Lefkowitz) who is frustrated over his life. Danny DeVito has a supporting part as a fellow Brooklynite. Rated R for sexual situations and profanity. 88m. **DIR:** Joseph Jacoby. **CAST:** John Lefkowitz, Linda De Coff, Danny DeVito. 1973

HYSTERICAL ★★ Zany horror spoof generates a sprinkling of laughs. This movie was supposed to make the Hudson Brothers the Marx Brothers of the 1980s. Rated PG. 87m. **DIR:** Chris Bearde. **CAST:** William Hudson, Mark Hudson, Brett Hudson, Cindy Pickett, Richard Kiel, Julie Newmar, Bud Cort, Robert Donner, Murray Hamilton, Clint Walker. 1983

I DON'T BUY KISSES ANYMORE ★★★½ Sweetheart of a romantic comedy. Jason Alexander stars as an overweight shoe salesman who thinks he's hit pay dirt when a college student shows an interest in him. What blossoms is true love and a film that revels in that celebration. Rated PG. 112m. **DIR:** Robert Mascarelli. **CAST:** Jason Alexander, Nia Peeples, Eileen Brennan, Lainie Kazan, Lou Jacobi. 1991

I LOVE LUCY (TV SERIES) ★★★★★ The archetypical TV sitcom. Domestic squabbles have never been more entertaining. Ricky's accent and temper, Lucy's schemes and ambitions, Ethel's submissiveness, Fred's parsimoniousness, all added up to surefire hilarity. The chemistry among the cast members was incredible. Episodes bear innumerable viewings. Classic moments include Lucy and Ethel toiling in a chocolate factory, Lucy stomping grapes, Lucy meeting William Holden, Ricky getting the news that he's a father, and Lucy selling a health tonic which happens to have a high alcohol content. Each tape 48m. **DIR:** William Asher. **CAST:** Lucille Ball, Desi Arnaz Sr., Vivian Vance, William Frawley. **1951–1956**

I LOVE MY WIFE 🦃 The problems of an upper-class couple and their ridiculous attempts to solve them. Rated PG. 95m. **DIR:** Mel Stuart. **CAST:** Elliott Gould, Brenda Vaccaro, Angel Tompkins, Dabney Coleman, Joan Tompkins. **1970**

I LOVE YOU AGAIN ★★★★ Master con artist William Powell awakes from a nine-year bout of amnesia and learns he has become a stuffy but successful small-town businessman about to be divorced by wife Myrna Loy. He recalls nothing of the nine years, yet wants to win back his wife and pull an oil scam on the town. Witty dialogue, hilarious situations, and just plain fun. B&W; 99m. **DIR:** W. S. Van Dyke. **CAST:** William Powell, Myrna Loy, Frank McHugh, Edmund Lowe, Carl "Alfalfa" Switzer. **1940**

I LOVE YOU ALICE B. TOKLAS! ★★★ Peter Sellers plays a lawyer-cum-hippie in this far-out comedy about middle-age crisis. Rated PG. 93m. **DIR:** Hy Averback. **CAST:** Peter Sellers, Leigh Taylor-Young, Jo Van Fleet. **1968**

I LOVE YOU TO DEATH ★★★★ Offbeat true-life murder comedy, in which loving wife Tracey Ullman decides to dispatch philandering husband Kevin Kline with the help of her mom (Joan Plowright), an admirer (River Phoenix), and two stoned-out hit men (William Hurt and Keanu Reeves). Funny, but not for all tastes. Rated R for profanity and violence. 96m. **DIR:** Lawrence Kasdan. **CAST:** Kevin Kline, Tracey Ullman, Joan Plowright, River Phoenix, William Hurt, Keanu Reeves, James Gammon, Victoria Jackson. **1990**

I MARRIED A WOMAN ★½ George Gobel plays an advertising man who is having difficulty holding on to both his biggest account and his wife, who feels he's not paying her enough attention. Angie Dickinson and John Wayne have walk-on parts. B&W/color; 80m. **DIR:** Hal Kanter. **CAST:** George Gobel, Diana Dors, Adolphe Menjou, Jessie Royce Landis, Nita Talbot, William Redfield, John McGiver. **1958**

I OUGHT TO BE IN PICTURES ★★★★ Neil Simon's best work since *The Goodbye Girl*, this heartwarming story stars Walter Matthau as a father who deserts his Brooklyn family. Dinah Manoff is the daughter who wants to be a movie star, and Ann-Margret is the woman who brings the two together. Rated PG for mild profanity and brief nudity. 107m. **DIR:** Herbert Ross. **CAST:** Walter Matthau, Ann-Margret, Dinah Manoff. **1982**

I WANNA HOLD YOUR HAND ★★★ A group of New Jersey teens try to get tickets to the Beatles' first appearance on the *Ed Sullivan Show*. This was one of the biggest money losers of 1978, but it's not that bad. Fast-paced and energetic, with a nice sense of period and some fine performances. Rated PG. 104m. **DIR:** Robert Zemeckis. **CAST:** Nancy Allen, Bobby DiCicco, Marc McClure, Theresa Saldana, Eddie Deezen, Will Jordan, Wendie Jo Sperber. **1978**

I WAS A MALE WAR BRIDE ★★★★ Cary Grant plays Henri Rochard, a real-life French officer who married an American WAC in post–World War II Germany just as she was to return to the United States. A great farce from beginning to end, with Grant a riot in drag attempting to board a ship full of war brides bound for America. B&W; 105m. **DIR:** Howard Hawks. **CAST:** Cary Grant, Ann Sheridan, Marion Marshall, Kenneth Tobey. **1949**

I WAS A TEENAGE TV TERRORIST 🦃 A teenager and his girlfriend pull a series of pranks designed to look like the work of terrorists. 85m. **DIR:** Stanford Singer. **CAST:** Julie Hanlon, Adam Nathan. **1985**

I WILL, I WILL...FOR NOW 🦃 A Santa Barbara sex clinic where "nothing is unnatural." Rated R. 96m. **DIR:** Norman Panama. **CAST:** Elliott Gould, Diane Keaton, Paul Sorvino, Victoria Principal, Robert Alda, Warren Berlinger. **1976**

IDENTITY CRISIS ★★ A witch fuses the soul of a murdered fashion designer with a rapper's body in this fluffy comedy. Rated R for profanity and nudity. 98m. **DIR:** Melvin Van Peebles. **CAST:** Mario Van Peebles, Ilan Mitchell-Smith. **1990**

IF... ★★★★ This is British director Lindsay Anderson's black comedy about English private schools and the revolt against their strict code of behavior taken to the farthest limits of the imagination. Malcolm McDowell's movie debut. Rated R. 111m. **DIR:** Lindsay Anderson. **CAST:** Malcolm McDowell, David Wood, Richard Warwick. **1969**

IF I HAD A MILLION ★★★★½ Wonderful episodic tale where wealthy Richard Bennett picks names from the telephone book, giving each person one million dollars. The two funniest segments star Charles Laughton and W. C. Fields. Both comic masterpieces. B&W; 90m. **DIR:** Various. **CAST:** Gary Cooper, W. C. Fields, Charles Laughton, George Raft, Richard Bennett, Mary Boland,

Frances Dee, Jack Oakie, Gene Raymond, Charlie Ruggles, Alison Skipworth. 1932

IF I WERE RICH ★★★ How to live and avoid paying bills while waiting for prosperity to return is the theme of this entertaining British comedy. Robert Donat falls for Wendy Barrie when he arrives to shut off her once-rich-but-now-bankrupt father Edmund Gwenn's electricity. The debonair Donat is a delight in this early pairing with Barrie. B&W; 63m. **DIR:** Zoltán Korda. **CAST:** Robert Donat, Wendy Barrie, Edmund Gwenn. 1933

IF IT'S TUESDAY, THIS MUST BE BELGIUM ★★★½ Plenty of laughs with a group of Americans on a wild eighteen-day bus tour of Europe, running from one mishap to another. Added fun with lots of guest stars in surprise cameos. Rated G. 99m. **DIR:** Mel Stuart. **CAST:** Suzanne Pleshette, Ian McShane, Mildred Natwick, Murray Hamilton, Michael Constantine, Norman Fell, Peggy Cass, Marty Ingels, Pamela Britton, Sandy Baron. 1969

I'LL DO ANYTHING ★★½ Writer-director James L. Brooks *badly* miscalculated in this saga of struggling Hollywood actor and single father Nick Nolte, whose stabs at cinematic fame are derailed by the need to care for his precocious daughter Whittni Wright. Although shooting for the vicious insider's humor of *The Player*, this overblown mess staggers beneath its own pretensions. Bad editing also betrays its origins as a musical—the songs were eliminated after they tested badly. Rated PG-13 for profanity and brief nudity. 115m. **DIR:** James L. Brooks. **CAST:** Nick Nolte, Albert Brooks, Julie Kavner, Joely Richardson, Tracey Ullman, Whittni Wright. 1994

I'M ALL RIGHT JACK ★★★½ British comedies can be marvelously entertaining, especially when they star Peter Sellers, as in this witty spoof of the absurdities of the labor movement carried to its ultimate extreme. B&W; 101m. **DIR:** John Boulting. **CAST:** Peter Sellers, Terry-Thomas, Ian Carmichael. 1960

I'M GONNA GIT YOU SUCKA! ★★★★ Keenen Ivory Wayans wrote and directed this uproariously funny parody of the blaxploitation flicks of the early Seventies. The gags run fast and loose, and the result is a satisfying laughfest. Rated R for language. 88m. **DIR:** Keenen Ivory Wayans. **CAST:** Keenen Ivory Wayans, Bernie Casey, Jim Brown, Isaac Hayes, Antonio Fargas, Steve James, John Vernon, Clu Gulager. 1989

I'M NO ANGEL ★★★★ One of her funniest films, Mae West had complete creative control over script, camera angles, costars, and director. She plays a circus performer who cons gullible old men out of their money. The highlight of the show is the courtroom scene with West acting as her own attorney and compromising the judge, as well as everyone else. B&W; 87m. **DIR:** Wesley Ruggles. **CAST:** Mae West, Cary Grant, Kent Taylor, Edward Arnold, Gregory Ratoff, Gertrude Michael, Dennis O'Keefe, Ralf Harolde. 1933

IMMORAL MR. TEAS, THE ★★★ After receiving an anesthetic at the dentist's office, middle-aged Mr. Teas discovers that he has the ability to see through women's clothing. Surprisingly well made, this was a huge hit and ushered in a whole era of nudie cuties, most with variations on the same plot. The nudity is tame by modern standards, and anyone who remembers the Fifties and Sixties should enjoy this as a nostalgic curiosity. 63m. **DIR:** Russ Meyer. **CAST:** W. Ellis Teas. 1959

IMPORTANCE OF BEING EARNEST, THE ★★★½ A peerless cast of stage professionals brings this version of Oscar Wilde's classic Victorian Era comedy of manners to vivid life in high style. Once again, the problem of Mr. Worthing's cloakroom origins delights with hilarious results. A very funny film. 95m. **DIR:** Anthony Asquith. **CAST:** Michael Redgrave, Edith Evans, Margaret Rutherford, Joan Greenwood, Michael Denison, Dorothy Tutin, Richard Wattis. 1952

IMPOSSIBLE YEARS, THE 🦃 Kids using bad words at school and having premarital sex, all done in bad taste. Inexplicably rated G. 92m. **DIR:** Michael Gordon. **CAST:** David Niven, Lola Albright, Chad Everett, Ozzie Nelson, Cristina Ferrare, Jeff Cooper, Don Beddoe. 1968

IMPROPER CHANNELS ★★ Story of an overeager social worker who accuses a father (Alan Arkin) of child abuse. Rated PG for language. 92m. **DIR:** Eric Till. **CAST:** Alan Arkin, Mariette Hartley, Monica Parker. 1981

IMPURE THOUGHTS ★★½ A group of friends who attended the same Catholic grammar school in the early Sixties meet after death and reminisce about their youths. Rated PG. 87m. **DIR:** Michael A. Simpson. **CAST:** Brad Dourif, Lane Davies, Terry Beaver, John Putch. 1986

IN-LAWS, THE ★★★★ This delightful caper comedy mixes mystery and action with the fun. Vince Ricardo (Peter Falk) is the mastermind behind a bold theft of engravings of U.S. currency from a Treasury Department armored car. Sheldon Kornpett (Alan Arkin) is a slightly neurotic dentist. Soon they're off on a perilous mission. Falk and Arkin make a great team, playing off each other brilliantly. Rated PG. 103m. **DIR:** Arthur Hiller. **CAST:** Peter Falk, Alan Arkin, Penny Peyser, Michael Lembeck. 1979

IN PERSON ★★★ Vivacious, shrewish film star flees to a resort incognito and meets a handsome stranger who is totally unimpressed when he learns who she really is. Enjoyable. B&W; 85m. **DIR:** William A. Seiter. **CAST:** Ginger Rogers, George Brent, Alan Mowbray, Grant Mitchell, Samuel S. Hinds, Edgar Kennedy. 1935

IN SOCIETY ★★½ Abbott and Costello are mistaken for pillars of upscale society. Imagine the possibilities. Slick, fast-paced comedy from their initial Universal period. B&W; 75m. **DIR:** Jean Yarbrough. **CAST:** Bud Abbott, Lou Costello, Arthur Treacher, Marion Hutton, Kirby Grant. 1944

IN THE MOOD ★★½ Patrick Dempsey plays a conniving teenager who becomes a media star by repeatedly marrying older women. Although this period (1940s) comedy has some funny bits and lines, the story is slapdash. Rated PG-13. 100m. **DIR:** Phil Alden Robinson. **CAST:** Patrick Dempsey, Talia Balsam, Beverly D'Angelo, Michael Constantine, Kathleen Freeman. 1987

IN THE SOUP ★★ Very bizarre movie in which an aspiring film writer finds an extremely strange man to help him finance his script. Don't expect to laugh during this film, unless you like off-the-wall humor. Not rated, but contains nudity and profanity. 96m. **DIR:** Alexandre Rockwell. **CAST:** Seymour Cassel, Steve Buscemi, Jennifer Beals, Will Patton, Stanley Tucci, Pay Moya, Jim Jarmusch, Carol Kane. 1992

IN THE SPIRIT ★★★½ Marlo Thomas stands out in a top-flight cast as a lovable New Age nut who involves a hapless married couple (Elaine May, Peter Falk) in murder and mayhem when her protégé, a prostitute (Jeannie Berlin), is found dead. Berlin, May's daughter, co-wrote the script. Rated R for profanity and violence. 95m. **DIR:** Sandra Seacat. **CAST:** Jeannie Berlin, Olympia Dukakis, Peter Falk, Melanie Griffith, Elaine May, Marlo Thomas. 1990

INCREDIBLE MR. LIMPET, THE ★★ What can you say about a film whose hero is a fishbowl fancier who wishes himself into a fish so he can help the U.S. Navy defeat enemy submarines during World War II? Don Knotts as Henry Limpet is guilty as charged. Although popular with children, this outré excursion into fantasy will leave most viewers scratching their scales and flapping their gills wondering why on earth it was ever made. 102m. **DIR:** Arthur Lubin. **CAST:** Don Knotts, Carole Cook, Jack Weston, Andrew Duggan, Larry Keating. 1964

INCREDIBLE ROCKY MOUNTAIN RACE, THE ★★★ This Western with a comic touch is about a race used by townspeople to get rid of two troublemakers. These troublemakers include Mark Twain (Christopher Connelly) and his archenemy, Mike Fink (Forrest Tucker). There is more comedy as the snags increase and the problems get out of hand. Rated G. 97m. **DIR:** James L. Conway. **CAST:** Christopher Connelly, Forrest Tucker, Larry Storch, Jack Kruschen, Mike Mazurki. 1985

INCREDIBLE SHRINKING WOMAN, THE ★★ This comedy, starring Lily Tomlin, falls prey to the law of diminishing returns. But to simply dismiss it as a failure would be inaccurate and unfair. This comic adaptation of Richard Matheson's classic science-fiction novel (*The Shrinking Man*) is not a bad movie. It's more like...well...the perfect old-fashioned Disney movie—a little corny and strained at times but not a total loss. Rated PG. 88m. **DIR:** Joel Schumacher. **CAST:** Lily Tomlin, Ned Beatty, Henry Gibson, Elizabeth Wilson, Charles Grodin, Pamela Bellwood, Mike Douglas, Mark Blankfield. 1981

INDIAN SUMMER ★★★ This amiable, warmhearted comedy is best described as *The Big Chill* goes to summer camp. An Ontario camp director invites his favorite kids from the "golden years" of the early 1970s back for a twenty-year reunion. It's a movie full of big grins and tolerable, skin-deep goo. Rated PG-13 for language, drug use, and simulated sex. 98m. **DIR:** Mike Binder. **CAST:** Alan Arkin, Matt Craven, Diane Lane, Bill Paxton, Elizabeth Perkins, Kevin Pollak, Sam Raimi, Vincent Spano, Julie Warner, Kimberly Williams. 1993

INDISCREET (1931) 🦃 Gloria Swanson trying to conceal her questionable past. B&W; 92m. **DIR:** Leo McCarey. **CAST:** Gloria Swanson, Ben Lyon, Arthur Lake. 1931

INDISCREET (1958) ★★½ Dated comedy about an on-again, off-again affair between rich actress Ingrid Bergman and playboy bachelor Cary Grant. These stars could make anything watchable, but this isn't one of their best. 100m. **DIR:** Stanley Donen. **CAST:** Cary Grant, Ingrid Bergman, Cecil Parker. 1958

INSIDE MONKEY ZETTERLAND ★★★ Monkey Zetterland is a former teen movie star turned scriptwriter. His extended family includes a mother who's a soap star, a hairdresser brother, a gay sister and her pregnant girlfriend, a pair of terrorists, and his wandering biker dad. The ensemble cast struggles gamely to rise above the erratic script. Rated R for adult situations, profanity, and brief violence. 93m. **DIR:** Jeffrey Levy. **CAST:** Steve Antin, Patricia Arquette, Sandra Bernhard, Sofia Coppola, Tate Donovan, Rupert Everett, Katherine Helmond, Bo Hopkins, Ricki Lake, Debi Mazar, Martha Plimpton. 1992

INSPECTOR GENERAL, THE ★★★★ In this classic comedy set in Russia of the 1800s, Danny Kaye is the town fool who is mistaken for a confidant of Napoleon. The laughs come when Danny is caught up in court intrigue and really has no idea what is going on. Kaye's talents are showcased in this film. 102m. **DIR:** Henry Koster. **CAST:** Danny Kaye, Walter Slezak, Elsa Lanchester. 1949

INSTANT KARMA 🦃 A young creative consultant for a television network looks for love. Not rated. 91m. **DIR:** Roderick Taylor. **CAST:** Craig Sheffer, David Cassidy, Chelsea Noble, Alan Blumenfeld. **1990**

INTERNATIONAL HOUSE ★★★½ An offbeat, must-see film involving a melting pot of characters gathered at the luxurious International House Hotel to bid on the rights to the radioscope, an early version of television. As usual, a Russian muddies the waters with cunning and craft, while an American bumbles to the rescue. W. C. Fields and Burns and Allen are in rare form throughout. B&W; 70m. **DIR:** A. Edward Sutherland. **CAST:** W. C. Fields, Peggy Hopkins Joyce, Baby Rose Marie, Cab Calloway, Stu Erwin, George Burns, Gracie Allen, Bela Lugosi, Franklin Pangborn, Sterling Holloway, Jeanne Marie. **1933**

INTERNATIONAL TOURNÉE OF ANIMATION VOL. I, THE ★★★½ Fine collection of animated shorts from the nineteenth International Tournée of Animation. This video package features some award-winning animation by filmmakers from around the world. Some of the best selections from this compilation are Marv Newland's *Anijam,* John Canemaker's *Bottom's Dream,* Osamu Tezuka's *Jumping,* and the Academy Award–winning *Anna & Bella,* by Dutch cartoonist Borge Ring. Amusing and inventive. 88m. **DIR:** Various. **1988**

INTERNATIONAL TOURNÉE OF ANIMATION VOL. II, THE ★★★★ Highly impressive collection of animated shorts from around the world featuring some of the best new animation around. Some of the compilations' best works are the Academy Award–winning short "A Greek Tragedy," from Belgium; "The Frog, The Dog and The Devil," from New Zealand; Bill Plympton's "Your Face"; and "Drawing on My Mind," by Bob Kurtz featuring dialogue and the voice of comic George Carlin. 86m. **DIR:** Various. **1989**

INVASION OF THE GIRL SNATCHERS 🦃 An assistant detective and a cult leader in the service of aliens from outer space do battle. Unrated; the film contains nudity and sexual suggestiveness. 90m. **DIR:** Lee Jones. **CAST:** Elizabeth Rush. **1973**

INVASION OF THE SPACE PREACHERS ★★½ Nerds camping in West Virginia help a beautiful female alien track bad guys from her planet. No big laughs, but a genial time waster. Rated R for nudity and profanity. 100m. **DIR:** Daniel Boyd. **CAST:** Jim Wolfe, Guy Nelson. **1990**

INVISIBLE WOMAN, THE ★★★ Featherweight sci-fi comedy as a scientist turns a fashion model invisible, but it's got the best cast of any Universal programmer of the 1940s. B&W; 72m. **DIR:** A. Edward Sutherland. **CAST:** John Barrymore, Virginia Bruce, John Howard, Charlie Ruggles, Margaret Hamilton, Oscar Homolka. **1941**

INVITATION TO THE WEDDING ★★ A feeble little British tale about a young American college student who falls in love with his best friend's sister, who just so happens to be engaged to an English war hero. John Gielgud offers the only comic relief as an Englishman-turned-Southern evangelist. 89m. **DIR:** Joseph Brooks. **CAST:** John Gielgud, Ralph Richardson, Paul Nicholas, Elizabeth Shepherd. **1973**

IRMA LA DOUCE ★★★ Gendarme Jack Lemmon gets involved with prostitute Shirley MacLaine in what director Billy Wilder hoped would be another MacLaine/Lemmon hit like *The Apartment.* It isn't. It's raw humor in glorious color. Send the "Silver Spoons" set off to bed before you screen this one. 142m. **DIR:** Billy Wilder. **CAST:** Shirley MacLaine, Jack Lemmon, Lou Jacobi, Herschel Bernardi. **1963**

ISHTAR 🦃 A bloated, disjointed, and ponderous megabuck vanity production. Rated PG-13 for language and brief nudity. 107m. **DIR:** Elaine May. **CAST:** Warren Beatty, Dustin Hoffman, Isabelle Adjani, Charles Grodin, Jack Weston, Tess Harper, Carol Kane. **1987**

IT (1927) ★★★ Advance promotion about *It* (read: sex appeal) made this clever little comedy about shop girl Clara Bow chasing and catching her boss Antonio Moreno a solid hit. It also boosted red-haired Brooklyn bombshell Clara to superstardom. Rising star Gary Cooper appears only briefly. Silent. B&W; 71m. **DIR:** Clarence Badger. **CAST:** Clara Bow, Antonio Moreno, William Austin, Lloyd Corrigan, Jacqueline Gadsden, Gary Cooper. **1927**

IT CAME FROM HOLLYWOOD ★★★ Dan Aykroyd, John Candy, Cheech and Chong, and Gilda Radner appear in comedy vignettes as the hosts of this watchable *That's Entertainment*–style compilation of the worst all-time (but hilarious) losers in *Plan 9 from Outer Space, Robot Monster, Batmen of Africa,* and *Untamed Women.* Rated PG for sexual references and scatological humor. 80m. **DIR:** Malcolm Leo, Andrew Solt. **CAST:** Dan Aykroyd, John Candy, Cheech and Chong, Gilda Radner. **1982**

IT HAPPENED ONE NIGHT ★★★★★ Prior to *One Flew over the Cuckoo's Nest,* this 1934 comedy was the only film to capture all the major Academy Awards. Clark Gable stars as a cynical reporter on the trail of a runaway heiress, Claudette Colbert. They fall in love, of course, and the result is vintage movie magic. B&W; 105m. **DIR:** Frank Capra. **CAST:** Clark Gable, Claudette Colbert, Ward Bond. **1934**

IT HAPPENS EVERY SPRING ★★★½ Great farce with chemistry professor Ray Milland accidentally developing a compound that, when applied, results in a baseball repulsing anything made of wood, including a bat. His major-league career as a pitcher is short-lived but lots of fun. B&W; 87m. **DIR:** Lloyd Bacon. **CAST:** Ray Milland, Jean Peters, Paul Douglas, Ed Begley Sr., Ted de Corsia, Ray Collins, Jessie Royce Landis, Alan Hale Jr. **1949**

IT SHOULD HAPPEN TO YOU ★★★½ Judy Holliday plays an actress who's desperate to garner publicity and hopes splashing her name across billboards all over New York City will ignite her career. The movie provides steady chuckles. Jack Lemmon makes an amusing screen debut. Holliday is hard to resist. B&W; 81m. **DIR:** George Cukor. **CAST:** Judy Holliday, Peter Lawford, Jack Lemmon, Michael O'Shea, Vaughn Taylor. **1954**

IT STARTED IN NAPLES ★★ Clark Gable and Sophia Loren together sounds good on paper but doesn't work in this predictable comedy about an American man trying to get custody of his Italian nephew. 100m. **DIR:** Melville Shavelson. **CAST:** Clark Gable, Sophia Loren, Vittorio De Sica. **1960**

IT STARTED WITH A KISS ★★★ A show girl looking for a rich husband marries an air force sergeant instead, then wants the marriage kept platonic until she is sure. Fred Clark, as a general, again steals the show. 104m. **DIR:** George Marshall. **CAST:** Glenn Ford, Debbie Reynolds, Eva Gabor, Fred Clark, Edgar Buchanan, Harry Morgan. **1959**

IT TAKES TWO ★★ This young boy's fantasy features George Newbern as a reluctant bridegroom who has an affair with a fast car and a hot blonde car dealer. Only teens may fully appreciate this trite sex comedy. Rated PG-13 for profanity and sexual situations. 79m. **DIR:** David Beaird. **CAST:** George Newbern, Kimberly Foster. **1988**

ITALIAN JOB, THE ★★★ An ex-con creates the world's biggest traffic jam in an attempt to steal millions in gold. The only problem is the mob doesn't like the idea. A fairly funny caper comedy. 99m. **DIR:** Peter Collinson. **CAST:** Michael Caine, Noel Coward, Benny Hill, Rossano Brazzi. **1969**

IT'S A BIG COUNTRY ★★★ Producer and cowriter Dore Schary's overboard but loving tribute to the United States is a grab bag of short stories (some cute but many pointless) glorifying the American way of life. The best has Ethel Barrymore set out to change our vital statistics because no one counted her in the last census. B&W; 89m. **DIR:** Clarence Brown, Don Hartman, John Sturges, Richard Thorpe, Charles Vidor, Don Weis, William Wellman. **CAST:** Ethel Barrymore, Keefe Brasselle, Gary Cooper, Nancy Davis, Van Johnson, Gene Kelly, Janet Leigh, Marjorie Main, Fredric March, George Murphy, William Powell, S. Z. Sakall, Lewis Stone, James Whitmore, Keenan Wynn. **1951**

IT'S A BUNDYFUL LIFE ★★★ From the television series *Married...With Children* comes this raunchy, irreverent Christmas special spoofing Frank Capra's classic *It's A Wonderful Life*. Sam Kinnison stars as Al Bundy's guardian angel. 47m. **DIR:** Gerry Cohen. **CAST:** Ed O'Neill, Katey Sagal, David Garron, Amanda Bearse, Christina Applegate, David Faustino, Sam Kinnison, Ted McGinley. **1989**

IT'S A COMPLEX WORLD ★★ Strange film involving a nightclub, politics, bad singing, terrorists, and bizarre characters. The narration doesn't help this plot that jumps all over the place. Rated R for violence and profanity. 81m. **DIR:** James Wolpaw. **CAST:** Stanley Mathis, Lou Albano. **1989**

IT'S A GIFT ★★★★★ In a class with the best of the comedies of the 1930s (including *Duck Soup, I'm No Angel, My Man Godfrey*), this classic was produced during the peak of Fields's association with Paramount and is his archetypal vehicle, peopled with characters whose sole purpose in life seems to be to annoy his long-suffering Harold Bissonette. A side-splitting series of visual delights. B&W; 73m. **DIR:** Norman Z. McLeod. **CAST:** W. C. Fields, Kathleen Howard, Baby LeRoy. **1934**

IT'S A GREAT LIFE ★★★ Dagwood and Blondie Bumstead sure could get away with silly story lines, and this is one of the silliest. Dagwood buys a horse because he misunderstood his instructions—he was told to buy a house. The players make it work. B&W; 75m. **DIR:** Frank Strayer. **CAST:** Penny Singleton, Arthur Lake, Danny Mummert, Hugh Herbert, Marjorie Ann Mutchie, Irving Bacon, Alan Dinehart. **1943**

IT'S A JOKE, SON! ★★ Radio's Senator Claghorn comes to life in the form of Kenny Delmar, whose bombastic talk and Old South attitude entertained millions on Fred Allen's popular network show. The blustering politician is hijacked by some underhanded rivals and only the strains of his beloved "Dixie" give him the strength to win the day. Cornball but fun. B&W; 63m. **DIR:** Ben Stoloff. **CAST:** Kenny Delmar, Una Merkel, June Lockhart, Kenneth Farrell, Douglass Dumbrille. **1947**

IT'S A MAD MAD MAD MAD WORLD ★★★★ Spencer Tracy and a cast made up of "Who's Who of American Comedy" are combined in this wacky chase movie to end all chase movies. Tracy is the crafty police captain who is following the progress of various money-mad citizens out to beat one another in discovering the buried hiding place of 350,000 stolen dollars. 154m. **DIR:** Stanley Kramer. **CAST:** Spencer Tracy, Milton Berle, Jonathan Winters, Buddy Hackett, Sid Caesar, Phil Silvers, Mickey Rooney, Peter Falk, Dick Shawn, Ethel Merman, Buster Keaton, Jimmy Durante, Edie Adams, Dorothy Provine, Terry-Thomas, William Demarest, Andy Devine. **1963**

IT'S IN THE BAG ★★★ The plot (if there ever was one) derives from the Russian fable about an impoverished nobleman on a treasure hunt. Continuity soon goes out the window, however, when the cast starts winging it in one hilarious episode after another. This is Fred Allen, acerbic and nasal as always, in his best screen comedy. B&W; 87m. **DIR:** Richard Wallace. **CAST:** Fred Allen, Jack Benny, Binnie Barnes, Robert Benchley, Victor Moore, Sidney Toler, Rudy Vallee, William Bendix, Don Ameche. **1945**

I'VE HEARD THE MERMAIDS SINGING ★★★ A slight but often engaging story about a naïve photographer (Sheila McCarthy) who longs to be a part of the elitist art world. The cloyingly whimsical ending is the only thunk in this nifty debut from director Patricia Rozema. Rated PG. 83m. **DIR:** Patricia Rozema. **CAST:** Sheila McCarthy, Paule Viallargeon, Anne-Marie Macdonald. **1987**

IZZY & MOE ★★★½ Together for the last time, Jackie Gleason and Art Carney are near-perfect as ex-vaudevillians who become New York Prohibition agents in this made-for-TV movie based on actual characters. The two stars still work beautifully together after all these years. 100m. **DIR:** Jackie Cooper. **CAST:** Jackie Gleason, Art Carney, Cynthia Harris, Zohra Lampert. **1985**

JABBERWOCKY ★★½ Monty Python fans will be disappointed to see only one group member, Michael Palin, in this British film. Palin plays a dim-witted peasant during the Dark Ages. A monster called Jabberwocky is destroying villages all over the countryside, so Palin tries to destroy the monster. There are some funny moments but nothing in comparison with true Python films. No MPAA rating. 100m. **DIR:** Terry Gilliam. **CAST:** Michael Palin, Max Wall, Deborah Fallender. **1977**

JACK BENNY PROGRAM, THE (TV SERIES) ★★★★ Following the formula that had made him a smash on radio, Jack Benny became a fixture on TV. Bolstered by the top-notch character actors who popped up on the show, Benny held the spotlight with a pregnant pause, a hand on the chin, or a shift of the eyes. Comic bits frequently revolved around Benny's stinginess and deadly violin playing. A host of stars visited the show over the years, appearing in songs and/or sketches. The roster on video includes Ernie Kovacs, Jayne Mansfield, Johnny Carson, Connie Francis, The Smothers Brothers, George Burns, Humphrey Bogart, Kirk Douglas, Fred Allen, Ann-Margret, and Bob Hope. B&W; 30m. **DIR:** Frederick de Cordova. **CAST:** Jack Benny, Mary Livingstone, Eddie "Rochester" Anderson, Dennis Day, Don Wilson, Mel Blanc. **1950–1965**

JACKIE CHAN'S POLICE FORCE 🦃 A lame, comedic kung fu mixture. Rated PG-13 for violence. 101m. **DIR:** Jackie Chan. **CAST:** Jackie Chan, Brigitte Lin. **1986**

JACKIE GLEASON'S HONEYBLOOPERS ★★★★ Wonderful flubs from the *Honeymooners* TV series and the comedy that results from attempts to cover them up. A must for *Honeymooners* fans. Not rated. 60m. **DIR:** Frank Satenstein. **CAST:** Jackie Gleason, Art Carney, Audrey Meadows, Joyce Randolph. **1984**

JACKIE MASON ON BROADWAY ★★½ Jackie Mason had a hit on Broadway with this one-man show, joking his way through life with broad strokes. It seems everyone gets on this guy's nerves. Moderately funny. Not rated. 60m. **DIR:** Dwight Hemion. **CAST:** Jackie Mason. **1988**

JANE AND THE LOST CITY ★★★½ World War II British comic-strip heroine, Jane, comes to life in the form of lovely Kristen Hughes. She must help England's war effort by finding the diamonds of Africa's Lost City before the Nazis get them. A treasure trove of chuckles. Rated PG for profanity. 94m. **DIR:** Terry Marcel. **CAST:** Kristen Hughes, Maud Adams, Sam Jones. **1987**

JANE AUSTEN IN MANHATTAN ★★ The team responsible for *A Room with a View* comes up empty with this satire about two off-Broadway producers battling for the rights to a little-known play written by Jane Austen when she was 12 years old. The infighting among the theatrical community is amusing, but the movie is predominantly cold and unmoving. Unrated. 108m. **DIR:** James Ivory. **CAST:** Anne Baxter, Robert Powell, Sean Young, Tim Choate. **1980**

JANE CAMPION SHORTS ★★★ Australian filmmaker Jane Campion made quite an impression at the 1986 Cannes Film Festival with these stylistic film shorts which were shot while she was a student at the Australian Film and TV school. All three films achieve a sense of comic irony, great emotional insight, and show a distinctive stylistic visual aproach. The video features: "Passionless Moments," "A Girl's Own Story," and "Peel." Not rated, but recommended for adult viewers. 49m. **DIR:** Jane Campion. **CAST:** Tim Pye, Katie Pye, Ben Martin. **1991**

JAY LENO'S AMERICAN DREAM ★★★½ Talented comedian Jay Leno takes an irreverent look at all that is Americana as he saunters through much of this video in a glossy silver sports coat. His commentary is salty and enjoyable because it hits so close to home. 49m. **DIR:** Ira Wohl. **CAST:** Jay Leno. **1986**

JEEVES AND WOOSTER (TV SERIES) ★★★★ P. G. Wodehouse fans will love these impeccably faithful renditions of tales about bumbling ne'er-do-well Bertie Wooster (Hugh Laurie) and his all-knowing retainer, Jeeves (Stephen Fry), who always manages to pull his master's bacon out of the most improbable fires. Aside from Wodehouse's piquant verbal byplay, there's nothing more delightful than watching Jeeves puncture the balloons of his aristocratic, stuffed-shirt employer...who never even perceives he's been humbled. Start with "Jeeves' Arrival," which first introduces the famous pair, and proceed from there. 52m. each episode. **DIR:** Robert Young. **CAST:** Stephen Fry, Hugh Laurie. **1990**

JEKYLL & HYDE—TOGETHER AGAIN ★★★ If you like offbeat, crude, and timely humor, you'll enjoy this 1980s-style version of Robert Louis Stevenson's horror classic. Though the film needs some editing, Mark Blankfield is a riot as the mad scientist. Rated R for heavy doses of vulgarity and sexual innuendo. 87m. **DIR:** Jerry Belson. **CAST:** Mark Blankfield, Bess Armstrong, Krista Erickson. **1982**

JERK, THE ★★★★ Steve Martin made a very funny starring debut in this wacky comedy. Nonfans probably won't like it, but for those who think he's hilarious, the laughs just keep on coming. Rated R. 94m. **DIR:** Carl Reiner. **CAST:** Steve Martin, Bernadette Peters, Bill Macy, Jackie Mason. **1979**

JERRY LEWIS LIVE 💔 One of the worst stand-up comedy tapes we've viewed so far. 73m. **DIR:** Arthur Forrest. **CAST:** Jerry Lewis. **1984**

JERSEY GIRL ★★★½ Winning fairy tale about Jersey girl Jami Gertz looking for Mr. Right in Manhattan. She literally runs into him when she sideswipes Dylan McDermott's Mercedes. He's everything she's looking for, but she reminds him of everything he's worked so hard to leave behind. But you know what they say about opposites. The fun is watching Gertz pursue her man against all odds. Funny, warm, and sweet. Rated PG-13 for language and adult situations. 95m. **DIR:** David Burton Morris. **CAST:** Jami Gertz, Dylan McDermott, Joseph Bologna, Star Jasper, Molly Price, Aida Turturro. **1993**

JET BENNY SHOW, THE ★★½ Peculiar spoof stars Jack Benny impersonator Steve Norman as a Buck Rogers–type hero accompanied on his adventures in outer space by a Rochester-like robot. The concept is as elusive as the humor, though fans of the old Jack Benny TV show may want to check it out. Unrated. 77m. **DIR:** Roger D. Evans. **CAST:** Steve Norman, Kevin Dees. **1975**

JIMMY HOLLYWOOD ★★ A struggling, manic actor goes ballistic when his car is burglarized. With the help of a cerebrally challenged buddy, he becomes America's first video vigilante by taping criminals at work and leaving the evidence and tied-up crooks for the cops. The self-obsessed thespian tries to parlay his new Bronson-with-a-camcorder fame into a career of sorts. This meandering, watery, oddball, socially redemptive comedy about the down side of Tinsel Town stardom just never gels. Rated R for language and violence. 110m. **DIR:** Barry Levinson. **CAST:** Joe Pesci, Christian Slater, Victoria Abril. **1994**

JINXED ★★½ Bette Midler is in peak form as a would-be cabaret singer who enlists the aid of a blackjack dealer (Ken Wahl) in a plot to murder her gambler boyfriend (Rip Torn) in this often funny black comedy. If it weren't for Midler, you'd notice how silly and unbelievable it all is. Rated R for profanity and sexual situations. 103m. **DIR:** Don Siegel. **CAST:** Bette Midler, Ken Wahl, Rip Torn, Benson Fong. **1982**

J-MEN FOREVER ★★ Firesign Theatre's Peter Bergman and Philip Proctor have taken footage from old films of the Thirties and Forties and dubbed in their own comic dialogue. It's funny at times but way too long for this type of treatment. Rated PG for profanity and violence. 75m. **DIR:** Richard Patterson. **CAST:** Peter Bergman, Philip Proctor. **1979**

JOCKS 💔 A tennis coach must make his goofy team champions. Rated R for nudity and obscenities. 90m. **DIR:** Steve Carver. **CAST:** Scott Strader, Perry Lang, Mariska Hargitay, Richard Roundtree, Christopher Lee. **1986**

JOE BOB BRIGGS—DEAD IN CONCERT ★★½ Like a manic Will Rogers, drive-in movie critic Joe Bob Briggs talks his way through subjects ranging from homosexuals to how he advertised for a wife through the classified section. Not extremely funny, but sometimes fun to watch. Unrated, but contains adult languauge. 65m. **DIR:** Jim Rowley. **CAST:** Joe Bob Briggs. **1985**

JOE PISCOPO LIVE! ★★★ This HBO concert was taped on the UCLA campus. Joe Piscopo showcases some of his characterizations as Robert De Niro (*Taxi Driver, Raging Bull*) and as Phil Donahue (to George Wallace's Oprah Winfrey). It's an uneven show and Piscopo sometimes appears to be entertaining himself more than the fans. 60m. **DIR:** David Grossman. **CAST:** Joe Piscopo, George Wallace. **1987**

JOE PISCOPO VIDEO, THE ★★½ This HBO special has some funny moments, most deriving from Joe Piscopo's impressions. But aside from a Frank Sinatra look-alike singing in a heavy-metal rock band and a "Thriller" spin-off where the ghouls popping up out of the graveyard are Jerry Lewis clones *à la The Nutty Professor*, the moments are delivered in a quick montage and then disappear for good. 60m. **DIR:** Jay Dubin. **CAST:** Joe Piscopo, Eddie Murphy, Joseph Bologna, Jan Hooks. **1984**

JOE VERSUS THE VOLCANO ★★★½ You have to be in the right mood to enjoy this featherweight comedy from writer-director John Patrick Shanley. When a millionaire offers Tom Hanks an expense account and a leisurely trip to the South Seas, Hanks accepts—even though it means jumping into a volcano. Meg Ryan is superb in three hilarious supporting roles. Rated PG for brief profanity. 94m. **DIR:** John Patrick Shanley. **CAST:** Tom Hanks, Meg Ryan, Lloyd Bridges, Robert Stack, Abe Vigoda, Dan Hedaya, Ossie Davis. 1990

JOHNNY BE GOOD 🦃 Anthony Michael Hall is a high school football player who is heavily recruited by every major college in the United States. Rated R for language, partial nudity, and sexual situations. 86m. **DIR:** Bud Smith. **CAST:** Anthony Michael Hall, Robert Downey Jr., Paul Gleason, Uma Thurman, Steve James, Seymour Cassel, Michael Greene, Robert Downey Sr. 1988

JOHNNY COME LATELY ★★★ A good showcase for James Cagney's feisty personality with a wholesome touch not often seen in today's movies. He plays a vagrant who happens onto a job on a small-town newspaper, and winds up playing cupid to the publisher's daughter and her boyfriend. B&W; 97m. **DIR:** William K. Howard. **CAST:** James Cagney, Grace George, Hattie McDaniel, Marjorie Lord, Marjorie Main. 1943

JOHNNY DANGEROUSLY 🦃 In this fitfully funny spoof of 1930s gangster movies, Michael Keaton and Joe Piscopo play rival crime lords. Directed by Amy Heckerling, it leaves the viewer with genuinely mixed feelings. Rated PG-13 for violence and profanity. 90m. **DIR:** Amy Heckerling. **CAST:** Michael Keaton, Joe Piscopo, Marilu Henner, Maureen Stapleton. 1984

JOHNNY SUEDE ★★½ Brad Pitt plays a lackluster, aimless adolescent who discovers a purpose in life when he's literally hit on the head with a pair of suede shoes. This low-budget comedy is from the surreal, off-the-wall school, and owes much to the early work of Jim Jarmusch (for whom Tom DiCillo was once a cinematographer). Only fans of cult films and the preciously weird need apply. 97m. **DIR:** Tom DiCillo. **CAST:** Brad Pitt, Catherine Keener, Calvin Levels, Alison Moir, Nick Cave, Tina Louise. 1992

JOSEPH ANDREWS ★★ The adventures of Joseph Andrews (Peter Firth) as he rises from lowly servant to personal footman. This is director Tony Richardson's second attempt to transform a Henry Fielding novel to film. Unfortunately, the first-rate cast cannot save this ill-fated attempt to restage *Tom Jones*. Rated R for sex and profanity. 99m. **DIR:** Tony Richardson. **CAST:** Ann-Margret, Peter Firth, Beryl Reid, Michael Hordern, Jim Dale, John Gielgud, Hugh Griffith, Wendy Craig, Peggy Ashcroft. 1977

JOSHUA THEN AND NOW ★★★★½ Based by screenwriter Mordecai Richler (*The Apprenticeship of Duddy Kravitz*) on his autobiographical novel of the same name, this little-known gem is blessed with humor, poignancy, and insight. James Woods is wonderful as Jewish writer Joshua Shapiro, whose life seems to be in shambles. He is a hard guy to keep down. Surviving an embarrassing upbringing by a gangster father (Alan Arkin in his funniest performance ever), Joshua nearly meets his match in the snobbish high society of his WASP wife (Gabrielle Lazure). Rated R for profanity, nudity, suggested sex. 118m. **DIR:** Ted Kotcheff. **CAST:** James Woods, Alan Arkin, Gabrielle Lazure, Michael Sarrazin, Linda Sorenson. 1985

JOY OF SEX, THE ★★ This comedy, about the plight of two virgins, male and female, in a sex-crazy age, has few offensive elements. But there is one problem: it isn't funny. Rated R for profanity, suggested sex, and scatological humor. 93m. **DIR:** Martha Coolidge. **CAST:** Michelle Meyrink, Cameron Dye, Lisa Langlois. 1984

JOY STICKS 🦃 A wealthy businessman wants to shut down the local video game room. Rated R. 88m. **DIR:** Greydon Clark. **CAST:** Joe Don Baker, Leif Green, Logan Ramsey. 1983

JULIA MISBEHAVES ★★★★ Delightful farce with Greer Garson as a London chorine, long separated from stuffy husband Walter Pidgeon and their refined daughter, Elizabeth Taylor, coming back into their lives for the marriage of the latter. Garson is wonderful in her only comic role, even allowing herself to become foil to a group of acrobats. B&W; 99m. **DIR:** Jack Conway. **CAST:** Greer Garson, Walter Pidgeon, Peter Lawford, Elizabeth Taylor, Cesar Romero, Lucile Watson, Nigel Bruce, Mary Boland, Henry Stephenson, Ian Wolfe, Veda Ann Borg. 1948

JUMPIN' JACK FLASH ★★½ Whoopi Goldberg's inspired clowning is the only worthwhile element in her first big-screen comedy. She plays a computer operator who finds herself involved in international intrigue. Rated R for profanity and violence. 100m. **DIR:** Penny Marshall. **CAST:** Whoopi Goldberg, Stephen Collins, John Wood, Carol Kane, James Belushi, Annie Potts, Peter Michael Goetz, Roscoe Lee Browne, Jeroen Krabbé, Jonathan Pryce. 1986

JUMPING JACKS ★★★ It's all Jerry Lewis antics as two nightclub entertainers join the parachute corps. Not on a par with *At War With The Army*. B&W; 96m. **DIR:** Norman Taurog. **CAST:** Dean Martin, Jerry Lewis, Mona Freeman, Don DeFore, Robert Strauss, Ray Teal. 1952

JUNE BRIDE ★★★½ A noted correspondent is forced to work for his ex-flame, now an editor of a woman's magazine. His cynicism causes complications with the bride and her family. Robert Montgomery, as the reporter, steals the show. B&W; 97m. **DIR:** Bretaigne Windust. **CAST:** Bette Davis, Robert Montgomery, Fay Bainter, Tom Tully, Mary Wickes, Jerome Cowan. 1948

JUST ONE OF THE GIRLS 💔 Lowbrow teen fantasy has Corey Haim cross-dressing on campus to avoid the school bully and get closer to the bully's sister. Exactly what you'd expect, but worse. Rated R for nudity and language. 94m. **DIR:** Michael Keusch. **CAST:** Corey Haim, Nicole Eggert, Cameron Bancroft, Gabe Khouth. **1993**

JUST ONE OF THE GUYS ★★★ A sort of reverse *Tootsie*, this surprisingly restrained teen-lust comedy stars Joyce Hyser as an attractive young woman who switches high schools and sexes. The premise is flimsy and forced, but director Lisa Gottlieb and her cast keep the viewer entertained. Rated PG-13 for nudity, violence, and profanity. 88m. **DIR:** Lisa Gottlieb. **CAST:** Joyce Hyser, Clayton Rohner, Billy Jacoby, Toni Hudson. **1985**

JUST TELL ME WHAT YOU WANT ★★ Alan King gives a fine performance in this otherwise forgettable film as an executive who attempts to get his mistress (Ali MacGraw) back. She's in love with a younger man (Peter Weller). Rated R. 112m. **DIR:** Sidney Lumet. **CAST:** Alan King, Ali MacGraw, Peter Weller, Myrna Loy, Keenan Wynn, Tony Roberts, Dina Merrill. **1980**

JUST YOU AND ME, KID ★★ The delights of George Burns as an ex-vaudeville performer do not mask the worthless plot in this tale of Burns's attempt to hide a young runaway (Brooke Shields) fleeing a drug dealer. Shields's inability to move with Burns's rhythm rapidly becomes annoying. Rated PG for mild language and brief nudity. 93m. **DIR:** Leonard Stern. **CAST:** George Burns, Brooke Shields, Ray Bolger, Lorraine Gary, Burl Ives. **1979**

K-9 ★★★ James Belushi is terrific as a maverick cop whose single-minded pursuit of a drug dealer (Kevin Tighe) makes him a less-than-desirable partner. Enter Jerry Lee, a feisty police dog who proves to be more than a match for Belushi. Rated PG-13 for profanity and violence. 95m. **DIR:** Rod Daniel. **CAST:** James Belushi, Mel Harris, Kevin Tighe. **1989**

KEATON RIDES AGAIN/RAILROADER ★★★★ Coupled delightfully in this Buster Keaton program are a biographical profile with interviews, and a solo opus of Buster in trouble on a handcar rolling along the seemingly endless tracks of the Canadian National Railway. Both were lovingly produced by the National Film Board of Canada less than a year before the great comic's life ended. B&W; 81m. **DIR:** John Spotton, Gerald Potterton. **CAST:** Buster Keaton. **1965**

KENTUCKY FRIED MOVIE ★★★ The first film outing of the creators of *Airplane!* is an on-again, off-again collection of comedy skits. Directed by John Landis, the best bits involve a Bruce Lee takeoff and a surprise appearance by Wally and the Beaver. Rated R. 78m. **DIR:** John Landis. **CAST:** Evan Kim, Master Bong SooHan, Bill Bixby, Donald Sutherland. **1977**

KENTUCKY KERNELS ★★½ Wheeler and Woolsey (a now-forgotten early Thirties comedy team) and *Our Gang/Little Rascals* star Spanky McFarland travel to the heart of Dixie to claim an inheritance. Breezy, slapstick comedy has aged surprisingly well. One of the first features directed by George Stevens. B&W; 75m. **DIR:** George Stevens. **CAST:** Bert Wheeler, Robert Woolsey, Mary Carlisle, Spanky McFarland. **1934**

KEY TO THE CITY ★★★½ Prim Loretta Young and roughneck Clark Gable meet at a mayor's convention in San Francisco, and a wacky and rocky romance follows. A much underrated movie with hilarious situations handled expertly by pros. Marilyn Maxwell's striptease is a hoot. B&W; 101m. **DIR:** George Sidney. **CAST:** Clark Gable, Loretta Young, Marilyn Maxwell, Frank Morgan, Lewis Stone, Raymond Burr, James Gleason, Raymond Walburn, Pamela Britton, Clinton Sundberg. **1950**

KEYSTONE COMEDIES, VOL. 1 ★★★ *Fatty's Faithful Fido, Fatty's Tintype Tangle*, and *Fatty's New Role*—three fast-moving bop-and-bash comedies in the celebrated Fatty series produced by Mack Sennett at Keystone Studios in 1915—compose this first of five volumes devoted to the famed silent comedian's artistry. *Fatty's Faithful Fido* is a comedy action gem. The dog comes close to stealing the show. Slapstick humor in the classic mold. B&W; 46m. **DIR:** Roscoe Arbuckle. **CAST:** Roscoe "Fatty" Arbuckle, Minta Durfee, Al St. John, Louise Fazenda, Edgar Kennedy, Joe Bordeaux. **1915**

KEYSTONE COMEDIES, VOL. 2 ★★★ Mack Sennett hit real reel pay dirt when he teamed rotund comic Roscoe Arbuckle and elfin comedienne Mabel Normand in a film series. These three examples—*Fatty and Mabel at the San Diego Exposition, Fatty and Mabel's Simple Life*, and *Mabel's Washday*—amply show why. B&W; 42m. **DIR:** Roscoe Arbuckle. **CAST:** Roscoe "Fatty" Arbuckle, Mabel Normand, Minta Durfee, Al St. John, Alice Davenport, Joe Bordeaux. **1915**

KEYSTONE COMEDIES, VOL. 3 ★★★ Four more stanzas in the screen lives of two of silent film's great comedic performers: Roscoe Arbuckle and Mabel Normand. They're all "watch springs and elastic" as they create marvelous mayhem in *Mabel Lost and Won, Wished on Mabel, Mabel, Fatty and the Law*, and *Fatty's Plucky Pup*. B&W; 58m. **DIR:** Roscoe Arbuckle. **CAST:** Roscoe "Fatty" Arbuckle, Mabel Normand, Minta Durfee, Dora Rogers, Alice Davenport, Al St. John, Owen Moore. **1915**

KEYSTONE COMEDIES, VOL. 4 ★★★ Three stanzas in the sidesplitting Fatty-and-Mabel slapstick series Mack Sennett connived and contrived between 1912 and 1916: *Mabel's Willful Way, That Little Band of Gold,* and *Mabel and Fatty's Married Life.* Mayhem and mirth only past masters of the double take and pratfall can muster. B&W; 44m. **DIR:** Roscoe Arbuckle. **CAST:** Roscoe "Fatty" Arbuckle, Mabel Normand, Edgar Kennedy, Glen Cavender, Ford Sterling, Mae Busch, Al St. John, Alice Davenport. **1915**

KEYSTONE COMEDIES, VOL. 5 ★★★ Fabled Mack Sennett's madcap mob of laugh-catchers dish up three more hilarious happy helpings of classic silent comedy: *Miss Fatty's Seaside Lovers, Court House Crooks,* and *Love Loot and Crash.* Keystone Studios' pride, roly-poly Roscoe Arbuckle, is a tubby terror in drag. B&W; 45m. **DIR:** Roscoe Arbuckle. **CAST:** Roscoe "Fatty" Arbuckle, Bill Bennett, Walter Reed, Edgar Kennedy, Harold Lloyd, Joe Bordeaux, Minta Durfee, Ford Sterling, Charles Arling, Joe Swickard, Dora Rogers, Nick Cogley, Charlie Chase, W. C. Hauber. **1915**

KID, THE/THE IDLE CLASS ★★★★ A skillful blend of comedy and pathos, *The Kid,* the first of Charles Chaplin's silent feature films, has his famous tramp alter ego adopting an abandoned baby boy whose mother, years later, suddenly appears to claim him. Chaplin is magnificent. Coogan's performance in the title role made him the first child superstar. Also on the bill: *The Idle Class,* a satire on the leisure of the rich involving mistaken identity. Silent. B&W; 86m. **DIR:** Charles Chaplin. **CAST:** Charlie Chaplin, Edna Purviance, Jackie Coogan. **1921**

KID FROM BROOKLYN, THE ★★★ Danny Kaye is fine as the comedy lead in this remake of Harold Lloyd's *The Milky Way.* He plays the milkman who becomes a prizefighter. Good family entertainment. 104m. **DIR:** Norman Z. McLeod. **CAST:** Danny Kaye, Virginia Mayo, Vera-Ellen, Steve Cochran, Eve Arden. **1946**

KID WITH THE BROKEN HALO, THE ★★ Sort of a *Different Strokes* meets *It's A Wonderful Life,* this television movie tells of a little angel forced to earn his wings by making things right for people in three vignettes. The film was actually an unsold pilot, and the fare is sweet and gentle enough. 100m. **DIR:** Leslie Martinson. **CAST:** Gary Coleman, Robert Guillaume, June Allyson, Ray Walston, Mason Adams, Telma Hopkins, Georg Stanford Brown, John Pleshette. **1982**

KILLER TOMATOES EAT FRANCE ★★★ Part four of the killer tomato trilogy is a cute spoof on just about everything. Dr. Mortimer Gangreen, played wonderfully by John Astin, breaks out of prison and tries to put a fake King Louie on the throne of France. Not rated, but contains humorous violence. 90m. **DIR:** John DeBello. **CAST:** Marc Price, Angela Visser, Steve Lundquist, John Astin. **1991**

KILLER TOMATOES STRIKE BACK 🦃 Third installment of the killer tomato saga features John Astin as Professor Gangreen attempting—once again—to dominate the world. Beyond corny, this reduces the original to an all-time low. Unrated. 88m. **DIR:** John DeBello. **CAST:** John Astin. **1990**

KIND HEARTS AND CORONETS ★★★★ A young man (Dennis Price) thinks up a novel way to speed up his inheritance—by killing off the other heirs. This is the central premise of this arresting black comedy, which manages to poke fun at mass murder and get away with it. Alec Guinness plays all eight victims. 104m. **DIR:** Robert Hamer. **CAST:** Dennis Price, Alec Guinness, Valerie Hobson. **1949**

KINDERGARTEN COP ★★★½ High-concept comedy has big Arnold Schwarzenegger playing an undercover narcotics detective who has to pose as a kindergarten teacher to get the goods on a nasty drug lord (Richard Tyson). If it weren't for all the violence, this could have been a fun film for the whole family. As it is, Schwarzenegger is often funny, and Pamela Reed does a bang-up job as his unpredictable partner. Rated PG-13 for violence. 111m. **DIR:** Ivan Reitman. **CAST:** Arnold Schwarzenegger, Penelope Ann Miller, Pamela Reed, Linda Hunt, Richard Tyson, Carroll Baker, Cathy Moriarty. **1990**

KING IN NEW YORK, A ★★½ Supposedly anti-American, this 1957 film by Charles Chaplin, not seen in the United States until 1973, was a big letdown to his fans, who had built their worship on *Easy Street, City Lights, Modern Times,* and *The Great Dictator.* It pokes fun at the 1950s, with its witch-hunts and burgeoning post-war technology. It is not the Chaplin of old, but just old Chaplin, and too much of him. B&W; 105m. **DIR:** Charles Chaplin. **CAST:** Charlie Chaplin, Dawn Addams, Michael Chaplin. **1957**

KING RALPH ★★★ When a freak accident wipes out the entire royal family, Las Vegas entertainer John Goodman is the sole heir to the English crown. With the help of Peter O'Toole and Richard Griffiths (in fine performances), Goodman's good-natured, lovable slob attempts to rise to the occasion. Amiably entertaining comedy. Rated PG for brief profanity. 97m. **DIR:** David S. Ward. **CAST:** John Goodman, Peter O'Toole, John Hurt, Camille Courdi, Richard Griffiths. **1991**

KISS ME GOODBYE ★★★ Sally Field plays a widow of three years who has just fallen in love again. Her first husband was an electrifying Broadway choreographer named Jolly (James Caan). Her husband-to-be is a slightly stuffy Egyptologist (Jeff Bridges). Before her wedding day, she receives a visit from Jolly's ghost, who is apparently upset about the approaching wedding. Rated PG for profanity and sexual situations. 101m. **DIR:** Robert Mulligan. **CAST:** Sally Field, James Caan, Jeff Bridges, Claire Trevor. **1982**

KISS ME, STUPID ★★★½ A skirt-chasing boozing singer (Dean Martin) stops in the town of Climax, Nevada, and is waylaid by a would-be songwriter. This sex farce is on its way to cult status. When released it was condemned by the Legion of Decency and panned by critics and the general public; but it's worth a second look. Scripted by I. A. L. Diamond and director Billy Wilder. B&W; 126m. **DIR:** Billy Wilder. **CAST:** Dean Martin, Kim Novak, Ray Walston, Felicia Farr, Cliff Osmond, Alice Pearce. **1964**

KISSES FOR MY PRESIDENT ★★★ With a little more care, this could have been a great comedy. As it is, there is some fun when Fred MacMurray, as the husband of the first woman president of the United States (Polly Bergen), falls heir to many of the tasks and functions handled by our first ladies. B&W; 113m. **DIR:** Curtis Bernhardt. **CAST:** Fred MacMurray, Polly Bergen, Arlene Dahl, Edward Andrews. **1964**

KLONDIKE ANNIE ★★★½ Mae West stars in this comedy as a shady lady who leaves the Barbary Coast for Alaska, where she takes on the identity of a zealous nun and finds out religion isn't as much of a sham as she thought. It's unusual for West, but she keeps it respectable—and so did the overzealous censors, who cut out all of her double-entendres. B&W; 78m. **DIR:** Raoul Walsh. **CAST:** Mae West, Victor McLaglen, Helen Jerome Eddy, Phillip Reed, Harold Huber. **1936**

KLUTZ, THE 🦃 A born loser is left holding the bag in a bank robbery he didn't commit. Poorly dubbed, low-budget French comedy. 87m. **DIR:** Pierre Rose. **CAST:** Louise Portal, Guy Provost. **1973**

KNACK...AND HOW TO GET IT, THE ★★★★ Ray Brooks plays the lad with a knack for handling the ladies. Michael Crawford is the novice who wants to learn. Rita Tushingham is the lass caught in the middle. A British sex comedy produced before sex comedies were fashionable, meaning there's more talk than action. But the talk is witty, the direction zesty and the acting close to perfection. B&W; 85m. **DIR:** Richard Lester. **CAST:** Michael Crawford, Ray Brooks, Donal Donnelly, Rita Tushingham, Charlotte Rampling, Peter Copley. **1965**

KNIGHTS AND EMERALDS ★★★½ A young drummer in a marching band in working-class Birmingham defies the racism of his family and friends when he takes up with a competing band of black youths. Original and endearing, sidestepping countless clichés into which it could easily have fallen. A good family item. Rated PG. 94m. **DIR:** Ian Emes. **CAST:** Christopher Wild, Beverly Hills, Warren Mitchell. **1986**

KNOCKOUTS 🦃 Slickly edited sexploitation film about coeds in a female boxing competition. Rated R for nudity. 91m. **DIR:** John Bowen. **CAST:** Brad Zutaut, Robert Thine, Tally. **1992**

KNOWHUTIMEAN? ★★★ A fun, if slightly repetitive, collection of Ernest commercials followed by a series of skits featuring Varney as a variety of Ernest's colorful ancestors. A must for Jim Varney fans. 57m. **DIR:** John R. Cherry III. **CAST:** Jim Varney. **1983**

KOTCH ★★★★ Walter Matthau is in top form as a feisty senior citizen who takes to the road when his family tries to put him in a retirement home. First-time director Jack Lemmon does himself proud with this alternately witty and warmly human comedy. Rated PG. 113m. **DIR:** Jack Lemmon. **CAST:** Walter Matthau, Deborah Winters, Felicia Farr, Charles Aidman. **1971**

KOVACS ★★★★ Ernie Kovacs was one of the most innovative forces in the early days of television. His ingenious approach to comedy revolutionized the medium, and its impact can still be felt today. This definitive anthology contains some of his best moments, including his famous "Mack the Knife" blackout segments. His career on television lasted from 1950 to 1962, when his life was cut short by a fatal car accident. B&W; 85m. **DIR:** Ernie Kovacs. **CAST:** Ernie Kovacs. **1971**

L.A. GODDESS ★★ Lust on a movie set as a studio executive falls for a star's stunt double. The comedic tone seems an afterthought to shore up the soft-core erotica. Available in R and unrated versions; contains sex and profanity. 92m./93m. **DIR:** Jag Mundhra. **CAST:** David Heavener, Kathy Shower, Jeff Conaway, Joe Estevez. **1993**

L.A. STORY ★★★★ In writer Steve Martin's *Manhattan*-style comedy about Los Angeles, a wacky weatherman (Martin) becomes disillusioned with his television job, his status-crazy girlfriend (Marilu Henner), and life in general until a British journalist (Martin's wife Victoria Tennant) brings romance back into his world. Great fun for Martin's fans, with a hilarious supporting performance by Sarah Jessica Parker as a gum-popping Valley Girl. Rated PG-13 for profanity. 95m. **DIR:** Mick Jackson. **CAST:** Steve Martin, Victoria Tennant, Richard E. Grant, Marilu Henner, Sarah Jessica Parker. **1991**

LADIES' MAN, THE ★★ Jerry Lewis plays a houseboy for an all-female boardinghouse in Hollywood. Lewis wrote, directed, and stars in this silly slapstick farce. Watch for an amusing cameo by George Raft. 106m. **DIR:** Jerry Lewis. **CAST:** Jerry Lewis, Helen Traubel, Kathleen Freeman, Hope Holiday, Pat Stanley. **1961**

LADY EVE, THE ★★★★ Barbara Stanwyck, Henry Fonda, and Charles Coburn are first-rate in this romantic comedy, which was brilliantly written and directed by Preston Sturges. Fonda is a rather simpleminded millionaire, and Stanwyck is the conniving woman who seeks to snare him. The results are hilarious. B&W; 94m. **DIR:** Preston Sturges. **CAST:** Barbara Stanwyck, Henry Fonda, Charles Coburn, William Demarest. 1941

LADY IS WILLING, THE ★★★½ Marlene Dietrich wants to adopt an abandoned baby she found but needs a husband of convenience. She decides on Fred MacMurray, a handy pediatrician. Lighweight comedy but the stars shine. B&W; 92m. **DIR:** Mitchell Leisen. **CAST:** Marlene Dietrich, Fred MacMurray, Aline MacMahon, Stanley Ridges, Arline Judge. 1942

LADYBUGS ★★ Dangerfield is an inept girls' soccer coach who convinces his fiancée's son to dress up like a girl and help run the team. Dangerfield's trademark one-liners are the best things about the film. Rated PG-13 for brief profanity and sexual innuendo. 91m. **DIR:** Sidney J. Furie. **CAST:** Rodney Dangerfield, Jackée, Jonathan Brandis, Ilene Graff, Vinessa Shaw, Tom Parks. 1992

LADYKILLERS, THE ★★★★½ England had a golden decade of great comedies during the 1950s. *The Ladykillers* is one of the best. Alec Guinness and Peter Sellers are teamed as a couple of small-time criminals who have devised what they believe to be the perfect crime. Unfortunately, their plans are thwarted by the sweetest, most innocent little old landlady you'd ever want to meet. Great fun! 87m. **DIR:** Alexander Mackendrick. **CAST:** Alec Guinness, Peter Sellers, Cecil Parker. 1955

LAS VEGAS HILLBILLYS 🖤 Hillbilly Ferlin Husky inherits a failing Las Vegas bar and makes it a success by turning it into Vegas' only country-and-western nightclub. The 1967 sequel *Hillbillys in a Haunted House,* is equally dismal. 90m. **DIR:** Arthur C. Pierce. **CAST:** Ferlin Husky, Jayne Mansfield, Mamie Van Doren, Sonny James, Richard Kiel. 1966

LAS VEGAS WEEKEND ★★ After getting kicked out of college, a nerdy computer whiz decides to take his foolproof blackjack system to Las Vegas. Mild comedy could have been funnier. Rated R for brief nudity. 82m. **DIR:** Dale Trevillion. **CAST:** Barry Hickey, Ray Dennis Steckler. 1985

LASER MAN, THE ★★★ A funny and inventive melting-pot comedy about a Chinese-American laser researcher living in Manhattan. However, the comedy is tempered by an incongruously serious subplot about arms dealers and the morality of scientific research. Not a total success, but worth seeing. 93m. **DIR:** Peter Wang. **CAST:** Marc Hayashi, Maryann Urbano, Tony Leung, Peter Wang, Sally Yeh. 1988

LAST AMERICAN VIRGIN, THE 🖤 Tawdry teen-sex. Rated R for sex. 92m. **DIR:** Boaz Davidson. **CAST:** Lawrence Monoson, Diane Franklin, Steve Antin, Joe Rubbo, Louisa Moritz. 1982

LAST FLING, THE ★★★ Cute made-for-TV movie about a philanderer (John Ritter) who finally finds his perfect match (Connie Sellecca) only to have her disappear. His attempts to find her are usually funny and often hilarious. 95m. **DIR:** Corey Allen. **CAST:** John Ritter, Connie Sellecca, Scott Bakula, Paul Sand, John Bennett Perry. 1986

LAST MARRIED COUPLE IN AMERICA, THE 🖤 Lamebrained little sex farce about one perfect couple's struggle to hold their own marriage together. Rated R for profanity and nudity. 103m. **DIR:** Gilbert Cates. **CAST:** Natalie Wood, George Segal, Arlene Golonka, Bob Dishy, Priscilla Barnes, Dom DeLuise, Valerie Harper. 1980

LAST NIGHT AT THE ALAMO ★★★★ On the night before the demolition of a run-down Houston bar, the regulars gather to mourn its passing. The satire of Kim Henkel's script, which targets machismo, is balanced by a real affection for these losers who depend on beer and bull to face the world. Recommended. Unrated, the film features plentiful profanity. 82m. **DIR:** Eagle Pennell. **CAST:** Sonny Davis. 1983

LAST OF MRS. CHENEY, THE ★★★ Jewel thieves in high society. This star-studded remake of Norma Shearer's 1929 hit version of Frederick Lonsdale's evergreen comedy falls a mite short, but is nonetheless worth watching. As always, Robert Montgomery and William Powell are urbanity in spades. Good show. B&W; 98m. **DIR:** Richard Boleslawski. **CAST:** Robert Montgomery, Joan Crawford, William Powell, Frank Morgan, Jessie Ralph, Benita Hume, Nigel Bruce. 1937

LAST OF THE RED HOT LOVERS 🖤 A married man uses his mother's apartment for amorous dalliances. Rated PG. 98m. **DIR:** Gene Saks. **CAST:** Alan Arkin, Paula Prentiss, Sally Kellerman. 1972

LAST POLKA, THE ★★★★ This made-for-HBO special features the unique Second City comedy of Yosh (John Candy) and Stan (Eugene Levy) Schmenge, a delightful pair of polka bandleaders, as they reminisce about their checkered musical careers. Fellow *SCTV* troupe members Catherine O'Hara and Rick Moranis add to this adept send-up of *The Last Waltz,* Martin Scorsese's documentary chronicling the final concert of real-life rock legends The Band. 60m. **DIR:** John Blanchard. **CAST:** John Candy, Eugene Levy, Catherine O'Hara, Rick Moranis. 1984

LAST REMAKE OF BEAU GESTE, THE 🦃 Vapid foreign legion comedy. Rated PG—sexual situations. 84m. **DIR:** Marty Feldman. **CAST:** Marty Feldman, Michael York, Ann-Margret, Trevor Howard. **1977**

LAST RESORT ★★½ Charles Grodin and family are off on vacation to Club Sand. Amid slapstick jokes and Grodin's exasperated yelling is an intermittently entertaining movie. Rated R for sex and language. 80m. **DIR:** Zane Buzby. **CAST:** Charles Grodin, Jon Lovitz, Robin Pearson Rose, Megan Mullally, John Ashton. **1985**

LAUREL AND HARDY: AT WORK ★★★½ This volume of the *Classics Collection* showcases three bits by the boys: "Towed in a Hole," "Busy Bodies," and "The Music Box." The selections are highly enjoyable, but the drawback, for those only vaguely familiar with the comedy-duo, might be the slow pace of the action. B&W; 75m. **DIR:** Hal Roach. **CAST:** Stan Laurel, Oliver Hardy. **1932–1933**

LAUREL AND HARDY CLASSICS, VOLUME 1 ★★★ This collection contains *The Music Box*, *County Hospital*, *The Live Ghost*, and *Twice Two*. *The Music Box* won an Oscar as the Best Short of 1932. In it, Stan Laurel and Oliver Hardy attempt to deliver a piano up a long flight of stairs to the home of Theodore Swarzenhoffen (Billy Gilbert). Other than that outstanding offering, this is a mediocre collection of L&H comedy. B&W; 90m. **DIR:** James Parrott, Charles R. Rogers. **CAST:** Stan Laurel, Oliver Hardy, Billy Gilbert, Charlie Hall. **1930**

LAUREL AND HARDY CLASSICS, VOLUME 2 ★★★★★ Packed with laughs in every minute, this collection contains *Blotto*, *Towed in a Hole*, *Brats*, and *Hog Wild*, four of the best short comedies produced by this classic team. While some of the situations might seem dated (sneaking out to drink booze during Prohibition and putting up a radio antenna), the development of the plots is flawless and transcends time. This is the best of the short-subject collections. B&W; 80m. **DIR:** James Parrott, George Marshall. **CAST:** Stan Laurel, Oliver Hardy, Stanley Sanford, Charlie Hall. **1930**

LAUREL AND HARDY CLASSICS, VOLUME 3 ★★½ Four more Laurel and Hardy short subjects: *Oliver the Eighth*, *Busy Bodies*, *Their First Mistake*, and *Dirty Work*. *Busy Bodies* is by far the best of the bunch, with a lumber-factory setting. B&W; 80m. **DIR:** Lloyd French, George Marshall. **CAST:** Stan Laurel, Oliver Hardy, Mae Busch, Charlie Hall. **1930**

LAUREL AND HARDY CLASSICS, VOLUME 4 ★★★ In *Another Fine Mess*, Stan Laurel and Oliver Hardy are trapped in a house when escaping from the police. *Laughing Gray* has them attempting to hide a forbidden dog in their room. *Come Clean* starts with a simple trip for ice cream, but after saving Mae Busch's life, Stan and Ollie can't get rid of her. *Any Old Port* pits them against Walter Long twice; once as the manager of a hotel and again as a boxer. This collection contains a consistently entertaining group of short subjects. B&W; 90m. **DIR:** James W. Horne, James Parrott. **CAST:** Stan Laurel, Oliver Hardy, Charlie Hall, James Finlayson, Walter Long, Mae Busch. **1930**

LAUREL AND HARDY CLASSICS, VOLUME 5 ★★★ Two good and two moderate comedies—*Perfect Day*, *Helpmates*, *Be Big*, and *Night Owls*, respectively—make up this tape. In *Helpmates*, the action develops from a simple idea: Ollie has to clean up the house so that his wife won't know he's hosted a party in her absence. From this simple beginning, laughs are many and well earned. B&W; 80m. **DIR:** James Parrott. **CAST:** Stan Laurel, Oliver Hardy, Edgar Kennedy, Anita Garvin. **1930**

LAUREL AND HARDY CLASSICS, VOLUME 6 ★★★★ A collection of top-notch comedies all: *Our Wife*, *The Fixer-Uppers*, *Them Thar Hills*, and *Tit for Tat*. *Them Thar Hills* is a marvelous blend of logic and silliness, with Stan and Ollie going to the mountains for Ollie's health and ending up in a tit-for-tat duel with Charlie Hall. The duel is resumed in *Tit for Tat*, the only sequel ever made by L&H. *Our Wife*, the weakest of the group, has a scene that forecasts the stateroom sequence in the Marx Brothers' *A Night at the Opera*. B&W; 80m. **DIR:** James W. Horne, Charles R. Rogers. **CAST:** Stan Laurel, Oliver Hardy, Mae Busch, Charlie Hall. **1930**

LAUREL AND HARDY CLASSICS, VOLUME 7 ★★½ A collection of two moderately funny films, *Thicker Than Water* and *Midnight Patrol*, and two well-done films, *Below Zero* and *Me and My Pal*. *Patrol* places Stan and Ollie in the police force. It may bear the distinction of having the most gruesome ending of any of their films. B&W; 80m. **DIR:** James Parrott, James W. Horne, Lloyd French, Charles R. Rogers. **CAST:** Stan Laurel, Oliver Hardy, Charlie Hall, James Finlayson. **1930**

LAUREL AND HARDY CLASSICS, VOLUME 8 ★★½ *Men o' War* is the standout of this collection. As sailors on leave, Laurel and Hardy attempt to impress two young ladies in Los Angeles' MacArthur Park. *One Good Turn* has them attempting to help an older woman save her home. *The Laurel and Hardy Murder Case*, the weakest film here, is a parody of murder mysteries. B&W; 70m. **DIR:** Lewis R. Foster, James W. Horne, James Parrott. **CAST:** Stan Laurel, Oliver Hardy, Stanley Sanford, Billy Gilbert. **1930**

LAUREL AND HARDY CLASSICS, VOLUME 9 ★★★½ In *Beau Hunks*, Stan Laurel and Oliver Hardy join the foreign legion. *Going Bye-Bye!* has Stan and Ollie attempting to leave town after offering testimony that convicts Walter Long; their escape includes the totally logical and classic line "Excuse me, please—my ear is full of milk." *Chickens Come Home* is an election-year saga. *Berth Marks* is the first Laurel and Hardy sound film. Despite its audio awkwardness, this video has some fine comedy pieces. B&W; 108m. **DIR:** James W. Horne, Charles R. Rogers, Lewis R. Foster. **CAST:** Stan Laurel, Oliver Hardy, Mae Busch, Charlie Hall, Jean Harlow, James Finlayson, Walter Long. **1930**

LAUREL AND HARDY ON THE LAM ★★★★½ A collection of four Laurel and Hardy shorts made when they were at their peak. "Another Fine Mess" was good enough to become their trademark film, while "Scram!," "One Good Turn," and "Going Bye-Bye" contain some of the funniest moments ever captured by the camera. A very enjoyable package. B&W; 95m. **DIR:** James Parrott, James W. Horne, Charles R. Rogers. **CAST:** Stan Laurel, Oliver Hardy, James Finlayson, Mae Busch, Billy Gilbert. **1930–34**

LAUREL AND HARDY'S LAUGHING 20S ★★★★ Another fine compilation by Robert Youngson, following *Days of Thrills and Laughter, The Golden Age of Comedy,* and *When Comedy was King*—with sidesplitting excerpts from silent films, primarily those of Stan Laurel and Oliver Hardy, from 1915 to 1928. B&W; 90m. **DIR:** Robert Youngson. **CAST:** Stan Laurel, Oliver Hardy, Charlie Chase, Edgar Kennedy. **1965**

LAVENDER HILL MOB, THE ★★★★★ Fun, fun, and more fun from this celebrated British comedy. Alec Guinness is a mousy bank clerk. He has a plan for intercepting the bank's armored-car shipment. With the aid of a few friends he forms an amateur robbery squad. Lo and behold, they escape with the loot. After all, the plan was foolproof. Or was it? B&W; 82m. **DIR:** Charles Crichton. **CAST:** Alec Guinness, Stanley Holloway, Sidney James, Alfie Bass. **1951**

LAWRENCEVILLE STORIES, THE ★★★½ Award-winning miniseries takes a humorous look at a turn-of-the-century boarding school. Owen Johnson's delightful short story collection sets the stage for endless pranks perpetuated by teenage boys. 180m. **DIR:** Allan A. Goldstein, Robert Iscove. **CAST:** Zach Galligan, Edward Herrmann, Robert Joy, Nicholas Rowe. **1988**

LEADER OF THE BAND ★★★ In this charming comedy Steve Landesberg plays an unemployed musician who becomes the band instructor for a group of misfits. Too much footage is devoted to marching-band performances, but all in all this film has general appeal. Rated PG for profanity. 90m. **DIR:** Nessa Hyams. **CAST:** Steve Landesberg, Gailard Sartain, Mercedes Ruehl. **1987**

LEAGUE OF GENTLEMEN, THE ★★★★ A British army officer assembles a group of other military retirees and plots a perfect robbery. One of those lighthearted thrillers where the joy comes from watching professionals pull off an incredibly detailed crime. B&W; 114m. **DIR:** Basil Dearden. **CAST:** Jack Hawkins, Nigel Patrick, Roger Livesey, Richard Attenborough, Bryan Forbes, Kieron Moore. **1961**

LEMON DROP KID, THE ★★★ Great group of character actors makes this Damon Runyon story of an incompetent bookie work like a charm. Fast-talking Bob Hope has the tailor-made leading role. Deadly Lloyd Nolan plays the guy putting the screws to Hope, and Marilyn Maxwell plays the girl caught in the middle. B&W; 91m. **DIR:** Sidney Lanfield. **CAST:** Bob Hope, Marilyn Maxwell, Lloyd Nolan, Jane Darwell, Andrea King, Fred Clark, Jay C. Flippen, William Frawley. **1951**

LEMON SISTERS, THE ★★ Engaging characters are in desperate need of a coherent story as three middle-aged, part-time lounge singers find their show-biz dreams slipping away in 1982 Atlantic City. Hollow comedy-cum-drama. Rated PG-13. 100m. **DIR:** Joyce Chopra. **CAST:** Diane Keaton, Carol Kane, Kathryn Grody, Rubén Blades, Aidan Quinn, Elliott Gould. **1990**

LENNY BRUCE PERFORMANCE FILM, THE ★★★★ This simple, straightforward solo showcases Lenny Bruce, the master of bitter satire, in all his gritty brilliance. Bruce was an original, a pioneer who paved the way for George Carlin, Richard Pryor, and all the rest. Also included is Bruce's color-cartoon parody of the Lone Ranger, "Thank You Masked Man." Otherwise, black and white. Rated R for language. 70m. **DIR:** John Magnuson. **CAST:** Lenny Bruce. **1968**

LEONARD PART 6 🦃 Bill Cosby, forced into saving the world, does so, but he can't save the picture. Rated PG. 83m. **DIR:** Paul Weiland. **CAST:** Bill Cosby, Tom Courtenay, Joe Don Baker, Moses Gunn. **1987**

LES PATTERSON SAVES THE WORLD ★★★ Barry Humphries, the immensely popular Australian comic best known here for his character Dame Edna Everage, plays both the good dame and Sir Les Patterson, a fat, flatulent, drunken ambassador from down under. The plot, a spy-movie spoof, holds together a string of outrageous slapstick gags involving bodily functions, ethnic humor, and sexual etiquette. Unrated; it's not for kids. 105m. **DIR:** George Miller. **CAST:** Barry Humphries, Pamela Stephenson. **1987**

LET IT RIDE ★★★½ One last binge at the racetrack by a chronic gambler (Richard Dreyfuss), who can't resist a hot tip on the horses, turns into a riotous fiasco in this breezy, modest comedy. Rated PG-13. 91m. **DIR:** Joe Pytka. **CAST:** Richard Dreyfuss, Teri Garr, David Johansen, Allen Garfield, Jennifer Tilly. **1989**

LET'S DO IT AGAIN ★★★½ After scoring with *Uptown Saturday Night*, Sidney Poitier and Bill Cosby decided to reteam for this tale of a couple of lodge brothers taking on the gangsters. Rated PG. 112m. **DIR:** Sidney Poitier. **CAST:** Sidney Poitier, Bill Cosby, Jimmie Walker, Calvin Lockhart, John Amos. **1975**

LET'S MAKE IT LEGAL ★★★ Claudette Colbert and Zachary Scott are the best players in this sophisticated comedy about marriage, divorce, and friendship. Marilyn Monroe shines in a supporting role. B&W; 74m. **DIR:** Richard Sale. **CAST:** Claudette Colbert, Marilyn Monroe, Macdonald Carey, Zachary Scott, Robert Wagner. **1951**

LETTER TO BREZHNEV ★★★½ This wistful, spunky little movie presents two young women of Liverpool who befriend a couple of Russian sailors. Teresa (played by Liverpool comedienne Margi Clarke) is just after some fun, but Elaine (Alexandra Pigg) falls in love with her sailor. Peter Firth plays Elaine's love and he's the quintessence of sweetness. Alexandra Pigg gives the film some street-talking sass, and Firth imbues it with adorable innocence. 95m. **DIR:** Chris Bernard. **CAST:** Alexandra Pigg, Alfred Molina, Peter Firth, Margi Clarke. **1985**

LIBELED LADY ★★★★★ Their fame as Nick and Nora Charles in the *Thin Man* series notwithstanding, this is the finest film to have paired William Powell and Myrna Loy. They take part in a deliciously funny tale of a newspaper that, when faced with a libel suit from an angered woman, attempts to turn the libel into irrefutable fact. Spencer Tracy and Jean Harlow lend their considerable support, and the result is a delight from start to finish. B&W; 98m. **DIR:** Jack Conway. **CAST:** William Powell, Myrna Loy, Spencer Tracy, Jean Harlow. **1936**

LICENSE TO DRIVE ★★★ Wildly improbable yet frenetically funny account of how young Les (Corey Haim) flunks his driver's license exam yet steals his grandfather's Cadillac for a hot date. Richard Masur is perfect as the quiet, sane father trying to deal with insanity. Rated PG-13 for profanity. 88m. **DIR:** Greg Beeman. **CAST:** Corey Haim, Corey Feldman, Carol Kane, Richard Masur, Heather Graham. **1988**

LIFE BEGINS FOR ANDY HARDY ★★★ Andy Hardy, fresh out of high school, tries on New York City for size, comes to grips with a mature woman, and learns a few big-city lessons before deciding college near home and hearth is best. The eleventh and one of the best in the series. B&W; 100m. **DIR:** George B. Seitz. **CAST:** Mickey Rooney, Judy Garland, Lewis Stone, Fay Holden, Ann Rutherford, Sara Haden. **1941**

LIFE OF BRIAN ★★★★ Religious fanaticism gets a real drubbing in this irreverent and often sidesplitting comedy, which features and was created by those Monty Python crazies. Graham Chapman plays the title role of a reluctant "savior" born in a manger just down the street from Jesus Christ's. Rated R for nudity and profanity. 93m. **DIR:** Terry Jones. **CAST:** Terry Jones, John Cleese, Eric Idle, Michael Palin, Terry Gilliam, Graham Chapman. **1979**

LIFE STINKS ★★½ A kinder, gentler Mel Brooks directed, cowrote, and stars in this message movie about a rich land developer who bets he can spend a month on the streets of Los Angeles. Even though the film is quite funny, he unfortunately tends to be a tad preachy. Rated PG-13 for profanity and suggested sex. 91m. **DIR:** Mel Brooks. **CAST:** Mel Brooks, Lesley Ann Warren, Jeffrey Tambor, Stuart Pankin, Howard Morris. **1991**

LIFE WITH FATHER ★★★★ A warm, witty, charming, nostalgic memoir of life and the coming of age of author Clarence Day in turn-of-the-century New York City. Centering on his staid, eccentric father (William Powell), the film is a 100 percent delight. Based on the long-running Broadway play. 118m. **DIR:** Michael Curtiz. **CAST:** William Powell, Irene Dunne, Edmund Gwenn, ZaSu Pitts, Jimmy Lydon, Elizabeth Taylor, Martin Milner. **1947**

LIFE WITH MIKEY ★★★½ The story of a former child star who runs a talent agency has built-in laugh spots. Especially with Michael J. Fox as the agent who needs a child star for a commercial or his agency will go under. Fox has a handle on comic reactions and gets to use them. Rated PG. 106m. **DIR:** James Lapine. **CAST:** Michael J. Fox, Nathan Lane, Cyndi Lauper, Christina Vidal. **1993**

LIKE FATHER, LIKE SON ★★ Father and son (Dudley Moore and Kirk Cameron) accidentally transfer brains. The film too often sinks to tasteless and juvenile stunts to spice up the lone idea. Rated PG-13. 99m. **DIR:** Rod Daniel. **CAST:** Dudley Moore, Kirk Cameron, Margaret Colin, Catharine Hicks, Sean Astin, Patrick O'Neal. **1987**

LI'L ABNER (1940) ★★ The first of two filmed versions of Al Capp's popular comic strip boasts a great cast of silent film's best clowns. B&W; 78m. **DIR:** Albert S. Rogell. **CAST:** Granville Owen, Martha Driscoll, Buster Keaton, Kay Sutton, Edgar Kennedy, Chester Conklin, Billy Bevan, Al St. John. **1940**

LILY IN LOVE ★★★★ Christopher Plummer is superb as an aging, egocentric actor who disguises himself as a younger man in an attempt to snag a plum role in a film written by his wife (Maggie Smith), and succeeds all too well. *Lily in Love* is a marvelously warm and witty adult comedy. Unrated, the film has some profanity. 105m. **DIR:** Karoly Makk. **CAST:** Christopher Plummer, Maggie Smith, Elke Sommer, Adolph Green. **1985**

LILY TOMLIN SPECIAL—VOL. I, THE ★★★ One of the first Lily Tomlin specials produced for television in the Seventies. Along with the laughs, there is an insightful skit with Richard Pryor about the way the poverty-stricken and disfranchised are sometimes treated. Not rated. 60m. **DIR:** Bill Davis. **CAST:** Lily Tomlin, Richard Pryor, Alan Alda, Judy Kahan. **1973**

LIMELIGHT ★★★½ Too long and too much Charlie Chaplin (who trimmed Buster Keaton's part when it became obvious he was stealing the film), this is nevertheless a poignant excursion. Chaplin is an aging music hall comic on the skids who saves a ballerina (Claire Bloom) from suicide and, while bolstering her hopes, regains his confidence. The score, by Chaplin, is haunting. B&W; 145m. **DIR:** Charles Chaplin. **CAST:** Charlie Chaplin, Claire Bloom, Buster Keaton, Sydney Chaplin, Nigel Bruce. **1952**

LIMIT UP ★★ Nancy Allen stars as a woman who wants to be a trader with Chicago's Mercantile Exchange. She's enticed by one of Satan's disciples into a contract for her soul. Harmless, predictable. Watch for cameos by Sally Kellerman and Ray Charles. Rated PG-13 for profanity. 88m. **DIR:** Richard Martini. **CAST:** Nancy Allen, Dean Stockwell, Brad Hall, Danitra Vance. **1989**

LINGUINI INCIDENT, THE ★★ David Bowie's even performance as a man desperate to get married can't compensate for Rosanna Arquette's annoyingly brittle portrayal of a would-be escape artist. The two join with hilarious Eszter Balint to rob an ultra-trendy restaurant. Rated R for profanity. 93m. **DIR:** Richard Shepard. **CAST:** Rosanna Arquette, David Bowie, Eszter Balint, André Gregory, Buck Henry, Marlee Matlin. **1992**

LISTEN TO YOUR HEART ★★★ This cute but predictable romantic comedy features a book editor (Tim Matheson) falling in love with his art director (Kate Jackson). Made for TV, this is unrated. 104m. **DIR:** Don Taylor. **CAST:** Kate Jackson, Tim Matheson, Cassie Yates, George Coe, Tony Plana. **1983**

LITTLE DARLINGS ★★ A story of the trials and tribulations of teen-age virginity, this film too often lapses into chronic cuteness. *Little Darlings* follows the antics of two 15-year-old outcasts—rich, sophisticated Ferris Whitney (Tatum O'Neal) and poor, belligerent Angel Bright (Kristy McNichol)—as they compete to "score" with a boy first. Rated R. 95m. **DIR:** Ronald F. Maxwell. **CAST:** Tatum O'Neal, Kristy McNichol, Matt Dillon, Armand Assante. **1980**

LITTLE GIANT ★★ Title refers to a vacuum cleaner that Lou Costello sells door to door. Bud Abbott's in the movie, too, but they don't have any scenes together. Were they feuding? Whatever the reason, the gimmick doesn't work. B&W; 91m. **DIR:** William A. Seiter. **CAST:** Bud Abbott, Lou Costello, Brenda Joyce. **1946**

LITTLE MURDERS ★★★★ Jules Feiffer's savagely black comedy details the nightmarish adventures of a mild-mannered New Yorker (Elliott Gould) who finds the world becoming increasingly insane and violent. What seemed like bizarre fantasy when *Little Murders* was originally released is today all too close to reality. Strangely, this makes the film easier to watch while taking away none of its bite. Terrific supporting performances by Vincent Gardenia, Elizabeth Wilson, and director Alan Arkin. Rated PG for violence and profanity. 107m. **DIR:** Alan Arkin. **CAST:** Elliott Gould, Marcia Rodd, Vincent Gardenia, Elizabeth Wilson, Donald Sutherland, Lou Jacobi, Alan Arkin. **1971**

LITTLE ROMANCE, A ★★★★½ Everyone needs *A Little Romance* in their life. This absolutely enchanting film by director George Roy Hill has something for everyone. Its story of two appealing youngsters (Thelonious Bernard and Diane Lane) who fall in love in Paris is full of surprises, laughs, and uplifting moments. Rated PG. 108m. **DIR:** George Roy Hill. **CAST:** Thelonious Bernard, Diane Lane, Laurence Olivier, Sally Kellerman, Broderick Crawford, David Dukes. **1979**

LITTLE SEX, A ★★ A New York director of television commercials can't keep his hands off his actresses, even though he's married to a beautiful, intelligent woman. This is a tepid romantic comedy. Rated R. 95m. **DIR:** Bruce Paltrow. **CAST:** Tim Matheson, Kate Capshaw, Edward Herrmann. **1982**

LITTLE SISTER ★★½ Likable comedy with Jonathan Silverman as a love-struck student who dons women's clothing in order to sneak into a sorority. Been-there, done-that comedy still manages to be quite entertaining. Rated PG-13 for sexual content. 94m. **DIR:** Jimmy Zeilinger. **CAST:** Jonathan Silverman, Alyssa Milano, George Newbern. **1991**

LITTLE TOUGH GUYS ★★ Offshoot of the popular Dead End Kids films for Warner Bros., this was the first in a series for Universal that would eventually redefine the gang's hard edges and turn them into the bumbling East Side Kids and finally the hopelessly inept Bowery Boys. Not as good as the earlier entries, this film is still far superior to the treatment the boys would receive from Monogram Pictures in the years ahead. B&W; 63m. **DIR:** Harold Young. **CAST:** Billy Halop, Huntz Hall, Gabriel Dell, Bernard Punsley, David Gorcey, Helen Parrish, Robert Wilcox, Marjorie Main. **1938**

LITTLE VEGAS ★★★★ A fantastic movie about a man (Anthony Denison) trying to escape from the mob-like life of his family. After the death of a matronly woman who was taking care of him, he must contend with the other residents of a small desert town who see him as a gigolo. Rated R for nudity and profanity. 91m. **DIR:** Perry Lang. **CAST:** Anthony Denison, Catherine O'Hara, Anne Francis, Michael Nouri, Perry Lang, John Sayles, Bruce McGill, Jerry Stiller. **1990**

LITTLE WHITE LIES ★★★ While on vacation in Rome, surgeon Tim Matheson and detective Ann Jillian meet and fall in love. Harmless fluff, pleasant diversion for a made-for-television feature. 95m. **DIR:** Anson Williams. **CAST:** Tim Matheson, Ann Jillian. **1989**

LIVE AT HARRAH'S ★★ Rip Taylor is the host for the on- and off-stage routines of Bill Cosby, Elaine Boozler, Dick Shawn, and Sammy King. This is a curiously uneven selection of material. Boozler and Shawn deliver adult humor and then Cosby comes onstage with an overly long routine with kids from the audience. 60m. **DIR:** Greg Stevens. **CAST:** Bill Cosby, Rip Taylor, Elayne Boosler, Dick Shawn, Sammy King. **1981**

LIVE FROM WASHINGTON—IT'S DENNIS MILLER ★★★½ Miller, who is best known for Weekend Update on *Saturday Night Live,* is given no restrictions on language or subject matter and takes full advantage of it. His routine is well paced, and he makes some very funny observations. TV newscaster Edwin Newman has a cameo at the beginning, advising the comedian about going to D.C. and playing to a tough audience. 60m. **DIR:** Paul Miller. **CAST:** Dennis Miller. **1988**

LIVIN' LARGE ★★½ In this hit-and-miss comedy, Terrence "T. C." Carson plays a young man devoted to getting on television. When his big break comes, his devotion to his career threatens to alienate his longtime friends. Rated R for profanity and violence. 96m. **DIR:** Michael Schultz. **CAST:** Terrence "T. C." Carson, Lisa Arrindell, Nathaniel Hall, Blanche Baker, Julia Campbell. **1991**

LIZZIES OF MACK SENNETT, THE ★★★ Three fast-moving, mirth-and-mayhem film funnies produced by the master of slapstick, Mack Sennett. Lots of thrills, spills, and impossible feats mark "Lizzies of the Field," "Leading Lizzie Astray," and "Love, Speed and Thrills." Silent. B&W; 51m. **DIR:** Roscoe Arbuckle. **CAST:** Roscoe "Fatty" Arbuckle, Minta Durfee, Chester Conklin, Mack Swain, Andy Clyde. **1915–1924**

LOBSTER MAN FROM MARS ★★ A sometimes funny comedy about a movie producer who, in need of a tax-sheltering flop, calls upon an amateur filmmaker and his sci-fi flick to save him. Old and overused jokes and sight gags cause this parody to flop more often than fly. Rated PG. 84m. **DIR:** Stanley Sheff. **CAST:** Tony Curtis, Deborah Foreman, Patrick Macnee, Billy Barty. **1990**

LOCAL HERO ★★★★½ A wonderfully offbeat comedy by Bill Forsyth. Burt Lancaster plays a Houston oil baron who sends Peter Riegert to the west coast of Scotland to negotiate with the natives for North Sea oil rights. As with *Gregory's Girl,* which was about a gangly, good-natured boy's first crush, this film is blessed with sparkling little moments of humor, unforgettable characters, and a warmly human story. Rated PG for language. 111m. **DIR:** Bill Forsyth. **CAST:** Burt Lancaster, Peter Riegert, Fulton MacKay. **1983**

LONELY GUY, THE ★★★ Steve Martin stars in this okay comedy as a struggling young writer. One day he comes home to find his live-in mate (Robyn Douglass) in bed with another man and becomes the "Lonely Guy" of the title. Only recommended for Steve Martin fans. Rated R for brief nudity and profanity. 90m. **DIR:** Arthur Hiller. **CAST:** Steve Martin, Robyn Douglass, Charles Grodin, Merv Griffin, Dr. Joyce Brothers. **1984**

LONELY IN AMERICA ★★★½ Bittersweet comedy concerns an East Indian man's rude awakening to the less inviting aspects of immigrating to the United States. Some of his experiences are more painful than hilarious and, as such, send home a message about compassion and tolerance. Rated PG-13 for sexual situations. 96m. **DIR:** Barry Alexander Brown. **CAST:** Ranjit Chowdhry, Adelaide Miller, Robert Kessler. **1990**

LONG, LONG TRAILER, THE ★★★ You might not love Lucy in this one, but you'll sure like her a lot. Ball and Desi Arnaz portray a couple not unlike the Ricardos. Their honeymoon trip is complicated by an impossibly long trailer. Once their dream vehicle, this trailer becomes a nightmare. 103m. **DIR:** Vincente Minnelli. **CAST:** Lucille Ball, Desi Arnaz Sr., Marjorie Main, Keenan Wynn. **1954**

LONGSHOT, THE (1985) 🦃 Dreck about small-time horse players. Rated PG. 110m. **DIR:** Paul Bartel. **CAST:** Tim Conway, Harvey Korman, Jack Weston, Ted Wass, Anne Meara, Stella Stevens, Jonathan Winters. **1985**

LOOK WHO'S LAUGHING ★★ Pretty weak comedy featuring radio favorites Edgar Bergen and Fibber McGee and Molly. Rather lean on laughs, except when Charlie McCarthy takes the spotlight. B&W; 78m. **DIR:** Allan Dwan. **CAST:** Edgar Bergen, Jim Jordan, Marion Jordan, Lucille Ball, Harold Peary. **1941**

LOOK WHO'S TALKING ★★★★ Hilarious adventure of an unmarried woman (Kirstie Alley) seeking the perfect father for her baby. John Travolta becomes the baby's unconventional sitter. Baby Mikey's humorous impressions from conception to age one are relayed through the offscreen voice of Bruce Willis. PG-13 for an opening sex-ed sequence of Mikey's conception. 100m. **DIR:** Amy Heckerling. **CAST:** Kirstie Alley, John Travolta, Olympia Dukakis, George Segal. **1989**

LOOK WHO'S TALKING TOO 🦃 A totally unfunny sequel that reunites the original cast but can't come up with the spark that made the first so enjoyable. Also featuring the voices of Bruce Willis, Roseanne Barr, and Damon Wayans. 81m. **DIR:** Amy Heckerling. **CAST:** John Travolta, Kirstie Alley, Olympia Dukakis, Elias Koteas. **1990**

LOOK WHO'S TALKING NOW 🦃 Precocious family dogs spar with voices supplied by Danny DeVito and Diane Keaton in this tired, insulting sequel. Rated PG. 97m. **DIR:** Tom Ropelewski. **CAST:** John Travolta, Kirstie Alley. **1993**

LOOKIN' TO GET OUT ★★★ This offbeat comedy stars Jon Voight and Burt Young as a couple of compulsive gamblers out to hit the fabled "big score" in Las Vegas. It does drag a bit in the middle. However, the first hour zips by before you know it, and the ending is a humdinger. Rated R for violence and profanity. 104m. **DIR:** Hal Ashby. **CAST:** Jon Voight, Burt Young, Ann-Margret, Bert Remsen. **1982**

LOOSE CANNONS ★★ Gene Hackman stars as a hard-nosed career policeman who gets stuck with the deranged Dan Aykroyd as a partner. Only a few funny scenes provided by Aykroyd, including one in which he imitates the Road Runner, save this uneven cop comedy. Rated R for profanity and violence. 90m. **DIR:** Bob Clark. **CAST:** Gene Hackman, Dan Aykroyd, Dom DeLuise, Ronny Cox, Nancy Travis, Robert Prosky, Paul Koslo. **1990**

LOOSE CONNECTIONS ★★★½ In this cult comedy, an Englishwoman (Lindsay Duncan) builds a car with two female friends so that they can attend a feminist convention in Germany. At the last minute, her friends back out, and she is forced to accept a goofy substitute (Stephen Rea) as her traveling companion. Offbeat entertainment. Rated PG for profanity. 90m. **DIR:** Richard Eyre. **CAST:** Stephen Rea, Lindsay Duncan. **1984**

LOOSE SHOES 🦃 Failed attempt to spoof B movies. Rated R. 73m. **DIR:** Ira Miller. **CAST:** Buddy Hackett, Howard Hesseman, Bill Murray, Susan Tyrrell, Avery Schreiber. **1977**

LOOT ★★ A hearse driver and his friend rob a bank and store the loot inside a coffin, setting off a slapstick, cliché-ridden comedy complete with a runaway funeral procession—and every graveyard quip in the book. Dated now, this was probably racy in its day. Not rated. 102m. **DIR:** Silvio Narizzano. **CAST:** Lee Remick, Richard Attenborough, Milo O'Shea, Hywel Bennett. **1972**

LORD LOVE A DUCK ★★★½ A cynic's delight that makes a big joke out of greed, lust, and egomania. Roddy McDowall plays a high school senior who helps classmate Tuesday Weld con her father, marry a hunk, become a movie star and—when she gets bored with everything else—become a widow. A lot of laughs, but not for every taste. B&W; 105m. **DIR:** George Axelrod. **CAST:** Roddy McDowall, Tuesday Weld, Lola Albright, Ruth Gordon, Max Showalter, Martin Gabel, Harvey Korman, Donald Murphy, Sarah Marshall. **1966**

LOSIN' IT ★★★ Better-than-average teen exploitation flick, this one has four boys off to Tijuana for a good time. Shelley Long ("Cheers") adds interest as a runaway wife who joins them on their journey. Rated R. 104m. **DIR:** Curtis Hanson. **CAST:** Tom Cruise, Shelley Long, Jackie Earle Haley, John Stockwell. **1982**

LOST AND FOUND ★★ After teaming up successfully for *A Touch of Class*, writer-director Melvin Frank and his stars, Glenda Jackson and George Segal, tried again. But the result was an unfunny comedy about two bickering, cardboard characters. Rated PG. 112m. **DIR:** Melvin Frank. **CAST:** Glenda Jackson, George Segal, Maureen Stapleton. **1979**

LOST AND FOUND CHAPLIN: KEYSTONE ★★★½ A pre–Little Tramp Charlie Chaplin vies with contemporary peer Roscoe Arbuckle in "The Masquerader" and "The Rounders," two of these three early short comedies produced by Mack Sennett at Keystone Studios. In the third, "Making A Living," Chaplin makes his screen debut as a slick con man. B&W; 60m. **DIR:** Henry Lehrman, Charles Chaplin. **CAST:** Charlie Chaplin, Virginia Kirtley, Minta Durfee, Roscoe "Fatty" Arbuckle, Fritz Schade, Al St. John. **1914**

LOST IN A HAREM ★★★ Two down-and-out traveling magicians attempt to save a singer from the clutches of a sheikh. Best bit is Costello locked up with a murderer who explains: "S-l-o-w-l-y, I turned." 89m. **DIR:** Charles F. Riesner. **CAST:** Bud Abbott, Lou Costello, Marilyn Maxwell, Douglass Dumbrille. **1944**

LOST IN ALASKA ★★ Gambling, mining, the Alaska gold rush, and anything else the writers could think of is tossed into this mess of a comedy, one of Abbott and Costello's weakest. B&W; 76m. **DIR:** Jean Yarbrough. **CAST:** Bud Abbott, Lou Costello, Tom Ewell, Mitzi Green. **1952**

LOST IN AMERICA ★★★★½ Writer-director-star Albert Brooks is one of America's great natural comedic resources. *Lost in America* is his funniest film to date. Some viewers may be driven to distraction by Brooks's all-too-true study of what happens when a "successful" and "responsible" married couple chucks it all and goes out on an *Easy Rider*–style trip across the country. Brooks makes movies about the things most adults would consider their worst nightmare. He cuts close to the bone and makes us laugh at ourselves in a very original way. If you can stand the pain, the pleasure is well worth it. Rated R for profanity and adult situations. 92m. **DIR:** Albert Brooks. **CAST:** Albert Brooks, Julie Hagerty, Garry Marshall. **1985**

LOST STOOGES, THE ★★★ Leonard Maltin narrates this compilation of early film appearances by Ted Healy and the Three Stooges in MGM musicals and two-reel fillers—before Moe Howard, Larry Fine, and Curly Howard broke off to make their successful series of shorts for Columbia. These excerpts are primarily of interest for their historical value, and even die-hard Stooges fans may find this program to be slow-going. Unrated, this direct-to-video release has Stooges-type violence. B&W; 68m. **DIR:** Mark Lamberti. **CAST:** Moe Howard, Larry Fine, Curly Howard, Ted Healy. **1990**

LOTS OF LUCK ★★ Made for Disney's cable channel, this mildly funny family film exposes the darker side of striking it rich. A family (Martin Mull and Annette Funicello play dad and mom) suddenly wins the lottery. Unfortunately they lose their friends and privacy. 88m. **DIR:** Peter Baldwin. **CAST:** Martin Mull, Annette Funicello, Fred Willard, Polly Holliday, Mia Dillon, Tracey Gold. **1985**

LOUIE ANDERSON: MOM! LOUIE'S LOOKING AT ME AGAIN! ★★★★ Young comic Louie Anderson combines perfect timing with unmistakable facial contortions to relive his hilariously troubled youth. His gun-toting father, babbling mom, and intimidated little brother, Tommy, come to life through Anderson's delightful routines. 60m. **DIR:** Jeffrey Weihe. **CAST:** Louie Anderson. **1987**

LOUISIANA PURCHASE ★★★½ Attempts are made to frame an honest fuddy-duddy senator (Victor Moore). Moore is a joy, but it is Bob Hope's classic filibuster that is the highlight of the movie. Based on an Irving Berlin musical; a few good songs were retained. 98m. **DIR:** Irving Cummings. **CAST:** Bob Hope, Vera Zorina, Victor Moore, Dona Drake, Raymond Walburn, Maxie Rosenbloom, Frank Albertson. **1941**

LOVE AMONG THE RUINS ★★★★ In this made-for-TV comedy-romance, Katharine Hepburn plays opposite Laurence Olivier. The delightful story focuses on the plight of an aging actress who is being sued by a young gigolo for breach of promise. Her situation is further complicated when the prominent barrister handling her defense turns out to be a lovestruck former suitor. 100m. **DIR:** George Cukor. **CAST:** Katharine Hepburn, Laurence Olivier, Leigh Lawson, Joan Sims. **1975**

LOVE AND DEATH ★★★★ This comedy set in 1812 Russia is one of Woody Allen's funniest films. Diane Keaton is the high-minded Russian with assassination (of Napoleon) in mind. Allen is her cowardly accomplice with sex on the brain. The movie satirizes not only love and death, but politics, classic Russian literature (Tolstoy's *War and Peace*), and foreign films, as well. Use of Prokofiev music enhances the piece. Rated PG. 82m. **DIR:** Woody Allen. **CAST:** Woody Allen, Diane Keaton, Harold Gould, Alfred Lutter, Zvee Scooler. **1975**

LOVE AT FIRST BITE ★★★★ The Dracula legend is given the comedy treatment in this amusing parody of horror films. George Hamilton plays the campy Count, who has an unorthodox way with the ladies. (In this case, it's Susan Saint James, much to the chagrin of her boyfriend, Richard Benjamin.) Even though the humor is heavy-handed in parts, you find yourself chuckling continually in spite of yourself. Rated PG. 96m. **DIR:** Stan Dragoti. **CAST:** George Hamilton, Susan Saint James, Richard Benjamin, Dick Shawn, Arte Johnson. **1979**

LOVE AT FIRST SIGHT 🦃 Dan Aykroyd tries for laughs as a blind man in love with a girl whose family won't have him for a son-in-law. Rated PG. 85m. **DIR:** Rex Bromfield. **CAST:** Mary Ann McDonald, Dan Aykroyd, Barry Morse. **1977**

LOVE AT LARGE ★★★★ Writer-director Alan Rudolph serves up a deliciously offbeat spoof of the mystery movie with his tale of a private eye (Tom Berenger) hired by a mysterious woman (Anne Archer). It's funny and intriguing; a movie buff's delight. Rated R for profanity and violence. 97m. **DIR:** Alan Rudolph. **CAST:** Tom Berenger, Elizabeth Perkins, Anne Archer, Kate Capshaw, Annette O'Toole, Ted Levine, Ann Magnuson, Neil Young. **1990**

LOVE AT STAKE 🦃 Attempted spoof of witchcraft and black-magic films is a dismal failure. Rated R for nudity and profanity. 88m. **DIR:** John Moffitt. **CAST:** Barbara Carrera, Bud Cort, Dave Thomas, Patrick Cassidy, Stuart Pankin. **1988**

LOVE CRAZY ★★★★ Crazy is right, in this screwball comedy where innocent William Powell is found by his wife (Myrna Loy) in a compromising situation with an old flame. She sues for divorce; he feigns insanity to keep her, carrying the act all the way to a lunacy hearing. B&W; 99m. **DIR:** Jack Conway. **CAST:** William Powell, Myrna Loy, Gail Patrick, Jack Carson, Florence Bates, Sidney Blackmer, Sig Ruman. **1941**

LOVE FINDS ANDY HARDY ★★★ In this fourth film of the series, the love that finds Mickey Rooney as Andy Hardy is then-teenager Lana Turner. As usual, it's an all-innocent slice of small-town American family life. B&W; 90m. **DIR:** George B. Seitz. **CAST:** Mickey Rooney, Lewis Stone, Fay Holden, Judy Garland, Cecilia Parker, Lana Turner, Ann Rutherford. **1938**

LOVE HAPPY ★★ The last Marx Brothers movie, this 1949 production was originally set to star only Harpo, but Chico and, later, Groucho were brought in to beef up its box-office potential. They should've known better. Only Groucho's ogling of then-screen-newcomer Marilyn Monroe makes it interesting for movie buffs. B&W; 91m. **DIR:** David Miller. **CAST:** The Marx Brothers, Marilyn Monroe, Raymond Burr. **1949**

LOVE HURTS ★★ Womanizer is forced into dealing with his irresponsible past when he finds his ex-wife and kids have moved in with his parents. Rated R for profanity and suggested sex. 110m. **DIR:** Bud Yorkin. **CAST:** Jeff Daniels, Judith Ivey, John Mahoney, Cynthia Sikes, Amy Wright, Cloris Leachman. **1989**

LOVE IN THE AFTERNOON ★★★★ Audrey Hepburn shares fantastic chemistry with both Maurice Chevalier and Gary Cooper in this film classic, which explores the love interests of an American entrepreneur and his lopsided involvement with a young French ingenue. When her doting father (a detective) is asked to investigate the American's love life, it makes for a touching, charming bit of entertainment that never loses its appeal. 130m. **DIR:** Billy Wilder. **CAST:** Gary Cooper, Audrey Hepburn, Maurice Chevalier, John McGiver. **1957**

LOVE LAUGHS AT ANDY HARDY ★★ America's all-American, lovable, irritating, well-meaning wimp comes home from World War II and plunges back into the same adolescent rut of agonizing young love. The change of times has made this cookie-cutter film very predictable, but it's fun anyway. B&W; 93m. **DIR:** Willis Goldbeck. **CAST:** Mickey Rooney, Lewis Stone, Fay Holden, Sara Haden, Bonita Granville. **1946**

LOVE NEST ★★½ An ex-GI returns home to find that his wife has purchased a run-down apartment building whose tenants come to dominate their lives. Mild comedy, mostly of interest to Marilyn Monroe completists. B&W; 84m. **DIR:** Joseph M. Newman. **CAST:** William Lundigan, June Haver, Frank Fay, Marilyn Monroe, Jack Paar. **1951**

LOVE ON THE RUN (1936) ★★★ When a foreign correspondent helps a publicity-shy heiress flee from her own wedding ceremony (sound familiar?), they become involved with spies and intrigue. Good escapism. B&W; 80m. **DIR:** W. S. Van Dyke. **CAST:** Joan Crawford, Clark Gable, Franchot Tone, Reginald Owen, William Demarest, Donald Meek, Billy Gilbert. **1936**

LOVE OR MONEY? ★★ A rising young real estate turk wrestles with his conscience. Should he nail the big deal or follow his heart down the path of love with his client's daughter? Trite comedy. Rated PG-13. 90m. **DIR:** Todd Hallowell. **CAST:** Timothy Daly, Haviland Morris, Kevin McCarthy, Shelley Fabares, David Doyle. **1988**

LOVE POTION #9 ★★★★ Dweeb, zero-charisma scientists Tate Donovan and Sandra Bullock trade in their beakers for romance when they down that famous love potion from gypsy Anne Bancroft. Funny, charming comedy finds new avenues for laughter. The complications are pretty typical, but the script and direction by Dale Launer are sharp and on the money. Rated PG-13 for sexual situations and language. 99m. **DIR:** Dale Launer. **CAST:** Tate Donovan, Sandra Bullock, Dale Midkiff, Anne Bancroft. **1992**

LOVED ONE, THE ★★★★½ A hilarious look at death, American style. The film centers around a naïve British poet, who finds himself in the California funeral industry that includes human and animal customers. Outstanding dark comedy that features an all-star cast with Jonathan Winters in a dual role as an unscrupulous clergyman and the director of a pet cemetery. Brilliantly written by Christopher Isherwood and Terry Southern. B&W; 116m. **DIR:** Tony Richardson. **CAST:** Robert Morse, Rod Steiger, Robert Morley, Jonathan Winters, Tab Hunter, Milton Berle, Lionel Stander, Anjanette Comer, Liberace, James Coburn, John Gielgud. **1965**

LOVELINES Dreadful teen comedy. Rated R for nudity, suggested sex, violence, and profanity. 93m. **DIR:** Rod Amateau. **CAST:** Michael Winslow, Greg Bradford, Mary Beth Evans. **1984**

LOVER COME BACK ★★★★ Rock Hudson and Doris Day are rival advertising executives battling professionally, psychologically, and sexually. A bright comedy that builds nicely. One of their best. Silly, innocent fun with a great supporting cast. 107m. **DIR:** Delbert Mann. **CAST:** Rock Hudson, Doris Day, Tony Randall, Edie Adams, Jack Oakie, Jack Kruschen, Ann B. Davis, Joe Flynn, Jack Albertson. **1961**

LOVERBOY Lame sex farce. Rated PG-13 for profanity and sexual situations. 98m. **DIR:** Joan Micklin Silver. **CAST:** Patrick Dempsey, Kate Jackson, Carrie Fisher, Barbara Carrera, Kirstie Alley, Robert Ginty. **1989**

LOVERS AND LIARS ★★½ The first thing that occurs to you while watching this film is a question: What's Goldie Hawn doing in a dubbed Italian sex comedy? Costarring Giancarlo Giannini it is a modestly entertaining piece of fluff tailored primarily for European tastes and, therefore, will probably disappoint most of Hawn's fans. Rated R. 96m. **DIR:** Mario Monicelli. **CAST:** Goldie Hawn, Giancarlo Giannini, Laura Betti. **1979**

LOVERS AND OTHER STRANGERS ★★★½ A funny film about young love, marriage, and their many side effects on others. Marks Diane Keaton's debut in pictures. The late Gig Young is a delight. 106m. **DIR:** Cy Howard. **CAST:** Gig Young, Diane Keaton, Bea

Arthur, Bonnie Bedelia, Anne Jackson, Harry Guardino, Richard Castellano, Michael Brandon, Cloris Leachman, Anne Meara. 1970

LOVES AND TIMES OF SCARAMOUCHE, THE 🦃 Michael Sarrazin, as Scaramouche, stumbles through this ridiculous swashbuckler. 92m. **DIR:** Enzo G. Castellari. **CAST:** Michael Sarrazin, Ursula Andress, Aldo Maccioni, Gian Carlo Prete. 1976

LOVESICK ★★★ You won't fall out of your seat laughing or grab a tissue to dab away the tears. But this movie, about a psychiatrist's (Dudley Moore) obsession with his patient (Elizabeth McGovern) does have its moments. Rated PG. 95m. **DIR:** Marshall Brickman. **CAST:** Dudley Moore, Elizabeth McGovern, Alec Guinness, John Huston. 1983

LOVING COUPLES ★★ The plot is that old and tired one, about two couples who swap partners for a temporary fling only to reunite by film's end happier and wiser for the experience. It's a premise that's been worn thin and is badly in need of retirement. Rated PG. 97m. **DIR:** Jack Smight. **CAST:** Shirley MacLaine, James Coburn, Susan Sarandon, Stephen Collins. 1980

LUCKY JIM ★★★ High jinks and antics at a small British university as a young lecturer tries to improve his lot by sucking up to his superior, but continually goofs. Acceptable adaptation of the Kingsley Amis novel. 95m. **DIR:** John Boulting. **CAST:** Ian Carmichael, Terry-Thomas, Hugh Griffith. 1957

LUCKY PARTNERS ★★★ Artist Ronald Colman wishes passing errand girl Ginger Rogers good luck, thereby touching off a chain of events ending in romance. Lightweight comedy with, for the time, raw touches. Ginger's naïve charm and Ronald's urbanity make for interesting interplay. B&W; 99m. **DIR:** Lewis Milestone. **CAST:** Ginger Rogers, Ronald Colman, Spring Byington, Jack Carson, Harry Davenport. 1940

LUCKY STIFF ★★★ Lovelorn Joe Alaskey can't believe his luck when he's picked up by gorgeous Donna Dixon and invited to her family's home for Christmas dinner. What he doesn't know is that he's the entree-to-be for this cannibal clan. Writer Pat Profft provides plenty of hilariously demented characters and funny one-liners. Rated PG. 82m. **DIR:** Anthony Perkins. **CAST:** Joe Alaskey, Donna Dixon, Jeff Kober. 1988

LUGGAGE OF THE GODS 🦃 A primitive tribe, unaware of the advances of man, is both delighted and frightened by an airplane emptying its cargo pit over their territory. Rated G. 78m. **DIR:** David Kendall. **CAST:** Mark Stolzenberg, Gabriel Barr, Gwen Ellison. 1983

LUNATIC, THE ★★★ Delicious comedy stars Paul Campbell as the title character, a freewheeling, free-loving reggae man who talks to trees and is generally considered an annoyance. Excellent musical sound track enhances the lush, natural beauty of the film and characters. Rated R for sexual situations. 93m. **DIR:** Lol Creme. **CAST:** Julie T. Wallace, Paul Campbell. 1992

LUNATICS: A LOVE STORY ★★★ Lunatic Theodore Raimi (brother of writer-director Sam) hides out in his apartment, afraid of the real world. When he accidentally connects on the phone with on-the-run Deborah Foreman, he sees his chance to escape his mental cell. Pretty wacky stuff, including some outrageous special effects. Rated PG-13 for language and surreal violence. 87m. **DIR:** Josh Becker. **CAST:** Theodore Raimi, Deborah Foreman, Bruce Campbell. 1992

LUNCH WAGON ★★½ The vehicle of the title belongs to three enterprising young women who set up near a construction site. Spirited drive-in comedy offers more laughs than most of its ilk along with the requisite jiggle. Rated R for nudity and profanity. 88m. **DIR:** Ernest Pintoff. **CAST:** Pamela Bryant, Rose Marie. 1980

LUPO ★★★ In this warmhearted comedy from Israel, Yuda Barkan is charming as Lupo, a cart driver. Like a modern Fiddler on the Roof, he's caught in the currents of change. His horse is killed by a car, his daughter is wooed by a rich banker's son, and the city plans to demolish the old shack he calls home. Rated G. 100m. **DIR:** Menahem Golan. **CAST:** Yuda Barkan, Gabi Amrani, Esther Greenberg. 1970

LUST IN THE DUST ★★ Tab Hunter and female impersonator Divine (who's anything but), who first teamed in *Polyester*, star in this so-so spoof of spaghetti Westerns, directed by Paul Bartel. The ad blurb tells all: "He rode the West. The girls rode the rest. Together they ravaged the land." Rated R for nudity, suggested sex, and violence. 86m. **DIR:** Paul Bartel. **CAST:** Tab Hunter, Divine, Lainie Kazan, Geoffrey Lewis, Henry Silva, Cesar Romero. 1985

LUV ★★ When talent the caliber of Jack Lemmon, Peter Falk, and Elaine May cannot breathe life into a film, then nothing can. The plot concerns three New York intellectuals and their tribulations. Who cares? 95m. **DIR:** Clive Donner. **CAST:** Jack Lemmon, Elaine May, Peter Falk, Severn Darden. 1967

M*A*S*H ★★★★½ Fans of the television series of the same name and *Trapper John, M.D.* may have a bit of trouble recognizing their favorite characters, but this is the original. One of eccentric film director Robert Altman's few true artistic successes, this release is outrageous good fun. Rated PG. 116m. **DIR:** Robert Altman. **CAST:** Elliott Gould, Donald Sutherland, Sally Kellerman, Tom Skerritt, Robert Duvall, Jo Ann Pflug, Bud Cort, Gary Burghoff. 1970

M*A*S*H* (TV SERIES) ★★★★ Nobody expected director Robert Altman's wry 1970 war comedy to translate well on the small screen, but a decade's worth of episodes and an impressive string of Emmy Awards proved the folly of that particular prediction. Alan Alda (Benjamin "Hawkeye" Pierce) and Wayne Rogers ("Trapper" John McIntyre) became perfectly acceptable substitutes for Elliott Gould and Donald Sutherland, and the series also introduced a host of supporting players—notably McLean Stevenson, as the bumbling Lieutenant Colonel Henry Blake—who eventually went on to successes of their own. (Gary Burghoff's anticipatory Corporal Radar O'Reilly was the only carryover from film to series.) Without belittling the ensemble cast's superb efforts, the series owes most of its success to Larry Gelbart's thoughtful and often poignant scripts. Definitely a television classic. Each tape includes two half-hour episodes. 52m. **DIR:** Hy Averback, Jackie Cooper, Gene Reynolds. **CAST:** Alan Alda, Wayne Rogers, McLean Stevenson, Loretta Swit, Larry Linville, Gary Burghoff. **1972–1983**

M*A*S*H: GOODBYE, FAREWELL, AMEN ★★★★ A beautiful send-off to one of the great television series. Alan Alda and company have finally seen the end of the Korean War and are headed home. This last episode is handled with the usual excellence that one has come to associate with the series. A must for "M*A*S*H" fans and those who think there is nothing worth watching on television. 120m. **DIR:** Alan Alda. **CAST:** Alan Alda, Harry Morgan, Loretta Swit, Jamie Farr. **1983**

MABEL AND FATTY ★★★ "He Did and He Didn't," "Mabel and Fatty Viewing the World's Fair at San Francisco," and "Mabel's Blunder" comprise this boffo trio of silent comedies in the classic Mack Sennett tradition. Mabel goes it alone in the third. Silent with music. B&W; 61m. **DIR:** Roscoe Arbuckle, Mack Sennett. **CAST:** Roscoe "Fatty" Arbuckle, Mabel Normand. **1916**

MACARONI ★★★★½ Wonderful Italian comedy-drama from the director of *A Special Day* and *Le Bal*. This one concerns an American executive (Jack Lemmon) who returns to Naples for a business meeting forty years after his stay there with the army. He is visited by an old friend (Marcello Mastroianni). Both Lemmon and Mastroianni deliver brilliant performances. Rated PG for profanity. 104m. **DIR:** Ettore Scola. **CAST:** Jack Lemmon, Marcello Mastroianni, Daria Nicolodi. **1985**

MACK SENNETT COMEDIES, VOL. 2 ★★★ "Fatty and Mabel Adrift," one of the finest Fatty Arbuckle and Mabel Normand films ever made, heads this quartet of foolery and foibles put together by two of silent comedy's kingpins, Mack Sennett and Hal Roach. Rounding out the pack are Sennett's "Mabel, Fatty, and the Law" and "Fatty's Tin-Type Tangle," and Roach's "Our Congressman," a spoof on political life. Silent. B&W; 84m. **DIR:** Roscoe Arbuckle. **CAST:** Roscoe "Fatty" Arbuckle, Mabel Normand, Al St. John, Minta Durfee, Edgar Kennedy, Louise Fazenda, Will Rogers. **1915–1924**

MAD ABOUT YOU ★★ Barely watchable heiress-on-the-move flick, features a millionaire's daughter dating three men simultaneously. Rated PG. 92m. **DIR:** Lorenzo Doumani. **CAST:** Claudia Christian, Joe Gian, Adam West, Shari Shattuck. **1988**

MAD MISS MANTON, THE ★★★ A group of high-society ladies led by Miss Manton (Barbara Stanwyck) help solve a murder mystery with comic results—sometimes. The humor is pretty outdated, and the brand of romanticism, while being in step with the 1930s, comes off rather silly in the latter part of the twentieth century. Henry Fonda plays a newspaper editor who falls in love with the mad Miss Manton. B&W; 80m. **DIR:** Leigh Jason. **CAST:** Barbara Stanwyck, Henry Fonda, Sam Levene, Frances Mercer, Stanley Ridges. **1938**

MAD WEDNESDAY ★★½ The great silent comedian Harold Lloyd stars in an update of his famous brash, go-getting 1920s straw-hatted, black-rimmed-glasses character. A good, but not well executed, idea. Originally issued in 1947 as *The Sin of Harold Diddlebrock* in the director's version. This was producer Howard Hughes's "improved" version. B&W; 90m. **DIR:** Preston Sturges. **CAST:** Harold Lloyd, Frances Ramsden, Jimmy Conlin, Raymond Walburn, Arline Judge, Lionel Stander, Rudy Vallee, Edgar Kennedy. **1950**

MADE FOR EACH OTHER ★★★★ This is a highly appealing comedy-drama centering on the rocky first years of a marriage. The young couple (Carole Lombard and James Stewart) must do battle with interfering in-laws, inept servants, and the consequences of childbirth. The real strength of this film lies in the screenplay, by Jo Swerling. It gives viewers a thoughtful and tasteful picture of events that we can all relate to. B&W; 100m. **DIR:** John Cromwell. **CAST:** Carole Lombard, James Stewart, Charles Coburn, Lucile Watson, Harry Davenport. **1939**

MADE IN AMERICA ★★★ Some of the funniest slapstick scenes ever filmed are in this movie, but they are used to cover up its serious themes rather than clarify them. The story of a black teenager who wants a father so badly she seeks out his identity against her mother's wishes. When the teen finds out her father was a sperm bank donor and is white, to boot, sparks fly in every direction. Rated PG. 118m. **DIR:** Richard Benjamin. **CAST:** Whoopi Goldberg, Ted Danson, Will Smith, Nia Long, Paul Rodriguez, Jennifer Tilly, Peggy Rea. **1993**

MADE IN HEAVEN (1948) ★★ This silly English comedy stars a very young Petula Clark. Following a tradition started by Henry VI, a local village holds an annual contest to determine if a couple can survive one year of unmarried married bliss. The hiring of a flirtatious, Hungarian maid complicates the matter. 90m. **DIR:** John Paddy Carstairs. **CAST:** David Tomlinson, Petula Clark, Sonja Ziemann, A. E. Matthews. **1948**

MADHOUSE (1990) ★★ Yuppie couple Kirstie Alley and John Larroquette find their dream house invaded and destroyed by unwanted houseguests. Only the game performances of Larroquette and Alley save this painful-to-watch comedy. Rated PG-13 for profanity and simulated sex. 100m. **DIR:** Tom Ropelewski. **CAST:** John Larroquette, Kirstie Alley, Alison La Placa, John Diehl, Jessica Lundy, Dennis Miller, Robert Ginty. **1990**

MADIGAN'S MILLIONS 🦃 Only the most fanatical Dustin Hoffman fans need bother with this tedious spy farce. 86m. **DIR:** Stanley Prager. **CAST:** Dustin Hoffman, Elsa Martinelli, Cesar Romero. **1967**

MAGIC CHRISTIAN, THE ★★★ A now-dated comedy about the world's wealthiest man (Peter Sellers) and his adopted son (Ringo Starr) testing the depths of degradation to which people will plunge themselves for money still has some funny scenes and outrageous cameos by Christopher Lee (as Dracula), Raquel Welch, and Richard Attenborough. Rated PG. 93m. **DIR:** Joseph McGrath. **CAST:** Peter Sellers, Ringo Starr, Christopher Lee, Raquel Welch, Richard Attenborough, Yul Brynner. **1970**

MAID, THE ★★★ Businessman Martin Sheen falls for businesswoman Jacqueline Bisset and becomes her maid to get closer to her in this sometimes predictable, but always entertaining, romantic comedy. Rated PG for mild profanity. 91m. **DIR:** Ian Toynton. **CAST:** Martin Sheen, Jacqueline Bisset, Jean-Pierre Cassel, James Faulkner. **1991**

MAID TO ORDER ★★½ This modern retelling of the Cinderella fable isn't much of a star vehicle for Ally Sheedy, who's constantly upstaged by the supporting players. She's a spoiled little rich girl whose hip fairy godmother (Beverly D'Angelo) turns her into a nonentity, forced to work for an honest dollar. Rated PG for language and brief nudity. 96m. **DIR:** Amy Jones. **CAST:** Ally Sheedy, Beverly D'Angelo, Michael Ontkean, Valerie Perrine, Dick Shawn, Tom Skerritt. **1987**

MAID'S NIGHT OUT, THE ★★ This energetic comedy tells of a millionaire's son (Allan Lane) who becomes a milkman for a month to win a bet with his self-made millionaire father (George Irving). Along the way, he meets Joan Fontaine. Lowbrow but fun. B&W; 64m. **DIR:** Ben Holmes. **CAST:** Joan Fontaine, Hedda Hopper, Allan "Rocky" Lane, Cecil Kellaway. **1938**

MAIN EVENT, THE 🦃 A limp boxing comedy that tried unsuccessfully to reunite the stars of *What's Up Doc?* Rated PG. 112m. **DIR:** Howard Zieff. **CAST:** Barbra Streisand, Ryan O'Neal, Paul Sand. **1979**

MAIN STREET TO BROADWAY ★★ The story of a young playwright's rise to success on Broadway is nothing you haven't seen before. The only attraction here is an endless array of cameo appearances by Ethel and Lionel Barrymore, Shirley Booth, Rex Harrison, Rodgers and Hammerstein, Mary Martin, Lilli Palmer, Cornel Wilde, and other notables of the theatre world. B&W; 102m. **DIR:** Tay Garnett. **CAST:** Tom Murton, Mary Murphy, Agnes Moorehead, Rosemary DeCamp, Tallulah Bankhead. **1953**

MAJOR BARBARA ★★★½ In the title role as a Salvation Army officer, Wendy Hiller heads a matchless cast in this thoughtful film of George Bernard Shaw's comedy about the power of money and the evils of poverty. Rex Harrison, as her fiancé, and Robert Newton, as a hard case with doubts about the honesty and motives of do-gooders, are excellent. B&W; 136m. **DIR:** Gabriel Pascal. **CAST:** Wendy Hiller, Rex Harrison, Robert Morley, Robert Newton, Emlyn Williams, Sybil Thorndike, Deborah Kerr. **1941**

MAJOR LEAGUE ★★★½ In this often funny but clichéd baseball comedy, the Cleveland Indians find themselves headed for oblivion when the new owner, former show girl Margaret Whitton, decides to put together the worst possible team. Tom Berenger, Charlie Sheen, and Corbin Bernsen are fine as three inept players, and character actor James Gammon shines as their coach. Rated R for profanity and violence. 95m. **DIR:** David S. Ward. **CAST:** Tom Berenger, Charlie Sheen, Corbin Bernsen, Margaret Whitton, James Gammon. **1989**

MAJOR LEAGUE II ★★ The sequel to the 1989 baseball hit is more of the same, with an almost identical plot and nearly the entire cast reprising their original roles (Omar Epps replaces Wesley Snipes). This time, though, the zest is gone—everyone looks tired and just a little embarrassed. Rated PG, but with profanity some may find offensive. 105m. **DIR:** David S. Ward. **CAST:** Charlie Sheen, Tom Berenger, Corbin Bernsen, James Gammon, David Keith, Omar Epps. **1994**

MAJORITY OF ONE, A ★★★★ In spite of terrible miscasting, the charm and wit of Leonard Spiegelgass's successful Broadway play shine through. Rosalind Russell tries very hard to play a typical Jewish mother and this just calls attention to her WASPishness. Sir Alec Guinness drops his "l's" and rolls his "r's" as a Japanese gentleman and gets laughs in the wrong places. Even so, the interracial romance has some delightful moments. Very predictable and obvious but fun. 156m. **DIR:** Mervyn LeRoy. **CAST:** Rosalind Russell, Alec Guinness, Madlyn Rhue, Ray Danton, Mae Questel, Sharon Hugeny, Alan Mowbray, Gary Vinson, Marc Mamo. 1961

MAKE A MILLION ★★★ In this Depression comedy, college economics professor Charles Starrett's radical ideas for sharing the wealth get him fired. He develops a plan that soon has him rolling in money—and attracting a greedy banker and others bent on getting in on the gravy. B&W; 66m. **DIR:** Lewis D. Collins. **CAST:** Charles Starrett, Pauline Brooks. 1935

MAKE MINE MINK ★★★★ Bright dialogue and clever situations make this crazy comedy from Britain highly enjoyable. An ex-officer, a dowager, and a motley crew of fur thieves team to commit larceny for charity. Gap-toothed Terry-Thomas is in top form in this one. 100m. **DIR:** Robert Asher. **CAST:** Terry-Thomas, Athene Seyler, Billie Whitelaw. 1960

MAKING MR. RIGHT ★★½ This mild satire, about a female image consultant who falls for the android she's supposed to be promoting, doesn't come close to the energy level of director Susan Seidelman's *Desperately Seeking Susan*. Rated PG-13. 98m. **DIR:** Susan Seidelman. **CAST:** John Malkovich, Ann Magnuson, Ben Masters, Glenne Headly, Laurie Metcalf, Polly Bergen, Hart Bochner. 1987

MAKING THE GRADE ★★½ A rich kid pays a surrogate to attend prep school for him. Typical teen-exploitation fare. Rated R. 105m. **DIR:** Dorian Walker. **CAST:** Judd Nelson, Jonna Lee, Carey Scott. 1984

MALCOLM ★★★★½ An absolutely charming Australian entry that swept that country's Oscars the year it was released. Colin Friels has the title role as an emotionally immature young man who, after he loses his job with a local rapid-transit company (for building his own tram with company parts), finds himself among thieves and loves it. 90m. **DIR:** Nadia Tess. **CAST:** Colin Friels, John Hargreaves, Lindy Davies, Chris Haywood. 1986

MALIBU BIKINI SHOP, THE 🦃 An exploitative romp about two brothers who inherit a bikini shop. Rated R for nudity and profanity. 90m. **DIR:** David Wechter. **CAST:** Michael David Wright, Bruce Greenwood, Barbara Horan, Debra Blee, Jay Robinson. 1985

MALIBU EXPRESS 🦃 The amazing thing about this film is how it managed to get an R rating when it is clearly soft porn. 101m. **DIR:** Andy Sidaris. **CAST:** Darby Hinton, Sybil Danning, Shelley Taylor Morgan, Brett Clark, Art Metrano. 1984

MAN CALLED SARGE, A 🦃 World War II misfits against Rommel's desert forces. Rated PG-13. 88m. **DIR:** Stuart Gillard. **CAST:** Gary Kroeger, Gretchen German, Jennifer Runyon, Marc Singer. 1990

MAN FROM PAINTED POST, THE ★★★½ Early Fairbanks actioner about a good bad man. Great stunts on horseback and with the lasso. Silent. 55m. **DIR:** Joseph E. Henabery. **CAST:** Douglas Fairbanks Sr., Eileen Percy, Frank Campeau. 1917

MAN IN THE WHITE SUIT, THE ★★★★★ In *The Man in the White Suit*, Alec Guinness is the perfect choice to play an unassuming scientist who invents a fabric that can't be torn, frayed, or stained! Can you imagine the furor this causes in the textile industry? This uniquely original script pokes fun at big business and big labor as they try to suppress his discovery. Joan Greenwood is a treasure in a supporting role. B&W; 84m. **DIR:** Alexander Mackendrick. **CAST:** Alec Guinness, Joan Greenwood, Cecil Parker. 1952

MAN OF FLOWERS ★★★★★ Kinky, humorous, and touching, this winner from Australia affirms Paul Cox (of *Lonely Hearts* fame) as one of the wittiest and most sensitive directors from Down Under. Norman Kaye is terrific as an eccentric old man who collects art and flowers and watches pretty women undress. To him these are things of beauty that he can observe but can't touch. Rated R for nudity. 90m. **DIR:** Paul Cox. **CAST:** Norman Kaye, Alyson Best, Chris Haywood, Werner Herzog. 1984

MAN THAT CORRUPTED HADLEYBURG, THE ★★★★★ Robert Preston shows up in Hadleyburg with a sack of gold. Would-be saints and holier-than-thou guardians of public decency are exposed as ordinary people with quite human failings in this delightfully sly adaptation of Mark Twain's acerbic story. Henry Fonda's introduction includes rare film footage of Twain. Unrated and suitable for family viewing. 40m. **DIR:** Ralph Rosenblum. **CAST:** Robert Preston, Fred Gwynne, Frances Sternhagen, Tom Aldredge. 1980

MAN TROUBLE ★★ A terrific cast is wasted in this inept comedy about a down-on-his-luck security expert. Jack Nicholson mugs shamelessly, while Beverly D'Angelo gives this supposed comedy's only funny performance. Rated PG-13 for profanity, simulated sex, and violence. 100m. **DIR:** Bob Rafelson. **CAST:** Jack Nicholson, Ellen Barkin, Harry Dean Stanton, Beverly D'Angelo, Michael McKean, Saul Rubinek, Viveka Davis, Veronica Cartwright, David Clennon, Paul Mazursky. 1992

MAN UPSTAIRS, THE ★★ An awkward performance by Ryan O'Neal doesn't help this stagy made-for-TV comedy about a prison escapee who hides in the home of an elderly woman (Katharine Hepburn). It's not an inspired teaming; their timing is off and the frequent attempts at humor fall flat. 95m. **DIR:** George Schaefer. **CAST:** Katharine Hepburn,

Ryan O'Neal, Henry Beckman, Helena Carroll, Brenda Forbes. 1992

MAN WHO CAME TO DINNER, THE ★★★★★ The classic George Kaufman and Moss Hart farce features Monty Woolley in his original Broadway role. High camp and high comedy result when a cynical newspaper columnist falls and supposedly breaks his leg. Bette Davis has a straight role as the secretary. Wacky and lots and lots of fun. 112m. **DIR:** William Keighley. **CAST:** Monty Woolley, Bette Davis, Ann Sheridan, Jimmy Durante, Mary Wickes, Reginald Gardiner, Grant Mitchell, Richard Travis, Billie Burke. 1941

MAN WHO LOVED WOMEN, THE (1983) ★★★ The first collaboration of Burt Reynolds, Julie Andrews, and her director-hubby, Blake Edwards, didn't sound like the kind of thing that would make screen history. And it isn't. But it is a pleasantly entertaining—and sometimes uproariously funny—adult sex comedy. The always likable Reynolds plays a guy who just can't say no to the opposite sex. Rated R for nudity and profanity. 110m. **DIR:** Blake Edwards. **CAST:** Burt Reynolds, Julie Andrews, Marilu Henner, Kim Basinger, Barry Corbin. 1983

MAN WHO WASN'T THERE, THE [turkey] Espionage and invisibility. This was originally released in 3-D. Rated R for nudity and language. 111m. **DIR:** Bruce Malmuth. **CAST:** Steve Guttenberg, Jeffrey Tambor, Lisa Langlois, Art Hindle, Vincent Baggetta. 1983

MAN WITH ONE RED SHOE, THE ★★★½ An American remake of the French comedy *The Tall Blond Man with One Black Shoe*, this casts Tom Hanks as a concert violinist who is pursued by a group of spies. Hanks is nearly the whole show. Jim Belushi (as his practical-joke-loving buddy) and Carrie Fisher (as an overly amorous flute player) also provide some hearty laughs. Rated PG for profanity and violence. 96m. **DIR:** Stan Dragoti. **CAST:** Tom Hanks, Dabney Coleman, Charles Durning, Lori Singer, James Belushi, Carrie Fisher, Edward Herrmann. 1985

MAN WITH TWO BRAINS, THE ★★★★ Steve Martin stars in this generally amusing takeoff of 1950s horror-sci-fi flicks as a scientist with a nasty wife (Kathleen Turner) and a sweet patient (the voice of Sissy Spacek). There's only one problem with the latter: all that's left of her is her brain. Rated R for nudity, profanity, and violence. 93m. **DIR:** Carl Reiner. **CAST:** Steve Martin, Kathleen Turner, David Warner, Paul Benedict. 1983

MANHANDLED ★★½ Disappointing vehicle for Gloria Swanson. Believe it or not, she's a department store salesclerk—but never fear, Swanson gets ample opportunities to model exotic gowns as she impersonates a Russian countess. Slick but routine. Silent. B&W; 70m. **DIR:** Allan Dwan. **CAST:** Gloria Swanson, Tom Moore. 1924

MANHATTAN ★★★★★ Reworking the same themes he explored in *Play It Again, Sam* and *Annie Hall*, Woody Allen again comes up with perhaps his greatest masterpiece. Diane Keaton returns as the object of his awkward but well-meaning affections. It's heartwarming, insightful, screamingly funny, and a feast for the eyes. The black-and-white cinematography of long-time Allen collaborator Gordon Willis recalls the great visuals of *Citizen Kane* and *The Third Man*. Rated R. B&W; 96m. **DIR:** Woody Allen. **CAST:** Diane Keaton, Woody Allen, Michael Murphy, Mariel Hemingway, Meryl Streep. 1979

MANHATTAN MURDER MYSTERY ★★★★ Joyous reunion for Woody Allen and Diane Keaton presents them as a married couple at odds over whether a neighbor has committed murder. She's sure of it, he thinks she's gone off the deep end, and the audience is almost too busy laughing to care. A cleverly constructed howdunit from Allen and Marshall Brickman, who previously collaborated on *Annie Hall* and *Manhattan*. Rated PG for brief violence. 108m. **DIR:** Woody Allen. **CAST:** Woody Allen, Diane Keaton, Alan Alda, Anjelica Huston, Jerry Adler, Joy Behar, Ron Rifkin. 1993

MANIFESTO ★★★½ A colorful, eccentric comedy from the director of *Montenegro* and *The Coca-Cola Kid*. It's a wacky tale of revolutionaries trying to alter the political system in a picturesque European country, circa 1920. Romance, misguided idealism, and ineptitude get in the way of all their efforts, but viewers have a lot of fun along the way. 96m. **DIR:** Dusan Makavejev. **CAST:** Camilla Soeberg, Alfred Molina, Eric Stoltz, Simon Callow, Lindsay Duncan. 1988

MANNEQUIN (1987) [turkey] MTV glitz and worn-out comedy bits. Rated PG. 90m. **DIR:** Michael Gottlieb. **CAST:** Andrew McCarthy, Kim Cattrall, Estelle Getty, G. W. Bailey, Meshach Taylor. 1987

MANNEQUIN TWO: ON THE MOVE ★★ William Ragsdale is a modern-day descendant of royalty who discovers that a department-store mannequin is really alive. Good comic turns by Terry Kiser as a dastardly count and Meshach Taylor, who reprises his role as an effeminate art director. Rated PG. 98m. **DIR:** Stewart Raffill. **CAST:** Kristy Swanson, William Ragsdale, Terry Kiser, Stuart Pankin, Meshach Taylor. 1991

MAN'S FAVORITE SPORT? ★★★ Comedy about a nonfishing outdoor-sports columnist who finds himself entered in an anglers' contest is fast and funny and provides Rock Hudson with one of his best roles. Screwball Paula Prentiss spends most of her time gumming up the works for poor Rock. The situations and dialogue are clever and breezy, employing director Howard Hawks's famous overlapping dialogue to maximum advantage. 120m. **DIR:** Howard Hawks. **CAST:** Rock Hudson, Paula Prentiss, John McGiver, Roscoe Karns, Maria Perschy, Charlene Holt. **1964**

MARATHON ★★½ In this comic examination of mid-life crisis, Bob Newhart becomes enamored with a woman he sees at a local running event, only to discover his true feelings. The uninspired direction and screenplay weaken the efforts of a veteran cast. Rated PG for mild language. 97m. **DIR:** Jackie Cooper. **CAST:** Bob Newhart, Herb Edelman, Dick Gautier, Anita Gillette, Leigh Taylor-Young, John Hillerman. **1985**

MARCH OF THE WOODEN SOLDIERS ★★★★ Originally titled *Babes in Toyland,* this film features Stan Laurel and Oliver Hardy as the toy-maker's assistants in the land of Old King Cole. Utterly forgettable songs slow down an otherwise enjoyable fantasy film. Stan and Ollie are integrated well into the storyline, finally saving the town from the attack of the boogeymen. B&W; 73m. **DIR:** Gus Meins. **CAST:** Stan Laurel, Oliver Hardy, Charlotte Henry. **1934**

MARRIAGE CIRCLE, THE ★★★★★ Arguably Ernst Lubitsch's best American silent. A comedy of erotic manners ensues when a professor tries to divorce his wife after seeing her flirt with the husband of her best friend. Silent. B&W; 104m. **DIR:** Ernst Lubitsch. **CAST:** Florence Vidor, Monte Blue, Marie Prevost, Adolphe Menjou. **1924**

MARRIED TO THE MOB ★★★★½ Imagine the amazing *Something Wild* with less menace, more humor, oddball set design to the nth degree, eccentric characters galore, and, as usual in a Jonathan Demme movie, music that sets the scene and the audience in motion. Michelle Pfeiffer plays a beautiful, innocent-yet-fatal femme, here doing her darnedest to extricate herself from the Long Island mob scene after her mobster husband is "iced"; Dean Stockwell is the threatening Don Juan don; Matthew Modine is the savior-nerd. Rated R for language and adult situations. 106m. **DIR:** Jonathan Demme. **CAST:** Michelle Pfeiffer, Matthew Modine, Dean Stockwell, Mercedes Ruehl. **1988**

MARRYING MAN, THE ★★½ Neil Simon's screenplay sprinkles laughs into the romance between a toothpaste heir and a torch singer. Stand-up comedian Paul Reiser does a fine job of delivering the best zingers as he narrates their on-again, off-again love story. Rated R for profanity, violence, and simulated sex. 115m. **DIR:** Jerry Rees. **CAST:** Kim Basinger, Alec Baldwin, Robert Loggia, Elisabeth Shue, Armand Assante, Paul Reiser, Fisher Stevens, Peter Dobson. **1991**

MARTIANS GO HOME 🦃 Some wisecracking aliens come to Earth. Rated PG-13 for adult language. 89m. **DIR:** David Odell. **CAST:** Randy Quaid, Margaret Colin, John Philbin, Anita Harris. **1990**

MARY HARTMAN, MARY HARTMAN (TV SERIES) ★★★★ This series was too off-the-wall for the networks, so producer Norman Lear sold it in syndication. Full of whimsy and satire, the show plunged into subjects considered taboo by normal sitcoms, such as impotence and marijuana, not to mention waxy yellow buildup. Louise Lasser, as Mary, fashioned a unique character with which a wide audience empathized. This series is definitely worth another look. 70m. **DIR:** Joan Darling, Jim Drake. **CAST:** Louise Lasser, Greg Mullavey, Mary Kay Place, Graham Jarvis, Victor Kilian, Debralee Scott, Martin Mull. **1976**

MASALA ★★★★ Silliness abounds in this delightfully funny domestic comedy. A distraught Indian woman living in Canada summons a Hindu god to help her dysfunctional family. Before the day is done, various family members will confront terrorists, marital woes, government agents, and a son who arrives with some interesting news. Multicultural effort is in English. Not rated, but contains adult situations, nudity, and strong language. 105m. **DIR:** Srinivas Krishna. **CAST:** Saeed Jaffrey, Srinivas Krishna, Zohra Segal. **1992**

MASTERMIND ★★★ Zero Mostel spoofs Charlie Chan in this 1969 comedy that wasn't released until 1976. It's better than it sounds, with in-jokes for old-movie buffs and lots of slapstick for the whole family. It's even rated G! 84m. **DIR:** Alex March. **CAST:** Zero Mostel, Bradford Dillman, Jules Munshin. **1976**

MASTERS OF MENACE ★★★ Cameos by Jim Belushi, John Candy, George Wendt, and Dan Aykroyd help this story of a young lawyer who must follow a motorcycle gang around and make sure they don't get into any trouble. He doesn't have any luck. Rated PG-13 for violence and profanity. 97m. **DIR:** Daniel Raskov. **CAST:** David Rasche, Catherine Bach, David L. Lander, Teri Copley, Ray Baker. **1990**

MATCHMAKER, THE ★★★★ Gabby Shirley Booth takes it upon herself to find a wife for rich merchant Paul Ford, but finds herself attracted to the stuffy old crank, and they end up an item. Young Anthony Perkins and Shirley MacLaine fall in love along the way, and everything ends up swell. This pleasant little comedy was written for the stage by Thornton Wilder, and it found its way to the stage and the screen again as *Hello Dolly.* B&W; 101m. **DIR:** Joseph Anthony. **CAST:** Shirley Booth, Paul Ford, Anthony Perkins, Shirley MacLaine, Robert Morse, Wallace Ford, Rex Evans, Russell Collins, Gavin Gordon. **1958**

MATILDA ★★★½ A cute comedy about a boxing kangaroo who becomes a legend in the sport. Elliott Gould plays a small-time booking agent who becomes the manager of the heavyweight marsupial. Sentimental at times and a bit corny, too, but worth the time. Recommended for family viewing. Rated G. 105m. **DIR:** Daniel Mann. **CAST:** Elliott Gould, Robert Mitchum, Clive Revill, Harry Guardino, Roy Clark, Lionel Stander, Art Metrano. **1978**

MATINEE ★★★★ Charlie Haas's screenplay is set during the Cuban Missile Crisis in Key West, where cigar-chomping John Goodman is staging a premiere of his latest masterwork: *Mant*—"Half Man, Half Ant, All Terror!" while the populace deals with the fear of impending nuclear war. The film-within-the-film (featuring genre veterans William Schallert and Robert Cornthwaite) is often hilarious, and Goodman's deft performance is complemented by a well-played, coming-of-age story. Rated PG for profanity. 97m. **DIR:** Joe Dante. **CAST:** John Goodman, Cathy Moriarty, Simon Fenton, Omri Katz, Kellie Martin, Lisa Jakub, Jesse White, Dick Miller, John Sayles, William Schallert, Robert Cornthwaite. **1993**

MATING GAME, THE ★★★★ A straight-as-an-arrow tax collector finds himself being wooed by both the farmer and his daughter, who have never seen any good reason to pay taxes. Great comedy, exceptional cast, with special mention for Fred Clark as the evil head of the Internal Revenue Service. 101m. **DIR:** George Marshall. **CAST:** Debbie Reynolds, Tony Randall, Paul Douglas, Fred Clark, Una Merkel, Philip Ober. **1951**

MATING SEASON, THE ★★★ An enjoyable romantic comedy set among the flora and fauna commonly inhabited by bird-watchers. When an emotional lady attorney resorts to bird-watching for relaxation, she meets a charming businessman. Affable little TV movie. 96m. **DIR:** John Llewellyn Moxey. **CAST:** Lucie Arnaz, Laurence Luckinbill, Swoosie Kurtz, Diane Stilwell, Joel Brooks. **1986**

MATTER OF PRINCIPLE, A ★★★★ Delightful tale about a selfish tyrant (Alan Arkin) who is suddenly overthrown by his much-put-upon wife (Barbara Dana, Arkin's real-life wife). She takes their eleven children after he destroys their first Christmas tree. Finally, he must wake up and think about someone besides himself. Unrated, but fine family entertainment. 60m. **DIR:** Gwen Arner. **CAST:** Alan Arkin, Barbara Dana, Tony Arkin. **1983**

MAXIE ★★ Cute but not particularly impressive fantasy about a conservative secretary (Glenn Close) who becomes possessed by the spirit of a flamboyant flapper (Close, too). The star is wonderful, but the predictable plot and the uninspired direction let her—and the viewer—down. Rated PG for suggested sex. 98m. **DIR:** Paul Aaron. **CAST:** Glenn Close, Mandy Patinkin, Ruth Gordon, Barnard Hughes, Valerie Curtin. **1985**

MAY WINE ★★★ Pleasant bedroom romp features a Parisian gynecologist (Guy Marchand) being shamelessly pursued by two Americans. The twist is that the two women are mother (Joanna Cassidy) and daughter (Lara Flynn Boyle). Contrived, but guaranteed to elicit a giggle or two. Rated R for nudity and language. 88m. **DIR:** Carol Wiseman. **CAST:** Joanna Cassidy, Guy Marchand, Lara Flynn Boyle, Paul Freeman. **1990**

ME AND HIM ★★ You'd think a comedy about a staid businessman who gets life lessons from his newly loquacious penis would offer a few laughs, and this does. *Very* few. There are songs, too, though not from *him.* Rated R for nudity and sexual situations. 94m. **DIR:** Doris Dörrie. **CAST:** Griffin Dunne, Ellen Greene, Carey Lowell, Craig T. Nelson, Mark Linn-Baker. **1987**

ME, MYSELF & I 🦃 Irritating comedy finds writer George Segal trying to make sense of neighbor JoBeth Williams's twin personalities. Dull and uninteresting. Rated R for language and adult situations. 97m. **DIR:** Pablo Ferro. **CAST:** George Segal, JoBeth Williams, Shelley Hack, Don Calfa. **1992**

MEANEST MAN IN THE WORLD, THE ★★★½ Jack Benny's best picture. He plays a lawyer who can't win a case, and decides the only way to get ahead in the world is to be rotten to people. The film is good satire that still holds true, and Benny plays the role to the hilt. B&W; 57m. **DIR:** Sidney Lanfield. **CAST:** Jack Benny, Priscilla Lane, Eddie "Rochester" Anderson, Edmund Gwenn, Anne Revere, Tor Johnson. **1943**

MEATBALLS ★★★½ Somehow, this *Animal House*-style comedy's disjointedness is easier to swallow than it should be. Elmer Bernstein's music gets sentimental in the right places, and star Bill Murray is fun to watch. Rated PG. 92m. **DIR:** Ivan Reitman. **CAST:** Bill Murray, Harvey Atkin, Kate Lynch, Chris Makepeace. **1979**

MEATBALLS PART II 🦃 Pitifully unfunny high jinks at summer camp. Rated PG for sexual references. 87m. **DIR:** Ken Wiederhorn. **CAST:** Richard Mulligan, Kim Richards, John Mengatti, Misty Rowe. **1984**

MEATBALLS III 🦃 Lousy. Rated R for nudity, profanity, and suggested sex. 94m. **DIR:** George Mendeluk. **CAST:** Sally Kellerman, Patrick Dempsey, Al Waxman, Shannon Tweed. **1987**

MEATBALLS 4 🦃 Hey kids, it's the old let's-save-the-summer-camp scenario one more time. Boring. Rated R for nudity and language. 84m. **DIR:** Bob Logan. **CAST:** Corey Feldman, Jack Nance, Sarah Douglas. **1992**

MEDUSA: DARE TO BE TRUTHFUL ★★★★½ Former MTV host Julie Brown takes on Madonna in this right-on made-for-cable spoof of the blonde one's infamous film of her celebrated tour. Brown is incredibly funny, capturing the arrogance and attitude with pinpoint accuracy. Not rated, but contains adult language. 54m. **DIR:** John Fortenberry. **CAST:** Julie Brown, Bob Goldthwait. **1992**

MEET THE APPLEGATES 🦃 A family of insects disguised as humans. Rated R for profanity and sexual themes. 90m. **DIR:** Michael Lehmann. **CAST:** Ed Begley Jr., Stockard Channing, Bobby Jacoby, Dabney Coleman. **1989**

MEET THE HOLLOWHEADS ★★ Five minutes of introduction would have saved viewers the first twenty minutes of confusion as we enter the lives of a family living in an unknown place and at an undisclosed time. Things don't really pick up until Mr. Hollowhead brings his villainous boss home to dinner. Rated PG-13 for sexual innuendo and gore. 87m. **DIR:** Tom Burman. **CAST:** John Glover, Nancy Mette, Richard Portnow, Anne Ramsey. **1988**

MELVIN AND HOWARD ★★★★★ This brilliantly directed slice-of-life film works marvelously well on two levels. On the surface, it's the entertaining tale of how Melvin Dummar (Paul LeMat) met Howard Hughes (Jason Robards)—or did he? Underneath, it's a hilarious spoof of our society. Mary Steenburgen costars in this triumph of American filmmaking, a rare gem that deserves to be seen and talked about. Rated R. 95m. **DIR:** Jonathan Demme. **CAST:** Paul LeMat, Jason Robards Jr., Mary Steenburgen, Pamela Reed. **1980**

MEMORIES OF ME ★★ A New York doctor (Billy Crystal) has a heart attack and decides to reevaluate his priorities as well as his stormy relationship with his father (Alan King). Rated PG-13 for profanity and adult situations. 104m. **DIR:** Henry Winkler. **CAST:** Billy Crystal, Alan King, JoBeth Williams. **1988**

MEN DON'T LEAVE ★★★★ Jessica Lange struggles to raise two precocious sons after their father dies in a freak accident. The death of a loved one is no laughing matter—unless we're referring to this remarkable movie from Paul Brickman, who waited six years after hitting it big with *Risky Business* to make his second film. Rated PG-13 for adult themes. 120m. **DIR:** Paul Brickman. **CAST:** Jessica Lange, Arliss Howard, Joan Cusack, Tom Mason, Kathy Bates. **1990**

MERMAIDS ★★★½ Terrific performances by Cher, Bob Hoskins, and Winona Ryder highlight this uneven but generally entertaining and decidedly offbeat comedy. Ryder is the confused 15-year-old daughter of the unpredictable Cher. A sort of *Harold and Maude* of the mother-daughter set, this one is not for all tastes. Rated PG-13 for profanity. 115m. **DIR:** Richard Benjamin. **CAST:** Cher, Bob Hoskins, Winona Ryder, Michael Schoeffling, Christina Ricci. **1990**

MERRY WIVES OF WINDSOR, THE ★★ A slow-moving stage production of Shakespeare's comedy of morals with the colorful Sir John Falstaff (Leon Charles) out to seduce two married women and have them support his habits. Interesting casting of Gloria Grahame as Mistress Page, but, overall, disappointing. A Bard Productions Ltd. release. 160m. **DIR:** Jack Manning. **CAST:** Leon Charles, Gloria Grahame, Valerie Sedle Snyder, Dixie Neyland, Joel Asher, John Houseman. **1970**

MERTON OF THE MOVIES ★★★★ Red Skelton enlivens a very dated script with the help of comedy genius Buster Keaton. Both of them devised the slapstick routines that freshen the story of a movie-theatre usher who climbs Hollywood's ladder of success with a gentle push from his friends. The show-business atmosphere is amiable and authentic, and the comedic timing is terrific. B&W; 83m. **DIR:** Robert Alton. **CAST:** Red Skelton, Virginia O'Brien, Gloria Grahame, Leon Ames, Alan Mowbray, Hubo Haas. **1947**

MEXICAN HAYRIDE ★★ Lou Costello chases swindler Bud Abbott to Mexico and dim-wittedly aids him. Substandard entry in the series. B&W; 77m. **DIR:** Charles Barton. **CAST:** Bud Abbott, Lou Costello, Virginia Grey, John Hubbard, Pedro De Cordoba, Fritz Feld. **1948**

MEXICAN SPITFIRE ★★★½ This is one of a series of second-feature comedies about a youngish businessman and his temperamental Mexican wife. Though the stars are Lupe Velez and Donald Woods, the simplistic plot shifts early on to the young man's accident-prone uncle Matt and his rich and proper boss Lord Epping, both of whom were played by the spaghetti-legged Ziegfeld comic Leon Errol. He's in top form here. B&W; 75m. **DIR:** Leslie Goodwins. **CAST:** Lupe Velez, Donald Woods, Leon Errol. **1939**

MGM'S THE BIG PARADE OF COMEDY ★★ Disappointing and disjointed; an incoherent grab bag of short scenes from comic silent and sound films, compiled by the usually dependable Robert Youngson. B&W; 100m. **DIR:** Robert Youngson. **CAST:** Stan Laurel, Oliver Hardy, Bud Abbott, Lou Costello, Marion Davies. **1963**

MIAMI SUPERCOPS 🦃 The stars of *They Call Me Trinity* ditch the Old West for Miami in this Italian import that's so bad, it's unbearable. Rated PG. 97m. **DIR:** Bruno Corbucci. **CAST:** Terence Hill, Bud Spencer. **1985**

MICKI & MAUDE ★★★★½ In this hysterically funny comedy Dudley Moore stars as a television personality who tries to juggle marriages to two women, Amy Irving and Ann Reinking. Directed by Blake Edwards, it's a triumph for filmmaker and cast alike. Rated PG-13 for profanity and suggested sex. 96m. **DIR:** Blake Edwards. **CAST:** Dudley Moore, Amy Irving, Ann Reinking, George Gaynes, Wallace Shawn. **1984**

MIDDLE-AGE CRAZY ★★★ Bruce Dern lives the lyrics of this pop song–turned-film, playing a fellow who shorts out upon reaching the mid-life crisis of his fortieth birthday. Wife Ann-Margret is abandoned for a football cheerleader, and the family car is pushed aside by a Porsche. Director John Trent resists the easy opportunity for cheap comedy, however, and treats the material with surprising compassion. Rated PG. 95m. **DIR:** John Trent. **CAST:** Bruce Dern, Ann-Margret, Graham Jarvis. **1980**

MIDNIGHT MADNESS 🦃 A midnight scavenger hunt. Rated PG. 110m. **DIR:** David Wechter, Michael Nankin. **CAST:** David Naughton, Debra Clinger, Eddie Deezen, Stephen Furst. **1980**

MIDNIGHT MOVIE MASSACRE ★★★ This is definitely a candidate for the midnight-movie cult crowd—set in 1956 while an audience of outrageous characters are watching a sci-fi movie. A real flying saucer lands outside, and the monster invades the theater. Gross fun, a crowd pleaser with surprisingly good photography and production. Unrated, with graphic violence and simulated sex. 86m. **DIR:** Mark Stock. **CAST:** Robert Clarke, Ann Robinson. **1986**

MIDSUMMER NIGHT'S DREAM, A (1968) ★★½ Special effects and countryside locales strangely distract from the overall hilarity of Shakespeare's spoof on love. Some of the most pun-filled lines are lost as some of the cast members confuse talking fast for authentic articulation. Diana Rigg is rather pathetic as the lovelorn Helena while Ian Holm's Puck provides laughs. Unrated; features Judi Dench as the Fairy Queen in very scanty attire. 124m. **DIR:** Peter Hall. **CAST:** Diana Rigg, David Warner, Ian Holm, Judi Dench, Ian Richardson. **1968**

MIDSUMMER NIGHT'S SEX COMEDY, A ★★½ Woody Allen's sometimes dull cinematic treatise—albeit sweet-natured, and beautifully photographed by Gordon Willis—on the star-writer-director's favorite subjects: sex and death. That's not to say *A Midsummer Night's Sex Comedy* doesn't have its humorous moments. Allen's fans will undoubtedly enjoy it. Rated PG for adult themes. 88m. **DIR:** Woody Allen. **CAST:** Woody Allen, Mia Farrow, José Ferrer, Julie Hagerty, Tony Roberts, Mary Steenburgen. **1982**

MIKEY AND NICKY ★★★ The story of a fateful day and the relationship of two small-time crooks who have been best friends since childhood. This hauntingly funny film slowly builds to its climax in the Elaine May tradition. Great acting from Peter Falk and John Cassavetes. Rated R for profanity. 119m. **DIR:** Elaine May. **CAST:** Peter Falk, John Cassavetes, Ned Beatty, Joyce Van Patten. **1976**

MILKY WAY, THE (1936) ★★★★ In this superb compendium of gags flowing from his character of a milkman who innocently decks the champion during a brawl, the great Harold Lloyd amply proves why he was such a success. Lloyd was a master comic craftsman. This is the finest of his few talking films. B&W; 83m. **DIR:** Leo McCarey. **CAST:** Harold Lloyd, Adolphe Menjou, Helen Mack. **1936**

MILLION DOLLAR MYSTERY 🦃 A gimmick film that originally offered $1 million to the first audience member who could put the movie's clues together. Rated PG. 95m. **DIR:** Richard Fleischer. **CAST:** Jamie Alcroft, Royce D. Applegate, Tom Bosley, Eddie Deezen, Rich Hall, Mack Dryden. **1987**

MILLION TO JUAN, A ★★ Comedian Paul Rodriguez plays a Hispanic father in L.A. working for his green card who receives a million-dollar check. The catch: he can only "use" it, not cash it. The film is well-intentioned, but the script (loosely adapted from a Mark Twain story) tries to be too many things—romantic comedy, social satire, rags-to-riches fantasy—and winds up a mess. Rated PG. 93m. **DIR:** Paul Rodriguez. **CAST:** Paul Rodriguez, Edward James Olmos, Richard "Cheech" Marin, Rubén Blades, Polly Draper. **1994**

MIRACLE BEACH ★★★ Delightful fantasy unfolds when an all-around loser finds a genie who can grant all his wishes. Rated R for nudity and simulated sex. 88m. **DIR:** Skott Snider. **CAST:** Dean Cameron, Ami Dolenz, Felicity Waterman, Noriyuki "Pat" Morita. **1991**

MIRACLE OF MORGAN'S CREEK, THE ★★★★½ All comic hell breaks loose when Betty Hutton finds herself pregnant following an all-night party, can't recall who the father is, and eventually gives birth to sextuplets. An audacious, daring Bronx cheer at American morals and ideals, this rollicking farce, cram-jammed with comic lines, is a real winner. B&W; 99m. **DIR:** Preston Sturges. **CAST:** Betty Hutton, Eddie Bracken, William Demarest, Diana Lynn, Brian Donlevy, Akim Tamiroff, Jimmy Conlin, Porter Hall. **1944**

MIRACLES ★★½ This film involves a sick little girl in a remote Mexican jungle, a doctor and his recently divorced wife in L.A., and a bungling burglar. The story revolves around the sometimes funny circumstances that bring all these characters together. Rated PG for language and mild violence. 90m. **DIR:** Jim Kouf. **CAST:** Tom Conti, Teri Garr, Paul Rodriguez, Christopher Lloyd. **1986**

MISADVENTURES OF BUSTER KEATON, THE ★★ The world-famous "Great Stone

Face" has his moments in this sound version of one of his classic silent comedies but falls short of what he did in his prime. Still, Keaton running a small theatre, bumbling and fumbling at every turn, is a delight to behold. B&W; 65m. **DIR:** Arthur Hilton. **CAST:** Buster Keaton, Marcia Mae Jones. **1950**

MISADVENTURES OF MR. WILT, THE ★★★½ Screwball British comedy about a man trying to explain to the police that he didn't kill his wife, but a life-size blow-up doll. Told in flashback, this is an effective little film that is hampered only by a disappointing ending. Rated R for profanity. 84m. **DIR:** Michael Tuchner. **CAST:** Griff Rhys Jones, Mel Smith, Alison Steadman, Diana Quick. **1989**

MISCHIEF ★★★ In this disarming coming-of-age comedy, Doug McKeon (*On Golden Pond*) plays Jonathan, whose hopes of romance are thwarted until Gene (Chris Nash, in an impressive debut), a kid from the big city, shows him how. Rated R for violence, profanity, nudity, and simulated sex. 93m. **DIR:** Mel Damski. **CAST:** Doug McKeon, Catherine Mary Stewart, Chris Nash, Kelly Preston, D. W. Brown. **1985**

MISS FIRECRACKER ★★★★ A wacky, colorful, feel-good movie about a young Mississippi woman whose hunger for self-respect takes her through the rigors of her hometown Yazoo City Miss Firecracker Contest. Holly Hunter is marvelous as the misguided woman, while Mary Steenburgen shines as her cousin. From the off-Broadway play by Beth (*Crimes of the Heart*) Henley. Rated PG. 102m. **DIR:** Thomas Schlamme. **CAST:** Holly Hunter, Mary Steenburgen, Tim Robbins, Alfre Woodard, Scott Glenn. **1989**

MISS GRANT TAKES RICHMOND ★★★ Lucille Ball plays a dizzy secretary who outwits a band of thieves and wins handsome William Holden (who looks just as baffled as he did years later guest-starring on *I Love Lucy*). Agreeable star vehicle has a stalwart supporting cast. B&W; 87m. **DIR:** Lloyd Bacon. **CAST:** Lucille Ball, William Holden, Janis Carter, James Gleason, Frank McHugh. **1949**

MISS RIGHT ★★ This vignettish, uneven sex comedy strongly resembles TV's *Love American Style*. A UPI correspondent in Rome (William Tepper) becomes involved with several beautiful women. Rated R for profanity and nudity. 98m. **DIR:** Paul Williams. **CAST:** William Tepper, Karen Black, Margot Kidder, Virna Lisi, Marie-France Pisier, Clio Goldsmith. **1988**

MISSIONARY, THE ★★★½ Monty Python's Michael Palin, who also wrote the script, plays a well-meaning American minister assigned the task of saving the souls of London's fallen women. Not a nonstop, gag-filled descent into absurdity like the Monty Python movies. It is, instead, a warmhearted spoof with the accent on character and very sparing but effective in its humor. Rated R. 90m. **DIR:** Richard Loncraine. **CAST:** Michael Palin, Maggie Smith, Denholm Elliott, Trevor Howard, Michael Hordern. **1982**

MR. AND MRS. SMITH ★★★★ This film deals with the love-hate-love relationship of Carole Lombard and Robert Montgomery, who play a couple who discover their marriage isn't legal. The bouncy dialogue by Norman Krasna is justly famous and includes some of the most classic comedy scenes ever. Directing this enjoyable farce, in his only pure comedy, is Alfred Hitchcock. B&W; 95m. **DIR:** Alfred Hitchcock. **CAST:** Carole Lombard, Robert Montgomery, Gene Raymond, Jack Carson. **1941**

MR. BASEBALL ★★★ Tom Selleck mugs his way through this fish-out-of-water comedy about an American major league baseball player who is sent to play in Japan. Rated PG-13 for profanity. 110m. **DIR:** Fred Schepisi. **CAST:** Tom Selleck, Ken Takakura, Dennis Haysbert. **1992**

MR. BILL LOOKS BACK ★★★ This is a collection of shorts taken from *Saturday Night Live* episodes. In each, Mr. Bill and his dog Spot are tormented by Mr. Hands and the evil Sluggo. Bill's adventures take him to Coney Island, Skid Row, a psychiatrist's office, the police station, and Sing Sing. There are some hilarious moments. 30m. **DIR:** Walter Williams. **CAST:** Animated. **1980**

MR. BILL'S REAL LIFE ADVENTURES ★★½ The hilarity of the clay figure's misfortunes doesn't quite translate with real-life characters. Peter Scolari as Mr. Bill, however, is terrific. Mr. Bill, his sweet wife Sally (Valerie Mahaffey), their son Billy, and dog Spot are tiny people who must battle not only the huge world around them but also their neighbors. 43m. **DIR:** Jim Drake. **CAST:** Peter Scolari, Valerie Mahaffey, Lenore Kasdorf, Michael McAnus. **1986**

MR. BLANDINGS BUILDS HIS DREAM HOUSE ★★★★ In this screwball comedy, Cary Grant plays a man tired of the hustle and bustle of city life. He decides to move to the country, construct his private Shangri-La, and settle back into a serene rural lifestyle. His fantasy and reality come into comic conflict. Myrna Loy is cast as his ever-patient wife in this very fine film. B&W; 94m. **DIR:** H. C. Potter. **CAST:** Cary Grant, Myrna Loy, Melvyn Douglas. **1948**

MR. DEEDS GOES TO TOWN ★★★★★ The quiet unassuming world of a contented New Englander (Gary Cooper) is severely tested when he inherits a fortune in this classic Frank Capra comedy. An amusing series of misadventures results when our hero's straightforward values are caught in a tug-of-war with the corruption of big city money and snobbishness. B&W; 120m. **DIR:** Frank

Capra. **CAST:** Gary Cooper, Jean Arthur, Douglass Dumbrille, Lionel Stander, George Bancroft. **1936**

MR. DESTINY ★★½ James Belushi plays a pencil pusher who believes he is a failure. Michael Caine, who can shape people's lives, shows him differently in this passable comedy that reminds one of *It's a Wonderful Life*. Rated PG-13 for profanity. 117m. **DIR:** James Orr. **CAST:** James Belushi, Linda Hamilton, Jon Lovitz, Hart Bochner, Michael Caine. **1990**

MR. HOBBS TAKES A VACATION ★★★ Somewhat against his better judgment, ever-patient James Stewart takes his wife Maureen O'Hara and their children and grandchildren on vacation. They wind up in a ramshackle old house on the Pacific Coast, and he winds up more hassled than when home or at work. Good acting and a clever script make this thin-plotted comedy amusing. 116m. **DIR:** Henry Koster. **CAST:** James Stewart, Maureen O'Hara, Marie Wilson, Fabian, John Saxon. **1962**

MR. MIKE'S MONDO VIDEO ★★★ This comedy special by former *Saturday Night Live* writer Michael O'Donoghue was originally slated to run on late-night network television, but NBC decided it was too outrageous—even offensive in some parts—to be broadcast. *Mr. Mike's Mondo Video* was then briefly released to theaters. In fact, it is kind of a time capsule of comedy and pop figures from the 1970s. It stands as a reminder of how far-out comedy got on television after years of safe, insipid sitcoms. 75m. **DIR:** Michael O'Donoghue. **CAST:** Michael O'Donoghue, Dan Aykroyd, Jane Curtin, Carrie Fisher, Teri Garr, Deborah Harry, Margot Kidder, Bill Murray, Laraine Newman, Gilda Radner, Julius LaRosa, Paul Shaffer, Sid Vicious. **1979**

MR. MOM ★★★★ Michael Keaton is hilarious as an engineer who loses his job at an automobile manufacturing plant and, when wife Teri Garr gets a high-paying job at an advertising agency, becomes a hopelessly inept househusband. The story is familiar and predictable, but Keaton's off-the-wall antics and boyish charm make it all seem fresh and lively. Rated PG for light profanity. 91m. **DIR:** Stan Dragoti. **CAST:** Michael Keaton, Teri Garr, Ann Jillian, Martin Mull. **1983**

MR. NORTH ★★★½ In this fantasy a young Yale graduate arrives in elite Newport, Rhode Island as a tutor and ends up touching the citizens in seemingly magical ways. Based on Thornton Wilder's novel, *Theophilus North,* and directed by the late John Huston's son, Danny, this small-scale piece of whimsy is a winner. Rated PG. 92m. **DIR:** Danny Huston. **CAST:** Anthony Edwards, Robert Mitchum, Lauren Bacall, Harry Dean Stanton, Anjelica Huston. **1988**

MR. PEABODY AND THE MERMAID ★★ This is *Splash*, 1940s-style. A married New Englander (William Powell) snags an amorous mermaid while fishing and transfers her to his swimming pool, with the expected results. B&W; 89m. **DIR:** Irving Pichel. **CAST:** William Powell, Ann Blyth, Irene Hervey. **1948**

MR. ROBERTS ★★★★½ A navy cargo ship well outside the World War II battle zone is the setting for this hit comedy-drama. Henry Fonda is Lieutenant Roberts, the first officer who helps the crew battle their ceaseless boredom and tyrannical captain (James Cagney). Jack Lemmon began his road to stardom with his sparkling performance as the irrepressible con-man Ensign Pulver. 123m. **DIR:** John Ford, Mervyn LeRoy. **CAST:** Henry Fonda, James Cagney, Jack Lemmon, William Powell, Ward Bond. **1955**

MR. SATURDAY NIGHT ★★★★ Billy Crystal gives a smashing performance in this poignant comedy chronicling fifty years in the life of a stand-up comedian. Costar David Paymer almost steals Crystal's show as his brother-manager who must put up with the increasingly irritating comic. Rated R for profanity. 119m. **DIR:** Billy Crystal. **CAST:** Billy Crystal, David Paymer, Julie Warner, Helen Hunt, Ron Silver, Jerry Orbach. **1992**

MR. SKITCH ★★★ Will Rogers, broke after a bank failure, heads West hoping to recoup at a gambling casino. A dollar wins him a bundle—that wife ZaSu Pitts promptly loses. Typical Rogers comedy fare sprinkled with quick quips and homespun philosophy. B&W; 70m. **DIR:** James Cruze. **CAST:** Will Rogers, ZaSu Pitts, Rochelle Hudson, Eugene Pallette. **1933**

MR. SYCAMORE 🦃 A mailman decides to turn into a tree. Peculiar and pointless. Unrated. 87m. **DIR:** Pancho Kohner. **CAST:** Jason Robards Jr., Sandy Dennis, Jean Simmons, Mark Miller. **1975**

MR. WINKLE GOES TO WAR ★★★ Edward G. Robinson is a henpecked bookkeeper who gets drafted into the army during World War II. As the saying goes, the army makes a man out of him. Like so many films of its time, *Mr. Winkle Goes to War* was part of the war effort, and as such, hasn't worn very well; what was considered heartfelt or patriotic back in the 1940s is now rendered maudlin or just corny. Still, the acting is excellent. B&W; 80m. **DIR:** Alfred E. Green. **CAST:** Edward G. Robinson, Ruth Warrick, Richard Lane, Robert Armstrong. **1944**

MRS. DOUBTFIRE ★★★★ Robin Williams is a howl as a father so desperate to be near his kids after separating from his wife that he masquerades as their elderly Irish nanny. Sally Field proves to be a terrific "straight man" for her costar, while the film smartly avoids the pitfalls found in the similarly themed *All I Want for Christmas*. Rated PG-13 for brief profanity and scatological humor. 125m. **DIR:** Chris Columbus. **CAST:** Robin Williams, Sally Field, Pierce Brosnan, Harvey Fierstein, Polly Holliday, Lisa Jakub, Matthew Lawrence, Mara Wilson, Robert Prosky, Anne Haney, Sydney Walker, Martin Mull. 1993

MO' MONEY ★★★½ Damon Wayans wrote and stars in this comedy about a small-time street hustler who falls in love and tries to go straight. There are some terrific moments of hilarity in this fast-paced, fun flick, which also features an impressive feature-film acting debut by Marlon Wayans. Rated R for profanity, nudity, and violence. 97m. **DIR:** Peter MacDonald. **CAST:** Damon Wayans, Marlon Wayans, Stacey Dash, Joe Santos, John Diehl. 1992

MOB BOSS ★★½ Sometimes funny gangster story about an aging don (William Hickey) who calls upon his absolutely useless son (Eddie Deezen) to take over the family business. Deezen's training as a mobster is hilarious. Rated R for nudity and profanity. 93m. **DIR:** Fred Olen Ray. **CAST:** Morgan Fairchild, Eddie Deezen, William Hickey, Don Stroud, Jack O'Halloran, Mike Mazurki, Stuart Whitman. 1990

MOB STORY ★★½ A moderately funny comedy-drama. A mob kingpin escapes to Winnipeg to stay with relatives. His attempts to train his nephew in the fine art of crime run afoul as his enemies track him down. Rated PG-13. 98m. **DIR:** Jancarlo Markiw, Gabriel Markiw. **CAST:** Margot Kidder, John Vernon, Kate Vernon, Al Waxman. 1988

MODERN GIRLS ★★★ Cynthia Gibb, Virginia Madsen, and Daphne Zuniga turn in fine individual performances as the *Modern Girls*, but this well-edited and visually striking film has some slow scenes among the funny. However, younger viewers should find it enjoyable overall. Rated PG-13 for profanity and sexual situations. 82m. **DIR:** Jerry Kramer. **CAST:** Cynthia Gibb, Virginia Madsen, Daphne Zuniga, Clayton Rohner, Stephen Shellen, Chris Nash. 1987

MODERN LOVE ★★ Robby Benson's ideal concept of marital bliss is marred by the realities of daily life. Some funny bits, but Benson's fantasies get unbelievably out of hand. (His real wife, Karla DeVito, is great as his harried film wife and a new mother.) Rated R for nudity. 110m. **DIR:** Robby Benson. **CAST:** Robby Benson, Karla DeVito, Burt Reynolds, Rue McClanahan. 1990

MODERN PROBLEMS ★★ In this passable comedy, directed by Ken (*The Groove Tube*) Shapiro, Chevy Chase plays an air traffic controller who may be permanently out to lunch. Rated PG because of its brief nudity and sexual theme. 91m. **DIR:** Ken Shapiro. **CAST:** Chevy Chase, Patti D'Arbanville, Mary Kay Place. 1981

MODERN ROMANCE ★★★★ Love may be a many-splendored thing for some people, but it's sheer torture for Robert Cole (Albert Brooks) in this contemporary comedy. Brooks wrote, directed, and starred in this very entertaining, often hilarious story about a self-indulgent, narcissistic Hollywood film editor whose love life has the stability of Mount St. Helens. Rated R. 93m. **DIR:** Albert Brooks. **CAST:** Albert Brooks, Kathryn Harrold, Bruno Kirby. 1981

MODERN TIMES ★★★★ Charlie Chaplin must have had a crystal ball when he created *Modern Times*. His satire of life in an industrial society has more relevance today than when it was made. Primarily it is still pure Chaplin, with his perfectly timed and edited sight gags. The story finds the Little Tramp confronting all the dehumanizing inventions of a futuristic manufacturing plant. B&W; 89m. **DIR:** Charles Chaplin. **CAST:** Charlie Chaplin, Paulette Goddard. 1936

MODERNS, THE ★★ This ironic look at the Paris art scene of the Twenties just isn't funny *enough*. Director Alan Rudolph is always poised at the crossroads of humorous seriousness, but in *The Moderns* he's got his vision in limbo too much of the time. Keith Carradine is good as an expatriate painter, and Wallace Shawn has the best lines as a gossip columnist. Unrated. 126m. **DIR:** Alan Rudolph. **CAST:** Keith Carradine, Linda Fiorentino, John Lone, Wallace Shawn, Genevieve Bujold, Geraldine Chaplin, Kevin J. O'Connor. 1988

MONDO TRASHO 🦃 This is not a sync-sound movie, and the 1950s rock 'n' roll, along with the occasional wild dubbed-over dialogue, gets tiresome after twenty minutes. Unrated, but this is equivalent to an X for violence, gore, and sex. 130m. **DIR:** John Waters. **CAST:** Divine, Mary Vivian Pearce, Mink Stole, David Lochary. 1971

MONEY FOR NOTHING ★★★★ The fact-based story of Joey Coyle, an unemployed Philadelphia dock worker who finds $1.2 million when it falls out of an armored car on its way to an Atlantic City casino. The film bends the facts somewhat—it has the satiric feel of a 1940s Preston Sturges farce—but it makes fine entertainment, fast-paced and well acted by an excellent cast. Rated R for profanity. 100m. **DIR:** Ramon Menendez. **CAST:** John Cusack, Debi Mazar, Michael Madsen, Maury Chaykin. 1993

MONEY PIT, THE ★★ In this gimmicky, contrived Steven Spielberg production, Tom Hanks plays a rock 'n' roll lawyer who falls in love with musician Shelley Long. When these lovebirds buy a fixer-upper, they encounter all sorts of problems. Rated PG for profanity and suggested sex. 90m. **DIR:** Richard Benjamin. **CAST:** Tom Hanks, Shelley Long, Alexander Godunov, Maureen Stapleton, Joe Mantegna, Philip Bosco, Josh Mostel. 1986

MONKEY BUSINESS (1931) ★★★★½ The Marx Brothers are stowaways on a cruise ship, deflating pomposity and confusing authority. This movie dispenses with needless subplots and stagy musical numbers. It's undiluted Marx zaniness, and one of the team's best films. B&W; 77m. **DIR:** Norman Z. McLeod. **CAST:** The Marx Brothers, Thelma Todd, Ruth Hall. **1931**

MONKEY BUSINESS (1952) ★★★★ A romping screwball comedy about a genius chemist (Cary Grant) who invents a formula that delays the aging process. A chimpanzee in the lab pours the formula in the public water fountain, causing all concerned to revert to adolescence. A minor classic. B&W; 97m. **DIR:** Howard Hawks. **CAST:** Cary Grant, Marilyn Monroe, Ginger Rogers, Charles Coburn, Hugh Marlowe, Larry Keating. **1952**

MONSIEUR BEAUCAIRE ★★★½ Bob Hope is King Louie XV's barber, tricked into impersonating a court dandy, not knowing an assassination is planned. Joan Caulfield is a beautiful chambermaid. Lots of laughs. Very loosely based on Booth Tarkington's novel. B&W; 93m. **DIR:** George Marshall. **CAST:** Bob Hope, Joan Caulfield, Patric Knowles, Marjorie Reynolds, Cecil Kellaway, Joseph Schildkraut, Reginald Owen, Constance Collier, Hillary Brooke. **1946**

MONSIEUR VERDOUX ★★★★ A trendsetting black comedy in which a dandified, Parisian Bluebeard murders wives for their money. Wry humor abounds. Charlie Chaplin is superb in the title role. But it's Martha Raye who steals the film—most decidedly in the rowboat scene. The genius that made Chaplin famous the world over shows throughout. B&W; 123m. **DIR:** Charles Chaplin. **CAST:** Charlie Chaplin, Martha Raye, Isobel Elsom, Marilyn Nash, William Frawley. **1947**

MONSTER A GO-GO 🦃 An astronaut is turned into a giant by radiation. B&W; 70m. **DIR:** Bill Rebane, Sheldon Seymour. **CAST:** Phil Morton, June Travis. **1965**

MONSTER HIGH 🦃 Inept, dull, and tasteless attempt to spoof the alien invader, end of the world, and monster genres—all of it taking place at a high school. Rated R for gore, language, and nudity. 84m. **DIR:** Rudiger Poe. **CAST:** Dean Iandoli. **1989**

MONSTER IN A BOX ★★★★ Nobody can sit and talk to the camera like Spalding Gray. In this, the monologist's second filmed stage performance, Gray discusses his brushes with life and death as he wrote his pseudoautobiographical novel *Impossible Vacation*. Rated PG-13 for profanity. 90m. **DIR:** Nick Broomfield. **CAST:** Spalding Gray. **1991**

MONTY PYTHON AND THE HOLY GRAIL ★★★½ The Monty Python gang assault the legend of King Arthur and his knights in this often uproariously funny, sometimes tedious, movie. Rated PG. 90m. **DIR:** Terry Gilliam. **CAST:** Terry Jones, Graham Chapman, John Cleese, Terry Gilliam, Michael Palin. **1974**

MONTY PYTHON LIVE AT THE HOLLYWOOD BOWL ★★★★ Hold on to your sides! Those Monty Python crazies are back with more unbridled hilarity. Rated R for profanity, nudity, and the best in bad taste. 73m. **DIR:** Terry Hughes. **CAST:** John Cleese, Eric Idle, Graham Chapman, Terry Jones, Michael Palin, Terry Gilliam. **1982**

MONTY PYTHON'S FLYING CIRCUS (TV SERIES) ★★★★ This is a series of videos featuring highlights from the popular English TV show of the early 1970s. All the madcap characters remain intact along with the innovative and trendsetting animation by Terry Gilliam. You don't have to be British to enjoy the various political asides and lampoons. You do have to like fast-paced, off-the-wall craziness. The talented cast also conceived and wrote all of the material. Each tape 60m. **DIR:** Ian McNaughton. **CAST:** Graham Chapman, John Cleese, Terry Gilliam, Eric Idle, Terry Jones, Michael Palin. **1970–1972**

MONTY PYTHON'S THE MEANING OF LIFE ★★★★ Those Monty Python goons perform a series of sketches on the important issues of life. According to Michael Palin, the film "ranges from philosophy to history to medicine to halibut—especially halibut." It's the English troupe's finest feature film to date—a heady mixture of satiric and surreal bits about the life cycle from birth to death. It may prove offensive to some and a sheer delight to others. Rated R for all manner of offensive goings-on. 103m. **DIR:** Terry Jones. **CAST:** John Cleese, Eric Idle, Graham Chapman, Terry Jones, Terry Gilliam. **1983**

MOON IS BLUE, THE ★★ It's hard to believe this comedy, based on a stage hit, was once considered highly controversial. We doubt that even your grandmother would be offended by this very moral film. The thin plot concerns a young woman who fends off two slightly aging playboys by repeatedly vowing to remain a virgin until married. B&W; 95m. **DIR:** Otto Preminger. **CAST:** William Holden, David Niven, Maggie McNamara, Tom Tully, Dawn Addams. **1953**

MOON OVER PARADOR ★★½ This misfired comedy thrusts Richard Dreyfuss, who plays a modestly successful actor, into the role of his career: impersonating the recently deceased dictator of an anonymous Caribbean country. Political strongman Raul Julia wants the charade to continue until he can take over smoothly. Everything rattles to a most unconvincing conclusion. Rated PG-13 for language and mild sexual themes. 105m. **DIR:** Paul Mazursky. **CAST:** Richard Dreyfuss, Raul Julia, Sonia Braga, Jonathan Winters, Fernando Rey, Polly Holliday. **1988**

MOONSTRUCK ★★★★½ Cher, Nicolas Cage, and a superb supporting cast enliven this delightful comedy about a group of Italian-Americans who find amore when the moon shines bright. *Moonstruck*, with its quirky humor and ensemble playing, reminds one of a Woody Allen comedy. Director Norman Jewison and screenwriter John Patrick Shanley manage to make one hilarious complication follow another. Rated PG for profanity and suggested sex. 102m. **DIR:** Norman Jewison. **CAST:** Cher, Nicolas Cage, Vincent Gardenia, Olympia Dukakis, Danny Aiello, Julie Bovasso, John Mahoney, Feodor Chaliapin. **1987**

MORE THE MERRIER, THE ★★★★ This delightful comedy is set in Washington, D.C., during the hotel and housing shortage of the hectic World War II years. Charles Coburn earned a supporting Oscar as the old curmudgeon trying to cope with the housing problem while advising Joel McCrea and Jean Arthur on how to handle their love life. (Cary Grant played Coburn's character when this was remade as *Walk, Don't Run.*) B&W; 104m. **DIR:** George Stevens. **CAST:** Joel McCrea, Jean Arthur, Charles Coburn. **1943**

MORGAN ★★★★ In this cult favorite, Vanessa Redgrave decides to leave her wacky husband (David Warner). He's a wild man who has a thing for gorillas (this brings scenes from *King Kong*). Nevertheless, he tries to win her back in an increasingly unorthodox manner. Deeply imbedded in the 1960s, this film still brings quite a few laughs. B&W; 97m. **DIR:** Karel Reisz. **CAST:** Vanessa Redgrave, David Warner, Robert Stephens, Irene Handl. **1966**

MORGAN STEWART'S COMING HOME ★★ Made before *Pretty in Pink* but released after it to take advantage of the impression Jon Cryer made in that John Hughes teen comedy. The young actor stars in this tepid comedy as a preppie who tries to reorder his family's priorities. Cryer has some good moments, and Lynn Redgrave is top-notch as his mom, but the laughs just aren't there. Rated PG-13. 92m. **DIR:** Alan Smithee. **CAST:** Jon Cryer, Lynn Redgrave, Viveka Davis, Paul Gleason, Nicholas Pryor. **1987**

MORON MOVIES ★★★ This tape, like its sequel, *More Moron Movies*, features nearly 150 brief gag films made by Len Cella, a man with a home movie camera and a very strange sense of humor. You can tell from the titles: "Jell-O Makes a Lousy Doorstop," "How to Know if You're Ugly." This hit-and-miss collection is best watched in small doses, though it's sometimes extremely funny. Unrated. 60m. **DIR:** Len Cella. **1985**

MORONS FROM OUTER SPACE ★★½ Four aliens from a distant planet crash-land on Earth, but their arrival is not a secret and they soon become international celebrities. The comedy comes from the fact that they're idiots and act accordingly. Unfortunately, the morons are not as funny as the viewer would hope. Rated PG for language. 78m. **DIR:** Mike Hodges. **CAST:** Griff Rhys Jones, Mel Smith, James B. Sikking, Dindsdale Landen. **1985**

MORTUARY ACADEMY ★★ Academic comedy fails to advance to the head of the class. The brothers Grimm (yes, that's their last name) must make it through the dreaded academy in order to inherit big bucks. Typical. Rated R for nudity, language, and some violence. 86m. **DIR:** Michael Schroeder. **CAST:** Christopher Atkins, Tracey Walter, Lynn Danielson, Mary Woronov, Perry Lang. **1992**

MOSCOW ON THE HUDSON ★★★★½ Robin Williams stars in this sweet, funny, sad, and sexy comedy as a Russian circus performer who, while on tour in the United States, decides to defect after experiencing the wonders of Bloomingdale's department store in New York. Paul Mazursky cowrote and directed this touching character study. Rated R for profanity, nudity, suggested sex, and violence. 115m. **DIR:** Paul Mazursky. **CAST:** Robin Williams, Maria Conchita Alonso, Cleavant Derricks. **1984**

MOTHER, JUGS, AND SPEED ★★★ Hang on tight! This is a fast and furious black comedy about a run-down ambulance service that puts body count ahead of patient welfare in the race to the hospital. Bill Cosby and Raquel Welch make an odd combination that clicks. There's also some scene-stealing hilarity from Larry Hagman as an oversexed driver. Rated R. 95m. **DIR:** Peter Yates. **CAST:** Bill Cosby, Raquel Welch, Larry Hagman, Harvey Keitel. **1976**

MOTORAMA ★★★★ Ten-year-old Jordan Christopher Michael takes off in a stolen car, questing for Motorama game cards and instant wealth. This darkly funny, extremely bizarre road movie features a strange supporting cast and gallons of imagination. For unusual tastes only. Rated R for profanity and brief nudity. 90m. **DIR:** Barry Shils. **CAST:** Jordan Christopher Michael, Flea, Meat Loaf, Drew Barrymore, Garrett Morris, Michael J. Pollard, Mary Woronov, Martha Quinn. **1991**

MOUSE THAT ROARED, THE ★★★★ Any film that features Peter Sellers at his peak can't help but be funny. In this British movie, a tiny European nation devises a foolproof method of filling its depleted treasury. It declares war on the United States with the intention of losing and collecting war reparations from the generous Americans. Even foolproof plans don't always go as expected...in this case with hilarious results. 83m. **DIR:** Jack Arnold. **CAST:** Peter Sellers, Jean Seberg, Leo McKern. **1958**

MOVERS AND SHAKERS ★★ This star-studded film starts off well but quickly falls apart. Walter Matthau plays a Hollywood producer who begins work on a movie project with only the title, *Love in Sex*, to start with. Charles Grodin plays the screenwriter who is commissioned to write the script, which is intended as a tribute to love. But with serious marital problems, Grodin is hardly the proper candidate. Rated PG for profanity. 80m. **DIR:** William Asher. **CAST:** Walter Matthau, Charles Grodin, Vincent Gardenia, Tyne Daly, Bill Macy, Gilda Radner, Steve Martin, Penny Marshall. **1985**

MOVIE MOVIE ★★★½ Clever, affectionate spoof of 1930s pictures presents a double feature: *Dynamite Hands* is a black-and-white boxing story; *Baxter's Beauties of 1933* is a lavish, Busby Berkeley–type extravaganza. This nostalgic package even includes a preview of coming attractions. Rated PG. 107m. **DIR:** Stanley Donen. **CAST:** George C. Scott, Trish Van Devere, Eli Wallach, Red Buttons, Barry Bostwick, Harry Hamlin, Barbara Harris, Art Carney, Ann Reinking, Kathleen Beller. **1978**

MOVIE STRUCK (A.K.A. PICK A STAR) ★★ Typical story about a young girl trying to break into pictures is brightened by a brief appearance by Stan Laurel and Oliver Hardy, who demonstrate the effectiveness of breakaway glass during a barroom confrontation with a tough. Strange musical numbers and some witty dialogue buoy this thin story a little, but Stan and Ollie are still the main reasons to catch this one—and there just isn't that much of them. B&W; 70m. **DIR:** Edward Sedgwick. **CAST:** Stan Laurel, Oliver Hardy, Jack Haley, Patsy Kelly. **1937**

MOVING ★★ Chalk this up as another disappointment from Richard Pryor. Pryor plays an out-of-work mass-transit engineer who finds a job in Idaho and must move his family from their home in New Jersey. Rated R for profanity and violence. 90m. **DIR:** Alan Metter. **CAST:** Richard Pryor, Beverly Todd, Dave Thomas, Dana Carvey, Randy Quaid, Rodney Dangerfield. **1988**

MOVING VIOLATIONS ★★ Neal Israel and Pat Proft, who brought us *Police Academy* and *Bachelor Party*, writhe again with another "subject" comedy—this time about traffic school. Star John Murray does a reasonable job of imitating his older brother, Bill. Rated PG-13 for profanity and suggested sex. 90m. **DIR:** Neal Israel. **CAST:** John Murray, Jennifer Tilly, James Keach, Wendie Jo Sperber, Sally Kellerman, Fred Willard. **1985**

MUCH ADO ABOUT NOTHING ★★★★ As with his marvelous *Henry V*, actor-producer-writer-director Kenneth Branagh again brings energy, accessibility and cinematic style to one of William Shakespeare's classic stories. Confirmed bachelor Benedick (Branagh) trades barbs with the caustic Beatrice (Emma Thompson), and young Claudio (Robert Sean Leonard) suspects duplicity on the part of the innocent Hero (Kate Beckinsale). Michael Keaton adds humor, as the English-mangling Dogberry. Great fun! Rated PG-13 for brief nudity and suggested sex. 110m. **DIR:** Kenneth Branagh. **CAST:** Kenneth Branagh, Michael Keaton, Robert Sean Leonard, Keanu Reeves, Emma Thompson, Denzel Washington, Kate Beckinsale, Brian Blessed, Imelda Staunton, Phyllida Law. **1993**

MUGSY'S GIRLS 🦃 A predictable bit of fluff about a sorority out to earn rent money through mud wrestling. Rated R for nudity and profanity. 87m. **DIR:** Kevin Brodie. **CAST:** Ruth Gordon, Laura Branigan, Eddie Deezen. **1985**

MUNSTERS' REVENGE, THE ★★★ More schlock than shock and chock full of predictable puns, this munster mash is super Saturday-morning fun. Most of the original players from the TV series are back, with outstanding guests like Sid Caesar as the curator of a wax museum. 96m. **DIR:** Don Weis. **CAST:** Fred Gwynne, Yvonne De Carlo, Al Lewis, Sid Caesar. **1981**

MURDER BY DEATH ★★★★ Mystery buffs will get a big kick out of this spoof of the genre, penned by Neil Simon. Peter Sellers, Peter Falk, David Niven, Maggie Smith, and James Coco play thinly disguised send-ups of famed fictional detectives who are invited to the home of Truman Capote to solve a baffling murder. Rated PG. 94m. **DIR:** Robert Moore. **CAST:** Peter Sellers, Peter Falk, David Niven, Maggie Smith, James Coco, Alec Guinness. **1976**

MURPHY'S LAWS OF GOLF ★★ Tom Poston hacks his way through a round of golf while being harassed by Murphy's Law. Everything that can go wrong does, and the result is only slightly funny. Even golfers may be disappointed. Not rated. 30m. **DIR:** David Wechter. **CAST:** Tom Poston, David Doyle, Richard Moll. **1989**

MUSCLE BEACH PARTY ★★ Everyone's favorite surfing couple, Frankie and Annette, and their beach buddies return for more fluff in the sun. This features the first screen appearance of Little Stevie Wonder. 94m. **DIR:** William Asher. **CAST:** Frankie Avalon, Annette Funicello, Buddy Hackett, Luciana Paluzzi, Don Rickles, John Ashley, Jody McCrea, Morey Amsterdam. **1964**

MUTANT ON THE BOUNTY ★★ Silly yet sometimes amusing sci-fi spoof about a research team on a spaceship. Not rated. 93m. **DIR:** Robert Torrance. **CAST:** John Roarke, Deborah Benson, John Furey. **1989**

MUTANTS IN PARADISE ★★½ Campus loser, roped into an experiment to create a "nuke-proof" man, becomes a local celebrity. Rambling student-made film has cute ideas but lacks the budget to flesh them out. For one thing, there aren't any mutants. Unrated;

contains no objectionable material. 77m. **DIR:** Scott Apostolou. **CAST:** Brad Greenquist, Anna Nicholas, Edith Massey, Ray "Boom Boom" Mancini. **1985**

MY AMERICAN COUSIN ★★★★ This delightful Canadian comedy-drama focuses on what happens when the dull life of 12-year-old Sandra (played by feisty newcomer Margaret Langrick) is invaded by her high-spirited 17-year-old relative, Butch (John Wildman), from California. A warm character study with a number of funny moments, this is a refreshing antidote to the mindless teen flicks so common today. Rated PG for mild sexuality. 110m. **DIR:** Sandy Wilson. **CAST:** Margaret Langrick, John Wildman, Richard Donat. **1986**

MY BEST FRIEND IS A VAMPIRE ★★ Teen romance with a twist: Our hero has just become a vampire. Abundant car-chase scenes should intrigue teen viewers. Rated PG for Jeremy's seduction by the sexy vampire. 90m. **DIR:** Jimmy Huston. **CAST:** Robert Sean Leonard, Cheryl Pollak, René Auberjonois, Fannie Flagg. **1986**

MY BEST GIRL ★★½ Typical sweet, sunshiny Mary Pickford fare, this is a small-town romantic comedy about a tried-and-true shop girl who falls in love with the new clerk. He's really the boss's son. Virtue is rewarded, of course. Silent. B&W; 60m. **DIR:** Sam Taylor. **CAST:** Mary Pickford, Charles "Buddy" Rogers, Lucien Littlefield, Hobart Bosworth. **1927**

MY BLUE HEAVEN ★★★ Steve Martin and Rick Moranis are fun to watch in this gangster comedy, which has Martin as a mob informer in the witness protection program and Moranis as the FBI agent assigned to watch over him. Don't expect to laugh uproariously. Rated PG-13 for profanity and violence. 95m. **DIR:** Herbert Ross. **CAST:** Steve Martin, Rick Moranis, Joan Cusack, Melanie Mayron, Carol Kane, Bill Irwin, Deborah Rush. **1990**

MY BOYFRIEND'S BACK ★★★½ Macabre, offbeat black comedy works deliciously well in its own little world. When love-struck nerd Andrew Lowery is shot saving Traci Lind's life, his dying wish is that she will accompany him to the prom. She agrees; he dies. Lowery keeps his date by returning from the dead, setting off some hilarious complications. Humor is derived mainly from his home life, and the interaction of his goofy parents (Edward Herrmann and Mary Beth Hurt). Rated PG-13 for comic gore and adult language. 85m. **DIR:** Bob Balaban. **CAST:** Andrew Lowery, Traci Lind, Mary Beth Hurt, Edward Herrmann, Paul Dooley, Cloris Leachman. **1993**

MY BREAKFAST WITH BLASSIE ★½ Former professional wrestling champion Fred Blassie and protégé Andy Kaufman discuss life, breakfast, and various ways of insulting people during a breakfast at a southern California coffee shop. Spoof on *My Dinner with Andre* is mildly amusing at first and the concept is reasonably clever, but even fans of the two performers will find the film tedious. 60m. **DIR:** Johnny Legend, Linda Lautrec. **CAST:** Andy Kaufman, Fred Blassie. **1983**

MY CHAUFFEUR ★★½ In this better-than-average (for the genre) soft-core sex comedy, an aggressive, slightly kooky young woman upsets things at an all-male limousine company. Rated R for oodles of nudity, leering dirty old men by the truckload, suggested sex, and profanity. Don't let the kids rent this while you're out playing poker. 97m. **DIR:** David Beaird. **CAST:** Deborah Foreman, Sam Jones, Howard Hesseman, E. G. Marshall, Sean McClory. **1986**

MY COUSIN VINNY ★★★★ A fledgling Brooklyn lawyer attempts to free his cousin, who has been arrested on a murder charge in backward Wahzoo City, Alabama. It's a movie you won't want to miss. Joe Pesci is terrific, and so is Marisa Tomei as his gum popping fiancée. Rated R for profanity and brief violence. 116m. **DIR:** Jonathan Lynn. **CAST:** Joe Pesci, Ralph Macchio, Marisa Tomei, Mitchell Whitfield, Fred Gwynne, Lane Smith, Austin Pendleton, Bruce McGill, Maury Chaykin. **1991**

MY DEAR SECRETARY ★★½ A comedy battle of quips and wits between writer Kirk Douglas and bestselling author Laraine Day. Both lose the picture to Keenan Wynn, who is a droll delight. B&W; 94m. **DIR:** Charles Martin. **CAST:** Laraine Day, Kirk Douglas, Helen Walker, Keenan Wynn, Alan Mowbray. **1948**

MY DEMON LOVER ★★★½ Scott Valentine is delightful as a lovable bum who is possessed by the devil. His infatuation with a very gullible Denny (Michelle Little) becomes complicated when he is transformed into a demon every time he gets amorous. Rated PG for simulated sex and mild gore. 87m. **DIR:** Charlie Loventhal. **CAST:** Scott Valentine, Michelle Little, Robert Trebor, Gina Gallego, Alan Fudge. **1987**

MY FATHER IS COMING ★★★ A young German woman living in Manhattan pretends to be married when her father pays a visit, then watches in amazement as the supposedly stuffy old man has an affair with a sex therapist. Amusing exploration of modern sexuality. Not rated; contains nudity and frank sexual discussions. B&W; 82m. **DIR:** Monika Treut. **CAST:** Shelley Kastner, Alfred Edel, Annie Sprinkle. **1991**

MY FATHER, THE HERO ★★★½ Genial, goofy Disney comedy is obviously intended to increase French superstar Gérard Depardieu's popularity in America. Though at first seemingly miscast, Depardieu is fine as the father of a feisty teenage girl. She tries to pass him off as her older lover while they're on vacation in order to appear sexy and sophisticated to a young suitor. It's charming, corny, and humorous all at the same time. Rated PG. **DIR:** Steve Miner. **CAST:** Gérard Depardieu, Katherine Heigl, Dalton James, Faith Prince, Stephen Tobolowsky, Emma Thompson. **1994**

MY FAVORITE BLONDE ★★★★ Funny outing with cowardly vaudeville star Bob Hope on his way to Hollywood. (His trained penguin just won a contract.) He becomes involved with a British secret agent and assassinations. B&W; 78m. **DIR:** Sidney Lanfield. **CAST:** Bob Hope, Madeleine Carroll, Gale Sondergaard, George Zucco. **1942**

MY FAVORITE BRUNETTE ★★★★½ Classic Bob Hope comedy with Bob as a photographer who, thanks to a case of mistaken identity, makes No. 1 on the death list of a gang of thugs, played beautifully by Peter Lorre, Lon Chaney Jr., John Hoyt, and Elisha Cook Jr. Bob tries every trick in the book to save his neck, as well as Dorothy Lamour's. A scream! B&W; 87m. **DIR:** Elliott Nugent. **CAST:** Bob Hope, Dorothy Lamour, Peter Lorre, Lon Chaney Jr., John Hoyt. **1947**

MY FAVORITE WIFE ★★★★★ Cary Grant and Irene Dunne teamed up for many hilarious films, but the best is this often-copied comedy. Grant is a widower about to be remarried when his long-lost and presumed-dead wife (Dunne) is rescued after years on an island with a handsome young scientist (Randolph Scott). The delightful complications that result make this one of the 1940s' best comedies. B&W; 88m. **DIR:** Garson Kanin. **CAST:** Cary Grant, Irene Dunne, Randolph Scott. **1940**

MY FAVORITE YEAR ★★★★½ This warmhearted, hilarious comedy is an affectionate tribute to the frenzied Golden Age of television, that period when uninhibited comics like Sid Caesar faced the added pressure of performing live. With superb performances all around and on-the-money direction by Richard Benjamin, it's a real treasure. Rated PG for slight profanity and sexual situations. 92m. **DIR:** Richard Benjamin. **CAST:** Peter O'Toole, Mark Linn-Baker, Joseph Bologna, Lainie Kazan, Bill Macy. **1982**

MY FRIEND IRMA ★★½ The plan to transpose a popular radio show about the "dumbest" of all "dumb blondes" to the screen went astray when it became the vehicle to introduce the team of Dean Martin and Jerry Lewis. The creator of the radio show, Cy Howard, coscripted, but he and his star, the lovely Marie Wilson, were all but lost in the shuffle. B&W; 113m. **DIR:** George Marshall. **CAST:** John Lund, Diana Lynn, Don DeFore, Marie Wilson, Dean Martin, Jerry Lewis, Hans Conried. **1949**

MY GEISHA ★★★ A Hollywood actress disguises herself as a geisha to convince her producer-husband to cast her in his Japan-based production of *Madame Butterfly.* Shirley MacLaine is delightful in an *I Love Lucy* sort of plot. 120m. **DIR:** Jack Cardiff. **CAST:** Shirley MacLaine, Yves Montand, Edward G. Robinson, Robert Cummings. **1962**

MY GRANDPA IS A VAMPIRE 🦃 Grandpa (Al Lewis) does not meet vampire criteria. He's able to survive in sunlight, doesn't suck blood, and performs a number of magic tricks. This film, made in New Zealand, takes the bite out of the would-be vampire thus reducing him to an ET-ish ghoul. Unrated, contains violence. 92m. **DIR:** David Blyth. **CAST:** Al Lewis. **1991**

MY LITTLE CHICKADEE ★★★★★ W. C. Fields and Mae West enter a marriage of convenience in the Old West. It seems the card sharp (Fields) and the tainted lady (West) need to create an aura of respectability before they descend upon an unsuspecting town. That indicates trouble ahead for the town, and lots of fun for viewers. B&W; 83m. **DIR:** Eddie Cline. **CAST:** W. C. Fields, Mae West, Dick Foran, Joseph Calleia. **1940**

MY LOVE FOR YOURS ★★★ An eager cast and a witty script make a passable entertainment of this otherwise trite story of a cool, self-assured career girl thawed by love. It's also known as *Honeymoon in Bali.* B&W; 99m. **DIR:** Edward H. Griffith. **CAST:** Madeleine Carroll, Fred MacMurray, Allan Jones, Helen Broderick, Akim Tamiroff, Osa Massen, John Qualen. **1939**

MY MAN ADAM ★★ Daydreaming teenager Raphael Sbarge gets a chance to live out his fantasies when he uncovers a sinister plot at school. Disappointing comedy has some clever moments but the plot seems slapped together. Rated R, though there's nothing really offensive. 84m. **DIR:** Roger L. Simon. **CAST:** Raphael Sbarge, Page Hannah, Dave Thomas, Veronica Cartwright. **1985**

MY MAN GODFREY (1936) ★★★★★ *My Man Godfrey* is one of the great screwball comedies of the 1930s. Carole Lombard plays the most eccentric member of an eccentric family. William Powell is the relatively sane portion of the formula. Carole finds him when she is sent to find a "lost man." Powell seems to fit the bill, since he's living a hobo's life on the wrong side of the tracks. B&W; 95m. **DIR:** Gregory La Cava. **CAST:** Carole Lombard, William Powell, Gail Patrick, Alice Brady, Eugene Pallette. **1936**

MY MAN GODFREY (1957) ★★½ Passable but otherwise doomed updating of the 1936 classic screwball comedy will play better for those not familiar with the original. The stars try. 92m. **DIR:** Henry Koster. **CAST:** June Allyson, David Niven, Jessie Royce Landis,

Robert Keith, Eva Gabor, Jay Robinson, Jeff Donnell, Martha Hyer. 1957

MY MOM'S A WEREWOLF ★★ When a bored housewife (Susan Blakely) succumbs to a charming stranger (John Saxon), she is horrified to find herself transforming into a werewolf. Now her daughter and her ghoulish pal must figure out how to transform Blakely back into dear old mom. PG for profanity and violence. 90m. DIR: Michael Fischa. CAST: Susan Blakely, John Saxon, Katrina Caspary, Ruth Buzzi. 1988

MY NEIGHBORHOOD ★★★ An offbeat comedy with a dark tone featuring director-actor Michell Kriegman as neurotic pub owner who invites strangers off the street to view bizarre, homemade videos. Original and recommended. 28m. DIR: Michael Kriegman. CAST: Michael Kriegman. 1982

MY NEW GUN ★★½ This droll comedy doesn't quite deliver on its entertaining premise, but it satisfies modestly, thanks to the principal players. Diane Lane stars as a yuppie housewife who doesn't quite know how to react when her husband (Stephen Collins) gives her a gun for protection. 100m. DIR: Stacy Cochran. CAST: Diane Lane, Stephen Collins, James LeGros, Tess Harper. 1992

MY STEPMOTHER IS AN ALIEN ★★½ A beautiful alien (Kim Basinger) comes to Earth to reverse the effects of a ray that has changed the gravity of her planet. Unfortunately, the creator of the ray (Dan Aykroyd) doesn't know how to re-create it. Thinking he is lying, she marries him to get the secret. A so-so farce with a predictably sweet ending. Rated PG-13. 108m. DIR: Richard Benjamin. CAST: Dan Aykroyd, Kim Basinger, Jon Lovitz, Alison Hannigan. 1988

MY TUTOR 🦃 A young man gets an education in more than just reading, writing, and 'rithmetic. Rated R for nudity and implied sex. 97m. DIR: George Bowers. CAST: Matt Lattanzi, Caren Kaye, Kevin McCarthy. 1983

MYRA BRECKENRIDGE ★★ Infamous film version of Gore Vidal's satiric novel about a gay movie buff who has a sex-change operation (turning him into Raquel Welch!). Not very good, but the prententious psychedelic style and parade of old movie stars in cameo roles make it a must-see for camp enthusiasts and Sixties nostalgists. Originally rated X, the brief nudity and sexual concerns would barely earn this an R today. 94m. DIR: Michael Sarne. CAST: Raquel Welch, Mae West, John Huston, Rex Reed, John Carradine, Farrah Fawcett, Tom Selleck. 1970

MYSTERY DATE ★★½ This teenage version of Martin Scorsese's *After Hours* is only moderately funny and is saved from total video-shelf hell by young star Ethan Hawke. Rated PG-13 for violence and profanity. 90m. DIR: Jonathan Wacks. CAST: Ethan Hawke, Teri Polo, Brian McNamara, Fisher Stevens, B. D. Wong. 1991

MYSTERY OF THE LEAPING FISH/CHESS FEVER ★★ Two mighty peculiar products from two very dissimilar geniuses of the cinema. Leaping Fish, the Fairbanks film, stems from his early days in Hollywood and looks very much like a Mack Sennett farce. He plays Coke Ennyday, a cocaine-taking detective. *Chess Fever*, the Pudovkin film, is a mild fantasy about chess players. Silent. 64m. DIR: V. I. Pudovkin. CAST: Douglas Fairbanks Sr., Vsevelod Pudovkin. 1916/1925

NADINE ★★★ A cute caper comedy. Kim Basinger is a not-so-bright hairdresser who finds herself involved in murder and mayhem. She enlists the aid of her estranged husband (Jeff Bridges). Rip Torn gives a fine performance as the chief villain. Rated PG for light violence and profanity. 95m. DIR: Robert Benton. CAST: Jeff Bridges, Kim Basinger, Rip Torn, Gwen Verdon, Glenne Headly, Jerry Stiller. 1987

NAKED GUN, THE ★★★★ Fans of the short-lived television series *Police Squad!* will love this full-length adventure featuring Leslie Nielsen's stiff-lipped Frank Drebin, the toughest—and clumsiest—cop in the universe. The writing and producing team of David Zucker, Jim Abrahams, and Jerry Zucker, also responsible for *Airplane,* have riddled this parody of 1960s television cop shows with countless sight gags, outrageous puns, and over-the-top characterizations. Rated PG-13 for language and mild sexual coarseness. 85m. DIR: David Zucker. CAST: Leslie Nielsen, George Kennedy, Priscilla Presley, Ricardo Montalban, O. J. Simpson, Nancy Marchand. 1988

NAKED GUN 2 1/2, THE ★★★½ The loony *Police Squad* gang is back in this wacky sequel to the smash-hit police parody. In this saga, the amazingly brain-dead Lt. Frank Drebin (Leslie Nielsen) gets involved in efforts to bust a criminal hatching a nefarious antiecology crime. The film lacks the zip of the original, but it's still a nutty romp. Rated PG-13 for profanity and adult humor. 88m. DIR: David Zucker. CAST: Leslie Nielsen, Priscilla Presley, Robert Goulet, George Kennedy, O. J. Simpson. 1991

NAKED GUN 33 1/3, THE—THE FINAL INSULT ★★½ TV's *Police Squad!* originators make their third regurgitation of utter comic chaos as klutzy cop Lt. Frank Drebin comes out of brief retirement to nab a mad bomber. This lampooning of prison movies and much, much more climaxes with Drebin being mistaken for Phil Donahue as he brings an Oscars telecast to its knees. Cameo surprises abound, but this romp is not as funny or crisply paced as its predecessors. Rated PG-13 for suggested sex and language. 83m.

DIR: Peter Segal. **CAST:** Leslie Nielsen, Priscilla Presley, Fred Ward, George Kennedy, O. J. Simpson. 1994

NAKED TRUTH ★★½ This oddball comedy involves a group of loonies who are brought together to get rid of the editor of a smutty magazine. Peter Sellers is good as a disgusting television celebrity and Terry-Thomas is very effective as a racketeer. This British picture was originally titled *Your Past Is Showing*. 92m. **DIR:** Mario Zampi. **CAST:** Terry-Thomas, Dennis Price, Peter Sellers, Shirley Eaton. 1957

NASTY HABITS ★★ *Nasty Habits* promises much more than it delivers. As a satire of the Watergate conspiracy, placed in a convent, it relies too heavily on the true incident for its punch. Rated PG, with some profanity. 96m. **DIR:** Michael Lindsay-Hogg. **CAST:** Glenda Jackson, Sandy Dennis, Susan Penhaligon, Edith Evans, Melina Mercouri. 1977

NASTY RABBIT ★★ Stilted *Blazing Saddles*–type parody is a curiosity piece, featuring Mexican bandits, Japanese soldiers, Nazi troopers, Indians, cowboys, and circus freaks, all rolled into one long-winded mess. 85m. **DIR:** James Landis. **CAST:** Arch Hall Jr., Richard Kiel. 1964

NATIONAL LAMPOON'S LOADED WEAPON 1 ✗ It's amazing that an action-comedy parody under the *National Lampoon* banner could be so lame and deadly dull, but this cop-action satire is a misfired groanfest. Rated PG-13 for violence and language. 97m. **DIR:** Gene Quintano. **CAST:** Emilio Estevez, Samuel L. Jackson, Jon Lovitz, Tim Curry, William Shatner, Whoopi Goldberg, Bruce Willis, Charlie Sheen, Kathy Ireland. 1993

NATIONAL LAMPOON'S CHRISTMAS VACATION ★★★ Chevy Chase glides charmingly through this frantic farce. This sequel to the two Lampoon *Vacation* flicks has the Griswold family staying home for the holidays and being invaded by bickering relatives. Randy Quaid excels as the ultimate slob. Rated PG-13 for scatological humor and profanity. 97m. **DIR:** Jeremiah S. Chechik. **CAST:** Chevy Chase, Beverly D'Angelo, Randy Quaid, Diane Ladd, John Randolph, E. G. Marshall. 1989

NATIONAL LAMPOON'S CLASS OF '86 ★★★ You've got to be in a *National Lampoon* frame of mind to enjoy this comedy revue, which means embracing the off-the-wall humor for which the magazine is noted. Though unrated, it's strictly adult fare. 86m. **DIR:** Jerry Adler. **CAST:** Rodger Bumpass, Veanne Cox, Annie Golden, Tommy Koenig, John Michael Higgins, Brian O'Connor. 1986

NATIONAL LAMPOON'S CLASS REUNION ✗ The graduating class of 1972 returns to wreak havoc on its alma mater. Rated R for nudity. 84m. **DIR:** Michael Miller. **CAST:** Gerrit Graham, Stephen Furst, Zane Buzby, Michael Lerner. 1982

NATIONAL LAMPOON'S EUROPEAN VACATION ✗ The sappy sequel to *Vacation*. Rated PG-13 for profanity. 95m. **DIR:** Amy Heckerling. **CAST:** Chevy Chase, Beverly D'Angelo, Dana Hill, Jason Lively, Eric Idle, Victor Lanoux, John Astin. 1985

NATIONAL LAMPOON'S LAST RESORT ✗ Made-for-video lame duck take on the old, "Hey gang, let's save the summer camp" premise. Teen has-beens Corey Haim and Corey Feldman save the day. Who will save us? Rated PG-13 for language and sexual situations. 91m. **DIR:** Rafal Zielinski. **CAST:** Corey Feldman, Corey Haim, Geoffrey Lewis, Robert Mandan. 1994

NATIONAL LAMPOON'S VACATION ★★★ Clark Griswold (Chevy Chase) goes on a disastrous vacation with his wife, Ellen (Beverly D'Angelo), and kids, Rusty (Anthony Michael Hall) and Audrey (Dana Barron). Rated R for nudity and profanity. 98m. **DIR:** Harold Ramis. **CAST:** Chevy Chase, Beverly D'Angelo, Anthony Michael Hall, Dana Barron, Christie Brinkley, John Candy. 1983

NAUGHTY NINETIES, THE ★★ Suitably attired for the period, the always eager Bud and Lou find themselves hip-deep in Mississippi riverboat gamblers. The pair's usual ripostes, including "Who's on First," prevail. The finale is tried-and-true slapstick. B&W; 76m. **DIR:** Jean Yarbrough. **CAST:** Bud Abbott, Lou Costello, Joe Sawyer, Alan Curtis, Rita Johnson, Lois Collier. 1945

NAVY BLUE AND GOLD ★★★ Familiar but entertaining story of three Annapolis middies learning (by way of the annual Army-Navy football game) the meaning of esprit de corps. Billie Burke is a particular delight. B&W; 94m. **DIR:** Sam Wood. **CAST:** Robert Young, James Stewart, Lionel Barrymore, Florence Rice, Billie Burke, Tom Brown, Samuel S. Hinds, Paul Kelly, Frank Albertson, Minor Watson. 1937

NEAR MISSES ★★½ Executive Judge Reinhold balances two wives and a secretary-girlfriend on the side, but his troubles really begin when he asks fellow coworker Casey Siemaszko to impersonate him when his yearly army reserve duty comes up. Rated PG-13 for profanity. 92m. **DIR:** Baz Taylor. **CAST:** Judge Reinhold, Casey Siemaszko, Rebecca Pauley, Cecile Paoli. 1990

NECESSARY ROUGHNESS ★★★★ While the premise of this football comedy is familiar—a group of losers banding together against almost impossible odds—the execution seems fresh. Not only is this a very funny comedy, it has something to say about the state of college athletics. Rated PG-13 for profanity. 104m. **DIR:** Stan Dragoti. **CAST:** Scott Bakula, Robert Loggia, Harley Jane Kozak, Sinbad, Hector Elizondo, Jason Bateman, Kathy Ireland, Larry Miller. 1991

NEIGHBORS ★★★½ This is a strange movie. John Belushi plays a suburban homeowner whose peaceful existence is threatened when his new neighbors (played by Dan Aykroyd and Cathy Moriarty) turn out to be complete wackos. It isn't a laugh-a-minute farce, but there are numerous chuckles and a few guffaws along the way. Rated R because of profanity and sexual content. 94m. **DIR:** John G. Avildsen. **CAST:** John Belushi, Dan Aykroyd, Cathy Moriarty, Kathryn Walker, Tim Kazurinsky. 1981

NERVOUS TICKS ★★★ Airline employee Bill Pullman tries to run off to Rio with married Julie Brown. Interesting for having been shot in "real time," but the plot is just too wacky. Rated R for violence, profanity, and nudity. 95m. **DIR:** Rocky Lang. **CAST:** Bill Pullman, Peter Boyle, Julie Brown, Brent Jennings, James LeGros. 1991

NEUROTIC CABARET ★★★ A strange and entertaining movie. The plot revolves around two people's attempts to get their movie made. Tammy Stones, who also penned the script, stars as a strip-joint dancer. An amusing vehicle played tongue in cheek. Rated R for nudity. 97m. **DIR:** John Woodward. **CAST:** Tammy Stones, Dennis Worthington. 1990

NEVER GIVE A SUCKER AN EVEN BREAK ★★★★ This is a wild and woolly pastiche of hilarious gags and bizarre comedy routines revolving around W. C. Fields's attempt to sell an outlandish script to a movie studio. Some of the jokes misfire, but the absurdity of the situations makes up for the weak spots. B&W; 71m. **DIR:** Eddie Cline. **CAST:** W. C. Fields, Gloria Jean, Leon Errol. 1941

NEVER WAVE AT A WAC ★★★ Ancestor of *Private Benjamin*, with Rosalind Russell as a spoiled socialite who joins the Women's Army Corps. Russell may be a bit old for the part, but she and dumb-blonde sidekick Marie Wilson provide some laughs. Also known as *The Private Wore Skirts*. B&W; 87m. **DIR:** Norman Z. McLeod. **CAST:** Rosalind Russell, Marie Wilson, Paul Douglas, Louise Beavers. 1952

NEW HOMEOWNER'S GUIDE TO HAPPINESS, THE ★★★ In this black comedy, Judge Reinhold is a new resident of suburbia who finds various means to silence the endless yapping of the neighborhood dogs that disrupt his paradise. As his pregnant wife, Demi Moore also knows how to handle the neighbors. This is the last half of a one-hour tape coupled with *Ron Reagan Is the President's Son*, which you should fast-forward through. 60m. **DIR:** Jonathan Cutler. **CAST:** Judge Reinhold, Demi Moore. 1988

NEW KIND OF LOVE, A ★★ A minor romantic comedy that gets one star for showcasing the real-life vibes between Paul Newman and Joanne Woodward. It gets another star for having Maurice Chevalier sing "Mimi" and "Louise." The rest of it gets zilch. 110m. **DIR:** Melville Shavelson. **CAST:** Paul Newman, Joanne Woodward, Maurice Chevalier, Thelma Ritter, Eva Gabor, George Tobias, Marvin Kaplan. 1963

NEW LEAF, A ★★★★ A rare (and wonderful) triple play from an American female talent: writer-director-star Elaine May makes an impressive mark with this latter-day screwball comedy, about a bankrupt rogue (Walter Matthau) who must find a rich woman to marry—within six weeks. His target turns out to be a clumsy botanist (May) seeking immortality by finding a new specimen of plant life (hence one element of the title). Rated PG for adult situations. 102m. **DIR:** Elaine May. **CAST:** Walter Matthau, Elaine May, Jack Weston, James Coco, William Redfield. 1971

NEW LIFE, A ★★★ This amusing examination of life after divorce will please writer-director Alan Alda's fans, but others may find the brew too reminiscent of Neil Simon and Woody Allen (both of whom have done better with similar material). After a fairly agreeable separation, Alda and Ann-Margret stumble into other relationships. Hal Linden gives a standout performance as Alda's happily promiscuous best friend. Rated PG-13 for language and sexual themes. 104m. **DIR:** Alan Alda. **CAST:** Alan Alda, Ann-Margret, Hal Linden, Veronica Hamel, John Shea, Mary Kay Place, Beatrice Alda. 1988

NEW WAVE COMEDY ★★ A comical hodgepodge offering everything from break-dancing hand puppets to an overly worldly Barbie doll impersonation. The only familiar faces in this eight-part comedy tape are those of Mark Weiner (*Saturday Night Live*), Margaret Smith, a deadpan stand-up comic who frequents the David Letterman set, and John Kassir, the 1985 comedy champ from *Star Search*. Strong language. 60m. **DIR:** Michael Kriegman. **CAST:** Mark Weiner, Eric Bogosian, Margaret Smith, John Kassir, Wayne Federman, Patty Rosborough, Jefferey Essman, Steve Sweeny. 1986

NEW YORK STORIES ★★★★½ Here's a wonderful creation that provides discriminating video viewers with three terrific movies for the price of one. Woody Allen's *Oedipus Wrecks* marks his long-awaited return to comedy. Starring Allen as a lawyer who cannot escape his mother's overbearing influence, it's a hilarious vignette. Francis Coppola's *Life Without Zoe* is a light but charming fantasy about a sophisticated youngster named Zoe (Heather McComb) and her adventures in New York City. The best of this splendid trio is Martin Scorsese's *Life Les-*

sons, about the obsessive love of a celebrated painter (Nick Nolte) for his protégée (Rosanna Arquette). Rated PG for profanity. 119m. **DIR:** Woody Allen, Francis Ford Coppola, Martin Scorsese. **CAST:** Woody Allen, Rosanna Arquette, Mia Farrow, Giancarlo Giannini, Julie Kavner, Heather McComb, Nick Nolte, Don Novello, Patrick O'Neal, Talia Shire. **1989**

NEXT TIME I MARRY ★★★ A madcap comedy about marriage with Lucille Ball as an heiress who marries the first man she sees in order to get her inheritance. Ball has a ball, and it's contagious. B&W; 80m. **DIR:** Garson Kanin. **CAST:** Lucille Ball, Lee Bowman, James Ellison, Mantan Moreland. **1938**

NICE DREAMS ★★★ Cheech and Chong, the counterculture kings of drug-oriented comedy, haven't run out of steam yet. Their third feature film doesn't have quite as many classic comic gems as its predecessors, but it's more consistently entertaining. Rated R for nudity and profanity. 87m. **DIR:** Thomas Chong. **CAST:** Cheech and Chong, Evelyn Guerrero, Pee-Wee Herman, Stacy Keach. **1981**

NICE GIRL LIKE ME, A 🦃 Dated Sixties comedy that was considered risqué for its time, but now seems silly and contrived. Rated PG. 91m. **DIR:** Desmond Davis. **CAST:** Barbara Ferris, Harry Andrews, Gladys Cooper. **1969**

NICE GIRLS DON'T EXPLODE ★★ Droll, slow-moving comedy about a girl (Michelle Meyrink) who causes spontaneous combustion of objects. William O'Leary as her current boyfriend is exceptional. Rated PG, the film contains some strong language and mild nudity. 92m. **DIR:** Chuck Martinez. **CAST:** Barbara Harris, Michelle Meyrink, William O'Leary, Wallace Shawn. **1987**

NICK DANGER IN THE CASE OF THE MISSING YOLK 🦃 The usually funny Firesign Theatre Players (Phil Austin, Peter Bergman, and Phil Proctor) don't quite make it with this one. A hillbilly family, the Yolks, are transported to a futuristic home. 60m. **DIR:** William Dear. **CAST:** Firesign Theatre Players, Wendy Cutler, Christy Kaatz. **1983**

NICKEL & DIME ★★ C. Thomas Howell, a con artist who tries to match "long lost" heirs with unclaimed estates, is saddled with obnoxious accountant Wallace Shawn. A jumble, but Shawn and Howell forge a strangely endearing odd-couple relationship. Rated PG for profanity. 96m. **DIR:** Ben Moses. **CAST:** C. Thomas Howell, Wallace Shawn. **1992**

NIGHT AFTER NIGHT ★★★★ Mae West's first movie is one of her funniest, and she only has a brief supporting role. The real star is George Raft as a rich hoodlum who tries to break into New York society during the Depression. West plays one of the hoodlum's former girlfriends, and she flounces in to turn society on its ear in this delightfully witty farce. B&W; 70m. **DIR:** Archie Mayo. **CAST:** George Raft, Constance Cummings, Alison Skipworth, Mae West, Wynne Gibson, Louis Calhern. **1932**

NIGHT AT THE OPERA, A ★★★★★ Despite the songs and sappy love story, the Marx Brothers (minus Zeppo) are in peak form in this classic musical comedy, which costars the legendary Margaret Dumont. B&W; 92m. **DIR:** Sam Wood. **CAST:** The Marx Brothers, Margaret Dumont, Kitty Carlisle, Allan Jones, Sig Ruman. **1935**

NIGHT BEFORE, THE ★★★ A senior prom date turns into a hilarious nightmare in this riveting, offbeat comedy. After waking up in an alley, a young man (Keanu Reeves) finds his date and wallet missing along with his father's sports car. And then things get surreal—in the style of *After Hours*. Rated R for language and violence. 85m. **DIR:** Thom Eberhardt. **CAST:** Keanu Reeves, Lori Loughlin, Theresa Saldana, Trinidad Silva. **1988**

NIGHT IN CASABLANCA, A ★★★ Although the formula was wearing thin by 1946, Groucho's wisecracks and the incomparable antics of Chico and Harpo still carry the film. Joining forces in post-WWII Casablanca, the brothers wreak havoc in the staid Hotel Casablanca. B&W; 85m. **DIR:** Archie Mayo. **CAST:** The Marx Brothers, Charles Drake, Lisette Verea, Lois Collier. **1946**

NIGHT IN THE LIFE OF JIMMY REARDON, A 🦃 Jimmy Reardon is a teenage sex fiend in 1962 Evanston, Illinois. Rated R for profanity and leering sexual content. 92m. **DIR:** William Richert. **CAST:** River Phoenix, Meredith Salenger, Ione Skye, Louanne, Ann Magnuson. **1988**

NIGHT OF THE LIVING BABES 🦃 Two men check out a new whorehouse, only to be abducted by the prostitutes, tormented by strippers, and threatened by a transvestite. 60m. **DIR:** Jon Valentine. **CAST:** Michelle McClellan, Connie Woods, Andrew Nichols. **1987**

NIGHT PATROL 🦃 A bumbling rookie policeman doubles as "The Unknown Comic," cracking jokes in Los Angeles comedy clubs while wearing a paper bag over his head. Rated R. 84m. **DIR:** Jackie Kong. **CAST:** Linda Blair, Pat Paulsen, Jaye P. Morgan, Jack Riley, Billy Barty, Murray Langston. **1985**

NIGHT SHIFT ★★★★ When a nerdish morgue attendant (Henry Winkler) gets talked into becoming a pimp by a sweet hooker (Shelley Long) and his crazed coworker (Michael Keaton), the result is uproarious comedy. While the concept is a little weird, director Ron Howard packs it with so many laughs and such appealing characters that you can't help but like it. Rated R for nudity, profanity, sex, and violence. 105m. **DIR:** Ron Howard. **CAST:** Henry Winkler, Shelley Long, Michael Keaton. **1982**

NIGHT THEY RAIDED MINSKY'S, THE ★★★½ Director William Friedkin's tale of a religious girl's (Britt Ekland) involvement, much to her father's dismay, with a burlesque comic (Jason Robards). It's a nice look at what early burlesque was like, with good performances by all. Rated PG. 99m. **DIR:** William Friedkin. **CAST:** Britt Ekland, Jason Robards Jr., Elliott Gould. **1968**

NIGHT TO REMEMBER, A (1943) ★★★★ This is a very interesting comedy-whodunit about a Greenwich Village mystery author and his wife who try to solve a real murder. Performances are wonderful and the direction is taut. B&W; 91m. **DIR:** Richard Wallace. **CAST:** Loretta Young, Brian Aherne, Jeff Donnell, William Wright, Sidney Toler, Gale Sondergaard. **1943**

NIGHT WE NEVER MET, THE ★★★½ A sophisticated comedy with strong players who understand the meaning of teamwork. Kevin Anderson time-shares his New York apartment to help pay the rent. Would-be lothario Matthew Broderick and unhappily married Annabella Sciorra rent on alternate days. You know in advance that they will find each other, but the fun is finding out how. Delightful dialogue. 99m. **DIR:** Warren Light. **CAST:** Matthew Broderick, Annabella Sciorra, Kevin Anderson, Jeanne Tripplehorn, Justine Bateman, Garry Shandling, Louise Lasser, Katharine Houghton. **1993**

9½ NINJAS ★★★ A slapstick spoof of ninja movies and *9 1/2 Weeks*. A nonexistent plot, but solid hilarity. Michael Phenice is terrific. Rated R for nudity. 82m. **DIR:** Aaron Worth. **CAST:** Michael Phenice. **1990**

NINE LIVES OF FRITZ THE CAT ★★½ A streetwise alley cat tries to escape his mundane existence in the sequel to the 1972 cult favorite, *Fritz the Cat*. Fritz is his usual witty, horny self. The animation is excellent and the film is written with a hip sense of humor. This is not Saturday-morning material, however, as there is a distinctly erotic tone to virtually every scene. Rated R for adult theme and language. 77m. **DIR:** Robert Taylor. **CAST:** Animated. **1974**

NINE TO FIVE ★★★★ In this delightful comedy, Jane Fonda almost ends up playing third fiddle to two marvelous comediennes, Lily Tomlin and Dolly Parton. (That's right, Dolly Parton!) The gifted singer-songwriter makes one of the brightest acting debuts ever in this hilarious farce about three secretaries who decide to get revenge on their sexist, egomaniacal boss (Dabney Coleman). Rated PG. 110m. **DIR:** Colin Higgins. **CAST:** Jane Fonda, Lily Tomlin, Dolly Parton, Dabney Coleman. **1980**

1941 🦃 Steven Spielberg laid his first multimillion-dollar egg with this unfunny what-if comedy about the Japanese attacking Los Angeles during World War II. Rated PG. 118m. **DIR:** Steven Spielberg. **CAST:** John Belushi, Dan Aykroyd, Toshiro Mifune, Christopher Lee, Slim Pickens, Ned Beatty, John Candy, Nancy Allen, Tim Matheson, Murray Hamilton, Treat Williams. **1979**

90 DAYS ★★★ A fine little comedy shot in documentary style. The narrator has sent for a Korean pen pal to come to be his wife in Canada. The resultant cultural differences are humorously explored. Not rated. 100m. **DIR:** Giles Walker. **CAST:** Stefas Wodoslavsky, Sam Grana. **1986**

92 IN THE SHADE ★★★ This wild and hilarious adaptation of first-time director Thomas McGuane's prize-winning novel concerns rival fishing-boat captains in Florida. Entire cast is first-rate in this sleeper. Rated R. 93m. **DIR:** Thomas McGuane. **CAST:** Peter Fonda, Warren Oates, Margot Kidder, Harry Dean Stanton, Burgess Meredith, Elizabeth Ashley, Sylvia Miles. **1975**

NINOTCHKA ★★★★★ "Garbo laughs," proclaimed the ads of its day; and so will you in this classic screen comedy. Greta Garbo is a Soviet commissar sent to Paris to check on the lack of progress of three bumbling trade envoys who have been seduced by the decadent trappings of capitalism. Melvyn Douglas, as a Parisian playboy, meets Garbo at the Eiffel Tower and plans a seduction of his own, in this most joyous of Hollywood comedies. B&W; 110m. **DIR:** Ernst Lubitsch. **CAST:** Greta Garbo, Melvyn Douglas, Bela Lugosi. **1939**

NO MAN OF HER OWN ★★★★ A big-time gambler marries a local girl on a bet and tries to keep her innocent of his activities. This vintage film has everything the average film fan looks for—drama, romance, and comedy. B&W; 85m. **DIR:** Wesley Ruggles. **CAST:** Clark Gable, Carole Lombard. **1932**

NO SMALL AFFAIR ★★½ A 16-year-old amateur photographer named Charles Cummings (Jon Cryer) falls in love with an up-and-coming 23-year-old rock singer, Laura Victor (Demi Moore). A mixture of delightfully clever and unabashedly stupid elements. Rated R for nudity, violence, and profanity. 102m. **DIR:** Jerry Schatzberg. **CAST:** Jon Cryer, Demi Moore. **1984**

NO SURRENDER ★★ Eccentric British film about a New Year's Eve party at a rundown nightclub in Liverpool. There is a moral subtext here, but little else that is engaging. Rated R. Contains violence and profanity. 100m. **DIR:** Peter Smith. **CAST:** Michael Angelis, Avis Bunnage, James Ellis, Tom Georgeson, Bernard Hill, Ray McAnally, Joanne Whalley, Elvis Costello. **1986**

NO TIME FOR SERGEANTS ★★★★ In this hilarious film version of the Broadway play by Ira Levin, young Andy Griffith is superb as a country boy drafted into the service. You'll scream with laughter as good-natured Will Stockdale (as portrayed by Andy on stage as well as here) proceeds to make a complete shambles of the U.S. Air Force through nothing more than sheer ignorance. B&W; 119m. **DIR:** Mervyn LeRoy. **CAST:** Andy Griffith, Nick Adams, Myron McCormick, Murray Hamilton, Don Knotts. **1957**

NOBODY'S FOOL 🦃 Despite its pedigree—a screenplay by playwright Beth Henley *(Crimes of the Heart)*—this film is a real disappointment. Rated PG-13 for mild violence. 107m. **DIR:** Evelyn Purcell. **CAST:** Rosanna Arquette, Eric Roberts, Mare Winningham, Jim Youngs, Louise Fletcher. **1986**

NOBODY'S PERFECT ★★½ *Some Like it Hot* redux. This time, the boy behind the skirt (Chad Lowe) is posing as the new girl on the tennis team. Rated PG-13 for language. 90m. **DIR:** Robert Kaylor. **CAST:** Chad Lowe, Gail O'Grady, Robert Vaughn. **1989**

NOBODY'S PERFEKT ★★ Three friends all undergoing psychoanalysis (Gabe Kaplan, Robert Klein, and Alex Karras) decide to extort $650.00 from the city of Miami to pay for their car, which was totaled because they ran into a large pothole. Along the way, they become heroes by capturing armored-car robbers. 96m. **DIR:** Peter Bonerz. **CAST:** Gabe Kaplan, Alex Karras, Robert Klein, Susan Clark, Paul Stewart, Alex Rocco. **1981**

NOCTURNA 🦃 This fourth-rate imitation of *Old Dracula* and *Love at First Bite* has Dracula's granddaughter moving to Manhattan. Rated R for nudity. 85m. **DIR:** Harry Tampa. **CAST:** Nai Bonet, John Carradine, Yvonne De Carlo, Sy Richardson. **1979**

NOISES OFF ★★★★ Hilarious adaptation of the play by Michael Frayn presents Michael Caine as a director struggling to get a saucy comedy and its sometimes sauced performers ready. Director Peter Bogdanovich and his all-star cast capture the total mania of a classic Marx Brothers movie. Rated PG-13 for humorous violence, brief profanity, and suggestive double entendres. 104m. **DIR:** Peter Bogdanovich. **CAST:** Carol Burnett, Michael Caine, Denholm Elliott, Julie Hagerty, Marilu Henner, Mark Linn-Baker, Christopher Reeve, John Ritter, Nicollette Sheridan. **1992**

NOOSE HANGS HIGH, THE ★★ One of the comedy team's lesser efforts, and they take a backseat to veteran laugh-getters in the supporting cast. The plot is about $50,000 of stolen money, with Abbott and Costello trying to get it back. B&W; 77m. **DIR:** Charles Barton. **CAST:** Bud Abbott, Lou Costello, Leon Errol, Cathy Downes, Mike Mazurki, Joseph Calleia, Fritz Feld. **1948**

NORMAN CONQUESTS, THE, EPISODE 1: TABLE MANNERS ★★★½ Alan Ayckbourn's clever trilogy is set in a family home in a small English town. The three segments each take place in a different part of the house but encompass the same span of time. Furthermore, each part is complete in itself, but blends with the others for a delightful experience. In the dining room, Norman (Tom Conti) tries to seduce his two sisters-in-law and draws the rest of the family into the tangle with surprising results. Sara (Penelope Keith) is a treat as she tries to organize meals and control the others. 108m. **DIR:** Herbert Wise. **CAST:** Richard Briers, Penelope Keith, Tom Conti, David Troughton, Fiona Walker, Penelope Wilton. **1980**

NORMAN CONQUESTS, THE, EPISODE 2: LIVING TOGETHER ★★★½ The parlor is the setting as the family gathers for the weekend. Norman (Tom Conti) keeps everyone on the run as he drinks, manipulates, and seduces. 93m. **DIR:** Herbert Wise. **CAST:** Richard Briers, Penelope Keith, Tom Conti, David Troughton, Fiona Walker, Penelope Wilton. **1980**

NORMAN CONQUESTS, THE, EPISODE 3: ROUND AND ROUND THE GARDEN ★★★½ A garden setting rounds out a zany weekend at an English house. As Norman (Tom Conti) pursues his wife's sister, Tom (David Troughton), the visiting vet, misinterprets the goings-on and embarrasses himself in the bargain. 106m. **DIR:** Herbert Wise. **CAST:** Richard Briers, Penelope Keith, Tom Conti, David Troughton, Fiona Walker, Penelope Wilton. **1980**

NORMAN...IS THAT YOU? ★★ This embarrassing look at homophobia has a skillful cast that deserved better. Redd Foxx tries too hard to be funny as a father who finds out his son is gay. The Motown sound track is much better than the plot. Rated PG for its discreet handling of an R-rated topic. 91m. **DIR:** George Schlatter. **CAST:** Redd Foxx, Pearl Bailey, Michael Warren, Jayne Meadows, Dennis Dugan. **1976**

NORMAN LOVES ROSE ★★★½ In this Australian-made comedy, Tony Owen plays a love-struck teenager who is enamored of his sister-in-law, Carol Kane. When she gets pregnant, the question of paternity arises. Lots of laughs in this one! Rated R. 98m. **DIR:** Henri Safran. **CAST:** Carol Kane, Tony Owen, Warren Mitchell. **1982**

NORMAN'S AWESOME EXPERIENCE 🦃 Boneheaded saga of a nuclear technician, a magazine-cover model, and an Italian photographer accidentally transported back to the Roman Empire. Unrated. 95m. **DIR:** Paul Donovan. **CAST:** Tom McCamus, Laurie Paton, Jacques Lussier. **1989**

NORTHERN EXTREMES ★★★ A tiny island secedes from Canada after losing its fishing rights and uses a deserted Soviet submarine to underscore the situation. Sharp satire of government and some quirky characterizations, but the tiny budget gets in the way. A good-hearted little comedy, even if the technical quality is extremely uneven. Rated PG for violence and sexual situations. 90m. **DIR:** Paul Donovan. **CAST:** Paul Gross, Denise Virieux. **1993**

NOT FOR PUBLICATION ★★½ A writer and a photographer attempt to break out of sleazy tabloid journalism by doing an investigative piece about high-level corruption. Playful, but not as distinctive as Paul Bartel's other works, such as *Eating Raoul* and *Lust in the Dust*. Rated PG for profanity. 87m. **DIR:** Paul Bartel. **CAST:** Nancy Allen, David Naughton, Laurence Luckinbill. **1984**

NOT QUITE HUMAN ★★★ Made for the Disney Channel, this is the first of a trilogy of films about a likable android (Jay Underwood) and his eccentric creator (Alan Thicke). After completing his "project," Thicke flees with his daughter and new "son" to escape toy-company leaders who want to transform the android into the ultimate war toy. Underwood is terrific as the amiable robot. Fun family viewing. 95m. **DIR:** Steven H. Stern. **CAST:** Alan Thicke, Jay Underwood, Robyn Lively, Joseph Bologna, Robert Harper. **1987**

NOT QUITE HUMAN 2 ★★★½ This second film in the Disney trilogy about Chip the android (Jay Underwood) is the most hilarious and heartwarming. Chip goes to college and falls in love with a beautiful android. He must also contend with a computer virus that threatens to destroy him. The gentle romance upgrades an otherwise zany family film. 92m. **DIR:** Eric Luke. **CAST:** Jay Underwood, Alan Thicke, Robyn Lively, Katie Barberi, Dey Young. **1989**

NOT QUITE PARADISE ★★ A disparate group of people from around the world volunteer to work on an Israeli kibbutz. Surprisingly mean-spirited movie resembles a teens-at-camp comedy, though it offers some laughs in spite of itself. Rated R for sexual humor. 105m. **DIR:** Lewis Gilbert. **CAST:** Sam Robards, Joanna Pacula. **1986**

NOTHING BUT TROUBLE (1944) ★★½ Stan Laurel and Oliver Hardy are the chef and the table server, bringing havoc to a society partygiver. Some good sight gags, but not enough. B&W; 69m. **DIR:** Sam Taylor. **CAST:** Stan Laurel, Oliver Hardy, Mary Boland. **1944**

NOTHING BUT TROUBLE (1991) ★★ Disappointing, gross comedy—aimed by writer-director Dan Aykroyd at the *Police Academy/Porky's* crowd—about New Yorkers Chevy Chase and Demi Moore setting off for Atlantic City and being arrested. Rated PG-13 for profanity and gore. 90m. **DIR:** Dan Aykroyd. **CAST:** Chevy Chase, Dan Aykroyd, John Candy, Demi Moore. **1991**

NOTHING PERSONAL 🦃 A romantic comedy about the fight to stop the slaughter of baby seals? Rated PG. 97m. **DIR:** George Bloomfield. **CAST:** Donald Sutherland, Suzanne Somers, Lawrence Dane, Roscoe Lee Browne, Dabney Coleman, Saul Rubinek, John Dehner. **1980**

NOTHING SACRED ★★★★ Ace scriptwriter Ben Hecht's cynical mixture of slapstick and bitterness, perfectly performed by Fredric March and Carole Lombard, makes this satirical comedy a real winner. Vermont innocent, Lombard, is mistakenly thought to be dying of a rare disease. A crack New York reporter (March) pulls out all the stops in exploiting her to near-national sainthood. The boy-bites-man scene is priceless. 75m. **DIR:** William Wellman. **CAST:** Carole Lombard, Fredric March, Walter Connolly, Charles Winninger. **1937**

NUDE BOMB, THE ★★ Maxwell Smart (Don Adams), of the *Get Smart!* television series, gets the big-screen treatment in this barely watchable spy spoof about a crazed villain's attempt at world domination—by vaporizing all clothing. This film endured some editing-room "touching up" by *Robot Monster* director Phil Tucker. Also known as *The Return of Maxwell Smart*. Rated PG. 94m. **DIR:** Clive Donner. **CAST:** Don Adams, Andrea Howard, Vittorio Gassman, Dana Elcar, Rhonda Fleming, Sylvia Kristel, Joey Forman, Norman Lloyd. **1980**

NUDITY REQUIRED 🦃 Two lowlifes pose as producers. Not rated, but contains nudity and profanity. 90m. **DIR:** John Bowman. **CAST:** Julie Newmar, Troy Donahue. **1990**

NUMBER ONE OF THE SECRET SERVICE ★★★ In this enjoyable spoof of James Bond films, secret agent Charles Blind attempts to stop evil Arthur Loveday from killing prominent international financiers. Rated PG. 87m. **DIR:** Lindsay Shonteff. **CAST:** Nicky Henson, Richard Todd, Aimi MacDonald, Geoffrey Keen, Sue Lloyd, Dudley Sutton, Jon Pertwee. **1970**

NUNS ON THE RUN ★★★★ In this hilarious farce, Eric Idle and Robbie Coltrane play lower-echelon English crooks who decide to rip off their boss and fly to Brazil. When their plan goes awry, they are forced to hide in a convent and disguise themselves as nuns. What writer-director Jonathan Lynn and his actors do with the premise will have you gasping for breath after fits of uproarious laughter, Rated PG-13 for profanity and sexual humor. 90m. **DIR:** Jonathan Lynn. **CAST:** Eric Idle, Robbie Coltrane, Janet Suzman. **1990**

NUTCASE 🦃 Wacky villains threaten to blow up New Zealand's volcanoes if they don't receive $5 million. 49m. **DIR:** Roger Donaldson. **CAST:** Nevan Rowe, Ian Watkin, Michael Wilson, Ian Mune. **1983**

NUTS IN MAY ★★★★★ A delightfully cynical British tale of Keith and his wife Candice-Marie, who take an arduous, event-filled camping vacation together. Keith is hideously domineering and possessive, torturing the timid Candice-Marie with exhausting hikes and tedious visits to places of little interest, but when Candice-Marie befriends a fellow camper, the plot really begins to sicken. 84m. **DIR:** Mike Leigh. **CAST:** Roger Sloman, Alison Steadman, Anthony O'Donnell. **1976**

NUTTY PROFESSOR, THE ★★★★ Jerry Lewis's funniest self-directed comedy, this release—a takeoff on Robert Louis Stevenson's *Dr. Jekyll and Mr. Hyde*—is about a klutz who becomes a smoothie when he drinks a magic formula. Reportedly, this was Lewis's put-down of former partner Dean Martin. 107m. **DIR:** Jerry Lewis. **CAST:** Jerry Lewis, Stella Stevens, Kathleen Freeman. **1963**

O.C. & STIGGS ★★★ Inspired by characters from *National Lampoon*, this offbeat film has two teenagers whose goal is to make life completely miserable for the local bigot (Paul Dooley), an obnoxious insurance magnate. Another energetic iconoclastic comedy from Robert Altman. Not rated. 109m. **DIR:** Robert Altman. **CAST:** Daniel H. Jenkins, Neill Barry, Paul Dooley, Jane Curtin, Martin Mull, Dennis Hopper, Ray Walston, Jon Cryer, Melvin Van Peebles. **1987**

OBJECT OF BEAUTY, THE ★★ The best things in life may be free, but you can't prove it to the Gold Card–flashing Jake and Tina, a jet-setting duo who've been living a life of incredible luxury. Played by John Malkovich and Andie MacDowell, they're the central characters in this inconsistent and somewhat flat comedy from writer-director Michael Lindsay-Hogg. Rated R. 110m. **DIR:** Michael Lindsay-Hogg. **CAST:** John Malkovich, Andie MacDowell, Rudi Davies. **1991**

ODD COUPLE, THE ★★★★ Walter Matthau as Oscar Madison and Jack Lemmon as Felix Unger bring Neil Simon's delightful stage play to life in this comedy. They play two divorced men who try living together. The biggest laughs come from the fact that Felix is "Mr. Clean" and Oscar is a total slob—they're constantly getting on each other's nerves. Rated G. 105m. **DIR:** Gene Saks. **CAST:** Walter Matthau, Jack Lemmon, John Fiedler, Herb Edelman. **1968**

ODD JOB, THE ★★½ Monty Python's Graham Chapman wrote and starred in this comedy about a depressed businessman who hires a hitman to kill him. When he decides that life is worth living after all, he finds that he can't cancel his contract. Full of oddball characters and silly situations, but somehow it never builds up a full head of steam. Unrated. 86m. **DIR:** Peter Medak. **CAST:** Graham Chapman, David Jason, Diana Quick, Bill Paterson, Simon Williams. **1978**

ODDBALL HALL 🦃 Jewel thieves masquerade as members of a fraternal order of do-gooders in this flat comedy of mistaken identities. Rated PG. 87m. **DIR:** Jackson Hunsicker. **CAST:** Don Ameche, Burgess Meredith, Bill Maynard. **1990**

ODDBALLS 🦃 Confusing comedy. Rated PG for obscenities and sexual situations. 92m. **DIR:** Miklos Lente. **CAST:** Foster Brooks, Michael Macdonald. **1984**

OFF BEAT ★★ This attempt at an old-fashioned romantic comedy succeeds as a romance, but as a comedy, it elicits only an occasional chuckle. One gains instant sympathy for captivating Meg Tilly's vulnerable big-city police officer. Rated PG. 100m. **DIR:** Michael Dinner. **CAST:** Meg Tilly, Judge Reinhold, Cleavant Derricks, Harvey Keitel. **1986**

OFF LIMITS (1953) ★★ Marilyn Maxwell adds a little "oomph" to this otherwise silly story of two army buddies and their antics. B&W; 89m. **DIR:** George Marshall. **CAST:** Bob Hope, Mickey Rooney, Marilyn Maxwell, Marvin Miller. **1953**

OFF THE MARK ★★★ This off-the-wall comedy centers around Mark Neely, who once hosted a Russian boy (Terry Farrell) in his home for a year. Now they're both grown up and competing in a triathlon. The two leads are a delight. 81m. **DIR:** Bill Berry. **CAST:** Mark Neely, Terry Farrell, Virginia Capers, Jon Cypher, Barry Corbin. **1986**

OFF THE WALL 🦃 A Tennessee speed demon (Rosanna Arquette) picks up two handsome hitchhikers. Rated R. 86m. **DIR:** Rick Friedberg. **CAST:** Paul Sorvino, Patrick Cassidy, Rosanna Arquette, Billy Hufsey, Mickey Gilley, Monte Markham. **1982**

OH! CALCUTTA! ★★ Only historians of the 1960s will have any reason to watch this, a videotaped performance of the musical revue that became infamous because it dealt with sex and featured onstage nudity. None of the sketches retain any humor or bite, a disappointment considering that the writers included Sam Shepard, John Lennon, Jules Feiffer, and Dan Greenberg. Unrated. 108m. **DIR:** Guillaume Martin Aucion. **CAST:** Raina Barrett, Mark Dempsey, Samantha Harper, Bill Macy. **1972**

OH DAD, POOR DAD—MAMA'S HUNG YOU IN THE CLOSET AND I'M FEELING SO SAD ★★★½ A cult favorite, and deservedly so. The plot has something to do with an odd young man (Robert Morse) whose mother (Rosalind Russell) drags him off on a vacation in the tropics with the boy's dead father. Morse excels in this unique, well-written, often hilarious film. 86m. **DIR:** Richard Quine. **CAST:** Rosalind Russell, Robert Morse, Barbara Harris, Jonathan Winters, Lionel Jeffries. **1967**

✓ **OH, GOD!** ★★★★ God is made visible to a supermarket manager in this modern-day fantasy. The complications that result make for some predictable humor, but the story is kept flowing by some inspired casting. Ageless George Burns is a perfect vision of a God for Everyman in his tennis shoes and golf hat. John Denver exudes the right degree of naïveté as the put-upon grocer. Rated PG. 104m. **DIR:** Carl Reiner. **CAST:** George Burns, John Denver, Teri Garr, Ralph Bellamy. **1977**

OH, GOD! BOOK II ★★ George Burns, as God, returns in this fair sequel and enters a little girl's life, assigning her the task of coming up with a slogan that will revive interest in him. So she comes up with "Think God" and begins her campaign. It's passable family fare. Rated PG. 94m. **DIR:** Gilbert Cates. **CAST:** George Burns, Suzanne Pleshette, David Birney, Louanne, Howard Duff. **1980**

OH, GOD, YOU DEVIL! ★★★½ George Burns is back as the wisecracking, cigar-smoking deity. Only this time he plays a dual role—appearing as the devil. Ted Wass is the songwriter who strikes a Faustian bargain with Burns's bad side. This delightful comedy-with-a-moral is guaranteed to lift your spirits. Rated PG for suggested sex and profanity. 96m. **DIR:** Paul Bogart. **CAST:** George Burns, Ted Wass, Roxanne Hart, Ron Silver, Eugene Roche. **1984**

OKLAHOMA ANNIE 🦃 Judy Canova chases varmints out of town and brings decency to her community. 90m. **DIR:** R. G. Springsteen. **CAST:** Judy Canova, John Russell, Grant Withers, Allen Jenkins, Almira Sessions, Minerva Urecal. **1952**

OLD SPANISH CUSTOM, AN ★★½ Set in Spain and filmed in England, this Buster Keaton sound comedy feature is best appreciated by diehard Keaton fans. Keaton is a bumbling yachtsman pursuing a scheming senorita. B&W; 56m. **DIR:** Adrian Brunel. **CAST:** Buster Keaton. **1935**

ON APPROVAL ★★★ Former Sherlock Holmes Clive Brook displays a confident hand at directing in this enjoyable farce about women who exchange boyfriends. Fun and breezy with terrific performances by some of England's best talents, this film gave beloved Beatrice Lillie one of her best screen roles. B&W; 80m. **DIR:** Clive Brook. **CAST:** Beatrice Lillie, Clive Brook, Googie Withers, Roland Culver. **1943**

ONCE AROUND ★★★½ If it weren't for off-putting, vulgar language and some skimpy character development, this offbeat comedy in the style of *Moonstruck* would be a real winner. As it is, there are some truly delightful and hilarious moments in its tale of a Boston woman (Holly Hunter) who finds romance in the arms of an oddball, middle-aged millionaire (Richard Dreyfuss). Rated R for profanity. 115m. **DIR:** Lasse Hallstrom. **CAST:** Richard Dreyfuss, Holly Hunter, Danny Aiello, Laura San Giacomo, Gena Rowlands. **1991**

ONCE BITTEN ★★★ Sly little vampire film about an ancient bloodsucker (Lauren Hutton) who can remain young and beautiful only by periodically supping on youthful male virgins. Likable Jim Carrey is her latest target, and their first few encounters (three's the magic number) leave him with an appetite for raw hamburgers and a tendency to sleep during the day so as to avoid sunlight. Rated PG-13 for sexual situations. 92m. **DIR:** Howard Storm. **CAST:** Lauren Hutton, Jim Carrey, Karen Kopins, Cleavon Little. **1985**

ONCE UPON A CRIME ★★ Obnoxious, all-star comedy about murder and mayhem in Monte Carlo. The few moments of funny work by the cast members make it tolerable, but why did director Eugene Levy have the actors scream nearly every line at the top of their lungs? Rated PG for profanity and goofy violence. 94m. **DIR:** Eugene Levy. **CAST:** John Candy, James Belushi, Cybill Shepherd, Sean Young, Richard Lewis, Ornella Muti, Giancarlo Giannini, George Hamilton. **1992**

ONCE UPON A HONEYMOON ★★½ In this travesty, one Cary Grant preferred to forget, he plays a newspaperman trying to get innocent stripteaser Ginger Rogers out of Europe as the German army advances. This amusing adventure-comedy is a bit dated, but Grant fans won't mind. B&W; 117m. **DIR:** Leo McCarey. **CAST:** Ginger Rogers, Cary Grant, Walter Slezak, Albert Dekker, Albert Basserman, Harry Shannon, John Banner. **1942**

ONE COOKS, THE OTHER DOESN'T ★★ Suzanne Pleshette is the driving force behind this TV movie about a woman who finds herself having to share quarters with her ex-husband and his youthful bride-to-be when he is unable to make ends meet in the realty business. Though high in dimple quotient, it's engaging enough. 100m. **DIR:** Richard Michaels. **CAST:** Suzanne Pleshette, Rosanna Arquette, Joseph Bologna, Oliver Clark. **1983**

ONE CRAZY NIGHT ★★★★ Five Australian teens are trapped in the basement of a Melbourne hotel housing the Beatles in 1964. During the course of the night, these very different people swap their ideas on hero worship, sexual fantasies, fears, and expectations. It has that *Breakfast Club* feel, but bittersweet humor and a fresh cast make for an appealing diversion. Rated PG-13 for profanity. 92m. **DIR:** Michael Pattinson. **CAST:** Beth Champion, Malcolm Kennard, Dannii Minogue, Willa O'Neill, Noah Taylor. **1991**

ONE CRAZY SUMMER ★★½ Star John Cusack and writer-director Savage Steve Holland of *Better Off Dead* are reunited in this weird, slightly sick, and sometimes stupidly funny comedy about a college hopeful

(Cusack) who must learn about love to gain entrance to an institute of higher learning. If you accept that silly premise, then you may get a few laughs. Rated PG. 94m. **DIR:** Savage Steve Holland. **CAST:** John Cusack, Demi Moore, Curtis Armstrong, Bob Goldthwait, Joe Flaherty, Tom Villard. **1986**

ONE IN A MILLION ★★★ Sonja Henie's film debut is only slightly dated. The center of the movie is her skating ability, and no one has ever topped her. She plays an unknown skater recruited to save a traveling show and winds up at Madison Square Garden with a proud papa, a handsome boyfriend, and an adoring public. B&W; 95m. **DIR:** Sidney Lanfield. **CAST:** Sonja Henie, Don Ameche, Adolphe Menjou, The Ritz Brothers, Jean Hersholt, Arline Judge, Ned Sparks, Dixie Dunbar, Borrah Minevich, Bess Flowers, Leah Ray. **1936**

ONE MORE SATURDAY NIGHT ★★★½ Al Franken and Tom Davis, who were writers and semiregulars on the original *Saturday Night Live* TV show, star in this enjoyable comedy, which they also wrote, about the problems encountered by adults and teenagers when trying to get a date on the most important night of the week. In its humane and decidedly offbeat way, *One More Saturday Night* is about the human condition in all its funny/sad complexity. Rated R for profanity and simulated sex. 95m. **DIR:** Dennis Klein. **CAST:** Al Franken, Tom Davis, Moira Harris. **1986**

ONE NIGHT IN THE TROPICS ★★½ Comics Abbott and Costello were brought in to enliven this revue-style romance with a few of their routines. They stole the movie, and it launched their screen careers. The nominal story line centers on a love triangle and Oscar Hammerstein, Jerome Kern, and Dorothy Fields wrote the songs. B&W; 82m. **DIR:** A. Edward Sutherland. **CAST:** Allan Jones, Nancy Kelly, Robert Cummings, Bud Abbott, Lou Costello, Leo Carrillo. **1940**

ONE NIGHT WITH DICE ★★★ The extremely raunchy comedian Andrew Dice Clay is seen in an early comedy club performance. The show is not bad if you can handle The Diceman's humor, which can be directed at just about any group of people but singles out women and homosexuals in particular. Not rated, but contains extreme profanity. 60m. **DIR:** Kevin Padden. **CAST:** Andrew Dice Clay. **1989**

ONE RAINY AFTERNOON ★★ Silly movie about a young man who causes a furor when he kisses the wrong girl during a performance in the theater. It's a pretty slight premise, but under the skillful hands of director Rowland V. Lee (*The Count of Monte Cristo, Son of Frankenstein*), it becomes entertaining fare. A fine supporting cast helps flesh out the thin story, and a young Ida Lupino makes for a lovely leading lady. B&W; 79m. **DIR:** Rowland V. Lee. **CAST:** Francis Lederer, Ida Lupino, Roland Young, Hugh Herbert, Erik Rhodes, Mischa Auer. **1936**

ONE TOUCH OF VENUS ★★ The Pygmalion myth gets the Hollywood treatment, long before *My Fair Lady*, although this is a wee bit diluted. Robert Walker plays a window decorator who becomes smitten, predictably, when a display statue of Venus comes to life in the form of Ava Gardner. The potentially entertaining premise is left flat by a script that lacks originality and wit. B&W; 90m. **DIR:** William A. Seiter. **CAST:** Robert Walker, Ava Gardner. **1948**

ONE, TWO, THREE ★★★½ James Cagney's "retirement" film (and his only movie with famed director Billy Wilder) is a nonstop, madcap assault on the audience. Wilder's questionable humor and odd plot about the clash between capitalism and communism could have spelled catastrophe for any other leading man, but veteran Cagney pulls it off with style. B&W; 108m. **DIR:** Billy Wilder. **CAST:** James Cagney, Arlene Francis, Horst Buchholz, Pamela Tiffin, Lilo Pulver, Red Buttons. **1961**

ONIONHEAD ★★ One of the few Andy Griffith comedies that doesn't work, but it's not his fault. He plays a country boy in the coast guard who is sent to the galley to learn to cook. Walter Matthau is his teacher, and their scenes together are fine. It's the silly slapstick scenes involving love-starved girls that turn the movie topsy-turvy. B&W; 110m. **DIR:** Norman Taurog. **CAST:** Andy Griffith, Walter Matthau, Erin O'Brien, Ray Danton, Felicia Farr, Joey Bishop, Joe Mantell, James Gregory, Claude Akins, Roscoe Karns. **1958**

ONLY THE LONELY ★★★½ Those *Home Alone* guys, writer John Hughes and director Chris Columbus, cooked up this follow-up to their surprise box-office smash. John Candy stars as a 38-year-old beat cop who falls in love with a mortician's daughter (Ally Sheedy), much to the disapproval of his feisty, opinionated Irish mother (a delightful performance by scene-stealer Maureen O'Hara). Rated PG-13 for profanity. 110m. **DIR:** Chris Columbus. **CAST:** John Candy, Maureen O'Hara, Ally Sheedy, Anthony Quinn, James Belushi, Kevin Dunn, Milo O'Shea, Bert Remsen, Macaulay Culkin. **1991**

ONLY TWO CAN PLAY ★★★½ Peter Sellers is fabulous as a frustrated but determined Don Juan with aspirations of wooing society woman Mai Zetterling. As in so many of his roles, Sellers is funny and appealing in every move and mood. And Zetterling is the perfect choice for the haughty object of his attentions. 106m. **DIR:** Sidney Gilliat. **CAST:** Peter Sellers, Mai Zetterling, Richard Attenborough, Virginia Maskell. **1962**

ONLY WITH MARRIED MEN ★★ This TV movie is a pleasant yet thoroughly predictable light sex comedy about a woman

(Michele Lee) who decides she will only date married men. She mistakes a bachelor (David Birney) for his married partner. 74m. **DIR:** Jerry Paris. **CAST:** David Birney, Michele Lee, Dom DeLuise, Judy Carne, Gavin MacLeod. **1974**

ONLY YOU ★★★ Enjoyable romantic romp features an adorable cast and some witty dialogue. Andrew McCarthy takes time off from his busy schedule to be with gorgeous Kelly Preston at a scenic seaside resort, where he meets cute Helen Hunt. Director Betty Thomas keeps everything light and charming. Rated PG-13 for language. 85m. **DIR:** Betty Thomas. **CAST:** Andrew McCarthy, Kelly Preston, Helen Hunt. **1991**

OPERATION PETTICOAT ★★★★ The ageless Cary Grant stars with Tony Curtis in this wacky service comedy. They are captain and first officer of a submarine that undergoes a madcap series of misadventures during World War II. Their voyage across the Pacific is further complicated when a group of navy women is forced to join the crew. 124m. **DIR:** Blake Edwards. **CAST:** Cary Grant, Tony Curtis, Dina Merrill, Gene Evans, Arthur O'Connell, Dick Sargent. **1959**

OPPORTUNITY KNOCKS ★★★ Mixing elements from *Trading Places* and *The Sting*, this is a big-screen sitcom designed to show off the talents of *Saturday Night Live* regular Dana Carvey. It does its job well. Carvey is a hoot as a con-man who lucks into a big score while hiding from a revenge-minded gangster. Rated PG-13 for profanity and adult humor. 95m. **DIR:** Donald Petrie. **CAST:** Dana Carvey, Robert Loggia, Todd Graff, Julia Campbell, Milo O'Shea, James Tolkan. **1990**

OPPOSITE SEX (AND HOW TO LIVE WITH THEM), THE 🦃 A waste of time and talent. The sexcapades of young singles are exploited more than they are explained in a laughless comedy about people who can't keep their hormones under control. The big scene is a "Strip Twister" dance scene followed by group wine tasting. Rated R for obvious reasons. 86m. **DIR:** Matthew Meshekoff. **CAST:** Arye Gross, Courteney Cox, Kevin Pollak, Julie Brown, Mitchell Ryan, Jack Carter, Phil Bruns, Mitzi McCall, B. J. Ward. **1993**

OPTIONS ★★ Modest little comedy features a nerdish contract man for TV movies treading the wilds of Africa—in complete suit and tie, plus briefcase!—to get the option on another life story. Rated PG for violence. 105m. **DIR:** Camilo Vila. **CAST:** Matt Salinger, Joanna Pacula, John Kani. **1988**

OSCAR (1991) ★★★ This farce features a perfectly capable comic performance from Sylvester Stallone as a gangster who promises his dying father (Kirk Douglas in a hilarious cameo) that he'll go straight. But complications make keeping his vow difficult. An all-star supporting cast help buoy the story, which often drags under John Landis's laid-back direction. Rated PG for brief profanity. 110m. **DIR:** John Landis. **CAST:** Sylvester Stallone, Ornella Muti, Peter Riegert, Vincent Spano, Tim Curry, Chazz Palminteri, Marisa Tomei, Elizabeth Barondes, Kirk Douglas, Don Ameche, Yvonne De Carlo, Eddie Bracken, Martin Ferrero, Harry Shearer, Linda Gray, William Atherton. **1991**

OTHER PEOPLE'S MONEY ★★★½ Danny DeVito has a field day as a ruthless corporate raider conniving to take over upstanding Gregory Peck's business while romancing Peck's daughter. It's a modern-day version of a Capra film, but in the Nineties it is not a forgone conclusion that the good guys will win. Adapted by screenwriter Alvin Sargent from the play by Jerry Sterner. Rated R for profanity. 103m. **DIR:** Norman Jewison. **CAST:** Danny DeVito, Gregory Peck, Penelope Ann Miller, Piper Laurie, Dean Jones. **1991**

OUR HOSPITALITY ★★★★ Based on the legendary Hatfield–McCoy feud, this period comedy has Buster Keaton as innocent and unsuspecting Willie McKay journeying south to claim his inheritance. Keaton's comic and daredevil antics are brilliant. Silent. B&W; 74m. **DIR:** Buster Keaton, John G. Blystone. **CAST:** Buster Keaton, Natalie Talmadge, Ralph Bushman, Michael Keaton, Buster Keaton Jr. **1923**

OUR MISS BROOKS (TV SERIES) ★★★ Desilu, basking in the success of *I Love Lucy*, adapted this likable vehicle for comedienne Eve Arden. The show, previously a hit on radio, stars Arden as Connie Brooks, a well-meaning English teacher at Madison High. Miss Brooks goes to extremes to earn the affection—or even the attention—of biology instructor Philip Boynton (Robert Rockwell). Each episode 30m. **DIR:** Al Lewis. **CAST:** Eve Arden, Gale Gordon, Robert Rockwell, Richard Crenna, Gloria McMillan, Jane Morgan. **1952–1957**

OUR RELATIONS ★★★½ Stan Laurel and Oliver Hardy play two sets of twins. One set are sailors; the other are happily married civilians. When the boys' ship docks in the same city, a hilarious case of mistaken identity occurs. Highly enjoyable, the film doesn't lag at all. It features excellent performances by James Finlayson, Alan Hale, and Sidney Toler. B&W; 74m. **DIR:** Harry Lachman. **CAST:** Stan Laurel, Oliver Hardy, James Finlayson, Alan Hale Sr., Sidney Toler. **1936**

OUT COLD ★★★ Dark comedy featuring Teri Garr as a sultry housewife who enlists the aid of John Lithgow after she puts her philandering husband on ice. Some hilarious moments in an otherwise uneven movie. Rated R for sexual situations and violence. 92m. **DIR:** Malcolm Mowbray. **CAST:** John Lithgow, Teri Garr, Randy Quaid. **1989**

OUT OF CONTROL 💔 A group of teenagers take off for an exciting weekend on a private island. Rated R for obscenities, nudity, and violence. 78m. **DIR:** Allan Holzman. **CAST:** Martin Hewitt, Betsy Russell, Jim Youngs. **1984**

OUT OF THE BLUE ★★★ A not-very-innocent young woman passes out in a naïve married man's apartment, making all sorts of trouble in this entertaining romantic comedy of errors and such. B&W; 84m. **DIR:** Leigh Jason. **CAST:** George Brent, Virginia Mayo, Ann Dvorak, Turhan Bey, Carole Landis. **1947**

OUT OF TOWNERS, THE ★★★ Jack Lemmon and Sandy Dennis star in this Neil Simon comedy of a New York City vacation gone awry. It's a good idea that doesn't come off as well as one would have hoped. Rated PG for language. 97m. **DIR:** Arthur Hiller. **CAST:** Jack Lemmon, Sandy Dennis, Sandy Baron, Anne Meara, Billy Dee Williams. **1970**

OUT ON A LIMB (1992) ★★ There are few laughs in this comedy about a corporate executive (Matthew Broderick) who has a disaster-fraught journey from the big city to his rural hometown. The rest of the cast seems to be struggling to ignore how ridiculous the whole thing is. Rated PG for profanity, nudity, and violence. 83m. **DIR:** Francis Veber. **CAST:** Matthew Broderick, Jeffrey Jones, Heidi Kling, John C. Reilly, Marian Mercer, Larry Hankin, David Margulies. **1992**

OUTLAW BLUES ★★½ Yet another of Peter Fonda's harmless but rather bland light comedies. He's an ex-con with a talent for songwriting but little in the way of industry smarts; he naïvely allows established country-western star James Callahan to make off with a few hits. Aided by backup singer Susan Saint James, in a charming little part, Fonda figures out how to succeed on his own. Rated PG for light violence and brief nudity. 100m. **DIR:** Richard T. Heffron. **CAST:** Peter Fonda, Susan Saint James, James Callahan, Michael Lerner. **1977**

OUTRAGEOUS ★★★★ A very offbeat and original comedy-drama concerning a gay nightclub performer's relationship with a pregnant mental patient. A different kind of love story, told with taste and compassion. Female impersonator Craig Russell steals the show. Take a chance on this one. Rated R. 100m. **DIR:** Richard Benner. **CAST:** Craig Russell, Hollis McLaren, Richert Easley. **1977**

OUTRAGEOUS FORTUNE ★★★★ Yet another delightfully inventive adult comedy from Disney's Touchstone arm, highlighted by a show-stealing performance by the Mae West of the 1980s: Bette Midler. Her strutting, strident would-be actress is a scream, a word that also describes the level at which she delivers her rapid-fire dialogue. Rated R for profanity. 100m. **DIR:** Arthur Hiller. **CAST:** Bette Midler, Shelley Long, Peter Coyote, Robert Prosky, John Schuck, George Carlin. **1987**

OUTTAKES 💔 Forrest Tucker is the narrator of this collection of blackouts and vignettes. Stupid beyond belief. Not rated, but contains nudity. 75m. **DIR:** Jack M. Sell. **CAST:** Forrest Tucker, Bobbi Weyler, Joleen Lutz. **1985**

OVER HER DEAD BODY ★★ Black comedy features Elizabeth Perkins and Judge Reinhold as adulterers who kill in self-defense when they're caught in the act. The whole film centers around Perkins's attempts to dump the body and make it look like an accident. Rated R for profanity and violence. 105m. **DIR:** Maurice Phillips. **CAST:** Elizabeth Perkins, Judge Reinhold, Maureen Mueller, Jeffrey Jones, Rhea Perlman. **1989**

OVER THE BROOKLYN BRIDGE ★★½ Elliott Gould stars in this occasionally interesting but mostly uneven slice-of-life story about a slovenly, diabetic Jewish luncheonette owner who dreams of getting out by buying a restaurant in downtown Manhattan. Rated R for nudity and profanity. 108m. **DIR:** Menahem Golan. **CAST:** Elliott Gould, Shelley Winters, Sid Caesar, Carol Kane, Burt Young, Margaux Hemingway. **1983**

OVER THE HILL ★★½ Unwanted widow Olympia Dukakis takes a road trip in the Australian outback. Its very oddness works in its favor, but the action drags and the ending is melodramatic. Rated PG for brief nudity. 102m. **DIR:** George Miller. **CAST:** Olympia Dukakis, Sigrid Thornton, Derek Fowlds, Aden Young. **1992**

OVERBOARD 💔 A haughty heiress falls off her yacht and loses her memory. Rated PG. 106m. **DIR:** Garry Marshall. **CAST:** Goldie Hawn, Kurt Russell, Edward Herrmann, Katherine Helmond. **1988**

OWL AND THE PUSSYCAT, THE ★★★★ Barbra Streisand plays a street-smart but undereducated prostitute who teams up with intellectual snob and bookstore clerk George Segal. The laughs abound as the two express themselves, through numerous debates. Rated R. 95m. **DIR:** Herbert Ross. **CAST:** Barbra Streisand, George Segal, Robert Klein. **1970**

PACK UP YOUR TROUBLES ★★★ Stan Laurel and Oliver Hardy join the army in World War I, with the usual disastrous results. After being discharged, they assume responsibility for a fallen comrade's young daughter and search for her grandparents. The plot line and scripting aren't as solid as in other films, but the boys squeeze out every laugh possible. B&W; 68m. **DIR:** George Marshall. **CAST:** Stan Laurel, Oliver Hardy. **1932**

PADDY ★★½ Excellent performances by all the actors, especially Des Cave in the title role, cannot save this rather confused coming-of-age comedy. Despite moments of true hilarity, the film remains at best mildly amusing. 97m. **DIR:** Daniel Haller. **CAST:** Des Cave, Milo O'Shea, Peggy Cass. **1969**

PALEFACE, THE ★★★★ Hope stars as a cowardly dentist who marries Calamity Jane (Jane Russell in rare form) and becomes, thanks to her quick draw, a celebrated gunslinger. It inspired a sequel, *Son of Paleface*, and a remake, *The Shakiest Gun in the West*, with Don Knotts, but the original is still tops. 91m. **DIR:** Norman Z. McLeod. **CAST:** Bob Hope, Jane Russell, Robert Armstrong. **1948**

PALM BEACH STORY, THE ★★★★ Preston Sturges was perhaps the greatest of all American writer-directors. This light story of an engineer's wife (Claudette Colbert) who takes a vacation from marriage in sunny Florida and encounters one of the oddest groupings of talented characters ever assembled may well be his best film. B&W; 90m. **DIR:** Preston Sturges. **CAST:** Claudette Colbert, Joel McCrea, Rudy Vallee, Mary Astor, Sig Arno, William Demarest, Franklin Pangborn, Jimmy Conlin. **1942**

PALM SPRINGS WEEKEND ★★ It's sun, fun, and romance as some wild guys and cool chicks take a break from higher education and Watusi themselves silly during spring break. Harmless fun. 100m. **DIR:** Norman Taurog. **CAST:** Troy Donahue, Connie Stevens, Stefanie Powers, Robert Conrad, Ty Hardin, Jack Weston, Andrew Duggan. **1963**

PALS ★★★ George C. Scott and Don Ameche are delightful as two senior citizens who stumble across a cache of drug money. Made-for-television. 100m. **DIR:** Lou Antonio. **CAST:** George C. Scott, Don Ameche, Sylvia Sidney. **1986**

PANAMA LADY ★★ Lucille Ball does her best to liven up this tired story about a saloon dancer stuck in the tropics with her pick of the local sweat-soaked swains. Future Saturday-matinee cowboy favorite Allan "Rocky" Lane plays the two-fisted hombre who whisks everybody's favorite redhead off to the romantic oil fields in the jungle that he calls home. This is a remake of *Panama Flo* (1932). B&W; 65m. **DIR:** Jack B. Hively. **CAST:** Lucille Ball, Allan "Rocky" Lane, Donald Briggs, Evelyn Brent, Abner Biberman. **1939**

PANDEMONIUM ★★★ After attacks on cheerleading camps across the nation, there is only one place left to learn—Bambi's Cheerleading School. In this parody of slasher movies, Carol Kane steals the show as Candy, a girl with supernatural powers who just wants to have fun. Tom Smothers is a displaced Canadian Mountie; Paul Reubens (currently Pee-Wee Herman) plays his assistant. Rated PG for obscenities. 82m. **DIR:** Alfred Sole. **CAST:** Carol Kane, Tom Smothers, Debralee Scott, Candy Azzara, Miles Chapin, Tab Hunter, Paul Reubens. **1980**

PANIC BUTTON ★★ Looking for a tax loss, a gangster bankrolls a film sure to be so bad that he'll lose money on it. Did Mel Brooks see this obscure comedy before he made *The Producers* (which is much funnier)? B&W; 90m. **DIR:** George Sherman. **CAST:** Maurice Chevalier, Eleanor Parker, Jayne Mansfield, Mike Connors, Akim Tamiroff. **1964**

PAPER MOON ★★★★★ Critic-turned-director Peter Bogdanovich ended his four-film winning streak—which included *Targets*, *The Last Picture Show*, and *What's Up Doc?*—with this comedy, starring Ryan O'Neal and Tatum O'Neal as a con man and a kid in the 1930s who get involved in some pretty wild predicaments and meet up with a variety of wacky characters. It's delightful entertainment from beginning to end. Rated PG. B&W; 102m. **DIR:** Peter Bogdanovich. **CAST:** Ryan O'Neal, Tatum O'Neal, Madeline Kahn, John Hillerman. **1973**

PARADISE MOTEL ★★★ Another teen romp, but with a surprise: the appealing cast can act. Gary Herschberger is a student whose father keeps moving the family around in pursuit of his get-rich schemes. The latest venture is the Paradise Motel. To gain acceptance, Herschberger loans out one of the rooms to the class stud. Rated R for language and nudity. 87m. **DIR:** Cary Medoway. **CAST:** Gary Herschberger, Robert Krantz, Joanna Leigh Stack. **1985**

PARADISIO 🦃 One of dozens of early Sixties nudie movies that went to ridiculous lengths to show naked women. Star Arthur Howard was Leslie's brother. B&W; 82m. **DIR:** Not Credited. **CAST:** Arthur Howard, Eva Waegner. **1961**

PARAMEDICS ★★½ A good guys–bad guys flick disguised as a sex comedy. Two paramedics are transferred to a nasty part of the city where a vicious gang is killing people to sell their organs. The comedy comes in the form of a mysterious beauty with a rather fatal sex drive. Rated PG-13 for sexual references. 91m. **DIR:** Stuart Margolin. **CAST:** George Newbern, Christopher McDonald, Lawrence Hilton-Jacobs, John Pleshette, James Noble, John P. Ryan. **1987**

PARAMOUNT COMEDY THEATRE, VOL. 1: WELL DEVELOPED ★★★★ Howie Mandel hosts this very funny comic review filmed live at the Magic Club in Hermosa Beach, California. A big plus is that the material is new, and in many cases it is quite hilarious. Bob Saget is very funny with a fast-paced off-the-wall delivery. Judy Carter combines magic and comedy. Bruce Mahler uses an accordion and piano effectively. Our favorite is Philip Wellford, whose juggling and unicycle skills are perfect complements for his witty delivery. There is some adult-oriented material. 65m. **DIR:** Joe Hostettler. **CAST:** Howie Mandel, Bob Saget, Judy Carter, Philip Wellford, Bruce Mahler. **1986**

PARAMOUNT COMEDY THEATRE, VOL. 2: DECENT EXPOSURES ★★★ Howie Mandel once again hosts live performances by four up-and-coming comedians. Marsha Warfield, from the *Night Court* cast, is a standout. Doug Ferrari makes a couple of good observations on modern hang-ups. Paul Feig comes off as a well-dressed Pee-Wee Herman. The best performance is by Joe Alaskey. His impressions are outstanding. 67m. **DIR:** Joe Hostettler. **CAST:** Howie Mandel, Marsha Warfield, Doug Ferrari, Paul Feig, Joe Alaskey. **1987**

PARAMOUNT COMEDY THEATER, VOL. 3: HANGING PARTY ★★★ Howie Mandel hosts this third tape in a stand-up comedy series. Rick Shyder steals the show; unfortunately he's on first and no one else can match him. Best of the rest: Mark McCollum with his comic musical impressions. Not rated, but contains adult language. 68m. **DIR:** Joe Hostettler. **CAST:** Howie Mandel, Rick Shyder, Mark McCollum. **1987**

PARDON MY SARONG ★★★ Two Chicago bus drivers are hired by a playboy to drive him to California, and somehow they end up on his yacht sailing the seas. Good musical interludes (including the Ink Spots) contribute to the success of this early A&C outing. B&W; 83m. **DIR:** Erle C. Kenton. **CAST:** Bud Abbott, Lou Costello, Robert Paige, Virginia Bruce, Lionel Atwill, William Demarest, Samuel S. Hinds. **1942**

PARDON US ★★★★ Stan Laurel and Oliver Hardy are sent to prison for selling home-brewed beer. They encounter all the usual prison stereotypical characters and play off them to delightful comedy effect. During an escape, they put on black faces and pick cotton along with blacks and Ollie sings "Lazy Moon." B&W; 55m. **DIR:** James Parrott. **CAST:** Stan Laurel, Oliver Hardy, Wilfred Lucas. **1931**

PARENTHOOD ★★★★★ Director Ron Howard returns to the kind of movie he does best, with emphasis on character and comedy, and the result is a heartwarming and hilarious winner. Steve Martin and Mary Steenburgen are superb as model parents coping with career and kids. There's fine support from Rick Moranis as a yuppie who pushes his 3-year-old daughter to learn Kafka and karate, Dianne Wiest as a Woodstock-goer coping with three troubled teens, and Jason Robards as the granddad who discovers that parenthood is a job for life. Rated PG-13 for profanity and sexual themes. 110m. **DIR:** Ron Howard. **CAST:** Steve Martin, Mary Steenburgen, Tom Hulce, Jason Robards Jr., Dianne Wiest, Rick Moranis, Martha Plimpton, Keanu Reeves. **1989**

PARENTS 🖤 Black comedy about a cannibalistic couple and their relationship with their suspicious young son. Rated R. 90m. **DIR:** Bob Balaban. **CAST:** Randy Quaid, Mary Beth Hurt, Sandy Dennis, Bryan Madorsky. **1989**

PARIS HOLIDAY ★★ Film-within-a-film show business story featuring Bob Hope and French comic Fernandel never gets off the ground. Statuesque Anita Ekberg succeeds in diverting attention from the two uncomfortable comedians. 101m. **DIR:** Gerd Oswald. **CAST:** Bob Hope, Fernandel, Anita Ekberg, Martha Hyer, Preston Sturges. **1957**

PARIS WHEN IT SIZZLES ★★★ Uneven story-within-a-story about a screenwriter (William Holden) who "creates" a Parisian fantasyland for himself and the assistant (Audrey Hepburn) with whom he's fallen in love. As the story progresses, they—and the viewer—have an increasingly difficult time distinguishing fact from scripted fiction. 110m. **DIR:** Richard Quine. **CAST:** William Holden, Audrey Hepburn, Noel Coward, Gregoire Aslan, Marlene Dietrich. **1954**

PARLOR, BEDROOM AND BATH ★★★ Some genuine belly laughs buoy this slight comedy about a bewildered bumpkin (Buster Keaton) at the mercy of some society wackos. Charlotte Greenwood works well with the Great Stone Face. B&W; 75m. **DIR:** Edward Sedgwick. **CAST:** Buster Keaton, Charlotte Greenwood, Reginald Denny, Cliff Edwards, Dorothy Christy, Joan Peers, Sally Eilers, Natalie Moorhead, Edward Brophy. **1932**

PARTNERS ★★★ Ryan O'Neal and John Hurt are two undercover detectives assigned to pose as lovers in order to track down the murderer of a gay man in this warm, funny, and suspenseful comedy-drama written by Francis Veber (*La Cage aux Folles*). Rated R for nudity, profanity, violence, and adult themes. 98m. **DIR:** James Burrows. **CAST:** Ryan O'Neal, John Hurt. **1982**

PARTY, THE ★★★ The closest Peter Sellers ever came to doing a one-man show on film. He plays an actor from India who mistakenly gets invited to a plush Hollywood party, where he falls all over himself and causes more mishaps and pratfalls than the Three Stooges. 99m. **DIR:** Blake Edwards. **CAST:** Peter Sellers, Claudine Longet, Denny Miller, Marge Champion, Gavin MacLeod. **1968**

PARTY ANIMAL 🖤 Not even a great rock sound track can save this despicable piece of sludge. Rated R for nudity and profanity. 78m. **DIR:** Harvey Hart. **CAST:** Mathew Causey, Robin Harlan. **1983**

PARTY CAMP ★★ Andrew Ross takes a job as a camp counselor with the object of turning the militarylike operation into party time for all. Just another teen romp with the usual caricatures, obligatory nudity, and titillation. Rated R. 96m. **DIR:** Gary Graver. **CAST:** Andrew Ross, Kerry Brennan, Peter Jason. **1986**

PARTY GIRLS (PARTY INC.) 🦃 Overdone film-within-a-film. Rated R for nudity, profanity, and sexual situations. 90m. **DIR:** Chuck Vincent. **CAST:** Marilyn Chambers. **1989**

PARTY PLANE 🦃 Naughty stewardesses save their failing company by entertaining male passengers with a striptease. Lame adolescent fantasy flick. Unrated, but with considerable nudity and profanity. 81m. **DIR:** Ed Hansen. **CAST:** Kent Stoddard. **1987**

PASS THE AMMO ★★★½ Tim Curry's deliciously scheming evangelist is merely one of the delights in this inventive satire of television sermonizing. Bill Paxton and Linda Kozlowski play a couple of good ol' folks who plot to "steal back" some inheritance money the televangelist bilked from her family. Rated PG-13 for language and violence. 93m. **DIR:** David Beaird. **CAST:** Tim Curry, Bill Paxton, Linda Kozlowski, Annie Potts, Glenn Withrow, Dennis Burkley. **1987**

PASSED AWAY ★★★ In this black comedy written and directed by Charlie Peters, members of an Irish family must set aside differences when the 70-year-old patriarch (Jack Warden) dies unexpectedly. The performances by a terrific cast of character actors make this movie worth seeing. Rated PG-13 for profanity. 96m. **DIR:** Charlie Peters. **CAST:** Bob Hoskins, Blair Brown, Tim Curry, Frances McDormand, William L. Petersen, Pamela Reed, Peter Riegert, Maureen Stapleton, Nancy Travis, Jack Warden. **1992**

PASSPORT TO PIMLICO ★★★½ One of a number of first-rate comedies turned out by Britain in the wake of World War II. A salty group of characters form their own self-governing enclave smack in the middle of London. Sly Margaret Rutherford and Stanley Holloway divide comedy chores with cricket-crazy Basil Radford and Naunton Wayne. B&W; 85m. **DIR:** Henry Cornelius. **CAST:** Margaret Rutherford, Stanley Holloway, Hermione Baddeley, Basil Radford, Naunton Wayne. **1948**

PAT AND MIKE ★★★ Cameo appearances by a host of tennis and golf greats, including Babe Didrikson and Don Budge, stud this five-iron tale of athlete Katharine Hepburn and promoter-manager Spencer Tracy at odds with each other on a barnstorming golf and tennis tour. As always, the Tracy and Hepburn chemistry assures good comedy. B&W; 95m. **DIR:** George Cukor. **CAST:** Spencer Tracy, Katharine Hepburn, Aldo Ray, William Ching. **1952**

PATERNITY ★★½ Buddy Evans (Burt Reynolds) decides to have a son—without the commitment of marriage—and recruits a music student working as a waitress (Beverly D'Angelo) to bear his child in this adult comedy. The first two-thirds provide belly laughs and chuckles. The problem comes with the unoriginal and predictable romantic ending. Rated PG because of dialogue involving sex and childbirth. 94m. **DIR:** David Steinberg. **CAST:** Burt Reynolds, Beverly D'Angelo, Norman Fell, Elizabeth Ashley, Lauren Hutton. **1981**

PATSY, THE ★★½ A very minor Jerry Lewis comedy, though the stellar supporting cast is fun to watch. This one is for Lewis fans only; new viewers to Jerry's type of comedy should take in *The Errand Boy* or *The Nutty Professor* first. 101m. **DIR:** Jerry Lewis. **CAST:** Jerry Lewis, Everett Sloane, Ina Balin, Keenan Wynn, Peter Lorre, John Carradine. **1964**

PAUL REISER OUT ON A WHIM ★★★½ Paul Reiser, the star of the TV series *My Two Dads,* combines his stand-up comedy routine with a minimovie. The movie is about a fantasy in which Reiser searches for a beautiful dreamlike lady who keeps reappearing and wanting to know the meaning of "the real thing." This featurette breaks the usual comedian-stand-up mold and makes *Out on a Whim* worth a viewing. 60m. **DIR:** Carl Gottlieb. **CAST:** Paul Reiser, Belinda Bauer, Brooke Adams, Elliott Gould, Carol Kane, Carrie Fisher, Teri Garr, Michael J. Pollard, Desi Arnaz Jr. **1988**

PCU ★★ At small Port Charles University (PCU, get it?), every special-interest group has its pet cause, and the ultrasensitive president (Jessica Walter) is persecuting the only fraternity that wants to have fun. It's a 1990s *Animal House*—only without John Belushi, and with too few laughs. Rated PG-13. 81m. **DIR:** Hart Bochner. **CAST:** Jeremy Piven, Chris Young, David Spade, Megan Ward, Sarah Trigger, Jessica Walter. **1994**

PEE-WEE HERMAN SHOW, THE ★★½ Adult fans of Pee-Wee Herman will fit right into his childish but risqué playhouse. Others will no doubt wonder what planet he's from. Unrated, but some of the humor is sexual in nature. 58m. **DIR:** Marty Callner. **CAST:** Pee-Wee Herman, Phil Hartman, Brian Seff. **1981**

PEE-WEE'S BIG ADVENTURE ★★★½ You want weird? Here it is. Pee-Wee Herman makes the jump from television to feature films with this totally bizarre movie about a man-size, petulant, 12-year-old goofball (Herman) going on a big adventure after his most prized possession—a bicycle—is stolen by some nasties. Rated PG for a scary scene and some daffy violence. 90m. **DIR:** Tim Burton. **CAST:** Pee-Wee Herman, Elizabeth Daily, Mark Holton, Diane Salinger. **1985**

PEGGY SUE GOT MARRIED ★★★★½ Some have called this film a *Back to the Future* for adults. This description is fine as far as it goes, but there is much more to the film. Wistful, and often joyously funny, it features Kathleen Turner as Peggy, a 43-year-old mother of two who is facing divorce. When she attends her twenty-fifth annual high school reunion, she is thrust back in time and gets a chance to change the course of her life. Rated PG-13 for profanity and suggested sex. 103m. **DIR:** Francis Ford Coppola. **CAST:** Kathleen Turner, Nicolas Cage, Barry Miller, Catharine Hicks, Joan Allen, Kevin J. O'Connor, Lisa Jane Persky, Barbara Harris, Don Murray, Maureen O'Sullivan, Leon Ames, John Carradine. **1986**

PENN & TELLER GET KILLED ★★★ Your appreciation for this bizarre comedy will depend upon your reaction to Penn & Teller, an abrasive comedy-magic team who specialize in fake gory magic tricks. While engaging in sick humor and magician debunking, our heroes discover that someone is trying to kill them. Like it or hate it, you have to admit that it's different. Rated R for violence and profanity. 90m. **DIR:** Arthur Penn. **CAST:** Penn Jillette, Teller, Caitlin Clarke, David Patrick Kelly. **1989**

PENN & TELLER'S CRUEL TRICKS FOR DEAR FRIENDS ★★★½ Comic magicians Penn & Teller show the viewer how to trick and swindle friends. Very inventive and likely to cause some serious embarrassment for the sucker these cons are pulled upon. Not rated. 59m. **DIR:** Art Wolff. **CAST:** Penn Jillette, Teller. **1987**

PEOPLE ARE FUNNY ★★½ From the Pine-Thomas B unit at Paramount comes this agreeable little comedy. Jack Haley is a small-town radio announcer who has aspirations to be a big-time radio personality. Inspired by the radio program that later became a successful television series with Art Linkletter as the host. B&W; 94m. **DIR:** Sam White. **CAST:** Jack Haley, Rudy Vallee, Ozzie Nelson, Art Linkletter, Helen Walker, Frances Langford. **1946**

PEOPLE WILL TALK ★★★★½ Wonderful witty story of a doctor whose mysterious background is being investigated by jealous peers at his university. Meanwhile, he marries a young girl who is about to have another man's child. Yes, it is a comedy, and a great one. B&W; 110m. **DIR:** Joseph L. Mankiewicz. **CAST:** Cary Grant, Jeanne Crain, Finlay Currie, Hume Cronyn, Walter Slezak, Sidney Blackmer, Will Wright, Margaret Hamilton, Billy House. **1951**

PERFECT FURLOUGH ★★ Perfectly forgettable fluff about soldier Tony Curtis (who is taking the leave for his entire unit, which is stationed in the Arctic). At least he gets to meet and eventually win Janet Leigh (Mrs. Tony Curtis at that time). 93m. **DIR:** Blake Edwards. **CAST:** Tony Curtis, Janet Leigh, Keenan Wynn, Linda Cristal, Elaine Stritch, Troy Donahue. **1958**

PERFECT LITTLE MURDER, A ★★ Amiable made-for-cable comedy stars Teri Garr as a housewife who overhears a murder plot in her small town and then must go undercover to prove it. Pleasant diversion as Garr and husband Robert Urich deal with her harebrained schemes. Rated PG for sexual innuendo. 94m. **DIR:** Anson Williams. **CAST:** Teri Garr, Robert Urich. **1990**

PERFECT MARRIAGE ★★ On their tenth wedding anniversary Loretta Young and David Niven suddenly decide they can't stand each other and go their separate, flirtatious ways. Dull. B&W; 87m. **DIR:** Lewis Allen. **CAST:** Loretta Young, David Niven, Eddie Albert, Charlie Ruggles, Virginia Field, Rita Johnson, ZaSu Pitts, Jerome Cowan, Ann Doran. **1947**

PERFECT MATCH, THE ★★ Although Marc McClure and Jennifer Edwards create some funny moments, the pacing and the dialogue are iffy in this romantic hodgepodge. The couple meets through a misleading personal ad—with both parties claiming to be something they're not. Rated PG for no apparent reason. 93m. **DIR:** Mark Deimel. **CAST:** Marc McClure, Jennifer Edwards, Diane Stilwell, Rob Paulsen, Karen Witter. **1987**

PERFECTLY NORMAL ★★★½ This is a relaxed, off-kilter Canadian comedy showcasing the entertaining English comic actor, Robbie Coltrane. He plays Alonzo Turner, a mysterious, eccentric stranger who enlivens the life of a dull brewery worker. Original and offbeat. Rated R for profanity. 101m. **DIR:** Yves Simoneau. **CAST:** Robbie Coltrane, Michael Riley. **1990**

PERILS OF PAULINE, THE (1947) ★★★ Betty Hutton plays Pearl White, the queen of the silent serials, in this agreeable little movie. The old-style chase scenes and cliffhanger situations make up for the overdose of sentimentality. 96m. **DIR:** George Marshall. **CAST:** Betty Hutton, John Lund, Billy DeWolfe, William Demarest, Constance Collier, Frank Faylen. **1947**

PERIOD OF ADJUSTMENT ★★★½ Newlyweds Jane Fonda and Jim Hutton start marriage on the wrong foot. Friend Anthony Franciosa, whose own marriage is on the rocks, attempts to straighten them out. Fine performances in a rare light comedy from Tennessee Williams. B&W; 111m. **DIR:** George Roy Hill. **CAST:** Anthony Franciosa, Jane Fonda, Jim Hutton, Lois Nettleton, John McGiver, Jack Albertson. **1962**

PERSONAL PROPERTY ★★★½ A clever comedy designed to make the most of two fiery sex symbols of their time, this comedy-drama marks the only teaming of Robert Taylor and Jean Harlow. The story is a silly setup of contrivances to get the two together. It works as a personality piece. B&W; 85m. **DIR:** W. S. Van Dyke. **CAST:** Jean Harlow, Robert Taylor, Reginald Owen, Una O'Connor, E. E. Clive, Cora Witherspoon. **1937**

PERSONAL SERVICES ★★★ The true-life story of Christine Painter, a British waitress who happened into a very successful career as a brothel madam. Julie Walters gives an all-out performance that's fascinating, but the movie's bluntness may be off-putting to most American viewers. It's rated R for language. 105m. **DIR:** Terry Jones. **CAST:** Julie Walters, Alec McCowen, Shirley Stelfox. **1987**

PERSONALS, THE ★★★½ Entertaining light comedy about a recently divorced Minneapolis man (Bill Schoppert) trying to get back in the dating game. Schoppert has the characteristics of Woody Allen, showing both pathos and a knack for one-liners. Rated PG for profanity. 90m. **DIR:** Peter Markle. **CAST:** Bill Schoppert, Karen Landry, Paul Eiding, Michael Laskin. **1983**

PETE 'N' TILLIE ★★ Bloated, morose mess features a chronically depressed Carol Burnett married to skirt chaser Walter Matthau. Matthau and Burnett never click, and fans of the duo are warned to steer clear. Rated PG for profanity. 100m. **DIR:** Martin Ritt. **CAST:** Walter Matthau, Carol Burnett, Geraldine Page, Barry Nelson. **1972**

PHILADELPHIA STORY, THE ★★★★★ This is one of the best comedies to come out of Hollywood. From the first scene, where Tracy Lord (Katharine Hepburn) deposits her ex-husband's (Cary Grant) golf clubs in a heap at her front door and in return, Grant deposits Hepburn in a heap right next to the clubs, the 1940s version of *The Taming of the Shrew* proceeds at a blistering pace. Grand entertainment. B&W; 112m. **DIR:** George Cukor. **CAST:** Katharine Hepburn, Cary Grant, James Stewart, Ruth Hussey, John Howard. **1940**

PICKLE, THE 🦃 This film is just as bad as the film-within-a-film that has-been director Danny Aiello makes in an attempt to revive his career. Extremely dreadful considering its pedigree. Rated R for language and nudity. 103m. **DIR:** Paul Mazursky. **CAST:** Danny Aiello, Dyan Cannon, Shelley Winters, Christopher Penn. **1993**

PICK-UP ARTIST, THE 🦃 An absolute mess. Rated PG-13 for language and sexual content. 81m. **DIR:** James Toback. **CAST:** Molly Ringwald, Robert Downey Jr., Dennis Hopper, Harvey Keitel. **1987**

PICKWICK PAPERS, THE ★★★ Arguably the best cinema condensation of Charles Dickens. Here recorded are the clever antics of Samuel Pickwick, Alfred Jingle, and Sam Weller as they move through their corner of mid-nineteenth-century England. 109m. **DIR:** Noel Langley. **CAST:** James Hayter, James Donald, Joyce Grenfell, Nigel Patrick, Hermione Baddeley. **1954**

PIECE OF THE ACTION, A ★★★ Third entry in the Bill Cosby–Sidney Poitier partnership (after *Uptown Saturday Night* and *Let's Do It Again*), this one showing Poitier's greater comfort on both sides of the camera. The story concerns a pair of rascals given one of Life's Awful Choices: prison, or a team-up with some social workers to help a group of ghetto kids. Rated PG. 135m. **DIR:** Sidney Poitier. **CAST:** Sidney Poitier, Bill Cosby, Denise Nicholas, James Earl Jones. **1977**

PILLOW TALK ★★★★ If you like the fluffy light comedy of Doris Day and Rock Hudson, this is their best effort. The ever-virginal Miss Day is keeping the wolves at bay. Tony Randall is excellent as the suitor who never wins the girl. 105m. **DIR:** Michael Gordon. **CAST:** Doris Day, Rock Hudson, Tony Randall, Thelma Ritter. **1959**

PINK CHIQUITAS, THE 🦃 An army of women turned sex-starved by a pink meteor. Rated PG-13 for language and sexual situations. 85m. **DIR:** Anthony Currie. **CAST:** Frank Stallone, Bruce Pirrie, Elizabeth Edwards, Eartha Kitt. **1987**

PINK FLAMINGOS ★★ *Pink Flamingos* is the story of Babs Johnson (Divine), the "filthiest person alive," and Connie and Raymond Marble (Mink Stole and David Lochary), two challengers who are jealous of Babs's notoriety. As in all of Waters' films, the point here is to shock. If this doesn't, nothing will. Due to violence, nudity, and very poor taste, we'd rate this one an X. 95m. **DIR:** John Waters. **CAST:** Divine, Mink Stole, David Lochary, Mary Vivian Pearce, Edith Massey. **1972**

PINK MOTEL 🦃 Phyllis Diller and Slim Pickens as owners of a less than prosperous motel. Unrated, this contains sexual situations. 90m. **DIR:** Mike MacFarland. **CAST:** Phyllis Diller, Slim Pickens, Terri Berland, Squire Fridell. **1982**

PINK NIGHTS 🦃 Yet another teen sex comedy. Rated PG for profanity. 87m. **DIR:** Phillip Koch. **CAST:** Shaun Allen, Kevin Anderson. **1985**

PINK PANTHER, THE ★★★½ Peter Sellers is featured in his first bow as Inspector Jacques Clouseau, the inept French detective, on the trail of a jewel thief known as the Phantom in this, the original *Pink Panther*. This release has some good—and even hilarious—moments. But the sequel, *A Shot in the Dark*, is better. 113m. **DIR:** Blake Edwards. **CAST:** Peter Sellers, David Niven, Capucine, Claudia Cardinale, Robert Wagner. **1964**

PINK PANTHER STRIKES AGAIN, THE ★★★½ Peter Sellers's fourth time out as the clumsy Inspector Clouseau. Clouseau's former supervisor, Herbert Lom, cracks up and tries to destroy the world with a superlaser. Meanwhile, he's hired a team of international killers to do away with Clouseau. One turns out to be Lesley-Anne Down, who falls in love with the diminutive Frenchman. Rated PG. 103m. **DIR:** Blake Edwards. **CAST:** Peter Sellers, Herbert Lom, Lesley-Anne Down, Burt Kwouk, Colin Blakely. **1976**

PIRATES 🦃 A turgid, overblown mess. Rated PG-13 for vulgarity. 117m. **DIR:** Roman Polanski. **CAST:** Walter Matthau, Cris Campion, Charlotte Lewis, Roy Kinnear. **1986**

PIZZA MAN ★★★ Pizza delivery guy Elmo Bunn is caught in the middle of a campy worldwide conspiracy. Occasionally clever political satire. Unrated, but with some violence. 90m. **DIR:** J. D. Athens. **CAST:** Bill Maher, Annabelle Gurwitch. **1992**

PLAIN CLOTHES ★★★½ A 24-year-old police detective (Arliss Howard) goes undercover as a high school student. From this not-very-promising plot, director Martha Coolidge and screenwriter A. Scott Frank have fashioned a marvelously tongue-in-cheek hybrid of mystery, teen comedy, and suspense thriller. Rated PG for profanity and violence. 100m. **DIR:** Martha Coolidge. **CAST:** Arliss Howard, Suzy Amis, George Wendt, Seymour Cassel, Abe Vigoda, Robert Stack, Harry Shearer. **1988**

PLANES, TRAINS AND AUTOMOBILES ★★★★ Although it tends to lose momentum in the last half, this screamingly funny film features Steve Martin and John Candy at the peak of their comedic powers. Martin is an uptight marketing executive en route from New York to Chicago to celebrate Thanksgiving with his family, only to end up on a bizarre cross-country odyssey with an obnoxious bozo played by Candy. Rated R for profanity. 100m. **DIR:** John Hughes. **CAST:** Steve Martin, John Candy, Michael McKean, Laila Robins, Martin Ferrero, Charles Tyner. **1987**

PLAY IT AGAIN, SAM ★★★★½ Woody Allen plays a movie columnist and feature writer who lives his life watching movies. Humphrey Bogart is his idol, and the film commences with the final scenes from *Casablanca*. Allen's wife leaves him, and the film revolves around some unsuccessful attempts by his friends (Diane Keaton and Tony Roberts) to set him up with a girl. In an age when funny movies may make you smile at best, this is an oasis of sidesplitting humor. Rated PG. 87m. **DIR:** Herbert Ross. **CAST:** Woody Allen, Diane Keaton, Tony Roberts, Jerry Lacy, Susan Anspach. **1972**

PLAYBOY OF THE WESTERN WORLD ★★★★ Everything about this story is fresh and inspiring, especially the dialogue and accents. A wonderful adaptation of the classic Irish play about a young woman and her fellow villagers falling in love with a handsome roguish stranger. 100m. **DIR:** Brian Desmond Hurst. **CAST:** Siobhan McKenna, Gary Raymond, Michael O'Brian. **1962**

PLAYER, THE ★★★★★ In his most accessible film since his triumphs with *M*A*S*H*, *McCabe and Mrs. Miller*, and *Nashville*, director Robert Altman uses Michael Tolkin's screenplay to savage the motion-picture industry in a deft dark comedy about a sleazy studio executive (Tim Robbins) who fears for his life when a screenwriter starts sending a series of threatening postcards. A must-see for movie buffs. Rated R for profanity, violence, and nudity. 123m. **DIR:** Robert Altman. **CAST:** Tim Robbins, Greta Scacchi, Fred Ward, Whoopi Goldberg, Peter Gallagher, Brion James, Cynthia Stevenson, Vincent D'Onofrio, Dean Stockwell, Richard E. Grant, Sydney Pollack, Lyle Lovett, Dina Merrill. **1992**

PLAYING FOR KEEPS 🦃 Teenagers inherit a dilapidated hotel and turn it into a rock 'n' roll resort for kids. Rated PG-13 for profanity, violence, nudity, and suggested sex. 103m. **DIR:** Bob Weinstein, Harvey Weinstein. **CAST:** Daniel Jordano, Matthew Penn, Leon W. Grant, Harold Gould, Jimmy Baio. **1986**

PLAYING THE FIELD 🦃 Moronic Italian comedy about an ambitious soccer referee. Poorly dubbed. Contains profanity and sexual situations. 90m. **DIR:** Louis D'Amico. **CAST:** Lando Buzzanca, Joan Collins. **1974**

PLAYMATES ★★★★ This is a very good romantic comedy about two divorced men who become friends and then secretly begin to date each other's ex-wife, with crazy results. Good cast, fine direction, and an energized screenplay by Richard Baer make this TV movie sparkle. 73m. **DIR:** Theodore J. Flicker. **CAST:** Alan Alda, Connie Stevens, Barbara Feldon, Doug McClure, Severn Darden, Roger Bowen, Eileen Brennan. **1972**

PLAZA SUITE ★★★★½ Walter Matthau is at his comic best as he re-creates three separate roles from Neil Simon's stage comedy. The movie is actually three tales of what goes on in a particular suite. Rated PG. 115m. **DIR:** Arthur Hiller. **CAST:** Walter Matthau, Maureen Stapleton, Barbara Harris, Lee Grant. **1971**

PLEASE DON'T EAT MY MOTHER! ★★ Uncredited remake of *Little Shop of Horrors* is even worse—and almost as funny. Middle-aged Henry Fudd (Buck Kartalian, who also directed under a pseudonym) takes time out from being a peeping Tom to feed murder victims to his man- (and woman-) eating plant. Cheesy but fun. Also known as *Hungry Pets*. Unrated; plentiful nudity. 98m. **DIR:** Jack Beckett. **CAST:** Buck Kartalian. **1972**

PLEASE DON'T EAT THE DAISIES ★★★ Witty David Niven meets his match when he crosses Doris Day's path and questions her ambitions. A clever comedy about a drama critic who copes with his wife's remodeling plans and a conniving actress friend at the same time. Based on Jean Kerr's bestseller and the basis for a TV series during the

1960s. 111m. **DIR:** Charles Walters. **CAST:** Doris Day, David Niven, Janis Paige, Spring Byington, Margaret Lindsay, Richard Haydn, Patsy Kelly, Jack Weston. **1960**

PLOT AGAINST HARRY, THE ★★★★ Shot in a casual black-and-white style that matches the material, this is a tale of the misadventures of an amiable Jewish racketeer, freshly released from prison. Witty satire on middle-class Jewish immigrant life. Unrated, but of PG-13 tone. B&W; 81m. **DIR:** Michael Roemer. **CAST:** Martin Priest. **1969**

POCKET MONEY ★★½ Cowpoke Paul Newman and con man Lee Marvin fall in with a calculating cattleman and spend the rest of the film getting themselves out of it. Likable enough but really doesn't go anywhere. 102m. **DIR:** Stuart Rosenberg. **CAST:** Paul Newman, Lee Marvin, Christine Belford, Strother Martin, Kelly Jean Peters, Wayne Rogers. **1972**

POCKETFUL OF MIRACLES ★★★ The term Capracorn could have been coined in response to this overly sentimental picture, basically a remake of the director's 1933 *Lady for a Day.* But Bette Davis is a delight as Apple Annie and Glenn Ford is winningly earnest as the producer who tries to turn her into a lady. Ann-Margret's film debut. 136m. **DIR:** Frank Capra. **CAST:** Bette Davis, Glenn Ford, Hope Lange, Thomas Mitchell, Peter Falk, Edward Everett Horton, Jack Elam, Ann-Margret. **1961**

POISON IVY (1985) ★★ Top talents save this banal TV movie about life at a summer camp. Michael J. Fox is the hip counselor; Nancy McKeon is an assistant nurse and Fox's love interest; and Robert Klein is the bombastic camp director. All right for star watching. 97m. **DIR:** Larry Elikann. **CAST:** Michael J. Fox, Nancy McKeon, Robert Klein, Caren Kaye, Jason Bateman, Adam Baldwin. **1985**

POLICE ACADEMY ★★ Here's another *Animal House*–style comedy that tries very hard to be funny. Sometimes it is, and sometimes it isn't. Rated R for nudity, violence, and profanity. 95m. **DIR:** Hugh Wilson. **CAST:** Steve Guttenberg, George Gaynes, Kim Cattrall, Bubba Smith, Michael Winslow, Andrew Rubin. **1984**

POLICE ACADEMY II: THEIR FIRST ASSIGNMENT ★★ Those inept would-be officers from Hugh Wilson's *Police Academy* return in this less funny but still box office–potent production. Episodic and silly. Rated PG-13 for profanity. 90m. **DIR:** Jerry Paris. **CAST:** Steve Guttenberg, Bubba Smith, David Graf, Michael Winslow, Bruce Mahler, Colleen Camp, Marion Ramsey, Howard Hesseman, George Gaynes. **1985**

POLICE ACADEMY III: BACK IN TRAINING 🦃 Moronic. Rated PG for silly violence and references to body parts. 90m. **DIR:** Jerry Paris. **CAST:** Steve Guttenberg, Bubba Smith, David Graf, Michael Winslow, Marion Ramsey, Leslie Easterbrook, Art Metrano, Tim Kazurinsky, Bob Goldthwait, George Gaynes. **1986**

POLICE ACADEMY 4: CITIZENS ON PATROL 🦃 Let's just say that if you liked the first three, there's no reason you shouldn't like the fourth. Rated PG for mild profanity. 87m. **DIR:** Jim Drake. **CAST:** Steve Guttenberg, Bubba Smith, Michael Winslow, David Graf, Tim Kazurinsky, Sharon Stone, G. W. Bailey, Bob Goldthwait. **1987**

POLICE ACADEMY 5—ASSIGNMENT: MIAMI BEACH 🦃 Silly fifth entry in the series. Rated PG for language and ribald humor. 90m. **DIR:** Alan Myerson. **CAST:** Bubba Smith, David Graf, Michael Winslow, Leslie Easterbrook, Marion Ramsey, Janet Jones, Matt McCoy, René Auberjonois. **1988**

POLICE ACADEMY 6: CITY UNDER SIEGE 🦃 Rated PG for violence and profanity. 87m. **DIR:** Peter Bonerz. **CAST:** Bubba Smith, Kenneth Mars, George Gaynes, David Graf, Michael Winslow, G. W. Bailey. **1989**

POLICE SQUAD! ★★★★ Originally a 1982 summer TV show, with only six episodes aired, this is now a minor cult classic. The folks who made *Airplane!* went all out on this. Each one of the episodes is hilarious, much funnier than the popular film *Police Academy.* 75m. **DIR:** Jim Abrahams, David Zucker, Jerry Zucker, Joe Dante, Reza S. Badiyi. **CAST:** Leslie Nielsen, Alan North. **1982**

POLISH VAMPIRE IN BURBANK, A ★★½ Low-budget, sophomoric horror-comedy that, nonetheless, provides a few laughs. Mark Pirro plays a "virgin" vampire. His sultry sister, another vampire, takes him out one night for a bite. One of those films that you giggle at, then feel very sheepish. Not rated, but contains sexual suggestion and some ghoulish violence. 84m. **DIR:** Mark Pirro. **CAST:** Mark Pirro, Lori Sutton, Eddie Deezen. **1985**

POLYESTER ★★ Anyone for bad taste? Female impersonator Divine and 1950s heartthrob Tab Hunter play lovers in this film by writer-producer-director John Waters (*Pink Flamingos*). A special gimmick called "Odorama" allowed viewers to experience the story's various smells via a scratch-and-sniff card. Rated R. 86m. **DIR:** John Waters. **CAST:** Divine, Tab Hunter, Edith Massey, Mary Garlington. **1981**

POOR LITTLE RICH GIRL, THE (1917) ★★★ Mary Pickford's main claim to fame was her uncanny ability to convincingly portray females many years her junior. She stunted her range by doing so again and again, but the public loved it and willingly paid for it. She earned high critical acclaim demonstrating her range in this sentimental comedy-drama. One critic said that she was

8 years old, then a haughty 16, with no warning or motivation for the mercurial change. Silent, with organ music. B&W; 64m. **DIR:** Maurice Tourneur. **CAST:** Mary Pickford. **1917**

POPE MUST DIET, THE 🦃 As a comedy, *The Pope Must Die* (retitled *The Pope Must Diet*) is about as unfunny as you can get. Director Peter Richardson delivers a pastiche of gags that will have you hitting the fast-forward button to find the good parts. There aren't any. Rated R for violence, profanity, and nudity. 90m. **DIR:** Peter Richardson. **CAST:** Robbie Coltrane, Beverly D'Angelo, Alex Rocco, Paul Bartel, Herbert Lom, Balthazar Getty, Peter Richardson. **1991**

POPI ★★½ Alan Arkin is Popi (Pappa), a hard-working if somewhat irresponsible Puerto Rican immigrant who comes up with a plan to provide his two young boys with new lives as Cuban refugees. Offbeat dramatic comedy, recommended only for families with older children. Rated G, although there is some violence and partial nudity. 115m. **DIR:** Arthur Hiller. **CAST:** Alan Arkin, Rita Moreno. **1969**

PORKY'S 🦃 Teenagers in a fateful trip to a redneck dive called Porky's. Rated R for vulgarity, nudity, and adult themes. 94m. **DIR:** Bob Clark. **CAST:** Dan Monahan, Mark Herrier, Wyatt Knight, Roger Wilson, Kim Cattrall, Scott Colomby. **1981**

PORKY'S II: THE NEXT DAY 🦃 This time, the lustful kids of Angel Beach High battle with the Ku Klux Klan. Rated R for the usual garbage. 95m. **DIR:** Bob Clark. **CAST:** Dan Monahan, Wyatt Knight, Mark Herrier, Roger Wilson, Kaki Hunter, Scott Colomby, Nancy Parsons, Edward Winter. **1983**

PORKY'S REVENGE 🦃 It's just more of the same stupidity. Rated R for profanity, suggested sex, and nudity. 90m. **DIR:** James Komack. **CAST:** Dan Monahan, Wyatt Knight, Tony Ganios, Mark Herrier, Kaki Hunter, Scott Colomby. **1985**

POSITIVELY TRUE ADVENTURES OF THE ALLEGED TEXAS CHEERLEADER-MURDERING MOM, THE ★★★½ Trashy tabloid docudramas, and the media feeding-frenzy that creates them, are indicted in this often hilarious made-for-cable account of the Texas housewife (superbly played by Holly Hunter) who placed a contract on her daughter's cheerleading rival. Director Michael Ritchie maintains the darkly farcical tone against which his stars chew up the scenery. Rated R for profanity. 99m. **DIR:** Michael Ritchie. **CAST:** Holly Hunter, Beau Bridges, Swoosie Kurtz, Gregg Henry, Matt Frewer. **1993**

POSTCARDS FROM THE EDGE ★★★★ Meryl Streep lets it all hang out—and even sings—in this outrageous, entertaining adaptation of Carrie Fisher's bestselling autobiographical book. A superb supporting cast contributes to this tale of an actress (Streep) whose drug dependence is getting out of hand, and so is her relationship with her show-biz mom (Shirley MacLaine). The result is a movie that sparkles with wit, energy, and surprises. Rated R for profanity, drug use, and suggested sex. 106m. **DIR:** Mike Nichols. **CAST:** Meryl Streep, Shirley MacLaine, Dennis Quaid, Gene Hackman, Richard Dreyfuss, Rob Reiner, Mary Wickes, Conrad Bain, Annette Bening, Gary Morton, C.C.H. Pounder. **1990**

POWWOW HIGHWAY ★★★½ Taking a lighthearted look at a serious subject isn't easy, but this film does an excellent job. The subject is mistreatment of Indians on American reservations, from poor housing and bad job conditions to deprivation of tribal cultures and history. Though not rated, this is geared to an adult audience. 91m. **DIR:** Jonathan Wacks. **CAST:** A. Martinez, Gary Farmer, Amanda Wyss. **1988**

PRAY TV (1980) ★★½ Dabney Coleman plays Marvin Fleece, penny-ante con man, who takes faltering TV station KRUD and turns it into K-GOD. A really funny satire on religion and television, betrayed only by a weak ending. Rated PG for language and general tastelessness. 92m. **DIR:** Rick Friedberg. **CAST:** Dabney Coleman, Archie Hahn, Joyce Jameson, Nancy Morgan, Roger E. Mosley, Marcia Wallace. **1980**

PRELUDE TO A KISS ★★★★ It's a dream marriage for both Alec Baldwin and Meg Ryan when they finally tie the knot, which begins to unravel in seminightmarish fashion when the bride is kissed by an old man with whom she swaps souls. A charming, low-key romance with nice performances from Baldwin and Ryan. Rated PG-13. 105m. **DIR:** Norman René. **CAST:** Alec Baldwin, Meg Ryan, Kathy Bates, Ned Beatty, Patty Duke, Sydney Walker. **1992**

PREP SCHOOL ★★½ This comedy-drama about a coed prep school in New England has the usual cast of characters. Familiar, but nicely performed. Rated PG-13 for profanity. 97m. **DIR:** Paul Almond. **CAST:** Leslie Hope, Andrew Sabiston. **1981**

PREPPIES 🦃 R-rated sexploitation. Rated R for nudity, simulated sex, and profanity. 90m. **DIR:** Chuck Vincent. **CAST:** Nitchie Barrett, Dennis Drake, Steven Holt, Katt Shea. **1984**

PRESIDENT'S ANALYST, THE ★★★★ Vastly underappreciated satire from writer-director Theodore J. Flicker, who concocts a wild tale concerning a psychiatrist (James Coburn) selected to be our president's "secret shrink." Coburn walks away with the picture, his wicked smile and piercing eyes becoming more and more suspicious as he falls prey to the paranoia of his elite assignment. Unrated; adult themes. 104m. **DIR:** Theodore J. Flicker. **CAST:** James Coburn, Godfrey Cambridge, Pat Harrington, Will Geer. **1967**

PRETTY SMART 🦃 Claptrap about a rebellious new student at an exclusive girls' school. Rated R. 84m. **DIR:** Dimitri Logothetis. **CAST:** Tricia Leigh Fisher, Lisa Lorient, Dennis Cole, Patricia Arquette. **1986**

PRETTY WOMAN ★★★★ Imagine Cinderella as a young Hollywood hooker. Now put Prince Charming in a fancy sports car driving down the strip. Welcome to this fluffy, funny comedy about the unlikeliest of love mates: a runaway (Julia Roberts) and a corporate raider (Richard Gere). Rated R for profanity and sex. 119m. **DIR:** Garry Marshall. **CAST:** Richard Gere, Julia Roberts, Ralph Bellamy, Laura San Giacomo. **1990**

PRIME OF MISS JEAN BRODIE, THE ★★★★★ Maggie Smith's first Oscar-winning performance fuels this delicious character study of a late 1930s Edinburgh schoolteacher who steers her young charges past the rocky shoals of life. Delightfully wacky and relentlessly eccentric, Smith is utterly captivating as the cosmopolitan instructor who interlaces studies with sex (priceless descriptions of her affairs, to be specific). Jay Presson Allen's deft script is drawn from Muriel Spark's novel, and rarely has the spirit of a book been so well captured on screen. Rated PG for frank dialogue. 166m. **DIR:** Ronald Neame. **CAST:** Maggie Smith, Robert Stephens, Celia Johnson, Pamela Franklin, Gordon Jackson. **1969**

PRINCE AND THE SHOWGIRL, THE ★★½ Romantic comedy about the attraction of a nobleman for an American show girl. Marilyn Monroe and Laurence Olivier's acting talents are in full flower, and they are fun to watch; however, they are so dissimilar that they never click. 117m. **DIR:** Laurence Olivier. **CAST:** Laurence Olivier, Marilyn Monroe, Sybil Thorndike, Jeremy Spencer. **1957**

PRINCE OF PENNSYLVANIA 🦃 Keanu Reeves portrays a morbid, morose teenager in a small Pennsylvania mining town. Rated R for nudity, violence, and profanity. 93m. **DIR:** Ron Nyswander. **CAST:** Fred Ward, Bonnie Bedelia, Keanu Reeves, Amy Madigan. **1988**

PRINCESS ACADEMY, THE 🦃 Another girls' school movie, in which the entire point is to cram in as many extraneous shower and bedroom scenes as possible. Rated R. 90m. **DIR:** Bruce Block. **CAST:** Eva Gabor, Lar Park Lincoln. **1987**

PRINCESS AND THE PIRATE, THE ★★★ A happy, hilarious Bob Hope howler. He and the beautiful Virginia Mayo are pursued by pirates and trapped by potentate Walter Slezak. Victor McLaglen is menacing as a buccaneer bent on their destruction. Walter Brennan is something else—a pirate? This one's lots of fun for all! 94m. **DIR:** David Butler. **CAST:** Bob Hope, Virginia Mayo, Victor McLaglen, Walter Brennan, Walter Slezak. **1944**

PRISONER OF SECOND AVENUE, THE ★★★★ Neil Simon blends laughter with tears in this film about an executive (Jack Lemmon) who loses his job and has a nervous breakdown. Anne Bancroft plays Lemmon's wife. Rated PG. 105m. **DIR:** Melvin Frank. **CAST:** Jack Lemmon, Anne Bancroft, Gene Saks, Elizabeth Wilson, Florence Stanley. **1975**

PRISONER OF ZENDA, THE (1979) ★★★½ Zany rendition of the classic tale of a look-alike commoner who stands in for the endangered king of Ruritania. A warm and hilarious film despite the lack of critical acclaim. Rated PG for language. 108m. **DIR:** Richard Quine. **CAST:** Peter Sellers, Lionel Jeffries, Elke Sommer, Lynne Frederick. **1979**

PRISONERS OF INERTIA ★★ Slow-paced comedy features newlyweds (Amanda Plummer and Christopher Rich) attempting to enjoy a Manhattan Sunday. *Inertia* describes the film's tempo. Rated R for nudity. 92m. **DIR:** J. Noyes Scher. **CAST:** Amanda Plummer, Christopher Rich, John C. McGinley. **1989**

PRIVATE AFFAIRS 🦃 This is one affair they ought to keep private! The rich and elite mingle among the Rome fashion circles, spinning their wheels and little else in this tiresome mess. Rated R. 104m. **DIR:** Francesco Massaro. **CAST:** Kate Capshaw, David Naughton, Michele Placido. **1988**

PRIVATE BENJAMIN ★★★★ This comedy is at its best in the first half, when Goldie Hawn, as a spoiled Jewish princess, joins the army. The last part of the movie gets a little heavy on the message end, but Hawn's buoyant personality makes it easy to take. Rated R for profanity, nudity, and implicit sex. 110m. **DIR:** Howard Zieff. **CAST:** Goldie Hawn, Eileen Brennan, Armand Assante, Robert Webber, Sam Wanamaker. **1980**

PRIVATE EYES, THE 🦃 Holmes and Watson send-up. Rated PG. 91m. **DIR:** Lang Elliott. **CAST:** Tim Conway, Don Knotts, Trisha Noble, Bernard Fox. **1980**

PRIVATE FUNCTION, A ★★★★ The Michael Palin/Maggie Smith team repeat the success of *The Missionary* with this hilarious film about a meek foot doctor and his socially aspiring wife who become involved with the black market during the food rationing days of post–World War II England when they acquire an unlicensed pig. The humor is open to those who like Monty Python, but is also accessible to audiences who do not find that brand of humor funny. Rated R. 96m. **DIR:** Malcolm Mowbray. **CAST:** Michael Palin, Maggie Smith, Denholm Elliott, Richard Griffiths. **1985**

PRIVATE LESSONS 🦃 Soft-porn comedy, about a wealthy, virginal teenage boy. Rated R because of nudity. 87m. **DIR:** Alan Myerson. **CAST:** Sylvia Kristel, Howard Hesseman, Eric Brown, Pamela Bryant. **1981**

PRIVATE LIVES ★★★½ A divorced couple meet by accident on their second honeymoons; soon they've abandoned their new spouses and run off, endlessly bickering and making up. Noel Coward's sparkling play stylishly filmed; laughs multiply by the minute. B&W; 84m. **DIR:** Sidney Franklin. **CAST:** Norma Shearer, Robert Montgomery, Reginald Denny, Una Merkel. **1931**

PRIVATE POPSICLE 🦃 In this fourth film featuring the Lemon Popsicle gang, a popular comedy team in Europe, we find the trio joining the Israeli army. 100m. **DIR:** Boaz Davidson. **CAST:** Yftach Katzur, Zachi Noy, Jonathan Segall. **1982**

PRIVATE RESORT ★★ This teen comedy features two young men (Rob Morror and Johnny Depp) seeking romance and excitement at a luxurious resort. Few funny moments. Rated R for nudity, obscenities, and sexual situations. 82m. **DIR:** George Bowers. **CAST:** Rob Morror, Johnny Depp, Tony Azito, Dody Goodman, Hector Elizondo. **1985**

PRIVATE SCHOOL 🦃 Enroll at your own risk. Rated R for nudity and profanity. 97m. **DIR:** Noel Black. **CAST:** Phoebe Cates, Martin Mull, Sylvia Kristel, Ray Walston, Julie Payne, Michael Zorek, Matthew Modine. **1983**

PRIVATE SNUFFY SMITH ★★ Cloned from the comic strip "Barney Google and Snuffy Smith," this grade B time passer has cantankerous hillbilly Snuffy being allowed to join up after saving the life of an army sergeant. Supporting player Jimmie Dodd went on to shepherd Disney's Mouseketeers. B&W; 67m. **DIR:** Eddie Cline. **CAST:** Bud Duncan, Edgar Kennedy, Doris Linden, Jimmie Dodd. **1942**

PRIVATES ON PARADE ★★★½ While this story of a gay USO-type unit in the British army is a comedy, it has its serious moments. These come when the unit accidentally runs into a gang of gunrunners. John Cleese is hilarious as the pathetic army major who's ignorant of the foul play that goes on under his nose. Rated PG-13 for adult situations and profanity. 107m. **DIR:** Michael Blakemore. **CAST:** John Cleese, Denis Quilley, Michael Elphick, Simon Jones, Joe Melia, John Standing, Nicola Pagett. **1983**

PRIZZI'S HONOR ★★★★★ This totally bent comedy is perhaps best described as *The Godfather* gone stark, raving mad. Jack Nicholson plays a Mafia hit man who falls in love with a mystery woman (Kathleen Turner), who turns out to be full of surprises. Perhaps the blackest black comedy ever made. It's a real find for fans of the genre. Rated R for nudity, suggested sex, profanity, and violence. 130m. **DIR:** John Huston. **CAST:** Jack Nicholson, Kathleen Turner, Robert Loggia, John Randolph, William Hickey, Anjelica Huston. **1985**

PROBLEM CHILD ★★ A bickering yuppie couple (John Ritter, Amy Yasbeck) decide to adopt a child so they can get invited to all the upscale kiddie birthday parties. They end up with a foul-mouthed, destructive youngster (Michael Oliver). Moronic combination of *Police Academy* and *The Exorcist.* Rated PG for vulgar language and violence. 81m. **DIR:** Dennis Dugan. **CAST:** John Ritter, Jack Warden, Michael Oliver, Gilbert Gottfried, Amy Yasbeck, Michael Richards. **1990**

PROBLEM CHILD 2 ★★ John Ritter and Michael Oliver return as Ben Healy and his devilish adopted son Junior in this sequel. Too bad the writers had to heap projectile vomiting and dog feces on the audience. Rated PG-13 for mild profanity and scatological humor. 91m. **DIR:** Brian Levant. **CAST:** John Ritter, Michael Oliver, Laraine Newman, Amy Yasbeck, Ivyann Schwan, Jack Warden. **1991**

PRODUCERS, THE ★★★★ Mel Brooks's first film as a director remains a laugh-filled winner. Zero Mostel stars as a sleazy Broadway promoter who, with the help of a neurotic accountant (Gene Wilder), comes up with a scheme to produce an intentional flop titled *Springtime for Hitler* and bilk its backers. The plan backfires, and the disappointed duo ends up with a hit and more troubles than before. Rated PG. 88m. **DIR:** Mel Brooks. **CAST:** Zero Mostel, Gene Wilder, Kenneth Mars, Dick Shawn, Lee Meredith, Christopher Hewett. **1968**

PROJECTIONIST, THE ★★ A projectionist in a New York movie palace escapes his drab life by creating fantasies, casting himself as the hero in various films. The movie intercuts new footage into old classics, a technique used later by Steve Martin in *Dead Men Don't Wear Plaid.* The film has surprisingly little entertainment value. Rated R for profanity and partial nudity. 85m. **DIR:** Harry Hurwitz. **CAST:** Chuck McCann, Ina Balin, Rodney Dangerfield. **1970**

PROMISE HER ANYTHING ★★½ Single mom Leslie Caron must find a father for her precocious son. Dated romp is a direct precursor to *Look Who's Talking*. 97m. **DIR:** Arthur Hiller. **CAST:** Warren Beatty, Leslie Caron, Robert Cummings, Keenan Wynn. **1965**

PROMISES, PROMISES 🦃 The only thing going for this film is the scenes of a next-to-totally-naked Jayne Mansfield. Silly and crude. 75m. **DIR:** King Donovan. **CAST:** Jayne Mansfield, Marie McDonald, Tommy Noonan, Mickey Hargitay, Fritz Feld. **1963**

PROMOTER, THE ★★★ Alec Guinness is clever, conniving, and all innocence in this comedy centering on a penniless young man who exploits every opportunity to get ahead in the world. Glynis Johns is delightful as the girl who believes in him. B&W; 88m. **DIR:** Ronald Neame. **CAST:** Alec Guinness, Glynis Johns, Valerie Hobson, Petula Clark. **1952**

PROTOCOL ★★★½ In this film, directed by Herbert Ross, Goldie Hawn is a lovable airhead who goes through a startling metamorphosis to become a true individual. Sound a little like *Private Benjamin*? You bet your blond movie actress. It's no classic. However, viewers could do a lot worse. Rated PG for violence, partial nudity, and adult situations. 96m. **DIR:** Herbert Ross. **CAST:** Goldie Hawn, Chris Sarandon, Richard Romanus, Cliff De Young, Gail Strickland. **1984**

PUCKER UP AND BARK LIKE A DOG ★★★½ Cute romantic comedy about a reclusive and shy painter who searches for the girl of his dreams while trying to display his paintings in public. Wendy O. Williams gives the title its kinkiness as a biker who shows him how to live a little. Rated R for violence and nudity. 74m. **DIR:** Paul Salvatore Parco. **CAST:** Jonathan Gries, Lisa Zane, Barney Martin, Robert Culp, Wendy O. Williams, Paul Bartel, Phyllis Diller, Isabel Sanford. **1989**

PULP ★★½ Sometimes funny, sometimes lame black comedy casts Michael Caine as a pulp mystery writer hired to pen the biography of retired film star and reputed mobster Mickey Rooney. Caine carries the film well enough, with his voice-over narration a nice Chandleresque touch, and Rooney is excellent in his few scenes, but the film never really catches fire. Rated PG for profanity and violence. 95m. **DIR:** Mike Hodges. **CAST:** Michael Caine, Mickey Rooney, Lionel Stander, Lizabeth Scott, Al Lettieri. **1972**

PURE LUCK ★★ In this Americanized version of Francis Veber's *Le Chevre*, Danny Glover plays a hapless detective assigned to work with a bumbling accountant in order to locate the world's most accident-prone heiress. The actors try hard, but it just ain't that funny, folks. Rated PG. 96m. **DIR:** Nadia Tass. **CAST:** Martin Short, Danny Glover, Sheila Kelley, Scott Wilson, Harry Shearer, Sam Wanamaker, Jorge Luke. **1991**

PURLIE VICTORIOUS ★★★½ Alan Alda made his film debut as a southern liberal in this good-humored comedy written by Ossie Davis. Davis and his wife, Ruby Dee, play an evangelist couple who try to convert an old barn into an integrated church. Their chief opposition comes from the bigot (Sorrel Booke) who owns the barn. Also known as *Gone Are the Days*. B&W; 93m. **DIR:** Nicholas Webster. **CAST:** Ossie Davis, Ruby Dee, Sorrell Booke, Alan Alda, Godfrey Cambridge, Beah Richards. **1963**

PURPLE ROSE OF CAIRO, THE ★★★★ Mia Farrow is a Depression-era housewife who finds her dreary day-to-day existence enlivened when a dashing, romantic hero walks off the screen and sweeps her off her feet. Like Woody Allen's *Zelig* and *Broadway Danny Rose*, this mixes humor with very human situations. The result is a very satisfying work. Rated PG for violence. 85m. **DIR:** Woody Allen. **CAST:** Mia Farrow, Jeff Daniels, Danny Aiello, Edward Herrmann, John Wood. **1985**

PURSUIT OF D. B. COOPER ★★½ The famous skyjacker is turned into a fun-loving good old boy in this hit-and-miss comedy starring Treat Williams, Robert Duvall, and Kathryn Harrold. If you liked *Smokey and the Bandit*, you'll probably enjoy this. Rated PG because of minimal violence and sexuality. 100m. **DIR:** Roger Spottiswoode. **CAST:** Treat Williams, Robert Duvall, Kathryn Harrold, Ed Flanders, Paul Gleason, R. G. Armstrong. **1981**

PUTNEY SWOPE ★★★★ This wildly funny film concerns a black man who takes over a Madison Avenue advertising firm. Alan Abel, Mel Brooks, and Allen Garfield appear in this zany parody of American lifestyles. Rated R. 88m. **DIR:** Robert Downey. **CAST:** Alan Abel, Mel Brooks, Allen Garfield, Pepi Hermine, Ruth Hermine, Antonio Fargas. **1969**

PYGMALION ★★★★½ This is an impeccable adaptation of George Bernard Shaw's classic play. The comedy is deliciously sophisticated. The performances are exquisite, particularly that of Leslie Howard, who'll make you forget Rex Harrison's Henry Higgins in an instant. As the professor's feisty Cockney pupil, Wendy Hiller is a delight. B&W; 95m. **DIR:** Anthony Asquith, Leslie Howard. **CAST:** Leslie Howard, Wendy Hiller, Wilfrid Lawson, Marie Lohr, David Tree. **1938**

PYRATES 💔 Real-life husband-and-wife Kevin Bacon and Kyra Sedgwick play a couple who ignite sparks whenever they have sex, setting fires. Too bad they couldn't turn up the heat in this one-joke effort. Rated R for nudity. 98m. **DIR:** Noah Stern. **CAST:** Kevin Bacon, Kyra Sedgwick. **1991**

QUEENS LOGIC ★★★ Maturity and contentment can arrive at any age, assuming, of course, they arrive at all. That's the theme of this rambling, uneven, but amiable coming-of-age comedy-drama. It's *thirtysomething* crossed with *Diner*. Rated R for profanity. 116m. **DIR:** Steve Rash. **CAST:** Joe Mantegna, Kevin Bacon, John Malkovich, Ken Olin, Linda Fiorentino, Jamie Lee Curtis. **1991**

QUICK CHANGE ★★★★½ Robbing a bank is easy for Bill Murray (who co-directed), Geena Davis, and Randy Quaid—three New Yorkers driven to desperate measures. It's the getaway that they find nearly impossible. Adapted from the 1981 novel by Jay Cronley, this fast-and-funny caper film benefits from Murray's off-the-cuff comedy style. Rated R. 98m. **DIR:** Bill Murray, Howard Franklin. **CAST:** Bill Murray, Geena Davis, Randy Quaid, Jason Robards Jr. **1990**

QUICK, LET'S GET MARRIED 💔 Made in 1964 but not released for seven years, this feeble farce has Ginger Rogers as the madam of a bordello conspiring to pull off a hoax on a supposedly innocent prostitute. 96m. **DIR:** William Dieterle. **CAST:** Ginger Rogers, Ray Milland, Barbara Eden, Walter Abel, Michael Ansara, Elliott Gould. **1971**

QUIET MAN, THE ★★★★★ John Ford's easygoing and marvelously entertaining tribute to the people and the land of Ireland. The story centers around an American ex-boxer (John Wayne) who returns to his native land, his efforts to understand the culture and people of a rural village, and especially his interest in taming a spirited colleen (Maureen O'Hara) in spite of the disapproval of her brother (Victor McLaglen). 129m. **DIR:** John Ford. **CAST:** John Wayne, Maureen O'Hara, Victor McLaglen, Barry Fitzgerald, Mildred Natwick, Arthur Shields, Ward Bond, Jack MacGowran. **1952**

RABBIT TEST The world's first pregnant man. Rated R—profanity. 84m. **DIR:** Joan Rivers. **CAST:** Billy Crystal, Roddy McDowall, Joan Prather. **1978**

RACHEL PAPERS ★★★½ Dexter Fletcher (who looks like a young Mick Jagger) plays an infatuated young man persistently pursuing the girl of his dreams (Ione Skye). When she finally acknowledges him, the film takes a decidedly serious and downhill turn. Rated R for profanity and nudity. 95m. **DIR:** Damian Harris. **CAST:** Dexter Fletcher, Ione Skye, Jonathan Pryce. **1989**

RADIO DAYS ★★★ One of writer-director Woody Allen's gentler fables, a pleasant little fantasy about people whose lives revolved around the radio during the days prior to World War II. This affectionate overview does for radio what *The Purple Rose of Cairo* did for the movies; unfortunately, many of the characters in his large ensemble cast get lost, and too much time is spent with others. Rated PG. 85m. **DIR:** Woody Allen. **CAST:** Mia Farrow, Seth Green, Julie Kavner, Josh Mostel, Michael Tucker, Dianne Wiest. **1987**

RAFFERTY AND THE GOLD DUST TWINS ★★½ Amusing and entertaining little film with Sally Kellerman and Mackenzie Phillips kidnapping a hapless Alan Arkin and forcing him to drive them to New Orleans from California. Good cast and pacing make up for simple plot. Rated PG for profanity. 92m. **DIR:** Dick Richards. **CAST:** Sally Kellerman, Mackenzie Phillips, Alan Arkin, Alex Rocco, Charles Martin Smith, Harry Dean Stanton. **1975**

RAGE OF PARIS, THE ★★★ Famed French star Danielle Darrieux made her U.S. film debut in this airy romantic comedy about mistaken identity and artful conniving. Deft direction steered the excellent cast through an engaging script. Good, clean fun all around. B&W; 78m. **DIR:** Henry Koster. **CAST:** Danielle Darrieux, Douglas Fairbanks Jr., Mischa Auer, Helen Broderick, Glenda Farrell, Louis Hayward, Harry Davenport, Samuel S. Hinds. **1938**

RAGS TO RICHES ★★ Joseph Bologna plays millionaire Nick Foley, who tries to soften his ruthless-businessman image by adopting six girls. This was a pilot for the TV series of the same name. 96m. **DIR:** Bruce Seth Green. **CAST:** Joseph Bologna, Tisha Campbell. **1986**

RAISING ARIZONA ★★★★ An almost indescribable lunatic comedy from the makers of *Blood Simple*. Nicolas Cage plays an ex-convict married to policewoman Holly Hunter. Both want children but cannot have any. So they decide to help themselves to one. What follows is a delightful, offbeat comedy that is extremely fast-paced, with eye-popping cinematography and decidedly different characters. Rated PG-13. 94m. **DIR:** Joel Coen. **CAST:** Nicolas Cage, Holly Hunter, Randall "Tex" Cobb, Trey Wilson, John Goodman, William Forsythe. **1987**

RAP MASTER RONNIE—A REPORT CARD ★★★ As indicated by the title, this is a look back at the Ronald Reagan presidency as seen through the eyes of writer Garry Trudeau. Jim Morris, who makes his living imitating Reagan, does a fine job here with the help of a supporting cast. This HBO special is unrated. 47m. **DIR:** Jay Dubin. **CAST:** Jim Morris, Jon Cryer, Carol Kane, Tom Smothers. **1988**

RARE CHAPLIN ★★★½ Three early Charlie Chaplin comedy pearls are strung together in this collection: "The Bank," in which janitor Charlie foils a bank burglary—in his dreams; "Shanghaied," a tale of skulduggery afloat; and "A Night in the Show," a film version of the British music hall sketch that introduced Chaplin to American vaudeville audiences. Silent with musical score. B&W; 55m. **DIR:** Charles Chaplin. **CAST:** Charlie Chaplin, Edna Purviance, Wesley Ruggles. **1915**

RAT PFINK A BOO BOO A loose parody of *Batman*, it has everything a bad-movie lover could ever want. 72m. **DIR:** Ray Dennis Steckler. **CAST:** Vin Saxon, Carolyn Brandt. **1965**

RATINGS GAME, THE ★★★★ Danny DeVito directs and leads an amiable cast in this comedy about a millionaire trying to break into the Hollywood scene with his rotten screenplays. When he falls in love with an employee from the Computron company (Rhea Perlman), they fix the TV ratings. Not rated, has profanity. 102m. **DIR:** Danny DeVito. **CAST:** Danny DeVito, Rhea Perlman, Gerrit Graham, Louis Giambalvo, Ronny Graham, Huntz Hall, Kevin McCarthy, John Megna, Michael Richards, Mark L. Taylor. **1984**

RAVISHING IDIOT, THE Thin plot concerns a spy out to steal NATO plans of ship movements. B&W; 110m. **DIR:** Edouard Molinaro. **CAST:** Anthony Perkins, Brigitte Bardot. 1965

REACHING FOR THE MOON (1917) ★★★ One of several products of the Douglas Fairbanks/Anita Loos/John Emerson triumvirate. Lots of brash, physical comedy and stunts in the early Fairbanks manner. Silent. B&W; 91m. **DIR:** John Emerson. **CAST:** Douglas Fairbanks Sr., Eileen Percy. 1917

REACHING FOR THE MOON (1931) ★★★ Robust and energetic Douglas Fairbanks plays a financier on whom liquor has an interesting effect. Edward Everett Horton is his valet and Bebe Daniels is the girl. B&W; 62m. **DIR:** Edmund Goulding. **CAST:** Douglas Fairbanks Sr., Bebe Daniels, Edward Everett Horton. 1931

REAL GENIUS ★★★ This is a mildly amusing comedy about a group of science prodigies (led by Val Kilmer) who decide to thwart the plans of their egomaniacal mentor (William Atherton). Director Martha Coolidge does her best to keep things interesting, but she can't overcome the predictability of the climax. Rated PG for profanity. 105m. **DIR:** Martha Coolidge. **CAST:** Val Kilmer, Gabe Jarret, Michelle Meyrink, William Atherton, Ed Lauter. 1985

REAL LIFE ★★★ Albert Brooks's fans will eat up this tasty satire parodying an unrelenting PBS series that put the day-to-day life of an American family under the microscope. In Brooks's film the typical family comes hilariously unglued under the omnipresent eye of the camera. The script (written by Brooks) eventually falters, but not before a healthy number of intelligent laughs are produced. Rated PG. 99m. **DIR:** Albert Brooks. **CAST:** Albert Brooks, Charles Grodin, Frances Lee McCain, J. A. Preston. 1979

REAL MEN ★★★ This action-filled comedy features James Belushi as an infallible Bond-like CIA agent. His latest mission is to protect his wimpish new partner (John Ritter) and make contact with powerful aliens. Rated PG-13 for profanity, violence, and brief nudity. 86m. **DIR:** Dennis Feldman. **CAST:** James Belushi, John Ritter, Bill Morey, Gail Barl, Barbara Barrie. 1987

REALLY WEIRD TALES ★★★ For cable fodder, these three odd short stories produced for HBO have their moments. Martin Short plays a hack lounge singer at a playboy's swank party in "All's Well That Ends Strange." "Cursed with Charisma" features John Candy as a hustler who takes the citizens of a small town for all they have. The last story, featuring Catherine O'Hara, is the best. "I'll Die Loving" is about a woman who is cursed with the odd power of loving people to death. Not rated, has profanity. 85m. **DIR:** Paul Lynch, Don McBrearty, John Blanchard. **CAST:** Joe Flaherty, John Candy, Catherine O'Hara, Martin Short, Dan Harron, Olivia D'Abo, Sheila McCarthy. 1986

RECKLESS KELLY ★★½ Australian comic Yahoo Serious returns in a spoof of the career of outlaw Ned Kelly, Australia's answer to Jesse James. Serious is an engaging performer, and the film is fast-paced, with bright, carnival-colored wide-screen photography (which will suffer on video). High-spirited and likable, it's just not funny. Rated PG. 80m. **DIR:** Yahoo Serious. **CAST:** Yahoo Serious, Melora Hardin, Alexei Sayle, Hugo Weaving, Kathleen Freeman. 1994

RECRUITS 💔 A sheriff hires hookers, thieves, and bums as deputies. Rated R. 90m. **DIR:** Rafal Zielinski. **CAST:** Alan Deveau, Annie McAuley. 1987

RED DWARF (TV SERIES) ★★★½ This wonderfully inventive British TV series is pure lunacy as the remnant crew of the *Red Dwarf*, a gigantic spaceship, hurtles through the universe millions of years in the future. Absolutely perfect casting, with Craig Charles as likable slob/hero Dave Lister and Chris Barrie as his obnoxious, repressed roommate. Each tape 84–90m. **DIR:** Ed Bye. **CAST:** Chris Barrie, Craig Charles, Danny John-Jules, Robert Llewellyn. 1988–1993

REEFER MADNESS ★★½ This 1930s anti-marijuana film is very silly, and sometimes funny. It's a cult film that really isn't as good as its reputation suggests. B&W; 67m. **DIR:** Louis J. Gasnier. **CAST:** Dave O'Brien, Dorothy Short, Warren McCollum, Lillian Miles, Carleton Young. 1936

REF, THE ★★★ Jewel thief Denis Leary soon regrets taking perennially bickering married couple Judy Davis and Kevin Spacey hostage in a ritzy neighborhood. It's supposed to be a black comedy, but it's just bleak at times, and lacks appealing characters. There are some very funny moments, though. Rated R for profanity and frank sexual discussions. 92m. **DIR:** Ted Demme. **CAST:** Denis Leary, Judy Davis, Kevin Spacey, Robert J. Steinmiller, Glynis Johns, Christine Baranski, Richard Bright, Adam Lefevre, Raymond J. Barry. 1994

REIVERS, THE ★★★★ Grand adaptation of the William Faulkner tale concerning a young boy (Mitch Vogel) who, with the help of his mischievous older friends (Steve McQueen and Rupert Crosse), "borrows" an automobile and heads for fun and excitement in 1905 Mississippi. The charming vignettes include a stopover in a brothel and a climactic horse race that could spell doom for the adventurers. Rated PG. 107m. **DIR:** Mark Rydell. **CAST:** Steve McQueen, Rupert Crosse, Will Geer, Sharon Farrell, Mitch Vogel, Michael Constantine. 1969

RELUCTANT DEBUTANTE, THE ★★★ Kay Kendall steals the show as the new stepmother of Rex Harrison's American-bred daughter. Angela Lansbury is deliciously vicious, as always, as Kendall's snooty cousin. 94m. **DIR:** Vincente Minnelli. **CAST:** Rex Harrison, Kay Kendall, Angela Lansbury, Sandra Dee, John Saxon. **1958**

RENTED LIPS 🦃 Martin Mull and Dick Shawn play inept documentary filmmakers (*Aluminum, Our Friend,* etc.) who agree to complete a porno film called *Halloween in the Bunker.* Rated R for profanity, nudity, and violence. 85m. **DIR:** Robert Downey. **CAST:** Martin Mull, Dick Shawn, Jennifer Tilly, Robert Downey Jr., June Lockhart, Pat McCormick, Eileen Brennan. **1988**

REPO MAN ★★★★ Wild, weird, and unpredictable, this film stars Emilio Estevez as a young man who gets into the repossession racket. Under the tutelage of Harry Dean Stanton (in a typically terrific performance), Estevez learns how to steal cars from people who haven't kept up their payments. Meanwhile, bizarre events lead them to an encounter with what may be beings from space. Those who occasionally like to watch something different will enjoy it. Rated R. 92m. **DIR:** Alex Cox. **CAST:** Emilio Estevez, Harry Dean Stanton, Vonetta McGee, Sy Richardson, Tracey Walter. **1984**

REPOSSESSED ★★★½ Linda Blair gets to make fun of the genre she is most associated with in this uproarious parody of *Exorcist*-style flicks. Nielsen is great as a priest who relates the story of a possessed housewife (Blair) and his attempts to exorcise the devil from within her. Rated PG-13 for language. 89m. **DIR:** Bob Logan. **CAST:** Linda Blair, Ned Beatty, Leslie Nielsen. **1990**

RESTLESS NATIVES ★★★½ Okay, so it's not perfect—the humor and the characterizations are broad and the thick, Scottish accents sometimes make the dialogue difficult to decipher. But that doesn't stop this film from being thoroughly entertaining. Two young Scots, disguised as a clown and a wolf-man, rob tourist buses and become national heroes in the process. Rated PG. 90m. **DIR:** Michael Hoffman. **CAST:** Vincent Friell, Joe Mulloney, Teri Lolly, Ned Beatty. **1986**

RETURN OF CAPTAIN INVINCIBLE, THE ★★½ Camp send-up of old comic-book-hero serials of the Thirties and Forties. Arkin is Captain Invincible, fighting crime and Nazis and preserving the American way of life. During the communist witch-hunt of the Fifties, though, the captain is accused of being a Red and quickly becomes a national disgrace. Alan Arkin flies high as Captain Invincible. Songs, special effects, and corny melodrama all combine to get you through the occasional dull bits. Rated PG for profanity and violence. 101m. **DIR:** Philippe Mora. **CAST:** Alan Arkin, Christopher Lee. **1984**

RETURN OF OCTOBER, THE ★★★ A girl thinks her uncle is reincarnated as the horse, October. This fun movie set the stage, tone, and sense of humor for body-switch movies that came along a generation later. 87m. **DIR:** Joseph H. Lewis. **CAST:** Glenn Ford, Terry Moore, James Gleason, May Whitty, Albert Sharpe, Henry O'Neill, Samuel S. Hinds, Nana Bryant, Jackie Gleason. **1948**

RETURN OF SPINAL TAP, THE ★★★★ The world's most lovable heavy-metal band is back in this wonderful follow-up to Rob Reiner's cult 1984 "rockumentary," *This Is Spinal Tap*. This time the boys are in their native England where they blend excellent live-concert footage (including some new songs), interviews with old friends, and recollections of their formative years. Great music and great fun. Not rated. 110m. **DIR:** Jim DiBergi. **CAST:** Christopher Guest, Michael McKean, Harry Shearer. **1993**

RETURN OF THE KILLER TOMATOES ★★½ The mad scientist, whose experiments caused the first tomato war, perfects his process that creates intelligent vegetable life. Although it lacks the spontaneous humor the original exhibited, this *Return* has its moments. Language may not be suitable for a younger audience. Rated PG. 99m. **DIR:** John DeBello. **CAST:** Anthony Starke, George Clooney, John Astin. **1988**

RETURN OF THE PINK PANTHER, THE ★★★★ Writer-director Blake Edwards and star Peter Sellers revived their Inspector Clouseau character for a new series of comic adventures beginning with this slapstick classic. There are many funny scenes as Sellers attempts to track down the Phantom (Christopher Plummer) while making life intolerable for the chief inspector (Herbert Lom). Rated PG. 113m. **DIR:** Blake Edwards. **CAST:** Peter Sellers, Christopher Plummer, Herbert Lom, Catherine Schell, Burt Kwouk, Peter Arne. **1975**

RETURN OF THE SECAUCUS 7 ★★★★½ Here's an absolute gem of a movie. Written, produced, and directed by John Sayles, it's a story about the reunion of seven friends ten years after they were wrongfully busted in Secaucus, New Jersey, while on their way to the last demonstration against the Vietnam war in Washington, D.C. It is a delicious blend of characterization, humor, and insight. No MPAA rating, but *Secaucus 7* has nudity, profanity, and implicit sex. 100m. **DIR:** John Sayles. **CAST:** Mark Arnott, Gordon Clapp, Maggie Cousineau, Adam Lefevre, Bruce MacDonald, Jean Passanante, Maggie Renzi. **1980**

RETURN TO MAYBERRY ★★½ Nostalgia time. Andy, Barney, and most of the gang are reunited in this TV-movie valentine to *The Andy Griffith Show.* The many plot lines include Opie's impending fatherhood,

Barney's campaign for sheriff, and the appearance of a monster in the lake. 95m. **DIR:** Bob Sweeney. **CAST:** Andy Griffith, Don Knotts, Ron Howard, Jim Nabors, George Lindsey, Aneta Corseaut, Betty Lynn. **1986**

REUBEN, REUBEN ★★★★½ A funny, touching, and memorable character study about an irascible Scottish poet, this film, directed by Robert Ellis Miller (*The Heart Is a Lonely Hunter*) and written by Julius J. Epstein (*Casablanca*), ranges from romantic to ribald, and from low-key believability to blistering black comedy. In short, it's a rare cinematic treat. First and foremost among the picture's assets is a superb leading performance by Tom Conti. Rated R for profanity and suggested sex. 101m. **DIR:** Robert Ellis Miller. **CAST:** Tom Conti, Kelly McGillis, Roberts Blossom, Cynthia Harris, E. Katherine Kerr, Joel Fabiani, Lois Smith. **1983**

REVENGE OF THE CHEERLEADERS 🦃 There were never any good *Cheerleaders* movies, but this one is about the worst of a bad bunch. Rated R for nudity and profanity. 88m. **DIR:** Richard Lerner. **CAST:** Jeril Woods, Rainbeaux Smith, Carl Ballantine, David Hasselhoff. **1976**

REVENGE OF THE NERDS ★★★ The title characters, Lewis (Robert Carradine) and Gilbert (Anthony Edwards), strike back at the jocks who torment them in this watchable, fitfully funny comedy. Rated R. 90m. **DIR:** Jeff Kanew. **CAST:** Robert Carradine, Anthony Edwards, Julie Montgomery, Curtis Armstrong, Ted McGinley, Michelle Meyrink, James Cromwell, Bernie Casey, Timothy Busfield. **1984**

REVENGE OF THE NERDS II: NERDS IN PARADISE 🦃 With this sequel, one assumes that the filmmakers were out for revenge against their audience. Rated PG-13 for profanity and tasteless humor. 95m. **DIR:** Joe Roth. **CAST:** Robert Carradine, Timothy Busfield, Curtis Armstrong, Larry B. Scott, Courtney Thorne-Smith, Anthony Edwards, Ed Lauter. **1987**

REVENGE OF THE NERDS III: THE NEXT GENERATION 🦃 The nerds take their act to television, giving new meaning to the term "boob tube." 93m. **DIR:** Roland Mesa. **CAST:** Robert Carradine, Ted McGinley, Curtis Armstrong, Morton Downey Jr. **1992**

REVENGE OF THE PINK PANTHER, THE ★★★★½ This is arguably the best of the slapstick series. It contains inspired bits penned by director Blake Edwards and played to perfection by Peter Sellers. Rated PG. 99m. **DIR:** Blake Edwards. **CAST:** Peter Sellers, Dyan Cannon, Robert Webber, Marc Lawrence, Herbert Lom, Burt Kwouk, Robert Loggia, Paul Stewart. **1978**

RHINESTONE 🦃 A country singer and a New York cabbie. Rated PG for profanity, sexual innuendo, and violence. 111m. **DIR:** Bob Clark. **CAST:** Sylvester Stallone, Dolly Parton, Richard Farnsworth, Ron Leibman. **1984**

RICH HALL'S VANISHING AMERICA ★★★ Rich Hall goes in search of the Junior Seed Sales Club. (When he was 8, he joined the club. He sold the seeds, but never got his prize of a Wilt Chamberlain basketball and hoop.) A number of guest stars are on hand for this look at a nostalgic era—a vanishing America. This enjoyable film was made for cable and is recommended for general audience viewing. 50m. **DIR:** Steve Rash. **CAST:** Rich Hall, M. Emmet Walsh, Peter Isacksen, Harry Anderson, Wilt Chamberlain. **1986**

RICH LITTLE—ONE'S A CROWD ★★½ Rich Little is both host and entire cast in a sort of "Greatest Hits" video album. Little is, of course, very good at his craft, but his self-written material is not always the best, and his unique talent wears a little thin after an hour or so. Not rated, but with mild profanity. 86m. **DIR:** Thomas E. Engel. **CAST:** Rich Little. **1988**

RICH LITTLE'S LITTLE SCAMS ON GOLF ★★ Rich Little's talents are wasted in this compendium of ways to cheat at golf. Extremely boring. Not rated. 44m. **DIR:** Kimberlie Chambers. **CAST:** Rich Little. **1991**

RICHARD LEWIS—"I'M EXHAUSTED" ★★½ A melancholy Richard Lewis supposedly collapses from exhaustion following his umpteenth performance. He feverishly flashes back to the stage from his hospital bed. Rapid-fire nightclub humor will either tickle your silly bone, or leave you, too...exhausted. Not rated. 57m. **DIR:** Bruce Gowers. **CAST:** Richard Lewis, Jackie Collins, Steve Allen, Larry King, Garry Shandling. **1988**

RICHARD LEWIS—"I'M IN PAIN CONCERT" ★★½ Richard Lewis is a bold, daring comic who tends to turn his mind inside out on stage. Reckless and risky, his neurotic improvisation seems honest, but lacks the manic mimicking of Robin Williams, a skill that would make this comedy concert far more entertaining. 60m. **DIR:** Charles Braverman. **CAST:** Richard Lewis, Billy Crystal, Robin Williams, Harold Ramis, Rob Reiner. **1986**

RICHARD PRYOR—HERE AND NOW ★★★★½ The popular comedian doing what he does best, stand-up comedy. Rated R for profanity. 83m. **DIR:** Richard Pryor. **CAST:** Richard Pryor. **1983**

RICHARD PRYOR—LIVE AND SMOKIN' ★★½ Disappointing comedy concert film featuring Richard Pryor. It's not boring, but Pryor is clearly unnerved by the presence of the film crew. While there are some nice bits, the laughs are few. Unrated, the film has profanity. 45m. **DIR:** Michael Blum. **CAST:** Richard Pryor. **1985**

RICHARD PRYOR—LIVE IN CONCERT ★★★★★ Richard Pryor's first live comedy performance film is still the best. Life has never been so sad and funny at the same time. Rated R for profanity. 78m. **DIR:** Jeff Margolis. **CAST:** Richard Pryor. **1979**

RICHARD PRYOR LIVE ON THE SUNSET STRIP ★★★ Richard Pryor's second concert film (and first film after his accidental burning) is highly watchable. *Live in Concert* and *Here and Now*, however, are superior. Rated R for nonstop profanity and vulgarity. 82m. **DIR:** Joe Layton. **CAST:** Richard Pryor. **1982**

RIDE 'EM COWBOY ★★★ Two hot-dog vendors find themselves in the wild West working on a dude ranch. Some funny bits, a good cast, and top musical numbers and talent (including Ella Fitzgerald) make this Abbott and Costello comedy one of the best in the series. B&W; 84m. **DIR:** Arthur Lubin. **CAST:** Bud Abbott, Lou Costello, Anne Gwynne, Dick Foran, Johnny Mack Brown, Samuel S. Hinds, Douglass Dumbrille. **1942**

RIDERS OF THE STORM 🦃 Dennis Hopper as the captain of an ancient B-29 that has been circling the country for fifteen years to broadcast an illegal television network. Rated R for nudity. 92m. **DIR:** Maurice Phillips. **CAST:** Dennis Hopper, Michael J. Pollard, Eugene Lipinski. **1987**

RIDING ON AIR ★★★ Lots of thrills and laughs in this topically dated comedy adventure about two small-town newspaper correspondents vying for the same girl and the scoop on a story. Joe E. Brown is, as always, warm, winning, and wholesome. B&W; 58m. **DIR:** Edward Sedgwick. **CAST:** Joe E. Brown, Florence Rice, Vinton Haworth, Guy Kibbee. **1937**

RIKKI AND PETE ★★★ An offbeat comedy from Australia. A geologist and her crazy brother abandon the city for the Australian outback. This film is a great crash course in living your own life. Highly engaging! Rated R for nudity and language. 101m. **DIR:** Nadia Tass. **CAST:** Nina Landis, Stephen Kearny, Bruce Spence, Bruno Lawrence. **1988**

RIO RITA ★★★ Vintage Bud Abbott and Lou Costello, with routines that somehow seem fresh and familiar at the same time. They stowaway in the trunk of a car thinking it is going to New York and end up at a Texas ranch infested with Nazi spies. B&W; 91m. **DIR:** S. Sylvan Simon. **CAST:** Bud Abbott, Lou Costello, Kathryn Grayson, John Carroll, Tom Conway, Barry Nelson. **1942**

RIPPING YARNS ★★★½ Wildly funny series featuring excellent writing by Monty Python members Michael Palin and Terry Jones. Palin is well cast in different roles as he romps through six vignettes that comically parody the social structure and history of the British empire. Originally produced for British TV, this double cassette features the following episodes: "Tomkin's Schooldays," "Escape from Stalag Luft 112B," "Golden Gordon," "The Testing of Eric Olthwaite," "Whinfrey's Last Case," and "The Curse of the Claw." Not rated. 180m. **DIR:** Jim Franklin, Alan Bell, Terry Hughes. **CAST:** Michael Palin. **1978**

RISKY BUSINESS ★★★★ An ordinarily well-behaved boy (Tom Cruise) goes wild when his parents are on vacation. His troubles begin when a gorgeous hooker (Rebecca DeMornay) who doesn't exactly have a heart of gold makes a house call. It's stylish, funny, and sexy—everything, in fact, that most movies of this kind generally are not. Rated R for nudity, profanity, and suggested sex. 99m. **DIR:** Paul Brickman. **CAST:** Tom Cruise, Rebecca DeMornay, Curtis Armstrong, Bronson Pinchot, Raphael Sbarge, Joe Pantoliano, Nicholas Pryor, Richard Masur. **1983**

RITA, SUE AND BOB TOO 🦃 This British flick follows a pair of best friends who lose their virginity to a man whose children they both baby-sit. Rated R for language. 90m. **DIR:** Alan Clarke. **CAST:** George Costigan, Siobhan Finneran, Michelle Holmes. **1986**

RITZ, THE ★★★★ This film is brimful of belly laughs that will leave you exhausted. After the death of his father-in-law, Jack Weston (as Geatano Proclo) flees Cleveland. His brother-in-law has put out a contract on him to prevent his inheriting any part of the family garbage business. His escape takes him to New York City and, by accident, a gay hotel called The Ritz. Rated R for profanity. 91m. **DIR:** Richard Lester. **CAST:** Jack Weston, Rita Moreno, Jerry Stiller, Kaye Ballard, F. Murray Abraham, Treat Williams. **1976**

ROAD LAWYERS AND OTHER BRIEFS ★★½ Three student-made films: "Road Lawyers," a *Mad Max* parody set in a future world where lawyers battle for clients; "Escape from Heaven," featuring an insufferable nun; and "Hairline," in which a man can't cope with losing his hair. Rounding out the package is a segment of the Fifties serial *Radar Men From the Moon* with new overdubbed (not very funny) dialogue. Unrated. 79m. **DIR:** Tim Doyle, James Desmarais, David Lipman, Robert Rhine. **1989**

ROAD TO BALI ★★★½ Excellent entry in the Bob Hope/Bing Crosby *Road* series. In this one the boys play a pair of vaudeville performers in competition for Dorothy Lamour, pursuing her to the South Seas island of Bali, where they must contend with all sorts of jungle dangers, from cannibalistic natives to various Hollywood stars who appear in hilarious (though very brief) cameos. The Humphrey Bogart scene is a classic. 90m. **DIR:** Hal Walker. **CAST:** Bob Hope, Bing Crosby, Dorothy Lamour, Murvyn Vye. **1952**

ROAD TO HONG KONG, THE ★★ Bob Hope and Bing Crosby play con men in this listless effort that involves international intrigue and space exploration. This was the last of the *Road* pictures, which means that Hope and Crosby made one *Road* picture too many. B&W; 91m. **DIR:** Norman Panama. **CAST:** Bing Crosby, Bob Hope, Joan Collins, Dorothy Lamour, Robert Morley, Peter Sellers. **1962**

ROAD TO RIO ★★★ More a straight comedy than madcap mayhem, this fifth *Road* show has Bob Hope and Bing Crosby hopping a boat to Rio de Janeiro. On board they meet and fall for Dorothy Lamour, who runs hot and cold because her wicked aunt (Gale Sondergaard) is hypnotizing her so she will accept an arranged marriage. Lots of laughs. B&W; 100m. **DIR:** Norman Z. McLeod. **CAST:** Bob Hope, Bing Crosby, Dorothy Lamour, Gale Sondergaard, Frank Faylen, Jerry Colonna, The Andrews Sisters. **1947**

ROAD TO RUIN (1991) ★★½ Decent romance features a playboy millionaire signing away his money in order to see if a beautiful model really loves him. Predictable time passer. Rated PG-13 for sexual situations. 94m. **DIR:** Charlotte Brandstrom. **CAST:** Peter Weller, Carey Lowell, Michel Duchaussoy. **1991**

ROAD TO SINGAPORE ★★★½ Two happy-go-lucky adventurers on the lam from responsibility end up in the tropics where they sing and perform with local lovely Dorothy Lamour, the object of their affection and rivalry. This breezy film was the first of seven pictures that cemented Bob Hope and Bing Crosby as a top comedy team and provided some of the easiest laughs of the 1940s. (This longtime Paramount property had at various times been considered for George Burns and Gracie Allen and then Fred MacMurray and Jack Oakie.) B&W; 85m. **DIR:** Victor Schertzinger. **CAST:** Bing Crosby, Bob Hope, Dorothy Lamour, Charles Coburn, Anthony Quinn, Jerry Colonna, Johnny Arthur, Miles Mander. **1940**

ROAD TO UTOPIA ★★★ The Klondike and a hunt for an Alaskan gold mine provide the background for this fourth of the seven *Roads* Bob Hope, Bing Crosby, and Dorothy Lamour traveled between 1940 and 1962. Rated the best of the bunch by fans, it's a mix of songs, sight gags, wisecracks, inside jokes, hoke, and the usual love triangle. B&W; 90m. **DIR:** Hal Walker. **CAST:** Bob Hope, Bing Crosby, Dorothy Lamour, Hillary Brooke, Douglass Dumbrille, Jack LaRue, Robert Benchley. **1945**

ROAD TO ZANZIBAR ★★★★ Bob Hope and Bing Crosby play two fast-talking con men always just ahead of the authorities and ready to chuck everything for a sob story from a female. The story takes the adventurers to Africa in search of a diamond mine (and Dorothy Lamour!), but the funniest moments come as Fearless Frazier (Hope) is talked into one outlandishly dangerous stunt after another. B&W; 90m. **DIR:** Victor Schertzinger. **CAST:** Bing Crosby, Bob Hope, Dorothy Lamour, Una Merkel, Eric Blore, Iris Adrian, Douglass Dumbrille, Joan Marsh, Luis Alberni, Leo Gorcey. **1941**

ROBIN HOOD: MEN IN TIGHTS ★★½ Director Mel Brooks's rude comic shtick seems pretty shopworn these days, although there are some genuine laughs in this send-up of swashbucklers. For more of the same, see *When Things Were Rotten*, Brooks's 1975 TV comedy featuring the same characters and ideas. Rated PG-13 for brief profanity, scatological humor, and sexual references. 104m. **DIR:** Mel Brooks. **CAST:** Cary Elwes, Richard Lewis, Roger Rees, Amy Yasbeck, Mark Blankfield, Dave Chappelle, Isaac Hayes, Megan Cavanaugh, Tracey Ullman, Patrick Stewart, Dom DeLuise, Dick Van Patten, Mel Brooks. **1993**

ROBIN WILLIAMS LIVE ★★★★ An always funny and sometimes hilarious live performance by one of comedy's premier talents. Irreverent and vulgar, Williams doesn't so much shock as he carefully picks sensitive factors of the human condition. He will then immediately switch to impressions of Jack Nicholson debating Clint Eastwood. In the funniest portion of the show, he attacks our sexual practices and mocks radio sex therapists. Not rated, but contains profanity and many sexual references. Recommended for adult audiences. 65m. **DIR:** Bruce Cowers. **CAST:** Robin Williams. **1986**

ROCK 'N' ROLL HIGH SCHOOL ★★★½ The stern new principal tries to turn a school into a concentration camp. The popular Riff (P. J. Soles) goes against the principal by playing loud Ramones music all the time. Meanwhile, boring Tom (Vincent Van Patten) has a crush on Riff. The film includes lots of laughs and good rock 'n' roll music—a cult favorite. Rated PG. 93m. **DIR:** Allan Arkush. **CAST:** P. J. Soles, Vincent Van Patten, Clint Howard, Dey Young, The Ramones. **1979**

ROCK 'N' ROLL HIGH SCHOOL FOREVER 🦃 Superlame sequel to the cult hit. Rated PG-13 for profanity. 94m. **DIR:** Deborah Brock. **CAST:** Corey Feldman, Mary Woronov, Larry Linville. **1990**

ROCK 'N' ROLL WRESTLING WOMEN VS. THE AZTEC MUMMY 🦃 Some folks found this old Mexican horror flick and attempted to turn it into a comedy by redubbing the dialogue, giving it a comical rock 'n' roll sound track, and retitling it. Not rated; has violence. B&W; 88m. **DIR:** René Cardona Sr., Manuel San Fernando. **CAST:** Lorena Velazquez, Armand Silvestre. **1986**

ROCKIN' RONNIE ★★★ Hilariously manic collage of Ronald Reagan's films, commercials, and political statements is irreverently blended. Slick, rapid-fire clips. 45m.

DIR: Stuart Samuels. **CAST:** Ronald Reagan, Nancy Reagan. **1986**

RODNEY DANGERFIELD: "IT'S NOT EASY BEING ME" ★★ Humdrum comic showcase for a new bunch of stand-up comedians. The show is hosted by Dangerfield, whose contributions are limited to a short routine, and screamingly unfunny buffer vignettes between the acts. Most of the show is badly edited to boot. Not rated; the movie contains vulgar language. 59m. **DIR:** Walter C. Miller. **CAST:** Rodney Dangerfield, Jeff Altman, Roseanne Arnold, Sam Kinnison, Bob Nelson, Jerry Seinfeld, Robert Townsend. **1986**

RODNEY DANGERFIELD—NOTHIN' GOES RIGHT ★★ Rodney Dangerfield introduces several aspiring stand-up comics at his comedy club, Dangerfield's, and provides "cameo" jokes between the acts. Robert Schimmel and Barry Sobel are the best of the bunch, but none of them is very funny, and much of the humor will be offensive to blacks, gays, foreigners, and especially women. Not rated, but there is much profanity and some very frank discussions of sex. 83m. **DIR:** Walter C. Miller. **CAST:** Rodney Dangerfield. **1988**

ROMANCE WITH A DOUBLE BASS ★★★½ Monty Python madman John Cleese stars in this delightfully silly vignette about a double-bass player and a princess who are caught naked in a pond when a thief makes off with their clothes. The ensuing romance will tickle and charm most adult viewers with its refreshing subtlety, but a word of caution for parents: This short will not win any awards for costume design. 40m. **DIR:** Robert Young. **CAST:** John Cleese, Connie Booth, Graham Crowden, Desmond Jones, Freddie Jones, Andrew Sachs. **1974**

ROMANTIC COMEDY ★★★ In this enjoyable comedy, based on the 1979 Broadway play, Dudley Moore and Mary Steenburgen star as two collaborating playwrights who, during their long association, suffer from "unsynchronized passion." Rated PG for profanity and suggested sex. 103m. **DIR:** Arthur Hiller. **CAST:** Dudley Moore, Mary Steenburgen, Frances Sternhagen, Janet Eilber, Robyn Douglass, Ron Leibman. **1983**

RON REAGAN IS THE PRESIDENT'S SON 🦃 Junior should leave the acting to papa. 60m. **DIR:** Jim Yukich. **CAST:** Ron Reagan. **1987**

ROOM SERVICE ★★★ After leaving his brothers (Groucho, Harpo, and Chico) to try movie producing, Zeppo Marx came up with this Broadway play about a foundering stage production and attempted to have it rewritten to suit his siblings' talents. He wasn't completely successful, but this romp does have its moments. Look for Lucille Ball and Ann Miller in early supporting roles. B&W; 78m. **DIR:** William A. Seiter. **CAST:** The Marx Brothers, Lucille Ball, Ann Miller. **1938**

ROSALIE GOES SHOPPING ★★★½ The *Bagdad Café* gang is back with another bit of quirky American-landscape comedy. German writer-director Percy Adlon and his talented German star Marianne Sägebrecht tackle consumer greed, credit card debt, and true love in this offbeat tale of an eccentric Little Rock, Arkansas family. Rated PG. 94m. **DIR:** Percy Adlon. **CAST:** Marianne Sägebrecht, Brad Davis. **1990**

ROSEANNE BARR SHOW, THE ★★★½ This HBO comedy special showcases Roseanne Barr in her stand-up routine and mixes in scenes with her family in the old mobile home. Made before her meteoric rise to stardom, this could have served as the inspiration for her hit TV series. Rated R for language not allowed on her weekly sitcom. 60m. **DIR:** Rocco Urbishi. **CAST:** Roseanne Arnold. **1987**

ROSEBUD BEACH HOTEL, THE 🦃 Colleen Camp and Peter Scolari take over her father's failing hotel and hire prostitutes as bellgirls to improve business. Rated R. 82m. **DIR:** Harry Hurwitz. **CAST:** Colleen Camp, Peter Scolari, Christopher Lee, Hamilton Camp, Eddie Deezen, Chuck McCann, Hank Garrett. **1985**

ROSENCRANTZ AND GUILDENSTERN ARE DEAD ★★★½ Filmization of Tom Stoppard's immensely witty Shakespearean spin-off, which changes the tone of *Hamlet* from tragedy to comedy. The screen version marks the playwright's debut as a director. Rated PG. 118m. **DIR:** Tom Stoppard. **CAST:** Gary Oldman, Tim Roth, Richard Dreyfuss. **1991**

ROUND NUMBERS ★★ A dowdy woman suspects her husband is cheating. Uneven and frequently amateurish sex comedy. Rated R for profanity and nudity. 98m. **DIR:** Nancy Zala. **CAST:** Kate Mulgrew, Samantha Eggar. **1992**

ROUND TRIP TO HEAVEN ★★½ Corey Feldman drags cousin Zach Galligan along to Palm Springs in a stolen Rolls to meet a super model. Typical chase film. Rated R for violence, nudity, and language. 97m. **DIR:** Alan Roberts. **CAST:** Corey Feldman, Zach Galligan, Ray Sharkey, Julie McCullough. **1991**

ROXANNE ★★★★½ Steve Martin's most effective and rewarding comedy since *All of Me*. Martin, who wrote the screenplay, based on Rostand's *Cyrano de Bergerac*, plays the big-nosed fire chief of a small town who befriends a professional firefighter (Rick Rossovich) who has come to help train the inept local firemen. While doing so, he meets and falls in love with the title character (Daryl Hannah) and soon enlists Martin's aid in wooing her with words. Rated PG for profanity and suggested sex. 107m. **DIR:** Fred Schepisi. **CAST:** Steve Martin, Daryl Hannah, Shelley Duvall, Rick Rossovich, Michael J. Pollard, Fred Willard. **1987**

RSVP ★★★ This is an out-and-out sex comedy with lots of nudity and sexual situations. An author has written a novel that turns out to be based on fact. The people who inspired the "characters" have been invited to a Hollywood party to celebrate the making of a movie from the book. The writing is lively, and the puns and gags are funny. Rated R for sexual situations and language that will be offensive to some. 87m. **DIR:** John Almo, Lem Almo. **CAST:** Ray Colbert, Veronica Hart, Carey Hayes. **1984**

RUBIN & ED ★★ Wannabe salesman Howard Hesseman must bring someone—anyone—to his success seminar. The only one he can convince is a very weird Sixties throwback (Crispin Glover) who insists on burying his cat on the way. Plain strange. Rated PG-13 for profanity. 82m. **DIR:** Trent Harris. **CAST:** Crispin Glover, Howard Hesseman, Karen Black, Michael Greene. **1991**

RUDE AWAKENING (1989) ★★★ In 1969 two draft dodgers (Cheech Marin and Eric Roberts) flee from the FBI and drop out to Central America until a twist of fate fans their liberal fires and propels them to New York City in 1989. Rated R for language. 100m. **DIR:** Aaron Russo. **CAST:** Richard "Cheech" Marin, Eric Roberts, Julie Hagerty, Robert Carradine, Buck Henry, Louise Lasser, Cindy Williams, Andrea Martin, Cliff De Young. **1989**

RUGGLES OF RED GAP ★★★★½ Charles Laughton is superb as Ruggles, the valet who is lost in a poker game by a continental gentleman (Roland Young) to Americans (Charlie Ruggles and Mary Boland). The latter take him from Paris to the wilds of 1908 Washington State. Hilarious. B&W; 92m. **DIR:** Leo McCarey. **CAST:** Charles Laughton, Mary Boland, Charlie Ruggles, ZaSu Pitts, Roland Young, Leila Hyams. **1935**

RULING CLASS, THE ★★★★ Superbly irreverent satire about upper-crust British eccentricities. Peter O'Toole plays the heir to a peerage who proves problematic because of his insane belief that he is Jesus Christ. Rated PG. 154m. **DIR:** Peter Medak. **CAST:** Peter O'Toole, Alastair Sim, Arthur Lowe, Harry Andrews, Coral Browne. **1972**

RUN FOR YOUR MONEY, A ★★★★ A pair of Welsh miners in London for a day get into more than their share of misadventures. One of the best of the Ealing Studios comedies—if you're a fan of British humor, this one's a must-see. B&W; 83m. **DIR:** Charles Frend. **CAST:** Alec Guinness, Meredith Edwards, Moira Lister, Donald Houston, Hugh Griffith. **1949**

RUNNING KIND, THE ★★★★ The straitlaced scion (David Packer) of an Akron, Ohio family takes the summer off from dad's law firm to follow a sexy, free-thinking rock drummer (Brie Howard) into the bowels of Los Angeles's punk scene. A marvelously inventive comedy from writer-director Max Tash. Rated R for profanity and brief violence. 90m. **DIR:** Max Tash. **CAST:** David Packer, Brie Howard. **1989**

RUNNING MATES (1992) ★★★ Political vulnerability is the topic of A. L. Appling's script, which concerns the fallout resulting from presidential candidate Ed Harris's growing involvement with children's book author Diane Keaton (whose condescending behavior wears thin *very* quickly). Alas, this made-for-cable romantic comedy concludes unsatisfyingly, without confronting this issue of privacy versus the public's right to know. 88m. **DIR:** Michael Lindsay-Hogg. **CAST:** Diane Keaton, Ed Harris, Ed Begley Jr., Ben Masters, Russ Tamblyn. **1992**

RUNNING WILD (1927) ★★ W. C. Fields is miscast and overplays his role of a toady worm suddenly turned (by hypnotism) into a coarse, violent lion—mean to family, friends, and dog. Far from vintage Fields, this film is a disappointing outing for his comic genius. Silent with titles. B&W; 68m. **DIR:** Gregory La Cava. **CAST:** W. C. Fields, Mary Brian, Claude Buchanan. **1927**

RUSSIANS ARE COMING, THE RUSSIANS ARE COMING, THE ★★★½ A Russian submarine runs aground off Nantucket Island, and the townspeople go gaga, not knowing what to do first, get guns or pour vodka. Cued by Alan Arkin's engaging portrayal of an out-of-his-depth Russian sailor, the cast delivers a solid comedy as cultures clash. With Jonathan Winters aboard, think wacky. 120m. **DIR:** Norman Jewison. **CAST:** Alan Arkin, Carl Reiner, Paul Ford, Theodore Bikel, Brian Keith, Jonathan Winters, Eva Marie Saint. **1966**

RUSSKIES ★★½ A sweet-natured Russian sailor (Whip Hubley) becomes stranded in Key West, Florida, when a raft capsizes and aborts a secret mission. He finds three youngsters who eventually agree to help him escape. The cast is appealing, but the laughs aren't frequent enough. Rated PG-13 for slight violence and profanity. 90m. **DIR:** Rick Rosenthal. **CAST:** Whip Hubley, Leaf Phoenix, Peter Billingsley, Charles Frank. **1987**

RUSTLER'S RHAPSODY ★★★ In this fun spoof of the singing cowboy movies of the 1930s, 1940s, and 1950s, Tom Berenger plays the horseback crooner of them all, Rex O'Herlihan. Viewers need to be familiar with the old B Westerns to get the jokes. If you are, it's a hoot. Rated PG for mild violence and slight profanity. 88m. **DIR:** Hugh Wilson. **CAST:** Tom Berenger, G. W. Bailey, Marilu Henner, Andy Griffith, Fernando Rey, Patrick Wayne. **1985**

RUTHLESS PEOPLE ★★★★½ Hollywood's only three-man directing team comes up with another comedy classic. Danny De-

Vito decides to murder his obnoxious wife, played by Bette Midler. But when he arrives home to carry out the deed, he discovers she has been abducted. The kidnappers demand fifty thousand dollars "or else." Exactly what DeVito has in mind, so he refuses to pay a cent. Rated R for nudity and profanity. 90m. **DIR:** Jim Abrahams, David Zucker, Jerry Zucker. **CAST:** Danny DeVito, Bette Midler, Judge Reinhold, Helen Slater, Anita Morris, Bill Pullman. **1986**

S.O.B. ★★★ Director Blake Edwards vents his resentment over Hollywood's treatment of him in the early 1970s in this failed attempt at satire. There are some good moments, but too few. Self-indulgent. Rated R. 121m. **DIR:** Blake Edwards. **CAST:** Julie Andrews, William Holden, Robert Preston, Richard Mulligan, Robert Vaughn, Loretta Swit, Larry Hagman, Craig Stevens, Shelley Winters, Rosanna Arquette. **1981**

SABRINA ★★★★ Elfin Audrey Hepburn shines in the title role. She's the simple chauffeur's daughter who is swept off her feet by wealthy rake William Holden. Humphrey Bogart, as Holden's business-minded brother, attempts to save her from the ne'er-do-well. Director Billy Wilder paces things with his usual deft touch. B&W; 113m. **DIR:** Billy Wilder. **CAST:** Audrey Hepburn, Humphrey Bogart, William Holden, John Williams. **1954**

SAD SACK, THE ★★½ Jerry Lewis in the army. That's all the plot there is in this better-than-average Lewis vehicle which, as usual, will please his fans and annoy all others. 98m. **DIR:** George Marshall. **CAST:** Jerry Lewis, David Wayne, Phyllis Kirk, Peter Lorre. **1957**

SAM KINNISON LIVE! ★★★½ Once a balls-of-fire preacher, Sam Kinnison, the crazed screaming comic, still divides audiences squarely in half. His fans, the believers, idolize him. Detractors think him loud, crude, and one-dimensional. His routines are anything but subtle. It's gonzo, frontal-assault humor, an aggressive take-no-prisoners approach that will leave you livid or laughing out loud. Rated R. 50m. **DIR:** Walter C. Miller. **CAST:** Sam Kinnison. **1987**

SAMANTHA ★★★ Upon learning she was adopted, a 21-year-old eccentric sets about to discover her "real" self. Martha Plimpton's acerbic lead performance helps to balance a too-cute script. A pleasant diversion. Rated PG for profanity. 101m. **DIR:** Stephen La Rocque. **CAST:** Martha Plimpton, Dermot Mulroney, Hector Elizondo, Mary Kay Place, Ione Skye. **1992**

SAME TIME NEXT YEAR ★★★★ Funny, touching film begins with an accidental meeting in 1951 between two married strangers at a rural California inn. Doris (Ellen Burstyn) is a young housewife from California, and George (Alan Alda) an accountant from New Jersey. Their meetings become an annual event. And through them, we see the changes in America and its people as we return to the same cottage every five years until 1977. Rated PG. 117m. **DIR:** Robert Mulligan. **CAST:** Ellen Burstyn, Alan Alda. **1978**

SAMMY AND ROSIE GET LAID ★★★★ Excellent sexual farce set in riot-torn East London concerns a young married couple who receive an unexpected visit from Sammy's father, an arrogant politician who is fleeing from a Middle Eastern country. His world becomes shaken up by the couple's sexually liberated, anarchic friends. Outrageous comedy from the creators of *My Beautiful Laundrette*. Not rated, but contains nudity and violence. 97m. **DIR:** Stephen Frears. **CAST:** Shashi Kapoor, Frances Barber, Claire Bloom, Ayub Khan Din. **1987**

SAPS AT SEA ★★★ Oliver Hardy contracts "hornophobia," and the only cure is rest and sea air. Comic timing is off and some of the jokes misfire, but enough of them work to make the movie enjoyable. B&W; 57m. **DIR:** Gordon Douglas. **CAST:** Oliver Hardy, Stan Laurel, Ben Turpin. **1940**

SARATOGA ★★★ When Jean Harlow learns her late father lost control of their racehorse farm to bookie Clark Gable, she plots to win it back. Harlow died during production; many scenes were completed by her stand-in. B&W; 92m. **DIR:** Jack Conway. **CAST:** Clark Gable, Jean Harlow, Lionel Barrymore, Frank Morgan, Walter Pidgeon, Una Merkel, Hattie McDaniel. **1937**

SATURDAY NIGHT LIVE ★★★½ *Saturday Night Live* was to the 1970s what *Your Show of Shows* was to the 1950s and *Rowan & Martin's Laugh-In* to the 1960s—a hit comedy-variety show that reflected the times. Its nucleus was The Not Ready For Prime Time Players, a group of talented yet struggling comedians assembled by producer Lorne Michaels. John Belushi, Chevy Chase, Dan Aykroyd, Bill Murray, and Jane Curtin all based successful careers on their initial fame earned on the show. 64m. **DIR:** Dave Wilson. **CAST:** John Belushi, Chevy Chase, Dan Aykroyd, Bill Murray, Gilda Radner, Jane Curtin, Laraine Newman, Garrett Morris, Steve Martin, Lily Tomlin, George Carlin, Richard Pryor, Ray Charles, Rodney Dangerfield. **1975–1980**

SATURDAY NIGHT SLEAZIES ★★ Each of these three volumes re-creates the experience of attending an adults-only movie house in the mid-1960s. Aside from two tacky movies whose plots range from ridiculously melodramatic to broadly comic, each tape features coming attractions and short subjects. Volume one features *College Girl Confidential* and *Suburban Confidential*; volume two, *Lady Godiva Meets Tom Jones* and *Bachelor's Dream*; volume three, *Motel Confidential* and *Office Love-In*. Unrated, but still not for kids of any age. Approximately 150m per tape. **DIR:** A. C. Stephen.

SAVAGES (1973) ★★★ James Ivory's offbeat look at society, in which a naked group of primitives find their sacrificial rites disrupted by a croquet ball. This discovery leads them to a deserted mansion where an odd cluster of events culminates in a transformation in which they are civilized. Unrated, contains nudity and violence. 108m. **DIR:** James Ivory. **CAST:** Lewis J. Stadlen, Anne Francine, Thayer David, Salome Jens. **1973**

SAVING GRACE ★★★★ The pope (Tom Conti), frustrated with his lack of freedom, finds himself in the small, depressed Italian village of Montepetra where he gets back to helping people on a one-on-one basis. *Saving Grace* is very good, showing moments of conflict with the human element exposed in all its emotions. Rated PG for violence and profanity. 112m. **DIR:** Robert M. Young. **CAST:** Tom Conti, Fernando Rey, Edward James Olmos, Giancarlo Giannini, Erland Josephson. **1986**

SAY ANYTHING ★★★½ So many things are right with this comedy-drama about first love that one can't help wincing when it takes a wrong turn. Yet everything else is honest in its depiction of a well-meaning, unexceptional guy (John Cusack) who falls in love with a seemingly unattainable beauty with brains (Ione Skye). It's a minor gem from first-time director Cameron Crowe, who wrote *Fast Times at Ridgemont High*. Rated PG-13 for suggested sex and profanity. 100m. **DIR:** Cameron Crowe. **CAST:** John Cusack, Ione Skye, John Mahoney. **1989**

SAY YES ★★½ A multimillionaire (Jonathan Winters) dies, leaving his estate to his son (Art Hindle) on the condition that he marry before his thirty-fifth birthday—only a day away. The comedy doesn't work most of the time, but the story is cute enough to tolerate. Rated PG-13 for sex, nudity, and profanity. 87m. **DIR:** Larry Yust. **CAST:** Art Hindle, Lissa Layng, Logan Ramsey, Jonathan Winters, Maryedith Burrell, Anne Ramsey. **1986**

SCANDALOUS (1983) ★★ Robert Hays plays an investigative reporter who gets mixed up with spies, con men, and murder in London. The cast includes Pamela Stephenson and John Gielgud, as a pair of con artists. Gielgud seems to be having a grand old time playing everything from an old Chinese man to the world's oldest punk rocker. Rated PG for profanity, nudity, and brief violence. 93m. **DIR:** Rob Byrum. **CAST:** Robert Hays, Pamela Stephenson, John Gielgud, Jim Dale, M. Emmet Walsh. **1983**

SCAVENGER HUNT 🦃 *It's a Mad Mad Mad Mad World* writhes again as a bunch of wackos run hither, thither, and yawn. Rated PG. 117m. **DIR:** Michael Schultz. **CAST:** Richard Benjamin, James Coco, Scatman Crothers, Ruth Gordon, Cloris Leachman, Roddy McDowall, Cleavon Little, Robert Morley, Richard Mulligan, Tony Randall, Vincent Price. **1979**

SCAVENGERS 🦃 Miami University professor and his ex-girlfriend against the CIA, KGB, and a local African drug kingpin. Rated PG-13 for violence. 94m. **DIR:** Duncan McLachlan. **CAST:** Kenneth Gilman, Brenda Bakke, Ken Gampu. **1988**

SCENES FROM A MALL ★★ It would be hard to imagine a drearier comedy than this uninspired tale of a married couple (Woody Allen, Bette Midler) breaking up and making up as they romp through a Beverly Hills shopping mall. Only the film's first twenty minutes—a sprightly introduction of the two main characters—make it worth watching. Rated R for profanity. 87m. **DIR:** Paul Mazursky. **CAST:** Bette Midler, Woody Allen, Bill Irwin. **1991**

SCENES FROM THE CLASS STRUGGLE IN BEVERLY HILLS ★★★★ Director Paul Bartel helms this bizarre sexual romp through the lives of the glamorous Tinseltown set. Jacqueline Bisset is delicious as a neurotic ex-sitcom star whose television comeback is complicated by her dead husband (Paul Mazursky), who keeps materializing while pledging his infernal love to her. This offbeat adult comedy is rated R for nudity and profanity. 95m. **DIR:** Paul Bartel. **CAST:** Jacqueline Bisset, Ray Sharkey, Ed Begley Jr., Paul Mazursky, Wallace Shawn, Robert Beltran. **1989**

SCHLOCK ★★★ Directed by and starring John Landis, this film is a spoof of not only "missing link" monster movies but other types of horror and science-fiction films. This is Landis's first film, and while it doesn't have the laughs of his later effort, *Animal House*, it does include some chuckles of its own. Rated PG. 80m. **DIR:** John Landis. **CAST:** John Landis, Saul Kahan, Joseph Piantadosi. **1971**

SCHOOL DAZE ★★★½ Writer-director Spike Lee tries to get people to wake up not only to the conflict in South Africa, but also the problems that exist among different factions of the black community. Too much time is spent on a silly subplot involving a college fraternity; however, the film features some first-rate production numbers and a fine musical score by the filmmaker's father, Bill Lee. Rated R for profanity and nudity. 120m. **DIR:** Spike Lee. **CAST:** Larry Fishburne, Giancarlo Esposito, Tisha Campbell, Spike Lee, Ossie Davis. **1988**

SCHOOL FOR SCANDAL ★★½ Richard Sheridan's eighteenth-century comedy about philandering and infidelity became a decent but basically crude and static film in this early adaptation. The limitations of early sound techniques are painfully obvious in this stage-bound presentation. B&W; 75m.

DIR: Maurice Elvey. CAST: Madeleine Carroll, Basil Gill, Ian Fleming. 1930

SCHOOL SPIRIT 🦃 Stupid high school flick about an obnoxious libido case (Tom Nolan) who dies in an auto accident and returns as a ghost. Not rated, but an easy R for nudity and profanity. 90m. DIR: Alan Holleb. CAST: Tom Nolan, Elizabeth Foxx, Larry Linville. 1985

SCOUNDREL, THE ★★★½ After his untimely death, an arrogant writer (Noel Coward) is sent back to earth to make amends for the grief he caused. The combination of Coward and dialogue by Ben Hecht and Charles MacArthur is to die for, even if the plot is thin. B&W; 78m. DIR: Ben Hecht, Charles MacArthur. CAST: Noel Coward, Julie Haydon, Stanley Ridges, Alexander Woollcott, Lionel Stander. 1935

SCREEN TEST 🦃 Teenage boys pose as film producers in order to audition beautiful women nude. Rated R. 84m. DIR: Sam Auster. CAST: Michael Allan Bloom, Robert Bundy. 1986

SCREWBALL ACADEMY 🦃 When a production company tries to make a movie in a small beachfront town, assorted loonies come out of the closet. Reuben Rose is former *SCTV* director John Blanchard under a pseudonym. Rated R for profanity. 90m. DIR: Reuben Rose. CAST: Colleen Camp, Kenneth Welsh. 1987

SCREWBALLS 🦃 Teen-lust comedy takes place at Taft and Adams Educational Center, otherwise known as "T&A High." Rated R for nudity and profanity. 80m. DIR: Rafal Zielinski. CAST: Peter Keleghan, Linda Speciale, Linda Shayne. 1983

SCROOGED ★★½ The power of Charles Dickens's uncredited source material and an energetic turn by Carol Kane as the Ghost of Christmas Present save this bloated comedy from total disaster. Bill Murray waltzes through his role as a venal television executive. Rated PG-13 for language. 101m. DIR: Richard Donner. CAST: Bill Murray, Karen Allen, John Forsythe, John Glover, Bob Goldthwait, Carol Kane, Robert Mitchum, Alfre Woodard. 1988

SEARCH FOR SIGNS OF INTELLIGENT LIFE IN THE UNIVERSE, THE ★★★★ As Trudy says in *The Search for Signs of Intelligent Life in the Universe*, reality "is nothing but a collective hunch." But the hunch that evolves from the fertile imaginations of actress Lily Tomlin and writer Jane Wagner is funny, perceptive, and right on target. Trudy, a bag lady in touch with alien life-forms, is just one of a dozen diverse characters brought to life in a bravura performance by Tomlin, cleverly adapted from her one-woman play. Rated PG-13. 109m. DIR: John Bailey. CAST: Lily Tomlin. 1991

SECOND CITY COMEDY SHOW, THE ★★ Those looking for a laugh-a-minute good time should look elsewhere. This basic waste of video is saved only by the presence of John Candy. With this tape we can see why he eventually joined the ranks of other Second City graduates on the big screen. Not rated. 60m. DIR: Perry Rosemond. CAST: John Candy, Fred Willard, Tim Kazurinsky, Gloria Gaynor. 1979

SECOND SIGHT ★★ Silly rip-off of *Ghostbusters* stars John Larroquette as the head of a detective agency that solves its cases with the help of a mystic (Bronson Pinchot). TV-sitcom–style shtick. Rated PG for profanity and violence. 85m. DIR: Joel Zwick. CAST: John Larroquette, Bronson Pinchot, Bess Armstrong, Stuart Pankin, John Schuck, James Tolkan. 1989

SECRET ADMIRER ★★½ A sweet-natured sex comedy that suffers from predictability, this stars C. Thomas Howell as a 16-year-old who, on the last day of school before summer vacation, receives an anonymous letter from a female who swears undying love. He hopes it's from the girl of his dreams (Kelly Preston) and decides to find out. Rated R for nudity, light violence, and profanity. 100m. DIR: David Greenwalt. CAST: C. Thomas Howell, Lori Loughlin, Kelly Preston, Dee Wallace, Cliff De Young, Fred Ward, Leigh Taylor-Young. 1985

SECRET CINEMA, THE ★★½ While working for a TV commercial production company in New York, Paul Bartel made this short film. It's a super-low-budget surreal comedy about a woman who becomes the victim of a diabolical director, who secrectly films her life with hidden cameras. Also on the program is a 7-minute erotic short called "Naughty Nurse." 37m. DIR: Paul Bartel. CAST: Amy Vane. 1967

SECRET DIARY OF SIGMUND FREUD, THE ★★★½ *The Secret Diary of Sigmund Freud* is a consistently humorous satire on the early life of Freud. Everyone in the cast looks to be having a swell time. Sexual and psychological jokes abound. That they are flamboyantly funny is no small feat. Rated PG. 129m. DIR: Danford B. Greene. CAST: Bud Cort, Carol Kane, Klaus Kinski, Marisa Berenson, Carroll Baker, Ferdinand Mayne, Dick Shawn. 1984

SECRET LIFE OF AN AMERICAN WIFE, THE ★★ Bored wife Anne Jackson decides to moonlight as a call girl. Her first client is her husband's employer. Husband walks in on wife and employer, etc. Director and writer George Axelrod had a cute idea, but it really doesn't gel. 93m. DIR: George Axelrod. CAST: Walter Matthau, Anne Jackson, Patrick O'Neal, Edy Williams, Richard Bull. 1968

SECRET LIFE OF WALTER MITTY, THE ★★★★ Based on James Thurber's story, this comedy presents Danny Kaye as a timid man who dreams of being a brave, glory-bound hero. This comedy provides plenty of laughs and enjoyable moments. 105m. **DIR:** Norman Z. McLeod. **CAST:** Danny Kaye, Virginia Mayo, Boris Karloff, Reginald Denny, Florence Bates, Ann Rutherford, Thurston Hall. **1947**

SECRET OF MY SUCCESS, THE ★★★½ The secret of this movie's success can be found in its ingredients: a witty script, vibrant direction, bouncy pop score, ingratiating star, and gifted supporting cast. Michael J. Fox is terrifically likable as a wildly ambitious Kansas lad who heads for New York City with plans to conquer the corporate world overnight. Rated PG-13. 110m. **DIR:** Herbert Ross. **CAST:** Michael J. Fox, Helen Slater, Margaret Whitton, Richard Jordan, Christopher Murney, John Pankow, Fred Gwynne. **1987**

SECRET POLICEMEN'S OTHER BALL, THE ★★★★ British comedians John Cleese, Graham Chapman, Michael Palin, and Terry Jones (of Monty Python) join with rock performers Sting, Eric Clapton, Jeff Beck, and Pete Townshend (of the Who) in a live performance to benefit Amnesty International. The comedy bits—which also feature Dudley Moore's former partner, Peter Cook—go from funny to hilarious, and the music is surprisingly effective. Rated R for profanity and adult themes. 91m. **DIR:** Julien Temple, Roger Graef. **CAST:** John Cleese, Graham Chapman, Michael Palin, Terry Jones, Eric Clapton, Jeff Beck, Pete Townshend, Peter Cook. **1982**

SECRET POLICEMAN'S PRIVATE PARTS, THE ★★★ Monty Python fans will find some of their favorite sketches in this Amnesty International production, but they have been executed elsewhere in better form. If you are a fan, you probably will enjoy it, but if you're less of an enthusiast, you might check out *Monty Python Live at the Hollywood Bowl* first. Rated R. 77m. **DIR:** Roger Graef, Julien Temple. **CAST:** John Cleese, Michael Palin, Terry Jones, Graham Chapman, Peter Cook, Terry Gilliam, Pete Townshend, Phil Collins, Donovan, Bob Geldof. **1984**

SECRET WAR OF HARRY FRIGG, THE ★★ A group of Allied generals has been captured by the Italians. In their vast wisdom, the high command chooses a disgruntled private (Paul Newman) to go behind the lines and free them. This is a very basic comedy, with few original laughs. Rated PG. 110m. **DIR:** Jack Smight. **CAST:** Paul Newman, Sylva Koscina, Andrew Duggan, James Gregory. **1968**

SEE NO EVIL, HEAR NO EVIL ★★★½ Richard Pryor and Gene Wilder play two handicapped buddies—one deaf, one blind—who find themselves running from cops and killers alike when they "witness" a murder. Forget the contrived, stale plot and enjoy the marvelous interplay between the stars. Rated R for profanity, nudity, and violence. 103m. **DIR:** Arthur Hiller. **CAST:** Gene Wilder, Richard Pryor, Joan Severance, Kevin Spacey. **1989**

SEEMS LIKE OLD TIMES ★★★ This slick, commercial package is much better than it deserves to be. It's another predictable Neil Simon sitcom packed with one-liners. But at least it's funny most of the time. Rated PG. 121m. **DIR:** Jay Sandrich. **CAST:** Goldie Hawn, Chevy Chase, Charles Grodin, Robert Guillaume, Harold Gould. **1980**

SEMI-TOUGH ★★ Semihumorous love triangle set in a professional football background is just not as funny as it should be. Some inspired moments and very funny scenes make it a highly watchable film (especially Lotte Lenya's guest bit as an untemptable masseuse), and the character actors are fine, but much of the humor relies on profanity and cruel situations. Rated R. 108m. **DIR:** Michael Ritchie. **CAST:** Burt Reynolds, Jill Clayburgh, Kris Kristofferson, Robert Preston, Bert Convy, Lotte Lenya. **1977**

SENATOR WAS INDISCREET, THE ★★★ A staid and irreproachable U.S. senator's diary disclosures cause considerable embarrassment in this satire. Urbane and suave as always, William Powell is perfect in the title role. B&W; 81m. **DIR:** George S. Kaufman. **CAST:** William Powell, Ella Raines, Peter Lind Hayes, Arleen Whelan, Hans Conried. **1947**

SEND ME NO FLOWERS ★★★ Typically bright and bubbly Doris Day vehicle has Rock Hudson as her hypochondriacal hubby, who, believing he is dying, keeps trying to find a mate for his increasingly flustered wife. This is a light, frothy comedy that provokes some solid chuckles, thanks to the two leads and Tony Randall's supporting turn. 100m. **DIR:** Norman Jewison. **CAST:** Rock Hudson, Doris Day, Tony Randall, Paul Lynde, Clint Walker, Hal March, Edward Andrews. **1964**

SENIORS, THE 🦃 Sophomoric. 87m. **DIR:** Rod Amateau. **CAST:** Jeffrey Byron, Gary Imhoff, Dennis Quaid, Priscilla Barnes, Edward Andrews, Alan Reed. **1978**

SENSUAL MAN, THE ★★ Unengaging dubbed comedy about the sexual exploits of an aristocratic young man (Giancarlo Giannini). Good cast never rises above the mediocre sexist script. Rated R for nudity and profanity. 98m. **DIR:** Marco Vicario. **CAST:** Giancarlo Giannini, Rossana Podesta, Lionel Stander. **1983**

SEPARATE VACATIONS ★★★½ This comedy about Richard, a bored husband (David Naughton) suddenly seeking romance outside his marriage, has some hilarious, if contrived, moments. Rated R for nudity and sexual situations. 92m. **DIR:** Michael Anderson. **CAST:** David Naughton, Jennifer Dale, Mark Keyloun, Tony Rosato. **1985**

SERIAL ★★★½ Harvey Holroyd (Martin Mull) finds it difficult to go with the flow, especially when he finds out his wife, Kate (Tuesday Weld), is having an affair with a Cuban poodle-groomer while his daughter, Joan (Jennifer McAlister), has joined a religious cult. That's when the problems really begin. Rated R. 86m. **DIR:** Bill Persky. **CAST:** Martin Mull, Tuesday Weld, Jennifer McAlister, Bill Macy, Tom Smothers, Christopher Lee. **1980**

SERIAL MOM ★★★★ Picture June Cleaver with a homicidal streak and you have Beverly Sutphin—a "perfect" mother driven to murder when her middle-class family life is even slightly jostled by outsiders. Of course, writer-director-trashmeister John Waters sees her murderous zeal as grisly fodder for yet another warped social comedy. He skewers the media for turning killers into celebrities and turns a one-note joke into a savagely funny romp that is definitely not for everyone. Rated R for simulated sex, language, violence, and gore. 97m. **DIR:** John Waters. **CAST:** Kathleen Turner, Sam Waterston, Ricki Lake, Matthew Lillard, Scott Wesley Morgan, Walt MacPherson. **1994**

SEVEN DAY'S LEAVE ★★ Lucille Ball and Victor Mature are paired up again in this light musical comedy about two sailors on leave who seek out romantic opportunities. Lucy's charisma is unfortunately undermined by a poor script and weak direction. Some good tunes are performed by the Freddy Martin and Les Brown bands. B&W; 87m. **DIR:** Tim Whelan. **CAST:** Lucille Ball, Victor Mature, Harold Peary. **1942**

SEVEN LITTLE FOYS, THE ★★★ Deftly tailored to Bob Hope, this biography of famed vaudevillian Eddie Foy and his performing offspring is gag-filled entertainment until death makes him a widower at odds with his talented brood. A classic scene with James Cagney as George M. Cohan has Hope dancing on a tabletop. All's well that ends well—in church! 95m. **DIR:** Melville Shavelson. **CAST:** Bob Hope, Milly Vitale, George Tobias, Billy Gray, James Cagney. **1955**

SEVEN MINUTES IN HEAVEN ★★½ When her only parent leaves town on business, 15-year-old Natalie (Jennifer Connelly) allows classmate Jeff (Byron Thames) to move into her home. Their relationship is purely platonic, but no one will believe them. Average but well-meant teen comedy. Rated PG for tastefully suggested sex. 95m. **DIR:** Linda Feferman. **CAST:** Jennifer Connelly, Byron Thames, Maddie Corman, Michael Zaslow. **1986**

SEVEN YEAR ITCH, THE ★★★★ This movie is Marilyn Monroe's most enjoyable comedy. Marilyn lives upstairs from average American Tom Ewell. It seems his wife has escaped the heat of their New York home by going on vacation. This leaves Tom alone and unprotected, and one visit from luscious neighbor Marilyn leads him on a Walter Mitty–style adventure that is a joy to behold. 105m. **DIR:** Billy Wilder. **CAST:** Tom Ewell, Marilyn Monroe, Oscar Homolka, Carolyn Jones. **1957**

SEVEN YEARS' BAD LUCK ★★★½ A welcome opportunity to sample the dapper comedic talents of the French master, Max Linder. He plays a bachelor who must endure all manner of misfortunes due (apparently) to the accidental smashing of a mirror. Plenty of slapstick comedy and screwball situations. Silent. B&W; 85m. **DIR:** Max Linder. **CAST:** Max Linder. **1920**

SEX AND THE SINGLE GIRL ★★★ A skin magazine editor makes a play for a lady psychologist by using all the ploys espoused in his magazine. A risqué premise handled in a tastefully entertaining way. 115m. **DIR:** Richard Quine. **CAST:** Tony Curtis, Natalie Wood, Lauren Bacall, Henry Fonda, Mel Ferrer, Larry Storch, Stubby Kaye, Edward Everett Horton. **1964**

SEX APPEAL ★★ A nerdish accountant makes an all-out attempt to attract the opposite sex with humorously disastrous results. Gratuitous sleaze mars an otherwise cute story. Rated R for nudity and profanity. 81m. **DIR:** Chuck Vincent. **CAST:** Louie Bonanno. **1986**

SEX ON THE RUN 🦃 This story of a sexually voracious Arabian sheikh is amazingly bad. 88m. **DIR:** François Legrand. **CAST:** Tony Curtis, Marisa Berenson, Britt Ekland. **1978**

SEX WITH A SMILE ★½ Silly, badly dubbed Italian film featuring five short stories on sexual misunderstandings. Marty Feldman's section produces some laughs. Rated R for nudity and sex. 100m. **DIR:** Sergio Martino. **CAST:** Marty Feldman, Edwige Fenech, Sydne Rome, Barbara Bouchet, Dayle Haddon. **1976**

SEXTETTE 🦃 A dreadful movie that documents the vulgar campiness of the nearly 80-year-old Mae West. Rated R. 91m. **DIR:** Ken Hughes, Irving Rapper. **CAST:** Mae West, Timothy Dalton, Dom DeLuise, Tony Curtis, Ringo Starr, George Hamilton, George Raft. **1978**

SGT. BILKO (TV SERIES) ★★★★½ Master Sergeant Ernie Bilko was indeed a master of bilking soldiers and civilians alike. His job was to helm the motor pool. But his mission in life was to con anyone who could cough up a buck or two. For Phil Silvers, this was the role of a lifetime. A superb supporting cast added to the hilarity. As the stern Colonel Hall, Paul Ford proved to be the perfect foil. The series, created by Nat Hiken, was one of the first of its era to frequently hire black actors. Originally named *You'll Never Get Rich*, it became *The Phil Silvers Show* and, finally, in syndication, *SGT. Bilko*. Two episodes are included per tape. B&W; 60m. each tape. **DIR:** Al DeCaprio. **CAST:** Phil Silvers,

Harvey Lembeck, Paul Ford, Joe E. Ross, Allan Melvin, Herbie Faye, Maurice Gosfield, Billy Sands, Elisabeth Fraser. **1955–1959**

SHADEY ★★½ Mildly entertaining British comedy about Shadey (Antony Sher), a man who has the ability to "think pictures onto film." These little movies turn out to be prophecies that are ultimately fulfilled. Plodding one moment, all-out bizarre the next. Rated PG-13 for violence and profanity. 90m. **DIR:** Philip Saville. **CAST:** Antony Sher, Billie Whitelaw, Patrick Macnee, Katherine Helmond. **1987**

SHAKES THE CLOWN ★★½ Stand-up comedian Bobcat Goldthwait makes his directorial debut with this clown-out-of-circus tale. Goldthwait is the clown who hits rock bottom. Former *Brady* mom Florence Henderson is downright hilarious as a clown groupie. Rated R for profanity. 88m. **DIR:** Bob Goldthwait. **CAST:** Bob Goldthwait, Julie Brown, Paul Dooley, Florence Henderson. **1991**

SHAKIEST GUN IN THE WEST, THE ★★ This picture is a remake of *The Paleface* with Don Knotts in the Bob Hope role. A fun family film. 100m. **DIR:** Alan Rafkin. **CAST:** Don Knotts, Barbara Rhoades, Jackie Coogan, Don Barry. **1968**

SHAME OF THE JUNGLE ★★½ French animated spoof of *Tarzan of the Apes* comes from Belgian artist Picha, and like the ground-breaking *Fritz the Cat*, goes for the jugular. Americanized by writers from *Saturday Night Live* and redubbed by comedians John Belushi, Bill Murray, and Christopher Guest, this cartoon is an all-out assault on good taste, with something to offend everyone. Funny in the right frame of mind. Rated R for language, cartoon nudity, and sex. 73m. **DIR:** Picha, Boris Szulzinger. **1975**

SHANGHAI SURPRISE 🦃 Madonna plays an uptight missionary in Shanghai, 1938. She recruits a con artist (Sean Penn) to help her recover eleven hundred pounds of opium. Rated PG. 93m. **DIR:** Jim Goddard. **CAST:** Sean Penn, Madonna, Paul Freeman, Richard Griffiths, Philip Sayer, Victor Wong. **1986**

SHE COULDN'T SAY NO ★★ An oil-rich woman (Jean Simmons) wishes to repay the citizens of her hometown of Progress, Arkansas for the kindnesses shown her in childhood. Her idea of showering the town with money is charitable, but disrupts the day-to-day life of the citizenry. Robert Mitchum, as the town doctor, seems out of place in this picture. B&W; 89m. **DIR:** Lloyd Bacon. **CAST:** Robert Mitchum, Jean Simmons, Arthur Hunnicutt, Edgar Buchanan. **1954**

SHE-DEVIL ★★★ Meryl Streep is a hoot as a snooty romance novelist who takes Ed Begley Jr., away from frumpy Roseanne Barr. The moments of mirth come as Barr methodically manages her wifely revenge. The story is predictable, and the pace is sometimes plodding and deliberate, but there are enough funny bits to make it worth watching. Rated PG-13 for profanity and suggested sex. 94m. **DIR:** Susan Seidelman. **CAST:** Meryl Streep, Roseanne Arnold, Ed Begley Jr., Sylvia Miles, Linda Hunt. **1989**

SHE DONE HIM WRONG ★★★★ Mae West woos Cary Grant in this comedy classic. She is a lady saloon keeper in the Gay Nineties. He is the undercover cop assigned to bring her in. She says, "Come up and see me sometime." He does, and the result is movie magic. B&W; 66m. **DIR:** Lowell Sherman. **CAST:** Mae West, Cary Grant, Gilbert Roland, Noah Beery Sr., Rochelle Hudson, Louise Beavers. **1933**

SHE GOES TO WAR ★★ Farfetched comedy-drama about a spoiled woman who takes her fiancé's place at the front. Loaded with stereotypes, coincidences, stilted dialogue, and miserable songs. B&W; 87m. **DIR:** Henry King. **CAST:** Eleanor Boardman, John Holland, Edmund Burke. **1929**

SHERLOCK JR. ★★★★ In this film about film, projectionist Buster Keaton dreams about being a detective and miraculously finds himself inside the film he is showing. The plot involves saving his beloved from the villain, but the real thrust and appeal of the film lies in brilliant camera tricks providing some of the greatest of silent comedy sight gags. Silent. B&W; 45m. **DIR:** Buster Keaton. **CAST:** Buster Keaton, Kathryn McGuire. **1924**

SHE'S BACK ★★½ Black comedy finds Carrie Fisher returning from the dead, edging her meek husband to seek retribution against the street thugs who iced her. Rated R for violence. 88m. **DIR:** Tim Kincaid. **CAST:** Carrie Fisher, Robert Joy. **1989**

SHE'S GOTTA HAVE IT ★★★★ A movie about a randy young woman who's "gotta have it" might seem a bit iffy. But independent filmmaker Spike Lee—who wrote, directed, and edited this unique narrative-quasidocumentary—set up the challenge for himself and then set out to succeed *con gusto*. The beautiful lady in question, Nola Darling, is played by Tracy Camilla Johns. Rated R for language and nudity. B&W; 100m. **DIR:** Spike Lee. **CAST:** Tracy Camilla Johns, Redmond Hicks, John Terrell, Spike Lee. **1986**

SHE'S HAVING A BABY ★★ Director John Hughes, champion of the teenage set, advanced from the breakfast club to the breakfast table in this bland account of a young newlywed couple, played by Kevin Bacon and Elizabeth McGovern. A major (and deserved) failure. Rated PG-13 for profanity, suggested sex, and sexual themes. 110m. **DIR:** John Hughes. **CAST:** Kevin Bacon, Elizabeth

McGovern, William Windom, James Ray, Holland Taylor. 1988

SHE'S OUT OF CONTROL 🦃 Tony Danza overplays the father of a 15-year-old girl who suddenly blossoms into a sexy young woman. Rated PG. 97m. **DIR:** Stan Dragoti. **CAST:** Tony Danza, Catharine Hicks, Wallace Shawn, Ami Dolenz. 1989

SHIRLEY VALENTINE ★★★★ Adult viewers will revel in this wise and witty movie. Pauline Collins is terrific as the title character, who one day decides to chuck it all and head for romance in the Greek Isles. Tom Conti is fun as the restaurant owner who woos the wacky but sympathetic heroine. Rated R for profanity and nudity. 160m. **DIR:** Lewis Gilbert. **CAST:** Pauline Collins, Tom Conti, Julia McKenzie, Joanna Lumley, Bernard Hill, Sylvia Syms. 1989

SHOCK TREATMENT 🦃 Forgettable sequel to *The Rocky Horror Picture Show*. Janet and Brad go on a TV game show and end up trying to escape from it. Rated PG. 94m. **DIR:** Jim Sharman. **CAST:** Jessica Harper, Cliff De Young, Richard O'Brien. 1981

SHOOT (1991) ★★½ Passable spoof of undercover greed features DeDee Pfeiffer as a ditzy photographer studying her crime boss's gambling operation. His real ace in the hole is a million-dollar pearl he plans to sell to the highest bidder. Surprise ending is too strange to be believed. Unrated; contains violence and criminial activity. 97m. **DIR:** Hugh Parks. **CAST:** DeDee Pfeiffer, Miles O'Keeffe, Christopher Atkins, Fred Ottaviano. 1991

SHOOT LOUD, LOUDER...I DON'T UNDERSTAND 🦃 Antique dealer confronts inept gunmen. Unrated, this film contains violence. 100m. **DIR:** Eduardo De Filippo. **CAST:** Marcello Mastroianni, Raquel Welch, Leopoldo Trieste. 1966

SHOOTING ELIZABETH ★★½ A husband tells his friend that he is going to kill his wife during their second honeymoon. Mundane plot and acting. Not rated. 96m. **DIR:** Baz Taylor. **CAST:** Jeff Goldblum, Mimi Rogers, Burt Kwouk. 1992

SHOP AROUND THE CORNER, THE ★★★★ A charming period comedy dealing with the lives of two people who work in the same Budapest shop and become loving pen pals. MGM later remade this picture as *In the Good Old Summertime*, and it formed the basis of the stage musical *She Loves Me*. B&W; 98m. **DIR:** Ernst Lubitsch. **CAST:** James Stewart, Margaret Sullavan, Frank Morgan, Joseph Schildkraut. 1939

SHORT TIME ★★★½ In this sometimes hilarious action-comedy, Dabney Coleman is a soon-to-retire police officer who is incorrectly diagnosed as having a terminal disease. He spends the last few days on the force attempting to get killed to leave his wife (Teri Garr) and son a substantial insurance settlement. Rated PG-13 for violence and profanity. 102m. **DIR:** Gregg Champion. **CAST:** Dabney Coleman, Matt Frewer, Teri Garr, Barry Corbin, Joe Pantoliano. 1990

SHOT IN THE DARK, A ★★★★ *A Shot in the Dark* is a one-man show, with Peter Sellers outdoing himself as the character he later reprised in *The Return of the Pink Panther*, *The Pink Panther Strikes Back*, and *The Revenge of the Pink Panther*. In this slapstick delight, Clouseau attempts to discover whether or not a woman (Elke Sommer) is guilty of murdering her lover. 101m. **DIR:** Blake Edwards. **CAST:** Peter Sellers, Elke Sommer, George Sanders, Burt Kwouk, Herbert Lom. 1964

SHOW PEOPLE ★★★★ Loosely based on the career of Gloria Swanson, this was the justly fabled Marion Davies's last silent film. Davies is warm and genuinely touching as innocent Polly Pepper, a young actress whose ambitions are thwarted at nearly every turn. As a satire on the industry, this is a glittering gem, right on the money. Charlie Chaplin, John Gilbert, May Murray, and Norma Talmadge are among a coterie of stars appearing as themselves. Silent. B&W; 81m. **DIR:** King Vidor. **CAST:** Marion Davies, William Haines, Polly Moran. 1928

SHOW-OFF, THE ★★½ The third version of George Kelly's play is the weakest, but Red Skelton has the right personality for the leading role. He plays an office clerk who will do anything to impress a girlfriend and winds up getting in big trouble. Most of the laughs are supplied by the supporting cast because, strangely, Skelton has more straight lines than punch lines. B&W; 84m. **DIR:** Harry Beaumont. **CAST:** Red Skelton, Marilyn Maxwell, Marjorie Main, Eddie "Rochester" Anderson, Leon Ames, Marshall Thompson, Grady Sutton, Lila Leeds. 1946

SHRIMP ON THE BARBIE ★★ The ordinarily watchable and funny Richard "Cheech" Marin is cast in this disappointing comedy as an unemployed Mexican-American who decides to try his luck in Australia. Rated PG-13 for profanity. 90m. **DIR:** Alan Smithee. **CAST:** Richard "Cheech" Marin, Emma Samms. 1990

SIBLING RIVALRY ★★★½ Kirstie Alley gives a hilarious performance as a woman whose first affair leads to disaster. By sheer force of combined will, director Carl Reiner and Alley turn a gimmicky, cutesy story into a genuinely amusing—albeit uneven—laughfest. Rated PG-13 for profanity. 89m. **DIR:** Carl Reiner. **CAST:** Kirstie Alley, Bill Pullman, Carrie Fisher, Jami Gertz, Sam Elliott, Scott Bakula, Frances Sternhagen, John Randolph, Ed O'Neill, Paul Benedict, Bill Macy. 1990

SIDEWALKS OF NEW YORK ★★ This Buster Keaton comedy would have made a very funny silent movie, but the actor gets bogged down with talk here. The camera lingers so long on his deadpan expression that the pace is irritatingly slow. The story of a rich playboy in love with a poor tenement girl turns into a sentimental cliché. B&W; 70m. **DIR:** Jules White, Zion Myers. **CAST:** Buster Keaton, Anita Page, Cliff Edwards, Syd Saylor, Clark Marshall, Frank Rowan, Frank La Rue. **1931**

SILENT MOVIE ★★★½ Mel Brooks's *Silent Movie* is another kitchen-sink affair, with Brooks going from the ridiculous to the sublime with a beautiful idea that bears more exploring. Silent films were the best for comedy, and Brooks, along with costars Marty Feldman, Dom De Luise, and Sid Caesar, supplies numerous funny moments. Rated PG. 86m. **DIR:** Mel Brooks. **CAST:** Mel Brooks, Marty Feldman, Dom DeLuise, Bernadette Peters, Sid Caesar, James Caan, Burt Reynolds, Paul Newman, Liza Minnelli, Anne Bancroft, Marcel Marceau, Harry Ritz, Ron Carey. **1976**

SILVER BEARS ★★ If *Silver Bears* was meant to be a comedy, it isn't funny. If it was meant to be a drama, it isn't gripping. It's boring. Michael Caine stars as a Mafia henchman sent to Switzerland to buy a bank. He's swindled and ends up buying two rooms over a pizza parlor. Rated PG. 113m. **DIR:** Ivan Passer. **CAST:** Michael Caine, Cybill Shepherd, Louis Jourdan, Martin Balsam, Stéphane Audran, Tom Smothers, David Warner. **1978**

SILVER STREAK (1976) ★★★★½ A fast-paced action story laced with comedy and stars such as Gene Wilder, Jill Clayburgh, and Richard Pryor. It will have you cheering, laughing, gasping, and jumping. *Streak* pits neurotic Wilder, sexy Clayburgh, and shifty Pryor against cool millionaire villain Patrick McGoohan and his evil henchman, Ray Walston, in a wild high-speed chase that brings back the train as a modern-day source for good thrillers. Rated PG. 113m. **DIR:** Arthur Hiller. **CAST:** Gene Wilder, Jill Clayburgh, Richard Pryor, Patrick McGoohan, Ray Walston, Ned Beatty, Richard Kiel. **1976**

SIMON ★★ Weird, weird comedy about an average guy (Alan Arkin) who is brainwashed into thinking he's a visitor from outer space. The film has some funny moments, but it just doesn't work as a whole. Rated PG. 97m. **DIR:** Marshall Brickman. **CAST:** Alan Arkin, Madeline Kahn, Austin Pendleton, William Finley, Fred Gwynne. **1980**

SIMPLE MEN ★★★ Director Hal Hartley's offbeat road movie is short on plot but long on eccentric behavior. Brothers Robert Burke and William Sage go looking for their father and encounter a cast of characters more off kilter than they are. One brother and the father are wanted by the law, but when they team up with mystery women Karen Sillas and Elina Lowensohn, their lives really become complicated. Rated R for language and adult situations. 105m. **DIR:** Hal Hartley. **CAST:** Robert Burke, William Sage, Karen Sillas, Elina Lowensohn, Mary Mackenzie. **1992**

SIN OF HAROLD DIDDLEBOCK (A.K.A. MAD WEDNESDAY) ★★★½ The result of a disastrous joint effort of director Preston Sturges, silent-screen great Harold Lloyd, and backer Howard Hughes is a much better film than popular Hollywood legend implies. This story about a middle-aged man fired from his job and set adrift with nothing but unfulfilled potential doesn't sound like a scream. However, Lloyd's bizarre antics redeem the character. Hughes rereleased it in 1950 as *Mad Wednesday* and edited it down to 79 minutes. B&W; 90m. **DIR:** Preston Sturges. **CAST:** Harold Lloyd, Frances Ramsden, Jimmy Conlin, Raymond Walburn, Edgar Kennedy, Arline Judge, Lionel Stander, Margaret Hamilton, Rudy Vallee. **1947**

SINFUL LIFE, A 🦃 An aging chorus girl must find a husband before she is declared an unfit mother by her daughter's teacher. Based on the stage play *Just Like the Pom Pom Girls.* Rated R for profanity. 90m. **DIR:** William Schreiner. **CAST:** Anita Morris, Rick Overton, Dennis Christopher. **1989**

SINGLES ★★★★ High marks to writer-director Cameron Crowe for this witty study of twentysomethings seeking romance and personal fulfillment in the Seattle rock scene. The central players often speak directly to the viewer while justifying their behavior. Crowe has a definite ear for the verbal byplay of young love, and his ensemble cast is superb. Rated PG-13 for profanity and suggested sex. 99m. **DIR:** Cameron Crowe. **CAST:** Bridget Fonda, Campbell Scott, Kyra Sedgwick, Matt Dillon, Sheila Kelley, Jim True, Bill Pullman. **1992**

SINGLETON'S PLUCK ★★★ In this gentle British comedy, a goose farmer, whose business has been shut down by a strike, decides to herd his gaggle to the slaughterhouse himself. Television reporters begin to cover his hundred-mile trip and he becomes a national figure. 93m. **DIR:** Richard Eyre. **CAST:** Ian Holm, Penelope Wilton. **1984**

SIRENS ★★★★ Straitlaced young minister Hugh Grant and his wife (Tara Fitzgerald) have their eyes opened when they visit a bohemian artist (Sam Neill) at his secluded mountain estate. Writer-director John Duigan's study of art, religion, and sexual repression manages to be thoughtful, erotic, and charmingly funny all at the same time. Rated R for nudity and mature themes. 94m. **DIR:** John Duigan. **CAST:** Hugh Grant, Tara Fitzgerald, Sam Neill, Elle MacPherson, Portia de Rossi, Kate Fischer. **1993**

SISTER ACT ★★★½ Fast-living nightclub singer Whoopi Goldberg has to hide out in a convent after she witnesses her gangster boyfriend (Harvey Keitel) preside over the killing of a police informant. Goldberg is a delight in this surprisingly funny and heartwarming romp. Rated PG for profanity. 100m. **DIR:** Emile Ardolino. **CAST:** Whoopi Goldberg, Maggie Smith, Kathy Najimy, Wendy Makkena, Mary Wickes, Harvey Keitel, Bill Nunn. **1992**

SISTER ACT 2: BACK IN THE HABIT ★★★½ Reacting to the surprise popularity of *Sister Act* with kids, the folks at Disney made this family-oriented, toned-down sequel. Sister Mary Clarence, Delores Van Cartier (Whoopi Goldberg), goes undercover as a music teacher at an inner-city school in an attempt to reach rebellious students. Very tame—the worst things these kids do is sing rap music in class and put glue on the teacher's chair—but charming. Rated PG for light profanity. 107m. **DIR:** Bill Duke. **CAST:** Whoopi Goldberg, Maggie Smith, Kathy Najimy, Mary Wickes, Wendy Makkena, Barnard Hughes, James Coburn, Michael Jeter, Robert Pastorelli, Brad Sullivan. **1993**

SITTING DUCKS 🦃 A mafia accountant and his pal steal a day's payroll and hit the road. Rated R for nudity and language. 90m. **DIR:** Henry Jaglom. **CAST:** Michael Emil, Zack Norman, Patrice Townsend, Richard Romanus. **1980**

SIX PACK 🦃 Kenny Rogers plays a footloose stock-car racer who is latched on to by six homeless, sticky-fingered kids. Rated PG for profanity. 110m. **DIR:** Daniel Petrie. **CAST:** Kenny Rogers, Diane Lane, Erin Gray, Barry Corbin. **1982**

SIXTEEN CANDLES ★★★★ Molly Ringwald stars in this fast and funny teen comedy as a high school student who is crushed when the whole family forgets her sixteenth birthday. Things, it seems to her, go downhill from there—that is, until the boy of her dreams suddenly starts showing some interest. Rated PG for profanity. 93m. **DIR:** John Hughes. **CAST:** Molly Ringwald, Paul Dooley, Blanche Baker, Edward Andrews, Anthony Michael Hall, Billie Bird. **1984**

SIZZLE BEACH, U.S.A. 🦃 Drive-in fodder about three girls who head to L.A. notable only as the debut of Kevin Costner (whose appearance isn't as prominent as the video box would lead you to believe). Rated R for nudity and sexual situations. 93m. **DIR:** Richard Brander. **CAST:** Terry Congie, Leslie Brander, Roselyn Royce, Kevin Costner. **1976**

SKI PATROL ★★ Comedy fluff about the antics of a group of misfit skiers who work for a popular resort. Never gets off the beginners' slope. Rated PG. 91m. **DIR:** Richard Correll. **CAST:** Roger Rose, Ray Walston, Martin Mull. **1990**

SKI SCHOOL ★★½ An obvious rip-off of *Animal House,* this teen comedy is nonetheless very funny thanks in part to Dean Cameron as the leader of a wacko class of ski bums. Not rated, but contains nudity and profanity. 85m. **DIR:** Damien Lee. **CAST:** Dean Cameron, Tom Breznahan, Patrick Laborteaux, Mark Thomas Miller. **1990**

SKIN DEEP ★★ Writer-director Blake Edwards tries for another sex farce in the *10* vein, but this one fails to rise to its potential. John Ritter's undeniable charm cannot compensate for the fact that his character—a womanizing alcoholic—is utterly lacking in redeeming social qualities. Viewers with raised consciousnesses are advised to stay away from this one. Rated R for nudity, profanity, and explicit sexual themes. 98m. **DIR:** Blake Edwards. **CAST:** John Ritter, Vincent Gardenia, Alyson Reed, Joel Brooks, Julianne Phillips, Don Gordon, Nina Foch. **1989**

SKYLINE ★★★ Antonio Resines plays a Spanish photographer named Gustavo who comes to New York seeking international fame. Once there, he struggles to learn English, find work, and pursue friendship and romance. In Spanish and English, with subtitles it would be excellent for bilingual viewers. The twist ending really gives one a jolt. We'd rate it PG for slight profanity. 84m. **DIR:** Fernando Colombo. **CAST:** Antonio Resines, Susana Ocana. **1984**

SLACKER ★★★★ Imagine if you will a movie that has ninety-seven roles of equal importance, yet never spends more than five minutes with any character. Meet *Slacker*. A rogue's gallery of deadbeats, pseudointellectuals and just-plain folks is presented in this semitwisted examination of attitudes among college students in Austin, Texas. It's surprisingly entertaining. Rated R for profanity. 97m. **DIR:** Richard Linklater. **1991**

SLAMMER GIRLS ★★ Spoof of women's prison films. A male reporter disguises himself as a woman to prove the heroine's innocence. A few funny bits, but many more that are plain stupid. Rated R for nudity and profanity. 82m. **DIR:** Chuck Vincent. **CAST:** Devon Jenkin, Jeff Eagle, Jane Hamilton. **1987**

SLAP SHOT ★★★★ When released in 1977, this comedy about a down-and-out hockey team was criticized for its liberal use of profanity. The controversy tended to obscure the fact that *Slap Shot* is a very funny, marvelously acted movie. Paul Newman, as an aging player-coach who's a loser in love and on the ice until he instructs the members of his team to behave like animals during their matches, has never been better. Rated R. 122m. **DIR:** George Roy Hill. **CAST:** Paul Newman, Strother Martin, Jennifer Warren, Lindsay Crouse, Melinda Dillon. **1977**

SLAPSTICK OF ANOTHER KIND 🦃 Jerry Lewis hasn't made a funny film in years, and this sci-fi spoof is no exception. Rated PG. 85m. **DIR:** Steven Paul. **CAST:** Jerry Lewis, Madeline Kahn, Marty Feldman. **1983**

SLAVE GIRLS FROM BEYOND INFINITY ★★ A pair of space bimbos in bikinis find themselves on a weird planet whose sole occupant hunts intergalactic visitors. Low budget, but with decent effects and lighting. Not nearly campy enough. Rated R for nudity. 80m. **DIR:** Ken Dixon. **CAST:** Elizabeth Cyton, Cindy Beal, Brinke Stevens. **1987**

SLAVES OF NEW YORK 🦃 Manhattan's downtown art scene. Rated R, with profanity and sexual situations. 125m. **DIR:** James Ivory. **CAST:** Bernadette Peters, Chris Sarandon, Mary Beth Hurt, Madeleine Potter. **1989**

SLEAZEMANIA ★★½ Rhino Video clip compilation devoted to preview trailers and excerpts from such bottom-of-the-barrel exploitation features as *Jailbait Babysitters* and *The Flesh Merchants*. Demented fun. B&W/color; 60m. **DIR:** Johnny Legend, Jeff Vilencia. **1986**

SLEAZEMANIA STRIKES BACK ★★½ More fast-paced, bad-taste trailers from movies—e.g., *Suburban Roulette*—you'd never be seen buying a ticket for. B&W/color; 60m. **DIR:** Johnny Legend, Jeff Vilencia. **1987**

SLEEPER ★★★★ Writer-star-director Woody Allen finally exhibited some true filmmaking talent with this 1973 sci-fi spoof. The frenetic gag-a-minute comedy style of Allen's earlier films was replaced by nice bits of character comedy. The most enjoyable of Allen's pre–*Annie Hall* creations. Rated PG. 88m. **DIR:** Woody Allen. **CAST:** Woody Allen, Diane Keaton, John McLiam, John Beck. **1973**

SLEEPLESS IN SEATTLE ★★★★ Writer-turned-director Nora Ephron touches all the bases with this witty, insightful romantic comedy reminiscent of her breakthrough hit as a screenwriter, *When Harry Met Sally*. When recently widowed Tom Hanks's plight is described during a radio talk show by his well-meaning son, soon-to-be-wed reporter Meg Ryan becomes obsessed with the idea of meeting him. Only true romantics need apply. Great score, too. Rated PG for brief profanity. 101m. **DIR:** Nora Ephron. **CAST:** Tom Hanks, Meg Ryan, Bill Pullman, Ross Malinger, Rosie O'Donnell, Gaby Hoffman, Victor Garber, Rita Wilson, Barbara Garrick, Carey Lowell, Dana Ivey, Rob Reiner. **1993**

SLIGHTLY HONORABLE ★★★ Wisecracks and red herrings provide the drawing cards in this fast-paced comedy-thriller. The plot's muddy, but basically it concerns a lawyer, Pat O'Brien, who is set up for a murder by crooked politician Edward Arnold. B&W; 85m. **DIR:** Tay Garnett. **CAST:** Pat O'Brien, Edward Arnold, Broderick Crawford, Evelyn Keyes, Phyllis Brooks, Eve Arden. **1939**

SLITHER ★★★ In this bizarre comedy the four leads are after a cache of stolen money, carrying them on a California odyssey with a house trailer in tow, pursued by two of the most ominous looking RVs ever built. Rated PG. 92m. **DIR:** Howard Zieff. **CAST:** James Caan, Sally Kellerman, Peter Boyle, Louise Lasser. **1973**

SLUGGER'S WIFE, THE ★★ The most shallow of Neil Simon's works to date, this is bad television situation comedy blown up to big-screen size. Darryl Palmer (Michael O'Keefe) is a self-centered baseball player who bullies his way into the affections of Debby Palmer (Rebecca DeMornay), a would-be rock star. Rated PG-13 for nudity and profanity. 105m. **DIR:** Hal Ashby. **CAST:** Michael O'Keefe, Rebecca DeMornay, Martin Ritt, Randy Quaid, Cleavant Derricks. **1985**

SLUMBER PARTY 57 🦃 In this sleazy, smutty movie, six girls sit around a camp fire and tell about the first time they "did it." Rated R. 89m. **DIR:** William A. Levey. **CAST:** Noelle North, Debra Winger, Rainbeaux Smith, Joe E. Ross. **1977**

SMALLEST SHOW ON EARTH, THE ★★★½ Warm, often hilarious comedy about a couple who inherit a run-down movie theater and its wacky attendants. Excellent performances by Peter Sellers and Margaret Rutherford. B&W; 80m. **DIR:** Basil Dearden. **CAST:** Peter Sellers, Bill Travers, Margaret Rutherford. **1957**

SMILE ★★★★ Don't miss this one; it's a true neglected classic. This backstage look at a teenage beauty pageant is great satirical fun every inch of the way, managing to be both tough-minded and soft-hearted. Rated PG. 113m. **DIR:** Michael Ritchie. **CAST:** Bruce Dern, Barbara Feldon, Michael Kidd, Geoffrey Lewis, Nicholas Pryor, Mario O'Brien, Colleen Camp, Joan Prather, Annette O'Toole, Melanie Griffith. **1975**

SMOKEY AND THE BANDIT ★★★½ *Smokey and the Bandit* may strain credibility, but it never stops being fun. The Bandit (Burt Reynolds) is an infamous independent trucker who is hired to transport four hundred cases of Coors beer from Texarkana, Texas, where it is legal, to Atlanta, Georgia, where it is not. Hold on to your hat. Rated PG for profanity. 97m. **DIR:** Hal Needham. **CAST:** Burt Reynolds, Pat McCormick, Jerry Reed, Sally Field, Mike Henry, Jackie Gleason, Paul Williams. **1977**

SMOKEY AND THE BANDIT II ★★ *Smokey II* is just more proof that "sequels aren't equal." But it isn't a total loss. Don't turn it off until the credits roll (although you may want to fast-forward). Outtakes featuring the stars flubbing their lines are spliced together at the end, and they're hilarious. Rated PG. 101m. **DIR:** Hal Needham. **CAST:** Burt Reynolds, Jerry Reed, Pat McCormick, Paul

Williams, Mike Henry, Jackie Gleason, Dom DeLuise. 1980

SMOKEY AND THE BANDIT III 🦃 The Bandit may be back, but it ain't Burt. Rated PG for nudity, profanity, and scatological humor. 86m. **DIR:** Dick Lowry. **CAST:** Jerry Reed, Jackie Gleason, Paul Williams, Pat McCormick. 1983

SMOKEY BITES THE DUST ★★½ Jimmy McNichol stars as a mischievous teenager who takes great delight in stealing cars and making buffoons out of the sheriff and his deputies. This is pretty standard car-chase action, but it does move along and there are some laughs along the way. Rated PG. 85m. **DIR:** Charles B. Griffith. **CAST:** Jimmy McNichol, Walter Barnes, John Blythe Barrymore, William Forsythe. 1981

SNAPPER, THE ★★★★½ The second film made from author Roddy Doyle's *Barrytown* trilogy (following *The Commitments*) is a delightful character study. The strong-willed daughter in a working-class family becomes pregnant and refuses to divulge the name of the father. Colm Meaney (of the *Star Trek* TV shows) is terrific as the befuddled father, and Ruth McCabe is equally memorable as the matriarch who must hold her family together with common sense and love. This is a gem! Rated R for frank discussions of sex and brief profanity. 95m. **DIR:** Stephen Frears. **CAST:** Colm Meaney, Ruth McCabe, Tina Kellegher, Colm O'Bryne, Pat Laffan. 1994

SO FINE ★★ This so-called sex comedy—about a fashion house (run by Ryan O'Neal and Jack Warden) that introduces a new line of designer jeans with see-through plastic inserts in the seat—is little more than a television situation comedy with leers. Rated R because of nudity and profanity. 91m. **DIR:** Andrew Bergman. **CAST:** Ryan O'Neal, Jack Warden, Richard Kiel, Fred Gwynne, Mike Kellin, David Rounds. 1981

SO I MARRIED AN AXE MURDERER ★★½ Mike Myers proves he can get some laughs outside of *Wayne's World* in this comedy about a modern-day beat poet's ill-fated marriage to butcher's assistant Nancy Travis. However, Myers doesn't register much charisma, especially when sharing scenes with dynamos like Travis, Anthony LaPaglia, Alan Arkin, and Charles Grodin. But there are some good moments in this paper-thin whodunit. Rated PG-13 for violence, suggested sex, nudity, and vulgarity. 94m. **DIR:** Thomas Schlamme. **CAST:** Mike Myers, Nancy Travis, Anthony LaPaglia, Amanda Plummer, Brenda Fricker, Matt Doherty, Charles Grodin, Alan Arkin, Phil Hartman, Debi Mazar, Michael Richards, Steven Wright. 1993

SO THIS IS PARIS ★★★ Some of Ernst Lubitsch's best comedies come from his first decade in Hollywood. This one is typically full of philanderings, flirtations, and erotic innuendo before two married couples eventually are reconciled. Silent. B&W; 70m. **DIR:** Ernst Lubitsch. **CAST:** Monte Blue, Patsy Ruth Miller, Myrna Loy. 1926

SO THIS IS WASHINGTON ★★½ From a park bench in Washington, D.C., Charles Lauck and Norris Goff, radio's cracker-barrel philosophers Lum and Abner, dispense common sense to senators and congressmen. Third in a series, this product of wartime mentality is a simpleminded feature aimed at warming the heart. B&W; 65m. **DIR:** Ray McCarey. **CAST:** Charles Lauck, Norris Goff, Alan Mowbray, Minerva Urecal. 1943

SOAPDISH ★★★½ Daytime soap operas get the raspberry in this often funny spoof, which features a fine performance by Sally Field as the embattled star of *The Sun Always Sets.* When a sex-crazed producer (Robert Downey Jr.) hires Field's former costar and lover Kevin Kline, the fur starts to fly. Kline is especially good as the hammy has-been, but the whole cast manages to do some lively work. Rated PG-13 for profanity. 97m. **DIR:** Michael Hoffman. **CAST:** Sally Field, Kevin Kline, Whoopi Goldberg, Robert Downey Jr., Cathy Moriarty, Elisabeth Shue, Teri Hatcher, Garry Marshall, Carrie Fisher. 1991

SOME GIRLS ★★★ European tale about a young man (Patrick Dempsey) invited to join a girl and her very strange family over the Christmas season. Concentrates more on character and dramatic depth than story development. Rated R for language, nudity, and simulated sex. 95m. **DIR:** Michael Hoffman. **CAST:** Patrick Dempsey, Jennifer Connelly, Lila Kedrova, Florinda Bolkan. 1988

SOME KIND OF HERO ★★ This Richard Pryor movie can't decide whether to tell the story of a Vietnam prisoner of war returning to American society or be another comedy caper film. As a result, it's neither very funny nor worth thinking about. Rated R for profanity, nudity, and violence. 97m. **DIR:** Michael Pressman. **CAST:** Richard Pryor, Margot Kidder, Ronny Cox, Olivia Cole. 1982

SOME KIND OF WONDERFUL ★★★★ Eric Stoltz stars as an affable lad who can't seem to make any headway with women. Unaware of the deep affection hurled in his direction by constant companion Mary Stuart Masterson (who all but steals the show), Stoltz sets his sights high on Lea Thompson. Perceptive, thoughtful viewing. Rated PG-13 for mature situations. 93m. **DIR:** Howard Deutch. **CAST:** Eric Stoltz, Mary Stuart Masterson, Lea Thompson, Craig Sheffer, John Ashton. 1987

SOME LIKE IT HOT ★★★★★ Billy Wilder's *Some Like It Hot* is the outlandish story of two men (Jack Lemmon and Tony Curtis) who accidentally witness a gangland slaying. They pose as members of an all-girl band in order to avoid the gangsters, who are now trying to silence them permanently.

Marilyn Monroe is at her sensual best as the band's singer. Joe E. Brown is also hilarious as a wealthy playboy who develops an attraction for an obviously bewildered Lemmon. B&W; 119m. **DIR:** Billy Wilder. **CAST:** Marilyn Monroe, Jack Lemmon, Tony Curtis, Joe E. Brown, George Raft, Pat O'Brien, Nehemiah Persoff, Mike Mazurki. **1959**

SOMETHING SHORT OF PARADISE ★★★ This romantic comedy is something short of perfect but still manages to entertain. Two New Yorkers (Susan Sarandon and David Steinberg) manage to find love and happiness together despite distractions from other conniving singles. Marilyn Sokol is great as one of the obstacles. Rated PG. 91m. **DIR:** David Helpern Jr. **CAST:** Susan Sarandon, David Steinberg, Marilyn Sokol, Jean-Pierre Aumont. **1979**

SOMETHING SPECIAL ★★★ Offbeat but surprisingly pleasant comedy about a 15-year-old girl named Milly (Pamela Segall) who is convinced that life would be easier if she were a boy. With the help of a magical potion and a solar eclipse, she manages to grow a penis. She changes her name to Willy to please her father and to satisfy her own curiosity. Rated PG-13. 90m. **DIR:** Paul Schneider. **CAST:** Patty Duke, Pamela Segall, Eric Gurry, Mary Tanner, John Glover, Seth Green. **1987**

SOMETHING WILD ★★★★½ Jeff Daniels stars as a desk-bound investment type whose idea of yuppie rebellion is stiffing a local diner for the price of a lunch. This petty larceny is observed by a mysterious woman (Melanie Griffith) who, to Daniels's relief and surprise, takes him not to the local police but to a seedy motel, where they share an afternoon that justifies the film's R rating. This moves from hilarious beginnings to true edge-of-the-seat terror. Rated R. 113m. **DIR:** Jonathan Demme. **CAST:** Jeff Daniels, Melanie Griffith, Ray Liotta, Margaret Colin, Tracey Walter. **1986**

SON-IN-LAW ★★★ Credit irrepressible Pauly Shore with keeping this hayseed comedy afloat, despite tired sight gags milked to death years ago on television's *Green Acres.* He plays a spaced-out valley guy who transforms the repressed and conservative parents of girlfriend Carla Gugino. Although terminally silly, the film delivers a solid, family-oriented moral. Rated PG-13 for sexual innuendo. 96m. **DIR:** Steve Rash. **CAST:** Pauly Shore, Carla Gugino, Lane Smith. **1993**

SON OF PALEFACE ★★★½ Bob Hope is in top shape as he matches wits with smooth villain Douglass Dumbrille and consistently loses, only to be aided by gun-totin' Jane Russell and government agent Roy Rogers. 95m. **DIR:** Frank Tashlin. **CAST:** Bob Hope, Jane Russell, Roy Rogers, Douglas Dumbrille, Bill Williams, Harry Von Zell, Iron Eyes Cody. **1952**

SON OF THE PINK PANTHER ★★ Writer-director Blake Edwards should quit while he's behind. Despite the usually funny Roberto Benigni (as Inspector Clouseau's illegitimate son), this leaden comedy loses its appeal after Bobby McFerrin's quirky rendition of Henry Mancini's "Pink Panther Theme." Rated PG for comic violence. 93m. **DIR:** Blake Edwards. **CAST:** Roberto Benigni, Herbert Lom, Claudia Cardinale, Jennifer Edwards, Robert Davi, Burt Kwouk. **1993**

SONS OF THE DESERT ★★★★★ In *Sons of the Desert,* Stan Laurel and Oliver Hardy scheme to get away from their wives and attend a lodge convention in Chicago. After persuading the wives that Ollie needs to sail to Honolulu for his health, they go to Chicago. The boat sinks on the way back from Hawaii, and the boys end up having to explain how they got home a day earlier than the other survivors (they ship-hiked). B&W; 69m. **DIR:** William A. Seiter. **CAST:** Stan Laurel, Oliver Hardy, Charlie Chase. **1933**

SORORITY BABES IN THE SLIMEBALL BOWL-O-RAMA ★★★½ A spoof of horror films. A group of kids break into a bowling alley and accidentally release a murderous little demon. Silly and with low production values, but it's a lot of gory fun. Rated R for nudity, violence, and profanity. 77m. **DIR:** David DeCoteau. **CAST:** Linnea Quigley, Andras Jones, Robin Rochelle. **1987**

SORROWFUL JONES ★★★ Bob Hope's first semiserious film, this is a remake of the 1934 Shirley Temple hit, *Little Miss Marker.* Bob, as a bookie, gets tangled up with nightclub singer Lucille Ball and an assortment of gangsters while baby-sitting a gambler's baby daughter. A good mix of wisecracks, fast action, and sentiment. B&W; 88m. **DIR:** Sidney Lanfield. **CAST:** Bob Hope, Lucille Ball, Mary Jane Saunders, Thomas Gomez, William Demarest, Bruce Cabot. **1949**

SOUL MAN ★★★ Los Angeles preppie Mark Watson (C. Thomas Howell) masquerades as a needy black to gain entrance to Harvard Law School. Director Steve Miner keeps things moving so fast one doesn't have time to consider how silly it all is. Rated PG-13 for profanity, suggested sex, and violence. 101m. **DIR:** Steve Miner. **CAST:** C. Thomas Howell, Rae Dawn Chong, James Earl Jones, Arye Gross, James B. Sikking, Leslie Nielsen. **1986**

SOUP FOR ONE ★★★ Marcia Strassman (formerly the wife on *Welcome Back Kotter*) stars as the dream girl to an often disappointed lover. Although there are a few slow-moving parts, it is a generally enjoyable comedy. Rated R for sexual themes. 87m. **DIR:** Jonathan Kaufer. **CAST:** Saul Rubinek, Marcia Strassman, Teddy Pendergrass. **1982**

SOUTHERN YANKEE, A ★★★ Red Skelton captures an elusive Confederate spy, then assumes his identity, going behind rebel lines with fake Union war plans. Some very good sight gags, reportedly devised by Buster Keaton. B&W; 90m. **DIR:** Edward Sedgwick. **CAST:** Red Skelton, Brian Donlevy, Arlene Dahl, John Ireland. **1948**

SPACEBALLS ★★ The plot loosely concerns planet Spaceball's attempt to "steal" the atmosphere from neighbor Druidia by kidnapping and ransoming off the royally spoiled Princess Vespa. The wacky Dark Helmet (Rick Moranis) is responsible for this dastardly plot, and he is opposed by rogue trader Lone Starr (Bill Pullman). Rated PG for mild profanity. 96m. **DIR:** Mel Brooks. **CAST:** Mel Brooks, John Candy, Rick Moranis, Bill Pullman, Daphne Zuniga, Dick Van Patten, George Wyner, Michael Winslow, Lorene Yarnell. **1987**

SPACED OUT ★★★ In this spoof of science-fiction films, the Earth is visited by an all-female crew on a broken-down spaceship. Three men and a woman are taken hostage and the discovery of the differences between men and women make for a watchable but raunchy comedy. This film is rated R for nudity and implied sex. 85m. **DIR:** Norman J. Warren. **CAST:** Barry Stokes, Tony Maiden, Glory Annen. **1985**

SPACESHIP 🦃 This "comedy" is all about an unwanted alien tagging along on a rocket full of idiots. Original title: *The Creature Wasn't Nice.* Rated PG. 88m. **DIR:** Bruce Kimmel. **CAST:** Cindy Williams, Bruce Kimmel, Leslie Nielsen, Gerrit Graham. **1981**

SPALDING GRAY: TERRORS OF PLEASURE ★★★★ Spalding Gray, the master storyteller, relates the humorous adventure of finding the perfect retreat and piece of land to call his own. This HBO special was filmed in concert, but some terrific editing takes you to the scenes he describes. The star of *Swimming to Cambodia* also describes his brief encounter with Hollywood. 60m. **DIR:** Thomas Schlamme. **CAST:** Spalding Gray. **1988**

SPEAK EASILY ★★½ Naïve college professor Buster Keaton is falsely informed that he has inherited a large sum of money and sets out to see the world. Along the way he befriends an itinerant theatre troupe, headed by Jimmy Durante. Tired and thin story. B&W; 82m. **DIR:** Edward Sedgwick. **CAST:** Buster Keaton, Jimmy Durante, Thelma Todd, Sidney Toler, Hedda Hopper, Edward Brophy, Henry Armetta. **1932**

SPIES, LIES, AND NAKED THIGHS ★★★½ If you laughed at *The In-Laws*, you should enjoy this similar made-for-TV movie. Harry Anderson plays an eccentric government agent who enlists skeptical interpreter Ed Begley Jr. in his quest to save the world from a maniac armed with...well, we won't spoil it. 100m. **DIR:** James Frawley. **CAST:** Harry Anderson, Ed Begley Jr., Linda Purl, Wendy Crewson. **1988**

SPIES LIKE US ★★½ Chevy Chase and Dan Aykroyd, who were co-stars on the original *Saturday Night Live* television show, appeared together on the big screen for the first time in this generally enjoyable comedy about two inept recruits in a U.S. intelligence organization's counterespionage mission. Rated PG for violence and profanity. 104m. **DIR:** John Landis. **CAST:** Chevy Chase, Dan Aykroyd, Bruce Davison, William Prince, Steve Forrest, Bernie Casey, Donna Dixon. **1985**

SPIKE & MIKE'S FESTIVAL OF ANIMATION ★★★★ Well-balanced compilation of animated short subjects that include two Academy Award–winning efforts: "Tango" and "Charade." Impressive representation of the medium includes everything from the hilarious "Snookles" and "Bambi Meets Godzilla" to the abstract "Primiti Too Taa." Unrated. 80m. **DIR:** Mike Gribble, Craig Decker. **1991**

SPIKE OF BENSONHURST ★★ Haphazard comedy-drama about life in a Mafia-run neighborhood in New York City. Sasha Mitchell stars as a young Italian boxer trying to get his big break. Rated R for nudity, violence, and profanity. 102m. **DIR:** Paul Morrissey. **CAST:** Sasha Mitchell, Ernest Borgnine, Sylvia Miles. **1989**

SPIRIT OF '76, THE ★★ Spoof of the Seventies has three people traveling back in time to bring back the Constitution—and thereby revive their dying culture. We found this comedy a disco drag, but it has its admirers. Rated PG for profanity. 82m. **DIR:** Lucas Reiner. **CAST:** David Cassidy, Olivia D'Abo, Leif Garrett, Barbara Bain, Julie Brown, Tommy Chong, Don Novello, Carl Reiner, Rob Reiner, Moon Zappa. **1991**

SPITE MARRIAGE ★★★★ Buster Keaton is a pants presser who masquerades as a millionaire to impress actress Dorothy Sebastian. When she is spurned by her lover, she marries Keaton out of spite, and he seeks to win her true love. Silent. B&W; 77m. **DIR:** Edward Sedgwick. **CAST:** Buster Keaton, Dorothy Sebastian. **1929**

SPLASH ★★★★★ An uproarious comedy about a young man (Tom Hanks) who unknowingly falls in love with a mermaid (Daryl Hannah). John Candy and Eugene Levy add some marvelous bits of comedy. Rated PG for profanity and brief nudity. 111m. **DIR:** Ron Howard. **CAST:** Tom Hanks, Daryl Hannah, John Candy, Eugene Levy, Dody Goodman, Richard B. Shull. **1984**

SPLITTING HEIRS ★★★★ Wonderfully silly comedy about two babies switched at birth, resulting in the wrong man becoming the sixteenth Duke of Bournemouth. Eric Idle is the real heir. When he discovers the truth about his heritage, he plots to murder the man who stole his title, Rick Moranis. Idle and Moranis play well off each other, while Idle's screenplay is a marvelous confection of comic situations and hilarious bits that recalls his TV spoof of the Beatles, *The Rutles*. Rated PG-13 for profanity, nudity, suggested sex, and violence. 88m. **DIR:** Robert Young. **CAST:** Eric Idle, Rick Moranis, John Cleese, Barbara Hershey, Catherine Zeta Jones, Sadie Frost, Stratford Johns. **1993**

SPOOKS RUN WILD 🦃 Bela Lugosi in another silly role that gives the aging East Side Kids a chance to humiliate him on-screen. B&W; 69m. **DIR:** Phil Rosen. **CAST:** Bela Lugosi, The East Side Kids, Dave O'Brien, Dennis Moore. **1941**

SPRING BREAK 🦃 Four guys on the make in Fort Lauderdale. R rating. 101m. **DIR:** Sean S. Cunningham. **CAST:** David Knell, Steve Bassett, Perry Lang, Paul Land. **1983**

SPRING FEVER 🦃 Canadian production is an unbelievably dull story about a rising young tennis star (Carling Bassett). Rated PG. 100m. **DIR:** Joseph L. Scanlan. **CAST:** Jessica Walter, Susan Anton, Frank Converse, Carling Bassett, Stephen Young. **1983**

SPY WITH A COLD NOSE, THE ★★★ This cute British spy spoof features Lionel Jeffries as an un-Bond-like counterintelligence agent. His plan to implant a microphone in the goodwill gift to the Soviets goes awry. The gift, a bulldog, may require an operation, and then the Soviets would be outraged. 113m. **DIR:** Daniel Petrie. **CAST:** Laurence Harvey, Daliah Lavi, Lionel Jeffries, Eric Sykes, Paul Ford. **1966**

S*P*Y*S 🦃 CIA agents assisting a Russian dancer wanting to defect to the West. 87m. **DIR:** Irvin Kershner. **CAST:** Donald Sutherland, Elliott Gould, Joss Ackland. **1974**

SQUEEZE, THE (1987) 🦃 Michael Keaton can always be counted on for at least a few laughs, but a few laughs is about all you get in this dreary comedy-thriller. It's rated PG-13 for language and violence. 101m. **DIR:** Roger Young. **CAST:** Michael Keaton, Rae Dawn Chong, Meat Loaf. **1987**

SQUEEZE PLAY ★★ Another Troma trauma from the world's cheapest movie studio, a proudly dumb comedy that transfers the battle of the sexes to a softball field. Strictly for the couchbound whose remote controls are broken. Rated R for vulgarity and brief nudity. 92m. **DIR:** Samuel Weil. **CAST:** Jim Harris. **1980**

STAGE DOOR ★★★★ A funny and tender taste of New York theatrical life. Katharine Hepburn and Ginger Rogers are two aspiring actresses who undergo the stifling yet stimulating life of a lodging house that caters to a vast array of prospective actresses. Eve Arden, Lucille Ball, and Ann Miller also take residence in this overcrowded and active boardinghouse. B&W; 92m. **DIR:** Gregory La Cava. **CAST:** Katharine Hepburn, Ginger Rogers, Eve Arden, Lucille Ball, Ann Miller. **1937**

STAND-IN ★★★ This send-up of Hollywood rubbed more than one Tinsel Town mogul the wrong way by satirizing front office studio manipulators. Eastern financial genius Leslie Howard is sent west to "stand in" for stockholders and find out why Colossal Pictures is heading for skidsville. B&W; 91m. **DIR:** Tay Garnett. **CAST:** Leslie Howard, Humphrey Bogart, Joan Blondell, Jack Carson, Alan Mowbray. **1937**

STAND-UP REAGAN ★★ Compilation of the ex-president's quips, jokes, and stories culled from speeches made during his presidency. Republicans will love it. Not rated. 40m. **DIR:** Drew Brown. **CAST:** Ronald Reagan. **1989**

STARDUST MEMORIES 🦃 Absolutely unwatchable Woody Allen film, his most chaotic and Bergmanesque attempt to claim that he can't stand his fans. Rated PG—profanity. B&W; 88m. **DIR:** Woody Allen. **CAST:** Woody Allen, Charlotte Rampling, Jessica Harper, Marie-Christine Barrault. **1980**

STARS AND BARS ★★ Inept comedy about a well-groomed British art expert who finds himself in a culture clash when he is sent to rural Georgia to acquire a priceless Renoir from an eccentric businessman. Pretty disappointing considering the fine cast. Rated R for nudity and profanity. 99m. **DIR:** Pat O'Connor. **CAST:** Daniel Day-Lewis, Harry Dean Stanton, Maury Chaykin, Joan Cusack, Keith David, Spalding Gray, Will Patton, Martha Plimpton, Steven Wright. **1988**

START THE REVOLUTION WITHOUT ME ★★★★ Gene Wilder and Donald Sutherland star in this hilarious comedy as two sets of twins who meet just before the French Revolution. Cheech and Chong's *The Corsican Brothers* covered the same ground. If you want to see the story done right, check this one out. Rated PG. 98m. **DIR:** Bud Yorkin. **CAST:** Gene Wilder, Donald Sutherland, Hugh Griffith, Jack MacGowran. **1970**

STARTING OVER ★★★★ Burt Reynolds and Jill Clayburgh are delightful in this Alan Pakula film about two lonely hearts trying to find romance in a cynical world. Candice Bergen is superb as Reynolds's off-key singer/ex-wife, whom he has trouble trying to forget in this winner. Rated R. 106m. **DIR:** Alan J. Pakula. **CAST:** Burt Reynolds, Jill Clayburgh, Candice Bergen, Charles Durning, Frances Sternhagen. **1979**

STATUE, THE 🦃 A Nobel Prize–winning linguist and a nude statue. Rated R for innuendos and nudity. 84m. **DIR:** Rod Amateau. **CAST:** David Niven, Virna Lisi, Robert Vaughn, John Cleese. **1971**

STAY TUNED ★★★ John Ritter is a couch potato who buys a devilish satellite dish from the prince of darkness himself. Before long, he and wife Pam Dawber are sucked into a nightmarish world of television where programs like "Meet the Mansons" and "Driving Over Miss Daisy" compete with game shows like "You Can't Win" and "Sadistic Hidden Videos." Warner Brothers' great Chuck Jones directs a wonderful segment with Ritter and Dawber as cartoon mice running from a robotic cartoon cat. Dopey fun for the TV generation. Rated PG for mild violence. 98m. **DIR:** Peter Hyams. **CAST:** John Ritter, Pam Dawber, Jeffrey Jones, Eugene Levy, David Tom, Heather McComb. **1992**

STEAGLE, THE ★★★ Black comedy about how a daydreaming college professor (Richard Benjamin) deals with his mortality during the Cuban missile crisis. The week-long living spree he goes on has some hilarious consequences, but the screenplay is not handled very well despite the excellent cast. Rated PG for profanity and sex. 94m. **DIR:** Paul Sylbert. **CAST:** Richard Benjamin, Cloris Leachman, Chill Wills, Susan Tyrrell, Peter Hobbs. **1971**

STEAMBOAT BILL JR. ★★★★½ Buster Keaton is at his comedic-genius best in this delightful silent film as an accident-prone college student who is forced to take over his father's old Mississippi steamboat. The climax features spectacular stunts by Keaton. It is truly something to behold—and to laugh with. Silent. B&W; 71m. **DIR:** Charles F. Reisner. **CAST:** Buster Keaton, Ernest Torrence, Marion Byron. **1928**

STEELYARD BLUES ★★★½ This is a quirky little film about a group of social misfits who band together to help one of their own against his government-employed brother. Jane Fonda, Donald Sutherland, and Peter Boyle seem to have fun playing the misfits. Boyle's imitation of Marlon Brando is a highlight. Rated PG for language. 93m. **DIR:** Alan Myerson. **CAST:** Jane Fonda, Donald Sutherland, Peter Boyle, Alan Myerson, Garry Goodrow. **1973**

STEVE MARTIN LIVE ★★★½ Though the bulk of this video offers a 1979 live performance that you've probably already seen in part on television, you'll enjoy this comedy video. If you're a fan of Martin's onstage bits, such as "King Tut" and "Happy Feet," the live segment is for you. Viewers are also offered a tasty helping of Martin's satirical wit in his comedic short, *The Absent Minded Waiter*, which was nominated for an Academy Award. 60m. **DIR:** Carl Gottlieb, Gary Weis. **CAST:** Steve Martin, Buck Henry, Teri Garr, David Letterman, Paul Simon, Alan King, Henny Youngman, Henry Winkler. **1986**

STEVEN WRIGHT LIVE ★★★½ For fans of the low-octane, extremely cerebral comic Steven Wright, this performance film is paradise. Wright delivers an endless stream of odd observations. He's funny, but an hour of deadpan is almost an eternity. 60m. **DIR:** Walter C. Miller. **CAST:** Steven Wright. **1985**

STEWARDESS SCHOOL 🦃 Perfectly awful stewardess comedy. Rated PG. 93m. **DIR:** Ken Blancato. **CAST:** Judy Landers, Wendie Jo Sperber, Sandahl Bergman, Brett Cullen, Mary Cadorette, Vicki Frederick, Vito Scotti, Donny Most. **1987**

STICK-UP, THE 🦃 The alternate title, *Mud*, seems more appropriate for this dreary romance-adventure set in 1935 England. 101m. **DIR:** Jeffrey Bloom. **CAST:** David Soul, Pamela McMyler. **1977**

STICKY FINGERS 🦃 Two struggling female musicians are handed $900,000 in dirty money by a drug-dealing friend. Rated PG-13 for language and sexual allusions. 89m. **DIR:** Catlin Adams. **CAST:** Helen Slater, Melanie Mayron, Eileen Brennan, Christopher Guest, Stephen McHattie, Shirley Stoler, Gwen Welles, Danitra Vance, Carol Kane. **1988**

STILL NOT QUITE HUMAN ★★½ While still delivering family fun, this made-for-cable film is the weakest and most unbelievable in the Disney trilogy. Chip's scientist father (Alan Thicke) is cloned by an evil scientist. Chip must find his real dad who is being tortured to reveal his computer technology secrets. 90m. **DIR:** Eric Luke. **CAST:** Alan Thicke, Jay Underwood, Christopher Neame, Rosa Nevin, Betsy Palmer. **1992**

STILL SMOKIN' 🦃 Shambles about a film festival in Amsterdam. Rated R for nudity and scatological humor. 91m. **DIR:** Thomas Chong. **CAST:** Cheech and Chong, Hansman In't Veld, Carol Van Herwijnen. **1983**

STIR CRAZY ★★★½ Richard Pryor and Gene Wilder work something close to a miracle, making something out of nothing or, at least, close to nothing. It's a simpleminded spoof of crime and prison movies with, of all things, a little *Urban Cowboy* thrown in. But you have so much fun watching the stars, you don't mind. Rated R. 111m. **DIR:** Sidney Poitier. **CAST:** Richard Pryor, Gene Wilder, Georg Stanford Brown, JoBeth Williams. **1980**

STITCHES 🦃 Med school students playing pranks. Rated R. 92m. **DIR:** Alan Smithee. **CAST:** Parker Stevenson, Geoffrey Lewis, Eddie Albert. **1985**

STOOGEMANIA 🦃 It's the story of Howard F. Howard (Josh Mostel), a man whose life is controlled by watching Three Stooges films. Not rated. 83m. **DIR:** Chuck Workman. **CAST:** Josh Mostel, Melanie Chartoff, Sid Caesar, Moe Howard, Curly Howard, Larry Fine, Shemp Howard. **1985**

STOP! OR MY MOM WILL SHOOT ★★★ Silly farce about a cop attempting to survive a visit by his overbearing mother. Anyone who is disappointed by this piece of fluff should have known better than to rent it in the first place. Rated PG. 87m. **DIR:** Roger Spottiswoode. **CAST:** Sylvester Stallone, Estelle Getty, JoBeth Williams, Roger Rees, Martin Ferrero, Gailard Sartain, Dennis Burkley. **1992**

STORM IN A TEACUP ★★★ The refusal of an old lady to pay for a dog license touches off this amusing farrago on love, politics, and life. Rex Harrison is, of course, smashing. The dialogue is the thing. B&W; 87m. **DIR:** Victor Saville, Ian Dalrymple. **CAST:** Vivien Leigh, Rex Harrison, Cecil Parker, Sara Allgood. **1937**

STRAIGHT TALK ★★★½ An Arkansas country girl decides to try her luck in Chicago, where she finds her gift for gab the ticket to success as a radio talk-show host. Dolly Parton and a superb supporting cast make every scene believable. Surprisingly good. Rated PG for profanity. 87m. **DIR:** Barnet Kellman. **CAST:** Dolly Parton, James Woods, Griffin Dunne, Michael Madsen, Philip Bosco, Jerry Orbach, John Sayles, Teri Hatcher, Spalding Gray, Charles Fleischer. **1992**

STRANGE BREW ★★★½ Okay, all you hosers and hoseheads, here come those *SCTV* superstars from the Great White North, Bob and Doug McKenzie (Rick Moranis and Dave Thomas) in their first feature film. Beauty, eh? A mad scientist employed by a brewery controls a group of mental patients by feeding them beer laced with a mind-controlling drug. Rated PG. 90m. **DIR:** Dave Thomas, Rick Moranis. **CAST:** Rick Moranis, Dave Thomas, Max von Sydow, Paul Dooley, Lynne Griffin. **1983**

STRANGER THAN PARADISE ★★★★½ In this superb independently made comedy, three oddball characters go on a spontaneous road trip through the United States, where they encounter boredom, routine problems, bad luck, and outrageous good fortune. The film, which won acclaim at the Cannes and New York film festivals, plays a lot like a Woody Allen comedy. It's a silly film for smart people. Rated R for profanity. B&W; 90m. **DIR:** Jim Jarmusch. **CAST:** John Lurie, Richard Edson, Eszter Balint. **1985**

STRICTLY BUSINESS ★★★ Frequent laughs, deft characterizations, and fine acting save what could have been little more than a paint-by-the-numbers movie about a streetwise office boy whose success in business is connected to the rise of a junior executive. Rated PG-13 for profanity and violence. 83m. **DIR:** Kevin Hooks. **CAST:** Tommy Davidson, Joseph C. Phillips, Halle Berry, Anne-Marie Johnson, David Marshall Grant, Jon Cypher. **1991**

STRIKE IT RICH ★★ Whirlwind romance results in a honeymoon at Monte Carlo for a prudish British accountant (Robert Lindsay) and his young wife (Molly Ringwald). Bland romantic comedy derived from a Graham Greene novel. Rated PG. 90m. **DIR:** James Scott. **CAST:** Robert Lindsay, Molly Ringwald, John Gielgud, Simon de la Brosse. **1990**

STRIKE UP THE BAND ★★★ This encore to *Babes in Arms* has ever-exuberant Mickey Rooney leading a high school band that would shade Glenn Miller's. Second banana Judy Garland sings. "Come on, kids, let's put on a show" in a different setting. B&W; 120m. **DIR:** Busby Berkeley. **CAST:** Mickey Rooney, Judy Garland, June Preisser, Paul Whiteman. **1940**

STRIPES ★★★★ It's laughs aplenty when *Saturday Night Live* graduate Bill Murray enlists in the army. But hey, as Murray might say, after a guy loses his job, his car, and his girl all in the same day, what else is he supposed to do? Thanks to Murray, Harold Ramis, and John Candy, the U.S. Army may never be the same. Warren Oates also is in top form as the no-nonsense sergeant. Rated R. 105m. **DIR:** Ivan Reitman. **CAST:** Bill Murray, Harold Ramis, John Candy, Warren Oates, P. J. Soles, Sean Young, John Larroquette. **1981**

STROKE OF MIDNIGHT ★★½ Filmed in Paris, this features Jennifer Grey as a drab high-fashion dresser who makes a Cinderella-type transformation after a fairy godmother rewards her for a good deed. Cute fantasy is okay time-passer. Rated PG for profanity. 102m. **DIR:** Tom Clegg. **CAST:** Jennifer Grey, Rob Lowe, Andrea Ferreol. **1990**

STROKER ACE ★★★ Film critics all over the country jumped on this car-crash-and-corn-pone comedy. It's not all that bad. About an egotistical, woman-chasing race-car driver, it's the same old predictable nonsense. Yet it's certain to please the audience it was intended for. Rated PG for sexual innuendo and violence. 96m. **DIR:** Hal Needham. **CAST:** Burt Reynolds, Ned Beatty, Jim Nabors, Loni Anderson, Parker Stevenson. **1983**

STRONG MAN, THE ★★★½ At one time silent comedy star Harry Langdon gave Charlie Chaplin, Buster Keaton, and Harold Lloyd a run for their money. *The Strong Man*, directed by a very young Frank Capra, is Langdon's best feature film. Langdon plays a young Belgian soldier who wistfully dreams of the American girl he has been corresponding with while bungling most of his assignments on the battlefield. Silent. B&W; 75m. **DIR:** Frank Capra. **CAST:** Harry Langdon, Priscilla Bonner, Robert McKim. **1926**

STUCK ON YOU 🦃 A dewinged Angel Gabriel is sent to Earth to help bring a couple back together. Rated R for nudity, obscenities, and simulated sex. 86m. **DIR:** Michael Herz, Samuel Weil. **CAST:** Professor Irwin Corey, Virginia Penta, Mark Mikulski. **1982**

STUDENT CONFIDENTIAL ★★½ A new school counselor helps some problem children with high IQs. *Student Confidential* does not speak to teens with the self-satisfaction of *The Breakfast Club* or the brutality of *River's Edge*, but it is far better than most teen films. Rated R for violence, profanity, and nudity. 92m. **DIR:** Richard Horian. **CAST:** Eric Douglas, Marlon Jackson, Ronee Blakley. **1987**

STUFF STEPHANIE IN THE INCINERATOR Excruciatingly bad stalk-and-hunt comedy that has nothing to do with an incinerator, but still deserves to get stuffed. Rated PG-13. 97m. **DIR:** Lloyd Kaufman. **CAST:** Catherine Dee. **1989**

SUBURBAN COMMANDO ★★½ Wrestler Hulk Hogan is extremely likable as an outer-space bounty hunter in this humorous comedy. Christopher Lloyd is a nebbish architect who learns to handle his boss with the help of Hogan's commando tactics. Rated PG. 85m. **DIR:** Burt Kennedy. **CAST:** Hulk Hogan, Christopher Lloyd, Shelley Duvall, Larry Miller, Jack Elam. **1991**

SULLIVAN'S TRAVELS ★★★★★ Pure genius produced this social comedy. It's the most beautifully witty and knowing spoof of Hollywood ever realized. Joel McCrea, playing a film director, decides to find out what life outside the Tinseltown fantasyland is really like. With only ten cents in his pocket, he sets out on his travels. Along the way, he acquires a fellow wanderer in the form of the lovely Veronica Lake. This is a genuine Hollywood classic. B&W; 90m. **DIR:** Preston Sturges. **CAST:** Joel McCrea, Veronica Lake, Robert Warwick, William Demarest, Franklin Pangborn, Porter Hall, Eric Blore, Jimmy Conlin. **1941**

SUMMER CAMP The madcaps in this case are teens invited to a reunion of their old summer camp. Rated R. 85m. **DIR:** Chuck Vincent. **CAST:** Michael Abrams, Jake Barnes. **1979**

SUMMER HOUSE, THE ★★★½ In the course of this relatively short film, director Waris Hussein makes mincemeat of Alice Thomas Ellis's novel, *The Clothes in the Wardrobe*. We're never quite sure what happened to sweet, hard-drinking Margaret (Lena Headey) in Egypt to upset her so much or why she agreed to marry the boorish Syl (David Threlfall), but Jeanne Moreau and Joan Plowright, as coconspirators in derailing the upcoming nuptials, are so deliciously oddball that the movie succeeds almost in spite of itself. Unrated, the film has brief moments of profanity, violence, and suggested sex. 83m. **DIR:** Waris Hussein. **CAST:** Jeanne Moreau, Joan Plowright, Julie Walters, Lena Headey, David Threlfall, Maggie Steed, John Wood, Gwenyth Strong, Catherine Schell. **1993**

SUMMER RENTAL ★★½ John Candy is watchable in his first film as star. Unfortunately, the film itself does not live up to his talents. It starts off well enough—with air traffic controller Candy exhibiting the kind of stress that causes his superiors to suggest a vacation—but after a fairly funny first hour, it sinks into the mire of plot resolution. Rated PG for profanity. 88m. **DIR:** Carl Reiner. **CAST:** John Candy, Richard Crenna, Karen Austin, Rip Torn, Kerri Green. **1985**

SUMMER SCHOOL ★★★★ This teen comedy does something almost unheard of for its genre—it bridges the generation gap and entertains young and old alike. Director Carl Reiner knows how to milk every scene for a laugh. Mark Harmon stars as a P.E. coach forced to teach remedial English in summer school. Rated PG-13 for obscenities and gore. 95m. **DIR:** Carl Reiner. **CAST:** Mark Harmon, Kirstie Alley, Nels Van Patten, Carl Reiner, Courtney Thorne-Smith, Lucy Lee Flippin, Shawnee Smith. **1987**

SUNSET LIMOUSINE John Ritter plays an out-of-work comic who must make something of himself before his girlfriend (Susan Dey) will take him back. Made for TV. 92m. **DIR:** Terry Hughes. **CAST:** John Ritter, Susan Dey, Martin Short, Paul Reiser, Audrie Neenan, Lainie Kazan. **1983**

SUNSHINE BOYS, THE ★★★★ *The Sunshine Boys* tells the story of two feuding ex-vaudeville stars who make a TV special. Walter Matthau, Richard Benjamin, and (especially) George Burns give memorable performances. Director Herbert Ross turns this adaptation of the successful Broadway play by Neil Simon into a celluloid winner. Rated PG. 111m. **DIR:** Herbert Ross. **CAST:** Walter Matthau, Richard Benjamin, George Burns, Lee Meredith, Carol Arthur, Howard Hesseman, Ron Rifkin. **1975**

SUPER, THE ★★★ Star Joe Pesci, as a slumlord sentenced to live in his dilapidated New York tenement building, makes this thin comedy easy to take. Without him, the silly, predictable story would be painful to watch. Rated R for profanity. 98m. **DIR:** Rod Daniel. **CAST:** Joe Pesci, Vincent Gardenia, Madolyn Smith, Rubén Blades. **1991**

SUPERGRASS, THE ★★ The reluctant hero (Adrian Edmondson) of this English farce pretends to be an important drug dealer in order to impress his girlfriend. Ultimately, the bloke is in way over his head. So-so comedy. 96m. **DIR:** Peter Richardson. **CAST:** Adrian Edmondson, Jennifer Saunders, Peter Richardson. **1987**

SUPPOSE THEY GAVE A WAR AND NOBODY CAME? ★★ In this comedy involving a confrontation between a rural town and a nearby military base, Brian Keith, Tony Curtis, and Ivan Dixon play three army buddies who take it upon themselves to stop the fighting. Some funny moments. Rated PG for adult themes. 113m. **DIR:** Hy Averback. **CAST:** Brian Keith, Ernest Borgnine, Suzanne Pleshette, Tom Ewell, Tony Curtis, Bradford Dillman, Ivan Dixon, Arthur O'Connell, Don Ameche. **1970**

SURE THING, THE ★★★½ This enjoyable romantic comedy, about two college freshmen who discover themselves and each other through a series of misadventures on the road, is more or less director Rob Reiner's updating of Frank Capra's *It Happened One Night*. John Cusack and Daphne Zuniga star as the unlikely protagonists. Rated PG-13 for profanity and suggested sex. 100m. **DIR:** Rob Reiner. **CAST:** John Cusack, Daphne Zuniga, Anthony Edwards, Boyd Gaines, Lisa Jane Persky. **1985**

SURF 2 ★★ Combination spoof of beach party and horror movies, with lunatic Eddie Deezen out for revenge on a group of surfers. Fitfully funny, with the best joke in the title: there is no *Surf 1*. Rated R for the obligatory topless beach bunnies. 91m. **DIR:** Randall Badat. **CAST:** Eddie Deezen, Linda Kerridge, Cleavon Little, Lyle Waggoner, Eric Stoltz, Corinne Bohrer, Ruth Buzzi. **1984**

SURPRISE PACKAGE ★★½ A change of pace for Yul Brynner as a high-living gambler deported to Greece, where he meets and decides to rob an exiled king (Noel Coward, who also sings the title song). So-so comedy, based on a novel by Art Buchwald. B&W; 100m. **DIR:** Stanley Donen. **CAST:** Yul Brynner, Mitzi Gaynor, George Coulouris, Noel Coward, Eric Pohlmann. **1960**

SURRENDER ★★★ Sally Field gives a sparkling performance as a confused woman in love with Michael Caine, Steve Guttenberg, and money, not necessarily in that order. Caine and Guttenberg are superb. At times contrived and a bit forced, overall, this is an enjoyable light comedy. Rated PG-13 for language and sex. 105m. **DIR:** Jerry Belson. **CAST:** Sally Field, Michael Caine, Steve Guttenberg, Peter Boyle, Julie Kavner, Jackie Cooper. **1987**

SURVIVING DESIRE ★★★ Kooky made-for-TV romance based on literary ideas rather than passion ignites between an untalented college professor (Martin Donovan) and his only attentive student (Mary Ward). Ward is a comic gem especially as she halfheartedly offers to help customers in a bookstore. Also included on the tape are two other Hal Hartley shorts *Theory of Achievement* and *Ambition*. 86m. **DIR:** Hal Hartley. **CAST:** Martin Donovan, Mary Ward, Matt Malloy, Rebecca Nelson. **1991**

SURVIVORS, THE ★★★½ This is an often funny movie about a goofy "survivalist" (Robin Williams), who is "adopted" by a service station owner (Walter Matthau) and pursued by a friendly but determined hit man (Jerry Reed). Generally a black comedy, this movie features a variety of comedic styles, and they all work. Rated R for vulgar language and violence. 102m. **DIR:** Michael Ritchie. **CAST:** Robin Williams, Walter Matthau, Jerry Reed, James Wainwright. **1983**

SUSAN SLEPT HERE ★★½ Screenwriter Dick Powell must keep a tight leash on the ultrahigh-spirited vagrant teenager he protects and falls for in the course of researching a script on juvenile delinquency. Amusing dialogue and lots of innuendo mark this otherwise pedestrian sex comedy. 98m. **DIR:** Frank Tashlin. **CAST:** Dick Powell, Debbie Reynolds, Anne Francis, Glenda Farrell. **1954**

SWAN, THE (1925) ★★½ While adored by a commoner, a princess is pursued by a playboy prince in this classic comedy-drama of manners drawn from the Ferenc Molnàr play. Silent. B&W; 112m. **DIR:** Dimitri Buchowetzki. **CAST:** Frances Howard, Adolphe Menjou, Ricardo Cortez. **1925**

SWEATER GIRLS 🦃 Teen sexcapade. Rated R for sex and language. 84m. **DIR:** Don Jones. **CAST:** Harry Moses, Meegan King, Noelle North, Kate Sarchet, Charlene Tilton. **1984**

SWEET LIBERTY ★★★★ Writer-director-star Alan Alda strikes again, this time with the story of a small-town historian (Alda) whose prize-winning saga of the Revolutionary War is optioned by Hollywood and turned into a movie. When the film crew descends on Alda's hometown for location shooting, predictable chaos erupts. Quite entertaining. Rated PG for mild sexual situations. 107m. **DIR:** Alan Alda. **CAST:** Alan Alda, Michael Caine, Michelle Pfeiffer, Bob Hoskins, Lise Hilboldt, Lillian Gish, Saul Rubinek, Lois Chiles, Linda Thorson. **1986**

SWEET LIES ★★ This so-called comedy contains little to laugh at, as Treat Williams plays an insurance investigator out to prove that a wheelchair-bound litigant is faking his injury. Ho-hum. Rated R for nudity and sexual situations. 96m. **DIR:** Nathalie Delon. **CAST:** Treat Williams, Joanna Pacula, Julianne Phillips. **1987**

SWEET REVENGE (1990) ★★★★ A newly divorced couple wrangle nonstop in this romantic comedy, originally telecast on cable. Lighthearted and pleasant, with some colorful European backgrounds. 89m. **DIR:** Charlotte Brandstrom. **CAST:** Carrie Fisher, John Sessions, Rosanna Arquette. **1990**

SWEET TALKER ★★★ Ex-convict Harry Reynolds (Bryan Brown) dupes the residents of an Australian village into investing in the excavation of a bogus sunken ship filled with gold. Harry befriends the local hotel owner's son, only to have the boy see him as a surrogate father. Charming story and good acting. Rated PG. 91m. **DIR:** Michael Jenkins. **CAST:** Bryan Brown, Karen Allen, Chris Haywood, Bill Kerr. **1990**

SWEET WILLIAM ★★★½ Sam Waterston and Jenny Agutter shine in this low-key adult comedy, which, while concerned with sex, doesn't feel the need to display any of it. She is attracted to his frenetic romanticism but slowly realizes that that same trait gets him into bed with every woman in sight. The women get the last laugh in this gentle British farce. Rated R for talk, not action. 92m. **DIR:** Claude Whatham. **CAST:** Sam Waterston, Jenny Agutter, Anna Massey, Tim Pigott-Smith. **1980**

SWIMMING TO CAMBODIA ★★★★ This low-budget movie consists of nothing more than actor-monologist Spalding Gray sitting at a desk while he tells about his experiences as a supporting actor in *The Killing Fields*. But seldom has so much come from so little. Gray is an excellent storyteller and his extended anecdotes—covering the political history of Cambodia, the filming of the movie, the sex and drugs available in Southeast Asia, and life in New York City—are often hilarious. Unrated. 87m. **DIR:** Jonathan Demme. **CAST:** Spalding Gray. **1987**

SWIMSUIT 🦃 Lousy made-for-TV movie about the search for a model for a new swimsuit line. 95m. **DIR:** Chris Thomson. **CAST:** William Katt, Catherine Oxenberg, Nia Peeples, Tom Villard, Jack Wagner, Billy Warlock, Cyd Charisse. **1989**

SWING HIGH, SWING LOW ★★½ Entertainers Carole Lombard and Fred MacMurray, stranded in Panama, get married, split, and fight ennui and a variety of troubles. This is a slanted-for-comedy remake of 1929's highly successful tearjerking backstage drama, *The Dance of Life*. B&W; 95m. **DIR:** Mitchell Leisen. **CAST:** Carole Lombard, Fred MacMurray, Dorothy Lamour, Charles Butterworth, Franklin Pangborn, Anthony Quinn. **1937**

SWING IT, SAILOR ★★ Envision two gobs after one gal, or make it two swabs after one skirt, and you've got this film figured out. Broad, roughhouse humor is the order of the day. The story is stale, but moves along at a decent clip. B&W; 61m. **DIR:** Raymond Connon. **CAST:** Wallace Ford, Isabel Jewell, Ray Mayer. **1937**

SWINGIN' SUMMER, A ★★ This is one of those swingin' Sixties flicks where three swingin' teens move to a swingin' summer resort for a swingin' vacation. They start up their own swingin' dance concert schedule and book big-name acts like Gary and the Playboys, the Rip Tides, and the Righteous Brothers. Raquel Welch debuts here and also sings. 82m. **DIR:** Robert Sparr. **CAST:** Raquel Welch, James Stacy, William Wellman Jr., Quinn O'Hara, Martin West. **1965**

SWISS MISS ★★★ Here we have Stan Laurel and Oliver Hardy in the Swiss Alps. A weak and uneven script is overcome by the stars, who seize several opportunities for brilliant comedy. For the most part, however, the film is mediocre. B&W; 72m. **DIR:** John G. Blystone. **CAST:** Stan Laurel, Oliver Hardy, Della Lind, Walter Woolf King, Eric Blore. **1938**

SWITCH ★★★ Writer-director Blake Edwards continues his exploration of the sexes with this story of a sleazy womanizer (Perry King) who is killed by his jilted ex-lovers only to come back as a woman. Ellen Barkin is wonderful as a male in a female body. Rated R for profanity and brief nudity. 104m. **DIR:** Blake Edwards. **CAST:** Ellen Barkin, Jimmy Smits, JoBeth Williams, Lorraine Bracco, Tony Roberts, Perry King, Bruce Payne. **1991**

SWITCHING CHANNELS ★★★ Effective performances by Kathleen Turner, Burt Reynolds, and Christopher Reeve enliven this fourth big-screen version of Ben Hecht and Charles MacArthur's *The Front Page*. More specifically a remake of Howard Hawks's 1940 comedy classic, *His Girl Friday*, *Switching Channels* switches from newspapers to television but keeps many of the elements of the original's plot. Rated PG for profanity. 113m. **DIR:** Ted Kotcheff. **CAST:** Kathleen Turner, Burt Reynolds, Christopher Reeve, Ned Beatty, Henry Gibson, Joe Silver. **1988**

TAKE DOWN ★★½ Earnest comedy-drama set in the arena of high school wrestling. It centers on two initially reluctant participants: an intellectual teacher-turned-coach and a fiery student. The movie has enough heart to carry it to victory. Rated PG. 107m. **DIR:** Kieth Merrill. **CAST:** Edward Herrmann, Kathleen Lloyd, Lorenzo Lamas, Maureen McCormick, Kevin Hooks, Stephen Furst. **1978**

TAKE THE MONEY AND RUN ★★★★ Woody Allen's first original feature is still a laugh-filled delight as the star-director plays an inept criminal in a story told in pseudo-documentary-style (à la *Zelig*). It's hilarious. Rated PG. 85m. **DIR:** Woody Allen. **CAST:** Woody Allen, Janet Margolin, Marcel Hillaire. **1969**

TAKE THIS JOB AND SHOVE IT ★★★½ Robert Hays stars as a rising corporate executive who returns, after a ten-year absence, to his hometown to take charge of a brewery where he once worked, and winds up organizing a revolt among his fellow employees. This contemporary comedy-drama is out to raise one's spirits, and it does just that. Rated PG. 100m. **DIR:** Gus Trikonis. **CAST:** Robert Hays, Art Carney, Barbara Hershey, Martin Mull, Eddie Albert. **1981**

TAKING CARE OF BUSINESS ★★★ Small-time crook James Belushi finds the Filofax of high-powered businessman Charles Grodin and takes over his business dealings, with predictable results. Wastes the talents of the two stars, mainly by not giving them enough scenes together. A harmless time killer. Rated R for profanity and sexual themes. 108m. **DIR:** Arthur Hiller. **CAST:** Charles Grodin, James Belushi. **1990**

TALK OF THE TOWN, THE ★★★★ Falsely accused of arson and murder, parlor radical Cary Grant escapes jail and holes up in a country house Jean Arthur is readying for law professor Ronald Colman. The radical and the egghead take to one another. Gifted direction and a brilliant cast make this topflight entertainment. B&W; 118m. **DIR:** George Stevens. **CAST:** Ronald Colman, Jean Arthur, Cary Grant, Edgar Buchanan, Glenda Farrell, Emma Dunn, Charles Dingle, Tom Tyler, Don Beddoe, Rex Ingram. **1942**

TALKIN' DIRTY AFTER DARK ★★½ Black comedy stars Martin Lawrence as a comedian who will do anything to land a spot at the infamous Dukie's nightclub, and that includes sleeping with the main man's main squeeze. Too much jive and not enough laughs. Rated R for language and nudity. 86m. **DIR:** Topper Carew. **CAST:** Martin Lawrence, John Witherspoon. **1991**

TALKING WALLS ★★ Offbeat, mildly interesting comedy-drama about a student who decides to do his thesis on sexual relationships by videotaping unwitting guests as they cavort in a sleazy Hollywood motel. Not rated, contains nudity, sex, and vulgar language. 85m. **DIR:** Stephen F. Verona. **CAST:** Stephen Shellen, Marie Laurin, Sybil Danning, Sally Kirkland, Barry Primus. **1987**

TALL GUY, THE ★★★½ Delightfullly whacked-out comedy about an American actor (Jeff Goldblum) stuck in a dead-end London gig as a foil for a loud, obnoxious, and egotistical comedian (Rowan Atkinson). This all changes when he falls in love with a no-nonsense nurse (Emma Thompson). Rated R for profanity and nudity. 90m. **DIR:** Mel Smith. **CAST:** Jeff Goldblum, Emma Thompson, Rowan Atkinson, Geraldine Jones. **1990**

TALL STORY ★★★ Jane Fonda makes a delightful college student who falls for a basketball player. This is Fonda's first movie and shows her flair for comedy. B&W; 90m. **DIR:** Joshua Logan. **CAST:** Jane Fonda, Anthony Perkins, Elizabeth Patterson, Ray Walston, Anne Jackson, Murray Hamilton, Gary Lockwood, Marc Connelly, Tom Laughlin. **1960**

TAMING OF THE SHREW, THE (1929) ★★★ The first royal couple of Hollywood costarred in this film while under the duress of a failing marriage. Mary Pickford is properly shrewish as Katharina; Douglas Fairbanks is smug, commanding, and virile as Petruchio. Critics liked it and the public flocked to see the famous duo have at the Bard. Director Sam Taylor gave Hollywood one of its enduring anecdotes by taking screen credit for additional dialogue. B&W; 66m. **DIR:** Sam Taylor. **CAST:** Mary Pickford, Douglas Fairbanks Sr., Dorothy Jordan. **1929**

TAMING OF THE SHREW, THE (1966) ★★★★½ This is a beautifully mounted comedy of the battle of the sexes. Petruchio (Richard Burton), a spirited minor nobleman of the Italian Renaissance, pits his wits against the man-hating Kate (Elizabeth Taylor) in order to win her hand. The zest with which this famous play is transferred to the screen can be enjoyed even by those who feel intimidated by Shakespeare. 126m. **DIR:** Franco Zeffirelli. **CAST:** Richard Burton, Elizabeth Taylor, Cyril Cusack, Michael York. **1966**

TAMING OF THE SHREW (1982) ★★★★ Inventive and laugh-filled, a stage production of Shakespeare's best-loved comedy as the ambitious Petruchio (Franklyn Seales) comes to wed himself well in Padua, choosing the fiery, mean-spirited Kate (Karen Austin) as his reluctant bride. Catch the running visual joke concerning Pisa. Released by Bard Productions Ltd. 115m. **DIR:** John Allison. **CAST:** Franklyn Seales, Karen Austin, Larry Drake, Kathryn Johnson, Bruce Davison, David Chemel. **1982**

TANNER '88 ★★★½ *Doonesbury* creator Garry Trudeau wrote this insightful tale of a dark-horse presidential candidate (played to perfection by Michael Murphy). Along the way Tanner runs into Bob Dole, Gary Hart, and Pat Robertson. Originally aired on HBO. 120m. **DIR:** Robert Altman. **CAST:** Michael Murphy, Pamela Reed, Cynthia Nixon, Kevin J. O'Connor, Daniel H. Jenkins. **1988**

TAPEHEADS ★★★ In this off-the-wall *Night Shift,* John Cusack plays a pretentious and obnoxious con man who convinces Tim Robbins, a video genius, to make music videos. Weird and funny viewing, and the chemistry between the two leads is perfect. Not rated; contains offensive language and sexual situations. 94m. **DIR:** Bill Fishman. **CAST:** John Cusack, Tim Robbins, Mary Crosby, Connie Stevens, Doug McClure, Lyle Alzado. **1988**

TATTLE TALE ★★½ C. Thomas Howell is a struggling actor whose ex-wife writes a "kiss and tell" book. Ally Sheedy is fabulous as the bitchy, egocentric hack, but Howell is lost amid silly disguises and a thin plot. Some clever moments but too unbelievable overall. Rated PG for profanity. 93m. **DIR:** Baz Taylor. **CAST:** C. Thomas Howell, Ally Sheedy. **1993**

TBONE N WEASEL ★★ Lame story follows the misadventures of two not-so-smart criminals. The film is played for laughs that never really come off. Stars try hard, but to no avail. 105m. **DIR:** Lewis Teague. **CAST:** Gregory Hines, Christopher Lloyd, Ned Beatty, Larry Hankin, Graham Jarvis. **1992**

TEACHERS ★★ This satirical look at a contemporary urban high school flunks as a film. Teachers will hate it because it's not serious enough; students will hate it because it's just terrible. It's no more interesting than a dull day in high school. Rated R for sexual innuendo, violence, and profanity. 106m. **DIR:** Arthur Hiller. **CAST:** Nick Nolte, JoBeth Williams, Judd Hirsch, Richard Mulligan, Ralph Macchio. 1984

TEACHER'S PET ★★★ Winsome journalism instructor Doris Day fascinates and charms hardboiled city editor Clark Gable in this near plotless but most diverting comedy of incidents. The two are terrific, but Gig Young, as the teacher's erudite but liquor-logged boyfriend, is the one to watch. B&W; 120m. **DIR:** George Seaton. **CAST:** Clark Gable, Doris Day, Gig Young, Mamie Van Doren, Nick Adams, Jack Albertson, Marion Ross. 1958

TEAHOUSE OF THE AUGUST MOON, THE ★★★½ The post–World War II Americanizing of Okinawa gets sent up in faultless style in this screen version of the 1952 Broadway stage comedy hit. Marlon Brando is amusing as the clever Okinawan interpreter who binds it all together, but it is blustering Paul Ford, from the stage production, who comes knife-edge close to stealing this memorable film. 123m. **DIR:** Daniel Mann. **CAST:** Marlon Brando, Glenn Ford, Eddie Albert, Machiko Kyo, Paul Ford. 1956

TED & VENUS ★★ Quirky, off-beat love story from director Bud Cort, who knows the territory well (he was Harold in *Harold & Maude*). This time he plays a poet whose fascination with the girl of his dreams forces him to go to extremes in order to get her attention. Some funny moments, but it's just too cordial to be crazy. Rated R for nudity and adult language. 100m. **DIR:** Bud Cort. **CAST:** Bud Cort, Carol Kane, James Brolin, Rhea Perlman, Andrea Martin, Martin Mull, Woody Harrelson. 1990

TEEN VAMP 🦃 High school nerd is transformed into a vampire by a bloodsucking prostitute. Rated R for violence and profanity. 87m. **DIR:** Samuel Bradford. **CAST:** Clu Gulager, Karen Carlson. 1988

TEEN WITCH ★★ Robyn Lively plays Louise, a high school wallflower who discovers on her sixteenth birthday that she has the powers of witchcraft. Some blandly catchy songs (by Larry Weir) are patched in for the music-video market. Rated PG-13 for mild profanity. 90m. **DIR:** Dorian Walker. **CAST:** Robyn Lively, Zelda Rubinstein, Dick Sargent, Shelley Berman. 1989

TELEPHONE, THE ★★ It's hard to like, but even harder to walk away from, this uneven comedy-drama. Whoopi Goldberg stars as an out-of-work actress who is more than a little nuts. Definitely for the midnight-movie junkie who will enjoy the bizarre ending. Rated R for profanity. 96m. **DIR:** Rip Torn. **CAST:** Whoopi Goldberg, Elliott Gould, Amy Wright, John Heard, Severn Darden. 1987

TELL IT TO THE JUDGE ★★★ Robert Cummings tries to talk ex-wife Rosalind Russell into remarrying him, not Gig Young. Amiable comedy coasts on star power. B&W; 87m. **DIR:** Norman Foster. **CAST:** Rosalind Russell, Robert Cummings, Gig Young, Marie McDonald, Louise Beavers. 1949

10 ★★★½ Ravel's "Bolero" enjoyed a renewed popularity, and Bo Derek rocketed to stardom because of this uneven but generally entertaining sex comedy, directed by Blake Edwards (*The Pink Panther*). Most of the film's funny moments come from the deftly timed physical antics of Dudley Moore, who plays a just-turned-40 songwriter who at long last meets the girl (Bo Derek) of his dreams—on her wedding day. Rated R. 122m. **DIR:** Blake Edwards. **CAST:** Dudley Moore, Bo Derek, Julie Andrews, Robert Webber. 1979

10 FROM YOUR SHOW OF SHOWS ★★★★ Ten skits from the early 1950s television program that set the pace for all variety shows. Granted, the style is dated and far from subtle, but as a joyful look at television's formative years, it can't be beat. Unrated. B&W; 92m. **DIR:** Max Liebman. **CAST:** Sid Caesar, Imogene Coca, Carl Reiner, Howard Morris, Louis Nye. 1973

TENDER TRAP, THE ★★★ Swinging bachelor Frank Sinatra takes aim at a young actress (Debbie Reynolds) who turns out less naïve (and more marriage-minded) than she seems. Sprightly stage-derived romantic comedy has clever dialogue, attractive stars, and a solid supporting cast. 111m. **DIR:** Charles Walters. **CAST:** Frank Sinatra, Debbie Reynolds, Celeste Holm, David Wayne, Carolyn Jones, Lola Albright. 1955

THAT CERTAIN THING ★★★ When a poor working-class girl (Viola Dana) marries a wealthy idler (Ralph Graves), they are cut off from his inheritance. Fairy-tale romance with more than a touch of the screwball comedies to come from director Frank Capra. Silent. B&W; 70m. **DIR:** Frank Capra. **CAST:** Viola Dana, Ralph Graves. 1928

THAT LUCKY TOUCH ★★★ This romantic comedy features unlikely neighbors falling in love. Roger Moore plays Michael Scott, a weapons merchant. Susannah York, on the other hand, is an antimilitary writer. Shelley Winters provides a few laughs as the airhead wife of a NATO general (Lee J. Cobb). Comparable with a PG, but basically pretty tame. 93m. **DIR:** Christopher Miles. **CAST:** Roger Moore, Susannah York, Shelley Winters, Lee J. Cobb, Sydne Rome. 1975

THAT SINKING FEELING ★★★★ Following Scottish director Bill Forsyth's box-office success with *Gregory's Girl* and *Local Hero,* his first feature was resurrected for release in America. It's a typically wry and dry comic affair about a group of unemployed young men deciding on a life of crime. The result is engaging silliness. Rated PG. 92m. **DIR:** Bill Forsyth. **CAST:** Robert Buchanan, John

Hughes, Billy Greenlees, Gordon John Sinclair. **1979**

THAT TOUCH OF MINK ★★★½ This 1962 romantic comedy is enjoyable, but only as escapist fare. Doris Day stars as an unemployed girl pursued by a wealthy businessman (Cary Grant). 99m. **DIR:** Delbert Mann. **CAST:** Doris Day, Cary Grant, Gig Young, Audrey Meadows, John Astin. **1962**

THAT UNCERTAIN FEELING ★★½ This is an amusing film about marital unrest until the midpoint, when the time-tried romantic triangle plot thins rather than thickens. Burgess Meredith all but filches the film in a supporting role. Merle Oberon is devastatingly beautiful, even when she has the hiccups—an important plot device. B&W; 86m. **DIR:** Ernst Lubitsch. **CAST:** Merle Oberon, Melvyn Douglas, Alan Mowbray, Burgess Meredith, Eve Arden, Sig Ruman. **1941**

THAT'S ADEQUATE ★★ This mock documentary rapidly exhausts its welcome. The sixty-year examination of the Adequate Pictures Studio includes glimpses of its many exploitation fiascos, such as *Singing in the Synagogue* and *Sigmund Freud in Sherwood Forest.* Rated R for raunchy language and brief nudity. 80m. **DIR:** Harry Hurwitz. **CAST:** Tony Randall, James Coco, Jerry Stiller, Anne Meara, Bruce Willis, Richard Lewis. **1989**

THAT'S LIFE ★★★ Jack Lemmon and Julie Andrews play a married couple enduring a torrent of crises during one fateful weekend. The film is a mixture of good and bad, funny and sad, tasteful and tasteless. That it ends up on the plus side is to the credit of its lead players. Rated PG-13 for profanity and scatological humor. 102m. **DIR:** Blake Edwards. **CAST:** Julie Andrews, Jack Lemmon, Sally Kellerman, Robert Loggia, Jennifer Edwards, Chris Lemmon. **1986**

THERE GOES THE NEIGHBORHOOD ★★★★ Prison shrink Jeff Daniels learns of $8.5 million of Mafia loot buried in the suburbs. Catherine O'Hara is the woman living over said loot. Quirky and cute, this breezy comedy is unpredictable and sweetly enjoyable. Rated PG-13 for profanity. 88m. **DIR:** Bill Phillips. **CAST:** Jeff Daniels, Catherine O'Hara, Dabney Coleman, Hector Elizondo, Judith Ivey, Rhea Perlman. **1992**

THERE'S A GIRL IN MY SOUP ★★½ Goldie Hawn hadn't completely shed her *Laugh-In* image when this British sex farce came out, and it didn't do her career any good. Quite a letdown, after her Oscar-winning performance in *Cactus Flower.* Peter Sellers is a middle-aged boob who falls in lust with flower child Hawn. A low point for all concerned. Rated R. 95m. **DIR:** Roy Boulting. **CAST:** Peter Sellers, Goldie Hawn, Diana Dors, Tony Britton. **1970**

THESE GIRLS WON'T TALK ★★ As a series of three silent short stories, this Mack Sennett–produced series is short of inspiration. The shorts are called *Her Bridal Nightmare, Campus Carmen,* and *As Luck Would Have It.* The most interesting thing about this compilation is seeing Carole Lombard long before she was a star. B&W; 50m. **DIR:** Mack Sennett. **CAST:** Colleen Moore, Carole Lombard, Betty Compson. **1920**

THEY ALL LAUGHED ★★★★ This is director Peter Bogdanovich at his best. A very offbeat comedy that looks at four New York private eyes' adventures and love lives. Final film of ex-Playboy bunny Dorothy Stratten. Worth a look. Rated PG. 115m. **DIR:** Peter Bogdanovich. **CAST:** Audrey Hepburn, Ben Gazzara, John Ritter, Dorothy Stratten. **1981**

THEY CALL ME BRUCE? ★★ In this unsophisticated kung fu comedy, Johnny Yune portrays an Asian immigrant who, because of his "resemblance" to Bruce Lee and an accidental exhibition of craziness (misinterpreted as martial arts expertise), gets a reputation as a mean man with fists and feet. But it is Ralph Mauro, playing Bruce's chauffeur, who steals the show. Rated PG. 88m. **DIR:** Elliot Hong. **CAST:** Johnny Yune, Ralph Mauro, Margaux Hemingway. **1982**

THEY GOT ME COVERED ★★½ Typical Bob Hope vehicle of the 1940s is full of gals, gags, goofy situations, snappy dialogue, and one-line zingers, and boasts an incredible supporting cast of great character actors and actresses. Thin story about spy nonsense in Washington, D.C., is secondary to the zany antics of Paramount's ski-nosed comedian. B&W; 95m. **DIR:** David Butler. **CAST:** Bob Hope, Dorothy Lamour, Lenore Aubert, Otto Preminger, Eduardo Ciannelli, Marion Martin, Donald MacBride, Donald Meek, Philip Ahn. **1943**

THEY STILL CALL ME BRUCE 🦃 Perhaps one of the least-anticipated sequels ever, this attempt by Korean comic Johnny Yune to follow up his 1982 nonhit *They Call Me Bruce?* is completely hopeless. It's rated PG for Yune's occasionally off-color humor. 91m. **DIR:** Johnny Yune, James Orr. **CAST:** Johnny Yune, David Mendenhall, Joey Travolta. **1987**

THIEF WHO CAME TO DINNER, THE ★★★ Silly stuff about Ryan O'Neal leading a double life: as a bookish computer programmer by day and a jewel thief by night. The film's most interesting performance comes from Jill Clayburgh in an early screen role. It's mindless fluff and inoffensive. Rated PG. 102m. **DIR:** Bud Yorkin. **CAST:** Ryan O'Neal, Jacqueline Bisset, Warren Oates, Jill Clayburgh, Charles Cioffi, Ned Beatty. **1973**

THINGS ARE TOUGH ALL OVER 🦃 Richard "Cheech" Marin and Tommy Chong up to no good. Rated R for profanity. 92m. **DIR:** Tom Avildsen. **CAST:** Cheech and Chong, Rikki Marin, Rip Taylor. **1982**

THINGS CHANGE ★★★★ Director David Mamet and his coscreenwriter, Shel Silverstein, have fashioned a marvelously subtle and witty comedy about an inept, low-level gangster (Joe Mantegna). He goes against orders to take an old shoe-shine "boy" (Don Ameche) on one last fling before the latter goes to prison for a crime he didn't commit. Rated PG for profanity and violence. 100m. **DIR:** David Mamet. **CAST:** Don Ameche, Joe Mantegna, Robert Prosky. **1988**

THINGS WE DID LAST SUMMER ★★½ A mixed bag used to supplement *Saturday Night Live* episodes in the show's first golden era, this features some of The Not Ready For Prime Time Players in skits of varying quality. The highlights are provided by John Belushi and Dan Aykroyd performing live in concert as the Blues Brothers. 50m. **DIR:** Gary Weis. **CAST:** John Belushi, Dan Aykroyd, Bill Murray, Gilda Radner, Garrett Morris, Laraine Newman. **1977**

THINK BIG ★★½ The perpetually late Barbarian Brothers (Peter and David Paul) are sent to L.A. to deliver a truckload of toxic waste, and a stowaway throws a wrench into their gears. Surprisingly good-natured in the dubious tradition of the all-star *Gumball Rally/Cannonball Run* films. PG-13. 86m. **DIR:** Jon Turteltaub. **CAST:** Martin Mull, Richard Moll, Michael Winslow, David Carradine, Richard Kiel, Ari Meyers, Claudia Christian, Peter Paul, David Paul. **1988**

THINKIN' BIG ★★ Soft-core beach romp with the usual horny teens heading for spring-break fun in the sun. Rated R for nudity. 94m. **DIR:** S. F. Brownrigg. **CAST:** Bruce Anderson, Nancy Buechler. **1986**

30 FOOT BRIDE OF CANDY ROCK, THE ★★ A nebbish inventor turns his girlfriend into a giant. A mild comedy with a certain amount of charm, this was the last film made by Columbia's B-picture unit, and Lou Costello's only feature film after breaking up with Bud Abbott. He died before the film was released. B&W; 75m. **DIR:** Sidney Miller. **CAST:** Lou Costello, Dorothy Provine, Gale Gordon, Charles Lane, Doodles Weaver. **1959**

30 IS A DANGEROUS AGE, CYNTHIA ★★ Dated British comedy features Dudley Moore as a pianist-composer who intends to find a bride and write a musical before he turns 30. 83m. **DIR:** Joseph McGrath. **CAST:** Dudley Moore, Suzy Kendall, Eddie Foy Jr., John Bird, Patricia Routledge. **1967**

THIS COULD BE THE NIGHT ★★★ A timid schoolteacher becomes a secretary to two nightclub owners and finds herself pursued by one of them. A fair try at a Damon Runyon atmosphere. Joan Blondell and J. Carrol Naish steal the movie. B&W; 103m. **DIR:** Robert Wise. **CAST:** Jean Simmons, Paul Douglas, Anthony Franciosa, Julie Wilson, Joan Blondell, J. Carrol Naish, ZaSu Pitts. **1957**

THIS HAPPY FEELING ★★ Curt Jurgens is an aging actor, Debbie Reynolds is the young girl who develops a crush on him, and John Saxon is Jurgens's handsome young neighbor who falls hard for Reynolds. The film is truly reflective of the 1950s, with its unreal colors and a musical score inundating every scene. Alexis Smith as "the other woman" is enjoyable. 92m. **DIR:** Blake Edwards. **CAST:** Debbie Reynolds, Curt Jurgens, John Saxon, Alexis Smith, Mary Astor, Estelle Winwood, Troy Donahue. **1958**

THIS IS MY LIFE ★★★ Sparkling dialogue and memorable characters help elevate this comedy about conflicting mother-daughter perspectives. The low spots involve onstage comedy routines by Mom (Julie Kavner). As with most movies about stand-up comics, these bits aren't really funny. Rated PG-13 for profanity. 94m. **DIR:** Nora Ephron. **CAST:** Julie Kavner, Samantha Mathis, Gaby Hoffman, Carrie Fisher, Dan Aykroyd. **1992**

THIS IS SPINAL TAP ★★★★½ This is one of the funniest movies ever made about rock 'n' roll. This is a satire of rock documentaries that tells the story of Spinal Tap, an over-the-hill British heavy-metal rock group that's fast rocketing to the bottom of the charts. *This Is Spinal Tap* isn't consistently funny, but does it ever have its moments. Some of the song lyrics are hysterical, and the performances are perfect. Rated R for profanity. 82m. **DIR:** Rob Reiner. **CAST:** Michael McKean, Christopher Guest, Harry Shearer, Rob Reiner. **1984**

THOSE DARING YOUNG MEN IN THEIR JAUNTY JALOPIES ★★★ Director Ken Annakin's follow up to *Those Magnificent Men In Their Flying Machines* lacks that certain spark it takes to make a classic, but there are some hilarious moments in this tale of a European road rally in the 1920s. Peter Cook and Dudley Moore as two very, very British officers are the best of the international cast. Rated G. 125m. **DIR:** Ken Annakin. **CAST:** Tony Curtis, Susan Hampshire, Peter Cook, Gert Fröbe, Dudley Moore, Terry-Thomas. **1969**

THOSE ENDEARING YOUNG CHARMS ★★★ Heroine Laraine Day brings smoothie Robert Young to bay and then to heel in this cliché-plotted, but sprightly played, romantic comedy. Public hunger for wholesome laughter and sentimental tears as World War II wound down made this a box-office bonanza. Ann Harding is perfect as the wise mother. B&W; 82m. **DIR:** Lewis Allen. **CAST:** Robert Young, Laraine Day, Bill Williams, Ann Harding, Anne Jeffreys, Lawrence Tierney. **1945**

THOSE MAGNIFICENT MEN IN THEIR FLYING MACHINES ★★★★ An air race between London and Paris in the early days of flight is this comedy's centerpiece. Around it hang an enjoyable number of rib-tickling vignettes. A large international cast, each get their chance to shine as the contest's zany participants. Terry-Thomas stands out as the hapless villain. 132m. **DIR:** Ken Annakin. **CAST:** Terry-Thomas, Stuart Whitman, Sarah Miles, Gert Fröbe. **1965**

THOUSAND CLOWNS, A ★★★★ Famous Broadway play comes to the screen with memorable performances by all the principals and standout jobs by Jason Robards as a talented nonconformist and Barry Gordon as his precocious ward. They struggle against welfare bureaucracy in order to stay together. Very funny in spots and equally poignant in others. B&W; 118m. **DIR:** Fred Coe. **CAST:** Jason Robards Jr., Barry Gordon, Barbara Harris, Martin Balsam, Gene Saks, William Daniels. **1965**

THREE AGES, THE ★★★½ Frozen-faced Buster Keaton coproduced and codirected this parody on the films of that master of excessiveness, Cecil B. DeMille. A funny and very enjoyable silent film. Not Keaton's best, but far from mundane. B&W; 89m. **DIR:** Buster Keaton, Eddie Cline. **CAST:** Buster Keaton, Wallace Beery, Oliver Hardy. **1923**

THREE AMIGOS ★★½ In this send-up of *The Cowboy Star,* Steve Martin, Chevy Chase, and Martin Short play three silent-screen cowboys who attempt to save a Mexican village from bloodthirsty banditos. Steve Martin, in particular, has some very funny moments. Overall, it's pleasant—even amusing—but nothing more. Rated PG. 105m. **DIR:** John Landis. **CAST:** Steve Martin, Chevy Chase, Martin Short, Alfonso Arau, Patrice Martinez, Joe Mantegna, Jon Lovitz. **1986**

THREE BROADWAY GIRLS ★★★ Three streetwise gold diggers stalk their prey among New York's socially prominent in this comedy adapted from Zoe Atkins's 1930 Broadway hit. Also titled *The Greeks Had a Word for Them.* B&W; 78m. **DIR:** Lowell Sherman. **CAST:** Joan Blondell, Ina Claire, Madge Evans, David Manners, Betty Grable. **1932**

THREE CHARLIES AND A PHONEY! ★★★ Two early Keystone comedies, "Recreation" and "His Musical Career," a special World War I bond sales promotion, "The Bond," and "His Day Out" make up this slapstick anthology. Silent. 1914–1918 with organ music; B&W; 69m. **DIR:** Charles Chaplin. **CAST:** Charlie Chaplin, Mack Swain, Edna Purviance, Sydney Chaplin.

THREE FOR BEDROOM C ★★★ Adequate farce that was the first film made by Gloria Swanson after her stunning comeback in *Sunset Boulevard.* She portrays a movie star who books a compartment on a train that is also occupied by a Harvard scientist. Predictable. 74m. **DIR:** Milton H. Bren. **CAST:** Gloria Swanson, James Warren, Fred Clark, Hans Conried, Margaret Dumont. **1952**

THREE FOR THE ROAD ★★ Dull comedy about a senator's aide (Charlie Sheen) who is assigned to take his employer's difficult daughter (Kerri Green) to a reform school. Rated PG. 95m. **DIR:** B.W.L. Norton. **CAST:** Charlie Sheen, Kerri Green, Alan Ruck, Sally Kellerman. **1987**

THREE FUGITIVES ★★★ France's current master of film comedy, Francois Veber, makes his American debut with this overly sentimental but often hilarious comedy about a hardened criminal (Nick Nolte) thrown together with a mute girl (Sarah Rowland Doroff) and her down-and-out dad (Martin Short) when the latter robs a bank and takes Nolte hostage. Rated PG-13 for profanity and violence. 90m. **DIR:** Francis Veber. **CAST:** Nick Nolte, Martin Short, James Earl Jones, Kenneth McMillan, Sarah Rowland Doroff. **1989**

THREE IN THE ATTIC ★★ Three women kidnap the college Lothario and get revenge by making him their sex slave. The titillating premise of this curio soon gives way to tired debates about relationships. Rated R. 91m. **DIR:** Richard Wilson. **CAST:** Christopher Jones, Yvette Mimieux, Judy Pace. **1968**

THREE IN THE CELLAR 🦃 Wes Stern as a college student who has just lost his scholarship. Unrated, this low-budget yawner contains nudity and sexual situations. 93m. **DIR:** Theodore J. Flicker. **CAST:** Wes Stern, Joan Collins, Larry Hagman, David Arkin, Judy Pace. **1970**

THREE MEN AND A BABY ★★★½ Tom Selleck, Steve Guttenberg, and Ted Danson are three carefree bachelors in this energetic remake of the French *Three Men and a Cradle.* The trio find an unexpected bundle at the door of their impeccably furnished apartment. The conclusion (changed from the French original) is hopelessly hokey, but getting there's a lot of fun. Rated PG for language. 102m. **DIR:** Leonard Nimoy. **CAST:** Tom Selleck, Steve Guttenberg, Ted Danson, Nancy Travis, Margaret Colin. **1987**

THREE MEN AND A LITTLE LADY ★★★ Amiable, lightweight sequel to *Three Men and a Baby,* in which the title trio (Tom Selleck, Steve Guttenberg, and Ted Danson) must confront the possibility of losing their ward when her mother (Nancy Travis) decides to marry. Rated PG for brief profanity. 106m. **DIR:** Emile Ardolino. **CAST:** Tom Selleck, Steve Guttenberg, Ted Danson, Nancy Travis, Robin Weisman, Christopher Cazenove. **1990**

THREE MEN ON A HORSE ★★★½ Frank McHugh, a timid greeting-card writer, handicaps winning horses as a hobby. Some small-time gamblers, led by Sam Levene, learn of his talent and turn it to their advantage. Stagy, but fun to watch. B&W; 87m. **DIR:** Mervyn LeRoy. **CAST:** Frank McHugh, Joan Blondell, Sam Levene, Guy Kibbee, Carol Hughes, Allen Jenkins, Edgar Kennedy, Eddie "Rochester" Anderson. **1936**

THREE MUSKETEERS, THE (1939) ★★★ The Ritz Brothers as Dumas's famous trio? Yes, it's true. As a comedy-musical, this picture rides a moderate course, sticking closely to the original story but never taking anything too seriously. Don Ameche is very sharp as D'Artagnan and Binnie Barnes is charming as Lady DeWinter. B&W; 73m. **DIR:** Allan Dwan. **CAST:** Don Ameche, The Ritz Brothers, Lionel Atwill, Binnie Barnes. **1939**

THREE NUTS IN SEARCH OF A BOLT 🦃 Three loonies, too poor to see a psychiatrist on their own, hire an out-of-work actor to pretend he has each of their symptoms. Not rated, but equal to PG-13 for nudity and adult situations. 78m. **DIR:** Tommy Noonan. **CAST:** Mamie Van Doren, Tommy Noonan, Paul Gilbert, Ziva Rodann. **1964**

THREE O'CLOCK HIGH ★★½ Director Phil Joanou leaves no doubt of his technical skill in his first film. Too bad his story is just a teen variation on *High Noon.* Jerry Mitchell (Casey Siemaszko) is an average high schooler who ends up having the worst day of his life. Rated PG-13 for profanity and violence. 95m. **DIR:** Phil Joanou. **CAST:** Casey Siemaszko, Anne Ryan, Richard Tyson, Jeffrey Tambor, Philip Baker Hall, John P. Ryan. **1987**

THREE STOOGES, THE (VOLUMES 1–10) ★★★★ The Three Stooges made 190 two-reel short subjects between 1934 and 1959. For over fifty years, people have either loved them or hated them. Those in the latter category should, of course, avoid these tapes. But if you are a fan, you'll find these collections the answer to a knucklehead's dream. Each cassette features three shorts of impeccable quality, transferred from brand-new, complete 35-mm prints. All of the films are from the classic "Curly" period, when the team was at the peak of its energy and originality. B&W; 60m. **DIR:** Various. **CAST:** Moe Howard, Curly Howard, Larry Fine. **1934**

THREE'S TROUBLE ★★★½ Screenwriter David Williamson often hits the bull's-eye with this warm, witty *Mr. Mom* Australian style. When a much put upon housewife hires a baby-sitter (handsome Steven Vidler), her know-it-all husband is forced to reassess his contributions to the family. Unrated, contains profanity. 93m. **DIR:** Chris Thomson. **CAST:** Jacki Weaver, John Waters, Steven Vidler. **1985**

THREESOME ★★ A woman (Lara Flynn Boyle) is assigned two male roommates in a college dorm. This clumsy film tries to mix leering sex farce with soulful sensitivity—*Porky's* meets *A Separate Peace.* The muttered dialogue is often inaudible. Rated R for profanity and simulated sex. 93m. **DIR:** Andrew Fleming. **CAST:** Lara Flynn Boyle, Stephen Baldwin, Josh Charles. **1994**

THRILL OF IT ALL, THE ★★★ Married life is perfect for housewife and mother Doris Day and doctor James Garner until she accepts a high-paying television commercial job in this witty observation of television, advertising, and domestic bliss, as scripted by Carl Reiner. 103m. **DIR:** Norman Jewison. **CAST:** Doris Day, James Garner, Arlene Francis, Edward Andrews, ZaSu Pitts, Elliott Reid, Reginald Owen, Alice Pearce. **1963**

THROW MOMMA FROM THE TRAIN ★★★ Gravel-voiced Anne Ramsey, as the titular Momma, is by far the best element of this comedy, which marks the directing debut of star Danny DeVito. He's a would-be writer in novelist Billy Crystal's class, and the two concoct a scheme to trade murders *à la* Hitchcock's *Strangers on a Train.* The finished film just doesn't provide the manic delight promised by its two stars. Rated PG-13 for language. 88m. **DIR:** Danny DeVito. **CAST:** Danny DeVito, Billy Crystal, Anne Ramsey, Kim Greist, Kate Mulgrew. **1987**

TIGER'S TALE, A 🦃 Grievously unfunny comedy about a not-so-bright teenage stud from Texas. Rated R for nudity. 97m. **DIR:** Peter Douglas. **CAST:** Ann-Margret, C. Thomas Howell, Charles Durning, Kelly Preston, William Zabka, Ann Wedgeworth, Tim Thomerson. **1988**

TIGHT LITTLE ISLAND ★★★★ A World War II transport laden with whiskey founders just off the shore of a Scottish island. Hilarious hell breaks loose as delirious lads and lassies seek to salvage the water of life before authorities can claim it. One of the great comedies that revived the British film industry after the war. B&W; 82m. **DIR:** Alexander Mackendrick. **CAST:** Basil Radford, Joan Greenwood, James Robertson Justice, Gordon Jackson. **1949**

TILT 🦃 Brooke Shields's third movie (after *Alice, Sweet Alice* and *Pretty Baby*) is a mess. Rated PG. 104m. **DIR:** Rudy Durand. **CAST:** Brooke Shields, Ken Marshall, Charles Durning, Geoffrey Lewis. **1978**

TIME OF THEIR LIVES, THE ★★½ Bearing more than a passing resemblance to *The Canterville Ghost* and *I Married a Witch,* this story of ghostly goings-on is one of Abbott and Costello's most unusual features. Costello plays a man mistakenly shot as a traitor during the Revolutionary War and doomed to haunt a Colonial mansion until proved innocent. B&W; 82m. **DIR:** Charles Barton. **CAST:** Bud Abbott, Lou Costello, Marjorie Reynolds, Binnie Barnes, John Shelton, Gale Sondergaard, Robert Barrat, Donald MacBride. **1946**

TIN MEN ★★★★ Writer-director Barry Levinson takes a simple subject—the vendetta between two aluminum-siding salesmen in the 1950s—and fashions it into an insightful, witty comedy. The tone is similar to Levinson's earlier *Diner.* He has elicited top-notch performances from his trio of stars. Barbara Hershey is convincing as she transforms her character from mousy pawn to attractive, assertive woman. Rated R. 110m. **DIR:** Barry Levinson. **CAST:** Richard Dreyfuss, Danny DeVito, Barbara Hershey. **1987**

TO BE OR NOT TO BE (1942) ★★★★½ After gaining early stardom in *Twentieth Century,* Carole Lombard returned to another black comedy and another role as an oddball theater performer, for the last film of her life. One of Hollywood's premier comedy directors, Ernst Lubitsch, coached excellent performances from Carole Lombard and costar Jack Benny in this hilarious farce about a theater couple who outwit the Nazis. B&W; 99m. **DIR:** Ernst Lubitsch. **CAST:** Carole Lombard, Jack Benny, Robert Stack. **1942**

TO BE OR NOT TO BE (1983) ★★★★ In this hilarious remake of the Jack Benny–Carole Lombard classic from 1942, Mel Brooks and Anne Bancroft are Polish actors who foil the Nazis at the outbreak of World War II. It's producer-star Brooks's best film since *Young Frankenstein* and was directed by Alan Johnson, who choreographed *Springtime for Hitler* for Brooks's first film, *The Producers*. Rated PG. 108m. **DIR:** Alan Johnson. **CAST:** Mel Brooks, Anne Bancroft, Charles Durning, Tim Matheson. **1983**

TO PARIS WITH LOVE ★★½ Alec Guinness stands out like a pumpkin in a pea patch in this average comedy about a rich and indulgent father who takes his son to gay Paree to learn the facts of life. 78m. **DIR:** Robert Hamer. **CAST:** Alec Guinness, Odile Versois, Austin Trevor, Vernon Gray. **1955**

TO SEE SUCH FUN ★★ This is a compilation of a vast number of comedy film clips from 1930 to 1970. Many of the clips illustrate the British love of puns, rhymes, and slapstick. Viewers hoping to see a lot of Peter Sellers, Benny Hill, and Marty Feldman clips will be disappointed because most of the footage comes from films of the 1930s and 1940s. 90m. **DIR:** Jon Scoffield. **CAST:** Peter Sellers, Marty Feldman, Benny Hill, Eric Idle, Margaret Rutherford, Alec Guinness, Dirk Bogarde, Spike Milligan, Norman Wisdom. **1977**

TOM, DICK AND HARRY ★★★½ An energetic comic delight has Ginger Rogers trying to decide which very eligible bachelor to have for her beau. The entire cast comes through with solid performances, but Phil Silvers almost walks off with the show in his role as an obnoxious ice-cream man. Garson Kanin's direction is sharp. B&W; 86m. **DIR:** Garson Kanin. **CAST:** Ginger Rogers, George Murphy, Burgess Meredith, Alan Marshal, Phil Silvers. **1941**

TOM JONES ★★★★★ Rarely has a movie captured the spirit and flavor of its times or the novel on which it was based. This is a rambunctious, witty, and often bawdy tale of a youth's misadventures in eighteenth-century England. Albert Finney is a perfect rascal as Tom. We joyously follow him through all levels of British society as he tries to make his fortune and win the lovely Sophie (Susannah York). The entire cast is brilliant. 129m. **DIR:** Tony Richardson. **CAST:** Albert Finney, Susannah York, Hugh Griffith, Edith Evans. **1963**

TOMMY CHONG ROAST, THE 🦃 A comedian whose chief claim to fame is bringing drug and flatulence jokes to the big screen. Rated R for language. 60m. **DIR:** Barry Glazer. **CAST:** Tommy Chong, Dick Shawn, Richard Belzer, Slappy White, Jerry Seinfeld, David Steinberg. **1986**

TONIGHT FOR SURE 🦃 One of two nudie movies that Francis Ford Coppola made while he was still a student at UCLA. 66m. **DIR:** Francis Ford Coppola. **CAST:** Don Kenney. **1962**

TOO MUCH SUN 🦃 Utterly tasteless comedy about the gay son and lesbian daughter of a multimillionaire (Howard Duff) whose will decrees that one or the other of his offspring must produce a son. Rated R for profanity and simulated sex. 97m. **DIR:** Robert Downey. **CAST:** Robert Downey Jr., Laura Ernst, Jim Haynie, Eric Idle, Ralph Macchio, Andrea Martin, Leo Rossi, Howard Duff. **1991**

TOOTSIE ★★★★★ Dustin Hoffman is Michael Dorsey, an out-of-work actor who disguises himself as a woman—Dorothy Michaels—to get a job and becomes a big star on a popular television soap opera. An absolute delight, *Tootsie* is hilarious, touching, and marvelously acted. Rated PG for adult content. 119m. **DIR:** Sydney Pollack. **CAST:** Dustin Hoffman, Bill Murray, Jessica Lange, Teri Garr, Dabney Coleman, Sydney Pollack, George Gaynes. **1982**

TOP SECRET ★★½ By the makers of *Airplane!*, this film makes up for its flimsy plot with one gag after another. Nick Rivers (Val Kilmer), a rock 'n' roll star, visits East Germany. There he falls in love with Hilary and becomes involved in the plot to free her scientist father. Lots of lively old Beach Boys and Elvis Presley tunes. Rated PG for some profanity and sexually oriented gags. 90m. **DIR:** Jim Abrahams, David Zucker, Jerry Zucker. **CAST:** Val Kilmer, Omar Sharif, Peter Cushing, Lucy Gutteridge. **1984**

TOPAZE (1933) ★★★½ John Barrymore gives one of his finest comic performances in this engaging film about a college professor who is innocently inveigled into a swindle and ends up turning the tables on the crooks. Witty and often moving. B&W; 80m. **DIR:** Harry D'Arrast. **CAST:** John Barrymore, Myrna Loy. **1933**

TOPPER ★★★★ This is the original feature of what became a delightful fantasy movie series and television series. Cary Grant and Constance Bennett are the Kirbys, a duo of social high livers who, due to an unfortunate auto accident, become ghosts. They now want to transfer their spirit of living the good life to a rather stodgy banker, the fellow they are now haunting, one Cosmo Topper (Roland Young). Good fun all around. B&W; 97m. **DIR:** Norman Z. McLeod. **CAST:** Cary Grant, Constance Bennett, Roland Young, Billie Burke. **1937**

TOPPER RETURNS ★★★ Cary Grant and Constance Bennett have gone on to their heavenly rewards, but Roland Young, as Cosmo Topper, is still seeing ghosts. This time the spooky personage is that of Joan Blondell, who helps our hero solve a murder in this entertaining comedy. B&W; 87m. **DIR:** Roy Del Ruth. **CAST:** Roland Young, Joan Blondell, Eddie "Rochester" Anderson, Carole Landis, Dennis O'Keefe, H. B. Warner. **1941**

TOPPER TAKES A TRIP ★★★ Second film in the original series finds Cosmo and Henrietta Topper on the French Riviera accompanied by their ghostly friend Marion Kirby, portrayed by the star of the original film, Constance Bennett. Topper and Marion pool forces to stop Mrs. Topper from being victimized by a smooth-talking confidence man. Cary Grant makes a brief appearance in a flashback sequence. Harmless fun. B&W; 85m. **DIR:** Norman Z. McLeod. **CAST:** Constance Bennett, Roland Young, Billie Burke, Alan Mowbray, Franklin Pangborn. **1939**

TOUCH AND GO ★★½ A comedy that sat on the shelf for two years. Chicago hockey player falls in love with the mother of a young delinquent who mugged him. Michael Keaton is appealing, Maria Conchita Alonso is fiery, and the script contains sharp dialogue, a few good laughs, and a number of sweet moments. Rated PG for profanity. 101m. **DIR:** Robert Mandel. **CAST:** Michael Keaton, Maria Conchita Alonso, Ajay Naidu. **1984**

TOUCH OF CLASS, A ★★★★★ In one of the best romantic comedies of recent years, George Segal and Glenda Jackson are marvelously paired as a sometimes loving—sometimes bickering—couple who struggle through an extramarital affair. They begin their oddball romance when he runs over one of her children while chasing a fly ball in a baseball game. Fine acting and witty dialogue. Rated PG. 105m. **DIR:** Melvin Frank. **CAST:** George Segal, Glenda Jackson, Paul Sorvino, Hildegard Neil. **1972**

TOUGH GUYS ★★★ This enjoyable movie features Burt Lancaster and Kirk Douglas as two flamboyant train robbers who are released from prison after thirty years to find they have no place in society. They decide to strike back by doing what they do best. It's featherweight, but the stars make it fun. Rated PG for light profanity, suggested sex, and mild violence. 103m. **DIR:** Jeff Kanew. **CAST:** Burt Lancaster, Kirk Douglas, Charles Durning, Alexis Smith, Dana Carvey, Darlanne Fluegel, Eli Wallach. **1986**

TOVARITCH ★★★½ A Russian duchess and her consort flee the revolution to Paris while entrusted with the tzar's fortune of forty billion francs. Too honest to spend any of it, they hire themselves out as domestics. Good farce. B&W; 98m. **DIR:** Anatole Litvak. **CAST:** Claudette Colbert, Charles Boyer, Basil Rathbone, Anita Louise, Melville Cooper, Isabel Jeans, Montagu Love, Curt Bois. **1937**

TOY, THE ★★ You would think any comedy that combines the talents of Richard Pryor and Jackie Gleason would have to be exceptionally good, to say nothing of funny. But that's simply not true of this movie, about a spoiled rich kid (Scott Schwartz) whose father (Gleason) allows him to buy the ultimate toy (Pryor). Rated PG for profanity and adult themes. 99m. **DIR:** Richard Donner. **CAST:** Richard Pryor, Jackie Gleason, Scott Schwartz, Ned Beatty. **1982**

TOYS 🦃 Idiotic waste of Robin Williams's talents. A toy manufacturer's whimsical, spacey son. Dad Donald O'Connor's death results in a battle between Williams and militaristic uncle Michael Gambon, who is bent on making lethal war toys. A rare misfire from director Barry Levinson. Rated PG-13 for violence. 121m. **DIR:** Barry Levinson. **CAST:** Robin Williams, Michael Gambon, Joan Cusack, Robin Wright, Donald O'Connor, Arthur Malet, Jack Warden. **1992**

TRADING HEARTS ★★★ A period charmer written by Frank Deford casts Raul Julia as a washed-up baseball player who's lured into the sedate Florida family life of a single mother and her precocious child. Predictable and occasionally schmaltzy, but entertaining. Rated PG. 88m. **DIR:** Neil Leifer. **CAST:** Raul Julia, Beverly D'Angelo, Nina Axelrod, Jenny Lewis. **1987**

TRADING PLACES ★★★★ Here's an uproarious comedy about what happens when uptight Philadelphia broker (Dan Aykroyd) and dynamic black street hustler (Eddie Murphy) change places. Rated R for nudity and profanity. 117m. **DIR:** John Landis. **CAST:** Dan Aykroyd, Eddie Murphy, Ralph Bellamy, Don Ameche, Jamie Lee Curtis, Denholm Elliot. **1983**

TRAIL OF THE PINK PANTHER, THE ★★½ Through the magic of editing, the late Peter Sellers "stars" as the bumbling Inspector Clouseau. Writer-director Blake Edwards uses outtakes of Sellers from previous films and combines them with new footage featuring David Niven, Herbert Lom, and Capucine. Disappointing. Rated PG for nudity and scatological humor. 97m. **DIR:** Blake Edwards. **CAST:** Peter Sellers, David Niven, Herbert Lom, Capucine, Robert Wagner. **1982**

TRANSYLVANIA 6-5000 ★★ Sometimes amusing but ultimately silly horror spoof focusing on an inept pair of tabloid reporters (Jeff Goldblum and Ed Begley Jr.) sent to Transylvania to investigate the Frankenstein monster. Rated PG for mild profanity. 93m. **DIR:** Rudy DeLuca. **CAST:** Jeff Goldblum, Ed Begley Jr., Joseph Bologna, Carol Kane, Jeffrey Jones, John Byner, Michael Richards. **1985**

TRANSYLVANIA TWIST ★★½ No horror movie is safe in this lampoon from producer Roger Corman. Scenes from classics like *Frankenstein* and *Dracula,* along with more recent entries in the genre (*Friday the 13th* and *Nightmare on Elm Street*) are parodied in this tale of the search for a book that will raise the "evil one." Rated PG-13. 82m. **DIR:** Jim Wynorski. **CAST:** Robert Vaughn, Teri Copley, Steve Altman, Angus Scrimm, Jay Robinson, Howard Morris, Steve Franken. **1990**

TRAVELS WITH MY AUNT ★★½ Director George Cukor's screen version of Graham Greene's comic novel is only slightly above average. Maggie Smith's overbearing and overplayed aunt knocks what could have been a delightful *Auntie Mame*–style farce completely off-kilter. Alec McCowen gives an affecting performance as the bank executive who finds his tidy world disrupted. Rated PG. 109m. **DIR:** George Cukor. **CAST:** Maggie Smith, Alec McCowen, Lou Gossett Jr., Robert Stephens, Cindy Williams. **1972**

TRENCHCOAT ★★ No one is what he appears to be in this inept spoof of the detective genre. While there are moments that evoke some chuckles, *Trenchcoat* rarely hits the mark. Rated PG. 91m. **DIR:** Michael Tuchner. **CAST:** Margot Kidder, Robert Hays, Daniel Faraldo. **1983**

TRICKS OF THE TRADE ★★ Short-on-laughs comedy features Cindy Williams as a well-to-do housewife involved with a Hollywood prostitute (Markie Post) after her husband is murdered in Post's apartment. Made for TV. 94m. **DIR:** Jack Bender. **CAST:** Cindy Williams, Markie Post, Scott Paulin, John Ritter. **1988**

TRIPLECROSS ★★★ Harmless made-for-TV comedy about a trio of former police detectives who, after being left sizable fortunes by a grateful crime victim, now battle each other as to who can solve the crime *du jour.* 97m. **DIR:** David Greene. **CAST:** Ted Wass, Markie Post, Gary Swanson, Shannon Wilcox, Barbara Horan, Robert Costanzo, Ric Mancini, Mike Genovese, Dennis Farina. **1985**

TROOP BEVERLY HILLS 🦃 Shelley Long as a ditsy Beverly Hills mom who agrees to act as the troop leader for her daughter's Wilderness Girls group. Rated PG. 105m. **DIR:** Jeff Kanew. **CAST:** Shelley Long, Craig T. Nelson, Betty Thomas, Mary Gross. **1989**

TROUBLE IN PARADISE ★★ Made for TV, a reworking of *Swept Away,* with a diplomat's widow and a roughneck Australian sailor castaway on a tropical island. When opposites begin to attract, drug smugglers intrude. A joy only for Raquel Welch watchers. 100m. **DIR:** Di Drew. **CAST:** Raquel Welch, Jack Thompson, Nicholas Hammond. **1988**

TROUBLE IN THE GLEN ★★ A white-haired, cigar-chomping Orson Welles in Scots kilts is farfetched, to say the least. The film turns on a feud over a closed road. Thoroughly scotched by poor pacing and a script that misses the mark. Deep-dyed Welles fans will like it. 91m. **DIR:** Herbert Wilcox. **CAST:** Orson Welles, Margaret Lockwood, Victor McLaglen, Forrest Tucker. **1953**

TROUBLE WITH ANGELS, THE ★★★ Rosalind Russell stars as the Mother Superior at the St. Francis Academy for Girls. Her serenity and the educational pursuits of the institution are coming apart at the seams due to the pranks of two rambunctious teenagers, Hayley Mills and June Harding. This comedy's humor is uninspired, but the warmth and humanity of the entire production make it worthwhile family viewing. 112m. **DIR:** Ida Lupino. **CAST:** Rosalind Russell, Hayley Mills, June Harding. **1966**

TROUBLE WITH HARRY, THE ★★★★ Shirley MacLaine made her film debut in this wickedly funny black comedy, directed by Alfred Hitchcock. This is the last of long-unseen screen works by the master of suspense to be rereleased, and the most unusual, because the accent is on humor instead of tension-filled drama. In it, a murdered man causes no end of problems for his neighbors in a peaceful New England community. Rated PG when it was rereleased. 100m. **DIR:** Alfred Hitchcock. **CAST:** John Forsythe, Edmund Gwenn, Shirley MacLaine, Mildred Natwick, Jerry Mathers. **1955**

TROUBLE WITH SPIES, THE ★★ Even Donald Sutherland's amiable charm can't save this inept secret-agent spoof, which makes no sense at all. Producer-director Burt Kennedy, who also adapted the script from Marc Lovell's *Apple Spy in the Sky,* lacks the simplest knowledge of pacing, shading, or tonal consistency. Rated PG-13 for partial nudity. 91m. **DIR:** Burt Kennedy. **CAST:** Donald Sutherland, Ned Beatty, Ruth Gordon, Lucy Gutteridge, Michael Hordern, Robert Morley. **1984**

TRUE IDENTITY ★★★ British comedian Lenny Henry makes his film debut in this generally enjoyable entry about an aspiring black actor who must masquerade as a white hit man. It's the little insights provided by director Charles Lane and the occasional big laughs from Henry's clowning that make this movie worth watching. Rated R for violence and profanity. 106m. **DIR:** Charles Lane. **CAST:** Lenny Henry, Frank Langella, Charles

Lane, J. T. Walsh, Anne-Marie Johnson, Andreas Katsulas, Michael McKean, Peggy Lipton. **1991**

TRUE LOVE ★★★★ A very funny yet sometimes painful look at the preparations for a New York wedding. From the engagement party to the wedding day, director Nancy Savoca finds all the comedy and drama involved between two people who probably shouldn't get married—and the family and friends around them. Rated R for profanity. 100m. **DIR:** Nancy Savoca. **CAST:** Annabella Sciorra, Ron Eldard. **1990**

TRUE STORIES ★★½ *True Stories* is Talking Heads leader David Byrne's satirical look at the imaginary town of Virgil, Texas. It's a mixture of *The National Enquirer* and deadpan cinematic humor. Some of the bits are truly funny, but the lethargic tone becomes an aggravating artistic conceit. Rated PG. 89m. **DIR:** David Byrne. **CAST:** David Byrne, John Goodman, Annie McEnroe, Swoosie Kurtz, Spalding Gray. **1986**

TRULY TASTELESS JOKES ★★ Not really as raunchy as the title suggests, this short video pretends to be a live version of the book of the same name. In reality it's merely a marketing ploy for the brief performances of many minor league comics. The format gives a nice, short sampling of a variety of routines, but there is neither continuity nor purpose. Rated R for language. 30m. **DIR:** Peter Robert. **CAST:** John Fox, Larry Reeb, Marsha Warfield, Ollie Joe Prater, Denny Johnston, The Legendary Wid. **1987**

TRUST ME ★★★ Ex-rocker Adam Ant is an L.A. art dealer who loves the high life, but is on the verge of bankruptcy. Observing that dead artists' works seem to sell better than live ones, he starts looking for some talent that might be suicidal or terminal. Interesting black comedy. Rated R for language. 94m. **DIR:** Bobby Houston. **CAST:** Adam Ant, Talia Balsam, Barbara Bain. **1989**

TULIPS [turkey] Canadian-made comedy casts Gabe Kaplan and Bernadette Peters as would-be suicides. Rated PG. 91m. **DIR:** Stan Ferris. **CAST:** Gabe Kaplan, Bernadette Peters, Henry Gibson, Al Waxman. **1981**

TUNE, THE ★★★ Animator Bill Plympton's first feature is a whimsical endeavor. He uses his trademark style to tell the tale of a songwriter at a creative crossroads, who gets swept into the imaginary world of Flooby Nooby. Plympton experiments with various musical styles, each one complimented by his strange, surreal animation. Most unusual. Not rated. 72m. **DIR:** Bill Plympton. **1993**

TUNE IN TOMORROW ★★★ Thoroughly enjoyable romp has young, impressionable Keanu Reeves falling for spinster aunt Barbara Hershey, while assisting writer Peter Falk on a radio serial. Free-wheeling adaptation of Mario Vargas Llosa's *Aunt Julia and the Scriptwriter*—worth turning the dial for. Rated PG-13 for profanity. 102m. **DIR:** Jon Amiel. **CAST:** Peter Falk, Keanu Reeves, Barbara Hershey, Bill McCutcheon. **1990**

TUNNEL OF LOVE, THE ★★★½ A mild sex farce, with Doris Day and Richard Widmark tied up in the adoption process. He considers adopting his own child as a result of his fling with social worker Gia Scala. B&W; 98m. **DIR:** Gene Kelly. **CAST:** Doris Day, Richard Widmark, Gig Young, Gia Scala. **1958**

TUNNELVISION ★★½ Here is a lightweight spoof of television. Sometimes it is funny, and other times it is just gross. The "stars," like Chevy Chase, have small bits. Still, there are some funny moments. *Tunnelvision* is like *The Groove Tube* in most respects, the good equally in proportion to the bad. Rated R. 67m. **DIR:** Neal Israel, Brad Swirnoff. **CAST:** Chevy Chase, Howard Hesseman, Betty Thomas, Laraine Newman. **1976**

TURNER AND HOOCH ★★★ *K-9* redux! Tom Hanks is a fussy police detective who finds himself stuck with a mean junkyard dog who is the only witness to a murder. Once again the Hanks magic elevates a predictable story into a fun film. Rated PG. 110m. **DIR:** Roger Spottiswoode. **CAST:** Tom Hanks, Mare Winningham. **1989**

TURTLE DIARY ★★★★½ Glenda Jackson and Ben Kingsley are absolutely delightful in this deliciously offbeat bit of British whimsy about urban life—of people living side by side but rarely touching. Jackson is Neaera Duncan, an author of children's books, while Kingsley is William Snow, a bookstore assistant. Both share an obsession for turtles and devise a plan to kidnap the shelled creatures, who are imprisoned in a nearby zoo, and release them into their natural habitat. Rated PG for nudity. 97m. **DIR:** John Irvin. **CAST:** Glenda Jackson, Ben Kingsley, Richard Johnson, Michael Gambon, Rosemary Leach, Eleanor Bron, Harriet Walter, Jeroen Krabbé. **1986**

TUTTLES OF TAHITI, THE ★★★ Captain Bligh goes native in this comedy of arch indolence and planned sloth in beautiful, bountiful Tahiti. Impoverished Charles Laughton and Florence Bates are rivals whose son Jon Hall and daughter Peggy Drake respectively fall in love. A good-natured, congenial film of leisure life. B&W; 91m. **DIR:** Charles Vidor. **CAST:** Charles Laughton, Jon Hall, Peggy Drake, Mala, Florence Bates, Alma Ross, Victor Francen, Curt Bois, Gene Reynolds. **1942**

TV CLASSICS: JIMMY DURANTE ★★★ Taken from the original Jimmy Durante show, this charming video also showcases the talents of Eddie Jackson, who belts out a rousing version of "Bill Bailey, Won't You Please Come Home," with Durante tickling the ivories. Includes Durante singing "September Song." Not rated. 30m. **DIR:** Sheldon Leonard. **CAST:** Jimmy Durante, Barbara Whiting, Eddie Jackson. **1987**

TV CLASSICS: LAUREL & HARDY 🦃 In what is perhaps the worst episode of TV's *This Is Your Life,* host Ralph Edwards humiliates classic clowns Stan Laurel and Oliver Hardy. 1950s; B&W; 30m. **DIR:** Ralph Edwards. **CAST:** Stan Laurel, Oliver Hardy.

TV CLASSICS: MILTON BERLE 🦃 This so-called TV classic is a not-too-cleverly disguised 30-minute commercial taken from the appropriately titled *Buick-Berle Show.* Not rated. 30m. **DIR:** Greg Garrison. **CAST:** Milton Berle, Carol Channing, Peter Lawford, Arnold Stang. **1987**

TV TURKEYS ★★½ Another compilation of forgotten television clips from the vault of Rhino Video, hosted by Skip Young, known from the sitcom *Leave It to Beaver.* This collection features clips from failed programs such as *The Arnold Stang Show, The Meanest Man in the World, The Buckskin Kid* (with an all-child cast as cowboys and Indians), and *Suicide Theatre.* B&W/color; 60m. **DIR:** Jeff Vilencia, Johnny Legend. **1985**

TV'S GREATEST BITS ★★½ This retrospective look at television in 1964, while not very well produced, is quite fun. Scenes from TV classics are included, as well as bits of trivia to get the brain working. Not rated. 53m. **DIR:** Chris Balton. **CAST:** Gary Owens, Bob Denver. **1986**

TWELVE CHAIRS, THE ★★★ Based on a Russian comedy fable about an impoverished nobleman seeking jewels secreted in one of a dozen fancy dining room chairs. Ron Moody is the anguished Russian, Dom DeLuise his chief rival in the hunt. Mel Brooks's direction keeps things moving with laughs. Rated G. 94m. **DIR:** Mel Brooks. **CAST:** Mel Brooks, Dom DeLuise, Frank Langella, Ron Moody. **1970**

TWENTIETH CENTURY ★★★★ A screwball-comedy masterpiece, scripted from the hit play by Ben Hecht and Charles MacArthur. Egocentric Broadway producer, John Barrymore, turns shop girl Carole Lombard into a star, gets dumped, and pulls out all stops to win her back during a cross-country train trip. The fun is fast and furious as the miles fly by. Barrymore and Lombard couldn't be funnier. B&W; 91m. **DIR:** Howard Hawks. **CAST:** Carole Lombard, John Barrymore, Roscoe Karns, Walter Connolly, Edgar Kennedy. **1934**

TWENTY BUCKS ★★½ Money—what it does to people and what people do with it—is the subject of this low-budget comedy-drama. A single twenty-dollar bill gets lost, found, stolen, lent, spent, and ironically shuffled about by a bag lady, teen skateboarder, emigrant chewing-gum magnate, bride and groom, stripper, crooks, and aspiring writer in a series of quirky, uneven vignettes. The tone of the picture is alternately whimsical and deadly serious—but not consistently memorable. Rated R for nudity, violence, and language. 91m. **DIR:** Keva Rosenfeld. **CAST:** Brendan Fraser, Christopher Lloyd, Steve Buscemi, Linda Hunt, Elisabeth Shue. **1994**

29TH STREET ★★★★ Imagine winning the first New York state lottery of $6.2 million and being unhappy about it—that's what happens to Frank Pesce (Anthony LaPaglia) in this warmhearted, often hilarious movie. Frank has always been lucky, and now it seems his luck may destroy his family. The real Pesce plays older brother Vito. Rated R for profanity and violence. 105m. **DIR:** George Gallo. **CAST:** Danny Aiello, Anthony LaPaglia, Lainie Kazan, Robert Forster. **1991**

TWINS ★★★★ Arnold Schwarzenegger and Danny DeVito play the title roles in this marvelously silly movie, which has the far-from-identical twins—products of a supersecret scientific experiment—meeting as adults after being separated at birth. This could easily have been a one-joke movie, but director Ivan Reitman and the stars keep it warm, funny, and fast-paced right up to the nicely satisfying conclusion. Rated PG for profanity and violence. 105m. **DIR:** Ivan Reitman. **CAST:** Arnold Schwarzenegger, Danny DeVito, Kelly Preston, Chloe Webb. **1988**

TWISTER ★★ Patriarch Harry Dean Stanton presides over a mansion filled with the spoiled, eccentric, and just plain lunatic members of his extended family. This adaptation of Mary Robison's *Oh* lacks the central point of view needed to make it palatable. Rated PG-13 for profanity. 95m. **DIR:** Michael Almereyda. **CAST:** Harry Dean Stanton, Suzy Amis, Crispin Glover, Dylan McDermott, Jenny Wright, Lois Chiles. **1988**

TWO-FACED WOMAN ★★★ Garbo's last film is better than its reputation. She has an infectious sense of humor as the woman who tests her husband's faithfulness by posing as her own seductive twin sister. Fast-moving, full of clever dialogue, and professionally acted by the entire cast. 94m. **DIR:** George Cukor. **CAST:** Greta Garbo, Melvyn Douglas, Constance Bennett, Roland Young, Robert Sterling, Ruth Gordon. **1941**

TWO FOR THE ROAD ★★★★ Clever editing and Frederic Raphael's inventive script highlight this delightful study of a marriage on the rocks, illuminated by deftly inserted flashbacks that occur each time the vacationing couple passes another car on the road. Albert Finney and Audrey Hepburn are the tempestuous lovers; the sweetly romantic score comes from Henry Mancini. 112m. **DIR:** Stanley Donen. **CAST:** Audrey Hepburn, Albert Finney, Jacqueline Bisset. **1967**

TWO HOUSES OF KEATON ★★★ Two of the Great Stone Face's two-reel comedies of the early 1920s paired for double the laughs. "The Play House" is a masterpiece of synchronization and multiple exposure in which Buster Keaton plays every role: cast, orchestra, and staff, in a minstrel show staged in Keaton's Opera House. In "The Electric House," the deadpan comic ingeniously creates a modern-day wonder by automating an entire house. Silent with musical score. B&W; 56m. **DIR:** Buster Keaton, Eddie Cline. **CAST:** Buster Keaton. **1921–1922**

TWO OF A KIND (1983) ★★ John Travolta and Olivia Newton-John, who first teamed on-screen in the box-office smash *Grease*, are reunited in this 1980s-style screwball comedy, which mixes clever ideas with incredibly stupid ones. Young viewers probably won't rave, but neither will they be too disappointed. Others, however, should stay away. Rated PG for profanity and violence. 87m. **DIR:** John Herzfeld. **CAST:** John Travolta, Olivia Newton-John, Charles Durning. **1983**

TWO-REELERS: COMEDY CLASSICS #1 ★★★ Offering a good look at the second-bill comedy shorts that filled out movie programs in the 1930s and 1940s, this trio of howlers is highlighted by "slow-burn" Edgar Kennedy jettisoning an obnoxious brother-in-law in "Feather Your Nest." In another two-reeler Jack Norton, the famous fumbling, mumbling drunk of numerous features, surprises his wife with a dog. B&W; 54m. **DIR:** Hal Yates, Harry Sweet. **CAST:** Edgar Kennedy, Jack Norton. **1933–1944**

TWO-REELERS: COMEDY CLASSICS #2 ★★★ Three more short comedy classics. In "Twin Husbands," rubber-legged, henpecked Leon Errol gets into big trouble when his twin brother comes to town. In "Chicken Feed," tubby, wheezing, sneezing Billy Gilbert invents a stove that can cook a meal in fifteen minutes. Long before microwaving, of course. Finally, in "False Roomers," an exasperated Edgar Kennedy is caught between a crazy tenant and a visit from his demanding uncle. B&W; 53m. **DIR:** Hal Yates, Leslie Goodwins. **CAST:** Leon Errol, Jason Robards Sr., Billy Gilbert, Edgar Kennedy, James Finlayson. **1938–1946**

TWO TOP BANANAS ★★½ Don Rickles and Don Adams bring burlesque back in this production of sketches, sight gags, one-liners, and song and dance. The two Dons are suited to this unsophisticated brand of comedy. Rated R for nudity and profanity. 45m. **DIR:** Phil Olsman. **CAST:** Don Rickles, Don Adams, Carol Wayne, Murray Langston. **1982**

TWO-WAY STRETCH ★★★★ Delightful British caper comedy about a group of thieves plotting to break out of their lenient prison just long enough to pull a huge robbery and then return to their cells, leaving them with the perfect alibi. First-rate. 84m. **DIR:** Robert Day. **CAST:** Peter Sellers, Wilfrid Hyde-White, David Lodge, Bernard Cribbins, Lionel Jeffries. **1961**

TWO WEEKS TO LIVE ★★½ This second of the Lum and Abner series has Abner (Norris Goff) agreeing to pilot a rocket ship to Mars because he thinks he is dying. Director St. Clair, who began in silent slapstick with Mack Sennett, keeps the pace breakneck with sight gags galore. B&W; 65m. **DIR:** Malcolm St. Clair. **CAST:** Chester Lauck, Norris Goff, Franklin Pangborn, Kay Linaker, Irving Bacon, Herbert Rawlinson. **1943**

UFORIA ★★★★ Like *Repo Man* and *Stranger Than Paradise*, this low-budget American film deserved better treatment than it was given. Cindy Williams is hilarious as a born-again Christian who believes that salvation will come to Earth in the form of a flying saucer. Harry Dean Stanton plays a crooked evangelist who exploits the Jesus-in-a-spaceship concept for every penny he can get. Rated PG for profanity. 100m. **DIR:** John Binder. **CAST:** Cindy Williams, Harry Dean Stanton, Fred Ward, Harry Carey Jr., Darrell Larson. **1984**

UHF ★★★½ Daydreamer George Newman (Weird Al Yankovic) finally lands in the right habitat: Channel 62, a UHF station with the lowest ratings in the country. What this station needs is fewer reruns of *Mister Ed* and *The Beverly Hillbillies* and more local talent! Like Emo Philips, the local wood-shop instructor who loses a digit in the buzz saw, and Stanley Spadowski (Michael Richards as the movie's real hero), station janitor turned kid-show host. Tastelessly innocent and funny. Rated PG-13 for profanity and violence. 95m. **DIR:** Jay Levey. **CAST:** "Weird Al" Yankovic, Victoria Jackson, Kevin McCarthy, Michael Richards, David Bowe, Anthony Geary, Billy Barty. **1989**

UNCLE BUCK ★★★★ If you enjoyed John Candy in *Planes, Trains and Automobiles*, you'll love him here as the slobbish *Uncle Buck* who is called upon to take care of his brother's three kids when their mother's father has a heart attack. The results are hilarious and heartwarming. Rated PG for profanity. 106m. **DIR:** John Hughes. **CAST:** John Candy, Amy Madigan, Jean Kelly. **1989**

UNDER THE RAINBOW ★★½ While this comedy is not quite jam-packed with laughs, it certainly keeps your interest. Set in 1938, the improbable story centers around the making of *The Wizard of Oz*, assassination attempts on a duke and duchess, the nefarious doings of Nazi and Japanese spies prior to World War II, and the life span of a dog named Streudel. Rated PG because of slight nudity and suggestive dialogue. 98m. **DIR:** Steve Rash. **CAST:** Chevy Chase, Carrie Fisher, Eve Arden, Joseph Maher. **1981**

UNDERCOVER BLUES ★★★ Sometimes stupid films are so charming that you can't help enjoying them—Ian Abrams's terminally silly update of *The Thin Man* is a perfect example. Kathleen Turner and Dennis Quaid play superspies Jane and Jeff Blue, called out of retirement and child-rearing to save the world from master villainess Fiona Shaw. Stanley Tucci steals the show as a frustrated street thug constantly bested by our nonchalant heroes. Rated PG-13 for cartoon violence and sensuality. 89m. **DIR:** Herbert Ross. **CAST:** Kathleen Turner, Dennis Quaid, Fiona Shaw, Stanley Tucci, Larry Miller, Obba Babatunde. **1993**

UNDERGROUND ACES 🦃 Big-city hotel parking attendants run amok. Rated PG for profanity and nudity. 93m. **DIR:** Robert Butler. **CAST:** Dirk Benedict, Melanie Griffith, Kario Salem, Robert Hegyes, Audrey Landers, Frank Gorshin. **1980**

UNFAITHFULLY YOURS (1948) ★★★ Symphony conductor Rex Harrison suspects his wife of infidelity and contemplates several solutions to his "problem." This film follows all the prerequisites of screwball comedies—mistaken identities, misinterpreted remarks. Harrison has fun, but his energy cannot sustain a film that runs about fifteen minutes too long. Unrated—family fare. B&W; 105m. **DIR:** Preston Sturges. **CAST:** Rex Harrison, Linda Darnell, Kurt Kreuger, Barbara Lawrence, Rudy Vallee, Lionel Stander. **1948**

UNFAITHFULLY YOURS (1984) ★★★ In this entertaining and sometimes hilarious remake of Preston Sturges's 1948 comedy, Dudley Moore plays a symphony orchestra conductor who suspects his wife (Nastassja Kinski) of fooling around with a violinist (Armand Assante) and decides to get revenge. Rated PG for nudity and profanity. 96m. **DIR:** Howard Zieff. **CAST:** Dudley Moore, Nastassja Kinski, Armand Assante, Albert Brooks. **1984**

UNKISSED BRIDE 🦃 Tom Kirk plays the groom who passes out every time he and his wife (Anne Helm) contemplate lovemaking. 82m. **DIR:** Jack H. Harris. **CAST:** Tommy Kirk, Danica d'Hondt, Anne Helm, Jacques Bergerac, Joe Pyne. **1966**

UP! ★★★ One of Russ Meyer's most bizarre efforts, combining lumberjacks, a mad killer, and Adolf Hitler in a small town—with the director's usual Amazonian women. It's a pointless but amusing parody loaded with extreme (though unbelievable) violence and sex. Like all of his films, it's edited faster than any MTV video. Unrated, but better hide it from the kids. 80m. **DIR:** Russ Meyer. **CAST:** Robert McLane. **1976**

UP IN ARMS ★★½ Danny Kaye's first film will not disappoint his fans, as he sings and mugs his way through the war. Dinah Shore loves the hypochondriac Kaye; the war takes a backseat to entertainment. 105m. **DIR:** Elliott Nugent. **CAST:** Danny Kaye, Dinah Shore, Dana Andrews, Constance Dowling. **1944**

UP IN SMOKE ★★★★ This is Cheech and Chong's first, and best, film. Forget about any plot as Cheech and Chong go on the hunt for good weed, rock 'n' roll, and good times. Several truly hysterical moments, with Stacy Keach's spaced-out cop almost stealing the show. Rated R for language, nudity, and general raunchiness. 87m. **DIR:** Lou Adler. **CAST:** Cheech and Chong, Strother Martin, Stacy Keach, Edie Adams, Tom Skerritt. **1978**

UP THE ACADEMY 🦃 This was *Mad* magazine's first and only attempt to emulate *National Lampoon*'s film success. Rated R for profanity and general disgustingness. 88m. **DIR:** Robert Downey. **CAST:** Ron Leibman, Wendell Brown, Ralph Macchio, Tom Citera, Tom Poston, Stacey Nelkin, Barbara Bach. **1980**

UP THE CREEK (1958) ★★★★ Left in charge of an unimportant naval base without a commanding officer, junior officer Peter Sellers turns it into a fountain for personal money-making schemes. Dryly funny British farce with a plethora of amusing supporting players. 86m. **DIR:** Val Guest. **CAST:** Peter Sellers, David Tomlinson, Wilfrid Hyde-White, Vera Day, Lionel Jeffries. **1958**

UP THE CREEK (1984) ★★★ Two stars from *Animal House*, Tim Matheson ("Otter") and Stephen Furst ("Flounder"), are reunited in this mostly entertaining raft-race comedy. It doesn't beg you to laugh at it the way *Police Academy* does. Matheson is charismatic enough to carry the film. Rated R for nudity, profanity, scatalogical humor, and violence. 95m. **DIR:** Robert Butler. **CAST:** Tim Matheson, Stephen Furst, Dan Monahan, John Hillerman, James B. Sikking, Tom Nolan. **1984**

UP THE DOWN STAIRCASE ★★★½ Sandy Dennis perfectly captures the flighty teacher of Bel Kaufman's hilarious novel about the New York City high school scene, but the students and minor plot crises do not wear as well as her performance. Although Dennis smoothly enacts the teacher we'd all like to have, Tad Mosel's script never quite catches the book's inspired lunacy. 124m. **DIR:** Robert Mulligan. **CAST:** Sandy Dennis, Eileen Heckart, Jean Stapleton. **1967**

UP THE SANDBOX ★★ A weird, uneven comedy about a neglected housewife (Barbra Streisand). Its fantasy sequences are among the strangest ever put on film. Rated R. 97m. **DIR:** Irvin Kershner. **CAST:** Barbra Streisand, David Selby, Jane Hoffman. **1972**

UP YOUR ALLEY 🦃 L.A. street dwellers. Rated R for profanity. 90m. **DIR:** Bob Logan. **CAST:** Linda Blair, Murray Langston, Ruth Buzzi. **1988**

UP YOUR ANCHOR 🦃 Ever wonder what one of the beach films of the 1960s or *Love Boat* would be like with nudity and rampant sexual encounters? 89m. **DIR:** Dan Wolman. **CAST:** Yftach Katzur, Zachi Nay. **1985**

UPHILL ALL THE WAY 🦃 Ridiculous film concerns two down-and-outers mistaken for bank robbers. Rated PG. 86m. **DIR:** Frank Q. Dobbs. **CAST:** Roy Clark, Mel Tillis, Glen Campbell. **1985**

UPTOWN SATURDAY NIGHT ★★★½ Sidney Poitier (who also directed), Bill Cosby, Harry Belafonte, Richard Pryor, and Flip Wilson head an all-star cast in this enjoyable comedy about a couple of buddies (Poitier and Cosby) who get into all sorts of trouble. Rated PG. 104m. **DIR:** Sidney Poitier. **CAST:** Sidney Poitier, Bill Cosby, Harry Belafonte, Richard Pryor, Flip Wilson. **1974**

USED CARS ★★★★ This is a riotous account of two feuding used-car businesses. Jack Warden and Kurt Russell are both excellent in this overlooked comedy. Fine support is offered by Frank McRae, Gerrit Graham, and Deborah Harmon. Rated R for language, nudity, and some violence. 111m. **DIR:** Robert Zemeckis. **CAST:** Jack Warden, Kurt Russell, Frank McRae, Gerrit Graham, Deborah Harmon. **1980**

USED PEOPLE ★★★½ Shirley MacLaine and Marcello Mastroianni are up to their tried-and-true tricks in this story of an Italian ne'er-do-well whose love for a Jewish woman is given full flower when her husband dies. The old pros manage to carry if off. Rated PG-13 for profanity and suggested sex. 116m. **DIR:** Beeban Kidron. **CAST:** Shirley MacLaine, Marcello Mastroianni, Jessica Tandy, Kathy Bates, Marcia Gay Harden, Sylvia Sidney, Bob Dishy, Joe Pantoliano. **1992**

UTILITIES ★★★½ Despite some rather crude humor once in a while, this modest comedy has a lot of charm and the heart of a Frank Capra film. Robert Hays plays a fed-up social worker who turns vigilante against the public utility companies. Rated PG for profanity and sex. 94m. **DIR:** Harvey Hart. **CAST:** Robert Hays, Brooke Adams, John Marley. **1983**

VAGRANT, THE ★★½ Bill Paxton is a Yuppie homeowner driven out of his mind by an intrusive, repulsive derelict. This weird, low-budget flick is riddled with a black humor that turns eerie as Paxton unravels. Not for everyone. Rated R for profanity and violence. 91m. **DIR:** Chris Walas. **CAST:** Bill Paxton, Michael Ironside. **1992**

VALET GIRLS 🦃 Valet Girls taking on the Fraternity Parkers as they compete for a job at a lecherous Hollywood mogul's home. Unrated, but contains nudity. 83m. **DIR:** Rafal Zielinski. **CAST:** Meri D. Marshall, John Terlesky. **1983**

VALLEY GIRL ★★★½ The story of a romance between a San Fernando Valley girl and a Hollywood punker, *Valley Girl* claims the distinction of being one of the few teen movies directed by a woman: Martha Coolidge. And, perhaps for that reason, it's a little treasure: a funny, sexy, appealing story that contains something for nearly everyone. Rated R. 95m. **DIR:** Martha Coolidge. **CAST:** Nicolas Cage, Deborah Foreman, Colleen Camp, Frederic Forrest, Lee Purcell. **1983**

VALS, THE ★★ Not as totally grody as one would expect, this teen flick features bored valley girls who transform from shopaholics into charitable drug busters. Rated R for profanity. 96m. **DIR:** James Polakof. **CAST:** Jill Carroll, Elena Stratheros. **1982**

VAMPIRE OVER LONDON 🦃 This is one of many titles appended to Bela Lugosi's last British film, shot as *Old Mother Riley Meets the Vampire*, and starring Arthur Lucan as the washerwoman character he designed decades earlier for a drag act on the music hall circuit. Finally released in the United States in the Sixties as *My Son, the Vampire*. B&W; 74m. **DIR:** John Gilling. **CAST:** Bela Lugosi, Arthur Lucan. **1952**

VAN, THE 🦃 Inept teenager uses his impressive new van to seduce bimbos. Rated PG. 92m. **DIR:** Sam Grossman. **CAST:** Stuart Getz, Danny DeVito. **1976**

VASECTOMY ★★½ A bank vice president (Paul Sorvino) is having plenty of family problems. After bearing their eighth child, his wife urges him to have a vasectomy while other family members are stealing from his bank. This comedy is rated R for nudity and obscenities. 92m. **DIR:** Robert Burge. **CAST:** Paul Sorvino, Abe Vigoda, Cassandra Edwards, Lorne Greene. **1986**

VICE ACADEMY 🦃 Moronic retread of *Police Academy*. Rated R for nudity, violence, and profanity. 90m. **DIR:** Rick Sloane. **CAST:** Linnea Quigley, Ginger Lynn Allen. **1988**

VICE ACADEMY 2 🦃 More offensive nonsense with the female cop/buddies taking on a villainess named Spanish Fly. Rated R for nudity, violence, and profanity. 92m. **DIR:** Rick Sloane. **CAST:** Linnea Quigley, Ginger Lynn Allen. **1990**

VICE ACADEMY III 🦃 Former porn queen Ginger Lynn Allen is back for another dose of sophomoric laughs as a member of the Vice Academy squad. Rated R for nudity. 88m. **DIR:** Rick Sloane. **CAST:** Ginger Lynn Allen. **1991**

VICE VERSA ★★★½ Young Fred Savage nearly steals the show from Judge Reinhold in this surprisingly entertaining comedy about a father who changes bodies with his son. We've seen it all many times before in lesser films such as *Freaky Friday* and *Like Father, Like Son*. However, the writing of Dick

Clement and Ian De Frenais and the chemistry of the players make it seem almost fresh. Rated PG for profanity. 98m. **DIR:** Brian Gilbert. **CAST:** Judge Reinhold, Fred Savage, Swoosie Kurtz, Jane Kaczmarek, David Proval, William Prince. **1988**

VICTOR/VICTORIA ★★★★ Director Blake Edwards takes us on a funny, off-the-wall romp through 1930s Paris. Julie Andrews plays a down-on-her-luck singer who poses as a gay Polish count to make ends meet. Rated PG because of adult situations. 133m. **DIR:** Blake Edwards. **CAST:** Julie Andrews, James Garner, Robert Preston, Lesley Ann Warren. **1982**

VIRGIN HIGH 🦃 Inane tale of a girl sent to a Catholic boarding school in order to protect her virginity. Her boyfriend pursues her, disguising himself as a priest. Gratuitous sleaze downgrades an extremely mediocre teen romance. Rated R for nudity, sex, and profanity. 90m. **DIR:** Richard Gabai. **CAST:** Chris Dempsey, Burt Ward, Linnea Quigley, Tracy Dali. **1990**

VIRGIN QUEEN OF ST. FRANCIS HIGH, THE ★★★ This teen market release has more depth and interest than most in its genre. There's nothing much new in the first half hour, but the two leads, Joseph R. Straface and Stacy Christensen, have winning personalities. The ending is too pat and saccharine, though. Rated PG for profanity. 89m. **DIR:** Francesco Lucente. **CAST:** Joseph R. Straface, Stacy Christensen. **1988**

VIVA MAX! ★★★ Skip credibility and enjoy. Peter Ustinov is a contemporary Mexican general who leads his men across the border to reclaim the Alamo as a tourist attraction. Jonathan Winters all but steals this romp, playing a bumbling, confused National Guard officer in the face of an audacious "enemy." Rated G. 92m. **DIR:** Jerry Paris. **CAST:** Peter Ustinov, Jonathan Winters, Keenan Wynn, Pamela Tiffin. **1969**

VIVACIOUS LADY ★★★ Cultures clash when small-town professor James Stewart impulsively weds New York nightclub singer Ginger Rogers, brings her back to the campus, and cannot tell his father, upright and stuffy college president Charles Coburn, who the new lady is. B&W; 90m. **DIR:** George Stevens. **CAST:** Ginger Rogers, James Stewart, Charles Coburn, Frances Mercer, James Ellison, Beulah Bondi, Franklin Pangborn, Grady Sutton, Jack Carson, Willie Best. **1938**

VIXEN ★★½ Russ Meyer, functioning simultaneously as producer, scriptwriter, director, and camerman, turns out one of his best films with this bizarre satirical farce concerning a voluptuous young woman called Vixen (Erica Gavin) who has an unlimited appetite for sex. Contains a great deal of nudity and profanity. Recommended for adult viewing only. 70m. **DIR:** Russ Meyer. **CAST:** Erica Gavin, Garth Pillsbury, Harrison Page. **1968**

VOLUNTEERS ★★ This comedy reunites Tom Hanks and John Candy, who were so marvelously funny together in Ron Howard's *Splash*. However, this film about high jinks in the Peace Corps in Thailand circa 1962 has very little going for it. Hanks and Candy do their best, but the laughs are few and far between. Rated R for profanity, violence, and sexual innuendo. 105m. **DIR:** Nicholas Meyer. **CAST:** Tom Hanks, John Candy, Rita Wilson, Tim Thomerson, Gedde Watanabe. **1985**

WACKIEST SHIP IN THE ARMY, THE ★★★ A battered ship becomes an unlikely implement for World War II heroism. The situation is played mostly for laughs, but dramatic moments are smoothly included. Jack Lemmon sets his performance at just the right pitch. Ricky Nelson is amiable and amusing. 99m. **DIR:** Richard Murphy. **CAST:** Jack Lemmon, Ricky Nelson, John Lund, Chips Rafferty, Tom Tully, Joby Baker, Warren Berlinger. **1960**

WACKO 🦃 Excruciating parody of *Halloween*. Rated PG. 90m. **DIR:** Greydon Clark. **CAST:** Joe Don Baker, Stella Stevens, George Kennedy, Jeff Altman. **1981**

WACKY WORLD OF WILLS AND BURKE, THE ★★½ Incongruously lighthearted parody of the true story of the explorers who set out to cross Australia by camel in 1860. (A straight version of the ill-fated expedition, *Burke and Wills*, was made at the same time as this.) Some funny Monty Python-ish satire will be lost on those unfamiliar with Australian history. Unrated. 97m. **DIR:** Bob Weis. **CAST:** Garry McDonald, Kim Gyngell, Nicole Kidman, Colin Hay. **1985**

WAITRESS 🦃 This awful comedy features three waitresses working in a most unsanitary restaurant. Rated R for nudity, profanity, and simulated sex. 85m. **DIR:** Samuel Weil, Michael Herz. **CAST:** Jim Harris, Carol Drake, Carol Bever. **1981**

WALK, DON'T RUN ★★★ During the summer Olympics in Tokyo, Samantha Eggar agrees to share her apartment in the crowded city with businessman Cary Grant and athlete Jim Hutton. Happy, wholesome havoc results. Cary Grant's last film, a remake of 1943's *The More the Merrier*. 114m. **DIR:** Charles Walters. **CAST:** Cary Grant, Samantha Eggar, Miiko Taka, Jim Hutton, John Standing, George Takei. **1966**

WALK LIKE A MAN 🦃 Unfunny, forced attempt at a comic version of *The Jungle Book*. Rated PG-13 for language. 86m. **DIR:** Melvin Frank. **CAST:** Howie Mandel, Christopher Lloyd, Cloris Leachman, Amy Steel. **1987**

WALTZ OF THE TOREADORS ★★★★ The unique Peter Sellers is superb as a retired military officer who can't subdue his roving eye. Margaret Leighton is fine, as always. Dany Robin is adorable. It's saucy and sex-shot, but intellectually stimulating nonetheless. A charming film, and not just for Sellers's fans. 105m. **DIR:** John Guillermin. **CAST:** Peter Sellers, Margaret Leighton, Dany Robin. **1962**

WALTZES FROM VIENNA ★★ Alfred Hitchcock...directing a musical? Not really. This biopic of the Strauss family is more of a romantic comedy. By any category, it's a misfire. Unrated; suitable for family viewing. B&W; 80m. **DIR:** Alfred Hitchcock. **CAST:** Jessie Matthews, Esmond Knight, Edmund Gwenn. **1933**

WAR OF THE ROSES, THE ★★★★★ A brilliant black comedy from director Danny DeVito, this frightening and funny film stars Michael Douglas and Kathleen Turner as a couple whose marriage collapses into a vicious divorce battle over material possessions. The acting is superb, and the direction is stunning. Rated R for profanity, seminudity, and violence. 100m. **DIR:** Danny DeVito. **CAST:** Michael Douglas, Kathleen Turner, Danny DeVito, Marianne Sägebrecht, Sean Astin, G. D. Spradlin, Peter Donat. **1989**

WATCH THE BIRDIE ★★½ Red Skelton runs a photo shop and, with a borrowed newsreel camera, unknowingly films crooks. Passable family fodder. B&W; 71m. **DIR:** Jack Donohue. **CAST:** Red Skelton, Arlene Dahl, Ann Miller. **1950**

WATER ★★★ In this delightful British comedy, Michael Caine is the governor of the small English colony located on the island of Cascara. The governor's wife (Brenda Vaccaro) is bored until an oil company sends out a famous actor to film a commercial. Pleasant craziness accompanied by a great sound track featuring the music of Eddy Grant, and a jam session with Ringo Starr, George Harrison, and Eric Clapton. Rated PG-13. 91m. **DIR:** Dick Clement. **CAST:** Michael Caine, Brenda Vaccaro, Valerie Perrine, Fred Gwynne. **1986**

WATERMELON MAN ★★ A bigoted white man wakes up one morning and finds himself black. Using the late, great black comedian Godfrey Cambridge in the title role shows that someone in production had his head on right. The film makes a statement. Trouble is, it makes it over and over and over again. Rated R. 97m. **DIR:** Melvin Van Peebles. **CAST:** Godfrey Cambridge, Estelle Parsons. **1970**

WAY BACK HOME 🦃 Whatever cornball charm this folksy little radio-related oddity can claim relies on rural amusements, songs, hymns, and a plot line old as the hills. Bette Davis was originally billed seventh. B&W; 81m. **DIR:** William A. Seiter. **CAST:** Bette Davis, Phillips Lord, Frankie Darro. **1932**

WAY OUT WEST ★★★★★ Stan Laurel and Oliver Hardy travel west to deliver a gold mine map to the daughter of a friend. The map is given to an imposter, and the boys have to retrieve it and ensure correct delivery. A delightful, marvelous film that demonstrates the team's mastery of timing and characterization. B&W; 65m. **DIR:** James W. Horne. **CAST:** Stan Laurel, Oliver Hardy, Sharon Lynn. **1937**

WAYNE'S WORLD ★★★½ Mike Myers and Dana Carvey re-create and flesh out their characters from the recurring *Saturday Night Live* sketch in this comedy that will appeal primarily to the show's fans. The familiar story has our heroes fighting a sleazy promoter to maintain the integrity of their cable show when it is moved to commercial television. Rated PG-13 for profanity and sexual humor. 95m. **DIR:** Penelope Spheeris. **CAST:** Mike Myers, Dana Carvey, Rob Lowe, Tia Carrere, Brian Doyle-Murray, Lara Flynn Boyle, Ed O'Neill, Colleen Camp, Donna Dixon, Alice Cooper, Meat Loaf. **1992**

WAYNE'S WORLD 2 ★★ More idiocy from the goofy head-banger hosts of cable-access TV—but not as infectiously funny. *Saturday Night Live* characters Wayne Campbell and Garth Algar return as rock-culture Peter Pans in a world of babe-olas, party maximas, and thrashing guitars. They stage a massive rock concert (Waynestock) amid misadventures filled with more movie spoofs than memorable laughs. Rated PG-13 for language and suggested sex. 91m. **DIR:** Stephen Surjik. **CAST:** Mike Myers, Dana Carvey, Tia Carrere, Olivia D'Abo, Aerosmith, Christopher Walken, Chris Farley, Kim Basinger, James Hong. **1993**

WE THINK THE WORLD OF YOU ★★★½ A bittersweet British comedy, set in the 1950s, and based on the autobiographical novel by Joseph R. Ackerley. Alan Bates plays a frustrated and emotionally abused homosexual who can't seem to reconcile his relationship with an ex-sailor/ex-con (Gary Oldman). This is a quirky, gentle, offbeat film, elevated by strong performances. Rated PG. 100m. **DIR:** Colin Gregg. **CAST:** Alan Bates, Gary Oldman, Frances Barber, Max Wall. **1988**

WEBBER'S WORLD ★★★½ Better than one might expect. Desperately in need of cash, a dysfunctional family agrees to turn their everyday lives into a twenty-four-hour-a-day cable show. The Webbers' televised arguments and sexual liaisons make them a hit, but son David Arquette isn't so sure he wants the notoriety. Some moments are downright hilarious. Not rated; contains nudity, adult situations, and strong language. 109m. **DIR:** Brad Marlowe. **CAST:** Jeffrey Tambor, Rita Taggart, Jennifer Tilly, David Arquette, Brian Bloom, Caroline Goodall, Robby Benson. **1993**

WEDDING, A ★★★ This is one of those *almost* movies—one that has enough good things about it to recommend, but that could have been so much better. During the late 1970s, director Robert Altman's films had begun to lose their focus, as this film demonstrates. The story deals with a wedding between two relatively wealthy families and the comic implications that follow. Fine acting keeps things afloat. Rated PG. 125m. **DIR:** Robert Altman. **CAST:** Carol Burnett, Desi Arnaz Jr., Geraldine Chaplin, Vittorio Gassman, Lillian Gish, Lauren Hutton, Paul Dooley, Howard Duff, Pam Dawber, Dina Merrill, John Considine. **1978**

WEDDING BANQUET, THE ★★★½ Gentle, Woody Allen-esque comedy about a New York real estate dealer who agrees to marry one of his tenants to help her get a green card and put an end to his parents' attempts to find him "the perfect Chinese wife." This is all done with the knowledge and consent of his male lover. Things go reasonably well until Mom and Dad decide to fly over from Taiwan for the festivities. Little character moments and surprises make *The Wedding Banquet* very enjoyable. Unrated, the film has brief profanity and suggested sex. 112m. **DIR:** Ang Lee. **CAST:** Winston Chao, May Chin, Mitchell Lichtenstein. **1993**

WEDDING PARTY, THE 🦃 Plodding and irksome, this is about a groom who develops cold feet. Filmed in 1963, but not released until 1969; B&W; 92m. **DIR:** Cynthia Munroe, Wilford Leach, Brian De Palma. **CAST:** Robert De Niro, Jill Clayburgh, Jennifer Salt. **1969**

WEDDING REHEARSAL ★★ There's not much magic or comedy in this shaky farce. Director Alexander Korda shows poor directorial technique in this story of an officer whose grandmother plans to get him married. You can catch the whole thing with one eye closed and your favorite radio station on. B&W; 84m. **DIR:** Alexander Korda. **CAST:** Roland Young, George Grossmith, John Loder, Lady Tree, Wendy Barrie, Maurice Evans, Merle Oberon. **1932**

WEEKEND AT BERNIE'S ★★½ In this tolerable comedy with some hilarious moments, Andrew McCarthy and Jonathan Silverman play upwardly mobile young executives all set to have a wild, wild weekend at their boss's swank beach house—until they find the murdered body of said boss. Terry Kiser steals the show as the dead man, which gives you an idea of how silly it all is. Rated PG-13 for profanity and tasteless humor. 110m. **DIR:** Ted Kotcheff. **CAST:** Andrew McCarthy, Jonathan Silverman, Catherine Mary Stewart, Terry Kiser. **1989**

WEEKEND AT BERNIE'S II ★★½ More of the same as yuppie junior executives Andrew McCarthy and Jonathan Silverman resurrect their dead boss (Terry Kiser) for another adventure. The plot is pretty lame, but Kiser is hilarious. He shows more life as a corpse—made more animate this time by a voodoo spell—than his supposedly livelier costars. Rated PG for light profanity and silly violence. 89m. **DIR:** Robert Klane. **CAST:** Andrew McCarthy, Jonathan Silverman, Terry Kiser, Barry Bostwick, Tom Wright, Steve James, Troy Beyer. **1993**

WEEKEND PASS 🦃 A quartet of stupid sailors on shore leave in Los Angeles. Rated R. 92m. **DIR:** Lawrence Bassoff. **CAST:** D. W. Brown, Peter Ellenstein, Patrick Hauser, Chip McAllister. **1984**

WEEKEND WARRIORS ★★ Mildly amusing, excessively wacky tale of Hollywood actors, writers, and singers circa 1961—avoiding combat by enlisting in the reserves. Rated R for profanity and sexual innuendo. 90m. **DIR:** Bert Convy. **CAST:** Chris Lemmon, Lloyd Bridges, Vic Tayback, Graham Jarvis, Tom Villard. **1986**

WEIRD SCIENCE ★★★ In this wacky comedy by writer-director John Hughes, two put-upon nerds (Anthony Michael Hall and Ilan Mitchell-Smith), desperate for a date, cop an idea from James Whale's *Frankenstein* and create a sexy woman via computer. Thus begins a roller coaster ride of hit-and-miss humor as the nerds get class fast. Rated PG-13 for slight violence, partial nudity, and profanity. 94m. **DIR:** John Hughes. **CAST:** Anthony Michael Hall, Kelly LeBrock, Ilan Mitchell-Smith. **1985**

WELCOME HOME, ROXY CARMICHAEL ★★★★ Although shunned at the box office, Karen Leigh Hopkins's, perceptive and poignant little tale says a great deal about friendship, love, and the dangers of putting aside grim reality for the more seductive lure of idol worship. Winona Ryder stars as Dinky Bossetti, a small-town girl attaching special significance to the return of Roxy Carmichael, a local legend who fled as a teenager and achieved fame and fortune on the West Coast. Rated PG-13 for language. 98m. **DIR:** Jim Abrahams. **CAST:** Winona Ryder, Jeff Daniels, Laila Robins, Dinah Manoff. **1990**

WELCOME TO 18 🦃 This low-budget film's only point of interest is that it marks the big-screen debut of Mariska Hargitay, the daughter of Jayne Mansfield. Rated PG-13 for profanity and nudity. 91m. **DIR:** Terry Carr. **CAST:** Mariska Hargitay, Courtney Thorne-Smith, Jo Ann Willette. **1986**

WE'RE NO ANGELS (1955) ★★½ The *New York Times* dubbed this "a slow, talky reprise of the delightful stage comedy" and was right. Three Devil's Island convicts "adopt" an island family and protect it against an uncle it can do without. There is a roguishness about the trio that almost makes them endearing, but the film does drag. 106m. **DIR:** Michael Curtiz. **CAST:** Humphrey

Bogart, Peter Ustinov, Aldo Ray, Basil Rathbone, Joan Bennett, Leo G. Carroll. 1955

WE'RE NO ANGELS (1989) ★★★½ The screenplay by David Mamet is a goofy send-up of the old Warner Bros. gangster melodramas, with Robert De Niro and Sean Penn mugging it up as a couple of escaped convicts mistaken for priests, who find themselves involved in a miracle. Director Neil Jordan couldn't decide whether he was making a crime-drama or a comedy. However, De Niro and Penn (and James Russo's bravura, Cagney-style turn as the bad guy) are winners. Rated PG-13 for nudity, profanity, and violence. 106m. **DIR:** Neil Jordan. **CAST:** Robert De Niro, Sean Penn, Demi Moore, James Russo, Ray McAnally, Hoyt Axton, Wallace Shawn, Bruno Kirby. 1989

WE'RE NOT MARRIED ★★★½ Assorted couples learn their marriages were performed illegally, so now they have certain options. Great episodic comedy. B&W; 85m. **DIR:** Edmund Goulding. **CAST:** Fred Allen, Eve Arden, Eddie Bracken, Louis Calhern, Paul Douglas, Zsa Zsa Gabor, Mitzi Gaynor, Marilyn Monroe, Victor Moore, Ginger Rogers, David Wayne. 1952

WE'RE TALKING SERIOUS MONEY ★★ Two con artists cheat a mob boss in New York and end up running to California. Unbelievable characters and bad acting make this a disappointing film. Rated PG-13 for profanity and violence. 92m. **DIR:** James Lemmo. **CAST:** Dennis Farina, Leo Rossi, Fran Drescher. 1991

WET AND WILD SUMMER 🦃 Vulgar Aussie version of Frankie-and-Annette beach movies is sexist, badly acted, and buffoonish. Rated R for nudity, profanity, and general bad taste. 95m. **DIR:** Maurice Murphy, Martin McGrath. **CAST:** Christopher Atkins, Elliott Gould, Julian McMahon, Rebecca Cross. 1993

WHAT ABOUT BOB? ★★★½ Fitfully hilarious tale of a deranged but lovable neurotic (Bill Murray) who attaches himself to the family of a high-profile psychiatrist (Richard Dreyfuss) while they're on vacation. Murray is typically goofy, but Dreyfuss gives a masterfully comic performance. Rated PG for brief profanity. 97m. **DIR:** Frank Oz. **CAST:** Bill Murray, Richard Dreyfuss, Julie Hagerty, Charlie Korsmo. 1991

WHAT DO YOU SAY TO A NAKED LADY? 🦃 Allen Funt's R-rated version of *Candid Camera*. 90m. **DIR:** Allen Funt. **CAST:** Allen Funt, Richard Roundtree. 1970

WHAT! NO BEER? ★★½ Then topical, now dated comedy, with Jimmy Durante pulling his friend, taxidermist Buster Keaton, and his money, into a plan to brew beer and have it ready for sale upon the end of Prohibition. Not enough deadpan Keaton antics. B&W; 66m. **DIR:** Edward Sedgwick. **CAST:** Buster Keaton, Jimmy Durante, Roscoe Ates, Edward Brophy, John Miljan. 1933

WHAT PRICE GLORY ★★★ James Cagney is Captain Flagg, Dan Dailey is Sergeant Quirt in this rough-and-tumble tale of rivalry in romance set against the sobering background of World War I in France. The feisty pair of Marines vies for the affections of adorable Charmaine (Corinne Calvet). Between quarrels, they fight in the trenches. 109m. **DIR:** John Ford. **CAST:** James Cagney, Dan Dailey, Corinne Calvet, William Demarest, Robert Wagner, Marisa Pavan, James Gleason. 1952

WHAT'S EATING GILBERT GRAPE? ★★★½ Small-town grocery clerk—the passive anchor of an odd Iowa family—cares for his 500-pound recluse mom and mentally challenged brother. He's having an affair with a married store customer when he gets an emotional jump start from a free-spirited, vacationing lass. This midwestern *Fellini's Mayberry*, if you will, is about how personal happiness can take a backseat to family responsibility. It's a strange, sad, melancholy story that is also sometimes very funny. Rated PG-13 for suggested sex and language. 118m. **DIR:** Lasse Hallstrom. **CAST:** Johnny Depp, Leonardo DiCaprio, Juliette Lewis, Mary Steenburgen, Kevin Tighe, John C. Reilly, Crispin Glover. 1994

WHAT'S NEW, PUSSYCAT? ★★★ Peter O'Toole is a fashion editor who can't stop becoming romantically involved with his models. In spite of a strong supporting cast, this dated 1960s "hip" comedy has few genuine laughs. Mostly, it's just silly. 108m. **DIR:** Clive Donner. **CAST:** Peter Sellers, Peter O'Toole, Woody Allen, Ursula Andress, Romy Schneider, Capucine, Paula Prentiss. 1965

WHAT'S UP, DOC? ★★★★ A virtual remake of Howard Hawks's classic *Bringing Up Baby*, with Ryan O'Neal and Barbra Streisand representing the Cary Grant and Katharine Hepburn roles, this manages to recapture much of the madcap charm and nonstop action of the original story. O'Neal is the studious scientist delightfully led astray by a dizzy Streisand, who keeps forcing herself into his life. The zany final chase through the streets of San Francisco is one of filmdom's best. Rated G. 94m. **DIR:** Peter Bogdanovich. **CAST:** Ryan O'Neal, Barbra Streisand, Kenneth Mars, Austin Pendleton. 1972

WHAT'S UP FRONT 🦃 Silly comedy features a determined nerd selling bras door-to-door. Unrated. 90m. **DIR:** Bob Whealing. **CAST:** Tommy Holden, Marilyn Manning. 1963

WHAT'S UP, TIGER LILY? ★★★ A dreadful Japanese spy movie has been given a zany English-language sound track by Woody Allen in one of his earliest movie productions. You are left with an offbeat spoof of the whole genre of spy films. The results are often amusing, but its one-joke premise gets rather tedious before it's over. 80m. **DIR:** Woody Allen. **CAST:** Tatsuya Mihashi, Miya Hana, Woody Allen. **1966**

WHEEL OF FORTUNE ★★½ John Wayne in a screwball comedy? Yep. Also titled *A Man Betrayed,* the surprise is that this low-budget production is watchable. B&W; 83m. **DIR:** John H. Auer. **CAST:** John Wayne, Frances Dee, Ward Bond. **1941**

WHEELER DEALERS, THE ★★★½ Texas millionaires risk huge sums without getting their grins or ten-gallon hats out of place. James Garner is at his delightfully devious best in this briskly paced romp. Lee Remick is a treat for the eyes. A gang of talented character actors lends strong support. 106m. **DIR:** Arthur Hiller. **CAST:** Lee Remick, James Garner, Jim Backus, Phil Harris, Chill Wills, John Astin, Louis Nye. **1963**

WHEN COMEDY WAS KING ★★★★ A nostalgic, sidesplitting look back to the screen comedy days of yesteryear when absurdity and the sight gag reigned supreme. This clutch of classic comedy scenes from silent days is outstanding. B&W; 81m. **DIR:** Robert Youngson. **CAST:** Charlie Chaplin, Buster Keaton, Gloria Swanson, Mabel Normand, Oliver Hardy, Stan Laurel. **1960**

WHEN HARRY MET SALLY ★★★★½ Wonderful character comedy stars Billy Crystal and Meg Ryan as longtime acquaintances who drift from mild animosity to friendship to love. Director Rob Reiner skillfully tickles our funny bones and touches our hearts with this semiautobiographical tale, which was scripted by Nora Ephron. Rated R for profanity and suggested sex. 110m. **DIR:** Rob Reiner. **CAST:** Billy Crystal, Meg Ryan, Carrie Fisher, Bruno Kirby. **1989**

WHEN THE CLOUDS ROLL BY ★★★★ If you have to choose *the* outstanding example of the precostume Douglas Fairbanks comedies, surely this is it. It's a satire on hypochondriacs. The highlight is a chase in a revolving room and a subsequent scuffle in slow-motion photography. Silent. B&W; 77m. **DIR:** Victor Fleming. **CAST:** Douglas Fairbanks Sr. **1919**

WHEN THINGS WERE ROTTEN (TV SERIES) ★★★ This compilation of three episodes from the short-lived television series of the same name is sure to please fans of *Blazing Saddles*–style humor. Dick Gautier's nearly serious portrayal of Robin Hood is a perfect foil for the slapstick antics of the rest of the cast. 78m. **DIR:** Coby Ruskin, Marty Feldman, Peter Bonerz. **CAST:** Dick Gautier, Dick Van Patten, Bernie Kopell, Richard Dimitri, Henry Polic II, Misty Rowe, David Sabin. **1975**

WHEN WOMEN HAD TAILS ★★ Italian comedy about five cavemen discovering the delightful difference of the sexes when pretty Senta Berger suddenly appears in their midst. Despite plenty of potential, this farce falls flat. Rated R for language and nudity. 99m. **DIR:** Pasquale Festa Campanile. **CAST:** Senta Berger, Frank Wolff, Giuliano Gemma, Lando Buzzanca. **1970**

WHEN WOMEN LOST THEIR TAILS ★★½ Most of the cast of *When Women Had Tails* returns in a much more sophisticated sex comedy set in prehistoric times. This slapstick sequel takes a broader view, poking fun at the earliest manifestations of civilization. The Stone Age jabs are still silly, but many of the observations are surprisingly enlightening. Rated R. 94m. **DIR:** Pasquale Festa Campanile. **CAST:** Senta Berger, Frank Wolff, Lando Buzzanca, Francesco Mule. **1971**

WHEN'S YOUR BIRTHDAY? ★★★ Joe E. Brown stars as a student of astrology who doubles as a boxer. The stars tell him when he'll win in the ring. Unfortunately, a gangster gets wind of his abilities and tries to turn them to his own ends. It's all a showcase for Brown, though Edgar Kennedy steals his scenes with his hilarious slow burn. B&W; 76m. **DIR:** Harry Beaumont. **CAST:** Joe E. Brown, Marian Marsh, Edgar Kennedy, Margaret Hamilton. **1937**

WHERE THE BOYS ARE ★★★ Connie Francis warbled the title tune and made her movie debut in this frothy, mildly entertaining film about teenagers doing what's natural during Easter vacation in Fort Lauderdale. It's miles ahead of the idiotic remake. 99m. **DIR:** Henry Levin. **CAST:** Dolores Hart, George Hamilton, Yvette Mimieux, Jim Hutton, Barbara Nichols, Connie Francis. **1960**

WHERE THE BOYS ARE '84 🦃 Poor remake. Rated R. 96m. **DIR:** Hy Averback. **CAST:** Lisa Hartman, Russell Todd, Lorna Luft, Lynn-Holly Johnson, Wendy Schaal, Howard McGillin, Louise Sorel. **1984**

WHERE THE BUFFALO ROAM 🦃 Horrendous film about the exploits of gonzo journalist Hunter S. Thompson. Rated R. 96m. **DIR:** Art Linson. **CAST:** Bill Murray, Peter Boyle, Bruno Kirby, René Auberjonois, R. G. Armstrong, Rafael Campos, Leonard Frey. **1980**

WHERE WERE YOU WHEN THE LIGHTS WENT OUT? 🦃 Bad attempt at farce and sexual mix-ups and misunderstandings. Backfires all the way. 94m. **DIR:** Hy Averback. **CAST:** Doris Day, Robert Morse, Terry-Thomas, Patrick O'Neal, Lola Albright, Steve Allen, Jim Backus, Ben Blue, Pat Paulsen. **1968**

WHERE'S POPPA? ★★★★ One of George Segal's best comic performances is found in this cult favorite. Ruth Gordon costars as the senile mother whom Segal tries to scare into having a cardiac arrest. Director Carl Reiner's son, Rob, makes a short appearance as a fervent draft resister. Rated R. 82m. **DIR:** Carl Reiner. **CAST:** George Segal,

Ruth Gordon, Trish Van Devere, Ron Leibman, Rae Allen, Vincent Gardenia, Barnard Hughes, Rob Reiner, Garrett Morris. **1970**

WHICH WAY IS UP? ★★★★ This irreverent, ribald farce reunites the talented comedy team of director Michael Shultz and star Richard Pryor (*Greased Lightning*) for one of the funnier movies of the 1970s. Pryor plays three major roles. His ability to create totally separate and distinctive characters contributes greatly to the success of this oft-tried but rarely believable gimmick. Rated R. 94m. **DIR:** Michael Schultz. **CAST:** Richard Pryor, Lonette McKee, Margaret Avery, Dolph Sweet, Morgan Woodward. **1977**

WHICH WAY TO THE FRONT? 🦃 Jerry Lewis directs and stars in this pathetic story about a rich 4-F American who enlists other such unfortunates into a military unit to combat Nazi Germany. 96m. **DIR:** Jerry Lewis. **CAST:** Jerry Lewis, John Wood, Jan Murray, Kaye Ballard, Robert Middleton, Paul Winchell, Gary Crosby. **1970**

WHIFFS 🦃 Army private is a human guinea pig suffering annoying side effects from biological and chemical-weapons testing. Not rated. 92m. **DIR:** Ted Post. **CAST:** Elliott Gould, Eddie Albert, Jennifer O'Neill, Harry Guardino. **1975**

WHISTLING IN BROOKLYN ★★★ Red Skelton returns as the radio sleuth, The Fox, this time pursued by the police from one Brooklyn landmark to another, and ending up at Ebbets Field pitching against the Dodgers. More slapstick than usual. B&W; 87m. **DIR:** S. Sylvan Simon. **CAST:** Red Skelton, Ann Rutherford, Rags Ragland, Jean Rogers, Ray Collins, Henry O'Neill, William Frawley, Sam Levene. **1943**

WHISTLING IN DIXIE ★★★½ Red Skelton's second outing as the radio detective, The Fox, plunges him and his bride into mysterious doings at an old southern mansion. Some good chills mixed in with lots of laughs. B&W; 74m. **DIR:** S. Sylvan Simon. **CAST:** Red Skelton, Ann Rutherford, George Bancroft, Guy Kibbee. **1942**

WHISTLING IN THE DARK ★★★½ Red Skelton is a radio criminologist, The Fox, noted for devising and solving ingenious crimes. He's pursued and kidnapped by Conrad Veidt, who wants him to construct a perfect murder. Lots of laughs in Skelton's first starring role, aided and abetted by the hilariously sinister Veidt. B&W; 77m. **DIR:** S. Sylvan Simon. **CAST:** Red Skelton, Conrad Veidt, Ann Rutherford, Virginia Grey, Rags Ragland, Eve Arden, Henry O'Neill, Reed Hadley. **1941**

WHITE MEN CAN'T JUMP ★★★★ As with writer-director Ron Shelton's *Bull Durham*, this movie about a pair of hoop hustlers (Wesley Snipes, Woody Harrelson) is smart, sassy, sexy, and rich in characterization. Deceptively adept at basketball, Harrelson arrives in Venice, California, to hook up with local hotshot Snipes for a big score. The dialogue is lightning fast, and the performances are just as electric. Rated R for profanity, nudity, and brief violence. 115m. **DIR:** Ron Shelton. **CAST:** Wesley Snipes, Woody Harrelson, Rosie Perez, Tyra Ferrell. **1992**

WHO AM I THIS TIME? ★★★½ The new girl in town, Helene Shaw (Susan Sarandon), gets a part in the local theater group production of *A Streetcar Named Desire* opposite Harry Nash (Christopher Walken). Dreadfully shy, Harry only comes to life in every part he plays on the stage. Helene sets out to win him. This is a pleasing Kurt Vonnegut Jr. story played by a capable cast. 60m. **DIR:** Jonathan Demme. **CAST:** Susan Sarandon, Christopher Walken, Robert Ridgely. **1982**

WHO DONE IT? ★★½ Standard Abbott and Costello programmer about a pair of soda jerks who witness an on-the-air murder during a radio broadcast and pose as detectives. William Gargan and William Bendix. B&W; 75m. **DIR:** Erle C. Kenton. **CAST:** Bud Abbott, Lou Costello, Patric Knowles, William Gargan, Louise Allbritton, William Bendix, Thomas Gomez, Jerome Cowan. **1942**

WHO FRAMED ROGER RABBIT ★★★★½ In this innovative and vastly entertaining motion picture, which seamlessly blends animated characters with live action, cartoon character Roger Rabbit (voice by Charles Fleischer) is accused of murder and turns to a hardboiled private detective (Bob Hoskins) for help. As with his *Back to the Future* and *Romancing the Stone*, director Robert Zemeckis has come up with a wonderful movie for all ages. Rated PG for vulgar language. 103m. **DIR:** Robert Zemeckis. **CAST:** Bob Hoskins, Christopher Lloyd, Joanna Cassidy, Stubby Kaye. **1988**

WHO IS KILLING THE GREAT CHEFS OF EUROPE? ★★★★ Scripter Peter Stone (*Charade*), working from Nan and Ivan Lyons' deliciously funny novel, whips up a droll entrée in that most difficult of genres: the comic mystery. Internationally renowned dessert chef Jacqueline Bisset wins a commission as the final course in the meal of the century, while fending off the boorish advances of her ex-husband George Segal, a fast-food mogul hoping to open a chain of garish joints in old-world European locales. Rated PG for imaginative violence. 112m. **DIR:** Ted Kotcheff. **CAST:** George Segal, Jacqueline Bisset, Robert Morley, Jean-Pierre Cassel, Madge Ryan. **1978**

WHOLLY MOSES! ★★½ *Wholly Moses!* pokes fun at Hollywood biblical epics in a rapid-fire fashion. While the film is sometimes very funny, it is also loaded with a fair share of predictable, flat, and corny moments. It's so-so viewing fare. Rated R. 109m.

DIR: Gary Weis. **CAST:** Dudley Moore, Richard Pryor, Laraine Newman, James Coco, Paul Sand, Jack Gilford, Dom DeLuise, John Houseman, Madeline Kahn, David L. Lander, John Ritter. 1980

WHOOPEE BOYS, THE 🦃 A pair of obnoxious—and supposedly lovable—misfits attempt to save a school for needy children. Rated R for profanity. 94m. **DIR:** John Byrum. **CAST:** Michael O'Keefe, Paul Rodriguez, Lucinda Jenney, Denholm Elliott, Eddie Deezen. 1986

WHOOPS APOCALYPSE ★★½ This overlong but sometimes rewarding British comedy consists of a news coverage spoof on events leading up to World War III. The plot centers around the theft of a U.S. nuclear bomb. Many viewers may get fidgety during the second, less successful half. Unrated, it contains nudity and obscene language. 137m. **DIR:** John Reardon. **CAST:** John Barron, John Cleese, Richard Griffiths, Peter Jones, Barry Morse. 1981

WHO'S GOT THE ACTION? ★★ One of Lana Turner's less glamorous roles teams her with Dean Martin in a spoof of gambling movies. The twist is that they are married, and she tries to keep his gambling losses in the family by being his bookie—incognito, of course. When he starts winning, she has to sell her assets to pay him. The comic twists are diluted by the posturing of the stars. 93m. **DIR:** Daniel Mann. **CAST:** Lana Turner, Dean Martin, Walter Matthau, Eddie Albert, Margo, Nita Talbot, Paul Ford. 1962

WHO'S HARRY CRUMB? 🦃 Inept private eye Harry Crumb bumbles his way through the case of a kidnapped heiress. Rated PG-13 for profanity and suggested sex. 87m. **DIR:** Paul Flaherty. **CAST:** John Candy, Jeffrey Jones, Annie Potts, Tim Thomerson, Barry Corbin. 1989

WHO'S MINDING THE MINT? ★★★½ When a U.S. Mint employee (Jim Hutton) accidentally destroys thousands of newly printed bills, a group of misfits bands together to help him out. This film is often hilarious and always enjoyable. 97m. **DIR:** Howard Morris. **CAST:** Milton Berle, Jim Hutton, Dorothy Provine, Joey Bishop, Walter Brennan, Jamie Farr, Victor Buono. 1967

WHO'S THAT GIRL 🦃 A warped, pseudoremake of the 1938 comedy classic *Bringing Up Baby*. Rated PG for profanity. 95m. **DIR:** James Foley. **CAST:** Madonna, Griffin Dunne, Haviland Morris, John McMartin, John Mills. 1987

WHO'S THE MAN? ★★★ Two inept Harlem haircutters reluctantly become inept Harlem cops and investigate the murder of their former barbershop boss in this funny, sassy, streetwise comedy but MTV rap hosts Doctor Dre and Ed Lover bring to the party the most rhythmic and natural comic chemistry since Cheech and Chong. Rated R for language. 100m. **DIR:** Ted Demme. **CAST:** Doctor Dre, Ed Lover, Jim Moody, Denis Leary, Colin Quinn, Badja Djola, Cheryl James, Andre Blake, Rozwill Young. 1993

WHO'S WHO ★★★★★ This brilliant, ascerbic comedy deals with the violent differences in lifestyle and attitude that exist within the British class system. A pathetic, vacuous clerk in a stockbroker's office is obsessed with the aristocracy, who regard his social advances with facial expressions similar to the expressions of those who have just discovered fresh canine excrement on their shoes. Brilliant. Not rated. 75m. **DIR:** Mike Leigh. **CAST:** Bridget Kane, Sam Kelly, Simon Chandler, Adam Norton, Philip Davis. 1978

WILD LIFE, THE ★★ From some of the same people who brought you *Fast Times at Ridgemont High* comes a film set in a world where your "cool" is measured by how many cigarettes you can smoke (and eat) and how many girls you can bed. Christopher Penn offers a believable performance as the leader of a pack of teens trying to grow up too fast. Rated R for suggested sex and language. 96m. **DIR:** Art Linson. **CAST:** Christopher Penn, Lea Thompson, Rick Moranis, Randy Quaid, Ilan Mitchell-Smith. 1984

WILD WEST (1993) ★★½ Offbeat comedy about a group of Pakistani country-and-western musicians eking out a living in West London while hoping to travel to Nashville and make it big. Perhaps this British style of outrageous comedy doesn't travel well, but there is something in this film to offend nearly everyone. Unrated, the film has profanity, violence, and suggested sex. 85m. **DIR:** David Attwood. **CAST:** Naveen Andrews, Sarita Choudhury. 1993

WILDCATS ★★ Standard Goldie Hawn vehicle, with her playing high school football coach to a rowdy group of inner-city kids who need to prove their worth as much as she needs to raise her self-esteem and prove her skill to chauvinistic athletic directors. Director Michael Ritchie shows little of the tension he brought to *The Bad News Bears*. Rated R for nudity and language. 107m. **DIR:** Michael Ritchie. **CAST:** Goldie Hawn, Swoosie Kurtz, James Keach, Nipsey Russell, Woody Harrelson, M. Emmet Walsh. 1986

WILDER NAPALM ★★★ Everything works in this quirky comedy except the show-offy script, which wants to be screwball but is merely screwed up. Two feuding brothers, both in love with the same woman, share the power to start fires at will. Eventually everything in this movie turns out to be window dressing covering a brick wall. Rated PG-13 for sexual situations. 110m. **DIR:** Glenn Gordon Caron. **CAST:** Debra Winger, Dennis Quaid, Arliss Howard, Jim Varney, M. Emmet Walsh, Glenn Gordon Caron. 1993

WILLIE AND PHIL ★★½ Director Paul Mazursky's "hip" take on Truffaut's *Jules and Jim,* this story of a love triangle now seems quite dated. Margot Kidder is the love interest of two best friends who share her affections for nine years. Kidder's character is generally unsympathetic and, as a result, much of the film seems artificial. Rated R for nudity and profanity. 116m. **DIR:** Paul Mazursky. **CAST:** Michael Ontkean, Margot Kidder, Ray Sharkey, Jan Miner. **1980**

WIMPS 🦃 *Animal House* meets *Cyrano de Bergerac*. Rated R for language, nudity, and sexual situations. 94m. **DIR:** Chuck Vincent. **CAST:** Louie Bonanno, Deborah Blaisdell, Jim Abele, Jane Hamilton. **1986**

WIN, PLACE OR STEAL 🦃 Slow, boring comedy about three aging adolescents who prefer playing the ponies to working. Unrated. 88m. **DIR:** Richard Bailey. **CAST:** Dean Stockwell, Russ Tamblyn, Alex Karras, McLean Stevenson. **1972**

WINGS OF FAME ★★★ Peter O'Toole delivers a deliciously droll performance as Cesar Valetin, an actor who's being stalked by Brian Smith, a young fan played by Colin Firth. When Brian kills Valetin during a film festival, he finds Valetin and himself trapped in a spiritual hotel where the famous and near-famous go after they die. The film takes great delight in exposing pretentions and how they relate to those we put on a pedestal. Insightful, imaginative, and very funny. Rated R for adult language and situations. 109m. **DIR:** Otakar Votocek. **CAST:** Peter O'Toole, Colin Firth, Marie Trintignant. **1990**

WISE GUYS ★★★½ Director Brian De Palma, apparently tired of derivative Hitchcockian thrillers, returned to his roots with this send-up of gangster movies. Danny DeVito and Joe Piscopo play Harry and Moe, a couple of goofball syndicate gofers. When they muck up a bet on the ponies; as punishment, the boss secretly instructs each to kill the other. Inexplicably rated R for language. 91m. **DIR:** Brian De Palma. **CAST:** Danny DeVito, Joe Piscopo, Harvey Keitel, Ray Sharkey, Dan Hedaya. **1986**

WISH YOU WERE HERE ★★★★ The heroine of this British production is a foulmouthed, promiscuous 16-year-old (superbly played by Emily Lloyd), who raises hackles in the straitlaced world of 1940s England. Her story is shocking, funny, and ultimately touching. Writer-director David Leland has created a hilarious comedy. Rated R for profanity, nudity, and simulated sex. 92m. **DIR:** David Leland. **CAST:** Emily Lloyd, Tom Bell, Jesse Birdsall, Geoffrey Durham, Pat Heywood. **1987**

WISHFUL THINKING ★★ A recluse receives a magical notebook. With it, he can have anything he wants, and he wants a beautiful woman. Sight gags are overdone. Unrated, but contains nudity and violence. 94m. **DIR:** Murray Langston. **CAST:** Murray Langston, Michelle Johnson, Ruth Buzzi, Billy Barty, Ray "Boom Boom" Mancini. **1992**

WISTFUL WIDOW OF WAGON GAP, THE ★★★ Back in the old West a salesman accidentally kills a man and finds that legally he must support the widow and her six children. This doesn't sound like a comedy, but when the salesman is Lou Costello and the widow is Marjorie Main laughs come easily. B&W; 77m. **DIR:** Charles Barton. **CAST:** Bud Abbott, Lou Costello, Marjorie Main, Audrey Young, George Cleveland, Gordon Jones, William Ching. **1947**

WITCHES' BREW ★★ Margret (Teri Garr) and her two girlfriends have been dabbling in witchcraft to help their university professor husbands to succeed. It's supposed to be a horror spoof but turns out to be more of a horror rip-off of *Burn Witch Burn*! Lana Turner has a small role as the witchcraft mentor to the three young women. Rated PG. 98m. **DIR:** Richard Shoor, Herbert L. Strock. **CAST:** Richard Benjamin, Teri Garr, Lana Turner, Kathryn Leigh Scott. **1980**

WITCHES OF EASTWICK, THE ★★★★½ In this wickedly funny comedy, Jack Nicholson gives one of his finest—and funniest—performances as a self-described "horny little devil" who comes to a tiny hamlet at the behest of three women (Cher, Susan Sarandon, and Michelle Pfeiffer). Only trouble is, these "witches" have no idea of what they've done until it is very nearly too late. Rated R for profanity and suggested sex. 121m. **DIR:** George Miller. **CAST:** Jack Nicholson, Cher, Susan Sarandon, Michelle Pfeiffer, Veronica Cartwright, Richard Jenkins. **1987**

WITH HONORS ★★★ Joe Pesci plays a homeless philosopher who teaches blue-blooded Harvard student Brendan Fraser about life and compassion. The story is predictable, even when it takes a tearjerking turn, but Pesci's cocky charm and the remarkably attractive supporting ensemble keep things interesting. Rated PG-13 for profanity and mild nudity. 96m. **DIR:** Alek Keshishian. **CAST:** Joe Pesci, Brendan Fraser, Moira Kelly, Patrick Dempsey, Josh Hamilton, Gore Vidal. **1994**

WITH SIX YOU GET EGGROLL ★★ Widow Doris Day has three kids; widower Brian Keith has a daughter. They get together. Awwwww! *Bachelor Father* meets *Mother Knows Best.* The two stars refer to Doris and Brian, neither of whom helped their cause with this turkey. Strictly a picture for the 1960s. Unrated. 99m. **DIR:** Howard Morris. **CAST:** Doris Day, Brian Keith, Barbara Hershey. **1968**

WITHNAIL AND I ★★★★ A funny but sometimes grim comedy set in the Great Britain of the late 1960s. Two friends, whose decadent life-style of booze and drugs has hit bottom, try to make a new start by taking a holiday in the country. The performances are excellent, period details are perfect, and the movie is well made. Rated R for profanity and adult themes. 110m. **DIR:** Bruce Robinson. **CAST:** Richard E. Grant, Paul McGann, Richard Griffiths. **1987**

WITHOUT A CLUE ★★★★ In this delightful send-up of Conan Doyle's mysteries, it is revealed that Holmes was nothing more than a fictional creation of the real crime-fighting genius, Dr. John H. Watson (Ben Kingsley). The Great Detective was actually an inept, clumsy, and often inebriated actor, Reginald Kincaid (Michael Caine), hired by Watson. An overlooked gem of a comedy. Rated PG for violence. 106m. **DIR:** Thom Eberhardt. **CAST:** Michael Caine, Ben Kingsley, Jeffrey Jones, Lysette Anthony, Paul Freeman, Nigel Davenport, Peter Cook. **1988**

WITHOUT LOVE ★★★★ Widow Katharine Hepburn enters into a marriage of convenience with scientist Spencer Tracy. Great fun, with this wonderful team being matched every step of the way by wisecracking Lucille Ball and likable, lush Keenan Wynn. B&W; 111m. **DIR:** Harold S. Bucquet. **CAST:** Spencer Tracy, Katharine Hepburn, Lucille Ball, Keenan Wynn, Patricia Morison, Felix Bressart. **1945**

WITHOUT RESERVATIONS ★★★ Wartime comedy about authoress Claudette Colbert and her plan to turn soldier John Wayne into the leading man of her filmed novel is light and enjoyable and sprinkled with guest appearances by Hollywood celebrities. This is hardly the kind of war film in which one would expect to find John Wayne, but the Duke makes the best of a chance to act under top director Mervyn LeRoy (who was in a slump during this period). B&W; 107m. **DIR:** Mervyn LeRoy. **CAST:** John Wayne, Claudette Colbert, Don DeFore, Phil Brown, Thurston Hall, Louella Parsons. **1946**

WITHOUT YOU I'M NOTHING ★★★★ Comedian and social satirist Sandra Bernhard stars in an adaptation (cowritten with director John Boskovich) of her celebrated one-woman show. Not for the prudish or easily offended, but there are many thought-provoking laughs as Bernhard pokes wicked fun at middle-class life, love, and sexual politics. Rated R for profanity. 89m. **DIR:** John Boskovich. **CAST:** Sandra Bernhard. **1990**

WIZ KID, THE ★★ Teenage high jinks find young computer whiz Martin Forbes cloning himself so his hipper alter self can make out with the prettiest girl in school. Predictable problems don't help this obviously dubbed foreign import. Rated PG for adult situations. 90m. **DIR:** Gloria Behrens. **CAST:** Martin Forbes, Gary Forbes, Heiner Lauterbach. **1993**

WIZARD OF SPEED AND TIME, THE ★★★ Based on Mike Jittlov's own difficulties in breaking into show business, this tongue-in-cheek success story features him producing a special-effects masterpiece on a shoestring budget. Silly gags and slapstick surround five stop-motion shorts. Rated PG for language. 92m. **DIR:** Mike Jittlov. **CAST:** Mike Jittlov, Paige Moore, Richard Kaye, Philip Michael Thomas. **1986**

WOMAN IN RED, THE ★★★★ Gene Wilder's funniest film in years, this is best described as a bittersweet romantic comedy. Wilder, who also adapted the screenplay and directed, plays an advertising executive and heretofore happily married man who becomes obsessed with a beautiful woman. The results are hilarious. Rated PG-13 for partial nudity, brief violence, and profanity. 87m. **DIR:** Gene Wilder. **CAST:** Gene Wilder, Charles Grodin, Joseph Bologna, Gilda Radner, Judith Ivey, Michael Huddleston, Kelly LeBrock. **1984**

WOMAN OF DISTINCTION, A ★★★½ Though minor, this is really a quite enjoyable film. Rosalind Russell portrays a college dean who must face a tough decision involving a professor (Ray Milland). Familiar but fun. B&W; 85m. **DIR:** Edward Buzzell. **CAST:** Rosalind Russell, Ray Milland, Edmund Gwenn, Janis Carter, Francis Lederer. **1950**

WOMAN OF THE YEAR ★★★★★ This is the film that first teamed Spencer Tracy and Katharine Hepburn, and it's impossible to imagine anybody else doing a better job. He's a sports reporter; she's a famed political journalist who needs to be reminded of life's simple pleasures. Like baseball...and her attempts to learn the game are priceless. The witty script garnered an Oscar for Ring Lardner Jr. and Michael Kanin. Unrated—family fare. B&W; 112m. **DIR:** George Stevens. **CAST:** Spencer Tracy, Katharine Hepburn, Fay Bainter, Reginald Owen, William Bendix. **1942**

WOMEN, THE ★★★★½ Director George Cukor and some of Hollywood's finest female stars combine for a winning screen version of Claire Booth's stage hit. This look at the state of matrimony is great entertainment. The script is full of witty, stinging dialogue. B&W; 132m. **DIR:** George Cukor. **CAST:** Norma Shearer, Joan Crawford, Rosalind Russell, Joan Fontaine, Paulette Goddard. **1939**

WOMEN'S CLUB, THE ♥ Rated R for profanity, brief nudity, and excessive sexual situations. 89m. **DIR:** Sandra Weintraub. **CAST:** Michael Paré, Maud Adams, Eddie Velez. **1986**

WONDER MAN ★★★ Deftly doubling, Danny Kaye plays identical twins with personalities as far apart as the polar regions. One, Buzzy Bellew, is a brash, irrepressible nightclub comic; his mirror, Edwin Dingle, is a mousy double-dome full of tongue-twisting erudition. Identities are switched, of course. Thin on plot, this is mostly a tailored showcase for Kaye's brilliant talents. 98m. **DIR:** H. Bruce Humberstone. **CAST:** Danny Kaye, Vera-Ellen, Virginia Mayo, Donald Woods, S. Z. Sakall, Allen Jenkins, Edward Brophy. **1945**

WORKING GIRL ★★★★ A clever, sophisticated comedy with grit, *Working Girl* makes up for a lack of all-out belly laughs with the ring of truth. Melanie Griffith is terrific as the good-hearted gal attempting to work her way up in the brokerage business. She is thwarted in this by her scheming boss, Sigourney Weaver, until Harrison Ford, as a high-powered deal maker rides to the rescue. Weaver is marvelously sinister and Ford is properly perplexed, but it is Griffith who steals the show. Rated R for nudity and profanity. 120m. **DIR:** Mike Nichols. **CAST:** Harrison Ford, Sigourney Weaver, Melanie Griffith, Alec Baldwin, Joan Cusack. **1988**

WORKING STIFFS ★★★ This video is composed of the first three episodes of the 1979 TV series about two brothers working as janitors. Good scripts and great timing between the two leads make you wonder why it was canceled. Unrated. 75m. **DIR:** Penny Marshall, Norman Abbott. **CAST:** James Belushi, Michael Keaton. **1979**

WORLD OF ABBOTT AND COSTELLO, THE ★★★ Compilation of Abbott and Costello's best film footage is well handled, with many of their classic scenes intact: the frog in the soup, Lou in the wrestling ring, Lou meeting Dracula, and of course "Who's on First?" Would've been better without the narration, but the film never fails to entertain. Add one star if you're a fan. B&W; 79m. **DIR:** Jack E. Leonard. **CAST:** Bud Abbott, Lou Costello, various guest stars. **1965**

WORLD OF HENRY ORIENT, THE ★★★★ A quirky comedy for the whole family. Peter Sellers is a woman-crazy New York pianist who finds himself being followed by two teenage girls who have come to idolize him. Loads of fun, with a great performance by Angela Lansbury. 106m. **DIR:** George Roy Hill. **CAST:** Peter Sellers, Paula Prentiss, Angela Lansbury, Phyllis Thaxter. **1964**

WORLD'S GREATEST LOVER, THE ★★½ Gene Wilder plays a would-be silent-movie star who tests for the part of the "new Valentino" while his wife (Carol Kane) runs off with the real Rudolph. Dom De Luise is around to brighten things up, but writer-director Wilder's ideas of what's funny aren't quite right. Rated PG. 89m. **DIR:** Gene Wilder. **CAST:** Gene Wilder, Carol Kane, Dom DeLuise, Fritz Feld, Carl Ballantine, Michael Huddleston, Matt Collins, Ronny Graham. **1977**

WORTH WINNING 🦃 TV weatherman thinks he's the ultimate ladies' man. Rated PG-13 for profanity and suggested sex. 104m. **DIR:** Will Mackenzie. **CAST:** Mark Harmon, Madeleine Stowe, Lesley Ann Warren, Maria Holvoe, Mark Blum, Andrea Martin, David Brenner. **1989**

WRONG ARM OF THE LAW, THE ★★★★ Peter Sellers is hilarious as Pearly Gates, the Cockney leader of a group of bandits. Sellers and his gang join forces with police inspector Parker (Lionel Jeffries) after a group of Australians pose as police and capture Sellers's stolen goods. This British comedy contains enough to keep most viewers in stitches. B&W; 94m. **DIR:** Cliff Owen. **CAST:** Peter Sellers, Lionel Jeffries, Bernard Cribbins, Davy Kaye, Nanette Newman. **1962**

WRONG BOX, THE ★★★★ Some of Britain's best-known comics appear in this screwball farce about two zany families who battle over an inheritance in Victorian England. The film borders on black humor as the corpse of a wealthy brother is shuffled all over London by the contending parties—headed by John Mills and Ralph Richardson. Dudley Moore, Peter Sellers, and Peter Cook are just a few of the funnymen who give cameo performances in the delightful comedy. 105m. **DIR:** Bryan Forbes. **CAST:** John Mills, Ralph Richardson, Dudley Moore, Peter Sellers, Peter Cook, Michael Caine, Nanette Newman, Wilfrid Lawson, Tony Hancock. **1966**

WRONG GUYS, THE ★★ Low-energy farce about the camping-trip reunion of a 1962 Cub Scout Troop. The troop is mistaken for FBI agents by a crazed convict, and therein lies the comedy. Rated PG for language and comic-book violence. 86m. **DIR:** Danny Bilson. **CAST:** Louie Anderson, Richard Lewis, Richard Belzer, Franklin Ajaye, Tim Thomerson, John Goodman, Brion James, Ernie Hudson, Alice Ghostley, Kathleen Freeman. **1988**

WRONG IS RIGHT ★★★★ Sean Connery, as a globe-trotting television reporter, gives what may be the best performance of his career, in this outrageous, thoroughly entertaining end-of-the-world black comedy, written, produced, and directed by Richard Brooks. It's an updated combination of *Network* and *Dr. Strangelove*, and wickedly funny. Rated R because of profanity and violence. 117m. **DIR:** Richard Brooks. **CAST:** Sean Connery, Robert Conrad, George Grizzard, Katharine Ross, G. D. Spradlin, John Saxon, Henry Silva, Leslie Nielsen, Robert Webber, Rosalind Cash, Hardy Krüger, Dean Stockwell, Ron Moody. **1982**

YEAR IN PROVENCE, A ★★★★½ Based on Peter Mayle's delightful book, this four-part TV series is a visual, breezy delight. John Thaw and Lindsay Duncan are the British escapees who set up house in the south of France and chronicle their first year. Humorous and full of élan, but it presents a caricatured British view of the French villagers. Not rated. Four 90-minute episodes. **DIR:**

David Tucker. **CAST:** John Thaw, Lindsay Duncan. **1992**

YEAR OF THE COMET ★★½ In this slightly silly romantic adventure-comedy, Penelope Ann Miller finds a huge bottle of the world's finest and rarest wine—Lafitte 1811—only to have to rely on a boorish troubleshooter (Timothy Daly) to keep it out of the hands of thieves. This determinedly lightweight film was written by William Goldman. Rated PG-13 for profanity and violence. 91m. **DIR:** Peter Yates. **CAST:** Penelope Ann Miller, Timothy Daly, Louis Jourdan, Art Malik, Ian Richardson. **1992**

YELLOW CAB MAN, THE ★★★½ Red Skelton is a bumbling cabdriver who develops a process for a new unbreakable safety glass. Crooks see the potential and come after it. Good sight gags. B&W; 85m. **DIR:** Jack Donohue. **CAST:** Red Skelton, Gloria De Haven, Walter Slezak, Edward Arnold, James Gleason, Jay C. Flippen. **1950**

YELLOWBEARD ★★½ This pirate comedy barely contains a boatload of laughs under the directorship of first-timer Mel Damski. Rated PG for profanity, nudity, violence, gore, and scatological humor. 101m. **DIR:** Mel Damski. **CAST:** Graham Chapman, Eric Idle, John Cleese, Peter Cook, Cheech and Chong, Peter Boyle, Madeline Kahn, Marty Feldman, Kenneth Mars. **1983**

YO-YO MAN ★★★★ This is ostensibly an instruction video on the development of yo-yo skills, but it is much more. The actual instruction consists of the basic tricks, tips on using the yo-yo, plus advanced skills that are great fun to watch and can be accomplished with practice. There are clips from *The Smothers Brothers Comedy Hour* series and new footage with Tommy Smothers and yo-yo expert Daniel Volk. Dick Smothers adds narrative and humor, and there is a catchy sound track. 38m. **DIR:** David Grossman. **CAST:** Tom Smothers, Dick Smothers, Daniel Volk. **1988**

YOU BET YOUR LIFE (TV SERIES) ★★★½ Over the years, two different game formats were devised for this show, but it was the interview segment that made the program a winner. In grilling the contestants, who ranged from average folks to celebrities to bizarre characters, Groucho Marx invariably got off a number of clever quips. B&W; 30m. **DIR:** Robert Dwan, Bernie Smith. **CAST:** Groucho Marx, George Fenneman. **1950–1961**

YOU CAN'T CHEAT AN HONEST MAN ★★★½ Nearly plotless, this is, star W. C. Fields admitted, "a jumble of vaudeville skits"—which, nonetheless, brings together, with hilarious results, a cast of exquisite comedians. Fields fans will relish it all, of course. B&W; 76m. **DIR:** George Marshall. **CAST:** W. C. Fields, Edgar Bergen, Constance Moore, Mary Forbes, Thurston Hall, Eddie "Rochester" Anderson. **1939**

YOU CAN'T FOOL YOUR WIFE ★★★ A disillusioned Lucille Ball leaves her husband (James Ellison) and then tries to patch things up at a costume party. This is an average comedy with Ball playing two parts. B&W; 68m. **DIR:** Ray McCarey. **CAST:** Lucille Ball, Robert Coote, James Ellison. **1940**

YOU CAN'T HURRY LOVE ★★ A young man leaves Ohio to live with his hip cousin in Los Angeles. There he meets assorted women through a video dating service. Rated R for nudity and profanity. 92m. **DIR:** Richard Martini. **CAST:** David Leisure, Scott McGinnis, Anthony Geary, Bridget Fonda, Frank Bonner, Kristy McNichol. **1987**

YOU CAN'T TAKE IT WITH YOU (1938) ★★★★★ Frank Capra's adaptation of the beloved Kaufman and Hart stage classic continues to charm audiences. The fun starts when James Stewart and Jean Arthur fall in love and announce their desire to wed. This zany romp won 1938's Oscar for best picture. B&W; 126m. **DIR:** Frank Capra. **CAST:** James Stewart, Lionel Barrymore, Jean Arthur, Edward Arnold, Spring Byington, Mischa Auer, Ann Miller. **1938**

YOU CAN'T TAKE IT WITH YOU (1984) ★★★★½ Filmed on one set before a live audience, this Pulitzer Prize-winning Kaufman and Hart play features Jason Robards as the head of a very eccentric family. Now they must be on their best behavior to meet the parents of their daughter's beau. 116m. **DIR:** Kirk Browning. **CAST:** Jason Robards Jr., George Rose, Elizabeth Wilson, Colleen Dewhurst. **1984**

YOU'LL FIND OUT ★★★ Three titans of terror—Boris Karloff, Peter Lorre, and Bela Lugosi—menace bandleader Kay Kyser and heiress Helen Parrish in this silly but amiable comedy. Kyser isn't much of a screen personality, but director David Butler keeps the comedy, music, and suspense nicely balanced. B&W; 97m. **DIR:** David Butler. **CAST:** Kay Kyser, Peter Lorre, Boris Karloff, Bela Lugosi, Dennis O'Keefe, Helen Parrish. **1940**

YOUNG AT HEART COMEDIANS, THE ★★ Some of America's most famous comedians join together for this cable special. Moderately funny but dated material marks their routines. Not rated. 77m. **DIR:** Joe Hostettler. **CAST:** Carl Ballantine, Shelley Berman, Norm Crosby, Jackie Gayle, George Gobel, Jackie Vernon, Henny Youngman, David Brenner. **1984**

YOUNG DOCTORS IN LOVE ★★★ This comedy attempts to do for medical soap operas what *Airplane!* did for disaster movies—and doesn't quite make it. Director Garry Marshall has nevertheless created an enjoyable movie for open-minded adults. The R-rated film is a bit too raunchy and suggestive for the younger set. 95m. **DIR:** Garry Marshall. **CAST:** Michael McKean, Sean Young, Harry Dean Stanton, Patrick Macnee, Hector Elizondo, Dabney Coleman, Pamela Reed, Michael Richards, Taylor Negron, Saul Rubinek, Titos Vandis. 1982

YOUNG EINSTEIN 🦃 Einstein discovers how to split the atom and thus puts the bubbles into beer. Rated PG. 91m. **DIR:** Yahoo Serious. **CAST:** Yahoo Serious. 1989

YOUNG FRANKENSTEIN ★★★★½ This is one of Mel Brooks's best. *Young Frankenstein* is the story of Dr. Frankenstein's college professor descendant who abhors his family history. This spoof of the old Universal horror films is hilarious from start to finish. Rated PG. B&W; 105m. **DIR:** Mel Brooks. **CAST:** Gene Wilder, Marty Feldman, Peter Boyle, Teri Garr, Madeline Kahn, Cloris Leachman, Kenneth Mars, Richard Haydn, Gene Hackman. 1974

YOUNG IN HEART, THE ★★★½ This delightful romp has a fortune-hunting family finding a change of heart when they meet a nice old lady, appropriately named Miss Fortune. The entire cast is wonderful in this lavish production. 91m. **DIR:** Richard Wallace. **CAST:** Janet Gaynor, Douglas Fairbanks Jr., Paulette Goddard, Roland Young, Billie Burke. 1938

YOUNG NURSES IN LOVE 🦃 A foreign spy poses as a nurse to steal the sperm from the sperm bank that was donated by world leaders, celebrities, and geniuses. Rated R for nudity. 82m. **DIR:** Chuck Vincent. **CAST:** Jeanne Marie. 1989

YOUNG ONES, THE ★★★ Three episodes of the inventive, anarchic British TV series (you may have seen it on MTV) about a quartet of impoverished college students. Raucous, obnoxious, shrill—and often very funny. 96m. **DIR:** Geoffrey Posner. **CAST:** Rik Mayall, Adrian Edmondson, Nigel Planer, Alexei Sayle. 1982

YOUR FAVORITE LAUGHS FROM AN EVENING AT THE IMPROV ★★ Clips from various performers onstage at The Improv. Quick jokes are not always funny, and this tape suffers for it. Not rated. 59m. **DIR:** Ron Kantor. **CAST:** Harry Anderson, Sandra Bernhard, Elayne Boosler, Billy Crystal, Rich Hall, Michael Keaton, Harvey Korman, Howie Mandel, Paul Rodriguez, Dick Shawn, David Steinberg, Steven Wright. 1986

YOU'RE A BIG BOY NOW ★★★★½ Francis Ford Coppola not only directed this (his first) film but also wrote the screenplay. Peter Kastner, the product of overprotective parents, learns about life from streetwise go-go dancer Elizabeth Hartman. Fast-paced and very entertaining. 96m. **DIR:** Francis Ford Coppola. **CAST:** Peter Kastner, Elizabeth Hartman, Geraldine Page, Julie Harris, Rip Torn, Michael Dunn, Tony Bill, Karen Black. 1966

YOURS, MINE AND OURS ★★★ A widow with eight children marries a widower with ten of his own. This works as a harbinger of *The Brady Bunch.* Wholesome but never sterile or overly sentimental, this comedy-drama is probably Lucille Ball's best post-*I Love Lucy* vehicle. Rated G. 111m. **DIR:** Melville Shavelson. **CAST:** Lucille Ball, Henry Fonda, Van Johnson, Tom Bosley. 1968

ZANY ADVENTURES OF ROBIN HOOD, THE ★★ Made-for-TV spoof of the legendary hero of Sherwood Forest. George Segal is likable as Robin Hood. Okay time passer but nothing more. 90m. **DIR:** Ray Austin. **CAST:** George Segal, Morgan Fairchild, Roddy McDowall, Janet Suzman. 1984

ZAPPED! ★★ A campy takeoff on high school movies that doesn't work. *Zapped* is a bore. Rated R for nudity and sexual situations. 96m. **DIR:** Robert J. Rosenthal. **CAST:** Scott Baio, Willie Aames, Felice Schachter, Heather Thomas, Scatman Crothers, Robert Mandan, Greg Bradford. 1982

ZAPPED AGAIN ★★½ A new student inspires the science club to take on the jocks. His secret potion allows him to defy the law of gravity and manipulate people and things around him. As teen comedies go, this is not too bad. Rated R for nudity, profanity, and violence. 93m. **DIR:** Doug Campbell. **CAST:** Todd Eric Andrews, Kelli Williams, Linda Blair, Lyle Alzado. 1989

ZELIG ★★★★★ Woody Allen plays Leonard Zelig, a remarkable man who can fit anywhere in society because he can change his appearance at will. The laughs come fast and furious in this account of his adventures in the 1920s, when he became all the rage and hung out with the likes of F. Scott Fitzgerald, Jack Dempsey, and Babe Ruth. Allen seamlessly weds black-and-white newsreel footage with his humorous tale, allowing Zelig to be right in the thick of history. Rated PG. B&W; 79m. **DIR:** Woody Allen. **CAST:** Woody Allen, Mia Farrow. 1984

ZOMBIES ON BROADWAY ★★ Near-poverty row comedy starring Wally Brown and Alan Carney. The dim-witted duo portray press agents trying to book a zombie—a scheme that drops them into Bela Lugosi's clutches. B&W; 68m. **DIR:** Gordon Douglas. **CAST:** Wally Brown, Alan Carney, Bela Lugosi, Anne Jeffreys. 1945

ZOO GANG, THE ★★ An oddball gang of crooks sets out to discover whether crime pays and winds up with more than it bargained for. Distinguished by Ben Vereen's excellent performance. Rated PG-13 for violence. 96m. **DIR:** John Watson, Pen Densham. **CAST:** Ben Vereen, Jason Gedrick, Eric Gurry. 1985

ZOO RADIO ★★ This sophomoric comedy deals with dueling Los Angeles radio stations. A continuous stream of one-line jokes and sight gags—some work, some don't. Rated R for strong language. 88m. **DIR:** M. Ray Roach. **CAST:** Peter Feig, Ron Dickinson, David Pires, Terra Mays. **1990**

ZORRO, THE GAY BLADE ★★★★ Here's another delight from (and starring) actor-producer George Hamilton. As with *Love at First Bite*, in which Hamilton played a slightly bent Count Dracula to great effect, the accent in *Zorro, the Gay Blade* is on belly-wrenching laughs...and there are plenty of them. Rated PG because of sexual innuendo. 93m. **DIR:** Peter Medak. **CAST:** George Hamilton, Lauren Hutton, Brenda Vaccaro, Ron Leibman, Donovan Scott. **1981**

ZOTZ! ★★★½ Charming, underrated little fantasy about a college professor (Tom Poston) who finds a magical coin blessed with three bizarre powers: sudden pain, slow motion, and explosive destruction. An excellent opportunity for Poston to control a film in one of his rare leading parts. Give this a try; you won't be disappointed. B&W; 87m. **DIR:** William Castle. **CAST:** Tom Poston, Jim Backus, Julia Meade. **1962**

DOCUMENTARY

ACTS OF VIOLENCE ★★ Chop-licking shockumentary that profiles a cross section of society's more repellent murderers. Grim and gruesome; *60 Minutes* this ain't. Unrated. 72m. **DIR:** Imre Horvath. **1988**

AFRICA BLOOD AND GUTS ★★ Another shockumentary from the production team that created *Mondo Cane*. This film crudely explores tribal violence, the slaughter of wild animals, and the racial and political turbulence throughout Africa. It contains scenes of graphic, realistic violence; sensitive viewers should exercise caution. 90m. **DIR:** Gualtiero Jacopetti. **1983**

ALWAYS FOR PLEASURE ★★★★½ Les Blank has beautifully captured the true spirit of the Mardi Gras festival, a celebration of life through the rollicking, sensual ritual of music and dance. This remarkable piece of filmmaking features great traditional American ethnic music in the form of Dixieland jazz, blues, and rock 'n' roll. Blank's cinematography is a standout, creating the mood of a surreal fun house. 58m. **DIR:** Les Blank. **1979**

AMERICAN DREAM ★★★★ Oscar-winning documentary about the Local P-9 (meat packers) union in Austin, Minnesota, and their struggle to renegotiate wages with the Hormel Corporation. The local union bypasses its international chapter and hires a corporate image consultant. A good mix of interviews between the strikers, Hormel executives, and the international chapter. This documentary lets the viewers decide for themselves which side they should take. Rated PG-13 for profanity. 98m. **DIR:** Barbara Kopple. **1990**

AMERICAN FILM INSTITUTE LIFE ACHIEVEMENT AWARDS, THE ★★★½ When the American Film Institute Board of Trustees established a Life Achievement Award in 1973, the following criteria were established: "The recipient should be one whose talent has in a fundamental way advanced the film art; whose accomplishment has been acknowledged by scholars, critics, professional peers, and the general public; and whose work has stood the test of time." Director John Ford, who received the first of these awards that same year, became the first of an ever-expanding roster of great men and women from the world of cinema. The awards ceremonies follow a standard format: introductions and tributes by a stellar assortment of friends and coworkers, an assemblage of clips from the honored individual's career, and a final speech of thanks by the recipient. each. 68–97m. **DIR:** Various. **CAST:** James Cagney, Orson Welles, Bette Davis, Henry Fonda, John Ford, Alfred Hitchcock, James Stewart, Fred Astaire, John Huston, Lillian Gish, Gene Kelly, Billy Wilder, Jack Lemmon. **1973–1988**

AMERICAN GANGSTER, THE ★★ This brief overview of our most notorious "wise guys" takes us back to their early years of nickels and dimes to their heyday and beyond. Several famous crime bosses are featured; and because it helps to separate the facts from the fiction surrounding them, this documentary would probably make an interesting companion rental to any number of recently released mobster flicks. Unrated, but deals with mature themes and subject matter. 45m. **DIR:** Ben Burtt. **1992**

ANDY WARHOL: SUPERSTAR ★★★★ Thoroughly fascinating exploration of the pop icon's life and times, featuring a bevy of celebrities stepping forward with their recollections. Director Chuck Workman's film is like a time capsule filled with precious memories. 87m. **DIR:** Chuck Workman. **1991**

ANIMALS ARE BEAUTIFUL PEOPLE ★★★½ South African filmmaker Jamie Uys takes a pixilated perspective on wildlife documentaries in this sporadically hilarious film. Rated G. 92m. **DIR:** Jamie Uys. **1974**

ATHENS, GA. ★★★½ The right mixture of interviews and raw live footage, plus a pounding rock sound track and a dash of trash make this documentary must-viewing. Playful and witty, the film is tightly edited with a focus that flows gracefully from stage to Georgia street scenes, providing a grand view of the essence of Athens. 82m. **DIR:** Tony Gayton. **1987**

ATOMIC CAFE, THE ★★ Beyond being an interesting cultural document, this feature-length compilation of post–World War II propaganda, documentary, and newsreel footage on American attitudes toward the atomic bomb has little to offer. No MPAA rating. The film has no objectionable material, though some of the footage featuring casualties of atomic bomb explosions is quite graphic. B&W; 88m. **DIR:** Kevin Rafferty, Jayne Loader, Pierce Rafferty. **1982**

BACKSTAGE AT THE KIROV ★★★★ Documentary about Leningrad's Kirov Ballet, where dancers are rigorously trained for their art from an early age. Even nonfans will find themselves led to a better appreciation of ballet through interviews with the dancers. In fact, if you're looking for an introduction to ballet, you can't do better than this. 78m. **DIR:** Derek Hart. **1983**

BARAKA ★★★½ This often exhilarating, nonverbal "guided meditation" on the interconnectedness of our planet is a smorgasbord of exotic sights, sounds, and music. Similar to *Koyaanisqatsi*, which director Ron Fricke also photographed and coedited, this kaleidoscopic plunge into nature, history, and religious rites was gleaned from ninety hours of 70mm film shot in twenty-four countries. Footage includes time-lapse photography of a Tokyo intersection, stunning desert and rain forest locales, and visits to a Holocaust memorial and the burning Kuwait oil fields. The title is an ancient Sufi word translated as blessing, or breath, or essence of life. Unrated. 83m. **DIR:** Ron Fricke. **1993**

BEACH BOYS, THE: AN AMERICAN BAND ★★½ Even the most fervent fans of the country's number-one surf group are likely to be a bit disappointed by this "authorized biography," directed by Malcolm Leo (*This Is Elvis*). Only occasionally catches a wave. Rated G. 90m. **DIR:** Malcolm Leo. **CAST:** The Beach Boys, Al Jardine, Bruce Johnston, Mike Love. **1984**

BEATLES, THE: THE FIRST U.S. VISIT ★★★★ This excellent day-by-day audiovisual account of the Fab Four's historical 1964 debut American tour is riveting. The Beatles are captured in their limos, hotel rooms, and in transit. Besides their legendary appearances on the Ed Sullivan Show, everyone's favorite pop band is seen performing ten other tunes. 83m. **DIR:** Albert Maysles, David Maysles, Kathy Dougherty, Susan Froemke. **1992**

BERLIN—SYMPHONY OF A GREAT CITY ★★★★★ This is the granddaddy of all cityscape documentaries. A portrait of Berlin from dawn to midnight, following the street sweepers, the office workers, the pedestrians, the nightlife bustle, and good-night yawns. A masterpiece. Silent. B&W; 70m. **DIR:** Walther Ruttmann. **1927**

BEST BOY ★★★★★ Filmmaker Ira Wohl spent three years tracking his retarded cousin Philly who, at the age of 52, began to prepare for life away from his parents. The result is a moving and uplifting film about the pains and rewards of coping with life on your own. Oscar winner for best documentary. Unrated. 110m. **DIR:** Ira Wohl. **1979**

BIG BANG, THE ★★★½ For his first documentary, feature film director James Toback has assembled a widely varying collection of individuals—some famous, some not—for entertaining, honest, and open discussions of philosophical questions. Eccentric, enjoyable, thought-provoking. Rated R, with profanity. 81m. **DIR:** James Toback. **1990**

BLAST 'EM ★★★★ Enjoyable, insightful documentary focuses on those who specialize in ambush photojournalism—the paparazzi. They're the folks who will do anything to get a celebrity's photo. A who's who of Hollywood's "A" players do their best to avoid the cameras, and their efforts make this delightful documentary compelling viewing. Not rated, but contains strong language. 103m. **DIR:** Joseph Blasioli. **1992**

BORNEO ★★★★ Husband-and-wife explorers Martin and Osa Johnson spent twenty-five years exploring and making documentary films about then-uncharted areas of the world. In this one, their last (Martin Johnson was killed in a plane crash when they returned), the pair explore the primitive island of Borneo. Comic commentary in some sequences will help hold the kids' attention, and the unusual animals (flying snakes, land-roving fish, and some very odd-looking monkeys) will delight the whole family. B&W; 76m. **DIR:** Martin Johnson, Osa Johnson. **1937**

BRIEF HISTORY OF TIME, A ★★★★ Errol Morris, creator of the explosive documentary *The Thin Blue Line* returns with a quieter, more reflective, but equally brilliant film. The movie entertainingly explores the life of Stephen Hawking, the severely disabled genius whose bestselling book of the same title explored the world of physics, time, and evolution. The hypnotic score is by Philip Glass. Unrated. 84m. **DIR:** Errol Morris. **1992**

BRING ON THE NIGHT 🦃 Obnoxious, self-serving documentary about popular rock star Sting (formerly of The Police). Rated PG-13. 97m. **DIR:** Michael Apted. **CAST:** Sting, Omar Hakim, Darryl Jones, Kenny Kirkland, Branford Marsalis. **1985**

BROKEN NOSES ★★★ Young boxers seen through the admiring camera eye of Bruce Weber, set to an atmospheric jazz score. Weber manages to evoke an atmosphere of lyrical charm through his study of the boxer Andy Minister, who emerges as a likable, somewhat naïve character. Not rated. 75m. **DIR:** Bruce Weber. **1987**

BROTHER'S KEEPER ★★★★ The strange case of upstate New York's Ward brothers makes for an intriguing documentary. The four aged brothers lived and worked together on a small dairy farm. When one of the brothers is found dead in bed, and one of the remaining three is charged with murder, their lives change forever. Joe Berlinger and Bruce Sinofsky make their feature-film debut with this impressively detailed examination of the case, and of the brothers' incredible life-style. 116m. **DIR:** Joe Berlinger, Bruce Sinofsky. **1992**

BRUCE LEE: CURSE OF THE DRAGON ★★★ Rare footage and a slick style will appeal to Lee fans. The focus is on his work and his athletic prowess, although his childhood and untimely death are probed. Addendum about Lee's deceased son, Brandon, seems slightly tacky. Narrated by George Takei. Not rated. 90m. **DIR:** Fred Weintraub, Tom Khun. **CAST:** Bruce Lee, James Coburn, Linda Emery Lee, Brandon Lee, Chuck Norris. **1993**

BRUTES AND SAVAGES ★★ Arthur Davis takes his cameras into the South American landscape, recording the various rituals performed by different Indian tribes. Unfortunately these brutal and erotic depictions of primitive cultures lack real power and drift into camp, especially with the director's ridiculous narration. Unrated, but contains graphic violence. 91m. **DIR:** Arthur Davis. **1977**

BURDEN OF DREAMS ★★★★★ Documentary specialist Les Blank unearthed a rare treasure in Ecuador, where Werner Herzog was laboring for years to make *Fitzcarraldo*, a lavish film depicting a man's obsessive quest to bring fine opera to the jungle. Shooting on location, among fighting tribes, Herzog's task becomes a parallel quest of compulsion. This would be dreamlike material for any documentary, but Blank logged the overtime to make the metaphors meaningful, more powerful even than Herzog did in *Fitzcarraldo*. Unrated. 94m. **DIR:** Les Blank. **CAST:** Werner Herzog, Klaus Kinski, Mick Jagger, Jason Robards Jr., Claudia Cardinale. **1982**

BUSTER KEATON: A HARD ACT TO FOLLOW ★★★★★ Offered in three parts, this is a truly superb narrative study of Buster Keaton's matchless stone-faced comic genius. The episodes, titled "From Vaudeville to Movies," "Star without a Studio," and "A Genius Recognized," chronicle Buster Keaton's amazing and mercurial career from near start to close with compassion, insight, and captivating accuracy. A unique opportunity to see one of the greats of the silent screen at work. B&W/color; each part. 52m. **DIR:** Kevin Brownlow, David Gill. **1987**

BUSTER KEATON RIDES AGAIN ★★★ Narrated by Donald Britain, this inside look at Buster Keaton's career shows how he worked, planned, and thought. Excerpts from a number of his silent comedies and the Canadian Railways promotion film, "The Railrodder," illustrate his comic technical brilliance. B&W; 56m. **DIR:** John Spotton, Gerald Potterton. **CAST:** Buster Keaton. **1965**

CALIFORNIA REICH ★★★ Fascinating, unsettling documentary about the Nazi organization in California. Made by two Stanford University grads, the film ultimately connects today's resurgence of Nazism to Hitler. Not rated; contains rough language and gang violence. 55m. **DIR:** Walter F. Parkes, Keith F. Critchlow. **1977**

CANNIBAL ISLAND 🦃 Primitive, cheerfully racist antique mixes generic safari footage and staged reenactments—some of it dating back to the 1920s—with a few seconds of an apparently genuine cannibal barbecue. B&W; 60m. **DIR:** Not Credited. **1956**

CAUTION: FUNNY MEN AT WORK ★★★ Typical Mack Sennett mayhem and mirth mark this quartet of short comedies: "Sailor, Beware," "A Strong Revenge," "A Sea Dog's Tale," and "The Channel Swimmer." As usual, slapstick predominates. Silent. B&W; 59m. **DIR:** Mack Sennett. **CAST:** Mabel Normand, Ford Sterling, Billy Bevan, Andy Clyde, Eddie Quillan. **1913–1928**

CELEBRATING BIRD: THE TRIUMPH OF CHARLIE PARKER ★★★★ Fascinating documentary that chronicles jazz legend Charlie Parker's career through interviews and live performances. Parker, nicknamed Bird, created a new style of jazz before his untimely death at 34. Other jazz greats—Dizzy Gillespie, Charles Mingus, and Thelonius Monk—add to the pleasure. 58m. **DIR:** Gary Giddins, Kendrick Simmons. **CAST:** Charlie Parker. **1987**

CHARIOTS OF THE GODS ★★ Based on Erich Von Daniken's bestselling book, this German production presents the theory that centuries ago Earth was visited by highly advanced space folks. The film is a nice travelogue, but its theories are never proved. Of minor interest only. Rated G. 98m. **DIR:** Harald Reinl. **1974**

CHARLES BUKOWSKI TAPES 🦃 Celebrated underground writer Charles Bukowski is captured in a semialcoholic stupor in and around his North Hollywood home. Unrated, the tapes contain mucho profanity. 240m. **DIR:** Barbet Schroeder. **1987**

CHICKEN RANCH ★★★ This documentary about the brothel that was the setting for the musical *The Best Little Whorehouse in Texas* presents a different picture of prostitution. Although shot in a cinema verité style—the workers and customers speak for themselves, with no passing of judgment by the filmmakers—the movie paints a relentlessly grim picture of the oldest profession. Unrated. 84m. **DIR:** Nick Broomfield, Sandi Sissel. **1983**

CHILDREN OF THEATRE STREET, THE ★★★½ Grace Kelly narrates this documentary about the Kirov School of Ballet, where children who meet rigorous criteria are isolated from the world (including their families) and trained intensively. Bring this home with *Backstage at the Kirov* for the perfect ballet double feature. 92m. **DIR:** Robert Dornhelm. **1978**

CHUCK BERRY HAIL! HAIL! ROCK 'N' ROLL ★★★★★ Put simply, this is the greatest rock 'n' roll concert movie ever made. Anyone who has ever kissed, danced, or just tapped feet to the classic songs written by Chuck Berry will love it. They're all here: "Maybellene," "Roll Over Beethoven," "Memphis," "Nadine," "No Particular Place to Go"...Keith Richards, Eric Clapton, Julian Lennon, and Linda Ronstadt are just some of the singers and players who back Berry during his sixtieth-birthday-tribute concert at St. Louis's Fox Theatre. Rated PG. 120m. **DIR:** Taylor Hackford. **CAST:** Chuck Berry, Keith Richards, Bo Diddley, Little Richard, Eric Clapton, Linda Ronstadt, Johnnie Johnson. **1987**

CIVIL WAR, THE ★★★★★ Weaving an eloquent tapestry of letters, diaries, war dispatches, and contemporary newspaper reports, with academic opinion, award-winning director-producer Ken Burns brings the Civil War of 1861–1865 vividly to life in epic proportion. A brilliant tour de force. Unforgettable. B&W/color; 660m. **DIR:** Ken Burns. **1990**

CIVIL WAR JOURNAL ★★★★ This beautifully produced, made-for-cable documentary sparkles with fascinating stories of the American Civil War. Using photographs, artwork, and diaries, historians put the events and politics into perspective with a compelling narrative of a dark and troubling time. Hosted by Danny Glover. Made for TV. 650m. **DIR:** Donna E. Lusitana, Craig Haffner. **1993**

COMIC BOOK CONFIDENTIAL ★★★½ The history and pop-culture charms of the comic book are explored in this entertaining documentary by a Canadian filmmaker and comic-book buff. The leading lights of comic books—Marvel's Stan Lee, Robert Crumb, Jack Kirby, etc.—are interviewed. 90m. **DIR:** Ron Mann. **CAST:** Lynda Barry, Robert Crumb, Will Eisner, William M. Gaines, Stan Lee, Jack Kirby. **1988**

COMMON THREADS: STORIES FROM THE QUILT ★★★★ In *Common Threads: Stories from the Quilt*, AIDS becomes a shared ground for survivors of loved ones. They fashion a giant quilt with the names of the deceased stitched into each design. This stirring documentary is not only a tribute to the dead and dying, it is a study of how parents, lovers, and friends of victims have learned to deal constructively with loss—and to bring the impact of AIDS to the public. Unrated. 80m. **DIR:** Rob Epstein, Jeffrey Friedman. **1990**

COMPLEAT BEATLES, THE ★★★★ Even experts on the life and times of the Fab Four are likely to find something new and enlightening. Furthermore, while not a consistent work, this film provides something of interest for fans and nonfans. 119m. **DIR:** Patrick Montgomery. **CAST:** Malcolm McDowell, The Beatles. **1982**

CONNECTIONS 2 ★★★★ This sequel to writer-producer James Burke's fascinating 1980 series is every bit as provocative, and every bit as scholarly. Those lacking strong scientific and political backgrounds may find Burke's often arcane logic hard to follow as he draws lines between apparently dissimilar inventions. Basically, all technical achievements produce ripples: anesthesia leading to explosives, rifles leading to typewriters and then office computers. Viewed as an educational experience, this ten-tape series is invaluable, as Burke's style and presentation make history and science palatable. Each tape 30m. **DIR:** Mike Slee. **1994**

COUSIN BOBBY ★★★★ Filmmaker Jonathan Demme hadn't seen his second cousin, the Reverend Robert Castle, for thirty years until a family reunion inspired him to make this film. A socially conscious minister, Castle believes that one man can make a difference: in modern footage, we see him leading a congregation in Harlem and fighting institutionalized racism. A small gem. Unrated; no objectionable material. 70m. **DIR:** Jonathan Demme. **1992**

COVER UP (1988) ★★★ This leftist political propaganda piece puts together news clips and interviews to paint a picture of deception on the part of U.S. government officials in Central America. The scope is narrow and conclusions are often farfetched, yet the low-budget documentary offers an eye-opening overview of covert operations. Unrated. 76m. **DIR:** Barbara Trent. **1988**

CRIME INC. ★★★★ Outstanding documentary series from the BBC chronicles the often violent dark underworld of organized crime. Revealing profiles of Al Capone and other mobsters of yesteryear and today are drawn from secret police surveillance films, home movies, and interviews with ex-Mafia gang members. This series can be viewed in seven different episodes. B&W/color; 357m. **DIR:** Ken Craig, Ian Stuttard. **1984**

CRY OF REASON, THE ★★★★★ An impassioned and enlightening documentary about courage and sacrifice in the face of South Africa's apartheid policies. The Oscar-nominated film profiles Beyers Naude, a white Afrikaner minister who gave up a promising career and a powerful position in the white community to stand with the blacks against apartheid. 60m. **DIR:** Robert

Bilheimer. **CAST:** Beyers Naude, Desmond Tutu. **1986**

D.O.A.: A RIGHT OF PASSAGE ★★★ Must-see documentary for anyone interested in the London punk music scene of the late 1970s. The technical quality is (suitably) crude, and the film's highlight, a rare interview with Sex Pistol Sid Vicious and his girlfriend Nancy Spungen, makes *Sid and Nancy* look like Sunday tea with your Aunt Betty. Unrated; the film contains profanity. 93m. **DIR:** Lech Kowalski. **1981**

D. W. GRIFFITH, FATHER OF FILM ★★★★★ David Wark Griffith transformed what began as a crude novelty into an art form of worldwide impact. This three-cassette documentary tells his story through rare film clips, unique still photographs, and incisive interviews with key figures in his career, including leading ladies Lillian Gish and Blanche Sweet, and writer Anita Loos. It was Griffith who masterminded films that gave the medium stature and influence. A truly fine narrative study well worth viewers' time and attention. 153m. **DIR:** Kevin Brownlow, David Gill. **1993**

DADDY AND THE MUSCLE ACADEMY ★★★ Documentary exploring the life, lifestyle, and influences of gay artist Tom of Finland, known for his series of erotic, larger-than-life macho men. Utilizing interviews, works of art, and real-life canvases, it celebrates the life of the man who came to be known as the "gay Vargas." In English and Finnish with English subtitles. Not rated, but contains nudity and adult situations. 55m. **DIR:** Ilppo Pohjola. **1992**

DANCE ON FIRE ★★★ Doors leader Jim Morrison is captivating as the focal point in *Dance on Fire,* which succeeds in succinctly portraying one of the 1960s' top rock groups. A combination of Elektra Records promotional clips, new videos, TV-show appearances, and concert footage. The hi-fi stereo sound is outstanding, having been digitally mastered and mixed from the original master tapes. 65m. **DIR:** Ray Manzarek. **CAST:** Jim Morrison, The Doors. **1985**

DARIO ARGENTO'S WORLD OF HORROR ★★½ By far one of the better documentaries about horror films, this thorough study (by Argento acolyte Soavi) follows the Italian director-writer through various stages in the genesis of *Suspiria, Inferno, Demons,* and other popular shockers. While the film takes a rather adoring approach, it ultimately lets the viewer make up his own mind about the audacious Argento. Unrated, but with explicit gore. 76m. **DIR:** Michele Soavi. **1985**

DEAR AMERICA: LETTERS HOME FROM VIETNAM ★★★★ This docudrama traces the Vietnam conflict from 1964 to 1973 through the eyes of American soldiers writing to their loved ones at home. The live footage has been so carefully selected that you forget that the letter you are hearing is being read by an actor instead of the person on the screen. Offscreen narration by a *Who's Who* of actors, including Robert De Niro, Ellen Burstyn, Tom Berenger, Michael J. Fox, Sean Penn, Martin Sheen, and Robin Williams. Rated PG. 86m. **DIR:** Bill Couturie. **1988**

DECEMBER 7TH: THE MOVIE ★★★ Cinematographer Gregg Toland, commissioned by the Navy Department to prepare a documentary on the Pearl Harbor attack, instead made this feature-length film where the military, in the form of Walter Huston as Uncle Sam, was criticized for being unprepared in the Pacific. The navy suppressed the film, editing it to a 34-minute short, which, on its own, won an Oscar as best documentary. A curiosity and, as such, recommended. B&W; 82m. **DIR:** John Ford, Gregg Toland. **CAST:** Walter Huston, Harry Davenport. **1943**

DECLINE OF WESTERN CIVILIZATION, THE ★★★★ The L.A. punk scene captured at its 1979 peak, before MTV and the music industry sanitized it into oblivion (and made the stinging title seem sarcastic). Director Penelope Spheeris is both a fan of the music and an objective observer of the scene, which she depicts in engrossing detail. Unrated; the film contains profanity. 100m. **DIR:** Penelope Spheeris. **1981**

DECLINE OF WESTERN CIVILIZATION, PART II—THE METAL YEARS ★★★ An unrevealing but fun documentary about the jaded world of heavy-metal musicians and fans. Director Penelope Spherris, who previously explored punk, takes a safe, unchallenging stance as she explores the music and its makers. 90m. **DIR:** Penelope Spheeris. **CAST:** Ozzy Osbourne, Alice Cooper. **1988**

DINOSAUR! ★★★★ Walter Cronkite narrates this fascinating and enjoyable four-tape collection of the Art & Entertainment presentation chronicling the rise and fall of the mighty dinosaur. A very popular subject presented with an emphasis on detail and entertainment. each. 60m. **DIR:** Jim Black, Christopher Rowley. **1991**

DIRECTED BY ANDREI TARKOVSKY ★★★★ Penetrating look at director Andrei Tarkovsky, one of the most internationally acclaimed Soviet filmmakers. This documentary is a revealing portrait of the director who was ill with cancer while working on his last film *The Sacrifice.* In Swedish and Russian with English subtitles. Not rated. 100m. **DIR:** Michal Leszczykowski. **1988**

DISTANT HARMONY: PAVAROTTI IN CHINA ★★★ This documentary of Luciano Pavarotti's 1986 tour of the People's Republic of China has all the predictably superb music and scenery one would expect. Director DeWitt Sage cleverly juxtaposes Chinese and

Western cultures and includes a plethora of bright, optimistic Chinese children in doing so. Nevertheless, the unbelievably mediocre sound and film print and Pavarotti's own all-too-intrusive ego mar this production. 90m. **DIR:** DeWitt Sage. **1987**

DIVINE MADNESS ★★★½ Here's the sassy, unpredictable Bette Midler as captured in concert by director Michael Ritchie. Some of it is great; some of it is not. It helps if you're a Midler fan. Rated R for profanity. 95m. **DIR:** Michael Ritchie. **CAST:** Bette Midler. **1980**

DON'T LOOK BACK ★★★ A documentary account directed by D. A. Pennebaker of folksinger/poet ("guitarist," he calls himself) Bob Dylan on a 1965 tour of England. The tedium of travel and pressures of performing are eased by relaxing moments with fellow travelers Joan Baez, Alan Price, and (briefly) Donovan. Shot in striking black and white, with excellent sound quality. Unrated, it contains some vulgarity. B&W; 96m. **DIR:** D. A. Pennebaker. **CAST:** Bob Dylan, Joan Baez, Donovan, Alan Price. **1967**

DOORS, THE: A TRIBUTE TO JIM MORRISON ★★½ The life of Jim Morrison, rock's dark visionary poet of the prepsychedelic Sixties, gets a complete review through interviews, live performances, and conceptual footage in this fascinating music profile. But unless you're a die-hard Doors fan, this hour-long journey could seem excessive. The songs include "The End," "Moonlight Drive," "Touch Me," "When the Music's Over," and "Unknown Soldier." 60m. **DIR:** Ray Manzarek. **CAST:** Jim Morrison, The Doors. **1988**

DOORS, THE SOFT PARADE ★★ For die-hard Doors fans this tape is sheer heaven. Directed by Doors member Ray Manzarek, it's a collection of backstage clips and performances by the band, including the infamous Miami concert. Songs include "The Changeling," "Wishful Sinner," "Wild Child," "Build Me a Woman," "The Unknown Soldier," "The Soft Parade," and "Hello I Love You." Not rated. 50m. **DIR:** Ray Manzarek. **1969**

DOPE MANIA ★★ Collectively, this odd grouping of exploitation films deserves a higher rating than any of them could muster individually, meaning this is a cream-of-the-crap collection. Previews and snippets from 1950s anti-drug films provide most of the fun in this mishmash. B&W; 60m. **DIR:** Johnny Legend, Jeff Vilencia. **1987**

DOWN AND OUT IN AMERICA ★★★★ Oscar-winning documentary about the "new poor," working-class people who have been caught on the downward spiral into poverty. Actress-turned-director Lee Grant makes it clear that these people are not isolated cases, but victims of conditions that affect more and more American families every year. Unrated. 60m. **DIR:** Lee Grant. **1985**

DRACULA: A CINEMATIC SCRAPBOOK ★★★ Footage from all the classic-film accounts of Transylvania's noted fanged ghoul (save Coppola's) comprise this historical tour of the sanguinary adventures of literature's and legend's greatest vampire. Foremost, of course, is the portrayal of the count by Bela Lugosi. 60m. **DIR:** Ted Newsom. **1991**

ELVIS '56 ★★★★ Impressive documentary traces the evolution of Elvis Presley from naïve teenage rocker to jaded superstar—all in the space of one year. Narrated by Levon Helm (of The Band), the film uses television appearances, newsreel footage, publicity stills, and recordings to re-create the pivotal year in Elvis's career and life. 60m. **DIR:** Alan Raymond, Susan Raymond. **CAST:** Documentary. **1987**

ELVIS FILES, THE 🦃 Inane and completely one-sided pseudodocumentary by writer Gail Brewer-Giorgio on the myth that Elvis Presley faked his own death and is living in hiding, possibly in Kalamazoo. Unrated. B&W/Color; 55m. **DIR:** Laurette Healey. **1990**

ELVIS ON TOUR ★★½ So-so documentary follows the King on his U.S. tour. Main focus is on concert footage, with very little exposed about the man behind the legend. For a more candid look at the great one, check out *Elvis: That's The Way It Is*. 93m. **DIR:** Pierre Adidge, Robert Abel. **1972**

ELVIS—THAT'S THE WAY IT IS ★★★★½ Col. Tom Parker insisted that Elvis make this documentary about his concert at the International Hotel in Las Vegas. It was one of Col. Parker's wisest decisions because it showcased his personality better than any of his thirty-one feature-length films. 107m. **DIR:** Denis Sanders. **1970**

EPIC THAT NEVER WAS, THE ★★★ Produced for British television, this extraordinary account of the aborted filming of Robert Graves's epic novel *I, Claudius* focuses on the clash of egos and philosophies that ultimately destroyed the project. B&W; 74m. **DIR:** Bill Duncalf. **CAST:** Charles Laughton, Josef von Sternberg, Merle Oberon, Flora Robson, Robert Newton, Emlyn Williams. **1965**

EVENING WITH MARLENE DIETRICH, AN ★★★ The legendary Marlene Dietrich is captured in this unique concert, filmed in 1972 for British television at the New London Theatre. Performing here at 71, Dietrich still has charismatic grace and eloquence. This concert, her last performance before a live audience, will be a treat for her most devoted fans. 50m. **DIR:** Not Credited. **CAST:** Marlene Dietrich. **1988**

EXILES, THE ★★★ An examination of the exodus of Europe's intellectuals under the looming threat of Nazi Germany in the 1930s. Skillfully interweaving interviews, archival footage, and re-creation, director Richard Kaplan follows a host of individuals through often harrowing escapes to influential new lives in America as artists, scientists, and teachers. 116m. **DIR:** Richard Kaplan. **1990**

FABULOUS VILLAINS, THE ★★½ From the first filming of the Frankenstein monster in 1906 to Batman's villainous enemy The Joker, and Freddy Kruger, this mixture of silent and sound clips, publicity stills, and trailers, documents the famous and infamous villains and monsters of motion pictures. Even Popeye's Bluto is included. 58m. **DIR:** James Gordon. **1992**

FACES OF DEATH I & II 🦃 These two gruesome video programs are the ultimate in tasteless exploitation. Both feature graphic, uncensored footage of death autopsies, suicides, executions, and the brutal slaughter of animals. 88/84 minutes. **DIR:** Rosilyn T. Scott. **1983**

FALL OF THE ROMANOV DYNASTY, THE ★★ A silent documentary montage of the events that occurred in Russia between 1912 and 1917. No doubt innovative in its day, this now has little to offer. Only for the intense historians. 90m. **DIR:** Esther Shub. **1927**

FANTASY FILM WORLDS OF GEORGE PAL, THE ★★★ Documentary of the film career of George Pal, the father of screen sci-fi. Poorly written and edited, the film is more than saved by the excellent interviews and film clips, dating back to vintage Pal *Puppetoons*, produced in the Thirties for Paramount. *Destination Moon* is extensively covered, as well as the classic *When Worlds Collide* and *The War of the Worlds*. Narrated by Paul Frees. 93m. **DIR:** Arnold Leibovit. **CAST:** Rod Taylor, Charlton Heston, Yvette Mimieux, Ray Bradbury, Roy Disney, Walter Lantz, Ray Harryhausen, Gene Roddenberry. **1985**

FINAL FOUR: THE MOVIE ★★★★ This astute compilation of the National Collegiate Athletic Association's hallowed basketball finals tracks the championship playoffs from 1939 to the present, with clips and close-ups that provide not only an insight into what it takes to be in the four best college teams in the nation but also an interesting study of the game's transitions. Updated annually. A must-see for basketball fans. 90m. **DIR:** Not Credited. **1988**

FLYING SAUCERS OVER HOLLYWOOD ★★★★ Everything you could ever want to know about *Plan 9 from Outer Space*, popularly known as "the worst movie of all time." This entertaining tape features interviews with friends and associates of *Plan 9* creator Edward D. Wood Jr., rare footage of other Wood projects, and commentary from Wood admirers, including Joe Dante and Sam Raimi. 111m. **DIR:** Mark Patrick Carducci. **1992**

FOREVER JAMES DEAN ★★★★ Anyone remotely interested in the mecurial star James Dean will want to see this documentary—tracing Dean's career from his first Pepsi commercial to the final scene in *Giant*. From Emmy-winning filmmaker Ara Chekmayan. 69m. **DIR:** Ara Chekmayan. **1988**

FRANKENSTEIN: A CINEMATIC SCRAPBOOK ★★★ Admirers of Victor Frankenstein and his monster will love this unique horror history collection of previews and swatches from Edison's 1910 film to Gene Wilder's hilarious send-up, *Young Frankenstein*. Really a must for every horror collector. 60m. **DIR:** Ted Newsom. **1991**

FROM MAO TO MOZART ★★★★½ Violinist Isaac Stern's concert tour of Red China is the subject of this warm and perceptive Academy Award–winning documentary. 88m. **DIR:** Murray Lerner. **CAST:** Isaac Stern, David Golub, Tan Shuzhen. **1980**

GAP-TOOTHED WOMEN ★★★ Independent filmmaker Les Blank's amusing poetic homage to women is a clever exploration into the female image and pressures to conform to ideals of mass media. Not rated. 30m. **DIR:** Les Blank. **1987**

GARLIC IS AS GOOD AS 10 MOTHERS ★★★½ Filmmaker Les Blank's tasty journey into the history, consumption, cultivation, and culinary powers of garlic. A must-see for garlic connoisseurs. Not rated. 51m. **DIR:** Les Blank. **1977**

GENERAL IDI AMIN DADA ★★★★ Barbet Schroeder often makes films about people you wouldn't want to spend much time with—*Barfly, Reversal of Fortune*—but never more so than in this documentary about murderous Ugandan dictator Idi Amin. Amin cooperated fully in the making of this film, which nevertheless shows him to be an extremely bizarre, self-inflated despot. Mesmerizingly weird. Unrated. 90m. **DIR:** Barbet Schroeder. **1975**

GIMME SHELTER ★★★★ This documentary chronicles the events leading up to and including the now-infamous free Rolling Stones concert in 1969 at the Altamont Speedway outside San Francisco. It's the dark side of Woodstock, with many unforgettable scenes, including the actual murder of a spectator by the Hell's Angels in front of the stage as the Stones are playing. Rated R for violence, language, and scenes of drug use. 91m. **DIR:** David Maysles, Albert Maysles, Charlotte Zwerin. **CAST:** The Rolling Stones, Melvin Belli. **1970**

GIRL TALK ★★ A less-than-thorough examination of serious issues raised in this profile of three young, independent Boston women. Never contrasting that limited view with their peers in the inner city. Unrated, but has nudity and profanity. 85m. **DIR:** Kate Davis. **1987**

GIZMO! ★★★★½ A collection of short films of daredevils, flying machines, and enthusiastic inventors demonstrating their questionable benefits to mankind. It's up to the audience to decide whether these people were complete morons or just ahead of their time. A delightful, often hysterical celebration of the American spirit. Rated G. B&W; 77m. **DIR:** Howard Smith. **1977**

GOSPEL ★★★★ Featuring many of the top stars of black gospel music, this is a joyous, spirit-lifting music documentary that contains the highlights of a five-and-a-half-hour concert filmed in June 1981 at Oakland Paramount Theater. The spirited performances might even make a believer out of you—that is, if you aren't already. Rated G. 92m. **DIR:** David Levick, Frederick A. Rizenberg. **CAST:** Mighty Clouds of Joy, Clark Sisters, Walter Hawkins and the Hawkins Family, Shirley Caesar, Rev. James Cleveland. **1982**

GRASS ★★★★ Fascinating documentary of a journey spearheaded by explorers-filmmakers Cooper and Schoedsack, who follow a tribe of Persian nomads on their annual livestock pilgrimage. It's easy to see how the directors later brought such authority to *King Kong* and their other fictional movies. Followed two years later by *Chang*. B&W; 70m. **DIR:** Merian C. Cooper, Ernest B. Schoedsack, Marguerite Harrison. **1925**

GRATEFUL DEAD MOVIE, THE ★★★½ Dead Heads will undoubtedly love this combination of backstage, concert, and animated psychedelic scenes. Supervised by Dead lead guitarist-vocalist Jerry Garcia, it's a laughable look at the mechanics and magic of rock. The uninitiated and unconverted may find it tedious. 131m. **DIR:** Jerry Garcia, Leon Gast. **CAST:** Grateful Dead. **1976**

GREAT AMERICAN WEST ★★★★★ Director John Ford and actor John Wayne return to Monument Valley to reminisce, relive memories, and pay loving homage to the nine classic Westerns Ford lensed there. Clips of several are utilized in this TV special originally titled *The American West of John Ford*. Indeed, Ford is remembered today as he wished to be, "a guy that made Westerns." 55m. **DIR:** Denis Sanders. **CAST:** John Wayne, Henry Fonda, James Stewart, John Ford, Andy Devine. **1973**

GREAT TOY TRAIN LAYOUTS OF AMERICA (VOLUMES 1–6) ★★★★ Toy and scale-model electric trains of all ages and gauges abound in this brilliantly produced series spotlighting thirteen of the finest private collections of operating layouts in the United States. Narrated by Jeffery Smith. Approximately 55m. per volume. **DIR:** Tom McComas, Jim Touhy. **1988–1993**

GREY GARDENS ★★★★ A hilarious, tragic portrait of two endearing, eccentric recluses: Edith Bouvier Beale and her grown daughter, Little Edie (aunt and first cousin of Jackie Onassis). This offbeat documentary beautifully captures psychological drama between mother and daughter while they rehash the past behind the walls of a decaying East Hampton mansion. Not rated. 94m. **DIR:** David Maysles, Albert Maysles, Ellen Hovde, Muffie Meyer. **1976**

GUNS OF AUGUST, THE ★★★★ Classic documentary based on Barbara Tuchman's book takes a thorough look at the causes and effects of World War I. This intelligent analysis of an event whose effects are still being felt features much rare historical footage. B&W; 99m. **DIR:** Nathan Kroll. **1964**

HAPPY ANNIVERSARY 007: 25 YEARS OF JAMES BOND ★★★★ Roger Moore hosts this engaging tribute to superspy James Bond, which scripter Richard Schickel cleverly divides into segments reflecting 007's diverse experiences: dangerous train trips, briefings with Q and his gadgets, deadly skiing excursions, bizarre death traps, and his limitless fund of arcane knowledge. 59m. **DIR:** Mel Stuart. **CAST:** Sean Connery, Roger Moore, George Lazenby, Timothy Dalton. **1987**

HARLAN COUNTY, U.S.A. ★★★★½ This Oscar-winning documentary concerning Kentucky coal miners is both tragic and riveting. Its gripping scenes draw the audience into the world of miners and their families. Superior from start to finish. Rated PG. 103m. **DIR:** Barbara Kopple. **1977**

HAROLD LLOYD: THE THIRD GENIUS ★★★★ History chronicles three patent geniuses of comedy film: Charlie Chaplin, Buster Keaton, and lesser-known Harold Lloyd, who certainly deserves his place in the line. Generous clips from his films and interviews with friends, associates, and Lloyd himself make this well worth viewing. B&W; 120m. **DIR:** Kevin Brownlow, David Gill. **1989**

HEARTS AND MINDS ★★★★★ Unforgettable Oscar-winning documentary about the effects of the Vietnam War on the people of that country. Without narration or commentary, filmmaker Peter Davis juxtaposes scenes of the ruined country with interviews of military leaders. Rated R. 112m. **DIR:** Peter Davis. **1974**

HEARTS OF DARKNESS ★★★★★ Using 60 hours of footage shot by Eleanor Coppola during the 238 days of principal photography in the Philippines for husband Francis's *Apocalypse Now* (as well as after-the-fact interviews with its cast and crew), Fax

Bahr and George Hickenlooper give us unprecedented insight into the moviemaking process and the on-location madness that almost destroyed the controversial Vietnam War film and its creator. A must-see for film buffs. Unrated; the film has profanity and graphic scenes of native rituals during which animals are slain. 96m. **DIR:** Fax Bahr, George Hickenlooper. **1992**

HEAT IS ON: THE MAKING OF MISS SAIGON, THE ★★★ All the trials and tribulations of getting the musical *Miss Saigon* to the stage are chronicled in this engrossing look at the writing, scoring, casting, choreographing, and rehearsal time put into the big-budget show. Unfortunately, there is no narration. Also unfortunate is the small amount of actual music this tape gives its audience. Not rated, but contains profanity. 75m. **DIR:** David Wright. **1991**

HEAVEN ★★★ Weird collage assembled by actress Diane Keaton mixes footage from old movies with interviews of assorted oddballs who talk about what they think Heaven will be like. Love it or hate it, it's certainly different. Unrated. 80m. **DIR:** Diane Keaton. **1987**

HEAVY PETTING ★★★½ The dating and sexual rituals of the 1960s are explored in this often funny and always entertaining documentary, which weds comments by celebrities with footage from movies and television shows of the era. Unrated, the film has profanity and sexual descriptions. 75m. **DIR:** Obie Benz, Josh Waletzsky. **CAST:** David Byrne, Sandra Bernhard, Allen Ginsberg, William S. Burroughs, Spalding Gray, Ann Magnuson, Josh Mostel, Laurie Anderson. **1989**

HELGA PICTURES, THE ★★★★ Charlton Heston hosts this fine program that explores the work of American artist Andrew Wyeth and his famous Helga paintings. Filmed on location in Chadds Ford on the Kuerner farm, where many of the pictures were painted. Not rated. 36m. **DIR:** Dennis Powers. **1979**

HELL'S ANGELS FOREVER ★★½ A documentary on the notorious biker organization; mostly a feature-length endorsement rather than an objective profile. Early portion, tracing the Hells Angels' origins in post–World War II, working-class California, is best. Rated R for profanity. 87m. **DIR:** Richard Chase, Kevin Keating, Leon Gast. **1983**

HELLSTROM CHRONICLE, THE ★★★★ This 1971 pseudodocumentary features fantastic close-up cinematography of insects and their ilk underpinning a story line by Dr. Hellstrom (Lawrence Pressman), which contends the critters are taking over. Despite the dumb premise, *The Hellstrom Chronicle* remains a captivating film. Rated G. 90m. **DIR:** Walon Green. **CAST:** Lawrence Pressman. **1971**

HERDSMEN OF THE SUN ★★★★ Shot in the desolate, drought-stricken Sahara, this fascinating documentary explores the bizarre rituals of the nomadic Woodabe tribe. German director Werner Herzog continues his obsession with primitive cultures and creates a one-of-a-kind, hypnotic film experience. In French and Peul with English subtitles. Unrated; the film has brief nudity. 52m. **DIR:** Werner Herzog. **1990**

HERE'S LOOKING AT YOU, WARNER BROTHERS ★★★★ Documentarian par excellence David L. Wolper scores again, this time with a fascinating glimpse at the studio founded in 1904 by four brothers—Harry, Jack, Sam, and Albert—convinced of cinema's entertainment potential. Aside from clips featuring stars from John Barrymore to Pee-Wee Herman, Robert Guenette's lovingly scripted tribute includes some truly fascinating screen tests—Marlon Brando, Paul Newman, James Dean, and a 21-year-old Orson Welles. 108m. **DIR:** Robert Guenette. **CAST:** Clint Eastwood, Barbra Streisand, Goldie Hawn, Steven Spielberg, Chevy Chase. **1991**

HIGH LONESOME—THE STORY OF BLUEGRASS MUSIC ★★★ Archival photos, film footage, and interviews with America's top bluegrass musicians chart and celebrate the evolution of bluegrass music from its folk roots. This combination history lesson and concert collage—narrated by Mac ("the voice with the heart") Wiseman—is both entertaining and educational. Unrated. 95m. **DIR:** Rachel Liebling. **CAST:** Bill Monroe, Ralph Stanely, Earl Scruggs, Mac Wiseman, Jimmy Martin, Sam Bush, Alison Krauss. **1993**

HOLLYWOOD ★★★★ First-class documentary series on the silent-film era was made for British television. It includes interviews with Gloria Swanson, Lillian Gish, Douglas Fairbanks Jr., Buster Keaton and King Vidor. The titles in this thirteen-cassette release include *The Pioneers, In the Beginning, Single Beds and Double Standards, Hollywood Goes to War, Hazard of the Game, Swanson and Valentino, The Autocrats, Comedy—A Serious Business, Out West, The Man with the Megaphone, Star Treatment,* and *End of an Era.* B&W; 9052m. **DIR:** David Gill, Kevin Brownlow. **1979**

HOLLYWOOD CLOWNS, THE ★★★★ Glenn Ford narrates this anthology of comedy film clips featuring Buster Keaton, W.C. Fields, Charlie Chaplin, Harold Lloyd, Abbott and Costello, Laurel and Hardy, Danny Kaye, Red Skelton, the Marx Brothers, Martin and Lewis, Betty Hutton, and Bob Hope. A fine tribute to some great performers. 60m. **DIR:** Bill Gleason. **1985**

HOT PEPPER ★★★★ Penetrating look into the life of Louisiana zydeco–music legend Clifton Chenier. Filmmaker Les Blank follows the Cajun-French accordionist through the sweaty dance halls and along the streets and into the homes of family and friends. Another excellent documentary from Blank. 54m. **DIR:** Les Blank, Maureen Gosling. **CAST:** Clifton Chenier. **1980**

HOTEL TERMINUS: THE LIFE AND TIMES OF KLAUS BARBIE ★★★★½ A fascinating film chronicle of the life of Nazi SS Captain Klaus Barbie, the "Butcher of Lyon," responsible for the deportation and death of thousands of Jews, and the brutal torture of French Resistance members. Oscar winner as best documentary. In English and French, German, and Spanish with English subtitles. Unrated, but with graphic discussion of torture, so parental discretion is advised. B&W/Color; 267m. **DIR:** Marcel Ophuls. **1988**

HUGH HEFNER: ONCE UPON A TIME ★★★ An involving examination of the changing moral values of America in the past four decades as seen through the eyes of publisher-philosopher Hugh Hefner, creator of *Playboy* magazine. A surprisingly candid documentary that eschews nudity. 88m. **DIR:** Robert Heath. **1992**

I LOVE TOY TRAINS ★★★★ Adults and kids alike will love this captivating look at toy trains in action. The sights and sounds include model trains, tiny lights, and great accessory action including log loading and coal tippling, plus spectacular scenes from fabulous layouts. For anyone, young or old, ever excited by a toy train. 30m. **DIR:** Tom McComas. **1993**

I'M ALMOST NOT CRAZY: JOHN CASSAVETES—THE MAN AND HIS WORK ★★★★ Penetrating look at filmmaker-actor John Cassavetes, whose low-budget American movies earned the praise of film directors and critics internationally. His working methods are explored on the set of *Love Streams* (his final screen bid). Cassavetes's brutal, uncompromising approach to his craft is brilliantly captured by Michael Ventura. Not rated, but contains some profanity. 60m. **DIR:** Michael Ventura. **1989**

IMAGINE: JOHN LENNON ★★★★★ Superb documentary chronicles the life, times, and untimely death of rock 'n' roll icon John Lennon. Carefully selected footage from the career of the Beatles is combined with television interviews and never-before-seen film of Lennon's private life for a remarkably insightful and emotionally moving work. Rated R for nudity and profanity. 103m. **DIR:** Andrew Solt. **CAST:** John Lennon, Yoko Ono, George Harrison. **1988**

IMPROPER CONDUCT ★★★★½ An astonishing view of Fidel Castro's terrifying regime is found in this uncompromising documentary by Academy Award–winning cinematographer Nestor Almendros. Cuban refugees discuss their experiences within the labor concentration camps and jails. This provocative work is undoubtedly the best film to date on the Cuban revolution. Not rated. In Spanish with English narration and subtitles. 112m. **DIR:** Nestor Almendros, Orlando Jimenez Leal. **1984**

INCIDENT AT OGLALA ★★★★ Director Michael Apted and the Native Americans interviewed in this documentary make a compelling case for a retrial of Leonard Peltier, a leader in the American Indian Movement who is now serving two consecutive life terms for his alleged murder of two FBI agents during a confrontation. Apted somewhat fictionalized the conflicts between traditionalist Indians and their "mixed-blood" tribal leaders in *Thunderheart,* which should be viewed before watching this heartrending documentary. Rated PG. 93m. **DIR:** Michael Apted. **1992**

INCREDIBLE STORY OF DOGS, THE ★★★★ Superior BBC/A&E collaboration focuses on man's diverse interactions with canines. Dogs are pampered and abused, adored and abhorred, fed and even eaten in this worldwide tour. Originally Jack Perkins and his four-legged friend introduced each segment of this six-part series. Three volumes, each 100m. **DIR:** Bradley Adams, Geoff Deehan, Franc Roddam, Andrew Jackson, Michael Waldman, Charles Davies, Pratap Rughani. **1993**

IT'S ALL TRUE ★★★★½ This fresh glimpse of Orson Welles's three aborted 1942 docudramas about Latin American culture—commissioned to promote President Roosevelt's Good Neighbor Policy—sadly reminds us of all the great films Welles never made. His unfinished shorts about a Mexican boy and his bull, the samba, and four Brazilian fishermen on a social protest voyage are mixed with interviews of the legendary filmmaker and his associates. The result is part travelogue, part historic treasure, and part passion play. Rated G. 89m. **DIR:** Richard Wilson, Myron Meisel, Bill Krohn. **CAST:** Orson Welles. **1993**

JAMES DEAN ★★½ Interesting look at actor James Dean through rare film clips and interviews with relatives, friends, and fellow actors. 90m. **DIR:** Claudio Masenza. **1983**

JANIS ★★★ The most comprehensive documentary study of flower child Janis Joplin, this is filled with poignant memories and electrifying performances. Rated R for language. 96m. **DIR:** Howard Alk, Seaton Findlay. **CAST:** Documentary. **1974**

JAZZ ON A SUMMER'S DAY ★★★★★ Superb jazz documentary catches the highpoints of the 1956 Newport Jazz Festival. Director Bert Stern mixes inspired photography with peak performances for a truly evocative time capsule. 84m. **DIR:** Bert Stern. **CAST:** Louis Armstrong, Mahalia Jackson, Chuck

Berry, Dinah Washington, Thelonious Monk, Gerry Mulligan, George Shearing, Chico Hamilton, Anita O'Day, Jack Teagarden, Big Maybelle. **1959**

JERRY LEE LEWIS—I AM WHAT I AM ★★½ It's easy to find faults with this low-budget look at rock's wild man of music. Not all the footage matches the music, and the script is rather macabre as it races through the disastrous decade when Lewis lost two sons and two wives. Still, we recommend it as a companion to *Great Balls of Fire*. 60m. **DIR:** Mark Hall. **CAST:** Jerry Lee Lewis, Johnny Cash, Paul Anka, Roy Orbison, Jimmy Swaggert, Mickey Gilley, Ronnie Wood. **1989**

JIMI HENDRIX ★★★★ Jimi Hendrix, the undisputed master of psychedelia, is captured brilliantly through concert footage and candid film clips in this excellent all-around 1973 rockumentary. The film explores Hendrix's career through interviews and rare concert footage of his performances from London's Marquee Club in 1967, and the Monterey Pop, Woodstock, and Isle of Wight festivals. Director Gary Weis was responsible for some great film shorts on *Saturday Night Live*. 103m. **DIR:** Gary Weis. **CAST:** Jimi Hendrix, Billy Cox, Mitch Mitchell, Eric Clapton, Pete Townshend, Little Richard, Dick Cavett. **1984**

JOHN HUSTON—THE MAN, THE MOVIES, THE MAVERICK ★★★★★ A wonderful, robust, and entertaining documentary biography of the great director, compiled from rare home movies, film clips, and interviews, narrated by Robert Mitchum (who speaks from a fantasy attic of engrossing Huston memorabilia). John Huston was an utterly fascinating eccentric and adventurer. This TV biography is a superb tribute. 129m. **DIR:** Frank Martin. **1989**

KIDS ARE ALRIGHT, THE ★★★½ More a documentary detailing the career of British rock group the Who than an entertainment, this film by Jeff Stein still manages to capture the spirit of rock 'n' roll. Rated PG. 108m. **DIR:** Jeff Stein. **CAST:** The Who, Ringo Starr, Steve Martin, Tom Smothers. **1979**

KING TUT: THE FACE OF TUTANKHAMUN ★★★½ The four 50-minute segments of this documentary produced for A&E are hosted by series writer and historian Christopher Frayling. The length stretches somewhat beyond the material, but some dazzling artifacts are showcased as the historical and apocryphal aspects of the boy king are unraveled. Not rated. 200m. **DIR:** Derek Towers, David Wallace. **1992**

KOKO: A TALKING GORILLA ★★★ Does a gorilla that has been taught a three-hundred-plus-word vocabulary have civil rights? That's one of the arguments raised as this film looks at the efforts of a psychology researcher to keep the ape, borrowed from the San Francisco Zoo, which she has taught to "speak" (via sign language). 82m. **DIR:** Barbet Schroeder. **1978**

KOYAANISQATSI ★★★★ The title is a Hopi Indian word meaning "crazy life, life in turmoil, life disintegrating, life out of balance, a state of life that calls for another way of living." In keeping with this, director Godfrey Reggio contrasts scenes of nature to the hectic life of the city. There is no plot or dialogue. Instead, the accent is on the artistic cinematography, by Ron Fricke, and the score, by Philip Glass. It's a feast for the eyes and ears. No MPAA rating. 87m. **DIR:** Godfrey Reggio. **1983**

LADIES SING THE BLUES, THE ★★★★ Some of the finest ladies of blues are beautifully represented here in great archival footage. Even though the narration is weak, the music is powerful and sweet. Standout Billie Holiday is backed by brilliant sidemen Coleman Hawkins, Lester Young, and Ben Webster as they groove together on "Fine and Mellow." 60m. **DIR:** Tom Jenz. **CAST:** Billie Holiday, Dinah Washington, Bessie Smith, Lena Horne, Peggy Lee, Sarah Vaughan. **1989**

LAST CALL AT MAUD'S ★★★ Informative, sentimental documentary covering the closing of the famous San Francisco lesbian bar is actually a funny, sad history of lesbianism over the last fifty years. Utilizing nostalgic newsreels, newspaper clippings, and documentary footage, this fond farewell remains a positive statement despite its sad subject. Unrated; contains mature themes. 77m. **DIR:** Paris Poirer. **1993**

LAST PARTY, THE ★★★½ Robert Downey Jr. is the host of this satiric, in-your-face documentary chronicling the 1992 presidential race. Downey finds plenty to poke fun at and recruits some famous names and faces to help him try to find meaning at the Democratic and Republican National Conventions. You know the participants in this celluloid mirror are politicians because they keep making donkeys out of themselves. Not rated, but contains strong language. 96m. **DIR:** Martin Benjamin, Marc Levin. **1993**

LAST WALTZ, THE ★★★★ Director Martin Scorsese's (*Taxi Driver*) superb film of The Band's final concert appearance is an unforgettable celebration of American music. Rated PG. 117m. **DIR:** Martin Scorsese. **CAST:** The Band, Bob Dylan, Neil Young, Joni Mitchell, Van Morrison, Eric Clapton, Neil Diamond, Muddy Waters. **1978**

LAUREL & HARDY: A TRIBUTE TO "THE BOYS" ★★★ Hosted by Dom DeLuise, this look at the careers of Stan Laurel and Oliver Hardy is primarily useful as an introduction to children of the joys provided by the two great screen clowns. Features comments on the team's comedy style by Johnny

Carson, Steve Allen, Walter Matthau, Henny Youngman, the Smothers Brothers, Rich Little, Robert Klein, Bronson Pinchot, and Professor Irwin Corey. 120m. **DIR:** Jeff Weinstock, Gene Rosow. **1991**

LEGEND OF LOBO, THE ★★★ An animal adventure film told from the perspective of Lobo, a wolf, this is one of the excellent nature films produced by Disney in the 1950s and 1960s. Although the story is highly fictionalized to create dramatic impact, this is both an entertaining and informative film. 67m. **DIR:** Not Credited. **1962**

LEGENDS ★★½ Sometimes fascinating, sometimes unsettling look at celebrity impersonators on the nightclub circuit and the promoter who has shaped their lives. An interesting study of celebrity obsession from the point of view of both entertainers and fans. Not rated. 54m. **DIR:** Ilana Bar-Din. **CAST:** John Stuart, Susan Griffiths, Jonathon von Brana, Monica Maris. **1992**

LEGENDS OF COMEDY ★★★★ A galaxy of comedy greats, from silent and sound film, radio and television, populate this three-volume retrospective covering fifty years of side-splitting routines and punch lines. They're all here: Charlie Chaplin, Buster Keaton, W. C. Fields, Laurel and Hardy, the Marx Brothers, Edgar Bergen, the Three Stooges, Bob Hope, Mae West, Jackie Gleason, Jack Benny, Eddie Cantor, Burns and Allen, Red Skelton, Lucille Ball, and many more. 165m. **DIR:** John C. Feld. **1920–1970**

LEGENDS OF THE AMERICAN WEST (SERIES) ★★★½ Rare photos, diaries, interviews with relatives of the legends, movie clips, and reenactments are used to give a factual account of the American West and the famous characters we have known through myth and legend. *Jesse James, Billy The Kid,* and *Wyatt Earp and the Gunfighters* are the best with fine use of memorabilia, photos, and new facts. The uneven *Cowboys and Indians* emphasizes truth over movie distortion, and the Indians get a fair shake for once. *The West Remembered* is disappointing. Unrated. each. 30m. **DIR:** Marina Amoruso. **1992**

LET IT BE ★★★½ The last days of the Beatles are chronicled in this cinema verité production, which was originally meant to be just a documentary on the recording of an album. What emerges, however, is a portrait of four men who have outgrown their images and, sadly, one another. There are moments of abandon, in which they recapture the old magic, but overall, the movie makes it obvious that the Beatles would never get back to where they once belonged. Rated G. 80m. **DIR:** Michael Lindsay-Hogg. **CAST:** The Beatles. **1970**

LET'S GET LOST ★★★★★ The music and the volatile, self-destructive personality of Chet Baker are explored in this artful, invigorating, and controversial documentary feature from photographer-filmmaker Bruce Weber. This film, which justifiably earned an Oscar nomination, depicts Baker in what turned out to be the last year of his life, as he meanders through performances, recording sessions, and self-centered encounters with women, fans, and family. B&W; 120m. **DIR:** Bruce Weber. **CAST:** Chet Baker. **1989**

LET'S SPEND THE NIGHT TOGETHER ★★★½ In this concert film, directed by Hal Ashby, the Rolling Stones are seen rockin' and rollin' in footage shot during the band's 1981 American tour. It's a little too long—but Stones fans and hard-core rockers should love it. Rated PG for suggestive lyrics and behavior. 94m. **DIR:** Hal Ashby. **CAST:** The Rolling Stones. **1982**

LISTEN UP: THE LIVES OF QUINCY JONES ★★★ In imagining a documentary on the highly influential musician, composer, arranger, and producer Quincy Jones, one would expect a celebration of the music he created with Miles Davis, Michael Jackson, Frank Sinatra, Ella Fitzgerald, Ray Charles, Sarah Vaughan, Barbra Streisand, Dizzy Gillespie, and other major talents. But what there is of this comes in short, unsatisfying snippets. Rated PG-13 for profanity. 111m. **DIR:** Ellen Weisbrod. **1991**

LONG WAY HOME, THE ★★★ Director Michael Apted turns his cameras on Russian rock 'n' roller Boris Grebenshikov, whose musical odyssey is both tune-filled and inspirational. From Leningrad to New York to Los Angeles, the cameras document Russia's equivalent of Bruce Springsteen. Musical cameos by Dave Stewart, Annie Lennox, and Chrissie Hynde. Unrated. 82m. **DIR:** Michael Apted. **1989**

LOUISIANA STORY, THE ★★★ This last film by noted documentarian Robert Flaherty dramatizes the effect of oil development on the lives of a young boy, his family, and his pet raccoon in Louisiana. Score by Virgil Thomson, played by the Philadelphia Symphony Orchestra. B&W; 79m. **DIR:** Robert Flaherty. **1948**

MAD DOGS AND ENGLISHMEN ★★★½ Joe Cocker and friends, including Rita Collidge and Leon Russell, put together one of the zaniest rock tours ever in the early 1970s, leaving a legendary trail of drugs and groupies in their wake. Fortunately, the superstar group was also able to function on stage, and this movie effectively captures the spirit of the 1970 tour. Performances of "With a Little Help from My Friends," "Superstar," and "Feeling Alright" can be considered rock classics. 118m. **DIR:** Pierre Adidge. **CAST:** Joe Cocker, Leon Russell, Rita Coolidge. **1972**

MAKING OF A LEGEND—*GONE WITH THE WIND* ★★★★ Though some film purists object to Ted Turner's colorization of film classics, they have to acknowledge that he's supported the creation of first-rate documentaries *about* Hollywood. This feature documentary uses David O. Selznick's many memos, other letters, and the remembrances of survivors to reconstruct the creation of the most popular Hollywood film of all time. Produced by Selznick's sons, and written by David Thomson, it's must viewing for *GWTW's* many fans. 120m. **DIR:** David Hinton. **1989**

MAN WHO SAW TOMORROW, THE ★★★½ Orson Welles narrates and appears in this fascinating dramatization of the prophecies of sixteenth-century poet, physician, and psychic Michel de Nostradamus. Nostradamus was astonishingly accurate and, in some cases, actually cited names and dates. His prediction for the future is equally amazing—and, sometimes, terrifying. Rated PG. 90m. **DIR:** Robert Guenette. **CAST:** Orson Welles (narrator). **1981**

MAN WITH A MOVIE CAMERA ★★★★ Russian directors pioneered the use of inventive editing techniques in the Twenties. This experimental documentary shows off many of those methods. The subject matter here is the making of a movie about the city of Moscow, and we follow from initial production to public screening. Sixty years later, the craft demonstrated here is still impressive. B&W; 60m. **DIR:** Dziga Vertov. **1927**

MANCE LIPSCOMB: A WELL-SPENT LIFE ★★★★ Les Blank's stirring portrait of Texas songster Mance Lipscomb is a moving tribute to a legendary bluesman. Lipscomb's crafty, bottleneck-slide guitar style is reminiscent of country-blues giant Furry Lewis and contemporary Texas-blues great Lightnin' Hopkins. 44m. **DIR:** Les Blank. **1981**

MARX BROTHERS IN A NUTSHELL, THE ★★★★ Narrated by Gene Kelly, this anthology of clips from Marx Brothers films, interviews, and rare outtakes was originally broadcast on public TV as a tribute. On stage or off, Groucho is as comically caustic as always. A collector's gem. 100m. **DIR:** Richard Patterson. **CAST:** The Marx Brothers, Margaret Dumont. **1990**

MASTERS OF ANIMATION ★★★★★ This remarkable glimpse into the world of animation took over ten years to complete. A four-volume tape set represents the peak achievements by some of the most gifted artists from over thirteen countries around the world. Produced and directed by John Halas, award-winning animator. 348m. **DIR:** John Halas. **1986**

MASTERS OF COMIC BOOK ART ★★★ Science fiction author Harlan Ellison narrates this hit-and-miss documentary on comic-book artists Will Eisner, Harvey Kurtzman, Jack Kirby, Steve Ditko, Neal Adams, Berni Wrightson, Moebius, Frank Miller, Dave Sim, and Art Spiegelman. Some of the interviews, such as those with Adams and Wrightson, are very informative and insightful, while others are disappointing. Unrated. 60m. **DIR:** Ken Viola. **1987**

MEMORIES OF HOLLYWOOD ★★★ With the help of Jack Haley Jr., Douglas Stewart compiled clips from over fifty films, silents through the Fifties. Although there is absolutely no dialogue, viewers will enjoy identifying the myriad acting greats—including John Wayne, Shirley Temple, Loretta Young, Bette Davis, Joan Bennett, Buster Keaton, José Ferrer, Ronald Reagan, and Bob Hope. Academy Award–winning musical scores supply the only sound track. Great fun! B&W; 47m. **DIR:** Douglas M. Stewart Jr. **1990**

MESSIN' WITH THE BLUES ★★★★ Recorded live on June 28, 1974, at the Montreux Jazz Festival in Switzerland, this fine documentary records master bluesman Muddy Waters leading his disciples (Junior Wells, Buddy Guy, Pinetop Perkins, and Bill Wyman) through a fine set of Chicago boogie. A set by Wells and Guy kicks off the tape. 54m. **DIR:** Jean Bovon. **1974**

MILLHOUSE: A WHITE COMEDY ★★★ Meant to ridicule then President Richard Milhous Nixon, this collection of live footage follows his political career from 1948 to 1970, focusing on six political fiascos, any one of which could have destroyed a less determined man. B&W; 93m. **DIR:** Emile De Antonio. **1971**

MINDWALK ★★★ A trio of archetypes—a scientist (Liv Ullmann), a politician (Sam Waterston), and a poet (John Heard)—discuss the current "crisis in perspective," which comes from the discovery, in physics, that the old, "mechanistic" way of looking at life (thinking about living things in terms of their components) should be replaced by a more holistic view. More of a lecture than a movie, *Mindwalk* will fascinate those who appreciate novelist-turned-screenwriter Fritjof Capra's theories. Rated PG. 111m. **DIR:** Berndt Capra. **CAST:** Liv Ullmann, Sam Waterston, John Heard, Ione Skye. **1991**

MINGUS ★★★ Revealing portrait of Charles Mingus, the great bassist, considered to be one of the most influentual figures in jazz. Most of this film was shot in his cluttered New York loft as he awaited eviction in the wake of a legal tangle with the city. B&W; 58m. **DIR:** Thomas Reichmann. **1968**

MISSISSIPPI BLUES ★★★★★ French film director Bertrand Tavernier joins American author Robert Parrish on a spellbinding odyssey through the deep South. Tavernier and his French camera crew beautifully capture the true spirit of the South through the religious fervor of the black evangelical movement. Some great location photography laced with a rich blues sound track. In English and French with English subtitles. 92m. **DIR:** Bertrand Tavernier, Robert Parrish. **CAST:** Roosevelt Barnes, Joe Cooper, Hayword Mills. **1987**

MOANA OF THE SOUTH SEAS ★★★★★ Encouraged by the success of Robert Flaherty's classic *Nanook of the North*, Jesse L. Lasky dispatched Flaherty to the South Seas to document the disappearing culture of the Samoans. Even if some of the sequences—notably the famous tattoo ritual—were staged, the film still remains breathtakingly beautiful. Silent. B&W; 76m. **DIR:** Robert Flaherty. **1926**

MONDO CANE ★★★ One of the oddest movies ever made (the title means *A Dog's World*), this Italian film inspired a deluge of shockumentaries throughout the 1960s and the 1970s. In many vignettes—some scenes are real while others are patently staged—we are given a cook's tour of human eccentricities, from the "cargo cults" of New Guinea to a southern California pet cemetery. Believe it or not, the beautiful song "More" was introduced in this movie. Not rated; unsuitable for children. 105m. **DIR:** Gualtiero Jacopetti. **1963**

MONDO CANE II ★★ Disappointing sequel to the controversial and bizarre cult documentary released in 1963. Again the strange and fascinating world of human ritual is explored but without the intensity or the humor that the first film managed to create. Not rated; contains violence and nudity. 90m. **DIR:** Gualtiero Jacopetti. **1964**

MONDO TOPLESS ★★½ Silly Russ Meyer "documentary" is nothing more than scenes of topless dancers going through their paces in various outdoor locations. What makes it amusing are the inane narration (a Meyer trademark) and the frenetic editing, which makes it look like an hour-long MTV video. Unrated; there is no sex or even sexual suggestiveness, just nonstop toplessness. 60m. **DIR:** Russ Meyer. **1966**

MONKEY PEOPLE ★★ Science would like us to recognize similarities between ourselves and our close simian cousins, but there can be no doubt which of us has the more fulfilling niche on this planet. Even though Susan Sarandon lends her credible talents as a narrator here, watching them, at length, perform the more mundane aspects of survival—eating, sleeping, and other monkey stuff—is like having the batteries of a remote die before you can zap past a cable nature show. 85m. **DIR:** Gerard Vienne. **1990**

MONTEREY POP ★★★★ Despite its ragged sound by today's digital standards, *Monterey Pop* is a historical masterpiece. A chance to see legendary Sixties soloists and groups in their prime far outweighs any technical drawbacks. This was the concert that kicked off 1967's Summer of Love, and with it, a generation of mega-performer shows that culminated in Woodstock. 72m. **DIR:** D. A. Pennebaker. **CAST:** Jimi Hendrix, Otis Redding, The Who, The Animals, Jefferson Airplane, Janis Joplin, Country Joe and the Fish, The Mamas and the Papas, Booker T. and the MGs, Ravi Shankar. **1969**

MORE MILTON BERLE'S MAD WORLD OF COMEDY ★★★ In this Jack Haley Jr. production, Milton Berle interviews comedy greats Dick Martin, Pat Buttram, Mort Sahl, and Eddie Quillan to find out what makes people laugh. Clips from comedic geniuses are used throughout the show. Among the best are Jackie Gleason, Abbott and Costello, Mike Nichols and Elaine May, Rowan and Martin, Buster Keaton, Will Rogers, and Charlie Chaplin. Berle maintains a serious demeanor despite the clowning around of professional funnymen. Contains some vintage B&W footage. 67m. **DIR:** Jim Washburn. **CAST:** Milton Berle, Dick Martin, Pat Buttram, Mort Sahl, Eddie Quillan. **1974**

MOTHER TERESA ★★★★★ Many consider her to be a living saint and her selfless dedication to the world's sick of heart, body, mind, and soul seems to justify that claim. Mother Teresa is, at the very least, a heroic figure who simply believes that "we must all be holy in what we do." Five years in the making, this documentary lets an extraordinary life speak for itself. Unrated, this film has shocking scenes of poverty and starvation. 83m. **DIR:** Ann Petrie, Jeanette Petrie. **1987**

MOVIE MAGIC ★★★ This is an all-too-short look behind the scenes at how the astounding special effects were created for films like *Die Hard*, *Ghostbusters*, *The Abyss*, and others. Special-effects gurus like Rick Baker, Richard Edlund, and Randall William Cook are interviewed. Not rated. 30m. **DIR:** Stephen Rocha. **1990**

MYSTERY, MR. RA ★★ Filmmaker Frank Cassenti captures Sun Ra and his band during rehearsals and rare concert footage from Sun Ra's remarkable Afro-psychedelic music circus. Disappointing look at the thirty-five-year-career of this remarkable musician, bandleader, philosopher, and shaman. 51m. **DIR:** Frank Cassenti. **CAST:** Sun Ra. **1983**

NANOOK OF THE NORTH ★★★★ Crude and primitive as the conditions under which it was made, this direct study of Eskimo life set the standard for and has remained the most famous of the early documentary films. A milestone in stark realism; the walrus hunt sequence is especially effective. B&W; 55m. **DIR:** Robert Flaherty. **1922**

NIGHT AND FOG, THE ★★★★ Graphic footage of the Nazi death camps makes this sad, shockingly painful documentary one of the most personal and effective of all studies of Hitler's final solution. Beautifully composed, this film juxtaposes still photographs and Allied footage of gruesome spectacles. In French with English subtitles. 32m. **DIR:** Alain Resnais. 1955

NO NUKES ★★★½ Entertaining record of the MUSE concerts presented for five nights at Madison Square Garden to benefit the antinuclear movement. Your enjoyment will depend on appreciation of the artists involved, but the rare footage of Bruce Springsteen in concert is electrifying. While the picture is grainy, the stereo sound track is excellent. Rated PG for profanity. 103m. **DIR:** Julian Schlossberg, Dan Goldberg, Anthony Potenza. **CAST:** Jackson Browne, Crosby Stills and Nash, The Doobie Brothers, John Hall, Gil Scott-Heron, Bonnie Raitt, Carly Simon, Bruce Springsteen, James Taylor, Jessie Colin Young. 1980

NOTEBOOK ON CITIES AND CLOTHES ★★★½ One of German director Wim Wender's free-form visual diaries, this one was prompted by his interest in Japanese fashion-designer Yohji Yamamoto and by the new video technology that would figure in his next film, *Until the End of the World*. A fascinating glimpse into the mind of a filmmaker as he develops a project. 80m. **DIR:** Wim Wenders. 1990

NOTES FOR AN AFRICAN ORESTES ★★★½ Inspired by the Greek myth of Orestes, filmmaker Pier Paolo Pasolini turns his lens on the remote villages in Africa. He photographs crowded marketplaces and documents local rituals while keeping a director's notebook on the Third World. Music performed by Gato Barbieri. Not rated. B&W; 75m. **DIR:** Pier Paolo Pasolini. 1970

ORNETTE—MADE IN AMERICA ★★★★ This critically acclaimed documentary by film and video artist Shirley Clark is a revealing portrait of jazz musician Ornette Coleman, one of the most innovative forces in contemporary music. He is captured in performance in his hometown, Fort Worth, Texas. It's a sensational performance with the local symphony orchestra. The stunning music is juxtaposed with interviews and rare early performances that feature jazz musicians Charley Haden, Don Cherry, and Ornette's son Darnel. 80m. **DIR:** Shirley Clarke. **CAST:** Ornette Coleman. 1987

OSCAR'S GREATEST MOMENTS: 1971 TO 1991 ★★★★ Twenty years of memorable highlights from Academy Awards presentations fill this nostalgic, star-studded scrapbook. Look back at winners and runners-up, famous acceptance speeches, funniest moments—including the streaker running onstage behind David Niven. Also: production numbers, great scenes, legendary honorary recipients. Lots of memories here. Karl Malden is your host. 110m. **DIR:** Jeff Margolis. 1992

OSSIAN: AMERICAN BOY-TIBETAN MONK ★★★½ Fascinating documentary about a four-year-old American boy who enters a Tibetan Buddhist monastery. Shot on location in Nepal, the film follows him through a day of study and play with his teachers, mother, and fellow monks. 28m. **DIR:** Tom Anderson. 1990

PALAZZOLO'S CHICAGO ★★★ Filmmaker Tom Palazzolo's hypnotic journey through the human landscape of Chicago is both fascinating and entertaining. Some of his best works in this two-volume collection include a short about a tattooed lady who performs at a carnival, a senior citizens' picnic, and a deli owner who prods his customers through terror tactics. Not rated. 125m. **DIR:** Tom Palazzolo. 1988

PANAMA DECEPTION, THE ★★★★ This blistering, Oscar-winning documentary chronicles the events leading to the U.S. invasion of Panama, actually a crusade designed to renegotiate the treaty that would have given Panama control of the strategically critical Panama Canal by the year 2000. Although these often grim images are laced with explicit footage of burned children and civilians crushed by tanks, the most chilling fact to emerge is that the U.S. mainstream media were duped into reporting only what the Reagan and Bush administrations wanted them to see...a truly terrifying example of information control. Unrated, but contains graphic violence. 91m. **DIR:** Barbara Trent. 1992

PARIS IS BURNING ★★★★ This superb documentary takes us through the public and private domain of poor black and Hispanic gays in New York City who vamp at lavish balls. At these events, participants imitate fashion models, Marines, Wall Street brokers, and other figures culled from magazine advertisements. Rated R for some nudity. 78m. **DIR:** Jennie Livingston. 1990

PAUL BOWLES IN MOROCCO ★★★ Interesting portrait of American composer and author Paul Bowles, who has lived and worked in Tangier, Morocco since the 1940s. The film captures the author's world of crowded bazaars, snake charmers, religious ecstatics, and the exotic world of North Africa. 57m. **DIR:** Gary Conklin. 1970

PAUL MCCARTNEY AND WINGS—ROCK SHOW ★★½ Paul McCartney covers most of his hits in this concert recorded at the Seattle King Dome during Wings' 1976 world tour. But unless you're a big fan, this unimaginatively shot film (underlit and grainy) will probably put you to sleep. McCartney and his band perform most of the music in a lifeless manner. 102m. **DIR:** Paul McCartney. **CAST:** Paul McCartney. **1991**

PEOPLE VS. ZSA ZSA GABOR, THE This poor excuse for a documentary features live footage of Zsa Zsa Gabor's trial for assaulting Beverly Hills police officer Paul Kramer. Includes additional footage of reporters greeting the outspoken Gabor each day outside the courtroom. 60m. **DIR:** Uncredited. **1989**

PHANTOM INDIA ★★★★★ Louis Malle's epic film is a timeless journey through the mystical, exotic landscape of India. He takes the viewer on a tour of a nation in modern transition illuminating on such topics as the movie industry, a dancing school, a birth-control clinic, and esoteric cults. One of the most remarkable films ever made about India. 364m. **DIR:** Louis Malle. **1968**

PLOW THAT BROKE THE PLAINS, THE ★★★★ Written, directed, and produced by master documentarian Pare Lorentz, with a musical score by Virgil Thomson, this cornerstone film is a moving and dramatic account of man's abuse of America's Great Plains: Grass is its heroine, sun and wind its villain, its players nameless farmers whose farming practices produced the Dust Bowl and the Oklahoma-Kansas-Nebraska exodus. Coupled with it is "Night Mail," the John Grierson film tribute to the British postal and railway systems. B&W; 49m. **DIR:** Pare Lorentz. **1934–1936**

POLE TO POLE ★★★★ Second world tour hosted and narrated by Michael Palin is another winner. Covering 23,000 miles, he takes us from Finland to Antarctica. Always witty, Palin infuses learning with laughter. A four-volume series, this TV miniseries can be viewed in segments or as a Palin viewfest. 400m. **DIR:** Roger Mills. **CAST:** Michael Palin. **1992**

PORTRAIT OF JASON ★★★★ Celebrated independent filmmaker Shirley Clarke's penetrating glimpse into the life of a street hustler is a provocative, daring study in human tragedy. Not rated, but contains profanity and violence. B&W; 105m. **DIR:** Shirley Clarke. **1967**

POWAQQATSI ★★★★ Director Godfrey Reggio's follow-up to *Koyaanisqatsi* is a sumptuous treat for the eyes and the ears. Subtitled *Life in Transformation*, it combines gorgeous cinematography with exquisite music by Philip Glass. Like its predecessor, it's an engaging but sobering look at the cost of what some call progress. 99m. **DIR:** Godfrey Reggio. **1988**

POWER OF MYTH, THE ★★★★ Author-philosopher Joseph Campbell explores the world of mythology and its reflection on contemporary society in these six absorbing one-hour episodes originally aired on PBS and hosted by Bill Moyers. Campbell discusses death as rebirth as in the myth of the buffalo and the story of Christ. The individual episodes are *The Heroes Adventure, The Message of the Myth, The First Storytellers, Sacrifice and Bliss, Love and the Goddess,* and *Mask of Eternity.* 360m. **DIR:** Bill Moyers. **1988**

PRIVATE CONVERSATIONS: ON THE SET OF DEATH OF A SALESMAN ★★★★½ This provocative documentary goes behind the scenes of the production of Arthur Miller's acclaimed *Death of a Salesman.* Dustin Hoffman demonstrates his unique gift while perfecting the character of Willie Loman. This riveting study in filmmaking won the Grand Prize at the 1986 United States Film Festival. Not rated. 82m. **DIR:** Christian Blackwood. **CAST:** Dustin Hoffman, Arthur Miller, John Malkovich, Volker Schlondorff. **1986**

RAY CHARLES: THE GENIUS OF SOUL ★★★★★ Superb made-for-TV documentary about Ray Charles's music and personal life. The clips of Charles performing his groundbreaking style of music—which wed gospel, jazz, and blues to create soul music—are reason enough to watch this entry in PBS's "American Masters" series. Through narration and interviews writer-director Yvonne Smith gives viewers an uncompromising, in-depth and well-rounded look at a complex, brilliant man. David "Fathead" Newman, Dr John, Hank Crawford, Billy Joel, Willie Nelson, and Billy Preston are among those interviewed. 60m. **DIR:** Yvonne Smith. **1991**

RED SKELTON: A CAREER OF LAUGHTER ★★★ This fond look at Red Skelton's years on TV and in the movies was once more aptly titled *Red Skelton: A Comedy Scrapbook.* The video doesn't trace his career so much as piece together classic bits that help make up this very thorough sampler of his many comedy personas. Narrated by Mike Eagan. 71m. **DIR:** Sandy Oliveri, Paul Harris. **CAST:** Red Skelton, Bing Crosby, Jack Benny, Peter Lorre, George Raft. **1992**

RING OF FIRE ★★★★ Fascinating journey into the primitive, exotic, and mysterious islands of Indonesia by two filmmakers, brothers Lorne and Lawrence Blair. This ten-year voyage is a personal and spiritual odyssey through worlds where ancient myths and bizarre rituals still flourish. Four episodes: Vol. 1, "Spice Island Saga"; Vol. 2; "Dance of the Warriors"; Vol. 3; "East of Krakatoa"; Vol. 4; "Dream Wanderers of Borneo." 208m. **DIR:** Lawrence Blair. **1988**

ROAD CONSTRUCTION AHEAD ★★★★ Praised by the *New York Times* and *Wall Street Journal*, this award-winning documentary on road construction for children is terrific from the very first frame. Kids are fascinated by tractors, backhoes, graders, earth movers, and mammoth dump trucks, and they're all here, accurately presented in thrilling action. 30m. **DIR:** Fred Levine. 1993

ROAD SCHOLAR ★★★½ Filmmaker Roger Weisberg follows Romanian-born poet Andrei Codrescu on a coast-to-coast drive in an old Cadillac convertible. What Codrescu discovers—an amazing range of personalities, eccentrics, and crackpots—makes for an amusing, ironic, and rather sweet-tempered ride, with Codrescu's wry commentary an added pleasure. Not rated. 83m. **DIR:** Roger Weisberg, Jean De Segonzac. **CAST:** Andrei Codrescu. 1993

ROGER & ME ★★★★ Michael Moore's controversial documentary about the growing despair, homelessness, and crime in Flint, Michigan, where more than 30,000 autoworkers were left unemployed by the closing of General Motors plants. Scathingly funny and ultimately sobering. Rated R for brief profanity. 106m. **DIR:** Michael Moore. 1989

ROY ROGERS, KING OF THE COWBOYS ★★★★ This entertaining Dutch documentary follows the exploits of director Thys Ockersen, as he explores his boyhood obsession with cowboy star Roy Rogers. We see a few moments of old Roy Rogers movies with Dutch subtitles, and then come with Ockersen to America. His travels take him to a Western movie convention (and a meeting with the now-aged Lash LaRue), to Roy and Trigger's footprints at Graumen's Chinese Theatre in Los Angeles, and on to the Roy Rogers Museum in Portsmouth, Ohio. 80m. **DIR:** Thys Ockersen. 1992

SALESMAN ★★★★ Wildly funny, landmark documentary that follows a group of Bible salesmen through New York and Florida in the late 1960s. A great insight into the saga of the American salesman. B&W; 85m. **DIR:** Albert Maysles, David Maysles. 1968

SANS SOLIEL ★★★★ This visual essay shows filmmaker Chris Marker's feelings about the world we live in (or on). While even Marker admits that the meanings are occasionally too personal for viewers, the photography (mostly of overindustrialized Japan and primitive Africa, but also Iceland, France, and California) is always mesmerizing. 100m. **DIR:** Chris Marker. 1982

SAY AMEN, SOMEBODY ★★★★ This is a joyful documentary about gospel singers Thomas A. Dorsey and Willie Mae Ford Smith. Two dozen gospel songs make this modest film a treat for the ears as well as the eyes and soul. Rated G. 100m. **DIR:** George T. Nierenberg. **CAST:** Thomas A. Dorsey, Willie Mae Ford Smith, Sallie Martin. 1982

SENSE OF LOSS, A ★★ Marcel Ophuls (*The Sorrow and the Pity*) turns his attention to the troubles in Northern Ireland with diminished effect. As it was made over fifteen years ago, it will confuse more than illuminate viewers. Unrated. 135m. **DIR:** Marcel Ophuls. 1972

SHERMAN'S MARCH ★★★★ In 1981 Boston-based documentary filmmaker Ross McElwee received a $9,000 grant to make a movie about the effects of General William Tecumseh Sherman's bloody march on the South. Then McElwee's girlfriend left him. He made the film, but *Sherman's March* is only tangentially about that historic figure. Subtitled "A Meditation on the Possibility of Romantic Love in an Era of Nuclear Weapons Proliferation," it mostly deals with the filmmaker's hilarious search for the meaning of life and someone to love. Unrated, the film has brief nudity. 150m. **DIR:** Ross McElwee. 1987

SHOAH ★★★★ Monumental documentary of enormous cumulative effect has no less a subject than the causes of Hitler's "final solution," the murder of six million Jews. One complaint: it really could have been a bit shorter. In French with English subtitles. 570m. **DIR:** Claude Lanzmann. 1985

SHOCKING ASIA ★★½ Gross as it is, this West Germany–Hong Kong coproduction remains one of the more legitimate shockumentaries to follow *Mondo Cane*. No rating, but strictly X-level. 120m. **DIR:** Emerson Fox. 1985

SHOCKING ASIA 2 ★★ Although it's subtitled *The Last Taboo*, this sadist's eye view of the Orient is mostly just leftover footage from the first *Shocking Asia*. As explicit as its predecessor. 120m. **DIR:** Emerson Fox. 1985

SIGN O' THE TIMES ★★ This two-hour fiesta of funk is exquisitely filmed (mainly during a Holland performance) and features superb sound. The concert sequences are connected by dreamlike vignettes that, while equally beautiful, add little to what is essentially an hour and a half of MTV. Rated PG-13 for suggested sex. 85m. **DIR:** Prince. **CAST:** Prince, Sheila E., Cat. 1987

SIGNATURES OF THE SOUL ★★★ Fascinating documentary hosted by Peter Fonda that explores the ritual and human obsession with tattoos. This bizarre art form is viewed through different cultures in America, Japan, and New Zealand. Not rated. 60m. **DIR:** Geoff Steven. 1987

SKY ABOVE, THE MUD BELOW, THE ★★★★★ Gripping record of a trek by French explorers across the then-uncharted island of New Guinea, a land teeming with weird animals, unnavigable terrain, and primitive natives. A priceless record of one of this planet's last frontiers. Dubbed. 92m. **DIR:** Pierre-Dominique Gaisseau. 1961

SO FAR ★★★ Modern video techniques make this Grateful Dead film a bit more lively than those past. The band's psychedelic music is accentuated with colorful visual effects and clever editing. Little attention is paid to the infamous "Dead Heads," but this is a movie about the band, not the scene that accompanies it. 55m. **DIR:** Len Dell'Amico, Jerry Garcia. **CAST:** Grateful Dead. **1987**

SOFT PARADE, THE ★★★½ The Door's keyboardist Ray Manzarek couldn't groove to director Oliver Stone's take on that classic rock band. So Manzarek directed his own documentary, replete with plenty of fresh material and insight. The film's centerpiece is the band's last TV appearance in 1969 and several never-before-seen interviews. Unrated. 50m. **DIR:** Ray Manzarek. **CAST:** Jim Morrison, The Doors. **1991**

SONG REMAINS THE SAME, THE ★★★ If any band is truly responsible for the genre of "heavy-metal" music, it is Led Zeppelin. Although this movie is a must for Zeppelin fans, the untrained ear may find numbers such as the twenty-three-minute version of "Dazed and Confused" a bit tedious. Rated PG. 136m. **DIR:** Peter Clifton, Joe Massot. **CAST:** Led Zeppelin, Peter Grant. **1976**

SORROW AND THE PITY, THE ★★★★★ Probably the most revealing work in any medium on the subject of collaboration in World War II. Marcel Ophuls carefully and intimately examines the residents of a French town that spent the war partly under Vichy rule and partly under the Nazis. Despite its great length, there is not a single wasted moment in this perfectly realized documentary. 270m. **DIR:** Marcel Ophuls. **1970**

SOUNDSTAGE: BLUES SUMMIT IN CHICAGO ★★★★ Homage is paid to blues great Muddy Waters in this music-packed documentary. Willie Dixon, Koko Taylor, Dr. John, Mike Bloomfield, Junior Wells, Johnny Winter, Nick Gravenites, and Buddy Miles are among the students who sit in with the master of Chicago blues, who beams with pleasure at the high quality of the music. Good interview footage, too. Made for TV. 58m. **DIR:** Dave Erdman. **1974**

SPIES (1992) ★★★★ History buffs and secret-agent fans will love this intriguing twenty-six–volume series that blends archival footage, simulations, and interviews (with those few participants still alive) to document scores of heinous and provocative examples of actual espionage. The entire twentieth century is covered, from Mata Hari's dangerous dance between the French and Germans during World War I to U.S. Navy official John Walker's astonishing seventeen years as a KGB spy during the 1950s and '60s. The subjects are fascinating, the presentation calculated to shock and amaze. Each tape 22m. **DIR:** Anthony Ross Potter. **1992**

STATE OF THE ART OF COMPUTER ANIMATION, THE ★★½ Lack of structure hurts this collection of the best in computer animation from around the world. Prime segments are a minidocumentary about the making of a computer-animated commercial and a *Dire Straits* music video. Interesting if you're a fan of computer animation. 60m. **DIR:** Various. **1988**

STOP MAKING SENSE ★★★★ Jonathan Demme's *Stop Making Sense* has been called a star vehicle. Filmed over a three-night period in December 1983 at Hollywood's Pantages Theater, the movie is a straight recording of a Talking Heads concert that offers the movie audience front-row-center seats. It offers great fun for the band's fans. Rated PG for suggestive lyrics. 88m. **DIR:** Jonathan Demme. **CAST:** Talking Heads. **1984**

STRAIGHT TIME: HE WROTE IT FOR CRIMINALS ★★ Combination of how Dustin Hoffman's film *Straight Time* was shot, and the life story of the film's writer Edward Bunker. Inspirational story of a reformed bank robber who writes novels about crime for prisoners. Not rated. 24m. **DIR:** Marino Colmano. **1977**

STREETWISE ★★★★★ A powerful, emotionally compelling glimpse into the lives of displaced homeless youths surviving as pimps, prostitutes, muggers, panhandlers, and small-time drug dealers on the streets of Seattle. This Oscar nominee explores its disturbing theme with great sensitivity while creating a portrait of a teenage wasteland. Highly recommended. Not rated, but contains violence and profanity. 92m. **DIR:** Martin Bell, Mary Ellen Mark, Cheryl McCall. **1985**

STRIPPER (1985) ★★★ At the First Annual Strippers' Convention in Las Vegas, several young women discuss their reasons for working in this profession. Rated R for nudity. 90m. **DIR:** Jerome Gary. **CAST:** Janette Boyd, Sara Costa. **1985**

SWEET HOME CHICAGO ★★★★★ The story of Chicago's Chess Records and its timeless blues recordings is told with admirable attention to detail by filmmakers Alan and Susan Raymond. Rare footage of performances by the label's pacesetters—Muddy Waters, Howlin' Wolf, Sonny Boy Williamson, John Lee Hooker, Otis Spann, Buddy Guy, Chuck Berry, and Willie Dixon, among others—is integrated with anecdote-packed interviews for a one-of-a-kind viewing experience. Blues fans will want to own it. Made for video. 64m. **DIR:** Alan Raymond, Susan Raymond. **1993**

SYMPATHY FOR THE DEVIL 🦃 Several uncompleted sessions on the title song and documentary-style footage of black guerrillas with machine guns seem to be all that compose this boring film from director Jean-

Luc Godard. 92m. **DIR:** Jean-Luc Godard. **CAST:** The Rolling Stones. **1970**

TEENAGE CONFIDENTIAL A rip-off, advertised as "an in-depth study," wherein Mamie Van Doren introduces a couple of short, juvenile delinquency documentaries from the 1940s, followed by "Previews of Coming Attractions" of rock 'n' roll, high school, and biker movies that packed the drive-ins during the 1950s. B&W/Color; 60m. **DIR:** Various. **1987**

THANK YOU AND GOODNIGHT ★★½ Filmmaker Jan Oxenberg mixes footage of her grandmother dying in a hospital with scenes of herself recounting her childhood memories and examining her current identity. Oxenberg's humor and inventiveness mitigate the narcissistic premise, but watching an old woman die makes for extremely unpleasant viewing. Unrated. 82m. **DIR:** Jan Oxenberg. **1991**

THAT'S DANCING ★★★★ This is a glorious celebration of dance on film. From ballet to breakin', from Fred Astaire to Busby Berkeley, from James Cagney (in *Yankee Doodle Dandy*) to Marine Jahan (Jennifer Beals's stand-in in *Flashdance*), this one has it all. Rated G. 105m. **DIR:** Jack Haley Jr. **CAST:** Mikhail Baryshnikov, Ray Bolger, Sammy Davis Jr., Gene Kelly, Liza Minnelli. **1985**

THAT'S ENTERTAINMENT ★★★★★ *That's Entertainment* is a feast of screen highlights. Culled from twenty-nine years of MGM classics, this release truly has something for everybody. Taken from Metro-Goldwyn-Mayer's glory days when it boasted "more stars than there are in heaven," nearly every sequence is a showstopper. Rated G. 135m. **DIR:** Jack Haley Jr. **CAST:** Judy Garland, Fred Astaire, Frank Sinatra, Gene Kelly, Esther Williams. **1974**

THAT'S ENTERTAINMENT PART II ★★★★ More wonderful scenes from the history of MGM highlight this compilation, hosted by director Gene Kelly and Fred Astaire. It's a real treat for film buffs. Rated G. 132m. **DIR:** Gene Kelly. **CAST:** Gene Kelly, Fred Astaire. **1976**

THAT'S ENTERTAINMENT! III ★★★★½ This fourth compilation of old MGM musical routines feels, quite naturally, a bit repetitious, but it's gussied up with the expected treasury of outtakes, previously unseen production numbers, and behind-the-scenes footage. Add the best of such beloved stars as Judy Garland, Fred Astaire, and Eleanor Powell, and it's proof positive why MTV will never be MGM. Rated G. 113m. **DIR:** Bud Friedgen, Michael J. Sheridan. **CAST:** June Allyson, Cyd Charisse, Lena Horne, Howard Keel, Gene Kelly, Ann Miller, Debbie Reynolds, Mickey Rooney, Esther Williams. **1994**

THELONIOUS MONK: STRAIGHT, NO CHASER ★★★★ An extraordinary document of one of the great innovators in modern jazz. If Monk remains ultimately baffling, this is still a brave and absorbing examination. Rare footage of studio sessions and road tours is intercut with interviews with members of Monk's family and his associates. B&W/color; 90m. **DIR:** Michael Blackwood, Christian Blackwood. **1989**

THIN BLUE LINE, THE ★★★★ Fascinating look into the 1976 murder of a Dallas policeman that led to a highly debated conviction of a drifter. Filmmaker Errol Morris's terrifying account of this incident raises some serious questions about the misuse of our current justice system. Not rated. 90m. **DIR:** Errol Morris. **1988**

35 UP ★★★★½ When he's not working on mainstream films, English director Michael Apted returns to the brilliant, ongoing documentary with which he first made his reputation. The filming of the lives and times of a select group of fourteen English men and women. They've been interviewed and depicted on film at seven-year intervals, starting when they were seven, in 1963. You don't have to be familiar with earlier segments to gain a lot from *35 Up*. Unrated. 127m. **DIR:** Michael Apted. **1991**

THIS IS ELVIS ★★★★ *This Is Elvis* blends film footage of the "real" Elvis with other portions, played by convincing stand-ins. The result is a warm, nostalgic portrait of a man who touched the hearts of young and old throughout the world. Rated PG because of slight profanity. 101m. **DIR:** Malcolm Leo, Andrew Solt. **CAST:** Elvis Presley, David Scott, Paul Boensh III. **1981**

THREE SONGS OF LENIN ★★ An emotionally charged epitaph to Lenin, divided by three songs and accompanying footage of the man and his time. In Russian with English subtitles. 62m. **DIR:** Dziga Vertov. **1934**

THROUGH THE WIRE ★★★★ A chilling portrait of three uncompromising women who were convicted of politically motivated crimes. This brilliant award-winning PBS documentary is narrated by Susan Sarandon. A must-see! 77m. **DIR:** Nina Rosenblum. **1990**

THUNDERBOLT ★★★ This documentary is concerned with the exploits in World War II of the P-47 Thunderbolt, a tactical fighter plane. Unlike William Wyler's previous documentary, *The Memphis Belle* (an account of the last bombing run of the famous B-17 bomber), this movie fails to convey the same compelling sense of mission and camaraderie. James Stewart narrates. 45m. **DIR:** William Wyler. **1947**

TIBET ★★★ Splendid cinematography and an arresting score by Mark Isham turn this travelogue into a stunning tour de force in the style of *Koyaanisqatsi*. Sticklers for plot will be disappointed, for this is a visual and audio masterpiece of mystical images. 50m. **DIR:** Stanley Dorfman. **1988**

TONG TANA ★★★★ A visually stunning look at the Penans (a tribe of people on the island nation of Borneo), as they fight against big business. Not rated. In Swedish with English subtitles. 88m. **DIR:** Jan Roed. **1990**

TRIUMPH OF THE WILL ★★★★½ World-renowned German documentary of the rise of Hitler's Third Reich is a masterpiece of propaganda and remains a chilling testament to the insanity that can lurk in great art. Director Leni Riefenstahl created a powerful and noble image of a German empire that was already threatening Europe and would eventually engulf the world in a devastating war. B&W; 110m. **DIR:** Leni Riefenstahl. **1935**

TRIUMPH, TRAGEDY & REBIRTH: THE STORY OF THE SPACE SHUTTLE ★★ It's hard to believe a documentary on the space shuttle—and all the highs and lows of that program—could be boring, but this uninspired film is proof positive. The people at *National Geographic* shouldn't be worried. Not rated. 54m. **DIR:** Don Barrett. **1988**

TRUTH OR DARE ★★★★ Pop superstar Madonna allowed first-time filmmaker Alek Keshishian complete access—both onstage and backstage—to her 1990 Blond Ambition tour. The result is a fascinating, not-so-flattering look at one of contemporary music's true phenomena. Rated R for nudity and profanity. 118m. **DIR:** Alek Keshishian. **CAST:** Madonna, Warren Beatty, Sandra Bernhard, Kevin Costner. **1991**

28 UP ★★★★★ A riveting and innovative British documentary that follows the woes and wonders of fourteen young people, reuniting them for new interviews every seven years. The result is a movie that exposes human vulnerability, while exposing the ludicrous and pompous British class system. Not rated. 120m. **DIR:** Michael Apted. **1985**

25 X 5: THE CONTINUING HISTORY OF THE ROLLING STONES ★★★★★ The definitive history lesson on the Rolling Stones. Using extensive interviews and rare never-before-seen video footage, director Nigel Finch chronicles twenty-five years of the band—beginning in the early Sixties and ending with the Steel Wheels Tour. No rating. Contains adult language and brief nudity. 130m. **DIR:** Nigel Finch. **1989**

TWO BY SCORSESE ★★★ Interesting duet of early works by Martin Scorsese, one of the most prolific American film directors. *Italianamerican*, made in 1974, is a penetrating look at the filmmakers' parents. *The Big Shave*, made in 1968, is a black comedy musical about a man having a bloody shave to the tune of Bunny Berigan's "I Can't Get Started." Not rated, but contains mild violence. 54m. **DIR:** Martin Scorsese. **1991**

U2: RATTLE AND HUM ★★★★½ *U2: Rattle and Hum* is more than just a concert movie. It's an eloquent cry for change. The Irish rock quartet and 26-year-old director Phil Joanou have combined forces to create a remarkably moving screen work. Filmed in black and white and color during the group's American tour in support of its groundbreaking *Joshua Tree* album, it captures the excitement of the live shows while underlining U2's timely message. Rated PG-13 for profanity. 99m. **DIR:** Phil Joanou. **CAST:** U2. **1988**

UNDERGROUND (1976) ★★★ This documentary features interviews with members of the radical Weather Underground. Whether or not you agree with their views, they are discussed intelligently, making this an invaluable document for any study of recent radical politics. 88m. **DIR:** Emile De Antonio, Mary Lampson, Haskell Wexler. **1976**

UNKNOWN CHAPLIN ★★★★ In three parts—"My Happiest Years," "The Great Director," and "Hidden Treasures"—this is a fascinating excursion into the creative techniques and art of Charlie Chaplin. James Mason narrates. B&W; each part. 60m. **DIR:** Kevin Brownlow, David Gill. **1983**

VANISHING PRAIRIE, THE ★★★½ Award-winning true-life adventure from Walt Disney ranks with *The Living Desert* as the finest (and certainly most widely seen) nature film of the 1950s. Beautifully photographed, this is a fun but sobering movie the whole family can enjoy. 75m. **DIR:** James Algar. **1954**

VELVET UNDERGROUND, THE: VELVET REDUX—LIVE MCMXCIII ★★★★★ The best concert film since *Stop Making Sense*, filmed in Paris during a reunion tour by the 1960s band that most influenced the music of the 1980s and 1990s. Best known for intense, anarchic songs chronicling the dark urban underside of the 1960s, the Velvets also had a softer side that shows in tunes as gorgeous as anything that ever came out of an AM radio. 90m. **DIR:** Declan Lowney. **CAST:** Lou Reed, John Cale, Sterling Morrison, Maureen Tucker. **1993**

VERNON, FLORIDA ★★★ Weirdos of the world seem to have united and set up housekeeping in Vernon, Florida. This unique and off-the-wall film comes from the strange vision of director Errol Morris. In this slice of life, the viewers become acquainted with (and amused by) the citizens of this slightly off-center small town. Not rated. 60m. **DIR:** Errol Morris. **1988**

VINCENT: THE LIFE AND DEATH OF VINCENT VAN GOGH ★★★★ Australian filmmaker Paul Cox combines painter Vincent van Gogh's "Dear Theo" letters with stunning visuals—juxtaposing van Gogh's paintings with luscious scenery—for a deeply satisfying portrait of the brilliant but tortured artist. John Hurt does an excellent job of narrating. Truly impressive. 110m. **DIR:** Paul Cox. **1987**

VISIONS OF LIGHT: THE ART OF CINEMATOGRAPHY ★★★★ Marshall McLuhan once wrote that the literate person of the future would be visually literate. This documentary look at the work of great cinematographers is a step in that direction. Through interviews and stunning clips, we learn of the contributions, aspirations, and art of great movie cameramen, from Nestor Almendros to Ernest Dickerson. If you like movies, you'll love this tribute to the men who film them. 90m. **DIR:** Arnold Glassman, Todd McCarthy, Stuart Samuels. **CAST:** Nestor Almendros, John Baijley, Michael Ballhaus, Ernest Dickerson. **1992**

VOICES OF SARAFINA ★★★★ A robust, feature-length documentary that details the personal stories of the performers and creators of *Sarafina,* the antiapartheid Broadway hit musical from South Africa. Directed by English filmmaker Nigel Noble, it's not only a record of the unique stage show but also a gentle, affecting portrayal of the performers and their amazing ability to maintain hope and strength in the face of racism at home. The music is by Hugh Masakela and other South Africans. 90m. **DIR:** Nigel Noble. **CAST:** Hugh Masakela. **1988**

W. C. FIELDS STRAIGHT UP ★★★★ Narrated by Dudley Moore and featuring interviews and comments by W. C. Fields's grandson, old friends, associates, and admirers, this documentary on the life and career of America's foremost curmudgeon is a winner throughout. Excerpts from Fields's films bring the master comedian back to robust, hilarious life. B&W; 60m. **DIR:** Robert B. Weide. **1990**

WAR ROOM, THE ★★★★ Nominated for an oscar for best documentary in 1993, this film follows Bill Clinton's 1992 presidential campaign staff (including James Carville and George Stephanopoulos) from the first primary to the acceptance speech. The viewer gets a firsthand look at the inner workings of a campaign, including mudslinging. Very well done and quite fascinating. Rated PG for profanity. 96m. **DIR:** Chris Hegedus, D. A. Pennebaker. **1993**

WASN'T THAT A TIME! ★★★★★ This is a folk music documentary about the Weavers' last reunion, as narrated wryly by group member Lee Hays. What really sets this apart from all the rest is the wealth of superb archival footage, all used in the proper proportion and sequence. The finale is the final reunion concert, and what a glorious and joyful event that was. Rated G. 78m. **DIR:** Jim Brown. **CAST:** The Weavers, Pete Seeger, Lee Hays, Ronnie Gilbert, Fred Hellerman, Arlo Guthrie, Don McLean, Holly Near, Mary Travers, Harry Reasoner, Studs Turkel. **1981**

WHO ARE THE DEBOLTS AND WHERE DID THEY GET 19 KIDS? ★★★★★ This Academy Award–winning documentary features Dorothy and Bob Debolt and their nineteen children—some natural, most adopted. Their family is unique not only for its great size but for the multiple physical disabilities their adopted children have, the positive way these problems are dealt with, and the fantastic organizational system under which their daily lives are run. This is an excellent and inspirational film. Rated G. 73m. **DIR:** John Korty. **1978**

WOLFMAN: A CINEMATIC SCRAPBOOK ★★★ Followers of the ill-fated Lawrence Talbot and other cinematic characters cursed by the bite of the werewolf will thoroughly enjoy this roundup centering on the hairy changeling personified by Lon Chaney Jr. and Michael Landon, among others. 60m. **DIR:** Ted Newsom. **1991**

WONDER OF IT ALL ★★★½ This nature documentary takes you on an armchair cruise around the world. You will observe animals in their natural environment interacting with members of their own and other species. While Disney nature films include superior photography, this is still worth a watch by animal and nature lovers. Rated G. 47m. **DIR:** Arthur R. Dubs. **1982**

WONDERFUL WIZARD OF OZ, THE: THE MAKING OF A MOVIE CLASSIC ★★★★ Hosted by Angela Lansbury, this lush and satisfying peek at Ozmania covers it all, from behind-the-scenes gossip to casting and technical problems. There is rare footage, archival interviews, foreign-language versions of the movie, and a look at the impact of the book by L. Frank Baum. A drier, though still intriguing, collection of outtakes and interviews is tacked onto the end. 52m. **DIR:** Jack Haley Jr. **CAST:** Judy Garland, Margaret Hamilton, Ray Bolger, Jack Haley, Liza Minnelli, Harold Arlen. **1990**

WOODSTOCK ★★★½ Woodstock is probably, along with *Gimme Shelter*, the most important film documentation of the late 1960s counterculture in the United States. The bulk of the film consists of footage of the bands and various other performers who played at the festival. There are some great split-screen sequences and some imaginative interviews. Well worth viewing. Rated R. 184m. **DIR:** Michael Wadleigh. **CAST:** Country Joe and the Fish, Jimi Hendrix, Jefferson Airplane. **1970**

WOODY GUTHRIE—HARD TRAVELIN' ★★★½ Woody Guthrie's musical presence will be felt for many years. This tribute traces his brilliant songwriting career from the dust bowl of the Midwest to California in the early 1940s. Many performers, including Joan Baez and Arlo Guthrie, Woody's son, sing and discuss the Guthrie influence on their own music. 74m. **DIR:** Jim Brown. **CAST:** Hoyt Axton, Joan Baez, Judy Collins, Pete Seeger, Arlo Guthrie. 1984

YESSONGS ★★★ A favorite on the midnight-movie circuit, *Yessongs* provides an interesting look at the glittery overindulgences of rock in the early 1970s. Formed in 1968, Yes fought for credibility with its suitelike, classical brand of rock, which utilized high vocal harmonies. By the time this concert was filmed in 1973, the band was one of rock's top draws. 70m. **DIR:** Peter Neal. **CAST:** Yes. 1974

ZIGGY STARDUST AND THE SPIDERS FROM MARS 🦃 Only the most devoted David Bowie fans will enjoy this documentary, filmed July 3, 1973, at London's Hammersmith Odeon Theatre. Rated PG for suggestive lyrics. 90m. **DIR:** D. A. Pennebaker. **CAST:** David Bowie. 1982

DRAMA

AARON LOVES ANGELA ★★★ This Harlem love affair features a black youth (Kevin Hooks) falling for a sweet Puerto Rican girl (Irene Cara). Their relative innocence contrasts with the drug-dealing violence around them. Rated R for violence and profanity. 99m. **DIR:** Gordon Parks Jr. **CAST:** Moses Gunn, Kevin Hooks, Irene Cara, Ernestine Jackson, Robert Hooks. **1975**

ABE LINCOLN IN ILLINOIS ★★★★ Based on Sherwood Anderson's Broadway play, this is a reverent look at the early career and loves of the sixteenth president. As contrasted to John Ford's *Young Mr. Lincoln*, this is a more somber, historically accurate, and better-acted version. B&W; 110m. **DIR:** John Cromwell. **CAST:** Raymond Massey, Ruth Gordon, Gene Lockhart, Mary Howard. **1934**

ABIGAIL'S PARTY ★★★★★ A superb slice of acerbic British social commentary. Beverly is a gin-sodden shrew with middle-class aspirations, who holds a small get-together for the neighbors. This movie is like an English version of *Who's Afraid of Virginia Woolf*, a group of adults congregate, imbibe vast amounts of alcohol, and squirm-inducing disaster ensues. 105m. **DIR:** Mike Leigh. **CAST:** Alison Steadman. **1977**

ABOUT LAST NIGHT ★★★★ A slick adaptation of David Mamet's play, *Sexual Perversity in Chicago*. Demi Moore and Rob Lowe meet for a one-night stand and then realize they *like* each other. Jim Belushi and Elizabeth Perkins turn in solid performances, but the film belongs to Moore. Rated R for nudity and explicit adult situations. 113m. **DIR:** Edward Zwick. **CAST:** Rob Lowe, Demi Moore, James Belushi, Elizabeth Perkins, George DiCenzo. **1986**

ABOVE THE RIM ★★½ Two brothers clash as they try to influence a morally struggling young man in this Manhattan melodrama about inner-city crime, broken dreams, and one high-school athlete's attempt to climb out of the dangerous Harlem street scene. The laws and rhythms of the street are brought to life by a magnetic cast, but this bold bite out of the dark side of the Big Apple has a familiar taste to it. Rated R for violence and language. 96m. **DIR:** Jeff Pollack. **CAST:** Duane Martin, Leon, Tupac Shakur, Bernie Mac, Marlon Wayans. **1994**

ABRAHAM LINCOLN ★★★★ A milestone in many ways, this episodic film is legendary director Griffith's first "talkie," Hollywood's first sound biography of an American, the first attempt to cover Lincoln's life from cradle to grave, and the first about the martyred president to include the Civil War. Walter Huston's peerless performance in the title role dominates throughout. B&W; 91m. **DIR:** D. W. Griffith. **CAST:** Walter Huston, Una Merkel, Kay Hammond, Ian Keith, Hobart Bosworth, Jason Robards Sr., Henry B. Walthall. **1930**

ABSOLUTION ★★½ Slow-moving but interesting tale of a priest's emotional and physical battle with one of his students at an English school for boys. As the priest, Richard Burton gives his usual compelling performance. Nice plot twist at the end. Not rated, but contains violence. 91m. **DIR:** Anthony Page. **CAST:** Richard Burton, Dominic Guard, Andrew Keir, Billy Connolly. **1977**

ACCEPTABLE RISKS ★★★ Heavy-handed message film about the risks a chemical plant poses to the inhabitants of a new housing development. Unbelievable amount of carelessness by plant workers and blind greed by owners reduces this TV movie to near sci-fi rather than gritty docudrama. 97m. **DIR:** Rick Wallace. **CAST:** Brian Dennehy, Kenneth McMillan, Christine Ebersole, Cicely Tyson. **1986**

ACCIDENT ★★★★ Harold Pinter's complicated play retains its subtleties in this sometimes baffling British film. Dirk Bogarde is excellent as a married professor pursuing an attractive student. There are enough twists and turns in the characters' actual desires to maintain your complete attention. 105m. **DIR:** Joseph Losey. **CAST:** Dirk Bogarde, Stanley Baker, Jacqueline Sassard, Michael York. **1967**

ACCIDENTAL TOURIST, THE ★★★★ William Hurt and Kathleen Turner team again with director Lawrence Kasdan (they worked together on *Body Heat*) for this compelling adaptation of Anne Tyler's novel. Hurt's the writer of travel guides who distances himself from everybody—including wife Kathleen Turner—after the death of their young son; Geena Davis is the earthy, colorful free spirit who tries to break through his wall of self-imposed isolation. Filled with strong emotional highs and lows, and highlighted by a superb supporting cast. Rated PG. 120m. **DIR:** Lawrence Kasdan. **CAST:** William Hurt, Kathleen Turner, Geena Davis, Bill Pullman, Amy Wright, David Ogden Stiers, Ed Begley Jr. **1988**

ACCUSED, THE ★★★★ Superb, emotionally intense retelling of the precedent-setting New Bedford, Massachusetts, gang-rape case, with Jodie Foster as an innocent but definitely not saintly victim, and Kelly McGillis as a tough DA. An excellent and wrenching film. Rated R for adult themes, language, nudity, and sexual violence. 105m. **DIR:** Jonathan Kaplan. **CAST:** Jodie Foster, Kelly McGillis, Bernie Coulson, Steve Antin, Leo Rossi, Woody Brown. **1988**

ACROSS THE TRACKS ★★★★ Two brothers compete for a scholarship in a county track championship. The sound track is excellent, the acting is convincing, and the screenplay deals with believable, real-life situations. Rated PG. 101m. **DIR:** Sandy Tung. **CAST:** Rick Schroder, Brad Pitt, Carrie Snodgress. **1990**

ACT, THE ★★★ A comedy-drama with a convoluted plot of political chicanery, double cross, and robbery. The overall quality is erratic and yet this ends up being a good effort from a veteran cast. Trivia fans may note John Sebastian's involvement in the musical score. Rated R for sexual situations and language. 90m. **DIR:** Sig Shore. **CAST:** Robert Ginty, Sarah Langenfeld, Jill St. John, Eddie Albert, Pat Hingle. **1982**

ACT OF PASSION ★★ In this made-for-television movie, Marlo Thomas plays a single woman who picks up a stranger (Kris Kristofferson) at a party. She is subsequently subjected to harassment by the police and the press when the man turns out to be a suspected terrorist. Harsh and blatantly exaggerated. 95m. **DIR:** Simon Langton. **CAST:** Marlo Thomas, Kris Kristofferson, Jon De Vries, David Rasche, Linda Thorson, Edward Winter, George Dzundza. **1984**

ACT OF VENGEANCE ★★★★ In this first-rate drama, a suprisingly effective Charles Bronson plays Jock Yablonski, an honest man who wants to turn his coal-miners union around. When he runs for union president against the thoroughly corrupt incumbent (played brilliantly by Wilford Brimley), the threatened leader resorts to strong-arm tactics. Excellent supporting cast. Not rated, but contains violence and profanity. 97m. **DIR:** John Mackenzie. **CAST:** Charles Bronson, Ellen Burstyn, Wilford Brimley, Hoyt Axton, Ellen Barkin. **1985**

ACTORS AND SIN ★★½ *Actors and Sin* is actually two short films. *Actor's Blood* is a drama starring Edward G. Robinson as the devoted father of a successful Broadway actress (Marsha Hunt). *Woman's Sin* is a comedy starring Eddie Albert as an irrepressible Hollywood agent who finds a winning screenplay but loses its author. B&W; 86m. **DIR:** Ben Hecht, Lee Garmes. **CAST:** Edward G. Robinson, Eddie Albert, Marsha Hunt, Alan Reed, Dan O'Herlihy. **1952**

ADAM ★★★★ Daniel J. Travanti and JoBeth Williams deliver fine performances in this chillingly real account of John and Reve Williams's search for their missing 6-year-old son, Adam. A quite believable picture, detailing the months of uncertainty and anguish that surrounded the child's disappearance from a department store. This ordeal resulted in the formation of the Missing Children's Bureau. Made for television. 97m. **DIR:** Michael Tuchner. **CAST:** Daniel J. Travanti, JoBeth Williams, Richard Masur. **1983**

ADAM AT 6 A.M. ★★★ In his second film, Michael Douglas—in a coming-of-age role—leaves his California professorship to find his roots in rural Missouri. There he falls in love with a small-town girl (Lee Purcell) while working as a road laborer. Ending is a gem! Rated PG for violence. 100m. **DIR:** Robert Scheerer. **CAST:** Michael Douglas, Lee Purcell, Joe Don Baker, Grayson Hall. **1970**

ADAM HAD FOUR SONS ★★★★ This classic has it all: good acting, romance, seduction, betrayal, tears, and laughter. Ingrid Bergman plays the good governess, and Susan Hayward plays the seductive hussy who tries to turn brother against brother. Warner Baxter offers a fine performance as Adam, the father. B&W; 81m. **DIR:** Gregory Ratoff. **CAST:** Ingrid Bergman, Warner Baxter, Susan Hayward. **1941**

ADJUSTER, THE ★★ Elias Koteas stars as an insurance adjuster. His wife is obsessed with the pornography and violence she views every day as a film censor. Another couple enter their lives—a wealthy duo who spend all their money and time on elaborate sex games. If you're looking for clarity and plot, abandon faith, all ye who enter here. 102m. **DIR:** Atom Egoyan. **CAST:** Elias Koteas, Arsinée Khanjian, Maury Chaykin, Gabrielle Rose. **1992**

ADULTRESS, THE 🦃 Abysmal film about an impotent husband who hires a gigolo to service his wife. 85m. **DIR:** Norbert Meisel. **CAST:** Tyne Daly, Eric Braeden, Greg Morton. **1973**

ADVENTURE ★★½ Flat and slow-moving romantic drama has a rough merchant sailor involved with a staid librarian. Neither Joan Blondell nor Thomas Mitchell (in his patented drunk Irishman role) can save this one. B&W; 125m. **DIR:** Victor Fleming. **CAST:** Clark Gable, Greer Garson, Joan Blondell, Thomas Mitchell, Tom Tully, John Qualen, Lina Romay, Harry Davenport. **1946**

ADVENTURES OF GALLANT BESS ★★ Minor melodrama about a man who seems to be more in love with his horse than he is with the woman in his life. The photography is quite good and the performances are passable, but it is still only fair. 73m. **DIR:** Lew Landers. **CAST:** Cameron Mitchell, Audrey Long, Fuzzy Knight. **1948**

ADVENTURES OF MARK TWAIN, THE (1944) ★★★½ This very episodic tale follows Samuel Clemens (Fredric March) from boyhood and young manhood on his beloved Mississippi River to recognition as a writer and lecturer. A nice bit of license is taken when he is involved in a frog-jump contest with Bret Harte (John Carradine). B&W; 130m. **DIR:** Irving Rapper. **CAST:** Fredric March, Alexis Smith, Donald Crisp, Alan Hale Sr., C. Aubrey Smith, John Carradine, Walter Hampen, Joyce Reynolds, Percy Kilbride. **1944**

ADVENTURES OF NELLIE BLY, THE ★★ In this made-for-television film, Linda Purl shines as a reporter who uncovers serious problems in factories and insane asylums. The script unfortunately is weak and the direction is uninspired. 100m. **DIR:** Henning Schellerup. **CAST:** Linda Purl, Gene Barry, John Randolph, Raymond Buktenica, J. D. Cannon. **1981**

ADVISE AND CONSENT ★★★½ An engrossing adaptation of Allen Drury's bestseller about behind-the-scenes Washington. Fine performances abound among the familiar faces that populate Otto Preminger's vision of the U.S. Senate as it is called upon to confirm a controversial nominee for Secretary of State (Henry Fonda). Easily the most riveting is Charles Laughton, at his scene-stealing best, as a smiling old crocodile of a southern senator. B&W; 140m. **DIR:** Otto Preminger. **CAST:** Henry Fonda, Don Murray, Charles Laughton, Franchot Tone, Lew Ayres, Walter Pidgeon, Peter Lawford, Paul Ford, Burgess Meredith, Gene Tierney. **1962**

AFFAIR, THE ★★★ Touching, honest story of a crippled songwriter (Natalie Wood) tentatively entering into her first love affair—with an attorney (Robert Wagner). This is an unusually well-acted, sensitively told TV movie. 74m. **DIR:** Gilbert Cates. **CAST:** Natalie Wood, Robert Wagner, Bruce Davison, Kent Smith, Pat Harrington. **1973**

AFFAIR IN TRINIDAD ★★★ Sultry, enticing café singer Rita Hayworth teams with brother-in-law Glenn Ford to trap her husband's murderer. The two fall in love en route. 98m. **DIR:** Vincent Sherman. **CAST:** Glenn Ford, Rita Hayworth, Alexander Scourby, Torin Thatcher. **1952**

AFFAIR TO REMEMBER, AN ★★★★ Leo McCarey's gorgeous, haunting remake of his Oscar-nominated *Love Affair*. Cary Grant and Deborah Kerr have a shipboard romance, then part for six months. They agree to meet atop the Empire State Building at the end of the year, but an accident prevents it. 115m. **DIR:** Leo McCarey. **CAST:** Cary Grant, Deborah Kerr, Richard Denning, Cathleen Nesbitt, Robert Q. Lewis. **1957**

AFRICAN DREAM, AN ★★★★ Powerful film about a British-educated black man (John Kani) who returns to Africa as a teacher. Enter Kitty Aldridge as a joyful young woman who has just become a part of the nearby British colony, circa 1906. Inspirational portrayal of two people who dare to dream of a better world. Rated PG for violence. 94m. **DIR:** John Smallcombe. **CAST:** Kitty Aldridge, John Kani. **1990**

AFRICAN QUEEN, THE ★★★★★ Humphrey Bogart and Katharine Hepburn star in this exciting World War I adventure film. Bogart's a drunkard, and Hepburn's the spinster sister of a murdered missionary. Together they take on the Germans and, in doing so, are surprised to find themselves falling in love. 106m. **DIR:** John Huston. **CAST:** Humphrey Bogart, Katharine Hepburn, Peter Bull, Robert Morley, Theodore Bikel. **1951**

AFTER JULIUS ★★½ Slow-paced British soap about a widow and the effect her husband's death has on her and her daughters. Unrated, but contains nudity. 150m. **DIR:** John Glenister. **CAST:** Faith Brook, John Carson, Cyd Hayman. **1978**

AFTER THE PROMISE ★★ An uneducated laborer (Mark Harmon) loses custody of his sons following the death of his ailing wife. His efforts to get them back lead him down a road of red tape. Shamelessly maudlin and predictable TV movie. 93m. **DIR:** David Greene. **CAST:** Mark Harmon, Diana Scarwid, Donnelly Rhodes. **1987**

AFTER THE SHOCK ★★ A telemovie depicting the heroics of a group of Bay Area residents after the October 17, 1989 earthquake. Gary Sherman shot the movie with a home-movie, you-are-there feel. 92m. **DIR:** Gary A. Sherman. **CAST:** Scott Valentine, Jack Scalia, Yaphet Kotto. **1990**

AFTERBURN ★★★★★ Made-for-cable drama doesn't get much better than this scathing indictment of government air force contracts, and the lengths to which life-threatening mistakes will be buried beneath red tape. Laura Dern superbly handles her role as fiery Janet Harduvel, who single-handedly forced General Dynamics to acknowledge that the F-16 fighter plane that killed her husband went down due to faulty design, rather than "pilot error." 103m. **DIR:** Robert Markowitz. **CAST:** Laura Dern, Robert Loggia, Michael Rooker, Vincent Spano. **1992**

AGAINST THE WALL ★★★★ This crackling thriller dramatizes the events leading to 1971's Attica Prison riots, which ultimately resulted in forty-three deaths, as seen through the eyes of impressionable new guard Kyle MacLachlan. Scripter Ron Hutchinson is careful not to paint all prisoners as misunderstood saints and all guards as unrepentant sadists, but there's little doubt the situation deteriorated due to political opportunism. It's hard to tear your eyes from the screen. Rated R for violence, profanity, and nudity. 111m. **DIR:** John Frankenheimer. **CAST:** Kyle MacLachlan, Samuel L. Jackson, Clarence Williams III, Frederic Forrest, Harry Dean Stanton. **1994**

AGE OF INNOCENCE, THE ★★★★ If nothing else, *The Age of Innocence* proves that Martin Scorsese can make a classy motion picture. Daniel Day-Lewis and Michelle Pfeiffer are star-crossed lovers in this romance that also examines the mores and morals of New York in the 1870s. As good as Lewis and Pfeiffer are, the film belongs to the luminous Winona Ryder, who plays Lewis's patient and formidable fiancée. Narrated by Joanne Woodward. Rated PG for suggestion of impropriety. 133m. **DIR:** Martin Scorsese. **CAST:** Daniel Day-Lewis, Michelle Pfeiffer, Winona Ryder, Geraldine Chaplin, Alec McCowen, Richard E. Grant, Mary Beth Hurt, Stuart Gordon, Robert Sean Leonard, Sian Phillips, Carolyn Farina, Michael Gough, Miriam Margoyles, Alexis Smith, Jonathan Pryce, Norman Lloyd. **1993**

AGE-OLD FRIENDS ★★★★½ This poignant study of aging, adapted by Bob Larbey from his Broadway play *A Month of Sundays*, makes a superb vehicle for star Hume Cronyn. While enthusiastically flirting with his kind young nurse or testily enduring his monthly Inspection Day—a visit from his estranged daughter—Cronyn's crusty codger puts his effort and concern into the well-being of best friend Vincent Gardenia. 90m. **DIR:** Allan Kroeker. **CAST:** Hume Cronyn, Vincent Gardenia, Tandy Cronyn, Esther Rolle. **1989**

AGENCY ★★ Despite the presence of Robert Mitchum, this Canadian feature about a power struggle in the world of advertising doesn't convince. Rated PG. 94m. **DIR:** George Kaczender. **CAST:** Robert Mitchum, Lee Majors, Saul Rubinek, Valerie Perrine. **1981**

AGNES OF GOD ★★★ This fascinating drama features tour-de-force performances by Jane Fonda, Anne Bancroft, and Meg Tilly. Tilly's character, the childlike novice of an extremely sheltered convent, is discovered one night with the bloodied body of a baby. Psychiatrist Fonda is sent to determine Tilly's sanity in anticipation of a court hearing; Bancroft, as the Mother Superior, struggles to prevent the young girl's loss of innocence. Rated PG-13 for subject matter. 101m. **DIR:** Norman Jewison. **CAST:** Jane Fonda, Anne Bancroft, Meg Tilly, Anne Pitoniak, Winston Rekert. **1985**

AGONY AND THE ECSTASY, THE ★★★ Handsomely mounted but plodding historical drama based on Irving Stone's best-selling novel about Pope Julius II (Rex Harrison) engaging Michelangelo (Charlton Heston) to paint the ceiling of the Sistine Chapel. Heston overacts and the direction is heavy-handed. 140m. **DIR:** Carol Reed. **CAST:** Charlton Heston, Rex Harrison, Diane Cilento, Harry Andrews. **1965**

AIRPORT ★★★★ The daddy of them all, this *Grand Hotel* in the air is slick, enjoyable entertainment. Taking place on a fateful winter night, it miraculously rises above some stiff performances and an often hackneyed plot. Rated G. 137m. **DIR:** George Seaton. **CAST:** Burt Lancaster, Dean Martin, Helen Hayes, Jacqueline Bisset, Van Heflin, Jean Seberg, George Kennedy. **1970**

AIRPORT 1975 🦃 Poor sequel. Rated PG. 106m. **DIR:** Jack Smight. **CAST:** Charlton Heston, George Kennedy, Karen Black, Sid Caesar, Helen Reddy. **1974**

AIRPORT '77 🦃 If you've seen one *Airport*, you've seen them all. Rated PG for violence. 113m. **DIR:** Jerry Jameson. **CAST:** Jack Lemmon, Lee Grant, George Kennedy, Christopher Lee. **1977**

AIRPORT '79: THE CONCORDE 🦃 Bring your own airsickness bag. Rated PG. 113m. **DIR:** David Lowell Rich. **CAST:** Alain Delon, Robert Wagner, Susan Blakely, George Kennedy, Eddie Albert, Cicely Tyson. **1979**

ALAMO BAY ★★★★ French director Louis Malle once again looks at the underbelly of the American dream. This time, he takes us to the Gulf Coast of Texas in the late 1970s where Vietnamese refugees arrived, expecting the land of opportunity, and came face-to-face, instead, with the Ku Klux Klan. Rated R for nudity, violence, and profanity. 105m. **DIR:** Louis Malle. **CAST:** Ed Harris, Amy Madigan, Ho Nquyen, Donald Moffat. **1985**

ALAN AND NAOMI ★★ Well-intentioned but muddled story about a high school student in the Forties and his attempts to help a victim of Nazi terrorism. The performances add a level of quality, but they are thwarted by the funereal tone and an inexcusably abrupt conclusion. Rated PG for mature themes. 98m. **DIR:** Sterling Vanwagenen. **CAST:** Lukas Haas, Vanessa Zaoui, Michael Gross, Amy Aquino, Kevin Connolly, Zohra Lampert. **1992**

ALEXANDER THE GREAT ★★★½ The strange, enigmatic, self-possessed Macedonian conqueror of Greece and most of the civilized world of his time rides again. Richard Burton, with his enthralling voice and uniquely hypnotic eyes, dominates an outstanding cast in this lavish epic. 141m. **DIR:** Robert Rossen. **CAST:** Richard Burton, Fredric March, Claire Bloom, Danielle Darrieux. **1956**

ALICE ADAMS ★★★★ Life and love in a typical mid-American small town when there were still such things as concerts in the park and ice-cream socials. Hepburn is a social-climbing girl wistfully seeking love while trying to overcome the stigma of her father's lack of money and ambition. High point of the film is the dinner scene, at once a comic gem and painful insight into character. B&W; 99m. **DIR:** George Stevens. **CAST:** Katharine Hepburn, Fred MacMurray, Evelyn Venable, Fred Stone, Frank Albertson, Hattie McDaniel, Charley Grapewin, Hedda Hopper. **1935**

ALICE DOESN'T LIVE HERE ANYMORE ★★★★½ The feature film that spawned the television series *Alice* is a memorable character study about a woman (Ellen Burstyn, who won an Oscar for her performance) attempting to survive after her husband's death has left her penniless and with a young son to support. The hard-edged direction by Martin Scorsese adds grit to what might have been a lightweight yarn. Rated PG for profanity and violence. 113m. **DIR:** Martin Scorsese. **CAST:** Ellen Burstyn, Kris Kristofferson, Harvey Keitel, Billy Green Bush, Alfred Lutter, Jodie Foster, Vic Tayback, Diane Ladd. **1975**

ALICE'S RESTAURANT ★★★½ This film was based on Arlo Guthrie's hit record of the same name. Some insights into the 1960s counterculture can be found in this story of Guthrie's attempt to stay out of the draft. Some fine acting by a basically unknown cast. Rated PG for language and some nudity. 111m. **DIR:** Arthur Penn. **CAST:** Arlo Guthrie, Pat Quinn, James Broderick, Michael McClanathan, Geoff Outlaw, Tina Chen. **1969**

ALIVE ★★★½ This gripping adaptation of Piers Paul Read's bestseller benefits from Frank Marshall's crackling direction and a reasonably unflinching script from John Patrick Shanley (*Moonstruck*). After a horrifyingly realistic plane crash in the Andes, the surviving members of a South American rugby team eventually steel themselves to the requirements of staying alive. Rated R for language. 123m. **DIR:** Frank Marshall. **CAST:** Ethan Hawke, Vincent Spano, Josh Hamilton, Brucy Ramsay. **1993**

ALL ABOUT EVE ★★★★★ The behind-the-scenes world of the New York theater is the subject of this classic. The picture won several Academy Awards, including best picture, but it is Bette Davis as Margo Channing whom most remember. The dialogue sparkles, and the performances are of high caliber. B&W; 138m. **DIR:** Joseph L. Mankiewicz. **CAST:** Bette Davis, Anne Baxter, Marilyn Monroe, George Sanders, Celeste Holm, Gary Merrill. **1950**

ALL FALL DOWN ★★½ Sporadically powerful William Inge soap opera about the love affair of a young man (Warren Beatty) and an older woman (Eva Marie Saint), with a subplot about the man's adoring younger brother (Brandon de Wilde). Slightly overlong and handicapped by the puritanical Hollywood production code of the time. B&W; 110m. **DIR:** John Frankenheimer. **CAST:** Warren Beatty, Eva Marie Saint, Karl Malden, Angela Lansbury, Brandon de Wilde. **1962**

ALL GOD'S CHILDREN ★★ Forced busing to achieve educational integration is the crux of this story of two families, one white and one black. The cast is excellent, but a wandering script makes comprehension difficult. Rated PG for violence. 107m. **DIR:** Jerry Thorpe. **CAST:** Richard Widmark, Ned Beatty, Ossie Davis, Ruby Dee. **1980**

ALL MINE TO GIVE ★★★ Reaching for the heartstrings, this melodrama follows the lives of a Scottish family in 1850s Wisconsin. The backwoods life is brutal and by the film's midpoint both the mother and father have died and left the oldest child the task of parceling out his little brothers and sisters to the far-flung neighbors. A fairly decent weeper. 102m. **DIR:** Allen Reisner. **CAST:** Glynis Johns, Cameron Mitchell, Patty McCormack, Hope Emerson. **1957**

ALL MY SONS ★★★½ An excellent adaptation of the Arthur Miller play. A family must deal with the death of one son in World War II and the father's profit made by selling plane parts during the war. James Whitmore is the guilt-ridden father, Michael Learned his distraught wife. Made for TV. 122m. **DIR:** Jack O'Brien. **CAST:** James Whitmore, Aidan Quinn, Michael Learned, Joan Allen. **1986**

ALL QUIET ON THE WESTERN FRONT (1979) ★★★½ This is a television remake of the 1930 film, which was taken from Erich Maria Remarque's classic antiwar novel. It attempts to recall all the horrors of World War I, but even the great detail issued to this film can't hide its TV mentality and melodramatic characters. Despite this major flaw, the film is watchable for its rich look and compelling story. 126m. **DIR:** Delbert Mann. **CAST:** Richard Thomas, Ernest Borgnine, Donald Pleasence, Ian Holm, Patricia Neal, Keith Carradine. **1979**

ALL THE KING'S MEN ★★★★ Broderick Crawford and Mercedes McCambridge won Academy Awards for their work in this adaptation of Robert Penn Warren's Pulitzer Prize–winning novel about a corrupt politician's ascension to power. The film retains its relevance and potency. B&W; 109m. **DIR:** Robert Rossen. **CAST:** Broderick Crawford, Joanne Dru, John Ireland, Mercedes McCambridge, John Derek. **1949**

ALL THE RIGHT MOVES ★★★½ Tom Cruise (*Risky Business*) stars in this entertaining coming-of-age picture as a blue-collar high school senior trying to get out of a

Pennsylvania mill town by way of a football scholarship. Rated R for profanity, sex, and nudity. 91m. **DIR:** Michael Chapman. **CAST:** Tom Cruise, Craig T. Nelson, Christopher Penn, Lea Thompson. **1983**

ALL THIS AND HEAVEN TOO ★★★★ Based on a true murder case, this film, set in Paris in 1840, casts Bette Davis as the governess who wins Charles Boyer's heart. Barbara O'Neil is the uncaring mother and obsessed wife who becomes jealous. When she is found murdered, Davis and Boyer become prime suspects. A classic. B&W; 121m. **DIR:** Anatole Litvak. **CAST:** Bette Davis, Charles Boyer, Jeffrey Lynn, Barbara O'Neil, Virginia Weidler, Henry Daniell, Ann Todd, June Lockhart, Harry Davenport. **1940**

ALLIGATOR SHOES ★★ This is pretty much a home movie by two brothers, Gary and Clay Borris. Although their characters here are grownup, they still live at home. When their mentally disturbed aunt moves in, trouble arises. This drama becomes strained before its fatal conclusion. Unrated. 98m. **DIR:** Clay Borris. **CAST:** Gary Borris, Clay Borris, Ronalda Jones, Rose Mallais-Borris. **1982**

ALMOS' A MAN ★★½ You'll have trouble finding firm moral ground in this adaptation of Richard Wright's short story about a boy (LeVar Burton) impatient to achieve adulthood. The conclusion leaves an unpleasant taste. Introduced by Henry Fonda; unrated and suitable for family viewing. 51m. **DIR:** Stan Lathan. **CAST:** LeVar Burton, Madge Sinclair, Robert DoQui, Christopher Brooks, Garry Goodrow. **1976**

ALMOST BLUE ★★½ Jazz saxophonist Michael Madsen is overwhelmed with grief after his wife dies. He attempts to soothe his troubled soul by immersing himself in his music and new girlfriend Lynette Walden, but they only remind him of his loss. Moody and atmospheric, the film is rather downbeat, but that's the blues. Rated R for language and adult situations. 98m. **DIR:** Keoni Waxman. **CAST:** Michael Madsen, Lynette Walden. **1992**

ALOHA SUMMER ★★★½ Chris Makepeace stars as a middle-class, Italian-American teenager who goes to the Hawaiian islands with his family in 1959. Once there, he learns important lessons about life and love. Instead of being just another empty-headed teen exploitation flick, *Aloha Summer* is blessed with sensitivity and insight. Rated PG for violence. 97m. **DIR:** Tommy Lee Wallace. **CAST:** Chris Makepeace, Don Michael Paul, Tia Carrere. **1988**

ALONE IN THE NEON JUNGLE ★★★★ Suzanne Pleshette is top-notch in this superior made-for-TV crime-drama about a woman police captain, heading up the tough Los Angeles Southeast Precinct, called "the sewer." Excellent writing pits Pleshette and her force against drugs and gangs, and a cop killer still on the loose. 90m. **DIR:** Georg Stanford Brown. **CAST:** Suzanne Pleshette, Danny Aiello, Joe Morton. **1991**

ALPHABET CITY 💔 Pretentious movie set in Manhattan's Lower East Side. Rated R for profanity, nudity, and violence. 98m. **DIR:** Amos Poe. **CAST:** Vincent Spano, Kate Vernon, Michael Winslow, Zohra Lampert, Raymond Serra. **1984**

ALWAYS (1989) ★★★★ Steven Spielberg's transcendent remake of *A Guy Named Joe* is touching, funny, life-affirming, and lightweight. Richard Dreyfuss is in top form as a daredevil pilot who dies after saving the life of his buddy (John Goodman). Holly Hunter is the girl Dreyfuss leaves behind—until, that is, he comes back as a guardian angel to a fledgling pilot. Rated PG for brief profanity. 106m. **DIR:** Steven Spielberg. **CAST:** Richard Dreyfuss, Holly Hunter, John Goodman, Audrey Hepburn, Brad Johnson. **1989**

AMAZING GRACE AND CHUCK 💔 Paranoid fantasy about what happens when a 12-year-old Little Leaguer (Joshua Zuehlke) decides to give up baseball in protest of nuclear arms. Rated PG. 115m. **DIR:** Mike Newell. **CAST:** Jamie Lee Curtis, Alex English, Gregory Peck, William L. Petersen, Dennis Lipscomb, Lee Richardson. **1987**

AMAZING HOWARD HUGHES, THE ★★ Howard Hughes was amazing, but little in this account of his life and career would so indicate. Best portrayal is Ed Flanders as longtime, finally turned-upon associate Noah Dietrich. An ambitious TV production that falls short of the mark. 215m. **DIR:** William A. Graham. **CAST:** Tommy Lee Jones, Ed Flanders, Tovah Feldshuh, Sorrell Booke, Lee Purcell, Arthur Franz. **1977**

AMAZING MR. X ★★★ This drama about a bogus medium and the woman he plans to hoodwink is leisurely paced but well written and acted by a solid cast. A pleasant surprise. B&W; 78m. **DIR:** Bernard Vorhaus. **CAST:** Turhan Bey, Cathy O'Donnell, Lynn Bari. **1948**

AMAZING TRANSPLANT, THE 💔 Preposterous melodrama about a penis transplant that turns a young man into a rapist and murderer. Not rated. 80m. **DIR:** Louis Silverman. **CAST:** Juan Fernandez. **1970**

AMBASSADOR, THE ★★★½ *The Ambassador* confronts the Arab-Israeli conflict with a clear head and an optimistic viewpoint. Robert Mitchum plays the controversial U.S. ambassador to Israel, who tries to solve the Palestinian question while being criticized by all factions. Rock Hudson (in his last big-screen role) is the security officer who saves the ambassador's life. Rated R for violence, profanity, sex, and nudity. 97m. **DIR:** J. Lee

Thompson. **CAST:** Robert Mitchum, Rock Hudson, Ellen Burstyn, Fabio Testi, Donald Pleasence. **1984**

AMBUSH MURDERS, THE ★★★ Formulaic TV adaptation of a true story. The title refers to the killing of two California policemen in a black neighborhood. A black activist is framed and it's up to hardworking lawyer James Brolin to get him acquitted. Intermittently engrossing. 98m. **DIR:** Steven H. Stern. **CAST:** James Brolin, Dorian Harewood, Amy Madigan, Antonio Fargas. **1982**

AMERICAN ANTHEM 🦃 Starring 1984 Olympic gold medal gymnast Mitch Gaylord, this film features superb gymnastics. Rated PG. 100m. **DIR:** Albert Magnoli. **CAST:** Mitch Gaylord, Janet Jones, Michelle Phillips. **1986**

AMERICAN BLUE NOTE ★★★ Offbeat nostalgic tale about struggling jazz musicians, circa 1960. Peter MacNicol, in an engaging performance, plays the ever-hopeful but constantly thwarted bandleader who desperately tries to keep his quintet together. Rated PG-13 for profanity. 96m. **DIR:** Ralph Toporoff. **CAST:** Peter MacNicol, Charlotte d'Amboise, Trini Alvarado. **1989**

AMERICAN BOYFRIENDS ★★★½ Precocious Canadian Sandy Wilcox, last seen as the gawky 12-year-old of *My American Cousin*, has matured in this sequel from writer-director Sandy Wilson. This time Sandy attends the wedding of her cousin Butch (John Wildman) in Portland, Oregon. Margaret Langrick, as Sandy, has added drop-dead cuteness to her spunky personality; but Wilson's story has a decidedly bittersweet tone. Rated PG-13 for sexual connotations. 90m. **DIR:** Sandy Wilson. **CAST:** Margaret Langrick, John Wildman. **1989**

AMERICAN CLOCK, THE ★★★★ Telling and thought-provoking look at the stock-market crash of 1929 and the great depression that followed. Engrossing story line, vivid characterizations, and wonderful performances make this a winner based on the Arthur Miller stage play. Made for cable television. 95m. **DIR:** Bob Clark. **CAST:** Kelly Preston, John Randolph, David Strathairn, Joanna Miles, Darren McGavin, Mary McDonnell, Estelle Parsons, Yaphet Kotto, Eddie Bracken, Jim Dale, Tony Roberts, Roberts Blossom, Loren Dean. **1993**

AMERICAN FLYERS ★★★½ Another bicycle-racing tale from writer Steve Tesich (*Breaking Away*), who correctly decided he could milk that theme at least one more time. Kevin Costner and David Marshall Grant star as estranged brothers who get to know and like each other again during a grueling three-day overland race. Rated PG-13 for brief nudity and language. 113m. **DIR:** John Badham. **CAST:** Kevin Costner, David Marshall Grant, Rae Dawn Chong, Alexandra Paul, Janice Rule, John Amos. **1985**

AMERICAN GIGOLO ★★ This story of a male hooker, Julian Kay (Richard Gere), who attends to the physical needs of bored, rich, middle-aged women in Beverly Hills, may be something different. But who needs it? This is sensationalism in the guise of social comment, though it has some incidental humor and impressive performances by Gere and Lauren Hutton. Rated R for explicit depictions of a low lifestyle. 117m. **DIR:** Paul Schrader. **CAST:** Richard Gere, Lauren Hutton, Hector Elizondo, Nina Van Pallandt. **1980**

AMERICAN HEART ★★★½ Tough, realistic film follows the volatile relationship of a recently released convict and his 15-year-old son. As the father and son attempt reconciliation, they are drawn into life on the streets. Movie benefits greatly from gritty location filming and memorable performances, especially Jeff Bridges and Edward Furlong. Rated R for violence and language. 117m. **DIR:** Martin Bell. **CAST:** Jeff Bridges, Edward Furlong, Lucinda Jenney, Don Harvey. **1991**

AMERICAN ME ★★★★★ Brilliant directorial debut by Edward James Olmos has him adopting the storytelling style of his mentor, director Robert M. Young, in depicting thirty years in the life of an East Los Angeles Latino family. Olmos stars as the pivotal character, a hardened criminal who finds his soul too late. A cinema milestone. Rated R for violence, nudity, and profanity. 126m. **DIR:** Edward James Olmos. **CAST:** Edward James Olmos, William Forsythe, Pepe Serna, Danny De La Paz, Evelina Fernandez. **1992**

AMERICANA ★★½ Strange, offbeat film about a Vietnam veteran (director David Carradine) who attempts to rebuild a merry-go-round in a rural Kansas town and meets with hostility from the locals. Carradine attempts to make a statement about rebuilding America, but this gets lost in the impressionistic haze of his film. Rated PG for violence and profanity. 90m. **DIR:** David Carradine. **CAST:** David Carradine, Barbara Hershey, Michael Greene, Bruce Carradine, John Blythe Barrymore. **1981**

AMIN: THE RISE AND FALL 🦃 Idi Amin during his reign of terror in Uganda. Rated R for violence, nudity, and profanity. 101m. **DIR:** Richard Fleischer. **CAST:** Joseph Olita. **1981**

AMONG THE CINDERS ★★½ A teenager (Paul O'Shea) holds himself responsible for the accidental death of a friend, and it takes a trip to the wilds with his grandfather (Derek Hardwick) to pull him out of it. This coming-of-age drama from New Zealand has its good moments, but these are outnumbered by the unremarkable ones. Rated R for nudity, profanity, suggested sex, and brief gore. 105m. **DIR:** Rolf Haedrick. **CAST:** Paul O'Shea, Derek Hardwick. **1985**

AMONGST FRIENDS ★★★★ Writer-director Rob Weiss's compelling little study of youth led astray makes excellent use of its cast of newcomers. Steve Parlavecchio shines as one of three Long Island teenagers seduced by the easy money of organized crime. Given its humble origins, this is a far more palatable modern gangster drama than *Goodfellas*. Rated R for profanity, violence, and nudity. 88m. **DIR:** Rob Weiss. **CAST:** Steve Parlavecchio, Joseph Lindsey, Patrick McGaw, Mira Sorvino. **1993**

AMY FISHER STORY, THE ★★½ The best of the made-for-television movies about the Long Island Lolita, whose affair with auto mechanic Joey Buttafuoco led her to shoot Buttafuoco's wife, Mary Jo. Drew Barrymore effectively captures the spirit of the tempting teen, but steamy footage added for video features a body double. Not rated, but contains adult situations. 96m. **DIR:** Andy Tennant. **CAST:** Drew Barrymore, Anthony Denison, Harley Jane Kozak. **1993**

ANASTASIA ★★★½ Ingrid Bergman earned her second Oscar for the title role of the young woman who looks amazingly like Anastasia, Czar Nicholas's daughter. (The entire royal family was supposedly assassinated). Is she or isn't she Anastasia? A compelling drama. 105m. **DIR:** Anatole Litvak. **CAST:** Ingrid Bergman, Yul Brynner, Helen Hayes, Akim Tamiroff. **1956**

ANASTASIA: THE MYSTERY OF ANNA ★★½ Star-studded cast can't compensate for the uninspired performance by Amy Irving in the title role of this TV miniseries. She plays the mysterious woman who appeared six years after the Romanov Royalty of Russia were annihilated, claiming to have survived. Rex Harrison plays her staunchest adversary as the current head of the Romanov family. Costuming and music are superior. 208m. **DIR:** Marvin J. Chomsky. **CAST:** Amy Irving, Rex Harrison, Edward Fox, Olivia de Havilland, Omar Sharif, Susan Lucci. **1986**

AND BABY MAKES SIX ★★★ Colleen Dewhurst is a middle-aged mother who becomes pregant. It's too much for her loving husband (Warren Oates), who just doesn't want the responsibility of another child. A wonderful cast proved this made-for-TV movie good enough to produce a sequel, *Baby Comes Home*. 104m. **DIR:** Waris Hussein. **CAST:** Colleen Dewhurst, Warren Oates, Mildred Dunnock, Maggie Cooper, Timothy Hutton. **1979**

AND GOD CREATED WOMAN (1987) 🦃 Rebecca DeMornay is unbelievable as a convict who tries to go straight. Rated R for language, nudity, and simulated sex. 97m. **DIR:** Roger Vadim. **CAST:** Rebecca DeMornay, Vincent Spano, Frank Langella, Donovan Leitch. **1987**

AND I ALONE SURVIVED ★★½ In this TV movie Blair Brown stars as Lauren Elder, the only survivor of a plane crash in California's Sierra Nevada mountains. Based on a true event, the film tends toward the overdramatic and begs for better characterizations. Still, Brown does give a fine performance. 100m. **DIR:** William A. Graham. **CAST:** Blair Brown, David Ackroyd, Vera Miles, G. D. Spradlin. **1978**

AND JUSTICE FOR ALL ★★★½ This is a bristling black comedy starring Al Pacino as a lawyer who becomes fed up with the red tape of our country's legal system. It's both heartrending and darkly hilarious—but not for all tastes. Rated R. 117m. **DIR:** Norman Jewison. **CAST:** Al Pacino, Jack Warden, John Forsythe, Craig T. Nelson. **1979**

AND NOTHING BUT THE TRUTH ★★★ A British film about a TV news magazine—an Anglo *A Current Affair*. Glenda Jackson stars as a documentary filmmaker who must confront a sometimes exploitative reporter (well played by Jon Finch). Superficial but interesting. 90m. **DIR:** Karl Francis. **CAST:** Glenda Jackson, Jon Finch, Kenneth Colley. **1982**

AND THE BAND PLAYED ON ★★★★½ A gripping adaptation of journalist Randy Shilt's book about the early days of the AIDS epidemic. Matthew Modine leads an all-star cast as a scientist with the Center for Disease Control who must battle bureaucracy and ignorance to show that AIDS is everyone's problem, not just that of homosexuals. Part detective thriller, part tearjerker, this film drives home its message from the harrowing opening scenes to the final saddening montage. Rated PG-13 for adult themes. 140m. **DIR:** Roger Spottiswoode. **CAST:** Matthew Modine, Alan Alda, Phil Collins, Richard Gere, Anjelica Huston, Steve Martin, Ian McKellen, Lily Tomlin. **1993**

ANDERSONVILLE TRIAL, THE ★★★★½ Based on MacKinley Kantor's Pulitzer Prize novel, this made-for-TV play tells the story of Andersonville, the notorious Georgia prison where 50,000 northern soldiers suffered and close to 14,000 died. This is one of the great accounts of the Civil War. 150m. **DIR:** George C. Scott. **CAST:** Martin Sheen, William Shatner, Buddy Ebsen, Richard Basehart, Cameron Mitchell, Jack Cassidy. **1970**

ANDY WARHOL'S BAD ★★★½ Carroll Baker stars in this nasty and very sick outing from producer Andy Warhol. She plays a tough mama who runs a squad of female hit men out of her cheery suburban home. Into this strange company comes Perry King as a mysterious stranger who boards there until he completes his "mission." The film has gore, violence, and nudity. 107m. **DIR:** Jed Johnson. **CAST:** Carroll Baker, Perry King, Susan Tyrrell. **1977**

ANGEL AT MY TABLE, AN ★★★★★ New Zealand filmmaker Jane Campion followed her eccentric comedy-drama, *Sweetie*, with this brilliant, affecting, and perceptive portrait of writer Janet Frame. Based on Frame's autobiographic trilogy, the film details her emotional journey through a quirky childhood, a misdiagnosis of mental illness, and a severe, lifelong shyness. Though the film is long, it never seems too long because of its intelligence and style and humanity. If you liked *My Left Foot*, you should love this story of an exceptional artist. Rated R for profanity and sexual frankness. 145m. **DIR:** Jane Campion. **CAST:** Kerry Fox, Alexia Keogh, Karen Fergusson. **1991**

ANGEL CITY ★★★ A family is forced to leave their West Virgina farm and travel to Florida in search of work. Exploited by a corrupt labor-camp boss, the family members open the gates for all the immigrant workers to escape and start their lives again. Made for television. 100m. **DIR:** Philip Leacock. **CAST:** Jennifer Warren, Jennifer Jason Leigh, Mitchell Ryan. **1980**

ANGEL ON MY SHOULDER (1946) ★★★★ In a break from his big-budget prestige screen biographies of the period, Paul Muni stars in this entertaining fantasy as a murdered gangster who makes a deal with the devil. He wants to return to his human form. He gets his wish and spends his time on Earth—as a judge—trying to outwit Satan. B&W; 101m. **DIR:** Archie Mayo. **CAST:** Paul Muni, Anne Baxter, Claude Rains, George Cleveland, Onslow Stevens. **1946**

ANGEL ON MY SHOULDER (1980) ★★★ Remade-for-television update of the 1946 Paul Muni fantasy about a wrongly murdered gangster returned to Earth on a Satanic errand. Genial comedy-drama. 100m. **DIR:** John Berry. **CAST:** Peter Strauss, Richard Kiley, Barbara Hershey, Janis Paige. **1980**

ANGELA ★★ Sophia Loren's 5-month-old son is kidnapped by feisty mob king John Huston. Twenty years pass, and she falls in love with a much younger man. Could the bond be more than originally thought? Turgid. 90m. **DIR:** Boris Sagal. **CAST:** Sophia Loren, Steve Railsback, John Huston, John Vernon. **1977**

ANGELIC CONVERSATION ★★ Eclectic filmmaker and painter Derek Jarman delves into a very personal perspective of his world. A mythic figure summons his inner self to join him on a spiritual quest. Boring, heavy-handed self-indulgence saturated with personal passions and vivid visual fantasies. Liberally laced with narrations of Shakespearean sonnets by Judi Dench. 80m. **DIR:** Derek Jarman. **CAST:** Paul Reynolds, Phillip Williamson. **1985**

ANGELO, MY LOVE ★★★★ Robert Duvall wrote and directed this loosely scripted, wonderfully different movie about a streetwise 11-year-old gypsy boy. Duvall reportedly conceived the project when he spotted the fast-talking, charismatic Angelo Evans on a New York street and decided he ought to be in pictures. Rated R for profanity. 115m. **DIR:** Robert Duvall. **CAST:** Angelo Evans, Michael Evans. **1983**

ANGELS OVER BROADWAY ★★★ Codirected by legendary newsmen and playwrights Ben Hecht and Lee Garmes, this tale of streetwise Douglas Fairbanks's efforts to save would-be suicide John Qualen is full of great dialogue and pithy comments on life. But it lacks the charm that would mark it as a true classic. Recommended for its dialogue, as well as its odd tone. B&W; 80m. **DIR:** Ben Hecht, Lee Garmes. **CAST:** Douglas Fairbanks Jr., Rita Hayworth, Thomas Mitchell, John Qualen. **1940**

ANGIE ★★★★ Emotionally involved tale of a Bensonhurst, NY, woman who becomes pregnant and begins questioning everything about her life—especially when she meets a witty, romantic Englishman (Stephen Rea) who's everything her working-class boyfriend (James Gandolfini) isn't. Geena Davis is excellent as the Italian-American heroine, who isn't always sympathetic but will touch something deep in viewers' hearts. There are some very funny moments as well. Rated R for adult subject matter. 108m. **DIR:** Martha Coolidge. **CAST:** Geena Davis, Stephen Rea, James Gandolfini, Aida Turturro, Philip Bosco, Jenny O'Hara. **1994**

ANIMAL FARM ★★½ Serious, sincere animated adaptation of George Orwell's ingenious satire concerning the follies of government. The treatment would have benefited from greater intensity. The attempt at creating an optimistic ending was ill-advised. Keep in mind the film isn't children's fare. 72m. **DIR:** John Halas, Joy Batchelor. **CAST:** Animated. **1954**

ANIMAL KINGDOM, THE ★★★½ The first filming of a Philip Barry play paved the way for his later *Holiday* and *Philadelphia Story* analyses of marriages, manners, and morals. Leslie Howard lets his hair down with bohemian girlfriend Ann Harding, but he marries snobbish Myrna Loy for appearance's sake, and it backfires. B&W; 85m. **DIR:** Edward H. Griffith. **CAST:** Leslie Howard, Myrna Loy, Ann Harding, William Gargan, Neil Hamilton, Ilka Chase, Henry Stephenson. **1932**

ANN VICKERS ★★★★ Rebuffed by Bruce Cabot, noble and self-sacrificing Irene Dunne scorns all men and turns to social service. Against all odds she seeks penal reform. A somewhat unique women's prison film in that the heroine is not a victimized inmate. B&W; 72m. **DIR:** John Cromwell. **CAST:** Irene Dunne, Bruce Cabot, Walter Huston, Conrad Nagel, Edna May Oliver, J. Carrol Naish. **1933**

ANNA • ★★★★ In this wonderfully offbeat turn on *All About Eve*, Sally Kirkland plays a former Czech film star struggling to find work in New York. Model Paulina Porizkova is fine as the refugee who remembers Kirkland's former glories and insinuates herself into the older woman's life only to surpass her successes in America. In English and Czech with subtitles. Rated PG-13 for nudity and profanity. 100m. **DIR:** Yurek Bogayevicz. **CAST:** Sally Kirkland, Paulina Porizkova, Robert Fields, Stefan Schnabel. **1987**

ANNA AND THE KING OF SIAM ★★★★ This original *King and I* boasts poignant performances that give the characters of Anna Leonowens and King Mongkut a different perspective. It's based on Margaret Landon's memoirs as a governess in the Siamese court during the last century. The story parallels the musical version, but with more details about individual family members. 128m. **DIR:** John Cromwell. **CAST:** Irene Dunne, Rex Harrison, Linda Darnell, Lee J. Cobb, Gale Sondergaard. **1946**

ANNA CHRISTIE (1922) ★★ Anna (Blanche Sweet) is a former prostitute whose struggle for a new life runs her afoul of two men—her father (George F. Marion) and a sailor (Matt Burke). Don't expect any of the edgy, sordid aspects of the Eugene O'Neill original. But Henry Sharp's solid camerawork nicely conveys the dockside scenes. Silent. B&W; 75m. **DIR:** John Griffith Wray. **CAST:** Blanche Sweet, George F. Marion, Matt Burke. **1922**

ANNA CHRISTIE (1930) ★★★★ Greta Garbo is mesmerizing and Marie Dressler hilariously memorable in this early sound classic adapted from Eugene O'Neill's play. The tag line for it in 1930 was "Garbo speaks!" And speak she does, uttering the famous line, "Gif me a viskey, ginger ale on the side, and don't be stingy, baby," while portraying a woman with a shady past. B&W; 90m. **DIR:** Clarence Brown. **CAST:** Greta Garbo, Charles Bickford, Marie Dressler. **1930**

ANNA KARENINA (1935) ★★★★ The forever fascinating, peerless Greta Garbo, a superb supporting cast headed by Fredric March, and the masterful direction of Clarence Brown make this film one of the actress's greatest, a true film classic. B&W; 95m. **DIR:** Clarence Brown. **CAST:** Greta Garbo, Fredric March, Basil Rathbone, Freddie Bartholomew, Maureen O'Sullivan, Reginald Denny, May Robson, Reginald Owen. **1935**

ANNA KARENINA (1947) ★★½ In this version of Tolstoy's classic story of a married woman madly in love with a military officer, Vivien Leigh is miscast as the heroine. Though she tries valiantly, she is overwhelmed by the role. An overly sentimental script doesn't help. B&W; 139m. **DIR:** Julien Duvivier. **CAST:** Vivien Leigh, Kieron Moore, Ralph Richardson, Sally Ann Howes, Michael Gough. **1947**

ANNA KARENINA (1985) ★★ Tolstoy's classic suffers in this tedious remake for television. Garbo did it best in 1935. Paul Scofield as Anna's husband, however, is worth the watch. 150m. **DIR:** Simon Langton. **CAST:** Jacqueline Bisset, Paul Scofield, Christopher Reeve, Ian Ogilvy. **1985**

ANNAPOLIS STORY, AN ★★ John Derek and Kevin McCarthy vie for the hand of Diana Lynn in this formula service academy yarn of rigid training, lights out, bed check, and romance. 81m. **DIR:** Don Siegel. **CAST:** John Derek, Diana Lynn, Kevin McCarthy. **1955**

ANNE OF AVONLEA ★★★★ Anne Shirley matures and falls in love in this sequel to *Anne of Green Gables*, which scripter-director Kevin Sullivan has helmed with the same devotion to period authenticity. 224m. **DIR:** Kevin Sullivan. **CAST:** Megan Follows, Colleen Dewhurst, Wendy Hiller. **1987**

ANNE OF GREEN GABLES (1985) ★★★★ This delightful film, based on L. M. Montgomery's classic novel, is set in 1908 on Canada's Prince Edward Island. Anne (Megan Follows) is a foster child taken in by Matthew (Richard Farnsworth) and Marilla Cuthbert (Colleen Dewhurst), who mistakenly expect her to be a farmhand. Unrated; suitable for family viewing. 240m. **DIR:** Kevin Sullivan. **CAST:** Megan Follows, Richard Farnsworth, Colleen Dewhurst. **1985**

ANNE OF THE THOUSAND DAYS ★★★ The story of Anne Boleyn, Henry VIII's second wife and mother of Queen Elizabeth I, is given the big-budget treatment. Luckily, the tragic tale of a woman who is at first pressured into an unwanted union with England's lusty king, only to fall in love with him and eventually lose her head to court intrigue, is not lost beneath the spectacle. Genevieve Bujold's well-balanced performance of Anne carries the entire production. 146m. **DIR:** Charles Jarrott. **CAST:** Genevieve Bujold, Richard Burton, Anthony Quayle. **1969**

ANOTHER COUNTRY ★★★½ For this film, Julian Mitchell adapted his stage play about Guy Burgess, an Englishman who became a spy for Russia in the 1930s. Little in this story reportedly was based on fact. Still, Mitchell's postulations provide interesting viewing, and Rupert Everett's lead performance—as Guy "Bennett"—is stunning. Rated PG for suggested sex and profanity. 90m. **DIR:** Marek Kanievska. **CAST:** Rupert Everett, Colin Firth, Cary Elwes. **1984**

ANOTHER TIME, ANOTHER PLACE (1958) ★★ Ho-hum melodrama about American newspaperwoman whose brief affair with British journalist ends in tragedy when he dies during World War II. B&W; 98m. **DIR:** Lewis Allen. **CAST:** Lana Turner, Barry Sullivan, Glynis Johns, Sean Connery, Sidney James. **1958**

ANOTHER TIME, ANOTHER PLACE (1984) ★★★ In this British import set in 1944, a woman named Janie (Phyllis Logan) lives on a small farm in Scotland with her husband, Dongal (Paul Young), fifteen years her senior. As part of a war rehabilitation program, the couple welcomes three Italian POW's onto their place, and Janie falls in love. Rated PG. 118m. **DIR:** Michael Radford. **CAST:** Phyllis Logan, Paul Young. **1984**

ANOTHER WOMAN ★★★★ A subtle, purposely enigmatic yet engrossing portrait of a woman reassessing her own identity and purpose. Gena Rowlands is superb as a college professor whose life is not as solid as she assumes. When she overhears another woman (Mia Farrow) in a session with her psychoanalyst, Rowlands begins to have doubts. Rated PG. 81m. **DIR:** Woody Allen. **CAST:** Gena Rowlands, Gene Hackman, Ian Holm, Mia Farrow, John Houseman, Blythe Danner, Sandy Dennis. **1988**

ANTHONY ADVERSE ★★★½ Fredric March, in the title role, wanders around early nineteenth-century America and Mexico, sowing oats, and buckling swash, in this all-stops-out romantic blockbuster. B&W; 136m. **DIR:** Mervyn LeRoy. **CAST:** Fredric March, Olivia de Havilland, Anita Louise, Donald Woods, Edmund Gwenn, Claude Rains, Louis Hayward, Gale Sondergaard, Henry O'Neill. **1936**

ANTONY AND CLEOPATRA (1973) ★★ Marginal film interpretation of Shakespeare's play. Obviously a tremendous amount of work on Charlton Heston's part, casting himself as Antony, but the film is lacking in energy. Rated PG. 160m. **DIR:** Charlton Heston. **CAST:** Charlton Heston, Hildegard Neil, Eric Porter, Fernando Rey, John Castle. **1973**

ANTONY AND CLEOPATRA (1981) ★★★½ Timothy Dalton and Lynn Redgrave are fine as Marc Antony and Cleopatra in this filmed stage production of Shakespeare's tale of passion, war, and betrayal in Egypt and Rome. John Carradine is outstanding as the soothsayer who foretells it all. A Bard Productions Ltd. release. 183m. **DIR:** Lawrence Carra. **CAST:** Timothy Dalton, Lynn Redgrave, Nichelle Nichols, John Carradine, Anthony Geary, Barrie Ingham, Walter Koenig, Brian Kerwin, Kim Miyori. **1981**

ANY MAN'S DEATH ★★½ John Savage plays a traumatized Vietnam-vet-turned-journalist sent to Africa. He discovers a strange scientist (William Hickey) whose human experiments have killed thousands. Confusing kaleidoscope of events leaves more questions than answers. Rated R for profanity and violence. 105m. **DIR:** Tom Clegg. **CAST:** John Savage, William Hickey, Mia Sara, Ernest Borgnine. **1989**

ANY NUMBER CAN PLAY ★★★½ Wonderful cast in an absorbing drama revolving around the personal and professional problems of honest gambling-house owner Clark Gable. Marjorie Rambeau is a standout. Screenplay by Richard Brooks. B&W; 112m. **DIR:** Mervyn LeRoy. **CAST:** Clark Gable, Alexis Smith, Wendell Corey, Audrey Totter, Darryl Hickman, Frank Morgan, Lewis Stone, Barry Sullivan, Mary Astor, Marjorie Rambeau, Leon Ames, Edgar Buchanan, William Conrad. **1949**

ANZACS ★★★★ The ANZACS (Australian/New Zealand Army Corps) join the British in World War I to stir up a few stuffed shirts among the very stiff English. Emphasis is upon the friendship and loyalty among the Australians. Paul Hogan provides a few moments of comic relief. A powerful war film that dwells on the people involved, not the machinery. Made for television, this is unrated but deals with mature subject matter. 165m. **DIR:** George Miller. **CAST:** Andrew Clark, Paul Hogan, Megan Williams. **1985**

APPLAUSE ★★★★½ This is a remarkable early sound-era movie. Filmed at actual New York locations, it tells the story of a fading vaudeville star (Helen Morgan) who loses the love of her daughter and is jilted by her lowly boyfriend. A smashing success. B&W; 78m. **DIR:** Rouben Mamoulian. **CAST:** Helen Morgan, Joan Peers. **1929**

APPRENTICESHIP OF DUDDY KRAVITZ, THE ★★★ Richard Dreyfuss, in an early starring role, is the main attraction in this quirky little comedy about a poor Jewish lad from a Montreal ghetto. The story is full of cruel and smart-assed humor, a trait that haunts Dreyfuss to this day. Ultimately, the film is too long and too shrill. Rated PG for sexual content. 121m. **DIR:** Ted Kotcheff. **CAST:** Richard Dreyfuss, Jack Warden, Micheline Lanctot, Denholm Elliott, Randy Quaid. **1974**

ARCH OF TRIUMPH ★★★ In Paris before the Nazis arrive, a refugee doctor meets and falls in love with a woman with a past in this long, slow-paced, emotionless drama. It's sad, frustrating, tedious, and sometimes murky, but fans of the principal players will forgive and enjoy. B&W; 120m. **DIR:** Lewis Milestone. **CAST:** Ingrid Bergman, Charles Boyer, Charles Laughton, Louis Calhern. **1948**

ARENA BRAINS 🦃 This experimental short is not rated, but contains nudity and profanity. 34m. **DIR:** Robert Longo. **CAST:** Ray Liotta, Eric Bogosian, Sean Young. **1988**

ARRANGEMENT, THE 🦃 The cast is the only real reason for watching this tedious talkfest. Rated R for language. 127m. **DIR:** Elia Kazan. **CAST:** Kirk Douglas, Deborah Kerr, Faye Dunaway, Richard Boone. **1969**

ARROGANT, THE 🦃 A waitress and a philosophy-spouting motorcyclist. There's enough profanity, violence, and nudity to earn an R rating. 86m. **DIR:** Philippe Blot. **CAST:** Gary Graham, Sylvia Kristel. **1987**

ARROWSMITH ★★★★ Mellifluous-voiced Ronald Colman is a young, career-dedicated research doctor tempted by the profits of commercialism in this faithful rendering of Sinclair Lewis's noted novel of medicine. Helen Hayes is his first wife—doomed to die before he sees the light. This is the first film to center seriously on a doctor's career and raise the question of professional integrity and morality versus quick money and social status. B&W; 101m. **DIR:** John Ford. **CAST:** Ronald Colman, Helen Hayes, Richard Bennett, DeWitt Jennings, Beulah Bondi, Myrna Loy. **1931**

ARTHUR'S HALLOWED GROUND ★★ An elderly British gent stands his ground against the system in order to protect his beloved land. A good premise, until one realizes the bit of turf in question is a field on which to play cricket! 88m. **DIR:** Freddie Young. **CAST:** Michael Elphick, Jimmy Jewel, David Swift. **1973**

ARTICLE 99 ★★★½ VA hospitals take it on the chin in scripter Ron Cutler's acerbic blend of *M*A*S*H* and *Catch-22,* which concerns a governmental regulation denying treatment to veterans who cannot prove their injuries are war-related. Cutler's stinging satire eventually yields to a dubiously happy ending, but getting there is a lot of fun. Rated R for profanity and graphic medical procedures. 98m. **DIR:** Howard Deutch. **CAST:** Ray Liotta, Kiefer Sutherland, Forest Whitaker, John C. McGinley, Lea Thompson, John Mahoney, Kathy Baker, Eli Wallach. **1992**

AS IS ★★½ How AIDS affects family and loved ones is dealt with in a thoughtful manner as Robert Carradine portrays a homosexual who contracts the disease. Jonathan Hadary is the lover who stands by him. Although not preachy, the film does suffer from staginess. Not rated, but the whole concept is adult in nature, and some coarse language is used. 86m. **DIR:** Michael Lindsay-Hogg. **CAST:** Robert Carradine, Jonathan Hadary, Joanna Miles, Alan Scarfe, Colleen Dewhurst. **1986**

AS SUMMERS DIE ★★★½ A very leisurely story set in Georgia, 1959, concerns a southern aristocratic family's attempt to wrest control of land given to a black woman years earlier, because oil deposits have been found on it. Plot line is nothing new but the performances by a veteran cast carry this HBO film. Bette Davis has some touching moments as a woman whose mental competency is challenged. 87m. **DIR:** Jean-Claude Tramont. **CAST:** Scott Glenn, Jamie Lee Curtis, Bette Davis, John Randolph, Ron O'Neal, Bruce McGill, John McIntire, Beah Richards. **1987**

AS YOU DESIRE ME ★★ Greta Garbo plays an amnesiac, and her attempt to be sexy means putting on a blond wig. It works only up to a point. Based on a play by Pirandello, the film remains resolutely stage bound. B&W; 71m. **DIR:** George Fitzmaurice. **CAST:** Greta Garbo, Erich Von Stroheim, Melvyn Douglas, Owen Moore, Hedda Hopper. **1932**

ASH WEDNESDAY ★★½ Elizabeth Taylor plays an aging woman who undergoes a painful cosmetic make-over in order to make herself more appealing to husband Henry Fonda. This disjointed morality play has some good moments, but offensive close-ups of the facial operation and the melodramatic predictability of the story eventually work against it. Rated R. 99m. **DIR:** Larry Peerce. **CAST:** Elizabeth Taylor, Henry Fonda, Helmut Berger, Keith Baxter, Margaret Blye, Monique Van Vooren. **1973**

ASPEN EXTREME ★★★½ Despite its party-hearty appearance, writer-director Patrick Hasburgh's impressive little B movie at times veers dangerously close toward intelligence and wit. Paul Gross and Peter Berg leave dead-end jobs in Detroit to hire on as Aspen ski instructors, where the former's California-style good looks make an immediate impression with predatory rich lady Finola Hughes. Rated PG-13 for profanity and suggested sex. 117m. **DIR:** Patrick Hasburgh. **CAST:** Paul Gross, Peter Berg, Finola Hughes, Teri Polo, William Russ. **1993**

ASSASSIN OF YOUTH (A.K.A. MARIJUANA) ★★ This silly, low-budget exploitation film tells the story of a courageous young reporter who goes undercover to infiltrate the marijuana cult that has been wreaking havoc with a local town. Cornball humor gives this an extra edge on most films of this nature. B&W; 67m. **DIR:** Elmer Clifton. **CAST:** Luana Walters, Arthur Gardner, Earl Dwire. **1936**

ASSASSINATION OF TROTSKY, THE 🦃 Richard Burton as the exiled Soviet leader. A chaotic yawner. Rated R. 102m. **DIR:** Joseph Losey. **CAST:** Richard Burton, Alain Delon, Romy Schneider. **1972**

ASSAULT AT WEST POINT ★★★ Although based on a reprehensible actual event, misfired casting prevents this film from consuming us with the rage felt by writer-director Harry Moses. Newcomer Seth Gilliam remains too detached as Johnson Whittaker, the first black cadet accepted at West Point, whose military career was derailed after he was assaulted . . . *and "proved" to have beaten himself unconscious.* The usually excellent Sam Waterston is uncomfortably stiff as Whittaker's defense attorney, and the story never quite connects. Rated PG for mild profanity and brief violence. 95m. **DIR:** Harry Moses. **CAST:** Samuel L. Jackson, Sam Waterston, Seth Gilliam, John Glover, Josef Sommer, Mason Adams. **1994**

AT PLAY IN THE FIELDS OF THE LORD 🦃 A boring movie without redeeming social value in spite of its high-powered cast tells a dramatic story, but Babenco's overbearing style makes it unbearable to watch. Rated R for nudity and profanity. 186m. **DIR:** Hector Babenco. **CAST:** Kathy Bates, John Lithgow, Aidan Quinn, Tom Berenger, Daryl Hannah, Tom Waits. 1991

ATLANTIC CITY ★★★★★ This superb motion picture has all of the elements that made the films of Hollywood's golden age great—with a few appropriately modern twists tossed in. The screenplay, by John Guare—about a struggling casino worker (Susan Sarandon) who becomes involved in a drug deal—gives us powerful drama, wonderful characters, memorable dialogue, and delightfully funny situations. And the performances by Burt Lancaster, Sarandon, and Kate Reid, in particular, are top-notch. Rated R because of brief nudity and violence. 104m. **DIR:** Louis Malle. **CAST:** Burt Lancaster, Susan Sarandon, Kate Reid. 1981

ATTIC: THE HIDING OF ANNE FRANK ★★★★ The true story of Anne Frank seen from the viewpoint of Miep Gies, the woman who risked everything to hide the Jewish families during World War II. William Hanley's teleplay wonderfully depicts the events outside the attic and the harsh realities of the German occupation. Great performances all around, especially from Mary Steenburgen, who portrays Gies. 95m. **DIR:** John Erman. **CAST:** Mary Steenburgen, Paul Scofield, Huub Stapel, Eleanor Bron, Frances Cuka. 1988

ATTICA ★★★★ This made-for-TV account of the horrifying Attica prison riots of 1971 is a very detailed translation of Tom Wicker's bestselling book *A Time to Die.* Screenwriter James Henerson deserves kudos for this adaptation. The performances are uniformly excellent. 100m. **DIR:** Marvin J. Chomsky. **CAST:** Charles Durning, George Grizzard, Anthony Zerbe, Glynn Turman, Henry Darrow. 1980

AUTOBIOGRAPHY OF A PRINCESS ★★½ A captivating performance by Indian actress Madhur Jaffrey dominates this mundane, British teledrama about an exiled Indian princess and her father's ex-tutor (James Mason) sharing memories of colonial India. Unusual for a Merchant-Ivory production, this too-short film suffers from a lack of character development, uninspired dialogue, and an absence of lavish production quality. 59m. **DIR:** James Ivory. **CAST:** James Mason, Madhur Jaffrey. 1975

AUTOBIOGRAPHY OF MISS JANE PITTMAN, THE ★★★★★ This terrific television movie traces black history in America from the Civil War years to the turbulent civil rights movement of the 1960s. All this is seen through the eyes of 110-year-old ex-slave Jane Pittman (Cicely Tyson). The entire cast is superb, but Tyson still manages to tower above the others in the title role. There is no rating, but it should be noted that there are some violent scenes. 110m. **DIR:** John Korty. **CAST:** Cicely Tyson, Richard Dysart, Odetta, Michael Murphy, Thalmus Rasulala. 1974

AUTUMN LEAVES ★★½ Troubled middle-aged typist Joan Crawford is further anguished after marrying a younger man (Cliff Robertson) who proves to be mentally disturbed and already married. Run-of-the-mill Crawford fare. B&W; 108m. **DIR:** Robert Aldrich. **CAST:** Joan Crawford, Cliff Robertson, Vera Miles, Lorne Greene. 1956

AVALON ★★★★½ For the third film in his Baltimore trilogy, which also includes *Tin Men* and *Diner,* writer-director Barry Levinson has created what may come to be considered his masterpiece: a heart-tugging story of fifty years in the lives of three generations of Russian-Jewish immigrants. Armin Mueller-Stahl gives an unforgettable performance as the ultimate grandfather, whose honest values and love of family are slowly pushed out of fashion by something called progress. Rated PG for brief profanity. 126m. **DIR:** Barry Levinson. **CAST:** Armin Mueller-Stahl, Aidan Quinn, Elizabeth Perkins, Joan Plowright, Elijah Wood, Lou Jacobi. 1990

AVIATOR, THE ★★ This film, about a grumpy flyer (Christopher Reeve) during the 1920s who is forced to take a feisty passenger (Rosanna Arquette) on his mail route, is too similar to *High Road to China.* It has neither the high adventure nor the humor of the latter. Rated PG. 102m. **DIR:** George Miller. **CAST:** Christopher Reeve, Rosanna Arquette, Jack Warden, Scott Wilson, Tyne Daly, Sam Wanamaker. 1984

AWAKENING OF CASSIE, THE ★★ Rather dispassionate coming-of-age film about a country girl who brings her paintings to the Big Apple where she must choose between a childish sculptor and a married man. A Romance Theatre production introduced by Louis Jourdan. Unrated, this TV production is very tame. 97m. **DIR:** Jim Drake. **CAST:** P. J. Soles, David Hedison, Patty McCormack, Richard Deacon. 1982

AWAKENINGS ★★★★½ With *Big* Penny Marshall proved herself to be a gifted filmmaker. *Awakenings* is even better: a masterpiece of characterization. In a story based on true incident, a properly subdued Robin Williams plays a doctor who fights to use an experimental drug on a group of catatonic patients, whom he believes are "alive inside." Robert De Niro is the first recipient of this medication, and his transformation is miraculous. Rated PG-13 for profanity and light violence. 121m. **DIR:** Penny Marshall. **CAST:** Robert De Niro, Robin Williams, Julie Kavner, Ruth Nelson, John Heard, Penelope Ann Miller, Max von Sydow. 1990

BABE, THE ★★★★ In this old-fashioned, Hollywood-style bio-pic, John Goodman hits a home run as Babe Ruth. We like it better than *The Babe Ruth Story* because of its grit and seeming no-holds-barred honesty. The legend makes for a memorable motion picture. Rated PG for profanity. 115m. **DIR:** Arthur Hiller. **CAST:** John Goodman, Kelly McGillis, Trini Alvarado, Bruce Boxleitner, Peter Donat, J. C. Quinn. **1992**

BABE RUTH STORY, THE ★★ Bio-pic about baseball's most famous hero is long on sap and short on facts as it milks every situation for maximum sentimental value. The supporting cast is good, but William Bendix just doesn't make the grade as the immortal Bambino. B&W; 106m. **DIR:** Roy Del Ruth. **CAST:** William Bendix, Claire Trevor, Charles Bickford, Sam Levene, William Frawley, Stanley Clements. **1948**

BABY CAKES ★★★★ Ricki Lake is adorable as the plump girl who sets her sights on gorgeous Craig Sheffer, even though her friends and family tell her that someone of his caliber wouldn't be interested in her. This delightful film proves that beauty is more than skin-deep. Playful and inspiring, with both stars especially likable. 93m. **DIR:** Paul Schneider. **CAST:** Ricki Lake, Craig Sheffer, Betty Buckley, John Karlen. **1989**

BABY DOLL ★★★★ Set in hot, humid, sleazy Mississippi, this is the story of a child bride (Carroll Baker) who sleeps in a crib, her lusting, short-on-brains husband (Karl Malden), and a scheming business rival (Eli Wallach) determined to use and abuse them both. What else but a Tennessee Williams story? When first released, the film was condemned by the Legion of Decency. Baker's skimpy pajamas became fashionable. B&W; 114m. **DIR:** Elia Kazan. **CAST:** Carroll Baker, Eli Wallach, Karl Malden, Mildred Dunnock, Lonny Chapman, Rip Torn. **1956**

BABY FACE ★★★ Ambitious Barbara Stanwyck uses her looks and her charms to work her way from a saloon to a fancy salon in this mildly scandalous but eventually moralistic study. Stanwyck does a standout job, and her aggressive sexuality is pretty much implied despite the furor it raised with the censors of the day. B&W; 70m. **DIR:** Alfred E. Green. **CAST:** Barbara Stanwyck, George Brent, Donald Cook, Douglass Dumbrille, Margaret Lindsay, John Wayne. **1933**

BABY GIRL SCOTT ★★★½ Emotional and tragic story of older parents forced to deal with a dangerously small premature baby and doctors who overstep their boundaries. Well acted and quite gripping, though a bit melodramatic. Not rated. 97m. **DIR:** John Korty. **CAST:** Mary Beth Hurt, John Lithgow. **1987**

BABY, IT'S YOU ★★★★ Writer-director John Sayles has such an unerring sense of what's right in a scene and such a superb ear for dialogue that his movies often seem more like intimate documentaries than simple fiction. So it is with this enjoyable movie about the trials and tribulations of high school kids in Trenton, New Jersey, circa 1966. *Baby, It's You* is not only funny and touching, but also very sexy. Rated R for violence, profanity, and nudity. 105m. **DIR:** John Sayles. **CAST:** Rosanna Arquette, Vincent Spano. **1983**

BABY MAKER, THE ★★ Still timely if overwrought drama of a couple who hire Barbara Hershey to have a baby when it is discovered the wife is barren. Mediocre dialogue, too many beach scenes, and some not-so-interesting subsidiary characters drag this potentially exciting drama to a halt. One of Hershey's first roles. 109m. **DIR:** James Bridges. **CAST:** Barbara Hershey, Colin Wilcox-Horne, Scott Glenn, Sam Groom, Jeannie Berlin. **1970**

BABY THE RAIN MUST FALL ★★½ This confusing character study of a convict who is paroled and reunited with his family raises a lot of questions but answers none of them. B&W; 100m. **DIR:** Robert Mulligan. **CAST:** Steve McQueen, Lee Remick, Don Murray. **1965**

BACHELOR, THE ★★★ This exquisite period piece finds turn-of-the-century doctor Keith Carradine reexamining his life after his sister, upon whom he was very dependent, dies. He eventually finds friendship and then love with a widow, wonderfully played by Miranda Richardson. Set in England, with picture-postcard scenery and dignified performances throughout. Rated PG-13 for adult situations. 105m. **DIR:** Roberto Faenza. **CAST:** Keith Carradine, Miranda Richardson, Max von Sydow, Kristin Scott-Thomas. **1993**

BACK FROM ETERNITY ★★ No surprises in this rehash of similar films about a handful of people who survive a calamity (in this case, an airplane crash) and have to learn to cope with their predicament as well as with each other. Basically a potboiler that depends on stock footage and phony studio sets, this tired story limps along and gives Anita Ekberg plenty of opportunity to show off her torn blouse. B&W; 97m. **DIR:** John Farrow. **CAST:** Robert Ryan, Anita Ekberg, Rod Steiger, Phyllis Kirk. **1956**

BACK ROADS ★★★ Pug (Tommy Lee Jones) and prostitute (Sally Field) hitch and brawl down the back roads of the South in this sometimes raunchy, often hilarious romance-fantasy. Though it drags a bit, the performances by the two stars and an earthy, down-home charm make it worthwhile. Rated R. 94m. **DIR:** Martin Ritt. **CAST:** Sally Field, Tommy Lee Jones, David Keith. **1981**

BACK STREET ★★★ Third version of novelist Fannie Hurst's romantic tearjerker about clandestine love, with Susan Hayward as the noble mistress who stands by her lover even when he stupidly marries another woman. 107m. **DIR:** David Miller. **CAST:** Susan Hayward, John Gavin, Vera Miles. **1961**

BACK TO HANNIBAL: THE RETURN OF TOM SAWYER AND HUCKLEBERRY FINN ★★★ Decent guess at what Mark Twain's lovable scamps might have grown up to be. Tom, a Chicago lawyer, and Huck, a St. Louis reporter, return to their hometown when their friend, Jim, the former slave, is falsely accused of murder. Lacks the wit and ingenuity of Twain but remains reasonably entertaining. Made for the Disney channel, this is family fare. 95m. **DIR:** Paul Krasny. **CAST:** Raphael Sbarge, Paul Winfield, Mitchell Anderson, Megan Follows, William Windom, Ned Beatty. **1990**

BACKDOOR TO HEAVEN ★★★½ With superb performances from a talented cast, this strong social drama is somewhat dated but still compelling. A poor young man must make a choice: a lifetime of toil and repression or a career of crime. B&W; 86m. **DIR:** William K. Howard. **CAST:** Aline MacMahon, Wallace Ford, Stu Erwin, Van Heflin. **1939**

BACKSTREET DREAMS 🦃 Airheaded mush about a small-time mob enforcer. Rated R for violence and profanity. 104m. **DIR:** Rupert Hitzig. **CAST:** Brooke Shields, Jason O'Malley, Anthony Franciosa, Burt Young, Sherilyn Fenn, Nick Cassavetes, Elias Koteas. **1990**

BACKTRACK ★★★ An impressive ensemble cast, which includes uncredited cameos by Joe Pesci and Charlie Sheen, turns this quixotic, made-for-cable thriller into an intriguing curiosity. Electronic artist Jodie Foster witnesses a mob slaying, and then flees for her life from torpedo Dennis Hopper...who abandons the contract after falling in love with her. A bit overlong, but interesting. Contains profanity, violence, nudity, and kinky sexual overtones. 102m. **DIR:** Dennis Hopper. **CAST:** Dennis Hopper, Jodie Foster, Dean Stockwell, Vincent Price, John Turturro, Fred Ward, Bob Dylan. **1990**

BAD AND THE BEAUTIFUL, THE ★★★★½ Dynamite story of a Hollywood producer (Kirk Douglas) and his turbulent relations with a studio actress (Lana Turner). Along the way there are fine performances by all of the cast. It's old Hollywood gloss, and very good, indeed. Five Oscars for this gem. B&W; 118m. **DIR:** Vincente Minnelli. **CAST:** Lana Turner, Kirk Douglas, Gloria Grahame, Dick Powell, Barry Sullivan, Walter Pidgeon, Gilbert Roland. **1952**

BAD BOYS ★★★★½ A grimly riveting vision of troubled youth. Sean Penn and Esai Morales are Chicago street hoods sworn to kill each other in prison. It's exciting, thought-provoking, and violent, but the violence, for once, is justified and not merely exploitative. Rated R for language, violence, and nudity. 123m. **DIR:** Rick Rosenthal. **CAST:** Sean Penn, Esai Morales, Reni Santoni, Ally Sheedy, Jim Moody, Eric Gurry. **1983**

BAD DAY AT BLACK ROCK ★★★★ Spencer Tracy gives one of his greatest performances in this suspenseful, action-packed drama as a one-armed man who stirs up trouble when he arrives at a western town whose citizens have a guilty secret. Robert Ryan is superb as the main villain. Lee Marvin and Ernest Borgnine ooze menace as brutal, sadistic henchmen. 81m. **DIR:** John Sturges. **CAST:** Spencer Tracy, Robert Ryan, Anne Francis, Walter Brennan, Lee Marvin, Ernest Borgnine. **1955**

BAD GIRLS GO TO HELL ★★ Sleaze-film addict Joe Bob Briggs introduces another of Doris Wishman's Sixties drive-in weirdies. A dim-witted sexpot housewife is repeatedly ravaged by gross hairy men and lesbians amid tacky Fifties-living-room decor. Miniscule plot line features early doses of sadism and masochism with all the bawdiness of a suburban home movie. 98m. **DIR:** Doris Wishman. **CAST:** Gigi Darlene. **1965**

BAD LIEUTENANT ★★★½ Tough, raw, uncompromising police drama follows the last days of a corrupt New York police lieutenant as he works on a rape case involving a nun. Film pulls no punches in showing the physical as well as the moral corruption of the title character. Be forewarned, some scenes are extremely tough to watch. Rated NC-17 for nudity, drug use, language, violence, and moral deprivation. 96m. **DIR:** Abel Ferrara. **CAST:** Harvey Keitel, Victor Argo, Paul Calderon. **1992**

BAD SEED, THE ★★½ Despite the contrived ending and pathetically cutesy "curtain call," this story of a perfectly wicked child protected by her image is still capable of generating chills. Nancy Kelly may be more than a bit melodramatic as the concerned mother on a constant crying jag, but young Patty McCormack has that special cold beauty that makes her crimes all the more hideous. B&W; 129m. **DIR:** Mervyn LeRoy. **CAST:** Patty McCormack, Nancy Kelly, Henry Jones, Eileen Heckart, William Hopper. **1956**

BADGE OF THE ASSASSIN ★★★½ Fine reenactment of the pursuit, capture, and trial of three radical black men who killed two policemen in Harlem in 1971. James Woods and Yaphet Kotto are intense as the assistant DA and detective who must make their case stick against the three ruthless killers. Rated R for violence and profanity. 96m. **DIR:** Mel Damski. **CAST:** James Woods, Yaphet Kotto, Alex Rocco, David Harris. **1985**

BADLANDS ★★★★ Featuring fine performances by Sissy Spacek, Martin Sheen, and Warren Oates, this is a disturbing recreation of the Starkweather-Fugate killing spree of the 1950s. It is undeniably a work of intelligence and fine craftsmanship. However, as with Martin Scorsese's *Taxi Driver* and Bob Fosse's *Star 80, Badlands* is not an easy film to watch. Rated PG. 95m. **DIR:** Terence Malick. **CAST:** Martin Sheen, Sissy Spacek, Warren Oates, Ramon Bieri, Alan Vint. **1973**

BAIL JUMPER ★★★ A small-town thug and his ex-con girlfriend flee Missouri in search of the good life in New York City in this surreal love-on-the-run road movie. Bizarre romp through the American landscape that is reminiscent of David Lynch's *Wild at Heart* and Jim Jarmusch's *Mystery Train*. Not rated. 96m. **DIR:** Christian Faber. **CAST:** Eszter Balint, B. J. Spalding. **1989**

BAJA OKLAHOMA ★★ Lesley Ann Warren plays a tired bartender who dreams of success as a country-and-western songwriter. Willie Nelson and Emmylou Harris make cameo appearances as themselves. Made for HBO, this contains profanity, violence, and partial nudity. 100m. **DIR:** Bobby Roth. **CAST:** Lesley Ann Warren, Peter Coyote, Swoosie Kurtz, Billy Vera. **1988**

BALBOA 🦃 Tacky soap about a ruthless millionaire. Unrated; this film contains nudity. 92m. **DIR:** James Polakof. **CAST:** Tony Curtis, Carol Lynley, Steve Kanaly, Chuck Connors. **1982**

BALCONY, THE ★★★★ Jean Genet's hard-hitting surreal political fable is set in a brothel of illusion, where the customers take over real power during a revolution. Peter Falk sizzles in the role of a police chief who uses the whorehouse as a rallying point from which to suppress the revolution. Outrageous, poignant satire on the church and state, brilliantly performed by a top-notch cast. B&W; 87m. **DIR:** Joseph Strick. **CAST:** Shelley Winters, Peter Falk, Leonard Nimoy, Lee Grant. **1963**

BALLAD OF THE SAD CAFE, THE ★★★ Strangeness abounds in this visually appealing tale of a masochist's love for a hard, angular spinster. For its sparse content, the film has a deliberate slow-as-molasses pace, and in that time it takes many Southern stereotypes and turns them upside down. Based on the story by Carson McCullers. Rated PG-13 for violence. 100m. **DIR:** Simon Callow. **CAST:** Vanessa Redgrave, Keith Carradine, Rod Steiger. **1992**

BANG THE DRUM SLOWLY ★★★★ Robert De Niro and Michael Moriarty are given a perfect showcase for their acting talents in this poignant film, and they don't disappoint. The friendship of two baseball players comes alive as the team's star pitcher (Moriarty) tries to assist journeyman catcher (De Niro) in completing one last season before succumbing to Hodgkin's disease. The story may lead to death, but it is filled with life, hope, and compassion. Rated PG. 98m. **DIR:** John Hancock. **CAST:** Robert De Niro, Michael Moriarty, Vincent Gardenia. **1973**

BARABBAS ★★½ Early Dino De Laurentis opus is long on production, short on credibility. Standard gory religious spectacle follows the life of the thief Barabbas, whom Pilate freed when Jesus was condemned to die. Good cast of veteran character actors attempts to move this epic along, but fails. 144m. **DIR:** Richard Fleischer. **CAST:** Anthony Quinn, Jack Palance, Ernest Borgnine, Katy Jurado. **1962**

BARBARIAN AND THE GEISHA, THE 🦃 American ambassador to Japan during the nineteenth century finds romance with geisha. 105m. **DIR:** John Huston. **CAST:** John Wayne, Sam Jaffe, Eiko Ando. **1958**

BARBARIANS AT THE GATE ★★★★ The legacy of the 1980s—corporate greed—is brilliantly indited in Larry Gelbart's rollicking made-for-cable adaptation of Bryan Borrough and John Helyar's equally mesmerizing account of the Nabisco takeover. James Garner has a plum-starring role as "good ol' boy" F. Ross Johnson, the Nabisco CEO who battled the circling sharks in an effort to take control of the company he professed to love so dearly. Rated R for profanity. 107m. **DIR:** Glenn Jordan. **CAST:** James Garner, Jonathan Pryce, Peter Riegert, Joanna Cassidy, Fred Dalton Thompson, Mark Harelik. **1993**

BARBARY COAST, THE ★★★½ Big-budget Hollywood hokum drew its inspiration from Herbert Asbury's colorful history of early San Francisco, but tailored the book to fit the unique talents of its great cast. This story of femme fatale Miriam Hopkins and the men in her life is fun for the whole family and a treat for film buffs who like the look of the past as created on studio back lots. Look for David Niven in his first recognizable bit as a drunken tramp who gets thrown out of a tavern. B&W; 90m. **DIR:** Howard Hawks. **CAST:** Edward G. Robinson, Miriam Hopkins, Joel McCrea, Walter Brennan, Brian Donlevy, Frank Craven. **1935**

BAREFOOT CONTESSA, THE ★★★ A gaggle of Hollywood vultures headed by director Humphrey Bogart picks naïve dancer Ava Gardner out of a Madrid nightclub and proceeds to mold her into a film star. A simple unpretentious soul, she marries an impotent Italian nobleman (Rossano Brazzi), dies, and is buried by her chief mentor who tells her tragic story in flashback. A cynical, bizarre tale that never delivers what it promises. 128m. **DIR:** Joseph L. Mankiewicz. **CAST:** Humphrey Bogart, Ava Gardner, Edmond O'Brien, Marius Goring, Rossano Brazzi. **1954**

BARFLY ★★★★ Superb performances by Mickey Rourke and Faye Dunaway, as well as a dynamite jazz and R&B score, highlight this hip, flip, and often gruesomely funny semiautobiographical film written by

Charles Bukowski. Rourke and Dunaway drink their way from one sodden, sleazy misadventure to another, and director Barbet Schroeder makes it all seem to truly take place on the street—or is that the gutter? Rated R for profanity, suggested sex, and violence. 97m. **DIR:** Barbet Schroeder. **CAST:** Mickey Rourke, Faye Dunaway, Alice Krige, J. C. Quinn, Frank Stallone. **1987**

BARN BURNING ★★★★ A sterling adaptation of William Faulkner's short story. Oscar-winning scripter Horton Foote is responsible for this teleplay. Tommy Lee Jones is grand in a role that oozes menace. Introduced by Henry Fonda; unrated and suitable for family viewing. 40m. **DIR:** Peter Werner. **CAST:** Tommy Lee Jones, Diane Kagan, Shawn Whittington. **1980**

BARNUM (1987) ★★★ Above-average TV film looks at the greatest showman on Earth, P. T. Barnum, played to the hilt by Burt Lancaster. Nice atmosphere and sets lend to the overall effect, but this is Lancaster's show all the way. 94m. **DIR:** Lee Philips. **CAST:** Burt Lancaster, Hanna Schygulla. **1987**

BARRETTS OF WIMPOLE STREET, THE ★★★ Stagy but well-acted version of the romance between Robert Browning and Elizabeth Barrett under the watchful, jealous eye of her domineering father. First-rate cast triumphs over a slightly dated script. B&W; 110m. **DIR:** Sidney Franklin. **CAST:** Norma Shearer, Fredric March, Charles Laughton, Maureen O'Sullivan. **1934**

BARRY LYNDON ★★★ This period epic directed by Stanley Kubrick will please only the filmmaker's most fervent admirers. Although exquisitely photographed and meticulously designed, this three-hour motion picture adaptation of William Makepeace Thackeray's novel about an eighteenth-century rogue is a flawed masterpiece at best and is far too drawn out. However, it is worth watching for the lush cinematography by John Alcott. Rated PG for brief nudity and violence. 183m. **DIR:** Stanley Kubrick. **CAST:** Ryan O'Neal, Marisa Berenson, Patrick Magee, Hardy Krüger, Steven Berkoff, Gay Hamilton. **1975**

BARTLEBY ★★★½ Herman Melville's tale of a man who "would prefer not to" seems especially timely now. Paul Scofield is the unfortunate boss who, stuck with the inert Bartleby, is forced to fire him. Superior acting makes this thought-provoking tale both moving and believable. 79m. **DIR:** Anthony Friedman. **CAST:** Paul Scofield, John McEnery. **1970**

BASIC INSTINCT ★★ Cop Michael Douglas finds himself seduced (repeatedly) by bisexual heiress Sharon Stone, even though she's suspected of having committed a brutal ice-pick murder. Director Paul Verhoeven takes sex and violence to extremes, perhaps in an effort to cover up the TV-movie-of-the-week weakness of Joe Eszterhas's sleazy screenplay. Rated R for nudity, simulated sex, violence, and profanity. 130m. **DIR:** Paul Verhoeven. **CAST:** Michael Douglas, Sharon Stone, George Dzundza, Jeanne Tripplehorn, Stephen Tobolowsky. **1992**

BASTARD, THE ★★★ TV miniseries ably adapts part one of John Jakes's American Revolution saga. Numerous well-known stars pop in for cameo appearances, while Andrew Stevens takes the lead as the illegitimate son of a British nobleman. His hopes of sharing the man's wealth dashed, he heads for America. 189m. **DIR:** Lee H. Katzin. **CAST:** Andrew Stevens, Tom Bosley, Kim Cattrall, Patricia Neal, Olivia Hussey. **1978**

BATTERED ★★½ This TV docudrama will have you believing there are wife beaters lurking around every corner. The script is somewhat stiff and uninventive at times, but does offer a fairly accurate picture of the few alternatives open to the women in this desperate situation. 95m. **DIR:** Peter Werner. **CAST:** Mike Farrell, LeVar Burton, Karen Grassle, Joan Blondell, Howard Duff, Diana Scarwid. **1978**

BATTLE CIRCUS ★★ Humphrey Bogart and June Allyson are mismatched in this nonaction war picture. It's a soap opera about a military doctor arguing with and finally falling for a nurse on the Korean battlefield. Soggy. B&W; 90m. **DIR:** Richard Brooks. **CAST:** Humphrey Bogart, June Allyson, Keenan Wynn, Robert Keith, Steve Forrest, Philip Ahn, William Campbell. **1953**

BATTLEGROUND ★★★½ Made over the protests of MGM czar Louis B. Mayer, this rugged look at World War II's famous Battle of the Bulge was a resounding hit. Everything looks and sounds real. Oscars went to script and photography. B&W; 118m. **DIR:** William Wellman. **CAST:** Van Johnson, John Hodiak, Denise Darcel, Ricardo Montalban, George Murphy, James Whitmore. **1949**

BAXTER ★★½ Troubled schoolboy Scott Jacoby is treated by speech therapist Patricia Neal in this earnest British drama. Well-done for its type. Rated PG. 100m. **DIR:** Lionel Jeffries. **CAST:** Patricia Neal, Scott Jacoby, Jean-Pierre Cassel, Lynn Carlin, Britt Ekland. **1973**

BAY BOY, THE ★★★★½ The story of a brief period in an adolescent boy's life while growing up in a small mining town on the Nova Scotia coast during the mid-1930s. This film develops the character, including the sexual awakening, guilt, and terror, of Donald Campbell (Kiefer Sutherland). Liv Ullmann is well cast as Donald's mother. 104m. **DIR:** Daniel Petrie. **CAST:** Liv Ullmann, Kiefer Sutherland, Joe MacPherson. **1985**

BAYOU ROMANCE 🦃 A successful artist inherits a Louisiana plantation. 105m. **DIR:**

Alan Myerson. **CAST:** Annie Potts, Michael Ansara, Barbara Horan. **1982**

BEACHCOMBER, THE ★★★ This Somerset Maugham story of a dissolute South Seas beachcomber and the lady missionary who reforms him is sculptor's clay in the expert hands of Charles Laughton and Elsa Lanchester. He is delightful as the shiftless, conniving bum; she is clever and captivating as his Bible-toting nemesis. A scene at a bar is Laughton at his wily, eye-rolling, blustering best. B&W; 80m. **DIR:** Erich Pommer. **CAST:** Charles Laughton, Elsa Lanchester, Tyrone Guthrie, Robert Newton. **1938**

BEACHES ★★★★ Here's a terrific tear-jerker that casts Bette Midler and Barbara Hershey as two unlikely friends who enjoy a thirty-year relationship that's full of ups and downs. Fans of five-handkerchief films will love it. Midler is often hilarious as the show-biz-crazy Jewish gal who both loves and competes with WASPish heiress Hershey. See it if only for the mind-boggling performance of look-alike Mayim Bialik as the 11-year-old Midler, but be prepared to suspend your disbelief. Rated PG-13 for profanity and suggested sex. 120m. **DIR:** Garry Marshall. **CAST:** Bette Midler, Barbara Hershey, John Heard, Spalding Gray. **1988**

BEAU BRUMMELL (1924) ★★★★ John Barrymore scores a great success as the handsome dandy who works his way into the good graces of the Prince of Wales. Mary Astor is wonderful as Lady Alvanley. This is a must-see film for admirers of the silent film nearing its peak of perfection. Silent. B&W; 92m. **DIR:** Harry Beaumont. **CAST:** John Barrymore, Mary Astor, Irene Rich, Carmel Myers. **1924**

BEAU BRUMMELL (1954) ★★★½ Good telling of the on-again, off-again friendship and patronage between the Duke of Wales (later George IV) and court rogue and dandy, Beau Brummell. Stewart Granger is fine in the title role, and Elizabeth Taylor is beautiful, but the movie belongs to Peter Ustinov as the duke, and in a small role, Robert Morley as George III. 113m. **DIR:** Curtis Bernhardt. **CAST:** Stewart Granger, Elizabeth Taylor, Peter Ustinov, Robert Morley, James Donald, Rosemary Harris, Peter Bull. **1954**

BEAUTIFUL DREAMERS ★★★½ Rip Torn delivers a wonderful performance as poet Walt Whitman, who accompanies a young doctor back to his small town, where the outspoken Whitman's beliefs set the local townsfolk aback. While the rest of the cast is in tune with the vision, it's Torn who paints the brightest images in this intelligent film. Rated PG-13 for language. 108m. **DIR:** John Kent Harrison. **CAST:** Rip Torn, Colm Feore, Sheila McCarthy. **1991**

BEAUTY FOR THE ASKING 🦃 Beautician Lucille Ball creates a skin cream that sells millions. B&W; 68m. **DIR:** Glenn Tryon. **CAST:** Lucille Ball, Patric Knowles, Frieda Inescort, Donald Woods. **1939**

BECKET ★★★★ Magnificently acted spectacle of the stormy relationship between England's King Henry II (Peter O'Toole) and his friend and nemesis Archbishop Thomas Becket (Richard Burton). This visually stimulating historical pageant, set in twelfth-century England, garnered Oscar nominations for both its protagonists. 148m. **DIR:** Peter Glenville. **CAST:** Richard Burton, Peter O'Toole, Martita Hunt, Pamela Brown. **1964**

BECKY SHARP ★★½ Well-mounted historical drama of a callous young woman who lives for social success is lovely to look at in its original three-strip Technicolor. Fine performances by a veteran cast bolster this first sound screen adaptation of Thackeray's *Vanity Fair*. 83m. **DIR:** Rouben Mamoulian. **CAST:** Miriam Hopkins, Frances Dee, Cedric Hardwicke, Billie Burke, Alison Skipworth, Nigel Bruce. **1935**

BECOMING COLETTE ★★★ Beautifully photographed story chronicling the life of Colette, and the events that made her a world-famous author. From marriage to an older publisher to her introduction to decadent turn-of-the-century Paris, this film conveys a sumptuous eye for detail. Excellent performances from Mathilda May as the alluring Colette, Klaus Maria Brandauer as her husband, and Virginia Madsen as French actress Polaire. Rated R for nudity and adult situations. 97m. **DIR:** Danny Huston. **CAST:** Mathilda May, Klaus Maria Brandauer, Virginia Madsen, Paul Rhys. **1992**

BED AND BREAKFAST ★★★ After a man (Roger Moore) is washed up on the beach area in front of a house in Maine inhabited by widow Talia Shire and her mother-in-law, Colleen Dewhurst, the women's lives take some unexpected turns. Director Robert Ellis Miller and screenwriter Cindy Meyers examine the tender side of human relationships in a decidedly feminine fashion, while using just enough mystery and suspense to add an edge to their tale. Rated PG-13 for brief violence, suggested sex, and profanity. 96m. **DIR:** Robert Ellis Miller. **CAST:** Roger Moore, Talia Shire, Colleen Dewhurst, Ford Rainey. **1992**

BEDFORD INCIDENT, THE ★★★ A battle of wits aboard a U.S. destroyer tracking Soviet submarines off Greenland during the Cold War. Richard Widmark is a skipper with an obsession to hunt and hound a particular sub. A conflict develops between the captain and Sidney Poitier, a cocky magazine reporter along for the ride. B&W; 102m. **DIR:** James B. Harris. **CAST:** Richard Widmark, Sidney Poitier, Martin Balsam, Wally Cox, Eric Portman. **1965**

BEETHOVEN'S NEPHEW ★★½ This surreal drama by Paul Morrissey takes an incisive look at the dark side of Beethoven's genius. It's a convoluted period piece that follows the bizarre exploits of Beethoven's young nephew, Karl. Interesting performances, beautiful settings, and great costumes carry this film over the slow spots. Rated R. 103m. **DIR:** Paul Morrissey. **CAST:** Wolfgang Reichmann, Dietmar Prinz, Jane Birkin, Nathalie Baye, Mathieu Carriere. **1985**

BEHOLD A PALE HORSE ★★ Gregory Peck is miscast in this slow, talky, vague drama of a Loyalist holdout in post–Civil War Spain who continues to harass the Franco regime. 118m. **DIR:** Fred Zinnemann. **CAST:** Gregory Peck, Anthony Quinn, Omar Sharif. **1963**

BEING HUMAN ★★½ Writer-director Bill Forsyth's big-screen meditation on the plight of unexceptional men is neither funny (as were his earliest films) nor very dramatic. In his best sad-eyed fashion, Robin Williams plays five roles in five different historical settings, ranging from the Stone Age to modern times. A brief, humorous turn by John Turturro (as an inept Roman businessman) and a touching wrap-around story make this worth watching. Rated PG-13 for light profanity, brief violence, and suggested sex. 119m. **DIR:** Bill Forsyth. **CAST:** Robin Williams, Anna Galiena, Vincent D'Onofrio, Hector Elizondo, John Turturro, Lorraine Bracco, Lindsay Crouse, Helen Miller, Charles Miller, William H. Macy. **1994**

BELFAST ASSASSIN ★★½ This film, about an IRA hit man and a British antiterrorist who is ordered to track down the Irish assassin on his own turf, could have used a clipper-happy editor. The film takes a pro-IRA stand, yet is open-minded enough to see the other side of the story. Not rated, but the equivalent of a PG for sex, violence, and profanity. 130m. **DIR:** Lawrence Gordon Clark. **CAST:** Derek Thompson, Ray Lonnen, Benjamin Whitrow. **1982**

BELIZAIRE THE CAJUN ★★★★ *Belizaire the Cajun* is a film that is atmospheric in the best sense of the word. The Louisiana bayou of the 1850s is richly re-created in a cadence of texture and deep, dark swampland colors, along with the rhythms of Cajun accents and full-bodied folk music (score by Michael Doucet). Armand Assante is Belizaire, an herbal doctor who finds himself in a mess of trouble because of his affection for his childhood sweetheart and his efforts to save a friend from persecution. 114m. **DIR:** Glen Pitre. **CAST:** Armand Assante, Gail Youngs, Michael Schoeffling, Stephen McHattie, Will Patton. **1986**

BELL JAR, THE ★★★ Based on the novel by Sylvia Plath about the mental breakdown of an overachiever in the world of big business in the 1950s, this film has a strong lead performance by Marilyn Hassett and thoughtful direction by her husband, Larry Peerce. But the overriding melancholy of the subject matter makes it difficult to watch. Barbara Barrie is also memorable in a key supporting role. Rated R. 107m. **DIR:** Larry Peerce. **CAST:** Marilyn Hassett, Julie Harris, Anne Jackson, Barbara Barrie, Robert Klein. **1979**

BELLS OF ST. MARY'S, THE ★★★★½ An effective sequel to *Going My Way*, also directed by Leo McCarey, this film has Bing Crosby returning as the modern-minded priest once again up against a headstrong opponent, Mother Superior (played by Ingrid Bergman). While not as memorable as his encounter with hard-headed older priest Barry Fitzgerald in the first film, this relationship—and the movie as a whole—does have its viewing rewards. B&W; 126m. **DIR:** Leo McCarey. **CAST:** Bing Crosby, Ingrid Bergman, Ruth Donnelly. **1945**

BELLY OF AN ARCHITECT, THE ★★ Dreamlike, symbolism-laced story of an American architect (Brian Dennehy) trying to deal with hypocrisy in his art and in his life while working on a project in Italy. His efforts take on an urgency when he begins to suspect that he's dying of cancer. Alternately artful and pretentious, the film is most interesting as a showcase for Dennehy. 108m. **DIR:** Peter Greenaway. **CAST:** Brian Dennehy, Chloe Webb, Lambert Wilson. **1987**

BELOVED ENEMY ★★★½ This stylish film concerns a beautiful woman (Merle Oberon) in love with a young leader in the Irish revolution (Brian Aherne). Great supporting cast adds panache to this crackerjack Samuel Goldwyn production. B&W; 86m. **DIR:** H. C. Potter. **CAST:** Merle Oberon, Brian Aherne, Karen Morley, David Niven. **1936**

BELOW THE BELT ★★★½ This agreeable low-budget feature is short on technical polish but long on heart. It's a semidocumentary about a waitress (Regina Baff) who tries to become a professional wrestler, taking advice from ex-champ Mildred Burke (playing herself). There's even a *Rocky*ish finale. Made in 1974, but not released until 1980. Rated R. 91m. **DIR:** Robert Fowler. **CAST:** Regina Baff, Mildred Burke, John C. Becher, Shirley Stoler, Dolph Sweet, Ric Mancini. **1980**

BEN-HUR (1926) ★★★★ Colossal in every sense of the word, this greatest of silent film spectacles is still a winner today. Years in production, it cost a staggering $4 million and was two years being edited. The chariot-race and sea-battle scenes are unsurpassed. Ramon Novarro as Ben-Hur and Francis X. Bushman as Messala gave the performances of their careers. B&W; 116m. **DIR:** Fred Niblo. **CAST:** Ramon Novarro, Francis X. Bushman, May McAvoy, Betty Bronson, Carmel Myers. **1926**

BENNY GOODMAN STORY, THE ★★★ If you enjoy good big-band music and don't mind a few errors in biographical fact, then this big brassy picture is a must for you. Steve Allen as Benny Goodman does a fine job. Watch for some other great performers in cameos. 116m. **DIR:** Valentine Davies. **CAST:** Steve Allen, Donna Reed, Teddy Wilson, Herbert Anderson, Gene Krupa, Robert F. Simon. **1955**

BERLIN AFFAIR, THE ★★ Uneven erotic psychodrama about a Japanese art student in prewar 1938 Germany who becomes involved in a bizarre love triangle with the wife of a politically affluent German diplomat and her husband. Though heavy on eroticism, the film is lean on story and character motivation. Rated R for nudity and profanity. 97m. **DIR:** Liliana Cavani. **CAST:** Gudrun Landgrebe, Kevin McNally, Mio Takaki. **1985**

BERNADETTE ★★ This long, slow-moving French film features an almost too glamorous Sydney Penny as the impoverished young girl chosen to be the messenger at Lourdes. Rated PG for profanity. 120m. **DIR:** Jean Delannoy. **CAST:** Sydney Penny, Michelle Simonnett. **1987**

BEST LITTLE GIRL IN THE WORLD, THE ★★★★½ This gut-wrenching teleplay about a girl, portrayed by Jennifer Jason Leigh who suffers from anorexia nervosa pulls no punches; some of the drama is hard to take, but if you can make it through the film's end, you'll feel rewarded. This was originally an after-school special. The entire cast turns in great performances. The equivalent of a PG for intense drama. 90m. **DIR:** Sam O'Steen. **CAST:** Jennifer Jason Leigh, Charles Durning, Eva Marie Saint, Jason Miller. **1986**

BEST MAN, THE ★★★★ Sharp characterizations bring to life this drama of disparate political types jockeying for position and endorsement at a presidential convention. Thoroughly engrossing. B&W; 102m. **DIR:** Franklin J. Schaffner. **CAST:** Henry Fonda, Cliff Robertson, Edie Adams, Margaret Leighton, Shelley Berman, Lee Tracy, Ann Sothern. **1964**

BEST YEARS OF OUR LIVES, THE ★★★★★ What happens when the fighting ends and warriors return home is the basis of this eloquent, compassionate film. William Wyler takes his time and guides a superb group of players through a tangle of postwar emotional conflicts. Harold Russell's first scene has lost none of its impact. Keep in mind World War II had just ended when this film debuted. B&W; 170m. **DIR:** William Wyler. **CAST:** Myrna Loy, Fredric March, Teresa Wright, Dana Andrews, Virginia Mayo, Harold Russell, Cathy O'Donnell. **1946**

BETHUNE ★★★½ This biographical teleplay gets off to a slow start, but delivers an absorbing story and masterful acting. It's the biography of Norman Bethune, the Canadian hero who served as a doctor in the combat between China and Japan. 88m. **DIR:** Eric Till. **CAST:** Donald Sutherland, Kate Nelligan, David Gardner, James Hong. **1984**

BETRAYAL (1978) ★★½ Based on a true incident, this soapy TV movie concerns a young woman who has an affair with her psychiatrist. What could have been revealing and vital breaks down into conventional melodrama. 100m. **DIR:** Paul Wendkos. **CAST:** Lesley Ann Warren, Rip Torn, Richard Masur, Peggy Ann Garner, Ron Silver, Bibi Besch. **1978**

BETRAYAL (1983) ★★★★★ Harold Pinter's play about the slow death of a marriage has been turned into an intelligent and innovative film that begins with the affair breaking apart and follows it backward to the beginning. Jeremy Irons and Patricia Hodge are superb. Rated R for profanity. 95m. **DIR:** David Jones. **CAST:** Jeremy Irons, Ben Kingsley, Patricia Hodge. **1983**

BETSY, THE ★★ A classic example of how to waste loads of talent and money. The Harold Robbins novel about a wealthy family in the auto manufacturing business was trashy to start with, but after Hollywood gets done with it, not even Laurence Olivier can save this debacle. Rated R. 125m. **DIR:** Daniel Petrie. **CAST:** Laurence Olivier, Tommy Lee Jones, Robert Duvall, Katharine Ross, Lesley-Anne Down, Jane Alexander. **1978**

BETWEEN FRIENDS ★★½ Two middle-aged divorcées meet and gradually form a life-sustaining friendship. This made-for-cable feature occasionally gets mired in melodramatic tendencies, but its two charismatic stars make it well worth watching. Unrated. 100m. **DIR:** Lou Antonio. **CAST:** Elizabeth Taylor, Carol Burnett, Barbara Rush, Stephen Young, Henry Ramer. **1983**

BETWEEN HEAVEN AND HELL 🦃 This one is closer to Hell, mainly because it's all talk and no action. Broderick Crawford plays a sadistic drill sergeant who browbeats spoiled recruit Robert Wagner. It's all been done before and better. 94m. **DIR:** Richard Fleischer. **CAST:** Robert Wagner, Terry Moore, Broderick Crawford, Brad Dexter, Buddy Ebsen, Scatman Crothers, Skip Homeier. **1956**

BETWEEN TWO WOMEN ★★★★ For this TV movie Colleen Dewhurst won an Emmy as the mother-in-law from Hell. After her severe stroke, she is cared for by her much-maligned daughter-in-law (Farrah Fawcett). Remarkably moving and believable. 95m. **DIR:** Jon Avnet. **CAST:** Colleen Dewhurst, Farrah Fawcett, Michael Nouri, Steven Hill. **1986**

BETWEEN WARS 🦃 Australian offering about an idealistic doctor. 97m. **DIR:** Michael Thornhill. **CAST:** Corin Redgrave, Arthur Dingham, Judy Morris. **1985**

BEULAH LAND ★★★½ A generational look at the life of a southern plantation family. The saga carries you through the Civil

War and its aftermath. A polished TV production with a strong cast, all of whom turn in fine performances. 267m. **DIR:** Virgil Vogel, Harry Falk. **CAST:** Lesley Ann Warren, Michael Sarrazin, Eddie Albert, Hope Lange, Don Johnson, Meredith Baxter-Birney. **1980**

BEVERLY HILLS MADAM 🦃 In this TV movie, Faye Dunaway is madam Lil Hutton, whose carefully cultivated reputation is being threatened by her own call girls. 97m. **DIR:** Harvey Hart. **CAST:** Faye Dunaway, Louis Jourdan, Donna Dixon, Robin Givens, Terry Farrell, Marshall Colt. **1986**

BEVERLY HILLS 90210 ★★ Pilot movie for the Fox TV series introduces America to a whole new generation of teen idols. The film explores the problems faced by the Walsh family from Minnesota when they relocate to America's city of glamour. About as socially relevant as a Clearasil commercial. 90m. **DIR:** Tim Hunter. **CAST:** Jason Priestley, Shannen Doherty, Jennie Garth, Ian Ziering, Gabrielle Carteris, Maxwell Caulfield, Josh Mostel, Richard Cummings Jr. **1990**

BEYOND REASON ★★★ Telly Savalas shows his stuff in this sensitve film, which he wrote and directed. He plays an iconoclastic psychologist who slowly loses touch with reality. Though thought-provoking and touching throughout, the story gets a little muddy from time to time and finishes unsatisfyingly. 88m. **DIR:** Telly Savalas. **CAST:** Telly Savalas, Diana Muldaur, Marvin Laird. **1985**

BEYOND THE FOREST ★★ Too much Bette Davis spoils this mix of greed, adultery, abortion, and murder, even if she does utter the classic line, "What a dump!" Snarling and whining, Davis gives a performance that turns the murky-plotted film into a melodramatic mess even her most devoted fans reject. B&W; 96m. **DIR:** King Vidor. **CAST:** Bette Davis, Joseph Cotten, David Brian, Ruth Roman, Minor Watson, Regis Toomey. **1949**

BEYOND THE LIMIT ★★ Dull, unconvincing adaptation of *The Honorary Consul*, Graham Greene's novel about love and betrayal in an Argentinian town stars Michael Caine as a kidnapped diplomat and Richard Gere as the doctor in love with his wife. It'll take you beyond your limit. Rated R. 103m. **DIR:** John Mackenzie. **CAST:** Michael Caine, Richard Gere, Bob Hoskins, Elpidia Carrillo. **1983**

BEYOND THE VALLEY OF THE DOLLS 🦃 This was rated X when it came out, but by today's standards it's an R for gratuitous nudity and profanity. 109m. **DIR:** Russ Meyer. **CAST:** Dolly Read, Cynthia Myers, Marcia McBroom. **1970**

BIBLE, THE ★★★ An overblown all-star treatment of five of the early stories in the Old Testament. Director John Huston gives this movie the feel of a Cecil B. De Mille spectacle, but there is little human touch to any of the stories. This expensively mounted production forgets that in the Bible, individual accomplishments are equally relevant to grandeur. 174m. **DIR:** John Huston. **CAST:** Michael Parks, Ulla Bergryd, Richard Harris, John Huston, Ava Gardner. **1966**

BIG BLUFF, THE 🦃 A young woman with a terminal disease marries a gigolo who plots to murder. B&W; 70m. **DIR:** W. Lee Wilder. **CAST:** John Bromfield, Martha Vickers, Robert Hutton, Rosemarie Bowe. **1955**

BIG BUSINESS GIRL ★★★ One of Hollywood's first career-girl movies and a star vehicle for Loretta Young and Joan Blondell. The comedy-drama mixes career problems with romantic dilemmas and is aimed primarily at a female audience with elements Hollywood still uses to appeal to women today. B&W; 75m. **DIR:** William A. Seiter. **CAST:** Loretta Young, Joan Blondell, Ricardo Cortez, Jack Albertson, Dorothy Christy, Bobby Gordon. **1931**

BIG CHILL, THE ★★★★½ As with John Sayles's superb *Return of the Secaucus 7*, this equally impressive and thoroughly enjoyable film by writer-director Lawrence Kasdan concerns a weekend reunion of old friends, all of whom have gone on to varied life-styles after once being united in the hip, committed 1960s. It features a who's who of today's hot young stars as the friends. Rated R for nudity and profanity. 103m. **DIR:** Lawrence Kasdan. **CAST:** Tom Berenger, William Hurt, Glenn Close, Jeff Goldblum, JoBeth Williams, Kevin Kline, Mary Kay Place, Meg Tilly. **1983**

BIG JIM MCLAIN ★★ This relic of the McCarthy era has John Wayne and James Arness as two-fisted investigators for the House Un-American Activities Committee. Clumsy and dull. B&W; 90m. **DIR:** Edward Ludwig. **CAST:** John Wayne, James Arness, Nancy Olson, Veda Ann Borg, Hans Conried. **1952**

BIG LIFT, THE ★★½ Montgomery Clift gives an emotionally charged performance as an air force pilot who becomes romantically involved with a young German girl in post–World War II Berlin. Excellent location photography gives a lift to this uneven melodrama. B&W; 120m. **DIR:** George Seaton. **CAST:** Montgomery Clift, Paul Douglas, Cornell Borchers, O. E. Hasse. **1950**

BIG PARADE, THE ★★★★★ A compelling depiction of World War I, this silent film has long been recognized as King Vidor's masterpiece. As the saying goes, it has everything: romance, humor, love, tragedy, and suspense. B&W; 126m. **DIR:** King Vidor. **CAST:** John Gilbert, Renée Adorée, Hobart Bosworth. **1925**

BIG STREET, THE ★★½ Though somewhat too sentimental at times, this Damon Runyon story of a busboy's (Henry Fonda) sincere devotion to a couldn't-care-less-for-him nightclub singer (Lucille Ball) is often touching and lively. Lucille Ball gives her best big-screen performance and you couldn't ask for a better gangster than Barton MacLane. B&W; 88m. **DIR:** Irving Reis. **CAST:** Henry Fonda, Lucille Ball, Hans Conried, Barton MacLane, Agnes Moorehead, Ray Collins, Sam Levene, Louise Beavers. **1942**

BIG TOWN, THE ★★ Chicago, circa 1957. A talented small-town boy (Matt Dillon) with a penchant for crapshooting goes off to the big city. But the production loses focus and drive. Rated R for language, nudity, and sex. 110m. **DIR:** Ben Bolt. **CAST:** Matt Dillon, Diane Lane, Tommy Lee Jones, Bruce Dern, Tom Skerritt, Lee Grant, Suzy Amis. **1987**

BIG WEDNESDAY ★★ Only nostalgic surfers with more than a little patience will enjoy this ode to the beach by writer-director John Milius. Rated PG. 120m. **DIR:** John Milius. **CAST:** Jan-Michael Vincent, Gary Busey, William Katt, Lee Purcell, Patti D'Arbanville. **1978**

BIG WHEEL, THE ★★½ Smart-mouthed Mickey Rooney rises from garage mechanic to champion racing-car driver in this well-worn story worn thinner by a poor script and poorer direction. More than 20 of the film's 92 minutes are given over to earsplitting scenes of high-speed racing. B&W; 92m. **DIR:** Edward Ludwig. **CAST:** Mickey Rooney, Thomas Mitchell, Spring Byington, Allen Jenkins, Michael O'Shea. **1949**

BIGAMIST, THE ★★★ Ida Lupino stepped behind the camera to direct several underrated *film noir* excursions in the early Fifties, of which this is among the best. Title character Edmond O'Brien is neurotic, not conventionally villainous. Lupino's only acting role in one of her directing efforts. B&W; 80m. **DIR:** Ida Lupino. **CAST:** Edmond O'Brien, Joan Fontaine, Ida Lupino, Edmund Gwenn, Jane Darwell, Kenneth Tobey. **1953**

BILL ★★★★½ Extremely moving drama based on the real-life experiences of Bill Sackter, a retarded adult forced to leave the mental institution that has been his home for the past forty-five years. Mickey Rooney won an Emmy for his excellent portrayal of Bill. Dennis Quaid plays a filmmaker who offers kindness to Bill as he tries to cope with life on the "outside." Unrated. 100m. **DIR:** Anthony Page. **CAST:** Mickey Rooney, Dennis Quaid, Largo Woodruff. **1981**

BILL OF DIVORCEMENT, A ★★★½ Melodramatic weeper about a man's return to his family after confinement in a mental hospital rises above the material due to a stunning cast and deft direction by Hollywood master George Cukor. Katharine Hepburn in her first film really carries this somewhat overwrought soap opera. B&W; 70m. **DIR:** George Cukor. **CAST:** John Barrymore, Billie Burke, Katharine Hepburn, David Manners, Bramwell Fletcher, Henry Stephenson, Paul Cavanagh, Elizabeth Patterson. **1932**

BILL: ON HIS OWN ★★★½ This is the sequel to the 1981 drama *Bill*. Mickey Rooney continues his role as Bill Sackter, a mentally retarded adult forced to live on his own after spending forty-five years in an institution. Helen Hunt costars as the college student who tutors him. It doesn't have quite the emotional impact that *Bill* carried, but it's still good. 104m. **DIR:** Anthony Page. **CAST:** Mickey Rooney, Helen Hunt, Teresa Wright, Dennis Quaid, Largo Woodruff. **1983**

BILLIONAIRE BOYS CLUB ★★½ Severely edited version of the miniseries starring Judd Nelson as Joe Hunt, a notorious commodities broker-cum-murderer. Nelson conveys Hunt's hypnotic personality and greed, though the production is saddled with unimaginative editing and tinny music. Based on an actual Los Angeles murder case. Made for TV. 94m. **DIR:** Marvin J. Chomsky. **CAST:** Judd Nelson, Ron Silver. **1987**

BILLY BATHGATE ★★★★½ A compelling gangster movie with superb performances, this work, based by screenwriter Tom Stoppard on the novel by E. L. Doctorow, concerns the odyssey of young Billy Bathgate (Loren Dean) who goes from being a poor street kid in 1935 to a coveted position in the crime organization of crazy, big-time hood Dutch Schultz (Dustin Hoffman). Rated R for violence, nudity, and profanity. 106m. **DIR:** Robert Benton. **CAST:** Dustin Hoffman, Nicole Kidman, Bruce Willis, Steven Hill, Loren Dean, Steve Buscemi, Stanley Tucci. **1991**

BILLY BUDD ★★★½ Herman Melville's brooding, allegorical novel of the overpowering of the innocent is set against a backdrop of life on an eighteenth-century British warship. The plight of a young sailor subjected to the treacherous whims of his ship's tyrannical first mate is well-acted throughout. It is powerful filmmaking and succeeds in leaving its audience unsettled and questioning. B&W; 112m. **DIR:** Peter Ustinov. **CAST:** Terence Stamp, Robert Ryan, Peter Ustinov. **1962**

BILLY GALVIN ★★★½ Surprisingly good slice-of-life drama about steelworkers in Boston. Karl Malden is excellent as Jack Galvin, a hard-bitten steelworker who doesn't want his son, Billy (Lenny Von Dohlen, also excellent), to follow in his footsteps. Rated PG for language. 99m. **DIR:** John Gray. **CAST:** Karl Malden, Lenny Von Dohlen, Toni Kalem, Keith Szarabajka, Alan North, Barton Heyman, Joyce Van Patten. **1986**

BILLY LIAR ★★★★ Poignant slices of English middle-class life are served expertly in this finely played story of a lazy young man who escapes dulling routine by retreating into fantasy. The eleven minutes Julie Christie is on screen are electric and worth the whole picture. B&W; 96m. **DIR:** John

Schlesinger. **CAST:** Tom Courtenay, Julie Christie, Finlay Currie, Ethel Griffies, Mona Washbourne. **1963**

BIRD MAN OF ALCATRAZ ★★★★ In one of his best screen performances, Burt Lancaster plays Robert Stroud, the prisoner who became a world-renowned authority on birds. B&W; 143m. **DIR:** John Frankenheimer. **CAST:** Burt Lancaster, Karl Malden, Thelma Ritter, Telly Savalas. **1962**

BIRDY ★★★★½ Matthew Modine and Nicolas Cage give unforgettable performances in this dark, disturbing, yet somehow uplifting study of an odd young man named Birdy (Modine) from South Philadelphia who wants to be a bird. That way he can fly away from all his troubles—which worsen manifold after a traumatic tour of duty in Vietnam. Rated R for violence, nudity, and profanity. 120m. **DIR:** Alan Parker. **CAST:** Matthew Modine, Nicolas Cage, John Harkins, Sandy Baron, Karen Young, Bruno Kirby. **1985**

BIRTH OF A NATION, THE ★★★★ Videotape will probably be the only medium in which you will ever see this landmark silent classic. D. W. Griffith's epic saga of the American Civil War and its aftermath is today considered too racist in its glorification of the Ku Klux Klan ever to be touched by television or revival theaters. This is filmdom's most important milestone (the first to tell a cohesive story) but should only be seen by those emotionally prepared for its disturbing point of view. B&W; 158m. **DIR:** D. W. Griffith. **CAST:** Lillian Gish, Mae Marsh, Henry B. Walthall, Miriam Cooper. **1915**

BITCH, THE 🦃 Joan Collins has the title role in this fiasco, an adaptation of sister Jackie Collins's book. Rated R. 93m. **DIR:** Gerry O'Hara. **CAST:** Joan Collins, Kenneth Haigh, Michael Coby. **1979**

BITTER HARVEST (1981) ★★★★ In this made-for-television film based on a true incident, Ron Howard gives an excellent performance as an at-first panicky and then take-charge farmer whose dairy farm herd becomes sick and begins dying. His battle to find out the cause of the illness (chemicals in the feed), provides for scary, close-to-home drama. Good supporting cast. 104m. **DIR:** Roger Young. **CAST:** Ron Howard, Art Carney, Richard Dysart. **1981**

BITTER MOON ★★ Roman Polanski again assaults audience sensibilities with this lurid psychodrama about self-destructive obsession and sexual terrorism. On a Mediterranean cruise, an unsuccessful American novelist in a wheelchair shocks and seduces a starchy Englishman with perverse details of his relationship with his French wife. This ludicrous portrait of decayed love and sadomasochism—adapted from Pascal Bruckner's novel *Lunes de Fiel*—is visually seductive but not as darkly funny as intended. Rated R for simulated sex and language. 139m. **DIR:** Roman Polanski. **CAST:** Peter Coyote, Hugh Grant, Emmanuelle Seigner, Kristin Scott-Thomas. **1994**

BITTER TEA OF GENERAL YEN, THE ★★★★ An American joins her missionary fiancé in China and finds herself drawn to a Chinese warlord who takes her prisoner. When released this movie was panned by reviewers upset by the interracial theme. A historical note: This film was chosen to open New York's Radio City Music Hall. B&W; 89m. **DIR:** Frank Capra. **CAST:** Barbara Stanwyck, Nils Asther, Gavin Gordon, Lucien Littlefield, Toshia Mori, Richard Loo, Walter Connolly. **1933**

BITTERSWEET LOVE 🦃 Young married couple discover that they are a half brother and sister. Rated PG. 92m. **DIR:** David Miller. **CAST:** Lana Turner, Robert Lansing, Celeste Holm, Robert Alda, Meredith Baxter-Birney. **1976**

BLACK FURY ★★★★ Paul Muni is excellent as Joe Radek, an apolitical eastern European immigrant coal miner who unwittingly falls into the middle of a labor dispute. The acting is good, but the film doesn't reach its happy ending in a logical manner, so things just seem to fall into place without any reason. B&W; 95m. **DIR:** Michael Curtiz. **CAST:** Paul Muni, Karen Morley, William Gargan, Barton MacLane. **1935**

BLACK HAND, THE ★★ Gene Kelly offers a fine dramatic performance as a young man who must avenge the murder of his father. He becomes embroiled in the machinations of the Black Hand, (a.k.a. the Mafia) at the turn of the century. 93m. **DIR:** Richard Thorpe. **CAST:** Gene Kelly, J. Carrol Naish, Teresa Celli. **1950**

BLACK LIKE ME ★★★ Based on the book by John Griffin, this film poses the question: What happens when a white journalist takes a drug that turns his skin black? James Whitmore plays the reporter, who wishes to experience racism firsthand. Somewhat provocative at its initial release, but by today's standards, a lot of the punch is missing. B&W; 107m. **DIR:** Carl Lerner. **CAST:** James Whitmore, Roscoe Lee Browne, Will Geer, Sorrell Booke. **1964**

BLACK MAGIC (1949) ★★½ Orson Welles revels in the role of famous eighteenth-century charlatan Count Cagliostro—born Joseph Balsamo, a peasant with imagination and a flair for magic, hypnosis, and the power of superstition. The story is of Cagliostro's attempt to gain influence and clout in Italy using his strange and sinister talents. The star codirected (without credit). B&W; 105m. **DIR:** Gregory Ratoff. **CAST:** Orson Welles, Akim Tamiroff, Nancy Guild, Raymond Burr, Frank Latimore. **1949**

BLACK MARBLE, THE ★★★ A Los Angeles cop (Robert Foxworth) and his new partner (Paula Prentiss) attempt to capture a dog snatcher (Harry Dean Stanton) who is demanding a high ransom from a wealthy dog lover. Along the way, they fall in love. Based on Joseph Wambaugh's novel. Rated PG—language and some violence. 110m. **DIR:** Harold Becker. **CAST:** Paula Prentiss, Harry Dean Stanton, Robert Foxworth. **1980**

BLACK NARCISSUS ★★★½ Worldly temptations, including those of the flesh, create many difficulties for a group of nuns starting a mission in the Himalayas. Superb photography makes this early postwar British effort a visual delight. Unfortunately, key plot elements were cut from the American prints by censors. 99m. **DIR:** Michael Powell. **CAST:** Deborah Kerr, Jean Simmons, David Farrar, Flora Robson, Sabu. **1947**

BLACK ORCHID, THE ★★½ Sophia Loren plays the widow of a criminal and Anthony Quinn is the businessman who is romancing her in this patchy weeper. B&W; 96m. **DIR:** Martin Ritt. **CAST:** Sophia Loren, Anthony Quinn, Ina Balin, Peter Mark Richman. **1959**

BLACK PANTHER, THE ★★½ In 1974 Donald Neilson (Donald Sumpter), known as the Black Panther, robbed a series of post offices and killed their employees. Neilson also plotted the kidnapping of a wealthy teenage heiress that went awry. *The Black Panther* portrays Neilson's actions in such a matter-of-fact fashion that it removes all the horror. Still, some good action and a few intense scenes. Not rated, has violence and nudity. 90m. **DIR:** Ian Merrick. **CAST:** Donald Sumpter, Debbie Farrington, Marjorie Yates, David Swift. **1977**

BLACK ROBE ★★★★ Thought-provoking drama follows the struggle of Jesuit priest Father LaForgue (Lothaire Bluteau) as he journeys through the frozen Canadian wilderness in 1634 with the help of Algonquian Indians who become increasingly distrustful of the strange man they call "Blackrobe." This impressive motion picture manages to examine Christianity and tribal beliefs without trivializing either. Rated R for violence, nudity, and simulated sex. 105m. **DIR:** Bruce Beresford. **CAST:** Lothaire Bluteau, Aden Young, Sandrine Holt, August Schellenberg. **1991**

BLACK SISTER'S REVENGE ★★½ Shamefully, a new title and cover art imply that the movie is a blaxploitation action-adventure. In reality, it's a serious drama, originally titled *Emma Mae,* about a black girl from Georgia struggling to fit in with other kids in an L.A. ghetto. It's a low-budget movie lacking technical flair, but it deserves more attention than the misleading advertising is going to bring it. Not rated. 100m. **DIR:** Jamaa Fanaka. **CAST:** Jerri Hayes, Ernest Williams II. **1976**

BLACKBOARD JUNGLE, THE ★★★★ Glenn Ford plays a high school instructor who desperately tries to reach some emotionally turbulent youths in the New York school system. Hard-hitting, gritty drama. Excellent adaptation of Evan Hunter's powerful novel. B&W; 101m. **DIR:** Richard Brooks. **CAST:** Glenn Ford, Anne Francis, Vic Morrow, Sidney Poitier. **1955**

BLADES OF COURAGE ★★★½ Christianne Hirt is a Canadian ice skater with a promising future in the Olympics. Unfortunately she is assigned a coach who employs ruthless methods to achieve what he desires. Aside from the stereotyped pushy mother, this is a realistic film that reveals the effort involved in developing a champion. It is well acted with some choice figure-skating numbers. Unrated. 98m. **DIR:** Randy Bradshaw. **CAST:** Christianne Hirt, Colm Feore, Stuart Hughes, Rosemary Dunsmore. **1988**

BLAME IT ON THE NIGHT 🦃 Mick Jagger cowrote the original story for this movie but wisely chose not to appear in it. It's a trite tale of a rock singer who discovers he has a 13-year-old son. Rated PG-13. 85m. **DIR:** Gene Taft. **CAST:** Nick Mancuso, Byron Thames, Leslie Ackerman, Dick Bakalyan. **1984**

BLAZE ★★ Paul Newman stars as progressive Louisiana governor Earl Long in this late 1950s story of back-room politics and Long's affair with Bourbon Street stripper Blaze Starr. The look behind the scandalous headlines of yesteryear never really ignites. Rated R. 108m. **DIR:** Ron Shelton. **CAST:** Paul Newman, Lolita Davidovich. **1989**

BLEAK HOUSE ★★★★ First-rate adaptation of Charles Dickens's novel was made for the BBC as a miniseries. The skilled cast is headed by Diana Rigg and Denholm Elliott. Superb sets, costumes, and photography add to the period flavor. A must-see for Dickens aficionados. Made for TV. 391m. **DIR:** Ross Devenish. **CAST:** Diana Rigg, Denholm Elliott, Peter Vaughan, T. P. McKenna. **1985**

BLESS THE BEASTS AND CHILDREN 🦃 A group of misfit teenagers at a ranch resort rebel against their counselors to save a nearby herd of buffalo. Rated R for explicit violence. 109m. **DIR:** Stanley Kramer. **CAST:** Billy Mumy, Barry Robins, Miles Chapin, Ken Swofford, Jesse White, Vanessa Brown. **1972**

BLIND DATE (1984) ★★ Not to be confused with the comedies of the same name, this *Blind Date* is about a man who gets a reprieve from his sightless existence through the miraculous effects of an experimental machine. He uses his newfound perceptions to stalk a psychotic killer through some extremely visual Greek locations. Beyond the sights and decent acting, however, the story tends to plod. Rated R for violence. 100m. **DIR:** Nico Mastorakis. **CAST:** Joseph Bottoms, Keir Dullea, Kirstie Alley, James Daughton. **1984**

BLIND HUSBANDS ★★★ A doctor and his wife are in an Alpine village so that he can do some mountain climbing. His wife falls prey to the attentions of a suave Austrian army officer who seduces her. In addition to directing and starring, Erich Von Stroheim adapted the screenplay from his own story and designed the sets. A shocker when first released. Silent. B&W; 98m. **DIR:** Erich Von Stroheim. **CAST:** Sam de Grasse, Francis Billington, Erich Von Stroheim, Gibson Gowland. **1919**

BLIND SPOT ★★★★ In this *Hallmark Hall of Fame* presentation, Joanne Woodward does an outstanding job of portraying a strong-headed congresswoman who must cope with the death of her drug-addicted top aide who is also her son-in-law. Laura Linney is superb as Phoebe, Woodward's drug-addicted and pregnant daughter who wants to lead her own life. The story line is quite moving and shows the viewer how each character feels. Rated PG-13 for drug use. 99m. **DIR:** Michael Toshiyuki Uno. **CAST:** Joanne Woodward, Laura Linney, Reed Edward Diamond, Fritz Weaver. **1993**

BLOCKHOUSE, THE 🦃 Set during World War II, this hideous drama follows the exploits of a group of workers who become trapped in a German army bunker. 90m. **DIR:** Clive Rees. **CAST:** Peter Sellers, Charles Aznavour, Peter Vaughan, Jeremy Kemp. **1973**

BLONDE ICE ★★ Odd, obscure melodrama about an unbalanced woman who makes a career of killing her husbands and boyfriends because she likes the attention she gets. (Not to mention the money.) Another long-forgotten curiosity revived for video. 73m. **DIR:** Jack Bernhard. **CAST:** Leslie Brooks, Robert Paige, Walter Sands, John Holland, James Griffith. **1949**

BLONDE VENUS 🦃 This is a rambling, incomprehensible piece of glitzy fluff. B&W; 90m. **DIR:** Josef von Sternberg. **CAST:** Marlene Dietrich, Cary Grant, Herbert Marshall. **1932**

BLOOD AND SAND (1922) ★★★½ One of Rudolph Valentino's most successful vehicles, although it lacks the action and pacing of his best pictures, *Son of the Sheik* and *The Eagle*. Silent. B&W; 80m. **DIR:** Fred Niblo. **CAST:** Rudolph Valentino, Nita Naldi, Lila Lee. **1922**

BLOOD AND SAND (1941) ★★★ The "Moment of Truth" is not always just before the matador places his sword, as Tyrone Power learns in this classic story of a poor boy who rises to fame in the bullring. Linda Darnell loves him, Rita Hayworth leads him on, in this colorful remake of a 1922 Valentino starrer. 123m. **DIR:** Rouben Mamoulian. **CAST:** Tyrone Power, Rita Hayworth, Anthony Quinn, Linda Darnell, Nazimova, John Carradine. **1941**

BLOOD MONEY (1933) ★★★ This highly engaging film features an excellent cast in a story about an underworld bailbondsman who falls for a thrill-seeking socialite. His life becomes complicated by another female cohort. B&W; 65m. **DIR:** Rowland Brown. **CAST:** George Bancroft, Frances Dee, Judith Anderson, Chick Chandler, Blossom Seeley. **1933**

BLOOD OF OTHERS, THE ★★ A disappointment, considering the talent involved (in front of *and* behind the camera), this made-for-cable miniseries is a generally unconvincing adaptation of a Simone de Beauvoir novel about a doomed love affair in the occupied Paris of World War II. 176m. **DIR:** Claude Chabrol. **CAST:** Jodie Foster, Michael Ontkean, Sam Neill, Stéphane Audran, Jean-Pierre Aumont, Lambert Wilson, Micheline Presle. **1984**

BLOOD RED 🦃 Sicilian grape farmers feud with a tycoon over land in 1850 California. Rated R for violence and nudity. 102m. **DIR:** Peter Masterson. **CAST:** Eric Roberts, Giancarlo Giannini, Dennis Hopper, Burt Young. **1989**

BLOOD TIES (1987) ★★ Brad Davis is an innocent American engineer blackmailed into assassinating his cousin, an anticrime justice in Sicily. Not rated, but contains strong language, violence, and nudity. 98m. **DIR:** Giacomo Battiato. **CAST:** Brad Davis, Tony Lo Bianco, Vincent Spano, Barbara de Rossi, Ricky Tognazzi, Michael Gazzo. **1987**

BLOOD VOWS: THE STORY OF A MAFIA WIFE ★★★½ A fairy-tale romance between a beautiful orphan (Melissa Gilbert) and a dashing lawyer (Joe Penny) results in a nightmarish prison for her after they marry. It seems his clan needs him back home for a war between Mafia families and, she can't deal with the violence or the restrictions put on mob women. Some chilling moments. Originally shown as a TV movie. 104m. **DIR:** Paul Wendkos. **CAST:** Melissa Gilbert, Joe Penny, Talia Shire, Eileen Brennan. **1987**

BLOODBROTHERS ★★★½ Richard Gere and Marilu Henner take top honors in this drama. Plot revolves around a family of construction workers and the son (Gere) who wants to do something else with his life. Rated R. 116m. **DIR:** Robert Mulligan. **CAST:** Richard Gere, Paul Sorvino, Tony Lo Bianco, Marilu Henner. **1978**

BLOODLINE 🦃 Audrey Hepburn falls heir to a pharmaceutical fortune in this inexcusably repulsive montage of bad taste and incoherence. Rated R for sex scenes. 116m. **DIR:** Terence Young. **CAST:** Audrey Hepburn, Ben Gazzara, James Mason, Omar Sharif. **1979**

BLUE CHIPS ★★★ University-basketball coach is tempted to flush his squeaky-clean recruitment ethics down the toilet after suffering through his first losing season in a long career. Writer Ron Shelton (*White Men Can't Jump*) paints an ugly picture of a collegiate system filled with money-laundering alumni with deep pockets and blue-chip players who brazenly solicit under-the-table perks. The movie transcends several sports clichés by plunging deep into the aesthetics of the game and is packed with familiar NBA faces. Rated PG-13 for language. 108m. **DIR:** William Friedkin. **CAST:** Nick Nolte, Shaquille O'Neal, J. T. Walsh, Anfernee Hardaway, Alfre Woodard, Matt Nover, Mary McDonnell. **1994**

BLUE COLLAR ★★★★½ This film delves into the underbelly of the auto industry by focusing on the fears, frustrations, and suppressed anger of three factory workers, superbly played by Richard Pryor, Harvey Keitel, and Yaphet Kotto. It is the social comment and intense drama that make this a highly effective and memorable film. Good music, too. Rated R for violence, sex, nudity, and profanity. 114m. **DIR:** Paul Schrader. **CAST:** Richard Pryor, Harvey Keitel, Yaphet Kotto. **1978**

BLUE HEAVEN 🦃 New York TV executive threatened by a severe problem with alcohol. Not rated, but contains violence and strong language. 100m. **DIR:** Kathleen Dowdey. **CAST:** Leslie Denniston, James Eckhouse. **1984**

BLUE HOTEL ★★ Unsatisfying interpretation of Stephen Crane's short story. David Warner chews the scenery as a stranger in town who fears his life will be taken by the other guests of the hotel he occupies. The entire silly affair, which flirts with the notion of predestination, revolves around a card game. Introduced by Henry Fonda; unrated and suitable for family viewing. 55m. **DIR:** Ján Kadár. **CAST:** David Warner, James Keach, John Bottoms, Rex Everhart. **1984**

BLUE KNIGHT, THE (1973) ★★★½ William Holden gives an excellent, Emmy-winning performance as the hero of Joseph Wambaugh's bestselling novel. *The Blue Knight* chronicles the last four days in the life of an aging L.A. street cop. Lee Remick is superb as Holden's girlfriend. Originally made for television and cut down from a four-part, 200-minute presentation. Not rated. 103m. **DIR:** Robert Butler. **CAST:** William Holden, Lee Remick, Joe Santos, Sam Elliott, David Moody, Jamie Farr. **1973**

BLUE KNIGHT, THE (1975) ★★ This is the second made-for-TV production based on Joseph Wambaugh's bestselling book. In this rendering, George Kennedy assumes the role of tough L.A. cop Bumper Morgan, who is searching frantically for a cop killer. The story is average, but Kennedy gives a typically strong portrayal. 78m. **DIR:** J. Lee Thompson. **CAST:** George Kennedy, Alex Rocco, Verna Bloom, Glynn Turman. **1975**

BLUE LAGOON, THE ★★½ Two things save *The Blue Lagoon* from being a complete waste: Nestor Almendros's beautiful cinematography and the hilarious dialogue. Unfortunately, the laughs are unintentional. The screenplay is a combination of *Swiss Family Robinson* and the story of Adam and Eve, focusing on the growing love and sexuality of two children stranded on a South Sea island. Rated R for nudity and suggested sex. 101m. **DIR:** Randal Kleiser. **CAST:** Brooke Shields, Christopher Atkins, Leo McKern, William Daniels. **1980**

BLUE SKIES AGAIN ★★ A sure-fielding, solid-hitting prospect tries to break into the lineup of a minor league team. There's just one problem: The determined ball player is a female. Nothing more than a routine grounder. Rated PG. 96m. **DIR:** Richard Michaels. **CAST:** Harry Hamlin, Robyn Barto, Mimi Rogers, Kenneth McMillan, Dana Elcar. **1983**

BLUEBERRY HILL ★★ Carrie Snodgress plays a neurotic mother in 1956. Her daughter finds out the truth about her deceased father and also discovers, that she has inherited his piano skills. *Zzzzz.* Rated R for nudity and language. 93m. **DIR:** Strathford Hamilton. **CAST:** Carrie Snodgress, Margaret Avery, Matt Lattanzi. **1987**

BLUME IN LOVE ★★★★ Sort of the male version of *An Unmarried Woman*, this Paul Mazursky film is the heartrending, sometimes shocking tale of a lawyer (George Segal) who can't believe his wife (Susan Anspach) doesn't love him anymore. He tries everything to win her back (including rape), and the result is a drama the viewer won't soon forget. Superb performances by Segal, Anspach, and Kris Kristofferson (as the wife's new beau) help immensely. Rated R for suggested sex, profanity, and violence. 117m. **DIR:** Paul Mazursky. **CAST:** George Segal, Susan Anspach, Kris Kristofferson, Marsha Mason, Shelley Winters. **1973**

BOBBY DEERFIELD ★★★½ In this film, a racing driver (Al Pacino) becomes obsessed with the cause of how a competitor was seriously injured in an accident on the track. In a visit to the hospitalized driver, he meets a strange lady (Marthe Keller) and has an affair. Rated PG. 124m. **DIR:** Sydney Pollack. **CAST:** Al Pacino, Marthe Keller, Romolo Valli. **1977**

BODIES, REST & MOTION ★★½ Set in a Southwest desert city, this ponderous comedy-drama looks at the dreams and disillusionment of twentysomethings. Phoebe Cates, Bridget Fonda, and Eric Stoltz contribute a consistent charm. Rated R for adult situations and language. 93m. **DIR:** Michael Steinberg. **CAST:** Phoebe Cates, Bridget Fonda, Tim Roth, Eric Stoltz. **1993**

BODY AND SOUL (1947) ★★★★★ The best boxing film ever, this is an allegorical work that covers everything from the importance of personal honor to corruption in politics. It details the story of a fighter (John Garfield) who'll do anything to get to the top—and does, with tragic results. Great performances, gripping drama, and stark realism make this a must-see. B&W; 104m. **DIR:** Robert Rossen. **CAST:** John Garfield, Lilli Palmer, Hazel Brooks, Anne Revere, William Conrad. **1947**

BODY AND SOUL (1981) ★★★ Okay remake of the 1947 boxing classic. It's not original, deep, or profound, but entertaining. However, the original, with John Garfield, is better. Rated R for violence and profanity. 100m. **DIR:** George Bowers. **CAST:** Leon Isaac Kennedy, Jayne Kennedy, Perry Lang. **1981**

BODY MOVES 🦃 This dance flick is about as formulaic as you can get. Two dance troupes suffer through infighting on their way to a final showdown in the local dance contest. Rated PG-13 for profanity. 98m. **DIR:** Gerry Lively. **CAST:** Kirk Rivera. **1990**

BODYGUARD, THE ★★★ Lawrence Kasdan originally wrote *The Bodyguard* in 1972 with Steve McQueen in mind, and Kevin Costner attempts a homage to the charismatic action star as the protector to singer-actress Whitney Houston. The result proved extremely popular with filmgoers, so who are we to argue? While Houston is just fine in her big-screen debut, Costner's impersonation of McQueen seems cold rather than cool. So, if you're so inclined, enjoy. Rated R for profanity, suggested sex, and violence. 129m. **DIR:** Mick Jackson. **CAST:** Kevin Costner, Whitney Houston, Gary Kemp, Bill Cobbs, Ralph Waite. **1992**

BOGIE ★★½ Boring biography of Humphrey Bogart unconvincingly enacted by Bogie and Bacall look-alikes. Too much time is spent on the drinking and temper problems of Bogie's third wife, Mayo Methot, and not enough time is spent on Lauren Bacall. Kathryn Harrold, as Bacall, is so bad, however, that it's probably a blessing her part is small. 100m. **DIR:** Vincent Sherman. **CAST:** Kevin J. O'Connor, Kathryn Harrold, Ann Wedgeworth, Patricia Barry. **1980**

BOLERO (1984) 🦃 American heiress in the 1920s trying to lose her virginity. 106m. **DIR:** John Derek. **CAST:** Bo Derek, George Kennedy, Andrea Occhipinti, Ana Obregon, Olivia D'Abo. **1984**

BONFIRE OF THE VANITIES ★★ Tom Wolfe's novel has been shaped into a trivial, cartoon-style movie by director Brian De Palma. This savage comedy about the very rich bumping heads with the very poor in New York City boasts great photography by Vilmos Zsigmond, but the characters aren't very interesting, especially if you liked the book. Rated R for some nudity and violence. 126m. **DIR:** Brian De Palma. **CAST:** Bruce Willis, Tom Hanks, Melanie Griffith, Saul Rubinek, Morgan Freeman. **1990**

BONJOUR TRISTESSE ★★★ Jean Seberg is a spoiled teenager who tries to ruin the affair between her widowed father (David Niven) and his mistress (Deborah Kerr) in this dated soap opera. Kerr gives a fine performance and Niven is just right as the suave playboy, but Otto Preminger failed again to make a star of Seberg. Not rated. 94m. **DIR:** Otto Preminger. **CAST:** Deborah Kerr, David Niven, Jean Seberg, Mylene Demongeot. **1958**

BOOM TOWN ★★★★ Big-budget MGM star vehicle has buddies Clark Gable and Spencer Tracy striking it rich, going broke, and striking it rich again in the oil fields of the Southwest. Great fun. B&W; 116m. **DIR:** Jack Conway. **CAST:** Clark Gable, Spencer Tracy, Hedy Lamarr, Chill Wills, Frank Morgan, Lionel Atwill. **1940**

BOOST, THE ★★ The controversy surrounding the off-screen, *Fatal Attraction*-style relationship between James Woods and Sean Young is certainly more interesting than the movie itself. Woods gives a typically high-powered performance in this uncomfortably intense drama as a Beverly Hills investment broker who begins to use cocaine and loses control. The story lacks coherence. Rated R for nudity, profanity and drug use. 96m. **DIR:** Harold Becker. **CAST:** James Woods, Sean Young, Steven Hill. **1989**

BORDER RADIO 🦃 A disillusioned rock star steals a large sum of performance money owed to him by a sleazy club owner. Not rated, but contains profanity and violence. B&W; 89m. **DIR:** Allison Anders, Dean Lent, Kurt Voss. **CAST:** Chris D., Luana Anders. **1988**

BORN AGAIN 🦃 President Nixon's special counsel Charles Colson. Rated PG. 110m. **DIR:** Irving Rapper. **CAST:** Dean Jones, Anne Francis, Jay Robinson, Dana Andrews. **1978**

BORN INNOCENT ★★★ Rape with a broomstick marked this made-for-television film a shocker when first aired. The scene has been toned down, but the picture still penetrates with its searing story of cruelty in a juvenile detention home. Linda Blair does well as the runaway teenager. Joanna Miles is excellent as a compassionate teacher whose heart lies with her charges. It's strong stuff. 100m. **DIR:** Donald Wrye. **CAST:** Linda Blair, Kim Hunter, Joanna Miles. **1974**

BORN OF FIRE ★★ A classical concert flutist (Peter Firth) journeys to the Middle East in hopes of finding the reason for his father's death. The flutist only becomes embroiled in the same drama that befell his father. A boring, confusing story. Contains sex, nudity, and violence. 84m. **DIR:** Jamil Dehlaui. **CAST:** Peter Firth, Suzan Crowley, Stefan Kalipha. **1987**

BORN ON THE FOURTH OF JULY ★★★½ Tom Cruise's superb performance is the reason to watch this overblown screen biography of Vietnam veteran and antiwar activist Ron Kovic. Characters suddenly appear and disappear. Despite all this, Kovic's tale is a powerful one, and Cruise's breakthrough performance makes it memorable. Rated R for profanity, nudity, simulated sex, and violence. 135m. **DIR:** Oliver Stone. **CAST:** Tom Cruise, Kyra Sedgwick, Willem Dafoe, Raymond J. Barry, Tom Berenger. **1989**

BORN TO BE BAD ★★★ Conniving opportunist Joan Fontaine scrambles for a secure foothold in life while stepping on anything or anyone in her way. Although more than a bit melodramatic, Nicholas Ray's adult look at sexual relationships was ahead of its time and still has impact today. B&W; 94m. **DIR:** Nicholas Ray. **CAST:** Joan Fontaine, Robert Ryan, Joan Leslie, Zachary Scott, Mel Ferrer. **1950**

BORN TO WIN ★★★½ In one of his best performances, George Segal plays a New York junkie with a $100-a-day habit. Ivan Passer's direction is more inventive than successful, and the film often seems to be going in several directions. But the acting makes up, including a brief appearance by a young Robert De Niro. Also known as *Addict*. Rated R for profanity. 90m. **DIR:** Ivan Passer. **CAST:** George Segal, Karen Black, Hector Elizondo, Paula Prentiss, Jay Fletcher, Robert De Niro. **1971**

BOSS' SON, THE ★★★ Enjoyable drama about a young man's passage to adulthood. Our hero jumps at the chance to run the family factory. But when Dad decides his son must earn his way to the top, the boy learns what it truly means to earn a living. A little slow but rewarding. Unrated. 102m. **DIR:** Bobby Roth. **CAST:** Asher Brauner, Rita Moreno, Rudy Solari, Henry G. Sanders, James Darren, Piper Laurie. **1978**

BOSTONIANS, THE ★★★ A visually striking but dry production from Merchant Ivory Productions. Most of the sparks of conflict come not from the tortured love affair between Christopher Reeve and Madeleine Potter or the main theme of women's fight for equality, but from the few scenes of direct confrontation between Reeve and Vanessa Redgrave. The setting is Boston during the Centennial. 120m. **DIR:** James Ivory. **CAST:** Christopher Reeve, Vanessa Redgrave, Jessica Tandy, Madeleine Potter, Nancy Marchand, Wesley Addy, Linda Hunt, Nancy New, Jon Van Ness, Wallace Shawn. **1984**

BOULEVARD NIGHTS ★★ Well-intentioned but dramatically dull account of a Chicano youth's desire to break out of East Los Angeles. Richard Yniguez is sincere in the lead role and Danny De La Paz is sympathetic as his brother, but the whole thing comes across like a preachy soap opera. Rated R for violence and profanity. 102m. **DIR:** Michael Pressman. **CAST:** Richard Yniguez, Marta Du Bois, Danny De La Paz, Carmen Zapata, Victor Millan. **1979**

BOULEVARD OF BROKEN DREAMS ★★★½ A famous Hollywood screenwriter returns home to Australia to win back his wife and daughter. Good acting, a wonderful plot, interesting side plots, and superb supporting characters make this a very enjoyable film, except for several unnecessary musical interludes. Rated PG-13 for profanity and frontal nudity. 95m. **DIR:** Pino Amenta. **CAST:** John Waters, Penelope Stewart, Kim Gyngell, Nicki Paull, Andrew McFarlane, Kevin Miles. **1988**

BOUND BY HONOR ★★★ Taylor Hackford's often exciting and emotional drama, portraying aspects of modern Chicano immigrant life through the stories of three young East Los Angeles men, in the late 1970s and 1980s. Unfortunately, at nearly three hours, the film seems at least 30 minutes too long. The film may also remind viewers of Edward James Olmos's superior *American Me*. Jessie Borrego is memorable as a Chicano artist who finds salvation with the paintbrush. Rated R, with strong violence and profanity. 172m. **DIR:** Taylor Hackford. **CAST:** Damian Chapa, Jessie Borrego, Benjamin Bratt. **1993**

BOUND FOR GLORY ★★★★ David Carradine had one of the best roles of his career as singer-composer Woody Guthrie. Film focuses on the depression years when Guthrie rode the rails across America. Director Hal Ashby explores the lives of those hit hardest during those times. Haskell Wexler won the Oscar for his beautiful cinematography. Rated PG. 147m. **DIR:** Hal Ashby. **CAST:** David Carradine, Ronny Cox, Melinda Dillon, Randy Quaid, Gail Strickland, Ji-Tu Cumbuka, John Lehne. **1976**

BOXOFFICE 🖤 From lousy nightclubs to the big time. Not rated, but contains language and nudity. 92m. **DIR:** Josef Bogdanovich. **CAST:** Robin Clark, Monica Lewis, Carole Cortne, Eddie Constantine, Aldo Ray, Edie Adams, Peter Hurkos. **1981**

BOY IN BLUE, THE ★★★ Nice little screen biography of Ned Hanlan (Nicolas Cage), the famed Canadian lad who owned the sport of international sculling (rowing) for ten years during the end of the nineteenth century. Although the picture plays like a thin retread of *Rocky*—particularly with respect to its music—the result is no less inspirational. Inexplicably rated R for very brief nudity and coarse language. 97m. **DIR:** Charles Jarrott. **CAST:** Nicolas Cage, Christopher Plummer, Cynthia Dale, David Naughton. **1986**

BOY IN THE PLASTIC BUBBLE, THE ★★ John Travolta has his hands full in this significantly altered television adaptation of the boy who, because of an immunity deficiency, must spend every breathing moment in a sealed environment. Vapid stuff needlessly mired with sci-fi jargon. Unrated. 100m. **DIR:** Randal Kleiser. **CAST:** John Travolta, Glynnis O'Connor, Ralph Bellamy, Robert Reed, Diana Hyland, Buzz Aldrin. **1976**

BOY WHO COULD FLY, THE ★★★★ Writer-director Nick Castle has created a marvelous motion picture which speaks to the dreamer in all of us. His heroine, Milly (Lucy Deakins), is a newcomer to a small town where her neighbor, Eric (Jay Underwood), neither speaks nor responds to other people. All he does is sit on his roof and pretend to fly. Rated PG for dramatic intensity. 114m. **DIR:** Nick Castle. **CAST:** Lucy Deakins, Jay Underwood, Bonnie Bedelia, Fred Savage, Colleen Dewhurst, Fred Gwynne, Mindy Cohn. **1986**

BOY WITH GREEN HAIR, THE ★★★ A young war orphan's hair changes color, makes him a social outcast, and brings a variety of bigots and narrow minds out of the woodwork in this food-for-thought fable. The medium is the message in this one. 82m. **DIR:** Joseph Losey. **CAST:** Dean Stockwell, Robert Ryan, Barbara Hale, Pat O'Brien. **1948**

BOYS IN THE BAND, THE ★★★ Widely acclaimed film about nine men who attend a birthday party and end up exposing their lives and feelings to one another in the course of the night. Eight of the men are gay; one is straight. One of the first American films to deal honestly with the subject of homosexuality. Sort of a large-scale *My Dinner with André* with the whole film shot on one set. Rated R. 119m. **DIR:** William Friedkin. **CAST:** Kenneth Nelson, Peter White, Leonard Frey, Cliff Gorman. **1970**

BOYS NEXT DOOR, THE ★★★ This story of two alienated teenage youths, Charlie Sheen and Maxwell Caulfield, going on a killing spree in Los Angeles, makes for some tense viewing. Sheen and Caulfield decide to go to L.A. Once in the city, one violent encounter spawns another. Beware: This one is extremely graphic in its depiction of violence. Rated R. 88m. **DIR:** Penelope Spheeris. **CAST:** Charlie Sheen, Maxwell Caulfield, Hank Garrett, Patti D'Arbanville, Christopher McDonald, Moon Zappa. **1985**

BOYS' TOWN ★★★★ Spencer Tracy gives one of his most memorable performances in this MGM classic about Father Flanagan and his struggle to give orphans and juvenile delinquents a chance at life. Overtly manipulative, but rewarding. B&W; 93m. **DIR:** Norman Taurog. **CAST:** Spencer Tracy, Mickey Rooney, Henry Hull. **1938**

BOYZ N THE HOOD ★★★★½ Although *Boyz N the Hood* may appear to be an exploitation flick about gang violence, it is far from being so. This powerful drama, which marks the directing debut of 23-year-old John Singleton, is a responsible, heart-tugging tale of a modern tragedy, focusing on a group of young men and women caught in the war zone of south central Los Angeles. Rated R for profanity, violence, and nudity. 111m. **DIR:** John Singleton. **CAST:** Ice Cube, Cuba Gooding Jr., Morris Chestnut, Larry Fishburne, Nia Long, Tyra Ferrell. **1991**

BRAMBLE BUSH, THE ★★ Soap opera about a doctor who pulls the plug on his terminally ill best friend while having an affair with the sick buddy's wife. There are enough subplots for an afternoon full of daytime dramas in this mildly diverting movie. 93m. **DIR:** Daniel Petrie. **CAST:** Richard Burton, Angie Dickinson, Barbara Rush, Tom Drake, James Dunn, Henry Jones. **1960**

BRASS ★★ Routine made-for-TV cop thriller starring Carroll O'Connor as a top New York City police officer and a politically sensitive kidnap-murder case. The pilot for a proposed series. 94m. **DIR:** Corey Allen. **CAST:** Carroll O'Connor, Lois Nettleton, Jimmy Baio, Paul Shenar. **1985**

BREAK OF DAWN ★★★½ Based on a true story, this chronicles Pedro J. Gonzalez's entry to the United States in 1928 and his rapid rise to popularity as the first Mexican radio show host. When his influence over the East L.A. population threatens the racist DA, he's framed for rape. Low-budget, yet convincing. In English and Spanish with English subtitles when needed. Unrated, contains mature themes. 100m. **DIR:** Isaac Artenstein. **CAST:** Oscar Chavez, Tony Plana, Maria Rojo, Pepe Serna. **1988**

BREAK OF HEARTS ★★½ Mediocre drama about a struggling composer and her troubled marriage to highly acclaimed symphony conductor. Some good acting makes up for the predictable script. B&W; 80m. **DIR:** Phillip Moeller. **CAST:** Katharine Hepburn, Charles Boyer, John Beal. **1935**

BREAKFAST AT TIFFANY'S ★★★★ An offbeat yet tender love story of a New York writer and a fey party girl. Strong performances are turned in by George Peppard and Audrey Hepburn. Hepburn's Holly Golightly is a masterful creation that blends the sophistication of a Manhattan "escort" with the childish country girl of her roots. Henry Mancini's score is justly famous, as it creates much of the mood for this wistful story. 115m. **DIR:** Blake Edwards. **CAST:** Audrey Hepburn, George Peppard, Patricia Neal, Buddy Ebsen, Mickey Rooney, Martin Balsam. 1961

BREAKING HOME TIES ★★★ Texas farm family drama, set in the 1950s, in which the proud father sends his only son off to college in the big city. Well-written TV drama with believable characters and good acting. 95m. **DIR:** John Wilder. **CAST:** Jason Robards Jr., Eva Marie Saint, Doug McKeon, Erin Gray, Claire Trevor. 1987

BREAKING POINT ★★★½ Decent World War II espionage thriller, this remake of *36 Hours* features Corbin Bernsen as a top U.S. intelligence officer who becomes the victim of an elaborate Nazi plot. Made for cable, this is unrated but contains mature themes. 90m. **DIR:** Peter Markle. **CAST:** Corbin Bernsen, Joanna Pacula, John Glover, David Marshall Grant. 1989

BREAKING THE RULES ★★★½ Three friends reunite and learn that one of them is dying of cancer. They take a cross-country trip to California and meet an unusual woman along the way. Annie Potts is brilliant as Mary, the wacky artist who wants to beautify the country. Rated PG-13 for profanity and suggested sex. 100m. **DIR:** Neal Israel. **CAST:** Jason Bateman, C. Thomas Howell, Jonathan Silverman, Annie Potts, Krista Tesreau. 1991

BREAKING UP IS HARD TO DO ★★ Superficial made-for-TV movie about six men, all recently divorced, going through the usual trials and tribulations as they try to heal the wounds. 96m. **DIR:** Lou Antonio. **CAST:** Ted Bessell, Jeff Conaway, Robert Conrad, Billy Crystal, Tony Musante, David Ogden Stiers. 1979

BREATHING LESSONS ★★★★ Joanne Woodward steals the show in this, the 180th *Hallmark Hall of Fame*. Woodward plays a whimsical, meddling woman who tries to make things right but usually makes matters worse. James Garner, excellent as her long-suffering husband, resigns himself to their unpredictable but lasting relationship. Based on Ann Tyler's novel, this film focuses on relationships rather than actions and events and has a surprisingly powerful effect on viewers. 93m. **DIR:** John Erman. **CAST:** James Garner, Joanne Woodward, Paul Winfield, Joyce Van Patten. 1994

BREATHLESS (1983) 🦃 Richard Gere plays a car thief hunted by police. Rated R for nudity, profanity, and violence. 100m. **DIR:** Jim McBride. **CAST:** Richard Gere, Valerie Kaprisky, Art Metrano, John P. Ryan. 1983

BRIAN'S SONG ★★★★★ This is one of the best movies ever made originally for television. James Caan is Brian Piccolo, a running back for football's Chicago Bears. His friendship for superstar Gale Sayers (Billy Dee Williams) becomes a mutually stimulating rivalry on the field and inspirational strength when Brian is felled by cancer. As with any quality film that deals with death, this movie is buoyant with life and warmth. Rated G. 73m. **DIR:** Buzz Kulik. **CAST:** James Caan, Billy Dee Williams, Jack Warden, Judy Pace, Shelley Fabares. 1970

BRIDE WORE RED, THE ★★ A trampy club singer pretends to be a society debutante, and all the rich guys fall in love with her. Joan Crawford played so many street girls who posed as classy ladies, her movies became a cliché. This is probably the definitive one. B&W; 103m. **DIR:** Dorothy Arzner. **CAST:** Joan Crawford, Franchot Tone, Robert Young, Billie Burke, Reginald Owen, Dickie Moore, George Zucco. 1937

BRIDESHEAD REVISITED ★★★★ Evelyn Waugh's massive novel of British upper-class decadence gets royal treatment in this adaptation from John Mortimer (*Rumpole of the Bailey*), who captures every nuance of Waugh's indictment of the wealthy. Jeremy Irons stars as the impressionable Oxford youth bedazzled by Sebastian Flyte (Anthony Andrews), youngest of the ill-fated Marchmain family. Irons quickly falls in love with this odd group, but their embrace nearly proves more than he can handle. Unrated; includes frank sexual themes and brief nudity. 388m. **DIR:** Charles Sturridge, Michael Lindsay-Hogg. **CAST:** Jeremy Irons, Anthony Andrews, Diana Quick, Laurence Olivier, Claire Bloom, John Gielgud, Stéphane Audran, Mona Washbourne, John Le Mesurier, Simon Jones. 1981

BRIDGE AT REMAGEN, THE ★★★ Solid World War II drama concerns the German attempt to hold or blow up one of the last remaining bridges leading into the fatherland. Well-done action sequences keep things moving along at a good pace. Not a great film, but it should fill the bill for fans of the genre. 115m. **DIR:** John Guillermin. **CAST:** George Segal, Ben Gazzara, Robert Vaughn, E. G. Marshall, Bradford Dillman, Peter Van Eyck. 1969

BRIDGE OF SAN LUIS REY, THE ★★½ Five people meet death when an old Peruvian rope bridge collapses. This snail's-pace, moody version of Thornton Wilder's fatalistic 1920s novel traces their lives. Not too hot, and neither was the 1929 version. B&W; 85m. **DIR:** Rowland V. Lee. **CAST:** Lynn Bari, Nazimova, Louis Calhern, Akim Tamiroff, Francis Lederer, Blanche Yurka, Donald Woods. 1944

BRIDGE TO NOWHERE ★★½ Five streetwise city kids head to the rough-and-rugged country for a fun-filled weekend. Once they trespass on the land of an extremely vicious and violent man (Bruno Lawrence), they are forced to fight for survival. Parental discretion advised. 87m. **DIR:** Ian Mune. **CAST:** Bruno

Lawrence, Alison Routledge, Margaret Umbers, Philip Gordon. 1986

BRIDGE TO SILENCE ★★½ Sincere performances by a talented cast, including Marlee Matlin in her first speaking role, cannot quite overcome a melodramatic story in which a deaf woman (Matlin) nearly loses custody of her daughter to the mother (Lee Remick) who never understood her. Made for television. 95m. **DIR:** Karen Arthur. **CAST:** Marlee Matlin, Lee Remick, Josef Sommer, Michael O'Keefe. 1989

BRIEF ENCOUNTER (1945) ★★★★½ In this evergreen classic, a chance meeting in a railroad station results in a doomed, poignant love affair between two lonely people married to others. Celia Johnson is the woman, Trevor Howard the man. A compassionate look at the innocence of sudden, unforeseen romance. David Lean's direction results in a moving, memorable film for all time. B&W; 85m. **DIR:** David Lean. **CAST:** Celia Johnson, Trevor Howard, Stanley Holloway, Joyce Carey, Cyril Raymond. 1945

BRIEF ENCOUNTER (1974) ★★½ This is a remake of the 1945 classic film that was based on Noel Coward's play *Still Life*. It tells the story of two married strangers who meet in a British train terminal and fall into a short-lived but intense romance. This made-for-television production suffers in comparison. 103m. **DIR:** Alan Bridges. **CAST:** Richard Burton, Sophia Loren. 1974

BRIG, THE ★★½ One of the more self-conscious efforts of the American New Cinema of the 1960s, adapted from a stage play set in a Marine Corps prison. With almost no dialogue, the film conveys the dehumanizing aspects of life as a prisoner. But even at this abbreviated length (it was originally 120m.), it's hard to watch. B&W; 57m. **DIR:** Jonas Mekas, Adolfas Mekas. **CAST:** Warren Finnerty. 1965

BRIGHT ANGEL ★★★½ Thoroughly engrossing film follows a young woman's attempt to free her brother from jail. A real sleeper that grabs hold and refuses to let go right up to its uncompromising conclusion. Rated R for language, nudity, and violence. 94m. **DIR:** Michael Fields. **CAST:** Dermot Mulroney, Lili Taylor, Mary Kay Place, Bill Pullman, Burt Young, Valerie Perrine, Sam Shepard. 1991

BRIGHT LIGHTS, BIG CITY ★★ Films grappling with the evils of substance abuse run the risk of glamorizing the subject they intend to criticize, and that is precisely the problem with this adaptation of Jay McInerney's novel (even though he wrote his own screenplay). Rated R for language and graphic drug emphasis. 110m. **DIR:** James Bridges. **CAST:** Michael J. Fox, Kiefer Sutherland, Phoebe Cates, Swoosie Kurtz, Frances Sternhagen, John Houseman, Jason Robards Jr., Dianne Wiest, William Hickey. 1988

BROADWAY BILL ★★★ One of Frank Capra's favorite films and one of the few he remade in later years. Warner Baxter stars as a horse owner who cares more about animals than his superficial family. He shirks family responsibility and his inheritance to train his favorite horse, Broadway Bill. Capra's remake was called *Riding High* and starred Bing Crosby. B&W; 90m. **DIR:** Frank Capra. **CAST:** Warner Baxter, Myrna Loy, Helen Vinson, Walter Connolly, Frankie Darro, Jason Robards Sr., Lucille Ball, Ward Bond, Dennis O'Keefe, Margaret Hamilton, Alan Hale Sr., Lynne Overman, Douglass Dumbrille. 1934

BROKEN ANGEL ★★ Distraught parents find their world turned upside down when their daughter disappears after a gang fight during her senior prom. Made for TV movie that superficially skims the surface of parental trust and love. 94m. **DIR:** Richard T. Heffron. **CAST:** William Shatner, Susan Blakely, Roxann Biggs, Brock Peters. 1992

BROKEN BLOSSOMS ★★★½ The tragic story of a young Chinese boy's unselfish love for a cruelly mistreated white girl. Lillian Gish is heart-twisting as the girl; Richard Barthelmess's portrayal of the Chinese boy made him an overnight star. Donald Crisp, later famous in warm and sympathetic roles, is the unfortunate girl's evil tormentor. Silent. B&W; 68m. **DIR:** D. W. Griffith. **CAST:** Lillian Gish, Richard Barthelmess, Donald Crisp. 1919

BROKEN STRINGS ★★½ A strangely humorous all-black melodrama in which the son of a paralyzed and embittered concert violinist tries to earn the cost of an operation by singing jazz. B&W; 60m. **DIR:** Bernard B. Ray. **CAST:** Clarence Muse, Sybil Lewis, Stymie Beard. 1940

BRONX TALE, A ★★★★ Robert De Niro makes an impressive directorial debut with this atmospheric, exquisitely detailed character study of a youngster torn between his hardworking, bus-driver dad (De Niro) and the flashy mobster (played superbly by screenwriter Chazz Palminteri) who rules their Bronx neighborhood. It's hard-edged at times—disturbingly so in segments on racial hatred—but ultimately rewarding. Rated R for violence and profanity. 122m. **DIR:** Robert De Niro. **CAST:** Robert De Niro, Chazz Palminteri, Joe Pesci, Lillio Brancato, Francis Capra, Taral Hicks. 1993

BROTHER JOHN ★★ In this not-so-heavenly melodrama, Sidney Poitier stars as an angel who returns to his Alabama hometown to see how things are going. He steps into bigotry and labor troubles. Not one of Poitier's best. Rated PG. 94m. **DIR:** James Goldstone. **CAST:** Sidney Poitier, Paul Winfield, Will Geer, Beverly Todd, Bradford Dillman. 1971

BROTHER SUN, SISTER MOON ★★★★ Alec Guinness stars as the Pope in this movie about religious reformation. This film shows a young Francis of Assisi starting his own church. He confronts the Pope and rejects the extravagant and pompous ceremonies of the Catholic Church, preferring simple religious practices. Rated PG. 121m. **DIR:** Franco Zeffirelli. **CAST:** Graham Faulkner, Judi Bowker, Alec Guinness. **1973**

BROTHERHOOD, THE ★★ A *Godfather* predecessor, *The Brotherhood* stars Kirk Douglas and Alex Cord as Italian brothers who inherit their father's criminal empire. Douglas doesn't make a convincing Italian, but the story is good and overcomes the poor casting and cinematography. Not rated, contains violence and mild profanity. 96m. **DIR:** Martin Ritt. **CAST:** Kirk Douglas, Alex Cord, Irene Papas, Luther Adler, Susan Strasberg, Murray Hamilton. **1968**

BROTHERHOOD OF JUSTICE ★★ Rich teenagers decide to band together after their high school is vandalized. Yuppie *Death Wish*. Ninety minutes of bad dialogue, but the message is worth something. Rated PG for violence. 97m. **DIR:** Charles Braverman. **CAST:** Keanu Reeves, Kiefer Sutherland, Lori Loughlin, Billy Zane. **1986**

BROTHERS KARAMAZOV, THE ★★★ Director Richard Brooks, who also scripted, and a fine cast work hard to give life to Russian novelist Fyodor Dostoyevsky's turgid account of the effect of the death of a domineering father on his disparate sons: a fun lover, a scholar, a religious zealot, and an epileptic. Studio promotion called it absorbing and exciting. It is, but only in flashes. 146m. **DIR:** Richard Brooks. **CAST:** Yul Brynner, Claire Bloom, Lee J. Cobb, Maria Schell, Richard Basehart, William Shatner, Albert Salmi. **1957**

BROTHERS OF THE WILDERNESS 🦃 Amateur production attempts to build a story around cute footage of a small boy and a wolf-dog. Unfortunately, the plot, dialogue, and acting are incredibly wooden. Rated G; contains no objectionable material. 60m. **DIR:** David Michael Hillman. **CAST:** George Randall, Charles Kivette, Mark Sawicki, Alina Szpak, George Bamber. **1983**

BROWNING VERSION, THE ★★★★ Michael Redgrave, in perhaps his greatest performance, is an aging teacher betrayed by his wife and disliked by his students, forced into early retirement by illness. He feels his whole life has been a failure. Fine adaptation by Terence Rattigan of his play. B&W; 90m. **DIR:** Anthony Asquith. **CAST:** Michael Redgrave, Jean Kent, Nigel Patrick, Wilfrid Hyde-White, Ronald Howard, Bill Travers. **1951**

BRUBAKER ★★★ Robert Redford stars as Henry Brubaker, a reform-minded penologist who takes over a decrepit Ohio prison, only to discover the state prison system is even more rotten than its facilities. The film begins dramatically enough, with Redford masquerading as one of the convicts. After that, its dramatic impact lessens. Rated R. 132m. **DIR:** Stuart Rosenberg. **CAST:** Robert Redford, Yaphet Kotto, Jane Alexander, Murray Hamilton. **1980**

BUD AND LOU ★★★ Made-for-TV movie explores the tensions between comedians Bud Abbott (Harvey Korman) and Lou Costello (Buddy Hackett). Based, we assume, on the excellent book of the same name by Bob Thomas, this film is at its best when examining the poignant offscreen relationship between the two funnymen. Its greatest flaw is that the stars are unable to make the duo's most celebrated routines even amusing. 99m. **DIR:** Robert C. Thompson. **CAST:** Harvey Korman, Buddy Hackett, Michele Lee, Arte Johnson, Robert Reed. **1978**

BUDDY SYSTEM, THE ★★ In the middle of this movie, the would-be novelist (Richard Dreyfuss) takes his unbound manuscripts to the edge of the sea and lets the wind blow the pages away. He should have done the same thing with the screenplay for this mediocre romantic comedy. The plot is that old chestnut about a fatherless little kid (Wil Wheaton) who helps his mom (Susan Sarandon) and an eligible man (Dreyfuss) get together. Rated PG for profanity. 110m. **DIR:** Glenn Jordan. **CAST:** Richard Dreyfuss, Susan Sarandon, Nancy Allen, Wil Wheaton. **1984**

BUDDY'S SONG ★★★½ Roger Daltrey delivers a surprisingly strong performance as a loser who takes hope in his son's singing career. Very watchable albeit painfully so at times. Rated R for nudity, profanity, and violence. 107m. **DIR:** Claude Whatham. **CAST:** Roger Daltrey, Chesney Hawkes, Sharon Duce, Michael Elphick. **1991**

BUFFALO JUMP ★★★½ Enjoyable, family-oriented Canadian drama stars Wendy Crewson as a young woman who inherits a ranch in the middle of nowhere. She rises to the challenge and learns some very valuable lessons about growing up. Pleasant affair. Not rated. 97m. **DIR:** Eric Till. **CAST:** Wendy Crewson, Paul Gross. **1989**

BUGSY ★★★★½ Warren Beatty gives a flamboyant, explosive performance as gangster Benjamin "Bugsy" Siegel. Charming, shrewd, and given to fits of uncontrollable temper and violence, Siegel becomes obsessed with the creation of Las Vegas, an expensive project that puts him dangerously at odds with his partners. A stellar cast and superb direction by Barry Levinson make this an outstanding gangster movie. Rated R for violence, brief profanity, and nudity. 135m. **DIR:** Barry Levinson. **CAST:** Warren Beatty, Annette Bening, Harvey Keitel, Ben Kingsley, Elliott Gould, Joe Mantegna, Bebe Neuwirth, Wendy Phillips, Richard Sarafian, Bill Graham. **1991**

BUNNY'S TALE, A ★★★ Engaging comedy-drama stars Kirstie Alley as feminist author Gloria Steinem, who became a Bunny at a Playboy Club in order to get the real story behind the Hugh Hefner empire. Her experiences make for major entertainment, and this made-for-TV film never slips into the peekaboo trap it easily could have. 97m. **DIR:** Karen Arthur. **CAST:** Kirstie Alley, Cotter Smith, Deborah Van Valkenburgh, Joanna Kerns, Delta Burke. **1985**

BURKE AND WILLS ★★ Like most Australian period movies, this historical drama about a failed attempt to travel through the uncharted interior of nineteenth century Australia is meticulously produced, but ends up being more exhausting than entertaining. It's also about 45 minutes too long. It's rated PG-13 for language and brief nudity. 140m. **DIR:** Graeme Clifford. **CAST:** Jack Thompson, Nigel Havers, Greta Scacchi. **1987**

BURN! ★★★★ Marlon Brando's performance alone makes *Burn!* worth watching. Seldom has a star so vividly and memorably lived up to his promise as acting great, and that's what makes this film a must-see. Brando plays Sir William Walker, an egotistical mercenary sent by the British to instigate a slave revolt on a Portuguese-controlled sugar-producing island. He succeeds all too well by turning José Dolores (Evaristo Marquez) into a powerful leader and soon finds himself back on the island, plotting the downfall of his Frankenstein monster. Rated PG. 112m. **DIR:** Gillo Pontecorvo. **CAST:** Marlon Brando, Evaristo Marquez, Renato Salvatori. **1969**

BURNING BED, THE ★★★★ Farrah Fawcett is remarkably good in this made-for-TV film based on a true story. She plays a woman reaching the breaking point with her abusive and brutish husband, well played by Paul LeMat. Fawcett not only proves she can act, but that she has the capacity to pull off a multilayered role. Believable from start to finish, this is a superior television film. 105m. **DIR:** Robert Greenwald. **CAST:** Farrah Fawcett, Paul LeMat, Richard Masur, Grace Zabriskie. **1984**

BURNING SECRET ★★ A cool, overly restrained mystery-romance, set in an Austrian health spa in the years between the world wars. Faye Dunaway and Klaus Maria Brandauer star as emotionally crippled strangers who meet when Brandauer befriends her young son. Remarkably short on passion. Rated PG. 110m. **DIR:** Andrew Birkin. **CAST:** Faye Dunaway, Klaus Maria Brandauer. **1988**

BUS IS COMING, THE ★★★ The message of this production is: racism (both black and white) is wrong. In this film, Billy Mitchell (Mike Sims) is a young black soldier who returns to his hometown after his brother is murdered. Billy's white friend encourages him to investigate the death of his brother, while his black friends want to tear the town down. The acting is not the greatest, but the film does succeed in making its point. Rated PG for violence. 102m. **DIR:** Wendell J. Franklin. **CAST:** Mike Simms, Stephanie Faulkner, Burl Bullock. **1971**

BUSINESS AS USUAL ★★ Glenda Jackson plays a dress-shop manager fired after going to bat for an employee who's been sexually harrassed by a higher-up. Writer-director Lezli-An Barrett's script covers a wide range of issues but never develops any dramatic tension or strong characters. Rated PG. 89m. **DIR:** Lezli-An Barrett. **CAST:** Glenda Jackson, John Thaw, Cathy Tyson, Mark McGann, James Hazeldine. **1987**

BUSTED UP ★★½ A story about a local-circuit bare-fisted fighter and a nightclub singer. Typical plot, average acting, but professionally produced and technically polished. Rated R for violence and language. 93m. **DIR:** Conrad E. Palmisano. **CAST:** Irene Cara, Paul Coufos, Tony Rosato, Stan Shaw. **1986**

BUSTER ★★★ Pop star Phil Collins makes his film debut in this enjoyable story about the British Great Train Robbery of 1963. Collins is Buster Edwards, who became a folk hero after he and his cronies pulled off the greatest robbery in the history of England. It's enjoyable fare and an interesting character study. Rated R for language and brief nudity. 93m. **DIR:** David Greene. **CAST:** Phil Collins, Julie Walters, Sheila Hancock. **1988**

BUSTER AND BILLIE ★★ A handsome high school boy falls in love with a homely but loving girl in the rural South. Set in the 1940s, the film has an innocent, sweet quality until it abruptly shifts tone and turns into a mean-spirited revenge picture. Rated R for violence and nudity. 100m. **DIR:** Daniel Petrie. **CAST:** Jan-Michael Vincent, Joan Goodfellow, Pamela Sue Martin, Clifton James. **1974**

BUT NOT FOR ME ★★½ Clark Gable does a credible job as an aging Broadway producer who feels the ravages of time in both his professional career and private life. Predictable comedy-drama but the leading players (especially Lilli Palmer) and a title song by Ella Fitzgerald help. B&W; 105m. **DIR:** Walter Lang. **CAST:** Clark Gable, Carroll Baker, Lilli Palmer, Lee J. Cobb, Barry Coe, Thomas Gomez, Charles Lane. **1959**

BUTTERFIELD 8 ★★★ Severe illness helped sway votes her way when Elizabeth Taylor copped an Oscar for her by-the-numbers portrayal of a big-ticket call girl who wants to go straight after finding someone she thinks is Mr. Right. Adapted from the John O'Hara novel. 109m. **DIR:** Daniel Mann. **CAST:** Elizabeth Taylor, Laurence Harvey, Eddie

Fisher, Dina Merrill, Mildred Dunnock, Betty Field. 1960

BUTTERFLIES ARE FREE ★★★★ Edward Albert is a blind youth determined to be self-sufficient in spite of his overbearing mother and the distraction of his will-o'-the-wisp next-door neighbor (Goldie Hawn). This fast-paced comedy benefits from some outstanding performances, none better than that by Eileen Heckart. Her concerned, protective, and sometimes overloving mother is a treasure to behold. Rated PG. 109m. **DIR:** Milton Katselas. **CAST:** Goldie Hawn, Edward Albert, Eileen Heckart, Mike Warren. 1972

BUTTERFLY ★★ Sex symbol Pia Zadora starts an incestuous relationship with her father (Stacy Keach). Orson Welles, as a judge, is the best thing about this film. Rated R. 107m. **DIR:** Matt Cimber. **CAST:** Pia Zadora, Stacy Keach, Orson Welles, Lois Nettleton. 1982

BY DAWN'S EARLY LIGHT ★★★ This slick adaptation of William Prochnau's *Trinity's Child*, unfolds like an updated *Fail-Safe*. Nuclear terrorists trick the Soviet Union into believing the U.S. has struck first, and the reprisal is launched before the mistake is detected. Unrated made-for-cable film; contains profanity. 104m. **DIR:** Jack Sholder. **CAST:** Powers Boothe, Rebecca DeMornay, James Earl Jones, Martin Landau, Darren McGavin, Jeffrey DeMunn, Peter MacNicol, Rip Torn. 1990

BY DESIGN ★★½ Patty Duke plays a lesbian fashion designer who decides she'd like to have a baby. She attempts to get pregnant by a heterosexual man. Interesting subject matter gets an uneven result. Rated R. 88m. **DIR:** Claude Jutra. **CAST:** Patty Duke, Sara Botsford, Saul Rubinek. 1981

BYE BYE, BABY 🦃 Bizarre twist on Noel Coward's *Private Lives*. The film was clearly shot simultaneously in English and Italian, with dialogue that sounds like badly translated Esperanto. Rated R for nudity. 90m. **DIR:** Enrico Oldoini. **CAST:** Carol Alt, Luca Barbareschi, Brigitte Nielsen, Jason Connery. 1989

CABIN IN THE COTTON ★★★ An ambitious young sharecropper is educated by and then works for a rich landowner. His loyalties are challenged when he learns of widespread theft by tenant farmers. Worth the price of rental to hear vixen Bette Davis utter the immortal, and often misquoted line: "Ah'd *like* ta' kiss ya, but ah jus' washed mah hair." B&W; 78m. **DIR:** Michael Curtiz. **CAST:** Richard Barthelmess, Bette Davis, Dorothy Jordan, Russell Simpson. 1932

CABIN IN THE SKY ★★★ One of Hollywood's first general-release black films and Vincente Minnelli's first feature. Eddie Anderson shows acting skill that was sadly and too long diluted by his playing foil for Jack Benny. Ethel Waters, as always, is superb. The film is a shade racist, but bear in mind that it was made in 1943, when Tinsel Town still thought blacks did nothing but sing, dance, and love watermelon. B&W; 100m. **DIR:** Vincente Minnelli. **CAST:** Eddie "Rochester" Anderson, Lena Horne, Ethel Waters, Rex Ingram, Louis Armstrong. 1943

CACTUS ★★★½ Have patience with this warm and witty tale of a French lady (Isabelle Huppert) injured in an auto accident while visiting Australia. A young blind man helps her adjust to her diminishing eyesight. The supporting cast and Australian locale add to this story of growth and awareness. 96m. **DIR:** Paul Cox. **CAST:** Isabelle Huppert, Robert Menzies, Norman Kaye. 1986

CADDIE ★★★★ This is an absorbing character study of a woman who struggles to support herself and her children in Australia in the 1920s. Thanks greatly to the star's performance, it is yet another winner from down under. MPAA unrated, but contains mild sexual situations. 107m. **DIR:** Donald Crombie. **CAST:** Helen Morse, Takis Emmanuel, Jack Thompson, Jacki Weaver. 1976

CADENCE ★★½ Well-meant film about the evils of racism is skewed by director Martin Sheen's overly sympathetic portrait of a prejudiced stockade commander who attempts to use newcomer Charlie Sheen to spy on his cell mates, all of whom are black. More notable for good intentions than dramatic power. Rated PG-13 for profanity and violence. 97m. **DIR:** Martin Sheen. **CAST:** Charlie Sheen, Martin Sheen, Larry Fishburne, Michael Beach, Ramon Estevez. 1991

CAESAR AND CLEOPATRA ★★½ George Bernard Shaw's wordy play about Rome's titanic leader and Egypt's young queen. Claude Rains and Vivien Leigh are brilliant. 127m. **DIR:** Gabriel Pascal. **CAST:** Claude Rains, Vivien Leigh, Stewart Granger, Francis L. Sullivan, Flora Robson. 1946

CAINE MUTINY, THE ★★★★ Superb performances by Humphrey Bogart, Van Johnson, José Ferrer, and Fred MacMurray, among others, make this adaptation of Herman Wouk's classic novel an absolute must-see. This brilliant film concerns the hard-nosed Captain Queeg (Bogart), who may or may not be slightly unhinged, and the subsequent mutiny by his first officer and crew, who are certain he is. Beautifully done, a terrific movie. 125m. **DIR:** Edward Dmytryk. **CAST:** Humphrey Bogart, José Ferrer, Van Johnson, Robert Francis, Fred MacMurray. 1954

CAINE MUTINY COURT MARTIAL, THE ★★★★ Splendid adaptation of Herman Wouk's brilliant Pulitzer Prize–winning novel. Brad Davis comes aboard in the Humphrey Bogart role as Queeg, whose unorthodox actions aboard the U.S.S. *Caine* forced his crew to mutiny. Director Robert Altman keeps everything shipshape, and evokes outstanding performances from the enlisted men. Rated PG. 100m. **DIR:** Robert Altman. **CAST:** Brad Davis, Eric Bogosian, Jeff Daniels, Peter Gallagher, Michael Murphy. **1988**

CAL ★★★★ This superb Irish film, which focuses on "the troubles" in Northern Ireland, stars John Lynch as Cal, a teenage boy who wants to sever his ties with the IRA. This turns out to be anything but easy, as the leader tells him, if he isn't for them, he's against them. Cal hides out at the home of Marcella (Helen Mirren, in a knockout of a performance). She's the widow of a policeman he helped murder. Nevertheless, they fall in love. Rated R for sex, nudity, profanity, and violence. 102m. **DIR:** Pat O'Connor. **CAST:** Helen Mirren, John Lynch, Donal McCann. **1984**

CALIFORNIA DREAMING ★★ Wimpy film about a dork from Chicago trying to fit into the California life-style. The cast is good, but the story is maudlin and slow-moving. Rated R for partial nudity. 93m. **DIR:** John Hancock. **CAST:** Glynnis O'Connor, Seymour Cassel, Dennis Christopher, Tanya Roberts. **1979**

CALIGULA 🦃 A $15 million porno flick with big stars. Rated X for every excess imaginable. 156m. **DIR:** Tinto Brass. **CAST:** Malcolm McDowell, Peter O'Toole, Teresa Ann Savoy, Helen Mirren. **1980**

CALL OF THE WILD (1992) ★★★ Fairly loyal to Jack London's best-selling novel, this drama focuses on the many changes a domesticated dog must undergo after being stolen for arctic sledding. Rick Schroder is the only human to show him genuine kindness after his ordeal begins. High production values and authentic location shots are a plus. Unrated, contains simulated animal abuse. 97m. **DIR:** Alan Smithee. **CAST:** Rick Schroder, Gordon Tootoosis, Duncan Fraser, Mia Sara. **1992**

CALL TO GLORY ★★★½ Engrossing pilot episode for a short-lived TV series. Set in the early 1960s, it follows an air force officer's family through the events of the Kennedy presidency. The taut script ably balances the story of their struggle to deal with military life and still retains the flavor of a historical chronicle of the times. This uniformly well -acted and -directed opening show promised much quality that was unfortunately unfulfilled in later episodes. 97m. **DIR:** Thomas Carter. **CAST:** Craig T. Nelson, Cindy Pickett, Keenan Wynn, Elisabeth Shue, David Hollander. **1984**

CALLIE AND SON ★★½ Syrupy drama about a poor waitress who becomes the queen of a Texas publishing empire. On the way, she is reunited with her long-lost son. Sometimes halfway engrossing; sometimes really disturbing. 150m. **DIR:** Waris Hussein. **CAST:** Lindsay Wagner, Jameson Parker, Dabney Coleman, Andrew Prine, Michelle Pfeiffer, James Sloyan. **1981**

CAMILLE ★★★★ Metro-Goldwyn-Mayer's lavish production of the Dumas classic provided screen goddess Greta Garbo with one of her last unqualified successes and remains the consummate adaptation of this popular weeper. The combined magic of the studio and Garbo's presence legitimized this archaic creaker about a dying woman and her love affair with a younger man (Robert Taylor, soon to be one of MGM's biggest stars). B&W; 108m. **DIR:** George Cukor. **CAST:** Greta Garbo, Robert Taylor, Lionel Barrymore, Henry Daniell, Laura Hope Crews, Elizabeth Allan, Lenore Ulric, Jessie Ralph. **1936**

CAN YOU HEAR THE LAUGHTER? THE STORY OF FREDDIE PRINZE ★★½ Freddie Prinze was a Puerto Rican comedian who rose from the barrio to television superstardom in a relatively brief time. His premiere achievement was a starring role in *Chico and The Man,* with Jack Albertson. Sympathetic, but no punches are pulled on the facts surrounding his death. 106m. **DIR:** Burt Brinckerhoff. **CAST:** Ira Angustain, Kevin Hooks, Randee Heller, Julie Carmen. **1979**

CANDIDATE, THE ★★★½ Michael Ritchie expertly directed this incisive look at a political hopeful (Robert Redford) and the obstacles and truths he must confront on the campaign trail. Rated PG. 109m. **DIR:** Michael Ritchie. **CAST:** Robert Redford, Peter Boyle, Don Porter, Allen Garfield. **1972**

CANDY MOUNTAIN ★★★★ Mediocre musician (Kevin J. O'Connor) takes to the highway in search of a legendary guitar craftsman Elmore Silk. Celebrated photographer and underground filmmaker Robert Frank joins screenwriter Rudy Wurlitzer to create an engaging, offbeat, visually beautiful film. Rated R for nudity and profanity. 90m. **DIR:** Robert Frank, Rudy Wurlitzer. **CAST:** Kevin J. O'Connor, Harris Yulin, Tom Waits, Bulle Ogier, David Johansen, Leon Redbone, Joe Strummer, Dr. John. **1987**

CANDYMAN, THE (1968) 🦃 English drug peddler in Mexico City plots to kidnap the child of an American movie star. 98m. **DIR:** Herbert J. Leder. **CAST:** George Sanders, Leslie Parrish. **1968**

CAPTAIN NEWMAN, M.D. ★★★ The movie fluctuates between meaningful laughter and heavy drama. An excellent ensemble neatly maintains the balance. Gregory Peck is at his noble best as a sympathetic army psychiatrist. The film's most gripping performance comes from Bobby Darin, who plays a psychotic. 126m. **DIR:** David Miller. **CAST:** Gregory Peck, Angie Dickinson, Tony Curtis, Eddie Albert, Jane Withers, Bobby Darin, Larry Storch. **1963**

CAPTAINS COURAGEOUS ★★★★★ This is an exquisite adaptation of Rudyard Kipling's story about a spoiled rich kid who falls from an ocean liner and is rescued by fishermen. Through them, the lad learns about the rewards of hard work and genuine friendship. Spencer Tracy won a well-deserved best-actor Oscar for his performance as the fatherly fisherman. B&W; 116m. **DIR:** Victor Fleming. **CAST:** Spencer Tracy, Freddie Bartholomew, Lionel Barrymore, Melvyn Douglas, Mickey Rooney. **1937**

CAPTIVE ★★½ A rich man's daughter is kidnapped by a trio of young European anarchists whose only purpose is to convert her to their way of thinking. Arty but obscure. Unrated, but contains nudity, suggested sex, and violence. 95m. **DIR:** Paul Mayersberg. **CAST:** Irina Brook, Oliver Reed. **1986**

CAPTIVE HEART ★★★★½ Exciting, well-written, marvelously performed story that examines the plight of British POWs and their Nazi captors. A superior job by all involved. B&W; 108m. **DIR:** Basil Dearden. **CAST:** Michael Redgrave, Rachel Kempson, Basil Radford, Jack Warner. **1946**

CAPTIVE HEARTS ★★½ Quiet little drama about two bomber crewmen (Chris Makepeace and Michael Sarrazin) shot down over a small Japanese town in the waning days of World War II. Makepeace is in over his head with this role, but Pat Morita, as the village elder, and Sarrazin carry the picture. Rated PG for language and violence. 102m. **DIR:** Paul Almond. **CAST:** Noriyuki "Pat" Morita, Chris Makepeace, Michael Sarrazin. **1988**

CARAVAGGIO ★★★★ Derek Jarman's extraordinary and revealing film is based on the life and art of Caravaggio, perhaps the greatest of Italian post-Renaissance painters. This controversial biography explores the artist's life, which was troubled by extremes of passion and artistic radicalism. Not rated; contains nudity, profanity, and violence. 97m. **DIR:** Derek Jarman. **CAST:** Nigel Terry, Sean Bean, Tilda Swinton, Spencer Leigh, Michael Gough. **1986**

CARAVANS 🦃 An American diplomat is sent to the Middle East to bring back the daughter of an American politician. Rated PG. 123m. **DIR:** James Fargo. **CAST:** Anthony Quinn, Michael Sarrazin, Jennifer O'Neill, Christopher Lee, Joseph Cotten, Barry Sullivan, Jeremy Kemp. **1978**

CARDINAL, THE ★★★ Director Otto Preminger's epic view of a vital and caring young Catholic priest's rise from a backwoods clergyman to cardinal. Alternately compelling and shallow. Watch for the late Maggie McNamara in her last role. 175m. **DIR:** Otto Preminger. **CAST:** Tom Tryon, Romy Schneider, Carol Lynley, John Huston. **1963**

CAREER ★★★★ Anthony Franciosa delivers a surprisingly powerful performance as an actor for whom success is always just beyond reach. In his pursuit for the one big part, he sacrifices his personal happiness and youth. Exemplary supporting performances by Dean Martin and Carolyn Jones. B&W; 105m. **DIR:** Joseph Anthony. **CAST:** Anthony Franciosa, Dean Martin, Shirley MacLaine, Carolyn Jones, Joan Blackman. **1959**

CAREFUL HE MIGHT HEAR YOU ★★★★½ A child's-eye view of the harsh realities of life, this Australian import is a poignant, heartwarming, sad, and sometimes frightening motion picture. A young boy named P.S. (played by 7-year-old Nicholas Gledhill) gets caught up in a bitter custody fight between his two aunts. While the movie does tend to become a tearjerker on occasion, it does so without putting off the viewer. Rated PG for suggested sex and violence. 116m. **DIR:** Carl Schultz. **CAST:** Robyn Nevin, Nicholas Gledhill, Wendy Hughes, John Hargreaves. **1983**

CARNAL KNOWLEDGE ★★★★ The sexual dilemmas of the modern American are analyzed and come up short in this thoughtful film. Jack Nicholson and singer Art Garfunkel are college roommates whose lives are followed through varied relationships with the opposite sex. Nicholson is somewhat of a stinker, and one finds oneself more in sympathy with the women in the cast. Rated R. 96m. **DIR:** Mike Nichols. **CAST:** Jack Nicholson, Candice Bergen, Art Garfunkel, Ann-Margret. **1971**

CARNIVAL STORY ★★ Familiar story of rivalry between circus performers over the affections of the girl they both love. No real surprises. Filmed in Germany. 95m. **DIR:** Kurt Neumann. **CAST:** Anne Baxter, Steve Cochran, Jay C. Flippen, George Nader. **1954**

CARNY ★★★★ This film takes us behind the bright lights into the netherworld of the "carnies," people who spend their lives cheating, lying, and stealing from others yet consider themselves superior to their victims. Gary Busey, Jodie Foster, Robbie Robertson are all outstanding. The accent in *Carny* is on realism with disenchanted losers who live only from day to day. Rated R. 107m. **DIR:** Robert Kaylor. **CAST:** Gary Busey, Jodie Foster, Robbie Robertson, Meg Foster, Bert Remsen. **1980**

CAROLINA SKELETONS ★★★ Lou Gossett Jr., adept as usual, stars in this fact-based story about a war hero's return to a southern town in search of the truth behind his brother's execution years earlier. Quality performances from Gossett and Bruce Dern. Made for cable. Rated R for profanity and violence. 94m. **DIR:** John Erman. **CAST:** Lou Gossett Jr., Bruce Dern. **1992**

CARPETBAGGERS, THE ★★★ Howard Hughes–like millionaire George Peppard makes movies, love, and enemies in the Hollywood of the 1920s and 1930s. Alan Ladd, as a Tom Mix clone, helps in this, his last picture. Carroll Baker is steamy. Very tame compared with the porno-edged Harold Robbins novel. 150m. **DIR:** Edward Dmytryk. **CAST:** George Peppard, Alan Ladd, Audrey Totter, Carroll Baker, Robert Cummings, Lew Ayres, Martin Balsam, Archie Moore. **1964**

CARRIE (1952) ★★★★ Theodore Dreiser's *Sister Carrie*: Jennifer Jones in the title role and Laurence Olivier as her morally blinded married lover make this tale a classic. Basil Ruysdael is perfect in a bit as Olivier's unyielding employer. B&W; 118m. **DIR:** William Wyler. **CAST:** Jennifer Jones, Laurence Olivier, Eddie Albert, Basil Ruysdael, Miriam Hopkins. **1952**

CARRINGTON, V. C. ★★★ Everybody's Englishman David Niven gives one of the finest performances of his career. A stalwart British army officer, accused of stealing military funds, undertakes to conduct his own defense. This is a solid, engrossing drama. Filmed in England and released heavily cut in the United States under the title *Court Martial*. B&W; 105m. **DIR:** Anthony Asquith. **CAST:** David Niven, Margaret Leighton, Noelle Middleton, Laurence Naismith, Victor Maddern, Maurice Denham. **1955**

CASABLANCA ★★★★★ A kiss may be just a kiss and a sigh just a sigh, but there is only one *Casablanca*. Some misguided souls tried to remake this classic in 1980 as *Caboblanco*, but film lovers are well advised to accept no substitutes. The original feast of romance and pre–World War II intrigue is still the best. Superb performances by Humphrey Bogart and Ingrid Bergman, Paul Henreid, Claude Rains, Peter Lorre, and Sydney Greenstreet, and the fluid direction of Michael Curtiz combined to make it an all-time classic. B&W; 102m. **DIR:** Michael Curtiz. **CAST:** Humphrey Bogart, Ingrid Bergman, Claude Rains, Paul Henreid, Peter Lorre, Sydney Greenstreet. **1942**

CASE OF DEADLY FORCE, A ★★★★ Richard Crenna plays a determined attorney who helps a victim's family win the first-ever "wrongful death" suit against the Boston Police Department after an innocent black man is shot to death. Based on a true story of police corruption and violence, this drama is surprisingly taut and packs an emotional punch. Made for TV. 95m. **DIR:** Michael Miller. **CAST:** Richard Crenna, John Shea, Tate Donovan. **1986**

CASE OF LIBEL, A ★★★★★ Slick, superb made-for-cable adaptation of Henry Denker's famed Broadway play, which itself is taken from the first portion of Louis Nizer's excellent biography, *My Life in Court*. The story closely follows the legendary Westbrook Pegler–Quentin Reynolds libel suit, wherein columnist Pegler had attempted to smear Reynolds's reputation with a series of vicious lies. Ed Asner plays the lawyer and Daniel J. Travanti the columnist. Ranks with the finest courtroom dramas on film. Unrated. 92m. **DIR:** Eric Till. **CAST:** Edward Asner, Daniel J. Travanti, Gordon Pinsent, Lawrence Dane. **1984**

CASINO ★★ This pedestrian telemovie features former *Mannix* star Mike Connors as the action-oriented owner of a plush hotel and casino. 100m. **DIR:** Don Chaffey. **CAST:** Mike Connors, Gene Evans, Barry Van Dyke, Gary Burghoff, Joseph Cotten, Lynda Day George, Robert Reed, Barry Sullivan. **1980**

CASS TIMBERLANE ★★ Sinclair Lewis's story of a prominent judge married to a voluptuous younger woman turns into a silly, superficial soap opera. Spencer Tracy and Lana Turner are mismatched as the judge and his wife. B&W; 119m. **DIR:** George Sidney. **CAST:** Spencer Tracy, Lana Turner, Zachary Scott, Mary Astor, Tom Drake, Albert Dekker. **1947**

CASSANDRA CROSSING, THE 🦃 A plague-infested train heads for a weakened bridge. Rated PG. 127m. **DIR:** George Pan Cosmatos. **CAST:** Richard Harris, Sophia Loren, Burt Lancaster, Ava Gardner, Martin Sheen. **1977**

CAST THE FIRST STONE ★★★ When schoolteacher Jill Eikenberry is raped and becomes pregnant, she decides to keep the baby despite public protest. When school officials doubt her version of the story, they dismiss her. Eikenberry fights back by hiring lawyer Richard Masur, who not only helps her win the case, but helps restore her dignity as well. Riveting made-for-television movie. 94m. **DIR:** John Korty. **CAST:** Jill Eikenberry, Lew Ayres, Richard Masur, Elizabeth Ruscio, Joe Spano. **1990**

CASTAWAY ★★ Nicolas Roeg adds some surreal touches to this otherwise mediocre film about a wealthy publisher (Oliver Reed) who advertises for a woman to live with him for a year on a deserted tropical island. His dreams of animal passion turn into domestic doldrums when his companion (Amanda Donohoe) opts for celibacy. Rated R for profanity, nudity, and simulated sex. 118m. **DIR:** Nicolas Roeg. **CAST:** Oliver Reed, Amanda Donohoe. **1987**

CASTLE, THE ★★★½ This highly metaphorical story from Franz Kafka's incomplete novel is translated literally here and makes for a very strange and humorous affair. Maximillian Schell is a land surveyor who is employed by the mysterious inhabitants of a castle, only to be denied access to the place once he arrives there. Not rated, has sex and nudity. 89m. **DIR:** Rudolf Noelte. **CAST:** Maximilian Schell, Cordula Trantow, Trudik Daniel. **1983**

CASUALTIES OF LOVE: THE LONG ISLAND LOLITA STORY ★★ One of a trio of made-for-TV movies that exploited the alleged affair between teenager Amy Fisher and auto mechanic Joey Buttafuoco. The acting by the two leads is surprisingly good. 94m. **DIR:** John Herzfeld. **CAST:** Jack Scalia, Alyssa Milano, Leo Rossi, Phyllis Lyons. **1993**

CASUALTIES OF WAR ★★★★ Michael J. Fox turns in an exceptional performance in this thought-provoking Vietnam War drama as the lone dissenter during his squad's rape and murder of a Vietnamese girl. Director Brian De Palma graphically brings home the horror of a war without purpose and heroes without valor. Rated R for violence, simulated sex, and profanity. 106m. **DIR:** Brian De Palma. **CAST:** Michael J. Fox, Sean Penn, Don Harvey, John C. Reilly. **1989**

CAT ON A HOT TIN ROOF (1958) ★★★★ This heavy drama stars Elizabeth Taylor as the frustrated Maggie and Paul Newman as her alcoholic, ex-athlete husband. They've returned to his father's (Big Daddy, played by Burl Ives) home upon hearing he's dying. They are joined by Newman's brother, Gooper, and his wife, May, and their many obnoxious children. 108m. **DIR:** Richard Brooks. **CAST:** Elizabeth Taylor, Paul Newman, Burl Ives, Jack Carson. **1958**

CAT ON A HOT TIN ROOF (1985) ★★★½ Updated rendition of the famed Tennessee Williams play strikes to the core in most scenes but remains oddly distanced in others. The story itself is just as powerful as it must have been in 1955, with its acute examination of a family under stress. Jessica Lange is far too melodramatic as Maggie the Cat; it's impossible to forget she's acting. Things really come alive, though, when Big Daddy (Rip Torn) and Brick (Tommy Lee Jones) square off. The play ends on what is for Williams an uncharacteristically optimistic note. A near miss. Unrated, has sexual situations. 140m. **DIR:** Jack Hofsiss. **CAST:** Jessica Lange, Tommy Lee Jones, Rip Torn, Kim Stanley, David Dukes, Penny Fuller. **1985**

CATERED AFFAIR, THE ★★★½ Bette Davis portrays a woman from the Bronx who is determined to give her daughter a big wedding. This Paddy Chayefsky drama, which he adapted from his teleplay, has much of the realistic flavor of his classic *Marty*. B&W; 93m. **DIR:** Richard Brooks. **CAST:** Bette Davis, Ernest Borgnine, Debbie Reynolds, Barry Fitzgerald, Rod Taylor. **1956**

CATHERINE THE GREAT ★★ Stodgy spectacle from Great Britain is sumptuously mounted but takes its own time in telling the story of the famed czarina of Russia and her (toned-down) love life. Elisabeth Bergner in the title role lacks a real star personality, and dashing Douglas Fairbanks Jr. and sage Flora Robson provide the only screen charisma evident. Fair for a historical romance, but it won't keep you on the edge of your seat. B&W; 92m. **DIR:** Paul Czinner. **CAST:** Elisabeth Bergner, Douglas Fairbanks Jr., Flora Robson, Joan Gardner, Gerald Du Maurier. **1934**

CATHOLICS ★★★★½ This film has Martin Sheen playing the representative of the Father General (the Pope). He comes to Ireland to persuade the Catholic priests there to conform to the "new" teachings of the Catholic Church. The Irish priests and monks refuse to discard traditional ways and beliefs. Trevor Howard is excellent as the rebellious Irish abbot. 78m. **DIR:** Jack Gold. **CAST:** Trevor Howard, Martin Sheen, Raf Vallone, Andrew Keir. **1973**

CAUGHT ★★★ Starry-eyed model Barbara Bel Geddes marries neurotic millionaire Robert Ryan, who proceeds to make her life miserable. His treatment drives her away and into the arms of young doctor James Mason. B&W; 88m. **DIR:** Max Ophüls. **CAST:** Robert Ryan, Barbara Bel Geddes, James Mason, Natalie Schafer, Ruth Brady, Curt Bois, Frank Ferguson. **1949**

CAVALCADE ★★★★½ A richly detailed pageant of life in London between 1900 and 1930, this film is as innovative as it was when it was declared best picture of 1933. The drama of relationships focuses on the way World War I affected their lives. A truly remarkable film. B&W; 111m. **DIR:** Frank Lloyd. **CAST:** Clive Brook, Diana Wynyard, Ursula Jeans, Margaret Lindsay, Bonita Granville, Billy Bevan, Una O'Connor, Beryl Mercer, Frank Lawton. **1933**

CEASE FIRE ★★★½ An answer to the comic book–style heroism of *Rambo* and the *Missing in Action* movies, *Cease Fire* is a heartfelt, well-acted, and touching drama about the aftereffects of Vietnam and the battle still being fought by some veterans. Don Johnson stars as Tim Murphy, a veteran whose life begins to crumble after fifteen years of valiant effort at fitting back into society. Rated R for profanity and violence. 97m. **DIR:** David Nutter. **CAST:** Don Johnson, Lisa Blount, Robert F. Lyons, Richard Chaves, Chris Noel. **1985**

CELEBRITY ★★★½ Three high school buddies go too far on a drunken binge, with one of them raping a country girl. This crime binds the three as they go on with their lives. Each gains fame in a different medium (writing, acting, and preaching). Twenty-five years later, they're reunited in a highly publicized trial. This sudsy TV miniseries will have you glued to your set. 313m. **DIR:** Paul Wendkos. **CAST:** Michael Beck, Joseph Bottoms, Ben Masters. **1984**

CELIA, CHILD OF TERROR ★★★ Misleadingly promoted on video as a horror movie (the original title was simply *Celia*), this Australian import is about a 9-year-old girl having trouble adjusting to life in a conservative suburb after her beloved grandmother dies. Unrated, but not suitable for young children. 110m. **DIR:** Ann Turner. **CAST:** Rebecca Smart. **1989**

CEMENT GARDEN, THE ★★ This oddball little film is definitely not for everyone. Four children in working-class England find themselves suddenly orphaned and, to avoid being separated, the kids bury Mama's corpse in concrete in the basement. Sixteen-year-old Jack (Andrew Robertson) has decidedly unbrotherly feelings about his nubile older sister (Charlotte Gainsbourg). Given the subject matter, the film avoids overt sensationalism, but it's dreary, spiritless, and extremely ugly to look at. Not rated, but contains profanity, incest, and other sexual activity. 101m. **DIR:** Andrew Birkin. **CAST:** Andrew Robertson, Charlotte Gainsbourg, Sinead Cusack, Alice Coulthard, Ned Birkin. **1993**

CEMETERY CLUB, THE ★★★½ Ellen Burstyn, Olympia Dukakis, and Diane Ladd are excellent as three widows who have trouble adjusting to life without their husbands. Screenwriter Ivan Menehell, who penned the original play, is not entirely successful in translating his snappy bits of stage repartee into screen action. Rated PG-13 for profanity. 107m. **DIR:** Bill Duke. **CAST:** Ellen Burstyn, Olympia Dukakis, Diane Ladd, Danny Aiello, Lainie Kazan, Jeff Howell, Christina Ricci, Bernie Casey, Wallace Shawn. **1993**

CENTERFOLD GIRLS Insane brute spends his time killing beautiful, exotic models. Rated R. 93m. **DIR:** John Peyser. **CAST:** Andrew Prine, Tiffany Bolling, Aldo Ray, Ray Danton, Jeremy Slate. **1974**

CERTAIN SACRIFICE, A Two drifters fall in love. Rated R for language, nudity, violence. 58m. **DIR:** Stephen Jon Lewicki. **CAST:** Jeremy Pattnosh, Madonna. **1985**

CHAIN LIGHTNING ★★ A slow-moving story about a World War II veteran who volunteers to test-fly a new jet during peacetime. But Bogart isn't the type to play a wimp, so the movie is not very credible. B&W; 94m. **DIR:** Stuart Heisler. **CAST:** Humphrey Bogart, Eleanor Parker, Raymond Massey, Richard Whorf, James Brown, Fay Baker, Morris Ankrum. **1950**

CHAIN OF DESIRE Intended as a message film about AIDS, this fails to engage or involve the viewer on any level. The film consists of just one sexual encounter after another. Unrated; contains profanity, sex, and drug use. 107m. **DIR:** Temistocles Lopez. **CAST:** Linda Fiorentino, Elias Koteas, Malcolm McDowell, Tim Guinee, Grace Zabriskie. **1993**

CHAINED ★★★ A typical potboiler from the 1930s that still radiates the vibes between Clark Gable and Joan Crawford. In this one he plays a macho South American rancher. The swimming scene with Gable and Crawford has as much sex appeal as an R-rated movie without nudity, just knowing looks. B&W; 75m. **DIR:** Clarence Brown. **CAST:** Clark Gable, Joan Crawford, Otto Kruger, Stu Erwin, Mickey Rooney, Akim Tamiroff, Una O'Connor. **1934**

CHAINED FOR LIFE This murder drama featuring Siamese twins Daisy and Violet Hilton is certainly one of the saddest and most exploitative feature films of all. Cheap and embarrassing, this tawdry attempt to cash in on a physical deformity is long, boring, and in terrible taste. B&W; 81m. **DIR:** Harry Fraser. **CAST:** Daisy Hilton, Violet Hilton. **1951**

CHAINS OF GOLD ★★★½ A crusading social worker combs Los Angeles to find a young friend kidnapped by a particularly nasty drug-running street gang. The somewhat chaotic script comes from four hands (including John Travolta's), but director Rod Holcomb maintains a snappy pace that circumvents a few glaring inconsistencies. Made for cable; rated R for language and violence. 95m. **DIR:** Rod Holcomb. **CAST:** John Travolta, Marilu Henner, Bernie Casey, Hector Elizondo, Joey Lawrence. **1991**

CHALK GARDEN, THE ★★★ Adapted from the play of the same name by Enid Bagnold. The plot centers around a spoiled brat (Hayley Mills) who is the bane of her grandmother's (Edith Evans) life until she is made to see the light of day by the new governess (Deborah Kerr). Sensational acting all around. 106m. **DIR:** Ronald Neame. **CAST:** Deborah Kerr, Edith Evans, Hayley Mills, John Mills, Elizabeth Sellars. **1964**

CHALLENGE OF A LIFETIME ★★★ A depressed middle-aged woman decides to pick herself up by training for the Hawaiian Ironman competition. Worth seeing for the always-fun Penny Marshall and underground star Mary Woronov in a rare TV appearance. Not rated; contains no objectionable material. 95m. **DIR:** Russ Mayberry. **CAST:** Penny Marshall, Richard Gilliland, Mary Woronov, Jonathan Silverman, Paul Gleason, Cathy Rigby, Mark Spitz. **1985**

CHAMELEON STREET ★★★★ *Chameleon Street* is not an address; he's a man: a real-life Detroit imposter named William Douglas Street. And this quirky, entertaining film tells his story. A fascinating, offbeat screen portrait by writer-director-star Wendell B. Harris Jr., it details how Street successively posed as a *Time* magazine reporter, a physician who actually performs surgery, an attorney who befriends Detroit Mayor Coleman Young, a foreign-exchange college student from France, and other purely bogus individuals. Rated R. 98m. **DIR:** Wendell B. Harris Jr. **CAST:** Wendell B. Harris Jr. **1989**

CHAMP, THE (1931) ★★★★ Wallace Beery is at his absolute best in the Oscar-winning title role of this tearjerker, about a washed-up fighter and his adoring son

(Jackie Cooper) who are separated against their will. King Vidor manages to make even the hokiest bits of hokum work in this four-hankie feast of sentimentality. B&W; 87m. **DIR:** King Vidor. **CAST:** Wallace Beery, Jackie Cooper, Irene Rich. **1931**

CHAMP, THE (1979) ★★★½ This remake is a first-class tearjerker. Billy Flynn (Voight), a former boxing champion, works in the backstretch at Hialeah when not drinking or gambling away his money. His son, T.J. (Schroder), calls him "Champ" and tells all his friends about his father's comeback, which never seems to happen. Rated PG. 121m. **DIR:** Franco Zeffirelli. **CAST:** Jon Voight, Faye Dunaway, Rick Schroder, Jack Warden. **1979**

CHAMPAGNE 🦃 Alfred Hitchcock regarded this silent feature as one of his worst films, and who are we to disagree? B&W; 69m. **DIR:** Alfred Hitchcock. **CAST:** Betty Balfour, Gordon Harker. **1928**

CHAMPION ★★★★ One of Hollywood's better efforts about the fight game. Kirk Douglas is a young boxer whose climb to the top is accomplished while forsaking his friends and family. He gives one of his best performances in an unsympathetic role. B&W; 100m. **DIR:** Mark Robson. **CAST:** Kirk Douglas, Arthur Kennedy, Ruth Roman. **1949**

CHAMPIONS ★★★★ The touching true story of English steeplechase jockey Bob Champion (John Hurt), who fought a desperate battle against cancer to win the 1981 Grand National. Rated PG. 113m. **DIR:** John Irvin. **CAST:** John Hurt, Edward Woodward, Jan Francis, Ben Johnson. **1984**

CHANEL SOLITAIRE ★★ This half-hearted rendering of the rise to prominence of French designer Coco Chanel (played by fragile Marie-France Pisier) is long on sap and short on plot. For the terminally romantic only. Rated R. 120m. **DIR:** George Kaczender. **CAST:** Marie-France Pisier, Timothy Dalton, Rutger Hauer, Karen Black, Brigitte Fossey. **1981**

CHANGE OF HABIT ★★ In direct contrast to the many comedy-musicals that Elvis Presley starred in, this drama offers a more substantial plot. Elvis plays a doctor helping the poor in his clinic. Mary Tyler Moore plays a nun who is tempted to leave the order to be with Elvis. Rated G. 93m. **DIR:** William A. Graham. **CAST:** Elvis Presley, Mary Tyler Moore, Barbara McNair, Jane Elliot, Edward Asner. **1970**

CHANTILLY LACE ★★★½ This modern spin on Clare Boothe's *The Women* gets considerable mileage from its high-octane ensemble cast but ultimately disappoints because of its improvisational nature. Director-coplotter Linda Yellen encouraged her seven stars to develop their own dialogue but failed to provide enough structure. It's entertaining to watch these ladies discuss men, relationships, and jobs, but the third act is self-indulgently maudlin. Rated R for profanity, brief nudity, simulated sex. 105m. **DIR:** Linda Yellen. **CAST:** Lindsay Crouse, Jill Eikenberry, Martha Plimpton, Ally Sheedy, Talia Shire, Helen Slater, JoBeth Williams. **1993**

CHAPLIN ★★★½ Robert Downey Jr. does an impressive impersonation of Charlie Chaplin in this well-intentioned and often well-acted bio-pic. Unfortunately, director Richard Attenborough takes almost a scandal-sheet approach, forgetting what made Chaplin so important was the movies he made. Worth seeing for Downey and equally impressive turns by Kevin Kline (as Douglas Fairbanks Sr.) and Geraldine Chaplin (as his mentally ill mother). Rated PG-13 for profanity and nudity. 145m. **DIR:** Richard Attenborough. **CAST:** Robert Downey Jr., Dan Aykroyd, Geraldine Chaplin, Kevin Dunn, Anthony Hopkins, Milla Jovovich, Moira Kelly, Kevin Kline, Diane Lane, Penelope Ann Miller, Paul Rhys, John Thaw, Marisa Tomei, Nancy Travis, James Woods. **1992**

CHAPTER TWO ★★★½ In *Chapter Two*, writer Neil Simon examines the problems that arise when a recently widowed author courts and marries a recently divorced actress. George Schneider (James Caan) is recovering from the death of his wife when he strikes up a whirlwind courtship with actress Jennie MacLaine (Marsha Mason). They get married, but George is tormented by the memory of his first, beloved wife. Rated PG. 124m. **DIR:** Robert Moore. **CAST:** James Caan, Marsha Mason, Valerie Harper, Joseph Bologna. **1979**

CHARIOTS OF FIRE ★★★★★ Made in England, this is the beautifully told and inspiring story of two runners (Ian Charleson and Ben Cross) who competed for England in the 1924 Olympics. An all-star supporting cast—Ian Holm, John Gielgud, Dennis Christopher (*Breaking Away*), Brad Davis (*Midnight Express*), and Nigel Davenport—and taut direction by Hugh Hudson help make this a must-see motion picture. Rated PG, the film has no objectionable content. 123m. **DIR:** Hugh Hudson. **CAST:** Ben Cross, Ian Charleson, Nigel Havers, Nicolas Farrell, Alice Krige, Ian Holm, John Gielgud, Dennis Christopher, Brad Davis, Nigel Davenport. **1981**

CHASE, THE (1946) ★★ If the tempo were faster and the writing tighter, this film might have been interesting. As it is, it staggers along. The plot is quite predictable as Michele Morgan runs away from her husband. B&W; 86m. **DIR:** Arthur Ripley. **CAST:** Robert Cummings, Michele Morgan, Peter Lorre, Steve Cochran. **1946**

CHASE, THE (1966) ★★½ Convoluted tale of prison escapee (Robert Redford) who returns to the turmoil of his Texas hometown. The exceptional cast provides flashes of brilliance, but overall, the film is rather dull. Redford definitely showed signs of his superstar potential here. 135m. **DIR:** Arthur Penn. **CAST:** Robert Redford, Jane Fonda, Marlon Brando, Angie Dickinson, Janice Rule, James Fox, Robert Duvall, E. G. Marshall, Miriam Hopkins, Martha Hyer. **1966**

CHASING DREAMS ★★★ Here's another film made before a current top-billed player's stardom. In this case Kevin Costner is in and out of the story within the first five minutes. We're left with a low-budget, but very appealing, tearjerker. While Costner's away at college, his slightly younger brother must work on the farm, care for their ill youngest brother, and somehow sneak in baseball practice. Rated PG for profanity. 96m. **DIR:** Sean Roche, Therese Conte. **CAST:** David Brown, Jim Shane, Kevin Costner. **1981**

CHATTAHOOCHEE ★★★★ British actor Gary Oldman gives a brilliant performance as an American war hero who attempts a bizarre suicide and ends up in the nightmarish Chattahoochee State Mental Hospital. Once inside, he devotes himself to exposing the horrific treatment of the patients. Rated R for brutality, nudity, and profanity. 98m. **DIR:** Mick Jackson. **CAST:** Gary Oldman, Dennis Hopper, Frances McDormand, Pamela Reed, Ned Beatty, M. Emmet Walsh. **1990**

CHEATIN' HEARTS ★★★★ Gorgeously photographed, multilayered story of three strong women and the men in their lives, in the "new" West. Sally Kirkland must come to terms with her philandering husband (James Brolin) and a new life as her two daughters make their own way in the world. Intriguing look, if a bit slow, at adult choices and the resulting consequences. Rated R for profanity and nudity. 88m. **DIR:** Rod McCall. **CAST:** Sally Kirkland, James Brolin, Kris Kristofferson, Pamela Gidley. **1993**

CHECKERED FLAG ★★½ A race car driver must face his ex-friend after stealing his girlfriend. An overdose of macho get-even feats serve as annoying distractions until the two learn to work together on a winning team. Unrated, contains nudity, profanity, and violence. 100m. **DIR:** John Glen, Michael Levine. **CAST:** Bill Campbell, Rob Estes, Amanda Wyss, Carrie Hamilton, Pernell Roberts. **1990**

CHEERS FOR MISS BISHOP ★★★ Nostalgic, poignant story of a schoolteacher in a midwestern town who devotes her life to teaching. A warm reassuring film in the tradition of *Miss Dove* and *Mr. Chips*. B&W; 95m. **DIR:** Tay Garnett. **CAST:** Martha Scott, William Gargan, Edmund Gwenn, Sterling Holloway, Sidney Blackmer. **1941**

CHERNOBYL: THE FINAL WARNING ★★★ Well-intended look at the Chernobyl nuclear power plant disaster in Russia. This telefilm takes a close look at one family affected by the accident, as well as the broad impact it had and continues to have on the entire world. 94m. **DIR:** Anthony Page. **CAST:** Jon Voight, Jason Robards Jr., Sammi Davis, Annette Crosbie, Ian McDiarmid. **1991**

CHERRY, HARRY AND RAQUEL ★★★½ One of Russ Meyer's best movies, even though he lost several reels after he finished shooting and had to pad the film out at the last minute with purposely silly commentary by a woman wearing nothing but an Indian headdress. Forget the plot about a drug-running sheriff (the wonderful Charles Napier) in New Mexico. Novelist Tom Wolfe wrote the screenplay. Rated X in 1969, though it would get an R nowadays. 71m. **DIR:** Russ Meyer. **CAST:** Charles Napier. **1969**

CHICAGO JOE AND THE SHOWGIRL ★★ Based on the real-life Cleft Chin Murder Case in 1944 London, this disappointing thriller stars Kiefer Sutherland as a U.S. serviceman who teams up with an English dancer (Emily Lloyd) for a crime spree that ends in one murder and another attempted murder. Rated R for violence and profanity. 103m. **DIR:** Bernard Rose. **CAST:** Kiefer Sutherland, Emily Lloyd, Patsy Kensit, Liz Fraser, Alexandra Pigg. **1990**

CHILD BRIDE OF SHORT CREEK ★★ Based on a true account, this is the story of a polygamist community in Arizona disbanded by the police. Made for TV. 100m. **DIR:** Robert Michael Lewis. **CAST:** Christopher Atkins, Diane Lane, Conrad Bain, Dee Wallace. **1981**

CHILD IS WAITING, A ★★★ Difficult to watch but emotionally satisfying. Judy Garland, in a brilliant performance, is a worker at a hospital treating mentally retarded children. 102m. **DIR:** John Cassavetes. **CAST:** Burt Lancaster, Judy Garland, Gena Rowlands, Steven Hill, Paul Stewart. **1963**

CHILDREN OF A LESSER GOD ★★★★★ Based on the Tony Award–winning play by Mark Medoff, this superb film concerns the love that grows between a teacher (William Hurt) for the hearing-impaired and a deaf woman (Oscar-winner Marlee Matlin). The performances are impeccable, the direction inspired, and the story unforgettable. Considering the problems inherent in telling its tale, this represents a phenomenal achievement for first-time film director Randa Haines. Rated R for suggested sex, profanity, and adult themes. 118m. **DIR:** Randa Haines. **CAST:** William Hurt, Marlee Matlin, Piper Laurie, Philip Bosco. **1986**

CHILDREN OF AN LAC, THE ★★★★ Just before the fall of Saigon in 1975, three women did the next to impossible: They managed the escape of hundreds (perhaps thousands) of Vietnamese children. One of these women was actress Ina Balin, who plays herself here. The performances and production values of this made-for-television film are very good. 100m. **DIR:** John Llewellyn Moxey. **CAST:** Ina Balin, Shirley Jones, Beulah Quo, Alan Fudge, Ben Piazza. **1980**

CHILDREN OF RAGE ★★½ This little-seen film deserves credit for doing something that few were willing to do at the time it was made: look beyond the actions of Palestinian terrorists to try to understand their motives. Unfortunately, good intentions don't compensate for lack of drama in this talky story about an Israeli doctor who attempts to open lines of communications with terrorists. Unrated, the film contains violence. 106m. **DIR:** Arthur Allan Seidelman. **CAST:** Helmut Griem, Olga Georges-Picot, Cyril Cusack, Simon Ward. **1975**

CHILDREN OF SANCHEZ, THE ★★★ Anthony Quinn stars as a poor Mexican worker who tries to keep his large family together. This well-intentioned film is slightly boring. Rated PG. 126m. **DIR:** Hall Bartlett. **CAST:** Anthony Quinn, Dolores Del Rio. **1978**

CHILDREN OF TIMES SQUARE, THE ★★★ A baby-faced teenage runaway is suddenly confronted with the pimps and drug dealers who prey on the desperate newcomers to New York City. Violent, powerful, made-for-TV message film. 95m. **DIR:** Curtis Hanson. **CAST:** Howard Rollins Jr., Joanna Cassidy, David Ackroyd, Larry B. Scott. **1986**

CHILDREN'S HOUR, THE ★★★½ Originally this was a moderately well-received play by Lillian Hellman, which director William Wyler filmed in 1937 (as *These Three*). Not satisfied with his first attempt, Wyler directed this remake about rumored lesbianism in a school for girls. Good performances from a veteran cast. B&W; 107m. **DIR:** William Wyler. **CAST:** Audrey Hepburn, Shirley MacLaine, James Garner, Miriam Hopkins, Veronica Cartwright, Fay Bainter. **1962**

CHILLY SCENES OF WINTER ★★★★ You'll probably find this excellent little film in the comedy section of your local video store, but don't be fooled; it's funny all right, but it has some scenes that evoke the true pain of love. John Heard plays a man in love with a married woman (Mary Beth Hurt). She also loves him, but is still attached to her husband. Rated PG for language and sex. 96m. **DIR:** Joan Micklin Silver. **CAST:** John Heard, Mary Beth Hurt, Peter Riegert, Kenneth McMillan, Gloria Grahame. **1979**

CHIMES AT MIDNIGHT ★★★½ Known also as *Falstaff*, this arresting film combines parts of five of the Bard's plays in which the popular, indelible Sir John Falstaff appears. Orson Welles as the famous roly-poly tosspot is superb, but the film is hampered by its anemic budget. Ralph Richardson narrates. B&W; 115m. **DIR:** Orson Welles. **CAST:** Orson Welles, Jeanne Moreau, Margaret Rutherford, John Gielgud, Keith Baxter, Alan Webb, Walter Chiari. **1967**

CHINA BEACH (TV SERIES) ★★★½ Television pilot film for Emmy Award–winning dramatic series. Set at a medical base in Vietnam, this is basically *M*A*S*H* without the laughs. Dana Delaney shines as a nurse who has seen so much that she's becoming numb. Sixties songs are a plus. 97m. **DIR:** Rod Holcomb. **CAST:** Dana Delany, Nan Woods, Michael Patrick Boatman, Tim Ryan, Chloe Webb. **1988**

CHINA CRY ★★★★ Based on the autobiography by Nora Lamm, this gripping drama is the story of one woman's struggle for justice in 1950s Communist China. Julia Nickson-Soul gives an outstanding performance as the adult version of the lead character, whose idyllic, privileged life as the daughter of a doctor (James Shigeta) is all but destroyed after the Japanese invade Shanghai in 1941. Rated PG-13. 103m. **DIR:** James F. Collier. **CAST:** Julia Nickson, Russell Wong, James Shigeta, France Nuyen. **1991**

CHINA GATE ★★½ A romantic triangle develops in North Vietnam in the late Fifties. Not bad, but Angie Dickinson and Lee Van Cleef as Asians just don't cut it. B&W; 95m. **DIR:** Samuel Fuller. **CAST:** Angie Dickinson, Gene Barry, Nat King Cole, Lee Van Cleef. **1957**

CHOCOLATE WAR, THE ★★★½ Actor Keith Gordon makes an impressive directorial debut with this comedy-drama about a bereaved student (Ilan Mitchell-Smith) facing the horrors of a sadistic teacher (John Glover) and a secret society of students at his Catholic high school. Some excellent performances and a story that keeps you fascinated. Rated R for profanity and violence. 103m. **DIR:** Keith Gordon. **CAST:** John Glover, Ilan Mitchell-Smith, Wally Ward, Adam Baldwin, Bud Cort. **1989**

CHOICE, THE ★★ Abortion is the controversy in this made-for-television film. Susan Clark stars as a mother who must help her daughter make the critical decision on whether to have an abortion or not. Too sentimental, but the performances are commendable. 100m. **DIR:** David Greene. **CAST:** Susan Clark, Mitchell Ryan, Jennifer Warren. **1981**

CHOIRBOYS, THE 🦃 Despite its stellar ensemble cast, this remains one of the worst police dramas ever lensed. Rated R for profanity and raunch. 119m. **DIR:** Robert Aldrich. **CAST:** Charles Durning, Lou Gossett Jr., Perry King, Randy Quaid, Burt Young, James Woods, Blair Brown. **1977**

CHOSEN, THE ★★★★★ *The Chosen* is a flawless, arresting drama illustrating the conflict between friendship and family loyalty experienced by two young men. Based on the novel of the same name by Chaim Potok, the story, centering on Jewish issues, transcends its setting to attain universal impact. Rated G. 105m. **DIR:** Jeremy Paul Kagan. **CAST:** Robby Benson, Rod Steiger, Maximilian Schell. **1978**

CHRISTMAS TO REMEMBER, A ★★★★ Grandpa Larson (Jason Robards), who never got over his son's death, resents his grandson's visit. His unkind manner toward the boy convinces the youngster that he must run away. Eva Marie Saint plays Grandma Larson, who rebuffs her husband for his cruelty. Joanne Woodward makes a cameo appearance. Unrated, this provides fine family entertainment comparable with a G rating. 96m. **DIR:** George Englund. **CAST:** Jason Robards Jr., Eva Marie Saint, Joanne Woodward. **1979**

CHRISTMAS WIFE, THE ★★★½ Jason Robards delivers his usual superior performance as a newly widowed man who goes to a lonely hearts agency. Julie Harris, as his arranged date, has quite a little secret to hide. Fine seasonal heart-warmer created for HBO. 73m. **DIR:** David Jones. **CAST:** Jason Robards Jr., Julie Harris, Don Francks. **1988**

CHRISTMAS WITHOUT SNOW, A ★★★★ John Houseman and the entire cast shine in this beautiful made-for-TV story about a dictatorial choirmaster, a newly divorced woman, a church choir, and their combined problems while rehearsing for a performance of Handel's *Messiah* oratorio. Definitely worth viewing. 100m. **DIR:** John Korty. **CAST:** John Houseman, Ramon Bieri, James Cromwell, Valerie Curtin. **1980**

CHRISTOPHER STRONG ★★½ Katharine Hepburn's second film, this one gave her her first starring role. She is a record-breaking flyer who falls passionately in love with a married man she cannot have. High-plane soap opera. Kate's legions of fans will love it, however. B&W; 77m. **DIR:** Dorothy Arzner. **CAST:** Katharine Hepburn, Colin Clive, Billie Burke, Helen Chandler, Jack LaRue. **1933**

CIAO! MANHATTAN 🦃 Far more pornographic than any skin flick, this sleazy, low-budget release features Edie Sedgwick, a onetime Andy Warhol "superstar," in a grotesque parody of her life. 84m. **DIR:** John Palmer, David Weisman. **CAST:** Edie Sedgwick, Isabel Jewell, Baby Jane Holzer, Roger Vadim, Viva, Paul America. **1983**

CINDERELLA LIBERTY ★★★½ Marsha Mason earned an Oscar nomination as a feisty Seattle hooker with a worldly-wise 11-year-old son in this quirky little romance, which also stars James Caan as a sailor who learns to love them both. The plot is predictable, but the performances are genuinely touching. Rated R for profanity and sexual themes. 117m. **DIR:** Mark Rydell. **CAST:** James Caan, Marsha Mason, Eli Wallach. **1973**

CIRCLE OF LOVE 🦃 This is a terrible rehash of Max Ophuls's *La Ronde*. 105m. **DIR:** Roger Vadim. **CAST:** Jane Fonda, Jean-Claude Brialy, Maurice Ronet, Jean Sorel, Anna Karina. **1964**

CIRCLE OF TWO 🦃 Eccentric artist develops a romantic—but somehow platonic—relationship with a teenage girl. Rated PG for nudity. 105m. **DIR:** Jules Dassin. **CAST:** Richard Burton, Tatum O'Neal, Kate Reid, Robin Gammell. **1980**

CIRCUS WORLD 🦃 Even John Wayne can't help this sappy soap opera set under the big top. 135m. **DIR:** Henry Hathaway. **CAST:** John Wayne, Rita Hayworth, Claudia Cardinale, John Smith, Lloyd Nolan, Richard Conte. **1964**

CITADEL, THE ★★★½ Superb acting by a fine cast marks this adaptation of novelist A. J. Cronin's story of an impoverished doctor who temporarily forsakes his ideals. B&W; 112m. **DIR:** King Vidor. **CAST:** Robert Donat, Rosalind Russell, Ralph Richardson, Rex Harrison, Emlyn Williams, Francis L. Sullivan, Felix Aylmer, Mary Clare, Cecil Parker. **1938**

CITIZEN COHN ★★★★★ James Woods is the ultimate unstoppable force in this mesmerizing made-for-cable account of attorney Roy Cohn's meteoric rise to power. Blessed with a viciously prideful mother (Lee Grant), the anti-Semitic and blatantly homophobic Cohn (who was both Jewish and gay) quickly learned how to dominate by intimidation. David Franzoni's fascinating script unfolds in flashback, as Cohn lies dying of AIDS in a hospital bed. 110m. **DIR:** Frank Pierson. **CAST:** James Woods, Joe Don Baker, Joseph Bologna, Ed Flanders, Frederic Forrest, Lee Grant, Pat Hingle. **1992**

CITIZEN KANE ★★★★★ What can you say about the film considered by many to be the finest picture ever made in America? The story of a reporter's quest to find the "truth" about the life of a dead newspaper tycoon closely parallels the life of William Randolph Hearst. To 1940s audiences, the plot may have seemed obscured by flashbacks, unusual camera angles, and lens distortion. After forty years, however, most of these film tricks are now commonplace, but the story, the acting of the Mercury Company cast, Gregg Toland's camera work, and Bernard Herrmann's score haven't aged a bit. This picture is still a very enjoyable experience for first-time viewers, as well as for those who have seen it ten times. B&W; 119m. **DIR:** Orson Welles. **CAST:** Orson Welles, Joseph Cotten, Everett Sloane, Agnes Moorehead, Ray Collins, George Coulouris, Ruth Warrick. **1941**

CITY FOR CONQUEST ★★★½ James Cagney gives another outstanding performance as a self-sacrificing man who gives his all in the boxing ring to advance the career of his musician brother. Everyone shines in this curious blend of beautiful music and crime melodrama. B&W; 101m. **DIR:** Anatole Litvak. **CAST:** James Cagney, Ann Sheridan, Arthur Kennedy, Frank Craven, Donald Crisp, Frank McHugh, George Tobias, Jerome Cowan, Anthony Quinn, Lee Patrick, Blanche Yurka, Elia Kazan. **1940**

CITY OF HOPE ★★★★½ Whereas most movies are comparable to short stories, this miraculous piece of cinema is closer to a novel. Divided into two main stories, writer-director-star John Sayles's brilliant screenplay is about modern-day city life and the corruption found therein. There are no good guys or bad guys, just folks who are trying to survive. With a superb cast enlivening even the smallest parts, the result is a motion picture with uncommon resonance. Rated R for profanity and violence. 129m. **DIR:** John Sayles. **CAST:** Vincent Spano, Tony Lo Bianco, Joe Morton, John Sayles, Angela Bassett, David Strathairn, Maggie Renzi, Anthony Denison, Kevin Tighe, Barbara Williams. **1991**

CITY OF JOY ★★★★ A disillusioned American surgeon (Patrick Swayze) goes to India and discovers purpose in life in poverty-stricken Calcutta. Swayze's character and story are a bit contrived, but the film is saved by Om Puri's superb performance as a fearful farmer who becomes a hero. Rated PG-13 for profanity and violence. 134m. **DIR:** Roland Joffe. **CAST:** Patrick Swayze, Pauline Collins, Om Puri, Art Malik. **1992**

CITY THAT NEVER SLEEPS ★★★½ Dated but delectable film about a Chicago policeman (Gig Young) who decides to leave his wife and the force to run away with a cheap show girl. In a corny device, the city talks to us—via an offscreen narrator—to introduce its citizens and explain its purpose in society. Unrated, it contains violence. B&W; 90m. **DIR:** John H. Auer. **CAST:** Gig Young, Mala Powers, Edward Arnold, William Talman. **1953**

CITY WITHOUT MEN ★★ Wan drama of women who live in a boardinghouse near the prison where their husbands are serving time. Good cast, but otherwise forgettable. B&W; 75m. **DIR:** Sidney Salkow. **CAST:** Linda Darnell, Michael Duane, Sara Allgood, Glenda Farrell, Margaret Hamilton. **1943**

CIVIL WAR DIARY ★★★½ This low-budget family film is a fairly realistic account of a Civil War-era clan, as told by its youngest member. The story centers on the home front at a time when the older males are choosing sides and leaving the farm. Unrated, but with violence. 82m. **DIR:** Kevin Meyer. **CAST:** Todd Duffey, Miriam Byrd-Nethery, Holis McCarthy. **1990**

CIVILIZATION ★★★ Though little-known today, Thomas Ince was one of the first great American film producers and *Civilization* was his crowning effort. Seeing the overwhelming response to D. W. Griffith's epic *Birth of a Nation,* Ince decided to abandon the short Westerns and dramas that made him wealthy. Instead, he put all his efforts into this moralistic antiwar blockbuster. Unfortunately for Ince, America entered Word War I after the sinking of the *Lusitania* and *Civilization* died at the box office. Silent with intertitles. B&W; 102m. **DIR:** Thomas Ince. **CAST:** Howard Hickman, Enid Markey, Lola May. **1916**

CLAIRE OF THE MOON ★★½ Two women with conflicting points of view are roommates at a writers' retreat. They get on each other's nerves until a seminar conducted by a congenial, openly gay lecturer launches them into a sexual relationship. Controversial film is well acted and directed, but not for all tastes. Unrated, but contains nudity, simulated sex, and profanity. 92m. **DIR:** Nicole Conn. **CAST:** Trisha Todd, Karen Trumbo, Daimon Craig, Faith DeVitt. **1992**

CLARA'S HEART ★★½ Despite a wonderful performance by Whoopi Goldberg, this is a strangely unaffecting drama about a Jamaican maid who helps a youngster (Neil Patrick Harris) come to terms with life. The characters are so unsympathetic, though, that the viewer cannot help but lose interest. PG-13 for profanity. 107m. **DIR:** Robert Mulligan. **CAST:** Whoopi Goldberg, Michael Ontkean, Kathleen Quinlan, Spalding Gray, Beverly Todd, Neil Patrick Harris. **1988**

CLARENCE DARROW ★★★★ This television adaptation of the stage play is a tour de force for Henry Fonda. Highlights from the career of one of the most gifted legal minds ever to pace the courtrooms of America. 81m. **DIR:** John Rich. **CAST:** Henry Fonda. **1978**

CLASH BY NIGHT ★★★½ Intense, adult story is a dramatist's dream but not entertainment for the masses. Barbara Stanwyck gives another of her strong characterizations as a woman with a past who marries amiable Paul Douglas only to find herself gravitating toward tough but sensual Robert Ryan. Gritty realism and outstanding performances make this a slice-of-life tragedy that lingers in the memory. B&W; 105m. **DIR:** Fritz Lang. **CAST:** Barbara Stanwyck, Paul Douglas, Robert Ryan, Marilyn Monroe, Keith Andes, J. Carrol Naish. **1952**

CLASS OF '44 ★★★ Sequel to the very popular *Summer of '42* proves once again it's tough to top the original. Gary Grimes and Jerry Houser are back again. This time we follow the two through college romances. No new ground broken, but Grimes is very watchable. Rated PG. 95m. **DIR:** Paul Bogart. **CAST:** Gary Grimes, Jerry Houser, William Atherton, Deborah Winters. **1973**

CLASS OF MISS MACMICHAEL, THE ★★ British film about obnoxious students battling obnoxious teachers. Mixes *The Black-*

board Jungle, *To Sir with Love*, and *Teachers* without expanding on them. Loud and angry, but doesn't say much. Rated R for profanity. 91m. **DIR:** Silvio Narizzano. **CAST:** Glenda Jackson, Oliver Reed, Michael Murphy. **1978**

CLAUDIA ★★ Tame British soaper concerning the traumatized wife of a wealthy control-freak who escapes her husband's dominance. She starts a new life and falls in love with a young musician, but hubby tracks her down. Not rated, but equivalent to PG-13. 88m. **DIR:** Anwar Kawadri. **CAST:** Deborah Raffin, Nicholas Ball. **1985**

CLEAN AND SOBER ★★★★ Michael Keaton gives a brilliant performance in this highly effective drama as a hotshot executive who wakes up one morning to find that his life is totally out of control. He checks into a drug rehabilitation center to dry out and discovers the shocking truth about himself. An impressive filmmaking debut for Glenn Gordon Caron, creator of television's *Moonlighting*. Rated R for violence and profanity. 124m. **DIR:** Glenn Gordon Caron. **CAST:** Michael Keaton, Morgan Freeman, M. Emmet Walsh, Kathy Baker. **1988**

CLEOPATRA (1934) ★★★★ One of the most opulent and intelligent films Cecil B. De Mille ever directed. Its success arises in large part from historical accuracy and the superb peformances by all the principals. B&W; 95m. **DIR:** Cecil B. DeMille. **CAST:** Claudette Colbert, Warren William, Henry Wilcoxon, C. Aubrey Smith. **1934**

CLEOPATRA (1963) ★★★★ This multimillion-dollar, four-hour-long extravaganza created quite a sensation when released. Its all-star cast includes Elizabeth Taylor (as Cleopatra) and Richard Burton (as Marc Antony). The story begins when Caesar meets Cleopatra in her native Egypt and she has his son. Later she comes to Rome to join Caesar when he becomes the lifetime dictator of Rome. Marc Antony gets into the act as Cleopatra's Roman lover. 243m. **DIR:** Joseph L. Mankiewicz. **CAST:** Elizabeth Taylor, Richard Burton, Rex Harrison, Roddy McDowall, Pamela Brown. **1963**

CLOCK, THE ★★★ Dated but still entertaining film directed by Judy Garland's then-husband, Vincente Minnelli. Judy stars as a working girl who meets and falls in love with soldier Robert Walker. He's on a forty-eight-hour leave, so they decide to make the most of the time they have together. 90m. **DIR:** Vincente Minnelli. **CAST:** Judy Garland, Robert Walker, James Gleason, Keenan Wynn. **1945**

CLOSE MY EYES ★★½ Love triangles don't get much more startling than this alternately cold, bitchy, sensitive, and beguiling British drama about incest between a brother and his older, married sister. The acting is superb, with Alan Rickman stealing scenes as the filthy rich husband who suspects his wife is having an affair. Rated R for nudity, profanity, and sexual themes. 109m. **DIR:** Stephen Poliakoff. **CAST:** Alan Rickman, Saskia Reeves, Clive Owen. **1991**

CLOSE TO HOME ★★½ Canadian docudrama focuses on the link from child abuse and neglect to teen runaways and prostitution. A bit heavy-handed but still an effective message to parents. 93m. **DIR:** Rick Beairsto. **CAST:** Daniel Allman. **1985**

CLOSER, THE ★★½ Danny Aiello reprises his stage role as a businessman whose pending retirement sets into motion an evening of high stakes for those anxious to succeed him. Aiello is the one to watch here. Rated R for profanity. 86m. **DIR:** Dimitri Logothetis. **CAST:** Danny Aiello, Michael Paré, Justine Bateman, Diane Baker, Joe Cortese. **1990**

CLOUD WALTZING ★★★ Beautiful photography and a respectable performance by Kathleen Beller are the highlights of this telefilm. The story is only marginal. Beller stars as an American journalist who is sent to France to do an exclusive interview with a hard-nosed French wine maker. She uses many ploys, including a hot-air balloon ride, to get her interview and finally her man. 103m. **DIR:** Gordon Flemyng. **CAST:** Kathleen Beller, François-Eric Gendron. **1987**

CLOUDS OVER EUROPE ★★½ Handsome test pilot Laurence Olivier teams up with a man from Scotland Yard to discover why new bombers are disappearing in this on-the-verge-of-war thriller. B&W; 82m. **DIR:** Tim Whelan. **CAST:** Laurence Olivier, Valerie Hobson, Ralph Richardson. **1939**

CLOWN, THE ★★★ Red Skelton in a dramatic role? Yes, it's true. In this film, a reworking of *The Champ*, he portrays a comedian who wins the love of his estranged son. Skelton is commendable and Tim Considine is excellent as the son. This film has an average story line but is well performed. B&W; 91m. **DIR:** Robert Z. Leonard. **CAST:** Red Skelton, Jane Greer, Tim Considine, Loring Smith. **1953**

CLUB, THE (1985) ★★★ A highly paid rookie joins an Australian football team whose last championship was twenty years ago. A powerful story of winning and losing, of business and loyalty, and of determination. Intense and polished. Rated PG for profanity and violence. 93m. **DIR:** Bruce Beresford. **CAST:** Jack Thompson, Harold Hopkins, Graham Kennedy, John Howard. **1985**

CLUB MED ★½ Another tired retread of the *Fantasy Island/Love Boat/Hotel* scenario. 104m. **DIR:** Bob Giraldi. **CAST:** Jack Scalia, Linda Hamilton, Patrick Macnee, Bill Maher. **1986**

COACH 🦃 A root-for-the-underdog basketball saga without heart. 100m. **DIR:** Bud Townsend. **CAST:** Cathy Lee Crosby, Michael Biehn, Keenan Wynn. **1978**

COCAINE FIENDS ★★ Grim drama about drug addiction follows two women down their path to dependency. Better acted than most cheap morality tales. B&W; 74m. **DIR:** William A. O'Connor. **CAST:** Lois January, Sheila Manners, Noel Madison. **1936**

COCAINE: ONE MAN'S SEDUCTION ★★★½ Though this is not another *Reefer Madness*, the subject could have been handled a little more subtly. Still, the melodrama is not obtrusive enough to take away from Dennis Weaver's brilliant performance as a real estate salesman who gets hooked. Not rated, but the equivalent of a PG for adult subject matter. 97m. **DIR:** Paul Wendkos. **CAST:** Dennis Weaver, Karen Grassle, Pamela Bellwood, James Spader, David Ackroyd, Jeffrey Tambor. **1983**

COCKTAIL 🦃 Tom Cruise, as the fast-rising newcomer of the glass-and-bottle set. Rated R for language and brief nudity. 104m. **DIR:** Roger Donaldson. **CAST:** Tom Cruise, Bryan Brown, Elisabeth Shue, Laurence Luckinbill. **1988**

COHEN AND TATE ★★ Roy Scheider stars as a burned-out Mafia hit man. He contracts for one last job: the kidnapping of a 9-year-old boy (Harley Cross) who has witnessed the murder of his informant parents by the mob. Rated R for violence and profanity. 86m. **DIR:** Eric Red. **CAST:** Roy Scheider, Adam Baldwin, Harley Cross. **1989**

COLD HEAVEN ★★½ In this moody, murky melodrama, the unfaithful wife of a physician watches in horror as her mate is run over by a speedboat near Acapulco. His body then disappears from a hospital autopsy slab! Rated R for profanity and nudity. 105m. **DIR:** Nicolas Roeg. **CAST:** Theresa Russell, Mark Harmon, James Russo, Talia Shire, Will Patton, Richard Bradford. **1992**

COLD ROOM, THE 🦃 This made-for-television movie is a waste of good material. George Segal plays a writer who travels to East Germany, only to run into the secret police and radicals. 95m. **DIR:** James Dearden. **CAST:** George Segal, Amanda Pays, Warren Clarke, Anthony Higgins. **1984**

COLD SASSY TREE ★★★ Small-town drama reflects on the lives of residents of Cold Sassy Tree—a rural community built on the site of a former sassafras grove, and still isolated with a post–Civil War mentality in the early 1900s. Good performances and well-meaning sentimentality abound. This cable TV-movie is not rated. 97m. **DIR:** Joan Tewkesbury. **CAST:** Faye Dunaway, Richard Widmark, Frances Fisher, Neil Patrick Harris. **1989**

COLDITZ STORY, THE ★★★½ Tight direction, an intelligent script, and a terrific cast make this one of the most compelling British dramas of the 1950s and one of the best prison films of all time. John Mills is outstanding as the glue that keeps the escape plans together, but the entire crew works well together. B&W; 97m. **DIR:** Guy Hamilton. **CAST:** John Mills, Eric Portman, Lionel Jeffries, Bryan Forbes, Ian Carmichael, Theodore Bikel, Anton Diffring, Richard Wattis. **1957**

COLLECTION, THE ★★★★ A superb cast shines in this British television adaptation of the Harold Pinter play about the consequences of an unusual romantic triangle. The stars bring a professional elegance and extra viewer interest to the downbeat story. Made for TV. 64m. **DIR:** Michael Apted. **CAST:** Alan Bates, Malcolm McDowell, Helen Mirren, Laurence Olivier. **1975**

COLLECTOR'S ITEM ★★★½ This erotic suspense-drama is a surprise sleeper. Tony Musante meets up with gorgeous Laura Antonelli whom he had seduced sixteen years earlier. The actors give intense performances and Antonelli just may have found a role model in Glenn Close of *Fatal Attraction* fame. Unrated, but strictly adult fare with nudity and profanity. 99m. **DIR:** Giuseppe Patroni Griffi. **CAST:** Tony Musante, Laura Antonelli, Florinda Bolkan. **1988**

COLOR ME DEAD ★★½ An innocent accountant (Tom Tryon) gets caught in the middle of an illegal uranium robbery and is poisoned with a deadly slow-working drug. He tries to find out why he was murdered. Carolyn Jones is effective as Tryon's girlfriend-secretary and gives the story poignancy; but the screenplay is wanting. Not rated, the film contains violence. 91m. **DIR:** Eddie Davis. **CAST:** Tom Tryon, Carolyn Jones, Rick Jason. **1969**

COLOR OF MONEY, THE ★★★★ A sequel to *The Hustler*, this film features outstanding performances by Paul Newman as the now-aging pool champion and Tom Cruise as his protégé. The story may be predictable, even clichéd, but the actors make it worth watching. Rated R for nudity, profanity, and violence. 117m. **DIR:** Martin Scorsese. **CAST:** Paul Newman, Tom Cruise, Mary Elizabeth Mastrantonio, Helen Shaver, John Turturro. **1986**

COLOR PURPLE, THE ★★★★★ Steven Spielberg's adaptation of Alice Walker's Pulitzer Prize–winning novel about the growth to maturity and independence of a mistreated black woman is one of those rare and wonderful movies that can bring a tear to the eye, a lift to the soul, and joy to the heart. Walker's story, set between 1909 and 1947 in a small town in Georgia, celebrates the qualities of kindness, compassion, and love. Rated PG-13 for violence, profanity, and suggested sex. 130m. **DIR:** Steven Spielberg. **CAST:** Whoopi Goldberg, Danny Glover, Adolph Caesar, Margaret Avery, Oprah Winfrey, Rae Dawn Chong, Akosua Busia. **1985**

COLORS ★★★★ Robert Duvall gives a powerhouse performance in this hard-hitting police drama. He's a cool, experienced cop who attempts to teach his young, hotheaded partner (Sean Penn) how to survive in East Los Angeles. Penn manages to match Duvall and director Hopper holds it all together, although he does go overboard in the sex and violence department. Rated R for language, profanity, suggested sex, and nudity. 119m. **DIR:** Dennis Hopper. **CAST:** Sean Penn, Robert Duvall, Maria Conchita Alonso, Randy Brooks, Don Cheadle. **1988**

COME BACK AFRICA ★★★½ Lionel Rogosin, director of the extraordinary *On the Bowery*, has created another overwhelming portrait of human tragedy in this drama about a black South African who loses a series of jobs while trying to keep his residency in Johannesburg. Exploited by a racist bureaucracy, the central character is forced to endure the horrible conditions of the hazardous coal mines. Not rated, but recommended to adult viewers. B&W; 83m. **DIR:** Lionel Rogosin. **1959**

COME BACK, LITTLE SHEBA ★★★★ A maudlin, emotionally anguished housewife dreams of long past, happier days while her small world and drunken husband are upset by a younger woman. Shirley Booth made her screen debut and won an Oscar for her work here. Cast against type, Burt Lancaster as the husband matches her all the way. B&W; 99m. **DIR:** Daniel Mann. **CAST:** Shirley Booth, Burt Lancaster, Terry Moore, Richard Jaeckel. **1952**

COME BACK TO THE FIVE AND DIME, JIMMY DEAN, JIMMY DEAN ★★★½ This film concerns the twenty-year reunion of the Disciples of James Dean, a group formed by high school friends from a small Texas town after *Giant* was filmed on location nearby. Their get-together forces the members to confront the lies they have been living since those innocent days. Though a surreal work that deals with broken dreams and crippling illusions, *Jimmy Dean* is highlighted by some excellent comedy and a terrific performance by Cher. Unrated, the film contains profanity and mature subject matter. 110m. **DIR:** Robert Altman. **CAST:** Sandy Dennis, Cher, Karen Black, Sudie Bond, Kathy Bates, Marta Heflin. **1982**

COME SEE THE PARADISE ★★★ One of the great tragedies of World War II was the internment of American citizens who were of Japanese descent. British writer-director Alan Parker attempts to put a human face on this regrettable piece of U.S. history, but he isn't wholly successful. Rated R for violence, nudity, and profanity. 133m. **DIR:** Alan Parker. **CAST:** Dennis Quaid, Tamlyn Tomita, Sab Shimono. **1990**

COMEBACK KID, THE ★★ John Ritter plays a down-and-out major leaguer who ends up coaching a group of street kids. Mediocre made-for-TV movie. 97m. **DIR:** Peter Levin. **CAST:** John Ritter, Doug McKeon, Susan Dey, Jeremy Licht, James Gregory. **1980**

COMEDIAN, THE ★★★★★ Originally aired live as a *Playhouse 90* drama, this film features Mickey Rooney as Sammy Hogarth, a ruthless, egomaniacal comedy star. His insatiable desire for unconditional adoration and obedience from those closest to him makes life a nightmare for his humiliated brother Lester (Mel Torme) and gag writer (Edmond O'Brien). Rod Serling's tight screenplay and the outstanding performances combine to make this an undated classic. B&W; 90m. **DIR:** John Frankenheimer. **CAST:** Mickey Rooney, Mel Torme, Edmond O'Brien, Kim Hunter. **1957**

COMEDIANS, THE ★★ In this drama, Elizabeth Taylor and Richard Burton inadvertently become involved in the political violence and unrest of Haiti under Papa Doc Duvalier. The all-star cast does little to improve an average script—based on Graham Greene's novel. 160m. **DIR:** Peter Glenville. **CAST:** Elizabeth Taylor, Richard Burton, Alec Guinness, Peter Ustinov, Paul Ford, Lillian Gish, James Earl Jones, Cicely Tyson. **1967**

COMIC, THE (1969) ★★★★ There's a bit of every famous silent film funny man—Chaplin, Keaton, Arbuckle, Langdon, and Lloyd—in this engrossing account of a beloved reel comedian who's an egocentric heel in real life. Dick Van Dyke is peerless in the title character. Well planned and executed, this is a gem of its genre. Beautifully handled, the closing minutes alone are worth the entire film. Rated PG. 96m. **DIR:** Carl Reiner. **CAST:** Dick Van Dyke, Mickey Rooney, Michele Lee, Cornel Wilde, Nina Wayne, Pert Kelton, Jeannine Riley. **1969**

COMIC, THE (1985) 🦃 Set in a police state of the near future, an aspiring comic kills a popular entertainer in order to get a chance to perform in his stead. Unrated; brief nudity. 90m. **DIR:** Richard Driscoll. **CAST:** Steve Munroe. **1985**

COMING HOME ★★★★½ Jane Fonda, Jon Voight, and Bruce Dern give superb performances in this thought-provoking drama about the effect the Vietnam War has on three people. Directed by Hal Ashby, it features a romantic triangle with a twist: Fonda, the wife of a gung-ho officer, Dern, finds real love when she becomes an aide at a veteran's hospital and meets a bitter but sensitive paraplegic, Voight. Rated R. 127m. **DIR:** Hal Ashby. **CAST:** Jane Fonda, Jon Voight, Bruce Dern, Robert Carradine, Robert Ginty, Penelope Milford. **1978**

COMING OUT OF THE ICE ★★★½ An engrossing made-for-television movie based on a true story. An American spends thirty-eight years in a Soviet prison camp for not renouncing his American citizenship. 97m.

DIR: Waris Hussein. **CAST:** John Savage, Willie Nelson, Ben Cross, Francesca Annis. 1987

COMMAND DECISION ★★★½ Tense, gripping look at the psychology and politics of waging war under pressure. Confrontation and anguish color this engrossing drama, based on the stage hit. B&W; 112m. **DIR:** Sam Wood. **CAST:** Clark Gable, Walter Pidgeon, Van Johnson, Brian Donlevy, Charles Bickford, John Hodiak, Edward Arnold, John McIntire. 1948

COMMON BONDS ★★ The prison system helps rehabilitate a born loser by chaining him to a handicapped man's wheelchair. Airheaded message drama. Unrated, but with profanity and violence. 109m. **DIR:** Allan A. Goldstein. **CAST:** Rae Dawn Chong, Michael Ironside, Brad Dourif. 1991

COMMON LAW, THE ★★½ Constance Bennett has a field day as a kept woman who dumps her older lover and becomes painter Joel McCrea's model. True love wins out in the end, naturally. Predictable melodrama. B&W; 72m. **DIR:** Paul Stein. **CAST:** Constance Bennett, Joel McCrea, Hedda Hopper, Marion Shilling. 1931

COMMON LAW CABIN ★★ Melodrama set at an isolated fishing cabin on the Colorado River, where the guests include sex-starved women, ineffectual husbands, and an escaped bank robber. Not as over the top as such later Russ Meyer films as *Vixen*, *Cherry*, and *Harry and Raquel*. Unrated, but a mild R equivalent for brief nudity and violence. 70m. **DIR:** Russ Meyer. **CAST:** Ken Swofford. 1967

COMPETITION, THE ★★★½ Richard Dreyfuss and Amy Irving star in this exquisitely crafted and completely enjoyable romance about two classical pianists who, while competing for top honors in a recital program, fall in love. Lee Remick and Sam Wanamaker add excellent support. Watch it with someone you love. Rated PG. 129m. **DIR:** Joel Oliansky. **CAST:** Richard Dreyfuss, Amy Irving, Lee Remick, Sam Wanamaker. 1980

COMPULSION ★★★½ Superb characterizations add up to first-rate melodrama in this retelling of the infamous 1924 Leopold-Loeb murder case. Orson Welles is brilliant as the brooding defense attorney. B&W; 103m. **DIR:** Richard Fleischer. **CAST:** Orson Welles, Bradford Dillman, Dean Stockwell, Diane Varsi, Martin Milner, E. G. Marshall. 1959

CON ARTISTS, THE 🦃 What could have been a lark turns into a ho-hum caper. 87m. **DIR:** Sergio Corbucci. **CAST:** Anthony Quinn, Capucine. 1977

CONCRETE ANGELS ★★ Set in 1964 Toronto, this downbeat teen drama revolves around several friends trying to put together a band to enter in a competition. Separate stories of the boys are spun off, told with more realism than most teen films about the early Sixties. Unrated, but an R equivalent. 97m. **DIR:** Carlo Liconti. **CAST:** Joseph Dimambro, Luke McKeehan. 1987

CONCRETE JUNGLE, THE (1962) (A.K.A. THE CRIMINAL) ★★★ Grim, claustrophobic prison drama is tightly directed and well acted (especially by the underrated Stanley Baker), and remains one of the best films of its kind as well as one of director Joseph Losey's most satisfying works. Often referred to in filmographies as *The Criminal*, this uncompromising look at life "inside" boasts gutsy, believable performances. B&W; 86m. **DIR:** Joseph Losey. **CAST:** Stanley Baker, Margit Saad, Sam Wanamaker, Gregoire Aslan, Jill Bennett, Laurence Naismith, Edward Judd. 1962

CONFESSIONS OF A HITMAN 🦃 Extremely boring. A dying hit man is being chauffeured to Las Vegas to avenge the death of his father; along the way he telephones people to confess past transgressions. Rated R for violence and profanity. 93m. **DIR:** Larry Leahy. **CAST:** James Remar, Michael Wright, Emily Longstreth. 1992

CONFESSIONS OF A POLICE CAPTAIN 🦃 Heavy-handed melodrama wastes a fine performance by Martin Balsam as a good cop amid an avalanche of corruption. This Italian-made film is given to excess. Rated PG. 102m. **DIR:** Damiano Damiani. **CAST:** Martin Balsam, Franco Nero, Marilu Tolo. 1971

CONFESSIONS OF A VICE BARON 🦃 Fly-by-night film chronicling the rise and fall of a vice baron. B&W; 70m. **DIR:** Harvey Thew. **CAST:** Willy Castello. 1942

CONNECTION (1973) ★★★½ Charles Durning steals the show in this made-for-television movie. As an out-of-work newspaperman desperately in need of money, he becomes the intermediary between an insurance company and a high-priced jewel thief. Taut direction and a literate script help. 73m. **DIR:** Tom Gries. **CAST:** Charles Durning, Ronny Cox, Zohra Lampert, Dennis Cole, Dana Wynter. 1973

CONNECTION, THE (1961) ★★★★ A group of junkies await the arrival of their heroin dealer while a documentary filmmaker records their withdrawal symptoms. A classic of the American avant-garde cinema, filmed in real time and featuring a topflight jazz score. B&W; 103m. **DIR:** Shirley Clarke. **CAST:** William Redfield, Warren Finnerty, Garry Goodrow, Roscoe Lee Browne. 1961

CONQUEST ★★★ A better-than-average Greta Garbo picture because she isn't the whole show. Charles Boyer plays Napoleon—and Garbo is Marie Walewska, his Polish mistress. This is the story of how they met and why he deserted Josephine for her. B&W; 112m. **DIR:** Clarence Brown. **CAST:** Greta

Garbo, Charles Boyer, May Whitty, Reginald Owen, Alan Marshal, Henry Stephenson, Leif Erickson. 1937

CONRACK ★★★★ In this sleeper, based on a true story, Jon Voight plays a dedicated white teacher determined to bring the joys of education to deprived blacks inhabiting an island off the coast of South Carolina. Rated PG. 107m. **DIR:** Martin Ritt. **CAST:** Jon Voight, Paul Winfield, Hume Cronyn, Madge Sinclair. 1974

CONSENTING ADULTS (1985) ★★★½ Based on a bestselling novel by Laura Z. Hobson, this made-for-TV film tells the story of an all-American family when their son proclaims his homosexuality. It is told with taste and style. 100m. **DIR:** Gilbert Cates. **CAST:** Marlo Thomas, Martin Sheen, Talia Balsam, Barry Tubb, Ben Piazza. 1985

CONSOLATION MARRIAGE ★★★ Slow-moving but well-made (for early talkie) soap opera about two jilted sweethearts (Irene Dunne and Pat O'Brien) who marry each other on the rebound, then their old lovers come back. Stilted dialogue is a drawback, but the film remains interesting for the early performances of the stars. Unrated, but suitable for all audiences. B&W; 81m. **DIR:** Paul Sloane. **CAST:** Irene Dunne, Pat O'Brien, John Halliday, Myrna Loy. 1931

CONSPIRACY: THE TRIAL OF THE CHICAGO 8 ★★★ Docudrama-style made-for-cable-TV movie about the notorious court proceedings that followed the riots of the 1968 Democratic convention. Solid performances by a top-notch cast. 118m. **DIR:** Jeremy Paul Kagan. **CAST:** Robert Carradine, Elliott Gould, Martin Sheen, Robert Loggia. 1987

CONTRACT FOR LIFE: THE S.A.D.D. STORY ★★★½ Based on the work of real-life hockey coach Bob Anastas, this chronicles the creation of Students Against Driving Drunk. After two of his all-stars are killed while driving drunk, Anastas (beautifully played by Stephen Macht) inspires his students to band together to prevent similar tragedies. Well done! 46m. **DIR:** Joseph Pevney. **CAST:** Stephen Macht. 1984

CONVICTED ★★★ Fact-based drama focuses on inadequacies in the judicial system when family man John Larroquette is accused of being a rapist and sentenced to five years in prison. Wife Lindsay Wagner spends five years searching for the truth in this inspiring made-for-TV tale of truth and justice. 94m. **DIR:** David Lowell Rich. **CAST:** John Larroquette, Lindsay Wagner, Carroll O'Connor, Burton Gilliam. 1990

CONVOY (1940) ★★★½ Excellent documentary-style, stiff-upper-lip British film about the daily danger faced by the officers and crew of cargo convoys and the warships that protect them. Producer Michael Balcon gave this movie his customary stamp of authenticity and humanity. B&W; 95m. **DIR:** Pen Tennyson. **CAST:** Clive Brook, John Clements, Judy Campbell, Edward Chapman, Michael Wilding, Charles Farrell, Albert Lieven. 1940

COOL AS ICE 🦃 Vanilla Ice's first starring role as a motorcycle rider who woos a small-town girl proves he is an even worse actor than he is a rap singer. If that's possible. Rated PG for profanity. 91m. **DIR:** David Kellogg. **CAST:** Vanilla Ice, Kristin Minter, Michael Gross, Sidney Lassick, Dody Goodman, Candy Clark. 1991

COOL BLUE ★★ Bumbling artist meets mysterious siren in urban bohemia. Miscast, labored, and pitifully unbelievable, *Cheers* star Woody Harrelson looks as if he needs a few belts. Rated R. 90m. **DIR:** Mark Mullen, Richard Shepard. **CAST:** Woody Harrelson. 1988

COOPERSTOWN ★★★★ Superior baseball fantasy focuses on a bitter ex-ball player, who is unhappy because he hasn't been inducted into the hall of fame. He is visited by the ghost of a friend who died on the eve of his own induction. Beautifully acted and directed. Film is truly touching and captures the essence of baseball. 108m. **DIR:** Charles Haid. **CAST:** Alan Arkin, Hope Lange, Graham Greene, Ed Begley Jr., Josh Charles, Ann Wedgeworth. 1992

COQUETTE ★★★ A sticky soap opera that looks hokey today, but it wowed audiences in 1929. Mary Pickford won an Oscar for the role of a college girl who lies in court to get her father off. He was charged with murder, and the film itself is a Flapper Age melodrama that set a pattern for so-called women's movies. B&W; 81m. **DIR:** Sam Taylor. **CAST:** Mary Pickford, Matt Moore, Johnny Mack Brown, Louise Beavers. 1929

CORN IS GREEN, THE (1945) ★★★★ Bette Davis leads a winning cast in this well-mounted film of British playwright-actor Emlyn Williams's drama of education vs. coal in a rough-edged Welsh mining village. John Dall is the young miner whom schoolteacher Davis grooms to win a university scholarship. B&W; 114m. **DIR:** Irving Rapper. **CAST:** Bette Davis, John Dall, Joan Lorring, Nigel Bruce, Rhys Williams, Mildred Dunnock. 1945

CORN IS GREEN, THE (1979) ★★★½ Based on Emlyn Williams's play and directed by George Cukor, this telefilm stars Katharine Hepburn. She gives a tour-de-force performance as the eccentric spinster-teacher who helps a gifted young man discover the joys of learning. 100m. **DIR:** George Cukor. **CAST:** Katharine Hepburn, Ian Saynor, Bill Fraser, Patricia Hayes, Anna Massey. 1979

CORNBREAD, EARL AND ME ★★½ A fine cast of black performers is ill served by this overdone drama about racism. A gifted basketball player is mistakenly killed by the police. It's a familiar plot directed with little inspiration by Joseph Manduke. Rated R. 95m. **DIR:** Joseph Manduke. **CAST:** Moses Gunn, Bernie Casey, Rosalind Cash, Madge Sinclair. **1975**

CORREGIDOR 🦃 An early World War II movie made on the cheap, and it shows. Elissa Landi is the girl in a romantic triangle. There isn't any action whatever. B&W; 73m. **DIR:** William Nigh. **CAST:** Elissa Landi, Donald Woods, Otto Kruger, Frank Jenks, Ian Keith, Wanda McKay. **1943**

COUNT OF MONTE CRISTO, THE (1912) ★★★ The famous Irish actor James O'Neill, father of playwright Eugene, is captured for posterity in his popular interpretation of the Alexandre Dumas story. An unmoving camera is focused onstage, and O'Neill is supremely hammy, but this is an invaluable record of a bygone time. Silent. B&W; 90m. **DIR:** Edwin S. Porter. **CAST:** James O'Neill. **1912**

COUNTDOWN ★★★ This lesser-known Robert Altman film finds James Caan and Robert Duvall as American astronauts preparing for a moon shot. Realistic scenes and great acting—well worth watching. Unrated. 101m. **DIR:** Robert Altman. **CAST:** James Caan, Robert Duvall, Charles Aidman. **1968**

COUNTRY ★★★★ A quietly powerful movie about the plight of farmers struggling to hold on while the government and financial institutions seem intent on fostering their failure. *Country* teams Jessica Lange and Sam Shepard on-screen, for the first time since the Oscar-nominated *Frances*, in a film as topical as today's headlines. Rated PG. 109m. **DIR:** Richard Pearce. **CAST:** Jessica Lange, Sam Shepard, Wilford Brimley, Matt Clark. **1984**

COUNTRY GIRL, THE (1954) ★★★★½ Bing Crosby and Grace Kelly give terrific performances in this little-seen production. Crosby plays an alcoholic singer who wallows in self-pity until he seizes a chance to make a comeback. Kelly won an Oscar for her sensitive portrayal of his wife. B&W; 104m. **DIR:** George Seaton. **CAST:** Bing Crosby, Grace Kelly, William Holden, Anthony Ross. **1954**

COUNTRY GIRL, THE (1982) ★★★½ Cable TV remake of Clifford Odets's tragic play pales somewhat compared to the Bing Crosby–Grace Kelly rendition. In this filmed stage-play version Dick Van Dyke is the alcoholic actor who has one last chance at a comeback. Ken Howard is the brash young director who blames Van Dyke's wife (Faye Dunaway) for the actor's decline. 137m. **DIR:** Gary Halvorson. **CAST:** Faye Dunaway, Dick Van Dyke, Ken Howard. **1982**

COUNTRYMAN ★★★½ A strange and fun film following the adventures of a young marijuana-smuggling woman (Kristian Sinclair) whose airplane crash-lands in Jamaica. She is rescued by Countryman and led to safety. Lots of Rasta humor and supernatural happenings keep the viewer entertained. *Countryman* also has a great reggae music sound track. Rated R for nudity and adult themes. 103m. **DIR:** Dickie Jobson. **CAST:** Hiram Keller, Kristian Sinclair. **1984**

COURAGEOUS DR. CHRISTIAN, THE ★★½ In this episode in the Dr. Christian series, Jean Hersholt again plays the saintlike physician. Predictable but pleasing. B&W; 67m. **DIR:** Bernard Vorhaus. **CAST:** Jean Hersholt, Dorothy Lovett, Robert Baldwin, Tom Neal. **1940**

COURAGEOUS MR. PENN ★★ Stilted title of this bloodless biography of religious leader William Penn is indicative of the mediocrity of the entire production. B&W; 79m. **DIR:** Lance Comfort. **CAST:** Clifford Evans, Deborah Kerr. **1943**

COURT-MARTIAL OF BILLY MITCHELL, THE ★★★ In 1925, Army General Billy Mitchell was court-martialed for calling the army and the navy almost treasonous for their neglect of military air power after World War I. Gary Cooper is marvelous as Mitchell, but the show is almost stolen by prosecuting attorney Rod Steiger. 100m. **DIR:** Otto Preminger. **CAST:** Gary Cooper, Rod Steiger, Charles Bickford, Ralph Bellamy, Elizabeth Montgomery, Jack Lord, Peter Graves, Darren McGavin. **1955**

COURT-MARTIAL OF JACKIE ROBINSON, THE ★★★½ Well-made television drama examines baseball great Jackie Robinson's battles against racism in the army from 1942 to 1944. Andre Braugher is very good as the young Robinson, with veterans Ruby Dee and Bruce Dern lending stellar support in small but important roles. 94m. **DIR:** Larry Peerce. **CAST:** Andre Braugher, Daniel Stern, Ruby Dee, Stan Shaw, Paul Dooley, Bruce Dern. **1990**

COURTESANS OF BOMBAY ★★★★ Fascinating mix of documentary and fiction explores the lives of impoverished Indian women who support themselves through a combination of performing and prostitution. Made for British television, the film is chiefly concerned with the social context of a society that encourages such life-styles. Unrated; the subject matter is discreetly handled but too frank for young children. 73m. **DIR:** Ismail Merchant, James Ivory, Ruth Prawer Jhabvala. **CAST:** Saeed Jaffrey. **1983**

COURTNEY AFFAIR, THE ★★★ British family saga stretching across four and a half decades: 1900–1945. Classy soap opera in which a housemaid marries money and trades the backstairs for the drawing room. B&W; 112m. **DIR:** Herbert Wilcox. **CAST:** Anna Neagle, Michael Wilding, Coral Browne. **1947**

COURTSHIP ★★★★ A touching and engrossing period play (set in 1915) from the pen of Horton Foote, whose superb dialogue makes this tale of a young woman's coming-of-age easy to believe. A wonderful transport back to the more chivalrous days of yesteryear. No rating. 85m. **DIR:** Howard Cummings. **CAST:** Hallie Foote, Amanda Plummer, Rochelle Oliver, Michael Higgins, William Converse-Roberts. **1987**

COWARD OF THE COUNTY ★★★ This made-for-TV film is based on Kenny Rogers's hit song. He plays a World War II Georgia preacher with a pacifist nephew. When the nephew's girlfriend is raped, he's put to the ultimate test of his nonviolent beliefs. The acting and setting are believable, making this a film worth viewing. 110m. **DIR:** Dick Lowry. **CAST:** Kenny Rogers, Frederic Lehne, Largo Woodruff, Mariclare Costello, Ana Alicia. **1981**

COWBOY AND THE BALLERINA, THE ★★ This telemovie is romance at its most basic. Lee Majors plays a former world-champion rodeo rider who meets a Russian ballerina (Leslie Wing) who is attempting to defect. Corny but adequate time passer. 100m. **DIR:** Jerry Jameson. **CAST:** Lee Majors, Leslie Wing, Christopher Lloyd, Anjelica Huston. **1984**

CRACKER FACTORY ★★★★ This made-for-TV drama features Natalie Wood as Cassie Barrett, an alcoholic housewife who loses her grip on reality. Her long-suffering husband, Charlie (Peter Haskell), silently offers support while she spends her rehabilitation in the Cracker Factory, a mental institution. Unrated, but the mature topic warrants parental discretion. 95m. **DIR:** Burt Brinckerhoff. **CAST:** Natalie Wood, Peter Haskell, Shelley Long, Vivian Blaine, Perry King. **1979**

CRAIG'S WIFE ★★★ In her first film success, Rosalind Russell is brilliant as Harriet Craig, the wife of the title, a heartless domestic tyrant whose neurotic preference for material concerns over human feelings alienates all around her. John Boles is her long-suffering, slow-to-see-the-light husband. B&W; 75m. **DIR:** Dorothy Arzner. **CAST:** Rosalind Russell, John Boles, Billie Burke, Jane Darwell, Thomas Mitchell, Alma Kruger. **1936**

CRASH OF FLIGHT 401 ★★ Based on fact, this made-for-television movie tells the story of the disastrous airliner crash in the Florida Everglades in December of 1972 and the eventful rescue of seventy-three survivors. Routine. 100m. **DIR:** Barry Shear. **CAST:** William Shatner, Eddie Albert, Adrienne Barbeau. **1978**

CRAZY FROM THE HEART ★★★ Made-for-cable comedy-drama looks at the relationship between a Texas high school principal and a Mexican janitor. As they become more fond of each other, the pressures of an interracial affair come to bear. A little sugary at times, but still manages to keep focused on the main issues. 96m. **DIR:** Thomas Schlamme. **CAST:** Christine Lahti, Rubén Blades, William Russ, Louise Latham, Mary Kay Place, Tommy Muniz. **1991**

CRAZY IN LOVE ★★★ Holly Hunter shares an island home with her mother and grandmother, whose bitter experiences with men may be a bad influence on Hunter's marriage. Minor but enjoyable romantic drama. Not rated; contains no objectionable material. 93m. **DIR:** Martha Coolidge. **CAST:** Holly Hunter, Gena Rowlands, Bill Pullman, Julian Sands, Herta Ware, Frances McDormand. **1992**

CRAZY MOON ★★ This is another entry in the *Harold and Maude* genre: neurotic, alienated young man gets his act together when he falls in love with a spunky disabled woman who is managing to cope with real problems. Rated PG-13. 89m. **DIR:** Allan Eastman. **CAST:** Kiefer Sutherland, Vanessa Vaughan. **1986**

CREATOR ★★ This film, about a scientist (Peter O'Toole) who is attempting to bring back to life the wife who died thirty years before, during childbirth, is, at first, a very witty and occasionally heart-tugging comedy. However, in its last third, it turns into a sort of second-rate tearjerker. Rated R for nudity, profanity, and simulated sex. 108m. **DIR:** Ivan Passer. **CAST:** Peter O'Toole, Mariel Hemingway, Vincent Spano, Virginia Madsen, David Ogden Stiers, John Dehner. **1985**

CRIME AND PUNISHMENT (1935) ★★★★ The most faithful film version of the Dostoyevski novel, this film makes good use of atmospheric lighting, dramatic shadows, and eerie mood music. Peter Lorre stars as Raskolnikov, a mild-mannered man who unwittingly becomes a murderer. He successfully escapes the police, but his conscience takes over. Thought-provoking as well as entertaining. B&W; 88m. **DIR:** Josef von Sternberg. **CAST:** Peter Lorre, Edward Arnold, Marian Marsh, Elisabeth Risdon, Mrs. Patrick Campbell. **1935**

CRIME OF PASSION ★★½ The story of a tough newspaperwoman who will do anything to hold onto her man is a good showcase for Barbara Stanwyck. But it's a contrived and predictable movie, the type she made many times during her long career. The film has more suggestive scenes than usual for its era. B&W; 85m. **DIR:** Gerd Oswald. **CAST:** Barbara Stanwyck, Sterling Hayden, Raymond Burr, Fay Wray, Royal Dano, Stuart Whitman. **1957**

CRIMES AND MISDEMEANORS ★★★★★ In what may be Woody Allen's masterpiece, Martin Landau plays a successful doctor who attempts to call a halt to a foolish affair. However, his mistress (Anjelica Huston) proves to be emotionally unstable and refuses to let him go. On the periphery of this serious study of morality are Allen's antics as a documentary filmmaker hired by his egotistical brother-in-law (Alan Alda) to make a movie about the latter's career as a TV sitcom king. Rated PG-13 for adult themes. 104m. **DIR:** Woody Allen. **CAST:** Martin Landau, Woody Allen, Alan Alda, Mia Farrow, Anjelica Huston, Jerry Orbach, Sam Waterston. **1989**

CRIMES OF PASSION 🦃 By day she's a highly paid fashion designer; by night, she's a kinky high-priced hooker. Rated R for nudity, suggested sex, profanity, and violence. 107m. **DIR:** Ken Russell. **CAST:** Kathleen Turner, Anthony Perkins, John Laughlin. **1984**

CRIMINAL CODE, THE ★★★★ A powerful performance by Boris Karloff as a revenge-minded convict, elevates this Howard Hawks release from interesting to memorable. It's a lost classic that deserves its release on video. The story involves a district attorney (impressively played by Walter Huston) who overzealously pursues his job, with the result that an innocent man (Phillips Holmes) is sent to prison. B&W; 83m. **DIR:** Howard Hawks. **CAST:** Boris Karloff, Walter Huston, Phillips Holmes. **1931**

CRIMINAL JUSTICE ★★ Writer-director Andy Wolk's disagreeably vague and stridently preachy telescript is partly salvaged by Forest Whitaker's masterful lead performance as a felon accused of robbing and knifing a young woman, whose veracity (as the only witness) is never sufficiently questioned. Unrated, but with considerable profanity. 90m. **DIR:** Andy Wolk. **CAST:** Forest Whitaker, Anthony LaPaglia, Rosie Perez, Jennifer Grey. **1990**

CRISIS AT CENTRAL HIGH ★★★★½ In the late Fifties Little Rock, Arkansas, was rocked by the integration of the school system. This television film is a retelling of those events as seen through the eyes of teacher Elizabeth Huckaby, one of the principal characters involved. Joanne Woodward is simply wonderful as the caught-in-the-middle instructor. 125m. **DIR:** Lamont Johnson. **CAST:** Joanne Woodward, Charles Durning, Henderson Forsythe, William Russ. **1981**

CRISSCROSS (1992) ★★★ Some fine performances highlight this slice-of-life character study about a 12-year-old boy who discovers the shocking truth about his mother's nighttime job. Screenwriter Scott Sommer adds some interesting touches to this tale set in the Sixties, but director Chris Menges directs in too laid-back a fashion. Rated R for profanity, nudity, and violence. 100m. **DIR:** Chris Menges. **CAST:** Goldie Hawn, Arliss Howard, James Gammon, Keith Carradine, David Arnott, J. C. Quinn, Steve Buscemi. **1992**

CROMWELL ★★ Richard Harris hams it up again in this overblown historical melodrama. A fine cast founders amid tradition-soaked locations and beautiful backgrounds. The accoutrements and design are splendid, but the story is lacking and Harris's performance is inept. 145m. **DIR:** Ken Hughes. **CAST:** Richard Harris, Alec Guinness, Robert Morley, Frank Finlay, Dorothy Tutin, Timothy Dalton, Patrick Magee. **1970**

CROOKED HEARTS ★★ The talents of an ensemble cast are showcased in this slow-paced story of a family's struggle to give each other room to grow. The film resembles movies adapted from John Irving novels, only here, the surreal humor and irony are missing. Rated R for profanity and partial nudity. 113m. **DIR:** Michael Bortman. **CAST:** Vincent D'Onofrio, Jennifer Jason Leigh, Peter Berg, Cindy Pickett, Juliette Lewis, Marg Helgenberger, Peter Coyote. **1991**

CROSS COUNTRY ★★ Michael Ironside plays Detective Ed Roersch, who pursues Richard Beymer following the murder of an expensive call girl. Although this movie involves prostitution, blackmail, murder, and deceit, it still manages to bore. Rated R for nudity, sex, profanity, and violence. 95m. **DIR:** Paul Lynch. **CAST:** Richard Beymer, Nina Axelrod, Michael Ironside, Brent Carver. **1983**

CROSS CREEK ★★★½ About the life of 1930s author Marjorie Kinnan Rawlings (Mary Steenburgen), this watchable release illustrates how Rawlings's relationships with backwoods folks inspired her novels, particularly *The Yearling* and *Jacob's Ladder*. Rated PG for brief violence. 122m. **DIR:** Martin Ritt. **CAST:** Mary Steenburgen, Rip Torn, Peter Coyote, Dana Hill. **1983**

CROSSING, THE ★★ Australian melodrama about a young woman in a romantic triangle forced into choosing between life in a small town with her current boyfriend or with his best friend who left town to pursue a career in the art world. Clichéd. Rated R for nudity and profanity. 92m. **DIR:** Russell Crowe. **CAST:** Russell Crowe, Robert Mammone, Danielle Spencer. **1992**

CROSSING DELANCEY ★★★★½ Amy Irving has the role of her career as the independent New Yorker scrutinized by Susan Sandler's deft and poignant screenplay (adapted from her own stage play). Irving has a bookstore job that brings her into close contact with the pretentious members of the Big Apple's literary scene; she fulfills deeper needs with visits to her feisty grandmother (Reizl Bozyk). Grandmother has matchmaking plans, specifically involving Irving with street vendor Peter Riegert, whose flawless timing is one of the many highlights here. Rated PG for language and mild sexual themes. 97m. **DIR:** Joan Micklin Silver. **CAST:** Amy Irving, Peter Riegert, Reizl Bozyk, Jeroen Krabbé, Sylvia Miles. **1988**

CROSSING THE BRIDGE ★★★ Gutsy, credible performances give this 1970s coming-of-age story a raw edge as three Detroit buddies get jolted into adulthood when a plan to smuggle hash across the Canadian border goes sour. Written and directed with apparent autobiographical clarity by Mike Binder. Rated R for language and violence. 103m. **DIR:** Mike Binder. **CAST:** Josh Charles, Jason Gedrick, Stephen Baldwin, Cheryl Pollack, Richard Edson. **1992**

CROSSING THE LINE (1990) ★★½ When a motorcycle accident puts his best friend in a coma, rich kid Rick Hearst takes the heat. Exciting race footage sets the pace for this domestic drama about sibling rivalry. Rated R for strong language. 94m. **DIR:** Gary Graver. **CAST:** John Saxon, Rick Hearst, Jon Stafford, Cameron Mitchell. **1990**

CROSSING THE LINE (1991) ★★★ An unemployed coal miner (Liam Neeson) gets involved with illegal bare-knuckle boxing and hoodlums in this Scottish drama. The brawling is gritty and glamourless in an intriguing story that ends with a surprising turn of events. Rated R for violence. 94m. **DIR:** David Leland. **CAST:** Liam Neeson, Joanne Whalley, Ian Bannen, Billy Connolly, Hugh Grant. **1991**

CROWD, THE ★★★★½ Director King Vidor's pioneering slice-of-life story of a working-class family in a big city during the Jazz Age still holds up beautifully after sixty years. James Murray, in his only major movie, gives an extraordinary performance as a hardworking clerk who never seems to get ahead. Not rated; suitable for all but the youngest children. B&W; 90m. **DIR:** King Vidor. **CAST:** James Murray, Eleanor Boardman. **1928**

CRUEL SEA, THE ★★★½ The ever-changing and unpredictable wind-lashed sea is the star of this gripping documentary-style adventure about a stalwart British warship during World War II. B&W; 121m. **DIR:** Charles Frend. **CAST:** Jack Hawkins, Virginia McKenna, Stanley Baker, Donald Sinden. **1953**

CRY FOR LOVE, A ★★★½ Taut teledrama about two people—one an alcoholic, the other addicted to uppers—who, through some very real difficulties, fall in love. Their attempts to help each other over the crises of substance abuse draw them closer together. 100m. **DIR:** Paul Wendkos. **CAST:** Susan Blakely, Powers Boothe, Gene Barry, Edie Adams, Lainie Kazan, Charles Siebert. **1980**

CRY FREEDOM ★★★★½ Director Richard Attenborough and screenwriter John Briley's superb film about South African apartheid begins by chronicling the growing friendship between nonviolent black leader Steve Biko (Denzel Washington) and white newspaperman Donal Woods (Kevin Kline). When Biko is brutally murdered, Woods must fight to tell the truth to the rest of the world. Rated PG for violence. 130m. **DIR:** Richard Attenborough. **CAST:** Kevin Kline, Penelope Wilton, Denzel Washington, Ian Richardson. **1987**

CRY IN THE DARK, A ★★★★½ A chilling, superbly acted true-life drama set in 1980 Australia, this film features Meryl Streep and Sam Neill as the parents of an infant who is stolen by a wild dog while they are camping out—or so they say. The authorities begin to doubt their story and the Australian people begin spreading rumors that the baby was killed in a sacrificial rite. Thus begins this harrowing motion picture. Rated PG-13 for mature themes. 120m. **DIR:** Fred Schepisi. **CAST:** Meryl Streep, Sam Neill, Charles Tingwell. **1988**

CRY IN THE WIND ★★★ David Morse is a bitterly lonely mountain man who kidnaps shy and pretty schoolgirl Megan Follows. Though effectively harsh, the flick only touches the surface of what was the largest manhunt in Pennsylvania history. 95m. **DIR:** Charles Correll. **CAST:** David Morse, Megan Follows, David Soul. **1991**

CRY, THE BELOVED COUNTRY ★★★★ A touching film about the problems of apartheid in South Africa with Sidney Poitier and Canada Lee exceptionally good as preachers fighting prejudice in their homeland. Based on Alan Paton's controversial novel of the same name and the inspiration for the Kurt Weill musical drama, *Lost in the Stars*. B&W; 105m. **DIR:** Zoltán Korda. **CAST:** Sidney Poitier, Canada Lee, Joyce Carey, Charles Carson, Geoffrey Keen. **1952**

CRY VENGEANCE 🦃 An ex-cop set up as a fall guy seeks revenge. B&W; 83m. **DIR:** Mark Stevens. **CAST:** Mark Stevens, Martha Hyer, Skip Homeier, Joan Vohs, Douglas Kennedy. **1954**

CRYING GAME, THE ★★★★★ Brilliant, adult-oriented motion picture by writer-director Neil Jordan casts sad-eyed Stephen Rea as an IRA volunteer assigned to guard British soldier Forest Whitaker, and that's when the plot's ingenious twists and turns begin. Newcomer Jaye Davidson makes a startling film debut. This evocative exploration of the human condition should be on every serious film buff's must-see list. Rated R for violence, profanity, and nudity. 113m. **DIR:** Neil Jordan. **CAST:** Stephen Rea, Miranda Richardson, Forest Whitaker, Jaye Davidson, Jim Broadbent, Ralph Brown, Adrian Dunbar. **1992**

CRYSTAL HEART 🦃 A young man with a rare illness falls in love with an aspiring rock singer. Rated R. 103m. **DIR:** Gil Bettman. **CAST:** Tawny Kitaen, Lee Curreri, Lloyd Bochner. **1987**

CUL-DE-SAC ★★★ Early Roman Polanski black comedy, about hoods on the lam who briefly victimize a man and his luscious young wife. Early Polanski is just like later Polanski...an acquired taste. One of the director's first films in English. B&W; 111m. **DIR:** Roman Polanski. **CAST:** Donald Pleasence, Françoise Dorleac, Lionel Stander, Jack MacGowran, Jacqueline Bisset. **1966**

CUT AND RUN 🦃 A television journalist in South America covering a bloody cocaine war. Rated R for violence, profanity, and nudity. 87m. **DIR:** Ruggero Deodato. **CAST:** Lisa Blount, Leonard Mann, Willie Aames, Richard Lynch, Richard Bright, Michael Berryman, John Steiner, Karen Black. **1985**

CUTTING EDGE, THE ★★★½ Ice-hockey player D. B. Sweeney reluctantly becomes the figure-skating partner of ice queen Moira Kelly. Few surprises, but those who thaw at the idea of a love story will find it entertaining. Rated PG for profanity. 101m. **DIR:** Paul Michael Glaser. **CAST:** D. B. Sweeney, Moira Kelly, Roy Dotrice, Dwier Brown, Terry O'Quinn. **1992**

CYRANO DE BERGERAC (1950) ★★★★ Charming, touching story of steadfast devotion and unrequited love done with brilliance and panache. As the fearless soldier of the large nose, José Ferrer superbly dominates this fine film. Mala Powers is beautiful as his beloved Roxanne. William Prince, who now often plays heavies, makes Christian a proper, handsome, unimaginative nerd. B&W; 112m. **DIR:** Michael Gordon. **CAST:** José Ferrer, Mala Powers, William Prince. **1950**

D.I., THE ★★★ Jack Webb embodies the tough, no-nonsense drill instructor so commonly associated with the Marine Corps in this straightforward story of basic training and the men that it makes (or breaks). Don Dubbins plays the troublesome recruit who makes life miserable for Webb; many other roles are played by real-life members of the armed services. B&W; 106m. **DIR:** Jack Webb. **CAST:** Jack Webb, Don Dubbins, Lin McCarthy, Monica Lewis, Jackie Loughery, Virginia Gregg. **1957**

D.P. ★★★★ The shattering loss of innocence by war's true victims—children—is examined in this Emmy-winning adaptation of Kurt Vonnegut's poignant story. Julius Gordon is one of many orphans cared for by nuns in post–World War II Germany, a truly "displaced person" because he is the only boy with black skin. Unrated; suitable for family viewing. 60m. **DIR:** Alan Bridges. **CAST:** Stan Shaw, Rosemary Leach, Julius Gordon. **1985**

D. W. GRIFFITH SHORTS VOL. 1–12 ★★½ Vintage collection of film shorts by D. W. Griffith. This 12-volume set contains some of Griffith's earliest work. It is hardly as complex or photographed as interestingly as his feature films of the 1920s. Silent. 1908–1914; B&W; 1440m. **DIR:** D. W. Griffith.

D. W. GRIFFITH TRIPLE FEATURE ★★★ Kentucky dreamer and failed playwright David Wark Griffith was the American film industry's first great mover and shaker. Three fine examples of his early short films make up this feature: *The Battle of Elderbush Gulch, Iola's Promise,* and *The Goddess of Sagebrush Gulch.* Silent. B&W; 50m. **DIR:** D. W. Griffith. **CAST:** Mae Marsh, Lillian Gish, Charles West, Blanche Sweet, Mary Pickford. **1922**

DA ★★★★ New York City playwright Martin Sheen returns to his Irish home when his adoptive father (Barnard Hughes) dies. While in the house in which he was raised, Sheen relives his less-than-idyllic youth with the help of his father's cantankerous ghost. Both sentimental and uncompromising, this special film benefits from a performance of a lifetime by Hughes and one of nearly equal merit by Sheen. Rated PG for profanity. 96m. **DIR:** Matt Clark. **CAST:** Barnard Hughes, Martin Sheen, William Hickey, Doreen Hepburn. **1988**

DAD ★★★★ In this wonderful weeper, Ted Danson is a successful businessman who attempts to make an emotional connection with his 75-year-old father (Jack Lemmon) before it is too late. Writer-director Gary David Goldberg, who adapted the novel by William Wharton, doesn't let us off easy. Rated PG. 116m. **DIR:** Gary David Goldberg. **CAST:** Jack Lemmon, Ted Danson, Olympia Dukakis, Kathy Baker, Kevin Spacey, Ethan Hawke. **1989**

DAISY MILLER ★★ This limp screen adaptation of a story by the great novelist Henry James is more a study on rambling dialogue than on the clashing of two cultures. Rated G. 93m. **DIR:** Peter Bogdanovich. **CAST:** Cybill Shepherd, Barry Brown, Cloris Leachman, Mildred Natwick, Eileen Brennan. **1974**

DAKOTA (1988) ★★★ Outstanding cinematography highlights this run-of-the-mill story of a troubled teen on the run. Lou Diamond Phillips is the teen who works off a debt by training horses on a Texas farm. In the process he learns he must also face his past. Rated PG-13. 90m. **DIR:** Fred Holmes. **CAST:** Lou Diamond Phillips, Dee Dee Morton. **1988**

DAMAGE ★★ When Stephen Fleming—a respected British Parliament member—meets his son's new girlfriend, he's overcome by a sexual obsession that sends his entire world into a tragic tailspin. A high-gloss soap that is as cold and detached as the enigmatic woman at its lurid core. Rated R for language, nudity, and violence. 100m. **DIR:** Louis Malle. **CAST:** Jeremy Irons, Juliette Binoche, Miranda Richardson, Rupert Graves, Leslie Caron, Ian Bannen. **1993**

DANCE, FOOLS, DANCE ★★½ Joan Crawford plays a determined young woman who becomes a crime reporter and tries to make her reputation by bringing gangster Clark Gable to justice. The sparks fly—and their torrid teaming and some risqué bits of business rescue this precode melodrama from the stale plot line. B&W; 81m. **DIR:** Harry Beaumont. **CAST:** Joan Crawford, Clark Gable, Cliff Edwards, Natalie Moorhead. **1931**

DANCE HALL RACKET 🦃 Lenny Bruce plays creepy killer Vincent, bodyguard to a vice lord. B&W; 60m. **DIR:** Phil Tucker. **CAST:** Lenny Bruce. **1953**

DANCE WITH A STRANGER ★★★★½ A superbly acted, solidly directed import, this British drama is a completely convincing tale of tragic love. Newcomer Miranda Richardson makes a stunning film debut as the platinum-blonde hostess in a working-class nightclub who falls in love with a self-indulgent, upper-class snob (Rupert Everett). The screenplay was based on the true story of Ruth Ellis, who, on July 13, 1955, was hanged at London's Holloway prison for shooting her lover outside a pub. Rated R for profanity, nudity, sex, and violence. 102m. **DIR:** Mike Newell. **CAST:** Miranda Richardson, Rupert Everett, Ian Holm, Matthew Carroll. **1985**

DANCERS ★★½ Only lovers of ballet will enjoy this wafer-thin drama, since its latter half is devoted solely to an American Ballet Theatre production of *Giselle*. The minimal attempt at parallel storytelling concerns the conceited company star-director and the dancer who falls under his spell. Rated PG for sexual themes. 99m. **DIR:** Herbert Ross. **CAST:** Mikhail Baryshnikov, Leslie Browne. **1987**

DANCING IN THE DARK ★★½ Interesting drama about Edna Cormick (Martha Henry) who—after twenty years of being the ideal housewife, finds her life torn apart in a few short hours. From her hospital bed, Edna reconstructs the events that led up to her act of vengeance. Although this film is extremely slow-moving, feminists are likely to appreciate it. Rated PG-13. 93m. **DIR:** Leon Marr. **CAST:** Martha Henry, Neil Munro, Rosemary Dunsmore. **1986**

DANGER LIGHTS ★★★ Louis Wolheim plays a tough-as-nails rail-yard boss who befriends hobo Robert Armstrong and jeopardizes his chances with a young Jean Arthur, who is "almost" a fiancée. This story, done many times before and since, works well against the backdrop of a railroad world that is now largely gone. B&W; 73m. **DIR:** George B. Seitz. **CAST:** Louis Wolheim, Jean Arthur, Robert Armstrong, Hugh Herbert. **1930**

DANGEROUS ★★ One of the weakest movies to earn its star an Oscar. Bette Davis plays a former stage star-turned-alcoholic rescued by an idealistic architect (Franchot Tone). B&W; 78m. **DIR:** Alfred E. Green. **CAST:** Bette Davis, Franchot Tone, Alison Skipworth, Margaret Lindsay, John Eldredge, Dick Foran. **1935**

DANGEROUS COMPANY ★★ The true story of convict Ray Johnson, who lived in and out of prison for years until his reform. Excellent acting saves what would otherwise be a tedious biography. 100m. **DIR:** Lamont Johnson. **CAST:** Beau Bridges, Carlos Brown, Karen Carlson, Kene Holiday, Ralph Macchio. **1982**

DANGEROUS LIAISONS ★★★★ Based on the classic French novel *Les Liaisons Dangereuses*, this exquisitely filmed story of competitive sexual gamesmanship between two ex-lovers is charged with sensual energy. The cast, led by a marvelously brittle Glenn Close and John Malkovich, is first rate. There's a sumptuous rhythm to the language and a lush setting that beautifully captures upper-class, eighteenth-century France. Rated R. 120m. **DIR:** Stephen Frears. **CAST:** Glenn Close, John Malkovich, Michelle Pfeiffer, Mildred Natwick, Swoosie Kurtz. **1989**

DANGEROUS LIFE, A ★★½ Interesting made-for-cable portrayal of the Philippine uprising against Ferdinand and Imelda Marcos during the mid-Eighties. Gary Busey plays a reporter stationed in Manila when all hell breaks loose. Unrated, but some violence. 163m. **DIR:** Robert Markowitz. **CAST:** Gary Busey, Rebecca Gilling, James Handy. **1988**

DANGEROUS RELATIONS ★★★½ Don't be misled by the sensationalistic sleeve art—this apparently lurid prison drama is actually a thoughtful tale about an estranged father and son (Lou Gossett Jr. and Blair Underwood) attempting to make peace while forced to serve their parole under the same roof. Walter Halsey Davis's intelligent script suffers only from uneven direction by Georg Stanford Brown, who elicits what may be Rae Dawn Chong's most awkward performance ever. Made for TV. 93m. **DIR:** Georg Stanford Brown. **CAST:** Lou Gossett Jr., Blair Underwood, Rae Dawn Chong, David Harris, Clarence Williams III. **1993**

DANGEROUS SUMMER, A 🦃 Set in Australia, this film deals with a posh resort damaged by fire and the subsequent investigation. Unrated; the film has violence and profanity. 100m. **DIR:** Quentin Masters. **CAST:** James Mason, Tom Skerritt, Ian Gilmour, Wendy Hughes. **1984**

DANGEROUS WOMAN, A ★★½ Oddball drama doesn't quite gel around Debra Winger's would-be bravura performance as a mentally impaired but well-meaning woman whose carefully constructed life begins falling apart. An affair with a new handyman brings romance, while an unjust accusation of stealing calls up more volatile emotions. The film lacks a cohesive dramatic structure and distinct point of view. Rated R for profanity, violence, and simulated sex. 99m. **DIR:**

Stephen Gyllenhaal. **CAST:** Debra Winger, Barbara Hershey, Gabriel Byrne, David Strathairn, Laurie Metcalf, Chloe Webb, John Terry, Jan Hooks, Paul Dooley, Viveka Davis, Richard Riehle. **1993**

DANIEL ★★½ Sidney Lumet directed this disappointing and ultimately depressing screen version of E. L. Doctorow's thinly veiled account of the Rosenberg case of thirty years ago, in which the parents of two young children were electrocuted as spies. If it weren't for Timothy Hutton's superb performance in the title role (as one of the children), *Daniel* would be much less effective. Rated R for profanity and violence. 130m. **DIR:** Sidney Lumet. **CAST:** Timothy Hutton, Mandy Patinkin, Lindsay Crouse, Edward Asner, Amanda Plummer. **1983**

DANIELLE STEELE'S "FINE THINGS" ★★ Condensed television miniseries based on bestseller by author Danielle Steel. Too much soap and not enough opera in this tale of newlyweds, D. W. Moffett and Tracy Pollan, who discover she suffers from the most incurable of miniseries diseases. Ho-hum, but costar Cloris Leachman has some nice moments. 145m. **DIR:** Tom Moore. **CAST:** D. W. Moffett, Tracy Pollan, Noley Thornton, Cloris Leachman, Darrell Larson. **1990**

DANNY BOY (1941) ★★ Estranged from her husband and small son, a singer searches for them, only to find that they have become street musicians. Overly sentimental, but the music is nice enough. B&W; 80m. **DIR:** Oswald Mitchell. **CAST:** Ann Todd, Wilfrid Lawson. **1941**

DANNY BOY (1982) ★★★★ A young saxophone player witnesses the brutal murder of two people and becomes obsessed with understanding the act. Set in Ireland, this movie is enhanced by haunting musical interludes that highlight the drama of the people caught up in the Irish "troubles." There are flaws, most notably in some of the coincidences, but the overall effect is mesmerizing. Rated R. 92m. **DIR:** Neil Jordan. **CAST:** Stephen Rea, Marie Kean, Ray McAnally, Donal McCann. **1982**

DANTE'S INFERNO ★★½ This early film by director Ken Russell exhibits great cinematic style but falls short in dramatic execution. The movie focuses on the morose and brilliant poet and painter Dante Gabriel Roth, played by Oliver Reed with comic pathos. Not very engaging. Unrated, but recommended for adult viewers. B&W; 90m. **DIR:** Ken Russell. **CAST:** Oliver Reed. **1968**

DARK CITY ★★★ Noirish melodrama has cynical bookie Charlton Heston (in his first Hollywood film) on the run from a psychotic gangster with a grudge. Noteworthy for the cast, particularly Jack Webb (in a villainous role!) and his future *Dragnet* sidekick Harry Morgan. B&W; 88m. **DIR:** William Dieterle. **CAST:** Charlton Heston, Jack Webb, Lizabeth Scott, Viveca Lindfors, Dean Jagger, Don DeFore, Harry Morgan, Ed Begley Sr., Mike Mazurki. **1950**

DARK CORNER, THE ★★★½ Released from prison after being framed by his partner, private eye Mark Stevens finds he is being dogged by a man in a white suit. Before he can fathom why, he finds his ex-partner's body under his bed, and the police once again closing in. His secretary, Lucille Ball, helps unravel the sinister murder scheme. Above-average *film noir*. B&W; 99m. **DIR:** Henry Hathaway. **CAST:** Mark Stevens, Clifton Webb, Lucille Ball, William Bendix, Kurt Kreuger. **1946**

DARK OBSESSION ★★ Painful to watch and ultimately pointless, this focuses on a sadistic husband's obsession with controlling his wife. Released with two ratings; NC17 and R, this contains nudity, profanity, and violence. 97m. **DIR:** Nick Broomfield. **CAST:** Amanda Donohoe, Gabriel Byrne, Douglas Hodge, Ian Carmichael, Michael Hordern. **1990**

DARK PAST, THE ★★ A psychotic killer escapes from prison and a psychologist attempts to convince the hood to give himself up. Lee J. Cobb is marvelous as the psychiatrist and William Holden is wonderful as the bad guy. Nina Foch is top-notch as Holden's moll. A remake of *Blind Alley*. 75m. **DIR:** Rudolph Maté. **CAST:** William Holden, Lee J. Cobb, Nina Foch, Adele Jergens. **1948**

DARK RIVER: A FATHER'S REVENGE ★★★ When his daughter dies, a man stands alone to prove the town's leading industry is to blame. This better-than-average TV film covers some familar territory, but contains some exceptional performances. 95m. **DIR:** Michael Pressman. **CAST:** Mike Farrell, Tess Harper, Helen Hunt. **1989**

DARK TIDE ★★½ Brigitte Bako's atrocious acting mars what might have been a reasonably taut erotic thriller containing—for once—a nice balance between dramatic tension and soft-core groping. She's the catalyst who turns island thugs against researcher Chris Sarandon, who ignores imminent danger while collecting venom from incredibly malicious sea snakes. Rated R for profanity, nudity, violence, rape, and simulated sex. 94m. **DIR:** Luca Bercovici. **CAST:** Brigitte Bako, Richard Tyson, Chris Sarandon. **1993**

DARK VICTORY ★★★★ This Warner Bros. release gave Bette Davis one of her best roles, as a headstrong heiress who discovers she has a brain tumor. A successful operation leads to a love affair with her doctor (George Brent). In the midst of all this bliss, Davis learns the tragic truth: surgery was only a halfway measure, and she will die in a year. Sure it's corny. But director Edmund Goulding, Davis, and her costars make it work. B&W; 106m. **DIR:** Edmund Goulding. **CAST:** Bette Davis, George Brent, Humphrey Bogart, Ronald Reagan, Geraldine Fitzgerald. **1939**

DARK WATERS ★★½ Muddled story of orphaned girl(?), Merle Oberon, and her strange and terrifying experiences in the bayou backwaters of Louisiana is atmospheric, but fails to deliver enough of a story to justify its moody buildup. But the supporting players (along with the misty bogs) really carry the ball in this film. B&W; 90m. **DIR:** André de Toth. **CAST:** Merle Oberon, Franchot Tone, Thomas Mitchell, Fay Bainter, Rex Ingram, John Qualen, Elisha Cook Jr. **1944**

DARLING ★★★★ John Schlesinger's direction is first-rate, and Julie Christie gives an Oscar-winning portrayal of a ruthless model who bullies, bluffs, and claws her way to social success, only to find life at the top meaningless. B&W; 122m. **DIR:** John Schlesinger. **CAST:** Julie Christie, Dirk Bogarde, Laurence Harvey, Jose Luis de Villalonga. **1965**

DAUGHTERS OF THE DUST ★★★★ Writer-director Julie Dash's *Daughters of the Dust* is an absolutely gorgeous motion picture. Set in 1902 on one of the sea islands off Georgia and North Carolina, it plays like a series of vintage photographs set to music and combined with dramatic sequences. The story centers around a final ceremony being held prior to an African-American family's journey North. Fascinating. Unrated, the film has no objectionable material. 113m. **DIR:** Julie Dash. **CAST:** Adisa Anderson, Cheryl Lynn Bruce, Cora Lee Day. **1992**

DAVID AND BATHSHEBA ★★ Mediocre biblical epic with a polished cast nearly defeated by mundane script. Normally reliable director Henry King can't breathe life into this soporific soap opera. 116m. **DIR:** Henry King. **CAST:** Gregory Peck, Susan Hayward, Raymond Massey, Kieron Moore. **1951**

DAVID AND LISA ★★★½ Mentally disturbed teenagers (Keir Dullea and Janet Margolin) meet and develop a sensitive emotional attachment while institutionalized. Abetted by Howard DaSilva as their understanding doctor, Dullea and Margolin make this study highly watchable. Independently produced, this one was a sleeper. B&W; 94m. **DIR:** Frank Perry. **CAST:** Keir Dullea, Janet Margolin, Howard DaSilva, Neva Patterson, Clifton James. **1962**

DAVID COPPERFIELD ★★★★½ A first-rate production of Charles Dickens's rambling novel about a young man's adventures in nineteenth-century England. W. C. Fields and Edna May Oliver are standouts in an all-star cast. B&W; 100m. **DIR:** George Cukor. **CAST:** Freddie Bartholomew, Frank Lawton, Lionel Barrymore, W. C. Fields, Edna May Oliver, Basil Rathbone. **1935**

DAWNING, THE ★★★½ Leisurely paced coming-of-age film focuses on a naïve Irish girl whose life changes when she meets a renegade IRA leader. Seaside shots are spectacular as well as haunting. Equivalent to a PG for violence. 97m. **DIR:** Robert Knights. **CAST:** Anthony Hopkins, Rebecca Pidgeon, Trevor Howard, Jean Simmons. **1988**

DAY IN OCTOBER, A ★★½ WWII drama set in Nazi-occupied Denmark, about efforts to evacuate Danish Jews into neutral Sweden. Competently made film seems overly familiar, despite the efforts of a strong cast. Rated PG. 97m. **DIR:** Kenneth Madsen. **CAST:** D. B. Sweeney, Kelly Wolf, Tovah Feldshuh. **1992**

DAY OF THE LOCUST, THE ★★★★½ This drama is both extremely depressing and spellbinding. It shows the unglamorous side of Hollywood in the 1930s. The people who don't succeed in the entertainment capital are the focus of the film. Rated R. 144m. **DIR:** John Schlesinger. **CAST:** Donald Sutherland, Karen Black, Burgess Meredith, Bo Hopkins, William Atherton. **1975**

DAY ONE ★★★ Television tackles the creation of the nuclear bomb as American scientists work on the Manhattan Project. Stellar cast helps this true story, which is rich in production values and benefits from a riveting screenplay. Not rated. 141m. **DIR:** Joseph Sargent. **CAST:** Brian Dennehy, David Strathairn, Michael Tucker, Richard Dysart, David Ogden Stiers. **1989**

DAY THAT SHOOK THE WORLD, THE ★★★ A slow start can't reduce one's fascination with the shocking incident—the assassination of Austria's Archduke Ferdinand and his wife—that resulted in World War I. Rated R for violence, including disturbing hunting scenes and graphic torture footage. 111m. **DIR:** Veljko Bulajic. **CAST:** Christopher Plummer, Maximilian Schell, Florinda Bolkan. **1978**

DAYS OF HEAVEN ★★★★½ Each frame of *Days of Heaven* looks like a page torn from an exquisitely beautiful picture book. The film begins in the slums of Chicago, where Bill (Richard Gere) works in a steel mill. He decides to take Abby (Brooke Adams), his girl, and Linda (Linda Manz), his young sister, to the Texas Panhandle to work in the wheat fields at harvest time. That's the beginning of an idyllic year that ends in tragedy. Rated PG. 95m. **DIR:** Terence Malick. **CAST:** Richard Gere, Brooke Adams, Sam Shepard, Linda Manz. **1978**

DAYS OF WINE AND ROSES ★★★½ In this saddening film, Jack Lemmon and Lee Remick shatter the misconceptions about middle-class alcoholism. B&W; 117m. **DIR:** Blake Edwards. **CAST:** Jack Lemmon, Lee Remick, Charles Bickford, Jack Klugman. **1962**

DAYS OF WINE AND ROSES, THE (TELEVISION) ★★★½ Unpolished but still excellent television original from which the 1962 film was adapted. Cliff Robertson is the up-and-coming executive and Piper Laurie, his pretty wife, whose lives are shattered by alcoholism. Written for the *Playhouse 90* series, *The Days of Wine and Roses* is introduced by Julie Harris and framed with interviews with the featured players. B&W; 90m. **DIR:** John Frankenheimer. **CAST:** Cliff Robertson, Piper Laurie. **1958**

DAZED AND CONFUSED ★★★½ Although it's hard to view the "silly Seventies" with the same nostalgia George Lucas gave the Sixties in *American Graffiti*, writer-director Richard Linklater makes a game effort. Employing a cast of mostly unknowns, Linklater shows how the final day of high school in 1976 affects the outgoing seniors and incoming freshmen. While not to all tastes, this whimsical ensemble drama contains occasional truths and a lot of heart. Rated R for profanity and drug use. 103m. **DIR:** Richard Linklater. **CAST:** Jason London, Rory Cochrane, Adam Goldberg, Anthony Rapp, Sasha Jenson, Milla Jovovich, Michelle Burke. **1993**

D-DAY THE SIXTH OF JUNE ★★ Slow-moving account of the Normandy invasion in World War II. Story concentrates on Allied officers Robert Taylor's and Richard Todd's romantic and professional problems. 106m. **DIR:** Henry Koster. **CAST:** Robert Taylor, Richard Todd, Dana Wynter, Edmond O'Brien. **1956**

DEAD, THE ★★★★★ John Huston's final bow is an elegant adaptation of James Joyce's short story about a party given by three women for a group of their dearest friends. During the evening, conversation drifts to those people, now dead, who have had a great influence on the lives of the guests and hostesses at the party. Huston, who died before the film was released, seems to be speaking to us from beyond the grave. This is one of his best. Rated PG. 81m. **DIR:** John Huston. **CAST:** Anjelica Huston, Donal McCann, Ingrid Craigie, Dan O'Herlihy, Marie Kean, Donal Donnelly, Sean McClory. **1987**

DEAD AHEAD: THE EXXON VALDEZ DISASTER ★★★★ First-rate advocacy cinema from scripter Michael Baker, who documents the ecological disaster that resulted when the Exxon Valdez dumped 11 million gallons of oil into Alaska's Prince William Sound. John Heard, as the site's leading environmental champion, is appropriately outraged; Christopher Lloyd has the tougher role as the Exxon bureaucrat sacrificed as the incident's scapegoat. 88m. **DIR:** Paul Seed. **CAST:** John Heard, Christopher Lloyd, Ron Frazier, Michael Murphy, Rip Torn. **1992**

DEAD END ★★★ Many famous names combined to film this story of people trying to escape their oppressive slum environment. Humphrey Bogart is cast in one of his many gangster roles from the 1930s. Joel McCrea conforms to his Hollywood stereotype by playing the "nice guy" architect, who dreams of rebuilding New York's waterfront. B&W; 93m. **DIR:** William Wyler. **CAST:** Humphrey Bogart, Sylvia Sidney, Joel McCrea, Claire Trevor. **1937**

DEAD MAN OUT ★★★ Awaiting execution, an inmate on Death Row (Rubén Blades) goes mad. This creates a problem for the state, since an insane man cannot be executed. The state-appointed psychiatrist (Danny Glover) contemplates whether or not he should declare Ben sane again in time for him to die. Ron Hutchinson's teleplay is riveting, and Glover and Blades deliver fine performances. Not rated. 87m. **DIR:** Richard Pearce. **CAST:** Danny Glover, Rubén Blades, Larry Block, Samuel L. Jackson, Sam Stone, Maria Ricossa, Ali Giron, Val Ford. **1988**

DEAD POETS SOCIETY ★★★½ Robin Williams offers an impressive change-of-pace as an unorthodox English teacher. He inspires a love of poetry and intellectual freedom in his students at a strict, upscale New England prep school. Though not entirely satisfying in its resolution, the film offers much of the heart and mood of *Goodbye, Mr. Chips* and *The Prime of Miss Jean Brodie*. Richly textured by Australian filmmaker Peter Weir. Rated PG. 124m. **DIR:** Peter Weir. **CAST:** Robin Williams, Robert Sean Leonard, Norman Lloyd, Ethan Hawke. **1989**

DEAD SOLID PERFECT ★★★★ Dan Jenkins's witty golf fable becomes an equally engaging made-for-cable film, with Randy Quaid starring as a second-stringer desperate to have his shot at success. Jenkins and coscripter-director Bobby Roth deftly capture the boring routine of cross-country tours. 93m. **DIR:** Bobby Roth. **CAST:** Randy Quaid, Kathryn Harrold, Larry Riley, Corinne Bohrer, Jack Warden. **1988**

DEADLINE (1987) ★★★ Christopher Walken is good as a reporter covering the conflict in Beirut, finding himself becoming personally involved when he falls for a German nurse working for the rebels. This film is very much in the vein of *Salvador* and *Under Fire*, but cannot duplicate their tension. Rated R. 100m. **DIR:** Nathaniel Gutman. **CAST:** Christopher Walken, Hywel Bennett. **1987**

DEADLINE USA ★★★★ In this hard-hitting newspaper drama, Humphrey Bogart plays an editor who has to fight the city's underworld while keeping the publisher (superbly portrayed by Ethel Barrymore) from giving in to pressure and closing the paper down. While Kim Hunter is wasted in the small role as Bogart's ex-wife, the picture has much to recommend it. B&W; 87m. **DIR:**

Richard Brooks. **CAST:** Humphrey Bogart, Kim Hunter, Ethel Barrymore. **1952**

DEADLY ENCOUNTER (1975) 🦃 A rich woman schemer. Rated R for sexual talk. 90m. **DIR:** R. John Hugh. **CAST:** Dina Merrill, Carl Betz, Leon Ames. **1975**

DEADLY WEAPONS 🦃 Joe Bob Briggs introduces another of the worst (or best) of Doris Wishman's Sixties sleazoids, featuring the imposing Chesty Morgan (73 inches) and porno legend Harry Reems in a soggy excuse for a crime-drama. Rated R. 90m. **DIR:** Doris Wishman. **CAST:** Chesty Morgan, Harry Reems, Greg Reynolds. **1972**

DEALERS 🦃 Boring British rip-off of *Wall Street.* Rated R for violence and profanity. 92m. **DIR:** Colin Bucksey. **CAST:** Rebecca De-Mornay, Paul McGann, Derrick O'Connor. **1989**

DEATH DRUG ★★ A truthful yet cliché-filled movie about a promising young musician who starts using angel dust. Although the drug PCP deserves any bad rap it gets, this movie is a mediocre effort. Not rated, but fairly inoffensive. 73m. **DIR:** Oscar Williams. **CAST:** Philip Michael Thomas, Vernee Watson, Rosalind Cash. **1986**

DEATH IN VENICE ★★ Slow, studied film based on Thomas Mann's classic novel about an artist's quest for beauty and perfection. The good cast seems to move through this movie without communicating with one another or the audience. Visually absorbing, but lifeless. Adult language, adult situations throughout. Rated PG. 130m. **DIR:** Luchino Visconti. **CAST:** Dirk Bogarde, Marisa Berenson, Mark Burns, Silvana Mangano. **1971**

DEATH OF A CENTERFOLD ★★ This made-for-TV film chronicles the brutal murder of Playboy playmate Dorothy Stratten. Bob Fosse's *Star 80* does a much better job. Unrated. 100m. **DIR:** Gabrielle Beaumont. **CAST:** Jamie Lee Curtis, Robert Reed, Bruce Weitz. **1981**

DEATH OF A PROPHET ★★½ Docudrama combines live footage of Sixties civil rights movement among black Americans as well as interviews with people who were close to Malcolm X. Morgan Freeman reenacts Malcolm X during the twenty-four hours prior to his assassination. Freeman portrays Malcolm X as a patient, religious man who believed there was an African connection with the quality of life black Americans could enjoy. Unrated, contains violence. 60m. **DIR:** Woodie King Jr. **CAST:** Morgan Freeman, Yolanda King, Mansoor Najee-ullah, Sam Singleton. **1991**

DEATH OF A SALESMAN ★★★★ Impressive TV version of the Arthur Miller play. Dustin Hoffman is excellent as the aging, embittered Willy Loman, who realizes he has wasted his life and the lives of his family. Kate Reid is his long-suffering wife and Charles Durning is the neighbor. Thoughtful and well produced. 135m. **DIR:** Volker Schlondörff. **CAST:** Dustin Hoffman, Kate Reid, John Malkovich, Stephen Lang, Charles Durning. **1985**

DEATH OF A SCOUNDREL ★★★ If anyone could portray a suave, debonair, conniving, ruthlessly charming, amoral, despicable, notorious, manipulating cad, it was George Sanders. He does so to a *tee* in this portrait of the ultimate rake—based on the life of financier Serge Rubenstein. 119m. **DIR:** Charles Martin. **CAST:** George Sanders, Zsa Zsa Gabor, Tom Conway, Yvonne De Carlo, Nancy Gates, Coleen Gray, Victor Jory, John Hoyt. **1956**

DEATH OF A SOLDIER ★★½ Based on a true story. In 1942 an American GI stationed in Australia murdered three Melbourne women. The incident aggravated U.S.–Australian relations, and General MacArthur ordered the execution of the serviceman to firm up Allied unity. James Coburn plays a major who believes the GI isn't sane enough to stand trial. Rated R for profanity, violence, and nudity. 93m. **DIR:** Philippe Mora. **CAST:** James Coburn, Bill Hunter, Reb Brown, Maurie Fields. **1985**

DEATH OF ADOLF HITLER, THE ★★★ Made-for-British-television dramatization of the last ten days of the dictator's life, all spent in the underground bunker where he received the news of Germany's defeat. Frank Finlay is excellent as Hitler, avoiding the usual stereotypes. The low-key nature of the production renders it eerie, but strangely unmoving. Not rated. 107m. **DIR:** Rex Firkin. **CAST:** Frank Finlay, Caroline Mortimer, Ray McAnally. **1972**

DECEMBER ★★★ Intelligent, thoughtful drama unfolds on the day after Pearl Harbor has been bombed by the Japanese. Five New England prep school friends gather to discuss the implications of the event, and how it will affect them. Compelling. Rated PG. 92m. **DIR:** Gabe Torres. **CAST:** Wil Wheaton, Brian Krause, Balthazar Getty, Chris Young. **1991**

DECEPTION (1946) ★★★½ A better-than-average Bette Davis melodrama, with Claude Rains as a domineering orchestra conductor who imposes his will on musician Davis. The leads make this detergent drama work with their intensity and apparent desire to one-up each other in front of the camera. 110m. **DIR:** Irving Rapper. **CAST:** Bette Davis, Paul Henreid, Claude Rains. **1946**

DECORATION DAY ★★★★★ This superior adaptation of John William Corrington's novel finds retired judge James Garner investigating a mystery when an old friend (Bill Cobbs) refuses to accept a long overdue Medal of Honor. Originally produced as a television *Hallmark Hall of Fame* special, this stirring character study benefits from superb performances—particularly by Garner—and first-rate production values. 91m. **DIR:** Robert Markowitz. **CAST:** James Garner, Bill Cobbs, Judith Ivey, Ruby Dee, Larry Fishburne. **1991**

DEDICATED MAN, A ★★ Haunting British romance about a workaholic who asks a lonely spinster to pose as his wife. All goes well until she starts asking questions about his past. The *Romance Theatre* presentation will disappoint viewers hoping for high passions. 50m. **DIR:** Robert Knights. **CAST:** Alec McCowen, Joan Plowright, Christopher Irving. **1982**

DEER HUNTER, THE ★★★★★ Five friends—Michael (Robert De Niro), Stan (John Cazale), Nick (Christopher Walken), Steven (John Savage), and Axel (Chuck Aspergen)—work at the dangerous blast furnace in a steel mill of the dingy Mid-Atlantic town of Clairton, Pennsylvania, in 1968. At quitting time, they make their way to their favorite local bar to drink away the pressures of the day. For Michael, Nick, and Steven it is the last participation in the ritual. In a few days, they leave for Vietnam, where they find horror and death. What follows is a gripping study of heroism and the meaning of friendship. Rated R for profanity and violence. 183m. **DIR:** Michael Cimino. **CAST:** Robert De Niro, John Cazale, John Savage, Meryl Streep, Christopher Walken. **1978**

DEFIANT ONES, THE ★★★★ Director Stanley Kramer scored one of his few artistic successes with this compelling story about two escaped convicts (Tony Curtis and Sidney Poitier) shackled together—and coping with mutual hatred—as they run from the authorities in the South. B&W; 97m. **DIR:** Stanley Kramer. **CAST:** Tony Curtis, Sidney Poitier, Theodore Bikel, Charles McGraw, Lon Chaney Jr. **1958**

DEJA VU 🦃 Stupid story about reincarnation. Rated R. 91m. **DIR:** Anthony Richmond. **CAST:** Jaclyn Smith, Shelley Winters, Claire Bloom, Nigel Terry. **1984**

DELIBERATE STRANGER, THE ★★★ Mark Harmon is impressive in his first major role as serial killer Ted Bundy in this better-than-average TV movie. The script for all the time it spends depicting Bundy's crimes doesn't provide enough insight into what made Bundy tick. 192m. **DIR:** Marvin J. Chomsky. **CAST:** Mark Harmon, Frederic Forrest, George Grizzard, Ben Masters, Glynnis O'Connor, M. Emmet Walsh, John Ashton. **1986**

DELINQUENT DAUGHTERS ★½ A reporter and a cop decide to find out just what's going on with today's kids after a high school girl commits suicide. Slow-moving cheapie that is merely a hyped-up dud. B&W; 71m. **DIR:** Albert Herman. **CAST:** June Carlson, Fifi D'Orsay, Teala Loring. **1944**

DELUSION (1991) ★★★ A computer whiz, having just embezzled $480 thousand, heads for Reno, picks up a Las Vegas show girl and her boyfriend (who is a hit man for the mob). Very odd little movie, but some will find this a real gem. Rated R for profanity, nudity, and violence. 99m. **DIR:** Carl Colpaert. **CAST:** Jim Metzler, Jennifer Rubin, Kyle Secor, Robert Costanzo, Jerry Orbach, Tracey Walter. **1991**

DEMETRIUS AND THE GLADIATORS 🦃 Film centers on the search for the robe that Christ wore before he was crucified. Overblown. 101m. **DIR:** Delmer Daves. **CAST:** Victor Mature, Susan Hayward, Debra Paget, Michael Rennie, Anne Bancroft, Ernest Borgnine, Richard Egan, Jay Robinson. **1954**

DEMPSEY ★★★ Treat Williams plays Jack Dempsey, World Heavyweight Champion boxer from 1919 to 1926. Stylish and with riveting plot twists. As Dempsey's first wife, Sally Kellerman is particularly effective. Not rated, contains violence and profanity. 110m. **DIR:** Gus Trikonis. **CAST:** Treat Williams, Sam Waterston, Sally Kellerman, Victoria Tennant, Peter Mark Richman, Jesse Vint. **1983**

DENIAL ★★★ Erotic tale of free-spirited young woman Robin Wright whose chance encounter with hunky artist Jason Patric turns her life upside down. Wright leaves to regain her identity, only to be consumed by Patric's memory. Rated R for nudity. 103m. **DIR:** Erin Dignam. **CAST:** Jason Patric, Robin Wright, Barry Primus, Rae Dawn Chong. **1991**

DESCENDING ANGEL ★★★★ First-rate made-for-cable thriller about a resourceful fellow (Eric Roberts) who begins to suspect his fiancée's Romanian father (George C. Scott) might have allied himself with Hitler's Nazis during World War II. The theme may be a bit shopworn, but the execution is superb. Unrated, but with violence, profanity, and brief nudity. 98m. **DIR:** Jeremy Paul Kagan. **CAST:** George C. Scott, Eric Roberts, Diane Lane, Jan Rubes. **1990**

DESERT BLOOM ★★★ This poignant study of awakening adolescence and family turmoil is effectively set against a backdrop of 1950 Las Vegas, as the atomic age dawns. The story unfolds slowly but sensitively. Thirteen-year-old Annabeth Gish gives a remarkably complex performance as a brilliant girl who must cope with an abusive stepfather, an ineffectual mother, and a sexpot aunt. Rated PG. 106m. **DIR:** Eugene Corr. **CAST:** Jon Voight, JoBeth Williams, Ellen Barkin, Allen Garfield, Annabeth Gish. **1986**

DESERT HEARTS ★★★½ A sensitive portrayal of the evolving relationship between a young, openly lesbian woman and a quiet university professor ten years her senior in 1959. Patricia Charbonneau and Helen Shaver superbly set off the development of their individual and joint characters. Some may find the explicit love scenes upsetting, but the humor and characterization entirely overrule any objection, and the bonus of 1950s props and sets is a treat. Rated R for profanity and sex. 90m. **DIR:** Donna Deitch. **CAST:** Helen Shaver, Patricia Charbonneau, Audra Lindley, Gwen Welles, Dean Butler. **1986**

DESERT RATS, THE ★★★★ Very good World War II drama focuses on the British North African campaign against the German forces, led by Field Marshal Rommel. Richard Burton heads a small, outnumbered unit charged with holding a strategic hill while facing the enemy onslaught. Tough, realistic. B&W; 88m. **DIR:** Robert Wise. **CAST:** Richard Burton, Robert Newton, James Mason, Chips Rafferty. **1953**

DESIRE ★★ Dull story about a common Scottish fisherman and a globe-trotting feminist. They fell in love when they were young, and whenever they meet again, their love is always rekindled. Not rated, but contains profanity and simulated sex. 108m. **DIR:** Andrew Birkin. **CAST:** Greta Scacchi, Vincent D'Onofrio, Anais Jeanneret, Hanns Zischler, Barbara Jones. **1993**

DESIRE UNDER THE ELMS ★★ A hard-hearted New England farmer (Burl Ives) brings home an immigrant bride (Sophia Loren), who promptly falls into the arms of his weakling son (Anthony Perkins). Eugene O'Neill's play was already ponderously dated by the time it was filmed, and Loren (whose command of English was still shaky) is miscast. B&W; 114m. **DIR:** Delbert Mann. **CAST:** Burl Ives, Sophia Loren, Anthony Perkins, Frank Overton, Pernell Roberts, Anne Seymour. **1958**

DESIRÉE ★★ A romantic tale of Napoleon's love for 17-year-old seamstress Desirée Clary. Marlon Brando bumbles about as Napoleon in this tepid travesty of history. 110m. **DIR:** Henry Koster. **CAST:** Marlon Brando, Jean Simmons, Merle Oberon, Michael Rennie, Cameron Mitchell, Isobel Elsom, John Hoyt, Cathleen Nesbitt. **1954**

DESPERATE JOURNEY ★★½ Average WWII propaganda film follows the exploits of an RAF bomber crew that is shot down while on a special mission over Poland. They escape and begin a treacherous and sometimes humorous journey across Germany, trying to return to England. B&W; 106m. **DIR:** Raoul Walsh. **CAST:** Errol Flynn, Ronald Reagan, Alan Hale Sr., Arthur Kennedy, Raymond Massey. **1942**

DETECTIVE, THE (1968) ★★★ A disgusted NYPD detective (Frank Sinatra), railroads the wrong man into the electric chair while seeking a homosexual's killer. He loses his job and leaves his nympho wife (Lee Remick). Filmed on location in New York, this is one of the first hard-look-at-a-cop's life films. 114m. **DIR:** Gordon Douglas. **CAST:** Frank Sinatra, Lee Remick, Al Freeman Jr., Jacqueline Bisset, Ralph Meeker, Jack Klugman, Robert Duvall, William Windom. **1968**

DEVIL AND DANIEL WEBSTER, THE ★★★★ This wickedly witty tale, based on a Stephen Vincent Benét story, delivers some potent messages. Edward Arnold, so often cast as a despicable villain, is riveting as the noble Webster. This eloquent hero must defend ingenuous James Craig in a bizarre courtroom. Both of their immortal souls are at stake. Opposing Webster is Mr. Scratch, also known as the Devil. Walter Huston gives a dazzling performance in the role. B&W; 85m. **DIR:** William Dieterle. **CAST:** Edward Arnold, Walter Huston, James Craig, Anne Shirley, Jane Darwell, Simone Simon, Gene Lockhart. **1941**

DEVIL AT 4 O'CLOCK, THE ★★★ This script may be weak and predictable, but the acting of Spencer Tracy and Frank Sinatra make this a watchable motion picture. Tracy is a priest who is in charge of an orphanage. When their island home is endangered by an impending volcanic eruption, he seeks the aid of a group of convicts headed by Sinatra. 126m. **DIR:** Mervyn LeRoy. **CAST:** Spencer Tracy, Frank Sinatra, Kerwin Mathews, Jean-Pierre Aumont. **1961**

DEVILS, THE ★★★★ Next to *Women in Love*, this is director Ken Russell's best film. Exploring witchcraft and politics in France during the seventeenth century, it's a mad mixture of drama, horror, camp, and comedy. Ugly for the most part (with several truly unsettling scenes), it is still fascinating. Rated R. 109m. **DIR:** Ken Russell. **CAST:** Oliver Reed, Vanessa Redgrave, Dudley Sutton, Max Adrian, Gemma Jones. **1971**

DEVIL'S PARTY, THE 🦃 Insipid melodrama. B&W; 65m. **DIR:** Ray McCarey. **CAST:** Victor McLaglen, Paul Kelly, William Gargan. **1938**

DEVOTION ★★½ Watchable but far-fetched tale about a rich young woman who poses as a dowdy nanny in order to get close to the man of her dreams. All goes well until his wife comes between them. B&W; 81m. **DIR:** Robert Milton. **CAST:** Ann Harding, Leslie Howard, O. P. Heggie. **1931**

DIAMOND HEAD ★★ Domineering Hawaiian plantation boss Charlton Heston comes close to ruining his family with his dictatorial ways. The lush scenery is the only credible thing in this pineapple opera. 107m. **DIR:** Guy Green. **CAST:** Charlton Heston, Yvette Mimieux, George Chakiris, France Nuyen, James Darren. **1963**

DIANE ★★ Lana Turner's swan song at MGM, the studio that developed her star power, and Roger Moore's Hollywood debut. She played the mistress of a sixteenth-century French king, and he played the king. Lots of court intrigue, pageantry, and aimless talk. 110m. **DIR:** David Miller. **CAST:** Lana Turner, Roger Moore, Marisa Pavan, Henry Daniell, Taina Elg, Cedric Hardwicke, Torin Thatcher, Ian Wolfe, Gene Reynolds. **1956**

DIARY OF A MAD HOUSEWIFE ★★★ Most women will detest Jonathan (Richard Benjamin), the self-centered, social climber husband of Tina (Carrie Snodgress). He has had an affair and also lost all their savings in a bad investment. Tina, a college graduate, has been unhappily stuck at home for years with their two children. She finally finds happiness in an affair with George (Frank Langella). Profanity, sex, and nudity are included in this film. 94m. **DIR:** Frank Perry. **CAST:** Richard Benjamin, Carrie Snodgress, Frank Langella. **1970**

DIARY OF A TEENAGE HITCHHIKER ★★ Trite dialogue and an inappropriate score lessen the impact of this made-for-TV drama documenting the dangers of hitchhiking for young women. Inferior. 96m. **DIR:** Ted Post. **CAST:** Charlene Tilton, Dick Van Patten, Katherine Helmond, James Carroll Jordan, Katy Kurtzman, Dominique Dunne, Craig T. Nelson. **1979**

DIARY OF ANNE FRANK, THE ★★★★½ Excellent adaptation of the Broadway play dealing with the terror Jews felt during the Nazi raids of World War II. Two families are forced to hide in a Jewish sympathizer's attic to avoid capture by the Nazis. Anne (Millie Perkins) is the teenage girl who doesn't stop dreaming of a better future. Shelley Winters won an Oscar for her role as the hysterical Mrs. Van Daan, who shares sparse food and space with the Frank family. B&W; 170m. **DIR:** George Stevens. **CAST:** Millie Perkins, Joseph Schildkraut, Shelley Winters. **1959**

DIARY OF FORBIDDEN DREAMS ★★½ A bizarre variation on the classic fantasy *Alice In Wonderland*, this concerns a beautiful young woman (Sydne Rome) who becomes lost in a remote area of the Italian Riviera. The film suffers from too many diversions that create a complete mess. Rated R for nudity and language. 94m. **DIR:** Roman Polanski. **CAST:** Hugh Griffith, Marcello Mastroianni, Sydne Rome. **1981**

DIFFERENT STORY, A ★★★½ Perry King and Meg Foster play homosexuals who realize their romances are just not clicking. They fall in love with each other, marry, grow rich, and, eventually, dissatisfied. King and Foster are genuinely funny and appealing. Rated PG. 107m. **DIR:** Paul Aaron. **CAST:** Perry King, Meg Foster, Valerie Curtin, Peter Donat. **1979**

DIM SUM: A LITTLE BIT OF HEART ★★★★ *Dim Sum* is an independently made American movie about the tension and affection between a Chinese mother and daughter living in San Francisco's Chinatown. The film moves quietly, but contains many moments of humor. The restraint of the mother, who wants her daughter to marry, and the frustration of the daughter, who wants to live her life as she chooses, are beautifully conveyed by real-life mother and daughter Laureen and Kim Chew. Victor Wong, as a rambunctious uncle, is a gas. Rated PG. 88m. **DIR:** Wayne Wang. **CAST:** Laureen Chew, Kim Chew, Victor Wong. **1985**

DINGAKA ★★★½ Cultures collide in this South African film as Masai warrior Ken Gampu tracks his daughter's killer to a metropolis and comes face-to-face with civilized justice. Spectacularly filmed by writer-producer Jamie Uys, this impressive movie features knockout performances by African film star Gampu as the accused and Stanley Baker as his attorney. 98m. **DIR:** Jamie Uys. **CAST:** Stanley Baker, Juliet Prowse, Ken Gampu, Bob Courtney. **1965**

DINO ★★ Sal Mineo plays a troubled teen. Brian Keith is the savvy psychologist who helps him understand his emotions in this utterly predictable film. The street jargon is strained. B&W; 96m. **DIR:** Thomas Carr. **CAST:** Sal Mineo, Brian Keith, Susan Kohner, Frank Lovejoy, Joe De Santis. **1957**

DISCOVERY PROGRAM ★★★★ Marvelous collection of four short stories including the 1987 Oscar winner for best short film, "Ray's Male Heterosexual Dance Hall," which spoofs networking executives. "The Open Window" is also a comedy featuring a would-be actor who goes off the deep end when he can't get a good night's sleep. Unrated, contains profanity, violence, and nudity. 106m. **DIR:** Bryan Gordon, Damian Harris, Rupert Wainwright, Steve Anderson. **CAST:** Eric Stoltz, James Spader. **1987**

DISHONORED ★★★½ Sin and sex are the real stars of this Marlene Dietrich movie. She plays a World War I Austrian spy who tangles with an overly amorous Russian agent. Dietrich's second Hollywood vehicle was the first to make good use of her mystique. B&W; 91m. **DIR:** Josef von Sternberg. **CAST:** Marlene Dietrich, Victor McLaglen, Lew Cody, Gustav von Seyffertitz, Warner Oland. **1931**

DISPLACED PERSON, THE ★★★★ Man's cruel, ugly side is exposed in this adaptation of Flannery O'Connor's brutal short story. Irene Worth is a struggling Georgia farm widow who allows a Polish World War II refugee and his family to live and work on her land. The woman's initially sympathetic feelings gradually mirror those of her other worthless laborers, who fear that their lives of relative laziness are jeopardized by this "unwanted foreigner." Introduced by Henry Fonda; unrated and suitable for family viewing. 58m. **DIR:** Glenn Jordan. **CAST:** Irene Worth, John Houseman, Shirley Stoler, Lane Smith, Robert Earl Jones. **1976**

DISRAELI ★★★½ Worth seeing solely for George Arliss's Oscar-winning performance, *Disraeli* shows how pretentious movies became when the talkies arrived. He plays the wily English prime minister who outwits the Russians in a fight over the Suez Canal. B&W; 89m. **DIR:** Alfred E. Green. **CAST:** George Arliss, Florence Arliss, Joan Bennett, Anthony Bushell. **1929**

DISTANT THUNDER (1988) ★★½ After roaming the wilds of the Pacific Northwest with his Vietnam-vet buddies for several years, ex-soldier John Lithgow decides to return to civilization and find the son (Ralph Macchio) he hasn't seen in over a decade. Lithgow struggles valiantly with the downbeat material, but Macchio is miscast and no help at all. Rated R for violence and profanity. 114m. **DIR:** Rick Rosenthal. **CAST:** John Lithgow, Ralph Macchio. **1988**

DISTANT VOICES/STILL LIVES ★★★★★ An impressionistic memory film, based on the director's family memories and history. Set in England in the late 1940s, it explores the relationships and emotions of a middle-class family as they undergo domestic brutality, failed marriages, and the pains of life. The film's rich humanity and its unique use of a robust musical score overcome its cynicism. Offbeat and original. 85m. **DIR:** Terence Davies. **CAST:** Freda Dowie, Pete Postlethwaite, Angela Walsh, Dean Williams. **1988**

DIVE BOMBER ★★★ The planes and acting styles date this one pretty badly, but the story line, about a military doctor working on ways to prevent blackouts while flying, is still intriguing. 133m. **DIR:** Michael Curtiz. **CAST:** Errol Flynn, Fred MacMurray, Ralph Bellamy, Alexis Smith, Craig Stevens, Robert Armstrong, Regis Toomey. **1941**

DIVING IN ★★ A feel-good movie about a teenager's ambition to make his high school diving team and overcome a fear of heights. Predictable. Rated PG-13. 92m. **DIR:** Strathford Hamilton. **CAST:** Burt Young, Matt Lattanzi, Matt Adler, Kristy Swanson. **1990**

DIVORCE HIS: DIVORCE HERS ★★½ This less-than-exceptional TV movie follows the breakup of a marriage in which both partners explain what they think led to the failure of their marriage. The talents of Elizabeth Taylor and Richard Burton are barely tapped. 144m. **DIR:** Waris Hussein. **CAST:** Richard Burton, Elizabeth Taylor, Carrie Nye, Barry Foster, Gabriele Ferzetti. **1972**

DIVORCEE, THE ★★ Dated melodrama about a woman with loose morals. Silly by today's standards, this was racy when made and earned Norma Shearer a best-actress Oscar. A curiosity piece with a good cast. B&W; 83m. **DIR:** Robert Z. Leonard. **CAST:** Norma Shearer, Robert Montgomery, Chester Morris, Conrad Nagel, Florence Eldridge. **1930**

DO THE RIGHT THING ★★★★½ Writer-director-star Spike Lee's controversial study of the deep-rooted racism in America starts off as a hilarious multicharacter comedy and evolves into a disturbing, thought-provoking, and timely drama. The events take place during the hottest day of the year in a one-block area of the Brooklyn neighborhood of Bedford-Stuyvesant, where tensions exist among the blacks, Italians, and Koreans who live and work there. Rated R for violence, profanity, and nudity. 120m. **DIR:** Spike Lee. **CAST:** Danny Aiello, Ossie Davis, Ruby Dee, Richard Edson, Giancarlo Esposito, Spike Lee, Bill Nunn, John Savage, John Turturro. **1989**

DOCKS OF NEW YORK, THE ★★★★ A solid drama of love and death on a big-city waterfront. Rough-edged George Bancroft rescues would-be suicide Betty Compson, marries her, clears her of a murder charge, and goes to jail for her. The direction is masterful, the camera work and lighting superb in this, one of the last silent films to be released. B&W; 60m. **DIR:** Josef von Sternberg. **CAST:** George Bancroft, Betty Compson, Olga Baclanova, Mitchell Lewis. **1928**

DOCTOR, THE ★★★★ A doctor discovers the sore throat that's been bothering him is actually cancer, and, in becoming a patient, experiences the dehumanizing effects of the medical establishment. An effective drama with a superlative star performance by William Hurt. Rated PG-13 for profanity and scenes of surgery. 128m. **DIR:** Randa Haines. **CAST:** William Hurt, Christine Lahti, Elizabeth Perkins, Mandy Patinkin, Adam Arkin, Charlie Korsmo, Wendy Crewson, Bill Macy. **1991**

DR. BETHUNE ★★★★ Big-budget story of the Canadian doctor who is revered in China for the many lives he saved when that country fought Japan. Donald Sutherland played the same character in the TV-movie *Bethune* (also on video), and he emphasizes the man's larger-than-life qualities, both positive and negative, in this unusually absorbing biography. Not rated; contains adult themes. 115m. **DIR:** Phillip Borsos. **CAST:** Donald Sutherland, Helen Mirren, Helen Shaver, Colm Feore, Anouk Aimée. **1990**

DR. CHRISTIAN MEETS THE WOMEN 🦃 Kindly old Dr. Christian takes on a diet charlatan in this stanza of the film series. B&W; 60m. **DIR:** William McGann. **CAST:** Jean Hersholt, Dorothy Lovett, Edgar Kennedy, Frank Albertson, Veda Ann Borg, Rod La Rocque. **1940**

DR. FAUSTUS ★★ Richard Burton is the man who sells his soul and Elizabeth Taylor is Helen of Troy in this weird adaptation of Christopher Marlowe's retelling of the ancient legend. Strictly for Taylor and Burton fans. 93m. **DIR:** Richard Burton. **CAST:** Richard Burton, Elizabeth Taylor. **1968**

DOCTOR QUINN MEDICINE WOMAN ★★★ This pilot film for Jane Seymour's

TV series is surprisingly riveting. Seymour convincingly plays a Boston doctor who goes west to start her practice. Scorned by the rugged pioneers she encounters, she must seek ways to prove her talents to them. Unrated; contains violence. 94m. **DIR:** Jeremy Paul Kagan. **CAST:** Jane Seymour, Joe Lando, Diane Ladd, Guy Boyd, Colm Meaney. **1992**

DR. ZHIVAGO ★★★★ An epic treatment was given to Boris Pasternak's novel of romance and revolution in this film. Omar Sharif is Zhivago, a Russian doctor and poet whose personal life is ripped apart by the upheaval of the Russian Revolution. The screenplay is choppy and overlong and is often sacrificed to the spectacle of vast panoramas, detailed sets, and impressive costumes. These artistic elements, along with a beautiful musical score, make for cinema on a grand scale, and it remains a most watchable movie. 176m. **DIR:** David Lean. **CAST:** Omar Sharif, Julie Christie, Geraldine Chaplin, Rod Steiger, Alec Guinness, Tom Courtenay. **1965**

DOCTORS' WIVES 🦃 Trashy film that focuses on the seedy side of being a doctor's wife. Rated PG. 100m. **DIR:** George Schaefer. **CAST:** Gene Hackman, Richard Crenna, Carroll O'Connor, Janice Rule, Dyan Cannon, Cara Williams. **1971**

DODSWORTH ★★★★ Walter Huston, in the title role, heads an all-star cast in this outstanding adaptation of the Sinclair Lewis novel. Auto tycoon Samuel Dodsworth is the epitome of the classic American self-made man. His wife is an appearance-conscious nouveau riche snob. An intelligent, mature script, excellent characterizations, and sensitive cinematography make this film a modern classic. B&W; 101m. **DIR:** William Wyler. **CAST:** Walter Huston, Ruth Chatterton, Mary Astor, David Niven, Spring Byington, Paul Lukas, John Payne, Maria Ouspenskaya. **1936**

DOGFIGHT ★★½ River Phoenix is one of a group of Marines who stage an "ugly date" contest on the eve of their departure to Vietnam. Even though the premise is incredibly mean-spirited, this is actually a fairly entertaining flick. Rated R for profanity and brief violence. 95m. **DIR:** Nancy Savoca. **CAST:** River Phoenix, Lili Taylor, Richard Panebianco, Anthony Clark, Mitchell Whitfield, Holly Near. **1991**

DOLLMAKER, THE ★★★★ Jane Fonda won an Emmy for her intensely quiet portrayal of a mother of five in 1940s Kentucky. As a devoted mother, her only personal happiness is sculpting dolls out of wood. When her husband is forced to take work in Detroit, their relocation causes many personal hardships and setbacks. The story is beautifully told. This made-for-TV movie is unrated, but it provides excellent family entertainment. 140m. **DIR:** Daniel Petrie. **CAST:** Jane Fonda, Levon Helm, Amanda Plummer, Susan Kingsley, Ann Hearn, Geraldine Page. **1984**

DOLL'S HOUSE, A (1973) ★★★ Jane Fonda is quite good in this screen version of Henrik Ibsen's play about a liberated woman in the nineteenth century, and her struggles to maintain her freedom. Pacing is a problem at times, but first-class acting and beautiful sets keep the viewer interested. 103m. **DIR:** Joseph Losey. **CAST:** Jane Fonda, David Warner, Trevor Howard. **1973**

DOLL'S HOUSE, A (1989) ★★★★ A spoiled housewife (Claire Bloom), confident that her husband adores her, is in for a rude awakening when a past transgression resurfaces and threatens her carefree existence. Fine rendition of Ibsen's masterpiece. Rated G. 96m. **DIR:** Patrick Garland. **CAST:** Claire Bloom, Anthony Hopkins, Ralph Richardson, Denholm Elliott. **1989**

DOMINICK AND EUGENE ★★★★½ Fraternal twin brothers Dominick and Eugene Luciano have big plans for the future. Eugene (Ray Liotta), an ambitious medical student, plans to take care of Dominick (Tom Hulce), who is considered "slow" but nonetheless has been supporting them by working as a trash collector. All "Nicky" wants is to live in a house by a lake where he and his brother can be together. This is a deeply touching film; superbly directed and acted. Rated PG-13 103m. **DIR:** Robert M. Young. **CAST:** Tom Hulce, Ray Liotta, Jamie Lee Curtis, Robert Levine. **1988**

DOMINO ★★ Artsy Italian film delves into the surreal as it follows Brigitte Nielsen in her quest for love. She's been looking in all the wrong places and now thinks she's found it in the voice of an obscene caller. Rated R for nudity and countless sexual situations. 96m. **DIR:** Ivana Massetti. **CAST:** Brigitte Nielsen. **1989**

DON JUAN ★★★ The now-legendary Great Profile John Barrymore is at the top of his hand-kissing, cavalier womanizing form in this entertaining romantic adventure. The first silent released with canned music and sound effects. Silent. B&W; 111m. **DIR:** Alan Crosland. **CAST:** John Barrymore, Mary Astor, Estelle Taylor, Myrna Loy. **1926**

DON'T CRY, IT'S ONLY THUNDER ★★★★ Here is one of those "little" movies that slipped by without much notice yet is so satisfying when discovered by adventurous video renters. A black market wheeler-dealer (Dennis Christopher), lining his pockets behind the lines during the Vietnam War is forced to aid some Asian nuns and their ever-increasing group of Saigon street orphans. The results are predictably heartwarming and occasionally heartbreaking, but the film never drifts off into sentimental melodrama. Rated PG. 108m. **DIR:**

Peter Werner. **CAST:** Dennis Christopher, Susan Saint James. **1982**

DON'T MESS WITH MY SISTER 🦃 A young man trapped in a forced marriage. Unrated; contains profanity, violence, and sexual situations. 85m. **DIR:** Meir Zarchi. **CAST:** Joe Perce, Jeannine Lemay. **1985**

DOUBLE EDGE ★★ Faye Dunaway plays an aggressive New York reporter on assignment in Jerusalem. She realizes that there are no clear-cut answers. Dunaway is believable as she struggles with both her toughness and vulnerability. Unrated; contains sex and violence. 96m. **DIR:** Amos Kollek. **CAST:** Faye Dunaway, Amos Kollek, Shmuel Shiloh, Muhamad Bakri. **1992**

DOUBLE EXPOSURE (1989) ★★★ This biographical film about Depression-era photographer Margaret Bourke-White has a familiar plot: strong woman fights for equality in a man's profession. Exceptional performances save this telefilm from mediocrity. 94m. **DIR:** Lawrence Schiller. **CAST:** Farrah Fawcett, Frederic Forrest, David Huddleston, Jay Patterson. **1989**

DOUBLE LIFE, A ★★★★ Ronald Colman gives an Oscar-winning performance as a famous actor whose stage life begins to take over his personality and private life, forcing him to revert to stage characters, including Othello, to cope with everyday situations. Brilliantly written by Garson Kanin and Ruth Gordon, and impressively acted by a standout cast. Top treatment of a fine story. B&W; 104m. **DIR:** George Cukor. **CAST:** Ronald Colman, Edmond O'Brien, Shelley Winters, Ray Collins. **1947**

DOUBLE REVENGE ★★½ Tough Guy Joe Dallesandro bungles a small-town robbery, resulting in the death of a local businessman's wife. You guessed it—everybody wants revenge. Rated R. 96m. **DIR:** Armand Mastroianni. **CAST:** Leigh McCloskey, Joe Dallesandro, Nancy Everhard, Theresa Saldana, Richard Rust. **1988**

DOUBLE STANDARD 🦃 A prolific circuit-court justice gets caught leading a double family life. Made for TV. 95m. **DIR:** Louis Rudolph. **CAST:** Robert Foxworth, Pamela Bellwood, Michele Greene. **1988**

DOUBLE THREAT ★★ An aging screen queen (Sally Kirkland) becomes concerned when her gigolo/costar gets interested in her young body double. Tricky behind-the-scenes thriller boasts a few unexpected twists. Available in R and unrated versions; both feature profanity, nudity, and sexual situations. 94m./96m. **DIR:** David A. Prior. **CAST:** Sally Kirkland, Andrew Stevens, Sherri Rose, Chick Vennera, Richard Lynch, Anthony Franciosa. **1992**

DOUBLECROSSED ★★★½ Dennis Hopper is a casting agent's dream come true as a drug smuggler-turned-DEA informant in this fascinating fact-based study. Hopper's beguiling con artist is impossible to dislike. Rated R for violence and relentlessly foul language. 111m. **DIR:** Roger Young. **CAST:** Dennis Hopper, Robert Carradine, Richard Jenkins, Adrienne Barbeau, G. W. Bailey. **1991**

DOWN TO THE SEA IN SHIPS ★★★ The plot involving a family of whalers has appeal, but vivid scenes filmed at sea aboard real New England whalers out of Bedford make it worthwhile. B&W; 83m. **DIR:** Elmer Clifton. **CAST:** William Walcott, Marguerite Courtot, Clara Bow. **1922**

DOWNHILL RACER ★★★½ Robert Redford struggles with an unappealing character, in this study of an Olympic skier. But Gene Hackman is excellent as the coach, and the exciting scenes of this snow sport hold the film together. Rated PG. 101m. **DIR:** Michael Ritchie. **CAST:** Robert Redford, Gene Hackman, Camilla Sparv. **1969**

DRAGON SEED ★★½ This study of a Chinese town torn asunder by Japanese occupation is taken from the novel by Nobel Prize winner Pearl S. Buck. It's occasionally gripping but in general too long. B&W; 145m. **DIR:** Jack Conway, Harold S. Bucquet. **CAST:** Katharine Hepburn, Walter Huston, Turhan Bey, Hurd Hatfield. **1944**

DREAM OF KINGS, A ★★★★ Anthony Quinn turns in an unforgettable performance in this powerful and touching drama set in Chicago's Greek community. He plays an earthy, proud father determined to raise enough money to flee from America to Greece with his ailing young son. A moving character study. Not rated. 111m. **DIR:** Daniel Mann. **CAST:** Anthony Quinn, Irene Papas, Inger Stevens, Sam Levene, Val Avery. **1969**

DREAM OF PASSION, A ★★★½ Melina Mercouri plays a Greek actress who is preparing to play Medea. As a publicity stunt, she goes to a prison to meet a real-life Medea. Ellen Burstyn is brilliant as the American prisoner who has killed her three children in order to take revenge on her husband. Rated R. 106m. **DIR:** Jules Dassin. **CAST:** Melina Mercouri, Ellen Burstyn, Andreas Voutsinas, Despo Diamantidou. **1978**

DREAM STREET ★★ Good struggles with evil in this sentimental morality tale of London's infamous Limehouse slum. Two brothers, in love with the same girl, vie for her attentions. Good eventually wins. Silent. B&W; 138m. **DIR:** D. W. Griffith. **CAST:** Carol Dempster, Charles Emmett Mack, Ralph Graves, Tyrone Power Sr., Morgan Wallace. **1921**

DREAM TO BELIEVE ★★★ If you like *Flashdance*, *Rocky*, and the *World Gymnastics Competition*, you'll love this Cinderella story. It's the soap drama of a teenage girl who, against physical odds, turns herself into an accomplished gymnast. No rating. 96m. **DIR:** Paul Lynch. **CAST:** Olivia D'Abo, Rita Tushingham, Keanu Reeves. **1985**

DREAMER ★★ Small-towner Tim Matheson pursues his dream: to become a champion bowler. As exciting as a film about bowling can be. (Which is to say, not very.) Rated PG. 86m. **DIR:** Noel Nosseck. **CAST:** Tim Matheson, Susan Blakely, Jack Warden. **1979**

DRESS GRAY ★★★★★ Extremely well-made TV miniseries about the closing of ranks at a military academy after an unpopular plebe is murdered. Alec Baldwin is the beleaguered cadet who refuses to be the scapegoat or let the investigation die. Compelling Gore Vidal script is enhanced by a stellar cast. Not rated, but contains mild profanity. 192m. **DIR:** Glenn Jordan. **CAST:** Alec Baldwin, Hal Holbrook, Eddie Albert, Lloyd Bridges, Susan Hess. **1986**

DRESSER, THE ★★★★★ Peter Yates directed this superb screen treatment of Ronald Harwood's play about an eccentric stage actor (Albert Finney) in wartime England and the loyal valet (Tom Courtenay) who cares for him, sharing his triumphs and tragedies. Rated PG for language. 118m. **DIR:** Peter Yates. **CAST:** Albert Finney, Tom Courtenay, Edward Fox, Zena Walker. **1983**

DRESSMAKER, THE ★★★½ In London during World War II, a teenage girl lives with two maiden aunts, one who tries to insulate her and one who encourages her to enjoy herself. Worth seeing for the performances of three superb actresses (including Jane Horrocks in her debut), though the ending is a bit perfunctory. Unrated, with sexual discussions that put this above the heads of young children. 90m. **DIR:** Jim O'Brien. **CAST:** Joan Plowright, Billie Whitelaw, Jane Horrocks, Tim Ransom. **1988**

DRIVER'S SEAT, THE ★★ Tedious Italian-made drama featuring Elizabeth Taylor in one of her less memorable performances as a psychotic woman with a death wish. Rated PG. 101m. **DIR:** Giuseppe Patroni Griffi. **CAST:** Elizabeth Taylor, Ian Bannen, Mona Washbourne, Andy Warhol. **1973**

DRIVING MISS DAISY ★★★★★ Alfred Uhry's stage play is brought to stunning, emotionally satisfying life by director Bruce Beresford and his superb cast. The story concerns the twenty-five-year relationship of the feisty Miss Daisy (Jessica Tandy) and a wise, wily chauffeur, Hoke (Morgan Freeman). Dan Aykroyd is remarkably effective as Daisy's doting son. Rated PG for profanity. 99m. **DIR:** Bruce Beresford. **CAST:** Morgan Freeman, Jessica Tandy, Dan Aykroyd, Patti LuPone, Esther Rolle. **1989**

DROWNING BY NUMBERS ★★ Director Peter Greenaway brings us another exercise in excess and esoteric glibness. Three women, all friends and all three with the same first name, extract revenge on their sadistic husbands by drowning them. Rated R for violence, profanity, and nudity. 121m. **DIR:** Peter Greenaway. **CAST:** Joan Plowright, Juliet Stevenson, Joely Richardson. **1988**

DRUGSTORE COWBOY ★★★★½ A gritty, often shocking examination of life on the edge, this superb character study features Matt Dillon in a terrific performance as the leader of a gang of drug users in the 1960s. Dillon and his cohorts keep their habits fed by robbing drugstores until their luck runs out. Rated R for profanity and violence. 100m. **DIR:** Gus Van Sant. **CAST:** Matt Dillon, Kelly Lynch, James Remar, William S. Burroughs. **1989**

DRUM 🦃 Sweaty, sexed-up continuation of *Mandingo*, Kyle Onstott's lurid tale of plantation life in the pre–Civil War South. 110m. **DIR:** Steve Carver. **CAST:** Ken Norton, Warren Oates, Pam Grier, John Colicos, Yaphet Kotto. **1976**

DRY WHITE SEASON, A ★★★★ Donald Sutherland stars as a white schoolteacher in South Africa who slowly becomes aware of what apartheid means to black people. Director Euzhan Palcy, who worked with screenwriter Collin Welland on adapting the novel by André Brink, sometimes allows things to become melodramatic, especially the film's main villain (Jurgen Prochnow). Overall, however, she tells a powerful, upsetting story in a riveting, unforgettable way. Rated R for violence and profanity. 106m. **DIR:** Euzhan Palcy. **CAST:** Donald Sutherland, Janet Suzman, Jurgen Prochnow, Zakes Mokae, Susan Sarandon, Marlon Brando. **1989**

DRYING UP THE STREETS 🦃 Canadian exposé of drugs and prostitution. Unrated. 90m. **DIR:** Robin Spry. **CAST:** Sarah Torgov, Don Francks, Len Cariou, Calvin Butler. **1984**

DUDES ★★ Billed as the first punk-rock Western, this film starts off well as a comedy about three New York City rockers (Jon Cryer, Daniel Roebuck and Flea) who decide to go to California in hopes of finding a better life. After the first goofy 20 minutes, *Dudes* abruptly turns violent. Rated R for violence and profanity. 90m. **DIR:** Penelope Spheeris. **CAST:** Jon Cryer, Catherine Mary Stewart, Daniel Roebuck, Flea, Lee Ving. **1988**

DUEL OF HEARTS ★★ Lush TV adaptation of Barbara Cartland's bestseller. A free-spirited woman falls for a handsome lord and takes a position as his mother's companion. Dim romantic adventure, but the cast rises to the occasion. 95m. **DIR:** John Hough. **CAST:** Alison Doody, Michael York, Geraldine Chaplin, Benedict Taylor, Richard Johnson. **1990**

DUET FOR ONE ★★★ As an English virtuoso violinist with multiple sclerosis, Julie Andrews gives an outstanding performance in this high-class tearjerker. Alan Bates is her sympathetic but philandering husband. Max von Sydow is the psychiatrist who atttempts to help her. And Rupert Everett plays her protégé who shuns the classical world for big-time show biz. Rated R. 110m. **DIR:** Andrei Konchalovsky. **CAST:** Julie Andrews, Alan Bates, Max von Sydow, Rupert Everett. **1987**

DUMB WAITER, THE ★★ This TV adaptation of Harold Pinter's absurdist drama will probably not appeal to general audiences. Two hit men (John Travolta and Tom Conti) await their latest assignment in a deserted restaurant's basement. 60m. **DIR:** Robert Altman. **CAST:** John Travolta, Tom Conti. **1987**

DUNERA BOYS, THE ★★★★ Bob Hoskins is sensational in this harrowing war drama about a group of Jewish refugees who are ironically suspected of being German informants by the British army. They are shipped to a prison camp in Australia on the HMT *Dunera*. A film of great intelligence and humanity. Rated R for violence and profanity. 150m. **DIR:** Greg Snedon. **CAST:** Joe Spano, Bob Hoskins, Warren Mitchell. **1987**

DUST ★★ A Bergmanesque tale of a lonely South African farmer's daughter and her descent into madness after she kills her abusive father. Jane Birkin does a commendable job as the bitter farm maid, but the film is very moody, with lots of mumbled lines and long still shots. Not rated, but contains violence and suggested sex. 87m. **DIR:** Marion Hansel. **CAST:** Jane Birkin, Trevor Howard. **1985**

DUTCH GIRLS 🦃 British field-hockey team grappling with rites of puberty. Rated R for suggested sex. 83m. **DIR:** Giles Foster. **CAST:** Bill Paterson, Colin Firth, Timothy Spall. **1985**

DYING YOUNG ★★½ A free-spirited, working-class woman finds herself falling in love with the scion of a wealthy San Francisco family after she's hired to help him recover from the side effects of chemotherapy treatments. Julia Roberts and Campbell Scott elevate this uninspired *Love Story* clone. Rated R for profanity. 110m. **DIR:** Joel Schumacher. **CAST:** Julia Roberts, Campbell Scott, Vincent D'Onofrio, Colleen Dewhurst, David Selby, Ellen Burstyn. **1991**

EARLY FROST, AN ★★★★½ This timely, extremely effective drama focuses on a family's attempt to come to grips with the fact that their son is not only gay but has AIDS as well. Gena Rowlands, one of Hollywood's most neglected actresses, and Aidan Quinn take the acting honors as mother and son. One of those rare television movies that works on all levels, it is highly recommended. 100m. **DIR:** John Erman. **CAST:** Gena Rowlands, Ben Gazzara, Aidan Quinn, Sylvia Sidney, John Glover. **1985**

EAST OF EDEN (1955) ★★★★★ The final portion of John Steinbeck's renowned novel of miscommunication and conflict between a father and son was transformed into a powerful, emotional movie. James Dean burst onto the screen as the rebellious son in his first starring role. Jo Van Fleet received an Oscar for her role as Kate, a bordello madam and Dean's long-forgotten mother. 115m. **DIR:** Elia Kazan. **CAST:** James Dean, Jo Van Fleet, Julie Harris, Raymond Massey, Burl Ives. **1955**

EAST OF EDEN (1982) ★★★½ This above-average television miniseries maintains the integrity of the source material by John Steinbeck without dipping too far into pathos. One major change: the focus shifts from the two sons who crave Papa's affection, to the deliciously evil woman—Jane Seymour—who twists them all around her little finger. Stick with the 1955 original. Unrated. 240m. **DIR:** Harvey Hart. **CAST:** Jane Seymour, Timothy Bottoms, Bruce Boxleitner, Warren Oates, Anne Baxter, Lloyd Bridges, Howard Duff. **1982**

EAST OF ELEPHANT ROCK ★★ This story of the 1948 British struggle to maintain a Far Eastern colony focuses on a new governor general's takeover after his predecessor is murdered by terrorists. The film is slow-paced and burdened with soap-opera overtones. Rated R. 93m. **DIR:** Don Boyd. **CAST:** John Hurt, Jeremy Kemp, Judi Bowker. **1981**

EAST SIDE, WEST SIDE ★★½ A middling adaptation of Marcia Davenport's best-seller, with Barbara Stanwyck married to James Mason who is fooling around with Ava Gardner, but Stanwyck hangs in there trying to win back his love. This is a rare chance to see Nancy Davis (Reagan) in action. B&W; 108m. **DIR:** Mervyn LeRoy. **CAST:** Barbara Stanwyck, James Mason, Van Heflin, Ava Gardner, Cyd Charisse, Nancy Davis, Gale Sondergaard. **1949**

EASY LIVING ★★★½ Shorn of the clichés one usually expects from movies about over-the-hill athletes, this picture offers a realistic account of an aging professional football player (Victor Mature) coming to terms with the end of a long career and a stormy home life. Lucille Ball and Lizabeth Scott are wonderful as the understanding secretary and shrewish wife, respectively. B&W; 77m. **DIR:** Jacques Tourneur. **CAST:** Victor Mature, Lucille Ball, Lizabeth Scott, Sonny Tufts. **1949**

EASY RIDER ★★★½ Time has not been kind to this 1969 release, about two drifters (Peter Fonda and Dennis Hopper) motorcycling their way across the country only to be confronted with violence and bigotry. Jack Nicholson's keystone performance, however, still makes it worth watching. Rated R.

94m. **DIR:** Dennis Hopper. **CAST:** Peter Fonda, Dennis Hopper, Jack Nicholson, Karen Black, Luana Anders. **1969**

EASY VIRTUE ★★ In this melodrama, based loosely on a Noel Coward play, the wife of an alcoholic falls in love with a younger man who commits suicide. Her past life prevents her from leading a normal life. Considering the directorial credit, this is close to dull. A British production. B&W; 73m. **DIR:** Alfred Hitchcock. **CAST:** Isabel Jeans, Franklyn Dyall, Ian Hunter. **1927**

EAT A BOWL OF TEA ★★★★ This little domestic charmer, set in New York's post-World War II Chinatown, concerns the trouble that brews between a young Chinese-American veteran (Russell Wong) and the girl (Cora Miao) he meets and marries during a brief visit to China. Scripter Judith Rascoe has faithfully adapted Louis Chu's novel. Rated PG-13 for sexual themes. 114m. **DIR:** Wayne Wang. **CAST:** Cora Miao, Russell Wong, Victor Wong, Lau Siu Ming. **1989**

EATING ★★★★ A group of women talk about food, sex, and self-esteem. A highly entertaining social drama evocative of some of Woody Allen's more serious work. 110m. **DIR:** Henry Jaglom. **CAST:** Nelly Alard, Lisa Richards, Frances Bergen, Mary Crosby, Gwen Welles. **1991**

EBONY TOWER, THE ★★★ Sir Laurence Olivier is well cast as an aging artist who shields himself from the world outside his estate in this fine screen adaptation of the John Fowles novel. This absorbing British TV drama is not rated, but it contains some partial nudity. 80m. **DIR:** Robert Knights. **CAST:** Laurence Olivier, Greta Scacchi. **1986**

ECHO PARK ★★★ Tom Hulce, Susan Dey, and Michael Bowen star as three young show-biz hopefuls living in one of Los Angeles's seedier neighborhoods. Director Robert Dornhelm and screenwriter Michael Ventura have some interesting things to say about the quest for fame, and the stars provide some memorable moments. Rated R for nudity, profanity, and violence. 93m. **DIR:** Robert Dornhelm. **CAST:** Susan Dey, Tom Hulce, Michael Bowen, Christopher Walker, Shirley Jo Finney, John Paragon, Richard "Cheech" Marin, Cassandra Peterson. **1986**

ECHOES IN THE DARKNESS ★★★½ This Joseph Wambaugh crime-drama is based on the 1979 true-life murder of schoolteacher Susan Reinert (Stockard Channing). It's a toned-down TV movie devoid of most of the usual Wambaugh grit. At just under four hours, it takes quite a commitment for one night's viewing. Not rated. 234m. **DIR:** Glenn Jordan. **CAST:** Peter Coyote, Robert Loggia, Stockard Channing, Peter Boyle, Gary Cole, Treat Williams, Cindy Pickett. **1987**

EDDY DUCHIN STORY, THE ★★½ Overly sentimental telling of the troubled professional and family life of pianist-bandleader Eddy Duchin. Many fine piano renditions of the standards of the era ("Body and Soul," "Sweet Sue"), and Duchin's theme song, "Chopin Nocturne in E Flat," all dubbed by Carmen Cavallaro. 123m. **DIR:** George Sidney. **CAST:** Tyrone Power, Kim Novak, Victoria Shaw, James Whitmore, Rex Thompson. **1956**

EDEN (TV SERIES) ★★ This erotic soap opera is brought to you by the folks at *Playboy* and features one of the best-looking casts on the small screen. The story (such as it is) centers on Eden, a beach resort where guests, staff, and hormones run wild. Not rated, contains nudity and sexual situations. Each tape 98m. **DIR:** Victor Lobl. **CAST:** Barbara Alyn Woods, Steve Chase, Darcy DeMoss. **1993**

EDISON, THE MAN ★★★½ The second half of MGM's planned two-part tribute to Thomas Alva Edison (following by months the release of *Young Tom Edison*). Spencer Tracy is perfect as the great inventor from young manhood through age 82. Great family viewing. B&W; 107m. **DIR:** Clarence Brown. **CAST:** Spencer Tracy, Rita Johnson, Lynne Overman, Charles Coburn, Gene Lockhart, Henry Travers. **1940**

EDUCATION OF SONNY CARSON, THE ★★★ This grim but realistic movie is based on the autobiography of Sonny Carson, a ghetto-raised black youth whose life was bounded by gangs, drugs, and crime. There's no upbeat happy ending and no attempt to preach, either; the film simply shows ghetto life for the frightening hell it is. Rated R. 104m. **DIR:** Michael Campus. **CAST:** Rony Clanton, Don Gordon, Joyce Walker, Paul Benjamin. **1974**

EDWARD AND MRS. SIMPSON ★★★ This miniseries does a commendable, if overlong, job of capturing the romance between a manipulative American divorcée and a rather simpleminded king. Talky in that inimitable *Masterpiece Theatre* style, but by the end we are quite convinced Mrs. Simpson saved the future of the English monarchy by keeping Edward VIII off the throne. Originally aired as seven episodes on PBS, it has been released in a truncated version on video. Unrated. 270m. **DIR:** Waris Hussein. **CAST:** Edward Fox, Cynthia Harris. **1980**

EDWARD II ★★★ Derek Jarman's bizarre, medieval costume drama—the characters speak in rich Elizabethan prose while wearing mostly modern attire—grabs Christopher Marlowe's sixteenth century play *(The Troublesome Reign of Edward II)* by the throat and heaves it kicking and screaming into the 1990s. The story about the downfall of England's openly gay king skewers sexual obsessions, repression, and politics with an intriguing sense of timelessness and moral decay, but is definitely not for everyone. Rated R for profanity, nudity, and violence. 90m. **DIR:** Derek Jarman. **CAST:** Steven Waddington, Andrew Tiernan, Tilda Swinton, Nigel Terry. **1992**

EFFICIENCY EXPERT, THE ★★★ Echoes of *Local Hero* are present in this offbeat film about British efficiency expert Anthony Hopkins plying his trade in 1960s Australia and beginning to question his own efficacy. While this film doesn't have the charm and truly off-the-wall humor of director Bill Forsyth's cult comedy, it is generally enjoyable. Rated PG for violence. 96m. **DIR:** Mark Joffe. **CAST:** Anthony Hopkins, Ben Mendelsohn, Toni Collette, Bruno Lawrence, Rebecca Rigg. **1992**

EGYPTIAN, THE ★★½ With the exception of Edmund Purdom, most of the cast is ill-used in this highly atmospheric, bumpy biblical spectacle centering on a physician. 140m. **DIR:** Michael Curtiz. **CAST:** Jean Simmons, Edmund Purdom, Victor Mature, Gene Tierney, Peter Ustinov, Michael Wilding. **1954**

84 CHARING CROSS ROAD ★★½ Anne Bancroft manages to act manic even while reading books in this true story based on the life of Helene Hanff, a writer and reader who begins a twenty-year correspondence with a London bookseller (Anthony Hopkins). Along with her orders for first editions, Hanff sends witty letters and care packages to the employees during the hard postwar times. Hanff and the bookseller begin to rely on the correspondence, yet never get to meet. Rated PG for language. 99m. **DIR:** David Jones. **CAST:** Anne Bancroft, Anthony Hopkins, Judi Dench, Maurice Denham. **1986**

EIGHT MEN OUT ★★★★½ Writer-director John Sayles scores a home run with this baseball drama about the 1919 Black Sox scandal—when members of the Chicago White Sox conspired to throw the World Series. A superb ensemble cast, which includes Sayles as Ring Lardner, shines in this true-life shocker, with David Strathairn and John Cusack giving standout performances. Rated PG for profanity. 120m. **DIR:** John Sayles. **CAST:** Charlie Sheen, John Cusack, Christopher Lloyd, D. B. Sweeney, David Strathairn, Michael Lerner, Clifton James, John Sayles, Studs Terkel. **1988**

ELEANOR: FIRST LADY OF THE WORLD ★★★ Jean Stapleton's Eleanor Roosevelt will either charm you or grate on your nerves in this made-for-TV movie. But either way, you'll be inspired by the story of Mrs. Roosevelt's determination. 102m. **DIR:** John Erman. **CAST:** Jean Stapleton, E. G. Marshall, Coral Browne, Joyce Van Patten. **1982**

ELECTRIC HORSEMAN, THE ★★★ Directed by Sydney Pollack, *The Electric Horseman* brought the third teaming of Jane Fonda and Robert Redford on the screen. The result is a winsome piece of light entertainment. Redford plays Sonny Steele, a former rodeo star who has become the unhappy spokesman for Ranch Breakfast, a brand of cereal. He's always in trouble and in danger of blowing the job—until he decides to rebel. Rated PG. 120m. **DIR:** Sydney Pollack. **CAST:** Robert Redford, Jane Fonda, Valerie Perrine, Willie Nelson, John Saxon, Nicolas Coster. **1979**

ELEMENT OF CRIME, THE ★★★ Uneven attempt at *film noir*, about an ex-cop who returns to a postnuclear Europe to uncover the mystery of a serial killer who preys on young girls. Brilliant camera work shot entirely in sepia tone is not enough to sustain interest. Unrated, but contains nudity and violence. 105m. **DIR:** Lars von Trier. **CAST:** Michael Elphick, Esmond Knight. **1988**

ELENI ★★★ Interesting film adaptation of Nicholas Gage's factual book *Eleni*. In 1948, during the civil war in Greece, a small mountain village is terrorized by a group of Communist guerrillas. Eleni Gatzoyiannis (Kate Nelligan) defies the Communists and their attempts to abduct her children and is subsequently tortured and executed in cold blood. Eleni's son Nicholas Gage (John Malkovich) returns to Greece after many years as a reporter for the *New York Times*, devoting his life there to unmasking her killers. Rated PG for language and violence. 116m. **DIR:** Peter Yates. **CAST:** Kate Nelligan, John Malkovich, Linda Hunt. **1985**

ELEPHANT MAN, THE (1980) ★★★★ Though it has its flaws, this film is a fascinating and heartbreaking study of the life of John Merrick, a hopelessly deformed but kind and intelligent man who struggles for dignity. John Hurt is magnificent in the title role. Rated PG. B&W; 125m. **DIR:** David Lynch. **CAST:** Anthony Hopkins, John Hurt, Anne Bancroft, Wendy Hiller, Freddie Jones. **1980**

ELEPHANT MAN, THE (1982) ★★★★ Unlike the David Lynch film, this is a straight adaptation (made for television) of the Broadway play about the hideously deformed Victorian John Merrick. Philip Anglim plays Merrick without makeup, using only pantomime to suggest his appearance, and his performance is tremendously moving. 112m. **DIR:** Jack Hofsiss. **CAST:** Philip Anglim, Kevin Conway, Penny Fuller. **1982**

ELEPHANT WALK ★★ Elizabeth Taylor plays the bride of a Ceylon tea planter (Peter Finch) bewildered by her new home and carrying on with the hired hand (Dana Andrews). Dull, unconvincing drama; the climactic elephant stampede is too little, too late. 103m. **DIR:** William Dieterle. **CAST:** Elizabeth Taylor, Peter Finch, Dana Andrews, Abraham Sofaer. **1954**

ELLIS ISLAND ★★★ This TV miniseries, of the soap-opera variety, follows the lives of three immigrants who come to the United States at the turn of the century. All struggle to find acceptance, happiness, and success in the promised land. 310m. **DIR:** Jerry London. **CAST:** Richard Burton, Faye Dunaway, Ben Vereen, Melba Moore, Ann Jillian, Greg Martyn, Peter Riegert. **1984**

ELMER GANTRY ★★★★ Burt Lancaster gives one of his most memorable performances in this release as a phony evangelist who, along with Jean Simmons, exploits the faithful with his fire-and-brimstone sermons. Arthur Kennedy is the reporter out to expose their operation in this screen version of Sinclair Lewis's story set in the Midwest of the 1920s. 145m. **DIR:** Richard Brooks. **CAST:** Burt Lancaster, Jean Simmons, Dean Jagger, Arthur Kennedy, Shirley Jones. **1960**

ELUSIVE PIMPERNEL, THE ★★½ Lesser remake of the 1934 swashbuckling adventure, *The Scarlet Pimpernel.* David Niven pales in comparison to Leslie Howard's portrayal of the death-defying savior. Not enough action to sustain viewer interest. 107m. **DIR:** Michael Powell. **CAST:** David Niven, Margaret Leighton, Cyril Cusack, Jack Hawkins. **1950**

ELVIS—THE MOVIE ★★★★ A fictional account of Elvis Presley's rise to stardom, it probes deeply into the family life of rock 'n' roll's king. This TV movie should rate highly with fans of Elvis, as well as those just interested in a good story. Excellent voice recreation by Ronnie McDowell. 117m. **DIR:** John Carpenter. **CAST:** Kurt Russell, Shelley Winters, Pat Hingle, Melody Anderson, Season Hubley, Charlie Hodge, Ellen Travolta, Ed Begley Jr. **1979**

EMILY ★★ This British film was Koo Stark's premiere in soft-core porn. She plays a teenager returning home from boarding school who finds out that her mother is a well-paid prostitute. This bit of news upsets Emily momentarily, but she manages to create her own sexual world with a female painter, the painter's husband, and her boyfriend, James. Lots of nudity and sex. Rated R. 87m. **DIR:** Henry Herbert. **CAST:** Koo Stark. **1982**

EMPEROR JONES, THE ★★★½ This liberal version of Eugene O'Neill's prize-winning play invents entire sections that were written to capitalize on star Paul Robeson's fame as a singer as well as an introductory piece that provides a background for Robeson's character, the doomed Jones. This is still an interesting and sometimes strong film despite the drastic changes. Surviving prints that have been transferred to tape are not always in the best of condition, so quality will vary on this title. B&W; 72m. **DIR:** Dudley Murphy. **CAST:** Paul Robeson, Dudley Digges, Frank Wilson. **1933**

EMPIRE OF THE SUN ★★★½ J. G. Ballard's harrowing autobiographical examination of life in a World War II Japanese prison camp has been given the Hollywood treatment by director Steven Spielberg, who took his film crew to Shanghai for some stunning location work. Young Christian Bale stars as Ballard's boyhood self, who winds up in a concentration camp for four years. Too much surface gloss prevents this from being a genuine classic, but it nonetheless contains scenes of surprising power and poignancy. Rated PG for language and intensity. 145m. **DIR:** Steven Spielberg. **CAST:** Christian Bale, John Malkovich, Miranda Richardson, Nigel Havers. **1987**

EMPTY CANVAS, THE ★★ Would-be painter Horst Buchholz falls for gold-digging model Catherine Spaak. Maudlin pap. B&W; 118m. **DIR:** Damiano Damiani. **CAST:** Bette Davis, Horst Buchholz, Catherine Spaak, Daniela Rocca, Georges Wilson. **1964**

ENCHANTED COTTAGE, THE ★★★½ An engrossing blend of romance, fantasy, and melodrama. Robert Young gives one of his best big-screen performances as a battle-scarred World War II veteran. Dorothy McGuire offers a beautifully realized portrayal of a young woman whose inner loveliness is hidden beneath a painfully plain exterior. As the blind friend who sees so much more than everyone else, Herbert Marshall is as suave as ever. B&W; 91m. **DIR:** John Cromwell. **CAST:** Dorothy McGuire, Robert Young, Herbert Marshall, Spring Byington, Hillary Brooke. **1945**

ENCORE ★★★ Somerset Maugham introduces three of his short stories in this sequel to *Trio.* The best of the three is "Gigolo and Gigolette" in which trapeze artist Glynis Johns begins to feel used by her husband as he promotes her death-defying act. The other two ("The Ant and the Grasshopper" and "Winter Cruise") are more humorous. B&W; 85m. **DIR:** Harold French, Pat Jackson, Anthony Pelissier. **CAST:** Glynis Johns, Nigel Patrick, Kay Walsh, Roland Culver, Ronald Squire, Peter Graves. **1952**

END OF INNOCENCE, THE ★★ Serio-comic story of a woman, driven over the edge who "finds herself" only after a drug overdose. All that saves the film are occasional flashes of style and self-mockery from first-time feature director Dyan Cannon (who also wrote). Rated R for profanity and sexual situations. 92m. **DIR:** Dyan Cannon. **CAST:** Dyan Cannon, John Heard, George Coe, Rebecca Schaeffer, Billie Bird, Viveka Davis. **1990**

END OF THE LINE ★★★ Financed as a labor of love by executive producer and co-star Mary Steenburgen, this first film by director Jay Russell features Wilford Brimley as a railroad worker who, with buddy Levon

Helm, steals a train engine to protest the closing of the freight depot where he has worked for thirty-eight years. The skilled performances will keep you interested right to the end of the line. Rated PG for profanity. 105m. **DIR:** Jay Russell. **CAST:** Wilford Brimley, Levon Helm, Kevin Bacon, Bob Balaban, Barbara Barrie, Mary Steenburgen, Holly Hunter, Bruce McGill, Howard Morris. **1988**

END OF THE ROAD ★★ Stacy Keach plays a college graduate who falls out of society, receives help from an unorthodox psychotherapist named Doctor D (James Earl Jones), then becomes intimately involved with a married couple. The imagery can be compelling, but the finale is too graphic. Rated X (by 1960s standards) but more like a hard R for sex, nudity, and adult themes. 110m. **DIR:** Aram Avakian. **CAST:** Stacy Keach, Harris Yulin, Dorothy Tristan, James Earl Jones. **1969**

ENDLESS GAME, THE ★★ With a creakily indifferent tone, writer-director Bryan Forbes's cold war–styled spy thriller overdoses on the residual cynicism of a once-vibrant genre. Albert Finney stars as a retired agent summoned back to learn why aged members of a disbanded European operation are being killed. Unrated; explicit dialogue, brief nudity, and violence. 120m. **DIR:** Bryan Forbes. **CAST:** Albert Finney, George Segal, Anthony Quayle, Nanette Newman. **1990**

ENDLESS LOVE ★★ Though this story of a teenage love affair has all the elements of a great romance, it is marred by implausibility and inconsistency. The film improves as it progresses and even offers some compelling moments, but not enough to compensate for its flaws. Rated R because of sex and nudity. 115m. **DIR:** Franco Zeffirelli. **CAST:** Brooke Shields, Martin Hewitt, Shirley Knight, Don Murray. **1981**

ENEMIES—A LOVE STORY ★★★★ Director Paul Mazursky achieves a delicate mixture of drama and comedy in his adaptation of the novel by Isaac Bashevis Singer. Set in New York in 1949, the film focuses on the hectic life of Holocaust survivor and womanizer Herman Broder (Ron Silver). Rated R for profanity, nudity, and simulated sex. 120m. **DIR:** Paul Mazursky. **CAST:** Ron Silver, Anjelica Huston, Lena Olin, Margaret Sophie Stein, Alan King, Paul Mazursky. **1989**

ENGLISHMAN ABROAD, AN ★★★★ Much acclaimed BBC production dramatizing actress Coral Browne's actual Moscow encounter with an exiled British diplomat accused of spying for the Russians. Alan Bates is witty, sarcastic, and ultimately tragic as the infamous Guy Burgess—longing for some taste of the England now so unattainable to him. A superb script by Alan Bennett. 63m. **DIR:** John Schlesinger. **CAST:** Alan Bates, Coral Browne, Charles Gray. **1988**

ENOLA GAY: THE MEN, THE MISSION, THE ATOMIC BOMB ★★★ In this made-for-TV drama, Patrick Duffy plays Paul Tibbets, the man in charge of the plane that dropped the atomic bomb over Hiroshima. The film delves into the lives and reactions of the crew members in a fairly effective manner. 150m. **DIR:** David Lowell Rich. **CAST:** Billy Crystal, Kim Darby, Patrick Duffy, Gary Frank, Gregory Harrison. **1980**

ENTERTAINER, THE ★★★★ Laurence Olivier is brilliant as Archie Rice, a self-deceiving, low-moraled, small-talent vaudeville song-and-dance man in this slice-of-life drama based on the play written especially for him by John Osborne. Constantly nagged about his failures, insulated by audiences, and careless of all who love him, Archie is finally brought down by a raging ego that demands undeserved admiration. Olivier reveled in the role, declaring, "It's what I really am. I am not Hamlet." 97m. **DIR:** Tony Richardson. **CAST:** Laurence Olivier, Brenda de Banzie, Joan Plowright, Roger Livesey, Alan Bates, Albert Finney. **1960**

EQUINOX (1993) ★★½ Oodles of glossy style and a fine Matthew Modine performance aren't quite enough to maintain intense interest in this enigmatic, surreal tale of twin brothers—timid, shy writer, Henry, and mean-spirited criminal, Freddy. Lara Flynn Boyle costars as a woman who draws the brothers together. Though writer-director Rudolph offers intriguing ideas, he's never quite clear or passionate enough to bring the ideas home. Rated R, with profanity. 100m. **DIR:** Alan Rudolph. **CAST:** Matthew Modine, Lara Flynn Boyle, Fred Ward. **1993**

ERIC ★★★★ This made-for-TV movie is the true story of Eric Lund, a teenager with a promising athletic future who becomes terminally ill. John Savage, in the title role, gives a meaningful portrayal of a young man who refuses to give up. Patricia Neal, as the mother, gives the kind of warm, sensitive performance she is noted for, and there is a fine supporting cast. 100m. **DIR:** James Goldstone. **CAST:** Patricia Neal, John Savage, Claude Akins, Sian Barbara Allen, Mark Hamill, Nehemiah Persoff. **1975**

ESCAPE ME NEVER ★★★ A blend of colorful personalities keeps this one afloat. Since it isn't typical of any of the major stars involved, it's interesting to see how a sophisticated composer handles his loveless marriage and his passionate love of music. B&W; 105m. **DIR:** Peter Godfrey. **CAST:** Errol Flynn, Ida Lupino, Eleanor Parker, Gig Young, Reginald Denny, Isobel Elsom, Albert Basserman, Ludwig Stossel. **1947**

ESCAPE TO BURMA 🦃 A tea plantation, wild animals, and a hunted man seeking refuge. B&W; 87m. **DIR:** Allan Dwan. **CAST:** Barbara Stanwyck, Robert Ryan, David Farrar, Murvyn Vye. **1955**

ESCAPE TO LOVE ★★★ This adventurous romance pits a beautiful American student (Clara Perryman) and her lover against the Polish KGB as they speed on a train toward Paris. Their passion increases to a point where they must both reach a life-changing decision. 105m. **DIR:** Herb Stein. **CAST:** Clara Perryman. **1982**

ESCAPE TO THE SUN ★★★ Two young university students try to escape from the oppressive Soviet Union under the watchful eyes of the KGB. They try first for an exit visa; only one visa is issued, and one of the students is taken into custody. The two are forced to make a heroic escape to the West. Rated PG for violence. 94m. **DIR:** Menahem Golan. **CAST:** Laurence Harvey, Josephine Chaplin, John Ireland, Jack Hawkins. **1972**

ESCAPIST, THE 🦃 Real-life escape artist, Bill Shirk, plays himself in this exhibition of his talents through multiple escapes. Unrated, the film contains nudity and simulated sex. 87m. **DIR:** Eddie Beverly Jr. **CAST:** Bill Shirk, Peter Lupus. **1983**

ETERNALLY YOURS ★★★ A stellar cast of accomplished scene stealers deftly brings off this iffy story of a magician (David Niven) and his wife (Loretta Young), who thinks his tricks are overshadowing their marital happiness. B&W; 95m. **DIR:** Tay Garnett. **CAST:** Loretta Young, David Niven, C. Aubrey Smith, ZaSu Pitts, Billie Burke, Eve Arden, Hugh Herbert, Broderick Crawford. **1939**

ETERNITY 🦃 A reincarnated goodie-two-shoes battling his greedy brother. Rated R for nudity and simulated sex. 122m. **DIR:** Steven Paul. **CAST:** Jon Voight, Armand Assante, Wilford Brimley, Eileen Davidson. **1990**

ETHAN FROME ★★★★ Edith Wharton's austere novel about nineteenth-century Puritan values and doomed love is given an equally austere film treatment in this longish but well-acted drama. Liam Neeson is memorable as the title character, a deformed recluse. Joan Allen plays Frome's bitter wife while Patricia Arquette is the breath of fresh air who steals his heart and seals his fate. A bit severe, chilly, and static for some viewers—others will love its literary purity. Either way, Neeson is a revelation. Rated PG. 147m. **DIR:** John Madden. **CAST:** Liam Neeson, Patricia Arquette, Joan Allen, Katharine Houghton. **1993**

EUREKA ★★★★½ Another stunner from Nicolas Roeg. *Eureka* is about an ambitious gold miner (Gene Hackman) who makes his fortune in the snowbound Canadian wilderness, then retires to his very own Caribbean island. Rated R for sex, nudity, violence, and profanity. 130m. **DIR:** Nicolas Roeg. **CAST:** Gene Hackman, Theresa Russell, Rutger Hauer, Jane Lapotaire, Mickey Rourke, Ed Lauter, Joe Pesci. **1983**

EUROPEANS, THE ★★★★ This intelligent, involving adaptation of the Henry James novel is another wonder from director James Ivory. Lee Remick is one of two free-thinking, outspoken foreigners who descend on their Puritan relatives in nineteenth-century New England. The result is a character-rich study of a clash of cultures. Rated PG. 90m. **DIR:** James Ivory. **CAST:** Lee Remick, Robin Ellis, Wesley Addy, Tim Choate, Lisa Eichhorn, Tim Woodward, Kristin Griffith. **1979**

EVELYN PRENTICE ★★★ Myrna Loy kills a blackmailer and her unknowing lawyer husband defends another woman accused of the crime. Strangely remote movie saved by a twist ending and the debut of Rosalind Russell. B&W; 80m. **DIR:** William K. Howard. **CAST:** William Powell, Myrna Loy, Una Merkel, Rosalind Russell, Harvey Stephens, Isabel Jewell, Edward Brophy, Jessie Ralph. **1934**

EVERLASTING SECRET FAMILY, THE ★★½ Strange Australian film about a secret society of powerful men who choose teenage boys to be their possessions. Unrated, but contains nudity and sexual situations. 93m. **DIR:** Michael Thornhill. **CAST:** Arthur Dignam, Mark Lee, Heather Mitchell, John Meillon. **1988**

EVERSMILE NEW JERSEY 🦃 Daniel Day-Lewis shows little of the talent he displayed in *My Left Foot*. Here he plays a traveling dentist. As exciting as getting teeth pulled. Rated PG. 103m. **DIR:** Carlos Sorin. **CAST:** Daniel Day-Lewis, Mirjana Jokovic. **1989**

EVERY TIME WE SAY GOODBYE ★★★ A change-of-pace role for Tom Hanks, who stars as an American pilot in WWII Jerusalem who falls in love with a young Jewish girl. Hanks brings a certain well-rounded realism to this dramatic part, injecting the seriousness with humor, and Cristina Marsillach is very subtle as the Jewish girl. Rated PG-13 for mild profanity, brief nudity, and mature themes. 97m. **DIR:** Moshe Mizrahi. **CAST:** Tom Hanks, Cristina Marsillach, Benedict Taylor. **1987**

EVERYBODY'S ALL-AMERICAN ★★★½ Though a bit long-winded at times, this story (based on a book by *Sports Illustrated*'s Frank Deford) is a must-see for anyone who believes professional athletes have it made. Dennis Quaid is the college football hero who believes he can go on catching passes as a professional forever. Since he can't, and catching passes pays the bills, he soon finds himself unable to cope. Jessica Lange (as Quaid's wife) and Timothy Hutton round out an unnecessary love triangle. Rated R for profanity and suggested sex. 122m. **DIR:** Taylor Hackford. **CAST:** Dennis Quaid, Jessica Lange, Timothy Hutton, John Goodman. **1988**

EX-LADY ★★ Early women's lib, with Bette Davis reluctantly marrying her lover, knowing it will take the romance out of their relationship. Nothing much. B&W; 67m. **DIR:** Robert Florey. **CAST:** Bette Davis, Gene Raymond, Frank McHugh. **1933**

EXECUTION OF PRIVATE SLOVIK, THE ★★★★ Superior made-for-television film chronicles the fate of American soldier Eddie Slovik, who was executed for desertion during World War II. Intelligent teleplay, powerful performances, and sensitive direction. 120m. **DIR:** Lamont Johnson. **CAST:** Martin Sheen, Ned Beatty, Gary Busey, Charles Haid, Mariclare Costello. **1974**

EXECUTIONER'S SONG, THE ★★★½ Pulitzer Prize novelist Norman Mailer's made-for-television adaptation of his engrossing account of convicted killer Gary Gilmore's fight to get Utah to carry out his death sentence. The performances of Tommy Lee Jones and Rosanna Arquette are electrifying. Unrated. 200m. **DIR:** Lawrence Schiller. **CAST:** Tommy Lee Jones, Rosanna Arquette, Christine Lahti, Eli Wallach. **1982**

EXECUTIVE ACTION ★★★★ This forceful film, based on Mark Lane's book *Rush to Judgment*, features a fascinating look at possible reasons for the assassination of John F. Kennedy. Rated PG. 91m. **DIR:** David Miller. **CAST:** Burt Lancaster, Robert Ryan, Will Geer, Gilbert Green, John Anderson. **1973**

EXECUTIVE SUITE ★★★★ An all-star cast is top-notch in this film about the world of corporate life. Based on Cameron Hawley's novel, the drama examines the intense power struggles in big business with honesty and panache. B&W; 104m. **DIR:** Robert Wise. **CAST:** William Holden, June Allyson, Barbara Stanwyck, Fredric March, Louis Calhern, Walter Pidgeon, Shelley Winters, Dean Jagger, Nina Foch, Paul Douglas. **1954**

EXODUS ★★½ The early days of Israel are seen through the eyes of various characters, in this epic, adapted from the novel by Leon Uris. Directed by the heavy-handed Otto Preminger, its length and plodding pace caused comic Mort Sahl to quip, "Otto, let my people go," at a preview. 213m. **DIR:** Otto Preminger. **CAST:** Paul Newman, Eva Marie Saint, Ralph Richardson, Peter Lawford, Lee J. Cobb, Sal Mineo, Jill Haworth. **1960**

EXTREME JUSTICE ★★★ Intelligent performances and a disturbing story line ripped from current headlines are nearly sabotaged by director Mark L. Lester's emphasis on ludicrous violence and gratuitous mayhem. Bad-boy cop Lou Diamond Phillips gets assigned to an LAPD "Death Squad" headed by old buddy Scott Glenn; our heroes then watch and wait while slimeballs jeopardize innocent civilians, all in the name of securing a "righteous collar"... or, more often than not, "justified shooting." Rated R for rape, violence, profanity, nudity, and drug use. 95m. **DIR:** Mark L. Lester. **CAST:** Lou Diamond Phillips, Scott Glenn, Chelsea Field, Yaphet Kotto, Ed Lauter. **1993**

EXTREMITIES ★★½ This well-meant but difficult-to-watch thriller casts Farrah Fawcett (in a first-rate performance) as a single woman who is brutalized in her own home by a homicidal maniac (James Russo). When she manages to outwit her attacker, she must decide between bloody revenge and human compassion. Robert M. Young directs this adaptation by William Mastrosimone of his play with authority and realism. Rated R for violence. 100m. **DIR:** Robert M. Young. **CAST:** Farrah Fawcett, James Russo, Diana Scarwid, Alfre Woodard. **1986**

EYE ON THE SPARROW ★★★ Mare Winningham and Keith Carradine star in this fact-based made-for-TV drama about a blind couple trying to buck the system and become adoptive parents. Winningham's performance is especially forceful, but both actors are amazingly convincing. 94m. **DIR:** John Korty. **CAST:** Mare Winningham, Keith Carradine, Conchata Ferrell. **1987**

F.I.S.T. ★★ It's too bad that *F.I.S.T.* is so predictable and cliché-ridden, because Sylvester Stallone gives a fine performance. As Johnny Kovak, leader of the Federation of Interstate Truckers, he creates an even more poignant character than Rocky Balboa. It is ironic that Stallone, after being favorably compared with Marlon Brando, should end up in a film so similar to *On the Waterfront*...and with Rod Steiger yet! Rated PG. 145m. **DIR:** Norman Jewison. **CAST:** Sylvester Stallone, Rod Steiger, Peter Boyle, Melinda Dillon, David Huffman, Tony Lo Bianco. **1978**

FABULOUS BAKER BOYS, THE ★★★★½ This deliciously sultry character study concerns a pair of mildly contentious piano-playing brothers (played by offscreen brothers Jeff and Beau Bridges) who, in an effort to revitalize a lounge act mired in tired old standards, hire a feisty singer (Michelle Pfeiffer). She becomes the catalyst that prompts age-old regrets to surface. Rated R for language. 113m. **DIR:** Steve Kloves. **CAST:** Jeff Bridges, Michelle Pfeiffer, Beau Bridges, Jennifer Tilly. **1989**

FACE IN THE CROWD, A ★★★★ A sow's ear is turned into a silk purse in this Budd Schulberg story, scripted by the author, of a television executive who discovers gold in a winsome hobo she molds into a tube star. But all that glitters is not gold. A fine cast makes this a winning film, which brought Andy Griffith and Lee Remick to the screen for the first time. B&W; 125m. **DIR:** Elia Kazan. **CAST:** Andy Griffith, Patricia Neal, Lee Remick, Anthony Franciosa, Walter Matthau, Kay Medford. **1957**

FAKEOUT ★★ A Las Vegas singer goes to jail instead of ratting on her boyfriend. Later, agreeing to falsely testify in exchange for her freedom, she becomes a target for death. Not rated, but contains violence. 89m. **DIR:** Matt Cimber. **CAST:** Telly Savalas, Pia Zadora, Desi Arnaz Jr., Larry Storch. **1982**

FALCON AND THE SNOWMAN, THE ★★★★★ In this powerful motion picture, Timothy Hutton and Sean Penn give stunning performances as two childhood friends who decide to sell United States secrets to the Russians. Based on a true incident, this release—to its credit—makes no judgments. The viewer is left to decide what's right and wrong, and whether Boyce met with justice. It is not an easy decision to make. Rated R for violence and profanity. 131m. **DIR:** John Schlesinger. **CAST:** Timothy Hutton, Sean Penn, Pat Hingle, Lori Singer, Richard Dysart. **1985**

FALL OF THE ROMAN EMPIRE, THE ★★★★ During the early and mid-1960s, Hollywood looked to the history books for many of its films. Director Anthony Mann has fashioned an epic that is a feast for the eyes and does not insult the viewers' intelligence. *The Fall of the Roman Empire* has thrilling moments of action and characters the viewer cares about. 149m. **DIR:** Anthony Mann. **CAST:** Sophia Loren, James Mason, Stephen Boyd, Alec Guinness, Christopher Plummer, John Ireland, Mel Ferrer. **1964**

FALLEN ANGEL ★★★½ This made-for-television drama deals with the controversial topic of child pornography. A young girl, Jennifer (played by Dana Hill), is pushed into pornography by a so-called adult friend, Howard (played by Richard Masur). Jennifer sees no hope of getting out of her predicament, because she can't communicate with her mother (played by Melinda Dillon). Very timely topic! 100m. **DIR:** Robert Michael Lewis. **CAST:** Dana Hill, Richard Masur, Melinda Dillon, Ronny Cox, David Hayward. **1981**

FALLEN ANGELS ★★★★ High marks to this two-volume anthology series that put impressive talent behind and in front of the camera to adapt some of the moodiest short fiction of the 1940s. Each tale is set in or near seamy World War II–era Los Angeles locales and involves the sort of characters made famous by Raymond Chandler and Cornell Woolrich. The private eyes talk tough, the women are hard as nails, and the cops are always on the take or on the lam. Unrated, with considerable violence and strong sexual content. 90m. **DIR:** Steven Soderbergh, Jonathan Kaplan, Phil Joanou, Tom Hanks, Tom Cruise, Alfonso Cuaron. **CAST:** Laura Dern, Gary Busey, Bonnie Bedelia, James Woods, Tom Hanks, Peter Gallagher, Gary Oldman, Joe Mantegna, Bruno Kirby, Isabella Rossellini, Alan Rickman. **1993**

FALLEN IDOL, THE ★★★★ A small boy hero-worships a household servant suspected of murdering his wife in this quiet Graham Greene thriller. Largely told from the child's point of view, this one is pulse-raising. As always, the late Ralph Richardson is great. Bernard Lee later became "M" in the Bond films. B&W; 94m. **DIR:** Carol Reed. **CAST:** Ralph Richardson, Michele Morgan, Bobby Henrey, Jack Hawkins, Bernard Lee. **1948**

FALLEN SPARROW, THE ★★★ In this sometimes confusing but generally engrossing film, John Garfield is a veteran of the Spanish Civil War whose wartime buddy is later murdered by Fascists in New York City. Many powerful scenes and strong performances make this one of Garfield's best films. 94m. **DIR:** Richard Wallace. **CAST:** John Garfield, Maureen O'Hara, Walter Slezak, Patricia Morison, Martha O'Driscoll. **1943**

FALLING DOWN ★★★★ Defense worker Michael Douglas is mad as hell, and he's not going to take it anymore. So he goes on an impromptu reign of terror in East Los Angeles. Detective Robert Duvall is the only one who has a clue what's going on. *Falling Down* has been misinterpreted as endorsing violence, but director Joel Schumacher and screenwriter Ebbe Roe Smith have, above all, created a thoughtful and believable character study. Rated R for violence and profanity. 112m. **DIR:** Joel Schumacher. **CAST:** Michael Douglas, Robert Duvall, Barbara Hershey, Rachel Ticotin, Frederic Forrest, Tuesday Weld, Lois Smith. **1993**

FALLING FROM GRACE ★★★★ Famous country singer finds that going home again may not be such a good idea after all. During a family visit to his rural Indiana hometown, he rekindles a relationship with an old girlfriend who not only married his brother, but also is having an affair with their dad. This opens a Pandora's box of festering regrets and emotional wounds that writer Larry McMurtry installs with a sense of truth rarely found in films today. Rated PG-13 for profanity. 101m. **DIR:** John Mellencamp. **CAST:** John Mellencamp, Mariel Hemingway, Kay Lenz, Claude Akins, Dub Taylor. **1992**

FALLING IN LOVE ★★★ Robert De Niro and Meryl Streep are fine as star-crossed lovers who risk their marriages for a moment of passion. Thanks to the uneven direction of Ulu Grosbard and an unbelievable story by Michael Cristofer, the stars' performances are the only outstanding features in this watchable love story. Rated PG for profanity and adult situations. 107m. **DIR:** Ulu Grosbard. **CAST:** Robert De Niro, Meryl Streep, Harvey Keitel. **1984**

FALSE ARREST ★★★ Based on a 1981 Arizona case, this features Donna Mills being falsely accused of killing her husband's partner. Perjuring witnesses land her in the slammer. Her only hope is proving that even the DA lied to get her convicted. Believable and well-done with Mills at her best. Unrated; contains nudity and violence. 102m. **DIR:** Bill L. Norton. **CAST:** Donna Mills, Robert Wagner, Steven Bauer, James Handy, Lane Smith. **1991**

FAMILY BUSINESS ★★½ Despite the high-powered cast of Sean Connery, Dustin Hoffman, and Matthew Broderick, this is a disappointing drama about a three-generation crime family from director Sidney Lumet. Rated R for profanity and violence. 116m. **DIR:** Sidney Lumet. **CAST:** Sean Connery, Dustin Hoffman, Matthew Broderick. **1989**

FAMILY LIFE ★★★½ A middle-class British girl strives to break free of her parents, who resort to increasingly severe measures to keep her under their control. Powerful drama filmed in a near-documentary style. Unrated. 95m. **DIR:** Kenneth Loach. **CAST:** Sandy Ratcliff, Bill Dean. **1971**

FAMILY MATTER, A ★★★ Handsome production values elevate this standard Mafia soap opera. Supermodel Carol Alt plays a Mafia princess bent on revenge, not realizing that the man she loves is the same one who killed her father. Syndicated television feature also known as *Vendetta*. Unrated. 112m. **DIR:** Stuart Margolin. **CAST:** Carol Alt, Eric Roberts, Burt Young, Eli Wallach, Nick Mancuso. **1990**

FAMILY PRAYERS ★★★½ Poignant coming-of-age drama introduces Tzvi Ratner-Stauber as a 13-year-old trying to make sense of his life. When his parents (Joe Mantegna and Anne Archer) start questioning their marriage, he must discard youth for adulthood. In the process he learns some valuable lessons, especially from his eccentric aunt, wonderfully played by Patti LuPone. Rated PG for language. 109m. **DIR:** Scott Rosenfelt. **CAST:** Joe Mantegna, Anne Archer, Paul Reiser, Allen Garfield, Patti LuPone, Tzvi Ratner-Stauber. **1991**

FAMILY UPSIDE DOWN, A ★★★ A touching, all too real drama about a previously self-sufficient couple whose age makes them dependent on their grown children. Hayes, Duke, and Zimbalist were nominated, and Astaire won an Emmy for this affecting made-for-television film. 100m. **DIR:** David Lowell Rich. **CAST:** Helen Hayes, Fred Astaire, Efrem Zimbalist Jr., Patty Duke. **1978**

FAMILY VIEWING ★★★★ Canadian filmmaker Atom Egoyan has created a brilliant surreal portrait of a dysfunctional family in this absorbing character study. The story centers around a troubled young man who attempts to piece together the events that lead to the disappearance of his mother. Not rated, but recommended for adults. 86m. **DIR:** Atom Egoyan. **CAST:** David Hemblen. **1988**

FANNY (1961) ★★★★ Leslie Caron is a beautiful and lively Fanny in this 1961 film. She plays a young girl seeking romance with the boy she grew up with. Unfortunately, he leaves her pregnant as he pursues a life at sea. 133m. **DIR:** Joshua Logan. **CAST:** Leslie Caron, Maurice Chevalier, Charles Boyer, Horst Buchholz, Baccaloni, Lionel Jeffries. **1961**

FANNY HILL: MEMOIRS OF A WOMAN OF PLEASURE 🦃 Tame adaptation of the famous erotic novel about an innocent girl who finds shelter in a house of prostitution. Unrated. B&W; 104m. **DIR:** Russ Meyer. **CAST:** Letitia Roman, Miriam Hopkins. **1965**

FANTASIES 🦃 A female Walter Mitty. Rated R for brief nudity. 81m. **DIR:** John Derek. **CAST:** Bo Derek, Peter Hooten, Anna Alexiadis. **1984**

FAR AND AWAY ★★★★ Director Ron Howard's sweeping tale of Irish immigrants who come to America in search of land in the late 1800s is truly an entertaining saga. Tom Cruise and his real-life wife Nicole Kidman play a bickering couple from different social classes who find themselves adrift in the New World. Look for the letter-boxed edition to more fully enjoy Howard's grand vision. Rated PG-13 for violence and profanity. 140m. **DIR:** Ron Howard. **CAST:** Tom Cruise, Nicole Kidman, Thomas Gibson, Robert Prosky, Barbara Babcock, Colm Meaney, Eileen Pollock, Michelle Johnson. **1992**

FAR FROM THE MADDING CROWD ★★★★ The combination of the world-class director and a stellar British cast makes this Thomas Hardy adaptation a lovely, intelligent epic. Julie Christie plays a country girl who becomes entangled in the lives of three diverse men. Cinematographer-now-director Nicolas Roeg beautifully captured the rustic countryside. 169m. **DIR:** John Schlesinger. **CAST:** Julie Christie, Terence Stamp, Alan Bates, Peter Finch. **1967**

FAR PAVILIONS, THE ★★★ In this romantic adventure, Ben Cross plays Ash, a young British officer in imperial India. Oddly enough, he had been raised as an Indian until he was eleven. As an adult, he is reunited with his childhood friend the Princess Anjuli (Amy Irving). Despite her impending marriage to the elderly Rajaha (Rossano Brazzi), Ash and Anjuli fall in love. Rated PG for sex and violence. 108m. **DIR:** Peter Duffell. **CAST:** Ben Cross, Amy Irving, Omar Sharif, Christopher Lee, Benedict Taylor, Rossano Brazzi. **1983**

FAREWELL TO ARMS, A ★★★★ Ernest Hemingway's well-crafted story of doomed love between a wounded ambulance driver and a nurse in Italy during World War I. Adolphe Menjou is peerless, Helen Hayes dies touchingly, and Gary Cooper strides away in the rain. B&W; 78m. **DIR:** Frank Borzage. **CAST:** Helen Hayes, Gary Cooper, Adolphe Menjou, Mary Philips, Jack LaRue. **1932**

FAST-WALKING ★★★½ This one is definitely not for everyone, but if you are adventurous, it may surprise you. James Woods plays a prison guard whose yearning for the good life leads him into a jailbreak scheme. Film plays for black comedy and generally succeeds. Rated R for violence, language, nudity. 116m. **DIR:** James B. Harris. **CAST:** James Woods, Kay Lenz, Tim McIntire, Robert Hooks, Susan Tyrrell. **1983**

FAT CITY ★★★★½ This neglected treasure is perhaps the best film ever made about boxing. Tank-town matches between hopefuls and has-beens along California's Central Valley keep Stacy Keach and Jeff Bridges in hamburger and white port. A classic piece of Americana and one of John Huston's greatest achievements. Rated PG. 96m. **DIR:** John Huston. **CAST:** Stacy Keach, Jeff Bridges, Susan Tyrrell, Nicholas Colasanto, Candy Clark. **1972**

FAT MAN AND LITTLE BOY ★★½ In spite of its historically significant story line—the World War II development of the atomic bomb—this film remains curiously flat and distanced. The clash between military chief General Leslie R. Groves (Paul Newman) and scientific genius J. Robert Oppenheimer (Dwight Schultz) seems mannered and forced. Rated PG-13 for intensity. 126m. **DIR:** Roland Joffe. **CAST:** Paul Newman, Dwight Schultz, Bonnie Bedelia, John Cusack, Laura Dern, Natasha Richardson. **1989**

FATAL VISION ★★★★½ This excellent TV miniseries is based on the actual case of convicted murderer, Dr. Jeffrey MacDonald. In 1970, MacDonald (Gary Cole) murdered his pregnant wife and two daughters. Although he denies the charges, his father-in-law (Karl Malden) becomes suspicious and helps to convict him. 198m. **DIR:** David Greene. **CAST:** Karl Malden, Gary Cole, Eva Marie Saint, Gary Grubbs, Mitchell Ryan, Andy Griffith. **1984**

FATHERS & SONS ★★★½ Mystical overtones enhance this drama of a teenager in jeopardy (Rory Cochrane) and his widower dad (Jeff Goldblum), who tries to shield his son from life's more painful lessons as the boy becomes entangled with a local drug dealer. Slow going, but atmospheric, well-acted, and artfully directed. Rated PG for profanity, sexuality, and brief nudity. 109m. **DIR:** Paul Mones. **CAST:** Jeff Goldblum, Rory Cochrane, Rosanna Arquette, Joie Lee. **1992**

FATHER'S REVENGE, A ★★★★ When his daughter, a flight assistant, is taken hostage in Germany by terrorists, a high school basketball coach (Brian Dennehy) decides to take matters into his own hands. The often-seen Dennehy is given one of his better-written roles in this TV movie, and he does a terrific job with it. 93m. **DIR:** John Herzfeld. **CAST:** Brian Dennehy, Ron Silver, Joanna Cassidy, Anthony Valentine. **1987**

FBI STORY, THE ★★★ A glowing history of the FBI from Prohibition to the cold war, through the career of a fictitious agent (James Stewart). Some good episodes reminiscent of Warner Bros.' G-Man pictures of the Thirties, but with too many forays into Stewart's family life. Not rated, but with lots of gunplay. 149m. **DIR:** Mervyn LeRoy. **CAST:** James Stewart, Vera Miles, Larry Pennell, Nick Adams, Murray Hamilton, Diane Jergens. **1959**

FEAR (1955) ★★ Neither star Ingrid Bergman nor her then-husband director Roberto Rossellini are able to save this tired drama of an indiscreet wife being blackmailed by her lover's ex. As ever, Bergman scores personally. B&W; 91m. **DIR:** Roberto Rossellini. **CAST:** Ingrid Bergman, Kurt Kreuger, Mathias Wiemann. **1955**

FEAR STRIKES OUT ★★½ Anthony Perkins stars in this compelling, if melodramatic, biography of baseball player Jim Piersall, whose dramatic mental breakdown during the season was played to a national audience. Elmer Bernstein's music is particularly effective, but a little more baseball and a bit less psychology would have helped this film. B&W; 81m. **DIR:** Robert Mulligan. **CAST:** Anthony Perkins, Karl Malden, Norma Moore, Adam Williams, Perry Wilson, Peter J. Votrian. **1957**

FEARLESS (1993) ★★★★ Director Peter Weir returns to the kind of otherwordly theme with which he began his career in Australia. Like *The Last Wave* and *Picnic at Hanging Rock*, this is an offbeat exploration of mankind's spiritual side, focusing on Jeff Bridges's inability to resume his normal, day-to-day life after surviving a plane crash. This fascinating and rewarding movie may pose more questions than it answers, but it's highly satisfying. Rated R for profanity and violence. 124m. **DIR:** Peter Weir. **CAST:** Jeff Bridges, Isabella Rossellini, Rosie Perez, Tom Hulce, John Turturro, Benicio Del Toro, Deirdre O'Connell, John De Lancie. **1993**

FEDORA ★★★★ This marvelous ball-of-twine mystery is writer-director Billy Wilder's bookend to his 1950 classic *Sunset Boulevard*. Down-on-his-luck producer William Holden flies to a Greek isle to lure a Garbo-like actress out of retirement. This is not an old man's dismissal of Hollywood as many believe; in fact, it is Wilder's last great film. 114m. **DIR:** Billy Wilder. **CAST:** William Holden, Marthe Keller, Hildegarde Neff, José Ferrer. **1978**

FELLOW TRAVELER ★★½ What could have been a gripping drama, set amid the horror and persecution of Hollywood's McCarthyesque witch-hunts, loses its momentum when Michael Eaton's script descends into pop psycho-babble. Ron Silver stars as a screenwriter who, while hiding in England (where he fled, rather than testify before the House Un-American Activities Committee), learns that his best friend has committed suicide—after some dealings with HUAC. Made for HBO. 91m. **DIR:** Philip Saville. **CAST:** Ron Silver, Hart Bochner, Imogen Stubbs, Daniel J. Travanti. **1989**

FEMALE JUNGLE ★★ A suitably sleazy, low-rent crime potboiler that was one of Jayne Mansfield's first movies. Lawrence Tierney is a police detective stalking a killer. One of the few features directed by Roger Corman stock-company actor Bruno VeSota. Alternate title: *The Hangover*. B&W; 56m. **DIR:** Bruno VeSota. **CAST:** Jayne Mansfield, Lawrence Tierney, John Carradine, Kathleen Crowley. **1956**

FEVER PITCH ★★ Ryan O'Neal plays a sports journalist writing about gambling. To research his story, O'Neal becomes a gambler, loses his wife, endangers his job, and becomes involved with a sleazy bookie. Rated R for profanity and violence. 95m. **DIR:** Richard Brooks. **CAST:** Ryan O'Neal, Catharine Hicks, Giancarlo Giannini, Bridgette Anderson, Chad Everett, John Saxon, William Smith. **1985**

FIELD, THE ★★★★ Richard Harris gives a superb performance in this drama, which is not unlike the dark side of John Ford's *The Quiet Man*. Tom Berenger plays an American who comes to Ireland in search of his roots and with plans to modernize the country, which include buying and paving a piece of fertile land lovingly tended by Harris and his son (Sean Bean). Rated PG-13 for violence and profanity. 107m. **DIR:** Jim Sheridan. **CAST:** Richard Harris, John Hurt, Sean Bean, Tom Berenger, Brenda Fricker, Frances Tomelty. **1990**

FIFTH MONKEY, THE ★★★ Ben Kingsley is upstaged by four chimpanzees in this uplifting adventure. Kingsley plays a Brazilian peasant desperately trying to earn enough money to marry the woman he loves by selling snakeskins. Rated PG-13 for violence. 93m. **DIR:** Eric Rochat. **CAST:** Ben Kingsley. **1990**

55 DAYS AT PEKING ★★ A lackluster big-screen adventure about the Boxer Revolt in 1900. Charlton Heston, David Niven, and the rest of the large cast seem made of wood. 150m. **DIR:** Nicholas Ray. **CAST:** Charlton Heston, Ava Gardner, David Niven, John Ireland. **1963**

FIGHTING FATHER DUNNE ★★★½ Inspirational, at times tearjerking, tale of one priest's effort to care for the homeless boys of St. Louis in 1905. You'll be amazed by the clever priest's ability to acquire supplies and services with goodwill instead of hard cash. B&W; 93m. **DIR:** Ted Tetzlaff. **CAST:** Pat O'Brien, Barry Fitzgerald, Darryl Hickman. **1948**

FIGHTING MAD ★★★ A quiet, unassuming farmer (Peter Fonda) is driven to distraction by a ruthless businessman who wants to assume his property. Instead of a free-for-all of violence and car crashes (as in other Fonda films of the time), this ranks as an in-depth character study. Rated R for violence. 90m. **DIR:** Jonathan Demme. **CAST:** Peter Fonda, Lynn Lowry, John Doucette, Philip Carey, Scott Glenn, Kathleen Miller. **1976**

FIGHTING SULLIVANS, THE ★★★★ This based-on-fact story of five brothers who died together when the cruiser *Juneau* was torpedoed by emotionally devastated World War II moviegoers. Many cinema owners decided not to show it because of the effect on those who had lost loved ones. The early scenes of the boys growing up in Waterloo, Iowa is fine Americana, but be forewarned: the ending has some of the saddest, most heart-wrenching moments ever filmed. Also released as *The Sullivans*. B&W; 111m. **DIR:** Lloyd Bacon. **CAST:** Thomas Mitchell, Anne Baxter, Selena Royle, Ward Bond, Bobby Driscoll. **1944**

FINAL VERDICT ★★★ Based on true events, this is a slow-paced account of one girl's adoration of her lawyer father (Treat Williams). Set in Los Angeles, circa 1919, this made-for-TV film does an above-average job. 93m. **DIR:** Jack Fisk. **CAST:** Treat Williams, Glenn Ford, Olivia Burnett, Ashley Crow, Raphael Sbarge. **1991**

FINDERS KEEPERS, LOVERS WEEPERS 🦃 Trite melodrama about two adulterous couples. Unrated, but an R equivalent for some nudity. 71m. **DIR:** Russ Meyer. **CAST:** Paul Lockwood. **1968**

FINGERS ★★★★ Harvey Keitel gives an electric performance as a would-be concert pianist who is also a death-dealing collector for his loan-sharking dad. Extremely violent and not for all tastes, but there is an undeniable fascination toward the Keitel character and his tortured life. Rated R. 91m. **DIR:** James Toback. **CAST:** Harvey Keitel, Jim Brown, Tisa Farrow, Michael Gazzo. **1978**

FINISH LINE ★★ Pressured by his coach-father to excel, a high school athlete begins using steroids. Well-meaning drama, made for cable TV, is as predictable as most TV movies. Unrated. 96m. **DIR:** John Nicolella. **CAST:** James Brolin, Josh Brolin, Mariska Hargitay, Billy Vera. **1989**

FINISHING SCHOOL ★★★½ A poor little rich girl finds true love with a med student. Surprisingly progressive, this film was codirected and written by a woman—Wanda Tuchock—rare, indeed, for the 1930s. Some scenes are melodramatic and attitudes are dated, but overall the film remains engrossing. B&W; 73m. **DIR:** Wanda Tuchock, George Nicholls Jr. **CAST:** Frances Dee, Billie Burke, Ginger Rogers, Bruce Cabot, John Halliday. **1934**

FIRE DOWN BELOW ★★★ Rita Hayworth is a lady of dubious background and virtue on a voyage between islands aboard a tramp steamer owned by adventurers Robert Mitchum and Jack Lemmon, both of whom chase her. A below-decks explosion traps one of the partners. The plot is familiar, contrived, but entertaining just the same. 116m. **DIR:** Robert Parrish. **CAST:** Rita Hayworth, Robert Mitchum, Jack Lemmon, Herbert Lom, Anthony Newley. **1957**

FIRE WITH FIRE ★★ What hath Shakespeare wrought? The true story of a girl's Catholic school that invited the residents of a neighboring boy's reform school to a dance. Another good girl/bad boy melodrama wherein misunderstood teens triumph against all odds. Craig Sheffer and Virginia Madsen are appealing, but the plot is laughable. Rated PG-13 for mild sex and language. 103m. **DIR:** Duncan Gibbins. **CAST:** Craig Sheffer, Virginia Madsen, Jon Polito, Kate Reid, Jean Smart. **1986**

FIRES WITHIN ★★ Boring love triangle involving an American fisherman, a Cuban refugee, and a Cuban political prisoner. Writer Cynthia Cidre failed to create a film with either believable characters and/or an engaging plot. 90m. **DIR:** Gillian Armstrong. **CAST:** Jimmy Smits, Greta Scacchi, Vincent D'Onofrio, Luis Avalos. **1991**

FIRST AFFAIR ★★★ Melissa Sue Anderson stars as a naïve Harvard scholarship student. She finds herself romantically inclined toward her English professor's husband. A strong entourage of actors helps make this an insightful commentary about the difficulties of keeping a marriage together, and the pain of losing one's innocence. Made for television. 100m. **DIR:** Gus Trikonis. **CAST:** Loretta Swit, Melissa Sue Anderson, Joel Higgins, Charley Lang, Kim Delaney, Amanda Bearse. **1983**

FIRST LOVE ★★ A somber movie about a college student who is unlucky in love. While the film has an interesting cast, sharp dialogue, and a refreshingly honest story, it's basically muddleheaded. Rated R for nudity and language. 92m. **DIR:** Joan Darling. **CAST:** William Katt, Susan Dey, John Heard, Beverly D'Angelo, Robert Loggia. **1977**

FIRST MONDAY IN OCTOBER ★★★ This is a Walter Matthau picture, with all the joys that implies. As he did in *Hopscotch*, director Ronald Neame allows Matthau, who plays a crusty Supreme Court justice, to make the most of every screen moment. Jill Clayburgh plays the first woman appointed to the Supreme Court. Rated R for nudity and profanity. 98m. **DIR:** Ronald Neame. **CAST:** Walter Matthau, Jill Clayburgh, Barnard Hughes, Jan Sterling. **1981**

FIRSTBORN ★★★★ An emotionally charged screen drama that deftly examines some topical, thought-provoking themes, this stars Teri Garr as a divorced woman who gets involved with the wrong man (Peter Weller) to the horror of her two sons. Rated PG for profanity and violence. 100m. **DIR:** Michael Apted. **CAST:** Teri Garr, Peter Weller. **1984**

FISH HAWK ★★★ Excellent drama about an Indian (Will Sampson) who befriends a young farm boy in turn-of-the-century rural America. Sampson has a drinking problem, which he kicks in an effort to return to his former life. Rated G; contains very mild profanity. 95m. **DIR:** Donald Shebib. **CAST:** Will Sampson, Don Francks, Charles Fields, Chris Wiggins. **1984**

FIVE CAME BACK ★★★ A plane carrying the usual mixed bag of passengers goes down in the jungle. Only five of the group will survive. The cast, fine character players all, makes this melodrama worthwhile, though it shows its age. B&W; 75m. **DIR:** John Farrow. **CAST:** Chester Morris, Wendy Barrie, John Carradine, Allen Jenkins, Joseph Calleia, C. Aubrey Smith, Patric Knowles, Lucille Ball. **1939**

FIVE CORNERS ★★★½ Most viewers will feel a little *Moonstruck* after watching this bizarre comedy-drama written by John Patrick Shanley. Jodie Foster stars as a young woman who attempts to get help from the tough-guy-turned-pacifist (Tim Robbins) who saved her from being raped by an unhinged admirer (John Turturro) when the latter is released from prison. Moments of suspense and hard-edged realism are effectively mixed with bits of offbeat comedy. Rated R for violence and adult themes. 92m. **DIR:** Tony Bill. **CAST:** Jodie Foster, Tim Robbins, John Turturro. **1988**

FIVE DAYS ONE SUMMER ★★★ This is an old-fashioned romance, with Sean Connery as a mountain climber caught in a triangle involving his lovely niece and a handsome young guide. Two handkerchiefs and a liking for soap operas are suggested. Rated PG for adult situations. 108m. **DIR:** Fred Zinnemann. **CAST:** Sean Connery, Anna Massey, Betsy Brantley, Lambert Wilson. **1983**

FIVE EASY PIECES ★★★★½ Shattering drama concerns Jack Nicholson's return to his family home after years of self-imposed exile. Playing a once promising pianist who chose to work in the oil fields, Nicholson has rarely been better; his fully shaded character with its explosions of emotion are a wonder to behold. One of the gems of the Seventies. The chicken-salad scene in the diner is now a classic. Rated R. 90m. **DIR:** Bob Rafelson. **CAST:** Jack Nicholson, Karen Black, Susan Anspach, Billy Green Bush, Sally Struthers, Ralph Waite, Fannie Flagg. **1970**

FIXER, THE ★★★★½ This excellent adaptation of Bernard Malamud's bestseller is hard to watch because of stark brutality and heart-tugging performances. In Czarist Russia anti-Semitism was almost the law of the land. A Jewish man is suspected of killing a young boy because, supposedly, Jews drink the blood of children. He is tortured to get him to confess, then the government assigns a lawyer to his case. Rated PG. 130m. **DIR:** John Frankenheimer. **CAST:** Alan Bates, Dirk Bogarde, Elizabeth Hartman, Hugh Griffith, Georgia Brown, David Warner, Ian Holm. **1968**

FLAMINGO ROAD ★★★½ A typical Joan Crawford soap opera with her dominating the weak men in her life. In this one she plays a carnival dancer who intrigues Zachary Scott and David Brian in a small town where the carnival stops. Fast-moving melodrama. B&W; 94m. **DIR:** Michael Curtiz. **CAST:** Joan Crawford, David Brian, Sydney Greenstreet, Zachary Scott, Gladys George. **1949**

FLESH 🦃 Joe Dallesandro as a street hustler who can't stay away from transvestites, sleazy women, and drugs. Not rated, contains nudity and profane language. 90m. **DIR:** Paul Morrissey. **CAST:** Joe Dallesandro, Geraldine Smith, Patti D'Arbanville, Candy Darling. **1968**

FLESH AND BONE ★★★½ In the prologue to writer-director Steve Kloves's suspenseful, thought-provoking film, a young boy named Arliss becomes an unwilling accomplice to murder when his father uses him in a robbery that goes awry. Years later, the adult Arliss (Dennis Quaid) is a self-employed businessman who drifts from place to place, seemingly in an attempt to avoid memories of his dark past. An act of kindness toward a pretty stranger (Meg Ryan) sets in motion an inexorable chain of events that leads to a day of reckoning. Offbeat drama is not for all tastes. Rated R for violence, profanity, nudity, and simulated sex. 127m. **DIR:** Steve Kloves. **CAST:** Dennis Quaid, Meg Ryan, James Caan, Gweneth Paltrow, Scott Wilson, Christopher Rydell. **1993**

FLESH AND THE DEVIL ★★★ Story of a woman who flaunts moral conventions by pursuing a third man while married to two others. The sensual pairing of sultry Greta Garbo with suave John Gilbert electrifies this film. B&W; 103m. **DIR:** Clarence Brown. **CAST:** Greta Garbo, John Gilbert. **1927**

FLIGHT FROM VIENNA ★★★ Theodore Bikel gets to demonstrate the range of his acting abilities as a Hungarian official trying to defect to the West. B&W; 54m. **DIR:** Denis Kavanagh. **CAST:** Theodore Bikel, John Bentley, Donald Gray. **1956**

FLIGHT OF BLACK ANGEL ★★½ This potentially intriguing made-for-cable thriller, about a renegade fighter pilot with a stolen tactical nuclear weapon, turns unsavory and relentlessly stupid at the halfway point. Training instructor Peter Strauss takes it personally when one of his former students, believing himself a self-styled "Angel of the Lord," uses real missiles on trainees and then heads out on a mission to annihilate Las Vegas. Rated R for language violence. 102m. **DIR:** Jonathan Mostow. **CAST:** Peter Strauss, William O'Leary. **1991**

FLIM-FLAM MAN, THE ★★★ A con man (George C. Scott) teaches an army deserter (Michael Sarrazin) the art of fleecing yokels. Scott is an altogether charming, wry, winning rascal in this improbable, clever film, which is highlighted by a spectacular car-chase scene. 104m. **DIR:** Irvin Kershner. **CAST:** George C. Scott, Michael Sarrazin, Sue Lyon, Harry Morgan, Jack Albertson. **1967**

FLIRTING ★★★★ This Australian comedy-drama is the second film in writer-director John Duigan's projected trilogy about the coming-of-age of an adolescent named Danny. In the first film, *The Year My Voice Broke*, we meet the boy in a small town in the Australian outback. In *Flirting*, Danny is now at an all-boys boarding school, across a lake from an all-girls school. Amid the typical prep school studies, socials, and antics, Danny is surpised to find himself falling for a young Ugandan girl. If you've yet to discover these two Duigan films, they're genuine sleepers. 96m. **DIR:** John Duigan. **CAST:** Noah Taylor, Thankie Newton, Nicole Kidman. **1992**

FOOL FOR LOVE ★★★½ Writer-star Sam Shepard's disturbing, thought-provoking screenplay is about people who, as one of his characters comments, "can't help themselves." Shepard plays a cowboy-stuntman who is continuing his romantic pursuit of Kim Basinger in spite of her objections. For open-minded adults who appreciate daring, original works. Rated R for profanity and violence. 107m. **DIR:** Robert Altman. **CAST:** Sam Shepard, Kim Basinger, Harry Dean Stanton, Randy Quaid. **1986**

FOOLISH WIVES ★★★★ Anticipating Orson Welles by two decades, director and star Erich Von Stroheim also wrote, produced, codesigned, and cocostumed this stark and unsettling account of a sleazy rogue's depraved use of women to achieve his aims. Von Stroheim is brilliant as the oily, morally corrupt, bogus nobleman plying his confidence game against the naïve rich in post–World War I Monaco and Monte Carlo. The final scene is a masterful simile. Silent. B&W; 107m. **DIR:** Erich Von Stroheim. **CAST:** Erich Von Stroheim, Mae Busch, Rudolph Christians. **1921–1922**

FOOLS 🦃 An aging star of horror pictures falls in love with the beautiful wife of an attorney. Rated PG. 97m. **DIR:** Tom Gries. **CAST:** Jason Robards Jr., Katharine Ross, Scott Hylands. **1970**

FOOLS OF FORTUNE ★★ The troubles in Northern Ireland turn the idyllic childhood of Willie Clinton into a nightmare, and as an adult he plots his revenge. Based on the novel by William Trevor, this is a profoundly disturbing drama that features good perfomances but is of an intensity that makes it nearly unwatchable. Rated PG-13 for violence. 109m. **DIR:** Pat O'Connor. **CAST:** Mary Elizabeth Mastrantonio, Iain Glen, Julie Christie, Michael Kitchen, Sean McClory. **1990**

FOR KEEPS The serious issue of teen pregnancy is irresponsibly trivialized. Rated PG-13 for frank language. 98m. **DIR:** John G. Avildsen. **CAST:** Molly Ringwald, Randall Batinkoff, Kenneth Mars, Brenda Vaccaro, Conchata Ferrell, Miriam Flynn. **1988**

FOR LADIES ONLY ★★★ A young, good-looking farm-belt guy goes to New York to become a star. He finally turns to stripping to make more money. This stale, TV film is a predictable morality play made fresher with the role reversal. 94m. **DIR:** Mel Damski. **CAST:** Gregory Harrison, Lee Grant, Louise Lasser, Dinah Manoff. **1981**

FOR LOVE ALONE ★★★½ An Australian girl is frustrated by the romantic double standard of the 1930s. Helen Buday plays the lovelorn student willing to waste her life on her selfish professor (Hugo Weaving) until she meets a dashing banker (Sam Neill). Buday and Neill are excellent, but Weaving offers a very wooden performance. Rated PG for partial nudity and simulated sex. 102m. **DIR:** Stephen Wallace. **CAST:** Helen Buday, Sam Neill, Hugo Weaving. **1985**

FOR LOVE OF ANGELA ★★ A beautiful jewelry clerk falls in love with the store owner's son. His meddling mom tries to break them up. Originally made for commercial TV, this film has numerous cuts and breakaways that are most distracting. 105m. **DIR:** Rudy Vejar. **CAST:** Sarah Rush, Barbara Mallory, David Winn, Margaret Fairchild, Dr. Joyce Brothers. **1982**

FOR QUEEN AND COUNTRY ★★★½ A taut, tragic combination of social commentary and ghetto thriller focusing on racism in contemporary England. American actor Denzel Washington is superb as a black working-class British soldier who returns home from military service to find himself restricted to a second-class life. Rated R. 108m. **DIR:** Martin Stellman. **CAST:** Denzel Washington, Amanda Redman, George Baker. **1989**

FOR US THE LIVING: THE MEDGAR EVERS STORY ★★★★ Assassinated civil-rights activist Medgar Evers is profiled in this inspirational drama. Adapted from Evers's wife's biography, this film gives a look at the total person, not just the legends surrounding him. Originally made for television, this is unrated. 90m. **DIR:** Michael Schultz. **CAST:** Howard Rollins Jr., Irene Cara, Margaret Avery, Roscoe Lee Browne. **1983**

FOR YOUR LOVE ONLY ★★ European beauty Nastassja Kinski stars as a young student who has an affair with her teacher, which leads to murder and blackmail. Pretty dull soap opera made for German television and released theatrically in 1982. Not rated, but contains sexual situations and violence. 97m. **DIR:** Wolfgang Petersen. **CAST:** Nastassja Kinski, Christian Quadflieg. **1976**

FORBIDDEN ★★★ Made-for-cable film about a gentile woman who falls in love with a Jewish man during World War II: a crime in Hitler's Germany. Enough suspense here to keep the viewer attentive, but not enough atmosphere to make it as intense as the melodramatic sound track assumes it to be. Not rated, but the equivalent of a PG for some violence and light sex. 114m. **DIR:** Anthony Page. **CAST:** Jacqueline Bisset, Jurgen Prochnow, Irene Worth, Peter Vaughan. **1984**

FORBIDDEN LOVE Silly made-for-TV love story involving a sexy older woman and a young man. 100m. **DIR:** Steven H. Stern. **CAST:** Yvette Mimieux, Andrew Stevens, Lisa Lucas, John Considine. **1982**

FORBIDDEN SUN Lauren Hutton as an ex-Olympian who coaches a group of young female hopefuls on the isle of Crete. Rated R for violence and adult situations. 88m. **DIR:** Zelda Barron. **CAST:** Lauren Hutton, Cliff De Young, René Estevez. **1989**

FORCE OF EVIL ★★★ A lawyer (John Garfield) abandons his principles and goes to work for a racketeer in this somber, downbeat story of corruption and loss of values. Compelling story and acting compensate for some of the heavy-handedness of the approach. A good study of ambition and the different paths it leads the characters on. B&W; 78m. **DIR:** Abraham Polonsky. **CAST:** John Garfield, Thomas Gomez, Roy Roberts, Marie Windsor. **1948**

FORCED MARCH ★★★ Chris Sarandon is a deteriorating American Method actor portraying Miklos Radnoti, in a movie about the Hungarian poet's ordeal at a Jewish labor camp. As a film about the making of a film it is engaging at times—especially as it relates each character's dedication to the project. Not rated. 104m. **DIR:** Rick King. **CAST:** Chris Sarandon, Renee Soutendijk, Josef Sommer, John Seitz. **1989**

FORD: THE MAN & THE MACHINE ★★½ This TV biography of Henry Ford runs out of gas long before the film does. Canadian effort stars Cliff Robertson as the grandfather of the automobile, only to let senility slip in and affect the script. Episodic storytelling revs its engine for those interested in such fare, but doesn't flesh out the story enough for a full road trip. 210m. **DIR:** Allan Eastman. **CAST:** Cliff Robertson, Hope Lange, Michael Ironside, Heather Thomas, R. H. Thomson. **1987**

FOREIGN AFFAIRS ★★★ Opposites attract in this light, warm story of a college professor and a sanitation engineer who meet in England and fall in love. Stars rise above familiar story line and keep interest level up. 106m. **DIR:** Jim O'Brien. **CAST:** Joanne Woodward, Brian Dennehy, Eric Stoltz, Stephanie Beacham, Ian Richardson. **1993**

FOREVER AMBER ★★★½ After much tampering by censors, Kathleen Winsor's (then) lusty bestseller made it to the screen. Linda Darnell plays ambitious tavern wench Amber St. Clare, who seduces all in sight until she becomes the mistress of Charles II. First-rate production and cast. 140m. **DIR:** Otto Preminger. **CAST:** Linda Darnell, Cornel Wilde, Richard Greene, George Sanders, Glenn Langan, Richard Haydn, Jessica Tandy, Anne Revere, John Russell, Leo G. Carroll, Margaret Wycherly. **1947**

FOREVER AND A DAY ★★★★ A morale builder during World War II and worth seeing for its cast, this film is a series of episodes linked together by a regal house in war-torn London. An American with British ancestry (Kent Smith) visits the house with plans to take it over. B&W; 104m. **DIR:** René Clair, Robert Stevenson, Herbert Wilcox, Victor Saville, Cedric Hardwicke, Edmund Goulding. **CAST:** Kent Smith, Charles Laughton, Anna Neagle, Ray Milland, Claude Rains, Ida Lupino, Merle Oberon, Brian Aherne, Victor McLaglen, Robert Cummings, Buster Keaton, Elsa Lanchester. **1943**

FOREVER YOUNG (1983) ★★ This slow-moving British soap opera features a handsome priest who is idolized by a lonely boy. Unrated, but brief nudity and mature themes would make it comparable with a PG. 85m. **DIR:** David Drury. **CAST:** James Aubrey, Nicholas Gecks, Alec McCowen. **1983**

FORGOTTEN, THE ★★★½ Six Vietnam Green Beret POWs are released after seventeen years only to be put through more torture by U.S. officials. A disturbing psychological thriller, this made-for-cable TV movie has violence and some strong language. 96m. **DIR:** James Keach. **CAST:** Keith Carradine, Steve Railsback, Stacy Keach. **1989**

FORGOTTEN PRISONERS ★★★ The horrors of life in a Turkish prison are vividly depicted in this gut-wrenching made-for-cable drama that focuses on human rights. Ron Silver is excellent as a lawyer hired by Amnesty International. 92m. **DIR:** Robert Greenwald. **CAST:** Ron Silver, Hector Elizondo, Roger Daltrey. **1990**

FORT APACHE—THE BRONX ★★★½ Jarring violence surfaces throughout this story about New York's crime-besieged South Bronx, but absorbing dramatic elements give this routine cops-and-criminals format gutsy substance. Paul Newman, as an idealistic police veteran, proves his screen magnetism hasn't withered with time. The supporting cast is top-notch. Rated R for violence, profanity, and sexual references. 125m. **DIR:** Daniel Petrie. **CAST:** Paul Newman, Ken Wahl, Edward Asner, Kathleen Beller, Rachel Ticotin. **1981**

FORTRESS (1985) ★★½ In this drawn-out story of a mass kidnapping in the Australian outback, Rachel Ward is passable as a teacher in a one-room school. She is abducted along with her students, ranging in age from about 6 to 14. The story centers around their attempts to escape. 90m. **DIR:** Arch Nicholson. **CAST:** Rachel Ward, Sean Garlick, Rebecca Rigg. **1985**

FORTUNE AND MEN'S EYES ★★½ Well acted but unpleasant and ultimately an exploitative look at homosexuality in prison. Rated R for violence and suggested sex. 102m. **DIR:** Harvey Hart. **CAST:** Wendell Burton, Michael Greer, Zooey Hall. **1971**

FORTUNES OF WAR ★★★ Based on Olivia Manning's novels, *Balkan Trilogy* and *Levant Trilogy*, this BBC epic focuses on the effects of World War II on a nonmilitary British couple living in Romania. The husband is attracted to rebel factions and lofty ideals, while his wife must focus on daily life and reality. Slow-moving and overlong. 335m. **DIR:** James Cellan Jones. **CAST:** Kenneth Branagh, Emma Thompson, Ronald Pickup, Rupert Graves. **1987**

49TH PARALLEL, THE ★★★★ Rich suspense drama about a World War II German U-boat sunk off the coast of Canada whose crew makes it to shore and tries to reach safety in neutral territory. The cast is first-rate, the characterizations outstanding. Original story won an Oscar. B&W; 105m. **DIR:** Michael Powell. **CAST:** Laurence Olivier, Anton Walbrook, Eric Portman, Leslie Howard, Raymond Massey, Finlay Currie, Glynis Johns. **1941**

FOUNTAINHEAD, THE ★★½ Gary Cooper tries his best in this Ayn Rand novel, brought to the screen without any of the book's vitality or character development. "Coop" is cast as Howard Roark, a Frank Lloyd Wright-type architect whose creations are ahead of their time and therefore go unappreciated. Patricia Neal is the love interest. B&W; 114m. **DIR:** King Vidor. **CAST:** Gary Cooper, Patricia Neal, Raymond Massey, Kent Smith, Robert Douglas. **1949**

FOUR DAUGHTERS ★★★★½ Widower Claude Rains helps his daughters through the ups and downs of small-town romance in this irresistible tearjerker from a Fannie Hurst novel. Great cast, with John Garfield a standout in his first film. B&W; 90m. **DIR:** Michael Curtiz. **CAST:** Claude Rains, Rosemary Lane, Lola Lane, Priscilla Lane, Gale Page, John Garfield. **1938**

FOUR DAYS IN JULY ★★★ A stark, cold realistic view of war-torn Northern Ireland, concentrating on two couples: one Catholic, and one Protestant. Irish accents may be difficult, but the almost intrusive nature of this "fly-on-the-wall" directorial style makes it worth the effort. 99m. **DIR:** Mike Leigh. **CAST:** Brid Brennan, Desmond McAleer, Charles Lawson, Paula Hamilton. **1984**

FOUR FRIENDS ★★ Arthur Penn directed and Steve Tesich (*Breaking Away*) wrote this interesting but ultimately disappointing film about America as seen through the eyes of a young immigrant (Craig Wasson) and the love he shares with two friends for a freethinking young woman (Jodi Thelen). Rated R because of violence, nudity, and profanity. 114m. **DIR:** Arthur Penn. **CAST:** Craig Wasson, James Leo Herlihy, Jodi Thelen. **1981**

FOUR IN A JEEP ★★½ Just after World War II, Vienna was a city divided into four nationally divided zones. This picture deals with a police patrol made up of American, Soviet, British, and French troops who clash over cases with which they must deal. It's not a terribly exciting film, but it does evoke some emotion about this tragic episode in postwar history. B&W; 96m. **DIR:** Leopold Lindtberg. **CAST:** Viveca Lindfors, Ralph Meeker. **1951**

FOUR SEASONS, THE ★★★½ Written and directed by Alan Alda, this film focuses on the pains and joys of friendship shared by three couples who are vacationing together. Despite a flawed and uneven script, the characters have been skillfully drawn and convincingly played by an excellent cast. *Four Seasons* is by no means perfect, yet it is an appealing, uplifting piece of entertainment. Rated PG. 117m. **DIR:** Alan Alda. **CAST:** Alan Alda, Carol Burnett, Len Cariou, Sandy Dennis, Rita Moreno, Jack Weston. **1981**

FOURTH WISE MAN, THE ★★★½ A surprisingly well-done fable about a physician who sets out to join three other notables in a quest to witness the birth of the Messiah, but this fourth wise man (Martin Sheen) encounters stumbling blocks along the way. Stylishly produced TV movie. 72m. **DIR:** Michael Ray Rhodes. **CAST:** Martin Sheen, Alan Arkin, Eileen Brennan, Ralph Bellamy, Richard Libertini, Harold Gould, Lance Kerwin, Adam Arkin. **1985**

FOURTH WISH, THE ★★★★ This moving Australian tearjerker features a 12-year-old boy dying of leukemia. His father's desire to grant his final wishes gets progressively harder to arrange. Wonderful story of a father's love, but be prepared with a box of Kleenex nearby. Not rated. 120m. **DIR:** Don Chaffey. **CAST:** John Meillon, Robert Bettles, Robyn Nevin. **1976**

FOXES ★★★ Adrian Lyne directed this fitfully interesting film, about four young women who share an apartment in Los Angeles. The cast is good but somehow it all falls flat. Rated R. 106m. **DIR:** Adrian Lyne. **CAST:** Jodie Foster, Sally Kellerman, Cherie Currie, Randy Quaid, Scott Baio. **1980**

FOXFIRE ★★★★½ Jessica Tandy is mesmerizing in this *Hallmark Hall of Fame* presentation. She plays an elderly Appalachian woman who must choose between her beloved mountaintop cabin and a new home with her son and his children. Hume Cronyn is the ghost of her late husband whom Tandy keeps very much alive, and John Denver is the singing son who wants to care for her. The Blue Ridge Mountains are as much a part of this lovely film as Tandy's thoughtful performance. Rated PG. 118m. **DIR:** Jud Taylor. **CAST:** Jessica Tandy, Hume Cronyn, John Denver. **1987**

FOXFIRE LIGHT 🦃 A love triangle in the Ozarks. Badly written. Rated PG for adult situations. 102m. **DIR:** Allen Baron. **CAST:** Leslie Nielsen, Tippi Hedren, Lara Parker, Barry Van Dyke, Burton Gilliam. **1982**

FOXTROT ★★½ Peter O'Toole plays a European aristocrat who escapes World War II when he takes a yacht to a deserted island and sets up residence with his wife (Charlotte Rampling), his ship's captain (Max von Sydow), and his servant (Jorge Luke). *Foxtrot* centers on the wastes of the leisure class even in a time of war. Rated R for sex, nudity, and violence. 91m. **DIR:** Arturo Ripstein. **CAST:** Peter O'Toole, Charlotte Rampling, Max von Sydow, Jorge Luke, Helena Rojo, Claudio Brook. **1975**

FRAMED (1930) ★★★ Atmospheric melodrama that makes the most of lighting, shadows, and sexy situations. The story is your basic melodrama: girl wants revenge on the man who shot her father but falls for the killer's son instead. One of the first gangster melodramas of the 1930s. B&W; 71m. **DIR:** George Archainbaud. **CAST:** Evelyn Brent, Regis Toomey, Ralf Haralde. **1930**

FRANCES ★★★★½ Director Howard Hawks called Frances Farmer "the best actress I ever worked with." However, the Seattle-born free-thinker was never allowed to reign as a star in Hollywood. This chilling, poignant motion picture explains why. Jessica Lange is superb as the starlet who snubs the power structure at every turn and pays a horrifying price for it. Kim Stanley is also impressive as Frances's mother, a money- and fame-hungry hag who uses her daughter. Sam Shepard is the one person who loves Frances for who and what she really is. An unforgettable film. Rated R. 139m. **DIR:** Graeme Clifford. **CAST:** Jessica Lange, Kim Stanley, Sam Shepard, Jeffrey DeMunn. **1982**

FRANCIS GARY POWERS: THE TRUE STORY OF THE U-2 SPY INCIDENT ★★★½ In this made-for-television movie, the infamous 1960 U-2 spy plane shoot down over Russia is dramatized. The best performances in this true story are supplied by the supporting cast. Based on U-2 pilot Francis Gary Powers's book, it's worth viewing. 120m. **DIR:** Delbert Mann. **CAST:** Lee Majors, Noah Beery Jr., Nehemiah Persoff, Brooke Bundy, William Daniels, James Gregory, Lew Ayres. **1976**

FRANKIE AND JOHNNY (1934) 🦃 Poorly acted costume drama inspired by the now-legendary love-triangle song. B&W; 66m. **DIR:** Chester Erskine. **CAST:** Helen Morgan, Chester Morris, Lilyan Tashman. **1934**

FRANKIE AND JOHNNY (1991) ★★★½ It's the supporting characters in this angst-ridden Terrence McNally drama who make it such a treat. Set primarily in a diner, *Frankie and Johnny* offers occasionally deft and delicious servings of one-liners; but Al Pacino and Michelle Pfeiffer are somehow not quite right in their roles as unlikely lovers. Rated R for profanity and nudity. 117m. **DIR:** Garry Marshall. **CAST:** Al Pacino, Michelle Pfeiffer, Hector Elizondo, Kate Nelligan, Nathan Lane, Jane Morris. **1991**

FREE SOUL, A ★★½ Primarily a showcase for Lionel Barrymore, who won an Oscar for his role of a cantankerous attorney. The character is based on Adela Rogers St. John's father, a lawyer known for his colorful but irascible ways. Remade as *The Girl Who Had Everything*. With Elizabeth Taylor. B&W; 89m. **DIR:** Clarence Brown. **CAST:** Clark Gable, Lionel Barrymore, Norma Shearer, Leslie Howard, James Gleason. **1931**

FREE, WHITE, AND 21 ★★ A southern black man is accused of raping a white woman who is working for the civil rights movement. The main attraction of this dated movie is that it is made in a pseudodocumentary style—as a trial during which the testimony is shown in the form of flashbacks. Interesting, though very overlong. B&W; 102m. **DIR:** Larry Buchanan. **CAST:** Frederick O'Neal, Annalena Lund. **1963**

FRENCH LIEUTENANT'S WOMAN, THE ★★★★★ A brilliant adaptation of John Fowles' bestseller, starring Meryl Streep as the enigmatic title heroine and Jeremy Irons as her obsessed lover. Victorian and modern attitudes on love are contrasted in this intellectually and emotionally engrossing film. Rated R because of sexual references and sex scenes. 123m. **DIR:** Karel Reisz. **CAST:** Meryl Streep, Jeremy Irons, Leo McKern, Hilton McRae, Emily Morgan. **1981**

FRENCH QUARTER ★★½ Everyone in the cast plays two characters, one in modern times and one at the turn of the century, in this drama set in New Orleans. Both stories are connected by voodoo magic, as a woman discovers she is the reincarnation of a prostitute. Slow-moving but intriguing. Rated R for sexual situations. 101m. **DIR:** Dennis Kane. **CAST:** Bruce Davison, Virginia Mayo. **1977**

FRENCH WOMAN, THE ★★ Laughable erotic thriller loosely based on the best-selling memoirs of Madame Claude, who operated a "modeling agency" of high-priced hookers. Rated R for nudity. 97m. **DIR:** Just Jaeckin. **CAST:** Françoise Fabian, Murray Head, Dayle Haddon, Klaus Kinski, Robert Webber. **1977**

FRESH HORSES ★★ Adult version of *Pretty in Pink*. Molly Ringwald continues as the kid from the wrong side of the tracks, only this time there's nothing upbeat about her. Andrew McCarthy is once again typecast as a middle-class nice guy. Rated PG-13 for profanity and violence. 106m. **DIR:** David Anspaugh. **CAST:** Molly Ringwald, Andrew McCarthy, Patti D'Arbanville. **1988**

FRIED GREEN TOMATOES ★★★★ Adapted from Fannie Flagg's novel, *Fried Green Tomatoes at the Whistle Stop Café*, this touching motion picture is essentially the story of friendships between two sets of women. Kathy Bates is the put-upon, overweight housewife who finds herself in the rec room of a senior citizens' home listening to Jessica Tandy's tales of the Depression-era adventures of Mary Stuart Masterson and Mary-Louise Parker. It's wonderful. Rated PG-13 for profanity and violence. 120m. **DIR:** Jon Avnet. **CAST:** Kathy Bates, Mary Stuart Masterson, Mary-Louise Parker, Jessica Tandy, Cicely Tyson, Chris O'Donnell, Stan Shaw, Gailard Sartain, Lois Smith. **1991**

FRIENDLY FIRE ★★★★ A gripping account of an American couple who run into government indifference when they attempt to learn the truth about their son's death—by American artillery fire—in Vietnam. Based on a true story. Both Carol Burnett and Ned Beatty give smashing performances as the grieved couple. Picture won four Emmy awards. Not rated; made for TV. 180m. **DIR:** David Greene. **CAST:** Carol Burnett, Ned Beatty, Sam Waterston, Timothy Hutton. **1979**

FRIENDLY PERSUASION ★★★★ Jessamyn West's finely crafted novel of a Quaker family beset by the realities of the Civil War in southern Indiana is superbly transferred to film by an outstanding cast guided by gifted direction. 140m. **DIR:** William Wyler. **CAST:** Gary Cooper, Dorothy McGuire, Marjorie Main, Anthony Perkins, Robert Middleton, Richard Eyer. **1956**

FRINGE DWELLERS, THE ★★★★ Bruce Beresford, the Australian filmmaker who directed *Breaker Morant* and *Tender Mercies*, has a tendency to make movies that have rambling stories but fascinating characters and rich performances. That description fits this production, which follows the domestic problems of a family of Aborigines who move from a shantytown to a clean and proper suburban neighborhood. It's an intriguing, touching, but nonsentimental look at a race of people unfamiliar to most Americans. It's rated PG for language. 98m. **DIR:** Bruce Beresford. **CAST:** Justine Saunders, Kristina Nehm, Bob Maza. **1987**

FROM HERE TO ETERNITY (1953) ★★★★★ This smoldering drama, depicting the demands of military life just before America's involvement in World War II, earned the Academy Award for best picture of 1953. This riveting classic includes the historic on-the-beach love scene that turned a few heads during its time. And no wonder! Director Fred Zinnemann took chances with this realistic portrait of the U.S. military. B&W; 118m. **DIR:** Fred Zinnemann. **CAST:** Burt Lancaster, Montgomery Clift, Deborah Kerr, Frank Sinatra, Donna Reed, Ernest Borgnine. **1953**

FROM HERE TO ETERNITY (1979) ★★★ William Devane and Natalie Wood find playtime during wartime in this watchable TV remake of the 1953 movie classic. This glossy melodrama depicts army-base life and a general sense of moral chaos brought on by World War II. 110m. **DIR:** Buzz Kulik. **CAST:** Natalie Wood, William Devane, Steve Railsback, Kim Basinger. **1979**

FROM THE TERRACE ★★ Overblown denouncement of the struggle for success and the almighty dollar is just so much Technicolor trash despite the luminous presence of Paul Newman and Joanne Woodward. 144m. **DIR:** Mark Robson. **CAST:** Paul Newman, Joanne Woodward, Myrna Loy, Ina Balin, Leon Ames, Elizabeth Allen, Barbara Eden, George Grizzard, Patrick O'Neal, Felix Aylmer. **1960**

FRONT, THE ★★★★ Focusing on the horrendous blacklist of entertainers in the 1950s, this film manages to drive its point home with wit and poignance. This film is about writers who find a man to submit their scripts to after they have been blacklisted. Woody Allen plays the title role. Rated PG. 94m. **DIR:** Martin Ritt. **CAST:** Woody Allen, Zero Mostel, Andrea Marcovicci, Joshua Shelley, Georgann Johnson. **1976**

FUGITIVE, THE (1947) ★★★ Intriguing John Ford version of Graham Greene novel is a flawed minor masterpiece. Complex story about a self-doubting priest escaping a relentless police lieutenent in Mexico where the government strives to control the Catholic church. B&W; 99m. **DIR:** John Ford. **CAST:** Henry Fonda, Dolores Del Rio, Pedro Armendariz, J. Carrol Naish, Leo Carrillo, Ward Bond, Robert Armstrong, John Qualen. **1947**

FUGITIVE, THE (TV SERIES) ★★★★ Wildly popular TV series that featured an innocent man (David Janssen) falsely convicted of murdering his wife and sentenced to death. Escaping, he becomes both pursuer and pursued as he seeks the one-armed man he saw at the scene of the crime while evading a single-minded police lieutenant (Barry Morse). Each episode features well-known stars, most of whom try to help the likable Janssen. Volumes 1 to 5, 105m. each. **DIR:** Richard Donner, William A. Graham, Jerry Hopper. **CAST:** David Janssen, Barry Morse, Bill Raisch, Mickey Rooney, Suzanne Pleshette, Susan Oliver, Ron Howard, Kurt Russell, John McIntire. **1963–1966**

FUGITIVE KIND, THE ★★ This picture takes Tennessee Williams's stage play *Orpheus Descending*, shakes it up, and lets a new story line fall out. Marlon Brando is a wanderer who woos southern belles while strumming a guitar. As one of the wooed, Joanne Woodward gives a fine performance. B&W; 135m. **DIR:** Sidney Lumet. **CAST:** Marlon Brando, Joanne Woodward, Anna Magnani, Victor Jory. **1959**

FUGITIVE ROAD 🦃 Erich Von Stroheim as a border guard helping immigrants escape to America. 69m. **DIR:** Frank Strayer. **CAST:** Erich Von Stroheim. **1934**

FULFILLMENT ★★ When an impotent farmer senses his wife's attraction to his visiting brother, he suggests that she sleep with the other man to conceive the child they can't have. Self-serious made-for-TV drama, originally shown as *The Fulfillment of Mary Gray*. Unrated, the film features sexual situations. 96m. **DIR:** Piers Haggard. **CAST:** Cheryl Ladd, Ted Levine, Lewis Smith. **1989**

FULL EXPOSURE ★★ Seedy, made-for-TV crime-drama features Anthony Denison as a police detective on a case involving a murdered call girl and her missing video diary of clients. He's teamed with rookie Lisa Hartman, and things really heat up when she goes undercover as a call girl and finds herself attracted to the lifestyle. Not rated. 95m. **DIR:** Noel Nosseck. **CAST:** Lisa Hartman, Anthony Denison, Jennifer O'Neill, Vanessa Williams. **1989**

FULL METAL JACKET ★★★★ Stanley Kubrick and Vietnam? How can that combination miss? Well, it does and it doesn't. Kubrick scores higher in smaller moments than in scenes seemingly intended to be climactic. Don't be surprised if days later, fragments of what you saw and heard are still with you. Particularly memorable is Lee Ermey as Gunnery Sgt. Hartman. Rated R for violence and some inventive and colorful profanity. 120m. **DIR:** Stanley Kubrick. **CAST:** Matthew Modine, Adam Baldwin, Vincent D'Onofrio, R. Lee Ermey, Dorian Harewood, Arliss Howard, Ed O'Ross. **1987**

FUN DOWN THERE 🦃 Extremely low-budget saga of a small-town dork who comes to New York City to explore his homosexual tendencies. Unrated, contains nudity and profanity. 89m. **DIR:** Roger Stigilano. **CAST:** Michael Waite, Nickolas Nagurney. **1988**

FURY ★★★★ A stranger in a small town (Spencer Tracy) becomes the innocent victim of a lynch mob and turns into a one-man mob himself when he luckily survives. The script gets a bit contrived toward the end, but it's still powerful stuff, brutally well directed by Fritz Lang. B&W; 94m. **DIR:** Fritz Lang. **CAST:** Sylvia Sidney, Spencer Tracy, Walter Abel, Edward Ellis, Bruce Cabot, Walter Brennan. **1936**

FUTZ ★★ Once controversial, now merely a curiosity piece, this film adaptation of an avant-garde play by New York's famed La Mama troupe is like something out of a time capsule. There's no real plot, but it's set in a farm community where one farmer is ostracized for falling in love with his prize pig Amanda. Unrated, contains nudity and sexual situations. 92m. **DIR:** Tom O'Horgan. **CAST:** Seth Allen, Sally Kirkland. **1969**

GABRIEL OVER THE WHITE HOUSE ★★★ A corrupt politician becomes president and then experiences a change of heart, soul, and mind. A highly moralistic fable intended as a tribute to FDR and a condemnation of the presidents who preceded him. Acted with sincerity and directed with a sentimental hand. B&W; 87m. **DIR:** Gregory La Cava. **CAST:** Walter Huston, Franchot Tone, Jean Parker, Karen Morley, Dickie Moore, C. Henry Gordon, Samuel S. Hinds. **1933**

GABY, A TRUE STORY ★★★★ Rachel Levin gives a smashing portrayal of a brilliant young woman trapped in a body incapacitated by cerebral palsy. Based on the true-life drama of Gabriela Brimmer. Assisted by a screenplay that steers clear of maudlin situations, the cast delivers powerful performances. Rated R for profanity and sexual frankness. 120m. **DIR:** Luis Mandoki. **CAST:** Liv Ullmann, Norma Aleandro, Robert Loggia, Rachel Levin, Lawrence Monoson, Robert Beltran. **1987**

GAL YOUNG 'UN ★★★ Set in the early 1900s, this charming low-budget film focuses on a young man who woos a lonely, elderly (and comparatively rich) widow. He cons her into marriage with his boyish charm and uses her money to set up his own moonshine still. Featuring fine performances and good use of locations, this film is not rated. 105m. **DIR:** Victor Nunez. **CAST:** Dana Peru, David Peck, J. Smith-Cameron. **1986**

GALLANT HOURS, THE ★★★½ This is not an action epic, but a thoughtful view of the ordeal of command, with James Cagney in a fine performance as Fleet Admiral William F. Halsey, Jr. Done in semidocumentary style, following Halsey's command from 1942 through the battle of Guadalcanal. B&W; 111m. **DIR:** Robert Montgomery. **CAST:** James Cagney, Dennis Weaver, Ward Costello, Richard Jaeckel. **1960**

GALLIPOLI ★★★★½ Add this to the list of outstanding motion pictures from Australia and the very best films about war. Directed by Peter Weir this appealing character study, which is set during World War I, manages to say more about life on the battlefront than many of the more straightforward pictures in the genre. Rated PG because of violence. 110m. **DIR:** Peter Weir. **CAST:** Mark Lee, Mel Gibson, Robert Grubb, Tim McKenzie, David Argue. **1981**

GAMBLE ON LOVE ★★ Las Vegas provides the backdrop for this slow-moving film. Liz (Beverly Garland) inherits a casino from her father and falls in love with the brash casino manager. This relationship leads to an explosive climax. 105m. **DIR:** Jim Balden. **CAST:** Beverly Garland. **1982**

GAMBLER, THE (1974) ★★★½ This gritty film features James Caan in one of his best screen portrayals as a compulsive, self-destructive gambler. Director Karel Reisz keeps the atmosphere thick with tension. Always thinking he's on the edge of a big score, Caan's otherwise intelligent college professor character gets him deeper and deeper into trouble. It's a downer, but still worth watching. Rated R. 111m. **DIR:** Karel Reisz. **CAST:** James Caan, Paul Sorvino, Lauren Hutton, Jacqueline Brooks, Morris Carnovsky. **1974**

GAMBLER AND THE LADY, THE 🦃 This British production dramatizes the troubles of a gambler who falls in love with a beautiful woman. B&W; 71m. **DIR:** Patrick Jenkins. **CAST:** Dane Clark, Kathleen Byron, Naomi Chance. **1952**

GAME OF LOVE, THE ★★½ A group of people (young, old, single, married, and divorced) congregate at a local night spot in this routine romantic drama. Ken Olin is the bar owner who oversees the whole scene and gives out advice. Rated PG for adult themes. 94m. **DIR:** Bobby Roth. **CAST:** Ken Olin, Ed Marinaro, Max Gail, Robert Rusler, Belinda Bauer, Tracy Nelson, Jack Blessing, Gerrit Graham, Janet Margolin, Brynn Thayer. **1987**

GANDHI ★★★★★ One of the finest screen biographies in the history of motion pictures, this film, by Richard Attenborough, chronicles the life of the deceased Indian leader (Ben Kingsley). Running three hours, it is an old-style "big" picture, with spectacle, great drama, superb performances, and, as they used to say, a cast of thousands. Yet for all its hugeness, *Gandhi* achieves a remarkable intimacy. Afterward, viewers feel as if they have actually known—and, more important, been touched by—the man Indians called the "Great Soul." Rated PG for violence. 188m. **DIR:** Richard Attenborough. **CAST:** Ben Kingsley, Candice Bergen, Edward Fox, John

Gielgud, Martin Sheen, John Mills, Trevor Howard, Saeed Jaffrey, Roshan Seth. 1982

GANGSTER, THE ★★½ Slow-moving film about a gang boss with an attitude just doesn't make the grade despite a great cast and realistic locales. B&W; 82m. **DIR:** Gordon Wiles. **CAST:** Barry Sullivan, Belita, Joan Lorring, Akim Tamiroff, Harry Morgan, John Ireland, Sheldon Leonard, Elisha Cook Jr., Leif Erickson, Charles McGraw. 1947

GANGSTER'S BOY ★★½ Jackie Cooper's first dramatic role uses every cliché possible to showcase his boyish appeal. His role of the school valedictorian ostracized by his classmates when they learn that his father was a bootlegger was intended to make him the James Dean of his day. It didn't. B&W; 79m. **DIR:** William Nigh. **CAST:** Jackie Cooper, Robert Warwick, Betty Blythe. 1938

GANGSTER'S LAW 🦃 Mafia story filmed in Italy. Dubbed. 89m. **DIR:** Siro Marcellini. **CAST:** Klaus Kinski, Maurice Poli, Suzy Andersen, Max Delys. 1986

GARDEN, THE ★★★ Uncompromising film from controversial director Derek Jarman tackles the Church's persecution of homosexuality by depicting the passion play as a celebration of life between two male lovers. Jarman's juxtaposition of traditional events and those experienced by the lovers makes for a visual feast, but some may find the comparison sacrilegious. Not rated, but contains nudity and adult situations. 90m. **DIR:** Derek Jarman. **CAST:** Tilda Swinton, Johnny Mills, Phillip MacDonald, Roger Cook, Kevin Collins. 1990

GARDEN OF ALLAH, THE ★★ Gloriously photographed, yawnable yarn of romance in the Algerian boondocks. However, the early Technicolor—which won a special Oscar—is outstanding. Could be retitled: *Marlene's Manhunt.* 80m. **DIR:** Richard Boleslawski. **CAST:** Marlene Dietrich, Charles Boyer, Tilly Losch, John Carradine, Basil Rathbone, Joseph Schildkraut. 1936

GARDENS OF STONE ★★★½ A poignant drama examining the self-described toy soldiers who officiate at military funerals at Virginia's Fort Myer, adjacent to Arlington National Cemetery. The setting is the Vietnam 1960s, and James Caan stars as a disillusioned sergeant. D. B. Sweeney is excellent as the young recruit who is taken under Caan's wing, but James Earl Jones walks away with his every scene as the poetically foulmouthed Sergeant Major "Goody" Nelson. Rated R for profanity. 111m. **DIR:** Francis Ford Coppola. **CAST:** James Caan, Anjelica Huston, James Earl Jones, D. B. Sweeney, Dean Stockwell, Mary Stuart Masterson, Dick Anthony Williams, Lonette McKee, Sam Bottoms. 1987

GAS, FOOD, LODGING ★★★★½ Richard Peck's insightful coming-of-age novel gets first-rate treatment from scripter-director Allison Anders, who has fashioned a superb study of three women frustrated by their dead-end lives in a small New Mexico town. Harried single mom Brooke Adams works as a waitress while trying to find time for her two daughters. Great performances all around. Rated R for profanity and simulated sex. 100m. **DIR:** Allison Anders. **CAST:** Brooke Adams, Ione Skye, Fairuza Balk, James Brolin. 1992

GATHERING, THE ★★★★ Winner of the Emmy for outstanding TV drama special of 1977–1978, this powerful tearjerker features Ed Asner as Adam Thornton. He returns to the family he abandoned after learning that he's dying. The reunion with his family occurs at Christmas and succeeds mainly because his estranged wife (Maureen Stapleton) encourages her children to forgive and forget the past. 104m. **DIR:** Randal Kleiser. **CAST:** Edward Asner, Maureen Stapleton, Lawrence Pressman. 1977

GATHERING, PART II, THE ★★★½ Picking up two years after *The Gathering,* this sequel opens with Kate (Maureen Stapleton) managing her late husband's business. When she falls in love with a business tycoon, she decides to break the news to her grown children over Christmas dinner. 104m. **DIR:** Charles S. Dubin. **CAST:** Maureen Stapleton, Rebecca Balding, Efrem Zimbalist Jr., Jameson Parker. 1979

GATHERING STORM 🦃 Winston Churchill's life from 1937 to the start of World War II. 72m. **DIR:** Herbert Wise. **CAST:** Richard Burton, Virginia McKenna, Robert Hardy, Ian Bannen. 1974

GENE KRUPA STORY, THE ★★ A fictionalized biography of the late great drummer Gene Krupa. The film borrows facts when needed. Krupa's addiction to drugs is handled with delicacy. B&W; 101m. **DIR:** Don Weis. **CAST:** Sal Mineo, Susan Kohner, Susan Oliver, James Darren, Yvonne Craig, Red Nichols. 1959

GENTLEMAN BANDIT, THE ★★★ Ralph Waite gives a convincing portrait of Father Pagano, who was accused of a series of armed robberies in 1978. This made-for-TV biography chronicles his ordeal when mistakenly identified by seven eyewitnesses. Good viewing. 96m. **DIR:** Jonathan Kaplan. **CAST:** Ralph Waite, Julie Bovasso, Jerry Zaks, Joe Grifasi, Estelle Parsons, Vincent Spano. 1981

GENTLEMAN JIM ★★★★½ Errol Flynn has a field day in this beautifully filmed biography of heavyweight champion Jim Corbett. Always cocky and light on his feet, Flynn is a joy to behold and will make those who considered him a star instead of a actor think twice. Ward Bond is equally fine as John L. Sullivan. Said to have been Flynn's favorite role. B&W; 104m. **DIR:** Raoul Walsh. **CAST:** Errol Flynn, Jack Carson, Alan Hale Sr., Alexis Smith. **1942**

GENTLEMEN'S AGREEMENT ★★★½ A writer doing a feature on anti-Semitism passes himself off as a Jew. Along with the anticipated problems, he gets surprising reactions from friends and coworkers. With 1947's *Crossfire* this was a Hollywood pacesetter in attacking bigotry, but it has lost some bite. Oscars for the best picture, director Elia Kazan, and supporting actress Celeste Holm. B&W; 118m. **DIR:** Elia Kazan. **CAST:** Gregory Peck, Dorothy McGuire, John Garfield, Celeste Holm, Anne Revere, June Havoc, Albert Dekker, Jane Wyatt, Dean Stockwell, Sam Jaffe. **1947**

GEORGE MCKENNA STORY, THE ★★★½ Based on a true story, a new principal tries to make a gang-ridden high school a better place to learn. He gains the respect of the students and most of the faculty, but a few teachers try to have him removed. Denzel Washington does a nice job of portraying the compassionate principal, and Lynn Whitfield is wonderful as his neglected wife. Not rated, but contains violence. 93m. **DIR:** Eric Laneville. **CAST:** Denzel Washington, Lynn Whitfield, Akosua Busia, Richard Masur. **1986**

GEORGE WASHINGTON ★★★½ Sweeping made-for-TV chronicle of George Washington (Barry Bostwick) as surveyor and fighter in the French and Indian Wars through his years as commander of the victorious colonial army. Some dull home scenes at Mount Vernon but there are ample battles and some fascinating revelations of the infighting among the "professional" generals who surrounded him. Bostwick seems to grow more sure of his role as the movie progresses, perhaps as it should be. Based on the books of James Thomas Flexner. A sequel, *George Washington: The Forging of a Nation*, followed. 408m. **DIR:** Buzz Kulik. **CAST:** Barry Bostwick, Patty Duke, David Dukes, Jaclyn Smith, Lloyd Bridges, José Ferrer, Hal Holbrook, Trevor Howard, Jeremy Kemp, Richard Kiley, Stephen Macht, James Mason, Rosemary Murphy, Clive Revill, Robert Stack, Anthony Zerbe. **1984**

GEORGE WASHINGTON: THE FORGING OF A NATION ★★★½ A fine made-for-TV sequel to 1984's *George Washington*, with Barry Bostwick again impressive as the reluctant first president of the United States. The film covers his two terms in office and the myriad problems he faced as the leader of a new nation. Jeffrey Jones and Richard Bekins are outstanding as Thomas Jefferson and Alexander Hamilton, whose jealousy of each other almost destroyed the leader they served and admired. 210m. **DIR:** William A. Graham. **CAST:** Barry Bostwick, Patty Duke, Jeffrey Jones, Richard Bekins, Penny Fuller, Lise Hilboldt. **1986**

GEORGIA, GEORGIA ★★ This film, adapted by Maya Angelou from one of her stories, is a dated but fairly interesting study of racism. The story centers around the relationship between a white photographer and a black singer. If you get mildly involved with this movie, stay with it. Rated R. 91m. **DIR:** Stig Bjorknan. **CAST:** Diana Sands, Dirk Benedict, Minnie Gentry, Roger Furman. **1972**

GETTING OF WISDOM, THE ★★★★ Out of Australia, this better-than-average rites-of-passage story of an unrefined country girl (Susannah Fowle) who gets sent off to school in the city displays all the qualities of top-notch directing. The girl is easy prey for her more sophisticated, yet equally immature classmates. The story takes place in the mid-1800s and is taken from the classic Australian novel by Henry Handel Richardson. Not rated, but the equivalent of a G. 100m. **DIR:** Bruce Beresford. **CAST:** Susannah Fowle, Sheila Helpmann, Patricia Kennedy, Hilary Ryan. **1980**

GETTING OVER 🦃 This low-budget black exploitation flick is so poorly lit that it's hard to discern the facial expressions of the actors. Unrated; it contains profanity. 108m. **DIR:** Bernie Rollins. **CAST:** John Daniels, Gwen Brisco, Paulette Gibson. **1980**

GETTING PHYSICAL ★★★½ Alexandra Paul plays Nadine, a pudgy junk-food addict who decides to toughen up after her purse is stolen. Couch potatoes can vicariously experience the joy of Nadine's transformation from chubby wimp to lean bodybuilder. A must-see for everyone who dreams about a fitter life-style. Made for television, this is unrated and very mild. 95m. **DIR:** Steven H. Stern. **CAST:** Alexandra Paul, Sandahl Bergman, David Naughton. **1984**

GETTING STRAIGHT ★★½ During the campus riots of the 1960s, Hollywood jumped on the bandwagon with such forgettable films as *The Strawberry Statement* and *R.P.M.* Add *Getting Straight* to the list. Elliott Gould plays a "hip" graduate student caught up in campus unrest. It now seems like an odd curio. Rated PG. 124m. **DIR:** Richard Rush. **CAST:** Elliott Gould, Candice Bergen, Max Julien, Jeff Corey, Robert F. Lyons. **1970**

GETTYSBURG ★★ Civil War buffs will revel in the authenticity writer-director Ronald F. Maxwell brings to this epic film, while all others will find it overlong and lethargic. That said, the sections in the first half of the movie featuring Jeff Daniels and Sam Elliott are superb. Rated PG for violence. 248m. **DIR:** Ronald F. Maxwell. **CAST:** Tom Berenger, Jeff Daniels, Sam Elliott, Martin Sheen, Richard Jordan, Stephen Lang, C. Thomas Howell, Kevin Conway, Andrew Prine, John Diehl, Richard Anderson, Maxwell Caulfield, Timothy Scott, George Lazenby. **1993**

GHOST (1990) ★★★ This generally diverting romantic-fantasy-comedy-drama casts Patrick Swayze as a murder victim who tries to protect his wife (Demi Moore) from his killers with the help of a psychic (Whoopi Goldberg). The scenes between Swayze and Moore are designed to be ultraromantic, Goldberg's scenes are played for laughs, and the crimes are hard-edged. Director Jerry Zucker isn't always successful in balancing so many elements and tones. Rated PG-13 for violence, suggested sex, and profanity. 105m. **DIR:** Jerry Zucker. **CAST:** Patrick Swayze, Demi Moore, Whoopi Goldberg, Tony Goldwyn. **1990**

GHOST IN MONTE CARLO, A ★★ Weak, flimsy period piece mystery concerns revenge and intrigue among the royalty in beautiful Monte Carlo. 93m. **DIR:** John Hough. **CAST:** Sarah Miles, Oliver Reed, Christopher Plummer, Samantha Eggar, Ron Moody, Fiona Fullerton, Lysette Anthony. **1990**

GIANT ★★★½ The third part of director George Stevens's American Trilogy, which also included *Shane* and *A Place in the Sun*, this 1956 release traces the life of a cattle rancher through two generations. Although the lead performances by Elizabeth Taylor, Rock Hudson, and James Dean are unconvincing when the stars are poorly "aged" with make-up, *Giant* is still a stylish, if overlong movie that lives up to its title. 198m. **DIR:** George Stevens. **CAST:** James Dean, Rock Hudson, Elizabeth Taylor, Carroll Baker, Dennis Hopper. **1956**

GIDEON'S TRUMPET ★★★★ Henry Fonda is the chief delight in this factual account of Clarence Earl Gideon, who was thrown into prison in the early 1960s for a minor crime—and denied a legal counsel because he could not afford to pay for one. Gideon boned up on the laws of our land and concluded that everybody was entitled to a lawyer, whether or not such was affordable. This made-for-TV movie accurately follows Anthony Lewis's source book. Unrated; suitable for family viewing. 104m. **DIR:** Robert Collins. **CAST:** Henry Fonda, John Houseman, José Ferrer. **1980**

GIFT OF LOVE, THE ★★ Inspired by, but bearing very little resemblance to, O. Henry's short-story masterpiece "The Gift of the Magi," this fluffy TV special features Marie Osmond and Timothy Bottoms as star-crossed lovers. Osmond's acting skills are minimal, but her turn-of-the-century gowns are splendid. 96m. **DIR:** Don Chaffey. **CAST:** Marie Osmond, Timothy Bottoms, James Woods, June Lockhart. **1978**

GILDA ★★★★ Glenn Ford plays a small-time gambler who goes to work for a South American casino owner and his beautiful wife, Gilda (Rita Hayworth). When the casino owner disappears and is presumed dead, Ford marries Hayworth and they run the casino together. All goes well until the husband returns, seeking revenge against them. There is some violence in this film. B&W; 110m. **DIR:** Charles Vidor. **CAST:** Glenn Ford, Rita Hayworth, George Macready, Joseph Calleia, Steven Geray. **1946**

GIN GAME, THE ★★★★½ A sensitive, insightful, and touchingly funny, award-winning Broadway play taped live in London with its two original stars. The enchanting performances are highlighted with superb simplicity in this two-character play that explores the developing relationship between two senior citizens. Unrated, but freely sprinkled with profanity. 82m. **DIR:** Mike Nichols. **CAST:** Jessica Tandy, Hume Cronyn. **1984**

GINGER IN THE MORNING ★★½ A lonely salesman, Monte Markham, picks up a hitchhiker, Sissy Spacek, and romance blossoms in this okay romantic comedy. No great revelations about human nature will be found in this one, just harmless fluff that will be forgotten soon after it's been viewed. 89m. **DIR:** Gordon Wiles. **CAST:** Sissy Spacek, Monte Markham, Slim Pickens, Susan Oliver, Mark Miller. **1973**

GIRL, THE ★★★ A strange and disturbing European film analyzing the seduction of a powerful attorney by a 14-year-old schoolgirl. Lust, passion, and murder become the norm. Unfortunately, what might have been a very powerful film becomes slow and plods to the finish. Though no rating is available, there is ample sex and nudity throughout the film. 104m. **DIR:** Arne Mattson. **CAST:** Franco Nero, Bernice Stegers, Clare Powney, Christopher Lee. **1986**

GIRL FROM PETROVKA, THE ★★★ American journalist Hal Holbrook falls in love with Russian Goldie Hawn while on assignment in the Soviet Union. The manipulative script often becomes overly melodramatic, but the film still works as an effective tearjerker. Something about Hawn's guileless, resourceful character is impossible to resist, and the story's conclusion packs a surprising punch. Rated PG for adult situations. 104m. **DIR:** Robert Ellis Miller. **CAST:** Goldie Hawn, Hal Holbrook, Anthony Hopkins. **1974**

GIRL IN BLUE, THE ★★½ Trifling romantic drama about a man obsessed with a woman he glimpsed fleetingly years before. Filmed in Montreal. Unrated, the movie contains brief nudity and sexual situations. 105m. **DIR:** George Kaczender. **CAST:** David Selby, Maud Adams. **1973**

GIRL WHO HAD EVERYTHING, THE ★★ A dated melodrama obviously produced to capitalize on Elizabeth Taylor's beauty. She plays the daughter of a lawyer, and she falls in love with a criminal her father is slated to defend in court. Good performances; weak script. B&W; 69m. **DIR:** Richard Thorpe. **CAST:** Elizabeth Taylor, William Powell, Fernando Lamas, Gig Young, James Whitmore. **1953**

GIRLFRIENDS ★★★★ Realistic film about a young Jewish woman who learns to make it on her own after her best friend/roommate leaves to get married. Melanie Mayron's performance is the highlight of this touching and offbeat comic-drama. Rated PG. 88m. **DIR:** Claudia Weill. **CAST:** Melanie Mayron, Anita Skinner, Eli Wallach, Christopher Guest, Viveca Lindfors. **1978**

GIRLS OF HUNTINGTON HOUSE ★★ With Shirley Jones as the teacher in a halfway house for unwed young mothers-to-be, this made-for-TV story explores the plight of a group of young women trying to make a most difficult decision. Simplistic dialogue and plot developments help to water down the impact of this one. 73m. **DIR:** Alf Kjellin. **CAST:** Shirley Jones, Sissy Spacek, Mercedes McCambridge, Pamela Sue Martin. **1973**

GIVE 'EM HELL, HARRY! ★★★★ This is the film version of James Whitmore's wonderful portrayal of President Harry S. Truman. Taken from the stage production, the film is a magnificent tribute and entertainment. Rated PG. 102m. **DIR:** Steve Binder. **CAST:** James Whitmore. **1975**

GLADIATOR ★★★ A middle-class kid moves to the tough South Side of Chicago, where he gets involved with the world of illegal underground boxing. Some down-and-dirty fight scenes and the presence of character actors Brian Dennehy, Robert Loggia, and Ossie Davis make this film more than a clone of *Rocky*. Rated R for violence, profanity, and nudity. 98m. **DIR:** Rowdy Herrington. **CAST:** James Marshall, Cuba Gooding Jr., Robert Loggia, Ossie Davis, Brian Dennehy, John Heard. **1992**

GLASS HOUSE, THE ★★★★ This powerful prison drama is based on a story by Truman Capote. An idealistic new prison guard (Clu Gulager) is overwhelmed by the gang violence within the prison. Alan Alda plays a new prisoner who becomes the target of a violent gang leader (Vic Morrow). R for sex and violence. 89m. **DIR:** Tom Gries. **CAST:** Vic Morrow, Clu Gulager, Billy Dee Williams, Dean Jagger, Alan Alda. **1972**

GLASS MENAGERIE, THE ★★★★ Director Paul Newman made this impressive screen drama to immortalize wife Joanne Woodward's excellent portrayal of faded southern belle Amanda Winfield, whose strong opinions tend to make her adventure-hungry son (John Malkovich) miserable, and drive her shy daughter (Karen Allen) deeper within herself. This is the best film version to date of Tennessee Williams's semiautobiographical play. Rated PG. 134m. **DIR:** Paul Newman. **CAST:** Joanne Woodward, John Malkovich, Karen Allen, James Naughton. **1987**

GLEN OR GLENDA ★★ Incredible film by the incomparably *inept* Edward D. Wood Jr., tells the powerful story of a young transvestite who finally summons up the courage to come out of the closet and ask his fiancée if he can wear her sweater. B&W; 67m. **DIR:** Edward D. Wood Jr. **CAST:** Bela Lugosi, Dolores Fuller, Daniel Davis, Lyle Talbot, Timothy Farrell, George Weiss. **1953**

GLENGARRY GLEN ROSS ★★★★★ Powerhouse performances and a blistering script highlight David Mamet's adaptation of his own Pulitzer-winning stage play, set during 24 frantic hours in the lives of four rapacious real estate salesmen. Al Pacino and Jack Lemmon are the two central players, the former a relaxed "closer" able to entice anybody into anything, the latter increasingly frantic over a lengthy bad streak. Rated R for relentless profanity. 120m. **DIR:** James Foley. **CAST:** Al Pacino, Jack Lemmon, Ed Harris, Alan Arkin, Kevin Spacey, Jonathan Pryce, Alec Baldwin. **1992**

GLORY ★★★★★ If nothing else, *Glory* rights a terrible wrong. It brings to light the fact that black soldiers fought valiantly on the side of the Union during the Civil War. Yet this excellent film is more than an important lesson in history; it is also a fully involving antiwar movie blessed with unforgettable scenes and scintillating actors (including Oscar-recipient Denzel Washington). Rated R for violence and brief profanity. 202m. **DIR:** Edward Zwick. **CAST:** Matthew Broderick, Denzel Washington, Cary Elwes, Morgan Freeman. **1989**

GO FOR BROKE! ★★★½ This a paean to the grit and guts of the Japanese-Americans who comprised the 442nd Regiment during World War II. Their gallantry and team spirit, in the face of homefront prejudice and battlefront horror, earned them a nation's respect and presidential citation for outstanding accomplishments in combat. 90m. **DIR:** Robert Pirosh. **CAST:** Van Johnson, Warner Anderson. **1951**

GOD BLESS THE CHILD ★★★★ Inspiring made-for-TV drama about one man's fight to insure that a homeless mother and her daughter get the help and find the dignity they deserve. Mare Winningham delivers a heartbreaking performance as the woman abandoned in a new city by her husband. Winningham struggles to raise her daughter under extreme circumstances, and social worker Dorian Harewood changes their lives in this roller coaster of emotions. Grace Johnston will steal your heart as the understanding daughter. Not rated. 93m. **DIR:** Larry Elikann. **CAST:** Mare Winningham, Dorian Harewood, Grace Johnston. **1988**

GODDESS, THE ★★★ A lonely girl working in a Maryland five-and-dime dreams of film stardom, goes to Hollywood, clicks in a minor role, and makes the big time, only to find it all bittersweet. Stage star Kim Stanley, largely ignored by Hollywood, does well in the title role, though she was far from suited for it. Paddy Chayefsky supposedly based his screenplay on Marilyn Monroe. B&W; 105m. **DIR:** John Cromwell. **CAST:** Kim Stanley, Lloyd Bridges, Betty Lou Holland, Joyce Van Patten, Steven Hill. **1958**

GODFATHER, THE ★★★★★ Mario Puzo's popular novel comes to life in artful fashion. Filmed in foreboding tones, the movie takes us into the lurid world of the Mafia. Marlon Brando won an Oscar for his performance, but it's Al Pacino who grabs your attention with an unnerving intensity. Rated R. 175m. **DIR:** Francis Ford Coppola. **CAST:** Marlon Brando, Al Pacino, James Caan, Richard Castellano, John Cazale, Diane Keaton, Talia Shire, Robert Duvall, Sterling Hayden, John Marley, Richard Conte, Al Lettieri. **1972**

GODFATHER, PART II, THE ★★★★★ This is a sequel that equals the quality of the original, an almost unheard-of circumstance in Hollywood. Director Francis Ford Coppola skillfully meshes past and present, intercutting the story of young Don Corleone (Robert De Niro), an ambitious, immoral immigrant, and his son Michael (Al Pacino), who lives up to his father's expectations, turning the family's crime organization into a sleek, cold, modern operation. This gripping film won seven Academy Awards. Rated R. 200m. **DIR:** Francis Ford Coppola. **CAST:** Al Pacino, Robert Duvall, Diane Keaton, Robert De Niro, John Cazale, Talia Shire, Lee Strasberg, Michael Gazzo. **1974**

GODFATHER, PART III, THE ★★★★½ From the first frame of this operatic, Shakespeare-influenced final chapter in the screen's finest gangster epic, we are thrust back into the larger-than-life world of the Corleone family. It is two decades after the "modern-day" events in *Part II*, and Michael (a brilliant performance by Al Pacino) has managed to move the family interests out of crime and into legitimate enterprises. But sinister forces lurking within his empire compel Michael to revert to the old, violent ways—with tragic consequences. Rated R for violence and profanity. 163m. **DIR:** Francis Ford Coppola. **CAST:** Al Pacino, Diane Keaton, Talia Shire, Andy Garcia, Eli Wallach, Joe Mantegna, Sofia Coppola, George Hamilton, Richard Bright, Helmut Berger, Don Novello, John Savage. **1990**

GODFATHER EPIC, THE ★★★★★ Few screen creations qualify as first-class entertainment and cinematic art. Francis Ford Coppola's *The Godfather* series unquestionably belongs in that category. Yet as good as *The Godfather* and *The Godfather, Part II* are, they are no match for *The Godfather Epic*. A compilation of the two films with extra scenes added, it is nothing less than a masterwork. By editing the two films together in chronological order, for the videotape release of *The Godfather Epic*, Coppola has created a work greater than the sum of its parts. See it! Rated R. 380m. **DIR:** Francis Ford Coppola. **CAST:** Marlon Brando, Talia Shire, James Caan, Robert Duvall, John Cazale, Al Pacino, Diane Keaton, Robert De Niro. **1977**

GOD'S LITTLE ACRE ★★★★ This is a terrific little film focusing on poor Georgia farmers. Robert Ryan gives one of his best performances as an itinerant farmer. Aldo Ray, Jack Lord, and Buddy Hackett lend good support. B&W; 110m. **DIR:** Anthony Mann. **CAST:** Robert Ryan, Aldo Ray, Tina Louise, Jack Lord, Fay Spain, Buddy Hackett. **1958**

GOING MY WAY ★★★★½ Bing Crosby won the best-actor Oscar in 1944 for his delightful portrayal of the easygoing priest who finally wins over his strict superior (Barry Fitzgerald, who also won an Oscar for his supporting role). Leo McCarey wrote and directed this funny, heartwarming character study and netted two Academy Awards for his efforts, as well as crafting the year's Oscar-winning best picture. B&W; 130m. **DIR:** Leo McCarey. **CAST:** Bing Crosby, Barry Fitzgerald, Rise Stevens, Gene Lockhart, Frank McHugh. **1944**

GOLD OF NAPLES, THE ★★★½ A charming quartet of vignettes: Sophia Loren as a wife who cheats on her pizza-baker husband; demon cardplayer Vittorio De Sica being put down by a clever child; Toto as a henpecked husband; and Silvana Mangano playing a married whore whose marital arrangement is more than passing strange. B&W; 107m. **DIR:** Vittorio De Sica. **CAST:** Sophia Loren, Vittorio De Sica, Toto, Silvana Mangano. **1954**

GOLDEN BOY ★★★★ William Holden made a strong starring debut in this screen adaptation of Clifford Odet's play about a musician who becomes a boxer. Though a bit dated today, Holden and costar Barbara Stanwyck still shine. B&W; 100m. **DIR:** Rouben Mamoulian. **CAST:** William Holden, Barbara Stanwyck, Adolphe Menjou, Lee J. Cobb. **1939**

GOLDEN HONEYMOON, THE ★★★★ Delightful adaptation of Ring Lardner's deft and biting story. James Whitmore steals the show as talkative Charley Tate, a crusty old windbag married fifty happy years to his patient wife, Lucy (Teresa Wright). While celebrating their golden anniversary in Florida, she meets up with an old flame, and Charley feels the need to prove that Lucy didn't choose the wrong fella fifty years back. Introduced by Henry Fonda; unrated and suitable for family viewing. 52m. **DIR:** Noel Black. **CAST:** James Whitmore, Teresa Wright, Stephen Elliott, Nan Martin. **1980**

GONE WITH THE WIND ★★★★★ The all-time movie classic with Clark Gable and Vivien Leigh as Margaret Mitchell's star-crossed lovers in the final days of the Old South. Need we say more? 222m. **DIR:** Victor Fleming. **CAST:** Clark Gable, Vivien Leigh, Leslie Howard, Olivia de Havilland, Thomas Mitchell, Hattie McDaniel. 1939

GOOD EARTH, THE ★★★★ Nobel Prize novelist Pearl Buck's engrossing, richly detailed story of a simple Chinese farm couple whose lives are ruined by greed is impressively brought to life in this milestone film. Luise Rainer won the second of her back-to-back best-actress Oscars for her portrayal of the ever-patient wife. The photography and special effects are outstanding. B&W; 138m. **DIR:** Sidney Franklin. **CAST:** Paul Muni, Luise Rainer, Keye Luke, Walter Connolly, Jessie Ralph. 1937

GOOD FATHER, THE ★★★★½ In this brilliant British import, Anthony Hopkins is a walking time bomb. A separation from his wife has left him on the outside of his son's life. Hopkins's reaction is so extreme that he is haunted by nightmares. Director Mike Newell lays on the suspense artfully with this device while detailing the revenge Hopkins plots against the wife of a friend who is in similar circumstances. Rated R for profanity, suggested sex, and stylized violence. 90m. **DIR:** Mike Newell. **CAST:** Anthony Hopkins, Jim Broadbent, Harriet Walter, Simon Callow, Joanne Whalley. 1986

GOOD FIGHT, THE ★★½ Christine Lahti and Terry O'Quinn elevate this courtroom drama above the clichés as divorced attorneys drawn back together after she takes on an impossible case. The chemistry between the two explodes when their love of the law clears the way for a rekindled romance. The best moments take place in the courtroom and not the bedroom. Not rated. 91m. **DIR:** John David Coles. **CAST:** Christine Lahti, Terry O'Quinn, Kenneth Welsh, Lawrence Dane. 1992

GOOD MORNING...AND GOODBYE! ★★ One of Russ Meyer's more obscure movies, and one of the duller ones as well. Unsatisfied wife Alaina Capri fools around until her older husband (Stuart Lancaster) is magically cured of his impotence. Dated—and unrated. 78m. **DIR:** Russ Meyer. **CAST:** Alaina Capri, Stuart Lancaster. 1967

GOOD MORNING, BABYLON ★★★ This follows the misadventures of two brothers who come to America to find their fortunes as artists and find jobs on the production of D. W. Griffith's silent classic, *Intolerance*. The movie has moments of lyrical beauty and its story is sweet. But the dialogue has been translated from Italian in an occasionally awkward fashion. Rated PG-13 for nudity and profanity. 115m. **DIR:** Paolo Taviani, Vittorio Taviani. **CAST:** Vincent Spano, Joaquim de Almeida, Greta Scacchi, Charles Dance. 1987

GOOD MORNING, VIETNAM ★★★½ Robin Williams stars as disc jockey Adrian Cronauer, who briefly ruled Saigon's Armed Forces Radio in 1965. Williams's improvisational monologues are the high points in a film that meanders too much, but Forest Whitaker also shines. Rated R for language and violence. 120m. **DIR:** Barry Levinson. **CAST:** Robin Williams, Forest Whitaker, Tung Thanh Tran, Chintara Sukapatana, Bruno Kirby, Robert Wuhl, J. T. Walsh. 1987

GOOD MOTHER, THE ★★ Single mom Anna (Diane Keaton) finds romance with an irresistible Irish artist (Liam Neeson). Anna's ex-husband accuses the artist of sexually abusing his daughter. This film will make you speculate on the rightness or wrongness of Anna's sexually open child-rearing techniques. Rated R for nudity and obscenities. 104m. **DIR:** Leonard Nimoy. **CAST:** Diane Keaton, Jason Robards Jr., Ralph Bellamy, Liam Neeson, James Naughton. 1988

GOOD WIFE, THE 🦃 One woman's yearning for sexual fulfillment. Rated R. 97m. **DIR:** Ken Cameron. **CAST:** Rachel Ward, Bryan Brown, Sam Neill, Steven Vidler. 1987

GOODBYE AGAIN ★★½ Francoise Sagan melodrama starring Ingrid Bergman as a fashion designer who uses callow Tony Perkins to make noncommittal boyfriend Yves Montand jealous. The Paris settings and capable cast make it painless. Look for Diahann Carroll. 120m. **DIR:** Anatole Litvak. **CAST:** Ingrid Bergman, Anthony Perkins, Yves Montand, Jessie Royce Landis, Peter Bull, Diahann Carroll. 1961

GOODBYE, MR. CHIPS (1939) ★★★★½ Robert Donat creates one of filmdom's most heartwarming roles as Chips, the Latin teacher of an English boys' school. The poignant movie follows Chips from his first bumbling, early teaching days until he becomes a beloved school institution. Greer Garson was introduced to American audiences in the rewarding role of Chips's loving wife. B&W; 114m. **DIR:** Sam Wood. **CAST:** Robert Donat, Greer Garson, John Mills. 1939

GOODBYE, NORMA JEAN ★★★ A depiction of Norma Jean Baker's travels along the rocky road to superstardom as Marilyn Monroe. Her only motivation in life is her dream of becoming a star. Rated R for nudity. 95m. **DIR:** Larry Buchanan. **CAST:** Misty Rowe, Terrence Locke, Patch Mckenzie. 1975

GOODBYE PEOPLE, THE ★★★★ This unashamedly sentimental film is a delight. Martin Balsam is memorable as a man attempting to realize the dream of many years by rebuilding his Coney Island hot dog stand. Pamela Reed and Judd Hirsch, as the young people who help him, turn in outstanding performances, and the hot dog stand itself is a fantastic structure. 104m. **DIR:** Herb Gardner. **CAST:** Judd Hirsch, Martin Balsam, Pamela Reed, Ron Silver, Michael Tucker, Gene Saks. **1984**

GOODFELLAS ★★★★★ No punches are pulled in this violent, mesmerizing movie, which covers thirty years in the life of a Mafia family. Based on the book by Nicholas Pileggi, it features Ray Liotta as a half-Irish, half-Sicilian kid from Brooklyn who achieves his life's ambition of being a gangster when he is adopted by a local "family" headed by Paul Sorvino. Rated R for violence, profanity, and depictions of drug use. 148m. **DIR:** Martin Scorsese. **CAST:** Robert De Niro, Joe Pesci, Ray Liotta, Lorraine Bracco, Paul Sorvino. **1990**

GORE VIDAL'S LINCOLN ★★★★ Fine made-for-TV adaptation of Gore Vidal's novel depicting Lincoln as more of a politician than an idealist. Sam Waterston makes a decent Lincoln but Mary Tyler Moore delivers the performance of a lifetime as a mentally unstable Mary Todd Lincoln. The film focuses on the four years between Lincoln's presidential election and his assassination. Unrated, but contains violence and gore in multiple Civil War battle scenes. 118m. **DIR:** Lamont Johnson. **CAST:** Sam Waterston, Mary Tyler Moore, Richard Mulligan, Ruby Dee, Stephen Culp, Tom Brennan, Gregory Cooke. **1988**

GORGEOUS HUSSY, THE ★★ This tale of an innkeeper's daughter who wins the hearts of various political guests is the kind of movie that flickers in the bedrooms of insomniacs at three in the morning. B&W; 103m. **DIR:** Clarence Brown. **CAST:** Joan Crawford, Lionel Barrymore, Robert Taylor, Franchot Tone, Melvyn Douglas, James Stewart. **1936**

GORILLAS IN THE MIST ★★★★ Sigourney Weaver stars in this impressive biopic about Dian Fossey, the crusading primatologist whose devotion to the once nearly extinct mountain gorillas of central Africa led to her murder. Rather than present Fossey as a saint, director Michael Apted, screenwriter Anna Hamilton Phelan, and Weaver take great pains to show her complexity. There are some truly unforgettable scenes of Fossey's interaction with the gorillas. Rated PG-13 for profanity, suggested sex, and violence. 129m. **DIR:** Michael Apted. **CAST:** Sigourney Weaver, Bryan Brown, Julie Harris, John Omirah Miluwi. **1988**

GRADUATE, THE ★★★★½ Mike Nichols won an Academy Award for his direction of this touching, funny, unsettling, and unforgettable release about a young man (Dustin Hoffman, in his first major role) attempting to chart his future and develop his own set of values. He falls in love with Katharine Ross, but finds himself seduced by her wily, sexy mother, Anne Bancroft (as Mrs. Robinson). Don't forget the superb sound track of songs by Paul Simon and Art Garfunkel. 105m. **DIR:** Mike Nichols. **CAST:** Dustin Hoffman, Anne Bancroft, Katharine Ross. **1967**

GRAND CANYON ★★★★½ Writer-director Lawrence Kasdan picks up ten years later with the baby-boom generation he first examined in *The Big Chill*. Through a collection of vignettes of daily life, a superb cast portrays what it's like to be 40 in the Nineties. No motion picture is flawless, but this funny, touching, and insightful character study comes pretty close. Rated R for profanity, nudity, and violence. 134m. **DIR:** Lawrence Kasdan. **CAST:** Danny Glover, Kevin Kline, Steve Martin, Mary McDonnell, Mary-Louise Parker, Alfre Woodard. **1991**

GRAND HOTEL ★★★★ World War I is over. Life in the fast lane has returned to Berlin's Grand Hotel, crossroads of a thousand lives, backdrop to as many stories. This anthology of life at various levels won an Oscar for best picture. B&W; 113m. **DIR:** Edmund Goulding. **CAST:** John Barrymore, Greta Garbo, Wallace Beery, Joan Crawford, Lionel Barrymore, Lewis Stone. **1932**

GRAND ISLE ★★★ While on vacation on an island paradise, Kelly McGillis discovers the passion inside of her reawakened when she encounters several men. Handsome production features a gorgeous cast and scenery. Contains nudity and simulated sex. 94m. **DIR:** Mary Lambert. **CAST:** Kelly McGillis, Julian Sands, Glenne Headly, Ellen Burstyn. **1991**

GRAND PRIX ★★½ The cars, the drivers, and the race itself are the real stars of this international epic, beautifully filmed on locations throughout Europe. The four interrelated stories of professional adversaries and their personal lives intrude on the exciting footage of the real thing. Yves Montand, though, does a credible job in what is basically a big-budget soap opera with oil stains. 179m. **DIR:** John Frankenheimer. **CAST:** James Garner, Eva Marie Saint, Yves Montand, Toshiro Mifune, Brian Bedford, Jessica Walter, Antonio Sabato, Adolfo Celi. **1966**

GRANDVIEW, U.S.A. ★★ *Grandview, U.S.A.* is a coming-of-age study lacking in depth and characterization. Rated R for nudity, violence, and profanity. 97m. **DIR:** Randal Kleiser. **CAST:** Jamie Lee Curtis, C. Thomas Howell, Patrick Swayze, Jennifer Jason Leigh, Ramon Bieri, Carole Cook, Troy Donahue, William Windom. **1984**

GRAPES OF WRATH, THE ★★★★★ Henry Fonda stars in this superb screen adaptation of the John Steinbeck novel about farmers from Oklahoma fleeing the Dust Bowl and poverty of their home state only to be confronted by prejudice and violence in California. It's a compelling drama beautifully acted by the director's stock company. B&W; 129m. **DIR:** John Ford. **CAST:** Henry Fonda, John Carradine, Jane Darwell, Russell Simpson, Charley Grapewin, John Qualen. **1940**

GREASER'S PALACE ★★½ You'll either love or hate this one, a retelling of the passion of Christ set in a small western town. Sometimes inventive, sometimes maddening. Not rated. 91m. **DIR:** Robert Downey. **CAST:** Allan Arbus, Luana Anders, Herve Villechaize, Don Calfa. **1972**

GREAT DAN PATCH, THE ★★★ The story of the greatest trotting horse of them all. Good racing scenes. An opera for horse lovers. B&W; 94m. **DIR:** Joseph M. Newman. **CAST:** Dennis O'Keefe, Gail Russell, Ruth Warrick, Charlotte Greenwood. **1949**

GREAT DAY ★★½ Eleanor Roosevelt's impending trip to Great Britain is the background for this tribute to England's women during wartime. Effective quasi-documentary. B&W; 94m. **DIR:** Lance Comfort. **CAST:** Eric Portman, Flora Robson, Sheila Sim. **1945**

GREAT EXPECTATIONS (1946) ★★★★½ A penniless orphan becomes a gentleman through the generosity of a mysterious patron. The second of three film versions of Charles Dickens's classic story. Made at the close of World War II, this version is by far the finest from all standpoints: direction, script, cast, photography, art direction. B&W; 118m. **DIR:** David Lean. **CAST:** John Mills, Alec Guinness, Valerie Hobson, Bernard Miles, Finlay Currie, Martita Hunt, Jean Simmons. **1946**

GREAT EXPECTATIONS (1988) ★★★★ Fine BBC production of Charles Dickens's classic tale about a boy named Pip. This broadcast takes special care to include every plot convolution (and there are many!). While literary enthusiasts will rejoice in this, most casual viewers will be fidgeting with impatience. Best to watch this in two sittings! 300m. **DIR:** Julian Amyes. **CAST:** Stratford Johns, Gerry Sundquist, Joan Hickson. **1988**

GREAT EXPECTATIONS—THE UNTOLD STORY ★★½ This story should *never* have been told. We follow Magwitch, the escaped convict who befriends the little boy in Charles Dickens's *Great Expectations*, as he changes to a rich gentleman in Australia. Not rated. 102m. **DIR:** Tim Burstall. **CAST:** John Stanton, Sigrid Thornton, Robert Coleby, Noel Ferrier. **1987**

GREAT FLAMARION, THE ★★★ Schemer Mary Beth Hughes suckers vaudeville trick-shot artist Erich Von Stroheim into murdering her husband and leaves him to take the fall while she flees with Dan Duryea. Nothing new in the plot line, but Von Stroheim's performance is reward enough. B&W; 78m. **DIR:** Anthony Mann. **CAST:** Erich Von Stroheim, Mary Beth Hughes, Dan Duryea. **1945**

GREAT GABBO, THE ★★★½ Cinema giant Erich Von Stroheim gives a tour-de-force performance as a brilliant but cold ventriloquist whose disregard for the feelings of others comes back to haunt him when he realizes that he has lost the affection of a girl he has come to love. This is a film that lingers in the memory and rates with other fine films about ventriloquism like *Dead Of Night* and *Magic*. B&W; 89m. **DIR:** James Cruze. **CAST:** Erich Von Stroheim, Betty Compson, Don Douglas. **1929**

GREAT GATSBY, THE ★★★ This is a well-mounted, well-acted film that is, perhaps, a bit overlong. However, Robert Redford, the mysterious title character, is marvelous as Gatsby. Bruce Dern is equally memorable as the man who always has been rich and selfish. Rated PG. 144m. **DIR:** Jack Clayton. **CAST:** Robert Redford, Mia Farrow, Karen Black, Sam Waterston, Bruce Dern. **1974**

GREAT GUY ★★ Depression film about a feisty inspector crusading against corruption in the meat-packing business. Not vintage James Cagney… but okay. B&W; 75m. **DIR:** John G. Blystone. **CAST:** James Cagney, Mae Clarke, Edward Brophy. **1936**

GREAT IMPOSTOR, THE ★★★½ The amazing story of Ferdinand Demara is told in engrossing style by director Robert Mulligan. Demara, with natural charm and uncanny adaptability, successfully managed to pose as everything from a clergyman to a doctor. The role is a tour de force for Tony Curtis. Compelling and seasoned with dark humor. 112m. **DIR:** Robert Mulligan. **CAST:** Tony Curtis, Edmond O'Brien, Arthur O'Connell, Gary Merrill. **1960**

GREAT LIE, THE ★★★ Prime soap opera in the tradition of Bette Davis's *The Old Maid*, but this time she is the bitchy one who takes over someone else's child. Mary Astor (an Oscar winner for supporting actress) plays a concert pianist who marries Davis's former lover, George Brent, The marriage turns out to be illegal, and, before they can get married again Brent crashes in the jungle. B&W; 102m. **DIR:** Edmund Goulding. **CAST:** Bette Davis, George Brent, Mary Astor, Hattie McDaniel, Lucile Watson, Jerome Cowan, Grant Mitchell. **1941**

GREAT LOS ANGELES EARTHQUAKE, THE ★★½ The big one hits Los Angeles in this condensed version of the television miniseries. Characters get lost in the trim, leaving only victims of the overblown special effects. Joe Spano is especially embarrassing as the city official afraid to cry wolf. 106m. **DIR:** Larry Elikann. **CAST:** Joanna Kerns, Dan Lauria, Alan Autry, Ed Begley Jr., Joe Spano. **1990**

GREAT LOVE EXPERIMENT, THE ★★ This HBO Family Playhouse special features a nerdy teen who becomes the guinea pig for the in group. To her surprise, she is suddenly pursued by three cool guys and made over by the most popular girl in the senior class. For teens only. 45m. **DIR:** Claudia Weill. **CAST:** Tracy Pollan. **1982**

GREAT SANTINI, THE ★★★★ Robert Duvall's superb performance in the title role is the most outstanding feature of this fine film. The story of a troubled family and its unpredictable patriarch (Duvall), it was released briefly in early 1980 and then disappeared. But thanks to the efforts of the New York film critics, it was rereleased with appropriate hoopla and did well at the box office. Rated PG for profanity and violence. 116m. **DIR:** Lewis John Carlino. **CAST:** Robert Duvall, Blythe Danner, Michael O'Keefe. **1980**

GREAT WALLENDAS, THE ★★★ In this made-for-television movie, Lloyd Bridges stars as the head of the Wallenda family of high-wire artists. Bridges gives one of his most convincing performances as he keeps the spirit and determination of the family alive through their many tragedies. 104m. **DIR:** Larry Elikann. **CAST:** Lloyd Bridges, Britt Ekland, Taina Elg, John van Dreelen, Cathy Rigby, Michael McGuire. **1978**

GREAT WHITE HOPE, THE ★★★ Compelling, emotional character study of the first black heavyweight champion, Jack Johnson, with a supercharged performance by James Earl Jones in the main role. Jones is supported by an equally great cast in this portrait of a man doomed by the prejudice of his society. Rated PG. 101m. **DIR:** Martin Ritt. **CAST:** James Earl Jones, Jane Alexander, Lou Gilbert, Hal Holbrook. **1970**

GREATEST, THE ★★ Muhammad Ali plays himself in this disjointed screen biography, which is poorly directed by Tom Gries. Even the supporting performances don't help much. Rated PG. 101m. **DIR:** Tom Gries. **CAST:** Muhammad Ali, Ernest Borgnine, John Marley, Robert Duvall, James Earl Jones, Roger E. Mosley. **1977**

GREATEST SHOW ON EARTH, THE ★★★★ The 1952 Oscar winner for best picture succeeds in the same manner as its subject, the circus; it's enjoyable family entertainment. Three major stories of backstage circus life all work and blend well in this film. 153m. **DIR:** Cecil B. DeMille. **CAST:** Betty Hutton, James Stewart, Charlton Heston, Cornel Wilde, Dorothy Lamour, Gloria Grahame. **1952**

GREATEST STORY EVER TOLD, THE ★★★ Although this well-meant movie is accurate to the story of Jesus, the viewer tends to be distracted by its long running time and the appearance of Hollywood stars in unexpected roles. 141m. **DIR:** George Stevens. **CAST:** Max von Sydow, Charlton Heston, Carroll Baker, Angela Lansbury, Sidney Poitier, Telly Savalas, José Ferrer, Van Heflin, Dorothy McGuire, John Wayne, Ed Wynn, Shelley Winters. **1965**

GREED ★★★★★ One of the greatest silent films, this is the stark, brilliant study of the corruption of a decent, simple man by the specter of poverty and failed dreams. Gibson Gowland is superb as the bumbling self-taught dentist who marries spinster ZaSu Pitts, loses his trade, and succumbs to avarice-based hatred leading to murder. A masterpiece. Silent. B&W; 133m. **DIR:** Erich Von Stroheim. **CAST:** Gibson Gowland, ZaSu Pitts, Jean Hersholt. **1924**

GREEK TYCOON, THE ★★½ When this film was first shown, it stimulated much controversy and interest, because it promised to tell all about the Aristotle Onassis and Jackie Kennedy romance. Anthony Quinn borrows from his *Zorba the Greek* role to be a convincingly macho and callous Greek shipping tycoon. Unfortunately, the plot was neglected and the story comes across as grade-B soap. Rated R. 106m. **DIR:** J. Lee Thompson. **CAST:** Anthony Quinn, Jacqueline Bisset, Raf Vallone, Edward Albert, Charles Durning, Camilla Sparv, James Franciscus. **1978**

GREEN DOLPHIN STREET ★★ Plodding drama about two sisters, Lana Turner and Donna Reed, in romantic pursuit of the same man, Van Heflin. Special effects, including a whopper of an earthquake, won an Oscar, but do not a film make. B&W; 141m. **DIR:** Victor Saville. **CAST:** Lana Turner, Donna Reed, Van Heflin, Edmund Gwenn, Frank Morgan, Richard Hart. **1947**

GREEN PASTURES ★★★★ A fine all-black cast headed by Rex Ingram as de Lawd brings Marc Connelly's classic fable of life in heaven vividly to the screen. A unique viewing experience. B&W; 90m. **DIR:** William Keighley, Marc Connelly. **CAST:** Rex Ingram, Eddie "Rochester" Anderson. **1936**

GREEN PROMISE, THE ★★★ The hard life of farmers and their families is explored in this surprisingly involving and well-acted film. Walter Brennan gives his usual first-rate performance as the patriarch who toils over and tills the land. B&W; 93m. **DIR:** William D. Russell. **CAST:** Marguerite Chapman, Walter Brennan, Robert Paige, Natalie Wood. **1949**

GRIEVOUS BODILY HARM ★★½ This Australian drama is a well-woven tale about a police detective trying to find his missing wife. The acting is first-rate, as is the script, but director Mark Joffe lets the pace drag from time to time. Rated R. 135m. **DIR:** Mark Joffe. **CAST:** Colin Friels, John Waters, Bruno Lawrence, Shane Briant. **1988**

GRIFFIN AND PHOENIX: A LOVE STORY ★★★½ Strange, haunting tearjerker about two dying people in love with one another and with life. Jill Clayburgh and Peter Falk in the title roles win hearts hands-down and lift spirits as gloom and doom close in. Made for TV. 100m. **DIR:** Daryl Duke. **CAST:** Peter Falk, Jill Clayburgh, Dorothy Tristan. **1976**

GRIFTERS, THE ★★★★ A savagely funny and often shocking adaptation by Donald E. Westlake of Jim Thompson's hard-boiled novel, this black comedy is like a grotesque version of *The Sting*. Anjelica Huston, John Cusack, and Annette Bening are clever crooks who cheat their way through life until the inevitable catches up with them. Rated R for violence, nudity, and profanity. 119m. **DIR:** Stephen Frears. **CAST:** Anjelica Huston, John Cusack, Annette Bening, Pat Hingle, Henry Jones, J. T. Walsh, Charles Napier, Stephen Tobolowsky, Gailard Sartain. **1990**

GRISSOM GANG, THE ★★★ Lurid crime-drama set in the 1920s. A wealthy heiress (Kim Darby) is kidnapped by a family of grotesque rednecks whose leader (Scott Wilson) falls in love with her. This gritty, violent film receives comically uneven direction from Robert Aldrich. Rated R. 127m. **DIR:** Robert Aldrich. **CAST:** Kim Darby, Scott Wilson, Irene Dailey, Tony Musante, Robert Lansing. **1971**

GROSS ANATOMY ★★★ Sort of a *Paper Chase* for med school, this focuses on the very likable son of a fisherman who must accept or reject the cutthroat competition among his peers. A bit contrived but still watchable. Rated PG-13 for profanity. 107m. **DIR:** Thom Eberhardt. **CAST:** Matthew Modine, Daphne Zuniga, Christine Lahti. **1989**

GROUP, THE ★★★ Based on the book by Mary McCarthy about the lives and loves of eight female college friends. Overlong, convoluted semi-sleazy fun. The impressive cast almost makes you forget it's just a catty soap opera. So watch it anyway. 150m. **DIR:** Sidney Lumet. **CAST:** Joan Hackett, Elizabeth Hartman, Shirley Knight, Joanna Pettet, Jessica Walter, James Broderick, Larry Hagman, Richard Mulligan, Hal Holbrook. **1966**

GROWN-UPS ★★ Originally made for cable TV, this theatre piece by cartoonist Jules Feiffer revolves around a writer (Charles Grodin) and his difficulties with his family. Feiffer's dialogue is sharply observed, but there's no real story, and the characters' continual bickering never leads anywhere. 106m. **DIR:** John Madden. **CAST:** Charles Grodin, Martin Balsam, Marilu Henner, Jean Stapleton. **1985**

GUARDIAN, THE (1984) ★★★½ When the tenants of an upper-class New York City apartment house become fed up with the violence of the streets intruding on their building, they hire a live-in guard (Louis Gossett Jr.). While he does manage to rid the building of lawbreakers, some begin to question his methods. This HBO made-for-cable film is notches above most cable fare. Profanity and violence. 102m. **DIR:** David Greene. **CAST:** Martin Sheen, Lou Gossett Jr., Arthur Hill. **1984**

GUESS WHO'S COMING TO DINNER ★★★ This final film pairing of Spencer Tracy and Katharine Hepburn was also one of the first to deal with interracial marriage. Though quite daring at the time of its original release, this movie, directed by the heavy-handed Stanley Kramer, seems rather quaint today. Still, Tracy and Hepburn are fun to watch, and Sidney Poitier and Katharine Houghton (Hepburn's niece) make an appealing young couple. 108m. **DIR:** Stanley Kramer. **CAST:** Spencer Tracy, Katharine Hepburn, Sidney Poitier, Katharine Houghton, Cecil Kellaway, Beah Richards, Virginia Christine. **1967**

GUEST IN THE HOUSE ★★★ This grim melodrama features Anne Baxter as an emotionally disturbed girl who turns an idyllic household into a chaotic nightmare. An engrossing psychological thriller. B&W; 121m. **DIR:** John Brahm. **CAST:** Anne Baxter, Ralph Bellamy, Aline MacMahon, Ruth Warrick, Jerome Cowan. **1944**

GUILTY AS SIN ★★ A courtroom melodrama about a lady lawyer who falls for her handsome client. But the movie is an uneven blend of star power and director's disinterest. 120m. **DIR:** Sidney Lumet. **CAST:** Rebecca DeMornay, Don Johnson, Stephen Lang, Jack Warden. **1993**

GUILTY BY SUSPICION ★★★★ Robert De Niro is marvelous as a Hollywood director who loses his home and ability to make a living after refusing to testify against his friends at a hearing of the House Un-American Activities Committee during the blacklist period of the Fifties. Riveting film by producer-turned-writer-director Irwin Winkler. Rated PG-13 for profanity. 105m. **DIR:** Irwin Winkler. **CAST:** Robert De Niro, Annette Bening, George Wendt, Patricia Wettig, Sam Wanamaker, Ben Piazza, Gailard Sartain, Stuart Margolin, Martin Scorsese. **1991**

GULAG ★★½ This engrossing tale of an American athlete shipped to a Soviet prison camp works at odd moments in spite of a preposterous script. On the other hand, the escape sequence is clever and quite exciting. 120m. **DIR:** Roger Young. **CAST:** David Keith, Malcolm McDowell. **1985**

GUN IN THE HOUSE, A ★★★½ This TV movie stars Sally Struthers as a woman being tried for the handgun murder of a man who broke into her house. Struthers excels in the role. An above-average drama. 100m. **DIR:** Ivan Nagy. **CAST:** Sally Struthers, David Ackroyd, Jeffrey Tambor, Dick Anthony Williams, Millie Perkins. **1981**

GUNCRAZY (1992) 🦃 Small-town bad girl Drew Barrymore's love letters to young convict James LeGros brings him to town upon parole, whereupon the two shoot up the locals. Growin' up sure is hard to do. Rated R for violence, suggested sex, and profanity. 96m. **DIR:** Tamra Davis. **CAST:** Drew Barrymore, James LeGros, Rodney Harvey, Joe Dallesandro, Michael Ironside, Ione Skye. **1992**

GUY NAMED JOE, A ★★★★ Enchanting film has a dead WWII pilot (Spencer Tracy) coming back to Earth from heaven to aid a young aviator (Van Johnson) with his love life and combat missions. MGM pulls out all the stops with a blockbuster cast and high production values. Tracy's performance is sublime. B&W; 120m. **DIR:** Victor Fleming. **CAST:** Spencer Tracy, Van Johnson, Irene Dunne, Ward Bond, Lionel Barrymore, James Gleason. **1943**

GYPSY ANGELS 🦃 Even die-hard fans eager to see Vanna White in a blink-and-you'll-miss-it topless scene won't care about this romance between an Atlanta stripper and a stunt pilot. Rated R. 92m. **DIR:** Alan Smithee. **CAST:** Vanna White, Gene Bicknell, Richard Roundtree, Tige Andrews, Marilyn Hassett, Lyle Waggoner. **1989**

GYPSY BLOOD ★★½ This adaptation of the Prosper Merimee story *Carmen* vaulted both director Ernst Lubitsch and star Pola Negri to the front rank of the European film scene. It has been called the first major postwar German release on the international scene. The title was changed to *Gypsy Blood* for American distribution. Silent. B&W; 104m. **DIR:** Ernst Lubitsch. **CAST:** Pola Negri. **1918**

HAIL, HERO! ★★ Dated, uneven film features an overly rambunctious Michael Douglas (in his first film) returning home to announce his enlistment during the Vietnam War. Rated PG. 100m. **DIR:** David Miller. **CAST:** Michael Douglas, Arthur Kennedy, Peter Strauss, Teresa Wright. **1969**

HAIRY APE, THE ★★★ Eugene O'Neill's play about an animallike coal stoker on an ocean liner. The hairy ape falls in love with a heartless socialite passenger who at once is captivated and repulsed by his coarse approach to life. William Bendix is fascinating in the title role. B&W; 90m. **DIR:** Alfred Santell. **CAST:** William Bendix, Susan Hayward, John Loder. **1944**

HALLELUJAH! ★★★★ Dated in technique but up-to-date in story and acting, this is the first major movie with an all-black cast. The plot revolves around a preacher who has lost his fight with temptation too many times. Irving Berlin wrote the song, "Waiting at the End of the Road," expressly for the film. B&W; 106m. **DIR:** King Vidor. **CAST:** Nina Mae McKinney, Daniel Hayner. **1929**

HAMBONE AND HILLIE ★★★ A delightful story of love and loyalty between an old woman (Lillian Gish) and her dog and constant companion, Hambone. While boarding a flight in New York to return to Los Angeles, Hambone is accidentally lost. And so begins a three-thousand-mile cross-country trip filled with perilous freeways, wicked humans, and dangerous animals. Rated PG. 97m. **DIR:** Roy Watts. **CAST:** Lillian Gish, Timothy Bottoms, Candy Clark, O. J. Simpson, Robert Walker. **1984**

HAMBURGER HILL ★★½ In dealing with one of the bloodiest battles of the Vietnam War, director John Irvin and screenwriter Jim Carabatsos have made a film so brutally real that watching it is an endurance test. Although well acted and well made, it is more like a shocking documentary than a work of fiction. Rated R for violence and profanity. 112m. **DIR:** John Irvin. **CAST:** Anthony Barrile, Michael Patrick Boatman, Don Cheadle, Michael Dolan, Don James, Dylan McDermott, M. A. Nickles, Harry O'Reilly, Tim Quill, Courtney B. Vance, Steven Weber, Daniel O'Shea. **1987**

HAMLET (1948) ★★★★★ In every way a brilliant presentation of Shakespeare's best-known play masterminded by England's foremost player. Superb in the title role, Laurence Olivier won the 1948 Oscar for best actor, and (as producer) for best picture. A high point among many is Stanley Holloway's droll performance as the First Gravedigger. B&W; 150m. **DIR:** Laurence Olivier. **CAST:** Laurence Olivier, Basil Sydney, Eileen Herlie, Jean Simmons, Felix Aylmer, Terence Morgan, Peter Cushing, Stanley Holloway. **1948**

HAMLET (1969) ★★★ Nicol Williamson gives a far more energetic portrayal of the famous Dane than the noted Oscar-winning performance of Laurence Olivier. Worth seeing for comparison of interpretations. An exceptional supporting cast adds to the allure of this low-budget adaptation. 113m. **DIR:** Tony Richardson. **CAST:** Nicol Williamson, Gordon Jackson, Anthony Hopkins, Judy Parfitt, Marianne Faithfull, Mark Dignam. **1969**

HAMLET (1990) ★★★★½ Kenneth Branagh's *Henry V* proved that Shakespeare adaptations could be accessible to mainstream audiences and still remain faithful to the source. Director Franco Zefirelli's *Hamlet* continues this tradition, with Mel Gibson bringing great vitality and physicality to the role of the Bard's most poignant hero. Rated PG for violence. 135m. **DIR:** Franco Zeffirelli. **CAST:** Mel Gibson, Glenn Close, Alan Bates, Ian Holm, Paul Scofield, Helena Bonham Carter. **1990**

HANDFUL OF DUST, A ★★★★ Based on Evelyn Waugh's masterpiece, *A Handful of Dust* is a deliciously staged drama of actions and fate. Set in post–World War I England

and the jungles of South America, this film presents two aristocrats searching along different paths for happiness. Superb ensemble playing. 118m. **DIR:** Charles Sturridge. **CAST:** James Wilby, Rupert Graves, Kristin Scott Thomas, Anjelica Huston, Alec Guinness. **1988**

HANGING ON A STAR 🦃 Deborah Raffin is the persistent and savvy road agent for a promising group of unknown musicians. Rated PG. 93m. **DIR:** Mike MacFarland. **CAST:** Lane Caudell, Deborah Raffin, Wolfman Jack. **1978**

HANGMEN ALSO DIE ★★★★ Brian Donlevy plays the assassin charged with killing a Nazi stooge in Prague. Gene Lockhart is the scapegoat. One of Fritz Lang's best movies. B&W; 134m. **DIR:** Fritz Lang. **CAST:** Brian Donlevy, Walter Brennan, Anna Lee, Gene Lockhart, Dennis O'Keefe. **1943**

HANNA'S WAR ★★★½ Powerful true story of a brave Jewish girl who is recruited by the British to rescue captured British fliers during WWII. Maruschka Detmers plays the brave Hanna who, though tortured brutally after her own capture, refuses to divulge military secrets. Rated PG-13 for violence. 148m. **DIR:** Menahem Golan. **CAST:** Maruschka Detmers, Ellen Burstyn, Anthony Andrews, Donald Pleasence. **1988**

HANOI HILTON, THE 🦃 A prisoner-of-war camp during the Vietnam War. Rated R for profanity and extreme violence. 130m. **DIR:** Lionel Chetwynd. **CAST:** Michael Moriarty, Paul LeMat, David Soul, Jeffrey Jones, Lawrence Pressman. **1987**

HANOVER STREET ★★ Action director Peter Hyams is out of his element with this melodramatic World War II drama, which consists mostly of an unlikely tryst between American soldier Harrison Ford and (married) British nurse Lesley-Anne Down. Overblown and mawkish. Rated PG. 109m. **DIR:** Peter Hyams. **CAST:** Harrison Ford, Lesley-Anne Down, Christopher Plummer, Alec McCowen. **1979**

HARD CHOICES ★★★ Independently made low-budget feature starts out as a drama about a social worker's efforts to free a boy she believes has been unjustly imprisoned. But it loses plausibility when she falls in love with him and helps him escape. Unrated; contains nudity, violence, and profanity. 90m. **DIR:** Rick King. **CAST:** Margaret Klenck, Gary McCleery, John Seitz, John Sayles, Martin Donovan, Spalding Gray. **1984**

HARD PROMISES ★★★ A woman divorces her husband while he is away on a twelve-year trip, only to have him turn up right before she remarries. Rated PG for profanity. 95m. **DIR:** Martin Davidson. **CAST:** Sissy Spacek, William L. Petersen, Brian Kerwin, Mare Winningham, Jeff Perry. **1991**

HARD TRAVELING ★★ California, 1940. A struggling farm couple battle the odds to survive. Slow-moving saga. Rated PG. 99m. **DIR:** Dan Bessie. **CAST:** J. E. Freeman, Ellen Geer, Barry Corbin. **1985**

HARD WAY, THE (1942) ★★★★ Ida Lupino proved she could carry the whole show as a disgruntled woman who hates her life and wants to make sure her sister has a better one. She manipulates her sister's life and destroys just about everyone else around them. Hardcore melodrama and exceptionally good. B&W; 108m. **DIR:** Vincent Sherman. **CAST:** Ida Lupino, Joan Leslie, Dennis Morgan, Jack Carson, Roman Bohnen, Faye Emerson, Gladys George, Julie Bishop. **1942**

HARDER THEY FALL, THE ★★★½ This boxing drama is as mean and brutal as they come. A gentle giant is built up, set up, and brought down by a collection of human vultures while sportswriter Humphrey Bogart flip-flops on the moral issues. The ring photography is spectacular. Don't expect anything like *Rocky*. B&W; 109m. **DIR:** Mark Robson. **CAST:** Humphrey Bogart, Rod Steiger, Jan Sterling, Mike Lane, Max Baer, Jersey Joe Walcott. **1956**

HARDHAT AND LEGS ★★★ The scene is New York City. Kevin Dobson is a horse-playing Italian construction worker who whistles at nice gams. Sharon Gless is democratic upper class. The twain meet, and sparks fly. It's all cheerful and upbeat and works because of first-rate acting. Made for television. 104m. **DIR:** Lee Philips. **CAST:** Kevin Dobson, Sharon Gless. **1980**

HAREM ★★★½ Nastassja Kinski is a stockbroker who is abducted by a wealthy OPEC oil minister (Ben Kingsley) and becomes a part of his harem. A bittersweet tale of a lonely dreamer and his passion for a modern woman. Not rated, but has violence, profanity, and nudity. 107m. **DIR:** Arthur Joffe. **CAST:** Nastassja Kinski, Ben Kingsley, Robbin Zohra Segal. **1985**

HARLEY ★★★ Lou Diamond Phillips stars as Harley, an L.A. motorcycle hood who gets sent to a Texas ranch instead of a juvenile detention center. Good family film. Rated PG. 80m. **DIR:** Fred Holmes. **CAST:** Lou Diamond Phillips. **1985**

HARLOW ★★ One of two films made in 1965 that dealt with the life of the late film star and sex goddess Jean Harlow. Carroll Baker simply is not the actress to play Harlow, and the whole thing is a trashy mess. 125m. **DIR:** Gordon Douglas. **CAST:** Carroll Baker, Peter Lawford, Red Buttons, Mike Connors, Raf Vallone, Angela Lansbury, Martin Balsam, Leslie Nielsen. **1965**

HARMONY CATS ★★ Mediocre morality play about an out-of-work symphony violinist who, as a last resort, teams up with a country and western group. Obviously out of his league, Jim Byrnes begins to get into the swing of things. Hee-haw! Not rated, but contains strong language and adult situations. 104m. **DIR:** Sandy Wilson. **CAST:** Kim Coates, Jim Byrnes, Lisa Brokop. **1993**

HARRAD EXPERIMENT, THE ★★ Uninvolving adaptation of Robert Rimmer's well-intentioned bestseller about an experimental college that makes sexual freedom the primary curriculum. The film is attractive as a novelty item because of erotic scenes between Don Johnson and Laurie Walters. Rated R. 88m. **DIR:** Ted Post. **CAST:** Don Johnson, James Whitmore, Tippi Hedren, Bruno Kirby, Laurie Walters. **1973**

HARRY AND SON ★★★ A widower (Paul Newman) can land a wrecking ball on a dime but can't seem to make contact with his artistically inclined son, Howard (Robby Benson), in this superb character study. Directed, coproduced, and cowritten by Newman, it's sort of a male *Terms of Endearment*. Rated PG for nudity and profanity. 117m. **DIR:** Paul Newman. **CAST:** Paul Newman, Robby Benson, Joanne Woodward, Ellen Barkin, Ossie Davis, Wilford Brimley. **1984**

HARRY AND TONTO ★★★★ Art Carney won an Oscar for his tour-de-force performance in this character study, directed by Paul Mazursky. In a role that's a far cry from his Ed Norton on Jackie Gleason's *The Honeymooners*, the star plays an older gentleman who, with his cat, takes a cross-country trip and lives life to the fullest. Rated R. 115m. **DIR:** Paul Mazursky. **CAST:** Art Carney, Ellen Burstyn, Chief Dan George, Geraldine Fitzgerald, Larry Hagman, Arthur Hunnicutt. **1974**

HASTY HEART ★★★½ Made for Showtime pay cable, this version of the 1949 movie with Ronald Reagan is corny as all getout, but is still pretty effective. In an army hospital in Burma during WWII, a proud Scottish soldier (Gregory Harrison) doesn't know that he has only a few weeks to live. He refuses to accept the hospitality of the other soldiers in the ward, all of whom know of his approaching death. Get out your handkerchiefs! 135m. **DIR:** Martin Speer. **CAST:** Gregory Harrison, Cheryl Ladd, Perry King. **1983**

HAUNTED SUMMER ★★ Though visually stunning, this story of the meeting between Lord Byron and Percy Shelley (that eventually led to Mary Shelley's tale *Frankenstein*) is just too weird to be taken seriously. Full of sexual innuendo and drug-induced tripping, this is definitely one for fans of period pieces only. Rated R. 106m. **DIR:** Ivan Passer. **CAST:** Philip Anglim, Laura Dern, Alice Krige, Eric Stoltz, Alex Winter. **1988**

HAUNTING OF JULIA, THE ★★ A vague, confused story of a young mother whose daughter chokes to death. In this otherwise pedestrian film there are sporadic spots of quality, mostly in Tom Conti's scenes. Rated R for profanity. 96m. **DIR:** Richard Loncraine. **CAST:** Mia Farrow, Keir Dullea, Tom Conti. **1981**

HAVANA ★★ Despite a very promising and involving first hour, this *Casablanca*, Cuban style, bogs down in political polemics and a predictable plot as out-for-himself gambler Robert Redford finds himself falling in love with a politically involved widow (Lena Olin). Rated R for profanity, violence, and nudity. 130m. **DIR:** Sydney Pollack. **CAST:** Robert Redford, Lena Olin, Alan Arkin, Raul Julia, Tomas Milian, Tony Plana. **1990**

HAWAII ★★★★ All-star epic presentation of Part III of James Michener's six-part novel of the same title. Excellent performances by Max von Sydow and Julie Andrews as the early 1800s missionaries to Hawaii, as well as by Richard Harris as the sea captain who tries to woo Andrews away. 171m. **DIR:** George Roy Hill. **CAST:** Julie Andrews, Max von Sydow, Richard Harris, Gene Hackman, Carroll O'Connor. **1966**

HAWKS ★★★★ This neglected treasure concerns a couple of feisty patients—Timothy Dalton and Anthony Edwards—in a hospital terminal ward. The macabre gallows humor may be difficult for mainstream tastes, but Dalton's often enraged battle with life is utterly compelling. With music by the Bee Gees (and Barry Gibb takes cocredit for the story idea). Rated R for profanity and brief nudity. 103m. **DIR:** Robert Ellis Miller. **CAST:** Timothy Dalton, Anthony Edwards. **1989**

HEARST AND DAVIES AFFAIR, THE ★★★ From William Randolph Hearst's and Marion Davies's first meeting at the Ziegfeld Follies to his death, this made-for-TV original takes the viewer through their entire affair—told from Davies's point of view. The mise-en-scène is beautiful, since the film was shot on location at Hearst Castle. Both Robert Mitchum and Virginia Madsen deliver fine performances as the title couple. Not rated. 95m. **DIR:** David Lowell Rich. **CAST:** Robert Mitchum, Virginia Madsen, Fritz Weaver, Doris Belack. **1985**

HEART ★★ A down-and-out boxer (Brad Davis) makes a comeback. This is well-worn territory and *Heart* has little new to offer. Rated R for violence and profanity. 93m. **DIR:** James Lemmo. **CAST:** Brad Davis, Jesse Doran, Sam Gray, Robinson Frank Adu, Steve Buscemi, Frances Fisher. **1987**

HEART BEAT ★★★★ *Heart Beat* is a perfect title for this warm, bittersweet visual poem on the beat generation by writer-director John Byrum. It pulses with life and emotion, intoxicating the viewer with a rhythmic flow of stunning images and superb performances by Nick Nolte, Sissy Spacek, and John Heard. The story begins with the cross-country adventure that inspired Jack Kerouac's *On the Road*. Rated R. 109m. **DIR:** John Byrum. **CAST:** Nick Nolte, Sissy Spacek, John Heard, Ray Sharkey, Ann Dusenberry. **1980**

HEART IS A LONELY HUNTER, THE ★★★★ This release features Alan Arkin in a superb performance, which won him an Academy Award nomination. In it, he plays a sensitive and compassionate man who is also a deaf-mute. Rated G. 125m. **DIR:** Robert Ellis Miller. **CAST:** Alan Arkin, Sondra Locke, Laurinda Barrett, Stacy Keach, Chuck McCann, Cicely Tyson. **1968**

HEART LIKE A WHEEL ★★★★ This top-notch film biography of racing-champion Shirley Muldowney features a marvelous performance by Bonnie Bedelia as the first woman to crack the National Hot Rod Association's embargo against female competitors. Rated PG for profanity. 113m. **DIR:** Jonathan Kaplan. **CAST:** Bonnie Bedelia, Beau Bridges, Leo Rossi, Hoyt Axton, Bill McKinney, Dean Paul Martin, Dick Miller. **1983**

HEART OF A CHAMPION: THE RAY MANCINI STORY ★★★ Made-for-TV movie of the life of Ray "Boom Boom" Mancini focuses on his quest for the lightweight boxing title. His drive is intensified by his desire to bring pride to his father, who could have had a shot at the title had he not been called to serve in World War II. Fight sequences staged by Sylvester Stallone. 100m. **DIR:** Richard Michaels. **CAST:** Robert Blake, Doug McKeon, Mariclare Costello. **1985**

HEART OF DARKNESS ★★½ Slow-moving and sometimes incoherent made-for-TV interpretation of Joseph Conrad's novel concerning an ivory company representative who may or may not have gone mad at his isolated African outpost, and the steamboat captain sent to find him. Conrad's novel is served far better by director Francis Ford Coppola's *Apocalypse Now*. 104m. **DIR:** Nicolas Roeg. **CAST:** Tim Roth, John Malkovich, Isaach De Bankee, James Fox, Morten Faldaas, Iman. **1994**

HEART OF DIXIE, THE ★★ With its heart in the right place but its head lost in the clouds *The Heart of Dixie* only manages to satisfy on two levels: its 1957 period details of the South, which is struggling to maintain its slipping grip on antebellum grandeur; and a small, tight performance by Treat Williams. The film centers on the activities of a group of sorority sisters at Alabama's Randolph University and their Big-Daddy-in-training lugs of boyfriends. Rated PG for mild violence and reasonably oblique sexual discussions. 110m. **DIR:** Martin Davidson. **CAST:** Ally Sheedy, Virginia Madsen, Phoebe Cates, Don Michael Paul, Treat Williams. **1989**

HEART OF JUSTICE ★★★½ Engrossing drama follows a reporter's attempt to piece together the reason a popular author was murdered by a wealthy socialite. Film plays like an Alfred Hitchcock movie with very fine performances by all involved. 108m. **DIR:** Bruno Barreto. **CAST:** Dennis Hopper, Eric Stoltz, Jennifer Connelly, Bradford Dillman, William H. Macy, Dermot Mulroney, Vincent Price, Joanna Miles, Harris Yulin. **1993**

HEART OF THE STAG ★★★★ The shocking subject matter of *Heart of the Stag*—forced incest—could have resulted in an uncomfortable film to watch. However, New Zealander Michael Firth, who directed the movie and conceived the story, handles it expertly, and the result is a riveting viewing experience. Rated R for violence, profanity, and sexual situations. 94m. **DIR:** Michael Firth. **CAST:** Bruno Lawrence, Terence Cooper, Mary Regan. **1983**

HEARTACHES ★★★ A touching, yet lighthearted, film about love, friendship, and survival, *Heartaches* follows the trials and tribulations of a young pregnant woman (Annie Potts), who is separated from her husband (Robert Carradine), and the kooky girlfriend she meets on the bus (Margot Kidder). The Canadian film is rated R for a minimal amount of sex, which is handled discreetly. 93m. **DIR:** Donald Shebib. **CAST:** Robert Carradine, Margot Kidder, Annie Potts, Winston Rekert, George Touliatos. **1981**

HEARTBREAK HOTEL ★★★ In this bit of none-too-convincing whimsy, Charlie Schlatter plays an aspiring rock guitarist who kidnaps Elvis Presley (David Keith). Keith does a terrific job of impersonating Presley, and director Chris Columbus's script has some warmly funny moments, but the movie cannot overcome its preposterous premise. Rated PG-13 for profanity and violence. 100m. **DIR:** Chris Columbus. **CAST:** David Keith, Tuesday Weld, Charlie Schlatter, Chris Mulkey. **1988**

HEARTBREAKERS ★★★½ Two men in their thirties, Arthur Blue (Peter Coyote) and Eli Kahn (Nick Mancuso), friends since childhood, find their relationship severely tested when each is suddenly caught up in his own fervent drive for success. Rated R for simulated sex and profanity. 106m. **DIR:** Bobby Roth. **CAST:** Peter Coyote, Nick Mancuso, Max Gail, Kathryn Harrold. **1984**

HEARTS OF FIRE 🦃 A girl who dreams of becoming a rock star. Rated R for brief nudity and profanity. 95m. **DIR:** Richard Marquand. **CAST:** Fiona, Bob Dylan, Rupert Everett, Julian Glover. **1987**

HEARTS OF THE WORLD ★★★ This World War I epic, a propaganda film, was made to convince the United States to enter the conflict and aid Britain and France. Actual battle footage from both sides in the conflict is interwoven with the story of a young man going to war and the tragic effects on his family and village. Silent. B&W; 122m.

DIR: D. W. Griffith. **CAST:** Lillian Gish, Dorothy Gish, Robert Harron, Ben Alexander. **1918**

HEAT (1972) ★★★ One of Andy Warhol's better film productions is this steamy tale of an unemployed actor (Joe Dallesandro) whose involvement with a neurotic has-been actress (Sylvia Miles) has tragicomic results. A low-budget homage to *Sunset Boulevard* that even non-Warhol fans may enjoy. Excellent music score composed and performed by John Cale. Rated R for nudity and language. 100m. **DIR:** Paul Morrissey. **CAST:** Sylvia Miles, Joe Dallesandro, Andrea Feldman, Pat Ast. **1972**

HEAT AND DUST ★★★★ Two love stories—one from the 1920s and one from today—are entwined in this classy, thoroughly enjoyable soap opera about two British women who go to India and become involved in its seductive mysteries. Julie Christie stars as a modern woman retracing the steps of her great-aunt (Greta Scacchi), who fell in love with an Indian ruler (played by the celebrated Indian star Shashi Kapoor). Rated R for nudity and brief violence. 130m. **DIR:** James Ivory. **CAST:** Julie Christie, Greta Scacchi, Shashi Kapoor, Christopher Cazenove, Julian Glover, Susan Fleetwood. **1983**

HEAT AND SUNLIGHT ★★★★ Electrifying, narratively risky drama featuring director Rob Nilsson as a photographer who is overwhelmed with jealousy and obsession. Visually stunning, with a great sound track by David Byrne and Brian Eno. Rated R for nudity and profanity. B&W; 98m. **DIR:** Rob Nilsson. **CAST:** Rob Nilsson. **1987**

HEAT WAVE ★★★½ Cable television film depicting the Watts riots of the early Seventies. Blair Underwood plays a young black *L.A. Times* employee given his chance at reporting when it becomes apparent that white journalists cannot get into the Watts area to cover the riots. Engrossing fact-based account. 96m. **DIR:** Kevin Hooks. **CAST:** Blair Underwood, Cicely Tyson, James Earl Jones, Margaret Avery. **1990**

HEATWAVE ★★★ Judy Davis plays an idealistic liberal opposed to proposed real estate developments. Davis's crusade leads to her involvement in a possible kidnap-murder and a love affair with the young architect of the housing project she's protesting. Unrated. 99m. **DIR:** Phillip Noyce. **CAST:** Judy Davis, Richard Moir, Chris Haywood, Bill Hunter, Anna Jemison. **1983**

HEAVEN AND EARTH (1993) ★★★ Oliver Stone returns to Vietnam once too often, this time focusing on one woman's Dickensian ordeals. She survives the French and American invasions, and then tackles life in the gluttonous United States after marrying a war-weary sergeant who, in a bit of near comical overkill, becomes violently homicidal. Although Hiep Thi Le and Tommy Lee Jones are sensational in the lead roles, their characters are lost amid Stone's bombastic visual diatribes. Rated R for violence, profanity, nudity, and rape. 140m. **DIR:** Oliver Stone. **CAST:** Hiep Thi Le, Tommy Lee Jones, Joan Chen, Haing S. Ngor, Debbie Reynolds. **1993**

HEAVEN IS A PLAYGROUND ★★★½ A Chicago slum has one thing going for it: a basketball coach determined to take kids off the streets and onto college campuses. Enter a young white lawyer who helps the coach vanquish an unethical promoter. Rated R for profanity and violence. 104m. **DIR:** Randall Fried. **CAST:** Mike Warren, D. B. Sweeney, Richard Jordan. **1991**

HEAVEN ON EARTH ★★★★ Scripters Margaret Atwood and Peter Pearson pay tribute to a bit of Canadian history with this poignant look at the thousands of orphaned "home children" shipped from England to work as indentured slaves...or, if they were lucky, to be adopted into loving families. Suitable for family viewing. 82m. **DIR:** Allan Kroeker. **CAST:** R. H. Thompson, Sian Leisa Davies. **1986**

HEAVEN TONIGHT ★★★½ This British import is a slick contemporary retelling of *A Star Is Born*, with John Waters as an aging rocker frustrated by his inability to generate the headlines he did twenty years earlier, and Guy Pearce as his capable, soft-spoken son, whose musical star is on the rise. Frank Howson and Alister Webb's script contains considerable truth and a lot of heart. Rated R for profanity and drug use. 97m. **DIR:** Pino Amenta. **CAST:** John Waters, Rebecca Gilling, Kim Gyngell, Guy Pearce. **1993**

HEAVY TRAFFIC ★★★ Ralph Bakshi's follow-up to *Fritz the Cat* is a mixture of live action and animation. Technically outstanding, but its downbeat look at urban life is rather unpleasant to watch. Rated R for profanity, nudity, and violence. 76m. **DIR:** Ralph Bakshi. **CAST:** Animated. **1973**

HEDDA ★★★★ Screenwriter-director Trevor Nunn creates a fine adaptation of Henrik Ibsen's *Hedda Gabler*. Glenda Jackson presides as a coldhearted, power-hungry manipulator who toys with the lives and emotions of those around her. Jackson's costars—members of the Royal Shakespeare Company—match her fine performance. 103m. **DIR:** Trevor Nunn. **CAST:** Glenda Jackson, Timothy West, Peter Eyre, Patrick Stewart. **1975**

HEIRESS, THE ★★★★½ This moving drama takes place in New York City in the mid-1800s. Olivia de Havilland is excellent (she won an Oscar for this performance) as a plain but extraordinarily rich woman who is pursued by a wily gold digger (played by Montgomery Clift). Ralph Richardson is great as her straitlaced father. B&W; 115m. **DIR:** William Wyler. **CAST:** Olivia de Havilland,

Montgomery Clift, Ralph Richardson, Miriam Hopkins, Vanessa Brown, Mona Freeman, Ray Collins. **1949**

HEIST, THE ★★★½ Fun revenge film features Pierce Brosnan as a framed con seeking to even the score with his former racetrack partner (Tom Skerritt). There are so many twists and turns in the plot that you will be guessing the final outcome until the closing shot. Unrated HBO film features violence. 97m. **DIR:** Stuart Orme. **CAST:** Pierce Brosnan, Tom Skerritt, Wendy Hughes. **1989**

HELL TO ETERNITY ★★★ A trimly told and performed antiprejudice, antiwar drama based on the life of World War II hero Guy Gabaldon, a Californian raised by Japanese-American parents. Jeffrey Hunter and Sessue Hayakawa share acting honors as the hero and the strong-minded Japanese commander who confronts him in the South Pacific. Lots of battle scenes. B&W; 132m. **DIR:** Phil Karlson. **CAST:** Jeffrey Hunter, David Janssen, Vic Damone, Patricia Owens, Sessue Hayakawa. **1960**

HELTER SKELTER ★★★★ The story of Charles Manson's 1969 murder spree is vividly retold in this excellent TV movie. Steve Railsback is superb as the crazed Manson. Based on prosecutor Vincent Bugliosi's novel, this is high-voltage stuff. Unrated and too intense for the kids. 114m. **DIR:** Tom Gries. **CAST:** George DiCenzo, Steve Railsback, Nancy Wolfe, Marilyn Burns. **1976**

HELTER-SKELTER MURDERS, THE 🦃 Sensationalistic account of the Tate murders. Rated R for graphic violence. B&W/color; 83m. **DIR:** Frank Howard. **CAST:** Debbie Duff. **1988**

HENRY & JUNE ★★½ Good direction doesn't offset mediocre acting and an excruciatingly boring script in this oft-melodramatic story about expatriate author Henry Miller and his personal problems with sex. Based on Anais Nin's memoirs, it was the first release under the new NC-17 rating code, though could have squeaked through with an R. 136m. **DIR:** Phil Kaufman. **CAST:** Fred Ward, Uma Thurman, Maria de Medeiros, Kevin Spacey, Richard E. Grant. **1990**

HENRY V (1944) ★★★★★ The first of Olivier's three major film forays into Shakespeare (the others are *Hamlet* and *Richard III*), this production blazed across screens like a meteor. A stirring, colorful film, full of sound and fury, and all the pageantry one expects from English history brought to vivid life. Olivier won an honorary Oscar for acting, directing, and producing. In a word: superb. 137m. **DIR:** Laurence Olivier. **CAST:** Laurence Olivier, Robert Newton, Leslie Banks, Felix Aylmer, Renée Asherson, Leo Genn. **1944**

HENRY V (1989) ★★★★★ What star-adapter-director Kenneth Branagh has done with Shakespeare's *Henry V* on screen is nothing short of miraculous. Not better, but different, than Laurence Olivier's 1944 production, Branagh's version truly does "ascend the brightest heaven of invention," as promised in the film's stunning prologue. In chronicling young King Henry's war against France, Branagh has created a movie as exciting as *Star Wars* and infinitely more satisfying. Like Akira Kurosawa's *Ran*, it is a Shakespearean adaptation on an epic scale and one of the best films of its kind. Rated PG for violence. 138m. **DIR:** Kenneth Branagh. **CAST:** Kenneth Branagh, Derek Jacobi, Paul Scofield, Judi Dench, Ian Holm, Emma Thompson, Robert Stephens, Geraldine McEwan, Alec McCowen. **1989**

HENRY: PORTRAIT OF A SERIAL KILLER ★★★★ Chillingly real and brutally explicit, this profile of a murderous drifter and his former prison pal emerges as a quasi-documentary that dwells so deep in the psychopathic mind of its title character one almost expects disclaimers to parade across the screen. Unrated, but filled with violence and raw brutality. 90m. **DIR:** John McNaughton. **CAST:** Michael Rooker. **1990**

HERO, THE ★★ Richard Harris distinguishes himself neither as actor nor as director in this mawkish sports drama. He plays a soccer star getting on in years who agrees to throw a game for money. Not the freshest of story lines. Not rated. 97m. **DIR:** Richard Harris. **CAST:** Richard Harris, Romy Schneider, Kim Burfield. **1971**

HERO AIN'T NOTHIN' BUT A SANDWICH, A ★★½ Heartfelt, uneven black soap opera—a typical latter-day Ralph Nelson production. The director of *Lilies of the Field* lays it on thick in this sentimental adaptation of Alice Childress's book about a black ghetto teen's drug problem. 105m. **DIR:** Ralph Nelson. **CAST:** Cicely Tyson, Paul Winfield, Larry B. Scott, Glynn Turman. **1978**

HEROES ★★★½ Henry Winkler is excellent in this compelling story of a confused Vietnam vet traveling cross-country to meet a few of his old war buddies. MCA Home Video has elected to alter the film's closing theme for this release. Removing the emotionally charged "Carry on Wayward Son" by Kansas in favor of a teary generic tune somewhat diminishes the overall impact of the movie. Rated PG for mild language and violence. 113m. **DIR:** Jeremy Paul Kagan. **CAST:** Henry Winkler, Sally Field, Harrison Ford, Val Avery. **1977**

HEROES FOR SALE ★★★ Warner Bros., noted for gangster films, also turned out many social conscience dramas during the Great Depression, and this is a good one. Richard Barthelmess, more a Poor Soul than an Everyman, suffers morphine addiction caused by war injuries, the loss of a business in the industrial revolution, the death of his wife in a labor riot, and unjust imprisonment as a radical. Grim going, but fine performances. B&W; 71m. **DIR:** William Wellman. **CAST:** Richard Barthelmess, Aline MacMahon, Loretta Young. **1933**

HESTER STREET ★★★★ Beautifully filmed look at the Jewish community in nineteenth-century New York City. Film focuses on the relationship of a young couple, he turning his back on the old Jewish ways while she fights to hold on to them. Fine performances and great attention to period detail make this very enjoyable. Rated PG. B&W; 92m. **DIR:** Joan Micklin Silver. **CAST:** Carol Kane, Steven Keats, Mel Howard. **1975**

HEY GOOD LOOKIN' 🦃 Boring animated film about street gangs of New York City during the 1950s. Rated R. 86m. **DIR:** Ralph Bakshi. **CAST:** Animated. **1983**

HEY, I'M ALIVE! ★★½ TV movie based on a true story of two people who survived a plane crash in the Yukon, then struggled to stay alive until rescuers could locate them. Well-acted, though nothing you haven't seen before. 74m. **DIR:** Lawrence Schiller. **CAST:** Edward Asner, Sally Struthers. **1975**

HIDDEN AGENDA ★★★★ Frances McDormand is a member of a panel investigating British atrocities in Northern Ireland who is caught up in the cover-up of the death of her boyfriend at the hands of British soldiers. This is a wonderful conspiracy flick concerning the rise to power of British Prime Minister Margaret Thatcher. An added touch of realism is supplied by director Kenneth Loach's documentary-style filmmaking. Rated R for violence and profanity. 105m. **DIR:** Kenneth Loach. **CAST:** Frances McDormand, Brian Cox, Brad Dourif, Mai Zetterling. **1990**

HIDE IN PLAIN SIGHT ★★★½ James Caan is a tire factory laborer whose former wife marries a two-bit hoodlum. The hood turns informant and, under the Witness Relocation Program, is given a secret identity. Caan's former wife and their two children are spirited off to points unknown. Caan's subsequent quest for his kids becomes a one-man-against-the-system crusade in this watchable movie. Rated PG. 98m. **DIR:** James Caan. **CAST:** James Caan, Jill Eikenberry, Robert Viharo, Joe Grifasi. **1980**

HIDING PLACE, THE ★★½ A professional cast gives depth and feeling to this true story of two Dutch women who are sent to a concentration camp for hiding Jews from the Nazis during World War II. This film was produced by Reverend Billy Graham's Evangelistic Association. 145m. **DIR:** James F. Collier. **CAST:** Julie Harris, Eileen Heckart, Arthur O'Connell. **1975**

HIGH AND THE MIGHTY, THE ★★★½ Spencer Tracy was originally set to play the lead role in this early, prototypical entry in the disaster-film genre, but dropped out before filming began. This is how producer John Wayne ended up starring in one of the most popular films of his career as Dan Roman, a veteran pilot with a tragic past. Although slow-going at times, this *Grand Hotel* in the air has more than enough fine moments generated by a cast of familiar faces to keep the viewer's interest. 147m. **DIR:** William Wellman. **CAST:** John Wayne, Claire Trevor, Laraine Day, Robert Stack, Jan Sterling, Phil Harris, Robert Newton, David Brian, Paul Kelly, Sidney Blackmer, Julie Bishop, John Howard, Wally Brown, Ann Doran, John Qualen, Paul Fix, George Chandler, Douglas Fowley, Regis Toomey, Carl "Alfalfa" Switzer, William Schallert, Karen Sharpe, John Smith. **1954**

HIGH SCHOOL CONFIDENTIAL! ★★½ A narcotics officer sneaks into a tough high school to bust hopheads. Incredibly naïve treatment of drug scene is bad enough, but it's the actors' desperate attempts to look "hip" that make the film an unintentional laugh riot. B&W; 85m. **DIR:** Jack Arnold. **CAST:** Russ Tamblyn, Jan Sterling, John Drew Barrymore, Mamie Van Doren. **1958**

HIGH TIDE ★★★★ Judy Davis gives a superb performance as a rock 'n' roll singer stranded in a small Australian town when she loses her job in a band and her car breaks down all in the same day. She winds up staying in a trailer park only to encounter by accident the teenage daughter she deserted following the death of her husband. The offbeat but moving *High Tide* reunites Davis with her *My Brilliant Career* director, Gillian Armstrong, for some truly impressive results. Rated PG. 102m. **DIR:** Gillian Armstrong. **CAST:** Judy Davis, Jan Adele, Claudia Karvan, Colin Friels. **1987**

HILL, THE ★★★★ Powerful drill-sergeant-from-hell film, this zeroes in on the psychological and mental agony faced by a group of British military prisoners. Sean Connery is excellent as the latest victim of the break-their-spirits program. 122m. **DIR:** Sidney Lumet. **CAST:** Sean Connery, Harry Andrews, Ian Hendry, Ossie Davis, Michael Redgrave. **1965**

HINDENBURG, THE 🦃 Another disaster movie whose major disaster is its own script. Rated PG. 125m. **DIR:** Robert Wise. **CAST:** George C. Scott, Anne Bancroft, William Atherton, Roy Thinnes, Burgess Meredith, Charles Durning. **1975**

HIROSHIMA: OUT OF THE ASHES ★★★★ This superior TV-movie rendition of the atomic bombing of Hiroshima allows us to see things from the perspective of those who were there. An ironic twist of fate places freed POWs among the ruins. Rated

PG-13 for violence. 98m. **DIR:** Peter Werner. **CAST:** Max von Sydow, Judd Nelson, Noriyuki "Pat" Morita, Mako, Ben Wright. **1990**

HISTORY IS MADE AT NIGHT ★★★ A preposterous film, but...Colin Clive is a sadistic jealous husband whose wife, Jean Arthur, falls for Parisian headwaiter Charles Boyer. He tries to frame the headwaiter for a murder he himself committed. He fails. Insanely determined to destroy the lovers, he arranges for his superliner to hit an iceberg! B&W; 97m. **DIR:** Frank Borzage. **CAST:** Charles Boyer, Jean Arthur, Colin Clive, Leo Carrillo. **1937**

HITLER ★★ Richard Basehart plays Adolf Hitler in this rather slow-moving, shallow account of *der Führer*'s last years. You're better off watching a good documentary on the subject. 107m. **DIR:** Stuart Heisler. **CAST:** Richard Basehart, Cordula Trantow, Maria Emo, John Mitchum. **1962**

HITLER—DEAD OR ALIVE 🦃 Paroled gangster and his henchmen accept a $1 million offer to assassinate Hitler. B&W; 72m. **DIR:** Nick Grindé. **CAST:** Ward Bond, Warren Hymer, Paul Fix. **1942**

HITLER, THE LAST TEN DAYS ★★ This film should hold interest only for history buffs. It is a rather dry and tedious account of the desperate closing days of the Third Reich. Alec Guinness gives a capable, yet sometimes overwrought, performance as the Nazi leader from the time he enters his underground bunker in Berlin until his eventual suicide. Rated PG. 108m. **DIR:** Ennio De-Concini. **CAST:** Alec Guinness, Simon Ward, Adolfo Celi, Diane Cilento. **1973**

HITLER'S DAUGHTER 🦃 Made-for-cable drama suggests one of Hitler's mistresses produced a girl-child, who was then trained by Nazi-nasties to revive the Fourth Reich in our United States. Rated R for language and violence. 88m. **DIR:** James A. Contner. **CAST:** Patrick Cassidy, Melody Anderson, Veronica Cartwright, Kay Lenz. **1990**

HOFFA ★★★★ Though it leaves several questions about its subject's past and family life unaddressed, this screen biography of labor leader Jimmy Hoffa is nonetheless a tour de force for director Danny DeVito and star Jack Nicholson. The film does not whitewash the events that led to Hoffa's rise to power. Instead, it maintains a kind of moral ambiguity reminiscent of Francis Ford Coppola's *The Godfather* movies. Screenplay by David Mamet. Rated R for profanity, violence, and nudity. 140m. **DIR:** Danny DeVito. **CAST:** Jack Nicholson, Danny DeVito, Armand Assante, J. T. Walsh, John C. Reilly, Frank Whaley, Kevin Anderson, John P. Ryan, Robert Prosky, Natalija Nogulich, Nicholas Pryor, Paul Guilfoyle, Karen Young, Cliff Gorman. **1992**

HOLD THE DREAM ★★★ This made-for-TV sequel to *A Woman of Substance* finds an aging Emma Harte (Deborah Kerr) turning over her department-store empire to her granddaughter, Paula (Jenny Seagrove). The rest of the family has plans to steal the business for themselves. Not as captivating as *Woman of Substance*, this sequel will still manage to entertain patrons of the soaps. 180m. **DIR:** Don Sharp. **CAST:** Jenny Seagrove, Deborah Kerr, Stephen Collins, James Brolin. **1986**

HOLD YOUR MAN ★★★★ One of the best examples of a movie that succeeds because of the vibes between its stars, this one holds your attention from start to finish. The two leads play a gangster and a gun moll who trade barbs, insults, and kisses with equal displays of passion. B&W; 87m. **DIR:** Sam Wood. **CAST:** Jean Harlow, Clark Gable, Dorothy Burgess, Guy Kibbee, Stu Erwin, Elizabeth Patterson. **1933**

HOLIDAY AFFAIR ★★★ Two highly different men court a pretty widow with a young son in this Christmas season story. A warm and friendly film for devotees of romantic melodrama. B&W; 87m. **DIR:** Don Hartman. **CAST:** Janet Leigh, Robert Mitchum, Wendell Corey. **1949**

HOLLYWOOD HEARTBREAK ★★½ Decent, but all too familiar, tale of a Hollywood hopeful. This time the twist is that instead of a gorgeous starlet, the protagonist is a male writer. Unrated, but contains profanity. 80m. **DIR:** Lance Dickson. **CAST:** Mark Moses, Carol Mayo Jenkins, Ron Karabatsos. **1990**

HOLOCAUST ★★★★½ This Emmy-winning miniseries is one of the finest programs ever produced for television. The story follows the lives of two German families during the reign of Hitler's Third Reich. Everyone in front of and behind the camera does a stunning job. This is a must-see. 570m. **DIR:** Marvin J. Chomsky. **CAST:** Tom Bell, Michael Moriarty, Tovah Feldshuh, Meryl Streep, Fritz Weaver, David Warner. **1978**

HOME FOR CHRISTMAS ★★★ Unbelievable, yet touching, made-for-TV tale of a young girl's desire to receive a grandfather for Christmas. Mickey Rooney plays the homeless man she's chosen. 96m. **DIR:** Peter McCubbin. **CAST:** Mickey Rooney, Chantellese Kent, Simon Richards, Lesley Kelly. **1990**

HOME FROM THE HILL ★★★★ Melodramatic film focuses on a wealthy but dysfunctional southern family. Robert Mitchum is the philandering patriarch. George Hamilton and George Peppard debut as Mitchum's grown sons. Downbeat but well acted and directed. 151m. **DIR:** Vincente Minnelli. **CAST:** Robert Mitchum, Eleanor Parker, George Hamilton, George Peppard, Luana Patten. **1959**

HOME OF OUR OWN, A ★★★ A single mother (Kathy Bates) and her six kids move into an abandoned farmhouse in Idaho, making a deal with the owner to fix it up and eventually buy it from him. There's a crisis every ten minutes, and not much happens that you haven't seen before, but the actors carry the film, especially Edward Furlong and Clarissa Lessig as the two older children. Rated PG. 102m. **DIR:** Tony Bill. **CAST:** Kathy Bates, Edward Furlong, Clarissa Lessig, Soon-Teck Oh, Tony Campisi. **1993**

HOME OF THE BRAVE ★★★ This is one of the first films dealing with blacks serving in the military during World War II. The story finds James Edwards on a mission in the Pacific and deals with the racial abuse that he encounters from his own men. The good plot of this film could use some more action, yet it is still worth watching. B&W; 85m. **DIR:** Mark Robson. **CAST:** James Edwards, Steve Brodie, Jeff Corey, Douglas Dick. **1949**

HOME, SWEET HOME ★★½ Henry B. Walthall is John Howard Payne in this fanciful biography of the famous composer. Lillian Gish is his faithful, long-suffering sweetheart. Denied happiness in life, the lovers are united as they "fly" to heaven. Silent. B&W; 80m. **DIR:** D. W. Griffith. **CAST:** Henry B. Walthall, Lillian Gish, Dorothy Gish, Mae Marsh, Spottiswoode Aitken, Miriam Cooper, Robert Harron, Donald Crisp, Blanche Sweet, Owen Moore. **1914**

HOMEBOY ★★ This slow-moving, moody drama about a washed-up cowboy prizefighter is engorged with down-and-out characters. Mickey Rourke stars as the maverick boxer who drinks, smirks, and mumbles his way to one last shot as a top middleweight contender. The raunchy, atmospheric sound track is by Eric Clapton and Michael Kamen. Rated R for profanity and violence. 118m. **DIR:** Michael Seresin. **CAST:** Mickey Rourke, Christopher Walken, Debra Feuer, Kevin Conway. **1988**

HOMEBOYS ★★ Mexican-Americans are portrayed as ruthless drug dealers in this urban piece about how a cop can be torn between his job and his love for his brother. The young cast does a fair job in this low-budget production. Unrated, but with nudity and profanity. 91m. **DIR:** Lindsay Norgard. **CAST:** Todd Bridges, David Garrison. **1992**

HOMECOMING (1948) ★★ In this post–WWII melodrama, Clark Gable, Lana Turner, and Anne Baxter are glamorous. If they had something to do other than talk and stare, they might have had a better movie. It's about an army surgeon who has a romance with his nurse while both are in the trenches. Even with Gable and Turner as the illicit lovers, the movie isn't as good as it should have been. B&W; 113m. **DIR:** Mervyn LeRoy. **CAST:** Clark Gable, Lana Turner, Anne Baxter, John Hodiak, Ray Collins, Cameron Mitchell, Gladys Cooper, Marshall Thompson. **1948**

HOMECOMING, THE (1973) ★★★★ Michael Jayston brings his wife, Vivien Merchant, home to meet the family after several years of separation. His father and two brothers are no-holds-barred Harold Pinter characters. If you like drama and Pinter, you'll want to check out this American Film Theater production, which has outstanding direction by Peter Hall. 111m. **DIR:** Peter Hall. **CAST:** Cyril Cusack, Ian Holm, Michael Jayston, Vivien Merchant, Terrence Rigby, Paul Rogers. **1973**

HOMER AND EDDIE ★★★ Outstanding performance by James Belushi as a retarded man trying to return to his dying father despite the fact that his father has disowned him. Whoopi Goldberg plays a sociopathic woman who gives Belushi the ride of a lifetime. Rated R for profanity and violence. 102m. **DIR:** Andrei Konchalovsky. **CAST:** James Belushi, Whoopi Goldberg, Karen Black, Anne Ramsey. **1989**

HOMEWORK 🦃 High school teacher seduces one of her students. Rated R for nudity. 90m. **DIR:** James Beshears. **CAST:** Joan Collins, Shell Kepler, Wings Hauser, Betty Thomas. **1982**

HONKYTONK MAN ★★★★ Clint Eastwood stars as an alcoholic, tubercular country singer headed for an audition at the Grand Ole Opry during the depths of the Depression. A bittersweet character study, it works remarkably well. You even begin to believe Eastwood in the role. The star's son, Kyle Eastwood, makes an impressive film debut. Rated PG for strong language and sexual content. 122m. **DIR:** Clint Eastwood. **CAST:** Clint Eastwood, Kyle Eastwood, John McIntire. **1982**

HONOR THY FATHER ★★ A movie version of the real-life internal Mafia war that took place during the late 1960s among members of the Bonanno crime family. Weak. Not rated, but contains violence. 97m. **DIR:** Paul Wendkos. **CAST:** Joseph Bologna, Brenda Vaccaro, Raf Vallone. **1973**

HOODLUM PRIEST, THE ★★★½ Don Murray gives a sincere performance as Father Charles Dismis Clark, a Jesuit priest who devotes himself to helping newly released convicts reenter society. The focus is on one young parolee (Keir Dullea, in his debut) who has trouble finding his way. Murray coproduced. B&W; 101m. **DIR:** Irvin Kershner. **CAST:** Don Murray, Keir Dullea, Larry Gates, Logan Ramsey, Don Joslyn, Cindi Wood. **1961**

HOOSIERS ★★★★½ *Hoosiers* is the most satisfying high school basketball movie in years. Gene Hackman is the new coach—with a mysterious past—at Hickory High. His unorthodox methods rankle the locals and his fellow teachers (particularly frosty Barbara Hershey), not to mention the undisciplined team members. But before you can say hoosiermania, the team is at the 1951 state championships. It doesn't hurt, either, that the realistic script is based on a true Indiana Cinderella story. Rated PG. 114m. **DIR:** David Anspaugh. **CAST:** Gene Hackman, Barbara Hershey, Dennis Hopper, Sheb Wooley. **1986**

HOPE AND GLORY ★★★★½ Writer-producer-director John Boorman's much-praised film chronicles his boyhood experiences during the London blitz. Rather than the horror story one might expect, it is a marvelously entertaining, warm, and thoughtful look backward. Blessed with vibrant characters, cultural richness, and a fresh point of view, it never fails to fascinate. Rated PG-13 for profanity and suggested sex. 113m. **DIR:** John Boorman. **CAST:** Sarah Miles, David Hayman, Derrick O'Connor, Susan Wooldridge, Sammi Davis, Ian Bannen, Sebastian Rice Edwards, Jean-Marc Barr. **1987**

HOSTAGES ★★½ Bernard MacLaverty's well-meaning made-for-cable account of the five-year hostage crisis in Lebanon suffers from simplified characters and events compressed past the point of conveying much drama. No doubt this superficial tone results from the lack of participation by those who were there. Director David Wheatley also elicits very little passion from his strong ensemble cast. The result is oddly uninvolving. 96m. **DIR:** David Wheatley. **CAST:** Colin Firth, Ciaran Hinds, Jay O. Sanders, Josef Sommer, Harry Dean Stanton, Kathy Bates, Natasha Richardson. **1993**

HOSTILE TAKE OVER ★★★½ Apt direction by George Mihalka elevates what would be another psycho-on-the-loose cheapie. David Warner plays a lonely employee who holds three colleagues hostage. A tense thriller rated R for nudity, profanity, and violence. 93m. **DIR:** George Mihalka. **CAST:** David Warner, Michael Ironside, Kate Vernon, Jayne Eastwood. **1988**

HOT SHOT ★★★½ More than just a soccer version of *The Karate Kid*, this film of a young man's conquest of adversity stands on its own. Jim Youngs is a rich kid who runs away to Rio de Janeiro, where he pursues his idol, Pelé, the greatest soccer player of all time. An enjoyable family film and a must for soccer fans. Rated PG. 94m. **DIR:** Rick King. **CAST:** Jim Youngs, Pelé, Billy Warlock, Weyman Thompson, Mario Van Peebles. **1986**

HOT SPELL ★★★ Entertaining thoughts of leaving her for a younger woman, macho husband Anthony Quinn has anguishing housewife Shirley Booth sweating out this near remake of *Come Back, Little Sheba*. Booth invokes empathy, Quinn again proves his depth of talent, Shirley MacLaine shows why stardom soon was hers; but a soap opera is a soap opera. B&W; 86m. **DIR:** Daniel Mann. **CAST:** Shirley Booth, Anthony Quinn, Shirley MacLaine, Earl Holliman, Eileen Heckart. **1958**

HOT SPOT ★★½ Director Dennis Hopper keeps the *Hot Spot* on simmer when it needs to boil over with tension and excitement. Don Johnson is semicomatose as a lowlife who drifts into a small Texas town where he robs the local bank and gets involved with two women, one bad (Virginia Madsen) and one innocent (Jennifer Connelly). Rated R for simulated sex, nudity, profanity, and violence. 129m. **DIR:** Dennis Hopper. **CAST:** Don Johnson, Virginia Madsen, Jennifer Connelly, Charles Martin Smith, Bill Sadler, Jerry Hardin, Barry Corbin. **1990**

HOTEL ★★½ This film is based on Arthur Hailey's bestseller, which eventually spawned a TV series. In its *Airport*-style story, a number of characters and events unfold against the main theme of Melvyn Douglas's attempt to keep from selling the hotel to a tycoon who would modernize and change the landmark. 125m. **DIR:** Richard Quine. **CAST:** Rod Taylor, Catherine Spaak, Melvyn Douglas, Karl Malden, Richard Conte, Michael Rennie, Merle Oberon, Kevin McCarthy. **1967**

HOTEL NEW HAMPSHIRE, THE ★★ Based on John Irving's novel, this muddled motion picture has its moments. Beau Bridges stars as the head of a family that weathers all sorts of disasters. Rated R for profanity. 110m. **DIR:** Tony Richardson. **CAST:** Beau Bridges, Jodie Foster, Rob Lowe, Nastassja Kinski, Amanda Plummer. **1984**

HOTEL RESERVE ★★½ Intrigue and romance are the chief ingredients of this lightweight spy melodrama set just before the outbreak of World War II in a fancy resort hotel. B&W; 80m. **DIR:** Victor Hanbury. **CAST:** James Mason, Lucie Mannheim, Herbert Lom, Patricia Medina. **1944**

HOUDINI ★★★½ Tony Curtis is quite good in this colorful but sketchy account of the famed illusionist. Enjoyable fluff makes up for lack of substance with good period atmosphere and dandy reenactments of Houdini's most famous escapes. 106m. **DIR:** George Marshall. **CAST:** Tony Curtis, Janet Leigh, Ian Wolfe, Torin Thatcher. **1953**

HOURS AND TIMES ★★★★½ This short (60-minute) feature marks an auspicious debut for writer-director Christopher Munch. It's an impressive, wonderfully intimate drama that supposes what might have gone on between John Lennon and his manager, Brian Epstein, during a weekend in 1963, when they flee the insanity of Beatlemania for a little solitude in Barcelona. David Angus and Ian Hart are fabulous as the fabled rock star and his manager. B&W; 60m. **DIR:** Christopher Munch. **CAST:** David Angus, Ian Hart, Stephanie Pack. **1992**

HOUSE ACROSS THE BAY, THE ★★½ An airplane designer (Walter Pidgeon) swipes the waiting wife (Joan Bennett) of a gangster (George Raft) while Raft is paying his dues in the joint. Then he gets out.... Classic Raft film. Tense, exciting, but familiar. Lloyd Nolan plays a shyster very well. B&W; 86m. **DIR:** Archie Mayo. **CAST:** George Raft, Joan Bennett, Lloyd Nolan, Gladys George, Walter Pidgeon. **1940**

HOUSE OF CARDS ★★★★ Strange but gripping drama about a young girl who retreats into her mind after seeing her father fall to his death. Frantic, her mother, Kathleen Turner, calls in psychiatrist Tommy Lee Jones to help reach the girl, but everything they try seems to make the situation worse. Heartrending. Rated PG-13 for adult situations. 109m. **DIR:** Michael Lessac. **CAST:** Kathleen Turner, Tommy Lee Jones, Asha Menina, Shiloh Strong, Esther Rolle, Park Overall, Michael Horse. **1993**

HOUSE OF STRANGERS ★★★½ Well-acted, engrossing tale of the fall of a wealthy banker's family. Edward G. Robinson plays the patriarch whose four sons are now at odds with him and each other for various reasons. B&W; 101m. **DIR:** Joseph L. Mankiewicz. **CAST:** Edward G. Robinson, Luther Adler, Richard Conte, Susan Hayward. **1949**

HOUSE OF THE SEVEN GABLES, THE ★★★★½ The only rendition of the Nathaniel Hawthorne classic made during the talkie era thus far, and a good one. Vincent Price and George Sanders one-up each other with cynical dialogue and scenery-chewing, and the script is faithful to the book. The story of a jealous man who sends an innocent man to prison is hauntingly photographed and uses replicas of the nineteenth-century New England house that inspired it. B&W; 90m. **DIR:** Joe May. **CAST:** Vincent Price, Margaret Lindsay, George Sanders, Nan Grey, Alan Napier, Dick Foran. **1940**

HOUSE OF THE SPIRITS, THE ★★½ Even a high-powered cast cannot save this sketchy depiction of seventy years in the history of an unnamed country (reportedly Chile) as seen by three generations of aristocracy. The on-screen collaboration of Meryl Streep and Glenn Close seems to consist only of a few brief scenes, while top-billed Jeremy Irons's accent makes his dialogue sound dubbed. Not quite an all-out embarrassment, but close. Rated R for violence, profanity, nudity, and simulated sex. 138m. **DIR:** Bille August. **CAST:** Jeremy Irons, Meryl Streep, Glenn Close, Winona Ryder, Antonio Banderas, Vanessa Redgrave, Armin Mueller-Stahl, Maria Conchita Alonso, Sarita Choudhury. **1994**

HOUSE ON GARIBALDI STREET ★★ Run-of-the-mill suspense tale chronicling the abduction of Nazi war criminal Adolf Eichmann by Israelis in South America. Effectively performed, though. 104m. **DIR:** Peter Collinson. **CAST:** Martin Balsam, Topol, Janet Suzman, Leo McKern. **1979**

HOUSEKEEPING ★★★ Director Bill Forsyth makes superbly quirky movies, and *Housekeeping*, based on Marilynne Robinson's novel, is a worthy addition to his body of work. Christine Lahti plays a contented transient who comes to the Pacific Northwest to care for her two orphaned nieces. Lahti makes the offbeat moments resound with weird humor. Rated PG. 112m. **DIR:** Bill Forsyth. **CAST:** Christine Lahti, Andrea Burchill, Sarah Walker. **1987**

HOUSEWIFE ★★ When a would-be rapist and thief breaks into the house of a well-to-do Beverly Hills couple, he unleashes the tensions that exist beneath the surface of their well-ordered lives. Exploitative drama with a cast that deserves better. Rated R for violence and sexual situations. 95m. **DIR:** Larry Cohen. **CAST:** Yaphet Kotto, Andrew Duggan, Joyce Van Patten, Jeannie Berlin. **1972**

HOW GREEN WAS MY VALLEY ★★★★★ This 1941 best-picture Oscar winner is a tribute to the lasting value of a family's love. Director John Ford also won an Oscar for the way he brings out the soul of Richard Llewellyn's bestseller, which concerns a Welsh mining family, as seen through the eyes of its youngest member (Roddy McDowall, in one of his most famous child-star roles). 118m. **DIR:** John Ford. **CAST:** Walter Pidgeon, Maureen O'Hara, Roddy McDowall, Donald Crisp, John Loder, Barry Fitzgerald. **1941**

HOWARDS END ★★★★★ Two relatively liberated middle-class sisters become entangled with the members of an upper-crust British family. The creative team that adapted E. M. Forster's *Room with a View* and *Maurice* saved the best for this magnificent Forster adaptation. This Merchant-Ivory adaptation is a gorgeous, intelligent, and engrossing story of the first decade of the Twentieth century, and is propelled through distinctive, well-defined characters, rich dialogue, elements of delicious irony, and evocative locales. Rated PG. 140m. **DIR:** James Ivory. **CAST:** Emma Thompson, Anthony Hopkins, Vanessa Redgrave, Helena Bonham Carter, James Wilby, Samuel West. **1992**

HOWARDS OF VIRGINIA, THE ★★ Tiring, too-long retelling of the Revolutionary War centering on an aristocratic Virginia family. In the Cary Grant filmography, it is just plain awful. B&W; 117m. **DIR:** Frank Lloyd. **CAST:** Cary Grant, Martha Scott, Cedric Hardwicke, Alan Marshal, Richard Carlson, Paul Kelly, Anne Revere, Irving Bacon. **1940**

HUCKSTERS, THE ★★ Exposé of the advertising business is as vapid as the products pushed by the advertisers in this overlong melodrama. A mature Clark Gable, recently returned from duty in World War II, heads a stunning but ultimately wasted cast that includes Deborah Kerr and Ava Gardner as the two gals who want him. B&W; 115m. **DIR:** Jack Conway. **CAST:** Clark Gable, Deborah Kerr, Sydney Greenstreet, Adolphe Menjou, Ava Gardner, Keenan Wynn, Edward Arnold, Frank Albertson, Douglas Fowley. **1947**

HUD ★★★★★ In one of his most memorable performances, Paul Newman stars as the arrogant ne'er-do-well son of a Texas rancher (Melvyn Douglas) who has fallen on hard times. Instead of helping his father, Hud drunkenly pursues the family's housekeeper (Patricia Neal), who wants nothing to do with him. When asked, Newman dubbed this one "pretty good." An understatement. B&W; 112m. **DIR:** Martin Ritt. **CAST:** Paul Newman, Patricia Neal, Melvyn Douglas, Brandon de Wilde. **1963**

HUMAN COMEDY, THE ★★★½ California author William Saroyan's tender and touching story of life in a small valley town during World War II is a winner all around in this compassionate, now-nostalgic film. Mickey Rooney shines as the Western Union messenger verging on manhood. A sentimental slice of life, comic and tragic. B&W; 118m. **DIR:** Clarence Brown. **CAST:** Mickey Rooney, Frank Morgan, "Butch" Jenkins, Ray Collins, Darryl Hickman, Marsha Hunt, Fay Bainter, Donna Reed, James Craig, Van Johnson. **1943**

HUMAN DESIRE ★★★½ Broderick Crawford turns in a compelling performance as a hot-tempered husband who kills an innocent man with whom he suspects his wife of having an affair. Fritz Lang's remake of Jean Renoir's *La Bête Humaine*. B&W; 90m. **DIR:** Fritz Lang. **CAST:** Glenn Ford, Broderick Crawford, Gloria Grahame, Edgar Buchanan. **1954**

HUMAN HEARTS ★★½ Old-fashioned story of a criminally manipulated big-city woman who comes between a devoted father and son. Set in a peaceful village in Arkansas. Handkerchief material. Silent. B&W; 99m. **DIR:** King Baggott. **CAST:** House Peters, Russell Simpson, Mary Philbin. **1922**

HUMORESQUE ★★★★ Terrific dialogue highlights this wonderfully trashy story of a talented violinist (John Garfield) who sells his soul and body to a wealthy, older woman (Joan Crawford) who promises to further his career. Witty, sophisticated, and lavish in its production values, this is a weeper par excellence. 125m. **DIR:** Jean Negulesco. **CAST:** Joan Crawford, John Garfield, Oscar Levant, J. Carrol Naish, Craig Stevens. **1946**

HUNT FOR THE NIGHT STALKER ★★★ Involving made-for-television police drama that follows the exploits of the two detectives who diligently pursued serial killer Richard Ramirez, whose reign of terror put southern California in a panic. Good performances and painstaking detail. Also known as *Manhunt: Search for the Night Stalker*. 100m. **DIR:** Bruce Seth Green. **CAST:** Richard Jordan, A. Martinez, Lisa Eilbacher. **1989**

HUNTER'S BLOOD 🦃 *Deliverance*, but without any of that film's tension or acting. Rated R for language and violence. 101m. **DIR:** Robert C. Hughes. **CAST:** Sam Bottoms, Clu Gulager, Kim Delaney, Mayf Nutter, Ken Swofford, Joey Travolta. **1987**

HUNTING ★★★ Torrid drama finds rich, attractive John Savage playing with the emotions of both friends and business associates. When he lures young, married Kerry Armstrong into an affair, blackmail and murder ensue. Rated R for nudity and violence. 97m. **DIR:** Frank Howson. **CAST:** John Savage, Kerry Armstrong, Guy Pearce, Rebecca Rigg. **1991**

HURRICANE, THE (1937) ★★★ One of early Hollywood's disaster films. The lives and loves of a group of stereotyped characters on a Pacific island are interrupted by the big wind of the title. The sequences involving people are labored, but the special effects of the hurricane make this picture worth watching. B&W; 102m. **DIR:** John Ford. **CAST:** Jon Hall, Dorothy Lamour, Raymond Massey, Mary Astor. **1937**

HUSBANDS AND LOVERS 🦃 Seemingly endless and pointless film features Joanna Pacula as a selfish wife who demands weekends off to spend with her abusive lover. Comes in R and unrated versions, both containing violence and nudity. 94m. **DIR:** Mauro Bolognini. **CAST:** Julian Sands, Joanna Pacula, Tcheky Karyo. **1991**

HUSBANDS AND WIVES ★★★½ Off-camera events eclipsed this Woody Allen comedy-drama during its initial release, detracting from the power of an often brilliant study of marriages under stress. Judy Davis is simply magnificent as a fault-finding shrew. While the characters are uniformly excellent, the film is severely compromised by Carlo Di Palma's headache-inducing hand-held camera (intended to suggest a documentary approach). Rated R for profanity. 107m. **DIR:** Woody Allen. **CAST:** Woody Allen, Mia Farrow, Judy Davis, Sydney Pollack, Juliette Lewis, Liam Neeson. **1992**

HUSSY ★★ Both the talented British actress Helen Mirren and director Matthew Chapman (his debut) usually do much better work than in this dreary melodrama about a nightclub hostess and part-time prostitute. Chapman succeeds at re-creating the oppressive atmosphere of a seedy British nightclub all too well. Rated R for nudity. 95m. **DIR:** Matthew Chapman. **CAST:** Helen Mirren, John Shea. **1980**

HUSTLER, THE ★★★★★ This film may well contain Paul Newman's best screen performance. As pool shark Eddie Felson, he's magnificent. A two-bit hustler who travels from pool room to pool room taking suckers—whom he allows to win until the stakes get high enough, then wipes them out—Felson decides to take a shot at the big time. He challenges Minnesota Fats (nicely played by Jackie Gleason) to a big money match. B&W; 135m. **DIR:** Robert Rossen. **CAST:** Paul Newman, Jackie Gleason, Piper Laurie, George C. Scott, Murray Hamilton, Myron McCormick. **1961**

HUSTLING ★★★★ An investigative report delves into the world of big-city prostitution in this adult TV movie. Fine performances and a good script place this above the average TV film. 100m. **DIR:** Joseph Sargent. **CAST:** Lee Remick, Jill Clayburgh, Alex Rocco, Monte Markham. **1975**

I AM A CAMERA ★★★½ Julie Harris is perfect as the easy, good-time English bohemian Sally Bowles in this finely honed film clone of the play adapted by John Van Druten from novelist Christopher Isherwood's autobiographical stories about pre-World War II Berlin. The Broadway and screen versions ultimately became the musical *Cabaret*. 98m. **DIR:** Henry Cornelius. **CAST:** Julie Harris, Laurence Harvey, Shelley Winters, Ron Randell, Patrick McGoohan. **1955**

I AM A FUGITIVE FROM A CHAIN GANG ★★★★ Dark, disturbing, and effective Paul Muni vehicle. The star plays an innocent man who finds himself convicted of a crime and brutalized by a corrupt court system. An unforgettable film. B&W; 90m. **DIR:** Mervyn LeRoy. **CAST:** Paul Muni, Glenda Farrell, Helen Vinson, Preston Foster. **1932**

I AM THE CHEESE ★★½ A teenager who has witnessed the death of his parents is confined to a psychiatric hospital where doctors try to get him to deal with his tragedy. The dime-store psychology is the only drawback to this well-played movie. Rated PG. 95m. **DIR:** Robert Jiras. **CAST:** Robert MacNaughton, Hope Lange, Don Murray, Robert Wagner, Cynthia Nixon, Lee Richardson. **1983**

I AM THE LAW ★★★ This slick but somewhat silly crime melodrama stars Edward G. Robinson as a crusading district attorney out to get a group of mobsters headed by a corrupt civic leader. B&W; 83m. **DIR:** Alexander Hall. **CAST:** Edward G. Robinson, Barbara O'Neil, John Beal, Wendy Barrie, Otto Kruger, Marc Lawrence. **1938**

I, CLAUDIUS ★★★★★ This PBS series brilliantly recounts the history of the Roman Empire—the reign of Augustus, the infamous cruelty of Tiberius and his successor, Caligula, and the reign of the mild and amiable Claudius. One of the most popular *Masterpiece Theater* presentations. 780m. **DIR:** Herbert Wise. **CAST:** Derek Jacobi, Sian Phillips, Brian Blessed, John Hurt. **1976**

I HEARD THE OWL CALL MY NAME ★★★½ In this mystical tale of love and courage, Tom Courtenay beautifully portrays Father Mark Brian, a young Anglican priest whose bishop, played by Dean Jagger, sends him to make his mark. He finds himself among the proud Indians of the Northwest. Rated G. 79m. **DIR:** Daryl Duke. **CAST:** Tom Courtenay, Dean Jagger, Paul Stanley. **1973**

I KNOW WHY THE CAGED BIRD SINGS ★★★½ Based on writer Maya Angelou's memoirs of her early life in the Depression years in the South. Often very touching and effective, this made-for-TV film details the author's reaction to her parents' divorce and the struggle of her grandparents to raise her and her brother. 100m. **DIR:** Fielder Cook. **CAST:** Diahann Carroll, Ruby Dee, Esther Rolle, Roger E. Mosley. **1979**

I LIVE MY LIFE ★★★ A wealthy young woman falls in love with an archaeologist while on a cruise. Charming romantic drama. B&W; 97m. **DIR:** W. S. Van Dyke. **CAST:** Joan Crawford, Brian Aherne, Frank Morgan, Aline MacMahon. **1935**

I LIVE WITH ME DAD ★★★ Yes, the title is correct. That's what a poor Australian boy keeps repeating to the various child-welfare and police authorities who try to take him from his father. Unrated. 86m. **DIR:** Paul Moloney. **CAST:** Haydon Samuels, Rebecca Gibney. **1985**

I LOVE N. Y. 🦃 Scott Baio plays a hotheaded photographer who falls for a famous actor's daughter. Rated R for profanity. 100m. **DIR:** Alan Smithee. **CAST:** Scott Baio, Christopher Plummer, Jennifer O'Neill. **1988**

I MARRIED A CENTERFOLD ★★½ When a nerdish engineer bets $500 that he can meet Miss November, a centerfold, he not only finds her, but the two fall in love. Made for TV. 100m. **DIR:** Peter Werner. **CAST:** Teri Copley, Timothy Daly, Diane Ladd, Anson Williams. **1984**

I NEVER PROMISED YOU A ROSE GARDEN ★★★½ Kathleen Quinlan plays a schizophrenic teenager seeking treatment from a dedicated psychiatrist in this well-acted but depressing drama. Rated R. 96m. **DIR:** Anthony Page. **CAST:** Bibi Andersson, Kathleen Quinlan, Diane Varsi. **1977**

I NEVER SANG FOR MY FATHER ★★★★½ A depressing but finely crafted film about a man (Gene Hackman) who must deal with the care of his elderly father (Melvyn Douglas). Everyone in this touching film does a superb job. Based on a play of the same name by Robert Anderson. Rated PG. 93m. **DIR:** Gilbert Cates. **CAST:**

Melvyn Douglas, Gene Hackman, Estelle Parsons, Dorothy Stickney. **1970**

I POSED FOR PLAYBOY 🦃 Three women pose nude and must live with the repercussions. Slow, bland, and listless melodrama. Rated R for nudity and profanity. 103m. **DIR:** Stephen Stafford. **CAST:** Lynda Carter, Michele Greene, Amanda Peterson. **1991**

I REMEMBER MAMA ★★★½ Irene Dunne is Mama in this sentimental drama about an engaging Norwegian family in San Francisco. Definitely a feel-good film for the nostalgic-minded. Hearts of gold all the way! B&W; 148m. **DIR:** George Stevens. **CAST:** Irene Dunne, Barbara Bel Geddes, Oscar Homolka, Philip Dorn, Ellen Corby. **1948**

I STAND CONDEMNED ★★★ A jealous suitor frames a rival in order to have a clear field for the affections of the woman both love. Not much here, except a young and dashing Laurence Olivier in one of his first films. B&W; 75m. **DIR:** Anthony Asquith. **CAST:** Harry Baur, Laurence Olivier, Robert Cochran. **1935**

I WANT TO LIVE! ★★★ Pulling all stops out, Susan Hayward won an Oscar playing antiheroine B-girl Barbara Graham in this shattering real-life drama. Stupidly involved in a robbery-murder, Graham was indicted, railroaded to conviction, and executed at California's infamous San Quentin State Prison in 1955. To sit through this one you have to be steel-nerved or supremely callous, or both. B&W; 120m. **DIR:** Robert Wise. **CAST:** Susan Hayward, Simon Oakland, Virginia Vincent, Theodore Bikel. **1958**

I WANT WHAT I WANT ★★ The search for emotional and sexual identity is the focal point of this British production about a man who undergoes a sex-change operation and falls in love. Although the subject matter is still controversial today, this film is remarkably tame. 97m. **DIR:** John Dexter. **CAST:** Anne Heywood, Harry Andrews, Jill Bennett, Michael Coles, Nigel Flatley. **1972**

ICE CASTLES ★★½ Alexis Wintson (Lynn-Holly Johnson) is a girl from a small midwestern town who dreams of skating in the Olympics. No matter how fetching and believable Johnson may be, nothing can surmount the soggy sentimentality of this cliché-ridden work. Rated PG. 109m. **DIR:** Donald Wrye. **CAST:** Robby Benson, Lynn-Holly Johnson, Colleen Dewhurst, Tom Skerritt. **1979**

ICE PALACE ★★★½ Film adaptation of Edna Ferber's soap-opera saga about Alaska's statehood. Zeb Kennedy (Richard Burton) fights against statehood while Thor Storm (Robert Ryan) devotes his life to it. Beautifully acted, particularly by Carolyn Jones as the woman both men love. 144m. **DIR:** Vincent Sherman. **CAST:** Richard Burton, Robert Ryan, Carolyn Jones, Martha Hyer, Jim Backus. **1960**

IDIOT'S DELIGHT ★★★½ An all-star cast makes memorable movie history in this, the last antiwar film produced before World War II erupted. Norma Shearer is at her best as a Garbo-like fake-Russian-accented mistress companion of munitions tycoon Edward Arnold. Clark Gable is her ex, a wisecracking vaudeville hoofer. With other types, they are stranded in a European luxury hotel as war looms. B&W; 105m. **DIR:** Clarence Brown. **CAST:** Clark Gable, Norma Shearer, Edward Arnold, Charles Coburn, Burgess Meredith, Laura Hope Crews, Joseph Schildkraut, Virginia Grey. **1938**

IDOL DANCER, THE ★★½ A drunken Yankee beachcomber befriends a young native girl on an island in the South Seas. B&W; 76m. **DIR:** D. W. Griffith. **CAST:** Richard Barthelmess, Clarine Seymour, Creighton Hale. **1920**

IF EVER I SEE YOU AGAIN 🦃 Fresh from his success with *You Light Up My Life*, writer-director-composer Joe Brooks threw together this celluloid love poem to model Shelley Hack. Rated PG. 105m. **DIR:** Joseph Brooks. **CAST:** Joe Brooks, Shelley Hack, Jimmy Breslin, George Plimpton. **1978**

IF YOU COULD SEE WHAT I HEAR ★★ The film is supposedly the biography of blind singer/composer Tom Sullivan. You'd have to be not only blind but deaf and, most of all, dumb to appreciate this one. Rated PG. 103m. **DIR:** Eric Till. **CAST:** Marc Singer, R. H. Thompson, Sarah Torgov, Shari Belafonte-Harper, Douglas Campbell. **1982**

IKE: THE WAR YEARS ★★ Robert Duvall is D-day commander General Dwight Eisenhower, and Lee Remick is his wartime romance Kay Summersby, in this tedious retelling of high-echelon soldiering and whitewashed hanky-panky during the European phase of World War II. Trimmed drastically from an original six-hour miniseries. 196m. **DIR:** Melville Shavelson, Boris Sagal. **CAST:** Robert Duvall, Lee Remick, J. D. Cannon, Darren McGavin. **1978**

ILL MET BY MOONLIGHT ★★★ In 1944 on the island of Crete, the British hatch a plot to kidnap a German general and smuggle him to Cairo. This sets off a manhunt with twenty thousand German troops and airplanes pursuing the partisans through Crete's mountainous terrain. B&W; 105m. **DIR:** Michael Powell. **CAST:** Dirk Bogarde, Marius Goring, David Oxley, Cyril Cusack. **1957**

ILLEGALLY YOURS 🦃 A bumbling jury member falls for the plaintiff in a murder case. Rated PG. 102m. **DIR:** Peter Bogdanovich. **CAST:** Rob Lowe, Colleen Camp, Kenneth Mars, Kim Myers. **1988**

ILLICIT ★★ A sexy title for a dull movie about a loose-living woman who tries to settle down until she gets bored with marriage. The same story is better presented in the Bette Davis remake called *Ex-Lady*. B&W; 81m. **DIR:** Archie Mayo. **CAST:** Barbara Stanwyck, Joan Blondell, Charles Butterworth, Ricardo Cortez, James Rennie. **1931**

I'M A FOOL ★★★ Ron Howard stars as a naïve young man who abandons his Ohio home for life on the road as a horse trainer. His desperate attempts to make himself worthy in the eyes of the opposite sex escalate until he's passing himself off as the son of a fabulously wealthy man. From a Sherwood Anderson story. Introduced by Henry Fonda; unrated and suitable for family viewing. 38m. **DIR:** Noel Black. **CAST:** Ron Howard, Amy Irving, John Light. **1976**

I'M DANCING AS FAST AS I CAN 🦃 Based on documentary filmmaker Barbara Gordon's bestselling autobiography, which dealt with her valiant—and sometimes horrifying—struggle with Valium addiction. Rated PG for profanity. 107m. **DIR:** Jack Hofsiss. **CAST:** Jill Clayburgh, Nicol Williamson, Geraldine Page. **1981**

IMAGE, THE ★★★★½ Ratings-hungry telejournalists turn a critical eye on themselves in this crackling topical drama—a study of a network news star who begins to believe his own reviews. This made-for-cable movie is unrated, but contains explicit language and brief nudity. 89m. **DIR:** Peter Werner. **CAST:** Albert Finney, John Mahoney, Kathy Baker, Swoosie Kurtz, Marsha Mason. **1990**

IMAGE OF PASSION 🦃 In this unimpressive romance, a young advertising executive begins a passionate affair with a male stripper. 105m. **DIR:** Susan Orlikoff-Simon. **CAST:** James Horan, Susan D. Shaw. **1982**

IMAGEMAKER, THE ★★★½ Intriguing exposé on the selling of American politicians. Michael Nouri plays a deposed political power maker whose life is threatened when he plans to tell all. Anne Twomey plays the TV reporter who had ruined his previous career. Rated R for nudity, violence, and profanity. 93m. **DIR:** Hal Weiner. **CAST:** Michael Nouri, Anne Twomey, Jerry Orbach, Jessica Harper, Farley Granger. **1985**

IMITATION OF LIFE ★★★½ Earnest performances and gifted direction make this soap-operaish, Fannie Hurst tearjerker tolerable viewing. Lana Turner is a fame-greedy actress who neglects her daughter for her career. Juanita Moore is her black friend whose daughter repudiates her heritage and breaks her mother's heart by passing for white. 124m. **DIR:** Douglas Sirk. **CAST:** Lana Turner, John Gavin, Sandra Dee, Dan O'Herlihy, Susan Kohner, Troy Donahue, Robert Alda, Juanita Moore. **1959**

IMMEDIATE FAMILY ★★★½ Unable to have children, a wealthy couple decide to adopt a teenager's baby. Meeting the girl and her boyfriend proves to be both touching and humorous. Rated PG-13 for adult topic. 100m. **DIR:** Jonathan Kaplan. **CAST:** Glenn Close, James Woods, Mary Stuart Masterson, Kevin Dillon. **1989**

IMMORTAL BATTALION, THE (A.K.A. THE WAY AHEAD) ★★★½ Based on an idea conceived by Lt. Col. David Niven, this highly effective wartime semidocumentary follows his attempts to turn a group of newly activated civilians into a combat team. This gem skillfully mixes training and combat footage with filmed sequences to create a powerful mood while delicately balancing great performances. 91m. **DIR:** Carol Reed. **CAST:** David Niven, Stanley Holloway, Raymond Huntley, Peter Ustinov, Trevor Howard, Leo Genn, James Donald. **1944**

IMMORTAL SERGEANT, THE ★★★½ Henry Fonda gives a solid performance as a corporal in the Canadian army, attached to the British Eighth Army in North Africa during World War II. During a battle with Nazi troops, his squad sergeant is killed and he is forced into command. From a novel by John Brophy. B&W; 91m. **DIR:** John M. Stahl. **CAST:** Henry Fonda, Maureen O'Hara, Thomas Mitchell, Allyn Joslyn, Reginald Gardiner, Melville Cooper. **1943**

IMMORTAL STORY ★★★★ A powerful, cynical old man tries to turn a myth into reality by hiring people to enact it for his amusement. Made for French television, this adaptation of a short story by Isak Dinesen shows a subtler and more contemplative side of director Orson Welles, not the brash youth who made *Citizen Kane*. 63m. **DIR:** Orson Welles. **CAST:** Orson Welles, Jeanne Moreau, Roger Coggio, Fernando Rey. **1968**

IMPOSTER, THE 🦃 Con artist in a private war against juvenile drug dealers. Not rated. 95m. **DIR:** Michael Pressman. **CAST:** Anthony Geary, Billy Dee Williams, Lorna Patterson, Penny Johnson, Jordan Charney. **1984**

IMPROMPTU ★★★★ George Sand, the female novelist with the men's pants and stylish cigars, and Frederic Chopin, the Polish composer, pianist, and all-around sensitive soul, were the talk of Paris as they embarked on a most unusual and passionate affair. That's the subject of this extravagant and entertaining period romance spiced with unexpected comedy and lovely music. Rated PG-13. 109m. **DIR:** James Lapine. **CAST:** Judy Davis, Hugh Grant, Mandy Patinkin, Bernadette Peters, Julian Sands, Emma Thompson. **1991**

IN A MOMENT OF PASSION 🦃 This laughably melodramatic clunker, with Chase Masterson simply awful as a Hollywood ingenue cuddling up to killer Maxwell Caulfield, plays like a student film given ill-advised mainstream distribution. Rated R for profanity, violence, and nudity. 100m. **DIR:** Zbigniew Kaminski. **CAST:** Maxwell Caulfield, Chase Masterson, Vivian Schilling. **1993**

IN A SHALLOW GRAVE ★★ Michael Biehn stars as a disfigured World War II vet who returns to an empty home and life. Patrick Dempsey is a drifter who becomes a messenger between Biehn and his ex-fiancée (Maureen Mueller). The resulting love triangle, both heterosexual and homosexual, is too short on plot, and the movie ends without an ending. Rated R. 92m. **DIR:** Kenneth Bowser. **CAST:** Michael Biehn, Patrick Dempsey, Michael Beach, Maureen Mueller. **1988**

IN BETWEEN 🦃 Boring minimalist film that depicts feminine isolation. B&W; 30m. **DIR:** Wade Novy. **CAST:** Maggie McOmie. **1979**

IN COUNTRY ★★★½ A Kentucky teenager (Emily Lloyd) tries to understand the Vietnam War and why her father had to die in this uneven but well-intentioned and ultimately powerful film. Bruce Willis gives an effective performance as Lloyd's uncle, a Vietnam vet who has never fully recovered from his combat experience. Rated R for brief violence and profanity. 106m. **DIR:** Norman Jewison. **CAST:** Bruce Willis, Emily Lloyd, Joan Allen, Kevin Anderson, Richard Hamilton, Judith Ivey, Peggy Rea. **1989**

IN DANGEROUS COMPANY 🦃 Unexciting, glitzy Sidney Sheldon-ish piece has Tracy Scoggins as a beautiful woman who uses her body to square one bad guy off against the other. Rated R for nudity, simulated sex, violence, and language. 92m. **DIR:** Reuben Preuss. **CAST:** Tracy Scoggins, Cliff De Young, Chris Mulkey, Henry Darrow, Richard Portnow, Steven Keats. **1988**

IN LOVE WITH AN OLDER WOMAN ★★½ San Francisco lawyer John Ritter falls in love with a woman fifteen years older than him. They move in together. Made-for-TV movie (can't you tell?), though not bad. 96m. **DIR:** Jack Bender. **CAST:** John Ritter, Karen Carlson, Jamie Rose, Jeff Altman. **1982**

IN NAME ONLY ★★★½ This is a classic soap opera. Cary Grant is desperately in love with sweet and lovely Carole Lombard. Unfortunately, he's married to venomous Kay Francis. You can't help but get completely wrapped up in the skillfully executed story. B&W; 102m. **DIR:** John Cromwell. **CAST:** Carole Lombard, Cary Grant, Kay Francis, Charles Coburn, Helen Vinson, Peggy Ann Garner. **1939**

IN OLD CHICAGO ★★★★ Tyrone Power attempts to control Chicago through corruption and vice while his brother, Don Ameche, heads a reform movement. Fast-moving story leading to a spectacular re-creation of the 1871 fire. Supporting Oscar for Alice Brady as their mother (Mrs. O'Leary), who owns the cow that kicks over the lantern that . . . B&W; 95m. **DIR:** Henry King. **CAST:** Tyrone Power, Alice Faye, Don Ameche, Alice Brady, Andy Devine, Brian Donlevy, Phyllis Brooks, Tom Brown, Sidney Blackmer, Rondo Hatton. **1938**

IN PRAISE OF OLDER WOMEN 🦃 A man's reflections on his various affairs. Rated R. 108m. **DIR:** George Kaczender. **CAST:** Tom Berenger, Karen Black, Susan Strasberg, Alexandra Stewart. **1978**

IN SEARCH OF ANNA 🦃 Pseudo-art movie about an ex-con and a flaky model. 94m. **DIR:** Esben Storm. **CAST:** Richard Moir, Judy Morris, Chris Hayward, Bill Hunter. **1977**

IN SEARCH OF HISTORIC JESUS 🦃 Low-budget reenactments of key events in Jesus' life. Rated G. 91m. **DIR:** Henning Schellerup. **CAST:** John Rubinstein, John Anderson, Morgan Brittany, Nehemiah Persoff, John Hoyt. **1979**

IN SELF DEFENSE 🦃 Linda Purl testifies against a crazed murderer after the police promise her protection they can't provide in this unimaginative, overacted thriller. Rated PG for substance abuse and violence. 94m. **DIR:** Bruce Seth Green. **CAST:** Linda Purl, Yaphet Kotto, Billy Drago. **1987**

IN THE NAME OF THE FATHER ★★★★ Star Daniel Day-Lewis and director Jim Sheridan of *My Left Foot* reteam for this political thriller, based on the true story of Gerry Conlon, an Irish youth accused of a crime he didn't commit. Conlon is enjoying the freewheeling lifestyle of the swinging '60s in London and has an antiestablishment attitude, but he isn't guilty of the terrorist bombing for which he and his equally innocent father are arrested. Emma Thompson adds vitality to the courtroom scenes as she attempts to prove their innocence. Riveting and brilliantly acted. Rated R for violence and profanity. 125m. **DIR:** Jim Sheridan. **CAST:** Daniel Day-Lewis, Emma Thompson, Pete Postlethwaite. **1993**

IN THIS OUR LIFE ★★★½ The best Bette Davis movies are those in which she must work to keep the spotlight, such as when paired with skillful Olivia de Havilland. They play sisters in love with the same man (Dennis Morgan). Humphrey Bogart and the cast of *The Maltese Falcon* have walk-ons in a bar scene. B&W; 97m. **DIR:** John Huston. **CAST:** Bette Davis, Olivia de Havilland, Dennis Morgan, Charles Coburn, George Brent, Hattie McDaniel, Frank Craven, Billie Burke, Lee Patrick. **1942**

IN TROUBLE 🦃 Canadian film about a young woman who finds herself pregnant and unmarried. Not rated, but contains brief nudity. 82m. **DIR:** Gilles Carle. **CAST:** Julie Lachapelle, Jacques Cohen, Daniel Pilon. **1967**

IN WHICH WE SERVE ★★★★★ Noel Coward wrote, produced, directed, and acted in this, one of the most moving wartime portrayals of men at sea. It is not the stirring battle sequences that make this film stand out but the intimate human story of the crew, their families, and the ship they love. A great film in all respects. B&W; 115m. **DIR:** Noel Coward, David Lean. **CAST:** Noel Coward, John Mills, Michael Wilding. **1942**

INCIDENT, THE (1967) ★★★½ Gritty inner-city horror story takes place on a late-night subway ride as two young thugs (Martin Sheen and Tony Musante, in their first film) terrorize each of the passengers. Definitely worth a watch! Unrated, but contains violence. B&W; 99m. **DIR:** Larry Peerce. **CAST:** Tony Musante, Martin Sheen, Beau Bridges, Donna Mills, Gary Merrill, Thelma Ritter, Ruby Dee. **1967**

INCIDENT, THE (1989) ★★★½ During World War II, a small-town lawyer (Walter Matthau) finds himself railroaded by a powerful judge (Harry Morgan) into defending an accused murderer (Peter Firth). The problem is that Matthau's client is a German soldier from a nearby POW camp, where he allegedly killed the town doctor (Barnard Hughes), who was also the lawyer's longtime friend. Well-done. Made for TV. 94m. **DIR:** Joseph Sargent. **CAST:** Walter Matthau, Harry Morgan, Robert Carradine, Susan Blakely, Peter Firth, Barnard Hughes. **1989**

INCIDENT AT DARK RIVER ★★ Predictable environmental-pollution teledrama is nonetheless enjoyable, due largely to reliable Mike Farrell (who also wrote the story). A battery factory is dumping nasty things in the river out back—and denying everything. 94m. **DIR:** Michael Pressman. **CAST:** Mike Farrell, Tess Harper, Helen Hunt. **1989**

INCONVENIENT WOMAN, AN ★★ Dominick Dunne's celebrated novel arrives as a made-for-TV soap opera with murder, double crosses, and plenty of scenery chewing. Great cast makes the best of a mediocre situation. 126m. **DIR:** Larry Elikann. **CAST:** Rebecca DeMornay, Jason Robards Jr., Jill Eikenberry, Peter Gallagher. **1991**

INCREDIBLE JOURNEY OF DR. MEG LAUREL, THE ★★★½ In this made-for-television film, Lindsay Wagner gives her usual solid performance as Meg Laurel. From humble beginnings as an orphan from the Appalachian Mountains, she becomes a doctor. After graduating from Harvard Medical School, she sets up practice in 1930s Boston. But Wagner decides to return to the mountain people and administer the latest in medical procedures. 150m. **DIR:** Guy Green. **CAST:** Lindsay Wagner, Jane Wyman, Dorothy McGuire, James Woods, Gary Lockwood, Charles Tyner, Andrew Duggan, Brock Peters, John C. Reilly. **1978**

INCREDIBLE SARAH, THE ★★ As the legendary French actress Sarah Bernhardt—in her time the toast of Paris, London, and New York—Glenda Jackson tears passions to tatters, to very rags. Theatre history buffs may like this pseudobiography. 106m. **DIR:** Richard Fleischer. **CAST:** Glenda Jackson, Daniel Massey, Yvonne Mitchell. **1976**

INDECENT BEHAVIOR 🦃 Viewer beware—the title tells all in this potboiler about a wealthy client of a sex therapist who overdoses on a designer drug. Rated R for nudity, simulated sex, profanity, and violence. 93m. **DIR:** Lawrence Landoff. **CAST:** Shannon Tweed, Gary Hudson, Jan-Michael Vincent, Brad Sanders, Penny Peyser, Robert Sampson, George Shannon, Lawrence Hilton-Jacobs. **1993**

INDECENT OBSESSION, AN ★★★ A bleak, intense view of the results of war. Wendy Hughes is the compassionate nurse for shell-shocked British soldiers and other war-torn crazies. A sensitive adaptation of Colleen McCullough's bestseller. Not rated, but contains violence, nudity, and profanity. 100m. **DIR:** Lex Marinos. **CAST:** Wendy Hughes, Gary Sweet, Richard Moir. **1985**

INDECENT PROPOSAL ★★½ Good performances cannot save this brainless soap opera. Extremely wealthy Robert Redford offers $1 million to married Demi Moore if she'll spend the night with him. Naturally, Moore and her hubby, a whining, less-than-effective Woody Harrelson, are in deep financial trouble and the rest of the film is just as predictable. Rated R for profanity, nudity, and simulated sex. 113m. **DIR:** Adrian Lyne. **CAST:** Robert Redford, Demi Moore, Woody Harrelson, Oliver Platt, Seymour Cassel. **1993**

INDEPENDENCE DAY ★★★★ Excellent little story about a young woman (Kathleen Quinlan) who wants to leave the stifling environment of her hometown. She's helped and hindered by a growing attachment to David Keith, a garage mechanic with his own problems. Rated R for violence and sex. 110m. **DIR:** Robert Mandel. **CAST:** David Keith, Kathleen Quinlan, Richard Farnsworth, Frances Sternhagen, Cliff De Young, Dianne Wiest. **1983**

INDIAN RUNNER, THE ★★★½ As a first-time director, actor Sean Penn has fashioned a movie that's not unlike one of his better performances—edgy, rough-hewn, daring, passionate, and fascinating. His movie revolves around the conflicts arising from two brothers as unalike as Cain and Abel. Though a box-office failure, *The Indian Runner* offers hope for a substantial directorial career from Penn. Rated R, with profanity and violence. 125m. **DIR:** Sean Penn. **CAST:** David Morse, Viggo Mortensen, Valeria Golino, Patricia Arquette, Charles Bronson, Sandy Dennis. **1991**

INDISCRETION OF AN AMERICAN WIFE ★★½ One hour and three minutes of emotional turmoil played out against the background of Rome's railway station as adultress Jennifer Jones meets her lover, Montgomery Clift, for the last time. B&W; 63m. **DIR:** Vittorio De Sica. **CAST:** Jennifer Jones, Montgomery Clift, Gino Cervi, Richard Beymer. **1954**

INFORMER, THE ★★★★ John Ford's classic about a slow-witted Irish pug (Victor McLaglen), who turns his friend in for money to impress his ladylove and gets his comeuppance from the IRA, has lost none of its atmospheric punch over the years. McLaglen is superb, and the movie lingers in your memory long after the credits roll. B&W; 91m. **DIR:** John Ford. **CAST:** Victor McLaglen, Heather Angel, Preston Foster. **1935**

INHERIT THE WIND ★★★★★ In this superb film based on the stage play of the notorious Scopes monkey trial, a biology teacher is put on trial for teaching the theory of evolution. The courtroom battle that actually took place between Clarence Darrow and William Jennings Bryan could not have been more powerful or stimulating than the acting battle put on by two of America's most respected actors—Spencer Tracy and Fredric March. B&W; 127m. **DIR:** Stanley Kramer. **CAST:** Spencer Tracy, Fredric March, Gene Kelly, Dick York, Claude Akins. **1960**

INKWELL, THE ★★ This amateurish coming-of-age story has its heart in the right place, but it's a dramatic and comic mess. A decent but troubled African-American teen from New York City and his parents spend their 1976 summer vacation with affluent relatives on Martha's Vineyard. The fashions—especially the bell-bottomed, polyester jumpsuits—are a scream. But the film never draws a credible bead on its characters or the relationships between the shy teen, his ex-Black Panther father and Republican uncle, and his mom and moody grandmother. Rated R for language and suggested sex. 112m. **DIR:** Matty Rich. **CAST:** Larenz Tate, Suzzanne Douglas, Joe Morton, Glynn Turman, Jada Pinkett. **1994**

INN OF THE SIXTH HAPPINESS, THE ★★★★ Superb acting marks this heartwarming biography of China missionary Gladys Aylward (Ingrid Bergman). The movie opens with her determined attempt to enter the missionary service and follows her to strife-torn China. The highlight is her cross-country adventure as she leads a group of orphans away from the war zone. 158m. **DIR:** Mark Robson. **CAST:** Ingrid Bergman, Curt Jurgens, Robert Donat. **1958**

INNER CIRCLE, THE ★★★½ This drama, released within weeks of the dismantling of the Soviet Union, comes along to remind us of the coldly cruel totalitarianism of Josef Stalin. Tom Hulce stars as Ivan Sanshin, a young KGB projectionist who is shocked and thrilled to find himself selected as chief projectionist for the movie buff and dictator. The fact that it's based on a true story, and was filmed entirely in the Kremlin and other parts of Russia, lends authenticity and impact. Rated PG-13. 137m. **DIR:** Andrei Konchalovsky. **CAST:** Tom Hulce, Lolita Davidovich, Bob Hoskins. **1991**

INQUIRY, THE ★★ Italian-made film about the investigation by a Roman official (Keith Carradine) into the resurrection of Christ. Carradine is fine but Harvey Keitel makes an uneasy Pontius Pilate because of his tough-guy accent. Not rated; contains some nudity and violence. 106m. **DIR:** Damiano Damiani. **CAST:** Keith Carradine, Harvey Keitel, Phyllis Logan. **1986**

INSERTS 🦃 Dreary film about a once-great 1930s film director now making porno movies. Rated R. 99m. **DIR:** John Byrum. **CAST:** Richard Dreyfuss, Jessica Harper, Bob Hoskins, Veronica Cartwright. **1976**

INSIDE DAISY CLOVER ★★ Natalie Wood plays a teenager who wants to be a star. Robert Redford is the matinee idol she marries to get her name in the gossip columns. A grim story about Hollywood that has better performances than plot. 128m. **DIR:** Robert Mulligan. **CAST:** Natalie Wood, Robert Redford, Christopher Plummer, Roddy McDowall, Ruth Gordon. **1964**

INSIDE MOVES ★★★★ This is a film that grows on you as the heartwarming story unfolds. With a unique blend of humor and insight, director Richard Donner and screenwriters Valerie Curtin and Barry Levinson provide a captivating look into a very special friendship. John Savage plays a man who, after failing at suicide, succeeds at life with the help of some disabled friends. Rated PG. 113m. **DIR:** Richard Donner. **CAST:** John Savage, David Morse, Amy Wright, Tony Burton. **1980**

INSIDE OUT (1986) ★★½ Compelling drama that tackles agoraphobia, the fear of open spaces. Elliott Gould stars as a man who fears leaving his New York apartment; his only contact with the outside world are the phone and delivery services. Rated R for profanity. 87m. **DIR:** Robert Taicher. **CAST:** Elliott Gould, Howard Hesseman, Jennifer Tilly, Dana Elcar. **1986**

INSIDE THE THIRD REICH ★★★½ This made-for-TV miniseries is based on the autobiography of Albert Speer, the German architect who became Hitler's chief builder. Rutger Hauer portrays Speer as a man obsessed with the opportunity to build extensively while being blissfully unaware of the horrors of war around him. 250m. **DIR:** Marvin J. Chomsky. **CAST:** Rutger Hauer, Derek Jacobi, Blythe Danner, John Gielgud, Ian Holm, Elke Sommer, Trevor Howard, Robert Vaughn. **1982**

INSIGNIFICANCE ★★ Michael Emil's absolutely wonderful impersonation of Albert Einstein makes this film worth seeing. In 1954 Marilyn Monroe comes to visit Einstein in his hotel room to explain the theory of relativity to him. Charming, but it eventually loses its uniqueness as it incorporates disjunctive symbolic flashbacks into the narrative. Rated R. 110m. **DIR:** Nicolas Roeg. **CAST:** Michael Emil, Theresa Russell, Gary Busey, Tony Curtis, Will Sampson. **1985**

INSPIRATION ★★★ Greta Garbo plays a Parisian model and courtesan with whom an aspiring politician becomes infatuated, even though aware of and troubled by her past. The high rating is for the legion of Garbo fans; others may find it dated and dull. B&W; 74m. **DIR:** Clarence Brown. **CAST:** Greta Garbo, Robert Montgomery, Lewis Stone, Marjorie Rambeau. **1931**

INTERIORS ★★★★ Woody Allen tips his hat to Swedish director Ingmar Bergman with this very downbeat drama about a family tearing itself apart. Extremely serious stuff, with fine performances by all. Allen shows he can direct more than comedy. Rated R for language. 99m. **DIR:** Woody Allen. **CAST:** Diane Keaton, E. G. Marshall, Geraldine Page, Richard Jordan, Sam Waterston. **1978**

INTERMEZZO (1939) ★★★★ A love affair between a married concert violinist and a young woman doesn't stray very far from the standard eternal love triangle. This classic weeper has more renown as the English-language debut of Ingrid Bergman. B&W; 70m. **DIR:** Gregory Ratoff. **CAST:** Leslie Howard, Ingrid Bergman, Cecil Kellaway. **1939**

INTERNS, THE ★★★ This melodrama of the lives of interns in an American hospital has it all. The new doctors must deal with death, drugs, abortions, and personal problems. Competently acted and directed. B&W; 130m. **DIR:** David Swift. **CAST:** Cliff Robertson, Michael Callan, James MacArthur, Nick Adams, Suzy Parker, Buddy Ebsen, Telly Savalas. **1962**

INTERSECTION 🦃 Vancouver architect floundering in a midlife crisis watches chunks of his life pass before him during a nasty rural auto accident. Rated R for sex, nudity, and language. 105m. **DIR:** Mark Rydell. **CAST:** Richard Gere, Sharon Stone, Lolita Davidovich, Martin Landau, David Selby. **1994**

INTERVAL ★★ Merle Oberon's last feature film is a weepy story of a woman who tours the world trying to find her one true love while attempting to forget her past. Passable, but hardly a distinguished finale for Oberon's career. Rated PG. 84m. **DIR:** Daniel Mann. **CAST:** Merle Oberon, Robert Wolders, Claudio Brook, Russ Conway. **1973**

INTIMATE CONTACT ★★★ Claire Bloom and Daniel Massey are wonderful as an affluent couple confronted with the specter of AIDS. A sobering account of a family's attempt to deal with this tragic disease. Rate PG. 159m. **DIR:** Waris Hussein. **CAST:** Claire Bloom, Daniel Massey, Sylvia Syms, Mark Kingston, Maggie Steed. **1987**

INTIMATE POWER ★★★ This is the true story of a French girl sold into slavery who becomes the sultan's favorite. She bears him a male heir and then proceeds to instill in her son the rights of the Turkish people hoping for reform when he becomes sultan. Rated R for violence and nudity. 104m. **DIR:** Jack Smight. **CAST:** F. Murray Abraham, Maud Adams. **1989**

INTIMATE STRANGERS ★★ Dennis Weaver and Sally Struthers are a husband and wife who permit a lack of self-esteem to drag them into the dark areas of psychological warfare and wife beating. Melvyn Douglas is outstanding and Tyne Daly was nominated for an Emmy Award for her work in this made-for-TV film. 120m. **DIR:** John Llewellyn Moxey. **CAST:** Dennis Weaver, Sally Struthers, Tyne Daly, Larry Hagman, Melvyn Douglas. **1977**

INTO THE NIGHT ★★½ Packed with cinematic in-jokes and guest appearances by more than a dozen film directors, this is a film fan's dream. Unfortunately, it might also be a casual viewer's nightmare. Jeff Goldblum and Michelle Pfeiffer stumble into international intrigue and share a bizarre and deadly adventure in contemporary Los Angeles. Rated R for violence and profanity. 115m. **DIR:** John Landis. **CAST:** Jeff Goldblum, Michelle Pfeiffer, Paul Mazursky, Kathryn Harrold, Richard Farnsworth, Irene Papas, David Bowie, Dan Aykroyd. **1985**

INTOLERANCE ★★★★ This milestone silent epic tells and blends four stories of injustice, modern and ancient. The sets for the Babylonian sequence were the largest ever built for a film. One scene alone involved 15,000 people and 250 chariots. The acting is dated, but the picture presents a powerful viewing experience. B&W; 123m. **DIR:** D. W. Griffith. **CAST:** Lillian Gish, Bessie Love, Mae Marsh, Elmo Lincoln, Tully Marshall, Eugene Pallette, Tod Browning, Monte Blue, Robert Harron, Constance Talmadge, Erich Von Stroheim. **1916**

INTRUDER, THE (1961) ★★★½ Gripping film about a racist (William Shatner) who attempts to block court-ordered integration in a small-town school. Shatner's performance is very good, and the finale is especially intense. A.k.a. *Shame* and *I Hate Your Guts.* Not rated. B&W; 80m. **DIR:** Roger Corman. **CAST:** William Shatner, Leo Gordon, Jeanne Cooper. **1961**

INTRUDER IN THE DUST ★★★★★ One of the best adaptations of a William Faulkner novel, this was one of the first movies to take a stand on racial issues. Basically, it's the story of the lynching of an African-American by rednecks in the South. It deals as much with the reaction of the white population as it does with that of the black community. B&W; 88m. **DIR:** Clarence Brown. **CAST:** David Brian, Juano Hernandez, Claude Jarman Jr., Will Geer, Elizabeth Patterson, Porter Hall, Charles Kemper. **1949**

IRAN DAYS OF CRISIS ★★★ Fact-based account of the Iranian takeover of the American embassy in Tehran and the subsequent hostage crisis. Engrossing, thought-provoking film boasts good performances and realistic locales. Made for cable. 183m. **DIR:** Kevin Connor. **CAST:** Jeff Fahey, George Grizzard, Arliss Howard, Alice Krige, Tony Goldwyn, Daniel Gélin, Valerie Kaprisky. **1991**

IRISHMAN, THE ★★★½ Excellent Australian drama set in the 1920s. An immigrant Irish worker, who has made a living in rough territory with his team of horses, refuses to recognize progress in the form of a gas-driven truck that will put him out of business. His unwillingness to adapt tears apart his family, who wants to back him up but recognizes that he is wrong. 108m. **DIR:** Donald Crombie. **CAST:** Michael Craig, Simon Burke, Robyn Nevin, Lou Brown. **1978**

IRON & SILK ★★★ Mark Salzman's experiences in China to master martial arts jump from book to the big screen in a film that's filled with visual splendor and compelling characters. Cultures clash in a winning way as Salzman forsakes his western ways to become more in tune with his surroundings. Rated PG. 94m. **DIR:** Shirley Sun. **CAST:** Mark Salzman. **1990**

IRON DUKE, THE ★★★★ A thoroughly English stage actor, George Arliss did not make this, his first British film, until late in the decade he spent in the Hollywood studios. His Duke of Wellington, victor over Napoleon at Waterloo, is picture perfect. Buffs will particularly enjoy a younger Felix Aylmer, later Polonius in Laurence Olivier's 1948 *Hamlet*. B&W; 88m. **DIR:** Victor Saville. **CAST:** George Arliss, A. E. Matthews, Emlyn Williams, Felix Aylmer, Gladys Cooper. **1936**

IRON MAJOR, THE ★★½ Decent Hollywood bio-pic about disabled World War I hero Frank Cavanaugh, who became a trophy-winning college football coach. Loaded with sentiment, spunk, and humor. B&W; 90m. **DIR:** Ray Enright. **CAST:** Pat O'Brien, Ruth Warrick, Robert Ryan, Leon Ames. **1943**

IRON TRIANGLE, THE ★★★ The Vietnam War seen through the eyes of a hard-boiled American captain (Beau Bridges, fine as always). Haing S. Ngor (Oscar winner for *The Killing Fields*) plays a small part as a Cong officer. Solid, blood-and-guts war drama bogs down in the middle but ends with a well-staged climactic battle. Rated R for graphic combat scenes and profanity. 94m. **DIR:** Eric Weston. **CAST:** Beau Bridges, Haing S. Ngor, Johnny Hallyday. **1988**

IRONCLADS ★★½ This TV movie dramatizes the historic sea battle between the *Monitor* and the *Merrimack*. History lesson is almost ruined with silly subplots. 94m. **DIR:** Delbert Mann. **CAST:** Virginia Madsen, Alex Hyde-White, Reed Edward Diamond, Philip Casnoff, E. G. Marshall, Fritz Weaver. **1991**

IRONWEED ★★★★½ William Kennedy's adaptation of his Pulitzer Prize–winning novel turns into a showcase for Jack Nicholson and Meryl Streep, both playing skid-row alcoholics. Director Hector Babenco superbly captures the grinding, hand-to-mouth dreariness of this Depression era tale, which traces the relationship of opportunity and convenience between the two leads. This may be Streep's finest hour; her complete descent into the part is riveting. Rated R for language, violence, and brief nudity. 144m. **DIR:** Hector Babenco. **CAST:** Jack Nicholson, Meryl Streep, Carroll Baker, Michael O'Keefe, Tom Waits, Fred Gwynne. **1987**

IRRECONCILABLE DIFFERENCES ★★½ Drew Barrymore plays a little girl who sues her self-centered, career-conscious parents—Ryan O'Neal and Shelley Long—for divorce. The laughs are few, but there are some effective scenes of character development. Rated PG for profanity and nudity. 101m. **DIR:** Charles Shyer. **CAST:** Drew Barrymore, Ryan O'Neal, Shelley Long. **1984**

IS PARIS BURNING? ★★★ A spectacular war movie that plays like a newsreel with famous stars in bit parts. The story of the liberation of Paris, and the Nazi attempt to burn it to the ground is dramatic, moving, and educational. B&W; 175m. **DIR:** René Clement. **CAST:** Kirk Douglas, Glenn Ford, Orson Welles, Jean-Paul Belmondo, Charles Boyer, Leslie Caron, Yves Montand, Simone Signoret, Robert Stack, Jean-Pierre Cassel, Claude Dauphin, Gert Fröbe, Daniel Gélin, Alain Delon. **1966**

ISADORA (1966) ★★ Messy attempt to depict the personality of dancer Isadora Duncan. Director Ken Russell is up to his usual excessive antics in this unengaging account of the famous dancer. B&W; 67m. **DIR:** Ken Russell. **CAST:** Vivian Pickles. **1966**

ISADORA (1969) ★★★ A straightforward biography of American modern dance pioneer Isadora Duncan. Vanessa Redgrave ably carries the burden of bringing this eccentric, early flower child to life. Unfortunately she is often undone by a script that drags, becomes repetitious, and rambles. 138m. **DIR:** Karel Reisz. **CAST:** Vanessa Redgrave, James Fox, Jason Robards Jr. **1969**

ISLAND IN THE SKY ★★½ Pilot John Wayne is forced to land his C-47 on the frozen, uncharted tundra of Labrador. Talky, slow-moving drama. B&W; 109m. **DIR:** William Wellman. **CAST:** John Wayne, Lloyd Nolan, Walter Abel, James Arness, Andy Devine, Allyn Joslyn, Jimmy Lydon, Harry Carey Jr., Hal Baylor, Sean McClory, Regis Toomey, Paul Fix, George Chandler, Bob Steele, Darryl Hickman, Mike Connors, Carl "Alfalfa" Switzer. **1953**

ISLAND OF DESIRE ★★ A trio become involved in a romantic triangle when they are marooned on an island during World War II. The whole thing is substandard, but Linda Darnell is still worth watching. 103m. **DIR:** Stuart Heisler. **CAST:** Linda Darnell, Tab Hunter, Donald Gray. **1952**

ISLAND OF THE BLUE DOLPHINS ★★★ Alone on an island, a girl and her brother struggle to survive. When attacked by wild dogs, the girl manages to befriend the fiercest one. This adventure will be especially interesting for 7- to 12-year-olds. 93m. **DIR:** James B. Clark. **CAST:** Celia Kaye, George Kennedy, Larry Domasin. **1964**

ISLANDER, THE ★★★ A young girl grapples with sexism and diminished expectations in a quiet fishing village of Norwegian immigrants along the shores of Lake Michigan. Quaint coming-of-age film. Rated PG. 99m. **DIR:** Nany Thurow. **CAST:** Kit Wholihan, Jeff Weborg. **1988**

ISLANDS IN THE STREAM ★★★ *Islands in the Stream* is really two movies in one. The first part is an affecting and effective look at a broken family. The second is a cheap action-adventure. Thomas Hudson (George C. Scott), a famous painter and sculptor, lives the life of a recluse in the Bahamas. His only companions are his seagoing crew of Joseph and Eddy. One summer, his three sons Tom, Andy, and Davy arrive to see him for the first time in four years. Rated PG for violence and profanity. 105m. **DIR:** Franklin J. Schaffner. **CAST:** George C. Scott, Julius W. Harris, David Hemmings, Brad Savage, Hart Bochner, Claire Bloom. **1977**

ISTANBUL: KEEP YOUR EYES OPEN ★★ A father searches for his daughter in this very odd drama. Director Mats Ahern leads his cast around and around, eventually leading them, and the audience, into confusion. Rated PG-13. 88m. **DIR:** Mats Ahern. **CAST:** Timothy Bottoms, Twiggy, Robert Morley. **1990**

IT RAINED ALL NIGHT THE DAY I LEFT ★★½ Tony Curtis and Louis Gossett Jr. play two small-time weapons salesmen who are ambushed in Africa. They go to work for a recently widowed woman (Sally Kellerman) who controls all the water in this extremely hot and dry region. Because she blames the natives for her husband's death, she rations their water. Rated R for sex and violence. 100m. **DIR:** Nicolas Gessner. **CAST:** Lou Gossett Jr., Sally Kellerman, Tony Curtis. **1978**

IT'S A WONDERFUL LIFE ★★★★½ Have you ever wished you'd never been born? What if that wish were granted? That's the premise of Frank Capra's heartbreaking, humorous, and ultimately heartwarming *It's a Wonderful Life*. James Stewart was tapped for the lead role right after he left the service at the end of World War II. The story is about a good man who is so busy helping others that life seems to pass him by. B&W; 129m. **DIR:** Frank Capra. **CAST:** James Stewart, Donna Reed, Lionel Barrymore, Thomas Mitchell, Ward Bond, Henry Travers. **1946**

IT'S GOOD TO BE ALIVE ★★★½ The tragedy of a great athlete being struck down in the prime of his career is dealt with in this story of Brooklyn Dodgers catcher Roy Campanella (Paul Winfield). Campanella had two spectacular seasons with the Dodgers before being permanently crippled from the waist down in a car accident in 1958. *It's Good to Be Alive* focuses on Campanella's struggle with self-respect after the wreck. A good companion piece to *Brian's Song*. 100m. **DIR:** Michael Landon. **CAST:** Paul Winfield, Lou Gossett Jr., Ruby Dee, Ramon Bieri, Lloyd Gough. **1974**

IT'S MY TURN ★★ Jill Clayburgh is a college professor confused about her relationship with live-in lover Charles Grodin, a Chicago real estate salesman. Then she meets baseball player Michael Douglas. They fall in love. The viewer yawns. Rated R. 91m. **DIR:** Claudia Weill. **CAST:** Jill Clayburgh, Michael Douglas, Beverly Garland, Charles Grodin. **1980**

I'VE ALWAYS LOVED YOU ★★★ A lavish musical featuring Arthur Rubinstein on the sound track performing selections by Rachmaninoff, Tchaikovsky, Beethoven, Chopin, Liszt, Wagner, and Mendelssohn—to underscore the romance of an arrogant orchestra conductor and the lady pianist who upstages him. It was seen by very few people when released. The UCLA archivally restored print is an obvious labor of love as it restores the vibrant Technicolor and provides a clean sound track. 117m. **DIR:** Frank Borzage. **CAST:** Catherine McLeod, Philip Dorn, Maria Ouspenskaya, Felix Bressart, Elizabeth Patterson, Vanessa Brown, Adele Mara, Fritz Feld, Stephanie Bachelor, Cora Witherspoon. **1946**

IVORY HUNTERS ★★★½ Powerful made-for-cable drama reveals the horrors of elephants mutilated for their tusks. Manages to make its point without overt preaching. John Lithgow plays an author in Nairobi to find his missing researcher. There he meets a dedicated field biologist (Isabella Rossellini) and a police inspector (James Earl Jones) waging their own wars against poachers. 94m. **DIR:** Joseph Sargent. **CAST:** John Lithgow, Isabella Rossellini, James Earl Jones, Tony Todd. **1990**

JACK KNIFE MAN, THE ★★★★ A lonely old river rat finds his life changed for the better by an orphan boy left in his care. Better than the hokey plot sounds, with believable characterizations and impressively atmospheric direction by a young King Vidor. Silent with musical score. B&W; 86m. **DIR:** King Vidor. **CAST:** Fred Turner, Harry Todd, Bobby Kelso, Florance Vidor. **1920**

JACK LONDON ★★ Episodic, fictionalized account of the life of one of America's most popular authors is entertaining enough, but one wishes that a more accurate, detailed biography of this fabulous man were available on film. Heavily influenced by the anti-Japanese sentiment rampant at the time of its release, the colorful and tragic tale of the poor boy who gained and alienated the love of America and the world cries out to be remade in today's more permissive and investigative atmosphere. B&W; 94m. **DIR:** Alfred Santell. **CAST:** Michael O'Shea, Susan Hayward, Osa Massen, Harry Davenport, Frank Craven, Virginia Mayo. **1943**

JACK THE BEAR ★★★★ The joys and horrors of childhood are explored in this insightful film, which stars Danny DeVito as a local TV personality—he hosts monster movies—attempting to raise his two sons after the tragic death of his wife. The title character is his eldest son, a preteen whose adventures with first love and new friends are darkened by the specter of a psychotic neighbor, well played by Gary Sinise. Rated PG for brief profanity and violence. 99m. **DIR:** Marshall Herskovitz. **CAST:** Danny DeVito, Robert J. Steinmiller, Miko Hughes, Gary Sinise, Art La Fleur, Stefan Gierasch, Erica Yohn, Julia Louis-Dreyfus, Reese Witherspoon, Bert Remsen. **1993**

JACKIE ROBINSON STORY, THE ★★★★ This is one of the best baseball films ever—the biography of Jackie Robinson, first black to play in the major leagues. The performances (including Mr. Robinson as himself) are very good, and the direction is sharp. B&W; 76m. **DIR:** Alfred E. Green. **CAST:** Jackie Robinson, Ruby Dee, Minor Watson, Louise Beavers. **1950**

JACKKNIFE ★★★★ Ed Harris and Kathy Baker star as brother and sister in this drama about veterans who suffer from post-Vietnam stress syndrome. Robert De Niro plays another vet who comes into their lives, causing volatile changes. Rated R, with profanity and violence. 102m. **DIR:** David Jones. **CAST:** Robert De Niro, Ed Harris, Kathy Baker. **1989**

JACKSONS: AN AMERICAN DREAM, THE ★★★½ Though slanted in favor of its title characters, this made-for-TV movie features excellent performances by a star-studded cast as they act out the saccharine history of one of America's most talented dysfunctional families. Main attraction Michael is played by fifteen different actors as he ages. Not rated. 225m. **DIR:** Karen Arthur. **CAST:** Holly Robinson, Angela Bassett, Billy Dee Williams, Margaret Avery, Lawrence Hilton-Jacobs, Vanessa Williams. **1992**

JACOB I HAVE LOVED ★★★ Fine adaptation of Katherine Paterson's Newbery Award–winning book. Bridget Fonda portrays a tomboy who plays second fiddle to her glamorous and talented twin sister. Resentment turns to hatred until Fonda befriends an old sea captain. Originally shown on PBS's *Wonderworks* series. 57m. **DIR:** Victoria Hochberg. **CAST:** Bridget Fonda, Jenny Robertson, John Kellogg. **1989**

JAGGED EDGE ★★½ A publishing magnate (Jeff Bridges) is accused of the ritualistic slaying of his wife; an attorney (Glenn Close) is hired to defend him. They fall in love, conduct an affair during the trial(!), which is not noticed by the ambitious prosecutor (Peter Coyote) (!), and generally behave like total fools; during this, we and Close ponder the burning question: Did Bridges do the dirty deed? Too bad the story doesn't measure up. Rated R for violence. 108m. **DIR:** Richard Marquand. **CAST:** Glenn Close, Jeff Bridges, Peter Coyote, Robert Loggia, Leigh Taylor-Young. **1985**

JAMAICA INN ★★★ Not one of Alfred Hitchcock's best directorial efforts. But the cast makes it, just the same. Charles Laughton is Squire Pengallon, the evil chief of a band of cutthroats in Victorian England. Maureen O'Hara is a beautiful damsel in distress. B&W; 98m. **DIR:** Alfred Hitchcock. **CAST:** Charles Laughton, Maureen O'Hara, Leslie Banks, Emlyn Williams, Robert Newton, Mervyn Johns. **1939**

JAMES DEAN—A LEGEND IN HIS OWN TIME ★★½ Lackluster dramatization of actor James Dean's life as seen through the eyes of a friend. Stephen McHattie qualifies as a James Dean look-alike and gives a solid performance. This film features a fine supporting cast. 99m. **DIR:** Robert Butler. **CAST:** Michael Brandon, Stephen McHattie, Candy Clark, Amy Irving, Meg Foster, Jayne Meadows, Brooke Adams. **1976**

JAMES JOYCE'S WOMEN ★★★★½ *James Joyce's Women* is a delicious, verbally erotic movie. With Joyce as the writer and Fionnula Flanagan (writer and producer) as interpreter, things are bound to be intense. The film is virtually a one-woman show, with Flanagan portraying seven different characters from Joyce's life and works. The humor and sensuality will thrill Joyce fans. Rated R for nudity and sexual situations. 89m. **DIR:** Michael Pearce. **CAST:** Fionnula Flanagan, Timothy E. O'Grady, Chris O'Neill. **1985**

JANE DOE ★★½ A passable suspense movie about a woman who is brutally attacked and left for dead in a shallow grave. She survives with amnesia, so she can't identify her attacker. Made for TV. 96m. **DIR:** Ivan Nagy. **CAST:** Karen Valentine, William Devane, Eva Marie Saint, David Huffman. **1983**

JANE EYRE (1934) ★★ A willing second-tier cast and the passage of time make something of a curiosity of this classic story of a young orphan girl who grows up to become a governess. Tolerable. B&W; 70m. **DIR:** Christy Cabanne. **CAST:** Colin Clive, Virginia Bruce. **1934**

JANE EYRE (1944) ★★★★ Devotee's of Charlotte Brontë's romantic novel about a young woman leaving an orphans' home and being placed as a governess may be disappointed. But for others, the movie really starts with the appearance of Orson Welles and his interpretation of the moody and mysterious Edward Rochester. B&W; 96m. **DIR:** Robert Stevenson. **CAST:** Orson Welles, Joan Fontaine, Margaret O'Brien, Peggy Ann Garner, John Sutton, Sara Allgood, Henry Daniell, Agnes Moorehead, Elizabeth Taylor. **1944**

JANE EYRE (1983) ★★★★ This marvelous BBC production honors Charlotte Brontë's classic tale of courage and romance. A thrilling and thorough adaptation. Zelah Clarke plays the orphaned, mistreated, and unloved Jane who later falls for the darkly mysterious Mr. Rochester (Timothy Dalton). 239m. **DIR:** Julian Amyes. **CAST:** Timothy Dalton, Zelah Clarke. **1983**

JAVA HEAD 🦃 Tepid romance about a Chinese girl brought to a shipping village to marry an Englishman. B&W; 70m. **DIR:** J. Walter Ruben. **CAST:** Anna May Wong, Elizabeth Allan, Edmund Gwenn, John Loder, Ralph Richardson. **1935**

JAYNE MANSFIELD STORY, THE ★★ Loni Anderson gives only an average performance as 1950s blonde sex bomb Mansfield. Made for television. 100m. **DIR:** Dick Lowry. **CAST:** Loni Anderson, Arnold Schwarzenegger, Kathleen Lloyd. **1980**

JERICHO ★★★½ Paul Robeson plays a black soldier who is convicted of manslaughter for the accidental murder of his sergeant. He takes advantage of the kindness of officer Henry Wilcoxon to escape across the African desert and begin a new life. Absorbing study of revenge and human dignity. B&W; 77m. **DIR:** Thornton Freeland. **CAST:** Paul Robeson, Henry Wilcoxon, Wallace Ford. **1937**

JERICHO MILE, THE ★★★★ This tough, inspiring TV movie tells the story of a man, serving a life sentence at Folsom Prison, who dedicates himself to becoming an Olympic-caliber runner. Director Michael Mann makes sure the film is riveting and realistic at all times. 100m. **DIR:** Michael Mann. **CAST:** Peter Strauss, Roger E. Mosley, Brian Dennehy, Billy Green Bush, Ed Lauter, Beverly Todd. **1979**

JESSE ★★ By-the-numbers TV movie based on a true story about a small-town nurse who provides medical care in place of the often-absent regional doctor. The contrived dramatic conflict renders much of the story unbelievable. 100m. **DIR:** Glenn Jordan. **CAST:** Lee Remick, Scott Wilson, Richard Marcus, Albert Salmi. **1988**

JESSIE OWENS STORY, THE ★★★ This made-for-TV movie of the Olympic hero provides a provocative insight into the many behind-the-scenes events that plague people who are thrust into public admiration. Dorian Harewood is perfect in his performance of the not-always-admirable hero, a victim of his own inabilities and the uncontrollable events surrounding him. This film also holds up a mirror to our society's many embarrassing racial attitudes. 180m. **DIR:** Richard Irving. **CAST:** Dorian Harewood, Debbi Morgan, George Kennedy, Georg Stanford Brown, Tom Bosley, LeVar Burton. **1984**

JESUS ★★ More a Bible study than entertainment; this film is narrated by Alexander Scourby and the words are taken from the Good News Bible, the Book of Luke. Filmed in the Holy Land. 117m. **DIR:** Peter Sykes, John Kirsh. **CAST:** Brian Deacon, Rivka Noiman. **1979**

JESUS OF NAZARETH ★★★★ This vivid TV movie of the life of Jesus is beautifully directed by the poetic genius Franco Zefferelli. An outstanding cast gives warm and sensitive performances in what is the finest film to date of the familiar Bible story. It fills *three* cassettes but well worth the time. 371m. **DIR:** Franco Zeffirelli. **CAST:** Robert Powell, Anne Bancroft, James Mason, Rod Steiger, Olivia Hussey. **1976**

JEWEL IN THE CROWN, THE ★★★★★ Based on Paul Scott's *Raj Quartet*, this Emmy Award–winning series first aired on the BBC in fourteen episodes. It is a wonderful epic that depicts Britain's last years of power in India (1942–1947). The story revolves around the love of an Indian man, Hari Kumar (Art Malik), for a white woman, Daphne Manners (Susan Wooldridge), and the repercussions of their forbidden romance. The love-hate relationship of the English and the Indians is well depicted. Fine entertainment! 700m. **DIR:** Christopher Morahan, Jim O'Brien. **CAST:** Tim Pigott-Smith, Geraldine James, Peggy Ashcroft, Charles Dance, Susan Wooldridge, Art Malik, Judy Parfitt. **1984**

JEZEBEL ★★★★ Bette Davis gives one of her finest performances as a spoiled southern belle in this release. Devised by Warner Bros. as a consolation prize for their star, who was turned down when she tried for the role of Scarlett O'Hara, it's not as good a film as *Gone with the Wind*. But then, how many are? Directed by William Wyler, it brought Davis her second best-actress Oscar—and a well-deserved one at that. She's superb as the self-centered "Jezebel" who takes too long in deciding between a banker (Henry Fonda) and a dandy (George Brent) and loses all. B&W; 103m. **DIR:** William Wyler. **CAST:** Bette Davis, Henry Fonda, George Brent, Spring Byington. **1938**

JFK ★★★★ Director Oliver Stone's fascinating, three-hour-plus examination of the assassination of President John F. Kennedy attempts to disprove the contention that Lee Harvey Oswald was the lone killer. Kevin Costner leads a remarkable, all-star cast as Jim Garrison, the New Orleans district attorney who attempted to prosecute a local businessman (Tommy Lee Jones) for conspiracy in the Nov. 22, 1963, murder. Stone, a master of overstatement, is on his best behavior throughout most of the film, but there are moments of unnecessary sensationalism. Rated R for violence, profanity, and suggested sex. 190m. **DIR:** Oliver Stone. **CAST:** Kevin Costner, Sissy Spacek, Joe Pesci, Tommy Lee Jones, Gary Oldman, Jay O. Sanders, Michael Rooker, Laurie Metcalf, Gary Grubbs, John Candy, Jack Lemmon, Walter Matthau, Edward Asner, Donald Sutherland, Kevin Bacon, Brian Doyle-Murray, Sally Kirkland. **1991**

JFK: RECKLESS YOUTH ★★★ Patrick Dempsey delivers an exceptional performance as the young Kennedy, long before the White House. The conflicts that permeated his life, from his decision to disobey his father's wishes to the women and illness that plagued his life, come to the forefront in this made-for-TV miniseries. The emotional impact and production values are better-than-average. Not rated. 182m. **DIR:** Harry Winer. **CAST:** Patrick Dempsey, Terry Kinney, Loren Dean, Diana Scarwid, Andrew Lowery. **1993**

JILTING OF GRANNY WEATHERALL, THE 🦃 Depressing adaptation of the Katherine Anne Porter short story. Introduced by Henry Fonda; suitable for family viewing. 57m. **DIR:** Randa Haines. **CAST:** Geraldine Fitzgerald, Lois Smith. **1980**

JIM THORPE—ALL AMERICAN ★★★ This well-intentioned bio-pic stretches much of the truth in the sad story of American Indian athlete Jim Thorpe, Olympic medalist and professional baseball, football, and track star. Director Michael Curtiz places most of the audience sympathy with toothy Burt Lancaster, sidestepping Thorpe's own personal demons. Burt himself is in fine physical shape as he re-creates some of Thorpe's feats for the camera. B&W; 107m. **DIR:** Michael Curtiz. **CAST:** Burt Lancaster, Charles Bickford, Steve Cochran, Phyllis Thaxter, Dick Wesson. **1951**

JO JO DANCER, YOUR LIFE IS CALLING ★★★★½ In this brilliant show-biz biography, Richard Pryor plays Jo Jo Dancer, a well-known entertainer at the peak of his popularity and the depths of self-understanding and love. A drug-related accident puts Jo Jo in the hospital and forces him to reexamine his life. Rated R for profanity, nudity, suggested sex, drug use, violence, and unflinching honesty. 100m. **DIR:** Richard Pryor. **CAST:** Richard Pryor, Debbie Allen, Art Evans, Fay Hauser, Barbara Williams, Carmen McRae, Paula Kelly, Diahnne Abbott, Scoey Mitchell, Billy Eckstine, Wings Hauser, Michael Ironside. **1986**

JOAN OF ARC ★★★ Ingrid Bergman is touching and devout in this by-the-book rendering of Maxwell Anderson's noted play, but too much talk and too little action strain patience and buttocks. 100m. **DIR:** Victor Fleming. **CAST:** Ingrid Bergman, José Ferrer, Francis L. Sullivan, J. Carrol Naish, Ward Bond. **1948**

JOAN OF PARIS ★★ Allied fliers parachute into Nazi-held France and enlist a local barmaid to help them find their way to British Intelligence. It all made sense back in 1942, and this melodrama is strong on love, duty, and sacrifice, and thick with snarling Nazis and long-winded patriots. B&W; 93m. **DIR:** Robert Stevenson. **CAST:** Michele Morgan, Paul Henreid, Thomas Mitchell, Laird Cregar, May Robson, Alan Ladd. **1942**

JOE ★★★ Peter Boyle stars in this violent film about a bigot who ends up associating much more closely with the people he hates. Falling short in the storytelling, *Joe* is nevertheless helped along by top-notch acting. Rated R. 107m. **DIR:** John G. Avildsen. **CAST:** Peter Boyle, Dennis Patrick, Susan Sarandon. **1970**

JOE LOUIS STORY, THE ★★ Real-life boxer Coley Wallace brings some sense of authenticity to this all-too-familiar Hollywood sketch of an athlete's rise to fame. Newsreel footage elevates this otherwise routine low-budget bio-pic. B&W; 88m. **DIR:** Robert Gordon. **CAST:** Coley Wallace, Paul Stewart, Hilda Simms, James Edwards, John Marley. **1953**

JOEY BREAKER ★★★ An obnoxious, smooth-talking agent on the fast track to money and power falls in love with a waitress who is striving to complete her education as a nurse. Quirky, offbeat film benefits from the performances of its talented cast members. Rated R for nudity and profanity. 92m. **DIR:** Steven Starr. **CAST:** Richard Edson, Cedella Marley, Erik King, Gina Gershon. **1992**

JOHN AND THE MISSUS ★★★ The beautiful coast of Newfoundland provides the backdrop for this otherwise depressing Canadian film. A town loses its source of income when the local mine is closed. Gordon Pinsent plays a stubborn, courageous man who refuses the meager resettlement money the government offers. Rated PG for mature themes. 98m. **DIR:** Gordon Pinsent. **CAST:** Gordon Pinsent, Jackie Burroughs, Timothy Webber. **1987**

JOHN & YOKO: A LOVE STORY ★★ Episodic account of the John Lennon–Yoko Ono relationship—from the famous "Christ" remark in 1966 to his assassination in 1980—is marred by unbelievable characters and a condensed mix of fact and fabrication. The technical adviser was Lennon's friend, Elliot Minz (played briefly by David Baxt). Not rated. 180m. **DIR:** Sandor Stern. **CAST:** Mark McGann, Kim Miyori, Peter Capaldi, Richard Morant. **1989**

JOHNNY APOLLO ★★★★ Tyrone Power's father is exposed as a white-collar criminal; bitter Tyrone turns to crime himself and winds up in the same cell block as Dad. Tough, engrossing crime melodrama is solid entertainment all the way. B&W; 93m. **DIR:** Henry Hathaway. **CAST:** Tyrone Power, Dorothy Lamour, Edward Arnold, Lloyd Nolan, Charley Grapewin, Lionel Atwill. **1940**

JOHNNY BELINDA ★★★★ Jane Wyman won an Oscar for her remarkable performance as a deaf-mute farm girl. Her multidimensional characterization lifts this movie over mere melodrama. The many disasters that befall its put-upon heroine, including rape and trying to raise the resulting offspring in the face of community pressure, would be scoffed at in a lesser actress. B&W; 103m. **DIR:** Jean Negulesco. **CAST:** Jane Wyman, Lew Ayres, Charles Bickford, Agnes Moorehead. **1948**

JOHNNY EAGER ★★★★½ When the DA's daughter falls for a good-looking mobster, sparks fly. Few cops-and-robbers movies are as well cast as this one. Robert Taylor was no longer known as a pretty boy after playing the role of the gangster, and Lana Turner established her image as a sizzling sex symbol. Van Heflin earned a best-supporting-actor's Oscar for his role of the gangster with a conscience. B&W; 107m. **DIR:** Mervyn LeRoy. **CAST:** Lana Turner, Robert Taylor, Robert Sterling, Edward Arnold, Glenda Farrell, Patricia Dane, Barry Nelson, Van Heflin. **1941**

JOHNNY GOT HIS GUN ★★½ Featuring Timothy Bottoms as an American World War I soldier who loses his legs, eyes, ears, mouth, and nose after a German artillery shell explodes, this is a morbid, depressing antiwar film with flashes of brilliance. Rated PG. 111m. **DIR:** Dalton Trumbo. **CAST:** Timothy Bottoms, Marsha Hunt, Jason Robards Jr., Donald Sutherland, Diane Varsi, David Soul, Anthony Geary. **1971**

JOHNNY TIGER ★★½ Chad Everett is a half-breed Seminole, Robert Taylor is a sympathetic teacher, and Geraldine Brooks is a sympathetic doctor, all trying to reach some valid conclusion about the American Indians' role in the modern world. It's nothing to get excited about. 102m. **DIR:** Paul Wendkos. **CAST:** Robert Taylor, Geraldine Brooks, Chad Everett. **1966**

JOLLY CORNER, THE ★★★ The uncertainties of diverging career paths lie at the heart of this TV adaptation of the moody Henry James short story. Fritz Weaver returns to turn-of-the-century America after having lived abroad for thirty-five years, and he becomes obsessed by the memories contained within his ancestral home. Introduced by Henry Fonda; unrated and suitable for family viewing. 43m. **DIR:** Arthur Barron. **CAST:** Fritz Weaver, Salome Jens. **1975**

JONATHAN LIVINGSTON SEAGULL 🦃 Overblown and laughable. Rated G. 120m. **DIR:** Hall Bartlett. **1973**

JOSEPHINE BAKER STORY, THE ★★★★ Lynn Whitfield *owns* this ambitious, unblushingly sexy HBO biography of singer and dancer Josephine Baker, who scandalized the States with her uninhibited personality and erotic choreography. Rubén Blades and David Dukes are fine as two of the significant men in her life. Craig T. Nelson's riveting cameo as Walter Winchell reveals the newscaster in far less than his usual flattering light. Rated R for nudity. 134m. **DIR:** Brian Gibson. **CAST:** Lynn Whitfield, Rubén Blades, David Dukes, Kene Holiday, Craig T. Nelson, Lou Gossett Jr. **1991**

JOURNEY FOR MARGARET ★★★ A childless journalist in war-ravaged England falls for two little orphans, and he and his wife become involved with their future. Margaret O'Brien pushes all the emotional buttons in a phenomenal film debut. This is solid MGM wartime filmmaking at its propagandistic best. B&W; 81m. **DIR:** W. S. Van Dyke. **CAST:** Robert Young, Laraine Day, Fay Bainter, Nigel Bruce, Margaret O'Brien. **1942**

JOY HOUSE ★★½ Spooky and interesting, but ultimately only mildly rewarding, this film features Jane Fonda in one of her sexy French roles as a free-spirited waif attempting to seduce her cousin's chauffeur (Alain Delon). 98m. **DIR:** René Clement. **CAST:** Jane Fonda, Alain Delon, Lola Albright, Sorrell Booke. **1964**

JOY LUCK CLUB, THE ★★★★★ Amy Tan's sensational bestseller received first-rate treatment from director Wayne Wang and became the throat-catching film sensation of its year. Employing multiple flashbacks which never become confusing, Wang explores the turbulent lives of four uncompromising Chinese women, each of whom emerges from mainland China's male-dominated society to face the possibly greater challenge of coping with a now-grown daughter raised in the United States. The ensemble cast is superb, and each vignette manages to be more poignant and compelling than its predecessor. Rated R for violence, profanity, and strong sexual themes. 138m. **DIR:** Wayne Wang. **CAST:** Kieu Chinh, Ming-Na Wen, Tamlyn Tomita, Tsai Chin, France Nuyen, Lauren Tom, Lisa Lu, Rosalind Chao. **1993**

JOYLESS STREET ★★★ Greta Garbo has her first starring role as a young woman who succumbs to hard times in the decadent Vienna of World War I. Look for Marlene Dietrich in a cameo. B&W; 65m. **DIR:** G. W. Pabst. **CAST:** Greta Garbo, Asta Nielsen. **1925**

JOYRIDE ★★½ Four second-generation actors acquit themselves fairly well in this loosely directed drama about a quartet of youngsters who start off in search of adventure and find themselves turning to crime. Rated R. 92m. **DIR:** Joseph Ruben. **CAST:** Desi Arnaz Jr., Robert Carradine, Melanie Griffith, Anne Lockhart, Tom Ligon. **1977**

JUAREZ ★★★★ Warner Bros. in the 1930s and '40s seemed to trot out veteran actor Paul Muni every time they attempted to film a screen biography. This re-creation of the life of Mexico's famous peasant leader was no exception. Surrounded by an all-star cast, including Bette Davis and Brian Aherne, this big budget bio is well mounted and well intentioned. B&W; 132m. **DIR:** William Dieterle. **CAST:** Paul Muni, Bette Davis, Brian Aherne, Claude Rains, John Garfield. **1939**

JUDGE PRIEST ★★★½ A slice of Americana, and a good one. Life and drama in an old southern town, with all the clichés painted brilliantly. Will Rogers is fine. Stepin Fetchit is properly Uncle Tom. John Ford's sensitive direction makes this film one for the books. A touching, poignant portrait of community life lost and gone forever. B&W; 71m. **DIR:** John Ford. **CAST:** Will Rogers, Anita Louise, Stepin Fetchit, Henry B. Walthall, Tom Brown, Hattie McDaniel. **1934**

JUDGE STEPS OUT, THE ★★★½ A Boston judge (Alexander Knox) runs away from his increasingly empty life to find happiness as a short-order cook in California. He falls in love and must choose between responsibility and pleasure. B&W; 91m. **DIR:** Boris Ingster. **CAST:** Alexander Knox, Ann Sothern, George Tobias, Florence Bates, Frieda Inescort. **1949**

JUDGMENT ★★★★ The Catholic church takes a beating in this gripping teledrama, loosely lifted from an actual court case. The setting is a small-town Louisiana parish filled with staunch Catholics who idolize local priest David Strathairn (superb in a chilling role). Alas, the good father regards his altar boys with decidedly unhealthy affection. Rated PG-13 for frank sexual themes. 90m. **DIR:** Tom Topor. **CAST:** Keith Carradine, Blythe Danner, David Strathairn, Michael Faustino, Mitchell Ryan, Robert Joy, Jack Warden. **1990**

JUDGMENT AT NUREMBERG ★★★★ An all-star cast shines in this thoughtful social drama. During the late stages of the Nazi war crimes trial, an American judge (Spencer Tracy) must ponder the issue of how extensive is the responsibility of citizens for carrying out the criminal orders of their governments. B&W; 178m. **DIR:** Stanley Kramer. **CAST:** Spencer Tracy, Burt Lancaster, Maximilian Schell, Richard Widmark, Marlene Dietrich, Montgomery Clift, Judy Garland. **1961**

JUDGMENT IN BERLIN ★★★ Intelligent courtroom drama in the *Inherit the Wind* and *Judgment at Nuremberg* vein. An East German hijacks a Polish airliner and has it fly to West Berlin, where he seeks political asylum. Instead of offering safety, the U.S. government puts him on trial for terrorism. Martin Sheen as the no-nonsense judge carries the film. Rated PG for language. 110m. **DIR:** Leo Penn. **CAST:** Martin Sheen, Sam Wanamaker, Max Gail, Sean Penn. **1988**

JUDITH OF BETHULIA ★★★ The first American four-reel film designed for feature-length exhibition, this lavish biblical spectacle of deep emotional confict and deception brings together two stories: (1) the forty-day siege of the great Judean walled city of Bethulia and (2) the innocent lovers the siege engulfs and threatens. A brilliant example of early film drama presaging Cecil B. DeMille. Silent with musical score. B&W; 65m. **DIR:** D. W. Griffith. **CAST:** Blanche Sweet, Henry B. Walthall, Mae Marsh, Robert Harron, Lillian Gish, Dorothy Gish. **1914**

JUICE ★★★½ Spike Lee's cinematographer, Ernest R. Dickerson, makes his directorial debut with this gritty, downbeat chronicle of life on the streets of Harlem. Four friends edge around the outside of the law until the fateful moment when they finally step over the line and find themselves on the run. It's not unlike an inner-city version of *The Wild Bunch*. Rated R for profanity, violence, and suggested sex. 96m. **DIR:** Ernest R. Dickerson. **CAST:** Omar Epps, Jermaine Hopkins, Khalil Kain, Tupac Shakur. **1992**

JULIA ★★★★½ Alvin Sargent won an Oscar for his taut screen adaptation of the late Lillian Hellman's bestselling memoir *Pentimento*. It's a harrowing tale of Hellman's journey into Germany to locate her childhood friend who has joined in the resistance against the Nazis. Great performances by all cast members. Rated PG. 118m. **DIR:** Fred Zinnemann. **CAST:** Jane Fonda, Vanessa Redgrave, Jason Robards Jr., Maximilian Schell, Meryl Streep. **1977**

JULIA HAS TWO LOVERS 🦃 Daphna Kastner was unknown as a writer and actress before this horrid film, whose title is self-explanatory, and hopefully she will never be heard from again. Rated R for nudity and simulated sex. 87m. **DIR:** Bashar Shbib. **CAST:**

Daphna Kastner, David Duchovny, David Charles. **1990**

JULIUS CAESAR (1953) ★★★★ Cool, confident, star-bright performances mark this stirring, memorable mounting of Shakespeare's great classic of honor and the struggle for power in ancient Rome. A superb blend of eloquent language and judicious camera art. Standouts: John Gielgud as the cunning Cassius and Marlon Brando, whose fire-hot/ice-cold portrayal of Mark Antony alone makes the film worthwhile. B&W; 120m. **DIR:** Joseph L. Mankiewicz. **CAST:** Louis Calhern, Marlon Brando, James Mason, John Gielgud, Edmond O'Brien, Greer Garson, Deborah Kerr. **1953**

JULIUS CAESAR (1970) ★★ A good cast, but Shakespeare loses in this so-so rendering of ambition, greed, jealousy, and politics in toga Rome. 117m. **DIR:** Stuart Burge. **CAST:** Charlton Heston, Jason Robards Jr., John Gielgud, Robert Vaughn, Richard Chamberlain, Diana Rigg, Christopher Lee. **1970**

JUMPIN' AT THE BONEYARD ★★½ Two brothers accidentally meet for the first time in years and try to connect again. One is divorced and unemployed, the other a drug-addicted thief, and their visit to the Bronx slum where they grew up mirrors their bleak lives. Sometimes compelling but ultimately pointless and downbeat. Rated R for profanity and drug use. 107m. **DIR:** Jeff Stanzler. **CAST:** Tim Roth, Alexis Arquette, Danitra Vance, Samuel L. Jackson, Luis Guzman. **1992**

JUNGLE FEVER ★★★ Writer-director Spike Lee's story of an interracial romance between a married black architect (Wesley Snipes) and his single Italian-American secretary (Annabella Sciorra) has some terrific performances and unforgettable moments. Sad to say, you have to wade through quite a bit of tedium to get to them. Rated R for profanity, violence, and nudity. 135m. **DIR:** Spike Lee. **CAST:** Wesley Snipes, Annabella Sciorra, Spike Lee, Anthony Quinn, Ossie Davis, Ruby Dee, Lonette McKee, John Turturro, Tim Robbins, Brad Dourif. **1991**

JUNO AND THE PAYCOCK ★★½ Sean O'Casey's famous play gets the Hitchcock treatment, and the result is an intriguing blend of Irish melodrama and sinister moods. The setting is the Dublin uprising, the characters members of a poor family with more than its share of grief. A young unwed mother, an anticipated inheritance, and an unwise young man are the focus for various sorts of tragedy. B&W; 85m. **DIR:** Alfred Hitchcock. **CAST:** Sara Allgood, Edward Chapman, Sidney Morgan. **1929**

JUST A GIGOLO 🦃 Prussian aristocrat ends up as a disillusioned male prostitute. 96m. **DIR:** David Hemmings. **CAST:** David Bowie, Sydne Rome, Kim Novak, David Hemmings, Marlene Dietrich, Maria Schell, Curt Jurgens. **1978**

JUST ANOTHER GIRL ON THE I.R.T ★★★½ Powerful debut from director Leslie Harris, who draws a memorable performance out of Ariyan Johnson as a determined Brooklyn high-school student attempting to make a better life for herself. Her dreams of higher education take a backseat to reality when she finds herself pregnant. Excellent slice-of-life drama is sometimes funny, sometimes sad, but always interesting and well directed. Rated R for language and adult situations. 96m. **DIR:** Leslie Harris. **CAST:** Ariyan Johnson, Kevin Thigpen. **1993**

JUST BETWEEN FRIENDS ★★★½ Mary Tyler Moore stars in this big-screen soap opera as a homemaker happily married to Ted Danson. She meets TV news reporter Christine Lahti and they become friends. They have a lot in common—including being in love with the same man. Rated PG-13 for profanity and suggested sex. 115m. **DIR:** Allan Burns. **CAST:** Mary Tyler Moore, Christine Lahti, Sam Waterston, Ted Danson, Mark Blum. **1986**

JUST THE WAY YOU ARE ★★½ Kristy McNichol gives a fine performance as a pretty flautist who cleverly overcomes the need to wear a leg brace. But this deception brings an unexpected moment of truth. Even the plodding direction of Edouard Molinaro can't prevent this well-written work from occasionally being witty, and touching. Rated PG. 95m. **DIR:** Edouard Molinaro. **CAST:** Kristy McNichol, Michael Ontkean, Kaki Hunter. **1984**

JUSTINE ★★ Compressing all four volumes of Laurence Durrell's *Alexandria Quartet* into one film was an all-but-impossible task; to say that it was done here as well as it could be is faint praise. It is the story of a Middle Eastern prostitute who rises to a position of power in her country. Fans of the novels will be disappointed; those unfamiliar with the story will be confused. Rated R for nudity and sexual situations. 117m. **DIR:** George Cukor. **CAST:** Anouk Aimée, Dirk Bogarde, Robert Forster, Anna Karina, Philippe Noiret, Michael York, John Vernon, Jack Albertson, Cliff Gorman, Michael Constantine, Severn Darden. **1969**

KALIFORNIA ★★★★½ This *Bad Lands* for the 1990s is a tense, chilling psychodrama and darkly comic road movie. While visiting America's most infamous murder sites to develop material for a book, a liberal journalist and his photographer lover share a convertible and traveling expenses with a white-trash sociopath and his incredibly dumb girlfriend. The characters are brilliantly developed and interconnected during the trek, and the cast and hypnotic direction are superb. Rated R for sex, violence, and profanity. 117m. **DIR:** Dominic Sena. **CAST:** Brad Pitt, Juliette Lewis, David Duchovny, Michelle Forbes. **1993**

KANDYLAND ★★★ Fairly interesting story centers around a girl's desire to make a living at exotic dancing. The nice thing about this film is that it concentrates on the people involved, not the dances. Rated R for nudity, profanity, and violence. 94m. **DIR:** Robert Schnitzer. **CAST:** Sandahl Bergman, Kim Evenson. **1987**

KANGAROO ★★★★ Real-life husband and wife Colin Friels and Judy Davis give superb performances in this Australian film adaptation of the semiautobiographical novel by D. H. Lawrence. Writer Richard Somers (Friels), a thinly veiled version of Lawrence, finds himself vilified by critics in his native England for writing sexually suggestive novels and, with his German-born wife Harriet (Davis), journeys down under in search of a better life. Rated R for violence, nudity, and profanity. 100m. **DIR:** Tim Burstall. **CAST:** Colin Friels, Judy Davis, John Walton, Hugh Keays-Byrne. **1986**

KANSAS ★★ Lethargic melodrama has fresh-faced Andrew McCarthy teaming up with sleazy Matt Dillon, who cons him into robbing a bank. Rated R for profanity and violence. 105m. **DIR:** David Stevens. **CAST:** Matt Dillon, Andrew McCarthy, Leslie Hope, Kyra Sedgwick. **1988**

KARATE KID, THE ★★★★½ A heartwarming, surefire crowd pleaser, this believable and touching work about the hazards of high school days and adolescence will have you cheering during its climax and leave you with a smile on your face. You'll find yourself rooting for the put-upon hero, Daniel (Ralph Macchio), and booing the bad guys. Rated PG for violence and profanity. 126m. **DIR:** John G. Avildsen. **CAST:** Ralph Macchio, Noriyuki "Pat" Morita, Elisabeth Shue. **1984**

KARATE KID PART II, THE ★★★½ This second in the *Karate Kid* series begins moments after the conclusion of the first film. Mr. Miyagi (Noriyuki "Pat" Morita) receives word that his father, residing in Okinawa, is dying, so he drops everything and heads for home, with young Daniel (Ralph Macchio) along for the ride. Once in Okinawa, Miyagi encounters an old rival and an old love, while Daniel makes a new enemy and a new love. Rated PG for mild violence. 113m. **DIR:** John G. Avildsen. **CAST:** Ralph Macchio, Noriyuki "Pat" Morita, Nobu McCarthy, Martin Kove, William Zabka. **1986**

KARATE KID PART III, THE ★★ Back for the third time as Daniel "The Karate Kid" LaRusso, Ralph Macchio prepares to defend his championship. Even the watchable Pat Morita can't make this one a winner. Rated PG. 111m. **DIR:** John G. Avildsen. **CAST:** Ralph Macchio, Noriyuki "Pat" Morita, Martin Kove. **1989**

KATHERINE ★★★ This television movie follows Sissy Spacek from a middle-class young student to a social activist and finally to an underground terrorist. Spacek is very convincing in this demanding role. The movie tends to remind one of the Patty Hearst case and features good, solid storytelling. 100m. **DIR:** Jeremy Paul Kagan. **CAST:** Sissy Spacek, Art Carney, Henry Winkler, Jane Wyatt, Julie Kavner. **1975**

KEEPER OF THE CITY ★★½ Anthony LaPaglia flips out—too much abuse as a child—and embarks on a one-man crusade to rid Chicago of its aging crime lords. Lou Gossett's hardened and weary cop lifts this routine made-for-cable thriller slightly above other genre entries, no thanks to Gerald DePego's pedestrian adaptation of his own novel. 95m. **DIR:** Bobby Roth. **CAST:** Lou Gossett Jr., Anthony LaPaglia, Peter Coyote, Renee Soutendijk. **1992**

KEEPER OF THE FLAME ★★★★ In this second teaming of Spencer Tracy and Katharine Hepburn, he is a noted journalist who plans to write a tribute to a respected and admired patriot killed in a vehicle accident; she is the patriot's widow. Fine adult drama. B&W; 100m. **DIR:** George Cukor. **CAST:** Spencer Tracy, Katharine Hepburn, Richard Whorf, Margaret Wycherly, Forrest Tucker, Percy Kilbride, Darryl Hickman, Donald Meek, Howard DaSilva. **1942**

KENNEDY (TV MINISERIES) ★★★★ This outstanding made-for-TV miniseries is even more enjoyable when viewed in one sitting. This upfront portrait of John F. Kennedy from presidential campaign to assassination shows the warts as well as the charm and mystique of the entire Kennedy clan. The cast is excellent, with Martin Sheen as JFK, John Shea as RFK, and Vincent Gardenia particularly chilling as J. Edgar Hoover. An easy-to-swallow history lesson on Camelot. 278m. **DIR:** Jim Goddard. **CAST:** Martin Sheen, John Shea, Blair Brown, E. G. Marshall, Geraldine Fitzgerald, Vincent Gardenia. **1983**

KENNETH ANGER—VOLUME ONE ★★½ Filmmaker Kenneth Anger's collection of movie shorts are a bizarre invocation of his fusion of dreams and sexual desire. The works presented in this middling program are "Fireworks," "Rabbit's Moon," and "Eaux d'Artifice." Not rated, but contains explicit sexuality. 21m. **DIR:** Kenneth Anger. **CAST:** Kenneth Anger, Gordon Gray. **1953**

KENNETH ANGER—VOLUME TWO ★★★ Kenneth Anger's "Inauguration of the Pleasure Dome" is a surreal opera of mystical awakening inspired by the literary works of author Aleister Crowley. It is by far one of the avant-garde filmmaker's most hypnotic works. Not rated, but contains explicit sex.

38m. DIR: Kenneth Anger. CAST: Marjorie Cameron, Anais Nin, Kenneth Anger. 1954

KENNETH ANGER—VOLUME THREE ★★★ Kenneth Anger's third volume of collected film shorts are surreal comical reflections on Hollywood, decadence, and masculinity. Titles included in this program are "Kustom Kar," "Kommandos," "Puce Moment," and "Scorpio Rising." 37m. DIR: Kenneth Anger. CAST: Bruce Byron, Johnny Sapienza. 1965

KENNETH ANGER—VOLUME FOUR ★★ Kenneth Anger's fourth volume of film shorts focuses on paganism and satanic rituals. Music by Mick Jagger and Bobby Beausoleil. Program titles are "Invocation of My Demon Brother" and "Lucifier Rising." Not rated, but contains sex and violence. 39m. DIR: Kenneth Anger. CAST: Leslie Huggins, Marianne Faithfull, Donald Cammell. 1980

KENT STATE ★★★★ Disturbing docudrama traces the events leading up to the killing of four students by National Guardsmen during a 1970 antiwar protest. Objectively filmed, this TV movie is a memorable and effective history lesson. 180m. DIR: James Goldstone. CAST: Jane Fleiss, Charley Lang, Talia Balsam, Keith Gordon, John Getz, Jeff McCracken. 1981

KEY, THE ★★½ A strange, moody curio, directed in somber tones by British filmmaker Carol Reed, and noteworthy as the first British film to star Sophia Loren. She plays a kept woman who comes with the London flat belonging to a succession of tugboat captains during World War II. B&W; 125m. DIR: Carol Reed. CAST: William Holden, Sophia Loren, Trevor Howard, Oscar Homolka, Bernard Lee. 1958

KEY EXCHANGE ★★★ This movie is a good study of modern-day relationships. Brooke Adams and Ben Masters play a couple making a firm commitment in their relationship. Daniel Stern is hilarious as a friend of the couple who is going through his own domestic crisis. Rated R for language, sex, and nudity. 96m. DIR: Barnet Kellman. CAST: Brooke Adams, Ben Masters, Daniel Stern, Danny Aiello, Tony Roberts. 1985

KEYS TO THE KINGDOM, THE ★★★½ Gregory Peck is a Scottish priest in this bleak tale of poverty and despotism in 1930s war-torn China. As the missionary who bests the odds, Peck is fine. B&W; 137m. DIR: John M. Stahl. CAST: Gregory Peck, Vincent Price, Thomas Mitchell, Roddy McDowall. 1944

KID GALAHAD (1937) ★★★½ Solid gangster tale has fight promoter Edward G. Robinson discovering a boxer in bellhop Wayne Morris. It's prime Warner Bros. melodrama, deliciously played. Because of the Elvis Presley remake, this was retitled *The Battling Bellhop* for television. B&W; 101m. DIR: Michael Curtiz. CAST: Edward G. Robinson, Bette Davis, Humphrey Bogart, Wayne Morris, Harry Carey, Jane Bryan, William Haade, Ben Welden, Veda Ann Borg, Frank Faylen. 1937

KILL CRUISE ★★ Spur of the moment decision by an alcoholic yachtsman to sail to Barbados with two young British women leads to the predictable clash of passions. Listless voyage propelled only by capable performances and a twist ending. Rated R for violence, profanity, and nudity. 99m. DIR: Peter Keglevic. CAST: Jurgen Prochnow, Patsy Kensit, Elizabeth Hurley. 1990

KILLING CARS ★★ A car designer finds that the Berlin company he works for is going to shelve his environmentally safe automobile, so he sets out to sell the plans to someone who will manufacture the machine. Rated R for violence, nudity, and profanity. 104m. DIR: Michael Verhoeven. CAST: Jurgen Prochnow, Senta Berger, Bernhard Wicki, William Conrad, Daniel Gélin. 1986

KILLING 'EM SOFTLY ★★ George Segal is a down-and-out musician who kills the friend of a young singer (Irene Cara) in an argument over the death of his dog. While attempting to prove that Segal is not the killer, Cara falls in love with him. An interesting and well-acted story bogs down in the attempt to turn this film into a music video. The music is good, but it overpowers the story. Filmed in Canada. 90m. DIR: Max Fischer. CAST: George Segal, Irene Cara, Joyce Gordon, Barbara Cook. 1985

KILLING FIELDS, THE ★★★★★ Here's an unforgettable motion picture. Based on the experiences of *New York Times* correspondent Sidney Schanberg during the war in Cambodia and his friendship with Cambodian guide and self-proclaimed journalist Dith Pran (whom Schanberg fights to save from imprisonment), it is a tale of love, loyalty, political intrigue, and horror. The viewer cannot help but be jarred and emotionally moved by it. Rated R for violence. 142m. DIR: Roland Joffe. CAST: Sam Waterston, Haing S. Ngor, John Malkovich, Julian Sands, Craig T. Nelson. 1984

KILLING FLOOR, THE ★★★ Honest and forthright depiction of union squabbles in the Chicago stockyards during World War II. Credible performances and a well-honed script add to a realistic picture of working life in the sticky goo of a slaughterhouse operating under Dickensian stringency. Not rated. 117m. DIR: Bill Duke. CAST: Damien Leake, Moses Gunn, Alfre Woodard, Clarence Felder. 1984

KILLING HEAT ★★½ Uneven acting and a general lack of atmosphere hinder the screen adaptation of Doris Lessing's novel *The Grass is Singing*. Karen Black plays a city woman who marries a small-time farmer and slowly goes insane while trying to adapt herself to the rural life-style. Set in South Africa in the early 1960s. Not rated, but contains nudity and violence. 104m. **DIR:** Michael Raeburn. **CAST:** Karen Black, John Thaw, John Kani. **1984**

KILLING IN A SMALL TOWN ★★ Based on a true case, this just passable TV murder-of-the-week entry falls flat with Barbara Hershey internalizing the drab exterior of her character—ignoring the fact that she is also a passionate ax murderess. 95m. **DIR:** Stephen Gyllenhaal. **CAST:** Barbara Hershey, Brian Dennehy, John Terry, Richard Gilliland. **1990**

KILLING OF A CHINESE BOOKIE ★★★½ Downbeat character study stars Ben Gazzara as a small-time nightclub owner who finds himself in big-time trouble when he's coerced into murdering a Chinese crime lord to pay off a debt. Director John Cassavetes's most accessible film is nevertheless a meandering character study with shaky cinematography and a bit too much improvisation. At least it goes somewhere. Rated R for violence and profanity. 113m. **DIR:** John Cassavetes. **CAST:** Ben Gazzara, Timothy Carey, Seymour Cassel. **1976**

KILLING OF ANGEL STREET, THE ★★ The misleading title and packaging of *The Killing of Angel Street* makes it look like a teenage slasher flick, but the title refers to an actual street in a neighborhood in Australia. The plot involves the citizens' struggle to keep their homes from demolition by corrupt businessmen. 100m. **DIR:** Donald Crombie. **CAST:** Liz Alexander, John Hargreaves, Reg Lye. **1981**

KILLING OF RANDY WEBSTER, THE ★★ Hal Holbrook and Dixie Carter, his real-life wife, portray parents searching desperately for meaning in the death of their troubled teenage son. The boy steals a van, then leads Houston police on a wild chase. They fire as the boy pulls a gun. Or did he? Made for television. 90m. **DIR:** Sam Wanamaker. **CAST:** Hal Holbrook, Dixie Carter, Jennifer Jason Leigh, Sean Penn. **1985**

KILLING OF SISTER GEORGE, THE ★★½ Now that the initial controversy that swirled around this film's honest depiction of a lesbian relationship has died away, a retrospective viewing shows a passable yet uninspired story and wooden acting in its central performances. This stage play of an aging actress whose career and relationships are crumbling around her was not brought to the screen with much spirit. Rated R for nudity. 140m. **DIR:** Robert Aldrich. **CAST:** Beryl Reid, Susannah York, Coral Browne. **1968**

KIND OF LOVING, A ★★ This British romance features Alan Bates as a young man infatuated with a cute blonde at work. When she gets pregnant, he marries her and realizes how ill-prepared he was for this commitment. Unrated, this contains nudity and adult themes equivalent to an R. B&W; 107m. **DIR:** John Schlesinger. **CAST:** Alan Bates, Thora Hird, June Ritchie. **1962**

KING ★★★★ Paul Winfield and Cicely Tyson star as the Rev. Martin Luther King Jr. and Coretta Scott King in this outstanding docudrama of the martyred civil rights leader's murder-capped battle against segregation and for black human dignity. Director Abby Mann, who also scripted, interpolated actual newsreel footage with restaged confrontation incidents for maximum dramatic impact. 272m. **DIR:** Abby Mann. **CAST:** Paul Winfield, Cicely Tyson, Ossie Davis, Roscoe Lee Browne, Howard Rollins Jr., Cliff De Young, Dolph Sweet, Lonny Chapman. **1978**

KING DAVID ★★★ Only biblical scholars will be able to say whether the makers of *King David* remained faithful to the Old Testament. As a big-screen production, however, it is impressive. Directed by Australian filmmaker Bruce Beresford, it is one of the few responsible attempts at filming the Bible. Rated PG-13 for nudity and violence. 115m. **DIR:** Bruce Beresford. **CAST:** Richard Gere, Edward Woodward, Alice Krige, Denis Quilley. **1985**

KING LEAR (1971) ★★★½ Sturdy but truncated film adaptation of Shakespeare's play about a mad king and his cruel, power-hungry children. The Danish set location lends a disturbing air to this production, which features a powerful portrayal from Paul Scofield. 137m. **DIR:** Peter Brook. **CAST:** Paul Scofield, Irene Worth, Jack MacGowran, Alan Webb, Cyril Cusack, Patrick Magee. **1971**

KING LEAR (1982) ★★★ A good stage production of what is possibly Shakespeare's most tragic of tales. Mike Kellen is very good as the aging Lear, betrayed by his daughters, but acting honors go to Charles Aidman as the tortured Gloucester. David Groh is interesting as his plotting bastard son, Edmund. A Bard Productions Ltd. release. 182m. **DIR:** Alan Cooke. **CAST:** Mike Kellen, Darryl Hickman, Charles Aidman, David Groh, Joel Baily. **1982**

KING LEAR (1984) ★★★★ Produced for television, this version of Shakespeare's great tragedy of greed and lust for power became an instant classic, and promptly won an Emmy. A career-crowning achievement for Laurence Olivier. 158m. **DIR:** Michael Elliot. **CAST:** Laurence Olivier, Diana Rigg, Anna Calder-Marshall, Dorothy Tutin, Leo McKern, John Hurt, Robert Lindsay. **1984**

KING LEAR (1988) ★★★½ Patrick Magee stars in this Shakespearean tragedy about a foolish king who surrounds himself with treacherous flatterers while banishing those who remain true to him. Fine acting and glorious costumes and sets make this British television production most watchable. 110m. **CAST:** Patrick Magee, Ray Smith, Ronald Radd. 1988

KING OF COMEDY, THE ★★★★ This is certainly one of the most unusual movies of all time; a sort of black-comedy variation on creator Martin Scorsese's *Taxi Driver*. The star of that film, Robert De Niro, stars as aspiring comic Rupert Pupkin. In order to get his big break on television, Pupkin kidnaps a talk-show host (Jerry Lewis). Rated PG. 109m. **DIR:** Martin Scorsese. **CAST:** Robert De Niro, Jerry Lewis, Sandra Bernhard. 1983

KING OF KINGS, THE (1927) ★★★ Cecil B. DeMille was more than ready when he made this one. It's silent, but Hollywood's greatest showman displays his gift for telling a story with required reverence. Naturally, since it's by DeMille, the production is a lavish one. B&W; 115m. **DIR:** Cecil B. DeMille. **CAST:** H. B. Warner, Ernest Torrence, Jacqueline Logan, William Boyd, Joseph Schildkraut. 1927

KING OF KINGS (1961) ★★★ Well-told tale of the life of Christ, performed with understanding and compassion, though flawed by too much attention to the spectacular, rather than the spiritual. Has its moving moments, nonetheless. Narrated by Orson Welles. 168m. **DIR:** Nicholas Ray. **CAST:** Jeffrey Hunter, Siobhan McKenna, Robert Ryan, Hurd Hatfield, Viveca Lindfors, Rita Gam, Rip Torn, Royal Dano, George Coulouris. 1961

KING OF MARVIN GARDENS, THE ★★★ Jack Nicholson and Bruce Dern, at the peak of their young careers, play brothers involved in an Atlantic City swindle. Some entertaining theatrics, but once the novelty wears off, the film is overpoweringly depressing. Rated R for profanity, and brief nudity. 104m. **DIR:** Bob Rafelson. **CAST:** Jack Nicholson, Bruce Dern, Ellen Burstyn, Scatman Crothers. 1972

KING OF THE GYPSIES ★★★ Dave Stepanowicz (Eric Roberts) is the grandson of King Zharko Stepanowicz (Sterling Hayden), the patriarch of a gypsy tribe who is both intelligent and violent. Though Dave renounces his gypsy heritage, he is unable to escape it. The performances are uniformly excellent. Director Frank Pierson is the only one who can be held responsible for the film's lack of power. Rated R. 112m. **DIR:** Frank Pierson. **CAST:** Eric Roberts, Sterling Hayden, Susan Sarandon, Annette O'Toole, Brooke Shields, Shelley Winters. 1978

KING OF THE HILL ★★★★★ A. E. Hotchner's Depression-era memoirs are the basis for writer-director Steven Soderbergh's poignant study of childhood strength in the face of escalating tragedy. Young Jesse Bradford watches as his family is scattered, and then—when his father accepts a distant job—becomes the sole occupant of their seedy hotel rooms. Equal parts E. L. Doctorow, Jean Shepherd, and Ray Bradbury, this enthralling tale is populated with eclectic characters, all rendered splendidly by a masterful ensemble cast. Rated PG-13 for mild profanity and dramatic intensity. 103m. **DIR:** Steven Soderbergh. **CAST:** Jesse Bradford, Jeroen Krabbé, Lisa Eichhorn, Spalding Gray, Elizabeth McGovern, Karen Allen. 1993

KING OF THE MOUNTAIN ★★ The quest for success by a trio of buddies leads mostly to unexciting night races on Hollywood's winding Mulholland Drive and cliché backstabbing in the music business. Rated PG. 90m. **DIR:** Noel Nosseck. **CAST:** Harry Hamlin, Richard Cox, Joseph Bottoms, Dennis Hopper. 1981

KING OF THE ROARING TWENTIES ★★ The career (supposedly) of the notorious bookie who, among other things, fixed the 1919 World Series. No excitement or conviction; David Janssen is miscast. Not rated, but with the usual gangster gunplay. B&W; 106m. **DIR:** Joseph M. Newman. **CAST:** David Janssen, Dianne Foster, Jack Carson, Diana Dors, Mickey Rooney. 1961

KING, QUEEN AND KNAVE 🦃 Even with the wonderful grace and charm of David Niven, this story authored by Vladimir Nabokov is a dud. Not rated. 92m. **DIR:** Jerzy Skolimowski. **CAST:** David Niven, Gina Lollobrigida, John Moulder-Brown, Mario Adorf. 1972

KING RAT ★★★★ A Japanese prison camp in World War II is the setting for this stark drama of survival of the fittest, the fittest in this case being "King Rat" (George Segal), the opportunistic head of black-market operations within the compound. B&W; 133m. **DIR:** Bryan Forbes. **CAST:** George Segal, Tom Courtenay, James Fox, John Mills. 1965

KING RICHARD II ★★★½ David Birney is quite effective as Shakespeare's scheming, then remorseful Richard, in this well-made, filmed stage production. Acting honors are shared by Paul Shenar as his cousin, the betrayed and vengeful Bolingbroke (later Henry IV), and Peter MacLean as their uncle, the Duke of York. A Bard Productions Ltd. release. 172m. **DIR:** William Woodman. **CAST:** David Birney, Paul Shenar, Peter MacLean, Mary Joan Negro, Logan Ramsey, Nan Martin, Jay Robinson, Nicholas Hammond. 1982

KINGS GO FORTH ★★★★ A World War II melodrama with social consciousness. Frank Sinatra and Tony Curtis play two skirt chasers in the army who fall for the same girl (Natalie Wood). When they find out one of her parents is black, the true colors of the soldiers are revealed. B&W; 110m. **DIR:** Delmer Daves. **CAST:** Tony Curtis, Frank Sinatra, Natalie Wood, Leora Dana. 1958

KING'S ROW ★★★★★ A small American town at the turn of the century is the setting where two men (Ronald Reagan and

Robert Cummings) grow up to experience the corruption and moral decay behind the facade of a peaceful, serene community. This brilliantly photographed drama is close to being a masterpiece, thanks to exceptional performances by many of Hollywood's best character actors. B&W; 127m. **DIR:** Sam Wood. **CAST:** Ann Sheridan, Robert Cummings, Ronald Reagan, Claude Rains, Charles Coburn, Betty Field, Judith Anderson. **1941**

KING'S WHORE, THE ★★★ A European king is obsessed with a happily married woman who wants nothing to do with him. Good acting, but the story drags on too long. Rated R for profanity, nudity, and violence. 111m. **DIR:** Axel Corti. **CAST:** Timothy Dalton, Valeria Golino, Stephane Freiss, Margaret Tyzack, Feodor Chaliapin, Eleanor David, Paul Crauchet, Robin Renucci. **1990**

KIPPERBANG ★★½ This is another World War II coming-of-age saga, in the same category as *Hope and Glory, Empire of the Sun*, and *Au Revoir les Enfants*. Charming and wistful at times, it doesn't quite reach the heights. Rated PG. 80m. **DIR:** Michael Apted. **CAST:** John Albasiny, Alison Steadman. **1982**

KISMET (1944) ★★ Ronald Colman plays the beggar-of-beggars who cons his way into the Caliph's palace and romances Marlene Dietrich. The musical version has the same story line and the advantage of Moussorgsky's music to make it more romantic. 100m. **DIR:** William Dieterle. **CAST:** Ronald Colman, Marlene Dietrich, Edward Arnold, James Craig, Joy Page, Hugh Herbert, Florence Bates, Harry Davenport, Robert Warwick, Hobart Cavanaugh. **1944**

KISS, THE (1929) ★★★★ The kind of smooth, stylish, and sophisticated production that best represents the apex of the silent-film period. Irene (Greta Garbo) gets caught up in a messy domestic tangle of infidelity and murder. The highly stylized courtroom scenes (redolent of German Expressionism) and flashback sequences give the film a flamboyant, visually arresting look. B&W; 70m. **DIR:** Jacques Feyder. **CAST:** Greta Garbo, Conrad Nagel. **1929**

KISS OF DEATH ★★★★½ Finely crafted gangster film deals with convict Victor Mature infiltrating a gang run by psychopath Richard Widmark (in his film debut) so that Mature can obtain evidence on Widmark. Contains the now-famous scene of Widmark gleefully pushing a wheelchair-bound woman to her death down a flight of stairs. B&W; 98m. **DIR:** Henry Hathaway. **CAST:** Victor Mature, Richard Widmark, Brian Donlevy, Karl Malden, Coleen Gray. **1947**

KISS OF THE SPIDER WOMAN ★★★★ This first English-language film by Hector Babenco is a somber, brilliantly acted tale about a gay window dresser, Molina (William Hurt), and a revolutionary, Valentin (Raul Julia), who slowly begin to care for each other and understand each other's viewpoint while imprisoned together in a South American prison. It is stark, violent, and daring. Rated R for profanity, violence, and suggested sex. 119m. **DIR:** Hector Babenco. **CAST:** William Hurt, Raul Julia, Sonia Braga. **1985**

KISS SHOT ★★★ Single mom struggles after being laid off. In desperation, she hustles pool while being wooed by both her manager and a playboy. Solid performances and well-paced plot development maintain viewer interest. Rated PG for violence. 88m. **DIR:** Jerry London. **CAST:** Whoopi Goldberg, Dennis Franz, Dorian Harewood. **1989**

KITCHEN TOTO, THE ★★★★ Powerful, uncompromising drama about a 10-year-old black boy who becomes hopelessly caught in the middle of racial violence between East African tribesmen and white British colonists in 1952 Kenya. Brilliantly performed and directed. Rated PG. Contains violence and nudity. 90m. **DIR:** Harry Hook. **CAST:** Bob Peck, Phyllis Logan. **1988**

KITTY FOYLE ★★★★ Ginger Rogers, who became a star in comedies and musicals, went dramatic (and won an Oscar) in this three-hanky tearjerker about the troubled love life of an attractive secretary. Pure soap opera, but splendidly presented. B&W; 107m. **DIR:** Sam Wood. **CAST:** Ginger Rogers, Dennis Morgan, James Craig, Eduardo Ciannelli, Gladys Cooper, Ernest Cossart. **1940**

KLANSMAN, THE 🦃 Lee Marvin and Richard Burton fight the Klan in a southern town. Rated R. 112m. **DIR:** Terence Young. **CAST:** Lee Marvin, Richard Burton, Cameron Mitchell, O. J. Simpson, Lola Falana, Linda Evans. **1974**

KNIGHT WITHOUT ARMOUR ★★★ This melodrama, about a British national caught up in the Russian Revolution and his attempts to save aristocrat Marlene Dietrich, is filled with beautiful photography but remains basically a curiosity, one of the few American films to depict communism in the 1930s. Robert Donat is an unassuming, gentle hero. B&W; 107m. **DIR:** Jacques Feyder. **CAST:** Robert Donat, Marlene Dietrich, Miles Malleson, David Tree. **1937**

KNOCK ON ANY DOOR ★★★½ Before John Derek became a Svengali for Ursula Andress, Linda Evans, and Bo Derek, he was an actor—and a pretty good one, too, as he proves in this courtroom drama directed by Nicholas Ray. He's a kid who can't help having gotten into trouble, and Humphrey Bogart is the attorney who attempts to explain his plight to the jury. B&W; 100m. **DIR:** Nicholas Ray. **CAST:** John Derek, Humphrey Bogart, Susan Perry, Allene Roberts. **1949**

KNUTE ROCKNE—ALL AMERICAN ★★★ This is an overly sentimental biography of the famous Notre Dame football coach. But if you like football or you want to see Ronald Reagan show off his moves, it could hold your interest. Pat O'Brien has the central role, and he plays it with real gusto. B&W; 84m. **DIR:** Lloyd Bacon. **CAST:** Ronald Reagan, Pat O'Brien, Donald Crisp. **1940**

KOSTAS ★★½ A tormented Greek-Cypriot tries to find love with an Australian girl in England. Director Paul Cox has created a character study with little depth and too much tedium. Not for the easily bored. Rated R for suggested sex. 110m. **DIR:** Paul Cox. **CAST:** Takis Emmanuel, Wendy Hughes. **1979**

KRAMER VS. KRAMER ★★★★ Dustin Hoffman and Meryl Streep star in the Academy Award–winning drama about a couple who separate, leaving their only son in the custody of the father, who is a stranger to his child. Just when the father and son have learned to live with each other, the mother fights for custody of the child. *Kramer vs. Kramer* jerks you from tears to laughs and back again—and all the while you're begging for more. Rated PG. 104m. **DIR:** Robert Benton. **CAST:** Dustin Hoffman, Meryl Streep, Jane Alexander, Howard Duff, JoBeth Williams. **1979**

KRAYS, THE ★★★★ From British filmmaker Peter Medak comes this compelling, chilling portrait of Ronald and Reginald Kray, psychotic twins who ruled the London underworld in the 1960s. Features first-rate performances. Rated R for profanity and violence. 119m. **DIR:** Peter Medak. **CAST:** Billie Whitelaw, Gary Kemp, Martin Kemp, Susan Fleetwood. **1990**

L.A. LAW ★★★½ Above-average television movie introduced the cast of characters of the new successful series. Set in a high-powered Los Angeles law firm, *L.A. Law* is both compelling and humorous. A must for fans of the series. 97m. **DIR:** Gregory Holbit. **CAST:** Harry Hamlin, Susan Dey, Jimmy Smits, Michael Tucker, Jill Eikenberry, Richard Dysart, Corbin Bernsen, Alan Rachins, Susan Ruttan. **1987**

LADIES OF LEISURE ★★★ Gold-digger Barbara Stanwyck snares a rich fiancé, but her past reputation gets in the way. Dated melodrama, but worth seeing for the young Stanwyck. B&W; 98m. **DIR:** Frank Capra. **CAST:** Barbara Stanwyck, Ralph Graves, Lowell Sherman, Marie Prevost. **1930**

LADIES OF THE CHORUS ★★ The story of a chorus girl who tries to keep her young daughter from making romantic mistakes is pure detergent drama. A minor Marilyn Monroe musical, but her first major role so it's a curiosity piece. Adele Jergens is fine as the mother. B&W; 61m. **DIR:** Phil Karlson. **CAST:** Marilyn Monroe, Adele Jergens, Rand Brooks. **1949**

LADIES THEY TALK ABOUT ★★★ Bank robber Barbara Stanwyck is rehabilitated in prison by good-hearted Preston Foster. Pre-Production Code movie, adapted from the play *Women in Prison*, raised some eyebrows with its frank dialogue. B&W; 69m. **DIR:** Howard Bretherton, William Keighley. **CAST:** Barbara Stanwyck, Lyle Talbot, Preston Foster, Lillian Roth. **1933**

LADY BY CHOICE ★★★ The flip side of *Lady for a Day/ Pocketful of Miracles*, with Carole Lombard as a do-gooder who turns May Robson into a proper lady. Witty Depression comedy. B&W; 80m. **DIR:** David Burton. **CAST:** Carole Lombard, May Robson, Roger Pryor, Walter Connolly, Arthur Hohl. **1934**

LADY CAROLINE LAMB ★★ Without shame, this banal film victimizes the wife of an English politician who openly carried on with poet and womanizer Lord Byron. Writer-director Robert Bolt created this fiasco. 118m. **DIR:** Robert Bolt. **CAST:** Sarah Miles, Richard Chamberlain, John Mills, Laurence Olivier, Ralph Richardson, Margaret Leighton, Jon Finch. **1972**

LADY CHATTERLEY'S LOVER (1959) ★★ Cinematic telling of D. H. Lawrence's risqué novel. It concerns the wife of a crippled and impotent mine owner who has an affair with a handsome gamekeeper. It's not very good in any respect. A British-French coproduction. B&W; 101m. **DIR:** Marc Allegret. **CAST:** Danielle Darrieux, Leo Genn, Erno Crisa. **1959**

LADY CHATTERLEY'S LOVER (1981) ★★ A beautifully staged, but banal, version of the D. H. Lawrence classic. Rated R. 105m. **DIR:** Just Jaeckin. **CAST:** Sylvia Kristel, Nicholas Clay. **1981**

LADY FOR A DAY ★★★★ An elderly beggar woman elicits the aid of a petty mobster and an oddball assortment of New York down-and-outers. She needs to palm herself off as a society matron in order to convince a Spanish noble family to accept her daughter as a suitable mate for their son. Remade by Frank Capra as *Pocketful of Miracles*. B&W; 95m. **DIR:** Frank Capra. **CAST:** May Robson, Warren William, Guy Kibbee, Glenda Farrell, Walter Connolly. **1933**

LADY FOR A NIGHT 🦃 John Wayne plays second fiddle to Joan Blondell. She's a saloon singer fighting for a measure of respectability. B&W; 87m. **DIR:** Leigh Jason. **CAST:** John Wayne, Joan Blondell, Ray Middleton. **1941**

LADY FROM YESTERDAY, THE ★★ Made-for-TV movie with a less-than-original plot: an ex-soldier, now a happily married businessman, is shocked when the Vietnamese woman he had an affair with shows up on his doorstep, complete with the child he never knew they had. Viewers will be somewhat less surprised. 98m. **DIR:** Robert Day.

CAST: Wayne Rogers, Bonnie Bedelia, Pat Hingle, Tina Chen. **1985**

LADY GREY 🦃 A woman makes the long, hard climb to the top of the show-biz ladder, only to lose her soul along the way. Not rated, but an R equivalent for sexual situations. 100m. **DIR:** Worth Keeter. **CAST:** Ginger Alden. **1980**

LADY IN QUESTION ★★★ Brian Aherne plays a French merchant who acts as a juror on a murder trial where young Rita Hayworth is the defendant. After her eventual release, Aherne takes pity on her and brings her to his home to work and live while keeping her identity a secret from his family. Remake of the French film *Gribouille*. B&W; 78m. **DIR:** Charles Vidor. **CAST:** Brian Aherne, Rita Hayworth, Glenn Ford, Irene Rich, George Coulouris, Lloyd Corrigan, Evelyn Keyes. **1940**

LADY JANE ★★★½ Excellent costume political soap opera about Lady Jane Grey, accidental successor to the English throne. Helena Bonham Carter glows as Lady Jane, the strong-willed suffragist who engages in a power struggle with Mary I for the throne of England. Rated PG-13 for adult situations and violence. 140m. **DIR:** Trevor Nunn. **CAST:** Helena Bonham Carter, Cary Elwes, John Wood, Michael Hordern, Jill Bennett, Jane Lapotaire, Sara Kestleman, Patrick Stewart. **1985**

LADY L ★★ Too much style and not enough substance, with the preposterous premise that Sophia Loren would enter an in-name-only marriage with David Niven while dallying with anarchist Paul Newman. The movie is all posturing and posing and leads absolutely nowhere. 124m. **DIR:** Peter Ustinov. **CAST:** Sophia Loren, Paul Newman, Peter Ustinov, David Niven, Marcel Dalio, Claude Dauphin, Michel Piccoli. **1965**

LADY OF THE HOUSE ★★ Dyan Cannon stars in this TV dramatization of the life of Sally Stanford, Mayor of Sausalito, California. Cannon gives a better performance than usual, and Armand Assante is even better. 90m. **DIR:** Ralph Nelson, Vincent Sherman. **CAST:** Dyan Cannon, Armand Assante, Zohra Lampert, Susan Tyrrell. **1978**

LADY WINDERMERE'S FAN ★★★★½ This is a dynamite version of Oscar Wilde's play. The very enigmatic Mrs. Erlynne comes close to scandalizing all of London society. This is one of Ernst Lubitsch's best silent films. B&W; 80m. **DIR:** Ernst Lubitsch. **CAST:** Ronald Colman, May McAvoy, Irene Rich. **1925**

LAKE CONSEQUENCE ★★½ Arty smut-maven Zalman King turns producer for this melodramatic tale of a suburban housewife (Joan Severance) who slips into debauched sex with the tightly wired stud (Billy Zane) pruning the trees in her neighborhood. Lots of bare skin. Rated R for nudity and profanity. 85m. **DIR:** Rafael Eisenman. **CAST:** Billy Zane, Joan Severance, May Karasun. **1993**

LAND OF THE PHARAOHS ★★½ Joan Collins plays the cunning villainess in a story about ancient Egypt. Talky but colorful historical drama with a visual tour of Egypt in all its splendor. 106m. **DIR:** Howard Hawks. **CAST:** Jack Hawkins, Joan Collins, Sydney Chaplin, James Robertson Justice, Dewey Martin. **1955**

LARRY JORDAN LIVE FILM SHORTS ★★ Four experimental shorts by filmmaker Larry Jordan, best known for his innovative work in the field of animation. Unfortunately this offering contains none of the brilliance of his early animated films and may be of interest only to connoisseurs of the avant-garde. 32m. **DIR:** Larry Jordan. **1987**

LAS VEGAS STORY, THE 🦃 Las Vegas loser. B&W; 88m. **DIR:** Robert Stevenson. **CAST:** Jane Russell, Victor Mature, Vincent Price, Hoagy Carmichael, Jay C. Flippen, Brad Dexter. **1952**

LAST ANGRY MAN, THE ★★★½ Paul Muni, one of Hollywood's most respected actors, gave his final screen performance in this well-made version of Gerald Greene's novel about an aging family doctor in Brooklyn. The sentiment gets a little thick occasionally, but Muni's performance keeps it all watchable. Look for Godfrey Cambridge in a small role. Unrated, but suitable for the whole family. B&W; 100m. **DIR:** Daniel Mann. **CAST:** Paul Muni, David Wayne, Betsy Palmer, Luther Adler, Joby Baker. **1959**

LAST CALL ★★ William Katt has a business deal go sour, so he and Shannon Tweed pair up for a little sex and vengeance in this confusing drama about greed. Too much sex and not enough plot. Not rated, but contains violence and profanity. 90m. **DIR:** Jag Mundhra. **CAST:** William Katt, Shannon Tweed, Joseph Campanella, Stella Stevens. **1990**

LAST CHANTS FOR A SLOW DANCE 🦃 This existential drama was shot in super 8mm for $2 thousand, and never rises above the cost of the film stock. Not rated, but contains graphic violence and excessive profanity. 90m. **DIR:** Jon Jost. **CAST:** Tom Blair, Steve Woorhels, Mary Vollmer. **1983**

LAST COMMAND, THE (1928) ★★★★ German star Emil Jannings's second U.S. film has him portraying a czarist army commander who flees the Russian Revolution to America. Here, he sinks into poverty and winds up as a Hollywood extra. Art imitates life when he is cast to play a Russian general in a film directed by a former revolutionary (and former rival in love). William Powell plays the director, a stiff, unbending sadist bent upon humiliating Jannings. Silent. B&W; 80m. **DIR:** Josef von Sternberg. **CAST:**

Emil Jannings, William Powell, Evelyn Brent. **1928**

LAST DAYS OF CHEZ NOUS, THE ★★★★ Quirky, European-style comedy-drama from Australian director Gillian Armstrong focuses on a writer and her relationships with a French-born husband, troubled sister, and crochety father. Armstrong's low-key, believable and touching handling of the subject matter is what makes *The Last Days of Chez Nous* such a treasure. Unrated, the film has profanity and brief nudity. 96m. **DIR:** Gillian Armstrong. **CAST:** Lisa Harrow, Bruno Ganz, Kerry Fox, Miranda Otto, Kiri Paramore, Bill Hunter. **1993**

LAST DAYS OF PATTON, THE ★★★ A three-star adaptation of Ladislas Farago's book, which follows four-star General George S. Patton's 1945 peacetime career as commander of the Third Army, military governor of Bavaria, and finally as head of the Fifteenth Army. This made-for-TV sequel to George C. Scott's Oscar-winner lacks much of its predecessor's blood and guts. 146m. **DIR:** Delbert Mann. **CAST:** George C. Scott, Erika Hoffman, Eva Marie Saint, Richard Dysart, Murray Hamilton, Ed Lauter. **1985**

LAST DAYS OF POMPEII, THE (1935) ★★★ Roman blacksmith Preston Foster becomes a gladiator after tragedy takes his wife and baby. En route to fortune, he adopts the young son of one of his victims. In Judea, he sees but refuses to help Christ, who cures the boy following serious injury. Touched by Jesus, the boy grows up to help runaway slaves. Tremendous special effects. B&W; 96m. **DIR:** Ernest B. Schoedsack. **CAST:** Preston Foster, Basil Rathbone, Alan Hale Sr., Louis Calhern. **1935**

LAST DETAIL, THE ★★★★ Two veteran navy men (Jack Nicholson and Otis Young) are assigned to transport a young sailor to the brig for theft. They take pity on the naïve loser (Randy Quaid) and decide to show him one last good time. By opening the youngster's eyes to the previously unknown world around him, their kindness is in danger of backfiring in this drama. Rated R. 105m. **DIR:** Hal Ashby. **CAST:** Jack Nicholson, Otis Young, Randy Quaid, Michael Moriarty, Nancy Allen. **1973**

LAST EMPEROR, THE ★★★★★ An awe-inspiring epic that tells a heartrending, intimate story against a backdrop of spectacle and history. The screenplay by Mark Peploe and director Bernardo Bertolucci dramatizes the life of Pu Yi (John Lone), China's last emperor. When he was taken from his home at the age of 3 to become the all-powerful Qing Emperor, the youngster was ironically condemned to a lifetime of imprisonment. Rated PG-13 for violence, brief nudity, and frank sexuality. 160m. **DIR:** Bernardo Bertolucci. **CAST:** John Lone, Peter O'Toole, Joan Chen, Ying Ruocheng, Victor Wong, Dennis Dun. **1987**

LAST EXIT TO BROOKLYN ★★★★ Uli Edel's film is a dark, unflinching drama about mislaid dreams, unfulfilled expectations, and gritty survival, set in the midst of waterfront labor unrest in the Brooklyn of the early Fifties. Adapted from the cult 1964 novel by Hubert Selby Jr. Rated R, with strong violence and profanity. 102m. **DIR:** Uli Edel. **CAST:** Stephen Lang, Jennifer Jason Leigh, Peter Dobson, Ricki Lake, Jerry Orbach. **1990**

LAST GAME, THE ★★ Maudlin tale of an attractive and responsible clean-cut college kid who works two jobs, goes to school, and takes care of his blind father while his father dreams that one day his boy will play pro football. This movie is just too banal for recommendation. No MPAA rating, but equal to a PG for sex and profanity. 107m. **DIR:** Martin Beck. **CAST:** Howard Segal, Ed L. Grady, Terry Alden, Joan Hotchkis. **1980**

LAST HOLIDAY ★★★★ Alec Guinness is magnificent as a failed salesman told he has only months to live. He plans to quietly live out his time at a resort hotel, but becomes an important influence on the guests and staff. Bittersweet, witty story by J. B. Priestley. B&W; 88m. **DIR:** Henry Cass. **CAST:** Alec Guinness, Beatrice Campbell, Kay Walsh, Bernard Lee, Wilfrid Hyde-White. **1950**

LAST HURRAH, THE ★★★★ Spencer Tracy gives a memorable performance as an Irish-Catholic mayor running for office one last time. Jeffrey Hunter is Tracy's nephew, a cynical reporter who comes to respect the old man's values and integrity. B&W; 111m. **DIR:** John Ford. **CAST:** Spencer Tracy, Jeffrey Hunter, Dianne Foster, Pat O'Brien, Basil Rathbone, Donald Crisp, James Gleason, Edward Brophy, John Carradine, Wallace Ford, Frank McHugh, Jane Darwell. **1958**

LAST LIGHT ★★★★★ A masterful character study from first-time director Kiefer Sutherland, who also stars as an unrepentant killer. While waiting on death row, he finds an unlikely friend in prison guard Forest Whitaker. Robert Eisele's script offers no apologies for the murderer's brutality but makes a case for treating even the most heinous individual with dignity. You'll be riveted from the first few shocking frames. Rated R for violence and profanity. 104m. **DIR:** Kiefer Sutherland. **CAST:** Forest Whitaker, Kiefer Sutherland, Amanda Plummer, Kathleen Quinlan, Lynne Moody, Clancy Brown. **1993**

LAST MAN STANDING ★★★★ Surprisingly good prizefight film in which Vernon Wells plays a down-and-out boxer who attempts to find work outside the ring. The brutality of the fight game is well captured. Rated R for profanity and violence. 92m. **DIR:**

Damien Lee. **CAST:** Vernon Wells, William Sanderson, Franco Columbu. **1988**

LAST MILE, THE ★★★ No-win prison film (based on a stage play) is a claustrophobic foray into death row. This archetypal prison-break melodrama has a quiet dignity that elevates the dialogue between the inmates. Preston Foster as Killer Miles plays the toughest con in the block and the leader of the break attempt. B&W; 70m. **DIR:** Sam Bischoff. **CAST:** Preston Foster, Howard Phillips, George E. Stone, Paul Fix. **1932**

LAST MOVIE, THE 🦃 Dennis Hopper's abysmal follow-up to *Easy Rider* wastes a talented cast in this incoherent story about a film crew after they pull out of a small Peruvian village. Also known as *Chinchero*. Rated R for nudity and profanity. 108m. **DIR:** Dennis Hopper. **CAST:** Dennis Hopper, Julie Adams, Peter Fonda, Kris Kristofferson, Sylvia Miles, John Phillip Law, Samuel Fuller, Dean Stockwell. **1971**

LAST OF ENGLAND, THE ★★★★★ Painter-poet-filmmaker Derek Jarman has created a stunning visionary work that is a mysterious, well-crafted montage of image and sound, evoking a world of apocalyptic fury—filmed in Belfast and London. With a British strain of convulsive romanticism Jarman uses Super-8 lyricism, gay erotica, and old home movies to illustrate the fall of England. Not rated, but contains nudity and violence. B&W/color; 87m. **DIR:** Derek Jarman. **CAST:** Tilda Swinton, Spencer Leigh. **1987**

LAST OF HIS TRIBE, THE ★★★ Graham Greene contributes a moving and dignified interpretation of Ishi, the last free-living Yahi Indian who—in 1911 was taken to San Francisco and placed under the care of Professor Albert Kroeber (Jon Voight). While both actors (along with David Ogden Stiers's compassionate surgeon) make the most of their material, Stephen Harrigan's screenplay is marred by missed opportunities. Made for cable, with graphic surgical footage. Rated PG-13 for sexual frankness and explicit medical procedures. 90m. **DIR:** Harry Hook. **CAST:** Jon Voight, Graham Greene, David Ogden Stiers, Jack Blessing, Anne Archer. **1992**

LAST OF MRS. LINCOLN, THE ★★★★ Julie Harris shines in her portrayal of Mary Todd Lincoln during the last seventeen years of her life. Bearing enormous debts accumulated during her stay in the White House and denied a pension by the Senate because of her southern heritage, she eventually falls into penury and insanity. Michael Cristofer and Robby Benson play the two surviving Lincoln sons. Made for television. 117m. **DIR:** George Schaefer. **CAST:** Julie Harris, Michael Cristofer, Robby Benson, Patrick Duffy, Denver Pyle, Priscilla Morrill. **1984**

LAST PICTURE SHOW, THE ★★★★★ Outstanding adaptation of Larry McMurtry's novel about a boy's rites of passage in a small Texas town during the 1950s. Virtually all the performances are excellent due to the deft direction of Peter Bogdanovich, who assured his fame with this picture. Ben Johnson, as a pool-hall owner, and Cloris Leachman, as a lonely wife, deservedly won Oscars for their supporting performances. Rated R for brief nudity and adult situations. B&W; 118m. **DIR:** Peter Bogdanovich. **CAST:** Timothy Bottoms, Ben Johnson, Jeff Bridges, Cloris Leachman, Cybill Shepherd, Randy Quaid. **1971**

LAST PROSTITUTE, THE ★★★★ This heartwarming made-for-cable coming-of-age drama features two teenage boys seeking the services of an infamous prostitute. They're disappointed to find her retired from the business. Fine acting and directing make this an unforgettable gem. 93m. **DIR:** Lou Antonio. **CAST:** Sonia Braga, Wil Wheaton, Cotter Smith, David Kaufman. **1991**

LAST SAFARI ★★ Director Henry Hathaway's trademark machismo got the better of him in this dreary drama about an aging big-game hunter who escorts a young couple to Africa. 110m. **DIR:** Henry Hathaway. **CAST:** Stewart Granger, Kaz Garas. **1967**

LAST SUMMER ★★½ Engrossing tale of teen desires, frustrations, and fears, played out in disturbingly dark fashion. Bruce Davison and Cathy Burns are especially memorable in unusual roles. Rated R. 97m. **DIR:** Frank Perry. **CAST:** Richard Thomas, Barbara Hershey, Bruce Davison, Cathy Burns, Ralph Waite, Conrad Bain. **1969**

LAST TANGO IN PARIS ★★★ A middle-aged man (Marlon Brando) and a young French girl (Maria Schneider) have a doomed love affair. This pretentious sex melodrama was mainly notable for being banned when it first came out. Rated R for sex. 129m. **DIR:** Bernardo Bertolucci. **CAST:** Marlon Brando, Maria Schneider, Jean-Pierre Léaud. **1972**

LAST TEMPTATION OF CHRIST, THE ★★★ Martin Scorsese's well-intentioned adaptation of Nikos Kazantzakis's controversial novel suffers from the filmmaker's excesses. There are some unnecessary scenes of nudity and simulated sex. Nevertheless, what emerges is a heartfelt work that has some moments of true power—especially when the story's reluctant savior (Willem Dafoe) accepts his divine nature and begins to perform miracles. Rated R for nudity and violence. 164m. **DIR:** Martin Scorsese. **CAST:** Willem Dafoe, Harvey Keitel, Barbara Hershey, Harry Dean Stanton, David Bowie, Verna Bloom, Andre Gregory. **1988**

LAST TIME I SAW PARIS, THE ★★★ The Metro-Goldwyn-Mayer glitter shows clearly in this dramatic account of post–World War II Paris. This Paris, though, is filled with divorce, domestic quarrels, and jaded lives. Donna Reed gives the best performance. 116m. **DIR:** Richard Brooks. **CAST:** Van Johnson, Elizabeth Taylor, Donna Reed, Walter Pidgeon, Eva Gabor. **1954**

LAST TYCOON, THE ★★★ Tantalizing yet frustrating, this slow-moving attempt to film F. Scott Fitzgerald's last (and unfinished) book is a blockbuster conglomeration of talent at all levels, but appears to be a somewhat confusing collection of scenes and confrontations. Robert De Niro as Monroe Starr, the sickly motion picture magnate and the "last tycoon" gives another fine, understated performance. 125m. **DIR:** Elia Kazan. **CAST:** Robert De Niro, Robert Mitchum, Tony Curtis, Jeanne Moreau, Jack Nicholson, Donald Pleasence, Peter Strauss, Ray Milland, Ingrid Boulting, Dana Andrews, John Carradine. **1976**

LAST WINTER, THE 🦃 Kathleen Quinlan and Yona Elian are wives of Israeli soldiers missing in action during the Yom Kippur War of 1973. 92m. **DIR:** Riki Shelach. **CAST:** Kathleen Quinlan, Yona Elian, Stephen Macht. **1984**

LAST WORD, THE ★★★ When police try to evict him and his family from a rundown apartment building, inventor Danny Travis (Richard Harris) takes a police officer hostage. His goal is to get the attention of the newspapers so that he can expose the governor's crooked real estate racket and save his home. Likable comedy-drama in the Frank Capra mold. Rated PG. 105m. **DIR:** Roy Boulting. **CAST:** Richard Harris, Karen Black, Martin Landau, Dennis Christopher, Biff McGuire, Christopher Guest, Penelope Milford, Michael Pataki. **1979**

LATINO ★★ Master cinematographer Haskell Wexler tries his hand at writing and directing in this story of a Chicago Green Beret who questions the activities required of him in the Nicaraguan war. This is a fairly routine war story, with the exception of the protagonist being a Latin American. 108m. **DIR:** Haskell Wexler. **CAST:** Robert Beltran, Annette Cardona, Tony Plana. **1985**

LAUGHING AT LIFE ★★½ Fleeing the police, gunrunner Victor McLaglen deserts his family to knock about the world. Years later he meets his son. For McLaglen, this drama of sacrifice was practically drawn from his life before he took up acting. Two years later, he won an Oscar for best actor in *The Informer*. B&W; 68m. **DIR:** Ford Beebe. **CAST:** Victor McLaglen, Regis Toomey, Tully Marshall, Noah Beery Sr. **1933**

LAUGHING HORSE 🦃 A stranded traveler in the desert becomes a driver for a strange couple. 60m. **DIR:** Michael Blake. **CAST:** John Coinman, Irene Miracle. **1986**

LAUGHING SINNERS ★★½ In the first of their eight screen teamings, Clark Gable is a Salvation Army officer who "saves" Joan Crawford after she has been seduced and abandoned by a fast-talking traveling salesman. B&W; 72m. **DIR:** Harry Beaumont. **CAST:** Joan Crawford, Clark Gable, Neil Hamilton, Marjorie Rambeau, Roscoe Karns, Guy Kibbee, Cliff Edwards. **1931**

LAUREL AVENUE ★★★★ Compelling saga focuses on a close-knit family's struggle with changing values and increasing inner-city crime. Spanning three generations and an emotionally charged weekend, we're given a vivid—at times painful—glimpse into the struggles of each member. An HBO miniseries, with violence, profanity, drug use, and sexual situations. 160m. **DIR:** Carl Franklin. **CAST:** Mary Alice, Jay Brooks, Juanita Jennings, Scott Lawrence, Dan Martin. **1993**

LAW OF THE SEA ★★★ Wreck survivors are rescued by a sadistic sea captain, whose lust drives a woman to suicide. Creaky curiosity. B&W; 60m. **DIR:** Otto Brower. **CAST:** William Farnum. **1932**

LAZARUS SYNDROME, THE ★★ When the illicit practices of a hospital administrator drive another practitioner to distraction, he joins forces with a patient who just happens to be a journalist in order to expose the bad guy and his lackeys. Made for television. 90m. **DIR:** Jerry Thorpe. **CAST:** Lou Gossett Jr., Ronald Hunter, E. G. Marshall, Sheila Frazier. **1976**

LBJ: THE EARLY YEARS ★★★★ This superlative made-for-TV movie is the story of Lyndon Johnson from 1934, when he was first entering politics as a congressman's aide, to his swearing in as president aboard *Air Force One*. Randy Quaid and Patti LuPone as LBJ and Lady Bird are outstanding. 144m. **DIR:** Peter Werner. **CAST:** Randy Quaid, Patti LuPone, Morgan Brittany, Pat Hingle, Kevin McCarthy, Charles Frank. **1986**

LEAGUE OF THEIR OWN, A ★★★½ Director Penny Marshall's tribute to the first women's baseball league is a nice little movie that runs out of steam a bit in the last 45 minutes. Geena Davis is superb as "the natural" who finds herself caught in a battle of wills with sister/pitcher Lori Petty and the team's rummy coach, Tom Hanks, a one-time baseball great. The comedy bits by Madonna, Rosie O'Donnell, Megan Cavanaugh, and (seen all too briefly) Jon Lovitz help to buoy the film's melodramatic plotline. Rated PG. 118m. **DIR:** Penny Marshall. **CAST:** Tom Hanks, Geena Davis, Madonna, Lori Petty, Jon Lovitz, David Strathairn, Garry Marshall, Megan Cavanaugh, Rosie O'Donnell, Tracy Reiner, Bill Pullman. **1992**

LEAN ON ME ★★★★ Morgan Freeman gives a superb performance as real-life high school principal Joe Clark, who almost single-handedly converted Eastside High in Paterson, New Jersey, from a den of drugs, gangs, and corruption into an effective place of learning. Director John Avildsen has created a feel-good movie that conveys a timely message. Rated PG-13 for profanity and violence. 104m. **DIR:** John G. Avildsen. **CAST:** Morgan Freeman, Robert Guillaume, Beverly Todd. **1989**

LEAP OF FAITH ★★★½ The glorious gospel music is the main reason to catch Steve Martin's act as a dancin' preacher who decides to con the residents of a small town. Debra Winger plays the cynical right-hand man to Martin's phony faith healer. *Leap of Faith* pours on the sentimentality a bit thick, but the music—hallelujah! Rated PG-13 for profanity. 108m. **DIR:** Richard Pearce. **CAST:** Steve Martin, Debra Winger, Liam Neeson, Lolita Davidovich, Lukas Haas, Meat Loaf, Philip Seymour Hoffman, M. C. Gainey, Delores Hall, John Toles-Bay, Albertina Walker. **1992**

LEARNING TREE, THE ★★★★ In adapting his own novel about the coming-of-age of a young black man in Kansas circa 1920, photographer-turned-filmmaker Gordon Parks not only wrote and directed, but also produced the project and composed its musical score. The result is a uniquely personal vision. Rated PG for violence, profanity, and racial epithets. 107m. **DIR:** Gordon Parks Jr. **CAST:** Kyle Johnson, Alex Clarke, Estelle Evans, Dana Elcar. **1969**

LEATHER BOYS, THE ★★ Considered adult and controversial when first released in England, this slice-of-life drama about teenagers who marry for sex and settle into drab existences doesn't carry the weight it once did. Rather depressing, this film is an interesting look at life in London in the early 1960s, but it has dated badly. B&W; 108m. **DIR:** Sidney J. Furie. **CAST:** Rita Tushingham, Dudley Sutton, Colin Campbell. **1963**

LEAVE 'EM LAUGHING ★★★★½ Mickey Rooney is outstanding portraying real-life Chicago clown Jack Thum. Thum and his wife (played by Anne Jackson) cared for dozens of unwanted children. When Thum realizes he has terminal cancer, he falls apart and his wife must help him regain his inner strength and deal with reality. A real tearjerker! Made for TV, this is unrated. 104m. **DIR:** Jackie Cooper. **CAST:** Mickey Rooney, Anne Jackson, Red Buttons, William Windom, Elisha Cook Jr. **1981**

LEAVING NORMAL ★★★ In what could unkindly be called *Thelma and Louise II*, a tough, no-nonsense waitress (Christine Lahti) and a naïve young woman (Meg Tilly) fleeing an abusive husband go on a road trip from Normal, Wyoming, to the wilds of Alaska. The performances and a few surprises on the way help mitigate a now-too-familiar story. Rated R for profanity, violence, and nudity. 110m. **DIR:** Edward Zwick. **CAST:** Christine Lahti, Meg Tilly, Lenny Von Dohlen, James Gammon. **1992**

LEFT FOR DEAD 🦃 Contrived murder drama, staged in a series of flashbacks. Not rated, but contains violence, profanity, and nudity. 88m. **DIR:** Murray Markowitz. **CAST:** Elke Sommer, Donald Pilon, Chuck Shamata, George Touliatos. **1978**

LEGACY OF LIES ★★ Michael Ontkean portrays a good Chicago cop who is caught up in a politically motivated murder. Martin Landau plays his father, a crooked Chicago police officer who's willing to take the fall to prevent his son from becoming corrupt. Weak story line undermines this made-for-cable drama. 91m. **DIR:** Bradford May. **CAST:** Michael Ontkean, Martin Landau, Joe Morton, Patricia Clarkson, Chelcie Ross, Eli Wallach. **1992**

LEGEND OF THE LOST ★★ Cornball adventure-romance borrows several themes from *Treasure of the Sierra Madre* and doesn't improve upon them. John Wayne is a cynical soldier of fortune who escorts idealist Rossano Brazzi and prostitute Sophia Loren through the desert in search of ancient treasure. 107m. **DIR:** Henry Hathaway. **CAST:** John Wayne, Sophia Loren, Rossano Brazzi, Kurt Kasznar. **1957**

LEGEND OF VALENTINO ★★ TV movie released close to the fiftieth anniversary of the fabled actor's death adheres to some facts concerning the archetypal Latin lover, but still presents an unsatisfying and incomplete portrait. But this film still leaves too many questions either unanswered or glossed over. Not too bad for a TV movie. 100m. **DIR:** Melville Shavelson. **CAST:** Franco Nero, Suzanne Pleshette, Judd Hirsch, Lesley Ann Warren, Milton Berle, Yvette Mimieux, Harold J. Stone. **1975**

LENNY ★★★★★ Bob Fosse brilliantly directed this stark biography of self-destructive, controversial persecuted comic talent Lenny Bruce. Dustin Hoffman captures all those contrary emotions in his portrayal of the late 1950s and '60s stand-up comedian. Valerie Perrine is a treasure in her low-key role as Bruce's stripper wife. Rated R. B&W; 112m. **DIR:** Bob Fosse. **CAST:** Dustin Hoffman, Valerie Perrine, Jan Miner. **1974**

LEOPARD, THE ★★★★ Luchino Visconti's multigenerational spectacle of nineteenth-century Sicily has been restored on video, replacing the dubbed version that was cut by 40 minutes and presented to confused American audiences in the mid-1960s. Burt Lancaster is surprisingly effective as the formidable head of an Italian (!) dynasty. 205m. **DIR:** Luchino Visconti. **CAST:** Burt Lancaster, Alain Delon, Claudia Cardinale. **1963**

LEOPARD IN THE SNOW ★★ Silly romance between a spoiled rich girl and a maimed former race-car driver. The dialogue is slow and some scenes lead nowhere. The pluses include the driver's pet leopard and his butler Bolt (Jeremy Kemp). Rated PG for one scene in which our lovebirds *almost* become passionate. 89m. **DIR:** Gerry O'Hara. **CAST:** Keir Dullea, Susan Penhaligon, Kenneth More, Billie Whitelaw, Jeremy Kemp. **1977**

LES MISERABLES (1935) ★★★★ The most watchable and best acted of the many versions of Victor Hugo's story of good and evil. Fredric March steals a loaf of bread to survive, only to undergo a lifetime of torment. Charles Laughton is absolutely frightening as the personification of an uncaring legal system. B&W; 108m. **DIR:** Richard Boleslawski. **CAST:** Fredric March, Charles Laughton, Cedric Hardwicke, Florence Eldridge. **1935**

LES MISERABLES (1978) ★★★½ Lavish television version of Victor Hugo's classic tale of a petty thief's attempt to forget his past only to be hounded through the years by a relentless police inspector. Richard Jordan as the thief turned mayor and Anthony Perkins as his tormentor are extremely good. 150m. **DIR:** Glenn Jordan. **CAST:** Richard Jordan, Anthony Perkins, John Gielgud, Cyril Cusack, Flora Robson, Claude Dauphin. **1978**

LESS THAN ZERO 🦃 A movie meant to illuminate the meaninglessness of Los Angeles's post-college-crowd cool. Rated R for violence and profanity. 100m. **DIR:** Marek Kanievska. **CAST:** Andrew McCarthy, Jami Gertz, Robert Downey Jr., James Spader, Tony Bill, Nicholas Pryor, Michael Bowen. **1987**

LET HIM HAVE IT ★★★★★ One of the best films of 1991—a powerful tale of a miscarriage of justice in the London of 1952, based on the true story of two teens convicted of murdering a policeman. Peter Medak's film details how one of the kids, a sweet-natured, simpleminded adolescent, ended up on death row, when he shouldn't even have been tried. Rated R, with profanity and violence. 110m. **DIR:** Peter Medak. **CAST:** Chris Eccleston, Paul Reynolds, Tom Courtenay. **1991**

LET IT ROCK ★½ This ludicrous behind-the-scenes view of the music business features Dennis Hopper as a manic rock-music promoter. Rated R for nudity, profanity, and violence. 75m. **DIR:** Roland Klick. **CAST:** Dennis Hopper, Terrance Robay, David Hess. **1988**

LETHAL CHARM ★★ Familiar tale has White House correspondent Barbara Eden playing mentor to novice Heather Locklear, only to have Locklear take over Eden's life, her son, and eventually her job. When Locklear becomes volatile, Eden uses her investigative skills to get to the bottom of things. Ho-hum made-for-TV affair. Not rated. 92m. **DIR:** Richard Michaels. **CAST:** Barbara Eden, Heather Locklear. **1990**

LETHAL LOLITA—AMY FISHER: MY STORY 🦃 Trashy sensationalized made-for-TV movie about an immature 16-year-old girl and her scandalous affair with a married man. 93m. **DIR:** Bradford May. **CAST:** Ed Marinaro, Noelle Parker, Boyd Kestner, Pierrette Lynch, Kathleen Laskey. **1992**

LET'S GET HARRY ★★½ When an American (Mark Harmon) is kidnapped during a South American revolution, a group of his friends decide to bring him home. They hire a soldier of fortune (Robert Duvall) to lead them into the jungles of Colombia where, against all odds, they fight to bring Harry home. Rated R for violence and language. 98m. **DIR:** Alan Smithee. **CAST:** Robert Duvall, Gary Busey, Mark Harmon, Glenn Frey, Michael Schoeffling. **1986**

LETTER FROM AN UNKNOWN WOMAN ★★★ Disregarding the fact that concert pianist Louis Jourdan uses her without pity, beautiful Joan Fontaine stupidly continues to love him through the years. Romantic direction and smooth performances make the clichés work. B&W; 90m. **DIR:** Max Ophüls. **CAST:** Joan Fontaine, Louis Jourdan, Mady Christians, Art Smith, Erskine Sanford. **1948**

LETTER OF INTRODUCTION ★★★★ An essentially enjoyable melodrama, *Letter of Introduction* is the story of a young actress (Andrea Leeds) who seeks out the advice of an old actor (Adolphe Menjou). The aging star encourages her in her various endeavors. The relationship between the two lead characters is so real, so warm that it carries the film. B&W; 100m. **DIR:** John M. Stahl. **CAST:** Adolphe Menjou, Andrea Leeds, Edgar Bergen, George Murphy, Eve Arden, Rita Johnson, Ernest Cossart, Ann Sheridan. **1938**

LETTER TO THREE WIVES, A ★★★½ Three wives receive a letter from a friend saying that she has run off with one of their husbands. The viewer is then shown three stories that tell why each of the women's husbands might have left them. Very interesting screenplay and superb acting make this an enjoyable film. B&W; 103m. **DIR:** Joseph L. Mankiewicz. **CAST:** Jeanne Crain, Linda Darnell, Ann Sothern, Kirk Douglas, Paul Douglas, Barbara Lawrence, Jeffrey Lynn. **1949**

LETTERS TO AN UNKNOWN LOVER ★★★ A soldier who has been carrying on a romance through the mails with a Frenchwoman he has never met dies. When his friend escapes from a Nazi prison camp, he pretends to be the dead man in order to get the woman and her sister to hide him. This engrossing tale, a French and British coproduction, is unrated; it contains some nudity and sexual situations. 100m. **DIR:** Peter Duffell. **CAST:** Cherie Lunghi, Yves Beneyton, Mathilda May. **1985**

LIANNA ★★★★ The problem with most motion pictures about gays is they always seem to be more concerned with sex than love. In comparison, this film, written and directed by John Sayles stands as a remarkable achievement. About a married housewife named Lianna (Linda Griffiths) who decides to have an affair with, and eventually move in with, another woman (Jane Halloren), it is a sensitive study of one woman's life and loves. Rated R for nudity, sex, and profanity. 110m. **DIR:** John Sayles. **CAST:** Linda Griffiths, Jane Halloren, Jon De Vries, Jo Henderson. **1983**

LIAR'S MOON ★★★½ Two young lovers encounter unusually hostile resistance from their parents. Their elopement produces many of the expected problems faced by youths just starting out: limited finances, inexperience, and incompatibility. Rated PG for language. 106m. **DIR:** David Fisher. **CAST:** Matt Dillon, Cindy Fisher, Christopher Connelly, Hoyt Axton, Yvonne De Carlo, Susan Tyrrell. **1983**

LIBERATION OF L. B. JONES, THE 🦃 A wealthy black man is deluded into divorcing his wife because of her believed infidelity with a white cop. Rated R. 102m. **DIR:** William Wyler. **CAST:** Lola Falana, Roscoe Lee Browne, Lee J. Cobb, Lee Majors, Barbara Hershey. **1970**

LIES ★★★★ Ann Dusenberry plays a starving actress who gets sucked into a complicated and treacherous plan to gain the inheritance of a rich patient in a mental hospital. The plot is complicated and the good acting balances the intensity. The best part: a great performance by Gail Strickland, who plays a character you'll love to hate. Rated R for violence, sex, nudity, and profanity. 93m. **DIR:** Ken Wheat, Jim Wheat. **CAST:** Ann Dusenberry, Gail Strickland, Bruce Davison, Clu Gulager, Terence Knox, Bert Remsen. **1986**

LIES BEFORE KISSES ★★★ Above-average made-for-TV vengefest features Ben Gazzara being framed for the murder of a beautiful blackmailer. The setup is obvious, but who hates him enough to do this must be revealed. Satisfying ending. 93m. **DIR:** Lou Antonio. **CAST:** Jaclyn Smith, Ben Gazzara, Nick Mancuso, Greg Evigan. **1991**

LIFE AND ASSASSINATION OF THE KINGFISH, THE ★★★ A docudrama chronicling the life of flamboyant Louisiana politician Huey Long (Edward Asner). Told as a flashback, during the time Long lay dying from an assassin's bullet, this is an insightful look at an unforgettable time in U.S. history. 96m. **DIR:** Robert Collins. **CAST:** Edward Asner, Nicholas Pryor. **1976**

LIFE AND DEATH OF COLONEL BLIMP, THE ★★★★★ A truly superb film chronicling the life and times of a staunch for-king-and-country British soldier. Sentimentally celebrating the human spirit, it opens during World War II and unfolds through a series of flashbacks that reach as far back as the Boer War. Roger Livesey is excellent in the title role. Deborah Kerr portrays the four women in his life across four decades with charm and insight. Definitely a keeper. 163m. **DIR:** Michael Powell, Emeric Pressburger. **CAST:** Roger Livesey, Deborah Kerr, Anton Walbrook. **1943**

LIFE IN THE THEATER, A ★★★½ Wonderful acting by Jack Lemmon and Matthew Broderick and a witty script by David Mamet highlight this look at theatrical actors. Lemmon and Broderick deliver all the dialogue as the old pro and the promising newcomer. A real treat to watch. Made for TV. 94m. **DIR:** Gregory Mosher. **CAST:** Jack Lemmon, Matthew Broderick. **1993**

LIFE IS SWEET ★★★★½ Writer-director Mike Leigh is a social visionary, who prior to his first movie *High Hopes*, enthralled and captivated Britain with his made-for-television plays. This, his second movie, is a superlative portrait of a British family: a nurturing mother, a lovably blundering father, and two daughters. The complete spectrum of human emotion is covered and evoked as we observe the family members interact. Rated R for profanity, nudity, and simulated sex. 103m. **DIR:** Mike Leigh. **CAST:** Timothy Spall, Jane Horrocks, Alison Steadman, Jim Broadbent. **1991**

LIFE OF EMILE ZOLA, THE ★★★★ Paul Muni is excellent in the title role of the nineteenth-century novelist who championed the cause of the wrongly accused Captain Dreyfus (Joseph Schildkraut). A lavish production! B&W; 93m. **DIR:** William Dieterle. **CAST:** Paul Muni, Joseph Schildkraut, Gale Sondergaard, Gloria Holden, Donald Crisp, Louis Calhern. **1937**

LIFE OF HER OWN, A ★★ Can a career woman find love and still have a life of her own? If she looks like Lana Turner, she obviously can in this tearjerker about two models who want careers and husbands in that order. Sluggish pacing and pretentious dialogue make this movie look like a TV soap opera. B&W; 108m. **DIR:** George Cukor. **CAST:** Lana Turner, Ray Milland, Ann Dvorak, Barry Sullivan, Louis Calhern, Tom Ewell, Jean Hagen, Sara Haden, Phyllis Kirk. **1950**

LIFE ON THE MISSISSIPPI ★★★ A veteran riverboat pilot takes on a young apprentice. Good ensemble acting and beautiful location photography enhance this TV movie based on Mark Twain's novel about his own experiences during the glorious days of riverboats. 115m. **DIR:** Peter H. Hunt. **CAST:** Robert Lansing, David Knell, James Keane, Donald Madden. **1980**

LIFEGUARD ★★½ After his fifteen-year high school reunion, Sam Elliott begins to feel twinges of fear and guilt. How long can he go on being a lifeguard? Shouldn't he be making the move into a career with a future? The film is likable and easygoing, like its star. If your interest starts to drift, Elliott's charisma will pull you back. Rated PG. 96m. **DIR:** Daniel Petrie. **CAST:** Sam Elliott, Anne Archer, Kathleen Quinlan, Parker Stevenson, Stephen Young. **1976**

LIGHT IN THE JUNGLE, THE 🦃 Malcolm McDowell plays Dr. Albert Schweitzer as he brings medicine and music to Africa. Schweitzer, who won the Nobel Peace Prize in 1953, deserves a better bio than this static, sentimental, and unfulfilling bit of window dressing. Rated PG. 91m. **DIR:** Gray Hofmeyr. **CAST:** Malcolm McDowell, Susan Strasberg. **1990**

LIGHT OF DAY ★★½ The dead-end lives of a Cleveland bar band. There's Michael J. Fox as the guitarist willing to compromise in life for some stability. And there's his nihilistic sister (Joan Jett), the leader of the group who says that the beat of the music is all-important. Rated PG-13. 107m. **DIR:** Paul Schrader. **CAST:** Michael J. Fox, Gena Rowlands, Joan Jett, Jason Miller, Michael McKean. **1987**

LIGHT SLEEPER ★★★ 40-year-old drug delivery boy (Willem Dafoe) must come to terms with his future when his boss (Susan Sarandon) decides to shut down her upscale drug service. A very moody piece, with fine performances by Dafoe and Sarandon. Rated R for profanity and violence. 103m. **DIR:** Paul Schrader. **CAST:** Willem Dafoe, Susan Sarandon, Dana Delany, David Clennon, Mary Beth Hurt, Victor Garber, Jane Adams. **1992**

LIGHTNING OVER WATER ★★★½ This haunting film chronicles the final days in the life of American film director Nicholas Ray, whose movies include *Rebel Without a Cause*, *Johnny Guitar*, and *In a Lonely Place*. Wim Wenders presents a warm and gentle portrait of the director as he slowly dies from cancer. Filmed on location in Ray's loft in New York City. Poignant and unforgettable. 91m. **DIR:** Wim Wenders. **CAST:** Nicholas Ray, Wim Wenders. **1980**

LIGHTS, CAMERA, ACTION, LOVE ★★ This Romance Theatre production about an actress who must choose between a cameraman and her director could easily be dismissed for its poor acting, inane dialogue, and contrived plot. Its soap-opera style, however, may appeal to those hooked on either soaps or Harlequin romances. Introduced by Louis Jourdan. Unrated; contains no objectionable material. 97m. **DIR:** Jim Balden. **CAST:** Laura Johnson, Gary Hudson, Kathleen Nolan, Elissa Leeds, Robert Phelps. **1972**

LIGHTSHIP, THE ★★ The chief interest in this allegorical suspense drama is in seeing Robert Duvall play an over-the-top villain. But the story itself—a trio of sadistic bank robbers hijack a floating, anchored lighthouse and the ship's pacifist captain (Klaus Maria Brandauer) tries to stop his crew from fighting back—is short on suspense. Rated R. 90m. **DIR:** Jerzy Skolimowski. **CAST:** Robert Duvall, Klaus Maria Brandauer, Michael Lyndon. **1986**

LILIES OF THE FIELD (1930) ★★ Corinne Griffith loses custody of her child and finds a new life as a show girl. A real weepy in the most mawkish tarnished-woman tradition. Stolid and overwrought. B&W; 65m. **DIR:** Alexander Korda. **CAST:** Corinne Griffith, Ralph Forbes. **1930**

LILIES OF THE FIELD (1963) ★★★★ Sidney Poitier won an Academy Award for his portrayal of a handyman who happens upon a group of nuns who have fled from East Germany and finds himself building a chapel for them. With little or no buildup, the movie went on to become a big hit. B&W; 93m. **DIR:** Ralph Nelson. **CAST:** Sidney Poitier, Lilia Skala. **1963**

LILITH ★★ This is an intriguing, somber, frequently indecipherable journey into the darker depths of the human psyche. Warren Beatty is a young psychiatric therapist at a mental institute who falls in love with a beautiful schizophrenic patient (Jean Seberg), with tragic results. Visually impressive, it remains dramatically frustrating due to its ambiguous blending of sanity and madness. B&W; 114m. **DIR:** Robert Rossen. **CAST:** Warren Beatty, Jean Seberg, Peter Fonda, Kim Hunter, Anne Meacham, Jessica Walter, Gene Hackman. **1964**

LILLIE ★★★★ The fascinating, fashionable, passionate, scandal-marked life of Edwardian beauty Lillie Langtry, international stage star and mistress of Edward, Prince of Wales, heir to Queen Victoria, is colorfully told in this excellent PBS series of manners and mannerisms. 690m. **DIR:** Tony Wharmby. **CAST:** Francesca Annis, Peter Egan, Anton Rodgers. **1977**

LILY WAS HERE ★★½ Dutch film about a decent girl who plans to move to America with a wholesome soldier. When he is murdered, she leaves her coldhearted mother and decides to have the baby she's carrying. Melodramatic but watchable. Rated R for violence. 110m. **DIR:** Ben Verbong. **CAST:** Marion Van Thijn, Thom Hoffman, Monique van de Ven. **1989**

LINDBERGH KIDNAPPING CASE, THE ★★★ Still another look at one of this century's most famous and fascinating tragedies, this made-for-television version is above average. Anthony Hopkins rates four stars as Bruno Hauptmann, the man convicted and executed for the crime. 150m. **DIR:** Buzz Kulik. **CAST:** Cliff De Young, Anthony Hopkins, Joseph Cotten, Denise Alexander, Sian Barbara Allen, Martin Balsam, Peter Donat, Dean Jagger, Walter Pidgeon. **1976**

LION IN THE STREETS, A ★★★½ An overlooked, and neglected, movie with James Cagney as a southern hustler and con artist, making it big in politics, stepping on anyone and everyone he meets. In lesser hands than Cagney's, and his favorite director Raoul Walsh, this would be only so-so, but with them it packs a wallop. 88m. **DIR:** Raoul Walsh. **CAST:** James Cagney, Barbara Hale, Anne Francis, Jeanne Cagney, Lon Chaney Jr. **1953**

LION IN WINTER, THE ★★★★½ Acerbic retelling of the clash of wits between England's King Henry II (Peter O'Toole) and Eleanor of Aquitaine (Katharine Hepburn), adapted by James Goldman from his Broadway play. Hepburn won an Oscar for her part, and it's quite well played. The story's extended power struggle rages back and forth, with Henry and Eleanor striking sparks throughout. Rated PG. 135m. **DIR:** Anthony Harvey. **CAST:** Katharine Hepburn, Peter O'Toole, Anthony Hopkins, John Castle, Timothy Dalton. **1968**

LIP SERVICE ★★★½ This HBO film exposes the decline of TV news shows in an offbeat, at times hilarious, style. Old-timer Paul Dooley is forced to share his early morning show with a brash, brainless youngster (Griffin Dunne) who specializes in cheap theatrics. Contains profanity. 77m. **DIR:** W. H. Macy. **CAST:** Griffin Dunne, Paul Dooley. **1988**

LISTEN TO ME 🦃 Members of a college debating team take time out to find romance. Rated PG-13. 107m. **DIR:** Douglas Day Stewart. **CAST:** Kirk Cameron, Jami Gertz, Roy Scheider, Anthony Zerbe. **1989**

LITTLE ANNIE ROONEY ★★★ The title character is a teenaged street kid in braids, but America's Sweetheart, Mary Pickford, who played her, was 32 at the time. Pickford gets away with it—as she did in many of her films. As the daughter of a widowed New York cop, Annie keeps house, runs a street gang, and anguishes when her father is killed and her boyfriend is wrongly accused of the crime. Silent. B&W; 60m. **DIR:** William Beaudine. **CAST:** Mary Pickford, Spec O'Donnell, Hugh Fay. **1925**

LITTLE BOY LOST ★★★ Newspaperman Bing Crosby can't tell which kid is his as he searches for his son in a French orphanage following World War II. Get out the Kleenex. 95m. **DIR:** George Seaton. **CAST:** Bing Crosby, Claude Dauphin, Nicole Maurey. **1953**

LITTLE DORRIT ★★★★★ Told in two parts "Nobody's Fault" and "Little Dorritt's Story," this is a splendid six-hour production of Charles Dickens's most popular novel of his time. Derek Jacobi plays Arthur Clennam, a businessman whose life is forever changed when he meets the good-hearted heroine of the title (newcomer Sarah Pickering). An epic of human suffering, compassion, and triumph. Rated G. 356m. **DIR:** Christine Edzard. **CAST:** Alec Guinness, Derek Jacobi, Sarah Pickering, Joan Greenwood, Roshan Seth. **1988**

LITTLE FOXES, THE ★★★★ The ever-fascinating, ever-unique Bette Davis dominates this outstanding rendering of controversial playwright Lillian Hellman's drama of amoral family greed and corruption down South. Davis's ruthless matriarch, Regina, is the ultimate Edwardian bitch, for whom murder by inaction is not beyond the pale when it comes to achieving her desires. B&W; 116m. **DIR:** William Wyler. **CAST:** Bette Davis, Herbert Marshall, Teresa Wright, Richard Carlson, Dan Duryea. **1941**

LITTLE GLORIA...HAPPY AT LAST ★★★★ This TV miniseries focuses on the unhappy childhood of Gloria Vanderbilt and the tug-of-war surrounding her custody trial in 1934. It's hard not to pity the poor little rich girl as portrayed in William Haney's bestseller and adapted in this teleplay. Definitely worth a watch! 208m. **DIR:** Waris Hussein. **CAST:** Martin Balsam, Bette Davis, Michael Gross, Lucy Gutteridge, Glynis Johns, Angela Lansbury, Maureen Stapleton. **1982**

LITTLE LADIES OF THE NIGHT ★½ Linda Purl plays a teenage runaway who is forced into prostitution. TV-movie sexploitation. 100m. **DIR:** Marvin J. Chomsky. **CAST:** Linda Purl, David Soul, Lou Gossett Jr., Carolyn Jones, Paul Burke, Dorothy Malone. **1977**

LITTLE LORD FAUNTLEROY (1936) ★★★★ Far from a syrupy-sweet child movie, this is the affecting tale of a long-lost American heir (Freddie Bartholomew) brought to live with a hard-hearted British lord (C. Aubrey Smith) whose icy manner is warmed by the cheerful child. B&W; 98m. **DIR:** John Cromwell. **CAST:** Freddie Bartholomew, C. Aubrey Smith, Dolores Costello, Jessie Ralph, Mickey Rooney, Guy Kibbee. **1936**

LITTLE MEN (1940) 🦃 Louisa May Alcott's classic of childhood turned into a travesty. B&W; 84m. **DIR:** Norman Z. McLeod. **CAST:** Jack Oakie, Kay Francis, George Bancroft, Jimmy Lydon, Ann Gillis, William Demarest, Sterling Holloway, Isabel Jewell. **1940**

LITTLE MINISTER, THE ★★★½ An early effort in the career of Katharine Hepburn. This charming story, of a proper Scottish minister who falls in love with what he believes is a gypsy girl, is not just for Hepburn fans. B&W; 110m. **DIR:** Richard Wallace. **CAST:** Katharine Hepburn, Donald Crisp, John Beal, Andy Clyde. **1934**

LITTLE NOISES ★★ Low-budget, seemingly pointless film. A talentless writer sells the poems of a mute man as his own. Now he must deal with his conscience. Unrated. 80m. **DIR:** Jane Spencer. **CAST:** Crispin Glover, Tatum O'Neal, Rik Mayall, Tate Donovan. **1991**

LITTLE SWEETHEART ★★★ Not since *The Bad Seed* have we seen a little girl as deadly as 9-year-old Thelma (played by newcomer Cassie Barasch). She delves in blackmail of a couple on the run from a bank embezzlement job. Rated R for violence. 93m. **DIR:** Anthony Simmons. **CAST:** John Hurt, Karen Young, Cassie Barasch, Barbara Bosson. **1990**

LITTLE WOMEN (1933) ★★★★½ George Cukor's *Little Women* is far and away the best of the four film versions of Louisa May Alcott's timeless story of the March family. Katharine Hepburn is excellent as the tomboyish Jo. B&W; 115m. **DIR:** George Cukor. **CAST:** Katharine Hepburn, Spring Byington, Joan Bennett, Frances Dee, Jean Parker. **1933**

LITTLE WOMEN (1949) ★★½ Textbook casting and intelligent performances make this a safe second rendering of Louisa May Alcott's famous story of maturing young women finding romance in the nineteenth century. Technicolor is an enhancement, but the 1933 original is vastly superior. 121m. **DIR:** Mervyn LeRoy. **CAST:** June Allyson, Peter Lawford, Elizabeth Taylor, Mary Astor, Janet Leigh, Margaret O'Brien. **1949**

LIVE! FROM DEATH ROW ★★★ In this skillfully directed made-for-TV nail biter, Bruce Davison gives a high-powered performance as a condemned murderer who takes a tabloid reporter and her crew hostage just before his scheduled execution. Unrated; contains adult situations. 94m. **DIR:** Patrick Duncan. **CAST:** Bruce Davison, Joanna Cassidy, Jason Tomlins, Kathleen Wilhoite, Art La Fleur. **1992**

LIVING END, THE ★★★★ This hardcore, unsentimental road movie/romance between two HIV-positive gay men manages to be bizarre, bitter, *and* intriguing. Figuring they have nothing to lose, Craig Gilmore and Mike Dytri hit the road and act out their bad-boy fantasies amid provocative conversations. Tough to watch, but nihilism rarely looks this good. Not rated, but includes profanity, violence, nudity, and sexual situations. 85m. **DIR:** Gregg Araki. **CAST:** Craig Gilmore, Mike Dytri, Darcy Marta, Scot Goetz, Johanna Went, Mary Woronov. **1992**

LIVING PROOF: THE HANK WILLIAMS, JR., STORY 🦃 A miscast made-for-television stink bomb. 100m. **DIR:** Dick Lowry. **CAST:** Richard Thomas, Clu Gulager, Allyn Ann McLerie. **1983**

LIVING THE BLUES ★★ White suburban boy who wants to be a blues guitarist pesters the uncle of his inner-city girlfriend for a spot in his band. Well-intended but amateurish. Unrated; contains mild sexual situations. 78m. **DIR:** Alan Gorg. **CAST:** Michael Kerr, Galyn Gorg, Sam Taylor, Gwyn Gorg, Martin Raymond. **1986**

LOIS GIBBS AND THE LOVE CANAL ★★½ Marsha Mason is good as the housewife-turned-activist who fought for justice for residents of Niagara Falls after it was discovered that their homes were built over a toxic waste dump. But this made-for-TV movie tends to trivialize that real-life tragedy. 95m. **DIR:** Glenn Jordan. **CAST:** Marsha Mason, Bob Gunton, Penny Fuller. **1982**

LOLITA ★★★ A man's unconventional obsession for a "nymphet" is the basis for this bizarre satire. James Mason and Sue Lyon are the naughty pair in this film, which caused quite a stir in the 1960s but seems fairly tame today. B&W; 152m. **DIR:** Stanley Kubrick. **CAST:** James Mason, Sue Lyon, Shelley Winters, Peter Sellers. **1962**

LONDON KILLS ME ★★★ True-to-life portrayal of a London drug dealer who wants to get a real job, but must first buy decent shoes. If you can sit through the gritty first half, you'll actually start rooting for the main character. Rated R for violence and nudity. 107m. **DIR:** Hanif Kureishi. **CAST:** Justin Chadwick, Steven Mackintosh, Emer McCourt, Roshan Seth, Fiona Shaw, Brad Dourif. **1992**

LONDON MELODY ★★★ Intrigued by her beauty and spunk, a kindhearted diplomat secretly helps a struggling cockney street singer realize her ambitions by financing her musical training. Charming slice of London nightlife before World War II. B&W; 71m. **DIR:** Herbert Wilcox. **CAST:** Anna Neagle, Tullio Carminati. **1937**

LONELY HEARTS (1981) ★★★★½ A funny, touching Australian romantic comedy about two offbeat characters who fall in love. Peter (Norman Kaye) is a 50-year-old mama's boy who doesn't know what to do with his life when his mother dies. Then he meets Patricia (Wendy Hughes), a woman who has never had a life of her own. It's a warmly human delight. Rated R. 95m. **DIR:** Paul Cox. **CAST:** Norman Kaye, Wendy Hughes, Julia Blake. **1981**

LONELY HEARTS (1991) ★★★½ Eric Roberts plays an unscrupulous swindler who wines and dines lonely women before taking all their assets for bogus investments. Beverly D'Angelo cramps his style by clinging desperately to him. Suspenseful made-for-cable thriller. 109m. **DIR:** Andrew Lane. **CAST:** Eric Roberts, Beverly D'Angelo, Joanna Cassidy, Herta Ware. **1991**

LONELY LADY, THE 🦃 Pia Zadora as an aspiring writer who is used and abused by every man she meets. Rated R for violence, nudity, and profanity. 92m. **DIR:** Peter Sasdy. **CAST:** Pia Zadora, Lloyd Bochner, Bibi Besch. **1983**

LONELY PASSION OF JUDITH HEARNE, THE ★★★★ Maggie Smith gives a superb, seamless performance as Judith Hearne, an

Irish spinster in the 1950s sequestered from the carnal world by plainness and Catholicism. When she meets an Americanized Irishman (brilliantly portrayed by Bob Hoskins, New York accent and all), parts of her character's dormant personality spring to life. Rated R 115m. **DIR:** Jack Clayton. **CAST:** Maggie Smith, Bob Hoskins, Marie Kean, Wendy Hiller. **1987**

LONELYHEARTS ★★ A perfect example of how Hollywood can ruin great material. Montgomery Clift is tortured, Robert Ryan is cynical, and Maureen Stapleton is pitifully sex-starved in this disappointing adaptation of Nathaniel West's brilliant novel about an agony columnist who gets too caught up in a correspondent's life. Baloney! B&W; 101m. **DIR:** Vincent J. Donehue. **CAST:** Montgomery Clift, Robert Ryan, Myrna Loy, Maureen Stapleton, Dolores Hart, Jackie Coogan, Mike Kellin, Frank Overton, Onslow Stevens. **1958**

LONG AGO TOMORROW ★★★ Malcolm McDowell stars in this in-depth story about an arrogant soccer player who is paralyzed by a mysterious disease. A pretty young woman who shares the same disability is able to help him adapt. McDowell keeps the plot alive with a very believable performance. Rated PG. 116m. **DIR:** Bryan Forbes. **CAST:** Malcolm McDowell, Nanette Newman, Georgia Brown, Gerald Sim, Bernard Lee, Michael Flanders. **1970**

LONG DAY CLOSES, THE ★★★★½ This is another masterful and affecting stream-of-consciousness movie memoir from the creator of *Distant Voices/Still Lives*. Once again, he explores his rough-and-tumble, working-class English childhood. This later film spotlights his much warmer and loving feelings about his mother. Once again, colorful family members come and go, and the world is spiced with lovingly re-created songs of memory. Davies's movies are an acquired taste, but one well worth acquiring. 84m. **DIR:** Terence Davies. **CAST:** Marjorie Yates, Leigh McCormack, Anthony Watson. **1993**

LONG DAY'S JOURNEY INTO NIGHT (1962) ★★★★★ This superb film was based on Eugene O'Neill's play about a troubled turn-of-the-century New England family. Katharine Hepburn is brilliant as the drug-addict wife. Ralph Richardson is equally good as her husband, a self-centered actor. One of their sons is an alcoholic, while the other is dying of tuberculosis. Although depressing, it is an unforgettable viewing experience. B&W; 136m. **DIR:** Sidney Lumet. **CAST:** Katharine Hepburn, Ralph Richardson, Jason Robards Jr., Dean Stockwell. **1962**

LONG DAY'S JOURNEY INTO NIGHT (1987) ★★★★ Excellent television adaptation of Eugene O'Neill's harrowing drama about a New England family in deep crisis. The stunning direction by Jonathan Miller makes this almost the equal of the 1962 film. Jack Lemmon turns in another powerful performance. Recommended for mature audiences. 169m. **DIR:** Jonathan Miller. **CAST:** Jack Lemmon, Bethel Leslie, Peter Gallagher, Kevin Spacey. **1987**

LONG GONE ★★★★ This very likable film follows the exploits of a minor-league baseball team and their manager (William Petersen) during one magical season in Florida during the early Fifties. Insightful HBO-produced movie is not unlike *Bull Durham* in that both take a loving look at Americas's favorite pastime while dissecting other societal concerns. 110m. **DIR:** Martin Davidson. **CAST:** William L. Petersen, Virginia Madsen, Henry Gibson. **1987**

LONG GREY LINE, THE ★★★ John Ford stock company regulars Maureen O'Hara and Ward Bond join heartthrob Tyrone Power in this sentimental tale of a celebrated West Point athletic trainer, and his years of devoted service to the academy and its plebs before cheating scandals and racial bigotry. 138m. **DIR:** John Ford. **CAST:** Tyrone Power, Maureen O'Hara, Robert Francis, Ward Bond, Donald Crisp, Betsy Palmer. **1955**

LONG HAUL ★★ Blond bombshell Diana Dors entices unhappily married trucker Victor Mature into nefarious schemes. Limp British drama. B&W; 100m. **DIR:** Ken Hughes. **CAST:** Victor Mature, Patrick Allen, Diana Dors. **1957**

LONG HOT SUMMER, THE (1958) ★★★★ Paul Newman drifts into a Mississippi town and sets hearts aflutterin' and tongues awaggin' as he fascinates the womenfolk, alienates the menfolk, and aggravates Big Daddy Varner, the town's monied redneck, played by a corpulent Orson Welles. Based on parts of two short stories and one novel by William Faulkner, this hodgepodge of sex, sleaze, scandal, and suspicion is great fun. 115m. **DIR:** Martin Ritt. **CAST:** Paul Newman, Joanne Woodward, Orson Welles, Anthony Franciosa, Lee Remick, Angela Lansbury. **1958**

LONG HOT SUMMER, THE (1985) ★★★½ Don Johnson is a drifter who comes to a small southern town and upsets the routine of a family clan headed by patriarch Jason Robards. As well as being a moving, steamy tale of lust and greed, it also shows that director Stuart Cooper can get above-average performances from the likes of Johnson and Cybill Shepherd. This telemovie was originally shown in two parts. 208m. **DIR:** Stuart Cooper. **CAST:** Don Johnson, Jason Robards Jr., Cybill Shepherd, Judith Ivey, Ava Gardner, Wings Hauser. **1985**

LONG VOYAGE HOME, THE ★★★★½ Life in the merchant marine as experienced and recalled by Nobel Prize–winning playwright Eugene O'Neill. The hopes and dreams and comradeship of a group of seamen beautifully blended in a gripping, moving account of men, a ship, and the ever-enigmatic sea. The major characters are superbly drawn by those playing them. Definitely a must-see, and see-again, film. Classic. B&W; 105m. **DIR:** John Ford. **CAST:** John Wayne, Barry Fitzgerald, Thomas Mitchell, Mildred Natwick. **1940**

LONG WALK HOME, THE ★★★★ Superb performances by Sissy Spacek and Whoopi Goldberg highlight this absorbing drama about the first civil rights action: the Montgomery, Alabama, bus boycott of 1956. Rated PG for racial epithets and brief violence. 97m. **DIR:** Richard Pearce. **CAST:** Sissy Spacek, Whoopi Goldberg, Dwight Schultz, Ving Rhames, Dylan Baker. **1990**

LONGSHOT (1981) 🦃 A soccer star turns down a scholarship at a prestigious university in order to attend the football championships in Europe. 100m. **DIR:** E. W. Swackhamer. **CAST:** Leif Garrett, Ralph Seymour, Zoe Chaveau, Linda Manz. **1981**

LONGTIME COMPANION ★★★★ An accessible and affecting film that puts a much-needed human face on the tragedy of AIDS. An ensemble piece following the lives and relationships among nine gay New Yorkers and one woman friend over nine years. The cast is superb, with Bruce Davison especially memorable. The perceptive script is by playwright Craig Lucas. Rated R for profanity. 96m. **DIR:** Norman René. **CAST:** Bruce Davison, Campbell Scott, Dermot Mulroney, Mark Lamos, Patrick Cassidy, John Dossett, Mary-Louise Parker. **1990**

LOOK BACK IN ANGER (1958) ★★★★½ This riveting look into one of the "angry young men" of the 1950s has Richard Burton and Claire Bloom at their best. Burton exposes the torment and frustration these men felt toward their country and private life with more vividness than you may want to deal with, but if you're looking for a realistic recreation of the period, look no further. B&W; 99m. **DIR:** Tony Richardson. **CAST:** Richard Burton, Claire Bloom. **1958**

LOOK BACK IN ANGER (1980) ★★ Jimmy Porter is a failed trumpet player and lower-class intellectual who turns his dashed hopes into a symphony of verbal abuse played upon his wife and best friend. McDowell serves up a Porter who is smug and easy to despise, but his portrayal lacks the powerful rage of Richard Burton in the 1958 film version of this mid-Fifties stage smash. 101m. **DIR:** Lindsay Anderson. **CAST:** Malcolm McDowell, Lisa Banes, Fran Brill, Robert Brill, Raymond Hardie. **1980**

LOOK BACK IN ANGER (1989) ★★★★ Kenneth Branagh is brilliant as a detestable young man who constantly lashes out at his wife and business partner. This spellbinding adaptation of John Osborne's play was produced for British television. Unrated; contains profanity. 114m. **DIR:** David Jones. **CAST:** Kenneth Branagh, Emma Thompson, Gerard Horan, Siobhan Redmond. **1989**

LOOKING FOR MIRACLES ★★★½ The summer of 1935 marks the reunion of two brothers separated by poverty. Heartwarming family entertainment originally made for the Disney Channel. 104m. **DIR:** Kevin Sullivan. **CAST:** Greg Spottiswood, Zachary Bennett, Joe Flaherty. **1990**

LORD OF THE FLIES (1963) ★★★★ William Golding's grim allegory comes to the screen in a near-perfect adaptation helmed by British stage director Peter Brook. English schoolboys, stranded on an island and left to their own devices, gradually revert to the savage cruelty of wild animals. Visually hypnotic and powerful, something you just can't tear your eyes away from. The cast is outstanding, and what the film fails to take from Golding's symbolism, it compensates for with raw energy. B&W; 91m. **DIR:** Peter Brook. **CAST:** James Aubrey, Hugh Edwards, Tom Chapin. **1963**

LORD OF THE FLIES (1989) ★★ This 1989 Americanization of Sir William Golding's apocalyptic novel has the external trappings of a good film—lush scenery, and a fine cast of unknowns. But the depth and sensitivity of the 1963 Peter Brook version are blatantly missing. Rated R for profanity and violence. 120m. **DIR:** Harry Hook. **CAST:** Balthazar Getty. **1989**

LORDS OF DISCIPLINE, THE ★★★½ A thought-provoking film, *Lords* contains many emotionally charged and well-played scenes. David Keith stars as a student at a military academy who puts his life in danger by helping a black cadet being hazed. Rated R for profanity, nudity, and violence. 102m. **DIR:** Franc Roddam. **CAST:** David Keith, Robert Prosky, G. D. Spradlin, Rick Rossovich. **1983**

LORDS OF FLATBUSH, THE ★★½ Of all the leads, only Paul Mace didn't go on to bigger things. A stocky Sylvester Stallone shows promise as a character actor. Perry King is dashing. Susan Blakely is lovely. And Henry Winkler is particularly winning, playing an unexaggerated Fonzie-type character. The film provides a fairly satisfying blend of toughness and sentimentality, humor and pathos, as it tells a story of coming-of-age in 1950s New York. Rated PG. 88m. **DIR:** Stephen F. Verona, Martin Davidson. **CAST:** Perry King, Sylvester Stallone, Henry Winkler, Paul Mace, Susan Blakely. **1974**

LORENZO'S OIL ★★★★★ In a switch from his *Mad Max* films, doctor-turned-director George Miller uses the full force of his knowledge and skills to make gripping this emotionally powerful tale about a couple fighting for the life of their seriously ill son. In refusing to accept the verdict of a stodgy, entrenched medical establishment, the parents use every means possible to find a cure. Based on a true story. Rated PG-13 for profanity. 135m. **DIR:** George Miller. **CAST:** Nick Nolte, Susan Sarandon, Peter Ustinov, Kathleen Wilhoite. **1992**

LORNA ★★½ A sexually frustrated backwoods wife finds satisfaction with an escaped convict while her husband is away at work. Adult director Russ Meyer's first "serious" movie after his earlier nudie films, this atmospheric morality play will interest his fans, but may seem campy to some and dull to others. Unrated, it includes brief nudity and sexual situations. B&W; 78m. **DIR:** Russ Meyer. **CAST:** Lorna Maitland. **1964**

LORNA DOONE ★★★½ Beautiful, made-for-British-television adaptation of R. D. Blackmore's romantic novel stars Sean Bean and Polly Walker as star-crossed lovers whose union adds some kinks to a family feud. After his parents are killed, John Ridd vows to kill the Doone family, but unexpectedly falls for their daughter Lorna. Wonderfully romantic and steeped in period detail. Rated PG. 90m. **DIR:** Andrew Grieve. **CAST:** Sean Bean, Polly Walker, Clive Owen, Billie Whitelaw. **1990**

LOST! ★★★½ Even though it contains no nudity or violence, this is a movie that you should be careful about letting children see. Based on a true incident, it tells of three people adrift in the Pacific Ocean on an overturned boat. One, a religious zealot, feels that their plight is a test of God, and that they should do nothing to try to help themselves. Not rated. 94m. **DIR:** Peter Rowe. **CAST:** Kenneth Walsh, Helen Shaver, Michael Hogan. **1986**

LOST ANGELS ★★★★ Adam Horovitz ("King Ad Rock" of the Beastie Boys) makes an impressive dramatic debut as Tim Doolan, a misguided teenager who winds up in a Los Angeles psychiatric counseling center, where one of the staff psychiatrists (Donald Sutherland) wants to see the troubled youngsters properly treated. Director Hugh Hudson, who scored big with *Chariots of Fire*, is once again blessed with a good script. Rated R for language and violence. 121m. **DIR:** Hugh Hudson. **CAST:** Adam Horovitz, Donald Sutherland, Amy Locane, Don Bloomfield, Celin Weston, Graham Beckel. **1989**

LOST CAPONE, THE 🦃 Al Capone and his little-known brother, who became a lawman in Nebraska and fought the bootleggers sent by Brother Al. Dull television movie. 93m. **DIR:** John Gray. **CAST:** Adrian Pasdar, Ally Sheedy, Eric Roberts, Jimmie F. Skaggs. **1990**

LOST HORIZON ★★★★ Novelist James Hilton's intriguing story of a group of disparate people who survive an air crash and stumble on to a strange and haunting Tibetan land. One of the great classic films of the late 1930s. Long-missing footage has recently been restored, along with so-called lost scenes. B&W; 132m. **DIR:** Frank Capra. **CAST:** Ronald Colman, Jane Wyatt, John Howard, Edward Everett Horton, Margo, Sam Jaffe, Thomas Mitchell, Isabel Jewell, H. B. Warner. **1937**

LOST IN YONKERS ★★★★ Playwright Neil Simon wrote the screenplay for this adaptation of his Pulitzer and Tony Award–winning play about two brothers left with their crotchety old grandmother in the 1930s. Mercedes Ruehl is fabulous as the boys' aunt, a slightly dim-witted woman living with her mother (Irene Worth). Richard Dreyfuss also makes a fine impression as the boys' gangster uncle. Rated PG for adult themes. 110m. **DIR:** Martha Coolidge. **CAST:** Richard Dreyfuss, Mercedes Ruehl, Irene Worth, David Strathairn, Brad Stoll. **1993**

LOST LANGUAGE OF CRANES, THE ★★★ Set in England, this film deals with a homosexual who decides to tell his parents the truth, only to find out that his father has suppressed his own homosexuality for years. Eileen Atkins wonderfully portrays the mother who cannot accept her son's lifestyle and then loses her husband. Not rated, but contains homosexual activity. 85m. **DIR:** Nigel Finch. **CAST:** Brian Cox, Eileen Atkins, Angus Macfaden, Corey Parker, René Auberjonois, John Schlesinger, Cathy Tyson, Richard Warwick. **1992**

LOST MOMENT, THE ★★★½ A low-key, dark, offbeat drama based on Henry James's novel *The Aspern Papers*, which was based on a true story. A publisher (Robert Cummings), seeking love letters written by a long-dead great poet, goes to Italy to interview a very old lady and her niece. The old lady is spooky, the niece neurotic, the film fascinating. Those who know Cummings only from his TV series will be pleasantly surprised with his serious acting. B&W; 88m. **DIR:** Martin Gable. **CAST:** Robert Cummings, Susan Hayward, Agnes Moorehead, Eduardo Ciannelli. **1947**

LOST WEEKEND, THE ★★★★★ Gripping, powerful study of alcoholism and its destructive effect on one man's life. Arguably Ray Milland's best performance (he won an Oscar) and undeniably one of the most potent films of all time. Forty years after its release, the movie has lost none of its importance or effectiveness. Additional Oscars for best picture, director, and screenplay. B&W; 101m. **DIR:** Billy Wilder. **CAST:** Ray Milland, Jane Wyman, Philip Terry, Howard DaSilva, Frank Faylen. **1945**

LOUISIANA 🦃 Southern belle manages to destroy the lives of all around her. Made for television. 206m. **DIR:** Philippe de Broca. **CAST:** Margot Kidder, Ian Charleson, Victor Lanoux, Andrea Ferreol. **1984**

LOVE AND HATE ★★★ Based on *A Canadian Tragedy*, by Maggie Siggins, this powerful film looks at the life of a prominent Saskatchewan family. Kate Nelligan plays the battered wife who finally leaves, only to be terrorized by her husband (Kenneth Welsh). Not rated. 176m. **DIR:** Francis Mankiewicz. **CAST:** Kate Nelligan, Kenneth Welsh, Leon Pownall, Brent Carver. **1989**

LOVE AND WAR ★★★ An account of navy pilot Jim Stockdale's eight-year imprisonment in a North Vietnamese prison camp. James Woods is excellent as Stockdale; conveying uncertainty behind his undying patriotic loyalty. Painful but enlightening made-for-TV movie. 96m. **DIR:** Paul Aaron. **CAST:** James Woods, Jane Alexander, Haing S. Ngor. **1987**

LOVE AT THE TOP ★★★★ In this delightful film, Glynnis (Janis Paige) is at the top of her career as a lingerie designer. While being considered for promotion, she finds herself pitted against the son-in-law of the boss, a very romantic young man. Excellent. 105m. **DIR:** John Bowab. **CAST:** Janis Paige, Richard Young, Jim McKrell. **1982**

LOVE CHILD ★★★★ Although its ads gave *Love Child* the appearance of a cheapo exploitation flick, this superb prison drama is anything but. Directed by Larry Peerce, it is the gripping story of a young woman, Terry Jean Moore (Amy Madigan), who became pregnant by a guard in a women's prison in Florida and fought for the right to keep her baby. Rated R for profanity, nudity, sex, and violence. 96m. **DIR:** Larry Peerce. **CAST:** Amy Madigan, Beau Bridges, Mackenzie Phillips. **1982**

LOVE FIELD ★★★★ Michelle Pfeiffer is a 1960s Dallas housewife who models herself after Jacqueline Kennedy. When President John F. Kennedy is assassinated, Pfeiffer decides she has to attend the funeral. On the way, she encounters Dennis Haysbert, a black man traveling with his daughter. Pfeiffer and Haysbert (in a role originally given to Denzel Washington, who left the picture) are superb. Rated PG-13 for profanity and violence. 104m. **DIR:** Jonathan Kaplan. **CAST:** Michelle Pfeiffer, Dennis Haysbert, Stephanie McFadden, Brian Kerwin, Louise Latham, Peggy Rea. **1992**

LOVE HAS MANY FACES 🦃 Anachronistic, tame sex opera—filmed in Acapulco—with Lana Turner, Cliff Robertson and Hugh O'Brian. Unwatchable. 105m. **DIR:** Alexander Singer. **CAST:** Lana Turner, Cliff Robertson, Hugh O'Brian, Ruth Roman, Stefanie Powers, Virginia Grey. **1965**

LOVE IN THE PRESENT TENSE ★★½ Millie Perkins adds style and class to this Romance Theatre soap. A former model returns to New York to promote her daughter's career and falls for an irresistible photographer. Made for TV. 97m. **DIR:** Tony Mordente. **CAST:** Millie Perkins, Thomas MacGreevy, Deborah Foreman, Doris Roberts. **1982**

LOVE IS A MANY-SPLENDORED THING ★★★ Clichéd story of ill-starred lovers from two different worlds who don't make it. Jennifer Jones is a Eurasian doctor who falls in love with war correspondent William Holden during the Korean conflict. 102m. **DIR:** Henry King. **CAST:** Jennifer Jones, William Holden, Isobel Elsom, Richard Loo. **1955**

LOVE LEADS THE WAY ★★★★ This Disney TV movie features Timothy Bottoms in the true story of Morris Frank, the first American to train with a seeing-eye dog. Blinded while boxing, Frank at first refuses to accept his handicap and later resents the dog who offers to be his eyes. Fortunately, he adapts and later lobbies for acceptance of seeing-eye dogs throughout the United States. Bottoms turns in an exceptional performance as the struggling Frank. 99m. **DIR:** Delbert Mann. **CAST:** Timothy Bottoms, Eva Marie Saint, Arthur Hill, Susan Dey. **1984**

LOVE LETTERS ★★★★ In this impressive character study, the heroine, played by Jamie Lee Curtis, wonders aloud to her friend (Amy Madigan): "Sometimes it's right to do the wrong thing, isn't it?" Probing the emotions that lead to infidelity, *Love Letters* is a true adult motion picture. This concept is intelligently explored by writer-director Amy Jones. Rated R for graphic sex. 98m. **DIR:** Amy Jones. **CAST:** Jamie Lee Curtis, Amy Madigan, Bud Cort, James Keach. **1983**

LOVE MACHINE, THE ★★ A lust for power drives a television newscaster into the willing arms of the network president's wife. Pessimistic tale of the motivations that move the wheels of television news. Sexy, soapy adaptation of the Jacqueline Susann novel. Rated R. 108m. **DIR:** Jack Haley Jr. **CAST:** Dyan Cannon, John Phillip Law, Robert Ryan, Jackie Cooper, David Hemmings, Shecky Greene, William Roerick. **1971**

LOVE MATTERS ★★★ In spite of some preachiness, this little melodrama makes a few perceptive points on the hard work and dedication required for a successful marriage. Unfortunately, we don't see enough of distanced lovers Griffin Dunne and Annette O'Toole; too much time is wasted on the selfish antics of a shallow friend (Tony Goldwyn) and his latest sexual conquest. Rated R for profanity, nudity, and simulated sex. 97m. **DIR:** Eb Lottimer. **CAST:** Griffin Dunne, Tony Goldwyn, Annette O'Toole, Gina Gershon, Kate Burton, Gerrit Graham. **1993**

LOVE ON THE DOLE ★★★½ Based on Walter Greenwoods's novel, this film is about a London family trying to subsist during the Depression. A classy cast gives top-notch performances. 89m. **DIR:** John Baxter.

CAST: Deborah Kerr, Clifford Evans, Mary Merrall. 1941

LOVE STORY ★★★★ Unabashedly sentimental and manipulative, this film was a box-office smash. Directed by Arthur Hiller and adapted by Erich Segal from his best-selling novel, it features Ryan O'Neal and Ali MacGraw as star-crossed lovers who meet, marry, make it, and then discover she is dying. Rated PG. 99m. **DIR:** Arthur Hiller. **CAST:** Ryan O'Neal, Ali MacGraw, Ray Milland, John Marley. 1970

LOVE STREAMS ★★ A depressing story of a writer who involves himself in the lives of lonely women for inspiration, and his emotionally unstable sister, whom he takes in after a difficult divorce has left her without possession of her child. There are some funny moments and some heartfelt scenes, as well, but John Cassavetes's direction is awkward. Rated PG-13 for language and adult situations. 122m. **DIR:** John Cassavetes. **CAST:** John Cassavetes, Gena Rowlands, Diahnne Abbott, Seymour Cassel. 1984

LOVE STREET 🦃 Direct-to-video sleaze exists only so the female leads can disrobe in three short tales. Rated R for nudity, simulated sex, and profanity. 90m. **DIR:** Various. **CAST:** Christina Whitaker, Lisa Verlo, David Frailey. 1993

LOVE WITH A PERFECT STRANGER ★★ Chance encounters on a train, exotic international locations, carriage rides, curiously abandoned fine restaurants, and luxury hotels all create an atmosphere for romance. This Harlequin Romance has dialogue and interplay patterned after the popular books. This unrated British television production is suitable for any age. 98m. **DIR:** Desmond Davis. **CAST:** Marilu Henner, Daniel Massey. 1988

LOVE WITH THE PROPER STRANGER ★★★★ This neatly crafted tale of a pregnant young woman (Natalie Wood) and a restless trumpet player (Steve McQueen) offers generous portions of comedy, drama, and romance. Wood is at her most captivating. McQueen, veering a bit from his trademark cool, gives a highly engaging performance. Their relationship creates ample sparks. 100m. **DIR:** Robert Mulligan. **CAST:** Natalie Wood, Steve McQueen, Edie Adams, Herschel Bernardi, Tom Bosley. 1963

LOVE YOUR MAMA ★★ If good intentions and a conscientious heart were all it took, *Love Your Mama* would be a classic. *Love Your Mama* is a rough-hewn, amateurish-looking drama about a black family in the Chicago ghetto, held together through the love and hard work of the mother. It's too bad it wasn't more polished. Rated PG-13, with profanity. 92m. **DIR:** Ruby L. Oliver. **CAST:** Carol E. Hall, Audrey Morgan. 1993

LOVELESS, THE ★★ This could have been called *The Senseless* thanks to its lack of plot and emphasis on violence. It's a biker picture set in the 1950s and stars Willem Dafoe, who gives a good performance with the scant dialogue he's given. Though a poor tribute to *The Wild One*, this film does have a cult following. Rated R for violence, nudity and sex scenes. 85m. **DIR:** Kathryn Bigelow, Monty Montgomery. **CAST:** Willem Dafoe, Robert Gordon, Marin Kanter. 1984

LOVER, THE ★★★ Although director-coscenarist Jean-Jacques Annaud gives Marguerite Duras's infamous bestseller the serious treatment it deserves, the aggravatingly sparse story line seems mere window-dressing. French schoolgirl Jane March enters a relationship with twentysomething Chinese gentleman Tony Leung. Considerable arty coupling. Rated R for nudity and simulated sex. 110m. **DIR:** Jean-Jacques Annaud. **CAST:** Jane March, Tony Leung, Frederique Meininger. 1992

LOVERS' LOVERS ★★ Limp sex fantasy finds a couple trying to spice up their relationship by bringing another couple into their bedroom. They should have tried counseling. Rated R for nudity and language. 90m. **DIR:** Serge Rodnunsky. **CAST:** Serge Rodnunsky, Jennifer Ciesar, Cindy Parker, Ray Bennett. 1993

LOVERS OF THEIR TIME ★★ In this passable film, a married man (Edward Petherbridge) leads a boring life until he meets his dream love. 60m. **DIR:** Robert Knights. **CAST:** Edward Petherbridge, Cheryl Prime. 1986

LOVES OF CARMEN, THE ★★ Rita Hayworth plays an immoral gypsy hussy who ruins the life of a young Spanish officer (Glenn Ford). It's melodramatic and corny at times but still fun to see sparks fly between Hayworth as the beautiful vixen and an ever-so-handsome Ford. 98m. **DIR:** Charles Vidor. **CAST:** Rita Hayworth, Glenn Ford, Ron Randell, Victor Jory, Luther Adler, Arnold Moss. 1948

LOVE'S SAVAGE FURY 🦃 TV-movie attempt to re-create the passion of *Gone With the Wind*. 100m. **DIR:** Joseph Hardy. **CAST:** Jennifer O'Neill, Perry King, Raymond Burr, Connie Stevens. 1979

LOYALTIES ★★ In this Canadian-made drama, an upper-class Englishwoman reluctantly moves to a small town in one of the northwest provinces, where she becomes friends with her housekeeper, a hell-raising half-Indian woman. The story of the two women is well handled, but the movie turns into an unbelievable melodrama about the wife having to suffer for her husband's indiscretions. Rated R for violence and sexual situations. 98m. **DIR:** Anne Wheeler. **CAST:** Susan Wooldridge, Tantoo Cardinal, Kenneth Welsh. 1987

LUCAS ★★★★ Charming tale of young love, leagues above the usual teen-oriented fare due to an intelligent and compassionate script by writer-director David Seltzer. Corey Haim stars as a 14-year-old whiz kid "accelerated" into high school who falls in love, during the summer between terms, with 16-year-old Kerri Green. Rated PG-13 for language. 100m. **DIR:** David Seltzer. **CAST:** Corey Haim, Kerri Green, Charlie Sheen, Courtney Thorne-Smith, Winona Ryder. **1986**

LUCY AND DESI: BEFORE THE LAUGHTER ★★★ A warts-and-all portrayal of America's favorite couple of the 1960s, particularly distinguished by Frances Fisher's passionate turn as the redheaded queen of comedy. Not recommended for those who maintain the *I Love Lucy* image. Not rated. 96m. **DIR:** Charles Janot. **CAST:** Frances Fisher, Maurice Bernard. **1991**

LUST FOR LIFE ★★★½ A standout performance by Kirk Douglas, in the role of artist Vincent van Gogh, creates a rare, affecting portrait of a tormented man driven by the frenzied energy of passion. Unfortunately this overblown Hollywood production fails to exploit the beauty of some of the locations that inspired the paintings. 123m. **DIR:** Vincente Minnelli. **CAST:** Kirk Douglas, Anthony Quinn, James Donald, Pamela Brown. **1956**

LUTHER ★★★ Stacy Keach's gripping performance as Martin Luther is more than enough reason to see this otherwise turgid version of John Osborne's play (minimally adapted for this American Film Theater presentation) about the founder of Protestantism. Rated G. 108m. **DIR:** Guy Green. **CAST:** Stacy Keach, Patrick Magee, Hugh Griffith, Leonard Rossiter, Judi Dench, Maurice Denham. **1974**

LYDIA ★★★½ This sentimental treatment of the highly regarded French film *Carnet du Bal* is well acted and directed. It's the story of an elderly woman who has a reunion with four of her former loves. Merle Oberon's performance is one of her best. B&W; 104m. **DIR:** Julien Duvivier. **CAST:** Merle Oberon, Joseph Cotten, Edna May Oliver, Alan Marshal. **1941**

M.A.D.D.: MOTHERS AGAINST DRUNK DRIVING ★★½ True story of Candy Lightner and her struggle to establish M.A.D.D., the national anti-drunk driving organization. A convincing performance by Mariette Hartley as the California housewife whose life is thrown into turmoil and tragic heartbreak when her daughter is killed by a drunk driver. Above-average TV movie. 100m. **DIR:** William A. Graham. **CAST:** Mariette Hartley, Paula Prentiss, Bert Remsen, John Rubinstein, Cliff Potts, David Huddleston, Grace Zabriskie, Nicolas Coster. **1983**

M. BUTTERFLY ★★ Playwright David Henry Hwang's 1988 Tony-winning play, *M. Butterfly*, was based on the true story of a French diplomat tried and convicted of espionage in 1986 after having a twenty-year affair with a Chinese opera singer who turned out to be a spy—and a man. It's a fascinating tale, but one that is more suited to the illusions of the stage than the harsh reality of the camera. Despite a typically strong performance by Jeremy Irons, this screen adaptation fails to convince. Rated R for profanity, simulated sex, and violence. 101m. **DIR:** David Cronenberg. **CAST:** Jeremy Irons, John Lone, Barbara Sukowa, Ian Richardson. **1993**

MAC ★★★★ Writer-director-star John Turturro's tribute to the life and work ethic of his father, is a collection of real-life vignettes superbly acted and visualized. While not for all tastes, *Mac* is obviously a labor of love. Set in Queens in 1954 and focusing on three brothers who make the heartbreaking mistake of going into business together, it is an offbeat yet sometimes intensely moving film. Rated R for profanity, violence, and simulated sex. 118m. **DIR:** John Turturro. **CAST:** John Turturro, Michael Badalucco, Carl Capotoro, Katherine Borowitz, Ellen Barkin, John Amos, Olek Krupa. **1993**

MACARTHUR ★★★ Gregory Peck is cast as the famous general during the latter years of his long military career. It begins with his assumption of command of the Philippine garrison in World War II and continues through his sacking by President Truman during the Korean Conflict. The film takes a middle ground in its depiction of this complex man and the controversy that surrounded him. Peck's performance is credible, but the film remains uneven. Rated PG. 130m. **DIR:** Joseph Sargent. **CAST:** Gregory Peck, Dan O'Herlihy, Ed Flanders. **1977**

MACBETH (1948) ★★★ Shakespeare's noted tragedy, filmed according to a script by Orson Welles. Interesting movie—made on a budget of $700,000 in three weeks. Welles is an intriguing MacBeth, but Jeanette Nolan as his lady is out of her element. Edgar Barrier and Dan O'Herlihy are fine as Banquo and MacDuff. B&W; 105m. **DIR:** Orson Welles. **CAST:** Orson Welles, Roddy McDowall, Jeanette Nolan, Edgar Barrier, Dan O'Herlihy. **1948**

MACBETH (1961) ★★★½ As the crown-hungry Scottish thane Macbeth, Maurice Evans is superb and superbly abetted by Dame Judith Anderson, as the grasping, conniving Lady Macbeth. Another in the developing series of made-for-television *Hallmark Hall of Fame* programs being released on videocassette. B&W; 103m. **DIR:** George Schaefer. **CAST:** Maurice Evans, Judith Anderson. **1961**

MACBETH (1971) ★★★½ The violent retelling of this classic story was commissioned and underwritten by publisher Hugh Hefner. Shakespeare's tragedy about a man driven to self-destruction by the forces of evil is vividly brought to life by director Roman Polanski. Grim yet compelling, this version of one of our great plays is not for everyone and contains scenes that make it objectionable for children (or squeamish adults). 140m. **DIR:** Roman Polanski. **CAST:** Jon Finch, Francesca Annis, Martin Shaw, Nicholas Selby, John Stride. **1971**

MACBETH (1981) ★★½ Allowing for this being a film of a stage production, it is a disappointing and somewhat slow-moving telling of Shakespeare's tale. Interesting and offbeat casting. A Bard Productions Ltd. release. 150m. **DIR:** Arthur Allan Seidelman. **CAST:** Jeremy Brett, Piper Laurie, Simon MacCorkindale, Barry Primus, Millie Perkins, Alan Oppenheimer, Jay Robinson, Johnny Crawford. **1981**

MACK, THE ★★ Typical of the blaxploitation films of the early 1970s, a broadly overacted story about a southern California pimp. It gets two stars only because it's a fair example of the genre. Rated R for violence and language. 110m. **DIR:** Michael Campus. **CAST:** Richard Pryor, Max Julien, Roger E. Mosley, Don Gordon. **1973**

MAD BULL ★★½ A wrestler struggles to escape the sensationalism of his profession. Alex Karras is believable as a man haunted by the assassination of his tag-team brother. Schmaltzy at times, but enjoyable nonetheless. 100m. **DIR:** Walter Doniger, Len Steckler. **CAST:** Alex Karras, Susan Anspach, Nicholas Colasanto, Elisha Cook Jr., Danny Dayton. **1977**

MAD DOG AND GLORY ★★★★ Police photographer-detective Robert De Niro inadvertently saves the life of gangster Bill Murray and finds himself the recipient of a special favor: one week of the live-in charms of Uma Thurman. At first, De Niro wants no part of it, then he begins falling in love with Thurman—much to the chagrin of Murray. De Niro, Thurman, and Murray are excellent. Rated R for violence, profanity, and nudity. 97m. **DIR:** John McNaughton. **CAST:** Robert De Niro, Uma Thurman, Bill Murray, Kathy Baker, David Caruso, Mike Starr, Tom Towles. **1993**

MADAME BOVARY (1949) ★★★ Emma Bovary is an incurable romantic whose affairs of the heart ultimately lead to her destruction. Jennifer Jones is superb as Emma. Louis Jourdan plays her most engaging lover. Van Heflin portrays her betrayed husband. James Mason portrays Gustave Flaubert, on whose classic French novel the film is based. B&W; 115m. **DIR:** Vincente Minnelli. **CAST:** Jennifer Jones, Louis Jourdan, Van Heflin, James Mason. **1949**

MADAME CURIE ★★★★½ An excellent biography of the woman who discovered radium, balanced by a romantic retelling of her private life with her husband. The show belongs to Greer Garson and Walter Pidgeon in the third film to costar them and make the most of their remarkable chemistry. B&W; 124m. **DIR:** Mervyn LeRoy. **CAST:** Greer Garson, Walter Pidgeon, May Whitty, Henry Travers, Albert Basserman, Robert Walker, C. Aubrey Smith, Victor Francen, Reginald Owen, Van Johnson, Margaret O'Brien. **1943**

MADAME SATAN ★★★ A wealthy socialite tries to win her husband back from the arms of a chorus girl. Bizarre extravaganza in which the story only gets in the way of a lot of DeMille spectacularizing. B&W; 115m. **DIR:** Cecil B. DeMille. **CAST:** Kay Johnson, Reginald Denny, Lillian Roth, Roland Young. **1930**

MADAME SOUSATZKA ★★★ A flamboyant star turn from Shirley MacLaine fuels this gentle story about an eccentric piano teacher and the gifted prodigy (Navin Chowdhry) who comes to her for lessons in both music and life. As was true with Ruth Prawer Jhabvala's Oscar-winning script for *Room With a View,* her adaptation this time (of Bernice Rubens's novel) devotes equal time to richly drawn supporting characters: Peggy Ashcroft's wistful landlady and Twiggy's aspiring singer, among others. Rated PG-13 for language. 122m. **DIR:** John Schlesinger. **CAST:** Shirley MacLaine, Navin Chowdhry, Peggy Ashcroft, Twiggy. **1988**

MADAME X (1937) ★★★ One of the few versions of the famous stage play that relies on acting and characterization more than glamour and pretense. Character actress Gladys George adds heart, soul, and a lot of acting technique to the story of a diplomat's daughter who has a brief affair and is forced into prostitution because of it. B&W; 75m. **DIR:** Sam Wood. **CAST:** Gladys George, Warren William, John Beal, Reginald Owen, Henry Daniell, Phillip Reed, Ruth Hussey, Emma Dunn, Lynne Carver, Luis Alberni, George Zucco, Cora Witherspoon. **1937**

MADAME X (1966) ★★★ In this sentimental old chestnut, filmed six times since 1909, a woman is defended against murder charges by an attorney who is not aware he is her son. Lana Turner is good and is backed by a fine cast, but Technicolor and a big budget make this one of producer Ross Hunter's mistakes. Constance Bennett's last film. 100m. **DIR:** David Lowell Rich. **CAST:** Lana Turner, John Forsythe, Constance Bennett, Ricardo Montalban, Burgess Meredith. **1966**

MADE IN USA ★★½ Bonnie and Clyde-style drama about a couple of drifters who leave their brutal job as coal miners in Pennsylvania for the sunny horizon of California. While en route west they encounter sexy hitchhiker Lori Singer and embark on a crime spree. Good cast fails to lift this overdone crime-drama above mediocrity. Pretty disappointing. Rated R. 82m. **DIR:** Ken Friedman. **CAST:** Adrian Pasdar, Christopher Penn, Lori Singer. **1988**

MADEMOISELLE ★★★½ A lusty melodrama tailor-made for international sex-goddess Jeanne Moreau. She makes the most of her role as a sexually repressed schoolteacher who works out her frustration by committing a variety of crimes. She then seduces a woodcutter and claims he raped her and is the real crime doer in the community. *Then* she goes after the woodcutter's teenaged son. Outlandish but fascinating. B&W; 103m. **DIR:** Tony Richardson. **CAST:** Jeanne Moreau, Ettore Manni, Umberto Orsini, Keith Skinner, Mony Rey. **1966**

MADEMOISELLE FIFI ★★½ An allegory about Nazis inspired by two different Guy de Maupassant short stories. A bullish Prussian gets his comeuppance from a French laundress during the Franco-Prussian War. Alluring performances, but very predictable. B&W; 69m. **DIR:** Robert Wise. **CAST:** Kurt Kreuger, Simone Simon, John Emery, Alan Napier, Jason Robards Sr., Norma Varden. **1944**

MADWOMAN OF CHAILLOT, THE ★★ Self-conscious story about an eccentric who feels the world is better off without the greed of mercenary interests. Everyone looks embarrassed. Rated G because it is completely innocuous. 132m. **DIR:** Bryan Forbes. **CAST:** Katharine Hepburn, Charles Boyer, Yul Brynner, Danny Kaye, John Gavin, Nanette Newman, Giulietta Masina, Richard Chamberlain, Edith Evans, Paul Henreid, Donald Pleasence, Margaret Leighton, Oscar Homolka. **1969**

MAE WEST ★★★½ This TV biography features a very convincing Ann Jillian as siren Mae West. (Some poetic license has been taken in order to make this complimentary to West.) Roddy McDowall, as a female impersonator, trains West to be sultry, alluring, and ultradesirable while James Brolin plays the longtime love who offers her stability. 100m. **DIR:** Lee Philips. **CAST:** Ann Jillian, James Brolin, Roddy McDowall, Piper Laurie. **1982**

MAFIA PRINCESS 🦃 Susan Lucci plays the spoiled daughter of a Mafia crime lord. Made for TV. 100m. **DIR:** Robert Collins. **CAST:** Tony Curtis, Susan Lucci, Kathleen Widdoes, Chuck Shamata. **1986**

MAGDALENE ★★ This film plays like a Barbara Cartland romance novel with Nastassja Kinski as a beautiful woman who spurns the love of a powerful baron. Corny. Rated R for nudity. 89m. **DIR:** Monica Teuber. **CAST:** Nastassja Kinski, David Warner, Steve Bond, Franco Nero. **1990**

MAGIC TOWN ★★ After successfully collaborating with Frank Capra on some of his finest films, writer Robert Riskin teamed with director William Wellman for this mildly entertaining but preachy tale. An advertising executive (James Stewart) finds the perfect American community, which is turned topsy-turvy when the secret gets out. B&W; 103m. **DIR:** William Wellman. **CAST:** James Stewart, Jane Wyman, Ned Sparks. **1947**

MAGICIAN OF LUBLIN, THE 🦃 Superficial adaptation of Isaac Bashevis Singer's novel about a Jewish traveling magician in nineteenth-century Europe. Rated R for nudity. 105m. **DIR:** Menahem Golan. **CAST:** Alan Arkin, Louise Fletcher, Valerie Perrine, Shelley Winters, Lou Jacobi, Warren Berlinger, Lisa Whelchel. **1979**

MAGNIFICENT AMBERSONS, THE ★★★★★ Orson Welles's legendary depiction of the decline of a wealthy midwestern family and the comeuppance of its youngest member is a definite must-see motion picture. Much has been made about the callous editing of the final print by studio henchmen, but that doesn't change the total impact. It's still a classic. Special notice must be given to Welles and cameraman Stanley Cortez for the artistic, almost portraitlike, look of the film. B&W; 88m. **DIR:** Orson Welles. **CAST:** Joseph Cotten, Tim Holt, Agnes Moorehead. **1942**

MAGNIFICENT OBSESSION ★★★ Rock Hudson, a drunken playboy, blinds Jane Wyman in an auto accident. Stricken, he reforms and becomes a doctor in order to restore her sight in this melodramatic tearjerker. First filmed in 1935, with Irene Dunne and Robert Taylor. 108m. **DIR:** Douglas Sirk. **CAST:** Jane Wyman, Rock Hudson, Agnes Moorehead, Otto Kruger. **1954**

MAGNIFICENT YANKEE, THE ★★★½ Moving film biography of the Washington years of Oliver Wendell Holmes. The movie opens with his appointment to the Supreme Court in 1902 (at age 61) and closes just before his retirement in 1933. This also happens to be a charming love story. Louis Calhern was Oscar nominated for his portrayal. B&W; 80m. **DIR:** John Sturges. **CAST:** Louis Calhern, Ann Harding, Eduard Franz, Philip Ober, Ian Wolfe, Richard Anderson, Jimmy Lydon. **1950**

MAHABHARATA, THE ★★★★ An exquisite six-part Shakespearean-style production made in Paris for public television of the eighteen book Sanskrit epic of mankind's search for Dharma (truth). Dealing with the fortunes of rival ruling families, the Kauravas and Pandavas, this tale weaves historical elements and myth to expose man's ultimate choice between destiny and freedom. 222m. **DIR:** Peter Brook. **CAST:** Robert Langton-Lloyd. **1989**

MAHLER ★★½ Ken Russell's fantasy film about the biography of composer Gustav

Mahler. Robert Powell's portrayal of Mahler as a man consumed with passion and ambition is a brilliant one. Georgina Hale as Alma, Mahler's wife, is also well played. Unfortunately, the cast cannot give coherence to the script. 115m. **DIR:** Ken Russell. **CAST:** Robert Powell, Georgina Hale, Richard Morant. **1974**

MAHOGANY ★★ The highlight of this unimpressive melodrama is Diana Ross's lovely wardrobe. She plays a poor girl who makes it big as a famous model and, later, dress designer after Anthony Perkins discovers her. This one jerks more yawns than tears. Rated PG. 109m. **DIR:** Berry Gordy. **CAST:** Diana Ross, Anthony Perkins, Billy Dee Williams. **1975**

MAKE A WISH 🦃 Basil Rathbone is a jolly good composer. Henry Armetta, Leon Errol, and Donald Meek want to steal Basil's latest operetta. B&W; 80m. **DIR:** Kurt Neumann. **CAST:** Bobby Breen, Basil Rathbone, Marion Claire, Henry Armetta, Leon Errol, Donald Meek. **1937**

MAKE ME AN OFFER 🦃 A young woman makes her way to the top by becoming a quick study in the California real estate business. Made for television. 100m. **DIR:** Jerry Paris. **CAST:** Susan Blakely, Patrick O'Neal, Stella Stevens, John Rubinstein. **1980**

MAKING LOVE ★★ Kate Jackson discovers that her husband (Michael Ontkean) is in love with another...man (Harry Hamlin). Rated R because of adult subject matter, profanity, and implicit sexual activity. 113m. **DIR:** Arthur Hiller. **CAST:** Kate Jackson, Michael Ontkean, Harry Hamlin. **1982**

MALAREK ★★★ Victor Malarek's biographical novel (*Hey, Malarek*) exposes the abuse of teens in the Montreal Detention Center. As a rookie reporter, Malarek witnessed the cold-blooded shooting of an escaped teen. His investigation inspired his book and this film. Rated R for violence and profanity. 105m. **DIR:** Roger Cardinal. **CAST:** Elias Koteas, Kerrie Keane, Al Waxman, Michael Sarrazin. **1988**

MALCOLM X ★★★★★ Writer-director Spike Lee's most passionate film may also be his greatest. In chronicling the life of the black activist from his Harlem gangster years to his 1965 assassination at the age of 39 by followers of Elijah Muhammad, Lee pays scrupulous attention to detail and avoids the rambling, self-indulgent qualities that hampered his previous projects. At the heart of the film is a superb performance in the title role by Denzel Washington. Brilliant! Rated PG-13 for violence, suggested sex, and profanity. 193m. **DIR:** Spike Lee. **CAST:** Denzel Washington, Spike Lee, Angela Bassett, Albert Hall, Al Freeman Jr., Delroy Lindo, Kate Vernon, Lonette McKee. **1992**

MALTA STORY, THE ★★★ Set in 1942, this is about British pluck on the island of Malta while the British were under siege from the Axis forces and the effect the war has on private lives. Flight Lieutenant Ross's (Alec Guinness) love for a native girl (Muriel Pavlow) goes unrequited when his commanding officer (Anthony Steel) sends him on a dangerous mission. B&W; 103m. **DIR:** Brian Desmond Hurst. **CAST:** Alec Guinness, Jack Hawkins, Anthony Steel, Muriel Pavlow. **1953**

MAMBO ★★ Dated B movie features Silvano Mangano as an impoverished Venetian who seeks wealth and fame, first as a dancer and then as a count's wife. She has an annoying habit of thinking aloud rather than showing her emotions. B&W; 94m. **DIR:** Robert Rossen. **CAST:** Silvana Mangano, Michael Rennie, Shelley Winters, Vittorio Gassman. **1954**

MAN CALLED ADAM, A 🦃 A world-class jazz trumpet player can't live with the guilt of accidentally killing his wife and child. B&W; 103m. **DIR:** Leo Penn. **CAST:** Sammy Davis Jr., Louis Armstrong, Peter Lawford, Mel Torme, Frank Sinatra Jr., Lola Falana, Ossie Davis, Cicely Tyson. **1966**

MAN CALLED PETER, A ★★★½ This warm, winning film biography tells the story of Scottish clergyman Peter Marshall, who was appointed chaplain of the U.S. Senate. Beautifully played by Richard Todd and Jean Peters. 117m. **DIR:** Henry Koster. **CAST:** Richard Todd, Jean Peters, Marjorie Rambeau, Les Tremayne. **1955**

MAN FOR ALL SEASONS, A ★★★★★ This splendid film, about Sir Thomas More's heartfelt refusal to help King Henry VIII break with the Catholic church and form the Church of England, won the best-picture Oscar in 1966. Paul Scofield, who is magnificent in the title role, also won best actor. Directed by Fred Zinnemann and written by Robert Bolt, the picture also benefits from memorable supporting performances by an all-star cast. 120m. **DIR:** Fred Zinnemann. **CAST:** Paul Scofield, Wendy Hiller, Robert Shaw, Orson Welles, Susannah York. **1966**

MAN FROM LEFT FIELD, THE ★★★ Burt Reynolds directed and stars in this heartfelt made-for-TV drama about a homeless man who ends up coaching a ragtag kids' baseball team. Although a mystery to the locals and even himself, he begins to unlock his past and learns how he lost everything. Reba McEntire has some nice moments as a mom who helps him. Not too sweet, but inspiring. 96m. **DIR:** Burt Reynolds. **CAST:** Burt Reynolds, Reba McEntire. **1993**

MAN I LOVE, THE ★★★½ A moody melodramatic movie that benefits from sexy stars and sensational music by George Gershwin, Jerome Kern, and Johnny Green. Ida Lupino is sensuous as a streetwise cabaret singer who keeps mobsters at arm's length in order to protect her family. Not much story, but plenty of sophistication. B&W; 96m. **DIR:** Raoul Walsh. **CAST:** Ida Lupino, Robert Alda, Andrea King, Bruce Bennett, Dolores Moran, John Ridgely, Martha Vickers, Alan Hale Sr., Craig Stevens. **1946**

MAN IN GREY, THE ★★★ A tale of attempted husband-stealing that worked well to make the prey, James Mason, a star. Margaret Lockwood is the love thief who proves to intended victim Phyllis Calvert that with her for a friend she needs no enemies. Mason is a stand-out as the coveted husband. B&W; 116m. **DIR:** Leslie Arliss. **CAST:** Margaret Lockwood, James Mason, Phyllis Calvert, Stewart Granger, Martita Hunt. **1943**

MAN IN LOVE, A 🦃 European actress finds herself involved in an affair with an egotistical American film star. Rated R for nudity, profanity, and simulated sex. 108m. **DIR:** Diane Kurys. **CAST:** Peter Coyote, Greta Scacchi, Peter Riegert, Jamie Lee Curtis, Claudia Cardinale, John Berry. **1987**

MAN IN THE GRAY FLANNEL SUIT, THE ★★★½ The title of Sloan Wilson's novel became a catchphrase to describe the mindset of corporate America in the 1950s. Considering that, it's a pleasant surprise to find that Nunnally Johnson's film has hardly dated at all. 153m. **DIR:** Nunnally Johnson. **CAST:** Gregory Peck, Jennifer Jones, Fredric March, Marisa Pavan, Lee J. Cobb, Keenan Wynn, Gene Lockhart. **1956**

MAN IN THE MOON, THE ★★★★ About two sisters who fall in love with the same boy, this coming-of-age movie skillfully captures all the angst, joy, and heartbreak of adolescence and first love. It might have been a simple tearjerker if not for its remarkable sense of realism and honesty. Rated PG-13 for suggested sex and mature themes. 103m. **DIR:** Robert Mulligan. **CAST:** Sam Waterston, Tess Harper, Gail Strickland, Reese Witherspoon, Jason London, Emily Warfield. **1991**

MAN INSIDE, THE (1990) ★★ Well-intentioned drama about a crusader (Jurgen Prochnow) who goes undercover to expose a corrupt, muckraking West German newspaper that goes over the top a bit too often. Rated R for violence and profanity. 93m. **DIR:** Bobby Roth. **CAST:** Jurgen Prochnow, Peter Coyote, Dieter Laser, Nathalie Baye. **1990**

MAN OF A THOUSAND FACES ★★½ Sentimentalized, soap-opera bio-pic of Lon Chaney Sr., the screen's greatest horror star, dwells too much on his troubled private life and too little on films. James Cagney turns in a moving performance in the title role. Chaney's films, currently available on video, speak more eloquently without dialogue. 122m. **DIR:** Joseph Pevney. **CAST:** James Cagney, Dorothy Malone, Jane Greer, Marjorie Rambeau, Jim Backus, Robert Evans, Jeanne Cagney, Snub Pollard. **1957**

MAN OF PASSION, A ★★ Typical story of a young boy's coming-of-age. The young boy is left with his grandfather, a famous painter. There he learns about life and sex. Not rated, but contains nudity and simulated sex. 95m. **DIR:** J. Anthony Loma. **CAST:** Anthony Quinn, Maud Adams, Ramon Sheen, Ray Walston, Elizabeth Ashley. **1989**

MAN WHO BROKE 1000 CHAINS, THE ★★★★½ An excellent retelling of *I am a Fugitive from a Chain Gang* with Val Kilmer in the Paul Muni role. Kilmer's performance is as sharp as Muni's, and the supporting players, notably Charles Durning, are superb. Not rated, has violence and profanity. 113m. **DIR:** Daniel Mann. **CAST:** Val Kilmer, Sonia Braga, Charles Durning, Kyra Sedgwick, James Keach. **1987**

MAN WHO HAD POWER OVER WOMEN, THE ★★ This British picture, adapted from Gordon Williams's novel, takes a semi-serious look at a talent agency. A passable time filler, with some unexpected touches. Rated R. 89m. **DIR:** John Krish. **CAST:** Rod Taylor, James Booth, Carol White. **1970**

MAN WITH THE GOLDEN ARM, THE ★★★ This dated film attempts to be *The Lost Weekend* of drug-addiction movies. Frank Sinatra is the loser on the needle and the nod in sleazy Chicago surroundings. Eleanor Parker is his crippled wife. Kim Novak, in an early role, is the girl who saves him. As a study of those who say yes, it carries a small jolt. B&W; 119m. **DIR:** Otto Preminger. **CAST:** Frank Sinatra, Eleanor Parker, Kim Novak, Arnold Stang, Darren McGavin, Robert Strauss. **1955**

MAN WITHOUT A FACE, THE ★★★★ Touching drama from first-time director Mel Gibson about a 12-year-old boy who dreams of following in the footsteps of his deceased father by attending a prestigious military academy. When he fails to pass the entrance exam, the lad turns to a reclusive former teacher, whose scarred face and tragic past have caused him to be viewed as something of a monster by the other kids living in their coastal village. Rated PG-13 for brief profanity and sexual undertones. 114m. **DIR:** Mel Gibson. **CAST:** Mel Gibson, Margaret Whitton, Fay Masterson, Gaby Hoffman, Geoffrey Lewis, Richard Masur, Nick Stahl, Michael DeLuise. **1993**

MAN, WOMAN AND CHILD ★★★½ Here's a surprisingly tasteful and well-acted tearjerker written by Erich Segal. Martin Sheen stars as a married college professor who finds out he has a son in France, the result of an affair ten years before. Sheen decides to bring his son to America, which causes complications. Rated PG for language and adult situations. 99m. **DIR:** Dick Richards.

CAST: Martin Sheen, Blythe Danner, Sebastian Dungan. **1983**

MANDELA ★★★ Although Danny Glover and Alfre Woodard put heart and soul into their interpretations of South African activists Nelson and Winnie Mandela, Ronald Harwood's poorly balanced script sets events in a one-sided vacuum. A less involving drama than Richard Attenborough's *Cry Freedom*. Unrated; suitable for family viewing. 135m. **DIR:** Philip Saville. **CAST:** Danny Glover, Alfre Woodard, Warren Clarke, Julian Glover. **1987**

MANDINGO 🦃 Sick film concerning Southern plantations before the Civil War and the treatment of the black slaves. Rated R. 127m. **DIR:** Richard Fleischer. **CAST:** James Mason, Susan George, Perry King, Richard Ward, Brenda Sikes. **1975**

MANIONS OF AMERICA, THE ★★★★ A bit sudsy at times, this was originally televised as a miniseries. It is an absolutely absorbing saga of a rebellious Irish lad's life as an immigrant in the United States. His hotheadedness can only be matched by the willfulness and determination of his British wife. 360m. **DIR:** Joseph Sargent. **CAST:** Pierce Brosnan, Kate Mulgrew, David Soul, Linda Purl. **1981**

MANIPULATOR, THE 🦃 Schizophrenic movie makeup man abducts an actress. Rated R for violence, profanity, and nudity. 91m. **DIR:** Yabo Yablonsky. **CAST:** Mickey Rooney, Luana Anders, Keenan Wynn. **1971**

MANNEQUIN (1937) ★★★ Poor working girl sees only the riches of a self-made millionaire as a way to happiness, yet lets herself be manipulated by a cad. Pros at work. The song "Always And Always" was Oscar-nominated. B&W; 95m. **DIR:** Frank Borzage. **CAST:** Joan Crawford, Spencer Tracy, Alan Curtis, Ralph Morgan. **1937**

MANXMAN, THE 🦃 Afternoon soap operas are nothing compared to this howler, the last of director Alfred Hitchcock's silent films. B&W; 70m. **DIR:** Alfred Hitchcock. **CAST:** Carl Brisson, Malcolm Keen, Anny Ondra. **1929**

MAP OF THE HUMAN HEART ★★★★ With great cinematic panache, director Vincent Ward tells the epic story of a young Eskimo who falls in love with a woman of mixed race. Through decades, they encounter obstacles to their romance. Anne Parillaud is particularly compelling as the object of the naïve Eskimo lad's desire. The WWII flying sequences are dazzling. The film reminds us of the value of primitive cultures. Rated R for nudity and suggested sex. 95m. **DIR:** Vincent Ward. **CAST:** Anne Parillaud, Patrick Bergin, Jason Scott Lee, John Cusack, Jeanne Moreau. **1993**

MARAT/SADE ★★★★ Glenda Jackson made her film debut in this terrifying adaptation of Peter Weiss's play about a performance staged by some inmates of a French insane asylum, under the direction of the Marquis de Sade. Peter Brook's direction is superb, as he creates a dark, claustrophobic atmosphere. Great ensemble acting. Not for the squeamish. 115m. **DIR:** Peter Brook. **CAST:** Patrick Magee, Glenda Jackson, Ian Richardson. **1966**

MARCIANO ★★ This made-for-TV biofilm concentrates far too much on the private life of the only boxer ever to retire from the pugilistic sport world undefeated—Rocky Marciano. More footage should have been devoted to his professional fighting career. There's nothing special here. 100m. **DIR:** Bernard Kowalski. **CAST:** Tony Lo Bianco, Belinda Montgomery, Vincent Gardenia, Richard Herd. **1979**

MARIA'S LOVERS 🦃 A former World War II prisoner of war and his loving wife. Rated R for profanity, nudity, suggested sex, and violence. 105m. **DIR:** Andrei Konchalovsky. **CAST:** Nastassja Kinski, John Savage, Keith Carradine, Robert Mitchum, Vincent Spano, Bud Cort. **1985**

MARIE ★★★ Sissy Spacek plays real-life heroine Marie Ragghianti, whose courage and honesty brought about the fall of a corrupt administration in Tennessee. Marie is a battered housewife who leaves her cruel husband. Struggling to raise her three children, she eventually works her way up to becoming the state's first female parole board head. Rated PG-13 for violence and profanity. 100m. **DIR:** Roger Donaldson. **CAST:** Sissy Spacek, Jeff Daniels, Keith Szarabajka. **1986**

MARIE ANTOINETTE ★★★ A regal rendition of the queen who lost her head, but not her stature in history. The film traces the life of the Austrian princess who became queen of France, and covers the period when she had a romantic attachment for the Swedish Count Axel de Fersen (Tyrone Power). B&W; 149m. **DIR:** W. S. Van Dyke. **CAST:** Norma Shearer, Tyrone Power, Robert Morley, John Barrymore, Joseph Schildkraut, Gladys George, Anita Louise, Reginald Gardiner. **1938**

MARIJUANA 🦃 A woman's addiction to marijuana forces her into prostitution and other crimes. B&W; 58m. **DIR:** Dwain Esper. **CAST:** Harley Wood, Hugh McArthur. **1937**

MARILYN & BOBBY: HER FINAL AFFAIR 🦃 This made-for-cable original is just another boring, poorly acted account of the last days of Marilyn Monroe. Not rated. 95m. **DIR:** Bradford May. **CAST:** Melody Anderson, James F. Kelly, Jonathan Banks, Kristoffer Tabori, Geoffrey Blake, Thomas Wagner, Ian Buchanan, Tomas Millan, Richard Dysart. **1993**

MARJOE ★★★½ The life of evangelist-turned-actor Marjoe Gortner is traced in this entertaining documentary. Film offers the viewer a peek into the world of the traveling evangelist. When Marjoe gets his act going, the movie is at its best. At times a little stagy, but always interesting. Rated PG for language. 88m. **DIR:** Howard Smith, Sarah Kernochan. **CAST:** Marjoe Gortner. **1972**

MARJORIE MORNINGSTAR ★★★ Natalie Wood and Gene Kelly give fine performances in this adaptation of the novel by Herman Wouk. Wood falls for show biz and for carefree theatrical producer Kelly. As Wood's eccentric uncle, Ed Wynn almost steals the show. A fine score by Max Steiner. 123m. **DIR:** Irving Rapper. **CAST:** Gene Kelly, Natalie Wood, Ed Wynn, Claire Trevor, Everett Sloane, Martin Milner, Carolyn Jones. **1958**

MARK OF THE HAWK, THE 🦃 African man struggles to integrate his people into the societal mainstream. A snooze. 84m. **DIR:** Michael Audley. **CAST:** Sidney Poitier, Juano Hernandez, Eartha Kitt, John McIntire. **1958**

MARLENE ★★★★ In this documentary, director Maximilian Schell pulls off something close to a miracle: he creates an absorbing and entertaining study of Marlene Dietrich without ever having her on camera during the interviews. (She refused to be photographed.) Instead, we hear her famous husky voice talking about her life, loves, and movies as scenes from the latter—as well as newsreels and TV clips—play onscreen. 95m. **DIR:** Maximilian Schell. **CAST:** Marlene Dietrich, Maximilian Schell. **1985**

MARRIED MAN, A ★★ A love triangle leads to murder in this oh-so-British boudoir-and-drawing-room tale. Expect to yawn frequently during this made-for-TV feature. 200m. **DIR:** John Davies. **CAST:** Anthony Hopkins, Ciaran Madden, Lise Hilboldt, John Le Mesurier. **1984**

MARRIED PEOPLE, SINGLE SEX ★★★ Three couples find themselves struggling with their love lives. One couple wants to end their marriage. One wife turns outside her marriage for thrills, while another husband finds pleasure on the phone. It's *thirtysomething* with plenty of nudity and sex as everyone tries to come to terms with their impending mid-life crisis. Literate and sexy. Available in rated R and unrated version; both contain plenty of adult language, situations, and nudity. 110m. **DIR:** Mike Sedan. **CAST:** Chase Masterson, Josef Pilato, Bob Rudd, Darla Slavens, Teri Thompson. **1993**

MARRIED TO IT ★★½ Three New York City couples become friends while planning a school play for their children. Some funny and poignant bits, but ultimately doesn't live up to the sum of its parts. Rated R for profanity and nudity. 105m. **DIR:** Arthur Hiller. **CAST:** Beau Bridges, Stockard Channing, Robert Sean Leonard, Mary Stuart Masterson, Cybill Shepherd, Ron Silver. **1991**

MARRIED TOO YOUNG ★★ An uncredited Ed Wood contributed to the script of this drab potboiler about a teen couple whose life together goes downhill after they quit high school to get married. B&W; 76m. **DIR:** George Moskov. **CAST:** Harold Lloyd Jr., Trudy Marshall, Anthony Dexter. **1962**

MARTIN LUTHER ★★½ This biography of the cleric who broke with the Catholic Church and founded Protestantism is handsomely photographed but overly respectful—Luther seems too saintly, wasting the talents of Old Vic veteran Niall MacGinnis. B&W; 104m. **DIR:** Irving Pichel. **CAST:** Niall MacGinnis, John Ruddock. **1953**

MARTY ★★★★★ This heartwarming movie about a New York butcher captured the Academy Award for best picture and another for Ernest Borgnine's poignant portrayal. Two lonely people manage to stumble into romance in spite of their own insecurities and the pressures of others. B&W; 91m. **DIR:** Delbert Mann. **CAST:** Ernest Borgnine, Betsy Blair. **1955**

MARTY (TELEVISION) ★★★★ The original *Marty*, written for the *Goodyear Playhouse* by Paddy Chayefsky in 1953. Rod Steiger is tremendously sincere in his first starring role as the lonely butcher who meets a plain schoolteacher (Nancy Marchand) one night at the Waverly ballroom. Powerful, low-key drama, hardly hurt by the poor technical standards of the time. Hosted by Eva Marie Saint; interviews with the stars and the director thrown in for good measure. B&W; 60m. **DIR:** Delbert Mann. **CAST:** Rod Steiger, Nancy Marchand, Esther Minciotti, Joe Mantell, Betsy Palmer, Nehemiah Persoff. **1953**

MARVIN AND TIGE ★★★★ Touching story of a runaway (Gibran Brown) who finds a friend in a poor and lonely man (John Cassavetes). Cassavetes's beautiful loser character works so well with Brown's streetwise pomp that the tension created by the clash of personalities makes their eventual deep relationship that much more rewarding. Rated PG for a few profane words. 104m. **DIR:** Eric Weston. **CAST:** John Cassavetes, Gibran Brown, Billy Dee Williams, Denise Nicholas, Fay Hauser. **1982**

MARY AND JOSEPH: A STORY OF FAITH 🦃 One can wish for a good telling of the story of Mary, she of the Immaculate Conception, and the devout Joseph, chosen "parents" of Christ, but this TV movie is not it. Dull, badly acted, and sustains no interest either historically or religiously. 146m. **DIR:** Eric Till. **CAST:** Blanche Baker, Jeff East, Lloyd Bochner, Colleen Dewhurst. **1979**

MARY OF SCOTLAND ★★★★ Katharine Hepburn plays one of history's tragic figures in director John Ford's biography of the sixteenth-century queen of Scotland. Fredric March is Bothwell, her supporter (and eventual lover) in her battle for power. The last scene, where Mary confronts her English accusers in court, is so well acted and photographed, it alone is worth the price of the rental. B&W; 123m. **DIR:** John Ford. **CAST:** Katharine Hepburn, Fredric March, John Carradine. **1936**

MASADA ★★★★ A spectacular TV movie based on the famous battle of Masada during the Roman domination of the known world. Fine acting, especially by Peter O'Toole, and excellent production values elevate this one far above the average small-screen movie. Unrated. 131m. **DIR:** Boris Sagal. **CAST:** Peter O'Toole, Peter Strauss, Barbara Carrera. **1984**

MASK (1985) ★★★★★ They used to call them moving pictures, and few films fit this phrase as well as this one, starring Cher, Sam Elliott, and Eric Stoltz. The story of a teenage boy coping with a disfiguring disease, it touches the viewer's heart as few movies have ever done. *Mask* rises above simple entertainment with its uplifting true-life tale. Rated PG-13. 120m. **DIR:** Peter Bogdanovich. **CAST:** Cher, Sam Elliott, Eric Stoltz, Laura Dern. **1985**

MASS APPEAL ★★★★½ A first-rate discussion of the dichotomy between private conscience and mass appeal, this film finds a mediocre and worldly priest, Father Tim Farley (Jack Lemmon), walking a political tightrope between the young seminarian (Zeljko Ivanek) he has befriended and his superior, Monsignor Burke (Charles Durning). At times both comic and tragic, it is not only a fine memorial but also a splendid motion picture. Rated PG. 99m. **DIR:** Glenn Jordan. **CAST:** Jack Lemmon, Zeljko Ivanek, Charles Durning, Louise Latham, James Ray. **1984**

MASSACRE IN ROME ★★★½ Chilling drama about a priest (Marcello Mastroianni) opposing a Nazi colonel (Richard Burton) who must execute hundreds of Roman citizens in retaliation for the death by partisans of some Nazi troops. Rated PG for violence. 103m. **DIR:** George Pan Cosmatos. **CAST:** Richard Burton, Marcello Mastroianni, Leo McKern, John Steiner. **1973**

MASTER HAROLD AND THE BOYS ★★★★ An intense movie filmed in a single setting with a cast of three. Matthew Broderick gives a moving performance as a white English boy in 1950s South Africa. Zakes Mokae, in a brilliant portrayal as a black servant, tries to lead the boy gently toward manhood. Not rated, but contains profanity. 90m. **DIR:** Michael Lindsay-Hogg. **CAST:** Matthew Broderick, Zakes Mokae, John Kani. **1984**

MASTER RACE, THE ★★★ Hitler's Third Reich collapses. A dedicated Nazi officer escapes. His refusal to accept defeat becomes an engrossing study of blind obedience to immorality. B&W; 96m. **DIR:** Herbert J. Biberman. **CAST:** George Coulouris, Stanley Ridges, Osa Massen, Lloyd Bridges. **1944**

MATA HARI (1931) ★★★ Casting Greta Garbo as history's most alluring spy proved to be big box office. She captivated Ramon Novarro—*and* the audience! The legend's throaty voice is hypnotic. B&W; 90m. **DIR:** George Fitzmaurice. **CAST:** Greta Garbo, Ramon Novarro, Karen Morley, Lionel Barrymore, Lewis Stone. **1931**

MATEWAN ★★★★½ Writer-director John Sayles's masterpiece about the massacre of striking West Virginia coal miners in 1920 has both heart and humor. Chris Cooper is the soft-spoken union organizer who tries to avoid violence. James Earl Jones is the leader of a group of black workers who were shocked to find, too late, that they were brought in as scabs. And David Strathairn is memorable as the town sheriff who attempts to keep the peace. Rated PG-13 for violence and profanity. 132m. **DIR:** John Sayles. **CAST:** Chris Cooper, Will Oldham, Mary McDonnell, James Earl Jones, David Strathairn, Josh Mostel. **1987**

MATTER OF DEGREES, A ★★★ When a college threatens to change its progressive campus radio station to a more laid-back listening format, staff members and students revolt. Rated R for sexual situations. 90m. **DIR:** W. T. Morgan. **CAST:** Arye Gross, Judith Hoag, Tom Sizemore. **1990**

MATTER OF TIME, A 🦃 A penniless countess takes a country-bumpkin-come-to-the-big-city hotel chambermaid in hand. Rated PG. 99m. **DIR:** Vincente Minnelli. **CAST:** Liza Minnelli, Ingrid Bergman, Charles Boyer, Spiro Andros, Isabella Rossellini. **1976**

MATTERS OF THE HEART ★★ Made-for-cable melodrama concerning a talented college musician (Christopher Gartin) who falls in love with a world-famous pianist (Jane Seymour at her bitchiest)...who, naturally, has cancer! Brief nudity. 94m. **DIR:** Michael Ray Rhodes. **CAST:** Jane Seymour, Christopher Gartin, James Stacy, Geoffrey Lewis. **1990**

MAURICE ★★★ Based on E. M. Forster's long-suppressed, semiautobiographical novel, this film details the love of a middle-class college student (James Wilby) for his aristocratic classmate (Hugh Grant). A minor, but handsome film. Rated R for nudity and implied sex. 140m. **DIR:** James Ivory. **CAST:** James Wilby, Hugh Grant, Rupert Graves, Denholm Elliott. **1987**

MAX AND HELEN ★★★½ Thoughtful, often heartbreaking story looks at two victims of the Holocaust. Max (Treat Williams) tells his story to famed Nazi hunter Simon Wiesenthal (Martin Landau), who has located the camp commandant where Max and his fiancée Helen (Alice Krige) were held.

Made for cable TV. No rating, but contains scenes of torture and rape. 79m. **DIR:** Philip Saville. **CAST:** Martin Landau, Treat Williams, Alice Krige. **1990**

MAX DUGAN RETURNS ★★½ After spending many years in jail and gambling to big winnings, Max Dugan (Jason Robards) seeks his daughter (Marsha Mason) to bestow gifts upon her and her son. Though grateful, she finds it difficult to explain to her policeman-boyfriend, Donald Sutherland. The charm of this Neil Simon fable wears thin. Rated PG. 98m. **DIR:** Herbert Ross. **CAST:** Jason Robards Jr., Marsha Mason, Donald Sutherland. **1983**

MAYFLOWER MADAM ★★ TV-movie bio of Mayflower descendant and debutante Sydney Biddle Barrows. Though allegedly based on fact, the events depicted here seem strictly soap-operaish. 96m. **DIR:** Lou Antonio. **CAST:** Candice Bergen, Chris Sarandon, Chita Rivera. **1987**

MCCONNELL STORY, THE ★★½ Run-of-the-mill romanticized bio-pic of real-life jet-test pilot has Alan Ladd acting like a stick, June Allyson as his devoted wife tearfully waiting on the tarmac. 107m. **DIR:** Gordon Douglas. **CAST:** Alan Ladd, June Allyson, James Whitmore, Frank Faylen. **1955**

MCVICAR ★★★ In this interesting British film, Roger Daltrey (lead singer for the Who) portrays John McVicar, whose real-life escape from the high-security wing of a British prison led to him being named "public enemy No. 1." Rated R. 111m. **DIR:** Tom Clegg. **CAST:** Roger Daltrey, Adam Faith, Jeremy Blake. **1980**

ME & VERONICA 🦃 False sentiment as hard-living Patricia Wettig dumps her kids with sister Elizabeth McGovern just before she heads off to jail. Slow and uninteresting. Rated R for adult situations and language. 97m. **DIR:** Don Scardino. **CAST:** Elizabeth McGovern, Patricia Wettig, Michael O'Keefe. **1992**

MEAN STREETS ★★★★½ This impressive film by director Martin Scorsese has criminal realism and explosive violence. Robert De Niro gives a high-energy performance as a ghetto psycho in New York's Little Italy who insults a Mafia loan shark by avoiding payment. He then rips off the friend who tries to save him. This study of street life at its most savage is a cult favorite. Rated R. 110m. **DIR:** Martin Scorsese. **CAST:** Robert De Niro, Harvey Keitel, Amy Robinson, Robert Carradine, David Carradine. **1973**

MEDICINE MAN ★★★ For those of us who could derive enjoyment in watching Sean Connery in a dog-food commercial, this muddled adventure-drama will do just fine. While one would expect better from director John McTiernan, there's not much even Howard Hawks could do with this "politically correct" story about a crotchety scientist who finds and then loses a cure for cancer in the threatened rain forests of Brazil. Rated PG-13 for violence and profanity. 104m. **DIR:** John McTiernan. **CAST:** Sean Connery, Lorraine Bracco, José Wilker. **1992**

MEDIUM COOL ★★★★½ Robert Forster stars as a television news cameraman in Chicago during the 1968 Democratic convention. All the political themes of the 1960s are here—many scenes were filmed during the riots. Cinematographer Haskell Wexler's first try at directing is a winner. Highly recommended. Rated R for nudity and language. 110m. **DIR:** Haskell Wexler. **CAST:** Robert Forster, Verna Bloom, Peter Bonerz. **1969**

MEET DR. CHRISTIAN ★★ Folksy Jean Hersholt enacts the title role, meeting and besting medical crisis after medical crisis, in this first of six films translated from the popular 1930s radio series. B&W; 63m. **DIR:** Bernard Vorhaus. **CAST:** Jean Hersholt, Dorothy Lovett, Robert Baldwin, Paul Harvey, Marcia Mae Jones, Jackie Moran. **1939**

MEET JOHN DOE ★★★★ A penniless drifter (Gary Cooper) gets caught up in a newspaper publicity stunt. He is groomed and presented as the spokesman of the common man by powerful men who manipulate his every action for their own purposes. When he finally resists, he is exposed as a fraud. His fellow common men turn against him, or do they? Barbara Stanwyck is the newspaperwoman who first uses him and with whom he predictably falls in love. B&W; 132m. **DIR:** Frank Capra. **CAST:** Gary Cooper, Barbara Stanwyck, Walter Brennan, Spring Byington. **1941**

MEETING VENUS ★★½ Glenn Close enters the rarefied air of opera for a romantic film in the tradition of Ingrid Bergman's high-class romance, *Intermezzo*. She plays a world-class diva who falls hard for her conductor during the hectic rehearsals for a Parisian production of *Tannhauser*. The film, however, frequently has more in common with soap opera than grand opera. Rated PG-13. 120m. **DIR:** Istvan Szabo. **CAST:** Glenn Close, Neils Arestrup. **1991**

MEETINGS WITH REMARKABLE MEN ★★★★ The quest for spiritual truth and self-realization by Russian philosopher G. I. Gurdjieff (Dragan Maksimovic) is the subject of this intriguing work. Director Peter Brook concentrates on Gurdjieff's early days. Not rated. 102m. **DIR:** Peter Brook. **CAST:** Dragan Maksimovic, Mikica Dimitrijevic, Terence Stamp, Athol Fugard, Gerry Sundquist, Warren Mitchell. **1979**

MELANIE ★★★ This drama about an illiterate Arkansas woman trying to regain custody of her son from her ex-husband in California is full of clichés but works anyway thanks to sincere direction and performances. Singer Burton Cummings plays a washed-up rock star who helps Melanie and is redeemed in the process; he also contributed the musical score. Not rated, but the equivalent of a PG-13. 109m. **DIR:** Rex Bromfield. **CAST:** Glynnis O'Connor, Burton Cummings, Paul Sorvino, Don Johnson. **1982**

MELODY FOR THREE ★★ In the last (and weakest) of the Dr. Christian movies, the compassionate MD branches out into psychology by restoring a family torn apart by divorce. Gratuitous musical numbers only make this short feature seem longer than it is. 67m. **DIR:** Erle C. Kenton. **CAST:** Jean Hersholt, Fay Wray, Irene Ryan. **1941**

MELODY IN LOVE An innocent young girl comes to a fiery tropical island, where promiscuity seems to be the order of the day. 81m. **DIR:** Hubert Frank. **CAST:** Melody O'Bryan, Sasha Hehn. **1978**

MELODY MASTER ★★ This film, also known under the title of *New Wine* and *The Great Awakening*, is another one in a long line of tortured-composer melodramas. Alan Curtis gives a bland portrayal of Franz Schubert. There are some good comedy spots supplied by Binnie Barnes and Billy Gilbert. B&W; 80m. **DIR:** Reinhold Schunzel. **CAST:** Alan Curtis, Ilona Massey, Albert Basserman, Binnie Barnes, Billy Gilbert, Sterling Holloway, John Qualen, Sig Arno, Forrest Tucker. **1941**

MEMBER OF THE WEDDING, THE ★★★★ Julie Harris plays an awkward 12-year-old who is caught between being a child and growing up. She yearns to belong and decides to join her brother and his bride on their honeymoon. Her total introversion allows her to ignore the needs of her motherly nanny (brilliantly played by Ethel Waters) and her loyal cousin (Brandon de Wilde). Depressing but riveting. B&W; 91m. **DIR:** Fred Zinnemann. **CAST:** Julie Harris, Ethel Waters, Brandon de Wilde, Arthur Franz. **1953**

MEMORIAL DAY ★★★ Made-for-TV movie with stirring, sensitive performances by Mike Farrell, Robert Walden, and Edward Hermann. Farrell portrays a successful attorney who has a reunion with his former Vietnam combat buddies. The reunion awakens painful memories and a dark secret. Shelley Fabares plays Farrell's psychologist wife. Rated PG. 95m. **DIR:** Joseph Sargent. **CAST:** Mike Farrell, Shelley Fabares, Robert Walden, Edward Herrmann, Danny Glover, Bonnie Bedelia. **1988**

MEMPHIS ★★★ Engrossing thriller follows the kidnapping of the son of a black banker by three whites in the 1950s. Film boasts strong performances and a real eye for period detail. Made for cable. 93m. **DIR:** Yves Simoneau. **CAST:** Cybill Shepherd, J. E. Freeman, Richard Brooks, Moses Gunn. **1992**

MEMPHIS BELLE (1990) ★★★★ This spectacular British-American production about U.S. pilots in World War II was based on the 1943 documentary made during the war by Hollywood director William Wyler. The story concerns the twenty-fifth and final mission of the crew of the Memphis Belle, a giant B17 bomber that was known as a flying fortress in its day. Top-flight. Rated PG-13 for brief profanity and violence. 101m. **DIR:** Michael Caton-Jones. **CAST:** Matthew Modine, Eric Stoltz, Tate Donovan, D. B. Sweeney, Billy Zane, Sean Astin, Harry Connick Jr., Courtney Gains, John Lithgow, David Strathairn. **1990**

MEN, THE ★★★★ Marlon Brando's first film, this is about a paralyzed World War II vet trying to deal with his injury. A sensitive script and good acting make this film a classic. Better than *Coming Home* in depicting vets' feelings and attitudes about readjusting to society. B&W; 85m. **DIR:** Fred Zinnemann. **CAST:** Marlon Brando, Jack Webb, Teresa Wright. **1950**

MEN AT WORK ★★ Cool garbagemen discover a nefarious plot to pollute the environment in what is best described as *Police Academy Meets Big Green*. Better luck next time, boys! Rated PG-13 for violence and profanity. 98m. **DIR:** Emilio Estevez. **CAST:** Charlie Sheen, Emilio Estevez, Leslie Hope, Keith David, Dean Cameron, John Getz. **1990**

MEN IN LOVE ★★★½ Shot on video, this film presents a human, honest approach to the subject of AIDS. Sensitive, inspiring tale of a gay man who returns his lover's ashes to Hawaii for dispersal. There he meets his lover's friends, who console him. 87m. **DIR:** Marc Huestis. **CAST:** Doug Self, Joe Tolbe, Emerald Starr. **1990**

MEN OF BOYS TOWN ★★★ Spencer Tracy and Mickey Rooney are back again as Father Flanagan and Whitey Marsh in this sentimental sequel to MGM's *Boys Town*. Here a completely reformed Rooney is involved in rehabilitating kids and raising the money to keep the institution operating. Good family entertainment. B&W; 107m. **DIR:** Norman Taurog. **CAST:** Spencer Tracy, Mickey Rooney, Bobs Watson, Larry Nunn, Darryl Hickman, Lee J. Cobb, Mary Nash. **1941**

MEN OF RESPECT ★★ With Francis Ford Coppola making *The Godfather Part III* into a gangster version of Shakespeare's *King Lear*, it probably made sense to writer-director William Reilly to adapt *Macbeth* for a similarly styled film. Unlike Coppola's majestic movie, however, *Men of Respect* is dreary, overacted, and overwrought. Rated R for violence, profanity, and nudity. 122m. **DIR:** William Reilly. **CAST:** John Turturro, Katherine Borowitz, Dennis Farina, Peter Boyle, Rod Steiger, Lilia Skala, Steven Wright, Stanley Tucci. **1991**

MENACE ON THE MOUNTAIN ★★½ This lesser Disney coming-of-age film features Mitch Vogel as a spunky 14-year-old forced to become the man of the house. While his Confederate dad fights the Yankees during the Civil War, Vogel must face thieving deserters who threaten his family. The plot is weak, the dialogue insipid. Unrated; contains violence. 89m. **DIR:** Vincent McEveety. **CAST:** Mitch Vogel, Pat Crowley, Albert Salmi, Charles Aidman. **1970**

MENACE II SOCIETY ★★★★ Sobering, insightful film about the horrors of inner-city life focuses on the moral crisis confronting a teenage gang member, who attempts to turn life around with the help of a no-nonsense teacher and a straitlaced young woman. The filmmakers and actors do an excellent job of showing the audience the predicaments, pressure, and prejudices that can turn a basically decent kid into a cold-blooded killer. Powerful stuff. Rated R for violence, profanity, and simulated sex. 104m. **DIR:** Allen Hughes, Albert Hughes. **CAST:** Tyrin Turner, Jada Pinkett, Larenz Tate, Bill Duke, Charles S. Dutton, Samuel L. Jackson, Glenn Plummer. **1993**

MEN'S CLUB, THE ★★★ Fine performances by an all-star cast in this offbeat and disturbing film about a boy's night out that is turned into an exploration of men's attitudes toward women.The changes remain hidden inside the characters, although we can guess what has happened by their actions. Rated R for nudity, profanity, suggested sex, and violence. 93m. **DIR:** Peter Medak. **CAST:** Roy Scheider, Frank Langella, Harvey Keitel, Treat Williams, Richard Jordan, David Dukes, Craig Wasson, Stockard Channing, Ann Wedgeworth, Jennifer Jason Leigh, Cindy Pickett. **1986**

MERRY CHRISTMAS, MR. LAWRENCE ★★★½ Set in a prisoner-of-war camp in Java in 1942, this film, by Nagisa Oshima, focuses on a clash of cultures—and wills. Oshima's camera looks on relentlessly as a British officer (David Bowie), who refuses to cooperate or knuckle under, is beaten and tortured by camp commander Ryuichi Sakomoto. Rated R for violence, strong language, and adult situations. 122m. **DIR:** Nagisa Oshima. **CAST:** David Bowie, Ryuichi Sakamoto, Tom Conti. **1983**

MESSAGE, THE (MOHAMMAD, MESSENGER OF GOD) ★★½ Viewers expecting to see Mohammad in this three-hour epic will be disappointed.... He never appears on the screen. Instead, we see Anthony Quinn, as Mohammad's uncle, struggling to win religious freedom for Mohammad. The film tends to drag a bit and is definitely overlong. Rated PG. 180m. **DIR:** Moustapha Akkad. **CAST:** Anthony Quinn, Irene Papas, Michael Ansara, Johnny Sekka. **1977**

METROPOLITAN ★★★★½ In this deliciously different, independently made movie, writer-director-producer Whit Stillman allows viewers a glimpse at the fading preppie-debutante social scene of New York by introducing a middle-class outsider (Edward Clements) into this rarefied world. An accidental meeting brings Clements into the "Sally Fowler Rat Pack" where a nice girl (Carolyn Farina) develops an immediate crush on him. Rated PG-13 for profanity. 107m. **DIR:** Whit Stillman. **CAST:** Carolyn Farina, Edward Clements, Christopher Eigeman, Taylor Nicholas. **1990**

MIDDLE OF THE NIGHT ★★★ A melodrama about marriage that symbolized a moral awakening for middle-aged America in the late 1950s. Fine-tuned film treatment of Paddy Chayefsky's stage play. B&W; 119m. **DIR:** Delbert Mann. **CAST:** Fredric March, Kim Novak, Glenda Farrell, Martin Balsam, Lee Grant, Joan Copeland. **1959**

MIDNIGHT (1934) ★★ Based on a well-received stage play, this rather implausible melodrama concerns a jury foreman who insists on a death verdict in the case of a young woman who killed a cruel lover. The juror then has to turn his own daughter over to the authorities for the same crime. Its main appeal now is Humphrey Bogart in a supporting role as a slick gangster. B&W; 74m. **DIR:** Chester Erskine. **CAST:** O. P. Heggie, Sidney Fox, Henry Hull, Lynne Overman, Margaret Wycherly, Humphrey Bogart, Richard Whorf. **1934**

MIDNIGHT CLEAR, A ★★★★ With his filmmaking debut on *The Chocolate War*, actor-turned-director Keith Gordon showed great promise. That promise is fulfilled in this compelling antiwar drama about a group of young American soldiers sent on a reconnaissance mission into enemy territory during World War II. Based on William Wharton's autobiographical novel, this impressive film recalls the impact and filmmaking technique of Stanley Kubrick's *Paths of Glory*. Rated R for profanity and violence. 107m. **DIR:** Keith Gordon. **CAST:** Ethan Hawke, Kevin Dillon, Peter Berg, Arye Gross, Frank Whaley, Gary Sinise, John C. McGinley. **1992**

MIDNIGHT COWBOY ★★★★★ In this tremendous film, about the struggle for existence in the urban nightmare of New York's Forty-second Street area, Jon Voight and Dustin Hoffman deliver brilliant performances. The film won Oscars for best picture, best director, and best screenplay. Voight plays handsome Joe Buck, who arrives from Texas to make his mark as a hustler, only to be outhustled by everyone else, including the crafty, sleazy "Ratso," superbly played by Hoffman. Rated R. 113m. **DIR:** John Schlesinger. **CAST:** Jon Voight, Dustin Hoffman, Sylvia Miles, Barnard Hughes, Brenda Vaccaro. **1969**

MIDNIGHT DANCER ★★★ A young ballerina balances her artistic yearning with a night job in the chorus line of Club Paradise. Hints of gangsters, drugs, and seedy sex give this Australian film an honest coating of grit—rare among recent dance movies. Rated R. 97m. **DIR:** Pamela Gibbons. **CAST:** Deanne Jeffs, Mary Regan. **1987**

MIDNIGHT EXPRESS ★★★★½ This is the true story of Billy Hayes, who was busted for trying to smuggle hashish out of Turkey and spent five years in the squalor and terror of a Turkish prison. *Midnight Express* is not an experience easily shaken. Yet it is a film for our times that teaches a powerful and important lesson. Rated R. 121m. **DIR:** Alan Parker. **CAST:** Brad Davis, John Hurt, Randy Quaid. **1978**

MIKE'S MURDER ★★★ This could have been an interesting tale of a small-time Los Angeles drug dealer and part-time tennis pro involved in a drug rip-off. But a string of confusing plot devices, doesn't work. Rated R for violence, language, and nudity. 97m. **DIR:** James Bridges. **CAST:** Debra Winger, Mark Keyloun, Darrell Larson. **1984**

MILAGRO BEANFIELD WAR, THE ★★★ There are fine perfomances in this slight, but enjoyable comedy-drama in which a group of citizens from a small town attempt to save their way of life by fighting big-money interests. The story is simplistic but a real spirit lifter. Rated R for violence and profanity. 117m. **DIR:** Robert Redford. **CAST:** Rubén Blades, Richard Bradford, Sonia Braga, Julie Carmen, James Gammon, Melanie Griffith, John Heard, Daniel Stern, Christopher Walken, Chick Vennera. **1988**

MILDRED PIERCE ★★★★ Bored housewife Joan Crawford parlays waiting tables into a restaurant chain and an infatuation with Zachary Scott. Her spoiled daughter, Ann Blyth, hits on him. Emotions run high and taut as everything unravels in this A-one adaptation of James M. Cain's novel of murder and cheap love. Her performance in the title role won Joan Crawford an Oscar for best actress. B&W; 109m. **DIR:** Michael Curtiz. **CAST:** Joan Crawford, Jack Carson, Zachary Scott, Eve Arden, Ann Blyth, Bruce Bennett, George Tobias, Lee Patrick. **1945**

MILES FROM HOME ★★ Richard Gere and Kevin Anderson star as brothers in this uneven drama about tragic rural figures. The brothers' farm is lost to foreclosure. They respond by torching the place and heading off on a confused odyssey of crime and misadventure. Rated R for profanity and violence. 103m. **DIR:** Gary Sinise. **CAST:** Richard Gere, Kevin Anderson. **1988**

MILES TO GO ★★★ When she learns she is dying of cancer, a woman lays plans for the future of her family by seeking her own "replacement." Unusual premise is handled tastefully in this TV movie. 98m. **DIR:** David Greene. **CAST:** Jill Clayburgh, Tom Skerritt, Mimi Kuzyk. **1986**

MILL ON THE FLOSS, THE ★★★½ Geraldine Fitzgerald is Maggie and James Mason is Tom Tolliver in this careful and faithful adaptation of novelist George Eliot's story of ill-starred romance. B&W; 77m. **DIR:** Tim Whelan. **CAST:** Geraldine Fitzgerald, James Mason. **1939**

MILLER'S CROSSING ★★★★ Corrupt political boss (Albert Finney) of an eastern city severs ties with his best friend and confidant (Gabriel Byrne) in 1929 when they both fall for the same woman and find themselves on opposing sides of a violent gang war. An underworld code of ethics, protocol, and loyalty provides the ground rules for this very entertaining, slightly bent homage to past mobster films. Rated R for language and violence. 115m. **DIR:** Joel Coen. **CAST:** Gabriel Byrne, Marcia Gay Harden, John Turturro, Albert Finney, Jon Polito. **1990**

MILLIONS ★★ Spoiled young man whose ambitions outstrip his brainpower decides to make his fortune. Lots of sex cheapens the plot. Rated R for nudity and profanity. 90m. **DIR:** Carlo Vanzina. **CAST:** Billy Zane, Lauren Hutton, Carol Alt, Donald Pleasence, Alexandra Paul. **1991**

MIN AND BILL ★★★ Their first picture together as a team puts Marie Dressler and Wallace Beery to the test when the future of the waif (Dorothy Jordan) she has reared on the rough-and-tumble waterfront is threatened by the girl's disreputable mother, Marjorie Rambeau. Her emotional portrayal won Marie Dressler an Oscar for best actress and helped make the film the box-office hit of its year. B&W; 70m. **DIR:** George Hill. **CAST:** Marie Dressler, Wallace Beery, Dorothy Jordan, Marjorie Rambeau. **1931**

MINE OWN EXECUTIONER ★★★ Noted psychiatrist Burgess Meredith accepts ex-fighter pilot and Japanese prisoner of war Kieron Moore as a patient. He finds himself in the thick of a schizophrenic's hell, resulting in murder and suicide. Top-notch suspense. B&W; 105m. **DIR:** Anthony Kimmins. **CAST:** Burgess Meredith, Kieron Moore, Dulcie Gray. **1948**

MINIVER STORY, THE ★★½ Post–World War II sequel to the popular *Mrs. Miniver* has Greer Garson putting her family's affairs in order while hiding the fact that she is dying. Good performances by the stars, but it is really just pure soap opera. B&W; 104m. **DIR:** H. C. Potter. **CAST:** Greer Garson, Walter Pidgeon, John Hodiak, Leo Genn, Cathy O'Donnell, Reginald Owen, Peter Finch, Henry Wilcoxon. **1950**

MIRACLE, THE (1959) ★★★ In Spain in the early 1800s, a postulant nun deserts her order to search for a soldier she loves and becomes a noted gypsy, singer, and courtesan. Tries for deep religious meaning but misses the mark. 120m. **DIR:** Irving Rapper. **CAST:** Carroll Baker, Roger Moore, Walter Slezak, Vittorio Gassman, Katina Paxinou, Dennis King. **1959**

MIRACLE, THE (1990) ★★★ Two Irish teenagers (Niall Byrne and Lorraine Pilkington) while away their days fantasizing about people they encounter. When a mysterious woman (Beverly D'Angelo) arrives, Byrne takes it a step further only to find out that she's the mother he never knew. A pleasant surprise. Rated PG for profanity. 100m. **DIR:** Neil Jordan. **CAST:** Beverly D'Angelo, Niall Byrne, Donal McCann, Lorraine Pilkington. **1990**

MIRACLE IN THE WILDERNESS ★★ Heavy-handed message film spreads the "give peace a chance" motto. When settlers (Kris Kristofferson and Kim Cattrall) are kidnapped by vengeful Blackfeet Indians, Kristofferson's violent attempts to save his wife and child are in vain. Only Cattrall's gentle ways can free them. Preachy and unbelievable made-for-cable drama. 88m. **DIR:** Kevin Dobson. **CAST:** Kris Kristofferson, Kim Cattrall, John Dennis Johnston. **1991**

MIRACLE OF OUR LADY OF FATIMA, THE ★★★½ Remarkably well-told story of the famous appearance of the Virgin Mary in the small town of Fatima, Portugal. The Virgin appears to some farm children and they try to spread her word to a skeptical world. Not rated, but equivalent to a G. 102m. **DIR:** John Brahm. **CAST:** Gilbert Roland, Frank Silvera, Sherry Jackson. **1952**

MIRACLE OF THE BELLS, THE ★★★ A miracle takes place when a movie star is buried in her coal-mining hometown. Hard-bitten press agent Fred MacMurray turns mushy to see "the kid" gets the right send-off. The story is trite and its telling too long, but the cast is earnest and the film has a way of clicking. B&W; 120m. **DIR:** Irving Pichel. **CAST:** Fred MacMurray, Alida Valli, Frank Sinatra, Lee J. Cobb. **1948**

MIRACLE OF THE HEART ★★★ Made-for-TV sequel to the 1938 *Boys Town*, which featured Spencer Tracy as Father Flanagan. This time, Art Carney plays one of Flanagan's boys, who is now an older priest. Touching and heartwarming. 96m. **DIR:** Georg Stanford Brown. **CAST:** Art Carney, Casey Siemaszko, Jack Bannon, Darrell Larson. **1986**

MIRACLE ON ICE ★★½ This made-for-TV movie reenacts the American hockey victory at the 1980 Lake Placid Olympic Games. Karl Malden plays his usual tough-but-fair persona to the hilt as character-building coach Herb Brooks. 140m. **DIR:** Steven H. Stern. **CAST:** Karl Malden, Andrew Stevens, Steve Guttenberg, Jessica Walter. **1981**

MIRACLE WORKER, THE (1962) ★★★★½ Anne Bancroft and Patty Duke are superb when re-creating their acclaimed Broadway performances in this production. Patty Duke is the untamed and blind deaf-mute Helen Keller and Bancroft is her equally strong-willed, but compassionate, teacher. Their harrowing fight for power and the ultimately touching first communication make up one of the screen's great sequences. B&W; 107m. **DIR:** Arthur Penn. **CAST:** Anne Bancroft, Patty Duke, Andrew Prine. **1962**

MIRACLE WORKER, THE (1979) ★★★½ This made-for-TV biography features Patty Duke Austin as Anne Sullivan, teacher and friend of a disturbed deaf and blind girl. Melissa Gilbert takes the role of Helen Keller, which garnered an Oscar for Duke in 1962. This version is not quite as moving as the earlier one, but it's still worth watching. 100m. **DIR:** Paul Aaron. **CAST:** Patty Duke Austin, Melissa Gilbert, Charles Siebert. **1979**

MIRAGE ★★★ Some really fine scenes and top-notch actors enliven this slow but ultimately satisfying mystery thriller. Gregory Peck is David Stillwell, a man who has lost his memory. Occasionally snappy dialogue, with an interesting but overdone use of flashbacks. B&W; 108m. **DIR:** Edward Dmytryk. **CAST:** Gregory Peck, Diane Baker, Walter Matthau, Kevin McCarthy, Jack Weston, George Kennedy, Leif Erickson, Walter Abel. **1965**

MISFITS, THE ★★★ Arthur Miller's parable of a hope-stripped divorcée and a gaggle of her boot-shod cowpoke boyfriends shagging wild horses in the Nevada desert, this film was the last hurrah for Marilyn Monroe and Clark Gable. The acting is good, but the story line is lean. B&W; 124m. **DIR:** John Huston. **CAST:** Marilyn Monroe, Clark Gable, Montgomery Clift, Thelma Ritter, Eli Wallach, Estelle Winwood. **1961**

MISHIMA: A LIFE IN FOUR CHAPTERS ★★★★ By depicting this enigmatic writer's life through his art, filmmaker Paul Schrader has come close to illustrating the true heart of an artist. This is not a standard narrative biography but a bold attempt to meld an artist's life with his life's work. The movie is, as suggested in the title, divided into four parts: "Beauty," "Art," "Action," and the climactic "A Harmony of Pen and Sword." Rated R for sex, nudity, violence, and adult situations. 121m. **DIR:** Paul Schrader. **CAST:** Ken Ogata, Ken Swada, Yasusuka Brando. **1985**

MISPLACED ★★★ A modest but appealing independent film about the hurdles facing a teenage immigrant, newly arrived in America. Set in 1981, *Misplaced* is part coming-of-age tale and part cross-cultural drama. Unrated. 98m. **DIR:** Louis Yansen. **CAST:** John

Cameron Mitchell, Elzbieta Czyzewska, Viveca Lindfors. **1991**

MISS ROSE WHITE ★★★★ *Hallmark Hall of Fame* movie starring Kyra Sedgwick as a young Jewish career woman forced to confront her family's heritage and tragic past. Heartwarming with captivating performances by the entire cast. 95m. **DIR:** Joseph Sargent. **CAST:** Kyra Sedgwick, Maximilian Schell, Amanda Plummer, D. B. Sweeney, Penny Fuller, Milton Selzer. **1992**

MISS SADIE THOMPSON ★★½ A remake of *Rain*, the 1932 adaptation of Somerset Maugham's novel with Joan Crawford and Walter Huston, this production (with music) is notable only for the outstanding performance by Rita Hayworth in the title role. 91m. **DIR:** Curtis Bernhardt. **CAST:** Rita Hayworth, José Ferrer, Aldo Ray. **1953**

MISSILES OF OCTOBER, THE ★★★★½ This is a superbly cast, well-written, excitingly directed made-for-TV film dealing with the crucial decisions that were made during the Cuban missile crisis of October 1962. It follows the hour-by-hour situations that occurred when the U.S. government discovered that the Soviet Union was installing offensive missiles in Cuba. Gripping and realistic. 175m. **DIR:** Anthony Page. **CAST:** William Devane, Ralph Bellamy, Martin Sheen, Howard DaSilva. **1974**

MISSING ★★★★★ A superb political thriller directed by Costa-Gavras, this stars Jack Lemmon and Sissy Spacek as the father and wife of a journalist who disappears during a bloody South American coup. Rated R for violence, nudity, and profanity. 122m. **DIR:** Constantin Costa-Gavras. **CAST:** Jack Lemmon, Sissy Spacek, John Shea, Melanie Mayron, Janice Rule, David Clennon. **1982**

MISSION, THE ★★★½ Jeremy Irons plays a Spanish Jesuit who goes into the South American wilderness to build a mission in the hope of converting the Indians of the region. Robert De Niro plays a slave hunter who is converted and joins Irons in his mission. When Spain sells the colony to Portugal, they are forced to defend all they have built against the Portuguese aggressors. Rated PG for violence and sex. 125m. **DIR:** Roland Joffe. **CAST:** Jeremy Irons, Robert De Niro, Liam Neeson, Ray McAnally, Aidan Quinn. **1986**

MISSION OF THE SHARK ★★★ Though compelling, this film doesn't develop the characters of the Americans aboard the USS *Indianapolis* before they're struck by Japanese torpedoes in July 1945. Stacy Keach plays Captain Charles McVay, who ultimately is blamed for the deaths of over 800 men. Terrifying scenes of the men's struggle to survive for five days without food or water in the shark-infested ocean. Unrated; contains violence. 92m. **DIR:** Robert Iscove. **CAST:** Stacy Keach, Richard Thomas, Carrie Snodgress. **1991**

MISSION TO GLORY 🦃 The true story of Father Francisco Kin, the Spanish padre who helped develop California in the late seventeenth century. Rated PG for violence. 97m. **DIR:** Ken Kennedy. **CAST:** Ricardo Montalban, Cesar Romero, Rory Calhoun, Michael Ansara, Keenan Wynn, Richard Egan. **1979**

MISSISSIPPI BURNING ★★★★ Proving once again—as with *Midnight Express*—that he's the master of dramatic propaganda, Alan Parker presents this hair-raising account of what *might* have happened back in 1964 when three civil rights activists turned up missing in Mississippi. Laid-back Gene Hackman and by-the-book Willem Dafoe are the FBI agents in charge of the investigation. If good intentions excuse execution, then this is worthy fiction; at the very least, it allows Hackman to demonstrate his considerable range. Definitely not for the squeamish. Rated R for language and brutal violence. 125m. **DIR:** Alan Parker. **CAST:** Gene Hackman, Willem Dafoe, Frances McDormand, Brad Dourif, R. Lee Ermey. **1988**

MISSISSIPPI MASALA ★★★★ Director Mira Nair manages to achieve something of a miracle with this story of love between a black businessman (Denzel Washington) and an Indian immigrant (Sarita Choudhury) who become outcasts in the Deep South. A serious, insightful examination of racial prejudice wedded with heartwarming and sexy romance. Washington is particularly impressive. Rated R for profanity, nudity, and violence. 117m. **DIR:** Mira Nair. **CAST:** Denzel Washington, Roshan Seth, Sarita Choudhury, Charles S. Dutton, Tico Wells, Joe Seneca. **1991**

MR. AND MRS. BRIDGE ★★★★ Adapted from the novels *Mr. Bridge* and *Mrs. Bridge* by Evan S. Connell, this slice of Americana features marvelous performances by Paul Newman and Joanne Woodward, stunning detail in every frame, and an affecting chronicle of the lives and times of an upper-class WASP family. Composed of vignettes in the characters' lives, some of which are more compelling than others, it nonetheless adds up to a genuinely satisfying motion picture. Rated PG-13 for profanity. 127m. **DIR:** James Ivory. **CAST:** Paul Newman, Joanne Woodward, Blythe Danner, Simon Callow, Kyra Sedgwick, Robert Sean Leonard, Austin Pendleton. **1990**

MR. ARKADIN (A.K.A. CONFIDENTIAL REPORT) ★★½ Actor-writer-director Orson Welles confuses the audience more than he entertains them in this odd story of an amnesiac millionaire financier who hires an investigator to find his past. The intriguing story fails to translate effectively to the screen; even the efforts of a fine cast couldn't help Welles turn this into a critical or commerical success. B&W; 99m. **DIR:** Orson Welles. **CAST:** Orson Welles, Michael Redgrave, Akim Tamiroff, Patricia Medina, Mischa Auer. **1955**

MR. HALPERN AND MR. JOHNSON ★★★ Laurence Olivier plays a recently widowed Jewish manufacturer who, to his surprise, is asked to join a stranger named Johnson (Jackie Gleason) for a drink after the funeral. It seems that Johnson was once in love with the late Mrs. Halpern. What's more, they carried on a friendship for a number of years right up to just before her death. And therein lies the drama of this slight tale. 57m. **DIR:** Alvin Rakoff. **CAST:** Laurence Olivier, Jackie Gleason. **1983**

MISTER JOHNSON ★★★★ A poignant drama about the clash of cultures in the colonial western Africa of the 1920s. Adapted from Joyce Cary's 1939 novel, it follows the tragicomic exploits of a black African clerk named Johnson as he attempts to ingratiate himself into the lives and society of the ruling white colonialists. Rated PG-13. 102m. **DIR:** Bruce Beresford. **CAST:** Maynard Eziashi, Pierce Brosnan, Edward Woodward. **1991**

MR. JONES ★★ Doctor-patient romances don't get much more unconvincing than this. A wild-eyed, mysterious manic-depressive so infatuates a hospital shrink that she sacrifices her professional ethics for offscreen sex with her emotionally kinetic charge. The film's two stars keep the film promising, but the sterile love story doesn't do justice to its serious themes of emotional alienation and mental care. It's a tantalizing puzzle that has several missing pieces. Rated R for profanity. 110m. **DIR:** Mike Figgis. **CAST:** Richard Gere, Lena Olin. **1993**

MR. LOVE ★★½ Slow-moving yet interesting study of a middle-aged man who wins the love of women by being caring and encouraging. Barry Jackson is the soft-spoken British gardener who, stuck in a loveless marriage, seeks to befriend the lonesome women he encounters. Rated PG-13. 91m. **DIR:** Roy Battersby. **CAST:** Barry Jackson, Maurice Denham, Margaret Tyzack. **1985**

MR. SKEFFINGTON ★★★ Selfish and self-centered Bette Davis goes from reigning society beauty to hag in this typical soap opera of the upper crust—ranging across decades through feast and famine, indulgence and deceit. Time takes its toll on her. Then comes her one chance to do the right thing. Davis's performance is splendid. B&W; 147m. **DIR:** Vincent Sherman. **CAST:** Bette Davis, Claude Rains, Walter Abel, George Coulouris, Jerome Cowan, Gigi Perreau. **1944**

MR. SMITH GOES TO WASHINGTON ★★★★★ This Frank Capra classic is the story of a naïve senator's fight against political corruption. James Stewart stars as Jefferson Smith, the idealistic scoutmaster who is appointed to fill out the term of a dead senator. Upon arriving in the capitol, he begins to get a hint of the corruption in his home state. His passionate filibuster against this corruption remains one of the most emotionally powerful scenes in film history. B&W; 129m. **DIR:** Frank Capra. **CAST:** James Stewart, Jean Arthur, Claude Rains. **1939**

MR. WONDERFUL ★★★★ Fine ensemble acting highlights this sensitive and insightful study of relationships, something of an East Coast version of *The Big Chill*. Matt Dillon has the pivotal role of a Con Edison electrical worker who is being strapped by alimony payments. What's more, fiancée Mary-Louise Parker suspects he's still in love with ex-wife Annabella Sciorra. Rated PG-13 for brief profanity and simulated sex. 101m. **DIR:** Anthony Minghella. **CAST:** Matt Dillon, Annabella Sciorra, Mary-Louise Parker, William Hurt, Vincent D'Onofrio, David Barry Gray, Bruce Kirby, Dan Hedaya, Luis Guzman, Joanna Merlin, Jessica Harper, Adam LeFevre. **1993**

MISTRAL'S DAUGHTER ★★ This sudsy adaptation of Judith Krantz's novel features Stefanie Powers as the model and then mistress of a cynical artist (Stacy Keach). Made for television, this miniseries is unrated but contains partial nudity and simulated sex. 300m. **DIR:** Douglas Hickox. **CAST:** Stefanie Powers, Stacy Keach, Lee Remick, Timothy Dalton, Robert Urich, Stéphane Audran. **1984**

MISTRESS (1987) ★★ Sudsy coming-of-age melodrama about a mistress who must support herself after her wealthy lover dies. Made for TV, this contains adult themes. 96m. **DIR:** Michael Tuchner. **CAST:** Victoria Principal, Don Murray, Joanna Kerns, Kerrie Keane. **1987**

MISTRESS (1992) ★★★ A writer (Robert Wuhl) tries to get his long forgotten script made into a movie, while a trio of wealthy men attempt to get their mistresses shoehorned into acting roles. Barry Primus directs from his own story and deftly captures the games Hollywood wannabes play; similar to Robert Altman's *The Player*. Look for comic shenanigans from Robert De Niro. Rated PG. 109m. **DIR:** Barry Primus. **CAST:** Robert Wuhl, Robert De Niro, Martin Landau, Danny Aiello, Eli Wallach, Laurie Metcalf, Sheryl Lee Ralph, Jean Smart, Ernest Borgnine, Christopher Walken. **1992**

MRS. MINIVER ★★★★ This highly sentimental story of the English home front during the early years of World War II is one of the best examples of cinematic propaganda ever produced. It follows the lives of the Miniver family, especially Mrs. Miniver (Greer Garson), as they become enmeshed in a series of attempts to prove that there will always be an England. It won seven Academy Awards, including best picture. B&W;

134m. **DIR:** William Wyler. **CAST:** Greer Garson, Walter Pidgeon, Teresa Wright, May Whitty, Richard Ney, Henry Travers, Henry Wilcoxon, Reginald Owen. **1942**

MRS. PARKINGTON ★★★½ Over a sixty-year period a poor girl from a Nevada mining town becomes the matriarch of a powerful New York family. Fine performances from an outstanding cast, witty dialogue, and interesting subplots. Oscar nominations for Greer Garson and, in support, Agnes Moorehead. B&W; 124m. **DIR:** Tay Garnett. **CAST:** Greer Garson, Walter Pidgeon, Agnes Moorehead, Edward Arnold, Cecil Kellaway, Gladys Cooper, Frances Rafferty, Dan Duryea, Hugh Marlowe, Lee Patrick, Tom Drake, Rod Cameron, Selena Royle, Peter Lawford. **1944**

MRS. SOFFEL ★★½ We assume Australian director Gillian Armstrong's intent was to make more than a simple entertainment about a warden's wife (Diane Keaton) who helps two prisoners (Mel Gibson and Matthew Modine) escape. But she creates a shapeless "statement" about the plight of women at the turn of the century. Even the stars' excellent performances can't save it. Rated PG-13 for violence, suggested sex, and profanity. 112m. **DIR:** Gillian Armstrong. **CAST:** Diane Keaton, Mel Gibson, Matthew Modine, Edward Herrmann, Trini Alvarado. **1984**

MRS. WIGGS OF THE CABBAGE PATCH ★★ This sentimental twaddle about a poor but optimistic family from the wrong side of the tracks is a throwback to nineteenth-century stage melodrama, saved only by the presence of the great W. C. Fields, ZaSu Pitts, and a fine cast of character actors. If you are a Fields fan, beware—the much-put-upon comedian only appears in the last part of the film. Creaky. B&W; 80m. **DIR:** Norman Taurog. **CAST:** Pauline Lord, W. C. Fields, ZaSu Pitts, Evelyn Venable, Kent Taylor, Charles Middleton, Donald Meek. **1934**

MISUNDERSTOOD (1984) 🦃 A rich businessman raises two young sons who are traumatized by the sudden death of their mother. Rated PG for profanity. 91m. **DIR:** Jerry Schatzberg. **CAST:** Gene Hackman, Henry Thomas, Huckleberry Fox. **1984**

MISUNDERSTOOD (1988) ★★ This is an Italian production of the U.S. film release that starred Gene Hackman. The slow, depressing story did not need to be done twice. In this version, Anthony Quayle is a British consul in Italy. He is trying to raise his two sons following the death of his wife. The focus is on the father's relationship with the older son, which lacks understanding and compassion. The director, Luigi Comencini, takes far too long to reach the too late conclusion. Rated PG for adult themes. 101m. **DIR:** Luigi Comencini. **CAST:** Anthony Quayle, Stefano Colagrande, Georgia Moll. **1988**

MOCKERY ★★½ Silent-screen master of menace Lon Chaney Sr. stars in this MGM melodrama set during the Russian Revolution. Modern viewers may find it slow-going. Worth seeing for Chaney in a straight role, however, and for the stylish direction of Benjamin Christensen, which includes a chilling opening shot. B&W; 90m. **DIR:** Benjamin Christensen. **CAST:** Lon Chaney Sr., Barbara Bedford, Ricardo Cortez, Mack Swain. **1927**

MOLLY MAGUIRES, THE ★★★ The Molly Maguires were a group of terrorists in the 1870s who fought for better conditions for the Pennsylvania coal miners. In this dramatization, Sean Connery is their leader and Richard Harris is a Pinkerton detective who infiltrates the group. The film gives a vivid portrayal of the miners' dreadful existence. Performances are first-rate. A little long, but worth checking out. 123m. **DIR:** Martin Ritt. **CAST:** Sean Connery, Richard Harris, Samantha Eggar, Frank Finlay, Art Lund. **1970**

MOMMIE DEAREST ★★★½ At times this trashy screen version of Christine Crawford's controversial autobiography—which stars Faye Dunaway in an astounding performance as Joan Crawford—is so harrowing and grotesque you're tempted to stop the tape. But it's so morbidly fascinating you can't take your eyes off the screen. Rated PG. 129m. **DIR:** Frank Perry. **CAST:** Faye Dunaway, Diana Scarwid, Steve Forrest. **1981**

MONDO NEW YORK 🦃 A young girl observes the depravity and senselessness of New York City. Not rated, contains vile language and nudity. 83m. **DIR:** Harvey Keith. **CAST:** Joey Arias, Rick Aviles, Charlie Barnett. **1987**

MONEYTREE, THE ★★ A marijuana grower attempts to ply his trade despite a materialistic, disapproving girlfriend, cops, and rip-off artists. There are some bright moments among the predictable, poorly improvised, and preachy pro-drug ones. Unrated; the film has profanity, violence, and nudity. 94m. **DIR:** Alan Dienstag. **CAST:** Christopher Dienstag. **1991**

MONKEY GRIP ★★★½ One year in the life of a divorced mother as she struggles to keep some sense of herself while trying to support herself and her child and maintain a relationship with a drug-addicted musician. Possibly too slow for some tastes, but overall this Australian film offers a probing look at contemporary life-styles. Unrated; the film contains frank discussions of sex. 100m. **DIR:** Ken Cameron. **CAST:** Noni Hazlehurst, Colin Friels, Christina Amphlett. **1982**

MONSIGNOR 🦃 A Vatican priest seduces a student nun and makes deals with the Mafia to help the Church's finances. Rated R for profanity, nudity, and violence. 122m. **DIR:** Frank Perry. **CAST:** Christopher Reeve, Genevieve Bujold, Fernando Rey, Jason Miller. **1982**

MONSIGNOR QUIXOTE ★★★½ When a newly appointed monsignor (Alec Guinness) sets out on a holiday with a confirmed Communist (Leo McKern), the two form a strong friendship. Together they challenge corruption within the church. Guinness, playing Don Quixote's grandson, is an innocent idealist while McKern plays the crusty cynic. Made for HBO. 123m. **DIR:** Rodney Bennett. **CAST:** Alec Guinness, Leo McKern, Ian Richardson. **1985**

MONSOON 🦃 An American finds love in the arms of his fiancée's mysterious, jungle-wandering sister. 79m. **DIR:** Rod Amateau. **CAST:** Ursula Thiess, George Nader, Myron Healey, Diana Douglas, Ellen Corby. **1953**

MONTANA ★★½ Very slow-paced story of a Montana cattle-ranching family torn between the old values of the land and selling out to coal developers. Film loses its focus early on. Hit-and-miss script by Larry McMurtry doesn't help. Made for cable. 73m. **DIR:** William A. Graham. **CAST:** Richard Crenna, Gena Rowlands, Lea Thompson, Justin Deas, Elizabeth Berridge, Scott Coffey, Darren Calton, Peter Fonda. **1990**

MONTE CARLO ★★ Tacky TV miniseries features Joan Collins as a singing spy during World War II. If you enjoy soap operas, you won't mind. Scenery is a plus. 205m. **DIR:** Anthony Page. **CAST:** Joan Collins, George Hamilton, Lauren Hutton, Malcolm McDowell. **1986**

MONTENEGRO ★★★★ Susan Anspach stars as a discontented housewife who wanders into a Yugoslavian nightclub, finds herself surrounded by sex and violence, and discovers she rather likes it, in this outlandish, outrageous, and sometimes shocking black comedy. The laughs come with the realization that this movie is totally bonkers. Rated R because of profanity, nudity, sex, and violence. 98m. **DIR:** Dusan Makavejev. **CAST:** Susan Anspach, John Zacharias. **1981**

MONTH IN THE COUNTRY, A ★★★ Two emotionally scarred World War I veterans find themselves working for a month in a small Yorkshire village. The acting is flawless, but a gripping plot never quite materializes. Rated PG. 96m. **DIR:** Pat O'Connor. **CAST:** Colin Firth, Kenneth Branagh, Natasha Richardson. **1987**

MOON AND SIXPENCE, THE ★★★½ One of the better movies based on a Somerset Maugham novel. George Sanders is appropriately disillusioned as artist Charles Strickland, a character loosely based on real-life painter Paul Gauguin. He moves to Tahiti to fulfill his ambitions when the constrictions of European society get him down. B&W; 89m. **DIR:** Albert Lewin. **CAST:** George Sanders, Herbert Marshall, Florence Bates, Doris Dudley, Elena Verdugo, Albert Basserman, Eric Blore. **1942**

MOON IN SCORPIO 🦃 Three Vietnam War vets and their girlfriends go on a sailing trip that turns to horror. Not rated; has violence, profanity, and nudity. 90m. **DIR:** Gary Graver. **CAST:** Britt Ekland, John Phillip Law, William Smith. **1987**

MOON OVER HARLEM ★★½ Uneven melodrama featuring an all-black cast. The unlikely director is German émigré Edgar G. Ulmer, the visionary film poet who worked with F. W. Murnau and other German Expressionists. Ulmer has a considerable reputation among French critics. B&W; 77m. **DIR:** Edgar G. Ulmer. **CAST:** Bud Harris. **1939**

MOONRISE ★★ Being the son of a man hanged for murder isn't easy, and Danny (Dane Clark) has grown up with quite a chip on his shoulder. Very melodramatic. B&W; 90m. **DIR:** Frank Borzage. **CAST:** Dane Clark, Gail Russell, Lloyd Bridges, Ethel Barrymore. **1948**

MORE AMERICAN GRAFFITI ★★ Sequel to George Lucas's high-spirited, nostalgic *American Graffiti* lacks the charm of the original as it follows up on the lives of the various characters. There are a few bright moments, but a split-screen technique that didn't work when the film was initially released is even more annoying on video. Rated PG. 111m. **DIR:** B.W.L. Norton. **CAST:** Ron Howard, Paul Le-Mat, Candy Clark, Bo Hopkins, Cindy Williams, Charles Martin Smith, Mackenzie Phillips, Harrison Ford, Scott Glenn, Mary Kay Place, Rosanna Arquette. **1979**

MORNING GLORY (1933) ★★½ A naïve young actress comes to New York to find fame and romance. Based on the Zoe Akins play, the stagy film version hasn't aged well. But Katharine Hepburn is charismatic as the actress. She won her first Academy Award for this showy performance. B&W; 74m. **DIR:** Lowell Sherman. **CAST:** Katharine Hepburn, Adolphe Menjou, Douglas Fairbanks Jr., C. Aubrey Smith. **1933**

MORNING GLORY (1992) ★★½ Based on a book by LaVyrle Spencer, an ex-con applies for a job as the husband of a reclusive woman. Just when they fall in love, he's charged with killing a floozy. Unfortunately the story is very slow and boring. Rated PG-13 for profanity. 96m. **DIR:** Steven H. Stern. **CAST:** Christopher Reeve, Deborah Raffin, Lloyd Bochner, Nina Foch, Helen Shaver, J. T. Walsh. **1992**

MOROCCO ★★★ The fabulous and fabled Marlene Dietrich in her first Hollywood film. She's a cabaret singer stranded in exotic, sinister Morocco, who must choose between suave, rich Adolphe Menjou, or dashing French Legionnaire Gary Cooper. The scene at the oasis is classic 1930s cinematography. B&W; 92m. **DIR:** Josef von Sternberg. **CAST:** Gary Cooper, Adolphe Menjou, Marlene Dietrich. **1930**

MORTAL STORM, THE ★★★★ Phyllis Bottome's famous novel about the rise of Nazism makes good screen fare in spite of the screenwriter's apparent reluctance to call a spade a spade. Germany is never identified even though it is quite obvious in this story about a schoolteacher's family in the early days of World War II. Very well acted. B&W; 100m. **DIR:** Frank Borzage. **CAST:** James Stewart, Margaret Sullavan, Robert Young, Bonita Granville, Frank Morgan, Irene Rich, Dan Dailey, Tom Drake, Robert Stack, Maria Ouspenskaya, Gene Reynolds, Ward Bond. **1940**

MOSES ★★★ This biblical screen story of the Hebrew lawgiver is fairly standard as such films go. Burt Lancaster is well suited to play the stoic Moses. However, in trimming down this six-hour TV miniseries for video release, its makers lost most of the character development in the supporting roles. 141m. **DIR:** Gianfranco De Bosio. **CAST:** Burt Lancaster, Anthony Quayle, Irene Papas, Ingrid Thulin, William Lancaster. **1975**

MOSQUITO COAST, THE ★★★ In spite of the top-notch talent involved, this remains a flawed endeavor. Allie Fox (Ford) is a monomaniacal genius who can't bear what he perceives to be the rape of the United States, so he drags his wife and four children to the untamed wilderness of the Mosquito Coast in a self-indulgent attempt to mimic the Swiss Family Robinson. Rated PG. 117m. **DIR:** Peter Weir. **CAST:** Harrison Ford, Helen Mirren, River Phoenix, Conrad Roberts, Andre Gregory, Martha Plimpton. **1986**

MOTHER AND THE LAW, THE ★★★★★ One of the undisputed masterpieces of the silent cinema. This is the rarely seen complete version of the so-called modern episode to D. W. Griffith's *Intolerance*. A young husband (Bobby Harron) is unjustly indicted for murder and is saved only at the last minute in one of Griffith's most sensational last-minute-rescue climaxes. Silent. B&W; 93m. **DIR:** D. W. Griffith. **CAST:** Mae Marsh, Robert Harron. **1914**

MOULIN ROUGE ★★★★ Overlooked gem by director John Huston, with José Ferrer memorable as Henri de Toulouse-Lautrec, the famous nineteenth-century Parisian artist whose growth was stunted by a childhood accident. Lavish photography and Oscar-winning art direction and costumes make this a feast for the eyes. 123m. **DIR:** John Huston. **CAST:** José Ferrer, Zsa Zsa Gabor, Suzanne Flon, Christopher Lee, Peter Cushing. **1952**

MOUNTAIN, THE ★★★ Though this moralistic drama lacks punch, the fine performances of Spencer Tracy and Robert Wagner make it worth watching. They play mountaineering brothers risking a treacherous climb to find the wreckage of a passenger plane. 105m. **DIR:** Edward Dmytryk. **CAST:** Spencer Tracy, Robert Wagner, Claire Trevor, William Demarest, Richard Arlen, E. G. Marshall. **1956**

MUDHONEY ★★★★ A cult favorite from Russ Meyer about the exploits of some rural folks involved in the pursuit of cheap thrills and the meaning of life. Considered an adults-only film when released, it now seems quite tame. Plot has a local scum terrorizing Antoinette Cristiani, a deaf-and-dumb beautiful blonde until her rescue by Hal Hopper. Unrated, but an R rating would be in order because of some nudity and adult themes. B&W; 92m. **DIR:** Russ Meyer. **CAST:** Hal Hopper, Antoinette Cristiani. **1965**

MURDER ELITE ★★ Ali MacGraw plays a woman who, after losing all her money in America, comes back to her native England to start fresh. Meanwhile, there is a killer on the loose. The two stories ultimately collide, but MacGraw's uninspired acting and the poor direction make the film rather plodding. Not rated. 104m. **DIR:** Claude Whatham. **CAST:** Ali MacGraw, Billie Whitelaw, Hywel Bennett, Ray Lonnen. **1985**

MURDER IN COWETA COUNTY ★★★½ Andy Griffith is outstanding as a Georgia businessman who thinks he can get away with murder. Johnny Cash plays the determined sheriff who's willing to go to any lengths to prove Griffith's guilt. This made-for-TV suspense-drama was based on an actual Georgia murder that took place in 1948. 104m. **DIR:** Gary Nelson. **CAST:** Andy Griffith, Johnny Cash, Earl Hindman. **1983**

MURDER IN NEW HAMPSHIRE ★★½ Passable TV killer-of-the-week saga focuses on a video production teacher's plot to use her student as her husband's assassin. At times unbelievable, although this is based on fact. 93m. **DIR:** Joyce Chopra. **CAST:** Helen Hunt, Chad Allen, Larry Drake, Ken Howard, Howard Hesseman. **1992**

MURDER OF MARY PHAGAN, THE ★★★★ True story of 1913 Georgia governor John Slaton's fight to free a factory manager accused of killing a young girl. He has to fight a lynch mob determined to hang the factory manager because he was Jewish. This TV movie is long, but well worth seeing. 250m. **DIR:** William Hale. **CAST:** Jack Lemmon, Peter Gallagher, Richard Jordan, Robert Prosky, Kevin Spacey, Kathryn Walker, Paul Dooley, Rebecca Miller. **1988**

MURDER ON THE BAYOU ★★★½ German director Volker Schlondörff examines the American South, specifically the Bayou country of Louisiana, where an elderly black man (Lou Gossett Jr.) is suspected of killing a white racist. Marvelously well-acted TV movie, rich in character moments, and surprisingly upbeat given its subject matter. 91m. **DIR:** Volker Schlondörff. **CAST:** Lou

Gossett Jr., Richard Widmark, Holly Hunter, Joe Seneca, Will Patton, Woody Strode. 1987

MURDER SO SWEET ★★★ Better-than-average network teleflic "based on actual events," with dependable Harry Hamlin starring as hunkish good ol' boy Steve Catlin, an unrepentant ladies' man who loved 'em and left 'em . . . dead. Plucky Helen Shaver decides to take him down. Lurid boxart suggests otherwise, but this is pretty tame stuff. Rated PG for mild profanity. 94m. **DIR:** Larry Peerce. **CAST:** Harry Hamlin, Helen Shaver, Terence Knox, Ed Lauter, Faith Ford, Eileen Brennan. 1993

MURDER WITHOUT MOTIVE ★★★ Subtitled *The Edmund Perry Story* and based on Robert Sam Anson's book *Best Intentions*, this is the tragic account of a Harlem honor student's loneliness and frustration at an exclusive private high school. Curtis McClarin is convincing in the lead. Unrated; contains violence and drug use. 93m. **DIR:** Kevin Hooks. **CAST:** Curtis McClarin, Anna Maria Horsford, Carla Gugino, Christopher Daniel Barnes. 1991

MURDERERS AMONG US: THE SIMON WIESENTHAL STORY ★★★½ Powerful HBO reenactment of real-life Nazi concentration camp victim Simon Wiesenthal's postwar search for Nazi leaders. Among those he brings to justice are the notorious Adolf Eichmann and Franz Murer. Ben Kingsley is unforgettable as Wiesenthal. 155m. **DIR:** Brian Gibson. **CAST:** Ben Kingsley, Renee Soutendijk, Craig T. Nelson. 1989

MURPHY'S ROMANCE ★★★★ This sweet little love story marks the finest performance by James Garner. He's a crusty small-town pharmacist, a widower with no shortage of home-cooked meals but little interest in anything more permanent. Garner and Sally Field are great together, and the result is a complete charmer. Rated PG-13. 107m. **DIR:** Martin Ritt. **CAST:** Sally Field, James Garner, Brian Kerwin, Corey Haim. 1985

MURROW ★★★★ Compassionate HBO film about the famous radio and television journalist Edward R. Murrow, played brilliantly by Daniel Travanti. The film devotes most of its running time to the journalist's struggle against McCarthyism. 114m. **DIR:** Jack Gold. **CAST:** Daniel J. Travanti, Dabney Coleman, Edward Herrmann, John McMartin, David Suchet, Kathryn Leigh Scott. 1985

MUSIC OF CHANCE, THE ★★★ Dreamers Mandy Patinkin and James Spader enter a high-stakes poker game with two eccentric gamblers. When they lose, they are forced to build a wall to pay off their debt—once construction begins, all rhyme and reason end. Interesting cast makes this gambler's bluff pay off. Rated R for strong language. 98m. **DIR:** Philip Haas. **CAST:** James Spader, Mandy Patinkin, M. Emmet Walsh, Joel Grey, Charles Durning, Samantha Mathis. 1993

MUSIC SCHOOL, THE ★★★ The mathematical precision of music as a metaphor for the ideal life unattainable by mere mortals is the driving force behind this John Updike story. Ron Weyand stars as a typically angst-ridden Updike hero. The story unfolds through Updike's off-camera commentary. Introduced by Henry Fonda; aside from fleeting nudity, suitable for family viewing. 30m. **DIR:** John Korty. **CAST:** Ron Weyand, Dana Larsson, Cathleen Bauer. 1974

MUSSOLINI AND I ★★★ A weak and confusing narrative hinders this HBO film about the Fascist leader and his family's struggle with power. Bob Hoskins plays the Italian premier with a British accent; ditto for Anthony Hopkins who portrays Galeazzo Ciano, Italy's minister of foreign affairs and the dictator's brother-in-law. Still, the story is kept interesting despite its length. Not rated, but the equivalent of a PG for violence. 130m. **DIR:** Alberto Negrin. **CAST:** Anthony Hopkins, Susan Sarandon, Bob Hoskins, Annie Girardot, Barbara de Rossi, Vittorio Mezzogiorno, Fabio Testi, Kurt Raab. 1985

MY BEAUTIFUL LAUNDRETTE ★★★★½ In modern-day England, a young Pakistani immigrant is given a launderette by his rich uncle and, with the help of his punk-rocker boyfriend turns it into a showplace. A racist gang decides to close them down. British director Stephen Frears keeps things from becoming too heavy by adding deft touches of comedy. Rated R for profanity, suggested and simulated sex, and violence. 103m. **DIR:** Stephen Frears. **CAST:** Saeed Jaffrey, Roshan Seth, Daniel Day-Lewis, Gordon Warnecke, Shirley Anne Field. 1985

MY BODYGUARD ★★★★★ This is a wonderfully funny and touching movie. Fifteen-year-old Clifford Peache (Chris Makepeace) must face the challenges of public high school after nine years of private education. His classes are easy. It's his schoolmates who cause problems. Specifically, there's Moody (Matt Dillon), a nasty young thug who extorts money from the other students. Rated PG. 96m. **DIR:** Tony Bill. **CAST:** Chris Makepeace, Matt Dillon, Martin Mull, Ruth Gordon, Adam Baldwin. 1980

MY BOYS ARE GOOD BOYS ★★ It's good to see veteran actors Ralph Meeker and Ida Lupino again, but it's too bad the occasion is this low-budget effort. They play parents of juvenile delinquents who rob an armored car. Pretty mediocre. Rated PG. 90m. **DIR:** Bethel Buckalew. **CAST:** Ralph Meeker, Ida Lupino, Lloyd Nolan, David Doyle. 1978

MY BRILLIANT CAREER ★★★★½ A superb Australian import, *My Brilliant Career* is about a young woman clearly born before her time. It is the waning years of the nineteenth century, when the only respectable status for a woman is to be married. Sybylla Melvyn (Judy Davis), who lives with her family in the Australian bush, does not want to marry. She has "immortal longings." Rated G. 101m. **DIR:** Gillian Armstrong. **CAST:** Judy Davis, Sam Neill, Wendy Hughes. **1979**

MY DINNER WITH ANDRE ★★★★★ One of the most daring films ever made, this fascinating work consists almost entirely of a dinner conversation between two men. It's a terrific little movie. You'll be surprised how entertaining it is. No MPAA rating. The film has no objectionable material. 110m. **DIR:** Louis Malle. **CAST:** Andre Gregory, Wallace Shawn. **1981**

MY FIRST WIFE ★★★½ In the tradition of *Ordinary People, Kramer vs. Kramer*, and *Smash Palace* comes another film about the dissolution of a marriage. The story deals with a classical music programmer/composer who finds that his wife doesn't love him anymore. Rated PG for adult situations and language. 95m. **DIR:** Paul Cox. **CAST:** John Hargreaves, Wendy Hughes. **1985**

MY FORBIDDEN PAST ★★ Set in steamy New Orleans in 1890, this one's about Ava Gardner's cold-blooded attempts to buy married-man Robert Mitchum's affections with the help of an unexpected inheritance. His wife is killed. He's accused of her murder. Gardner, revealing her unsavory past in order to save him, wins his love. B&W; 81m. **DIR:** Robert Stevenson. **CAST:** Robert Mitchum, Ava Gardner, Janis Carter, Melvyn Douglas, Lucile Watson. **1951**

MY GIRL TISA ★★½ Tired story of a pretty, diligent immigrant girl's efforts to bring her father to New York from the old country. B&W; 95m. **DIR:** Elliott Nugent. **CAST:** Lilli Palmer, Sam Wanamaker, Akim Tamiroff, Alan Hale Sr., Stella Adler. **1948**

MY LEFT FOOT ★★★★★ Everything is right in the screen biography of handicapped Irish writer-artist Christy Brown who was afflicted with cerebral palsy from birth. Writer-director Jim Sheridan and coscripter Shane Connaughton tell Brown's story without once succumbing to cliché or audience manipulation. Oscar-winner Daniel Day-Lewis gives what may be the performance of his career. Rated R for profanity and violence. 119m. **DIR:** Jim Sheridan. **CAST:** Daniel Day-Lewis, Ray McAnally, Brenda Fricker, Fiona Shaw, Hugh O'Connor, Cyril Cusack. **1989**

MY LIFE ★★★ A career-obsessed public relations executive, dying of cancer, spends his last months making peace with his parents and videotaping himself for his unborn child. Solid, surefire performances from stars Michael Keaton and Nicole Kidman redeem this predictable disease-of-the-week tearjerker. Rated PG-13 for mild profanity and mature themes. 114m. **DIR:** Bruce Joel Rubin. **CAST:** Michael Keaton, Nicole Kidman, Michael Constantine, Haing S. Ngor. **1993**

MY LITTLE GIRL ★★ Familiar tale of a do-good rich kid's introduction to the real world. Mary Stuart Masterson stars as a 16-year-old high school student who volunteers to spend a summer working at a state-run shelter. The performances raise this (just barely) to the tolerable level. Rated R for violence and profanity. 118m. **DIR:** Connie Kaiserman. **CAST:** James Earl Jones, Geraldine Page, Mary Stuart Masterson, Anne Meara. **1986**

MY MOTHER'S SECRET LIFE ★★ Long-lost daughter turns up on Mom's doorstep. To her horror, Mom (Loni Anderson) turns out to be an expensive call girl. Hard to believe and just barely watchable. 94m. **DIR:** Robert Markowitz. **CAST:** Loni Anderson, Paul Sorvino, Amanda Wyss. **1984**

MY OLD MAN ★★★★ Excellent made-for-television adaptation of a short story by Ernest Hemingway about a down-on-his-luck horse trainer (Warren Oates) and the daughter (Kristy McNichol) who loves him even more than horses. Oates gives a fabulous performance; certainly one of the best of his too-brief career. Eileen Brennan lends support as a sympathetic waitress. Unrated; suitable for family viewing. 104m. **DIR:** John Erman. **CAST:** Warren Oates, Kristy McNichol, Eileen Brennan. **1979**

MY OLD MAN'S PLACE ★★ Outdated cliché-ridden melodrama about a soldier's return home from Vietnam bringing two army friends with him. The inevitable clash of wills and personalities leads to the film's deadly conclusion. Rated R for nudity, profanity, and violence. 92m. **DIR:** Edwin Sherin. **CAST:** Arthur Kennedy, Mitchell Ryan, William Devane, Michael Moriarty. **1973**

MY OWN PRIVATE IDAHO ★★★★ Stylishly photographed road movie about two young male street hustlers on their own personal vision quest. River Phoenix gives a heartfelt performance as a street prostitute who suffers from narcolepsy. Keanu Reeves plays a troubled bisexual youth from an affluent family. Moving, bittersweet movie. Rated R for nudity, profanity, and violence. 110m. **DIR:** Gus Van Sant. **CAST:** Keanu Reeves, River Phoenix, William Richert. **1991**

MY SWEET CHARLIE ★★★★ The fine performances of Patty Duke and Al Freeman Jr. make this made-for-TV drama especially watchable. Duke plays a disowned, unwed mom-to-be who meets a black lawyer being pursued by the police. They hit it off and manage to help each other. A must-see for viewers interested in drama with a social comment. 97m. **DIR:** Lamont Johnson. **CAST:** Patty Duke, Al Freeman Jr., Ford Rainey. **1969**

MY WICKED, WICKED WAYS ★★ Errol Flynn's fast-paced life is slowed down a bit for this TV movie. It seems to have lost its zest in the translation. But choosing Duncan Regehr to play Flynn was an inspiration. 142m. **DIR:** Don Taylor. **CAST:** Duncan Regehr, Barbara Hershey, Darren McGavin, Hal Linden. **1984**

MY WONDERFUL LIFE 🦃 Italian fantasy features Carol Alt in a series of abusive relationships, more nauseating than erotic. Rated R for nudity, profanity, and violence. 107m. **DIR:** Carlo Vanzina. **CAST:** Carol Alt, Elliott Gould, Jean Rochefort, Pierre Cosso. **1989**

MYSTERIOUS LADY, THE ★★★½ Greta Garbo plays Tania, a Russian spy who falls in love with an Austrian soldier, calling into question her political loyalties. Early Garbo vehicle whose preposterous love story and willfully arbitrary plot machinations nonetheless make for great fun. Silent. B&W; 84m. **DIR:** Fred Niblo. **CAST:** Greta Garbo, Conrad Nagel, Gustav von Seyffertitz. **1928**

MYSTERY TRAIN ★★★½ Offbeat character study that takes place in Memphis. The film centers around a couple of Japanese tourists with a penchant for Elvis nostalgia, an Italian woman who arrives to bury her murdered husband, and an unemployed Englishman who is breaking up with his American girlfriend. Some hilarious moments. Rated R for nudity and profanity. 110m. **DIR:** Jim Jarmusch. **CAST:** Youki Kaudoh, Masatochi Nagase, Joe Strummer, Screamin' Jay Hawkins. **1990**

MYSTIC PIZZA ★★★½ This coming-of-age picture has all of the right ingredients of a main-course favorite. The antics involve three women—two sisters and a friend—who work at a pizza parlor in the resort town of Mystic, Connecticut. The superb young players and the dazzling New England scenery are a slice of heaven. Rated R for language. 102m. **DIR:** Donald Petrie. **CAST:** Annabeth Gish, Julia Roberts, Lili Taylor, Vincent D'Onofrio, William R. Moses, Adam Storke. **1988**

NAIROBI AFFAIR ★★ Charlton Heston plays a safari photographer who is having an affair with his son's ex-wife (Maud Adams). Rated PG for violence. 95m. **DIR:** Marvin J. Chomsky. **CAST:** John Savage, Maud Adams, Charlton Heston. **1986**

NAKED ★★★★ A bleak, stark drama about Johnny, a homeless young man who roams the streets of London in search of sex and shelter, both of which he gets often. Numerous characters come and go, and most of them are emotionally manipulated or machinated by our young antihero. Disturbing and dazzling. Rated R for nudity and violence. 126m. **DIR:** Mike Leigh. **CAST:** David Thewlis, Lesley Sharp, Katrin Cartlidge, Greg Cruttwell. **1994**

NAKED CIVIL SERVANT, THE ★★★½ Exceptional film based on the biography of the famous English homosexual Quentin Crisp. John Hurt's remarkable performance earned him a British Academy Award for his sensitive portrayal. Not rated, but recommended for mature audiences. 80m. **DIR:** Jack Gold. **CAST:** John Hurt, Patricia Hodge. **1975**

NAKED COUNTRY, THE ★★★ A rancher, his lonely wife, and an alcoholic policeman form a deadly triangle in Australia's outback. Set in 1955, this beautifully filmed story is rooted in soap opera, but becomes a violent struggle with the aborigines that resonates with remorse. Rated R for nudity, profanity, and violence. 90m. **DIR:** Tim Burstall. **CAST:** John Stanton, Rebecca Gilling. **1992**

NAKED HEART, THE ★★ After five years in a convent, a young woman returns to her home in the frozen Canadian north and tries to decide which of her three suitors to marry. Filmed in Europe, this slow, somewhat depressing tale has little going for it. B&W; 96m. **DIR:** Marc Allegret. **CAST:** Michele Morgan, Kieron Moore, Françoise Rosay. **1950**

NAKED MAJA, THE ★★ Dull telling of the eighteenth-century romance between artist Francisco Goya and the duchess of Alba which led to their fall from grace with the Spanish court and the Catholic Church. 111m. **DIR:** Henry Koster. **CAST:** Ava Gardner, Anthony Franciosa, Amadeo Nazzari, Gino Cervi. **1958**

NAKED TANGO ★★★ In the 1920s, a young woman comes to Buenos Aires as a mail-order bride, only to find that she has been sold into white slavery by her intended husband. The film is an overheated melodrama of male-domination fantasies, but dark, moody photography and strong acting make it engrossing and hard to dismiss. Rated R for violence and sexual situations. 90m. **DIR:** Leonard Schrader. **CAST:** Vincent D'Onofrio, Mathilda May, Esai Morales, Fernando Rey, Josh Mostel. **1991**

NAKED VENUS ★★ Famed cult director Edgar G. Ulmer's last film is a slow-moving drama about an American artist whose marriage to a nudist-model is torn apart by his wealthy mother. The film explores the barriers of prejudice concerning nudist colonies. Not rated, but contains nudity. B&W; 80m. **DIR:** Edgar G. Ulmer. **CAST:** Patricia Conelle. **1958**

NAPOLEON (1955) 🦃 Boring. 115m. **DIR:** Sacha Guitry. **CAST:** Orson Welles, Maria Schell, Yves Montand, Erich Von Stroheim. **1955**

NAPOLEON AND JOSEPHINE: A LOVE STORY 🦃 TV miniseries. Armand Assante plays Napoleon from his pregeneral days until his exile. Jacqueline Bisset is his loving Josephine. 300m. **DIR:** Richard T. Heffron. **CAST:** Jacqueline Bisset, Armand Assante, Anthony Perkins, Stephanie Beacham. **1987**

NASHVILLE ★★★★★ Robert Altman's classic study of American culture is, on the surface, a look into the country-western music business. But underneath, Altman has many things to say about all of us. Great ensemble acting by Keith Carradine, Lily Tomlin, Ned Beatty, and Henry Gibson, to name just a few, makes this one of the great films of the 1970s. Rated R for language and violence. 159m. **DIR:** Robert Altman. **CAST:** Keith Carradine, Lily Tomlin, Ned Beatty, Henry Gibson, Karen Black, Ronee Blakley. **1975**

NATIVE SON ★★½ In this well-meant but muddled screen adaptation of Richard Wright's 1940 novel, a 19-year-old black youth (Victor Love) takes a job as a chauffeur to a wealthy white couple. His hopes for a brighter future are shattered when a tragic accident leads to the death of their daughter (Elizabeth McGovern) and he is accused of murder. Rated R for nudity, suggested sex, violence, and gore. 101m. **DIR:** Jerrold Freedman. **CAST:** Victor Love, Geraldine Page, Elizabeth McGovern, Matt Dillon, Oprah Winfrey, Akosua Busia, Carroll Baker, Art Evans, David Rasche, Lane Smith, John McMartin. **1986**

NATIVITY, THE ★★ Nicely filmed but dramatically unimpressive TV movie about Joseph's (John Shea) wooing of Mary (Madeline Stowe). Leo McKern is the mad King Herod. Not one of the top Biblical epics by a long shot. 97m. **DIR:** Bernard Kowalski. **CAST:** John Shea, Madeleine Stowe, Jane Wyatt, Paul Stewart, Leo McKern, John Rhys-Davies, Kate O'Mara. **1978**

NATURAL, THE ★★★★ A thoroughly rewarding, old-fashioned screen entertainment, this adaptation of Bernard Malamud's novel about an unusually gifted baseball player is a must-see. With its brilliant all-star cast, superb story, unforgettable characters, sumptuous cinematography, and sure-handed direction, this film recalls the Golden Age of Hollywood at its best. Rated PG for brief violence. 134m. **DIR:** Barry Levinson. **CAST:** Robert Redford, Robert Duvall, Glenn Close, Kim Basinger, Wilford Brimley, Richard Farnsworth, Robert Prosky, Joe Don Baker. **1984**

NATURAL ENEMIES ★★★★ Excellent study of domestic murder. Hal Holbrook plays a successful magazine editor who murders his wife and three children. Louise Fletcher is great as Holbrook's emotionally unstable wife. Depressing, to be certain, but worth watching. Rated R for violence, profanity, sex, nudity, and adult subject matter. 100m. **DIR:** Jeff Kanew. **CAST:** Hal Holbrook, Louise Fletcher, Viveca Lindfors, José Ferrer, Patricia Elliott. **1979**

NECESSARY PARTIES ★★★★ Clever film about a teenager who refuses to accept his parents' divorce. With the help of an idealistic part-time lawyer/full-time auto mechanic, the boy sues his folks as an affected third party. This sensitive presentation from TV's *Wonderworks* offers occasional chuckles. 109m. **DIR:** Gwen Arner. **CAST:** Alan Arkin, Mark Paul Gosselaar, Barbara Dana, Donald Moffat, Adam Arkin, Julie Hagerty. **1988**

NETWORK ★★★★★ "I'm mad as hell and I'm not going to take it anymore!" Peter Finch (who won a posthumous Academy Award for best actor), William Holden, Faye Dunaway, Robert Duvall, and Ned Beatty give superb performances in this black comedy about the world of television as penned by Paddy Chayefsky. It's a biting satire on the inner workings of this century's most powerful medium. Rated R. 121m. **DIR:** Sidney Lumet. **CAST:** Peter Finch, William Holden, Faye Dunaway, Robert Duvall, Ned Beatty. **1976**

NEVER FORGET ★★★½ Fact-based TV account of Jewish concentration camp survivor Mel Mermelstein's fight against the Institute for Historical Review, an organization that refused to accept the fact that the Holocaust ever took place. Leonard Nimoy has never been better. 94m. **DIR:** Joseph Sargent. **CAST:** Leonard Nimoy, Blythe Danner, Dabney Coleman, Paul Hampton. **1991**

NEVER LET GO ★★ Peter Sellers bombs out in his first dramatic role as a ruthless criminal in this thin story about car stealing. The sure acting of Mervyn Johns, longtime dependable supporting player, helps things but cannot begin to save the film. Nor can Richard Todd's efforts. B&W; 90m. **DIR:** John Guillermin. **CAST:** Peter Sellers, Richard Todd, Elizabeth Sellars, Carol White, Mervyn Johns. **1960**

NEVER LOVE A STRANGER 🦃 John Drew Barrymore as a young hustler whose success puts him on a collision course with his old boss and an eager district attorney. 91m. **DIR:** Robert Stevens. **CAST:** John Drew Barrymore, Lita Milan, Steve McQueen. **1958**

NEVER ON SUNDAY ★★★★ A wimpy egghead tries to make a lady out of an earthy, fun-loving prostitute. The setting is Greece; the dialogue and situations are delightful. Melina Mercouri is terrific. 91m. **DIR:** Jules Dassin. **CAST:** Melina Mercouri, Jules Dassin. **1960**

NEVER ON TUESDAY ★★★ Two best friends, leaving their boring hometown for sunny L.A., are stranded for two days in the desert with a beautiful girl. Unexpected cameo appearances by Charlie Sheen and Emilio Estevez. Rated R for nudity and simulated sex. 90m. **DIR:** Adam Rifkin. **CAST:** Claudia Christian, Andrew Lauer, Peter Berg. **1988**

NEVER TOO LATE ★★★½ The villain, a conniving jail official, cleverly frames the handsome young hero in order to steal his girl in this classic melodrama. Originally, on the stage, the play resulted in sweeping reforms in the British penal system in the mid-nineteenth century. B&W; 67m. **DIR:** David MacDonald. **CAST:** Tod Slaughter. **1937**

NEW CENTURIONS, THE ★★★★ *The New Centurions* is a blend of harsh reality and soap opera. The moral seems to be "It is no fun being a cop." Watching George C. Scott and Stacy Keach get their lumps, we have to agree. Rated R. 103m. **DIR:** Richard Fleischer. **CAST:** George C. Scott, Stacy Keach, Jane Alexander, Erik Estrada. **1972**

NEW YEAR'S DAY ★★★½ This gentle movie is a fairly intimate, if familiar, character study about three women who aren't quite ready to move out of the New York apartment that Henry Jaglom has recently been leased. The film explores younger women's attachments to older men, and vice versa. Maybe too slow paced for some people. Rated R for nudity and profanity. 90m. **DIR:** Henry Jaglom. **CAST:** Henry Jaglom, Maggie Jakobson, Gwen Welles, Irene Moore, Milos Forman. **1990**

NEWS AT ELEVEN ★★★★ Martin Sheen plays a news anchorman whose integrity is threatened by the demands of his ratings-crazed news director. This is a jolting reminder of the enormous power of the press, with Sheen delivering a superior performance. 95m. **DIR:** Mike Robe. **CAST:** Martin Sheen, Barbara Babcock, Sheree Wilson, Peter Riegert. **1985**

NEWSFRONT ★★★★ A story of a newsreel company from 1948 until technology brought its existence to an end, this is a warm and wonderful film about real people. It's an insightful glimpse at the early days of the news business, with good character development. Rated PG. 110m. **DIR:** Phillip Noyce. **CAST:** Bill Hunter, Wendy Hughes, Gerald Kennedy. **1978**

NEXT OF KIN (1984) ★★★½ A young man suffering from boredom and dissatisfaction with his upper-middle-class family undergoes video therapy with his parents. He becomes fascinated by a videotape of an Armenian family who feel guilty about surrendering their infant son to a foster home. Poignant look at a young WASP's displacement and response to his upper-middle-class role in Canadian society. Highly original filmmaking. Not rated. 74m. **DIR:** Atom Egoyan. **CAST:** Patrick Tierney. **1984**

NEXT STOP, GREENWICH VILLAGE ★★★★ One of writer-director Paul Mazursky's first attempts to dramatize his youth, this film is a seriocomic study of the eccentricities of Greenwich Villagers. Unique as well as entertaining. 109m. **DIR:** Paul Mazursky. **CAST:** Lenny Baker, Shelley Winters, Ellen Greene, Christopher Walken, Jeff Goldblum, Lou Jacobi, Lois Smith. **1976**

NEXT VOICE YOU HEAR, THE ★★½ Man's-man director William Wellman was an odd choice to direct this preachy tract—typical of Dore Schary's well-meaning but ponderous message pictures of the Fifties—in which the voice of God speaks to mankind via a radio broadcast. The solid performances by James Whitmore and Jeff Corey lend the film what strength it has. B&W; 83m. **DIR:** William Wellman. **CAST:** James Whitmore, Nancy Davis, Jeff Corey. **1950**

NICHOLAS AND ALEXANDRA ★★ This is an overlong, overdetailed depiction of the events preceding the Russian Revolution until the deaths of Czar Nicholas (Michael Jayston), his wife (Janet Suzman) and family. Some of the performances are outstanding, and the sets and costumes are top-notch. However, the film gets mired in trying to encompass too much historical detail. Rated PG. 183m. **DIR:** Franklin J. Schaffner. **CAST:** Michael Jayston, Janet Suzman, Tom Baker, Laurence Olivier, Michael Redgrave. **1971**

NICHOLAS NICKLEBY ★★★½ Proud but penniless young Nicholas Nickleby struggles to forge a life for himself and his family while contending with a money-mad scheming uncle and lesser villains. Good acting and authentic Victorian settings bring this classic Dickens novel to vivid screen life. Not quite in the mold of *Great Expectations*, but well above average. B&W; 108m. **DIR:** Alberto Cavalcanti. **CAST:** Derek Bond, Cedric Hardwicke, Sally Ann Howes, Cathleen Nesbitt. **1947**

NIGHT AND THE CITY (1950) ★★★★ Director Jules Dassin's drama is *film noir* at its best. Richard Widmark is the fight promoter, hustling up some action in London's East End, trying to make the score of a lifetime while keeping ahead of his debtors. Gene Tierney is splendid as the loyal girlfriend being taken for a ride. Plenty of mood and atmosphere permeate this entry. B&W; 95m. **DIR:** Jules Dassin. **CAST:** Richard Widmark, Gene Tierney, Googie Withers, Herbert Lom, Hugh Marlowe, Mike Mazurki. **1950**

NIGHT AND THE CITY (1992) ★★★½ Director Irwin Winkler's remake of Jules Dassin's 1950 *film noir* benefits from strong performances by Robert De Niro, Jessica Lange, and a distinguished cast of supporting players. The downbeat story has lawyer De Niro romancing the wife (Lange) of bar owner and longtime buddy Cliff Gorman while attempting to scam his way into the big time. Not a classic, but worth watching. Rated R for profanity and violence. 104m. **DIR:** Irwin Winkler. **CAST:** Robert De Niro, Jessica Lange, Cliff Gorman, Alan King, Jack Warden, Eli Wallach, Barry Primus, Gene Kirkwood. **1992**

NIGHT FULL OF RAIN, A ★★ After a series of stunning successes in the early Seventies, Italian director Lina Wertmuller began a downward slide with this film, her first attempt at an English-language movie. It details the ins and outs of the relationship between an independent woman (Candice Bergen) and her old-fashioned husband (Giancarlo Giannini). 104m. **DIR:** Lina Wertmuller. **CAST:** Giancarlo Giannini, Candice Bergen, Jill Eikenberry. **1978**

NIGHT IN HEAVEN, A 🦃 College teacher falls in lust with student-male stripper. Rated R for nudity, slight profanity, and simulated sex. 80m. **DIR:** John G. Avildsen. **CAST:** Lesley Ann Warren, Christopher Atkins, Robert Logan, Carrie Snodgress. **1983**

'NIGHT, MOTHER ★★ *'Night, Mother,* playwright Marsha Norman's argument in favor of suicide, is incredibly depressing material. Sissy Spacek plays a woman who has chosen to end her life. She decides to commit the act in her mother's house, with her mother there. We are only shown Spacek's unhappiness, and this limited manipulative view leaves us with nothing to do but wait uncomfortably for the outcome. Rated PG-13. 97m. **DIR:** Tom Moore. **CAST:** Sissy Spacek, Anne Bancroft. **1986**

NIGHT MUST FALL ★★★★ A suspenseful stage play makes a superbly suspenseful movie by letting the audience use its imagination. Robert Montgomery neatly underplays the role of the mad killer who totes his victim's head in a hatbox. Rosalind Russell is the girl who believes in him, but slowly learns the truth. B&W; 117m. **DIR:** Richard Thorpe. **CAST:** Robert Montgomery, Rosalind Russell, May Whitty, Alan Marshal, E. E. Clive, Kathleen Harrison. **1937**

NIGHT NURSE ★★★ No-nonsense Barbara Stanwyck plays the title role, using underworld contacts to safeguard two small children. A tough, taut melodrama that still works, thanks to its intriguing personalities. B&W; 73m. **DIR:** William Wellman. **CAST:** Barbara Stanwyck, Clark Gable, Ben Lyon, Joan Blondell, Charles Winninger. **1931**

NIGHT OF THE IGUANA, THE ★★★ In this film, based on Tennessee Williams's play, Richard Burton is a former minister trying to be reinstated in his church. Meanwhile, he takes a menial job as a tour guide, from which he gets fired. His attempted suicide is foiled and confusing. Finally, he finds other reasons to continue living. Sound dull? If not for the cast, it would be. B&W; 118m. **DIR:** John Huston. **CAST:** Richard Burton, Ava Gardner, Deborah Kerr, Sue Lyon. **1964**

NIGHT OF THE WILDING 🦃 As the movie repeats numerous times, *wilding* is slang for needless destruction both against people and property. Rated R for violence and nudity. 85m. **DIR:** Joseph Merhi. **CAST:** Erik Estrada, Joey Travolta. **1990**

NIGHT ON EARTH ★★★ Episodic film about four cabdrivers and their oddball encounters with an array of passengers on the same night in different countries. As with most of director Jim Jarmusch's films, the determinedly low-key and offbeat *Night on Earth* is a cinematic non sequitur, and only his fans will find it completely satisfying. Rated R for profanity. 128m. **DIR:** Jim Jarmusch. **CAST:** Gena Rowlands, Winona Ryder, Armin Mueller-Stahl, Giancarlo Esposito, Rosie Perez, Roberto Benigni. **1992**

NIGHT PORTER, THE 🦃 Sordid outing about an ex-Nazi and the woman he used to abuse sexually in a concentration camp. Lots of kinky scenes, including lovemaking on broken glass. Rated R for violence, nudity, and profanity. 115m. **DIR:** Liliana Cavani. **CAST:** Dirk Bogarde, Charlotte Rampling, Philippe Leroy, Gabriele Ferzetti, Isa Miranda. **1974**

NIGHT THE CITY SCREAMED, THE ★★ Made-for-TV movie shows how different urban characters react to a power blackout on a hot summer night. The best subplot follows rookie cops David Cassidy and Clifton Davis as they try to contain an outbreak of looting. Rated PG for mild violence. 96m. **DIR:** Harry Falk. **CAST:** Georg Stanford Brown, Raymond Burr, David Cassidy, Robert Culp, Clifton Davis, Don Meredith, Linda Purl. **1980**

NIGHT THE LIGHTS WENT OUT IN GEORGIA, THE ★★★½ Gutsy, lusty, and satisfying film about a country singer (Dennis Quaid) with wayward appetites and his level-headed sister-manager (Kristy McNichol) who run into big trouble while working their way to Nashville. The gritty Deep South settings, fine action, a cast of credible extras, some memorable musical moments, and a dramatic script with comic overtones add up to above-average entertainment. Rated PG. 120m. **DIR:** Ronald F. Maxwell. **CAST:** Kristy McNichol, Mark Hamill, Dennis Quaid, Don Stroud. **1981**

NIGHT TIDE ★★★ Dennis Hopper stars in this surreal fantasy about a young sailor on leave who falls in love with a mysterious woman posing as a mermaid in a seafront carnival. Avant-garde filmmaker Curtis Harrington, in his first feature, manages to create a mystical and nightmarish world in which his characters' true motivations are often obscured. Recommended for connoisseurs of the offbeat. B&W; 84m. **DIR:** Curtis Harrington. **CAST:** Dennis Hopper, Linda Lawson, Gavin Muir. **1961**

NIGHT TO REMEMBER, A (1958) ★★★★ Authenticity and credibility mark this documentarylike enactment of the sinking of the luxury passenger liner H.M.S. *Titanic* in deep icy Atlantic waters in April, 1912. Novelist Eric Ambler scripted from historian Walter Lord's meticulously detailed account of the tragedy. B&W; 123m. **DIR:** Roy Ward Baker. **CAST:** Kenneth More, Jill Dixon, David McCallum, Laurence Naismith, Honor Blackman, Frank Lawton, Alec McCowen, George Rose. **1958**

NIGHT TRAIN TO KATMANDU ★★ Standard family fare about two youngsters who are uprooted from their comfortable suburban home in the United States to live with their anthropologist parents in Nepal. There they get involved in the quest for the legendary City That Never Was. Nothing special. Not rated. 102m. **DIR:** Robert Wiemer. **CAST:** Pernell Roberts, Eddie Castrodad. **1988**

NIGHT VISITOR, THE (1970) ★★★ Revenge is the name of the game in this English-language Danish production. Max von Sydow plays an inmate in an insane asylum who comes up with a plan to escape for a single night and take revenge on the various people he believes are responsible for his current predicament. Performances are fine. Rated PG. 106m. **DIR:** Laslo Benedek. **CAST:** Max von Sydow, Liv Ullmann, Trevor Howard, Per Oscarsson, Rupert Davies. **1970**

NIGHT ZOO ★★★ An impressive, quirky French-Canadian film that brings together the unlikely combination of a tough, visceral, urban thriller and a sensitive, bittersweet story about the renewed love between a dying father and his grown son. The film moves from the dark streets of nighttime Montreal to a strange encounter with an elephant during a nocturnal visit to the zoo. Rated R, with strong violence and profanity. 107m. **DIR:** Jean-Claude Lauzon. **CAST:** Gilles Maheu, Roger Le Bel. **1987**

NIGHTBREAKER ★★★★ Effective message film takes us behind the scenes of nuclear tests on military personnel in Nevada, 1956. The atomic bomb horrors are both realistic and terrifying. Made for TV. 99m. **DIR:** Peter Markle. **CAST:** Emilio Estevez, Martin Sheen, Lea Thompson. **1989**

NIGHTMARE YEARS, THE ★★★★ William L. Shirer's first-person account of the rise of Hitler comes to life in this made-for-cable bio. Sam Waterston plays the daring American reporter in Berlin, Vienna, and France from 1934 to 1940. 474m. **DIR:** Anthony Page. **CAST:** Sam Waterston, Marthe Keller, Kurtwood Smith. **1989**

NIGHTS IN WHITE SATIN ★★½ Hokey Cinderella story has Prince Charming as an ace fashion photographer. The glass slippers are snapshots of a rags-dressed beauty who lives among the poor just a motorcycle ride from the photographer's elegant loft. Rated R for nudity. 99m. **DIR:** Michael Bernard. **CAST:** Kenneth Gilman, Priscilla Harris. **1987**

NIJINSKY ★★★ George de la Pena stars as the legendary dancer and Alan Bates is his lover, a Ballet Russe impresario. Herbert Ross (*The Turning Point*) is no stranger to ballet films. Here, he has assembled an outstanding cast and filmed them beautifully. Rated R. 125m. **DIR:** Herbert Ross. **CAST:** Alan Bates, George de la Pena, Leslie Browne, Jeremy Irons. **1980**

9½ WEEKS ★★ Somewhere between toning down the bondage and liberating the heroine, this movie's story definitely loses out to the imagery. Mickey Rourke is quite believable in the lead role of the masochistic seducer, but Kim Basinger does little more than look pretty. This couple makes steamy work of simple things like dressing and eating. Rated R for sex and violence. 113m. **DIR:** Adrian Lyne. **CAST:** Mickey Rourke, Kim Basinger, Margaret Whitton, David Branski, Karen Young. **1986**

NINE DAYS A QUEEN ★★★ This well-acted historical drama picks up after the death of Henry VIII and follows the frenzied and often lethal scramble for power that went on in the court of England. Lovely Nova Pilbeam plays Lady Jane Grey, the heroine of the title who is taken to the headsman's block by Mary Tudor's armies after a pathetic reign of only nine days. Tragic and moving, this British film was well received by critics when it premiered but is practically forgotten today. B&W; 80m. **DIR:** Robert Stevenson. **CAST:** Cedric Hardwicke, Nova Pilbeam, John Mills, Sybil Thorndike, Leslie Perrins, Felix Aylmer, Miles Malleson. **1936**

1900 ★★ This sprawling, self-conscious, exhausting film seems to revel in violence for its own sake. An insincere mishmash of scenes, *1900* chronicles the adventures of two young men set against the backdrop of the rise of fascism and socialism in Italy. The performances of Gérard Depardieu, Robert De Niro, and Dominique Sanda are lost in the all flashiness and bravado of Bernardo Bertolucci's direction. Rated R. 240m. **DIR:** Bernardo Bertolucci. **CAST:** Robert De Niro, Gérard Depardieu, Dominique Sanda, Burt Lancaster. **1976**

1918 ★★★ Minor-key slice-of-life film focuses on the denizens of a small Texas town in 1918. After introducing the main characters (including some based on members of his own family), screenwriter Horton Foote details the effects of a devastating epidemic of influenza that ravaged the town that year. The result is an almost academic but well-acted look at a bygone era. Rated PG. 94m. **DIR:** Ken Harrison. **CAST:** William Converse-Roberts, Hallie Foote, Matthew Broderick, Rochelle Oliver, Michael Higgins. **1984**

1969 ★★★ Writer-director Ernest Thompson's reminiscences of the flower-power era feature Kiefer Sutherland and Robert Downey Jr. as high school buddies who face the challenges of college and the abyss of military service in Vietnam. Thompson goes for too many larger-than-life moments in his directorial debut. But Sutherland and Bruce Dern create sparks as son and father, and the other actors are fine, too. Rated R for profanity, nudity, and violence. 105m. **DIR:** Ernest Thompson. **CAST:** Kiefer Sutherland, Robert Downey Jr., Bruce Dern,

Mariette Hartley, Winona Ryder, Joanna Cassidy. **1988**

NINTH CONFIGURATION, THE ★★★★½ This terse, intense film is not for everyone; a barroom brawl near the film's close is one of the most uncomfortable scenes in all of flickdom, but the plot, screenplay, and acting are top-notch. Stacy Keach plays a psychiatrist caring for Vietnam War veterans who suffer from acute emotional disorders. Rated R for profanity and violence. 115m. **DIR:** William Peter Blatty. **CAST:** Stacy Keach, Scott Wilson, Jason Miller, Ed Flanders, Neville Brand, George DiCenzo, Moses Gunn, Robert Loggia, Joe Spinell, Alejandro Rey, Tom Atkins. **1979**

NO BIG DEAL ★★ Kevin Dillon plays an underprivileged punk who makes a lot of nice friends between trips to juvenile hall. Low production values and limited acting don't help matters. 90m. **DIR:** Robert Charlton. **CAST:** Kevin Dillon, Christopher Gartin, Mary Joan Negro, Sylvia Miles, Tammy Grimes. **1984**

NO DRUMS, NO BUGLES ★★★ Because he refuses to kill, a West Virginian farmer (Martin Sheen) spends three years during the Civil War hiding in the Blue Ridge Mountains. Generally the movie is excellent; Sheen commands your interest in what is essentially a one-man show, and the nature photography is striking. It's ruined for the home viewer, though, by a terrible film-to-video transfer in which much of the wide-screen dimension has been compressed into the square television ratio. What a waste! Rated PG. 85m. **DIR:** Clyde Ware. **CAST:** Martin Sheen. **1971**

NO LOVE FOR JOHNNIE ★★★ This oddly titled drama is about a member of the British Parliament beset by problems in his personal and professional lives. Enjoyable for the performances by the outstanding character actors. B&W; 111m. **DIR:** Ralph Thomas. **CAST:** Peter Finch, Stanley Holloway, Mary Peach, Donald Pleasence, Billie Whitelaw, Dennis Price. **1961**

NO ONE CRIES FOREVER ★★★ Don't let the confusing start discourage you—this one gets better! An innocent South African girl is forced into prostitution. When she falls in love with a charming conservationist, her madam has her face disfigured and her boyfriend sets out in search of her. Contains violence and gore. 96m. **DIR:** Jans Rautenbach. **CAST:** Elke Sommer, Howard Carpendale, James Ryan. **1985**

NO TIME FOR SERGEANTS (TELEVISION) ★★½ Andy Griffith turns in a good performance as Will Stockdale, a Georgia hick drafted into the army in this 1955 comedy written especially for television by Ira Levin. Unfortunately, this type of physical comedy needs lots of rehearsal, something to which live television did not lend itself. Also, modern audiences have now been inundated with the innocent-turning-the-establishment-on-its-ear storyline, thereby dating the play. In this case, the theatrical movie is better. B&W; 60m. **DIR:** Alex Segal. **CAST:** Andy Griffith, Harry Clark, Robert Emhardt, Eddie Le Roy, Alexander Clark. **1955**

NOAH'S ARK ★★★ A silent epic that uses the Old Testament story of Noah as a simile for World War I. Several animals and bit players actually drowned during the spectacular flood sequence so the torment shown is authentic. The story is corny, but the special effects are excellent. B&W; 127m. **DIR:** Michael Curtiz. **CAST:** George O'Brien, Dolores Costello, Myrna Loy, Noah Beery Sr., Guinn Williams, Louise Fazenda. **1929**

NOBODY'S CHILDREN ★★★ This made-for-cable movie is based on the true story of an American couple who go to Romania to adopt a child. They must struggle with corrupt politicians, the black market, and the Romanian government bureaucracy. The story is all right, but too long. Not rated, but contains graphic news footage. 95m. **DIR:** David Wheatley. **CAST:** Ann-Margret, Jay O. Sanders, Dominique Sanda, Reiner Schoene, Clive Owen. **1994**

NONE BUT THE LONELY HEART ★★★ Old pro Ethel Barrymore won an Oscar for her sympathetic portrayal of a moody, whining cockney as Cary Grant's mother Ma Mott in this murky drama of broken dreams, thwarted hopes, and petty crime in the slums of London in the late 1930s. Nothing else like it in the Grant filmography. B&W; 113m. **DIR:** Clifford Odets. **CAST:** Cary Grant, Ethel Barrymore, Barry Fitzgerald, Jane Wyatt, June Duprez, Dan Duryea. **1944**

NOON WINE ★★★★½ The fickle nature of human opinion and its ability to savage a victim already down on his luck are the bitter lessons in this adaptation of Katharine Anne Porter's perceptive tale. Porter establishes a stable protagonist (Fred Ward) whose life eventually collapses after he generously provides work on his turn-of-the-century Texas farm for a taciturn loner (Stellan Skarsgard). Suitable for family viewing. 81m. **DIR:** Michael Fields. **CAST:** Fred Ward, Lise Hilboldt, Stellan Skarsgard, Pat Hingle, Jon Cryer. **1985**

NORMA RAE ★★★★ Sally Field won her first Oscar for her outstanding performance as a southern textile worker attempting to unionize the mill with the aid of organizer Ron Leibman. Film is based on a true story and has good eyes and ears for authenticity. Entire cast is first-rate. Rated PG, some language, minor violence. 113m. **DIR:** Martin Ritt. **CAST:** Sally Field, Ron Leibman, Pat Hingle, Beau Bridges. **1979**

NORTH AND SOUTH ★★★½ Epic, all-star TV miniseries detailing the events leading up to the Civil War springs vividly to life from the pages of John Jakes's bestselling historical novel. The human drama unfolds on both sides of the conflict, inside the war rooms and bedrooms, and tears apart two friends, played by Patrick Swayze and James Read. Not rated. 561m. **DIR:** Richard T. Heffron. **CAST:** Patrick Swayze, James Read, Kirstie Alley, David Carradine, Lesley-Anne Down, Robert Guillaume, Hal Holbrook, Gene Kelly. **1985**

NORTH DALLAS FORTY ★★★★½ Remarkably enough, *North Dallas Forty* isn't just another numbingly predictable sports film. It's an offbeat, sometimes brutal, examination of the business of football. A first-rate Nick Nolte stars. Rated R. 119m. **DIR:** Ted Kotcheff. **CAST:** Nick Nolte, Bo Svenson, G. D. Spradlin, Dayle Haddon, Mac Davis. **1979**

NORTH SHORE ★★½ Matt Adler plays an Arizona teen who desperately wants to make it in Hawaii's North Shore surfing pipeline. The pipeline shots are terrific. Rated PG for mild violence. 92m. **DIR:** William Phelps. **CAST:** Matt Adler, Nia Peeples, John Philbin, Gregory Harrison. **1987**

NORTHERN EXPOSURE (TV SERIES) ★★★★ Joshua Brand and John Folsey's quixotic little drama began as a routine fish-out-of-water tale and matured into a densely layered and often delightful account of the history and ongoing vitality of fictitious Cicely, Alaska (pop. 813). Rob Morrow is a droll bundle of neuroses forced into temporary servitude to repay the state of Alaska for medical school. While the talented ensemble cast makes the show an ongoing delight, it's hard to catch this program's rhythm on the basis of just one or two episodes; you'll do better to rent or buy 'em all. 52m. **DIR:** Various. **CAST:** Rob Morrow, Janine Turner, Barry Corbin, John Corbett, Darren E. Burrows, John Cullum, Cynthia Geary, Elaine Miles, Peg Phillips. **1990–93**

NORTHERN LIGHTS ★★★★ Produced, directed, and edited by Rob Nilsson and John Hanson, this independently made feature presents the rich chronicle of a group of Swedish farmers in North Dakota during the winter of 1915–16. Though the budget was a slight $330,000, the film is a triumph of craft and vision. No MPAA rating. B&W; 98m. **DIR:** John Hanson, Rob Nilsson. **CAST:** Robert Behling, Joe Spano. **1979**

NOT AS A STRANGER ★★★★ A testament to the medical profession that doesn't skirt on those with lack of ethics. Olivia de Havilland is somewhat self-conscious in a blonde wig and Swedish accent. But she tries hard as the nurse willing to put medical student Robert Mitchum through school by marrying him and caring for him. B&W; 135m. **DIR:** Stanley Kramer. **CAST:** Olivia de Havilland, Robert Mitchum, Charles Bickford, Frank Sinatra, Gloria Grahame, Lee Marvin, Broderick Crawford, Lon Chaney Jr., Harry Morgan, Virginia Christine. **1955**

NOT MY KID ★★★ Not just another disease-of-the-week vehicle. This telefilm is a well-written look at teenage drug abuse and the havoc it wreaks in a family. 100m. **DIR:** Michael Tuchner. **CAST:** George Segal, Stockard Channing, Andrew Robinson, Tate Donovan. **1985**

NOT WITHOUT MY DAUGHTER ★★★½ The true story of Betty Mahmoody, a Michigan housewife who accompanied her Iranian doctor-husband to his home country for a visit and found herself a prisoner. A terrific performance by Sally Field in the lead role makes it worth the watch. Rated PG-13 for violence and profanity. 115m. **DIR:** Brian Gilbert. **CAST:** Sally Field, Alfred Molina, Sheila Rosenthal, Roshan Seth. **1991**

NOTHING IN COMMON ★★★½ Tom Hanks plays a hotshot advertising executive who must deal with his increasingly demanding parents, who are divorcing after thirty-four years of marriage. Jackie Gleason gives a subtle, touching portrayal of the father. The film succeeds at making the difficult shift from zany humor to pathos. Rated PG for profanity and suggested sex. 120m. **DIR:** Garry Marshall. **CAST:** Tom Hanks, Jackie Gleason, Eva Marie Saint, Hector Elizondo, Barry Corbin, Bess Armstrong, Sela Ward. **1986**

NOW AND FOREVER 🦃 A boutique owner comes back from a clothes-buying trip to find that her husband has been accused of rape. Rated R for violence. 93m. **DIR:** Adrian Carr. **CAST:** Cheryl Ladd, Robert Coleby, Carmen Duncan. **1983**

NOW, VOYAGER ★★★½ Bette Davis plays a neurotic, unattractive spinster named Charlotte Vale; an ugly duckling, who, of course, blossoms into a beautiful swan. And it's all thanks to the expert counsel of her psychiatrist (Claude Rains) and a shipboard romance with a married man (Paul Henreid). Directed by Irving Rapper, it features the famous cigarette-lighting ritual that set a trend in the 1940s. B&W; 117m. **DIR:** Irving Rapper. **CAST:** Bette Davis, Claude Rains, Paul Henreid. **1942**

NOWHERE TO RUN (1989) ★★ This coming-of-age film is based on an actual series of murders in Caddo, Texas, during 1960. When paroled con (David Carradine) goes on a killing spree for revenge, six high school seniors find themselves swept into a world of corrupt politicians, crooked cops, and their own hormones. Rated R for violence and profanity. 87m. **DIR:** Carl Franklin. **CAST:** David Carradine, Jason Priestley, Henry Jones. **1989**

NUN'S STORY, THE ★★★ A record of a devoted nun's ultimate rebellion against vows of chastity, obedience, silence, and poverty, this Audrey Hepburn starrer was one of the big box-office hits of the 1950s. The wistful and winning Miss Hepburn shines. The supporting cast is excellent. 152m. **DIR:** Fred Zinnemann. **CAST:** Audrey Hepburn, Edith Evans, Peter Finch, Dean Jagger, Beatrice Straight, Colleen Dewhurst, Peggy Ashcroft, Mildred Dunnock. **1959**

NURSE EDITH CAVELL ★★★ The story of England's second most famous nurse, who helped transport refugee soldiers out of German-held Belgium during World War I. The film delivered a dramatically satisfying antiwar message just as World War II got under way. B&W; 95m. **DIR:** Herbert Wilcox. **CAST:** Anna Neagle, Edna May Oliver, George Sanders, ZaSu Pitts, H. B. Warner, May Robson, Robert Coote, Martin Kosleck, Mary Howard. **1939**

O LUCKY MAN! ★★★★ Offbeat, often stunning story of a young salesman (Malcolm McDowell) and his efforts and obstacles in reaching the top rung of the success ladder. Allegorical and surrealistic at times, this film takes its own course like a fine piece of music. Great acting by a great cast (many of the principals play multiple roles) makes this a real viewing pleasure. Some adult situations and language. Rated R. 173m. **DIR:** Lindsay Anderson. **CAST:** Malcolm McDowell, Rachel Roberts, Ralph Richardson, Alan Price, Lindsay Anderson. **1973**

O PIONEERS! ★★★½ Eons distant from her film debut in Kong's palm, a self-assured, strong Jessica Lange bests male sibling opposition and competition and the rigors of Nebraska farm life to win and prevail. The gait is slow, the mood a mite somber, but the aim is true. 100m. **DIR:** Glenn Jordan. **CAST:** Jessica Lange, David Strathairn, Tom Aldredge, Anne Heche, Heather Graham. **1992**

OBSESSED ★★★½ After her son is accidentally struck and killed by the car of an American businessman, a Montreal woman feels improperly served by the legal system and plots revenge. Intelligently written drama about grief and responsibility. Rated PG-13. 103m. **DIR:** Robin Spry. **CAST:** Kerrie Keane, Daniel Pilon, Saul Rubinek, Colleen Dewhurst, Alan Thicke. **1988**

OCTAVIA 🦃 A ridiculously sappy fairy tale that quickly falls into an exploitation mode. Rated R. 93m. **DIR:** David Beaird. **CAST:** Susan Curtis, Neil Kinsella, Jake Foley. **1982**

ODD ANGRY SHOT, THE ★★★ This low-key film about Australian soldiers stationed in Vietnam during the undeclared war is a good attempt to make sense out of a senseless situation as Bryan Brown and his comrades attempt to come to grips with the morality of their involvement in a fight they have no heart for. Odd, sometimes highly effective blend of comedy and drama characterize this offbeat war entry. Some violence; adult situations and language. 89m. **DIR:** Tom Jeffrey. **CAST:** Bryan Brown, John Hargreaves, Graham Kennedy. **1979**

ODE TO BILLY JOE ★★★ For those who listened to Bobbie Gentry's hit song and wondered why Billy Joe jumped off the Talahatchie Bridge, this movie tries to provide one hypothesis. Robby Benson plays Billy Joe with just the right amount of innocence and confusion to be convincing as a youth who doubts his sexual orientation. Rated PG. 108m. **DIR:** Max Baer. **CAST:** Robby Benson, Glynnis O'Connor, Joan Hotchkis. **1976**

OEDIPUS REX (1957) ★★½ Good adaptation of Sophocles's tragedy. Douglas Rain plays Oedipus, the doomed hero, who kills his father and marries his mother in fulfillment of the prophecy. 87m. **DIR:** Tyrone Guthrie. **CAST:** Douglas Rain, Douglas Campbell. **1957**

OF HUMAN BONDAGE (1934) ★★★★½ A young doctor (Leslie Howard) becomes obsessed with a sluttish waitress (Bette Davis), almost causing his downfall. Fine acting by all, with Davis an absolute knockout. No rating, but still a little adult for the kiddies. B&W; 83m. **DIR:** John Cromwell. **CAST:** Bette Davis, Leslie Howard, Alan Hale Sr., Frances Dee. **1934**

OF HUMAN BONDAGE (1964) ★★★★½ Excellent remake of the 1934 film with Bette Davis. This time Kim Novak plays Mildred Rogers, the promiscuous free spirit who becomes the obsession of Philip Carey (Laurence Harvey). Harvey's performance is wonderfully understated, and Novak plays the slut to the hilt without overdoing it. B&W; 100m. **DIR:** Ken Hughes. **CAST:** Kim Novak, Laurence Harvey, Robert Morley, Siobhan McKenna, Roger Livesey, Nanette Newman, Ronald Lacey. **1964**

OF HUMAN HEARTS ★★★½ A fine piece of Americana features Walter Huston as a backwoods traveling preacher whose son doesn't understand his faith and dedication to others. You'll even forgive the hokey ending with Abraham Lincoln (John Carradine) chiding selfish James Stewart for neglecting his mother. B&W; 100m. **DIR:** Clarence Brown. **CAST:** Walter Huston, James Stewart, Beulah Bondi, Guy Kibbee, Charles Coburn, John Carradine, Ann Rutherford, Charley Grapewin, Gene Lockhart, Clem Bevans, Gene Reynolds. **1938**

OF MICE AND MEN (1981) ★★★½ Robert Blake is George, Randy Quaid is big, dim-witted Lenny in this Blake-produced TV remake of the classic 1939 Burgess Meredith/Lon Chaney Jr. rendition of John Steinbeck's morality tale. While not as sensitive as the original, this version merits attention and appreciation. 125m. **DIR:** Reza S. Badiyi. **CAST:** Robert Blake, Randy Quaid, Lew Ayres, Pat Hingle, Cassie Yates. **1981**

OF MICE AND MEN (1992) ★★★★★ Actor-director Gary Sinise, working with a superb script from Horton Foote, delivers a hauntingly poignant adaptation of John Steinbeck's melancholy study of Depression-era California migrant workers. John Malkovich steals the film as the hulking Lenny, an inarticulate simpleton equally fascinated by puppies and pretty girls. Rated PG-13 for profanity and violence. 110m. **DIR:** Gary Sinise. **CAST:** Gary Sinise, John Malkovich, Casey Siemaszko, Ray Walston, Sherilyn Fenn. **1992**

OFFENCE, THE ★★★½ A series of child molestations causes London detective Sean Connery to go over the edge. Director Sidney Lumet tells the story in what is essentially a three-act play of Connery's confrontations with superior officer Trevor Howard, disillusioned wife Vivien Merchant, and, suspect Ian Bannen. It's a superbly played, disturbing character study. Rated R for violence and profanity. 122m. **DIR:** Sidney Lumet. **CAST:** Sean Connery, Trevor Howard, Vivien Merchant, Ian Bannen, Derek Newark. **1973**

OFFICE ROMANCES ★★ Slow-moving British soap. A plain, lonely country girl comes to work in London and is seduced by a selfish, married coworker. Ironically, she feels lucky to have been chosen by him. Unrated. 48m. **DIR:** Mary McMurray. **CAST:** Judy Parfitt, Ray Brooks. **1981**

OFFICER AND A GENTLEMAN, AN ★★★★½ Soap opera has never been art. However, this funny, touching, corny, and predictable movie, starring Richard Gere and Debra Winger, takes the genre as close to it as any of the old three-handkerchief classics. Director Taylor Hackford keeps just the right balance between the ridiculous and the sublime, making *An Officer and a Gentleman* one of the best of its kind. Rated R for nudity, profanity, and simulated sex. 125m. **DIR:** Taylor Hackford. **CAST:** Richard Gere, Debra Winger, Lou Gossett Jr., David Keith, Harold Sylvester. **1982**

OH, ALFIE 🦃 Alan Price is an uncaring ladies' man. Rated R for nudity. 99m. **DIR:** Ken Hughes. **CAST:** Alan Price, Jill Townsend, Joan Collins, Rula Lenska, Hannah Gordon. **1975**

OH, WHAT A NIGHT ★★★ Nostalgic soundtrack and innocent teen pranks highlight this better-than-average period piece about some 1950s teens trying to sow their wild oats. Young Corey Haim gets more than he bargained for when he falls for older woman Barbara Williams. Unexpectedly warm and sensitive. Made in Canada. Not rated, but contains adult situations. 93m. **DIR:** Eric Till. **CAST:** Corey Haim, Barbara Williams, Keir Dullea, Robbie Coltrane, Genevieve Bujold. **1992**

O'HARA'S WIFE ★★ Trite little tale about a businessman whose dead wife returns from the grave to help him along in life. Made for television. 87m. **DIR:** William Bartman. **CAST:** Edward Asner, Mariette Hartley, Jodie Foster, Tom Bosley. **1982**

OLD BOYFRIENDS 🦃 A woman decides to exact revenge on those men who made her past miserable. Rated R for profanity and violence. 103m. **DIR:** Joan Tewkesbury. **CAST:** Talia Shire, Richard Jordan, Keith Carradine, John Belushi, John Houseman, Buck Henry. **1979**

OLD ENOUGH 🦃 A prepubescent "coming-of-age" movie. Rated PG. 91m. **DIR:** Marisa Silver. **CAST:** Sarah Boyd, Rainbow Harvest, Neill Barry, Danny Aiello. **1984**

OLD GRINGO, THE ★★★ Based on the novel by Carlos Fuentes. Jane Fonda hesitantly portrays an American schoolteacher on a quest for adventure with Pancho Villa's army during the 1910 Mexican revolution. Gregory Peck is an aging expatriate journalist traveling along for the last ride of his life. This project shows more aesthetic sensitivity during battle scenes than in dialogue sequences. Rated R for adult language. 120m. **DIR:** Luis Puenzo. **CAST:** Jane Fonda, Gregory Peck, Jimmy Smits. **1989**

OLD MAID, THE ★★★½ Tearjerking film version of the Zoe Akins play based on the Edith Wharton novel about an unwed mother (Bette Davis) who gives up her daughter to be raised by a married cousin (Miriam Hopkins), and suffers the consequences. Hopkins works hard to upstage Davis. A solid box-office winner. B&W; 95m. **DIR:** Edmund Goulding. **CAST:** Bette Davis, Miriam Hopkins, George Brent, Donald Crisp. **1939**

OLD SWIMMIN' HOLE, THE ★★ Easygoing homage to small-town America focuses on young Jackie Moran's plans to become a doctor, and his and his mother's life in simpler times. Modest and pleasant enough. B&W; 78m. **DIR:** Robert McGowan. **CAST:** Marcia Mae Jones, Jackie Moran, Leatrice Joy, Charles Brown. **1940**

OLDEST LIVING GRADUATE, THE ★★★★ *The Oldest Living Graduate* features a memorable performance by Henry Fonda as the oldest living member of a prestigious Texas military academy. Cloris Leachman shines in her role of the colonel's daughter-in-law. The final moments of this teleplay are poignantly realistic. 90m. **DIR:** Jack Hofsiss. **CAST:** Henry Fonda, George Grizzard, Harry Dean Stanton, Penelope Milford, Cloris Leachman, David Ogden Stiers, Timothy Hutton. **1983**

OLIVER TWIST (1922) ★★★ Young Jackie Coogan, teamed with the legendary "Man of a Thousand Faces" Lon Chaney to portray, respectively, abused orphan Oliver Twist and literature's great manipulator of thieving children, Fagin, in this loose adaptation of Charles Dickens's enduring classic. Something of an oddity, this is one of at least eight film versions of the world-famous novel. Silent. B&W; 77m. **DIR:** Frank Lloyd. **CAST:** Jackie Coogan, Lon Chaney Sr., Gladys Brockwell, Esther Ralston. **1922**

OLIVER TWIST (1933) ★★ Low-budget version of the popular Charles Dickens story features some interesting performances and a few effective moments. This is a curiosity for students of literature or early sound film. Print quality is marginal. B&W; 77m. **DIR:** William Cowen. **CAST:** Dickie Moore, Irving Pichel, William "Stage" Boyd, Barbara Kent. **1933**

OLIVER TWIST (1948) ★★★★ Alec Guinness and Robert Newton give superb performances as the villains in this David Lean adaptation of the Charles Dickens story about a young boy who is forced into a life of thievery until he's rescued by a kindly old gentleman. B&W; 105m. **DIR:** David Lean. **CAST:** Alec Guinness, Robert Newton, John Howard Davies. **1948**

OLIVER'S STORY 🦃 Even if you loved *Love Story*, you'll find it difficult to like this lame sequel. Rated PG. 92m. **DIR:** John Korty. **CAST:** Ryan O'Neal, Candice Bergen, Nicola Pagett, Edward Binns, Ray Milland. **1978**

ON BORROWED TIME ★★★½ Lionel Barrymore is concerned about the future of his orphaned grandson. When death (Mr. Brink) calls, he tricks him up a tree and delays the inevitable. A rewarding fantasy. B&W; 98m. **DIR:** Harold S. Bucquet. **CAST:** Lionel Barrymore, Cedric Hardwicke, Beulah Bondi, Una Merkel, Bobs Watson, Henry Travers. **1939**

ON GOLDEN POND ★★★★★ Henry Fonda, Katharine Hepburn, and Jane Fonda are terrific in this warm, funny, and often quite moving film, written by Ernest Thompson, about the conflicts and reconciliations among the members of a family that take place during a fateful summer. Rated PG because of brief profanity. 109m. **DIR:** Mark Rydell. **CAST:** Henry Fonda, Katharine Hepburn, Jane Fonda, Doug McKeon. **1981**

ON THE BOWERY ★★★★ Gritty, uncompromising docudrama, dealing with life among the tragic street people of the Lower East Side in New York City. An extraordinary, agonizing glimpse into the world of the depraved alcoholic nomads whose lives become a constant daily struggle. Excellent black-and-white cinematography. B&W; 65m. **DIR:** Lionel Rogosin. **CAST:** Ray Sayler, Gorman Hendricks, Frank Mathews. **1956**

ON THE EDGE ★★★½ Bruce Dern gives a solid performance as a middle-aged runner hoping to regain the glory that escaped him twenty years earlier when he was disqualified from the 1964 Olympic trials. The race to test his ability is the grueling 14.2-mile annual Cielo Sea Race over California's Mount Tamalpais. The mobile camera action in the training and race sequences is very effective. Rated PG. 95m. **DIR:** Rob Nilsson. **CAST:** Bruce Dern, Bill Bailey, Jim Haynie, John Marley, Pam Grier. **1985**

ON THE MAKE ★★½ Well-intended but preachy movie about dating in the AIDS era. Teens obsessed with scoring at the local disco are heedless of such consequences as disease, pregnancy, and emotional numbness. Rated R for sexual situations and brief nudity. 74m. **DIR:** Samuel Herwitz. **CAST:** Steve Irlen, Mark McKelvey, Teresina, Kirk Baltz, Tara Leigh. **1989**

ON THE NICKEL ★★½ Ralph Waite, of TV's *The Waltons*, wrote, produced, and directed this drama about derelicts on L.A.'s skid row. It's a well-intentioned effort that is too unfocused and sentimental to work, though Donald Moffat's performance as a cleaned-up drunk is worth seeing. Rated R for rough language. 96m. **DIR:** Ralph Waite. **CAST:** Donald Moffat, Ralph Waite, Hal Williams, Jack Kehoe, Ellen Geer. **1980**

ON THE WATERFRONT ★★★★★ Tough, uncompromising look at corruption on the New York waterfront. Marlon Brando is brilliant as Terry Malloy, a one-time fight contender who is now a longshoreman. Led into crime by his older brother (Rod Steiger), Terry is disgusted by the violent tactics of boss Lee J. Cobb. Yet if he should turn against the crooks, it could mean his life. A classic film with uniformly superb performances. B&W; 108m. **DIR:** Elia Kazan. **CAST:** Marlon Brando, Eva Marie Saint, Karl Malden, Lee J. Cobb, Rod Steiger. **1954**

ON VALENTINE'S DAY ★★½ Horton Foote created this small-town love story about his own parents. A young couple (William Converse and Hallie Foote) tries to make ends meet after eloping. Her parents haven't spoken to her since they ran away, but all that is about to change. Rated PG. 106m. **DIR:** Ken Harrison. **CAST:** William Converse-Roberts, Hallie Foote, Michael Higgins, Steven Hill, Rochelle Oliver, Matthew Broderick. **1986**

ONASSIS: THE RICHEST MAN IN THE WORLD ★★½ Mediocre made-for-TV biography of Aristotle Onassis's life focusing on his rise to wealth and power and unhappy marriages. Raul Julia stands out in the lead but has little support from his female counterparts. 120m. **DIR:** Waris Hussein. **CAST:** Raul Julia, Jane Seymour, Anthony Quinn, Francesca Annis, Anthony Zerbe. **1990**

ONCE IN PARIS ★★★ Effervescent romantic comedy about a script doctor (Wayne Rogers) called to Paris to repair a screenplay. Once there, he falls in love and ends up ignoring his work. Sparkling writing perks up an old story. Rated PG for adult situations. 100m. **DIR:** Frank D. Gilroy. **CAST:** Wayne Rogers, Gayle Hunnicutt, Jack Lenoir, Tanya Lopert, Doris Roberts. **1978**

ONCE IS NOT ENOUGH Trash based on Jacqueline Susann's novel of jet-set sex. Rated R. 121m. **DIR:** Guy Green. **CAST:** Kirk Douglas, Alexis Smith, David Janssen, Deborah Raffin, George Hamilton, Melina Mercouri, Brenda Vaccaro. **1975**

ONE AGAINST THE WIND ★★★★ A British socialite (Judy Davis) risks her life to guide Allied soldiers through Nazi-occupied France in this Hallmark Hall of Fame drama. Based on an actual person, Davis is captivating as the complex woman whose life disintegrates as she saves lives, using only her wits and impeccable manners. Made for TV. 96m. **DIR:** Larry Elikann. **CAST:** Judy Davis, Sam Neill. **1991**

ONE AND ONLY, THE ★★★ Writer Steve Gordon got started with this tale of an obnoxious college show-off who eventually finds fame as a wrestling showboater. Henry Winkler was still struggling to find a big-screen personality, but his occasional character flaws often are overshadowed by Gordon's deft little script. Rated PG. 98m. **DIR:** Carl Reiner. **CAST:** Henry Winkler, Kim Darby, Herve Villechaize, Harold Gould, Gene Saks, William Daniels. **1978**

ONE DAY IN THE LIFE OF IVAN DENISOVICH ★★★ Tom Courtenay does a fine job as the title character, a prisoner in a Siberian labor camp. The famed novel by Alexander Solzhenitsyn is beautifully and bleakly photographed. Not an uplifting story, but a significant one. 100m. **DIR:** Caspar Wrede. **CAST:** Tom Courtenay, Espen Skjonberg, James Maxwell, Alfred Burke. **1971**

ONE FLEW OVER THE CUCKOO'S NEST ★★★★★ Not since Capra's *It Happened One Night* had a motion picture swept all the major Academy Awards. Jack Nicholson sparkles as Randall P. McMurphy, a convict who is committed to a northwestern mental institution for examination. While there, he stimulates in each of his ward inmates an awakening spirit of self-worth and frees them from their passive acceptance of the hospital authorities' domination. Louise Fletcher is brilliant as the insensitive head nurse. Rated R. 133m. **DIR:** Milos Forman. **CAST:** Jack Nicholson, Louise Fletcher, Will Sampson, Danny DeVito, Christopher Lloyd, Scatman Crothers, Brad Dourif. **1975**

ONE GOOD COP ★★★ When his partner is killed in a shoot-out with a drug-crazed criminal, detective Michael Keaton and his wife take in the partner's three daughters. Familiar material is handled well by a committed cast. Rated R for violence and profanity. 106m. **DIR:** Heywood Gould. **CAST:** Michael Keaton, René Russo, Anthony LaPaglia, Kevin Conway, Rachel Ticotin, Tony Plana. **1991**

ONE LAST RUN ★★ Male bonding theme is just an excuse for endless ski stunts. Unrated, contains profanity. 80m. **DIR:** Glenn Gebhard, Peter Winograd. **CAST:** Russell Todd, Craig Branham, Nels Van Patten, Ashley Laurence, Chuck Connors, Tracy Scoggins. **1990**

ONE MAGIC CHRISTMAS ★★★★½ Mary Steenburgen stars in this touching, feel-good movie as a young mother who has lost the spirit of Christmas. She regains it with the help of a Christmas angel (played by that terrific character actor Harry Dean Stanton). Rated G. 95m. **DIR:** Phillip Borsos. **CAST:** Mary Steenburgen, Harry Dean Stanton, Gary Basaraba, Arthur Hill, Ken Pogue. **1985**

ONE MAN'S WAR ★★★ A superb ensemble cast does not compensate for the bewildering lack of punch to Mike Carter and Sergio Toledo's fact-based account of a family's battle with the corrupt government of 1976 Paraguay. Anthony Hopkins is mesmerizing as the proud and stubborn Dr. Joel Filartiga, who believes political "connections" will protect his family. Made for cable TV. 91m. **DIR:** Sergio Toledo. **CAST:** Anthony Hopkins, Norma Aleandro, Fernanda Torres, Rubén Blades. **1991**

ONE MAN'S WAY ★★★ More a tribute than an in-depth biography of clergyman Norman Vincent Peale and his early ministry. Don Murray is fine in the title role and there is passion when he delivers some of Peale's actual sermons. Good insight into the questions raised by other clerics over his book, *The Power of Positive Thinking*. B&W; 105m. **DIR:** Denis Sanders. **CAST:** Don Murray, Diana Hyland, William Windom, Virginia Christine, Veronica Cartwright, Ian Wolfe. **1964**

ONE-NIGHT STAND Canadian made-for-TV adaptation of a stage play. Unrated; it's all talk and no action. 93m. **DIR:** Allan Winton King. **CAST:** Chapelle Jaffe, Brent Carver. **1977**

ONE ON ONE ★★★★ The harsh world of big-time college athletics is brought into clearer focus by this unheralded "little film." Robby Benson is a naïve small-town basketball star who has his eyes opened when he wins a scholarship to a large western university. He doesn't play up to his coach's expectations, and the pressure is put on to take away his scholarship. Rated R. 98m. **DIR:** Lamont Johnson. **CAST:** Robby Benson, Annette O'Toole, G. D. Spradlin. **1980**

ONE RUSSIAN SUMMER In czarist Russia of the eighteenth century, an anarchist peasant arrives at the estate of a brutish landowner to seek revenge. Rated R. 112m. **DIR:** Antonio Calenda. **CAST:** Oliver Reed, John McEnery, Claudia Cardinale, Carole André, Raymond Lovelock. **1973**

ONION FIELD, THE ★★★★ Solid screen version of Joseph Wambaugh's book about a cop (John Savage) who cracks up after his partner is murdered. James Woods and Franklyn Seales are memorable as the criminals. While not for all tastes, this film has a kind of subtle power and an almost documentarylike quality that will please those fascinated by true-crime stories. Rated R. 124m. **DIR:** Harold Becker. **CAST:** John Savage, James Woods, Franklyn Seales, Ted Danson, Ronny Cox, Dianne Hull. **1979**

ONLY WHEN I LAUGH ★★★ A brilliant but self-destructive actress (Marsha Mason) and her daughter (Kristy McNichol) reach toward understanding in this sometimes funny, sometimes tearful, but always entertaining adaptation by Neil Simon of his play *The Gingerbread Lady.* Rated R for profanity. 121m. **DIR:** Glenn Jordan. **CAST:** Marsha Mason, Kristy McNichol, James Coco, Joan Hackett. **1981**

OPENING NIGHT ★★★ Gena Rowlands delivers a potent performance as an actress coming to grips with her life on the opening night of her new play. Director John Cassavetes guides Rowlands through this emotional roller coaster with his usual improvisational style, giving Rowlands every opportunity to shine. The events leading up to and following the actual production provide the fine cast with plenty of room to strut their stuff. Rated PG-13 for language. 144m. **DIR:** John Cassavetes. **CAST:** Gena Rowlands, Ben Gazzara, Joan Blondell, Paul Stewart, Zohra Lampert. **1977**

OPERATION PACIFIC ★★★½ Action, suspense, comedy, and romance are nicely mixed in this fact-based film about the rush to perfect American torpedoes during World War II. John Wayne and Ward Bond are the navy men frustrated by the nonexploding, submerged missiles, and Patricia Neal is the nurse who can't quite decide whether or not she loves Wayne. B&W; 111m. **DIR:** George Waggner. **CAST:** John Wayne, Patricia Neal, Ward Bond, Scott Forbes, Philip Carey, Paul Picerni, Martin Milner, Jack Pennick, William Campbell. **1951**

OPERATOR 13 ★★★ Two of Hollywood's most glamorous players get in a romantic clinch similar to Scarlett O'Hara and Rhett Butler's five years before *Gone with the Wind.* Marion Davies plays a Yankee spy during the Civil War. Gary Cooper is a southern sympathizer. They square off against each other and love blooms. Very romantic, very flashy, and slightly dated. B&W; 86m. **DIR:** Richard Boleslawski. **CAST:** Marion Davies, Gary Cooper, Jean Parker, Katharine Alexander, Ted Healy, Hattie McDaniel, Russell Hardie, Fuzzy Knight, Douglass Dumbrille. **1934**

ORDEAL OF DR. MUDD, THE ★★★½ The true story of Dr. Samuel Mudd, who innocently aided the injured, fleeing John Wilkes Booth following Lincoln's assassination and was sent to prison for alleged participation in the conspiracy. Dennis Weaver's fine portrayal of the ill-fated doctor makes this film well worthwhile. More than a century passed before Mudd was cleared, thanks to the efforts of a descendant, newscaster Roger Mudd. Rated PG. 143m. **DIR:** Paul Wendkos. **CAST:** Dennis Weaver, Susan Sullivan, Richard Dysart, Arthur Hill. **1980**

ORDINARY HEROES ★★★ A moving love story about a young couple torn apart when the man (Richard Dean Anderson) is drafted into the army and sent to Vietnam. He returns from combat blinded and attempts to piece his broken life back together with his former girlfriend (Valerie Bertinelli). This absorbing drama gets its strength from strong performances by both leads. Rated PG. 90m. **DIR:** Peter H. Cooper. **CAST:** Richard Dean Anderson, Valerie Bertinelli, Doris Roberts. **1986**

ORDINARY MAGIC ★★★ Inspiring family film stars David Fox as an orphan who must leave India and live with his aunt in the United States. His interest in Indian culture and his practice of yoga make him a prime target for ridicule. When his aunt's house is scheduled for demolition, he wages a personal battle to save his new home. Glenne Headly lends nice support as the withdrawn aunt who comes alive. Not rated. 96m. **DIR:** Giles Walker. **CAST:** Glenne Headly, David Fox, Paul Anka. **1993**

ORDINARY PEOPLE ★★★★½ This moving human drama, which won the Academy Award for best picture of 1980, marked the directorial debut of Robert Redford...and an auspicious one it is, too. Redford elicits memorable performances from Mary Tyler Moore, Donald Sutherland, Timothy Hutton, and Judd Hirsch and makes the intelligent, powerful script by Alvin Sargent seem even better. Rated R for adult situations. 123m. **DIR:** Robert Redford. **CAST:** Mary Tyler Moore, Donald Sutherland, Timothy Hutton, Judd Hirsch, Elizabeth McGovern, Dinah Manoff, James B. Sikking. **1980**

ORIGINAL INTENT ★★ Preachy, heavy-handed film about a yuppie lawyer becoming aware of the homeless problem and trying to save a shelter from a greedy developer. Rated PG for profanity. 97m. **DIR:** Robert Marcarelli. **CAST:** Jay Richardson, Candy Clark, Martin Sheen, Kris Kristofferson, Vince Edwards, Robert DoQui. **1991**

ORLANDO ★★ The plight of women throughout the ages is examined in director Sally Potter's smug, off-putting screen adaptation of the novella by Virginia Woolf. It's visually stunning, but woe to anyone who expects to be entertained. Worst of all, Potter misuses gifted actress Tilda Swinton, who is expected to portray both a man and a woman. Balderdash. Rated PG-13 for violence, nudity, and suggested sex. 93m. **DIR:** Sally Potter. **CAST:** Tilda Swinton, Billy Zane, John Wood, Charlotte Valandrey, Heathcote Williams, Quentin Crisp, Peter Eyre, Thom Hoffman, Dudley Sutton. **1993**

ORPHAN TRAIN ★★★½ Inspirational tale of a young woman's desire to help thousands of orphans who were roaming the streets of New York in the 1850s. Realizing that her soup kitchen can't keep the kids out of trouble, she takes a group out west in hopes of finding farming families willing to adopt them. Originally shown on TV. 150m. **DIR:** William A. Graham. **CAST:** Jill Eikenberry, Kevin Dobson, Linda Manz, Glenn Close. **1979**

ORPHANS ★★★★ Based on the play by Lyle Kessler, this compact drama is a psychological thriller with a poignant twist. Albert Finney effectively portrays an affluent American gangster who does more than merely befriend two homeless young men—Treat, an angry delinquent (Matthew Modine), and Phillips (Kevin Anderson), his helpless younger brother. In a short time, he changes their lives. Rated R. 115m. **DIR:** Alan J. Pakula. **CAST:** Albert Finney, Matthew Modine, Kevin Anderson. **1987**

ORPHANS OF THE STORM ★★★½ Film's first master director blends fact and fiction, mixing the French Revolution with the trials and tribulations of two sisters—one blind and raised by thieves, the other betrayed by self-saving aristocrats. The plot creaks with age, but the settings and action spell good entertainment. Silent. B&W; 125m. **DIR:** D. W. Griffith. **CAST:** Lillian Gish, Dorothy Gish, Sidney Herbert, Sheldon Lewis, Monte Blue, Joseph Schildkraut, Creighton Hale, Morgan Wallace. **1922**

ORPHEUS DESCENDING ★★★½ Fascinatingly horrifying made-for-cable adaptation of Tennessee Williams's slice-of-southern-Gothic stage play. Vanessa Redgrave fails at an Italian accent, but when she abandons an overused hysterical laugh, she delivers her usual fine performance. Unrated, contains nudity, profanity, and violence. 117m. **DIR:** Peter Hall. **CAST:** Vanessa Redgrave, Kevin Anderson, Brad Sullivan. **1990**

OSCAR, THE (1966) 🦃 An unscrupulous actor advances his career at the expense of others. 119m. **DIR:** Russell Rouse. **CAST:** Stephen Boyd, Elke Sommer, Tony Bennett, Eleanor Parker, Ernest Borgnine, Joseph Cotten. **1966**

OTHELLO (1922) ★★★★ Despite the silence of this early version of the Shakespeare tragedy, the essence of the drama is effectively conveyed by memorable quotes on title cards, elaborate sets and costuming, and fine performances. Silent. B&W; 81m. **DIR:** Dimitri Buschowetzki. **CAST:** Emil Jannings, Werner Krauss, Lya de Putti. **1922**

OTHELLO (1952) ★★★★½ Months of high-tech restoration have done much to reverse the damage done by years of neglect to Orson Welles's cockeyed masterpiece. Shot entirely out of sequence over four years (whenever other acting jobs, including *The Third Man*, paid him enough to reassemble his cast and crew)—and under the most inhospitable circumstances—*Othello*, nevertheless, bears the unmistakable mark of the American genius. The sparest black-and-white cinematography, the monumental sets, the stark choral and instrumental music, and the reduced essence of Shakespeare are melded by the alchemist Welles into an unforgettable film experience. Best feature film, 1952 Cannes Film Festival. B&W; 91m. **DIR:** Orson Welles. **CAST:** Orson Welles, Suzanne Cloutier, Micheal MacLiammoir, Robert Coote, Fay Compton. **1952**

OTHELLO (1982) ★★★½ A fine stage production with William Marshall impressive as the valiant, but tragic Moor of Venice, Othello, tricked into madness and murder by his jealous aide, Iago (Ron Moody). Moody is magnificent as Shakespeare's greatest villain. Released by Bard Productions Ltd. 195m. **DIR:** Frank Melton. **CAST:** William Marshall, Ron Moody, Jenny Agutter, DeVeren Bookwalter, Peter MacLean, Jay Robinson. **1982**

OTHER SIDE OF MIDNIGHT, THE 🦃 Glossy soap opera derived from schlockmaster Sidney Sheldon's bestselling novel. Rated R. 165m. **DIR:** Charles Jarrott. **CAST:** Marie-France Pisier, John Beck, Susan Sarandon, Raf Vallone, Clu Gulager. **1977**

OTHER SIDE OF THE MOUNTAIN, THE ★★★ Absolutely heart-wrenching account of Jill Kinmont, an Olympic-bound skier whose career was cut short by a fall that left her paralyzed. Marilyn Hassett, in her film debut, makes Kinmont a fighter whose determination initially backfires and prompts some to have unreasonable expectations of her limited recovery. Rated PG. 103m. **DIR:** Larry Peerce. **CAST:** Marilyn Hassett, Beau Bridges. **1975**

OTHER SIDE OF THE MOUNTAIN, PART II, THE ★★ A sequel to the modest 1975 hit, the film continues the story of Jill Kinmont, a promising young skier who was paralyzed from the shoulders down in an accident. The tender romance, well played by Hassett and Bottoms, provides some fine moments. Rated PG. 100m. **DIR:** Larry Peerce. **CAST:** Marilyn Hassett, Timothy Bottoms, Nan Martin, Belinda Montgomery. **1978**

OUR DAILY BREAD ★★½ This vintage Depression social drama about an idealistic man organizing community farms and socialistic society is pretty creaky despite director King Vidor. Lead actor Tom Keene did better in cowboy films. B&W; 74m. **DIR:** King Vidor.

CAST: Tom Keene, Karen Morley, John Qualen, Addison Richards. **1934**

OUR DANCING DAUGHTERS ★★★ One of the most famous flaming-youth movies of the late 1920s, and the one that really got Joan Crawford on her way as a top star for MGM. She plays Diana, a vivacious flapper who jiggles a lot and takes frequent belts from her hip flask. Silent. B&W; 86m. **DIR:** Harry Beaumont. **CAST:** Joan Crawford, Johnny Mack Brown, Nils Asther. **1928**

OUR FAMILY BUSINESS ★★ Two sons take different tacks in surviving within a Mafia family. Sam Wanamaker and Ray Milland give strong performances in this generally slow, uninspired twist on the *Godfather* theme. Made for television. 74m. **DIR:** Robert Collins. **CAST:** Ted Danson, Sam Wanamaker, Vera Miles, Ray Milland. **1981**

OUR MODERN MAIDENS ★★★ Jazz age drama of love and infidelity bears more than a passing resemblance to *Our Dancing Daughters*, with Joan Crawford once again a flapper who makes a bad marriage. Ignore the story and enjoy the art deco sets and elaborate Adrian costumes. B&W; 75m. **DIR:** Jack Conway. **CAST:** Joan Crawford, Douglas Fairbanks Jr., Rod La Rocque, Anita Page. **1929**

OUR TIME 🦃 A stilted story about young women of the 1950s and their melodramatic sexual experiences has cardboard acting, a contrived script, and a slow, plodding pace. Rated PG. 90m. **DIR:** Peter Hyams. **CAST:** Pamela Sue Martin, Parker Stevenson, Betsy Slade, George O'Hanlon Jr., Karen Balkin. **1974**

OUR TOWN (1940) ★★★★ Superb performances from a top-flight cast add zest to this well-done adaptation of Thornton Wilder's play about life in a small town. B&W; 90m. **DIR:** Sam Wood. **CAST:** Frank Craven, William Holden, Martha Scott, Thomas Mitchell, Fay Bainter. **1940**

OUR TOWN (1980) ★★★½ Not as good as the 1940s theatrical version, this TV version of the award-winning play by Thornton Wilder is notable for the fine performance of Hal Holbrook. The simple telling of the day-to-day life of Grover's Corners is done with remarkable restraint. 100m. **DIR:** Franklin J. Schaffner. **CAST:** Ned Beatty, Sada Thompson, Ronny Cox, Glynnis O'Connor, Robby Benson, Hal Holbrook, John Houseman. **1980**

OUT OF AFRICA ★★★★½ Robert Redford and Meryl Streep are at the peaks of their considerable talents in this 1985 Oscar winner for best picture, a grand-scale motion picture also blessed with inspired direction, gorgeous cinematography, and a haunting score. An epic romance, it was based by Kurt Luedtke on the life and works of Isak Dinesen and concerns the love of two staunch individualists for each other and the land in which they live. Rated PG for a discreet sex scene. 160m. **DIR:** Sydney Pollack. **CAST:** Robert Redford, Meryl Streep, Klaus Maria Brandauer, Michael Kitchen, Malick Bowens, Michael Gough, Suzanna Hamilton. **1985**

OUT OF SEASON ★★ This British mood piece is full of atmosphere, but its strange love story, about a man who returns to England to find the woman with whom he had an affair twenty years before, is nothing more than average. Rated R. 90m. **DIR:** Alan Bridges. **CAST:** Vanessa Redgrave, Cliff Robertson, Susan George. **1975**

OUT ON A LIMB (1986) ★★½ This TV film recounts Shirley MacLaine's move into metaphysics, discovering who she is and where she came from. Much too long, but if you like MacLaine, you might be amused. 159m. **DIR:** Robert Butler. **CAST:** Shirley MacLaine, Charles Dance, John Heard, Anne Jackson, Jerry Orbach. **1986**

OUTLAW AND HIS WIFE, THE ★★★ In nineteenth-century Iceland a farmer is accused of stealing sheep and must retreat to the hills to escape capture. An amazing work for its time, this silent movie from Sweden was restored in 1986 and dons a full orchestral score. Unrated. B&W; 73m. **DIR:** Victor Sjöström. **CAST:** Victor Sjöström. **1917**

OUTRAGE! ★★★½ Compelling courtroom drama that takes on the judicial system with a vengeance. Robert Preston is superb as a man who readily admits to killing his daughter's murderer. Beau Bridges shines as his attorney. This made-for-television film tackles important issues without flinching. 100m. **DIR:** Walter Grauman. **CAST:** Robert Preston, Beau Bridges, Anthony Newley, Burgess Meredith, Linda Purl. **1986**

OUTSIDE THE LAW ★★★ Director Tod Browning's long association with the greatest of all character actors and one of the biggest stars of the silent screen began in 1921 when Lon Chaney supported female star Priscilla Dean in this crime-drama. The incomparable Chaney plays Black Mike, the meanest and smarmiest of hoodlums, as well as an old Chinese man, the faithful retainer to Miss Dean. Silent. B&W; 77m. **DIR:** Tod Browning. **CAST:** Priscilla Dean, Lon Chaney Sr., Ralph Lewis, Wheeler Oakman. **1921**

OUTSIDERS, THE 🦃 Based on S. E. Hinton's popular novel, this is a simplistic movie about kids from the wrong side of the tracks. Rated PG for profanity and violence. 91m. **DIR:** Francis Ford Coppola. **CAST:** C. Thomas Howell, Matt Dillon, Ralph Macchio, Emilio Estevez, Tom Cruise, Leif Garrett. **1983**

OVER THE EDGE ★★★★ An explosive commentary on the restlessness of today's youth, this film also serves as an indictment against America's hypocritically permissive society. The violence that was supposedly caused by the release of gang films like *The*

Warriors, *Boulevard Nights*, and *The Wanderers* caused the movie's makers to shelve it. However, Matt Dillon, who made his film debut herein, is now a hot property, and that's why this deserving movie is out on video. Rated R. 95m. **DIR:** Jonathan Kaplan. **CAST:** Matt Dillon, Michael Kramer, Pamela Ludwig. **1979**

OVER THE TOP ★★ Thoroughly silly effort. Sylvester Stallone stars as a compassionate trucker who only wants to spend time with the son (David Mendenhall) whom he left, years before, in the custody of his wife (Susan Blakely, in a thankless role) and her rich, iron-willed father (Robert Loggia, as a one-note villain). This clichéd story has little of interest. Rated PG for mild violence. 94m. **DIR:** Menahem Golan. **CAST:** Sylvester Stallone, Robert Loggia, Susan Blakely, David Mendenhall. **1987**

OVERINDULGENCE ★★ Rather tame rendition of the scandalous 1940s South African murder trial that shocked the world. A sordid tale of adultery, drugs, and child abuse is told by Juanita Carberry, one of the daughters of the decadent British settlers. Sir Jock Broughton is the accused murderer, and only Juanita knows the truth behind the sensational killing. A good dramatic story is done in by a lightweight script, amateurish direction, and mediocre acting. For substance, sophistication, and style covering the subject, check out *White Mischief*. Rated PG-13. 95m. **DIR:** Ross Devenish. **CAST:** Denholm Elliott, Holly Aird, Michael Bryne, Kathryn Pogson. **1987**

OXFORD BLUES ★★ Rob Lowe plays a brash American attending England's Oxford University. Writer-director Robert Boris has even worked in the sports angle, by making Lowe a rowing champ who has to prove himself. A formula picture. Rated PG-13. 93m. **DIR:** Robert Boris. **CAST:** Rob Lowe, Amanda Pays. **1984**

P.K. & THE KID ★★★ Molly Ringwald, in one of her earliest films, is running away from her abusive father, Alex Rocco. She hitches up with Paul LeMat, who is driving to California for the annual arm-wrestling championships. The characters are well developed, and you can see a star in the making. 90m. **DIR:** Lou Lombardo. **CAST:** Paul LeMat, Molly Ringwald, Alex Rocco, Esther Rolle, John Madden. **1985**

PAINTED VEIL, THE ★★★ A better-than-average Garbo melodrama because it has a better-than-average source. Somerset Maugham wrote the novel that inspired this sophisticated love story about a woman who cheats on her husband, then tries to make amends. B&W; 85m. **DIR:** Richard Boleslawski. **CAST:** Greta Garbo, George Brent, Herbert Marshall, Warner Oland, Jean Hersholt, Keye Luke, Cecilia Parker, Beulah Bondi. **1934**

PALM BEACH ★★★ Four different stories concerning troubled Australian teens converge at the title location, a popular Aussie beach. Fans of the new Australian cinema will want to take a look, though the accents may be a bit thick for others. Not rated. 88m. **DIR:** Albie Thomas. **CAST:** Nat Young, Ken Brown, Amanda Berry, Bryan Brown. **1979**

PALOOKA ★★½ First filmed version of Ham Fisher's popular *Joe Palooka* is an okay little film about country bumpkin Stu Erwin's rise to the top in the fight game. This film shares a niche with the other seldom-seen comic-strip film adaptations of the 1930s, and its availability on video is a pleasant gift to the fan who loves those tough and slightly goofy movies of the early 1930s. B&W; 86m. **DIR:** Ben Stoloff. **CAST:** Jimmy Durante, Stu Erwin, Lupe Velez, Marjorie Rambeau, Robert Armstrong, William Cagney, Thelma Todd, Mary Carlisle. **1934**

PANCHO BARNES ★★★½ The incredible true-life story of little-known Florence Pancho Barnes, portrayed fabulously by Valerie Bertinelli. This remarkable woman raced against Amelia Earhart, became a stunt pilot, and trained some of the most famous army boys to fly. Made for TV. 180m. **DIR:** Richard T. Heffron. **CAST:** Valerie Bertinelli, Ted Wass, James Stephens, Cynthia Harris, Geoffrey Lewis, Sam Robards. **1988**

PAPA'S DELICATE CONDITION ★★½ Somewhat stolid but pleasant enough story of family life in a small Texas town and the sometimes unpleasant notoriety brought to a family by their alcoholic patriarch, Jackie Gleason. Not as good a film as it was considered when released, this is still an enjoyable movie. 98m. **DIR:** George Marshall. **CAST:** Jackie Gleason, Glynis Johns, Charlie Ruggles, Laurel Goodwin, Charles Lane, Elisha Cook Jr., Juanita Moore, Murray Hamilton. **1963**

PAPER, THE ★★★★ Michael Keaton stars as an editor in director Ron Howard's ensemble comedy-drama about a New York daily tabloid newspaper. He has only a few hours to get the scoop on a murder and stop cost-conscious managing editor Glenn Close from printing a sensationalistic cover that implies two innocent youngsters are guilty. First-rate performances and comic touches turn what could have been overwrought melodrama into believable human drama. Rated R for profanity and violence. 110m. **DIR:** Ron Howard. **CAST:** Michael Keaton, Glenn Close, Marisa Tomei, Randy Quaid, Robert Duvall, Jason Robards Jr., Jason Alexander, Spalding Gray, Catherine O'Hara, Jack Kehoe, Clint Howard. **1994**

PAPER CHASE, THE ★★★★ John Houseman won the Oscar for best actor in a supporting role in 1973 with his first-rate performance in this excellent film. Timothy Bottoms stars as a law student attempting to earn his law degree in spite of a stuffy professor (Houseman). Rated PG. 111m. **DIR:** James Bridges. **CAST:** Timothy Bottoms, John Houseman, Lindsay Wagner. **1973**

PAPER LION ★★★½ Based on George Plimpton's book, this film tells the story of the author's exploits when he becomes an honorary team member of the Detroit Lions pro football team. Alan Alda is fine as Plimpton and Alex Karras is a standout in his support. 107m. **DIR:** Alex March. **CAST:** Alan Alda, Lauren Hutton, Alex Karras, David Doyle, Ann Turkel, Roger Brown. **1968**

PAPER MARRIAGE (1992) ★★ Silly tale of a Polish girl arriving in London to marry her fiancé. When his mom disapproves of the union, she marries an unemployed man. Problems naturally result in their bizarre marriage, but these are nothing compared to the effect that the emotionless actors have on the film. Unrated, contains sex, violence, and profanity. 90m. **DIR:** Krzysztof Lang. **CAST:** Gary Kemp, Joanna Trepechinska, Rita Tushingham. **1992**

PAPER WEDDING ★★★½ In order to save a political refugee from being deported, a single woman agrees to marry him. But the name-only marriage becomes real when the couple is forced to live together. This strong comedy was made before the similar *Green Card*, and the acting is excellent. Unrated, the film has suggested sex. 95m. **DIR:** Michel Brault. **CAST:** Genevieve Bujold, Manuel Aranguiz, Dorothee Berryman. **1989**

PARADISE (1991) ★★★½ When a 10-year-old boy spends the summer with an emotionally estranged couple, they all help each other overcome personal tragedies. Better than the movie-of-the-week-style crisis films it resembles, this film, adapted from the French *Le Grand Chemin* (*The Grand Highway*), has some very touching and funny moments. Rated PG-13 for profanity and nudity. 104m. **DIR:** Mary Agnes Donoghue. **CAST:** Don Johnson, Melanie Griffith, Elijah Wood, Thora Birch, Sheila McCarthy, Eve Gordon, Louise Latham. **1991**

PARADISE ALLEY 🦃 Turgid mess about three brothers hoping for a quick ride out of the slums. Rated PG for violence. 107m. **DIR:** Sylvester Stallone. **CAST:** Sylvester Stallone, Armand Assante, Lee Canalito. **1978**

PARIS BLUES ★★★½ Duke Ellington's superb jazz score enhances this drama. The action takes place in Paris where two jazz musicians (Paul Newman and Sidney Poitier) fall for two lovely tourists (Joanne Woodward and Diahann Carroll). What the plot lacks in originality is amply made up for by the fine music and outstanding cast. 98m. **DIR:** Martin Ritt. **CAST:** Paul Newman, Joanne Woodward, Diahann Carroll, Sidney Poitier, Louis Armstrong, Serge Reggiani. **1961**

PARIS, TEXAS ★★★★½ *Paris, Texas* is a haunting vision of personal pain and universal suffering, with Harry Dean Stanton impeccable as the weary wanderer who returns after four years to reclaim his son (Hunter Carson) and search for his wife (Nastassja Kinski). It is the kind of motion picture we rarely see, one that attempts to say something about our country and its people—and succeeds. Rated R for profanity and adult content. 144m. **DIR:** Wim Wenders. **CAST:** Harry Dean Stanton, Nastassja Kinski, Dean Stockwell, Aurore Clement, Hunter Carson. **1984**

PARIS TROUT ★★½ Pete Dexter's bleak take on 1949 Georgia gets first-cabin treatment but remains as inexplicably pointless as his novel. Dennis Hopper stars as the titular character, a venal and paranoid storekeeper who shoots and kills a young black girl and then dismisses the act as "nothing scandalous." Made-for-cable drama includes shocking violence and coarse language. 100m. **DIR:** Stephen Gyllenhaal. **CAST:** Dennis Hopper, Barbara Hershey, Ed Harris. **1991**

PARK IS MINE, THE ★★½ After his friend is killed, unstable Vietnam vet (Tommy Lee Jones) invades New York's Central Park and proclaims it to be his. Predictable ending. Pretty farfetched stuff. An HBO Film. 102m. **DIR:** Steven H. Stern. **CAST:** Tommy Lee Jones, Helen Shaver, Yaphet Kotto. **1985**

PARKER ADDERSON, PHILOSOPHER ★★★★ Man's ability to inflict torment even on those with nothing left to lose is the theme of this deft adaptation of the Ambrose Bierce short story. Harris Yulin stars as a Yankee spy caught red-handed by the ragtag troops of Douglas Watson's Confederate general. Introduced by Henry Fonda; suitable for family viewing. 39m. **DIR:** Arthur Barron. **CAST:** Harris Yulin, Douglas Watson, Darren O'Connor. **1974**

PARRISH ★★ Lust among the young and greed among the old in the tobacco fields of Connecticut. Karl Malden saves this. 140m. **DIR:** Delmer Daves. **CAST:** Troy Donahue, Claudette Colbert, Karl Malden, Dean Jagger, Connie Stevens, Diane McBain, Dub Taylor. **1961**

PARTING GLANCES ★★★★ Nick (Steve Buscemi), a rock singer, discovers he is dying of AIDS. Writer-director Bill Sherwood charts the effect this discovery has on Nick and his estranged lover, Michael (Richard Ganoung), who now lives with Robert (John Bolger). Subject matter aside, *Parting Glances* has a number of funny moments and is a life-affirming look at the gay life-style. 90m. **DIR:** Bill Sherwood. **CAST:** Richard Ganoung, John Bolger, Steve Buscemi, Adam Nathan, Kathy Kinney, Patrick Tull. **1986**

PARTY GIRL ★★★½ Crime-drama with lawyer Robert Taylor as a cunning mouthpiece for the mob in 1930s Chicago. All hell breaks loose when he decides to go legit. Familiar, but well produced. 99m. **DIR:** Nicholas Ray. **CAST:** Robert Taylor, Cyd Charisse, Lee J. Cobb, John Ireland, Kent Smith. **1958**

PASCALI'S ISLAND ★★★★ A quietly enigmatic film about town loyalties, hypocrisy, and broader philosophical issues of art and romanticism, as represented by three characters on a Greek island in 1908. Ben Kingsley is brilliant as a low-level bureaucrat and semispy who will never challenge what he does or why, even when it threatens to destroy everything he cares about. Rated PG-13. 101m. **DIR:** James Dearden. **CAST:** Ben Kingsley, Helen Mirren, Charles Dance. **1988**

PASSAGE TO INDIA, A ★★★★★ After an absence from the screen of fourteen years, British director David Lean returned triumphantly, with the brilliant *A Passage to India.* Based on the 1924 novel by E. M. Forster, it is a work that compares favorably with the filmmaker's finest. Ostensibly about the romantic adventures of a young Englishwoman in "the mysterious East" that culminate in a court trial (for attempted rape), it is also a multilayered, symbolic work about, in the words of Forster, "the difficulty of living in the universe." Rated PG. 163m. **DIR:** David Lean. **CAST:** Judy Davis, Victor Banerjee, Alec Guinness, Peggy Ashcroft. **1984**

PASSION FISH ★★★★★ John Sayles scores another triumph with this superb character study about a soap-opera actress who is left paralyzed after being hit by a cab in New York City. Embittered, she returns to her childhood home in the Louisiana swamplands. Alfre Woodard and an emerging friendship between the two emotionally scarred and scared women. The underrated David Strathairn adds more heart to this touching, but unsentimental story. Rated R for profanity. 134m. **DIR:** John Sayles. **CAST:** Mary McDonnell, Alfre Woodard, David Strathairn, Vondie Curtis-Hall, Angela Bassett, Maggie Renzi. **1992**

PASSION FLOWER ★★½ In Singapore, a young playboy banker gets tangled up with the married daughter of a prominent financial figure in the British and American business community. Nicol Williamson is dandy as a sadistic and manipulative father who has his daughter's lover right where he wants him. This made-for-television movie contains mild profanity. 95m. **DIR:** Joseph Sargent. **CAST:** Bruce Boxleitner, Barbara Hershey, Nicol Williamson. **1985**

PAST MIDNIGHT ★★★ Rutger Hauer stars as a parolee trying to get a new start after serving fifteen years in prison. Natasha Richardson is the social worker assigned to ease him back into society. But someone doesn't want Hauer free and starts terrorizing Richardson. Fine performances by Hauer and Richardson keep your attention away from the overworked plot. Rated R for nudity, violence, and profanity. 100m. **DIR:** Jan Eliasberg. **CAST:** Rutger Hauer, Natasha Richardson, Clancy Brown, Guy Boyd. **1991**

PASTIME ★★★★ Wonderfully entertaining film deals with a minor-league relief pitcher in the twilight of his career and his relationship with a shy rookie pitcher who appears to have the stuff to make the big leagues. William Russ gives a beautiful performance as the aging pitcher. Rated PG. 91m. **DIR:** Robin B. Armstrong. **CAST:** William Russ, Glenn Plummer, Noble Willingham, Jeffrey Tambor, Scott Plank, Deirdre O'Connell. **1991**

PATCH OF BLUE, A ★★★½ A blind white girl who does not know her compassionate boyfriend is black, and her overprotective mother, are deftly brought together in this corn-filled but touching story. Shelley Winters as the mother won her second Oscar. B&W; 105m. **DIR:** Guy Green. **CAST:** Sidney Poitier, Elizabeth Hartman, Shelley Winters, Wallace Ford, Ivan Dixon. **1965**

PATHS OF GLORY ★★★★★ A great antiwar movie! Kirk Douglas plays the compassionate French officer in World War I who must lead his men against insurmountable enemy positions, and then must defend three of them against charges of cowardice when the battle is lost. Adolphe Menjou and George Macready perfectly portray Douglas's monstrous senior officers. B&W; 86m. **DIR:** Stanley Kubrick. **CAST:** Kirk Douglas, Adolphe Menjou, George Macready, Timothy Carey, Ralph Meeker. **1957**

PATTERNS ★★★½ Ed Begley dominates this Rod Serling drama of manipulation and machinations in the executive suite. The classic corporate-power-struggle story has changed in recent years, dating this film somewhat, but the game people play to climb to the top is still fascinating. B&W; 83m. **DIR:** Fielder Cook. **CAST:** Van Heflin, Everett Sloane, Ed Begley Sr., Beatrice Straight. **1956**

PATTI ROCKS ★★★★ Controversial sequel to 1975's *Loose Ends* picks up twelve years later. Bill (Chris Mulkey) has been having an affair with Patti Rocks (Karen Landry), who has informed him that she is pregnant. A very human story with a genuine twist. Rated R for profanity, nudity, and simulated sex. 86m. **DIR:** David Morris. **CAST:** Chris Mulkey, John Jenkins, Karen Landry. **1987**

PATTON ★★★★★ Flamboyant, controversial General George S. Patton is the subject of this Oscar-winning picture. George C. Scott is spellbinding in the title role. Scott's brilliant performance manages to bring alive this military hero, who strode a fine line between effective battlefield commander and demigod. Rated PG. 169m. **DIR:** Franklin J.

Schaffner. **CAST:** George C. Scott, Karl Malden, Stephen Young, Tim Considine. **1970**

PATTY HEARST ★★★ Paul Schrader provides a restless, relentless, and often moving story of revolutionary idealism gone amok in this documentary-style drama of the kidnapping and subversion of Patty Hearst (Natasha Richardson). Richardson's rendition of Hearst is captivating, and William Forsythe and Frances Fisher are outstanding as Bill and Emily Harris. Yet the film leaves one with a lot of unanswered questions. Rated R for profanity, nudity, and violence. 108m. **DIR:** Paul Schrader. **CAST:** Natasha Richardson, William Forsythe, Ving Rhames, Frances Fisher. **1988**

PAUL'S CASE ★★ Eric Roberts's impassioned portrayal of the working-class youth from turn-of-the-century Pittsburgh is the only draw. The outcome will leave viewers wondering. Introduced by Henry Fonda; suitable for family viewing. 52m. **DIR:** Lamont Johnson. **CAST:** Eric Roberts, Michael Higgins, Lindsay Crouse. **1980**

PAWNBROKER, THE ★★★★★ This is a somber and powerfully acted portrayal of a Jewish man who survived the Nazi Holocaust, only to find his spirit still as bleak as the Harlem ghetto in which he operates a pawnshop. Rod Steiger gives a tour-de-force performance as a man with dead emotions who is shocked out of his zombielike existence by confronting the realities of modern urban life. B&W; 116m. **DIR:** Sidney Lumet. **CAST:** Rod Steiger, Geraldine Fitzgerald, Brock Peters. **1965**

PAY OR DIE ★★★½ Ernest Borgnine plays the fabled leader of the Italian Squad, New York's crack police detectives who dealt with the turn-of-the-century Black Hand. Borgnine and his fellow Italian-Americans use force and intimidation to combat the savage Mafia-connected hoodlums who extort and murder their own people in Little Italy. An underrated crime film. B&W; 110m. **DIR:** Richard Wilson. **CAST:** Ernest Borgnine, Zohra Lampert, Al Austin. **1960**

PAYDAY ★★★★ Bravura performance by Rip Torn as a hard-drinking, ruthless country singer who's bent on destroying himself and everyone around him. Gripping, emotionally draining drama. Rarely seen in theaters, this one is definitely worth viewing on tape. Rated R for language, nudity, sexual situations. 103m. **DIR:** Daryl Duke. **CAST:** Rip Torn, Ahna Capri, Elayne Heilveil, Michael C. Gwynne. **1973**

PEARL, THE ★★ John Steinbeck's heavy-handed parable about the value of wealth when compared with natural treasures is beautifully photographed and effectively presented, but the film suffers from the same shortcoming inherent in the book. The plight of the loving couple and their desperately ill son is relentlessly hammered home. 77m. **DIR:** Emilio Fernandez. **CAST:** Pedro Armendariz, Maria Elena Marques. **1948**

PEARL OF THE SOUTH PACIFIC 🦃 A dull film about murder in the tropics. 86m. **DIR:** Allan Dwan. **CAST:** Virginia Mayo, Dennis Morgan, David Farrar, Murvyn Vye. **1955**

PEDESTRIAN, THE ★★★½ The directorial debut for Maximilian Schell, this is a disturbing near masterpiece of drama exploring the realm of guilt and self-doubt that surrounds ex–World War II Nazis. Gustav Rudolph Sellner's haunting and quiet performance as an aging industrialist who is exposed as an ex-Nazi is a little tedious but thought-provoking in the outcome—much like the film itself. 97m. **DIR:** Maximilian Schell. **CAST:** Gustav Rudolph Sellner, Peter Hall, Maximilian Schell. **1974**

PENITENT, THE ★★ Raul Julia is a member of the Penitents, a religious cult that remembers the suffering of Christ by affixing one of its members to a cross and leaving him in the desert sun for an entire day—often to die as "God's will." Exploration of this intriguing milieu is set aside in favor of a silly soap opera about Julia's problem with his young wife and lusty pal. Rated PG for suggested sex. 90m. **DIR:** Cliff Osmond. **CAST:** Raul Julia, Armand Assante, Julie Carmen. **1988**

PENNY SERENADE ★★★★ Cary Grant and Irene Dunne are one of the most fondly remembered comedy teams in films such as *The Awful Truth* and *My Favorite Wife*. This 1941 film is a radical change of pace, for it is a ten-hankie tearjerker about a couple's attempt to have children. They are excellent in this drama far removed from their standard comic fare. B&W; 125m. **DIR:** George Stevens. **CAST:** Cary Grant, Irene Dunne, Edgar Buchanan. **1941**

PEOPLE VS. JEAN HARRIS ★★ A sedate reenactment of a lengthy trial transcript, shot entirely inside a courtroom. A long, long, boring trial. Made for TV. 147m. **DIR:** George Schaefer. **CAST:** Ellen Burstyn, Martin Balsam, Richard Dysart, Peter Coyote. **1981**

PERFECT ★★ In this irritatingly uneven and unfocused film, John Travolta stars as a *Rolling Stone* reporter out to do an exposé on the health-club boom. Jamie Lee Curtis is the aerobics instructor he attempts to spotlight in his story. Just another moralizing mess about journalistic ethics. Rated R for profanity, suggested sex, and violence. 120m. **DIR:** James Bridges. **CAST:** John Travolta, Jamie Lee Curtis, Jann Wenner, Marilu Henner, Laraine Newman. **1985**

PERFECT WITNESS ★★★★½ This crackling suspenser, first aired on HBO, puts family man Aidan Quinn into a crime-infested nightmare. After witnessing a mob-style execution and telling the police what he knows, Quinn receives threats; but when he backs down and changes his mind, special attorney Brian Dennehy tosses him into jail for perjury. Terry Curtis Fox and Ron Hutchinson have scripted the ultimate horror—personal vs. social responsibility—and Quinn plays the part to frustrated perfection. Laura Harrington is excellent as Quinn's wife, and Stockard Channing equally fine as Dennehy's assistant. 104m. **DIR:** Robert Mandel. **CAST:** Brian Dennehy, Aidan Quinn, Stockard Channing, Laura Harrington. **1989**

PERFECT WORLD, A ★★★★ Escaped convict Kevin Costner takes a young boy hostage and flees with Texas Ranger Clint Eastwood hot on his trail. You wouldn't expect such a serious-sounding film to contain moments of comedy, but that's one of the many pleasant surprises in this essentially downbeat morality play. Costner does a fine job of playing against type, and Eastwood tries a John Wayne turn as an aged-in-the-saddle professional for the first time with great success. Rated R for violence, profanity, and lewdness. 136m. **DIR:** Clint Eastwood. **CAST:** Kevin Costner, Clint Eastwood, Laura Dern, T. J. Lowther, Keith Szarabajka. **1993**

PERMANENT RECORD ★★½ This drama stars Keanu Reeves as Chris, whose best friend, a popular, talented, seemingly well-adjusted high school senior, commits suicide. The film focuses on the effects the suicide has on his closest friends and how they come to accept it. Rated PG-13. 92m. **DIR:** Marisa Silver. **CAST:** Keanu Reeves, Alan Boyce, Richard Bradford. **1988**

PERSECUTION 🦃 This tale of murder and deception never shows minimal signs of life. Rated R. 92m. **DIR:** Don Chaffey. **CAST:** Lana Turner, Trevor Howard, Ralph Bates. **1974**

PERSONAL BEST ★★★★ Oscar-winning screenwriter Robert Towne wrote, directed, and produced this tough, honest, and nonexploitive story about two women who are friends, teammates, and sometimes lovers (Mariel Hemingway, Patrice Donnelly) preparing for the 1980 Olympics. Hemingway's and Donnelly's stunning performances make the film an impressive achievement. Rated R for nudity, strong language, and drug use. 124m. **DIR:** Robert Towne. **CAST:** Mariel Hemingway, Patrice Donnelly, Scott Glenn. **1982**

PETER'S FRIENDS ★★★½ A *Big Chill*–style reunion of English theatrical types in this humorous and touching soufflé from Kenneth Branagh. Costar-screenwriter Rita Rudner's script doesn't always hit the mark, but the cast does. Rated R for profanity and nudity. 102m. **DIR:** Kenneth Branagh. **CAST:** Kenneth Branagh, Emma Thompson, Rita Rudner, Steven Fry, Hugh Laurie, Imelda Staunton, Alphonsia Emmanuel, Tony Slattery, Phyllida Law, Alex Lowe. **1993**

PETRIFIED FOREST, THE ★★★★½ This adaptation of the Robert Sherwood play seems a bit dated at first. It's about a gangster (Humphrey Bogart, in one of his first important screen roles) who holds a writer (Leslie Howard), a waitress (Bette Davis), and others hostage in a diner. The first-rate story, exquisite ensemble acting and taut direction by Archie Mayo soon mesmerize the viewer. B&W; 83m. **DIR:** Archie Mayo. **CAST:** Humphrey Bogart, Leslie Howard, Bette Davis, Dick Foran. **1936**

PETULIA ★★★★ A story of complex relationships that centers around a prominent doctor (George C. Scott) who gets involved with a kooky young socialite (Julie Christie). A brilliant tragicomedy, one of Richard Lester's major achievements. Rated R. 105m. **DIR:** Richard Lester. **CAST:** George C. Scott, Julie Christie, Richard Chamberlain, Shirley Knight, Joseph Cotten, Arthur Hill. **1968**

PEYTON PLACE ★★★★ A landmark movie from a landmark novel with Lana Turner in her Oscar-nominated role of unwed mother Constance MacKenzie. She lives a lie so that her daughter, Alison (Diane Varsi), will never know the facts of her life. But Alison discovers quite a few facts of her own as the movie explores the morals of small-town life, couple by couple. A much better movie than most of the sexier films released in the 1990s. 160m. **DIR:** Mark Robson. **CAST:** Lana Turner, Diane Varsi, Lloyd Nolan, Betty Field, Hope Lange, Arthur Kennedy, David Nelson, Terry Moore, Lee Philips, Russ Tamblyn, Leon Ames, Mildred Dunnock, Barry Coe, Lorne Greene. **1957**

PHAR LAP ★★★★½ Absolutely chilling (and true) account of the superb Australian racehorse that chewed up the track in the 1920s and early 1930s. Tom Burlinson, stars as the stable boy who first believed in, and then followed to fame, the indefatigable Phar Lap. This film's indictment of early horse-racing practices will make you shudder. Rated PG—very intense for younger children. 106m. **DIR:** Simon Wincer. **CAST:** Tom Burlinson, Ron Leibman, Martin Vaughn. **1984**

PHILADELPHIA ★★★★ Tom Hanks's Oscar-winning portrayal of an AIDS-infected attorney battling for his rights is the main draw in this heartfelt drama. Denzel Washington is equally good as the homophobic attorney who must confront his own prejudice and ignorance after he agrees to take on the case, in which Hanks alleges that he lost his job at a prestigious law firm because of discrimination. Ron Nyswaner's screenplay is a masterpiece of character development and suspense. Rated R for profanity and mature subject matter. 119m. **DIR:** Jonathan Demme. **CAST:** Tom Hanks, Denzel Washington, Jason Robards Jr., Mary Steenburgen, Antonio Banderas, Ron Vawter, Robert Ridgely, Charles Napier, Lisa Summerour. **1993**

PHONE CALL FROM A STRANGER ★★★ Fine acting by a stellar cast lifts this soap opera above the bubbles. Gary Merrill plays confessor to various fellow passengers on an ill-fated airline flight, and brings comfort and understanding to their families when most are killed in the crash. B&W; 96m. **DIR:** Jean Negulesco. **CAST:** Shelley Winters, Gary Merrill, Michael Rennie, Keenan Wynn, Bette Davis, Craig Stevens, Hugh Beaumont. **1952**

PIANO, THE ★★★★★ Director Jane Campion has created what may be her masterpiece in this mesmerizing film about a mute-by-choice Scotswoman (played entrancingly by Oscar-winner Holly Hunter) who journeys to the untamed jungles of nineteenth-century New Zealand to marry Sam Neill, a man she's never met. Once there, she is horrified to find her beloved piano left on the beach until a neighbor (Harvey Keitel) offers to let her play it in exchange for romantic favors. Electrifying and offbeat, this is one for lovers of pure and original cinema. Rated R for nudity, simulated sex, and brief violence. 121m. **DIR:** Jane Campion. **CAST:** Holly Hunter, Harvey Keitel, Sam Neill, Anna Paquin. **1993**

PIANO FOR MRS. CIMINO, A ★★★★ Blessed with great humor and a terrific performance by Bette Davis, this made-for-television film about growing old with dignity is manipulative at times. In light of all the wonderful moments, however, the contrivances don't seem so bad. Davis plays a widow who is institutionalized for senility. The film follows her through her recovery and her rebirth as a single, self-sufficient woman. 96m. **DIR:** George Schaefer. **CAST:** Bette Davis, Keenan Wynn, Alexa Kenin, Penny Fuller, Christopher Guest, George Hearn. **1982**

PICNIC ★★★★ This is one of the best films about small-town life ever lensed, blessed with a cast that makes it even more credible. William Holden plays a drifter who, while visiting old school chum Cliff Robertson, falls for his friend's fiancée (Kim Novak). Derived from the William Inge stage play. 115m. **DIR:** Joshua Logan. **CAST:** William Holden, Kim Novak, Rosalind Russell, Susan Strasberg, Arthur O'Connell, Cliff Robertson, Nick Adams. **1956**

PILOT, THE ★★½ Cliff Robertson directed and starred in this film about an airline pilot's struggle with alcohol. Robertson's directing is not as convincing as his acting. Rated PG for profanity. 98m. **DIR:** Cliff Robertson. **CAST:** Cliff Robertson, Frank Converse, Diane Baker, Gordon MacRae, Dana Andrews, Milo O'Shea, Edward Binns. **1979**

PING PONG ★★ A young lawyer must gather the feuding members of a large family in order to administer a dead man's will. The plot is merely an excuse to guide us around the Chinese section of London. Modestly appealing. Rated PG. 100m. **DIR:** Po-chih Leong. **CAST:** Lucy Sheen, David Yip. **1988**

PINKY ★★★½ Still powerful story of a light-skinned black girl. She has been passing for white, but her status becomes known when she returns home to a small Mississippi town. Straightforward handling and presentation of what was then rather explosive material. Outstanding performances. B&W; 102m. **DIR:** Elia Kazan. **CAST:** Jeanne Crain, Ethel Barrymore, Ethel Waters, William Lundigan, Arthur Hunnicutt. **1949**

PIPE DREAMS 🦃 A wife moves to Alaska to win back her estranged man who is working on the pipeline. Rated PG for violence, profanity, and adult subject matter. 89m. **DIR:** Stephen F. Verona. **CAST:** Gladys Knight, Barry L. Hankerson, Bruce French, Wayne Tippitt. **1976**

PITFALL ★★★ A tightly directed melodrama about a married man who strays and gets involved in a murder. Dick Powell made this one as a follow-up to *Murder, My Sweet*. This is the last movie Byron Barr made under that name; he changed it to Gig Young for future films. B&W; 84m. **DIR:** André de Toth. **CAST:** Dick Powell, Jane Wyatt, Lizabeth Scott, John Litel, Gig Young, Ann Doran, Raymond Burr, Dick Wessel. **1948**

PITTSBURGH ★★★ John Wayne still gets third billing in his second movie with Marlene Dietrich and Randolph Scott (following 1942's *The Spoilers*), but he dominates the screen as Pittsburgh Markham, an ambitious coal miner who risks it all to make his dreams come true. Interestingly, Pittsburgh is more of an opportunist than a hero, and this leads to another Wayne-Scott battle royale. Somewhat slow and awkward, this is still a step up from most of Wayne's would-be Republic A-pictures from the same era. B&W; 90m. **DIR:** Lewis Seiler. **CAST:** Marlene Dietrich, Randolph Scott, John Wayne, Frank Craven, Louise Allbritton, Thomas Gomez, Shemp Howard, Ludwig Stossel, Paul Fix. **1942**

PLACE CALLED TODAY, A 🦃 Political drama laid in a city beset by racial strife. Also on video as *City in Fear*. Rated R for nudity and violence. 103m. **DIR:** Don Schain. **CAST:** J. Herbert Kerr Jr., Lana Wood, Cheri Caffaro. **1972**

PLACE IN THE SUN, A ★★★★ Elizabeth Taylor, Montgomery Clift, and Shelley Winters are caught in a tragic love triangle, based on Theodore Dreiser's *An American Tragedy*. All three artists give first-rate performances. The story of a working-class man who falls for a wealthy girl is a traditional one, yet the eroticism conveyed in the scenes between Taylor and Clift keeps this production well above the standard. B&W; 122m. **DIR:** George Stevens. **CAST:** Elizabeth Taylor, Montgomery Clift, Shelley Winters, Keefe Brasselle, Raymond Burr, Anne Revere. **1951**

PLACE OF WEEPING ★★★½ The first film about the South African struggle made by South Africans, this drama follows the battle of one woman who, with the help of a white reporter, stands against the system of apartheid. Although this film is a bit slow-moving and obviously made on a low budget, its political importance cannot be denied. Rated PG. 88m. **DIR:** Darrell Roodt. **CAST:** James Whylie, Geina Mhlope, Charles Comyn. **1986**

PLACES IN THE HEART ★★★★★ Writer-director Robert Benton's *Places in the Heart* is a great film. Based on Benton's childhood memories in Waxahachie, Texas, the film stars Sally Field, Ed Harris, Lindsay Crouse, with special performances by John Malkovich and Danny Glover. Field plays Edna Spalding, a mother of two who is suddenly widowed. Almost immediately, she is pressured by the bank to sell her home and the surrounding property. Rated PG for suggested sex, violence, and profanity. 110m. **DIR:** Robert Benton. **CAST:** Sally Field, Ed Harris, Lindsay Crouse, John Malkovich, Danny Glover. **1984**

PLAGUE, THE ★★★★ The bubonic plague strikes a city in South America. A doctor (William Hurt), with the help of a French reporter and her videographer, battles both the disease and the local government. Raul Julia brilliantly portrays a local cab driver who isn't quite what he seems. A gripping story, well acted and directed. Rated R for nudity and violence. 105m. **DIR:** Luis Puenzo. **CAST:** William Hurt, Robert Duvall, Raul Julia, Sandrine Bonnaire, Jean-Marc Barr. **1993**

PLATINUM BLONDE ★★★★ Jean Harlow's namesake film shows her self-mocking style to advantage. She plays a rich girl who marries a poor newspaper reporter and drags herself up to his level of humanity. The story is similar to *It Happened One Night* but predated it by three years. B&W; 89m. **DIR:** Frank Capra. **CAST:** Jean Harlow, Loretta Young, Robert Williams. **1931**

PLATINUM HIGH SCHOOL ★★ Overheated nonsense, good for a few laughs. Mickey Rooney as a grieving father trying to uncover the conspiracy of silence behind his son's "accidental" death at an exclusive school. B&W; 93m. **DIR:** Charles Haas. **CAST:** Mickey Rooney, Terry Moore, Dan Duryea, Yvette Mimieux, Conway Twitty. **1960**

PLATOON ★★★★★ Writer-director Oliver Stone's Oscar-winning work is not just the best film made on the subject of Vietnam; it is a great cinematic work that stands high among the finest films ever made. Charlie Sheen is the well-meaning youth who volunteers for military service to become a real person instead of, in his words, "a fake human being." Not only does every step and noise bring the threat of death, but there is an intercompany war going on between the brutal Tom Berenger and the humanistic Willem Dafoe. Rated R for profanity, gore, and violence. 120m. **DIR:** Oliver Stone. **CAST:** Tom Berenger, Willem Dafoe, Charlie Sheen, Forest Whitaker, Francesco Quinn, John C. McGinley, Richard Edson. **1986**

PLAYBOYS, THE ★★★★ A sense of foreboding runs through this period piece, based on coscreenwriter Shane Connaughton's childhood reminiscences of traveling troupes who performed at Irish villages in the 1950s. Robin Wright is splendid as the freethinking single mother who comes into conflict with the locals—until she's rescued from her situation by a flamboyant actor (Aidan Quinn). Rated PG-13 for profanity and violence. 113m. **DIR:** Gillies Mackinnon. **CAST:** Albert Finney, Aidan Quinn, Robin Wright, Milo O'Shea, Alan Devlin. **1992**

PLAYERS 🦃 Ali MacGraw is the bored mistress of Maximilian Schell; she falls for tennis pro Dean Paul Martin. Rated PG—sexual situations. 120m. **DIR:** Anthony Harvey. **CAST:** Ali MacGraw, Dean Paul Martin, Maximilian Schell. **1979**

PLAYING FOR TIME ★★★★ This outstanding TV drama won numerous Emmy Awards. It's the true story of Fania Fenelon (Vanessa Redgrave) and a group of women prisoners in Auschwitz who survived by forming a small orchestra and performing for the Nazi officers. 148m. **DIR:** Daniel Mann. **CAST:** Vanessa Redgrave, Jane Alexander, Maud Adams, Viveca Lindfors, Shirley Knight. **1980**

PLEASURE PALACE ★★ No, this is not a porno flick—the characters in this made-for-TV movie are more like old-fashioned melodrama icons. Hope Lange plays an honest widowed casino owner (yea!) who is afraid she will loose her casino to an influential oil baron (boo!). Despite the lack of subtlety in characters, some of the gambling scenes have real tension in them. Not rated, but the equivalent of a PG for violence. 92m. **DIR:** Walter Grauman. **CAST:** Omar Sharif, Victoria Principal, Walter Grauman, J. D. Cannon, Gerald S. O'Loughlin, José Ferrer, Hope Lange. **1980**

PLENTY ★★★★ In this difficult but rewarding film, Meryl Streep is superb as a former member of the French Resistance who finds life in her native England increasingly maddening during the postwar reconstruction period. Rated R for profanity, suggested sex, and violence. 120m. **DIR:** Fred Schepisi. **CAST:** Meryl Streep, Charles Dance, Sam Neill, Tracey Ullman, John Gielgud, Sting, Ian McKellen. **1985**

PLOUGHMAN'S LUNCH, THE ★★ *The Ploughman's Lunch* is a morality piece about opportunism and exploitation portrayed through the world of journalism. The problem is that almost everyone in the film is a weasel. The point is to call attention to this fact, but it doesn't make for very enjoyable movie watching. Rated R. 107m. **DIR:** Richard Eyre. **CAST:** Jonathan Pryce, Tim Curry, Rosemary Harris, Frank Finlay, Charlie Dore. **1984**

POETIC JUSTICE ★★ Director John Singleton's follow-up to *Boyz N the Hood* is essentially a self-indulgent mess about the offbeat love affair between a self-styled poet (Janet Jackson, in her film debut) and a troubled young man (Tupac Shakur). Jackson's inexpressive performance is further hampered by her inappropriate, overdubbed readings of Maya Angelou's poetry. Overall, *Poetic Justice* plays like the first draft of a potentially worthwhile screenplay. Rated R for profanity, simulated sex, and violence. 108m. **DIR:** John Singleton. **CAST:** Janet Jackson, Tupac Shakur, Regina King, Joe Torry, Tyra Ferrell, Maya Angelou. **1993**

POINT BLANK ★★★★ This brutal crime-drama is one of the finest films of its type. Gangster Lee Marvin is double-crossed by his wife and crime partner, who shoot him and leave him for dead on Alcatraz Island—only to have him turn up a few years later, bent on revenge. Entire cast pulls out all of the stops; it's one of Lee Marvin's strongest performances. Rated R. 92m. **DIR:** John Boorman. **CAST:** Lee Marvin, Angie Dickinson, Lloyd Bochner, Keenan Wynn, Carroll O'Connor, John Vernon. **1967**

POINTSMAN, THE ★★★ A lady from Holland mysteriously disembarks from a train in the Scottish Highlands. The only person at the depot is the point man who resides at this isolated outpost. This most unusual film requires patience, but it has a strangely compelling attraction. The interesting characters, the fine photography, and the sensual development between the two leads keep you rapt until the end. Rated R for nudity and adult situations. 95m. **DIR:** Jos Stelling. **CAST:** Stephane Excoffier. **1988**

POISON ★★ Disturbing, at times disgusting, trilogy of stories spliced together jumping back and forth from one horror to the next. In one, a seven-year-old murders his father; another features a mad scientist whose experiment transforms him into a leper; and finally there's a cruel glimpse into a sadistic homosexual relationship behind prison bars. Unrated, contains nudity, violence, and profanity. 85m. **DIR:** Todd Haynes. **CAST:** Edith Meeks, Larry Maxwell, Susan Norman, Scott Renderer, James Lyons. **1990**

POOR LITTLE RICH GIRL: THE BARBARA HUTTON STORY 🦃 Farrah Fawcett plays the title role in this shallow but well-dressed biography of the unhappy American heiress. Edited down from a 250-minute TV miniseries, this is extremely choppy and superficial. Not rated, but contains profanity. 98m. **DIR:** Charles Jarrott. **CAST:** Farrah Fawcett, Bruce Davison, Kevin McCarthy, James Read. **1987**

POOR WHITE TRASH 🦃 Yankee architect clashes with the business (and moral) ethics of Louisiana developers. Unrated, but with nudity and violence. B&W; 90m. **DIR:** Harold Daniels. **CAST:** Peter Graves, Lita Milan, Douglas Fowley, Timothy Carey, Jonathan Haze. **1961**

POOR WHITE TRASH II 🦃 Not really a sequel to *Poor White Trash,* just another lousy thriller about an insane Vietnam veteran who starts slaughtering people. Rated R for violence. 83m. **DIR:** S. F. Brownrigg. **CAST:** Gene Ross. **1976**

POPE JOHN PAUL II ★★★★ Albert Finney is superb as the charismatic pontiff in this enactment of the Polish priest's adult life—from battles with Nazis and communism to his ascension to the throne of the Catholic church. Made for TV but with big-screen production values, the film represented Finney's American TV debut. 150m. **DIR:** Herbert Wise. **CAST:** Albert Finney, Nigel Hawthorne, Brian Cox, John McEnery, Ronald Pickup. **1984**

POPE OF GREENWICH VILLAGE, THE ★★★½ This watchable film focuses on the hard-edged misadventures of two Italian cousins, Paulie (Eric Roberts) and Charlie (Mickey Rourke). Paulie is a not-so-bright dreamer who's obviously headed for trouble, and Charlie, who is smart enough to know better, always seems to get caught up in the middle of his cousin's half-baked and dangerous rip-off schemes. Rated R for profanity and violence. 120m. **DIR:** Stuart Rosenberg. **CAST:** Eric Roberts, Mickey Rourke, Daryl Hannah, Geraldine Page. **1984**

PORK CHOP HILL ★★★★ This no-win look at the Korean conflict features tough yet vulnerable Gregory Peck as the man forced to hold an insignificant mound of earth against overwhelming hordes of communist Chinese. A great cast and master director Lewis Milestone elevate this story to epic status. B&W; 97m. **DIR:** Lewis Milestone. **CAST:** Gregory Peck, Harry Guardino, Rip Torn, Woody Strode, George Peppard, Bob Steele, James Edwards. **1959**

PORT OF NEW YORK ★★½ A female narcotics smuggler decides to play ball with the police and deliver her former colleagues to them. Yul Brynner is the head smuggler who wants to stop the squealing—fast. Gritty and engrossing. B&W; 82m. **DIR:** Laslo Benedek. **CAST:** Scott Brady, Richard Rober, K. T. Stevens, Yul Brynner. **1949**

PORTFOLIO 🦃 This has no plot—just a series of interviews endeavoring to make modeling look appealing. Rated R for profanity. 83m. **DIR:** Robert Guralnick. **CAST:** Carol Alt, Julie Wolfe, Patty Owen, Kelly Emberg, Paulina Porizkova. **1983**

PORTNOY'S COMPLAINT ★★ Amazing that anyone had the nerve to attempt to translate Philip Roth's infamous novel to the screen. The neurotic Jewish boy, who has a strange relationship with his mother and an obsession with sex, should be neutered. It's worth viewing only as a curiosity. Rated R for profanity and sex. 101m. **DIR:** Ernest Lehman. **CAST:** Richard Benjamin, Karen Black, Lee Grant, Jack Somack, Jeannie Berlin, Jill Clayburgh. **1972**

PORTRAIT, THE ★★★ Sentimental story focuses on the twilight years of an elderly couple, while their daughter attempts to finish a portrait of the two. It's nice to see two great stars at work. Considering the wealth of talent involved, this film is a disappointment. 108m. **DIR:** Arthur Penn. **CAST:** Gregory Peck, Lauren Bacall, Cecilia Peck, Paul McCrane. **1993**

PORTRAIT OF A SHOWGIRL ★★ This made-for-television film is another attempt to chronicle the life of Las Vegas show girls. They meet men, they lose men. They lose jobs, they get jobs. 100m. **DIR:** Steven H. Stern. **CAST:** Lesley Ann Warren, Rita Moreno, Dianne Kay, Tony Curtis, Barry Primus, Howard Morris. **1982**

PORTRAIT OF A STRIPPER ★★ A dancer is forced to strip to support her fatherless son, causing the authorities to label her an unfit mother. Originally made for TV, timid presentation will, no doubt, disappoint many drooling video renters. 100m. **DIR:** John A. Alonzo. **CAST:** Lesley Ann Warren, Edward Herrmann, Vic Tayback, Sheree North. **1979**

PORTRAIT OF JENNIE ★★★★ A talented, unsung artist achieves fame and success after meeting a mysterious young girl who just might not be real in this charming, somewhat supernatural love story based on Robert Nathan's novel. A first-rate cast and high production values. B&W; 86m. **DIR:** William Dieterle. **CAST:** Jennifer Jones, Joseph Cotten, Ethel Barrymore, Lillian Gish, David Wayne, Henry Hull. **1948**

PORTRAIT OF THE ARTIST AS A YOUNG MAN, A ★★★ Fair adaptation of James Joyce's autobiographical novel about the coming-of-age of a young man while attending a Dublin university. The character intensely questions the morals of his day, which include the Catholic Church and the tyranny of family and state. Excellent ensemble acting by a superb cast. Not rated. 93m. **DIR:** Joseph Strick. **CAST:** Bosco Hogan, T. P. McKenna, John Gielgud. **1977**

POSSESSED (1931) ★★★½ Wonderful melodrama featuring Joan Crawford as a beautiful gold digger who becomes Clark Gable's mistress. When he has a chance to run for governor, she must choose between her luxurious life-style and his chance for a political career. Don't confuse this with Crawford's efforts as a schizophrenic in the 1947 *Possessed*. This gem was released to celebrate MGM's Diamond Jubilee. B&W; 77m. **DIR:** Clarence Brown. **CAST:** Joan Crawford, Clark Gable, Wallace Ford. **1931**

POSSESSED (1947) ★★★ A cold and clinical account of loveless marriage, mysterious suicide, frustrated love for a scoundrel, murder, and schizophrenia. The much-maligned Joan Crawford heads a fine, mature cast and gives one of her finer performances as a mentally troubled nurse. Extremely watchable. The opening scene is a real grabber. B&W; 108m. **DIR:** Curtis Bernhardt. **CAST:** Van Heflin, Joan Crawford, Raymond Massey, Geraldine Brooks, Stanley Ridges. **1947**

POT O' GOLD ★★ An amusing time passer based on a one-time popular radio show. The plot concerns an enthusiastic young man's effort to get Horace Heidt and his orchestra on his uncle's radio program. Gee! B&W; 86m. **DIR:** George Marshall. **CAST:** James Stewart, Paulette Goddard, Horace Heidt, Charles Winninger, Mary Gordon. **1941**

POWER (1986) ★★★★ Sidney Lumet, who directed *Network*, once again takes viewers into the bowels of an American institution with this hard-edged study of the manipulation of the political process by market research and advertising. Richard Gere gives one of his better performances as a ruthless hustler who is given pause when the one politician he believes in (E. G. Marshall) becomes a pawn in the political power trade. Rated R for profanity, violence, and suggested sex. 111m. **DIR:** Sidney Lumet. **CAST:** Richard Gere, Julie Christie, Gene Hackman, Kate Capshaw, Denzel Washington, E. G. Marshall, Beatrice Straight. **1986**

POWER OF ONE, THE ★★★★½ Remarkably effective epic about a young man's fight against prejudice in South Africa. Set in the Thirties and Forties, *The Power of One* details the adventures of an English boy who survives being tormented by youthful Afrikaners with the help of two mentors, one white (Armin Mueller-Stahl) and one black (Morgan Freeman). Director John Avildsen uses the same combination of sports excitement and characterization that made *Rocky* so satisfying, and the result is stunning. Rated PG-13 for violence and profanity. 127m. **DIR:** John G. Avildsen. **CAST:** Stephen Dorff, Armin Mueller-Stahl, Morgan Freeman, John Gielgud, Fay Masterson, Daniel Craig, Dominic Walker, Alois Moyo, Ian Roberts, Marius Weyers. **1992**

POWER, PASSION, AND MURDER ★★ Hollywood of the late Thirties is the setting for a rising star's tragic affair with a married man. This telefilm is marred by daydreams of wanna-bes and has-beens. 104m. **DIR:** Paul Bogart. **CAST:** Michelle Pfeiffer, Brian Kerwin, Hector Elizondo. **1987**

PRAY TV (1982) ★★½ Interesting TV movie about a young minister (John Ritter) who comes under the spell of a charismatic televangelist (Ned Beatty). Beatty is superb, but Ritter's performance is lackluster. 96m. **DIR:** Robert Markowitz. **CAST:** John Ritter, Ned Beatty, Richard Kiley, Madolyn Smith, Louise Latham. **1982**

PREPPIE MURDER, THE ★★★ William Baldwin is convincingly creepy as convicted killer Robert Chambers in this chilling made-for-TV crime-drama. After he strangles his girlfriend, played by Lara Flynn Boyle, in Central Park, his perfect life begins to unravel, and a portrait of a monster begins to surface. Danny Aiello is the detective who pieces it all together. Not rated, but contains adult situations. 94m. **DIR:** John Herzfeld. **CAST:** Danny Aiello, William Baldwin, Lara Flynn Boyle, Joanna Kerns. **1990**

PRESENTING LILY MARS ★½ Stagestruck girl plugs her way to stardom. High points are when Judy Garland sings and The Tommy Dorsey and Bob Crosby bands. B&W; 104m. **DIR:** Norman Taurog. **CAST:** Judy Garland, Van Heflin, Richard Carlson, Marta Eggerth, Connie Gilchrist, Fay Bainter, Spring Byington, Marilyn Maxwell, Tommy Dorsey, Bob Crosby. **1943**

PRESSURE POINT ★★★½ During World War II, a black psychiatrist is assigned to evaluate a bigoted prisoner, jailed for sedition as a member of the American Nazi party. Interesting drama, fine performances, with a special nod to the underrated Bobby Darin. B&W; 91m. **DIR:** Hubert Cornfield. **CAST:** Sidney Poitier, Bobby Darin, Peter Falk, Carl Benton Reid. **1962**

PRESUMED GUILTY 🦃 A James Dean look-alike is paroled from prison for a crime he didn't commit only to return home to a number of disappointments. Not rated; the film includes violence and profanity. 91m. **DIR:** Lawrence Simone. **CAST:** Jack Vogel. **1991**

PRETTY BABY ★★★★ Forcing the audience to reexamine accepted concepts is just one of the effects of this brilliant work by Louis Malle. He is fascinated by Violet (Brooke Shields), the girl we see growing up in a whorehouse in New Orleans. For Violet, all that goes on around her is normal. Rated R. 109m. **DIR:** Louis Malle. **CAST:** Brooke Shields, Susan Sarandon, Keith Carradine, Frances Faye, Antonio Fargas. **1978**

PRETTY IN PINK ★★★★ Molly Ringwald is wonderful as a young woman "from the poor side of town" who falls in love with rich kid Andrew McCarthy. The feeling is mutual, but their peers do everything they can to keep them apart. It is that rare teenage-oriented release that can be enjoyed by adults. Rated PG-13 for profanity and violence. 96m. **DIR:** Howard Deutch. **CAST:** Molly Ringwald, Harry Dean Stanton, Jon Cryer, Andrew McCarthy, Annie Potts, James Spader. **1986**

PRETTY POISON ★★★★ Anthony Perkins gives one of his finest performances in this bizarre drama about a troubled arsonist who enlists a sexy high school girl (Tuesday Weld) in a wild scheme. This surreal black comedy is sparked by Weld's vivid performance and a highly original screenplay by Lorenzo Semple Jr. Not rated. 89m. **DIR:** Noel Black. **CAST:** Anthony Perkins, Tuesday Weld, Beverly Garland. **1968**

PRICELESS BEAUTY 🦃 Italian-style *I Dream of Jeannie*. Rated R for nudity and profanity. 94m. **DIR:** Charles Finch. **CAST:** Christopher Lambert, Diane Lane, Francesco Quinn, J. C. Quinn. **1989**

PRICK UP YOUR EARS ★★★★ The poignant love story at the center of *Prick Up Your Ears* will be touching to some and shocking to others. But this film about the rise to prominence of British playwright Joe Orton (Gary Oldman) and his relationship with Kenneth Halliwell (Alfred Molina) never fails to fascinate. Rated R for profanity and scenes of graphic sex. 110m. **DIR:** Stephen Frears. **CAST:** Gary Oldman, Alfred Molina, Vanessa Redgrave, Julie Walters, Wallace Shawn. **1987**

PRIDE AND PREJUDICE (1940) ★★★★ This film is an accurate adaptation of Jane Austen's famous novel. The story takes place in nineteenth-century England with five sisters looking for suitable husbands. B&W; 116m. **DIR:** Robert Z. Leonard. **CAST:** Greer Garson, Laurence Olivier, Maureen O'Sullivan, Marsha Hunt. **1940**

PRIDE AND PREJUDICE (1985) ★★★★ Marvelous BBC adaptation of Jane Austen's classic Victorian romance. Comic moments abound as a silly mother desperately tries to marry off her five daughters. Period costumes and English countryside and manor houses are authentic. 226m. **DIR:** Cyril Coke. **CAST:** Elizabeth Garvie, David Rintoul, Moray Watson, Priscilla Morgan. **1985**

PRIDE AND THE PASSION, THE ★★ Here is a supreme example of how miscasting can ruin a movie's potential. Frank Sinatra is horrible as the Spanish peasant leader of a guerrilla army during the Napoleonic era. He secures the services of a gigantic cannon and a British navy officer (Cary Grant) to fire it. Sophia Loren is also in the cast, primarily as window dressing. 132m. **DIR:** Stanley Kramer. **CAST:** Frank Sinatra, Cary Grant, Sophia Loren, Theodore Bikel. **1957**

PRIDE OF JESSE HALLMAN, THE ★★ This is a well-meant but sluggish account of the quest for literacy by the title character, who is played by country singer–songwriter Johnny Cash. Made for television. 99m. **DIR:**

Gary Nelson. **CAST:** Johnny Cash, Brenda Vaccaro, Eli Wallach, Ben Marley, Guy Boyd. **1981**

PRIDE OF ST. LOUIS, THE ★★½ The ups and downs of popular St. Louis Cardinals baseball player Dizzy Dean are affectionately chronicled in this warm and humorous sandlot-to-big-league bio. Dan Dailey is amusing and believable as the word-fracturing Dean. B&W; 92m. **DIR:** Harmon Jones. **CAST:** Dan Dailey, Joanne Dru, Richard Crenna, Hugh Sanders. **1952**

PRIDE OF THE BOWERY ★★ This offshoot of the famous Dead End Kids features Leo Gorcey and Bobby Jordan, two of the original "kids," along with Gorcey's brother David, who continued on and off for the rest of the series. Not quite as bad as their later efforts, this film still needs a dyed-in-the-wool East Side Kids fan to really enjoy it. B&W; 63m. **DIR:** Joseph H. Lewis. **CAST:** Leo Gorcey, Bobby Jordan, Donald Haines, Carleton Young, Kenneth Howell, David Gorcey. **1940**

PRIDE OF THE YANKEES, THE ★★★★★ Gary Cooper gives one of his finest performances as he captures the courageous spirit of New York Yankee immortal Lou Gehrig. This 1942 drama is a perfect blend of an exciting sports biography and a touching melodrama as we follow Gehrig's baseball career from its earliest playground beginnings until an illness strikes him down in his prime. Teresa Wright is just right in the difficult role of his loving wife. B&W; 127m. **DIR:** Sam Wood. **CAST:** Gary Cooper, Teresa Wright, Babe Ruth, Walter Brennan, Dan Duryea, Ludwig Stossel. **1942**

PRIEST OF LOVE ★★★★ The culmination of a decade-long quest to film the life of D. H. Lawrence (Ian McKellen) by producer-director Christopher Miles, *Priest of Love* is absorbing, brilliantly acted, and stunningly photographed. It deals with Lawrence's exile from his native England, where his books were generally reviled; his relationship with wife Frieda (Janet Suzman); and their final time together in Italy, where Lawrence wrote *Lady Chatterley's Lover*. Rated R for profanity and sex. 125m. **DIR:** Christopher Miles. **CAST:** Ian McKellen, Janet Suzman, Ava Gardner, John Gielgud, Penelope Keith, Jorge Rivero, Maurizio Merli. **1981**

PRIMARY MOTIVE ★★★ Judd Nelson comes on strong as a young press secretary who uncovers some dirt about his candidate's opposition. Business as usual in the political arena: double crosses, lies, intrigue. Rated R for language. 98m. **DIR:** Daniel Adams. **CAST:** Judd Nelson, Richard Jordan, Sally Kirkland, Justine Bateman, John Savage. **1992**

PRIMARY TARGET ★★ Vietnam 1977: a wealthy American's wife is kidnapped. Anyone watching for inconsistencies will have a field day, but writer-director Clark Henderson plays it soft with likable heroes and equally nefarious villains. Rated R for violence. 85m. **DIR:** Clark Henderson. **CAST:** John Calvin, Miki Kim, Joey Aresco. **1990**

PRIME SUSPECT 🦃 A young girl is murdered. A decent, honest, hardworking citizen becomes the prime suspect in the case. 100m. **DIR:** Noel Black. **CAST:** Mike Farrell, Teri Garr, Veronica Cartwright, Lane Smith, Barry Corbin, James Sloyan, Charles Aidman. **1982**

PRIMROSE PATH ★★★★ In one of her best dramatic roles, Ginger Rogers stars as a young woman from the wrong side of the tracks who cons Joel McCrea into marriage. A fine film with a literate script, deftly crafted characters, fine production values—and heart. B&W; 93m. **DIR:** Gregory La Cava. **CAST:** Ginger Rogers, Joel McCrea, Marjorie Rambeau, Henry Travers. **1940**

PRINCE OF BEL AIR ★★★ Ever-watchable Mark Harmon plays a pool cleaner who has his way with countless wealthy and beautiful women. Silly TV movie—but Kirstie Alley shines as Harmon's true love. 95m. **DIR:** Charles Braverman. **CAST:** Mark Harmon, Kirstie Alley, Robert Vaughn. **1985**

PRINCE OF THE CITY ★★★★ Director Sidney Lumet has created one of the screen's most intense character studies out of the true story of a corrupt New York narcotics cop, played wonderfully by Treat Williams. In becoming a government agent, the cop destroys the lives of his closest friends. Rated R because of violence and strong profanity. 167m. **DIR:** Sidney Lumet. **CAST:** Treat Williams, Jerry Orbach, Richard Foronjy. **1981**

PRINCE OF TIDES, THE ★★★½ Strong themes are explored in Barbra Streisand's second directorial effort, an adaptation of Pat Conroy's novel that is burdened with an attenuated ending. Yet this is easy to forgive, considering the superb performances. Streisand plays a psychiatrist attempting to delve into the deep psychological problems of the suicidal Melinda Dillon with the help of brother Nick Nolte. Rated R for profanity, violence, and simulated sex. 132m. **DIR:** Barbra Streisand. **CAST:** Barbra Streisand, Nick Nolte, Blythe Danner, Kate Nelligan, Jeroen Krabbé, Melinda Dillon, Jason Gould, George Carlin, Brad Sullivan. **1991**

PRINCES IN EXILE ★★★ A tough subject, teenagers with life-threatening diseases, is handled adroitly by a cast of unknowns and director Giles Walker. The plot has vestiges of teen movies but the film never slips over the edge and loses its humor or intelligence. Rated PG-13. 103m. **DIR:** Giles Walker. **CAST:** Zachary Ansley, Nicholas Shields, Stacy Mistysyn. **1990**

PRINCESS DAISY ★★½ If you enjoy sleaze and glitter, then you should be tickled by this made-for-TV rendition of Judith

Krantz's novel of a poor little rich girl. Stacy Keach and Claudia Cardinale give the best performances. 188m. **DIR:** Waris Hussein. **CAST:** Lindsay Wagner, Paul Michael Glaser, Robert Urich, Claudia Cardinale, Ringo Starr, Merete Van Kamp, Sada Thompson, Stacy Keach, Barbara Bach, Rupert Everett. **1983**

PRINCIPAL, THE ★★ Unrealistic treatment and poor writing sabotage this story of a renegade teacher (James Belushi) who, as punishment, is made principal of a high school where all the hardship cases from the other schools are relegated. Belushi doesn't do justice to his role, but Louis Gossett Jr. is good as the school's security chief. Rated R for language and violence. 110m. **DIR:** Christopher Cain. **CAST:** James Belushi, Lou Gossett Jr., Rae Dawn Chong, Michael Wright, Esai Morales. **1987**

PRISON FOR CHILDREN ★★★ Depressing, fact-based story of young offenders beaten down by a brutal system that tosses abandonded kids in with delinquents. This made-for-TV story is told with sensitivity but is on the sappy side. Especially touching is Raphael Sbarge as a countrified teen warehoused in a vicious juvenile prison. Not rated, but contains adult themes. 96m. **DIR:** Larry Peerce. **CAST:** Raphael Sbarge, Kenny Ransom, John Ritter, Betty Thomas, Jonathan Chapin, Josh Brolin. **1986**

PRISON STORIES: WOMEN ON THE INSIDE ★★★ This three-segment made-for-cable anthology directed by and starring women attempts to draw attention to problems facing prison mothers. Because of its TV production values, a lot of the grit is missing. As a result, real-life drama has been downplayed as the main characters turn into disposable stereotypes. Partial nudity, profanity, and violence. 94m. **DIR:** Penelope Spheeris, Donna Deitch, Joan Micklin Silver. **CAST:** Lolita Davidovich, Rachel Ticotin, Rae Dawn Chong, Annabella Sciorra. **1991**

PRISONER, THE ★★★★ Gripping political drama with outstanding performances by Alec Guinness and Jack Hawkins. Guinness portrays a cardinal being held as a political prisoner in a communist country. Jack Hawkins is the head of the secret police in charge of breaking down and brainwashing Guinness. Not rated. 91m. **DIR:** Peter Glenville. **CAST:** Alec Guinness, Jack Hawkins. **1955**

PRISONER OF HONOR ★★★★ Scripter Ron Hutchinson's fascinating account of 1895's Dreyfus Affair, which became a national scandal and an international embarrassment. Richard Dreyfuss, superbly proud and defiant as Colonel George Picquart, grows convinced that Captain Alfred Dreyfus was convicted of espionage simply because of being a Jew; the resulting investigation makes a public mockery of French justice. Compelling made-for-cable drama. 88m. **DIR:** Ken Russell. **CAST:** Richard Dreyfuss, Oliver Reed, Peter Firth, Jeremy Kemp, Brian Blessed, Lindsay Anderson. **1991**

PRISONERS OF THE SUN ★★★ This Australian drama offers a complex look at justice in the West versus the East, especially when it's clouded by political corruption. Bryan Brown plays an Australian military lawyer pressing war-crimes charges against Japanese officers and soldiers who killed hundreds of Australian POWs in a death camp during World War II. Rated R. 109m. **DIR:** Stephen Wallace. **CAST:** Bryan Brown, George Takei, Terry O'Quinn. **1991**

PRIVATE AFFAIRS OF BEL AMI, THE ★★★★ Nobody ever played a cad better than George Sanders, and this is his crowning achievement. He is the antihero in Guy de Maupassant's famous story of a charmer who loves the ladies and leaves them until it finally catches up with him. The ending is pure Hollywood. UCLA's Film Archive restored the original print for the video release. B&W; 112m. **DIR:** Albert Lewin. **CAST:** George Sanders, Angela Lansbury, Frances Dee, Ann Dvorak, Albert Basserman, John Carradine, Hugo Haas, Warren William, Marie Wilson. **1947**

PRIVATE HELL 36 ★★½ Tight, well-constructed story of two cops who skim money from a haul they have intercepted and have trouble living with it, is nicely acted by veteran performers. Ida Lupino, equally adept on either side of the camera, cowrote and produced this grim drama. B&W; 81m. **DIR:** Don Siegel. **CAST:** Ida Lupino, Steve Cochran, Howard Duff, Dean Jagger, Dorothy Malone. **1954**

PRIVATE LIFE OF DON JUAN, THE ★★ A vehicle for the aging Douglas Fairbanks, his last picture is set in seventeenth-century Spain. A famous lover (Fairbanks) fakes a suicide in order to make a comeback in disguise. It is somewhat tragic that the first great hero of the screen should have ended up in this disappointment. B&W; 90m. **DIR:** Alexander Korda. **CAST:** Douglas Fairbanks Sr., Merle Oberon, Binnie Barnes, Benita Hume, Joan Gardner, Melville Cooper. **1934**

PRIVATE LIFE OF HENRY THE EIGHTH, THE ★★★★ This well-paced historical chronicle of England's bluebeard monarch and his six wives was to be Britain's first successful entry into worldwide moviemaking. Charles Laughton's tour de force as the notorious king remains one of filmdom's greatest portrayals. Laughton's real-life spouse, Elsa Lanchester, plays Anne, the fourth wife. She manages to keep her head off the chopping block by humoring the volatile king during a memorable game of cards. B&W; 87m. **DIR:** Alexander Korda. **CAST:** Charles Laughton, Robert Donat, Merle Oberon, Elsa Lanchester, Binnie Barnes. **1933**

PRIVATE LIVES OF ELIZABETH AND ESSEX, THE ★★★½ Bette Davis is Queen Elizabeth and Errol Flynn is her dashing suitor in this enjoyable costume drama. 106m. **DIR:** Michael Curtiz. **CAST:** Bette Davis, Errol Flynn, Olivia de Havilland, Vincent Price, Donald Crisp, Nanette Fabray, Henry Daniell, Alan Hale Sr., Robert Warwick, Henry Stephenson. **1939**

PRIVATE MATTER, A ★★★★★ The abortion movement's roots are traced in scripter William Nicholson's unflinchingly forceful (and true) account. Sissy Spacek is compelling as Sherri Finkbine, who achieved prominence in the early Sixties as a host of the children's television show *Romper Room*. Although she and husband are quite eager for the arrival of their next child, Sherri learns that her use of thalidomide-based tranquilizers has almost certainly harmed her fetus. Attempts to handle the situation go awry when a strong sense of moral outrage prompts her to spread the news, in the hopes of warning other women. Made for cable. 89m. **DIR:** Joan Micklin Silver. **CAST:** Sissy Spacek, Aidan Quinn, Estelle Parsons, Sheila McCarthy. **1992**

PRIVATE WAR ★★ Former war hero goes to Vietnam as a DI for an elite military unit. Members of his squad meet with mysterious accidents before one member figures out the psychotic DI is responsible. Familiar territory. Rated R for violence and profanity. 95m. **DIR:** Frank DePalma. **CAST:** Martin Hewitt, Joe Dallesandro, Kimberly Beck. **1988**

PRIZE, THE ★★★★ A fast-moving thriller based on Irving Wallace's popular novel. Paul Newman plays a Nobel Prize winner in Stockholm who gets involved in espionage, a passionate affair, and politics. 136m. **DIR:** Mark Robson. **CAST:** Paul Newman, Edward G. Robinson, Elke Sommer, Anna Lee, Kevin McCarthy, Micheline Presle, Don Dubbins, Sergio Fantoni, Leo G. Carroll, Diane Baker, Virginia Christine, John Qualen. **1963**

PRIZE PULITZER, THE: THE ROXANNE PULITZER STORY ★★★ Uneven, but surprisingly sturdy telling of the divorce scandal of the 1980s. Made-for-TV bio-shocker. 95m. **DIR:** Richard A. Colla. **CAST:** Perry King, Courteney Cox, Chynna Phillips. **1989**

PRODIGAL, THE ★★★ Sexy stuff with Lana as a high priestess in biblical days who seduces Edmund Purdom and makes him wish he never left home. Somewhat silly and contrived but highly enjoyable thanks to a good cast. 114m. **DIR:** Richard Thorpe. **CAST:** Lana Turner, Edmund Purdom, Taina Elg, Neville Brand, Louis Calhern, Joseph Wiseman, Cecil Kellaway, James Mitchell. **1955**

PROGRAM, THE ★★★★ Director David S. Ward's best-written work since *The Sting*. This ensemble piece features Craig Sheffer as the troubled quarterback for Eastern State University who believes he has to engage in life-threatening stunts to cement his position of leadership. About the enormous pressure on participants in college sports, *The Program* has many richly drawn characters and situations. Rated R for profanity, violence, and drug use. 114m. **DIR:** David S. Ward. **CAST:** James Caan, Halle Berry, Omar Epps, Craig Sheffer, Kristy Swanson, Abraham Benrubi, Duane Davis. **1993**

PROMISE, THE ★★½ After a car accident, Kathleen Quinlan accepts money from her fiancé's mother to have extensive reconstructive surgery and never see him again. Destiny and true love override all obstacles in this obvious romance. Rated PG for mild profanity. 97m. **DIR:** Gilbert Cates. **CAST:** Kathleen Quinlan, Stephen Collins, Beatrice Straight. **1978**

PROMISED A MIRACLE ★★★ Although greater depth should have been brought to this TV movie, it remains a thought-provoking account of two Christian parents seeking a miracle from God—the faith healing of their diabetic son. Based on the book *We Let Our Son Die* by Larry Parker. 94m. **DIR:** Stephen Gyllenhaal. **CAST:** Rosanna Arquette, Judge Reinhold, Maria O'Brien. **1988**

PROMISED LAND ★★ *Promised Land* shows a segment from the lives of four young people, three of whom have just graduated from high school. And the film is all exposition and not much insight. Kiefer Sutherland is convincing as an insecure, misguided wanderer. Rated R for profanity. 101m. **DIR:** Michael Hoffman. **CAST:** Kiefer Sutherland, Meg Ryan, Jason Gedrick. **1988**

PROMISES IN THE DARK ★★★½ This film is about a young girl dying of cancer. Marsha Mason costars as her sympathetic doctor. Good movie, but very depressing! Rated PG. 115m. **DIR:** Jerome Hellman. **CAST:** Marsha Mason, Ned Beatty, Susan Clark, Michael Brandon, Kathleen Beller, Paul Clemens, Donald Moffat. **1979**

PROOF ★★★★ Blind since birth, Martin is convinced that his mother hated him for being blind and deceived him with her descriptions of what she saw. Now Martin hopes that he may trust someone to describe to him the countless photographs he takes—thereby giving him the proof of a long-dead mother's love. Add a psychosexual love triangle, intriguing cinematography, and original music, and we have the film that swept the 1991 Australian Film Institute Awards. Rated R for profanity and nudity. 90m. **DIR:** Jocelyn Moorhouse. **CAST:** Hugo Weaving, Genevieve Picot, Russell Crowe. **1991**

PROSPERO'S BOOKS ★★★ In this dense, ornate, relentlessly lush version of *The Tempest*, director Peter Greenaway shocks with graphic exactness, yet charms with lavish sets and Renaissance costumes designed by someone seemingly on LSD. Sir John Gielgud speaking Shakespeare's magnificent lines makes the film occasionally soar. Rated R for nudity and violence. 126m. **DIR:** Peter Greenaway. **CAST:** John Gielgud, Michael Clark, Isabelle Pasco, Michel Blanc. **1991**

PROVIDENCE ★★★★ Director Alain Resnais's first English-language film includes the great cast of Dirk Bogarde, John Gielgud, Ellen Burstyn, and David Warner. An old and dying writer (Gielgud) completing his last novel invites his family up for the weekend. The fast cutting between the writer's imagined thoughts and real life makes this film difficult to follow for some. Rated R. 104m. **DIR:** Alain Resnais. **CAST:** Dirk Bogarde, John Gielgud, Ellen Burstyn, David Warner, Elaine Stritch. **1977**

PSYCH-OUT ★★½ The psychedelic Sixties couldn't have been more outrageous. A pretty, deaf runaway ends up in Haight-Ashbury while searching for her missing brother. She encounters a rock musician (Jack Nicholson) with whom she falls in love. Too self-important to be taken seriously. Rated PG. 82m. **DIR:** Richard Rush. **CAST:** Susan Strasberg, Jack Nicholson, Adam Roarke, Dean Stockwell, Bruce Dern. **1968**

PT 109 ★★½ Cliff Robertson is John F. Kennedy in this monument to the former president's war adventures on a World War II PT boat. Robertson is credible, but the story is only interesting because of the famous people and events it represents. 140m. **DIR:** Leslie Martinson. **CAST:** Cliff Robertson, Robert Culp, Ty Hardin, James Gregory, Robert Blake, Grant Williams. **1963**

PUBERTY BLUES ★★★½ This film takes a frank look at the coming-of-age of two teenagers as they grow up on the beaches of Australia. The two girls become temporary victims of peer group pressure that involves drugs, alcohol, and sex. Unlike many other teenage films, *Puberty Blues* offers interesting insights into the rite of passage as seen from a female point of view. Rated R. 86m. **DIR:** Bruce Beresford. **CAST:** Nell Schofield, Jad Capelja. **1981**

PUDD'NHEAD WILSON ★★★½ Mark Twain's sometimes humorous but always entertaining tale of deceit is faithfully re-created in this American Playhouse production. When a rash of crimes are committed in a Midwest town, only Pudd'nhead Wilson and his newfangled fingerprinting theory can unearth the culprit. Fine slice of Americana! 90m. **DIR:** Alan Bridges. **CAST:** Ken Howard, Lise Hilboldt. **1984**

PUMP UP THE VOLUME ★★★ Unable to make friends at his new high school, teenager Christian Slater creates a charismatic alter ego with a pirate radio station set up in his bedroom. Director Alan Moyle's script is a little sketchy, but the film has a hip, youthful energy and the cast is uniformly strong. Rated R for language and nudity. 100m. **DIR:** Alan Moyle. **CAST:** Christian Slater, Scott Paulin, Samantha Mathis, Ellen Greene, James Hampton. **1990**

PUMPING IRON ★★★★ Very good documentary concerning professional bodybuilding. Arnold Schwarzenegger and Lou Ferrigno ("The Hulk") are at the forefront as they prepare for the Mr. Universe contest. Always interesting and at times fascinating. Rated PG for language. 85m. **DIR:** George Butler, Robert Fiore. **CAST:** Arnold Schwarzenegger, Lou Ferrigno, Matty and Victoria Ferrigno, Mike Katz. **1977**

PUMPING IRON II: THE WOMEN ★★★★½ This documentary on the 1983 Women's World Cup held at Caesar's Palace is more than just beauty and brawn. While it does seem to side with one contestant (and when you see Bev Francis's massive body, you'll know why), the film has all the passion and wit of a first-rate narrative. Not rated, but an equivalent of a PG. 107m. **DIR:** George Butler. **CAST:** Lori Bowen, Carla Dunlap, Bev Francis, Rachel McLish. **1985**

PUNCHLINE ★★★ An energetic performance from Tom Hanks can't quite compensate for the bewildering miscasting of Sally Field in this tribute to the hellishly difficult life of stand-up comics. Although Hanks superbly conveys the anguish of a failed med-school student with comedy in his blood, Field never convincingly captures the conservative housewife who yearns for more. Inexplicably rated R for language. 128m. **DIR:** David Seltzer. **CAST:** Tom Hanks, Sally Field, John Goodman, Mark Rydell. **1988**

PURCHASE PRICE, THE ★★★½ A good cast and skillful direction turn a predictable script into good entertainment. A torch singer trying to get away from her gangster boyfriend marries a perfect stranger. The stars make it believable. B&W; 74m. **DIR:** William Wellman. **CAST:** Barbara Stanwyck, George Brent, Lyle Talbot, David Landau. **1932**

PURE COUNTRY ★★★ Featuring nearly a dozen George Strait songs destined for extended jukebox play, this warmhearted story about a personable country singer is predictable but entertaining. Too bad Strait's down-home charm is buried under a pile of clichés. Rated PG for language. 112m. **DIR:** Christopher Cain. **CAST:** George Strait, Lesley Ann Warren, John Doe, Isabel Glasser, Rory Calhoun. **1992**

PURPLE HEART, THE ★★★★ Dana Andrews and Richard Conte are leaders of a group of American fliers who are captured by the Japanese after they bomb Tokyo and put on trial for war crimes. This fascinating film is a minor classic. B&W; 99m. **DIR:** Lewis Milestone. **CAST:** Dana Andrews, Richard

Conte, Farley Granger, Sam Levene, Tala Birell, Nestor Paiva. 1944

PURPLE HEARTS ★★ Anyone who can sit all the way through this Vietnam War-film romance deserves a medal. Ken Wahl stars as a surgeon in the United States Navy Medical Corps who falls in love with a nurse (Cheryl Ladd). There's an additional forty minutes of unnecessary and unoriginal story tacked on. Rated R for nudity, profanity, violence, and gore. 115m. **DIR:** Sidney J. Furie. **CAST:** Ken Wahl, Cheryl Ladd. 1984

PURPLE TAXI, THE ★★★ Fred Astaire, Edward Albert, and Philippe Noiret star in this exploration of angst, love, and friendship in Ireland, where a collection of expatriate characters impaled on memories and self-destructive compulsions work out their kinks before returning to various homelands. Fine backdrops in Ireland's "curtain of rain" and impressive acting. Rated R. 107m. **DIR:** Yves Boisset. **CAST:** Fred Astaire, Edward Albert, Philippe Noiret, Peter Ustinov, Charlotte Rampling, Agostina Belli. 1977

PURSUIT OF HAPPINESS, THE ★★★½ Although it will seem dated to many, this heartfelt drama about a young man standing up for his ideals is still worth a look. Michael Sarrazin is good as a student who runs afoul of the judicial system more for a bad attitude than for his actual crime. Robert Mulligan's direction is excellent, and the cast features many now-familiar faces in small roles. Rated PG. 85m. **DIR:** Robert Mulligan. **CAST:** Michael Sarrazin, Barbara Hershey, Robert Klein, Arthur Hill, E. G. Marshall, David Doyle, Barnard Hughes, Sada Thompson, Rue McClanahan, William Devane, Charles Durning. 1971

QB VII ★★★★ Leon Uris's hefty bestseller is vividly brought to life in this five-hours-plus made-for-television drama about a Polish expatriate doctor living in England who sues an American writer for libel when the writer accuses him of carrying out criminal medical activities for the Nazis during World War II. Anthony Hopkins is brilliant as the physician, Ben Gazzara is outraged and tenacious as the writer. Expect a powerful, engrossing ending. 312m. **DIR:** Tom Gries. **CAST:** Anthony Hopkins, Ben Gazzara, Leslie Caron, Lee Remick, Anthony Quayle. 1974

QUACKSER FORTUNE HAS A COUSIN IN THE BRONX ★★★★ This comedy-drama falls into the category of sleeper. Gene Wilder is delightful as an Irishman who marches to the beat of a different drummer. Margot Kidder is a rich American going to university in Dublin who meets and falls in love with him. Filmed in Ireland and rated R for nudity and language. 88m. **DIR:** Waris Hussein. **CAST:** Gene Wilder, Margot Kidder, Eileen Colga. 1970

QUALITY STREET ★★½ In early nineteenth-century England, a schoolteacher (Katharine Hepburn) worries about whether her youthful flame (Eric Blore) will return from war. A familiar story, but a fine cast elevates the proceedings. B&W; 84m. **DIR:** George Stevens. **CAST:** Katharine Hepburn, Joan Fontaine, Eric Blore, Franchot Tone. 1937

QUARTERBACK PRINCESS ★★½ True story of Tami Maida, the girl who came to a small Oregon town and managed to become a star on the football team as well as the homecoming queen. Helen Hunt is adequate as Tami; Don Murray is better as her supportive dad. Made for television. 96m. **DIR:** Noel Black. **CAST:** Helen Hunt, Don Murray, Barbara Babcock, Dana Elcar, John Stockwell. 1983

QUARTET (1948) ★★★★ A dramatization of W. Somerset Maugham's favorite stories: "The Facts of Life," "The Alien Corn," "The Kite," and "The Colonel's Lady." All four are immensely watchable. B&W; 120m. **DIR:** Ken Annakin, Arthur Crabtree, Harold French, Ralph Smart. **CAST:** Dirk Bogarde, Hermione Baddeley, Mervyn Johns, Cecil Parker, Basil Badford, Françoise Rosay, Susan Shaw, Naunton Wayne, Mai Zetterling. 1948

QUARTET (1981) ★★ In terms of acting, this is a first-rate film. Unfortunately, the pathetic characters that mope around in this period piece drag down any positive points. Isabelle Adjani plays the wife of a convicted criminal who ends up in a ménage à trois with a married couple, played by Alan Bates and Maggie Smith. Rated R for nudity. 101m. **DIR:** James Ivory. **CAST:** Isabelle Adjani, Alan Bates, Anthony Higgins, Maggie Smith. 1981

QUEEN CHRISTINA ★★★★ This haunting romance might be laughable if anyone but Greta Garbo were in it. She plays the controversial Swedish queen who gave up her throne for the sake of love (according to the movie). The last scene—of Garbo looking wistfully into the camera—has become her trademark. B&W; 97m. **DIR:** Rouben Mamoulian. **CAST:** Greta Garbo, John Gilbert, Lewis Stone, C. Aubrey Smith, Reginald Owen. 1933

QUEEN ELIZABETH ★★ Sarah Bernhardt stars as Queen Elizabeth I in this heavy-handed silent melodrama. The plot revolves around a love triangle involving the queen, the earl of Essex, and the countess of Nottingham. Silent. B&W; 46m. **DIR:** Henri Desfontanes. **CAST:** Sarah Bernhardt. 1927

QUEEN KELLY ★★★ Gloria Swanson used her clout to keep Erich Von Stroheim's *Queen Kelly* buried for nearly sixty years. This reconstructed version is but a shadow of the five-hour epic Von Stroheim had intended to make. The sumptuously mounted melodrama is fascinating—and often hilarious—for its indulgences, decadence, and outright perversity. Swanson plays a rebellious schoolgirl who is kidnapped from a convent and introduced to the pleasures of life by a debauched prince. Silent. B&W; 95m. **DIR:** Erich Von Stroheim. **CAST:** Gloria Swanson. **1928**

QUEEN OF HEARTS ★★★★ A comedy-drama with dialogue primarily in English but a sensibility that is very Italian. By running away from her marriage to a wealthy Sicilian, the beautiful Rosa (Anita Zagaria) sets in motion a tragic and funny tale of revenge. Unrated, the film has profanity and violence. 112m. **DIR:** Jon Amiel. **CAST:** Anita Zagaria, Joseph Long, Eileen Way. **1989**

QUEEN OF THE STARDUST BALLROOM ★★★★ Touching love story about a lonely widow (Maureen Stapleton) who finally finds Mr. Right (Charles Durning). Stapleton is outstanding. 100m. **DIR:** Sam O'Steen. **CAST:** Maureen Stapleton, Charles Durning, Michael Brandon, Michael Strong. **1975**

QUEENIE ★★★ Lavish television production based on Michael Korda's novel, a fictionalized story of the youth and early movie career of his real-life aunt, Merle Oberon. The opening scenes, set in early 1930s India, are more interesting than her adult years. 235m. **DIR:** Larry Peerce. **CAST:** Mia Sara, Kirk Douglas, Claire Bloom, Joel Grey, Martin Balsam, Sarah Miles, Topol, Kate Emma Davies. **1987**

QUESTION OF FAITH ★★★½ Made-for-TV tearjerker, originally aired under the title *Leap of Faith*. Superior cast, led by Anne Archer and Sam Neill, and literate script help this incurable disease movie to transcend the boundaries usually associated with such fare. 90m. **DIR:** Stephen Gyllenhaal. **CAST:** Anne Archer, Sam Neill, Frances Lee McCain, Louis Giambalvo, James Tolkan, Michael Constantine. **1993**

QUESTION OF HONOR, A ★★★★ Superior made-for-TV movie tells the true story of an honest New York narcotics officer who got caught in the middle of a federal drug scam and found himself accused of corruption. Based on a book by Sonny Grosso, the cop portrayed by Roy Scheider in *The French Connection*. Not rated. 134m. **DIR:** Jud Taylor. **CAST:** Ben Gazzara, Robert Vaughn, Paul Sorvino, Tony Roberts, Danny Aiello. **1982**

QUICKSILVER ★★ Wretched mess of a film. Kevin Bacon stars as a Wall Street wizard who blows it all one day and then puts his natural talents to work by becoming...a bicycle messenger! Rated PG for mild violence. 101m. **DIR:** Tom Donnelly. **CAST:** Kevin Bacon, Jami Gertz, Paul Rodriguez, Rudy Ramos, Larry Fishburne. **1986**

QUIET DAY IN BELFAST, A ★★★½ This fine Canadian message film reveals the hopelessness and insanity of Ireland's civil war. Margot Kidder plays Catholic twins, one in love with a British soldier. Unrated, but contains profanity, nudity, and violence. 92m. **DIR:** Milad Bessada. **CAST:** Margot Kidder, Barry Foster. **1978**

QUO VADIS (1951) ★★★ Colossal! Roman soldier Robert Taylor loves and pursues Christian maiden Deborah Kerr. It's Christians versus Nero and the lions in the eternal fight between good and evil. 171m. **DIR:** Mervyn LeRoy. **CAST:** Robert Taylor, Deborah Kerr, Peter Ustinov, Leo Genn, Finlay Currie, Patricia Laffan, Abraham Sofaer, Felix Aylmer, Buddy Baer. **1951**

QUO VADIS? (1985) ★★★ Lavish adaptation of Henryk Sienkiewicz's novel set during the reign of Nero. Klaus Maria Brandauer gives a brilliant performance as Nero in this made-for-Italian-television production. 200m. **DIR:** Franco Rossi. **CAST:** Klaus Maria Brandauer, Frederic Forrest, Cristina Raines, Francesco Quinn. **1985**

R.P.M. (REVOLUTIONS PER MINUTE) ★★ In this story set on a small-town college campus in the late 1960s, a liberal professor (Anthony Quinn) and his coed mistress (Ann-Margret) become involved in the efforts of a liberal student (Gary Lockwood) to have the professor made president of the university. Good intentions turn into campus unrest and violence. Rated R for violence. 92m. **DIR:** Stanley Kramer. **CAST:** Anthony Quinn, Ann-Margret, Gary Lockwood. **1970**

RABBIT RUN ★★ John Updike's novel concerning an ex–high school athlete's trouble adjusting to life off the field is brought to the screen in a very dull fashion. James Caan has the title role as the lost ex-jock. Supporting cast is good, but the script sinks everyone involved. 74m. **DIR:** Jack Smight. **CAST:** James Caan, Carrie Snodgress, Jack Albertson, Henry Jones, Anjanette Comer. **1970**

RACERS, THE ★★★ A reworking of *Champion* set in the world of car racers, with Kirk Douglas as the idealist who becomes a racing champion and then an unethical competitor. The photography at the racetrack is unusually effective. 112m. **DIR:** Henry Hathaway. **CAST:** Kirk Douglas, Gilbert Roland, Bella Darvi, Cesar Romero, Katy Jurado, Lee J. Cobb. **1955**

RACHEL, RACHEL ★★★½ Paul Newman's directorial debut focuses on a spinsterish schoolteacher (Joanne Woodward) and her awakening to a world beyond her job and her elderly mother's influence. This bittersweet story is perfectly acted by Woodward, with strong support by James Olson as her short-term lover and Estelle Parsons as her friend. Rewarding on all levels. Rated R. 101m. **DIR:** Paul Newman. **CAST:** Joanne Woodward, James Olson, Kate Harrington, Estelle Parsons. **1968**

RACHEL RIVER ★★★ *American Playhouse* presentation boasts a screenplay by *Or-*

dinary People author Judith Guest and an excellent cast in this tale of a lonely small-town woman who falls for the one guy in town who makes her happy. Watching these two opposites attract is magnetic. 97m. **DIR:** Sandy Smolan. **CAST:** Pamela Reed, Craig T. Nelson, Viveca Lindfors, James Olson. **1988**

RACING WITH THE MOON ★★★½ Sean Penn and Elizabeth McGovern star in this thoroughly entertaining and touching comedy-romance set during World War II. He's just a regular town boy who discovers he's fallen in love with one of the area's rich girls. But that doesn't stop him from trying to win her heart. Rated PG for nudity, profanity, suggested sex, and brief violence. 108m. **DIR:** Richard Benjamin. **CAST:** Sean Penn, Elizabeth McGovern, Nicolas Cage, John Karlen, Rutanya Alda, Carol Kane. **1984**

RACKET, THE ★★★ This pessimistic look at political corruption focuses on the steps honest police captain Robert Mitchum takes in order to bring underworld figure Robert Ryan to justice. Mitchum is a man alone as he confronts seemingly insurmountable opposition from both police and political higher-ups who want to keep things just as crooked as they are. B&W; 88m. **DIR:** John Cromwell. **CAST:** Robert Mitchum, Robert Ryan, Lizabeth Scott, William Talman, Ray Collins, Robert Hutton. **1951**

RADIO FLYER ★★ Two youngsters attempt to escape the terrors inflicted on them by their violent stepfather by turning their Radio Flyer wagon into a flying machine. The horrors of child abuse are ineffectively wed with innocent childhood fantasies in this disturbing film. A misfire. Rated PG-13 for violence and profanity. 114m. **DIR:** Richard Donner. **CAST:** Lorraine Bracco, John Heard, Elijah Wood, Joseph Mazzello, Adam Baldwin, Tom Hanks, Ben Johnson. **1992**

RAGE (1972) ★★★ This pits a lone man against the impersonal Establishment (in this instance the U.S. Army). This is not a happy film by any means, but it is an interesting one. Making his directorial debut, George C. Scott plays a peaceful sheep rancher whose son is the victim of military chemical testing. Seeking revenge, he sets out to nail those responsible. Rated PG. 104m. **DIR:** George C. Scott. **CAST:** George C. Scott, Martin Sheen, Richard Basehart, Barnard Hughes. **1972**

RAGE (1980) ★★★ David Soul travels through the agonies of intense therapy as a convicted rapist in this above-par TV-movie drama. Loaded with fine performances from an incredible cast. 100m. **DIR:** William A. Graham. **CAST:** David Soul, James Whitmore, Craig T. Nelson, Yaphet Kotto, Caroline McWilliams, Leo Gordon, Sharon Farrell, Vic Tayback. **1980**

RAGE OF ANGELS 🦃 Trashy TV movie. Unrated. 200m. **DIR:** Buzz Kulik. **CAST:** Jaclyn Smith, Ken Howard, Armand Assante, Ron Hunter, Kevin Conway. **1986**

RAGGEDY RAWNEY, THE ★★½ A quaint, modest effort most notable because its first-time writer-director is the superb Cockney actor, Bob Hoskins. He created this folk fable about Gypsies and a myth about a speechless madwoman with magical powers who follows the caravans about. 102m. **DIR:** Bob Hoskins. **CAST:** Bob Hoskins, Dexter Fletcher. **1988**

RAGING BULL ★★★★½ This is a tough, compelling film...in fact, a great one. Directed by Martin Scorsese and starring the incredible Robert De Niro, it's one movie you won't want to miss. In playing prizefighter Jake La Motta from his twenties through to middle age, De Niro undergoes a transformation that takes him from his normal weight of 150 to 212 pounds. That is startling in itself, but the performance he gives is even more startling—see it. Rated R. B&W; 128m. **DIR:** Martin Scorsese. **CAST:** Robert De Niro, Cathy Moriarty, Joe Pesci, Frank Vincent, Nicholas Colasanto, Theresa Saldana. **1980**

RAGTIME ★★★★½ James Cagney returned to the screen after an absence of twenty years in this brilliant screen adaptation of E. L. Doctorow's bestselling novel about New York City at the turn of the century. It's a bountifully rewarding motion picture. Rated PG for violence and nudity. 155m. **DIR:** Milos Forman. **CAST:** James Cagney, Brad Dourif, Pat O'Brien, Donald O'Connor, Elizabeth McGovern, Mary Steenburgen. **1981**

RAID ON ENTEBBE ★★★ Second of three dramas filmed in 1976–1977 about the daring Israeli commando assault on the Entebbe airport in Uganda, this TV movie avoids the soap-opera tone of the earlier *Victory at Entebbe* (also made for TV) and focuses on the action and power struggle between the Israelis and Idi Amin. More effective when it was initially shown, but it's still worth a watch. 150m. **DIR:** Irvin Kershner. **CAST:** Peter Finch, Charles Bronson, Horst Buchholz, Martin Balsam, John Saxon, Jack Warden, Yaphet Kotto. **1977**

RAILROADED ★★★ Future TV father Hugh Beaumont has his hands full as a police detective trying to run interference between gangster John Ireland and his intended victim Sheila Ryan. Tough, tight, and deadly, this early effort from director Anthony Mann oozes suspense and remains a fine example of American *film noir*, modestly budgeted and effectively conveyed. B&W; 71m. **DIR:** Anthony Mann. **CAST:** John Ireland, Sheila Ryan, Hugh Beaumont, Jane Randolph, Keefe Brasselle. **1947**

RAILWAY STATION MAN, THE ★★½ An offbeat love story set in Ireland involves painter Julie Christie with a red-haired, one-handed Donald Sutherland, who plays the title character. The two stars, working together twenty years after making *Don't Look Now*, make this TV movie watchable but cannot overcome a confusing subplot involving terrorists. 93m. **DIR:** Michael Whyte. **CAST:** Julie Christie, Donald Sutherland, John Lynch, Frank McCusker, Mark Tandy. **1993**

RAIN ★★★★ Joan Crawford plays island hussy Sadie Thompson in this depressing drama. Walter Huston is the preacher who wants to "save" her—for himself. B&W; 93m. **DIR:** Lewis Milestone. **CAST:** Joan Crawford, Walter Huston, William Gargan, Guy Kibbee, Walter Catlett, Beulah Bondi. **1932**

RAIN MAN ★★★★★ Dustin Hoffman gives the performance of his career as the autistic older brother of Tom Cruise, who plays (once again) a thoughtless, self-centered hustler with no room in his life for anything but money. Greed propels him to take a cross-country road trip with Hoffman, who inherited the bulk of Dad's vast estate. Barry Levinson deftly blends pathos with gentle humor that allows us to laugh with, but never at, Hoffman's autistic savant. Inexplicably rated R for occasional profanity. 140m. **DIR:** Barry Levinson. **CAST:** Dustin Hoffman, Tom Cruise, Valeria Golino. **1988**

RAIN PEOPLE, THE ★★★★ James Caan plays a retired football star who is picked up by a bored pregnant woman (played by Shirley Knight). She felt trapped as a housewife and ran away from her husband to be free. Directed by Francis Ford Coppola, this is an interesting, well-acted character study. Rated R. 102m. **DIR:** Francis Ford Coppola. **CAST:** James Caan, Shirley Knight, Robert Duvall, Tom Aldredge. **1969**

RAIN WITHOUT THUNDER ★★★½ Writer-director Gary Bennett has created an often-intriguing abortion rights drama with a decided pro-choice agenda. Set in a not-so-distant future when abortion is again illegal, *Rain Without Thunder* assumes a mock documentary style to tell the story of a mother and daughter charged with traveling to Sweden to obtain an abortion. The viewer's potential empathy for the film may be determined by his or her position on the volatile abortion issue. Rated PG-13, with profanity and adult issues. 87m. **DIR:** Gary Bennett. **CAST:** Jeff Daniels, Betty Buckley, Linda Hunt, Frederic Forrest, Graham Greene, Austin Pendleton. **1993**

RAINBOW, THE ★★★★ Director Ken Russell returns to D. H. Lawrence, the source of his great success, *Women in Love*. This time, he focuses on the companion novel, a prequel. Sammi Davis is wonderful as an adolescent English girl exposed to the ways of love at the hands of both a soldier and her teacher, and makes a decision to seek a more satisfying life for herself. Rated R. 102m. **DIR:** Ken Russell. **CAST:** Sammi Davis, Paul McGann, Glenda Jackson, Amanda Donohoe, David Hemmings, Christopher Gable. **1989**

RAINMAKER, THE ★★★½ Based on N. Richard Nash's play, the movie adaptation could easily have seemed confined, but the boundless intensity and energy of Burt Lancaster's performance as the smooth-talking con man gives the whole film an electric crackle. Katharine Hepburn has the magnetism to hold her own in the role of the spinster. 121m. **DIR:** Joseph Anthony. **CAST:** Burt Lancaster, Katharine Hepburn, Wendell Corey, Lloyd Bridges, Earl Holliman, Wallace Ford, Cameron Prud'homme. **1956**

RAINS CAME, THE ★★★ Louis Bromfield's epic novel of India has been turned into a so-so drama of forbidden romance between a white woman and an Indian doctor. A spectacular earthquake and tidal wave, but little more. Remade in 1955 as *The Rains of Ranchipur*. B&W; 104m. **DIR:** Clarence Brown. **CAST:** Myrna Loy, Tyrone Power, George Brent, Brenda Joyce, Nigel Bruce, Maria Ouspenskaya, Joseph Schildkraut, Jane Darwell, Marjorie Rambeau, Henry Travers, H. B. Warner. **1939**

RAINTREE COUNTY ★★★ Civil War melodrama with Elizabeth Taylor as a southern belle is two and one-half hours of showy tedium that wastes a fine cast and miles of film. Bestselling novel comes to the screen as an extended soap opera with little promise and fewer results. 168m. **DIR:** Edward Dmytryk. **CAST:** Elizabeth Taylor, Montgomery Clift, Eva Marie Saint, Nigel Patrick, Lee Marvin, Rod Taylor, Agnes Moorehead, Walter Abel, Rhys Williams. **1957**

RAISIN IN THE SUN, A (1961) ★★★★ A black family tries to escape from their crowded apartment life by moving to a house in an all-white neighborhood. Sidney Poitier delivers his usual outstanding performance in this film with a message about the limited opportunities open to blacks in the 1950s. B&W; 128m. **DIR:** Daniel Petrie. **CAST:** Sidney Poitier, Claudia McNeil, Ruby Dee, Diana Sands, Ivan Dixon, John Fiedler, Lou Gossett Jr. **1961**

RAISIN IN THE SUN, A (1988) ★★★★ Gripping TV remake of the 1961 classic, with Danny Glover replacing Sidney Poitier as the angry young man who's ready to explode. Esther Rolle superbly struggles to reunite her family by buying a home that just happens to be in an all-white neighborhood. 171m. **DIR:** Bill Duke. **CAST:** Danny Glover, Esther Rolle, Starletta Dupois. **1988**

RAMBLING ROSE ★★★★ Everything is just right in this film about a 13-year-old boy who falls in love with his 19-year-old nanny, a sexy ball of fire called Rose. Rose scorches everyone in her path in this uproariously funny, heart-tugging, and sexy release adapted from the semiautobiographical book by Calder Willingham. Rated R for profanity, nudity, and suggested sex. 112m. **DIR:** Martha Coolidge. **CAST:** Laura Dern, Robert Duvall, Diane Ladd, Lukas Haas, John Heard, Kevin Conway. **1991**

RANDOM HARVEST ★★★★ Ronald Colman and Greer Garson are at their best in this touching, tearful story. A shell-shocked World War I veteran is saved from oblivion by the compassion of a music-hall entertainer. A stellar cast supports. B&W; 124m. **DIR:** Mervyn LeRoy. **CAST:** Ronald Colman, Greer Garson, Philip Dorn, Henry Travers, Reginald Owen. **1942**

RAPE AND MARRIAGE: THE RIDEOUT CASE ★★ Despite the dramatic potential of its story line and a strong cast, this fact-based TV drama—about the infamous 1978 husband-wife rape case in Oregon—falls far short of answering any questions about the issues. 96m. **DIR:** Peter Levin. **CAST:** Mickey Rourke, Rip Torn, Linda Hamilton, Eugene Roche, Gail Strickland, Conchata Ferrell. **1980**

RAPPACCINI'S DAUGHTER ★★★★½ This Nathaniel Hawthorne tale concerns a university student who accepts new lodgings overlooking a beautiful and mysterious garden. What follows is a particularly spellbinding tale of love and tragedy. Introduced by Henry Fonda; unrated and suitable for family viewing. 57m. **DIR:** Dezso Magyar. **CAST:** Kristoffer Tabori, Kathleen Beller, Michael Egan, Leonardo Cimino. **1980**

RAPTURE, THE ★★★★ Mimi Rogers is riveting as a Los Angeles telephone operator who tires of mate-swapping and turns to a religious sect for spiritual guidance. Writer-director Michael Tolkin's bold approach to religious themes makes this tragic drama both a demanding and unforgettable experience. It's an amazing, disturbing story of squandered life, rebirth, and tested faith. Rated R for nudity and language. 102m. **DIR:** Michael Tolkin. **CAST:** Mimi Rogers, Kimberly Cullum, Patrick Bauchau. **1991**

RASPUTIN AND THE EMPRESS ★★½ Lionel Barrymore portrays the mad monk Rasputin (he's badly miscast), and siblings Ethel (in her sound-film debut) and John co-star in this overlong historical melodrama of court intrigue during the troubled reign of Nicholas and Alexandra in czarist Russia. B&W; 123m. **DIR:** Richard Boleslawski. **CAST:** John Barrymore, Ethel Barrymore, Lionel Barrymore, Ralph Morgan. **1932**

RATBOY ★★ Not a horror film but a satirical allegory directed by and starring Sondra Locke. Eugene, a boy with the face of a rat, is torn out of his peaceful existence in a dump by an unemployed window dresser (Locke). With her two brothers, she sets out to market the "ratboy" as a media star. Rated PG-13 for profanity and some violence. 104m. **DIR:** Sondra Locke. **CAST:** Sondra Locke, Robert Townsend, Louie Anderson, Gerrit Graham, Christopher Hewett. **1986**

RATTLE OF A SIMPLE MAN ★★★ One of the realistic, kitchen-sink dramas that were in vogue in England at the time, this resembles a British version of *Marty.* Middle-aged Percy, a virgin who lives with his mother, is goaded by his friends into a bet that he can't pick up and spend the night with an attractive waitress. In his attempt to do so, he finds love for the first time. B&W; 96m. **DIR:** Muriel Box. **CAST:** Harry H. Corbett, Diane Cilento, Michael Medwin. **1964**

RAZOR'S EDGE, THE (1946) ★★★★½ A long but engrossing presentation of Somerset Maugham's philosophical novel about a young man seeking the goodness in life. Full of memorable characterizations and scenes. Herbert Marshall steers the plot, playing the author. B&W; 146m. **DIR:** Edmund Goulding. **CAST:** Tyrone Power, Gene Tierney, Clifton Webb, Herbert Marshall, Anne Baxter, John Payne, Elsa Lanchester. **1946**

RAZOR'S EDGE, THE (1984) ★★★½ Bill Murray gives a finely balanced comic and dramatic portrayal as a man searching for meaning after World War I in this adaptation of W. Somerset Maugham's novel. The result is a richly rewarding film, which survives the unevenness of John Byrum's direction. Rated PG-13 for suggested sex, violence, and profanity. 128m. **DIR:** John Byrum. **CAST:** Bill Murray, Theresa Russell, Catharine Hicks, James Keach, Brian Doyle-Murray. **1984**

REAL AMERICAN HERO, THE ★½ Below-average TV movie does not do justice to slain sheriff Buford Pusser. Brian Dennehy plays Pusser, a frustrated law enforcer who will do anything—even risk his own life—to get the bad guys. Ken Howard plays a ruthless bar owner. *Walking Tall* says it all better. Not rated, but contains profanity and violence. 94m. **DIR:** Lou Antonio. **CAST:** Brian Dennehy, Forrest Tucker, Brian Kerwin, Ken Howard, Sheree North. **1978**

REALITY BITES ★★★½ This mordantly amusing, often tragic drama is the first to speak for the Generation X'ers, who now have their own cinematic statement à la *Easy Rider* and *The Big Chill*. College valedictorian Winona Ryder vacillates between financially successful dropout Ben Stiller (also making a stylish directorial debut) and philosophical Ethan Hawke, who coasts through life. The film's video verité cinematography is the perfect statement for the MTV generation, and the appealing young leads do a credible job. Rated PG-13 for profanity, drug use, and sexual frankness. 99m. **DIR:** Ben Stiller. **CAST:** Winona Ryder, Ethan Hawke, Ben Stiller, Janeane Garofalo, Steve Zahn. **1994**

REBECCA OF SUNNYBROOK FARM (1917) ★★½ Once again, the adult Mary Pickford successfully portrays a saucy teenager who wins love, respect, and prosperity in this rags-to-riches tearjerker based on the famous Kate Douglas Wiggin bestseller. Shirley Temple starred in a talkie version in 1938. Silent. B&W; 77m. **DIR:** Marshall Neilan. **CAST:** Mary Pickford, Eugene O'Brien, Helen Jerome Eddy. **1917**

REBEL (1985) During World War II, a Marine sergeant in Australia goes AWOL and falls in love with a nightclub singer. Rated R for profanity. 93m. **DIR:** Michael Jenkins. **CAST:** Matt Dillon, Debbie Byrne, Bryan Brown, Bill Hunter, Ray Barrett. **1985**

REBEL LOVE Yankee widow falls in love with a Confederate spy. Unrated; there is some mild sexual content. 84m. **DIR:** Milton Bagby Jr. **CAST:** Jamie Rose, Terence Knox, Fran Ryan, Charles Hill. **1986**

REBEL WITHOUT A CAUSE ★★★★★ This is the film that made James Dean a legend. Directed by Nicholas Ray, it is undoubtedly the classic film about juvenile delinquency. Featuring fine performances by Dean, Natalie Wood, and Sal Mineo as the teens in trouble, it has stood up surprisingly well over the years. 111m. **DIR:** Nicholas Ray. **CAST:** James Dean, Natalie Wood, Sal Mineo, Jim Backus, Ann Doran, Corey Allen, Edward Platt, Dennis Hopper, Nick Adams. **1955**

REBELS, THE ★★★ The second of John Jakes's bicentennial bestsellers to be converted into a TV miniseries, this is a step up from *The Bastard*. Much of the sleaze has been replaced with swashbuckling adventure thanks to Don Johnson and Doug McClure's contributions. Using America's history from 1775 to 1781 as a background, this allows us to experience the eventual triumph of our Continental army. 190m. **DIR:** Russ Mayberry. **CAST:** Andrew Stevens, Don Johnson, Doug McClure, Joan Blondell, Tanya Tucker. **1979**

RECKLESS (1935) ★★ Jean Harlow, terribly miscast as a Broadway musical star, marries troubled alcoholic playboy Franchot Tone, who feels she entrapped him and heads downhill toward suicide. William Powell stands by until needed. B&W; 97m. **DIR:** Victor Fleming. **CAST:** Jean Harlow, William Powell, Franchot Tone, May Robson, Rosalind Russell, Mickey Rooney. **1935**

RECKLESS (1984) ★★ A 1980s version of the standard 1950s "angry young man" movie, this features Aidan Quinn as a motorcycle-riding, mumbling (à la James Dean and Marlon Brando) outcast and Daryl Hannah as the "good girl." That should give you an idea of how original this movie is. Rated R for nudity, profanity, violence, and suggested sex. 90m. **DIR:** James Foley. **CAST:** Aidan Quinn, Daryl Hannah, Kenneth McMillan, Cliff De Young, Lois Smith, Adam Baldwin, Dan Hedaya. **1984**

RED BADGE OF COURAGE, THE ★★★½ Natural performances mark this realistic treatment of Stephen Crane's famous Civil War novel of a young soldier's initiation to battle. A John Huston classic, and a major film achievement by any standard. B&W; 69m. **DIR:** John Huston. **CAST:** Audie Murphy, Bill Mauldin, Royal Dano, Arthur Hunnicutt, Douglas Dick. **1951**

RED DUST ★★★★ *Red Dust* is one of those remarkable films where the performances of its stars propel a movie to classic status despite a rather uninspired story. A hackneyed story of a rubber plantation boss (Gable) who dallies with another man's wife only to return to the arms of a shady lady (Harlow) with the proverbial heart of gold. B&W; 83m. **DIR:** Victor Fleming. **CAST:** Clark Gable, Jean Harlow, Mary Astor, Donald Crisp, Gene Raymond, Tully Marshall. **1932**

RED-HEADED WOMAN ★★★½ Every female star on every major motion-picture lot wanted the plum role of the gal who followed her heart and her instincts to gain social prominence and a swell guy. Young Jean Harlow took the prize and made it her own in this pre-Code gem. B&W; 79m. **DIR:** Jack Conway. **CAST:** Jean Harlow, Chester Morris, Leila Hyams, Lewis Stone, Una Merkel, Henry Stephenson, May Robson. **1932**

RED KIMONO, THE A young lady is abandoned by her philandering husband and forced to become a scarlet woman. Silent. B&W; 95m. **DIR:** Walter Lang. **CAST:** Priscilla Bonner, Nellie Bly Baker, Mary Carr, Tyrone Power Sr. **1925**

RED KING, WHITE KNIGHT ★★½ Tom Skerritt's impeccable rendering of a retired and weary CIA agent brought back into the fold (initially as a dupe) enlivens Ron Hutchinson's dreary story about a rogue Soviet KGB official who plots against Gorbachev to retain the cold war status quo. Things also improve considerably when the brilliant Max von Sydow appears. Made for HBO; considerable violence and frank dialogue. 107m. **DIR:** Geoff Murphy. **CAST:** Tom Skerritt, Max von Sydow, Helen Mirren, Tom Bell, Barry Corbin. **1989**

RED LIGHT STING, THE ★★ Pale TV film about a young district attorney (Beau Bridges) who is assigned to buy a whorehouse to bring out an elusive big-time crook (Harold Gould). Not rated, but the equivalent of a PG for adult subject matter. 96m. **DIR:** Rod Holcomb. **CAST:** Farrah Fawcett, Beau Bridges, Harold Gould, Paul Burke, Alex Henteloff, Conrad Janis, James Luisi, Philip Charles MacKenzie. **1984**

RED MENACE, THE A sloppily written movie made to capitalize on the McCarthy menace with onetime *Our Miss Brooks* hero Robert Rockwell menaced by Communist sympathizers in a very unconvincing way.

B&W; 87m. **DIR:** R. G. Springsteen. **CAST:** Robert Rockwell, Betty Lou Gerson, Barbara Fuller, Hanne Axman. **1949**

RED NIGHTS 🦃 A New England youth with stars in his eyes heads out to Hollywood. Rated R. 89m. **DIR:** Izhak Hanooka. **CAST:** Christopher Parker, Brian Matthews, Jack Carter, William Smith. **1988**

RED SHOE DIARIES 🦃 Chic smut purveyor Zalman King hits rock bottom. A flightly young woman tests her boyfriend by sleeping with a kinky, hunky shoe salesman. An interminable bore. Nudity, graphic sex, and profanity spice this made-for-cable porn parade. 105m. **DIR:** Zalman King. **CAST:** David Duchovny, Brigitte Bako, Billy Wirth, Kai Wulfe, Brenda Vaccaro. **1992**

RED SHOE DIARIES II: DOUBLE DARE ★★ Three mediocre short subjects: two strangers meet every week for sexual intercourse; two people try to outdo each other in sex; a man and woman dare each other, via the fax machine, to perform sexual acts. Contains nudity, graphic sex, and profanity. 95m. **DIR:** Zalman King, Tibor Takacs. **CAST:** Steven Bauer, Joan Severance, Denise Crosby, Rob Knepper, Laura Johnson, Michael Woods, David Duchovny. **1992**

RED SHOE DIARIES 3: ANOTHER WOMAN'S LIPSTICK ★★ What started off as a hot and steamy series has been reduced to a peekaboo event thanks to lackluster stories. Here, three episodes explore different female fantasies, from making out with a delivery boy to laying rubber on a deserted highway. Ho-hum. Unrated, but contains adult situations and language. 90m. **DIR:** Zalman King, Ted Kotcheff, Rafael Eisenman. **CAST:** Maryam D'Abo, Nina Siemaszko, Christina Fulton, Richard Tyson. **1993**

RED SHOE DIARIES 4: AUTO EROTICA 🦃 Three more vapid examples of the nonerotic erotica that has flooded the cable market in recent years. Available in R and unrated formats, both with nudity and sexual situations. 83m. **DIR:** Michael Karbelnikoff, Alan Smithee, Zalman King. **CAST:** Ally Sheedy, David Duchovny, Sheryl Lee. **1994**

RED TENT, THE ★★½ Sean Connery heads an international cast in this slow-moving reconstruction of a polar expedition that ended in tragedy in 1928. The scope of the film and the trials faced by the party in their struggles for survival are enthralling, but too much reliance on flashbacks works against this one. 121m. **DIR:** Mikhail K. Kalatozov. **CAST:** Sean Connery, Claudia Cardinale, Hardy Krüger, Peter Finch, Massimo Girotti. **1970**

REDS ★★★★★ Warren Beatty produced, directed, cowrote, and starred in this $33 million American film masterpiece. This three-hour-plus film biography of left-wing American journalist John Reed (Beatty) and Louise Bryant (Diane Keaton) also features brilliant bits from Jack Nicholson, Gene Hackman, and Maureen Stapleton. Rated PG because of profanity, silhouetted sex scenes, and war scenes. 200m. **DIR:** Warren Beatty. **CAST:** Warren Beatty, Diane Keaton, Jack Nicholson, Gene Hackman, Edward Herrmann, Maureen Stapleton, Jerzy Kosinski. **1981**

REFLECTING SKIN, THE ★★★★ The innocence of a small boy is stripped away as he observes the strange and macabre characters that surround him. Life in a small town is magnified beyond reality into a surreal quasi-fantasy that brilliantly fuses the mind of the child and that of the adult, directly challenging our idealized notions of the innocence of childhood. A must for those who appreciate the work of David Lynch, and enjoy challenging alternative cinema. Rated R for violence and suggested sex. 98m. **DIR:** Philip Ridley. **CAST:** Viggo Mortensen, Lindsay Duncan, Jeremy Cooper. **1991**

REFLECTIONS IN A GOLDEN EYE ★★½ Very bizarre film concerning a homosexual army officer (Marlon Brando) stationed in the South. This very strange film very rarely works—despite a high-powered cast. 108m. **DIR:** John Huston. **CAST:** Marlon Brando, Elizabeth Taylor, Brian Keith, Julie Harris, Robert Forster. **1967**

REGARDING HENRY ★★★★ Harrison Ford gives one of his finest performances as Henry Turner, a successful, self-centered attorney who loses all memory of his past when a robber shoots him in the head with a small-caliber weapon. Annette Bening is equally fine as the wife who finds herself falling in love with the gentle, childlike man who emerges in her husband's body. Rated PG-13 for violence and profanity. 107m. **DIR:** Mike Nichols. **CAST:** Harrison Ford, Annette Bening, Bill Nunn, Donald Moffat, Nancy Marchand, Elizabeth Wilson. **1991**

REILLY: THE ACE OF SPIES ★★ Sam Neill is wasted in this slow-moving, so-called thriller about the first James Bond–type spy employed by the British. In 1901 Russia he manages not only to smuggle secret maps out of the country but also to lure a surly minister's young wife into his bed. Unrated, this made-for-TV production contains violence and nudity. 80m. **DIR:** Jim Goddard. **CAST:** Sam Neill, Leo McKern, Norman Rodway, Peter Egan. **1984**

REMAINS OF THE DAY ★★★★★ Anthony Hopkins and Emma Thompson give remarkable performances in this heartwrenching exploration of English reserve and unrequited love, a seamless blend of period detail and dramatic power from the creators of *A Room with a View* and *Howards End.* Hopkins is a gentleman's gentleman whose private life and longings are subjugated to his professional responsibilities; this very dedication leads to personal tragedy. Exquisite. Rated PG-13 for brief profanity. 134m. **DIR:** James Ivory. **CAST:** Anthony Hopkins, Emma Thompson, James Fox, Christopher Reeve, Peter Vaughan, Hugh Grant, Michel Lonsdale, Tim Pigott-Smith. **1993**

REMBRANDT ★★★★ This is one of the few satisfying movie biographies of an artist. The depiction of the famous Dutch painter and his struggle to maintain his artistic integrity is related with respectful restraint and attention to factual detail. Charles Laughton, as Rembrandt, is brilliant in what was for him an atypically low-key performance. B&W; 90m. **DIR:** Alexander Korda. **CAST:** Charles Laughton, Gertrude Lawrence, Elsa Lanchester. **1936**

REMEDY FOR RICHES ★★½ When not dispensing country medicine to his patients, kindly Dr. Christian keeps an eye out for their financial well-being by alerting them to a con man's phony oil scheme. Modest series entry with a parade of eccentric characters. 67m. **DIR:** Erle C. Kenton. **CAST:** Jean Hersholt, Dorothy Lovett, Edgar Kennedy. **1941**

RENO AND THE DOC ★★½ Though it has a slow start, this tale of two middle-aged men brought together by mental telepathy soon gains momentum. Ken Walsh plays Reno, a solitary mountain man who is induced by Doc (Henry Ramer) to enter the pro-ski tour. Mild nudity and obscenities. 88m. **DIR:** Charles Dennis. **CAST:** Kenneth Walsh, Henry Ramer, Linda Griffiths. **1984**

REPORT TO THE COMMISSIONER ★★★★ One of the best of the urban crime films to come out in the early Seventies. Michael Moriarty plays an innocent rookie in the New York Police Department. Not understanding the politics of the cop on the beat, he commits a series of errors that leads to his downfall. Look for Richard Gere in a small part as a pimp. Rated PG for violence, profanity, and nudity. 113m. **DIR:** Milton Katselas. **CAST:** Michael Moriarty, Yaphet Kotto, Susan Blakely, Hector Elizondo, Tony King, William Devane, Richard Gere. **1974**

REQUIEM FOR A HEAVYWEIGHT ★★★½ Anthony Quinn, Julie Harris, Jackie Gleason, Mickey Rooney, and Muhammad Ali (at that time Cassius Clay) give fine performances in this watchable film about boxing corruption. An over-the-hill boxer (Quinn) receives career counseling from a social worker (Harris). B&W; 100m. **DIR:** Ralph Nelson. **CAST:** Anthony Quinn, Julie Harris, Jackie Gleason, Mickey Rooney. **1962**

REQUIEM FOR A HEAVYWEIGHT (TELEVISION) ★★★★ Superb drama written for *Playhouse 90* by Rod Serling, about a washed-up heavyweight boxer (Jack Palance) who is forced to find a life outside the ring. Keenan Wynn is magnificent as his gruff, self-centered manager, and Ed Wynn is perfect as the trainer. One of the best live dramas to come out of the Golden Age of Television. Hosted by Jack Klugman, with interviews with the stars and background information on the show. B&W; 89m. **DIR:** Ralph Nelson. **CAST:** Jack Palance, Keenan Wynn, Kim Hunter, Ed Wynn, Ned Glass. **1956**

RESTLESS ★★ This Greek movie with Raquel Welch, originally titled *The Beloved,* was unknown until it appeared on video, and if you watch it, you'll know why. There's a lot of pretty island scenery, but the plot about housewife Raquel having an affair with a childhood friend is a guaranteed sleep inducer. Unrated; the film contains sexual situations and violence. 75m. **DIR:** George Pan Cosmatos. **CAST:** Raquel Welch, Richard Johnson, Flora Robson. **1972**

RESURRECTION ★★★★½ Ellen Burstyn's superb performance is but one of the topflight elements in this emotional powerhouse. After Burstyn loses her husband and the use of her legs in a freak automobile accident, she discovers she has the power to heal not only herself but anyone who is sick or crippled. Pulitzer Prize–winning playwright Sam Shepard is also memorable as the young hell-raiser who begins to believe she is Jesus reborn. Rated PG. 103m. **DIR:** Daniel Petrie. **CAST:** Ellen Burstyn, Sam Shepard, Richard Farnsworth, Roberts Blossom, Clifford David, Pamela Payton-Wright, Eva LeGallienne. **1980**

RETURN ★★ Right before her father's bid for the Arkansas governorship, Diana (Karlene Crockett) decides to find out about her grandfather's mysterious death. She meets a young man who relives her grandfather's life through hypnosis. Below-par mystery. Rated R for profanity, violence, and partial nudity. 78m. **DIR:** Andrew Silver. **CAST:** Karlene Crockett, John Walcutt, Anne Francis, Frederic Forrest. **1984**

RETURN OF PETER GRIMM, THE ★★★½ Enjoyable blend of *It's a Wonderful Life* and *A Christmas Carol* with the incomparable Lionel Barrymore as Peter Grimm, who dies and is given a second chance to return to Earth and reconcile his family and affairs. B&W; 82m. **DIR:** George Nicholls Jr. **CAST:** Lionel Barrymore, Helen Mack, Edward Ellis, Donald Meek. **1935**

RETURN OF THE SOLDIER, THE ★★★★★ During World War I, a soldier (Alan Bates) suffers shell shock and forgets the last twenty years of his life. His doctors must decide whether he should be allowed to enjoy what has resulted in a carefree second youth, or be brought back to real life and the responsibilities that go with it. Everyone in the cast is superb. Not rated, the film contains adult situations. 105m. **DIR:** Alan Bridges. **CAST:** Glenda Jackson, Julie Christie, Ann-Margret, Alan Bates, Ian Holm, Frank Finlay, Jeremy Kemp. **1985**

RETURN TO EDEN ★★★ This four-and-one-half-hour miniseries, originally made for Australian television, is a bit much to watch at one sitting. Fans of soaps, however, will find it holds their interest. A wealthy woman discovers that her handsome husband only married her for her money when he feeds her to the crocodiles. Miraculously surviving, she alters her appearance and sets about gaining revenge. Unrated, but with brief nudity. 259m. **DIR:** Karen Arthur. **CAST:** Rebecca Gilling, James Reyne, Wendy Hughes. **1983**

RETURN TO PEYTON PLACE ★★ A misfire that should have scored. The sequel to one of the most popular films of all time suffers from a bad case of miscasting. No one from the first film reappears in the sequel, and none of the players look or act at ease with their characters. 122m. **DIR:** José Ferrer. **CAST:** Eleanor Parker, Carol Lynley, Jeff Chandler, Robert Sterling, Tuesday Weld, Mary Astor, Bob Crane, Luciana Paluzzi, Brett Halsey, Gunnar Hellstrom. **1961**

RETURN TO THE BLUE LAGOON 🦃 The beautifully photographed scenes of a lush tropical island cannot salvage this lame sequel which basically rehashes the story of its 1980 predecessor. Rated PG-13 for nudity and brief violence. 101m. **DIR:** William A. Graham. **CAST:** Milla Jovovich, Brian Krause, Lisa Pelikan, Courtney Phillips, Garette Patrick Ratliff. **1991**

RETURN TO TWO-MOON JUNCTION ★★★ This languid girl-meets-boy erotic drama fulfills the genre's requirements—attractive performers, idyllic setting, and playfully sensual lovemaking—and is quite superior to its predecessor. Rated R for nudity, simulated sex, and profanity. 96m. **DIR:** Farhad Mann. **CAST:** Melinda Clarke, John Clayton Schafer, Louise Fletcher. **1994**

REUNION ★★★★ Jason Robards portrays an elderly Jew who returns to Germany fifty-five years after escaping the rise of Hitler in this touching film about letting go of the past by grasping the present. But Robards's scenes are just bookends to the central story of his character as a boy and the friendship that develops between him and a German aristocrat's son. Rated PG-13 for brief nudity. 110m. **DIR:** Jerry Schatzberg. **CAST:** Jason Robards Jr. **1991**

REUNION IN FRANCE ★★ A romantic melodrama that is badly dated, especially considering the fact that it top lines John Wayne and he doesn't get the girl in the last reel. Joan Crawford is a sophisticated Parisian who finds out her lover (Philip Dorn) is apparently collaborating with the Nazis. She switches her affections to an American flier (John Wayne) running from the Gestapo. B&W; 102m. **DIR:** Jules Dassin. **CAST:** Joan Crawford, John Wayne, Philip Dorn, Reginald Owen, John Carradine. **1942**

REVERSAL OF FORTUNE ★★★★ This absorbing drama is fueled by Ron Silver's portrayal of Alan Dershowitz, the fiercely driven Harvard law professor who accepted the challenge of defending the unloved and icily aristocratic Claus Von Bulow (rendered here with aloof arrogance by Oscar-winner Jeremy Irons). Glenn Close, as Sunny Von Bulow, contributes acerbic voice-over narration from her comatose state in a hospital bed. Rated R for language. 111m. **DIR:** Barbet Schroeder. **CAST:** Glenn Close, Jeremy Irons, Ron Silver, Annabella Sciorra, Uta Hagen. **1990**

REVOLUTION ★★ Director Hugh Hudson must have had good intentions going into this project, examining what it might have been like to be involved in the American Revolution. Unfortunately, his actors are so miscast and the script so ragged that Hudson's project stalls almost before it gets started. Rated R. 125m. **DIR:** Hugh Hudson. **CAST:** Al Pacino, Nastassja Kinski, Donald Sutherland. **1986**

RHAPSODY ★★★ A soap opera with classical music background. Elizabeth Taylor plays a woman involved with a violinist and a pianist. They take out their frustration with flamboyant concerts. 115m. **DIR:** Charles Vidor. **CAST:** Elizabeth Taylor, Vittorio Gassman, John Ericson, Louis Calhern, Michael Chekhov. **1954**

RHODES OF AFRICA ★★★ The annexation and assimilation of a culture and people for material gain is not a plot that could sell a film today, but flagrant exploitation of the wealth of South Africa is still timely. Location photography, a good cast, and a standout performance by Walter Huston as the visionary opportunist whose dreams of empire are barely blunted by his philanthropic efforts make this film palatable to modern audiences. B&W; 89m. **DIR:** Berthold Viertel. **CAST:** Walter Huston, Oscar Homolka, Basil Sydney, Peggy Ashcroft, Bernard Lee. **1936**

RICH AND FAMOUS ★★★★ Jacqueline Bisset and Candice Bergen star in this warm, witty, and involving chronicle of the ups, downs, joys, and heartbreak experienced by two friends during a twenty-year relationship. Hollywood great George Cukor directed in his inimitable style. Rated R because of profanity and sex. 117m. **DIR:** George Cukor. **CAST:** Jacqueline Bisset, Candice Bergen, David Selby, Hart Bochner, Steven Hill, Meg Ryan, Matt Lattanzi, Michael Brandon. **1981**

RICH AND STRANGE ★★½ This quirky little drama from Alfred Hitchcock concerns a bickering couple (Henry Kendall and Joan Barry) who come into money, take a world cruise, and suffer through a few minor adventures. The domestic squabbling, which forms the story's only true conflict, is far from Hitchcock's forte; this probably will be of interest only to the director's devotees.

Not rated; suitable for family viewing. B&W; 83m. **DIR:** Alfred Hitchcock. **CAST:** Henry Kendall, Joan Barry, Percy Marmont. **1932**

RICH GIRL ★★★ Jill Schoelen is the title character who strikes out on her own as a waitress in a nightclub. The best rich-girl-falls-in-love-with-a-guy-from-the-wrong-side-of-the-tracks film since *Dirty Dancing*. Rated R for profanity and mild violence. 96m. **DIR:** Joel Bender. **CAST:** Jill Schoelen, Don Michael Paul, Sean Kanan, Ron Karabatsos, Paul Gleason, Willie Dixon. **1991**

RICH IN LOVE ★★★★ Kathryn Erbe comes home from high school one day to find a note from her mother (Jill Clayburgh) to her father (Albert Finney) that says she has gone off "to start a second life." Skillful portrait of an American family crumbling from its core. Thought-provoking and insightful, it's a real gem. Rated PG-13 for profanity and nudity. 105m. **DIR:** Bruce Beresford. **CAST:** Albert Finney, Jill Clayburgh, Kathryn Erbe, Kyle MacLachlan, Piper Laurie, Ethan Hawke, Suzy Amis, Alfre Woodard. **1993**

RICH KIDS ★★ A poor screenplay plagues this movie about two kids going through puberty. A great cast helps. Also, there is an unforgettable heartfelt moment between mother and daughter (Kathryn Walker and Trini Alvarado). Rated PG for language. 97m. **DIR:** Robert M. Young. **CAST:** Trini Alvarado, Jeremy Levy, John Lithgow, Kathryn Walker, Terry Kiser, Paul Dooley. **1979**

RICHARD III ★★★★ Once again, as in *Henry V* and *Hamlet*, England's foremost player displays his near-matchless acting and directing skills in bringing Shakespeare to life on film. His royal crookback usurper is beautifully malevolent, a completely intriguing, smiling villain. The film fascinates from first to last. 161m. **DIR:** Laurence Olivier. **CAST:** Laurence Olivier, Ralph Richardson, John Gielgud, Claire Bloom. **1955**

RICHARD'S THINGS ★★ Gloomy drama about a widow who gets seduced by her late husband's girlfriend. Liv Ullmann plays the patsy as if she were on depressants. 104m. **DIR:** Anthony Harvey. **CAST:** Liv Ullmann, Amanda Redman, David Markham. **1980**

RIFFRAFF (1936) ★★ The give-and-take banter between Spencer Tracy and Jean Harlow is all that holds together this muddled melodrama about the relationship of two tough-as nails waterfront workers. A confusing script and an over-abundance of characters who are never knit into the central story. B&W; 89m. **DIR:** J. Walter Ruben. **CAST:** Spencer Tracy, Jean Harlow, Una Merkel, Joseph Calleia. **1936**

RIFF-RAFF (1992) ★★★★ The fringes of British society are explored in this documentary-like drama about homeless men doing laborer work at a construction site. *Riff-Raff* is an excellent example of independent filmmaking. Naturalistic humor offsets the inherent social commentary as director Ken Loach helps his cast create unforgettable characters. Unrated, the film has profanity, nudity, suggested sex, and violence. 96m. **DIR:** Kenneth Loach. **CAST:** Robert Carlyle, Emer McCourt, Richard Belgrave, Jimmy Coleman, George Moss, Ricky Tomlinson. **1993**

RIGHT HAND MAN, THE 🦃 A dying, disabled, nobleman's repressed love for his doctor's daughter. Rated R for nudity and suggested sex. 101m. **DIR:** Di Drew. **CAST:** Rupert Everett, Hugo Weaving, Arthur Dignam, Jennifer Claire. **1987**

RIGHT OF WAY ★★★★ This made-for-cable work deals with a rather unusual decision made by an old married couple, (Bette Davis and James Stewart) who have decided to commit suicide. Thus begins a battle between daughter (Melinda Dillon) and parents. The result is a surprisingly gripping character study. 106m. **DIR:** George Schaefer. **CAST:** James Stewart, Bette Davis, Melinda Dillon, Priscilla Morrill, John Harkins. **1983**

RIGHT STUFF, THE ★★★★★ From Tom Wolfe's bestseller about the early years of the American space program, writer-director Phil Kaufman has created an epic screen tribute to, and examination of the men (both test pilots and astronauts) who "pushed the outside of the envelope," and the women who watched and waited while the world watched them. Rated PG for profanity. 193m. **DIR:** Phil Kaufman. **CAST:** Sam Shepard, Scott Glenn, Ed Harris, Dennis Quaid, Barbara Hershey, Fred Ward, Kim Stanley, Veronica Cartwright, Pamela Reed, Donald Moffat, Levon Helm, Scott Wilson, Jeff Goldblum, Harry Shearer. **1983**

RING, THE ★★ Long before Sylvester Stallone turned boxing into a filmic event, Alfred Hitchcock toyed with the sports medium in this unremarkable melodrama. The story is little more than a love triangle between two boxing champions (Carl Brisson and Ian Hunter) and the woman loved by both (Lillian Hall-Davies). Not rated; suitable for family viewing. B&W; 73m. **DIR:** Alfred Hitchcock. **CAST:** Carl Brisson, Lillian Hall-Davies, Ian Hunter. **1927**

RING OF SCORPIO ★★½ Three women seek revenge on the drug smugglers who used them as pawns during their college days. The women's story is exciting, but the flashbacks are ineffective. Made for cable. 120m. **DIR:** Ian Barry. **CAST:** Catherine Oxenberg, Jack Scalia, Caroline Goodall. **1991**

RIPTIDE ★★★ A soap opera about the failings of the rich that was obviously made to help a Depression-era audience feel superior to those who still had money. It holds up because of good acting and directing, not good writing. The bored rich heroine dallies with a former lover while her husband is away. B&W; 90m. **DIR:** Edmund Goulding. **CAST:** Norma Shearer, Robert Montgomery, Herbert Marshall, Mrs. Patrick Campbell, Lilyan Tashman, Skeets Gallagher, Arthur Treacher, Ralph Forbes. **1934**

RISING SON ★★★½ Superb TV drama focuses on an auto-parts plant-manager's life after he is laid off. With a son not wanting to finish college and a wife going back to work against his will to help support the family, Brian Dennehy's character is forced to reevaluate his own life and beliefs. 96m. **DIR:** John David Coles. **CAST:** Brian Dennehy, Graham Beckel, Matt Damon, Ving Rhames, Piper Laurie. **1990**

RITA HAYWORTH: THE LOVE GODDESS ★★½ This lifeless attempt to re-create pinup queen Rita Hayworth's exciting life falls short of its goal. Beautiful Lynda Carter as Hayworth, however, keeps the viewer's attention. Made for television. 100m. **DIR:** James Goldstone. **CAST:** Lynda Carter, Michael Lerner, John Considine, Alejandro Rey. **1983**

RIVER, THE (1951) ★★★½ Beautiful locations enhance this lyrical drama about English children growing up in Bengal. This well-orchestrated character study is brilliantly directed by cinema master Jean Renoir and is equally blessed with rich color photography by his brother Claude. 99m. **DIR:** Jean Renoir. **CAST:** Nora Swinburne, Arthur Shields. **1951**

RIVER, THE (1984) ★★★½ Following as it does on the heels of two other first-rate farmer films, this work by director Mark Rydell often seems hopelessly unoriginal and, as a result, boring. As with *Country*, it deals with a farming family who must battle a severe storm and foreclosure proceedings. It simply has little new to say. Rated PG for nudity, violence, and profanity. 122m. **DIR:** Mark Rydell. **CAST:** Mel Gibson, Sissy Spacek, Scott Glenn. **1984**

RIVER OF UNREST ★★ Melodrama about the Sinn Fein rebellion in Ireland bears a strong resemblance to John Ford's classic *The Informer*, but there's more emphasis on the love story between Antoinette Cellier and the two men in her life. Good performances by a capable cast help this slow-moving story, which was based on a stage play. B&W; 69m. **DIR:** Brian Desmond, Walter Summers. **CAST:** John Lodge, John Loder, Antoinette Cellier, Niall MacGinnis, Clifford Evans. **1937**

RIVER RAT, THE ★★★½ Although essentially the story of the growing love between a long-separated father (Tommy Lee Jones), who has been in prison for thirteen years, and daughter (newcomer Martha Plimpton), this release is much more than a simple tearjerker. Writer-director Tom Rickman has invested his story with a grit and realism that set it apart from similar works. As a result, he's created a powerful, thought-provoking motion picture. Rated R for profanity and violence. 109m. **DIR:** Tom Rickman. **CAST:** Tommy Lee Jones, Martha Plimpton, Brian Dennehy. **1984**

RIVER RUNS THROUGH IT, A ★★★★ Robert Redford's elegiac coming-of-age story is based on the memoir by Norman Maclean. Brad Pitt is the young man who finds peace and comradeship in fly-fishing. Redford narrates the film, which compares favorably with his first directorial triumph, *Ordinary People*, in every way. Rated PG for profanity and nudity. 123m. **DIR:** Robert Redford. **CAST:** Brad Pitt, Craig Sheffer, Tom Skerritt, Brenda Blethyn, Emily Lloyd, Edie McClurg, Stephen Shellen. **1992**

RIVER'S EDGE ★★★½ This is a deeply disturbing film based on a real-life 1980 murder case. The teenage murderer in *River's Edge* takes his friends to see the corpse of his classmate-victim. The death becomes a secret bond among them until two decent kids (Keanu Reeves, Ione Skye) decide to do something about it. Rated R for violence, profanity, nudity, and simulated sex. 99m. **DIR:** Tim Hunter. **CAST:** Dennis Hopper, Crispin Glover, Keanu Reeves, Ione Skye, Roxana Zal, Daniel Roebuck, Tom Bower, Leo Rossi. **1987**

ROAD TO MECCA, THE ★★★★ An eccentric widow living in a small South African town has a spiritual revelation to build a large sculpture garden in her yard, made to resemble Mecca. This unusual film is adapted by Athol Fugard from his play. Unrated. 106m. **DIR:** Athol Fugard, Peter Goldsmid. **CAST:** Kathy Bates, Yvonne Bryceland, Athol Fugard. **1991**

ROAD TO RUIN, THE (1928) 🦃 A classic exploitation feature, this silent quickie is creaky and heavily moralistic. Silent. B&W; 45m. **DIR:** Norton S. Parker. **CAST:** Helen Foster, Grant Withers, Charles Miller. **1928**

ROAD TO YESTERDAY, THE ★★★ This is Cecil B. DeMille's first independent film. The plot involves reincarnation and modern characters who flash back historically to seventeenth-century England and explain their actions and feelings years later. The action sequences make this a compelling mix of melodrama and spectacle. Silent with musical score. B&W; 136m. **DIR:** Cecil B. DeMille. **CAST:** Joseph Schildkraut, William Boyd, Vera Reynolds, Sally Rand. **1925**

ROADSIDE PROPHETS ★★★★ Entrusted with the cremated remains of a man he barely knows, John Doe (of the rock group X) searches for the mythical Nevada town the man had once spoke of. Along the way he hooks up with a strange kid. A road movie with a difference. Rated R for profanity and nudity. 96m. **DIR:** Abbe Wool. **CAST:**

John Doe, Adam Horovitz, John Cusack, David Carradine, Arlo Guthrie, Timothy Leary. 1992

ROARING ROAD, THE ★★★ Car salesman Wallace Reid represents his company in a famous auto race. Lots of real racing footage. Silent. B&W; 57m. **DIR:** James Cruze. **CAST:** Wallace Reid. 1919

ROBE, THE ★★★★ Richard Burton is the Roman tribune charged with overseeing the execution of Christ in this story of his involvement with the followers of Christ and the effect the robe of Jesus has on all involved. It is a well-made film, and not heavy-handed in its approach. 135m. **DIR:** Henry Koster. **CAST:** Richard Burton, Victor Mature, Jean Simmons, Michael Rennie, Richard Boone, Dean Jagger, Dawn Addams, Jay Robinson. 1953

ROCKET GIBRALTAR ★★★ A bittersweet comedy-drama about the reunion of an eccentric family in the Hamptons, drawn by the 77th birthday of the patriarch. Burt Lancaster plays the elder, giving this slight, sentimental film credibility. Rated PG. 100m. **DIR:** Daniel Petrie. **CAST:** Burt Lancaster, Suzy Amis, John Glover, Bill Pullman. 1988

ROCKING HORSE WINNER, THE ★★★½ Impressive screen adaptation of D. H. Lawrence's disturbing story about a sensitive little boy's uncanny ability to predict racehorse winners by riding his rocking horse. B&W; 91m. **DIR:** Anthony Pelissier. **CAST:** Valerie Hobson, John Howard Davies, John Mills. 1949

ROCKY ★★★★★ Those put to sleep by the endless sequels in this series probably have forgotten the gentleness and dignity of this initial entry. Star Sylvester Stallone wrote the original script about Rocky Balboa, the painfully shy boxer who only "wants to go the distance" with champ Apollo Creed (Carl Weathers). The supporting cast is excellent—Burgess Meredith as the feisty trainer, Talia Shire as Rocky's girlfriend, and Burt Young as her brother. One of the ultimate feel-good films, and it works every time. Rated PG for violence. 119m. **DIR:** John G. Avildsen. **CAST:** Sylvester Stallone, Burgess Meredith, Talia Shire, Burt Young, Carl Weathers. 1976

ROCKY II ★★ The weakest entry in Sylvester Stallone's boxing series, about a down-and-out fighter attempting to prove himself through a rematch with the champ (Carl Weathers). Talia Shire, Burgess Meredith, and Burt Young reprise their series roles in this soaper in the ring. Rated PG. 119m. **DIR:** Sylvester Stallone. **CAST:** Sylvester Stallone, Carl Weathers, Talia Shire, Burgess Meredith, Burt Young. 1979

ROCKY III ★★★ Writer-director-star Sylvester Stallone's third entry in the Rocky Balboa series is surprisingly entertaining. Though we've seen it all before, Stallone manages to make it work. Rated PG for violence and mild profanity. 99m. **DIR:** Sylvester Stallone. **CAST:** Sylvester Stallone, Talia Shire, Burgess Meredith, Mr. T, Carl Weathers. 1982

ROCKY IV ★★★ Sylvester Stallone's Everyman returns to take on a massive Russian fighter (Dolph Lundgren) trained via computer and programmed to kill. The result is deliciously corny, enjoyably predictable entertainment. Rated PG for violence and profanity. 90m. **DIR:** Sylvester Stallone. **CAST:** Sylvester Stallone, Talia Shire, Burt Young, Carl Weathers, Brigitte Nielsen, Tony Burton, Michael Pataki, Dolph Lundgren. 1985

ROCKY V ★★★½ Rocky returns home from the Soviet Union to a hero's welcome but financial ruin, thanks to naïve business decisions by brother-in-law Paulie (Burt Young). The saga of Sylvester Stallone's Rocky Balboa concludes with a suitably subdued whisper. Rated PG-13. 104m. **DIR:** John G. Avildsen. **CAST:** Sylvester Stallone, Talia Shire, Burt Young, Burgess Meredith. 1990

RODEO GIRL ★★★★ Katharine Ross is Sammy, the wife of rodeo champ Will Garrett (Bo Hopkins). When she decides to try her hand at roping and bronco riding, she finds that she has the potential to be a rodeo champ. But complications arise when she discovers she is pregnant. Based on a true story. 92m. **DIR:** Jackie Cooper. **CAST:** Katharine Ross, Bo Hopkins, Candy Clark, Jacqueline Brooks, Wilford Brimley. 1980

ROE VS. WADE ★★★★ Winner of two Emmy Awards—for outstanding drama special and outstanding lead actress—this fine telefilm shows the abortion issue from the point of a down-and-out, unmarried woman (Holly Hunter). Amy Madigan, as Hunter's determined attorney, delivers an electrifyingly intense statement before the court justices. Contains frank adult discussion. 92m. **DIR:** Gregory Hoblit. **CAST:** Holly Hunter, Amy Madigan, Kathy Bates, Chris Mulkey, James Gammon. 1989

ROLL OF THUNDER, HEAR MY CRY ★★★½ Heartwarming tale of a black family struggling to get by in Depression-era Mississippi. Made for television, this was meant to be shown in three parts, and it's best viewed that way—the pace is a little too leisurely (especially for kids) to watch this in one sitting. 150m. **DIR:** Jack Smight. **CAST:** Claudia McNeil, Janet MacLachlan, Robert Christian, Morgan Freeman. 1978

ROMAN HOLIDAY ★★★★★ Amid the beauty and mystique of Rome, an American newspaperman (Gregory Peck) is handed a news scoop on the proverbial silver platter. A princess (Audrey Hepburn) has slipped away from her stifling royal lifestyle. In her efforts to hide as one of Rome's common people, she encounters Peck. Their amiable adventures provide the basis for a charming fantasy-romance. B&W; 119m. **DIR:** William Wyler. **CAST:** Gregory Peck, Audrey Hepburn, Eddie Albert. **1953**

ROMAN SPRING OF MRS. STONE, THE ★★ A sensitive, elegant middle-aged actress (Vivien Leigh) has retreated to Rome to get a new focus. Warren Beatty plays a sleek, surly, wet-lipped Italian gigolo out for what he can get with the help of a crass, waspish procuress (Lotte Lenya). Banal. 104m. **DIR:** Jose Quintero. **CAST:** Vivien Leigh, Warren Beatty, Lotte Lenya, Jill St. John. **1961**

ROMANCE ★★★ Greta Garbo, even miscast as an Italian singer, brings interest to this tale of a woman of questionable character finding herself pursued by a young minister. At the 1929–30 Academy Awards Garbo and director Clarence Brown were each nominated for this movie and *Anna Christie*; both lost. B&W; 79m. **DIR:** Clarence Brown. **CAST:** Greta Garbo, Lewis Stone, Gavin Gordon, Elliott Nugent. **1930**

ROMANCE IN MANHATTAN ★★★ Francis Lederer as a friendly, ebullient Czech immigrant deals bravely with an inhospitable New York City and wins the love of Ginger Rogers, who befriends him. She's good, but it's his picture. B&W; 78m. **DIR:** Stephen Roberts. **CAST:** Ginger Rogers, Francis Lederer, Donald Meek, Sidney Toler. **1935**

ROMANCE ON THE ORIENT EXPRESS 🦃 This British TV movie is ruined by insipid dialogue. 96m. **DIR:** Lawrence Gordon Clark. **CAST:** Cheryl Ladd, Stuart Wilson, John Gielgud. **1985**

ROMANTIC ENGLISHWOMAN, THE ★★★★ Though not a completely successful adaptation of Thomas Wiseman's novel this is likely to be vastly more engaging than anything on television on any given night. Casual infidelity among the wealthy intelligentsia is always at least voyeuristically satisfying. And here pulp novel writer Michael Caine actually impels his discontented, but presumably faithful, wife Glenda Jackson into an affair with gigolo Helmut Berger. Rated R for language, adult situations. 115m. **DIR:** Joseph Losey. **CAST:** Glenda Jackson, Michael Caine, Helmut Berger. **1975**

ROME ADVENTURE ★★★½ A soap opera produced just as Hollywood was getting sexier and starring two of the sexiest women of the 1960s: Suzanne Pleshette and Angie Dickinson. The locale is romantic Rome where a visiting schoolteacher has an affair with an aging playboy, then meets a man closer to her own age she likes better. The performances are especially good. 120m. **DIR:** Delmer Daves. **CAST:** Angie Dickinson, Troy Donahue, Suzanne Pleshette, Rossano Brazzi, Chad Everett, Hampton Fancher, Al Hirt, Constance Ford. **1962**

ROMEO AND JULIET (1936) ★★★ An almost literal translation of Shakespeare's classic romance, and it would have been better with some streamlining. Both Norma Shearer and Leslie Howard were much too old to play the young lovers, but they deliver the poetic dialogue with sincerity as well as emotion. John Barrymore and Basil Rathbone take acting honors, especially Barrymore as the hapless Mercutio. B&W; 126m. **DIR:** George Cukor. **CAST:** Norma Shearer, Leslie Howard, Basil Rathbone, Edna May Oliver, Andy Devine, John Barrymore, Reginald Denny, C. Aubrey Smith. **1936**

ROMEO AND JULIET (1968) ★★★★½ Franco Zeffirelli directed this excellent version of *Romeo and Juliet*. When it was filmed, Olivia Hussey was only 15 and Leonard Whiting was only 17, keeping their characters in tune with Shakespeare's hero and heroine. Rated PG. 138m. **DIR:** Franco Zeffirelli. **CAST:** Olivia Hussey, Leonard Whiting, John McEnery, Michael York, Milo O'Shea. **1968**

ROMEO AND JULIET (1983) ★★★½ A first-class stage production of Shakespeare's tale of the young "star-crossed" lovers, Romeo and Juliet. Esther Rolle is interesting, and quite good, as Juliet's nurse, but the acting honors go to Dan Hamilton as the spirited, fun-loving Mercutio. A Bard Productions Ltd. release. 165m. **DIR:** William Woodman. **CAST:** Alex Hyde-White, Blanche Baker, Esther Rolle, Dan Hamilton, Frederic Lehne, Alvah Stanley. **1983**

ROMEO AND JULIET (1988) ★★★½ Made for British television, this production of Shakespeare's timeless tale of star-crossed lovers is highly rewarding. Ann Hasson makes an especially sweet and beguiling Juliet. 360m. **DIR:** Joan Kemp-Welch. **CAST:** Christopher Neame, Ann Hasson, Peter Jeffrey, Peter Dyneley. **1988**

ROMERO ★★★½ An exquisitely understated and heartfelt performance by Raul Julia in the title role enlivens this somewhat heavy-handed political and religious message movie. It chronicles the struggle of Salvadoran Archbishop Oscar Romero, who was assassinated in 1980 by representatives of the repressive government the mild-mannered cleric had been forced to fight. Rated PG-13 for violence. 105m. **DIR:** John Duigan. **CAST:** Raul Julia, Richard Jordan, Ana Alicia, Eddie Velez, Tony Plana, Harold Gould. **1989**

ROOM AT THE TOP ★★★★★ John Braine's powerful novel, adapted for the screen by Neil Patterson, is a smashing success. Laurence Harvey is an opportunist who will stop at nothing, including a dalliance with his boss's daughter, to get to the top in the business world. A great cast and superb direction. This is a must-see film. B&W; 115m. **DIR:** Jack Clayton. **CAST:**

Laurence Harvey, Simone Signoret, Heather Sears, Hermione Baddeley. **1959**

ROOM 43 ★★ Cabbie Eddie Constantine battles a ring of white slavers after he falls in love with one of their victims, a French girl who needs his help to remain in England. Lukewarm crime tale, featuring Michael Caine and future trash novelist Jackie Collins in small roles. B&W; 85m. **DIR:** Alvin Rakoff. **CAST:** Eddie Constantine, Diana Dors, Odile Versois, Herbert Lom. **1959**

ROOM WITH A VIEW, A ★★★★★ This is a triumph of tasteful, intelligent filmmaking. Director James Ivory painstakingly recreates the mood, manners, and milieu of 1908 Edwardian England as he explores the consequence of a tour of Florence, Italy, taken by an innocently curious young woman (Helena Bonham Carter) and her persnickety, meddling aunt (Maggie Smith, in top form). Unrated, the film has one brief scene of violence and some male frontal nudity. 115m. **DIR:** James Ivory. **CAST:** Maggie Smith, Helena Bonham Carter, Denholm Elliott, Julian Sands, Daniel Day-Lewis, Simon Callow, Judi Dench, Rosemary Leach, Rupert Graves. **1986**

ROOTS ★★★★★ Unique in television history is this six-volume chronicle of eighteenth and nineteenth century black life from African enslavement to and beyond Civil War emancipation. Studded with stars, it is at once a triumph in every aspect—acting, writing, and production—and an illuminating look into a tragic side of American social history. Outstanding in a stellar cast are Lou Gossett Jr., as the wise and diplomatic antebellum house servant Fiddler, and Ben Vereen as the ebullient, post–Civil War freeman Chicken George. 540m. **DIR:** Marvin J. Chomsky. **CAST:** LeVar Burton, Edward Asner, Lloyd Bridges, Cicely Tyson, Lorne Greene, Ben Vereen, Sandy Duncan, Leslie Uggams, Chuck Connors, Burl Ives, Lou Gossett Jr. **1977**

ROOTS—THE GIFT ★★½ This made-for-TV spin-off from *Roots* and *Roots: The Next Generation* brings back Lou Gossett Jr. and LeVar Burton as Fiddler and Kunta Kunte to lead fellow slaves to freedom on Christmas Eve. Nice, but contrived. 100m. **DIR:** Kevin Hooks. **CAST:** Lou Gossett Jr., LeVar Burton, Michael Learned, Avery Brooks, Kate Mulgrew, Shaun Cassidy. **1988**

ROOTS: THE NEXT GENERATION ★★★★★ A seven-cassette, Emmy-winning continuation of *Roots*, television's most highly acclaimed dramatic series. An outstanding cast of 1,240, including fifty-three starring roles, follows the mesmerizing saga of slave Kunta Kinte's descendants forward from 1882 to post–World War II days, when author Alex Haley began the ancestral search for his "old African," and the beginning of his family. Like its predecessor, a fine, rewarding production. 686m. **DIR:** John Erman, Charles S. Dubin, Georg Stanford Brown, Lloyd Richards. **CAST:** Olivia de Havilland, Henry Fonda, Marlon Brando, Richard Thomas, Georg Stanford Brown, Ossie Davis, Dorian Harewood, James Earl Jones. **1979**

ROSE AND THE JACKAL, THE 🦃 TV movie concerning the Secret Service's attempt to stop Confederate espionage in Washington, D.C., at the outbreak of the Civil War. 95m. **DIR:** Jack Gold. **CAST:** Christopher Reeve, Madolyn Smith, Carrie Snodgress, Kevin McCarthy, Jeff Corey. **1990**

ROSE GARDEN, THE ★★★½ In modern-day Germany, a Holocaust survivor (Maximilian Schell) is arrested for assaulting a successful elderly businessman. Defense attorney (Liv Ullmann) discovers that the businessman was a former S.S. officer who presided over a brutal Nazi death camp and was responsible for the murder of dozens of children. Engrossing psychological drama. Rated PG-13 for violence. 152m. **DIR:** Fons Rademakers. **CAST:** Liv Ullmann, Maximilian Schell, Peter Fonda. **1990**

ROSE TATTOO, THE ★★★★ Making her American film debut, volatile Italian star Anna Magnani handily won a best-actress Oscar playing the widow obsessed by the memory of her stud husband. She finally lets go when she finds truck driver Burt Lancaster has a rose tattoo, the symbol of sexual prowess that the departed sported. Tangy and torrid. B&W; 117m. **DIR:** Daniel Mann. **CAST:** Anna Magnani, Burt Lancaster, Marisa Pavan, Ben Cooper, Jo Van Fleet, Virginia Grey. **1955**

ROSELAND ★★½ A somewhat overly respectful triptych set in the famous, now-tattered, New York dance palace. The three stories are quietly compelling, but only Christopher Walken (certainly a good enough dancer) and Don DeNatale (who was an emcee at Roseland) give the film any vim. 103m. **DIR:** James Ivory. **CAST:** Christopher Walken, Geraldine Chaplin, Teresa Wright, Lou Jacobi, Don DeNatale, Lilia Skala. **1977**

RUBY (1991) ★★★½ Superb performances help elevate this largely fictional account of the secret life of Dallas nightclub owner Jack Ruby, who became infamous for killing Lee Harvey Oswald. As with director John Mackenzie's classic British gangster film, *The Long Good Friday*, the characters and tense, realistic situations overcome the familiarity of certain key events. Rated R for violence and profanity. 100m. **DIR:** John Mackenzie. **CAST:** Danny Aiello, Sherilyn Fenn, Arliss Howard, Tobin Bell, David Duchovny, Richard Sarafian, Joe Cortese, Marc Lawrence. **1991**

RUBY GENTRY ★★★ An excellent cast and sensitive direction make this drama of a Carolina swamp girl's social progress better than might be expected. Its focus is the caste system and prejudice in a picturesque region of the great melting pot. B&W; 82m. **DIR:** King Vidor. **CAST:** Jennifer Jones, Charlton Heston, Karl Malden, Tom Tully. **1952**

RUBY IN PARADISE ★★★★ Engagingly offbeat character study about a young woman who leaves her husband and home in the Tennessee mountains for what she hopes will be a better life in Florida. The challenges faced by a young woman out on her own are thoughtfully presented in this well-made film, which benefits from an impressive big-screen debut by Ashley Judd. Rated R for brief profanity and simulated sex. 105m. **DIR:** Victor Nunez. **CAST:** Ashley Judd, Todd Field, Bentley Mitchum, Allison Dean, Dorothy Lyman, Betsy Douds, Felicia Hernandez. **1993**

RUMBLE FISH ★★ Francis Ford Coppola's black-and-white screen portrait of S. E. Hinton's second-rate novel about a teenage boy (Matt Dillon) seeking to escape his hellish life is a disappointing misfire. Rated R. B&W; 94m. **DIR:** Francis Ford Coppola. **CAST:** Christopher Penn, Tom Waits, Matt Dillon, Dennis Hopper, Vincent Spano, Mickey Rourke. **1983**

RUMOR MILL, THE ★★ Hokey soap opera played to the hilt by Elizabeth Taylor and Jane Alexander as rival gossip queens Louella Parsons and Hedda Hopper. Plenty of cat fights and eye-piercing high camp. Made-for-TV melodrama that originally aired as *Malice in Wonderland.* 94m. **DIR:** Gus Trikonis. **CAST:** Elizabeth Taylor, Jane Alexander, Richard Dysart. **1988**

RUN IF YOU CAN 🦃 An incomprehensible police thriller. Rated R for nudity and violence. 92m. **DIR:** Virginia Lively Stone. **CAST:** Martin Landau, Yvette Napir, Jerry Van Dyke. **1987**

RUNAWAY FATHER ★★ Made-for-TV true story stars Donna Mills as a wife out to prove that her missing husband faked his death in order to leave his family. Standard fare gets a boost from durable cast, including Jack Scalia as the scoundrel. Not rated. 94m. **DIR:** John Nicoella. **CAST:** Donna Mills, Jack Scalia, Chris Mulkey, Jenny Lewis, Priscilla Pointer. **1991**

RUNNER STUMBLES, THE ★★★ A good adaptation of Milan Stitt's play, which certainly did not deserve the scorching hatred generated during its brief box-office appearance. Dick Van Dyke plays a priest who falls in love with Kathleen Quinlan's appealing nun. The subject may make viewers uneasy, but the film is by no means tacky or exploitative. Rated PG for adult subject matter. 99m. **DIR:** Stanley Kramer. **CAST:** Dick Van Dyke, Kathleen Quinlan, Maureen Stapleton, Beau Bridges. **1979**

RUNNING AWAY ★★ Pointless WWII film features Sophia Loren and Sydney Penny as an Italian mother and daughter team traveling from what seemed a comparatively safe Rome to the mountains. Rated PG-13 for violence. 101m. **DIR:** Dino Risi. **CAST:** Sophia Loren, Sydney Penny, Robert Loggia, Andrea Occhipinti. **1989**

RUNNING BRAVE ★★★★ Robby Benson stars as Billy Mills, whose winning the ten-thousand meter race in the 1964 Olympics was one of the biggest upsets in sports history. The direction is pedestrian at best. But Benson's fine performance and the true-life drama of Mills's determination to set a positive example of achievement for his people—the Sioux and all Native Americans—is affecting. Rated PG for profanity. 105m. **DIR:** Donald Shebib. **CAST:** Robby Benson, Pat Hingle, Jeff McCracken. **1983**

RUNNING HOT ★★★ Eric Stoltz gives a very good performance as a 17-year-old sentenced to death row. The publicity of his case arouses the interest of 30-year-old Monica Carrico, who sends him love letters in prison. His escape and bizarre affair with her have serious consequences in this fast-paced drama. Rated R for sex, violence, language, and nudity. 88m. **DIR:** Mark Griffiths. **CAST:** Eric Stoltz, Stuart Margolin, Monica Carrico, Virgil Frye. **1983**

RUNNING MATES (1985) ★★ Stereotyped characters populate this story of two teenagers who fall in love, only to be torn apart when their respective fathers run against each other in an election. Rated PG for adult situations. 90m. **DIR:** Thomas L. Neff. **CAST:** Gregg Webb, Barbara Howard. **1985**

RUNNING ON EMPTY ★★★★ Extremely well-made film looks at a fugitive family that has been on the lam from the FBI for years. Unable to establish roots anywhere because of the constant fear of detection, parents Christine Lahti and Judd Hirsch must decide what to do when their son, River Phoenix, is accepted to the Juilliard School of Music. Rated PG-13. 116m. **DIR:** Sidney Lumet. **CAST:** Christine Lahti, Judd Hirsch, River Phoenix, Martha Plimpton. **1988**

RUNNING WILD (1955) ★★ Rookie cop William Campbell pretends to be a young tough to get the goods on an auto-theft gang headed by Keenan Wynn. Made to catch the teenage rock 'n' roll crowd. 81m. **DIR:** Abner Biberman. **CAST:** William Campbell, Mamie Van Doren, Keenan Wynn, Katherine Case, Jan Merlin, John Saxon. **1955**

RUSH ★★★ For her directorial debut, Lili Fini Zanuck (wife of producer Richard) chose a hard-edged story about undercover narcotics officers who become heavy users while busting other addicts in a small Texas town. It's downright dreary much of the time, with the fine acting of Sam Elliott and

Max Perlich adding several bright moments. Rated R for profanity, violence, and drug use. 120m. **DIR:** Lili Fini Zanuck. **CAST:** Jason Patric, Jennifer Jason Leigh, Sam Elliott, Max Perlich, Gregg Allman, Bill Sadler. **1991**

RUSSIA HOUSE, THE ★★★★ A British book publisher (Sean Connery) becomes involved in international espionage when a Russian woman (Michelle Pfeiffer) sends him an unsolicited manuscript. This first-rate adaptation of the John Le Carre novel is a thinking-person's spy movie. Rated R for profanity. 123m. **DIR:** Fred Schepisi. **CAST:** Sean Connery, Michelle Pfeiffer, Roy Scheider, Klaus Maria Brandauer, James Fox, John Mahoney, Michael Kitchen, J. T. Walsh, Ken Russell. **1990**

RYAN'S DAUGHTER ★★½ Acclaimed director David Lean took a critical beating with this release, about a spoiled woman (Sarah Miles) who shamelessly lusts after an officer (Christopher Jones). Robert Mitchum, as Miles's husband, is the best thing about this watchable misfire. Rated PG. 176m. **DIR:** David Lean. **CAST:** Sarah Miles, Christopher Jones, Robert Mitchum, Trevor Howard, John Mills, Leo McKern. **1970**

S.O.S. TITANIC ★★★ The "unsinkable" once again goes to her watery grave in this made-for-television docudrama compounded of fiction and fact. 105m. **DIR:** William Hale. **CAST:** David Janssen, Cloris Leachman, Susan Saint James, David Warner. **1979**

SADAT ★★★½ Although much of the great Egyptian statesman's life is left out of this two-part TV movie, what is seen is well-made and impressively acted, particularly by Lou Gossett Jr. as Sadat. 191m. **DIR:** Richard Michaels. **CAST:** Lou Gossett Jr., John Rhys-Davies, Madolyn Smith, Jeremy Kemp, Anne Heywood, Barry Morse, Nehemiah Persoff, Paul Smith, Jeffrey Tambor. **1983**

SADIE MCKEE ★★ A dated character study about a working girl who moves to the other side of the tracks, dragging her boyfriends behind her. This is the kind of movie Joan Crawford specialized in, but it is way out of style today. B&W; 89m. **DIR:** Clarence Brown. **CAST:** Joan Crawford, Franchot Tone, Edward Arnold, Gene Raymond, Esther Ralston, Leo G. Carroll, Akim Tamiroff. **1934**

SADIE THOMPSON ★★★ Screen legend Gloria Swanson is Somerset Maugham's famous South Seas floozy in this silent predecessor of the better-known 1932 Joan Crawford sound remake. Director-writer-costar Raoul Walsh more than holds his own against her, as reformer Lionel Barrymore resists but eventually succumbs to the sins of the flesh. B&W; 97m. **DIR:** Raoul Walsh. **CAST:** Gloria Swanson, Raoul Walsh, Lionel Barrymore. **1928**

SAILOR WHO FELL FROM GRACE WITH THE SEA, THE ★★ Much of Japanese culture remains misunderstood, and this inept adaptation of Yukio Mishima's novel is a perfect example. Kris Kristofferson doesn't have to stretch his limited abilities as an amiable sailor who falls in love with Sarah Miles. Rated R for violence and sex. 104m. **DIR:** Lewis John Carlino. **CAST:** Sarah Miles, Kris Kristofferson, Margo Cunningham, Earl Rhodes. **1976**

ST. BENNY THE DIP ★★ A good cast is about all that recommends this time-worn story of con artists who disguise their larceny behind clerics' robes and find themselves thinking clearer and walking the straight and narrow as a result of their contact with religion. B&W; 79m. **DIR:** Edgar G. Ulmer. **CAST:** Dick Haymes, Nina Foch, Roland Young, Lionel Stander, Freddie Bartholomew. **1951**

ST. ELMO'S FIRE ★★★ This film would have us believe a group of college graduates are, at the age of 22, all suffering from mid-life crises. However, fine acting by some of the screen's hottest young stars helps us forgive this off-kilter premise. The movie succeeds almost in spite of itself. Rated R for suggested sex, violence, nudity, and profanity. 110m. **DIR:** Joel Schumacher. **CAST:** Emilio Estevez, Rob Lowe, Andrew McCarthy, Demi Moore, Judd Nelson, Ally Sheedy, Mare Winningham, Martin Balsam, Andie MacDowell, Joyce Van Patten. **1985**

ST. HELENS ★★½ Very shallow look at the Mount St. Helens volcanic eruption and the following disasters. Art Carney plays Harry, the old man who refuses to move from his home. Pretty bland stuff. Rated PG for no particular reason. 90m. **DIR:** Ernest Pintoff. **CAST:** Art Carney, David Huffman, Cassie Yates, Albert Salmi, Ron O'Neal. **1981**

SAINT JACK ★★★ Although an interesting film, *Saint Jack* lacks power and a sense of wholeness. Ben Gazzara plays an oddly likable pimp plying his trade in Singapore in the 1970s who wants to become rich and powerful by running the classiest whorehouse in the Far East. Rated R. 112m. **DIR:** Peter Bogdanovich. **CAST:** Ben Gazzara, Denholm Elliott, James Villiers, Joss Ackland, Peter Bogdanovich, George Lazenby. **1979**

SAINT JOAN ★★ Even a screenplay by Graham Greene can't salvage Otto Preminger's dull screen version of George Bernard Shaw's intriguing play. Jean Seberg seems at a loss and the presence of such performers as Richard Widmark and John Gielgud, just remind one what could have been. B&W; 110m. **DIR:** Otto Preminger. **CAST:** Jean Seberg, Richard Widmark, Richard Todd, John Gielgud, Anton Walbrook, Harry Andrews, Felix Aylmer. **1957**

SAINT OF FORT WASHINGTON, THE ★★★½ Well-acted drama focuses on two homeless men struggling to survive both physically and spiritually on the mean streets of New York. Matt Dillon is an emotionally troubled photographer who finds himself protected by streetwise Danny Glover in a strong film that goes somewhat astray in the last half. Rated R for violence and profanity. 103m. **DIR:** Tim Hunter. **CAST:** Matt Dillon, Danny Glover, Rick Aviles, Nina Siemaszko, Ving Rhames, Joe Seneca, Harry Ellington. **1993**

SAKHAROV ★★★★ Compassionate story of the nuclear physicist and designer of the H-bomb, Andrei Sakharov (Jason Robards), who won the Nobel Peace Prize after waking up to the global terror of the nuclear gambit and contributing to the budding human rights movement in the Soviet Union during the late 1960s. 118m. **DIR:** Jack Gold. **CAST:** Jason Robards Jr., Glenda Jackson, Michael Bryant, Paul Freeman, Anna Massey, Joe Melia, Jim Norton. **1984**

SALLY OF THE SAWDUST ★★★★ W. C. Fields is at his brilliant best as the lovable con-man guardian of pretty Carol Dempster in this early film of his Broadway hit, *Poppy*. Knowing the identity of her wealthy grandparents, he works to restore her to her rightful place in society, does so after a variety of problems, and says farewell with the now-classic line—Fields's accepted credo—"Never give a sucker an even break." Silent. B&W; 91m. **DIR:** D. W. Griffith. **CAST:** Carol Dempster, W. C. Fields, Alfred Lunt. **1925**

SALOME (1923) ★★ Campy silent version of Oscar Wilde's play, *Salome's Dance of the Seven Veils*. Rejected and cursed by John the Baptist, Salome plans her revenge. B&W; 48m. **DIR:** Charles Bryant. **CAST:** Anna Nazimova. **1923**

SALOME (1953) ★★ Biblical belly dancer Salome (Rita Hayworth) offers herself up as a sacrifice to save John the Baptist (Stewart Granger). Inane. 103m. **DIR:** William Dieterle. **CAST:** Rita Hayworth, Stewart Granger, Judith Anderson, Charles Laughton, Cedric Hardwicke. **1953**

SALOME (1985) ★½ This is a strange mixture. It is the story of the famous temptress Salome, but in director Claude D'Anna's version the Roman soldiers are in World War II overcoats, there is an elevator in the palace, and the slaves are listening to portable radios. Whatever he had in mind, it doesn't make it. Rated R. 105m. **DIR:** Claude D'Anna. **CAST:** Jo Ciampa, Tomas Milian, Tim Woodward. **1985**

SALOME, WHERE SHE DANCED 🦃 Yvonne De Carlo plays an exotic dancer in the American West. 90m. **DIR:** Charles Lamont. **CAST:** Yvonne De Carlo, Rod Cameron, Walter Slezak, David Bruce, Albert Dekker, Marjorie Rambeau. **1945**

SALOME'S LAST DANCE ★★★★ Ken Russell pays homage to Oscar Wilde in this outrageous dark comedy that takes place in 1895 London. A group of eccentric actors enact Wilde's play *Salome* in the most bizarre setting imaginable: a brothel. Glenda Jackson is simply remarkable, and she's supported by an equally gifted cast in this brilliantly staged surreal fantasy. Rated R for nudity and profanity. 93m. **DIR:** Ken Russell. **CAST:** Glenda Jackson, Stratford Johns, Nickolas Grace, Douglas Hodge, Imogen Millais Scott. **1988**

SALT OF THE EARTH ★★★ Miners in New Mexico go on strike after a series of accidents and face a long, bitter battle. This once-controversial melodrama uses real mine workers in the cast and has a realistic feel. B&W; 94m. **DIR:** Herbert J. Biberman. **CAST:** Rosoura Revueltas, Will Geer. **1953**

SALUTE JOHN CITIZEN! ★★½ World War II home-front propaganda about how an ordinary British family copes with deprivations and does its part to pull for the war effort. Sort of a low-rent *Mrs. Miniver.* B&W; 74m. **DIR:** Maurice Elvey. **CAST:** Edward Rigby, Mabel Constanduroos, Stanley Holloway, Peggy Cummins. **1942**

SALVADOR ★★★★ James Woods plays screenwriter-photojournalist Richard Boyle in the latter's semiautobiographical account of the events that occurred in El Salvador circa 1980–81. It is a fascinating movie despite its flaws and outrageousness. Rated R for profanity, nudity, suggested sex, drug use, and violence. 120m. **DIR:** Oliver Stone. **CAST:** James Woods, John Savage, James Belushi, Michael Murphy, Elpidia Carrillo, Tony Plana, Cynthia Gibb. **1986**

SALVATION ★★★½ A punk's wife sends the family cash to a televangelist. Angered, the punk has his teenage sister-in-law seduce the preacher and then blackmails him into sharing his religious revenues. Beth B., who directed and shares writing and production credits, has delivered a raw, insightful film. Rated R for nudity and profanity. 80m. **DIR:** Beth B. **CAST:** Stephen McHattie, Dominique Davalos, Exene Cervenka. **1986**

SAMARITAN: THE MITCH SNYDER STORY ★★★★ Martin Sheen portrays a nonviolent activist named Mitch Snyder, who successfully convinces city officials to deal with the problems of the homeless. Sensitive made-for-TV biography. 90m. **DIR:** Richard T. Heffron. **CAST:** Martin Sheen, Roxanne Hart, Cicely Tyson. **1986**

SAM'S SON ★★★½ Written and directed by Michael Landon, this sweetly nostalgic semiautobiographical family film features Timothy Patrick Murphy as the young Eugene Orowitz (Landon's real name), whose parents, Sam (Eli Wallach) and Harriet (Anne Jackson), seem destined never to realize their fondest dreams until their son lends a hand. Rated PG for brief violence. 104m. **DIR:** Michael Landon. **CAST:** Timothy Patrick Murphy, Eli Wallach, Anne Jackson. **1984**

SAMSON AND DELILAH (1949) ★★★★ This Cecil B. DeMille extravaganza still looks good today. Hedy Lamarr plays the beautiful vixen Delilah, who robs Samson (Victor Mature) of his incredible strength. Dumb but fun. 128m. **DIR:** Cecil B. DeMille. **CAST:** Hedy Lamarr, Victor Mature, George Sanders, Angela Lansbury. **1949**

SAMSON AND DELILAH (1984) ★★½ An okay TV remake of the DeMille classic that had Victor Mature in the lead. This time, Mature plays Samson's father. Mature and the other veteran actors (Max von Sydow and José Ferrer) help to save the movie. Lots of action—lions, chains, and crumbling masonry. 100m. **DIR:** Lee Philips. **CAST:** Antony Hamilton, Belinda Bauer, Max von Sydow, Stephen Macht, Maria Schell, José Ferrer, Victor Mature. **1984**

SAN FRANCISCO ★★★★ In its heyday, MGM boasted it had more stars than were in the heavens, and it made some terrific star-studded movies as a result. Take this 1936 production, starring Clark Gable, Jeanette MacDonald, and Spencer Tracy, for example. It's entertainment of the first order, with special effects—of the San Francisco earthquake—that still stand up today. B&W; 115m. **DIR:** W. S. Van Dyke. **CAST:** Clark Gable, Jeanette MacDonald, Spencer Tracy. **1936**

SANDPIPER, THE 🦃 Corny love triangle. 116m. **DIR:** Vincente Minnelli. **CAST:** Richard Burton, Elizabeth Taylor, Eva Marie Saint, Charles Bronson. **1965**

SARA DANE ★★ Headstrong eighteenth-century girl manages to raise her status through marriages as well as wise business decisions. This Australian film's premise is very similar to *A Woman of Substance*. 150m. **DIR:** Rod Hardy, Gary Conway. **CAST:** Harold Hopkins, Brenton Whittle. **1981**

SARAH, PLAIN AND TALL ★★★★ Heartwarming story of a headstrong New England spinster who answers an ad for a mail-order wife placed by a stoic Kansas widower with two children. Sarah says she's not looking for love, but love and special courage win the day just when it seems all is lost. First in a series of videotape releases of *Hallmark Hall of Fame* television presentations. Rated G. 98m. **DIR:** Glenn Jordan. **CAST:** Glenn Close, Christopher Walken, Lexi Randall, Margaret Sophie Stein, Jon De Vries, Christopher Bell. **1991**

SATURDAY NIGHT AT THE PALACE ★★★ The fears and hatreds behind South Africa's policy of apartheid are explored in a microcosm in this intense South African film. It expands upon a real-life incident, a late-night confrontation between a white man and a black man at a suburban hamburger joint. Paul Slabolepszy, who plays the white antagonist, also wrote the screenplay. 87m. **DIR:** Robert Davies. **CAST:** Paul Slabolepszy, John Kani. **1988**

SAVAGE IS LOOSE, THE 🦃 Tedious tale strands a young man and his parents on an island for many years. Rated R. 114m. **DIR:** George C. Scott. **CAST:** George C. Scott, Trish Van Devere, John David Carson, Lee Montgomery. **1974**

SAVAGE MESSIAH ★★½ This flamboyant love story dramatized in the Ken Russell tradition of excess only works in part. The story of a French sculptor's affair with a much older Polish woman symbolizes the generation gap as well as the culture clash. It would have worked better as a morality play without Russell's overworked and self-indulgent camera tricks. Rated R. 100m. **DIR:** Ken Russell. **CAST:** Dorothy Tutin, Scott Anthony, Helen Mirren, John Justin, Michael Gough, Lindsay Kemp. **1972**

SAVE THE TIGER ★★★ Jack Lemmon won the Academy Award for best actor for his portrayal in this 1973 film as a garment manufacturer who is at the end of his professional and emotional rope. His excellent performance helps offset the fact that the picture is essentially a downer. Rated R. 101m. **DIR:** John G. Avildsen. **CAST:** Jack Lemmon, Jack Gilford, Thayer David. **1973**

SAY GOODBYE, MAGGIE COLE ★★★ A retired doctor reopens her practice in a tough Chicago neighborhood after her husband dies. Standard TV movie elevated by star Susan Hayward in her final performance. 74m. **DIR:** Jud Taylor. **CAST:** Susan Hayward, Darren McGavin, Michael Constantine, Beverly Garland. **1972**

SAYONARA ★★★★ Marlon Brando is an American airman who engages in a romance with a Japanese actress while stationed in Japan after World War II. His love is put to the test by each culture's misconceptions and prejudices. James A. Michener's thought-provoking tragedy-romance still holds up well. Red Buttons and Miyoshi Umeki deservedly won Oscars for their roles as star-crossed lovers "American Occupation"–style. 147m. **DIR:** Joshua Logan. **CAST:** Marlon Brando, Red Buttons, Miyoshi Umeki, Ricardo Montalban, James Garner. **1957**

SCANDAL ★★★★½ A remarkable motion picture, this British production takes on the Profumo affair of the 1960s and emerges as an uncommonly satisfying adult-oriented drama, rich in character and insight. John Hurt is superb as Stephen Ward, the London osteopath who groomed teenage Christine Keeler (Joanne Whalley-Kilmer) into the femme fatale who brought down the British Conservative government. Rated R for nudity, simulated sex, violence, and profanity. 105m. **DIR:** Michael Caton-Jones. **CAST:** John Hurt, Joanne Whalley, Bridget Fonda, Ian McKellen. **1989**

SCANDAL IN A SMALL TOWN ★★ Predictable (and misleadingly titled) drama starring Raquel Welch as a waitress who opposes an anti-Semitic schoolteacher. Cardboard characters and situations are the real scandal in this made-for-TV movie. 90m. **DIR:** Anthony Page. **CAST:** Raquel Welch, Christa Denton, Frances Lee McCain, Ronny Cox. **1989**

SCAR, THE ★★★★ Fans of hardboiled *film noir* will want to look for this lesser-known but memorable example of the genre. Paul Henreid plays two parts: a gambler fleeing from the police and a psychiatrist who is his exact double. The gambler plans to escape the law by killing the doctor and assuming his identity. Look for Jack Webb in a small role. B&W; 83m. **DIR:** Steve Sekely. **CAST:** Paul Henreid, Joan Bennett, Eduard Franz, Leslie Brooks, John Qualen. **1948**

SCARECROW ★★★ A real downer about two losers (Al Pacino and Gene Hackman) trying to make something of themselves, this drama is made watchable by the performances. Rated R. 115m. **DIR:** Jerry Schatzberg. **CAST:** Al Pacino, Gene Hackman, Eileen Brennan, Richard Lynch. **1973**

SCARLET DAWN ★★ The characters bounce between coping with the Russian Revolution and sex orgies in an uneven melodrama that is as heavy as the ornate sets and garish makeup on the faces of big-time stars who should have known better. More of a curiosity piece than a satisfying film. B&W; 80m. **DIR:** William Dieterle. **CAST:** Douglas Fairbanks Jr., Lilyan Tashman, Nancy Carroll, Earle Fox. **1932**

SCARLET EMPRESS, THE ★★★★½ This classic is a stunning cinematic achievement dominated by the seductive Marlene Dietrich. A naive, shy girl becomes a worldly wise woman adept at court intrigue as she goes from being the unwilling bride of Czar Peter and the empress of all the Russias. Visually impressive and marvelously detailed, this is a must-see movie. B&W; 110m. **DIR:** Josef von Sternberg. **CAST:** Marlene Dietrich, Louise Dresser, Sam Jaffe, John Lodge, Maria Sieber, C. Aubrey Smith, Gavin Gordon, Olive Tell, Jane Darwell, Jameson Thomas. **1934**

SCARLET LETTER, THE (1926) ★★★ Hester Prynne wears the scarlet letter A for adultery. Only her sadistic husband Roger knows that minister Arthur Dimmesdale is the father of her daughter, Pearl. Roger taunts Arthur, who plans to flee with Hester and the child but finally confesses his sin publicly. Silent. B&W; 80m. **DIR:** Victor Sjöström. **CAST:** Lillian Gish, Henry B. Walthall, Karl Dane, Lars Hanson. **1926**

SCARLET LETTER, THE (1934) ★★★ Twenties-flapper star Colleen Moore proved she had acting skill in this second version (first sound) of Nathaniel Hawthorne's great classic of love, hate, jealousy, and emotional blackmail in Puritan New England. As in the 1926 silent version, D. W. Griffith star Henry B. Walthall portrays the heartless persecutor Roger Chillingworth. B&W; 69m. **DIR:** Robert Vignola. **CAST:** Colleen Moore, Hardie Albright, Henry B. Walthall. **1934**

SCARLET STREET ★★★½ The director (Fritz Lang) and stars (Edward G. Robinson, Joan Bennett, and Dan Duryea) of the excellent *Woman in the Window* reteamed with less spectacular results for this film about a mild-mannered fellow (Robinson) seduced into a life of crime by a temptress (Bennett). B&W; 103m. **DIR:** Fritz Lang. **CAST:** Edward G. Robinson, Joan Bennett, Dan Duryea, Margaret Lindsay, Rosalind Ivan. **1945**

SCENES FROM THE GOLDMINE ★★½ Music industry exposé with Catherine Mary Stewart as a musician-composer who joins a rock band and falls in love with the lead singer. Even rock fans will find the band's performances somewhat synthetic. Rated R for sexual situations and profanity. 105m. **DIR:** Marc Rocco. **CAST:** Catherine Mary Stewart, Cameron Dye, Steve Railsback, Joe Pantoliano, Lee Ving, Lesley-Anne Down. **1987**

SCENT OF A WOMAN ★★★½ Al Pacino's over-the-top performance in this coming-of-age movie will delight some viewers and put off others. Pacino plays a foul-mouthed ex-serviceman who takes high school-age companion Chris O'Donnell on a last hurrah in New York City, where the older man intends to wine, dine, and have sex before committing suicide. Rated R for profanity and suggested sex. 157m. **DIR:** Martin Brest. **CAST:** Al Pacino, Chris O'Donnell, James Rebhorn, Gabrielle Anwar, Richard Venture. **1992**

SCHINDLER'S LIST ★★★★★ The story of one man's struggle to save the lives of one thousand Polish Jews during the Third Reich's implementation of Hitler's "final solution," this Oscar-winner for best picture may well be director Steven Spielberg's masterpiece. Skillfully shaded performances by Liam Neeson (whose Oskar Schindler evolves from a fast-living opportunist to a man of conscience) and Ben Kingsley bring humanity to this tale of real-life horror, which stands with *Judgment at Nuremberg* and *The Diary of Anne Frank* as one of the best films on the subject. Rated R for nudity and violence. 185m. **DIR:** Steven Spielberg. **CAST:** Liam Neeson, Ben Kingsley, Ralph Fiennes, Caroline Goodall, Jonathan Sagalle, Embeth Davidtz. **1993**

SCHOOL TIES ★★★★ Dick Wolf's thoughtful study of persecution for the teenage set, with Brendan Fraser just right as a 1950s-era high school senior who conceals his Jewish heritage hoping to cash in on his football skills. A compelling little sleeper. Rated PG-13 for profanity. 107m. **DIR:** Robert Mandel. **CAST:** Brendan Fraser, Chris O'Donnell, Andrew Lowery, Amy Locane, Peter Donat, Zeljko Ivanek. **1992**

SCORCHERS ★★ The lives of three women are tangled up in this poorly written and directed film. Not rated, but contains profanity and simulated sex. 80m. **DIR:** David Beaird. **CAST:** Faye Dunaway, James Earl Jones, Emily Lloyd, Jennifer Tilly, Denholm Elliott, James Wilder, Anthony Geary. **1991**

SCOTT OF THE ANTARCTIC ★★★★ This impeccable re-creation of the race to the South Pole superbly captures the unrelenting frustration of explorer Robert Scott's ill-fated final expedition. Gorgeously lensed and orchestrated by director Charles Frend. 110m. **DIR:** Charles Frend. **CAST:** John Mills, Derek Bond, Kenneth More, Christopher Lee. **1948**

SCROOGE (1935) ★★★ This little-known British version of Charles Dickens's classic *A Christmas Carol* is faithful to the original story and boasts a standout performance by Seymour Hicks, who also cowrote the screenplay. A truly enjoyable film, unjustly overshadowed by Alistair Sim's bravura performance as Scrooge in the venerated 1951 version. B&W; 78m. **DIR:** Henry Edwards. **CAST:** Seymour Hicks, Donald Calthrop, Robert Cochran, Maurice Evans. **1935**

SCRUBBERS ★★★½ Realistic depiction of life inside a girls' reform school. With an eye toward inspiring reform, this British film suggests that the well-intentioned but misguided treatment of troubled children puts them on a road to becoming permanently institutionalized. Rated R. 94m. **DIR:** Mai Zetterling. **CAST:** Amanda York, Elizabeth Edmonds. **1982**

SCRUPLES ★★½ Bestseller from author Judith Krantz gets the glossy TV soap-opera treatment: an ordinary woman is thrown for a loop when she inherits a conglomerate. Edited down from the television miniseries into feature-length. 100m. **DIR:** Robert Day. **CAST:** Priscilla Barnes, Shelley Smith, Vonetta McGee, Dirk Benedict, James Darren, Jessica Walter, Roy Thinnes. **1981**

SCUM ★★½ Harrowing look inside a British reform school. Rated R for violence and profanity. 98m. **DIR:** Alan Clarke. **CAST:** Ray Winstone, Mick Ford, John Judd, Phil Daniels, John Blundell. **1980**

SEA LION, THE ★★½ Stern sea story with hard-bitten Hobart Bosworth as a tyrannical ship's master who vents his pent-up hatred on the men in his charge. But romance rears its head and we find out that he's not all bad; he was just acting like a sadist because he had a broken heart. Silent. B&W; 50m. **DIR:** Rowland V. Lee. **CAST:** Hobart Bosworth, Bessie Love, Richard Morris. **1921**

SEARCH, THE ★★★★★ Heart-tugging story of the plight of displaced children in post–World War II Europe. One mother (Jarmila Novotna) searches for her son (Ivan Jandl), taken from her in a concentration camp. Montgomery Clift is an American soldier who finds and cares for the boy while the mother's search continues. B&W; 105m. **DIR:** Fred Zinnemann. **CAST:** Montgomery Clift, Aline MacMahon, Wendell Corey, Jarmila Novotna, Ivan Jandl. **1948**

SEARCH FOR BRIDEY MURPHY, THE ★★ Made quickly and cheaply (it shows) to cash in on the then-popular and controversial book by Morey Bernstein. Story of a woman under hypnosis who was able to recall her previous existence as a small girl in Ireland in the early 1800s. Dull. B&W; 84m. **DIR:** Noel Langley. **CAST:** Teresa Wright, Louis Hayward. **1956**

SEASON OF GIANTS, A ★★ Slow-moving, overly long TV bio of artist Michaelangelo. With a running time of over three hours, this is rough going. 195m. **DIR:** Jerry London. **CAST:** F. Murray Abraham, Steven Berkoff, John Glover, Ian Holm, Raf Vallone, Mark Frankel. **1991**

SECOND WOMAN, THE ★★★ Is Robert Young paranoid, or is the whole world crazy? Strange and violent occurrences are plaguing the life of this talented architect. Betsy Drake, smitten with the confused fellow, is the only onlooker who doesn't doubt his sanity. This dark drama maintains a steady undercurrent of suspense. B&W; 91m. **DIR:** James V. Kern. **CAST:** Robert Young, Betsy Drake, John Sutton. **1951**

SECRET, THE ★★★½ When it is discovered that an otherwise bright and talented 9-year-old boy cannot read, family ties begin to unravel in a small town on Cape Cod. Outstanding performances, assured direction, and insightful writing transform what could have been a typical "disease-of-the-week" TV movie about dyslexia into a touching human drama. Made for TV. 92m. **DIR:** Karen Arthur. **CAST:** Kirk Douglas, Bruce Boxleitner, Brock Peters, Linda Harrington, Jesse R. Tendler. **1992**

SECRET BEYOND THE DOOR ★★½ Master craftsman Fritz Lang does the best he can with this melodramatic potboiler about a lonely woman (Joan Bennett) who marries a mysterious stranger (Michael Redgrave) after a whirlwind courtship. Slowly she begins to suspect that her husband may be a murderer. B&W; 99m. **DIR:** Fritz Lang. **CAST:** Joan Bennett, Michael Redgrave. **1948**

SECRET CEREMONY ★★½ Typical Joseph Losey psychodrama about a psychotic girl (Mia Farrow) semikidnapping an aging streetwalker (Elizabeth Taylor) who reminds her of her dead mother. Robert Mitchum plays Farrow's lecherous stepfather. With its strong sexual undertones, this film is not for kids (and probably not for some adults). 108m. **DIR:** Joseph Losey. **CAST:** Elizabeth Taylor, Mia Farrow, Robert Mitchum, Peggy Ashcroft, Pamela Brown. **1968**

SECRET FRIENDS ★★★½ Dennis Potter, creator of *The Singing Detective*, made his feature directorial debut with this strange, challenging mind-game film. Alan Bates stars as an artist obsessed with doing away with his wife. Rewarding, if difficult, film. Bates, as usual, is superb. Unrated. 97m. **DIR:** Dennis Potter. **CAST:** Alan Bates, Gina Bellman, Frances Barber, Tony Doyle. **1992**

SECRET GAMES 🦃 A neglected wife gets a day job at a high-class cathouse and attracts an amorous psychopath. What we have here is a video for couples unaccustomed to sharing more explicit adult films. Rated R for nudity. 90m. **DIR:** Alexander Gregory Hippolyte. **CAST:** Martin Hewitt, Michele Brin, Delia Sheppard, Billy Drago. **1992**

SECRET HONOR ★★★★ This one-man show features Philip Baker Hall as Richard Nixon—drinking, swearing, and going completely over the top in his ravings, on such subjects as Castro, Kennedy, and Henry Kissinger. Fascinating, with Hall's performance a wonder. A one-of-a-kind movie from Robert Altman. Rated PG. 90m. **DIR:** Robert Altman. **CAST:** Philip Baker Hall. **1984**

SECRET LIFE OF JEFFREY DAHMER, THE ★★★ Fictional portrayal of the infamous serial killer is a low-budget effort that works despite its shortcomings. Carl Crew is magnetic as Dahmer, who invited unsuspecting men into his spider's web, took advantage of them, and then killed them. Most of the mayhem is offscreen but is effective nonetheless, giving us some insight about the loner who captivated the nation. Not rated, but contains violence, adult language, and situations. 100m. **DIR:** David R. Bowen. **CAST:** Carl Crew. **1993**

SECRET OBSESSIONS 🦃 Maudlin, morose, melodramatic yawner. Rated PG. 82m. **DIR:** Henri Vart. **CAST:** Julie Christie, Ben Gazzara, Patrick Bruel, Jean Carmet. **1988**

SECRET WEAPON ★★ A lab technician working on Israel's secret nuclear bomb capabilities decides to go public in order to stop the arms proliferation. Predictable and slowly paced TV movie. 95m. **DIR:** Ian Sharp. **CAST:** Karen Allen, Griffin Dunne, Jeroen Krabbé. **1990**

SECRETS ★★ Jacqueline Bisset's torrid sex scene is about the only interesting thing in this turgid soap opera. Rated R for nudity, suggested sex, and profanity. 86m. **DIR:** Philip Saville. **CAST:** Jacqueline Bisset, Per Oscarsson, Shirley Knight, Robert Powell. **1971**

SECRETS OF A MARRIED MAN 🦃 TV-movie involves William Shatner's attempt at conquering the final frontier of infidelity. 100m. **DIR:** William A. Graham. **CAST:** William Shatner, Cybill Shepherd, Michelle Phillips, Glynn Turman. **1984**

SEDUCERS, THE 🦃 San Francisco architect takes in two young women one rainy night and then can't get rid of them. Also on video under its original title, *Death Game*. Rated R for nudity and profanity. 90m. **DIR:** Peter Traynor. **CAST:** Sondra Locke, Seymour Cassel, Colleen Camp. **1977**

SEDUCTION OF JOE TYNAN, THE ★★★ Alan Alda plays Senator Joe Tynan in this story of behind-the-scenes romance and political maneuvering in Washington, D.C. Tynan must face moral questions about himself and his job. It's familiar ground for Alda but still entertaining. Rated PG for language and brief nudity. 107m. **DIR:** Jerry Schatzberg. **CAST:** Alan Alda, Barbara Harris, Meryl Streep, Rip Torn, Charles Kimbrough, Melvyn Douglas. **1979**

SEE YOU IN THE MORNING ★★★★ A touching character study. Jeff Bridges is a New York psychiatrist whose first marriage to model Farrah Fawcett crumbles, catching him off guard. A second marriage, to Alice Krige, seems more promising, but our hero has a number of obstacles to overcome. Rated PG-13 for profanity. 115m. **DIR:** Alan J. Pakula. **CAST:** Jeff Bridges, Alice Krige, Farrah Fawcett, Drew Barrymore, Lukas Haas, David Dukes, Frances Sternhagen, Linda Lavin. **1989**

SEEKERS, THE ★★ Most melodramatic and unbelievable TV production from the John Jakes's bicentennial series, this is part three of the Kent Family Chronicles. The original French immigrant is now a cynical man of wealth (Martin Milner) whose son (Randolph Mantooth) defies him by farming in Ohio. 189m. **DIR:** Sidney Hayers. **CAST:** Randolph Mantooth, Barbara Rush, Delta Burke, Edie Adams, Brian Keith, Martin Milner, George Hamilton, Hugh O'Brian, John Carradine, Gary Merrill, Ed Harris, Stuart Whitman. **1979**

SEIZE THE DAY ★★★ Robin Williams is watchable in this drama, but like so many comedians who attempt serious acting, he is haunted by his madcap persona. This PBS *Great Performances* entry casts Williams as Wilhelm "Tommy" Adler, the Jewish ne'er-do-well son of wealthy, unsympathetic Joseph Wiseman. The story concerns the disintegration of Tommy's life. 87m. **DIR:** Fielder Cook. **CAST:** Robin Williams, Joseph Wiseman, Jerry Stiller, Glenne Headly, John Fiedler, Tom Aldredge, Tony Roberts. **1986**

SENSATIONS 🦃 Odd-couple love story between a prostitute and a male stripper.

Rated R for strong sexual situations. 91m. **DIR:** Chuck Vincent. **CAST:** Rebecca Lynn, Blake Bahner. **1988**

SENSE OF FREEDOM, A ★★★ The true story of Jimmy Boyle, a violent Scottish criminal who refused to temper his viciousness during over a decade in various prisons. The film never attempts to make a hero out of Boyle, but neither does it offer any insight into his personality. A very well-made film from John Mackenzie, whose excellent *The Long Good Friday* featured a similar protagonist. Rated R. 81m. **DIR:** John Mackenzie. **CAST:** David Hayman, Alex Norton, Jake D'Arcy, Fulton MacKay. **1983**

SEPARATE BUT EQUAL ★★★★ In one of his finest performances, Sidney Poitier stars as Thurgood Marshall, the NAACP lawyer who took the fight for racial equality to the Supreme Court via the Brown vs. Board of Education case in 1954. Richard Kiley is marvelous as Chief Justice Earl Warren, and Burt Lancaster is typically dignified and believable as the opposing counsel. Gripping drama that originally aired as a two-parter on television. 200m. **DIR:** George Stevens Jr. **CAST:** Sidney Poitier, Burt Lancaster, Richard Kiley, Cleavon Little, John McMartin. **1991**

SEPARATE PEACE, A ★★★ Based on John Knowles's bestselling novel, this involving story of a young man's first glimpse of adult emotions and motivations—some say homosexual frustration—is watchable for plot and performance. Gene and Finny are prep school roommates at the beginning of World War II. Jealous of Finny's popularity, Gene betrays his roommate in a moment of anger and treachery, and is responsible for a crippling accident. Rated PG. 104m. **DIR:** Larry Peerce. **CAST:** John Heyl, Parker Stevenson, Peter Brush. **1972**

SEPARATE TABLES ★★★★★ This is a cable-television remake of the 1958 film with Burt Lancaster and Wendy Hiller. This time the work achieves a remarkable intimacy on tape with a top-notch British cast. Divided into two segments, this is a sort of British *Grand Hotel* room with Alan Bates and Julie Christie in dual roles. Richly engrossing adult entertainment. Rated PG for adult subject matter. 108m. **DIR:** John Schlesinger. **CAST:** Julie Christie, Alan Bates, Claire Bloom. **1983**

SEPTEMBER ★★★½ Woody Allen in his serious mode. Mia Farrow is superb as a troubled woman living in Vermont. Her houseguests are her hard-living mother (Elaine Stritch), her stepfather (Jack Warden), her best friend (Diane Wiest), and an aspiring writer (Sam Waterston). What transpires are subtle yet intense love-hate relationships. Rated PG. 82m. **DIR:** Woody Allen. **CAST:** Mia Farrow, Dianne Wiest, Sam Waterston, Denholm Elliott, Elaine Stritch, Jack Warden. **1987**

SEPTEMBER AFFAIR ★★½ Superficial romantic tale about two married people who are reported dead after a plane crash. This gives them their chance to conduct a love affair. Bonuses: nice photography on the isle of Capri and the famous Walter Huston recording of the title song. B&W; 104m. **DIR:** William Dieterle. **CAST:** Joseph Cotten, Joan Fontaine, Françoise Rosay, Jessica Tandy, Robert Arthur, Jimmy Lydon. **1950**

SEPTEMBER 30, 1955 ★★★½ Affecting, sentimental portrait of a group of young adults and how the death of movie star James Dean changes their lives. Richard Thomas gathers up his friends for a wake and then for a celebration of Dean's spirit that ends tragically before the evening is out. Rated PG for language and violence. 107m. **DIR:** James Bridges. **CAST:** Richard Thomas, Lisa Blount, Dennis Quaid, Tom Hulce, Dennis Christopher, Deborah Benson. **1977**

SERGEANT RYKER ★★★ This film revolves around the court-martial of Sergeant Ryker (Lee Marvin), a Korean War soldier. Ryker, accused of treason, is valiantly defended by his attorney (Bradford Dillman in a superb performance). Originally shown on television as *The Case Against Sergeant Ryker,* then released theatrically under the shortened title. 86m. **DIR:** Buzz Kulik. **CAST:** Lee Marvin, Bradford Dillman, Vera Miles, Peter Graves, Lloyd Nolan, Murray Hamilton. **1968**

SERPENT'S EGG, THE ★★ Two trapeze artists are trapped in Berlin during pre-Nazi Germany where they discover a satanic plot. Director Ingmar Bergman's nightmare vision is disappointing. 120m. **DIR:** Ingmar Bergman. **CAST:** Liv Ullmann, David Carradine, Gert Fröbe, James Whitmore. **1977**

SERPICO ★★★★ Al Pacino is magnificent in this poignant story of an honest man who happens to be a cop. The fact that this is a true story of one man's fight against corruption adds even more punch. Rated R. 130m. **DIR:** Sidney Lumet. **CAST:** Al Pacino, Tony Roberts, John Randolph, Biff McGuire, Jack Kehoe. **1973**

SERVANT, THE ★★★★ A conniving manservant (Dirk Bogarde) gradually dominates the life of his spoiled master in this psychological horror story. By preying on his sexual weaknesses, he is able to easily maneuver him to his will. The taut, well-acted adult drama holds your interest throughout, mainly because the shock value is heightened for the audience because of its plausibility. B&W; 115m. **DIR:** Joseph Losey. **CAST:** Dirk Bogarde, Sarah Miles, James Fox. **1963**

SESSIONS ★★★ Veronica Hamel poses as a career woman who also takes pleasure in being a high-priced call girl in the evening. Soap-opera drama? Yes, but that's what you expect in this made-for-TV movie. And it's done with class. 100m. **DIR:** Richard Pearce. **CAST:** Veronica Hamel, Jeffrey DeMunn, Jill Eikenberry. **1983**

SEVEN CITIES OF GOLD ★★★ Michael Rennie plays an incredibly pious Father Junípero Serra, struggling to set up his first mission in California. His love of the Indians contrasts sharply with the ruthless greed of the Spanish military leaders (played by Anthony Quinn and Richard Egan). Unrated, this contains violence. 103m. **DIR:** Robert D. Webb. **CAST:** Michael Rennie, Richard Egan, Anthony Quinn, Jeffrey Hunter, Rita Moreno. **1955**

SEVEN DAYS IN MAY ★★★★ A highly suspenseful account of an attempted military takeover of the U.S. government. After a slow buildup, the movie's tension snowballs toward a thrilling conclusion. This is one of those rare films that treat their audiences with respect. A working knowledge of the political process is helpful for optimum appreciation. Fredric March, as a president under pressure, heads an all-star cast, all of whom give admirable performances. B&W; 120m. **DIR:** John Frankenheimer. **CAST:** Burt Lancaster, Fredric March, Kirk Douglas, Ava Gardner, Edmond O'Brien, Martin Balsam. **1964**

SEVEN MINUTES, THE 🦃 Pornography is put on trial when a man claims that he was driven to commit rape after reading a sexy novel. Look for Tom Selleck in a small role. Rated R. 115m. **DIR:** Russ Meyer. **CAST:** Wayne Maunder, Marianne McAndrew, Jay C. Flippen, Edy Williams, Yvonne De Carlo, John Carradine. **1971**

SEVEN THIEVES ★★★ A rousing cops-and-robbers tale told from the robbers' viewpoint with Edward G. Robinson and Rod Steiger in top form. The setting is Monte Carlo, where thieves prosper and there is a lot of competition. B&W; 103m. **DIR:** Henry Hathaway. **CAST:** Edward G. Robinson, Rod Steiger, Eli Wallach, Joan Collins, Sebastian Cabot, Michael Dante, Alexander Scourby. **1960**

SEVENTH CROSS, THE ★★★★½ In 1936 Germany an anti-Nazi escapee from a concentration camp turns to friends for shelter and help in fleeing the country. Suspenseful, gripping drama. B&W; 111m. **DIR:** Fred Zinnemann. **CAST:** Spencer Tracy, Signe Hasso, Hume Cronyn, Jessica Tandy, Agnes Moorehead, Felix Bressart, George Macready, Ray Collins, Steven Geray, George Zucco. **1944**

SEVENTH VEIL, THE ★★★½ A young woman forsakes her family and chooses to become a musician, encountering many men along the way. Safe and satisfying, this middle-brow entertainment owes much of its success to a strong performance by James Mason and an Oscar-winning screenplay. Ann Todd is just right as the freethinking heroine. B&W; 94m. **DIR:** Compton Bennett. **CAST:** James Mason, Ann Todd, Herbert Lom, Hugh McDermott, Albert Lieven. **1945**

SEX AND THE COLLEGE GIRL ★★ This low-budget version of *Sex and the Single Girl* has two things going for it: the witty and informative intro by Joe Bob Briggs and the fact that it didn't force a happy ending. Unrated, but implied sex and immorality abound. 100m. **DIR:** Joseph Adler. **CAST:** Julie Sommars, Charles Grodin, John Gabriel, Richard Arlen, Luana Anders. **1964**

SEX, DRUGS, ROCK & ROLL ★★★★ Eric Bogosian stars as a succession of ten different characters in this aggressive, thought-provoking, often astonishing film version of his one-man off-Broadway show. Writer-actor Bogosian (of *Talk Radio* fame) creates full-bodied minidramas and comedies with varying, believable characters. Rated R, with strong profanity. 100m. **DIR:** John McNaughton. **CAST:** Eric Bogosian. **1991**

SEX, LIES AND VIDEOTAPE ★★★★½ Deliciously offbeat winner of the 1989 Palme d'Or at the Cannes Film Festival revolves around something as old-fashioned as the romantic triangle. However, the handling by writer-director Steven Soderbergh makes it seem fresh—as soft-spoken James Spader arrives to visit old college chum Peter Gallagher and ends up bringing to light Gallagher's affair with the sexy sister (Laura San Giacomo) of his slightly neurotic wife (Andie MacDowell). Rated R for simulated sex, profanity, and brief violence. 104m. **DIR:** Steven Soderbergh. **CAST:** James Spader, Andie MacDowell, Peter Gallagher, Laura San Giacomo. **1989**

SEX MADNESS 🦃 "Educational" film about the dangers of syphilis. B&W; 50m. **DIR:** Dwain Esper. **CAST:** None Credited. **1934**

SHACK-OUT ON 101 ★★★½ This odd blend of character study and espionage thriller, which takes place at a highway hash house, involves some of the most colorful patrons you'll ever run across. Perky Terry Moore plays the waitress who helps the authorities close in on the men who have sabotage plans for a local chemical plant, and Lee Marvin is at his most audacious as Slob, a name he does his best to live up to. B&W; 80m. **DIR:** Edward Dein. **CAST:** Frank Lovejoy, Terry Moore, Lee Marvin, Keenan Wynn, Whit Bissell. **1955**

SHADES OF LOVE: CHAMPAGNE FOR TWO ★★★ Enjoyable romp features a likable chef who becomes the unlikely roommate of a harried architect. Made for Canadian TV, this *Shades of Love* romance has more general audience appeal than anything found in the Romance Theatre collection. Unrated; contains mild profanity, nudity, and sex. 82m. **DIR:** Lewis Furey. **CAST:** Nicholas Campbell, Kirsten Bishop, Carol Ann Francis, Terry Haig. **1987**

SHADES OF LOVE: LILAC DREAM ★★ Mystery and romance combine in this tale of a young woman left brokenhearted. Then a storm leaves a man with no memory on the shore of her island. She nurses him back to health. Gradually, his past comes back to haunt him. 83m. **DIR:** Marc Voizard. **CAST:** Dack Rambo, Susan Almgren. **1987**

SHADES OF LOVE: SINCERELY, VIOLET ★★ In this mediocre story of love and romance, a professor (Patricia Phillips) becomes a cat burglar named Violet. She is caught in the act by Mark Janson (Simon MacCorkindale) who tries to reform her. 86m. **DIR:** Mort Ransen. **CAST:** Simon MacCorkindale, Patricia Phillips. **1987**

SHADES OF LOVE: THE ROSE CAFE ★★ Dreams can sometimes hide the truth, and in the case of Courtney Fairchild (Linda Smith), her dream of opening a restaurant has hidden her feelings for the men in her life. 84m. **DIR:** Daniele J. Suissa. **CAST:** Parker Stevenson, Linda Smith. **1987**

SHADOW BOX, THE ★★★ A fine cast and smooth direction highlight this powerful story of one day in the lives of three terminally ill patients at an experimental hospice in California. Adapted from the prize-winning Broadway stage play. 100m. **DIR:** Paul Newman. **CAST:** Joanne Woodward, Christopher Plummer, Valerie Harper, James Broderick, Melinda Dillon, Sylvia Sidney, John Considine. **1980**

SHADOW HUNTER ★★★ After a needlessly seamy prologue, writer-director J. S. Cardone's moody made-for-cable thriller settles comfortably into territory mined by mystery author Tony Hillerman. Burned-out big city cop Scott Glenn muffs an assignment to extradite a killer from a Navajo reservation, and then joins the forces tracking the escaped maniac...who can become a *skinwalker* and invade the dreams of his pursuers. Rated R for profanity, nudity, and violence. 98m. **DIR:** J. S. Cardone. **CAST:** Scott Glenn, Angela Alvarado, Robert Beltran. **1993**

SHADOW OF CHINA ★★★½ An idealistic Chinese revolutionary escapes to Hong Kong where he builds a financial empire. His dream of changing China through his business connections is threatened by the exposure of his early money-making schemes and his heritage. Rated PG-13 for violence. 100m. **DIR:** Mitsuo Yanagimachi. **CAST:** John Lone, Vivian Wu, Sammi Davis. **1991**

SHADOWLANDS ★★★★½ Based on screenwriter William Nicholson's play, this exquisite film chronicles the risque (for its time) love affair between author and lecturer C. S. Lewis (Anthony Hopkins) and an American fan/writer, Joy Gresham (Debra Winger). Seemingly total opposites, these two opinionated, strong-willed individuals strike sparks at every encounter, making for an emotionally fulfilling and memorable motion picture. Rated PG for brief profanity. 130m. **DIR:** Richard Attenborough. **CAST:** Anthony Hopkins, Debra Winger, Edward Hardwicke, John Wood, Michael Denison, Peter Firth. **1993**

SHADOWS ★★★ A zealous young minister takes it upon himself to convert the local Chinese laundrymen. Lon Chaney as Yen Sin gives a moving performance as the man who must confront the self-righteous churchman, played by Harrison Ford (no relation to today's star). A colorful cast of good character actors help to make this a thought-provoking film. Silent. B&W; 70m. **DIR:** Tom Forman. **CAST:** Lon Chaney Sr., Harrison Ford, Marguerite de la Motte, Walter Long. **1922**

SHADOWS AND FOG ★★ Only the parade of familiar faces engages much interest in this all-star, brooding misfire from writer-director-star Woody Allen. Ostensibly about a schnook (Allen) drafted by a vigilant committee to help capture a homicidal maniac, it's a meandering collage of angst-ridden moments. Rated PG-13 for violence. B&W; 86m. **DIR:** Woody Allen. **CAST:** Woody Allen, Kathy Bates, John Cusack, Mia Farrow, Jodie Foster, Fred Gwynne, Julie Kavner, Madonna, John Malkovich, Kenneth Mars, Kate Nelligan, Donald Pleasence, Lily Tomlin, Philip Bosco, Robert Joy, Wallace Shawn, Kurtwood Smith, Josef Sommer. **1992**

SHADOWS IN THE STORM ★★ Umpteenth version of a daydreaming nebbish's fatal obsession for a young beauty. Ned Beatty stars as a corporate librarian who meets vixen Mia Sara and finds himself going totally out of control. Rated R for violence and profanity. 90m. **DIR:** Terrell Tannen. **CAST:** Ned Beatty, Mia Sara. **1989**

SHAG, THE MOVIE ★★★½ This appealing film didn't get a fair shake on the big screen, which was surprising, considering the delightful cast and solid performances. It's set in Myrtle Beach, S.C., circa 1963, and chronicles a last fling by a covey of southern belles before their society debut takes them away from the realities of their age. The title, incidentally, connotes a popular dance style. Rated PG for brief nudity, the film is harmless enough for most age-groups. 96m. **DIR:** Zelda Barron. **CAST:** Phoebe Cates, Scott Coffey, Bridget Fonda, Annabeth Gish, Page Hannah, Tyrone Power Jr. **1989**

SHAKA ZULU ★★★½ A tremendously staged epic chronicling the rise of Shaka (Henry Cole) as the king of the Zulus. Set against the emergence of British power in Africa during the early nineteenth century, this film provides some valuable insights into comparative cultures. Despite some poor editing and an overly dramatic, inappropriate musical score, *Shaka Zulu* is quite rewarding. Unrated, this release contains graphic violence and frequent nudity. 300m.

DIR: William C. Faure. **CAST:** Edward Fox, Robert Powell, Trevor Howard, Fiona Fullerton, Christopher Lee, Henry Cole, Roy Dotrice, Gordon Jackson. **1986**

SHAKESPEARE WALLAH ★★★★ A family troupe of Shakespearean players performs to disinterested, dwinding audiences in the new India (*wallah* is Hindustani for *peddler*). Frustrated sensuality, social humiliation, dedication to a dying cause, and familial devotion are rendered here with the sensitivity and delicacy that we have come to expect from director James Ivory. Madhur Jaffrey won the best actress award at the Berlin Festival for her satiric rendering of a Bombay musical star. B&W; 114m. **DIR:** James Ivory. **CAST:** Shashi Kapoor, Geoffrey Kendall, Laura Liddell, Felicity Kendal, Madhur Jaffrey. **1964**

SHAKING THE TREE ★★½ This bland male-bonding film will seem familiar to anyone who's seen *Diner*. A lot of similar ground is covered in telling the story of a group of pals entering into a new era of responsibility as adults. PG-13 for profanity. 97m. **DIR:** Duane Clark. **CAST:** Arye Gross, Doug Savant, Steven Wilde, Courteney Cox, Gale Hansen. **1992**

SHAMING, THE ★★ A spinster schoolteacher is raped by a janitor and continues to have sex with him until she is exposed and then ostracized by the school. This film is rated R for sex. 90m. **DIR:** Marvin J. Chomsky. **CAST:** Anne Heywood, Donald Pleasence, Robert Vaughn, Carolyn Jones, Dorothy Malone, Dana Elcar. **1975**

SHAMPOO ★★★★ Star Warren Beatty and Robert Towne cowrote this perceptive comedy of morals, most of them bad, which focuses on a hedonistic Beverly Hills hairdresser played by Beatty. Although portions come perilously close to slapstick, the balance is an insightful study of the pain caused by people who try for no-strings-attached relationships. Rated R—sexuality and adult themes. 112m. **DIR:** Hal Ashby. **CAST:** Warren Beatty, Julie Christie, Lee Grant, Jack Warden, Goldie Hawn, Carrie Fisher. **1975**

SHANGHAI EXPRESS ★★★★ Marlene Dietrich's trademark role during the first stage of her Hollywood career has been copied by other would-be sex queens, but no one has ever equaled Dietrich's sultry appeal. She plays a woman of dubious reputation who causes the downfall of a Chinese warlord to save the life and reputation of the man she really loves. The story is loosely based on a Guy de Maupassant short story, but the style is strictly tailored to its star's mesmerizing personality. B&W; 80m. **DIR:** Josef von Sternberg. **CAST:** Marlene Dietrich, Warner Oland, Anna May Wong, Clive Brook, Eugene Pallette, Louise Closser Hale, Gustav von Seyffertitz. **1932**

SHANGHAI GESTURE, THE ★★ Camp melodrama—an excursion into depravity in mysterious Shanghai. Walter Huston wants to close the gambling casino run by Ona Munson, who has a hold over his daughter Gene Tierney. Atmospheric idiocy. B&W; 106m. **DIR:** Josef von Sternberg. **CAST:** Gene Tierney, Ona Munson, Walter Huston, Albert Basserman, Eric Blore, Victor Mature, Maria Ouspenskaya, Mike Mazurki. **1942**

SHATTERED (1972) ★★ Peter Finch plays a mild-mannered, neurotic businessman who picks up a hitchhiker (Linda Hayden) only to have her attach herself to him. As a result, he slowly begins to lose his sanity. Shelley Winters plays Finch's obnoxious wife. Like a lot of British thrillers, this one has little action until it explodes in the final fifteen minutes. Rated R for profanity and violence. 100m. **DIR:** Alastair Reid. **CAST:** Peter Finch, Shelley Winters, Colin Blakely, John Stride, Linda Hayden. **1972**

SHATTERED SPIRITS ★★★ Hard-hitting, made-for-television drama focuses on a father whose casual drinking problem turns into substance abuse with tragic results. When his drinking escalates to an uncontrollable rage, his family is torn apart. 93m. **DIR:** Robert Greenwald. **CAST:** Martin Sheen, Melinda Dillon, Matthew Laborteaux, Lukas Haas, Roxana Zal. **1986**

SHATTERED VOWS ★★★½ Based on a true story, this explores a young girl's commitment to become a nun—and her later decision to leave the convent. Made for TV. 95m. **DIR:** Jack Bender. **CAST:** Valerie Bertinelli, David Morse, Patricia Neal, Tom Parsekian. **1984**

SHEIK, THE ★★½ The story of an English lady abducted by a hot-blooded Arab promising illicit pleasure in the desert is tame today, but Rudolph Valentino made millions of female fans his love slaves. Predicted to flop by studio brass, this melodramatic blend of adventure and eroticism nonetheless catapulted the handsome Italian import to reigning stardom. Silent. B&W; 80m. **DIR:** George Melford. **CAST:** Rudolph Valentino, Agnes Ayres, Adolphe Menjou, Lucien Littlefield. **1921**

SHELTERING SKY, THE ★★½ So much is left unexplained in *The Sheltering Sky*, one cannot help but wonder if director Bernardo Bertolucci is trying to put something over on us. This tale of three aimless Americans becoming involved in an odd romantic triangle while enduring hardships in post–World War II North Africa mainly leaves one with the urge to read Paul Bowles's original novel and find out what the fuss was all about. Rated R for nudity, profanity, and simulated sex. 133m. **DIR:** Bernardo Bertolucci. **CAST:** Debra Winger, John Malkovich, Campbell Scott, Jill Bennett, Timothy Spall. **1990**

SHE'S DRESSED TO KILL ★★ Acceptable murder mystery concerning the deaths of high-fashion models. Eleanor Parker is excellent as a garish, once-renowned designer trying to stage a comeback. This made-for-TV movie was retitled *Someone's Killing the World's Greatest Models*. 100m. **DIR:** Gus Trikonis. **CAST:** Eleanor Parker, Jessica Walter, John Rubinstein, Jim McMullan, Corinne Calvet. **1979**

SHE'S IN THE ARMY NOW ★★★ The distributor has labeled this made-for-TV film a comedy, but there is very little to laugh about in the story of seven weeks of basic training in a women's squadron. Kathleen Quinlan as the appointed squadron leader and Jamie Lee Curtis as the streetwise recruit with problems are both very good. 97m. **DIR:** Hy Averback. **CAST:** Kathleen Quinlan, Jamie Lee Curtis, Melanie Griffith, Janet MacLachlan. **1981**

SHINING HOUR, THE ★★★ Soap opera about a nightclub entertainer (Joan Crawford) who fights for acceptance from her husband's small-town family with small-town values. An energetic film with good acting and a predictable plot. B&W; 81m. **DIR:** Frank Borzage. **CAST:** Joan Crawford, Margaret Sullavan, Melvyn Douglas, Robert Young, Fay Bainter, Hattie McDaniel, Allyn Joslyn, Frank Albertson. **1938**

SHINING SEASON, A ★★★ Fact-based story of track star and Olympic hopeful John Baker, (Timothy Bottoms) who, when stricken by cancer, devoted his final months to coaching a girls' track team. This is very familiar territory, but director Stuart Margolin keeps things above water most of the time. Bottoms is an engaging hero-victim. Made for television. 100m. **DIR:** Stuart Margolin. **CAST:** Timothy Bottoms, Allyn Ann McLerie, Ed Begley Jr., Rip Torn, Mason Adams. **1979**

SHINING THROUGH ★★★½ Working from the bestseller by Susan Isaacs, writer-director David Seltzer has come up with a clever and effective homage to the war films of the Forties that manages to re-create their charm and naïveté. Melanie Griffith is a wisecracking dame who figures out that her boss (Michael Douglas) is an American spy from what she's seen in movies like *The Immortal Storm* and *The Fighting 69th*. In no time, she's behind enemy lines in Nazi Germany attempting to gather information. Rated R for violence, profanity, and nudity. 125m. **DIR:** David Seltzer. **CAST:** Michael Douglas, Melanie Griffith, Liam Neeson, Joely Richardson, John Gielgud. **1992**

SHIP OF FOOLS ★★★★★ In 1933, a vast and varied group of characters take passage on a German liner sailing from Mexico to Germany amidst impending doom. The all-star cast features most memorable performances by Vivien Leigh (her last film) as the neurotic divorcée, Oskar Werner as the ship's doctor, who has an affair with the despairing Simone Signoret, Lee Marvin as the forceful American baseball player, and Michael Dunn as the wise dwarf. Superb screen adaptation of the Katherine Anne Porter novel of the same name. B&W; 150m. **DIR:** Stanley Kramer. **CAST:** Vivien Leigh, Oskar Werner, Simone Signoret, José Ferrer, Lee Marvin, George Segal, Michael Dunn, Elizabeth Ashley, Lilia Skala, Charles Korvin. **1965**

SHOCK, THE (1923) ★★★ The legendary Lon Chaney Sr. added yet another grotesque character to his growing closet of skeletons when he played Wilse Dilling. This decent crime melodrama, no different in plot than dozens of other films over the years, has the advantage of Chaney and an exciting climax consisting of a bang-up earthquake. Corny at times, this one is still a good bet if you're interested in silent films. B&W; 96m. **DIR:** Lambert Hillyer. **CAST:** Lon Chaney Sr., Christine Mayo. **1923**

SHOES OF THE FISHERMAN 🦃 A boring film about an enthusiastic pope who single-handedly attempts to stop nuclear war, starvation, and world strife. 157m. **DIR:** Michael Anderson. **CAST:** Anthony Quinn, Laurence Olivier, Oskar Werner, David Janssen, Vittorio De Sica, John Gielgud, Leo McKern, Barbara Jefford. **1968**

SHOOT THE MOON ★★ Why didn't they just call it *Ordinary People Go West*? Of course, this film isn't really a sequel to the 1980 Oscar winner. It's closer to a rip-off. None of the style, believability, or consistency of its predecessor. Rated R because of profanity, violence, and adult themes. 123m. **DIR:** Alan Parker. **CAST:** Albert Finney, Diane Keaton, Karen Allen, Dana Hill, Tracey Gold. **1982**

SHOOTING PARTY, THE ★★★★ This meditation on the fading English aristocracy is an acting showcase. All main characters are played with verve, or at least the verve one would expect from English nobility in the years preceding World War I. While nothing much happens here, the rich texture of the characters, the highly stylized sets, and the incidental affairs in the plot are enough to sustain the viewer. Not rated, but equivalent to a PG for partial nudity. 97m. **DIR:** Alan Bridges. **CAST:** James Mason, Edward Fox, Dorothy Tutin, John Gielgud, Gordon Jackson, Cheryl Campbell, Robert Hardy. **1985**

SHOPWORN ANGEL, THE ★★★½ Margaret Sullavan plays a callous and selfish actress who toys with the affections of shy soldier James Stewart until she is won over by his sincerity. Predictable, but this team is always a joy to watch. B&W; 85m. **DIR:** H. C. Potter. **CAST:** Margaret Sullavan, James Stewart, Walter Pidgeon, Hattie McDaniel, Nat Pendleton, Alan Curtis, Sam Levene. **1938**

SHORT CUTS ★★★★★ Maverick film director Robert Altman scores again with this superb film that intertwines several of Raymond Carver's short stories into a fascinating, thought-provoking panorama of modern-day life. The performances by a huge, all-star cast are uniformly excellent. Some viewers might be put off by the episodic, open-ended nature of the storytelling style. However, those looking for a work of substance that challenges and intrigues the mind will be knocked out. Rated R for profanity, nudity, and violence. 188m. **DIR:** Robert Altman. **CAST:** Andie MacDowell, Bruce Davison, Jack Lemmon, Julianne Moore, Matthew Modine, Anne Archer, Fred Ward, Jennifer Jason Leigh, Christopher Penn, Lili Taylor, Robert Downey Jr., Madeleine Stowe, Tim Robbins, Lily Tomlin, Tom Waits, Frances McDormand, Peter Gallagher, Annie Ross, Lori Singer, Lyle Lovett, Buck Henry, Huey Lewis. **1993**

SHORT EYES ★★★★ Film version of Miguel Pinero's hard-hitting play about a convicted child molester at the mercy of other prisoners. A brutal and frightening film. Excellent, but difficult to watch. Rated R for violence and profanity. 104m. **DIR:** Robert M. Young. **CAST:** Bruce Davison, Jose Perez. **1977**

SHOW THEM NO MERCY ★★★ Four gangsters snatch a child and are paid off in bills that can be traced. Nobody wins in this compelling drama about a kidnapping that goes sour. B&W; 76m. **DIR:** George Marshall. **CAST:** Rochelle Hudson, Bruce Cabot, Cesar Romero, Edward Norris, Edward Brophy. **1935**

SHY PEOPLE ★★★ Moody drama about a New York writer (Jill Clayburgh) who journeys to the Louisiana bayous to get family-background information from distant Cajun relatives. Barbara Hershey, in an offbeat role, plays a dominating Cajun mother. Clayburgh gives a strong performance, and Martha Plimpton as her troublemaking daughter is fine too. Rated R for language and sexual content. 118m. **DIR:** Andrei Konchalovsky. **CAST:** Barbara Hershey, Jill Clayburgh, Martha Plimpton, Merritt Butrick, John Philbin, Mare Winningham. **1987**

SID AND NANCY ★★★½ Leave it to Alex Cox, director of the suburban punk classic *Repo Man*, to try to make sense out of deceased punk rocker Sid Vicious and his girlfriend Nancy Spungen. Its compassionate portrait of the two famed nihilists is a powerful one, which nevertheless is not for everyone. Rated R for violence, sex, nudity, and adult subject matter. 111m. **DIR:** Alex Cox. **CAST:** Gary Oldman, Chloe Webb, Drew Schofield, David Hayman. **1986**

SIDE OUT ★★½ Peter Horton is a has-been volleyball pro with little going for him until he strikes up with C. Thomas Howell, who sparks his interest in a comeback. Some great contests with current pros Sinjin Smith and Randy Stoklos in this otherwise routine story. Rated PG-13. 103m. **DIR:** Peter Israelson. **CAST:** C. Thomas Howell, Peter Horton, Sinjin Smith, Randy Stoklos. **1990**

SIDEWALKS OF LONDON ★★★★ Street entertainer Charles Laughton puts pretty petty thief Vivien Leigh in his song-and-dance act, then falls in love with her. Befriended by successful songwriter Rex Harrison, she puts the streets and old friends behind her and rises to stage stardom while her rejected and dejected mentor hits the skids. Vivien Leigh is entrancing, and Charles Laughton is compelling and touching, in this dramatic sojourn in London byways. B&W; 85m. **DIR:** Tim Whelan. **CAST:** Vivien Leigh, Charles Laughton, Rex Harrison, Tyrone Guthrie. **1940**

SIGNAL 7 ★★★ Absorbing character study of two San Francisco cabbies features standout performances by Bill Ackridge and Dan Leegant. Entirely improvised, the film has a loose, almost documentary aproach. Unrated, but contains a lot of profanity. 92m. **DIR:** Rob Nilsson. **CAST:** Bill Ackridge, Dan Leegant. **1983**

SIGNS OF LIFE ★★★ When a shipyard goes out of business, its employees and owner are forced to face the inevitability of change. Rated PG-13 for profanity and violence. 95m. **DIR:** John David Coles. **CAST:** Arthur Kennedy, Beau Bridges, Vincent D'Onofrio, Kate Reid. **1989**

SILAS MARNER ★★★★ Fate is the strongest character in this BBC-TV adaptation of George Eliot's novel, although Ben Kingsley gives an excellent performance as the cataleptic eighteenth-century English weaver. Betrayed by his closest friend and cast out of the church, Marner disappears into the English countryside and becomes a bitter miser, only to have his life wonderfully changed when fate brings an orphan girl to his hovel. 97m. **DIR:** Giles Foster. **CAST:** Ben Kingsley, Jenny Agutter, Patrick Ryecart, Patsy Kensit. **1985**

SILENCE LIKE GLASS 🦃 Disease-of-the-week movie about a ballet dancer afflicted with cancer, a giant ego, and a clichéd screenplay. Rated R for profanity. 103m. **DIR:** Carl Schenkel. **CAST:** Jami Gertz, Martha Plimpton, George Peppard, Bruce Payne, Rip Torn, Gayle Hunnicutt, James Remar. **1990**

SILENCE OF THE NORTH ★★ There are some of us at the *Video Movie Guide* who would follow Ellen Burstyn anywhere. But Burstyn's narration here is pure melodrama, and ninety minutes of one catastrophe after the next is more tiring than entertaining. Burstyn portrays a woman who falls in love with a fur trapper, played by Tom Skerritt, and moves into the Canadian wilderness. Rated PG for violence. 94m. **DIR:** Allan Winton King. **CAST:** Ellen Burstyn, Tom Skerritt, Gordon Pinsent. **1981**

SILENT NIGHT, LONELY NIGHT ★★½ Slow-moving, but fairly interesting TV film about two lonely people (Lloyd Bridges and Shirley Jones) who share a few happy moments at Christmastime. Flashbacks to previous tragedies are distracting. Unrated. 98m. **DIR:** Daniel Petrie. **CAST:** Lloyd Bridges, Shirley Jones, Carrie Snodgress, Robert Lipton. **1969**

SILENT REBELLION ★★ Telly Savalas plays a naturalized American who goes back to his hometown in Greece to visit. But the cross-cultural experience is not always pleasant. Some poignant moments, but lots of dull ones, too. Not rated. 90m. **DIR:** Charles S. Dubin. **CAST:** Telly Savalas, Michael Constantine, Keith Gordon. **1982**

SILENT VICTIM ★★★½ Compelling true story follows distraught, pregnant wife Michele Greene, whose suicide attempt kills her unborn child. Her husband then sues her for performing an illegal abortion. Interesting idea gets plenty of mileage in the courtroom, where the issues of responsibility and morality are examined in gripping fashion. Rated R for language. 116m. **DIR:** Menahem Golan. **CAST:** Michele Greene, Kyle Secor, Alex Hyde-White, Ely Pouget. **1992**

SILENT VICTORY: THE KITTY O'NEIL STORY ★★★ Better-than-average TV biography of ace stuntwoman Kitty O'Neil, who overcame the handicap of being deaf to excel in her profession. Proof positive is O'Neil doubling Channing in the stunt scenes. 100m. **DIR:** Lou Antonio. **CAST:** Stockard Channing, James Farentino, Colleen Dewhurst, Edward Albert, Brian Dennehy. **1979**

SILKWOOD ★★★★ At more than two hours, *Silkwood* is a shift-and-squirm movie that's worth it. The fine portrayals by Meryl Streep, Kurt Russell, and Cher keep the viewer's interest. Based on real events, the story focuses on 28-year-old nuclear worker and union activist Karen Silkwood, who died in a mysterious car crash while she was attempting to expose the alleged dangers in the Oklahoma plutonium plant where she was employed. Rated R for nudity, sex, and profanity. 128m. **DIR:** Mike Nichols. **CAST:** Meryl Streep, Kurt Russell, Cher, Craig T. Nelson, Fred Ward, Sudie Bond. **1984**

SILVER CHALICE, THE ★★ Full of intrigue and togas, this film is notable only for two unnotable screen debuts by Paul Newman and Lorne Greene. 144m. **DIR:** Victor Saville. **CAST:** Jack Palance, Joseph Wiseman, Paul Newman, Virginia Mayo, Pier Angeli, E. G. Marshall, Alexander Scourby, Natalie Wood, Lorne Greene. **1954**

SILVER DREAM RACER ★★½ This so-so British drama features David Essex as a mechanic turned racer. He is determined to win not only the World Motorcycle Championship, but another man's girlfriend as well. Rated PG. 110m. **DIR:** David Wickes. **CAST:** David Essex, Beau Bridges, Cristina Raines, Clark Peters, Harry H. Corbett. **1980**

SILVER STREAK (1934) ★★ Interesting primarily for the vintage locomotives and the railway system as well as a good cast of unique personalities. B&W; 72m. **DIR:** Thomas Atkins. **CAST:** Charles Starrett, Sally Blane, Hardie Albright, William Farnum, Irving Pichel, Arthur Lake. **1934**

SIMBA ★★★★ In this hard-hitting drama, the ne'er-do-well brother (Dirk Bogarde) of a philanthropic doctor arrives in Kenya to find his brother has been murdered. Thought-provoking study of racial strife. 99m. **DIR:** Brian Desmond Hurst. **CAST:** Dirk Bogarde, Virginia McKenna, Basil Sydney. **1955**

SIMPLE JUSTICE ★★½ A team of madmen rob a bank, fatally shooting some and leaving a beautiful newlywed (Cady McClain) for dead. Her husband (Matthew Galle) and grandparents must cope with continued threats from the men who fear McClain will testify against them. Rated R for violence and profanity. 91m. **DIR:** Deborah Del Prete. **CAST:** Cesar Romero, Doris Roberts, Matthew Galle, Cady McClain. **1989**

SIN OF MADELON CLAUDET, THE ★★★★ The heroine's sin in this unabashed tearjerker is bearing a child out of wedlock. Her redemption lies in a lifetime of devotion and sacrifice. Helen Hayes's Oscar-winning performance is a distinct plus. B&W; 73m. **DIR:** Edgar Selwyn. **CAST:** Helen Hayes, Neil Hamilton, Lewis Stone, Marie Prevost, Karen Morley, Jean Hersholt, Robert Young. **1931**

SINCE YOU WENT AWAY ★★ This overlong, World War II soap opera doesn't hold together despite a great cast of stars and character actors, often in minor roles. Big-budget weeper tells of life on the home front. B&W; 152m. **DIR:** John Cromwell. **CAST:** Claudette Colbert, Joseph Cotten, Jennifer Jones, Shirley Temple, Monty Woolley, Lionel Barrymore, Robert Walker, Hattie McDaniel, Agnes Moorehead, Guy Madison. **1944**

SINCERELY YOURS 🦃 Ridiculous, sincerely. 115m. **DIR:** Gordon Douglas. **CAST:** Liberace, Joanne Dru, Dorothy Malone, William Demarest, Lurene Tuttle, Richard Eyer. **1955**

SINGLE BARS, SINGLE WOMEN 🦃 A dated film that pretends to know all about the singles scene. Made for TV. 100m. **DIR:** Harry Winer. **CAST:** Tony Danza, Paul Michael Glaser, Keith Gordon, Shelley Hack, Christine Lahti, Frances Lee McCain, Kathleen Wilhoite, Mare Winningham. **1984**

SINGLE ROOM FURNISHED 🦃 Jayne Mansfield's last movie was this lurid overwrought melodrama. 93m. **DIR:** Matt Cimber. **CAST:** Jayne Mansfield, Dorothy Keller, Fabian Dean. **1968**

SINGLE STANDARD, THE ★★ Tepid Greta Garbo vehicle that, like most avowedly feminist dramas of its time, fails to deliver on its initial premise. Garbo is a woman who tosses aside her wealth and social position to seek equality with an ex-prize fighter. Of interest primarily to Garbo completists who must see *everything*. Silent. B&W; 88m. **DIR:** John S. Robertson. **CAST:** Greta Garbo, Nils Asther, Johnny Mack Brown. **1929**

SINNERS IN PARADISE ★★½ Survivors of a plane crash find themselves on a tropical island, where they have plenty of time to reflect on their secrets and the things in their past that haunt them. An old idea is handled effectively. B&W; 65m. **DIR:** James Whale. **CAST:** Bruce Cabot, Madge Evans, Marion Martin, Gene Lockhart, John Boles, Milburn Stone, Don Barry. **1938**

SISTER-IN-LAW, THE ★★½ A struggling young singer is lured into drug smuggling by his brother's adulterous wife. Downbeat but occasionally interesting, at least as an early effort in the career of John Savage (who also wrote and sings a few songs). Rated R for nudity. 80m. **DIR:** Joseph Ruben. **CAST:** John Savage. **1974**

SISTER KENNY ★★ Rosalind Russell is noble and sincere in the title role of the Australian nurse who fought polio in the bush. But the telling of her life in this dull and slow box-office flop is tiresome. B&W; 116m. **DIR:** Dudley Nichols. **CAST:** Rosalind Russell, Alexander Knox, Dean Jagger, Charles Dingle, Philip Merivale, Beulah Bondi, John Litel. **1946**

SISTERS, THE (1938) ★★★★ This film offered Errol Flynn, after becoming a star, his first opportunity to play something besides a hero. He portrays a writer who, unable to make a success of himself, turns to the bottle for escape, breaking wife Bette Davis's heart. B&W; 98m. **DIR:** Anatole Litvak. **CAST:** Errol Flynn, Bette Davis, Alan Hale Sr., Donald Crisp, Anita Louise, Jane Bryan, Beulah Bondi, Dick Foran. **1938**

SIX DEGREES OF SEPARATION ★★★½ Fine performances elevate this uneven comedy-drama about a young man (Will Smith) who passes himself off as Sidney Poitier's son in order to gain access to the privileged world of wealthy couple Donald Sutherland and Stockard Channing. John Guare's screenplay, adapted from his Broadway play, gives us fascinating characters, but his story's hard edges rob the film of its potential charm. Rated R for profanity, violence, and suggested sex. 111m. **DIR:** Fred Schepisi. **CAST:** Stockard Channing, Will Smith, Donald Sutherland, Mary Beth Hurt, Bruce Davison, Heather Graham, Anthony Michael Hall, Eric Thal, Richard Masur, Ian McKellen. **1993**

SIX WEEKS ★★★½ Dudley Moore and Mary Tyler Moore star as two adults trying to make the dreams of a young girl—who has a very short time to live—come true in this tearjerker. Directed by Tony Bill, it's enjoyable for viewers who like a good cry. Rated PG for strong content. 107m. **DIR:** Tony Bill. **CAST:** Dudley Moore, Mary Tyler Moore, Katherine Healy, Joe Regalbuto. **1982**

SIX WIVES OF HENRY VIII, THE (TV SERIES) ★★★★ One of the first BBC costume dramas to appear on PBS, and still one of the best. What's really special is Keith Michell's virtuosic and sympathetic portrayal of the last Henry. Almost before your eyes, Henry is transformed from a handsome, brilliant young monarch to a corpulent, pitiable old tyrant. Each tape 90m. **DIR:** Naomi Capon. **CAST:** Keith Michell, Annette Crosbie, Dorothy Tutin, Anne Stallybrass. **1972**

'68 ★★ Hungarian immigrants settle in San Francisco, each with an idea of what America should be. While Dad tries to make it in the restaurant business, one son becomes an antiwar advocate as the other struggles with his homosexuality. This one redefines low budget. Rated R for nudity, violence, and profanity. 100m. **DIR:** Steven Kovacs. **CAST:** Eric Larson, Sandor Tecsi, Robert Locke, Terra Vandergaw, Neil Young. **1987**

SIZZLE 🦃 TV movie should be called *Fizzle*. 100m. **DIR:** Don Medford. **CAST:** Loni Anderson, John Forsythe, Michael Goodwin, Leslie Uggams, Roy Thinnes, Richard Lynch, Phyllis Davis. **1981**

SKAG ★★★½ Home-ridden to recuperate after being felled by a stroke, veteran steelworker Pete Skagska must deal with family problems, his own poor health, and the chance his illness may leave him impotent. In the title role, Karl Malden gives a towering, hard-driving performance as a man determined to prevail, no matter what the emotional cost. TV movie. 152m. **DIR:** Frank Perry. **CAST:** Karl Malden, Piper Laurie, Craig Wasson, Peter Gallagher, George Voskovec. **1980**

SKEEZER ★★½ Made-for-TV movie about a lonely young woman and her friendship with a mutt named Skeezer. This dog eventually helps her to reach emotionally disturbed children in a group home where she is a volunteer. Good for family viewing. 100m. **DIR:** Peter H. Hunt. **CAST:** Karen Valentine, Dee Wallace, Tom Atkins, Mariclare Costello. **1982**

SKIN ART ★★½ Tattoo artist Kirk Baltz makes a living branding Oriental prostitutes at a brothel in Manhattan. When he starts to fall for his latest masterpiece, she revives memories of his days as a Vietnam POW. His obsession to turn her into a living canvas reeks of *Tattoo,* starring Bruce Dern. Kinky but not erotic. Rated R for nudity, violence, and language. 90m. **DIR:** W. Blake Herron. **CAST:** Kirk Baltz, Ariane, Jake Webber, Nora Ariffin, Hil Cato. **1993**

SKOKIE ★★★ The threat of neo-Nazism comes to the small, predominantly Jewish town of Skokie, Illinois in the late 1970s. An all-star cast drives this well-written TV drama, which succeeds in portraying the two sides in unemotional terms. 121m. **DIR:** Herbert Wise. **CAST:** Danny Kaye, Brian Dennehy, Eli Wallach, Kim Hunter, Carl Reiner. **1981**

SKY IS GRAY, THE ★★★ Generosity comes from unexpected quarters in this languid TV adaptation of Ernest J. Gaines's melancholy study of a young boy's first exposure to racism, poverty, and pride in 1940s Louisiana. James Bond III is the youth, dragged to town by his strong-willed mother (Olivia Cole) to have an infected tooth removed. Introduced by Henry Fonda; suitable for family viewing. 46m. **DIR:** Stan Lathan. **CAST:** Olivia Cole, James Bond III, Margaret Avery, Cleavon Little, Clinton Derricks-Carroll. **1980**

SKYLARK ★★★½ *Hallmark Hall of Fame*'s sequel to *Sarah, Plain and Tall* combines high production values with wholesome entertainment. Glenn Close is terrific as the Maine-born, mail-order bride adapting to a difficult life on the Kansas plains. During a severe drought, she must comfort her husband (Christopher Walken) and stepchildren while coming to grips with her own ambiguous feelings about the land. Rated G. 98m. **DIR:** Joseph Sargent. **CAST:** Glenn Close, Christopher Walken, Lexi Randall, Christopher Bell. **1992**

SKYSCRAPER SOULS ★★★½ A one hundred-story office building is the setting for this *Grand Hotel*-type mélange of stories. Warren William is outstanding as the industrialist who seeks to control the entire building. B&W; 99m. **DIR:** Edgar Selwyn. **CAST:** Warren William, Maureen O'Sullivan, Gregory Ratoff, Anita Page, Jean Hersholt, Hedda Hopper. **1932**

SLATE, WYN, AND ME 🦃 Two sociopaths kidnap a woman who witnessed a murder they committed. Rated R for endless profanities and violence. 90m. **DIR:** Don McLennan. **CAST:** Sigrid Thornton, Simon Burke, Martin Sacks. **1987**

SLEEPING TIGER, THE ★★★½ A woman finds herself caught up in a tense triangular love affair with her psychiatrist husband and a cunning crook out on parole and released in her husband's custody. Dirk Bogarde gives a stunning performance as the ex-con. B&W; 89m. **DIR:** Joseph Losey. **CAST:** Alexis Smith, Alexander Knox, Dirk Bogarde. **1954**

SLENDER THREAD, THE ★★★½ Sidney Poitier is a psychology student working at a crisis clinic in Seattle. He fields a call from housewife Anne Bancroft, who has taken an overdose of barbiturates. Fine performances. B&W; 98m. **DIR:** Sydney Pollack. **CAST:** Sidney Poitier, Anne Bancroft, Telly Savalas, Steven Hill, Edward Asner, Dabney Coleman. **1965**

SLIGHTLY SCARLET ★★ Confused blend of romance, crime, and political corruption focuses on good girl falling for gang leader. Forget the story. Just watch the actors interplay. 99m. **DIR:** Allan Dwan. **CAST:** John Payne, Arlene Dahl, Rhonda Fleming, Kent Taylor. **1956**

SLOW BULLET 🦃 Vietnam veteran and his haunting memories of combat. Rated R for violence and nudity. 95m. **DIR:** Allen Wright. **CAST:** Jim Baskin. **1988**

SMALL CIRCLE OF FRIENDS, A ★½ Despite a solid cast, this story of campus unrest during the 1960s never comes together. As college students at Harvard, Karen Allen, Brad Davis, and Jameson Parker play three inseparable friends living and loving their way through protests and riots. Rated PG. 112m. **DIR:** Rob Cohen. **CAST:** Karen Allen, Brad Davis, Jameson Parker, Shelley Long, John Friedrich. **1980**

SMALL KILLING, A ★★★½ This above-average made-for-TV movie gains some of its appeal from the casting. Ed Asner is a cop going undercover as a wino and Jean Simmons is a professor posing as a bag lady. They're out to bust a hit man but manage to fall in love along the way. The supporting cast is equally wonderful. 100m. **DIR:** Steven H. Stern. **CAST:** Edward Asner, Jean Simmons, Sylvia Sidney, Andrew Prine. **1981**

SMALL SACRIFICES ★★★★ Farrah Fawcett delivers a fine but chilling performance as Diana Downs, the sociopathic mother who tried to kill her three children because her ex-boyfriend didn't like kids. John Shea brings intensity to the role of DA Frank Joziak who must protect the two surviving children while seeking a conviction of Downs. Absorbing made-for-TV movie. 159m. **DIR:** David Greene. **CAST:** Farrah Fawcett, John Shea, Ryan O'Neal, Gordon Clapp. **1989**

SMASH PALACE ★★★★ A scrap yard of crumpled and rusting automobiles serves as a backdrop to the story of a marriage in an equally deteriorated condition in this well-made, exceptionally acted film from New Zealand. Explicit sex and nude scenes may shock some viewers. It's a *Kramer vs. Kramer, Ordinary People*-style of movie that builds to a scary, nail-chewing climax. No MPAA rating; this has sex, violence, nudity, and profanity. 100m. **DIR:** Roger Donaldson. **CAST:** Bruno Lawrence, Anna Jemison, Greer Robson, Desmond Kelly. **1981**

SMASH-UP: THE STORY OF A WOMAN ★★★ Nightclub songbird Susan Hayward puts her songwriter husband's (Lee Bowman) career first. As he succeeds, she slips. His subsequent neglect and indifference make her a scenery-shedding bottle baby until near tragedy restores her sobriety and his attention. B&W; 103m. **DIR:** Stuart Heisler. **CAST:** Susan Hayward, Lee Bowman, Marsha Hunt, Eddie Albert, Carleton Young, Carl Esmond. **1947**

SMILE, JENNY, YOU'RE DEAD ★★★½ Neurotic obsession triggers murder and suspense in this exceptional pilot for *Harry O,* David Janssen's follow-up television series to *The Fugitive.* Definitely a keeper. 100m. **DIR:** Jerry Thorpe. **CAST:** David Janssen, Jodie Foster, Andrea Marcovicci, Howard DaSilva, Clu Gulager, John Anderson, Martin Gabel, Zalman King. **1974**

SMILIN' THROUGH (1932) ★★★½ The love of a soldier and an heiress is threatened by a crime his father committed against her family decades earlier. Satisfying fantasy-love story. Remade in 1941. B&W; 98m. **DIR:** Sidney Franklin. **CAST:** Norma Shearer, Fredric March, Leslie Howard, O. P. Heggie. **1932**

SMITHEREENS ★★★ An independently made feature (its budget was only $100,000), this work by producer-director Susan Siedelman examines the life of an amoral and aimless young woman (Susan Berman) living in New York. Rated R. 90m. **DIR:** Susan Seidelman. **CAST:** Susan Berman, Brad Rinn, Richard Hell, Roger Jett. **1982**

SMOKESCREEN ★★★ A fledgling ad executive, tired of being low man on the totem pole, becomes involved with a model who in turn involves him with a mob leader. Well acted and fairly well written, the film's main fault lies in its contrived ending. Rated R. 91m. **DIR:** Martin Lavut. **CAST:** Kim Cattrall, Matt Craven, Kim Coates, Dean Stockwell. **1990**

SMOOTH TALK ★★★★ Coltish Laura Dern owns this film, an uncompromising adaptation of the Joyce Carol Oates short story "Where Are You Going, Where Have You Been?" Dern hits every note as a sultry woman-child poised on the brink of adulthood and sexual maturity. Mary Kay Place does well as an exasperated mom, and Elizabeth Berridge is a sympathetic older sister. Rated PG-13 for language and sexual situations. 92m. **DIR:** Joyce Chopra. **CAST:** Laura Dern, Treat Williams, Mary Kay Place, Elizabeth Berridge, Levon Helm. **1985**

SNAKE PIT, THE ★★★★★ One of the first and best movies about mental illness and the treatment of patients in hospitals and asylums. Olivia de Havilland turns in an exceptional performance as a woman suffering from a nervous breakdown. Based on an autobiographical novel by Mary Jane Ward. B&W; 108m. **DIR:** Anatole Litvak. **CAST:** Olivia de Havilland, Mark Stevens, Leo Genn, Celeste Holm, Betsy Blair, Ruth Donnelly, Glenn Langan, Beulah Bondi, Leif Erickson. **1948**

SO ENDS OUR NIGHT ★★★★ Fredric March gives one of his best performances as a German trying to escape Nazi Germany but forced to return when he learns that his wife is terminally ill. One of the best movies to come from an Erich Maria Remarque novel. The movie was produced before Pearl Harbor and was dismissed by critics and public alike. After the United States entered the war, it was reissued to acclaim and still has strong entertainment value. B&W; 118m. **DIR:** John Cromwell. **CAST:** Fredric March, Margaret Sullavan, Glenn Ford, Frances Dee, Erich Von Stroheim, Anna Sten. **1941**

SODOM AND GOMORRAH ★★★ Better-than-average biblical epic concerning the twin cities of sin. Extremely long film contains good production values and performances. No rating, but film does contain scenes of violence and gore. 154m. **DIR:** Robert Aldrich. **CAST:** Stewart Granger, Stanley Baker, Pier Angeli, Rossana Podesta. **1963**

SOLDIER IN THE RAIN ★★★ *My Bodyguard* director Tony Bill is among the featured performers in this fine combination of sweet drama and rollicking comedy starring Steve McQueen, Jackie Gleason, and Tuesday Weld. Gleason is great as a high-living, worldly master sergeant, and McQueen is equally good as his protégé. B&W; 88m. **DIR:** Ralph Nelson. **CAST:** Steve McQueen, Tony Bill, Jackie Gleason, Tuesday Weld, Tom Poston. **1963**

SOLDIER'S HOME ★★★½ Melancholy adaptation of an Ernest Hemingway story. The war in question is World War I, "the war to end all wars," and young Harold Krebs (Richard Backus) learns, almost to his shame, that he'd prefer that the fighting continue; without it, he has no sense of purpose. Introduced by Henry Fonda; unrated and suitable for family viewing. 41m. **DIR:** Robert Young. **CAST:** Richard Backus, Nancy Marchand, Robert McIlwaine, Lisa Essary, Mark La Mura, Lane Binkley. **1976**

SOLDIER'S TALE, A ★★★ During World War II, romance develops between a British soldier (Gabriel Byrne) and a beautiful Frenchwoman (Marianne Basler) accused of collaborating with the Germans against the French Resistance. Ending is quite a surprise. Rated R for nudity, violence, and profanity. 95m. **DIR:** Larry Parr. **CAST:** Gabriel Byrne, Judge Reinhold, Marianne Basler. **1988**

SOLO 🦃 An uninteresting love story with forgettable characters. Rated PG. 90m. **DIR:** Tony Williams. **CAST:** Vincent Gil, Perry Armstrong. **1977**

SOLOMON AND SHEBA ★★★ High times in biblical times as Sheba vamps Solomon. The emphasis is on lavish spectacle. Eyewash, not brain food. 139m. **DIR:** King Vidor. **CAST:** Yul Brynner, Gina Lollobrigida, George Sanders. **1959**

SOME CALL IT LOVING 🦃 Jazz musician buys a "Sleeping Beauty" from a circus sideshow for his own perverse enjoyment. Rated R for nudity and language. 103m. **DIR:** James B. Harris. **CAST:** Zalman King, Carol White, Tisa Farrow, Richard Pryor, Logan Ramsey. **1974**

SOME CAME RUNNING ★★★½ Based on James Jones's novel of life in a midwestern town, this film offers an entertaining study of some rather complex characters. Shirley MacLaine gives a sparkling performance as the town's loose woman who's in love with Frank Sinatra. The story is not strong, but the performances are fine. 136m. **DIR:** Vincente Minnelli. **CAST:** Frank Sinatra, Dean Martin, Shirley MacLaine, Arthur Kennedy, Martha Hyer. **1958**

SOMEBODY HAS TO SHOOT THE PICTURE ★★★★ Two mesmerizing performances fuel this gripping made-for-cable indictment of the cruel and unusual treatment that often precedes capital punishment. Roy Scheider stars as a burned-out, Pulitzer Prize–winning photojournalist who accepts convict Arliss Howard's last wish: that his final moments be captured by a photographer. Unrated, but probably too intense for younger viewers. Rated R for language and intensity. 104m. **DIR:** Frank Pierson. **CAST:** Roy Scheider, Arliss Howard, Bonnie Bedelia, Robert Carradine. **1990**

SOMEBODY UP THERE LIKES ME ★★★★½ This is a first-rate biography. Boxer Rocky Graziano's career is traced from the back streets of New York to the heights of fame in the ring. It's one of the very best fight films ever made and features a sterling performance by Paul Newman. B&W; 113m. **DIR:** Robert Wise. **CAST:** Paul Newman, Pier Angeli, Everett Sloane, Sal Mineo, Eileen Heckart, Robert Loggia, Steve McQueen. **1956**

SOMEONE I TOUCHED ★★ The subject is VD as architect James Olson and pregnant wife Cloris Leachman trade accusations over who's to blame. The actors are far better than their material in this dated disease-of-the-week TV movie. 78m. **DIR:** Lou Antonio. **CAST:** Cloris Leachman, James Olson, Glynnis O'Connor, Andrew Robinson. **1975**

SOMEONE TO LOVE ★★ Danny (Henry Jaglom) decides to have a filmmaking–Valentine's Day party with single people explaining directly into the camera why they are alone. Orson Welles (in his last screen appearance) sits on the balcony, commenting. One small problem: This movie wallows in all there is to detest about the Los Angeles art scene. Rated R for language. 112m. **DIR:** Henry Jaglom. **CAST:** Henry Jaglom, Michael Emil, Andrea Marcovicci, Sally Kellerman, Orson Welles. **1986**

SOMETHING FOR EVERYONE ★★★ This sleeper about a manipulative, amoral young man (Michael York) and the lengths he goes to in order to advance himself might not be to everyone's tastes. Angela Lansbury gives one of her best performances as the down-on-her-luck aristocrat who falls victim to York's charms. Mature themes and situations make this film more suitable for an older audience. 112m. **DIR:** Harold Prince. **CAST:** Michael York, Angela Lansbury, Anthony Corlan, Jane Carr. **1970**

SOMETIMES A GREAT NOTION ★★★ Paul Newman plays the elder son of an Oregon logging family that refuses to go on strike with the other lumberjacks in the area. The family pays dearly for its unwillingness to go along. One scene in particular, which features Newman aiding Richard Jaeckel, who has been pinned in the water by a fallen tree, is unforgettable. Rated PG. 114m. **DIR:** Paul Newman. **CAST:** Paul Newman, Henry Fonda, Lee Remick, Michael Sarrazin, Richard Jaeckel. **1971**

SOMEWHERE I'LL FIND YOU ★★★★ A war picture that zeroes-in on the dangerous lives and loves of war correspondents in the heat of battle, this movie also has the distinction of Lana Turner's sexy allure and Clark Gable's obvious appreciation of it. They play war correspondents coping with their passions. Strong dramatic scenes set the tone for this WWII drama. B&W; 108m. **DIR:** Wesley Ruggles. **CAST:** Clark Gable, Lana Turner, Robert Sterling, Keenan Wynn, Reginald Owen, Charles Dingle, Lee Patrick, Patricia Dane. **1942**

SOMMERSBY ★★★★ French director Daniel Vigne's brilliant *The Return of Martin Guerre* is transferred to the post–Civil War South for this involving tale of redemption. Richard Gere is fine as the returning soldier who resumes his relationship with willing wife Jodie Foster and the running of his plantation while former acquaintances marvel at his new sense of honor and responsibility. *Sommersby* retains many of the outstanding qualities of the original. Rated PG-13 for nudity and violence. 120m. **DIR:** Jon Amiel. **CAST:** Richard Gere, Jodie Foster, Bill Pullman, James Earl Jones, William Windom. **1993**

SONG OF BERNADETTE, THE ★★★★ Four Oscars, including one to Jennifer Jones for best actress, went to this beautifully filmed story of the simple nineteenth-century French peasant girl, Bernadette Soubirous, who saw a vision of the Virgin Mary in the town of Lourdes. B&W; 156m. **DIR:** Henry King. **CAST:** Jennifer Jones, Charles Bickford, William Eythe, Vincent Price, Lee J. Cobb, Gladys Cooper, Anne Revere. **1943**

SONG OF LOVE ★★½ When the writers and producers acknowledge up front that they have taken "certain liberties," you can throw away all thoughts of a factual story of the marriage of Clara Wieck (Katharine Hepburn) to Robert Schumann (Paul Henreid) and their close friendship with young Johannes Brahms (Robert Walker). Close your eyes and listen to the piano interludes, dubbed, uncredited, by Arthur Rubinstein. B&W; 119m. **DIR:** Clarence Brown. **CAST:** Katharine Hepburn, Paul Henreid, Robert Walker, Henry Daniell, Henry Stephenson, Leo G. Carroll. **1947**

SONS OF THE SEA ★★½ Made and released in Great Britain as World War II began, this topical suspense-thriller drama involves the son of a naval commander with eyes-only clearance who unknowingly aids an enemy spy. Good show, but far better things were to come as the war progressed and England geared up its propaganda machine. B&W; 83m. **DIR:** Maurice Elvey. **CAST:** Leslie Banks, Kay Walsh, Mackenzie Ward, Cecil Parker. **1939**

SOONER OR LATER ★★ This made-for-TV romance may fascinate preteens. A 13-year-old girl (Denise Miller) sets her sights on a 17-year-old rock guitarist (Rex Smith). She pretends to be older and gets caught up in her lies. 100m. **DIR:** Bruce Hart. **CAST:** Denise Miller, Rex Smith, Morey Amsterdam, Judd Hirsch, Lynn Redgrave, Barbara Feldon. **1978**

SOPHIA LOREN: HER OWN STORY ★★½ Sophia Loren portrays herself in this television drama that chronicles her life from obscurity to international stardom. At times, it appears more like a self-parody. Interesting, but not compelling enough to justify its extreme length. 150m. **DIR:** Mel Stuart. **CAST:** Sophia Loren, John Gavin, Rip Torn. **1980**

SOPHIE'S CHOICE ★★★★★ A young, inexperienced southern writer named Stingo (Peter MacNicol) learns about love, life, and death in this absorbing, wonderfully acted, and heartbreaking movie. One summer, while observing the affair between Sophie (Meryl Streep), a victim of a concentration camp, and Nathan (Kevin Kline), a charming, but sometimes explosive biologist, Stingo falls in love with Sophie, a woman with deep, dark secrets. Rated R. 157m. **DIR:** Alan J. Pakula. **CAST:** Meryl Streep, Kevin Kline, Peter MacNicol. **1982**

SOPHISTICATED GENTS, THE ★★★½ Arguably one of the best TV movies ever made, this ensemble drama was based by Melvin Van Peebles on John A. Williams's book, *The Junior Bachelor Society*. A powerful production. 200m. **DIR:** Harry Falk. **CAST:** Bernie Casey, Rosey Grier, Robert Hooks, Ron O'Neal, Thalmus Rasulala, Raymond St. Jacques, Melvin Van Peebles, Dick Anthony Williams, Paul Winfield, Denise Nicholas. **1981**

SORROWS OF SATAN, THE ★★★ Lavish surreal drama about a struggling literary critic whose engagement to an impoverished writer becomes complicated by Satan in the form of a cunning wealthy gentleman. Visually impressive. B&W; 90m. **DIR:** D. W. Griffith. **CAST:** Adolphe Menjou, Carol Dempster, Ricardo Cortez, Lya de Putti. **1926**

SOUNDER ★★★★★ Beautifully made film detailing the struggle of a black sharecropper and his family. Director Martin Ritt gets outstanding performances from Cicely Tyson and Paul Winfield. When her husband is sent to jail, Tyson must raise her family and run the farm by herself while trying to get the eldest son an education. A truly moving and thought-provoking film. Don't miss this one. Rated G. 105m. **DIR:** Martin Ritt. **CAST:** Cicely Tyson, Paul Winfield, Kevin Hooks, Carmen Mathews, Taj Mahal, James Best, Janet MacLachlan. **1972**

SOUTH CENTRAL ★★★★ Tough, uncompromising urban drama about a father's attempts to keep his son out of gangs hits home and hits hard. Glenn Plummer delivers a powerful performance as a new father whose gang affiliation lands him in prison. While he counts the days until his release, his son grows up and becomes a pawn of his former gang. Now out of prison, Plummer will do everything he can to stay straight and win his son back. Explosive action coupled with hard-as-nails drama make this an exceptional film. Rated R for violence, language, and adult situations. 99m. **DIR:** Steve Anderson. **CAST:** Glenn Plummer, Carl Lumbly, Byron Keith Minns, LaRita Shelby, Kevin Best. **1992**

SOUTH OF RENO ★★★ This surreal psychodrama offers a compelling look at one man's struggle with desperation in a broiling Nevada backroads community. When he learns that his wife is carrying on an extramarital affair, he goes over the edge. Rated R; contains nudity, profanity, and violence. 98m. **DIR:** Mark Rezyka. **CAST:** Jeff Osterhage, Lisa Blount, Lewis Van Bergen, Joe Phelan. **1987**

SOUTHERNER, THE ★★★★ Stark life in the rural South before civil rights. Dirt-poor tenant farmer (Zachary Scott) struggles against insurmountable odds to provide for his family while maintaining his dignity. Visually a beautiful film, but uneven in dramatic continuity. Nonetheless, its high rating is deserved. B&W; 91m. **DIR:** Jean Renoir. **CAST:** Zachary Scott, Betty Field, J. Carrol Naish. **1945**

SOUVENIR ★★ Former German soldier returns to France for the first time in forty years to visit his daughter and come to terms with the guilt he feels. Christopher Plummer is wasted in this talky, predictable drama. Rated R for brief nudity. 93m. **DIR:** Geoffrey Reeve. **CAST:** Christopher Plummer, Catharine Hicks, Michel Lonsdale. **1988**

SPARROWS ★★★ The legendary Mary Pickford—"Our Mary" to millions during her reign as Queen of Hollywood when this film was made—plays the resolute, intrepid champion of a group of younger orphans besieged by an evil captor. Silent melodrama at its best, folks. B&W; 84m. **DIR:** William Beaudine. **CAST:** Mary Pickford, Gustav von Seyffertitz. **1926**

SPEAKING PARTS ★★★ Stylistically offbeat drama about an actor who supports himself by working as a housekeeper in a posh hotel. Canadian filmmaker Atom Egoyan combines the media of film and video technology to create a stunning visual display. Not rated, but contains nudity and profanity. 92m. **DIR:** Atom Egoyan. **CAST:** Michael McManus, Arsinée Khanjian, Gabrielle Rose. **1989**

SPENCER'S MOUNTAIN ★★½ Henry Fonda is fine as the head of a poor Wyoming family determined that his oldest son must go to college, but the movie is strangely unmoving. From the novel by Earl Hammer Jr., this is the basis for TV's *The Waltons*, and comparisons are inevitable. 118m. **DIR:** Delmer Daves. **CAST:** Henry Fonda, Maureen O'Hara, James MacArthur, Donald Crisp, Wally Cox, Virginia Gregg, Whit Bissell. **1963**

SPIRIT OF ST. LOUIS, THE ★★★★ Jimmy Stewart always wanted to portray Charles Lindbergh in a re-creation of his historic solo flight across the Atlantic. When he finally got his chance, at age 48, many critics felt he was too old to be believable. Stewart did just fine. The action does drag at times, but this remains a quality picture for the whole family. 138m. **DIR:** Billy Wilder. **CAST:** James Stewart, Patricia Smith, Murray Hamilton, Marc Connelly. **1957**

SPIRIT OF WEST POINT, THE ★★½ West Point football stars play themselves in this realistic saga of the Long Gray Line. B&W; 77m. **DIR:** Ralph Murphy. **CAST:** Felix "Doc" Blanchard, Anne Nagel, Alan Hale Sr., Tom Harmon. **1947**

SPITFIRE ★★★½ A girl (Katharine Hepburn) believes herself to have healing powers and is cast out from her Ozark Mountain home as a result. It's an interesting premise, and well-acted. B&W; 88m. **DIR:** John Cromwell. **CAST:** Katharine Hepburn, Robert Young, Ralph Bellamy, Sara Haden, Sidney Toler. **1934**

SPLENDOR IN THE GRASS ★★★★ Warren Beatty made his film debut in this 1961 film, as a popular, rich high school boy. Natalie Wood plays his less-prosperous girlfriend who has a nervous breakdown when he dumps her. A few tears shed by the viewer make this romantic drama all the more intriguing. 124m. **DIR:** Elia Kazan. **CAST:** Warren Beatty, Natalie Wood, Pat Hingle, Audrey Christie. **1961**

SPLIT DECISIONS ★★ Gene Hackman might have been hoping for an audience-pleasing sports film on a par with *Hoosiers* when he agreed to do this fight picture, but the result is another failed takeoff on the *Rocky* series. Pure melodrama: Hackman attempts to groom one son (Craig Sheffer) for the Olympics while fearing that he, like his older brother (Jeff Fahey), will opt for the easy money offered by sleazy fight promoters. Rated R for violence and profanity. 95m. **DIR:** David Drury. **CAST:** Gene Hackman, Craig Sheffer, Jeff Fahey, Jennifer Beals, John McLiam. **1988**

SPLIT IMAGE ★★★★ This is a very interesting, thought-provoking film about religious cults and those who become caught up in them. Michael O'Keefe plays a young man who is drawn into a pseudo-religious organization run by Peter Fonda. The entire cast is good, but Fonda stands out in one of his best roles. Rated R for language and nudity. 113m. **DIR:** Ted Kotcheff. **CAST:** Peter Fonda, James Woods, Karen Allen, Michael O'Keefe. **1982**

SPLIT SECOND (1953) ★★★ Tense film about an escaped convict who holds several people hostage in a deserted town has a lot working for it, including the fact that the place they're holed up in is a nuclear test site. B&W; 85m. **DIR:** Dick Powell. **CAST:** Stephen McNally, Alexis Smith, Jan Sterling, Paul Kelly, Richard Egan. **1953**

SPORTING CLUB, THE 🦃 An allegory of America that takes place at an exclusive hunting club. Look for Linda Blair in a small role. 104m. **DIR:** Larry Peerce. **CAST:** Robert Fields, Nicolas Coster, Margaret Blye, Jack Warden, Richard Dysart. **1971**

SPY IN BLACK, THE ★★★ Unusual espionage-cum-romance story of German agent Conrad Veidt and his love affair with British agent Valerie Hobson. British director Michael Powell brings just the right blend of duty and tragedy to this story, set in the turmoil of World War I. B&W; 82m. **DIR:** Michael Powell. **CAST:** Conrad Veidt, Valerie Hobson, Sebastian Shaw, June Duprez, Marius Goring. **1939**

SPY OF NAPOLEON ★★ Heavy-handed historical hokum finds Emperor Napoleon III using his illegitimate daughter to ferret out dissidents and enemies. Amusing enough and stars former silent-screen good guy Richard Barthelmess in a meaty role. B&W; 77m. **DIR:** Maurice Elvey. **CAST:** Richard Barthelmess, Dolly Hass. **1936**

SPY WHO CAME IN FROM THE COLD, THE ★★★★ Realism and stark authenticity mark this sunless drama of the closing days in the career of a British cold-war spy in Berlin. Richard Burton is matchless as embittered, burned-out Alec Leamas, the sold-out agent. No 007 glamour and gimmicks here.

112m. **DIR:** Martin Ritt. **CAST:** Richard Burton, Claire Bloom, Oskar Werner, Bernard Lee, George Voskovec, Peter Van Eyck, Sam Wanamaker. **1965**

SQUARE DANCE ★★★★ A coming-of-age drama about a 13-year-old Texas girl (Winona Ryder), *Square Dance* has so much atmosphere that you can almost smell the chicken-fried steaks. When the girl's loose-living mother (well played by Jane Alexander) takes her away from the comfort and care of her grandfather's (Jason Robards) ranch, the youngster's life goes from idyllic to hard-edged. Rated PG-13 for profanity and suggested sex. 110m. **DIR:** Daniel Petrie. **CAST:** Jason Robards Jr., Jane Alexander, Winona Ryder, Rob Lowe, Guich Koock. **1987**

SQUEEZE, THE (1977) ★★½ Stacy Keach plays an alcoholic detective whose ex-wife is kidnapped for a large ransom. Good performances do not save this mediocre film. Rated R for nudity and language. 106m. **DIR:** Michael Apted. **CAST:** Stacy Keach, David Hemmings, Edward Fox, Stephen Boyd, Carol White. **1977**

STACKING ★★★½ A cut above the righteous save-the-farm films that abound these days, because it doesn't allow for an overblown triumphant outcome and the performances are exquisite. Frederic Forrest is wonderful as a hard-drinking hired hand, and Christine Lahti really gets under the skin of her restless character. Rated PG. 95m. **DIR:** Martin Rosen. **CAST:** Christine Lahti, Frederic Forrest, Megan Follows, Jason Gedrick, Ray Baker, Peter Coyote. **1988**

STACY'S KNIGHTS ★★ Kevin Costner's career has come a long way since this early snoozer, sort of a cross between *The Karate Kid* and *The Sting* set at the blackjack tables of Reno. Rated PG. 95m. **DIR:** Jim Wilson. **CAST:** Andra Millian, Kevin Costner. **1982**

STAGE DOOR CANTEEN ★★ An all-star cast play themselves in this mildly amusing romance about the behind-the-scenes world of Broadway. Unless you enjoy looking at the many stage luminaries during their early years, you will find this entire film to be ordinary, predictable, and uninspired. B&W; 85m. **DIR:** Frank Borzage. **CAST:** William Terry, Cheryl Walkers, Katharine Hepburn, Harpo Marx, Helen Hayes, Count Basie, Edgar Bergen. **1943**

STAGE STRUCK (1958) ★★ Despite a fine cast—Susan Strasberg excepted—this rehash of *Morning Glory* is flat and wearisome. You don't really care to pull for the young actress trying to make her mark. The late Joan Greenwood's throaty voice, however, is sheer delight. 95m. **DIR:** Sidney Lumet. **CAST:** Henry Fonda, Susan Strasberg, Joan Greenwood, Herbert Marshall, Christopher Plummer. **1958**

STALIN ★★½ Robert Duvall's compelling portrayal of the infamous Soviet dictator is sabotaged by Paul Monash's haphazard script, which fails to provide the depth required to explain just how Stalin remained in power for so many years. Made for cable. 172m. **DIR:** Ivan Passer. **CAST:** Robert Duvall, Julia Ormond, Jeroen Krabbé, Joan Plowright, Maximilian Schell. **1992**

STAND AND DELIVER ★★★★½ A *Rocky*esque interpretation of high school math teacher Jaime Escalante's true-life exploits. Edward James Olmos stars as Escalante, a man who gave up a high-paying job in electronics to make a contribution to society. Recognizing that his inner-city students need motivation to keep them from a lifetime of menial labor, he sets them a challenge: preparation for the state Advanced Placement Test...in calculus. Rated PG for language. 105m. **DIR:** Ramon Menendez. **CAST:** Edward James Olmos, Lou Diamond Phillips, Rosana De Soto, Andy Garcia. **1988**

STAND BY ME (1986) ★★★★½ Based on Stephen King's novella, *The Body,* the story involves four young boys in the last days of summer and their search for the missing body of a young boy believed hit by a train. Morbid as it may sound, this is not a horror movie. Rather, it is a story of ascending to manhood. Sometimes sad and often funny. Rated R. 90m. **DIR:** Rob Reiner. **CAST:** Wil Wheaton, River Phoenix, Corey Feldman, Jerry O'Connell, Kiefer Sutherland, John Cusack, Richard Dreyfuss. **1986**

STANLEY AND IRIS ★★★ Jane Fonda stars as a recently widowed bakery worker who teaches an illiterate coworker (Robert De Niro) how to read. A predictable but likable low-key romance derived from Pat Banker's excellent novel, *Union Street.* Rated PG-13. 114m. **DIR:** Martin Ritt. **CAST:** Jane Fonda, Robert De Niro, Feodor Chaliapin, Martha Plimpton, Swoosie Kurtz, Harley Cross, Jamey Sheridan. **1990**

STANLEY AND LIVINGSTONE ★★★ When Spencer Tracy delivers the historic line, "Doctor Livingstone, I presume," to Cedric Hardwicke in this production, you know why he was such a great screen actor. His performance, as a reporter who journeys to Africa in order to find a lost Victorian explorer injects life and interest into what could have been just another stodgy prestige picture. B&W; 101m. **DIR:** Henry King. **CAST:** Spencer Tracy, Cedric Hardwicke, Richard Greene, Nancy Kelly. **1939**

STAR, THE ★★★ Bette Davis earned one of her ten Oscar nominations for her role of a has-been earnestly trying to make a comeback in show business. The story of a once-famous actress on the skids resembled her career at the time, and she makes more out of the role because of it. B&W;

89m. **DIR:** Stuart Heisler. **CAST:** Bette Davis, Sterling Hayden, Natalie Wood, Warner Anderson, Barbara Lawrence, June Travis, Minor Watson. **1952**

STAR 80 ★★★★ A depressing, uncompromising, but brilliantly filmed and acted portrait of a tragedy. Mariel Hemingway stars as Dorothy Stratten, the Playboy playmate of the year who was murdered in 1980 by the husband (an equally impressive portrayal by Eric Roberts) she had outgrown. The movie paints a bleak portrait of her life, times, and death. Rated R for nudity, violence, profanity, and sex. 102m. **DIR:** Bob Fosse. **CAST:** Mariel Hemingway, Eric Roberts, Cliff Robertson, Carroll Baker. **1983**

STAR IS BORN, A (1937) ★★★★ The first version of this thrice-filmed in-house Hollywood weeper, this is the story of an aging actor (Fredric March) whose career is beginning to go on the skids while his youthful bride's (Janet Gaynor) career is starting to blossom. Great acting and a tight script keep this poignant movie from falling into melodrama. 111m. **DIR:** William Wellman. **CAST:** Fredric March, Janet Gaynor, Adolphe Menjou, May Robson. **1937**

STAR IS BORN, A (1954) ★★★★½ Judy Garland's acting triumph is the highlight of this movie, which is considered to be the best version of this classic romantic tragedy. This one is well worth watching. James Mason is also memorable in the role originated by Fredric March. Be sure to get the full restored version. 154m. **DIR:** George Cukor. **CAST:** Judy Garland, James Mason, Charles Bickford, Jack Carson, Tommy Noonan. **1954**

STAR IS BORN, A (1976) ★★ The third and by far least watchable version of this venerable Hollywood war-horse has been sloppily crafted into a vehicle for star Barbra Streisand. The rocky romance between a declining star (Kris Kristofferson) and an up-and-coming new talent (Streisand) has been switched from the world of the stage to that of rock 'n' roll. Rated R. 140m. **DIR:** Frank Pierson. **CAST:** Barbra Streisand, Kris Kristofferson, Gary Busey, Oliver Clark. **1976**

STARLIGHT HOTEL ★★ Familiar tale, although with a new setting: 1929 New Zealand. A 12-year-old runaway bound for Australia heads across the New Zealand countryside. Rated PG for profanity and violence. 91m. **DIR:** Sam Pillsbury. **CAST:** Peter Phelps. **1987**

STARS LOOK DOWN, THE ★★★★ Classic film about a Welsh coal miner and his struggle to rise above his station and maintain his identity and the respect of his community is every bit as good today as it was when released. A coup for director Carol Reed and another great performance by Michael Redgrave as a man of quiet dignity and determination. Well worth the watching. B&W; 110m. **DIR:** Carol Reed. **CAST:** Michael Redgrave, Margaret Lockwood, Edward Rigby, Emlyn Williams, Cecil Parker. **1939**

STATE OF EMERGENCY ★★★★ Overcrowded inner-city emergency wards are the focus of this taut medical drama, which emphasizes the impending disintegration of the U.S. hospital network. Auto-accident victim Paul Dooley watches harried emergency-room surgeon Joe Mantegna wade through a nightmarish caseload, while administrators coldly consider measures to improve the hospital's financial profile by closing clinics. Performances are top-notch, but you won't be left with a good feeling. Rated R for profanity and graphic surgical procedures. 86m. **DIR:** Lesli Linka Glatter. **CAST:** Joe Mantegna, Lynn Whitfield, Melinda Dillon, Paul Dooley, Richard Beymer. **1994**

STATE OF GRACE ★★★ Intriguing first big-budget film from director Phil Joanou focuses on an undercover cop (Sean Penn) who comes back to his old neighborhood to bring down the Irish mob led by childhood friends Ed Harris and Gary Oldman. Oldman's performance is so over the top that he seems to have walked in from a John Waters or David Lynch movie. Rated R for violence, profanity, and nudity. 134m. **DIR:** Phil Joanou. **CAST:** Sean Penn, Ed Harris, Gary Oldman, Robin Wright, John Turturro, John C. Reilly, Burgess Meredith. **1990**

STATE OF THE UNION ★★★ This is a political fable about an American businessman who is encouraged by opportunities to run for the presidency, and leave his integrity behind in the process. Spencer Tracy and Katharine Hepburn are a joy to watch, as usual. B&W; 124m. **DIR:** Frank Capra. **CAST:** Spencer Tracy, Katharine Hepburn, Adolphe Menjou, Van Johnson, Angela Lansbury. **1948**

STATE'S ATTORNEY ★★½ John Barrymore is in good form in this barely believable story of a crooked lawyer who defends a prostitute as a lark and finds himself falling in love. Only in Hollywood, folks. B&W; 80m. **DIR:** George Archainbaud. **CAST:** John Barrymore, Helen Twelvetrees, William "Stage" Boyd. **1932**

STATIC ★★★ This highly offbeat drama explores isolation and alienation in human experience and the need to believe in something greater. The story centers around a would-be inventor (Keith Gordon) who attempts to enlighten people through a device that monitors images of Heaven. Surreal film falls somewhere between *Eraserhead* and *True Stories*. Rated R. 93m. **DIR:** Mark Romanek. **CAST:** Keith Gordon, Amanda Plummer, Bob Gunton. **1985**

STAY AS YOU ARE ★★★★ This film begins conventionally but charmingly as the story of a romance between a 20-year-old girl, Francesca (Nastassja Kinski), and Giulio (Marcello Mastroianni), a man old enough to be her father. It remains charming, but the charm becomes mingled with a controlled anguish when it becomes evident that Giulio may indeed be her father. No MPAA rating. 95m. **DIR:** Alberto Lattuada. **CAST:** Nastassja Kinski, Marcello Mastroianni, Francisco Rabal. **1978**

STAY HUNGRY ★★★★½ An underrated film dealing with a young southern aristocrat's (Jeff Bridges) attempt to complete a real estate deal by purchasing a bodybuilding gym. Bridges begins to appreciate the gym as well as getting some insights into his own life. Rated R for violence, brief nudity, and language. 103m. **DIR:** Bob Rafelson. **CAST:** Jeff Bridges, Sally Field, R. G. Armstrong, Arnold Schwarzenegger. **1976**

STAYING TOGETHER ★★★★ Skillfully directed by Lee Grant, this splendid character study focuses on the McDermott family and the fried-chicken restaurant they run in Ridgeway, South Carolina. You'll be pleasantly surprised at how deeply you become involved with the characters. Rated R for profanity, nudity, and suggested sex. 91m. **DIR:** Lee Grant. **CAST:** Sean Astin, Stockard Channing, Melinda Dillon, Jim Haynie, Levon Helm, Dinah Manoff, Dermot Mulroney, Tim Quill, Keith Szarabajka, Daphne Zuniga. **1989**

STEAL THE SKY ★★ In this pretentious, melodramatic misfire, first telecast on HBO, Ben Cross is an Iraqi jet pilot who is targeted by Israeli intelligence for its own purposes. Mariel Hemingway is the agent assigned to seduce him into cooperating. Not rated. 110m. **DIR:** John Hancock. **CAST:** Ben Cross, Mariel Hemingway. **1988**

STEALING HEAVEN ★★ Middle Ages story of a forbidden love between a member of the clergy and a beautiful young aristocrat—Abelard and Heloise. Lots of lust and guilt but little else to sustain the film. Rated R for nudity. 108m. **DIR:** Clive Donner. **CAST:** Derek de Lint, Kim Thomson, Denholm Elliott. **1988**

STEALING HOME ★★★½ Enjoyable and sporadically disarming character study about a gifted athlete (Mark Harmon) who renews his commitment to baseball after several years of aimless drifting. News reaches him that his one-time baby-sitter (Jodie Foster)—a freethinking rebel who was the one person who believed in him—has committed suicide. An ensemble cast does a fine job with this bittersweet tale. Foster is unforgettable. Rated PG-13 for profanity and suggested sex. 98m. **DIR:** Steven Kampmann, Will Aldis. **CAST:** Mark Harmon, Jodie Foster, Blair Brown, John Shea, Jonathan Silverman, Harold Ramis. **1988**

STEAMING ★★ Nell Dunn's play, *Steaming*, takes place in an English Turkish-style bathhouse where a group of women share their feelings about life. Vanessa Redgrave lends some needed reality to this sweaty gabfest. Rated R. 112m. **DIR:** Joseph Losey. **CAST:** Vanessa Redgrave, Sarah Miles, Diana Dors, Brenda Bruce, Felicity Dean. **1984**

STEEL MAGNOLIAS ★★★★½ Only a curmudgeon could resist falling in love with *Steel Magnolias*, which features an all-star cast in a classy tearjerker about the enduring friendships among six women in a small southern town. It's light and breezy at first, with Shirley MacLaine doing a wonderful job as the town grump. The story gradually becomes more serious and leads to an affecting, emotion-packed ending. Rated PG for brief profanity. 118m. **DIR:** Herbert Ross. **CAST:** Sally Field, Dolly Parton, Shirley MacLaine, Daryl Hannah, Olympia Dukakis, Julia Roberts, Sam Shepard, Tom Skerritt. **1989**

STELLA (1950) ★★ A family of screwballs and the suspicion of murder don't add up in this black comedy of errors. David Wayne believes he killed his uncle, buried the body, and forgot where. A moderately likable misfire. B&W; 83m. **DIR:** Claude Binyon. **CAST:** Ann Sheridan, Victor Mature, David Wayne, Leif Erickson, Frank Fontaine. **1950**

STELLA (1990) ★★ The Divine Miss M. takes a pratfall in this sudsy, airheaded remake of *Stella Dallas*. As in the original 1937 film, Bette Midler's Stella is a working-class gal who gives up her daughter to be raised by her wealthy father. Unfortunately for the film, the social conditions that existed during the Great Depression no longer prevail, and Stella's sacrifice seems stupid rather than noble. Rated PG-13 for profanity and frank sexual themes. 106m. **DIR:** John Erman. **CAST:** Bette Midler, John Goodman, Trini Alvarado, Stephen Collins, Marsha Mason. **1990**

STELLA DALLAS ★★★★ Barbara Stanwyck's title-role performance as the small-town vulgar innocent who sacrifices everything for her daughter got her a well-deserved Oscar nomination and set the standard for this type of screen character. John Boles is the elegant wealthy heel who does her wrong. Anne Shirley is Laurel, the object of her mother's completely self-effacing conduct. B&W; 111m. **DIR:** King Vidor. **CAST:** Barbara Stanwyck, Anne Shirley, John Boles, Alan Hale Sr., Tim Holt, Marjorie Main. **1937**

STEPPENWOLF ★★½ In this United States–Switzerland coproduction, director Fred Haines gives us an almost literal adaptation of Hermann Hesse's most widely read novel. It's a good try, but the source really isn't filmable. Rated PG. 105m. **DIR:** Fred Haines. **CAST:** Max von Sydow, Dominique Sanda, Pierre Clementi. **1974**

STERILE CUCKOO, THE ★★★★ Painfully poignant story about a dedicated young college lad (Wendell Burton) and the loopy young woman (Liza Minnelli) who, unable to handle people on their own terms, demands too much of those with whom she becomes involved. Minnelli's Pookie Adams won the actress a well-deserved Academy Award nomination. Rated PG for sexual situations. 107m. **DIR:** Alan J. Pakula. **CAST:** Liza Minnelli, Wendell Burton, Tim McIntire. **1969**

STEVIE ★★★★ Glenda Jackson gives a brilliant performance as reclusive poet Stevie Smith in this stagy, but still interesting, film. Mona Washbourne is the film's true delight as Smith's doting—and slightly dotty—aunt. Trevor Howard narrates and costars in this British release. Rated PG for brief profanity. 102m. **DIR:** Robert Enders. **CAST:** Glenda Jackson, Mona Washbourne, Trevor Howard, Alec McCowen. **1978**

STIGMA 🦃 An ex-medical student just out of prison battles prejudice and an epidemic of VD in a sheltered island community. 93m. **DIR:** David E. Durston. **CAST:** Philip Michael Thomas. **1972**

STOCKS AND BLONDES 🦃 A female college student researches a paper on corporate takeovers and unearths some dirty work. Rated R. 79m. **DIR:** Arthur Greenstands. **CAST:** Leigh Wood, Veronica Hart. **1984**

STOLEN HOURS ★★½ A fair remake of the classic 1939 Bette Davis tearjerker, *Dark Victory*. Susan Hayward is a fun-loving playgirl who learns she has only months to live and tries to make her limited time meaningful. Okay...if you haven't seen the original. 97m. **DIR:** Daniel Petrie. **CAST:** Susan Hayward, Michael Craig, Diane Baker, Edward Judd. **1963**

STOLEN LIFE, A ★★★ Bette Davis produced this film herself. It shows her histrionic talents off to good advantage because she plays twins—one good, the other bad. When one sister takes over the other's life, she also takes the boyfriend they both want. B&W; 109m. **DIR:** Curtis Bernhardt. **CAST:** Bette Davis, Glenn Ford, Dane Clark, Bruce Bennett, Charlie Ruggles, Walter Brennan. **1946**

STONE BOY, THE ★★★★★ A superb ensemble cast elevates this rural *Ordinary People*–style film about a boy who accidentally shoots the older brother he adores and begins losing touch with reality. It's a tough subject, exquisitely handled. For some reason, this fine film was never theatrically released on a wide scale. Rated PG for brief violence and some profanity. 93m. **DIR:** Christopher Cain. **CAST:** Robert Duvall, Frederic Forrest, Glenn Close, Wilford Brimley. **1984**

STORY OF A LOVE STORY ★★ In this offbeat and increasingly off-putting adaptation by screenwriter Nicholas Mosely of his novel *Impossible Object*, Alan Bates stars as an English novelist who becomes involved in an affair with a married Frenchwoman (Dominique Sanda). In English and French with some subtitles. Rated R for nudity and brief violence. 110m. **DIR:** John Frankenheimer. **CAST:** Alan Bates, Dominique Sanda, Evans Evans, Lea Massari, Michel Auclair. **1973**

STORY OF A THREE DAY PASS, THE ★★★½ A black soldier falls in love with a white French girl while on leave in Paris. First-time director Melvin Van Peebles makes the most of a shoestring budget on a project that contains only some of the rage that surfaced in his *Sweet Sweetback's Baadasssss Song*. 87m. **DIR:** Melvin Van Peebles. **CAST:** Harry Baird, Nicole Berger, Christian Marin. **1967**

STORY OF LOUIS PASTEUR, THE ★★★½ Master actor Paul Muni won an Oscar for his restrained portrayal of the famous French founder of bacteriology in this well-honed film biography. This is an honest, engrossing character study that avoids sentimentality. B&W; 85m. **DIR:** William Dieterle. **CAST:** Paul Muni, Josephine Hutchinson, Anita Louise, Donald Woods, Porter Hall, Akim Tamiroff. **1936**

STORY OF O, THE ★★ Adaptation of the French erotic novel. The filmmakers attempt to beautify what is basically a soft-core tale of bondage and sadomasochism. No matter how much Vaseline you apply to the camera lens, a nude whipping is still a nude whipping. Rated R (though it'd get an NC-17 today). 97m. **DIR:** Just Jaeckin. **CAST:** Udo Kier, Corinne Clery. **1975**

STORY OF RUTH, THE ★★★ Pagan priestess Ruth renounces her graven gods to embrace the true faith of Israel but finds acceptance rough going in this static retelling of the classic Bible story. 132m. **DIR:** Henry Koster. **CAST:** Elana Eden, Stuart Whitman, Tom Tryon, Peggy Wood, Viveca Lindfors, Jeff Marrow. **1960**

STRAIGHT OUT OF BROOKLYN ★★★½ Nineteen-year-old writer-producer-director Matty Rich makes a solid filmmaking debut with this thought-provoking drama about a black teenager (Lawrence Gilliard Jr.) who decides that robbing a local drug dealer is the best and quickest way to get his family out of the poverty-stricken housing projects of Red Hook in Brooklyn. Rated R for profanity, violence, and suggested sex. 91m. **DIR:** Matty Rich. **CAST:** George T. Odom, Lawrence Gilliard Jr., Matty Rich. **1991**

STRAIGHT TIME ★★★★ Well-told story of an ex-convict (Dustin Hoffman) attempting to make good on the outside only to return to crime after a run-in with his parole officer (M. Emmet Walsh). Hoffman's performance is truly chilling. A very grim and powerful film that was sadly overlooked on its initial release. Rated R for violence, nudity, and language. 114m. **DIR:** Ulu Grosbard. **CAST:** Dustin Hoffman, Harry Dean Stanton, Gary Busey, Theresa Russell, M. Emmet Walsh. **1978**

STRANGE AFFAIR OF UNCLE HARRY, THE ★★★★ George Sanders tried to get by the censors during the 1940s with several movies that bucked the system. This one cheats by changing the ending of Thomas Job's successful stage play about incest and murder. Hollywood kept the murder part, but you have to read between the lines to get the incest situation. The video print comes from a UCLA Archive restoration. B&W; 80m. **DIR:** Robert Siodmak. **CAST:** George Sanders, Geraldine Fitzgerald, Moyna McGill, Ella Raines, Sara Allgood, Samuel S. Hinds, Harry Von Zell. **1945**

STRANGE CARGO ★★★ *Strange* is the best way to describe this one, but the forceful and compelling personalities make it worth watching. Clark Gable leads a group of convicts out of Devil's Island in a daring escape. 105m. **DIR:** Frank Borzage. **CAST:** Clark Gable, Joan Crawford, Ian Hunter, Albert Dekker, Peter Lorre, Paul Lukas, Eduardo Ciannelli, J. Edward Bromberg. **1940**

STRANGE INTERLUDE (1932) ★★½ Eugene O'Neill's plays make heavy-handed movies, and this is one of the heaviest. Clark Gable and Norma Shearer play lovers who grow old together while married to other people. B&W; 110m. **DIR:** Robert Z. Leonard. **CAST:** Clark Gable, Norma Shearer, Robert Young, Maureen O'Sullivan, May Robson, Henry B. Walthall, Ralph Morgan. **1932**

STRANGE INTERLUDE (1988) ★★★★ Eugene O'Neill's complex love story is not for viewers seeking mindless entertainment, but for those willing to endure the considerable length, it offers ample rewards. Glenda Jackson plays a neurotic woman who, in the course of twenty-five years, manages to control the lives of the three men who love her. High-class soap opera. Unrated, this PBS production contains adult themes. 190m. **DIR:** Herbert Wise. **CAST:** Glenda Jackson, José Ferrer, David Dukes, Ken Howard, Edward Petherbridge. **1988**

STRANGE LOVE OF MARTHA IVERS, THE ★★★ Terrible title doesn't do this well-acted drama justice. Woman-with-a-past Barbara Stanwyck excels in this story of a secret that comes back to threaten her now-stable life and the lengths she must go to in order to ensure her security. Young Kirk Douglas in his film debut already charges the screen with electricity. B&W; 117m. **DIR:** Lewis Milestone. **CAST:** Barbara Stanwyck, Van Heflin, Kirk Douglas, Lizabeth Scott, Judith Anderson, Darryl Hickman. **1946**

STRANGE LOVE OF MOLLY LOUVAIN, THE ★★★½ A well-played melodrama with comic overtones and almost as much sexual innuendo as movies of the 1990s. An unwed mother dallies with gangsters of every stripe and color because she just plain likes men. B&W; 80m. **DIR:** Michael Curtiz. **CAST:** Ann Dvorak, Lee Tracy, Leslie Fenton, Richard Cromwell, Guy Kibbee, Mary Doran, Frank McHugh. **1932**

STRANGE WOMAN, THE ★★ Lusty tale of a woman who conspires with her stepson to kill her husband. A strange adaptation of the Ben Ames Williams bestseller, mainly because Hedy Lamarr looks better than she acts. She bought the rights to the book, selected cast and director, and listed herself as an associate producer. B&W; 100m. **DIR:** Edgar G. Ulmer. **CAST:** Hedy Lamarr, George Sanders, Gene Lockhart, Louis Hayward, Hillary Brooke, Rhys Williams, June Storey, Ian Keith. **1946**

STRANGERS ★★ Three mediocre vignettes. Too bad someone couldn't come up with just one good idea. Rated R for nudity and simulated sex. 90m. **DIR:** Daniel Vigne, Wayne Wang, Joan Tewkesbury. **CAST:** Linda Fiorentino, James Remar, François Montagut, Joan Chen, Lambert Wilson, Timothy Hutton. **1991**

STRANGERS IN GOOD COMPANY ★★★ Leisurely paced coming-of-age film of the geriatric set. A group of gray foxes are stuck in the wilderness when their tour bus breaks down. There they get to know each other while revealing their secret fears and desires. Enlightening Canadian film. Rated PG. 101m. **DIR:** Cynthia Scott. **CAST:** Alice Diabo, Constance Garneau. **1990**

STRANGERS IN THE CITY ★★★★ This forceful film set in a Manhattan slum paints a vivid picture of a Puerto Rican family struggling to adjust to life in a new country. When the proud father loses his job, other family members have to go to work to support themselves. The final third gives way to cheap melodrama, but the film is still well worth seeing. B&W; 83m. **DIR:** Rick Carrier. **CAST:** Robert Gentile, Camilo Delgado. **1961**

STRANGERS KISS ★★½ Offbeat film about the making of a low-budget movie, circa 1955. A strange romantic relationship between the male and female leads develops off-camera. A good script inspired by Stanley Kubrick's *Killer's Kiss* is quite absorbing despite some production flaws. Rated R for sexual situations. 94m. **DIR:** Matthew Chapman. **CAST:** Peter Coyote, Victoria Tennant, Blaine Novak, Dan Shor. **1984**

STRANGERS: THE STORY OF A MOTHER AND A DAUGHTER ★★★½ Bette Davis won an Emmy Award in this taut, made-for-television drama about a long-estranged daughter's sudden reentry into the life and home of her bitter, resentful mother. Gena Rowlands, as the daughter, holds her own matching Davis scene for scene. 100m. **DIR:** Milton Katselas. **CAST:** Bette Davis, Gena Rowlands, Ford Rainey, Royal Dano. **1979**

STRANGERS WHEN WE MEET ★★½ An all-star cast fails to charge this overblown soap opera about an unhappily married architect who falls in love with his beautiful neighbor. Evan Hunter derived the screenplay from his novel of the same name. Not rated. 117m. **DIR:** Richard Quine. **CAST:** Kirk Douglas, Kim Novak, Ernie Kovacs, Barbara Rush, Walter Matthau, Virginia Bruce, Kent Smith, Helen Gallagher. **1960**

STRAPLESS ★★★★ Deftly handled story of an American doctor in London who marries an enigmatic businessman in a moment of rapture, only to find him inscrutable and deceptive. Strong performances. Rated R. 99m. **DIR:** David Hare. **CAST:** Blair Brown, Bruno Ganz, Bridget Fonda. **1990**

STRAPPED ★★★ Although intelligently scripted by Dena Kleiman and artily helmed by actor Forest Whitaker (in his directorial debut), this slice of inner-city life is no different from any film by John Singleton, Spike Lee, or countless imitators: a bludgeoning indictment of failed social systems and no possible solutions. Bokeem Woodbine is quietly dignified as a young man whose efforts to help his pregnant, drug-dealing girlfriend are hampered by cop Michael Biehn and gun-dealer Craig Wasson. Rated R for incessant profanity and violence. 102m. **DIR:** Forest Whitaker. **CAST:** Bokeem Woodbine, Kia Joy Goodwin, Fredro, Paul McCrane, Craig Wasson, Michael Biehn. **1993**

STRATEGIC AIR COMMAND ★★½ Aviation and sports come together as professional baseball player Jimmy Stewart is called back to active service and forced to leave his career, his teammates, and his wife (June Allyson). Air force veterans and baseball fans will enjoy, but, otherwise, this is just routine studio fare. 114m. **DIR:** Anthony Mann. **CAST:** James Stewart, June Allyson, Frank Lovejoy, Barry Sullivan, Bruce Bennett, Rosemary DeCamp. **1955**

STRATTON STORY, THE ★★★★ Heartwarming true-life story of Chicago White Sox pitcher Monte Stratton, who lost a leg in a hunting accident at the height of his career. Fine performances in a "feel-good" movie. B&W; 106m. **DIR:** Sam Wood. **CAST:** James Stewart, June Allyson, Frank Morgan, Agnes Moorehead, Bill Williams. **1949**

STRAWBERRY BLONDE, THE ★★★ Sentimental flashback story of young man's unrequited love for *The Strawberry Blonde* (Rita Hayworth) is a change of pace for dynamic James Cagney and one of the most evocative period pieces produced in America about the innocent "Gay Nineties." Winsome Olivia de Havilland and a great cast of characters (including Alan Hale as Cagney's father) breathe life into this tragicomic tale. B&W; 97m. **DIR:** Raoul Walsh. **CAST:** James Cagney, Olivia de Havilland, Rita Hayworth, Alan Hale Sr., Jack Carson, George Tobias, Una O'Connor, George Reeves. **1941**

STRAWBERRY STATEMENT, THE ★★ Inane message film attempts to make some sense (and money) out of student dissidents and rebellion. Some good performances in this hodgepodge of comedy, drama, and youth-authority confrontations. Rated R. 103m. **DIR:** Stuart Hagmann. **CAST:** Kim Darby, Bruce Davison, Bob Balaban, James Kunen. **1970**

STREAMERS ★★★½ This tense film is about four recruits and two veterans awaiting orders that will send them to Vietnam. The six men are a microcosm of American life in the late 1960s and early 1970s. A powerful, violent drama, this film is not suitable for everyone. Rated R. 118m. **DIR:** Robert Altman. **CAST:** Matthew Modine, Michael Wright, Mitchell Lichtenstein. **1984**

STREET MUSIC ★★★½ An aspiring singer and her boyfriend, a tour guide, try to save a building full of senior citizens from eviction. Likable comedy-drama benefits from a realistic script and magnificent performances by Elizabeth Daily and Larry Breeding. Unrated; the film has sexual situations. 92m. **DIR:** Jenny Bowen. **CAST:** Elizabeth Daily, Larry Breeding, Ned Glass. **1981**

STREET OF FORGOTTEN WOMEN, THE ★★ Silent exploitation movie masquerading as an exposé of urban squalor and prostitution. Entertainingly absurd, with an appropriately melodramatic organ score: a must for bad-movie buffs. B&W; 55m. **DIR:** Unknown. **1927**

STREET SCENE ★★★½ Playwright Elmer Rice wrote the screenplay for this fine film version of his Pulitzer Prize–winning drama of life in the New York tenements and the yearning and anguish of the young and hopeful who are desperate to get out. The cast is excellent, the score classic Alfred Newman, the camera work outstanding. B&W; 80m. **DIR:** King Vidor. **CAST:** Sylvia Sidney, William Collier Jr., Beulah Bondi, David Landau, Estelle Taylor, Walter Miller. **1931**

STREET SMART ★★½ Christopher Reeve gives a listless performance as a magazine writer under pressure who fabricates the life story of a New York pimp. Problems arise when parallels with a real pimp under investigation by the DA surface. Morgan Freeman plays the pimp Fast Black with an electrifying mesh of elegance and sleaze. Rated R for language and theme. 97m. **DIR:** Jerry Schatzberg. **CAST:** Christopher Reeve, Kathy Baker, Mimi Rogers, Andre Gregory, Morgan Freeman. **1986**

STREET WARRIORS 🦃 A sleazy exploitation movie about Barcelona teens who rob and kill. 105m. **DIR:** J. Anthony Loma. **CAST:** Victor Petit, Frank Brana. **1977**

STREET WARRIORS II 🦃 This sequel is even worse; if there was ever any merit to this trash, it's been lost in the terrible dubbing. Contains nudity, simulated rape, and violence. 105m. **DIR:** J. Anthony Loma. **CAST:** Angel Fernandez Franco, Veronica Miriel. **1981**

STREETCAR NAMED DESIRE, A ★★★★★ Virtuoso acting highlights this powerful and disturbing drama based on the Tennessee Williams play. Vivien Leigh once again is the southern belle. Unlike Scarlett O'Hara, however, her Blanche DuBois is no longer young. She is a sexually disturbed woman who lives in a world of illusion. Her world begins to crumble when she moves in with her sister and brutish brother-in-law (Marlon Brando). B&W; 122m. **DIR:** Elia Kazan. **CAST:** Vivien Leigh, Marlon Brando, Kim Hunter, Karl Malden. **1951**

STREETFIGHT ★★ Originally released in 1975 as *Coonskin*, this mixture of animation and live action was labeled racist by many. The animation tells the tale in almost *Song of the South* characterizations of a young black country rabbit caught up in Harlem's drug world. Definitely a curiosity. Rated R. 89m. **DIR:** Ralph Bakshi. **CAST:** Barry White, Scatman Crothers, Philip Michael Thomas. **1987**

STREETS OF GOLD ★★★ This is a pleasant story about an ex-boxer (Klaus Maria Brandauer) who decides to regain his self-worth by passing on his skills to a pair of street boxers. Brandauer puts a lot of energy into his role, demonstrating shading and character depth far beyond what you'd expect from a routine story. Inexplicably rated R for mild language and violence. 95m. **DIR:** Joe Roth. **CAST:** Klaus Maria Brandauer, Adrian Pasdar, Wesley Snipes, Angela Molina. **1986**

STREETS OF L.A., THE ★★★½ Joanne Woodward plays a struggling real estate saleswoman who gets her new tires slashed by a group of angry Hispanics and decides to pursue them in the hopes of getting reimbursed. The acting is quite good even if the film is a low-budget production. A sensitive, rather quiet drama. Not rated, but contains violence. 94m. **DIR:** Jerrold Freedman. **CAST:** Joanne Woodward, Robert Webber, Michael C. Gwynne, Audrey Christie, Isela Vega, Pepe Serna, Miguel Pinero, Tony Plana. **1979**

STREETWALKIN' 🦃 Incoherent. Rated R for simulated sex, profanity, and violence. 84m. **DIR:** Joan Freeman. **CAST:** Julie Newmar, Melissa Leo, Leon Robinson, Antonio Fargas. **1985**

STRIPPER, THE (1963) ★★½ Somewhat engrossing account of an aging stripper (Joanne Woodward) falling in love with a teenager (Richard Beymer). Good performances by all, but the film tends to drag and become too stagy. Based on William Inge's play. 95m. **DIR:** Franklin J. Schaffner. **CAST:** Joanne Woodward, Richard Beymer, Claire Trevor, Carol Lynley, Robert Webber, Gypsy Rose Lee, Louis Nye. **1963**

STUD, THE 🦃 Sordid soft-core porn film concerning a young man's various affairs. Rated R. 95m. **DIR:** Quentin Masters. **CAST:** Joan Collins, Oliver Tobias. **1978**

STUDENT NURSES, THE ★★★ In their last year of schooling, four young women begin to experience life in the real world of medicine and men. The first of Roger Corman's successful *Nurse* movies, this is a well-written exploitation movie that you don't have to feel guilty about liking. Rated R for nudity. 85m. **DIR:** Stephanie Rothman. **CAST:** Elaine Giftos, Karen Carlson, Barbara Leigh. **1970**

STUDENT PRINCE IN OLD HEIDELBERG, THE ★★★★ The famous Lubitsch touch is in evidence in the story of a Bavarian prince eager to sow some wild oats. He enrolls at Heidelberg University, falls in love with a barmaid, and comes of age. Later versions with the famous Sigmund Romberg score turned the tale into a moodier romance. Silent. B&W; 105m. **DIR:** Ernst Lubitsch. **CAST:** Norma Shearer, Ramon Novarro, Jean Hersholt, Gustav von Seyffertitz. **1927**

STUDS LONIGAN ★★ Film version of James T. Farrell's landmark first novel is a major disappointment to those familiar with the *Studs Lonigan* trilogy. Depressing tale of a young man's slide into drunkenness and debauchery pulls most of the punches that the books delivered and ends up drastically changing the ending to a more conventional Hollywood fade-out. Memorable mainly for Jack Nicholson, miscast as the coldhearted Weary Reilly. B&W; 95m. **DIR:** Irving Lerner. **CAST:** Christopher Knight, Frank Gorshin, Jack Nicholson, Venetia Stevenson, Dick Foran, Jay C. Flippen, Carolyn Craig. **1960**

STUNT MAN, THE ★★★★½ Nothing is ever quite what it seems in this fast-paced, superbly crafted film. It's a Chinese puzzle of a movie and, therefore, may not please all viewers. Nevertheless, this directorial tour de force by Richard Rush has ample thrills, chills, suspense, and surprises for those with a taste for something different. Rated R. 129m. **DIR:** Richard Rush. **CAST:** Peter O'Toole, Steve Railsback, Barbara Hershey, Chuck Bail, Allen Garfield, Adam Roarke, Alex Rocco. **1980**

SUBJECT WAS ROSES, THE ★★★ A young soldier (Martin Sheen) returns home to his unhappily married parents (Patricia Neal, Jack Albertson). Well acted, especially by Neal in her first role after her near-fatal stroke. Vaudeville veteran Albertson won an Oscar. Rated G. 107m. **DIR:** Ulu Grosbard. **CAST:** Patricia Neal, Jack Albertson, Martin Sheen. **1968**

SUBURBAN ROULETTE 🦃 Showcased by Joe Bob Briggs, this piece of trash about wife swapping is tame and boring by today's standards. Not rated. 91m. **DIR:** Herschell Gordon Lewis. **CAST:** Elizabeth Wilkinson. **1967**

SUBURBIA ★★★ Penelope Spheeris, who directed the punk-rock documentary *Decline of Western Civilization,* did this low-budget film of punk rockers versus local rednecks and townspeople in a small suburban area. Not for all tastes, but a good little film for people who are bored with releases like *Cannonball Run II.* Rated R. 96m. **DIR:** Penelope Spheeris. **CAST:** Chris Pederson, Bill Coyne, Jennifer Clay. **1983**

SUCCESS IS THE BEST REVENGE ★★★½ Polish exile hustles to make a film about his native country while ignoring his own family problems. Director Jerzy Skolimowski, who dazzled us with the 1982 film *Moonlighting* is in good form with this biting drama. Not rated; but has violence, profanity, and nudity. 95m. **DIR:** Jerzy Skolimowski. **CAST:** Michael York, Anouk Aimée, Michael Lyndon, John Hurt, Jane Asher, Michel Piccoli. **1984**

SUDDENLY, LAST SUMMER ★★★ Another one of those unpleasant but totally intriguing forays of Tennessee Williams. Elizabeth Taylor is a neurotic girl being prodded into madness by the memory of her gay cousin's bizarre death, a memory that Katharine Hepburn, his adoring mother, wants to remain vague if not submerged. She prevails upon Montgomery Clift to make sure it does. B&W; 114m. **DIR:** Joseph L. Mankiewicz. **CAST:** Elizabeth Taylor, Montgomery Clift, Katharine Hepburn. **1959**

SUDIE & SIMPSON ★★★½ This finely etched portrait of racial intolerance in a small 1940s Georgia town shows how the friendship between kindly black Simpson (Lou Gossett Jr.) and sprite Sudie (Sara Gilbert) teaches the locals a lesson about understanding and prejudice. Things really heat up when Simpson is falsely accused of a crime, and Sudie comes to his rescue. Director Joan Tewkesbury gets excellent performances from all concerned in this made-for-TV movie. Not rated. 95m. **DIR:** Joan Tewkesbury. **CAST:** Lou Gossett Jr., Sara Gilbert, Frances Fisher, John Jackson. **1990**

SUGAR COOKIES 🦃 Two women are set up to be murdered by a porno filmmaker. Rated R for nudity, profanity, and violence. 89m. **DIR:** Michael Herz. **CAST:** Mary Woronov, Monique Van Vooren, Lynn Lowry. **1986**

SUGARLAND EXPRESS, THE ★★★★ A rewarding film in many respects, this was Steven Spielberg's first feature effort. Based on an actual incident in Texas during the late 1960s, a prison escapee and his wife try to regain custody of their infant child. Their desperation results in a madcap chase across the state with a kidnapped state trooper. Rated PG. 109m. **DIR:** Steven Spielberg. **CAST:** Goldie Hawn, Ben Johnson, Michael Sacks, William Atherton. **1974**

SUMMER AND SMOKE ★★½ Love-hungry spinster dominated by narrow-minded parents plays her cards wrong and can't turn a trick. Talky Tennessee Williams tale. Geraldine Page is fine, but one performance does not a hit make. 118m. **DIR:** Peter Glenville. **CAST:** Geraldine Page, Laurence Harvey, Una Merkel, Rita Moreno, John McIntire. **1961**

SUMMER CAMP NIGHTMARE ★★ Based on *The Butterfly Revolution* and misleadingly retitled to cash in on the teen-horror market, this is actually an antifascist parable similar to *Lord of the Flies.* A young counselor at a preteen summer camp stages a revolution, overthrowing the strict director and setting himself up in charge. The ambitious premise is never resolved satisfactorily, with a particularly anticlimactic ending. Rated PG-13 for violence and nudity. 88m. **DIR:** Bert L. Dragin. **CAST:** Chuck Connors, Charles Stratton. **1986**

SUMMER HEAT (1983) 🦃 Bruce Davison stars as a young sheepherder who, upon being sentenced to prison, attempts to escape with his new love. Rated R for violence, profanity, and implied sex. 101m. **DIR:** Jack Starrett. **CAST:** Bruce Davison, Susan George, Anthony Franciosa. **1983**

SUMMER HEAT (1987) 🦃 This is a barely lukewarm sex-and-soap sizzler. Rated R. 95m. **DIR:** Michie Gleason. **CAST:** Lori Singer, Bruce Abbott, Anthony Edwards, Clu Gulager, Kathy Bates. **1987**

SUMMER LOVERS 🦃 Study of a *ménage à trois* in Greece. Rated R for nudity, profanity, and implied sex. 98m. **DIR:** Randal Kleiser. **CAST:** Peter Gallagher, Daryl Hannah, Valerie Quennessen, Barbara Rush, Carole Cook. **1982**

SUMMER OF '42 ★★★★ Set against the backdrop of a vacationers' resort island off the New England coast during World War II. An inexperienced young man (Gary Grimes) has a crush on the 22-year-old bride (Jennifer O'Neill) of a serviceman. His stumbling attempts to acquire sexual knowledge are handled tenderly and thoughtfully. Rated PG. 102m. **DIR:** Robert Mulligan. **CAST:** Gary Grimes, Jennifer O'Neill, Jerry Houser, Oliver Conant, Christopher Norris, Lou Frizell. **1971**

SUMMER OF MY GERMAN SOLDIER ★★★★ Heartwarming tale of an open-minded girl's friendship with a German POW during World War II. Esther Rolle is superb as the family cook to whom the girl confides. Made for TV. 98m. **DIR:** Michael Tuchner. **CAST:** Kristy McNichol, Bruce Davison, Esther Rolle, Michael Constantine. **1978**

SUMMER PLACE, A ★★½ Big box-office bonanza for 1959 is a comparatively tame story of extramarital love and teenage infatuation. This mixed-audience melodrama made Troy Donahue and Sandra Dee household names. 130m. **DIR:** Delmer Daves. **CAST:** Dorothy McGuire, Richard Egan, Sandra Dee, Troy Donahue, Arthur Kennedy, Beulah Bondi, Constance Ford. **1959**

SUMMER SCHOOL TEACHERS ★★★ The usual Roger Corman *Nurse* movie formula: three young women of different backgrounds are devoted to their professions, but not so busy that they don't have time for a little love and lust. Director Barbara Peeters keeps it from being too exploitative, but never forgets who her true drive-in audience is. Rated R for nudity. 87m. **DIR:** Barbara Peeters. **CAST:** Candice Rialson, Pat Anderson, Dick Miller. **1975**

SUMMER STORY, A ★★★½ A farm girl (Imogen Stubbs) falls for a young London barrister (James Wilby). Can their odd coupling endure class-conscious turn-of-the-century England? Strong performances draw the viewer firmly into the story. Rated PG-13 for partial nudity. 97m. **DIR:** Piers Haggard. **CAST:** James Wilby, Imogen Stubbs, Susannah York, Kenneth Colley, Sophie Ward. **1989**

SUMMER TO REMEMBER, A ★★★½ Heartwarming story about a deaf-mute boy. When the boy befriends an intelligent orangutan, he begins to see beyond his closed world. Rated PG for no apparent reason. 98m. **DIR:** Robert Lewis. **CAST:** James Farentino, Louise Fletcher, Burt Young. **1984**

SUMMER WISHES, WINTER DREAMS 🦃 Manhattan housewife's depression. Rated PG. 95m. **DIR:** Gilbert Cates. **CAST:** Joanne Woodward, Martin Balsam, Sylvia Sidney, Dori Brenner. **1973**

SUMMERTIME ★★★★ Katharine Hepburn is a sensitive, vulnerable spinster on holiday in Venice. She falls in love with unhappily married shopkeeper Rossano Brazzi, and the romantic idyll is beautiful. David Lean's direction is superb, Jack Hildyard's cinematography excellent. 99m. **DIR:** David Lean. **CAST:** Katharine Hepburn, Rossano Brazzi, Edward Andrews, Darren McGavin, Isa Miranda. **1955**

SUN SHINES BRIGHT, THE ★★★ Lovable old curly-locked Charles Winninger steals the show in John Ford's remake of *Judge Priest*, his touching 1934 slice of small-town Americana. B&W; 92m. **DIR:** John Ford. **CAST:** Charles Winninger, Arleen Whelan, John Russell, Milburn Stone. **1953**

SUNDAY, BLOODY SUNDAY ★★★ Brilliant performances by Peter Finch and Glenda Jackson are the major reason to watch this very British three-sided love story; the sides are a bit different, though...both love Murray Head. Difficult to watch at times, but intriguing from a historical standpoint. Rated R for sexual situations. 110m. **DIR:** John Schlesinger. **CAST:** Peter Finch, Glenda Jackson, Murray Head, Peggy Ashcroft, Maurice Denham. **1971**

SUNDAY TOO FAR AWAY ★★★½ An Australian film about the life and lot of a sheepshearer down under circa 1956. Jack Thompson stars as Foley, a champion shearer who finds his mantle challenged. Unrated; the film has profanity, nudity, and violence. 100m. **DIR:** Ken Hannam. **CAST:** Jack Thompson, Max Cullen, John Ewart, Reg Lye. **1983**

SUNDOWN (1941) ★★½ Fairly entertaining British drama in Africa features Bruce Cabot as a Canadian and George Sanders as the army officer who replaces him. It seems that the local tribesmen are being armed by the Germans. Although there are some bursts of energy, this is still slow-going. B&W; 90m. **DIR:** Henry Hathaway. **CAST:** Gene Tierney, Bruce Cabot, George Sanders, Harry Carey, Cedric Hardwicke, Joseph Calleia, Reginald Gardiner, Marc Lawrence. **1941**

SUNDOWNERS, THE (1960) ★★★★ Robert Mitchum and Deborah Kerr were one of the great screen teams, and this is our choice as their best film together. The story of Australian sheepherders in the 1920s, it is a character study brought alive by Fred Zinnemann's sensitive direction, as well as by the fine acting of a superb cast. 113m. **DIR:** Fred Zinnemann. **CAST:** Robert Mitchum, Deborah Kerr, Peter Ustinov, Glynis Johns, Dina Merrill, Chips Rafferty. **1960**

SUNRISE ★★★★ Director F. W. Murnau's emotionally charged silent classic about a romantic triangle leading to attempted murder. Oscars went to star Janet Gaynor, cinematographers Karl Struss and Charles Rosher, and the film itself—which is stunning on a visual and narrative level. B&W; 110m. **DIR:** F. W. Murnau. **CAST:** George O'Brien, Janet Gaynor, Margaret Livingston, J. Farrell MacDonald. **1927**

SUNRISE AT CAMPOBELLO ★★★★★ Producer-writer Dore Schary's inspiring and heartwarming drama of Franklin Delano Roosevelt's public political battles and private fight against polio. Ralph Bellamy is FDR; Greer Garson is Eleanor. Both are superb. The acting is tops, the entire production sincere. Taken from Schary's impressive stage play, with all the fine qualities intact. 143m. **DIR:** Vincent J. Donehue. **CAST:** Ralph Bellamy, Greer Garson, Alan Bunce, Hume Cronyn. **1960**

SUNSET BOULEVARD ★★★★★ *Sunset Boulevard* is one of Hollywood's strongest indictments against its own excesses. It justly deserves its place among the best films ever made. William Holden plays an out-of-work gigolo-screenwriter who attaches himself to a faded screen star attempting a comeback. Gloria Swanson, in a stunning parody, is brilliant as the tragically deluded Norma Desmond. B&W; 110m. **DIR:** Billy Wilder. **CAST:** William Holden, Gloria Swanson, Erich Von Stroheim, Fred Clark, Jack Webb, Hedda Hopper, Buster Keaton. **1950**

SUNSET STRIP 🦃 And strip they do in this shabby tale of a young woman who has an affair with a club owner in L.A.'s exotic dance scene. Rated R for nudity and sex. 93m. **DIR:** Paul G. Volk. **CAST:** Jeff Conaway, Michelle Foreman. **1991**

SURE FIRE 🦃 Heavy-handed message film moves at a snail's pace. Two men choose different paths in life—one seeks material wealth while the other is content with his modest farm. Obvious cuts are a major distraction. Unrated; contains profanity and violence. 83m. **DIR:** Jon Jost. **CAST:** Tom Blair, Kristi Hager, Robert Ernst, Kate Dezina. **1990**

SURROGATE, THE ★★½ This bizarre film concerns a couple with marriage problems who seek counseling. A surrogate sex partner enters the picture. Fortunately, the stars are attractive. Rated R for nudity, simulated sex, profanity, and violence. 100m. **DIR:** Don Carmody. **CAST:** Art Hindle, Carole Laure, Shannon Tweed, Michael Ironside, Marilyn Lightstone, Jim Bailey. **1984**

SUSAN AND GOD ★★★ A strong cast bolsters this story of a woman who devotes herself to a new religious movement, pushing her newly adopted standards and beliefs on her family and friends. Fredric March is fine as her weak, alcoholic husband. B&W; 115m. **DIR:** George Cukor. **CAST:** Joan Crawford, Fredric March, Ruth Hussey, John Carroll, Rita Hayworth, Nigel Bruce, Marjorie Main, Gloria De Haven. **1940**

SUSAN LENOX: HER FALL AND RISE ★★★ Greta Garbo flees a brutish father eager to marry her off and takes refuge with Clark Gable. The melodramatic plot's tired, but Garbo and Gable give charged performances. B&W; 76m. **DIR:** Robert Z. Leonard. **CAST:** Greta Garbo, Clark Gable, Alan Hale Sr., Jean Hersholt. **1931**

SUZY ★★ Cary Grant plays a WWI pilot who falls for American show girl Jean Harlow. A spy story with charismatic performers who don't seem to connect. Not up to expectations. B&W; 99m. **DIR:** George Fitzmaurice. **CAST:** Jean Harlow, Cary Grant, Franchot Tone, Lewis Stone, Benita Hume, Una O'Connor. **1936**

SVENGALI (1983) ★★ Even stars like Peter O'Toole and Jodie Foster can't help this poorly scripted remake of the classic tale. Made for cable. 96m. **DIR:** Anthony Harvey. **CAST:** Peter O'Toole, Jodie Foster, Elizabeth Ashley, Larry Joshua, Holly Hunter. **1983**

SWAN, THE (1956) ★★★ First filmed with Frances Howard in 1925, then in 1930 with Lillian Gish, this Ferenc Molnar comedy, about a princess courted by a commoner while promised to a prince, gave Hollywood princess Grace Kelly ample time to act in reel life what she shortly became in real life. 112m. **DIR:** Charles Vidor. **CAST:** Grace Kelly, Louis Jourdan, Alec Guinness, Agnes Moorehead, Brian Aherne, Jessie Royce Landis, Estelle Winwood, Leo G. Carroll, Robert Coote. **1956**

SWAP, THE 🦃 Robert De Niro fans, don't waste your time. This hodgepodge uses a few minutes of film from an unreleased movie De Niro made in 1969 called *Sam's Song* to pad out a story about an ex-con looking for his brother's murderer. Rated R. 87m. **DIR:** John Shade, John Broderick, Jordon Leondopoulos. **CAST:** Robert De Niro, Jennifer Warren, Lisa Blount, Sybil Danning. **1980**

SWEET BIRD OF YOUTH (1962) ★★★★ Crowds lined up to see this near-perfect big screen translation of Tennessee Williams's steamy Broadway hit about a has-been film star and her lusty, fame-hungry young lover. Director and scripter Richard Brooks got the best out of everyone in a fine cast. Definitely not for the kiddies. 120m. **DIR:** Richard Brooks. **CAST:** Geraldine Page, Paul Newman, Shirley Knight, Rip Torn, Madeleine Sherwood, Ed Begley Sr., Mildred Dunnock. **1962**

SWEET BIRD OF YOUTH (1989) ★★★½ Gritty adaptation of Tennessee Williams's play features Elizabeth Taylor as a fading film star often in a drunken stupor. Hitting rock bottom she takes up with a handsome gigolo (Mark Harmon). She seeks a companion, but all he wants is her connections. Harmon's performance is powerful. Made for TV, but contains nudity, violence, and adult themes. 95m. **DIR:** Nicolas Roeg. **CAST:** Mark Harmon, Elizabeth Taylor, Cheryl Paris, Valerie Perrine. **1989**

SWEET COUNTRY 🦃 Chile under military rule after the murder of Allende. Rated R for violence and nudity. 105m. **DIR:** Michael Cacoyannis. **CAST:** Jane Alexander, John Cullum, Jean-Pierre Aumont, Irene Papas, Franco Nero, Carole Laure, Joanna Pettet, Randy Quaid. **1985**

SWEET 15 ★★★½ Marta's dream of a huge birthday celebration is shattered when her father fears he will be deported to Mexico in this fine family film first aired on PBS. Recommended. 110m. **DIR:** Victoria Hochberg. **CAST:** Karla Montana, Tony Plana. **1989**

SWEET HOSTAGE ★★ Congenial kidnapper Martin Sheen espouses poetry and simple common sense in trying to convince captive Linda Blair that a world awaits her away from the confines of the farm. Unrated. 93m. **DIR:** Lee Philips. **CAST:** Linda Blair, Martin Sheen. **1976**

SWEET LORRAINE ★★★★ There's a lot to like in this nostalgic stay at The Lorraine, a hotel in the Catskills. Maureen Stapleton is the owner of the 80-year-old landmark that may be seeing its last summer. It needs extensive repairs and developers are offering a tempting price. A perfect cast makes this small-scale film a huge success. Rated PG-13. 91m. **DIR:** Steve Gomer. **CAST:** Maureen Stapleton, Trini Alvarado, Lee Richardson, John Bedford Lloyd, Giancarlo Esposito. **1987**

SWEET LOVE, BITTER ★★ This film, adapted from the book *Night Song,* is loosely based on the life of Charlie Parker. Sax player (Dick Gregory) befriends a down-and-out college professor (Don Murray). Great jazz score (with Charles McPherson ghosting for Gregory on sax) and one hilarious pot-smoking scene are the only recommendations for this otherwise dated and cliché-ridden relic. Not rated, but contains some violence. B&W; 92m. **DIR:** Herbert Danska. **CAST:** Dick Gregory, Don Murray, Diane Varsi, Robert Hooks. **1966**

SWEET SMELL OF SUCCESS ★★★½ Burt Lancaster is superb as a ruthless newspaper columnist. Tony Curtis is equally great as the seedy press agent who will stop at nothing to please him. Outstanding performances by a great cast and brilliant cinematography by James Wong Howe perfectly capture the nightlife in Manhattan. Screenplay by Clifford Odets and Ernest Lehman. B&W; 96m. **DIR:** Alexander Mackendrick. **CAST:** Burt Lancaster, Tony Curtis, Martin Milner, Sam Levene, Barbara Nichols, Susan Harrison. **1957**

SWEETHEARTS' DANCE ★★★ From Ernest (*On Golden Pond*) Thompson, a delightful little movie about love and relationships. High school sweethearts Don Johnson and Susan Sarandon are a married couple whose marriage has stagnated. There are subplots about male bonding, best friends, and father-son relationships. Rated R for profanity. 101m. **DIR:** Robert Greenwald. **CAST:** Don Johnson, Susan Sarandon, Jeff Daniels, Elizabeth Perkins, Justin Henry. **1988**

SWEETIE ★★★½ Surrealistic first film by Australian writer-director Jane Campion recalls David Lynch's *Eraserhead* and *Blue Velvet* in its odd camera angles and bizarre characters. The title character (Genevieve Lemon) is a grotesque version of the spoiled daddy's girl. Rated R for profanity, nudity, and violence. 100m. **DIR:** Jane Campion. **CAST:** Genevieve Lemon, Karen Colston. **1990**

SWIMMER, THE ★★★★ A middle-aged man in a gray flannel suit who has never achieved his potential swims from neighbor's pool to neighbor's pool on his way home on a hot afternoon in social Connecticut. Each stop brings back memories of what was and what might have been. Burt Lancaster is excellent in the title role. Rated PG. 94m. **DIR:** Frank Perry. **CAST:** Burt Lancaster, Janet Landgard, Janice Rule, Joan Rivers, Tony Bickley, Marge Champion, Kim Hunter. **1968**

SWING KIDS ★★½ Jonathan Marc Feldman's Nazi-era drama can't quite figure out what it wants to be. The premise is certainly fascinating: young German "bop" fans resisted induction of the Hitler youth. Yet director Thomas Carter is sloppy: Kenneth Branagh's ominously chilling SS officer is undercut by *Hogan's Heroes*–style cartoon Nazis (reflecting the film's Disney origins). Not a complete botch, but pretty slipshod. Rated PG-13 for violence and profanity. 112m. **DIR:** Thomas Carter. **CAST:** Robert Sean Leonard, Christian Bale, Frank Whaley, Barbara Hershey, Kenneth Branagh. **1993**

SWING SHIFT ★★ Goldie Hawn stars in this disappointing 1940s-era romance as Kay Walsh, the girl who's left behind when her husband, Jack (Ed Harris), goes off to fight in World War II. Rated PG for profanity and suggested sex. 100m. **DIR:** Jonathan Demme. **CAST:** Goldie Hawn, Kurt Russell, Ed Harris, Fred Ward, Christine Lahti, Sudie Bond. **1984**

SWITCHED AT BIRTH ★★★½ Above-average made-for-TV miniseries chronicles the controversial true story of two baby girls swapped at birth. When tragedy strikes and one of the girls dies, it is discovered that her blood type doesn't match that of her parents, and the search for the truth begins. Long in the tooth, but entertaining nonetheless. 200m. **DIR:** Waris Hussein. **CAST:** Bonnie Bedelia, Brian Kerwin, Ariana Richards, Edward Asner, Eve Gordon. **1991**

SWOON ★★★★ *Swoon* follows in the footsteps of *Rope* and *Compulsion* as films inspired by the real-life exploits of 1920s Chicago college-boy killers, Nathan Leopold Jr. and Richard Loeb. The changing climate in America, though, allows Kalin to explore a heretofore ignored aspect of the story—that Leopold and Loeb were homosexual lovers. The film is an artful, wildly inventive example of low-budget guerilla filmmaking. It's stylish, original, and exciting. Rated R, with profanity and sexual content. B&W; 90m. **DIR:** Tom Kalin. **CAST:** Daniel Schlachet, Craig Chester, Ron Vawter, Michael Kirby. **1992**

SYBIL ★★★★ Sally Field is outstanding in this deeply disturbing but utterly fascinating made-for-TV drama of a young woman whose intense pyschological childhood trauma has given her seventeen distinct personalities. Joanne Woodward is the patient, dedicated psychiatrist who sorts it all out. 116m. **DIR:** Daniel Petrie. **CAST:** Joanne Woodward, Sally Field, William Prince. **1976**

SYLVESTER ★★★★ Director Tim Hunter does an admirable job with this hard-edged *National Velvet*–style drama about a tomboy (Melissa Gilbert) who rides her horse, Sylvester, to victory in the Olympics' Three-Day Event in Lexington, Kentucky. Gilbert is first-rate as the aspiring horsewoman, and Richard Farnsworth is his reliable, watchable self as her cantankerous mentor. Rated PG-13 for profanity and violence. 109m. **DIR:** Tim Hunter. **CAST:** Melissa Gilbert, Richard Farnsworth, Michael Schoeffling, Constance Towers. **1985**

SYLVIA ★★ *Sylvia* is about as underwhelming as a film can get and still have some redeeming qualities. Were it not for the fine performance by Eleanor David in the title role, this film about seminal educator Sylvia Ashton-Warner would be a muddled bore. It jumps from one event to another with little or no buildup or continuity. Rated PG for graphic descriptions of violence. 97m. **DIR:** Michael Firth. **CAST:** Eleanor David, Nigel Terry, Tom Wilkinson, Mary Regan. **1985**

SYLVIA SCARLETT ★★★½ The first screen teaming of Katharine Hepburn and Cary Grant lacks the sprightly pace and memorable humor of *Holiday* and *The Philadelphia Story*, which also were directed by George Cukor, but it's still a real find for fans of the stars. When Hepburn's con-man father (Edmund Gwenn) runs afoul of the law, they must quickly leave France while she masquerades as a boy to avert suspicion. B&W; 94m. **DIR:** George Cukor. **CAST:** Katharine Hepburn, Cary Grant, Brian Aherne, Edmund Gwenn. **1936**

T-MEN ★★½ Two undercover operatives for the Treasury Department infiltrate a master counterfeiting ring and find themselves on opposite sides when the lead starts to fly. Unable to save the life of his partner without exposing himself, agent Dennis O'Keefe courageously continues the work of both men. B&W; 92m. **DIR:** Anthony Mann. **CAST:** Dennis O'Keefe, Alfred Ryder, Mary Meade, Wallace Ford, June Lockhart, Charles McGraw, Jane Randolph. **1948**

TABLE FOR FIVE ★★★ Had it up to here with *Kramer vs. Kramer* clones about single parents coping with their kids? If you have, you'll probably decide to skip this movie—and that would be a shame, because it's a good one. Jon Voight stars as J. P. Tannen, a divorcé who takes his three youngsters on a Mediterranean cruise in hopes of getting back into their lives full-time. Rated PG for mature situations. 122m. **DIR:** Robert Lieberman. **CAST:** Jon Voight, Richard Crenna, Millie Perkins. **1983**

TABU ★★★½ Begun as a collaboration between F. W. Murnau and documentarian Robert Flaherty, this is an unusual but unique South Seas romance filmed with a combination of naturalistic settings and an expressionistic technique. A native girl falls in love with a young man despite the fact that she has been promised to the gods. Silent. 81m. **DIR:** F. W. Murnau. **CAST:** Anna Chevalier, Matahi. **1931**

TAILSPIN ★★★ Docu-style drama concerning the Soviet Union's tragic shooting down of Korean Airline's flight 007 over the Sea of Japan. A tactical error or an act of aggression? Made for TV. 82m. **DIR:** David Durlow. **CAST:** Michael Moriarty, Michael Murphy, Chris Sarandon, Harris Yulin. **1989**

TAKEN AWAY ★★ Valerie Bertinelli is a waitress/student who leaves her daughter alone one night and finds the child has become a ward of the state. Extremely manipulative, as the system set up to protect children rakes Bertinelli over the legal coals. Made as a movie of the week, and it shows. Not rated. 94m. **DIR:** John Patterson. **CAST:** Valerie Bertinelli, Kevin Dunn, Juliet Sorcey. **1989**

TAKING THE HEAT ★★★½ Gutsy cop Lynn Whitfield has her hands full in this entertaining thriller, when she's assigned to escort reluctant witness Tony Goldwyn to a court appointment. A routine trip across New York City becomes a nightmare thanks to a heat wave, a power blackout, and pursuing goons ordered by crime-lord Alan Arkin to eliminate Goldwyn. The leads get a lot of mileage out of Gary Hoffman and Dan Gordon's diverting script, and Tom Mankiewicz's directorial hand is appropriately light. Rated R for profanity, violence, nudity, and suggested sex. 90m. **DIR:** Tom Mankiewicz. **CAST:** Tony Goldwyn, Lynn Whitfield, George Segal, Peter Boyle, Will Patton, Alan Arkin. **1993**

TALE OF RUBY ROSE, THE ★★★ Rousing frontier adventure about a woman named Ruby Rose, who has lived her entire life in the backwoods of Tasmania. Then she takes a courageous journey in search of her grandmother, a trip that causes her to look to her inner self to survive a world she never knew existed. Exhilarating. Rated PG. 101m. **DIR:** Roger Scholes. **CAST:** Melita Jurisic, Chris Haywood. **1987**

TALE OF TWO CITIES, A (1935) ★★★★★ *A Tale of Two Cities* is a satisfactory rendition of Charles Dickens's novel. It is richly acted, with true Dickens flavor. Ronald Colman was ideally cast in the role of Sydney Carton, the English no-account who finds purpose in life amid the turmoil of the French Revolution. The photography in this film is one of its most outstanding features. The dark shadows are in keeping with the spirit of this somber Dickens story. B&W; 121m. **DIR:** Jack Conway. **CAST:** Ronald Colman, Basil Rathbone, Edna May Oliver, Elizabeth Allan. **1935**

TALE OF TWO CITIES (1967) ★★★½ Impressive detailed adaptation of the Charles Dickens novel that chronicles the turmoil of the French Revolution and features some good performances by a top-notch cast. 117m. **DIR:** Ralph Thomas. **CAST:** Dirk Bogarde,

Donald Pleasence, Christopher Lee, Dorothy Tutin. **1967**

TALE OF TWO CITIES, A (1980) ★★★ Acceptable version of the Dickens classic, though the other versions available on video are better. There's a topflight cast, but Chris Sarandon is a bit wan for Sydney Carlton. Not rated. 216m. **DIR:** Jim Goddard. **CAST:** Chris Sarandon, Peter Cushing, Kenneth More, Barry Morse, Flora Robson, Billie Whitelaw, Alice Krige. **1980**

TALE OF TWO CITIES, A (1991) ★★★★ This magnificent PBS production of Charles Dickens's classic lavishly re-creates the costumes and setting of France from 1767 to 1790. A self-imposed exile of French nobility (Xavier Deluc) finds himself helplessly drawn into the revolutionary madness of mob rule. 240m. **DIR:** Philippe Monnier. **CAST:** James Wilby, Xavier Deluc, Serena Gordon, Jean-Pierre Aumont. **1991**

TALENT FOR THE GAME ★★★½ Little-known film is a treasure trove of wonderful performances and memorable moments. The marvelous Edward James Olmos stars as a talent scout for the California Angels. An examination of life in modern America as compared with the values inherent in the game of baseball. Rated PG for profanity. 91m. **DIR:** Robert M. Young. **CAST:** Edward James Olmos, Lorraine Bracco, Jamey Sheridan, Terry Kinney, Jeff Corbett, Tom Bower, Janet Carroll, Felton Perry, Thomas Ryan. **1991**

TALES OF ORDINARY MADNESS 🦃 Ben Gazzara in the role of infamous drunken poet Charles Bukowski, who interacts with a strange assortment of women. Rated R for profanity and nudity. 107m. **DIR:** Marco Ferreri. **CAST:** Ben Gazzara, Ornella Muti, Susan Tyrrell, Tanya Lopert. **1983**

TALK RADIO ★★★★ Powerful story centers on a controversial Dallas radio talk-show host's rise to notoriety—and the ultimate price he pays for it. Eric Bogosian repeats his acclaimed Broadway stage performance as the radio host who badgers and belittles callers and listeners alike. A highly cinematic, fascinating film. Director Oliver Stone keeps his camera moving and the pace rapid throughout. Rated R. 110m. **DIR:** Oliver Stone. **CAST:** Eric Bogosian, Alec Baldwin, Ellen Greene, John Pankow, John C. McGinley. **1989**

TAMMY AND THE BACHELOR ★★★ Like Debbie Reynolds's number-one hit song *Tammy*, the movie is corny but irresistible. Ingenuous country girl Reynolds falls in love with injured pilot Leslie Nielsen and nurses him back to health. The romance and humor are sweet and charming. The movie's success led to sequels and a TV series. 89m. **DIR:** Joseph Pevney. **CAST:** Debbie Reynolds, Leslie Nielsen, Walter Brennan, Mala Powers, Fay Wray, Sidney Blackmer, Mildred Natwick, Louise Beavers. **1957**

TAMMY AND THE DOCTOR ★★ Cutesy romance between country gal Sandra Dee and young Peter Fonda is relatively harmless, but this is definitely a film with a limited audience. No muss, no fuss—in fact, not much of anything at all. 88m. **DIR:** Harry Keller. **CAST:** Sandra Dee, Peter Fonda, Macdonald Carey, Beulah Bondi, Margaret Lindsay, Reginald Owen, Adam West. **1963**

TAPS ★★★½ George C. Scott is an iron-jawed commander of a military academy and Timothy Hutton a gung ho cadet who leads a student revolt in this often exciting but mostly unbelievable and unnecessarily violent drama. Rated R. 118m. **DIR:** Harold Becker. **CAST:** George C. Scott, Timothy Hutton, Ronny Cox, Tom Cruise. **1981**

TARGET: FAVORITE SON ★★★ Television miniseries *Favorite Son* edited down to feature-length still packs quite a wallop for those into soap-opera politics. The usual collection of love, sex, politics, espionage, and assassination make this dramatic thriller as much fun as the real thing. 115m. **DIR:** Jeff Bleckner. **CAST:** Harry Hamlin, Linda Kozlowski, Robert Loggia, John Mahoney, Ronny Cox. **1988**

TARTUFFE ★★★ Let's be upfront about this one: It's a sophisticated version of Molière's play about religious hypocrisy. The satire is funny and biting, but this Royal Shakespeare Company production is not for everyone. The performances, especially Antony Sher's interpretation of Tartuffe, are brilliant, but very subtle. 110m. **DIR:** Bill Alexander. **CAST:** Antony Sher, Nigel Hawthorne, Alison Steadman. **1984**

TASK FORCE ★★½ Standard military soap opera tracing the development of the aircraft carrier. Predictable script, with all the usual heroics, but the stalwart cast holds it up. B&W; 116m. **DIR:** Delmer Daves. **CAST:** Gary Cooper, Jane Wyatt, Wayne Morris, Walter Brennan, Julie London, Jack Holt. **1949**

TASTE OF HONEY, A ★★★½ Offbeat comedy-drama memorably tells the story of a lower-class teenager (Rita Tushingham) made pregnant by a black sailor. Tough but tender, this piece of attempted social realism by new-wave British director Tony Richardson is based on a successful stage play. B&W; 100m. **DIR:** Tony Richardson. **CAST:** Rita Tushingham, Dora Bryan, Murray Melvin, Robert Stephens. **1961**

TATTOO 🦃 Simply the most vile, reprehensible, sexist, and misogynistic piece of tripe ever released under the guise of a mainstream film. Bruce Dern is a demented tattoo artist who kidnaps Maud Adams to use as a "living tableau." Rated R for gross violence and kinky sex. 103m. **DIR:** Bob Brooks. **CAST:** Bruce Dern, Maud Adams, John Getz. **1981**

TAXI DANCERS 🦃 Small-town girl must turn to dancing in a seedy club when her Hollywood dreams fail to materialize. Not rated, but contains adult situations, language, and violence. 97m. **DIR:** Norman Thaddeus Vane. **CAST:** Sonny Ladham, Robert Miano, Brittany McCrena, Michelle Hess. **1993**

TEA AND SYMPATHY ★★★★ Well-crafted story (from the Broadway play) of an introverted student who finds understanding and love with the wife of the school's headmaster. Sensitively directed and with convincing acting, this is a must-see film. 123m. **DIR:** Vincente Minnelli. **CAST:** Deborah Kerr, John Kerr, Leif Erickson, Edward Andrews, Darryl Hickman, Dean Jones. **1959**

TEAMSTER BOSS: THE JACKIE PRESSER STORY ★★★½ Brian Dennehy's larger-than-life performance as self-made Teamster president Jackie Presser fuels this strawberry-lensed TV adaptation of James Neff's *Mobbed Up*. Abby Mann's script works far too hard at glossing over the controversial figure's unpleasant qualities. Rated R for violence, suggested sex, and profanity. 110m. **DIR:** Alastair Reid. **CAST:** Brian Dennehy, Jeff Daniels, Maria Conchita Alonso, Eli Wallach, Robert Prosky, Donald Moffat. **1992**

TEARAWAY ★★ In this film from Australia, the young streetwise son of an alcoholic father rescues a rich girl from a gang of lecherous toughs. Regrettably, tragic but predictable events cause this otherwise gritty study to degenerate into another ordinary tale of revenge. Rated R for violence and strong language. 100m. **DIR:** Bruce Morrison. **CAST:** Matthew Hunter, Mark Pilisi. **1987**

TELL ME A RIDDLE ★★★½ Melvyn Douglas and Lila Kedrova give memorable performances as an elderly married couple whose relationship has grown bitter. Their love for each other is rekindled when they take a cross-country trip. This poignant drama marked the directorial debut of actress Lee Grant. Rated PG. 94m. **DIR:** Lee Grant. **CAST:** Melvyn Douglas, Lila Kedrova, Brooke Adams, Dolores Dorn, Zalman King. **1980**

TEMPEST (1928) ★★½ Set during the 1914 Bolshevik uprising in Russia, this richly romantic drama has army officer John Barrymore stepping out of place to court his aristocratic commandant's daughter. As a result, both are undone and must flee for their lives and love. Silent, with music track. B&W; 105m. **DIR:** Sam Taylor. **CAST:** John Barrymore, Camilla Horn, Louis Wolheim, George Fawcett. **1928**

TEMPEST (1982) 🦃 An architect has prophetic dreams. Rated PG; the film has nudity and profanity. 140m. **DIR:** Paul Mazursky. **CAST:** John Cassavetes, Gena Rowlands, Vittorio Gassman, Molly Ringwald, Susan Sarandon. **1982**

TEMPEST, THE (1983) ★★½ A slow-moving stage production of Shakespeare's tale of sorcery and revenge on a desolate island controlled by the mystical Prospero (Efrem Zimbalist Jr.). Zimbalist is interesting but very wooden in the role. A Bard Productions Ltd. release. 126m. **DIR:** William Woodman. **CAST:** Efrem Zimbalist Jr., William H. Bassett, Ted Sorel, Kay E. Kuter, Edward Edwards, Nicholas Hammond. **1983**

TEN COMMANDMENTS, THE (1923) ★★★ Master showman Cecil B. DeMille's monumental two-phase silent version of the Book of Exodus and the application of the Ten Commandments in modern life. Part One, set in ancient times, is in early color; Part Two, set in the modern (1923) period, is in black and white. Impressive special effects, including the parting of the Red Sea. In scope, this is the film that foreshadows DeMille's great spectacles of the sound era. B&W; 140m. **DIR:** Cecil B. DeMille. **CAST:** Theodore Roberts, Charles de Roche, Estelle Taylor, James Neill, Noble Johnson, Richard Dix, Rod La Rocque, Leatrice Joy, Nita Naldi. **1923**

TEN COMMANDMENTS, THE (1956) ★★★½ A stylish, visually stunning, epic-scale biblical study as only Cecil B. DeMille could make 'em (until William Wyler came along three years later with *Ben Hur*). Charlton Heston, as Moses, takes charge of "God's people" and wrests them from Egypt's punishing grasp. Heston's utter conviction holds the lengthy film together. Then, of course, there's the parting of the Red Sea—an effect that *still* looks great. Unrated; suitable for family viewing. 219m. **DIR:** Cecil B. DeMille. **CAST:** Charlton Heston, Yul Brynner, Edward G. Robinson, Cedric Hardwicke, John Derek, Anne Baxter, Debra Paget. **1956**

10 MILLION DOLLAR GETAWAY, THE ★★★½ Doug Feiden's published account of the infamous Lufthansa robbery is transformed by scripter Christopher Canaan into a slick (made-for-cable) character study that unequivocally proves that crime does not pay. The excellent cast is led by John Mahoney. Rated PG-13. 93m. **DIR:** James A. Contner. **CAST:** John Mahoney, Joseph Carberry, Terrence Mann, Karen Young, Tony Lo Bianco. **1991**

10 RILLINGTON PLACE ★★★★ This bleak true-crime drama is based on one of England's most famous murder cases and was actually shot in the house and the neighborhood where the crimes took place. The seamy squalor of the surroundings perfectly mirrors the poverty of mind and soul that allowed John Christy to murder and remain undetected for over ten years. 111m. **DIR:** Richard Fleischer. **CAST:** Richard Attenborough, Judy Geeson, John Hurt, Andre Morell. **1971**

TENDER COMRADE ★★★ This sentimental melodrama, in which Ginger Rogers ably portrays one of several wives left at home while their men are fighting in World War II, demonstrates that she was underrated as a dramatic actress. The film later attracted unwarranted controversy after its writer, Dalton Trumbo, and director, Edward Dmytryk, fell victim to the anticommunist blacklist. 102m. **DIR:** Edward Dmytryk. **CAST:** Ginger Rogers, Robert Ryan, Ruth Hussey. **1943**

TENDER MERCIES ★★★★★ Robert Duvall more than deserved his best-actor Oscar for this superb character study about a down-and-out country singer trying for a comeback. His Mac Sledge is a man who still has songs to sing, but barely the heart to sing them. That is, until he meets up with a sweet-natured widow (Tess Harper) who gives him back the will to live. Rated PG. 89m. **DIR:** Bruce Beresford. **CAST:** Robert Duvall, Tess Harper, Ellen Barkin. **1983**

TENDER YEARS, THE ★★½ The fight against cruelty to animals is at the heart of this sentimental film about a small-town minister who steals the dog his son loves, to save it from being used in illicit dogfighting. B&W; 81m. **DIR:** Harold Schuster. **CAST:** Joe E. Brown, Josephine Hutchinson, Charles Drake. **1948**

TENTH MAN, THE ★★★★ Superb made-for-TV adaptation of Graham Greene's novel starring Anthony Hopkins as a wealthy French attorney taken hostage by the Nazis during the occupation of France. When the French Resistance kills some Nazi officers, the Nazis order every tenth man held in prison executed in retaliation. Hopkins strikes a bargain when he becomes the tenth man. 87m. **DIR:** Jack Gold. **CAST:** Anthony Hopkins, Kristin Scott Thomas, Derek Jacobi, Cyril Cusack. **1992**

TENTH MONTH, THE ★★½ Tiresome overlong drama about a middle-aged divorcée who has an affair with a married man and becomes pregnant. Good performances by Carol Burnett and Keith Michell are the only bright spots in this made-for-TV film. 130m. **DIR:** Joan Tewkesbury. **CAST:** Carol Burnett, Keith Michell, Dina Merrill. **1979**

TERMINAL BLISS ★★½ A slow-moving and utterly depressing story of a group of rich teenagers who overindulge in drugs and angst. Despite its deep undercurrent of despair, this is a watchable film that will have you worried about the future of our youth. Rated R for violence, profanity, and drug use. 93m. **DIR:** Jordan Alan. **CAST:** Luke Perry, Timothy Owen. **1990**

TERMINI STATION ★★★½ Mom's a drunk, her daughter can't sustain relationships, and her son will sacrifice anything to get a promotion. Probing into this dysfunctional family's past reveals the root of everyone's problems. Colleen Dewhurst is terrific as the formerly passionate woman drowning her loneliness in a bottle. Unrated; this Canadian film contains profanity and violence. 105m. **DIR:** Allan Winton King. **CAST:** Colleen Dewhurst, Megan Follows, Gordon Clapp. **1989**

TERMS OF ENDEARMENT ★★★★ This stylish soap opera, written, produced, and directed by James L. Brooks, covers thirty years in the lives of a Houston matron, played by Shirley MacLaine, and her daughter, played by Debra Winger, who marries an English teacher with a wandering eye. Jack Nicholson is also on hand, to play MacLaine's neighbor, an astronaut with the wrong stuff. Rated PG for profanity and suggested sex. 132m. **DIR:** James L. Brooks. **CAST:** Shirley MacLaine, Debra Winger, Jack Nicholson, Danny DeVito, Jeff Daniels. **1983**

TERRY FOX STORY, THE ★★★ This made-for-HBO film chronicles the "Marathon of Hope" undertaken by amputee Terry Fox (Eric Fryer), who jogged 3,000 miles across Canada before collapsing in Ontario. Based on a true story, this uplifting film is helped by solid performances, direction, and writing. 96m. **DIR:** Ralph L. Thomas. **CAST:** Eric Fryer, Robert Duvall, Chris Makepeace, Rosalind Chao, Michael Zelniker. **1983**

TESS ★★★★½ A hypothetically beautiful adaptation of Thomas Hardy's late-nineteenth-century novel *Tess of the D'Urbervilles,* this is director Roman Polanski's finest artistic achievement. Nastassja Kinski is stunning as the country girl who is "wronged" by a suave aristocrat and the man she marries. The story unfolds at the pace of a lazy afternoon stroll, but Polanski's technical skills and the cinematography are spellbinding. Rated PG. 170m. **DIR:** Roman Polanski. **CAST:** Nastassja Kinski, Peter Firth, John Bett. **1979**

TEST OF LOVE, A ★★ This tearjerker, taken from the Australian bestselling novel *Annie's Coming Out,* vividly displays the love and determination a therapist (Angela Punch McGregor) has in fighting for the rights of Anne O'Farrell, a severely disabled teenager who was misdiagnosed as being retarded. Yet the makers of this movie lack the finesse it takes to make the antagonists of this story more than one-dimensional. Rated PG for profanity. 93m. **DIR:** Gil Brealey. **CAST:** Angela Punch McGregor, Drew Forsythe, Tina Arhondis. **1984**

TEST PILOT ★★★½ A top-notch cast playing believable characters made this drama of daredevils who try out new aircraft a big winner with critics and at the box office as World War II loomed. Cinematographer Ray June's aerial sequences are stunning. One of the biggest hits in MGM history. B&W; 118m. **DIR:** Victor Fleming. **CAST:** Clark Gable, Spencer Tracy, Myrna Loy, Marjorie Main, Lionel Barrymore, Louis Jean Heydt. **1938**

TEX ★★★★½ Matt Dillon, Jim Metzler, and Ben Johnson star in this superb coming-of-age adventure about the struggles and conflicts of two teenage brothers growing up in the Southwest without parental guidance. Rated PG for violence and mature situations. 103m. **DIR:** Tim Hunter. **CAST:** Matt Dillon, Jim Metzler, Ben Johnson, Emilio Estevez, Meg Tilly. **1982**

TEXASVILLE ★★★★ This much-maligned sequel to *The Last Picture Show* is surprisingly good—an absorbing tale of people facing the truth about themselves. The naïvité, manipulation, and hope that propelled the characters' lives in the original film (when they were decades younger) has given way to wisdom and sober truth. An uncommonly rich motion picture. Rated R for profanity. 125m. **DIR:** Peter Bogdanovich. **CAST:** Jeff Bridges, Cybill Shepherd, Annie Potts, Timothy Bottoms, Cloris Leachman, Randy Quaid, Eileen Brennan. **1990**

THAT CERTAIN WOMAN ★★½ A gangster's widow marries a weak alcoholic playboy, and his father forces an annulment. When they learn she has a child, they try to take him from her. Enough self-sacrifice by lovely Bette Davis to fill four movies. B&W; 96m. **DIR:** Edmund Goulding. **CAST:** Bette Davis, Henry Fonda, Ian Hunter, Donald Crisp, Anita Louise. **1937**

THAT CHAMPIONSHIP SEASON ★★½ Former high school basketball stars (Bruce Dern, Stacy Keach, Martin Sheen, and Paul Sorvino) and their coach (Robert Mitchum) get together for the twenty-fourth annual celebration of their championship season. While there's nothing wrong with a sobering look at broken dreams and the pain of midlife crisis, we've seen it all on screen before. Rated R for profanity, racial epithets, violence, and adult content. 110m. **DIR:** Jason Miller. **CAST:** Bruce Dern, Stacy Keach, Martin Sheen, Paul Sorvino, Robert Mitchum. **1982**

THAT COLD DAY IN THE PARK ★★ This claustrophobic study of an emotionally disturbed woman and her obsessive interest in a young man is just about as strange as they come. It nonetheless gives gifted Sandy Dennis one of her most memorable roles. This film focuses on repressed sexuality, but also hints at incest and other subjects considered taboo when this Canadian-made movie was released. 113m. **DIR:** Robert Altman. **CAST:** Sandy Dennis, Michael Burns, Suzanne Benton, John Garfield Jr., Luana Anders, Michael Murphy. **1969**

THAT FORSYTE WOMAN ★★ Greer Garson has the central role of a woman trapped in a marriage of convenience. She flaunts the rigid social taboos of nineteenth-century England. Based on the first book of John Galsworthy's epic *Forsyte Saga*. A dull movie with little conviction. B&W; 114m. **DIR:** Compton Bennett. **CAST:** Greer Garson, Errol Flynn, Janet Leigh, Walter Pidgeon, Robert Young, Harry Davenport. **1949**

THAT HAMILTON WOMAN ★★★½ The legendary acting duo of Mr. and Mrs. Laurence Olivier re-creates one of England's legendary romantic scandals: the love of naval hero Horatio Nelson for the alluring Lady Emma Hamilton. B&W; 128m. **DIR:** Alexander Korda. **CAST:** Vivien Leigh, Laurence Olivier. **1941**

THAT NIGHT ★★★ Nostalgic slice of life finds young Eliza Dushku acting as a go-between for popular Juliette Lewis and tough guy C. Thomas Howell. The year is 1961, and when Lewis becomes pregnant, it's up to Dushku to keep them together. Period soundtrack, an eye for detail, and sensitive, likable characters. Rated PG-13 for adult situations. 89m. **DIR:** Craig Bolotin. **CAST:** C. Thomas Howell, Juliette Lewis, Eliza Dushku. **1993**

THAT SUMMER OF WHITE ROSES ★★★ Guests at an isolated Yugoslavian summer resort clash with Nazis during WWII. A well-seasoned drama that simmers at the start, but eventually comes to a full boil. Rated R for profanity and violence. 98m. **DIR:** Rajko Grlic'. **CAST:** Tom Conti, Susan George, Rod Steiger. **1990**

THAT WAS THEN...THIS IS NOW ★★★★ Adapted from a novel by S. E. Hinton (*The Outsiders*; *Rumble Fish*). The cuteness and condescension that mar most coming-of-age films are laudably absent in its tale of two working-class teenagers (Emilio Estevez and Craig Sheffer) coming to grips with adulthood. A work that teens and adults alike can appreciate. Rated R for violence and profanity. 103m. **DIR:** Christopher Cain. **CAST:** Emilio Estevez, Craig Sheffer, Kim Delaney, Morgan Freeman, Larry B. Scott, Barbara Babcock. **1985**

THAT'S MY BABY 🦃 Unemployed man wants his career-oriented girlfriend to have his baby. Rated PG-13 for nudity. 97m. **DIR:** Edie Yolles, John Bradshaw. **CAST:** Timothy Webber, Sonja Smits. **1989**

THESE THREE ★★★★ A superb cast brings alive this story of two upright and decent schoolteachers victimized by the lies of a malicious student. Miriam Hopkins and Merle Oberon are the pair brutally slandered; Bonita Granville is the evil liar. Script by Lillian Hellman, loosely based on her play *The Children's Hour*, under which title the film was remade in 1961. B&W; 93m. **DIR:** William Wyler. **CAST:** Miriam Hopkins, Merle Oberon, Joel McCrea, Bonita Granville, Marcia Mae Jones. **1936**

THEY CALL IT SIN ★★½ A four-sided romance that uses top character stars to play stereotypes. The heroine is engaged to a womanizer, fights off an aging playboy, and cries on the shoulder of an uptight doctor in her search for lasting romance. Good but not great. B&W; 75m. **DIR:** Thornton Freeland. **CAST:** Loretta Young, George Brent, David Manners, Louis Calhern, Una Merkel, Helen Vincent, Nella Walker. **1932**

THEY CAME TO CORDURA ★★ This film, which examines the true character of the war hero, is not one of Gary Cooper's best. The story has Cooper in Mexico during World War I as one of six military men returning to base. The hardships they encounter on the way create the drama. The movie has a nice look, but just not enough action. 123m. **DIR:** Robert Rossen. **CAST:** Gary Cooper, Rita Hayworth, Van Heflin, Tab Hunter, Richard Conte. **1959**

THEY KNEW WHAT THEY WANTED ★★★ This film is a fine example of offbeat casting that somehow succeeds. Charles Laughton and Carole Lombard were required to submerge their usual histrionics in order to bring off a low-key little tragedy. The story is of the unrequited love of an Italian wine grower for the opportunistic hash house waitress that he marries. B&W; 96m. **DIR:** Garson Kanin. **CAST:** Charles Laughton, Carole Lombard, William Gargan, Harry Carey. **1940**

THEY LIVE BY NIGHT ★★★½ A seminal film dealing with youth, alienation, and the concept of the loner who operates outside the confines of conventional behavior and morality. This postwar crime drama gave American youth a minor cultural folk hero in Farley Granger and began the directing career of young Nicholas Ray, who would in turn provide the world with the ultimate image of teenage alienation: *Rebel Without a Cause*. B&W; 95m. **DIR:** Nicholas Ray. **CAST:** Farley Granger, Cathy O'Donnell, Howard DaSilva, Jay C. Flippen. **1949**

THEY MADE ME A CRIMINAL ★★½ John Garfield's film persona is a direct result of this Warner Bros. story about the redemption of a loner on the lam from the law for a crime he didn't commit. A great cast still doesn't change the fact that this remake of 1933's *The Life of Jimmy Dolan* is muddled and not too solidly constructed. B&W; 92m. **DIR:** Busby Berkeley. **CAST:** John Garfield, Claude Rains, Ann Sheridan, Gloria Dickson, The Dead End Kids, Ward Bond. **1939**

THEY MEET AGAIN ★★ In this film, the last in the popular Dr. Christian series about a snoopy small-town doctor, genial Jean Hersholt is upset because a man he feels is innocent is serving time. The good doctor finds out who embezzled the missing money. B&W; 69m. **DIR:** Erle C. Kenton. **CAST:** Jean Hersholt, Robert Baldwin, Neil Hamilton, Dorothy Lovett, Arthur Hoyt. **1941**

THEY SHOOT HORSES, DON'T THEY? ★★★★★ The desperation and hopelessness of the Great Depression are graphically shown in this powerful drama, through a pitiful collection of marathon dancers. Some of the group will endure this physical and mental assault on their human spirit; some will not. Jane Fonda, as a cynical casualty of the Depression, and Gig Young, as the uncaring master of ceremonies, give stunning performances. Rated PG. 121m. **DIR:** Sydney Pollack. **CAST:** Jane Fonda, Gig Young, Michael Sarrazin. **1969**

THEY WON'T BELIEVE ME ★★★½ Robert Young is a grade-A stinker in this classic *film noir* of deceit, mistaken murder, suicide, and doomed romance. Rita Johnson is especially fine as the wronged wife. B&W; 95m. **DIR:** Irving Pichel. **CAST:** Robert Young, Susan Hayward, Jane Greer, Rita Johnson, Tom Powers, Don Beddoe, Frank Ferguson. **1947**

THEY'RE PLAYING WITH FIRE 🦃 A high school student is seduced by a teacher in this gobbler. Rated R. 96m. **DIR:** Howard Avedis. **CAST:** Sybil Danning, Eric Brown, Andrew Prine. **1983**

THIEF OF HEARTS ★★★ A young, upwardly mobile married woman loses her intimate diary of sexual fantasies to a thief who has broken into her home. In an interesting premise, the woman becomes a willing participant in the thief's sexual manipulations without knowing that he is the man who stole her secrets. Rated R. 100m. **DIR:** Douglas Day Stewart. **CAST:** Steven Bauer, Barbara Williams. **1984**

THIEVES LIKE US ★★★★ A classic melodrama about gangsters that relies more on story and characters than gunfire and bloodshed. Robert Altman turns the story of survivors during the Depression into a heartfelt love story with sensitive acting and exceptional production values. It plays like a documentary and looks like a movie because of Altman's unique storytelling style. Rated R. 123m. **DIR:** Robert Altman. **CAST:** Keith Carradine, Shelley Duvall, Louise Fletcher, Bert Remsen, Tom Skerritt, John Schuck. **1974**

THING CALLED LOVE, THE ★★★½ River Phoenix, in his last role, is well cast as a frustrated singer trying to make it in Nashville. Director Peter Bogdanovich's film follows four young aspiring stars, and the exciting cast, fleshed out by real country stars, turns up the heat on and off the stage. Rated PG-13 for adult language and situations. 116m. **DIR:** Peter Bogdanovich. **CAST:** River Phoenix, Samantha Mathis, Sandra Bullock, Dermot Mulroney. **1993**

36 HOURS ★★★½ An intriguing psychological war-drama. James Garner, a designer of the secret Allied invasion plans, is kidnapped by Nazis and brainwashed into believing the war is long over. Rod Taylor is so likable as the doctor leading the ruse that you almost hope his plan succeeds. Remade for cable as *Breaking Point*. 115m. **DIR:**

George Seaton. **CAST:** James Garner, Eva Marie Saint, Rod Taylor, Werner Peters, Alan Napier. **1964**

THIRTY-TWO SHORT FILMS ABOUT GLENN GOULD ★★★★★ This innovative portrayal of the eccentric, controversial Canadian pianist—one of the greatest musicians of the twentieth century—won four Genie Awards (Canadian Oscars) including best picture and best director. Each elegant, fascinating vignette represents a distinct impression of the controversial musician from age four until his death in 1982 at the age of fifty. The film, linked to J. S. Bach's *Goldberg Variations,* one of Gould's most famous piano interpretations, is as refreshing and visionary as the man himself. Not rated. 90m. **DIR:** Francois Girard. **CAST:** Colm Feore. **1994**

THIS BOY'S LIFE ★★★ Young Tobias Wolff (Leonardo DiCaprio) travels from town to town with his mother (Ellen Barkin). She tries to do the right thing by marrying "a good provider" (Robert De Niro), and the boy's life slowly becomes a nightmare. Screenwriter Robert Getchell's adaptation of Wolff's autobiographical book skimps on character depth, leaving De Niro to play a one-dimensional brute in a good—but not great—film. Rated R for profanity, violence, nudity, and simulated sex. 114m. **DIR:** Michael Caton-Jones. **CAST:** Robert De Niro, Ellen Barkin, Leonardo DiCaprio, Chris Cooper. **1993**

THIS HAPPY BREED ★★★★ This slice of British nostalgia chronicles the lives of a working-class family from 1919 to 1939. Adapted from a Noel Coward play, this is an extraordinary film of collector caliber. 114m. **DIR:** David Lean. **CAST:** Robert Newton, Celia Johnson, John Mills, Kay Walsh, Stanley Holloway. **1944**

THIS LAND IS MINE ★★★ Charles Laughton performs another fine characterization, this time as a timid French teacher who blossoms as a hero when he is incited to vigorous action by the Nazi occupation. Time has dulled this wartime film, but the artistry of the director and players remains sharp. B&W; 103m. **DIR:** Jean Renoir. **CAST:** Charles Laughton, Maureen O'Hara, George Sanders, Walter Slezak. **1943**

THIS PROPERTY IS CONDEMNED ★★½ Marginal film interpretation of Tennessee Williams's play. Owen Legate (Robert Redford) is a stranger in town, there for the purpose of laying off local railroaders. Alva (Natalie Wood) is a flirtatious southern girl who casts her spell of romance on the stranger. 109m. **DIR:** Sydney Pollack. **CAST:** Natalie Wood, Robert Redford, Charles Bronson, Kate Reid, Robert Blake. **1966**

THIS SPORTING LIFE ★★★½ Richard Harris and Rachel Roberts shine in this stark, powerful look into the life and dreams of a Yorkshire coal miner who seeks to become a professional rugby player. The squeamish will not like all the game scenes. 129m. **DIR:** Lindsay Anderson. **CAST:** Rachel Roberts, Richard Harris, Colin Blakely. **1963**

THORNBIRDS, THE ★★★ Originally a ten-hour TV miniseries, this much-edited film is still worth a watch. Richard Chamberlain plays an ambitious priest who falls in love with an innocent, trusting young woman (Rachel Ward). It's all played out against shifting backgrounds of outback Australia, Vatican Rome, and idyllic Greece. This has been released for a limited time and copies may be hard to locate. 150m. **DIR:** Daryl Duke. **CAST:** Richard Chamberlain, Rachel Ward, Christopher Plummer, Bryan Brown, Barbara Stanwyck, Richard Kiley, Jean Simmons, John Friedrich, Philip Anglim. **1983**

THOSE GLORY GLORY DAYS ★★ A group of young girls idolize the members of their school's soccer team. Tired nostalgia from the British television anthology *First Love.* 77m. **DIR:** Philip Saville. **CAST:** Julia McKenzie, Elizabeth Spriggs. **1984**

THREADS ★★★★ Unforgettable British TV depiction of the effects of nuclear war on two small-town families makes *The Day After* look like a Hollywood musical. It doesn't indulge in shock or false sentimentality, rendering a chillingly plausible account of life after the end. 110m. **DIR:** Mick Jackson. **CAST:** Karen Meagher, Reece Dinsdale. **1984**

THREE CAME HOME ★★★ During World War II, British families residing in Borneo are forced into prison camps by Japanese troops. The courage and suffering of the confined women make for compelling drama. Claudette Colbert delivers one of her finest performances. 106m. **DIR:** Jean Negulesco. **CAST:** Claudette Colbert, Patric Knowles, Sessue Hayakawa. **1950**

THREE COMRADES ★★★½ Three friends in Germany have romantic designs on the same woman, and she has an incurable disease. A real weeper, but the acting is terrific. F. Scott Fitzgerald cowrote the screenplay with E. E. Paramore and got screen credit. It was Fitzgerald's only credit during his entire Hollywood stay. B&W; 98m. **DIR:** Frank Borzage. **CAST:** Robert Taylor, Margaret Sullavan, Robert Young, Franchot Tone, Monty Woolley, Lionel Atwill, Charley Grapewin, Guy Kibbee. **1938**

THREE FACES OF EVE, THE ★★★★★ This distinguised movie boasts Joanne Woodward's Oscar-winning performance as a woman with multiple personalities. Woodward progresses through all three personalities in one amazing scene. Based on a true-life case. 91m. **DIR:** Nunnally Johnson. **CAST:** Joanne Woodward, Lee J. Cobb, David Wayne, Vince Edwards. **1957**

THREE FACES WEST ★★★ John Wayne is the leader of a group of Dust Bowl farmers attempting to survive in this surprisingly watchable Republic release. Sigrid Gurie and Charles Coburn co-star as the European immigrants who show them what courage means. B&W; 79m. **DIR:** Bernard Vorhaus. **CAST:** John Wayne, Charles Coburn, Sigrid Gurie, Spencer Charters. **1940**

THREE OF HEARTS ★★★ A lesbian hires a male escort to break the heart of her former lover, but this film handles the premise with sensitivity, warmth, and humor. William Baldwin is endearing and Kelly Lynch is a revelation as the stereotype-busting lesbian. The buddy relationship the two develop makes the movie memorable. Rated R for language and suggested sex. 93m. **DIR:** Yurek Bogayevicz. **CAST:** William Baldwin, Kelly Lynch, Sherilyn Fenn, Joe Pantoliano, Gail Strickland. **1993**

THREE ON A MATCH ★★★ Tough direction, a nifty script, and snappy editing make a winner of this tale of the reunion of three slum girls who ignore superstition to tempt fate and court tragedy by lighting their cigarettes from the same match. Ann Dvorak lights up last, and is outstanding in an outstanding cast. B&W; 68m. **DIR:** Mervyn LeRoy. **CAST:** Joan Blondell, Bette Davis, Ann Dvorak, Humphrey Bogart, Glenda Farrell, Edward Arnold. **1932**

THREE SECRETS ★★★ Three women, each with her own reason for believing she is his mother, anxiously await the rescue of a five-year-old boy, the sole survivor of a plane crash in rugged mountains. B&W; 98m. **DIR:** Robert Wise. **CAST:** Eleanor Parker, Patricia Neal, Ruth Roman, Frank Lovejoy, Leif Erickson, Ted de Corsia. **1950**

THREE SOVEREIGNS FOR SARAH ♥ Salem witch trials. Supposedly a true story about the real motivations that led to this dark spot in American history. 171m. **DIR:** Philip Leacock. **CAST:** Vanessa Redgrave, Ronald Hunter, Patrick McGoohan, Will Lyman, Kim Hunter. **1987**

THUNDER IN THE CITY ★★ Time severely dates this comedy-drama about a brash, fast-talking American promotor (Edward G. Robinson) who goes to staid London to promote modern U.S. advertising methods. Nigel Bruce fared far better as Holmes's Dr. Watson. B&W; 85m. **DIR:** Marion Gering. **CAST:** Edward G. Robinson, Nigel Bruce, Ralph Richardson. **1937**

THURSDAY'S GAME ★★★ Engaging made-for-television film about two ordinary guys (Gene Wilder and Bob Newhart) who continue to get together on Thursday nights after their weekly poker game collapses. Both make the most of this small rebellion. The supporting cast is excellent. Unrated; adult themes. 74m. **DIR:** Robert Moore. **CAST:** Gene Wilder, Bob Newhart, Ellen Burstyn, Cloris Leachman, Rob Reiner, Nancy Walker, Valerie Harper. **1974**

TICKET TO HEAVEN ★★★ This Canadian film presents a lacerating look at the frightening phenomenon of contemporary religious cults. Nick Mancuso is riveting as the brainwashed victim. Saul Rubinek and Meg Foster are splendid in support. But R. H. Thompson almost steals the show as a painfully pragmatic deprogrammer. Nice touches of humor give the movie balance. Rated PG. 107m. **DIR:** Ralph L. Thomas. **CAST:** Nick Mancuso, Saul Rubinek, Meg Foster, Kim Cattrall, R. H. Thompson. **1981**

TIDY ENDINGS ★★★★ Tender, touching AIDS drama deals with the confrontation between the victim's wife, wonderfully played by Stockard Channing, and the man's gay lover, sensitively played by Harvey Fierstein. Both wife and lover must come to grips with each other, and what each other meant to the deceased. Insightful and human. 54m. **DIR:** Gavin Millar. **CAST:** Stockard Channing, Harvey Fierstein, Nathaniel Moreau, Jean De Baer. **1989**

TIGER BAY ★★★½ Young Hayley Mills began her film career—in a part originally written for a boy—as an imaginative girl who witnesses a murder and then befriends the killer. Since the child is a known liar, nobody believes her until events escalate to the point of desperation. Horst Buchholz is excellent as the remorseful murderer. A thoughtful drama for all ages. Unrated; suitable for family viewing. B&W; 105m. **DIR:** J. Lee Thompson. **CAST:** John Mills, Horst Buchholz, Hayley Mills, Yvonne Mitchell, Anthony Dawson. **1959**

TIGER WARSAW ★★ Members of a family torn apart by a tragic incident struggle through their lives—all the while unable to forgive and forget. Patrick Swayze is Tiger Warsaw, a man haunted by the memory of shooting his father. Vague film lacking in substance and direction. Rated R for violence and profanity. 92m. **DIR:** Amin Q. Chaudhri. **CAST:** Patrick Swayze, Barbara Williams, Lee Richardson, Piper Laurie. **1987**

TILL DEATH DO US PART ★★★½ Made-for-TV film based on Los Angeles DA Vincent Bugliosi's brilliant case against spouse killer Alan Palliko in 1966. All the evidence against Palliko and his gal pal was circumstantial. Suspenseful and spellbinding moments. Unrated contains violence and nudity. 93m. **DIR:** Yves Simoneau. **CAST:** Treat Williams, Arliss Howard, Rebecca Jenkins. **1991**

TILL THE END OF TIME ★★★ Three veterans of World War II come home to find life, in general and how it was when they left, considerably changed. Readjustment is tough, and the love they left has soured. A good drama. B&W; 105m. **DIR:** Edward

Dmytryk. **CAST:** Dorothy McGuire, Guy Madison, Robert Mitchum, Jean Porter. **1946**

TILL THERE WAS YOU ★★ A lackluster film about an American saxophonist (Mark Harmon) who goes to the island nation of Vanuatu. An almost plotless mystery. Rated PG-13 for violence and nudity. 94m. **DIR:** John Seale. **CAST:** Mark Harmon, Deborah Unger, Jeroen Krabbé, Briant Shane. **1991**

TIM ★★★★½ An unforgettable character study from down under, this features Mel Gibson in his film debut as a simpleminded young adult and Piper Laurie as the older woman who finds herself falling in love with him. Superb supporting performances by the Australian cast—especially Alwyn Kurts and Pat Evison, as Tim's parents. Rated PG for suggested sex. 108m. **DIR:** Michael Pate. **CAST:** Mel Gibson, Piper Laurie, Alwyn Kurts. **1979**

TIME FLIES WHEN YOU'RE ALIVE ★★★★ Actor Paul Linke's monologue chronicling his wife's battle with cancer and how it affected his family is a wonderful mix of humor and sorrow. Linke takes the audience on a roller coaster ride of emotions from heartbreaking tales of death and loss to amusing anecdotes celebrating life. Unrated, the film contains profanity. 80m. **DIR:** Roger Spottiswoode. **CAST:** Paul Linke. **1990**

TIME OF DESTINY, A ★★½ Old-fashioned tale of love, hate, and revenge set against the backdrop of World War II. William Hurt is the guilt-ridden son of a Basque family in San Diego out to avenge the accidental death of his father. Timothy Hutton is the subject of Hurt's revenge. Beautiful photography, terrific editing and pacing help keep you from noticing the weak spots in the familiar plot. Rated PG-13 for violence and profanity. 118m. **DIR:** Gregory Nava. **CAST:** William Hurt, Timothy Hutton, Melissa Leo, Stockard Channing. **1988**

TIME OF YOUR LIFE, THE ★★★½ Originally a prize-winning play by the brilliant William Saroyan. Director H. C. Potter and a talented group of actors have created a pleasing film about the diverse characters who are regulars at Nick's Saloon, Restaurant and Entertainment Palace on San Francisco's Barbary Coast. A charmer, this picture grows on you. B&W; 109m. **DIR:** H. C. Potter. **CAST:** James Cagney, Wayne Morris, Broderick Crawford, Jeanne Cagney, Ward Bond, Jimmy Lydon, Gale Page. **1948**

TIME TO KILL ★★ Nicolas Cage stars as Enrico, an Italian officer stationed in Africa who accidentally kills a woman. Rated R for violence and nudity. 100m. **DIR:** Giuliano Montaldo. **CAST:** Nicolas Cage. **1990**

TIME TO LOVE AND A TIME TO DIE, A ★★½ A well-intentioned but preachy and largely unsatisfying antiwar film adapted from the novel by Erich Maria Remarque who also portrays the professor. John Gavin is a German soldier who receives a furlough from the Russian front in 1944. He returns home to find his town a bombed-out shell and his parents missing. 133m. **DIR:** Douglas Sirk. **CAST:** John Gavin, Lilo Pulver, Jock Mahoney, Don DeFore, Keenan Wynn, Erich Maria Remarque, Jim Hutton, Klaus Kinski. **1958**

TIN MAN ★★★ For the most part, this is an intriguing drama about a deaf auto mechanic who invents a computer with which he can hear and speak. When he attempts to get the device manufactured, the computer company sets out to exploit him. Timothy Bottoms is extraordinary, and the story holds your attention, but the film is hurt by cardboard villains and a pat ending. Unrated. 95m. **DIR:** John G. Thomas. **CAST:** Timothy Bottoms, Deana Jurgens, John Phillip Law, Troy Donahue. **1983**

TO ALL MY FRIENDS ON SHORE ★★★★ The dreams of two working-class parents to move their family out of the city fade when they learn that their son has sickle-cell anemia. Much better than the usual disease-of-the-week TV movie, with strong performances and a heartfelt script. 75m. **DIR:** Gilbert Cates. **CAST:** Bill Cosby, Gloria Foster, Dennis Hines. **1972**

TO DANCE WITH THE WHITE DOG ★★★★ Hume Cronyn delivers the performance of a lifetime in this moving *Hallmark Hall of Fame* special. When his wife dies, he befriends a white dog only seen by him, and his daughters fear that he's losing his mind. Exceptional acting and superior production values do justice to Terry Kay's novel about eternal love. 95m. **DIR:** Glenn Jordon. **CAST:** Hume Cronyn, Jessica Tandy, Esther Rolle, Christine Baranski. **1993**

TO HEAL A NATION ★★★ Touching TV drama about the attempts of three Vietnam veterans to have the memorial wall built recounts the opposition and the enthusiasm. 100m. **DIR:** Michael Pressman. **CAST:** Eric Roberts, Glynnis O'Connor, Marshall Colt, Scott Paulin, Lee Purcell, Laurence Luckinbill. **1988**

TO KILL A MOCKINGBIRD ★★★★★ *To Kill a Mockingbird* is a leisurely paced, flavorful filming of Harper Lee's bestselling novel. Gregory Peck earned an Oscar as a small-town southern lawyer who defends a black man accused of rape. Mary Badham, Philip Alford, and John Megna are superb as Peck's children and a visiting friend who are trying to understand life in a small town. B&W; 129m. **DIR:** Robert Mulligan. **CAST:** Gregory Peck, Mary Badham, Philip Alford, John Megna. **1962**

TO KILL A PRIEST ★★ Set in Warsaw, Poland, in 1984, this story tells of a secret police officer (Ed Harris) obsessed with a Catholic priest (Christopher Lambert) who is aiding the Solidarity movement. An interesting story is hampered by a mishmash of French, American, and British accents. Rated R for violence and profanity. 117m. **DIR:** Agnieszka Holland. **CAST:** Christopher Lambert, Ed Harris, David Suchet, Joanne Whalley, Joss Ackland. **1990**

TO SIR WITH LOVE ★★★★ A moving, gentle portrait of the influence of a black teacher upon a classroom of poverty-ridden teenagers in London's East End, this stars Sidney Poitier, in one of his finest performances, as the teacher. He instills in his pupils a belief in themselves and respect for one another. 105m. **DIR:** James Clavell. **CAST:** Sidney Poitier, Judy Geeson, Christian Roberts, Suzy Kendall, Lulu. **1967**

TO SLEEP WITH ANGER ★★★★½ Writer-director Charles Burnett based much of this superb, offbeat film on the southern folktales told to him by his grandmother. Its most unusual character, Harry (Danny Glover), is what she called a trickster, "a man who comes to town to steal your soul, and you have to trick him out of it." Rated PG for profanity. 101m. **DIR:** Charles Burnett. **CAST:** Danny Glover, Paul Butler, Mary Alice, Carl Lumbly, Vonetta McGee, Richard Brooks, Sheryl Lee Ralph, Julius W. Harris. **1990**

TOAST OF NEW YORK, THE ★★★ Semiaccurate biography of legendary post-Civil War Wall Street wheeler-dealer James Fisk. But, even so, it is a good film. Edward Arnold superbly plays Fisk. Jack Oakie does a fine turn. Don't expect the Cary Grant you know and love, however. B&W; 109m. **DIR:** Rowland V. Lee. **CAST:** Edward Arnold, Cary Grant, Frances Farmer, Jack Oakie, Donald Meek, Clarence Kolb, Billy Gilbert. **1937**

TODAY WE LIVE ★★ A typical Joan Crawford movie of the 1930s, this film has all the right ingredients but doesn't come off well. It's set during World War I with Gary Cooper, Robert Young, and Franchot Tone competing for Crawford's affections between wartime exploits. The battle scenes are better than the love scenes and include some daredevil air sequences and a very exciting torpedo run. B&W; 113m. **DIR:** Howard Hawks. **CAST:** Gary Cooper, Joan Crawford, Robert Young, Franchot Tone, Roscoe Karns, Louise Closser Hale. **1933**

TODD KILLINGS, THE ★★½ Harrowing fact-based drama about a rebellious young murderer (Robert F. Lyons) and the alienated kids who protect him. This film offers a penetrating look into the pathological mind of 23-year-old killer who seeks out teenage girls. Shocking, disturbing portrait of a thrill-seeking psychopath. Rated R, contains nudity and violence. 93m. **DIR:** Barry Shear. **CAST:** Robert F. Lyons, Richard Thomas, Belinda Montgomery, James Broderick, Gloria Grahame, Holly Near, Edward Asner, Barbara Bel Geddes. **1971**

TOL'ABLE DAVID ★★½ Though it creaks a bit with age, this stalwart tale of good besting evil deserves attention and rewards it. Silent. B&W; 80m. **DIR:** King Vidor. **CAST:** Richard Barthelmess, Gladys Hulette, Ernest Torrence, Warner Richmond. **1921**

TOM BROWN'S SCHOOL DAYS (1940) ★★½ "Old school tie" story mixes top Hollywood production values and minor classic of British secondary schools into an enjoyable froth filled with all the clichés. Better than one would think and not the creaky old groaner it could have been. B&W; 86m. **DIR:** Robert Stevenson. **CAST:** Cedric Hardwicke, Freddie Bartholomew, Gale Storm, Jimmy Lydon, Josephine Hutchinson, Polly Moran, Billy Halop. **1940**

TOM BROWN'S SCHOOLDAYS (1950) ★★★½ Tom, played by John Howard Davies, brings a civilizing influence to his peers in this engaging account of life in a Victorian England boys' school. Robert Newton, of course, is superb. An excellent cast, under good direction, makes this a particularly fine film. B&W; 93m. **DIR:** Gordon Parry. **CAST:** Robert Newton, John Howard Davies, James Hayter, Hermione Baddeley. **1950**

TOMORROW ★★★★★ Robert Duvall gives yet another sensitive, powerful, and completely convincing performance in this superb black-and-white character study about a caretaker who finds himself caring for—in both senses—a pregnant woman (Olga Bellin) who turns up one day at the lumber mill where he works. Rated PG for violence. B&W; 103m. **DIR:** Joseph Anthony. **CAST:** Robert Duvall, Olga Bellin, Sudie Bond. **1972**

TOMORROW AT SEVEN ★★ Obscure murder drama pits crime novelist Chester Morris and bumbling policemen Allen Jenkins and Frank McHugh against the mysterious Ace, who sends his victims a calling card and tells them where to go to die, which they inevitably do. This routine whodunit has little to offer. B&W; 62m. **DIR:** Ray Enright. **CAST:** Chester Morris, Vivienne Osborne, Allen Jenkins, Frank McHugh, Henry Stephenson, Grant Mitchell, Charles Middleton. **1933**

TOMORROW IS FOREVER ★★★★ Orson Welles is tempermentally suited for the role of the man who has disappeared for twenty years. When he returns, he finds out his wife (Claudette Colbert) has remarried and has children by her second husband (George Brent). Weepy (but wonderful) melodrama. B&W; 105m. **DIR:** Irving Pichel. **CAST:** Claudette Colbert, Orson Welles, George Brent, Natalie Wood, Lucile Watson, Richard Long. **1946**

TOMORROW NEVER COMES 🦃 Absolutely brainless movie about a weirdo who goes on a rampage. Unrated; the film has violence. 109m. **DIR:** Peter Collinson. **CAST:** Oliver Reed, Susan George, Stephen McHattie, Raymond Burr, John Ireland, Donald Pleasence, Paul Koslo. **1977**

TOMORROW'S CHILD ★★ Made during television's cause-of-the-week period, this saga deals with the topics of in vitro fertilization and surrogate motherhood. *Remington Steele* charmer Stephanie Zimbalist is acceptably overwrought, as is most of the cast of familiar TV faces. 100m. **DIR:** Joseph Sargent. **CAST:** Stephanie Zimbalist, Arthur Hill, William Atherton, Bruce Davison, James Shigeta, Susan Oliver, Ed Flanders, Salome Jens. **1982**

TOO OUTRAGEOUS ★★ In this disappointing sequel to 1977's surprise hit *Outrageous*, Craig Russell reprises his role as the gay hairdresser, now having realized his dreams of becoming a successful female impersonator. Hollis McLaren is his schizophrenic friend. Rated R for language and sexual content. 100m. **DIR:** Richard Benner. **CAST:** Craig Russell, Hollis McLaren, David McIlwraith. **1987**

TORCH SONG ★★ A muddled melodrama made to show off Joan Crawford's form and figure when she was approaching fifty. She plays a tough chorus-girl-turned-Broadway-dancer. 90m. **DIR:** Charles Walters. **CAST:** Joan Crawford, Michael Wilding, Gig Young, Marjorie Rambeau, Harry Morgan. **1953**

TORCH SONG TRILOGY ★★★ Harvey Fierstein's prize-winning play of the same title couldn't be better suited to film, but this comedy-drama is not for everyone. Fierstein plays Arnold Beckoff, an insecure female impersonator looking for that one, all-encompassing relationship. Anne Bancroft is his unbending Jewish mama. The musical numbers in the gay nightclub are classy and clever. Rated R. 120m. **DIR:** Paul Bogart. **CAST:** Harvey Fierstein, Anne Bancroft, Matthew Broderick, Brian Kerwin. **1988**

TORCHLIGHT 🦃 Insecure husband becomes hopelessly addicted to cocaine. Rated R for explicit drug use and sadism. 90m. **DIR:** Thomas Wright. **CAST:** Pamela Sue Martin, Steve Railsback, Ian McShane, Al Corley. **1985**

TORN APART ★★½ An Israeli soldier and an Arab girl incur the wrath of their friends and families when they fall in love. Based on Chayym Zeldis's novel *A Forbidden Love*. A tolerable time-waster. Rated R for violence. 120m. **DIR:** Jack Fisher. **CAST:** Adrian Pasdar, Cecilia Peck. **1987**

TORN BETWEEN TWO LOVERS ★★★½ This made-for-TV romantic triangle features a married Lee Remick who finds herself having an affair with a divorced architect. She must finally tell her husband the truth and choose between the two. Nothing boring about this soap! 100m. **DIR:** Delbert Mann. **CAST:** Lee Remick, Joseph Bologna, George Peppard, Giorgio Tozzi. **1979**

TORRENTS OF SPRING 🦃 Beautifully photographed but uninvolving costume drama set in Europe during the 1840s. Rated R. 97m. **DIR:** Jerzy Skolimowski. **CAST:** Timothy Hutton, Nastassja Kinski, Valeria Golino, William Forsythe, Urbano Barberini. **1990**

TORTILLA FLAT ★★★½ A watered-down (understandable for the times) adaptation of John Steinbeck's lusty novel of a group of *paisanos* on the California coast, led by Spencer Tracy, whose main purpose in life is to avoid any form of work or responsibility. One, John Garfield, inherits two run-down houses and his outlook changes, much to the concern of his friends. B&W; 105m. **DIR:** Victor Fleming. **CAST:** Spencer Tracy, Hedy Lamarr, John Garfield, Frank Morgan, Akim Tamiroff, Sheldon Leonard. **1942**

TOUCHED ★★★ This sensitive drama involves the struggle of two young psychiatric patients who try to make it outside the hospital walls. Robert Hays and Kathleen Beller are terrific as the frightened couple who must deal with numerous unforeseen obstacles. Rated R for mature topic. 89m. **DIR:** John Flynn. **CAST:** Robert Hays, Kathleen Beller, Gilbert Lewis, Ned Beatty. **1982**

TOUCHED BY LOVE ★★★ Strong performances make this affecting sentimental drama about a teenage cerebral palsy victim given hope through correspondence with singer Elvis Presley. Deborah Raffin is excellent as the nurse who nurtures patient Diane Lane from cripple to functioning teenager. Originally titled *From Elvis with Love*. Rated PG. 95m. **DIR:** Gus Trikonis. **CAST:** Deborah Raffin, Diane Lane, Michael Learned, Cristina Raines, Mary Wickes, Clu Gulager, John Amos. **1980**

TOUGH GUYS DON'T DANCE ★★ Interesting but uneven attempt at *film noir*. Strenuous dialogue and bizarre acting make this excursion into experimental filmmaking confusing. Ryan O'Neal is an ex-con who wants to be a writer. Newcomer Debra Sundland is stunning as an obnoxious southern belle. Rated R for nudity, language, and violence. 110m. **DIR:** Norman Mailer. **CAST:** Ryan O'Neal, Isabella Rossellini, Wings Hauser, Debra Sundland, Frances Fisher. **1987**

TOWN LIKE ALICE, A ★★★★½ This outstanding PBS series is even more enjoyable to watch in one viewing than during a six-week period. It is the story of female British POWs in Malaysia and their incredible struggle. Helen Morse is wonderful as the one who takes charge to help maintain the sanity and welfare of the group. Bryan Brown is the soldier who risks his life to help the women and falls in love with Morse.

301m. **DIR:** David Stevens. **CAST:** Helen Morse, Bryan Brown, Gordon Jackson. **1980**

TOYS IN THE ATTIC ★★ A man brings his baby doll bride home to confront his two overly protective spinster sisters in this watered-down screen version of the Lillian Hellman stage play. As the sisters, Geraldine Page and Wendy Hiller are superb, as always. B&W; 90m. **DIR:** George Roy Hill. **CAST:** Dean Martin, Geraldine Page, Wendy Hiller, Yvette Mimieux, Gene Tierney, Nan Martin, Larry Gates. **1963**

TRACKS 🦃 A Vietnam War veteran escorts his dead buddy on a train cross-country and goes crazy in the process. Rated R. 90m. **DIR:** Henry Jaglom. **CAST:** Dennis Hopper, Taryn Power, Dean Stockwell, Topo Swope, Michael Emil. **1977**

TRAGEDY OF FLIGHT 103: THE INSIDE STORY, THE ★★★★ A tragic and riveting account of the events leading up to the destruction of Pan Am Flight 103, resulting in the deaths at Christmastime in 1988 of 270 people over Lockerbie, Scotland. This dramatized reconstruction exposes the inner workings of international terrorists, ineffectual cosmetic airport security, and how communication failures between intelligence agencies and airport officials have led to the loss of innocent lives. Made for TV. 89m. **DIR:** Leslie Woodhead. **CAST:** Peter Boyle, Ned Beatty, Vincent Gardenia. **1990**

TRAIN KILLER, THE ★★ The true story of Sylvester Matushka, the Hungarian businessman who was responsible for a number of train wrecks in 1931. What is frustrating about this film is that it prepares the viewer for political intrigue that is never fully explained by the end of the film. Towje Kleiner is superb as Dr. Epstein, investigator of the train wrecks. Not rated, but contains sex, nudity, and violence. 90m. **DIR:** Sandor Simo. **CAST:** Michael Sarrazin, Towje Kleiner. **1983**

TRAMP AT THE DOOR ★★★★ Poignant story of a transient who poses as a distant relative of a family to gain shelter and food from them. The script is solid, especially the stories that the tramp (played brilliantly by Ed McNamara) weaves for the astonished family. Not rated; for all ages. 81m. **DIR:** Allan Kroeker. **CAST:** Ed McNamara, August Schellenberg, Monique Mercure. **1985**

TRAPEZE ★★½ Overly familiar tale of professional (Burt Lancaster) who takes young protégé (Tony Curtis) under his wing only to have scheming opportunist Gina Lollobrigida come between them is okay but nothing out of the ordinary. Solid performances and competent stunts performed by the stars. 105m. **DIR:** Carol Reed. **CAST:** Burt Lancaster, Tony Curtis, Gina Lollobrigida, Katy Jurado, Thomas Gomez. **1956**

TRASH ★★½ Favorite Andy Warhol actor Joe Dallesandro faces the squalor of New York once again. This is one of Warhol's more palatable productions. It contains some truly amusing scenes and insightful dialogue, as well as good performances by Dallesandro and Holly Woodlawn, whose relationship is the highlight of the film. Nudity, language, and open drug use fill the frames of this freewheeling life study. 110m. **DIR:** Paul Morrissey. **CAST:** Joe Dallesandro, Holly Woodlawn, Jane Forth. **1970**

TRAVELING MAN ★★★½ John Lithgow puts heart and soul into this engaging portrayal of a congenial road-bound salesman pushing foam insulation. Lithgow winds up chaperoning a wet-behind-the-ears trainee (Jonathan Silverman)—who then makes a grab for his mentor's route. Originally made for cable, it is unrated, but contains nudity. 105m. **DIR:** Irvin Kershner. **CAST:** John Lithgow, Jonathan Silverman, John Glover, Margaret Colin. **1989**

TRAVELLING NORTH ★★★½ Fine Australian romance focuses on the love of two senior citizens. Touching, delightful, and definitely worth watching. Rated PG-13 for profanity and adult themes. 97m. **DIR:** Carl Schultz. **CAST:** Leo McKern, Julia Blake. **1988**

TREE GROWS IN BROOKLYN, A ★★★★ A richly detailed and sentimental evocation of working-class Brooklyn at the turn of the century. The story focuses on the happiness and tragedies of a poor family ruled by a kindly but alcoholic father and a strong-willed mother. B&W; 128m. **DIR:** Elia Kazan. **CAST:** Dorothy McGuire, James Dunn, Joan Blondell, Peggy Ann Garner, Lloyd Nolan, James Gleason. **1945**

TRESPASSES 🦃 A beautiful woman is raped by two degenerate transients while her banker husband watches. Rated R for nudity and violence. 90m. **DIR:** Adam Roarke, Loren Bivens. **CAST:** Ben Johnson, Robert Kuhn, Mary Pillot, Van Brooks, Adam Roarke. **1986**

TRIAL, THE ★★★½ A man in an unnamed country is arrested for an unexplained crime he is never told about. It is never made too clear to the audience, either. Orson Welles's unique staging and direction nevertheless make it all fascinating, if disturbing, entertainment. B&W; 118m. **DIR:** Orson Welles. **CAST:** Anthony Perkins, Jeanne Moreau, Romy Schneider, Orson Welles, Elsa Martinelli, Akim Tamiroff. **1963**

TRIAL OF THE CANTONSVILLE NINE, THE ★★ This film is a claustrophobic adaptation of a play about nine Baltimore antiwar protesters (two are priests), who faced trial in 1968. It's high-minded and self-righteous. 85m. **DIR:** Gordon Davidson. **CAST:** Ed Flanders, Douglas Watson, William Schallert, Peter Strauss, Richard Jordan, Barton Heyman. **1972**

TRIBES ★★★½ Long-haired peacenik Jan-Michael Vincent is drafted into the Marines and faces a tough time from drill instructor Darren McGavin. TV movie is far above the usual television schlock, with insightful script and solid acting. One of Vincent's best performances. Seems a bit dated by today's standards, but still worth a look. 74m. **DIR:** Joseph Sargent. **CAST:** Jan-Michael Vincent, Darren McGavin, Earl Holliman. **1970**

TRIBUTE ★★★½ A moving portrait of a man in crisis, *Tribute* bestows a unique gift to its audience: the feeling that they have come to know a very special man. Jack Lemmon stars as a Broadway press agent who has contracted a terminal blood disease and is feted by his friends in show business. Though adjusted to his fate, Lemmon finds that he has some unfinished business: to make peace with his son, Robby Benson. Rated PG. 121m. **DIR:** Bob Clark. **CAST:** Jack Lemmon, Robby Benson, Lee Remick, Colleen Dewhurst, John Marley. **1980**

TRIO ★★★★ Wonderful collection of Somerset Maugham's short stories, introduced by Maugham. Each has a nice twist ending. "The Verger" centers on a man's decisions after being fired for his illiteracy. "Mr. Know-All" is an obnoxious bore who is shunned by the others on his cruise. Finally, Michael Rennie and Jean Simmons co-star as TB patients who fall in love while they live in the sanitorium. B&W; 88m. **DIR:** Ken Annakin, Harold French. **CAST:** Jean Simmons, Michael Rennie, Nigel Patrick, Wilfrid Hyde-White. **1950**

TRIP, THE ★★ Peter Fonda plays a director of TV commercials who discovers the kaleidoscopic pleasures of LSD. This features outdated special effects and sensibilities. Screenplay by Jack Nicholson. 85m. **DIR:** Roger Corman. **CAST:** Peter Fonda, Susan Strasberg, Bruce Dern, Dennis Hopper, Dick Miller, Luana Anders, Peter Bogdanovich. **1967**

TRIP TO BOUNTIFUL, THE ★★★★½ In 1947, an elderly widow (wonderfully played by Oscar-winner Geraldine Page) leaves the cramped apartment where she lives with her loving but weak son (John Heard) and his demanding wife (Carlin Glynn) to return to Bountiful, the small town where she had spent her happy youth...unaware that it no longer exists. Along the way, she meets a kindred spirit (Rebecca DeMornay) and the film becomes a joyous celebration of life. Rated PG. 105m. **DIR:** Peter Masterson. **CAST:** Geraldine Page, John Heard, Carlin Glynn, Richard Bradford, Rebecca DeMornay. **1986**

TRIUMPH OF THE SPIRIT ★★★½ Willem Dafoe plays a Greek Jew imprisoned at Auschwitz who boxes for the entertainment of the Nazi officers. Dafoe's limp performance makes the film soft in the center, but the innate drama of the story, fine performances by Edward James Olmos and Robert Loggia, and Robert M. Young's firmly understated direction make it compelling. Rated R. 120m. **DIR:** Robert M. Young. **CAST:** Willem Dafoe, Edward James Olmos, Robert Loggia. **1990**

TROJAN WOMEN, THE ★★ This Greek-American film is worth seeing for the four female leads. Unfortunately, the plot (revolving around the Trojan War and their defeat) is lost. Rated PG. 105m. **DIR:** Michael Cacoyannis. **CAST:** Katharine Hepburn, Vanessa Redgrave, Genevieve Bujold, Irene Papas. **1972**

TROPIC OF CANCER ★★ Want to see what an X-rated movie looked like when major stars would appear in one and it wasn't box-office poison? Here you are. Henry Miller's account of a hedonistic American in Paris finds an eager interpreter in Rip Torn. Pretentious and dated. X-rated for profanity, full nudity, and simulated sex. 87m. **DIR:** Joseph Strick. **CAST:** Rip Torn, James Callahan, Ellen Burstyn. **1970**

TROUBLE ALONG THE WAY ★★★ Disillusioned, divorced ex–football coach John Wayne cares about only one thing: his young daughter. So when the Probation Bureau decides that he's an unfit father, Duke decides to fight back—by coaching a ragtag team for a run-down Catholic college. Sentimental Hollywood stuff played and directed with no-nonsense expertise. B&W; 110m. **DIR:** Michael Curtiz. **CAST:** John Wayne, Donna Reed, Charles Coburn, Sherry Jackson, Marie Windsor, Tom Tully, Leif Erickson, Chuck Connors. **1953**

TROUBLE IN MIND ★★★★ An ex-cop, Kris Kristofferson, is paroled from prison and returns to Rain City, hoping to rekindle his romance with café owner Genevieve Bujold. Once there, he falls in love with the wife (Lori Singer) of a thief (Keith Carradine). Director Alan Rudolph's ultrabizarre, semifuturistic tale is an unusual screen experience that almost defies description. Rated R. 111m. **DIR:** Alan Rudolph. **CAST:** Kris Kristofferson, Keith Carradine, Genevieve Bujold, Lori Singer, Joe Morton, Divine. **1986**

TRUE COLORS ★★★½ John Cusack and James Spader give impressive performances in this thought-provoking drama about how the desire for power corrupts a political hopeful. Strong support from Richard Widmark, as a hard-nosed senator, and Mandy Patinkin, as a sleazy developer, adds to this morality tale. Rated R for violence and profanity. 111m. **DIR:** Herbert Ross. **CAST:** John Cusack, James Spader, Richard Widmark, Imogen Stubbs, Mandy Patinkin. **1991**

TRUE HEART SUSIE ★★★ Lillian Gish and Robert Herron are sweethearts in a small, rural, bedrock-solid American town in this sentimental silent film account of a young girl's transition from scatterbrained, uninhibited adolescent to dignified, self-assured woman. Sensitive acting and directing make what could have been cloying mush a touching, charming excursion back to what are nostalgically recalled as "the good old days." B&W; 62m. **DIR:** D. W. Griffith. **CAST:** Lillian Gish, Robert Herron, Wilbur Higby, George Fawcett, Carol Dempster. **1919**

TRUE WEST ★★★★ Sam Shepard's powerful play about sibling rivalry and responsibility is masterfully performed by members of the Steppenwolf Theater Company for public television. John Malkovich stars as a reclusive drifter who returns home to make his brother, a Hollywood screenwriter, sit up and take notice. Not rated. 110m. **DIR:** Gary Sinise. **CAST:** John Malkovich, Gary Sinise. **1983**

TRUEBLOOD ★★½ Writer-director Frank Kerr gives a 1980s spin to urban underworld dramas of the 1940s like *The Naked City* and *Kiss of Death*. Jeff Fahey and Chad Lowe are brothers, estranged for ten years, who try to rebuild their relationship on the mean streets of Brooklyn. Rated R for profanity and graphic violence. 100m. **DIR:** Frank Kerr. **CAST:** Jeff Fahey, Chad Lowe. **1989**

TRULY, MADLY, DEEPLY ★★★★½ British writer-director Anthony Minghella's directorial debut is a truly, madly, deeply wonderful motion picture. Juliet Stevenson gives a remarkable performance as a young woman whose overpowering grief over the death of her lover turns to joy and maturity when he returns to help her back to the world of the living. Unrated, the film has brief profanity. 107m. **DIR:** Anthony Minghella. **CAST:** Juliet Stevenson, Alan Rickman, Bill Paterson, Michael Maloney. **1991**

TRUST ★★★★ Surprisingly touching tale of a pregnant high school dropout (whose father keels over dead with the baby news) and a somewhat older nihilistic electronics whiz (whose mother died giving birth to him). Surreal, but somehow believable. Rated R for language. 90m. **DIR:** Hal Hartley. **CAST:** Adrienne Shelly, Martin Donovan. **1991**

TRUTH ABOUT WOMEN, THE ★★½ Playboy Laurence Harvey flirts with every woman in sight in this comedy-drama. This British production has a fine cast, especially Julie Harris, and the production design is also quite good, but it's sooo slow. 98m. **DIR:** Muriel Box. **CAST:** Laurence Harvey, Julie Harris, Eva Gabor, Diane Cilento, Mai Zetterling, Wilfrid Hyde-White. **1958**

TRUTH OR DIE ★★★½ Tony Danza delivers a powerful performance as convicted killer Jerry Rosenberg, sentenced to the electric chair, who turns his life around while on death row. Made-for-TV film, also known as *Doing Life*. 100m. **DIR:** Gene Reynolds. **CAST:** Tony Danza, Lisa Langlois, Alvin Epstein, Jon De Vries. **1986**

TUCKER: A MAN AND HIS DREAM ★★★½ Francis Ford Coppola has always admired Preston Tucker, entrepreneurial genius and designer of the Tucker, a Forties automobile built to challenge the big three automakers. This homage to dreams stars Jeff Bridges, played with an almost comic-strip-style enthusiasm. This movie truly catches the spirit of postwar times when everything seemed possible. Rated PG for language. 130m. **DIR:** Francis Ford Coppola. **CAST:** Jeff Bridges, Frederic Forrest, Joan Allen, Dean Stockwell, Martin Landau, Mako, Lloyd Bridges, Christian Slater. **1988**

TUFF TURF ★★ A forgettable movie about young love as the new kid in town falls for a streetwise young woman with a dangerous lover. Rated R for violence, profanity, and suggested sex. 112m. **DIR:** Fritz Kiersch. **CAST:** James Spader, Kim Richards, Paul Mones. **1984**

TULSA ★★½ Typical potboiler has feisty Susan Hayward as a strong-willed woman intent on drilling oil wells on her property no matter who tries to interfere. Standard stock situations made more palatable by fine cast of character actors. 90m. **DIR:** Stuart Heisler. **CAST:** Susan Hayward, Robert Preston, Pedro Armendariz, Chill Wills, Ed Begley Sr. **1949**

TUNES OF GLORY ★★★★ Gripping drama of rivalry between embittered older soldier Alec Guinness and his younger replacement John Mills is a classic study of cruelty as Guinness loses no opportunity to bully and belittle the competent but less aggressive Mills. Superb acting highlights this tragic story. 107m. **DIR:** Ronald Neame. **CAST:** Alec Guinness, John Mills, Susannah York, Dennis Price, Duncan Macrae, Kay Walsh, Gordon Jackson, John Fraser, Allan Cuthbertson. **1960**

TUNNEL, THE 🦃 Married woman and her obsessive lover. Rated R for nudity, simulated sex, and violence. 99m. **DIR:** Antonio Drove. **CAST:** Jane Seymour, Peter Weller, Fernando Rey. **1987**

TURK 182 ★★ Timothy Hutton stars as a young man who embarks on a personal crusade against injustice. His older brother (Robert Urich), a fireman, has been denied his pension after being injured while saving a child from a burning building when he was off-duty. *Turk 182* is one of those manipulative movies thought by their makers to be surefire hits. It's anything but. Rated PG-13 for violence, profanity, and suggested sex. 102m. **DIR:** Bob Clark. **CAST:** Timothy Hutton, Robert Urich, Kim Cattrall, Robert Culp, Darren McGavin, Peter Boyle. **1985**

TURNING POINT, THE ★★★★½ Anne Bancroft and Shirley MacLaine have the meaty scenes in this well-crafted drama, as a pair of dancers both blessed and cursed with the aftermaths of their own personal turning points. Bancroft, forsaking family and stability, became a ballet star; MacLaine, forsaking fame and personal expression, embraced family and stability. Blended with the story is a series of beautifully rendered ballet sequences featuring Mikhail Baryshnikov, in his film debut. Great stuff, played with strength and conviction by all concerned. Rated PG for intensity of theme. 119m. **DIR:** Herbert Ross. **CAST:** Anne Bancroft, Shirley MacLaine, Mikhail Baryshnikov, Leslie Browne, Tom Skerritt. **1977**

TURTLE BEACH ★★★ Shocking images propel this sobering, thought-provoking movie about the plight of the Vietnamese boat people. Set on the east Malaysian coast, it depicts an ongoing human tragedy, which two women, a journalist and a courtesan attempt to stop. Rated R for violence, suggested sex, and nudity. 88m. **DIR:** Stephen Wallace. **CAST:** Greta Scacchi, Joan Chen, Jack Thompson, Art Malik, Norman Kaye. **1992**

12 ANGRY MEN ★★★★★ A superb cast under inspired direction makes this film brilliant in every aspect. Henry Fonda is the holdout on a jury who desperately seeks to convince his eleven peers to reconsider their hasty conviction of a boy accused of murdering his father. The struggle behind closed doors is taut, charged, and fascinating. B&W; 95m. **DIR:** Sidney Lumet. **CAST:** Henry Fonda, Lee J. Cobb, Ed Begley Sr., E. G. Marshall, Jack Klugman, Jack Warden, Martin Balsam, John Fiedler, Robert Webber, George Voskovec, Edward Binns, Joseph Sweeney. **1957**

TWENTY-ONE ★★★ Irreverent glimpse inside the life of an adventurous young woman (Patsy Kensit). Kensit carries on a monologue chronicling her simultaneous affairs with a drug addict and a married man. Rated R for nudity, violence, profanity, and drug use. 92m. **DIR:** Don Boyd. **CAST:** Patsy Kensit, Jack Shepherd, Patrick Ryecart. **1990**

TWICE IN A LIFETIME ★★★★★ Superior slice-of-life drama about a Washington mill worker (Gene Hackman) who reaches a mid-life crisis and decides that he and wife Ellen Burstyn can't sustain the magic anymore. That decision is helped by a sudden interest in local barmaid Ann-Margret, but the script isn't that simplistic. The cast is uniformly fine, the story poignant without being sugary. Rated R for adult situations. 111m. **DIR:** Bud Yorkin. **CAST:** Gene Hackman, Ann-Margret, Ellen Burstyn, Amy Madigan, Ally Sheedy, Brian Dennehy. **1985**

TWISTED: A STEP BEYOND INSANITY ★★★ A sadistic youth terrorizes his sister's baby-sitter by bombarding her with psychological warfare. A fairly effective low-budget thriller. Unrated, but has violence. 87m. **DIR:** Adam Holender. **CAST:** Lois Smith, Christian Slater, Tandy Cronyn. **1991**

TWISTED OBSESSION ★★ A screenwriter becomes infatuated with a film director's sister in this very offbeat tale of obsession and brother-sister domination. Unrated, but with nudity, profanity, and violence. 109m. **DIR:** Fernando Trueba. **CAST:** Jeff Goldblum, Miranda Richardson, Dexter Fletcher. **1990**

TWO FOR THE SEESAW ★★½ While reevaluating his life and previous marriage, a Nebraska attorney moves to New York City and has an affair with a quirky modern dancer. Candid dialogue and touching humor but a little too long to be fully recommended. B&W; 120m. **DIR:** Robert Wise. **CAST:** Robert Mitchum, Shirley MacLaine, Edmon Ryan, Elisabeth Fraser. **1962**

TWO MOON JUNCTION ★★ Two weeks before her marriage, a young, well-to-do southern woman falls for a muscular carnival worker. A pattern in their relationship soon develops. They argue, they make love, and then she cries. Rated R for nudity, profanity, and violence. 104m. **DIR:** Zalman King. **CAST:** Sherilyn Fenn, Richard Tyson, Louise Fletcher, Burl Ives, Kristy McNichol. **1988**

TWO OF A KIND (1982) ★★★★ This heartwarming TV film features George Burns as a discarded senior citizen and Robby Benson as his retarded grandson. The two come together when the boy decides to help his seemingly disabled grandpa play golf again. Cliff Robertson and Barbara Barrie play Benson's parents. All in all, this is a fine film with a positive message about family unity. 102m. **DIR:** Roger Young. **CAST:** George Burns, Robby Benson, Cliff Robertson, Barbara Barrie, Ronny Cox. **1982**

TWO WEEKS IN ANOTHER TOWN ★★½ Kirk Douglas is uptight as a former movie actor who had a bout with the bottle and is trying for a comeback. A downer based on an Irwin Shaw novel. 107m. **DIR:** Vincente Minnelli. **CAST:** Kirk Douglas, Edward G. Robinson, Cyd Charisse, Claire Trevor, George Hamilton, Daliah Lavi, Rosanna Schiaffino, George Macready, James Gregory, Leslie Uggams. **1962**

UGLY AMERICAN, THE ★★½ With Marlon Brando playing an American ambassador newly arrived at his Asian post, more is expected of this film than just a routine potboiler. However, the film attempts to focus on the political interworkings of Brando's struggle with rising communist elements, but fails to generate any excitement. 120m. **DIR:** George Englund. **CAST:** Marlon Brando, Pat Hingle, Sandra Church, Arthur Hill, Eiji Okada, Jocelyn Brando. **1963**

UN CHIEN ANDALOU ★★★★★ Possibly the only film ever made completely according to surrealist principles, this famous short consists of a series of shocking and humorous images designed to have no point or connection. Luis Buñuel and Salvador Dali wrote down some of their dreams, selected random incidents from them, and then photographed them. Sixty years later this seventeen-minute film retains the power to startle.

The videotape includes three other avant-garde shorts: *Ballet Mechanique, Regen (Rain), Uberfall,* and *The Hearts of Age,* by 19-year-old Orson Welles—all of interest to the serious cinema student. B&W; 74m. **DIR:** Luis Buñuel, Salvador Dali. **1928**

UNAPPROACHABLE, THE 🦃 A completely unwatchable film about a young man obsessed with a reclusive aging starlet. Not rated, but contains profanity. 100m. **DIR:** Krzysztof Zanussi. **CAST:** Leslie Caron, Daniel Webb, Leslie Magon. **1982**

UNBEARABLE LIGHTNESS OF BEING, THE ★★★★★ Philip Kaufman's *The Unbearable Lightness of Being* is one of the most playfully alive films ever made. Kaufman calls his film a "variation" of Milan Kundera's novel about Tomas, the womanizing neurosurgeon from Prague. What results is something poetic, erotic, funny, and exuberant. Rated R for sexual content. 164m. **DIR:** Phil Kaufman. **CAST:** Daniel Day-Lewis, Juliette Binoche, Lena Olin, Derek de Lint, Erland Josephson. **1988**

UNBELIEVABLE TRUTH, THE ★★½ When Robert Burke returns home after an extended vacation in prison, his presense gets the whole town talking. Off-beat film with an edge. Rated R for its profanity. 90m. **DIR:** Hal Hartley. **CAST:** Adrienne Shelly, Robert Burke, Christopher Cooke, Gary Sauer, Julia McNeal, Mark Bailey. **1990**

UNDER MILK WOOD ★★ Welsh poet Dylan Thomas's play loses its vitality in this slow, stuffy, dry, image-burdened film version. All the queen's men plus the beautiful Elizabeth Taylor, cannot infuse it with life. 90m. **DIR:** Andrew Sinclair. **CAST:** Elizabeth Taylor, Richard Burton, Peter O'Toole, Glynis Johns, Vivien Merchant, Sian Phillips. **1973**

UNDER THE BILTMORE CLOCK ★★★ This acceptable TV adaptation of F. Scott Fitzgerald's "Myra Meets His Family" presents Sean Young as a young woman who decides to marry for wealth; she then has the task of meeting fiancé Lenny Von Dohlen's eccentric family. 70m. **DIR:** Neal Miller. **CAST:** Sean Young, Lenny Von Dohlen, Barnard Hughes. **1985**

UNDER THE BOARDWALK 🦃 In this *West Side Story* update, the *lowks* (local dudes) take on the *vals* to see who will rule the local waves and babes. Rated R for violence and profanity. 102m. **DIR:** Fritz Kiersch. **CAST:** Danielle von Zerneck, Keith Coogan, Richard J. Paul, Sonny Bono. **1988**

UNDER THE CHERRY MOON ★★ Prince plays a gigolo-type singer who pursues a debutante, Mary (Kristin Scott Thomas). Rated PG-13 for language and mature theme. B&W; 100m. **DIR:** Prince. **CAST:** Prince, Jerome Benton, Steven Berkoff, Alexandra Stewart, Kristin Scott Thomas, Francesca Annis. **1986**

UNDER THE GUN 🦃 A hotheaded St. Louis cop comes to Los Angeles to investigate the murder of his brother. Rated R for language, violence, and nudity. 90m. **DIR:** James Sbardellati. **CAST:** Vanessa Williams, Sam Jones, John Russell. **1988**

UNDER THE VOLCANO ★★★★ Brilliant, but disturbing, adaptation of the Malcolm Lowry novel about a suicidal, alcoholic British consul in Mexico on the eve of World War II. Rated R for suggested sex, violence, and profanity. 109m. **DIR:** John Huston. **CAST:** Albert Finney, Jacqueline Bisset, Anthony Andrews. **1984**

UNDERCURRENT ★★ A bride (Katharine Hepburn) comes to realize her husband (Robert Taylor) is a scoundrel. Considering the talent involved, this is a peculiarly dull drama. B&W; 116m. **DIR:** Vincente Minnelli. **CAST:** Katharine Hepburn, Robert Taylor, Robert Mitchum, Edmund Gwenn, Jayne Meadows, Marjorie Main. **1946**

UNDERWORLD (1927) ★★★ After being rescued from prison by his moll and right-hand man, a gangster soon realizes that the two are having an affair. One of the first movies to look at crime through the gangster's point of view. Silent. B&W; 82m. **DIR:** Josef von Sternberg. **CAST:** George Bancroft, Evelyn Brent. **1927**

UNDERWORLD U.S.A. ★★★½ Impressive crime-drama from writer-director Sam Fuller about a man (Cliff Robertson) who, after witnessing his father's death at the hands of mobsters, develops a lifetime obsession to get even with the murderers. Great cinematography and exceptional performances rise above the weak script. B&W; 99m. **DIR:** Samuel Fuller. **CAST:** Cliff Robertson, Dolores Dorn. **1961**

UNEXPECTED ENCOUNTERS 🦃 This couples-only, after-hours rental is little more than a tease. Not rated (however there's partial nudity). 60m. **DIR:** Mannie Marshall. **CAST:** Giselle Wilder, Justin Dylan. **1988**

UNHOLY ROLLERS 🦃 Roller Derby flick. Enough profanity, nudity, and simulated sex to make it comparable to an R. 88m. **DIR:** Vernon Zimmerman. **CAST:** Claudia Jennings, Louis Quinn, Roberta Collins, Alan Vint. **1972**

UNMARRIED WOMAN, AN ★★★★★ Jill Clayburgh's Erica has settled into a comfortable rut and barely notices it when things begin to go wrong. One day, after lunch with her husband, Martin (Michael Murphy), she is shocked by his sobbing admission that he is in love with another woman. Her world is shattered. This first-rate film concerns itself with her attempts to cope with the situation. Rated R for sex, nudity, and profanity. 124m. **DIR:** Paul Mazursky. **CAST:** Jill Clayburgh, Michael Murphy, Alan Bates, Pat Quinn. **1978**

UNNATURAL CAUSES ★★★★ Alfre Woodard stars in this made-for-TV movie about a Veterans Administration counselor who takes up the cause of linking Agent Orange to stricken vets under her care. John Ritter gives a sensitive performance as one of the Vietnam vets. This fact-based story is given maximum impact thanks to the intelligent script of John Sayles. 100m. **DIR:** Lamont Johnson. **CAST:** John Ritter, Alfre Woodard, Patti LaBelle, John Sayles. **1986**

UNREMARKABLE LIFE, AN ★★★ Two elderly sisters who still live together in their family home find themselves at odds when one of them starts dating. Polished performances highlight what is an otherwise overwrought melodrama. Rated PG for racial epithets. 95m. **DIR:** Amin Q. Chaudhri. **CAST:** Patricia Neal, Shelley Winters, Mako. **1989**

UNSETTLED LAND 🦃 Israeli-made production concerning a commune of young Jews from Europe establishing a settlement in the Sinai Desert after World War I. Overblown saga. Rated PG for violence. 109m. **DIR:** Uri Barbash. **CAST:** Kelly McGillis, John Shea. **1987**

UNSPEAKABLE ACTS ★★★½ This TV dramatization of the landmark day-care sexual-abuse case in 1984 Miami features Jill Clayburgh and Brad Davis as the child psychologists who interviewed the abused children. Though disturbing, the film is a must-see for everyone seeking qualified child care. Contains mature themes. 94m. **DIR:** Linda Otto. **CAST:** Jill Clayburgh, Brad Davis, Season Hubley, Gregory Sierra. **1989**

UNTAMED HEART ★★★★ Tom Sierchio's poignant urban love story becomes a career-making vehicle for Marisa Tomei, in her first starring role. She's a perky Minneapolis twentysomething working as a waitress. She eventually connects with the diner's introverted busboy (Christian Slater, very good in a part completely unlike his usual work). Rated PG-13 for profanity. 102m. **DIR:** Tony Bill. **CAST:** Christian Slater, Marisa Tomei, Rosie Perez, Kyle Secor. **1993**

UNTIL SEPTEMBER ★★ A midwestern divorcée (Karen Allen) falls in love with a married Parisian banker (Thierry Lhermitte) during the summer vacation in this unabashed soap opera. Rated R. 95m. **DIR:** Richard Marquand. **CAST:** Karen Allen, Thierry Lhermitte, Christopher Cazenove. **1984**

UNTIL THEY SAIL ★★★½ Romantic drama about a quartet of sisters and the men they meet during World War II in New Zealand. Based on a James Michener novel, so there's plenty of meat to the story, including a murder and some mismatched lovers. B&W; 96m. **DIR:** Robert Wise. **CAST:** Paul Newman, Jean Simmons, Joan Fontaine, Sandra Dee, Piper Laurie, Dean Jones, Charles Drake, Patrick Macnee. **1957**

UP AGAINST THE WALL ★★ Black teenager has his moral code challenged when he moves from his mother's modest home to his brother's house in the affluent suburbs in this well-meaning but amateurish drama. Rated PG-13 for language and violence. 103m. **DIR:** Ron O'Neal. **CAST:** Marla Gibbs, Ron O'Neal, Stoney Jackson. **1991**

UPSTAIRS, DOWNSTAIRS ★★★★★ Life in a fashionable London town house between 1904 and 1930 is depicted with insight, wit, and charm through the activities and thoughts of the patrician family upstairs and the servants downstairs in this superb *Masterpiece Theater* series. The late Gordon Jackson is perfect as the unflappable butler Hudson, closely rivaled by Jean Marsh as the unpredictable maid Rose. 900m. **DIR:** Simon Langton. **CAST:** Gordon Jackson, Jean Marsh, Pauline Collins, Rachel Gurney, Ian Ogilvy, Raymond Huntley, Lesley-Anne Down. **1971**

UPTOWN NEW YORK ★★ Sobby melodrama about a doctor whose family forces him to jilt the girl he loves and marry for money. B&W; 80m. **DIR:** Victor Schertzinger. **CAST:** Jack Oakie, Shirley Grey. **1932**

URBAN COWBOY ★★★ The film is a slice-of-life *Saturday Night Fever*–like look at the after-hours life of blue-collar cowboys. Overall, the film works because of excellent directing by James Bridges and the fine acting of John Travolta, Debra Winger, and Scott Glenn. Rated PG. 132m. **DIR:** James Bridges. **CAST:** John Travolta, Debra Winger, Scott Glenn, Madolyn Smith, Charlie Daniels Band. **1980**

URGE TO KILL ★★★★ A top-notch cast shines in this drama about a convicted killer who, upon release from a mental institution, comes home to face prejudice and violent recriminations. Well written and acted, the film's focus is on the quality of justice versus the quality of mercy and what people will do to subvert both. Holly Hunter is outstanding as the sister of the murder victim. Not rated, but contains mature themes. 96m. **DIR:** Mike Robe. **CAST:** Karl Malden, Holly Hunter, Alex McArthur, Paul Sorvino, Catherine Mary Stewart, William Devane. **1984**

URINAL ★★★½ Structurally imaginative semidocumentary in which the ghosts of gay artists (including Sergey Eisenstein, Frida Kahlo, and Yukio Mishima) return to Canada to help combat police harassment of gays who meet in public washrooms. Not rated; contains nudity and strong sexual themes. 100m. **DIR:** John Greyson. **CAST:** Pauline Carey, Paul Bettis. **1988**

USERS, THE ★★ Another bloated TV movie boasts a fine cast and little else. Jaclyn Smith stars as a beautiful girl who plays a major role in the resurgence of a down-and-out movie star's career. Standard "television" production values and "television" dialogue do this one in. 125m. **DIR:** Joseph Hardy. **CAST:** Jaclyn Smith, Tony Curtis, Joan Fontaine, Red Buttons. **1978**

UTZ ★★★½ The director of *The Vanishing* here attempts a more subtle, complex film. Armin Mueller-Stahl stars as an obsessive collector of fine porcelain figures living in Prague. The Communist Czech government decides the collection belongs to the state. Peter Riegert costars as an American collector who unravels Utz's story in flashbacks, and the masterful Paul Scofield contributes a tasty bit as Utz's closest old friend. Though well acted, containing a strong finish, the film's narrative sags in the long middle portion. 101m. **DIR:** George Sluizer. **CAST:** Armin Mueller-Stahl, Brenda Fricker, Peter Riegert, Paul Scofield. **1992**

V.I.P.S, THE ★★★ The problems of an assortment of passengers stranded at a London airport get glossy treatment in this drama thrown together to cash in on the real-life romance of Elizabeth Taylor and Richard Burton. The stars are easily upstaged by the solid supporting cast, especially Maggie Smith and Oscar-winner Margaret Rutherford. Unrated. 119m. **DIR:** Anthony Asquith. **CAST:** Elizabeth Taylor, Richard Burton, Margaret Rutherford, Maggie Smith, Rod Taylor, Louis Jourdan, Orson Welles. **1963**

VALENTINO ★★½ This outrageous biography of one of the screen's greatest legends uses selective facts and historical settings in an attempt to isolate the real nature of the adulation of Rudolph Valentino. Director Ken Russell freely mixes truth and wild hallucinations. Rudolf Nureyev is somehow an apt choice to play Valentino, and the rest of the cast and production seems to fit. 132m. **DIR:** Ken Russell. **CAST:** Rudolf Nureyev, Leslie Caron, Michelle Phillips, Carol Kane, Felicity Kendal, Seymour Cassel, Huntz Hall, Alfred Marks, David De Keyser. **1977**

VALENTINO RETURNS ★★½ Small Town, U.S.A., 1955, proves too confining for Wayne Gibbs (Barry Tubb). He takes off in his new pink Cadillac and manages to take on a biker gang, ruin his car, and find love (lust) in short order. Rated R for violence, profanity, and nudity. 97m. **DIR:** Peter Hoffman. **CAST:** Frederic Forrest, Veronica Cartwright, Barry Tubb, Jenny Wright. **1988**

VALLEY OF THE DOLLS 🦃 Trash film of Jacqueline Susann's trashy bestseller about the effect of drugs (the *dolls* of the title) on ladies from show business and society. John Williams was Oscar-nominated for his score. 123m. **DIR:** Mark Robson. **CAST:** Barbara Parkins, Patty Duke, Sharon Tate, Susan Hayward, Paul Burke, Martin Milner, Lee Grant. **1967**

VALMONT ★★★★ Milos Forman took a great artistic risk in directing what amounts to a one-year-later remake of Stephen Frears's Oscar-winning *Dangerous Liaisons*, but the result is captivating, with a young cast bringing poignance and innocence to its tale of seduction and deceit. Rated R for nudity and violence. 137m. **DIR:** Milos Forman. **CAST:** Colin Firth, Annette Bening, Meg Tilly, Sian Phillips, Jeffrey Jones, Henry Thomas, Fabia Drake. **1989**

VANISHING ACT ★★★½ A tense psychological drama with a knockout ending. Mike Farrell's wife of one week is missing. He routinely reports this to town cop Elliot Gould. Before the investigation begins, the wife reappears. But Farrell says she's not his wife. Rated PG. 95m. **DIR:** David Greene. **CAST:** Mike Farrell, Margot Kidder, Elliott Gould, Fred Gwynne, Graham Jarvis. **1987**

VANITY FAIR 🦃 In updating Thackeray's classic *Vanity Fair*, screenwriter F. Hugh Herbert and director Chester M. Franklin have created a disaster. B&W; 78m. **DIR:** Chester M. Franklin. **CAST:** Myrna Loy, Conway Tearle, Barbara Kent, Anthony Bushell. **1938**

VELVET TOUCH, THE ★★★★½ This is a marvelous suspense-drama featuring Rosalind Russell as a stage actress. In a fit of rage, she kills her jealous producer, a blackmailer. Leo Rosten's screenplay crackles with spirit and polish. B&W; 97m. **DIR:** John Gage. **CAST:** Rosalind Russell, Leo Genn, Claire Trevor, Leon Ames, Sydney Greenstreet, Frank McHugh, Lex Barker. **1948**

VENICE/VENICE ★★★★ Henry Jaglom portrays a filmmaker at the Venice Film Festival doing the usual rounds of publicity until he's introduced to a female journalist from France. Their mutual interest continues through the festival and back at the filmmaker's home in Venice, California. (Hence, *Venice/Venice*). Highly enjoyable. Rated PG. 108m. **DIR:** Henry Jaglom. **CAST:** Henry Jaglom, Nelly Alard, Suzanne Bertish, Daphna Kastner, David Duchovny. **1992**

VERDICT, THE ★★★★½ In this first-rate drama, Paul Newman brilliantly plays an alcoholic Boston lawyer who redeems himself by taking on slick James Mason in a medical malpractice suit. Rated R for profanity and adult situations. 129m. **DIR:** Sidney Lumet. **CAST:** Paul Newman, James Mason, Charlotte Rampling, Jack Warden. **1982**

VERY EDGE, THE ★★★ An ex-model loses the child she is carrying after she is raped. Her trauma puts a strain on her marriage, while her attacker is still on the loose. Effective psychological suspense, marred slightly by a contrived ending. B&W; 82m. **DIR:** Cyril Frankel. **CAST:** Anne Heywood, Richard Todd, Jack Hedley, Maurice Denham, Patrick Magee. **1963**

VICTIM ★★★ One of the first films to deal with homosexuality, this well-made British effort has Dirk Bogarde as a lawyer confronting blackmailers who killed his lover. It was daring then, but not now. The story, though, is still interesting. B&W; 100m. **DIR:** Basil Dearden. **CAST:** Dirk Bogarde, Sylvia Syms, Dennis Price, John Barrie. **1961**

VIETNAM WAR STORY ★★★★ This is a collection of three outstanding episodes from HBO's short-term series. *The Pass* dramatizes one soldier's reluctance to return to duty. *The Mine* is about an independent soldier's reliance on others when he is trapped on a land mine. *Home* concerns disabled veterans in a hospital. All are heart-wrenching. There are no stars in the cast, but all performances are top-rate. Unrated, but for mature audiences. 90m. **DIR:** Kevin Hooks, Georg Stanford Brown, Ray Danton. **CAST:** Eriq La Salle, Nicholas Cascone, Tony Becker. **1988**

VIETNAM WAR STORY—PART TWO ★★★★ Three more segments of the HBO series: *An Old Ghost Walks the Earth*; *R&R* and *The Flagging*. Unrated, but for mature audiences. 90m. **DIR:** Michael Toshiyuki Uno, David Morris, Jack Sholder. **CAST:** Tim Guinee, Cynthia Bain. **1988**

VINCENT AND THEO ★★★★ Based on letters written by the celebrated painter Vincent van Gogh (Tim Roth) to his art-dealer brother, Theo (Paul Rhys), this is a first-rate cinematic biography; perhaps the best ever to be made about the life of a painter. Rated PG-13 for profanity and nudity. 138m. **DIR:** Robert Altman. **CAST:** Tim Roth, Paul Rhys, Johanna ter Steege. **1990**

VIOLETS ARE BLUE ★★★½ In this watchable screen soap opera, former sweethearts Sissy Spacek and Kevin Kline are reunited when she, a successful photojournalist, returns to her hometown. Their romance is rekindled although he is now married (to Bonnie Bedelia, who is terrific in her all-too-brief on-screen bits). Rated PG for suggested sex and light profanity. 89m. **DIR:** Jack Fisk. **CAST:** Sissy Spacek, Kevin Kline, Bonnie Bedelia, Augusta Dabney. **1986**

VIRGIN AND THE GYPSY, THE ★★★½ The title tells the tale in this stylish, effective screen adaptation of the D. H. Lawrence novella. Franco Nero and Joanna Shimkus exude sexual tension as the gypsy and his love, a minister's daughter. Rated R for nudity. 95m. **DIR:** Christopher Miles. **CAST:** Franco Nero, Joanna Shimkus, Honor Blackman, Mark Burns, Maurice Denham. **1970**

VIRGIN QUEEN, THE ★★★ Bette Davis reprises her memorable 1939 *Elizabeth and Essex* portrayal of Elizabeth I of England in this rehashing of majestic might and young love. This time around the queen dotes on Sir Walter Raleigh, who crosses her up, but survives to sail away to happiness. A fine example of Hollywood film history. 92m. **DIR:** Henry Koster. **CAST:** Bette Davis, Richard Todd, Joan Collins, Herbert Marshall. **1955**

VIRGIN SOLDIERS, THE ★★★★ This outstanding drama of young British recruits in 1950 Singapore has some great performances. Hywel Bennett is one of the recruits who is as green with his first sexual encounter as he is on the battlefield. 96m. **DIR:** John Dexter. **CAST:** Hywel Bennett, Nigel Patrick, Lynn Redgrave, Nigel Davenport. **1969**

VISION QUEST ★★★½ A young athlete makes good against all odds. If you can get past the familiarity of the plot, it isn't bad. It benefits particularly from a charismatic lead performance by Matthew Modine. Rated R for nudity, suggested sex, violence, and profanity. 96m. **DIR:** Harold Becker. **CAST:** Matthew Modine, Linda Fiorentino, Michael Schoeffling, Ronny Cox, Harold Sylvester. **1985**

VITAL SIGNS 💔 Third-year med students struggling through hospital training. Rated R for sexual situations and profanity. 102m. **DIR:** Marisa Silver. **CAST:** Jimmy Smits, Adrian Pasdar, Diane Lane. **1990**

VIVA ZAPATA! ★★★★½ This film chonicles Mexican revolutionary leader Emiliano Zapata from his peasant upbringing until his death as a weary, disillusioned political liability. Marlon Brando won an Oscar nomination for his insightful portrayal of Zapata. Anthony Quinn, as Zapata's brother, did manage to hold his own against the powerful Brando characterization and was rewarded with a supporting actor Oscar. B&W; 113m. **DIR:** Elia Kazan. **CAST:** Marlon Brando, Anthony Quinn, Jean Peters, Joseph Wiseman. **1952**

VOICES ★★★ A sentimental love story that manages to maintain a sensitive tone that ultimately proves infectious. Amy Irving stars as a deaf young woman who wants to become a dancer; Michael Ontkean is a young man who would rather be a singer. They meet, fall in love. The material is sugary, but Irving and Ontkean make it work. Rated PG for language and adult themes. 107m. **DIR:** Robert Markowitz. **CAST:** Amy Irving, Michael Ontkean, Herbert Berghof, Viveca Lindfors. **1979**

VOYAGE OF TERROR: THE ACHILLE LAURO AFFAIR ★★ Beware of falling asleep during this telefilm based on the true story of the hijacking of a cruise ship. The viewer views most of the ordeal through an older American couple. 95m. **DIR:** Alberto Negrin. **CAST:** Burt Lancaster, Eva Marie Saint, Rebecca Schaeffer, Bernard Fresson, Robert Culp. **1990**

VOYAGE OF THE DAMNED ★★★★ This fine drama takes place in 1939 as a shipload of Jewish refugees are refused refuge in Havana and are forced to return to Germany for certain imprisonment or death. Rated PG. 134m. **DIR:** Stuart Rosenberg. **CAST:** Oskar Werner, Faye Dunaway, Max von Sydow, Orson Welles, Malcolm McDowell, James Mason, Julie Harris, Lee Grant. **1976**

VOYAGE 'ROUND MY FATHER, A ★★★★ Writer John Mortimer, famed for creating British barrister Horace Rumpole, composed this play to honor his rather idiosyncratic father. Laurence Olivier, who essays the lead, turns eccentricity into an art form. The younger Mortimer is played by Alan Bates. Originally made for British television and suitable for family viewing. 85m. **DIR:** Alvin Rakoff. **CAST:** Laurence Olivier, Alan Bates, Jane Asher, Elizabeth Sellars. **1983**

VOYAGER ★★ Slow-moving tale of a man, the woman he loves, and the forbidden secret they share. Although well acted, this is a dull and soapy nostalgia piece. Rated PG-13 for adult themes. 113m. **DIR:** Volker Schlondörff. **CAST:** Sam Shepard, Julie Delpy, Barbara Sukowa. **1991**

WAIT UNTIL SPRING, BANDINI ★★★ Author John Fante's fond remembrance of his youth is lovingly brought to the screen in this nostalgic look at an immigrant family beating the odds in Colorado, circa 1920. Handsome production benefits from a warm cast, especially Joe Mantegna as the clan head. Rated PG for language. 102m. **DIR:** Dominique Deruddere. **CAST:** Joe Mantegna, Ornella Muti, Faye Dunaway, Burt Young, Daniel Wilson. **1989**

WAITING ★★★½ Imagine an Australian *Big Chill*, as told from a woman's perspective. Writer-director Jackie McKimmie has fashioned a charming tale of diverse female friends who come from around the world to help their friend with the forthcoming birth of her child. An entertaining film. 90m. **DIR:** Jackie McKimmie. **CAST:** Noni Hezelhurst, Deborra-Lee Furness. **1992**

WAITING FOR THE LIGHT ★★★½ A single mother of two children inherits and reopens a run-down roadside café. When her aunt, an ex–circus magician, pulls a nighttime prank on their mean-spirited neighbor, he mistakes it for a heavenly visit. Set during the uneasy time of the Cuban missile crisis, the troubled and the faithful flock to the scene of the "miracle," and business booms. Rated PG for profanity. 94m. **DIR:** Christopher Monger. **CAST:** Shirley MacLaine, Teri Garr, Vincent Schiavelli, Clancy Brown, John Bedford Lloyd. **1991**

WAITING FOR THE MOON ★★ Linda Hunt is Alice B. Toklas and Linda Bassett is Gertrude Stein in this idiosyncratic, self-indulgent, and frustrating film. The stars' performances are fine, but the impressionistic style of cowriter-director Jill Godmilow tends to be more irritating than artistic. Rated PG-13 for profanity and adult themes. 88m. **DIR:** Jill Godmilow. **CAST:** Linda Hunt, Linda Bassett, Bruce McGill, Andrew McCarthy, Bernadette Lafont. **1987**

WALK IN THE SPRING RAIN, A ★★½ Two well-into-middle-age people find romance while on vacation in the country. Their problem is that both are married to other people. From such a fine cast you expect more. Rated PG. 100m. **DIR:** Guy Green. **CAST:** Anthony Quinn, Ingrid Bergman, Fritz Weaver, Katherine Crawford. **1970**

WALK ON THE WILD SIDE ★★ Trashy tale of a young man's attempt to find his girlfriend, only to discover she's working in a New Orleans brothel. Extremely slow-paced film wastes a first-rate cast and a great musical score by Elmer Bernstein. For lovers of soap operas only. B&W; 114m. **DIR:** Edward Dmytryk. **CAST:** Laurence Harvey, Jane Fonda, Capucine, Barbara Stanwyck, Anne Baxter. **1962**

WALKER ★★★ True story of William Walker and his takeover of Nicaragua in 1855 by director Alex Cox. Ed Harris has a great time with the broad character of Walker and makes clear that power corrupts. For those with a taste for something out of the ordinary, *Walker* is worth viewing. Rated R for language nudity, and simulated sex. 98m. **DIR:** Alex Cox. **CAST:** Ed Harris, Richard Masur, René Auberjonois, Marlee Matlin, Sy Richardson, Peter Boyle. **1988**

WALL STREET ★★★★ The same energy and insight that propelled writer-director Oliver Stone's Oscar-winning *Platoon* helps make this look at double-dealing in the stock market much more entertaining than one would expect. Chief among its pleasures is Michael Douglas's deliciously evil character of Gordon Gekko, a hotshot financier who takes novice Bud Fox (Charlie Sheen) under his wing. Rated R for profanity, nudity, and violence. 120m. **DIR:** Oliver Stone. **CAST:** Michael Douglas, Charlie Sheen, Daryl Hannah, Martin Sheen, Terence Stamp, Sean Young, Hal Holbrook, James Spader. **1987**

WALLS OF GLASS ★★★½ A New York cabdriver who aspires to be an actor exposes us to the many characters of his life: his gambling family, his troubled youth, and the colorful customers in his cab. A truly warm and insightful drama with a bravura performance by Philip Bosco. Rated R for language. 85m. **DIR:** Scott Goldstein. **CAST:** Philip Bosco, Geraldine Page, Olympia Dukakis, William Hickey. **1988**

WANDERERS, THE ★★★★ This enjoyable film is set in the early 1960s and focuses on the world of teenagers. Though it has ample amounts of comedy and excitement, because it deals with life on the streets of the Bronx there is an atmosphere of ever-present danger and fear. The Wanderers are a gang of Italian-American youths who have banded together for safety and good times. Rated R. 113m. **DIR:** Phil Kaufman. **CAST:** Ken Wahl, John Friedrich, Karen Allen, Tony Ganios. **1979**

WAR AND PEACE (1956) ★★½ Mammoth international effort to film this classic novel results in an overlong, unevenly constructed melodrama. The massive battle scenes and outdoor panoramas are truly impressive, as are the performers on occasion. But the whole production seems to swallow up the principals and the action, leaving a rather lifeless film. 208m. **DIR:** King Vidor. **CAST:** Henry Fonda, Audrey Hepburn, Mel Ferrer, John Mills. **1956**

WAR AND REMEMBRANCE ★★★ Drawn-out sudsy TV docudrama is Herman Wouk's sequel to *Winds of War*. Action begins with Pearl Harbor and eventual battles with Hitler. 96–146m. **DIR:** Dan Curtis. **CAST:** Robert Mitchum, Jane Seymour, Polly Bergen, Hart Bochner, Victoria Tennant. **1988**

WAR GAME, THE ★★★★★ Pseudo-documentary depicts the events preceding and following a nuclear attack. Originally made for the BBC, which never ran it because it was thought to be too unsettling for viewers. Unrated. 47m. **DIR:** Peter Watkins. **1965**

WAR LOVER, THE ★★½ This is a very slow-moving account of pilots (Steve McQueen and Robert Wagner) in England during World War II. Both pilots are seeking the affections of the same woman. Nothing in the film raises it above the level of mediocrity. B&W; 105m. **DIR:** Philip Leacock. **CAST:** Steve McQueen, Robert Wagner, Shirley Anne Field. **1962**

WAR REQUIEM ★★★ Arty, at times surrealistic view of war as seen through the eyes of World War II soldiers, nurses, and children. All action is without dialogue using Wilfred Owen's poetry and Benjamin Britten's music with emotional and thought-provoking results. Unrated; contains violence. 92m. **DIR:** Derek Jarman. **CAST:** Laurence Olivier, Tilda Swinton, Owen Teale, Nathaniel Parker. **1988**

WARM NIGHTS ON A SLOW MOVING TRAIN ★★½ In this offbeat drama, Wendy Hughes portrays a schoolteacher who spends many of her nights as a prostitute on a passenger train in order to support her ailing, morphine-dependent brother. Rated R for simulated sex. 91m. **DIR:** Bob Ellis. **CAST:** Wendy Hughes, Colin Friels, Norman Kaye. **1989**

WARM SUMMER RAIN 🦃 Self-destructive woman botches a suicide attempt, flees to a roadside bar, purchases a five-legged iguana, uses it to belt a persistent fellow trying to pick her up, and then spends the rest of the film having her way with the same guy. Rated R for nudity. 96m. **DIR:** Joe Gayton. **CAST:** Kelly Lynch, Barry Tubb. **1989**

WARNING SHADOWS (1923) ★★★★ An insane husband's jealousy of his wife's lover comes to a head when a hypnotist performs a shadow play mirroring the trio's emotions and passions. A classic post–World War I German cinema drama laced with mystery, fantasy, romance, and psychological terror. Silent with English and German titles. B&W; 93m. **DIR:** Arthur Robison. **CAST:** Fritz Kortner, Ruth Weyher. **1923**

WASH, THE ★★★ A straightforward story of a fading marriage and the rekindling of love, unusual for the advanced age of its characters and the film's offbeat setting among Asian-Americans in California. The talented Mako is memorable as a gruff, seemingly unaffectionate retiree who can't understand why his wife (Nobu McCarthy) wants a separation. Rated PG. 100m. **DIR:** Michael Toshiyuki Uno. **CAST:** Mako, Nobu McCarthy. **1988**

WASHINGTON AFFAIR, THE ★★★ Jim Hawley (Tom Selleck) is an incorruptible federal agent who must award a government contract. Walter Nicholson (Barry Sullivan) tries to blackmail Hawley. There are enough surprises in this film to keep most viewers on the edge of their couch. Rated R for simulated sex. 104m. **DIR:** Victor Stoloff. **CAST:** Tom Selleck, Barry Sullivan, Carol Lynley. **1977**

WATCH IT ★★★ Peter Gallagher stars in this bittersweet drama about a young man who returns to his hometown to attempt a reconciliation with his male cousin. Moving in with the embittered relative and his roommates, Gallagher falls in love with his cousin's girlfriend. Rated R for nudity and profanity. 105m. **DIR:** Tom Flynn. **CAST:** Peter Gallagher, Suzy Amis, John C. McGinley, Jon Tenney, Cynthia Stevenson, Lili Taylor, Tom Sizemore. **1992**

WATCH ON THE RHINE ★★★★ Lillian Hellman's exposé of Nazi terrorism was brought from Broadway to the screen in first-rate form. Paul Lukas won a best-actor Oscar for his role of an underground leader who fled Germany for the United States, only to be hunted down by Nazi agents. Bette Davis is wonderful in what was one of her few small supporting roles. B&W; 114m. **DIR:** Herman Shumlin. **CAST:** Paul Lukas, Bette Davis, Geraldine Fitzgerald. **1943**

WATER ENGINE, THE ★★★½ What happens when an assembly-line worker invents an engine that runs on water for its only fuel is the main thrust of this fine drama written by David Mamet. Greed, back-stabbing, and other selfish motives come into play as word of the engine begins to circulate. Set in Chicago during the 1930's, the film boasts several very good performances and fine production values. 108m. **DIR:** Steven Schachter. **CAST:** Charles Durning, Patti LuPone, John Mahoney, Joe Mantegna, Treat Williams, William H. Macy, Joanna Miles. **1992**

WATERDANCE, THE ★★★★ Eric Stoltz, Wesley Snipes, and William Forsythe are superb in writer-codirector Neal Jimenez's fictionalized retelling of the aftermath of a hiking accident that left him permanently paralyzed from the waist down. Attention to detail, including what must be re-creations of events that happened during Jimenez's period of hospitalization, make for an absorbing, emotional, and often suprisingly humorous story of confronting the unthinkable. Rated R for profanity and violence. 106m. **DIR:** Neal Jimenez, Michael Steinberg. **CAST:** Eric Stoltz, Wesley Snipes, William Forsythe, Helen Hunt, Elizabeth Peña. **1992**

WATERFRONT ★★ Classic film villains John Carradine and J. Carrol Naish are properly menacing as Nazi spies who try to convert German-Americans to their cause in this low-budget wartime espionage drama. Uninspired. B&W; 68m. **DIR:** Steve Sekely. **CAST:** John Carradine, J. Carrol Naish, Terry Frost. **1944**

WATERLAND ★★★★ Jeremy Irons gives a superb performance as an Englishman suffering a nervous breakdown while teaching history at an American high school. At a loss to reach his disaffected students, let alone his increasingly manic-depressive wife, Irons turns to his past in an effort to explain the present. Rated R for nudity and profanity. 95m. **DIR:** Stephen Gyllenhaal. **CAST:** Jeremy Irons, Ethan Hawke, John Heard, Sinead Cusack, Grant Warnock, Lena Headley, David Morrissey. **1992**

WATERLOO ★★ Spectacular action and a confusing plot make a muddled movie. The story of Napoleon's defeat is staged in detail with the deft touch of Russia's Sergei Bondarchuk making it look larger than life. But the characters are cardboard and the dialogue lifeless. 123m. **DIR:** Sergei Bondarchuk. **CAST:** Rod Steiger, Orson Welles, Christopher Plummer, Jack Hawkins, Dan O'Herlihy, Virginia McKenna, Michael Wilding. **1971**

WATERLOO BRIDGE ★★★★ A five-hanky romance about the lives of two people caught up in the turmoil of World War II. This is a poignant tale of a beautiful ballerina (Vivien Leigh) who falls in love with a British officer (Robert Taylor) and how her life is altered when he leaves for the battlefields of Europe. This is one of Leigh's best performances, although she rarely gave a bad one. B&W; 103m. **DIR:** Mervyn LeRoy. **CAST:** Vivien Leigh, Robert Taylor, Lucile Watson. **1941**

WAY DOWN EAST ★★★ Classic story of a young woman ostracized by her family and community was an audience favorite of the early part of this century but old hat even by 1920, when this melodrama was released. Justly famous for the exciting and dangerous flight of the beautiful Lillian Gish across the ice floes, pursued and eventually rescued by stalwart yet sensitive Richard Barthelmess, this was one of classic director D. W. Griffith's last solid critical and commercial blockbusters. Silent. B&W; 119m. **DIR:** D. W. Griffith. **CAST:** Lillian Gish, Richard Barthelmess, Lowell Sherman. **1920**

WAY WE WERE, THE ★★★½ The popular theme song somewhat obscures the fact that this is a rather slow-moving romance about a Jewish girl (Barbra Streisand) who marries a WASPish writer (Robert Redford). The film has its moments, but a portion dealing with the McCarthy Communist witch-hunt falls flat. Rated PG. 118m. **DIR:** Sydney Pollack. **CAST:** Barbra Streisand, Robert Redford, Patrick O'Neal, Viveca Lindfors, Bradford Dillman, Lois Chiles. **1973**

WE ARE THE CHILDREN ★★★ This made-for-television story—about an American doctor (Ally Sheedy) who goes to famine-torn Ethiopia and meets up with a globe-trotting television reporter (Ted Danson)—suffers from preachiness. Despite that, Sheedy and Danson, along with Judith Ivey as a nun, give credible performances that make this a film worth watching. 92m. **DIR:** Robert M. Young. **CAST:** Ted Danson, Ally Sheedy, Judith Ivey, Zia Mohyeddin. **1987**

WEDDING IN WHITE ★★ It's World War II and Carol Kane is the young naïve daughter of an authoritative father who only shows affection for his son. The film succeeds in making you feel outrage, but is bleak from beginning to end. 103m. **DIR:** William Fruet. **CAST:** Donald Pleasence, Carol Kane, Doris Petrie. **1972**

WEDDING MARCH, THE ★★★½ The story is simple: the corrupt, money-hungry family of an Austrian prince forces him to forsake his true love, a penniless musician, and marry a dull, crippled heiress. The telling is incredibly overblown. Critics and big-city audiences acclaimed this film, but it laid eggs by the gross in the hinterlands. Silent. B&W; 140m. **DIR:** Erich Von Stroheim. **CAST:** Erich Von Stroheim, Fay Wray, ZaSu Pitts, George Fawcett. **1928**

WEEDS ★★★ Nick Nolte gives one of his finest performances in this uneven but generally rewarding film as a San Quentin inmate doing "life without possibility" until he secures his release by writing a play that impresses a reporter. Rated R for profanity, nudity, and violence. 115m. **DIR:** John Hancock. **CAST:** Nick Nolte, Lane Smith, William Forsythe, Joe Mantegna, Ernie Hudson. **1987**

WEEKEND AT THE WALDORF ★★★ 1932's *Grand Hotel* updated to World War II and transplanted to New York's classiest hotel. Can't touch the original, of course, but well made and polished to a fine gloss. B&W; 130m. **DIR:** Robert Z. Leonard. **CAST:** Ginger Rogers, Lana Turner, Walter Pidgeon, Van Johnson, Edward Arnold, Keenan Wynn, Robert Benchley. **1945**

WEEKEND WAR ★★ A group of National Guardsmen are assigned to repair a bridge in Honduras near the Nicaraguan border. Effective but bland antiwar drama. 100m. **DIR:** Steven H. Stern. **CAST:** Stephen Collins, Daniel Stern, Michael Beach, James Tolkan, Charles Haid. **1988**

WELCOME HOME ★★★½ This unjustly neglected drama makes ample use of Kris Kristofferson (in perhaps his best performance ever) as a Vietnam soldier presumed killed in action, who fourteen years later turns up in Thailand needing medical assistance. Once back stateside, he learns his wife has remarried. Rated R for language and brief nudity. 90m. **DIR:** Franklin J. Schaffner. **CAST:** Kris Kristofferson, JoBeth Williams, Sam Waterston, Brian Keith. **1990**

WELCOME TO L.A. ★★★½ Extremely well-made film concerning the disjointed love lives of several of Los Angeles's nouveaux riches. The film's focal point is songwriter Keith Carradine, whose romantic interludes set the wheels in motion. Entire cast is first-rate, with Richard Baskin's musical score the only drawback. Rated R. 106m. **DIR:** Alan Rudolph. **CAST:** Keith Carradine, Geraldine Chaplin, Harvey Keitel, Sally Kellerman, Sissy Spacek, Lauren Hutton. **1977**

WELL, THE ★★★ When a small black child becomes trapped in the bottom of a well, the gathering crowd's reactions say a lot about the small town in which they live. Powerful stuff. B&W; 85m. **DIR:** Leo Popkin, Russell Rouse. **CAST:** Harry Morgan, Barry Kelley, Ernest Anderson, Christine Larson. **1951**

WETHERBY ★★½ Buried under *Wetherby*'s dismally portentous attitudes about England and loneliness is a pretty interesting story. The film unfolds like a thriller, but it doesn't satisfy in the end. Vanessa Redgrave in the lead is characteristically excellent. 104m. **DIR:** David Hare. **CAST:** Vanessa Redgrave, Ian Holm, Judi Dench, Marjorie Yates, Joely Richardson, Tom Wilkinson, Stuart Wilson. **1985**

WHALE FOR THE KILLING, A ★★★ Peter Strauss's dramatic, powerful personal statement against the slaughter of whales off the rugged coast of Newfoundland. Based on Canadian environmentalist–nature writer Farley Mowat's noted book indicting the practice. Overlong, but engrossing, TV movie. 150m. **DIR:** Richard T. Heffron. **CAST:** Peter Strauss, Richard Widmark, Dee Wallace, Kathryn Walker, Bruce McGill. **1981**

WHALES OF AUGUST, THE ★★★ The joy of seeing two screen legends, Bette Davis and Lillian Gish, together in a film tailor-made for them is considerably muted by the uneventfulness of playwright David Barry's story. Essentially, we watch Davis and Gish play two elderly sisters who cope, bicker, and reminisce at their summer home on an island off the coast of Maine. Rated PG for profanity. 90m. **DIR:** Lindsay Anderson. **CAST:** Bette Davis, Lillian Gish, Vincent Price, Ann Sothern, Harry Carey Jr., Mary Steenburgen. **1987**

WHAT COMES AROUND ★★ Jerry Reed stars as a world-famous country-western singer who is strung out on booze and pills. Bo Hopkins plays the younger brother who kidnaps Reed to save him from his own self-destruction. This all-American action-comedy-drama features the country music of Jerry Reed. A must-see for his fans. Rated PG. 92m. **DIR:** Jerry Reed. **CAST:** Jerry Reed, Bo Hopkins, Barry Corbin, Arte Johnson. **1985**

WHAT PRICE HOLLYWOOD? ★★★★ This first production of *A Star Is Born* packs the same punch as the two more famous versions and showcases Constance Bennett as a tough but tender girl who wants to reach the top. Lowell Sherman plays the man with the connections who starts Constance on her way, but who eventually becomes a hindrance to her. Bennett seems somehow less martyred and long-suffering than either Janet Gaynor or Judy Garland, and that gives this version an edge that the others lack. B&W; 88m. **DIR:** George Cukor. **CAST:** Constance Bennett, Lowell Sherman, Neil Hamilton, Gregory Ratoff. **1932**

WHAT'S LOVE GOT TO DO WITH IT? ★★★★ The story of Ike and Tina Turner is based on Tina Turner's autobiography and stars two of Hollywood's most respected black performers. Even though biographical films can't rely on surprise elements, they can use strong personalities to advantage. Angela Bassett stars as Tina Turner from her teen years to the present. 120m. **DIR:** Brian Gibson. **CAST:** Angela Bassett, Larry Fishburne. **1993**

WHEN A MAN LOVES A WOMAN ★★★★ A weeper with a cast of pros who make it work. Meg Ryan plays Andy Garcia's alcoholic wife. She gets help, but it takes its toll on their marriage. They try to pick up the pieces, but it's tough on both of them. Rated PG-13 for mature themes. 122m. **DIR:** Luis Mandoki. **CAST:** Meg Ryan, Andy Garcia, C.C.H. Pounder, Tina Majorino, Mae Whitman. **1994**

WHEN HE'S NOT A STRANGER ★★★½ Date rape is sensitively handled in this made-for-TV drama. College freshman Annabeth Gish accepts an offer from popular John Terlesky to come up to his room and get acquainted, but what starts off innocently leads to a harrowing act. Gish must come to grips with the incident and seek the courage to fight back. Kevin Dillon is the friend who lends support. Not rated, but contains adult situations. 90m. **DIR:** John Gray. **CAST:** Annabeth Gish, Kevin Dillion, John Terlesky. **1989**

WHEN LADIES MEET ★★★½ A spasmodically delightful high-society romantic romp. A writer falls in love with her married publisher, much to the dismay of her jealous suitor, who befriends the publisher's wife and invites her to the writer's home for the weekend. B&W; 105m. **DIR:** Robert Z. Leonard. **CAST:** Joan Crawford, Robert Taylor, Greer Garson, Herbert Marshall, Spring Byington. **1941**

WHEN THE PARTY'S OVER ★★★★ Twenty-somethings share a house and some life lessons in this comedy-drama. At the center is Rae Dawn Chong, a successful businesswoman with a disastrous personal life. Though there are several intriguing characters, Fisher Stevens is especially good as a charismatic performance artist. Engrossing, but a bit rough around the edges. Rated R for profanity and sexual situations. 114m. **DIR:** Matthew Irmas. **CAST:** Rae Dawn Chong, Fisher Stevens, Elizabeth Berridge, Sandra Bullock, Kris Kamm, Brian McNamara. **1993**

WHEN THE TIME COMES ★★★ A 34-year-old woman dying from cancer decides to take her own life, much to the dismay of her friends and family. Better-than-average made-for-TV suds, thanks to a strong performance by Bonnie Bedelia. 94m. **DIR:** John Erman. **CAST:** Bonnie Bedelia, Brad Davis, Terry O'Quinn, Karen Austin. **1987**

WHEN THE WHALES CAME ★★★½ Paul Scofield plays a deaf islander known as the birdman because of his fine carvings. Befriended by two village children, the three must save a beached whale that the villagers are hungrily eyeing. Rated PG. 100m. **DIR:** Clive Rees. **CAST:** Helen Mirren, Paul Scofield, David Suchet, Jeremy Kemp. **1989**

WHEN WOLVES CRY 🖤 A 10-year-old boy is diagnosed as being terminally ill. Originally titled *The Christmas Tree*. Rated G. 108m. **DIR:** Terence Young. **CAST:** William Holden, Virna Lisi, Brook Fuller, Bourvil. **1983**

WHEN YOUR LOVER LEAVES 🖤 Valerie Perrine plays the other woman who's just lost out to her lover's wife. Hideous TV movie. 96m. **DIR:** Jeff Bleckner. **CAST:** Valerie Perrine, Betty Thomas, David Ackroyd, Ed O'Neill, Dwight Schultz. **1983**

WHERE ANGELS FEAR TO TREAD ★★★ Although still enjoyable, this is from Forster's less mature first novel, and British director Charles Sturridge fails to find the central core of the story or provide narrative urgency. Sturridge—whose reputation rests largely on his superb *Brideshead Revisited* adaptation for television—also fails to weave the comic and tragic elements into a seamless whole. However, this story of English arrogance and class attitude in Italy offers well-crafted performances, from Helena Bonham Carter (a veteran of three Forster films) and the irrepressible Judy Davis. Unrated. 112m. **DIR:** Charles Sturridge. **CAST:** Helena Bonham Carter, Judy Davis, Helen Mirren, Rupert Graves. **1991**

WHERE LOVE HAS GONE ★★ Hilariously anachronistic throwback to late-1940s "women's picture" histrionics, but the sleaze and vulgarity are vintage 1960s, as Joey Heatherton murders the lover of her mother, Susan Hayward. Adapted from Harold Robbins's novel, which echoed the Lana Turner–Johnny Stompanato killing, and anything else he could think of. Low camp. 114m. **DIR:** Edward Dmytryk. **CAST:** Bette Davis, Susan Hayward, Joey Heatherton, Michael Connors, Jane Greer. **1964**

WHERE THE DAY TAKES YOU ★★ This film switches between recorded interviews with a parolee and his life on the streets of Los Angeles. The viewer comes away feeling nothing for the characters in the film. Rated R for violence, profanity, and suggested sex. 107m. **DIR:** Marc Rocco. **CAST:** Sean Astin, Lara Flynn Boyle, Dermot Mulroney, Peter Dobson, Balthazar Getty, Kyle MacLachlan, Adam Baldwin, Nancy McKeon, Alyssa Milano, Leo Rossi, Rachel Ticotin, Laura San Giacomo, Christian Slater. **1992**

WHERE THE HEART IS 🖤 Mindless drivel about a successful demolition expert's fall from wealth. Rated R for profanity and adult situations. 111m. **DIR:** John Boorman. **CAST:** Dabney Coleman, Joanna Cassidy, Uma Thurman, Christopher Plummer. **1990**

WHERE THE SPIRIT LIVES ★★★ Stirring reenactment of Indian children in Canada being kidnapped and forced to live in terrifying residential schools in which physical, emotional, and sexual abuse were the order of the day. Michelle St. John stars as a defiant newcomer who decides that the only way to survive is to escape. Rated PG. 97m. **DIR:** Bruce Pittman. **CAST:** Michelle St. John, Anne-Marie Macdonald. **1989**

WHITE CARGO ★★½ Hedy Lamarr is Tondelayo, a sultry African native girl who sets about seducing a group of British plantation managers. Considered daring when released, the movie is pretty corny today. Lamarr has never been lovelier, reason enough to give this one a look. B&W; 90m. **DIR:** Richard Thorpe. **CAST:** Hedy Lamarr, Walter Pidgeon, Frank Morgan, Richard Carlson, Reginald Owen, Henry O'Neill. **1942**

WHITE CLIFFS OF DOVER, THE ★★★★ Taking advantage of the patriotic pro-British sentiment of World War II, MGM successfully crafted an all-star, big-budget tearjerker very similar in content and texture to their popular *Mrs. Miniver*. The movie follows Irene Dunne as an American woman who marries into English aristocracy. She and her family are forced to endure the hardships of two world wars. B&W; 126m. **DIR:** Clarence Brown. **CAST:** Irene Dunne, Alan Marshal, Roddy McDowall, Frank Morgan, C. Aubrey Smith, May Whitty, Van Johnson. **1943**

WHITE DOG ★★★ In this adaptation of the Romain Gary novel, Kristy McNichol finds a dog and decides to keep it—unaware that it has been trained by white supremacists to attack black people. An intriguing premise, although not entirely successful in the telling. Rated R for profanity and violence. 89m. **DIR:** Samuel Fuller. **CAST:** Kristy McNichol, Paul Winfield, Burl Ives, Jameson Parker, Lynne Moody, Marshall Thompson, Paul Bartel, Dick Miller, Parley Baer. **1982**

WHITE HUNTER BLACK HEART ★★★★ Director-star Clint Eastwood boldly impersonates flamboyant director John Huston (renamed John Wilson) in Peter Vietel's fictionalized account of the filming of *The African Queen*—during which Huston/Wilson is more interested in shooting an elephant than shooting his movie. Fascinating. Rated PG for profanity and violence. 112m. **DIR:** Clint Eastwood. **CAST:** Clint Eastwood, Jeff Fahey, George Dzundza, Marisa Berenson. **1990**

WHITE LEGION ★★ The White Legion were doctors who fought to find a cure for the yellow fever that plagued workers building the Panama Canal. Unfortunately, their story doesn't make for much of a movie; it's artificially padded with melodramatic situations. B&W; 81m. **DIR:** Karl Brown. **CAST:** Ian Keith, Tala Birell, Snub Pollard. **1936**

WHITE LIE ★★★★ Samuel Charters's *Louisiana Black* gets first-cabin treatment from director Bill Condon and scripter Nevin Schreiner, who send New York mayoral press adviser Gregory Hines to the Deep South to investigate the events that led to his father's lynching thirty years earlier. Hines finds sympathetic pediatrician Annette O'Toole...who may have her own reasons for getting involved. Made for cable, with highly unsettling images and attitudes. Rated PG-13 for mild profanity and mild violence. 93m. **DIR:** Bill Condon. **CAST:** Gregory Hines, Annette O'Toole, Bill Nunn, Gregg Henry. **1991**

WHITE MAMA ★★★ Aging widow Bette Davis, living on a shoestring in a condemned tenement, is befriended by a streetwise black youth (Ernest Harden) and becomes the mother he can't remember when she provides him with a home in return for protection. A good story, touchingly told. Made for TV. 105m. **DIR:** Jackie Cooper. **CAST:** Bette Davis, Ernest Harden, Eileen Heckart, Lurene Tuttle, Virginia Capers. **1980**

WHITE MISCHIEF ★★½ In the early Forties while Britain was being pounded to rubble by German bombs, a group of wealthy colonials carried on with alcohol, drugs, and spouse swapping in Kenya. A stunning backdrop—complete with giraffes roaming in the backyards of opulent mansions—is the film's greatest asset. But James Fox's script is flat. Rated R for language and explicit sex scenes. 100m. **DIR:** Michael Radford. **CAST:** Charles Dance, Sarah Miles, Greta Scacchi, John Hurt, Joss Ackland. **1987**

WHITE NIGHTS (1985) ★★★½ Russian defector and ballet star Mikhail Baryshnikov, finding himself back in the U.S.S.R., joins forces with American defector Gregory Hines to escape to freedom in this soap opera–styled thriller. The plot is contrived, but the dance sequences are spectacular. Rated PG-13 for violence and profanity. 135m. **DIR:** Taylor Hackford. **CAST:** Mikhail Baryshnikov, Gregory Hines, Geraldine Page, Jerzy Skolimowski, Isabella Rossellini. **1985**

WHITE PALACE ★★★ Twitchy, blank-eyed James Spader is a widowed yuppie who slowly falls for burger-slingin' country gal Susan Sarandon. It's one of those movies that is terrific in the early-to-middle scenes and just so-so in the conclusion. Rated R for nudity and profanity. 106m. **DIR:** Luis Mandoki. **CAST:** Susan Sarandon, James Spader, Jason Alexander, Kathy Bates, Eileen Brennan, Steven Hill, Renee Taylor. **1990**

WHITE ROSE, THE (1923) ★★★ Bessie Williams (Mae Marsh) is seduced and abandoned by an aristocratic Southerner (Ivor Novello). Sheer melodrama, although the production is salvaged by the soft-focus photography of Billy Bitzer and Hendrik Sartov. Not one of the major Griffith efforts, its appeal is limited to Griffith purists and silent-film specialists. Silent. B&W; 100m. **DIR:** D. W. Griffith. **CAST:** Mae Marsh, Carol Dempster, Ivor Novello. **1923**

WHITE SANDS ★★★½ Willem Dafoe is a small-town sheriff whose investigation of a murder leads him deep inside an FBI sting. Lots of plot twists and turns will keep viewers interested, although the middle of this film drags a bit. Rated R for violence, profanity, and nudity. 105m. **DIR:** Roger Donaldson. **CAST:** Willem Dafoe, Samuel L. Jackson, Mickey Rourke, Mary Elizabeth Mastrantonio, M. Emmet Walsh, Mimi Rogers. **1992**

WHITE SHADOWS IN THE SOUTH SEAS ★★½ Documentary director Robert Flaherty worked on this South Seas romance (ultimately without credit), which in certain ways is a more conventional dry run for his later *Tabu*. The location cinematography is this turgid soap opera's main strength. B&W; 88m. **DIR:** W. S. Van Dyke. **CAST:** Monte Blue, Raquel Torres. **1927**

WHITE SISTER, THE ★★★ Cheated out of an inheritance, Italian aristocrat Lillian Gish falls in love with an army officer. When he is reported dead, she joins a convent, only to be faced with renouncing her vows when he returns. Only about half of the original film remains, but that's more than enough. Silent. B&W; 68m. **DIR:** Henry King. **CAST:** Lillian Gish, Ronald Colman, Charles Lane, Juliette la Violette. **1923**

WHITE TOWER, THE ★★½ Symbolic melodrama of a weird group of people who attempt the ascension of an Alpine mountain. The action scenes are good, but the actors seem to walk through their parts. 98m. **DIR:** Ted Tetzlaff. **CAST:** Glenn Ford, Claude Rains, Alida Valli, Oscar Homolka, Cedric Hardwicke, Lloyd Bridges. **1950**

WHO KILLED BABY AZARIA? ★★★★ Made-for-Australian-TV version of the true story, told in the American *A Cry in the Dark*, about a woman accused of murdering a baby that she claims was dragged away by a wild dog in the outback. Less polished than the remake, but still compelling. Unrated. 96m. **DIR:** Judy Rymer. **CAST:** Elain Hudson, John Hamblin. **1983**

WHO SHOT PAT? 🦃 A plotless, nostalgic return to the narrator's last year at vocational school and the harsh realities of growing up in Brooklyn. Not rated, but contains profanity and violence. 111m. **DIR:** Robert Brooks. **CAST:** David Knight, Sandra Bullock. **1991**

WHORE ★★ This lurid walk on the wild side is just as harsh, brash, and uncompromising as the title implies. Sensationalism runs rampant as a streetwalker (Theresa Russell) talks directly into the camera between tricks about the intricacies of her profession, and hides out from her knife-wielding pimp. This film exists in both R and NC-17 versions, both due to profanity and explicit sexual content. 92m. **DIR:** Ken Russell. **CAST:** Theresa Russell, Benjamin Mouton, Antonio Fargas. **1991**

WHO'S AFRAID OF VIRGINIA WOOLF? ★★★★★ Edward Albee's powerful play about the love-hate relationship of a college professor and his bitchy wife was brilliantly transferred to the screen by director Mike Nichols. Elizabeth Taylor gives one of her best acting performances as Martha, a screeching bitch caught in an unfulfilled marriage. Richard Burton is equally stunning as the quiet, authoritative professor who must decide between abandoning or salvaging their marriage after a night of bitter recriminations and painful revelations. B&W; 129m. **DIR:** Mike Nichols. **CAST:** Elizabeth Taylor, Richard Burton, Sandy Dennis, George Segal. **1966**

WHO'S THAT KNOCKING AT MY DOOR? ★★★ All the trademark obsessional concerns—women, money, peer pressure—of better-known Martin Scorsese melodramas are evident in this first feature by the distinctive director. Harvey Keitel fumbles violently through his stormy relationship with a free-thinking, elusive young woman while shedding the shackles of strict Catholicism. B&W; 90m. **DIR:** Martin Scorsese. **CAST:** Zina Bethune, Harvey Keitel. **1968**

WHOSE CHILD AM I? 🦃 Artificial insemination is the pitiful excuse for this ridiculously sordid film. 90m. **DIR:** Lawrence Britten. **CAST:** Kate O'Mara, Paul Freeman, Edward Judd. **1974**

WHOSE LIFE IS IT, ANYWAY? ★★★★ Richard Dreyfuss is superb as a witty and intellectually dynamic sculptor who is paralyzed after an auto accident and fights for his right to be left alone to die. John Cassavetes and Christine Lahti costar as doctors in this surprisingly upbeat movie. Rated R. 118m. **DIR:** John Badham. **CAST:** Richard Dreyfuss, John Cassavetes, Christine Lahti, Bob Balaban, Kenneth McMillan, Kaki Hunter, Janet Eilber. **1981**

WHY SHOOT THE TEACHER? ★★★ Bud Cort stars in this intimate and simple film about a young instructor whose first teaching position lands him in the barren plains of Canada. Lean realism and bright dashes of humor give the picture some memorable moments, but this story develops with a disengaging slowness. Rated PG. 101m. **DIR:** Silvio Narizzano. **CAST:** Bud Cort, Samantha Eggar, Chris Wiggins, Gary Reineke. **1977**

WICKED LADY, THE (1945) ★★ Margaret Lockwood's scruples dip as low as her neckline in this somewhat tedious period piece about a vixen who masquerades as an outlaw. James Mason is appropriately evil as her companion in crime. B&W; 104m. **DIR:** Leslie Arliss. **CAST:** Margaret Lockwood, James Mason, Patricia Roc, Michael Rennie, Martita Hunt. **1945**

WIDE SARGASSO SEA ★★★½ Lush, gothic romance, based on Jean Rhys's celebrated novel, acts as a prequel to Charlotte Brontë's *Jane Eyre*. Nathaniel Parker is the Englishman who sets sail to Jamaica for an arranged marriage. His bride, the mysterious and sensual Karina Lombard, leads him on an erotic journey that crosses all boundaries and eventually leads to betrayal. Exotic locales, erotic sex, and handsome leads make this one hot film. Rated R and unrated versions available; both contain nudity and adult situations. 100m. **DIR:** John Duigan. **CAST:** Karina Lombard, Nathaniel Parker, Claudia Robinson, Michael York, Rachel Ward. **1993**

WIFE VS. SECRETARY ★★ Jean Harlow is a super secretary to publisher Clark Gable. Friends and family of his wife (Myrna Loy) convince her that Harlow is kept around for more than efficiency, so she files for divorce. B&W; 88m. **DIR:** Clarence Brown. **CAST:** Clark Gable, Jean Harlow, Myrna Loy, May Robson, James Stewart. **1936**

WILBY CONSPIRACY, THE ★★★½ This underappreciated political thriller tackled the issue of apartheid years before its worldwide recognition as a serious problem. Michael Caine stars as an apolitical Brit who gains social consciousness after encountering an idealistic revolutionary (Sidney Poitier). Somewhat implausible, but entertaining nonetheless. Rated PG. 104m. **DIR:** Ralph Nelson. **CAST:** Michael Caine, Sidney Poitier, Nicol Williamson. **1975**

WILD AT HEART ★★★ One's gag reflex gets a real workout in this off-the-edge movie about a pair of young lovers (Nicolas Cage, Laura Dern) on the run. Director David Lynch, explores the dark side of the American dream in a road picture that often seems to have been written and acted by the inmates of an insane asylum. Rated R for nudity, simulated sex, profanity, gore, and violence. 125m. **DIR:** David Lynch. **CAST:** Nicolas Cage, Laura Dern, Diane Ladd, Willem Dafoe, Isabella Rossellini, Harry Dean Stanton, Crispin Glover. **1990**

WILD DUCK, THE ★★½ Despite the cast, or maybe because of it, this poignant story of love and tragedy falls short of its ambitious mark. Jeremy Irons and Liv Ullmann are struggling parents whose child (Lucinda Jones) is slowly going blind. An idealistic friend (Arthur Dignam) complicates matters by unearthing truths that were better off buried. Derived from the classic Henrik Ibsen stage play. Rated PG for profanity. 96m. **DIR:** Henri Safran. **CAST:** Liv Ullmann, Jeremy Irons, Lucinda Jones, Arthur Dignam, John Meillon, Michael Pate. **1983**

WILD FLOWER ★★ A backwoods family tries to bring a mentally disabled girl (Patricia Arquette) out of her shell to join the rest of humanity. Although somewhat touching, this TV film tries to be all things and ends up never being compelling. 94m. **DIR:** Diane Keaton. **CAST:** Beau Bridges, Patricia Arquette, Susan Blakely, William McNamara. **1991**

WILD GUITAR An exploitative record company gets their comeuppance from hell-raising Arch Hall Jr., a motorcycle-riding rock 'n' roller who couldn't act if his life depended on it. Incredibly bad. 87m. **DIR:** Ray Dennis Steckler. **CAST:** Arch Hall Jr., Nancy Czar, William Watters (Arch Hall Sr.), Cash Flagg. **1962**

WILD IN THE COUNTRY ★★★ Elvis Presley is encouraged to pursue a literary career when counseled during his wayward youth. Most viewers will find it interesting to see Elvis in such a serious role. The supporting cast also—Hope Lange, Millie Perkins, John Ireland, and (especially) Tuesday Weld—add to the okay script. 114m. **DIR:** Philip Dunne. **CAST:** Elvis Presley, Hope Lange, Tuesday Weld, Millie Perkins, John Ireland. **1961**

WILD ORCHID ★★ Mickey Rourke does Rio de Janeiro in this sexual adventure that's as short on provocative eroticism as it is on plot. Screenplay by Patricia Louisianna Knap and director Zalman King. Rated R for language and nudity. 105m. **DIR:** Zalman King. **CAST:** Mickey Rourke, Carré Otis, Jacqueline Bisset. **1990**

WILD ORCHID 2: TWO SHADES OF BLUE ★★★ Not a sequel, but another exploration into the sexual awakening of a young woman. Nina Siemaszko stars as Blue, a teenage beauty sent off to live in a house of ill repute. How she redeems herself nicely offsets the decadence she must endure. Rated R for nudity, violence, and strong language. Unrated version contains more sexual content. The original *Wild Orchid* seems like a timeless classic by comparison. 111m. **DIR:** Zalman King. **CAST:** Wendy Hughes, Tom Skerritt, Robert Davi, Nina Siemaszko. **1992**

WILD ORCHIDS ★★★ A beautiful, young Greta Garbo is the highlight of this familiar story of tropic love. Plantation owner Lewis Stone busies himself with overseeing his property in Java, but local prince Nils Asther finds himself overseeing the owner's wife and the usual complications ensue. Silent. B&W; 103m. **DIR:** Sidney Franklin. **CAST:** Greta Garbo, Lewis Stone, Nils Asther. **1928**

WILD PARTY, THE (1929) ★★★ Legendary silent star Clara Bow, the "It" girl, made her talkie debut in this fast-paced story of a sexy, uninhibited college coed. Critics panned the film, but the public loved it, finding Bow's Brooklyn accent perfectly suited to her vivacious personality. B&W; 76m. **DIR:** Dorothy Arzner. **CAST:** Clara Bow, Fredric March, Jack Oakie. **1929**

WILD PARTY, THE (1975) ★★★½ This is a very grim look at how Hollywood treats its fading stars. James Coco plays a one-time comedy star trying to come back with a hit film. Raquel Welch plays Coco's girlfriend who plans a party for Hollywood's elite in order to push his film. The film is based on the career of Fatty Arbuckle. Rated R. 107m. **DIR:** James Ivory. **CAST:** James Coco, Raquel Welch, Perry King, David Dukes. **1975**

WILD RIDE, THE Early Jack Nicholson. Here he appears as a hedonistic hot-rodder who casually kills people. B&W; 63m. **DIR:** Harvey Berman. **CAST:** Jack Nicholson, Robert Bean. **1960**

WILD ROSE ★★ This low-budget film, shot in and around the Minnesota iron ore fields, floats between being a love story and a social commentary on mining conditions. By trying to cover all the bases, writer-director John Hanson fails to cover even one satisfactorily. 96m. **DIR:** John Hanson. **CAST:** Lisa Eichhorn, Tom Bower. **1984**

WILD THING ★★★½ Screenwriter (and sometimes director) John Sayles creates another wonderfully offbeat tale: A young boy witnesses the murder of his parents and escapes to grow up in the streets of New York as kind of an urban Tarzan. Lots of fun. Rated PG-13 for violence. 92m. **DIR:** Max Reid. **CAST:** Rob Knepper, Kathleen Quinlan, Robert Davi, Betty Buckley. **1987**

WILDFIRE (1988) ★★½ When a bank robbery goes wrong, a teen groom is imprisoned for eight years. In his absence his pregnant bride remarries a wealthy man. The imprisoned man returns for his woman with predictably disastrous results. Rated PG for profanity. 98m. **DIR:** Zalman King. **CAST:** Steven Bauer, Linda Fiorentino, Will Patton, Marshall Bell. **1988**

WILL, G. GORDON LIDDY ★★★½ Robert Conrad is transformed into the fanatic, strong-willed Watergate mastermind Liddy. The first half lacks excitement or revelation. Liddy's stay in prison, however, is a fascinating study. 100m. **DIR:** Robert Leiberman. **CAST:** Robert Conrad, Katherine Cannon, Gary Bayer, James Rebhorn. **1982**

WILLA ★★½ Made-for-TV movie has something of a cult reputation for feminist themes, but it's a pretty standard drama about a waitress who wants to become a trucker. 95m. **DIR:** Joan Darling, Claudio Guzman. **CAST:** Deborah Raffin, Clu Gulager, Cloris Leachman, Diane Ladd, Nancy Marchand, John Amos, Hank Williams Jr., Corey Feldman. **1979**

WILMA ★★½ This made-for-TV film chronicles the early years of Olympic star Wilma Rudolph (Cicely Tyson) and follows her career up to her winning the gold. Film fails to do justice to its subject matter. Lackluster production. 100m. **DIR:** Bud Greenspan. **CAST:** Cicely Tyson, Shirley Jo Finney, Joe Seneca, Jason Bernard. **1977**

WILSON ★★★★½ Outstanding film biography of the adult years of Woodrow Wilson (Alexander Knox) as dean of Princeton, governor of New Jersey, and president of the United States, with emphasis on World War I and his later determination to join the League of Nations. Winner of five Oscars, including Lamar Trotti's screenplay, with nominations for best picture, Knox's portrayal, and Henry King's direction. 154m. **DIR:** Henry King. **CAST:** Alexander Knox, Charles Coburn, Geraldine Fitzgerald, Thomas Mitchell, Ruth Nelson, Cedric Hardwicke, Vincent Price, William Eythe. **1944**

WIND, THE (1928) ★★★★ A gentle girl marries a brutish farmhand in order to escape from relatives who do not understand her sensitive nature. She finds no peace. As the girl, Lillian Gish joined Victor Seastrom (né Sjöström) in scoring an artistic triumph. An incredible film. Silent. B&W; 82m. **DIR:** Victor Sjöström. **CAST:** Lillian Gish, Lars Hanson, Montagu Love. **1928**

WINDMILLS OF THE GODS ★★★ Author Sidney Sheldon's bestselling novel gets the small-screen treatment, with mixed results. There's plenty to look at, from exotic locales, to Jaclyn Smith as a lady professor assigned as Ambassador to Romania. Cast is likable, locations are great, but film suffers from melodrama-itis. 95m. **DIR:** Lee Philips. **CAST:** Jaclyn Smith, Robert Wagner, Franco Nero, Ruby Dee, Ian McKellen. **1987**

WINDOM'S WAY ★★★ In this British drama set on an island in the Far East, a struggle ensues between the natives and plantation owners over civil rights. A doctor (Peter Finch) is enlisted as the spokesperson for the natives. Set against the backdrop of World War II, *Windom's Way* is enjoyable entertainment. 104m. **DIR:** Ronald Neame. **CAST:** Peter Finch, Mary Ure, Natasha Parry, Robert Flemyng, Michael Hordern, Marne Maitland, Gregoire Aslan. **1957**

WINDS OF JARRAH, THE ★★ At the close of World War II, an Englishwoman on the rebound from a bad love affair takes a position in Australia as a nanny. Her employer is a bitter, lonely man who hates women. Readers of paperback romances will guess what happens within the first two minutes, and the rest of the audience won't be far behind. Not rated. 78m. **DIR:** Mark Egerton. **CAST:** Terence Donovan, Sue Lyon, Harold Hopkins. **1983**

WINDS OF KITTY HAWK, THE ★★★★ This made-for-TV movie is beautifully photographed, quietly acted, and gives a wonderful insight into the lives of the Wright brothers and the period in which they lived. A treat for the entire family. 100m. **DIR:** E. W. Swackhamer. **CAST:** Michael Moriarty, David Huffman, Kathryn Walker. **1978**

WINDS OF WAR, THE ★★★½ Mega WWII epic follows the lives of a naval officer turned ambassador to Germany (Robert Mitchum) and his family from 1939 to 1941 with Hitler's conquests as a backdrop. Originally a TV miniseries, this adaptation of Herman Wouk's novel spared no expense in production and features dozens of well-known stars. 880m. **DIR:** Dan Curtis. **CAST:** Robert Mitchum, Polly Bergen, Jan-Michael Vincent, Ali MacGraw, John Houseman. **1983**

WINDY CITY ★★ Very uneven, very frustrating attempt to chronicle the story of a group of young adults who have known one another since they were kids. It has the feel of being based on real-life experiences but is embarrassingly true to rude and off-putting behavior most people would rather have private memories of. Rated R. 103m. **DIR:** Armyan Bernstein. **CAST:** John Shea, Kate Capshaw, Josh Mostel, Jeffrey DeMunn, Lewis J. Stadlen, James Sutorius. **1984**

WINGS OF EAGLES, THE ★★★★ An often moving bio-pic about navy-flier-turned-screenwriter Frank "Spig" Wead *(They Were Expendable)*, this film features fine dramatic performances from John Wayne and Maureen O'Hara. Features the usual John Ford elements of sentimentality and brawling slapstick, but there's also an underlying poignance that makes this a treat. 107m.

DIR: John Ford. **CAST:** John Wayne, Maureen O'Hara, Dan Dailey, Ward Bond, Ken Curtis, Edmund Lowe, Kenneth Tobey. **1957**

WINNING TEAM, THE ★★ This film biography of baseball pitcher Grover Cleveland Alexander would have worked better with a different cast. Ronald Reagan's inept acting is a distraction. B&W; 99m. **DIR:** Lewis Seiler. **CAST:** Doris Day, Ronald Reagan, Frank Lovejoy, Russ Tamblyn, Eve Miller, James Millican. **1952**

WINSLOW BOY, THE ★★★★ Robert Donat is superb as the proper British barrister defending a young naval cadet, wrongly accused of theft, against the overbearing pomp and indifferent might of the Crown. At stake in this tense Edwardian courtroom melodrama is the long-cherished and maintained democratic right to be regarded as innocent until proven guilty by a fair trial. Based on an actual 1912 case. B&W; 118m. **DIR:** Anthony Asquith. **CAST:** Robert Donat, Margaret Leighton, Cedric Hardwicke, Basil Radford, Frank Lawton, Wilfrid Hyde-White, Neil North. **1950**

WINTER KILLS ★★★★ An all-star cast is featured in this sometimes melodramatic, but often wry, account of a presidential assassination. Rated R. 97m. **DIR:** William Richert. **CAST:** Jeff Bridges, John Huston, Belinda Bauer, Richard Boone, Anthony Perkins, Toshiro Mifune, Sterling Hayden, Eli Wallach, Ralph Meeker, Dorothy Malone, Tomas Milian, Elizabeth Taylor. **1979**

WINTER MEETING ★★½ Talky, slow-moving story of a spinsterish writer falling for a war hero, learning he plans to join the priesthood. Jim Davis's debut. B&W; 115m. **DIR:** Bretaigne Windust. **CAST:** Bette Davis, Jim Davis, Janis Paige, John Hoyt, Florence Bates. **1948**

WINTER OF OUR DREAMS ★★ An all-too-typical soaper about a married man (Bryan Brown) who tries to help a lost soul (Judy Davis). This downbeat film has good acting but less-than-adequate direction. Rated R. 90m. **DIR:** John Duigan. **CAST:** Judy Davis, Bryan Brown, Cathy Downes. **1981**

WINTER PEOPLE ★★★½ Kelly McGillis's outstanding performance in this drama elevates what is essentially a Hatfields-and-McCoys rehash. Kurt Russell stars as a clock maker in the Depression who ends up in the Blue Ridge Mountains, where unwed mother McGillis is about to stir up the feudin' locals. Somehow, director Ted Kotcheff and his cast help us forget how silly *Winter People* is for most of its running time. Rated PG-13 for violence. 110m. **DIR:** Ted Kotcheff. **CAST:** Kurt Russell, Kelly McGillis, Lloyd Bridges, Mitchell Ryan. **1989**

WINTERSET ★★½ Heavy-duty drama of a bitter young man's efforts to clear his father's name boasts a great cast of distinguished character actors and marks the screen debut of the versatile Burgess Meredith. Long on moralizing and short on action. B&W; 78m. **DIR:** Alfred Santell. **CAST:** Burgess Meredith, Margo, Eduardo Ciannelli, John Carradine, Paul Guilfoyle, Stanley Ridges, Mischa Auer. **1936**

WIRED 🦃 John Belushi (Michael Chiklis) clambers from a body bag in the morgue after his fatal drug overdose and is escorted through his past by a Puerto Rican angel/cabbie (Ray Sharkey). Rated R. 112m. **DIR:** Larry Peerce. **CAST:** Michael Chiklis, J. T. Walsh, Patti D'Arbanville, Alex Rocco, Ray Sharkey. **1989**

WISE BLOOD ★★★★ While there are many laughs in this fascinating black comedy about a slow-witted country boy (Brad Dourif) who decides to become a man of the world, they tend to stick in your throat. This searing satire on southern do-it-yourself religion comes so close to the truth, it is almost painful to watch at times. Rated PG. 108m. **DIR:** John Huston. **CAST:** Brad Dourif, Harry Dean Stanton, Ned Beatty, Amy Wright, Dan Shor. **1979**

WITHOUT WARNING: THE JAMES BRADY STORY ★★★★ Scripter Robert Bolt, drawing from Mollie Dickenson's book *Thumbs Up*, provides Beau Bridges with a plum role. He's absolutely splendid as press secretary James Brady in this TV-movie recreation of John Hinckley's assassination attempt on Ronald Reagan, which left the president wounded and Brady crippled for life. As the self-avowed "North American brown bear" of the media, Bridges transcends the role and virtually *becomes* Jim Brady. 120m. **DIR:** Michael Toshiyuki Uno. **CAST:** Beau Bridges, Joan Allen, Bryan Clark, Steven Flynn, David Strathairn. **1991**

WIVES UNDER SUSPICION ★★★ Fanatical district attorney whose sole purpose in life is executing murderers is slapped into reality when a case he is prosecuting bears an uneasy similarity to his own situation at home. Warren William is fine as the zealous avenger, and Gail Patrick shines as his ignored and restless wife. B&W; 68m. **DIR:** James Whale. **CAST:** Warren William, Gail Patrick, William Lundigan, Constance Moore, Ralph Morgan, Samuel S. Hinds. **1938**

WIZARD OF LONELINESS, THE ★★★½ After his mom dies and his dad goes off to war (World War II), young Wendall Oler (Lukas Haas) is forced to live with his grandparents, aunt, uncle, and cousin. Good acting and excellent Forties sets and costumes add to John Nichols's thought-provoking novel. Rated PG-13 for violence and profanity. 110m. **DIR:** Jenny Bowen. **CAST:** Lukas Haas, Lea Thompson, John Randolph, Anne Pitoniak. **1988**

WOMAN CALLED GOLDA, A ★★★½ Ingrid Bergman won an Emmy for her outstanding performance as Israeli Prime Minister Golda Meir. Leonard Nimoy costars in this highly watchable film, which was originally made for TV. 200m. **DIR:** Alan Gibson. **CAST:** Ingrid Bergman, Judy Davis, Leonard Nimoy. **1982**

WOMAN CALLED MOSES, A ★★★ Cicely Tyson plays Harriet Tubman to perfection in this made-for-TV dramatization of her life. Unfortunately, this TV movie is soured by unnecessary narration by Orson Welles. 200m. **DIR:** Paul Wendkos. **CAST:** Cicely Tyson, Will Geer, Robert Hooks, James Wainwright, Hari Rhodes. **1978**

WOMAN HER MEN AND HER FUTON, A 🦃 Pointless film about a shallow woman who uses men for sex, money, and her career. She's so insipid and unsympathetic that it's painful to watch. Rated R for nudity, suggested sex, and profanity. 92m. **DIR:** Mussef Sibay. **CAST:** Jennifer Rubin, Lance Edwards, Grant Show, Robert Lipton. **1991**

WOMAN OF AFFAIRS, A ★★★ Young woman with wild tendencies loses her true love and enters into a disastrous marriage. Watered-down version of Michael Arelen's *The Green Hat*. Greta Garbo steals the show. Silent with synchronized score and effects. B&W; 90m. **DIR:** Clarence Brown. **CAST:** Greta Garbo, John Gilbert, Lewis Stone, Johnny Mack Brown, Douglas Fairbanks Jr., Hobart Bosworth. **1928**

WOMAN OF PARIS, A ★★★★ In this now-classic silent, a simple country girl (Edna Purviance) goes to Paris and becomes the mistress of a wealthy philanderer (Adolphe Menjou). In her wake follow her artist sweetheart and his mother. Director Charles Chaplin surprised everyone with this film by suddenly forsaking, if only momentarily, his Little Tramp comedy for serious caustic drama. B&W; 112m. **DIR:** Charles Chaplin. **CAST:** Edna Purviance, Adolphe Menjou, Henry Bergman. **1923**

WOMAN OF SUBSTANCE, A ★★★½ This TV miniseries retells Barbara Taylor Bradford's bestselling novel of love and revenge. Multimillionairess Emma Hart (Deborah Kerr) recalls her humble beginnings as a poor servant girl (Jenny Seagrove). Due to the length of this film it's broken down into three volumes (tapes). Volume I ("A Nest of Vipers") finds young Emma employed by the wealthy Fairleys. Volume II ("Fighting for the Dream") centers around Emma's struggle to survive in a new city, building a business for herself. In the final volume ("The Secret Is Revealed"), Emma finds the love of her life. Overall, this is fine entertainment. 300m. **DIR:** Don Sharp. **CAST:** Jenny Seagrove, Deborah Kerr, Barry Bostwick, John Mills, Barry Morse. **1984**

WOMAN REBELS, A ★★★★ Surprisingly valid today despite its 1936 vintage. Katharine Hepburn plays a rebellious woman of Victorian England who flaunts convention and becomes a fighter for women's rights. Van Heflin makes his film debut. B&W; 88m. **DIR:** Mark Sandrich. **CAST:** Katharine Hepburn, Herbert Marshall, Donald Crisp, Elizabeth Allan, Van Heflin. **1936**

WOMAN TIMES SEVEN ★★ Shirley MacLaine assays seven different roles in this episodic stew and is not as good as she could have been in any of them. There are some funny moments, but they do not a film make. 99m. **DIR:** Vittorio De Sica. **CAST:** Shirley MacLaine, Peter Sellers, Alan Arkin, Rossano Brazzi, Robert Morley, Michael Caine, Vittorio Gassman, Anita Ekberg. **1967**

WOMAN UNDER THE INFLUENCE, A ★★★★ Gena Rowlands is fascinating as a housewife mother swinging back and forth over the edge of insanity, with mood changes from vamp to childlike innocence. Peter Falk is her husband, trying to cope and be understanding, but often lashing out in utter frustration. The movie has been designated a "National Treasure" by the National Film Registry of the Library of Congress. Rated R for adult situations. 147m. **DIR:** John Cassavetes. **CAST:** Gena Rowlands, Peter Falk. **1974**

WOMAN WITH A PAST ★★★½ Forced to flee an abusive marriage with her two children, Pamela Reed (in a stellar performance) takes some drastic measures and becomes a fugitive of the law. After she establishes another identity, federal agents come knocking at her door and her perfect world begins to crumble. Torn from today's headlines, this film is a tour de force for Reed. Rated R for violence, language, and adult situations. 95m. **DIR:** Mimi Leder. **CAST:** Pamela Reed, Dwight Schultz, Richard Linebeck, Carrie Snodgress, Paul LeMat. **1994**

WOMAN'S FACE, A ★★★½ Joan Crawford is the heroine accused of villain Conrad Veidt's murder. Her personality undergoes an amazing transformation following plastic surgery in this taut, strongly plotted melodrama. B&W; 105m. **DIR:** George Cukor. **CAST:** Joan Crawford, Conrad Veidt, Melvyn Douglas, Osa Massen, Reginald Owen, Albert Basserman, Marjorie Main, Charles Quigley, Henry Daniell, George Zucco, Robert Warwick. **1941**

WOMAN'S TALE, A ★★★★★ A superb film from the highly individual Australian director, Paul Cox. It focuses on Martha, a modern, young-at-heart, fiercely independent woman, trapped in an 80-year-old body. This sensitive, humane, and gently profound film portrays Martha as she approaches the end of her life, refusing to give in to cynicism. Unrated. 94m. **DIR:** Paul Cox. **CAST:** Sheila Florance, Norman Kaye. **1992**

WOMEN & MEN: STORIES OF SEDUCTION ★★★★ Three short vignettes, adapted for HBO from noted American short stories, are given first-cabin treatment by cast and crew alike. Ernest Hemingway's "Hills Like White Elephants" is by far the best, with James Woods (as a Hemingway surrogate) and Melanie Griffith trying to pretend their relationship will continue unchanged after she has an abortion. Mary McCarthy's "The Man in the Brooks Brothers Suit" stars Elizabeth McGovern and Beau Bridges. Dorothy Parker's "Dusk Before Fireworks" stars Molly Ringwald and Peter Weller. A class act. 90m. **DIR:** Ken Russell, Frederic Raphael, Tony Richardson. **CAST:** Elizabeth McGovern, Beau Bridges, Peter Weller, Molly Ringwald, James Woods, Melanie Griffith. **1990**

WOMEN & MEN 2 ★★★★ The second entry in HBO's American short story anthology series follows a theme that finds well-meaning men at a crossroads. Carson McCullers's "A Domestic Dilemma" is by far the most poignant and shattering tale here, with Ray Liotta as a compassionate husband and father who cuts short his workdays because he cannot trust his children to the care of alcoholic wife Andie MacDowell. Irwin Shaw's "Return to Kansas City" finds Matt Dillon as a cautious boxer unwilling to take unnecessary risks. Finally, Scott Glenn plays author Henry Miller in "Mara," another of that writer's many bittersweet studies of Parisian streetwalkers. 90m. **DIR:** Walter Bernstein, Mike Figgis, Kristi Zea. **CAST:** Matt Dillon, Kyra Sedgwick, Ray Liotta, Andie MacDowell, Scott Glenn, Juliette Binoche. **1991**

WOMEN IN LOVE ★★★★½ Glenda Jackson won an Oscar for her performance in this British film. Two love affairs are followed simultaneously in this excellent adaptation of D. H. Lawrence's novel. Rated R. B&W; 129m. **DIR:** Ken Russell. **CAST:** Glenda Jackson, Oliver Reed, Alan Bates, Eleanor Bron, Jennie Linden, Alan Webb. **1970**

WOMEN OF BREWSTER PLACE, THE ★★★½ Marvelous made-for-TV soap about black women sharing a tenement and endless problems. Producer Oprah Winfrey comes across as a near saint both in raising her son and helping out the women around her. 195m. **DIR:** Donna Dietch. **CAST:** Oprah Winfrey, Jackée, Robin Givens, Cicely Tyson. **1989**

WOMEN OF VALOR ★★½ This made-for-television feature about a group of army nurses who are captured by the invading Japanese in the Philippines of early World War II is merely average, but the stars raise it up a notch. 100m. **DIR:** Buzz Kulik. **CAST:** Susan Sarandon, Kristy McNichol, Alberta Watson, Valerie Mahaffey. **1986**

WONDERLAND ★★★½ Meandering comedy-drama starts out as a romance between two gay teens, but turns into a thriller after they witness a gangland murder. Too overstuffed to be completely satisfying, though there are many nice bits. Originally known as *The Fruit Machine*. Rated R for sexual discussions. 103m. **DIR:** Philip Saville. **CAST:** Emile Charles, Tony Forsyth, Robert Stephens, Robbie Coltrane. **1988**

WOODEN HORSE, THE ★★★ Good casting and taut direction make this tale of British POWs tunneling out of a Nazi prison camp well worth watching. Made when memories were fresh, the film glows with reality as English cunning, grit, and timing vie with Nazi suspicion, assumed superiority, and complacency. B&W; 101m. **DIR:** Jack Lee. **CAST:** Leo Genn, David Tomlinson, Anthony Steel, Peter Finch. **1950**

WORD, THE ★★★ In a catacomb beneath Ostia, Italy, an archaeologist discovers an ancient manuscript that could cause chaos in the Christian world. The manuscript is said to contain the writings of Christ's younger brother, James the Just. A good story, with wonderful actors. Unrated. 188m. **DIR:** Richard Lang. **CAST:** David Janssen, John Huston, James Whitmore. **1978**

WORKING GIRLS ★★★★ The sex in this feminist docudrama about prostitution is about as appealing as the smell of dirty socks. The story, on the other hand, is compelling, thought-provoking, oddly touching, and often funny. The main character, Molly (Louise Smith), is a Yale graduate who lives with a female lover and is working toward becoming a professional photographer. Unrated, the film has simulated sex, profanity, nudity, and violence. 90m. **DIR:** Lizzie Borden. **CAST:** Louise Smith, Ellen McElduff. **1987**

WORLD ACCORDING TO GARP, THE ★★★★½ Director George Roy Hill and screenwriter Steven Tesich have captured the quirky blend of humor and pathos of John Irving's bestseller. The acting is impressive, with first-rate turns by Robin Williams (in the title role), Glenn Close as his mother, Jenny Fields, and John Lithgow as a kindly transsexual. Rated R for nudity, profanity, sexual situations, and violence. 136m. **DIR:** George Roy Hill. **CAST:** Robin Williams, Glenn Close, John Lithgow, Mary Beth Hurt, Hume Cronyn, Jessica Tandy, Swoosie Kurtz, Amanda Plummer. **1982**

WORLD APART, A ★★★½ Based on a true story, *A World Apart* is an emotionally charged drama about an anti-apartheid South African journalist (Barbara Hershey) who becomes the first white woman to be held under that country's infamous ninety-day detention law. Seen largely through the half-understanding eyes of the woman's daughter. The musical score enhances the searing brutality of this "world apart." Rated

PG. 135m. **DIR:** Chris Menges. **CAST:** Barbara Hershey, Jodhi May. **1988**

WORLD GONE MAD, THE ★★ This features Wall Street types of questionable character versus a district attorney and his investigators during the Prohibition era. A great cast, but the viewer loses interest. B&W; 73m. **DIR:** Christy Cabanne. **CAST:** Pat O'Brien, Evelyn Brent, Neil Hamilton, Mary Brian, Louis Calhern, J. Carrol Naish. **1933**

WORLD IS FULL OF MARRIED MEN, THE ★★ Neglected wife Carroll Baker sets out for revenge on her womanizing husband (Anthony Franciosa) in this pseudofeminist soap opera, written by Jackie Collins at her trashiest. Fun for those who don't take it too seriously. Rated R for sexual situations. 107m. **DIR:** Robert Young. **CAST:** Anthony Franciosa, Carroll Baker. **1979**

WORLD OF SUZIE WONG, THE ★★ William Holden is an artist living a bohemian life in Hong Kong. He falls in love with Nancy Kwan, a prostitute. Tepid and without much action. Nancy Kwan is very good, but she can't save the slow romantic melodrama. 129m. **DIR:** Richard Quine. **CAST:** William Holden, Nancy Kwan, Sylvia Syms, Michael Wilding, Laurence Naismith, Jackie Chan. **1960**

WRESTLING ERNEST HEMINGWAY ★★★½ Robert Duvall and Richard Harris show excellent teamwork in this easygoing drama about a Cuban barber and an Irish sea captain retired to a small Florida town. Director Randa Haines smooths out the aimless spots in Steve Conrad's episodic script, and the acting is first-rate. Sandra Bullock as a kindly waitress all but steals the show. Rated PG-13 for mild profanity. 122m. **DIR:** Randa Haines. **CAST:** Robert Duvall, Richard Harris, Sandra Bullock, Shirley MacLaine, Piper Laurie. **1993**

WRITTEN ON THE WIND ★★★½ Tame by today's standards, *Written on the Wind* still provides quite a few good moments and an Academy Award–winning performance by Dorothy Malone. Rock Hudson and Robert Stack play good friends who meet, respectively, Dorothy Malone who has a problem just saying no and Lauren Bacall who is nice and loves Stack but loves his oil-dipped money even more. High-quality Hollywood soap opera. 99m. **DIR:** Douglas Sirk. **CAST:** Rock Hudson, Lauren Bacall, Robert Stack, Dorothy Malone, Robert Keith. **1956**

WRONG MAN, THE (1993) ★★★★ Raymond Chandler's *film noir* sensibilities blend with Tennessee Williams's earthy sensuality in this delicious drama that finds ship-hand Kevin Anderson on the run for a murder he didn't commit. Things get worse when he encounters bickering John Lithgow and Rosanna Arquette; he's a nasty drunk and she's a cheerfully promiscuous tramp with no morals. A wonderfully eerie Los Lobos soundtrack provides superb counterpoint as the three debase themselves in every way imaginable. 98m. **DIR:** Jim McBride. **CAST:** Rosanna Arquette, Kevin Anderson, John Lithgow, Jorge Cervera Jr. **1993**

WUTHERING HEIGHTS (1939) ★★★★ Taken from the Emily Brontë novel, this is a haunting, mesmerizing film. Set on the murky, isolated moors, it tells the tale of Heathcliff, a foundling Gypsy boy who loves Cathy, the spoiled daughter of the house. Their affair, born in childhood, is doomed. As the star-crossed lovers, Laurence Olivier and Merle Oberon are impressive. B&W; 103m. **DIR:** William Wyler. **CAST:** Merle Oberon, Laurence Olivier, Flora Robson, David Niven. **1939**

WUTHERING HEIGHTS (1971) ★★★½ Inventive but not great rendition of Emily Brontë's classic about the star-crossed lovers, Heathcliff (Timothy Dalton) and Cathy (Anna Calder-Marshall). Dalton is especially good as Cathy's smoldering, abused, and later vengeful love. The 1939 version is still the best. Rated G. 105m. **DIR:** Robert Fuest. **CAST:** Timothy Dalton, Anna Calder-Marshall, Harry Andrews, Hugh Griffith. **1971**

X, Y AND ZEE 🦃 Pointless tale of sexual relationships. Rated R. 110m. **DIR:** Brian G. Hutton. **CAST:** Elizabeth Taylor, Michael Caine, Susannah York, Margaret Leighton, John Standing. **1972**

YANK IN THE RAF, A ★★½ Title is misleading in this story of an American pilot, Tyrone Power, enlisting in the British air force and falling in love with Betty Grable. Standard plot lines and lack of any real action do not help matters in this slow-moving, generally uninteresting film. 98m. **DIR:** Henry King. **CAST:** Tyrone Power, Betty Grable, Reginald Gardiner, John Sutton. **1941**

YANKS ★★★½ Director John Schlesinger re-created classic Hollywood, when smiling men went bravely off to battle while dedicated women stayed behind, in this World War II saga of England's reaction to young American GIs. Richard Gere (who cemented his pretty-boy image with this role) and Lisa Eichhorn handle the primary boy-meets-girl subplot, while William Devane and Vanessa Redgrave embark on a more subdued relationship. Rated R for nudity. 140m. **DIR:** John Schlesinger. **CAST:** Richard Gere, Vanessa Redgrave, William Devane, Lisa Eichhorn. **1979**

YEAR MY VOICE BROKE, THE ★★★★ A likable Australian coming-of-age drama with echoes of *The Last Picture Show* and the novels of S. E. Hinton. Though the film market has been saturated with adolescent dramas circa 1962, this movie's refreshing honesty makes it a welcome addition to the genre. Rated PG-13, with profanity and some mild sexual situations. 103m. **DIR:** John Duigan. **CAST:** Noah Taylor. **1988**

YESTERDAY'S HERO ★★★ Ian McShane plays a washed-up alcoholic ex-soccer star who wants to make a comeback. He gets assistance from his old flame (Suzanne Somers), a pop star, and her singing partner (Paul Nicolas). Not rated. 95m. **DIR:** Neil Leifer. **CAST:** Ian McShane, Adam Faith, Paul Nicolas, Suzanne Somers. **1979**

YOLANDA AND THE THIEF ★★ An exotic fantasy, staged with near-cloying opulence, and now a cult favorite. Down on his luck con man Fred Astaire finds beautiful, rich, convent-bred Lucille Bremer praying to her guardian angel. His eye on her money, he claims to be the angel. 108m. **DIR:** Vincente Minnelli. **CAST:** Fred Astaire, Lucille Bremer, Frank Morgan, Mildred Natwick, Ludwig Stossel, Leon Ames, Gigi Perreau. **1945**

YOU LIGHT UP MY LIFE ★★½ Pretty weak story concerning a young girl, Didi Conn, trying to make it in show business. Notable for the title song, film proves it's tough to make a hit song stretch into a feature film. Rated PG. 90m. **DIR:** Joseph Brooks. **CAST:** Didi Conn, Michael Zaslow, Joe Silver, Stephen Nathan. **1977**

YOU MUST REMEMBER THIS ★★½ Heavy-handed message film exposes the shameful portrayals of black actors in early films. Robert Guillaume delivers a wooden performance as a former film director who could not exploit his black actors. Though not overly entertaining, this—being a Wonderworks Production—is worthy of family viewing and discussion. Unrated; contains no objectionable material. 102m. **DIR:** Helaine Head. **CAST:** Robert Guillaume, Tim Reid, Maria Celedonio, Vonte Sweet, Vonetta McGee. **1992**

YOU ONLY LIVE ONCE ★★ About a three-time loser (Henry Fonda) who can't even be saved by the love of a good woman (Sylvia Sidney) because society won't allow him to go straight. This film is a real downer—recommended for Fonda fans only. B&W; 86m. **DIR:** Fritz Lang. **CAST:** Henry Fonda, Sylvia Sidney, William Gargan, Barton MacLane, Jerome Cowan, Margaret Hamilton, Ward Bond, Guinn Williams. **1937**

YOUNG AND WILLING ★★½ Hope springs eternal in the hearts of a gaggle of show business neophytes living and loving in a New York theatrical boardinghouse. Cute and entertaining, but formula. B&W; 82m. **DIR:** Edward H. Griffith. **CAST:** William Holden, Susan Hayward, Eddie Bracken, Barbara Britton, Robert Benchley. **1943**

YOUNG CATHERINE ★★★ Lavish cable-TV costume drama focuses on the early life of Russia's Catherine the Great and her ascent to the throne. Political intrigue and romance take center stage in this rather lengthy but always interesting film. 165m. **DIR:** Michael Anderson. **CAST:** Julia Ormond, Vanessa Redgrave, Christopher Plummer, Franco Nero, Marthe Keller, Maximilian Schell, Mark Frankel, Reece Dinsdale. **1991**

YOUNG GRADUATES 🦃 Misadventures of a high school girl who falls in love with her teacher. 99m. **DIR:** Robert Anderson. **CAST:** Patricia Wymer, Tom Stewart, Dennis Christopher. **1971**

YOUNG LIONS, THE ★★★½ The impact of love and war on young lives is the focus of this gripping drama of World War II told from the German and American points of view. Marlon Brando is superb as the Aryan soldier who comes to question his Nazi beliefs. Recommended. 167m. **DIR:** Edward Dmytryk. **CAST:** Marlon Brando, Montgomery Clift, Dean Martin, Hope Lange, Barbara Rush, May Britt, Maximilian Schell, Arthur Franz. **1958**

YOUNG LOVE, FIRST LOVE ★★ Boy loves girl, girl loves boy. Does girl love boy enough to go all the way? Nothing better to do? Then watch and find out. Valerie Bertinelli is supercute as the girl. Timothy Hutton is wasted as the boy with the sweats. Unrated. 100m. **DIR:** Steven H. Stern. **CAST:** Valerie Bertinelli, Timothy Hutton. **1979**

YOUNG MR. LINCOLN ★★★★½ Director John Ford's tribute to the Great Emancipator is splendidly acted by Henry Fonda in the title role, with typically strong support from a handpicked supporting cast. This homespun character study develops into a suspenseful courtroom drama for a rousing conclusion. B&W; 100m. **DIR:** John Ford. **CAST:** Henry Fonda, Alice Brady, Marjorie Weaver, Donald Meek, Richard Cromwell, Eddie Quillan, Milburn Stone, Ward Bond. **1939**

YOUNG NURSES, THE ★★ There's more sex than plot in the next-to-last of producer Roger Corman's *Nurse* movies. Look for director Sam Fuller in a cameo as a villainous doctor. Rated R for nudity. 77m. **DIR:** Clinton Kimbrough. **CAST:** Jean Manson, Ashley Porter, Dick Miller, Sally Kirkland, Mantan Moreland. **1973**

YOUNG PHILADELPHIANS, THE ★★★★ In this excellent film, Robert Vaughn stars as a rich young man accused of murder. Paul Newman, a young lawyer, defends Vaughn while pursuing society girl Barbara Rush. B&W; 136m. **DIR:** Vincent Sherman. **CAST:** Robert Vaughn, Paul Newman, Barbara Rush, Alexis Smith, Brian Keith, Adam West, Billie Burke, John Williams, Otto Kruger. **1959**

YOUNG TOM EDISON ★★★½ The first half of MGM's planned two-part tribute to Thomas Alva Edison (followed in months by *Edison, the Man*), geared to a subdued Mickey Rooney as the inquisitive teenage inventor. Mixture of fact and myth presented with respect. B&W; 86m. **DIR:** Norman Taurog. **CAST:** Mickey Rooney, Fay Bainter, George Bancroft, Virginia Weidler, Eugene Pallette, Clem Bevans. **1940**

YOUNG WINSTON ★★★ Rousing and thoroughly entertaining account of this century's man for all seasons, England's indomitable Winston Churchill. The film takes him from his often wretched school days to his beginnings as a journalist of resource and daring in South Africa during the Boer War, up to his first election to Parliament. Simon Ward is excellent in the title role. Rated PG. 145m. **DIR:** Richard Attenborough. **CAST:** Simon Ward, Anne Bancroft, Robert Shaw, John Mills, Jack Hawkins, Robert Flemyng, Patrick Magee, Laurence Naismith. **1972**

YOUNGBLOOD 🦃 Sensitive kid tries to make it in the world of hockey. Rated R for profanity, nudity, and violence. 110m. **DIR:** Peter Markle. **CAST:** Rob Lowe, Patrick Swayze, Cynthia Gibb, Ed Lauter, Jim Youngs, Fionnula Flanagan. **1986**

YUM-YUM GIRLS, THE ★★ Downbeat tale of young women who come to Manhattan to become models, only to discover they're expected to sleep their way into the business. The comic touches seem out of place in this inconsistent exploitation film. Rated R for nudity and sexual situations. 93m. **DIR:** Barry Rosen. **CAST:** Michelle Dawn, Carey Poe, Judy Landers, Tanya Roberts. **1976**

YURI NOSENKO, KGB ★★★½ This ably directed spy drama is based on the transcripts of public hearings, interviews, and published sources relating to the defection of KGB agent Yuri Nosenko in 1964. The filmmakers have filled in the gaps where direct evidence was unavailable. Tommy Lee Jones gives a tremendous performance as CIA agent Steve Daley. Oleg Rudnik is also good as Nosenko. 89m. **DIR:** Mick Jackson. **CAST:** Tommy Lee Jones, Josef Sommer, Ed Lauter, Oleg Rudnik. **1986**

ZABRISKIE POINT ★★½ An interesting but confusing story of a young college radical who shoots a policeman during a campus demonstration in the late 1960s. This film does not really say too much. Rated R. 112m. **DIR:** Michelangelo Antonioni. **CAST:** Mark Frechette, Daria Halprin, Rod Taylor. **1970**

ZANDALEE ★★ A sexually frustrated wife starts an affair with her husband's old friend. Unfortunately, writer Mari Kornhauser did a lousy job with an interesting idea. If you like graphic sex, you will love this film. Available in both R and unrated versions. 100m. **DIR:** Sam Pillsbury. **CAST:** Nicolas Cage, Judge Reinhold, Erika Anderson, Viveca Lindfors, Aaron Neville, Joe Pantoliano. **1990**

ZEBRAHEAD ★★★★½ Michael Rapaport is a white, Jewish kid who is preoccupied with black culture. This low-budget but well-made examination offers a truthful, often funny peek at teenagers in the 1990s and pulsates with a taut undercurrent of anger. Rated R for profanity, violence, and sexual situations. 102m. **DIR:** Anthony Drazan. **CAST:** Michael Rapaport, Ray Sharkey, DeShonn Castle, N'Bushe Wright. **1992**

ZED AND TWO NOUGHTS, A ★★ Bizarre, unpleasant, but beautifully photographed (by Sacha Vierny) oddity about a woman who loses her leg in an auto accident, then becomes involved with the husbands of two women killed in the same wreck. A good deal of frontal nudity earned the film its R rating. 115m. **DIR:** Peter Greenaway. **CAST:** Andrea Ferreol, Brian Deacon, Eric Deacon, Frances Barber, Joss Ackland. **1985**

ZELDA ★★ Silly, contrived drama of F. Scott Fitzgerald's romance and marriage to Zelda. Zelda descends into mental illness while attempting to steer Fitzgerald toward his writing and away from his drinking. Natasha Richardson gives it her all in the title role, but she can't save this drivel. Made for cable TV. 94m. **DIR:** Pat O'Connor. **CAST:** Timothy Hutton, Natasha Richardson, Jon De Vries, Spalding Gray, Rob Knepper. **1993**

ZELLY AND ME ★★ In this drama, we witness the turbulent life of a rich orphan played by Alexandra Johnes. She is overprotected and minus the knowledge of the ways of the real world. Isabella Rossellini and Glynis Johns are outstanding in secondary leads. The basic problem with this film, though, is that we never learn what happens to our orphan. Rated PG. 87m. **DIR:** Tina Rathborne. **CAST:** Isabella Rossellini, Alexandra Johnes, Glynis Johns, Kaiulani Lee. **1988**

ZEPPELIN ★★★ An emotionally wrought Michael York must choose between homeland and duty in this story of a German-born British aviator during World War I. Cast, design, and special effects blend to make this fine fare. 101m. **DIR:** Etienne Perier. **CAST:** Michael York, Elke Sommer, Marius Goring, Peter Carsten, Anton Diffring. **1971**

ZORBA THE GREEK ★★★★ A tiny Greek village in Crete is the home of Zorba, a zesty, uncomplicated man whose love of life is a joy to his friends and an eye-opener to a visiting stranger. Anthony Quinn is a delight as Zorba. Lila Kedrova was to win an Oscar for her poignant role as an aging courtesan in this drama. B&W; 146m. **DIR:** Michael Cacoyannis. **CAST:** Anthony Quinn, Alan Bates, Irene Papas, Lila Kedrova. **1963**

FOREIGN LANGUAGE

A.D. POLICE FILES, VOLS. 1–3 ★★★ Animated spin-off from the *Bubblegum Crisis* series that chronicles the cases of Mega Tokyo's special A.D. Police, who handle ultraviolent crimes. Dark and graphic, this series is not for younger audiences, but animation buffs will enjoy the fine artwork, music, and gritty stories. In Japanese with English subtitles. Not rated; contains violence and nudity. 40m. each **DIR:** Ikegami Takamasa. **1993**

A COEUR JOIE (HEAD OVER HEELS) 🦃 Sixties fluff about a woman torn between two men. Original title in its American release: *Two Weeks in September*. In French with English subtitles. 89m. **DIR:** Serge Bourguignon. **CAST:** Brigitte Bardot, Laurent Terzieff. **1967**

A NOS AMOURS ★★★ Winner of the Cesar (French Oscar) for best film of 1983, *A Nos Amours* examines the life of a working-class girl of 15 (Sandrine Bonnaire) who engages in one sexual relationship after another. In French with English subtitles. Rated R for nudity. 110m. **DIR:** Maurice Pialat. **CAST:** Sandrine Bonnaire, Dominique Besnehard, Maurice Pialat. **1983**

A NOUS LA LIBERTE ★★½ Louis and Emile are two prisoners who plan an escape. Only Louis gets away and, surprisingly, he becomes a rich, successful businessman. There are some slapstick segments, and many believe that this film was the inspiration for Charlie Chaplin's *Modern Times*. In French with English subtitles. B&W; 87m. **DIR:** René Clair. **CAST:** Raymond Cordy, Henri Marchand. **1931**

A PROPOS DE NICE ★★★★★ Brilliant surrealist documentary set in the famed resort town, contrasting the wealthy visitors who come there to play with the poverty-stricken natives. The first of only three films made by Jean Vigo reveals a level of humanism often missing in the avant garde. Photographed by Boris Kaufman, who rightfully deserves to be called the film's coauthor. Silent. 45m. **DIR:** Jean Vigo. **1930**

ABEL GANCE'S BEETHOVEN ★★★★ Originally titled *Un Grand Amour de Beethoven*, this contains some of Abel Gance's finest work with sound, especially in the scene at the Heiligenstadt Mill when Beethoven first begins to lose his hearing. In French with English subtitles. B&W; 116m. **DIR:** Abel Gance. **CAST:** Harry Baur, Annie Ducaux. **1937**

ACCATTONE ★★½ Director Pier Paolo Pasolini's first feature film adapted from his own novel follows the desperate existence of a pimp living in the slums of southern Italy. Lacks emotional depth and raw power. In Italian with (virtually unreadable) English subtitles. B&W; 116m. **DIR:** Pier Paolo Pasolini. **CAST:** Franco Citti. **1961**

ACCOMPANIST, THE ★★½ In Nazi-occupied Paris, a young pianist (Romane Bohringer) works for, and later flees to London with, a famous concert singer (Elena Safonova) and her manager/husband (Richard Bohringer, Romane's father). Lovely pastel photography and wonderful music (Mozart, Beethoven, Schubert, etc.), but it's a bit too measured and deliberate—not even World War II disturbs the tasteful serenity of it all. In French with English subtitles. Rated PG. 111m. **DIR:** Claude Miller. **CAST:** Richard Bohringer, Elena Safonova, Romane Bohringer, Samuel Labarthe, Julien Rassam. **1993**

ACES GO PLACES (1–3) (AKA MAD MISSION 1–3) ★★★½ These high-spirited slapstick spy capers center on a daredevil burglar. Best of the series is number 3, an over-the-top parody of *Mission Impossible* and James Bond. In Cantonese with English subtitles. Not rated; contains some strong violence. 94/100/110m. **DIR:** Eric Tsang, Tsui Hark. **CAST:** Samuel Hui, Sylvia Chang, Karl Maka. **1981–1984**

ACT OF AGGRESSION ★★½ After his wife and daughter are raped and murdered, Jean-Louis Trintignant takes the law into his own hands in this unpleasant Gallic contribution to the *Death Wish* genre. In French with English subtitles. Not rated; contains brief nudity and violence. 94m. **DIR:** Gilbert Pires. **CAST:** Jean-Louis Trintignant, Catherine Deneuve, Claude Brasseur. **1975**

ADORABLE JULIA ★★½ Somerset Maugham tale of a middle-aged stage actress who has an affair with a younger man while her husband waits in the wings. About as original as it sounds, though the cast lends it a bit of charm. Dubbed. Not rated. B&W; 97m. **DIR:** Alfred Weidenmann. **CAST:** Lilli Palmer, Charles Boyer, Jean Sorel. **1962**

ADVERSARY, THE ★★★ Vivid and disturbing account of a college graduate who has been out of work for months. Satyajit Ray's neorealist sense of tragedy is unforgettably dramatized in this heartfelt film. In Bengali with English subtitles. B&W; 110m. **DIR:** Satyajit Ray. **CAST:** Dhritiman Chatterjee. **1971**

AELITA: QUEEN OF MARS ★★★ Deeply esoteric entertainment here. A silent Russian movie concerning a disenchanted man who takes a spaceship to Mars to meet the woman of his dreams. He encounters a proletariat uprising on the planet and realizes daydreams are not all they seem. Silent. B&W; 113m. **DIR:** Yakov Protázanov. **CAST:** Yulia Solntseva. **1924**

AFTER THE REHEARSAL ★★★½ This Ingmar Bergman movie—originally made for Swedish television—is about a director (Erland Josephson) who is approached by a young actress with a proposition: she wants to have an affair with him. In Swedish with English subtitles. 72m. **DIR:** Ingmar Bergman. **CAST:** Erland Josephson. **1984**

AGE OF GOLD ★★★ Filmmaker Luis Buñuel's surrealist masterpiece is a savage assault on organized religion, the bourgeoisie, and social ethics. Salvador Dali contributed a few ideas to the production. In French with English subtitles. B&W; 62m. **DIR:** Luis Buñuel. **CAST:** Pierre Prevert, Gaston Modot, Lya Lys, Max Ernst. **1930**

AGUIRRE: WRATH OF GOD ★★★★ Klaus Kinski gives one of his finest screen performances as the mad, traitorous Spanish conquistador who leads an expedition through the South American wilds in a quest for the lost city of El Dorado. It's a spectacular adventure story. In German with English subtitles. Unrated, the film has violence. 94m. **DIR:** Werner Herzog. **CAST:** Klaus Kinski, Ruy Guerra, Del Negro, Helena Rojo. **1972**

AKIRA KUROSAWA'S DREAMS ★★★★ Celebrated Japanese director Akira Kurosawa delves into his dreams for this episodic motion picture. Like real dreams, Kurosawa's *Dreams* are snippets of situations and ideas. As such, they are often anti-climactic and even frustrating. Yet the images are breathtakingly beautiful. In Japanese with English subtitles. Rated PG. 120m. **DIR:** Akira Kurosawa. **CAST:** Akira Terao, Martin Scorsese. **1990**

ALBERTO EXPRESS ★★★½ When a young man leaves home, his father demands that he repay the costs of his upbringing before he starts his own family. Fifteen years later, with his wife pregnant, the son frantically struggles to find the money before she gives birth. Fast-paced comedy will have you laughing out loud. In Italian with English subtitles. 98m. **DIR:** Arthur Joffe. **CAST:** Sergio Castellitto, Nino Manfredi, Jeanne Moreau. **1990**

ALEXANDER NEVSKY ★★★★ Another classic from the inimitable Russian director Sergei Eisenstein (*Ivan the Terrible*; *Battleship Potemkin*), this film is a Soviet attempt to prepare Russia for the coming conflict with Hitlerian Germany via portrayal of Alexander Nevsky, a thirteenth-century Russian prince, and his victories over the Teutonic knights of that era. As with all state-commissioned art, the situations can be corny, but the direction is superb. In Russian with English subtitles. B&W; 105m. **DIR:** Sergei Eisenstein. **CAST:** Nikolai Cherkassov, Dmitri Orlov. **1938**

ALEXINA ★★½ Confusing erotic tale about a young woman who discovers she's not really a girl, after indulging in a relationship with another woman in this strange concoction of metamorphosis and identity crisis. Pretty baffling. Not rated, but contains nudity. In French with English subtitles. 98m. **DIR:** René Feret. **CAST:** Valerie Stroh, Bernard Freyd. **1991**

ALFRED HITCHCOCK'S BON VOYAGE AND AVENTURE MALGACHE ★★★ Alfred Hitchcock made these two intriguing propaganda films for the war effort and, strangely, they were never released to American audiences. More incredibly, only the first film had a brief theatrical run in France. *Bon Voyage* follows a downed RAF flyer and a Polish POW as they are passed from hand to hand by the French Resistance. In a series of double flashbacks, we find that one of the men is not what he seems. The long unseen *Aventure Malgache* chronicles the tensions in the French colony of Madagascar after the fall of France as a wily lawyer forms an underground organization. In French with English subtitles. B&W; 57m. **DIR:** Alfred Hitchcock. **CAST:** John Blythe, The Molière Players. **1944**

ALI: FEAR EATS THE SOUL ★★★½ Outrageous albeit touching story about a love affair between an old German floor washer and an inarticulate young Arab mechanic. Rainer Warner Fassbinder delicately explores this troubled relationship with deeply-felt humanism and cool irony. Winner of the International Critics' Prize at the Cannes Film Festival. In German with English subtitles. Not rated, but contains profanity and nudity. 94m. **DIR:** Rainer Werner Fassbinder. **CAST:** Brigitte Mira, El Hedi Ben Salem, Rainer Werner Fassbinder. **1974**

ALICE IN THE CITY ★★★ Another road movie from Wim Wenders. While touring the US, a German journalist stumbles upon a precocious 9-year-old girl who has been abandoned by her mother. Excellent eccentric tragicomedy. In German with English subtitles. B&W; 110m. **DIR:** Wim Wenders. **CAST:** Rudiger Vogler, Yella Rottlander, Lisa Kreuzer. **1974**

ALL SCREWED UP ★★★½ Minor but entertaining Lina Wertmuller comedy-drama about farmers confronted with the noise and chaos of life in the big city. Lacks subtlety. Rated PG. Dubbed in English. 105m. **DIR:** Lina Wertmuller. **CAST:** Luigi Diberti, Nino Bignamini. **1976**

ALL THESE WOMEN ★★ A comedy by Ingmar Bergman that is a not-so-subtle attack upon the legions of biographers who were pursuing him. The story is about a deceased cellist, Felix, who (we learn in a series of flashbacks) had been hounded by an erstwhile biographer. Bergman's first exercise in color, the movie suffers from a contrived, episodic structure. In Swedish with English subtitles. 80m. **DIR:** Ingmar Bergman. **CAST:** Bibi Andersson. **1964**

ALLEGRO NON TROPPO ★★★★ An animated spoof of Disney's *Fantasia* by Italian filmmaker Bruno Bozzetto, this release entertainingly weds stylish slapstick with the music of Debussy, Ravel, Vivaldi, Stravinsky, Dvorak, and Sibelius. Rated PG. 75m. **DIR:** Bruno Bozzetto. **CAST:** Animated. **1976**

ALPHAVILLE ★★★ Eddie Constantine portrays Lemmy Caution, French private eye extraordinaire, who is sent into the future to rescue a trapped scientist. It's a Dick Tracy–type of story with sci-fi leanings. In French with English subtitles. 98m. **DIR:** Jean-Luc Godard. **CAST:** Eddie Constantine, Anna Karina, Akim Tamiroff. **1965**

ALSINO AND THE CONDOR ★★ This is an earnest attempt to dramatize the conflict between the Central American governments and the Sandinista rebels in Nicaragua. The film revolves around the story of one young boy caught in the turmoil. Alan Esquivel is Alsino, the boy who escapes into a fantasy world of flight. 90m. **DIR:** Miguel Littin. **CAST:** Alan Esquivel, Dean Stockwell, Carmen Bunster. **1983**

AMARCORD ★★★★★ This landmark film is based on director Federico Fellini's reflections of his youth in a small town in prewar Italy. While celebrating the kinship that exists in the town, Fellini examines the serious shortcomings that would pave the route for fascism. Brilliantly photographed by Giuseppe Rotunno. Italian dubbed in English. 127m. **DIR:** Federico Fellini. **CAST:** Magali Noel, Bruno Zanin, Pupella Maggio. **1974**

AMBASSADOR MAGMA ★★ Dull artistry and an average story make this Japanese animated series rather tedious as Ambassador Magma, a giant golden robot, battles the evil would-be ruler of the universe and his army of weird demons. Dubbed in English. Not rated; contains violence. 70m. **DIR:** Yutaka Maseba. **1993**

AMERICAN FRIEND, THE ★★★★½ Tense story of an American criminal (Dennis Hopper) in Germany talking a picture framer into murdering a gangster. Extremely well-done, with lots of surprises. Cameo appearances by American film directors Sam Fuller and Nicholas Ray. Rated R for language, violence. 127m. **DIR:** Wim Wenders. **CAST:** Dennis Hopper, Bruno Ganz, Lisa Kreuzer, Gerard Blain. **1977**

AMERICAN SOLDIER, THE ★★★ A German-American Vietnam veteran is hired by the Munich police to murder local criminals. Slight but significant early film by Rainer Werner Fassbinder is at once an homage to and a critique of American crime-dramas, particularly as seen by German viewers. In German with English subtitles. Not rated. B&W; 80m. **DIR:** Rainer Werner Fassbinder. **CAST:** Karl Scheydt, Elga Sorbas, Margarethe Von Trotta, Rainer Werner Fassbinder. **1970**

AMORE ★★★★ Director Roberto Rossellini's homage to actress Anna Magnani features her in two short films that showcase her brilliant talent. In "The Human Voice," based on a one-act play by Jean Cocteau, she is alone on-screen, engaged in a telephone conversation with an unseen lover. "The Miracle," inspired by a story by Federico Fellini, features the Academy Award–winning actress in a small masterpiece about a peasant woman who must defend her belief that she has given birth to the new Messiah. It was condemned by the U.S. Catholic church, which resulted in a landmark U.S. Supreme Court decision that films are protected by the First Amendment. In Italian with English subtitles. B&W; 78m. **DIR:** Roberto Rossellini. **CAST:** Anna Magnani. **1948**

AND GOD CREATED WOMAN (1957) ★★½ Brigitte Bardot rose to international fame as the loose-moraled coquette who finds it hard to say no to an attractive male, especially a well-heeled one. Shot with as much of Bardot exposed as the law then allowed, this rather slight story works well. In French with English subtitles. 92m. **DIR:** Roger Vadim. **CAST:** Brigitte Bardot, Curt Jurgens, Jean-Louis Trintignant, Christian Marquand. **1957**

AND NOW, MY LOVE ★★★½ In biography-documentary style, director Claude Lelouch juxtaposes three generations of a family while depicting the moral, political, and artistic events that shaped the members' lives. All this is wonderfully designed to show how inevitable it is for two young people (played by André Dussolier and Marthe Keller) from different backgrounds to fall in love. Dubbed. 121m. **DIR:** Claude Lelouch. **CAST:** Marthe Keller, André Dussolier, Charles Denner. **1974**

AND THE SHIP SAILS ON ★★ Federico Fellini's heavily symbolic parable about a luxury liner sailing the Adriatic on the eve of

World War I was called by one critic "a spellbinding, often magical tribute to the illusions and delusions of art." That's one way of looking at it. We found it boring. However, Fellini fans may find it rewarding. In Italian with English subtitles. 138m. **DIR:** Federico Fellini. **CAST:** Freddie Jones, Barbara Jefford, Victor Poletti. **1984**

ANDREI RUBLEV ★★★★★ Considered by many to be the most important Russian film of the past thirty years, this epic is based on the life of Andrei Rublev, a monk and icon painter who wanders through a gruesome landscape, clinging to religious faith in the face of barbarism and pagan rituals in fifteenth-century Russia, then under the reign of Tartar invaders. Mesmerizing! In Russian with English subtitles. B&W; 185m. **DIR:** Andrei Tarkovsky. **CAST:** Andrej Mikhalkov, Andrei Tarkovsky. **1966**

ANGELE ★★★½ Absorbing character study that blends comedy with drama in a story about a young French girl who becomes bored with life in the country and is lured into a sleazy existence in Paris with an older street hustler. A poignant drama in the tradition of Jean Renoir. In French with English subtitles. B&W; 132m. **DIR:** Marcel Pagnol. **CAST:** Orane Demazis, Fernandel, Jean Servais. **1934**

ANGRY HARVEST ★★★★ This drama from director Agnieszka Holland features Fassbinder veterans Armin Mueller-Stahl and Elisabeth Trissenaar in a mesmerizing thriller about a Jewish woman who escapes from a train bound for the Nazi death camps. The film features brilliant performances. In German with English subtitles. Not rated, but contains nudity and violence. 102m. **DIR:** Agnieszka Holland. **CAST:** Armin Mueller-Stahl, Elisabeth Trissenaar. **1986**

ANTARCTICA ★★ *Antarctica* is the true story of a 1958 expedition. While in Antarctica, Japanese scientists encounter complications and are forced to return home, leaving their team of dogs behind to fend for themselves. The dogs are pretty good naturalistic actors, but you're not drawn to them as you are to the wolves of Carroll Ballard's *Never Cry Wolf*. Dubbed in English. 112m. **DIR:** Koreyoshi Kurahara. **CAST:** Ken Takakura, Tsunehiko Watase. **1984**

APARAJITO ★★★ In the second part of the chronicle of a Bengali family in the Apu trilogy, Apu's father brings the family to the holy city of Benares where his son begins his education and training. Fine ensemble acting. In Bengali with English subtitles. B&W; 108m. **DIR:** Satyajit Ray. **CAST:** Pinaki Sen Gupta, Smaran Ghosal. **1957**

APHRODITE ★★ In 1914, a group of jaded aristocrats meet on a Mediterranean island to reenact a mythological tale involving Aphrodite, the goddess of beauty. Pretty but pretentious soft-core erotica. Dubbed. Not rated; contains nudity. 96m. **DIR:** Robert Fuest. **CAST:** Horst Buchholz, Valerie Kaprisky, Capucine. **1982**

APPLESEED ★★★½ Japanese animation. Two SWAT team officers pursue a terrorist through the experimental city of Olympus in this satisfying tale. More emphasis on story makes this fast-paced, absorbing feature a real gem. In Japanese with English subtitles. Unrated; the film has violence. 70m. **DIR:** Kazuyashi Katayama. **1988**

AQUA E SAPONE ★★½ Would-be teacher, desperate for a job, poses as a priest in order to get a job tutoring a young American model. Bland comedy. In Italian with English subtitles. Unrated. 100m. **DIR:** Carlo Verdone. **CAST:** Carlo Verdone, Natasha Hovey, Florinda Bolkan. **1983**

ARABIAN NIGHTS (1974) ★★½ Pier Paolo Pasolini re-creates some of Scheherezade's original tales in this uneven but breathtaking film. Nudity is plentiful; violence is heavy-handed. In Italian with English subtitles. Rated X. 128m. **DIR:** Pier Paolo Pasolini. **CAST:** Franco Citti. **1974**

ARCADIA OF MY YOUTH 🦃 Captain Harlock and his avengers strike back against alien invaders in this maudlin, epic-length example of Japanese animation—twice the length, twice the incoherence, and more than twice the heroic/tragic death scenes. In Japanese with English subtitles. Not rated; contains violence. 130m. **DIR:** Tomoharu Katsumata. **1982**

ARIEL ★★★★ An out-of-work miner goes on a cross-country trip and encounters a mugging, false arrest, and an unexpected love affair that hints of domestic happiness. This black comedy won the National Society of Film Critics Best Foreign Film award. In Finnish with English subtitles. Unrated; the film has simulated sex. 74m. **DIR:** Aki Kaurismaki. **CAST:** Turo Pajala, Matti Pelloupaa. **1990**

ARMOUR OF GOD ★★★★½ In this big-budget, Indiana Jones–style adventure, archaeologist Jackie Chan agrees to secure the mystical "armour of God" for baddies who have kidnapped his ex-girlfriend. The stunt work and action scenes are phenomenal, even by Chan's high standards. In Cantonese with English subtitles. Not rated; contains comic violence. 98m. **DIR:** Jackie Chan. **CAST:** Jackie Chan, Alan Tam, Rosamund Kwan. **1987**

ARSENAL ★★ This imaginative, symbolic denouncement of war is rich in visual images, but takes too long to make its point. A collection of episodes that take place during the last part of World War I, this Russian offering lacks fire. B&W; 70m. **DIR:** Alexander Dovzhenko. **CAST:** Semyon Svashenko. **1929**

ASCENT TO HEAVEN (MEXICAN BUS RIDE) ★★★ A young man's wedding ceremony is interrupted so he can make a two-day bus journey to get his dying mother's will ratified. On the way, he encounters a variety of hilarious adventures and delays. A good light comedy, punctuated with Luis Buñuel's great surreal touches. In Spanish with English subtitles. B&W; 85m. **DIR:** Luis Buñuel. **CAST:** Lidia Prado, Esteban Marquez. **1951**

ASHES AND DIAMONDS ★★★★ The conflict between idealism and instinct is explored with great intensity in this story of a Polish resistance fighter who assassinates the wrong man at the end of World War II. Director Andrzej Wajda captures all the bitterness and disillusionment of political fanaticism in this powerful testament of the Polish people during the struggle that followed the war's end. In Polish with English subtitles. B&W; 102m. **DIR:** Andrzej Wajda. **CAST:** Zbigniew Cybulski. **1958**

ASSASSINS DE L'ORDRE, LES (LAW BREAKERS) ★★ Marcel Carné, who directed the 1944 classic *Children of Paradise*, slips into innocuousness with this less than riveting tale. Jacques Brel plays a judge who is trying to get to the bottom of corrupt police practices. 107m. **DIR:** Marcel Carné. **CAST:** Jacques Brel, Catherine Rouvel, Michel Lonsdale, Charles Denner, Didier Haudepin. **1971**

ASSAULT, THE ★★★★½ This Academy Award winner for best foreign language film deserves its praise. It is a tale of war and its inevitable impact. In Holland in 1945, a Nazi collaborator is murdered and the lives of the witnesses, a small boy in particular, are changed forever. Dubbed. 126m. **DIR:** Fons Rademakers. **CAST:** Derek de Lint, Marc van Uchelen, Monique van de Ven. **1986**

ASSOCIATE, THE ★★ Disappointing comedy about an unemployed bank clerk who schemes to murder his wealthy business partner. Michel Serrault is the only bright spot in this otherwise muddled comedy. In French with English subtitles. Not rated, but contains nudity and profanity. 94m. **DIR:** René Gainville. **CAST:** Michel Serrault, Claudine Auger, Catherine Alric. **1982**

AU REVOIR, LES ENFANTS ★★★★★ Louis Malle may have created his masterpiece with this autobiographical account of a traumatic incident in his youth that occurred in World War II France. Certainly this heartfelt and heartbreaking work about man's inhumanity to man is likely to remain his most unforgettable creation. Rated PG for strong themes. In French with English subtitles. 104m. **DIR:** Louis Malle. **CAST:** Gaspard Manesse, Raphael Fejto, Philippe Morier-Genoud, Francine Racette. **1987**

AUTUMN AFTERNOON, AN ★★★ Aging buddies discuss the fate of one of the men's daughters in this slow-moving drama. The group decides that an arranged marriage would be best for her. Although the film is dated, it is an often penetrating, insightful look into Japanese society and the era in which it is set. In Japanese with English subtitles. 112m. **DIR:** Yasujiro Ozu. **CAST:** Chishu Ryu, Shima Iwashita. **1962**

AUTUMN SONATA ★★★★★ Ingmar Bergman directed this superb Swedish release about the first meeting in seven years of a daughter (Liv Ullmann) with her difficult concert pianist mother (Ingrid Bergman). A great film. In Swedish and English. Rated PG. 97m. **DIR:** Ingmar Bergman. **CAST:** Ingrid Bergman, Liv Ullmann, Lena Nyman. **1978**

AVANT GARDE PROGRAM #2 ★★★ Fascinating collection of early silent experimental films by French and German surrealists. This program features René Clair's brilliant short, "Entr'acte," with music by Erik Satie, and Eggeling's "Symphonie Diagonale." Also on this program: Man Ray's "L'Étoile de Mer." B&W; 42m. **DIR:** René Clair, Man Ray, Eggeling. **CAST:** Erik Satie, Marcel Duchamp, Man Ray. **1924–1926**

AVIATOR'S WIFE, THE ★★★½ Not much happens in a film by French director Eric Rohmer, at least not in the traditional sense. In this typically Rohmer character study, a young law student (Philippe Marlaud) is crushed when he discovers his lover, Anne (Marie Riviere), in the company of another man and decides to spy on them. In French with English subtitles. Unrated; the film has no objectionable material. 104m. **DIR:** Eric Rohmer. **CAST:** Philippe Marlaud, Marie Riviere, Anne-Laure Marie. **1981**

AY, CARMELA! ★★½ One of Spain's most electrifying stars, Carmen Maura, joins forces with one of her nation's most invigorating directors, Carlos Saura, in this drama about the Spanish Civil War. The film offers insight and entertainment, but it's a mystery why all that electricity generates few sparks. In Spanish with English subtitles. Unrated. 103m. **DIR:** Carlos Saura. **CAST:** Carmen Maura. **1991**

BABETTE'S FEAST ★★★★ Writer-director Gabriel Axel's Oscar-winning adaptation of Isak Dinesen's short story has the kind of wistful warmth that makes it seem like a tale told by a wise old storyteller. It also has a pixilated quality that makes it good fun. The finale is a sumptuous dinner prepared by an expatriate French chef (Stéphane Audran) for a group of devout Danish Lutherans. It may be the funniest meal ever put on screen. In French and Danish with English subtitles. Rated G. 102m. **DIR:** Gabriel Axel. **CAST:** Stéphane Audran, Jean-Philippe Lafont, Jarl Kulle, Bibi Andersson. **1987**

BACKSTAIRS ★★★★ Superb example of the German Expressionist cinema. Its twisted sets and harsh extremes in lighting surround a grim tale of the violence that interrupts the love affair between a chambermaid and her lover. Silent. B&W; 44m. **DIR:** Leopold Jessner. **CAST:** William Dieterle. **1921**

BAD GIRLS (1969) ★★½ Weak erotic drama from Claude Chabrol about a love affair between a petty bourgeois woman and a beautiful young street artist. Poor chemistry among the characters, not one of Chabrol's better films. Lacks passion. Dubbed in English. Rated R for mild nudity. 97m. **DIR:** Claude Chabrol. **CAST:** Stéphane Audran, Jacqueline Sassard, Jean-Louis Trintignant. **1969**

BAD SLEEP WELL, THE ★★★★ A man seeks revenge for the murder of his father in this suspenseful tale of corruption. Akira Kurosawa remarkably captures the spirit of Forties crime-dramas in this engrossing film, based on an Ed McBain story. In Japanese with English subtitles. B&W; 152m. **DIR:** Akira Kurosawa. **CAST:** Toshiro Mifune, Masayuki Mori, Takashi Shimura. **1960**

BAKER'S WIFE, THE (1938) ★★★★ The new baker is coming to a town that has been without fresh-baked goods for too long. With great fanfare, the baker and his new wife arrive, but she has a roving eye. This comedy is a gem. In French with English subtitles. B&W; 124m. **DIR:** Marcel Pagnol. **CAST:** Raimu, Ginette Leclerc, Charles Moulin. **1938**

BALLAD OF A SOLDIER ★★★½ A soldier finds love and adventure on a ten-day pass to see his mother. This import features excellent cinematography and acting, and despite the always obvious Soviet propaganda, some piercing insights into the Russian soul. In Russian with English subtitles. B&W; 89m. **DIR:** Grigori Chukhrai. **CAST:** Vladimir Ivashov, Shanna Prokhorenko. **1959**

BALLAD OF NARAYAMA, THE ★★★★★ Based on one of the most unusual Japanese legends: a century ago in a remote mountain village in northern Japan, a local custom dictated that when a person reached 70 years old they were taken to Mount Narayama to die. A true masterpiece of Japanese cinema and a Grand Prize winner at the 1983 Cannes Film Festival. In Japanese with English subtitles. Not rated, but contains nudity and violence. 129m. **DIR:** Shohei Imamura. **CAST:** Ken Ogata. **1983**

BANANA COP ★★★ Engaging comedy about an Anglo-Chinese Scotland Yard inspector assigned to investigate a Chinatown murder. His wisecracking partner is played by Teddy Robin Kwan, the Eddie Murphy of Hong Kong. In Cantonese with English subtitles. Not rated, but contains violence. 96m. **DIR:** Po-Chih Leong. **CAST:** George Lam, Teddy Robin Kwan. **1984**

BAND OF OUTSIDERS ★★½ Disappointing *film noir* from director Jean-Luc Godard about a robbery that ends in the accidental death of a woman at the hands of her beautiful niece. This existential crime-drama suffers from an incoherent script. In French with English subtitles. Not rated. B&W; 97m. **DIR:** Jean-Luc Godard. **CAST:** Anna Karina, Sami Frey, Claude Brasseur. **1964**

BANDITS (1987) ★★★★ An imprisoned jewel thief sends his daughter to a Swiss boarding school while plotting to avenge his wife's murder. Once free, father and daughter reunite. The romance that develops between the charming daughter and a young thief is surprisingly moving. Superior acting and a plot that twists enough to keep viewers guessing. In French with English subtitles. Not rated, but contains brief nudity and violence. 98m. **DIR:** Claude Lelouch. **CAST:** Jean Yanne, Marie-Sophie Lelouch, Patrick Bruel, Charles Gerard. **1987**

BARITONE ★★★½ In 1933, a world-famous singer returns to Poland for the first time in twenty-five years. The infighting and scheming among his entourage, as well as the local officials, are meant as a parable of fascism, though this well-produced film is more enjoyable as a straightforward soap opera. In Polish with English subtitles. Not rated. 100m. **DIR:** Janusz Zaorski. **CAST:** Zbigniew Zapasiewicz. **1985**

BARJO ★★★ An oddball writer who obsessively catalogs everyday activities moves in with his sister and her husband and drives their emotional difficulties to the breaking point. Barjo's humorous investigations aren't well integrated with the black comedy of an impossible marriage between a man who wants order and a woman who wants "everything and its opposite," but both are amusing. In French with English subtitles. Rated R for sexual implications and discussions. 83m. **DIR:** Jerome Boivan. **CAST:** Hippolyte Giradot, Richard Bohringer, Anne Brochet. **1993**

BASILEUS QUARTET ★★★★★ When their leader dies, the remaining members of a renowned string quartet hire a young violinist to replace him. The presence of this aggressive, virile young man forces the three older men to confront what they have made of their own lives. An intelligent, literary film, flawlessly acted. Dubbed in English. Unrated, contains nudity and sexual situations. 105m. **DIR:** Fabio Carpi. **CAST:** Hector Alterio, Omero Antonutti, Pierre Malet, François Simon. **1982**

BATTLE ANGEL ★★★★ A young cybernetic girl becomes a successful bounty hunter in this animated tale. Outstanding artwork and bizarre characters give life to this cyberpunk adaptation of Kishiro Yukito's wildly successful comic. In Japanese with English subtitles. Not rated; contains nudity and violence. 70m. **DIR:** Hiroshi Fukutomi. **1993**

BATTLE OF ALGIERS ★★★★ This gut-wrenching Italian-Algerian pseudo-documentary about the war between Algerian citizens and their French "protectors" was released when America's involvement in Vietnam was still to reach its peak, but the parallels between the two stories are obvious. Covering the years from 1954 to 1962, this film is an emotional experience—it is not recommended for the casual viewer and is too strong for children. B&W; 123m. **DIR:** Gillo Pontecorvo. **CAST:** Yacef Saadi, Jean Martin, Brahim Haggiag. **1965**

BATTLESHIP POTEMKIN, THE ★★★★★ One of a handful of landmark motion pictures. This silent classic, directed by the legendary Sergei Eisenstein, depicts the mutiny of the crew of a Russian battleship and its aftermath. The directorial technique expanded the threshold of what was then standard cinema storytelling. The massacre of civilians on the Odessa Steps remains one of the most powerful scenes in film history. Silent. B&W; 65m. **DIR:** Sergei Eisenstein. **CAST:** Alexander Antonov, Vladimir Barsky. **1925**

BEATRICE ★★ In creating *Beatrice*, writer-director Bertrand Tavernier set out to demythologize the Middle Ages. He succeeds all too well with this repulsive, nightmarish movie in which the angelic title character (Julie Delpy) is raped and tortured by the demented father (Bernard Pierre Donnadieu) she once idolized. In French with English subtitles. Unrated, the film has nudity, violence, and simulated sex. 128m. **DIR:** Bertrand Tavernier. **CAST:** Bernard Pierre Donnadieu, Julie Delpy, Nils Tavernier. **1987**

BEAU PERE ★★★★ Patrick Dewaere stars again for French director Betrand Blier (*Get Out Your Handkerchiefs*) in this film, about a stepfather who falls in love with his adopted pubescent daughter. It could have been shocking—or just plain perverse. But *Beau Pere* is a bittersweet, thoroughly charming motion picture. In French with English subtitles. Unrated; the film has nudity, profanity, and adult themes. 120m. **DIR:** Bertrand Blier. **CAST:** Patrick Dewaere, Ariel Besse, Maurice Ronet, Nicole Garcia. **1982**

BEAUTY AND THE BEAST (1946) ★★★★★ This French classic goes far beyond mere retelling of the well-known fairy tale. Its eerie visual beauty and surrealistic atmosphere mark it as a genuine original. The tragic love story between Beauty (Josette Day) and the all-too-human Beast (Jean Marais) resembles a moving painting. In French with English subtitles. B&W; 90m. **DIR:** Jean Cocteau. **CAST:** Josette Day, Jean Marais. **1946**

BED AND SOFA ★★★★ During a housing shortage in Moscow a construction worker takes in an old friend. In the ensuing ménage à trois the worker's wife, now pregnant, turns her back on both the men in her life and leaves to make a new life for herself. A startling achievement, without precedent in the Soviet cinema. Silent. B&W; 73m. **DIR:** Abram Room. **CAST:** Nikolai Batalov, Vladimir Fogel. **1927**

BEFORE THE REVOLUTION ★★★½ Bernardo Bertolucci made this political drama at the age of twenty-two. The plot evolves around a young man who flirts with communism, while engaging in an incestuous relationship with his aunt. Great cinematography. In Italian with English subtitles. B&W; 110m. **DIR:** Bernardo Bertolucci. **CAST:** Adriana Asti, Francesco Barilli. **1962**

BEING AT HOME WITH CLAUDE ★★★ Complex, provocative study of the human psyche examines the murder of a young student, and the enigmatic male prostitute who confesses to the crime. During an intense interrogation, the truth about the shocking crime comes out, but not before we're subjected to a harrowing barrage of verbal abuse. In French with English subtitles. Not rated, but contains adult situations and language. 86m. **DIR:** Jean Beaudin. **CAST:** Roy Dupus, Jacques Godin, Jean-François Pinchette, Gaston Lepage. **1992**

BELLE EPOQUE ★★★★ An army deserter hiding out in the Spanish countryside of the 1930s becomes infatuated, one by one, with the four beautiful daughters of a crusty old artist. This eccentric, beautifully photographed movie won the 1993 Oscar for best foreign film. Delightfully ribald, strongly recommended for mature audiences only. In Spanish with English subtitles. Rated R for sexual scenes. 108m. **DIR:** Fernando Trueba. **CAST:** Jorge Sanz, Fernando Fernan Gomez, Ariadna Gil, Penelope Cruz. **1992**

BELLISSIMA ★★★ Luchino Visconti is known for such pioneering works as *Rocco and His Brothers*, *The Damned*, and *Death in Venice*. As for *Bellissima*, if you are programming an Anna Magnani festival, you might be interested in this oddly and determinedly lightweight comedy. The story is set in the Cinecitta Studios, where a search is on for the prettiest child in Rome. In Italian with English subtitles. B&W; 95m. **DIR:** Luchino Visconti. **CAST:** Anna Magnani, Walter Chiari, Tina Apicella. **1951**

BELLISSIMO: IMAGES OF THE ITALIAN CINEMA ★★★ A retrospective of the Italian cinema is explored from the early 1920s to the 1980s through film clips and interviews with various directors and actors. Filmmakers include Roberto Rossellini, Vittorio De Sica, Federico Fellini, Lina Wertmuller, and Sergio Leone. In Italian with English subtitles and English narration. 110m. **DIR:** Gianfranco Mingozzi. **1978**

BERLIN ALEXANDERPLATZ ★★★½ Remember the scene in *A Clockwork Orange* in which Malcolm McDowell's eyes are wired open and he is forced to watch movies? That's how we often felt when wading through the fifteen-and-a-half hours of Rainer Werner Fassbinder's magnum opus, *Berlin Alexanderplatz*. Not that this much-praised German television production doesn't have its moments of interest, and yes, even genius. But as with all of Fassbinder's films, *Berlin Alexanderplatz* also has its excesses and false notes. In German with English subtitles. Unrated. 930m. **DIR:** Rainer Werner Fassbinder. **CAST:** Gunter Lamprecht, Hanna Schygulla, Barbara Sukowa. **1983**

BEST INTENTIONS, THE ★★★★ Originally a six-hour miniseries for television, this Swedish import was cut almost in half for international theatrical distribution. However, Ingmar Bergman's story, set in 1909 and concerning the courtship and early years of his parents' marriage, remains intact, with the characterizations and situations fully explored. In Swedish with English subtitles. 186m. **DIR:** Bille August. **CAST:** Samuel Froler, Pernilla August, Max von Sydow. **1992**

BETTER TOMORROW, A ★★★½ Director John Woo reinvented the Hong Kong action film and began to attract world attention with this forceful melodrama that combines the action of classic Warner Brothers gangster films with the cynical sentimentality of spaghetti Westerns. In a supporting role, future star Chow Yun-Fat steals the movie. In Cantonese with English subtitles. Not rated; contains strong violence. 95m. **DIR:** John Woo. **CAST:** Leslie Cheung, Ti Lung, Chow Yun-Fat. **1986**

BETTER TOMORROW 2, A ★★★★½ The plot's tough to follow, and the subtitles are atrocious, but the high humor, unabashed melodrama, and roaring finale make this an action classic. Chow Yun-Fat duking it out with mafiosi in a Manhattan Chinese restaurant is a true delight. In Cantonese with English subtitles. Not rated; contains very strong violence. 100m. **DIR:** John Woo. **CAST:** Chow Yun-Fat, Leslie Cheung, Ti Lung. **1987**

BETTER TOMORROW 3, A: LOVE AND DEATH IN SAIGON ★★★½ This prequel set during the fall of Saigon has little to do with the two previous *Better Tomorrows*. Producer-director Tsui Hark is known for his incredible visual flamboyance and his interest in recent Asian history. This film features more of the latter, but action fans won't be displeased. In Cantonese with English subtitles. Not rated; contains strong violence. 100m. **DIR:** Tsui Hark. **CAST:** Chow Yun-Fat, Anita Mui, Tony Leung. **1987**

BETTY BLUE ★★ *Betty Blue* is about Betty, who is radically spontaneous and a bit wacko (we don't know why), and Zorg, the man she inspires to continue writing. The trick is not to think too much but instead to bask in Jean-Jacques Beineix's sensuous visual flair. In French with English subtitles. Rated R. 117m. **DIR:** Jean-Jacques Beineix. **CAST:** Jean-Hugues Anglade, Beatrice Dalle. **1986**

BEYOND FEAR ★★★ A man's wife and child are taken hostage by a band of outlaws, and he must work with the police to ensure the safety of his family in this compelling film. Rated R by mid-1970s standards due to violence and profanity (very little of both, actually). 92m. **DIR:** Yannick Andrei. **CAST:** Michel Bouquet, Michael Constantine, Marilu Tolo. **1975**

BEYOND OBSESSION ★★ Marcello Mastroianni and Eleonora Giorgi are strange bedfellows for American Tom Berenger in this confusing Italian film about hustling, obsession, and seduction. Dubbed. Not rated, has profanity and nudity. 116m. **DIR:** Liliana Cavani. **CAST:** Tom Berenger, Marcello Mastroianni, Eleonora Giorgi, Michel Piccoli. **1982**

BEYOND THE WALLS ★★½ This Israeli film pits Jewish and Arab convicts against each other with explosive consequences. A standard prison drama. Nominated for a best foreign film Oscar, it lost to *Dangerous Moves*. 103m. **DIR:** Uri Barbash. **CAST:** Arnon Zadok, Muhamad Bakri. **1984**

BICYCLE THIEF, THE ★★★★ Considered by critics an all-time classic, this touching, honest, beautifully human film speaks realistically to the heart with simple cinematic eloquence. A billposter's bicycle, on which his job depends, is stolen. Ignored by the police, who see nothing special in the loss, the anguished worker and his young son search Rome for the thief. In Italian with English subtitles. B&W; 90m. **DIR:** Vittorio De Sica. **CAST:** Lamberto Maggiorani, Lianella Carell, Enzo Staiola. **1949**

BIG DEAL ON MADONNA STREET ★★★★ Mario Monicelli directed this tale as a classic spoof of the perfect-crime film that depicts in great detail the elaborate planning and split-second timing involved in huge thefts. Monicelli's characters—who are attempting to burglarize a safe—also formulate intricate plans and employ precise timing, but everything they do results in humiliating disaster—providing a hilarious comedy of errors. In Italian with English subtitles. B&W; 91m. **DIR:** Mario Monicelli. **CAST:** Marcello Mastroianni, Vittorio Gassman, Toto, Renato Salvatori, Claudia Cardinale. **1960**

BILITIS ★★★★ A surprisingly tasteful and sensitive soft-core sex film, this details the sexual awakening of the title character, a 16-year-old French girl, while she spends the summer with a family friend. Rated R for nudity and simulated sex. 93m. **DIR:** David Hamilton. **CAST:** Patti D'Arbanville, Bernard Giraudeau, Mathieu Carriere. **1982**

BILLY ZE KICK ★★½ Uneven comedy-mystery about a bumbling cop who discovers that the fictitious tales he's been delivering to his daughter about a serial killer are beginning to spread throughout his own neighborhood as a reality. Stupid cartoonlike characters quickly become annoying and redundant. In French with English subtitles. Rated R for violence. 87m. **DIR:** Gérard Mordillat. **CAST:** Francis Perrin. **1985**

BIRCH WOOD ★★★★ A tubercular young pianist goes to rest at the forest home of his brother. The brother cannot accept the recent death of his wife, but the pianist sees his impending death as a natural part of life. A moving story, beautifully photographed in rural Poland. In Polish with English subtitles. 99m. **DIR:** Andrzej Wajda. **CAST:** Daniel Olbrychski. **1970**

BIRGIT HAAS MUST BE KILLED ★★★★★ It is hard to imagine a more perfect film than this spellbinding, French thriller-drama. Though its plot revolves around the assassination of a German terrorist (Birgit Haas) by a French counterspy organization, this film says as much about human relationships as it does espionage. In French with English subtitles. Unrated; the film contains well-handled violence and nudity. 105m. **DIR:** Laurent Heynemann. **CAST:** Philippe Noiret, Jean Rochefort, Lisa Kreuzer. **1981**

BITTER RICE ★★★ A steamy temperature-raiser in its day, this Italian neorealist drama of exploited rice workers—spiced up with some sex scenes—is tame and obvious today. Well directed, though, and as a curio, worth a look. B&W; 108m. **DIR:** Giuseppe De Santis. **CAST:** Silvana Mangano, Vittorio Gassman, Raf Vallone, Doris Dowling. **1948**

BITTER TEARS OF PETRA VON KANT, THE ★★★ A lesbian fashion designer falls in love with another woman and is met with betrayal when her lover has an affair with an American serviceman. Overlong drama gets a lift from solid performances and great cinematography by Michael Ballhaus, (*Raging Bull, The Last Temptation of Christ*). In German with English subtitles. Not rated, but contains nudity and profanity. 124m. **DIR:** Rainer Werner Fassbinder. **CAST:** Margit Carstensen, Hanna Schygulla. **1972**

BIZARRE, BIZARRE ★★★½ Frenetic farce set in Victorian England at the home of a writer of mystery novels. In French with English subtitles. 90m. **DIR:** Marcel Carné. **CAST:** Louis Jouvet, Françoise Rosay, Michel Simon, Jean-Pierre Aumont. **1937**

BIZET'S CARMEN ★★★★★ Julia Migenes-Johnson and Placido Domingo excel in this film adaptation of the opera by Georges Bizet. It is about a poor girl whose fierce independence maddens the men who become obsessed with her. In French with English subtitles. Rated PG for mild violence. 152m. **DIR:** Francesco Rosi. **CAST:** Placido Domingo, Julia Migenes-Johnson. **1985**

BLACK AND WHITE IN COLOR ★★★★ This whimsical film concerns a group of self-satisfied Frenchmen at a remote African trading post. The expatriates become stung by a fever of patriotism at the outbreak of World War I, and they organize a surprise assault on a nearby German fort. Excellent cast turns in outstanding performances in this sleeper that won an Oscar for best foreign film. In French with English subtitles. Not rated, but contains nudity, profanity, and violence. 90m. **DIR:** Jean-Jacques Annaud. **CAST:** Jean Carmet, Jacques Dufilho, Catherine Rouvel, Jacques Spiesser, Dora Doll. **1977**

BLACK GOD (WHITE DEVIL) ★★ Uneventful tale set in the impoverished northern Brazil, about a poor peasant who changes from a fanatical preacher into an honorable bandit. Poor film-to-video transfer and hard-to-read subtitles. In Portuguese with English subtitles. Not rated, but contains violence. 102m. **DIR:** Glauber Rocha. **CAST:** Yona Magalhaeds. **1964**

BLACK LIZARD ★★★ Strange tale in which a transvestite kidnaps a jeweler's daughter to ransom her for a rare jewel and to have her become one of his living dolls on his secret island. If you like the bizarre, you will enjoy this film. In Japanese with English subtitles. Not rated, but contains violence. 90m. **DIR:** Kinji Fukasaku. **CAST:** Akihiro Maru Yama, Yukio Mishima. **1968**

BLACK ORPHEUS ★★★★★ The Greek myth of Orpheus, the unrivaled musician, and his ill-fated love for Eurydice has been updated and set in Rio de Janeiro during carnival for this superb film. A Portuguese-French coproduction, it has all the qualities of a genuine classic. Its stunning photography captures both the magical spirit of the original legend and the tawdry yet effervescent spirit of Brazil. 98m. **DIR:** Marcel Camus. **CAST:** Breno Mello, Marpessa Dawn, Lea Garcia, Lourdes de Oliveira. **1959**

BLACK RAIN (1988) ★★★★ This winner at the Cannes Film Festival and best picture in Japan is a vivid portrait of the Hiroshima atomic bombing. It recounts the horror of the event and centers on the lives of one family five years later as they cope with radiation sickness. In Japanese with English subtitles. Unrated; too strong for youngsters. B&W; 123m. **DIR:** Shohei Imamura. **CAST:** Yoshiko Tanaka. **1988**

BLACK VENUS 🦃 Lavish nineteenth-century Parisian costumes and settings can't salvage this endless sex romp. Poorly dubbed. Rated R. 80m. **DIR:** Claude Mulot. **CAST:** Josephine Jacqueline Jones, Emiliano Redondo. **1983**

BLIND TRUST (POUVOIR INTIME) ★★★★ Four misfit robbers drive away with an armored car only to find a guard locked in the back with the money. Intense and fascinating. In French with English subtitles. Rated PG-13 for profanity and violence. 86m. **DIR:** Yves Simoneau. **CAST:** Marie Tifo, Pierre Curzi, Jacques Robert Gravel. **1987**

BLOOD FEUD ★★½ Marcello Mastroianni, a lawyer, and Giancarlo Giannini, a sleazy hood, compete for the romantic attentions of a beautiful Sicilian widow (Sophia Loren) in this abrasive, overblown potboiler in 1920s Italy. Dubbed in English. Not rated, but contains profanity and violence. B&W; 112m. **DIR:** Lina Wertmuller. **CAST:** Sophia Loren, Marcello Mastroianni, Giancarlo Giannini. **1979**

BLOOD OF A POET ★★½ This pretentious and self-centered first film by France's multitalented Jean Cocteau is also intriguing, provoking, and inventive. Cocteau stars in and narrates this highly personal excursion into a poet's inner life: his fears and obsessions, his relation to the world about him, and the classic poetic preoccupation with death. In French with English subtitles. B&W; 55m. **DIR:** Jean Cocteau. **CAST:** Jean Cocteau. **1930**

BLOOD WEDDING ★★★ Excellent ballet adaptation of Federico Garcia Lorca's classic tragedy is impeccably performed by a great, lavishly costumed cast in an empty rehearsal hall. Carlos Saura's direction gives this production a great sense of power and beauty. In Spanish with English subtitles. 72m. **DIR:** Carlos Saura. **CAST:** Antonio Gades, Cristina Hoyos. **1981**

BLUE (1993) ★★★½ A grieving French widow tries to sink into anonymity after her famous composer husband and child are killed in a car wreck. She becomes haunted by the unfinished personal and professional business of her dead spouse. Intoxicating imagery, classical music, and sensuality all induce a trancelike euphoria. For her frosty, somber performance, Juliette Binoche won the Venice Film Festival Best Actress award. In French with English subtitles. Rated R for nudity, sex, and language. 97m. **DIR:** Krzysztof Kieslowski. **CAST:** Juliette Binoche, Benoit Regent, Florence Pernel. **1993**

BLUE ANGEL, THE ★★★★★ This stunning tale about a straitlaced schoolteacher's obsession with a striptease dancer in Germany is the subject of many film classes. The photography, set design, and script are all top-notch, and there are spectacular performances by all. In German with English subtitles. B&W; 98m. **DIR:** Josef von Sternberg. **CAST:** Emil Jannings, Marlene Dietrich, Kurt Gerron. **1930**

BLUE COUNTRY ★★★½ A lighthearted comedy involving a nurse who leaves the city to enjoy a free and independent life in the country. She meets up with a bachelor who equally enjoys his freedom. Their encounters with the local townspeople provide amusing glimpses of French folk life. In French with English subtitles. 90m. **DIR:** Jean-Charles Tacchella. **CAST:** Brigitte Fossey, Jacques Serres, Ginette Garcin, Armand Meffre, Ginett Mathieu. **1977**

BLUE HOUR, THE ★★★½ Bittersweet German love story about a male prostitute who falls for his female neighbor after her bullish boyfriend walks out. Excellent performances highlight this improbable love story that looks at love from both sides. In German with English subtitles. Unrated, but contains nudity, sex, and frank language. 87m. **DIR:** Marcel Gisler. **CAST:** Andreas Herder, Dina Leipzig, Cristof Krix. **1991**

BLUE JEANS ★★ A group of French school boys takes a trip to England to try to lose their virginity. This dull film's only redemption is that one innocent boy learns a few of life's lessons. In French with English subtitles. Not rated, but contains profanity. 80m. **DIR:** Hughes des Rozier. **CAST:** Gilles Budin, Michel Gibet, Gabriel Cattand, Gerard Croce, Pierre Borizans. **1978**

BLUEBEARD (1963) ★★★½ Claude Chabrol, justifiably known as the Gallic Hitchcock, tells the story of the Frenchman who married and murdered eleven women in order to support his real family. Chabrol approaches the material in the same manner that Chaplin did in *Monsieur Verdoux*— as a satirical parable of capitalism. Not for all tastes, obviously, but well worth a look. Screenplay by Françoise Sagan. Original title *Landru*. Dubbed in English. 114m. **DIR:** Claude Chabrol. **CAST:** Charles Denner, Michele Morgan, Danielle Darrieux, Hildegarde Neff. **1963**

BOAT IS FULL, THE ★★★ Markus Imhoof's film about refugees from the Nazis trying to obtain refuge in Switzerland is tragic and extraordinarily effective. It could have been a better movie, but it could hardly have been more heartbreaking. No MPAA rating. 100m. **DIR:** Markus Imhoof. **CAST:** Tina Engel, Marin Walz. **1983**

BOB LE FLAMBEUR ★★★★★ This is an exquisite example of early French *film noir*. In it are all the trappings of the classic gangster movie. The most fascinating element of this import is the title character, Bob Montagne (Roger Duchesne), who plans to rob a casino of $800 million. In French with English subtitles. B&W; 102m. **DIR:** Jean-Pierre Melville. **CAST:** Roger Duchesne, Isabel Corey, Daniel Cauchy, Howard Vernon. **1955**

BOCCACCIO 70 ★★★★ As with its Renaissance namesake, this film tells stories—three of them, in fact, by three of Italy's greatest directors. Federico Fellini's entry, "The Temptation of Dr. Antonio," showcases

Anita Ekberg. The second playlet, by Luchino Visconti, is "The Bet," which features Romy Schneider as a not-so-typical housewife. "The Raffle," by Vittorio De Sica, is reminiscent of a dirty joke told badly, and it tends to cheapen the panache of the first two. In Italian with English subtitles. 165m. **DIR:** Federico Fellini, Luchino Visconti, Vittorio De Sica. **CAST:** Anita Ekberg, Sophia Loren, Romy Schneider, Tomas Milian. **1962**

BOLERO (1982) ★★ Like American Alan Rudolph, French director Claude Lelouch is an obsessive romantic whose admirers (a small cult in this country) seem to appreciate his fervent style more than his plots. In this case, even though *Bolero* is almost three hours long, there's little plot to speak of. The film spans fifty years in the lives of a number of characters who live for music. To confuse matters, most of the cast plays multiple roles. You'll either be mesmerized or bored stiff. 173m. **DIR:** Claude Lelouch. **CAST:** James Caan, Geraldine Chaplin, Robert Hossein, Nicole Garcia, Daniel Olbrychski, Richard Bohringer. **1982**

BOMBAY TALKIE ★★ An early effort from the team of producer Ismail Merchant, writer Ruth Prawer Jhabvala, and director James Ivory. (They finally hit it big in 1986 with *A Room With a View.*) In this drama, a British novelist (Jennifer Kendal) travels to India in search of romance, which she finds in the person of an Indian movie star (Shashi Kapoor). Pretty dull; the most fascinating parts have to do with the Indian film industry. 112m. **DIR:** James Ivory. **CAST:** Shashi Kapoor, Jennifer Kendal, Zia Mohyeddin. **1970**

BORDER STREET ★★★★ This hard-hitting Polish film is set in the ghettos into which Nazis forced Jews during the Third Reich and where many of them died for lack of food and medicine. There are a few lapses into low-grade melodrama, but mostly this is a gripping story that retains its power. 75m. **DIR:** Alexander Ford. **CAST:** M. Cwiklinska. **1950**

BOUDU SAVED FROM DROWNING ★★★★★ This is the original *Down and Out in Beverly Hills,* except that the tramp (the beloved Michel Simon) is saved by an antiquarian bookseller after a suicide attempt in the Seine—down and out in Paris. Unlike the play on which it was based and unlike the Hollywood version—both of which have the bum accept his responsibilities—*Boudu* is a celebration of joyful anarchy. A masterpiece. In French with English subtitles. B&W; 88m. **DIR:** Jean Renoir. **CAST:** Michel Simon, Charles Granval, Max Dalban, Jean Dasté. **1932**

BOYFRIENDS AND GIRLFRIENDS ★★★★ Another of French director Eric Rohmer's delightful "Comedies and Proverbs," this import deals with two beautiful young women who become friends and have romantic adventures with various lovers. As usual, not much happens in a dramatic sense, but no one can capture the moment like Rohmer, who has us fall in love with his characters as they fall in and out of love with each other. In French with English subtitles. 102m. **DIR:** Eric Rohmer. **CAST:** Emmanuelle Chaulet, Sophie Renoir, Anne-Laure Meury, Eric Viellard, François-Eric Gendron. **1987**

BREATHLESS (1959) ★★★★★ Richard Gere or Jean-Paul Belmondo? The choice should be easy after you see the Godard version of this story of a carefree crook and his "along for the ride" girlfriend. See it for Belmondo's performance as the continent's most charming crook, but while you're along for the ride, note just how well made a film can be. B&W; 89m. **DIR:** Jean-Luc Godard. **CAST:** Jean-Paul Belmondo, Jean Seberg. **1959**

BRINK OF LIFE ★★★ Early Ingmar Bergman film set entirely in a hospital maternity ward, where three women ponder their pregnancies and the relationships that preceded them. Rather bleak and naturalistic, this is an actors' piece, though Bergman still controls the film emotionally in subtle ways. In Swedish with English subtitles. B&W; 82m. **DIR:** Ingmar Bergman. **CAST:** Eva Dahlbeck, Ingrid Thulin, Bibi Andersson, Max von Sydow, Erland Josephson. **1957**

BUBBLEGUM CRASH, VOLS. 1–3 ★★★ Japanese animation. The Knight Sabers, unofficial superhero protectors of Mega Tokyo, are back in continuing new adventures based on the popular *Bubblegum Crisis* series. Though they have gotten on with their lives, the resourceful women reunite to meet the evil Voice and his nefarious minions. In Japanese with English subtitles. Unrated; contains violence and nudity. 45m. each. **DIR:** Noda Yasuyuki, Kiyotsumu Toshifumi, Fukushima Hiroyuki, Ishiodori Hiroshi. **1991**

BUBBLEGUM CRISIS—VOLS. 1–8 ★★★ Eight-part Japanese animated epic. Compelling stories with some visually stunning (albeit graphically violent) sequences involving the Knight Sabers and archenemies, the Boomers, genetically altered, Terminator-like mutants. This stylish series owes more than a passing nod to Ridley Scott's *Blade Runner.* In Japanese with English subtitles. Unrated with profanity and violence. 30–53m. each. **DIR:** Akiyama Katsuhito, Hayashi Hiroki, Oobari Masami, Takayama Fumihiko, Gooda Hiroaki. **1987–90**

BUFFET FROID (COLD CUTS) ★★★★ Outrageously funny surreal black comedy about three hapless murderers. This whimsical study in madness is laced with brilliant performances and great direction by Bertrand Blier. Highly engaging. In French with English subtitles. Not rated, but contains nudity, profanity, and violence. 95m. **DIR:** Bertrand Blier. **CAST:** Gérard Depardieu, Bernard Blier, Jean Carmet. **1979**

BURGLAR (1987) ★★★ Two unemployed brothers, beset by family problems, find an outlet in Leningrad's punk-rock scene. Nothing special, but worth seeing for a look at an underground musical culture that's not dominated by commercial interests. In Russian with English subtitles. Not rated. 101m. **DIR:** Valery Ogorodnikov. **CAST:** Konstantin Kinchev, Oleg Yelykomov. **1987**

BURMESE HARP, THE ★★★★ A haunting Japanese antiwar film about a soldier who, at the end of World War II, disguises himself as a monk and embarks on a soul-searching journey back to a mountain fortress where his comrades met their death. In Japanese with English subtitles. B&W; 116m. **DIR:** Kon Ichikawa. **CAST:** Shoji Yasui, Rentaro Mikuni. **1956**

BURN UP! ★★ Nothing overly original about this Japanese animated story. Three female police officers get embroiled in the investigation of a notorious white slaver, but obvious plotting undermines fair animation. Not rated; contains nudity and violence. 50m. **DIR:** Yasunori Ide. **1991**

BURNING COURT, THE ★★★ Variation on the haunted-house theme, with a family gathered at their cursed estate by a dying uncle. More stylized than scary. Dubbed in English. Not rated. B&W; 102m. **DIR:** Julien Duvivier. **CAST:** Jean-Claude Brialy, Nadja Tiller, Perrette Pradier. **1962**

BY THE BLOOD OF OTHERS ★★★ The town fathers of a small village search for a plan to rescue two women held hostage by a mentally disturbed young man. Like his father, novelist Georges Simenon, director Marc Simenon brings psychological depth to this suspense drama. In French with English subtitles. 95m. **DIR:** Marc Simenon. **CAST:** Mariangela Melato, Yves Beneyton, Bernard Blier. **1973**

BY THE LAW ★★★★ Adapted from Jack London's short story, "The Unexpected," this is a grim story of three trappers isolated by Alaskan storms and floods. Silent. Russian. B&W; 90m. **DIR:** Lev Kuleshov. **CAST:** Alexandra Khokhlova, Sergei Komarov, Vladimir Fogel. **1926**

BYE BYE BRAZIL ★★★½ This is a bawdy, bizarre, satiric, and sometimes even touching film that follows a ramshackle traveling tent show—the Caravana Rolidei—through the cities, jungle, and villages of Brazil. In Portuguese with English subtitles. Rated R. 110m. **DIR:** Carlos Diegues. **CAST:** José Wilker, Betty Faria. **1980**

CABEZA DE VACA ★★★★ Director Nicolas Echevarria draws on his experience as a documentary filmmaker for this engrossing study of Spanish explorer Alvar Nunez Cabeza de Vaca, who landed in Florida in 1528 and rose from an Indian slave to a respected shaman with another tribe. In Spanish with English subtitles. Rated R for violence and profanity. 112m. **DIR:** Nicolas Echevarria. **CAST:** Juan Diego. **1992**

CABINET OF DOCTOR CALIGARI, THE ★★★½ A nightmarish story and surrealistic settings are the main ingredients of this early German classic of horror and fantasy. Cesare, a hollow-eyed sleepwalker (Conrad Veidt), commits murder while under the spell of the evil hypnotist Dr. Caligari (Werner Krauss). Ordered to kill Jane, a beautiful girl (Lil Dagover), Cesare defies Caligari, and instead abducts her. Silent. B&W; 51m. **DIR:** Robert Wiene. **CAST:** Werner Krauss, Conrad Veidt, Lil Dagover. **1919**

CABIRIA ★★ This feature purportedly had a decisive influence on D. W. Griffith's epic ambitions. It made an international star out of Bartolomeo Pagano, whose role of strongman Maciste predated Schwarzenegger by many decades. Italian playwright Gabriele D'Annunzio lent his name—and some subtitles—to the picture. Silent. Italian. B&W; 95m. **DIR:** Giovanni Pastrone. **CAST:** Bartolomeo Pagano. **1914**

CAFE EXPRESS ★★★½ Chaplinesque comedy starring Nino Manfredi, best known in this country for *Bread and Chocolate*. He plays a similar character here, a vendor selling coffee on a commuter train. Because such sales are illegal, he is hounded by conductors and other petty types. A bit lightweight, but Manfredi is always fun to watch. 105m. **DIR:** Nanni Loy. **CAST:** Nino Manfredi, Adolfo Celi, Vittorio Mezzogiorno. **1980**

CAGED HEART, THE (L'ADDITION) ★★★ This absorbing French film has Bruno Winkler (Richard Berry) arrested for shoplifting when he tries to help a beautiful young woman (Victoria Abril). Once behind bars, he's accused of aiding a crime lord in his escape and shooting a guard. One can't help but get caught up in the story. Rated R for violence and profanity. 85m. **DIR:** Denis Amar. **CAST:** Richard Berry, Richard Bohringer, Victoria Abril. **1985**

CAMILA ★★★½ A romantic and true story of forbidden love in the classic tradition. Susu Pecoraro is Camila O'Gorman, the daughter of a wealthy aristocrat in Buenos Aires in the mid-1800s. Imanol Arias plays Ladislao Gutierrez, a Jesuit priest. In Spanish with English subtitles. Not rated, but with sex, nudity, and violence. 105m. **DIR:** Maria Luisa Bemberg. **CAST:** Susu Pecoraro, Imanol Arias, Hector Alterio, Mona Maris. **1984**

CAMILLE CLAUDEL ★★★★ Poignant, romantic tragedy based on the life of sculptor Camille Claudel. Isabelle Adjani gives an emotion-charged performance as the 21-year-old artist who becomes romantically involved with the great French sculptor Auguste Rodin in Paris during the late 1800s.

In French with English subtitles. Not rated, but contains nudity and is recommended for adults. 149m. **DIR:** Bruno Nuytten. **CAST:** Isabelle Adjani, Gérard Depardieu, Laurent Grevill, Alain Cuny. **1990**

CAMORRA ★★ Lina Wertmuller lacks her usual bite in this well-intentioned but conventional crime story. The movie details the efforts of an ex-prostitute to band the women of Naples together against the mobsters. Rated R for violence and sexual situations. 115m. **DIR:** Lina Wertmuller. **CAST:** Angela Molina, Francisco Rabal, Harvey Keitel. **1986**

CAMOUFLAGE ★★★★ Biting satire of Polish intellectuals focuses on a middle-aged professor and his callow young colleague. While much of the sting will be lost on non-Polish-speaking audiences, the humor comes across well. In Polish with English subtitles. Not rated. B&W; 106m. **DIR:** Krzysztof Zanussi. **CAST:** Zbigniew Zapasiewicz, Piotr Garlicki. **1977**

CANDIDE ★★★ Voltaire's classic tale of the wanderer trying to see the best in everything is updated to the World War II era with mixed results. Clever, but more talky than funny despite a top-flight French cast. Dubbed in English. B&W; 93m. **DIR:** Norbert Carbonnaux. **CAST:** Jean-Pierre Cassel, Daliah Lavi, Pierre Brasseur, Michel Simon, Jean Richard, Louis de Funes. **1960**

CANTERBURY TALES, THE ★★★½ Four of Chaucer's stories are adapted by Pier Paolo Pasolini in his inimitable style—gleefully offensive satire, with the Church the first of many targets. Not for the genteel. Rated X for nudity and simulated sex. 109m. **DIR:** Pier Paolo Pasolini. **CAST:** Hugh Griffith, Laura Betti, Tom Baker, Josephine Chaplin, Pier Paolo Pasolini. **1971**

CARNIVAL IN FLANDERS ★★★★ This sly drama about a village that postpones its destruction by collaborating with their conquerors was considered a poor statement to make to the rest of the world in light of what Nazi Germany and Italy were attempting to do to their neighbors. A clever, subtle work and one of Jacques Feyder's finest achievements, this classic is a conscious effort to recreate on celluloid the great paintings of the masters depicting village life during carnival time. Interesting on many levels. In French with English subtitles. B&W; 92m. **DIR:** Jacques Feyder. **CAST:** Françoise Rosay, Andre Alerme, Jean Murat, Louis Jouvet, Micheline Cheirel. **1936**

CARTOUCHE ★★★★ Great stuff: an eighteenth-century swashbuckler done with wit, incredible style, and an intoxicating passion for action and romance. Jean-Paul Belmondo and Claudia Cardinale head a band of brigands. In French with English subtitles. 115m. **DIR:** Philippe de Broca. **CAST:** Jean-Paul Belmondo, Claudia Cardinale, Odile Versois, Marcel Dalio, Philippe Lemaire. **1964**

CASANOVA (1976) ★★★½ Federico Fellini's account of the sexually bogus Venetian nobleman is a surreal journey into self-obsession and deviance. Casanova is depicted as a tedious braggart. In English and Italian with subtitles. Not rated, but contains nudity and profanity and is recommended for adult viewing. 139m. **DIR:** Federico Fellini. **CAST:** Donald Sutherland. **1976**

CAT, THE (LE CHAT) ★★★ Adaptation of the Georges Simenon novel about a long-married couple. Somewhere along the line their love turned to mutual loathing, and the husband transferred his affections to their pet cat. Not much happens, but watching Jean Gabin and Simone Signoret convey their feelings with almost no dialogue can be fascinating. In French with English subtitles. 88m. **DIR:** Pierre Granier-Deferre. **CAST:** Jean Gabin, Simone Signoret. **1971**

CAT AND MOUSE ★★★★½ Written, produced, and directed by Claude Lelouch, *Cat and Mouse* is a deliciously urbane and witty whodunit guaranteed to charm and deceive while keeping you marvelously entertained. The plot has more twists and turns than a country road, and the characters are...well...just slightly corrupt and totally fascinating. In French with English subtitles. Rated PG. 107m. **DIR:** Claude Lelouch. **CAST:** Michele Morgan, Jean-Pierre Aumont, Serge Reggiani, Valerie Lagrange. **1975**

CATHERINE & CO. ★★½ British-born Jane Birkin is one of France's most popular actresses, though this, one of her typical soft-core sex comedies, hardly shows why. She plays a young woman who, having drifted into an innocent sort of prostitution, decides to incorporate herself with four regular "stockholders." Rated R. 99m. **DIR:** Michel Boisrone. **CAST:** Jane Birkin, Patrick Dewaere, Jean-Claude Brialy, Jean-Pierre Aumont. **1975**

CAT'S PLAY ★★★★ A chaste friendship between a widow and a retired music teacher runs into trouble when one of her friends makes romantic gestures toward the man. A deliberately paced but lovely film. In Hungarian with English subtitles. 115m. **DIR:** Karoly Maak. **CAST:** Margit Dayka, Samu Balasz. **1974**

CELESTE ★★ Ponderously pedestrian, spasmodically amusing and touching, this tale concerns the blooming fondness between the author Marcel Proust and his maid, who says of him, "At times I feel like his mother, and at times his child." This movie is historically interesting, but ultimately bleak and lackluster. In German with English subtitles. Unrated. 107m. **DIR:** Percy Adlon. **CAST:** Eva Mattes, Jurgen Arndt. **1981**

CÉSAR ★★★★½ The final and best part of the Marseilles trilogy that includes *Marius* and *Fanny*. You can watch it on its own, but you won't enjoy it nearly as much unless you see all three parts: the cumulative effect is resoundingly emotional. In French with English subtitles. B&W; 117m. **DIR:** Marcel Pagnol. **CAST:** Raimu, Orane Demazis, Pierre Fresnay. **1933**

CÉSAR AND ROSALIE ★★★½ Beautifully orchestrated story of human passion about a woman (Romy Schneider) and her relationship with two lovers over a period of years. Excellent cast and a subtle screenplay and direction give strength to this comedy-drama. In French with English subtitles. Not rated. 104m. **DIR:** Claude Sautet. **CAST:** Yves Montand, Romy Schneider, Sami Frey, Umberto Orsini, Eva Marie Meineke. **1972**

CHAPAYEV ★★★ Although this was obviously designed as propaganda for the Bolshevik revolution, it is still well-made and entertaining, with a minimum of proselytizing. The film follows the overthrow of the czar from the point of view of Chapayev, a Russian general. In Russian with English subtitles. B&W; 95m. **DIR:** Sergei Vasiliev, Georgi Vasiliev. **CAST:** Boris Bobochkin. **1934**

CHEATERS, THE 🦃 A card cheat works for a Milan crime lord. Rated R for profanity, sex, and violence. 91m. **DIR:** Sergio Martino. **CAST:** Dayle Haddon, Luc Merenda, Lino Troisi, Enrico Maria Salerno. **1976**

CHIKAMATSU MONOGATARI ★★★★★ Because of a misunderstanding, a clerk and the wife of his employer are forced to flee their homes. One of Kenji Mizoguchi's masterpieces, a tragedy of ill-fated love in seventeenth-century Japan. In Japanese with English subtitles. Unrated. 110m. **DIR:** Kenji Mizoguchi. **CAST:** Kazuo Hasegawa, Kyoko Kagawa. **1954**

CHILDREN OF NATURE ★★★★ This enthralling look at old age was the first film from Iceland to receive an Oscar nomination for best foreign-language movie. It details the story of an elderly couple, abandoned by families into a nursing home. They escape one night, and head for the woman's homeland in Northern Iceland. In Icelandic with English subtitles. Unrated. 85m. **DIR:** Fridrik Thor Fridriksson. **CAST:** Gisli Halldorsson, Sigridur Hagalin, Bruno Ganz. **1991**

CHILDREN OF PARADISE, THE ★★★★★ Long beloved by connoisseurs the world over is this rich and rare film of infatuation, jealousy, deception, grief, murder, and true love lost forever—set in pre-1840 Paris. Brilliant performances carefully controlled by superb direction make this fascinating account of the timeless foibles of men and women a true cinema classic. As Baptiste, the mime, in love with an unattainable beautiful woman, Jean-Louis Barrault is matchless. In French with English subtitles. B&W; 188m. **DIR:** Marcel Carné. **CAST:** Jean-Louis Barrault, Arletty, Maria Casares, Pierre Brasseur, Albert Remay, Leon Larive. **1944**

CHINA IS NEAR ★★★½ Marco Bellocchio, infamous recently for the tiresome *Devil in the Flesh*, displays a talent for both sardonic humor and political satire in this early film. The main characters plot against each other to gain political office, sexual satisfaction, and financial security. Their various connivings eventually bring them together as a sort of large, squabbling family. In Italian with English subtitles. B&W; 110m. **DIR:** Marco Bellocchio. **CAST:** Glauco Mauri, Elda Tattoli. **1968**

CHINA, MY SORROW ★★★ In communist China, a mischievous boy is sent to a wilderness reeducation camp where he struggles with hardship and the penalties for nonconformity. A satisfying blend of tension and unexpected humor. In Mandarin with English subtitles. 86m. **DIR:** Dai Sijie. **CAST:** Guo Liang-Yi, Tieu Quan Nghieu, Vuong Han Lai, Sam Chi-Vy. **1989**

CHINESE GHOST STORY, A ★★★½ Atmospheric supernatural love story in ancient China where a young student takes shelter from a storm in a haunted temple where he falls for a beautiful ghost. Impressive special effects are laced with comical situations. In Cantonese with English subtitles. 93m. **DIR:** Ching Siu Tung. **CAST:** Leslie Cheung, Wong Tsu Hsien, Wu Ma. **1987**

CHINESE ROULETTE ★★★ A businessman, his wife, and their lovers are forced into an intense psychological game of truth telling by the couples' paraplegic daughter in this fascinating social satire. In German with English subtitles. Not rated, but contains nudity and profanity. 96m. **DIR:** Rainer Werner Fassbinder. **CAST:** Anna Karina, Margit Carstensen, Ulli Lommel, Brigitte Mira. **1976**

CHLOE IN THE AFTERNOON ★★★★ This film concludes director Eric Rohmer's series of "moral fables." It is a trifle featherweight and utterly charming. Will the faithful hero have an affair with bohemian Chloe (played deftly by singer-actress Zouzou)? In French with English subtitles. No rating. 97m. **DIR:** Eric Rohmer. **CAST:** Bernard Verley, Zouzou, Françoise Verley, Françoise Fabian, Beatrice Romand. **1972**

CHOCOLAT ★★★★ A subtle, sophisticated, remarkably restrained French look at the colonial life of the past in Africa, as viewed from the innocent perspective of an 8-year-old girl. Cecile Ducasse is memorable as the girl, whose story of growing racial awareness is told in flashback. In French with English subtitles. Rated PG-13 for profanity. 105m. **DIR:** Claire Dennis. **CAST:** Cecile Ducasse. **1989**

CHOICE OF ARMS, A ★★★ Yves Montand is a retired gangster who has chosen a peaceful life raising stud horses and giving his beautiful wife, Catherine Deneuve, all she could hope for. Gérard Depardieu is the convict who arrives seeking asylum. In French with subtitles; this film is unrated. 114m. **DIR:** Alain Corneau. **CAST:** Yves Montand, Gérard Depardieu, Catherine Deneuve, Michel Galabru, Gerard Lanvin. **1983**

CHRIST STOPPED AT EBOLI ★★ *Christ Stopped at Eboli* is based on a renowned Italian novel about Carlo Levi, a political exile who was punished in 1935 for his antifascist writings and exiled to a village in southern Italy. Irene Papas livens things up with her resounding laugh, but ultimately this quiet tale is forgettable. In Italian with English subtitles. 118m. **DIR:** Francesco Rosi. **CAST:** Gian Maria Volonté, Irene Papas, Alain Cuny, Lea Massari, François Simon. **1983**

CHRISTIANE F. ★★ Although quite interesting in places, this West German film dealing with young heroin addicts ultimately becomes a bore. In German with English subtitles. 124m. **DIR:** Uli Edel. **CAST:** Natja Brunkhorst, Thomas Haustein. **1981**

CHRONOPOLIS ★★★★ Highly original and imaginative science-fiction animation feature about a city lost in space where strange pharaoh-like immortals put an end to their deathless state by fabricating time, represented by metamorphosing white balls. Filmmaker Piotr Kamler took five years to complete this project. Not rated. In French with English subtitles. 70m. **DIR:** Piotr Kamler. **1982**

CIAO FEDERICO! ★★★ A revealing portrait of Federico Fellini at work, directing the actors who populate the unreal world of *Satyricon*. Immersed in the creative process, Fellini is captured by documentary filmmaker Gideon Bachmann. In English and Italian with English subtitles. Not rated. 55m. **DIR:** Gideon Bachmann. **CAST:** Federico Fellini, Martin Potter, Hiram Keller, Roman Polanski, Sharon Tate. **1971**

CIGARETTE GIRL FROM MOSSELPROM, THE ★★½ A man falls in love with a cigarette girl who unwittingly becomes a movie star, and in turn falls for the cameraman. Charming, quirky tale of unrequited love and unattained dreams. A clever ending makes this silent movie worth a look if your tastes are eclectic enough. Silent. B&W; 78m. **DIR:** Yuri Zhelyabuzhsky. **CAST:** Yulia Solntseva. **1924**

CINEMA PARADISO ★★★★ A pleasant sense of nostalgia pervades this Oscar winner for best foreign language film. Giuseppe Tornatore's story focuses on the love of a young boy—and indeed the entire Sicilian village where he lives—for movies. In Italian with English subtitles. Unrated, the film has profanity and suggested sex. 123m. **DIR:** Giuseppe Tornatore. **CAST:** Philippe Noiret, Jacques Perrin, Salvatore Cascio, Marco Leonardi. **1989**

CITY OF WOMEN ★★½ Marcello Mastroianni plays a middle-aged womanizer who follows a beautiful woman to a mansion, where he is held hostage. Federico Fellini's controversial film has been criticized as antifeminist, although it is really anti-everything. MPAA unrated, but contains profanity and nudity. 139m. **DIR:** Federico Fellini. **CAST:** Marcello Mastroianni, Ettore Manni. **1981**

CITY ON FIRE ★★★ Violent crime-drama about an undercover cop out to bust a syndicate of jewel thieves in Hong Kong. Pretty impressive screen action with an explosive climactic shoot-out. In Cantonese with English subtitles. Not rated, but contains violence and nudity. 98m. **DIR:** Ringo Lam. **CAST:** Chow Yun Fat. **1989**

CITY WAR ★★★ The stars of John Woo's *The Killer* are reteamed as a pair of cops stalked by a vengeful gangster. Neither the script nor the direction are up to Woo's standards, but the actors make this a satisfying thriller. In Cantonese with English subtitles. Not rated; contains strong violence. 100m. **DIR:** Sun Chung. **CAST:** Chow Yun-Fat, Danny Lee. **1988**

CLAIRE'S KNEE ★★★★★ There is no substitute for class, and director Eric Rohmer exhibits a great deal of it in this fifth film in a series entitled *Six Moral Tales*. The plot is simplicity itself. Jerome (Jean-Claude Brialy) renews his friendship with a writer (Aurora Cornu) whose roommate has two daughters; one is Claire. Jerome is intrigued by Claire but is obsessed with her knee—her right knee, to be specific. In French with English subtitles. PG rating. 103m. **DIR:** Eric Rohmer. **CAST:** Jean-Claude Brialy, Aurora Cornu, Beatrice Romand. **1971**

CLASSIC FOREIGN SHORTS: VOLUME 2 ★★★½ Excellent collection of foreign-film shorts by Europe's hottest movie directors. Featured in this collection is François Truffaut's early "Les Mistons," Jean-Luc Godard's first short, "All the Boys Named Patrick," Roman Polanski's "The Fat and the Lean," and "Two Men and a Wardrobe." Also: early featurettes by Michelangelo Antonioni ("U.N.") and Orson Welles ("Hearts of Age"). B&W; 100m. **DIR:** Jean-Luc Godard, Roman Polanski, Michelangelo Antonioni, François Truffaut, Orson Welles. **1989**

CLEAN SLATE (COUP DE TORCHON) ★★★★ Set during 1938 in a French West African colonial town, this savage and sardonic black comedy is a study of the circumstances under which racism and fascism flourish. Philippe Noiret stars as a simple-minded sheriff who decides to wipe out corruption. In French with English subtitles. Unrated; the film has nudity, implied sex, violence, profanity, and racial epithets. 128m. DIR: Bertrand Tavernier. CAST: Philippe Noiret, Isabelle Huppert, Stéphane Audran. 1981

CLEO FROM 5 TO 7 ★★★½ Filmed in real time, this new wave film follows 90 minutes in the life of a nightclub singer awaiting the results of a critical medical test. Sharp-eyed viewers can look for Jean-Luc Godard, Anna Karina, Sami Frey, Jean-Claude Brialy, and others as performers in a comedy film viewed by the protagonist. In French with English subtitles. Unrated. 90m. DIR: Agnes Varda. CAST: Corinne Marchand, Antoine Bourseiller, Michel Legrand. 1962

CLOCKMAKER, THE ★★★★ A small-town clock maker is stunned to learn that his son, whom he raised after the death of his wife, has committed a murder and is on the run from the police. Examining his life, he realizes how little he actually knows the boy. This strong, confident first film from Bertrand Tavernier, based on a Georges Simenon novel, features one of Philippe Noiret's finest performances. In French with English subtitles. Unrated. 105m. DIR: Bertrand Tavernier. CAST: Philippe Noiret, Jean Rochefort, Christine Pascal. 1973

CLOSE TO EDEN ★★★★ A visiting Russian's encounter with a family of farmers, descended from Genghis Khan, is the device director Nikita Mikhalkov uses to study the effects of modernization on Inner Mongolia. As this slow-moving film goes on, the events become increasingly surreal. In Mongol, Chinese, and Russian with English subtitles. Unrated, the film has violence and profanity. 106m. DIR: Nikita Mikhalkov. CAST: Badema, Bayaertu, Vladimir Gostukhin. 1991

CLOSELY WATCHED TRAINS ★★★★½ A bittersweet coming-of-age comedy-drama against a backdrop of the Nazi occupation of Czechoslovakia. A naïve young train dispatcher is forced to grow up quickly when asked to help the Czech underground. This gentle film is one of the more artistic efforts to come from behind the Iron Curtain. B&W; 91m. DIR: Jiri Menzel. CAST: Vaclav Neckar, Jitka Bendova. 1966

CLOWNS, THE ★★★★½ Federico Fellini's television documentary is a three-ring spectacle of fun and silliness, too. Here, style is substance, and the only substance worth noting is the water thrown onto the journalist who asks the cast of circus crazies, "What does it all mean?" In Italian with English subtitles. 90m. DIR: Federico Fellini. CAST: Mayo Morin, Lima Alberti. 1971

CLUB DES FEMMES ★★★ The romantic adventures of three young women who live in a plush mansion where no men are allowed were fairly shocking by 1930s American standards, but this lightweight import is just a diverting curio today. In French with English subtitles. B&W; 88m. DIR: Jacques Deval. CAST: Danielle Darrieux, Valentine Tessier. 1936

COLONEL REDL ★★½ The ponderous and deliberate nature of *Colonel Redl*, which tells the story of a pawn in a struggle for power in the Austro-Hungarian Empire just prior to World War I, keeps it from becoming a fully satisfying film. In German with English subtitles. Rated R for profanity, nudity, simulated sex, and violence. 144m. DIR: Istvan Szabo. CAST: Klaus Maria Brandauer, Armin Mueller-Stahl. 1985

COLOR OF POMEGRANATES, THE ★★★★ Visually rich but difficult film is best viewed as a mosaic epic of the spiritual history of Armenia, a nation long persecuted by its neighbors for its Christianity. The film, which went unseen for years while its creator was in a Soviet jail, is structured around incidents in the life of the eighteenth-century poet Sayat Nova. In Armenian with English subtitles. 73m. DIR: Sergi Parajanov. CAST: Sofico Chiaureli. 1969

COME AND SEE ★★★★ During World War II, a provincial teenager experiences the horrors of war as the Nazis ravage Byelorussia. In Russian with English subtitles. Unrated, but far too upsetting for children. 146m. DIR: Elem Klimov. CAST: Alexei Kravchenko, Olga Mironova. 1985

COMING UP ROSES ★★½ This offbeat comedy is about the efforts of a projectionist in a small mining village in south Wales to keep a local movie theatre open. Endearing characters performed with zest by an all-Welsh-speaking cast but the movie never rises above the poor film direction. In Welsh with English subtitles. Not rated. 90m. DIR: Stephen Bayly. CAST: Dafydd Hywel, Lola Gregory, Bill Paterson. 1986

COMMISSAR, THE ★★★★ A cinematic gift from Glasnost, it's a long-repressed Soviet film about a female Soviet officer and her relationship with a family of Jewish villagers. Challenging and innovative, it's a pro-Semitic film from the mid-Sixties that languished on a shelf for two decades before being freed by changing times. It surfaced in the U.S. in 1988. In Russian with English subtitles. 115m. DIR: Aleksandr Askoldov. CAST: Nonna Mordyukova. 1988

CONFIDENTIALLY YOURS ★★½ François Truffaut's last film is a stylized murder mystery in the tradition of Hitchcock, but it's only a lighthearted soufflé. Jean-Louis Trintignant plays a real estate agent framed for murder. Rated PG. In French with English subtitles. B&W; 110m. DIR: François Truffaut. CAST: Fanny Ardant, Jean-Louis Trintignant, Jean-Pierre Kalfon. 1983

CONFORMIST, THE ★★★★ Fascinating character study of Marcello Clerici (Jean-Louis Trintignant), a follower of Mussolini.

He becomes increasingly obsessed with conformity as he tries to suppress a traumatic homosexual experience suffered as a youth. He is forced to prove his loyalty to the fascist state by murdering a former professor who lives in exile. In French with English subtitles. Rated R for language and subject matter. 107m. **DIR:** Bernardo Bertolucci. **CAST:** Jean-Louis Trintignant, Stefania Sandrelli, Dominique Sanda, Pierre Clementi. **1971**

CONTEMPT ★★★½ A cult film to be, if it isn't already, this one takes a tongue-in-cheek, raised-eyebrow look at European moviemaking. Jack Palance is a vulgar producer; Fritz Lang, playing himself, is his director; Jean-Luc Godard plays Lang's assistant, and in directing this film turned it into an inside joke—in real (not reel) life, he held the film's producer Joseph E. Levine in contempt. 103m. **DIR:** Jean-Luc Godard. **CAST:** Brigitte Bardot, Jack Palance, Fritz Lang, Jean-Luc Godard, Michel Piccoli. **1963**

CONTRABAND ★★ A mediocre Italian gangster movie, dubbed into English. This time the main vice is contraband goods rather than hard drugs or prostitution. But the story is the same. 87m. **DIR:** Lucio Fulci. **CAST:** Fabio Testi, Ivana Monti. **1987**

CONTRACT ★★★★ Enjoyable and provocative satire takes place at the wedding party of the son of a well-to-do doctor. The arranged marriage is already off to a bad start, and things get steadily worse. In Polish with English subtitles. Unrated, the film features nudity. 111m. **DIR:** Krzysztof Zanussi. **CAST:** Leslie Caron, Maja Komorowska, Tadeusz Lomnicki. **1980**

CONVERSATION PIECE ★★ Burt Lancaster portrays a bewildered, reclusive professor whose life changes direction when he encounters a countess and her children. In Italian with English subtitles. 122m. **DIR:** Luchino Visconti. **CAST:** Burt Lancaster, Silvana Mangano, Helmut Berger, Claudia Cardinale. **1974**

COP AND THE GIRL, THE 🦃 Something is lost in the translation of this dubbed German film. Unrated, but contains profanity and violence. 95m. **DIR:** Peter Keglevic. **CAST:** Jurgen Prochnow, Annette Von Klier. **1987**

COUP DE GRACE ★★ In 1920, the daughter of a once-wealthy family falls in love with the militaristic leader of a group of soldiers. Mostly impenetrable pontificating on sex and politics, poorly adapted from a novel by Marguerite Yourcenar. In German with English subtitles. Unrated. 95m. **DIR:** Volker Schlondörff. **CAST:** Margarethe von Trotta, Matthias Habich, Mathieu Carriere. **1976**

COUSIN, COUSINE ★★★½ Marie-Christine Barrault and Victor Lanoux star in this beloved French comedy in the U.S., remade as *Cousins*. Married to others, they become cousins. Once the kissing starts, their relationship expands beyond the boundaries of convention. In French with English subtitles. 95m. **DIR:** Jean-Charles Tacchella. **CAST:** Marie-Christine Barrault, Victor Lanoux, Marie-France Pisier, Guy Marchand. **1975**

CRANES ARE FLYING, THE ★★★★ During World War II, a young woman is so shattered at the news of her lover's death that she agrees to marry a man she doesn't care for. Sublime, moving, and beautifully filmed, this little gem was named Best Film at Cannes. In Russian with English subtitles. B&W; 94m. **DIR:** Mikhail K. Kalatozov. **CAST:** Tatyana Samoilova, Alexei Batalov. **1957**

CRAZY FOR LOVE ★★½ Village-idiot Bourvil will come into an inheritance, but only if he can finish his grade-school education. Naturally, other family members try to ensure that he will fail. Innocuous slapstick comedy with Brigitte Bardot, in her first film, giving no indication of being a star in the making. In French with English subtitles. B&W; 80m. **DIR:** Jean Boyer. **CAST:** Bourvil, Jane Marken, Brigitte Bardot. **1953**

CRAZY RAY, THE ★★★½ René Clair's classic fantasy about a scientist's paralyzing ray is basically an experimental film. A handful of people who have not been affected by the ray take advantage of the situation and help themselves to whatever they want but eventually begin to fight among themselves. B&W; 60m. **DIR:** René Clair. **CAST:** Henri Rollan, Madeline Rodrigue, Albert Préjean. **1923**

CRICKET, THE ★★★½ A roadside café is the setting for this James M. Cain–like triangle involving an older woman, her new husband, and the woman's grown daughter. Although marketed as a steamy sex drama, it's considerably better than that, thanks to fine performances and probing direction by Alberto Lattuada. In Italian with English subtitles. Unrated; contains nudity and violence. 130m. **DIR:** Alberto Lattuada. **CAST:** Anthony Franciosa, Clio Goldsmith. **1982**

CRIES AND WHISPERS ★★★★★ Directed and written by Ingmar Bergman and hauntingly photographed by Sven Nykvist, this Swedish-language film tells a story of a dying woman, her two sisters, and a servant girl. Faultless performances make this an unforgettable film experience. Rated R. 106m. **DIR:** Ingmar Bergman. **CAST:** Harriet Andersson, Liv Ullmann, Ingrid Thulin, Kari Sylwan. **1972**

CRIME AND PUNISHMENT (1935) ★★★★ Excellent screen adaptation of Dostoyevski's complex, brooding novel. Director Pierre Chenal's poetic, surreal touch adds to the climate of dark realism in this tragedy about a murderer who struggles with his conscience after commiting a brutal, senseless crime. In French with English subtitles. B&W; 110m. **DIR:** Pierre Chenal. **CAST:** Harry Baur, Pierre Blanchar. **1935**

CRIME AND PUNISHMENT (1970) ★★★★ Another fine adaptation of Dostoyevski's story about an impoverished student living in squalor in a rooming house and murdering an old pawnbroker. Solid performances and a fine script. In Russian with English subtitles. B&W; 220m. **DIR:** Lev Kulijanov. **CAST:** Georgi Taratorkin. **1970**

CRIME OF MONSIEUR LANGE, THE ★★★★ Jean Renoir's compelling masterpiece sprang from the director's belief that the common man, by united action, could overcome tyranny. When the head of a printing press disappears with all of the firm's funds, the employees band together and raise enough money to go into business as a publisher of popular novelettes. In French with English subtitles. B&W; 90m. **DIR:** Jean Renoir. **CAST:** René Lefévre, Jules Berry. **1935**

CRIMINAL LIFE OF ARCHIBALDO DE LA CRUZ, THE ★★★★ Luis Buñuel's violently erotic satire about a perverted young aristocrat who believes a music box he owned as a child has the power to kill. This surreal black comedy is an uncompromising attack on the social, religious, and political ramifications of contemporary society. A must-see! In Spanish with English subtitles. Not rated. B&W; 91m. **DIR:** Luis Buñuel. **CAST:** Ernesto Alonso, Miroslava Stern. **1955**

CRONOS ★★★★ In this atmospheric Mexican vampire movie, a kindly old antique dealer discovers an alchemist's ancient, eternal-life device—and the thirst for blood that comes from using it. Rife with clever religious symbolism, satiric wit, and some tender family values, this subtle, intelligent chiller harks back to the Hammer horrors of the 1960s and Roger Corman's best Edgar Allan Poe pictures. In English and Spanish with English subtitles. Unrated, with limited graphic effects and gore. 92m. **DIR:** Guillermo del Toro. **CAST:** Federico Luppi, Ron Perlman, Claudio Brook, Tamara Shanath. **1993**

CROSS MY HEART (1991) ★★★★★ Jacques Fansten's bittersweet film spotlights the innocence, the pain, the insecurities, and the resilience of children. With surprising humor and rare sensitivity, the film examines the efforts of a group of children to comfort one of their own. In French with English subtitles. Unrated. 105m. **DIR:** Jacques Fansten. **1991**

CRUEL STORY OF YOUTH ★★★ Two bored middle-class teenagers set up a scheme to extort money from businessmen. Nagisa Oshima is clearly more interested in exploring Godardian techniques than in his emotionally bereft characters (though the approach is suited to them). An interesting but chilly film. In Japanese with English subtitles. B&W; 97m. **DIR:** Nagisa Oshima. **CAST:** Yusuke Kawazu, Miyuji Kuwano. **1960**

CRYSTAL TRIANGLE 🦃 Animated tale of an archaeologist who becomes involved in the search for "the message of God" while battling demons and Soviet and American spies. Truly inane. In Japanese with English subtitles. Not rated; contains violence and nudity. 86m. **DIR:** Seiji Okuda. **1987**

CUP FINAL ★★★★ This drama caused a stir in its native Israel, thanks to its refreshingly evenhanded examination of the relationship between an Israeli prisoner and a squad of PLO soldiers in 1982. The Israeli is taken prisoner, and then is shuttled across war-torn Lebanon with the PLO. In Hebrew with English subtitles. 107m. **DIR:** Eran Riklis. **CAST:** Moshe Ivgi. **1992**

CYRANO DE BERGERAC (1990) ★★★★★ This lavish French production is both ethereal and earthy, poetic and robust, a quintessential, cinematic new version of the classic play about an unattractive cavalier with the soul of perfect romance. The most charismatic and fascinating Gallic actor of the day—Gérard Depardieu—creates the definitive Cyrano. Rated PG. 135m. **DIR:** Jean-Paul Rappeneau. **CAST:** Gérard Depardieu, Anne Brochet, Vincent Perez, Jacques Weber. **1990**

DADDY NOSTALGIA ★★★ Enjoyable exploration of the relationship between a daughter and her dying father. Dirk Bogarde and Jane Birkin are magical as they try to work out their differences and come to understand and respect each other. Director Bertrand Tavernier scores again. In French with English subtitles. Rated PG. 105m. **DIR:** Bertrand Tavernier. **CAST:** Dirk Bogarde, Jane Birkin, Odette Laure. **1990**

DAGGER OF KAMUI, THE ★★★ The beautifully animated film from veteran director Rin Taro is wounded by a somewhat overlong (and sometimes terribly corny) story. Jiro, a young Ninja, is bent on discovering the secret that caused the death of his parents and threatens the destruction of the Tokugawa shogunate. In Japanese with English subtitles. Not rated; contains violence. 132m. **DIR:** Rin Taro. **1985**

DAMNED, THE ★★★½ Deep, heavy drama about a German industrialist family that is destroyed under Nazi power. This film is difficult to watch, as the images are as bleak as the story itself. In German with English subtitles. Rated R for sex. 155m. **DIR:** Luchino Visconti. **CAST:** Dirk Bogarde, Ingrid Thulin, Helmut Griem, Helmut Berger. **1969**

DANDELIONS 🦃 This German-made soft-porn film stars Rutger Hauer as a cold, sadistic leather boy. Made in 1974. Dubbed in English. 92m. **DIR:** Adrian Hoven. **CAST:** Rutger Hauer, Dagmar Lassander. **1987**

DANGAIO ★★★½ Japanese animation. Four psionically enhanced warriors learn to work together against an evil space pirate and his minions. Strong characterization and visuals add much to this above-average story. In Japanese with English subtitles. Unrated violence. 45m. **DIR:** Toshihiro Hirano. **1990**

DANGEROUS MOVES ★★★★½ Worthy of its Oscar for best foreign film of 1984, this French film about a chess match between two grand masters in Geneva is not just for fans of the game. Indeed, the real intensity that is created here comes from the sidelines: the two masters' camps, the psych-out attempts, the political stakes, and the personal dramas. Rated PG for adult situations and language. 95m. **DIR:** Richard Dembo. **CAST:** Michel Piccoli, Leslie Caron, Alexandre Arbatt, Liv Ullmann. **1984**

DANTON ★★★½ Polish director Andrzej Wajda takes the French revolutionary figure (well played by Gérard Depardieu) and the events surrounding his execution by onetime comrades and turns it into a parable of modern life. It may not be good history, but the film does provide food for thought. In French. Rated PG. 136m. **DIR:** Andrzej Wajda. **CAST:** Gérard Depardieu, Wojiech Pszoniak, Patrice Chereau. **1982**

DANZON ★★★★ Completely agreeable romantic drama about a thirty-something telephone operator who lives a shielded life with her teenage daughter in Mexico City. Her only foray into the world comes every Wednesday night when she dances the seductive *Danzon* with Carmello, her dance partner of six years. When he fails to appear one evening, she embarks on a journey of self-discovery and awakening in search of him. In Spanish with English subtitles. Rated PG. 103m. **DIR:** Maria Novaro. **CAST:** Maria Rojo, Blanca Guerra, Tito Vasconcelos, Carmen Salinas. **1992**

DARK EYES ★★★½ Based on several short stories by Anton Chekhov, *Dark Eyes* takes its title from a Russian ballad that fills the sound track. Marcello Mastroianni is wonderfully endearing as a dapper, lovestruck Italian who meets a young Russian woman at a spa and later in her village. The Russian scenery, replete with rolling hills at dawn and singing Gypsies, is a tourist's dream. In Italian with English subtitles. 118m. **DIR:** Nikita Mikhalkov. **CAST:** Marcello Mastroianni, Marthe Keller, Silvana Mangano. **1987**

DARK HABITS ★★ This surreal comedy features Carmen Maura as a nightclub singer. Director Pedro Almodóvar has a touch of Luis Buñuel without the depth or intelligence. This is fitfully funny, self-indulgent, and overlong. In Spanish with English subtitles. Unrated, but recommended for adults. 116m. **DIR:** Pedro Almodóvar. **CAST:** Carmen Maura. **1984**

DAS BOOT (THE BOAT) ★★★★★ During World War II, forty thousand young Germans served aboard Nazi submarines. Only ten thousand survived. This West German film masterpiece re-creates the tension and claustrophobic conditions of forty-three men assigned to a U-boat in 1941. This is the English-dubbed version. 150m. **DIR:** Wolfgang Petersen. **CAST:** Jurgen Prochnow, Herbert Gronemeyer. **1981**

DAY AND THE HOUR ★★ Drab war-drama, set in Nazi-occupied France, has widow Simone Signoret involved with American paratrooper Stuart Whitman. B&W; 115m. **DIR:** René Clement. **CAST:** Simone Signoret, Stuart Whitman, Genevieve Page, Michel Piccoli, Reggie Nalder. **1963**

DAY FOR NIGHT ★★★★★ One of the best of the film-within-a-film movies ever made, this work by the late François Truffaut captures the poetry and energy of the creative artist at his peak. In French with English subtitles. Beware of the badly dubbed English version. Rated PG. 120m. **DIR:** François Truffaut. **CAST:** Jacqueline Bisset, Jean-Pierre Léaud, François Truffaut. **1973**

DAY IN THE COUNTRY, A ★★★★ A young girl seduced on an afternoon outing returns to the scene fourteen years later, an unhappily married woman. Jean Renoir's lyrical impressionistic tragedy is based on a story by Guy de Maupassant. Mesmerizing cinematography by Claude Renoir and Henri Cartier-Bresson. In French with English subtitles. 40m. **DIR:** Jean Renoir. **CAST:** Sylvia Bataille, George Darnoux. **1935**

DAY OF WRATH ★★★½ Slow-moving, intriguing story of a young woman who marries an elderly preacher but falls in love with his son. Visually effective and well acted by all the principals, this film relies too much on symbolism but is still worthy as a study of hysteria and the motivations behind fear. B&W; 98m. **DIR:** Carl Dreyer. **CAST:** Lisbeth Movin, Thorkild Roose. **1944**

DAYDREAMER, THE (LE DISTRAIT) ★★★ This early vehicle for popular French comedian Pierre Richard, who also wrote and directed, is a hodgepodge of gags in varying comic styles. He plays a bumbler who lands a job at an ad agency and nearly destroys the place. In French with English subtitles. 80m. **DIR:** Pierre Richard. **CAST:** Pierre Richard, Bernard Blier, Maria Pacome, Marie-Christine Barrault. **1970**

DEATH OF A BUREAUCRAT ★★★ An entertaining black comedy about a man's struggle with the red tape of bureaucracy. He attempts to replace his dead relative in a graveyard after having to have him illegally exhumed. Delightful farce. In Spanish with

English subtitles. Unrated. B&W; 87m. **DIR:** Tomas Gutierrez Alea. **CAST:** Salvador Wood. **1966**

DEBAJO DEL MUNDO (UNDER EARTH) ★★★★ A Polish family's prosperous life is shattered when the German army invades their small farming community. This Spanish film captures the spirit of a family torn apart by war. A great cast gives compelling performances in this poignant drama. Dubbed in English. Rated R for profanity and graphic violence. 100m. **DIR:** Beda Docampo Feijoo, Juan Bautista Stagnaro. **CAST:** Sergio Renan. **1988**

DECAMERON, THE ★★★★ Earthy, vibrant adaptation of eight stories from the fourteenth-century work by Boccaccio. Probably Pier Paolo Pasolini's most purely enjoyable film. Dubbed in English. 111m. **DIR:** Pier Paolo Pasolini. **CAST:** Franco Citti. **1971**

DECLINE OF THE AMERICAN EMPIRE, THE ★★★★ Writer-director Denys Arcand focuses on two groups, one male and one female. Both reveal secrets about their lives. Rated R for profanity, nudity, and simulated sex. In French with English subtitles. 101m. **DIR:** Denys Arcand. **CAST:** Dominique Michel, Dorothee Berryman, Louise Portal. **1986**

DEDEE D'ANVERS ★★½ Simone Signoret's first starring role was as a prostitute in this melodrama. She works the docks but tries to get out of the life with the help of a kindly sailor. Pretty gloomy. In French with English subtitles. B&W; 95m. **DIR:** Yves Allegret. **CAST:** Simone Signoret, Marcel Pagliero, Bernard Blier. **1949**

DELICATESSEN ★★★½ In a post-apocalyptic world, a former circus clown comes to a town that has advertised for a butcher's assistant. What our hero doesn't know is that it's a short-term job, during which he'll be well fed until it's time for the boss to stock his shelves. Inventive black comedy will appeal enormously to some and offend others. In French with English subtitles. Unrated; the film has violence and nudity. 95m. **DIR:** Jean-Pierre Jeunet, Marc Caro. **CAST:** Marie-Laure Dougnac, Dominique Pinon, Karen Viard, Jean Claude Dreyfus. **1991**

DELUGE, THE (POTOP) ★★★ Overlong period piece set in the seventeenth century during the turbulent Polish-Swedish war. The story evolves around the stormy relationship between a barbaric soldier and a young gentlewoman. Based on the novel by Nobel Prize–winning author Henryk Sienkiewicz. In Polish with English subtitles. Not rated, but contains violence. 185m. **DIR:** Jerzy Hoffman. **CAST:** Daniel Olbrychski. **1973**

DELUSIONS OF GRANDEUR ★★★ In seventeenth-century Spain, a valet is given the job of royal tax collector and uses his position to boost taxes on the rich and give the money to the poor. Likable slapstick farce. In French with English subtitles. Unrated; contains no objectionable material. 85m. **DIR:** Gerard Oury. **CAST:** Yves Montand, Louis De Funes. **1971**

DEMONS IN THE GARDEN ★★★★ Fascinating portrait of a family damaged by fratricidal rivalries and morally wasted by corruption, as seen through the eyes of a young boy during post–Civil War Spain. Breathtaking cinematography by José Luis Alcaine. In Spanish with English subtitles. Not rated, but contains adult themes. 100m. **DIR:** Manuel Gutierrez Aragon. **CAST:** Angela Molina, Imanol Arias. **1982**

DERSU UZALA ★★★★½ This epic about the charting of the Siberian wilderness (circa 1900) is surprisingly as intimate in relationships and details as it is grand in vistas and scope. A Japanese-Russian coproduction, the second half of this Oscar winner is much better than the first. In Russian and Japanese with English subtitles. 140m. **DIR:** Akira Kurosawa. **CAST:** Maxim Munzuk, Yuri Solomin. **1974**

DESPAIR ★★★★ Karlovich (Dirk Bogarde), a Russian living in Germany in 1930, runs an unsuccessful chocolate factory. The stock market crash in America pushes his business into even deeper trouble, and he begins to lose touch with himself in a major way. Black comedy at its blackest. Rated R. 119m. **DIR:** Rainer Werner Fassbinder. **CAST:** Dirk Bogarde, Klaus Lowitsch. **1979**

DESTINY ★★★½ Fritz Lang's first important success is a triumph of style that delves into the nature of love. Consisting of interlocking stories, dream sequences, and nightmarish associations, Lang's fable tells the story of a young woman who challenges Death for the life of her lover but cannot bring herself to offer the sacrifices the grim one demands. Silent. B&W; 114m. **DIR:** Fritz Lang. **CAST:** Lil Dagover, Walter Janssen, Bernhard Goetzke, Rudolf Klein-Rogge. **1921**

DEVI (THE GODDESS) ★★★★ Excellent social satire from India's gifted Satyajit Ray. A deeply religious landowner becomes convinced that his beautiful daughter-in-law is the incarnation of the Hindu goddess Kali, to whom he becomes fanatically devoted. In Bengali with English subtitles. B&W; 96m. **DIR:** Satyajit Ray. **CAST:** Chhabi Biswas, Soumitra Chatterjee. **1960**

DEVIL HUNTER YOHKO ★★ Japanese animation. Imagine schoolgirl Yohko's surprise when she finds out that she is the next in a long line of Devil Hunters. This one is definitely not for children. In Japanese with English subtitles. Unrated; contains violence and nudity. 45m. **DIR:** Tetsuro Aoki. **1990**

DEVIL IN THE FLESH (1946) ★★★½ Story of an adulterous love affair between a young man and the wife of a soldier during World War I is moving and tragic. The mutual attraction of the two turns to passion after the girl's husband leaves for the front, and the growing guilt that they feel turns their love into torment. French with English subtitles. B&W; 110m. **DIR:** Claude Autant-Lara. **CAST:** Micheline Presle, Gérard Philipe, Denise Grey. **1946**

DEVIL IN THE FLESH (1987) 🦃 A story of two young lovers—a lanky student and a *Betty Blue*–like madwoman. In Italian with English subtitles. Rated X. 120m. **DIR:** Marco Bellocchio. **CAST:** Maruschka Detmers, Federico Pitzalis. **1987**

DEVILMAN VOL. 1–2 ★★ Vaguely reminiscent of the works of H. P. Lovecraft, this animated film has only a few points of interest. In order to defend the world from an impending demon invasion, two young men gain supernatural powers by becoming demons themselves. In Japanese with English subtitles. Not rated; contains violence and nudity. 55m. each. **DIR:** Tstutomu Iida. **1987–1990**

DEVIL'S EYE, THE ★★ Disappointing comedy. In order to cure the sty in his eye, the devil sends Don Juan (Jarl Kulle) from hell to breach a woman's chastity. Bibi Andersson plays Britt-Marie, the pastor's virgin daughter. 90m. **DIR:** Ingmar Bergman. **CAST:** Jarl Kulle, Bibi Andersson, Gunnar Björnstrand. **1960**

DIABOLICALLY YOURS ★★★ How would you like to wake up after an accident to find a beautiful wife and a luxurious mansion that you have no recollection of? Sound great? Unfortunately, it's the start of a nightmare. This French film is unrated, but contains violence. 94m. **DIR:** Julien Duvivier. **CAST:** Alain Delon, Senta Berger. **1967**

DIABOLIQUE ★★★★ This classic thriller builds slowly but rapidly gathers momentum along the way. Both wife and mistress of a headmaster conspire to kill him. This twisted plot of murder has since been copied many times. In French with English subtitles. B&W; 107m. **DIR:** Henri-Georges Clouzot. **CAST:** Simone Signoret, Vera Clouzot, Charles Vanel, Paul Meurisse. **1955**

DIARY OF A CHAMBERMAID (1946) ★★ Octave Mirbeau's once daring novel, *The Diary of a Chambermaid*, had most of its quirky and sensational elements watered down for this Hollywood version directed by Jean Renoir during his American sojourn in the 1940s. Not one of his better American films. B&W; 86m. **DIR:** Jean Renoir. **CAST:** Burgess Meredith, Paulette Goddard. **1946**

DIARY OF A CHAMBERMAID (1964) ★★★★ Excellent remake of Jean Renoir's 1946 film concerns the personal dilemma of a maid (Jeanne Moreau) caught in the grip of fascism in 1939 France. Director Luis Buñuel paints a cynical portrait of the bourgeoisie—a stunning character study. French dialogue with English subtitles. B&W; 95m. **DIR:** Luis Buñuel. **CAST:** Jeanne Moreau, Michel Piccoli, Georges Geret, Daniel Ivernel. **1964**

DIARY OF A COUNTRY PRIEST ★★★★ The slow pace at the beginning of this tale about a priest trying to minister to his parish might tend to put some viewers off. However, with Bresson's poetic style and camera work, the wait is well worth it. In French with English subtitles. B&W; 120m. **DIR:** Robert Bresson. **CAST:** Claude Laydu, Nicole Ladmiral, Nicole Maurey. **1950**

DIARY OF A LOST GIRL ★★★★ In this silent classic, Louise Brooks plays a young girl who is raped by her father's business partner (Fritz Rasp). Banished to a girls' reformatory, she eventually escapes, falling prey to the false sanctuary provided by a whorehouse madame. Those who maintain there is a docility to silent films may be surprised by the relatively mature subject matter in this film. B&W; 99m. **DIR:** G. W. Pabst. **CAST:** Louise Brooks, Joseph Rovensky, Fritz Rasp, André Roanne, Valeska Gert. **1929**

DIRTY DISHES ★★ The American-born daughter-in-law of Luis Buñuel makes her directorial debut with this mediocre comedy. A beautiful French housewife finds herself trapped in an uneventful marriage. This leads to an explosive encounter with a lecherous neighbor. Takes its theme from the superior *Diary of a Mad Housewife*. In French with English subtitles. Not rated. 99m. **DIR:** Joyce Buñuel. **CAST:** Pierre Santini, Liliane Roveryre, Liza Braconnier. **1982**

DIRTY PAIR: AFFAIR ON NOLANDIA 🦃 A ridiculously contrived and poorly animated story has two scantily clad female intergalactic troubleshooters investigating cases with very little brain power. Dubbed in English. Not rated; contains nudity, profanity, and violence. 57m. **DIR:** Masahara Okuwaki. **1985**

DISCREET CHARM OF THE BOURGEOISIE, THE ★★★★ Dinner is being served in this Luis Buñuel masterpiece, but the food never gets a chance to arrive at the table. Every time the hosts and guests try to begin the meal, some outside problem rises. Typically French, typically Buñuel, typically hilarious. Winner of the best foreign film Oscar for 1972. 100m. **DIR:** Luis Buñuel. **CAST:** Fernando Rey, Delphine Seyrig, Stéphane Audran, Bulle Ogier, Jean-Pierre Cassel, Michel Piccoli. **1972**

DISTANT THUNDER (1974) ★★★★ Outstanding drama by Satyajit Ray about the effects of a famine on the lives of various family members in World War II India. Beautiful cinematography sweeps the viewer through the desert landscapes of India. In Bengali with English subtitles. 92m. **DIR:** Satyajit Ray. **CAST:** Soumitra Chatterjee. **1974**

DIVA ★★★★ In this stunningly stylish suspense film by first-time director Jean-Jacques Beineix, a young opera lover unknowingly becomes involved with the underworld. Unbeknownst to him, he's in possession of some very valuable tapes—and the delightful chase is on. In French with English subtitles. Rated R for profanity, nudity, and violence. 123m. **DIR:** Jean-Jacques Beineix. **CAST:** Frederic Andrei, Wilhemenia Wiggins Fernandez. **1982**

DIVINE NYMPH, THE ★★½ This story of love and passion resembles an Italian soap opera at best. Laura Antonelli is the young beauty who is unfaithful to her fiancé. In Italian with English subtitles. Rated R for nudity. 89m. **DIR:** Giuseppe Patroni Griffi. **CAST:** Laura Antonelli, Terence Stamp, Marcello Mastroianni. **1977**

DIVORCE—ITALIAN STYLE ★★★½ Considered naughty in its day, now this Italian black comedy about a philandering husband's plans to rid himself of his wife simply plays as the fast, racy romp it is. Endlessly imitated in later, lesser rip-offs. Oscar for original screenplay. B&W; 104m. **DIR:** Pietro Germi. **CAST:** Marcello Mastroianni, Daniela Rocca, Stefania Sandrelli. **1962**

DO YOU REMEMBER DOLLY BELL? ★★★½ Delightful coming-of-age story set in 1960s Sarajevo, when stable political circumstances brought a flood of Western culture to Yugoslavia. In Serbo-Croatian with English subtitles. Not rated; mild sexual content. B&W; 106m. **DIR:** Emir Kusturica. **CAST:** Slavko Stimac, Mira Banjac. **1981**

DODES 'KA-DEN ★★★★ Akira Kurosawa's first color film is a spellbinding blend of fantasy and reality. The film chronicles the lives of a group of Tokyo slum dwellers that includes children, alcoholics, and the disabled. Illusion and imagination are their weapons as they fight for survival. In Japanese with English subtitles. 140m. **DIR:** Akira Kurosawa. **CAST:** Yoshitaka Zushi. **1970**

DOLL ★★★★ Per Oscarsson gives a remarkable performance as a lonely, depraved night watchman who steals a mannequin from a department store and engages in bizarre fantasies with it. Psychologically unsettling film. In Swedish with English subtitles. B&W; 94m. **DIR:** Arne Mattson. **CAST:** Per Oscarsson. **1962**

DOLLAR ★★ Three married couples bicker, flirt, separate, and unite all in one overblown weekend at a ski lodge. Noteworthy only for the radiant presence of a young Ingrid Bergman. In Swedish with English subtitles. B&W; 74m. **DIR:** Gustav Molander. **CAST:** Ingrid Bergman. **1938**

DONA FLOR AND HER TWO HUSBANDS ★★★★ A ribald Brazilian comedy about a woman (Sonia Braga) haunted by the sexy ghost of her first husband (José Wilker), who's anything but happy about her impending remarriage, this film inspired the Sally Field vehicle *Kiss Me Goodbye*. The original is better all around. In Portuguese with English subtitles. Unrated; the film has nudity. 106m. **DIR:** Bruno Barreto. **CAST:** Sonia Braga, José Wilker, Mauro Mendonca. **1978**

DONKEY SKIN (PEAU D'ÂNE) ★★★★ Looking for something different? The creator of *The Umbrellas of Cherbourg* also made this charming, colorful fairy tale for an adult audience. A princess, about to be forced to marry her own father, hides out as a scullery maid. Before long, though, the local Prince Charming sees through her drab disguise. *Donkey Skin* is a delightful combination of the real and the dreamlike that could easily have been unbearably cute in less skilled hands. Okay for kids, but not really intended for them. In French with English subtitles. 90m. **DIR:** Jacques Demy. **CAST:** Catherine Deneuve, Jean Marais, Jacques Perrin, Delphine Seyrig. **1970**

DONNA HERLINDA AND HER SON ★★★ This highly enjoyable, raunchy comedy explores the bizarre relationship a mother has with her sexually liberated homosexual son. It's a delightful comedy of manners featuring a memorable cast and a director with a great touch for deadpan humor. In Spanish with English subtitles. 90m. **DIR:** Jaime Humberto Hermosillo. **CAST:** Guadalupe Del Toro, Marco Antonio Trevino. **1986**

DOOMED MEGALOPOLIS, PARTS 1–4 ★★★ The evil, adept Kato wars with the forces of good as he seeks to unleash the slumbering spirit that guards Tokyo in this nicely executed animated horror story with strong, original visuals and a suspenseful plot. Fine animation. Dubbed in English. Not rated; contains violence and nudity. Each 50m. **DIR:** Rin Taro. **1992**

DOUBLE LIFE OF VERONIQUE, THE ★★★★ In this exquisite adult fairy tale, the luminous Irène Jacob plays the dual role of two identical women, one Polish and one French, who live parallel lives. It is an enigmatic but gorgeous film; one that often seems like a series of paintings come to life on-screen. In French and Polish with English subtitles. Unrated; the film has nudity and suggested sex. 105m. **DIR:** Krzysztof Kieslowski. **CAST:** Irène Jacob, Halina Gryglaszewska, Kalina Jedrusik. **1991**

DOUBLE SUICIDE ★★★★ Stunning portrait of erotic obsession and passion in turn-of-century Japan. Director Masahiro Shinoda explores sexual taboos in his story of a merchant and a geisha whose ill-fated love affair is orchestrated entirely by outside forces. This poignant drama is presented in the style of a Bunraku puppet play. In Japanese with English subtitles. Not rated. B&W; 105m. **DIR:** Masahiro Shinoda. **CAST:** Kichiemon Nakamura, Shima Iwashita. **1969**

DOWN AND DIRTY ★★★★ Brutal but brilliant black comedy about a slumlord of a shantytown in Rome. Nino Manfredi is excellent as a money-hoarding patriarch whose obsession with his stash leads to a plot by his wife and delinquent sons to kill him. In Italian with English subtitles. Not rated, but contains violence, profanity, and nudity. 115m. **DIR:** Ettore Scola. **CAST:** Nino Manfredi, Francesco Anniballi. **1976**

DRACULA (SPANISH VERSION) ★★★ The familiar tale of the bloodthirsty Count Dracula is enacted by a Spanish-speaking cast in this sister production to the famous 1931 American counterpart. This version was filmed at night using the same sets as the English-language production. The opening credits are evocative of the dread of the unknown; the camera is composed but fluid; the count actually rises from his coffin on camera, and the women (especially the unholy brides) are erotic and enticing. Bela Lugosi is still the consummate Dracula of the 1930s, but this overlong production has some memorable moments. In Spanish with English subtitles. B&W; 104m. **DIR:** George Melford. **CAST:** Carlos Villarias, Lupita Tovar, Pablo Alvarez Rubio. **1931**

DRAGON CHOW ★★★ Humorous and touching film about a Pakistani man living in West Germany. He lands a job in a mediocre Chinese restaurant where he strikes up a friendship with an Oriental waiter. Good slice-of-life character study. In German, Urdu, and Mandarin with English subtitles. Not rated. B&W; 75m. **DIR:** Jan Schuttes. **CAST:** Bhasker, Ric Young. **1987**

DRAGONS FOREVER ★★★½ A lawyer is persuaded to work against chemical plant owners who want to take over a site used by local fishermen. Amazing martial arts highlight this exciting comedy featuring Hong Kong's talented director-actor Jackie Chan. In Cantonese with English subtitles. Not rated, but contains violence. 88m. **DIR:** Samo Hung. **CAST:** Jackie Chan. **1988**

DREAMS ★★½ Fascinating but confusing drama about a photo agency head and her top model. In Swedish with English subtitles. B&W; 86m. **DIR:** Ingmar Bergman. **CAST:** Eva Dahlbeck, Harriet Andersson, Gunnar Björnstrand, Ulf Palme. **1955**

DRIFTING WEEDS ★★★★★ The leader of a troupe of traveling actors visits an old lover and his illegitimate son when the actors pass through a distant village. An exquisitely simple but moving drama from the master Japanese director Yasujiro Ozu. Also known as *Floating Weeds*. In Japanese with English subtitles. 119m. **DIR:** Yasujiro Ozu. **CAST:** Ganjiro Nakamura, Machiko Kyo. **1959**

DRUNKEN ANGEL ★★★★ Master director Akira Kurosawa here displays an early interest in good guys and bad guys. Toshiro Mifune is a petty gangster who learns from an idealistic slum doctor (Takashi Shimura) that he is dying of tuberculosis. In Japanese with English subtitles. B&W; 102m. **DIR:** Akira Kurosawa. **CAST:** Toshiro Mifune, Takashi Shimura. **1949**

DYBBUK, THE ★★★½ Eerie film version of a popular folk tale set in nineteenth-century Poland. A student kills himself when the father of the girl to whom he has been pledged in marriage breaks the promise in order to marry her into a rich family. The girl is then possessed by the spirit of the dead boy. A well-made film for its time and place. In Yiddish with English subtitles. 122m. **DIR:** Michael Wasynski. **CAST:** Abraham Morevski. **1938**

EARLY RUSSIAN CINEMA: BEFORE THE REVOLUTIONS (VOL. 1–10) ★★★★★ Soviet cinema didn't emerge fully formed from the heads of Eisenstein, Vertov, and Dovzhenko. Russia enjoyed a booming film industry prior to the revolution, but the Soviets found many of these films too cosmopolitan and removed them from circulation. This collection of twenty-eight works unearthed by Glasnost provides a fascinating look at a wide spectrum of pre-Soviet society. Silent. B&W; 695m. **DIR:** Evgenii Bauer, Ladislaw Starewicz, Yakov Protázanov. **1908–1918**

EARLY SUMMER ★★★½ Involved and involving story about a young woman rebelling against an arranged marriage in post–World War II Tokyo. Yasujiro Ozu, one of Japan's most respected directors, deftly presents this tale of culture clash, which won the Japanese Film of the Year Award in 1951. In Japanese with English subtitles. B&W; 135m. **DIR:** Yasujiro Ozu. **CAST:** Setsuko Hara. **1951**

EARRINGS OF MADAME DE..., THE ★★★★ A giddily romantic roundelay sparked by a pair of diamond earrings. They keep changing hands but always come back to haunt the fickle countess who owned them first. The style is a bit too lighthearted for what is ultimately a tragic story, but Max Ophüls imbues it with wit and technical flash. In French with English subtitles. 105m. **DIR:** Max Ophüls. **CAST:** Charles Boyer, Danielle Darrieux, Vittorio De Sica. **1953**

EARTH ★★★★ One of the last classic silent films, this short homage to the spirit of the collective farmer and his intangible ties to the land employs stunning camera shots. Certain scenes from the original print no longer exist, but what remains of this film tells a beautiful, moving story. Russian, silent. B&W; 56m. **DIR:** Alexander Dovzhenko. **CAST:** Semyon Svashenko. **1930**

EASTERN CONDORS ★★★★ À la *The Dirty Dozen*, a group of hardened criminals are sent to Vietnam on a suicide mission. Star-director Samo Hung, who usually plays comical parts, may be built like a cannonball, but he can move like one, too! In Cantonese with English subtitles. Not rated; contains strong violence. 100m. **DIR:** Samo Hung. **CAST:** Samo Hung, Yuen Biao, Haing S. Ngor. **1986**

ECLIPSE, THE ★★★½ A woman dissolves an affair with an older man, only to become involved with a self-centered young stockbroker in Rome's frenzied Borsa. Michelangelo Antonioni's meditation on doomed love has some good moments. Winner of the Grand Prize at Cannes. In Italian with English subtitles. B&W; 123m. **DIR:** Michelangelo Antonioni. **CAST:** Alain Delon, Monica Vitti, Francisco Rabal. **1962**

ECSTASY ★★½ Completely overshadowed since its release by the notoriety of Hedy Lamarr's nude scenes, this new packaging in video should shift the emphasis back to the film itself, which is basically a romance of illicit love. Filmed in pre-Hitler Czechoslovakia, this version is subtitled in English. B&W; 88m. **DIR:** Gustav Machaty. **CAST:** Hedy Lamarr, Aribert Mog. **1933**

EDITH AND MARCEL ★★★★ Based on the real life of famous torch singer Edith Piaf (Evelyn Bouix), this powerful musical-drama follows the passionate affair she had with champion boxer Marcel Cerdan (Marcel Cerdan Jr.). Director Claude Lelouch brings to life the stormy romance that captured the attention of the world. In French with English subtitles. 170m. **DIR:** Claude Lelouch. **CAST:** Evelyne Bouix, Marcel Cerdan Jr., Jacques Villeret, Francis Huster. **1983**

EGG ★★★ Delightful, bittersweet comedy from Holland about a quiet, illiterate baker who romances an awkward and lonely schoolteacher. In Dutch with English subtitles. 58m. **DIR:** Danniel Danniel. **CAST:** Johan Leysen, Marijke Veugelers. **1988**

8½ ★★★★★ Perhaps one of Federico Fellini's strongest cinematic achievements. *8 1/2* is the loose portrayal of a film director making a personal movie and finding himself trapped in his fears, dreams, and irresolutions. This brilliant exercise features outstanding performances, especially by Marcello Mastroianni. Dubbed into English. Not rated. B&W; 135m. **DIR:** Federico Fellini. **CAST:** Marcello Mastroianni, Anouk Aimée, Claudia Cardinale, Barbara Steele, Sandra Milo. **1963**

EIGHTIES, THE ★★ A somewhat disjointed, tepid film about the making of a musical. If you're suddenly seized by an uncontrollable urge to attend an experimental French acting workshop, then snap this one up. In French with English subtitles. Unrated; the film has nudity. 82m. **DIR:** Chantal Akerman. **CAST:** Aurore Clement, Magali Noel. **1983**

EIJANAIKA (WHY NOT?) ★★★★ *Why Not?* is set in the 1860s when Japan opened up to world trade after a military dictatorship, in power more than 700 years, was toppled, putting the emperor back in power and causing a rebellion by his subjects. Fascinating. In Japanese with English subtitles. Unrated, the film has nudity, profanity, and violence. 151m. **DIR:** Shohei Imamura. **CAST:** Shigeru Izumiya, Kaori Momoi, Ken Ogata, Mitsuko Baisho. **1981**

EL (THIS STRANGE PASSION) ★★★★ Surreal portrait of a wealthy and devout middle-aged man, who is driven to madness by his pathological jealousy and obsession with religious ritual. Director Luis Buñuel has created an ironic dramatization of the destructive effect obsession can have on marriage and sexuality. In Spanish with English subtitles. B&W; 82m. **DIR:** Luis Buñuel. **CAST:** Arturo De Cordova. **1952**

EL AMOR BRUJO ★★ This occasionally brilliant big-screen production of Manuel de Falla's ballet will appeal primarily to flamenco fans. The cast is excellent but overall the movie fails to fascinate. In Spanish with English subtitles. Rated PG for brief, stylized violence and references to sex in lyrics. 100m. **DIR:** Carlos Saura. **CAST:** Antonio Gades, Cristina Hoyos, Laura Del Sol. **1986**

EL BRUTO (THE BRUTE) ★★★½ Exceptional surreal drama from Luis Buñuel about a tough slaughterhouse laborer who is exploited by a tyrannical landowner. Some strange melodramatic twists laced with moments of irony make this Mexican film one of Buñuel's stronger efforts. Spanish dialogue with English subtitles. Not rated. B&W; 83m. **DIR:** Luis Buñuel. **CAST:** Pedro Armendariz, Katy Jurado, Andres Soler. **1952**

EL MARIACHI ★★★ This contemporary shoot-'em-up semi-spoofs spaghetti Westerns and Mexican action flicks. It's a visually choppy, grungy gem—shot on a fourteen-day, $7,000 schedule and cleaned up somewhat by Columbia Pictures before release—about a wandering Mexican musician who is pursued by thugs when he's mistaken for a rival hit man. In Spanish with English subtitles. Rated R for violence. 80m. **DIR:** Robert Rodriguez. **CAST:** Carlos Gallardo, Consuelo Gomez, Jaime de Hoyos, Peter Marquardt, Reinol Martinez. **1993**

EL NORTE ★★★★★ A rewarding story about two Guatemalans, a young brother and sister, whose American dream takes them on a long trek to El Norte—the United States. This American-made movie is funny, frightening, poignant, and sobering—a movie that stays with you. In Spanish with subtitles. Rated R for profanity and violence. 139m. **DIR:** Gregory Nava. **CAST:** Zaide Silvia Gutierrez, David Villalpando. **1983**

EL PROFESSOR HIPPIE ★★½ Veteran comedian Luis Sandrini plays a college professor who, because of his free-thinking attitudes and concerns for moral questions over matters of business, has more in common with his students than his colleagues. This gentle comedy is a real audience pleaser. In Spanish. 91m. **DIR:** Fernando Ayala. **CAST:** Luis Sandrini. **1969**

EL SUPER ★★★★ A funny and touching view of Cuban exiles living in a basement apartment during a cold winter in New York City. Raymundo Hidalgo-Gato turns in a strong performance as the superintendent who dreams of his homeland while struggling with the conditions of his new culture. In Spanish with English subtitles. Not rated. 80m. **DIR:** Leon Ichaso. **CAST:** Raymundo Hidalgo-Gato, Elizabeth Peña. **1979**

ELEGANT CRIMINAL, THE ★★★★ Handsomely produced true story of a nineteenth century intellectual who rebelled against his loveless upbringing by embarking on a life of crime, one designed to lead to his execution. In the title role, Daniel Auteuil is both charming and brutal, seductive and cold. Unrated, the film has violence and sexual situations. In French with English subtitles. 120m. **DIR:** Francis Girod. **CAST:** Daniel Auteuil, Jean Poiret, Marie-Armelle Deguy. **1990**

ELENA AND HER MEN ★★★ One of Jean Renoir's personal favorites, this musical fantasy is about the power of love, and the evil of dictators. Ingrid Bergman is supported by a fine cast in this enjoyable comedy-drama. Originally released in America as *Paris Does Strange Things*. In French with English subtitles. 98m. **DIR:** Jean Renoir. **CAST:** Ingrid Bergman, Jean Marais, Mel Ferrer, Juliette Greco. **1956**

ELEVATOR TO THE GALLOWS ★★★★ Marvelously twisted tale of murder and deceit features Jeanne Moreau as a wealthy woman plotting to have her husband killed by her lover. Her lover's getaway car is stolen by two teenagers who fit murder into their joyride, leaving the lover to take the rap. Jazz score by Miles Davis is perfect backdrop to nonstop decadence. (Also known as *Frantic.*) Unrated, in French with English subtitles. B&W; 87m. **DIR:** Louis Malle. **CAST:** Jeanne Moreau, Maurice Ronet, Georges Poujouly. **1957**

ELUSIVE CORPORAL, THE ★★★★½ Twenty-five years after he made his greatest masterpiece, *La Grande Illusion*, Renoir reexamines men in war with almost equally satisfying results. This time the soldiers are Frenchmen in a World War II prison camp. *The Elusive Corporal* is a delicate drama infused with considerable wit. In French with English subtitles. 108m. **DIR:** Jean Renoir. **CAST:** Jean-Pierre Cassel, Claude Brasseur, Claude Rich. **1962**

ELVIRA MADIGAN ★★★★ This is a simple and tragic story of a young Swedish officer who falls in love with a beautiful circus performer. Outstanding photography makes this film. Try to see the subtitled version. 89m. **DIR:** Bo Widerberg. **CAST:** Pia Degermark, Thommy Berggren. **1967**

EMMANUELLE ★★★ Sylvia Kristel became an international star as a result of this French screen adaptation of Emmanuelle Argan's controversial book about the initiation of a diplomat's young wife into the world of sensuality. In the soft-core sex film genre, this stands out as one of the best. Rated R for nudity. 92m. **DIR:** Just Jaeckin. **CAST:** Sylvia Kristel, Marika Green, Daniel Sarky, Alain Cuny. **1974**

EMMA'S SHADOW ★★★★ Enchanting story of an 11-year-old girl from wealthy parents who fakes her own kidnapping in the 1930s. Winner of the Danish best film award. In Danish with English subtitles. Unrated. 93m. **DIR:** Soeren Kragh-Jacobsen. **CAST:** Line Kruse, Borje Ahlstedt. **1988**

END OF ST. PETERSBURG, THE ★★★½ The story of a worker who gradually becomes aware of his duty to his class. He becomes a part of the 1917 Revolution. Although pure propaganda, this powerful indictment of czarist Russia has a fervor and sweep that transcends its message. Silent, with English intertitles. B&W; 75m. **DIR:** V. I. Pudovkin. **CAST:** Ivan Chuvelov. **1927**

ENTRE NOUS (BETWEEN US) ★★★★★ This down-to-earth, highly human story by director Diane Kurys concentrates on the friendship between two women, Madeline (Miou-Miou) and Lena (Isabelle Huppert), who find they have more in common with each other than with their husbands. It is an affecting tale the viewer won't soon forget. Rated PG for nudity, suggested sex, and violence. 110m. **DIR:** Diane Kurys. **CAST:** Miou-Miou, Isabelle Huppert, Guy Marchand. **1983**

EQUINOX FLOWER ★★★★ An interesting look at the Japanese custom of arranged marriages. Setsuko's parents had an arranged marriage and want the same for her; she, having found her own true love, rebels. In Japanese with English subtitles. Not rated, but suitable for all audiences. 115m. **DIR:** Yasujiro Ozu. **CAST:** Shin Saburi. **1958**

ERENDIRA ★★½ In this disturbing and distasteful black comedy, Irene Papas stars as a wealthy old woman who loses everything in a fire accidentally set by her sleepwalking granddaughter, Erendira (Claudia

Ohana). The grandmother turns her charge into a prostitute and insists that she earn back over $1 million. In Spanish with English subtitles. Unrated, the film has nudity, profanity, simulated sex, and violence. 103m. **DIR:** Ruy Guerra. **CAST:** Irene Papas, Claudia Ohana, Michel Lonsdale. **1983**

ETERNAL RETURN, THE ★★★ Interesting modern adaptation of the Tristan and Isolde legend from a script by Jean Cocteau. In French with English subtitles. B&W; 110m. **DIR:** Jean Delannoy. **CAST:** Jean Marais, Madeleine Sologne, Jean Murat. **1943**

EUROPA, EUROPA ★★★★ Based on the death-defying autobiography of Solomon Perel, this stunning film traces the author's real-life adventures during World War II in war-torn Europe. A Jewish teenager who first masquerades as a Communist and later is accepted into the Nazi Youth Party, Perel sees the war from all sides in this ironic, spine-tingling story. In German and Russian with English subtitles. Rated R for nudity. 115m. **DIR:** Agnieszka Holland. **CAST:** Marco Holschneider, Delphine Forest. **1990**

EVERY MAN FOR HIMSELF AND GOD AGAINST ALL ★★★★ Based on a real incident, the story of Kasper Hauser (Bruno S.) tells of a man who had been kept in confinement since birth. Hauser's appearance in Nuremberg in the 1820s was a mystery. He tried to adjust to a new society while maintaining his own vision. Also released as *The Mystery of Kasper Hauser*. In German with English subtitles. No MPAA rating. 110m. **DIR:** Werner Herzog. **CAST:** Bruno S., Walter Ladengast, Brigitte Mira. **1975**

EVERYBODY'S FINE ★★★★ Giuseppe Tornatore followed up his international sensation, *Cinema Paradiso,* with this more cynical, more complex, but quite affecting work. Marcello Mastroianni corrals a fabulous late-in-his-career role as an elderly widower who decides to travel about Italy, seeing his grown children. He's under the delusion that "everybody's fine," when in reality they've all gotten into various kinds of trouble or financial difficulty. In Italian with English subtitles. Unrated. 108m. **DIR:** Giuseppe Tornatore. **CAST:** Marcello Mastroianni, Michele Morgan. **1991**

EXTERMINATING ANGEL, THE ★★★★★ Luis Buñuel always did love a good dinner party. In *The Discreet Charm of the Bourgeoisie,* the dinner party never could get under way, and here the elite *après-opéra* diners find they cannot escape the host's sumptuous music room. This is a very funny film—in a very black key. In Spanish with English subtitles. B&W; 95m. **DIR:** Luis Buñuel. **CAST:** Silvia Pinal, Enrique Rambal. **1962**

EXTRAORDINARY ADVENTURES OF MR. WEST IN THE LAND OF THE BOLSHEVIKS, THE ★★ An American tourist (Podobed) finds some of the realities beyond the stereotypes of Soviet Russia. Offbeat and uneven. Silent. B&W; 55m. **DIR:** Lev Kuleshov. **CAST:** Podobed, Vsevelod Pudovkin. **1924**

EYES OF THE BIRDS ★★★★ Powerful fact-based psychological drama set in a supposedly model South American prison. A Red Cross investigation into prison conditions leads to reprisals. Unlike most prison movies, this film's effect comes from what it implies rather than what it shows. In French with English subtitles. 83m. **DIR:** Gabriel Auer. **CAST:** Roland Amastutz, Philippe Clevot. **1983**

EYES, THE MOUTH, THE 🦃 Story of a man (Lou Castel) who liberates his soul from the past and embraces life after his twin brother commits suicide. In Italian with English subtitles. Rated R for language and nudity. 100m. **DIR:** Marco Bellocchio. **CAST:** Lou Castel, Angela Molina, Emmanuelle Riva. **1983**

EYES WITHOUT A FACE ★★★★½ Georges Franju, one of the underrated heroes of French cinema, creates an austerely beautiful horror film about a plastic surgeon who, in systematic experiments, removes the faces of beautiful young women and tries to graft them onto the ruined head of his daughter. Imaginative cinematography by Eugen Shuftan with music by Maurice Jarre. Subtitled, not rated. (Originally released in America as *The Horror Chamber of Dr. Faustus.*) B&W; 102m. **DIR:** Georges Franju. **CAST:** Pierre Brasseur, Alida Valli, Edith Scob, Juliette Mayniel. **1960**

FACE OF ANOTHER, THE ★★★★ Excellent surreal drama that explores the dehumanization and identity crisis of a man disfigured in an accident. A great parable of the Frankenstein theme, with hauntingly erotic overtones. In Japanese with English subtitles. B&W; 124m. **DIR:** Hiroshi Teshigahara. **CAST:** Tatsuya Nakadai. **1966**

FAMILY, THE (1987) ★★★ This bustling, good-natured film, thick with anecdotes, covers the life of a man growing up in Italy from the turn of the century to the present. It is a celebration of family life. In Italian with English subtitles. The film has no objectionable material. 140m. **DIR:** Ettore Scola. **CAST:** Vittorio Gassman, Fanny Ardant, Stefania Sandrelli. **1987**

FAMILY GAME, THE ★★★★½ This is a very funny film about a modern Japanese family faced with the same problems as their Western counterparts. A teen with school problems, a father striving for middle-class affluency, and a new tutor who shakes things up result in what was voted best film of 1983 in Japan. With English subtitles. 107m. **DIR:** Yoshimitsu Morita. **CAST:** Yusaku Matsuda, Juzo Itami. **1983**

FANNY (1932) ★★★★ The middle part of a trilogy that began with *Marius* and ended with *César*, this can be viewed on its own. Young Marius leaves Marseilles to become a sailor, not knowing that his fiancée, Fanny, is pregnant. In his absence, she marries another man, who agrees to raise the child as his own. The film itself is static—it was conceived for the stage—but the performances are superb, particularly Raimu as Marius's father. The entire trilogy was condensed and remade in America as *Fanny* (1961). In French with English subtitles. B&W; 120m. **DIR:** Marc Allegret. **CAST:** Raimu, Orane Demazis, Pierre Fresnay. **1932**

FANNY AND ALEXANDER ★★★★★ Set in Sweden around the turn of the century, this movie follows the adventures of two children. Some have called this Ingmar Bergman's first truly accessible work. It is undeniably his most optimistic. In Swedish with English subtitles. Rated R for profanity and violence. 197m. **DIR:** Ingmar Bergman. **CAST:** Pernilla Allwin, Bertil Guve. **1983**

FARAWAY, SO CLOSE ★★★★ Sequel to director Wim Wenders's *Wings of Desire* focuses on the seriocomic adventures of the second angel (Otto Sanders) as he follows Bruno Ganz into the corporeal realm and falls prey to earthly temptation. Reportedly trimmed for American release, this import does not seem to have lost any important moments. Offbeat but heartwarming and thought-provoking. In English and German with English subtitles. Rated PG-13 for violence and profanity. 140m. **DIR:** Wim Wenders. **CAST:** Otto Sander, Peter Falk, Horst Buchholz, Willem Dafoe, Nastassja Kinski, Heinz Ruhmann, Bruno Ganz, Solveig Dommartin, Rudiger Volger, Lou Reed. **1993**

FAREWELL MY CONCUBINE ★★★½ This emotionally engorged, visually staggering epic is about a pair of male Peking opera stars whose commitment to art and each other is challenged throughout fifty years of civil war, foreign invasion, social revolution, political convulsions, and private squabbling. One performer, forced to forsake his true sexual identity both on and off the stage, becomes the odd player out in a volatile love triangle when his mentor marries a courtesan. This exotic backstage pass to the theatrical and political growing pains of China loses momentum after two hours but should not be missed. In Mandarin with English subtitles. Rated R. 154m. **DIR:** Chen Kaige. **CAST:** Leslie Cheung, Zhang Fengyi, Gong Li. **1993**

FATHER ★★★ Istvan Szabo, best known for the Oscar-winning *Mephisto*, directed this drama. A boy creates an elaborate fantasy about the heroism of his father, who was killed in World War II. As an adult, he is led to abandon his fantasies and examine the reality of his heritage. Slow-moving but provocative. In Hungarian with English subtitles. B&W; 89m. **DIR:** Istvan Szabo. **CAST:** Andras Balint, Miklos Gabor. **1966**

FAUST ★★★★★ The undisputed master of early German cinema, Friedrich W. Murnau triumphs once again with the legendary story of Faust. Gosta Ekman gives an excellent performance as Faust and Emil Jannings plays the Devil with comic pathos. Silent with English intertitles. B&W; 100m. **DIR:** F. W. Murnau. **CAST:** Emil Jannings, Gosta Ekman, Camilla Horn. **1926**

FEARLESS (1978) 🦃 This confusing, raunchy Italian film features Joan Collins as a rather inept striptease artist in Vienna. Unrated; it contains violence and nudity. 89m. **DIR:** Stelvio Massi. **CAST:** Joan Collins, Maurizio Merli. **1978**

FELLINI SATYRICON ★★★½ Federico Fellini's visionary account of ancient Rome before Christ is a bizarre, hallucinatory journey. Imaginative art direction, lavish costumes, and garish makeup create a feast for the eyes. Composer Nino Rota's brilliant score is another plus. Italian dialogue with English subtitles. Not rated, contains nudity and violence. 129m. **DIR:** Federico Fellini. **CAST:** Martin Potter, Hiram Keller, Gordon Mitchell, Capucine. **1969**

FELLINI'S ROMA ★★★★ Federico Fellini's odyssey through Rome is the director's impressionistic account of the city of his youth. With the help of a small film crew, Fellini explores the Italian capital with his own unique brand of visionary wit. A brilliant piece of moviemaking. In Italian with English subtitles. Not rated. 128m. **DIR:** Federico Fellini. **CAST:** Peter Gonzales, Marne Maitland, Federico Fellini. **1972**

FERNANDEL THE DRESSMAKER ★★ Using Fernandel as the hub, the film is a bit of whimsy about a gentleman's tailor who desires to become a world-famous couturier. Even with a lightweight plot, watching this famous comedian is certainly worth the time and effort to wade through the nonsense. In French with English subtitles. B&W; 84m. **DIR:** Jean Boyer. **CAST:** Fernandel, Suzy Delair, Françoise Fabian. **1957**

FIELD OF HONOR (1988) ★★ A nineteenth-century French saga about young men at war, with aspirations to the classic status of *The Red Badge of Courage*. Despite its aim at tragic symmetry, the film's muddled and meandering script causes it to fall short. Strangely uninvolving. In French with English subtitles. 89m. **DIR:** Jean-Pierre Denis. **CAST:** Cris Campion. **1988**

FIRE WITHIN, THE ★★★★ After his release from a sanatorium, a suicidal alcoholic looks for reasons not to kill himself. What sounds like a terribly depressing movie becomes a sharp study of a complex character in the hands of Louis Malle (who also scripted). In French with English subtitles. B&W; 121m. **DIR:** Louis Malle. **CAST:** Maurice Ronet, Lena Skerla, Jeanne Moreau, Alexandra Stewart. **1963**

FIREMAN'S BALL, THE ★★½ Highly acclaimed comedy of a small-town firemen's gathering that turns into a sprawling, ludicrous disaster. Fairly weak considering direction by Milos Forman. In Czech with English subtitles. 73m. **DIR:** Milos Forman. **CAST:** Jan Vostricil. **1968**

FIRES ON THE PLAIN ★★★★ Kon Ichikawa's classic uses World War II and soldiers' cannibalism as symbols for the brutality of man. *Fires on the Plain* is uncomplicated and its emotion intensely focused. It is a stark and disturbing vision. In Japanese with English subtitles. 105m. **DIR:** Kon Ichikawa. **CAST:** Eiji Funakoshi. **1959**

FIRST NAME: CARMEN ★★★ Jean-Luc Godard does a fabulous job portraying an eccentric filmmaker whose niece has hired him to direct a movie; actually, she is using him as a front for a terrorist attack. Slow-moving at times. In French with English subtitles. Not rated, but contains profanity and nudity. 85m. **DIR:** Jean-Luc Godard. **CAST:** Maruschka Detmers, Jacques Bonnaffe, Myriem Roussel, Jean-Luc Godard. **1983**

FITZCARRALDO ★★★½ For Werner Herzog, the making of this film was reportedly quite an ordeal. Watching it may be an ordeal for some viewers as well. In order to bring Caruso, the greatest voice in the world, to the backwater town of Iquitos, the title character (Klaus Kinski) decides to haul a large boat over a mountain. Unrated; this film has profanity. In German with English subtitles. 157m. **DIR:** Werner Herzog. **CAST:** Klaus Kinski, Claudia Cardinale. **1982**

FLIGHT OF THE EAGLE ★★★½ This Swedish production presents the true adventure of three foolhardy 1897 polar explorers (one played by Max von Sydow) who tried to conquer the Arctic in a balloon. In Swedish with English subtitles. Unrated; the film has some gore. 139m. **DIR:** Jan Troell. **CAST:** Max von Sydow. **1982**

FLIGHT OF THE INNOCENT ★★★★ When his family is murdered, a sweet-natured 10-year-old boy miraculously escapes, only to be pursued by the killers. Director Carlo Carlei's emotionally involving film unflinchingly examines a shocking, modern-day phenomenon: the kidnapping of children from well-to-do families in northern Italy by their southern neighbors, who hold their victims for ransom. In Italian with English subtitles. Rated R for violence and profanity. 115m. **DIR:** Carlo Carlei. **CAST:** Manuel Colao, Federico Pacifici, Sal Borgese, Giusi Cataldo, Lucio Zagaria, Massimo Lodolo, Francesca Neri, Jacques Perrin. **1993**

FLOR SYLVESTRE ★★★½ Mexican-born beauty Dolores Del Rio made many schlocky movies in America but had to return to her native country to appear in quality productions. This tale of two families torn apart by the Mexican revolution is one of the best. The story is a little corny, but beautifully photographed and directed. In Spanish with English subtitles. B&W; 94m. **DIR:** Emilio Fernandez. **CAST:** Dolores Del Rio, Pedro Armendariz, Emilio Fernandez. **1945**

FLUNKY, WORK HARD! ★★★ This short feature is the earliest surviving work of Japanese filmmaker Mikio Naruse. It's an odd mix about an insurance salesman struggling to provide for his wife and son. But it provides a priceless look at Japanese life before World War II. In Japanese with English subtitles. B&W; 28m. **DIR:** Mikio Naruse. **CAST:** Isamu Yamaguchi. **1931**

FOR A LOST SOLDIER ★★½ During World War II, a 12-year-old Dutch boy has an affair with a Canadian soldier in this film adapted from the autobiographical novel by Rudi van Dantzig. Director Roeland Kerbosch handles the controversial subject matter with taste, although there is a love scene that will shock all but the most open-minded of viewers. This Dutch import is undoubtedly one of the most professionally directed and acted gay love stories, but it is definitely not for everyone. In English and Dutch with subtitles. Unrated, the film has profanity, nudity, and simulated sex. 92m. **DIR:** Roeland Kerbosch. **CAST:** Jeroen Krabbé, Maarten Smit, Andrew Kelly. **1993**

FORBIDDEN GAMES ★★★★★ It has been said that *Forbidden Games* is to World War II what *Grand Illusion* is to World War I. The horror of war has never been more real than as portrayed here against the bucolic surroundings of the French countryside. At the nucleus of the plot is Paulette, played by 5-year-old Brigitte Fossey. Witnessing German troops kill her parents twists the girl, who acquires an attraction for the symbols of death. A truly tragic, must-see work. In French with English subtitles. B&W; 87m. **DIR:** René Clement. **CAST:** Brigitte Fossey, Georges Poujouly. **1951**

FOREVER MARY ★★★ A teacher in between assignments accepts a position at a notorious boys' reform school. His students are tough street kids with little hope of redemption. Updated version of *To Sir With Love*, Italian style. In Italian with English subtitles. Not rated, but contains violence and profanity. 100m. **DIR:** Marco Risi. **CAST:** Michele Placido, Claudio Amendola. **1989**

FORGET MOZART ★★ Poorly paced, surreal whodunit revolving around Mozart. But who killed him? In German with English subtitles. Unrated, contains nudity. 93m.

DIR: Salvo Luther. **CAST:** Armin Mueller-Stahl. **1986**

FORGOTTEN TUNE FOR THE FLUTE, A ★★★ This Glasnost romantic comedy is a little long and stumbles with a somewhat contrived ending, but it's a joy otherwise. It introduces to the West the vivacious and talented Tatyana Dogileva and is a perfect remedy for American movie watchers who think all Russian films are solemn enterprises at best, epic drags at worst. In Russian with English subtitles. 131m. **DIR:** Eldar Ryazanov. **CAST:** Tatyana Dogileva. **1988**

FORTUNE'S FOOL ★★½ Best known for his dramatic roles, Emil Jannings hams it up in this German comedy about a profiteering meat-packer. Jannings displays the gifts that made him a dominating screen figure. Silent. B&W; 60m. **DIR:** Reinhold Schunzel. **CAST:** Emil Jannings, Daguey Servaes, Reinhold Schunzel. **1925**

FORTY SEVEN RONIN ★★★½ A fascinating glimpse into the mentality of the Japanese during World War II, this two-volume cassette rates complete watching by completists only. The first volume is made from an old, scratchy print and is a slow-paced account of how a moment of anger over an insult to a powerful lord's honor brings terrible and unjust punishment. On the second tape, which has been made from a pristine 35mm. print, most of the events from part one are recapped as the lord's retainers plot and execute a daring revenge. In Japanese with English subtitles. Unrated; the film has brief violence. 112m. **DIR:** Kenji Mizoguchi. **CAST:** Chojuro Kawarsaki, Knemon Nakamura. **1942**

FOUR ADVENTURES OF REINETTE AND MIRABELLE ★★★½ French film that is actually slices of everyday life for two different girls—one naïve and one sophisticated. Not much plot; this is more of a character study. Slow-moving but pleasant. In French with English subtitles. 95m. **DIR:** Eric Rohmer. **CAST:** Joelle Miguel, Jessica Forde. **1986**

FOUR BAGS FULL ★★★★ In Nazi-occupied Paris, two scoundrels attempt to transport a contraband slaughtered pig across town. But when word of their cargo gets out, the Nazis are the least of their worries. First-rate comic thriller with a refreshingly cynical look at Frenchmen during the war. In French with English subtitles. Not rated. B&W; 90m. **DIR:** Claude Autant-Lara. **CAST:** Jean Gabin, Bourvil, Louis De Funes. **1956**

400 BLOWS, THE ★★★★★ Poignant story of a boy and the world that seems to be at odds with him is true and touching as few films have ever been. Powerful, tender, and at times overwhelmingly sad, this great film touches all the right buttons without being exploitative. In French with English subtitles. B&W; 99m. **DIR:** François Truffaut. **CAST:** Jean-Pierre Léaud, Patrick Auffay, Claire Maurier, Albert Remy. **1959**

FOURTH MAN, THE ★★★½ Jeroen Krabbe plays a gay alcoholic writer prone to hallucinations. Invited to lecture at a literary society, he meets a mysterious woman who he becomes convinced intends to kill him. *The Fourth Man* emerges as an atmospheric, highly original chiller. In Dutch with English subtitles. Unrated; the film has nudity, simulated sex, violence, and profanity. 128m. **DIR:** Paul Verhoeven. **CAST:** Jeroen Krabbé, Renee Soutendijk. **1984**

FOX AND HIS FRIENDS ★★½ Filmmaker Rainer Werner Fassbinder has the starring role as a lower-class carnival entertainer known as Fox, the Talking Head, who strikes it rich after a hard life by winning the lottery. His wealth attracts an elegant, bourgeois homosexual lover who proceeds to take advantage of him. In German with English subtitles. Not rated, but contains nudity and is recommended for adult viewers. 123m. **DIR:** Rainer Werner Fassbinder. **CAST:** Rainer Werner Fassbinder, Peter Chatel, Karlheinz Böhm, Harry Baer. **1975**

FRANZ 🦃 Leon falls in love with a woman named Leonie. He is tortured by his oppressive mother and his war memories. In French with English subtitles. 88m. **DIR:** Jacques Brel. **CAST:** Jacques Brel. **1972**

FREEZE—DIE—COME TO LIFE ★★★★ Vitaly Kanevski's gritty, uncomfortable look at the hard life in a part of the Soviet Union that's about as far from Moscow as one can get and still be in the USSR. It's the depressing, evocatively filmed story of two youngsters trying to overcome poverty and brutality in the bleak frozen terrain of the Soviet Orient. In Russian with English subtitles. Unrated. 105m. **DIR:** Vitaly Kanevski. **1990**

FRENCH CAN CAN ★★★ Jean Renoir's rich cinematic style is evident in this comedy-drama starring Jean Gabin as a nightclub owner. Renoir tosses his can-can artists at the viewer, seducing us with the consuming spectacle. In French with English subtitles. 93m. **DIR:** Jean Renoir. **CAST:** Jean Gabin. **1955**

FRENCH DETECTIVE, THE ★★★★ Suspenseful police drama featuring Lino Ventura as a tough, independent veteran cop who pursues a hood working for a corrupt politician. Solid performances by Ventura and Patrick Dewaere. In French with English subtitles. 93m. **DIR:** Pierre Granier-Deferre. **CAST:** Lino Ventura, Patrick Dewaere, Victor Lanoux, Jacques Serres. **1975**

FRENCH WAY, THE ★★ Famed burlesque dancer Josephine Baker appears as a café singer in this underdressed comedy about a boy and a girl who want to marry but can't. Baker begins to do her famous feather dance, but the ending is edited out. In French with English subtitles. B&W; 73m. **DIR:** Jacques De Baroncelli. **CAST:** Josephine Baker, Micheline Presle, Georges Marshall. **1952**

FRIDA ★★ Tedious, disjointed account of the life of Mexican painter Frida Kahlo, considered to be the most important woman artist of the twentieth century. The film desperately fails to give any insight into the artist's life, which was laced with human tragedy and self-obsession. In Spanish with English subtitles. Not rated, but contains mild nudity. 108m. **DIR:** Paul Leduc. **CAST:** Ofelia Medina. **1984**

FROM THE LIVES OF THE MARIONETTES ★★ This Ingmar Bergman film, which details the vicious sex murder of a prostitute by an outwardly compassionate and intelligent man, is a puzzle that never really resolves itself. Nevertheless, fans will no doubt consider it another triumphant essay on the human condition. B&W; 104m. **DIR:** Ingmar Bergman. **CAST:** Robert Atzorn, Christine Buchegger, Heinz Bennent. **1980**

FULL HEARTS AND EMPTY POCKETS ★★ A German youth in Rome begins with nothing and, through luck and happy coincidence, rises to a position of wealth and power. Forgettable European production will appeal only to those who can't resist another look at the streets of Rome. Dubbed in English. B&W; 88m. **DIR:** Camillo Mastrocinque. **CAST:** Thomas Fritsch, Alexandra Stewart, Gino Cervi, Senta Berger, Linda Christian, Françoise Rosay. **1963**

FULL MOON IN PARIS ★★ This French film from Eric Rohmer, does not sustain its momentum with this tale of a young girl's disillusionment with her live-in lover. Perhaps the problem is her self-absorption and lack of commitment, but you just don't seem to care about what happens. In French with English subtitles. 102m. **DIR:** Eric Rohmer. **CAST:** Pascale Ogier, Fabrice Luchini, Tcheky Karyo. **1984**

FUNERAL, THE ★★★½ An old man's sudden death creates hilarious havoc for his surviving family members in this engagingly offbeat comedy directed by Juzo Itami. The Japanese burial ritual becomes the stage where the younger generation struggles with the complex rituals of the traditional Buddhist ceremony. In Japanese with English subtitles. 124m. **DIR:** Juzo Itami. **CAST:** Nobuko Miyamoto, Tsutomu Yamazaki. **1987**

FUNNY DIRTY LITTLE WAR (NO HABRA MAS PENAS NI OLVIDO) ★★★ This allegorical, comedic piece begins in the small town of Colonia Vela. The comedy centers around the struggle between the Marxists and the Peronistas in 1974, shortly before the death of Juan Perón. The action quickly builds from a series of foolish misunderstandings to a very funny confrontation. Spanish with English subtitles. Not rated. 80m. **DIR:** Hector Olivera. **CAST:** Federico Luppi, Hector Bidonde. **1985**

GABRIELA ★★★ Sexy Sonia Braga is both cook and mistress for bar owner Marcello Mastroianni in this excellent adaptation of Brazilian novelist Jorge Amado's comic romp *Gabriela, Clove and Cinnamon*. In Portuguese with English subtitles. Rated R. 102m. **DIR:** Bruno Barreto. **CAST:** Sonia Braga, Marcello Mastroianni, Antonio Cantafora. **1983**

GALL FORCE ★★ Japanese animation. A wandering, boorish plot acts as a thin disguise for yet another "prepubescent-girls-get-naked-in-space" story. Occasional cleverness saves this from the turkey bin. In Japanese with English subtitles. Unrated; contains nudity. 86m. **DIR:** Katsuhito Akiyama. **1986**

GALL FORCE 2 ★★½ While marginally better than the original, this animated sequel still has little to recommend it other than some vivid artwork. In this one, Lufy, one of the heroines from the original, is brought back to life only to face the dilemma of continuing a bitter war or trying to save the last habitable world, Earth. In Japanese with English subtitles. Not rated; contains violence and nudity. 50m. **DIR:** Katsuhito Akiyama. **1987**

GAME IS OVER, THE ★★★ Emile Zola's novel *La Curée* was the basis for this adult story of a young woman who marries an older man but finds herself attracted to (and eventually sharing a bed with) his son. Well-acted, this film by Jane Fonda's then-husband Roger Vadim holds up well for today's audiences. In French. 96m. **DIR:** Roger Vadim. **CAST:** Jane Fonda, Peter McEnery, Michel Piccoli, Tina Marquand. **1966**

GAME OF SEDUCTION ★★ A professional killer accepts a bet that he cannot seduce a proper married woman. Tired continental erotica with a cast that should know better. Dubbed. Not rated; contains nudity and sexual situations. 81m. **DIR:** Roger Vadim. **CAST:** Sylvia Kristel, Nathalie Delon, Jon Finch. **1985**

GAMES OF COUNTESS DOLINGEN OF GRATZ, THE ★★½ Baffling drama concerning a schizoid woman (Carol Kane). She indulges in an exercise in reality and fantasy that centers around a little girl's erotic experience. The film's uneven narrative structure only adds to the confusion. In French with English subtitles. Not rated, but contains nudity. 110m. **DIR:** Catherine Binet. **CAST:** Georges Perec, Michel Lonsdale, Carol Kane. **1981**

GARDEN OF DELIGHTS, THE ★★★ Surreal comedy about a wealthy industrialist who suffers amnesia after a car accident. His greedy family attempts to gain the number of his Swiss bank account. In Spanish with English subtitles. 99m. **DIR:** Carlos Saura. **CAST:** José Luis Lopez Vasquez. **1970**

GARDEN OF THE FINZI-CONTINIS, THE ★★★★ Vittorio De Sica's adaptation of a Giorgio Bassani novel views the life of an aristocratic Jewish family's misfortune in Fascist Italy. Flawless acting by Dominique Sanda and Helmut Berger. One of De Sica's best. Rated R. 95m. **DIR:** Vittorio De Sica. **CAST:** Dominique Sanda, Helmut Berger, Lino Capolicchio, Fabio Testi. **1971**

GATE OF HELL ★★★★ Beautiful, haunting tale about a samurai who becomes a monk in twelfth-century Japan in order to atone for his crime of driving a married woman to suicide. Winner of the Academy Award for best foreign film of 1954. Director Teinosuke Kinugasa brilliantly re-creates medieval Japan. In Japanese with English subtitles. 86m. **DIR:** Teinosuke Kinugasa. **CAST:** Machiko Kyo. **1953**

GEISHA, A ★★★★ An aging geisha reluctantly agrees to train the daughter of her old patron. The two women initially do not get along, but the realization that theirs is a dying way of life unites them. A small-scale gem from one of Japan's finest directors. In Japanese with English subtitles. Not rated. B&W; 100m. **DIR:** Kenji Mizoguchi. **CAST:** Michiyo Kogure, Ayako Wakao. **1953**

GENERAL DELLA ROVERE ★★★★ Vittorio De Sica gives a first-rate performance as a small-time swindler who is arrested by the occupying German army and blackmailed into impersonating an executed Italian general. Brilliantly directed by Roberto Rossellini. In Italian with English subtitles. B&W; 130m. **DIR:** Roberto Rossellini. **CAST:** Vittorio De Sica, Hannes Messemer, Sandra Milo, Giovanna Ralli. **1957**

GENERATION, A ★★★ During World War II, two young men in occupied Warsaw join the Resistance. While Andrzej Wajda's first feature film was somewhat restrained by government involvement, it questions the difference between the official and apparent versions of Polish life. In Polish with English subtitles. Not rated. B&W; 90m. **DIR:** Andrzej Wajda. **CAST:** Tadeusz Lomnicki, Tadeusz Janezar, Roman Polanski. **1954**

GERTRUDE ★★★★½ A woman leaves her husband for a younger man. When her lover proves equally unsatisfying, she embarks on a series of affairs before realizing that true happiness lies within herself. Danish director Carl Dreyer's last film almost completely eliminates camera movement in order to force our attention onto what is happening between the characters. In Danish with English subtitles. 116m. **DIR:** Carl Dreyer. **CAST:** Nina Pens Rede, Bendt Rothe. **1963**

GERVAISE ★★★ Soap-opera fans will be the best audience for this adaptation of an Emile Zola novel. Set in 1850 Paris, the movie follows the sad life of a woman who is abandoned by her lover, unlucky in business, and sent into penury by her drunken husband. In French with English subtitles. B&W; 120m. **DIR:** René Clement. **CAST:** Maria Schell, François Perier, Suzy Delair. **1956**

GET OUT YOUR HANDKERCHIEFS ★★★½ Winner of the 1978 Academy Award for best foreign film, this stars Gérard Depardieu as a clumsy husband so desperate to make his melancholic wife happy and pregnant that he provides her with a lover (Patrick Dewaere). A mostly improbable existential drama. In French. Unrated, contains nudity. 108m. **DIR:** Bertrand Blier. **CAST:** Gérard Depardieu, Patrick Dewaere, Carole Laure. **1978**

GIANT ROBO ★★★★ Broadly played and beautifully drawn, this Japanese animated series blends the feel of traditional Saturday matinee serials with today's best animation. Super villains and heroes (including the radio-controlled Giant Robo and his boy master) clash over the fate of the world. Absolutely stunning animation with delightful characters and action. Dubbed in English. Not rated, but suitable for most audiences. 55m. each **DIR:** Yasuhiro Imagawa. **1992**

GIFT, THE ★★★ A 55-year-old bank worker (Pierre Mondy) decides to take early retirement. So his coworkers give him an unusual gift, an expensive hooker (Clio Goldsmith), who is asked to seduce him without his knowing her profession. An amiable sex comedy that most adult viewers will find diverting. In French with English subtitles. Rated R for nudity and profanity. 105m. **DIR:** Michel Lang. **CAST:** Clio Goldsmith, Pierre Mondy, Claudia Cardinale. **1982**

GINGER AND FRED ★★★★ Set in the bizarre world of a modern-television supernetwork, this Fellini fantasy presents Giulietta Masina and Marcello Mastroianni as Ginger and Fred—a dance couple of the late Forties who copied the style of Fred Astaire and Ginger Rogers. The two are reunited for *Here's to You*, a television extravaganza. *Ginger and Fred* is a brilliant satire of television and modern life. Rated PG-13 for profanity and adult themes. 127m. **DIR:** Federico Fellini. **CAST:** Marcello Mastroianni, Giulietta Masina, Franco Fabrizi. **1986**

GIRL FROM HUNAN ★★★ At the turn of the century, a Chinese woman's arranged marriage and her place in decent society are threatened by her opposition to the accepted moral standards of her community. This study of cultural taboos is one of the few films made in the People's Republic of China to be seen in this country. In Cantonese with English subtitles. Unrated. 99m. **DIR:** Xie Fei,

U Lan. **CAST:** Na Renhua, Liu Qing, Deng Xiaotuang. **1988**

GIRL WITH THE HATBOX, THE ★★ A greedy pig-faced employer gives his employee a lottery ticket instead of wages. She wins and subsequent opportunist advances from her employer. Slapstick, postrevolution esoterica. Silent. B&W; 67m. **DIR:** Boris Barnet. **CAST:** Anna Sten, Vladimir Fogel. **1927**

GO-MASTERS, THE ★★★★ An impressive coproduction from Japan and China. *The Go-Masters,* set primarily during the Sino-Japanese War, details the odyssey of a young man who becomes a champion player in the ancient art of Go at a heartrending price. A fascinating tale of obsession, heartbreak, and the tragedies of war. In Chinese and Japanese with English subtitles. Unrated, the film has violence. 123m. **DIR:** Junya Sato, Duan Ji-Shun. **CAST:** Sun Dao-Lin. **1984**

GOALIE'S ANXIETY AT THE PENALTY KICK ★★★ An athlete suffering from alienation commits a senseless murder for no apparent reason in this slow-moving, existential thriller. Arthur Brauss gives a moody performance. Excellent adaptation by Wim Wenders of the Peter Handke novel. In German with English subtitles. B&W; 101m. **DIR:** Wim Wenders. **CAST:** Arthur Brauss, Erika Pluhar. **1971**

GODS OF THE PLAGUE ★★ Incredibly boring drama about a professional killer who eludes a police manhunt with the help of his underworld friends. Hard-to-read subtitles. In German with English subtitles. Not rated, but contains graphic nudity. B&W; 92m. **DIR:** Rainer Werner Fassbinder. **CAST:** Hanna Schygulla, Margarethe von Trotta. **1970**

GOING PLACES ★★ Memorable only as one of Gérard Depardieu's first screen appearances. He and Patrick Dewaere play amiable lowlifes who dabble in petty thievery. Contains one of filmdom's most acutely uncomfortable scenes, when one of the young lads gets shot in the testicles. In French with English subtitles. Rated R for sex. 117m. **DIR:** Bertrand Blier. **CAST:** Gérard Depardieu, Patrick Dewaere, Miou-Miou, Jeanne Moreau, Isabelle Huppert, Brigitte Fossey. **1974**

GOLDEN COACH, THE ★★★★ Jean Renoir's little-known Franco-Italian masterpiece features Anna Magnani in a stunning performance as the leading lady of an eighteenth-century acting troupe touring South America. Magnani finds herself caught in a complex love triangle with a soldier, a vain bullfighter, and a viceroy who gives her a golden coach. In English. 95m. **DIR:** Jean Renoir. **CAST:** Anna Magnani. **1952**

GOLDEN DEMON ★★★ As a rule, most Japanese love stories are sad. *Golden Demon,* a story of true love broken by pride, tradition, and avarice, is an exception. The story of a poor young man, in love with his adopted parents' daughter, who loses her to a rich entrepreneur (an arranged marriage), is richly entertaining. In Japanese with English subtitles. 91m. **DIR:** Koji Shima. **CAST:** Jun Negami. **1953**

GOLEM, THE (HOW HE CAME INTO THE WORLD) (DER GOLEM, WIE ER IN DIE WELT) ★★★★ Director Paul Wegener plays the lead role as the Golem, an ancient clay figure from Hebrew mythology that is brought to life by means of an amulet activated by the magic word "Aemaet" (the Hebrew word for truth). In a story similar to *Frankenstein,* the man of clay roams through medieval Prague in a mystic atmosphere created by the brilliant cameraman Karl Freund. Silent. B&W; 70m. **DIR:** Paul Wegener. **CAST:** Paul Wegener. **1920**

GOLGOTHA ★★ Early, seldom-seen depiction of the passion of Jesus Christ was reverently filmed in France, where it was a big box-office success. Adapted from the four gospels of the New Testament, using only direct quotes for the lines spoken by Jesus. In French with English subtitles. B&W; 100m. **DIR:** Julien Duvivier. **CAST:** Robert le Vigan, Jean Gabin, Harry Baur. **1935**

GONZA THE SPEARMAN ★★★★ Powerful, classic tale of love, honor, and tragedy set in the early 1700s in Japan. Director Masahiro Shinoda's brilliant adaptation of well-known bunkaru playwright Monzaemon Chikamatsu's story features an equally impressive score by composer Toru Takemitsu. In Japanese with English subtitles. Not rated, but contains nudity and violence. 126m. **DIR:** Masahiro Shinoda. **CAST:** Hiromi Go. **1986**

GOODBYE EMMANUELLE ★★ One of the *Emmanuelle* soft-core series, *Goodbye Emmanuelle* takes place on a tropical island and concerns a succession of personal and sexual relationships among half a dozen men and women. The dubbing is tolerable. Rated R for sexual situations. 92m. **DIR:** François Letterier. **CAST:** Sylvia Kristel, Umberto Orsini, Jean Pierre Bouvier. **1979**

GOSPEL ACCORDING TO SAINT MATTHEW, THE ★★★★ Pier Paolo Pasolini's visionary account of Jesus Christ's spiritual struggle against the afflictions of social injustice. Shot on location throughout southern Italy with a cast of nonprofessional actors who possess a natural quality. This highly acclaimed film received a special jury prize at the Venice Film Festival. In Italian with English subtitles. B&W; 136m. **DIR:** Pier Paolo Pasolini. **CAST:** Enrique Irazoque. **1964**

GRAIN OF SAND, THE ★★★½ A struggling woman retreats to her hometown to search for an old love. Delphine Seyrig's strong performance is the highlight of this moving drama. In French with English subtitles. 90m. **DIR:** Pomme Meffre. **CAST:** Delphine Seyrig, Genevieve Fontanel. **1982**

GRAND ILLUSION ★★★★★ Shortly before Hitler plunged Europe into World War II, this monumental French film tried to examine why men submit to warfare's "grand illusions." We are taken to a German prison camp in World War I, where it becomes quite easy to see the hypocrisy of war while watching the day-to-day miniworld of camp life. This classic by Jean Renoir is a must-see for anyone who appreciates great art. B&W; 95m. **DIR:** Jean Renoir. **CAST:** Jean Gabin, Pierre Fresnay, Erich Von Stroheim, Marcel Dalio, Julien Carette. **1937**

GRAVE OF THE FIREFLIES ★★★★ Those who doubt that animation can successfully tell serious, meaningful stories should watch this wonderful animated feature. Young Seita and his little sister, homeless and orphaned during the final days of World War II, try desperately to survive in a time when food and aid are scarce. This story will break your heart. In Japanese with English subtitles. Not rated, but suitable for most audiences. 88m. **DIR:** Isao Takahata. **1988**

GREAT MADCAP, THE ★★½ To cure a rich man of his profligate ways, his family tricks him into thinking that his fortune has been lost. One of director Luis Buñuel's least interesting films, this features satirical themes that he would later redo. In Spanish with English subtitles. B&W; 90m. **DIR:** Luis Buñuel. **CAST:** Fernando Soler, Ruben Rojo. **1949**

GREAT, MY PARENTS ARE DIVORCING ★★★★ The French have a talent for dramatizing stories from a child's point of view. In this film, love and marriage and divorce are explored through the reactions of a group of children who unite as their real families are dissolving. Warmhearted film, offering laughs and wisdom in equal portions. In French with English subtitles. Unrated. 98m. **DIR:** Patrick Braoude. **CAST:** Patrick Braoude, Clementine Celarie, Patrick Bouchitey. **1992**

GREEN ROOM, THE ★★ Based on the writings of Henry James, this is a lifeless and disappointing film by François Truffaut about a writer who turns a dilapidated chapel into a memorial for World War I soldiers. Not the French filmmaker at his best. In French with English subtitles. Rated PG. 93m. **DIR:** François Truffaut. **CAST:** François Truffaut, Nathalie Baye, Jean Dasté. **1978**

GREEN WALL, THE ★★★★½ A young family, determined to escape the pressure of life in Lima, struggles against overwhelming obstacles to survive in the exotic, overgrown Peruvian jungle. Stunning cinematography by Mario Robles Godoy. In Spanish with English subtitles. 110m. **DIR:** Armando Robles Godoy. **CAST:** Julio Aleman. **1970**

GRIM REAPER, THE (1962) ★★★ Absorbing crime-drama about the violent death of a prostitute—as told through three different people. Pier Paolo Pasolini's script recalls *Rashomon*, with its series of flashbacks. Bernardo Bertolucci's first feature film. In Italian with English subtitles. B&W; 100m. **DIR:** Bernardo Bertolucci. **CAST:** Francesco Rulu. **1962**

GUNBUSTER—VOLS. 1–3 ★★ Japanese animation. A tedious, overwrought tale of duty and sacrifice in the Space Force. Quality animation. In Japanese with English subtitles. Unrated violence and illustrated nudity. 55–60m. each **DIR:** Hideaki Anno. **1989**

GUY: AWAKENING OF THE DEVIL ★★ Our heroes in this animated tribute to sex and violence are a pair of hard-boiled soldiers of fortune, one of whom gains the ability to mutate into a giant, apparently invulnerable creature. In Japanese with English subtitles. Available rated R or unrated, both with nudity and violence; the unrated version contains explicit sex. 40m. **DIR:** Yorihisa Uchida. **1990**

GUY II: SECOND TARGET ★★½ Guy and Raina, the terrible twosome of fortune hunters, go after a fortune hidden in the temple of a bizarre cult in this animated feature. Fans of the transforming-monster subgenre will enjoy this one. In Japanese with English subtitles. Not rated; contains violence, profanity, and brief nudity. 33m. **DIR:** Yorihisa Uchida. **1992**

GUYVER: OUT OF CONTROL ★★½ An early look at the origin of the Guyver superhero, this animated story tries to make up for its lack of detail with violent action but doesn't quite succeed. In Japanese with English subtitles. Not rated; contains violence and nudity. 55m. **DIR:** Hiroshi Watanabe. **1987**

HAIL MARY ★★★★ This story of the coming of Christ in modern times will offend only the most dogmatic Christians, or narrow-minded religious zealots. Godard's eye for the aesthetic gives this film a compassionate feel. *The Book of Mary*, a film by Anne-Marie Mieville, is the prologue and is equally beautiful. In French with English subtitles. Not rated; the equivalent of an R for nudity. 107m. **DIR:** Jean-Luc Godard. **CAST:** Myriem Roussel, Thierry Lacoste, Philippe Lacoste. **1985**

HAIRDRESSER'S HUSBAND, THE ★★★★ A 12-year-old boy has his first experience with sensuality in the chair of a local hairdresser. The warmth of the shampoo and the closeness of her body give birth to a romantic notion that leads the adult Antoine (Jean Rochefort) to marry a hairdresser (Anna Galiena). French writer-director Patrice Leconte takes a whimsical approach to the story. In French with English subtitles. Unrated, the film has simulated sex. 84m. **DIR:** Patrice Leconte. **CAST:**

Jean Rochefort, Anna Galiena, Roland Bertin. 1992

HALF OF HEAVEN ★★★★ A woman works her way up from poverty to power in this unusual import from Spain. Rosa (Angela Molina) almost seems to drift her way to the top as Madrid's most successful restaurateur, but there are deeper meanings in this often funny and always fascinating mix of magic, politics, and romance. Unrated, the film has brief violence. In Spanish with English subtitles. 127m. **DIR:** Manuel Gutierrez Aragon. **CAST:** Angela Molina, Margarita Lozano, Fernando Fernán-Gomez. 1987

HANNA K. 🦃 Jill Clayburgh is an Israeli lawyer appointed to defend a man who entered the country illegally in an attempt to reclaim the land where he grew up. Rated R for coarse language. 110m. **DIR:** Constantin Costa-Gavras. **CAST:** Jill Clayburgh, Jean Yanne, Gabriel Byrne, David Clennon. 1984

HANUSSEN ★★★★ In this German import based on a true story, Klaus Maria Brandauer is at the peak of his powers as a clairvoyant whose hypnotic, frightening talent for predicting the future both shocks and arouses the apathetic German public in the 1920s and 1930s. When his prophecies bring him to the attention of Adolf Hitler and the Nazi party, he finds his life in danger. In German with English subtitles. Rated R for violence and nudity. 117m. **DIR:** Istvan Szabo. **CAST:** Klaus Maria Brandauer, Erland Josephson, Walter Schmidinger. 1989

HAPPILY EVER AFTER ★★ For some unknown reason, a seemingly happy wife and mother takes off with a bisexual male prostitute in this Brazilian film. After *Dona Flor and Her Two Husbands*, director Bruno Barreto again presents a woman who seems to need two very different men in her life. In Portuguese with English subtitles. Unrated, but contains nudity and simulated sex. 108m. **DIR:** Bruno Barreto. **CAST:** Regina Duarte, Paulo Castelli. 1986

HAPPY NEW YEAR (LA BONNE ANNÉE) ★★★★ Delightful French crime caper mixed with romance and comedy. As two thieves plot a jewel heist, one (Lino Ventura) also plans a meeting with the lovely antique dealer (Françoise Fabian) who runs the shop next door to their target. Director Claude Lelouch's film blends suspense with engaging wit. Rated PG for profanity and sex. Available in French version or dubbed. 114m. **DIR:** Claude Lelouch. **CAST:** Lino Ventura, Françoise Fabian, Charles Gerard. 1974

HARVEST ★★★★ Simple but touching story of a man and woman struggling to survive in a deserted village. One of the great director's best loved films, though it does drag on a bit too long. In French with English subtitles. B&W; 129m. **DIR:** Marcel Pagnol. **CAST:** Gabriel Gabrio, Fernandel, Orane Demazis. 1937

HAWKS AND THE SPARROWS, THE ★★½ A father and his rambunctious son take a stroll that soon becomes a religious pilgrimage in this poetic comedy. The famous Italian comic Toto gives this lifeless story its brightest moments. In Italian with English subtitles. B&W; 90m. **DIR:** Pier Paolo Pasolini. **CAST:** Toto, Davoli Ninetto. 1966

HEAD AGAINST THE WALL ★★★ An unruly boy who blames his father for his mother's accidental death is sent to a mental hospital. Director Georges Franju shot much of this (his first feature-length film) in an actual insane asylum, and the sense of fatalistic foreboding may be a bit too oppressive for many viewers. In French with English subtitles. B&W; 98m. **DIR:** Georges Franju. **CAST:** Jean-Pierre Mocky, Pierre Brasseur, Anouk Aimée, Charles Aznavour. 1958

HEART OF GLASS ★★★★½ One of director Werner Herzog's most haunting and mystifying films. In a small village in preindustrial Germany, a glassblower dies, and the secret for his unique ruby glass is lost forever leaving the townspeople in hysteria. A remarkable, visionary film. In German with English subtitles. Not rated. 93m. **DIR:** Werner Herzog. **CAST:** Josef Bierbichler. 1976

HEAT OF DESIRE ★★ So many sex comedies are about married men who discover adultery brings new vitality, this plot has become a cinematic cliché. But this didn't stop director Luc Beraud from using it again in this disappointing film. In French with English subtitles. Unrated; the film has nudity and suggested sex. 91m. **DIR:** Luc Beraud. **CAST:** Patrick Dewaere, Clio Goldsmith, Jeanne Moreau, Guy Marchand. 1984

HEAVEN AND EARTH (1991) ★★★ Imagine the epic battles of the great Akira Kurosawa samurai epics, but without the rich philosophical dimension or tragic aura. This film lacks the emotional staying power of the master's work, but it is still rich in splendor. In Japanese with English subtitles. Rated PG-13. 106m. **DIR:** Haruki Kadokawa. **CAST:** Takaaki Enoki. 1991

HENRY IV ★★★ This Italian TV film is based on a Luigi Pirandello play. A modern aristocrat is thrown from his horse and then believes he is Emperor Henry IV. Twenty years pass and his past lover and a psychiatrist devise a plan to shake him back to reality. It's interesting, but seems long. In Italian with English subtitles. 95m. **DIR:** Marco Bellocchio. **CAST:** Marcello Mastroianni, Claudia Cardinale, Leopoldo Trieste. 1984

HEY, BABU RIBA ★★★½ Yugoslav version of *American Graffiti*. Poignant, funny reminiscence of four boys and a girl growing up in the early Fifties. The film has an easy charm. In Serbo-Croatian with English subtitles. Rated R for mild profanity, violence, and sex. 109m. **DIR:** Javan Acin. **CAST:** Gala Videnovic. **1986**

HIDDEN FORTRESS, THE ★★★★★ Toshiro Mifune stars in this recently reconstructed, uncut, and immensely entertaining 1958 Japanese period epic directed by Akira Kurosawa. George Lucas has openly admitted the film's influence on his *Star Wars* trilogy. *Hidden Fortress* deals with a strong-willed princess (à la Carrie Fisher in the space fantasy) and her wise, sword-wielding protector (Mifune in the role adapted for Alec Guinness). In Japanese with English subtitles. Unrated, the film has violence. B&W; 126m. **DIR:** Akira Kurosawa. **CAST:** Toshiro Mifune, Minoru Chiaki. **1958**

HIGH AND LOW ★★★★★ From a simple, but exquisitely devised detective story, Akira Kurosawa builds a stunning work of insight, humor, suspense, and social commentary. Toshiro Mifune is the businessman who must decide if he will pay a ransom to kidnappers who have taken his chauffeur's young son by mistake. A masterwork, featuring superb acting by two of the giants of Japanese cinema, Mifune and Tatsuya Nakadai. Based on Ed McBain's 87th Precinct novel *King's Ransom*. In Japanese with English subtitles. B&W; 143m. **DIR:** Akira Kurosawa. **CAST:** Toshiro Mifune, Tatsuya Nakadai, Tatsuya Mihashi, Tsutomu Yamazaki, Takashi Shimura. **1963**

HIGH HEELS (1972) ★★★ A French comedy to make you chuckle more often than not. A medical student marries the homely daughter of a hospital president to ensure himself a job. In French with English subtitles. Not rated, but recommended for viewers over 18 years of age. 90m. **DIR:** Claude Chabrol. **CAST:** Laura Antonelli, Jean-Paul Belmondo, Mia Farrow. **1972**

HIGH HEELS (1992) ★★★★ In this black comedy, the incandescent Victoria Abril plays the neurotic daughter of a self-absorbed film and stage star. When the mother returns to Spain after several years in Mexico, both women find themselves suspects in a murder investigation. It's funny, suspenseful, and oh-so-sexy. In Spanish with English subtitles. Unrated; the film has nudity, simulated sex, and violence. 115m. **DIR:** Pedro Almodóvar. **CAST:** Victoria Abril, Marisa Paredes, Miguel Bosé. **1991**

HIMATSURI ★★★★½ Metaphysical story about man's lustful and often destructive relationship with nature. Kinya Kitaoji plays a lumberjack in a beautiful seaboard wilderness which is about to be marred by the building of a marine park. Rated R for nudity and violence. 120m. **DIR:** Mitsuo Yanagimachi. **CAST:** Kinya Kitaoji. **1985**

HIROSHIMA, MON AMOUR ★★★★ A mind-boggling tale about two people: one, a Frenchwoman, the other, a male survivor of the blast at Hiroshima. They meet and become lovers. Together they live their pasts, present, and futures in a complex series of fantasies, and nightmares. In French with English subtitles. B&W; 88m. **DIR:** Alain Resnais. **CAST:** Emmanuelle Riva, Bernard Fresson, Eiji Okada. **1959**

HOLES, THE ★★ Obscure French satire about a group of misanthropes who live in the Paris sewers. Francophiles will want to see it for the cast, but there's little else to recommend it. Dubbed in English. Unrated. 94m. **DIR:** Pierre Tchernia. **CAST:** Michel Serrault, Michel Galabru, Charles Denner, Philippe Noiret, Gérard Depardieu. **1973**

HOLIDAY HOTEL ★★★ It's August, and all of France is going on vacation for the entire month. The cast of this fast-paced comedy is heading toward the Brittany coast. Michel Lang keeps the tempo moving with clever farcical bits and dialogue. Partially in English, the movie has an R rating due to nudity and profanity. 109m. **DIR:** Michel Lang. **CAST:** Sophie Barjac, Daniel Ceccaldi, Michel Grellier, Guy Marchand. **1978**

HOLY INNOCENTS ★★★★ This moving drama explores the social class struggles in a remote farming community during Franco's rule of Spain. It's a sensitive and compelling look into the struggle of the rural lower class against the wealthy landowners. This critically acclaimed film earned acting awards at the Cannes Film Festival for Alfredo Landa and Francisco Rabal. In Spanish with English subtitles. 108m. **DIR:** Marcel Camus. **CAST:** Alfredo Landa, Francisco Rabal. **1984**

HOME AND THE WORLD ★★★★★ Satyajit Ray's critically acclaimed, harrowing account of the coming-of-age of an Indian woman. She falls in love with her husband's best friend, an organizer against British goods. This fascinating portrait of Bengali life was based on the Nobel Prize–winning novel by Rabindranath Tagore. In Bengali with English subtitles. Not rated. 130m. **DIR:** Satyajit Ray. **CAST:** Soumitra Chatterjee, Victor Banerjee. **1984**

HORSE, THE ★★★ Grim tale of a father and son from a small village forced to travel to Istanbul to find work. Their struggles and the conditions in which the impoverished must live are realistically portrayed. Unrated, but far too bleak for kids. In Turkish with English subtitles. 116m. **DIR:** Ali Ozgenturk. **CAST:** Genco Erkal. **1982**

HORSE OF PRIDE, THE ★★ Unconvincing study of peasant life set in Brittany at the turn of the century, as seen through the eyes of a young boy. In French with English subtitles. Unrated. 118m. **DIR:** Claude Chabrol.

CAST: Jacques Dufilho, Bernadette Lesache, François Cluzet. **1980**

HORSE THIEF, THE ★★★★ The mysterious barren landscape of Tibet becomes the setting for a tribal drama of theft, ostracism, and horrible retribution. Beautifully photographed amidst a series of Buddhist rituals captured wordlessly. In Mandarin with English subtitles. Not rated. 88m. **DIR:** Tian Zhuangzhuang. **CAST:** Tseshang Rigzin. **1987**

HOT HEAD ★★½ Patrick Dewaere stars in this so-so French comedy about a freewheeling soccer athlete who gets kicked off the team after an incident with a star player, finds himself drifting in the streets, and eventually is framed for a rape he didn't commit. Dubbed (poorly) in English. Rated R for nudity. 90m. **DIR:** Jean-Jacques Annaud. **CAST:** Patrick Dewaere, France Dougnac, Dorothee Jemma. **1978**

HOUR OF THE STAR ★★★ A homely, dull-witted girl from the Brazilian countryside comes to São Paulo. She gets a job as a typist (even though she can neither type nor spell) while dreaming of a better life such as she has seen in the movies. Relentlessly depressing. In Portuguese with English subtitles. Unrated. 96m. **DIR:** Suzana Amaral. **CAST:** Marcelia Cartaxo. **1977**

HOUR OF THE WOLF ★★★★ Ingmar Bergman's surreal, claustrophobic look into the personality of a tormented artist. Bizarre hallucinations shape the artist's world, creating a disturbing vision that seems at times completely out of control. Probably the closest Bergman has ever come to creating a horror film. In Swedish with English subtitles. B&W; 89m. **DIR:** Ingmar Bergman. **CAST:** Max von Sydow, Liv Ullmann, Ingrid Thulin. **1968**

HOUSE OF ANGELS ★★★½ British director Colin Nutley has somehow tapped into the Swedish sensibility, becoming a popular filmmaker in his adopted country. This offbeat comedy examines the culture clash that occurs when the leather-clad granddaughter of a recently deceased landowner roars into town on a motorcycle to claim her inheritance and shocks the stuffy locals with her openly decadent lifestyle. Not for all tastes. In Swedish with English subtitles. Rated R for profanity, nudity, and simulated sex. 119m. **DIR:** Colin Nutley. **CAST:** Helena Bergstrom, Rikard Wolff, Sven Wollter, Viveka Sidahl, Per Oscarsson. **1993**

HOUSEHOLDER, THE ★★★★ Engaging low-budget comedy about a naïve young man and woman learning to adjust to their arranged marriage. The first collaboration by the legendary team of producer Ismail Merchant, writer Ruth Prawer Jhabvala and director James Ivory, aided by an uncredited Satyajit Ray as editor. In English. B&W; 100m. **DIR:** James Ivory. **CAST:** Shashi Kapoor. **1963**

HOW FUNNY CAN SEX BE? ★★½ Mediocre anthology featuring eight tales about love and sex. Giancarlo Giannini and Laura Antonelli liven up their segments, but you might want to fast-forward through some of the others. Rated R for nudity. 97m. **DIR:** Dino Risi. **CAST:** Giancarlo Giannini, Laura Antonelli. **1976**

HUMAN CONDITION, THE, PART ONE: NO GREATER LOVE ★★★★ Based on a popular Japanese bestseller, *The Human Condition*, tells the story of a sensitive, compassionate man who tries to maintain his humanity through the spiraling horrors of World War II. Part One opens in 1943, just as the war is beginning to go badly for Japan. The film is quite long, but never dull, with breathtaking wide-screen photography (the film is available in a letter box video format). The fractured-English subtitles are the only drawback. Unrated. B&W; 200m. **DIR:** Masaki Kobayashi. **CAST:** Tatsuya Nakadai, Michiyo Aratama, Chikage Awashima. **1958**

HUMAN CONDITION, THE, PART TWO: THE ROAD TO ETERNITY ★★★½ Director Masaki Kobayashi's epic film trilogy continues, with hero Kaji entering the imperial army in the closing months of World War II. Despite his doubts about Japanese war aims, he proves a good soldier and acquits himself bravely. Unlike the first film in the trilogy, this one ends with a cliff-hanger. Not rated, but not for children or squeamish adults. B&W; 180m. **DIR:** Masaki Kobayashi. **CAST:** Tatsuya Nakadai. **1959**

HUMAN CONDITION, THE, PART THREE: A SOLDIER'S PRAYER ★★★★ Director Masaki Kobayashi's magnum opus comes to its shattering conclusion as Kaji, his unit wiped out in battle, leads a band of stragglers and refugees through the Manchurian wilderness. Acting, cinematography, and editing are all first-rate in this heartwrenching tale of Japan's darkest days. Not rated. B&W; 190m. **DIR:** Masaki Kobayashi. **CAST:** Tatsuya Nakadai. **1961**

HUMANOID, THE ★★★ Japanese animation set on a far-off and idyllic planet. The title character is a "young" humanoid that is just beginning to understand and participate in human relationships. Unfortunately, "her" life is suddenly disturbed by a scheming villain. In Japanese with English subtitles. 45m. **DIR:** Shin-Ichi Masaki. **1986**

HUNGARIAN FAIRY TALE, A ★★★★½ An imaginative and affecting tale from Hungary, blending myth, social satire, and a Dickensian story of a Budapest orphan. Filmed in stunning black and white, and employing little dialogue. In Hungarian with English subtitles. 97m. **DIR:** Gyula Gazdag. **CAST:** David Vermes. **1988**

HUNGER (1966) ★★★★ Hauntingly funny portrait of a starving writer in Norway, circa 1890. The would-be writer explores his fantasies as he stumbles through the streets penniless. Per Oscarsson turns in a brilliant performance that netted him the best actor award at the Cannes Film Festival. A must-see! In Swedish with English subtitles. B&W; 100m. **DIR:** Henning Carlsen. **CAST:** Per Oscarsson, Gunnel Lindblom. **1966**

HUNT, THE ★★★½ A powerful, uncompromising meditation on violence, about three veterans of the Spanish Civil War who hunt rabbits a generation later in the same hills across which they fought. In Spanish with English subtitles. Not rated, but contains graphic violence. B&W; 92m. **DIR:** Carlos Saura. **CAST:** Ismael Merlo. **1954**

HUNTER IN THE DARK ★★★ Japan circa 1750: dissatisfied with their corrupt government, Japanese warriors create underground groups that wield Mafia-type power. Some brilliant shots of Ezo, the perfect land acquisition. Letter-boxed, which makes reading subtitles easy. In Japanese with English subtitles. Unrated, contains nudity, violence, and profanity. 138m. **DIR:** Hideo Gosha. **CAST:** Tatsuya Nakadai. **1979**

I AM CURIOUS BLUE ★★ Both *I Am Curious Yellow* and *Blue* were derived from the same footage, shot by director Vilgot Sjoman in the late Sixties. When the finished product turned out to be too long, he turned it into two movies instead. Ergo, *Curious Blue* is less a sequel than simply more of the same meandering inquiry into social issues, punctuated by an occasional naked body. In Swedish with English subtitles. Unrated; the movie features frank but unerotic sex. B&W; 103m. **DIR:** Vilgot Sjoman. **CAST:** Lena Nyman, Vilgot Sjoman, Borje Ahlstedt. **1968**

I AM CURIOUS YELLOW ★½ This Swedish import caused quite an uproar when it was released in the mid-1960s, because of its frontal nudity and sexual content. It seems pretty dull today. There isn't much of a plot built around the escapades of a young Swedish sociologist whose goal in life appears to be having sex in as many weird places as she can. In Swedish with English subtitles. B&W; 121m. **DIR:** Vilgot Sjoman. **CAST:** Lena Nyman, Borje Ahlstedt. **1967**

I KILLED RASPUTIN 🦃 It can't have been easy, but they actually managed to make a completely boring movie about Rasputin, the peasant monk who gained control over the czar of Russia in the period prior to the Russian Revolution. Actually, Rasputin isn't in it that much, and when he is they've cleaned up his act. Dubbed in English. 95m. **DIR:** Robert Hossein. **CAST:** Gert Fröbe, Peter McEnery, Geraldine Chaplin, Ivan Desny. **1967**

I LOVE YOU (EU TE AMO) ★★★ This release, starring Brazilian sexpot Sonia Braga, is a high-class hard-core—though not close-up—sex film with pretensions of being a work of art. And if that turns you on, go for it. Unrated, the film has nudity and profanity. 104m. **DIR:** Arnaldo Jabor. **CAST:** Sonia Braga, Paulo Cesar Pereio. **1982**

I SENT A LETTER TO MY LOVE ★★★ Simone Signoret and Jean Rochefort star as sister and brother in this absorbing study of love, devotion, loneliness, and frustration. After Signoret places a personal ad (requesting male companionship) in the local paper, Rochefort responds—and they begin a correspondence, via mail, that brings passion and hope to their otherwise empty lives. In French with English subtitles. 96m. **DIR:** Moshe Mizrahi. **CAST:** Simone Signoret, Jean Rochefort, Delphine Seyrig. **1981**

I VITELLONI ★★★★ Five men in a small town on the Adriatic become discontented and restless. Stunning cinematography highlights this consideration of rootlessness, a central theme that runs throughout Fellini's work. In Italian with English subtitles. B&W; 104m. **DIR:** Federico Fellini. **CAST:** Franco Interlenghi, Alberto Sordi, Franco Fabrizi. **1953**

I WAS STALIN'S BODYGUARD ★★★★½ Fascinating, controversial documentary about the last surviving personal bodyguard of Josef Stalin. Filmmaker Semeon Arranovitch brilliantly weaves together firsthand testimony with rare footage, including Stalin's home movies, creating a penetrating glimpse into a violent, repressive era of the Soviet Union. In Russian with English subtitles. Not rated. 73m. **DIR:** Semeon Arranovitch. **1990**

ICICLE THIEF, THE ★★★★½ Writer-director-actor Maurizio Nichetti has been called the Woody Allen of Italy, so it's appropriate that he's now made a wonderful film combining some of the ideas of *Purple Rose of Cairo* with the technical virtuosity of *Zelig*. A delightfully inventive parody-satire, this explores the ability of movies to carry us into other worlds. In Italian with English subtitles. Unrated. 90m. **DIR:** Maurizio Nichetti. **CAST:** Maurizio Nichetti. **1990**

ICY BREASTS ★★★ Detective Alain Delon discovers that his beautiful client has been killing the men in her life. Effective suspense-drama. In French with English subtitles. 105m. **DIR:** Georges Lautner. **CAST:** Alain Delon, Mirelle Darc. **1975**

IDIOT, THE ★★★★★ Early gem by Akira Kurosawa based on the novel by Dostoyevski about the confrontation between a demented ruffian and a holy fool prince. Akira Kurosawa transports this tale of madness and jealousy to postwar Japan and places it among blizzards and claustrophobic, madly lit interiors. Highly recommended! In Japanese with English subtitles. B&W; 166m. **DIR:** Akira Kurosawa. **CAST:**

Toshiro Mifune, Masayuki Mori, Setsuko Hara. **1951**

IKIRU ★★★★½ *Ikiru* is the Japanese infinitive *to live.* The film opens with a shot of an X ray; a narrator tells us the man—an Everyman—is dying of cancer. But a dream flickers to life, and his last years are fulfilled by a lasting accomplishment. *Ikiru* packs a genuine emotional wallop. In Japanese with English subtitles. B&W; 143m. **DIR:** Akira Kurosawa. **CAST:** Takashi Shimura. **1952**

IL BIDONE ★★★ Broderick Crawford gives a strong performance in this nearly forgotten film by Federico Fellini, about an aging con man who realizes his lifetime of selfishness has only made his existence meaningless. In Italian with English subtitles. B&W; 92m. **DIR:** Federico Fellini. **CAST:** Broderick Crawford, Richard Basehart, Giulietta Masina, Franco Fabrizi. **1955**

IL GRIDO ★★½ Drab film about a worker and his child wandering around rural Italy. Also known as *The Outcry.* In Italian with English subtitles. 102m. **DIR:** Michelangelo Antonioni. **CAST:** Steve Cochran, Alida Valli, Betsy Blair. **1957**

IL LADRO DI BAMBINI (STOLEN CHILDREN) ★★★★★ An 11-year-old girl and her younger brother are taken away from their mother, who has been supporting the family from her daughter's earnings as a prostitute. It falls to a young, good-hearted military officer to escort the youngsters to a children's home, and he turns the trip into a rediscovery of love and happiness for both of them. Both hard-edged and heartwarming, this is a brilliant motion picture. In Italian with English subtitles. 116m. **DIR:** Gianni Amelio. **CAST:** Enrico Lo Verso, Valentina Scalici, Guiseppe Ieracitano. **1992**

ILLUSION TRAVELS BY STREETCAR ★★★ Two employees of a municipal public transport company in Mexico City are dissatisfied with their superiors, so they withdraw an old tram, get drunk at a local festival, and take one last trip through the town. Light comedy from director Luis Buñuel during his prolific Mexican cinema period. In Spanish with English subtitles. 90m. **DIR:** Luis Buñuel. **CAST:** Lilia Prado, Carlos Navarro, Agustin Isunza. **1953**

I'M THE ONE YOU'RE LOOKING FOR ★★★★ A beautiful model is raped, then becomes curiously obsessed with her attacker, willing to endure anything and anyone to find him. Set in the seedy, seething atmosphere of Barcelona, this is a fascinating exploration of the macabre aspect of human sexual longing. In Spanish with English subtitles. Rated R for nudity. 85m. **DIR:** Jaime Chavarri. **CAST:** Patricia Adrian. **1988**

IMMORTAL BACHELOR, THE ★★ A female juror hearing the case of a cleaning woman who killed her cheating husband fantasizes about the dead man. But for the well-known cast, this Italian comedy would never have been imported. Dubbed in English. Unrated, but a PG equivalent. 95m. **DIR:** Marcello Fondato. **CAST:** Giancarlo Giannini, Monica Vitti, Vittorio Gassman, Claudia Cardinale. **1979**

IN A GLASS CAGE ★★ Horrifying film about an ex-Nazi doctor, now confined to an iron lung, who is tracked down by a young man who survived his sexual tortures. Made with great skill but overwrought—few will be able to stomach it. In Spanish with English subtitles. Unrated; definitely not for children. 112m. **DIR:** Agustin Villaronga. **CAST:** Gunter Meisner, David Sust. **1986**

IN NOME DEL PAPA RE (IN THE NAME OF THE POPE-KING) ★★★★ A compelling drama of intrigue, political conflict, and murder. In 1867, as Italian patriots fight to unify their country, an affluent public official's resignation is complicated when his son becomes a prime suspect in the bombing of a military barrack. Nino Manfredi's performance netted him a best actor award at the Paris Film Festival. In Italian with English subtitles. Not rated, but contains profanity and violence. 115m. **DIR:** Luigi Magni. **CAST:** Nino Manfredi. **1987**

IN THE REALM OF PASSION ★★★ Nagisa Oshima, Japan's most controversial director, scores some high and low points with this erotic, metaphysical ghost story about a woman who, along with her lover, kills her husband only to suffer a haunting by his vengeful spirit. Excellent performances by both leads along with some impressive atmospheric cinematography. In Japanese with English subtitles. Not rated, but contains nudity and violence. 108m. **DIR:** Nagisa Oshima. **CAST:** Kazuko Yoshiyuki, Tatsuya Fuji. **1980**

IN THE REALM OF THE SENSES ★★ Uneasy blend of pornography and art in this tale of sexual obsession. Director Nagisa Oshima delves into the mystery of human sexuality, but comes away with a shallow pretentious result. In Japanese with English subtitles. Rated X for its depiction of sex. 104m. **DIR:** Nagisa Oshima. **CAST:** Tatsuya Fuji, Eiko Matsuda. **1976**

IN THE WHITE CITY ★★★ A naval mechanic leaves his ship in Lisbon. He wanders the city, photographing it with his Super-8 camera, and sends the films back to his wife to explain why he won't come home. An elegantly photographed but slow-moving mood piece. In French with English subtitles. Not rated. 108m. **DIR:** Alain Tanner. **CAST:** Bruno Ganz, Teresa Madruga. **1983**

INDOCHINE ★★★★½ Set in French Indochina in 1930, this exquisite import chronicles the violent changes that led to the creation of Vietnam from the ruins of colonialism. Catherine Deneuve is superb in the pivotal role of an Asian-born, French-descended owner of a rubber plantation. In French with English subtitles. Rated PG-13 for violence, nudity, and profanity. 155m. **DIR:** Regis Wargnier. **CAST:** Catherine Deneuve, Vincent Perez, Linh Dan Pham, Jean Yanne. **1992**

INFERNAL TRIO, THE ★★★½ Lurid, stylishly gruesome black comedy about a sociopathic lawyer (Michel Piccoli) who, after seducing two sisters, enlists them to marry and murder victims and defraud their insurance companies. Based on an actual police case. In French with English subtitles. Not rated, but contains violence and nudity. 100m. **DIR:** Francis Girod. **CAST:** Romy Schneider, Michel Piccoli, Andrea Ferreol. **1974**

INHERITORS, THE 🦃 A teenage boy with a troubled family life stumbles into a neo-Nazi group, which trains him in the use of weapons and how and who to hate. A German film, this production didn't survive its trip overseas. 90m. **DIR:** Walter Bannert. **CAST:** Nicholas Vogel. **1984**

INNOCENCE UNPROTECTED ★★★★ Controversial Yugoslavian filmmaker Dusan Makavejev took a 1942 melodrama (the first feature film made in the Serb language), restored and recut it, and added new interviews with its director and cast. He then used it as the basis for a singular collage incorporating other elements of contemporary political importance. The result is alternately ironic, satirical, and serious, but always compelling. In Serb with English subtitles. Not rated. 78m. **DIR:** Dusan Makavejev. **1968**

INNOCENT, THE ★★★★ Some rate this as the most beautiful of all Luchino Visconti's films. Set in a nineteenth-century baronial manor, it's the old tale of the real versus the ideal, but beautifully done. In Italian with English subtitles. Rated R due to some explicit scenes. 115m. **DIR:** Luchino Visconti. **CAST:** Laura Antonelli, Giancarlo Giannini, Jennifer O'Neil. **1976**

INSECT WOMAN ★★★★ Sachiko Hidari gives an emotionally supercharged performance that gained her a best actress award at the Berlin Film Festival. In this harrowing drama, she plays an impoverished country girl who escapes a brutal existence by fleeing to Tokyo where she finds success as a madam. Director Shohei Imamura weaves a dark and often humorous story with shocking overtones. Winner of Japanese film awards for best actress, director, and film. In Japanese with English subtitles. B&W; 123m. **DIR:** Shohei Imamura. **CAST:** Sachiko Hidari. **1963**

INTERMEZZO (1936) ★★★★ Original version of the story about an affair between young pianist Ingrid Bergman and married violinist Gosta Ekman. Long unseen (David O. Selznick suppressed it when he remade it in Hollywood three years later), this rediscovery is a video treasure for Bergman fans. In Swedish with English subtitles. B&W; 88m. **DIR:** Gustav Molander. **CAST:** Gosta Ekman, Ingrid Bergman. **1936**

INTERROGATION ★★★★ A cabaret singer is imprisoned after sleeping with a military officer. This is a harrowing drama of one woman's struggle to survive unyielding cruelty and atrocious living conditions. Upon completion, this movie was banned by the Polish government, until the director managed to smuggle it out of the country. A gem. In Polish with English subtitles. Unrated; the film has nudity and violence. 118m. **DIR:** Richard Bugajski. **CAST:** Krystyna Janda, Adam Ferency, Agnieszka Holland. **1982**

INVESTIGATION ★★★ When the village tannery owner (Victor Lanoux) kills his wife to marry his pregnant girlfriend (Valerie Mairesse), a meticulous inspector comes to investigate. His Columbo-ish tactics pick up the film's pace and turn a so-so melodrama into a delightful winner. In French with English subtitles. Rated R for violence. 116m. **DIR:** Etienne Perier. **CAST:** Victor Lanoux, Jean Carmet, Valerie Mairesse, Michel Robin. **1979**

INVISIBLE ADVERSARIES ★★½ Controversial avant-garde film about a Viennese photographer who believes that extraterrestrial beings are taking over the minds of her fellow citizens while raising their level of human aggression. This dark satire is interesting but uneven. In German with English subtitles. Not rated, but contains explicit nudity and graphic violence. 112m. **DIR:** Valie Export. **CAST:** Susanne Wild, Peter Weibel. **1977**

INVITATION AU VOYAGE ★★★½ Here is a strange but watchable French import with plenty of suspense and surprises for those willing to give it a chance to work its unusual magic. Peter Del Monte's film allows the viewer to make assumptions and then shatters those conceptions with a succession of inventive twists and revelations. In French with English subtitles. Rated R for adult content. 100m. **DIR:** Peter Del Monte. **CAST:** Laurent Malet, Aurore Clement, Mario Adorf. **1982**

IP5: THE ISLAND OF PACHYDERMS ★★ This is another beautiful but confusing film from Jean-Jacques Beineix, the artful but enigmatic creator of *Diva*, *Betty Blue*, and *The Moon in the Gutter*. This tells of two Parisian street kids, a teenage Hispanic graffiti artist and an 11-year-old black street rapper. They steal a car, only to discover an elderly man asleep in the backseat. He teaches them mysterious lessons about nature and life. Since he's played by the masterful Yves Montand in his last performance, this portion of *IP5* is moving, even if its meaning is seldom clear. In French with English subtitles. 119m. **DIR:** Jean-Jacques Beineix. **CAST:**

Yves Montand, Olivier Martinez, Sekkou Sail, Geraldine Pailhas. 1992

IPHIGENIA ★★★★★ A stunning film interpretation of the Greek classic *Iphigenia in Aulis*. Irene Papas is brilliant as Clytemnestra, the caring and outraged mother. Intense score by Mikos Theodorakis. In Greek with English subtitles. No MPAA rating. 127m. **DIR:** Michael Cacoyannis. **CAST:** Irene Papas. 1978

IREZUMI (SPIRIT OF TATTOO) ★★★★½ An erotic tale of obsession that calls forth the rebirth of a near-dead art. A woman defies cultural taboos and gets her back elaborately tattooed to fulfill her mate's obsession. Rated R for nudity. 88m. **DIR:** Yoichi Takabayashi. **CAST:** Masayo Utsunomiya, Tomisaburo Wakayama. 1983

ISTANBUL 🦃 A grungy American with a mysterious past meets a penniless student in Belgium and involves him in a kidnapping. This English-dubbed thriller from France is hampered by the hammy overacting of Brad Dourif. Rated R for nudity, profanity, and sexual situations. 90m. **DIR:** Marc Didden. **CAST:** Brad Dourif, Dominique Deruddere, Ingrid De Vos. 1985

ITALIAN STRAW HAT, THE ★★★ The future happiness of newlyweds is threatened when the groom must find a replacement for a straw hat eaten by a horse. Failure means fighting a duel with the lover of the married woman who was wearing the hat. A silent classic with English intertitles and musical score. B&W; 72m. **DIR:** René Clair. **CAST:** Albert Préjean, Olga Tschechowa. 1927

IVAN THE TERRIBLE—PART I & PART II ★★★★★ Considered among the classics of world cinema, this certainly is the most impressive film to come out of the Soviet Union. This epic biography of Russia's first czar was commissioned personally by Joseph Stalin to encourage acceptance of his harsh and historically similar policies. World-renowned director Sergei Eisenstein, instead, transformed what was designed as party propaganda into a panoramic saga of how power corrupts those seeking it. B&W; 188m. **DIR:** Sergei Eisenstein. **CAST:** Nikolai Cherkassov, Ludmila Tselikovskaya. 1945

J'ACCUSE ★★★★ Director Abel Gance's remake of this classic silent film shows the horrors of war as it affects two friends, soldiers in love with the same woman. Cinematically rich, with an unforgettable sequence showing war casualties rising from their graves. In French with English subtitles. B&W; 95m. **DIR:** Abel Gance. **CAST:** Victor Francen, Jean Max. 1938

JACKO AND LISE 🦃 This film should have been called *Jacko and Freddie* because most of it concerns Jacko and his pal Freddie escaping responsibility and adulthood by doing juvenile things. In French. Rated PG. 92m. **DIR:** Walter Bal. **CAST:** Laurent Malet, Annie Girardot, Michel Montanary, Evelyne Bouix, Françoise Arnoul. 1975

JAMON, JAMON ★★½ A male model is hired to woo a young woman by her well-to-do mother, who disapproves of the girl's love for the son of the town prostitute. This film was named best picture at the Venice Film Festival, but we thought it was little more than a silly sex comedy with a soap-opera-style plot. In Spanish with English subtitles. Unrated, the film has nudity, simulated sex, profanity, and violence. 95m. **DIR:** Bigas Luna. **CAST:** Anna Galiena, Stefania Sandrelli, Javier Bardeem, Penelope Cruz. 1993

JAZZMAN ★★★½ Good-humored, accessible story about a classically trained Soviet musician who tries to start a jazz combo in the 1930s. In Russian with English subtitles. Not rated. 95m. **DIR:** Karen Chakhnazarov. **CAST:** Igor Skoliar, Alexandre Pankratov-Tchiorny. 1983

JE VOUS AIME (I LOVE YOU ALL) ★★ Some films are so complicated and convoluted you need a viewer's guide while watching them. So it is with this flashback-ridden French import. About a 35-year-old woman, Alice (Catherine Deneuve), who finds it impossible to keep a love relationship alive, it hops, skips, and jumps back and forth through her life. No MPAA rating; the film has sexual situations and nudity. 105m. **DIR:** Claude Berri. **CAST:** Catherine Deneuve, Jean-Louis Trintignant, Serge Gainsbourg. 1981

JEAN DE FLORETTE ★★★★★ This is a sort of French *Days of Heaven*, an epic set close to the land, specifically the hilly farm country of Provence. Land is the central issue around which the action swirls. Yves Montand is spellbinding as an ambitious, immoral farmer who dupes his city-bred neighbor Jean de Florette (played by the equally impressive Gérard Depardieu). The rest of the story is told in *Manon of the Spring*. In French with English subtitles. Rated PG. 122m. **DIR:** Claude Berri. **CAST:** Yves Montand, Gérard Depardieu, Daniel Auteuil. 1987

JENNY LAMOUR ★★★★ Without each other's knowledge, a venal cabaret singer and her doting husband try to cover up what they believe to be their involvement in a murder. But a dogged policeman (a wonderfully sardonic performance by Louis Jouvet) is determined to discover the truth. Witty, atmospheric, and professional. Dubbed. B&W; 105m. **DIR:** Henri-Georges Clouzot. **CAST:** Louis Jouvet, Suzy Delair, Bernard Blier. 1947

JESUS OF MONTREAL ★★★★½ Denys Arcand, the French-Canadian writer-director, finds original things to say with a not totally original idea—that the actor playing Jesus in a modern-day passion play may, in fact, *be* Jesus. Lothaire Bluteau is superb in the title role. In French with English subtitles. Rated R for profanity. 119m. **DIR:** Denys Arcand. **CAST:** Lothaire Bluteau, Denys Arcand. **1990**

JOHNNY STECCHINO ★★ This is a silly slapstick farce of mistaken identity that was the most popular film at the Italian box office up till that time. Roberto Benigni directs and plays the dual roles of a tough mafioso and a timid look-alike bus driver. When the shy driver is mistaken for a mob boss, his life is changed dramatically. The overlong film offers wacky, simplistic humor, not unlike a Jerry Lewis movie with an Italian accent. In Italian with English subtitles. 122m. **DIR:** Roberto Benigni. **CAST:** Roberto Benigni, Nicoletta Braschi, Paolo Bonacelli. **1992**

JOKE OF DESTINY ★★ Italian audiences may have laughed uproariously at this new film by director Lina Wertmuller. However, American viewers are unlikely to get the joke. In Italian with English subtitles. Rated PG for profanity. 105m. **DIR:** Lina Wertmuller. **CAST:** Ugo Tognazzi, Piera Degli Esposti, Gastone Moschin. **1984**

JONAH WHO WILL BE 25 IN THE YEAR 2000 ★★★½ A provocative, Swiss-French character study, centering on eight people thrust together by the social and political events of the late 1960s. The title obliquely refers to the unborn child carried by the pregnant Myriam Boyer. Mature, playful, and entertaining, it is bookended by the same director's *No Man's Land.* In French with English subtitles. Rated PG. 115m. **DIR:** Alain Tanner. **CAST:** Jean-Luc Bideau, Rufus, Miou-Miou, Jacques Denis, Dominique Labourier, Myriam Boyer, Roger Jendly. **1976**

JOSEPHA ★★ Infidelity ruins the professional and personal lives of a married pair of actors. Writer Christopher Frank adapted his own novel but can't get this self-serious drama to work on screen. Dubbed. Not rated; sexual situations. 100m. **DIR:** Christopher Frank. **CAST:** Claude Brasseur, Miou-Miou, Bruno Cremer. **1983**

JOUR DE FêTE ★★½ Jacques Tati is the focal point of this light comedy loosely tied to the arrival of a carnival in a small village. As François, the bumbling postman, Tati sees a film on the heroism of the American postal service and tries to emulate it on his small rural route. In French with subtitles. B&W; 81m. **DIR:** Jacques Tati. **CAST:** Jacques Tati, Guy Decomble, Paul Frankeur. **1949**

JOURNEY OF HOPE ★★★★ Swiss director Xavier Koller's Oscar-winning film chronicles the harrowing journey of a family of Kurds who attempt to leave the abject poverty of their Turkish village for the "promised land" of Switzerland. Based in part on fact and in part on Koller's imaginings, this is nevertheless a gripping motion picture. In Kurdish, Turkish, German, and Italian. Unrated, the film contains subject matter too harsh for children. 110m. **DIR:** Xavier Koller. **CAST:** Necmettin Cobanoglu. **1990**

JU DOU ★★★★★ This Oscar-nominated Chinese film is a lovely, sensual, ultimately tragic tale of illicit love in the strict, male-dominated feudal society of rural China, circa 1920. On visual imagery alone, the film would be worthy of attention. In Chinese with English subtitles. Unrated. 93m. **DIR:** Zhang Yimou. **CAST:** Gong Li, Li Baotian. **1990**

JUD SUSS *Jud Suss (The Jew, Suss)* is infamous as the most rabid of the anti-Semitic films made by the Nazis under personal supervision of propaganda minister Joseph Goebbels. It depicts "the Jewish menace" in both symbolic and overt terms in a story about a wandering Jew who enters a small European country and nearly brings it to ruin. Any serious student of cinema should see it as an example of the medium's enormous power to proselytize; it's an extreme and hateful version of what art does every day. In German with English subtitles. B&W; 97m. **DIR:** Veidt Harlan. **CAST:** Ferdinand Marian, Werner Krauss. **1940**

JUDEX ★★★½ This remake of a serial from the early days of cinema will make you laugh out loud one moment and become misty-eyed with nostalgia the next. Based on an old potboiler by Feuillade and Bernede, *Judex* ("the judge") is an enjoyable adventure of a superhero who is lovable, human, and fallible. In French with English subtitles. B&W; 103m. **DIR:** Georges Franju. **CAST:** Channing Pollock, Jacques Jouanneau, Edith Scob, Michel Vitold, Francine Berge. **1963**

JUDGE AND THE ASSASSIN, THE ★★★ In nineteenth-century France, a rural judge tries to ascertain whether a serial killer is insane or merely faking to escape execution. Interesting but ultimately vague (at least to American eyes) historical drama. In French with English subtitles. Unrated; brief nudity. 130m. **DIR:** Bertrand Tavernier. **CAST:** Philippe Noiret, Michel Galabru, Jean-Claude Brialy, Isabelle Huppert. **1976**

JULES AND JIM ★★★★★ Superb character study, which revolves around a bizarre ménage à trois. It is really a film about wanting what you can't have and not wanting what you think you desire once you have it. In French with English subtitles. B&W; 104m. **DIR:** François Truffaut. **CAST:** Oskar Werner, Jeanne Moreau, Henri Serre. **1961**

JULIET OF THE SPIRITS ★★★★★ The convoluted plot in this classic centers around a wealthy wife suspicious of her cheating husband. Giulietta Masina (in real life, Mrs. Fellini) has never been so tantalizingly innocent with her Bambi eyes. This is Fellini's first attempt with color. 148m. **DIR:** Federico

Fellini. **CAST:** Giulietta Masina, Sandra Milo, Valentina Cortese, Sylva Koscina. **1965**

JUNE NIGHT ★★★½ Ingrid Bergman gives a harrowing performance in this well-crafted melodrama about a young woman who changes her identity in order to escape the scars of a violent incident at the hands of a former lover. This poignant film gives viewers a chance to experience a young Bergman before her success in Hollywood. In Swedish with English subtitles. B&W; 90m. **DIR:** Per Lindberg. **CAST:** Ingrid Bergman. **1940**

JUPITER'S THIGH ★★★★½ The delightful *Dear Inspector* duo is back in this delicious sequel directed by Philippe de Broca (*King of Hearts*). This time, the lady detective (Annie Girardot) and her Greek archaeologist lover (Philippe Noiret) get married and honeymoon—where else?—in Greece. But they aren't there long before they find themselves caught up in mayhem. It's great fun, served up with sophistication. In French with English subtitles. 90m. **DIR:** Philippe de Broca. **CAST:** Annie Girardot, Philippe Noiret. **1983**

KAGEMUSHA ★★★★★ A 70-year-old Akira Kurosawa outdoes himself in this epic masterpiece about honor and illusion. Kurosawa popularized the samurai genre—which has been described as the Japanese equivalent of the Western—in America with his breathtaking, action-packed films. *Kagemusha* is yet another feast for the eyes, heart, and mind. Rated PG. 159m. **DIR:** Akira Kurosawa. **CAST:** Tatsuya Nakadai. **1980**

KAMERADSCHAFT ★★★½ In this classic, the story development is slow, but the concept is so strong, and the sense of cross-cultural camaraderie so stirring that the film remains impressive. The story concerns French miners getting trapped by a mine disaster, with German miners attempting a daring rescue. In German and French with English subtitles. B&W; 87m. **DIR:** G. W. Pabst. **CAST:** George Chalia, David Mendaille, Ernest Busch. **1931**

KAMIKAZE 89 ★★★ The late Rainer Werner Fassbinder stars in this bizarre fantasy-thriller set in a decadent German city in 1989. A bomb has been planted in the headquarters of a giant conglomerate and a police lieutenant (Fassbinder) has very little time to locate it. In German with English subtitles. 90m. **DIR:** Wolf Gremm. **CAST:** Rainer Werner Fassbinder, Gunther Kaufmann, Brigitte Mira, Franco Nero. **1983**

KANAL ★★★★ Andrzej Wajda's compelling war drama about the Polish resistance fighters during World War II brought international acclaim to the Polish cinema. This film explores the dreams, the despair, and the struggle of a generation who refused to be held captive in their own land by the Nazi war machine in 1944. In Polish with English subtitles. B&W; 96m. **DIR:** Andrzej Wajda. **CAST:** Teresa Izewska. **1957**

KAOS ★★★½ Italian writer-directors Paolo and Vittorio Taviani adapted four short stories by Luigi Pirandello for this sumptuously photographed film about peasant life in Sicily. For all its beauty and style, this is a disappointing, uneven work. The first two stories are wonderful, but the final pair leave a lot to be desired. In Italian with English subtitles. Rated R for nudity and violence. 188m. **DIR:** Paolo Taviani, Vittorio Taviani. **CAST:** Margarita Lozano, Enrica Maria Mudugno, Omero Antonutti. **1986**

KATIE'S PASSION ★★ The story of a poor country girl's struggle to survive in Holland during the economic crisis of the 1880s. Director Paul Verhoeve misses the mark with this saga. Rutger Hauer delivers a rather lackluster performance as a vain banker. Not much passion, or anything else here. In Dutch with English subtitles. 107m. **DIR:** Paul Verhoeven. **CAST:** Rutger Hauer, Monique van de Ven. **1988**

KIDNAP SYNDICATE, THE ★★ James Mason plays a millionaire whose child has been kidnapped. Luc Merenda is the poor father of a child who has been taken along with Mason's. Director Fernando Di Leo tries to juxtapose the irony of the two fathers, but it comes off like a trite melodrama with lots of blood spilling and profanity. 105m. **DIR:** Fernando Di Leo. **CAST:** James Mason, Luc Merenda, Valentina Cortese. **1976**

KIKA ★★★★ Just when you thought Spanish bad boy Pedro Almodóvar had run out of naughty shock strategies, along comes *Kika*. Nominally about a none-too-bright woman who loves both a photographer and his American stepfather, who may be a murderer, the story is really just an excuse to poke fun at our morbid, media-fed fascination with serial criminals. The film includes what can only be called the silliest rape scene ever staged, though it's still bound to outrage many viewers. In English and Spanish with English subtitles. Unrated, with lots of slapstick sex, nudity, and some violence. 95m. **DIR:** Pedro Almodóvar. **CAST:** Veronica Forque, Peter Coyote, Victoria Abril, Alex Casanovas, Rossy De Palma. **1993**

KILLER, THE ★★★★★ John Woo's best film, a preposterously perfect mix of Sam Peckinpah firepower and Douglas Sirk melodrama—with both raised to the nth degree. As an honorable assassin trying to get out of the business, Chow Yun-Fat oozes charisma. Woo's impeccable pacing and incredible action choreography create an operatic intensity that leaves you feeling giddy. Available both dubbed and in Cantonese with English subtitles. Unrated; very strong violence. 102m. **DIR:** John Woo. **CAST:** Chow Yun-Fat, Sally Yeh, Danny Lee. **1989**

KIMAGURE ORANGE ROAD, VOLS. 1–4 ★★★ Japanese animation. It is difficult to categorize this engrossing series as there are so many different elements involved in the stories. Essentially, this is a drama centering around a young man's relationship with two different girls. In Japanese with English subtitles. Unrated; contains nudity. 50m. **DIR:** Morikawa Shigeru. **1988**

KIMAGURE ORANGE ROAD: THE MOVIE ★★★½ Japanese animation. Two of the young characters from the Orange Road series have gone on to college where they confront their feelings for one another, much to the dismay of the third corner of their love triangle. Absorbing drama series. In Japanese with English subtitles. Unrated; contains nudity. 70m. **DIR:** Mochizuki Tomomichi. **1988**

KINDERGARTEN ★★★½ Poet Yevgenii Yevtushenko wrote and directed this film based on his own childhood memories of life in Moscow during World War II, especially the evacuation of the city as the Nazis approached. The chaos as seen through childlike eyes is compelling, even strangely beautiful. In Russian with English subtitles. Not rated. 159m. **DIR:** Yevgenii Yevtushenko. **1983**

KING OF HEARTS ★★★★½ Philippe de Broca's wartime fantasy provides delightful insights into human behavior. A World War I Scottish infantryman (Alan Bates) searching for a hidden enemy bunker enters a small town that, after being deserted by its citizens, has been taken over by inmates of an insane asylum. In French with English subtitles. No MPAA rating. 102m. **DIR:** Philippe de Broca. **CAST:** Alan Bates, Genevieve Bujold. **1966**

KINGS OF THE ROAD ★★★★ This is the film that put the new-wave German cinema on the map. Wim Wenders's classic road tale of wanderlust in Deutschland centers on a traveling movie projectionist-repairman who encounters a hitchhiker who is depressed following the collapse of his marriage. The men form an unusual relationship while en route from West to East Germany. A truly astonishing film with a great rock 'n' roll score. In German with English subtitles. B&W; 176m. **DIR:** Wim Wenders. **CAST:** Rudiger Vogler, Hanns Zischler, Lisa Kreuzer. **1976**

KNIFE IN THE WATER ★★★★ Absolutely fascinating feature-film debut for director Roman Polanski. A couple off for a sailing holiday encounter a young hitchhiker and invite him along. The resulting sexual tension is riveting, the outcome impossible to anticipate. In many ways, this remains one of Polanski's finest pictures. In Polish with English subtitles. Unrated; the film has sexual situations. B&W; 94m. **DIR:** Roman Polanski. **CAST:** Leon Niemczyk, Jolanta Umecka, Zygmunt Malanowicz. **1962**

KOJIRO ★★★★ This first-rate semisequel to director Hiroshi Inagaki's *Samurai Trilogy* casts Tatsuya Nakadai as the fabled master swordsman, Musashi Miyamoto, whose exploits made up the three previous films. But he is not the main character here. Instead, the focus is on Kojiro (Kikunosuke Onoe), whose goal is to become the greatest swordsman in all Japan and thus follow the trail blazed by Miyamoto. In Japanese with English subtitles. Unrated; the film contains violence. 152m. **DIR:** Hiroshi Inagaki. **CAST:** Kikunosuke Onoe, Yuriko Hoshi, Tatsuya Nakadai. **1967**

KRIEMHILDE'S REVENGE ★★★★ This is a perfect sequel to the splendid *Siegfried.* Watch them both in one sitting if you get the chance. Siegfried's vengeful lover Kriemhilde raises an army to atone for his death. Beautifully photographed and edited, this international success placed German cinema in the vanguard of filmmaking. Silent. B&W; 95m. **DIR:** Fritz Lang. **CAST:** Margarete Schon, Rudolf Klein-Rogge, Paul Richter, Bernhard Goetzke. **1925**

KWAIDAN ★★★★ An anthology of ghost stories adapted from books by Lafcadio Hearn, an American writer who lived in Japan in the late nineteenth century. Colorful, eerie, and quite unique, it's one of the most visually stunning horror films ever produced. The movie isn't for children, though—it could induce nightmares. In Japanese with English subtitles. 164m. **DIR:** Masaki Kobayashi. **CAST:** Michiyo Aratama, Keiko Kishi, Tatsuya Nakadai. **1963**

L'ANGE (THE ANGEL) ★★★ Strange concoction of the bizarre and grotesque make up this metaphysical animation feature depicting murderous phantasms stuck in a parallel universe. This film contains some dazzling images; too bad they found their way into an incoherent movie. In French with English subtitles. Not rated, but contains nudity and violence. 70m. **DIR:** Patrick Bokanowski. **1982**

L'ANNÉE DES MEDUSES 🦃 If Jackie Collins were French, she'd probably be churning out stuff like this. On the Riviera, a young girl competes with her mother for the pick of the season's hunk crop. In French with English subtitles. Unrated, but loaded with nudity and soft-core sex. 110m. **DIR:** Christopher Frank. **CAST:** Valerie Kaprisky, Bernard Giraudeau, Caroline Cellier. **1986**

L'ARGENT ★★★★★ Robert Bresson's last film, almost a fable, charts the inexorable moral degradation of a man condemned for a crime he didn't commit. Like all of this great director's work, *L'Argent* demands close attention, but rewards it with unforgettable images of overpowering emotional resonance. In French with English subtitles. Not rated. 90m. **DIR:** Robert Bresson. **CAST:** Christian Patey, Sylvie van den Elsen. **1983**

L'ATALANTE ★★★ The ocean and the elements form a backdrop for director Jean Vigo's surrealistic exercise. A disjointed but intriguing journey into the mind of an artist. Vigo died before his thirtieth birthday, shortly after completing *L'Atalante*, robbing the world of a promising filmmaker. In French with English subtitles. B&W; 82m. **DIR:** Jean Vigo. **CAST:** Michel Simon, Jean Dasté, Dita Parlo. **1934**

L'AVENTURA ★★★★ A girl disappears on a yachting trip, and while her lover and best friend search for her, they begin a wild romantic affair. Antonioni's penetrating study of Italy's bored and idle bourgeoisie contains some staggering observations on spiritual isolation and love. Winner of the Special Jury Award at Cannes. Italian with English subtitles. B&W; 145m. **DIR:** Michelangelo Antonioni. **CAST:** Monica Vitti, Gabriele Ferzetti, Lea Massari. **1960**

LA BALANCE ★★★★ *La Balance* is an homage of sorts to the American cop thriller. It turns the genre inside out, however, by focusing on the plight of two unfortunates—a prostitute (Nathalie Baye) and a petty criminal (Philippe Léotard)—who get caught in a vise between the cops and a gangland chief. The result is a first-rate crime story. In French with English subtitles. Rated R for nudity, profanity, and violence. 102m. **DIR:** Bob Swaim. **CAST:** Nathalie Baye, Philippe Léotard, Richard Berry, Maurice Ronet. **1982**

LA BELLE NOISEUSE ★★★★ As one wag put it, this four-hour art film is *really* about watching paint dry. Yet, it's also a fascinating, often-enthralling examination of the creative process. Its subject is the relationship between a gorgeous woman and the retired painter she inspires to return to painting. He's played by the remarkable Michel Piccoli, and the scenes in which he nervously contemplates reentering the painful world of creation make the film's four-hour running time a small price to pay. In French with English subtitles. 240m. **DIR:** Jacques Rivette. **CAST:** Michel Piccoli, Jane Birkin, Emmanuelle Beart, Marianne Denicourt, David Bursztein. **1991**

LA BêTE HUMAINE ★★★★½ Remarkable performances by Jean Gabin, Fernand Ledoux, and Simone Simon, along with Jean Renoir's masterful editing and perfectly simple visuals, elevate a middling and grim Emile Zola novel to fine cinema. The artistry of *La Bête Humaine*, a film about duplicity and murder, transcends what could have been a seedy little tale. In French with English subtitles. B&W; 99m. **DIR:** Jean Renoir. **CAST:** Jean Gabin, Julien Carette, Fernand Ledoux, Jean Renoir, Simone Simon. **1938**

LA BOUM ★★★ A teenager (Sophie Marceau) discovers a whole new world open to her when her parents move to Paris. Her new set of friends delight in giving "boums"—French slang for big parties. Although this film seems overly long, many scenes are nevertheless tender and lovingly directed by Claude Pinoteau. In French with English subtitles. No MPAA rating. 100m. **DIR:** Claude Pinoteau. **CAST:** Sophie Marceau, Brigitte Fossey, Claude Brasseur. **1980**

LA CAGE AUX FOLLES ★★★★ A screamingly funny French comedy and the biggest-grossing foreign-language film ever released in America, this stars Ugo Tognazzi and Michel Serrault as lovers who must masquerade as husband and wife so as not to obstruct the marriage of Tognazzi's son to the daughter of a stuffy bureaucrat. In French with English subtitles. Rated PG for mature situations. 110m. **DIR:** Edouard Molinaro. **CAST:** Ugo Tognazzi, Michel Serrault. **1978**

LA CAGE AUX FOLLES II ★★ This follow-up to the superb French comedy is just more proof "sequels aren't equals." In French with English subtitles. Rated PG for mature situations. 101m. **DIR:** Edouard Molinaro. **CAST:** Ugo Tognazzi, Michel Serrault. **1981**

LA CAGE AUX FOLLES III, THE WEDDING Pathetic and dreadful second sequel to *La Cage Aux Folles*. Rated PG-13. 88m. **DIR:** Georges Lautner. **CAST:** Michel Serrault, Ugo Tognazzi, Stéphane Audran. **1986**

LA CHIENNE ★★★★ Jean Renoir's first sound feature stars Michel Simon as a married man who finds himself involved with a prostitute after rescuing her from a beating by her pimp. Remade by Fritz Lang in 1945 as *Scarlet Street*. In French with English subtitles. B&W; 95m. **DIR:** Jean Renoir. **CAST:** Michel Simon, Janie Mareze. **1931**

LA DOLCE VITA ★★★★ Federico Fellini's surreal journey through Rome follows a society journalist (Marcello Mastroianni) as he navigates a bizarre world in which emotions have been destroyed by surface realities, moral conventions, and unresolved guilts. This film is considered a landmark in cinematic achievement. In Italian with English subtitles. Not rated. B&W; 175m. **DIR:** Federico Fellini. **CAST:** Marcello Mastroianni, Anouk Aimée, Anita Ekberg, Barbara Steele, Nadia Gray. **1960**

LA FEMME NIKITA ★★★★ Luc Besson's stylishly inventive, ultraviolent, high-energy thriller about the recruitment of a convicted drug addict to be a secret service assassin. This visceral thriller isn't for the squeamish, but action fans who also like to think and who have a sense of style ought to love it. In French with English subtitles. Rated R. 117m. **DIR:** Luc Besson. **CAST:** Anne Parillaud, Jean-Hugues Anglade, Tcheky Karyo. **1991**

LA GRANDE BOURGEOISE ★★ This should be a suspenseful film about a brother who murders his sister's lackluster husband. However, the movie's primary concern is with costume and soft-focus lenses so that even the lukewarm emotions are overshadowed. In Italian with English subtitles. 115m. **DIR:** Mauro Bolognini. **CAST:** Catherine Deneuve, Giancarlo Giannini, Fernando Rey. **1974**

LA LECTRICE (THE READER) ★★★ Clever comedy for ultraliterary types, with Miou-Miou at her charming best as a woman who hires herself out as a professional reader. She becomes a confidante, booster, adviser, and friend to a collection of loners, loonies, and emotionally unstable individuals. In French with English subtitles. 98m. **DIR:** Michel Deville. **CAST:** Miou-Miou, Maria Casares, Patrick Chesnais. **1989**

LA MARSEILLAISE ★★★★ Though its plot is somewhat uneven, *La Marseillaise* contains many beautiful sequences. This documentarylike story (and Jean Renoir's call to his countrymen to stand fast against the growing threat of Hitler) parallels the rise of the French Revolution with the spread of the new rallying song as 150 revolutionary volunteers from Marseilles march to Paris and join with others to storm the Bastille. In French with English subtitles. B&W; 130m. **DIR:** Jean Renoir. **CAST:** Pierre Renoir, Louis Jouvet, Julien Carette. **1937**

LA NUIT DE VARENNES ★★½ An ambitious and imaginative, but ultimately disappointing, film of King Louis XVI's flight from revolutionary Paris in 1791 as seen through the sensibilities of Casanova (Marcello Mastroianni), Restif de la Bretonne (Jean-Louis Barrault), and Tom Paine (Harvey Keitel). All these folks do is talk, talk, talk. In French with English subtitles. Rated R for nudity, sex, and profanity. 133m. **DIR:** Ettore Scola. **CAST:** Marcello Mastroianni, Jean-Louis Barrault, Harvey Keitel. **1983**

LA PASSANTE ★★½ Romy Schneider is featured in a dual role as Elsa, a German refugee, and as Lina, the wife of a contemporary world leader. This story centers on the relationship of two lovers caught up in a drama of political intrigue in France. Both Schneider and Michel Piccoli give excellent performances in this otherwise slow-moving thriller. In French with English subtitles. Contains nudity and violence; recommended for adult viewing. 106m. **DIR:** Jaques Rouffio. **CAST:** Romy Schneider, Michel Piccoli, Maria Schell. **1983**

LA PETITE BANDE ★★★ A group of bored London schoolchildren stow away across the English Channel and wreak havoc in France. Like a Steven Spielberg adventure (grownup villains eventually threaten the kids) without the special effects. There is no dialogue, just a persistent musical score. Unrated, but okay for children. 91m. **DIR:** Michel Deville. **CAST:** Andrew Chandler, Helene Dassule. **1983**

LA PURITAINE ★★★★ Penetrating drama played out in an empty theatre where the artistic manager prepares for the homecoming of the daughter who ran away a year earlier. He ensembles a group of young actresses of his troupe in order to have them impersonate behavioral aspects of his daughter. Brilliant cinematography by William Lubtchansky. In French with English subtitles. Not rated, but is recommended for adult viewers. 90m. **DIR:** Jacques Doillon. **CAST:** Michel Piccoli, Sandrine Bonnaire. **1986**

LA RONDE ★★★ It would be hard to imagine any film more like a French farce than *La Ronde,* in spite of its Austrian origins. This fast-paced, witty look at amours and indiscretions begins with the soldier (Serge Reggiani) and lady of easy virtue (Simone Signoret). Their assignation starts a chain of events that is charmingly risqué. In French with English subtitles. B&W; 97m. **DIR:** Max Ophüls. **CAST:** Anton Walbrook, Serge Reggiani, Simone Simon, Simone Signoret, Daniel Gelin, Danielle Darrieux. **1950**

LA SIGNORA DI TUTTI ★★ A famous actress attempts suicide, and we are taken on a retrospective journey through her life. Her beauty enchants and intoxicates men, who go as far as committing suicide to prove their love. Tacky, dated, and laughable at times, but with a hint of naïve historical charm that just barely saves it from the dreaded poultry symbol. In Italian with English subtitles. B&W; 89m. **DIR:** Max Ophüls. **CAST:** Isa Miranda. **1934**

LA STRADA ★★★★★ This is Fellini's first internationally acclaimed film. Gelsomina (Giulietta Masina), a simpleminded peasant girl, is sold to a circus strongman (Anthony Quinn), and as she follows him on his tour through the countryside, she falls desperately in love with him. She becomes the victim of his constant abuse and brutality until their meeting with an acrobat (Richard Basehart) dramatically changes the course of their lives. B&W; 94m. **DIR:** Federico Fellini. **CAST:** Giulietta Masina, Anthony Quinn, Richard Basehart. **1954**

LA TRAVIATA ★★★★ Franco Zeffirelli set out to make an opera film of Verdi's *La Traviata* that would appeal to a general audience as well as opera buffs, and he has handsomely succeeded. He has found the right visual terms for the pathetic romance of a courtesan compelled to give up her aristocratic lover. The score is beautifully sung by Teresa Stratas, as Violetta and Placido Domingo, as Alfredo. In Italian, with English subtitles. Rated G. 112m. **DIR:** Franco Zeffirelli. **CAST:** Teresa Stratas, Placido Domingo. **1982**

LA TRUITE (THE TROUT) ★★★ Sometimes disjointed story of a young girl who leaves her rural background and arranged marriage to climb the rocky path to success in both love and business. Although director Joseph Losey generally has the right idea, *La Truite*, in the end, lacks warmth and a sense of cohesion. In French with English subtitles. Rated R. 100m. **DIR:** Joseph Losey. **CAST:** Lissette Malidor, Isabelle Huppert, Jacques Spiesser. **1982**

LA VIE CONTINUE ★★ Soap-operaish story about a woman trying to build a new life for herself and her children after her husband dies suddenly. The American remake, *Men Don't Leave*, was actually much better. Dubbed in English. Unrated. 93m. **DIR:** Moshe Mizrahi. **CAST:** Annie Girardot, Jean-Pierre Cassel, Pierre Dux, Michel Aumont. **1981**

LABYRINTH OF PASSION ★★ Unengaging screwball comedy about the misadventures of a nympho punk rockette, an incestuous gynecologist, and a desperate empress in search of sperm from a member of the imperial family of Iran. In Spanish with English subtitles. Rated R for nudity and profanity. 100m. **DIR:** Pedro Almodóvar. **CAST:** Celia Roth, Imanol Arias, Antonio Banderas. **1983**

LACEMAKER, THE ★★★½ Isabelle Huppert had her first major role here as a shy young Parisian beautician who falls in love with a university student while on vacation. But when they try to keep the affair going back in Paris, class differences drive them apart. Huppert's sympathetic performance pulls the film through occasional patches of pathos. In French with English subtitles. Unrated; the film features sexual situations. 107m. **DIR:** Claude Goretta. **CAST:** Isabelle Huppert, Yves Beneyton. **1977**

LADIES ON THE ROCKS ★★★ Had Thelma and Louise taken to the stage instead of a life of crime, their adventures might have resembled this amusing low-key comedy. Two women tour rural Denmark with their male-bashing cabaret show. In Danish with English subtitles. Not rated; contains adult themes and sexual situations. 100m. **DIR:** Christian Braad Thomsen. **CAST:** Helle Ryslinge, Annemarie Helger. **1983**

LADY ON THE BUS ★★ Story of a shy bride who is frigid on her wedding night. She first turns to her husband's friends and then strangers she meets on buses. Marginal comedy. In Portuguese with English subtitles. Rated R for sex. 102m. **DIR:** Neville D'Almeida. **CAST:** Sonia Braga. **1978**

LADY WITH THE DOG, THE ★★★½ In this film based on a short story by Anton Chekhov, a Moscow banker and the wife of a Saratov politician begin their affair while on holiday at the turn of the century. This is a quietly elegant and gentle Russian film with English subtitles. B&W; 89m. **DIR:** Josef Heifits. **CAST:** Iya Savvina, Alexei Batalov. **1960**

LAND WITHOUT BREAD ★★★ A powerful documentary from director Luis Buñuel about the impoverished people living in the Las Hurdes region of Spain. In Spanish with English subtitles. B&W; 45m. **DIR:** Luis Buñuel. **1932**

LARKS ON A STRING ★★★½ Love blooms for a young couple in a reeducation camp, and their fellow detainees decide to give them a wedding and honeymoon under the noses of the camp authorities. This high-spirited comedy was banned by Soviet authorities until Glasnost. In Czech with English subtitles. Not rated. B&W; 96m. **DIR:** Jiri Menzel. **CAST:** Vera Kresadlova, Vaclav Neckar. **1969**

LAST FIVE DAYS, THE ★★★½ During the Nazi reign, a brother and sister are placed in jail to be questioned. The sister encounters Else, a prison clerk, who is awaiting her own trial. The viewer experiences the despair of the sister's last five days and her emotional encounter with Else and other anti-Hitler sympathizers. In German with English subtitles. Not rated, suitable for all audiences. 115m. **DIR:** Percy Adlon. **CAST:** Irm Hermann, Lena Stolze, Will Spindler, Hans Hirschmuller, Philip Arp, Joachim Bernhard. **1982**

LAST LAUGH, THE ★★★★ Historically recognized as the first film to exploit the moving camera, this silent classic tells the story of a lordly luxury hotel doorman who is abruptly and callously demoted to the menial status of a washroom attendant. Deprived of his job and uniform, his life slowly disintegrates. Emil Jannings gives a brilliant performance. B&W; 74m. **DIR:** F. W. Murnau. **CAST:** Emil Jannings. **1924**

LAST METRO, THE ★★★½ Catherine Deneuve and Gérard Depardieu star in this drama about a Parisian theatrical company that believes "the show must go on" despite the restrictions and terrors of the Nazis during their World War II occupation of France. This film has several nice moments and surprises that make up for its occasional dull spots and extended running time. Rated PG. 133m. **DIR:** François Truffaut. **CAST:** Catherine Deneuve, Gérard Depardieu, Jean Poiret. **1980**

LAST SUPPER, THE ★★★ Uncompromising drama based on an incident from eighteenth-century Cuban history about a petit-bourgeois slaveholder who decides to improve his soul by instructing his slaves in the glories of Christianity. He invites twelve of them to participate in a reenactment of the Last Supper in hopes of instilling Christian ideals. In Spanish with English subtitles. Not rated, but contains violence and nudity. 110m. **DIR:** Tomas Gutierrez Alea. **CAST:** Nelson Villagra. **1976**

LAST YEAR AT MARIENBAD ★★★ This film provides no middle ground—you either love it or you hate it. The confusing story is about a young man (Giorgio Albertazzi) finding himself in a monstrous, baroque hotel trying to renew his love affair with a woman who seems to have forgotten that there is an affair to renew. The past, present, and future all seem to run parallel, cross over, and converge. In French with English subtitles. B&W; 93m. **DIR:** Alain Resnais. **CAST:** Delphine Seyrig, Giorgio Albertazzi, Sacha Pitoeff. **1962**

LATE CHRYSANTHEMUMS ★★★★★ With limited options available to them, four aging geisha try to plan for their futures. Beautifully acted, realistic but never melodramatic; a wonderful film from Mikio Naruse, an overlooked (outside of his own country) master of the Japanese cinema. In Japanese with English subtitles. B&W; 101m. **DIR:** Mikio Naruse. **CAST:** Haruko Sugimura. **1954**

LATE SPRING ★★★★★ Afraid that his grown daughter will become an old maid, a widower pretends that he wishes to remarry to persuade her to leave home. Yasujiro Ozu made a number of films with a similar theme, but this is the best. In Japanese with English subtitles. 107m. **DIR:** Yasujiro Ozu. **CAST:** Setsuko Hara, Chishu Ryu. **1949**

LATE SUMMER BLUES 🦃 Trite, contrived sentimentality, and the acting ability of dried flattened roadkill. In Hebrew with English subtitles. Unrated. 101m. **DIR:** Renen Schorr. **CAST:** Dor Zweigen Bom. **1987**

LAUGH FOR JOY ★★★ Delightful comedy of errors set on New Year's Eve. Anna Magnani plays a film extra who complicates things for a pickpocket (Ben Gazzara). Also released on videocassette under the title *Passionate Thief*, which is dubbed in English. In Italian with English subtitles. B&W; 106m. **DIR:** Mario Monicelli. **CAST:** Anna Magnani, Ben Gazzara, Toto, Fred Clark. **1954**

LAW OF DESIRE ★★★ Spain's Pedro Almodóvar likes to play with the clichés of movie melodrama in a manner that endears him to movie buffs. This film first gained him wide attention in the U.S. A gay movie director who wants to live as passionately as his transsexual brother (now his sister). He gets his wish in this topsy-turvy farce. In Spanish with English subtitles. Unrated, but an R equivalent. 100m. **DIR:** Pedro Almodóvar. **CAST:** Eusebio Poncela, Carmen Maura, Antonio Banderas, Miguel Molina. **1986**

L'ETAT SAUVAGE (THE SAVAGE STATE) ★★★ Engrossing political thriller set in 1960s Africa after independence from colonial rule. A government official returns looking for his wife, who is living with a powerful black minister in the new government. A genuine sexual potboiler. In French with English subtitles. Not rated, but contains nudity and violence. 111m. **DIR:** Francis Girod. **CAST:** Jacques Dutronc, Marie-Christine Barrault, Michel Piccoli. **1978**

LE BAL ★★★★ European history of the last half century is reduced to some fifty popular dance tunes—and a variety of very human dancers—in this innovative and entertaining film. This unusual import eschews dialogue for tangos, fox trots, and jazz to make its points. Scola chronicles the dramatic changes in political power, social behavior, and fashion trends from the 1930s to the present without ever moving his cameras out of an art deco ballroom. No MPAA rating; the film has brief violence. 109m. **DIR:** Ettore Scola. **1983**

LE BEAU MARIAGE ★★★★ A young woman decides it is high time she got married. She chooses the man she wants, a busy lawyer, and tells her friends of their coming wedding. He knows nothing of this, but she is confident. That is the premise in this film by French director Eric Rohmer. In French with English subtitles. Rated R. 100m. **DIR:** Eric Rohmer. **CAST:** Beatrice Romand, Arielle Dombasle, André Dussolier. **1982**

LE BEAU SERGE ★★ An ailing theology student, home for a rest cure, is reunited with his boyhood friend, who is now an alcoholic stuck in an unhappy marriage. Vague drama is of interest only as an early example of the French new wave. In French with English subtitles. Unrated. 97m. **DIR:** Claude Chabrol. **CAST:** Gerard Blain, Jean-Claude Brialy, Bernadette Lafont. **1958**

LE BONHEUR ★★ Extremely boring story about happiness. A husband is happy with his wife, but becomes even happier when he takes a mistress. In French with English subtitles. Not rated, but contains nudity and graphic sex. 77m. **DIR:** Agnes Varda. **CAST:** Jean-Claude Druou, Claire Druou, Marie-France Boyer. **1978**

LE BOUCHER (THE BUTCHER) ★★★★ French director Claude Chabrol's mini-masterwork about a hunt for a serial killer in provincial France. Jean Yanne is the ex-army butcher who may or may not be the murderer. Prim schoolmistress Stéphane Audran (director Chabrol's wife) is irresistibly drawn to him. There are a few affectionate Hitchcock touches, but mostly, this ball-of-twine thriller is Chabrol's own, and that is its considerable strength. English subtitles (beware of the dubbed version). Rated R for violence. 94m. **DIR:** Claude Chabrol. **CAST:** Stéphane Audran, Jean Yanne, Antonio Passalia, Mario Beccaria. **1969**

LE BOURGEOIS GENTILHOMME ★★ This adaptation of Molière's satire about a social climber is a recording of the stage performance, and will seem static and overacted to most viewers. Worth checking out for Molière enthusiasts and French language classes, but not recommended for general audiences. In French with English subtitles. 97m. **DIR:** Jean Meyer. **CAST:** Jean Meyer, Louis Seigner, Jacques Charon. **1958**

LE CAS DU DR. LAURENT ★★½ Dated tale about a kindly old doctor who tries to introduce modern methods of medicine and sanitation to the residents of a small farming village. In particular, he tries to ease the suffering of women as they endure childbirth. Noteworthy for the performance of Gabin as the doctor and for footage of an actual childbirth. In French. B&W; 88m. **DIR:** Jean-Paul Le Chanois. **CAST:** Jean Gabin, Nicole Courcel, Sylvia Monfort. **1957**

LE CAVALEUR ★★★★ A poignantly philosophical, yet witty and often hilarious farce about the perils of the middle-aged heartbreak kid. Our cad about town is unerringly portrayed by Jean Rochefort as a classical pianist trying to juggle his art and the many past, present, and possible future women in his life. Nudity but generally innocent adult situations. 106m. **DIR:** Philippe de Broca. **CAST:** Jean Rochefort, Annie Girardot. **1980**

LE CHÊVRE (THE GOAT) ★★½ The stars of *Les Compères*, Pierre Richard and Gérard Depardieu, romp again in this French comedy as two investigators searching for a missing girl in Mexico. While this import may please staunch fans of the stars, it is far from being a laugh riot. In French with English subtitles. Unrated; the film has profanity and violence. 91m. **DIR:** Francis Veber. **CAST:** Pierre Richard, Gérard Depardieu, Michel Robin, Pedro Armendariz Jr. **1981**

LE COMPLOT (THE CONSPIRACY) ★★★½ Complex political thriller, based on true events, about an explosive game of espionage between leftist rebels, the police, and Gaullist patriots. Quite suspenseful. In French with English subtitles. Rated R for profanity and violence. 120m. **DIR:** René Gainville. **CAST:** Jean Rochefort, Michel Bouquet, Marina Vlady. **1973**

LE CORBEAU ★★★★ Citizens of a French provincial town are upset to find that someone is on to all their guilty secrets and is revealing them in a series of poison pen letters. An intelligent, involving thriller, remade in the United States as *The Thirteenth Letter*. Also known as *The Raven*. In French with English subtitles. 91m. **DIR:** Henri-Georges Clouzot. **CAST:** Pierre Fresnay, Pierre Larquey. **1943**

LE CRABE TAMBOUR ★★½ Hard-to-follow story of the exploits of a French naval officer over a span of two decades. The beautiful wide-screen photography is diminished on video, and even French historians will have difficulty navigating the complexities of the plot. In French with English subtitles. Unrated. 120m. **DIR:** Pierre Schoendoerffer. **CAST:** Jean Rochefort, Claude Rich, Jacques Perrin. **1977**

LE DÉPART ★★★ Jean-Pierre Léaud, best known from François Truffaut's semiautobiographical films *The 400 Blows* and *Love on the Run*, stars as another disaffected youth. He's desperately trying to borrow or rent a Porsche so that he can enter a race. Zany comedy is noteworthy for Léaud's performance and as an early effort by Polish director Jerzy Skolimowski. In French with English subtitles. Unrated. B&W; 89m. **DIR:** Jerzy Skolimowski. **CAST:** Jean-Pierre Léaud, Catherine Isabelle Duport. **1967**

LE DOULOS ★★★★ Outstanding, complex crime-drama about a police informer who attempts to expose a violent underworld crime ring. An excellent homage to American gangster films of the 1940s. Brilliant cinematography and sizzling performances by a great cast make this suspenseful thriller a film classic. In French with English subtitles. B&W; 105m. **DIR:** Jean-Pierre Melville. **CAST:** Jean-Paul Belmondo, Serge Reggiani, Michel Piccoli. **1961**

LE GAI SAVIOR (THE JOY OF KNOWLEDGE) ★★ Incomprehensible film about two aliens. The poor extraterrestrials may have had better luck if they hadn't landed in this movie. In French with English subtitles. 96m. **DIR:** Jean-Luc Godard. **CAST:** Jean-Pierre Léaud, Juliet Berto. **1965**

LE GENTLEMAN D'ESPOM (DUKE OF THE DERBY) ★★★ This lighthearted look at the sport of kings gives veteran French film star Jean Gabin ample chance to shine as the title character, an aged, suave snob living by his wits and luck handicapping and soliciting bets from the rich. Everything is fine until, eager to impress an old flame, he passes a bad check. B&W; 83m. **DIR:** Jacques Juranville. **CAST:** Jean Gabin, Madeleine Robinson, Paul Frankeur. **1962**

LE GRAND CHEMIN (THE GRAND HIGHWAY) ★★★★ A delightful film about an 8-year-old Parisian boy's summer in the country. Along with his friend Martine (Vanessa Guedj), Louis (played by director Jean-Loup Hubert's son Antoine) learns about the simple pleasures and terrors of life and love. This is great cinema for old and young alike, despite some nudity. In French with English subtitles. 104m. **DIR:** Jean-Loup Hubert. **CAST:** Vanessa Guedj, Antoine Hubert, Richard Bohringer, Anemone. **1988**

LE JOUR SE LEVE (DAYBREAK) (1939) ★★★ An affecting, atmospheric French melodrama by the director of the classic *Children of Paradise*. Jean Gabin plays a man provoked to murder his lover's seducer. There is some brilliant, sensuous moviemaking here. The existing print lacks sufficient subtitling but is still worth viewing. B&W; 85m.

DIR: Marcel Carné. **CAST:** Jean Gabin, Jules Berry, Arletty, Jacqueline Laurent. **1939**

LE MAGNIFIQUE ★★★ A writer of spy novels imagines himself as his own character, a James Bond type, with the girl next door as his trusty sidekick. Though it never builds up a full head of steam, this French comedy holds your interest through the dull stretches. Written by Francis Verber (*La Cage Aux Folles, Three Fugitives*). In French with English subtitles. 93m. **DIR:** Philippe de Broca. **CAST:** Jean-Paul Belmondo, Jacqueline Bisset. **1974**

LE MILLION ★★★★ Made more than fifty years ago, this delightful comedy about the efforts of a group of people to retrieve an elusive lottery ticket is more applicable to American audiences of today than it was when originally released. René Clair's classic fantasy-adventure is freewheeling and fun. Subtitled in English. B&W; 85m. **DIR:** René Clair. **CAST:** Annabella, René Lefévre. **1931**

LE PETIT AMOUR ★★½ Romantic comedy based on a short story by Jane Birkin about a 40-year-old divorcée who falls for a 15-year-old schoolboy. Mediocre, but with good performances. In French with English subtitles. Rated R for nudity. 80m. **DIR:** Agnes Varda. **CAST:** Jane Birkin, Mathieu Demy, Charlotte Gainsbourg. **1987**

LE PLAISIR ★★½ Max Ophüls (*La Ronde*) adapts three ironic stories by Guy de Maupassant with his customary style, most evident in his extremely mobile camera work. However, the stories themselves are mediocre and not really up to the elaborate treatment. In French with English subtitles. B&W; 97m. **DIR:** Max Ophüls. **CAST:** Jean Gabin, Danielle Darrieux, Simone Simon. **1952**

LE REPOS DU GUERRIER (WARRIOR'S REST) ★★★★ Brigitte Bardot plays a proper French girl who rescues a sociopathic drifter from a suicide attempt. The drifter immediately takes over Bardot's life, ruining her reputation and abusing her verbally and emotionally, yet denying her attempts to form a real relationship. This is a precursor of *The Servant, 9 1/2 Weeks,* and other frank observations of sexual obsession. In French. 98m. **DIR:** Roger Vadim. **CAST:** Brigitte Bardot, Robert Hossein, James Robertson Justice, Jean-Marc Bory. **1962**

LE SCHPOUNTZ ★★★½ Country doofus Fernandel, convinced that he's the next Charles Boyer, tries to break into the movies in this consistently funny satire of the film world. In French with English subtitles. B&W; 140m. **DIR:** Marcel Pagnol. **CAST:** Fernandel, Orane Demazis, Charpin, Robert Vattier, Pierre Brasseur. **1938**

LE SECRET ★★★ Jean-Louis Trintignant plays an escapee from a psychiatric prison who finds shelter with a reclusive writer and his wife by persuading them that he has been tortured for information. Fine performances, a tense atmosphere, and music by Ennio Morricone make this worth your while. In French with English subtitles. Unrated. 100m. **DIR:** Robert Enrico. **CAST:** Jean-Louis Trintignant, Marlene Jobert, Philippe Noiret. **1974**

LE SEX SHOP ★★★★ Wry, satirical film about an owner of a failing little bookstore, who converts his business into a sex shop, where he peddles pornographic books and sexual devices in order to make ends meet. Excellent social-sexual satire. In French with English subtitles. Not rated, but contains nudity and profanity. 90m. **DIR:** Claude Berri. **CAST:** Claude Berri, Juliet Berto. **1973**

LEAVES FROM SATAN'S BOOK ★★ Carl Dreyer's second film is a surprising mixture of leering and posturing clichés. The story tells of Satan's appearance in four different disguises to perform his unholy temptations. Beautiful sets and effective character types, but hopelessly melodramatic stereotypes. Silent. B&W; 165m. **DIR:** Carl Dreyer. **CAST:** Helge Nissen, Jacob Texiere. **1919**

L'ECOLE BUISSONNIERE ★★★½ A teacher with modern ideas goes to work for a small village, and now the once bored students are excited about going to school. A few elders in the village decide that the new teacher is a bad influence on the children; they make a bet with him, the stakes being his job. You'll be rooting for the teacher in this nicely portrayed, neo-realist film. In French with English subtitles. B&W; 84m. **DIR:** Jean-Paul Le Chanois. **CAST:** Bernard Blier, Juliette Faber, Pierre Coste. **1951**

LEGEND OF SURAM FORTRESS, THE ★★★★ Idiosyncratic retelling of a medieval Georgian legend about the attempt to build a fortress to repel invaders. Difficult to comprehend (unless you know a lot about Georgian folklore), the film's many striking images make for a memorable viewing experience. In Georgian with English subtitles. 87m. **DIR:** Sergi Parajanov, Dodo Abashidze. **CAST:** Levan Uchaneishvili. **1984**

LEGEND OF THE EIGHT SAMURAI ★★ Shizu is the princess who leads her warriors into battle against a giant centipede, ghosts, and a nearly immortal witch. An interesting story line, but derivative, slow in spots, badly dubbed, and disappointing. Unrated, has moderate violence. 130m. **DIR:** Haruki Kaduwara. **CAST:** Hiroku Yokoshimaru, Sonny Chiba. **1984**

LENINGRAD COWBOYS GO AMERICA 🦃 Don't waste 80 minutes of your life watching this horrible Finnish farce about an eccentric Finnish polka band that tours the United States. In Finnish with English subtitles. Rated PG-13 for language. 80m. **DIR:** Aki Kaurismaki. **CAST:** Matti Pelloupaa. **1989**

LEOLO ★★★★ This surreal memoir of growing up poor in Montreal's ghetto owes much to Fellini. Highly original, *Leolo* alternates between images of great beauty and great coarseness. The boy at the center of the story is fed up with a bizarre family life. He creates a fantasy background, concluding that he was accidentally fathered by an Italian peasant in a wacky accident that has to be seen to be believed. (You may never buy a tomato again at a public market.) *Leolo* gets many points for originality and audacity, but it's not for the easily offended. In French with English subtitles. Rated R, with profanity, scatological humor, and sexual situations. 107m. **DIR:** Jean-Claude Lauzon. **CAST:** Maxime Collin, Ginetta Reno, Julien Guiomar. **1993**

LES ABYSSES ★★★ Straightforward adaptation of the notorious murder case that inspired Jean Genet's *The Maids*. Two sisters try to stop the sale of a vineyard that is their only means of support; when they fail, they kill the owner for whom they have worked all their lives. In French with English subtitles. B&W; 90m. **DIR:** Nico Papatakis. **CAST:** Francine Berge, Colette Berge. **1963**

LES BICHES ★★★ This story revolves around Frederique and Why, two lesbian lovers in love with the same man. Good music, but the acting could be better. In French with English subtitles. Not rated, but contains profanity. 104m. **DIR:** Claude Chabrol. **CAST:** Jean-Louis Trintignant, Jacqueline Sassard, Stéphane Audran. **1968**

LES CHOSES DE LA VIE ★★★½ A hospitalized businessman, injured in an automobile accident, reflects on his relationship with his wife and mistress. Mediocre drama gets a lift from a strong cast. In French with English subtitles. 90m. **DIR:** Claude Sautet. **CAST:** Romy Schneider, Michel Piccoli, Lea Massari. **1970**

LES COMPERES ★★★★ Pierre Richard and Gérard Depardieu star in this madcap French comedy as two strangers who find themselves on the trail of a runaway teenager. Both think they're the father—it was the only way the boy's mother could think of to enlist their aid. In French with English subtitles. Rated PG for profanity and brief violence. 90m. **DIR:** Francis Veber. **CAST:** Pierre Richard, Gérard Depardieu. **1984**

LES COUSINS ★★★½ Innocent country lad, in Paris for the first time to attend university, moves in with his unscrupulous cousin. Melancholy study of big-city decadence directed with a cold, clear eye by Claude Chabrol. In French with English subtitles. Unrated. 110m. **DIR:** Claude Chabrol. **CAST:** Gerard Blain, Jean-Claude Brialy, Juliette Mayniel. **1958**

LES GRANDES GUEULES (JAILBIRDS' VACATION) ★★½ This comedy-drama about parolees working on a backwoods sawmill would be better if it were shorter and the extended fistfight scenes were cut measurably. Otherwise, the "jailbirds" are a lively, entertaining bunch. In French with English subtitles. 125m. **DIR:** Robert Enrico. **CAST:** Lino Ventura, Bourvil, Marie Dubois. **1965**

LES LIAISONS DANGEREUSES ★★★ Complex, amoral tale of a diplomat and his wife whose open marriage and numerous affairs eventually lead to tragedy. Well photographed and acted (especially by Jeanne Moreau), this adult and downbeat film fluctuates at times between satire and comedy and depression, but overall the experience is pretty grim. In French with English subtitles. B&W; 108m. **DIR:** Roger Vadim. **CAST:** Gérard Philipe, Jeanne Moreau, Jeanne Valerie, Annette Vadim, Simone Renant, Jean-Louis Trintignant. **1959**

LES MISERABLES (1957) ★★★★ The length weakens the story, but this is probably the most complete film version of Victor Hugo's novel. The story of a detective's relentless pursuit of a man for stealing bread inspired many modern chase films. In French with English subtitles. B&W; 210m. **DIR:** Jean-Paul L. Chanois. **CAST:** Jean Gabin, Daniele Delorme, Bourvil, Bernard Blier, Gianni Esposito. **1957**

LES RENDEZ-VOUS D'ANNA ★★★★ Anna is a film director who lives a life of desultory detachment while traveling through Europe. She indulges in anonymous sex and is plagued by people talking relentlessly about themselves, to whom she listens with comically placid disinterest. A fascinating movie, shot with flawless fluidity. In French with English subtitles. Rated R for nudity. 120m. **DIR:** Chantal Akerman. **CAST:** Aurore Clement, Helmut Griem, Magali Noel, Lea Massari, Jean-Pierre Cassel. **1978**

LES TRICHEURS ★★½ A roulette addict tries to break his habit with the help of a woman he meets at the tables. Lackluster gambling drama, set in the casinos of Europe. In French with English subtitles. Unrated. 93m. **DIR:** Barbet Schroeder. **CAST:** Jacques Dutronc, Bulle Ogier, Kurt Raab. **1984**

LES VIOLONS DU BAL ★★★ Clever movie combines the story of director-star Michel Drach's childhood (in France under the Nazi occupation) and his attempts as an adult to film the story. Engaging coming-of-age story. In French with English subtitles. 108m. **DIR:** Michel Drach. **CAST:** Michel Drach, Jean-Louis Trintignant, Marie-Jose Nat. **1974**

LES VISITEURS DU SOIR ★★★ In medieval France, the devil sends two of his servants to disrupt the engagement party of a baron's daughter. A handsome but lightweight morality play. In French with English subtitles. B&W; 110m. **DIR:** Marcel Carné.

CAST: Arletty, Jules Berry, Marie Dea, Alain Cuny. 1942

LESSON IN LOVE, A ★★★ Gunnar Björnstrand plays a philandering gynecologist who realizes that his long-suffering wife is the woman he loves the most, and he sets out to win her back. This is a little ponderous for a true romantic comedy, but good writing and good acting move the film along and provide some funny yet realistic situations. In Swedish with subtitles. B&W; 97m. **DIR:** Ingmar Bergman. **CAST:** Gunnar Björnstrand, Eva Dahlbeck, Harriet Andersson. 1954

LETTERS FROM THE PARK ★★★★ Charming love story à la *Cyrano de Bergerac* features Victor La Place as a sensitive man who writes letters professionally in Cuba in 1913. Hired by an awkward young man who prefers hot air balloons to poetry, he begins a romantic correspondence which becomes real for him. Originally made for Spanish television, this contains mature themes. In Spanish with English subtitles. 85m. **DIR:** Tomas Gutierrez Alea. **CAST:** Victor La Place, Ivonne Lopez, Miguel Paneque. 1988

L'HOMME BLESSÉ (THE WOUNDED MAN) ★★★½ Lurid sexual psychodrama about a withdrawn young man's obsession for a street hustler he meets by chance. His frustrated lust builds until it finds its shocking release. A powerful and disturbing piece of cinema for adults only. In French with English subtitles. Not rated; contains profanity, nudity, and violence. 90m. **DIR:** Patrice Chereau. **CAST:** Jean-Hugues Anglade, Vittorio Mezzogiorno, Roland Bertin, Lisa Kreuzer. 1988

LIARS, THE ★★ A woman and her lover pose as mother and son to gain the confidence of a rich man and then murder him for his money. Dreary melodrama. In French with English subtitles. B&W; 92m. **DIR:** Edmond Gréville. **CAST:** Dawn Addams, Jean Servais, Claude Brasseur. 1964

LIEBELEI ★★★★ A young lieutenant's love for a Viennese girl is disrupted when he is provoked to a duel by a baron (who mistakenly believes the young man in love with his wife). One of the first masterworks by Max Ophüls, a touching evocation of imperial Vienna. A minor masterpiece. In German with English subtitles. B&W; 88m. **DIR:** Max Ophüls. **CAST:** Magda Schneider, Wolfgang Liebeneiner. 1933

LIFE AND NOTHING BUT ★★★★★ Director Bertrand Tavernier's brilliant antiwar film focuses on a group of people attempting to find the bodies of dead soldiers—husbands, fathers, and other loved ones—after World War I. This rich tapestry of human emotions has all the elements of a true classic: unforgettable characters, romance, suspense, and magnificent visuals. Philippe Noiret, so wonderful in *Cinema Paradiso,* adds another great characterization to his list of credits. In French with English subtitles. Rated PG. 135m. **DIR:** Bertrand Tavernier. **CAST:** Philippe Noiret, Sabine Azema. 1989

LIFE OF OHARU ★★★★½ All but unknown in this country, Japanese director Kenji Mizoguchi was one of the great artists of the cinema. This story, of a woman in feudal Japan who, after disgracing the honor of her samurai father, is sold into prostitution, may seem somewhat melodramatic to Western audiences. But Mizoguchi's art rested in his formalistic visual style, consisting of carefully composed shots, long takes, and minimal editing. In Japanese with English subtitles. B&W; 136m. **DIR:** Kenji Mizoguchi. **CAST:** Kinuyo Tanaka, Toshiro Mifune. 1952

LIFE ON A STRING ★★★½ A blind musician can regain his sight only by so devoting his life to music that he breaks one thousand strings while playing his banjo. While the plot of this Chinese fable is occasionally obscure, director Chen Kaige (*Farewell My Concubine*) provides breathtaking scenery and an unforgettable battle scene. Unrated; contains no objectionable material. 110m. **DIR:** Chen Kaige. **CAST:** Liu Zhong Yuan, Huang Lei. 1990

LIKE WATER FOR CHOCOLATE ★★★★ Romance, fantasy, comedy, and drama blend in delicious fashion. Based on the celebrated novel by Laura Esquivel, the movie depicts a young woman whose engagement is thwarted by her selfish mother. The frustrated woman transfers her passion into her cooking, which takes on a supernatural quality. There is a magical aura to the film, which is also extremely sensual. In Spanish with English subtitles. Rated R for nudity and suggested sex. 113m. **DIR:** Alfonso Arau. **CAST:** Lumi Cavazos, Marco Leonardi, Regina Torne, Mario Ivan Martinez. 1993

LILI MARLEEN ★★★½ The popular song of the Forties and the wartime adventures of the singer of the song, who became known as Lili to the German troops, are the basis for this engrossing film. In German with English subtitles. Rated R because of nudity and implied sex. 120m. **DIR:** Rainer Werner Fassbinder. **CAST:** Hanna Schygulla, Giancarlo Giannini, Mel Ferrer. 1981

LITTLE THEATRE OF JEAN RENOIR, THE ★★★ The great director's last film (actually made for television) is better seen as a postscript to his long career. The three segments (plus a musical interlude from Jeanne Moreau) remind the viewer of his best work rather than recapitulating it. In French with English subtitles. 100m. **DIR:** Jean Renoir. **CAST:** Jeanne Moreau, Jean Carmet, Fernand Sardou, Pierre Olaf, Françoise Arnoul. 1969

LITTLE THIEF, THE ★★★★ François Truffaut was working on this script, sort of a female version of *The 400 Blows,* at the time of his death; it was completed and filmed by his friend Claude Miller. Charlotte Gainsbourg gives a strong performance as a rebellious adolescent girl, struggling to raise herself after she is abandoned by her mother. In French with English subtitles. Unrated; features adult themes. 104m. **DIR:** Claude Miller. **CAST:** Charlotte Gainsbourg, Didier Bezace. **1989**

LITTLE VERA ★★★ Glasnost takes a front-row-center seat in this angst-ridden drama about the thoroughly modern Moscowite Vera. Her alcoholic father and ineffectual mother constantly worry about Vera's untraditional ways. She falls in love and moves her fiancé into the family's tight quarters. This is the first widely released Soviet film to show present-day teenage culture—plus—simulated sex. In Russian with English subtitles. Not rated. 130m. **DIR:** Vasily Pichul. **CAST:** Natalya Negoda. **1989**

LITTLE WORLD OF DON CAMILLO, THE ★★★ The emotional and often grim struggle between Church and State has never been more humanely or lovingly presented than in the novels of Giovanni Guareschi, expertly brought to life in this gentle, amusing film. The great French comedian Fernandel captures the essence of the feisty priest who is a perpetual thorn in the side of the communist mayor of his village and parish. B&W; 96m. **DIR:** Julien Duvivier. **CAST:** Fernandel, Gino Cervi, Sylvie, Franco Interlenghi. **1953**

LIVING ON TOKYO TIME ★★★★ *Living on Tokyo Time* explores an Asian-American culture clash from the Japanese point of view. Kyoko (Minako Ohashi), a young woman, comes from Japan to San Francisco. She agrees to a marriage of convenience with a junk-food-eating Japanese-American who wants to be a rock star. The result is a warmhearted character study blessed with insight and humor. In English and Japanese with subtitles. 83m. **DIR:** Steven Okazaki. **CAST:** Minako Ohashi, Ken Nakagawa. **1987**

L'ODEUR DES FAUVES (SCANDAL MAN) 🦃 A hack photographer-reporter earns his living digging up *National Enquirer*–type stories. 86m. **DIR:** Richard Balducci. **CAST:** Maurice Ronet, Josephine Chaplin, Vittorio De Sica. **1986**

LOBSTER FOR BREAKFAST ★★½ Screwball comedy Italian style about the loves and misadventures of a toilet salesman. In Italian with English subtitles. Not rated, but contains profanity and nudity. 93m. **DIR:** Giorgio Capitani. **CAST:** Janet Agren, Claudine Auger. **1982**

LOLA (1960) ★★★★ Jacques Demy adapts the intoxicating camera pyrotechnics and style of Max Ophüls (to whom the film is dedicated) in this unjustly forgotten new wave classic starring Anouk Aimée as a cabaret singer romantically involved with three men. A delight. In French with English subtitles. Unrated. 91m. **DIR:** Jacques Demy. **CAST:** Anouk Aimée, Marc Michel. **1960**

LOLA (1982) ★★★★ Viewers can't help but be dazzled and delighted with *Lola*, the late Rainer Werner Fassbinder's offbeat remake of *The Blue Angel*. Centering his story on a singer-prostitute named Lola (Barbara Sukowa), Fassbinder reveals a cynical view of humanity. Rated R. In German with English subtitles. 114m. **DIR:** Rainer Werner Fassbinder. **CAST:** Barbara Sukowa, Armin Mueller-Stahl, Mario Adorf. **1982**

LOLA MONTES ★★★★★ A dazzlingly beautiful film. Mirroring the fragmented flashbacks in which the heroine, now reduced to a circus act, recounts her love affairs through nineteenth-century Europe, Max Ophüls's camera swoops and spins through the entire span of the expanded screen, retained in the video's letter box format. In French with English subtitles. Unrated. 110m. **DIR:** Max Ophüls. **CAST:** Martine Carol, Peter Ustinov, Anton Walbrook, Oskar Werner. **1955**

LOS OLVIDADOS ★★★★★ Luis Buñuel marks the beginning of his mature style with this film. Hyperpersonal, shocking, erotic, hallucinogenic, and surrealistic images are integrated into naturalistic action: two youths of the Mexican slums venture deeper and deeper into the criminal world until they are beyond redemption. In Spanish with English subtitles. B&W; 88m. **DIR:** Luis Buñuel. **CAST:** Alfonso Mejia, Roberto Cobo. **1950**

LOST HONOR OF KATHARINA BLUM, THE ★★★ Angela Winkler's performance as Katharina Blum is the central force behind Schlondörff's interpretation of Heinrich Boll's novel. Katharina Blum is a poor, young housekeeper who spends one night with a suspected political terrorist. Her life is thereby ruined by the police and the media. In German with English subtitles. Rated R. 97m. **DIR:** Volker Schlondörff. **CAST:** Angela Winkler. **1977**

LOULOU ★★★½ In this mixture of unabashed eroticism and deeply felt romanticism Isabelle Huppert and Gérard Depardieu play lovers who embark on a freewheeling relationship. Lustful, explosive sexual psychodrama. In French with English subtitles. Rated R for nudity and profanity. 110m. **DIR:** Maurice Pialat. **CAST:** Isabelle Huppert, Gérard Depardieu, Guy Marchand. **1980**

LOVE ★★★★ Rich character study of two long-suffering women thrown together to enact the final chapter of the older woman's life. Lili Darvas is excellent as the fragile but feisty elder. In Hungarian with English subtitles. B&W; 92m. **DIR:** Karoly Makk. **CAST:** Lili Darvas, Mari Torocsik. **1971**

LOVE AND ANARCHY ★★★★★ Giancarlo Giannini gets to eat up the screen with this role. Comic, tragic, and intellectually stimulating, this is Wertmuller's best film. Giannini is bent on assassinating Mussolini right after the rise of fascism but somehow gets waylaid. A classic. Rated R for sexual situations, language, and some nudity. 117m. **DIR:** Lina Wertmuller. **CAST:** Giancarlo Giannini, Mariangela Melato. **1973**

LOVE AND THE FRENCHWOMAN ★★★ Seven short films about women at different stages of life. Lightweight stuff, but not without some charming and comical moments. Dubbed. B&W; 135m. **DIR:** Henri Decoin, Jean Delannoy, Michel Boisrone, René Clair, Henri Verneuil, Christian-Jacque, Jean-Paul Le Chanois. **CAST:** Annie Girardot, Martine Lambert, Michel Serrault, Jean-Paul Belmondo. **1960**

LOVE IN GERMANY, A ★★ During World War II, the Germans bring in Polish POWs to do menial labor. Frau Kopp (Hanna Schygulla) hires a young Polish POW. The first half of the film is effective, but the second half receives an excessively sensational treatment, ultimately diminishing the flavor and appeal. In French with English subtitles. Rated R for violence and nudity. 107m. **DIR:** Andrzej Wajda. **CAST:** Hanna Schygulla, Marie-Christine Barrault, Bernhard Wicki. **1984**

LOVE MEETINGS ★★ Messy, unorganized documentary that explores the sexual attitudes of Italians in the early 1960s. Featuring interviews with philosophers, poets, students, clergymen, farmers, factory workers, and children. Dated material with completely unreadable English subtitles. B&W; 90m. **DIR:** Pier Paolo Pasolini. **1964**

LOVE OF JEANNE NEY ★★★ A romance between a French girl and a Russian Communist is thwarted at every turn. Lots of action in this Russian Revolution–set tale. Silent. B&W; 102m. **DIR:** G. W. Pabst. **CAST:** Brigitte Helm. **1926**

LOVE ON THE RUN (1979) ★★★½ François Truffaut's tribute to himself. *Love on the Run* is the fifth film (*400 Blows*; *Love at Twenty*, *Stolen Kisses*; *Bed & Board*) in the series for character Antoine Doinel (Jean-Pierre Léaud). Now in his thirties and on the eve of divorce, Doinel rediscovers women. Light romantic work filled with humor and compassion. In French with English subtitles. Rated PG. 93m. **DIR:** François Truffaut. **CAST:** Jean-Pierre Léaud, Claude Jade, Marie-France Pisier. **1979**

LOVE SONGS (PAROLES ET MUSIQUE) ★★ Christopher Lambert plays a bisexual rock singer having an affair with a woman (Catherine Deneuve). Pointless and frequently incomprehensible. Dubbed (execrably) into English. 107m. **DIR:** Elie Chouraqui. **CAST:** Catherine Deneuve, Christopher Lambert, Nick Mancuso, Richard Anconina, Jacques Perrin. **1985**

LOVE WITHOUT PITY 🦃 Extremely dull film involving an arrogant man who treats women like trash until he falls in love with a woman who treats him the same. In French with English subtitles. Rated R for language. 88m. **DIR:** Adeline Lecallier. **CAST:** Hippolyte Girardot, Mireille Perrier. **1989**

LOVERS, THE (1958) ★★ Notorious in the early Sixties, when it was prosecuted in the U.S. for obscenity, this French drama looks mighty tame now. All the fuss was over an extended lovemaking scene between rich wife Jeanne Moreau and a young man she has just met. What little interest the film retains is in its wide-screen photography, which is lost in the transfer to home video, anyway. In French with English subtitles. B&W; 90m. **DIR:** Louis Malle. **CAST:** Jeanne Moreau, Alain Cuny, Jean-Marc Bory. **1958**

LOVERS (1992) ★★★★ Just out of General Franco's army, a young soldier makes wedding plans with his virginal fiancée—when he's not involved in steamy sex and shady scams with his new landlady. In Spanish with English subtitles. Unrated, the film contains profanity, nudity, and violence. 103m. **DIR:** Vicente Aranda. **CAST:** Victoria Abril, Jorge Sanz, Maribel Verdu. **1992**

LOVERS ON THE BRIDGE ★★★★ This audacious film elevates the story of two homeless lovers to an artful exploration of love, need, and values. Beautifully crafted, the film follows the on-again, off-again relationship of two people who live on Paris's Pont-Neuf Bridge, when they're not trying to find food or emotional sustenance in the cold world. In French with English subtitles. 126m. **DIR:** Léos Carax. **CAST:** Denis Lavant, Juliette Binoche. **1992**

LOVES OF A BLONDE ★★★½ This dark comedy from Milos Forman centers on a young girl working in a small-town factory who pursues a musician. Often hilarious. In Czechoslovakian with English subtitles. B&W; 88m. **DIR:** Milos Forman. **CAST:** Hana Brejchova, Josef Sebanek. **1965**

LOVES OF THREE QUEENS ★★ A three-hour Italian epic starring Hedy Lamarr as three of history's most memorable women—Guinevere, Empress Josephine, Helen of Troy—was chopped down to less than half its original length for American release, so don't expect it to make a lot of sense. Dubbed. 80m. **DIR:** Marc Allegret. **CAST:** Hedy Lamarr. **1953**

LOWER DEPTHS (1936) ★★★★ Another poignant observation by Jean Renoir about social classes. This time the director adapts Maxim Gorky's play about an impoverished thief (brilliantly performed by Jean Gabin) who meets a baron and instructs him in the joys of living without material wealth. In French with English subtitles. 92m. **DIR:** Jean Renoir. **CAST:** Jean Gabin, Louis Jouvet. 1936

LOWER DEPTHS, THE (1957) ★★★★ Brilliant adaptation of Maxim Gorky's play about a group of destitute people surviving on their tenuous self-esteem, while living in a ghetto. Akira Kurosawa explores this crippled society with tolerance, biting humor, and compassion. In Japanese with English subtitles. B&W; 125m. **DIR:** Akira Kurosawa. **CAST:** Toshiro Mifune. 1957

LUMIERE 🦃 The only thing this film illuminates is Jeanne Moreau's pretentiousness. In French. 95m. **DIR:** Jeanne Moreau. **CAST:** Jeanne Moreau, Francine Racette, Bruno Ganz, François Simon, Lucia Bose, Keith Carradine. 1976

LUNATICS & LOVERS ★★ Tepid morality play stars Marcello Mastroianni as a wealthy aristocrat whose delusions upset the locals. When a musician attempts to replace his imaginary wife with the real thing, chaos ensues. In Italian with English subtitles. Rated PG. 92m. **DIR:** Flavio Mogherini. **CAST:** Marcello Mastroianni, Lino Toffalo, Claudia Mori, Lino Morelli. 1975

LUPIN III: TALES OF THE WOLF (TV SERIES) ★★★ Taken from the popular Japanese series, these episodes feature the animated adventures of cunning cat-burglar Wolf and his crafty comrades. With plenty of action and lighthearted fun, *Lupin* will be enjoyed by animation fans who value cleverness over graphic violence. Dubbed in English. Not rated, but suitable for most audiences (some brief illustrated nudity). 30m. each **DIR:** Hayao Miyazaki. 1977

LUZIA ★★½ Modern Western features a young woman seeking revenge for her parents' murder. She begins working as a cowhand at the ranch of the powerful men responsible for making her an orphan. Slow moving and a bit too melodramatic. Unrated, contains nudity, violence, and profanity. In Portuguese with English subtitles. 112m. **DIR:** Fabio Barreto. **CAST:** Claudia Ohana, Thales Pan Chacon, Luzia Falcao. 1988

M ★★★★★ A child-killer is chased by police, and by other criminals who would prefer to mete out their own justice. Peter Lorre, in his first film role, gives a striking portrayal of a man driven by uncontrollable forces. A classic German film, understated, yet filled with haunting images. Beware of videocassettes containing badly translated, illegible subtitles. In German, with English subtitles. Unrated. B&W; 99m. **DIR:** Fritz Lang. **CAST:** Peter Lorre, Gustav Grundgens. 1931

MACARIO ★★★★ Excellent poetic fable based on a story by the mysterious author B. Traven (*The Treasure of the Sierra Madre*). Tarso Ignacio Lopez gives a deeply felt performance as an impoverished woodcutter. One of the most honored Mexican films, and the first to earn an Oscar nomination. In Spanish with English subtitles. B&W; 91m. **DIR:** Roberto Gavaldon. **CAST:** Tarso Ignacio Lopez, Pina Pellicer. 1960

MACARTHUR'S CHILDREN ★★ This import deals with effects of Japan's occupation by America, on a group of youngsters and adults living on a tiny Japanese island. Rated PG for profanity and suggested sex. In Japanese with English subtitles. 120m. **DIR:** Masahiro Shinoda. **CAST:** Takaya Yamauchi, Yoshiyuki Omori. 1984

MADAME BOVARY (1934) ★★★ Valentine Tessier is superb in the role of a woman who is half swan and half goose in director Jean Renoir's charming offbeat version of Flaubert's great novel. In French with English subtitles. B&W; 96m. **DIR:** Jean Renoir. **CAST:** Pierre Renoir, Valentine Tessier. 1934

MADAME BOVARY (1991) ★★★★ This gorgeously filmed, spectacularly designed adaptation of Gustave Flaubert's once-controversial novel features a stunning performance by Isabelle Huppert as Emma Bovary, who uses marriage to escape the boredom of a provincial life and then turns into an adultress when seeking escape from her unimaginative spouse. A soap opera to be sure, but on a grand, impressive scale. In French with English subtitles. Unrated; this import has suggested sex. 131m. **DIR:** Claude Chabrol. **CAST:** Isabelle Huppert, Jean-François Balmer, Christophe Malavoy. 1991

MADAME ROSA ★★★★★ This superbly moving motion picture features Simone Signoret in one of her greatest roles. It is a simple, human story that takes place six flights up in a dilapidated building where a once-beautiful prostitute and survivor of Nazi concentration camps cares for the children of hookers. No MPAA rating. 105m. **DIR:** Moshe Mizrahi. **CAST:** Simone Signoret, Sammy Den Youb, Claude Dauphin. 1977

MADEMOISELLE STRIPTEASE ★★½ Lightweight comedy made just before Brigitte Bardot became an international sensation. She plays a free spirit sent to Paris, where romance and trouble lurk. Brief nudity scenes were trimmed for American release (and this video). Dubbed in English. B&W; 100m. **DIR:** Marc Allegret. **CAST:** Brigitte Bardot, Daniel Gélin, Robert Hirsch. 1956

MADO ★★★½ The midlife crisis of a French businessman sparks this complex, intelligent look at social unrest in modern France. In French with English subtitles. Not rated; contains sexual situations. 130m. **DIR:** Claude Sautet. **CAST:** Michel Piccoli, Romy Schneider, Charles Denner, Ottavia Piccolo. 1976

MADOX-01 ★★★ Japanese animation. Havoc ensues when a university student trapped in a high-tech military attack unit (Madox-01) runs afoul of a psychotic tank commander. Superior animation. In Japanese with English subtitles. Unrated with violence and mild profanity. 48m. **DIR:** Aramaki Nobuyuki. **1989**

MAEDCHEN IN UNIFORM ★★★★ At once a fascinating and emotionally disturbing film, this German classic turns mainly on the love of a sexually repressed young girl for a compassionate female teacher in a state-run school. Remade in 1958 with Romy Schneider and Lili Palmer. In German with English subtitles. B&W; 90m. **DIR:** Leontine Sagan. **CAST:** Emilia Unda, Dorothea Wieck. **1931**

MAGIC FLUTE, THE ★★★★ Ingmar Bergman's highly imaginative and richly stylized presentation of Mozart's last opera. The camera starts from a position within the audience at an opera house, but after the curtain rises, it moves freely within and around the stage. The adaptation remains highly theatrical, and quite magical, and the music, of course, is glorious. Sung in Swedish with English subtitles. Unrated. 150m. **DIR:** Ingmar Bergman. **1974**

MAGIC GARDEN, THE ★★★ Charming South African comedy featuring an amateur cast. A sum of money stolen from a church keeps finding its way into the hands of people who need it! A good family movie. Also known as *Pennywhistle Blues*. B&W; 63m. **DIR:** Donald Swanson. **CAST:** Tommy Ramokgopa. **1952**

MAGICIAN, THE ★★★ Dark and somber parable deals with the quest for an afterlife by focusing on confrontation between a mesmerist and a magician. This shadowy allegory may not be everyone's idea of entertainment, but the richness of ideas and the excellent acting of director Ingmar Bergman's fine stable of actors make this a compelling film. Subtitled in English. B&W; 102m. **DIR:** Ingmar Bergman. **CAST:** Max von Sydow, Ingrid Thulin, Gunnar Björnstrand, Bibi Andersson. **1959**

MAITRESSE ★★★ A normal young man becomes involved with a professional dominatrix. Odd film is neither exploitative nor pornographic, but it sure is peculiar. In French with English subtitles. Unrated, but the subject matter marks it as adults-only territory. 110m. **DIR:** Barbet Schroeder. **CAST:** Gérard Depardieu, Bulle Ogier, Andre Rouyer. **1975**

MAKE ROOM FOR TOMORROW ★★★ More a collection of mildly humorous events than an out-and-out comedy. Victor Lanoux plays a father going through a mid-life crisis. Rated R for language and nudity. 104m. **DIR:** Peter Kassovitz. **CAST:** Victor Lanoux, Jane Birkin, Georges Wilson. **1982**

MALICIOUS ★★★½ Italian beauty Laura Antonelli is hired as a housekeeper for a widower and his three sons. Not surprisingly, she becomes the object of affection for all four men—particularly 14-year-old Nino. Rated R. 98m. **DIR:** Salvatore Samperi. **CAST:** Laura Antonelli, Turi Ferro, Alessandro Momo, Tina Aumont. **1974**

MALOU ★★★ Moving drama of a woman's search for the truth about the marriage between her French mother and a German Jew during Hitler's terrifying reign. The story unfolds through a rich tapestry of flashbacks. In German with English subtitles. Not rated. 94m. **DIR:** Jeanine Meerapfel. **CAST:** Ingrid Caven, Helmut Griem. **1983**

MAMA, THERE'S A MAN IN YOUR BED ★★★★ This is a somewhat unlikely but sweet and funny romantic tale of a white Parisian executive and his unexpected love for the black cleaning woman at his office. Daniel Auteuil (the slow-witted nephew Ugolin in *Jean de Florette*) stars. In French with English subtitles. Unrated but of a PG-13 quality, with adult situations. 108m. **DIR:** Coline Serreau. **CAST:** Daniel Auteuil, Firmine Richard. **1990**

MAMA TURNS 100 ★★★ A comparatively lighthearted attack on Franco's Spain from Carlos Saura. He reunites the cast of his 1972 *Anna and the Wolves* for this similar story of a greedy family battling among themselves. The humor is hit-and-miss, and the social analysis may be lost on American audiences. In Spanish with English subtitles. Unrated. 115m. **DIR:** Carlos Saura. **CAST:** Geraldine Chaplin. **1979**

MAN AND A WOMAN, A ★★★★ This is a superbly written, directed, and acted story of a young widow and widower who fall in love. Anouk Aimée and race-car driver Jean-Louis Trintignant set this film on fire. A hit in 1966 and still a fine picture. Dubbed into English. 102m. **DIR:** Claude Lelouch. **CAST:** Anouk Aimée, Jean-Louis Trintignant, Pierre Barouh, Valerie Lagrange. **1966**

MAN AND A WOMAN, A: 20 YEARS LATER 🦃 The director of this movie took his 1966 *A Man and a Woman* and, after twenty years, assembled the original lead actors and created a monster. In French. Rated PG. 112m. **DIR:** Claude Lelouch. **CAST:** Anouk Aimée, Jean-Louis Trintignant, Richard Berry. **1986**

MAN BITES DOG ★★ Several brilliant cinematic shots cannot justify this sick spoof of the documentary. A camera crew follows a cold-blooded killer on his brutal daily routine. Unsettling and difficult to watch. Rated NC-17, this contains countless acts of violence as well as profanity, sex, and gore. In French with English subtitles. B&W; 96m. **DIR:** Rémy Belvaux. **CAST:** Benoit Poelvoorde, Rémy Belvaux, Jenny Drye, Malou Madou. **1992**

MAN FACING SOUTHEAST ★★★½ A haunting, eerie mystery in which an unknown man—possibly an alien—inexplicably appears in the midst of a Buenos Aires psychiatric hospital. Rich with Christian symbolism, this film leaves one wondering who is really sick—society or those society finds insane. Some nudity and sexual situations. In Spanish with English subtitles. 105m. **DIR:** Eliseo Subiela. **CAST:** Lorenzo Quinteros, Hugo Soto. **1987**

MAN FROM NOWHERE, THE ★★★½ A henpecked small-town man seizes the opportunity to move to Rome and start a new life when he is mistakenly reported dead. Stylish, ironic comedy, based on a Luigi Pirandello novel and (unusually, for the time) filmed on location in Italy. In French with English subtitles. B&W; 98m. **DIR:** Pierre Chenal. **CAST:** Pierre Blanchar, Isa Miranda, Ginette Leclerc. **1937**

MAN LIKE EVA, A ★★ Curious but unsatisfying film is a thinly disguised biography of German filmmaker Rainer Werner Fassbinder, here played by a woman. A poorly written movie. In German with English subtitles. Unrated. 92m. **DIR:** Radu Gabrea. **CAST:** Eva Mattes, Lisa Kreuzer. **1984**

MAN OF IRON ★★★★ This work of fiction set against the backdrop of stark truth in Communist Poland shows the dramatic events that bridged the Gdańsk student rebellions of the 1960s and the Solidarity strikes of 1980. The story is told through the eyes of a journalism student looking for evidence of political skulduggery. In Polish with English subtitles. Rated PG. 140m. **DIR:** Andrzej Wajda. **CAST:** Jerzy Radziwilowicz, Krystyna Janda, Marian Opiana, Irene Byrska. **1981**

MAN OF MARBLE ★★★★ Epic film that reconstructs the life of a Polish laborer, a forgotten heroic figure, through his political efforts against the Stalinist power structure of the 1950s. Engrossing. In Polish with English subtitles. Not rated. B&W/color; 160m. **DIR:** Andrzej Wajda. **CAST:** Jerzy Radziwilowicz, Krystyna Janda. **1977**

MAN RAY CLASSIC SHORTS ★★½ Abstract photographer-artist Man Ray uses animation, superimposition, and lens distortions in these early silent experimental films shot in and around 1920s Paris. Interesting cinematography gets redundant at times. With French subtitles. Silent. B&W; 45m. **DIR:** Man Ray. **1924–1926**

MAN WHO LOVED WOMEN, THE (1977) ★★★★ The basis for a 1983 Blake Edwards film starring Burt Reynolds, this comedy-drama from François Truffaut has more irony and bite than the remake. Beginning with the protagonist's funeral, the movie examines why he wants and needs women so much, and why they respond to him as well. Like most Truffaut films, it has a deceptively light tone. In French with English subtitles. 119m. **DIR:** François Truffaut. **CAST:** Charles Denner, Brigitte Fossey, Leslie Caron, Nathalie Baye. **1977**

MANON ★★½ Disappointing update of a classic love story takes place during the German occupation of France. The two stars are rather wan, leaving the gritty depiction of war-torn Paris as the film's sole saving grace. In French with English subtitles. Unrated. 90m. **DIR:** Henri-Georges Clouzot. **CAST:** Cecile Aubrey, Michel Auclair. **1951**

MANON OF THE SPRING ★★★★★ For its visual beauty alone, this sequel to *Jean de Florette* is a motion picture to savor. But it has a great deal more to offer. Chief among its pleasures are superb performances by Yves Montand and Daniel Auteuil. A fascinating tale of revenge and unrequited love. In French with English subtitles. Rated PG-13 for nudity. 113m. **DIR:** Claude Berri. **CAST:** Yves Montand, Daniel Auteuil, Emmanuelle Beart, Elisabeth Depardieu. **1987**

MARIUS ★★★ This French movie is a marvelous view of the working class in Marseilles between the wars. The story revolves around Marius (Pierre Fresnay) and his love for Fanny (Orane Demazis), the daughter of a fish store proprietess. The poetic essence of the film is captured with style as Marius ships out to sea, unknowingly leaving Fanny with child. In French with English subtitles. B&W; 125m. **DIR:** Alexander Korda. **CAST:** Raimu, Pierre Fresnay, Orane Demazis, Alida Rouffe. **1931**

MARQUIS ★★★ Weird, weird, weird French satire based on the writings of de Sade, in which the marquis and his jailers are played by actors in animal masks and his stories are enacted (quite graphically in some instances) with Claymation figures. In French with English subtitles. Not rated, but definitely not for kids. 88m. **DIR:** Henri Xhonneux. **CAST:** Philippe Bizot, Gabrielle van Damme. **1989**

MARRIAGE OF MARIA BRAUN, THE ★★½ *The Marriage of Maria Braun* is probably Rainer Werner Fassbinder's easiest film to take because it's basically straightforward and stars the sensual and comedic Hanna Schygulla. She plays Maria Braun, a tough cookie who marries a Wehrmacht officer whom she loses to the war and then prison. The film is full of Fassbinder's overly dramatic, sordid sexual atmosphere. It can be both funny and perverse. In German. Rated R. 120m. **DIR:** Rainer Werner Fassbinder. **CAST:** Hanna Schygulla, Klaus Lowitsch, Ivan Desny. **1979**

MARRIED WOMAN, A ★★★ One of Jean-Luc Godard's most conventional films, a study of a Parisian woman who doesn't know if the father of her unborn child is her husband or her lover. In French with English subtitles. 94m. **DIR:** Jean-Luc Godard. **CAST:** Macha Meril, Philippe Leroy, Bernard Noel. **1964**

MARY MY DEAREST ★★ A magician converts a thief, marries him, and has him join her in a traveling show. She inadvertently hitches a ride with people being transported to an insane asylum where she becomes trapped. Poorly acted and very depressing. In Spanish with English subtitles. Not rated, but contains nudity and suggested sex. 100m. **DIR:** Jaime Humberto Hermosillo. **CAST:** Maria Rojo, Hector Bonilla, Ana Ofelia Morguia. **1983**

MASCULINE FEMININE ★★★ Jean-Luc Godard's eleventh film is an uneven attempt at exploring the relationship between a young Parisian radical, effectively portrayed by Jean-Pierre Leaud, and a slightly promiscuous woman (Chantal Goya) in fifteen discontinuous, contrapuntal vignettes. Good camera work and interesting screenplay lose strength in a muddled and disjointed story. In French with English subtitles. B&W; 103m. **DIR:** Jean-Luc Godard. **CAST:** Jean-Pierre Léaud, Chantal Goya, Catherine Isabelle Duport, Marlene Jobert. **1966**

MASQUERADE (1986) ★★★½ Bizarre psychodrama about a famous young actor who, disillusioned by his popularity, escapes into a world where reality and fantasy become obscured. Unconventional, stylistic approach by director Janusz Kijowski (one of Poland's new-wave filmmakers). In Polish with English subtitles. 102m. **DIR:** Janusz Kijowski. **CAST:** Boguslaw Linda. **1986**

MASTER OF THE HOUSE (DU SKAL AERE DIN HUSTRU) ★★★★ In this funny satire of middle-class life, a wife runs away from her husband, a chauvinist pig who treats her brutally. Later, the wife is reunited with her husband after an old nurse has taught him a lesson. Silent. B&W; 81m. **DIR:** Carl Dreyer. **CAST:** Johannes Meyer, Astrid Holm. **1925**

MATADOR ★★★★ Mind-boggling psychosexual melodrama carried to hilarious extremes by director Pedro Almodóvar. The story centers around a lame ex-bullfighter who derives sexual gratification from murder. In Spanish with English subtitles. Rated R for nudity and violence. 107m. **DIR:** Pedro Almodóvar. **CAST:** Assumpta Serna, Antonio Banderas, Carmen Maura. **1988**

MAY FOOLS ★★★★ An upper-class French family (and a few hangers-on) gather for their mother's funeral at a country estate, just as the 1968 Paris student riots seem to be setting off another French Revolution. A leisurely comedy-drama from director Louis Malle (cowriting with Jean-Claude Carrière). Rated R for profanity, nudity, and simulated sex. 105m. **DIR:** Louis Malle. **CAST:** Michel Piccoli, Miou-Miou, Michel Duchaussoy, Harriet Walter, Bruno Carette, Paulette Dubost. **1989**

MAYERLING ★★★ Fine-tuned, convincing performances mark this French-made romantic tragedy based upon Austrian Crown Prince Rudolph's ill-starred clandestine love for court lady-in-waiting Countess Marie Vetsera, in 1889. A 1969 British remake stinks by comparison. In French with English subtitles. B&W; 91m. **DIR:** Anatole Litvak. **CAST:** Charles Boyer, Danielle Darrieux, Suzy Prim. **1936**

MEDEA ★★★★ Maria Callas enacts the title role in this film adaptation of Euripides' tragedy. The diva is an exciting screen presence. In Italian with English subtitles. Rated R for nudity and violence. 100m. **DIR:** Pier Paolo Pasolini. **CAST:** Maria Callas. **1970**

MEDITERRANEO ★★★★ In 1941, several misfit soldiers arrive on a Greek isle. The men, none very gung ho about their mission, are to hold and protect the island for Mussolini and the cause of fascism. A pleasant, bittersweet fable. In Italian with English subtitles. Unrated; the film has profanity and nudity. 90m. **DIR:** Gabriele Salvatores. **CAST:** Diego Abatantuono, Claudio Biagli, Giuseppi Cederna, Claudio Bisio. **1991**

MELO ★★★ An offering of quiet, subtle charms, one of those typically French chamber romances in which small gestures or glances speak volumes. It's a straightforward exploration of a romantic triangle, set in the world of contemporary classical music, and features a memorable, César-winning performance by Sabine Azema. In French with English subtitles. 112m. **DIR:** Alain Resnais. **CAST:** Sabine Azema, Pierre Arditi, Fanny Ardant, André Dussolier. **1988**

MELODIE EN SOUS-SOL (THE BIG GRAB) ★★★ Fresh from prison, aging gangster Jean Gabin makes intricate and elaborate plans to score big by robbing a major Riviera gambling casino. Alain Delon joins him in conniving their way to the casino vault by seducing a show girl to gain vital backstage access. Gabin, as the cool, experienced ex-convict, and Delon, as his young, upstart, eager partner, are part-perfect. In French with English subtitles. Originally released in U.S. as *Any Number Can Win*. B&W; 118m. **DIR:** Henri Verneuil. **CAST:** Jean Gabin, Alain Delon, Viviane Romance, Carla Marlier. **1963**

MEMORIES OF A MARRIAGE ★★★★ Sensitive film allows a mild-mannered husband to reflect on his married life through a series of revealing flashbacks. In each scene, his wife is passionate, stubborn, or charitable—but never lukewarm. In Danish with English subtitles. Unrated, contains mature themes. 90m. **DIR:** Kaspar Rostrup. **CAST:** Ghita Norby, Frits Helmuth, Rikke Bendsen, Henning Moritzen. **1989**

MEMORIES OF UNDERDEVELOPMENT ★★★ In the early 1960s, a Europeanized Cuban intellectual too lazy to leave Miami and too eccentric to fit into Cuban society engages in a passionate sexual affair with a beautiful young woman. A scathing satire on sex and politics. In Spanish with English subtitles. B&W; 97m. **DIR:** Tomas Gutierrez Alea. **CAST:** Sergio Corrieri. **1968**

MEN... ★★★★ In this tongue-in-cheek anthropological study by German writer-director Doris Dörrie, a hotshot advertising executive, who has been having a fling with his secretary, is outraged to discover that his wife has a lover. Devastated at first, he finally decides to get even, and his revenge is one of the most inventive and hilarious ever to grace the screen. In German with English subtitles. Unrated; the film has profanity. 99m. **DIR:** Doris Dörrie. **CAST:** Uwe Ochenknecht, Ulrike Kriener, Heiner Lauterbach. **1985**

MÉNAGE ★★★ Two down-and-outers (Michel Blanc and Miou-Miou) are taken in by a flamboyant thief (Gérard Depardieu), who introduces them to a life of crime and kinky sex in this alternately hilarious and mean-spirited comedy. The first half of this bizarre work is enjoyable, but the acceptance of the last part will depend on the taste—and tolerance—of the viewer. In French, with English subtitles. Unrated; the film has profanity, violence, nudity, and simulated sex. 84m. **DIR:** Bertrand Blier. **CAST:** Gérard Depardieu, Michel Blanc, Miou-Miou, Bruno Cremer. **1986**

MEPHISTO ★★★★★ Winner of the 1981 Academy Award for best foreign-language film, this brilliant movie, by Hungarian writer-director Istvan Szabo, examines the conceits of artists with devastating honesty and insight. Klaus Maria Brandauer, in a stunning performance, plays an actor whose overwhelming desire for artistic success leads to his becoming a puppet of the Nazi government. The film has nudity and violence. In German with English subtitles. 135m. **DIR:** Istvan Szabo. **CAST:** Klaus Maria Brandauer, Krystyna Janda. **1981**

MERCHANT OF FOUR SEASONS, THE ★★ Melodramatic character study about a fruit peddler who drinks himself to death. This slice-of-life soap opera gone amok lacks emotional power. In German with English subtitles. Not rated, but contains nudity and profanity. 88m. **DIR:** Rainer Werner Fassbinder. **CAST:** Irm Hermann, Hanna Schygulla. **1972**

MERCI LA VIE ★★ Even one of France's greatest filmmakers, Bertrand Blier, is entitled to an occasional miscue. This saga of two young women on an odyssey of self-discovery, is often aimless, frequently enigmatic and surreal in its use of time shifts. *Merci la Vie* romps through a confusing world of the mind. In French with English subtitles. 117m. **DIR:** Bertrand Blier. **CAST:** Charlotte Gainsbourg, Anouk Grinberg, Gérard Depardieu, Michel Blanc, Jean-Louis Trintignant. **1991**

MILKY WAY, THE (1970) ★★★★ Haunting comedy about two men making a religious pilgrimage through France. Excellent supporting cast and outstanding direction by Luis Buñuel. French dialogue with English subtitles. Not rated. 102m. **DIR:** Luis Buñuel. **CAST:** Paul Frankeur, Laurent Terzieff, Alain Cuny, Bernard Verley, Michel Piccoli, Delphine Seyrig. **1970**

MIRACLE IN MILAN ★★★½ A baby found in a cabbage patch grows up to be Toto the Good, who organizes a shantytown into the perfect commune. Or so he had hoped, but it is not to be—even with the help of the old lady who found him, now an angel of mercy. This fantasy by Vittorio De Sica also delivers a message of social satire and innocence. Winner of the Cannes Grand Prix and the New York Film Critics' Circle best foreign film awards. In Italian with English subtitles. B&W; 96m. **DIR:** Vittorio De Sica. **CAST:** Francesco Golisano, Paolo Stoppa. **1951**

MIRACLE IN ROME ★★★ Spanish TV film adaptation of Gabriel García Marquez's intriguing tale of one man's struggle with sainthood. Frank Ramirez plays the bereaved father who's lost his vivacious 7-year-old daughter. Heartwarming, though morbid, insight into a man's undying love and devotion for his innocent child. In Spanish with English subtitles. 76m. **DIR:** Lisandro Duque Naranjo. **CAST:** Frank Ramirez. **1988**

MIRROR, THE ★★★★ A young boy is hypnotized in an attempt to cure a chronic stutter in this poetic mixture of dream and reality by the Soviet Union's most visionary film director, Andrei Tarkovsky. Brilliant use of color and black-and-white cinematography. Mesmerizing. In Russian with English subtitles. 90m. **DIR:** Andrei Tarkovsky. **CAST:** Margarita Terekhova. **1976**

MISS JULIE ★★ An impetuous young Swedish countess rejected by her fiancé flirts with and then seduces a handsome servant. Brooding melodrama based on a Strindberg play becomes a very tedious experience. In Swedish with English subtitles. Not rated, but contains nudity. B&W; 90m. **DIR:** Alf Sjoberg. **CAST:** Anita Bjork, Ulf Palme, Max von Sydow. **1950**

MISS MARY ★★★½ A good knowledge of the history of Argentina—specifically between the years 1930 and 1945—will help viewers appreciate this biting black comedy. Julie Christie gives a marvelous performance as a British governess brought to the South American country to work for a wealthy family. Through her eyes, in a series of flashbacks, we see how the corrupt aristocracy slowly falls apart. In both English and Spanish. Rated R for profanity, nudity, and suggested and simulated sex. 100m.

DIR: Maria Luisa Bemberg. **CAST:** Julie Christie, Nacha Guevara, Tato Pavlovsky. **1987**

MISSISSIPPI MERMAID ★★★ Interesting drama about a wealthy industrialist living on an island who orders a bride by mail. All this eventually leads to deception and murder. Solid performances by Jean-Paul Belmondo and Catherine Deneuve. In French with English subtitles. Not rated. 123m. **DIR:** François Truffaut. **CAST:** Jean-Paul Belmondo, Catherine Deneuve, Michel Bouquet. **1969**

MR. HULOT'S HOLIDAY ★★★½ A delightfully lighthearted film about the natural comedy to be found in vacationing. Jacques Tati plays the famous Monsieur Hulot, who has some silly adventures at a seaside resort. Although partially dubbed in English, this film has a mime quality that is magical. B&W; 86m. **DIR:** Jacques Tati. **CAST:** Jacques Tati, Nathale Pascaud. **1953**

MR. KLEIN ★★★½ Dark-sided character study of a Parisian antique dealer who buys artwork and personal treasures from Jews trying to escape Paris in 1942. He (Alain Delon) finds himself mistaken for a missing Jew of the same name. Rated PG. Available in French version. 123m. **DIR:** Joseph Losey. **CAST:** Alain Delon, Jeanne Moreau, Juliet Berto, Michel Lonsdale, Jean Bouise, Francine Berge. **1976**

MR. VAMPIRE (VOL. 1–4) ★★★½ This Chinese vampire movie is a surreal and hilarious romp filled with remarkable martial arts and bizarre special effects laced with great slapstick and vampire erotica. Director Lau Koon Wai has created a bloodsucker who sports long purple fingernails and yellow fangs and, when not levitating, hops like a bunny. In Chinese with English subtitles. Not rated, but contains violence and nudity. 375m. **DIR:** Wong Kee Hung, Law Lit, Sung Kam Shing. **CAST:** Ricky Hui, Yuen Biao, Richard Ng. **1986–1988**

MISTRESS, THE (1953) ★★★½ Tragic tale of a Japanese woman trapped in a life as mistress to a greedy Shylock. When she falls in love with a medical student, her reputation causes nothing but heartache and sorrow. In Japanese with English subtitles. B&W; 106m. **DIR:** Shiro Toyoda. **CAST:** Hideko Takamine, Hiroshi Akutagawa. **1953**

MON ONCLE ANTOINE ★★★½ Above-average coming-of-age story about a boy in rural Canada during the 1940s. In French with English subtitles. Unrated, but fine for the entire family. 110m. **DIR:** Claude Jutra. **CAST:** Jacques Gagnon, Claude Jutra. **1971**

MON ONCLE D'AMERIQUE ★★★★ In this bizarre French comedy, director Alain Resnais works something close to a miracle: he combines intelligence with entertainment. On one level, *Mon Oncle d'Amerique* is a delectable farce with the requisite ironies, surprise complications, and bittersweet truths. Underneath, it is a thought-provoking scientific treatise—by biologist Henri Laborit—on the human condition. In French with English subtitles. Rated PG. 123m. **DIR:** Alain Resnais. **CAST:** Gérard Depardieu, Nicole Garcia, Roger Pierre. **1980**

MONIKA ★★ Young Harriet Andersson is Monika, a sultry, precocious teenager who escapes her poverty with the help of a young man. Pretty dull stuff. Also known by the title *Summer With Monika*. In Swedish with English subtitles. B&W; 82m. **DIR:** Ingmar Bergman. **CAST:** Harriet Andersson. **1952**

MONSIEUR HIRE ★★★★ A grouchy recluse, already suspected of murder, spies on his lovely neighbor; is he working up to kill again? Slow-moving but suspenseful, beautifully photographed and acted. In French with English subtitles. Rated PG-13 for subtle eroticism. 88m. **DIR:** Patrice Leconte. **CAST:** Michel Blanc, Sandrine Bonnaire, Luc Thuillier, Eric Berenger. **1990**

MONSIEUR VINCENT ★★★★ Winner of a special Academy Award, this is a moving, beautifully photographed biography of St. Vincent de Paul, patron saint of social workers. Even if you don't think you'd be interested in the subject matter, it's worth seeing for the performance of Pierre Fresnay, one of France's greatest actors. In French with English subtitles. 73m. **DIR:** Maurice Cloche. **CAST:** Pierre Fresnay, Aimée Clairiond, Jean Debucourt. **1949**

MOON IN THE GUTTER, THE 🦃 A pretentious, self-consciously artistic bore that seems to defy any viewer to sit through it. Rated R for profanity, nudity, and violence. In French with subtitles. 126m. **DIR:** Jean-Jacques Beineix. **CAST:** Gérard Depardieu, Nastassja Kinski, Victoria Abril. **1983**

MOONLIGHTING (1983) ★★★★½ This film, a political parable criticizing the Soviet Union's suppression of Solidarity in Poland, may sound rather heavy, gloomy, and dull. It isn't. Written and directed by Jerzy Skolimowski, it essentially focuses on four Polish construction workers remodeling a flat in London. Give it a look. In Polish with English subtitles. Rated PG for very brief nudity. 97m. **DIR:** Jerzy Skolimowski. **CAST:** Jeremy Irons, Eugene Lipinski. **1983**

MORE ★★★½ A German youth, on the road after finishing college, becomes enamored of a free-spirited American girl in Paris. Barbet Schroeder's first film as a director, this grim portrait of directionless young people is ironically best remembered for its Pink Floyd score. In English. Unrated, contains nudity. 110m. **DIR:** Barbet Schroeder. **CAST:** Mimsy Farmer, Klaus Grunberg. **1969**

MOSCOW DOES NOT BELIEVE IN TEARS ★★★★ For all its rewards, *Moscow Does*

Not Believe in Tears requires a bit of patience on the part of the viewer. The first hour of this tragic comedy is almost excruciatingly slow. But once it gets deeper into the story, you're very glad you toughed it out. MPAA unrated, but contains brief nudity and brief violence. 152m. **DIR:** Vladimir Menshov. **CAST:** Vera Alentova, Irina Muravyova. **1980**

MOTHER ★★★★ This is a beautifully shot black-and-white movie about a working-class mother who must raise her family after her husband's death in post–World War II. While the story appears to be simple, there is great depth in each character. This was voted Japan's best film in 1952. In Japanese with English subtitles. B&W; 98m. **DIR:** Mikio Naruse. **CAST:** Kinuyo Tanaka. **1952**

MOTHER KUSTERS GOES TO HEAVEN ★★★ When a German factory worker kills his boss and then commits suicide, his widow must deal with the convoluted aftermath. Emotionally and politically charged, this potent, pro-communist tract was banned by the Berlin Film Festival. In German with English subtitles. Rated R for adult themes. 108m. **DIR:** Rainer Werner Fassbinder. **CAST:** Brigitte Mira, Ingrid Caven, Margit Carstensen. **1975**

MOUCHETTE ★★★★ Director Robert Bresson's unique cinematic style has never been more evident than in this heartfelt drama. The story depicts the hardships of a young peasant girl who desperately attempts to transcend a brutal household where she lives with her alcoholic, bootlegger father and brothers. In French with English subtitles. Not rated. 90m. **DIR:** Robert Bresson. **CAST:** Nadine Nortier. **1966**

MOZART BROTHERS, THE ★★½ This surrealistic film about a zany director's insane production of *Don Giovanni* owes far more to the Marx Brothers than the music of Mozart. Étienne Glaser is splendid as the spacy director. However refreshing, the plot is not developed beyond the initial sniggers. In Swedish with English subtitles. Unrated. 111m. **DIR:** Suzanne Osten. **CAST:** Étienne Glaser, Philip Zanden. **1986**

MURIEL ★★★★ Like *Last Year at Marienbad*, this stylized Alain Resnais film is largely about the burden of memory, as experienced by four interlinked characters. Difficult and demanding, it is composed of many short, overlapping scenes. But for those who accept its challenge, the emotional payoff can be extraordinary. In French with English subtitles. 116m. **DIR:** Alain Resnais. **CAST:** Delphine Seyrig, Jean-Pierre Kérien, Nita Klein. **1963**

MURMUR OF THE HEART ★★★ Director Louis Malle's story of a sickly French teenager and his youthful, free-spirited mother in the 1950s gets off to a wonderful start, then runs out of steam in its second half as the two check into a health resort. Still, it has charm, wit, and style to spare. Not rated, but Malle's treatment of a single act of incest may raise American eyebrows, although the subject is very tastefully handled. In French with English subtitles. 118m. **DIR:** Louis Malle. **CAST:** Lea Massari, Benoit Ferreux, Daniel Gélin, Michel Lonsdale. **1971**

MUSIC TEACHER, THE ★★★★★ Belgian director and co-scenarist Gerard Corbiau weave an incredibly sensual story of the love of a gifted singer (Anne Roussel) for her music teacher (José Van Dam). Superb acting, exquisite cinematography, and great music. In French with English subtitles. Rated PG for suggested sex. 100m. **DIR:** Gerard Corbiau. **CAST:** José Van Dam, Anne Roussel, Philippe Volter. **1989**

MY BEST FRIEND'S GIRL ★★★ A philosophical comedy about two best but very different friends who find themselves in love with the same girl. Isabelle Huppert marvelously plays the sultry object of both men's desire, but the real gem of this film is the performance of Coluche, who falls in love with his best friend's girl. In French with English subtitles. Nudity and simulated sex. 99m. **DIR:** Bertrand Blier. **CAST:** Isabelle Huppert, Thierry Lhermitte, Coluche. **1984**

MY FATHER'S GLORY ★★★★★ French filmmaker Yves Robert's remarkable *My Father's Glory* is the unforgettable chronicle of author and filmmaker Marcel Pagnol's idyllic remembrances of his childhood. The most commonplace events are made to seem magical in this import and its sequel, *My Mother's Castle*. Not since *Jean de Florette* and *Manon of the Spring* has a French filmmaker so artfully mined a literary source. Bravo! In French with English subtitles. Rated G. 110m. **DIR:** Yves Robert. **CAST:** Philippe Caubère, Nathalie Roussel, Thérèse Liotard, Didier Pain. **1991**

MY LIFE AS A DOG ★★★★★ This charming, offbeat, and downright lovable import from Sweden is a big surprise. It tells of a young boy in 1950s Sweden who's shipped off to a country village when his mother becomes seriously ill. There, as he tries to come to terms with his new life, he encounters a town filled with colorful eccentrics and a young tomboy who becomes his first love. In Swedish with English subtitles. 101m. **DIR:** Lasse Hallstrom. **CAST:** Anton Glanzelius. **1987**

MY LIFE TO LIVE ★★★ Early piece of ground-breaking cinema by Jean-Luc Godard features Anna Karina as a young woman who leaves her husband to become an actress but eventually turns to prostitution. As with any Jean-Luc Godard film, the point is not so much the plot as the director's relentless experimentation with film technique and probing of social issues. In French with English subtitles. B&W; 85m. **DIR:** Jean-Luc Godard. **CAST:** Anna Karina, Saddy Rebbot. **1963**

MY MOTHER'S CASTLE ★★★★★ More glorious adventures for young Marcel Pagnol in the exquisite sequel to *My Father's Glory*. Once again, filmmaker Yves Robert brings out all of the suspense, humor, and heartbreak in this autobiographical tale. In French with English subtitles. Rated PG. 98m. **DIR:** Yves Robert. **CAST:** Philippe Caubère, Nathalie Roussel, Thérèse Liotard, Didier Pain, Jean Rochefort. **1991**

MY NAME IS IVAN ★★★★ The title character is a 12-year-old boy who works as a scout for the Soviet army during World War II. An affecting study of the horrors of war. Young Kolya Burlaiev is remarkable as Ivan. In Russian with English subtitles. Unrated. 84m. **DIR:** Andrei Tarkovsky. **CAST:** Kolya Burlaiev, Valentin Zubkov. **1963**

MY NEW PARTNER ★★★★ Walrus-faced Philippe Noiret is hilarious in this French comedy that swept the César Awards (the French Oscars). He plays a corrupt but effective police detective who is saddled with a new partner, an idealistic young police-academy graduate. Hollywood would never make a comedy this cynical about police work; they've seldom made one as funny either. In French with English subtitles. Rated R for nudity and sexual situations. 106m. **DIR:** Claude Zidi. **CAST:** Philippe Noiret, Thierry Lhermitte, Regine. **1984**

MY NIGHT AT MAUD'S ★★★★ *My Night at Maud's* was the first feature by Eric Rohmer to be shown in the United States. It is the third film of the cycle he called *Six Moral Tales*. A man is in love with a woman, but his eyes wander to another. However, the transgression is only brief, for, according to Rohmer, the only true love is the love ordained by God. Beautifully photographed in black and white, the camera looks the actors straight in the eye and captures every nuance. In French with English subtitles. B&W; 105m. **DIR:** Eric Rohmer. **CAST:** Jean-Louis Trintignant, Françoise Fabian, Marie-Christine Barrault. **1970**

MY OTHER HUSBAND ★★★★ At first, this French import starring the marvelous Miou-Miou seems rather like a scatterbrained, faintly funny retread of the old person-with-two-spouses comedy plot. But it goes on to become an affecting, sweetly sad little treasure. In French with English subtitles. Rated PG-13 for profanity. 110m. **DIR:** Georges Lautner. **CAST:** Miou-Miou, Roger Hanin, Eddy Mitchell. **1981**

MY 20TH CENTURY ★★★★ Two long-separated twins are reunited on the Orient Express on New Year's Eve, 1899. Though completely different—one is a vain young woman, the other a fiery revolutionary—both are lovers of the same man. A witty look at the genesis of our era, with two wonderful performances by Dorotha Segda as both sisters. In Hungarian with English subtitles. Not rated. B&W; 104m. **DIR:** Ildiko Enyedi. **CAST:** Dorotha Segda, Oleg Jankovskij. **1988**

MY UNCLE (MON ONCLE) ★★★★ The second of Jacques Tati's cinematic romps as Mr. Hulot (the first was the famous *Mr. Hulot's Holiday*), this delightful comedy continues Tati's recurrent theme of the common man confronted with an increasingly mechanized and depersonalized society. (It's also the only Tati film to win the Academy Award for best foreign film.) 116m. **DIR:** Jacques Tati. **CAST:** Jacques Tati, Jean-Pierre Zola. **1958**

MYSTERIES ★★★ Rutger Hauer plays an affluent foreigner in a seaside village who becomes obsessed by a local beauty. This intriguing drama is hampered by poorly dubbed dialogue. Not rated, but has sex and nudity. 93m. **DIR:** Paul de Lussanet. **CAST:** Sylvia Kristel, Rutger Hauer, David Rappaport, Rita Tushingham, Andrea Ferreol. **1984**

MYSTERY OF ALEXINA, THE ★★★★ True story of a sexually ambiguous young man, raised in the nineteenth century as a woman, who becomes aware of his true identity only when he falls in love with a young woman. The script doesn't answer all the questions it raises, but there's more than enough to compel your interest. In French with English subtitles. 84m. **DIR:** René Feret. **CAST:** Philippe Vuillemin, Valerie Stroh. **1985**

MYSTERY OF PICASSO, THE ★★★★★ Pablo Picasso conceives, prepares, sketches, and paints fifteen canvasses—all of which were destroyed after the film was completed. A one-of-a-kind look at the artistic process, sensitively directed with exquisite music and photography (by Claude Renoir). In French with English subtitles. 85m. **DIR:** Henri-Georges Clouzot. **1956**

NAIS ★★★ A hunchbacked laborer helps the girl he loves in her romance with the son of a rich landowner. Though he only wrote the screenplay (adapted from an Émile Zola story), this touching film bears the unmistakable stamp of Marcel Pagnol. In French with English subtitles. B&W; 95m. **DIR:** Raymond Leboursier. **CAST:** Fernandel, Jacqueline Pagnol. **1945**

NANA ★★½ Adaptation of Émile Zola's oft-filmed story about the girl who will do anything to get out of the slums. This handsomely produced vehicle for Martine Carol (wife of director Christian-Jaque) is otherwise undistinguished. In French with English subtitles. 120m. **DIR:** Christian-Jacque. **CAST:** Martine Carol, Charles Boyer. **1955**

NAPOLEON (1927) ★★★★★ Over a half century after its debut, *Napoleon* remains a visual wonder, encompassing a number of filmmaking techniques, some of which still seem revolutionary. The complete film—as pieced together by British film historian Kevin Brownlow over a period of twenty years—is one motion picture event no lover of the art form will want to miss even on the small screen without the full effect of its spectacular three-screen climax. B&W; 235m. **DIR:** Abel Gance. **CAST:** Albert Dieudonné, Antonin Artaud. **1927**

NASTY GIRL, THE ★★★★★ This Oscar-nominated film is the most highly original movie to come out of Germany since the glory days of Fassbinder and Herzog. And the key to its freshness is its unique blend of charming, upbeat comedy with a serious topic: the scars and guilt from the Nazi era that still run deep in modern German life. In German with English subtitles. Unrated. 96m. **DIR:** Michael Verhoeven. **CAST:** Lena Stolze. **1990**

NAZARIN ★★★★★ A priest is cast out of his church for giving shelter to a prostitute. A remarkable film by Luis Buñuel that presents a clever variation of the Don Quixote theme, applied to religion and hypocrisy. This surrealistic comedy won the Grand Prize at the Cannes Film Festival. In Spanish with English subtitles. B&W; 92m. **DIR:** Luis Buñuel. **CAST:** Francisco Rabal. **1958**

NEA (A YOUNG EMMANUELLE) ★★★ In this French sex comedy, a young girl, Sybille Ashby (Ann Zacharias), stifled by the wealth of her parents, turns to anonymously writing erotic literature via firsthand experience. A relatively successful and entertaining film of its kind, this has sex and adult themes. In French with English subtitles. Rated R. 103m. **DIR:** Nelly Kaplan. **CAST:** Sami Frey, Ann Zacharias, Micheline Presle. **1978**

NEO-TOKYO ★★ This collection of short animated stories is a rather uneven showcase for three of Japan's premiere animation directors. Two of the features are merely exercises in self-indulgence, but the last, "An Order to Stop Construction" from *Akira* director Katsuhiro Otomo, is definitely worth seeing. In Japanese with English subtitles. Not rated; contains some graphic violence. 50m. **DIR:** Rin Taro, Yoshiaki Kawajiri, Katsumi Otomo. **1986**

NEST, THE (1981) ★★½ *The Nest* is the story of a tragic relationship between a 60-year-old widower and a 12-year-old girl. The movie takes a far too romantic view of the widower's sacrifices to the friendship. Hector Alterio as the older man has a warm and inviting face and voice. He is the one who enlists our sympathies. In Spanish with English subtitles. 109m. **DIR:** Jaime De Arminan. **CAST:** Hector Alterio, Ana Torrent. **1981**

NEWS FROM HOME 🦃 Sandwiched between the spectacular and seedy elements of New York, there is the mundane, to which we are treated in huge elongated slices. If you want something exciting to happen while watching this, look out the window. In French with English subtitles. Unrated. 85m. **DIR:** Chantal Akerman. **1991**

NEXT SUMMER ★★★½ This romantic comedy features some of France's top stars in a story about a family in which personal frustrations conflict with passions in the quest for power and beauty. Excellent performances by a top-notch cast. In French with English subtitles. Not rated. 100m. **DIR:** Nadine Trintignant. **CAST:** Claudia Cardinale, Fanny Ardant, Philippe Noiret, Marie Trintignant, Jean-Louis Trintignant. **1986**

NEXT YEAR IF ALL GOES WELL ★★★ Innocuous comedy about a pair of cohabitating lovers trying to decide whether to take the leap into marriage. Likable performances by Isabelle Adjani and Thierry Lhermitte. Dubbed. Rated R for brief nudity. 95m. **DIR:** Jean-Loup Hubert. **CAST:** Isabelle Adjani, Thierry Lhermitte. **1981**

NIGHT AND DAY (1991) ★★★½ The meter's constantly running during this sharp-edged comedy about a woman who keeps two lovers. They're both cab drivers—one works the night shift, the other the day shift. She alternates between them and finds that she actually loves both men and her situation. Erotic and unconventional. In French with English subtitles. Not rated, but contains sexual situations. 90m. **DIR:** Chantal Akerman. **CAST:** Guilaine Londez, Thomas Langmann, Francois Negret. **1991**

NIGHT IS MY FUTURE ★★★½ In this early Ingmar Bergman film, a film that at the same time is dark in mood but bright with promise of things to come, we meet a blinded military veteran (Birger Malmsten) who is at war with the world and with himself due to his handicap. Through the selfless efforts of a maid, he learns to accept his problems and make a new life for himself. In Swedish with English subtitles. B&W; 87m. **DIR:** Ingmar Bergman. **CAST:** Mai Zetterling, Birger Malmsten. **1947**

NIGHT OF THE SHOOTING STARS ★★½ Made by Paolo and Vittorio Taviani, this Italian import is about the flight of peasants from their mined village in pastoral Tuscany during the waning days of World War II. Despite its subject matter, the horrors of war, it is a strangely unaffecting—and ineffective—motion picture. In Italian with English subtitles. Unrated; the film has violence. 116m. **DIR:** Paolo Taviani, Vittorio Taviani. **CAST:** Omero Antonutti, Margarita Lozano. **1982**

NIGHTS OF CABIRIA ★★★★ Federico Fellini's seventh film can be hailed as a tragicomic masterpiece. The story focuses on an impoverished prostitute (Giulietta Masina) living on the outskirts of Rome, who is continuously betrayed by her faith in human nature. Masina gives an unforgettable performance. In Italian with English subtitles. B&W; 110m. **DIR:** Federico Fellini. **CAST:** Giulietta Masina, Amadeo Nazzari, François Perier. **1957**

NO REGRETS FOR OUR YOUTH ★★★★ Poignant drama of feminist self-discovery set against the backdrop of a militarist Japanese society. Setsuko Hara gives a harrowing performance as a spoiled housewife who becomes enlightened to the hypocrisy of politics when her lover, a disaffected leftist, is arrested and executed for espionage. In Japanese with English subtitles. B&W; 110m. **DIR:** Akira Kurosawa. **CAST:** Setsuko Hara, Takashi Shimura. **1946**

NOSFERATU ★★★★ A product of the German Expressionist era, *Nosferatu* is a milestone in the history of world cinema. Director F. W. Murnau seems to make the characters jump out at you. With his skeletal frame, rodent face, long nails, and long, pointed ears, Max Schreck is the most terrifying of all screen vampires. Silent. B&W; 63m. **DIR:** F. W. Murnau. **CAST:** Max Schreck, Gustav von Waggenheim. **1922**

NOTORIOUS NOBODIES ★★★½ Eight vignettes based on true events take place on the same day in different countries and show the range of human-rights violations that occur every day. The film's power comes from its wide-spread canvas. While individual scenes may be dramatically weak, the cumulative effect is much more than the sum of its parts. Subtitled. Unrated; contains violence. 102m. **DIR:** Stanislav Stanojevic. **1985**

NOUS N'IRONS PLUS AU BOIS ★★ A group of young French Resistance fighters harass German troops in a forest held by the Germans. They capture a young German soldier who falls in love with a French girl. Aside from the presence of Marie-France Pisier, there's little here likely to interest an American audience. In French with English subtitles. 90m. **DIR:** Georges Dumoulin. **CAST:** Marie-France Pisier, Siegfried Rauch, Richard Leduc. **1969**

NUDO DI DONNA (PORTRAIT OF A WOMAN, NUDE) ★★★ Nino Manfredi stars in this Italian comedy as a husband shocked to discover his wife (Eleonora Giorgi) may have posed nude for a painting. Told the model was a hooker, the skeptical Manfredi attempts to discover the truth in this madcap import. In Italian with English subtitles. Unrated. 112m. **DIR:** Nino Manfredi. **CAST:** Nino Manfredi, Eleonora Giorgi. **1982**

NUN, THE (LA RELIGIEUSE) ★★ Forced into a nunnery by her family's poverty, a young woman tries to maintain her personal dignity despite physical and sexual abuse. While this is new-wave director Jacques Rivette's most accessible film, it still isn't easygoing. A serious film that is a chore to watch. In French with English subtitles. B&W; 140m. **DIR:** Jacques Rivette. **CAST:** Anna Karina, Lilo Pulver, Francisco Rabal. **1965**

OBLOMOV ★★★★ This thoroughly delightful film has as its main character Oblomov, a man who has chosen to sleep his life away. Then along comes a childhood friend who helps him explore a new meaning of life. A beautifully crafted triumph for director Nikita Mikhalkov (*A Slave of Love*). In Russian with English subtitles. MPAA unrated. 146m. **DIR:** Nikita Mikhalkov. **CAST:** Oleg Tabakov, Elena Soloyei. **1980**

OCCURRENCE AT OWL CREEK BRIDGE, AN ★★★½ This fascinating French film looks at the last fleeting moments of the life of a man being hanged from the bridge of the title during the American Civil War. This memorable short film works on all levels. B&W; 22m. **DIR:** Robert Enrico. **CAST:** Roger Jacquet, Anne Cornaly. **1962**

OCTOBER ★★★★ Sergei Eisenstein's contribution to the tenth anniversary of the Russian Revolution of 1917 is as dazzling in its imagery and cutting as it is perversely obscure in its storyline. The events leading up to the storming by the Cossacks of the Winter Palace are refracted through a sensibility more interested in what he called "Intellectual Cinema" than in routine plot formulas—making it perhaps more interesting to film history buffs than casual viewers. In America retitled *Ten Days that Shook the World.* Silent. B&W; 85m. **DIR:** Sergei Eisenstein. **CAST:** V. Nikandrov, N. Popov. **1928**

ODD OBSESSION ★★ An aging man hopes to revive his waning potency. In Japanese with often incomplete or confusing English subtitles. Unrated, it contains off-camera sex. 107m. **DIR:** Kon Ichikawa. **CAST:** Machiko Kyo, Tatsuya Nakadai. **1960**

OEDIPUS REX (1967) ★★ Disappointing adaptation of Sophocles' tragedy, offered in both contemporary and historical settings. Visually satisfying, but too excessive and unengaging. In Italian with English subtitles. Not rated, but contains nudity and violence. 110m. **DIR:** Pier Paolo Pasolini. **CAST:** Franco Citti, Silvana Mangano, Alida Valli, Julian Beck. **1967**

OFFICIAL STORY, THE ★★★★★ This winner of the Oscar for best foreign-language film unforgettably details the destruction of a middle-class Argentinian family. The beginning of the end comes when the wife (brilliantly played by Norma Aleandro) suspects that her adopted baby daughter may be the orphan of parents murdered during the "dirty war" of the 1970s. In Spanish with English subtitles. Unrated, the film has violence. 110m. **DIR:** Luis Puenzo. **CAST:** Norma Aleandro, Hector Alterio, Analia Castro. **1985**

OLD TESTAMENT, THE 🦃 In this boring Italian epic, the Jews of Jerusalem are ruled by cruel Syrians. They flee, gather strength in the desert, and reclaim their city. Unrated. 88m. **DIR:** Gianfranco Parolini. **CAST:** Susan Paget, Brad Harris, Bridgette Corey. **1963**

OLDEST PROFESSION, THE ★★½ Jean-Luc Godard's contribution, the final of six segments in this omnibus comedy about prostitution through the ages, is worth seeing. But the rest resembles a Gallic version of *Love, American Style*. In French with English subtitles. Unrated. 97m. **DIR:** Franco Indovina, Mauro Bolognini, Philippe de Broca, Michel Pfleghar, Claude Autant-Lara, Jean-Luc Godard. **CAST:** Elsa Martinelli, Gastone Moschin, Raquel Welch, Anna Karina, Jean-Pierre Léaud. **1967**

OLIVIER, OLIVIER ★★★★ An unusual French mystery of loss and identity, exploring themes similar to those in *The Return of Martin Guerre* and *Sommersby*, from Agnieszka Holland, the creator of *Europa Europa*. Once again, a person returns to a family after an absence of several years, and questions arise about his identity. Is he who we desperately want to believe he is? The story is contemporary and the missing person is a child. And Holland's writing and direction incorporate elements of fable and parapsychology. Rated R, with profanity, violence, and sexual material, including incest. 110m. **DIR:** Agnieszka Holland. **CAST:** Gregoire Colin, Marina Golovine. **1992**

ON TOP OF THE WHALE ★★½ Confusing, nonlinear metaphysical drama about an anthropologist who attempts to unravel the mystery concerning two Indians who speak a strange language made up of only a few phrases. Shot in five languages that only add to the film's confusion. In Dutch with English subtitles. Not rated, but contains profanity and violence. 93m. **DIR:** Raul Ruiz. **CAST:** Willeke Van Ammelrooy. **1982**

ONE ARABIAN NIGHT ★★ Heavy-handed screen version of the stage pantomine, *Sumurun*, by Max Reinhardt. The title character is the mistress of a sheikh who prefers romance with his son. Silent. B&W; 85m. **DIR:** Ernst Lubitsch. **CAST:** Pola Negri. **1920**

ONE DEADLY SUMMER ★★★ Isabelle Adjani stars as a promiscuous young woman who returns to a small village to seek revenge on three men who beat and raped her mother many years before. Exceptionally well acted, especially by Alain Souchon as her sympathetic boyfriend, and veteran European actress Suzanne Flon as his slightly crazy aunt. In French with English subtitles. Rated R for nudity and violence. 133m. **DIR:** Jean Becker. **CAST:** Isabelle Adjani, Alain Souchon, François Cluzet, Suzanne Flon, Manuel Gelin. **1983**

ONE SINGS, THE OTHER DOESN'T ★★½ Labeled early on as a feminist film, this story is about a friendship between two different types of women spanning 1962 to 1976. When they meet again at a women's rally after ten years, they renew their friendship. 105m. **DIR:** Agnes Varda. **CAST:** Valerie Mairesse, Thérèse Liotard. **1977**

ONE WILD MOMENT ★★★★ In French director Claude Berri's warm and very sensitive film, a middle-aged man (Jean-Pierre Marielle) is told by his best friend's daughter that she's in love with him. Enjoy the story (which was adapted by director Stanley Donen for *Blame it on Rio*) as it should be told, as delicately and thoughtfully handled by Berri. In French with English subtitles. Unrated, the film has nudity, and profanity. 90m. **DIR:** Claude Berri. **CAST:** Jean-Pierre Marielle, Victor Lanoux. **1980**

ONE WOMAN OR TWO ★★★½ Gérard Depardieu plays an anthropologist digging for "the missing link." Dr. Ruth debuts as a philanthropist whose money will continue the search. And Sigourney Weaver is the advertising executive who almost ruins the entire project. Wonderful acting and superb dialogue are the highlights of this French turn on *Bringing Up Baby*. In French with English subtitles. 95m. **DIR:** Daniel Vigne. **CAST:** Sigourney Weaver, Gérard Depardieu, Dr. Ruth Westheimer. **1987**

ONIBABA ★★★★½ Director Kaneto Shindo's brilliantly photographed, savage tale of lust and survival in war-ravaged medieval Japan. A mother and daughter are drawn into deep conflict over a cunning warrior, who seduces the younger one, causing the mother to seek violent revenge. In Japanese with English subtitles. Not rated, but contains nudity and is recommended for adults. B&W; 103m. **DIR:** Kaneto Shindo. **CAST:** Nobuko Otowa. **1964**

ONLY ONE NIGHT ★★★½ Ingrid Bergman plays a woman courted by a circus performer who feels he is really beneath her station. She thinks so, too, and makes sure he doesn't forget it. One of her last Swedish films, and one of the films her new Hollywood bosses didn't dare remake because of the suggestive material. B&W; 89m. **DIR:** Gustav Molander. **CAST:** Ingrid Bergman, Edvin Adolphson. **1939**

OPEN CITY ★★★★½ Stunning study of resistance and survival in World War II Italy was the first important film to come out of postwar Europe and has been considered a classic in realism. Co-scripted by a young Federico Fellini, this powerful story traces the threads of people's lives as they interact and eventually entangle themselves in the shadow of their Gestapo-controlled "open city." In Italian with English subtitles. B&W; 105m. **DIR:** Roberto Rossellini. **CAST:** Aldo Fabrizi, Anna Magnani. **1946**

OPEN DOORS ★★★★ A sturdy and slow-moving but engrossing Italian drama about a stubbornly determined judge attempting to establish justice in a courtroom dominated by Fascist dictates. It earned an Oscar nomination as best foreign-language film. In Italian with English subtitles. 109m. **DIR:** Gianni Amelio. **CAST:** Gian Maria Volonté. **1991**

OPERA DO MALANDRO ★★★ A homage to the Hollywood musicals of the Forties, this vibrant, stylish film is set in Rio's seedy back streets on the eve of the Pearl Harbor invasion. The story is about a gangster whose search for the American dream is disrupted by his love for a beautiful Brazilian girl. In Portuguese with English subtitles. 108m. **DIR:** Ruy Guerra. **CAST:** Edson Celulari, Claudia Ohana. **1987**

ORDET ★★★★½ Possibly the greatest work of Carl Dreyer, the Danish director whose films (*The Passion of Joan of Arc, Day of Wrath*) demonstrate an intellectual obsession with the nature of religious faith in the modern world. In this drama, based on a play written by a priest who was murdered by the Nazis, characters in a small, God-fearing town wrestle between two varieties of faith, one puritanical, the other life affirming. In Danish with English subtitles. B&W; 125m. **DIR:** Carl Dreyer. **CAST:** Henrik Malberg. **1955**

ORIANE ★★★ A taut gothic romance about a young woman who returns to a hacienda inherited from her aunt only to find herself caught up in a mystery concerning past events. Fina Torres scores some high marks in her first feature film that won the coveted Camera d'Or at Cannes in 1985. In Spanish and French with English subtitles. Not rated, but contains nudity. 88m. **DIR:** Fina Torres. **CAST:** Doris Wells. **1985**

ORPHEUS ★★★½ Jean Cocteau's surreal account of the Greek myth with Jean Marais as Orpheus, the successful, envied, and despised poet who thrusts himself beyond mortality. Maria Casares costars as the lonely, troubled, passionate Death. Cocteau's poetic imagery will pull you deep into the fantasy. In French with English subtitles. B&W; 86m. **DIR:** Jean Cocteau. **CAST:** Jean Marais, Maria Casares. **1949**

OSAKA ELEGY ★★★★ Excellent dramatic comedy that realistically shows the exploitation of women in Japanese society. Isuzu Yamada plays a tough, sassy working girl who is continuously taken advantage of by men notorious for their greed and spinelessness. In Japanese with English subtitles. B&W; 75m. **DIR:** Kenji Mizoguchi. **CAST:** Isuzu Yamada. **1936**

OSSESSIONE ★★★★★ James M. Cain's *The Postman Always Rings Twice* as adapted to Italian locations. The fatal triangle here is a dissatisfied wife, a vulgar husband, and the inevitable charming stranger. A landmark in the development of both *film noir* and Italian neorealism. In Italian with English subtitles. B&W; 135m. **DIR:** Luchino Visconti. **CAST:** Clara Calamai, Massimo Girotti. **1942**

OTAKU NO VIDEO ★★★ Incredibly dense with inside jokes and industry references, this tongue-in-cheek animated entry may be too esoteric for the casual viewer but any rabid animation fan (or *otaku*) will find it hysterically funny. The Japanese subculture of animation enthusiasts (somewhat comparable to *Star Trek* fans in this country) is examined through an animated story interspersed with live, mock interviews of fans and statistical charts. In Japanese with English subtitles. Not rated; contains nudity. 100m. **DIR:** Mori Takeshi. **1991**

OVERCOAT, THE ★★★ Based on a story by Gogol, this Russian film tells the story of an office clerk who is content with his modest life and ambitions until he buys a new overcoat and enters on an upward track. Entertaining satire. In Russian with English subtitles. B&W; 78m. **DIR:** Alexi Batalov. **CAST:** Rolan Bykov. **1960**

OVERSEAS ★★★½ Three French sisters share their joys and tragedies over an eighteen-year period (1946–1964) in Algeria. The native uprising forces each to say good-bye to her innocence. Lively musical score and touching moments are marred by confusing time jumps. Unrated, but contains nudity, violence, and profanity. In French with English subtitles. 96m. **DIR:** Brigitte Rouan. **CAST:** Nicole Garcia, Marianne Basler, Brigitte Rouan, Philippe Galland. **1992**

PADRE PADRONE ★★★½ Although slow-moving, this low-budget film is a riveting account of a young Sardinian's traumatizing relationship with his overbearing father in a patriarchal society. The son bears the brutality, but eventually breaks the emotional bonds. This quietly powerful film depends on the actors for its punch. In Sardinian (Italian dialect) with English subtitles. 114m. **DIR:** Vittorio Taviani, Paolo Taviani. **CAST:** Omero Antonutti, Saverio Marioni. **1977**

PAIN IN THE A—, A ★★ A professional hit man (Lino Ventura) arrives in Montpellier, Italy, to kill a government witness who is set to testify against the mob. This unfunny slapstick comedy was adapted by director Billy Wilder for the equally disappointing *Buddy, Buddy* with Jack Lemmon and Walter Matthau. In French with English subtitles. Rated PG for light violence. 90m. **DIR:** Edouard Molinaro. **CAST:** Lino Ventura, Jacques Brel. **1973**

PAINTED FACES ★★★★ Many of Hong Kong's top stars trained at the Peking Opera School. This docudrama tribute to the now-closed school, set in the 1960s, shows the rigorous training and strict discipline students received there, as well as the amazing results. In Cantonese with English subtitles. Not rated. 100m. **DIR:** Alex Law. **CAST:** Samo Hung, Kam-bo, Chang Pei-pei. 1987

PAISAN ★★★½ Six separate stories of survival are hauntingly presented by writer Federico Fellini and director Roberto Rossellini in this early postwar Italian film. Shot on the streets and often improvised, this strong drama exposes the raw nerves brought on by living in a battleground. B&W; 90m. **DIR:** Roberto Rossellini. **CAST:** Carmela Sazio, Robert Van Loon, Gar Moore. 1946

PALOMBELLA ROSSA ★★★½ A Fellini-inspired water-polo game becomes the waiting room for a politician's life after he has an auto accident. Michele (Nanni Moretti) finds himself searching for life's answers, while desperately trying to stay afloat during the game of his life. Truly inspired moments set against a surreal backdrop make this comedy a winner. In Italian with English subtitles. Not rated. 87m. **DIR:** Nanni Moretti. **CAST:** Nanni Moretti, Alfonso Santagata, Claudio Morganti, Asia Argento. 1989

PANDORA'S BOX ★★★★½ Here is a gem from the heyday of German silent screen Expressionism. The film follows a winning yet amoral temptress, Lulu (a sparkling performance by Louise Brooks). Without concerns or inhibitions, Lulu blissfully ensnares a variety of weak men, only to contribute to their eventual downfall. B&W; 131m. **DIR:** G. W. Pabst. **CAST:** Louise Brooks, Fritz Kortner. 1929

PANIQUE ★★★½ Based on a thriller by Georges Simenon, this gripping story features Michel Simon as a stranger who is framed for murder. A taut film comparable to the best of the chase *noir* genre so prevalent in French and American cinema of the mid-1940s. In French with English subtitles. B&W; 87m. **DIR:** Julien Duvivier. **CAST:** Michel Simon, Viviane Romance. 1946

PANTALOONS ★★★ In this period comedy, horse-faced Fernandel gets a chance to fill in for his master, Don Juan. Unfortunately, the circumstances are so hectic that he can't take advantage of any of the women who so want to be conquered by the great lover, even if he looks somewhat less dashing than they'd imagined. Dubbed. 93m. **DIR:** John Berry. **CAST:** Fernandel, Carmen Sevilla, Fernando Rey. 1957

PAPER MARRIAGE (1988) ★★½ Martial arts star Samo Hung plays an out-of-work Chinese boxer in Canada who reluctantly accepts a promise to marry a Hong Kong girl. Though highly uneven, the film has some funny moments. In Cantonese with English subtitles. Not rated, but contains violence. 102m. **DIR:** Samo Hung. **CAST:** Samo Hung, Maggie Cheung. 1988

PARADE ★★½ Sadly, the great comedian Jacques Tati's last film is his least distinguished work. He plays host to a group of circus performers in this semidocumentary that is little more than a footnote in his filmography. In French with English subtitles. 85m. **DIR:** Jacques Tati. **CAST:** Jacques Tati. 1974

PARDON MON AFFAIRE ★★★★ Enjoyable romantic comedy about a middle-class, happily married man (Jean Rochefort) who pursues his fantasy of meeting a beautiful model (Anny Duperey) and having an affair. Later remade in America as *The Woman in Red*. In French with English subtitles. Rated PG. 105m. **DIR:** Yves Robert. **CAST:** Jean Rochefort, Claude Brasseur, Anny Duperey, Guy Bedos, Victor Lanoux. 1976

PARDON MON AFFAIRE, TOO! ★★ Lukewarm comedy of infidelity and friendship. The focus is on four middle-aged men who share their troubles and feelings about their marriages and sex lives. No real laughs. In French with English subtitles. 110m. **DIR:** Yves Robert. **CAST:** Jean Rochefort, Claude Brasseur, Guy Bedos, Victor Lanoux, Daniele Delorme. 1977

PARDON MY TRUNK ★★½ An Italian schoolteacher (Vittorio De Sica), struggling against poverty does a good deed for a visiting Hindu prince. In gratitude, the Indian sends him a gift: a baby elephant. De Sica's performance elevates what otherwise would have been merely a silly slapstick exercise. Also known as *Hello Elephant!* Dubbed in English. B&W; 85m. **DIR:** Gianni Franciolini. **CAST:** Vittorio De Sica, Maria Mereader, Sabu, Nando Bruno. 1952

PARIS BELONGS TO US ★★ The first film directed by Jacques Rivette and the first feature-length release in the French new wave. Quite a *cause célèbre* in 1957, it is now something of a museum piece, a testament to the initial, tentative, highly self-conscious experimentations of the generation. The plot, which is quite incomprehensible, seems essentially to be the story of a young actress who becomes involved in a murderous intrigue hatched by an American novelist. In French with English subtitles. B&W; 135m. **DIR:** Jacques Rivette. **CAST:** Betty Schneider, Daniel Crohem, Jean-Claude Brialy. 1957

PARTNER ★★★ Bernardo Bertolucci apes Godard with less than optimal results in this story of a shy youth who creates an alternative self that possesses the qualities he lacks. Occasionally incoherent. In Italian and French with English subtitles. Unrated. 112m. **DIR:** Bernardo Bertolucci. **CAST:** Pierre Clementi, Tina Aumont, Stefania Sandrelli. 1968

PASSION (1919) ★★★ Combining realism with spectacle, this account of famous eighteenth-century French courtesan Madame Du Barry was the first German film to earn international acclaim after World War I. As a result, the director and the stars received Hollywood contracts. The film is still recognized as the best of seven made about the subject between 1915 and 1954. Silent. B&W; 134m. **DIR:** Ernst Lubitsch. **CAST:** Pola Negri, Emil Jannings. **1919**

PASSION FOR LIFE ★★★ An enthusiastic young teacher in a provincial school fights resistance from parents and his fellow teachers to introduce more effective new methods. Unsurprising but effective drama. In French with English subtitles. B&W; 89m. **DIR:** Jean-Paul Le Chanois. **CAST:** Bernard Blier, Juliette Faber. **1949**

PASSION OF ANNA, THE ★★★★½ One of Ingmar Bergman's greatest works is also one of his bleakest, an unflinching look into man's capacity for self-destruction. Four people are thrown together on an isolated island. Their interactions reveal their needs and insecurities, as well as the defenses they have developed. Bergman distances viewers from the film just as the characters try to distance themselves from others. In Swedish with English subtitles. Not rated. 101m. **DIR:** Ingmar Bergman. **CAST:** Liv Ullmann, Bibi Andersson, Max von Sydow, Erland Josephson. **1969**

PASSION OF JOAN OF ARC, THE ★★★★★ This is simply one of the greatest films ever made. Its emotional intensity is unsurpassed. Faces tell the tale of this movie. Maria Falconetti's Joan is unforgettable. Silent. B&W; 114m. **DIR:** Carl Dreyer. **CAST:** Maria Falconetti, Eugene Silvain, Antonin Artaud. **1928**

PASSION OF LOVE ★★★★ In 1862 Italy just after the war, a decorated captain (Bernard Giraudeau) is transferred to a faraway outpost, where he becomes the love object of his commander's cousin (Valeria D'Obici). What follows is a fascinating study of torment. Dubbed in English and unrated. 117m. **DIR:** Ettore Scola. **CAST:** Valeria D'Obici, Bernard Giraudeau, Laura Antonelli, Bernard Blier, Jean-Louis Trintignant, Massimo Girotti. **1982**

PASSIONATE THIEF, THE (1961) ★★ This less-than-hilarious Italian comedy is poorly dubbed. Ben Gazzara plays a thief at a New Year's Eve party. His suave attempts at removing the jewels are thwarted when Anna Magnani shows up and decides that he's interested in her. Monotonous. B&W; 100m. **DIR:** Mario Monicelli. **CAST:** Ben Gazzara, Anna Magnani, Toto, Fred Clark, Edy Vessel. **1961**

PATHER PANCHALI ★★★★ The first part of Satyajit Ray's *Apu* trilogy shows Apu's boyhood in an impoverished Bengal village after his father is forced to leave the family in order to seek work. Ray, who had no experience in filmmaking when he began, commands your attention with a lack of cinematic trickery, telling a universal story with a pure and unaffected style. The trilogy also includes *Aparajito* and *The World of Apu*. In Bengali with English subtitles. 112m. **DIR:** Satyajit Ray. **CAST:** Subir Banerji, Karuna Banerji. **1954**

PATHFINDER ★★★½ Brutal film about peaceful tribesmen being ruthlessly slaughtered by a savage group of scavengers. Action takes place in icy Norway with a treacherous chase through snow-covered mountains. Unrated, contains violence and nudity. In Lapp with English subtitles. 88m. **DIR:** Nils Gaup. **CAST:** Mikkel Gaup. **1987**

PATTES BLANCHES (WHITE PAWS) ★★★★ Engrossing melodrama about a reclusive aristocrat ridiculed in a small fishing community over a pair of white shoes he is fond of wearing. A well-crafted film by Jean Gremillon. In French with English subtitles. 92m. **DIR:** Jean Gremillon. **CAST:** Paul Bernard, Suzy Delair. **1987**

PAULINE AT THE BEACH ★★★★ The screen works of French writer-director Eric Rohmer are decidedly unconventional. In this, one of his "Comedies and Proverbs," the 14-year-old title character (Amanda Langlet) shows herself to have a better sense of self and reality than the adults around her. In French with English subtitles. Rated R for nudity. 94m. **DIR:** Eric Rohmer. **CAST:** Amanda Langlet, Arielle Dombasle, Pascal Greggory, Feodor Atkine. **1983**

PEARLS OF THE CROWN, THE ★★★½ This featherweight historical extravaganza was presented as a celebration of the coronation of England's George VI, but it was clearly an excuse for writer-codirector Sacha Guitry to concoct choice scenes for some of the best theatrical actors in France. Some of the bits are delightful, but some drag on. In English, and in French and Italian with English subtitles. B&W; 120m. **DIR:** Sacha Guitry, Christian-Jacque. **CAST:** Sacha Guitry, Renée Saint-Cyr, Arletty, Raimu. **1937**

PEKING OPERA BLUES ★★★★½ The circuslike Peking Opera provides an appropriately colorful backdrop for this period adventure that brings three dissimilar young women together to battle an evil general. High-spirited fun. In Cantonese with English subtitles. Not rated; contains violence. 98m. **DIR:** Tsui Hark. **CAST:** Lin Ching Hsia, Sally Yeh, Cherie Chung. **1986**

PELLE THE CONQUEROR ★★★★★ Bille August's superb drama casts Max von Sydow as a Swedish widower who takes his young son to Denmark in the hope of finding a better life. Once there, they must endure even harder times. In Danish and Swedish with English subtitles. Unrated, the film has nudity, violence, and profanity. 138m. **DIR:** Bille August. **CAST:** Max von Sydow, Pelle Hvenegaard. **1988**

PEOPLE'S HERO ★★★ Taken as a hostage during someone else's botched bank holdup, a cunning gangster turns the situation to his advantage. Hong Kong thriller downplays the usual firepower for plot, though the ending is explosive. In Cantonese with English subtitles. Not rated; contains strong violence. 82m. **DIR:** Yee Tung-shing. **CAST:** Ti Lung, Tony Leung, Ronald Wong. 1987

PEPE LE MOKO ★★★½ Algiers criminal Pepe Le Moko (Jean Gabin) is safe just as long as he remains in the city's picturesque, squalid native quarter. His passionate infatuation with a beautiful visitor from his beloved Paris, however, spells his doom. In French with English subtitles. B&W; 93m. **DIR:** Julien Duvivier. **CAST:** Jean Gabin, Mireille Balin, Gabriel Gario, Marcel Dalio. 1937

PEPI, LUCI, BOM AND OTHER GIRLS ★★★ The plot, a satirical pastiche of melodramatic clichés, is less important than the nonstop swipes at bourgeois society in Pedro Almodóvar's first film. Crudely made on an amateur budget, this will be of interest mainly to fans of his later films. In Spanish with English subtitles. Not rated; contains sexual situations. 80m. **DIR:** Pedro Almodóvar. **CAST:** Carmen Maura, Felix Rotaeta. 1980

PERFUMED NIGHTMARE ★★★★ Hilarious, poignant view of the impact of American cultural colonialism through the eyes of a young Philippine man. Brilliant meditation on the American dream shot on super 8mm for less than $10,000. Winner of the International Critics Award at the Berlin Film Festival. In Tagalog with English dialogue and subtitles. 91m. **DIR:** Kidlat Tahimik. 1983

PERIL ★★ Nicole Garcia plays the wife of a wealthy businessman who is having an affair with their daughter's guitar instructor (Christophe Malavoy). Filmmaker Michel Deville aims too high in his direction with French new wave–like scene cuts. In French with English subtitles. Rated R for nudity, violence, profanity, and adult subject matter. 100m. **DIR:** Michel Deville. **CAST:** Christophe Malavoy, Nicole Garcia, Richard Bohringer, Anemone, Michel Piccoli. 1985

PERSONA ★★★ Liv Ullmann gives a haunting performance as an actress who suddenly becomes mute and is put in the charge of a nurse (Bibi Andersson). The two women become so close that they change personalities. Ingmar Bergman's use of subtle split-screen effects dramatizes the metaphorical quality of this quiet film. In Swedish with English subtitles. B&W; 81m. **DIR:** Ingmar Bergman. **CAST:** Liv Ullmann, Bibi Andersson, Gunnar Björnstrand. 1966

PETIT CON ★★ France's equivalent of our American teenage-boy-in-heat flicks, with a few differences. The film tries for a serious side involving the trauma that Michel (Bernard Brieux) is causing his family. In French with English subtitles. Rated R. 90m. **DIR:** Gerard Lauzier. **CAST:** Guy Marchand, Caroline Cellier, Bernard Brieux, Souad Amidou. 1986

PHANTOM CHARIOT ★★ The legend of the Coachman of Death being replaced each year by the last man to die on December 31 is used here to drive home a sermon on the evils of drink. In its day the use of multiple-layered flashbacks and double-exposure techniques made this Swedish silent a great success; today, alas, it only seems tedious and unendurably slow-paced. Silent. B&W; 83m. **DIR:** Victor Sjöström. **CAST:** Victor Sjöström. 1920

PHANTOM OF LIBERTY, THE ★★ A kaleidoscope of satirical vignettes composed of outrageous riddles, jokes, and associations all mocking mankind's inexplicable willingness to enslave itself in order to be "free." A big disappointment from Luis Buñuel whose use of tricks from his other films make this one seem clichéd. In French with English subtitles. 104m. **DIR:** Luis Buñuel. **CAST:** Jean-Claude Brialy, Adolfo Celi, Michel Piccoli, Monica Vitti. 1974

PHEDRE ★★½ The performance of Marie Bell, the great French tragedienne, is the only reason to dig out this abbreviated adaptation of the Greek myth about the queen who fell in love with her stepson and caused her husband's death. The production is stagy. Poorly served by the subtitles. In French with English subtitles. 93m. **DIR:** Pierre Jourdan. **CAST:** Marie Bell, Jacques Dacqumine, Claude Giraud. 1968

PICNIC ON THE GRASS ★★★ Director Jean Renoir's tribute to French Impressionism takes place in the beautiful countryside as a scientific outing turns into a drunken reverie. In French with English subtitles. 92m. **DIR:** Jean Renoir. **CAST:** Paul Meurisse, Catherine Rouvel, Jacqueline Morane. 1959

PIERROT LE FOU ★★★½ Complex drama about a man who leaves his rich wife and runs off with a beautiful young woman who is fleeing some gangsters. Shot on location throughout the south of France, this existential character drama will fascinate some viewers while boring others. In French with English subtitles. 110m. **DIR:** Jean-Luc Godard. **CAST:** Jean-Paul Belmondo, Anna Karina, Samuel Fuller, Jean-Pierre Léaud. 1965

PIGSTY ★★★ This dark fable of bourgeois repression links the stories of two extremely unconventional people—a medieval soldier forced into cannibalism and a modern young man whose alienation from society leads him to bestiality. Skillfully made, though obscure. In Italian with English subtitles. Not rated; contains strong material and is not for children. 90m. **DIR:** Pier Paolo

Pasolini. **CAST:** Pierre Clementi, Franco Citti, Jean-Pierre Léaud, Ugo Tognazzi. **1969**

PIXOTE ★★★★ In Rio, half the population is younger than 18. Kids, only 10 or 12 years old, become thieves, beggars, and prostitutes. *Pixote* is the story of one of these unfortunates. For some viewers it may be too powerful and disturbing, yet it is not the least bit exploitative or exaggerated. Rated R for violence, explicit sex, and nudity. 127m. **DIR:** Hector Babenco. **CAST:** Fernando Ramos Da Silva, Marilia Pera. **1981**

PLAYTIME ★★★½ Mr. Hulot is back again in this slapstick comedy as he attempts to keep an appointment in the big city. Paris and all of its buildings, automobiles, and population seem to conspire to thwart Mr. Hulot at every turn, and there are plenty of visual gags. The subtitled American release version is over thirty minutes shorter than the original French release. 108m. **DIR:** Jacques Tati. **CAST:** Jacques Tati. **1967**

POISONOUS PLANTS ★★ A disillusioned journalist gets caught up in the lives of a teenage prostitute, a man falsely imprisoned for murder, and a botanist who raises poisonous plants. Unengaging drama set in contemporary Poland. In Polish with English subtitles. Not rated. 70m. **DIR:** Robert Glinsky. **CAST:** Boguslaw Linda. **1975**

POLICE ★★½ Dull crime-drama about a tough French cop (Gérard Depardieu), who becomes emotionally involved with a beautiful drug dealer (Sophie Marceau). Not much chemistry between the central characters. In French with English subtitles. Not rated, but contains nudity and profanity. 113m. **DIR:** Maurice Pialat. **CAST:** Gérard Depardieu, Sophie Marceau, Richard Anconina, Sandrine Bonnaire. **1985**

POLICE STORY III—SUPER COP ★★★★ With fantastic stunts, snappy touches of comedy, international locales, and a likable lead actor, this Hong Kong import comes extremely close to matching action films such as *Lethal Weapon*. Jackie Chan is a Hong Kong cop who goes undercover in Communist China in an effort to flush out a nasty drug lord. Chan—who does all his own stunts—really makes this a winner. In Cantonese with English subtitles. Unrated, the film contains violence and brief profanity. 100m. **DIR:** Stanley Tong. **CAST:** Jackie Chan, Michelle Yeoh, Maggie Cheung, Ken Tsang, Yuen Wah, Bill Tung, Josephine Koo. **1992**

POOL HUSTLERS, THE ★★★ Comedy-drama about an amateur pool player out to take the title away from the national champion. In Italian with English subtitles. Unrated, the film has sexual situations. 101m. **DIR:** Maurizio Ponzi. **CAST:** Francesco Nuti. **1983**

PORNOGRAPHERS, THE ★★★★ A small-time porno filmmaker struggles to cope with the corrupt sexual ways of his family, the world outside, and himself. A brilliant black comedy that explores contemporary Japanese society with a kinky, perverse, irrational vision. In Japanese with English subtitles. B&W; 128m. **DIR:** Shohei Imamura. **CAST:** Shoichi Ozawa. **1966**

PORT OF CALL ★★★ When a seaman begins working on the docks, he falls in love with a suicidal young woman. The woman has had an unhappy childhood and a wild past, which has given her a bad reputation. This drama seems dated today. In Swedish with English subtitles. B&W; 100m. **DIR:** Ingmar Bergman. **CAST:** Nine-Christine Jonsson, Bengt Eklund. **1948**

PORTRAIT OF TERESA ★★★½ Controversial emotionally charged drama about a disenchanted housewife who becomes involved with political and cultural groups in a postrevolutionary Cuban society. In Spanish with English subtitles. Not rated, but contains profanity and violence. 115m. **DIR:** Pastor Vega. **CAST:** Daisy Granados. **1979**

PRINCESS TAM TAM ★★★½ The best of several movies featuring legendary ecdysiast Josephine Baker. She plays an African girl brought to Paris by a writer who passes her off as an Indian princess. In French with English subtitles. B&W; 77m. **DIR:** Edmond Gréville. **CAST:** Josephine Baker, Albert Préjean. **1935**

PRINCESS YANG KWEI FEI ★★★½ Color is used with great effect in this big-budget epic of eighth-century China. When the current empress dies, the emperor falls in love with and marries a servant girl. But her life is ruined by jealous members of the royal court. In Japanese with English subtitles. 91m. **DIR:** Kenji Mizoguchi. **CAST:** Masayuki Mori, Machiko Kyo. **1955**

PRISON ON FIRE ★★★★ Sent to prison for killing a man in self-defense, a white-collar worker learns how to survive with the aid of a more hardened prisoner (Asian superstar Chow Yun-Fat). Ringo Lam, one of Hong Kong's top directors, keeps everything moving in this entertaining thriller. In Cantonese with English subtitles. Not rated; contains strong violence. 98m. **DIR:** Ringo Lam. **CAST:** Chow Yun-Fat, Leung Ka Fai. **1987**

PRIX DE BEAUTE (BEAUTY PRIZE) ★★★★★ Directly after making *Pandora's Box* and *Diary of a Lost Girl*, Louise Brooks made one other memorable movie, this early French sound film. She plays an ambitious young beauty contestant who aspires to a movie career. Her actions, however, infuriate her jealous husband. In French with English subtitles. B&W; 97m. **DIR:** Augusto Genina. **CAST:** Louise Brooks. **1930**

PROJECT A (PART I) ★★★ Vintage Jackie Chan period comedy full of Buster

Keaton-style slapstick and martial arts action. Chan plays a Marine cadet in turn-of-the-century Hong Kong, who battles smugglers and pirates operating on the South China Sea. Remarkable stunts, brilliantly choreographed. In Cantonese with English subtitles. Not rated. 95m. **DIR:** Jackie Chan. **CAST:** Jackie Chan, Samo Hung. **1983**

PROJECT A (PART II) ★★★½ Jackie Chan returns as Dragon Ma, the only uncorrupt cop in turn-of-century Hong Kong, where he finds himself at odds with the Chinese syndicate. As usual, the brilliantly staged martial arts battles are laced with comedy. In Cantonese with English subtitles. Not rated. 101m. **DIR:** Jackie Chan. **CAST:** Jackie Chan, Maggie Cheung. **1987**

PROJECT A-KO ★★★ Another of the more lighthearted entries in the Japanese animation wave, the story here revolves around a simple rivalry for the friendship of a dopey kid named C-Ko as disputed by the two heroines, A-Ko and B-Ko, who both happen to possess superhuman powers. In Japanese with English subtitles. Unrated with violence and illustrated nudity. 86m. **DIR:** Katsuhiko Nishijima. **1986**

QUATORZE JULIET ★★★★ Paris had no better publicist than René Clair, whose early films were delightfully simple musical fantasies of living in that city. *Quatorze Juliet* follows two young lovers—a taxi driver and a flower peddler—as they come into contact with different citizens and neighborhoods of Paris. In French with English subtitles. B&W; 85m. **DIR:** René Clair. **CAST:** Annabella, George Rigaud. **1932**

QUERELLE ★★½ In this depressing rendering of Jean Genet's story, Brad Davis stars in the title role as a young sailor whose good looks set off a chain reaction. This is a disturbing and depressing portrait of terminally unhappy people. In German with English subtitles. Rated R for nudity and obscenity. 120m. **DIR:** Rainer Werner Fassbinder. **CAST:** Rainer Werner Fassbinder, Brad Davis, Franco Nero, Jeanne Moreau. **1982**

QUESTION OF SILENCE, A ★★★★½ After an unusual murder is committed, three women, all strangers to one another, stand trial for the same crime. A woman psychiatrist is appointed to the case after the three openly display their hostilities toward male-dominated society. Rated R for profanity. Available in original Dutch or dubbed. 92m. **DIR:** Marleen Gorris. **CAST:** Cox Habbema, Nelly Frijda. **1983**

QUI ETES-VOUS, MR. SORGE? (SOVIET SPY) 🦃 This is a docudrama about the case of Richard Sorge, a German WWII journalist who, records show, was hanged as a Soviet spy in 1944. In French with English subtitles. 130m. **DIR:** André Girard. **CAST:** Thomas Holtzman, Keiko Kishi. **1961**

RAISE THE RED LANTERN ★★★★½ Chinese director Zhang Yimou's magnificent film chronicles the life of a 1920s maiden who, at her mother's urgings, agrees to marry a wealthy man. She becomes "Fourth Mistress" in a house where being the master's favorite means all. Based on a novel by Su Tong. In Mandarin with English subtitles. Unrated; the film has suggested sex and violence. 125m. **DIR:** Zhang Yimou. **CAST:** Gong Li. **1991**

RAMPARTS OF CLAY ★★★★ Terse but hauntingly beautiful documentary-style film set against the harsh background of a poor North African village. A young woman (Leila Schenna) struggles to free herself from the second-class role imposed on her by the village culture, much as the village tries to liberate itself from subservience to the corporate powers that control its salt mines. In Arabic with English subtitles. Rated PG. 87m. **DIR:** Jean-Louis Bertucelli. **CAST:** Leila Schenna and the villagers of Tehouda, Algeria. **1970**

RAN ★★★★★ This superb Japanese historical epic tells the story of a sixteenth-century warlord's time of tragedy. Based on Shakespeare's *King Lear,* this is yet another masterwork from Akira Kurosawa. It is stunningly photographed and acted, and blessed with touches of glorious humor and hair-raising battle sequences. In Japanese with English subtitles. Rated R for violence and suggested sex. 160m. **DIR:** Akira Kurosawa. **CAST:** Tatsuya Nakadai, Akira Terao. **1985**

RANMA 1/2 (TV SERIES) ★★★½ Despite a dubbed English soundtrack, the *Ranma 1/2* episodes are still quite entertaining. Ranma and his father, Genma, both avid martial-arts students, have fallen afoul of ancient curses that periodically change one into a young girl and the other into a giant panda. Another quirky series from Rumiko Takahashi (*Rumik World, Urusei Yatsura*). Dubbed in English. Not rated; contains some brief nudity. Each 50m. **DIR:** Tsutomu Shibayama. **1985–1987**

RAPE OF LOVE (L'AMOUR VIOLÉ) ★★★★ A graphic rape scene may scare some viewers away from this French export, but that would be unfortunate. *Rape of Love* is a telling account of one woman's quest to come to terms with her tragic experience. In French with English subtitles. Not rated, but has graphic violence, nudity, and profanity. 111m. **DIR:** Yannick Bellon. **CAST:** Nathalie Nell, Alain Foures. **1979**

RASCALS, THE ★★★ Two kids (Bernard Brieux and Thomas Chabrol) go through school together trying to beat the system. Taking place in the German-occupied France of 1942, *The Rascals* deals with the coming-of-age themes we have seen many times. But the film's nationalistic subtext, which results in a triumphant ending, is, perhaps, a new one. In French with English subtitles. Rated R for sex and nudity. 93m. **DIR:** Bernard Revon. **CAST:** Bernard Brieux, Thomas Chabrol, Pascale Rocard. **1979**

RASHOMON ★★★★★ After a violent murder and rape is committed by a bandit, four people tell their own different versions of what happened. Set in medieval Japan, this examination of truth and guilt is charged with action. The combination of brilliant photography, stellar acting, direction, and script won this Japanese classic the Oscar for best foreign film. B&W; 83m. **DIR:** Akira Kurosawa. **CAST:** Toshiro Mifune, Machiko Kyo, Masayuki Mori. **1951**

RASPUTIN ★★★★ Controversial film that was suppressed by the Soviet Union for nearly a decade. Director Elem Klimov brilliantly captures the rise of the illiterate "prophet" who sparked the Russian Revolution. In Russian with English subtitles. Not rated but contains nudity and violence. 107m. **DIR:** Elem Klimov. **CAST:** Alexei Petrenko. **1985**

RAVEN TENGU KABUTO ★★★½ High-tech gadgetry meets samurai sword in this animated video entry as Japanese mythology is blended skillfully with dark science fiction. Kabuto, the wandering swordsman, matches his sword and mystic arts against an evil sorceress. In Japanese with English subtitles. Unrated, with violence and nudity. 45m. **DIR:** Buichi Terasawa. **1992**

RED AND THE WHITE, THE ★★★★ Hungarian director Miklos Jancso creates a bleak and startling film of the senseless slaughter and sheer absurdity of war. The film depicts the bloody encounters between Russia's Bolshevik Red Army and the counterrevolutionary forces in central Russia during the Civil War of 1918. In Russian with English subtitles. 92m. **DIR:** Miklos Jancso. **CAST:** Tibor Molnar, Andreas Kozak, Josef Madaras. **1968**

RED BEARD ★★★★½ In the early nineteenth century, a newly graduated doctor hopes to become a society doctor. Instead, he is posted at an impoverished clinic run by Dr. Niide (Toshiro Mifune), whose destitute patients affectionately call him "Red Beard." Akira Kurosawa, at one of his directorial pinnacles, describes his film as a "monument to the goodness in man." In Japanese with English subtitles. B&W; 185m. **DIR:** Akira Kurosawa. **CAST:** Toshiro Mifune. **1965**

RED DESERT ★★★★ An acutely depressed married woman (Monica Vitti) finds her life with an industrial-engineer husband to be demanding. Photographed in the industrial wasteland of northern Italy by Carlo Di Palma, this film remains one of the most beautiful of director Michelangelo Antonioni's works. Italian with English subtitles. 116m. **DIR:** Michelangelo Antonioni. **CAST:** Monica Vitti, Richard Harris. **1964**

RED KISS (ROUGE BAISER) ★★★½ In 1952 France, a teenage girl raised by leftist parents is caught between her upbringing and a romance with an apolitical news photographer. Autobiographical tale is reminiscent of the films of Diane Kurys, with an added political dimension. In French with English subtitles. Unrated; brief sexual situations. 110m. **DIR:** Vera Belmont. **CAST:** Charlotte Valandrey, Lambert Wilson, Marthe Keller, Gunter Lamprecht. **1985**

RED LION ★★★ Toshiro Mifune is well cast as a man who impersonates a military officer in order to return to his village in grand style. Once there, he must liberate his followers from an oppressive government. In Japanese with English subtitles. 115m. **DIR:** Kihachi Okamoto. **CAST:** Toshiro Mifune, Shima Iwashita. **1969**

RED SORGHUM ★★★★★ A superb pastoral epic from the People's Republic of China and the winner of the Golden Bear at the 1988 Berlin Film Festival. The story relates a passionate folk tale about village wine makers who fight against interloping Japanese invaders. Lyrical and affecting drama. In Chinese with English subtitles. 91m. **DIR:** Zhang Yimou. **CAST:** Gong Li, Jian Weng, Liu Ji. **1988**

REGINA ★★★ This strange psychological drama features Ava Gardner as a nagging wife and mother who is obsessed with keeping her 36-year-old son at home with her. Anthony Quinn is the much-put-upon husband. An Italian film, this is unrated but contains mature themes. 86m. **DIR:** Jean-Yves Prate. **CAST:** Anthony Quinn, Ava Gardner, Ray Sharkey, Anna Karina. **1983**

REINCARNATION OF GOLDEN LOTUS, THE ★★★★★ In this compelling and tastefully erotic Hong Kong production, a woman (Joi Wong) murdered by a powerful lord in ancient times uses reincarnation as a way of exacting revenge. In Chinese with English subtitles. Unrated, the film has violence and nudity. 99m. **DIR:** Clara Law. **CAST:** Joi Wong. **1989**

REMBRANDT—1669 ★★★ From his start at painting dead bodies for a surgeon, to his ultimate bankruptcy and death, this film portrays Rembrandt's life in a dark and almost voiceless story. Although the characters are well portrayed by all the actors, the plot moves along too slowly. In Dutch with English subtitles. Not rated, but contains nudity. 114m. **DIR:** Jos Stelling. **CAST:** Frans Stelling, Ton de Koff, Aye Fil. **1977**

RENDEZ-VOUS ★★★ Provocative French import paints a rather unsettling portrait of alienated youth. Juliette Binoche is captivating as a promiscuous young woman wandering the Paris nightlife scene. In French with English subtitles. Unrated, the film contains nudity, profanity, and violence. 82m. **DIR:** André Téchiné. **CAST:** Juliette Binoche, Lambert Wilson, Wadeck Stanczak, Jean-Louis Trintignant. **1985**

REPENTANCE ★★★ Set in Georgia in the Soviet Union, this richly varied film presents a central character who personifies all European villains—a cross, most obviously, between Stalin and Hitler. The film is not only a brutally direct comment on evil in politics, but a marvelous study of Georgian life. No rating but there are violent scenes. In Russian with English subtitles. 151m. **DIR:** Tenghiz Abuladze. **CAST:** Avtandil Makharadze. **1987**

REPORT ON THE PARTY AND THE GUESTS, A ★★★★ Kafkaesque parable about a group of party guests who suffer a mean practical joke at the hands of their host. The cast is comprised of prominent Prague artists and intellectuals, and many of the references will be lost on American viewers, but the overall allegory is clear. In Czech with English subtitles. Not rated. B&W; 71m. **DIR:** Jan Nemec. **CAST:** Ivan Vyskocil, Jan Klusak, Josef Skvorecky. **1966**

REQUIEM FOR DOMINIC ★★★ Torn from the headlines, *Requiem for Dominic* is a powerful and riveting true story of revolution and the inhumane treatment of prisoners. When a Romanian political exile looks into the disappearance of his childhood friend, he discovers that he is being held prisoner for the murder of eighty innocent workers. In German with English subtitles. Rated R for violence. 88m. **DIR:** Robert Dornhelm. **CAST:** Felix Mitterer. **1991**

RETURN OF MARTIN GUERRE, THE ★★★★½ Brilliantly absorbing account of an actual sixteenth-century court case in which a man returns to his family and village after years away at the wars, only to have his identity questioned. Gérard Depardieu and Nathalie Baye give outstanding, carefully restrained performances. In French with English subtitles. No MPAA rating. 111m. **DIR:** Daniel Vigne. **CAST:** Gérard Depardieu, Nathalie Baye, Roger Planchon. **1982**

RETURN OF THE TALL BLOND MAN WITH ONE BLACK SHOE, THE ★★½ This sequel to the original *Tall Blond Man...* is, unfortunately, inferior. But it's still a delight to watch Pierre Richard go through his comic paces. Once again his reactions to what he's faced with are the reason to see this. In French with English subtitles. No MPAA rating. 84m. **DIR:** Yves Robert. **CAST:** Pierre Richard, Mireille Darc, Jean Rochefort. **1974**

REVOLT OF JOB, THE ★★★★ In this moving account of the Holocaust in rural Hungary, an old Jewish couple awaiting the inevitable Nazi takeover adopt a gentile orphan boy to survive them. Nominated for best foreign-language film in 1983's Academy Awards. In Hungarian with English subtitles. No rating. 97m. **DIR:** Imre Gyongyossy. **CAST:** Fereno Zenthe, Hedi Tenessy. **1983**

RHAPSODY IN AUGUST ★★★ In another screen poem not unlike his *Dreams,* Japanese director Akira Kurosawa looks back on the bombing of Nagasaki during World War II through the eyes of four Japanese youngsters. Richard Gere has a brief but effective role. In Japanese with English subtitles. 98m. **DIR:** Akira Kurosawa. **CAST:** Sachiko Murase, Hisashi Igawa, Richard Gere. **1992**

RIDING BEAN ★★★★ Japanese animation. Highly amusing tale set in (of all places) Chicago and involving a special courier named Bean, who, with the aid of a supercar and female assistant, takes on bad guys and a bumbling police force. In Japanese with English subtitles. Unrated with violence, profanity, and illustrated nudity. 46m. **DIR:** Tanaka Masahiro, Kamijoo Osamu, Oohira Hiroya, Okuda Tadashi. **1989**

RIKISHA-MAN ★★★★ In turn-of-the-century Japan, an uneducated rickshaw puller looks out for a boy whose father has died. Rewarding human story with a typically strong performance by Toshiro Mifune. In Japanese with English subtitles. 105m. **DIR:** Hiroshi Inagaki. **CAST:** Toshiro Mifune. **1958**

RIKYU ★★★★ This poignant film, which won a special jury award at the Cannes Film Festival, explores the struggle between art and power in sixteenth century Japan. The central character, Sen-no Rikyu, refined the art of the tea ceremony, lifting it to aesthetic, spiritual heights. A beautifully crafted character study with fine ensemble acting. In Japanese with English subtitles. Unrated. 116m. **DIR:** Hiroshi Teshigahara. **CAST:** Rentaro Mikuni, Tsutomu Yamazaki. **1990**

RISE OF LOUIS XIV, THE ★★ Slow-paced docudrama chronicles King Louis XIV's acquisition of power over corrupt French noblemen. He is portrayed as a wise ruler despite his reputation. Lack of action, however, makes this import nearly impossible to sit through. In French with English subtitles. 100m. **DIR:** Roberto Rossellini. **CAST:** Jean-Marie Patte, Raymond Jourdan. **1966**

ROADS TO THE SOUTH ★★★½ Sequel to *La Guerre Est Finie* reteams screenwriter Jorge Semprun and actor Yves Montand to give us an update on the antifacist exile (played to perfection by Montand) after he's joined the establishment enough to become a wealthy writer. In French with English subtitles. Unrated, but contains profanity and violence. 100m. **DIR:** Joseph Losey. **CAST:** Yves Montand, Laurent Malet, Miou-Miou, Jose Luis Gomez. **1978**

ROBERT ET ROBERT ★★★★½ A brilliant French film about two lonely but very different men (Charles Denner and Jacques Villeret) who strike up a tenuous friendship while waiting for their respective computer dates. It is a bittersweet tale of loneliness and compassion. No MPAA rating. 105m. **DIR:** Claude Lelouch. **CAST:** Charles Denner, Jacques Villeret, Jean-Claude Brialy, Macha Meril, Regine. **1978**

ROCCO & HIS BROTHERS ★★★★ Compelling drama about a mother and her five sons who leave their peasant home in the south of Italy for the big city. One of Luchino Visconti's strongest screen efforts. In Italian with English subtitles. B&W; 170m. **DIR:** Luchino Visconti. **CAST:** Alain Delon, Annie Girardot, Renato Salvatori, Claudia Cardinale. **1960**

ROOTS SEARCH ★★ Japanese animation. A spaceship crew is stalked and killed by an alien presence in this often graphically violent thriller. In Japanese with English subtitles. Unrated; contains violence and nudity. 45m. **DIR:** Hisashi Sugai. **1986**

RORRET ★★★ Movie buffs will enjoy this odd thriller about the murderous owner of a revival theater, if only to spot the various re-created scenes from classic suspense films. But it's a gimmick that never really leads anywhere. In Italian with English subtitles. 103m. **DIR:** Fulvio Wetzl. **CAST:** Lou Castel, Anna Galiena. **1988**

ROUND-UP, THE ★★★★ In 1868, Hungarian police looking for the leaders of a political uprising subject a group of suspects to psychological warfare. A powerful, austere work; one of the most influential films in Hungarian cinema. In Hungarian with English subtitles. Not rated. B&W; 94m. **DIR:** Miklos Jancso. **CAST:** Janos Gorbe, Tibor Molnar. **1965**

RULES OF THE GAME, THE ★★★★★ This is Jean Renoir's masterful comedy farce that deftly exposes the moral bankruptcy of the French upper classes. A manor house is the location for a party as the shallowness of each guest is brilliantly exposed. B&W; 110m. **DIR:** Jean Renoir. **CAST:** Marcel Dalio, Nora Gregor, Mila Parely. **1939**

RUMIK WORLD: FIRETRIPPER ★★ In this animated feature, a young girl with the unexplained ability to time travel lives in two worlds—feudal and modern-day Japan. Not as engrossing as others in the *Rumik World* series, but it does have a few points of interest. In Japanese with English subtitles. Not rated; contains brief nudity. 50m. **DIR:** Osamu Uemura. **1992**

RUMIK WORLD: LAUGHING TARGET ★★★ A suspenseful animated story of love and demonic possession (not a strange combination when compared to other Japanese animation) that moves along with the excellent pacing we expect from the *Rumik World* series. Most viewers will find this exploration of the Japanese occult world a refreshing change of pace. In Japanese with English subtitles. Not rated; contains violence and brief nudity. 50m. **DIR:** Tohru Matsuzono. **1992**

RUMIK WORLD: THE SUPERGAL ★★★ Japanese animation. One of four stories from Rumiko Takahashi's imaginative *Rumik World* universe. Maris, a young woman in the service of the Space Police, lives in perpetual debt because of the inadvertent destruction of property brought about by her incredible strength. When assigned to rescue the kidnapped son of a billionaire, Maris sees her chance to finally get out of hock. In Japanese with English subtitles. Unrated; contains nudity. 50m. **DIR:** Kazuyashi Katayama, Tomoko Konparu. **1992**

SACCO AND VANZETTI ★★★★ Excellent historical drama recounts the trial and eventual execution of Sacco and Vanzetti, the Italian immigrants who were convicted of murder in 1921. The case was a *cause célèbre* at the time, since many felt that they were condemned on the basis of their politics rather than on the weak evidence against them. Whether or not the film persuades you, it poses powerful questions about the American system of justice. Dubbed in English. Rated PG. 121m. **DIR:** Giuliano Montaldo. **CAST:** Gian Maria Volonté, Riccardo Cucciolla, Cyril Cusack, Milo O'Shea. **1971**

SACRIFICE, THE ★★★★ In this Andrei Tarkovsky film, the actors do most of the work that expensive special effects would accomplish in an American film with a similar theme. During an approaching world holocaust, we don't see devastation. Rather, the camera carefully records the various emotional reactions of six people in a house in the secluded countryside. Actors' faces and unpredictable actions mirror horror, pathos, and even grim humor as the plot twists in a surprisingly supernatural direction. In Swedish with English subtitles. Unrated; the film has suggested sex. 145m. **DIR:** Andrei Tarkovsky. **CAST:** Erland Josephson, Susan Fleetwood, Valerie Mairesse, Allan Edwall. **1986**

SACRILEGE ★★ Controversial drama where sin and lust take place behind the walls of a convent. An illicit affair between a nun and a nobleman escalates to a dangerous climax. Lavishly produced erotica. In Italian with English subtitles. Not rated, but contains nudity and violence and is recommended for adults. 104m. **DIR:** Luciano Odorisio. **CAST:** Myriem Roussel, Alessandro Gassman. **1990**

SALAAM BOMBAY! ★★★★½ In the most potent film about street children since Hector Babenco's *Pixote,* director Mira Nair takes us on a sobering, heartrending tour of the back alleys and gutters of India. It is there that young Krishna (Shafiq Syed) must struggle to survive among the drug dealers, pimps, and prostitutes. In Hindi with English subtitles. Unrated, the film has profanity, violence, and suggested sex. 113m. **DIR:** Mira Nair. **CAST:** Shafiq Syed, Sarfuddin Qurrassi. **1988**

SALO: 120 DAYS OF SODOM A shocking, repulsive film set during World War II in Italy, where a group of bourgeois Fascists brutalize and sexually degrade teenagers. In Italian with English subtitles. Not rated, but contains scenes of graphic sex and violence. 115m. **DIR:** Pier Paolo Pasolini. **CAST:** Paolo Bonacelli. **1975**

SALUT L'ARTISTE ★★★½ A struggling middle-aged actor, who works primarily in commercials, tries to reconcile with his ex-wife. Bittersweet comedy about the eternal appeal of show business, with Marcello Mastroianni perfectly cast as a man finally realizing that his dreams are unlikely to come true. In French with English subtitles. Not rated; contains brief nudity. 96m. **DIR:** Yves Robert. **CAST:** Marcello Mastroianni, Françoise Fabian, Jean Rochefort. **1973**

SAMURAI REINCARNATION ★★ Weak adventure yarn about a shogunate warrior who rises from the dead. Gory Japanese metaphysical drama. In Japanese with English subtitles. Not rated, but contains nudity and graphic violence. 122m. **DIR:** Kinji Fukasaku. **1981**

SAMURAI SAGA ★★★ Toshiro Mifune is in top form as a gallant samurai who challenges a powerful warrior clan in 1599 Japan while getting caught up in a love triangle involving a beautiful princess. Great action sequences. In Japanese with English subtitles. B&W; 112m. **DIR:** Hiroshi Inagaki. **CAST:** Toshiro Mifune. **1959**

SAMURAI TRILOGY, THE ★★★★★ This brilliant and cinematically beautiful three-deck epic by director Hiroshi Inagaki tells the story of the legendary Japanese hero Musashi Miyamoto, a sixteenth-century samurai who righted wrongs in the fashion of Robin Hood and Zorro. Toshiro Mifune is impeccable as Miyamoto, whom we follow from his wild youth through spiritual discovery to the final battle with his archenemy, Sasaki Kojiro (Koji Tsuruta). The samurai film for the uninitiated. In Japanese with English subtitles. B&W; 303m. **DIR:** Hiroshi Inagaki. **CAST:** Toshiro Mifune, Koji Tsuruta. **1954**

SAND AND BLOOD ★★½ Brooding drama that explores the relationship between a young, gifted matador and a cultivated doctor-musician. Both leads give exceptional performances that get lost in this slow-moving drama. In French with English subtitles. Not rated, but contains nudity and violence. 101m. **DIR:** Jeanne Labrune. **CAST:** Patrick Catalifo, Sami Frey. **1987**

SANDAKAN NO. 8 ★★★★ Penetrating drama about a female journalist who becomes friends with an old woman who had been sold into prostitution and sent to Borneo in the early 1900s. Winner at the Berlin Film Festival and nominated for an Academy Award. In Japanese with English subtitles. Not rated, but is recommended for adult viewers. 121m. **DIR:** Kei Kumai. **CAST:** Kinuyo Tanaka. **1974**

SANJURO ★★★★½ First-rate sequel to *Yojimbo* has the original "Man With No Name" (Toshiro Mifune) again stirring up trouble in feudal Japan. He is recruited by several young would-be samurai as their teacher and leader in exposing corruption in their clan. In his usual gentle manner, Mifune wreaks all sorts of havoc while occasionally warning, "Watch it, I'm in a bad mood." In Japanese with English subtitles. B&W; 96m. **DIR:** Akira Kurosawa. **CAST:** Toshiro Mifune, Tatsuya Nakadai, Takashi Shimura. **1962**

SANSHIRO SUGATA ★★★½ In this vintage film directed by Akira Kurosawa, Sanshiro Sugata (Susumu Fujita) is among the strongest practitioners of judo, but spiritually he is weak. Can he find inner strength and purity? This is an elegant film about spiritual triumph. In Japanese with English subtitles. B&W; 82m. **DIR:** Akira Kurosawa. **CAST:** Susumu Fujuita, Takashi Shimura. **1943**

SANSHO THE BAILIFF ★★★ This beautifully photographed tale presents the suffering and heroism of a mother who is separated from her two children by a brutal man called Sansho. A poetic film that exhibits the humanism for which director Kenji Mizoguchi is well-known. In Japanese with English subtitles. B&W; 125m. **DIR:** Kenji Mizoguchi. **CAST:** Kinuyo Tanaka. **1954**

SARDINE: KIDNAPPED ★★★ Intriguing adventure set on the Italian island of Sardinia. Peasants have traditionally obtained land by kidnapping members of wealthy families and ransoming them for land. One family has the courage to stand up to the bandits and informs the police. Directed by a former documentary filmmaker, this English-dubbed film benefits from a realistic look. 110m. **DIR:** Gianfranco Mingozzi. **CAST:** Franco Nero, Charlotte Rampling. **1968**

SAVAGE NIGHTS ★★½ Writer-director-star Cyril Collard died of AIDS shortly after this film about a young bisexual filmmaker with AIDS, torn between an unstable teenage girl and a shallow young pretty boy, came out. That offscreen tragedy made the film a hit in France, but, despite some fine scenes and good acting, the story loses momentum and seems much longer than it is. In French with English subtitles. Rated R for mature themes and sexual scenes. 126m. **DIR:** Cyril Collard. **CAST:** Cyril Collard, Romane Bohringer, Carlos Lopez. **1992**

SAWDUST AND TINSEL ★★★½ A traveling circus is the background for this study of love relationships between a circus manager, the woman he loves, and her lover. Director Ingmar Bergman scores some emotional bull's-eyes in this early effort. Love triangle leads to a powerful climax, somewhat reminiscent of *The Blue Angel*. B&W; 95m. **DIR:** Ingmar Bergman. **CAST:** Harriet Andersson, Anders Ek. **1953**

SCARLET LETTER (1973) ★★★½ Wim Wenders's stunning psychological portrait of bigotry and isolation, this follows a story about the social sanctions imposed upon a woman suspected of adultery in seventeenth-century Salem, Massachusetts. Based on Nathaniel Hawthorne's classic novel, this film version is given some fine contemporary touches by Wenders. In German with English subtitles. 90m. **DIR:** Wim Wenders. **CAST:** Senta Berger, Lou Castel, Hans-Christian Blech, Yella Rottlander. **1973**

SCENE OF THE CRIME (1987) ★★★ *Scene of the Crime* is a romantic thriller with an Oedipal angle. A nightclub owner (Catherine Deneuve) and her son get caught up in an increasingly dangerous attempt to safeguard a criminal. This watchable movie could use fast pacing and less obvious camera pyrotechnics. In French with English subtitles. 90m. **DIR:** André Téchiné. **CAST:** Catherine Deneuve, Danielle Darrieux, Wadeck Stanczak, Victor Lanoux. **1987**

SCENES FROM A MARRIAGE ★★★★★ Director Ingmar Bergman successfully captures the pain and emotions of a marriage that is disintegrating. Several scenes are extremely hard to watch because there is so much truth to what is being said. Originally a six-part film for Swedish television, the theatrical version was edited by Bergman. Believable throughout, this one packs a real punch. In Swedish. No rating (contains some strong language). 168m. **DIR:** Ingmar Bergman. **CAST:** Liv Ullmann, Erland Josephson, Bibi Andersson. **1973**

SCENT OF GREEN PAPAYA, THE ★★★ The first Vietnamese nominee for the Best Foreign Film Oscar tells the story of a young serving girl in Saigon who grows up to be the servant, and later the lover, of a composer. The film is exquisitely photographed and graceful, but the elliptical, allusive style makes it a bit slow-moving and uneventful. In Vietnamese with English subtitles. Not rated, but suitable for mature general audiences. 103m. **DIR:** Tran Anh Hung. **CAST:** Tran Nu Yen-Khe, Lu Man San, Truong Thi Loc, Nguyen Anh Hoa. **1993**

SCORPION WOMAN, THE ★★★½ An interesting and intelligent May-December story with an ironic twist. A woman judge has an affair with a 23-year-old law trainee. Believable characters highlight what might have been soap-opera material. In German with English subtitles. Not rated. 101m. **DIR:** Susanne Zanke. **CAST:** Angelica Domrose, Fritz Hammel. **1989**

SECRETS OF A SOUL ★★ A chemistry professor is troubled by dream images and premonitions of murder when he learns his wife's cousin is returning from India. This early attempt to convert psychoanalysis into cinematic entertainment was bound to suffer from heavy-handed and simplistic imagery (but then, was *Spellbound* any better twenty years later?). Germany. Silent. 94m. **DIR:** G. W. Pabst. **CAST:** Werner Krauss. **1926**

SECRETS OF WOMEN (WAITING WOMEN) ★★★½ Infidelity is the theme of this early Ingmar Bergman film. Three wives (Anita Bjork, May Britt, and Eva Dahlbeck) who are staying at a summerhouse recount adventures from their marriages. Clearly illustrates Bergman's talent for comedy and was his first commercial success. B&W; 107m. **DIR:** Ingmar Bergman. **CAST:** Anita Bjork, Jarl Kulle, Eva Dahlbeck, Gunnar Björnstrand, May Britt, Birger Malmsten. **1952**

SEDUCED AND ABANDONED ★★★½ This raucous Italian film takes wonderfully funny potshots at Italian life and codes of honor. It centers on a statute of Italian law that absolves a man for the crime of seducing and abandoning a girl if he marries her. This is one of the funniest movies exposing the stratagems of saving face. In Italian with English subtitles. B&W; 118m. **DIR:** Pietro Germi. **CAST:** Saro Urzi, Stefania Sandrelli. **1964**

SEDUCTION, THE: CRUEL WOMAN 🦃 Artsy-looking film about a dominatrix who stages S&M perfomances for customers in Berlin. In German with English subtitles. Not rated, but contains graphic sex and violence. 84m. **DIR:** Elfi Mikesch, Monika Treut. **CAST:** Pina Bausch. **1985**

SEDUCTION OF MIMI, THE ★★★★ Giancarlo Giannini gives an unforgettable performance as the sad-eyed Mimi, a Sicilian who migrates to the big city. He soon gets into trouble because of his obstinate character and his simple mind. Like all Wertmuller's films, sex and politics are at the heart of her dark humor. Includes one of the funniest love scenes ever filmed. Rated R for language and sex. 89m. **DIR:** Lina Wertmuller. **CAST:** Giancarlo Giannini, Mariangela Melato, Agostina Belli. **1974**

SENSUOUS NURSE, THE 🦃 A wealthy aristocrat has a heart attack and his two fortune-hunting, conniving nephews decide to help their lecherous uncle meet his maker. This dubbed Italian comedy is a dud. Rated R for nudity. 76m. **DIR:** Nello Rossati. **CAST:** Ursula Andress, Jack Palance, Duilio Del Prete, Luciana Paluzzi. **1978**

SEVEN BEAUTIES ★★★★★ Winner of many international awards, this Italian film classic is not what the title might suggest. *Seven Beauties* is actually the street name for a small-time gangster, played by Giancarlo Giannini. We watch him struggle and survive on the streets and in a World War II German prisoner-of-war camp. Excellent! Rated R. 115m. **DIR:** Lina Wertmuller. **CAST:** Giancarlo Giannini, Fernando Rey, Shirley Stoler. **1976**

SEVEN DEADLY SINS, THE ★★★ This collection of seven episodes illustrating the capital sins has its moments, but it should have been much better. Best is Jean-Luc Godard's segment on Laziness, with Eddie Constantine as a movie star more interested in his clothes than sex. In French with English subtitles. B&W; 113m. **DIR:** Sylvain Dhomme, Eugene Ionesco, Max Douy, Edouard Molinaro, Philippe de Broca, Jacques Demy, Jean-Luc Godard, Roger Vadim, Claude Chabrol. **CAST:** Claude Brasseur, Jean-Louis Trintignant, Eddie Constantine, Jean-Pierre Aumont, Sami Frey, Jean-Claude Brialy, Claude Berri. **1961**

SEVEN SAMURAI, THE ★★★★★ This Japanese release—about seven swordsmen coming to the aid of a besieged peasant village—is one of those rare screen wonders that seems to end much too soon. Its timeless and appealing story served as the basis for *The Magnificent Seven* and other American films. In Japanese with English subtitles. Unrated; the film has violence. B&W; 197m. **DIR:** Akira Kurosawa. **CAST:** Toshiro Mifune, Takashi Shimura. **1954**

SEVENTH SEAL, THE ★★★★½ This is considered by many to be Ingmar Bergman's masterpiece. It tells the story of a knight coming back from the Crusades. He meets Death, who challenges him to a chess match, the stakes being his life. The knight is brilliantly played by Max von Sydow. In Swedish with English subtitles. B&W; 96m. **DIR:** Ingmar Bergman. **CAST:** Max von Sydow, Bibi Andersson, Gunnar Björnstrand. **1956**

SHADOWS OF FORGOTTEN ANCESTORS ★★★★ A brilliant, epic story of star-crossed lovers set against the panoramic background of the Carpathian mountains. A visual masterpiece. In Russian with English subtitles. 99m. **DIR:** Sergi Parajanov. **CAST:** Ivan Mikolaichuk, Larisa Kadochnikova. **1964**

SHAMELESS OLD LADY, THE ★★★★½ Bertolt Brecht's reminiscences of his grandmother provided the basis for this comedy about a 70-year-old woman, wonderfully played by the great character actress Sylvie. A joyous movie. In French with English subtitles. 95m. **DIR:** Rene Allio. **CAST:** Sylvie, Malka Ribovska, Victor Lanoux. **1965**

SHAOLIN TEMPLE ★★★★ The best kung fu film since *Enter the Dragon*, this period piece, set in seventh-century China, traces the history of the Shaolin Temple. It stars the country's top martial arts experts, yet characterization and plot are not slighted. In Chinese with English subtitles. Unrated; the film has violence. 111m. **DIR:** Chang Hsin Yen. **CAST:** Li Lin Jei. **1982**

SHEEP HAS FIVE LEGS ★★★★ The beloved French comedian Fernandel plays six roles in one of his funniest movies: five identical brothers and their father. The humor doesn't come from the plot but from watching Fernandel juggle six comic characters. Great for families, if your kids don't mind a few subtitles. B&W; 92m. **DIR:** Henri Verneuil. **CAST:** Fernandel. **1954**

SHEER MADNESS ★★★½ The growing friendship between two women threatens to overwhelm their respective marriages in this complex, intelligently made film. Somewhat slow, but worth the effort. In German with English subtitles. Unrated. 110m. **DIR:** Margarethe von Trotta. **CAST:** Hanna Schygulla, Angela Winkler. **1985**

SHIN HEINKE MONOGATARI ★★★ Fans of the great Kenji Mizoguchi may be disappointed to find that this film is a historical samurai adventure rather than a story of oppressed women, his usual subject. Not one of Mizoguchi's best, though his striking use of color is memorable. In Japanese with English subtitles. 113m. **DIR:** Kenji Mizoguchi. **CAST:** Raizo Ichikawa. **1955**

SHOESHINE ★★★★ Neorealist classic about two boys whose friendship gets them through hard times in Rome during the Nazi occupation. But in a harsh jail, their relationship falters. Winner of a special Academy Award. In Italian with English subtitles. 93m. **DIR:** Vittorio De Sica. **CAST:** Rinaldo Smerdoni, Franco Interlenghi. **1946**

SHOGUN ASSASSIN ★★★ This film will rate a zero for the squeamish and close to five for fans of the nineteen-film "Baby Cart" series, so popular in Japan in the 1970s. The color red predominates in this meticulously reedited, rescripted, rescored (by Mark Lindsay), and English-dubbed version of the original *Baby-Cart at the River Styx*: swords enter bodies at the most imaginative angles; a body count is impossible; all records are broken for bloodletting. Rated R for the violence, which really is fairly aesthetic. 90m. **DIR:** Kenji Misumi, David Weisman, Robert Hous. **CAST:** Tomisaburo Wakayama. **1980**

SHOOT THE PIANO PLAYER ★★★½ Singer Charles Aznavour plays to perfection the antihero of this minor masterpiece directed by François Truffaut. Don't look for plot, unity of theme, or understandable mood transitions. This one's a brilliantly offbeat mix of crime, melodrama, romance, and slapstick. In French with English subtitles. B&W; 85m. **DIR:** François Truffaut. **CAST:** Charles Aznavour, Marie Dubois, Nicole Berger, Michele Mercier. **1962**

SHOP ON MAIN STREET, THE ★★★★ This film finds a Jewish woman removed from her small business and portrays her growing relationship with the man who has been put in charge of her shop. Set among the turbulent days of the Nazi occupation of Czechoslovakia, this tender film depicts the instincts of survival among the innocent pawns of a brutal war. A moving film. B&W; 128m. **DIR:** Ján Kadár. **CAST:** Elmar Klos, Josef Kroner, Ida Kaminska. **1964**

SIEGFRIED ★★★★ Vivid, spectacular story of young god Siegfried, whose conquests and eventual murder form an intrinsic part of Teutonic legend, this nationalistic triumph for German director Fritz Lang was the most ambitious attempt to transfer folklore to film and proved an international success. Moody sets and photography give this movie an otherworldly feeling and evoke just the right atmosphere. Silent. B&W; 100m. **DIR:** Fritz Lang. **CAST:** Paul Richter, Margarete Schon, Theodor Loos, Bernhard Goetzke. **1923**

SILENCE, THE ★★ *The Silence* is one of Ingmar Bergman's more pretentious and claustrophobic films. Two sisters who are traveling together stop for a time in a European hotel. The film is laden with heavy-handed symbolism and banal dialogue. In Swedish with English subtitles. 95m. **DIR:** Ingmar Bergman. **CAST:** Ingrid Thulin, Gunnel Lindblom, Birger Malmsten. **1963**

SILENT MOBIUS ★★ This animated story of futuristic ghostbusters is almost interesting at times, but in the end it's only mediocre. In a twenty-first–century metropolis, a group of psychic policewomen track down evil spirits that infest the city. Dubbed. Not rated; contains nudity and graphic violence. 50m. **DIR:** Michitaka Kikuchi. **1991**

SIMON OF THE DESERT ★★★★½ One has the feeling that *Simon of the Desert* is a short film because Luis Buñuel simply ran out of money (and tacked on a fairly unsatisfactory ending). It is, however, impossible to deny the sly pleasure we have with St. Simon Stylites, the desert anchorite who spent thirty-seven years atop a sixty-foot column (circa A.D. 400) preaching to Christian flocks and avoiding temptation—particularly with knockout Silvia Pinal, as the devil. Good nasty fun for aficionados and novices alike. In Spanish with English subtitles. B&W; 40m. **DIR:** Luis Buñuel. **CAST:** Claudio Brook, Silvia Pinal. **1965**

SIMPLE STORY, A ★★★½ Marie (Romy Schneider) is pregnant and decides to have an abortion. At forty, she is forced to reevaluate her life and her relationships with men. Rewarding film is paced very slowly and plot is interwoven with subplots of other characters in distress. One of Romy Schneider's best performances. In French with English subtitles. No MPAA rating. 110m. **DIR:** Claude Sautet. **CAST:** Romy Schneider, Bruno Cremer, Claude Brasseur, Roger Pigaut. **1978**

SINCERELY CHARLOTTE ★★★ Caroline Huppert directs her sister Isabelle in this intriguing tale of a woman with a shady past. Isabelle finds herself in trouble with the law and seeks the help of her old lover, who's now married. It's the interaction between these three characters that is fun and enticing. In French with English subtitles. 92m. **DIR:** Caroline Huppert. **CAST:** Isabelle Huppert, Neils Arestrup, Christine Pascal, Luc Beraud. **1986**

SINGING THE BLUES IN RED ★★★½ An oppressed East German protest singer is forced to defect and ply his trade in the West, only to discover new avenues of repression in the capitalist system. Exactingly scripted in English with German subtitles. Not rated. 110m. **DIR:** Kenneth Loach. **CAST:** Gerulf Pannach. **1989**

SIX IN PARIS (PARIS VUE PAR . . .) ★★★ Six *nouvelle vague* directors contributed short 16mm films about a Paris neighborhood to this collection. The shorts by Eric Rohmer and Claude Chabrol foreshadow their more mature work, though the rest is thin (Jean-Luc Godard's effort is particularly trivial). In French with English subtitles. 98m. **DIR:** Jean Douchet, Jean Rouch, Jean-Daniel Pollet, Eric Rohmer, Jean-Luc Godard, Claude Chabrol. **CAST:** Barbet Schroeder, Joanna Shimkus, Stéphane Audran, Claude Chabrol. **1965**

SLAVE OF LOVE, A ★★★★½ Shortly after the Bolshevik revolution, a crew of silent filmmakers attempt to complete a melodrama while fighting the forces of the changing world around them. This examines the role of the bourgeois as Olga (Elena Solovei) changes from matinee idol to revolutionary. Politically and emotionally charged. In Russian with English subtitles. Unrated. 94m. **DIR:** Nikita Mikhalkov. **CAST:** Elena Soloyei, Rodion Nakhapetov, Alexandar Kalyagin. **1978**

SLEAZY UNCLE, THE ★★★ Italian comedy features Vittorio Gassman as a lecherous old man. At times repulsive, there is something to be said for Gassman's obvious love of life. In Italian with English subtitles. Unrated, contains profanity and sexual innuendo. 104m. **DIR:** Franco Brusati. **CAST:** Vittorio Gassman, Giancarlo Giannini, Andrea Ferreol. **1991**

SLEEPING CAR MURDERS, THE ★★★★ An all-star French cast and crisp direction from Costa-Gavras (his first film) make this a first-rate thriller. Yves Montand stars as the detective investigating the case of a woman found dead in a sleeping compartment of a train when it pulls into Paris. Soon other occupants of the car are found murdered as well. In French with English subtitles. B&W; 92m. **DIR:** Constantin Costa-Gavras. **CAST:** Yves Montand, Simone Signoret, Pierre Mondy, Michel Piccoli, Jean-Louis Trintignant, Charles Denner. **1966**

SLIGHTLY PREGNANT MAN, A ★★ This French comedy features Marcello Mastroianni as the first pregnant man. The reversal of parenting roles provides a few laughs and the surprise ending is worth the wait in an otherwise ho-hum film. Unrated, this film contains adult subject matter. In French with subtitles. 92m. **DIR:** Jacques Demy. **CAST:** Catherine Deneuve, Marcello Mastroianni, Mireille Mathieu. **1973**

SMALL CHANGE ★★★★★ One of François Truffaut's best pictures, this is a charming and perceptive film viewing the joys and sorrows of young children's lives in a small French town. Wonderfully and naturally acted by a cast of young children. French. 104m. **DIR:** François Truffaut. **CAST:** Geary Desmouceaux, Philippe Goldman. **1976**

SMILES OF A SUMMER NIGHT ★★★★★ Nowhere in Ingmar Bergman's amazing *oeuvre,* perhaps nowhere in cinema, is there such a classic of carnal comedy. An elegant roundelay that is, at heart, an enlightened boudoir farce. Used as the basis of Stephen Sondheim's *A Little Night Music.* In Swedish with English subtitles. B&W; 106m. **DIR:** Ingmar Bergman. **CAST:** Ulla Jacobsson, Gunnar Björnstrand, Eva Dahlbeck, Harriet Andersson, Jarl Kulle. **1955**

SNOW COUNTRY ★★★½ A painter's romance with a lovely geisha is complicated by various friends and acquaintances. Fine Japanese love story set amidst the snowbanks of an isolated village. In Japanese with English subtitles. B&W; 134m. **DIR:** Shiro Toyoda. **CAST:** Ryo Ikebe. **1957**

SOFIE ★★★½ The great Norwegian actress Liv Ullmann directs her first film, a slow-moving but affecting family saga in turn-of-the-century Sweden. We follow the life of the title character, an enterprising and independent Jewish woman. Ullmann learned a lot from Ingmar Bergman, and layers in textures of family warmth, humor, and mystery, as well as a masterful performance by Bergman veteran Erland Josephson as Sofie's beloved father. The film could benefit from about a 20-minute reduction. In Swedish with English subtitles. 146m. **DIR:** Liv Ullmann. **CAST:** Karen-Lise Mynster, Erland Josephson, Ghita Norby. **1993**

SOFT SKIN, THE ★★★½ For some critics, *The Soft Skin* ranks as one of the new-wave master's worst; for some it remains one of his best. As usual, the truth lies in between. What keeps this from being at least a minor classic is the less-than-fresh plot. In French with English subtitles. 118m. **DIR:** François Truffaut. **CAST:** Jean Desailly, Nelly Benedetti, Françoise Dorleac. **1964**

SOIS BELLE ET TAIS-TOI (JUST ANOTHER PRETTY FACE) ★★★ This French import tries to be a lighthearted, romantic adventure, but doesn't focus itself properly. Mylene Demongeot is Virginie, an 18-year-old orphan who runs away from a reformatory and falls in with a jewel-smuggling gang. Jean-Paul Belmondo and Alain Delon, both in their first film roles, are members of the teenage gang. In French with English subtitles. B&W; 110m. **DIR:** Marc Allegret. **CAST:** Mylene Demongeot, Henri Vidal, René Lefévre, Jean-Paul Belmondo, Alain Delon. **1958**

SOL BIANCA ★★★★ After the pirate ship *Sol Bianca* unknowingly takes on a passenger, the five-woman crew of freebooters set their sights on a new prize: the "Gnosis," a treasure beyond price. Unfortunately the obstacle in their path, a tyrannical emperor, is determined to keep the treasure. Japanese animation from the director of *Bubblegum Crisis.* In Japanese with English subtitles. Unrated, with violence and profanity. 60m. **DIR:** Akiyama Katsuhito. **1990**

SOLARIS ★★★★ Based on a story by noted Polish author Stanislaw Lem, this motion picture explores the workings of a man's mind and how he deals with visions from his past. A space station situated over a water-covered planet has become almost deserted, and a scientist is sent to unravel the mysteries surrounding the death of a doctor on board the station. A milestone in the history of science-fiction cinema. In Russian with English subtitles. Unrated. 167m. **DIR:** Andrei Tarkovsky. **CAST:** Donatas Banionis, Natalya Bondarchuk. **1972**

SOLDIER OF ORANGE ★★★★★ Rutger Hauer became an international star as a result of his remarkable performance in this Dutch release, in which he plays one of four college buddies galvanized into action when the Nazis invade the Netherlands. This is an exceptional work; an exciting, suspenseful, and intelligent war adventure. In several languages and subtitled. Rated R for nudity, profanity, implied sex, and violence. 165m. **DIR:** Paul Verhoeven. **CAST:** Rutger Hauer, Peter Faber, Jeroen Krabbé. **1979**

SOLDIER OF THE NIGHT 🦃 This Israeli movie about a man who kills soldiers by night while working in a toy store by day has some psychological thriller elements, but its plodding story line and poor dubbing make it almost impossible to watch. Not rated, has nudity, violence, and profanity. 89m. **DIR:** Dan Wolman. **CAST:** Iris Kaner, Hillel Neeman, Yftach Katzur. **1984**

SONG OF THE EXILE ★★★★ A recent graduate of a British university returns home to Hong Kong where she is reunited with her mother and a battle of wills begins. One of the most beautiful and astonishing motion pictures of the new Asian cinema, this is director Ann Hui's finest achievement to date. In Mandarin and Japanese with English subtitles. Unrated. 100m. **DIR:** Ann Hui. **CAST:** Shwu Sen Chang, Maggie Cheung. **1990**

SORCERESS, THE (1988) ★★★½ Visually rich, enthralling tale set in a small village in medieval France about a priest on a search for those still practicing pagan rituals. Unfortunately, the English-dubbed version kills some of the film's impact. 98m. **DIR:** Suzanne Schiffman. **CAST:** Tcheky Karyo, Christine Boisson, Jean Carmet. **1988**

SOTTO SOTTO ★★★ A sexy, raucous, hilarious farce about a woman who finds herself romantically drawn to her best friend's husband. This leads to comically disastrous results. Good entertainment, especially for hard-core fans of Lina Wertmuller. In Italian with English subtitles. 104m. **DIR:** Lina Wertmuller. **CAST:** Enrico Montesano, Veronica Lario. **1984**

SPAGHETTI HOUSE ★★ Five Italian restaurant employees are held hostage in a food storage room by three crooks. Most of the film is lighthearted, though—and, unfortunately, light-headed. In Italian with English subtitles. Not rated, contains violence and profanity. 103m. **DIR:** Giulio Paradisi. **CAST:** Nino Manfredi, Rita Tushingham. **1985**

SPECIAL DAY, A ★★★★ Antonietta (Sophia Loren), a slovenly housewife, and Gabriele (Marcello Mastroianni), a depressed homosexual, meet in the spring of 1938—the same day Hitler arrives in Rome. Their experience together enriches but does not change the course of their lives. In Italian with English subtitles. No MPAA rating. 106m. **DIR:** Ettore Scola. **CAST:** Sophia Loren, Marcello Mastroianni. **1977**

SPETTERS ★★★★½ A study of the dreams, loves, discoveries, and tragedies of six young people in modern-day Holland, this is yet another tough, uncompromising motion picture from Paul Verhoeven. Though the sex scenes are more graphic than anything we've ever had in a major American movie, *Spetters* is never exploitative. MPAA-unrated, it contains violence, profanity, nudity. 115m. **DIR:** Paul Verhoeven. **CAST:** Hans Van Tongeren, Toon Agterberg, Renee Soutendijk. **1980**

SPICES ★★★½ This spirited, feminist fable from India stars Smita Patil (two-time winner of India's National Best Actress Award) in the role of an impoverished woman who struggles against oppression. Excellent direction and fine performances by some of India's top-name stars. In Hindi with English subtitles. Not rated. 98m. **DIR:** Ketan Mehta. **CAST:** Smita Patil. **1986**

SPIDER'S STRATAGEM, THE ★★★★ Compelling mystery about a young man who returns to a small Italian town where his father was murdered thirty years earlier. One of director Bernardo Bertolucci's most stunning cinematic works. In Italian with English subtitles. Not rated. 97m. **DIR:** Bernardo Bertolucci. **CAST:** Giulio Brogi, Alida Valli, Tino Scotti. **1970**

SPIES (1928) ★★★★ Thrilling, imaginative drama of the underworld and the dark doings of espionage agents is one of the finest of all such films and remains a classic of the genre as well as a terrific adventure movie. The camera moves in and out among the shadowy doings of the spies and their pursuers like a silent spider weaving all the components together. The final chase provides a fitting climax to this topflight entertainment from Fritz Lang. Silent. B&W; 90m. **DIR:** Fritz Lang. **CAST:** Rudolf Klein-Rogge, Gerda Maurus, Willy Fritsch, Fritz Rasp. **1928**

SPIRIT OF THE BEEHIVE, THE ★★★★ A disturbing cinematic study of the isolation of an individual. Ana Torrent gives an unforgettable performance as a lonely girl who enters the world of fantasy when she sees the 1931 *Frankenstein* and falls in love with the monster. By far one of the most haunting films ever made about children. In Spanish with English subtitles. Not rated. 95m. **DIR:** Victor Erice. **CAST:** Fernando Fernán Gomez, Ana Torrent. **1974**

SPRING SYMPHONY ★★ *Spring Symphony* is a routine presentation of the lives of German composer Robert Schumann and celebrated pianist Clara Wieck. The film portrays emotion in fairy-tale fashion, simplistic and overstated. The music is the star of this show. Dubbed in English. Rated PG. 102m. **DIR:** Peter Schamoni. **CAST:** Nastassja Kinski, Herbert Gronemeyer, Bernhard Wicki. **1984**

SPUTNIK ★★★ The memorable character actor Mischa Auer (remember the artist who imitated a gorilla in *My Man Godfrey*?) costars in this French comedy about an animal lover trying to protect a dog and a mouse that escaped from a Russian satellite. Pleasant family comedy. B&W; 80m. **DIR:** Jean Dreville. **CAST:** Noel-Noel, Denise Grey, Mischa Auer. **1960**

STALKER ★★★★ In a decrepit future, a guide takes a scientist and a writer into the mysterious "Zone," site of a meteor crash, to find a source of great extraterrestrial knowledge. Definitely not for *Star Wars* fans, this adaptation of a Stanislaw Lem novel moves slowly but is filled with unforgettably beautiful images. In Russian with English subtitles. Not rated. 161m. **DIR:** Andrei Tarkovsky. **CAST:** Alexander Kaidanovsky, Anatoly Solanitsin. **1979**

STATE OF SIEGE ★★★★ This is a highly controversial but brilliant film about the kidnapping of an American A.I.D. official by left-wing guerrillas in Uruguay. The film follows step-by-step how U.S. aid is sent to fascist countries through the pretext of helping the economy and strengthening democracy. No MPAA rating. 120m. **DIR:** Constantin Costa-Gavras. **CAST:** Yves Montand, O. E. Hasse, Renato Salvatori. **1973**

STATE OF THINGS, THE ★★★★½ Absorbing account of a film crew stranded on an island in Portugal during the production of a movie dealing with the aftermath of a nuclear holocaust. Running out of money and film stock, the German director, who is a parody of Wim Wenders, attempts to locate an American producer who is on the lam from loan sharks. In German and English. B&W; 120m. **DIR:** Wim Wenders. **CAST:** Allen Garfield, Samuel Fuller, Paul Getty III, Viva, Roger Corman, Patrick Bauchau. **1983**

STATELINE MOTEL ★★ This Italian-made film involves a jewelry store robbery by a ruthless killer (Eli Wallach) and his handsome partner, Floyd (Fabio Testi). Not much to the film except the surprise ending featuring Barbara Bach. The film is dubbed and rated R for nudity, violence, sexual situations, and obscenities. 87m. **DIR:** Maurizio Lucidi. **CAST:** Ursula Andress, Eli Wallach, Barbara Bach, Fabio Testi, Massimo Girotti. **1975**

STATION, THE ★★★ Adaptation of a popular Italian stage play takes place during one evening at a small railway station, as the manager meets a beautiful heiress on the run from her fiancé. Fresh, well-acted comic romance. In Italian with English subtitles. Not rated. 92m. **DIR:** Sergio Rubini. **CAST:** Sergio Rubini, Margherita Buy. **1990**

STAVISKY ★★★★ Complex drama about a crafty French swindler and a brilliant con man, whose financial exploits in the Thirties brought on riots that helped topple a government. With a superb musical score by Stephen Sondheim and dazzling cinematography by Sacha Vierny. In French with English subtitles. 117m. **DIR:** Alain Resnais. **CAST:** Jean-Paul Belmondo, Anny Duperey, Charles Boyer, Gérard Depardieu. **1974**

STILTS, THE (LOS ZANCOS) ★★★½ This film, about an aged playwright and professor (Fernando Fernán Gomez) who falls in love with a young actress (Laura Del Sol), is occasionally melodramatic. Her unwillingness to commit herself to him gives the film its tension, and the acting is good enough to overcome most of the overwrought moments. In Spanish with English subtitles. Not rated, but contains nudity. 95m. **DIR:** Carlos Saura. **CAST:** Laura Del Sol, Fernando Fernán Gomez, Francisco Rabal, Antonio Banderas. **1984**

STOLEN KISSES ★★★★★ This is François Truffaut's third film in the continuing story about Antoine Doinel (Jean-Pierre Léaud) which began with *400 Blows*. Like the other films in the series, this work resembles Truffaut's autobiography as he romantically captures the awkwardness of Doinel and his encounters with women. This delightful comedy is often considered one of Truffaut's best movies. In French with English subtitles. 90m. **DIR:** François Truffaut. **CAST:** Jean-Pierre Léaud, Delphine Seyrig, Michel Lonsdale, Claude Jade, Daniel Ceccaldi. **1968**

STORM OVER ASIA ★★★★ Also known as *The Heir to Genghis Khan*, this masterpiece is from the great Russian director, Vsevolod Pudovkin. It tells the story of a young Mongol hunter who is discovered to be the heir of the great Khan. A superb example of the formal beauty of the silent film. Silent. B&W; 102m. **DIR:** V. I. Pudovkin. **CAST:** Valeri Inkizhinov. **1928**

STORMY WATERS ★★★★ Tough rescue-ship captain Jean Gabin braves stormy waters to save hauntingly beautiful Michele Morgan. They then have a passionate love affair. This film is a fine example of French cinema at its pre–WWII zenith. 75m. **DIR:** Jean Gremillon. **CAST:** Jean Gabin, Michele Morgan, Madeleine Renaud, Fernand Ledoux. **1941**

STORY OF ADELE H, THE ★★★½ This basically simple story of author Victor Hugo's daughter, who loves a soldier in vain, is surprisingly textured and intriguing. Slow, exquisite unfolding of many-layered love story is arresting and pictorially beautiful. Nicely done. Some adult situations. In French with English subtitles. Rated PG. 97m. **DIR:** François Truffaut. **CAST:** Isabelle Adjani, Bruce Robinson. **1975**

STORY OF BOYS AND GIRLS ★★★★ Italian director Pupi Avati serves up a spicy, thought-provoking slice of life as thirty-plus participants in an engagement party indulge in a mouth-watering, eighteen-course meal. Set in pre–World War II Italy, this delicious import provides a feast of fascinating characters while examining the attitudes that led to the rise of fascism. In Italian with English subtitles. Unrated; the film has scenes of simulated sex. 92m. **DIR:** Pupi Avati. **CAST:** Felice Andreasi, Angiola Baggi. **1991**

STORY OF FAUSTA, THE ★★★ A Brazilian woman, sick of her lazy and abusive husband, seeks the easy way out by befriending a wealthy old man. The more she mistreats her rescuer, the more anxious he is to please her. The humor here is deeply black. In Portuguese with English subtitles. Unrated, contains violence, profanity, and nudity. 90m. **DIR:** Bruno Barreto. **CAST:** Betty Faria, Daniel Filho, Brandao Filho. **1988**

STORY OF QIU JU, THE ★★★★★ The masterful Zhang Yimou, the first Chinese director to acquire a western following, here makes his first film about contemporary Chinese life. Yimou's frequent star, Gong Li, plays a woman who goes through many levels of government bureaucracy to achieve justice in a minor incident. Her husband has been kicked by the village chief. Viewers can observe both the marvelous and mundane in modern Chinese life. And Gong Li proves again that she's one of the world's greatest actresses. This film is just the change of pace Zhang Yimou needed to demonstrate his versatility and multifaceted skills. In Chinese with English subtitles. Rated PG. 100m. **DIR:** Zhang Yimou. **CAST:** Gong Li, Lei Lao Sheng, Liu Pei Qi. **1993**

STORY OF WOMEN, THE ★★★★ Excellent political drama from director Claude Chabrol based on a true story about the last woman to be guillotined in France, at the onset of World War II. Isabelle Huppert delivers a powerful performance as an abortionist who becomes the victim of an indifferent society. This riveting performance won her the best-actress prize at the Venice Film Festival. In French with English subtitles. 112m. **DIR:** Claude Chabrol. **CAST:** Isabelle Huppert, François Cluzet. **1988**

STRAIGHT FOR THE HEART ★★★ Covering Contra atrocities in Nicaragua, a Canadian photographer copes by repressing his emotional reactions. But when he returns home, he finds that detachment difficult to shake. A grim but involving drama, featuring splendid Montreal locations. In French with English subtitles. Not rated. 92m. **DIR:** Lea Pool. **CAST:** Matthias Habich, Johanne-Marie Tremblay. **1988**

STRANGER, THE (1992) ★★★★½ *The Stranger* tells of a middle-class Calcutta husband and wife whose lives are disrupted when the wife's long-lost and unknown-to-them uncle arrives at the doorstep. The final film of the great Satyajit Ray, who died in 1992, is an entertaining, affecting modern-day fable, offering Ray's thoughtful views on families, cultural tradition, and the flaws in modern civilization. Though probably not Ray's most polished or profound work, this is an apt reminder of his place among the master filmmakers of the world. In Bengali with English subtitles. 120m. **DIR:** Satyajit Ray. **CAST:** Mamata Shankar, Deepankar Dey, Utpal Dutt. **1992**

STRAY DOG ★★★★ In a fascinatingly detailed portrait of postwar Tokyo, a young detective (Toshiro Mifune) desperately searches the underworld for his stolen service revolver. Akira Kurosawa has created a tense thriller in the tradition of early Forties crime-dramas. In Japanese with English subtitles. Not rated. B&W; 122m. **DIR:** Akira Kurosawa. **CAST:** Toshiro Mifune, Takashi Shimura. **1949**

STREET, THE ★★½ Lured by the fantasy and excitement of the street—a metaphor for elusive freedom—a husband leaves his monotonous home and is caught up in a life of gambling and murder. Classic German progenitor of a more realistic style. Silent. B&W; 87m. **DIR:** Karl Grune. **CAST:** Eugen Klopfer. **1923**

STREET OF SHAME ★★★★ A penetrating study of love and sex that honestly examines the dreams and problems of a group of prostitutes living in a Tokyo brothel. In his final film, Japan's master director Kenji Mizoguchi creates a stirring portrait of communal life among women trapped in a harsh and degrading existence. In Japanese with English subtitles. B&W; 88m. **DIR:** Kenji Mizoguchi. **CAST:** Machiko Kyo. **1956**

STRIKE ★★★★ Shot in a documentarylike style, this drama about a labor dispute during the czarist era was Sergei Eisenstein's first feature film. Advanced for its time and using techniques Eisenstein would perfect in his later masterpieces, *Strike* remains a remarkable achievement and still holds one's interest today. Silent. B&W; 82m. **DIR:** Sergei Eisenstein. **CAST:** Grigori Alexandrov, Alexander Antonov. **1924**

STROMBOLI ★★ This potboiler from the director of *Open City* is a brooding, sometimes boring movie about an attractive woman who marries a fisherman and attempts to adjust. Even Ingrid Bergman (by this time married to Rossellini) couldn't salvage this film. Subtitled. B&W; 81m. **DIR:** Roberto Rossellini. **CAST:** Ingrid Bergman, Mario Vitale. **1950**

STROSZEK ★★★★ Werner Herzog's hilarious, poignant vision of three misfits—a drunk, a soulful prostitute, and an eccentric old man—who leave Berlin and follow the American dream to rural Wisconsin. This funny, richly perceptive look at the American experience through the eyes of three German outcasts won international critical acclaim. In German with English subtitles. Not rated. 108m. **DIR:** Werner Herzog. **CAST:** Bruno S., Eva Mattes, Clemens Scheitz. **1977**

STUDENT OF PRAGUE ★★★★ One of the most important films in silent German Expressionist cinema. The film is based on the myths of the Doppelgänger and Faust legends. Brilliantly photographed. Silent with English titles. B&W; 45m. **DIR:** Henrik Galeen. **CAST:** Conrad Veidt, Werner Krauss. **1926**

SUBWAY ★★ The stunning Isabelle Adjani plays a young wife who becomes involved with a streetwise rogue played by Christopher Lambert. The plot is not very clear and the bad jokes don't help. Fast-paced action scenes keep the film interesting, but they all lead nowhere. In French with English subtitles. Rated R for profanity and violence. 110m. **DIR:** Luc Besson. **CAST:** Isabelle Adjani, Christopher Lambert, Richard Bohringer. **1985**

SUBWAY TO THE STARS ★★★ A near triumph of style over substance by a gifted Brazilian filmmaker. A musician searching for his girlfriend is guided through a nightmarish, Dante's Inferno-like labyrinth of Rio de Janeiro nightlife. Fascinating but overlong. 103m. **DIR:** Carlos Diegues. **CAST:** Guilherme Fontes. **1987**

SUGARBABY ★★★½ In this decidedly offbeat comedy-drama from West German filmmaker Percy Adlon, an overweight morgue attendant (Marianne Sägebrecht) finds new meaning in her life when she falls in love with a subway driver. In German with English subtitles. Unrated; the film has nudity. 86m. **DIR:** Percy Adlon. **CAST:** Marianne Sägebrecht. **1986**

SUGARCANE ALLEY ★★★★★ Set in Martinique of the 1930s, this superb French import examines the lives led by black sugarcane plantation workers. Specifically, it focuses on the hopes and dreams of José (Garry Cadenat), an 11-year-old orphan with a brilliant mind, which just may be the key to his breaking the bonds of slavery. In French with English subtitles. Unrated, the film has some scenes of violence. 100m. **DIR:** Euzhan Palcy. **CAST:** Garry Cadenat, Darling Legitimus. **1983**

SUMMER ★★★★ Eric Rohmer's fifth of his six-part *Comedies and Proverbs* is the slight but emotionally resonant tale of Delphine (Marie Riviere), a Paris secretary whose vacation plans are suddenly ruined. Like the previous films in the series, *Summer* requires a commitment on the part of the viewer. Ultimately, the story touches your heart. In French with English subtitles. Rated R for nudity and profanity. 98m. **DIR:** Eric Rohmer. **CAST:** Marie Riviere, Lisa Heredia, Beatrice Romand. **1986**

SUMMER INTERLUDE ★★★½ An aging ballerina recalls a lost love from her youth and she learns through her newly reawakened memories to cope successfully with her present life. Perhaps Ingmar Bergman's first major film, and one of his most beautifully lyric. In Swedish with English subtitles. B&W; 90m. **DIR:** Ingmar Bergman. **CAST:** May Britt. **1950**

SUMMER NIGHT ★★★ The full title is *Summer Night, with Greek Profile, Almond Eyes and Scent of Basil*, and it's a semisequel-reprise of Wertmuller's *Swept Away...*, with Mariangela Melato in a similar role as a rich industrialist who captures a terrorist and holds him prisoner on a secluded island. Wertmuller fans will be disappointed; it covers nothing she hasn't done better before. Nonfans with lower expectations can enjoy it. In Italian with English subtitles. Rated R for nudity and sexual situations. 94m. **DIR:** Lina Wertmuller. **CAST:** Mariangela Melato, Michele Placido. **1987**

SUMMER VACATION: 1999 🦃 Pubescent awakenings, hormones, homicide, and acting so inept there should be some kind of penalty to prevent it. In Japanese with English subtitles. Unrated. 90m. **DIR:** Shusuke Kaneko. **CAST:** Eri Miyagian. **1988**

SUNDAY IN THE COUNTRY, A ★★★★ Filmed like an Impressionist painting, this is a romantic look at French family life in pre-World War II France. Bertrand Tavernier won the best-director prize at the 1984 Cannes Film Festival for this delightful drama. In French with English subtitles. Rated G. 94m. **DIR:** Bertrand Tavernier. **CAST:** Louis Ducreux, Michel Aumont, Sabine Azema. **1984**

SUNDAYS AND CYBÈLE ★★★★ A shell-shocked soldier, who feels responsible for the death of a young girl in the war, seeks redemption through a friendship with a 12-year-old orphan. But he fails to see the suspicion with which the authorities view their relationship. Superb acting and direction mark this Oscar winner for best foreign film. In French with English subtitles. B&W; 110m. **DIR:** Serge Bourguignon. **CAST:** Hardy Krüger, Patricia Gozzi. **1962**

SUNDAY'S CHILDREN ★★★★★ Though Ingmar Bergman retired from film directing, he's continued to write beautiful scripts, usually exploring aspects of his childhood or the lives of his parents. This is a gem, entrusted into the hands of his son, director Daniel Bergman, and tells of the summer of Ingmar's eighth year, when he came to know his minister father. The film is full of the warmth, the moments of fear, the mystical and the mysterious, and is a true "Bergman film" in every way. In Swedish with English subtitles. 117m. **DIR:** Daniel Bergman. **CAST:** Thommy Berggren, Lena Endre, Henrik Linnros. **1993**

SUSANNA ★★ This lurid soap opera from Luis Buñuel concerns a voluptuous young girl who escapes from a reformatory and hides out with a plantation family. Unfortunately, this movie lacks Buñuel's comic surreal touch in exploiting his characters' obsessions. In Spanish with English subtitles. Not rated. B&W; 82m. **DIR:** Luis Buñuel. **CAST:** Rosita Quintana, Fernando Soler. **1951**

SUSPENDED ★★★½ Falsely accused and sentenced to death in Stalinist Poland, an ex-army officer escapes from prison and is hidden by a woman he met during the war. Their underground relationship becomes a metaphor for political repression in this provocative drama. In Polish with English subtitles. Not rated. 92m. **DIR:** Waldemar Kyzystek. **CAST:** Krystyna Janda, Jerzy Radziwilowicz. **1986**

SWANN IN LOVE ★★★★ Slow-moving but fascinating film portrait of a Jewish aristocrat (Jeremy Irons) totally consumed by his romantic and sexual obsession with an ambitious French courtesan (Ornella Muti). It's definitely not for all tastes. However, those who can remember the overwhelming ache of first love may find it worth watching. In French with English subtitles. Rated R for nudity and suggested sex. 110m. **DIR:** Volker Schlondörff. **CAST:** Jeremy Irons, Ornella Muti, Alain Delon, Fanny Ardant, Marie-Christine Barrault. **1985**

SWEET MOVIE 🦃 Incoherent, surreal comedy centers around a wealthy South African mining tycoon who purchases a virgin bride, then continues to exploit her sexually. In English and French with English subtitles. Not rated, but contains sexually explicit material. 97m. **DIR:** Dusan Makavejev. **CAST:** Carole Laure, Pierre Clementi, Sami Frey. **1974**

SWEPT AWAY ★★★½ The full title is *Swept Away by an Unusual Destiny in the Blue Sea in August*, and what this Italian import addresses is a condescending, chic goddess who gets hers on a deserted island. In Italian with English subtitles. Rated R. 116m. **DIR:** Lina Wertmuller. **CAST:** Giancarlo Giannini, Mariangela Melato. **1975**

SWIMMING POOL, THE 🦃 This slow-moving French film features Alain Delon, Romy Schneider, and Maurice Ronet in a love triangle that leads to homicide. Dubbed into English. Unrated, but contains nudity. 85m. **DIR:** Jacques Deray. **CAST:** Alain Delon, Romy Schneider, Maurice Ronet, Jane Birkin. **1970**

SWORD OF DOOM ★★★ Tatsuya Nakadai gives a fascinating performance as a brutal samurai, whose need to kill alienates even his once-devoted father. Several stories are interwoven in this film, but, suprisingly, at least two are left unresolved. This will make it disappointing—and confusing—for all but the most devoted fans of Japanese action movies. In Japanese with English subtitles. 122m. **DIR:** Kihachi Okamoto. **CAST:** Tatsuya Nakadai, Toshiro Mifune. **1967**

SYLVIA AND THE PHANTOM ★★★★ A delightful story concerning ghosts and the fantasies of a young lady living with her family in a castle. As the story begins, we meet Sylvia on the eve of her sixteenth birthday and find that she fantasizes about the portrait of her grandmother's lover and the rumors that he haunts the castle. In French with English subtitles. 97m. **DIR:** Claude Autant-Lara. **CAST:** Odette Joyeux, François Perier, Julien Carette. **1950**

TALE OF SPRINGTIME, A ★★★ A French schoolteacher is befriended by a young woman. She then becomes entangled in touchy family affairs when she's romantically paired with the girl's father. Eric Rohmer's passion for intelligent, witty discourse and subtle tension continues in a story he says "deals less with what people do than with what is going on in their minds while they are doing it." This is the third installment in his sophisticated *Tales of the Four Seasons* film series. In French with English subtitles. Rated PG. 107m. **DIR:** Eric Rohmer. **CAST:** Anne Teyssedre, Florence Darel, Hugues Quester. **1992**

TALES OF PARIS ★★½ Lightweight omnibus film featuring four stories of young women and their romantic escapades in Paris. The last segment is the most memorable, if only for a chance to see 19-year-old Catherine Deneuve in one of her first films. B&W; 85m. **DIR:** Marc Allegret, Jacques Poitrenaud, Michel Boisrone, Claude Barma. **CAST:** Dany Saval, Dany Robin, Jean Poiret, Catherine Deneuve, Johnny Hallyday. **1962**

TALL BLOND MAN WITH ONE BLACK SHOE, THE ★★★★ If you're looking for an entertaining, easy-to-watch comedy, this is one of the best. Pierre Richard plays the bumbling blond man to hilarious perfection, especially when it comes to physical comedy. The story involves spies, murder, a mysterious sexy woman, and plenty of action. Highly recommended, but try to see the original version, with subtitles, not the dubbed version. Rated PG. 90m. **DIR:** Yves Robert. **CAST:** Pierre Richard, Bernard Blier, Mireille Darc. **1972**

TAMPOPO ★★★★ This Japanese spoof of the Italian spaghetti Western (which was, in turn, a spin-off of the samurai movie) shows a female diner owner (Nobuko Miyamoto) learning how to make perfect noodles. As silly as it sounds, this is a wonderful movie full of surprises. In Japanese with English subtitles. Unrated but with nudity and brief violence. 95m. **DIR:** Juzo Itami. **CAST:** Nobuko Miyamoto. **1987**

TANGO BAR ★★★ Part musical, part documentary, part romantic-triangle love story, this film employs all those elements to detail the historical and cultural importance of the tango. Raul Julia and Ruben Juarez play two tango performers who are reunited. In Spanish with English subtitles. 90m. **DIR:** Marcos Zurinaga. **CAST:** Raul Julia, Valeria Lynch, Ruben Juarez. **1988**

TATIE DANIELLE ★★★½ While in the process of destroying the lives and home of her great-nephew and his sweet-natured wife, a cranky old lady manages to make them look like the culprits. This black comedy is exceedingly dark, and, therefore, not for all tastes. In French with English subtitles. Unrated; the film has profanity and nudity. 107m. **DIR:** Étienne Chatiliez. **CAST:** Tsilla Chelton, Catherine Jacob, Isabelle Nanty, Neige Dolsky, Eric Prat. **1991**

TAXI BLUES ★★★★½ This Russian film details the volatile love-hate relationship between a fiercely independent, undisciplined Jewish jazz artist and a stern, muscular, narrow-minded cabdriver. It's as aggressive and stimulating as the hard-driving sax solos that permeate the sound track. In Russian with English subtitles. Unrated. 100m. **DIR:** Pavel Lounguine. **CAST:** Piotr Zaitchenko, Piotr Mamonov. **1991**

TAXI ZUM KLO (TAXI TO THE TOILET) ★★★½ Sexually explicit film by and about Frank Ripploh, a restless and promiscuous gay elementary schoolteacher in Berlin. Ripploh pulls absolutely no punches in his portrait of his sexual encounters, and that should be a fair warning. Get through the sex, however, and the humor will seem refreshing compared to a lot of other films that try to capture gay life. In German with English subtitles. Not rated, but contains profanity and frank sexual content. 92m. **DIR:** Frank Ripploh. **CAST:** Frank Ripploh, Bernd Broaderup. **1981**

TAXING WOMAN, A ★★★ After exposing the world to the inner workings of the noodle business in *Tampopo*, director Juzo Itami focused on Japan's nasty Internal Revenue Service. Nobuko Miyamoto plays a hard-line tax inspector. Nicely offbeat. In Japanese with English subtitles. Unrated, with adult themes. 118m. **DIR:** Juzo Itami. **CAST:** Nobuko Miyamoto, Tsutomu Yamazaki. **1988**

TAXING WOMAN'S RETURN, A ★★★ In this follow-up to his 1987 hit, director Juzo Itami scores another high. This time the diligent heroine, tax inspector Nobuko Miyamoto, tackles a corrupt fundamentalist religious order. In Japanese with English subtitles. Rated R for nudity and violence. 127m. **DIR:** Juzo Itami. **CAST:** Nobuko Miyamoto. **1988**

TCHAO PANTIN ★★★★½ Violent *film noir* about an ex-cop suffering from alienation as a result of the tragic death of his son from narcotics. He befriends a young stranger who deals heroin. The two form an odd relationship that eventually leads to disaster. This movie swept the French Oscars. In French with English subtitles. 94m. **DIR:** Claude Berri. **CAST:** Coluche, Richard Anconina, Philippe Léotard. **1985**

TEN LITTLE GALL FORCE/SCRAMBLE WARS ★★★ This animated double feature is a sound spoof of the genre in a "superdeformed" format (caricatures of animated characters). The first feature includes animated "outtakes" of *Gall Force* and a live-action short about the story's creator Shonora Kenichi. In the second, characters from three different animation stories compete in a contest reminiscent of *Cannonball Run*. In Japanese with English subtitles. Not rated; contains nudity and violence. 67m. **DIR:** Yatagai Kenichi, Fukushima Hiroyuki. **1988**

TENDRES COUSINES ★★ Okay soft-core sex comedy about two pubescent cousins. Directed by renowned photographer, David Hamilton. In French with English subtitles. Rated R. 90m. **DIR:** David Hamilton. **CAST:** Thierry Tevini, Anja Shute. **1980**

TEOREMA ★★★ The title translates as *Theorem*, which indicates the mathematical style of this attack on bourgeois values. A handsome young man enters the home of a middle-class family, whose members are unable to cope with life after he leaves. In Italian with English subtitles. Unrated, but contains strong sexual content. 93m. **DIR:** Pier Paolo Pasolini. **CAST:** Terence Stamp, Silvana Mangano, Massimo Girotti. **1968**

TESTAMENT OF ORPHEUS, THE ★★★ Jean Cocteau's last film, it marks the final installment of an Orpheus Trilogy, began with *The Blood of the Poet* (1930) and continued with *Orpheus* (1949). While its nonlinear sequence of events is quite incomprehensible, the fifteen episodes are generally concerned with an eighteenth-century poet (Jean Cocteau) who dies and is reborn into modern times. In French with English subtitles. 80m. **DIR:** Jean Cocteau. **CAST:** Jean Cocteau, Jean Marais. **1959**

TETSUO: THE IRON MAN ★★★ There's hardly any story in this hyperkinetic cult hit about an office worker mutating into a part-human, part-metal being. Grotesque makeup, stop-action animation, and time-lapse photography make this the perfect visual equivalent of the industrial-music soundtrack. In Japanese with English subtitles. B&W; 67m. **DIR:** Shinya Tsukamoto. **CAST:** Tomorrow Taguchi, Kei Fujiwara. **1989**

THAT MAN FROM RIO ★★★★ This fast-moving comedy-action-thriller about a stolen artifact—with Jean-Paul Belmondo as a cross between James Bond and Indiana Jones—never lets up. In French with English subtitles. 115m. **DIR:** Philippe De Broca. **CAST:** Jean-Paul Belmondo, Françoise Dorleac, Simone Renant, Adolfo Celi. **1964**

THAT OBSCURE OBJECT OF DESIRE ★★★★½ Luis Buñuel's last film cunningly combines erotic teasing, wit, and social comment. Mathieu (Fernando Rey) is a 50-year-old man who falls hopelessly in love with a young woman. Buñuel, a master of surrealism, tantalizes the viewer by casting two actresses to play the heroine and a third actress to do the voice of both. Rated R for profanity and nudity. 100m. **DIR:** Luis Buñuel. **CAST:** Fernando Rey, Carole Bouquet, Angela Molina. **1977**

THERESE ★★★★½ French director Alain Cavalier's breathtakingly beautiful *Therese* is the story of St. Theresa of Lisieux, who entered a Carmelite nunnery in the late nineteenth century at the age of 15 and lived there for eight years until she died of tuberculosis. She was declared a saint by Pope Pius XI in 1925, twenty-eight years after her death. In French with English subtitles. 90m.

DIR: Alain Cavalier. **CAST:** Catherine Mouchet, Helene Alexandridis. **1986**

THERESE AND ISABELLE ★★ Two French schoolgirls keep their growing sexual attraction for each other a secret until they take a holiday together. Considered daring at the time of its release. In French with English subtitles. Unrated, but this might earn an R rating today because of nudity and story content. 102m. **DIR:** Radley Metzger. **CAST:** Essy Persson, Anna Gael, Barbara Laage, Anne Vernon. **1968**

THIRD SOLUTION, THE 🦃 Don't let the (usually) talented cast sucker you into sampling this laughably convoluted, poorly dubbed Italian political melodrama. Rated R for violence and brief nudity. 113m. **DIR:** Pasquale Squiteri. **CAST:** F. Murray Abraham, Treat Williams, Danny Aiello, Rita Rusic. **1989**

38 VIENNA BEFORE THE FALL ★★★ The romance between a Jewish theatrical producer and a beautiful Aryan woman becomes threatened by the prejudicial climate of pre-Nazi Germany. In German with English subtitles. Rated R for nudity, profanity, and violence. 97m. **DIR:** Wolfgang Gluck. **CAST:** Tobias Engel, Sunnyi Melles. **1989**

36 FILLETTE ★★★ A sexually charged comedy-drama from France, about a 14-year-old girl and her frustrated efforts to cast off her virginity. Delphine Zentout is most impressive as the girl. The title is a reference to a French adolescent dress size. In French with English subtitles. 92m. **DIR:** Catherine Breillat. **CAST:** Delphine Zentout, Etienne Chicot. **1988**

THIS MAN MUST DIE ★★★★ Claude Chabrol pays homage to Alfred Hitchcock with this outstanding thriller about a man who sets out to find the hit-and-run driver responsible for the death of his son. Complications ensue as the father encounters the murderer's sister, whom he seduces. A riveting shocker with a startling climax. Dubbed into English. 112m. **DIR:** Claude Chabrol. **CAST:** Michel Duchaussoy, Jean Yanne, Caroline Cellier. **1970**

THIS SPECIAL FRIENDSHIP ★★½ At a boys' boarding school, a relationship between an older student and a younger, innocent boy is broken up by teachers. Once-controversial story of homoeroticism now seems merely sentimental and self-consciously sensitive. In French with English subtitles. B&W; 105m. **DIR:** Jean Delannoy. **CAST:** Francis Lacombrade, Didier Haudepin, Michel Bouquet. **1964**

THOMAS GRAAL'S BEST CHILD ★★★★ The best of the Thomas Graal films. Newlyweds Victor Sjöström and Karin Molander bicker about the best ways to rear their child. Among the many subjects satirized is the so-called liberated woman of contemporary Sweden. Silent. B&W; 94m. **DIR:** Mauritz Stiller. **CAST:** Victor Sjöström, Karin Molander. **1918**

THOMAS GRAAL'S BEST FILM ★★★★ One of a popular series of Thomas Graal films, all starring Sjöström and his wife. They all presented satiric jabs at contemporary life, much in the same way as today's television sitcoms do. In this one Graal is a screenwriter distracted by a romance with a rich man's daughter. Sweden. Silent. B&W; 67m. **DIR:** Mauritz Stiller. **CAST:** Victor Sjöström, Karin Molander. **1917**

THREE BROTHERS ★★★★★ Francesco Rosi directed this thoughtful, emotionally powerful movie that details the effect of a mother's recent death on her family. A drama with great insight and compassion. In Italian with English subtitles. Unrated; the film has a few scenes of violence. 113m. **DIR:** Francesco Rosi. **CAST:** Philippe Noiret, Michele Placido, Vittorio Mezzogiorno. **1980**

317TH PLATOON, THE ★★★ Near the end of the French involvement in Vietnam, a group of soldiers tries to make its way back to its squadron after a failed offensive. Filmed in Cambodia, this is an eerie precursor to recent American films about Vietnam. In French with English subtitles. 100m. **DIR:** Pierre Schoendoerffer. **CAST:** Jacques Perrin, Bruno Cremer. **1965**

THREE MEN AND A CRADLE ★★★★ In this sweet-natured character study from France, three high-living bachelors become the guardians of a baby girl. In addition to turning their life-styles inside out, she forces them to confront their values—with heartwarming results. Rated PG for profanity and nudity. In French with English subtitles. 105m. **DIR:** Coline Serreau. **CAST:** Roland Giraud, Michel Boujenah, André Dussolier. **1985**

THREE STRANGE LOVES ★★½ Three former ballerinas struggle to find happiness in their private lives. Ingmar Bergman's gloomy style is the perfect backdrop for the disappointment and heartache the women face. In Swedish with subtitles that flicker by at a pace suitable only for a speed reader. B&W; 84m. **DIR:** Ingmar Bergman. **CAST:** Eva Henning, Birger Malmsten. **1949**

THREEPENNY OPERA, THE ★★★★ Classic gangster musical features mob leader Mack the Knife, his moll, and the hordes of the underworld. This Bertolt Brecht satire (with music by Kurt Weill), although not too popular with the Nazis or their predecessors, is always a favorite with the audience. B&W; 113m. **DIR:** G. W. Pabst. **CAST:** Rudolph Forster, Lotte Lenya, Reinhold Schunzel, Carola Neher. **1931**

THRONE OF BLOOD ★★★★★ Japanese director Akira Kurosawa's retelling of *Mac-*

beth may be the best film adaptation of Shakespeare ever made. Kurosawa uses the medium to present Shakespeare's themes in visual images. When Birnam Wood literally comes to Dunsinane, it is a truly great moment you would have believed could only happen in the limitless landscapes of a dream. In Japanese with English subtitles. B&W; 105m. **DIR:** Akira Kurosawa. **CAST:** Toshiro Mifune, Minoru Chiaki, Takashi Shimura. **1957**

THROUGH A GLASS DARKLY ★★ Two siblings compete for their father's love. The father, who happens to be a famous writer, sits back and observes. Ingmar Bergman goes overboard this time with endless monologues on God and love. In Swedish with English subtitles, this film is unrated but contains mature themes. B&W; 90m. **DIR:** Ingmar Bergman. **CAST:** Harriet Andersson, Gunnar Björnstrand, Max von Sydow. **1961**

TIE ME UP! TIE ME DOWN! ★★★½ From Spain's hot cult director Pedro Almodóvar, concerning the unorthodox romance between a soft-core porno star named Marina (Victoria Abril) and a recently released psychiatric patient named Ricky (Antonio Banderas.) This film exists in both R and unrated versions, due to profanity and explicit sexual content. In Spanish with English subtitles. 105m. **DIR:** Pedro Almodóvar. **CAST:** Victoria Abril, Antonio Banderas. **1990**

TIGER AND THE PUSSYCAT, THE ★★½ Male menopause comedy-drama of middle-aged Vittorio Gassman entranced with Ann-Margret, an American student living and loving in Italy. Pretty dated; the stars make it bearable. In English. Unrated, with some innocuous sex talk. 105m. **DIR:** Dino Risi. **CAST:** Ann-Margret, Vittorio Gassman, Eleanor Parker. **1967**

TILL MARRIAGE DO US PART ★★ Although a slight Italian sex comedy, its star, Laura Antonelli, is as delicious as ever. It's a treat for her fans only. Rated R. 97m. **DIR:** Luigi Comencini. **CAST:** Laura Antonelli. **1974**

TIME OF THE GYPSIES ★★★★ A young psychic gypsy boy learns the meaning of life the hard way. Absorbing character study, brilliantly photographed. The film weaves magical realism, visual humor, and pathos. A must-see! In Yugoslavian with English subtitles. Rated R. 136m. **DIR:** Emir Kusturica. **CAST:** Igraju, Davor Dujmovic, Bora Todorovic. **1989**

TIME OUT FOR LOVE ★★ Romantic roundelay with Jean Seberg as an American girl who gets caught in the middle of a failed love affair between a race driver and a suicidal fashion designer. In French with English subtitles. 93m. **DIR:** Jean Valère. **CAST:** Jean Seberg, Micheline Presle. **1961**

TIME STANDS STILL ★★½ This Hungarian export dwells so much on the "art for art's sake" credo that it nearly destroys some of the life the film tries to depict. *Time Stands Still* is about restless youths at the threshold of adulthood in Hungary. The film is presented in the original language with subtitles. Not rated, but the equivalent of an R for nudity and language. 99m. **DIR:** Peter Gothar. **CAST:** Ben Barenholtz, Albert Schwartz. **1982**

TIMES TO COME ★★★ When an innocent man is accidentally shot during a demonstration, this act hurls him into a nightmarish world where he must struggle to survive. A futuristic city plagued with political unrest and violence provides the backdrop for this baffling science-fiction thriller. In Spanish with English subtitles. Unrated; the film has profanity, nudity, and violence. 98m. **DIR:** Gustavo Mosquera. **CAST:** Hugo Soto, Juan Leyrado. **1988**

TIN DRUM, THE ★★★★½ Günter Grass's bizarre tale of 3-year-old Oskar, who stops growing as the Nazis rise to power in Germany. Oskar expresses his outrage by banging on a tin drum. This unique film has a disturbing dreamlike quality, while its visuals are alternately startling and haunting. *The Tin Drum* won an Academy Award for best foreign film. In German, with English subtitles. Rated R for nudity and gore. 142m. **DIR:** Volker Schlondörff. **CAST:** David Bennent, Mario Adorf, Angela Winkler, Daniel Olbrychski. **1979**

TITO AND ME ★★★★ In 1954 Yugoslavia, Zoran, a 10-year-old underachiever tries to impress a girl and finds himself on a state-sponsored hike through the homeland of President Tito. Political satire shares the screen with broad comedy, as Zoran's extended family lives in an apartment that's far too small for them. In Croatian with English subtitles. Unrated; contains no objectionable material. 104m. **DIR:** Goran Markovic. **CAST:** Dimitrie Vojnov, Lazar Ristovski. **1992**

TO FORGET VENICE ★★★★ Character-driven drama puts two pairs of gay lovers (one male, one female) in a quiet country house for a weekend. Prompted by the death of the woman who raised three of them, they are forced to come to grips with their lives. Beautifully acted. Dubbed in English. 110m. **DIR:** Franco Brusati. **CAST:** Erland Josephson, Mariangela Melato, Eleonora Giorgi, David Pontremoli. **1979**

TOKYO DECADENCE ★★★½ Decadent study of a 22-year-old Tokyo call girl who longs for a better life but must perform kinky sex in order to survive. Ali (Miho Nikhaido) sees her life as a steady stream of deviate johns. Then she meets a dominatrix who opens the door to her dreams. The degradation Ali is forced to endure makes for kinky viewing. In Japanese with English subtitles. Rated NC-17 for strong sexual content. 92m. **DIR:** Ryu Murakami. **CAST:** Miho Nikhaido, Sayoko Amano, Chie Sema. **1991**

TOKYO-GA ★★★ German filmmaker Wim Wenders presents an absorbing film diary of his visit to Japan, where he attempts to define his relationship to a culture and city he knows only through the cinematic work of Yasujiro Ozu, the director of *Tokyo Story*. A great introspective account of Ozu's career is much of the film's focus. In Japanese with English subtitles. 92m. **DIR:** Wim Wenders. **CAST:** Chishu Ryu, Yuharu Atsuta, Werner Herzog. **1983**

TOKYO STORY ★★★★★ Yasujiro Ozu's overpowering masterpiece is a deeply felt human drama about an elderly couple who travel to Tokyo, where they are unenthusiastically received by their grown-up children. Outstanding black-and-white cinematography brilliantly captures the landscape of Tokyo. In Japanese with English subtitles. B&W; 139m. **DIR:** Yasujiro Ozu. **CAST:** Chishu Ryu, Chiyeko Higashiyama. **1953**

TONI ★★★★ Of the Italian neorealists, only Luchino Visconti is known to have been aware of this film before 1950, but in story, style, and mood, *Toni* anticipates the methods of the future master postwar directors. A love quadrangle, a murder, a trial, an execution, a confession—these are the everyday elements director Jean Renoir chose to show as objectively as possible. No studio sets were used, and many citizens of the town where *Toni* was shot filled out the cast. Renoir was proud of his film (something of an experiment), and it holds up well. In French with English subtitles. B&W; 90m. **DIR:** Jean Renoir. **CAST:** Charles Blavette, Max Dalban. **1934**

TONIO KROGER ★★ This adaptation of Thomas Mann's semiautobiographical novel, about a young writer wandering Europe while trying to choose between bourgeois comfort and the excitement of the unchained life, never comes alive on screen. In German with English subtitles. 92m. **DIR:** Rolf Thiele. **CAST:** Jean-Claude Brialy, Najda Tiller, Werner Heinz, Gert Fröbe. **1965**

TOO BEAUTIFUL FOR YOU ★★★★½ Bertrand Blier's subtle, surprising French comedy about an offbeat romantic triangle. Gérard Depardieu stars as a married automobile dealer who falls for the rather dowdy secretary who works in his office. In French with English subtitles. Rated R for profanity. 91m. **DIR:** Bertrand Blier. **CAST:** Gérard Depardieu, Carole Bouquet, Josiane Balasko. **1990**

TOO SHY TO TRY ★★★ Director Pierre Richard stars in this romantic comedy about a man who takes a crash course in romance after meeting the girl of his dreams. Some genuinely funny moments. In French with English subtitles. Not rated, but contains nudity. 89m. **DIR:** Pierre Richard. **CAST:** Pierre Richard, Aldo Maccioni, Jacques François. **1982**

TOPAZE (1951) ★★★★ Another version of Marcel Pagnol's perennially popular satirical play (it was also adapted as a vehicle for John Barrymore and Peter Sellers) about a lowly schoolteacher who is dismissed from his job but finds success in the business world. The best and most faithful adaptation of the play makes a fine showcase for French-comedian Fernandel. In French with English subtitles. Not rated. B&W; 135m. **DIR:** Marcel Pagnol. **CAST:** Fernandel, Marcel Vallee, Jacqueline Pagnol. **1951**

TOPSY TURVY ★★ A conservative young man finds his world turned topsy-turvy when a swinging neighbor girl takes him on vacation. This European sex comedy, dubbed into English is mediocre. 90m. **DIR:** Edward Fleming. **CAST:** Lisbet Dahl, Ebbe Rode. **1984**

TOTO THE HERO ★★★★ In Belgian director Jaco Van Dormael's inventive black comedy, a cranky old man's reveries are made to seem the universal story of modern man. Toto's reminiscences are colored by his perspective, which, as the story unfolds, is proven to be somewhat askew. Rated PG-13 for nudity and violence. 90m. **DIR:** Jaco Van Dormael. **CAST:** Michel Bouquet, Mireille Perrier. **1991**

TOUS LES MATINS DU MONDE ★★★ Music for its own sake is the prevailing metaphor in Alain Corneau's sumptuously photographed biography of little-known seventeenth-century viol player and composer Monsieur de Sainte Colombe (Jean-Pierre Marielle, properly dour). Although talented, Sainte Colombe regarded public performance as an act which corrupted music's purity. Music lovers will be awed by the richly textured sound track, but mainstream viewers are apt to nod off during this *extremely* slow drama. Unrated, with brief nudity and simulated sex. 114m. **DIR:** Alain Corneau. **CAST:** Jean-Pierre Marielle, Gérard Depardieu, Anne Brochet, Guillaume Depardieu, Caroline Sihol, Carole Richert. **1993**

TOUTE UNE NUIT ★★ Overly fragmented movie about the various stages and states of relationships. The end product is ultimately creatively arid. Not one of Akerman's finer efforts. In French with English subtitles. Rated R for nudity. 90m. **DIR:** Chantal Akerman. **CAST:** Aurore Clement, Tcheky Karyo. **1983**

TRAGEDY OF A RIDICULOUS MAN ★★★½ A wealthy businessman struggles with the most difficult decision of his life: Should he sell his beloved cheese factory to raise the ransom money for his kidnapped son, or should he assume that his son has already been murdered? Ugo Tognazzi won the Cannes best-actor award for his role as the distraught father. In Italian with English subtitles. Unrated, but contains nudity and profanity. 117m. **DIR:** Bernardo Bertolucci. **CAST:** Ugo Tognazzi, Anouk Aimée, Laura Morante, Victor Cavallo. **1981**

TREASURE OF ARNE ★★ Swedish master Mauritz Stiller forsook his flair for comedy and wrought this grim tale of crime, guilt, and sacrifice—famous in its day but unrelievedly tedious today. Based on Selma Lagerlöf's tale about escaped prisoners who steal a treasure with a curse on it. Silent. B&W; 100m. **DIR:** Mauritz Stiller. **CAST:** Richard Lund, Mary Johnson, Hjalmar Selander. **1919**

TREE OF THE WOODEN CLOGS, THE ★★★★★ Stunning, epic masterpiece about the hardships in the life of a community of peasants in northern Italy, just before the turn of the century. In Italian with English subtitles. Not rated. 185m. **DIR:** Ermanno Olmi. **CAST:** Luigi Ornaghi, Francesca Moriggi, Omar Brignoli. **1978**

TRISTANA ★★★★ Luis Buñuel's hilarious, surreal drama about a young woman who becomes a victim of her own captivating beauty as she becomes the object of desire between two men. The film is a brilliant examination of moral decay through the dispassionate eye of Luis Buñuel. In Spanish with English subtitles. Not rated. 98m. **DIR:** Luis Buñuel. **CAST:** Catherine Deneuve, Fernando Rey, Franco Nero. **1970**

TURKISH DELIGHT ★★★½ Those already familiar with the work of Dutch director Paul Verhoeven (*Spetters, The 4th Man*) will be the most appreciative audience for this drama about a bohemian artist and his wife. Others may be put off by the graphic sexuality and crude behavior. Dubbed in English. 96m. **DIR:** Paul Verhoeven. **CAST:** Rutger Hauer, Monique van de Ven. **1974**

25, FIREMEN'S STREET ★★★★ The troubled history of post–World War II Hungary is recounted in the memories of people living in an old house slated for demolition. Political upheavals take on personal resonance in this innovative, fascinating film. In Hungarian with English subtitles. Unrated. 93m. **DIR:** Istvan Szabo. **CAST:** Rita Bekes. **1973**

TWENTY-FOUR EYES ★★★½ Beauty and innocence are lost as war and progress intrude upon a rural village in this poignant, touching drama. The story concerns a progressive schoolteacher from Tokyo who changes the lives of students in an elementary school on a remote island off Japan in the late 1920s. In Japanese with English subtitles. B&W; 158m. **DIR:** Teinosuke Kinugasa. **CAST:** Keisuke Kinoshita, Chishu Ryu. **1954**

TWIST AND SHOUT ★★★★½ An exceptional coming-of-age story about two friends, a drummer with a pseudo-Beatles group, and a quiet sort with severe problems at home, circa 1964. It is a true-to-life movie that will leave no viewer unmoved. In Danish with English subtitles. Unrated; the film has profanity, nudity, and suggested sex. 99m. **DIR:** Bille August. **CAST:** Adam Tonsberg, Lars Simonsen. **1986**

TWO DAUGHTERS ★★★★ Satyajit Ray's beautiful two-part film is based on tales by Nobel Prize–winning author Rabindranath Tagore. With Chekhovian delicacy and pathos, Ray explores the hopes and disappointments of two young women experiencing first love. Ray's stories transcend the surface of Indian culture while creating a universally felt character study. In Bengali with English subtitles. B&W; 114m. **DIR:** Satyajit Ray. **CAST:** Anil Chatterjee, Chandana Bannerjee, Soumitra Chatterjee. **1961**

TWO ENGLISH GIRLS ★★★★½ Twenty-two minutes were recently added to this very civilized and rewarding film. Set in pre–World War I Europe and based on the Henri-Pierre Roché novel (his only other being *Jules et Jim,* the modern flip side of the arrangement here), Truffaut's work has Frenchman Léaud the object of two English sisters' desire. In French with English subtitles. 130m. **DIR:** François Truffaut. **CAST:** Jean-Pierre Léaud, Kiki Markham, Stacey Tendeter. **1972**

TWO MEN AND A WARDROBE ★★★½ Roman Polanski's award-winning short made while he was a student at the Polish Film Institute is a bitter parable blending slapstick and the absurd. Two men emerge from the sea sporting a single wardrobe. Also included in the package is a second short, *The Fat and the Lean,* an outrageously funny attack on governmental tyranny. Silent. B&W; 35m. **DIR:** Roman Polanski. **CAST:** Henlyk Kluga, Jakub Goldberg. **1958**

TWO OF US, THE ★★★½ This story of generational and religious differences joins an 8-year-old Jewish boy (Alain Cohen) and an irascible Catholic grandpa (Michel Simon). The boy is fleeing Nazi-occupied France in 1944 and comes to live with the anti-Semitic old man who is a family friend's relative. Beautifully acted, this is a different kind of movie for parents to enjoy with their older children. In French with English subtitles. 86m. **DIR:** Claude Berri. **CAST:** Alain Cohen, Michel Simon. **1968**

TWO WOMEN ★★★★ In the performance that won her an Oscar, Sophia Loren is a widow who, with her 13-year-old daughter, escapes war-torn Rome, eventually finding solace in her native village. This uncompromising drama was a Grand Prize winner at the Cannes Film Festival. In Italian with English subtitles. Not rated. 99m. **DIR:** Vittorio De Sica. **CAST:** Sophia Loren, Eleanora Brown, Jean-Paul Belmondo, Raf Vallone. **1960**

UBU AND THE GREAT GIDOUILLE ★★★½ Impressive animation feature by world-renowned animator Jan Lenica, loosely based on Alfred Jarry's bizarre play that recounts the grotesque adventures of Père Ubu, who with his ignorance and greed seizes the throne of Poland and tyrannizes the people. A masterpiece of animation and black humor. In French with English subtitles. Not rated. 80m. **DIR:** Jan Lenica. **1979**

UGETSU ★★★★½ Set in sixteenth-century Japan, this film follows the lives of two Japanese peasants as their quest for greed and ambition brings disaster upon their families. There is a fine blending of action and comedy in this ghostly tale. In Japanese with English subtitles. 94m. **DIR:** Kenji Mizoguchi. **CAST:** Machiko Kyo, Masayuki Mori. **1953**

UMBERTO D ★★★★★ *Umberto D* seems as poignant now as when it was initially released. Quite simply, the plot centers upon a retired civil servant trying to maintain some sort of dignity and life for himself and his dog on his meager government pension. The film is agonizingly candid. A Vittorio De Sica masterpiece. In Italian with English subtitles. B&W; 89m. **DIR:** Vittorio De Sica. **CAST:** Carlo Battisti, Maria Pia Casilio. **1955**

UMBRELLAS OF CHERBOURG, THE ★★★★ Simply the most romantic film to come from France in the 1960s. Catherine Deneuve made her first popular appearance, and we've been madly in love with her ever since. Simple story—boy meets girl—but played against a luxuriously photographed backdrop. Exquisite score from Michel Legrand. Watch this with somebody you love. 91m. **DIR:** Jacques Demy. **CAST:** Catherine Deneuve, Nino Castelnuovo, Marc Michel. **1964**

UN COEUR EN HIVER ★★★★½ The delicacy and detail with which the French view romantic relationships often make for intoxicating viewing, as amply evidenced by this superb study of heartbreak. Violin-maker Jean Autevil sets out to steal the affections of the luminous Emmanuelle Beart, a concert violinist, from his married partner (André Dussollier), thus setting in motion a tragic chain of events. Enhanced by the glorious music of Ravel's sonatas and trios. In French with English subtitles. Unrated, the film has profanity, suggested sex, and light violence. **DIR:** Claude Sautet. **CAST:** Daniel Auteuil, Emmanuelle Beart, André Dussolier, Elisabeth Bourgnine, Brigitte Catillon, Maurice Garrel, Myriam Boyer. **1993**

UN SINGE EN HIVER (A MONKEY IN WINTER) ★★½ Alcoholic Jean Gabin vows to swear off if he and his wife survive the bombing of their village during World War II. They do, and he does. Years pass. A young version of Gabin arrives and rekindles the older man's memories of drink and dreams. In French with English subtitles. Originally released in the U.S. as *A Monkey in Winter*. Marred by murky photography. B&W; 105m. **DIR:** Henri Verneuil. **CAST:** Jean Gabin, Jean-Paul Belmondo, Suzanne Flon, Paul Frankeur, Noel Roquevert. **1962**

UNDER THE ROOFS OF PARIS ★★★★ This simple Parisian love story of a street singer and a young girl is less important for its plot than for its style: at a time when most movies were overdosing on dialogue, director René Clair used music and other types of sound to advance his story. It is also, like most of Clair's films, a charming depiction of his home city. In French with English subtitles. B&W; 92m. **DIR:** René Clair. **CAST:** Albert Préjean, Pola Illery. **1929**

UNDER THE SUN OF SATAN ★★ Though well-acted and emotionally complex, this drama about a wavering French priest will only reach viewers willing to wade through the film's murky, slow-moving style. In French with English subtitles. Unrated. 97m. **DIR:** Maurice Pialat. **CAST:** Gérard Depardieu, Sandrine Bonnaire, Maurice Pialat. **1987**

UNE PARTIE DE PLAISIR ★★★ Life and art uncomfortably commingle in this loosely fictionalized look at the troubled marriage of Paul Gegauff, director Claude Chabrol's usual scriptwriter. Gegauff plays himself (opposite his real ex-wife)—one can only hope that the brutal behavior he displays here was exaggerated. (A few years later, he was murdered by his second wife.) Occasionally fascinating, it may leave the viewer feeling voyeuristic. In French with English subtitles. Not rated. 100m. **DIR:** Claude Chabrol. **CAST:** Paul Gegauff, Danielle Gegauff. **1975**

UNFINISHED PIECE FOR THE PLAYER PIANO, AN ★★★★ Based on the writing of Anton Chekhov, this film is alive with intimate character portraits. A group of aristocrats gather for an annual family reunion where they find their traditional values and way of life are slipping away, poisoned by their own excesses. Alexander Kalyagin delivers a fine performance as Misha, a man suddenly and painfully self-aware. In Russian with English subtitles. 100m. **DIR:** Nikita Mikhalkov. **CAST:** Alexander Kalyagin, Elena Soloyei, Yevgenta Clushenko, Oleg Tabakov. **1977**

URANUS ★★★★ Sumptuous character study of a group of villagers immediately following the Nazi occupation of France. Gérard Depardieu is sensational as Leopold, a scoundrel, lover, poet, and owner of a small bar. The town has been torn into three camps: those who joined the Nazis, those who joined the resistance, and those who just minded their own business. Now all three factions must live together. In French with English subtitles. Not rated, but contains nudity and violence. 100m. **DIR:** Claude Berri. **CAST:** Gérard Depardieu, Michel Blanc,

Jean-Pierre Marielle, Philippe Noiret, Michel Galabru. 1992

UROTSUKIDOJI: LEGEND OF THE OVERFIEND ★★★ An unbelievably violent and perverse animated Japanese feature based on *The Wandering Kid* comics and representative of the violent/erotic subgenre. Every three-thousand years the Overfiend returns to unite the three separate worlds of man, demon, and animal-man—but is the creature a healer or a destroyer? Dubbed in English. Rated NC-17; contains explicit sexual scenes and violence. 108m. An unrated director's cut is also available combined with *Urotsukidoji II* and runs 40 minutes longer. **DIR:** Hideki Takayama. 1989

UROTSUKIDOJI II: LEGEND OF THE DEMON WOMB ★★ Less interesting than the original, this animated sequel absolutely ignores the story line of *Legend of the Overfiend*. Now in the form of a mild-mannered college student, the Overfiend must deal with his beloved cousin, who has become the Evil King and is being manipulated by the crazed son of a Nazi scientist. Sound ridiculous? It is. Dubbed in English. Unrated; contains gratuitous violence and explicit sexual scenes. 88m. A director's cut of this film combines this with *Urotsukidoji: Legend of the Overfiend* and runs 40 extra minutes. **DIR:** Hideki Takayama. 1991

URUSEI YATSURA (TV SERIES) VOLS. 1–45 ★★★½ Japanese animation. Entertaining mixture of love triangles, humor, and science fiction. The main characters include teenage Romeo, Ataru Morobishi, his main girlfriend, Shinobu, and Lum, the alien princess who lives in Ataru's closet. In Japanese with English subtitles. 80m. **DIR:** Kazuo Yamazaki, Yuuji Moriyama. 1980–1982

URUSEI YATSURA: BEAUTIFUL DREAMER ★★★★ Japanese animation. This is the second movie from the *Urusei Yatsura* collection. Strong, constantly developing characterizations make these feature films consistently enjoyable and a delightful change from the giant robots that transform into everything but the kitchen sink. In Japanese with English subtitles. Unrated. 90m. **DIR:** Oshii Mamoru. 1984

URUSEI YATSURA: INABA THE DREAMMAKER ★★★½ Japanese animation. The further adventures of Ataru, Shinobu, and Lum as they are presented with several of their possible futures, not all of which are desirable. Holds to the high standards of comedy found in the original series episodes and movies. In Japanese with English subtitles. 57m. **DIR:** Dezuki Tetsu. 1987

URUSEI YATSURA: ONLY YOU ★★★★ Japanese animation. How long has our hero Ataru had his obsession with girls? Find out as his associates plan to attend a reunion with his first flirtation. The fast-paced story line is reminiscent of Blake Edwards's early Pink Panther films. In Japanese with English subtitles. 101m. **DIR:** Kazuo Yamazaki, Yuuji Moriyama. 1983

URUSEI YATSURA: REMEMBER LOVE ★★★★ Japanese animation. Once again, Ataru's twisted charm enmeshes him in extraterrestrial difficulties and involves his associates in situations that stretch the imagination. The vocal characterizations, expressive artwork, and excellent subtitling allow the viewer to easily follow the story. In Japanese with English subtitles. 93m. **DIR:** Kazuo Yamazaki. 1985

VAGABOND ★★★½ French new wave writer-director Agnes Varda's dispassionate but beautifully photographed "investigation"—via flashbacks—of a young misfit's meandering trek through the French countryside features a superb performance by Sandrine Bonnaire. Her *Vagabond* is presented as rude, lazy, ungrateful. Yet in some subliminal way the film draws one into the alienation that fuels this outsider's journey into death. In French with English subtitles. Rated R for profanity and suggested sex. 105m. **DIR:** Agnes Varda. **CAST:** Sandrine Bonnaire, Macha Meril. 1986

VALENTINA ★★★ Subtle drama based on a novel by Ramon Sender about Jose Garce's love for Valentina that lasted from childhood until his death. Produced by Anthony Quinn. In Spanish with English subtitles. 90m. **DIR:** Antonio J. Betancor. **CAST:** Jorge Sanz, Paloma Gomez. 1984

VALLEY, THE ★★½ The plot of this dated movie—hip young people travel to New Guinea—is forgettable. But the exquisite Nestor Almendros photography and the Pink Floyd score make it a pleasant viewing experience. In French with English subtitles. Unrated; contains nudity and sexual situations. 114m. **DIR:** Barbet Schroeder. **CAST:** Bulle Ogier, Jean-Pierre Kalfon, Michael Gothard. 1972

VAMPIRE PRINCESS MIYU ★★ Spiritual investigator Himiko encounters strange happenings in two melodramatic, animated tales of the occult, Japanese style. In Japanese with English subtitles. 60m. **DIR:** Toshihiro Hirano. 1988

VAMPIRES, THE (1915) ★★★★ Generally considered the crowning achievement of Louis Feuillade, who took the form of the movie serial to its peak. The Vampires are a gang of costumed criminals led by the beautiful Musidora. Accused of glorifying crime, Feuillade and cast actually improvised much of the action in this ten-part silent serial. Still impressive today. B&W; 420m. **DIR:** Louis Feuillade. **CAST:** Musidora, Edouard Mathe. 1915–1916

VAMPYR ★★★★★ Director Carl Dreyer believed that horror is best implied. By relying on the viewer's imagination, he created a classic. A young man at a very bizarre inn, discovers an unconscious woman who had been attacked by a vampire in the form of an old woman. This outstanding film is one of the few serious films of the macabre. B&W; 68m. **DIR:** Carl Dreyer. **CAST:** Julian West, Sybille Schmitz. **1931**

VAN GOGH ★★ If they keep telling the story of Vincent van Gogh, perhaps somebody will finally get it right. Maurice Pialat did not get it right in this long, dull exercise. Pialat's point with the story of the famous painter, is to emphasize the mundane. It's a noble idea, but how do you make the mundane interesting for observers? Especially for nearly three hours? In French with English subtitles. 158m. **DIR:** Maurice Pialat. **CAST:** Jacques Dutronc, Bernard Le Coq, Gérard Sety, Alexandra London. **1991**

VANISHING, THE (1988) ★★★★★ Superb thriller as well as an insightful portrait of a sociopath. The mysterious disappearance of his girlfriend leads Rex (Gene Bervoets) on an obsessive quest that results in a confrontation with her killer (Bernard Pierre Donnadieu). The movie is quite unique. Its finely wrought, creepy tone does not rely on standard gothic clichés. The violence (including an unforgettable ending) is understated. Donnadieu's portrayal of the villain quietly freezes the blood. In Dutch and French with English subtitles. Rated R for adult content. 107m. **DIR:** George Sluizer. **CAST:** Bernard Pierre Donnadieu, Gene Bervoets, Johanna ter Steege. **1988**

VARIETY ★★★★★ A milestone of cinema art. It tells a simple, tragic tale of a famous and conceited vaudeville acrobat whose character flaw is cowardice; a clever and entirely unscrupulous girl; and a trusting waterfront circus boss—made a fool of by love—who murders because of that hollow love. The cast is incredible, the cinematography superb. Silent. B&W; 104m. **DIR:** E. A. Dupont. **CAST:** Emil Jannings, Lya de Putti. **1925**

VARIETY LIGHTS ★★★★ This is Federico Fellini's first film, though it's not entirely his. (It's codirected by Alberto Lattuada.) Still, Fellini fans will recognize themes of fantasy and illusion and the pursuit of impossible-to-capture dreams, as well as the presence of the sublime Giulietta Masina. In Italian with English subtitles. 93m. **DIR:** Federico Fellini, Alberto Lattuada. **CAST:** Peppino De Filippo, Carla Del Poggio, Giulietta Masina. **1950**

VENGEANCE IS MINE (1979) ★★★★ Terrifying, complex portrait of a mass murderer, played with chilling detachment by Ken Ogata. Shohei Imamura, Japan's most controversial director, has created a nightmarish film that is both poignant and disturbing in its depiction of a psychopathic mind at work. In Japanese with English subtitles. Not rated but contains scenes of graphic violence and nudity. 129m. **DIR:** Shohei Imamura. **CAST:** Ken Ogata. **1979**

VENUS WARS, THE ★★★★ Outstanding example of the art of Japanese animation, certainly one of the finest available in America. Set on barren Venus in the twenty-first century, the story follows young Hiro and his friends, members of a racing team. All the excitement of *Akira*, with a better (and more coherent) story. In Japanese with English subtitles. Unrated; contains violence. 104m. **DIR:** Yoshikazu Yasuhiko. **1989**

VERONIKA VOSS ★★ A famous German actress tries to revive her flagging career with alcohol and drugs in this final addition to Rainer Werner Fassbinder's trilogy about the collapse of the West German postwar dream. While technically a well-made movie, Fassbinder's point is lost amid the bleak shadow life of the losers he so skillfully captures. In German with English subtitles. Rated R. 105m. **DIR:** Rainer Werner Fassbinder. **CAST:** Rosel Zech, Hilmar Thate. **1982**

VERY CURIOUS GIRL, A ★★★ A village girl who has been sexually exploited by the town fathers gets revenge by charging for her "services." Broad (sometimes too broad) social satire. In French with English subtitles. Rated R for sexual content. 105m. **DIR:** Nelly Kaplan. **CAST:** Bernadette Lafont, Georges Geret, Michel Constantin. **1970**

VERY OLD MAN WITH ENORMOUS WINGS, A ★★★★ A winged man lands inexplicably in a tiny Colombian village. People flock in droves to the new attraction, and a huge carnival is born, spewed forth from the womb of human superstition and curiosity. A frenetically frenzied furor full of fantastic, colorful absurdity. In Spanish with English subtitles. Rated R for nudity and simulated sex. 90m. **DIR:** Fernando Birri. **CAST:** Daisy Granados, Asdrubal Melendez. **1988**

VERY PRIVATE AFFAIR, A ★★★ Bardot fan, or just never had a chance to see her? In this romantic drama she plays a famous movie star who can no longer cope with notoriety, so she retreats from public scrutiny. Marcello Mastroianni is equally appealing as a director coming to her aid. In French with English subtitles. 95m. **DIR:** Louis Malle. **CAST:** Brigitte Bardot, Marcello Mastroianni. **1962**

VIGIL ★★★ After the death of her father, a New Zealand farm girl observes the positive changes in her family brought on by the arrival of a young drifter. Compelling film is rich in visual imagery and texture. 90m. **DIR:** Vincent Ward. **CAST:** Penelope Stewart, Fiona Kay, Frank Whitten, Bill Kerr. **1984**

VINCENT, FRANÇOIS, PAUL AND THE OTHERS ★★★★★ A deeply moving film about friendship as a band of buddies survive marriage, affairs, and career challenges. Claude Sautet, one of France's most respected directors, gets superb performances from leading and supporting roles. Don't miss this one! In French with English subtitles. Unrated. 118m. **DIR:** Claude Sautet. **CAST:** Yves Montand, Michel Piccoli, Serge Reggiani, Gérard Depardieu, Stéphane Audran, Marie Dubois. **1974**

VIOLENCE AT NOON ★★★½ Complex drama about two rape victims and their rapist set against the socialist movement in postwar Japan. Director Nagisa Oshima explores the pathology of a society in which the criminal and victim reside. In Japanese with English subtitles. B&W; 100m. **DIR:** Nagisa Oshima. **CAST:** Saeda Kawaguchi, Akiko Koyama, Kei Sato. **1966**

VIRGIN SPRING, THE ★★★★★ Ingmar Bergman's scenario is based on a fourteenth-century Swedish legend. Accompanied by her jealous older stepsister, a young girl is raped and killed while on a journey to her church—and the three killers make the mistake of seeking shelter with the parents. Won an Oscar for best foreign language film. In Swedish with English subtitles. B&W; 87m. **DIR:** Ingmar Bergman. **CAST:** Max von Sydow, Birgitta Pettersson, Gunnel Lindblom. **1960**

VIRIDIANA ★★★★★ Angelic Viridiana (Silvia Pinal) visits her sex-obsessed uncle (Fernando Rey) prior to taking her religious vows. The film was an amazing *cause célèbre* at the time. *Viridiana*—much to Spain's and the Catholic Church's consternation—won the Palme d'Or at Cannes. In Spanish with English subtitles. B&W; 90m. **DIR:** Luis Buñuel. **CAST:** Silvia Pinal, Fernando Rey, Francisco Rabal, Margarita Lozano. **1961**

VIRUS KNOWS NO MORALS, A ★★★½ A comedy about AIDS may sound like the ultimate in tastelessness, but gay filmmaker Rosa von Praunheim's aim is to educate audiences while making them laugh. This loosely structured film, featuring a nonprofessional cast, makes fun of the public misconceptions and hysteria surrounding the disease. In German with English subtitles. Unrated. 82m. **DIR:** Rosa von Praunheim. **CAST:** Rosa von Praunheim, Dieter Dicken, Eva Kurz. **1985**

VIVA MARIA! ★★★★ Great slapstick and hilarious situations abound as two song-and-dance girls traveling with a carnival become involved with Mexican revolutionaries during the time of Pancho Villa. A fast-moving comedy gem. In French with English subtitles. 125m. **DIR:** Louis Malle. **CAST:** Jeanne Moreau, Brigitte Bardot, George Hamilton, Paulette Dubost. **1965**

VOLERE VOLARE ★★★½ A sexy woman who makes her living fulfilling fantasies falls in love with a nerdy cartoon sound man in this delightful romp. Like *Who Framed Roger Rabbit*, this hilarious comedy skillfully mixes live action and animation. Maurizio Nichetti writes, directs, and stars as the sound genius. In Italian with English subtitles. Rated R for nudity and sexual situations. 92m. **DIR:** Guido Manuli, Maurizio Nichetti. **CAST:** Maurizio Nichetti, Angela Finocciaro, Mariella Valentini, Patrizio Roversi. **1991**

VOLPONE ★★★★ Filmed in 1939, this superb screen version of Shakespeare contemporary Ben Jonson's classic play of greed was not released until after World War II, by which time star Harry Baur, a titan of French cinema, was mysteriously dead, having been, it is supposed, killed by the Nazis in 1941. Aided by his avaricious and parasitic servant, Mosca, Volpone, an old Venetian, pretends he is dying and convinces his greedy friends that each of them is his heir. Volpone and Mosca spin a web of lies until they are caught. In French with English subtitles. B&W; 80m. **DIR:** Maurice Tourneur. **CAST:** Harry Baur, Louis Jouvet. **1939**

VOULEZ VOUS DANSER AVEC MOI? (WILL YOU DANCE WITH ME?) 🦃 This is another interminable Brigitte Bardot film, one in which a marital squabble lands her in the center of a murder investigation. In French with English subtitles. 89m. **DIR:** Michel Boisrone. **CAST:** Brigitte Bardot, Henri Vidal, Dawn Addams, Noel Roquevert. **1959**

VOYAGE EN BALLON (STOWAWAY TO THE STARS) ★★★ This endearing French film is somewhat of a follow-up to *The Red Balloon* (also directed by Albert Lamorisse and starring son Pascal, this time allowing that boy to ascend into the clouds—in the basket of a hot air balloon). Unfortunately, Lamorisse *pegravere* is a far better director than writer, and this film lacks the drama needed to sustain its greater length. Unrated, suitable for family viewing. 82m. **DIR:** Albert Lamorisse. **CAST:** Andrè Gille, Maurice Baquet, Pascal Lamorisse. **1959**

VOYAGE IN ITALY ★★★ A married couple drives through Italy to inspect a property they have inherited. Removed from their usual routine, they begin to inspect their life together. Much admired by fans of director Roberto Rossellini, this slow neorealist drama is recommended only for the most patient viewers. In English. B&W; 97m. **DIR:** Roberto Rossellini. **CAST:** Ingrid Bergman, George Sanders. **1953**

WAGES OF FEAR, THE ★★★★★ This masterpiece of suspense pits four seedy and destitute men against the challenge of driving two nitroglycerin-laden trucks over crude and treacherous Central American mountain roads to quell a monstrous oil-well fire. Incredible risk and numbing fear ride along as the drivers, goaded by high wages, cope with dilemma after dilemma. In French with English subtitles. B&W; 128m. **DIR:** Henri-Georges Clouzot. **CAST:** Yves Montand, Charles Vanel, Peter Van Eyck, Vera Clouzot. 1953

WALL, THE ★★★★ Based-on-fact story of life in a brutal Turkish prison where prisoners of all ages, genders, and types (political and criminal) are incarcerated together. Director Yilmaz Guney spent much of his life in such prisons before escaping in 1981. Unrated, but too brutal for children. 117m. **DIR:** Yilmaz Guney. **CAST:** Tuncel Kurtiz. 1983

WANDERER, THE ★★½ An exciting newcomer turns a girl's life upside down, but her loyalty to him is a mystery since a more worthwhile man loves her. Marvelous music and imaginative surreal sequences cannot completely compensate for the slow pace and confusion that permeate this arty film. In French with English subtitles. 107m. **DIR:** Jean Gabriel Albicocco. **CAST:** Brigitte Fossey, Jean Blaise, Alain Noury. 1967

WANNABES ★★½ Japanese animation. This one does have a certain charm. The *Wannabes* are a duo of determined women wrestlers that become the unknowing test subjects of genetic research. Sounds like a stretch (and it is), but it has the flavor of a Fifties drive-in classic. In Japanese with English subtitles. Unrated. 45m. **DIR:** Masuzumi Matsumiya. 1986

WANNSEE CONFERENCE, THE ★★★★ This is a fascinating historical drama about a meeting held on January 20, 1942, with the fourteen members of Hitler's hierarchy. Wannsee is the Berlin suburb where they met to decide "the final solution" to the Jewish problem. Chillingly told from the actual minutes taken at the conference. A must-see film. In German with subtitles. 87m. **DIR:** Keinz Schirk. **CAST:** Dietrich Mattausch. 1984

WANTON CONTESSA, THE ★★★★½ Luchino Visconti—aristocrat by birth, Marxist by conviction—offers one of the lushest and most expressive Italian films ever made (known there as *Senso*). The large-budget spectacular is operatic in scope and look. Venice, 1866. A countess (the alluring Alida Valli) finds herself passionately in love with a young Austrian officer (Farley Granger). Dubbed in English (with dialogue by Tennessee Williams and Paul Bowles). 120m. **DIR:** Luchino Visconti. **CAST:** Alida Valli, Farley Granger, Massimo Girotti. 1954

WAR AND PEACE (1968) ★★★★★ Many film versions of great books take liberties that change important plot situations, and more. This Academy Award–winning Soviet production stays as close to the book as possible, making it terribly long, but one of the greatest re-creations of great literature ever done. It took five years to make at enormous cost; it is a cinematic treasure. Poorly dubbed. 373m. **DIR:** Sergei Bondarchuk. **CAST:** Lyudmila Savelyeva, Sergei Bondarchuk. 1968

WARRIORS FROM THE MAGIC MOUNTAIN ★★★ While caught in the middle of one of ancient China's senseless wars, a young soldier falls through a hole and finds himself on a quest to save the Earth from evil spirits. Filled with fantastic martial arts stunts and impressive special effects. In Cantonese with English subtitles. Not rated, but contains violence. 95m. **DIR:** Tsui Hark. **CAST:** Richard Ng. 1983

WAXWORKS ★★★ A young poet dreams about the wax figures he sees in a fair booth: an Oriental sultan (Harun-al-Rashid), Ivan the Terrible, and Jack the Ripper. Outstanding example of the German Expressionist cinema in the 1920s. Silent. B&W; 63m. **DIR:** Paul Leni. **CAST:** William Dieterle, Emil Jannings, Conrad Veidt, Werner Krauss. 1924

WE ALL LOVED EACH OTHER SO MUCH ★★★★ Exceptional high-spirited comedy about three friends and their lives and loves over the course of three decades. A wonderful homage to Fellini, De Sica, and postwar neorealism. In Italian with English subtitles. 124m. **DIR:** Ettore Scola. **CAST:** Nino Manfredi, Vittorio Gassman, Stefania Sandrelli. 1977

WE THE LIVING ★★½ Weak adaptation of Ayn Rand's compelling novel about a headstrong young Soviet woman who becomes romantically involved with a counterrevolutionary. In Italian with English subtitles. Not rated. B&W; 174m. **DIR:** Goffredo Alessandrini. **CAST:** Fosco Giachetti, Alida Valli, Rossano Brazzi. 1942

WEDDING, THE ★★★★ A wedding between a farm girl and a poet works as an allegory of the internal problems that have troubled Poland for centuries. One of director Andrzej Wajda's most cinematic films, its atmospheric virtuosity will be appreciated even by those who find its themes too obscure. In Polish with English subtitles. Not rated. B&W; 103m. **DIR:** Andrzej Wajda. **CAST:** Eva Zietek, Daniel Olbrychski, Wojiech Pszoniak. 1972

WEDDING IN BLOOD ★★★★ As in the best of Hitchcock, no one can be trusted in this elegantly perverse murder mystery. Two unhappily married people having an affair plan to rid themselves of their spouses. The spouses, however, have their own plans. In French with English subtitles. 98m. **DIR:** Claude Chabrol. **CAST:** Michel Piccoli, Stéphane Audran, Claude Pieplu. 1973

WEDDING IN GALILEE, A ★★★★★ A Palestinian village elder is determined to give his son a grand traditional wedding, but to do so he must agree to invite the occupying Israeli leaders as guests of honor. Exceptional drama works on many levels. Filmed on location in the occupied West Bank. In Arabic and Hebrew with English subtitles. Unrated, the film contains nudity. 113m. **DIR:** Michel Khleifi. **CAST:** Ali Mohammed El Akili. **1987**

WEEKEND ★★★ Jean-Luc Godard's apocalyptic film can best be described as a dark comic vision of the decline and fall of consumer society through the eyes of a young perverted bourgeois couple. Recommended only for hard-core fans of Godard. Others may find this movie too disgusting and very confusing. In French with English subtitles. Not rated, but contains sexual situations and violence. 105m. **DIR:** Jean-Luc Godard. **CAST:** Mireille Darc, Jean-Pierre Léaud, Jean Yanne. **1967**

WELL-DIGGER'S DAUGHTER, THE ★★★½ A well digger disowns his daughter when she is seduced and abandoned, but they are reunited by his assistant. As in all of the films of Marcel Pagnol, a melodramatic story becomes something greater. In French with English subtitles. B&W; 142m. **DIR:** Marcel Pagnol. **CAST:** Raimu, Fernandel, Charpin. **1940**

WESTFRONT 1918 ★★★★ G. W. Pabst's first sound film chronicles the agonies suffered by four French soldiers sent to the French front during the last months of World War I. Brilliant use of mobile camera gives the battle scenes a shocking look of realism. In German with English subtitles. B&W; 98m. **DIR:** G. W. Pabst. **CAST:** Gustav Diessl. **1930**

WHAT HAVE I DONE TO DESERVE THIS? ★★★★ Outrageously funny black comedy about a working-class housewife who struggles to maintain her sanity while keeping her crazy family afloat. This perverse fable on contemporary life is superbly directed by Pedro Almodóvar and features a brilliant performance by Carmen Maura. In Spanish with English subtitles. Not rated, but contains nudity and profanity. 100m. **DIR:** Pedro Almodóvar. **CAST:** Carmen Maura. **1984**

WHEN A WOMAN ASCENDS THE STAIRS ★★★★½ As in many of his films, Mikio Naruse examines a woman trying to make her own way in the world, in this case a bar hostess struggling with debt and loneliness. Clearly influenced by Hollywood melodramas of the 1950s, he adapts their conventions (including the wide-screen format, preserved in this letter-boxed video transfer) to good effect. In Japanese with English subtitles. B&W; 110m. **DIR:** Mikio Naruse. **CAST:** Hideko Takamine. **1960**

WHEN FATHER WAS AWAY ON BUSINESS ★★★ Seen through the eyes of a young boy, the film deals with the sudden disappearance of a father from a family. Tension mounts when it becomes clear that it is the father's brother-in-law who turned him in and had him sent to a work camp. The film received the Palm D'Or at the 1985 Cannes Film Festival. Rated R for sex and nudity. In Slavic with English subtitles. 144m. **DIR:** Emir Kusturica. **CAST:** Moreno De Bartolli, Miki Manojlovic. **1985**

WHERE THE GREEN ANTS DREAM ★★★★ Another stark, yet captivating vision from perhaps the most popular director of current German cinema. The film, set in Australia, is basically an ecological tug of war between progress and tradition, namely uranium mining interests against aborigines and their practices. 100m. **DIR:** Werner Herzog. **CAST:** Bruce Spence, Ray Barrett, Norman Kaye. **1984**

WHERE'S PICCONE? ★★★★ Highly entertaining comedy starring Giancarlo Giannini as a small-time hustler searching for a respectable Italian businessman who inexplicably vanished in an ambulance on the way to the hospital. In Italian with English subtitles. Not rated, but contains nudity, violence, and profanity. 110m. **DIR:** Nanni Loy. **CAST:** Giancarlo Giannini. **1984**

WHITE NIGHTS (1957) ★★★★ In this stylish melodrama, a shy young man encounters a mysterious girl whose lover has not returned from a journey across the sea. Based on a story by Dostoyevski. In Italian with English subtitles. B&W; 107m. **DIR:** Luchino Visconti. **CAST:** Marcello Mastroianni, Maria Schell, Jean Marais. **1957**

WHITE ROSE, THE (1983) ★★★ *The White Rose* is based on a true story about a group of youths in wartime Germany who revolted against Hitler by printing and distributing subversive leaflets to the public. All of the young actors are good, especially Lena Stolze, who plays the main protagonist. In German. 108m. **DIR:** Michael Verhoeven. **CAST:** Lena Stolze, Wulf Kessler, Martin Benrath. **1983**

WHITE SHEIK, THE ★★★ A warm salute to romantic movie heroes. When a recently wed couple go to Rome, the bride sneaks off to a movie set where her idol, the White Sheik, is making a film. Federico Fellini manages to create an original cinematic piece with great satirical precision. In Italian with English subtitles. B&W; 86m. **DIR:** Federico Fellini. **CAST:** Brunella Bovo, Leopoldo Trieste, Alberto Sordi, Giulietta Masina. **1952**

WIDOW COUDERC ★★★ Tense, well-acted thriller about a small-town woman's affair with an escaped killer. From a novel by Georges Simenon. In French with English subtitles. Unrated; contains no objectionable material. 92m. **DIR:** Pierre Granier-Deferre. **CAST:** Simone Signoret, Alain Delon. **1974**

WIFE! BE LIKE A ROSE! ★★★★ A young woman travels from Tokyo to rural

Japan in search of her father, hoping to persuade him to abandon his mistress and return home to his wife. Gentle comedy-drama. In Japanese with English subtitles. B&W; 73m. **DIR:** Mikio Naruse. **CAST:** Sachiko Chiba. **1935**

WIFEMISTRESS ★★★½ Marcello Mastroianni stars as a husband in hiding, and Laura Antonelli as his repressed wife. When Mastroianni is falsely accused of murder, he hides out in a building across the street from his own home. His wife, not knowing where he is, begins to relive his sexual escapades. There are some comic moments as the former philandering husband must deal with his wife's new sexual freedom. 110m. **DIR:** Marco Vicario. **CAST:** Marcello Mastroianni, Laura Antonelli, Leonard Mann. **1977**

WILD CHILD, THE (L'ENFANT SAUVAGE) ★★★★ Based on fact. In 1798 a boy, believed to be about 12, is found running wild in the French woods, apparently abandoned there when little more than an infant. A doctor-teacher of deaf mutes, sensitively played by director François Truffaut, takes over the task of domesticating the snarling, bewildered youth. Completely absorbing from start to finish. In French with English subtitles. Unrated, but suitable for all. B&W; 86m. **DIR:** François Truffaut. **CAST:** François Truffaut, Jean-Pierre Cargol. **1970**

WILD STRAWBERRIES ★★★★ This film is probably Ingmar Bergman's least ambiguous. Superbly photographed and acted, the film tells the story of an elderly professor facing old age and reviewing his life's disappointments. The use of flashbacks is very effective. B&W; 90m. **DIR:** Ingmar Bergman. **CAST:** Victor Sjöström, Ingrid Thulin, Bibi Andersson, Gunnar Björnstrand. **1957**

WINDOW SHOPPING ★★★ With tongue firmly entrenched in cheek, this French musical-comedy of romantic error concerns Lilli, the belle of the shopping mall. Somewhat like a cross between *Romeo and Juliet* and *Grease*, this buoyant movie is a cinematographic curiosity piece. In French with English subtitles. Rated R for nudity. 96m. **DIR:** Chantal Akerman. **CAST:** Delphine Seyrig, Myriam Boyer, Fanny Cottençon, Charles Denner, John Berry. **1986**

WINGS OF DESIRE ★★★★ Angels see in black-and-white; mortals see in color. Wim Wenders's follow-up to *Paris, Texas* is a stark and moving story set in Berlin about two angels (Bruno Ganz and Otto Sander) who travel through the city listening to people's thoughts. Ganz grows weary of comforting others and decides to reenter the world as a human. Rated PG-13 for adult subject matter. In German and French with English subtitles. 130m. **DIR:** Wim Wenders. **CAST:** Bruno Ganz, Solveig Dommartin, Curt Bois, Peter Falk, Otto Sander. **1988**

WINTER LIGHT ★★★ Second film in director Bergman's "faith" trilogy (it follows *Through a Glass Darkly* and precedes *The Silence*) centers on a disillusioned priest who attempts to come to grips with his religion and his position in the inner workings of the church. This effort to explore the psyche of a cleric is a thoughtful, incisive drama with great performances. In Swedish with English subtitles. B&W; 80m. **DIR:** Ingmar Bergman. **CAST:** Ingrid Thulin, Gunnar Björnstrand, Max von Sydow, Gunnel Lindblom. **1962**

WITCHCRAFT THROUGH THE AGES (HAXAN) ★★★½ After seventy years of notoriety, this controversial film is still unique as one of the most outrageous movies of all time. Envisioned by director Benjamin Christensen as a study of black magic, witchcraft, and demonology from the Middle Ages to the present, this silent Scandinavian epic fluctuates between lecture material and incredibly vivid footage that gave the censors ulcers in the 1920s. There is a version available with William Burroughs reading the narration; other prints are captioned in English. B&W; 82m. **DIR:** Benjamin Christensen. **CAST:** Maren Pedersen. **1921**

WOLF AT THE DOOR ★★ Pompous and heavy-handed, *Wolf at the Door* gnaws away at painter Paul Gauguin's life in a rather self-conscious fashion, despite some beautiful photography. Predictable and ponderous, and Gauguin's love life with 13-year-old girls is downright depressing. English-dubbed. 94m. **DIR:** Henning Carlsen. **CAST:** Donald Sutherland, Fanny Bastien. **1987**

WOLVES, THE ★★★ Three gangsters fight for survival in this stylish but slightly overlong *yakuza* story set in pre–World War II Japan, when the old samurai-based ways were beginning to collapse. In Japanese with English subtitles. Not rated. 132m. **DIR:** Hideo Gosha. **CAST:** Tatsuya Nakadai. **1981**

WOMAN IN FLAMES, A ★★★★ A male and a female prostitute fall in love and decide to set up shop in the same household, insisting that their business trysts will not interfere with their personal relationship. If erotic drama and bizarre twists are your fancy, this should be your film. Rated R for sexual situations and language. 104m. **DIR:** Robert Van Ackeren. **CAST:** Gudrun Landgrebe, Mathieu Carriere. **1984**

WOMAN IN THE DUNES ★★★★★ An entomologist collecting beetles on the dunes misses his bus back to the city. Some locals offer him assistance, and he is lowered by a ladder down into a sand pit where he finds a woman willing to provide food and lodging in her shack. The ladder is removed, however, and he is trapped. A classic thriller. In Japanese with English subtitles. B&W; 123m. **DIR:** Hiroshi Teshigahara. **CAST:** Eiji Okada. **1964**

WOMAN IN THE MOON (A.K.A. GIRL IN THE MOON; BY ROCKET TO THE MOON) ★★★ Fritz Lang's last silent film is actually a futuristic melodrama written by his wife and collaborator, Thea von Harbou. Although much of the action takes place on the moon (and is obviously shot on indoor sets), this film remains stuck to a story that could have taken place just as easily on Earth. Admired by science-fiction aficionados for Lang's imaginative visual sense, not the content of the story. German, silent. B&W; 115m. **DIR:** Fritz Lang. **CAST:** Gerda Maurus, Willy Fritsch, Fritz Rasp, Gustav von Waggenheim. **1929**

WOMAN IS A WOMAN, A ★★★★ One of Jean-Luc Godard's most accessible movies is built around a love triangle involving a stripper (Anna Karina, whom Godard married after filming), her lover, and his best friend. Unlike much of Godard's later work, this tribute cum parody of Hollywood musicals keeps your attention even when the literal meaning is unclear. In French with English subtitles. 85m. **DIR:** Jean-Luc Godard. **CAST:** Anna Karina, Jean-Paul Belmondo, Jean-Claude Brialy, Jeanne Moreau. **1961**

WOMAN NEXT DOOR, THE ★★★★½ François Truffaut is on record as one of the greatest admirers of Alfred Hitchcock, and the influence shows in his gripping, well-made film about guilt, passion, and the growing influence of a small sin that grows. In French with English subtitles. MPAA unrated, but contains nudity and violence. 106m. **DIR:** François Truffaut. **CAST:** Gérard Depardieu, Fanny Ardant, Henri Garcin. **1981**

WOMAN WITHOUT LOVE, A ★★★ Absorbing melodrama about a neglected housewife who indulges in an affair with an engineer only to return to her wealthy old husband. Twenty years later, the husband leaves a fortune to her son's lover, causing a family castastrophe. In Spanish with English subtitles. Not rated. B&W; 91m. **DIR:** Luis Buñuel. **CAST:** Rosario Granados, Julio Villarreal. **1952**

WOMEN ON THE VERGE OF A NERVOUS BREAKDOWN ★★★★ Delightful Spanish comedy features Carmen Maura as a pregnant soap-opera star who has just been dumped by her longtime lover. A madcap farce. In Spanish with bright yellow English subtitles. Rated R for profanity. 88m. **DIR:** Pedro Almodóvar. **CAST:** Carmen Maura, Fernando Guillen, Antonio Banderas. **1988**

WONDERWALL ★★½ Experimental curiosity piece depicts the fantasies of an entomologist as he spies on the woman in the apartment next to his. Electronic music score by George Harrison. Unrated, the film includes some nudity. 93m. **DIR:** Joe Massot. **CAST:** Jack MacGowran, Jane Birkin, Irene Handl. **1968**

WORLD OF APU, THE ★★★★ This is the concluding part of director Satyajit Ray's famed *Apu* trilogy covering the life and growth of a young man in India. In this last film, Apu marries and helps bring life into the world himself, completing the cycle amid realizations about himself and his limitations in this world. This movie and its predecessors form a beautiful tapestry of existence in a different culture and were among the most influential of all Indian films for many years. In Bengali with English subtitles. B&W; 103m. **DIR:** Satyajit Ray. **CAST:** Soumitra Chatterjee, Sharmila Tagore, Alok Charkravarty, Swapan Mukherji. **1959**

WORLD OF STRANGERS, A ★★★ When a London publisher is transferred to South Africa, he finds new friends among both the black and white communities, gradually becoming aware of the tensions and inequities around him. An intelligent and often disturbing treatment from the novel by Nadine Gordimer. B&W; 89m. **DIR:** Henning Carlsen. **CAST:** Zakes Mokae, Gideon Nxomalo, Evelyn Frank, Ivan Jackson. **1962**

WOYZECK ★★★½ Powerful yet uneven adaptation of Georg Buchner's haunting, absurd opera. Klaus Kinski plays a man who plunges into madness and murder. In German with English subtitles. Not rated, but contains nudity and violence. 82m. **DIR:** Werner Herzog. **CAST:** Klaus Kinski, Eva Mattes. **1978**

WR: MYSTERIES OF THE ORGANISM ★★★★ Once-controversial film still has an anarchic kick, with too many ideas flying around to catch them all in one viewing. Writer-director Dusan Makavejev mixes documentary and fictional elements to explore the theories of sexologist Wilhelm Reich, with a number of amusing detours along the way. In Serbian with English subtitles. Unrated. 84m. **DIR:** Dusan Makavejev. **CAST:** Milena Dravic, Jagoda Kaloper. **1971**

WRONG MOVE, THE ★★ Rudiger Vogler is cast as a would-be writer in this slow-moving character drama. It concerns a soul-searching odyssey across Germany by a diverse group of misfits. Initially absorbing, yet too disconcerting to recommend. German with English subtitles. 103m. **DIR:** Wim Wenders. **CAST:** Rudiger Vogler, Hanna Schygulla, Nastassja Kinski. **1978**

WUTHERING HEIGHTS (1953) ★★½ This is Luis Buñuel's film of the Emily Brontë classic. This Spanish version in no way measures up to the 1939 original. The Richard Wagner music, however, is perfect for the melodramatic performances. 90m. **DIR:** Luis Buñuel. **CAST:** Iraseme Dilian, Jorge Mistral. **1953**

YEAR OF THE QUIET SUN ★★★★ A beautifully orchestrated meditation on the nature of love, this import is about a Polish widow after World War II who becomes romantically involved with an American soldier during a war-crimes investigation. In Polish with English subtitles. 106m. **DIR:** Krzysztof Zanussi. **CAST:** Scott Wilson, Maja Komorowska. **1985**

YELLOW EARTH ★★★★ In 1939, a communist soldier is sent to a remote province to collect folk songs and learn about rural life. The first film from director Chen Kaige (*Farewell My Concubine*) is a small work of beautiful simplicity, in which the faces of characters communicate to the viewer feelings they cannot share with each other. In Chinese with English subtitles. Unrated, contains no objectionable material. 89m. **DIR:** Chen Kaige. **CAST:** Xue Bai, Wang Xueqi. **1984**

YESTERDAY, TODAY AND TOMORROW ★★★½ Hilarious three-vignette romp teaming Sophia Loren and Marcello Mastroianni. The first (and best) story features Loren as an impoverished woman who continues to have babies in order to avoid a jail sentence, with Mastroianni as her husband who gives in to the scheme. Italian dubbed into English. 119m. **DIR:** Vittorio De Sica. **CAST:** Sophia Loren, Marcello Mastroianni, Tina Pica. **1964**

YOJIMBO ★★★★½ Viewed from different perspectives, *Yojimbo* ("bodyguard") is: the most devastating comedy ever made; Kurosawa's parody of the American Western; or his satire on the United States and Soviet Union's achieving peace through nuclear proliferation. Toshiro Mifune, an unemployed samurai in nineteenth-century Japan, sells his services to two rival merchants, each with killer gangs that are tearing the town apart. The film is boisterous—*lots* of bones crunching and samurai swords flashing and slashing—and exuberant. (Remade by Sergio Leone as *A Fistful of Dollars.*) No rating, but very violent. B&W; 110m. **DIR:** Akira Kurosawa. **CAST:** Toshiro Mifune, Eijiro Tono. **1961**

YOL ★★★½ Winner of the Grand Prix at the Cannes Film Festival, this work, by Turkish filmmaker and political prisoner Yilmaz Gurney, follows several inmates of a minimum-security prison who are granted a few days' leave, telling their stories in parallel scenes. Gurney—who smuggled instructions out of prison to his trusted assistants, then escaped from prison and edited the film—was hailed at Cannes for creating an eloquent protest against suppression and totalitarian government. Unrated, the film has violence and suggested sex. 111m. **DIR:** Serif Goren. **CAST:** Tarik Akin, Serif Sezer. **1982**

Z ★★★★ Director Costa-Gavras first explored political corruption in this taut French thriller. Yves Montand plays a political leader who is assassinated. Based on a true story. Academy Award for best foreign film. Well worth a try. No rating, with some violence and coarse language. 127m. **DIR:** Constantin Costa-Gavras. **CAST:** Yves Montand, Irene Papas, Jean-Louis Trintignant, Charles Denner. **1969**

ZATOICHI: MASSEUR ICHI AND A CHEST OF GOLD ★★★ Popular samurai series from Japan features a blind swordsman—masseur on an endless quest through the Japanese countryside. In this adventure Zatoichi travels to pay his respects at the grave of a gambler he killed years ago. Zatoichi and a luckless local *yakuza* boss are framed for robbery and murder. The unusual premise of Zatoichi's character requires the viewer to suspend a certain amount of disbelief for enjoyment, but it's well worth it. In Japanese with English subtitles. Not rated, but contains violence. 83m. **DIR:** Kazuo Ikehiro. **CAST:** Shintaro Katsu, Mikiko Tsubouchi, Machiko Hasgawa, Kenzaburo Joh, Shogo Shimada. **1964**

ZATOICHI: THE BLIND SWORDSMAN AND THE CHESS EXPERT ★★★★ The ragged, endearing character of the long-running Japanese series, *Zatoichi*, returns. This time he befriends another samurai while on a gambling junket to Mt. Fuji. During the ship's voyage, Zatoichi incurs the wrath of gangsters when he wins all their money gambling. Watch for the amusing scene of Zatoichi outfoxing the young hoods during a dice game. In Japanese with English subtitles. Not rated, but contains violence. 87m. **DIR:** Kenji Misumi. **CAST:** Shintaro Katsu, Mikio Narita, Chizu Hayashi, Kaneko Iwasaski, Gayo Kamamoto. **1965**

ZATOICHI: THE BLIND SWORDSMAN'S VENGEANCE ★★★★ Wandering blind swordsman—masseur Zatoichi chances upon a gang of thieves robbing a dying man. After Zatoichi drives off the thieves, the dying man entrusts to him a bag of money to be delivered to someone named Taichi in a village just up the road. When Zatoichi finally locates the mysterious Taichi, he finds more than he bargained for. Unique blend of action, comedy, and drama gives these films a Zen-like quality. In Japanese with English subtitles. Not rated, but contains violence. 83m. **DIR:** Tokuzo Tanaka. **CAST:** Shintaro Katsu, Shigero Amachi, Mayumi Ogawa, Kei Sato, Jun Hamamura. **1966**

ZATOICHI VS. YOJIMBO ★★★½ Two of the giants of the Japanese samurai genre square off in this comic entry in the long-running blind-swordsman series. Shintaro Katsu is Zatoichi, an almost superhuman hero. The story is a send-up of Akira Kurosawa's *Yojimbo,* with Toshiro Mifune doing a comedic turn on his most famous character. It's fun for fans, but far from classic. In Japanese with English subtitles. 116m. **DIR:**

Kihachi Okamoto. **CAST:** Shintaro Katsu, Toshiro Mifune. **1970**

ZAZIE DANS LE METRO ★★★★ Hilarious, offbeat tale of a foulmouthed 11-year-old who comes to Paris to visit her drag-queen uncle (Philippe Noiret). Freewheeling fun. In French with English subtitles. 92m. **DIR:** Louis Malle. **CAST:** Catherine Demongeot, Philippe Noiret. **1960**

ZENTROPA ★★★ This dream-state surreal odyssey, whose chief attribute is style, follows a young man into a new job as a railway conductor in Germany immediately after the end of World War II. Often enigmatic and challenging, this Danish film uses the railway as a complex metaphor for the emerging of Europe after the war. Stunning photography, process shots, computer-generated graphics, and startling imagery abound. Note: *Zentropa* was titled *Europa* in its European release, but was retitled in America to avoid confusion with *Europa, Europa*. In Danish with English subtitles. 114m. **DIR:** Lars von Trier. **CAST:** Jean-Marc Barr, Barbara Sukowa, Lawrence Hartman, Udo Kier, Eddie Constantine. **1991**

ZERAM ★★ A female bounty hunter with a powerful computer must go into another universe to capture an evil alien being. Two stooges from the power company are accidently transported with her and must help her battle the alien. Dubbed in English. Not rated, but contains excessive violence and gore. 92m. **DIR:** Keita Amamiya. **CAST:** Yuko Moriyama, Kunihiko Ida, Yukijiro Hotaru. **1991**

ZERO FOR CONDUCT ★★★★½ This unique fantasy about the rebellion of boys in a French boarding school is told from the point of view of the students and provides perhaps the purest picture in the history of cinema of what authority appears to be to young minds. This all too short gem was sadly one of only four films made by terminally ill director Jean Vigo, at the age of 29. Banned across the Continent when first released, this 50-year-old film provided much of the story line for Lindsay Anderson's 1969 update *If*... In French with English subtitles. B&W; 44m. **DIR:** Jean Vigo. **CAST:** Jean Dasté. **1933**

ZVENIGORA ★★★★ Prompted by their grandfather's stories, two young peasants dream of the legendary treasure buried in the hills of Zvenigora. Alexander Dovzhenko was the cinema's great epic poet, and in this, his first feature, he seamlessly blends mythology and his own personal beliefs with the history of the Ukraine. Silent. B&W; 73m. **DIR:** Alexander Dovzhenko. **1928**

HORROR

ABOMINABLE DR. PHIBES, THE ★★★½ Stylish horror film features Vincent Price in one of his best latter-day roles as a man disfigured in a car wreck taking revenge. Rated PG. 93m. **DIR:** Robert Fuest. **CAST:** Vincent Price, Joseph Cotten, Hugh Griffith, Terry-Thomas. **1971**

AFTER MIDNIGHT ★★ University students taking a course on fear form a study group to tell each other scary stories. The film has a few thrills and chills, but it suffers from its lack of originality. Rated PG-13 for violence and profanity. 98m. **DIR:** Ken Wheat, Jim Wheat. **CAST:** Pamela Segall, Marc McClure, Marg Helgenberger. **1989**

AGAINST ALL ODDS (KISS AND KILL, BLOOD OF FU MANCHU) The evil Fu Manchu hatches another dastardly plan for world domination. A complete bore. Rated PG. 93m. **DIR:** Jess (Jesus) Franco. **CAST:** Christopher Lee, Richard Greene, Shirley Eaton. **1968**

ALBINO African terrorists, led by an albino chief, frighten natives. Unrated. 96m. **DIR:** Jurgen Goslar. **CAST:** Christopher Lee, Trevor Howard, James Faulkner, Sybil Danning. **1976**

ALCHEMIST, THE Mixed-up melodrama about a century-old curse and the girl who breaks it. Rated R. 84m. **DIR:** Charles Band. **CAST:** Robert Ginty, Lucinda Dooling. **1985**

ALICE, SWEET ALICE (COMMUNION AND HOLY TERROR) ★★ A 12-year-old girl goes on a chopping spree. Brooke Shields only has a small role in this, her first film. But after the success of *Pretty Baby*, the distributor changed the title, gave Brooke top billing, and rereleased this uninteresting thriller. Rated R for violence. 96m. **DIR:** Alfred Sole. **CAST:** Brooke Shields, Tom Signorelli, Paula E. Sheppard, Lillian Roth. **1977**

ALIEN PREY This savage alien is on a protein mission. This film contains sexual and cannibalistic scenes, making it unsuitable for the squeamish. 85m. **DIR:** Norman J. Warren. **CAST:** Barry Stokes, Sally Faulkner. **1984**

ALISON'S BIRTHDAY ★★½ A slow but interesting Australian horror story. A young girl is told by her father's ghost to leave home before her nineteenth birthday, but as you may guess, she's summoned back days before the big day, and things get nasty. 99m. **DIR:** Ian Coughlan. **CAST:** Joanne Samuel, Lou Brown. **1984**

ALLIGATOR ★★★½ The wild imagination of screenwriter John Sayles invests this comedy-horror film with wit and style. It features Robert Forster as a cop tracking down a giant alligator. It's good, unpretentious fun, but you have to be on your toes to catch all the gags (be sure to read the hilarious graffiti). Rated R. 94m. **DIR:** Lewis Teague. **CAST:** Robert Forster, Michael Gazzo, Robin Riker, Perry Lang, Jack Carter, Bart Braverman, Henry Silva, Dean Jagger. **1980**

ALLIGATOR II ★★½ An evil land developer prevents cops from stopping the ground-breaking ceremonies of his lakefront project, despite the fact that a mutant alligator is making lunch of anyone near the lake. Doesn't have the bite of the original John Sayles script, but manages to dig its teeth into you nonetheless. Rated R for violence. 94m. **DIR:** Brandon Clark. **CAST:** Joseph Bologna, Dee Wallace, Richard Lynch, Steve Railsback. **1990**

ALONE IN THE DARK The inmates of a New Jersey mental institution break out to terrorize a doctor and his family. Rated R. 92m. **DIR:** Jack Sholder. **CAST:** Jack Palance, Donald Pleasence, Martin Landau, Dwight Schultz, Deborah Hedwall, Erland Van Lidth. **1982**

AMERICAN GOTHIC ★★★½ Inventive, chilling, and atmospheric horror film pits a group of vacationers on a remote island against a grotesque, creepy family headed by Ma and Pa (Rod Steiger and Yvonne De Carlo). The latter's children, middle-aged adults who act and dress like kids, delight in killing off the newcomers one by one. An absence of gore and an emphasis on characterization make this an uncommonly satisfying film for horror buffs. Rated R for violence and profanity. 90m. **DIR:** John Hough. **CAST:** Rod Steiger, Yvonne De Carlo, Michael J. Pollard. **1988**

AMERICAN WEREWOLF IN LONDON, AN ★★★½ Director John Landis weaves humor, violence, and the classic horror elements of suspense in the tale of the two American travelers who find more than they bargained for on the English moors. Rated R for violence, nudity, and gore. 97m. **DIR:** John Landis. **CAST:** David Naughton, Jenny Agutter, Griffin Dunne. **1981**

AMITYVILLE HORROR, THE A better title for this turgid mishmash would be *The Amityville Bore*. Avoid it. Rated R. 117m. **DIR:** Stuart Rosenberg. **CAST:** James Brolin, Margot Kidder, Rod Steiger. **1979**

AMITYVILLE II: THE POSSESSION ★★ Okay, so it's not a horror classic. But thanks to tight pacing, skillful special effects, and fine acting, *Amityville II: The Possession* is a fairly suspenseful flick. Rated R for violence, implied sex, light profanity, and adult themes. 104m. **DIR:** Damiano Damiani. **CAST:** Burt Young, Rutanya Alda, James Olson, Moses Gunn. **1982**

AMITYVILLE III: THE DEMON In this soggy second sequel to *The Amityville Horror*, Tony Roberts plays a reporter who investigates the infamous house. Rated PG for violence and gore. 105m. **DIR:** Richard Fleischer. **CAST:** Tony Roberts, Candy Clark, Robert Joy, Tess Harper, Lori Loughlin, Meg Ryan. **1983**

AMITYVILLE 4: THE EVIL ESCAPES ★★ Rest easy: the most famous haunted house on Long Island and the subject of three earlier films is now demon free. Unfortunately, the evil has relocated to Jane Wyatt's California homestead. Ridiculous TV movie. 95m. **DIR:** Sandor Stern. **CAST:** Patty Duke, Jane Wyatt, Norman Lloyd. **1989**

AMITYVILLE CURSE, THE ★★½ The famous house of hell shakes its walls and rattles its floors for the fifth time. In this chapter, three young couples have purchased the dreadful dwelling. Naturally, things aren't what they should be. Rated R. 92m. **DIR:** Tom Berry. **CAST:** Kim Coates. **1989**

AMITYVILLE 1992: IT'S ABOUT TIME A possessed mantel clock takes its toll on an unsuspecting suburban family. This sixth installment of *The Amityville Horror* series has fair effects, but it hasn't any real suspense. Rated R for nudity, violence, and profanity. 95m. **DIR:** Tony Randel. **CAST:** Stephen Macht, Shawn Weatherly, Megan Ward, Damon Martin, Nita Talbot. **1992**

AMITYVILLE: A NEW GENERATION Low-budget and none-too-creative. The ancient Amityville evil is now lurking behind a strange-looking mirror in the possession of a young artist. Rated R for profanity, nudity, and violence. 92m. **DIR:** John Murlowski. **CAST:** Ross Partridge, Julia Nickson, David Naughton, Richard Roundtree, Terry O'Quinn. **1993**

AMSTERDAMNED When a psycho killer comes up from the depths of the Amsterdam canals seeking prey, a Dutch cop and his buddy, a scuba-diving expert, try to reel him in. Rated R for violence. 114m. **DIR:** Dick Maas. **CAST:** Huub Stapel, Monique van de Ven. **1988**

AND NOW THE SCREAMING STARTS ★★★ Frightening British horror film about a young newlywed couple moving into a house haunted by a centuries-old curse on the husband's family. Well-done, with a great cast, but occasionally a bit too bloody. Rated R. 87m. **DIR:** Roy Ward Baker. **CAST:** Peter Cushing, Stephanie Beacham, Herbert Lom, Patrick Magee, Ian Ogilvy. **1973**

ANDY WARHOL'S DRACULA Companion piece to Andy Warhol's equally revolting version of *Frankenstein*. Rated X for excessive violence and kinky sex. 93m. **DIR:** Paul Morrissey. **CAST:** Udo Kier, Joe Dallesandro, Vittorio De Sica, Roman Polanski. **1974**

ANDY WARHOL'S FRANKENSTEIN Blood and gore gush at every opportunity. Rated R for obvious reasons. 94m. **DIR:** Paul Morrissey. **CAST:** Joe Dallesandro, Monique Van Vooren, Udo Kier. **1974**

ANGUISH ★★★★ This horror-thriller is actually a movie within a movie. The first portion deals with a mother and son's odd relationship that has him murdering people for their eyes, while the second portion is actually about an audience watching the film and being terrorized by an unknown killer. *Not* recommended for those with weak stomachs. Rated R. 85m. **DIR:** Bigas Luna. **CAST:** Zelda Rubinstein, Michael Lerner. **1988**

ANTS! *Ants!* is just another haunting remnant of boring filmmaking from the *Movie of the Week* closet. 88m. **DIR:** Robert Sheerer. **CAST:** Robert Foxworth, Lynda Day George, Suzanne Somers, Myrna Loy, Brian Dennehy. **1977**

APE, THE ★★ Boris Karloff finished out his contract with Monogram Studios with this story about a doctor who discovers a cure for polio that requires spinal fluid from a human being. Not too many thrills, but Karloff is always worth watching. B&W; 61m. **DIR:** William Nigh. **CAST:** Boris Karloff, Gertrude Hoffman. **1940**

APE MAN, THE ★★ Bela Lugosi was one of the great horror film stars. However, the monster-movie boom stopped short in 1935, leaving the Hungarian actor out of work. When shockers came back in vogue four years later, Lugosi took any and every role he was offered. The result was grade-Z pictures such as this one, about a scientist (Lugosi) attempting to harness the physical power of apes for humankind. Too bad. B&W; 64m. **DIR:** William Beaudine. **CAST:** Bela Lugosi, Louise Currie, Wallace Ford, Minerva Urecal. **1943**

APOLOGY ★★★ This psycho-suspense film features Lesley Ann Warren as a bizarre artist who starts an anonymous phone service to get ideas. People call the recording and confess a sin they've committed. All goes well until a caller begins killing people in order to have something to be sorry for. Made for cable TV, this is unrated but it contains obscenities, gore, and simulated sex. 98m. **DIR:** Robert Bierman. **CAST:** Lesley Ann Warren, Peter Weller, George Loros, John Glover, Christopher Noth. **1986**

APPOINTMENT, THE Story of a father cursed by his evil daughter. Unrated, the film has some violence. 90m. **DIR:** Lindsey C. Vickers. **CAST:** Edward Woodward, Jane Merrow. **1982**

APPRENTICE TO MURDER ★★½ This film of the occult was inspired by a true story in Pennsylvania in 1927. Donald Sutherland appears as a religious leader with healing and mystical powers. Chad Lowe, in his desperation to get help for his alcoholic father, falls prey to Sutherland's powers. Rated PG-13 for language and violence. 97m. **DIR:** Ralph L. Thomas. **CAST:** Donald Sutherland, Chad Lowe, Mia Sara, Rutanya Alda, Eddie Jones, Mark Burton. **1987**

APRIL FOOL'S DAY ★★★ A group of college kids are invited to a mansion on a desolate island by a rich girl named Muffy St. John. They read Milton, quote Boswell, play practical jokes, and get killed off in a nice, orderly fashion. Not really a horror film; more of a mystery à la *Ten Little Indians*. Rated R for violence and profanity. 90m. **DIR:** Fred Walton. **CAST:** Jay Baker, Deborah Foreman, Griffin O'Neal, Amy Steel. **1986**

ARACHNOPHOBIA ★★★★ Steven Spielberg protégé and longtime producer Frank Marshall does a splendid job with the *Jaws* formula in this crackerjack thriller about a small-town doctor (Jeff Daniels) and a Rambo-style exterminator (John Goodman) attempting to find and kill a huge South American spider, which has been producing a passle of deadly offspring. It's both funny and scary; a delightful roller-coaster ride of guffaws and gasps. Rated PG-13 for mild violence. 103m. **DIR:** Frank Marshall. **CAST:** Jeff Daniels, John Goodman, Harley Jane Kozak. **1990**

ARMY OF DARKNESS ★★★½ This third film in writer-director Sam Raimi's *Evil Dead* series is by far the most polished. That's not to say it's the best, but the mixture of comedy and mayhem make it a good old time. Film fanatics will cherish some of Raimi's nods to famous fantastic films. Rated R for violence. 83m. **DIR:** Sam Raimi. **CAST:** Bruce Campbell, Embeth Davidtz, Marcus Gilbert, Ian Abercrombie, Richard Grove. **1993**

ARNOLD ★★ A delightful cast cannot save this rather muddled mess of murder and mirth. Stella Stevens, married to a corpse, suddenly discovers her costars meeting their maker in a variety of strange ways reminiscent of *The Abominable Dr. Phibes*. Rated PG for violence. 100m. **DIR:** Georg Fenady. **CAST:** Roddy McDowall, Elsa Lanchester, Stella Stevens, Farley Granger, Victor Buono, John McGiver, Shani Wallis. **1973**

ASTRO-ZOMBIES John Carradine as a mad scientist killing to obtain body parts for his new creation. 83m. **DIR:** Ted V. Mikels. **CAST:** Wendell Corey, John Carradine, Rafael Campos. **1967**

ASYLUM ★★★★ A first-rate horror anthology from England featuring fine performances. Four seemingly unrelated stories of madness by Robert Bloch are interwoven, leading to a nail-biting climax. Rated PG. 92m. **DIR:** Roy Ward Baker. **CAST:** Barbara Parkins, Sylvia Syms, Peter Cushing, Barry Morse, Richard Todd, Herbert Lom, Patrick Magee. **1972**

ASYLUM OF SATAN Girdler's first feature contains mucho sadism. Rated R. 82m. **DIR:** William Girdler. **CAST:** Charles Kissinger, Carla Borelli. **1972**

ATOM AGE VAMPIRE Badly dubbed Italian timewaster with cheese-ball special effects and a tired premise. B&W; 71m. **DIR:** Anton Giulio Masano. **CAST:** Alberto Lupo, Susanne Loret. **1960**

ATTACK OF THE CRAB MONSTERS ★★★ Neat Roger Corman low-budget movie, seemed scarier when you were a kid, but it's still a lot of fun. A remote Pacific atoll is besieged by a horde of giant land crabs that, upon devouring members of a scientific expedition, absorb their brains and acquire the ability to speak in their voices. B&W; 64m. **DIR:** Roger Corman. **CAST:** Richard Garland, Pamela Duncan, Mel Welles, Russell Johnson, Ed Nelson. **1957**

ATTACK OF THE 50-FOOT WOMAN (1958) ★★★ One of the best "schlock" films from the 1950s. Allison Hayes stars as a woman who is kidnapped by a tremendous bald alien and transformed into a giant herself. Duddy special effects only serve to heighten the enjoyment of this kitsch classic. B&W; 66m. **DIR:** Nathan Juran. **CAST:** Allison Hayes, William Hudson, Yvette Vickers. **1958**

ATTACK OF THE GIANT LEECHES ★★ Engagingly bad, lurid programmer—originally double-billed with *A Bucket of Blood*—about an Everglades town plagued by the title monsters. Cheesy fun from an imaginative B-movie director. B&W; 62m. **DIR:** Bernard Kowalski. **CAST:** Ken Clark, Yvette Vickers, Bruno Ve Sota. **1959**

ATTACK OF THE SWAMP CREATURE In one of Elvira's "Thriller Video" movies, we're subjected to the story of a mad scientist who turns himself into a giant, man-eating, walking catfish. 96m. **DIR:** Arnold Stevens. **CAST:** Frank Crowell, Patricia Robertson. **1985**

ATTIC, THE ★★ Rather slow-moving and routine story concerning a young woman (Carrie Snodgress) fighting to free herself from the clutches of her crippled, almost insane, father. Tries to be deep and psychological and falls flat on its face. Rated PG. 97m. **DIR:** George Edwards. **CAST:** Carrie Snodgress, Ray Milland. **1979**

AUDREY ROSE 🦃 Plodding melodrama about a man who annoys a couple by claiming that his dead daughter has been reincarnated as their live one. Rated PG. 113m. **DIR:** Robert Wise. **CAST:** Marsha Mason, Anthony Hopkins, John Beck. **1977**

AUNTIE LEE'S MEAT PIES ★★½ Good for Auntie Lee, played by Karen Black. Business is booming, and she sends out her four adorable nieces (former *Playboy* Playmates) to fetch fresh ingredients, including motorists, highway patrolmen, hitchhikers. Tongue-in-cheek black comedy is mildly entertaining. Rated R for nudity, violence, and language. 100m. **DIR:** Joseph F. Robertson. **CAST:** Karen Black, Noriyuki "Pat" Morita, Huntz Hall, Michael Berryman. **1992**

AUTOPSY 🦃 The story involves a young medical student doing graduate study in a morgue. Rated R for nudity and graphic violence. 90m. **DIR:** Armando Crispino. **CAST:** Mimsy Farmer, Raymond Lovelock, Barry Primus. **1976**

AVENGING CONSCIENCE, THE ★★½ Edgar Allan Poe's short stories provide the inspiration for this tale of a young writer (Henry B. Walthall) obsessed with Poe. Faced with the choice of continued patronage from his strict uncle or marriage with the "Annabel Lee" (Blanche Sweet) of his dreams, our tortured hero subjects his uncle to the tortures suggested by Poe's stories. Interesting historically, this silent feature is most effective in atmospheric chills. B&W; 78m. **DIR:** D. W. Griffith. **CAST:** Henry B. Walthall, Blanche Sweet, Mae Marsh, Robert Harron, Ralph Lewis. **1914**

AWAKENING, THE ★★½ In this mediocre horror flick, Charlton Heston plays an Egyptologist who discovers the tomb of a wicked queen. The evil spirit escapes the tomb and is reincarnated in Heston's newborn daughter. A bit hard to follow. Rated R for gore. 102m. **DIR:** Mike Newell. **CAST:** Charlton Heston, Susannah York, Jill Townsend, Stephanie Zimbalist. **1980**

B.O.R.N. ★★ *B.O.R.N.* (Body Organ Replacement Network) involves the same concept as *Coma*. The body organ black marketeers are at it again, only this time they're kidnapping healthy, unsuspecting people right off the street. Rated R for profanity, nudity, gore. 98m. **DIR:** Ross Hagen. **CAST:** Ross Hagen, Hoke Howell, P. J. Soles, William Smith. **1988**

BABY, THE ★★★ Extremely odd film by veteran director Ted Post about a teenager who has remained an infant all his life (yes, he still lives in his crib) and with his insane, overprotective mother. Eerily effective chiller is entertaining, though many will undoubtedly find it repulsive and ridiculous. Rated PG. 80m. **DIR:** Ted Post. **CAST:** Ruth Roman, Marianna Hill, Anjanette Comer. **1974**

BABYSITTER, THE ★★★½ Outside of some glaring plot flaws, *The Babysitter* is an effectively eerie film. Stephanie Zimbalist is Joanna, a woman hired as a housekeeper (not a babysitter). But Joanna is no Mary Poppins. Not rated, has violence. 96m. **DIR:** Peter Medak. **CAST:** Patty Duke, William Shatner, Quinn Cummings, David Wallace, Stephanie Zimbalist, John Houseman. **1980**

BAD BLOOD ★★★ Absolutely terrifying thriller, thanks to Ruth Raymond's performance as the psychotic mother who lusts after her long-lost son. Linda Blair has the unfortunate role of her much-abused daughter-in-law. Rated R for nudity and violence. 103m. **DIR:** Chuck Vincent. **CAST:** Ruth Raymond, Gregory Patrick, Linda Blair. **1988**

BAD DREAMS 🦃 Tale of a young woman awakened from a thirteen-year coma only to be haunted and hunted by the ghost of a maniacal leader of a hippie cult. Rated R for violence, gore, and profanity. 90m. **DIR:** Andrew Fleming. **CAST:** Jennifer Rubin, Bruce Abbott, Richard Lynch, Harris Yulin. **1988**

BAD RONALD ★★ Scott Jacoby lives secretly in a hidden room his mother builds for him after he kills a taunting peer. When Mama passes on, a new family moves into the place. Intriguing but tedious made-for-TV movie. 72m. **DIR:** Buzz Kulik. **CAST:** Scott Jacoby, Kim Hunter, Pippa Scott, Dabney Coleman. **1978**

BASKET CASE ★★★ Comedy and horror are mixed beautifully in this weird tale of a young man and his deformed Siamese twin out for revenge against the doctors who separated them. Gruesomely entertaining and highly recommended for shock buffs. Rated R. 91m. **DIR:** Frank Henenlotter. **CAST:** Kevin Van Hentenryck, Terri Susan Smith. **1982**

BASKET CASE 2 🦃 Shameless sequel. Rated R for violence and nudity. 90m. **DIR:** Frank Henenlotter. **CAST:** Kevin Van Hentenryck, Heather Rattray. **1990**

BASKET CASE 3: THE PROGENY ★★★ Bad is a relative term. And with this second sequel featuring the "Times Square Freak Twins" Duane and Belial Bradley, bad means good—in a sickening sort of way. The brothers head south for the delivery of Belial's mutant offspring. Along for the ride is the weirdest bunch of creatures this side of the Cantina scene in *Star Wars*. Rated R for violence, profanity, gore, and simulated mutant sex. 90m. **DIR:** Frank Henenlotter. **CAST:** Annie Ross, Kevin Van Hentenryck. **1992**

BAT PEOPLE 🦃 A young biologist on his honeymoon is bitten by a bat and is slowly transformed into a flying, blood-hungry rodent. Originally titled *It Lives by Night*. It sucks under any name. Rated R. 95m. **DIR:** Jerry Jameson. **CAST:** Stewart Moss, Marianne McAndrew, Michael Pataki. **1974**

BATTLE SHOCK ★★ Ralph Meeker portrays an artist who becomes involved in a murder while working in Mexico. Janice Rule is his doting wife. An uneven suspenser also known under the title of *A Woman's Devotion*. 88m. **DIR:** Paul Henreid. **CAST:** Ralph Meeker, Janice Rule, Rosenda Monteros, Paul Henreid. **1956**

BEAKS THE MOVIE 🦃 Hitchcock made birds menacing. *Beaks* makes them at times unintentionally funny and at other times too gruesome to watch. 86m. **DIR:** René Cardona Jr. **CAST:** Christopher Atkins, Michelle Johnson. **1987**

BEAST IN THE CELLAR, THE ★★ Boring story about a pair of aging sisters (well played by veterans Beryl Reid and Flora Robson) with something to hide. Their deranged, deformed brother is down there, and he wants out! Weak. Rated R. 87m. **DIR:** James Kelly. **CAST:** Beryl Reid, Flora Robson, T. P. McKenna, John Hamill. **1971**

BEAST MUST DIE, THE ★★ A millionaire hunter invites a group of guests to an isolated mansion. One of them is a werewolf he intends to destroy. A tame, talky reworking of Agatha Christie's *Ten Little Indians*. Rated PG. 98m. **DIR:** Paul Annett. **CAST:** Calvin Lockhart, Peter Cushing, Charles Gray, Anton Diffring. **1974**

BEAST OF THE YELLOW NIGHT ★★ Having played the hero in several Filipino Blood Island, mad-scientist movies, John Ashley here takes on the mantle of the villain. This Jekyll-and-Hyde effort is as cheesy as his earlier tropical thrillers, but the sporadic mayhem may keep you amused. Rated R. 87m. **DIR:** Eddie Romero. **CAST:** John Ashley, Mary Wilcox, Eddie Garcia. **1970**

BEAST WITH FIVE FINGERS, THE ★★★ Some eerie moments with the severed hand of a deceased pianist running loose in a mansion, choking people left and right. Another high-camp, wide-eyed performance by Peter Lorre. Fine special effects. B&W; 89m. **DIR:** Robert Florey. **CAST:** Robert Alda, Peter Lorre, Andrea King, J. Carrol Naish. **1947**

BEAST WITHIN, THE 🦃 This unbelievably gory movie consists mainly of one grisly murder after another. Rated R. 90m. **DIR:** Philippe Mora. **CAST:** Ronny Cox, Bibi Besch, Paul Clemens, Don Gordon. **1982**

BEDLAM ★★★ One of the lesser entries in the Val Lewton–produced horror film series at RKO, this release still has its moments as the courageous Anna Lee tries to expose the cruelties and inadequacies of an insane asylum run by Boris Karloff, who is first-rate, as usual. B&W; 79m. **DIR:** Mark Robson. **CAST:** Boris Karloff, Anna Lee, Ian Wolfe, Richard Fraser, Jason Robards Sr. **1946**

BEES, THE 🦃 Despite all temptation to label this a honey of a picture, it's a drone that will probably give viewers the hives. Rated PG. 83m. **DIR:** Alfredo Zacharias. **CAST:** John Saxon, John Carradine. **1978**

BEFORE I HANG ★★★ Neat little thriller has Boris Karloff as a goodhearted doctor who creates an age-retardant serum. Trouble begins when he tests it on himself, with horrible side effects. Nicely done, the film benefits from a good supporting performance by horror veteran Edward Van Sloan. B&W; 71m. **DIR:** Nick Grindé. **CAST:** Boris Karloff, Evelyn Keyes, Bruce Bennett, Pedro De Cordoba, Edward Van Sloan. **1940**

BEHIND LOCKED DOORS 🦃 Sleazy, near-plotless thriller about a nutcase who kidnaps young women for sexual "research." Unrated, but an R equivalent for nudity and rape. 79m. **DIR:** Charles Romine. **CAST:** Joyce Denner, Eve Reeves, Daniel Garth, Ivan Hagar. **1974**

BEING, THE 🦃 Water contaminated with nuclear waste spawned a beast that likes to shove itself *through* people. Rated R for gore and nudity. 82m. **DIR:** Jackie Kong. **CAST:** Martin Landau, José Ferrer, Dorothy Malone, Ruth Buzzi. **1984**

BELIEVERS, THE ★★★½ Martin Sheen portrays a recently widowed father whose son is chosen as a sacrifice to a voodoo cult running rampant in New York. John Schlesinger is not the best director for a thriller of this type, but in this case the quality of the acting, the snap of the writing, and the strength of the story build the suspense nicely and provide a striking climax. Rated R for language, nudity, and nightmarism. 110m. **DIR:** John Schlesinger. **CAST:** Martin Sheen, Helen Shaver, Robert Loggia, Richard Masur, Elizabeth Wilson, Lee Richardson, Harris Yulin, Jimmy Smits. **1987**

BEN 🦃 The only thing going for this silly sequel to *Willard* is an awkwardly charming title song performed by a young Michael Jackson (a love song for a rat, no less). Rated PG for violence. 95m. **DIR:** Phil Karlson. **CAST:** Arthur O'Connell, Lee Montgomery, Rosemary Murphy. **1972**

BERSERK ★★★½ Effectively staged thriller stars Joan Crawford as the owner of a once-great circus now on its last legs—until a number of accidental deaths of the performers starts packing 'em in. Joan comes under suspicion immediately when the cops begin counting the box-office receipts. Could she be guilty? 96m. **DIR:** Jim O'Connolly. **CAST:** Joan Crawford, Ty Hardin, Michael Gough, Diana Dors, Judy Geeson. 1967

BERSERKER Silly slasher in which a Viking demon, is reincarnated in his descendants. Rated R for nudity, violence, gore, and simulated sex. 85m. **DIR:** Jeff Richard. **CAST:** Joseph Alan Johnson. 1987

BEST OF DARK SHADOWS, THE ★★½ Lack of narration will leave viewers confused as this *Dark Shadows* compilation jumps from one teaser to another. We meet vampires, a werewolf, a witch, ghosts, and a Jekyll and Hyde character without benefit of the background leading to these shocking devlopments. B&W/color; 30m. **DIR:** Lela Swift, Henry Kapland, John Sedwick. **CAST:** Jonathan Frid, David Selby, Joan Bennett, Kate Jackson, Lara Parker, Kathryn Leigh Scott. 1965–1971

BEST OF SEX AND VIOLENCE ★★ A quickie video containing unrelated clips from low-budget exploitation films. A certain sleazy charm. Unrated, the film has profanity, nudity, and, of course, sex and violence. 76m. **DIR:** Ken Dixon. **CAST:** Hosted by John Carradine. 1981

BEYOND DARKNESS Hokey spooker about a priest and his family who move into an old house haunted by witches burned at the stake. Rated R for violence. 90m. **DIR:** Clyde Anderson. **CAST:** David Brandon. 1992

BEYOND EVIL A luxurious mansion happens to be haunted. Rated R. 94m. **DIR:** Herb Freed. **CAST:** John Saxon, Lynda Day George, Michael Dante. 1980

BEYOND THE DOOR Sick rip-off of *The Exorcist* has Juliet Mills as a woman possessed by guess what. Rated R. 94m. **DIR:** Ovidio Assonitis (Oliver Hellman). **CAST:** Juliet Mills, Richard Johnson, David Colin Jr. 1975

BEYOND THE DOOR 2 ★★ Why, why, why? Actually, this semisequel is much better than the original mainly because its director was the famed Mario Bava. This time a young boy becomes possessed by the unseen power of hell, and many die. Alternate title: *Shock*. Rated R. 92m. **DIR:** Mario Bava. **CAST:** Daria Nicolodi, John Steiner, David Colin Jr. 1979

BEYOND THE DOOR 3 A college student falls victim to the prince of darkness in this unscary horror yarn with laughable special effects. Rated R for profanity, nudity, and violence. 94m. **DIR:** Jeff Kwitny. **CAST:** Mary Kohnert. 1991

BIG FOOT Legendary monster comes down from the hills and beats the hell out of everybody. 94m. **DIR:** Robert F. Slatzer. **CAST:** John Carradine, Joi Lansing, John Mitchum, Chris Mitchum. 1971

BIKINI ISLAND Inane, low-budget T&A flick focuses on five swimsuit models stalked on an exotic location shoot. A number of likely suspects emerge but, of course, are red herrings. Rated R for nudity, violence, and profanity. 90m. **DIR:** Anthony Markes. **CAST:** Holly Floria, Jackson Robinson. 1991

BILLY THE KID MEETS THE VAMPIRES Billy the Kid takes a vacation and meets up with some of the lousiest actors and actresses this side of Mars. Not rated. 118m. **DIR:** Steve Postal. **CAST:** Michael K. Saunders, Debra Orth, Angela Shepard. 1991

BILLY THE KID VS. DRACULA Hokey horror film casts John Carradine as the famous vampire, on the loose in a small western town. 95m. **DIR:** William Beaudine. **CAST:** John Carradine, Chuck Courtney, Melinda Plowman, Virginia Christine, Harry Carey Jr. 1966

BIRDS, THE ★★★★ Alfred Hitchcock's *The Birds* is an eerie, disturbing stunner, highlighted by Evan Hunter's literate adaptation of Daphne Du Maurier's ominous short story. Rod Taylor and Tippi Hedren are thrown into an uneasy relationship while our avian friends develop an appetite for something more substantial than bugs and berries. Although quite fantastic, the premise is made credible by Hitchcock's unswerving attention to character; the supporting cast is excellent. Unrated, but may be too intense for younger viewers. 120m. **DIR:** Alfred Hitchcock. **CAST:** Rod Taylor, Tippi Hedren, Jessica Tandy, Suzanne Pleshette, Veronica Cartwright, Ethel Griffies. 1963

BIRDS II, THE: LAND'S END This idiotic sequel to Hitchcock's classic is a complete mess, with inane plotting, overwrought acting, and a climax that feels like the camera just ran out of film. Director Rick Rosenthal was disgusted enough to hide behind the alias Alan Smithee. Rated R for violence and profanity. 87m. **DIR:** Rick Rosenthal. **CAST:** Brad Johnson, Chelsea Field, James Naughton, Jan Rubes, Tippi Hedren. 1994

BLACK CAT, THE (1934) ★★★★ A surrealistic, strikingly designed horror-thriller that has become a cult favorite thanks to its pairing of Boris Karloff and Bela Lugosi. Lugosi has one of his very few good-guy roles as a concerned citizen who gets drawn into a web of evil that surrounds Karloff's black magic. Available on a videocassette double feature with *The Raven*. B&W; 70m. **DIR:** Edgar G. Ulmer. **CAST:** Boris Karloff, Bela Lugosi, Jacqueline Wells. 1934

BLACK CAT, THE (1981) ★★ Feline gore from Lucio Fulci, made when he was the most prolific of the low-budget Italian exploitation-horror directors. A very loose Poe adaptation. Rated R for violence. 92m. **DIR:** Lucio Fulci. **CAST:** Patrick Magee, Mimsy Farmer, David Warbeck. 1981

BLACK CHRISTMAS ★★★ During the holiday season, members of a sorority house fall victim to the homicidal obscene phone-caller living in their attic. Margot Kidder is quite convincing as a vulgar, alcoholic college kid with asthma. Atmospheric and frightening. Try to remember that it came before *Halloween* and *When A Stranger Calls*. Rated R. 99m. **DIR:** Bob Clark. **CAST:** Olivia Hussey, Keir Dullea, Margot Kidder, John Saxon. **1975**

BLACK DEVIL DOLL FROM HELL ★★ Direct-to-video melodrama in which a miniature voodoo doll goes on a gruesome rampage. Most of the time, sluggish and predictable. Not rated. 70m. **DIR:** Chester T. Turner. **CAST:** Rickey Roach. **1984**

BLACK DRAGONS 🦃 A silly film about Japanese agents who are surgically altered to resemble American businessmen and chiefs of industry. B&W; 62m. **DIR:** William Nigh. **CAST:** Bela Lugosi, Joan Barclay, Clayton Moore. **1949**

BLACK MAGIC TERROR 🦃 This Japanese horror is the story of a young woman jilted by her lover who turns to black magic for her violent revenge. Not rated, but contains some nudity and violence. 85m. **DIR:** L. Sujio. **CAST:** Suzanna. **1985**

BLACK ROOM, THE (1935) ★★★ Boris Karloff is excellent as twin brothers with an age-old family curse hanging over their heads. Well-handled thriller never stops moving. B&W; 67m. **DIR:** Roy William Neill. **CAST:** Boris Karloff, Marian Marsh, Robert Allen, Katherine DeMille, Thurston Hall. **1935**

BLACK ROOM, THE (1985) 🦃 A philandering husband rents an apartment from a couple who kill the adulterous man's girlfriends. Rated R for nudity. 88m. **DIR:** Norman Thaddeus Vane. **CAST:** Stephen Knight, Cassandra Gavioca. **1985**

BLACK ROSES ★★½ Black Roses is the name of a hard-rock group that comes to sleepy Mill Basin for a concert. Soon, the concert hall becomes a hell on Earth. Want to see a guy get sucked into a wall-mounted speaker? It's here. Rated R for violence, nudity, and language. 90m. **DIR:** John Fasano. **CAST:** John Martin, Ken Swofford. **1988**

BLACK SABBATH ★★★½ Above-average trio of horror tales given wonderful atmosphere by director Mario Bava. Boris Karloff plays host and stars in the third story, a vampire opus entitled "The Wurdalak." One of the others, "A Drop of Water," is based on a story by Chekhov; the third, "The Telephone," involves disconnected calls of the worst sort. 99m. **DIR:** Mario Bava. **CAST:** Boris Karloff, Mark Damon, Suzy Andersen. **1964**

BLACK SUNDAY (1961) ★★★★ Italian horror classic about the one day each century when Satan roams the Earth. Brilliant cinematography and art direction help establish a chilling, surreal atmosphere in this tale of a witch who swears vengeance on the offspring of those who brutally killed her centuries ago. B&W; 83m. **DIR:** Mario Bava. **CAST:** Barbara Steele, John Richardson, Ivo Garrani, Andrea Checci. **1961**

BLACKENSTEIN 🦃 Tasteless and grotesque entry in the subgenre of blaxploitation horror films. Rated R for violence and nudity. 92m. **DIR:** William A. Levey. **CAST:** John Hart, Joe DiSue. **1973**

BLACULA ★★★½ An old victim (William Marshall) of Dracula's bite is loose in modern L.A. Surprisingly well-done shocker. Fierce and energetic, with a solid cast. Rated R for violence. 92m. **DIR:** William Crain. **CAST:** William Marshall, Denise Nicholas, Vonetta McGee, Thalmus Rasulala. **1972**

BLADES 🦃 Really dull slice-and-dice raunch about a power mower from hell. Rated R for violence and profanity. 101m. **DIR:** Thomas R. Randinella. **CAST:** Robert North. **1989**

BLOB, THE (1958) ★★★ This was Steve McQueen's first starring role. He plays a teenager battling parents and a voracious hunk of protoplasm from outer space. Long surpassed by more sophisticated sci-fi, it's still fun to watch. 86m. **DIR:** Irvin S. Yeaworth Jr. **CAST:** Steve McQueen, Aneta Corseaut, Olin Howlin. **1958**

BLOB, THE (1988) ★★★★ Frightening and occasionally comedic remake of the 1958 cult classic. This time around, Kevin Dillon and Shawnee Smith battle the gelatinous ooze as it devours the inhabitants of a small ski resort. The best horror remake since *The Fly*. A thrill ride for those with the stomach to take it. Rated R for profanity and state-of-the-art gruesomeness. 95m. **DIR:** Chuck Russell. **CAST:** Kevin Dillon, Shawnee Smith, Donovan Leitch, Jeffrey DeMunn, Candy Clark, Joe Seneca. **1988**

BLOOD AND BLACK LACE ★★½ This sometimes frightening Italian horror film features a psychotic killer eliminating members of the modeling industry with gusto. Decent entry in the genre from specialist Mario Bava. 88m. **DIR:** Mario Bava. **CAST:** Cameron Mitchell, Eva Bartok. **1964**

BLOOD AND ROSES 🦃 The ghost of a centuries dead vampire possesses a young woman in an attempt to fulfill an ancient curse. Although artistically filmed, the script shuns almost all vampire lore. 74m. **DIR:** Roger Vadim. **CAST:** Mel Ferrer, Elsa Martinelli, Annette Vadim. **1960**

BLOOD BEACH 🦃 Poor horror story of mysterious forces sucking people down into the sand. Rated R. 89m. **DIR:** Jeffrey Bloom. **CAST:** John Saxon, Marianna Hill, Otis Young. **1981**

BLOOD BEAST TERROR, THE ★★ The performances of genre stalwarts Peter Cushing and Robert Flemyng—as a scientist investigating hideous murders and the doctor whose moth-woman daughter is committing them—help elevate this tepid British horror. The monster is laughable. 88m. **DIR:** Vernon Sewell. **CAST:** Peter Cushing, Robert Flemyng. 1967

BLOOD CASTLE (1970) Original title: *Scream of the Demon Lover.* Lamebrain hack-'em-up set against pseudogothic backdrop. Rated R. 97m. **DIR:** J. L. Merino. **CAST:** Erna Schurer, Agostina Belli. 1970

BLOOD CASTLE (1972) ★★ Adaptation of the real-life saga of Elisabeth Bathory, a seventeenth-century Hungarian countess who bathed in virgin blood in the belief it kept her young and beautiful. This Spanish-Italian coproduction inserts enough exploitable elements to ensure an R rating. Also known as *The Legend of Blood Castle.* 87m. **DIR:** Jorge Grau. **CAST:** Lucia Bose, Ewa Aulin. 1972

BLOOD DINER Two brothers kill women to obtain body parts for a demonic ceremony. Unrated, but filled with violence, nudity, and gore. 88m. **DIR:** Jackie Kong. **CAST:** Rick Burks, Carl Crew. 1987

BLOOD FEAST First and most infamous of the drive-in gore movies bolsters practically nonexistent plot of crazed murderer with gallons of director Herschell Gordon Lewis's patented stage blood. 75m. **DIR:** Herschell Gordon Lewis. **CAST:** Connie Mason, Thomas Wood. 1963

BLOOD FREAK Howlingly bad Florida horror about a hippie biker who turns into—appropriately—a turkey monster. Rated R. 86m. **DIR:** Brad F. Grinter. **CAST:** Steve Hawkes. 1971

BLOOD FRENZY ★★ In this made-for-video horror-thriller, a psychotherapist takes a group of her patients into the desert for a retreat. Predictably, someone starts killing them off one by one. Who is the killer? Who cares? Unrated; the movie contains violence. 90m. **DIR:** Hal Freeman. **CAST:** Wendy MacDonald, Hank Garrett, Lisa Loring. 1987

BLOOD HOOK While attending a fishing tournament, several teenagers are murdered by a killer who uses a giant fishhook to reel in his catch. Not rated, but contains graphic violence and brief nudity. 85m. **DIR:** James Mallon. **CAST:** Mark Jacobs, Lisa Todd. 1986

BLOOD LINK All his life, a prominent physician has had strange hallucinations about older women being brutally murdered. He discovers that he is seeing through the eyes of his Siamese twin. Rated R for nudity and violence. 98m. **DIR:** Alberto De Martino. **CAST:** Michael Moriarty, Penelope Milford, Cameron Mitchell. 1983

BLOOD MANIA R-rated wonder, which features greedy heirs, an inheritance, and an unscrupulous physician. 90m. **DIR:** Robert Vincent O'Neil. **CAST:** Peter Carpenter, Maria De Aragon. 1971

BLOOD MOON ★★ Video retitling of *The Werewolf versus the Vampire Woman,* with Paul Naschy as his recurring character from Spanish horror movies, the tortured lycanthrope Waldemar. Naschy's cheapjack efforts merge Universal-style nostalgic monster ingredients with the sexploitation demands of the Seventies. Idiotic but watchable. Rated R. 86m. **DIR:** Leon Klimovsky. **CAST:** Paul Naschy, Patty Shepard. 1970

BLOOD OF DRACULA ★★ Okay American-international teen horror about a troubled girl who comes under the vampiric (and vaguely lesbian) influence of a sinister teacher. Occasionally atmospheric, but never scary. B&W; 68m. **DIR:** Herbert L. Strock. **CAST:** Sandra Harrison. 1957

BLOOD OF DRACULA'S CASTLE Quite possibly the worst Dracula movie ever made. The film has a werewolf, a hunchback, women in chains, human sacrifices, a laughable script, and a ten-dollar budget. Rated PG. 84m. **DIR:** Al Adamson, Jean Hewitt. **CAST:** John Carradine, Paula Raymond, Alex D'Arcy, Robert Dix. 1967

BLOOD OF THE VAMPIRE ★★½ Pretty good imitation Hammer horror flick (from the vintage period of British gothic shockers), with Donald Wolfit as the title fiend. Semicampy fun, with some genuine thrills, but the direction is too flat for the film to be taken seriously. Even worse, all source prints for its video release are faded almost to sepia, robbing the film of its once gorgeous color. 87m. **DIR:** Henry Cass. **CAST:** Barbara Shelley, Donald Wolfit, Vincent Ball. 1958

BLOOD ON SATAN'S CLAW ★★★ Fun, frightening horror film set in seventeenth-century England. A small farming community is besieged by the devil himself, who succeeds in turning the local children into a coven of witches. Familiar story is presented in a unique manner by director Piers Haggard, helped by excellent period detail and clever effects. Not for the kids, though. Rated R. 93m. **DIR:** Piers Haggard. **CAST:** Patrick Wymark, Barry Andrews, Linda Hayden, Simon Williams. 1971

BLOOD ORGY OF THE SHE DEVILS Ritualistic murders. Rated PG. 73m. **DIR:** Ted V. Mikels. **CAST:** Lila Zaborin, Tom Pace. 1972

BLOOD RAGE When a 10-year-old boy kills a stranger at a drive-in movie, he escapes punishment by blaming his twin brother. It played movie houses and cable TV as *Nightmare at Shadow Woods.* Rated R.

83m. **DIR:** John Grissmer. **CAST:** Louise Lasser, Mark Soper. **1983**

BLOOD RELATIONS Repugnant gore-fest features three generations of a wealthy family lusting after a beautiful gold digger. Rated R for nudity, violence, and gore. 88m. **DIR:** Graeme Campbell. **CAST:** Jan Rubes, Kevin Hicks, Lynne Adams, Ray Walston. **1987**

BLOOD ROSE Murky, grade-C horror from France was billed as "the first sex-horror film" for its U.S. release. Rated R. 87m. **DIR:** Claude Mulot. **CAST:** Philippe Lemaire, Anny Duperey, Howard Vernon. **1969**

BLOOD SALVAGE Psychotic family preys on distressed motorists, abducting them and then selling their vital organs to a demented doctor. Too bad the folks behind this mess couldn't give it a brain. Rated R for violence and profanity. 90m. **DIR:** Tucker Johnstone. **CAST:** Danny Nelson, Lori Birdsong, Ray Walston, John Saxon, Evander Holyfield. **1989**

BLOOD SCREAMS ★★½ Atmospheric thriller about a sleepy Mexican village that harbors a deep, dark secret that surfaces to torment two Americans. Rated R for nudity and violence. 75m. **DIR:** Glenn Gebhard. **CAST:** Russ Tamblyn, Stacey Shaffer. **1988**

BLOOD SISTERS A group of sorority girls must spend the night in a haunted house with a maniac. Rated R for nudity. 85m. **DIR:** Roberta Findlay. **CAST:** Amy Brentano, Shannon McMahon. **1987**

BLOOD SPATTERED BRIDE, THE ★★ Sheridan Le Fanu's *Carmilla* gets another reworking in this intermittently stylish exploitation movie from Spain. Although the climax was heavily censored by U.S. distributors, it's still R-rated. 95m. **DIR:** Vicente Aranda. **CAST:** Simon Andreu, Maribel Martin, Alexandra Bastedo. **1974**

BLOOD SPELL A modern-day evil sorcerer possesses his son in an attempt to gain immortality. Rated R for graphic violence. 87m. **DIR:** Deryn Warren. **CAST:** Anthony Jenkins. **1987**

BLOOD SUCKERS FROM OUTER SPACE ★★ Low-budget horror spoof about an alien virus that causes people to vomit up their guts, turning them into sneaky zombies out to suck the innards from hapless victims. Although sometimes funny, the film is uneven. Not rated, but contains profanity and partial nudity. 79m. **DIR:** Glenn Coburn. **CAST:** Thom Meyer, Pat Paulsen. **1984**

BLOOD TIES (1993) ★★½ This interesting bite on the vampire legend finds a group of former blood suckers trying to fit into society. Into their Los Angeles lair comes a teenager whose parents were murdered by vampire killers, now hot on his trail. The group must decide whether to fight back or flee, great fodder for moral arguments and exciting close calls. Rated R for sexuality, violence, and strong language. 93m. **DIR:** Jim McBride. **CAST:** Harley Venton, Patrick Bauchau, Bo Hopkins, Michelle Johnson, Jason London. **1993**

BLOODBEAT This cheap supernatural flick tries to pass off the idea that a samurai ghost is haunting the backwoods of an American wilderness. 84m. **DIR:** Fabrice A. Zaphiratos. **CAST:** Helen Benton, Terry Brown. **1985**

BLOODLUST: SUBSPECIES III ★★ This better-than-expected continuation of the vampire series features impressive, gory special effects. Anders Hove returns as vampire Radu, pitting two sisters against each other in a battle over their souls. Rated R for language, nudity, and violence. 81m. **DIR:** Ted Nicolaou. **CAST:** Anders Hove, Melanie Shatner, Denice Duff, Kevin Blair. **1993**

BLOODMOON ★★ Okay British slasher features a deranged private school teacher who kills couples at the nearby lovers' lane. It seems he transfers his anger at his unfaithful wife onto his promiscuous female students. Rated R for nudity, violence, and gore. 104m. **DIR:** Alec Mills. **CAST:** Loon Lissek. **1989**

BLOODSTONE: SUBSPECIES II ★★★½ A lovely college student is bitten by a vampire and spends most of the movie cringing from her shiveringly ugly master. Enjoy the comic-book sensibilities, imaginative direction, and the dark sense of humor permeating this low-budget howler. Rated R for violence and profanity. 107m. **DIR:** Ted Nicolaou. **CAST:** Anders Hove, Denice Duff. **1993**

BLOODSUCKERS, THE ★★½ Lots of blood, gory special effects, and some good humor. Not bad for this type of film. Also known as *Return from the Past* and *Dr. Terror's Gallery of Horrors*. Not for the squeamish. 84m. **DIR:** David L. Hewitt. **CAST:** Lon Chaney Jr., John Carradine. **1967**

BLOODSUCKING FREAKS (THE INCREDIBLE TORTURE SHOW) This putrid film is an endurance test for even the most hard-core horror buffs. The scene where one of the maniacs sucks a woman's brains out with a straw has to be one of the most repulsive moments ever put on film. Rated R for nudity and violence. 89m. **DIR:** Joel M. Reed. **CAST:** Seamus O'Brian, Niles McMaster. **1978**

BLOODSUCKING PHARAOHS IN PITTSBURGH ★★ Campy horror farce comparable to *Night of the Living Dead* meets *Rocky Horror Picture Show*. This time a cult killer sleazes about the city, slicing up victims with a chain saw. 89m. **DIR:** Alan Smithee. **CAST:** Jake Dengel. **1991**

BLOODTHIRSTY BUTCHERS As the title suggests, an extremely violent series of murders is committed in very gruesome fashion. Rated R. 80m. **DIR:** Andy Milligan. **CAST:** John Miranda, Annabella Wood. **1970**

BLOODTIDE 🦃 Cheap horror film about bizarre rituals on a Greek isle. Rated R. 82m. **DIR:** Richard Jeffries. **CAST:** James Earl Jones, José Ferrer, Lila Kedrova. **1984**

BLOODY BIRTHDAY 🦃 Three children, born during an eclipse of the moon, run amok, killing everyone in sight. Rated R. 85m. **DIR:** Edward Hunt. **CAST:** Susan Strasberg, José Ferrer, Lori Lethin, Joe Penny. **1986**

BLOODY MOON ★★ A high-body-count exploitation horror film, this is one of the more perfunctory outings by Jess (Jesus) Franco, and thus one of his least revolting. Women are stabbed, choked, and in one memorable instance, buzz-sawed to death. A gory clip was used in Pedro Almodóvar's *Matador*. Rated R. 83m. **DIR:** Jess (Jesus) Franco. **CAST:** Olivia Pascal, Christoph Moosbrugger. **1981**

BLOODY NEW YEAR ★★½ Five teenagers become stranded on an abandonded island resort that's caught in a time warp. Zombie ghosts begin to pop up, first taunting the kids, then terrorizing, and finally killing them. Fairly well produced and boasting some decent special effects. Rated R for violence and nudity. 90m. **DIR:** Norman J. Warren. **CAST:** Suzy Aitchison, Colin Heywood, Cathrine Roman. **1987**

BLOODY PIT OF HORROR ★★ Nudie photographers and their comely models run afoul of a psycho who thinks he's the reincarnated Crimson Executioner when they visit a supposedly abandoned castle for a photo session. A laugh riot, if you've got a sick sense of humor—otherwise, steer clear. 74m. **DIR:** Max Hunter (Massimo Pupillo). **CAST:** Mickey Hargitay. **1965**

BLOODY WEDNESDAY ★★½ A peculiar psychological horror story whose prime attraction is that it never gets predictable. After a man suffers a nervous breakdown, his brother sets him up as the caretaker of a vacant hotel. Unfortunately, the story is never satisfactorily resolved. Not rated. 97m. **DIR:** Mark G. Gilhuis. **CAST:** Raymond Elmendorf, Pamela Baker. **1985**

BLUE MONKEY ★★★ A small city hospital becomes contaminated by a patient infected by an unknown insect that causes terminal gangrene as it gestates eggs. One of these insects becomes mutated and grows to huge proportions. A low-budget film, this movie sometimes has the charm, humor, and suspense of classics like *The Thing* and *Them*. Rated R for violence and language. 98m. **DIR:** William Fruet. **CAST:** Steve Railsback, Susan Anspach, Gwynyth Walsh, John Vernon, Joe Flaherty, Robin Duke. **1987**

BLUE VELVET ★★★★½ In this brilliant but disturbing film, Kyle MacLachlan and Laura Dern play youngsters who become involved in the mystery surrounding nightclub singer Isabella Rossellini. It seldom lets the viewer off easy, yet it is nevertheless a stunning cinematic work. Rated R for violence, nudity, and profanity. 120m. **DIR:** David Lynch. **CAST:** Kyle MacLachlan, Isabella Rossellini, Dennis Hopper, Laura Dern, Dean Stockwell. **1986**

BLUEBEARD (1944) ★★★ Atmospheric low-budget thriller by resourceful German director Edgar G. Ulmer gives great character actor John Carradine one of his finest leading roles as a strangler who preys on women. B&W; 73m. **DIR:** Edgar G. Ulmer. **CAST:** John Carradine, Jean Parker, Nils Asther, Ludwig Stossel, Iris Adrian. **1944**

BLUEBEARD (1972) ★★½ Richard Burton stars in *Bluebeard*, a film with its tongue planted firmly in cheek. The legend of the multiple murderer is intermingled with Nazi lore to come out as a reasonably convincing foray into a combination of black comedy and classic horror films. Rated R. 125m. **DIR:** Edward Dmytryk. **CAST:** Richard Burton, Raquel Welch, Karin Schubert, Joey Heatherton. **1972**

BODY COUNT 🦃 An unexceptional thriller about a man committed to a mental institution by relatives who want his money. He escapes, and the title should clue you in as to what happens next. Not rated. 93m. **DIR:** Paul Leder. **CAST:** Bernie White, Marilyn Hassett, Dick Sargent, Greg Mullavey. **1988**

BODY MELT 🦃 Those folks down under have a thing for gross-out horror films, but the plot disintegrates faster than the people in this film. This is no *Dead Alive*—it's just dead. Rated AO; contains extreme violence, nudity, adult situations, and strong language. 82m. **DIR:** Philip Brophy. **CAST:** Gerard Kennedy, Andrew Daddo, Ian Smith, Regina Gaigalas. **1993**

BODY PARTS ★★ Maurice Renard's classic short story, "The Hands of Orlac," gets hauled out one more time for this ludicrous update from gore-hound Eric Red. Criminal psychologist Jeff Fahey loses his right arm and then receives another—from a serial killer—thanks to the miracles of modern science. Rated R for profanity and outrageous gruesomeness. 88m. **DIR:** Eric Red. **CAST:** Jeff Fahey, Kim Delaney, Brad Dourif, Lindsay Duncan. **1991**

BODY SNATCHER, THE ★★★★ Boris Karloff gives one of his finest performances in the title role of this Val Lewton production, adapted from the novel by Robert Louis Stevenson. Karloff is a sinister grave robber who provides dead bodies for illegal medical research and then uses his activities as blackmail to form a bond of "friendship" with the doctor he services, Henry Daniell (in an equally impressive turn). B&W; 77m. **DIR:** Robert Wise. **CAST:** Henry Daniell, Boris Karloff, Bela Lugosi. **1945**

BOG 🦃 Unlucky group of people on an excursion into the wilderness run into the recently defrosted monster Bog. Rated PG. 87m. **DIR:** Don Keeslar. **CAST:** Gloria De Haven, Aldo Ray, Marshall Thompson. **1983**

BOGGY CREEK II ★★ Pseudo-documentary schlockmaster Charles B. Pierce is at it again in this basic retelling of the search for a legendary swamp monster in southern Alabama. Cut-rate production values abound. Rated PG. 93m. **DIR:** Charles B. Pierce. **CAST:** Cindy Butler, Chuck Pierce. **1983**

BONEYARD, THE ★★ An aging detective and lady psychic team up to solve some grisly goings-on at the local mortuary. Their investigation leads them to the city morgue, where three possessed corpses plague them. Bizarre. 98m. **DIR:** James Cummins. **CAST:** Ed Nelson, Norman Fell, Phyllis Diller. **1990**

BOOGEYMAN, THE ★★★½ Despite the lame title, this is an inventive, atmospheric fright flick about pieces of a broken mirror causing horrifying deaths. Good special effects add to the creepiness. Rated R for violence and gore. 86m. **DIR:** Ulli Lommel. **CAST:** Suzanna Love, Michael Love, John Carradine. **1980**

BOOGEYMAN 2, THE 🦃 Cheapo sequel. Rated R for violence and gore. 79m. **DIR:** Bruce Starr. **CAST:** Suzanna Love, Shana Hall, Ulli Lommel. **1983**

BOSTON STRANGLER, THE ★★★ True account, told in semidocumentary style, of Beantown's notorious deranged murderer, plumber Albert De Salvo. Tony Curtis gives a first-class performance as the woman killer. 120m. **DIR:** Richard Fleischer. **CAST:** Tony Curtis, Henry Fonda, Mike Kellin, Murray Hamilton, Sally Kellerman, Hurd Hatfield, George Kennedy, Jeff Corey. **1968**

BOWERY AT MIDNIGHT 🦃 *Very* cheaply made story about a maniac on a killing spree in the Bowery. B&W; 63m. **DIR:** Wallace Fox. **CAST:** Bela Lugosi, John Archer, Wanda McKay, Tom Neal. **1942**

BOXING HELENA ★★ In this horrific, voyeuristic story of obsession, domination, and sexual inadequacy, a pathetic surgeon amputates the arms and legs of a bitchy temptress and imprisons her in his mansion. Writer-director Jennifer Chambers Lynch shoots for the same hypererotic, surreal, and dark feel that mark the films of her father, *Twin Peaks*'s David Lynch. It's visually seductive and surprisingly goreless but emotionally sterile. Rated R for nudity, sex, and profanity. 105m. **DIR:** Jennifer Chambers Lynch. **CAST:** Julian Sands, Sherilyn Fenn, Bill Paxton, Kurtwood Smith, Art Garfunkel. **1993**

BOYS FROM BROOKLYN, THE 🦃 Absolutely hilarious bomb with Bela Lugosi as a mad scientist turning people into apes on a forgotten island. Better known as *Bela Lugosi Meets a Brooklyn Gorilla*, a much more appropriate title. B&W; 72m. **DIR:** William Beaudine. **CAST:** Bela Lugosi, Duke Mitchell, Sammy Petrillo. **1952**

BRAIN, THE (1988) ★★½ Hokey special effects take away from this shocker about a TV psychologist (David Gale) and his alien brain. The brain (eyes, nose, and long, sharp teeth added) starts munching anyone who gets in the way. Occasionally entertaining, this is one film that never reaches its potential. Rated R for violence and mild gore. 94m. **DIR:** Edward Hunt. **CAST:** Tom Breznahan, Cyndy Preston, David Gale. **1988**

BRAIN DAMAGE ★★½ A wisecracking giant worm escapes from its elderly keepers and forces a teenager to kill people. Although the low budget hampers the special effects, the offbeat execution makes this worth a look for horror fans. Rated R for sexual situations and graphic violence. 90m. **DIR:** Frank Henenlotter. **CAST:** Rich Herbst, Gordon MacDonald. **1988**

BRAIN OF BLOOD 🦃 A mad doctor performs brain transplants and creates a hulking monster. 83m. **DIR:** Al Adamson. **CAST:** Kent Taylor, John Bloom, Regina Carroll, Grant Williams. **1971**

BRAINIAC, THE ★★★ Mexi-monster stuff about a nobleman, executed as a warlock in 1661, who comes back to life to seek revenge on the descendants of those who killed him. Every so often he transforms himself into a monster with a long, snaky tongue to suck out people's brains. With their low-production values and indifferent dubbing, most Mexican horror films are good only for camp value. This one has those same flaws, but you'll also find it has some eerily effective moments. 77m. **DIR:** Chano Urveta. **CAST:** Abel Salazar. **1961**

BRAINSCAN ★★ After a teenager plays a video game in which he commits murder, real killings exactly like the ones in his "game" begin to occur. This none-too-original rehash of the Freddy Krueger films is doggedly predictable, with cheap special effects and a double cop-out ending. Rated R for gore. 96m. **DIR:** John Flynn. **CAST:** Edward Furlong, Frank Langella, T. Ryder Smith, Amy Hargreaves. **1994**

BRAINWAVES ★★★ A young San Francisco wife and mother undergoes brain surgery as a result of an accident. An experimental brain wave transfer is performed in an attempt to restore her to a normal life, producing startling results since the brain waves came from a murder victim. Rated R for some nudity and mild violence. 83m. **DIR:** Ulli Lommel. **CAST:** Keir Dullea, Suzanna Love, Vera Miles, Percy Rodrigues, Paul Wilson, Tony Curtis. **1982**

BRAM STOKER'S DRACULA ★★½ Vlad the Impaler, a.k.a. Dracula, becomes a tragic figure in Francis Ford Coppola's visually opulent but overwrought version of the famous vampire tale. Some offbeat casting and an overemphasis on sex and nudity. Rated R for nudity, gore, and violence. 130m. **DIR:** Francis Ford Coppola. **CAST:** Gary Oldman, Winona Ryder, Anthony Hopkins, Keanu Reeves, Richard E. Grant, Cary Elwes, Bill Campell, Tom Waits, Sadie Frost. **1992**

BRIDE, THE ★½ This remake of James Whale's classic 1935 horror-comedy of the macabre, *Bride of Frankenstein*, has some laughs. But these, unlike in the original, are unintentional. Rock singer Sting makes a rather stuffy, unsavory Dr. Charles (?!) Frankenstein, and Jennifer Beals is terribly miscast as his second creation. Rated PG-13 for violence, suggested sex, and nudity. 119m. **DIR:** Franc Roddam. **CAST:** Sting, Jennifer Beals, Geraldine Page, Clancy Brown, Anthony Higgins, David Rappaport. **1985**

BRIDE OF FRANKENSTEIN ★★★★★ This is a first-rate sequel to *Frankenstein*. This time, Henry Frankenstein (Clive) is coerced by the evil Dr. Praetorius (Ernest Thesiger in a delightfully weird and sinister performance) into creating a mate for the monster. B&W; 75m. **DIR:** James Whale. **CAST:** Boris Karloff, Colin Clive, Valerie Hobson, Dwight Frye, Ernest Thesiger, Elsa Lanchester. **1935**

BRIDE OF RE-ANIMATOR ★★★ Not as effective but just as bloodily wacked out, this sequel brings back most of the cast and crew behind the first film to wreak more havoc at Miskatonic University. Fans of the first *Re-Animator* won't want to miss it. Not rated, but contains profanity, nudity, and gore. 99m. **DIR:** Brian Yuzna. **CAST:** Bruce Abbott, Jeffrey Combs, David Gale, Claude Earl Jones. **1989**

BRIDE OF THE GORILLA ★★ Love and marriage on a jungle plantation give Raymond Burr more than he bargained for as he falls victim to an evil curse. Intermittently engrossing. B&W; 65m. **DIR:** Curt Siodmak. **CAST:** Raymond Burr, Barbara Payton, Lon Chaney Jr., Tom Conway, Paul Cavanagh, Woody Strode. **1951**

BRIDE OF THE MONSTER ★★ Another incredibly inept but hilarious film from Ed Wood Jr., this stinker uses most of the mad scientist clichés and uses them poorly as a cadaverous-looking Bela Lugosi tries to do fiendish things to an unconscious (even while alert) Loretta King. This bottom-of-the-barrel independent monstrosity boasts possibly the worst special-effects monster of all time, a rubber octopus that any novelty store would be ashamed to stock. B&W; 69m. **DIR:** Edward D. Wood Jr. **CAST:** Bela Lugosi, Tor Johnson, Tony McCoy, Loretta King. **1955**

BRIDES OF DRACULA ★★★½ The depraved son of a debauched noblewoman is held prisoner by her to spare the countryside his blood lust. When a pretty young teacher sets him free, his mother is the first victim of his reign of terror. David Peel is the blond vampire and Peter Cushing reprises his role as Dr. Van Helsing in this nicely acted Hammer Films horror entry. 85m. **DIR:** Terence Fisher. **CAST:** Peter Cushing, David Peel, Martita Hunt, Yvonne Monlaur, Freda Jackson, Miles Malleson, Mona Washbourne. **1960**

BRIDES OF THE BEAST 🦃 First entry in a dreadful trio of Filipino Blood Island, mad-scientist potboilers. Original title: *Brides of Blood*. 85m. **DIR:** Eddie Romero, Gerardo de Leon. **CAST:** John Ashley, Kent Taylor, Beverly Hills. **1968**

BRIGHTON STRANGLER, THE ★★½ John Loder runs amok after a Nazi bomb destroys the London theatre where he has been playing a murderer in a drama. Stunned in the explosion, he confuses his true identity with the character he has been playing. A chance remark by a stranger sends him off to the seaside resort of Brighton, where he performs his stage role for real! B&W; 67m. **DIR:** Max Nosseck. **CAST:** John Loder, June Duprez, Miles Mander, Rose Hobart, Ian Wolfe. **1945**

BRIMSTONE AND TREACLE ★★★ Sting plays an angelic-diabolic young drifter who insinuates himself into the home lives of respectable Denholm Elliott and Joan Plowright in this British-made shocker. Rated R. 85m. **DIR:** Richard Loncraine. **CAST:** Denholm Elliott, Joan Plowright, Suzanna Hamilton, Sting. **1982**

BROOD, THE ★★ Fans of director David Cronenberg will no doubt enjoy this offbeat, grisly horror tale about genetic experiments. Others need not apply. Rated R. 90m. **DIR:** David Cronenberg. **CAST:** Oliver Reed, Samantha Eggar, Art Hindle. **1979**

BROTHERHOOD OF SATAN 🦃 Ridiculous thriller about a small town taken over by witches and devil worshipers. Rated PG. 92m. **DIR:** Bernard McEveety. **CAST:** Strother Martin, L. Q. Jones, Charles Bateman, Ahna Capri. **1971**

BROTHERLY LOVE ★★★½ A revenge melodrama. Judd Hirsch plays twin brothers, one a respectable businessman, the other a sociopath. When the latter is released from a mental ward, he vows to ruin his brother. This TV movie is not rated, but contains some violence. 94m. **DIR:** Jeff Bleckner. **CAST:** Judd Hirsch, Karen Carlson, George Dzundza, Barry Primus, Lori Lethin, Josef Sommer. **1985**

BROTHERS IN ARMS ★★ Adequate slasher features backwoods crazies hunting humans as part of their religious rituals. A terrifying, suspense-filled chase with plenty of bloodshed. Rated R for extreme violence.

95m. **DIR:** George Jay Bloom III. **CAST:** Todd Allen, Jack Starrett. **1988**

BRUTE MAN, THE ★★ A homicidal maniac escapes from an asylum. Unmemorable, standard B-movie stuff, notable mainly as a showcase for actor Rondo Hatton. *The Brute Man* was Hatton's last film. He died in the year of its release, at the age of 42. B&W; 60m. **DIR:** Jean Yarbrough. **CAST:** Tom Neal, Rondo Hatton, Jane Adams. **1946**

BUCKET OF BLOOD, A ★★★ A funny beatnik spoof—and horror-movie lampoon—in the style of the original *Little Shop of Horrors*, put together by the same creative team. Dick Miller is a nerdy sculptor whose secret is pouring wet clay over the bodies of murder victims; the resulting, contorted sculptures make him a superstar among the cognoscenti. B&W; 66m. **DIR:** Roger Corman. **CAST:** Dick Miller, Barboura Morris, Ed Nelson, Anthony Carbone. **1959**

BUG ★★½ Weird horror film with the world, led by Bradford Dillman, staving off masses of giant mutant beetles with the ability to commit arson, setting fire to every living thing they can find. Rated PG for violence. 100m. **DIR:** Jeannot Szwarc. **CAST:** Bradford Dillman, Joanna Miles, Richard Gilliland. **1975**

BULLIES 🦃 A family moves to a small town that happens to be run by a murderous family of moonshiners. Rated R for graphic violence and profanity. 96m. **DIR:** Paul Lynch. **CAST:** Jonathan Crombie, Janet Laine Green, Olivia D'Abo. **1985**

BURIAL GROUND 🦃 A scientist's study inadvertently unearths the burial place of the living dead. Contains nudity and violence. 85m. **DIR:** Andrea Bianchi. **CAST:** Karin Well, Gian Luigi Chirizzi, Simone Mattioli. **1979**

BURIED ALIVE (1984) ★★ If *Psycho*'s Norman Bates wasn't loony enough for you, here's another demented taxidermist who takes necrophilia to extremes that are gross even for Italian gore films. This is probably the slickest, most compulsively watchable effort by bad taste auteur Joe D'Amato. Rated R. 90m. **DIR:** Joe D'Amato (Aristede Massaccesi). **CAST:** Sam Modesto, Ann Cardin. **1984**

BURNING, THE 🦃 Similar to many other blood feasts of late, it's the story of a summer camp custodian who, savagely burned as a result of a teenage prank, comes back years later for revenge. Rated R. 90m. **DIR:** Tony Maylam. **CAST:** Brian Matthews, Leah Ayres, Brian Backer. **1981**

BURNT OFFERINGS ★★ Good acting cannot save this predictable horror film concerning a haunted house. Rated PG. 115m. **DIR:** Dan Curtis. **CAST:** Oliver Reed, Karen Black, Burgess Meredith, Bette Davis, Lee Montgomery, Eileen Heckart. **1976**

C.H.U.D. ★★ The performances by John Heard and Daniel Stern make this cheapo horror film watchable. C.H.U.D. (Cannibalistic Humanoid Underground Dwellers) are New York City bag people who have been exposed to radiation and start treating the other inhabitants of the city as lunch. Rated R for violence, profanity, and gore. 88m. **DIR:** Douglas Cheek. **CAST:** John Heard, Daniel Stern, Christopher Curry. **1984**

C.H.U.D. II (BUD THE C.H.U.D.) 🦃 This is not a sequel at all, but a thinly disguised *Return of the Living Dead III*. Rated R for violence. 84m. **DIR:** David Irving. **CAST:** Brian Robbins, Gerrit Graham, Robert Vaughn, Bianca Jagger, June Lockhart, Norman Fell. **1989**

CAMERON'S CLOSET ★★★ A young boy with psychic powers unwittingly unleashes a demon in his closet. The above-par special effects, by Oscar winner Carlo Rambaldi (*E.T.* and *Alien*), and an ever-growing tension makes this a neat little supernatural thriller. Not rated, but contains violence. 90m. **DIR:** Armand Mastroianni. **CAST:** Cotter Smith, Mel Harris, Tab Hunter, Chuck McCann, Leigh McCloskey. **1989**

CAMPUS CORPSE, THE 🦃 College fraternity hazing gets out of hand when a pledge is accidentally killed. Rated PG for mild violence and language. 92m. **DIR:** Douglas Curtis. **CAST:** Jeff East, Brad Davis, Charles Martin Smith. **1977**

CANDLES AT NINE ★★ Old-dark-house mystery about a young woman who inherits a fortune from a great-uncle she hardly knew, with the stipulation that she has to spend a month living in his gloomy mansion. Musical star Jessie Matthews was the draw for this British film that is competently made but unexceptional. B&W; 84m. **DIR:** John Harlow. **CAST:** Jessie Matthews, John Stuart, Beatrix Lehmann. **1944**

CANDYMAN (1992) ★★★★ A very scary flick set in the slums of Chicago, *Candyman* concerns a mythical hook-handed killer who can be called forth by looking in a mirror and chanting his name five times. Virginia Madsen researches the Candyman's story and finds out he is all too real. Rated R for violence, profanity and nudity. 101m. **DIR:** Bernard Rose. **CAST:** Virginia Madsen, Tony Todd, Xander Berkeley, Kasi Lemmons, Vanessa Williams, Michael Culkin. **1992**

CANNIBAL 🦃 Originally titled *The Last Survivor*, this stomach churner is among the first (and worst) Italian exploitation potboilers about safaris that run afoul of Amazon cannibals. Rated R. 90m. **DIR:** Ruggero Deodato. **CAST:** Massimo Foschi, Me Me Lai, Ivan Rassimov. **1976**

CANNIBAL CAMPOUT 🦃 Direct-to-video sleazefest that turns out to be a homegrown (and ho-hum) horror, rather than another generic Italian cannibal flick. Not rated. 89m. **DIR:** Jon McBride. **CAST:** Jon McBride. **1988**

CANNIBAL HOLOCAUST ★★ An expedition follows a previous safari of filmmakers into the Amazon. They find some film cans near a village and view the horrific contents in New York. The farthest reaches of exploitation are explored in this most extreme—and disturbing—entry in the late-Seventies cannibal movie subgenre, directed by the field's pioneer auteur. Unrated, but with graphic violence. 95m. **DIR:** Ruggero Deodato. **CAST:** Francesca Ciardi, Luca Barbareschi, Robert Kerman. **1979**

CAPTAIN KRONOS: VAMPIRE HUNTER ★★★½ British film directed by the producer of *The Avengers* television show. It's an unconventional horror tale about a sword-wielding vampire killer. An interesting mix of genres. Good adventure, with high production values. Rated PG for violence. 91m. **DIR:** Brian Clemens. **CAST:** Horst Janson, John David Carson, Caroline Munro, Shane Briant. **1974**

CARMILLA ★★★★ This tale from the cable TV series *Nightmare Classics* features a lonely southern girl (Ione Skye) befriending a stranger (Meg Tilly) who just happens to be a vampire. Some positively chilling scenes!! Unrated, contains gore and violence. 52m. **DIR:** Gabrielle Beaumont. **CAST:** Ione Skye, Meg Tilly, Roddy McDowall, Roy Dotrice. **1989**

CARNIVAL OF BLOOD 🦃 Boring horror mystery about a series of murders committed at New York's Coney Island. 87m. **DIR:** Leonard Kirman. **CAST:** Earle Edgerton, Judith Resnick, Burt Young. **1976**

CARNIVAL OF SOULS ★★★½ Creepy film made on a shoestring budget in Lawrence, Kansas, concerns a girl who, after a near-fatal car crash, is haunted by a ghoulish, zombielike character. Extremely eerie, with nightmarish photography, this little-known gem has a way of getting to you. Better keep the lights on. B&W; 80m. **DIR:** Herk Harvey. **CAST:** Candace Hilligoss, Sidney Berger. **1962**

CARNOSAUR ★★½ Writer-director Adam Simon's unpleasantly bleak, end-of-the-world chiller winds up as nothing more than a laughably crude *Jurassic Park* rip-off. Mad scientist Diane Ladd genetically alters chicken eggs so that human females will give birth to dinosaurs, effectively terminating our reign on Earth. Has Colonel Sanders heard about this one? Rated R for gore and profanity. 83m. **DIR:** Adam Simon. **CAST:** Diane Ladd, Raphael Sbarge, Jennifer Runyon, Clint Howard. **1993**

CARPATHIAN EAGLE ★★ Murdered men begin popping up with their hearts cut out. A police detective scours the town and racks his brain looking for the killer, not realizing how close he is. What all this has to do with the title is never resolved in this addition to Elvira's Thriller Video. 60m. **DIR:** Francis Megahy. **CAST:** Anthony Valentine, Suzanne Danielle, Sian Phillips. **1982**

CARPENTER, THE ★★★ Once you realize writer Doug Taylor and director David Wellington had their tongues planted firmly in cheek, you will enjoy this tale of a neglected wife, after a mental breakdown, moving into an unfinished country home where a mysterious night carpenter becomes her protector. Not a spoof, just handled with style and wit. Unrated, but has gore, profanity, and nudity. 87m. **DIR:** David Wellington. **CAST:** Wings Hauser, Lynn Adams. **1989**

CARRIE (1976) ★★★★½ *Carrie* is the ultimate revenge tale for anyone who remembers high school as a time of rejection and ridicule. The story follows the strange life of Carrie White (Sissy Spacek), a student severely humiliated by her classmates and stifled by the Puritan beliefs of her mother (Piper Laurie), a religious fanatic. Rated R for nudity, violence, and profanity. 97m. **DIR:** Brian De Palma. **CAST:** Sissy Spacek, Piper Laurie, John Travolta, Nancy Allen, Amy Irving. **1976**

CARRIER 🦃 Small-town teenage outcast suddenly becomes a carrier of an unknown disease that consumes living organisms on contact. Rated R for violence and profanity. 99m. **DIR:** Nathan J. White. **CAST:** Gregory Fortescue, Steve Dixon. **1987**

CARS THAT EAT PEOPLE (THE CARS THAT ATE PARIS) ★★★ Peter Weir began with this weird black comedy-horror film about an outback Australian town where motorists and their cars are trapped each night. Rated PG. 90m. **DIR:** Peter Weir. **CAST:** John Meillon, Terry Camilleri, Kevin Miles. **1975**

CASSANDRA 🦃 Lifeless psychic thriller about an Australian woman plagued by a nightmare of her mother's gruesome suicide. Rated R for violence and nudity. 94m. **DIR:** Colin Eggleston. **CAST:** Tessa Humphries, Shane Briant. **1987**

CASTLE OF BLOOD ★★★ Grand fun: the best of the black-and-white Italian horrors ground out in the Sixties following Mario Bava's wild *Black Sunday*. A stranger (George Riviere) meets Edgar Allan Poe in a tavern, and the author bets him he can't spend the night alone in a haunted mansion. Who could resist? U.S. TV title: *Castle of Terror*. B&W; 84m. **DIR:** Anthony M. Dawson. **CAST:** Barbara Steele, George Riviere. **1964**

CASTLE OF EVIL 🦃 Take an electronic humanoid, a dead scientist, some faulty wiring, what appears to be a good cast, and throw them together with a budget that must have run into the tens of dollars and you get this pathetic suspense movie. 81m. **DIR:** Francis D. Lyon. **CAST:** Virginia Mayo, Scott Brady, David Brian, Hugh Marlowe. **1966**

CASTLE OF FU MANCHU The worst Fu Manchu film ever made. 92m. **DIR:** Jess (Jesus) Franco. **CAST:** Christopher Lee, Richard Greene, Maria Perschy. **1968**

CASTLE OF THE CREEPING FLESH Knee-slapper of a bad Eurotrash horror opus, witlessly enlivened by open-heart surgery footage. Once (incorrectly) credited to director Jess Franco, rather than the actual culprit—leading man Adrian Hoven. Not rated. 90m. **DIR:** Percy G. Parker. **CAST:** Adrian Hoven, Janine Reynaud, Howard Vernon. **1968**

CASTLE OF THE LIVING DEAD ★★½ What makes this otherwise run-of-the-mill horror yarn worth watching are some impressive scenes toward the end. They were added by Michael Reeves, a young Englishman who directed several powerful horror films before his suicide. Christopher Lee plays a count who preserves people with an embalming formula. Donald Sutherland, in his film debut, plays two parts, including an old witch woman! B&W; 90m. **DIR:** Herbert Wise. **CAST:** Christopher Lee, Philippe Leroy, Donald Sutherland. **1964**

CAT PEOPLE (1942) ★★★★ Simone Simon, Kent Smith, and Tom Conway are excellent in this movie about a shy woman (Simon) who believes she carries the curse of the panther. Jacques Tourneur knew the imagination was stronger and more impressive than anything filmmakers could show visually and played on it with impressive results. B&W; 73m. **DIR:** Jacques Tourneur. **CAST:** Simone Simon, Kent Smith, Tom Conway. **1942**

CAT PEOPLE (1982) ★★ While technically a well-made film, *Cat People* spares the viewer nothing—incest, bondage, bestiality. It makes one yearn for the films of yesteryear, which achieved horror through implication. Rated R for nudity, profanity, and gore. 118m. **DIR:** Paul Schrader. **CAST:** Nastassja Kinski, Malcolm McDowell, John Heard, Annette O'Toole, Ed Begley Jr., Ruby Dee, Scott Paulin. **1982**

CATHY'S CURSE A young girl is possessed by the spirit of her aunt, who died in an automobile accident as a child. 90m. **DIR:** Eddy Matalon. **CAST:** Alan Scarfe, Randi Allen. **1976**

CAT'S EYE ★★★½ Writer Stephen King and director Lewis Teague, who brought us *Cujo,* reteam for this even better horror release: a trilogy of terror in the much-missed *Night Gallery* anthology style. It's good, old-fashioned, tell-me-a-scary-story fun. Rated PG-13 for violence and gruesome scenes. 98m. **DIR:** Lewis Teague. **CAST:** James Woods, Robert Hays, Kenneth McMillan, Drew Barrymore, Candy Clark, Alan King. **1985**

CAULDRON OF BLOOD Boris Karloff plays a blind sculptor who uses the skeletons of women his wife has murdered as the foundations for his projects. 95m. **DIR:** Edward Mann (Santos Alocer). **CAST:** Boris Karloff, Viveca Lindfors, Jean-Pierre Aumont. **1968**

CAVE OF THE LIVING DEAD An Interpol inspector and a witch join forces to locate some missing girls. 89m. **DIR:** Akos von Ratony. **CAST:** Adrian Hoven, Karin Field, Erika Remberg, Wolfgang Preiss, John Kitzmiller. **1964**

CELLAR, THE ★★★ An ancient Indian demon, called upon to rid the world of the white man, resides in the basement of a rural farmhouse. When a young boy comes to visit his divorced father, no one believes his story about the hideous creature. A relatively scary monster movie directed by the man who brought us the wonderful *Night of the Demons.* Rated PG-13 for violence. 90m. **DIR:** Kevin S. Tenney. **CAST:** Patrick Kilpatrick, Suzanne Savoy, Ford Rainey. **1990**

CELLAR DWELLER Typical junk about a hideous, satanic monster. Not rated, but contains violence. 78m. **DIR:** John Carl Buechler. **CAST:** Deborah Mullowney, Vince Edwards, Yvonne De Carlo. **1987**

CHAIR, THE ★★½ Atmospheric movie about a psychologist (James Coco) who sets up shop in an abandoned prison and runs tests on a select group of inmates. More spooky than scary. Rated R for profanity, violence, and gore. 94m. **DIR:** Waldemar Korzenioswsky. **CAST:** James Coco, Trini Alvarado, Paul Benedict, John Bentley, Stephen Geoffreys. **1989**

CHAMBER OF FEAR Another of the Mexican films featuring footage of Boris Karloff shot in Los Angeles just before his death (see *Sinister Invasion*). 87m. **DIR:** Juan Ibanez, Jack Hill. **CAST:** Boris Karloff. **1968**

CHAMBER OF HORRORS ★★½ A mad killer stalks 1880s Baltimore. Two wax-museum owners attempt to bring him to justice. Originally produced as a television pilot titled House of Wax, but it was considered too violent. Tame and silly. 99m. **DIR:** Hy Averback. **CAST:** Patrick O'Neal, Cesare Danova, Wilfrid Hyde-White, Suzy Parker, Tony Curtis, Jeanette Nolan. **1966**

CHANGELING, THE ★★★★ This ghost story is blessed with everything a good thriller needs: a suspenseful story, excellent performances by a top-name cast, and well-paced solid direction by Peter Medak. The story centers around a composer whose wife and daughter are killed in a tragic auto accident. Rated R. 109m. **DIR:** Peter Medak. **CAST:** George C. Scott, Trish Van Devere, Melvyn Douglas, Jean Marsh, Barry Morse. **1979**

CHARLIE BOY 🦃 Charlie Boy is an African fetish, inherited by a young British couple, that will take care of all your problems—usually by killing them. 60m. **DIR:** Robert Young. **CAST:** Leigh Lawson, Angela Bruce. **1982**

CHEERLEADER CAMP 🦃 Another dumb teenage slasher flick, this time set at a resort for cheerleaders. Rated R for nudity and violence. 89m. **DIR:** John Quinn. **CAST:** Betsy Russell, Leif Garrett, Lucinda Dickey. **1987**

CHILD OF DARKNESS, CHILD OF LIGHT ★★ Two American teenage girls become pregnant while remaining virgins; according to Church prophecy, one will bear the child of God and the other will spawn the son of Satan...but which is which? What hath *The Omen* wrought? Dedicated performances save this produced-for-TV Catholic chiller from complete turkeydom. Rated PG-13. 85m. **DIR:** Marina Sargenti. **CAST:** Anthony Denison, Brad Davis, Paxton Whitehead, Sydney Penny, Sela Ward. **1991**

CHILDREN, THE 🦃 Terrible film about kids marked by a radioactive accident while they were on a school bus. Rated R. 89m. **DIR:** Max Kalmanowicz. **CAST:** Martin Shaker, Gil Rogers, Gale Garnett. **1980**

CHILDREN OF THE CORN 🦃 Yet another adaptation of a Stephen King horror story. A young couple come to a midwestern farming town where a young preacher with mesmerizing powers has instructed all the children to slaughter adults. Rated R for violence and profanity. 93m. **DIR:** Fritz Kiersch. **CAST:** Peter Horton, Linda Hamilton, R. G. Armstrong, John Franklin. **1984**

CHILDREN OF THE CORN II: THE FINAL SACRIFICE 🦃 A sour-pussed teen cult leader instigates more violence in this follow-up to Stephen King's original short story. Rated R for violence, simulated sex, and the world's most gruesome nosebleed. 94m. **DIR:** David F. Price. **CAST:** Terence Knox, Paul Scherrer, Rosalind Allen, Ned Romero. **1993**

CHILDREN OF THE DAMNED ★★½ Inevitable, but disappointing, sequel to the 1960 sleeper, *Village of the Damned.* Worldwide, only six of the alien children have survived, so the children band together. B&W; 90m. **DIR:** Tony Leader. **CAST:** Ian Hendry, Alan Badel, Barbara Ferris, Alfred Burke. **1963**

CHILDREN OF THE FULL MOON 🦃 Even the curvaceous horror hostess Elvira and her off brand of humor can't salvage this cross between *Rosemary's Baby* and *The Wolf-man.* 60m. **DIR:** Tom Clegg. **CAST:** Christopher Cazenove, Celia Gregory, Diana Dors. **1982**

CHILDREN OF THE NIGHT ★★★ Stylish horror-thriller goes right for the jugular in grand fashion. Peter DeLuise stars as a teacher who's summoned to the small town of Allburg when one of his friends claims that he has two female vampires locked up in a bedroom. Plenty of great, gory effects, and some splendid, campy acting. Rated R for violence and language. 92m. **DIR:** Tony Randel. **CAST:** Peter DeLuise, Karen Black, Maya McLaughlin, Ami Dolenz. **1992**

CHILDREN SHOULDN'T PLAY WITH DEAD THINGS 🦃 Typical "evil dead" entry; amateur filmmakers work in a spooky graveyard and make enough noise to, well, wake the dead. Rated PG. 85m. **DIR:** Bob Clark. **CAST:** Alan Ormsby, Anya Ormsby, Jeffrey Gillen. **1972**

CHILD'S PLAY ★★½ Hokey, violent horror film finds a dying criminal putting his soul into a doll. When a mother buys the doll for her son's birthday, predictable mayhem occurs. Good special effects and some humorous dialogue keep this one from becoming routine. Rated R. 87m. **DIR:** Tom Holland. **CAST:** Catharine Hicks, Chris Sarandon, Brad Dourif. **1988**

CHILD'S PLAY 2 ★★★ Chucky, the psychopathic doll from the 1988 original, returns to wreak more havoc as he attempts to transfer his demented soul into the body of a little boy. Effects wizard Kevin Yagher's new Chucky puppet adds to the terror. Rated R for violence and profanity. 88m. **DIR:** John Lafia. **CAST:** Alex Vincent, Jenny Agutter, Gerrit Graham, Christine Elise, Grace Zabriskie, Brad Dourif. **1990**

CHILD'S PLAY 3 ★★ A mess of molten plastic at the end of *Child's Play 2,* Chucky the killer doll is resurrected eight years later when the new CEO of the toy company that manufactured the Good Guys dolls resumes production. Chucky once again sets out to trade souls with Andy, now a teenaged cadet at a state-run military school. Rated R for violence and profanity. 89m. **DIR:** Jack Bender. **CAST:** Justin Whalin, Brad Dourif. **1991**

CHILLER ★★★ A wealthy corporate widow's heir prematurely thaws out at a cryogenics facility. This made-for-TV sci-fi-horror film sketchily explores the possibility of life after death. Fright-master Wes Craven does a fair job of building suspense. 100m. **DIR:** Wes Craven. **CAST:** Michael Beck, Paul Sorvino, Jill Schoelen, Beatrice Straight, Laura Johnson. **1985**

CHILLING, THE 🦃 Frozen bodies in a cryogenics facility are charged back to life during a lightning storm. A truly horrible experience. Rated R for profanity. 91m. **DIR:** Jack A. Sunseri, Deland Nuse. **CAST:** Linda Blair, Dan Haggerty, Troy Donahue. **1991**

CHOPPER CHICKS IN ZOMBIETOWN ★★½ A mad mortician is killing people and reanimating their bodies to work in a mine. A parody of both biker movies and zombie flicks from the crazies at Troma Inc. Rated R for profanity and violence. 84m. **DIR:** Dan Hoskins. **CAST:** Jamie Rose, Vicki Frederick, Ed Gale, Don Calfa, Martha Quinn. **1991**

CHOPPING MALL ★★½ A group of teenagers hold the ultimate office party at the local shopping mall. At midnight it is impenetrably sealed and security droids, armed with high-tech weaponry, go on patrol, incapacitating any unauthorized personnel. This film has a good sense of humor and good visual effects. Rated R for nudity, profanity, and violence. 77m. **DIR:** Jim Wynorski. **CAST:** Kelli Maroney, Tony O'Dell, John Terlesky, Russell Todd. **1986**

CHRISTINE ★★★½ Novelist Stephen King and director John Carpenter team up for topflight, tasteful terror with this movie about a 1958 Plymouth Fury with spooky powers. It's scary without being gory; a triumph of suspense and atmosphere. Rated R for profanity and violence. 111m. **DIR:** John Carpenter. **CAST:** Keith Gordon, John Stockwell, Alexandra Paul, Harry Dean Stanton, Robert Prosky, Christine Belford, Roberts Blossom. **1983**

CHRISTMAS EVIL 🦃 A toy factory employee goes slowly insane. Not rated, but the equivalent of an R rating for sex and violence. 91m. **DIR:** Lewis Jackson. **CAST:** Brandon Maggart, Jeffrey DeMunn. **1983**

CHURCH, THE ★★½ Horror impresario Dario Argento wrote this tale of demons entombed under a Gothic cathedral who are let loose during a renovation project. Not rated, but contains violence, profanity, and gore. 110m. **DIR:** Michele Soavi. **CAST:** Hugh Quarshie, Tomas Arana, Feodor Chaliapin. **1991**

CIRCUS OF FEAR 🦃 For its U.S. theatrical release, this tired Edgar Wallace mystery was shorn of half an hour, retitled *Psycho Circus,* and issued in black and white—but don't expect its video restoration to do anything but make its flaws more obvious. B&W; 90m. **DIR:** John Llewellyn Moxey. **CAST:** Christopher Lee, Suzy Kendall, Klaus Kinski. **1967**

CIRCUS OF HORRORS ★★★ British thriller about a renegade plastic surgeon using a circus as a front. After making female criminals gorgeous, he enslaves them in his Temple of Beauty. When they want out, he colorfully offs them. Well made with good performances. This is the more violent European version. 87m. **DIR:** Sidney Hayers. **CAST:** Anton Diffring, Erika Remberg, Yvonne Romain, Donald Pleasence. **1960**

CITY IN PANIC 🦃 A brutal killer stalks the city streets, murdering homosexuals. Not rated, but contains nudity and graphic violence. 85m. **DIR:** Robert Bouvier. **CAST:** Dave Adamson. **1987**

CITY OF THE WALKING DEAD 🦃 Yet another Italian *Dawn of the Dead* rip-off. Originally released as *Nightmare City.* Rated R. 92m. **DIR:** Umberto Lenzi. **CAST:** Hugo Stiglitz, Laura Trotter, Francisco Rabal, Mel Ferrer. **1980**

CLASS OF 1984 ★★½ Violent punkers run a school. A new teacher arrives and tries to change things, but his pregnant wife is raped. He takes revenge by killing all the punkers. Rated R for violence. 93m. **DIR:** Mark L. Lester. **CAST:** Perry King, Merrie Lynn Ross, Roddy McDowall, Timothy Van Patten. **1982**

CLASS OF NUKE 'EM HIGH 🦃 The makers of *The Toxic Avenger* strike again in this poor black comedy–monster movie. Rated R for nudity, profanity, and graphic violence. 84m. **DIR:** Richard W. Haines, Samuel Weil. **CAST:** Janelle Brady, Gilbert Brenton. **1987**

CLASS OF NUKE 'EM HIGH 2: SUBHUMANOID MELTDOWN ★★ Bad acting, scantily clad women, gross special effects, and a totally off-the-wall plot are all parts of this tongue-in-cheek flick from the wackos at Troma Inc. Remember, it's *supposed* to be this bad. Rated R for violence, profanity, and nudity. 96m. **DIR:** Eric Louzil. **CAST:** Brick Bronsky, Lisa Gaye. **1991**

CLOWNHOUSE ★★½ Novices willing to try a relatively bloodless horror flick might give this little programmer a try. Writer-director Victor Salva's script is strictly by the numbers as it sets the stage for three brothers to fight for their lives against three clowns (actually lunatics from a local asylum). Rated R for profanity and mild violence. 81m. **DIR:** Victor Salva. **CAST:** Nathan Forrest Winters. **1989**

CLUB, THE (1993) ★★ At their high-school prom six teens' deepest, darkest fears become reality. They'll have the devil to pay as they are initiated into a deadly club. Nifty special effects help save this routine shocker. Rated R for violence, language, and adult situations. 88m. **DIR:** Brenton Spencer. **CAST:** Joel Wyner, Kim Coates, Andrea Roth, Rino Romano, Kelli Taylor. **1993**

COLOR ME BLOOD RED 🦃 An artist discovers the perfect shade of red for his paintings. Unrated; the film has violence. 70m. **DIR:** Herschell Gordon Lewis. **CAST:** Don Joseph. **1965**

COMING SOON ★★★½ A compilation of scenes and trailers from Universal Studio's most famous and infamous horror and suspense films. There's also some behind-the-scenes interviews and production clips. A must for anyone who loves going to the movies and seeing those coming attractions. Not rated, but suitable for all audiences. 55m. **DIR:** John Landis. **CAST:** Jamie Lee Curtis. **1983**

COMMITTED ★★★ Jennifer O'Neill stars as a nurse who is tricked into committing herself into a mental institution. O'Neill is reasonably convincing as the single sane person in a sea of insanity. Rated R for violence. 101m. **DIR:** William A. Levey. **CAST:** Jennifer O'Neill, Robert Forster, Ron Palillo. **1990**

CONFESSIONS OF A SERIAL KILLER ★★½ Based on the exploits of serial killer Henry Lee Lucas, this shocker shot in semi-documentary form is realistically gritty and hard to watch, but compelling nonetheless. The film manages to repulse with every murder. Robert A. Burns is appropriately creepy as the person confessing. Not rated, but contains violence, nudity, and strong language. 85m. **DIR:** Mark Blair. **CAST:** Robert A. Burns, Dennis Hill. **1987**

CONQUEROR WORM, THE ★★★ In this graphic delineation of witch-hunting in England during the Cromwell period, Vincent Price gives a sterling performance as Matthew Hopkins, a self-possessed and totally convincing witch finder. The production values are very good considering the small budget. A must-see for thriller fans. 88m. **DIR:** Michael Reeves. **CAST:** Vincent Price, Ian Ogilvy, Hilary Dwyer. **1968**

CONTAGION ★★ When a traveling salesman is trapped in a rural mansion for a night, he comes under the influence of its reclusive owner. First, he must prove himself worthy by committing a murder. Rambling, unsatisfying thriller. Not rated. 90m. **DIR:** Karl Zwicky. **CAST:** John Doyle, Nicola Bartlett. **1988**

CORPSE GRINDERS, THE This silly horror comedy about two cat-food makers who use human corpses in their secret recipe has a cult reputation as one of those so-bad-it's-good movies. 72m. **DIR:** Ted V. Mikels. **CAST:** Sean Kenney, Monika Kelly. **1972**

CORPSE VANISHES, THE Hokey pseudoscientific thriller about crazed scientist Bela Lugosi and his efforts to keep his elderly wife young through transfusions from young girls. B&W; 64m. **DIR:** Wallace Fox. **CAST:** Bela Lugosi, Luana Walters, Tristram Coffin, Minerva Urecal, Elizabeth Russell. **1942**

CORRIDORS OF BLOOD ★★★ Kindly surgeon (Boris Karloff) in nineteeth-century London tries to perfect anesthesia and becomes addicted to narcotics. In a mental fog, he is blackmailed by grave robbers. A suprisingly effective thriller originally withheld from release in the United States for five years. 86m. **DIR:** Robert Day. **CAST:** Boris Karloff, Francis Matthews, Adrienne Corri, Betta St. John, Nigel Green, Christopher Lee. **1957**

COSMIC MONSTERS, THE ★★ Low-budget horror from Great Britain. Giant carnivorous insects invade our planet. An alien in a flying saucer arrives to save the day. The effects are cheap. B&W; 75m. **DIR:** Gilbert Gunn. **CAST:** Forrest Tucker, Gaby André. **1958**

COUNT DRACULA ★★½ Christopher Lee dons the cape once again in this mediocre version of the famous tale about the undead fiend terrorizing the countryside. Rated R. 98m. **DIR:** Jess (Jesus) Franco. **CAST:** Christopher Lee, Herbert Lom, Klaus Kinski. **1970**

COUNT YORGA, VAMPIRE ★★★ Contemporary vampire terrorizes Los Angeles. Somewhat dated, but a sharp and powerful thriller. Stars Robert Quarry, an intense, dignified actor who appeared in several horror films in the early 1970s, then abruptly left the genre. Rated R for violence. 91m. **DIR:** Bob Kelljan. **CAST:** Robert Quarry, Roger Perry, Donna Anders, Michael Murphy. **1970**

CRATER LAKE MONSTER, THE Inexpensive, unimpressive film about a prehistoric creature emerging from the usually quiet lake of the title and raising hell. Rated PG. 89m. **DIR:** William R. Stromberg. **CAST:** Richard Cardella, Glenn Roberts. **1977**

CRAVING, THE A witch burned at the stake hundreds of years ago comes back to life and resurrects her werewolf henchman to do her dirty work. Rated R for violence and nudity. 93m. **DIR:** Jack Molina. **CAST:** Paul Naschy. **1980**

CRAWLERS Dreadful, low-budget effort. Tree roots exposed to toxic chemicals change into vicious vines. Rated R for sex, violence, and language. 94m. **DIR:** Martin Newlin. **CAST:** Jason Saucier, Mary Sellers. **1993**

CRAWLING EYE, THE ★★★ Acceptable horror-thriller about an unseen menace hiding within the dense fog surrounding a mountaintop. A nice sense of doom builds throughout, and the monster remains unseen (always the best way) until the very end. B&W; 85m. **DIR:** Quentin Lawrence. **CAST:** Forrest Tucker, Janet Munro. **1958**

CRAWLING HAND, THE Low-budget tale of a dismembered hand at large in a small town. B&W; 89m. **DIR:** Herbert L. Strock. **CAST:** Peter Breck, Rod Lauren, Kent Taylor. **1963**

CRAWLSPACE Terrible imitation of the classic *Peeping Tom*, with Klaus Kinski as a sadistic landlord who engages in murder and voyeurism. Rated R. 82m. **DIR:** David Schmoeller. **CAST:** Klaus Kinski, Talia Balsam. **1986**

CRAZED A demented man living in a boardinghouse becomes obsessed with a young woman. Not rated, but contains violence and profanity. 88m. **DIR:** Richard Cassidy. **CAST:** Laslo Papas, Belle Mitchell, Beverly Ross. **1984**

CRAZIES, THE ★★ A military plane carrying an experimental germ warfare virus crashes near a small midwestern town, releasing a plague of murderous madness. George Romero attempts to make a statement about martial law while trying to capitalize on the success of his cult classic, *Night of the Living Dead*. Rated R. 103m. **DIR:** George A. Romero. **CAST:** Lane Carroll, W. G. McMillan, Lynn Lowry, Richard Liberty. **1975**

CRAZY FAT ETHEL II 🦃 Schlocky, sophomoric attempt at a slasher film with Priscilla Alden in the title role as an obese lunatic released from an asylum and terrorizing a half-way house. Not rated, but contains (ridiculous) violence. 70m. **DIR:** Nick Phillips. **CAST:** Priscilla Alden, Michael Flood. **1987**

CREATURE FROM BLACK LAKE ★★ This is another forgettable, cliché-ridden horror film. Dennis Fimple and John David Carson play two college students who go to the swamps of Louisiana in search of the missing link. Through the reluctant help of the locals, they come face-to-face with a man in an ape suit. Rated PG. 97m. **DIR:** Joy N. Houck Jr. **CAST:** Jack Elam, Dub Taylor, Dennis Fimple, John David Carson. **1979**

CREATURE FROM THE BLACK LAGOON ★★★½ In the remote backwaters of the Amazon, members of a scientific expedition run afoul of a vicious prehistoric man-fish inhabiting the area and are forced to fight for their lives. Excellent film (first in a trilogy) features true-to-life performances, a bone-chilling score by Joseph Gershenson, and beautiful, lush photography that unfortunately turns to mud in the murky 3-D video print. 79m. **DIR:** Jack Arnold. **CAST:** Richard Carlson, Julie Adams, Richard Denning, Nestor Paiva, Antonio Moreno, Whit Bissell. **1954**

CREATURE WALKS AMONG US, THE ★★½ Surprisingly imaginative, intermittently scary second sequel to *Creature from the Black Lagoon* shows what would happen if the Amazon gill man were surgically altered to enable him to breathe on land. For once, the lengthy passages between monster attacks aren't boring. B&W; 78m. **DIR:** John Sherwood. **CAST:** Jeff Morrow, Rex Reason, Leigh Snowden. **1956**

CREEPER, THE ★★ A feline phobia almost sends the daughter of a research scientist clawing up the walls. Dad's conducting experiments on cats—that's right, cats—for a mysterious miracle serum. Silly. 64m. **DIR:** Jean Yarbrough. **CAST:** Onslow Stevens, Eduardo Ciannelli. **1948**

CREEPERS ★★ Plodding Italian production casts Jennifer Connelly as a young girl with the ability to communicate with, and control, insects. She must use her little friends to track down the maniac who's been murdering students at the Swiss girls' school she's attending. Rated R for gore. 82m. **DIR:** Dario Argento. **CAST:** Jennifer Connelly, Donald Pleasence, Daria Nicolodi, Dalila Di Lazzaro. **1985**

CREEPING FLESH, THE ★★★ Peter Cushing and Christopher Lee are top-notch, in this creepy tale about an evil entity accidentally brought back to life by an unsuspecting scientist. While not as good as the stars' Hammer Films collaborations this will still prove pleasing to their fans. Rated PG. 91m. **DIR:** Freddie Francis. **CAST:** Peter Cushing, Christopher Lee, Lorna Heilbron. **1972**

CREEPOZOIDS 🦃 A post-apocalyptic sci-fi–horror yarn about military deserters who find an abandoned science lab that has a bloodthirsty monster wandering in the halls. Rated R for violence, nudity, and profanity. 72m. **DIR:** David DeCoteau. **CAST:** Linnea Quigley, Ken Abraham. **1987**

CREEPSHOW ★★★★ Stephen King, the modern master of printed terror, and George Romero, the director who frightened unsuspecting moviegoers out of their wits with *Night of the Living Dead*, teamed for this funny and scary tribute to the E.C. horror comics of the 1950s. Like *Vault of Horror* and *Tales from the Crypt*, two titles from that period, it's an anthology of ghoulish bedtime stories. Rated R for profanity and gore. 120m. **DIR:** George A. Romero. **CAST:** Hal Holbrook, Adrienne Barbeau, Fritz Weaver, Leslie Nielsen, Stephen King. **1982**

CREEPSHOW 2 ★★ Three tales of horror and terror based on short stories by Stephen King and a screenplay by George Romero should have turned out a lot better than this. "Ol' Chief Wooden Head" stars George Kennedy and Dorothy Lamour as senior citizens in a slowly dying desert town. "The Raft" concerns four friends whose vacation at a secluded lake turns into a nightmare. "The Hitchhiker" features Lois Chiles as a hit-and-run driver. Rated R for nudity, violence, and profanity. 92m. **DIR:** Michael Gornick. **CAST:** Lois Chiles, George Kennedy, Dorothy Lamour. **1987**

CRIME OF DR. CRESPI, THE ★★ Moody poverty-row item whose main distinction is its casting, principally Erich Von Stroheim as a vengeful surgeon. B&W; 63m. **DIR:** John H. Auer. **CAST:** Erich Von Stroheim, Dwight Frye, Paul Guilfoyle. **1935**

CRIMES AT THE DARK HOUSE ★★ Wilkie Collins's *The Woman in White* served as the source material for this typically florid, over-the-top outing for Britain's Tod Slaughter, the king of eye-rolling camp. B&W; 61m. **DIR:** George King. **CAST:** Tod Slaughter. **1940**

CRIMES OF STEPHEN HAWKE, THE ★★ The cast is a bit better than usual for this, one of Tod Slaughter's early outings, in which a serial killer and a charitable money-lender share a deadly secret. But Slaughter's grandiosely overdone style is, as ever, an acquired taste. B&W; 65m. **DIR:** George King. **CAST:** Tod Slaughter, Marjorie Taylor, Eric Portman. **1936**

CRIMINALLY INSANE ★★ This debut outing for Priscilla Alden's obese psychopath, Crazy Fat Ethel, should cure any compulsive overeaters in the audience. A sequel followed thirteen years later (*Crazy Fat Ethel*

II). Not rated. 61m. **DIR:** Nick Phillips. **CAST:** Priscilla Alden. **1974**

CRITTERS ★★★½ This mild horror film with its hilarious spots could become a cult classic. In it, eight ravenous critters escape from a distant planet and head for Earth. Two futuristic bounty hunters pursue them, and the fun begins. Rated PG-13 for gore and profanity. 90m. **DIR:** Stephen Herek. **CAST:** Dee Wallace, M. Emmet Walsh, Scott Grimes, Don Opper, Terrence Mann. **1986**

CRITTERS 2: THE MAIN COURSE ★★ *Critters 2* takes off where the first one ended, but dwells too much on a dopey subplot. Rated PG-13 for violence and profanity. 87m. **DIR:** Mick Garris. **CAST:** Scott Grimes, Liane Curtis, Don Opper, Barry Corbin, Terrence Mann. **1987**

CRITTERS 3 🦃 Those ferocious fur balls from outer space are back for more, this time inhabiting an apartment building. Low rent all the way. Rated PG-13 for violence. 86m. **DIR:** Kristine Peterson. **CAST:** Christopher Cousins, Joseph Cousins, Don Opper. **1991**

CRITTERS 4 ★★ Ferocious fur balls are back for a bigger bite of the pie. Go figure! Rated PG-13 for violence. 94m. **DIR:** Rupert Harvey. **CAST:** Don Opper, Paul Whitthorne, Angela Bassett, Brad Dourif. **1991**

CROCODILE 🦃 An island paradise is turned into a hellhole by a giant crocodile. Not rated, but contains profanity and violence. 95m. **DIR:** Sompote Sands. **CAST:** Nat Puvanai. **1981**

CROW, THE ★★★★ The accidental death of Brandon Lee during production did not prevent director Alex Proyas from making a genuinely gripping, comic-book horror-thriller. Lee plays a musician who comes back from the dead to wreak vengeance on the urban criminals who killed him and his fiancée. Looking like the Joker and distributing bloody justice, our hero stalks a darkly lit hellscape of decaying tenements (excellent miniature models here), maddening noise (ditto the superb sound mix), and sadistic sociopathy. Terrific, if gruesome, excitement throughout. Rated R for violence, language, brief nudity, and drug use. 97m. **DIR:** Alex Proyas. **CAST:** Brandon Lee, Ernie Hudson, Michael Wincott, David Patrick Kelly, Jon Polito. **1994**

CRUCIBLE OF HORROR ★★★½ Intense story of a violent, domineering man (Michael Gough in one of his better roles) who drives his passive wife and nubile daughter to murder. The suspense and terror build unrelentingly. Keep the lights on! Rated R. 91m. **DIR:** Viktors Ritelis. **CAST:** Michael Gough, Yvonne Mitchell. **1971**

CRUCIBLE OF TERROR 🦃 A demented sculptor coats his female victims with molten bronze in this lame British offering. Rated R. 79m. **DIR:** Ted Hooker. **CAST:** Mike Raven, Mary Maude, James Bolam. **1971**

CRY OF THE BANSHEE ★★ Uninspired film casts Vincent Price as a witch-hunting magistrate whose family is threatened when a curse is placed upon his house by practitioners of the old religion. Price fared much better in the similar *The Conqueror Worm*. Rated R for violence and nudity. 87m. **DIR:** Gordon Hessler. **CAST:** Vincent Price, Elisabeth Bergner, Hugh Griffith. **1970**

CRYPT OF THE LIVING DEAD 🦃 Arguably the worst of a trilogy of horror films directed by Ray Danton, this modern vampire opus—originally titled *Hannah, Queen of Vampires*—is cheap and predictable. Rated R. 83m. **DIR:** Ray Danton. **CAST:** Andrew Prine, Mark Damon, Patty Sheppard. **1972**

CRYSTAL FORCE 🦃 Distraught over the death of her father, a woman buys a crystal centerpiece that turns out to be the gateway for a rather troublesome, antisocial demon. Rated R for violence and nudity. 82m. **DIR:** Laura Keats. **CAST:** Katherine McCall, John Serrdakue, Tony C. Burton. **1990**

CTHULHU MANSION 🦃 A magician unleashes the devil's foot soldiers on a group of thugs hiding out at his home. Probably the world's worst adaptation of an H. P. Lovecraft concept. Rated R for profanity and violence. 92m. **DIR:** Juan Piquer Simon. **CAST:** Frank Finlay, Marcia Layton, Brad Fisher. **1990**

CUJO ★★★½ Stephen King's story of a mother and son terrorized by a rabid Saint Bernard results in a movie that keeps viewers on the edge of their seats. Rated R for violence and language. 91m. **DIR:** Lewis Teague. **CAST:** Dee Wallace, Danny Pintauro, Daniel Hugh-Kelly, Christopher Stone. **1983**

CULT OF THE COBRA ★★ An Asian high priestess goes to Manhattan to seek vengeance on the American soldiers who defiled her temple. Don't confuse this drab thriller with the camp favorite *Cobra Woman*. B&W; 80m. **DIR:** Francis D. Lyon. **CAST:** Faith Domergue, Richard Long, Marshall Thompson, Kathleen Hughes, Jack Kelly. **1955**

CURSE, THE 🦃 A meteor crashes and infects the water of a small town with alien parasites. Rated R for violence. 92m. **DIR:** David Keith. **CAST:** Wil Wheaton, John Schneider, Claude Akins. **1987**

CURSE II—THE BITE 🦃 Not even closely related to the first movie. Not rated, but contains violence and gore. 97m. **DIR:** Fred Goodwin. **CAST:** Jill Schoelen, J. Eddie Peck, Jamie Farr, Bo Svenson. **1988**

CURSE III: BLOOD SACRIFICE ★★ After her sister interrupts the ritual killing of a goat by a group of African natives, a farmer's wife (Jenilee Harrison) must face a curse placed on her by the village's witch doctor.

Christopher Lee portrays a local doctor who may or may not have something to do with it. Too bad. Rated R for profanity, nudity, and violence. 91m. **DIR:** Sean Burton. **CAST:** Christopher Lee, Jenilee Harrison. **1990**

CURSE IV: THE ULTIMATE SACRIFICE ★★★ This pseudosequel, originally called *Catacombs*, is a surprisingly stylish low-budget thriller. The memorable Feodor Chaliapin has a supporting role here. He's an aging patriarch who befriends his aide, a young priest troubled by a premature mid-life crisis. To make matters worse, a beautiful schoolteacher has invaded the brotherly order, and there's an ancient evil lurking below in the catacombs. Rated R, but fairly tame except for some blood, violence, and subject matter. 84m. **DIR:** David Schmoeller. **CAST:** Timothy Van Patten, Laura Schaefer, Jeremy West, Ian Abercrombie, Feodor Chaliapin. **1993**

CURSE OF FRANKENSTEIN, THE ★★★½ Hammer Films' version of the Frankenstein story about a scientist who creates a living man from the limbs and organs of corpses. Peter Cushing gives a strong performance as the doctor, with Christopher Lee his equal as the sympathetic creature. Some inspired moments are peppered throughout this well-handled tale. 83m. **DIR:** Terence Fisher. **CAST:** Peter Cushing, Christopher Lee, Robert Urquhart. **1957**

CURSE OF KING TUT'S TOMB, THE 🦃 Made-for-TV misfire concerning the mysterious events surrounding the opening of King Tut's tomb. 100m. **DIR:** Philip Leacock. **CAST:** Eva Marie Saint, Robin Ellis, Raymond Burr, Harry Andrews, Tom Baker. **1980**

CURSE OF THE BLACK WIDOW ★★ Made-for-TV movie with a recycled script and a cast that seems to have been plucked from an unshot *Love Boat* installment. Who's the killer that's leaving victims draped in gooey webbing? Only director Dan Curtis's familiarity with the genre gives this telefilm some bounce. 100m. **DIR:** Dan Curtis. **CAST:** Anthony Franciosa, Donna Mills, Patty Duke, June Allyson. **1977**

CURSE OF THE BLUE LIGHTS 🦃 Teenagers must find a way to escape from an underground world populated by demons. Unrated, but gory enough for an R rating. 96m. **DIR:** John H. Johnson. **CAST:** Brent Ritter. **1989**

CURSE OF THE CAT PEOPLE, THE ★★★ When Val Lewton was ordered by the studio to make a sequel to the successful *Cat People*, he came up with this gentle fantasy about a child who is haunted by spirits. Not to be confused with the 1980s version of *Cat People*. B&W; 70m. **DIR:** Gunther Von Fristch, Robert Wise. **CAST:** Simone Simon, Kent Smith, Jane Randolph, Elizabeth Russell. **1944**

CURSE OF THE CRYING WOMAN, THE ★★½ One of the better Mexican monster movies released straight to TV by American International Pictures in the 1960s. The film's visual style appears to have been influenced by *Nosferatu* and *Black Sunday*. B&W; 74m. **DIR:** Rafael Baledon. **CAST:** Rosita Arenas, Abel Salazar. **1961**

CURSE OF THE DEMON ★★★★½ Horrifying tale of an American occult expert, Dr. Holden (Dana Andrews), traveling to London to expose a supposed devil cult led by sinister Professor Karswell (Niall MacGinnis). Unfortunately for Holden, Karswell's cult proves to be all too real as a demon from hell is dispatched by the professor to put an end to the annoying investigation. Riveting production is a true classic of the genre. B&W; 96m. **DIR:** Jacques Tourneur. **CAST:** Dana Andrews, Peggy Cummins, Niall MacGinnis, Maurice Denham. **1958**

CURSE OF THE HOUSE SURGEON, THE 🦃 This tripe—about a pseudoexorcist for homes—makes *Plan 9 from Outer Space* look like *Citizen Kane*. Not rated. 113m. **DIR:** Steve Postal. **CAST:** Kendrick Kaufman, Jennifer Tuck, Angela Shepard, Angel Langley, Maurice Postal. **1991**

CURSE OF THE LIVING DEAD ★★★ More commonly available on video as *Kill, Baby, Kill*. It's the great Mario Bava's closing essay in gothic horror, a tremendously atmospheric supernatural mystery about a Transylvanian village and the doctor who tries to free it from a hideous curse in which murder victims are found with gold coins imbedded in their hearts. Slow-paced, but stay with it. 75m. **DIR:** Mario Bava. **CAST:** Giacomo Rossi-Stuart. **1966**

CURSE OF THE WEREWOLF, THE ★★★½ After being brutally raped in a castle dungeon by an imprisoned street beggar, a young woman gives birth to a son with a strange appetite for blood. His heritage remains a mystery until adulthood, whereupon he begins transforming into a wolf as the full moon rises. Oliver Reed is fine in the role of the werewolf, one of his earliest screen performances. 91m. **DIR:** Terence Fisher. **CAST:** Oliver Reed, Clifford Evans, Yvonne Romain, Anthony Dawson. **1961**

CURTAINS 🦃 A movie actress gets herself committed to a mental institution as preparation for an upcoming film. Rated R. 89m. **DIR:** Jonathan Stryker. **CAST:** John Vernon, Samantha Eggar, Linda Thorson, Anne Ditchburn. **1983**

CUTTING CLASS ★★ A mass murderer is on the loose at a local high school. Sound familiar? Well...it is. Rated R for violence and profanity. 91m. **DIR:** Raspo Pallenberg. **CAST:** Donovan Leitch, Jill Schoelen, Brad Pitt, Roddy McDowall, Martin Mull. **1989**

CYCLOPS, THE ★★½ Low-budget whiz Bert I. Gordon does it again with this cheaply made but effective film about a woman (Gloria Talbott) whose brother is transformed into a big, crazy monster by—what else?—radiation. Neat little movie. B&W; 75m. **DIR:** Bert I. Gordon. **CAST:** James Craig, Lon Chaney Jr., Gloria Talbott. **1957**

DAMIEN: OMEN II ★★★½ In this first sequel to *The Omen*, William Holden plays the world's richest man, Richard Thorn. In the previous picture, Richard's brother is shot by police while attempting to kill his son, who he believed to be the Antichrist, son of Satan. *Damien: Omen II* picks up seven years later. Rated R. 107m. **DIR:** Don Taylor. **CAST:** William Holden, Lee Grant, Lew Ayres, Sylvia Sidney. **1978**

DANCE OF DEATH Don't waste your time. Not rated. 75m. **DIR:** Juan Ibanez. **CAST:** Boris Karloff, Andres Garcia. **1971**

DANSE MACABRE ★★ Filmed on location in the Soviet Union, this horror film features Robert Englund as an American choreographer working at a world-renowned ballet college. When girls from around the world are allowed to enroll, trouble begins. One by one they are murdered. Rated R for nudity, violence, and profanity. 97m. **DIR:** Greydon Clark. **CAST:** Robert Englund. **1991**

DARK, THE ★★ A deadly alien. Rated R. 92m. **DIR:** John "Bud" Cardos. **CAST:** William Devane, Cathy Lee Crosby, Richard Jaeckel, Keenan Wynn, Vivian Blaine. **1979**

DARK HALF, THE ★★★½ Director George Romero also penned the screenplay for this Stephen King tale of a writer and his homicidal pseudonym. When threatened with the exposure of his literary alter ego, writer Timothy Hutton sees his chance to rid himself and his family of that dark side. But that alter ego manifests itself as a really nasty killer bent on revenge. Romero does a good job layering on the tension, but the overall film is hampered by flat characters. Rated R for violence and profanity. 115m. **DIR:** George A. Romero. **CAST:** Timothy Hutton, Amy Madigan, Michael Rooker, Julie Harris, Robert Joy, Kent Broadhurst, Beth Grant, Rutanya Alda, Tom Mardirosian. **1993**

DARK NIGHT OF THE SCARECROW ★★★ Despite its hasty beginning that fails to set up a strong premise for the pivotal scene of the movie, *Dark Night of the Scarecrow* is a chilling film that mixes the supernatural with a moral message. The film borrows some ideas from such films as *To Kill a Mockingbird* and *Of Mice and Men*. 100m. **DIR:** Frank DeFelitta. **CAST:** Charles Durning, Tonya Crowe, Jocelyn Brando. **1981**

DARK PLACES ★★★½ Christopher Lee and Joan Collins play two fortune hunters trying to scare away the caretaker (Robert Hardy) of a dead man's mansion so they can get to the bundle of cash stashed in the old house. The film has a sophisticated psychological twist to it that is missing in most horror films of late, but the cardboard bats on clearly visible wires have got to go! Rated PG for gore and profanity. 91m. **DIR:** Don Sharp. **CAST:** Christopher Lee, Joan Collins, Herbert Lom, Robert Hardy, Jane Birkin, Jean Marsh. **1973**

DARK POWER, THE A house over the graveyard of some ancient Mexican warriors. Not rated. 87m. **DIR:** Phil Smoot. **CAST:** Lash LaRue, Anna Lane Tatum. **1985**

DARK SANITY A formerly institutionalized housewife comes home and begins to have dark psychic visions of doom. Not rated, but contains violence. 89m. **DIR:** Martin Greene. **CAST:** Aldo Ray. **1982**

DARK SECRET OF HARVEST HOME, THE ★★½ Novelist-actor Tom Tryon's bewitching story of creeping horror gets fair treatment in this dark and foreboding film of Janus personalities and incantations in picturesque New England. 118m. **DIR:** Leo Penn. **CAST:** Bette Davis, Rosanna Arquette, David Ackroyd, Michael O'Keefe. **1978**

DARK SHADOWS (TV SERIES) ★★★ A truly different soap opera, this includes a bona fide vampire—one Barnabas Collins (convincingly portrayed by Jonathan Frid). Volumes 1 to 4, for example, begin with a greedy grave robber who gives the vampire new life, and culminate with the vampire's choosing a local girl for his bride. Mysterious, frightening, and atmospheric. B&W; each. 105–120m. **DIR:** John Sedwick, Lela Swift. **CAST:** Jonathan Frid, Joan Bennett, Kathryn Leigh Scott, John Karlen, Alexandra Moltke. **1966–1967**

DARK SIDE, THE ★★★ Extremely seedy street thriller in which a naïve New York cabbie falls for a pretty girl on the run from a pair of ruthless porn-film merchants who specialize in snuff movies. Rated R for brutality and language. 95m. **DIR:** Constantino Magnatta. **CAST:** Tony Galati, Cyndy Preston. **1987**

DARK TOWER A supernatural entity starts killing people. Rated R for violence and profanity. 91m. **DIR:** Ken Barnett. **CAST:** Michael Moriarty, Jenny Agutter, Theodore Bikel, Carol Lynley, Anne Lockhart, Kevin McCarthy. **1987**

DAUGHTER OF DR. JEKYLL ★★ Okay horror film about a girl (Gloria Talbott) who thinks she's inherited the famous dual personality. B&W; 71m. **DIR:** Edgar G. Ulmer. **CAST:** Gloria Talbott, John Agar, Arthur Shields, John Dierkes. **1957**

DAUGHTER OF HORROR The longest sixty minutes of your life. B&W; 60m. **DIR:**

John Parker. **CAST:** Adrienne Barrett, Bruno Ve Sota. **1955**

DAUGHTERS OF DARKNESS ★★★ Slick, handsomely mounted, and often genuinely eerie updating of the Elisabeth Bathory legend. Amid kinky trappings and soft-focus camera work, a wealthy woman vampire seduces a young couple at a European spa. Dated, but still striking and original. Rated R. Available in 87- and 96-m. versions of varying explicitness. **DIR:** Harry Kumel. **CAST:** Delphine Seyrig, Daniele Ouimet, John Karlen, Fons Rademakers. **1971**

DAUGHTERS OF SATAN Modern-day witches. Rated R for nudity and violence. 96m. **DIR:** Hollingsworth Morse. **CAST:** Tom Selleck, Barra Grant. **1972**

DAWN OF THE DEAD ★★★★ This film is the sequel to *Night of the Living Dead.* The central characters are three men and one woman who try to escape from man-eating corpses. As a horror movie, it's a masterpiece, but if you have a weak stomach, avoid this one. Rated R. 126m. **DIR:** George A. Romero. **CAST:** David Emge, Ken Foree, Scott Reiniger, Tom Savini. **1979**

DAWN OF THE MUMMY Archaeologists open up an accursed tomb. Not rated, but contains graphic violence. 93m. **DIR:** Frank Agrama. **CAST:** Brenda King. **1981**

DAY OF JUDGMENT, A ★★½ After the local preacher leaves for lack of a congregation (maybe because none of them can act), the nasties of a small town are taught their lesson by the grim reaper. Not rated, but contains violence. 101m. **DIR:** C.D.H. Reynolds. **CAST:** William T. Hicks. **1981**

DAY OF THE ANIMALS Nature goes nuts after the Earth's ozone layer is destroyed. Rated R for violence, profanity, and gore. 98m. **DIR:** William Girdler. **CAST:** Christopher George, Lynda Day George, Richard Jaeckel, Leslie Nielsen, Michael Ansara, Ruth Roman. **1977**

DAY OF THE DEAD ★★ The third film in George A. Romero's *Dead* series doesn't hold up to its predecessors. Like earlier films in the series, *Day of the Dead* portrays graphic scenes of cannibalism, dismemberment, and other gory carnage. Unlike the other films, this one has no truly likable characters to root for. Not rated, but contains scenes of violence. 100m. **DIR:** George A. Romero. **CAST:** Lori Cardille, Terry Alexander, Richard Liberty, Joe Pilato. **1985**

DEAD ALIVE ★★★½ Over-the-top New Zealand gorefest is so disgusting, it's hilarious. When shy and introverted Timothy Balme's doting mother is bitten by a Sumatran rat monkey, she begins to exhibit zombielike traits, including eating the flesh of the undead. Before you know it, the house is zombie central, and the lengths Balme must go through to alleviate the problem are extreme, to say the least. Rated R for violence, gore, and language; unrated version contains buckets more gore. 85m. /97m. **DIR:** Peter Jackson. **CAST:** Timothy Balme, Diana Penalver, Elizabeth Moody. **1992**

DEAD AND BURIED ★★ This muddled venture by the creators of *Alien* (Ronald Shusett and Dan O'Bannon) involves a series of gory murders, and the weird part is that the victims seem to be coming back to life. The puzzle is resolved during the suspenseful, eerie ending—definitely the high point of the movie. Rated R for violence. 92m. **DIR:** Gary A. Sherman. **CAST:** James Farentino, Melody Anderson, Jack Albertson, Dennis Redfield. **1981**

DEAD DON'T DIE, THE George Hamilton must take on the Zombie Master in order to clear his dead brother's name. Made for TV. 76m. **DIR:** Curtis Harrington. **CAST:** George Hamilton, Ray Milland, Joan Blondell, Linda Cristal, Ralph Meeker. **1975**

DEAD EYES OF LONDON ★★½ A German remake of the Bela Lugosi chiller *The Human Monster.* Once again the director of a home for the blind uses the place as a front for criminal activities. Interesting vehicle for Klaus Kinski, who gives a great maniacal performance. Even so, the film lacks the eerie atmosphere of the original. B&W; 104m. **DIR:** Alfred Vohrer. **CAST:** Klaus Kinski, Karin Baal. **1961**

DEAD HEAT ★★ In this so-so but gory spoof of the living-dead genre, Treat Williams and Joe Piscopo star as a pair of L.A. police detectives who find the mastermind behind a group of robberies that are being committed by criminals brought back from the dead. The special effects are pretty good, but 60 percent of the jokes fall flat. Rated R for violence and profanity. 86m. **DIR:** Mark Goldblatt. **CAST:** Treat Williams, Joe Piscopo, Lindsay Frost, Darren McGavin, Vincent Price, Keye Luke. **1988**

DEAD MEN WALK ★★ Master character actor George Zucco makes the most of one of his few leading roles, a dual one at that, in this grade-Z cheapie about vampires and zombies. B&W; 67m. **DIR:** Sam Newfield. **CAST:** George Zucco, Mary Carlisle, Nedrick Young, Dwight Frye. **1943**

DEAD OF NIGHT (1945) ★★★★½ The granddaddy of the British horror anthologies still chills today, with the final sequence—in which ventriloquist Michael Redgrave fights a losing battle with his demonic dummy—rating as an all-time horror classic. The other stories are told almost as effectively. B&W; 104m. **DIR:** Alberto Cavalcanti, Basil Dearden, Robert Hamer, Charles Crichton. **CAST:** Mervyn Johns, Michael Redgrave, Sally Ann Howes, Miles Malleson, Googie Withers, Basil Radford. **1945**

DEAD OF NIGHT (1977) ★★ This trilogy of shockers written by Richard Matheson has some interesting twists, but is far inferior to his other achievements. Elvira is host on this, another in her "Thriller Video" series. 76m. **DIR:** Dan Curtis. **CAST:** Ed Begley Jr., John Hackett, Patrick Macnee. **1977**

DEAD RINGERS ★★½ Director and co-scripter David Cronenberg toys intriguingly with the connective link between identical twins until the film sinks into a depressing spiral of depravity and gratuitous gore. Jeremy Irons is superb as both halves of twin gynecologists specializing in fertility. Rated R for graphic medical procedures, sexual themes, and unsettling violence. 115m. **DIR:** David Cronenberg. **CAST:** Jeremy Irons, Genevieve Bujold, Heidi Von Palleske, Stephen Lack. **1988**

DEAD ZONE, THE ★★★★ This is an exciting adaptation of the Stephen King suspense novel about a man who uses his psychic powers to solve multiple murders and perhaps prevent the end of the world. Rated R for violence and profanity. 103m. **DIR:** David Cronenberg. **CAST:** Christopher Walken, Brooke Adams, Tom Skerritt, Herbert Lom, Martin Sheen. **1983**

DEADLY BLESSING 🦃 A strange religious sect. Rated R because of nudity and bloody scenes. 102m. **DIR:** Wes Craven. **CAST:** Maren Jensen, Susan Buckner, Sharon Stone, Lois Nettleton, Ernest Borgnine, Jeff East. **1981**

DEADLY EYES 🦃 Grain full of steroids creates rats the size of small dogs. Rated R for gore, nudity, and simulated sex. 87m. **DIR:** Robert Clouse. **CAST:** Sam Groom, Sara Botsford, Scatman Crothers. **1982**

DEADLY FRIEND ★★ A teenage whiz revives his murdered girlfriend by inserting a computer chip into her brain. The girl becomes a robot-zombie and kills people. This would-be thriller has much in common with its title character. It's cold, mechanical, and brain-dead. Rated R for violence. 99m. **DIR:** Wes Craven. **CAST:** Matthew Laborteaux, Michael Sharrett, Kristy Swanson. **1986**

DEADLY OBSESSION ★★ This contrived, uneven thriller is about a disfigured psychopath who dwells in the tunnels and caves beneath a wealthy private college. He terrorizes the campus inhabitants in an effort to extort large sums of money. Rated R, contains nudity and violence. 93m. **DIR:** Jeno Hodi. **CAST:** Jeffrey R. Iorio. **1988**

DEADLY SANCTUARY 🦃 Two newly orphaned sisters fall prey to prison, prostitution, murder, and a torturous hellfire club. 93m. **DIR:** Jess (Jesus) Franco. **CAST:** Sylva Koscina, Mercedes McCambridge, Jack Palance, Klaus Kinski, Akim Tamiroff. **1970**

DEADMATE ★★½ Writer-director Straw Weisman concocts a spooky and bizarre tale about a woman who marries a mortician unaware that he, and most of the town, like to do strange things to dead bodies. Not rated, but contains violence and nudity. 93m. **DIR:** Straw Weisman. **CAST:** Elizabeth Manning, David Gregory, Lawrence Brockius, Adam Wahl, Judith Mayes, Kelvin Keraga. **1988**

DEADTIME STORIES 🦃 Bizarre, ghoulish versions of fairy tales. 89m. **DIR:** Jeffrey S. Delman. **CAST:** Scott Valentine. **1987**

DEAR DEAD DELILAH 🦃 Delilah (Agnes Moorehead) is about to die, but there's a fortune buried somewhere on her property that her loony relatives will do anything to get ahold of. Rated R for blood. 90m. **DIR:** John Farris. **CAST:** Agnes Moorehead, Will Geer, Michael Ansara, Dennis Patrick. **1972**

DEATH CURSE OF TARTU 🦃 Seminole witch doctor and his rebirth as a monster. 84m. **DIR:** William Grefe. **CAST:** Fred Pinero. **1967**

DEATH DREAMS ★★★ The ghost of a little girl tries to communicate the identity of her killer to her grieving mother. No one believes her. A well-acted, made-for-TV mystery. 94m. **DIR:** Martin Donovan. **CAST:** Christopher Reeve, Fionnula Flanagan, Marg Helgenberger. **1992**

DEATH NURSE 🦃 Infantile, microscopically budgeted flick about a fat nurse and her psychotic brother. Not rated, but contains violence. 70m. **DIR:** Nick Phillips. **CAST:** Priscilla Alden, Michael Flood. **1987**

DEATH SPA ★★½ A disturbing gore flick about the dead wife of a health-spa owner who makes things unbearable for him and the patrons of his state-of-the-art spa. Not rated, but contains violence, nudity, profanity, and gore. 89m. **DIR:** Michael Fischa. **CAST:** William Bumiller, Brenda Bakke, Merritt Butrick, Robert Lipton, Alexa Hamilton, Rosalind Cash, Shari Shattuck. **1990**

DEATH VALLEY ★★ Paul LeMat and Catharine Hicks star in this okay horror film about a vacation that turns into a nightmare. Rated R for violence and gore. 87m. **DIR:** Dick Richards. **CAST:** Paul LeMat, Catharine Hicks, Stephen McHattie, Wilford Brimley. **1982**

DEATH WARMED UP ★★ In this winner of the 1984 Grand Prix International Festival of Fantasy and Science Fiction Films, a psycho doctor is transforming patients into mutant killers, until a former patient comes after revenge. Rated R for violence, nudity, and profanity. 83m. **DIR:** David Blyth. **CAST:** Michael Hurst, Margaret Umbers, David Leitch. **1983**

DEATH WEEKEND ★★ Don Stroud is chillingly convincing as a vicious sadist who, with the help of two demented pals, terrorizes lovers Brenda Vaccaro and Chuck Shamata at their *House by the Lake*, which was the film's theatrical title. Director William

Fruet dwells too much on the cruelty. As a result, the film is uncomfortable to watch. Rated R for violence and profanity. 89m. **DIR:** William Fruet. **CAST:** Brenda Vaccaro, Don Stroud, Chuck Shamata. **1977**

DEATHDREAM ★★★½ The underrated director Bob Clark made some interesting low-budget movies in his native Canada before gaining commercial success (and critical scorn) with the *Porky's* series. This unsettling horror tale, an update of "The Monkey's Paw" as a comment on the Vietnam War and modern family life, is one of his best. It's a creepy mood piece, also known as *Dead of Night*. Rated R. 88m. **DIR:** Bob Clark. **CAST:** John Marley, Richard Backus, Lynn Carlin, Anya Ormsby. **1972**

DEATHMOON 🦃 A simple-minded telefilm about a businessman who is cursed by an old crone and turns into a werewolf. Not rated. 90m. **DIR:** Bruce Kessler. **CAST:** Robert Foxworth, Charles Haid, France Nuyen. **1985**

DEATHSHIP ★★ This story of a modern-day lost *Dutchman* involves a World War II battleship—haunted by those who died on it. The ship destroys any seagoing vessels it can find because it needs blood. There are a few chills along the way, but not enough. Rated R for violence and brief nudity. 91m. **DIR:** Alvin Rakoff. **CAST:** George Kennedy, Richard Crenna, Nick Mancuso, Sally Ann Howes, Kate Reid, Saul Rubinek. **1980**

DEEP RED (1975) ★★★ Another stylish and brutal horror-mystery from Italian director Dario Argento. His other works include *The Bird with the Crystal Plumage* and *Suspiria*. Like those, this film is slim on plot and a bit too talky, but Argento builds tension beautifully with rich atmosphere and driving electronic music. Rated R for violence. 98m. **DIR:** Dario Argento. **CAST:** David Hemmings, Daria Nicolodi, Gabriele Lavia. **1975**

DEEPSTAR SIX 🦃 A secret navy underwater colonization project goes awry. Rated R for violence and profanity. 105m. **DIR:** Sean S. Cunningham. **CAST:** Taurean Blacque, Nancy Everhard, Greg Evigan, Miguel Ferrer, Nia Peeples, Matt McCoy, Cindy Pickett. **1989**

DEF BY TEMPTATION ★★★ A divinity student is tempted by a seductive succubus who wants his soul. This independently produced horror-comedy is entertaining and well acted by its all-black cast. Rated R for profanity and violence. 95m. **DIR:** James Bond III. **CAST:** James Bond III, Kadeem Hardison, Melba Moore. **1990**

DEMENTIA 13 ★★★ Early Francis Coppola film is a low-budget shocker centering on a family plagued by violent ax murders that are somehow connected with the death of the youngest daughter many years before. Acting is standard, but the photography, creepy locations, and weird music are what make this movie click. Produced by Roger Corman. B&W; 75m. **DIR:** Francis Ford Coppola. **CAST:** William Campbell, Luana Anders, Patrick Magee. **1963**

DEMON BARBER OF FLEET STREET, THE ★★½ Long before Vincent Price was the embodiment of evil, there was Tod Slaughter, master of the Grand Guignol school of lip-smacking villainy and star of many bloody thrillers. Partially based on a true occurrence, this popular folktale tells the story of Sweeney Todd, an amoral barber who cuts the throats of his clients. Seldom seen in America since World War II, this influential film was a great success for the flamboyant Slaughter and provides the basis for the recent musical theater hit. B&W; 76m. **DIR:** George King. **CAST:** Tod Slaughter, Bruce Seton. **1936**

DEMON IN MY VIEW, A ★★★ One of Anthony Perkins' last roles was a psycho. But this time his reign of terror takes place in Europe, where he is a mild apartment dweller who is hiding a murderous past. A fine, edgy performance by Perkins highlights this intelligent thriller. Rated R for violence. 98m. **DIR:** Petra Hafter. **CAST:** Anthony Perkins. **1992**

DEMON KEEPER ★★ Creaky, haunted-house thriller. Fake medium Edward Albert summons up a real spirit and unleashes a demon. The special effects are better than usual, but the dialogue is frightfully unfunny. Rated R for horror, violence and language. 90m. **DIR:** Joe Tornatore. **CAST:** Dirk Benedict, Edward Albert, Katrina Maltby, Mike Lane. **1994**

DEMON LOVER, THE 🦃 College kids and bikers get involved with a Satanist. Rated R for nudity, profanity, and violence. 87m. **DIR:** Donald G. Jackson. **CAST:** Christmas Robbins, Gunnar Hansen, Sonny Bell. **1976**

DEMON OF PARADISE 🦃 An ancient sea creature awakened from its slumber. Rated R for brief nudity and violence. 84m. **DIR:** Cirio H. Santiago. **CAST:** Kathryn Witt, William Steis, Laura Banks. **1987**

DEMON WIND ★★★ After one of the dumbest reasons ever to go to a spooky house, a group of young people are systematically dispatched. Some great one-liners and slimy special effects. Rated R for violence, nudity, and gore. 97m. **DIR:** Charles Philip Moore. **CAST:** Eric Larson, Francine Lapensee, Bobby Johnson. **1990**

DEMONIAC 🦃 Director Jess Franco plays the lead himself in this dreary affair (originally titled *Ripper of Notre Dame* and, in a hard-core-porn version, *Exorcism & Black Masses*). Rated R. 87m. **DIR:** Jess (Jesus) Franco. **CAST:** Jess Franco, Lina Romay, Oliver Mathot. **1979**

DEMONIC TOYS 🦃 An army of toys is brought to life by a demon. A plastic baby doll's wisecracks are the only highlight of this film. Unrated, but has profanity and violence. 86m. **DIR:** Peter Manoogian. **CAST:** Tracy Scoggins, Bentley Mitchum. **1991**

DEMONOID 🦃 A couple who unearth a severed hand while working in a Mexican mine. Rated R for graphic violence. 78m. **DIR:** Alfredo Zacharias. **CAST:** Samantha Eggar, Stuart Whitman. **1981**

DEMONS ★★★ Selected at random, people on the street are invited to an advance screening of a new horror film. When the members of the audience try to escape, they find themselves trapped. Although much of the acting is poor and some story elements are plain stupid, this actually is a very frightening movie. Not rated, but features graphic violence and adult language. 89m. **DIR:** Lamberto Bava. **CAST:** Urbano Barberini. **1986**

DEMONS 2 🦃 Cross between George Romero's zombies and *The Evil Dead* attacking the inhabitants of a high-rise apartment building. Not rated, but an R equivalent for violence and gore. 88m. **DIR:** Lamberto Bava. **CAST:** David Knight, Nancy Brilli. **1987**

DEMONS OF LUDLOW, THE 🦃 An eastern seaboard community haunted by an old piano that is possessed. Not rated, but the equivalent of an R for nudity, profanity, violence, and gore. 83m. **DIR:** Bill Rebane. **CAST:** Paul Von Hausen. **1983**

DEMONS OF THE MIND ★★½ One of the last significant Hammer films before the British horror factory's demise in 1976. A Bavarian nobleman, fearing his children are possessed, keeps them locked away. Gillian Hills, in a role intended for Marianne Faithfull, is especially effective. Rated R. 89m. **DIR:** Peter Sykes. **CAST:** Paul Jones, Yvonne Mitchell, Gillian Hills. **1972**

DEMONSTONE ★★ In Manila a beautiful woman is possessed by an evil spirit bent on frying assorted gang members. Throw in Jan-Michael Vincent as an ex-Marine and all hell breaks loose. Rated R for adult language, violence, and nudity. 90m. **DIR:** Andrew Prowse. **CAST:** R. Lee Ermey, Jan-Michael Vincent, Nancy Everhard. **1989**

DERANGED ★★★ Murder is the result, when a woman slowly loses her senses and begins to confuse illusion with reality. Low-budget mind-bender is borrowed from Polanski's *Repulsion*, but holds its own, thanks to director Chuck Vincent's visual trickery and innate sense of black humor. Rated R for nudity. 85m. **DIR:** Chuck Vincent. **CAST:** Jane Hamilton, Jennifer Delora, Paul Siederman, Jamie Gillis. **1987**

DESTROYER 🦃 Lyle Alzado has the title role as a maniacal serial killer that the electric chair can't stop. Rated R for gratuitous violence, language, and nudity. 93m. **DIR:** Robert Kirk. **CAST:** Lyle Alzado, Anthony Perkins, Deborah Foreman, Clayton Rohner. **1988**

DEVIL BAT, THE ★★ Pretty fair thriller from PRC gives us Bela Lugosi as yet another bloodthirsty mad scientist who trains oversize rubber bats to suck blood from selected victims by use of a scent. B&W; 69m. **DIR:** Jean Yarbrough. **CAST:** Bela Lugosi, Suzanne Kaaren, Dave O'Brien, Guy Usher. **1941**

DEVIL BAT'S DAUGHTER ★★ Unimaginative sequel to *Devil Bat* finds heroine Rosemary La Planche fearing for her sanity as her father spends more and more of his time experimenting with those darn bats.... Low-budget bore. B&W; 66m. **DIR:** Frank Wisbar. **CAST:** Rosemary La Planche, Michael Hale, Molly Lamont. **1946**

DEVIL DOG: THE HOUND OF HELL 🦃 This made-for-television movie is even more ridiculous than the title implies. 95m. **DIR:** Curtis Harrington. **CAST:** Richard Crenna, Yvette Mimieux, Victor Jory, Ken Kercheval. **1976**

DEVIL DOLL, THE (1936) ★★★½ This imaginative fantasy-thriller pits crazed Lionel Barrymore and his tiny "devil dolls" against those who have done him wrong. Although not as original an idea now as it was then, the acting, special effects, and director Tod Browning's odd sense of humor make this worth seeing. B&W; 79m. **DIR:** Tod Browning. **CAST:** Lionel Barrymore, Maureen O'Sullivan, Frank Lawton, Henry B. Walthall. **1936**

DEVIL DOLL (1963) ★★ Isn't it amazing how many horror movies have been made with the same story of a ventriloquist's dummy occupied by a human soul? This low-key British version has some creepy moments as Hugo the dummy stalks his victims with a knife, but lackadaisical direction holds the movie back. B&W; 80m. **DIR:** Lindsay Shonteff. **CAST:** Bryant Halliday, William Sylvester, Yvonne Romain. **1963**

DEVIL GIRL FROM MARS 🦃 Messenger (the Devil Girl) sent from her native planet to kidnap Earth men for reproductive purposes. B&W; 76m. **DIR:** David MacDonald. **CAST:** Patricia Laffan, Hazel Court, Hugh McDermott. **1955**

DEVIL IN THE HOUSE OF EXORCISM, THE ★★ Originally titled *House of Exorcism*. Not as crummy as everybody says it is, but no Oscar candidate, either. Producer Alfred Leone took some footage from *Lisa and the Devil* and footage shot by Mario Bava, added some scenes shot by himself, and cobbled together this noisy *Exorcist* rip-off. Bava hides behind the pseudonym Mickey Lion. Rated R. 93m. **DIR:** Mario Bava. **CAST:** Elke Sommer, Robert Alda, Telly Savalas. **1975**

DEVIL WITHIN HER, THE 🦃 Hilariously bad at times, plodding the rest. Rated R for violence, nudity, and profanity. 90m. **DIR:** Peter Sasdy. **CAST:** Joan Collins, Donald Pleasence,

Eileen Atkins, Ralph Bates, Caroline Munro, John Steiner. 1975

DEVIL'S COMMANDMENT, THE ★★★ Serious horror fans should make an effort to find this movie, which marked the beginning of the revival of the gothic horror film in Europe. Another version of the story of Countess Bathory, who tried to salvage her youth with the blood of young women, the film was sliced up by both its Italian and American distributors. The distinctive visual sense of director Riccardo Freda (assisted by cinematographer Mario Bava) is still compelling. Dubbed in English. B&W; 71m. **DIR:** Riccardo Freda. **CAST:** Gianna Maria Canale, Antoine Balpetre, Paul Muller. 1956

DEVIL'S GIFT, THE 🦃 Ultralow-budget and uncredited rip-off of Stephen King's short story "The Monkey." Not rated. 112m. **DIR:** Kenneth Berton. **CAST:** Bob Mendlesolin. 1984

DEVIL'S MESSENGER, THE ★★ A film of note for its curio value only. Lon Chaney plays the devil (in a dark, short-sleeved sport shirt!), who takes pity on a young suicide victim and sends her back to Earth to lure sinners to their doom. An uncredited Curt Siodmak (*Donovan's Brain*) worked on the script. B&W; 72m. **DIR:** Herbert L. Strock. **CAST:** Lon Chaney Jr., Karen Kadler, John Crawford. 1961

DEVIL'S RAIN, THE ★★½ Great cast in a fair shocker about a band of devil worshipers at large in a small town. Terrific makeup, especially Ernest Borgnine's! Rated PG for language and violence. 85m. **DIR:** Robert Fuest. **CAST:** Ernest Borgnine, Ida Lupino, William Shatner, Eddie Albert, Tom Skerritt, Keenan Wynn, John Travolta. 1975

DEVIL'S UNDEAD, THE ★★★½ A surprisingly entertaining and suspenseful release starring the two kings of British horror, Christopher Lee and Peter Cushing, as a sort of modern-day Holmes and Watson in a tale of demonic possession. Rated PG. 91m. **DIR:** Peter Sasdy. **CAST:** Christopher Lee, Peter Cushing, Georgia Brown, Diana Dors. 1979

DEVIL'S WEDDING NIGHT, THE ★★ Say this for the Italians: even when their movies stink, they pack them with exploitable ingredients. Here, it's vampire queen Sara Bay (Rosalba Neri before she Anglicized her name), disrobing at every opportunity just as she did in *Lady Frankenstein*, and seducing knuckleheaded twin brothers, both played by Mark Damon. Rated R. 85m. **DIR:** Paul Solvay. **CAST:** Sara Bay, Mark Damon, Frances Davis. 1973

DEVONSVILLE TERROR, THE ★★★ Three witches are killed in Devonsville in 1683, and one of them places a curse on the townspeople. Flash forward to the present. This film has good performances, high production values, and a scary script that is not based on special effects. Rated R for nudity, violence, mild gore. 97m. **DIR:** Ulli Lommel. **CAST:** Paul Wilson, Suzanna Love, Donald Pleasence. 1983

DIARY OF A MADMAN 🦃 Unatmospheric adaptation of Guy de Maupassant's *The Horla*—with Vincent Price as a murderous sculptor. 96m. **DIR:** Reginald LeBorg. **CAST:** Vincent Price, Nancy Kovack, Ian Wolfe. 1963

DIE! DIE! MY DARLING! ★★½ This British thriller was Tallulah Bankhead's last movie. She plays a crazed woman who kidnaps her late son's fiancée for punishment and salvation. Grisly fun for Bankhead fans, but may be too heavy-handed for others. Unrated, the film has violence. 97m. **DIR:** Silvio Narizzano. **CAST:** Tallulah Bankhead, Stefanie Powers, Peter Vaughan, Donald Sutherland. 1965

DIE, MONSTER, DIE! 🦃 A slow-moving H. P. Lovecraft adaptation about a young man (Nick Adams) visiting his fiancée's family estate. 80m. **DIR:** Daniel Haller. **CAST:** Boris Karloff, Nick Adams, Suzan Farmer. 1965

DIE SCREAMING, MARIANNE 🦃 Graphic horror film concerns a young girl (Susan George) who is pursued by numerous crazies. Rated R. 99m. **DIR:** Pete Walker. **CAST:** Susan George, Barry Evans. 1972

DINOSAURUS! ★★½ Workers at a remote construction site accidentally stumble upon a prehistoric brontosaurus, tyrannosaurus rex, and a caveman (all quite alive) while excavating the area. Sure, the monsters look fake, and most of the humor is unintentional, but this film is entertaining nonetheless. 85m. **DIR:** Irvin S. Yeaworth Jr. **CAST:** Ward Ramsey, Paul Lukather. 1960

DISCIPLE OF DEATH 🦃 Bargain basement, overly ambitious British satanism romp. Rated R. 84m. **DIR:** Tom Parkinson. **CAST:** Mike Raven, Ronald Lacey. 1972

DISTORTIONS ★★½ The crazy plot developments in the final fifteen minutes of the film—about a widow (Olivia Hussey) being held captive by her wicked aunt (Piper Laurie)—make this rather contrived film interesting. Rated PG for violence. 98m. **DIR:** Armand Mastroianni. **CAST:** Steve Railsback, Olivia Hussey, Piper Laurie, Rita Gam, Edward Albert, Terence Knox, June Chadwick. 1987

DISTURBANCE, THE 🦃 Perfectly dreadful tale of a psychotic trying to come to grips with himself while slaughtering the requisite nubile young women. Unrated; the film has violence and profanity. 81m. **DIR:** Cliff Guest. **CAST:** Timothy Greeson. 1989

DR. ALIEN 🦃 Aliens assume human form and conduct experiments on a high school boy. Rated R for nudity and profanity. 90m. **DIR:** David DeCoteau. **CAST:** Billy Jacoby, Judy Landers, Arlene Golonka, Troy Donahue. 1988

DOCTOR AND THE DEVILS, THE ★★★ This film, based on a true story, with an original screenplay by Dylan Thomas, is set in England in the 1800s. Dr. Cook (Timothy Dalton) is a professor of anatomy, who doesn't have enough corpses to use in class demonstrations. Not for the squeamish. Rated R for language, simulated sex, and violence. 93m. **DIR:** Freddie Francis. **CAST:** Timothy Dalton, Jonathan Pryce, Twiggy, Julian Sands, Stephen Rea, Phyllis Logan, Beryl Reid, Sian Phillips. **1985**

DR. BLACK AND MR. HYDE Dr. Black develops a serum to cure his kidney ailment that turns him into a monster with white skin. Rated R. 88m. **DIR:** William Crain. **CAST:** Bernie Casey, Rosalind Cash. **1976**

DR. BUTCHER, M.D. (MEDICAL DEVIATE) Italian cannibal-zombie movie, and you know what that means—gore galore. Rated R. Dubbed in English. 80m. **DIR:** Frank Martin. **CAST:** Ian McCulloch, Alexandra Cole. **1979**

DR. CALIGARI Purportedly an update-parody of the German classic, this self-consciously bizarre movie is all gaudy art design and no plot. Rated R for sexual obsessions. 80m. **DIR:** Stephen Sayadian. **CAST:** Madeleine Reynal. **1989**

DR. CYCLOPS ★★★ Oscar-nominated special effects dominate this tale of a brilliant physicist (Albert Dekker) in the remote jungles of Peru. He shrinks a group of his colleagues to miniature size in order to protect his valuable radium discovery. Entertaining film is best remembered as one of the earliest Technicolor horror movies, with lush photography and an effective performance by Dekker. 75m. **DIR:** Ernest B. Schoedsack. **CAST:** Albert Dekker, Janice Logan, Charles Halton, Thomas Coley, Victor Kilian. **1940**

DR. DEATH: SEEKER OF SOULS ★★½ Dr. Death discovered how to cheat death one thousand years ago by periodically transferring his soul into another body. He's willing to share his talents with others, too. The makers of this low-rent terror tale had a tongue-in-cheek sense of humor, and it shows. Look for a cameo by head Stooge Moe Howard. Rated R, though pretty tame by current standards. 87m. **DIR:** Eddie Saeta. **CAST:** John Considine, Barry Coe, Cheryl Miller, Florence Marly, Jo Morrow. **1973**

DR. FRANKENSTEIN'S CASTLE OF FREAKS Italian exploitation film with Rossano Brazzi, Michael Dunn, and Edmond Purdom at the nadir of their careers. Rated R. 89m. **DIR:** Robert H. Oliver. **CAST:** Rossano Brazzi, Michael Dunn, Edmund Purdom. **1973**

DR. GIGGLES An escaped lunatic with a medical fixation employs stainless-steel technology to dispatch the usual libidinous teenagers. Tiresome low-rent shocker. Malpractice all the way. Rated R for violence and gore. 95m. **DIR:** Manny Coto. **CAST:** Larry Drake, Holly Marie Combs, Glenn Quinn, Cliff De Young, Richard Bradford. **1992**

DOCTOR GORE Cheap horror movie about a demented surgeon who, after the death of his wife, sets about assembling the perfect woman with parts taken from other women. Rated R. 91m. **DIR:** Pat Patterson. **CAST:** J. G. "Pat" Patterson. **1975**

DOCTOR HACKENSTEIN Boring rip-off of *Re-Animator*, as well as all those Frankenstein flicks. Rated R for nudity and violence. 88m. **DIR:** Richard Clarke. **CAST:** David Muir, Stacey Travis. **1988**

DR. JEKYLL AND MR. HYDE (1920) ★★★½ Still considered one of the finest film versions of Robert Louis Stevenson's story, this features John Barrymore in a bravura performance as the infamous doctor who becomes a raging beast. Barrymore always prided himself on changing into the dreadful Hyde by contorting his body rather than relying on heavy makeup. Silent. B&W; 63m. **DIR:** John S. Robertson. **CAST:** John Barrymore, Martha Mansfield, Nita Naldi, Louis Wolheim, Charles Lane. **1920**

DR. JEKYLL AND MR. HYDE (1932) ★★★★½ Fredric March's Oscar-winning performance is the highlight of this terrific horror film, which is also the best of the many versions of Robert Louis Stevenson's classic tale of good and evil. The direction by Rouben Mamoulian is exquisite. B&W; 98m. **DIR:** Rouben Mamoulian. **CAST:** Fredric March, Miriam Hopkins, Rose Hobart. **1932**

DR. JEKYLL AND MR. HYDE (1941) ★★★ A well-done version of Robert Louis Stevenson's classic story about a good doctor who dares to venture into the unknown. The horror of his transformation is played down in favor of the emotional and psychological consequences. Spencer Tracy and Ingrid Bergman are excellent, the production lush. B&W; 114m. **DIR:** Victor Fleming. **CAST:** Spencer Tracy, Ingrid Bergman, Lana Turner, Donald Crisp, C. Aubrey Smith, Sara Allgood. **1941**

DR. JEKYLL AND SISTER HYDE ★★ One of many variations on a Jack the Ripper theme, this one has a mad scientist driven to terrible deeds with slightly different results. Contains far too many midnight scenes in foggy old London Town. No rating, but contains violence and nudity. 94m. **DIR:** Roy Ward Baker. **CAST:** Ralph Bates, Martine Beswick, Gerald Sim. **1971**

DR. JEKYLL'S DUNGEON OF DEATH The great-grandson of the original Dr. Jekyll spends the entire movie in his basement, injecting the family serum into unwilling specimens. Rated R. 88m. **DIR:** James Woods. **CAST:** James Mathers. **1982**

DOCTOR OF DOOM 🦃 Mexican wrestling women battling a simian fiend. B&W; 77m. **DIR:** René Cardona Sr. **CAST:** Lorena Velazquez. **1962**

DR. PHIBES RISES AGAIN ★★★½ Good-natured terror abounds in this fun sequel to *The Abominable Dr. Phibes*, with Vincent Price reprising his role as a disfigured doctor desperately searching for a way to restore his dead wife to life. Entertaining. Rated PG for mild violence. 89m. **DIR:** Robert Fuest. **CAST:** Vincent Price, Robert Quarry, Peter Jeffrey, Fiona Lewis, Peter Cushing, Hugh Griffith, Terry-Thomas, Beryl Reid. **1972**

DR. TARR'S TORTURE DUNGEON ★★½ A reporter investigating an insane asylum in nineteenth-century France discovers that the director, whose therapy includes having patients act out their obsessions, is really one of the inmates. Much better than the usual Mexican schlock. Rated R for sex and violence. 88m. **DIR:** Juan Lopez Moctezuma. **CAST:** Claudio Brook, Ellen Sherman. **1972**

DR. TERROR'S HOUSE OF HORRORS ★★★ Good anthology horror entertainment about a fortune teller (Peter Cushing) who has some frightening revelations for his clients. A top-flight example of British genre moviemaking. 98m. **DIR:** Freddie Francis. **CAST:** Peter Cushing, Christopher Lee, Roy Castle, Donald Sutherland. **1965**

DOCTOR X ★★★½ From mayhem to murder, from cannibalism to rape—this picture offers it all. Dr. X is played with panache by Lionel Atwill. Lee Tracy is the reporter who tries valiantly to uncover and expose the mysterious doctor. This piece of vintage horror is a sure bet. 80m. **DIR:** Michael Curtiz. **CAST:** Lionel Atwill, Preston Foster, Fay Wray, Lee Tracy. **1932**

DOGS OF HELL 🦃 Low-budget thriller about a rural sheriff and a pack of rottweilers. Originally filmed in 3-D, the movie is rated R for profanity and graphic violence. 90m. **DIR:** Worth Keeter. **CAST:** Earl Owensby. **1982**

DOLLS ★★½ During a fierce storm, six people are stranded at the home of a kindly old doll maker and his wife. One by one, they are attacked by malevolent little creatures in funny outfits. (No, not Campfire Girls.) *Dolls* is from the same people who made *Re-Animator* and *From Beyond*. Rated R for violence. 77m. **DIR:** Stuart Gordon. **CAST:** Stephen Lee, Guy Rolfe, Hilary Mason. **1987**

DOLLY DEAREST ★★½ When an American family takes ownership of a run-down Mexican doll factory, they find that their new lease in life is no *Child's Play*. As luck would have it, the factory sits next to an ancient burial ground. Rated R for violence. 94m. **DIR:** Maria Lease. **CAST:** Rip Torn, Sam Bottoms, Denise Crosby. **1991**

DON'T ANSWER THE PHONE ★★ Also known as *The Hollywood Strangler*, this unpleasantly brutal exploitation quickie might have been better in more competent hands. Rated R for violence and nudity. 94m. **DIR:** Robert Hammer. **CAST:** James Westmoreland. **1981**

DON'T BE AFRAID OF THE DARK ★★★ Scary TV movie as newlyweds Kim Darby and Jim Hutton move into a weird old house inhabited by eerie little monsters who want Kim for one of their own. The human actors are okay, but the creatures steal the show. 74m. **DIR:** John Newland. **CAST:** Kim Darby, Jim Hutton, Pedro Armendariz Jr., William Demarest. **1973**

DON'T GO IN THE HOUSE 🦃 A mom-obsessed killer grows up wanting to set pretty young women on fire. Rated R. 82m. **DIR:** James Ellison. **CAST:** Dan Grimaldi. **1980**

DON'T GO IN THE WOODS 🦃 There's an ax-wielding maniac prowling the wilds of Utah. Rated R. 90m. **DIR:** James Bryan. **1981**

DON'T GO TO SLEEP ★★½ Supernatural thriller goes the distance but comes up short as the deceased daughter of a couple returns from the grave in order to reunite her family—on the other side. Made-for-television suspense works because of above-average cast. 100m. **DIR:** Richard Lang. **CAST:** Dennis Weaver, Valerie Harper, Ruth Gordon, Robert Webber. **1982**

DON'T LOOK IN THE BASEMENT ★★½ When the director of an insane asylum is murdered by one of the inmates, his assistant takes over. But that doesn't put an end to the murders. This is one horror movie in which the low budget actually helps; the lack of professionalism in the production gives it a disturbingly eerie aura. Rated R for violence. 95m. **DIR:** S. F. Brownrigg. **CAST:** William McGee. **1973**

DON'T OPEN TILL CHRISTMAS ★★½ A crazed maniac mutilates and kills bell-ringing Santas, and no one has a clue to the killer's identity, not even the filmmakers. But even with this problem, there is still a good bit of suspense. Not rated, but contains graphic violence and profanity. 86m. **DIR:** Edmund Purdom. **CAST:** Edmund Purdom, Caroline Munro, Gerry Sundquist. **1985**

DOOM ASYLUM 🦃 A man responsible for his wife's accidental death inhabits an old abandoned asylum. Not rated, but contains nudity and graphic violence. 77m. **DIR:** Richard Friedman. **CAST:** Patty Mullen, Ruth Collins. **1987**

DOPPELGANGER: THE EVIL WITHIN ★★ Drew Barrymore is either a schizoid murderer or actually has the evil counterpart she claims. A few chills before it deteriorates into drive-in hell. Rated R for profanity, violence, and nudity. 105m. **DIR:** Avi Nesher. **CAST:** Drew Barrymore, George Newbern. **1992**

DORIAN GRAY Horrid updating of the Oscar Wilde classic novel. Fascinating story has never been more boring, with some good actors wasted. Alternate title: *The Secret of Dorian Gray.* Rated R. 93m. **DIR:** Massimo Dallamano. **CAST:** Helmut Berger, Richard Todd, Herbert Lom. **1970**

DORM THAT DRIPPED BLOOD, THE The only good thing about this film is the title. Rated R for violence. 84m. **DIR:** Jeffrey Obrow, Stephen Carpenter. **CAST:** Pamela Holland, Stephen Sachs. **1981**

DRACULA (1931) ★★★★ Bela Lugosi found himself forever typecast after brilliantly bringing to life the bloodthirsty Transylvanian vampire of the title in this 1931 genre classic, directed by Tod Browning. His performance and that of Dwight Frye as the spider-eating Renfield still impress even though this early talkie seems somewhat dated today. B&W; 75m. **DIR:** Tod Browning. **CAST:** Bela Lugosi, Dwight Frye, David Manners, Helen Chandler, Edward Van Sloan. **1931**

DRACULA (1973) ★★★★ Surprisingly effective made-for-television version of Bram Stoker's classic tale has Jack Palance as a sympathetic count trapped by his vampirism. Director Dan Curtis and scripter Richard Matheson had previously collaborated on the excellent *The Night Stalker* telefilm and work together equally well here. 99m. **DIR:** Dan Curtis. **CAST:** Jack Palance, Simon Ward, Nigel Davenport, Pamela Brown, Fiona Lewis. **1973**

DRACULA (1979) ★★½ This *Dracula* is a film of missed opportunities. Frank Langella makes an excellent Count Dracula. It's a pity he has so little screen time. The story, for the uninitiated, revolves around the activities of a bloodthirsty vampire who leaves his castle in Transylvania for fresh hunting in London. Rated R. 109m. **DIR:** John Badham. **CAST:** Frank Langella, Laurence Olivier, Donald Pleasence, Jan Francis. **1979**

DRACULA AND SON ★★ French vampire spoof was probably much funnier before the inane English dubbing was added. The Dracula family looks for a new home after the Communists run them out of their Transylvanian home. Rated PG. 88m. **DIR:** Edouard Molinaro. **CAST:** Christopher Lee, Bernard Ménez. **1976**

DRACULA HAS RISEN FROM THE GRAVE ★★½ Freddie Francis took over the directorial reins from Terence Fisher for Hammer Films's third Dracula-Christopher Lee vehicle, and the result, while visually striking (Francis is an Oscar-winning cinematographer), is a major step down dramatically. A tepid revenge plot has the Count going after the niece of a monsignor. Rated G. 92m. **DIR:** Freddie Francis. **CAST:** Christopher Lee, Veronica Carlson, Rupert Davies, Barry Andrews. **1968**

DRACULA RISING After 500 years, a reincarnated woman is saved from an evil vampire by the wonderful vampire who loved her before; a good idea sucked dry by poor acting. Rated R for violence and nudity. 85m. **DIR:** Fred Gallo. **CAST:** Christopher Atkins, Stacey Travis, Doug Wert, Tara McCann. **1992**

DRACULA VS. FRANKENSTEIN Dracula's eternal search for blood. Pretty bad. Rated R. 90m. **DIR:** Al Adamson. **CAST:** J. Carrol Naish, Lon Chaney Jr., Jim Davis. **1971**

DRACULA'S DAUGHTER ★★★½ The lady in the title tries to break her addiction to human blood after she exorcises and burns the remains of her dead sire—but the cure doesn't take. This brooding film is stylish and creates its own strange mood through imaginative sets, art design, music, and compelling performances by Gloria Holden as the unhappy undead and Irving Pichel as her dour but dedicated servant. B&W; 69m. **DIR:** Lambert Hillyer. **CAST:** Gloria Holden, Otto Kruger, Marguerite Churchill, Edward Van Sloan, Irving Pichel. **1936**

DRACULA'S GREAT LOVE ★★ Anyone who isn't familiar with the cinematic exploits of Spanish horror film star Paul Naschy (Jacinto Molina to all you bilingual fans) may not want to begin here. Barrel-chested, hirsute Pablo is better suited to werewolves—in such romps as *Fury of the Wolfman*—than Transylvania's seducer. Some of this film's extensive nudity was cut, but it's still R-rated. 83m. **DIR:** Javier Aguirre. **CAST:** Paul Naschy, Haydee Politoff. **1972**

DRACULA'S LAST RITES (1980) The vampires here (none named Dracula) are the mortician, police chief, and doctor in a small town. Originally called *Last Rites.* Rated R. 88m. **DIR:** Domonic Paris. **CAST:** Patricia Lee Hammond, Gerald Fielding. **1980**

DRACULA'S WIDOW ★★ The bloodsucking lord of Transylvania is dead, but his estranged wife doesn't believe it. She tracks down the last remaining descendant of Jonathan Harker, who assures her of her spouse's demise. She then goes on a rampage, slaughtering a satanic vampire cult in hopes of finding Dracula's remains. Rated R for violence and nudity. 86m. **DIR:** Christopher Coppola. **CAST:** Josef Sommer, Sylvia Kristel, Lenny Von Dohlen, Stefan Schnabel. **1988**

DRIFTER, THE ★★ A successful businesswoman picks up a hitchhiker and they have a one-night stand. Afterward he refuses to leave her alone and her life is in jeopardy. Perhaps with a better script this could have been a reverse *Fatal Attraction.* Rated R for violence, nudity, and profanity. 89m. **DIR:** Larry Brand. **CAST:** Kim Delaney, Timothy Bottoms, Miles O'Keeffe. **1988**

DRILLER KILLER, THE 🦃 A maniac named Reno falls for his roommate. When rejected by her, he goes crazy. Not rated; contains violence, gore, and profanity. 84m. **DIR:** Abel Ferrara. **CAST:** Carolyn Mare, Jimmy Laine. **1979**

DRIVE-IN MASSACRE ★★½ If you're in the mood for a slasher movie, you could do worse than this ultralow-budget gorefest. The title says it all: Psycho killer bumps off patrons at a drive-in movie, but there are some bits that will please anyone who has ever spent summer nights at an outdoor cinema. Rated R for gore and nudity. 78m. **DIR:** Stuart Segall. **CAST:** Jake Barnes, Adam Lawrence. **1976**

DUNWICH HORROR, THE 🦃 Torpid horror-thriller made when folks didn't know that it's impossible to adapt H. P. Lovecraft. Dean Stockwell foreshadowed his hammy role in *Dune* with this laughable portrayal of a warlock. Rated PG for violence. 90m. **DIR:** Daniel Haller. **CAST:** Sandra Dee, Dean Stockwell, Sam Jaffe, Ed Begley Sr., Talia Shire. **1970**

DUST DEVIL ★★★ A South African devil arises from the desert to stalk hapless (and hopeless) victims. Moody and gory, this great-looking horror flick is too slow and artsy for its own good, and disjointed editing undermines creepy ritualism and eye-catching settings. Rated R for strong violence, sexuality, and language. 87m. **DIR:** Richard Stanley. **CAST:** Robert Burke, Chelsea Field, Zakes Mokae, Rufus Swart. **1992**

EATEN ALIVE ★★ Director Tobe Hooper's follow-up to *The Texas Chainsaw Massacre* has a similar theme but is less successful. The owner of a run-down Louisiana motel kills whoever wanders into his corner of the swamp, with the aid of a large, hungry alligator. Hooper was one of the inventors of the modern horror film, which emphasizes random violence, but this is often sloppy. Horror buffs will want to see it, anyway, for a cast that includes Neville Brand, Mel Ferrer, Stuart Whitman, and the future Freddy Krueger, Robert Englund. Rated R for strong violence. 97m. **DIR:** Tobe Hooper. **CAST:** Neville Brand, Mel Ferrer, Carolyn Jones, Marilyn Burns, William Finley, Stuart Whitman, Robert Englund. **1976**

EDGE OF SANITY ★★ Anthony Perkins is retooling his psychopathic screen persona again in this handsome-looking but mediocre British production of *Dr. Jekyll and Mr. Hyde*. No new twists on this old theme, but plenty of sexy girls and sordid violence. Rather forgettable. Not rated, this uncensored version is recommended for adults only. 86m. **DIR:** Gerard Kikoine. **CAST:** Anthony Perkins, Glynis Barber, David Lodge. **1989**

EEGAH! 🦃 Teenage caveman gets the hots for brain-dead babe. 90m. **DIR:** Nicholas Merriwether (Arch W. Hall Sr.). **CAST:** Arch Hall Jr., Richard Kiel, Marilyn Manning, William Watters (Arch Hall Sr.). **1962**

ELVES 🦃 Santa's little helpers are genetically mutated by former Nazi scientists. Unrated; the film has violence, nudity, and profanity. 89m. **DIR:** Jeff Mandel. **CAST:** Dan Haggerty, Deanna Lund. **1989**

EMERALD JUNGLE ★★ Originally titled *Eaten Alive by Cannibals,* this fitfully entertaining entry in the Italian cannibal parade was given its video moniker in the hope it would steal some of the thunder from John Boorman's unrelated *The Emerald Forest.* Heavily cut for U.S. release, but still plenty gross. Rated R. 90m. **DIR:** Umberto Lenzi. **CAST:** Robert Kerman, Janet Agren, Mel Ferrer. **1980**

EMPIRE OF THE DARK ★★ Run-of-the-mill devil flick concerning a Los Angeles police officer (writer-director-star Steve Barkett) who saves his baby son from a demonic cult. Twenty years later he and the now-grownup son must battle the cult again. Not rated, but contains violence and profanity. 93m. **DIR:** Steve Barkett. **CAST:** Steve Barkett, Richard Harrison. **1991**

ENDLESS DESCENT 🦃 A group of otherworldly genetic mutants in a sub-aquarian chamber. Not rated, but contains violence, profanity, and gore. 79m. **DIR:** Juan Piquer Simon. **CAST:** Jack Scalia, R. Lee Ermey, Ray Wise, Deborah Adair. **1989**

ENTITY, THE 🦃 Barbara Hershey stars as a woman who is sexually molested by an invisible, sex-crazed demon. Rated R for nudity, profanity, violence, and rape. 115m. **DIR:** Sidney J. Furie. **CAST:** Barbara Hershey, Ron Silver, Jacqueline Brooks. **1983**

EQUINOX (THE BEAST) ★★ Good special effects save this unprofessional movie about college students searching for their archaeology professor. On their search, they must face monsters and the occult. Rated PG. 82m. **DIR:** Jack Woods. **CAST:** Edward Connell, Barbara Hewitt. **1971**

ERASERHEAD ★★★ Weird, weird movie...director David Lynch created this nightmarish film about Henry Spencer (Jack Nance), who, we assume, lives in the far (possibly post-apocalyptic) future when everyone is given a free lobotomy at birth. Nothing else could explain the bizarre behavior of its characters. B&W; 90m. **DIR:** David Lynch. **CAST:** Jack Nance, Charlotte Stewart, Jeanne Bates. **1978**

EROTIKILL ★★ The indefatigable Spanish director Jess Franco—who's made so many cheap exploitation pictures, even *he* can't remember them all—is at the helm, and, briefly, in the cast of this raunchy opus about a female bloodsucker (Lina Romay) prowling the decadent Riviera. Definitely not for the kiddies, or the easily offended. You can find an even more explicit U.S. video edition under the title *Loves of Irina*. Rated R. 90m. **DIR:** Jess (Jesus) Franco. **CAST:** Lina Romay, Jack Taylor, Alice Arno. **1981**

EVICTORS, THE 🦃 A family who obviously didn't see *The Amityville Horror* move into a haunted house. Rated PG. 92m. **DIR:** Charles B. Pierce. **CAST:** Michael Parks, Jessica Harper, Vic Morrow. **1979**

EVIL, THE ★★★ Psychologist Richard Crenna, his wife, and some of his students are trapped in an old mansion where an unseen force kills them off one by one. It's your basic haunted-house story with one added twist: the devil himself makes a memorable appearance in the person of Victor Buono, a choice bit of casting. Rated R for violence and nudity. 89m. **DIR:** Gus Trikonis. **CAST:** Richard Crenna, Joanna Pettet, Andrew Prine, Cassie Yates, Victor Buono, Mary Louise Weller. **1978**

EVIL CLUTCH 🦃 She's a babe, she's a beast, she's a good time, until you get her aroused, and then the monster in her comes out. Most men wouldn't know the difference. Rated R for violence and nudity. 88m. **DIR:** Andreas Marfori. **CAST:** Caralina C. Tassoni, Diego Ribon, Luciano Crovato. **1988**

EVIL DEAD, THE ★★★★ Five college students spending the weekend at a cabin in the Tennessee woods accidentally revive demons who possess their bodies. This low-budget wonder isn't much in the plot department, but it features lots of inventive, energetic camera work and plenty of hysterically gruesome special effects. Most of the violence is committed against unfeeling demons, so it's not that hard to take, though a sequence in which a woman is molested by a tree (!) is in poor taste. Unrated, but the black-humored violence isn't for children. 86m. **DIR:** Sam Raimi. **CAST:** Bruce Campbell, Ellen Sandweiss. **1982**

EVIL DEAD 2 ★★★½ The original *Evil Dead* didn't have a lot of plot, and the sequel has even less. Ash, the survivor of the first film, continues to battle demons in the cabin in the woods. A few lost travelers happen by to provide additional demon fodder. It's more of a remake than a sequel, except that this time director Sam Raimi has explicitly fashioned it as a tribute to one of his greatest influences: the Three Stooges. The overt slapstick may turn off some horror fans. Unrated, it contains nonstop violence and gore. 85m. **DIR:** Sam Raimi. **CAST:** Bruce Campbell, Sarah Barry. **1987**

EVIL LAUGH 🦃 A typical slasher film about college students spending the weekend in an abandoned house while a crazed serial killer stalks and kills them. Rated R for violence and nudity. 90m. **DIR:** Dominick Brascia. **CAST:** Steven Bad, Dominick Brascia. **1986**

EVIL MIND, THE (A.K.A. THE CLAIRVOYANT) ★★★ Nicely mounted story of fake mentalist who realizes that his phony predictions are actually coming true. The elegant Claude Rains gives a fine performance as a man who has inexplicably acquired a strange power and finds himself frightened by it. Interesting and fun. B&W; 80m. **DIR:** Maurice Elvey. **CAST:** Claude Rains, Fay Wray, Mary Clare. **1934**

EVIL OF FRANKENSTEIN, THE ★★½ A weaker entry in Hammer Films's popular Frankenstein series pits Dr. Frankenstein (Peter Cushing) against an underhanded hypnotist (Peter Woodthorpe). Good production values and handsome set pieces, but the monster makeup is silly and the script convoluted. 98m. **DIR:** Freddie Francis. **CAST:** Peter Cushing, Duncan Lamont, Peter Woodthorpe. **1964**

EVIL SPAWN 🦃 An antiaging serum turns a vain actress into a giant werebug. Not rated, with nudity, violence, and sexual situations. 88m. **DIR:** Kenneth J. Hall. **CAST:** Bobbie Bresee, John Carradine. **1987**

EVIL SPIRITS 🦃 Tongue-in-cheek humor fails to save this low-budget shocker about a landlady whose backyard is overcrowded with the buried bodies of her tenants. Rated R for nudity and violence. 95m. **DIR:** Gary Graver. **CAST:** Arte Johnson, Karen Black, Robert Quarry. **1991**

EVIL SPIRITS IN THE HOUSE 🦃 Everything about this shot-on-video production about a father and daughter vacationing in a secluded cabin is incompetent. Lame acting, a poor script, and terrible direction. Not rated. 114m. **DIR:** Steve Postal. **CAST:** Larry Wallace, Jennifer Filkins, Angela Shepard, Dawn Chappel. **1990**

EVIL TOWN 🦃 In a quaint mountain town, a mad doctor is keeping the citizens from aging at the expense of young tourists. Rated R for violence, nudity, and language. 88m. **DIR:** Edward Collins. **CAST:** James Keach, Dean Jagger, Robert Walker, Michele Marsh. **1987**

EVILS OF THE NIGHT 🦃 Vampires from outer space hire two idiot mechanics to kidnap teenagers for them. Rated R for nudity, simulated sex, and violence. 85m. **DIR:** Mardi Rustam. **CAST:** Neville Brand, Aldo Ray, John Carradine, Tina Louise, Julie Newmar, Karrie Emerson, Tony O'Dell. **1985**

EVILSPEAK 🦃 A devil-worshiping medieval Spanish priest brought into modern times by a student on a computer. Rated R for nudity, violence, and gore. 89m. **DIR:** Eric Weston. **CAST:** Clint Howard, R. G. Armstrong, Joe Cortese, Claude Earl Jones. **1982**

EXORCIST, THE ★★★★½ A sensation at the time of its release, this horror film—directed by William Friedkin (*The French Connection*)—has lost some of its punch because of the numerous imitations it spawned. An awful sequel, *Exorcist II: The Heretic*, didn't help much either. Rated R. 121m. **DIR:** William Friedkin. **CAST:** Ellen Burstyn, Max von Sydow, Linda Blair, Jason Miller, Lee J. Cobb. **1973**

EXORCIST II: THE HERETIC 🦃 The script is bad, the acting poor, and the direction lacking in pace or conviction. Rated R for violence and profanity. 110m. **DIR:** John Boorman. **CAST:** Richard Burton, Linda Blair, Louise Fletcher, James Earl Jones, Max von Sydow. **1977**

EXORCIST III: LEGION ★★ This time priests discover some unutterable evil and turn to detective George C. Scott for help. Rated R for all sorts of ghastly stuff. 108m. **DIR:** William Peter Blatty. **CAST:** George C. Scott, Ed Flanders, Brad Dourif. **1990**

EXPOSED ★★ Nastassja Kinski stars in this mediocre and confusing film as a high-priced fashion model whose constant exposure in magazines and on television has made her the target for the sometimes dangerous desires of two men. Former ballet star Rudolph Nureyev is also featured. Rated R. 100m. **DIR:** James Toback. **CAST:** Nastassja Kinski, Rudolf Nureyev, Harvey Keitel, Ian McShane. **1983**

EYE OF THE DEMON 🦃 A yuppie couple relocates to a New England island. TV movie originally titled *Bay Coven*. 92m. **DIR:** Carl Schenkel. **CAST:** Tim Matheson, Pamela Sue Martin, Barbara Billingsley, Woody Harrelson, Susan Ruttan. **1987**

EYEBALL 🦃 Vacationers on a tour bus are murdered. Rated R for violence and nudity. 87m. **DIR:** Umberto Lenzi. **CAST:** John Richardson. **1977**

EYES OF A STRANGER ★★ *The Love Boat*'s Julie, Lauren Tewes, plays a reporter who decides to track down a psychopathic killer. Lots of blood and some sexual molestation. Rated R. 85m. **DIR:** Ken Wiederhorn. **CAST:** Lauren Tewes, Jennifer Jason Leigh. **1981**

EYES OF FIRE ★★★ Old-West settlers accused of witchcraft are surrounded by woods made from the souls of earlier settlers—and the witch who cast the spell upon them. Above-average special-effects highlight this original tale. Rated R for violence and nudity; 90m. **DIR:** Avery Crounse. **CAST:** Dennis Lipscomb, Rebecca Stanley, Guy Boyd. **1983**

FACE AT THE WINDOW, THE ★★½ Tod Slaughter produced and starred in a number of lurid gothic plays that barnstormed through the English provinces in the 1920s and eventually were made into low-budget horror films. This one, about a fiendish killer in 1880s Paris, was the most cinematic, and thus probably the best. Worth seeing as a curio, but it still drags, even at barely an hour. B&W; 65m. **DIR:** George King. **CAST:** Tod Slaughter, Marjorie Taylor, John Warwick. **1939**

FADE TO BLACK (1980) ★★★ Movie buffs and horror fans will especially love *Fade to Black*, a funny, suspenseful, and entertaining low-budget film that features Dennis Christopher in a tour-de-force performance. Christopher plays Eric Binford, an odd young man who spends most of his time absorbing films. His all-night videotaping sessions and movie orgies only make him out of step with other people his age, and soon Eric goes over the edge. Rated R. 100m. **DIR:** Vernon Zimmerman. **CAST:** Dennis Christopher, Linda Kerridge, Tim Thomerson, Morgan Paull, Marya Small. **1980**

FALL OF THE HOUSE OF USHER, THE (1949) ★★ Low-budget, semiprofessional adaptation of the famous horror tale. Produced in England, it is by turns amateurish, tedious, and genuinely scary. B&W; 74m. **DIR:** Ivan Barnett. **CAST:** Gwen Watford, Kaye Tendeter, Irving Steen. **1949**

FALL OF THE HOUSE OF USHER, THE (1960) ★★★½ Imagination and a chilling sense of the sinister make this low-budget Roger Corman version of Edgar Allan Poe's famous haunted-house story highly effective. Vincent Price is without peer as Usher. 79m. **DIR:** Roger Corman. **CAST:** Vincent Price, Mark Damon, Myrna Fahey. **1960**

FALL OF THE HOUSE OF USHER, THE (1979) 🦃 Edgar Allan Poe tale is tacky, inept, and dull. Rated PG. 101m. **DIR:** Stephen Lord. **CAST:** Martin Landau, Robert Hays, Charlene Tilton, Ray Walston. **1979**

FATAL GAMES 🦃 In a school for young athletes, a murderer begins eliminating the students, using a javelin. Not rated, but contains explicit nudity and violence. 88m. **DIR:** Michael Elliot. **CAST:** Sally Kirkland, Lynn Banashek, Teal Roberts. **1984**

FATAL PULSE 🦃 A house full of sorority girls. Not rated, but contains nudity, violence, and profanity. 90m. **DIR:** Anthony Christopher. **CAST:** Michelle McCormick, Ken Roberts. **1988**

FEAR IN THE NIGHT (DYNASTY OF FEAR) ★★★½ Effective British shocker about a teacher and his off-balance bride at a desolate boys' school. Another suspensful offering from Hammer Films. Rated PG. 94m. **DIR:** Jimmy Sangster. **CAST:** Ralph Bates, Judy Geeson, Peter Cushing, Joan Collins. **1972**

FEAR NO EVIL 🦃 The story of the satanic high school student hell-bent on destroying a senior class. Rated R. 96m. **DIR:** Frank LaLoggia. **CAST:** Stephan Arngrim, Elizabeth Hoffman. **1981**

FEARLESS VAMPIRE KILLERS, OR, PARDON ME, BUT YOUR TEETH ARE IN MY

NECK, THE ★★★★ Roman Polanski playfully revamps Transylvanian folklore as an elderly, nutty professor (Jack MacGowran) and his mousy protégé (Polanski) hunt down a castle-dwelling bloodsucker who has kidnapped the buxom daughter (Sharon Tate) of a lecherous innkeeper. Ressurected in Polanski's originally intended length, this misadventure of two of the most unlikeliest of heroes gushes with ghoulish, offbeat humor. 111m. **DIR:** Roman Polanski. **CAST:** Roman Polanski, Jack MacGowran, Alfie Bass, Sharon Tate, Ferdinand Mayne. **1966**

FIEND 🦃 An excruciatingly bad, zero-budget, one-man zombie movie about a chubby maniac. Rated R. 90m. **DIR:** Don Dohler. **CAST:** Don Leifert. **1980**

FIEND WITHOUT A FACE ★★★½ Surprisingly effective little horror chiller with slight overtones of the "Id" creature from *Forbidden Planet*. Scientific thought experiment goes awry and creates nasty creatures that look like brains with coiled tails. Naturally, they eat people. Story builds to a great climax. B&W; 74m. **DIR:** Arthur Crabtree. **CAST:** Marshall Thompson, Kim Parker, Terry Kilburn. **1958**

FIFTH FLOOR, THE 🦃 College lass is mistakenly popped into an insane asylum. Rated R for violence and nudity. 90m. **DIR:** Howard Avedis. **CAST:** Bo Hopkins, Dianne Hull, Patti D'Arbanville, Mel Ferrer, Sharon Farrell. **1980**

FINAL CONFLICT, THE ★★ The third and last in the *Omen* trilogy, this disturbing but passionless film concerns the rise to power of the son of Satan, Damien Thorn (Sam Neill), and the second coming of the Saviour. It depends more on shocking spectacle than gripping tension for its impact. Rated R. 108m. **DIR:** Graham Baker. **CAST:** Sam Neill, Rossano Brazzi, Don Gordon, Lisa Harrow, Mason Adams. **1981**

FINAL EXAM 🦃 A mad slasher hacks his way through a college campus. Rated R. 90m. **DIR:** Jimmy Huston. **CAST:** Joel S. Rice. **1981**

FINAL TERROR, THE ★★ Rachel Ward and Daryl Hannah weren't big stars when they made this mediocre low-budget slasher flick for onetime B-movie king Sam Arkoff and now they probably wish they hadn't. Rated R for brief nudity and violence. 82m. **DIR:** Andrew Davis. **CAST:** Rachel Ward, Daryl Hannah, John Friedrich, Adrian Zmed. **1981**

FIRESTARTER ★★★½ Stephen King writhes again. This time, Drew Barrymore stars as the gifted (or is that haunted) child of the title, who has the ability—sometimes uncontrollable—to ignite objects around her. David Keith is the father who tries to protect her from the baddies. *Firestarter* is suspenseful, poignant, and sometimes frightening entertainment that goes beyond its genre. Rated R for violence. 115m. **DIR:** Mark L. Lester. **CAST:** David Keith, Drew Barrymore, George C. Scott, Martin Sheen. **1984**

FIRST POWER, THE 🦃 Repulsive thing-that-wouldn't-die trash. Rated R. 100m. **DIR:** Robert Resnikoff. **CAST:** Lou Diamond Phillips, Tracy Griffith, Jeff Kober, Mykel T. Williamson, Dennis Lipscomb. **1990**

FLESH AND BLOOD SHOW, THE 🦃 Sluggish, gory British horror about a failed actor. Rated R. 96m. **DIR:** Pete Walker. **CAST:** Ray Brooks. **1972**

FLESH EATERS, THE ★★ This is the notorious cult horror epic—rarely available, even on video, in its uncut form—about a mad scientist (Martin Kosleck) who unleashes voracious organisms into the waters surrounding his tropical island laboratory. A seminal gore film, scripted by comics writer Arnold Drake, it'll have you chuckling at its amateurish performances one minute, then gagging at its surprisingly vivid special effects in the next. B&W; 87m. **DIR:** Jack Curtis. **CAST:** Martin Kosleck, Rita Morley. **1964**

FLESH EATING MOTHERS ★★ Tepid mix of gore and gags in a suburb where adulterous mothers become infected with a virus that turns them into cannibalistic zombies. Unrated, comic violence. 90m. **DIR:** James Aviles Martin. **CAST:** Robert Lee Oliver, Donatella Hecht. **1988**

FLESH FEAST 🦃 Veronica Lake was working as a waitress in Florida when she coproduced and starred in this film about a plastic surgeon who uses maggots as a unique form of dermabrasion. Rated R. 72m. **DIR:** Brad F. Grinter. **CAST:** Veronica Lake. **1970**

FLESHBURN ★★★½ An Indian who left five men in the desert to die breaks out of an insane asylum to hunt down and wreak his revenge against the psychiatrists who sentenced him. This film promises to be more than exploitation, and it does not let you down. Rated R for profanity and violence. 91m. **DIR:** George Gage. **CAST:** Sonny Landham, Steve Kanaly, Karen Carlson. **1983**

FLY, THE (1958) ★★★★ Classic horror film builds slowly but really pays off. A scientist (Al Hedison, soon to become David) experimenting with unknown forces turns himself into the hideous title character. Impressive production with top-notch acting and real neat special effects. 94m. **DIR:** Kurt Neumann. **CAST:** David Hedison, Patricia Owens, Vincent Price, Herbert Marshall. **1958**

FLY, THE (1986) ★★★½ A brilliant research scientist, Seth Brundle (Jeff Goldblum), has developed a way to transport matter. One night, thoroughly gassed, he decides to test the device on himself. Unfortunately, a pesky housefly finds its way into the chamber with the scientist. It must also be said that this otherwise entertaining update simply falls apart at the conclusion. Rated R for gore and slime. 100m. **DIR:** David Cronenberg. **CAST:** Jeff Goldblum, Geena Davis, John Getz. **1986**

FLY II, THE ★½ This sequel to David Cronenberg's masterfully crafted 1986 horror remake *The Fly* doesn't have the right chemistry. The weak, unbelievable story centers around the birth of an heir (Eric Stoltz) to the original fly. This one doesn't fly. Rated R for violence, adult situations, and profanity. 104m. **DIR:** Chris Walas. **CAST:** Eric Stoltz, Daphne Zuniga, Lee Richardson, John Getz. **1989**

FLYING SERPENT, THE ★★ Mad doctor Zucco keeps mythological Mexican bird Quetzalcoatl (the same monster that turns up, much bigger, in Larry Cohen's *Q*) in a cage, periodically letting it out to attack his enemies. One of the all-time great, unintentional laugh riots from poverty-row studio PRC, directed by Sam Newfield under one of his many pseudonyms, Sherman Scott. B&W; 59m. **DIR:** Sam Newfield. **CAST:** George Zucco, Ralph Lewis. **1946**

FOG, THE ★★★ This is one of those *almost* movies. Director John Carpenter is on familiar ground with this story of nineteenth-century colonists back from the dead, terrorizing a modern-day fishing village. The lack of any real chills or surprises makes this one a nice try but no cigar. Rated R. 91m. **DIR:** John Carpenter. **CAST:** Adrienne Barbeau, Jamie Lee Curtis, John Houseman, Hal Holbrook, Janet Leigh. **1980**

FORBIDDEN WORLD ★★ Jesse Vint was rescued from the obscurity of his deep-space death in *Silent Running*, and his reward was a starring role in this rip-off of *Alien* in which an experimental food stuff starts killing the inhabitants of a space colony. Rated R for violence. 77m. **DIR:** Allan Holzman. **CAST:** Jesse Vint, Dawn Dunlap, June Chadwick, Linden Chiles. **1982**

FORCED ENTRY Gas-station attendant kills women because his mother beat him when he was young. Original title: *The Last Victim*. Rated R. 88m. **DIR:** Jim Sotos. **CAST:** Ron Max, Tanya Roberts, Nancy Allen. **1975**

FOREST, THE Waste of time. Unrated. 90m. **DIR:** Don Jones. **CAST:** Dean Russell, Michael Brody. **1983**

FOREVER EVIL After his friends are massacred, the sole survivor tracks down the cult of the demon god who killed them. Not rated. 107m. **DIR:** Roger Evans. **CAST:** Red Mitchell, Tracey Hoffman. **1987**

FRANKENHOOKER ★★ In order to replace his girlfriend, a budding scientist decides to place her head on the various body parts of unfortunate streetwalkers in this low-budget gorefest. Not rated, but contains violence, profanity, nudity, and gore. 85m. **DIR:** Frank Henenlotter. **CAST:** James Lorinz, Patty Mullen, Louise Lasser, Shirley Stoler. **1990**

FRANKENSTEIN (1931) ★★★★ Despite all the padding, grease paint, and restrictive, awkward costuming, Boris Karloff gives a strong, sensitive performance in this 1931 horror classic—with only eyes and an occasional grunt to convey meaning. It still stands as one of the great screen performances. B&W; 71m. **DIR:** James Whale. **CAST:** Colin Clive, Mae Clarke, Boris Karloff, John Boles. **1931**

FRANKENSTEIN (1973) ★★½ Bo Svenson's sympathetic portrayal of the monster is the one saving grace of this essentially average made-for-TV retelling of Mary Wollstonecraft Shelley's horror tale. 130m. **DIR:** Glenn Jordan. **CAST:** Robert Foxworth, Susan Strasberg, Bo Svenson, Willie Aames. **1973**

FRANKENSTEIN (1984) ★★★ Solid made-for-TV adaptation of Mary Shelley's often filmed tale. Robert Powell gives a believable performance as a young Dr. Frankenstein, whose creation (David Warner) runs amok. Fine period flavor, crisp direction, and an excellent cast headed by Warner and John Gielgud. 81m. **DIR:** James Ormerod. **CAST:** Robert Powell, David Warner, Carrie Fisher, John Gielgud, Terence Alexander, Susan Wooldridge. **1984**

FRANKENSTEIN (1992) ★★★ Taking some liberties with Mary Shelley's classic tale, this film at least portrays the creature sympathetically. Randy Quaid is the much hunted being who implores his creator (Patrick Bergin) to help him find peace in a threatening world. Lush forest footage is a plus; plot inconsistencies a minus. Made for cable; contains violence, gore, and nudity. 117m. **DIR:** David Wickes. **CAST:** Patrick Bergin, Randy Quaid, John Mills, Lambert Wilson, Fiona Gillies. **1992**

FRANKENSTEIN AND THE MONSTER FROM HELL ★★ The release of Hammer veteran Terence Fisher's final directorial effort would be a major event, but for one thing: this is a censored TV print, not the R-rated original. But the out-of-print Japanese Laserdisc merits three stars. 93m. **DIR:** Terence Fisher. **CAST:** Peter Cushing, Shane Briant, Madeline Smith, Dave Prowse, Patrick Troughton, Bernard Lee. **1974**

FRANKENSTEIN ISLAND A group of men stranded on a remote island stumble upon a colony of young women in leopard-skin bikinis. Rated PG. 89m. **DIR:** Jerry Warren. **CAST:** John Carradine, Robert Clarke, Steve Brodie, Cameron Mitchell, Andrew Duggan. **1981**

FRANKENSTEIN MEETS THE SPACE MONSTER The Frankenstein here is actually an android named Frank sent into outer space by NASA. Also known as *Mars Invades Puerto Rico*. B&W; 75m. **DIR:** Robert Gaffney.

CAST: James Karen, Nancy Marshall, Robert Reilly. 1965

FRANKENSTEIN MEETS THE WOLF MAN ★★★½ As the title suggests, two of Universal's most famous monsters clash in this series horror film. Very atmospheric, with beautiful photography, music, set design, and special effects. Only drawback is Bela Lugosi's overblown portrayal of the Frankenstein monster. B&W; 73m. DIR: Roy William Neill. CAST: Lon Chaney Jr., Patric Knowles, Bela Lugosi, Ilona Massey, Maria Ouspenskaya. 1943

FRANKENSTEIN 1970 🦃 Boris Karloff as the great-grandson of the famous doctor, attempting to create a monster of his own. B&W; 83m. DIR: Howard W. Koch. CAST: Boris Karloff, Tom Duggan, Jana Lund, Don Barry. 1958

FRANKENSTEIN UNBOUND ★★½ Director Roger Corman makes his comeback with this twisted retelling of the Frankenstein legend in which a scientist from the year 2031 is sucked back in time and meets up with author Mary Godwin (soon to be Mary Shelley), as well as the infamous Dr. Victor Frankenstein. Rated R for violence and gore. 90m. DIR: Roger Corman. CAST: John Hurt, Raul Julia, Bridget Fonda, Jason Patric. 1990

FRANKENSTEIN'S DAUGHTER 🦃 The makeup is ridiculous, the sets are cheap, and the performers need to be oiled. B&W; 85m. DIR: Richard Cunha. CAST: John Ashley, Sandra Knight, Donald Murphy, Harold Lloyd Jr. 1958

FREAKMAKER ★★ Retitled video version of a badly washed-out print of the British horror shocker, *Mutations*. Mad doctor Donald Pleasence botches one experiment in genetics after another. This wildly sadistic movie is buoyed by its own tastelessness, which includes exploiting some real sideshow performers in a way Tod Browning never imagined. Rated R. 92m. DIR: Jack Cardiff. CAST: Donald Pleasence, Tom Baker, Michael Dunn. 1973

FREAKS ★★★★ This legendary "horror" movie by Tod Browning is perhaps the most unusual film ever made and certainly one of the most unsettling. Based on Tod Robbins's *Spurs*, this is the story of a circus midget who falls in love with a statuesque trapeze artist and nearly becomes her victim as she attempts to poison him for his money. Incensed by her betrayal of their little friend, the armless, legless, pinheaded "freaks" exact their revenge. B&W; 64m. DIR: Tod Browning. CAST: Wallace Ford, Leila Hyams, Olga Baclanova, Roscoe Ates. 1932

FREDDY'S DEAD: THE FINAL NIGHTMARE ★★★ In what has been promised as the last film in the *Nightmare on Elm Street* series of films, the audience gets just what is expected. A new batch of teenagers is served up for slaughter, only this time they are led by an adult who just happens to be Freddy Krueger's daughter. The finale was in 3-D in the theatres and something is lost in the video transfer. Rated R for violence and profanity. 96m. DIR: Rachel Talalay. CAST: Robert Englund, Lisa Zane, Yaphet Kotto. 1991

FREEWAY MANIAC 🦃 Matricidal maniac escapes from an insane asylum, not once but twice. *Playboy* cartoonist Gahan Wilson wrote this turkey. 94m. DIR: Paul Winters. CAST: Loren Winters, James Courtney. 1988

FRENCHMAN'S FARM ★★½ A fairly tame Australian import about a female law student who has a psychic experience and witnesses a murder that took place forty years earlier. Some good suspense, but the psychic-encounter scene is overdone. Rated R for language and violence. 86m. DIR: Ron Way. CAST: Tracy Tainsh, Ray Barrett, Norman Kaye, John Meillon. 1986

FRIDAY THE 13TH ★★★ The original slasher flick. A group of Crystal Lake camp counselors are systematically murdered by a masked maniac. Not much of a plot, just the killer hacking and slashing his way through the dwindling counselor population. Fine makeup effects by master Tom Savini highlight this spatterfest that has fostered many imitations and a series of (to date) eight Jason Voorhees slice-and-dicers. Rated R for gore. 95m. DIR: Sean S. Cunningham. CAST: Betsy Palmer, Adrienne King, Harry Crosby, Kevin Bacon. 1980

FRIDAY THE 13TH, PART II ★★ This sequel to the box-office hit of the same name is essentially the *Psycho* shower scene repeated ad nauseum. A group of young people are methodically sliced and diced by Jason, the masked maniac. Though the makeup effects in this rehash were reportedly toned down, there is still enough blood for gore hounds. Rated R for gruesomeness, no matter how toned-down. 87m. DIR: Steve Miner. CAST: Amy Steel, John Furey, Adrienne King, Betsy Palmer. 1981

FRIDAY THE 13TH, PART III ★★ More gruesome ax, knife, and meat-cleaver murders occur at sunny Crystal Lake. Works the same as the first two, though for the theatrical release it had the hook of being in 3-D. The video isn't in 3-D, so Jason is just his old two-dimensional self hacking and hewing his way through another unlucky group of campers. Won't they ever learn? Rated R for obvious reasons. 96m. DIR: Steve Miner. CAST: Dana Kimmel, Paul Kratka. 1982

FRIDAY THE 13TH—THE FINAL CHAPTER ★★★ It has been said that the only reason makeup master Tom Savini agreed to work on this film was that it gave him a chance to kill Jason, the maniacal killer whom he created in the original film. Well, Jason does die. Oh, boy! Does he ever! But not before dispatching a new group of teenagers. Savini's work is the highlight of this flick, which is really just a rehash of the first three. Rated R for extreme gruesomeness. 90m. **DIR:** Joseph Zito. **CAST:** Kimberly Beck, Corey Feldman, Peter Barton, Joan Freeman. **1984**

FRIDAY THE 13TH, PART V—A NEW BEGINNING 🦃 Well, they did it. The producers promised *Friday the 13th—The Final Chapter* would be the last of its kind. They lied. Rated R for graphic violence and simulated sex. 92m. **DIR:** Danny Steinmann. **CAST:** John Shepherd, Melanie Kinnaman, Richard Young. **1985**

FRIDAY THE 13TH, PART VI: JASON LIVES ★★★ It may be hard to believe, but this fifth sequel to the unmemorable *Friday the 13th* is actually better than all those that preceded it. Of course this thing is loaded with violence, but it is also nicely buffered by good comedy bits and one-liners. Rated R for language and violence. 85m. **DIR:** Tom McLoughlin. **CAST:** Thom Mathews, Jennifer Cooke. **1986**

FRIDAY THE 13TH, PART VII: THE NEW BLOOD ★★½ Jason returns, only this time someone's waiting for him: a mentally disturbed teenage girl with telekinetic powers. The result is a bloodbath as the two battle to decide who will star in Part VIII. A decent sequel with a little less gore than usual. Rated R for violence, language, and nudity. 90m. **DIR:** John Carl Buechler. **CAST:** Lar Park Lincoln, Terry Kiser. **1988**

FRIDAY THE 13TH, PART VIII: JASON TAKES MANHATTAN ★★ Fans of the series may be disappointed with the lack of blood in this seventh sequel. Jason torments a group of teenagers aboard a cruise ship and then takes to the streets of the Big Apple. Rated R for violence and profanity. 100m. **DIR:** Rob Hedden. **CAST:** Jensen Daggett, Scott Reeves, Peter Mark Richman. **1989**

FRIGHT NIGHT ★★★★½ Charley Brewster (William Ragsdale) is a fairly normal teenager save one thing: he's convinced his neighbor, Jerry Dandrige (Chris Sarandon), is a vampire—and he is! So Charley enlists the aid of former screen vampire hunter Peter Vincent (Roddy McDowall), and the result is a screamingly funny horror spoof. Rated R for nudity, profanity, and gore. 105m. **DIR:** Tom Holland. **CAST:** Chris Sarandon, William Ragsdale, Roddy McDowall, Amanda Bearse, Stephen Geoffreys. **1985**

FRIGHT NIGHT II ★★★ Charley Brewster (William Ragsdale) is back, after undergoing some psychiatric counseling from his original *Fright Night* encounter with the vampire next door. Like its predecessor, *Fright Night II* takes a fang-in-cheek attitude toward horror flicks, but it isn't the certifiable spoof the original was. Rated R for profanity, violence, and brief nudity. 90m. **DIR:** Tommy Lee Wallace. **CAST:** William Ragsdale, Roddy McDowall, Traci Lynn, Julie Carmen, Jonathan Gries. **1989**

FRIGHTMARE 🦃 An eccentric horror-movie star is called back from the dead. Not rated; this film contains some violence. 86m. **DIR:** Norman Thaddeus Vane. **CAST:** Luca Bercovici, Jennifer Starret, Nita Talbot. **1982**

FROGS ★★ In this fair horror film, Ray Milland has killed frogs, so frogs come to kill his family. The whole cast dies convincingly. Rated PG. 91m. **DIR:** George McCowan. **CAST:** Ray Milland, Sam Elliott, Joan Van Ark. **1972**

FROM BEYOND ★★★ A lecherous scientist and his assistant create a machine that stimulates a gland in the brain that allows one to see into another dimension. Then the fun begins—with better-than-average special effects, scary-looking monsters, and suspenseful horror. Made by the creators of *Re-Animator.* Not rated, but contains graphic violence and brief nudity. 89m. **DIR:** Stuart Gordon. **CAST:** Jeffrey Combs, Barbara Crampton, Ken Foree. **1986**

FROM BEYOND THE GRAVE ★★★ One of the best Amicus horror anthologies, this features Peter Cushing as the owner of a curio shop, Temptations Ltd., where customers get more than they bargain for. A strong cast of character actors enlivens this fine adaptation of four R.Chetwynd-Hayes stories: "The Gate Crasher," "An Act of Kindness," "The Elemental," and "The Door." Rated PG. 97m. **DIR:** Kevin Connor. **CAST:** Peter Cushing, Margaret Leighton, Ian Bannen, David Warner, Donald Pleasence, Lesley-Anne Down, Diana Dors. **1973**

FROM THE DEAD OF NIGHT ★★½ After a near-death experience, Lindsay Wagner is pursued by spirits of the dead. For a made-for-TV movie, this one has some pretty scary moments—if only it didn't take so long to get to them. 190m. **DIR:** Paul Wendkos. **CAST:** Lindsay Wagner, Bruce Boxleitner, Robin Thomas, Diahann Carroll, Robert Prosky. **1989**

FROZEN TERROR ★★½ Pretty good spaghetti horror from the son of the late horror maestro, Mario Bava. Bava *fils* unfortunately hasn't lived up to the promise displayed here. The video title (the film's original moniker was *Macabro*) refers to the unbalanced leading lady's prize possession: the head of her departed lover, stored in the refrigerator. Rated R. 91m. **DIR:** Lamberto Bava. **CAST:** Bernice Stegers. **1980**

FULL ECLIPSE ★★★ This horror yarn never quite takes off, in spite of a clever premise. Dedicated cop Mario Van Peebles is recruited by an elite assault squad comprised of—surprise!—drug-induced werewolves, who really put the bite on bad guys. Unresolved moral conflicts and a sloppy finale ultimately sabotage what could have been a great thriller. Rated R for violence, profanity, and strong sexual content. 93m. **DIR:** Anthony Hickox. **CAST:** Mario Van Peebles, Patsy Kensit, Anthony Denison, Jason Beghe, Bruce Payne. 1993

FUNHOUSE, THE ★★½ Looking for a watchable modern horror film? Then welcome to *The Funhouse*. This film about a group of teens trapped in the carnival attraction of the title proves that buckets of blood and severed limbs aren't essential elements to movie terror. Rated R. 96m. **DIR:** Tobe Hooper. **CAST:** Elizabeth Berridge, Cooper Huckabee, Miles Chapin, Largo Woodruff, Sylvia Miles. 1981

FURY, THE ★★★ *The Fury* is a contemporary terror tale that utilizes the average-man-against-the-unknown approach that made Hitchcock's suspense films so effective. In the story, Kirk Douglas is forced to take on a super-powerful government agency which has kidnapped his son (Andrew Stevens), who has psychic powers. It's a chiller. Rated R. 118m. **DIR:** Brian De Palma. **CAST:** Kirk Douglas, Andrew Stevens, Amy Irving, Fiona Lewis, John Cassavetes, Charles Durning. 1978

FURY OF THE WOLF MAN ★★ Fifth of a popular Spanish series featuring the sympathetic werewolf Waldemar Daninsky. Badly dubbed, but high production values make it watchable. Unrated; the film has violence. 85m. **DIR:** José Maria Zabalza. **CAST:** Paul Naschy. 1971

FUTURE HUNTERS 🦃 A warrior from the future travels back to the present. Rated R for violence, profanity, and nudity. 96m. **DIR:** Cirio H. Santiago. **CAST:** Robert Patrick. 1985

FUTURE-KILL 🦃 Frat boys run into a gang of punks—one of whom has been exposed to radiation. Rated R for profanity, nudity, and gore. 83m. **DIR:** Ronald W. Moore. **CAST:** Edwin Neal, Marilyn Burns. 1984

GANJASAURUS REX 🦃 A prodrug propaganda film about a prehistoric monster that awakens when the authorities begin burning marijuana crops. Not rated. 88m. **DIR:** Ursi Reynolds. **CAST:** Paul Bassis, Dave Fresh, Rosie Jones. 1988

GATE, THE ★★ A film that insists that children shouldn't play heavy-metal records with satanic messages. The kids in this film do and so unlock a gate to an ancient netherworld. Not very scary, this film exhibits outstanding special effects. Rated PG-13 for mild violence and profanity. 85m. **DIR:** Tibor Takacs. **CAST:** Stephen Dorff. 1987

GATE II ★★ Special effects and acting lift this film above its mediocre story. Basically a rehash of the original: teenagers open the door to the netherworld and then must fight evil spirits. Rated R for violence, profanity, and suggested sex. 90m. **DIR:** Tibor Takacs. **CAST:** Louis Tripp, Simon Reynolds, James Villemaire, Pamela Segall. 1992

GATES OF HELL 🦃 Italian imitation of *Dawn of the Dead*. Unrated; it played in theatres with an unofficial X rating. 93m. **DIR:** Lucio Fulci. **CAST:** Christopher George, Janet Agren. 1983

GHASTLY ONES, THE 🦃 Members of a family, reunited for the reading of their dead father's will, are murdered by a mysterious killer. Unrated; the movie has lots of fake-looking gore. 81m. **DIR:** Andy Milligan. **CAST:** Don Williams, Maggie Rogers. 1969

GHIDRAH, THE THREE-HEADED MONSTER ★★★ A giant egg from outer space crashes into Japan and hatches the colossal three-headed flying monster of the title. It takes the combined forces of Godzilla, Rodan, and Mothra to save Tokyo. Good Japanese monster movie is marred only by dumb subplot of evil agent out to kidnap a Martian princess. 85m. **DIR:** Inoshiro Honda. **CAST:** Yosuke Natsuki, Yuriko Hoshi, Hiroshi Koizumi. 1965

GHOST, THE (1963) ★★★ Barbara Steele is a faithless wife who poisons her husband, only to have him return and exact revenge. Entertaining Italian gothic that's a sequel of sorts to the same director's *The Horrible Dr. Hitchcock*. A must for devotees of Italian chillers, with splendidly atmospheric camera work. 93m. **DIR:** Robert Hampton (Riccardo Freda). **CAST:** Barbara Steele, Peter Baldwin. 1963

GHOST CHASE ★★ Teen filmmakers are taken on by a ruthless movie mogul after one of the boys inherits some seemingly worthless trinkets from his grandfather. Decent special effects, but acting and dialogue are lifeless. Rated PG for profanity. 89m. **DIR:** Roland Emmerich. **CAST:** Jason Lively, Tim McDaniel, Jill Whitlow, Paul Gleason. 1988

GHOST IN THE MACHINE ★★½ Fans of the *Nightmare on Elm Street* films should enjoy this high-tech variation, where a dying serial killer infiltrates a mainframe computer. No surprises, and the special effects are a bit cheap, but the film is efficiently packaged. Rated R for violence. 95m. **DIR:** Rachel Talalay. **CAST:** Karen Allen, Chris Mulkey, Ken Thorley. 1993

GHOST OF FRANKENSTEIN ★★★½ Dr. Frankenstein's second son takes a crack at monster rehabilitation and all's well until Ygor shares his thoughts (literally). This was the fourth Frankenstein film from Universal Studios and the beginning of the series' skid to programmer status. Luckily, Bela Lugosi is back as Ygor, the supporting cast is good, the music score is first-rate, and there are enough dynamic set pieces to liven up the story. B&W; 67m. **DIR:** Erle C. Kenton.

CAST: Lon Chaney Jr., Cedric Hardwicke, Ralph Bellamy, Lionel Atwill, Bela Lugosi. **1942**

GHOST SHIP ★★½ Creaky but occasionally spooky British tale of a couple who buy a ship only to discover it is haunted by the ghosts of some unhappy previous owners. Unrated. B&W; 69m. **DIR:** Vernon Sewell. **CAST:** Dermot Walsh, Hazel Court, Joss Ackland. **1951**

GHOST STORY 🦃 This film, based on the bestselling novel by Peter Straub, is about as frightening as an episode of *Sesame Street*. Rated R because of shock scenes involving rotting corpses and violence. 110m. **DIR:** John Irvin. **CAST:** John Houseman, Douglas Fairbanks Jr., Melvyn Douglas, Fred Astaire, Alice Krige, Craig Wasson, Patricia Neal. **1981**

GHOST TOWN ★★ A passable time waster mixing two genres, the horror film and the Western. Modern-day deputy (Franc Luz) with a penchant for the Old West stumbles into a satanic netherworld: ghost town in the middle of the Arizona desert. Rated R for nudity, violence, and profanity. 85m. **DIR:** Richard Governor. **CAST:** Franc Luz, Catherine Hickland, Bruce Glover. **1988**

GHOSTRIDERS ★★ Just before being hanged in 1886, a notorious criminal puts a curse on the preacher responsible for his execution. One hundred years later he and his gang return to wreak vengeance on the preacher's descendants. Rated R for violence and language. 85m. **DIR:** Alan L. Stewart. **CAST:** Bill Shaw. **1987**

GHOUL, THE (1933) ★★½ Trading on the success he achieved in *Frankenstein* and *The Mummy*, Boris Karloff plays an Egyptologist seeking eternal life through a special jewel. He dies and the jewel is stolen, bringing him back from the dead to seek revenge on the thief. B&W; 73m. **DIR:** T. Hayes Hunter. **CAST:** Boris Karloff, Cedric Hardwicke, Ernest Thesiger, Ralph Richardson, Kathleen Harrison. **1933**

GHOUL, THE (1975) ★★½ "Stay out of the garden, dear, there's a flesh-eating monster living there." One of Peter Cushing's many horror films. No gore, but not boring, either. Rated R. 88m. **DIR:** Freddie Francis. **CAST:** Peter Cushing, John Hurt, Gwen Watford. **1975**

GHOULIES 🦃 Gruesome. Rated PG-13 for violence and sexual innuendo. 87m. **DIR:** Luca Bercovici. **CAST:** Peter Liapis, Lisa Pelikan, John Nance. **1985**

GHOULIES II 🦃 Dreadful sequel that dramatizes the further adventures of those mischievous little demons. Rated PG-13 for violence. 89m. **DIR:** Albert Band. **CAST:** Damon Martin, Royal Dano. **1987**

GHOULIES III 🦃 Third chapter in the series finds the ghoulish slime-balls creating havoc at a local university. Like this movie, they flunk out! Rated R for violence. 94m. **DIR:** John Carl Buechler. **CAST:** Kevin McCarthy, Evan Mackenzie. **1989**

GIANT GILA MONSTER, THE 🦃 Slimy, slow-moving monster lizard prowls the Texas countryside. B&W; 74m. **DIR:** Ray Kellogg. **CAST:** Don Sullivan. **1959**

GIRL SCHOOL SCREAMERS 🦃 Mansion is inhabited by demonic spirits. Not rated, but contains nudity and violence. 85m. **DIR:** John P. Finegan. **CAST:** Mollie O'Mara. **1985**

GIRLY 🦃 A bizarre tale about the killing exploits of a demented English family. Rated R for suggested sex. 101m. **DIR:** Freddie Francis. **CAST:** Vanessa Howard, Michael Bryant, Ursula Howells, Pat Heywood, Robert Swann. **1987**

GODSEND, THE 🦃 Cheaply rips off *The Exorcist* and *The Omen* in its tale of a demented daughter. Rated R. 93m. **DIR:** Gabrielle Beaumont. **CAST:** Cyd Hayman, Malcolm Stoddard, Angela Pleasence. **1979**

GODZILLA, KING OF THE MONSTERS ★★★½ First, and by far the best, film featuring the four-hundred-foot monstrosity that was later reduced to a superhero. Here he's all death and destruction, and this movie really works, thanks to some expert photographic effects and weird music. B&W; 80m. **DIR:** Inoshiro Honda, Terry Morse. **CAST:** Raymond Burr, Takashi Shimura. **1956**

GODZILLA 1985 🦃 Once again, the giant Japanese lizard tramples cars and crushes tall buildings in his search for radioactive nutrition. Rated PG. 91m. **DIR:** Kohji Hashimoto, R. J. Kizer. **CAST:** Raymond Burr, Keiji Kobayashi. **1985**

GODZILLA VS. GIGAN 🦃 A basic rehash of previous Godzilla movies, only this time much more boring. 89m. **DIR:** Jun Fukuda. **CAST:** Hiroshi Ishikawa. **1972**

GODZILLA VS. MECHAGODZILLA ★★ For Godzilla fans only. An enemy from space builds a metal Godzilla in an effort to take over the world. Godzilla is pressed into action to destroy the beast. Rated PG. 82m. **DIR:** Jun Fukuda. **CAST:** Masaaki Daimon. **1975**

GODZILLA VS. MONSTER ZERO ★★★ Pretty good monster movie has an alien civilization "borrowing" Godzilla and Rodan to help defeat the hometown menace Monster Zero (known previously and since as Ghidrah). 90m. **DIR:** Inoshiro Honda. **CAST:** Nick Adams, Akira Takarada. **1966**

GODZILLA VS. MOTHRA ★★★ Fine Godzilla movie pits the "king of the monsters" against archenemy Mothra for its first half, later has him taking on twin caterpillars recently hatched from the moth's giant egg. Excellent battle scenes in this one, with Godzilla's first appearance a doozy. 90m.

DIR: Inoshiro Honda. **CAST:** Akira Takarada, Yuriko Hoshi, Hiroshi Koizumi. **1964**

GODZILLA VS. THE SEA MONSTER Godzilla must tackle a giant, rotten-looking crab monster. 85m. **DIR:** Jun Fukuda. **CAST:** None Credited. **1966**

GODZILLA'S REVENGE ★★ In his dreams, a young boy visits Monster Island and learns about self-respect from Godzilla's son. Goofy kid's movie, assembled from scenes made for other Godzilla films. Rated G. 92m. **DIR:** Inoshiro Honda. **CAST:** Kenji Sahara. **1969**

GOLIATH AND THE VAMPIRES ★★ A horde of barbarians who drink blood, torture their victims, and dissolve amid puffs of blue smoke are the formidable adversaries for Goliath (actually, Maciste) in this colorful, mindlessly enjoyable sword-and-sandal fantasy. U.S. television title: *The Vampires*. 91m. **DIR:** Giacomo Gentilomo. **CAST:** Gordon Scott, Jacques Sernas, Gianna Maria Canale. **1964**

GOODNIGHT, GOD BLESS British entry in the slasher sweepstakes has a maniacal killer dressed in priest's garb. Not rated, but contains violence and sexual suggestion. 100m. **DIR:** John Eyres. **CAST:** Emma Sutton, Frank Rozelaar Goleen. **1988**

GORATH An out-of-control planet headed for Earth is the subject of this Japanese science-fiction flick. 77m. **DIR:** Inoshiro Honda. **CAST:** None Credited. **1964**

GORE-MET, ZOMBIE CHEF FROM HELL A 600-year-old cannibal high priest wreaks gruesome havoc. No rating, but extremely graphic gore and sex. 90m. **DIR:** Don Swan. **CAST:** Theo Depuay. **1987**

GORGO ★★★½ Unpretentious thriller from England has a dinosaur-type monster captured and put on display in London's Piccadilly Circus, only to have its towering two-hundred-foot parent destroy half the city looking for it. Brisk pacing and well-executed effects. 76m. **DIR:** Eugene Lourie. **CAST:** Bill Travers, William Sylvester, Vincent Winter, Martin Benson. **1961**

GORGON, THE ★★★ Peter Cushing and Christopher Lee take on a Medusa-headed monster in this British Hammer Films chiller. A good one for horror buffs. 83m. **DIR:** Terence Fisher. **CAST:** Peter Cushing, Christopher Lee, Richard Pasco, Barbara Shelley. **1964**

GOTHIC ★★ Director Ken Russell returns to his favorite subject—the tortured artist—for this look at what may have happened that spooky evening in 1816 when Lord Byron, poet Percy Shelley, his fiancée Mary, her stepsister Claire, and Byron's ex-lover Dr. Polidori spent the evening together, attempting to scare each other. What the viewer gets is the usual Russell bag of tricks: insane hallucinations, group sex, scenes of gruesome murders, and much, much more. Rated R. 90m. **DIR:** Ken Russell. **CAST:** Gabriel Byrne, Julian Sands, Natasha Richardson, Timothy Spall. **1986**

GRADUATION DAY ★★ A high school runner dies during a competition. Soon someone begins killing all her teammates. Plenty of violence in this one. Rated R. 96m. **DIR:** Herb Freed. **CAST:** Christopher George, Michael Pataki, E. J. Peaker. **1981**

GRAVE OF THE VAMPIRE Baby bloodsucker grows up to search for his father and discover his birthright. 95m. **DIR:** John Hayes. **CAST:** William Smith, Michael Pataki. **1972**

GRAVE SECRETS ★★ A woman, tormented by what she believes are ghosts, hires a parapsychologist in this not-too-scary supernatural flick. Rated R for violence and profanity. 90m. **DIR:** Donald P. Borchers. **CAST:** Paul LeMat, Renee Soutendijk, David Warner, Lee Ving, John Crawford. **1989**

GRAVEYARD SHIFT (1987) New York cabbie expects more than a tip. Rated R. 90m. **DIR:** Gerard Ciccoritti. **CAST:** Silvio Oliviero, Helen Papas. **1987**

GREAT ALLIGATOR, THE Italian exploitation cheapie about a resort community and the monster alligator that dines on its inhabitants. Rated R. 91m. **DIR:** Sergio Martino. **CAST:** Barbara Bach, Mel Ferrer, Claudio Cassinelli. **1979**

GRIM PRAIRIE TALES ★★★ Two plains travelers, one a city dweller and the other a trail-weary bounty hunter, exchange stories of horror while they camp on the open prairie. Their freaky tales will test your ability to suspend belief, but all are fun to watch. Rated R for violence, profanity, and gore. 87m. **DIR:** Wayne Coe. **CAST:** James Earl Jones, Brad Dourif, William Atherton, Lisa Eichhorn, Marc McClure, Scott Paulin. **1990**

GRIM REAPER, THE (1980) The cannibal and zombie subgenres are combined in a single cheap movie by a director—Joe D'Amato (née Aristide Massaccesi) who has dabbled in each. Rated R. 87m. **DIR:** Joe D'Amato (Aristede Massaccesi). **CAST:** Tisa Farrow, Saverio Vallone. **1980**

GRIZZLY ★★ Another "nature runs amok" film with Christopher George going up against an eighteen-foot killer bear this time out. Some taut action, but the movie has no style or pizzazz. Rated PG for violence. 92m. **DIR:** William Girdler. **CAST:** Christopher George, Andrew Prine, Richard Jaeckel. **1976**

GROTESQUE Psychotic punks looking for a treasure. Rated R for violence and nudity. 80m. **DIR:** Joe Tornatore. **CAST:** Linda Blair, Tab Hunter, Charles Dierkop. **1987**

GRUESOME TWOSOME 🦃 *Sweeney Todd*–style parody about a wig maker and her homicidal son. 72m. **DIR:** Herschell Gordon Lewis. **CAST:** Elizabeth David, Chris Martel. **1967**

GUARDIAN, THE (1990) 🦃 Los Angeles couple finds out the hard way that the attractive, charming nanny they've hired is a tree-worshiping druid. Rated R for language, violence, and nudity. 93m. **DIR:** William Friedkin. **CAST:** Jenny Seagrove, Dwier Brown. **1990**

GUARDIAN OF THE ABYSS 🦃 Uneventful devil-worship flick from England. 50m. **DIR:** Don Sharp. **CAST:** Ray Lonnen. **1985**

H-MAN, THE ★★★ Unintentional humor makes this low-budget Japanese monster movie a near comedy classic. A boat wanders into a nuclear-test zone, mutating a crew member into a horrible water monster. With some of the lamest special effects ever filmed, this is guaranteed to make even the most humorless individual crack a smile. Not rated, but suitable for all ages. 79m. **DIR:** Inoshiro Honda. **CAST:** Yumi Shirakawa. **1959**

HALF HUMAN 🦃 From the director of *Godzilla* comes an abominable snowman terrorizing Mount Fuji. B&W; 78m. **DIR:** Inoshiro Honda. **CAST:** John Carradine, Morris Ankrum. **1958**

HALLOWEEN ★★★★½ This is a surprisingly tasteful and enjoyable slasher film. Director John Carpenter puts the accent on suspense and atmosphere rather than blood and guts, as in other films of this kind. The story revolves around the escape of a soulless maniac who returns to the town where he murdered his sister. Rated R. 93m. **DIR:** John Carpenter. **CAST:** Jamie Lee Curtis, Donald Pleasence, Nancy Loomis, P. J. Soles, Charles Cyphers. **1978**

HALLOWEEN II ★★★ This respectable sequel picks up where the original left off: with the boogeyman on the prowl and Jamie Lee Curtis running for her life. Rated R because of violence and nudity. 92m. **DIR:** Rick Rosenthal. **CAST:** Jamie Lee Curtis, Donald Pleasence, Charles Cyphers, Jeffrey Kramer, Lance Guest. **1981**

HALLOWEEN III: SEASON OF THE WITCH ★★½ A maniacal mask manufacturer in northern California provides kiddies with devilishly designed pumpkin masks. Not a true sequel to the gruesome *Halloween* twosome, but still watchable. Rated R. 96m. **DIR:** Tommy Lee Wallace. **CAST:** Tom Atkins, Stacey Nelkin, Dan O'Herlihy. **1983**

HALLOWEEN IV: THE RETURN OF MICHAEL MYERS ★★★ The makers of this third sequel to John Carpenter's ground-breaking *Halloween* obviously tried to create a quality horror film and for the most part they've succeeded. Director Dwight H. Little commendably puts the accent on atmosphere and suspense in detailing the third killing spree of Michael Myers (a.k.a. The Shape). Donald Pleasence returns as Myers's nemesis, Dr. Loomis, to hunt down this fiendish foe. Rated R for violence and profanity. 88m. **DIR:** Dwight H. Little. **CAST:** Donald Pleasence, Ellie Cornell, Danielle Harris. **1988**

HALLOWEEN V: THE REVENGE OF MICHAEL MYERS ★★ What started off as the story of a truly frightening killer (the unstoppable Michael Myers) has become a run-of-the-mill slasher series. Tedious. Rated R for violence. 89m. **DIR:** Dominique Othenin-Girard. **CAST:** Donald Pleasence, Ellie Cornell, Danielle Harris, Beau Starr. **1989**

HAND, THE 🦃 Thumbs down on this dull film. Rated R. 104m. **DIR:** Oliver Stone. **CAST:** Michael Caine, Andrea Marcovicci, Annie McEnroe, Bruce McGill. **1981**

HANDS OF THE RIPPER ★★★½ First-rate period horror—the last great offering of Britain's Hammer Films—speculates what might have happened if Jack the Ripper had had a daughter who grew up unknowingly emulating her murderous dad. A literate script, fine performances, and astute direction by then-promising Peter Sasdy. Rated R. 85m. **DIR:** Peter Sasdy. **CAST:** Eric Porter, Angharad Rees, Jane Merrow. **1971**

HAPPY BIRTHDAY TO ME ★★ After surviving a tragic car accident that killed her mother, a young woman (Melissa Sue Anderson) suffers recurrent blackouts. During these lapses of consciousness, other students at her exclusive prep school are murdered in bizarre and vicious ways. Story coherence and credibility take a backseat to all the bloodletting. Rated R. 108m. **DIR:** J. Lee Thompson. **CAST:** Melissa Sue Anderson, Glenn Ford, Matt Craven. **1981**

HARD ROCK ZOMBIES ★★½ The title pretty much says it all: After being murdered while on the road, the members of a heavy-metal band are brought back from the dead as zombies. Amusing in a goofy way, though shoddy special-effects makeup brings it down a notch. Rated R for violence and gore. 94m. **DIR:** Krishna Shah. **CAST:** E. J. Curcio, Sam Mann. **1985**

HARD TO DIE 🦃 "Hard to watch" is a more appropriate title for this silly slashfest. Five girls taking inventory don sexy lingerie then become victims. Pictures on video box include two women who weren't even in the film. Rated R for nudity, profanity, violence, and gore. 81m. **DIR:** Jim Wynorski. **CAST:** Orville Ketchum, Robyn Harris, Melissa Moore, Debra Dare, Forrest J. Ackerman, Lindsay Taylor. **1990**

HATCHET FOR THE HONEYMOON 🦃 A psychotic killer fashion mogul hacks up brides with a... guess what. Rated PG for violence. 90m. **DIR:** Mario Bava. **CAST:** Stephen Forsythe, Dagmar Lassander, Laura Betti. **1974**

HAUNTED CASTLE ★★★ Based on the novel by Rudolf Stratz, this complex chiller takes place in a northern German castle shrouded in a mysterious, haunting atmosphere. Great cinematography and set design make for an impressive spectacle. Silent. B&W; 56m. **DIR:** F. W. Murnau. **CAST:** Paul Hartmann, Olga Tschechowa. **1921**

HAUNTED PALACE, THE ★★★½ Although the title of this horror film, one of the best in a series of American-International Pictures releases directed by Roger Corman, was taken from a poem by Edgar Allan Poe, Charles Beaumont's screenplay was based on a story, "The Case of Charles Dexter Ward," written by H. P. Lovecraft. It's better than average Corman, with Vincent Price nicely subdued as the descendant of an ancient warlock. 85m. **DIR:** Roger Corman. **CAST:** Vincent Price, Debra Paget, Lon Chaney Jr., Elisha Cook Jr., Leo Gordon. **1963**

HAUNTED STRANGLER, THE ★★★½ Boris Karloff is well cast in this effective story of a writer who develops the homicidal tendencies of a long-dead killer he's been writing about. Gripping horror film. B&W; 81m. **DIR:** Robert Day. **CAST:** Boris Karloff, Anthony Dawson, Elizabeth Allan. **1958**

HAUNTING, THE ★★★★ Long considered one of the most masterly crafted tales of terror ever brought to the screen, this gripping triumph for Robert Wise still packs a punch. Julie Harris and Claire Bloom are outstanding as they recognize and finally confront the evil that inhabits a haunted house. Based on Shirley Jackson's classic *The Haunting of Hill House*. B&W; 112m. **DIR:** Robert Wise. **CAST:** Julie Harris, Claire Bloom, Richard Johnson, Russ Tamblyn, Fay Compton, Lois Maxwell. **1963**

HAUNTING FEAR 🦃 Tedious Edgar Allan Poe–inspired romp, based on *Premature Burial*, is premature on chills as husband and mistress attempt to drive wife insane. Exactly what you'd expect from sleaze-master director Fred Olen Ray. Unrated, but contains violence. 88m. **DIR:** Fred Olen Ray. **CAST:** Jan-Michael Vincent, Karen Black. **1991**

HAUNTING OF MORELLA, THE 🦃 Bad acting and directing help to mutilate this movie in which a mother's curse is placed upon her baby daughter. Rated R for violence and nudity. 82m. **DIR:** Jim Wynorski. **CAST:** David McCallum, Nicole Eggert, Christopher Halsted. **1989**

HE KNOWS YOU'RE ALONE ★★ There's a killer on the loose, specializing in brides-to-be. His current target for dismemberment is pretty Amy (Caitlin O'Heany). While stalking his special prey, the killer keeps his knife sharp by decimating the population of Staten Island. Rated R. 94m. **DIR:** Armand Mastroianni. **CAST:** Don Scardino, Caitlin O'Heaney, Elizabeth Kemp, Tom Hanks. **1981**

HEAD, THE (1959) ★★ Magnificently atmospheric and surreal West German mad scientist shocker with a much stronger plot than most films of its ilk—notably the Edgar Wallace series—could boast. Classically gothic and fogbound, this fascinating oddity follows the horrific events that result when a mad scientist becomes victim of his most daring experiment. B&W; 92m. **DIR:** Victor Trivas. **CAST:** Horst Frank, Michel Simon. **1959**

HEARSE, THE 🦃 This film is about a satanic pact between an old woman and her lover. Rated PG. 100m. **DIR:** George Bowers. **CAST:** Trish Van Devere, Joseph Cotten, David Gautreaux, Donald Hotton. **1980**

HELL HIGH 🦃 Students playing cruel practical jokes pick on the wrong victim, who summons demons from her past to do her bidding. The real cruel joke is having to sit through this film. Rated R for violence. 84m. **DIR:** Douglas Grossman. **CAST:** Christopher Stryker, Christopher Cousins, Jason Brill, Maureen Mooney. **1986**

HELL NIGHT ★★ Linda Blair (*The Exorcist*) returns to the genre that spawned her film career in this low-budget horror flick about fraternity and sorority pledges spending the night in a mansion "haunted" by a crazed killer. Rated R. 101m. **DIR:** Tom DeSimone. **CAST:** Linda Blair, Vincent Van Patten, Peter Barton, Jenny Neuman. **1981**

HELLBOUND: HELLRAISER II ★★½ People without skin! If that doesn't either pique your interest or turn you away, nothing will. A psychiatric patient, who is lost in a world of puzzles, unleashes the nasty Cenobites (introduced in *Hellraiser*). Clive Barker protégé Tony Randel makes everything a bit overwhelming, but it's all good, clean, gruesome fun. Rated R for gore. 96m. **DIR:** Tony Randel. **CAST:** Clare Higgins, Ashley Laurence, Kenneth Cranham. **1988**

HELLGATE ★★ A band of badly scripted teenagers on holiday search for adventure in a legendary ghost town—unfortunately peopled by the nasty living dance-hall dead. Feeble camp humor and tepid special effects sink this lightly erotic post-teen horror. Rated R. 96m. **DIR:** William A. Levey. **CAST:** Ron Palillo, Abigail Wolcott, Evan J. Klisser. **1989**

HELLHOLE 🦃 A young woman witnesses her mother's murder and psychosomatically loses her memory. Rated R for violence and nudity. 90m. **DIR:** Pierre DeMoro. **CAST:** Ray Sharkey, Judy Landers, Marjoe Gortner, Edy Williams. **1985**

HELLMASTER 🦃 Long-thought-dead professor John Saxon returns to his alma mater to continue his experiments turning students into mutants. The final exam has got to be a bummer. Unrated, but contains horror violence. 99m. **DIR:** Douglas Schulze. **CAST:** John Saxon, David Emge. **1990**

HELLO, MARY LOU: PROM NIGHT II Another tedious exploitation flick about a girl who returns from the grave to get revenge on her killers. Rated R for violence, nudity, and language. 96m. **DIR:** Bruce Pittman. **CAST:** Lisa Schrage, Wendy Lyon, Michael Ironside. **1987**

HELLRAISER ★★½ In his directing debut, Clive Barker adapts his short story and proves even the author can't necessarily bring his work to life on the screen. The story is about a man who acquires a demonic Rubik's Cube. Although imbued with marvelous visuals, the film has little of the intensity of a Barker novel. Rated R for violence, sex, and adult language. 90m. **DIR:** Clive Barker. **CAST:** Andrew Robinson, Clare Higgins, Ashley Laurence. **1987**

HELLRAISER 3: HELL ON EARTH ★★★ Pinhead returns, only this time he's brought some new friends and they don't want to go back where they came from. Combine gory (and very imaginative) special effects and a slightly off-center story and you have one that should please fans, but make others sick. Rated R for profanity, simulated sex, and graphic violence. 90m. **DIR:** Anthony Hickox. **CAST:** Terry Ferrell, Doug Bradley, Paula Marshall, Kevin Bernhardt, Ashley Laurence. **1992**

HIDE AND GO SHRIEK ★★ Slasher film that's a cut above the others because of the acting. Eight high school seniors, four boys and four girls, celebrate their graduation by partying in a deserted furniture store. Their plans are interrupted by a psychotic killer. Not rated, contains nudity and extreme violence. 94m. **DIR:** Skip Schoolnik. **CAST:** George Thomas, Brittain Frye. **1987**

HIDEOUS SUN DEMON, THE Robert Clarke directed and also stars as the scientist turned into a lizard-like monster by radiation. B&W; 74m. **DIR:** Robert Clarke. **CAST:** Robert Clarke, Patricia Manning. **1959**

HIGH DESERT KILL ★★ A group of deer hunters are stalked, a la *Predator*, in this third-rate knockoff. Marc Singer and Anthony Geary meet old man Chuck Connors in the high desert of Arizona and soon find the only animals left in their area are themselves. Made for cable. 93m. **DIR:** Harry Falk. **CAST:** Marc Singer, Anthony Geary, Chuck Connors, Micah Grant. **1989**

HIGHWAY TO HELL ★★★★ Two young lovers get caught in an inter-dimensional speed trap, and are sent straight to hell. Fast-paced writing and action, as well as large dashes of humor and sight gags, make this an entertaining thriller. Rated R for violence and profanity. 100m. **DIR:** Ate De Jong. **CAST:** Patrick Bergin, Chad Lowe, Kristy Swanson, Richard Farnsworth. **1991**

HILLS HAVE EYES, THE City folk have inherited a silver mine and are stopping on their way to California to check it out. That's when a ghoulish family comes crawling out of the rocks. Rated R for violence and profanity. 89m. **DIR:** Wes Craven. **CAST:** Susan Lamer, Robert Houston, Virginia Vincent, Russ Grieve, Dee Wallace. **1977**

HILLS HAVE EYES, THE: PART TWO This really lame sequel wouldn't scare the most timid viewer. Rated R for violence and profanity (mild by horror standards). 86m. **DIR:** Wes Craven. **CAST:** John Laughlin, Michael Berryman. **1984**

HITCHER, THE ★★★ C. Thomas Howell plays a young, squeamish California-bound motorist who picks up a hitchhiker, played by Rutger Hauer, somewhere in the desert Southwest. What transpires is action that will leave you physically and emotionally drained. If you thought *The Terminator* was too violent, this one will redefine the word for you. Rated R. 96m. **DIR:** Robert Harmon. **CAST:** Rutger Hauer, C. Thomas Howell, Jeffrey DeMunn, Jennifer Jason Leigh. **1986**

HITCHHIKER (SERIES), THE ★★★ Stories culled from HBO anthology series are included in this compilation of tapes. Reminiscent of *The Twilight Zone* TV series, the stories always have a supernatural background and a moral. The direction is first-rate, as is the acting, but sometimes the stories are a bit shallow. Not rated, but contains adult language, violence, and nudity. Each tape 90m. **DIR:** Roger Vadim, Paul Verhoeven, Carl Schenkel, Phillip Noyce, Mai Zetterling, Richard Rothstein, David Wickes, Mike Hodges. **CAST:** Page Fletcher, Harry Hamlin, Karen Black, Gary Busey, Geraldine Page, Margot Kidder, Darren McGavin, Susan Anspach, Peter Coyote, Barry Bostwick, Willem Dafoe, M. Emmet Walsh, Tom Skerritt, Steve Collins, Shannon Tweed, Robert Vaughn, Sybil Danning, Michael O'Keef. **1985**

HITCHHIKERS Female hitchhikers rob the motorists who stop to pick them up. Rated R for nudity, profanity, and simulated sex. 87m. **DIR:** Ferd Sebastian. **CAST:** Misty Rowe, Norman Klar, Linda Avery. **1971**

HOLLYWOOD CHAINSAW HOOKERS ★★ Easily Fred Olen Ray's best film (which admittedly is saying very little), this is not the rip-off its title suggests. Ray delivers a campy, sexy, *very* bloody parody about attractive prostitutes who dismember their unsuspecting customers. Both gory and tedious. Rated R. 90m. **DIR:** Fred Olen Ray. **CAST:** Gunnar Hansen, Linnea Quigley. **1988**

HOLLYWOOD MEATCLEAVER MASSACRE Cheesy hack-'em-up about a vengeful demon. Amateurish and inept. Rated R. 87m. **DIR:** Evan Lee. **CAST:** Christopher Lee, Larry Justin. **1975**

HOLLYWOOD STRANGLER MEETS THE SKID ROW SLASHER 🦃 Psycho wanders around L.A. taking photos of amateur models and then strangling them. Rated R for nudity, violence, and gore. 72m. **DIR:** Wolfgang Schmidt. **CAST:** Pierre Agostino, Carolyn Brandt. 1982

HOLOCAUST 2000 🦃 The Antichrist plans to destroy the world, using nuclear reactors. Rated R. 96m. **DIR:** Alberto De Martino. **CAST:** Kirk Douglas, Agostina Belli, Simon Ward, Anthony Quayle. 1978

HOMEBODIES ★★★ A cast of aging screen veterans liven up this offbeat thriller about a group of senior citizens who turn into a hit squad when faced with eviction. Director Larry Yust keeps things moving at a lively pace and even manages a few bizarre twists in the final scenes. Rated PG for violence, language. 96m. **DIR:** Larry Yust. **CAST:** Douglas Fowley, Ruth McDevitt, Ian Wolfe. 1974

HONEYMOON ★★★½ A Frenchwoman (Nathalie Baye) goes on what appears to be a carefree New York vacation with her boyfriend (Richard Berry). However, he is busted for smuggling cocaine, and she is set for deportation. She goes to an agency that arranges marriages of convenience. She is assured that she will never see her new American "husband"—only to have him show up and refuse to leave her alone. Rated R for profanity, nudity, and violence. 98m. **DIR:** Patrick Jamain. **CAST:** Nathalie Baye, John Shea, Richard Berry, Peter Donat. 1987

HONEYMOON MURDERS 🦃 A couple honeymoons at a possessed country cottage in this inept attempt at a horror movie. Not rated. 114m. **DIR:** Steve Postal. **CAST:** Dave Knapp, Angela Shepard. 1990

HORRIBLE DR. HICHCOCK, THE ★★½ Barbara Steele, first lady of Sixties Italian horror, stars as Robert Flemyng's naïve second wife, who's unaware of his plans to use her in a plot to revive her late predecessor. The U.S. version of this above-average Italian period-horror shocker is severely handicapped by its distributor's cutting of twelve minutes from the movie—mostly to eliminate details of the title character's obsession with necrophilia. The British release print (available as *The Terror of Dr. Hichcock* from some video companies) is slightly longer. 76m. **DIR:** Robert Hampton (Riccardo Freda). **CAST:** Barbara Steele, Robert Flemyng. 1962

HORRIBLE HORROR ★★½ Beloved 1950s *Shock Theater* host Zacherley (a.k.a. John Zacherle) is in vintage form for this direct-to-video compilation of clips, outtakes, and trailers from mostly awful horror movies. The dumb framing device will have you fast-forwarding through Zacherley's routines after about twenty minutes and slowing down to savor vignettes from *The Brainiac, Killers from Space, Devil Bat, She Demons,* and dozens more. Not rated. 110m. **DIR:** David Bergman. **CAST:** Zacherley (host). 1987

HORROR EXPRESS ★★★★ Director Eugenio Martin creates a neat shocker about a prehistoric manlike creature terrorizing a trans-Siberian train when he is awakened from his centuries-old tomb. Lively cast includes a pre-Kojak Telly Savalas in the role of a crazed Russian Cossack intent on killing the thing. Rated R. 88m. **DIR:** Eugenio Martin. **CAST:** Peter Cushing, Christopher Lee, Telly Savalas. 1972

HORROR HOSPITAL ★★ A crazy doctor (Michael Gough) performing gruesome brain experiments at a remote English hospital runs into trouble when a nosy young couple begins snooping around. Slow-moving gorefest. Rated R for violence and blood. 84m. **DIR:** Anthony Balch. **CAST:** Michael Gough, Robin Askwith, Dennis Price. 1973

HORROR HOTEL ★★★ Christopher Lee is a sinister teacher who urges a female student to research a witchcraft thesis at a New England village that's the perfect embodiment of Lovecraftian isolation. A good cast, screenwriter George Baxt (*Circus of Horrors*), and some top technicians—including legendary cinematographer Desmond Dickinson (Olivier's *Hamlet*)—overcome a tiny budget and make this witchcraft saga a miniclassic of the British horror renaissance. B&W; 76m. **DIR:** John Llewellyn Moxey. **CAST:** Dennis Lotis, Betta St. John, Christopher Lee, Venetia Stevenson. 1960

HORROR OF DRACULA ★★★★½ This is the one that launched Hammer Films's popular Dracula series, featuring Christopher Lee in the first—and best—of his many appearances as the Count and Peter Cushing as his archnemesis Van Helsing. A stylish, exciting reworking of Bram Stoker's classic story of a bloodthirsty vampire on the prowl from Transylvania to London and back again. Genuinely scary film, with a hell of an ending, too. 82m. **DIR:** Terence Fisher. **CAST:** Christopher Lee, Peter Cushing, Michael Gough, Melissa Stribling, Miles Malleson. 1958

HORROR OF FRANKENSTEIN ★★★★ Young medical student, fed up with school, decides to drop out and continue his studies alone. So what if his name just happens to be Frankenstein and he just happens to be making a monster? Good entry in the series has many ghoulish sequences, along with some welcome touches of humor. Recommended. Rated R. 95m. **DIR:** Jimmy Sangster. **CAST:** Ralph Bates, Kate O'Mara, Veronica Carlson, Dennis Price. 1970

HORROR OF PARTY BEACH, THE 🦃 A really horrendous horror film about radioactive lizard-like monsters. 72m. **DIR:** Del Tenney. **CAST:** John Scott, Alice Lyon. 1964

HORROR OF THE ZOMBIES 🦃 When Spain's ongoing series of Knights Templar zombie movies was issued as one of VidAmerica's "World's Worst Videos," someone took out what little gore there was. The original version is available on Super Video. Rated R. 90m. **DIR:** Amando de Ossorio. **CAST:** Maria Perschy, Jack Taylor. **1971**

HORROR RISES FROM THE TOMB ★★ Five hundred years after an evil knight is beheaded, he returns to make trouble for his descendants when they visit the family castle. Tired shocks, though better than many of the slasher cheapies on the video racks. Unrated, with the usual violence and tepid gore. 80m. **DIR:** Carlos Aured. **CAST:** Paul Naschy, Emma Cohen. **1972**

HORROR SHOW, THE ★★½ Executed killer Brion James haunts the family of the cop who captured him, turning their dreams into deadly nightmares. Standard horror yarn goes for shocks at the expense of logic. Rated R for strong violence. 95m. **DIR:** James Isaac. **CAST:** Lance Henriksen, Brion James, Rita Taggart, Alvy Moore. **1989**

HORRORS OF BURKE AND HARE 🦃 Witless rehash of the exploits of Edinburgh's famed body snatchers, with the emphasis on R-rated gore. 91m. **DIR:** Vernon Sewell. **CAST:** Harry Andrews, Derren Nesbitt. **1971**

HOSPITAL MASSACRE 🦃 Another *Halloween* clone, this one is set in a hospital where a psycho killer murders everyone in an attempt to get revenge on the girl who laughed at his Valentine's Day card twenty years before. Rated R for nudity and gore. 88m. **DIR:** Boaz Davidson. **CAST:** Barbi Benton, Chip Lucia, Jon Van Ness. **1982**

HOUSE ★★½ A comedy-thriller about an author who moves into an old mansion left to him by an aunt who committed suicide. The cast is good, but the shocks are predictable, crippling the suspense. Rated R for violence and profanity. 93m. **DIR:** Steve Miner. **CAST:** William Katt, George Wendt, Kay Lenz, Richard Moll. **1986**

HOUSE II: THE SECOND STORY ★★ In this unwarranted sequel to *House*, a young man inherits a mansion and invites his best friend to move in with him. A series of humorous and mysterious events lead the two to exhume the grave of the young man's great-grandfather, who is magically still alive. Rated PG-13 for foul language and some violence. 88m. **DIR:** Ethan Wiley. **CAST:** Arye Gross, Jonathan Stark, Royal Dano, Bill Maher, John Ratzenberger. **1987**

HOUSE IV ★★½ A famous horror writer dies and leaves his wife and daughter the old family home, but his half brother has other plans. Soon the whole family is up to their necks in spooky goings on. Rated R for nudity and violence. 94m. **DIR:** Lewis Abernathy. **CAST:** Terri Treas, Scott Burkholder, William Katt. **1991**

HOUSE BY THE CEMETERY ★★ One of the better latter-day spaghetti horrors, this merging of *The Amityville Horror* and *The Innocents* actually has some suspense to go along with the explicit gore. But don't let the kids see it. Rated R. 86m. **DIR:** Lucio Fulci. **CAST:** Katherine MacColl. **1981**

HOUSE OF DARK SHADOWS ★★★ Gore and murder run rampant throughout this film based on the TV soap *Dark Shadows*. Barnabas Collins (Jonathan Frid), a particularly violent vampire, will stop at nothing to be reunited with Josette, his fiancée 200 years ago. Rated PG for violence. 98m. **DIR:** Dan Curtis. **CAST:** Jonathan Frid, Kathryn Leigh Scott, Grayson Hall, Joan Bennett. **1970**

HOUSE OF DRACULA ★★½ The classic Universal Pictures monsters get together for one last rampage before their final bow in *Abbott and Costello Meet Frankenstein*. Scientist Onslow Stevens falls under the spell of Count Dracula (John Carradine) while Larry Talbot (Lon Chaney Jr.), a.k.a. the Wolfman, seeks to end the horror once and for all. The movie's nostalgia value makes it fun to watch, as do Carradine and Chaney, but it is by no means a classic. B&W; 67m. **DIR:** Erle C. Kenton. **CAST:** Lon Chaney Jr., John Carradine, Martha O'Driscoll, Lionel Atwill, Onslow Stevens, Glenn Strange, Jane Adams, Ludwig Stossel. **1945**

HOUSE OF EXORCISM, THE 🦃 Incomprehensible. Rated R for profanity, nudity, gore, and violence. 93m. **DIR:** Mickey Lion, Mario Bava. **CAST:** Telly Savalas, Robert Alda, Elke Sommer. **1975**

HOUSE OF FRANKENSTEIN ★★★½ Universal Pictures' first all-star monsterfest may have signaled the beginning of the end as far as the company's reign of horror, but it's nevertheless a very enjoyable film for fans of old-time chillers. Boris Karloff is excellent as the mad scientist who escapes from an insane asylum and proceeds to wreak havoc on his enemies with the expert help of Dracula (John Carradine, in his first and best appearance in the role), the Wolfman (Lon Chaney Jr.) and the Frankenstein monster (Glenn Strange). Sit back and enjoy on a rainy night. B&W; 71m. **DIR:** Erle C. Kenton. **CAST:** Boris Karloff, J. Carrol Naish, Lon Chaney Jr., John Carradine, Lionel Atwill, George Zucco, Glenn Strange, Anne Gwynne, Elena Verdugo, Sig Ruman. **1944**

HOUSE OF PSYCHOTIC WOMEN 🦃 The "World's Worst Videos" version of this already cut (for U.S. release) Spanish shocker about a sex murderer. Rated R. 90m. **DIR:** Carlos Aured. **CAST:** Paul Naschy, Diana Lorys. **1973**

HOUSE OF SEVEN CORPSES, THE ★★½ Veteran cast almost saves this minor yarn about a film crew shooting a horror movie in a foreboding old mansion. Semi-entertaining nonsense. Rated PG. 90m. **DIR:** Paul Harrison. **CAST:** John Ireland, Faith Domergue, John Carradine. **1973**

HOUSE OF THE DEAD 🦃 A young man stranded in a haunted house finds he is not alone. 90m. **DIR:** Knute Allmendinger. **CAST:** John Ericson, Charles Aidman, Bernard Fox. **1980**

HOUSE OF THE LONG SHADOWS ★★★ This is the good old-fashioned–type horror film that doesn't rely on blood and gore to give the viewer a scare. This gothic thriller is a great choice for horror fans who still like to use their imaginations. Rated PG. 102m. **DIR:** Pete Walker. **CAST:** Vincent Price, John Carradine, Christopher Lee, Desi Arnaz Jr., Peter Cushing. **1984**

HOUSE OF USHER, THE 🦃 Boring retelling of the Edgar Allan Poe classic. Rated R for violence and profanity. 92m. **DIR:** Alan Birkinshaw. **CAST:** Oliver Reed, Donald Pleasence, Romy Windsor. **1990**

HOUSE OF WAX ★★★½ Vincent Price stars as a demented sculptor who, after losing the use of his hands in a fire, turns to murder in this above-average horror film. 88m. **DIR:** André de Toth. **CAST:** Vincent Price, Phyllis Kirk, Carolyn Jones. **1953**

HOUSE OF WHIPCORD 🦃 A pair of elderly Brits kidnap voluptuous young singles and torture them. Rated R. 102m. **DIR:** Pete Walker. **CAST:** Barbara Markham, Patrick Barr, Ray Brooks. **1974**

HOUSE ON HAUNTED HILL ★★★ Vincent Price is at his most relaxed and confident in this fun fright flick about the wealthy owner of a creepy old fortress who offers a group a fortune if they can survive a night there. Humorous at times, deadly serious at others. B&W; 75m. **DIR:** William Castle. **CAST:** Vincent Price, Carol Ohmart, Richard Long, Elisha Cook Jr., Carolyn Craig, Alan Marshal. **1958**

HOUSE ON SKULL MOUNTAIN 🦃 Relatives gathered in an old, dark house for the reading of a will are killed off one by one. Rated PG. 89m. **DIR:** Ron Honthaner. **CAST:** Victor French, Mike Evans. **1974**

HOUSE ON SORORITY ROW 🦃 A group of college girls takes over their sorority and kills the house mother. Rated R. 90m. **DIR:** Mark Rosman. **CAST:** Eileen Davidson. **1983**

HOUSE ON TOMBSTONE HILL, THE ★★ College students take up residence in a cursed mansion, and become prey to the old lady who guards the attic. Unknown cast gives their all in this creaky thriller. Unrated, but contains nudity and violence. 92m. **DIR:** J. Riffel. **CAST:** Mark Zobian. **1988**

HOUSE THAT BLED TO DEATH, THE ★★ Marginally scary horror film about a house that is possessed. Possessed by what or who? Don't ask us—the film refuses to give up the reason for all the blood that keeps shooting out of the pipes, or the various bloody members that show up in the fridge now and then. Not rated, but would probably merit a PG for violence and gore. 50m. **DIR:** Tom Clegg. **CAST:** Nicholas Ball. **1985**

HOUSE THAT DRIPPED BLOOD, THE ★★★½ All-star horror-anthology high jinks adapted from the stories of Robert Bloch. It's not quite on a par with the pioneering British release *Dead of Night*, but it'll do. Best segment: a horror star (Jon Pertwee) discovers a vampire's cape and finds himself becoming a little too convincing in the role of a bloodsucker. Rated PG. 102m. **DIR:** Peter Duffell. **CAST:** Christopher Lee, Peter Cushing, Denholm Elliott, Jon Pertwee, Ingrid Pitt. **1970**

HOUSE THAT VANISHED, THE ★★ Exploitative suspense tale about a woman who sees a murder but can't convince anyone that it happened. There's a lot of nudity and an underdeveloped plot in this British-made film, which was fifteen minutes longer when it was originally released as *Scream and Die*. Rated R. 84m. **DIR:** Joseph Larraz. **CAST:** Andrea Allan. **1973**

HOUSE WHERE EVIL DWELLS, THE ★★ Depressing little horror romp with a Japanese background. In a savagely violent opening, a young samurai swordsman discovers the amorous activities of his less-than-faithful wife, and a gory fight ensues. This traps some really angry spirits in the house, which Edward Albert and Susan George move into centuries later. Rated R for nudity, violence, and language. 91m. **DIR:** Kevin O'Connor. **CAST:** Edward Albert, Susan George, Doug McClure. **1985**

HOUSEKEEPER, THE ★★★ A slightly demented housekeeper is driven over the edge by a Bible-thumping ex-hooker and proceeds to kill the family she works for. A suspenseful atmosphere moves the film along. Rated R for violence. 97m. **DIR:** Ousama Rawi. **CAST:** Rita Tushingham, Rose Petty, Jackie Burroughs. **1987**

HOW TO MAKE A MONSTER 🦃 Hollywood makeup artist goes off the deep end. B&W/color; 75m. **DIR:** Herbert L. Strock. **CAST:** Robert H. Harris, Paul Brinegar, Gary Conway, Gary Clarke, Malcolm Atterbury. **1958**

HOWLING, THE ★★★★ *The Howling* has every spooky scene you've ever seen, every horror movie cliché that's ever been overspoken, and every guaranteed-to-make-'em-jump, out-of-the-dark surprise that Hollywood ever came up with for its scary movies. It also has the best special effects since *Alien* and some really off-the-wall humor. Rated R for gruesome adult horror. 91m. **DIR:** Joe Dante. **CAST:** Dee Wallace, Christopher Stone, Patrick Macnee, Dennis Dugan, Slim Pickens, John Carradine. **1981**

HOWLING II...YOUR SISTER IS A WEREWOLF 🦃 Poor follow-up to *The Howling*. Rated R for nudity, blood, and gore. 91m. **DIR:** Philippe Mora. **CAST:** Christopher Lee, Reb Brown, Annie McEnroe, Sybil Danning. **1984**

HOWLING III ★★½ Werewolves turn up in Australia, only these are marsupials. A sociologist falls in love with one of them and tries to save the whole tribe. The story focuses more on character than gore, and you find yourself strangely engrossed. Rated PG-13 for brief nudity and violence. 95m. **DIR:** Philippe Mora. **CAST:** Barry Otto. **1987**

HOWLING IV 🦃 Werewolves are scarce in this third sequel about a woman haunted by the ghost of a nun who was killed by one of the lycanthropes. Rated R for violence and nudity. 94m. **DIR:** John Hough. **CAST:** Romy Windsor, Michael Weiss, Antony Hamilton. **1988**

HOWLING V—THE REBIRTH ★★★½ A group of people gather at a castle that has been shut for 500 years—for a rather fun game of who's the werewolf. Only the title has any relation to the previous movies in the series. Enjoyable. Rated R for violence and nudity. 99m. **DIR:** Neal Sundstrom. **CAST:** Philip Davis. **1989**

HOWLING VI: THE FREAKS ★★½ A carnival freak show is the scene of a battle between a vampire and the werewolf-drifter who pursues him. Special effects that leave a lot to be desired diminish this really strange entry in the long-running werewolf series. Rated R for violence and profanity. 102m. **DIR:** Hope Perello. **CAST:** Brendan Hughes, Michele Matheson, Sean Gregory Sullivan, Antonio Fargas, Carol Lynley. **1990**

HUMAN DUPLICATORS, THE ★★ Alien giant Richard Kiel comes to Earth to create identical duplicates of its populace but falls in love instead. Hokey, cheap, and badly acted. 82m. **DIR:** Hugo Grimaldi. **CAST:** George Nader, Barbara Nichols, Hugh Beaumont, George Macready, Richard Arlen, Richard Kiel. **1965**

HUMAN MONSTER, THE (DARK EYES OF LONDON) ★★★ Creaky but sometimes clever suspense thriller about a humanitarian (Bela Lugosi) who may not be as philanthropic as he seems. Strange murders have been occurring in the vicinity of his charitable facility. This preposterous Edgar Wallace story has its moments. B&W; 73m. **DIR:** Walter Summers. **CAST:** Bela Lugosi, Hugh Williams, Greta Gynt, Edmon Ryan. **1939**

HUMANOIDS FROM THE DEEP ★★★ As in *Jaws*, beach goers are terrified by water beasts in this science-fiction film. This time, it's underwater vegetable monsters. This is a never-a-dull-moment thriller. Rated R. 80m. **DIR:** Barbara Peeters. **CAST:** Doug McClure, Ann Turkel, Vic Morrow. **1980**

HUMONGOUS 🦃 Idiotic teenagers become shipwrecked on an island whose only inhabitant is a hairy, murderous mutant. Rated R for violence. 90m. **DIR:** Paul Lynch. **CAST:** Janet Julian, David Wallace. **1982**

HUNCHBACK ★★★½ Handsome TV adaptation of Victor Hugo's novel *The Hunchback of Notre Dame*, with Anthony Hopkins in fine form as the tragic Quasimodo. Excellent supporting cast and stunning set design make this version of the classic one to cherish. 150m. **DIR:** Michael Tuchner. **CAST:** Anthony Hopkins, Derek Jacobi, Lesley-Anne Down, Robert Powell, John Gielgud, David Suchet, Tim Pigott-Smith. **1982**

HUNCHBACK OF NOTRE DAME, THE (1923) ★★★★½ Although it has been remade, with varying degrees of success, in the sound era, no film has surpassed the Lon Chaney version in screen spectacle or in the athletic excellence of moviedom's "man of a thousand faces." A musical score has been added. B&W; 108m. **DIR:** Wallace Worsley. **CAST:** Lon Chaney Sr., Patsy Ruth Miller, Ernest Torrence. **1923**

HUNCHBACK OF NOTRE DAME, THE (1939) ★★★★ In this horror classic, Charles Laughton gives a tour-de-force performance as the deformed bell ringer who comes to the aid of a pretty gypsy (Maureen O'Hara). Cedric Hardwicke and Edmond O'Brien also give strong performances in this remake of the silent film. B&W; 117m. **DIR:** William Dieterle. **CAST:** Charles Laughton, Thomas Mitchell, Maureen O'Hara, Edmond O'Brien, Cedric Hardwicke. **1939**

HUNGER, THE (1983) ★★ Arty and visually striking yet cold, this kinky sci-fi horror film features French actress Catherine Deneuve as a seductive vampire. Her centuries-old boyfriend (David Bowie) is about to disintegrate, so she picks a new lover (Susan Sarandon). Rated R for gore, profanity, and nudity. 94m. **DIR:** Tony Scott. **CAST:** Catherine Deneuve, David Bowie, Susan Sarandon, Cliff De Young. **1983**

HUSH...HUSH, SWEET CHARLOTTE ★★★ Originally planned as a sequel to *What Ever Happened to Baby Jane?*, reuniting stars of that movie Bette Davis and Joan Crawford, this effort was filmed with Bette opposite her old Warner Bros. cell mate—Olivia de Havilland. This time they're on opposite sides of the magnolia bush, with Olivia trying to drive poor Bette, who's not all there to begin with, mad. B&W; 133m. **DIR:** Robert Aldrich. **CAST:** Bette Davis, Olivia de Havilland, Joseph Cotten, Agnes Moorehead, Cecil Kellaway, Mary Astor, Bruce Dern. **1965**

I BURY THE LIVING ★★½ Rash of sudden deaths among cemetery plot owners gives mortuary manager Richard Boone grave suspicions he has the power to "put the lid" on his clients. Murder mystery with supernatural overtones is complemented by imaginative design and cinematography. B&W; 76m. **DIR:** Albert Band. **CAST:** Richard Boone, Theodore Bikel, Peggy Maurer, Herbert Anderson. **1958**

I DISMEMBER MAMA Great title—horrible movie. Rated R for violence and nudity. 86m. **DIR:** Paul Leder. **CAST:** Zooey Hall, Greg Mullavey. **1972**

I, MADMAN ★★ A bookstore employee (Jenny Wright) becomes so engrossed in a horror novel that she begins living its terrors. This film provides the same kind of tacky entertainment found in such masterpieces of ineptitude as *Plan 9 from Outer Space* and *Robot Monster.* Rated R for violence, simulated sex, and profanity. 95m. **DIR:** Tibor Takacs. **CAST:** Jenny Wright, Clayton Rohner. **1989**

I MARRIED A VAMPIRE Boring nonsense, more about a country girl's adventures in the big city than a horror flick. 85m. **DIR:** Jay Raskin. **CAST:** Rachel Golden, Brendan Hickey. **1983**

I SPIT ON YOUR CORPSE A team of larcenous females goes on a killing spree across the country. Not rated, but contains nudity and violence. 88m. **DIR:** Al Adamson. **CAST:** Georgina Spelvin. **1974**

I SPIT ON YOUR GRAVE After being brutally raped by a gang of thugs (one of whom is retarded), a young woman takes sadistic revenge. Most videotapes of this title contain the longer X-rated version. Rated R or X. 88m. **DIR:** Meir Zarchi. **CAST:** Camille Keaton. **1981**

I WALKED WITH A ZOMBIE ★★★★½ Director Jacques Tourneur made this classic horror film, involving voodoo and black magic, on an island in the Pacific. One of the best of its kind, this is a great Val Lewton production. B&W; 69m. **DIR:** Jacques Tourneur. **CAST:** Frances Dee, Tom Conway, James Ellison. **1943**

I WAS A TEENAGE FRANKENSTEIN ★★ A descendant of the infamous Dr. Frankenstein sets up shop in America and pieces together a new creature out of hotrod-driving teenagers. This follow-up to *I Was A Teenage Werewolf* is campy fun with mad scientist Whit Bissell uttering lines like "Answer me, you fool! I know you have a civil tongue in your head. I sewed it there myself!" B&W/color; 72m. **DIR:** Herbert L. Strock. **CAST:** Whit Bissell, Phyllis Coates, Robert Burton, Gary Conway. **1957**

I WAS A TEENAGE WEREWOLF ★★½ All things considered (the low budget, the demands of the teen/drive-in genre), this is a pretty good exploitation monster movie. Buoyed by Michael Landon's passionate performance and Gene Fowler Jr.'s energetic direction (which opens the film with a fist thrown straight at the audience). B&W; 70m. **DIR:** Gene Fowler Jr. **CAST:** Michael Landon, Yvonne Lime, Whit Bissell. **1957**

I WAS A TEENAGE ZOMBIE A drug pusher is murdered and his body thrown into a river contaminated by a nuclear power plant. Not rated, but contains violence, adult language, and brief nudity. 90m. **DIR:** John Elias Michalakis. **CAST:** Michael Rubin, Steve McCoy. **1986**

ILSA, HAREM KEEPER OF THE OIL SHIEKS Second *Ilsa* continues the cycle's attempt to squeeze more profits out of the porn audience by adding graphic violence and slick production values to the already explicit (if soft-core) sex. Rated R. 92m. **DIR:** Don Edmunds. **CAST:** Dyanne Thorne. **1978**

ILSA, SHE WOLF OF THE SS A disturbing portrait of a Nazi concentration-camp commandant and her insatiable need for both sex and violent torture. Sicko filmmaking. Not rated, but contains nudity and extreme violence. 92m. **DIR:** Don Edmunds. **CAST:** Dyanne Thorne. **1974**

ILSA, THE WICKED WARDEN Also titled: *Greta the Mad Butcher, Ilsa—Absolute Power.* Rated R. 90m. **DIR:** Jess (Jesus) Franco. **CAST:** Dyanne Thorne, Lina Romay, Jess Franco. **1980**

I'M DANGEROUS TONIGHT An Aztec ceremonial cloak serves as a catalyst for murders in a small college town. Originally aired on cable TV. 92m. **DIR:** Tobe Hooper. **CAST:** Madchen Amick, R. Lee Ermey, Anthony Perkins, Dee Wallace. **1990**

IMMORTAL SINS ★★ Heir to a Spanish castle is also the last male in his cursed line. This atmospheric thriller would be more effective if it were focused more on the antagonism between the heir's wife and a mysterious woman hoping to set their marriage asunder. Rated R for simulated sex. 80m. **DIR:** Herve Hachuel. **CAST:** Cliff De Young, Maryam D'Abo, Shari Shattuck. **1992**

IN THE SHADOW OF KILIMANJARO This is the supposedly true story of what happened in Kenya when ninety thousand baboons went on a killing spree because of the 1984 drought. Rated R for violence. 97m. **DIR:** Raju Patel. **CAST:** John Rhys-Davies, Timothy Bottoms, Irene Miracle, Michele Carey. **1986**

INCREDIBLE TWO-HEADED TRANSPLANT, THE A sadistic killer's head is grafted to the body of a dim-witted giant. Rated PG. 88m. **DIR:** Anthony M. Lanza. **CAST:** Bruce Dern, Pat Priest, Casey Kasem. **1971**

INCREDIBLY STRANGE CREATURES WHO STOPPED LIVING AND BECAME MIXED-UP ZOMBIES, THE 🦃 This movie doesn't live up to its title; how could it? It was later released as *Teenage Psycho Meets Bloody Mary.* 81m. **DIR:** Ray Dennis Steckler. **CAST:** Cash Flagg, Brett O'Hara, Carolyn Brandt, Atlas King. **1965**

INCUBUS, THE 🦃 About a spate of sex murders in a small town. Rated R for all manner of gruesome goings-on. 90m. **DIR:** John Hough. **CAST:** John Cassavetes, Kerrie Keane, Helen Hughes, John Ireland. **1982**

INDESTRUCTIBLE MAN ★★ Lon Chaney looks uncomfortable in the title role of an electrocuted man brought back to life who seeks revenge on the old gang who betrayed him. Nothing new has been added to the worn-out story, unless you want to count the awful narration, which makes this passable thriller seem utterly ridiculous at times. B&W; 70m. **DIR:** Jack Pollexfen. **CAST:** Lon Chaney Jr., Marian Carr, Ross Elliott, Casey Adams. **1956**

INFERNO ★★ This Italian horror flick is heavy on suspense but weak on plot. Leigh McCloskey is the hero who comes to help his sister when she discovers that her apartment is inhabited by an ancient evil spirit. Voices are dubbed, even American actor McCloskey's, and something may have been lost in the translation. Rated R for gore. 83m. **DIR:** Dario Argento. **CAST:** Eleonora Giorgi, Leigh McCloskey, Gabriele Lavia. **1978**

INFESTED 🦃 Wood ticks pumped up on herbal steroids crawl under the skin of forest visitors in this low-budget horrorama. Rated R for violence, gore, and language. 85m. **DIR:** Tony Randel. **CAST:** Rosalind Allen, Ami Dolenz, Seth Green, Virginya Keehne, Ray Oriel, Alfonso Ribeiro, Peter Scolari, Dina Dayrit, Michale Medeiros, Barry Lynch, Clint Howard. **1993**

INITIATION, THE ★★ A particularly gruesome story involving psychotic terror and lots of gore. In a quest to rid herself of a recurring nightmare, a young coed becomes involved in a bloody reality. Rated R. 97m. **DIR:** Larry Stewart. **CAST:** Vera Miles, Clu Gulager, James Read, Daphne Zuniga. **1984**

INITIATION OF SARAH, THE ★★ Adequate TV movie features Kay Lenz as a young college girl being victimized by other students during initiation, and her subsequent revenge upon acquiring supernatural powers. Hokey thriller should have been better, judging from the cast. 100m. **DIR:** Robert Day. **CAST:** Kay Lenz, Shelley Winters, Kathryn Crosby, Morgan Brittany, Tony Bill. **1978**

INNOCENT BLOOD ★★★ Director John Landis returns to his roots with this mostly amusing spin on vampire lore, which finds sultry Anne Parillaud as a selective bloodsucker who feeds only on those deserving to die. Rated R for gore, profanity, explicit sex, and nudity. 112m. **DIR:** John Landis. **CAST:** Anne Parillaud, Robert Loggia, Anthony LaPaglia, Don Rickles. **1992**

INTRUDER (1988) ★★ A bloodthirsty killer is locked in a supermarket with employees preparing for a going-out-of-business sale. Slasher fans should find this amusing. Rated R for violence and profanity. 90m. **DIR:** Scott Spiegel. **CAST:** Elizabeth Cox, Danny Hicks, René Estevez. **1988**

INVASION EARTH: THE ALIENS ARE HERE ★★ Comedic aliens take over a cinema presenting a sci-fi film festival, subverting humans into blank-eyed underwear-clad zombies. But some kids get wise to the scheme and try to put a stop to it before it's too late. Unfunny as comedy, but with great clips of classic sci-fi and horror films from years past. Not rated, but suitable for most age-groups. 84m. **DIR:** George Maitland. **CAST:** Janis Fabian, Christian Lee. **1987**

INVASION OF THE BLOOD FARMERS 🦃 The residents of a secluded New York town are really modern-day Druids. Rated PG. 84m. **DIR:** Ed Adlum. **CAST:** Cynthia Fleming. **1972**

INVASION OF THE FLESH HUNTERS ★★★ A new twist on the zombie flick. This time these guys aren't dead. They just have a cannibalistic disease brought back from Southeast Asia. Good effects. Not rated. 90m. **DIR:** Anthony M. Dawson. **CAST:** John Saxon. **1982**

INVISIBLE GHOST 🦃 Bela Lugosi as an unwitting murderer, used by his supposedly dead wife to further her schemes. B&W; 64m. **DIR:** Joseph H. Lewis. **CAST:** Bela Lugosi, Polly Ann Young, John McGuire, Betty Compson, Jack Mulhall. **1941**

INVISIBLE MAN, THE ★★★★½ Claude Rains goes unseen until the finish in his screen debut. He plays Jack Griffin, the title character in H. G. Wells's famous story of a scientist who creates an invisibility serum—with the side effect of driving a person slowly insane. Frightening film could initially be mistaken for a comedy, with large chunks of humor in the first half, turning deadly serious thereafter. B&W; 71m. **DIR:** James Whale. **CAST:** Claude Rains, Gloria Stuart, Una O'Connor, Henry Travers, E. E. Clive, Dwight Frye. **1933**

INVISIBLE MAN RETURNS ★★★ Convicted of his brother's murder and condemned to die, Vincent Price is injected with a serum that renders him invisible and aids in his effort to catch the real killer. John Fulton's special effects and a top-notch cast make this, the second in Universal's series, another one of their winning chillers. B&W; 81m. **DIR:** Joe May. **CAST:** Cedric Hardwicke,

Vincent Price, Nan Grey, John Sutton, Alan Napier, Cecil Kellaway. 1940

INVISIBLE RAY, THE ★★★ Boris Karloff and Bela Lugosi are teamed in this interesting story. A brilliant research scientist (Karloff), experimenting in Africa, is contaminated by a hunk of radioactive meteor landing nearby and soon discovers that his mere touch can kill. Neat Universal thriller features first-rate effects and good ensemble acting. B&W; 81m. **DIR:** Lambert Hillyer. **CAST:** Boris Karloff, Bela Lugosi, Frances Drake, Frank Lawton. 1936

INVISIBLE STRANGLER A murderer on death row discovers he has a psychic power to make himself invisible. Not rated, but contains graphic violence. 85m. **DIR:** John Florea. **CAST:** Robert Foxworth, Stefanie Powers, Elke Sommer. 1984

INVITATION TO HELL A family visits a posh vacation resort, only to be seduced by a beautiful Satan worshiper. Bland telefilm. 96m. **DIR:** Wes Craven. **CAST:** Robert Urich, Joanna Cassidy, Susan Lucci, Kevin McCarthy. 1984

ISLAND, THE Michael Caine as a reporter investigating the mysterious disappearances of pleasure craft and their owners in the Caribbean. Rated R. 113m. **DIR:** Michael Ritchie. **CAST:** Michael Caine, David Warner, Angela Punch McGregor. 1980

ISLAND CLAWS ★★ As science-fiction horror thrillers go, this one is about average. *Attack of the Killer Crabs* would have been a more appropriate title, though. Dr. McNeal (Barry Nelson) is a scientist who is experimenting to make larger crabs as a food source. Rated PG for violence. 91m. **DIR:** Hernan Cardenas. **CAST:** Robert Lansing, Barry Nelson, Steve Hanks, Nita Talbot. 1980

ISLAND OF LOST SOULS ★★★★ This seminal horror melodrama of the 1930s still has the power to thrill and enthrall, thanks to its otherworldly atmosphere (an exotic, sexy, yet claustrophobic tropical island) and sequences of unbridled, sadistic horror. H. G. Wells's *The Island of Dr. Moreau* is the basis for this tense chiller in which a shipwreck victim, the unwilling "guest" of the exiled doctor (Charles Laughton), discovers Moreau speeding up evolution to transform jungle beasts into humans...sort of. A classic. B&W; 70m. **DIR:** Erle C. Kenton. **CAST:** Charles Laughton, Richard Arlen, Leila Hyams, Bela Lugosi, Kathleen Burke, Stanley Fields. 1933

ISLAND OF TERROR ★★★ On an island off the coast of Ireland, scientists battle lab-created, turtlelike mutants that live on human bone marrow. Fun thriller with some terrifically queasy sound effects. 87m. **DIR:** Terence Fisher. **CAST:** Peter Cushing, Edward Judd, Carole Gray. 1966

ISLAND OF THE LOST ★★½ A scientist and his family become shipwrecked on an island inhabited by assorted beasts with genetic disorders. Not rated, but contains mild violence. 92m. **DIR:** John Florea. **CAST:** Richard Greene, Luke Halpin, Mart Hulswit, Robin Mattson. 1968

ISLE OF THE DEAD ★★★½ Atmospheric goings-on dominate this typically tasteful horror study from producer Val Lewton. A group of people are stranded on a Greek island during a quarantine. Star Boris Karloff is, as usual, outstanding. B&W; 72m. **DIR:** Mark Robson. **CAST:** Boris Karloff, Ellen Drew, Jason Robards Sr. 1945

IT (1991) ★★★½ Although scripters Lawrence D. Cohen and Tommy Lee Wallace do a superb job setting up the events of Stephen King's lengthy bestseller, the ultimate payoff—when It is finally given a form—is quite disappointing. That's a shame, because this teleplay's first half is perhaps the best King adaptation ever lensed. Made for TV, but probably too intense for very young viewers. 192m. **DIR:** Tommy Lee Wallace. **CAST:** Harry Anderson, Dennis Christopher, Richard Masur, Annette O'Toole, Tim Reid, John Ritter, Richard Thomas, Tim Curry. 1991

IT CAME FROM BENEATH THE SEA ★★★★ Ray Harryhausen's powerhouse special effects light up the screen in this story of a giant octopus from the depths of the Pacific that causes massive destruction along the North American coast as it makes its way toward San Francisco. A little talky at times, but the brilliantly achieved effects make this a must-see movie even on the small screen. B&W; 80m. **DIR:** Robert Gordon. **CAST:** Kenneth Tobey, Faith Domergue, Donald Curtis, Ian Keith. 1955

IT LIVES AGAIN ★★★ In an effort to outdo the original *It's Alive!*, this film has three mutated babies on the loose, and everybody in a panic. Doesn't quite measure up to its predecessor, but still successful due to another fine makeup job by Rick Baker. Rated R. 91m. **DIR:** Larry Cohen. **CAST:** Frederic Forrest, Kathleen Lloyd, John P. Ryan, John Marley, Andrew Duggan. 1978

IT'S ALIVE! ★★★½ This camp classic about a mutated baby with a thirst for human blood has to be seen to be believed. Convincing effects work by Rick Baker and a fantastic score by Bernard Herrmann make this film one to remember. Rated PG. 91m. **DIR:** Larry Cohen. **CAST:** John P. Ryan, Sharon Farrell, Andrew Duggan, Guy Stockwell, Michael Ansara. 1974

IT'S ALIVE III: ISLAND OF THE ALIVE ★★½ In this sequel, the mutant babies are sequestered on a desert island, where they reproduce and make their way back home to wreak havoc. Although this is a surprisingly strong entry in the *Alive* series, it suffers from some sloppy effects and mediocre acting. Rated R for violence. 95m. **DIR:** Larry Cohen. **CAST:** Michael Moriarty, Karen Black, Gerrit Graham, James Dixon. **1986**

J.D.'S REVENGE ★★★½ A gangster, murdered in 1940s New Orleans, returns from the dead thirty-five years later, possessing the body of a law student in his quest for revenge. Surprisingly well-crafted low-budget thriller. Rated R for strong violence and profanity. 95m. **DIR:** Arthur Marks. **CAST:** Glynn Turman, Joan Pringle, Lou Gossett Jr. **1976**

JACK THE RIPPER (1959) ★★ This thoroughly fictionalized rendering of the exploits of Whitechapel's mass murderer hasn't aged well. B&W; 84m. **DIR:** Robert S. Baker, Monty Berman. **CAST:** Lee Patterson, Eddie Byrne, George Rose. **1959**

JAR, THE 🦃 A man is haunted by a demon in a jar. 90m. **DIR:** Bruce Toscano. **CAST:** Gary Wallace, Karen Sjoberg. **1984**

JASON GOES TO HELL: THE FINAL FRIDAY ★★★ Fans of the *Friday the 13th* films will enjoy this ninth and final (?) trip to the infamous Crystal Lake. We wouldn't reveal anything by saying Jason is killed in this movie. He's been killed so often it is hard to keep track. Suffice to say, some loose ends are made tighter, and a rather intriguing explanation for Jason's evil is offered. Watch to the very end for something we wouldn't dream of giving away. Rated R for violence, profanity, and plenty of gore. 88m. **DIR:** Adam Marcus. **CAST:** John D. LeMay, Kari Keegan, Kane Hodder, Steven Williams, Steven Culp, Erin Gray, Allison Smith, Kipp Marcus. **1993**

JAWS ★★★★★ A young Steven Spielberg (27 at the time) directed this 1975 scare masterpiece based on the Peter Benchley novel. A large shark is terrorizing the tourists at the local beach. The eerie music by John Williams heightens the tension to underscore the shark's presence and scare the audience right out of their seats. Roy Scheider, Robert Shaw, and Richard Dreyfuss offer outstanding performances. Rated PG. 124m. **DIR:** Steven Spielberg. **CAST:** Roy Scheider, Robert Shaw, Richard Dreyfuss, Lorraine Gary, Murray Hamilton. **1975**

JAWS 2 ★★★ Even though it's a sequel, *Jaws 2* delivers. Police chief Martin Brody (Roy Scheider) believes there's a shark in the waters off Amity again, but his wife and employers think he's crazy. Rated PG. 120m. **DIR:** Jeannot Szwarc. **CAST:** Roy Scheider, Lorraine Gary, Murray Hamilton, Jeffrey Kramer. **1978**

JAWS 3 ★★ Among those marked for lunch in this soggy, unexciting sequel are Lou Gossett Jr., Dennis Quaid, and Bess Armstrong. They look bored. You'll be bored. Rated PG. 97m. **DIR:** Joe Alves. **CAST:** Lou Gossett Jr., Dennis Quaid, Bess Armstrong, Simon MacCorkindale. **1983**

JAWS OF DEATH, THE ★★ Low-rent *Jaws* clone features Jaeckel as a shark breeder who rents his finny friends out to Florida aquariums. But when he finds out that the sharks are being exploited, he seeks revenge. Better than *Jaws: The Revenge*, but not by much. 93m. **DIR:** William Grefe. **CAST:** Richard Jaeckel, Jennifer Bishop, Harold Sakata. **1976**

JAWS OF SATAN ★★ Satan himself breezes into town in the form of a cobra seeking revenge on a priest whose ancestors persecuted the Druids. What the viewer gets is this movie from hell, disguised as a rough-hewn horror film. Rated R for gore. 92m. **DIR:** Bob Claver. **CAST:** Fritz Weaver, Gretchen Corbett, Jon Korkes. **1984**

JAWS: THE REVENGE 🦃 This third sequel is lowest-common-denominator filmmaking, a by-the-numbers effort. Rated PG-13. 89m. **DIR:** Joseph Sargent. **CAST:** Lorraine Gary, Lance Guest, Michael Caine, Mario Van Peebles, Karen Young. **1987**

JENNIFER ★★ A carbon copy of *Carrie*—but with snakes. Jennifer is a sweet, innocent child on a poor-kid's scholarship at an uppity school for rich girls. She is tormented until she is harassed into a frenzy. What's the catch? Jennifer was raised by a cult of religious fanatics who believe that God has given her the power to command reptiles. Rated PG. 90m. **DIR:** Brice Mack. **CAST:** Lisa Pelikan, Bert Convy, Nina Foch, John Gavin, Wesley Eure. **1978**

JESSE JAMES MEETS FRANKENSTEIN'S DAUGHTER 🦃 The feeble plot pits hero Jesse James against the evil daughter of the infamous doctor of the title. 88m. **DIR:** William Beaudine. **CAST:** John Lupton, Estelita, Cal Bolder, Jim Davis. **1966**

JOHN CARPENTER PRESENTS: BODY BAGS ★★½ Writer-director John Carpenter's gleeful sense of humor and cameo appearances by the likes of Tom Arnold and Roger Corman can't save this *Tales from the Crypt* wannabe. Although laced with the appropriate gore, two of the three stories are strictly dullsville. The third, blessed with a grand performance by Stacy Keach as a fellow horrified by encroaching baldness, brings new meaning to a full-bodied head of hair. Rated R for profanity, nudity, simulated sex, and gobs o' gore. 95m. **DIR:** John Carpenter. **CAST:** Robert Carradine, Stacy Keach, David Warner, Sheena Easton, Deborah Harry, Mark Hamill, Twiggy. **1993**

JUNIOR 🦃 Despicable sadomasochism. Not rated, but contains violence, nudity, and profanity. 80m. **DIR:** Jim Henley. **CAST:** Linda Singer. **1984**

KEEP, THE ★★ A centuries-old presence awakens in an old castle. Rated R for nudity and violence. 96m. **DIR:** Michael Mann. **CAST:** Ian McKellen, Alberta Watson, Scott Glenn, Jurgen Prochnow. **1983**

KEEPER, THE ★★ The owner of an insane asylum preys on the wealthy families of his charges. Rated R. 96m. **DIR:** T. Y. Drake. **CAST:** Christopher Lee, Sally Gray. **1984**

KILLER KLOWNS FROM OUTER SPACE ★★★½ Lon Chaney once opined that "there is nothing more frightening than a clown after midnight." This low-budget sci-fi–horror thriller from the Chiodo brothers proves that claim with this high-style mixture of camp, comedy, and chills. The title pretty much says it all, but the results are more entertaining than one might expect. Rated PG-13 for profanity and violence. 90m. **DIR:** Stephen Chiodo. **CAST:** Grant Cramer, Suzanne Snyder, John Allen Nelson, Royal Dano, John Vernon. **1988**

KILLING SPREE ★★ This low-budget bloodfest about a jealous husband who kills the imagined suitors of his wife does contain some unique death scenes. But the lighting is often overbearing, and it's hard to hear what the actors (who aren't very good anyway) are saying. Unrated, the film contains violence. 88m. **DIR:** Tim Ritter. **CAST:** Asbestos Felt. **1987**

KINDRED, THE Derivative horror film, which steals its creature from *Alien* and its plot from any one of a hundred run-of-the-razor slasher flicks. Rated R for profanity, violence, and gore. 95m. **DIR:** Jeffrey Obrow, Stephen Carpenter. **CAST:** David Allen Brooks, Amanda Pays, Rod Steiger, Kim Hunter. **1987**

KING KONG (1933) ★★★★★ This classic was one of early sound film's most spectacular successes. The movie, about the giant ape who is captured on a prehistoric island and proceeds to tear New York City apart until his final stand on the Empire State Building, is the stuff of which legends are made. Its marriage of sound, music, image, energy, pace, and excitement made *King Kong* stand as a landmark film. B&W; 100m. **DIR:** Merian C. Cooper, Ernest B. Schoedsack. **CAST:** Robert Armstrong, Fay Wray, Bruce Cabot, Frank Reicher, Noble Johnson. **1933**

KING KONG (1976) ★★ This remake, starring Jeff Bridges and Jessica Lange, is a pale imitation of the 1933 classic. For kids only. Rated PG for violence. 135m. **DIR:** John Guillermin. **CAST:** Jeff Bridges, Jessica Lange, Charles Grodin. **1976**

KING KONG LIVES Romance of the resuscitated Kong and his new love, Lady Kong. Rated PG-13 for violence. 105m. **DIR:** John Guillermin. **CAST:** Brian Kerwin, Linda Hamilton, John Ashton, Peter Michael Goetz. **1986**

KING KONG VS. GODZILLA ★★ King Kong and Godzilla duke it out atop Mount Fuji in this East meets West supermonster movie. Here, though, Kong is a junkie hooked on some wild jungle juice. The bouts are quite humorous. Not rated. 91m. **DIR:** Inoshiro Honda. **CAST:** Michael Keith, Tadao Takashima, Kenji Sahara. **1963**

KING OF KONG ISLAND Spanish mad scientist melodrama. 92m. **DIR:** Robert Morris. **CAST:** Brad Harris, Esmerelda Barros, Marc Lawrence. **1968**

KING OF THE ZOMBIES Typical mad scientist–zombie movie with evil genius attempting to create an invulnerable army of mindless slaves. B&W; 67m. **DIR:** Jean Yarbrough. **CAST:** Dick Purcell, Joan Woodbury, Mantan Moreland, John Archer. **1941**

KINGDOM OF THE SPIDERS ★★★ William Shatner stars in this unsuspenseful thriller with lurid special effects. The title tells it all. Rated PG. 94m. **DIR:** John "Bud" Cardos. **CAST:** William Shatner, Tiffany Bolling, Woody Strode. **1977**

KISS, THE (1988) ★★ An African voodoo priestess (Joanna Pacula) is looking for an heir. So she invades the lives of her dead sister's family. That old black magic just ain't there. Rated R for nudity and violence. 105m. **DIR:** Pen Densham. **CAST:** Joanna Pacula, Meredith Salenger. **1988**

KISS MEETS THE PHANTOM OF THE PARK Flaccid made-for-TV movie about the heavy-metal group and a loony amusement park handyman. 100m. **DIR:** Gordon Hessler. **CAST:** Peter Criss, Ace Frehley, Gene Simmons, Paul Stanley. **1978**

KISS OF THE TARANTULA Unhinged girl obliterates her enemies with the help of some eight-legged friends. Rated PG for mild gore. 85m. **DIR:** Chris Munger. **CAST:** Suzanne Ling, Eric Mason. **1972**

LADY FRANKENSTEIN Joseph Cotten ill-used as Baron Frankenstein attempting once again to create life in yet another silly-looking assemblage of spare parts. Rated R for violence. 84m. **DIR:** Mel Welles. **CAST:** Joseph Cotten, Mickey Hargitay. **1971**

LAIR OF THE WHITE WORM Ken Russell writhes again, disgustingly perverse and snidely campy. Rated R. 99m. **DIR:** Ken Russell. **CAST:** Amanda Donohoe, Hugh Grant, Sammi Davis, Catherine Oxenberg, Peter Capaldi. **1988**

LAND OF THE MINOTAUR ★★ Peter Cushing, in one of his few truly villainous roles, plays the leader of a bloodthirsty devil cult that preys on tourists in modern Greece. Already slow-paced, this low-budget creature feature is gravely handicapped by its American distributor's decision to cut six minutes of nudity and violence, thereby ensuring a

PG rating. What remains is picturesque but tame. Brian Eno composed and performs the eerie electronic score. 88m. **DIR:** Costa Carayiannis. **CAST:** Peter Cushing, Donald Pleasence. **1976**

LAST HORROR FILM, THE 🦃 Mama's boy obsessed with a horror-movie actress goes on a killing spree at the Cannes Film Festival. Rated R for violence. 87m. **DIR:** David Winters. **CAST:** Caroline Munro, Joe Spinell. **1984**

LAST HOUSE ON DEAD END STREET 🦃 Raunchy, grade-Z exploitation item about snuff filmmakers. Rated R. 90m. **DIR:** Victor Janos. **CAST:** Steven Morrison, Janes Sorley. **1977**

LAST HOUSE ON THE LEFT 🦃 Two teenage girls are tortured and killed by a sadistic trio. Graphic torture and humiliation scenes rate this one an R at best. 91m. **DIR:** Wes Craven. **CAST:** David Hess, Lucy Grantham, Sandra Cassel. **1972**

LEATHERFACE—THE TEXAS CHAINSAW MASSACRE III ★★½ Some light comedy helps break up the terror in this story of two travelers who make the mistake of stopping in Texas for directions. Not as scary as the first film in the series and not as bloody as the second. Rated R for violence. 87m. **DIR:** Jeff Burr. **CAST:** Viggo Mortensen, William Butler, Ken Foree. **1989**

LEECH WOMAN, THE ★★ The neglected wife of a cosmetics researcher discovers an African potion that can restore her faded youth, but she has to kill young men to obtain the "secret ingredient." Coleen Gray gives an all-out performance, but there's too much setup and too little payoff. B&W; 77m. **DIR:** Edward Dein. **CAST:** Coleen Gray, Grant Williams, Gloria Talbott. **1959**

LEGACY, THE ★★ A young American couple (Katharine Ross and Sam Elliott) staying at a mysterious English mansion discover that the woman has been chosen as the mate for some sort of ugly, demonic creature upstairs. Rated R for violence and language. 100m. **DIR:** Richard Marquand. **CAST:** Katharine Ross, Sam Elliott, John Standing, Roger Daltrey. **1979**

LEGACY OF HORROR 🦃 Another of Andy Milligan's lethally dull and thoroughly amateurish shockers, a remake of his own *The Ghastly Ones.* Rated R. 90m. **DIR:** Andy Milligan. **CAST:** Elaine Bois, Chris Broderick. **1978**

LEGEND OF BOGGY CREEK ★★ One of the better "mystery of" docudramas, which were the rage of the early 1970s, this supposedly true story focuses on a monster that lurks in the swamps of Arkansas. Rated PG. 95m. **DIR:** Charles B. Pierce. **CAST:** Willie E. Smith, John P. Nixon. **1972**

LEGEND OF HELL HOUSE, THE ★★★½ Richard Matheson's riveting suspense tale of a group of researchers attempting to survive a week in a haunted house in order to try to solve the mystery of the many deaths that have occurred there. Jarring at times, with very inventive camera shots and a great cast headed by Roddy McDowall as the only survivor of a previous investigation. Rated PG for violence. 95m. **DIR:** John Hough. **CAST:** Roddy McDowall, Pamela Franklin, Gayle Hunnicutt, Clive Revill. **1973**

LEGEND OF THE WEREWOLF ★★ Peter Cushing's ever-professional performance is the only noteworthy element. British werewolf movie. Unrated, but the equivalent of PG-13. 90m. **DIR:** Freddie Francis. **CAST:** Peter Cushing, Ron Moody, Hugh Griffith. **1974**

LEPRECHAUN 🦃 No luck of the Irish for writer-director Mark Jones, whose abysmal little fright flick concerns a nasty Lucky Charms refugee. Nothing but blarney. Rated R for violence and profanity. 92m. **DIR:** Mark Jones. **CAST:** Warwick Davis, Jennifer Aniston, Ken Olandt, Mark Holton. **1993**

LET'S SCARE JESSICA TO DEATH ★★ A young woman staying with some odd people out in the country witnesses all sorts of strange things, like ghosts and blood-stained corpses. Is it real, or some kind of elaborate hoax? The title tells it all in this disjointed terror tale, though it does contain a few spooky scenes. Rated PG. 89m. **DIR:** John Hancock. **CAST:** Zohra Lampert, Barton Heyman. **1971**

LEVIATHAN ★★ The crew of an undersea mining platform comes across a sunken Soviet ship that has been scuttled in an effort to keep some genetic experiment gone awry away from the world. What the miners encounter is part *Alien,* part *20,000 Leagues Under the Sea,* part *The Thing.* Since these other films are so much better, it's best to leave this one alone. Rated R for violence. 98m. **DIR:** George Pan Cosmatos. **CAST:** Peter Weller, Richard Crenna, Amanda Pays, Daniel Stern, Ernie Hudson, Meg Foster, Lisa Eilbacher, Hector Elizondo. **1989**

LIFT, THE ★★★ Grizzly supernatural thriller about a demonic elevator that mysteriously claims the lives of innocent riders. The film mixes dark humor with the macabre. This Dutch-made horror film was a major box-office hit in Europe. Rated R for nudity and graphic violence. In Dutch with English subtitles. Also available in a dubbed version. 95m. **DIR:** Dick Maas. **CAST:** Huub Stapel. **1985**

LIGHTNING INCIDENT, THE 🦃 Absolutely laughable saga of a psychic woman (Nancy McKeon) whose newborn son is kidnapped by voodoo cultists. Moderately violent; made for cable. Rated R for language and violence. 90m. **DIR:** Michael Switzer. **CAST:** Nancy McKeon, Tantoo Cardinal, Elpidia Carrillo, Polly Bergen, Tim Ryan. **1991**

LINK ★★½ A student (Elisabeth Shue) takes a job with an eccentric anthropology professor (Terence Stamp) and finds herself menaced by a powerful, intelligent ape named Link. The story leaves a number of questions unanswered, but the film can be praised for taking the old cliché of an ape being on the loose and making it surprisingly effective. Rated R for profanity, brief nudity, and violence. 103m. **DIR:** Richard Franklin. **CAST:** Terence Stamp, Elisabeth Shue. **1986**

LITTLE SHOP OF HORRORS, THE (1960) ★★★★ Dynamite Roger Corman superquickie about a meek florist shop employee (Jonathan Haze) who inadvertently creates a ferocious man-eating plant. This horror-comedy was filmed in two days and is one of the funniest ever made. B&W; 72m. **DIR:** Roger Corman. **CAST:** Jonathan Haze, Mel Welles, Jackie Joseph, Jack Nicholson, Dick Miller. **1960**

LOCH NESS HORROR, THE 🦃 Japan isn't the only country that has monsters that look like muppets. Rated PG. Has some violence. 93m. **DIR:** Larry Buchanan. **CAST:** Barry Buchanan, Sandy Kenyon. **1982**

LONE WOLF ★★ Small-town students investigate a series of gory murders and discover a werewolf. Better than many such low-budget efforts, but barely worth seeing unless you're an avid lycanthrophile. Unrated, the film has some violence and gore. 96m. **DIR:** John Callas. **CAST:** Dyann Brown, Kevin Hart, Jamie Newcomb, Ann Douglas, Tom Henry. **1989**

LONG WEEKEND ★★★½ This Australian film is a must-see for environmentalists. We are introduced to a couple who carelessly start a forest fire, run over a kangaroo, senselessly destroy a tree, shoot animals for the sport of it, and break an eagle's egg. Then nature avenges itself. Unrated, this contains obscenities, nudity, and gore. 95m. **DIR:** Colin Eggleston. **CAST:** John Hargreaves, Briony Behets. **1986**

LOST BOYS, THE ★★ In this vampire variation on *Peter Pan*, director Joel Schumacher seems more interested in pretty shots and fancy costumes than atmosphere and plot. The story has Jason Patric falling in with a group of hip bloodsuckers led by Kiefer Sutherland. Rated R for violence, suggested sex, and profanity. 98m. **DIR:** Joel Schumacher. **CAST:** Jason Patric, Dianne Wiest, Corey Haim, Barnard Hughes, Edward Herrmann, Kiefer Sutherland, Jami Gertz, Corey Feldman. **1987**

LOST PLATOON 🦃 World War II vet begins to suspect that The Lost Platoon are actually vampires, fighting their way through two centuries of war. Pretty anemic for an action-horror film. Unrated, but contains violence. 91m. **DIR:** David A. Prior. **CAST:** David Parry, Ted Prior. **1989**

LOST TRIBE, THE 🦃 A story about twin brothers involved in smuggling, adultery, and murder. Not rated, but contains violence. 96m. **DIR:** John Laing. **CAST:** John Bach, Darien Takle, Emma Takle. **1983**

LOVE BUTCHER 🦃 A series of grisly murders of young women are committed by a deranged psycho. Rated R. 84m. **DIR:** Mikel Angel, Don Jones. **CAST:** Erik Stern. **1983**

LURKERS 🦃 Hopelessly meandering tale about an abused young girl haunted by the forces of evil. Rated R for violence and nudity. 95m. **DIR:** Roberta Findlay. **CAST:** Christine Moore, Gary Warner. **1988**

LUST FOR A VAMPIRE ★★★ All-girls school turns out to be a haven for vampires, with a visiting writer (Michael Johnson) falling in love with one of the undead students (Yutte Stensgaard). Atmospheric blending of chills and fleshy eroticism combined with a terrific ending. Rated R. 95m. **DIR:** Jimmy Sangster. **CAST:** Suzanna Leigh, Michael Johnson, Ralph Bates, Barbara Jefford, Yutte Stensgaard. **1970**

MACABRE SERENADE ★★ One of the four Mexican films featuring footage of Boris Karloff but assembled after his death (see *Sinister Invasion*), this is the best of a bad lot. He plays a toy maker whose creations seek revenge on his evil relatives after his death. There's a sloppily cut version also on video called *Dance of Death*; it originally played theatres as *House of Evil*. 75m. **DIR:** Juan Ibanez, Jack Hill. **CAST:** Boris Karloff. **1968**

MACISTE IN HELL ★★ Italian musclehero Maciste (Kirk Morris), the *real* hero of dozens of sword-and-sorcery epics with bogus Hercules titles appended for U.S. release, anachronistically pops up in medieval Scotland(!), where he combats a vengeful witch. 78m. **DIR:** Riccardo Freda. **CAST:** Kirk Morris, Helene Chanel. **1962**

MAD AT THE MOON ★★ Bizarre, confused horror-Western stars Mary Stuart Masterson as a young woman forced by her mother into marriage with a well-to-do rancher. When her husband turns out to be a werewolf, it's up to the man she loves to save her life. An arty misfire. Rated R for violence, simulated sex, and nudity. 98m. **DIR:** Martin Donovan. **CAST:** Mary Stuart Masterson, Hart Bochner, Fionnula Flanagan, Cec Verrell, Stephen Blake. **1992**

MAD DOCTOR OF BLOOD ISLAND, THE 🦃 He's experimenting with a chlorophyll-based fountain-of-youth solution—which turns people into green monsters instead. Rated PG. 88m. **DIR:** Eddie Romero, Gerardo de Leon. **CAST:** John Ashley. **1968**

MAD LOVE ★★★½ Colin Clive plays a gifted pianist who loses his hands in a rail accident, and finds that the hands miraculously grafted to his wrists by Peter Lorre belonged to a murderer and follow the impulses of the former owner. This complex story of obsession is a murder mystery with an odd twist. A compelling study of depravity. B&W; 67m. **DIR:** Karl Freund. **CAST:** Peter Lorre, Colin Clive, Frances Drake, Ted Healy, Sara Haden, Edward Brophy, Keye Luke. **1935**

MAD MONSTER 🦃 Scientist George Zucco is mad and Glenn Strange is the monster he creates in order to get even with disbelievers. B&W; 77m. **DIR:** Sam Newfield. **CAST:** Johnny Downs, George Zucco, Anne Nagel, Glenn Strange. **1942**

MADHOUSE (1972) ★★★ Vincent Price and Peter Cushing share more screen time in their third film together (following *Scream and Scream Again* and *Dr. Phibes Rises Again*, thus lifting it above most horror movies of its decade. In a story slightly reminiscent of the superior *Theatre of Blood*, Price plays an actor who is released from a hospital after suffering a nervous breakdown, only to discover that his TV-series alter ego, Dr. Death, is living up to his name. Rated PG for violence. 92m. **DIR:** Jim Clark. **CAST:** Vincent Price, Peter Cushing, Robert Quarry, Adrienne Corri, Linda Hayden. **1972**

MADHOUSE (1987) ★★½ When a woman's deranged twin escapes from the loony bin and crashes her sibling's party, you can imagine the blood fest that results. Although the story sounds simple, there are some surprises. Stylishly filmed and well acted, with a bigger budget this might have been a classic. As it is, it's worth a look. Not rated, but contains violence. 93m. **DIR:** Ovidio Assonitis (Oliver Hellman). **CAST:** Trish Everly, Michael MacRae. **1987**

MAKE THEM DIE SLOWLY 🦃 South American cannibals. Not rated; contains nudity, profanity, and extreme violence. 92m. **DIR:** Umberto Lenzi. **CAST:** John Morghen, Lorainne DeSelle. **1984**

MAMMA DRACULA 🦃 A horror–black comedy that fails on both counts. Not rated, but contains nudity and adult situations. 93m. **DIR:** Boris Szulzinger. **CAST:** Louise Fletcher, Maria Schneider, Marc-Henri Wajnberg, Alexander Wanberg, Jess Hahn. **1988**

MAN AND THE MONSTER, THE ★★ The Mexican monster movies that were made in the late 1950s at the Churubusco-Azteca Studios are an acquired taste. Their crisp, black-and-white photography is richly atmospheric, but production values are meager and acting is mediocre. This one, a Jekyll-Hyde potboiler involving a musician who changes into a hairy beast at inconvenient times, is directed by the man who made this odd subgenre's best films. B&W; 74m. **DIR:** Rafael Baledon. **CAST:** Enrique Rabal, Abel Salazar. **1958**

MAN BEAST 🦃 A search for the Abominable Snowman. B&W; 72m. **DIR:** Jerry Warren. **CAST:** Rock Madison, Virginia Maynor. **1955**

MAN THEY COULD NOT HANG, THE ★★★ Boris Karloff's fine performance carries this fast-paced tale of a scientist executed for murder and brought back to life and his bizarre plan of revenge on the judge and jury who convicted him. B&W; 72m. **DIR:** Nick Grindé. **CAST:** Boris Karloff, Lorna Gray, Robert Wilcox. **1939**

MAN WHO LIVED AGAIN, THE ★★★ One of Karloff's rare British films of the 1930s, this is an initially slow-moving, mad scientist melodrama about mind transference, which gradually builds to a potent second half. B&W; 61m. **DIR:** Robert Stevenson. **CAST:** Boris Karloff, Anna Lee, John Loder. **1936**

MAN WITH TWO HEADS 🦃 This semiremake of *Dr. Jekyll & Mr. Hyde* is loaded with gore and guts. Rated R. 80m. **DIR:** Scott Williams. **1982**

MANFISH 🦃 Probably the only low-budget attempt to cash in on calypso music using Edgar Allan Poe, boats, and fish. 76m. **DIR:** W. Lee Wilder. **CAST:** John Bromfield, Lon Chaney Jr., Victor Jory, Barbara Nichols. **1956**

MANHATTAN BABY 🦃 An archaeologist's daughter is possessed by an Egyptian demon. This film lacks the style and substance of some other Italian horror features. Unrated, but with lots of fake blood. 90m. **DIR:** Lucio Fulci. **CAST:** George Hacker, Christopher Connelly, Martha Taylor. **1992**

MANIA ★★★½ After *The Body Snatcher* (1945), this powerful British melodrama is the best fictional reworking of the scandalous saga of Edinburgh's Dr. Robert Knox and his clandestine pact with grave robbers Burke and Hare. Cushing, as Knox, is dagger-sharp as always, and the direction of Gilling evenly balances the requisite sensationalism with a mature script. B&W; 87m. **DIR:** John Gilling. **CAST:** Peter Cushing, June Laverick, Donald Pleasence. **1959**

MANIAC (1934) ★★ Legendary film about a mad doctor and his even madder assistant knocked 'em dead at the men's clubs and exploitation houses in the 1930s and 1940s, but it seems pretty mild compared to today's color gorefests. Not rated. B&W; 52m. **DIR:** Dwain Esper. **CAST:** Bill Woods, Horace Carpenter. **1934**

MANIAC (1980) 🦃 A plethora of shootings, stabbings, decapitations, and scalpings. Rated R for every excess imaginable. 87m. **DIR:** William Lustig. **CAST:** Joe Spinell, Caroline Munro, Gail Lawrence, Kelly Piper, Tom Savini. **1980**

MANIAC COP 🦃 A deranged killer cop is stalking the streets of New York. Rated R for violence, nudity, and adult situations. 92m.

DIR: William Lustig. **CAST:** Tom Atkins, Bruce Campbell, Richard Roundtree, William Smith, Sheree North. **1988**

MANIAC COP 2 ★★★ This sequel resurrects the homicidal cop out to avenge his unwarranted incarceration in Sing-Sing. Viciously maimed in prison, he sets out to dispatch any responsible party (and a few just for the hell of it). Rated R for violence, profanity, and gore. 90m. **DIR:** William Lustig. **CAST:** Robert Davi, Claudia Christian, Michael Lerner, Bruce Campbell, Clarence Williams III, Leo Rossi. **1990**

MANIAC COP 3: BADGE OF SILENCE ★★★ When a fellow police officer is wounded in action and then framed, the undead Maniac Cop sets out to clear her name, systematically eliminating all those who stand in the way. He seems to be rather inexact in his methods (to be expected from a moldering corpse, we suppose). Rated R for violence. 85m. **DIR:** William Lustig. **CAST:** Robert Davi, Robert Z'dar, Caitlin Dulany, Gretchen Becker, Jackie Earle Haley. **1993**

MANITOU, THE 🦃 Hilariously hokey film about a woman who by some strange trick of chance is growing an ancient Indian out of her neck! Rated PG. 104m. **DIR:** William Girdler. **CAST:** Tony Curtis, Susan Strasberg, Michael Ansara, Ann Sothern, Burgess Meredith, Stella Stevens. **1978**

MAN'S BEST FRIEND (1993) ★★ A genetically engineered guard dog runs amok when a crusading TV reporter, thinking she is rescuing him from vivisection, smuggles him home. Plenty of nasty shocks, with dumb characters doing the usual dumb things and getting their throats ripped out. Rated R for violence. 87m. **DIR:** John Lafia. **CAST:** Ally Sheedy, Lance Henriksen. **1993**

MANSTER, THE ★★½ Peter Dyneley plays a skirt-chasing, alcoholic reporter who falls victim to a Japanese mad scientist's experiments, eventually becoming a two-headed monster. A trash film must-see, with a welcome bonus: it's genuinely creepy in addition to being lurid. It's also got a unique *technical* hook: it's not a dubbed import, but one of the first international coproductions. B&W; 72m. **DIR:** George Breakston, Kenneth Crane. **CAST:** Peter Dyneley, Jane Hylton. **1962**

MARDI GRAS FOR THE DEVIL ★★½ Twenty years after his father was killed, a cop finds the murderer, who rips his victims' hearts out, is after him. Unfortunately, the killer is the devil, who just may be unstoppable. Don't even try to find a plot. Not rated, but contains nudity and graphic sex. 95m. **DIR:** David A. Prior. **CAST:** Robert Davi, Michael Ironside, Lesley-Anne Down, Lydie Denier, Mike Starr, Lillian Lehman, Margaret Avery, John Amos. **1993**

MARK OF CAIN ★★★ Though this film overdoes the eerie music and protracted conversations, it is a compelling tale about twin brothers. A graphic murder sets the plot in motion. A lovely old home surrounded by breathtaking winter scenery is the principal setting. 90m. **DIR:** Bruce Pittman. **CAST:** Robin Crew, Wendy Crewson, August Schellenberg. **1984**

MARK OF THE BEAST, THE 🦃 An anthropologist avenges her twin sister's ritual murder. Ineptly written and acted. Not rated, but contains nudity, profanity, violence, and simulated sex. 88m. **DIR:** Jeff Hathcock. **CAST:** Bo Hopkins, Richard Hill, Sheila Cann. **1990**

MARK OF THE DEVIL 🦃 A sadistic German-British film about an impotent, overachieving witch finder. Notorious as the only movie in history to offer free stomach-distress bags to every patron. Rated R. 96m. **DIR:** Michael Armstrong. **CAST:** Herbert Lom, Udo Kier, Reggie Nalder. **1970**

MARK OF THE DEVIL, PART 2 🦃 After the frolic of the original *Mark of the Devil*, what's left for this sequel to the notorious, medieval witch-hunting saga? Not much. Rated R. 88m. **DIR:** Adrian Hoven. **CAST:** Anton Diffring, Jean-Pierre Zola, Reggie Nalder, Erica Blanc. **1972**

MARK OF THE VAMPIRE ★★★½ MGM's atmospheric version of *Dracula*, utilizing the same director and star. This time, though, it's Count Mora (Bela Lugosi) terrorizing the residents of an old estate along with his ghoulish daughter (Carol Borland). Lionel Barrymore is the believer who tries to put an end to their nocturnal activities. B&W; 61m. **DIR:** Tod Browning. **CAST:** Lionel Barrymore, Elizabeth Allan, Bela Lugosi, Lionel Atwill, Carol Borland. **1935**

MARTIN ★★★ Director George Romero creates a good chiller with a lot of bloodcurdling power about a young man who thinks he's a vampire. This is very well-done. Rated R. 95m. **DIR:** George A. Romero. **CAST:** John Amplas, Lincoln Maazel. **1978**

MARY, MARY, BLOODY MARY ★★ A bloody and grisly film depicting the horror of vampirism and mass murder. A beautiful vampire and artist, Mary (Cristina Ferrare), goes to Mexico to fulfill her need for blood. This film is rated R for nudity, violence, and gore. 95m. **DIR:** Juan Lopez Moctezuma. **CAST:** Cristina Ferrare, David Young, Helena Rojo, John Carradine. **1987**

MASK, THE (1961) 🦃 Low-budget chiller, shot in 3-D, about a psychiatrist who discovers an ancient ritual mask that causes violent hallucinations. B&W; 85m. **DIR:** Julian Roffman. **CAST:** Paul Stevens, Claudette Nevins. **1961**

MASQUE OF THE RED DEATH, THE (1964) ★★★ The combination of Roger Corman, Edgar Allan Poe, and Vincent Price meant first-rate (though low-budget) horror films in the early 1960s. This was one of the best. Price is deliciously villainous. 86m. **DIR:** Roger Corman. **CAST:** Vincent Price, Hazel Court, Jane Asher, David Weston, Patrick Magee. **1964**

MASQUE OF THE RED DEATH (1989) ★★★ A fine rendition of the classic Edgar Allan Poe story of paranoia and death. Producer Roger Corman adds a smattering of sex and violence, but what elevates this film are the sumptuous sets and costumes. Rated R. 83m. **DIR:** Larry Brand. **CAST:** Patrick Macnee, Jeff Osterhage. **1989**

MASSACRE AT CENTRAL HIGH ★★★ Low-budget production has a teenager exacting his own brand of revenge on a tough gang who are making things hard for the students at a local high school. This violent drama has a lot going for it, except for some goofy dialogue. Otherwise, nicely done. Rated R. 85m. **DIR:** Renee Daalder. **CAST:** Andrew Stevens, Kimberly Beck, Derrel Maury, Robert Carradine. **1976**

MAUSOLEUM Housewife wreaks devastation on assorted victims because of a demonic possession. Rated R. 96m. **DIR:** Jerry Zimmerman, Michael Franzese. **CAST:** Bobbie Bresee, Marjoe Gortner. **1983**

MAXIMUM OVERDRIVE Chaotic mess, loosely based on Stephen King's short story "Trucks." 97m. **DIR:** Stephen King. **CAST:** Emilio Estevez, Pat Hingle, Laura Harrington, Yeardley Smith, Ellen McElduff, J. C. Quinn. **1986**

MAZES AND MONSTERS ★★ *Mazes and Monsters,* a TV movie, portrays the lives of several college students whose interest in a Dungeons and Dragons type of role-playing game becomes hazardous. If you're into this sword-and-sorcery stuff, rent *Ladyhawke* instead. 103m. **DIR:** Steven H. Stern. **CAST:** Tom Hanks, Chris Makepeace, Wendy Crewson, David Wallace, Lloyd Bochner, Peter Donat, Louise Sorel, Susan Strasberg. **1982**

MEATEATER, THE An abandoned movie house is haunted by a mad killer. Unrated; the film contains violence and gore. 85m. **DIR:** Derek Savage. **CAST:** Peter M. Spitzer. **1979**

MEDUSA TOUCH, THE ★★★ Born with the power to kill by will, Richard Burton goes completely out of control after someone almost beats him to death. This is a strange, disturbing film. Burton is effective, but Lee Remick is out of place as his psychiatrist. Rated R. 110m. **DIR:** Jack Gold. **CAST:** Richard Burton, Lee Remick, Gordon Jackson, Lino Ventura, Harry Andrews. **1978**

MEPHISTO WALTZ, THE ★★ Satanism and the transfer of souls are at the heart of this needlessly wordy and laughably atmospheric chiller. The thin material—and the viewer's patience—are stretched about twenty minutes too long. Rated R for violence. 108m. **DIR:** Paul Wendkos. **CAST:** Alan Alda, Jacqueline Bisset, Curt Jurgens. **1971**

MERIDIAN ★★★½ This Italian throwback to their horror flicks of the Sixties comes complete with haunted castle and the group of wandering sideshow performers who focus on the beautiful castle mistress (Sherilyn Fenn). The added twist is a Beauty and the Beast theme with British actor Malcolm Jamieson playing twins—one evil, one good. Rated R for nudity, violence, and gore. 90m. **DIR:** Charles Band. **CAST:** Sherilyn Fenn, Malcolm Jamieson, Hilary Mason, Alex Daniels. **1990**

METAMORPHOSIS Scientist performs DNA tests on himself—with predictably disastrous results. Rated R for gratuitous blood, violence, and shadowed nudity. 93m. **DIR:** G. L. Eastman. **CAST:** Gene Le Brock. **1989**

METEOR MONSTER Former Universal horror siren Anne Gwynne shielding her idiot son—who has been changed into a hairy monster by a meteor shower. Original title: *Teenage Monster.* B&W; 65m. **DIR:** Jacques Marquette. **CAST:** Anne Gwynne, Stuart Wade, Gloria Castillo. **1958**

MICROWAVE MASSACRE The title says it all. Rated R for violence, nudity, and profanity. 75m. **DIR:** Wayne Betwick. **CAST:** Jackie Vernon. **1979**

MIDNIGHT (1980) Two college guys and a female hitchhiker end up in a town plagued by a family of Satan worshipers. Rated R for violence and profanity. 91m. **DIR:** John Russo. **CAST:** Lawrence Tierney, Melanie Verlin, John Amplas. **1980**

MIDNIGHT CABARET Satanic time waster. Rated R for nudity and violence. 93m. **DIR:** Pece Dingo. **CAST:** Lisa Hart Carroll, Michael Des Barres, Paul Drake, Laura Harrington. **1988**

MIDNIGHT HOUR ★★★ High school students recite an ancient curse as a Halloween prank and unintentionally release demons from hell and the dead from their graves. Enjoyable cross between *Night of the Living Dead* and *An American Werewolf in London,* helped along by humor and a lively cast. Rated R for gore, violence, and profanity. 87m. **DIR:** Jack Bender. **CAST:** Shari Belafonte-Harper, LeVar Burton, Lee Montgomery, Dick Van Patten, Kevin McCarthy. **1986**

MIDNIGHT KISS ★★ A murderer who removes the blood from his victims is running loose, so a female detective is used as bait and is attacked. She cannot believe that vampires exist, until she becomes one herself. Extremely bad dialogue and horrible acting really take a bite out of this picture. In R-rated and not rated versions; contains profanity, violence, and nudity. 85m. **DIR:** Joel Bender. **CAST:** Michelle Owens, Gregory A. Greer, Michael McMillin, Robert Milano, B. J. Gates, Michael Shawn. **1992**

MIDNIGHT'S CHILD ★★ Run-of-the-mill, made-for-TV thriller with cult member Olivia D'Abo taking a job as a nanny in order to abduct her charge to be the bride of Satan. She doesn't rock the cradle, but manages to stir up the household a bit. Not rated. 89m. **DIR:** Colin Bucksey. **CAST:** Marcy Walker, Cotter Smith, Olivia D'Abo, Elissabeth Moss. **1992**

MIKEY ★★★½ Talk about problem children. Young Mikey, played by Brian Bonsall, has a real attitude problem. When he feels unloved, he murders his parents, and then moves on to the next foster home. This bad seed continues his reign of terror until he falls for the girl next door. Rated R for violence, nudity, and language. 92m. **DIR:** Dennis Dimster-Denk. **CAST:** John Diehl, Lyman Ward, Brian Bonsall, Josie Bissett. **1992**

MILL OF THE STONE WOMEN ★★★ A fascinating one-shot, made in Holland by French and Italian filmmakers, about a mad professor who turns women into statues. Visually innovative, scary, and original. 63m. **DIR:** Giorgio Ferroni. **CAST:** Pierre Brice, Wolfgang Preiss, Scilla Gabel. **1960**

MIND KILLER ★★ A nerdy library worker uncovers a manuscript about the power of positive thinking. Soon he has the power to control minds and to lift objects mentally. But the power has its drawbacks, turning him into a monster. The movie is low-budget, but the filmmakers try hard. Not rated, but contains adult language and situations. 84m. **DIR:** Michael Krueger. **CAST:** Joe McDonald. **1987**

MIND SNATCHERS, THE ★★★ Christopher Walken plays a nihilistic U.S. soldier in West Germany who is admitted to a mental institution. He finds out later the hospital is actually a laboratory where a German scientist is testing a new form of psychological control. Walken's performance is excellent and the idea is an interesting one, but the film moves slowly. Rated PG for violence and profanity. 94m. **DIR:** Bernard Girard. **CAST:** Christopher Walken, Ronny Cox, Joss Ackland, Ralph Meeker. **1972**

MIRROR MIRROR ★★½ An awkward teenage girl uses black magic, gained from an arcane mirror, to avenge herself on her cruel classmates. The film tries hard, but there's no payoff. Rated R for violence and profanity. 105m. **DIR:** Marina Sargenti. **CAST:** Karen Black, Rainbow Harvest, Yvonne De Carlo, William Sanderson. **1990**

MIRROR OF DEATH 🦃 An abused woman takes up voodoo as therapy. Not rated, but has violence, gore, and profanity. 85m. **DIR:** Deryn Warren. **CAST:** Julie Merrill. **1987**

MISERY ★★★★ In this black-comedy thriller, James Caan stars as a popular novelist, who is kept captive by his most ardent fan (Kathy Bates, who scored a best-actress Oscar)—who just happens to be a psychopath. As written by Academy Award–winner William Goldman, it's the best Stephen King adaptation since Reiner's *Stand By Me*. Rated R for profanity and violence. 104m. **DIR:** Rob Reiner. **CAST:** James Caan, Kathy Bates, Richard Farnsworth, Frances Sternhagen, Lauren Bacall. **1990**

MOM 🦃 A television reporter tries to protect his family and the community from his mother, a flesh-eating ghoul. Rated R for violence and profanity. 95m. **DIR:** Patrick Rand. **CAST:** Mark Thomas Miller, Art Evans, Mary McDonough, Jeanne Bates. **1990**

MONGREL 🦃 Young Jerry has dreams in which he turns into a weredog and mutilates innocent people. Unrated, with lots of fake gore. 90m. **DIR:** Robert A. Burns. **CAST:** Terry Evans, Aldo Ray. **1982**

MONKEY SHINES: AN EXPERIMENT IN FEAR ★★★ A virile young man doesn't take too readily to becoming a paralytic overnight, immobilized and wheelchair-bound. Enter Ella, a superintelligent (through the miracle of modern science) monkey who is brought in to help with absolutely everything, including revenge. Genuine amusement—and some decent chills—for aficionados of the genre. Rated R for violence, sex, and terror. 115m. **DIR:** George A. Romero. **CAST:** Jason Beghe, Kate McNeil, John Pankow, Joyce Van Patten. **1988**

MONOLITH MONSTERS, THE ★★★ Fragments of a meteor grow to enormous proportions when exposed to moisture in the Arizona desert. The good script has a novel premise, but B production values hold it back. B&W; 78m. **DIR:** John Sherwood. **CAST:** Grant Williams, Lola Albright, Les Tremayne. **1957**

MONSTER, THE ★★★ Horror buffs who grew up seeing tantalizing stills from this Lon Chaney Sr. vehicle in monster magazines may be disappointed initially to find that it's a comedy. But there is atmosphere to spare, and Chaney—as a mad scientist and the title fiend—is a bonus. B&W; 86m. **DIR:** Roland West. **CAST:** Lon Chaney Sr., Gertrude Olmstead. **1925**

MONSTER CLUB, THE ★★★½ Better-than-average series of horror tales by Ronald Chetwynd-Hayes, linked by a sinister nightclub where the guys 'n' ghouls can hang out. All the stories keep tongue firmly in cheek and involve imaginary creatures of mixed parentage, such as a "shadmonk," borne of a vampire and werewolf. Rated PG for violence. 97m. **DIR:** Roy Ward Baker. **CAST:** Vincent Price, John Carradine, Donald Pleasence, Stuart Whitman, Britt Ekland, Simon Ward. **1981**

MONSTER DOG 🦃 Alice Cooper's music video, shown in the first five minutes of the film, is the only part of this release worth watching. Unrated; the film has violence. 88m. **DIR:** Clyde Anderson. **CAST:** Alice Cooper, Victoria Vera. **1986**

MONSTER FROM GREEN HELL ★★ Giant rubber wasps on the rampage in Africa. Our heroes battle a lethargic script to the death. In an attempt to revive the audience, the last reel of the movie was filmed in color. Big deal. B&W/color; 71m. **DIR:** Kenneth Crane. **CAST:** Jim Davis, Barbara Turner, Eduardo Ciannelli. **1957**

MONSTER FROM THE OCEAN FLOOR, THE A legendary sea monster is discovered off the coast of Mexico. B&W; 64m. **DIR:** Wyott Ordung. **CAST:** Anne Kimball, Stuart Wade, Wyott Ordung. **1954**

MONSTER IN THE CLOSET ★★½ Horror spoof about a music-loving, bloodthirsty mutant that inhabits people's closets. Some jokes bomb, but most hit home. John Carradine is priceless in his short role. Rated PG for profanity and brief nudity. 100m. **DIR:** Bob Dahlin. **CAST:** Donald Grant, Denise Dubarry, Claude Akins, Henry Gibson, John Carradine, Stella Stevens. **1987**

MONSTER MAKER, THE ★★ A scientist conducting experiments in glandular research accidentally injects a pianist with a serum that causes his body to grow abnormally large, especially his hands. Low-budget thriller does very little. B&W; 64m. **DIR:** Sam Newfield. **CAST:** J. Carrol Naish, Ralph Morgan, Wanda McKay, Sam Flint, Glenn Strange. **1944**

MONSTER OF PIEDRAS BLANCAS, THE This monstrosity features a human-shaped sea creature with a penchant for separating humans from their heads. B&W; 71m. **DIR:** Irvin Berwick. **CAST:** Les Tremayne, Forrest Lewis. **1958**

MONSTER ON THE CAMPUS ★★ The blood of a prehistoric fish turns a university professor into a murderous ape-beast. Below-average effort from sci-fi specialist Jack Arnold. B&W; 77m. **DIR:** Jack Arnold. **CAST:** Arthur Franz, Joanna Moore, Judson Pratt, Troy Donahue. **1959**

MONSTER SQUAD, THE ★★★ A group of kids form a club to help combat an infiltration of monsters in their town. What unfolds is a clever mixture of Hollywood sci-fi monster effects and a well-conceived spoof of horror movies, past and present. Rated PG-13 for violence. 82m. **DIR:** Fred Dekker. **CAST:** Andre Gower, Duncan Regehr, Stan Shaw, Tommy Noonan. **1987**

MONSTER WALKS, THE ★★½ This independently produced creaker contains most of the elements popular in old-house horror shows of the late 1920s and early 1930s, including deadly apes, secret passages, gloomy storms, and thoroughly petrified ethnic types. Tolerably funny if you overlook the racist portrayal by Sleep 'n' Eat (Willie Best). B&W; 57m. **DIR:** Frank Strayer. **CAST:** Rex Lease, Vera Reynolds, Mischa Auer, Sheldon Lewis, Willie Best. **1932**

MOON OF THE WOLF ★★ Another ABC Movie of the Week makes it to video. Disappointing yarn of the search for a werewolf on the loose in Louisiana. Good acting by the leads, but there's not enough action or excitement to sustain interest. 73m. **DIR:** Daniel Petrie. **CAST:** David Janssen, Barbara Rush, Bradford Dillman, John Beradino. **1972**

MORTUARY All the standard elements of profanity, gore, nudity, blood, and sex have been thrown together. Rated R. 91m. **DIR:** Howard Avedis. **CAST:** Christopher George, Lynda Day George. **1984**

MOTEL HELL ★★½ "It takes all kinds of critters to make Farmer Vincent Fritters!" Ahem! This above-average horror-comedy stars Rory Calhoun (who overplays grandly) as a nice ol' farmer who has struck gold with his dried pork treats. His secret ingredient happens to be human flesh. Rated R for violence. 102m. **DIR:** Kevin Connor. **CAST:** Rory Calhoun, Nancy Parsons, Paul Linke, Nina Axelrod, Elaine Joyce. **1980**

MOTHER'S DAY This slasher has a twist: a "loving" mother has trained her sons to kidnap and torture innocent victims. Rated R for nudity, profanity, and violence. 98m. **DIR:** Charles Kaufman. **CAST:** Nancy Hendrickson, Deborah Luce. **1980**

MOUNTAINTOP MOTEL MASSACRE A deranged widow accidentally kills her daughter, and she takes her guilt out on the guests who stay at her hotel. Rated R for violence and brief nudity. 95m. **DIR:** Jim McCullough. **CAST:** Bill Thurman, Anna Chappell. **1983**

MULTIPLE MANIACS A homage to gore king Herschell Gordon Lewis's *Two Thousand Maniacs*. Unrated, but the equivalent of an X. B&W; 70m. **DIR:** John Waters. **CAST:** Divine, Mink Stole, Paul Swift, Cookie Mueller, David Lochary, Mary Vivian Pearce, Edith Massey. **1971**

MUMMY, THE (1932) ★★★★ First-rate horror-thriller about an Egyptian mummy returning to life after 3,700 years. Boris Karloff plays the title role in one of his very best performances. Superb makeup, dialogue, atmosphere, and direction make this one an all-time classic. B&W; 73m. **DIR:** Karl Freund. **CAST:** Boris Karloff, Zita Johann, David Manners, Edward Van Sloan. **1932**

MUMMY, THE (1959) ★★★½ Excellent updating of the mummy legend. Christopher Lee is terrifying as the ancient Egyptian awakened from his centuries-old sleep to take revenge on those who desecrated the tomb of his beloved princess. Well-photographed, atmospheric production is high-quality entertainment. 88m. **DIR:** Terence

Fisher. **CAST:** Peter Cushing, Christopher Lee, Yvonne Furneaux. **1959**

MUMMY AND THE CURSE OF THE JACKALS, THE This Las Vegas–based monster mess was unfinished and theatrically unreleased, and remains unwatchable. Not rated. 86m. **DIR:** Oliver Drake. **CAST:** Anthony Eisley, Martina Pons, John Carradine. **1967**

MUMMY'S CURSE, THE ★★½ In Universal's final *Mummy* movie, the monster turns up in the Louisiana bayou, where high priests Peter Coe and Martin Kosleck send him on a rampage. Unoriginal but creepy and fast-paced. B&W; 62m. **DIR:** Leslie Goodwins. **CAST:** Lon Chaney Jr., Peter Coe, Virginia Christine, Martin Kosleck. **1944**

MUMMY'S GHOST, THE ★★½ Universal Pictures' screenwriters used one new wrinkle in each of their otherwise routine *Mummy* chillers. In this one, the gimmick is the climactic fate of the heroine. Also, check out John Carradine as the mad high priest. B&W; 60m. **DIR:** Reginald LeBorg. **CAST:** Lon Chaney Jr., John Carradine, Ramsay Ames, Robert Lowery. **1944**

MUMMY'S HAND, THE ★★★ A pair of carnival barker archaeologists team up with a magician's daughter and go into the grave-robbing business. Their efforts bring them within a bandage width of the shambling mummy and the evil priest who brings the dead back to life. Tom Tyler makes a good mummy and the film has chills. B&W; 67m. **DIR:** Christy Cabanne. **CAST:** Dick Foran, Peggy Moran, Wallace Ford, Eduardo Ciannelli, Tom Tyler, George Zucco. **1940**

MUMMY'S TOMB, THE ★★½ This sequel to *The Mummy's Hand* was Lon Chaney Jr.'s first *Mummy* movie for Universal. Egyptian high priest Turhan Bey revives the Mummy at a New England museum and sends him on a rampage. Note: This 1993 video release is missing the scene in which Mary Gordon is murdered. B&W; 61m. **DIR:** Harold Young. **CAST:** Lon Chaney Jr., Elyse Knox, John Hubbard, Turhan Bey. **1942**

MUNCHIE In this silly sequel, a magical imp (the voice of Dom DeLuise) helps an unpopular youngster through some difficult childhood traumas. Although adults may find little substance here, children may be mildly entertained. Rated PG for violence. 85m. **DIR:** Jim Wynorski. **CAST:** Loni Anderson, Andrew Stevens, Arte Johnson. **1991**

MUNCHIES Harvey Korman has dual parts as an archaeologist who discovers a junk-food-eating creature, and as a con artist who kidnaps the little critters. Rated PG for sexual innuendo. 83m. **DIR:** Bettina Hirsch. **CAST:** Harvey Korman, Charles Stratton, Alix Elias. **1987**

MURDER IN THE RED BARN ★★ Fairly typical Tod Slaughter production for unsophisticated audiences, dealing with the exploits of a lecherous (and murderous) squire. B&W; 67m. **DIR:** Milton Rosmer. **CAST:** Tod Slaughter, Sophie Stewart. **1936**

MURDER ON LINE ONE ★★ Standard horror flick set in London. This time, the murderer films the killings and gets his kicks rewatching his work—transgressor of the VCR age. Rated R for violence and bloodshed. 103m. **DIR:** Anders Palm. **CAST:** Emma Jacobs, Peter Blake. **1990**

MURDERS IN THE RUE MORGUE (1932) ★★½ Very little of Edgar Allan Poe's original story is evident in this muddled and perverse story of Dr. Mirakle and his efforts to mate his companion (an ape) with the leading lady of the film. Bela Lugosi as the evil doctor grimaces often and wears a black cape. B&W; 92m. **DIR:** Robert Florey. **CAST:** Bela Lugosi, Sidney Fox, Leon Ames, Arlene Francis, Noble Johnson. **1932**

MURDERS IN THE RUE MORGUE (1971) ★★ Members of a horror theatre troupe in nineteenth-century Paris are dispatched systematically by a mysterious fiend. Good cast, nice atmosphere, but confusing and altogether too artsy for its own good. Rated PG. 87m. **DIR:** Gordon Hessler. **CAST:** Jason Robards Jr., Herbert Lom, Michael Dunn, Lilli Palmer, Christine Kaufmann, Adolfo Celi. **1971**

MURDERS IN THE ZOO ★★★ Wild, pre-Code horror from Paramount. Lionel Atwill is a zookeeper who's also a jealous husband. In the first scene, set in the Asian jungle, he sews his wife's lover's mouth shut, leaving him to die in the jungle. Back home, he dumps one victim into a crocodile pool, and kills another with snake venom. Lurid fun—not for the kiddies, even now. B&W; 64m. **DIR:** A. Edward Sutherland. **CAST:** Lionel Atwill, Charlie Ruggles, Randolph Scott, Gail Patrick, John Lodge, Kathleen Burke. **1933**

MUTANT Idiocy. Rated R for violence. 100m. **DIR:** John "Bud" Cardos. **CAST:** Bo Hopkins, Wings Hauser, Jennifer Warren, Cary Guffey, Lee Montgomery. **1983**

MUTILATOR, THE More gore galore as a psycho kills off his sons' friends when they visit the family island. Rated R. 86m. **DIR:** Buddy Cooper. **CAST:** Matt Mitler. **1984**

MY BLOODY VALENTINE ★★ Candy boxes stuffed with bloody human hearts signal the return of a legendary murderous coal miner to Valentine Bluffs. This film provides a few doses of excitement and a tidal wave of killings. Rated R. 91m. **DIR:** George Mihalka. **CAST:** Paul Kelman, Lori Hallier, Neil Affleck. **1981**

MY SISTER, MY LOVE ★★★ Offbeat story concerns two loving, but unbalanced, sisters who eliminate anyone who tries to come between them. Good acting all around and a perverse sense of style are just two elements that make this movie click. Alternate title—*The Mafu Cage*. Rated R. 99m. **DIR:** Karen Arthur. **CAST:** Carol Kane, Lee Grant, Will Geer, James Olson. **1979**

MYSTERY OF THE WAX MUSEUM ★★★ Dated but interesting tale of a crippled, crazed sculptor (the ever-dependable Lionel Atwill) who murders people and displays them in his museum as his own wax creations. Humorous subplot really curbs the attention, but stick with it. One of the earliest color films, it is often shown on television in black and white. 77m. **DIR:** Michael Curtiz. **CAST:** Lionel Atwill, Fay Wray, Glenda Farrell, Frank McHugh. **1933**

NAVY VS. THE NIGHT MONSTERS, THE Homicidal plants scheme to take over the world. 90m. **DIR:** Michael Hoey. **CAST:** Mamie Van Doren, Anthony Eisley, Pamela Mason, Bobby Van. **1966**

NEAR DARK ★★★½ A stylish story of nomadic vampires. A girl takes a fancy to a young stud and turns him into a vampire, forcing him to join the macabre family. His problem is that he can't bring himself to make his first kill. It's the character development and acting that make this movie worthwhile. Rated R for violence and language. 95m. **DIR:** Kathryn Bigelow. **CAST:** Adrian Pasdar, Jenny Wright, Tim Thomerson, Jenette Goldstein, Lance Henriksen, Bill Paxton. **1987**

NECROMANCER ★★ A sorceress possesses a young woman, using her to kill men and steal their life forces. Violence and bloodshed abound unfortunately, but not much suspense. Rated R for graphic violence and nudity. 88m. **DIR:** Dusty Nelson. **CAST:** Elizabeth Cayton, Russ Tamblyn. **1988**

NECROPOLIS A 300-year-old witch, looking pretty good for her age, is resurrected in New York City. Rated R. 96m. **DIR:** Bruce Hickey. **CAST:** Lee Anne Baker. **1987**

NEEDFUL THINGS ★★★★ In the small town of Castle Rock, Maine, a mysterious stranger opens a curio shop that seems to have something for everyone. Just one problem: The owner is actually the Devil, and he only trades for souls. He turns the locals against each other, setting off a chain reaction of murder and mayhem that culminates in an explosive finale between evil (a devilish Max von Sydow) and the law, played by Ed Harris. Viciously tongue-in-cheek. Rated R for strong violence and adult language. 113m. **DIR:** Fraser Heston. **CAST:** Max von Sydow, Ed Harris, Bonnie Bedelia, J. T. Walsh, Amanda Plummer. **1993**

NEON MANIACS ★★½ Ancient evil beings are released into present-day New York, killing everyone in their path. Three teenagers learn the demons' weakness and go on a crusade to destroy them. With good special effects, original creatures, and lots of scares, this film is worth a look. Rated R for violence. 90m. **DIR:** Joseph Mangine. **CAST:** Allan Hayes, Leilani Sarelle. **1985**

NEST, THE (1988) ★★★½ A skin-rippling tale of a genetic experiment gone awry. Flesh-eating cockroaches are on the verge of overrunning a small island and they are not about to let anything stand in their way. What's worse, they're mutating into a form of whatever they consume. Special effects are above par and definitely not for the squeamish. Rated R. 88m. **DIR:** Terence H. Winkless. **CAST:** Robert Lansing, Lisa Langlois, Franc Luz, Stephen Davies, Nancy Morgan. **1988**

NESTING, THE ★★ Tolerable haunted-house film about a writer (Robin Groves) who rents a house in the country so as to get some peace and quiet. But guess what. You got it—the house is plagued with undead spirits. Rated R for nudity and violence. 104m. **DIR:** Armand Weston. **CAST:** Robin Groves, Christopher Loomis, John Carradine, Gloria Grahame. **1980**

NETHERWORLD ★★★ The heir to a Louisiana mansion is asked to bring his father back from the dead as a condition of the deed. The film creates a sort of ornithological voodooist mythology. Unrated, but has profanity and brief nudity. 87m. **DIR:** David Schmoeller. **CAST:** Michael Bendetti, Denise Gentile, Anjanette Comer. **1991**

NEW KIDS, THE Two easygoing kids try to make friends at a new high school. Their attempt is thwarted by the town bully. Rated R for profanity, nudity, and violence. 96m. **DIR:** Sean S. Cunningham. **CAST:** Shannon Presby, Lori Loughlin, James Spader. **1985**

NEW YEAR'S EVIL A crazy killer stalks victims at a televised New Year's Eve party. Rated R for all the usual reasons. 90m. **DIR:** Emmett Alston. **CAST:** Roz Kelly, Kip Niven, Chris Wallace. **1980**

NEW YORK RIPPER, THE Explicitly gory—yet dull—Italian horror about a sex murderer. R rating (four minutes were cut to avoid an X). 88m. **DIR:** Lucio Fulci. **CAST:** Jack Hedley. **1982**

NEXT OF KIN (1987) Boring Australian suspense film has a young heiress inheriting her mother's mansion. Not rated; contains nudity, simulated sex, and violence. 90m. **DIR:** Tony Williams. **CAST:** Jackie Kerin, John Jarratt. **1987**

NICK KNIGHT ★★★ Pilot movie for the TV series stars Rick Springfield as a vampire turned detective for the Los Angeles Police Department. 94m. **DIR:** Farhad Mann. **CAST:** Rick Springfield, John Kapelos, Robert Harper, Richard Fancy, Laura Johnson, Michael Nader. **1991**

NIGHT ANGEL ★★ Predictable horror fare about a soul-searching seductress raising some hell when she poses as a fashion model. She violently dispatches plenty of weak-willed men. Rated R for nudity. 90m. **DIR:** Dominique Othenin-Girard. **CAST:** Isa Andersen, Linden Ashby, Debra Feuer, Karen Black. **1990**

NIGHT BREED ★★ Great monsters, fantastic makeup effects, exploding action—and very little plot. Horror writer Clive Barker's second turn as director lacks cohesion as it runs through the Canadian wilderness in search of a serial killer and an ancient tribe of monsters called the Night Breed. Rated R for violence. 97m. **DIR:** Clive Barker. **CAST:** Craig Sheffer, David Cronenberg, Charles Haid. **1989**

NIGHT CREATURE 🦃 Grade-Z film has Donald Pleasence playing a half-crazed adventurer who captures a killer leopard and brings the creature to his private island. Rated PG. 83m. **DIR:** Lee Madden. **CAST:** Donald Pleasence, Nancy Kwan, Ross Hagen. **1978**

NIGHT GALLERY ★★★ Pilot for the TV series. Three tales of terror by Rod Serling told with style and flair. Segment one is the best, with Roddy McDowall eager to get his hands on an inheritance. Segment two features Joan Crawford as a blind woman with a yearning to see. Segment three, involving a paranoid war fugitive, is the least of the three. 98m. **DIR:** Boris Sagal, Steven Spielberg, Barry Shear. **CAST:** Roddy McDowall, Joan Crawford, Richard Kiley. **1969**

NIGHT LIFE ★★★½ Four teenage corpses come back to life to haunt a young mortuary employee in this funny zombie picture. The corpses just want to party, and that they do until Scott Grimes can do away with them in grisly fashion. Rated R for violence, profanity, and gore. 92m. **DIR:** David Acomba. **CAST:** Scott Grimes, Cheryl Pollak, Anthony Geary, Alan Blumenfeld, John Astin. **1990**

NIGHT OF BLOODY HORROR 🦃 When a young man is released from a mental institution, a series of gory murders begins. Not rated. 89m. **DIR:** Joy N. Houck Jr. **CAST:** Gerald McRaney. **1969**

NIGHT OF DARK SHADOWS ★★ The new owner of a spooky mansion is haunted by his ancestors. Barnabas Collins is nowhere to be found in this second film based on the original *Dark Shadows* TV series. Given that the series itself is on video, there's no reason to bother with this tired leftover. Rated PG. 97m. **DIR:** Dan Curtis. **CAST:** David Selby, Lara Parker, Kate Jackson, Grayson Hall. **1971**

NIGHT OF THE BLOODY APES 🦃 A doctor revives his son with a heart transplant from a gorilla. 82m. **DIR:** René Cardona Sr. **CAST:** José Elias Moreno. **1968**

NIGHT OF THE BLOODY TRANSPLANT 🦃 Not to be confused with *Night of the Bloody Apes*—although both films resort to open-heart surgery footage to wake up the audience—this is an amateurish soap opera about a renegade surgeon. Rated R. 90m. **DIR:** David W. Hanson. **CAST:** Dick Grimm. **1986**

NIGHT OF THE COBRA WOMAN ★★ Former underground filmmaker Andrew Meyer (not to be confused with the utterly untalented Andy Milligan) coauthored and directed this sleazy, often boring, but nonetheless watchable drive-in horror flick, shot in the Philippines for Roger Corman. Rated R. 85m. **DIR:** Andrew Meyer. **CAST:** Marlene Clark, Joy Bang. **1972**

NIGHT OF THE CREEPS ★★★½ A film derived from virtually every horror movie ever made, this does a wonderful job paying homage to the genre. The story involves an alien organism that lands on Earth and immediately infects someone. Some thirty years later, when this contaminated individual is accidentally released, he wanders into a college town spreading these organisms in some rather disgusting ways. Not rated, but contains violence. 89m. **DIR:** Fred Dekker. **CAST:** Jason Lively, Steve Marchall, Jill Whitlow, Tom Atkins, Dick Miller. **1986**

NIGHT OF THE DEATH CULT ★★½ This is one of a popular series of Spanish horror movies concerning the Templars, blind medieval priests who rise from the dead when their tombs are violated. The film contains nudity, violence, and gore, though as a whole it is more subdued than American zombie movies. 85m. **DIR:** Amando de Ossorio. **CAST:** Victor Petit, Maria Kosti. **1975**

NIGHT OF THE DEMON 🦃 This is a boring little bomb of a movie with an intriguing title and nothing else. 97m. **DIR:** James C. Wasson. **CAST:** Michael Cutt, Jay Allen. **1983**

NIGHT OF THE DEMONS ★★★ A great creaky-house movie about a group of teenagers who hold a séance in an abandoned mortuary. What they conjure up from the dead is more than they bargained for. Rated R for violence and nudity. 90m. **DIR:** Kevin S. Tenney. **CAST:** William Gallo. **1989**

NIGHT OF THE DEVILS 🦃 Tepid modern-vampire melodrama. It's based on the same Tolstoy story that inspired the Boris Karloff sequence in *Black Sabbath*. No rating, but contains moderate violence and sex. English dubbed. 82m. **DIR:** Giorgio Ferroni. **CAST:** Gianni Garko, Agostina Belli, Mark Roberts. **1972**

NIGHT OF THE GHOULS ★★ From the director of *Plan 9 from Outer Space* and *Glen or Glenda* comes a film so bad it was never released. Not nearly as enjoyably bad as Edward Wood's other work, but definitely worth a look for movie buffs. For the record, two young innocents stumble upon a haunted house (filled with some very tiresome bad actors). B&W; 75m. **DIR:** Edward D. Wood Jr. **CAST:** Kenne Duncan, Criswell. **1958**

NIGHT OF THE HOWLING BEAST ★★ The Wolfman meets the Abominable Snowman. Paul Naschy is the horror king of Spain, but after his movies have been chopped up and dubbed for American release, it's pretty hard to see why. Unrated, but the equivalent of a light R. 87m. **DIR:** Miguel Iglesias Bonns. **CAST:** Paul Naschy. **1975**

NIGHT OF THE LIVING DEAD (1968) ★★★★ This gruesome low-budget horror film still packs a punch for those who like to be frightened out of their wits. It is an unrelenting shockfest laced with touches of black humor that deserves its cult status. B&W; 96m. **DIR:** George A. Romero. **CAST:** Duane Jones, Judith O'Dea, Keith Wayne. **1968**

NIGHT OF THE LIVING DEAD (1990) ★★★½ This remake, directed by makeup master Tom Savini and produced by George Romero, combines all the terror of the 1968 original with 1990 special effects. Surprisingly, Savini, known for his realistic effects in *Dawn of the Dead* and *Friday the 13th*, doesn't pile the blood on. Rated R for violence, profanity, and gore. 96m. **DIR:** Tom Savini. **CAST:** Tony Todd. **1990**

NIGHT OF THE WALKING DEAD 🦃 Dull medieval horror-drama about a silver-haired vampire nobleman and his buxom female victims. Made in Spain, and poorly dubbed into English. No rating, but contains gore. 84m. **DIR:** Leon Klimovsky. **CAST:** Emma Cohen, Carlos Ballesteros. **1975**

NIGHT OF THE ZOMBIES 🦃 It's just one long cannibal feast. Rated R for violence and gore. 101m. **DIR:** Vincent Dawn. **CAST:** Frank Garfield, Margie Newton. **1983**

NIGHT SCREAMS 🦃 Three escaped convicts crash a teenage party. Not rated, but contains graphic violence and nudity. 85m. **DIR:** Allen Plone. **CAST:** Janette Allyson Caldwell, Joe Manno, Ron Thomas. **1986**

NIGHT STALKER, THE (1971) ★★★★ A superb made-for-television chiller about a modern-day vampire stalking the streets of Las Vegas. Richard Matheson's teleplay is tight and suspenseful, with Darren McGavin fine as the intrepid reporter on the bloodsucker's trail. 73m. **DIR:** John Llewellyn Moxey. **CAST:** Darren McGavin, Carol Lynley, Claude Akins. **1971**

NIGHT STALKER, THE (1986) ★★★ A Vietnam veteran hits the street, brutally murdering prostitutes. An over-the-hill, alcoholic police detective pursues him. The acting is uneven, but the suspense is solid. Worth a look. Rated R for nudity, profanity, and graphic violence. 91m. **DIR:** Max Kleven. **CAST:** Charles Napier, Michelle Reese, Joe Gian, Leka Carlin. **1986**

NIGHT TO DISMEMBER, A ★★ A must for bad-movie buffs, this insanely disjointed slasher movie features almost no dialogue, actors whose hairstyles and clothes change in mid-scene, and a tacked-on narration desperately trying to make sense of it all. Unrated, but with nudity and hilariously bad gore effects. 70m. **DIR:** Doris Wishman. **CAST:** Samantha Fox. **1983**

NIGHT TRAIN TO TERROR ★★ Segments from three bad horror movies are condensed (which improves them considerably) and introduced by actors playing God and Satan. It's still pretty bad, but the edited stories are fast-moving and sleazily entertaining. See if you can recognize Richard "Bull" Moll (in two segments) with his hair. Rated R for nudity, graphic violence, and gore. 93m. **DIR:** John Carr, Jay Schlossberg-Cohen. **CAST:** Cameron Mitchell, John Phillip Law, Marc Lawrence, Richard Moll. **1985**

NIGHT WARNING ★★ As in many gory movies, the victims and near victims have a convenient and unbelievable way of hanging around despite clear indications they are about to get it. Consequently, *Night Warning*, in spite of good performances, is an unremarkable splatter film. Rated R for violence. 96m. **DIR:** William Asher. **CAST:** Jimmy McNichol, Bo Svenson, Susan Tyrrell. **1982**

NIGHT WATCH ★★ In this so-so suspense-thriller, Elizabeth Taylor stars as a wealthy widow recovering from a nervous breakdown. From her window, she seems to witness a number of ghoulish goings-on. But does she? The operative phrase here after a while is "Who cares?" Rated PG. 98m. **DIR:** Brian G. Hutton. **CAST:** Elizabeth Taylor, Laurence Harvey, Billie Whitelaw, Robert Lang, Tony Britton. **1973**

NIGHTCOMERS, THE ★★½ Strange prequel to *The Turn of the Screw*, this uneven effort contains some fine acting and boasts some truly eerie scenes, but is hampered by Michael Winner's loose direction and a nebulous story line. Marlon Brando is in good form as the mysterious catalyst, but this murky melodrama still lacks the solid story and cohesiveness that could have made it a true chiller. Rated R. 96m. **DIR:** Michael Winner. **CAST:** Marlon Brando, Stephanie Beacham, Thora Hird, Harry Andrews. **1971**

NIGHTLIFE ★★★½ A doctor finds a beautiful patient with a strange taste for blood in this funny and scary horror show, made for cable. Keith Szarabajka, as a doctor, steals the show by being both spooky and comically warped. Great fun. 90m. **DIR:** Daniel Taplitz. **CAST:** Maryam D'Abo, Ben Cross, Keith Szarabajka. **1989**

NIGHTMARE AT NOON 🦃 A group of renegade scientists testing a germ-warfare virus. Rated R for violence. 96m. **DIR:** Nico Mastorakis. **CAST:** Wings Hauser, Bo Hopkins, George Kennedy, Brion James. **1987**

NIGHTMARE CASTLE ★★ Barbara Steele plays two roles in this lurid Italian shocker about a faithless wife and the gory revenge exacted by her jealous husband. Routine theatrics, atmospherically photographed—and cut by fifteen minutes for its U.S. release. B&W; 90m. **DIR:** Mario Caiano. **CAST:** Barbara Steele, Paul Muller, Helga Line. **1965**

NIGHTMARE CIRCUS ★★ A young man who was abused as a child abducts women and chains them in the family barn. This graphically violent low-budget R-rater was the first theatrical feature by the now highly respected director Alan Rudolph. Also titled *Barn of the Living Dead* and *Terror Circus*. 86m. **DIR:** Alan Rudolph. **CAST:** Andrew Prine, Sherry Alberoni. **1973**

NIGHTMARE HOUSE 🦃 Previously available on video under its original title *Scream, Baby, Scream*, the movie is rated R for violence and brief nudity. 83m. **DIR:** Joseph Adler. **CAST:** Ross Harris. **1969**

NIGHTMARE IN BLOOD ★★ A film that's fun for genre fans only. A horror-movie star appears at a horror convention that people are dying to get into. The twist is he isn't just playing a vampire in his films; he *is* one. The cassette box says "filmed in and around picturesque San Francisco," and most viewers will think that's the best thing about it. Not rated, but contains mild bloodletting. 92m. **DIR:** John Stanley. **CAST:** Jerry Walter, Barrie Youngfellow, Kerwin Mathews. **1975**

NIGHTMARE IN WAX (CRIMES IN THE WAX MUSEUM) 🦃 Cameron Mitchell plays a disfigured ex–makeup man running a wax museum in Hollywood. Rated PG. 91m. **DIR:** Bud Townsend. **CAST:** Cameron Mitchell, Anne Helm, Scott Brady. **1969**

NIGHTMARE ON ELM STREET, A ★★★★ Wes Craven directed this clever shocker about a group of teenagers afflicted with the same bad dreams. Horror movie buffs, take note. Rated R for nudity, violence, and profanity. 91m. **DIR:** Wes Craven. **CAST:** John Saxon, Ronee Blakley, Heather Langenkamp, Robert Englund. **1985**

NIGHTMARE ON ELM STREET 2, A: FREDDY'S REVENGE 🦃 Another teen exploitation film. Rated R for nudity, language, and gore. 83m. **DIR:** Jack Sholder. **CAST:** Mark Patton, Kim Myers, Clu Gulager, Hope Lange. **1985**

NIGHTMARE ON ELM STREET 3, A: THE DREAM WARRIORS 🦃 Freddy is at it again. Rated R. 97m. **DIR:** Chuck Russell. **CAST:** Robert Englund, Heather Langenkamp, Patricia Arquette, Craig Wasson. **1987**

NIGHTMARE ON ELM STREET 4, A: THE DREAM MASTER ★★ America's favorite child-molesting burn victim Freddy Krueger (Robert Englund) is back in this fourth installment of the hit series. Freddy's favorite pastime, killing teenagers in their dreams, is played to the hilt with fantastic special effects. Rated R for violence and gore. 97m. **DIR:** Renny Harlin. **CAST:** Robert Englund, Lisa Wilcox. **1988**

NIGHTMARE ON ELM STREET 5: THE DREAM CHILD ★★★ This fifth installment in the series is a wild ride filled with gruesome makeup effects and mind-blowing visuals. Never mind that Freddy's return is not explained. (He was supposedly killed in part 4). This time he enters the dreams of the heroine's unborn child, attempting to place the souls of those he kills into the fetus. Rated R for violence, profanity, and plenty o' gore. 91m. **DIR:** Stephen Hopkins. **CAST:** Robert Englund, Lisa Wilcox. **1989**

NIGHTMARE ON THE 13TH FLOOR 🦃 Haunted hotel chiller. This made-for-cable movie has minimal violence. Rated PG-13. 85m. **DIR:** Walter Grauman. **CAST:** Michele Greene, Louise Fletcher, James Brolin, John Karlen. **1990**

NIGHTMARE SISTERS 🦃 The spirit of a succubus possesses three straitlaced sorority girls. Rated R for nudity and simulated sex. 83m. **DIR:** David DeCoteau. **CAST:** Linnea Quigley. **1988**

NIGHTMARE WEEKEND 🦃 An incomprehensible film about a scientist who invents a computer system that can transform solid inorganic objects into deadly weapons. Rated R for graphic violence and nudity. 88m. **DIR:** H. Sala. **CAST:** Debbie Laster, Debra Hunter, Lori Lewis. **1985**

NIGHTMARES ★★ Four everyday situations are twisted into tales of terror in this mostly mediocre horror film in the style of *Twilight Zone–the Movie* and *Creepshow*. Rated R for violence and profanity. 99m. **DIR:** Joseph Sargent. **CAST:** Cristina Raines, Emilio Estevez, Lance Henriksen. **1983**

NIGHTWING 🦃 Absolutely laughable tale, derived from an abysmal Martin Cruz Smith novel, about a flock (herd? pack?) of vampire bats. Rated PG. 105m. **DIR:** Arthur Hiller. **CAST:** David Warner, Kathryn Harrold, Nick Mancuso, Strother Martin. **1979**

976-EVIL ★★★½ Actor Robert Englund makes his directorial debut with this tale of a wimpish teenager who slowly becomes possessed by a 976 "Horrorscope" number. Englund gives his film a genuinely eerie feel without missing his chance to throw in a little comedy. Rated R for violence. 92m. **DIR:** Robert Englund. **CAST:** Jim Metzler, Stephen Geoffreys, Sandy Dennis, Robert Picardo. **1989**

976-EVIL II: THE ASTRAL FACTOR ★★ An occult-oriented telephone service assists a murderer in astrally projecting himself from jail so that he may continue his killing spree. A fair sequel. Rated R for graphic violence, profanity, and nudity. 93m. **DIR:** Jim Wynorski. **CAST:** Rene Assa, Brigitte Nielsen, Patrick O'Bryan. **1991**

NOMADS ★★★ In this thought-provoking and chilling shocker, Pierce Brosnan is a French anthropologist who discovers a secret society of malevolent ghosts living in modern-day Los Angeles. In doing so, he incurs their wrath and endangers the life of a doctor (Lesley-Anne Down). Rated R for profanity, nudity, and violence. 95m. **DIR:** John McTiernan. **CAST:** Lesley-Anne Down, Pierce Brosnan, Adam Ant, Mary Woronov. **1986**

NOT OF THIS EARTH ★★★ Purposely trashy remake of a Roger Corman sci-fi classic from the Fifties. Plenty of action, campy comedy, and sex to hold your interest. Traci Lords is a private nurse assigned to administer blood transfusions to a mysterious, wealthy patient. Once she starts nosing around, the fun starts. Rated R for nudity, simulated sex, and violence. 82m. **DIR:** Jim Wynorski. **CAST:** Traci Lords, Arthur Roberts. **1988**

OASIS OF THE ZOMBIES 🦃 Awful chopped-up version of a European movie. Zombies guard a Nazi treasure buried in the desert. Dubbed. Unrated; contains violence. 94m. **DIR:** Jess Franco. **CAST:** Manuel Gelin, Eduardo Fajardo, Lina Romay, Antonio Mayans. **1982**

OBLONG BOX, THE ★★ This little gothic horror is nothing to shiver about. Although it is taken from an Edgar Allan Poe short story, it can't escape the clichés of its genre: grave robbers, screaming women (with close-up shots of their widening eyes), lots of cleavage, and of course, the hero's bride to be, who is unaware of her betrothed's wrongdoings. Sound familiar? Rated R (but more like a PG by today's standards) for violence. 91m. **DIR:** Gordon Hessler. **CAST:** Vincent Price, Christopher Lee, Rupert Davies, Sally Geeson. **1969**

OCTAMAN ★★ Dull low-budget effort with a group of vacationers under attack by a funny-looking walking octopus-man created by a very young Rick Baker, who has since gone on to much bigger and better things. Rated PG for mild violence. 90m. **DIR:** Harry Essex. **CAST:** Kerwin Mathews, Pier Angeli, Jeff Morrow. **1971**

OF UNKNOWN ORIGIN ★★½ Flashes of unintentional humor enliven this shocker, about a suburban family terrorized in their home by a monstrous rat. Contains some inventive photography and effects, but mediocre acting and forgettable music. Bring on the exterminator! Rated R. 88m. **DIR:** George Pan Cosmatos. **CAST:** Peter Weller, Jennifer Dale, Lawrence Dane. **1983**

OFFERINGS 🦃 *Halloween* clone about a psychotic teen who escapes from a mental hospital and pursues cannibalistic activities. Rated R for gore. 92m. **DIR:** Christopher Reynolds. **CAST:** Loretta Leigh Bowman, Elizabeth Greene, G. Michael Smith, Jerry Brewer. **1989**

OFFSPRING, THE ★★★★ Four scary and original short stories are tied together by the narration of an old man (Vincent Price) who lives in a small town that seems to make people kill. Well written and acted, with decent special effects. Horror fans will love this. Rated R for violence and brief nudity. 99m. **DIR:** Jeff Burr. **CAST:** Vincent Price, Clu Gulager, Terry Kiser. **1986**

OLD DARK HOUSE, THE ★★ This messy, comedy-cum-chills rehash of the 1932 James Whale horror classic (which is still unavailable except in bootleg video versions) demonstrates mainly that William Castle, who directed the film, and Hammer Films, which coproduced it, were unsuited to collaboration. 86m. **DIR:** William Castle. **CAST:** Tom Poston, Robert Morley, Janette Scott, Joyce Grenfell, Mervyn Johns. **1963**

OMEN, THE ★★★★ This, first of a series of movies about the return to Earth of the devil, is a real chiller. In the form of a young boy, Damien, Satan sets about reestablishing his rule over man. A series of bizarre deaths points to the boy. Rated R. 111m. **DIR:** Richard Donner. **CAST:** Gregory Peck, Lee Remick, Billie Whitelaw, David Warner. **1976**

OMEN IV: THE AWAKENING 🦃 Made-for-TV continuation finds the devil continuing his reign of terror. 97m. **DIR:** Jorge Montesi, Dominique Othenin-Girard. **CAST:** Michael Lerner, Faye Grant, Michael Woods. **1992**

ONE DARK NIGHT ★★½ Meg Tilly and Adam "Batman" West star in this story of a young woman (Tilly) who is menaced by an energy-draining ghost. Rated R. 89m. **DIR:** Tom McLoughlin. **CAST:** Meg Tilly, Adam West, Robin Evans, Elizabeth Daily. **1983**

OPEN HOUSE 🦃 This slasher movie features some particularly repellent and sadistic murders, along with nudity and sexual situations. A definite R. 95m. **DIR:** Jag Mundhra. **CAST:** Joseph Bottoms, Adrienne Barbeau, Rudy Ramos, Tiffany Bolling. **1987**

ORACLE, THE ★★ A woman discovers that the last occupant of her new apartment was a murder victim. Reaching out from beyond the grave, he tries to force her to avenge his death. Better than average for this sort of low-budget chiller, with some effective shocks and a few interesting plot twists. Rated R for gore. 94m. **DIR:** Roberta

Findlay. **CAST:** Caroline Capers Powers, Roger Neil. 1985

ORCA ★★★ Where *Jaws* was an exaggerated horror story, *Orca* is based on the tragic truth. Motivated by profit, Richard Harris and his crew go out with a huge net and find a family of whales. He misses the male and harpoons the female, who dies and aborts, leaving her huge mate to wreak havoc on the tiny seaport. Rated PG. 92m. **DIR:** Michael Anderson. **CAST:** Richard Harris, Keenan Wynn, Will Sampson, Bo Derek, Robert Carradine, Charlotte Rampling. 1977

ORGY OF THE DEAD There's no plot to speak of, as the "Emperor of the Dead" (Criswell) holds court in a graveyard. Not rated. 82m. **DIR:** A. C. Stephen. **CAST:** Criswell, Pat Barringer, William Bates. 1965

OTHER, THE ★★★½ Screenwriter Thomas Tryon, adapting his bestselling novel, raises plenty of goose bumps. This supernatural tale of good and evil, as personified by twin brothers, creates a genuinely eerie mood. Legendary acting coach Uta Hagen contributes a compelling performance. Director Robert Mulligan, keeping the emphasis on characterizations, never allows the suspense to lag. 100m. **DIR:** Robert Mulligan. **CAST:** Uta Hagen, Diana Muldaur, Chris Udvarnoky, Martin Udvarnoky, John Ritter. 1972

OTHER HELL, THE An Italian film about a convent inhabited by the devil. Rated R for graphic violence and nudity. 88m. **DIR:** Stephan Oblowsky. **CAST:** Franca Stoppi, Carlo De Meio. 1980

OUT OF THE DARK Contrived thriller about a psychotic killer who systematically eliminates beautiful women who work at an erotic phone service. Rated R for profanity, nudity, and violence. 89m. **DIR:** Michael Schroeder. **CAST:** Cameron Dye, Karen Black, Bud Cort, Divine, Paul Bartel. 1989

OUTING, THE A teenage girl is possessed by a demon and convinces her friends to spend the night in her father's museum. Not rated but contains brief nudity and graphic violence. 87m. **DIR:** Tom Daley. **CAST:** Deborah Winters, James Huston, Danny D. Daniels. 1986

OVEREXPOSED ★★ Gorefest surrounds a beautiful soap opera star (Catherine Oxenberg) when the people closest to her are killed one after another. Rated R for nudity, violence, and gore. 80m. **DIR:** Larry Brand. **CAST:** Catherine Oxenberg, David Naughton, Jennifer Edwards, Karen Black. 1990

PACK, THE ★★ Slightly above-average horror film about a pack of dogs that goes wild and tries to kill two families. Rated R. 99m. **DIR:** Robert Clouse. **CAST:** Joe Don Baker, Hope Alexander Willis, Richard B. Shull, R. G. Armstrong. 1977

PALE BLOOD ★★ A suave vampire tries to catch the psycho giving his breed a bad name. Usual vampire exploitation flick, this bloodsucker begins on a creepy note but falters under a lousy script and a lopsided amount of violence against women. Rated R for profanity, violence, and nudity. 93m. **DIR:** Dachin Hsu. **CAST:** George Chakiris, Wings Hauser, Pamela Ludwig. 1990

PAPERHOUSE ★★★★ In this original film from England, a lonely, misunderstood 11-year-old girl (Charlotte Burke) begins retreating into a fantasy world. Her world turns nightmarish when it starts to take over her dreams and a flu-like disease keeps making her faint. Visually impressive, well-acted, and intelligent fare. Rated PG-13 for violence. 94m. **DIR:** Bernard Rose. **CAST:** Charlotte Burke, Glenne Headly, Ben Cross. 1989

PARASITE ★★½ If director Charles Band intended a film that would sicken its audience, he succeeded. Memorable scenes include parasites bursting through the stomach of one victim and the face of another. Rated R. 85m. **DIR:** Charles Band. **CAST:** Robert Glaudini, Demi Moore, Luca Bercovici, Vivian Blaine, Tom Villard. 1982

PATRICK ★★½ This film revolves around Patrick, who has been in a coma for four years. He is confined to a hospital, but after a new nurse comes to work on his floor he begins to exhibit psychic powers. Some violence, but nothing extremely bloody. Rated PG. 96m. **DIR:** Richard Franklin. **CAST:** Susan Penhaligon, Robert Helpmann. 1979

PENPAL MURDERS A man's pen pal comes for a visit and unfortunately waits until the end of this stinker to kill the cast. Not rated. 118m. **DIR:** Steve Postal. **CAST:** Jay Brockman, Jennifer Tuck, Angela Shepard. 1991

PEOPLE UNDER THE STAIRS, THE ★★★ A young boy from the ghetto gets more than he bargained for when he breaks into a house looking for money to help his cancer-stricken mother. It seems the home owners are a couple, with more than a few screws loose, who keep a group of boys locked in their basement. Hybrid of *Dawn of the Dead* and *Die Hard*. Rated R for violence and profanity. 102m. **DIR:** Wes Craven. **CAST:** Brandon Adams, Everett McGill, Wendy Robie, Ving Rhames, Kelly Jo Minter. 1991

PERFECT BRIDE, THE ★★ Nut-cake Sammi Davis, reacting violently to a childhood trauma (finally revealed after three ponderous flashbacks), repeatedly becomes engaged to nice young fellows, only to murder them on the eve of the wedding day. Plucky Kelly Preston senses something amiss. Made-for-cable chiller. 90m. **DIR:** Terrence O'Hara. **CAST:** Sammi Davis, Kelly Preston, Linden Ashby, John Agar. 1991

PET SEMATARY ★★★½ This scarefest is the most faithful film adaptation of a Stephen King novel yet. A young doctor moves his family to an idyllic setting in the Maine woods. The calm is shattered when first the family's cat and then their son are killed on the nearby highway. If you can bear this, you'll love the all-out terror that follows. Rated R for violence. 102m. **DIR:** Mary Lambert. **CAST:** Dale Midkiff, Fred Gwynne, Denise Crosby. **1989**

PET SEMATARY TWO ★★ This disappointing gorefest returns to that cryptic Maine burial ground. Young Edward Furlong hopes to return his mother to life...in spite of having seen his best friend's dog and stepfather revived as savage killers. So much for common sense. Rated R for violence and profanity. 102m. **DIR:** Mary Lambert. **CAST:** Edward Furlong, Anthony Edwards, Clancy Brown, Jared Rushton, Jason McGuire. **1992**

PHANTASM ★★½ This strange mixture of horror and science fiction, while not an outstanding film by any account, does provide viewers with several thrills and unexpected twists. If you like to jump out of your seat, watch this alone with all the lights out. R-rated after scenes were cut from the original X-rated version. 87m. **DIR:** Don Coscarelli. **CAST:** Michael Baldwin, Bill Thornbury, Reggie Bannister. **1979**

PHANTASM II ★★ After ten years, the Tall Man (Angus Scrimm) is back, and he's nastier than ever. No longer is he merely looting cemeteries to enslave the dead for his fiendish purposes. He's also going after the living. But the heroes from the first film are hot on his trail. Lacks the wit, style, and originality of its predecessor. Rated R for nudity, profanity, and graphic violence. 90m. **DIR:** Don Coscarelli. **CAST:** James LeGros, Reggie Bannister, Angus Scrimm. **1988**

PHANTOM CREEPS, THE ★★½ This Saturday-afternoon crowd pleaser features a crazed scientist, a giant robot, an invisibility belt, and a meteorite fragment that can render an entire army immobile—just about anything a kid can ask for in a serial. Good fun. B&W; 12 chapters. **DIR:** Ford Beebe, Saul Goodkind. **CAST:** Bela Lugosi, Regis Toomey. **1939**

PHANTOM OF DEATH ★★ A concert pianist, dying of a rare disease that causes rapid aging, takes out his frustration on women from his past by hacking them to pieces. Donald Pleasence and Michael York are old pros, but the direction is flat and any suspense is worn quickly into the ground. Not rated, but contains nudity and violence. 95m. **DIR:** Ruggero Deodato. **CAST:** Michael York, Edwige Fenech, Donald Pleasence. **1987**

PHANTOM OF THE OPERA (1925) ★★★★★ Classic silent horror with Lon Chaney Sr. in his most poignant and gruesome role. This 1925 sample of Chaney's brilliance—he was truly the "man of a thousand faces"—still has enough power to send chills up your spine. Enjoy. B&W; 79m. **DIR:** Rupert Julian. **CAST:** Lon Chaney Sr., Mary Philbin, Norman Kerry. **1925**

PHANTOM OF THE OPERA (1943) ★★★ Overabundance of singing hurts this otherwise good remake of the 1925 silent. The well-known story concerns a Paris opera house being terrorized by a disfigured composer (Claude Rains) whose best works have been stolen. Acting is great, production values are high, but that singing has got to go! 92m. **DIR:** Arthur Lubin. **CAST:** Claude Rains, Susanna Foster, Nelson Eddy, Edgar Barrier, Miles Mander, Hume Cronyn. **1943**

PHANTOM OF THE OPERA (1962) ★★½ Herbert Lom plays the title role as much for sympathy as scares in this low-key remake from England's Hammer Studios. Otherwise, the plot doesn't vary much from the preceding versions. 84m. **DIR:** Terence Fisher. **CAST:** Herbert Lom, Heather Sears, Thorley Walters, Michael Gough. **1962**

PHANTOM OF THE OPERA (1989) ★★ This muddled retread owes more to the slasher genre than to Gaston Leroux. Although Jill Schoelen makes an appealing heroine, she seems far too intelligent to so casually accept the attention of the heard-but-not-seen guardian angel who lurks beneath the Opera House. He, of course, is none other than serial killer Robert Englund—hiding behind a suitably gory facial-skin mask. Rated R for violence and brief nudity. 93m. **DIR:** Dwight H. Little. **CAST:** Robert Englund, Jill Schoelen, Alex Hyde-White. **1989**

PHANTOM OF THE MALL—ERIC'S REVENGE ★★ A killer seeks revenge on the developers who burned down his house and accidentally disfigured him while clearing the way for a new shopping mall. Good characters make this slasher flick marginally entertaining. Rated R for nudity. 91m. **DIR:** Richard Friedman. **CAST:** Derek Rydall, Jonathan Goldsmith, Rob Estes, Morgan Fairchild. **1988**

PHANTOM OF THE RITZ ★★½ Taking its cue from *Phantom of the Opera* and *Phantom of the Paradise*, this campy little comedy kicks off in 1952 with a drag race that ends in tragedy. Then it's off to 1992, with entrepreneur Peter Bergman reopening the infamous Ritz theatre. His plans for a gala opening are jeopardized when he realizes that an evil presence is making the rounds. Fun in a cheap sort of way, with the legendary Coasters lending musical support. Rated R for violence. 89m. **DIR:** Allen Plone. **CAST:** Peter Bergman, Deborah Van Valkenburgh. **1988**

PICTURE MOMMY DEAD ★★ The tragic death of her mother causes a young girl to lose her memory. Afterward, she is possessed by the spirit of her late mommy. Ooh!

Meanwhile the father, Don Ameche, marries again. Thus a rather silly battle ensues between stepmom and stepdaughter. Good acting; too bad the script isn't better. 88m. **DIR:** Bert I. Gordon. **CAST:** Don Ameche, Martha Hyer, Zsa Zsa Gabor, Signe Hasso, Susan Gordon. **1966**

PICTURE OF DORIAN GRAY, THE ★★★★ The classic adaptation of Oscar Wilde's famous novel, this features Hurd Hatfield giving a restrained performance in the title role of a young man whose portrait ages while he remains eternally youthful. Though talky and slow-moving, this film nevertheless keeps you glued to the screen. A few key scenes shot in Technicolor for effect. B&W/color; 110m. **DIR:** Albert Lewin. **CAST:** George Sanders, Hurd Hatfield, Donna Reed, Angela Lansbury, Peter Lawford. **1945**

PIECES 🦃 This movie promises, "You don't have to go to Texas for a chain-saw massacre!" While not rated by the MPAA, the picture would probably qualify for an X. 85m. **DIR:** Juan Piquer Simon. **CAST:** Christopher George, Lynda Day George, Edmund Purdom. **1983**

PIGS 🦃 Mental patient meets human-scarfing swine. Unrated, film contains violence. 79m. **DIR:** Marc Lawrence. **CAST:** Jesse Vint, Jim Antonio, Marc Lawrence. **1973**

PIN ★★★½ Superb psychological thriller from the screenwriter of *The Amityville Horror* about a schizophrenic youth who develops a mad fixation with a medical dummy called Pin. David Hewlett is excellent as the manic youth torn between fantasy and reality. Rated R for nudity and violence. 103m. **DIR:** Sandor Stern. **CAST:** David Hewlett, Terry O'Quinn. **1989**

PIRANHA ★★★ Director Joe Dante and writer John Sayles sent up *Jaws* in this nifty, gag-filled horror film. Full of scares and chuckles. Rated R. 92m. **DIR:** Joe Dante. **CAST:** Bradford Dillman, Kevin McCarthy, Heather Menzies, Keenan Wynn. **1978**

PIRANHA PART TWO: THE SPAWNING ★★ Sequel to *Piranha* by the man who would later grace us with *The Terminator*. A mutated strain of piranha (with the ability to fly, no less) launches an air and sea tirade of violence against a group of vacationers at a tropical resort. Rated R for mild gore. 88m. **DIR:** James Cameron. **CAST:** Tricia O'Neil, Steve Marachuk, Lance Henriksen, Leslie Graves. **1981**

PIT AND THE PENDULUM, THE (1961) ★★★ More stylish, low-budget Edgar Allan Poe–inspired terror with star Vincent Price and director Roger Corman reteaming for this release. This is for fans of the series only. 80m. **DIR:** Roger Corman. **CAST:** Vincent Price, John Kerr, Barbara Steele, Luana Anders, Anthony Carbone. **1961**

PIT AND THE PENDULUM, THE (1991) ★★ Gorefest claims to be based on Edgar Allan Poe's short story, but actually bears little resemblance to it. When a sympathetic woman tries to stop the beating of a small boy by Spanish Inquisition guards, she's imprisoned for witchcraft. Rated R for nudity, profanity, torture, and gore. 97m. **DIR:** Stuart Gordon. **CAST:** Lance Henriksen, Rona De Ricci, Jonathan Fuller, Jeffrey Combs. **1991**

PLANET OF THE VAMPIRES ★★ After landing on a mysterious planet, astronauts are possessed by formless alien vampires trying to reach Earth. An Italian-Spanish production, also known as *Demon Planet*. The film is plodding and poorly dubbed. Watch director Mario Bava's *Black Sunday* instead. 86m. **DIR:** Mario Bava. **CAST:** Barry Sullivan, Norma Bengell, Angel Aranda. **1965**

PLAYGIRL KILLER, THE 🦃 An insane painter kills his models and stores them in deep freeze. This Canadian film is unrated. 90m. **DIR:** Enrick Santamaran. **CAST:** William Kirwin, Jean Christopher, Neil Sedaka. **1968**

PLAYROOM ★★ Bizarre plot unfolds when an immortal prince draws a young archaeologist back to the site of his parents' murder. Adequate. Rated R for nudity, profanity, violence, and gore. 87m. **DIR:** Manny Coto. **CAST:** Lisa Aliff, Aron Eisenberg, Christopher McDonald, Vincent Schiavelli. **1989**

PLEDGE NIGHT ★★★½ A nicely original horror movie about a group of fraternity guys who are menaced by the ghost of a pledge killed in their house twenty years ago. Inspired special effects keep this from being just another dead-slasher movie. Not rated, but contains violence, nudity, and profanity. 90m. **DIR:** Paul Ziller. **CAST:** Todd Eastland, Shannon McMahon, Joey Belladonna, Will Kempe. **1988**

PLUTONIUM BABY 🦃 A heroic, shape-changing mutant squares off with his evil counterpart in New York City. Not rated, but contains violence and nudity. 85m. **DIR:** Ray Hirschman. **CAST:** Patrick Molloy, Danny Guerra. **1987**

POLTERGEIST ★★★★★ The ultimate screen ghost story, *Poltergeist* is guaranteed to raise goose pimples while keeping viewers marvelously entertained. A sort of *Close Encounters* of the supernatural, it's a scary story about the plight of a suburban family whose home suddenly becomes a house of horrors. Rated PG for tense situations. 114m. **DIR:** Tobe Hooper. **CAST:** Craig T. Nelson, JoBeth Williams, Beatrice Straight, Dominique Dunne. **1982**

POLTERGEIST II: THE OTHER SIDE ★★ Mere months (screen time) after their last film adventure, the stalwart Freeling family is up to its eyeballs in spooks again—although the ghosts stay backstage while another collection of effects parades before the audience. The whole project collapses under its own weight. Rated PG-13 for violence. 92m. **DIR:** Brian Gibson. **CAST:** JoBeth Williams, Craig T. Nelson, Heather O'Rourke, Oliver Robins, Zelda Rubinstein, Will Sampson, Geraldine Fitzgerald. **1986**

POLTERGEIST III 🦃 Little Carol Ann (Heather O'Rourke) moves to Chicago to attend a school for gifted children with mental disorders. Rated PG-13 for violence. 90m. **DIR:** Gary A. Sherman. **CAST:** Tom Skerritt, Nancy Allen, Heather O'Rourke, Zelda Rubinstein. **1988**

POOR GIRL, A GHOST STORY ★★ Strange, mildly interesting tale of a young governess being pursued by both her young pupil and his father. Soon a ghost takes over her actions. Made for Canadian TV, this is unrated but contains sexual situations. 52m. **DIR:** Michael Apted. **CAST:** Lynne Miller, Angela Thorne, Stuart Wilson. **1975**

POPCORN ★★★½ A film student discovers her weird dreams are rooted in an old horror flick. Wonderfully entertaining chiller set during a festival of scare movies. Tom Villard is both humorous and frightening as a classmate who tries to kill the entire class. Rated R for violence and profanity. 93m. **DIR:** Mark Herrier. **CAST:** Jill Schoelen, Tom Villard, Dee Wallace, Kelly Jo Minter, Tony Roberts, Ray Walston. **1991**

POSSESSED, THE (1977) ★★ A not-too-scary *Exorcist* clone. James Farentino is a defrocked priest who travels around in search of evil and is drawn to a girls' school. Made-for-TV demonic possession flick. 75m. **DIR:** Jerry Thorpe. **CAST:** James Farentino, Claudette Nevins, Eugene Roche, Harrison Ford, Ann Dusenberry, Diana Scarwid, Joan Hackett. **1977**

POSSESSION 🦃 French-German coproduction. Rated R for nudity, violence, and gore. 80m. **DIR:** Andrzei Zulawski. **CAST:** Isabelle Adjani, Sam Neill, Heinz Bennent. **1984**

POWER, THE (1980) 🦃 Aztec idol is unearthed by some youngsters, who must face the consequences. Rated R for profanity, violence, and gore. 87m. **DIR:** Jeffrey Obrow, Stephen Carpenter. **CAST:** Susan Stokey, Warren Lincoln, Lisa Erickson. **1980**

PREMATURE BURIAL, THE ★★ A medical student's paranoia about being buried alive causes his worst fears to come true. Roger Corman's only Poe-derived film without Vincent Price. Lacking Price's playful and hammy acting style, it all seems too serious. 81m. **DIR:** Roger Corman. **CAST:** Ray Milland, Hazel Court, Richard Ney, Heather Angel. **1962**

PREMONITION, THE ★★½ Well-written but turgidly directed terror film about a young adopted girl kidnapped by her natural mother. The girl's adoptive parents turn to ESP to locate her, and fall into a strange world. Not rated, but has intense situations and some violence. 94m. **DIR:** Robert Schnitzer. **CAST:** Sharon Farrell, Richard Lynch, Jeff Corey, Danielle Brisebois. **1975**

PREY, THE 🦃 Six young hikers go up into the woods, where they run into a ghoul. Yum. Rated R for nudity and violence. 80m. **DIR:** Edwin Scott Brown. **CAST:** Debbie Thurseon, Steve Bond, Lori Lethin, Jackie Coogan. **1980**

PRIMAL RAGE 🦃 An experiment on a college campus goes awry. Rated R for violence and profanity. 91m. **DIR:** Vittorie Rambaldi. **CAST:** Patrick Lowe, Bo Svenson. **1988**

PRIME EVIL ★★½ A band of priests in New York City are actually disciples of Satan. A bloody sacrifice every thirteen years grants them immortality. Passable horror film has decent suspense and contains violent acts without being awash in gore. Rated R. 87m. **DIR:** Roberta Findlay. **CAST:** William Beckwith, Christine Moore. **1989**

PRINCE OF DARKNESS 🦃 Priest learns about a canister hidden below an unused church and suspects he's found Satan's resting place. Rated R for violence and language. 110m. **DIR:** John Carpenter. **CAST:** Donald Pleasence, Jameson Parker, Victor Wong, Lisa Blount, Dennis Dun, Alice Cooper. **1987**

PRISON 🦃 An old prison is haunted by the vengeful ghost of a man executed in 1964. Rated R for language and violence. 102m. **DIR:** Renny Harlin. **CAST:** Lane Smith, Chelsea Field, Andre de Shields, Lincoln Kilpatrick. **1988**

PRIVATE PARTS ★★ When a teenage runaway seeks refuge at her aunt's San Francisco hotel, she finds that the residents can get downright deadly, as well as kinky. Mildly entertaining for fans of hack-and-slash erotic thrillers. Rated R for violence and nudity. 86m. **DIR:** Paul Bartel. **CAST:** Ann Ruymen, Lucille Benson, John Ventantonio. **1972**

PRIZE WINNING FILMS OF JAN SVANKMAJER, THE ★★★★★ Excellent collection of award-winning shorts by the masterful Czech animator whose brilliant, mesmerizing films have earned him international attention. He uses a wide assortment of techniques in his surreal universe. Included in this collection are "Dimensions in Dialogue," "The Last Trick," "Punch and Judy," and "Jabberwocky." Not rated, but definitely recommended for adults only. 54m. **DIR:** Jan Svankmajer. **1964–1982**

PROM NIGHT ★★ This okay slasher flick has a group of high school students being systematically slaughtered as payment for the accidental death of one of their friends when they were all children. Rated R. 92m. **DIR:** Paul Lynch. **CAST:** Jamie Lee Curtis, Leslie Nielsen, Casey Stevens. **1980**

PROM NIGHT III—LAST KISS ★★½ Prom queen from hell Mary Lou Maloney returns to her old high school to knock 'em dead. Done with some style and humor. Watch for the jukebox from hell. Rated R for nudity, violence, and profanity. 97m. **DIR:** Ron Oliver, Peter Simpson. **CAST:** Tom Conlon, Cyndy Preston. **1989**

PROM NIGHT IV—DELIVER US FROM EVIL ★★½ A religious fanatic stalks four teens he feels have transgressed the law of God. Really no different from a zillion other recent horror movies, but it's moderately well-done of its type. (It has, however, nothing to do with the other three *Prom Night* entries.) Rated R for violence. 95m. **DIR:** Clay Borris. **CAST:** Nikki De Boer, Alden Kane. **1991**

PROPHECY 🦃 Dull ecological horror film about a mutated beast that inhabits a northeastern American forest. Rated PG. 95m. **DIR:** John Frankenheimer. **CAST:** Talia Shire, Robert Foxworth, Armand Assante, Richard Dysart, Victoria Racimo. **1979**

PSYCHIC KILLER ★★ This is a completely ordinary thriller about a man who acquires psychic powers. *Psychic Killer* doesn't take itself seriously and that's a plus, but it's not sufficiently engrossing. Rated PG. 89m. **DIR:** Ray Danton. **CAST:** Jim Hutton, Paul Burke, Julie Adams, Nehemiah Persoff, Neville Brand, Aldo Ray, Della Reese. **1975**

PSYCHO ★★★★★ The quintessential shocker, which started a whole genre of films about psychotic killers enacting mayhem on innocent victims, still holds up well today. If all you can remember about this film is its famous murder of Janet Leigh in the shower, you might want to give it a second look. Anthony Perkins's performance and the ease with which Hitchcock maneuvers your emotions make *Psycho* far superior to the numerous films that tried to duplicate it. B&W; 109m. **DIR:** Alfred Hitchcock. **CAST:** Anthony Perkins, Janet Leigh, Vera Miles, John Gavin, John McIntire, Simon Oakland, John Anderson, Frank Albertson, Patricia Hitchcock, Martin Balsam. **1960**

PSYCHO II ★★★½ Picking up where Alfred Hitchcock's original left off, this sequel begins with Norman Bates (Anthony Perkins) being declared sane after twenty-two years in an asylum. Old Normie goes right back to the Bates Motel, and strange things begin to happen. Directed with exquisite taste and respect for the old master by Richard Franklin. It's suspenseful, scary, and funny. Rated R for profanity and violence. 113m. **DIR:** Richard Franklin. **CAST:** Anthony Perkins, Vera Miles, Meg Tilly, Robert Loggia, Dennis Franz, Hugh Gillin. **1983**

PSYCHO III ★★ Second follow-up to *Psycho* works mainly because actor-director Anthony Perkins understands poor Norman Bates inside and out. Although lensed beautifully by Bruce Surtees, the film fails in the most critical area: creating suspense. Rated R for gory violence. 93m. **DIR:** Anthony Perkins. **CAST:** Anthony Perkins, Diana Scarwid, Jeff Fahey, Hugh Gillin. **1986**

PSYCHO 4: THE BEGINNING ★★★ Once more into the Bates Motel, dear friends... Scripter Joseph Stefano, who adapted Robert Bloch's novel for Hitchcock's original *Psycho*, returns with this made-for-cable tale purporting to explain why poor Norman Bates (Anthony Perkins) became such a monster. Rated R for sex, nudity, and violence. 95m. **DIR:** Mick Garris. **CAST:** Anthony Perkins, Henry Thomas, Olivia Hussey, C.C.H. Pounder. **1990**

PSYCHO GIRLS ★★★ Over-the-top horror parody will appeal most to avid horror fans, who will appreciate the black humor. A writer of mystery novels holds a dinner party that is disrupted by a psychotic woman. Rated R for violence and nudity. 90m. **DIR:** Gerard Ciccoritti. **CAST:** John Haslett Cuff, Darlene Wignacci. **1986**

PSYCHO SISTERS ★★★★ After her husband is killed, a woman goes to stay with her sister—her sister who has only recently emerged from an insane asylum and is still hearing their dead mother's voice. This film is a classic of the early 1970s horror/gore/exploitation cycle. Rated PG for mild violence. 76m. **DIR:** Reginald LeBorg. **CAST:** Susan Strasberg, Faith Domergue, Charles Knox Robinson. **1972**

PSYCHOMANIA ★★ This British-made film is about a motorcycle gang. They call themselves the Living Dead because they committed a group suicide and only came back to life through a pact with the devil. The film moves slowly and includes lots of violence. Rated R. 95m. **DIR:** Don Sharp. **CAST:** George Sanders, Nicky Henson, Mary Larkin, Patrick Holt, Beryl Reid. **1971**

PSYCHOPATH, THE 🦃 The host of a children's television show spends his spare time killing parents who abuse their kids. Rated PG. 84m. **DIR:** Larry Brown. **CAST:** Tom Basham, John Ashton. **1973**

PSYCHOS IN LOVE ★★½ This film is an *Eating Raoul*-style horror comedy. Joe is a bar owner who has no trouble meeting women and getting dates. The problem is that he is a psychopath who ends up killing them—generally when he finds out they like grapes! This made-for-video movie has lots of gore and nudity. 88m. **DIR:** Gorman Bechard. **CAST:** Carmine Capobianco, Debi Thibeault, Frank Stewart. **1985**

PULSE 🦃 Cliff De Young against some incredibly vicious electrical pulses. Rated PG-13. 90m. **DIR:** Paul Golding. **CAST:** Cliff De Young, Roxanne Hart, Joey Lawrence, Matthew Lawrence, Charles Tyner, Dennis Redfield. **1988**

PUMA MAN, THE 🦃 Humorless Italian junk about a man given extraordinary powers to fight evil. 80m. **DIR:** Alberto De Martino. **CAST:** Donald Pleasence, Sydne Rome. **1980**

PUMPKINHEAD 🦃 A backwoods witch. Rated R for violence. 87m. **DIR:** Stan Winston. **CAST:** Lance Henriksen, Jeff East. **1989**

PUPPET MASTER, THE ★★★½ Highly effective chiller about a puppet maker (William Hickey) who uses an ancient Egyptian power to breed life into his demonic dolls. After his untimely death by suicide, a group of psychics tries to locate these terrifying toys. Excellent animation and special effects by David Allen (*Willow, Batteries Not Included*). Rated R for nudity and graphic violence. 90m. **DIR:** David Schmoeller. **CAST:** Paul LeMat, Irene Miracle, William Hickey. **1989**

PUPPET MASTER II ★★½ The diabolically deadly dolls from the first film resurrect their dead creator and go on another rampage. Moderately scary. Rated R for violence, profanity, and mild gore. 90m. **DIR:** David Allen. **CAST:** Elizabeth MacLellan, Collin Bernsen, Gregory Webb, Charlie Spradling, Steve Welles, Nita Talbot. **1990**

PUPPET MASTER III: TOULON'S REVENGE ★★½ In this second sequel, we go back and watch how Toulon and his killer puppets murder Nazis and escape from World War II Germany. Rated R for violence and profanity. 95m. **DIR:** David DeCoteau. **CAST:** Guy Rolfe, Ian Abercrombie, Sarah Douglas, Richard Lynch. **1991**

PUPPET MASTER FOUR ★★ Excellent special effects and creative animation remain the highlights in this continuing series. In this chapter, a genius whiz kid and friends conduct experiments in the abandoned hotel where viewers were first introduced to the lifelike puppets. This one will remind viewers of the old Saturday afternoon matinee serial chapterplays, à la Flash Gordon and Commando Cody. Rated R for violence, nudity, and profanity. 80m. **DIR:** Jeff Burr. **CAST:** Gordon Currie, Chandra West, Jason Adams, Teresa Hill, Guy Rolfe. **1993**

Q ★★★★ This is an old-fashioned giant monster film. The stop-motion animation is excellent, the acting (done tongue-in-cheek) is perfect. The story revolves around the arrival of a giant flying lizard in New York City. A series of ritualistic murders follow and point to the monster being Quetzelcoatl (the flying serpent god of the Aztecs). Rated R. 93m. **DIR:** Larry Cohen. **CAST:** Michael Moriarty, David Carradine, Candy Clark, Richard Roundtree, James Dixon. **1982**

QUEEN VICTORIA AND THE ZOMBIES 🦃 Queen Victoria and Prince Albert come from outer space to spend some time in a vacation cabin in this awful horror-comedy. Not rated. 118m. **DIR:** Steve Postal. **CAST:** Charlotte Leslie, Kendrick Kaufman, Eddie Crew, Jennifer Tuck, Angela Shepard, Melanie Lee, Maurice Postal. **1990**

QUEST, THE ★★ Henry Thomas plays a young boy living in Australia who has reason to believe that a monster lives in a small lake not far from his home. He sets out to prove the creature's existence—or to expose it as a fraud. Though slow, this film has decent acting. Rated PG. 94m. **DIR:** Brian Trenchard-Smith. **CAST:** Henry Thomas, Tony Barry, John Ewart. **1985**

RABID ★★ This horror flick has become a cult favorite despite many repulsive scenes. In it, porn queen Marilyn Chambers lives on human blood after a motorcycle accident operation. For fans of director David Cronenberg only. Rated R. 90m. **DIR:** David Cronenberg. **CAST:** Marilyn Chambers, Joe Silver, Patricia Gage. **1977**

RABID GRANNIES ★★★ A birthday party for two old ladies turns into a zombiefest thanks to a present sent by the family Satanist. Gruesome special effects are the name of the game in this over-the-top horror movie. Unrated, but not for kids or the squeamish. 83m. **DIR:** Emmanuel Kervyn. **CAST:** Catherine Aymerie, Caroline Braekman. **1989**

RACE WITH THE DEVIL ★★ Good cast and exciting chase sequences can't save this muddled yarn. It's about two couples who accidentally intrude on a witches' sacrificial ceremony. Rated PG for violence. 88m. **DIR:** Jack Starrett. **CAST:** Warren Oates, Peter Fonda, Loretta Swit, Lara Parker. **1975**

RAISING CAIN 🦃 Psychological thrillers don't come much sillier than this hopelessly muddled study of a demented child psychologist (John Lithgow, *way* over the top) who kidnaps small children. A real low for director Brian De Palma. Rated R for violence and profanity. 95m. **DIR:** Brian De Palma. **CAST:** John Lithgow, Lolita Davidovich, Steven Bauer, Frances Sternhagen. **1992**

RATS 🦃 Italian-made gore-a-thon set in the future after The Bomb has destroyed civilization. Dubbed in English. Unrated, but loaded with violence. 97m. **DIR:** Vincent Dawn. **CAST:** Richard Raymond, Alex McBride. **1983**

RATS ARE COMING!, THE WEREWOLVES ARE HERE!, THE 🦃 England is besieged by a pack of werewolves in the 1800s. Rated R. 92m. **DIR:** Andy Milligan. **CAST:** Hope Stansbury, Jackie Skarvellis. **1972**

RAVEN, THE (1935) ★★★★ Solid Universal Pictures horror-thriller casts Bela Lugosi as a mad scientist who is obsessed with the writings of Edgar Allan Poe. Boris Karloff is the hapless fugitive Lugosi deforms in order to carry out his evil schemes. Unlike many of the 1930s horror classics, this one has retained its suspense and drama. Available on a double-feature videocassette with *Black Cat*. B&W; 62m. **DIR:** Louis Friedlander. **CAST:** Boris Karloff, Bela Lugosi, Irene Ware, Lester Matthews, Samuel S. Hinds. **1935**

RAVEN, THE (1963) ★★★★ The best of the Roger Corman–directed Edgar Allan Poe adaptations, this release benefits from a humorous screenplay by Richard Matheson and tongue-in-cheek portrayals by Boris Karloff, Vincent Price, and Peter Lorre. Look for Jack Nicholson in an early role as Lorre's son. 86m. **DIR:** Roger Corman. **CAST:** Boris Karloff, Vincent Price, Peter Lorre, Jack Nicholson, Hazel Court. **1963**

RAWHEAD REX ★★½ A satanic demon is accidentally unearthed and begins to wreak havoc on a small village in Ireland. The acting and script are both low caliber, but worth watching if you like raunch. Rated R for profanity, nudity, and plenty-o'-gore. 89m. **DIR:** George Pavlou. **CAST:** David Dukes, Kelly Piper, Niall Toibin. **1986**

RAZORBACK ★★★½ This Australian film, concerning a giant pig that is terrorizing a small Aussie village, surprises the viewer by turning into a great little film. The special effects, photography, editing, and acting are great. Rated R. 95m. **DIR:** Russell Mulcahy. **CAST:** Gregory Harrison. **1983**

RE-ANIMATOR ★★★★ Stylishly grotesque and gory filming of H. P. Lovecraft's "Herbert West, Reanimator" hits the mark. This is Grand Guignol in the classic sense as we follow brilliant young medical student Herbert West in his deranged efforts to bring the dead back to life. Some outrageous scenes highlight this terror entry and, although very well-done, it's not for the squeamish. 86m. **DIR:** Stuart Gordon. **CAST:** Bruce Abbott, Barbara Crampton, David Gale, Robert Sampson, Jeffrey Combs. **1985**

REASON TO DIE ★★ A razor fiend is tracked by a bounty hunter, after a series of erotic slicings. Typical slasher, though at least high-voltage actor Wings Hauser is the protagonist. Unrated. 96m. **DIR:** Tim Spring. **CAST:** Wings Hauser. **1989**

RED-BLOODED AMERICAN GIRL ★★½ A quirky story about a scientist (Andrew Stevens) who is called upon to reverse the effects of a new drug that causes vampirism. Rated R for language, violence, and nudity. 90m. **DIR:** David Blyth. **CAST:** Heather Thomas, Andrew Stevens, Lydie Denier, Christopher Plummer, Kim Coates. **1990**

REINCARNATE, THE 🦃 A lawyer will live forever, as long as he can find a new body to inhabit when his present one dies. Rated PG. 89m. **DIR:** Don Haldane. **CAST:** Jack Creley, Jay Reynolds. **1971**

REINCARNATION OF PETER PROUD, THE 🦃 Turgid direction, contrived plot. Rated R for considerable nudity. 104m. **DIR:** J. Lee Thompson. **CAST:** Michael Sarrazin, Jennifer O'Neill, Margot Kidder, Cornelia Sharpe. **1975**

REJUVENATOR, THE ★★★ This flick begins by resembling *Re-Animator* in more than just name, but it soon takes on a life of its own. A rich woman funds a doctor's research into reversing the aging process in hopes he will discover a way to make her young again. Some very nasty side effects occur. Above-average special effects make this a must for horror-film fans. Rated R for extreme violence. 90m. **DIR:** Brian Thomas Jones. **CAST:** Vivian Lanko, John MacKay. **1988**

RELENTLESS II: DEAD ON ★★ Meg Foster and Leo Rossi reprise their roles from *Relentless*. A woman and her child were menaced by a serial killer at the end of that film. This one shows what effect it had on that child. Very bloody and violent, but also exciting and suspenseful. Rated R for violence, nudity, and tension. 93m. **DIR:** Michael Schroeder. **CAST:** Ray Sharkey, Meg Foster, Leo Rossi, Marc Poppel, Dale Dye, Miles O'Keeffe. **1991**

REMOTE CONTROL ★★½ The manager of a video-rental outlet learns that many of his customers are being brutally murdered after watching a certain cassette. Rated R for violence and profanity. 88m. **DIR:** Jeff Lieberman. **CAST:** Kevin Dillon, Jennifer Tilly, Deborah Goodrich. **1987**

REPULSION ★★★★½ This brilliant British production, the first English-language film directed by Roman Polanski, is a classic chiller. Catherine Deneuve plays a sexually repressed, mentally ill young girl who is terrified of men. Left alone at her sister's home for a weekend, she suffers a series of severe hallucinations that finally lead her to commit murder. B&W; 105m. **DIR:** Roman Polanski. **CAST:** Catherine Deneuve, Ian Hendry, Yvonne Furneaux, John Fraser, Patrick Wymark. **1965**

REST IN PIECES 🦃 A young couple inherit an old Spanish estate occupied by murderous Satanists. Not rated, but contains graphic violence and nudity. 90m. **DIR:** Joseph Braunsteen. **CAST:** Scott Thompson, Lorin Jean, Dorothy Malone, Patty Shepard. **1987**

RESURRECTED, THE ★★★ An enjoyable tongue-in-cheek production of H. P. Lovecraft's *The Case of Charles Dexter Ward*. The wife of a reclusive doctor asks a detective to find out what her husband has been doing in the lab late at night. Planted firmly in the dark comic tradition of the other Lovecraft-based films: *The Re-animator* and *From Beyond*. Rated R for gore and profanity. 108m. **DIR:** Dan O'Bannon. **CAST:** Chris Sarandon, John Terry, Jane Sibbett. **1991**

RETRIBUTION ★★ In this supernatural thriller, a mild-mannered, down-and-out artist attempts suicide at the same moment a small-time hood is tortured to death. The artist becomes possessed by the soul of the hood and then proceeds to avenge his murder. Low-budget shocker with an inadequate script. Rated R for violence and profanity. 109m. **DIR:** Guy Magar. **CAST:** Dennis Lipscomb, Leslie Wing, Hoyt Axton. **1988**

RETURN OF DRACULA ★★½ Until Hammer Films revived him, Count Dracula wasn't seen much in the 1950s, but this above-average outing is one of the exceptions. Francis Lederer takes the title role, assuming a European painter's identity in order to bleed modern California dry. Video release includes a color climax. B&W; 77m. **DIR:** Paul Landres. **CAST:** Francis Lederer, Norma Eberhardt, Ray Stricklyn. **1958**

RETURN OF THE ALIEN'S DEADLY SPAWN, THE ★★ Blood-filled horror film about alien creatures from outer space who kill and destroy anyone and everything that gets in their way. Lots of gore, ripped flesh, and off-the-wall humor. For people who like sick movies. Rated R for profanity and gore. 90m. **DIR:** Douglas McKeown. **CAST:** Charles George Hildebrandt. **1984**

RETURN OF THE APE MAN ★★★ Scientists Bela Lugosi and John Carradine revive a Neanderthal man, who soon goes on a rampage. Above-average Monogram poverty-row programmer, just fast-paced (and poker-faced) enough to be diverting. B&W; 68m. **DIR:** Phil Rosen. **CAST:** Bela Lugosi, John Carradine. **1944**

RETURN OF THE EVIL DEAD ★★ This Spanish zombie shocker has nothing to do with Sam Raimi's *Evil Dead* films. It's one of the entries in de Ossorio's intermittently scary Blind Dead cycle (see also *Horror of the Zombies*), retitled for U.S. release. A few scenes of the rotting undead stalking their victims have a claustrophobic quality that foreshadows John Carpenter's *The Fog*. Rated R. 85m. **DIR:** Amando de Ossorio. **CAST:** Victor Petit. **1975**

RETURN OF THE FLY, THE ★★★ In this fine sequel to *The Fly*, the son of the original insect makes the same mistake as his father...with identical results. Effective film benefits from stark black-and-white photography and solid effects. Watch out for the guinea-pig scene! B&W; 80m. **DIR:** Edward L. Bernds. **CAST:** Vincent Price, Brett Halsey, David Frankham. **1959**

RETURN OF THE LIVING DEAD, THE ★★★★ Extremely gory horror film produced with a great deal of style and ample amounts of comedy as well. The residents of a small New Orleans cemetery are brought back to life after accidental exposure to a strange chemical, and they're hungry...for human brains. Rated R for violence, nudity, and language. 91m. **DIR:** Dan O'Bannon. **CAST:** Clu Gulager, James Karen, Don Calfa, Thom Mathews. **1985**

RETURN OF THE LIVING DEAD PART II ★★ The dead have once again risen from their long slumber and are hungry for human brains. A drum of special gas that seems to reanimate the dead has been discovered by a trio of children. They unwittingly loose the gas on the unsuspecting town. Definitely an R rating for the violence and language. 90m. **DIR:** Ken Wiederhorn. **CAST:** James Karen, Thom Mathews, Dan Ashbrook. **1988**

RETURN OF THE LIVING DEAD 3 ★★★ Love never dies, at least not in this sequel. When Curt's girlfriend Mindy dies, he drags her body to a top-secret government lab where his father works on reanimating the dead. Curt revives Mindy, but when she starts craving human flesh, their relationship becomes strained. Goofy humor, outrageous special effects, and a likable cast make this series worth reviving. Rated R for nudity, language, and extreme violence. 96m. **DIR:** Brian Yuzna. **CAST:** J. Trevor Edmond, Mindy Clarke, Sarah Douglas, Kent McCord. **1993**

RETURN OF THE SWAMP THING ★★★ The big, green monster-hero comes out of the swamp to do battle once again with evil scientist Louis Jourdan, while Heather Locklear is the object of his affections. Unlike the first film, which was also based on the DC Comics character. You're not supposed to take this sequel seriously. Rated PG-13. 87m. **DIR:** Jim Wynorski. **CAST:** Louis Jourdan, Heather Locklear, Dick Durock. **1989**

RETURN OF THE VAMPIRE, THE ★★★ Set during World War II, this surprisingly good vampire tale has the supposedly destroyed fiend, Armand Tesla (Bela Lugosi), unearthed by a German bombing raid on London. B&W; 69m. **DIR:** Lew Landers, Kurt Neumann. **CAST:** Bela Lugosi, Frieda Inescort, Nina Foch, Miles Mander, Matt Willis. **1943**

RETURN TO BOGGY CREEK 🦃 A cheap and boring sequel about a mysterious creature that stalks the swamps of a small fishing community. Rated PG. 87m. **DIR:** Tom Moore. **CAST:** Dawn Wells. **1978**

RETURN TO HORROR HIGH 🦃 A group of filmmakers go back to a high school where a series of murders took place. Rated R for nudity, profanity, and violence. 95m. **DIR:** Bill Froechlich. **CAST:** Vince Edwards, Alex Rocco, Brendan Hughes, Scott Jacoby, Lori Lethin, Philip McKeon. **1987**

RETURN TO SALEM'S LOT, A 🦃 A divorced father, recently reunited with his teenage son, goes back to the town of his birth to find that its inhabitants are vampires. Rated R for nudity and violence. 101m.

DIR: Larry Cohen. CAST: Michael Moriarty, Samuel Fuller, Andrew Duggan, Evelyn Keyes. 1987

REVENGE OF THE CREATURE ★★ Even as sequels go, this follow-up to *Creature from the Black Lagoon* is disappointing. Scientists capture him and take him to Florida, he gets loose, and they kill him. Only the ferocity of some of the murders and Clint Eastwood's screen debut as a dim-witted lab assistant break the monotony. B&W; 82m. DIR: Jack Arnold. CAST: John Agar, Lori Nelson, John Bromfield, Clint Eastwood. 1955

REVENGE OF THE DEAD 💔 Talky Italian film with misleading title. Rated R for violence and profanity. 98m. DIR: Pupi Avati. CAST: Gabriele Lavia, Anne Canovas. 1984

REVENGE OF THE RED BARON ★★ A modicum of suspense saves this hokey thriller about a veteran flying ace (Mickey Rooney) who shot down the infamous Red Baron. Now in a wheelchair, Rooney must fight to save his family from a model biplane possessed by the spirit of the dead pilot. The plane creates havoc, but the film mostly creates laughs. Rated PG-13 for violence. 90m. DIR: Robert Gordon. CAST: Mickey Rooney, Toby Maguire, Cliff De Young, Laraine Newman, Ronnie Schell. 1994

REVENGE OF THE STEPFORD WIVES 💔 A TV sequel to the suspense classic. 95m. DIR: Robert Fuest. CAST: Arthur Hill, Don Johnson, Sharon Gless, Mason Adams, Audra Lindley. 1980

REVENGE OF THE TEENAGE VIXENS FROM OUTER SPACE 💔 This attempt to re-create the corny invader films of the 1950s nearly succeeds, but why bother? This time four hot chicks from outer space start hitting on high-school boys, so the boys' girlfriends decide to take the vixens on. Not rated. 83m. DIR: Jeff Ferrell. CAST: Lisa Schwedop, Howard Scott, Amy Crumpacker, Sterling Ramberg. 1985

REVENGE OF THE ZOMBIES ★★½ As soon as the Hollywood back-lot native walks across the foggy bog in baggy underwear and begins to wail "Whoooooo," you know this is going to be one of those films. And it sure is, with mad scientist John Carradine, his zombie wife Veda Ann Borg (in her best role), do-gooders Gale Storm and Robert Lowery, and "feets do yo' stuff" Mantan Moreland aiding escaping zombies and Nazis in this low-budget howler. B&W; 61m. DIR: Steve Sekely. CAST: John Carradine, Robert Lowery, Gale Storm, Veda Ann Borg, Mantan Moreland, Bob Steele. 1943

REVOLT OF THE ZOMBIES ★★ Following the unexpected success of their independently produced *White Zombie* in 1932, brothers Edward and Victor Halperin found themselves making another zombie movie in 1936. Lacking the style and imagination of their earlier effort, this quasi-supernatural story involves the use of a stupor-inducing potion that turns Cambodian troops into dull-eyed slaves. For curiosity seekers only. B&W; 65m. DIR: Victor Halperin. CAST: Dean Jagger, Roy D'Arcy, Dorothy Stone, George Cleveland. 1936

RIPPER, THE 💔 In this poorly filmed modernization of the Jack the Ripper legend, a college professor finds a ring, originally belonging to the nineteenth-century killer. 104m. DIR: Christopher Lewis. CAST: Tom Schreier, Wade Tower. 1985

ROBOT MONSTER ★★ Take a desolate-looking canyon outside of Los Angeles, borrow Lawrence Welk's bubble machine, and add a typical family on an outing and a man dressed in a gorilla suit wearing a diving helmet, and you have a serious competitor for the worst movie of all time. This absurd drama of the last days of Earth and its conquest by robot gorillas has long been considered the most inept of all science-fiction films. A must-see for all fans of truly terrible films. B&W; 63m. DIR: Phil Tucker. CAST: George Nader, Gregory Moffett, Claudia Barrett. 1953

ROCK 'N' ROLL NIGHTMARE 💔 Members of a heavy-metal band are killed by a mysterious presence. Unrated; the film contains violence and nudity. 89m. DIR: John Fasano. CAST: Jon-Mikl Thor, Paula Francescatto, Rusty Hamilton. 1987

ROCKTOBER BLOOD ★★ The ghost of a rock star, executed for murder, returns from the dead to avenge himself upon his former band members. The film starts off well and ends decently, but the middle wanders aimlessly. Non-horror fans will probably find this tedious. Rated R for violence, nudity, and profanity. 88m. DIR: Ferd Sebastian, Beverly Sebastian. CAST: Tray Loren. 1984

ROSEMARY'S BABY ★★★★ Mia Farrow is a young woman forced by her husband (John Cassavetes) into an unholy arrangement with a group of devil worshipers. The suspense is sustained as she is made aware that people around her are not what they seem. Ruth Gordon is priceless in her Oscar-winning role as one of the seemingly normal neighbors. Rated R. 136m. DIR: Roman Polanski. CAST: Mia Farrow, John Cassavetes, Ruth Gordon, Ralph Bellamy, Elisha Cook Jr., Maurice Evans, Patsy Kelly. 1968

RUBY (1977) ★★ A sleazy drive-in is the setting for this unexciting horror film about a young girl possessed by the homicidal ghost of a dead gangster. Rated R for gore. 84m. DIR: Curtis Harrington. CAST: Piper Laurie, Stuart Whitman, Roger Davis. 1977

RUDE AWAKENING (1982) ★★½ In another of Elvira's "Thriller Video" series, and one of the best, a real estate broker finds himself sucked into dreams that seem like reality; or is it the other way around? It sounds standard, but it's better than you would think. 60m. **DIR:** Peter Sasdy. **CAST:** Denholm Elliott, James Laurenson, Pat Heywood. **1982**

RUN STRANGER RUN ★★★½ Ron Howard plays a teenager searching for his biological parents in a seaside town. Once there, he discovers that some of the town inhabitants have been disappearing. Unfortunately, the disappearances are closely linked to his past. Overall, this film keeps viewer interest without dwelling on the slash-'em-up theme. Rated PG for gore. 92m. **DIR:** Darren McGavin. **CAST:** Patricia Neal, Cloris Leachman, Ron Howard, Bobby Darin. **1973**

RUNESTONE ★★★ An ancient Norse runestone that contains a mythical demon is unearthed and brought to New York City. When an archaeologist discovers its forbidden curse, not even the police can stop the carnage. Rated R for violence, profanity, and nudity. 105m. **DIR:** Willard Carroll. **CAST:** Peter Riegert, Joan Stevenson, William Hickey, Tim Ryan, Lawrence Tierney, Chris Young, Alexander Godunov. **1990**

RUSH WEEK ★★ A reporter (Pamela Ludwig) gets a scoop on murdered models and gets herself in the most ridiculously suicidal situations to follow her leads. Rated R for nudity, violence, and gore. 96m. **DIR:** Bob Bralver. **CAST:** Dean Hamilton, Pamela Ludwig, Gregg Allman, Roy Thinnes. **1989**

S. S. HELL CAMP 🦃 Cheap, incredibly gross Eurotrash stomach-turner set in a Nazi compound. No rating, but sexually explicit and very sadistic. 88m. **DIR:** Ivan Katansky. **CAST:** Macha Magall, John Braun. **1985**

SADIST, THE 🦃 A serial killer and his girlfriend terrorize three teachers stranded in the middle of nowhere. Not rated, but contains some violence. B&W; 90m. **DIR:** James Landis. **CAST:** Arch Hall Jr., Helen Hovey, Marilyn Manning. **1963**

SALEM'S LOT ★★★★ This story of vampires in modern-day New England is one of the better adaptations of Stephen King's novels on film. Some real chills go along with an intelligent script in what was originally a two-part TV movie. 112m. **DIR:** Tobe Hooper. **CAST:** David Soul, James Mason, Reggie Nalder, Lance Kerwin, Elisha Cook Jr., Ed Flanders. **1979**

SANTA SANGRE ★★★½ A disturbed young man who kills at the bequest of his armless mother. A weird and often wonderful surreal thriller that looks like a slasher film made by Federico Fellini with Salvador Dali as art director. Rated R for strong violence and sexual content. 124m. **DIR:** Alejandro Jodorowsky. **CAST:** Axel Jodorowsky, Guy Stockwell. **1990**

SATANIC RITES OF DRACULA, THE ★★½ Substantially better than the previous year's appalling *Dracula A.D. 1972,* this is the final Hammer Films *Dracula* outing to star Lee and Cushing as the count and his arch-foe, Professor Van Helsing. Actually it's Van Helsing's *grandson*, since this film is set in modern London. Rated R for nudity and gore. 88m. **DIR:** Alan Gibson. **CAST:** Christopher Lee, Peter Cushing, Freddie Jones. **1973**

SATAN'S CHEERLEADERS 🦃 Cheerleaders run afoul of a cult of Satanists. Rated PG. 92m. **DIR:** Greydon Clark. **CAST:** Kerry Sherman, John Ireland, Yvonne De Carlo, John Carradine, Jack Kruschen. **1977**

SATAN'S PRINCESS ★★ An ex-cop turned private detective takes on a missing-persons case that leads him straight to a centuries-old demoness, who kills people as often as she changes her wardrobe. Amateurish. Rated R for violence. 90m. **DIR:** Bert I. Gordon. **CAST:** Robert Forster, Lydie Denier, Caren Kaye. **1989**

SATAN'S SCHOOL FOR GIRLS ★★½ Originally made as an ABC Movie of the Week, this decent shocker concerns a series of apparent suicides at a prominent girls' school, but we all know better. Good acting and some creepy atmosphere, but the typical TV ending falls flat. 74m. **DIR:** David Lowell Rich. **CAST:** Pamela Franklin, Kate Jackson, Roy Thinnes, Cheryl Ladd. **1973**

SATURDAY NIGHT SHOCKERS ★★★ Each of these four tapes includes a pair of cheapo horror movies, cartoons, short subjects, and coming attractions, all from the Thirties, Forties, and Fifties. Thus seen in their proper context, these trash classics are much more entertaining than they would be if viewed alone. The titles (all reviewed separately in this book) are: Volume 1, *The Creeping Terror* and *Chained for Life*; Volume 2, *Manbeast* and *Human Gorilla*; Volume 3, a Todd Slaughter double feature of *Murders in the Red Barn* and *A Face at the Window*; and Volume 4, *Mesa of Lost Women* and *The Monster of Piedras Blancas*. Unrated; no objectionable content. Each tape is approximately 150m. **DIR:** Various.

SATURDAY THE 14TH 🦃 Richard Benjamin and Paula Prentiss star in this low-budget horror comedy about a family that moves into a haunted house. Rated PG. 75m. **DIR:** Howard R. Cohen. **CAST:** Richard Benjamin, Paula Prentiss, Jeffrey Tambor, Rosemary DeCamp. **1981**

SAVAGE BEES, THE ★★½ Above-average thriller about a plague of African killer bees wreaking havoc on New Orleans during Mardi Gras. Oscar-winner Ben Johnson gives dramatic punch to this made-for-TV chiller. Some good thrills. 99m. **DIR:** Bruce Geller. **CAST:** Ben Johnson, Michael Parks, Horst Buchholz. **1976**

SAVAGE INTRUDER, THE An aging film star hires a male nurse who turns out to be a psycho. 90m. **DIR:** Donald Wolfe. **CAST:** Miriam Hopkins, John David Garfield, Gale Sondergaard. **1977**

SAVAGE WEEKEND ★★ Several couples head out from the big city into the backwoods to watch a boat being built, but they are killed off one by one. The only reason this movie earns any stars is for talented actor William Sanderson's performance as a demented lunatic who may or may not be the killer. Rated R for nudity, simulated sex, and violence. 88m. **DIR:** John Mason Kirby. **CAST:** Christopher Allport, James Doerr, Marilyn Hamlin, William Sanderson. **1979**

SAVAGES (1974) ★★★ Man hunts man! Sam Bottoms is guiding Andy Griffith on a hunt in the desert when Griffith goes bananas and begins a savage, relentless pursuit of Bottoms. A sandy rendition of the famous short story, "The Most Dangerous Game." Thrilling, suspenseful, and intriguing to watch. Made for TV. 78m. **DIR:** Lee H. Katzin. **CAST:** Andy Griffith, Sam Bottoms, Noah Beery Jr., James Best. **1974**

SCALPEL Plastic surgeon transforms a young accident victim into the spitting image of his missing daughter to pull an inheritance swindle. Rated R. 96m. **DIR:** John Grissmer. **CAST:** Robert Lansing, Judith Chapman, Arlen Dean Snyder, Sandy Martin. **1976**

SCALPS ★★ Early effort from Florida poverty-row director Fred Olen Ray shows him still imitating better-financed Hollywood filmmakers. Presence of experienced character actors lends novelty value to horror thriller about resurrected Indian ghost and its teenage prey. Rated R. 82m. **DIR:** Fred Olen Ray. **CAST:** Kirk Alyn, Carol Borland. **1983**

SCANNERS ★★★½ From its first shocking scene—in which a character's head explodes, spewing blood, flesh, and bone all over—*Scanners* poses a challenge to its viewers: How much can you take? Shock specialist David Cronenberg wrote and directed this potent film, about a bloody war among people with formidable extrasensory powers. Rated R. 102m. **DIR:** David Cronenberg. **CAST:** Jennifer O'Neill, Patrick McGoohan, Stephen Lack, Lawrence Dane. **1981**

SCANNERS 2: THE NEW ORDER ★★½ Pretty much the same old thing, with a new breed of scanners roaming the streets, causing people to hemorrhage and explode. Good guy scanners David Hewlett and Deborah Raffin attempt to stop the bad guy scanners from controlling the city. Rated R for violence. 102m. **DIR:** Christian Duguay. **CAST:** David Hewlett, Deborah Raffin. **1991**

SCANNERS 3: THE TAKEOVER This third installment is distant from David Cronenberg's original vision. Dull. Rated R for nudity and profanity. 101m. **DIR:** Christian Duguay. **CAST:** Liliana Komorowska, Valerie Valois, Steve Parrish. **1992**

SCARECROWS ★★★★ This is something rare—a truly frightening horror film, loaded with suspense, intelligent writing, and decent acting. The story involves a group of military deserters who have ripped off a federal money exchange and are flying south in a stolen cargo plane. They land in a secluded wilderness of cornfields filled with...scarecrows. Not recommended for the squeamish, but horror fans will find this to be a feast. Not rated, but contains graphic violence. 88m. **DIR:** William Wesley. **CAST:** Ted Vernon, Michael Simms, Richard Vidan. **1988**

SCARED STIFF A newly married couple move into an old house cursed by a voodoo priest. Rated R for violence. 85m. **DIR:** Richard Friedman. **CAST:** Andrew Stevens, Mary Page Keller. **1986**

SCARED TO DEATH ★★ This tepid thriller is noteworthy primarily because it is Bela Lugosi's only color film, not for the lukewarm story about a woman who dies without a traceable cause. Plenty of hocus-pocus, red herrings, and hypnosis. Directed by Christy Cabanne, a silent film pioneer. 65m. **DIR:** Christy Cabanne. **CAST:** Bela Lugosi, Douglas Fowley, Joyce Compton, George Zucco, Nat Pendleton. **1946**

SCARS OF DRACULA ★★★ A young couple searching for the husband's brother follow the trail to Dracula's castle, and soon regret it. Compares well with other films in the series, thanks primarily to Christopher Lee's dynamite portrayal of the Count, and the first-rate direction of horror veteran Roy Ward Baker. Rated R. 94m. **DIR:** Roy Ward Baker. **CAST:** Christopher Lee, Dennis Waterman, Christopher Matthews. **1970**

SCHIZO A deranged night worker freaks out when his favorite figure skater announces her wedding plans. Rated R. 109m. **DIR:** Pete Walker. **CAST:** Jack Watson, Lynne Frederick, John Leyton. **1976**

SCHIZOID This is an unimaginative slasher flick with typically gory special effects. Rated R. 91m. **DIR:** David Paulsen. **CAST:** Klaus Kinski, Marianna Hill, Craig Wasson, Christopher Lloyd. **1980**

SCREAM A group of vacationing friends spend the night in a ghost town. Rated R. 86m. **DIR:** Byron Quisenberry. **CAST:** Woody Strode, John Ethan Wayne, Hank Worden, Alvy Moore, Gregg Palmer. **1982**

SCREAM AND SCREAM AGAIN ★★★½ A top-notch cast excels in this chilling, suspenseful story of a crazed scientist (Vincent Price) attempting to create a race of superbeings while a baffled police force copes with a series of brutal murders that may or may not be related. Complex film benefits from polished performances. Based on the novel *The Disoriented Man,* by Peter Saxon. Rated PG for violence, language, and brief nudity. 95m. **DIR:** Gordon Hessler. **CAST:** Vincent Price, Peter Cushing, Christopher Lee, Christopher Matthews, Michael Gothard. **1970**

SCREAM, BLACULA, SCREAM 🦃 William Marshall returns as the black vampire, Blacula, in this unimpressive sequel. Rated R. 96m. **DIR:** Bob Kelljan. **CAST:** William Marshall, Pam Grier, Michael Conrad. **1973**

SCREAM FOR HELP 🦃 A suspense-thriller about a teenage girl whose stepfather is trying to kill her and her mother. Rated R for nudity, profanity, and violence. 95m. **DIR:** Michael Winner. **CAST:** Rachel Kelly, David Brooks. **1986**

SCREAM GREATS, VOL. 1 ★★★ The first in a projected series by *Starlog Magazine*. A documentary on horror-effects master Tom Savini. Gory highlights are featured from many of his movies, including *Friday the 13th*, *Creepshow*, and *Dawn of the Dead.* Savini shows his secrets and explains his techniques. Unrated, contains massive but clinical gore. 60m. **DIR:** Damon Santostefano. **1986**

SCREAM OF THE DEMON LOVER (1976) 🦃 Michigan-based Satanism bloodbath is at least over and done with quickly. Rated R. 71m. **DIR:** Donald G. Jackson, Jerry Younkins. **CAST:** Gunnar Hansen. **1976**

SCREAMERS 🦃 An uncharted island, a mad doctor, a crazy inventor, and a bunch of underpaid extras in native costumes. Rated R. 90m. **DIR:** Sergio Martino, Dan T. Miller. **CAST:** Claudio Cassinelli, Richard Johnson, Joseph Cotten. **1979**

SCREAMING SKULL, THE 🦃 The old saw about a greedy husband trying to drive his wife crazy. B&W; 68m. **DIR:** Alex Nicol. **CAST:** John Hudson, Peggy Webber, Alex Nicol. **1958**

SEASON OF THE WITCH 🦃 Also known as *Hungry Wives*. Rated R. 90m. **DIR:** George A. Romero. **CAST:** Jan White, Ray Lane. **1972**

SEDUCTION, THE 🦃 This is a silly suspense film about a lady newscaster stalked by an unbalanced admirer. Rated R for nudity and violence. 104m. **DIR:** David Schmoeller. **CAST:** Morgan Fairchild, Andrew Stevens, Vince Edwards, Michael Sarrazin. **1982**

SEE NO EVIL ★★★½ Chilling yarn follows a young blind woman (Mia Farrow) as she tries to escape the clutches of a ruthless killer who has done away with her entire family at their quiet country farm. Mia Farrow is very convincing as the maniac's next target. Rated PG for tense moments. 90m. **DIR:** Richard Fleischer. **CAST:** Mia Farrow, Dorothy Alison, Robin Bailey. **1971**

SEIZURE ★★★ In Oliver Stone's directorial debut, an author of horror stories has a recurring dream about the murder of his houseguests by a trio of diabolical characters. Dream and reality intersect. Definitely a respectable chiller. Rated PG. 93m. **DIR:** Oliver Stone. **CAST:** Jonathan Frid, Martine Beswick, Herve Villechaize, Troy Donahue. **1974**

SENDER, THE ★★★ Those who like their horror movies with a little subtlety should have a look at this low-key but effective yarn. A young man brought to a hospital after he attempts suicide is discovered to have telepathic powers. Because of his emotional disturbances, he is unable to control himself and unleashes his nightmares into the minds of doctors and patients. Rated R for violence. 91m. **DIR:** Roger Christian. **CAST:** Kathryn Harrold, Zeljko Ivanek, Shirley Knight, Paul Freeman. **1982**

SENTINEL, THE 🦃 A woman unknowingly moves into an apartment building over the gates of hell. Rated R for nudity, profanity, and violence. 93m. **DIR:** Michael Winner. **CAST:** Chris Sarandon, Cristina Raines, Martin Balsam, John Carradine, José Ferrer, Ava Gardner, Arthur Kennedy, Burgess Meredith, Sylvia Miles, Deborah Raffin, Eli Wallach. **1977**

SERPENT AND THE RAINBOW, THE ★★★½ Loosely based on the nonfiction book of the same name, this is about a sociologist who goes to Haiti to bring back a potion that reportedly resurrects the dead. Rated R for violence, language, and nudity. 98m. **DIR:** Wes Craven. **CAST:** Bill Pullman, Cathy Tyson, Zakes Mokae, Paul Winfield. **1988**

SERVANTS OF TWILIGHT ★★★ Dean R. Koontz's *Twilight* is the source of this fast-paced, made-for-cable spin on *The Omen,* which features Bruce Greenwood as a dedicated private detective determined to save a little boy from a maniacal cult whose leader believes him to be the Antichrist. Violence and subdued sexual themes. 95m. **DIR:** Jeffrey Obrow. **CAST:** Bruce Greenwood, Belinda Bauer, Grace Zabriskie, Richard Bradford, Jack Kehoe. **1991**

SEVEN BROTHERS MEET DRACULA, THE ★★½ Hammer Film's last Dracula movie was a coproduction with the Shaw Brothers of Hong Kong, known mainly for their kung fu films. A martial arts–horror-fantasy about Professor Van Helsing fighting a vampire cult in China. An interesting attempt, but unless you are a kung fu fan, this entry will seem all too silly. Rated R; this feature was originally titled *Legend of the Seven Golden Vampires*. 88m. **DIR:** Roy Ward Baker. **CAST:** Peter Cushing, David Chaing, Julie Ege. **1973**

SEVEN DOORS OF DEATH ★★ This is the American release title (trimmed to obtain an R rating) of *The Beyond,* a stylishly gross Italian horror shocker about a Louisiana hotel situated on one of seven mythical gateways to hell. Even R-rated, this atmospheric shocker is incredibly gruesome. 86m.

DIR: Lucio Fulci. **CAST:** Katherine MacColl, David Warbeck. **1981**

SEVENTH SIGN, THE ★★★½ Finely crafted suspense film with Demi Moore portraying a woman whose unborn baby is threatened by the biblical curse of the Apocalypse. Moore is superb and Jurgen Prochnow is perfect as the avenging angel. Rated R for language and shock effects. 94m. **DIR:** Carl Schultz. **CAST:** Demi Moore, Michael Biehn, Jurgen Prochnow, John Heard. **1988**

SEVENTH VICTIM, THE ★★★ Innocent Kim Hunter stumbles onto a New York City coven of devil worshipers in this eerie thriller-chiller ancestor of *Rosemary's Baby*. Leave the lights on. B&W; 71m. **DIR:** Mark Robson. **CAST:** Tom Conway, Kim Hunter, Jean Brooks, Evelyn Brent, Hugh Beaumont, Isabel Jewell, Barbara Hale. **1943**

SEVERED ARM, THE ★★½ Before being rescued, a group of trapped mine explorers cut off the arm of one of the men as food for the others. Many years later, the survivors of the expedition are systematically slaughtered. This low-budget independent production is fairly suspenseful, though the acting is often listless and the gore a bit excessive. Rated R. 86m. **CAST:** Paul Carr, Deborah Walley, Marvin Kaplan. **1973**

SEVERED TIES ★★½ Outrageous special effects punctuate this campy horror film about a brilliant scientist who has found a way to regenerate limbs. He becomes the first recipient of his new discovery. Rated R for violence and language. 85m. **DIR:** Damon Santostefano. **CAST:** Oliver Reed, Elke Sommer, Garrett Morris, Billy Morrissette. **1992**

SHADOW PLAY ★★ Dee Wallace Stone plays a Manhattan playwright who is obsessed by the tragic death of her fiancé seven years earlier. Indeed, she becomes possessed by his ghost, which inspires her to write awful poetry. Rated R for profanity and violence. 101m. **DIR:** Susan Shadburne. **CAST:** Dee Wallace, Cloris Leachman, Ron Kuhlman, Barry Laws. **1986**

SHADOWZONE ★★½ A NASA dream-research experiment goes awry, releasing beings from a different dimension. Good gore effects highlight this suspenseful tale. Rated R for violence and gore. 88m. **DIR:** J. S. Cardone. **CAST:** David Beecroft, James Hong, Shawn Weatherly, Louise Fletcher. **1989**

SHE BEAST, THE ★★½ It's undeniably crude and extremely low-budget, but this Italian-Yugoslavian horror chiller about a reincarnated witch shouldn't be dismissed. It marked the filmmaking debut of Michael Reeves. 74m. **DIR:** Michael Reeves. **CAST:** Ian Ogilvy, Barbara Steele, Mel Welles. **1966**

SHE CREATURE, THE ★★½ American-International's answer to *Creature from the Black Lagoon* mixes Fifties reincarnation hocus-pocus with conventional monster lore. The eye-filling title beast is the finest creation of zero-budget makeup master Paul Blaisdell, who recycled the same suit for *Voodoo Woman* and *Ghost of Dragstrip Hollow*. B&W; 77m. **DIR:** Edward L. Cahn. **CAST:** Marla English, Tom Conway, Chester Morris. **1957**

SHE DEMONS A crazed Nazi scientist holds an uncharted island in a grip of terror. B&W; 80m. **DIR:** Richard Cunha. **CAST:** Irish McCalla, Tod Griffin, Victor Sen Yung, Gene Roth. **1958**

SHE FREAK, THE An uncredited remake of the classic *Freaks*. B&W; 87m. **DIR:** Byron Mabe. **CAST:** Claire Brennan, Lee Raymond. **1966**

SHE WAITS ★★ Producer-director Delbert Mann tries hard but cannot breathe any real thrills into this pedestrian tale of a young wife (Patty Duke) who becomes possessed by the spirit of her husband's first wife. Made-for-TV mediocrity. 74m. **DIR:** Delbert Mann. **CAST:** Patty Duke, David McCallum, Lew Ayres, Beulah Bondi, Dorothy McGuire. **1971**

SHINING, THE ★★½ A struggling writer (Jack Nicholson) accepts a position as the caretaker of a large summer resort hotel during the winter season. The longer he and his family spend in the hotel, the more Nicholson becomes possessed by it. Considering the talent involved, this is a major disappointment. Director Stanley Kubrick keeps things at a snail's pace, and Nicholson's performance approaches high camp. Rated R for violence and language. 146m. **DIR:** Stanley Kubrick. **CAST:** Jack Nicholson, Shelley Duvall, Scatman Crothers. **1980**

SHOCK (1946) ★★★ Highly effective thriller features Vincent Price in an early performance as a murderer—in this case he's a psychiatrist who murders his wife and is then forced to silence a witness through drugs and hypnosis. This minor classic provided the framework for many subsequent suspense movies. B&W; 70m. **DIR:** Alfred Werker. **CAST:** Vincent Price, Lynn Bari, Reed Hadley, Pierre Watkin, Frank Latimore. **1946**

• **SHOCK! SHOCK! SHOCK!** A sorry spoof of slasher flicks about an escaped mental patient who gets involved in a jewel theft. Not rated, but contains profanity and violence. B&W; 60m. **DIR:** Todd Rutt. **CAST:** Brad Isaac. **1988**

SHOCK WAVES (DEATH CORPS) Vacationers stumble upon a crazed army of underwater zombies. Rated PG. 86m. **DIR:** Ken Wiederhorn. **CAST:** Peter Cushing, Brooke Adams, John Carradine. **1977**

SHOCK'EM DEAD ★★ What starts out as an entirely lame scare flick ends as a completely lame scare flick. But in between are some truly frightening shocks as we see a wimp sell his soul to the devil in return for becoming the greatest rock star in the world. Rated R for violence, profanity, and gore. 94m. **DIR:** Mark Freed. **CAST:** Traci Lords, Aldo Ray, Troy Donahue. **1990**

SHOCKER ★★ Wes Craven introduces Horace Pinker, a maniacal TV repairman with a Freddy Kreuger personality and special powers. He spends his evenings hacking up families. Rated R for violence, profanity, and gore. 110m. **DIR:** Wes Craven. **CAST:** Mitch Pileggi, Michael Murphy. **1989**

SHOUT, THE (1979) ★★★ Enigmatic British chiller about a wanderer's chilling effect on an unsuspecting couple. He possesses the ancient power to kill people by screaming. Well made, with an excellent cast. The film may be too offbeat for some viewers. Rated R. 87m. **DIR:** Jerzy Skolimowski. **CAST:** Alan Bates, Susannah York, John Hurt, Robert Stephens, Tim Curry. **1979**

SHRIEK OF THE MUTILATED 🦃 College students looking for the Yeti find cannibals instead. Rated R. 92m. **DIR:** Michael Findlay. **CAST:** Alan Brock, Jennifer Stock. **1974**

SHRIEKING, THE 🦃 Tedious wannabe horror-action flick about Indian witchcraft used on some good old boys on motorcycles. Rated PG for violence. 93m. **DIR:** Leo Garen. **CAST:** Keith Carradine, Gary Busey, Scott Glenn. **1974**

SIDE SHOW ★★½ A young boy runs away to join the circus and discovers alcoholism, sex, and racial prejudice. When he witnesses a murder, he has to stay one step ahead of the killer. Not rated, but may not be suited for younger audiences. 98m. **DIR:** William Conrad. **CAST:** Lance Kerwin, Anthony Franciosa, Red Buttons, Connie Stevens. **1986**

SILENT MADNESS 🦃 Escaped maniac terrorizes a college campus. Rated R for nudity, violence, and profanity. 93m. **DIR:** Simon Nuchtern. **CAST:** Belinda Montgomery, Viveca Lindfors, Sidney Lassick. **1985**

SILENT NIGHT, BLOODY NIGHT ★★★ Give this one an extra star for originality, even if it's not that well produced. Lawyer Patrick O'Neal and girlfriend Mary Woronov spend a few nights in an old house that he is trying to sell. But the place used to be an insane asylum, and it has quite an interesting history. Rated R, it may be a bit too strong for kids. 88m. **DIR:** Theodore Gershuny. **CAST:** Patrick O'Neal, John Carradine, Mary Woronov. **1973**

SILENT NIGHT, DEADLY NIGHT 🦃 This is the one that caused such a commotion among parents' groups for its depiction of Santa Claus as a homicidal killer. No rating, but contains gobs of nudity and violent bloodshed. 92m. **DIR:** Charles E. Sellier Jr. **CAST:** Lilyan Chauvin, Gilmer McCormick, Robert Brian Wilson, Toni Nero. **1984**

SILENT NIGHT, DEADLY NIGHT PART 2 🦃 The first half of this sequel is composed almost entirely of flashback scenes from the earlier movie. Rated R for nudity and gore. 88m. **DIR:** Lee Harry. **CAST:** Eric Freeman, James L. Newman, Elizabeth Cayton. **1987**

SILENT NIGHT, DEADLY NIGHT 4—INITIATION ★★★ This fourth installment doesn't have any relation to the previous three films. Supernatural story that just happens to take place around Christmas. Rated R for violence and profanity. 90m. **DIR:** Brian Yuzna. **CAST:** Maud Adams, Tommy Hinkley, Allyce Beasley, Clint Howard. **1990**

SILENT NIGHT, DEADLY NIGHT 5: THE TOY MAKER 🦃 An old toymaker named Joe Peto and his oddball son Pino, make deadly toys designed to kill their child owners. A twisted but silly attempt at horror. Rated R for violence, profanity, and simulated sex. 90m. **DIR:** Martin Kitrosser. **CAST:** Mickey Rooney, Jane Higginson. **1991**

SILENT SCREAM ★★½ This is a well-done shock film with a semi-coherent plot and enough thrills to satisfy the teens. Rated R. 87m. **DIR:** Denny Harris. **CAST:** Yvonne De Carlo, Barbara Steele, Avery Schreiber, Rebecca Balding. **1980**

SILVER BULLET ★★★★ A superior Stephen King horror film, this release moves like the projectile after which it was named. From the opening scene, in which a railroad worker meets his gruesome demise at the claws of a werewolf, to the final confrontation between our heroes (Gary Busey and Corey Haim) and the hairy beast, it's an edge-of-your-seat winner. Rated R for violence and gore. 90m. **DIR:** Daniel Attias. **CAST:** Gary Busey, Everett McGill, Corey Haim, Megan Follows, James Gammon, Robin Groves. **1985**

SIMON, KING OF THE WITCHES 🦃 Modern-day warlock lives in a Los Angeles sewer. Rated R. 90m. **DIR:** Bruce Kessler. **CAST:** Andrew Prine, Brenda Scott. **1971**

SINISTER INVASION 🦃 Boris Karloff filmed scenes for this Mexican horror film just before his death. Also available in a truncated version, *Alien Terror*. 88m. **DIR:** Juan Ibanez, Jack Hill. **CAST:** Boris Karloff. **1968**

SINS OF DORIAN GRAY, THE ★★ This modern-day version of Oscar Wilde's famous horror tale manages to disappoint at nearly every turn. Only the plot—about a beautiful woman who sells her soul for eternal youth and then watches a video screen test of herself age and decay—manages to fascinate. Made for television. 98m. **DIR:** Tony Maylam. **CAST:** Anthony Perkins, Belinda Bauer, Joseph Bottoms, Olga Karlatos, Michael Ironside. **1983**

SISTER, SISTER ★★★ A gothic thriller set in the Louisiana bayou. Jennifer Jason Leigh is a frail lass who is haunted by a demon lover and taken care of by an overprotective older sister (Judith Ivey). Rated R for violence, nudity, simulated sex, and profanity. 91m. **DIR:** Bill Condon. **CAST:** Eric Stoltz, Jennifer Jason Leigh, Judith Ivey, Dennis Lipscomb, Anne Pitoniak. **1988**

SKEETER Mutant mosquitoes suck the life out of this low-rent nature-gone-awry thriller. Badly directed and poorly acted. Rated R for violence, language, and sexual situations. 95m. **DIR:** Clark Brandon. **CAST:** Tracy Griffith, Jim Youngs, Charles Napier, Michael J. Pollard. **1993**

SKULL, THE ★★★★ A collector of occult memorabilia covets the death's-head of the infamous Marquis de Sade. Based on a fine Robert Bloch short story, this imaginative fantasy is the apex of the Amicus Productions horror cycle of the 1960s. The modern-day setting helps rather than hinders. 83m. **DIR:** Freddie Francis. **CAST:** Peter Cushing, Patrick Wymark, Christopher Lee, Jill Bennett, Nigel Green, Patrick Magee. **1965**

SKULLDUGGERY A costume store employee inherits a Satanic curse that sends him on a killing rampage. Not rated, but would earn a PG for violence and profanity. 95m. **DIR:** Ota Richter. **CAST:** Thom Haverstock, Wendy Crewson. **1983**

SLASHER ★★ This routine Italian police melodrama, with former Hitchcock leading man Farley Granger hunting a serial killer, has been released in the United States under three titles: *Slasher*, *The Slasher Is the Sex Maniac*, and, finally, in a hard-core version (for the mid-seventies porno chic audience, with unrelated sex scenes having nothing to do with Granger) called *Penetration*. You don't need to race out and track down any of them. Rated R. 100m. **DIR:** Roberto Montero. **CAST:** Farley Granger. **1974**

SLAUGHTER HIGH ★★ Ten years after disfiguring a schoolmate, several former high school friends attend a deadly reunion. The rest of the film is fairly predictable. The ending is a welcome change from the norm, though, and it's nice to see horror queen Caroline Munro still working. Not rated, but contains graphic violence and adult situations. 91m. **DIR:** George Dugdale. **CAST:** Caroline Munro, Simon Scuddamore. **1986**

SLAUGHTER OF THE VAMPIRES A hunted vampire bites the neck of a beautiful victim. Italian would-be thriller. B&W; 81m. **DIR:** Roberto Mauri. **CAST:** Walter Brandi. **1971**

SLAUGHTERHOUSE A disturbed man butchers people as if they were farm animals. Rated R for violence and profanity. 85m. **DIR:** Rick Roessler. **CAST:** Joe Barton, Sherry Rendorf. **1987**

SLAUGHTERHOUSE ROCK Typical schlock shocker about a kid who becomes possessed by a spirit from Alcatraz. Rated R for nudity and violence. 90m. **DIR:** Dimitri Logothetis. **CAST:** Nicholas Celozzi. **1988**

SLEEPAWAY CAMP This bloody, disgusting film is one that will make you appreciate the fast-forward feature on your VCR. 88m. **DIR:** Robert Hiltzik. **CAST:** Mike Kellin, Paul DeAngelo. **1983**

SLEEPAWAY CAMP II: UNHAPPY CAMPERS ★★½ Gory and funny sequel about naughty kids being slaughtered by a puritanical camp counselor. Rated R for nudity, violence, and profanity. 81m. **DIR:** Michael A. Simpson. **CAST:** Pamela Springsteen, René Estevez, Brian Patrick Clarke. **1988**

SLEEPAWAY CAMP III Angela (Pamela Springsteen), the murderous happy camper, returns to Camp Happy Woods. Rated R for violence and nudity. 80m. **DIR:** Michael A. Simpson. **CAST:** Pamela Springsteen, Michael J. Pollard. **1988**

SLEEPING CAR, THE ★★ Haunted railway car converted into a rental home just may be the death of a disenchanted journalist. Stale one-liners and cheapie special effects weaken this potentially fascinating horror-comedy. Rated R for violence, language, and nudity. 96m. **DIR:** Douglas Curtis. **CAST:** David Naughton, Kevin McCarthy, Jeff Conaway. **1990**

SLITHIS ★★ Okay horror tale of a gruesome monster, derived from garbage and radiation in southern California, and his reign of terror. While earnestly done, the film just can't overcome its budget restrictions. Actual on-screen title: *Spawn of the Slithis*. Rated PG. 92m. **DIR:** Stephen Traxler. **CAST:** Alan Blanchard, Judy Motulsky. **1978**

SLUGS, THE MOVIE Mutated slugs infest a small town, devouring anyone they can crawl across. Rated R for violence and brief nudity. 90m. **DIR:** Juan Piquer Simon. **CAST:** Michael Garfield, Kim Terry, Patty Shepard. **1988**

SLUMBER PARTY MASSACRE A mass murderer has escaped from a mental hospital and is killing young girls with a power drill. Rated R for nudity and graphic violence. 77m. **DIR:** Amy Jones. **CAST:** Michele Michaels, Robin Stille, Michael Villella. **1982**

SLUMBER PARTY MASSACRE II ★★ The driller killer is back, but this time he appears as the ghost of a 1950s rock star. His weapon: a heavy-metal guitar with a high-powered drill extending from the neck. The producers tried to be original, but they didn't go far enough. Maybe next time. Rated R for violence, nudity, and profanity. 90m. **DIR:** Deborah Brock. **CAST:** Crystal Bernard. **1987**

SLUMBER PARTY MASSACRE 3 The driller killer is back yet again, boring holes into kicking and screaming scantily clad girls. Predictable gory schlock. Not rated, but contains nudity, profanity, and violence.

80m. **DIR:** Sally Mattison. **CAST:** Keely Christian, M. K. Harris, David Greenlee. **1990**

SNAKE PEOPLE 🦃 In this Mexican movie with scenes of Boris Karloff shot just before his death, the ailing actor plays a rich man whose niece is kidnapped by demon worshipers. 90m. **DIR:** Juan Ibanez, Jack Hill. **CAST:** Boris Karloff. **1968**

SNOW CREATURE, THE 🦃 Abominable Snowman movie is one of the weakest of the batch that hit American theatres in the mid-1950s. B&W; 70m. **DIR:** W. Lee Wilder. **CAST:** Paul Langton, Leslie Denison. **1954**

SNOWBEAST 🦃 Hokey white Sasquatch–Abominable Snowman makes life miserable on the slopes. 100m. **DIR:** Herb Wallerstein. **CAST:** Bo Svenson, Yvette Mimieux, Robert Logan, Clint Walker, Sylvia Sidney. **1977**

SNUFF 🦃 Dull garbage cynically passed off in its theatrical debut as a genuine snuff movie—actually nothing more than an Argentinian drug smuggling pic, capped with obviously fake disemboweling climax filmed in a New York apartment. Not rated. 82m. **DIR:** Michael Findlay. **1974**

SOCIETY ★★½ Every child's worst nightmare comes true for a Beverly Hills teenager who is plunged into a nightmarish world of ritual sacrifice and monstrous cruelty. Rated R for violence, profanity, and nudity. 99m. **DIR:** Brian Yuzna. **CAST:** Billy Warlock, Devin DeVasquez, Evan Richards. **1992**

SOLE SURVIVOR ★★ A gory remake of a fine English suspense thriller of the same title—about the lone survivor of an airplane crash, haunted by the ghosts of those who died in the tragedy. A psychic tries to help this haunted woman by keeping the ghosts from killing her. Although there are some chills, this version pales in comparison to its predecessor—with Robert Powell and Jenny Agutter. Rated R for sexual situations and violence. 85m. **DIR:** Thom Eberhardt. **CAST:** Anita Skinner, Kurt Johnson. **1985**

SOMETHING WEIRD 🦃 Tedious and bloodless time waster about a burn victim who finds he has gained extrasensory powers. There's also a subplot about a witch who restores his looks. None of it makes sense. 83m. **DIR:** Herschell Gordon Lewis. **CAST:** Tony McCabe, Elizabeth Lee. **1967**

SOMETIMES AUNT MARTHA DOES DREADFUL THINGS ★★ Weird obscurity about a killer hiding out from the police by holing up in a Miami beach house dressed as a woman. He has an indecisive young male lover whom he passes off as his nephew. There are a few touches of black comedy, but not enough. Rated R for nudity. 95m. **DIR:** Thomas Casey. **CAST:** Abe Zwick, Scott Lawrence, Robin Hughes. **1971**

SOMETIMES THEY COME BACK ★★★½ Chilling made-for-TV thriller gets good mileage from Stephen King's book. Tim Matheson is superb as the high school teacher who returns to his hometown thirty years after his brother died in a freak accident. The bullies responsible, who also died in the accident, come back one by one to seek revenge against Matheson. 97m. **DIR:** Tom McLoughlin. **CAST:** Tim Matheson, Brooke Adams, Robert Rusler. **1991**

SON OF BLOB (BEWARE! THE BLOB) ★★ Larry Hagman made this sequel to *The Blob* in his low period between *I Dream of Jeannie* and *Dallas*. It looks like he just got some friends together and decided to have some fun. The result is rather lame. Rated PG. 88m. **DIR:** Larry Hagman. **CAST:** Robert Walker, Godfrey Cambridge, Carol Lynley, Larry Hagman, Cindy Williams, Shelley Berman, Gerrit Graham, Dick Van Patten. **1972**

SON OF DRACULA (1943) ★★★½ Moody horror film features Lon Chaney's only turn as the Count, this time stalking a southern mansion as Alucard (spell it backward). Compelling, highly original Universal chiller boasts several eye-catching effects, dazzling camera work by George Robinson. B&W; 80m. **DIR:** Robert Siodmak. **CAST:** Lon Chaney Jr., Louise Allbritton, Robert Paige, Evelyn Ankers, Frank Craven, J. Edward Bromberg. **1943**

SON OF FRANKENSTEIN ★★★★½ A strong cast (including Boris Karloff in his last appearance as the monster) makes this second sequel to *Frankenstein* memorable. This time, Henry Frankenstein's son Wolf (Basil Rathbone) revives the dormant monster with the help of insane shepherd Ygor (Bela Lugosi, in his most underrated performance). Impressive, intelligent production scores highly in all departments, with the stark lighting and photography rating a special mention. B&W; 99m. **DIR:** Rowland V. Lee. **CAST:** Boris Karloff, Basil Rathbone, Bela Lugosi, Lionel Atwill, Josephine Hutchinson. **1939**

SON OF GODZILLA ★★ Juvenile production has the cute offspring of one of Japan's biggest stars taking on all sorts of crazy-looking monsters, with a little help from Dad. Good special effects and miniature sets make this at least watchable, but the story is just too goofy for its own good. Recommended viewing age: 2 and under. Rated PG. 86m. **DIR:** Jun Fukuda. **CAST:** Tadao Takashima, Kenji Sahara. **1969**

SON OF KONG, THE ★★★½ To cash in on the phenomenal success of *King Kong*, the producers hastily rushed this sequel into production using virtually the same cast and crew. Carl Denham (Robert Armstrong) returns to Skull Island only to find King Kong's easygoing son trapped in a pool of quicksand. Denham saves the twelve-foot albino gorilla, who becomes his protector. B&W; 70m. **DIR:** Ernest B. Schoedsack. **CAST:** Robert Armstrong, Helen Mack, Victor Wong, John Marston, Frank Reicher. **1933**

SONNY BOY ★★½ If you've ever wanted to see David Carradine in drag, you're in luck. As Pearl, he's the mother of a monstrous family that terrorizes a small desert town. You decide whether this one is funny on purpose or just bad: either way, it's pretty bizarre. Rated R for violence and gore. 98m. **DIR:** Robert Martin Carroll. **CAST:** David Carradine, Paul Smith, Brad Dourif, Sidney Lassick. **1987**

SORORITY HOUSE MASSACRE Features a vengeful killer slashing the sexy residents of a sorority house. Rated R for profanity, nudity, and violence. 74m. **DIR:** Carol Frank. **CAST:** Angela O'Neill, Wendy Martel. **1986**

SORORITY HOUSE MASSACRE 2 Lame hack-and-slash thriller about busty babes fighting off a bloodthirsty killer while in various states of undress. Typical shock horror, nearly plotless and badly acted. Not rated, but contains nudity, profanity, and graphic violence. 80m. **DIR:** Jim Wynorski. **CAST:** Robin Harris, Melissa Moore. **1992**

SOULTAKER ★★ Four teenagers are thrust into a realm between Earth and Heaven after a car accident. Mediocre, but with a solid ending. Rated R for violence. 94m. **DIR:** Michael Rissi. **CAST:** Joe Estevez, Vivian Schilling. **1990**

SPASMS ★★★ If it were not for the poor acting, this would be a top-notch horror film. Oliver Reed plays a millionaire trophy hunter who, on a hunting trip in a tropical jungle, becomes cursed by a giant monster-like snake. Peter Fonda plays the special psychologist who is hired to examine him. When the serpent is brought back to the hunter, the tension rises as the body count goes up. Not rated, but contains profanity, nudity, and gore. 92m. **DIR:** William Fruet. **CAST:** Peter Fonda, Oliver Reed, Kerrie Keane, Al Waxman, Marilyn Lightstone. **1982**

SPECIAL EFFECTS Low-budget horror about a film director who murders a would-be actress. Unrated; the film has nudity and violence. 90m. **DIR:** Larry Cohen. **CAST:** Zoe Tamerlis, Eric Bogosian, Brad Rjin, Kevin J. O'Connor. **1984**

SPECTERS Archaeologists uncover an ancient tomb in Rome. Not rated, but contains violence and brief nudity. 95m. **DIR:** Marcello Avallone. **CAST:** Donald Pleasence, John Pepper, Erna Schurer. **1987**

SPELLBINDER The obsession of a lawyer for a young woman who is a Satanist. Rated R for profanity, nudity, and violence. 99m. **DIR:** Janet Greek. **CAST:** Timothy Daly, Kelly Preston, Rick Rossovich, Audra Lindley. **1988**

SPELLCASTER Music television contest winners are brought to a castle to vie for a $1-million check. Tame little romp. Rated R for profanity. 83m. **DIR:** Rafal Zielinski. **CAST:** Richard Blade, Gail O'Grady, Adam Ant. **1991**

SPHINX (1981) ★★ This is a watchable film...but not a good one. Taken from the tedious novel by Robin Cook (*Coma*), it concerns the plight of an Egyptologist (Lesley-Anne Down) who inadvertently runs afoul of the underworld. Directed by Franklin J. Schaffner. Rated PG. 117m. **DIR:** Franklin J. Schaffner. **CAST:** Lesley-Anne Down, Frank Langella, Maurice Ronet, John Gielgud. **1981**

SPIDER BABY ★★½ Lon Chaney Jr. plays a chauffeur caring for a family of homicidal mental defectives. An odd little film, just quirky enough to interest fans of the weird. B&W; 81m. **DIR:** Jack Hill. **CAST:** Lon Chaney Jr., Carol Ohmart, Quinn Redeker. **1964**

SPIRIT OF THE DEAD ★★★½ Originally titled *The Asphyx*, slightly edited for videocassette. Interesting tale of a scientist who discovers the spirit of death possessed by all creatures. If the spirit is trapped, its owner becomes immortal. Well-made British film with sincere performances. Rated PG for mild violence. 82m. **DIR:** Peter Newbrook. **CAST:** Robert Stephens, Robert Powell, Jane Lapotaire. **1972**

SPIRITS ★★½ Group of psychic researchers investigate a supposedly haunted house where a series of murders took place ten years before. Erik Estrada plays a doubting priest who must face off against the evil. As usual, things go bump in the night. Rated R for violence and nudity. 94m. **DIR:** Fred Olen Ray. **CAST:** Erik Estrada, Robert Quarry, Brinke Stevens, Oliver Darrow, Carol Lynley. **1990**

SPLATTER UNIVERSITY Typical slasher film featuring students having sex and then getting hacked to pieces. Rated R for profanity, brief nudity, and violence. 78m. **DIR:** Richard W. Haines. **CAST:** Francine Forbes, Ric Randig. **1985**

SPONTANEOUS COMBUSTION Government experiment turns Brad Dourif into a human flame thrower, but the film extinguishes itself long before any sparks ignite. Sorry effort from director Tobe Hooper. Rated R for violence. 97m. **DIR:** Tobe Hooper. **CAST:** Brad Dourif, Cynthia Bain, Melinda Dillon, Dick Butkus, Jon Cypher. **1990**

SPOOKIES Zombies of all varieties maim and kill people trapped in an old mansion. Rated R for violence and profanity. 85m. **DIR:** Eugine Joseph, Thomas Doran, Brenden Faulkner. **CAST:** Felix Ward, Dan Scott. **1985**

SQUIRM Ugly film has hordes of killer worms attacking a small town. Rated PG.

92m. **DIR:** Jeff Lieberman. **CAST:** Don Scardino, Patricia Pearcy. **1976**

STANLEY ★★ A crazy Vietnam vet (Chris Robinson) uses deadly snakes to destroy his enemies in this watchable, though rather grim, horror yarn. Rated PG for violence and unpleasant situations. 106m. **DIR:** William Grefe. **CAST:** Chris Robinson, Alex Rocco, Susan Carroll, Steve Alaimo. **1972**

STEPFATHER II ★★ A misfire because it obviously tries to take advantage of its predecessor. The psychotic killer from the first film starts the same routine all over again by posing as a marriage counselor and preying on unsuspecting divorcées and widows. Rated R for gratuitous violence. 86m. **DIR:** Jeff Burr. **CAST:** Terry O'Quinn, Meg Foster, Henry Brown, Jonathan Brandis, Caroline Williams, Mitchell Laurance. **1989**

STEPFATHER III: FATHER'S DAY ★★ Make room for daddy once again, as the world's worst father returns after escaping from an insane asylum, having had his face surgically altered. Obviously the filmmaker hasn't heard of family values. Rated R for violence and language. 109m. **DIR:** Guy Magar. **CAST:** Robert Wrightman, Priscilla Barnes, Season Hubley. **1992**

STEPHEN KING'S GRAVEYARD SHIFT ★★ Based on a short story from King's *Night Shift* collection, this is a disappointing film about workers who are menaced by a giant mutant rat-bat while cleaning a factory basement. Rated R for violence, profanity, and gore. 90m. **DIR:** Ralph S. Singleton. **CAST:** David Andrews, Kelly Wolf, Stephen Macht, Brad Dourif, Andrew Divoff. **1990**

STEPHEN KING'S NIGHT SHIFT COLLECTION 🦃 In this so-called collection, featuring two short-story adaptations from Stephen King's book, *Night Shift*, we see again how hard it is to bring King's writing to the screen. 61m. **DIR:** Frank Durabont, Jeffrey C. Schiro. **CAST:** Michael Cornelison, Dee Croxton, Brion Libby. **1986**

STEPHEN KING'S SLEEPWALKERS ★★ An incestuous mother-son duo stalk virginal young women to feed their vampirelike hunger in this film of an original script from Stephen King. This film differs from his books in that it lacks all the things that make a Stephen King novel a Stephen King novel: fully fleshed out characters interacting in a cohesive plot. Rated R for violence, profanity, and gore. 91m. **DIR:** Mick Garris. **CAST:** Brian Krause, Madchen Amick, Alice Krige, Jim Haynie, Cindy Pickett, Ron Perlman. **1992**

STOLEN FACE ★★★ Early Hammer Films sleeper from the British studio's greatest director, Terence Fisher. Imported American lead Paul Henreid plays a noted plastic surgeon who remakes a female convict's face into the image of a woman he loved and lost. Taut and imaginative low-budget item. B&W; 72m. **DIR:** Terence Fisher. **CAST:** Paul Henreid, Lizabeth Scott, Andre Morell, Mary Mackenzie. **1952**

STONES OF DEATH 🦃 Nothing new here: teenagers getting knocked off one by one by supernatural forces. Rated R for nudity, profanity, and violence. 95m. **DIR:** James Bagle. **CAST:** Zoe Carides, Tom Jennings, Eric Oldfield. **1988**

STRAIT-JACKET ★★★½ Chilling vehicle for Joan Crawford as a convicted ax murderess returning home after twenty years in an insane asylum, where it appears she was restored to sanity. But was she? Genuinely frightening film features one of Joan's most powerful performances. George Kennedy is almost as good in an early role as a farmhand. B&W; 89m. **DIR:** William Castle. **CAST:** Joan Crawford, Diane Baker, Leif Erickson, George Kennedy. **1964**

STRANGE BEHAVIOR ★★★½ Michael Murphy stars as the police chief of Galesburg, Illinois, who suddenly finds himself inundated by unexplained knife murders. In all, this offbeat film is a true treat for horror-movie fans and other viewers with a yen for something spooky. Rated R. 98m. **DIR:** Michael Laughlin. **CAST:** Michael Murphy, Marc McClure, Dan Shor, Fiona Lewis, Louise Fletcher, Arthur Dignam. **1981**

STRANGE CASE OF DR. JEKYLL AND MR. HYDE, THE (1968) ★★ The offbeat casting of Jack Palance in the title role(s) is the main attraction in this taped-for-television production. Charles Jarrott directs with the same ponderous hand he brought to *Anne of the Thousand Days* and *Mary, Queen of Scots*, but the distinguished supporting cast is a plus. Not rated. 96m. **DIR:** Charles Jarrott. **CAST:** Jack Palance, Denholm Elliott, Torin Thatcher, Oscar Homolka, Leo Genn, Billie Whitelaw. **1968**

STRANGE CASE OF DR. JEKYLL AND MR. HYDE, THE (1989) ★★★½ Surprisingly effective entry in Shelley Duvall's Nightmare Classics series, this does not rely on a Hulk-like transition of Dr. Jekyll (Anthony Andrews) to terrify viewers. Instead, Andrews brilliantly creates two personalities—one timid, the other frightfully uninhibited—that refuse to overlap. Unrated, contains violence. 55m. **DIR:** Michael Lindsay-Hogg. **CAST:** Anthony Andrews, George Murdock, Laura Dern, Nicholas Guest. **1989**

STRANGENESS, THE 🦃 The Gold Spike Mine is haunted by a creature from down deep inside the Earth. Unrated. 90m. **DIR:** David Michael Hillman. **CAST:** Dan Lunham, Terri Berland. **1985**

STRANGER IS WATCHING, A ★★ A psychotic killer kidnaps two young ladies and keeps them prisoner in the catacombs beneath Grand Central Station. This commuter's nightmare is an ugly, dimly lit suspenser. Rated R. 92m. **DIR:** Sean S. Cunningham. **CAST:** Kate Mulgrew, Rip Torn, James Naughton. **1982**

STRANGER WITHIN, THE A housewife is mysteriously impregnated, and her unborn child begins to have a strange effect on her personality. Typical TV tripe. Not rated. 74m. **DIR:** Lee Philips. **CAST:** Barbara Eden, George Grizzard, Joyce Van Patten, David Doyle. **1979**

STRANGLER OF THE SWAMP ★★ Ghostly revenge story about a ferryman who was unjustly lynched and who hangs his murderers one by one is atmospheric and eerie but bogged down by a cheap budget and an unnecessary love story. Considered a minor classic among fantasy fans. B&W; 60m. **DIR:** Frank Wisbar. **CAST:** Rosemary La Planche, Robert Barrat, Blake Edwards, Charles Middleton. **1946**

STRAYS This bargain-basement critter entry attempts—and fails—to make deadly menaces of cuddly house cats. Supermom Kathleen Quinlan just looks foolish retreating in fear from a water-soaked tabby. Made for cable. Rated R for violence. 83m. **DIR:** John McPherson. **CAST:** Kathleen Quinlan, Timothy Busfield, Claudia Christian. **1991**

STREET TRASH Filmed in New York's Lower East Side, it focuses on street transients who consume a new brew that's been spiked by the military and go on a gory killing spree. 90m. **DIR:** Jim Muro. **CAST:** Bill Chepil, Jane Arakawa. **1987**

STRIPPED TO KILL II Slasher sleazoid at its worst, this investigation into a series of murders is a poor excuse for endless exotic dances and a razor-wielding psycho's rampage. Rated R for nudity, violence, and profanity. 85m. **DIR:** Katt Shea Ruben. **CAST:** Maria Ford. **1989**

STUDENT BODIES ★★½ This comedy-horror release has something extra, because it is a parody of blood-and-guts films. Rated R. 86m. **DIR:** Mickey Rose. **CAST:** Kristin Ritter, Matthew Goldsby, Joe Flood. **1981**

STUFF, THE A scrumptious, creamy dessert devours from within all those who eat it. Rated R for gore and profanity. 93m. **DIR:** Larry Cohen. **CAST:** Michael Moriarty, Andrea Marcovicci, Garrett Morris, Paul Sorvino, Danny Aiello. **1985**

SUBSPECIES ★★★ Two vampire brothers—one good, one evil—fight for a bloodstone left by their father. This interesting twist on the vampire legend suffers from bad acting, but benefits by holding true to many aspects of vampire lore. Not rated, but contains violence, profanity, and mild gore. 90m. **DIR:** Ted Nicolaou. **CAST:** Michael Watson, Laura Tate, Angus Scrimm. **1990**

SUMMER OF FEAR ★★ Confine Wes Craven to television and his horrific abilities fly out the window. A set-upon Linda Blair is the tormented target. Originally telecast as *Stranger In Our House*. 100m. **DIR:** Wes Craven. **CAST:** Linda Blair, Macdonald Carey, Carol Lawrence, Jeff East, Lee Purcell, Jeremy Slate, Jeff McCracken. **1978**

SUNDOWN (1990) ★★½ Purgatory is a small desert community established by a group of vampires fed up with the old ways. They manufacture their own blood and use sun block. A new generation of bloodsuckers decides enough is enough and declares war. Unique slant on the vampire legend starts off promisingly, but then gets batty toward the end. Rated R for nudity and violence. 104m. **DIR:** Anthony Hickox. **CAST:** David Carradine, Maxwell Caulfield, Morgan Brittany, Bruce Campbell, John Ireland. **1990**

SUPERNATURALS, THE ★★★½ A group of modern-day soldiers face off against Civil War Confederate zombies. The commanding officer (Nichelle Nichols) must find the secret to exorcise these evil spirits before they kill her and her men. Good scary entertainment. Rated R for graphic violence. 91m. **DIR:** Armand Mastroianni. **CAST:** Nichelle Nichols, Maxwell Caulfield, Talia Balsam, LeVar Burton. **1988**

SUSPIRIA ★★★★ Now classic art-horror chiller is even more fearsome in the uncut version, with a delicate lead performance by Jessica Harper, ingenious photography by Luciano Tivoli, and a relentlessly disturbing score by the Goblins. A timid American girl enrolls in a prudish European ballet academy, only to discover it's staffed by a coven of witches who trim the roster with frightening regularity. Malevolent atmosphere steers clear of the usual camp and is genuinely apprehensive, though the satisfying resolve may leave you wondering why the heroine didn't change schools a lot earlier. Not rated. 97m. **DIR:** Dario Argento. **CAST:** Jessica Harper, Stefania Casini, Joan Bennett, Alida Valli, Flavio Bucci, Udo Kier. **1977**

SWAMP THING ★★ Kids will love this movie, about a monster-hero—part plant, part scientist—who takes on a supervillain (Louis Jourdan) and saves heroine Adrienne Barbeau. But adults will no doubt find it corny. Based on the popular 1972 comic book of the same name. Rated PG, it has some tomato-paste violence and brief nudity. 91m. **DIR:** Wes Craven. **CAST:** Louis Jourdan, Adrienne Barbeau, Ray Wise, David Hess. **1982**

SWARM, THE Inept. Rated PG. 116m. **DIR:** Irwin Allen. **CAST:** Michael Caine, Katharine Ross, Richard Widmark, Henry Fonda, Olivia de Havilland, Richard Chamberlain, Fred MacMurray. **1978**

TALE OF A VAMPIRE ★★★★ Julian Sands plays a scholarly vampire who thinks he's found love again in Suzanna Hamilton, a woman similar to his long-dead paramour. Archenemy Kenneth Cranham arrives and casts a pall of tragic romanticism over the lovers. Slow but effectively moody in a gothic, gory manner. Rated R for violence and gore. 93m. **DIR:** Shimako Sato. **CAST:** Julian Sands, Suzanna Hamilton, Kenneth Cranham. **1993**

TALES FROM THE CRYPT ★★★½ Excellent anthology has five people gathered in a mysterious cave where the keeper (Ralph Richardson) foretells their futures, one by one, in gruesome fashion. Director Freddie Francis keeps things moving at a brisk pace, and the performances are uniformly fine, most notably Peter Cushing's in one of the better segments—"Poetic Justice." Don't miss it. Rated PG. 92m. **DIR:** Freddie Francis. **CAST:** Peter Cushing, Joan Collins, Ralph Richardson. **1972**

TALES FROM THE CRYPT (SERIES) ★★★½ Three creepy tales told with tongue firmly in cheek just as the original comic books were. Walter Hill's *The Man Who Was Death* chronicles an electric-chair executioner who takes his job just a little too far. Robert Zemeckis adds a new dimension to the demented Santa Claus idea with his tale *'Twas the Nite Before*. Richard Donner concludes the trio with *Dig That Cat...He's Real Gone*, about a man with nine lives who doesn't keep an accurate count of them. Not rated, but contains violence. 90m. **DIR:** Walter Hill, Robert Zemeckis, Richard Donner. **CAST:** Bill Sadler, Mary Ellen Trainor, Larry Drake, Joe Pantoliano, Robert Wuhl. **1989**

TALES FROM THE DARKSIDE, THE MOVIE ★★★ This horror anthology (inspired by the hit TV series) features a few exceptional moments and a lot of more mundane horror-film conventions. Rated R for violence and profanity. 90m. **DIR:** John Harrison. **CAST:** Deborah Harry, Christian Slater, David Johansen, William Hickey. **1990**

TALES FROM THE DARKSIDE, VOL. I ★★ The first installment in this ongoing series of TV-episode compilations is the only one worth bothering with, largely because of the three stories adapted: Stephen King's "Word Processor of the Gods," and Harlan Ellison's "D'Jinn, No Chaser," and "Slippage." The penny-ante budget doesn't help, though. 70m. **DIR:** Michael Gornick. **1985**

TALES OF TERROR ★★★ An uneven anthology of horror stories adapted from the works of Edgar Allan Poe. Directed by Roger Corman, it does have a few moments. 90m. **DIR:** Roger Corman. **CAST:** Vincent Price, Basil Rathbone, Peter Lorre, Debra Paget. **1962**

TALES THAT WITNESS MADNESS ★★★ Black-comic horror anthology featuring four stories told by an asylum keeper to a new psychiatrist. Most memorable is the third, in which Joan Collins fights for her husband's affections against his new lover: a possessed tree! Rated R for minor grossness. 90m. **DIR:** Freddie Francis. **CAST:** Donald Pleasence, Jack Hawkins, Suzy Kendall, Joan Collins, Kim Novak. **1973**

TARANTULA ★★★ Pretty good entry in the giant-bug subgenre of 1950s horror and science-fiction films. Heroic John Agar must deal with a mountain-sized arachnid created by well-meaning Leo G. Carroll's super-growth formula. Don't blink during the final scenes—Clint Eastwood has a *very* brief bit as the fighter pilot who brings the beastie down. B&W; 80m. **DIR:** Jack Arnold. **CAST:** John Agar, Mara Corday, Leo G. Carroll, Eddie Parker, Clint Eastwood. **1955**

TARANTULAS—THE DEADLY CARGO ★★ A small town is terrorized by a bumper crop of spiders in this TV movie that wastes too much time setting the viewer up for scare scenes which, when they finally arrive, aren't especially scary. 100m. **DIR:** Stuart Hagmann. **CAST:** Claude Akins, Charles Frank, Deborah Winters, Howard Hesseman. **1977**

TASTE OF BLOOD, A [turkey] The most ambitious film by Herschell Gordon Lewis, "The Godfather of Gore." The plot involves an American descendant of Dracula. 120m. **DIR:** Herschell Gordon Lewis. **CAST:** Bill Rogers. **1967**

TASTE THE BLOOD OF DRACULA ★★★ This fourth entry in Hammer Films's *Dracula* cycle is a big improvement after *Dracula Has Risen from the Grave*, but there's a problem: where's Dracula? We're almost half an hour into the movie before three Victorian family men revive the Count (unwittingly, natch). Stylish and creepy, but with more for the indefatigable Chris Lee to do, this might've been a four-star film. Rated PG. 95m. **DIR:** Peter Sasdy. **CAST:** Christopher Lee, Linda Hayden, Geoffrey Keen, Anthony Higgins, Roy Kinnear, Ralph Bates, Gwen Watford, John Carson, Isla Blair. **1970**

TEEN ALIEN [turkey] A group of kids put on a Halloween spook show in an abandoned mining mill. Rated PG for mild violence. 88m. **DIR:** Peter Senelka. **CAST:** Vern Adix. **1988**

TEEN WOLF [turkey] Pitifully bad film about a teenager who discovers he has the ability to change into a werewolf. Rated PG. 95m. **DIR:** Rod Daniel. **CAST:** Michael J. Fox, James Hampton, Scott Paulin. **1985**

TEEN WOLF, TOO [turkey] In this painfully dull sequel, the original Teen Wolf's cousin goes to college on a sports scholarship. Rated PG. 95m. **DIR:** Christopher Leitch. **CAST:** Jason Bateman, Kim Darby, John Astin, James Hampton. **1987**

TEENAGE ZOMBIES [turkey] Stodgy tale of teenagers stranded on an island where a lady scientist is conducting experiments. B&W;

71m. DIR: Jerry Warren. CAST: Don Sullivan, Katherine Victor. 1957

TELL-TALE HEART, THE ★★½ Fascinating, if extremely low-budget, study in sexual obsession and murder. A shy recluse, lured out of his dismal life-style by the new woman in his Victorian neighborhood, goes murderously mad when he spies her bedding down (shades of *Rear Window!*) with his best pal. B&W; 81m. DIR: Ernest Morris. CAST: Laurence Payne, Adrienne Corri, Dermot Walsh. 1961

TEMP, THE ★★ There's been kids from hell. Cops from hell. Dates from hell. And nannies from hell. Now comes the temporary office assistant from you know where—a femme fatale way beyond bitch who is just as efficient and sexy as she may be ruthless and insane. More of a slick crowd teaser than an actual thriller. Rated R for language and violence. 100m. DIR: Tom Holland. CAST: Lara Flynn Boyle, Timothy Hutton, Dwight Schultz, Oliver Platt, Faye Dunaway. 1993

TEMPTER, THE 🦃 Lurid Italian demonic-possession flick about a crippled woman who is the reincarnation of a witch. Rated R for profanity and violence. 96m. DIR: Alberto De Martino. CAST: Carla Gravina, Mel Ferrer, Arthur Kennedy. 1978

TENTACLES 🦃 Rotten monster movie from Italy about a phony-looking octopus attacking and devouring some famous Hollywood stars. Rated PG. 90m. DIR: Ovidio Assonitis (Oliver Hellman). CAST: John Huston, Shelley Winters, Henry Fonda, Bo Hopkins, Cesare Danova. 1977

TERMINAL CHOICE ★★ If it's blood you want, you'll get your money's worth with this one—by the gallons! There's some real tension in this film about a hospital staff that secretly bets on the mortality of its patients—not exactly family entertainment. Rated R for nudity, language, and plenty of gore. 98m. DIR: Sheldon Larry. CAST: Joe Spano, Diane Venora, David McCallum, Robert Joy, Don Francks, Nicholas Campbell, Ellen Barkin. 1984

TERMINAL MAN, THE ★★ A dreary adaptation of the crackling novel by Michael Crichton, although George Segal tries hard to improve the film's quality. He stars as a paranoid psychotic who undergoes experimental surgery designed to quell his violent impulses; unfortunately (and quite predictably), he becomes even worse. Rated R for violence. 104m. DIR: Mike Hodges. CAST: George Segal, Joan Hackett, Jill Clayburgh. 1974

TERROR, THE 🦃 This is an incomprehensible sludge of mismatched horror scenes even Boris Karloff can't save. 81m. DIR: Roger Corman. CAST: Boris Karloff, Jack Nicholson, Sandra Knight. 1963

TERROR AT LONDON BRIDGE ★★ Jack the Ripper is mystically resurrected in contemporary Arizona and goes on a killing spree in the British-style tourist trap. Only one man suspects that this is more than the work of a serial killer, and he must convince someone before it's too late. Predictable made-for-TV movie with some schlock gore effects. 96m. DIR: E. W. Swackhamer. CAST: David Hasselhoff, Stepfanie Kramer, Randolph Mantooth, Adrienne Barbeau. 1985

TERROR AT THE OPERA ★★½ In this stylish and suspenseful Italian production, a beautiful young diva is terrorized by a hooded maniac who makes her watch him murder the members of her opera company. An intense musical score, realistic effects, and the killer's brutality make this a disturbing experience. The movie fizzles out with a senseless conclusion. Unrated, but with extreme violence and some nudity. 107m. DIR: Dario Argento. CAST: Cristina Marsillach, Ian Charleson, Daria Nicolodi. 1991

TERROR AT THE RED WOLF INN ★★★ This is a sometimes ghoulishly funny horror-comedy about a college student who is chosen as the winner of a free vacation at an inn owned by a sweet old couple. Not all of the scenes work, but we guarantee it will give you the willies and the sillies. Rated R. (Also known as *The Folks at the Red Wolf Inn* and *Terror House*.) 98m. DIR: Bud Townsend. CAST: Linda Gillin, Arthur Space, John Neilson, Mary Jackson. 1972

TERROR CREATURES FROM THE GRAVE ★★½ Grade-Z title tacked onto what is actually a fairly stately, decorous Barbara Steele vehicle from Italy. She plays the wife of an occult scientist who summons zombies from the grounds of their Gothic estate. Atmospheric and fun. B&W; 83m. DIR: Ralph Zucker (Massimo Pupillo). CAST: Barbara Steele, Walter Brandi. 1966

TERROR IN THE AISLES ★★★ Donald Pleasence and Nancy Allen host this basically enjoyable compilation film of the most graphic scenes from seventy-five horror films. Rated R for violence, profanity, nudity, and suggested sex. 82m. DIR: Andrew Kuehn. CAST: Donald Pleasence, Nancy Allen. 1984

TERROR IN THE HAUNTED HOUSE ★★★ Although the title of this movie makes it sound as if it's a horror film, it is actually a psychological thriller along the Hitchcock line. It is the story of a young newlywed woman who has a recurring nightmare about a house she has never seen. She fears that something in the attic will kill her. The terror starts when her new husband takes her from Switzerland, where she has been since childhood, to the United States and...the house in her horrid dream. 90m. DIR: Harold Daniels. CAST: Gerald Mohr, Cathy O'Donnell. 1958

TERROR IN THE SWAMP 🦃 A Sasquatch-like creature is stalking the swamp. Rated

PG for violence. 87m. **DIR:** Joe Catalanotto. **CAST:** Billy Holiday. **1984**

TERROR IN THE WAX MUSEUM ★★ The all-star cast from yesteryear looks like a sort of Hollywood wax museum. Their fans will suffer through this unsuspenseful murder mystery. Rated PG. 93m. **DIR:** Georg Fenady. **CAST:** Ray Milland, Broderick Crawford, Elsa Lanchester, Maurice Evans, Shani Wallis, John Carradine, Louis Hayward, Patric Knowles. **1973**

TERROR OF MECHAGODZILLA ★★ Another outlandish Godzilla epic from the 1970s with the big guy battling his own robot double, Mechagodzilla. Nothing special, but a lot of flashy effects and explosions. As always, the kids will love it. Rated G. 89m. **DIR:** Inoshiro Honda. **CAST:** Katsuhiko Sasaki. **1978**

TERROR OUT OF THE SKY ★★ This made-for-television film is a sequel to *The Savage Bees* (1976). Here two bee experts and a gung ho pilot try everything to stop another infestation of the flying killers in the United States. Stick with the original. 100m. **DIR:** Lee H. Katzin. **CAST:** Efrem Zimbalist Jr., Dan Haggerty, Tovah Feldshuh, Lonny Chapman, Ike Eisenmann, Steve Franken. **1978**

TERROR STALKS THE CLASS REUNION ★★ The closing of a school on a German army base attracts a couple of psychos, one of whom still has a deadly crush on a former teacher. Geraint Wyn Davies captures Kate Nelligan, chains her to his wall, and plans their wedding. This Mary Higgins Clark story is clichéd, but Nelligan's performance is interesting. Rated PG for violence. 95m. **DIR:** Clive Donner. **CAST:** Jennifer Beals, Kate Nelligan, Geraint Wyn Davies. **1992**

TERROR TRAIN ★★★★ This is perhaps the best slasher film made in recent years. The story involves a New Year's Eve frat party taking place on a moving train, with everyone having a great time until students start showing up murdered. This film relies on true suspense and good performances for its thrills. Rated R for violence. 97m. **DIR:** Roger Spottiswoode. **CAST:** Ben Johnson, Jamie Lee Curtis, Hart Bochner, David Copperfield. **1980**

TERROR WITHIN, THE ★★½ A moderately scary terror film in the *Alien* mold. A group of scientists deep underground are the only people left after a plague wipes out mankind. Rated R for violence and profanity. 89m. **DIR:** Tierry Notz. **CAST:** George Kennedy, Andrew Stevens. **1988**

TERROR WITHIN 2, THE 🦃 It's sort of *Alien* meets *Mad Max Beyond Thunderdome* this time around as scientists battle superhuman mutants and a killer virus. Dopey. Rated R for nudity, profanity, and violence. 89m. **DIR:** Andrew Stevens. **CAST:** Andrew Stevens, Stella Stevens, Chick Vennera, R. Lee Ermey, Burton Gilliam. **1990**

TEXAS CHAINSAW MASSACRE, THE ★★★ This, the first film about a cannibalistic maniac by horror specialist Tobe Hooper, went pretty much unnoticed in its original release. That's probably because it sounds like the run-of-the-mill drive-in exploitation fare. While it was made on a very low budget, it nevertheless has been hailed as a ground-breaking genre work by critics and film buffs and became a cult classic. Rated R for extreme violence. 83m. **DIR:** Tobe Hooper. **CAST:** Marilyn Burns, Gunnar Hansen, Edwin Neal. **1974**

TEXAS CHAINSAW MASSACRE 2, THE ★★½ Leatherface is back! In fact, so is most of the family in this maniacal sequel. Dennis Hopper stars as a retired lawman out to avenge the gruesome murder of his nephew, and Caroline Williams plays the disc jockey who helps him locate the butchers. Unrated, but loaded with repulsive gore. 95m. **DIR:** Tobe Hooper. **CAST:** Dennis Hopper, Caroline Williams. **1986**

THEATRE OF BLOOD ★★★★ Deliciously morbid horror-comedy about a Shakespearean actor (Vincent Price) who, angered by the thrashing he receives from a series of critics, decides to kill them in uniquely outlandish ways. He turns to the Bard for inspiration, and each perceived foe is eliminated in a manner drawn from one of Shakespeare's plays. Rated R for violence. 104m. **DIR:** Douglas Hickox. **CAST:** Vincent Price, Diana Rigg, Robert Morley. **1973**

THEATRE OF DEATH ★★½ Mildly interesting mystery succeeds mainly due to Christopher Lee's assured performance and some well-timed scares as a series of gruesome murders is committed in Paris with an apparent connection to the local theatre company. Good title sequence deserves mention. 90m. **DIR:** Samuel Gallu. **CAST:** Christopher Lee, Julian Glover, Lelia Goldoni. **1967**

THERE'S NOTHING OUT THERE ★★★ Independent filmmaker Rolf Kanefsky sends up haunted house, hockey-mask groaners. His teens visiting a cabin in the middle of nowhere are in for a surprise. Sure, there's the alien creature patroling the woods, but there's also plenty of humor. One low-budget entry that defies its origins. Not rated, but contains nudity and adult language. 91m. **DIR:** Rolf Kanefsky. **CAST:** Craig Peck, Wendy Bednarz. **1990**

THEY ★★★ Rudyard Kipling's eerie short story gets stretched too far in this study of a distraught father (Patrick Bergin) who can't stop grieving for his dead daughter. He's got good reason, since the girl's spirit seems to be trapped in a house owned by weird southern mystic Vanessa Redgrave. Although everybody tries hard, there's just not enough plot to keep this feature going. Rated PG. 100m. **DIR:** John Korty. **CAST:** Patrick Bergin, Vanessa Redgrave, Valerie Mahaffey. 1993

THEY CAME FROM WITHIN ★★★ This is David Cronenberg's commercial feature-film debut. Even at this early stage in his career, his preoccupation with violence and biological rebellion is very much in evidence. Slimy, disgusting parasites invade the sterile orderliness of a high-rise apartment complex, turning the inhabitants into raving sex maniacs. Rated R. 87m. **DIR:** David Cronenberg. **CAST:** Paul Hampton, Joe Silver, Lynn Lowry, Barbara Steele. 1975

THEY LIVE ★★ The first two-thirds of this science-fiction–horror hybrid is such harebrained fun that one is truly disappointed when it falls apart at the end. Roddy Piper is a drifter in the not-so-distant future who discovers that the human population of Earth is being hypnotized into subservience by alien-created television signals. Rated R for nudity and violence. 95m. **DIR:** John Carpenter. **CAST:** Roddy Piper, Keith David, Meg Foster. 1988

THEY SAVED HITLER'S BRAIN 🦃 This bargain-basement bomb is actually a used movie since a major portion of it was lifted from an entirely different film made ten years earlier. B&W; 74m. **DIR:** David Bradley. **CAST:** Walter Stocker, Audrey Caire, Carlos Rivas, John Holland, Marshall Reed, Nestor Paiva. 1963

THIRST 🦃 An innocent young woman is kidnapped by a Satanic brotherhood and subjected to diabolical torture. Rated R for nudity and violence. 96m. **DIR:** Rod Hardy. **CAST:** Chantal Contouri, David Hemmings, Henry Silva, Rod Mullinar. 1988

THIRSTY DEAD, THE 🦃 Charles Mansonesque figure lives in the jungle and sacrifices young women in bloody rituals. Rated PG. 90m. **DIR:** Terry Becker. **CAST:** John Considine, Jennifer Billingsley. 1975

13 GHOSTS ★★★ Lighthearted horror tale of an average family inheriting a haunted house complete with a creepy old housekeeper (Margaret Hamilton) who may also be a witch, and a secret fortune hidden somewhere in the place. William Castle directs with his customary style and flair. Pretty neat. B&W; 88m. **DIR:** William Castle. **CAST:** Charles Herbert, Donald Woods, Martin Milner, Rosemary DeCamp, Jo Morrow, Margaret Hamilton. 1960

THIRTEENTH FLOOR, THE ★★ A young girl watches as her ruthless politician father has a man and his son executed. Years later, on the run from her father, she takes refuge in the same building where the killing took place. She soon discovers it's haunted by the spirit of the murdered boy. Rated R for violence and profanity. 86m. **DIR:** Chris Roach. **CAST:** Lisa Hensley, Tim McKenzie. 1990

THOU SHALT NOT KILL...EXCEPT 🦃 A violent cult (complete with a Charles Manson look-alike) goes on a killing spree. Not rated, but has violence, profanity, and comic-book gore. 84m. **DIR:** Josh Becker. **CAST:** Brian Schulz, Tim Quill, Sam Raimi. 1987

3 X 3 EYES, VOLS. 1–4 ★★★ Japanese animation. Bizarre but intriguing horror series. Pai, the last surviving member of her mythic three-eyed race, goes in search of the artifact that will at last transform her into a human being. Violent but entertaining. 30m. each. **DIR:** Daisuke Nishio. 1991

THREE ON A MEATHOOK 🦃 Hillbilly horror about a rural psychopath and his reign of terror. Can't decide if it's a spoof or a conventional gore movie. Rated R. 90m. **DIR:** William Girdler. **CAST:** Charles Kissinger. 1973

THRILL KILLERS, THE 🦃 Psycho killer Cash Flagg (a.k.a. writer–director Ray Dennis Steckler) and three escaped mental patients meet up at a diner, where they terrorize the patrons. Pretty dull. B&W; 69m. **DIR:** Ray Dennis Steckler. **CAST:** Cash Flagg, Liz Renay, Carolyn Brandt, Atlas King. 1965

THRONE OF FIRE, THE 🦃 The son of Satan must overthrow the king and marry his daughter to sit upon the legendary Throne of Fire. Not rated, but contains violence that might be unsuitable for younger viewers. 91m. **DIR:** Franco Prosperi. **CAST:** Sabrina Siani. 1973

TICKET OF LEAVE MAN, THE ★★ British horror star Tod Slaughter gleefully plays a maniacal killer who swindles rich philanthropists with a phony charity organization he has established. Slaughter single-handedly presided as Great Britain's unofficial hobgoblin during the 1930s and early 1940s. The majority of his films have been unavailable for years in America. B&W; 71m. **DIR:** George King. **CAST:** Tod Slaughter, John Warwick, Marjorie Taylor. 1937

TICKS ★★½ Why waste any effort on unimportant things like original characters or believable acting? Just cut right to the scary stuff—giant, bloodthirsty ticks. Anyone frightened by creepy-crawly critters will be cringing. Rated R for violence and gore. 85m. **DIR:** Tony Randel. **CAST:** Rosalind Allen, Ami Dolenz, Seth Green, Peter Scolari. 1993

TIME WALKER 🦃 Egyptologist accidentally brings an ancient mummy back to life. Avoid it. Rated PG. 83m. **DIR:** Tom Kennedy. **CAST:** Ben Murphy, Nina Axelrod, Kevin Brophy, Shari Belafonte-Harper. 1982

TINTORERA 🦃 Interminable *Jaws* rip-off. Rated R for gore and T&A. 91m. **DIR:** René Cardona Jr. **CAST:** Susan George, Hugo Stiglitz, Fiona Lewis. 1977

TO ALL A GOOD NIGHT ★★ In this typical slasher film, a group of young teenage girls gets away from supervision, and the mad killer shows up with a sharp weapon. A slightly above-average film of its genre. Rated R; has nudity, violence, and profanity. 90m. **DIR:** David Hess. **CAST:** Jennifer Runyon, Forrest Swenson. **1983**

TO DIE FOR ★★ Tooth-and-neck story stays fairly close to traditional vampire values, as warring brothers resolve a 500-year-old family feud in downtown L.A. Rated R for nudity and profanity. 94m. **DIR:** Deran Sarafian. **CAST:** Steve Bond, Sydney Walsh, Amanda Wyss, Duane Jones, Scott Jacoby, Brendan Hughes. **1989**

TO DIE FOR 2: SON OF DARKNESS ★★ The 500-year-old bloodsuckers are back, and it's up to the hero from the first film to put an end to their horror once and for all. Rated R for violence, profanity, and nudity. 95m. **DIR:** David F. Price. **CAST:** Rosalind Allen, Steve Bond, Scott Jacoby, Michael Praed, Amanda Wyss. **1991**

TO SLEEP WITH A VAMPIRE ★★★ Better-than-average slant on the vampire legend finds lonely bloodsucker Scott Valentine longing for the pleasures of daylight. When he meets lonely stripper Charlie Spradling, he finds a willing tutor. As the night comes to a close, the two have a difficult decision to make. Stylish thriller with fangs. Rated R for nudity, violence, and adult situations. 81m. **DIR:** Adam Friedman. **CAST:** Scott Valentine, Charlie Spradling, Richard Zobel, Ingrid Vold. **1993**

TO THE DEVIL, A DAUGHTER ★★★½ Dennis Wheatley wrote a number of books on the occult. This film was based on one of them, and it is his influence that raises this above the average thriller. Another plus is the acting. Richard Widmark gives an understated and effective performance as occult novelist John Verney, who finds himself pitted against Satanists. Rated R; the film contains nudity, profanity, and violence in small quantities. 95m. **DIR:** Peter Sykes. **CAST:** Richard Widmark, Christopher Lee, Honor Blackman, Denholm Elliott, Nastassja Kinski. **1976**

TOMB, THE ★★ Typical high-energy (and low-budget) Fred Olen Ray production, with the veteran stars on hand for B-movie marquee value, while a largely unknown young cast handles the strenuous mayhem. The plot centers on a curse that follows the desecrators of an Egyptian tomb. Rated R. 84m. **DIR:** Fred Olen Ray. **CAST:** Cameron Mitchell, John Carradine, Fred Olen. **1985**

TOMB OF LIGEIA ★★★ A grieving widower is driven to madness by the curse of his dead wife. This was Roger Corman's final Poe-inspired movie. The most subtle and atmospheric entry in the series, it was photographed by Nicolas Roeg on sets left over from *Becket*. The screenplay was by Robert Towne, who went on to write *Chinatown*. 81m. **DIR:** Roger Corman. **CAST:** Vincent Price, Elizabeth Shepherd. **1964**

TOMB OF TORTURE 🦃 A young woman, haunted by dreams that she lived a past life as an evil countess, visits the abandoned castle of the countess. Italian shocker, which is dubbed in English. B&W; 88m. **DIR:** Anthony Kristye. **CAST:** Annie Albert. **1966**

TOMBS OF THE BLIND DEAD ★★★ First entry in an entertaining exploitation-horror series, centering on the periodic resurrection of thirteenth-century Knights Templar and their quest for victims. Visually breathtaking—and one of the few examples of a Spanish horror film that has appeal for U.S. viewers. Rated R. 86m. **DIR:** Amando de Ossorio. **CAST:** Oscar Burner. **1971**

TORSO ★★½ Who's bumping off (and hacking apart) the pretty coeds at an Italian university? It takes forever to find out in this mechanical stalk-and-slash melodrama. However, the film springs to life for a climactic battle to the death between hero and masked villain. Rated R. 86m. **DIR:** Sergio Martino. **CAST:** Suzy Kendall, John Richardson, Tina Aumont, Luc Merenda. **1973**

TORTURE CHAMBER OF BARON BLOOD, THE ★★ Boring Italian production is basically nonsense as a long-dead nobleman (Joseph Cotten) is inadvertently restored to life, only to (naturally) embark on a horrendous killing spree. Worth watching for Mario Bava's unique directorial style. Originally titled *Baron Blood*. Rated R. 90m. **DIR:** Mario Bava. **CAST:** Joseph Cotten, Elke Sommer, Massimo Girotti. **1972**

TORTURE CHAMBER OF DR. SADISM, THE ★★ Based on Poe's "The Pit and the Pendulum," this German production has Christopher Lee as a count who lures Lex Barker and Karin Dor to his foreboding castle. Although containing some good shock scenes, *Torture Chamber* doesn't live up to its source material or title. Not rated, but contains violence and torture. 90m. **DIR:** Harald Reinl. **CAST:** Christopher Lee, Lex Barker, Karin Dor. **1967**

TORTURE DUNGEON 🦃 Unwatchable garbage from Andy Milligan, Staten Island's *auteur,* whose forays into medieval horror have all the entertainment value of a lobotomy. Rated R. 80m. **DIR:** Andy Milligan. **CAST:** Susan Cassidy, Jeremy Brooks. **1970**

TORTURE GARDEN ★★★½ A group of patrons at a carnival sideshow has their possible futures exposed to them by a screwball barker (Burgess Meredith) who exclaims, "I've promised you horror...and I intend to keep that promise." He does more than this in this frightening film laced with plenty of shock, plot twists, and intense situations. Rated PG. 93m. **DIR:** Freddie Francis. **CAST:** Burgess Meredith, Jack Palance, Beverly Adams,

Peter Cushing, Maurice Denham, Robert Hutton. **1968**

TOWER OF LONDON (1939) ★★★½ Basil Rathbone really sinks his teeth into the role of Richard III (and some of the scenery) in this historical drama about the evil prince's bloody rise to power. Despite a weak ending, *Tower of London* is an enjoyable movie of terror. In one of his all-too-rare leading roles, Rathbone is wonderful to watch, as are Boris Karloff (properly menacing as the executioner, Mord) and Vincent Price (as the conniving but ineffectual Duke of Clarence). B&W; 92m. **DIR:** Rowland V. Lee. **CAST:** Basil Rathbone, Boris Karloff, Vincent Price, Barbara O'Neil, Ian Hunter, Nan Grey, Leo G. Carroll, Miles Mander. **1939**

TOWER OF LONDON (1962) ★★★ A bloody update of the 1939 classic. Vincent Price plays Richard III, who systematically murders everyone who stands in his way to the throne of England. One can feel the chills crawling up the spine. Roger Corman's melodramatic style works well in this gothic setting. Not rated. B&W; 79m. **DIR:** Roger Corman. **CAST:** Vincent Price, Michael Pate, Joan Freeman. **1962**

TOWER OF SCREAMING VIRGINS, THE ★★ Lush, stately, sex-filled, and often sadistic medieval horror—supposedly based on an Alexander Dumas novel—set in and around a Gothic castle and its chamber of tortures. Despite the ad copy and lurid box art, the virgins are a bunch of young *men*, who fall prey to a sinister group of femmes fatales. Rated R. 89m. **DIR:** François Legrand. **CAST:** Terry Torday, Jean Piat, Uschi Glas. **1971**

TOXIC AVENGER, THE ★★★ Just another "nerdy pool attendant tossed into a tub of toxic waste becomes mutant crimefighter" picture. Actually, this low-budget horror spoof has a number of inspired moments. If you are looking for sick humor and creative bloodshed. Enjoy. Rated R for violence. 100m. **DIR:** Michael Herz, Samuel Weil. **CAST:** Mitchell Cohen. **1985**

TOXIC AVENGER PART II, THE ★★½ The makers of the original are back with another tounge-in-cheek bloodfest. Toxie goes to Japan in search of the man who might be his father. Not as bad as it sounds but just as weird. Rated R for violence and nudity. 96m. **DIR:** Michael Herz, Lloyd Kaufman. **CAST:** Ron Fazio, Lisa Gaye. **1989**

TOXIC AVENGER PART III: THE LAST TEMPTATION OF TOXIE, THE ★★★½ With nothing to do after ridding the town of Tromaville of all the bad guys, the Toxic Avenger unknowingly gets a job promoting a corporation bent on polluting the world. It's all in good fun. An unrated version runs a minute longer. Rated R for violence, profanity, and nudity. 102m. **DIR:** Michael Herz, Lloyd Kaufman. **CAST:** Ron Fazio, Lisa Gaye. **1989**

TRACK OF THE MOON BEAST 🦃 A mineralogist comes into contact with a fragment of a meteor. 90m. **DIR:** Richard Ashe. **CAST:** Chase Cordell. **1976**

TRANSMUTATIONS ★★ Much-lauded horror writer Clive Barker disowned this, the first of his stories to be filmed. A retired London mobster, searching for his missing girlfriend, discovers an underground society of mutants, the victims of drug experiments. The strong cast has little to do, and the story is more mystery than horror. Rated R. 103m. **DIR:** George Pavlou. **CAST:** Larry Lamb, Denholm Elliott, Nicola Cowper, Steven Berkoff, Miranda Richardson, Ingrid Pitt. **1985**

TRAP THEM AND KILL THEM 🦃 Originally titled *Emmanuelle and the Last Cannibals*, this gross out extravaganza merges the sexploitation *Emmanuelle* series of porn pictures with the Italian cannibal horror genre. Unrated, but sexually explicit and very gruesome. 85m. **DIR:** Joe D'Amato (Aristede Massaccesi). **CAST:** Laura Gemser, Gabriele Tinti, Susan Scott. **1977**

TRAUMA ★★ American cast gets lost in this weak effort from noted Italian horror-director Dario Argento. A woman is traumatized when she sees her parents decapitated by a serial killer. Argento keeps things creepy, but the film is slow and the characters are uninteresting. Unrated and R-rated versions available; unrated contains more gore. 106m. **DIR:** Dario Argento. **CAST:** James Russo, Frederick Forrest, Brad Dourif, Piper Laurie, Christopher Rydell, Asia Argento. **1992**

TREMORS ★★★★½ Here's a terrific, old-fashioned monster movie with great performances, a witty and suspenseful screenplay, and masterful direction. Kevin Bacon and Fred Ward are hilarious as a couple of independent cusses. One day our heroes discover a decapitated sheep rancher and his gruesomely devoured flock, and are forced to fight for their lives against a pack of flesh-eating, giant worms. Rated PG-13 for light profanity and remarkably limited violence. 90m. **DIR:** Ron Underwood. **CAST:** Kevin Bacon, Fred Ward, Finn Carter, Michael Gross, Reba McEntire, Victor Wong. **1990**

TRICK OR TREAT (1982) 🦃 A slow-moving mess about a baby-sitter and a spoiled brat on Halloween. Not rated, but contains violence and profanity. 90m. **DIR:** Gary Graver. **CAST:** Peter Jason, Chris Graver, David Carradine, Carrie Snodgress, Steve Railsback. **1982**

TRICK OR TREAT (1986) ★★½ Perhaps it was inevitable that someone would make a horror film about the supposed Satanic messages found in heavy-metal rock music. While not a classic of the genre, *Trick or Treat* is both clever and funny. Marc Price's performance is one of the film's pluses. Rated R for profanity, nudity, suggested sex, and violence. 97m. **DIR:** Charles Martin Smith. **CAST:**

Marc Price, Doug Savant, Elaine Joyce, Gene Simmons, Ozzy Osbourne. 1986

TRILOGY OF TERROR ★★★ Karen Black stars in this trio of horror stories, the best of which is the final episode, about an ancient Indian doll coming to life and stalking Black. It's often very frightening, and well worth wading through the first two tales. Originally made as an ABC Movie of the Week. 78m. **DIR:** Dan Curtis. **CAST:** Karen Black, Robert Burton, John Karlen. **1974**

TROLL II Flat sequel-of-sorts to producer Charles Band's original spoof. Family unleashes malevolent specter who wreaks havoc before being banished to late-night cable outlets everywhere. Rated PG-13 for violence. 95m. **DIR:** Drago Floyd. **CAST:** Michael Stephenson, Connie McFarland. **1992**

TURN OF THE SCREW, THE (1989) ★★★ This chilling entry in Shelley Duvall's *Nightmare Classics* features Amy Irving as the heroine of Henry James's novel. As a new governess, she tries to instill her two new charges with morality. In the process she must take on the evil spirit that possesses them. Unrated, but contains nudity and violence. 55m. **DIR:** Graeme Clifford. **CAST:** Amy Irving, David Hemmings, Balthazar Getty, Micole Mercurio. **1989**

TURN OF THE SCREW (1992) ★★★★ Updated to the 1960s, this is an intense and intelligent adaptation of Henry James's moody masterpiece. Julian Sands hires Patsy Kensit to tutor his odd niece and nephew, without revealing the secrets of his country house. Heavy doses of eroticism help build the tension to a creepy, albeit overly symbolic conclusion. Rated R for brief nudity and simulated sex. 95m. **DIR:** Rusty Lemorande. **CAST:** Patsy Kensit, Stéphane Audran, Julian Sands, Marianne Faithfull. **1992**

TWICE-TOLD TALES ★★ With all his usual feeling, Vincent Price lurks, leers, and hams his nefarious way through a trilogy of nineteenth-century novelist Nathaniel Hawthorne's most vivid horror stories, including *The House of the Seven Gables.* 119m. **DIR:** Sidney Salkow. **CAST:** Vincent Price, Sebastian Cabot, Joyce Taylor, Brett Halsey, Beverly Garland, Mari Blanchard. **1963**

TWILIGHT PEOPLE Mad scientist on remote island dabbles with things better left unfilmed. Rated R for violence. 84m. **DIR:** Eddie Romero. **CAST:** John Ashley, Jan Merlin, Pam Grier. **1972**

TWILIGHT ZONE—THE MOVIE ★★★ A generally enjoyable tribute to the 1960s television series created by Rod Serling, this film, directed by Steven Spielberg, John Landis, Joe Dante, and George Miller, is broken into four parts. Miller brings us the best: a tale about a white-knuckled air traveler (John Lithgow) who sees a gremlin doing strange things on the wing of a jet. Rated PG. 102m. **DIR:** Steven Spielberg, John Landis, Joe Dante, George Miller. **CAST:** Vic Morrow, Scatman Crothers, Kathleen Quinlan, John Lithgow, Dan Aykroyd, Albert Brooks. **1983**

TWINS OF EVIL ★★★ *Playboy* magazine's first twin Playmates, Madeleine and Mary Collinson, were tapped for this British Hammer Films horror entry about a good girl and her evil, blood-sucking sister. Peter Cushing adds class to what should in theory have been a forgettable exploitation film but provides surprisingly enjoyable entertainment for genre buffs. Rated R for nudity, violence, and gore. 85m. **DIR:** John Hough. **CAST:** Peter Cushing, Madeleine Collinson, Mary Collinson, Dennis Price. **1972**

TWISTED NIGHTMARE A group of young people at a camp near a lake are menaced by a mysterious homicidal maniac. Sound familiar? Rated R for violence. 95m. **DIR:** Paul Hunt. **CAST:** Rhonda Gray, Cleve Hall. **1982**

TWITCH OF THE DEATH NERVE ★★★ Also known as *Bay of Blood, Carnage,* and *Last House on the Left, Part II,* this is the ultimate splatter film, and it comes from an unexpected source: Mario Bava. The director was Italy's pioneer horror stylist, blending elegant visuals with gothic gore. In contrast, this *Ten Little Indians* clone is jarringly contemporary and features the most bloodletting ever in a non–X-rated shocker. Rated R. 87m. **DIR:** Mario Bava. **CAST:** Claudine Auger, Chris Avran, Laura Betti. **1970**

TWO EVIL EYES ★★ A two-part Edgar Allan Poe film shot in Pittsburgh. The first story, George Romero's version of "The Facts in the Case of M. Valdemar," is a total washout—shrill, derivative, and boring. The second, Dario Argento's adaptation of "The Black Cat," has some narrative shortcomings (principally its ending), but contains a powerful performance by Harvey Keitel and offers a scary study in obsession. 121m. **DIR:** Dario Argento, George A. Romero. **CAST:** Harvey Keitel, Adrienne Barbeau, E. G. Marshall, John Amos. **1990**

2,000 MANIACS Full of cruel tortures and mutilation, this drive-in hit was the prototype of today's sick-humor slasher films. 84m. **DIR:** Herschell Gordon Lewis. **CAST:** Thomas Wood, Jeffrey Allen. **1964**

UNBORN, THE Title says it all: another ferocious fetus movie that's unfortunately stillborn. Rated R for nudity, violence, and profanity. 84m. **DIR:** Rodman Flender. **CAST:** Brooke Adams, Jeff Hayenga, James Karen, K. Callan, Jane Cameron. **1991**

UNBORN II, THE Ferocious fetus returns for more mayhem, as Mom and a friend try to stop a fanatic from destroying the offspring. Just as bad as the first one.

Rated R for violence and language. 84m. **DIR:** Rick Jacobson. **CAST:** Michele Greene, Scott Valentine, Robin Curtis, Michael James McDonald. **1994**

UNCANNY, THE 🦃 A paranoid writer tells three tales of cat-related horror. Rated R. 88m. **DIR:** Denis Heroux. **CAST:** Peter Cushing, Ray Milland, Susan Penhaligon, Joan Greenwood, Donald Pleasence, Samantha Eggar, John Vernon. **1977**

UNDERSTUDY, THE: GRAVEYARD SHIFT II ★★ Silvio Oliviero returns in this sequel, playing an actor who gets the lead role in a vampire film without the rest of the cast knowing he really *is* a vampire. Rated R for nudity and gore. 88m. **DIR:** Gerard Ciccoritti. **CAST:** Wendy Gazelle, Mark Soper, Silvio Oliviero. **1988**

UNDERTAKER AND HIS PALS, THE 🦃 A mortician and two diner owners team up in a money-making venture, using human legs, breasts, etc., as the daily specials. Unrated. 70m. **DIR:** David C. Graham. **CAST:** Ray Dannis. **1967**

UNEARTHLY, THE 🦃 Mad scientist goes back into the lab to torture more innocent victims. 73m. **DIR:** Brooke L. Peters. **CAST:** John Carradine, Allison Hayes, Myron Healey. **1957**

UNHOLY, THE 🦃 A priest attempts to battle a demon that prolongs its existence by killing sinners in the act of sinning. Rated R for gore, nudity, and profanity. 99m. **DIR:** Camilo Vila. **CAST:** Ben Cross, Hal Holbrook, Ned Beatty, Trevor Howard, William Russ. **1988**

UNINVITED, THE (1987) 🦃 A group of college kids take staff jobs on a yacht and spend their spring break cruising to the Caribbean. Rated R for violence and nudity. 92m. **DIR:** Greydon Clark. **CAST:** George Kennedy, Alex Cord, Clu Gulager, Toni Hudson. **1987**

UNNAMABLE, THE ★★★ College students spend the night in a haunted house in this adaptation of an H. P. Lovecraft short story. While there, the promiscuous teens must contend with a family curse and a monstrous she-beast that delights in tearing humans limb from limb. There's a fair amount of good humor and some genuine chills. Horror fans should have a good time. Not rated, but contains nudity and graphic violence. 87m. **DIR:** Jean Paul Ouellette. **CAST:** Charles King, Mark Kinsey Stephenson, Alexandra Durrell. **1988**

UNNAMABLE II, THE ★★ Sequels are usually worse than the originals, and this is no exception. A 300-year-old winged demon is separated from the body and soul of the young, beautiful woman. So, of course, a bloody chase ensues. Not rated, but contains violence and nudity. 95m. **DIR:** Jean Paul Ouellette. **CAST:** John Rhys-Davies, Mark Kinsey Stephenson, Julie Strain, Peter Breck, David Warner. **1992**

UNSANE ★★★½ American fans of stylish Italian director Dario Argento have been awaiting his 1984 film *Tenebrae* for years. Although it never played theatrically in this country, it snuck onto video with a new title, *Unsane*. A mystery novelist discovers that a series of killings seems to be based on those in his latest book. Argento's trademarks—violent murders, a complex plot, and a pulsing synthesizer score—are all here in abundance. Unrated; the film contains nudity and violence. 92m. **DIR:** Dario Argento. **CAST:** Anthony Franciosa, Daria Nicolodi, John Saxon, Giuliano Gemma, John Steiner. **1984**

UNSEEN, THE 🦃 A cellar-dwelling invisible critter which does what you'd expect. Rated R. 89m. **DIR:** Peter Foleg. **CAST:** Barbara Bach, Sidney Lassick, Stephen Furst. **1981**

UP FROM THE DEPTHS 🦃 Perfunctory remake of *Creature from the Haunted Sea*. Rated R. 80m. **DIR:** Charles B. Griffith. **CAST:** Sam Bottoms, Susanne Reed, Virgil Frye. **1979**

VAMP ★★★ Effective comedy shocker concerns a pair of college kids (Chris Makepeace and Robert Rusler) who must find a stripper for a big party being thrown that night. Upon arriving at the After Dark Club, the duo quickly decide on the outrageous Katrina (Grace Jones), little realizing that she is a vicious, bloodthirsty vampire in disguise. Rated R for gore and brief nudity. 93m. **DIR:** Richard Wenk. **CAST:** Chris Makepeace, Grace Jones, Robert Rusler, Sandy Baron, Gedde Watanabe, Dedee Pfeiffer. **1986**

VAMPIRE, THE ★★½ Here it is, the first in a long line of late-Fifties/early-Sixties Mexican monster movies—all of them variously atmospheric, technically primitive, culturally eccentric..., and often compulsively watchable. German Robles was Mexico's Christopher Lee, although this first of his many vampire movies was shot a full year before Lee's *Horror of Dracula* debut. B&W; 84m. **DIR:** Fernando Mendez. **CAST:** German Robles, Abel Salazar. **1957**

VAMPIRE AT MIDNIGHT ★★ A young woman becomes the object of adoration of a brutal vampire posing as a motivational psychologist. This tries hard to be a character study rather than a horror movie, but it misses the mark. Rated R for violence and nudity. 94m. **DIR:** Greggor McClatchy. **CAST:** Jason Williams, Gustav Vintas, Leslie Milne, Jenie Moore, Robert Random. **1988**

VAMPIRE BAT, THE ★★★ Prolific director Frank Strayer gave low-rent Majestic Studios their biggest hit with this eerie thriller reminiscent of the great horror films. Lionel Atwill and Fay Wray reunite to share the screen with distinguished Melvyn Douglas as a skeptical magistrate out to solve several mysterious deaths. It seems the victims have all been drained of blood and great hordes of bats have been hovering about.... B&W; 63m. **DIR:** Frank Strayer. **CAST:** Lionel Atwill, Fay Wray, Melvyn Douglas, Dwight Frye, Maude Eburne. **1933**

VAMPIRE HAPPENING 🦃 A Hollywood sexpot vacations in Europe and learns her grandmother was a vampire. Not rated. 97m. **DIR:** Freddie Francis. **CAST:** Pia Degermark, Ferdinand Mayne, Thomas Hunter. **1971**

VAMPIRE HOOKERS 🦃 Aging vampire lords over a bevy of beauteous bloodsuckers. (Also known as *Sensuous Vampires.*) Rated R for violence and nudity. 82m. **DIR:** Cirio H. Santiago. **CAST:** John Carradine. **1979**

VAMPIRE HUNTER D ★★ Japanese animation. Stylized, rather stiff animation and below-average dubbing mar an otherwise passable feature set in a world where vampires and demons range freely. D, a half-vampire himself, protects a young woman. Unrated; contains violence and nudity. 80m. **DIR:** Toyoo Ashida. **1985**

VAMPIRE LOVERS, THE ★★★ Hammer Films of England revitalized the Frankenstein and Dracula horror series in the late 1950s. But by 1971, when *Vampire Lovers* was released, Hammer's horrors had become passé. Even adding sex to the mix, as the studio did in this faithful screen version of Sheridan LeFanu's *Camilla*, didn't help much. Nonetheless, sexy Ingrid Pitt makes a voluptuous vampire. Rated R for violence, nudity, suggested sex, and gore. 88m. **DIR:** Roy Ward Baker. **CAST:** Ingrid Pitt, Peter Cushing, Pippa Steele, Madeleine Smith, George Cole, Dawn Addams, Kate O'Mara. **1971**

VAMPIRES ALWAYS RING TWICE 🦃 A couple attempts to get away from it all and find themselves trying to get away from Postal vampires. Bottom of the barrel. Not rated. 118m. **DIR:** Steve Postal. **CAST:** Alan Ramey, Jennifer Tuck, Angela Shepard. **1990**

VAMPIRES FROM OUTER SPACE 🦃 An undead bride from the planet Cirrus takes her unwitting groom to a strange island in this entirely amateurish shot-on-video production. Not rated. 114m. **DIR:** Steve Postal. **CAST:** Alan Ramey, Angela Shepard, Jennifer Tuck. **1990**

VAMPIRE'S KISS 🦃 A ranting, obnoxious literary agent becomes convinced that he is a vampire. Rated R for violence, profanity, and brief nudity. 103m. **DIR:** Robert Bierman. **CAST:** Nicolas Cage, Maria Conchita Alonso, Jennifer Beals, Elizabeth Ashley. **1989**

VAMPYRES ★★½ This tale of two beautiful female vampires living in an old mansion and sharing their male victims sexually before drinking their blood was considered pornographic in its time. It's pretty tame by current standards, and also easier to appreciate as a piece of serious, if low-budget, erotica. There are two versions available on video; the longer, unrated one has elongated sexual situations, though both feature abundant nudity. 87m. **DIR:** Joseph Larraz. **CAST:** Marianne Morris, Anulka, Murray Brown, Brian Deacon, Bessie Love. **1974**

VARAN, THE UNBELIEVABLE ★★½ Another Godzilla rip-off with better-than-average effects. B&W; 70m. **DIR:** Inoshiro Honda. **CAST:** Jerry Baerwitz, Myron Healey, Tsuruko Kobayashi. **1962**

VAULT OF HORROR ★★ British sequel to *Tales from the Crypt* boasts a fine cast and five short stories borrowed from the classic EC comics line of the early 1950s, but delivers very little in the way of true chills and atmosphere. Not nearly as effective as the earlier five-story thriller *Dr. Terror's House of Horrors* and not as much fun as the most recent homage to the EC horror story, *Creepshow*. Rated R. 87m. **DIR:** Roy Ward Baker. **CAST:** Daniel Massey, Anna Massey, Terry-Thomas, Glynis Johns, Curt Jurgens, Dawn Addams, Tom Baker, Denholm Elliott, Michael Craig, Edward Judd. **1973**

VELVET VAMPIRE, THE ★★ Marginally unconventional low-budget horror about a young married couple vampirized by a sultry femme fatale. A few scenes are effective, but overall film is so slackly paced that it never generates any suspense. Rated R. 79m. **DIR:** Stephanie Rothman. **CAST:** Sherry Miles, Michael Blodgett, Celeste Yarnall. **1971**

VENOM 🦃 This combination horror film and police thriller doesn't really work as either. Rated R for nudity and violence. 98m. **DIR:** Piers Haggard. **CAST:** Nicol Williamson, Klaus Kinski, Susan George, Oliver Reed, Sterling Hayden, Sarah Miles. **1982**

VIDEODROME ★★½ Director David Cronenberg strikes again with a clever, gory nightmare set in the world of television broadcasting. James Woods and Deborah Harry (of the rock group Blondie) star in this eerie, occasionally sickening horror film about the boss (Woods) of a cable TV station. Rated R for profanity, nudity, violence, gore, and pure nausea. 88m. **DIR:** David Cronenberg. **CAST:** James Woods, Deborah Harry, Sonja Smits. **1983**

VILLAGE OF THE DAMNED ★★★★ A science-fiction thriller about twelve strangely emotionless children all born at the same time in a small village in England. Sanders plays their teacher, who tries to stop their plans for conquest. This excellent low-budget film provides chills. B&W; 78m. **DIR:** Wolf Rilla. **CAST:** George Sanders, Barbara Shelley, Michael C. Gwynne. **1960**

VILLAGE OF THE GIANTS ★★ Utterly ridiculous story of a gang of teenage misfits taking over a small town after they ingest a bizarre substance and grow to gigantic heights. What makes this worth watching, though, are the famous faces of the many young stars-to-be. 80m. **DIR:** Bert I. Gordon. **CAST:** Tommy Kirk, Beau Bridges, Ron Howard, Johnny Crawford. **1965**

VIRGIN AMONG THE LIVING DEAD, A 🦃 Available only in a severely cut version, this sub-gothic, damsel-in-distress snoozer is an atypical entry from its director's most prolific period—although the undead attack footage was shot eight years later by Jean Rollin during the making of *Zombie Lake,* and spliced in to make this English-language print releasable! 90m. **DIR:** Jess (Jesus) Franco. **CAST:** Christina von Blanc, Anne Libert, Howard Vernon. **1971**

VIRGIN OF NUREMBERG 🦃 A hooded killer lurking in an ancient German castle. (Alternate title: *Horror Castle.*) 82m. **DIR:** Anthony M. Dawson. **CAST:** Rossana Podesta, George Riviere, Christopher Lee. **1963**

VISITING HOURS 🦃 Here's a Canadian production that actually forces the viewer to wallow in the degradation, humiliation, and mutilation of women. Rated R for blood, gore, violence, and general unrelenting ugliness. 103m. **DIR:** Jean-Claude Lord. **CAST:** Lee Grant, William Shatner, Linda Purl, Michael Ironside. **1982**

VISITORS, THE ★★ An American family moves to Sweden, and strange things begin to happen in their new home. While the climax of this standard possessed-house movie is above par, it's too bad the rest is so boring. Rated R for violence and profanity. 102m. **DIR:** Joakim Ersgard. **CAST:** Keith Berkeley, Lena Endre, John Force, John Olsen, Joanna Berg, Brent Landiss, Patrick Ersgard. **1989**

VOODOO DAWN ★★ The old story of good versus evil played out in a small town in the South. Two college buddies take a road trip to visit a friend, who unfortunately is in the process of being transformed into a zombie. Rated R for violence and nudity. 83m. **DIR:** Steven Fierberg. **CAST:** Raymond St. Jacques, Theresa Merritt, Gina Gershon. **1990**

VOODOO DOLLS 🦃 Tender, young schoolgirls are seduced by the spirit residents of their old private academy. Rated R for profanity, nudity, suggested sex, and violence. 90m. **DIR:** Andre Pelletier. **CAST:** Maria Stanton. **1990**

VOODOO WOMAN ★★ Typical—if irresistible—American-International mixture of phony sets, too much talk, and an occasional outburst of mayhem as a jungle monster (AIP's *She Creature* suit, slightly reworked) is summoned by mad scientist Tom Conway. B&W; 77m. **DIR:** Edward L. Cahn. **CAST:** Marla English, Tom Conway, Mike Connors. **1957**

VULTURES ★★ A murder mystery with slasher undertones. Poorly written and acted, but has some suspense. Not rated, but contains graphic violence and adult situations. 101m. **DIR:** Paul Leder. **CAST:** Stuart Whitman, Greg Mullavey, Carmen Zapata, Yvonne De Carlo, Maria Perschy. **1983**

WARLOCK (1988) ★★★ An ancient witch-hunter follows an evil warlock to the streets of contemporary Los Angeles. Some great one-liners and a streamlined story help this entry. Rated R for violence, profanity, and gore. 102m. **DIR:** Steve Miner. **CAST:** Julian Sands, Lori Singer, Richard E. Grant, Mary Woronov, Allan Miller, Anna Levine, David Carpenter. **1988**

WARLOCK: THE ARMAGEDDON 🦃 The son of Satan returns for the final battle between good and evil in this rock-bottom stinker. Rated R for extreme violence and gore. 93m. **DIR:** Anthony Hickox. **CAST:** Julian Sands, Joanna Pacula. **1993**

WARLORDS 🦃 Genetic engineering goes awry in a postnuclear holocaust world. Rated R for graphic violence and profanity. 87m. **DIR:** Fred Olen Ray. **CAST:** David Carradine, Sid Haig, Ross Hagen, Robert Quarry. **1988**

WARNING SIGN ★★★ This is a passable science-fiction thriller about what happens when an accident occurs at a plant, producing a particularly virulent microbe for germ warfare. Rated R for violence and gore. 99m. **DIR:** Hal Barwood. **CAST:** Sam Waterston, Kathleen Quinlan, Yaphet Kotto, Jeffrey DeMunn, Richard Dysart, G. W. Bailey, Rick Rossovich. **1985**

WASP WOMAN 🦃 Laughable cult favorite centers around a cosmetics magnate who turns into a wasp-monster. B&W; 66m. **DIR:** Roger Corman. **CAST:** Susan Cabot, Anthony Eisley, Barboura Morris. **1960**

WATCH ME WHEN I KILL 🦃 Sylvia Kramer plays a woman who is witness to a murder and is now in danger of becoming one of the killer's next victims. Dubbed in English. Not rated; has violence and profanity. 94m. **DIR:** Anthony Bido. **CAST:** Richard Stewart, Sylvia Kramer. **1981**

WATCHER IN THE WOODS, THE ★★ This typical teenage gothic plot (family moves into old mansion and strange things begin to happen) is completely obscure and ends by defiantly refusing to explain itself. Rated PG because of minor violence. 84m. **DIR:** John Hough. **CAST:** Bette Davis, Lynn-Holly Johnson, Carroll Baker, David McCallum. **1980**

WATCHERS II ★★★ Huge fun for animal lovers, as a computer-literate dog aids a hapless couple in thwarting the activities of a murderous runaway biological experiment, reminiscent of Ridley Scott's *Alien.* Littered with classic horror homage, including a climax under L.A.'s storm drains. Rated R. 101m. **DIR:** Tierry Notz. **CAST:** Marc Singer,

Tracy Scoggins, Irene Miracle, Mary Woronov. 1989

WAXWORK ★★★ In this thrilling tongue-in-cheek horror film, six college students are invited to a midnight show at a mysterious wax museum. The sets of wax figures, famous monsters and killers, are missing one ingredient that can bring them all back to life: a dead victim. Rated R. 100m. **DIR:** Anthony Hickox. **CAST:** Zach Galligan, Deborah Foreman, Michelle Johnson, Miles O'Keeffe, Patrick Macnee, David Warner. **1988**

WAXWORK II: LOST IN TIME ★★ The two survivors of the previous film embark on a journey through time and meet various famous movie monsters. Fairly entertaining, especially to fans of classic horror films. Not rated, but contains violence. 104m. **DIR:** Anthony Hickox. **CAST:** Zach Galligan, Alexander Godunov, Bruce Campbell. **1991**

WELCOME TO SPRING BREAK ★★ Two of the least reputable movie genres—beach party and slasher—meet as an executed biker returns from the dead to wreak vengeance. *Where the Boys Are* it ain't. Rated R for violence and nudity. 92m. **DIR:** Harry Kirkpatrick. **CAST:** Nicolas de Toth, Sarah Buxton, Michael Parks, John Saxon. **1989**

WE'RE GOING TO EAT YOU! ★★ A gross, stylish horror-comedy about an island inhabited by cannibals and the predictably grisly fate that awaits those who stray into their clutches. If you thought there was nothing new in the cannibal subgenre, see this wild low-budget item. Not rated, but with plenty of gore on an NC-17 level. 90m. **DIR:** Tsui Hark. **1980**

WEREWOLF IN A GIRL'S DORMITORY 🦃 About a monster who's bumping off the staff and students at an exclusive academy. The dubbing of this Italian-Austrian coproduction and the reediting to introduce a trashy pop tune eliminate whatever suspense it may once have possessed. B&W; 84m. **DIR:** Richard Benson (Paolo Heusch). **CAST:** Carl Schell, Barbara Lass, Curt Lowens. **1961**

WEREWOLF OF LONDON ★★★ Universal's first attempt at a werewolf film is full of fog, atmosphere, and laboratory shots but short on chills and horror. Henry Hull just doesn't make the grade when his fangs grow. B&W; 75m. **DIR:** Stuart Walker. **CAST:** Henry Hull, Warner Oland, Valerie Hobson, Lester Matthews, Spring Byington. **1935**

WEREWOLF OF WASHINGTON ★★ Dean Stockwell plays the president's press secretary, who becomes a werewolf after a visit to eastern Europe. Although it was made at the height of the Watergate scandal, this satire is surprisingly lacking in bite. Stockwell gives a game performance, but the script doesn't give him much to work with. Rated PG. 90m. **DIR:** Milton Moses Ginsberg. **CAST:** Dean Stockwell, Biff McGuire, Clifton James, Michael Dunn. **1973**

WEREWOLVES ON WHEELS 🦃 Cursed bikers become werewolves. The worst of two genres. Rated R for nudity and violence. 85m. **DIR:** Michel Levesque. **CAST:** Steven Oliver, Barry McGuire, Billy Gray. **1971**

WHAT EVER HAPPENED TO BABY JANE? ★★★½ One of the last hurrahs of screen giants Bette Davis and Joan Crawford in a chillingly unpleasant tale of two aged sisters. Davis plays a former child movie star who spends her declining years dreaming of lost fame and tormenting her sister (Crawford). Victor Buono deserves special notice in a meaty supporting role. B&W; 132m. **DIR:** Robert Aldrich. **CAST:** Bette Davis, Joan Crawford, Victor Buono. **1962**

WHAT WAITS BELOW 🦃 A group of military and scientific researchers explore a cave and find a race of mutants. Rated PG: 88m. **DIR:** Don Sharp. **CAST:** Robert Powell, Lisa Blount, Richard Johnson, Anne Heywood, Timothy Bottoms. **1983**

WHATEVER HAPPENED TO AUNT ALICE? ★★★½ Entertaining black comedy about an eccentric woman (impeccably performed by Geraldine Page) who stays wealthy by killing off her housekeepers and stealing their savings. Ruth Gordon is equally impressive as an amateur sleuth trying to solve the missing-persons mystery. 101m. **DIR:** Lee H. Katzin. **CAST:** Geraldine Page, Ruth Gordon, Rosemary Forsyth, Robert Fuller, Mildred Dunnock. **1969**

WHAT'S THE MATTER WITH HELEN? ★★★½ Circa 1930, Debbie Reynolds and Shelley Winters flee to Hollywood to escape public hounding after their sons are involved in a brutal murder. They soon begin to fear they may have been followed by someone with revenge in mind. Good suspense and a fine feel for the era. Rated PG. 101m. **DIR:** Curtis Harrington. **CAST:** Debbie Reynolds, Shelley Winters, Dennis Weaver, Agnes Moorehead. **1971**

WHEN THE SCREAMING STOPS ★★★ A woman who lives under the Rhine must turn into a monster and eat people's hearts to remain the ruler of a magnificent underwater kingdom. Cheap monster effects and amateur gore do not detract from the wild story. Rated R for violence and nudity. 86m. **DIR:** Amando de Ossorio. **CAST:** Tony Kendall, Helga Line. **1974**

WHISPER KILLS, A 🦃 Weak made-for-TV slasher film about a killer who warns the potential victim by phone before the inevitable murder. 96m. **DIR:** Christian I. Nyby II. **CAST:** Loni Anderson, Joe Penny, June Lockhart. **1988**

WHITE PONGO (A.K.A. BLOND GORILLA) 🦃 Reverently referred to by fans of genre films as the worst of all crazed-gorilla–missing link jungle movies. B&W; 74m. **DIR:** Sam Newfield. **CAST:** Richard Fraser, Lionel Royce, Al Ebon, Gordon Richards. **1945**

WHITE ZOMBIE ★★★★ This eerie little thriller is the consummate zombie film, with hordes of the walking dead doing the bidding of evil Bela Lugosi as their overseer and master. A damsel-in-distress story with a new twist, this independently produced gem features sets and production standards usually found in films by the major studios. A minor classic, with a standout role by Lugosi. B&W; 73m. **DIR:** Victor Halperin. **CAST:** Bela Lugosi, Madge Bellamy, Robert Frazer. **1932**

WHO SLEW AUNTIE ROO? ★★ Ghoulish horror version of *Hansel and Gretel*, with Shelley Winters as the madwoman who lures two children (Mark Lester and Chloe Franks) into her evil clutches. Rated R for violence. 89m. **DIR:** Curtis Harrington. **CAST:** Shelley Winters, Mark Lester, Chloe Franks, Ralph Richardson, Lionel Jeffries, Hugh Griffith. **1971**

WICKED, THE ★★½ The Terminus family are bloodsuckers who are more than thrilled when strangers visit their quaint small town. Okay shocker. Rated R for nudity and violence. 87m. **DIR:** Colin Eggleston. **CAST:** Brett Cumo, Richard Morgan, Angela Kennedy, John Doyle. **1987**

WICKED STEPMOTHER, THE 🦃 A lame horror-comedy about an old woman who moves in with a family and turns their lives upside down with her evil powers. Rated PG-13 for profanity. 95m. **DIR:** Larry Cohen. **CAST:** Bette Davis, Barbara Carrera, Richard Moll, Tom Bosley. **1989**

WICKER MAN, THE ★★★★½ An anonymous letter that implies a missing girl has been murdered brings Sergeant Howie of Scotland Yard, to Summerisle, an island off the coast of England. Lord Summerisle, the ruler and religious leader of the island, seems to take it all as a joke, so Howie swears to find the truth. Rated R. 95m. **DIR:** Robin Hardy. **CAST:** Edward Woodward, Christopher Lee, Britt Ekland, Diane Cilento, Ingrid Pitt. **1973**

WILD BEASTS, THE ★★½ After PCP infects their water supply, animals and children go on a rampage killing anyone in sight. Made in Europe, where they must not have any animal-rights laws. Not rated, but contains violence and nudity. 92m. **DIR:** Franco Prosperi. **CAST:** John Aldrich. **1985**

WILLARD ★★½ This worked far better as a novel. Bruce Davison plays a put-upon wimp who identifies more with rodents than people. When nasty Ernest Borgnine becomes too unpleasant, Davison decides to make him the bait in a better rattrap. It was destined to get worse in the sequel, entitled *Ben*. Rated PG—mild violence. 95m. **DIR:** Daniel Mann. **CAST:** Bruce Davison, Ernest Borgnine, Sondra Locke. **1971**

WILLIES, THE ★★½ Lies, tall tales, and boyish machismo abound in this silly yet watchable movie as three kids try to out gross each other with wild stories. Rated PG-13. 92m. **DIR:** Brian Peck. **CAST:** James Karen, Sean Astin, Kathleen Freeman, Jeremy Miller. **1990**

WITCHBOARD ★★ Some good moments buoy this horror film about a group of people who play with a Ouija board at a party and find themselves haunted into becoming murderers and victims. Rated R for profanity and violence. 100m. **DIR:** Kevin S. Tenney. **CAST:** Todd Allen, Tawny Kitaen, Stephen Nicholas, Kathleen Wilhoite, Rose Marie. **1987**

WITCHBOARD 2 🦃 Wannnabe artist moves into a new apartment, toys with an abandoned Ouija board, and unleashes the spirit of a murdered former tenant. A sequel "which bored, too." Rated R for nudity, violence, and profanity. 96m. **DIR:** Kevin S. Tenney. **CAST:** Ami Dolenz, Timothy Gibbs, Laraine Newman. **1993**

WITCHCRAFT 🦃 A new mother can't understand the strange nightmares she begins to have after she moves in with her mother-in-law. R rating. 90m. **DIR:** Robert Spera. **CAST:** Anat Topol-Barzilai. **1988**

WITCHCRAFT II 🦃 This sequel to the original *Witchcraft* is as lame and ridiculous as its predecessor. Rated R for violence, profanity, and simulated sex. 88m. **DIR:** Mark Woods. **CAST:** Charles Solomon. **1990**

WITCHCRAFT III, THE KISS OF DEATH ★★ Two forces of evil confront each other over the love of a woman in this extremely sexy plot thinly disguised as a horror movie. Offers great-looking young men, sex kittens with breast implants, and mediocre-to-bad acting. Rated R for language. 85m. **DIR:** R. L. Tillmans. **CAST:** Charles Solomon. **1991**

WITCHCRAFT IV 🦃 A lawyer is lured into the world of witchcraft and devil worship, and seeks the help of a stripper. As banal as it sounds. Rated R for nudity. 92m. **DIR:** Kevin Morrissey. **CAST:** Charles Solomon, Julie Strain. **1992**

WITCHCRAFT V: DANCE WITH THE DEVIL ★★ Caine (David Huffman), chief cook and bottle washer for Satan, uses unwilling warlock William (Marklen Kennedy) to bring about the release of his evil master. You find yourself wishing that Caine could open the gates of Hell so something interesting would happen. Rated R for violence, nudity, and sexual situations. 94m. **DIR:** Talun Hsu. **CAST:** Marklen Kennedy, Carolyn Taye-Loren, Nicole Sassaman, David Huffman. **1993**

WITCHERY ★★ A fairly typical, somewhat suspenseful, demonic-possessions flick about a group of real estate speculators trapped in a haunted hotel. Unrated. 96m. **DIR:** Martin Newlin. **CAST:** David Hasselhoff, Linda Blair, Catherine Hickland. **1988**

WITCHING, THE (NECROMANCY) ♥ An embarrassment. Rated PG. 82m. **DIR:** Bert I. Gordon. **CAST:** Orson Welles, Pamela Franklin, Michael Ontkean, Lee Purcell. **1972**

WITCHING TIME ★★ Another entry from "Thriller Video," hosted by TV's Elvira, "Mistress of the Dark." The owner of an English farmhouse is visited by a previous occupant, a seventeenth-century witch. Unfortunately for him, after three hundred years, the old gal is hot to trot. Originally filmed for the British television series *Hammer House of Horror*. Unrated; nudity edited out of the print used for this cassette. 60m. **DIR:** Don Leaver. **CAST:** Jon Finch, Patricia Quinn, Prunella Gee, Ian McCulloch. **1985**

WITCH'S MIRROR, THE ★★ One of the better entries in the early-Sixties rash of low-budget Mexican horror movies that will bore the pants off some viewers, while entertaining the devotees. In the nineteenth century, the mirror of the title curses an unscrupulous surgeon. Weird and atmospheric, but unevenly dubbed into English. B&W; 75m. **DIR:** Chano Urveta. **CAST:** Rosita Arenas, Armando Calvo. **1960**

WITCHTRAP ★★ This story takes place in a mansion haunted by its former owner, who practiced Satanic rituals in the attic. When the new owner hires a team of expert psychics to rid the mansion of its evil, a horrifying chain of events occurs. Rated R for nudity and profanity. 92m. **DIR:** Kevin S. Tenney. **CAST:** James W. Quinn, Kathleen Bailey, Linnea Quigley. **1989**

WIZARD OF GORE, THE ♥ Blood and guts galore as a sideshow magician takes the old "saw the girl in half" trick a bit too far. Rated R. 80m. **DIR:** Herschell Gordon Lewis. **CAST:** Ray Sager. **1982**

WOLF MAN, THE ★★★★★ Classic horror film featuring a star-making performance by Lon Chaney Jr. as Lawrence Talbot (a role he would go on to play five times). Upon attempting to save a young woman from a wolf's vicious attack, Talbot is bitten by the animal. He discovers that it was not an ordinary wolf, but a werewolf, and that now he too will become a bloodthirsty creature of the night whenever the full moon rises. B&W; 70m. **DIR:** George Waggner. **CAST:** Lon Chaney Jr., Evelyn Ankers, Claude Rains, Patric Knowles, Ralph Bellamy, Bela Lugosi, Maria Ouspenskaya, Warren William. **1941**

WOLFEN ★★ The best features of this sluggish horror film are its innovative visual work and actors who make the most of an uneven script. Directed by Michael Wadleigh, *Wolfen* follows a sequence of mysterious murders that are sometimes disturbingly bloody. This explains the R rating. 115m. **DIR:** Michael Wadleigh. **CAST:** Albert Finney, Diane Venora, Gregory Hines, Tommy Noonan, Edward James Olmos, Dick O'Neill. **1981**

WOLFMAN ♥ A young man inherits his ancestral home, only to be transformed into a wolfman by a cult of Satanists. Not rated, but contains violence. 91m. **DIR:** Worth Keeter. **CAST:** Earl Owensby. **1978**

WORLD OF THE VAMPIRES ★★ One of the weaker Mexican-monster movies imported and dubbed into English by K. Gordon Murray, this convoluted melodrama *looks* marvelously atmospheric, but collapses midway along. Unintentionally funny. B&W; 85m. **DIR:** Alfonso Corona. **CAST:** Guillermo Murray. **1960**

WORM EATERS, THE ♥ Stomach-turning flick about southern town infested with night crawlers. Not rated. 75m. **DIR:** Herb Robins. **1977**

WRAITH, THE ★★ A small town in Arizona is visited by a spirit taking revenge on a gang of road pirates. Some nice car wrecks and explosions. Car buffs will like the Wraith Mobile. A typical shallow revenge picture without style, substance, or surprises. Rated PG. 93m. **DIR:** Mike Marvin. **CAST:** Charlie Sheen, Randy Quaid, Clint Howard, Griffin O'Neal. **1986**

XTRO ♥ Grotesquely slimy sci-fi horror flick with an idiotic plot that revolves around a series of repulsive bladder effects. Rated R. 84m. **DIR:** Harry Davenport. **CAST:** Philip Sayer, Bernice Stegers, Maryam D'Abo. **1982**

ZERO BOYS, THE ♥ A survival-game team of three college buddies truck out to the backwoods and ride straight into a murderous game of hide-and-seek. Rated R. 89m. **DIR:** Nico Mastorakis. **CAST:** Daniel Hirsch, Kelli Maroney, Nicole Rio. **1985**

ZOLTAN—HOUND OF DRACULA ♥ Dracula's faithful servant journeys to Los Angeles in search of the last surviving member of the Dracula clan. Rated R for violence. 85m. **DIR:** Albert Band. **CAST:** Michael Pataki, Reggie Nalder, José Ferrer. **1977**

ZOMBIE ♥ Gruesome, gory, and ghastly unauthorized entry in George Romero's zombie series. Rated X for gore and nudity. 91m. **DIR:** Lucio Fulci. **CAST:** Tisa Farrow, Ian McCulloch, Richard Johnson. **1979**

ZOMBIE HIGH ♥ Low-rent horror movie set at a prep school where the administration consists of 100-year-old men who have kept their youth through a potion made with live brain tissue obtained from their students. Rated R. 93m. **DIR:** Ron Link. **CAST:** Virginia Madsen, Richard Cox, James Wilder. **1987**

ZOMBIE ISLAND MASSACRE 🦃 Tourists in the Caribbean run into a pack of natives practicing voodoo. Rated R for violence, profanity, and nudity. 89m. **DIR:** John Carter. **CAST:** David Broadnax, Rita Jenrette. **1984**

ZOMBIE LAKE 🦃 Third Reich storm troopers return from their watery graves in this cheesy Eurotrash gorefest. Rated R. 90m. **DIR:** Jean Rollin. **CAST:** Howard Vernon. **1982**

ZOMBIE NIGHTMARE ★★ This film—about an innocent boy who is killed by some "savage suburban teens" only to rise again as a zombie to avenge his murder—tries to be more mystical than gory. But it never becomes atmospheric enough to be interesting. Rated R for violence and profanity. 89m. **DIR:** Jack Brauman. **CAST:** Adam West, Tia Carrere, Linda Singer. **1986**

ZOMBIES OF MORA TAV ★★ Laughable, low-budget time waster about zombies and sunken treasure. Shows how dull zombies were before *Night of the Living Dead*. Unrated, but timid enough for your aunt Sally. B&W; 70m. **DIR:** Edward L. Cahn. **CAST:** Gregg Palmer, Allison Hayes. **1957**

MUSICAL

ABSOLUTE BEGINNERS ★★★★ *Absolute Beginners* is based on the cult novel by Colin MacInnes, who chronicled the musical and social scene in London during the pivotal summer of 1958. Occasionally the accents are too thick and the references too obscure for Americans, but the overall effect is an unequivocal high. Rated PG-13 for stylized, but rather intense, violence and some profanity. 107m. **DIR:** Julien Temple. **CAST:** Eddie O'Connell, Patsy Kensit, David Bowie, James Fox, Ray Davies, Anita Morris, Sade Adu, Mandy Rice-Davies. **1986**

AFFAIRS OF DOBIE GILLIS, THE ★★★★ This delightful college comedy that is sexy but not obvious about it focuses on an overamorous undergrad who dates girls in spite of their parents' objections. Good songs and lively dances by solid pros lift this one above the ordinary. B&W; 74m. **DIR:** Don Weis. **CAST:** Debbie Reynolds, Bobby Van, Bob Fosse, Hans Conried, Lurene Tuttle. **1953**

AIRHEADS 🦃 A metal band takes a radio station hostage until it plays a demo tape. Poor performances, gimmicky direction, and shallow characters make this movie a dud. Rated PG-13 for language. 115m. **DIR:** Michael Lehmann. **CAST:** Brendan Fraser, Steve Buscemi, Adam Sandler, Joe Mantegna. **1994**

ALEXANDER'S RAGTIME BAND ★★★★★ The first all-star epic musical to feature classic Irving Berlin tunes. The story of a Nob Hill elitist who starts a ragtime band on the Barbary Coast is a suitable setting for over two dozen Berlin songs composed between World War I and the early days of World War II. Tyrone Power glamorizes the setting, while the music and the nostalgia element still have the magic to involve an audience emotionally. B&W; 105m. **DIR:** Henry King. **CAST:** Alice Faye, Tyrone Power, Don Ameche, Ethel Merman, Jack Haley, Dixie Dunbar. **1938**

ALICE (1981) 🦃 In this bizarre adaptation of *Alice in Wonderland*, Alice falls for a jogger called Rabbit. Unrated. 80m. **DIR:** Jerzy Gruza, Jacek Bromski. **CAST:** Sophie Barjac, Jean-Pierre Cassel, Susannah York, Paul Nicholas. **1981**

ALICE THROUGH THE LOOKING GLASS (1966) ★★★½ Another version of Lewis Carroll's immortal classic? Why not? When you've got such a talented cast working with a great story, you've got a winner. In this made-for-TV version, Alice makes an attempt to become the Queen of Wonderland by visiting the Royal Castle. 72m. **DIR:** Alan Handley. **CAST:** Ricardo Montalban, Judy Rolin, Nanette Fabray, Robert Coote, Agnes Moorehead, Jack Palance, Jimmy Durante, Tom Smothers, Dick Smothers, Roy Castle, Richard Denning. **1966**

ALL THAT JAZZ ★★★★ While it may not be what viewers expect from a musical, this story of a gifted choreographer, Joe Gideon (Roy Scheider, in his finest performance), who relentlessly drives himself to exhaustion is daring, imaginative, shocking, and visually stunning. Rated R. 123m. **DIR:** Bob Fosse. **CAST:** Roy Scheider, Ann Reinking, Jessica Lange. **1979**

AMADEUS ★★★★★ F. Murray Abraham, who won an Oscar for his performance, gives a haunting portrayal of Antonio Salieri, the court composer for Hapsburg Emperor Joseph II. A second-rate musician, Salieri felt jealousy and admiration for the young musical genius Wolfgang Amadeus Mozart (Tom Hulce), who died at the age of thirty-five—perhaps by Salieri's hand. It's a stunning film full of great music, drama, and wit. Rated PG for mild violence. 158m. **DIR:** Milos Forman. **CAST:** Tom Hulce, F. Murray Abraham, Elizabeth Berridge. **1984**

AMERICAN HOT WAX ★★★½ Though facts may be in short supply in this bio-pic of pioneer rock disc jockey Alan Freed, abundant energy and spirit make this movie a winner. Tim McIntire gives a remarkable performance as Freed. Rated PG. 91m. **DIR:** Floyd Mutrux. **CAST:** Tim McIntire, Fran Drescher, Jay Leno, John Lehne, Laraine Newman, Jeff Altman, Chuck Berry, Jerry Lee Lewis. **1978**

AMERICAN IN PARIS, AN ★★★★★ One of Gene Kelly's classic musicals, this Oscar-winning best picture features the hoofer as the free-spirited author of the title. The picture is a heady mixture of light entertainment and the music of George Gershwin. 115m. **DIR:** Vincente Minnelli. **CAST:** Gene Kelly, Leslie Caron, Nina Foch, Oscar Levant. **1951**

ANCHORS AWEIGH ★★★ A somewhat tedious and overlong dance film that is perked up by a few truly impressive numbers, none finer than Gene Kelly's duet with an animated Jerry the mouse (of Tom and Jerry fame). Unrated; suitable for family viewing. 140m. **DIR:** George Sidney. **CAST:** Gene Kelly, Frank Sinatra, Kathryn Grayson, Dean Stockwell. **1945**

ANNA KARENINA (1974) ★★★½ Based on Tolstoy's novel, this ballet was choreographed by and stars Maya Plisetskaya, the Bolshoi's great prima ballerina. Her husband, Rodion Shchedrin, composed the music. This is an imaginative and visually interesting film, as the camera and direction are creative rather than just filming a staged ballet performance. 81m. **DIR:** Margarita Pilichino. **CAST:** Bolshoi Ballet. **1974**

ANNIE ★★★★ A sparkling $40 million movie musical based on the Broadway production of the long-running comic strip *Little Orphan Annie.* Ten-year-old Aileen Quinn is just fine in the title role. Rated PG for brief profanity. 128m. **DIR:** John Huston. **CAST:** Albert Finney, Carol Burnett, Bernadette Peters, Edward Herrmann, Aileen Quinn. **1982**

ANNIE GET YOUR GUN ★★★½ Lavish, fast-moving transfer of Irving Berlin's stage hit to film with Annie Oaklie (Betty Hutton), Frank Butler (Howard Keel), Buffalo Bill Cody (Louis Calhern) and Sitting Bull (J. Carrol Naish) singing and shooting up a storm. "Anything You Can Do" and "There's No Business Like Show Business" are two of the musical highlights. Oscar for the score of Adolph Deutsch and Roger Edens. 107m. **DIR:** George Sidney. **CAST:** Betty Hutton, Howard Keel, Louis Calhern, Keenan Wynn, Edward Arnold, J. Carrol Naish. **1950**

APRIL IN PARIS ★★½ State department employee Ray Bolger mistakenly asks a chorus girl (Doris Day) to represent America at a festival of the arts in Paris, and the obvious complications arise. The often (usually) misused Bolger gets to shine in one good number, "We're Going To Ring the Bell Tonight." 101m. **DIR:** David Butler. **CAST:** Doris Day, Ray Bolger, Claude Dauphin. **1952**

ARIA ★★ High expectations are dashed in this unexpectedly boring collection of vignettes made by different directors using opera segments as a creative springboard. A few good moments, but the overall impression is about as memorable as a few hours of MTV. Rated R for nudity. 90m. **DIR:** Robert Altman, Bruce Beresford, Bill Bryden, Jean-Luc Godard, Derek Jarman, Franc Roddam, Nicolas Roeg. **CAST:** Buck Henry, John Hurt, Anita Morris, Bridget Fonda, Theresa Russell. **1988**

AROUND THE WORLD ★★½ Bandleader Kay Kyser entertains the troops during World War II by hamming it up with an endless number of corny puns and gags. The offstage antics of the performers are highlighted by an electrifying duel between Mischa Auer and an offended nobleman. B&W; 80m. **DIR:** Allan Dwan. **CAST:** Kay Kyser, Mischa Auer, Joan Davis. **1943**

ATHENA ★★ A minor musical about an eccentric family who believe regular exercise and eating all your vegetables will make your vocal chords strong. The plot is weak, but the personalities are impressive. 96m. **DIR:** Richard Thorpe. **CAST:** Jane Powell, Debbie Reynolds, Vic Damone, Edmund Purdom, Steve Reeves, Virginia Gibson, Louis Calhern, Linda Christian, Carl Benton Reid, Evelyn Varden. **1954**

BABES IN ARMS ★★★ Richard Rodgers and Lorenz Hart wrote the musical from which this film was taken—although most of the songs they wrote are absent. But never mind; Mickey and Judy sing, dance, and prance up a storm! B&W; 96m. **DIR:** Busby Berkeley. **CAST:** Mickey Rooney, Judy Garland, June Preisser, Guy Kibbee, Charles Winninger, Henry Hull, Margaret Hamilton. **1939**

BABES ON BROADWAY ★★½ Raising funds for underprivileged children is the excuse for this musical extravaganza showcasing Mickey Rooney and Judy Garland, both of whom shine despite a trite plot. See it for the songs. B&W; 118m. **DIR:** Busby Berkeley. **CAST:** Mickey Rooney, Judy Garland, Fay Bainter, Virginia Weidler, Richard Quine, Donna Reed. **1941**

BACK TO THE BEACH 🦃 Annette and Frankie are married, in their 40's, live in Ohio, and have two children with behavioral problems. Rated PG for language. 88m. **DIR:** Lyndall Hobbs. **CAST:** Frankie Avalon, Annette Funicello, Connie Stevens, Lori Loughlin. **1987**

BACKBEAT ★★★★ Before they became the Fab Four, the Beatles were a quintet—guitarists John Lennon, Paul McCartney, and George Harrison, backed by painter-turned-bass-player Stuart Sutcliffe and drummer Pete Best. *Backbeat* is an involving dramatization of the close friendship between Lennon (superbly played by Ian Hart of *Hours and Times*) and Sutcliffe (Stephen Dorff), and how it is tested during the band's apprenticeship in seamy Hamburg, Germany. Rated R for profanity, nudity, simulated sex, and brief violence. 100m. **DIR:** Iain Softley. **CAST:** Stephen Dorff, Sheryl Lee, Ian Hart, Kai Wiesinger, Jennifer Ehl, Gary Bakewell, Chris O'Neill, Scot Williams. **1994**

BALALAIKA ★★★ Cabaret singer Ilona Massey wins the heart of cossack Nelson Eddy. The plot is just a tool to introduce some wonderful musical numbers, but Massey is impressive in her American debut. B&W; 102m. **DIR:** Reinhold Schunzel. **CAST:** Nelson Eddy, Ilona Massey, Charlie Ruggles, Frank Morgan, Lionel Atwill, C. Aubrey Smith, Philip Terry, George Tobias, Joyce Compton. **1939**

BAND WAGON, THE ★★★★ One of Vincente Minnelli's best grand-scale musicals and one of Fred Astaire's most endearing roles. He plays a Hollywood has-been who decides to try his luck onstage. This is the film that gave us "That's Entertainment." Unrated—family fare. 112m. **DIR:** Vincente Minnelli. **CAST:** Fred Astaire, Cyd Charisse, Jack Buchanan, Nanette Fabray, Oscar Levant. **1953**

BARKLEYS OF BROADWAY, THE ★★★ As a film team, Ginger Rogers and Fred Astaire parted in 1939. This final pairing, the result of Judy Garland's inability to make the picture, does not favorably compare with earlier efforts. Harry Warren's score, while augmented by a great George Gershwin number, is not up to snuff. Nevertheless, the film was a critical and commercial hit. 109m. **DIR:** Charles Walters. **CAST:** Fred Astaire, Ginger Rogers, Oscar Levant. **1949**

BARNUM (1986) ★★★ Made-for-television adaptation of Cy Coleman-Michael Stewart Broadway hit. Michael Crawford as flamboyant promoter Phineas T. Barnum is mesmerizing, tracing Barnum's life, from his humble beginnings to creating the Barnum and Bailey Circus. 113m. **DIR:** Terry Hughes. **CAST:** Michael Crawford. **1986**

BATHING BEAUTY ★★½ One of MGM's best remembered musicals emerges dripping wet from the mists of time as a series of waterlogged vignettes flaunt new discovery Esther Williams. She plays a college girl who's crazy about songwriter Red Skelton, and jumps into a swimsuit as frequently as he dresses in drag in order to further the intrigue. 101m. **DIR:** George Sidney. **CAST:** Esther Williams, Red Skelton, Basil Rathbone, Margaret Dumont, Bill Goodwin, Jean Porter, Nana Bryant, Donald Meek, Harry James. **1944**

BEACH BLANKET BINGO ★★½ The fifth in the series, and the last true "Beach Party" film. Basically, it's the same old stuff: stars on their way up (Linda Evans) or on their way down (Buster Keaton) or at their peak (Frankie and Annette), spouting silly dialogue and singing through echo chambers. But it's one of the best of the series, whether you're laughing with it or at it. 98m. **DIR:** William Asher. **CAST:** Frankie Avalon, Annette Funicello, Paul Lynde, Harvey Lembeck, Don Rickles, Linda Evans, Jody McCrea, Marta Kristen, John Ashley, Deborah Walley, Buster Keaton. **1965**

BEACH PARTY ★★½ Bob Cummings, a bearded, sheltered anthropologist, studies the wild dating and mating habits of beach-bound teens. He ends up courting Annette Funicello to make Frankie Avalon jealous. Cummings has his moments, as does Harvey Lembeck, as the biker Eric Von Zipper. 101m. **DIR:** William Asher. **CAST:** Robert Cummings, Dorothy Malone, Frankie Avalon, Annette Funicello, Harvey Lembeck, Jody McCrea, John Ashley, Morey Amsterdam. **1963**

BEAT STREET 💔 A hackneyed plot, about kids breaking into show biz. Rated PG for profanity and violence. 106m. **DIR:** Stan Lathan. **CAST:** Rae Dawn Chong, Guy Davis. **1984**

BECAUSE YOU'RE MINE ★★½ When an opera star is drafted into the army, his training sergeant turns out to be a fan who has (surprise!) a sister with operatic ambitions. Forget the plot, just enjoy Mario Lanza's gifted voice. 101m. **DIR:** Alexander Hall. **CAST:** Mario Lanza, James Whitmore, Doretta Morrow, Jeff Donnell, Dean Miller, Paula Corday. **1952**

BELLE OF NEW YORK, THE ★★ A fantasy set at the turn of the century, this frothy film was a box-office failure about which, in his autobiography, Fred Astaire snaps: "The less said about it the better." Harry Warren's score—assembled from earlier hits—is terrific, though none of the songs have survived as standards. 82m. **DIR:** Charles Walters. **CAST:** Fred Astaire, Vera-Ellen, Marjorie Main, Keenan Wynn. **1952**

BELLS ARE RINGING ★★ This filmed version of the Broadway musical pits answering-service operator Judy Holliday against Dean Martin in an on-again, off-again love circle. Nothing new or exciting storywise here, but Fred Clark and Eddie Foy ham it up enough to hold your interest. 127m. **DIR:** Vincente Minnelli. **CAST:** Judy Holliday, Dean Martin, Fred Clark, Eddie Foy Jr. **1960**

BERT RIGBY, YOU'RE A FOOL ★★★ Musical-comedy star Robert Lindsay, who won a Tony for *Me and My Girl*, plays an English coal miner obsessed with the great musicals of Fred Astaire and Gene Kelly. When a strike is called at the mine, he decides to take a shot at making it as a song-and-dance man. Director Carl Reiner also scripted. There is some profanity, but the R rating seems excessive. 94m. **DIR:** Carl Reiner. **CAST:** Robert Lindsay, Cathryn Bradshaw, Robbie Coltrane, Jackie Gayle, Anne Bancroft, Corbin Bernsen. **1989**

BEST FOOT FORWARD ★★★½ Film star Lucille Ball accepts military cadet Tommy Dix's invitation to his school's annual dance. The film introduced June Allyson and Nancy Walker and gave numerous high schools a fight song by adapting its biggest hit, "Buckle Down, Winsocki." Wholesome family fun. 95m. **DIR:** Edward Buzzell. **CAST:** Lucille Ball, William Gaxton, Virginia Weidler, Tommy Dix, June Allyson, Nancy Walker, Gloria De Haven. **1943**

BEST LITTLE WHOREHOUSE IN TEXAS, THE ★★½ Dolly Parton and Burt Reynolds in a so-so version of the Broadway play, whose title explains all. Rated R for nudity, profanity, and sexual situations. 114m. **DIR:** Colin

Higgins. **CAST:** Burt Reynolds, Dolly Parton, Dom DeLuise, Charles Durning. 1982

BETTE MIDLER—ART OR BUST ★★★★ Bette Midler exudes more talent in this hour-and-a-half special than most entertainers do in a lifetime. Included are clips from her last bathhouse show and her more recent concert performances. Not rated, but contains adult language. 82m. **DIR:** Thomas Schlamme. **CAST:** Bette Midler. 1984

BIKINI BEACH ★★ This silly film captures Frankie Avalon and Annette Funicello in their best swim attire. A group of kids who always hang out at the beach try to prevent a man from closing it. Ho-hum. 100m. **DIR:** William Asher. **CAST:** Frankie Avalon, Annette Funicello, Keenan Wynn, Don Rickles. 1964

BIRD ★★★★½ Clint Eastwood's *Bird* soars with a majesty all its own. About the life of legendary saxophonist Charlie "Bird" Parker, it is the ultimate jazz movie. It features Parker's inspired improvised solos in abundance, while telling the story of the brilliant but troubled and drug-addicted artist. Parker is solidly played by Forest Whitaker. Rated R for profanity and drug use. 140m. **DIR:** Clint Eastwood. **CAST:** Forest Whitaker, Diane Venora, Samuel E. Wright, Keith David. 1988

BITTER SWEET ★★ Redeemed only by the lilting songs of Noel Coward, this tragic story of a violinist's romance with a dancer was the MacDonald-Eddy team's first financial failure, and it augered the end of their long reign. 92m. **DIR:** W. S. Van Dyke. **CAST:** Jeanette MacDonald, Nelson Eddy, George Sanders, Herman Bing, Felix Bressart, Ian Hunter, Sig Ruman, Veda Ann Borg. 1940

BLACK TIGHTS ★★★½ There are several attractive performers in this British film that aficionados of dance should not miss: Cyd Charisse, Zizi Jeanmaire, and in her last film before retirement, Moira Shearer. It's a good film that even those who are not dance groupies might enjoy. The film is also known under the French title *Un, Deux, Trois, Quatre!* 140m. **DIR:** Terence Young. **CAST:** Cyd Charisse, Zizi Jeanmaire, Moira Shearer, Roland Petit Dance Company. 1960

BLUE HAWAII ★★★½ In this enjoyable Elvis Presley flick, the star plays a returning soldier who works with tourists against his mom's (Angela Lansbury) wishes. 101m. **DIR:** Norman Taurog. **CAST:** Elvis Presley, Joan Blackman, Angela Lansbury, Iris Adrian. 1962

BODY ROCK 🦃 A youngster from the South Bronx sees break dancing as his ticket to the big time. Rated PG-13. 93m. **DIR:** Marcelo Epstein. **CAST:** Lorenzo Lamas, Vicki Frederick, Cameron Dye, Ray Sharkey. 1984

BORN TO DANCE ★★★ A curiosity piece because Jimmy Stewart croons "Easy to Love" without the help of a ghost singer on the sound track. The real star is Cole Porter, who wrote some of his most enduring melodies for the film. Eleanor Powell proves she has no peers when it comes to tap dancing. 105m. **DIR:** Roy Del Ruth. **CAST:** Eleanor Powell, James Stewart, Una Merkel, Buddy Ebsen, Virginia Bruce, Frances Langford, Reginald Gardiner. 1936

BOY FRIEND, THE ★★★ Ken Russell, at his least self-indulgent and most affectionate, provides a plucky parody of Twenties musicals. The inventiveness and opulence call to mind the work of Busby Berkeley. Twiggy's performance is engaging. Rated G. 110m. **DIR:** Ken Russell. **CAST:** Twiggy, Christopher Gable, Max Adrian, Tommy Tune, Glenda Jackson. 1971

BREAKIN' ★★ The dancing scenes are wonderful but as a whole, *Breakin'* is pretty lame. The film would have us believe that jazz dancer Kelly (Lucinda Dickey) could hook up with street dancers Ozone ("Shabba-Doo") and Turbo ("Boogaloo Shrimp") to win dance contests and finally break (no pun intended) into big-time show biz. Rated PG for profanity and violence. 90m. **DIR:** Joel Silberg. **CAST:** Lucinda Dickey, Adolfo Quinones, Michael Chambers, Ben Lokey. 1984

BREAKIN' 2 ELECTRIC BOOGALOO ★★½ This sometimes exhilarating break-dancing movie is better than the original. This time, Kelly (Lucinda Dickey), Ozone (Adolfo "Shabba-Doo" Quinones), and Turbo (Michael "Boogaloo Shrimp" Chambers) put on a show to save a local arts center for children. Rated PG for brief violence and suggested sex. 90m. **DIR:** Sam Firstenberg. **CAST:** Lucinda Dickey, Adolfo Quinones, Michael Chambers. 1984

BREAKING GLASS ★★½ British film about a new wave singer's rise to the top, at the expense of personal relationships. Hazel O'Connor's heavy music isn't for all tastes, and the plot line is as old as film itself, but the actors are sincere. 104m. **DIR:** Brian Gibson. **CAST:** Phil Daniels, Hazel O'Connor, Jon Finch, Jonathan Pryce. 1980

BREAKING THE ICE ★★ In this improbable meld of music and ice skating, Bobby Breen gets a job singing at a Philadelphia rink, and meets skating moppet Irene Dare. B&W; 79m. **DIR:** Eddie Cline. **CAST:** Bobby Breen, Charlie Ruggles, Dolores Costello, Billy Gilbert, Margaret Hamilton. 1938

BRIGADOON ★★★★ This enchanting musical stars Van Johnson and Gene Kelly as two Americans who discover Brigadoon, a Scottish village with a life span of only one day for every hundred years. In the village, Kelly meets Cyd Charisse, and they naturally dance up a storm. 108m. **DIR:** Vincente Minnelli. **CAST:** Gene Kelly, Van Johnson, Cyd Charisse, Elaine Stewart, Barry Jones. 1954

BROADWAY MELODY, THE ★★ Prototype of all the backstage musical romances. Two sisters (Anita Page and Bessie Love) run afoul of big-city corruption when they leave the sticks to pursue their destinies in New York. Stolid acting and awkward sound-recording techniques are mostly unrelieved, although the "Singin' in the Rain" number (the first of many times the song will be heard in MGM musicals) still packs a rough kind of charm. Somehow it won an Oscar as the year's best picture. B&W; 104m. **DIR:** Harry Beaumont. **CAST:** Anita Page, Bessie Love, Charles King. **1929**

BROADWAY MELODY OF 1936 ★★★ Backstage musical comedy. Obnoxious gossip columnist Jack Benny tries to use dancer Eleanor Powell to harass producer Robert Taylor. Forget the plot and enjoy the singing and dancing—including Taylor's rendition of "I've Got a Feelin' You're Foolin'," the only time he sang on-screen in his own voice. B&W; 110m. **DIR:** Roy Del Ruth. **CAST:** Jack Benny, Eleanor Powell, Robert Taylor, Una Merkel, Buddy Ebsen. **1935**

BROADWAY MELODY OF 1938 ★★½ Fifteen-year-old Judy Garland stops the show in this tuneful musical anthology when she sings the now legendary "Dear Mr. Gable" version of "You Made Me Love You." The finale stretches credibility until it snaps as Eleanor Powell, in top hat and tails, dances with a division of chorus boys before a neon skyline. B&W; 110m. **DIR:** Roy Del Ruth. **CAST:** Robert Taylor, Eleanor Powell, George Murphy, Binnie Barnes, Sophie Tucker, Judy Garland, Buddy Ebsen, Willie Howard, Billy Gilbert. **1937**

BROADWAY MELODY OF 1940 ★★★ Fine performances redeem this otherwise tired tale of friendship and rivalry between dancing partners. The dancing of course, is flawless; the Cole Porter songs are outstanding. B&W; 102m. **DIR:** Norman Taurog. **CAST:** Fred Astaire, Eleanor Powell, George Murphy, Frank Morgan, Ian Hunter. **1940**

BROADWAY RHYTHM ★★½ A reworking of Jerome Kern's last Broadway musical, *Very Warm for May*, with one of the finest songs Kern ever wrote, "All the Things You Are." The routine plot pits ex-vaudevillian performers against the new breed of singers. B&W; 114m. **DIR:** Roy Del Ruth. **CAST:** George Murphy, Ginny Simms, Gloria De Haven, Lena Horne, Hazel Scott, Tommy Dorsey, Charles Winninger, Ben Blue. **1943**

BROADWAY SERENADE ★★★ A musical aimed strictly at Jeanette MacDonald fans. She does all the singing as a woman at odds with her husband and her career. The splashy finale was directed by Busby Berkeley. B&W; 113m. **DIR:** Robert Z. Leonard. **CAST:** Jeanette MacDonald, Lew Ayres, Ian Hunter, Frank Morgan, Virginia Grey, Rita Johnson, William Gargan. **1929**

BUDDY HOLLY STORY, THE ★★★★½ Gary Busey's outstanding performance as Buddy Holly makes this one of the few great rock 'n' roll movies. Not only does he convincingly embody the legend from Lubbock, Texas, he also sings Holly's songs—including "That'll Be the Day," "Not Fade Away," and "It's So Easy"—with style and conviction. Backed by Don Stroud and Charles Martin Smith, who also play and sing impressively. Rated PG. 114m. **DIR:** Steve Rash. **CAST:** Gary Busey, Don Stroud, Charles Martin Smith, Dick O'Neill. **1978**

BY THE LIGHT OF THE SILVERY MOON ★★★ More trouble for the Winfield family in this sequel to *On Moonlight Bay*, with innocent Leon Ames suspected by his family of being involved with a French actress. Post-WWI setting, with many familiar songs from that period. 102m. **DIR:** David Butler. **CAST:** Doris Day, Gordon MacRae, Leon Ames, Rosemary DeCamp, Billy Gray, Mary Wickes, Russell Arms. **1953**

BYE BYE BIRDIE ★★★ A rock star's approaching appearance in a small town turns several lives upside down in this pleasant musical-comedy. Based on the successful Broadway play, this is pretty lightweight stuff, but a likable cast and good production numbers make it worthwhile. No rating; okay for the whole family. 112m. **DIR:** George Sidney. **CAST:** Dick Van Dyke, Ann-Margret, Janet Leigh, Paul Lynde, Bobby Rydell. **1963**

CABARET ★★★★★ This classic musical-drama takes place in Germany in 1931. The Nazi party has not yet assumed complete control, and the local cabaret unfolds the story of two young lovers, the ensuing mood of the country, and the universal touch of humanity. Everything is handled with taste—bisexual encounters, the horrors of the Nazi regime, and the bawdy entertainment of the nightclub. "Host" Joel Grey is brilliant. Michael York and Liza Minnelli are first-rate. So is the movie. Rated PG. 128m. **DIR:** Bob Fosse. **CAST:** Liza Minnelli, Michael York, Helmut Griem, Joel Grey. **1972**

CAIRO ★★★½ One of Jeanette MacDonald's last films, and she gets to warble with a woman singer instead of her leading man. Ethel Waters costars in this spoof of wartime spy melodramas. Robert Young provides the obligatory romantic interest, but the chief highlight is the music. B&W; 101m. **DIR:** W. S. Van Dyke. **CAST:** Jeanette MacDonald, Ethel Waters, Robert Young, Dooley Wilson, Reginald Owen. **1942**

CALAMITY JANE (1953) ★★★ A legend of the Old West set to music for Doris Day, who mends her rootin', tootin' ways in order to lasso Howard Keel. The song "Secret Love" copped an Oscar. Cute 'n' perky. 101m.

DIR: David Butler. CAST: Doris Day, Howard Keel, Allyn Ann McLerie, Philip Carey. 1953

CAMELOT ★★★ The legend of King Arthur and the Round Table—from the first meeting of Arthur (Richard Harris) and Guinevere (Vanessa Redgrave) to the affair between Guinevere and Lancelot (Franco Nero), and finally the fall of Camelot—is brought to life in this enjoyable musical. 178m. DIR: Joshua Logan. CAST: Richard Harris, Vanessa Redgrave, Franco Nero, David Hemmings, Lionel Jeffries. 1967

CAN-CAN ★★★ Frank Sinatra plays an 1890s French attorney defending Shirley MacLaine's right to perform the risqué can-can in a Parisian nightclub. The stars appear, at times, to be walking through their roles. Cole Porter songs include "I Love Paris," "C'est Magnifique" and the wonderful "Just One of Those Things." 131m. DIR: Walter Lang. CAST: Shirley MacLaine, Frank Sinatra, Maurice Chevalier, Juliet Prowse, Louis Jourdan. 1960

CAN'T HELP SINGING ★★★★½ A spirited Western with music by Jerome Kern, this is the only Technicolor film Deanna Durbin made. Songs include the title number, "Californi-yay," "More and More," and "Swing Your Sweetheart." All told, a delight. 89m. DIR: Frank Ryan. CAST: Deanna Durbin, Robert Paige, Akim Tamiroff, David Bruce, June Vincent, Clara Blandick, Ray Collins, Leonid Kinskey. 1944

CAN'T STOP THE MUSIC 🦃 Despite the title, the music of the Village People was stopped cold by this basically awful musical about show biz. Rated PG. 118m. DIR: Nancy Walker. CAST: The Village People, Valerie Perrine, Bruce Jenner, Steve Guttenberg, Paul Sand, Tammy Grimes, June Havoc, Jack Weston, Barbara Rush, Leigh Taylor-Young. 1980

CAREFREE ★★★ In this blend of music, slapstick situations, and romantic byplay, Ginger Rogers is a crazy, mixed-up girl-child who goes to psychiatrist Fred Astaire for counsel. His treatment results in her falling in love with him. While trying to stop this, he falls in love with her. Of course they dance! It's more screwball comedy than musical. B&W; 80m. DIR: Mark Sandrich. CAST: Fred Astaire, Ginger Rogers, Ralph Bellamy, Jack Carson. 1938

CARMEN JONES ★★★★ An exceptionally well-staged adaptation of Oscar Hammerstein's updating of the famous opera with Georges Bizet's music intact. As in the opera, a flirt causes a soldier to go off the deep end because of his passion for her, but the main event is the music. The cast includes celebrity singers, but their voices were dubbed to suit the operatic range of the music. 105m. DIR: Otto Preminger. CAST: Dorothy Dandridge, Harry Belafonte, Pearl Bailey, Diahann Carroll, Brock Peters, Roy Glenn, Olga James. 1954

CARNIVAL ROCK 🦃 This tedious tale about a nightclub offers little enjoyment. Great music, though, by the Platters and David Houston. 80m. DIR: Roger Corman. CAST: Susan Cabot, Dick Miller, Brian Hutton. 1958

CAROUSEL ★★★★★ A unique blend of drama and music with the eloquent Rodgers and Hammerstein score performed by the best of both Hollywood and the Metropolitan Opera. Molnar's famous story of *Liliom*, the carnival barker who gets one day to prove he's worthy of Heaven, is transferred to Maine, where majestic backdrops add emotional emphasis. Exceptional. 128m. DIR: Henry King. CAST: Gordon MacRae, Shirley Jones, Gene Lockhart, Cameron Mitchell, Barbara Ruick, Claramae Turner, Robert Rounseville, Jacques d'Amboise. 1956

CAT AND THE FIDDLE, THE ★★★★ Jeanette MacDonald sings "The Night Was Made for Love," and the screen comes alive with romance. Ramon Novarro costars in a tuneful rendition of a Jerome Kern operetta about a struggling composer who gets upset because MacDonald sings "She Didn't Say Yes" in response to his romantic overtures. B&W; 90m. DIR: William K. Howard. CAST: Jeanette MacDonald, Ramon Novarro, Frank Morgan, Jean Hersholt, Charles Butterworth. 1934

CHOCOLATE SOLDIER, THE ★★ Nelson Eddy and Rise Stevens play husband and wife opera stars whose marriage is skidding in this clever, winning remake of the Lunt-Fontanne hit, *The Guardsman*. Delightful. B&W; 102m. DIR: Roy Del Ruth. CAST: Nelson Eddy, Rise Stevens, Florence Bates, Nigel Bruce. 1941

CHORUS LINE, A ★★★★ The screen version of Michael Bennett's hit Broadway musical allows the viewer to experience the anxiety, struggle, and triumph of a group of dancers auditioning for a stage production. Director Richard Attenborough gracefully blends big production numbers with intimate moments. Rated PG for profanity and sexual descriptions. 120m. DIR: Richard Attenborough. CAST: Michael Douglas, Alyson Reed, Terrence Mann, Audrey Landers, Jan Gan Boyd. 1985

CINDERELLA (1964) ★★★ This film is a reworking of the live 1957 CBS broadcast of the Rodgers and Hammerstein musical that featured the young Julie Andrews. The score is unchanged with the exception of an additional "Loneliness of Evening," which had been cut from *South Pacific*. A charming show for the entire family. 100m. DIR: Charles S. Dubin. CAST: Lesley Ann Warren, Stuart Damon, Ginger Rogers, Walter Pidgeon, Celeste Holm. 1964

CINDERELLA (1987) ★★★★ The immortal fairy tale is set to music by Sergei Prokofiev and performed by the world-acclaimed Berlin Comic Opera Ballet. The beautiful Hannelore Bey and Roland Gawlick as the principals provide a balance to the comedy of the rest of the ballet corps. 75m. **DIR:** Tom Schilling. **CAST:** Berlin Comic Opera Ballet. **1987**

CINDERFELLA ★★ This musical version of the oft-told fairy tale has little to recommend it. Adapted for the talents of star Jerry Lewis, it will only appeal to his fans. 91m. **DIR:** Frank Tashlin. **CAST:** Jerry Lewis, Anna Maria Alberghetti, Ed Wynn. **1960**

CLAMBAKE ★★★ This typical Elvis Presley musical-romance has a *Prince and the Pauper* scenario. Elvis, an oil baron's son, trades places with Will Hutchins, a penniless water-ski instructor, in order to find a girl who'll love him for himself and not his money. When Elvis falls for a gold-digging Shelley Fabares, he must compete with Bill Bixby, the playboy speedboat racer. 100m. **DIR:** Arthur H. Nadel. **CAST:** Elvis Presley, Shelley Fabares, Will Hutchins, Bill Bixby, Gary Merrill, James Gregory. **1967**

COAL MINER'S DAUGHTER ★★★★½ Sissy Spacek gives a superb, totally believable performance in this film biography of country singer Loretta Lynn. The title role takes Spacek from Lynn's impoverished Appalachian childhood through marriage at thirteen up to her mid-thirties and reign as the "First Lady of Country Music." Rated PG. 125m. **DIR:** Michael Apted. **CAST:** Sissy Spacek, Tommy Lee Jones, Beverly D'Angelo, Levon Helm. **1980**

COLLEGE SWING ★★★½ One of Betty Grable's first major musicals, this film kids collegiates and intellectual attitudes by showing what happens when Gracie Allen inherits a small-town college and staffs it with vaudeville performers. Some hummable tunes by Frank Loesser, a witty Preston Sturges script. B&W; 86m. **DIR:** Raoul Walsh. **CAST:** Bob Hope, Betty Grable, George Burns, Gracie Allen, Martha Raye, Ben Blue, Robert Cummings, John Payne, Jerry Colonna. **1938**

COLOR ME BARBRA ★★ *Color Me Barbra,* Streisand's second TV special, doesn't hold a candle to her first, *My Name Is Barbra.* 60m. **DIR:** Dwight Hemion. **CAST:** Barbra Streisand. **1966**

COMEBACK ★★★½ Real-life rock singer Eric Burdon (lead singer of the Animals) stars in this rock 'n' roll drama. Burdon plays a white blues singer trying to get back on top. 96m. **DIR:** Christel Buschmann. **CAST:** Eric Burdon. **1982**

COMMITMENTS, THE ★★★★ The music is wonderful in this R&B musical about a Dublin promoter (Robert Arkins) who decides to put together the ultimate Irish soul band. Andrew Strong is particularly amazing as the soulful lead vocalist. Rated R for profanity. 125m. **DIR:** Alan Parker. **CAST:** Robert Arkins, Michael Aherne, Angeline Ball, Maria Doyle, Dave Finnegan, Bronagh Gallagher, Felim Gormley, Glen Hansard, Dick Massey, Johnny Murphy, Kenneth McCluskey, Andrew Strong. **1991**

COVER GIRL ★★★ Beautiful Rita Hayworth, a performer in Gene Kelly's nightclub act, must choose between a fabulous gig as a *Vanity* magazine cover girl—which may lead to a future with a millionaire producer—or life with an extremely petulant, chauvinistic Kelly. Let's-put-on-a-show scenario works well. B&W; 107m. **DIR:** Charles Vidor. **CAST:** Rita Hayworth, Gene Kelly, Phil Silvers, Eve Arden. **1944**

CROSSOVER DREAMS ★★★★ Rubén Blades plays a popular Latino musician who tries his talents at the big time. The price he pays for his efforts is high. And while this may all sound like one big movie cliché, it's now time to add that the cast put in performances that redefine the story, giving this trite tale a bite that will surprise the viewer. 85m. **DIR:** Leon Ichaso. **CAST:** Rubén Blades, Shawn Elliot, Elizabeth Peña, Tom Signorelli, Frank Robles. **1985**

CROSSROADS ★★★½ A superb blues score by guitarist Ry Cooder highlights this enjoyable fantasy about an ambitious young bluesman (Ralph Macchio) who "goes down to the crossroads," in the words of Robert Johnson, to make a deal with the devil for fame and fortune. Most viewers will enjoy the performances, the story, and the music in this all-too-rare big-screen celebration of the blues and its mythology. Rated R for profanity, suggested sex, and violence. 105m. **DIR:** Walter Hill. **CAST:** Ralph Macchio, Joe Seneca, Jami Gertz, Joe Morton, Dennis Lipscomb, Harry Carey Jr. **1986**

CRY-BABY 🦃 John Waters's flimsy remake of *Hairspray* features Johnny Depp as a *drape* from the bad side of town. Rated PG-13 for violence and profanity. 89m. **DIR:** John Waters. **CAST:** Johnny Depp, Amy Locane, Polly Bergen, Susan Tyrrell, Iggy Pop, Ricki Lake, Traci Lords, Troy Donahue, Joey Heatherton, David Nelson, Patty Hearst, Joe Dallesandro, Willem Dafoe. **1990**

CURLY TOP ★★★ Millionaire songwriter John Boles adopts moppet Shirley Temple who plays matchmaker when he falls in love with her sister Rochelle Hudson. Almost too-cute Shirley sings "Animal Crackers in My Soup." Arthur Treacher provides his usual droll humor. B&W; 74m. **DIR:** Irving Cummings. **CAST:** Shirley Temple, John Boles, Rochelle Hudson, Jane Darwell, Arthur Treacher. **1935**

DADDY LONG LEGS ★★★½ The oft-told tale of the wealthy playboy secretly arranging the education of a poor orphaned waif, is, as expected, secondary to the song and dance. Leslie Caron has a natural grace not seen in many of Fred Astaire's partners; their dances seem to flow. A highlight is Fred's drumstick solo in "History Of The Beat." Academy Award nominations for Johnny Mercer's "Something's Got To Give" and the scoring by Alfred Newman. 126m. **DIR:** Jean Negulesco. **CAST:** Fred Astaire, Leslie Caron, Terry Moore, Thelma Ritter. **1955**

DAMES ★★★ Music, songs, dancing, great Busby Berkeley numbers. Plot? Know the one about backing a Broadway musical? But, gee, it's fun to see and hear Joan Blondell, Dick Powell, Ruby Keeler, ZaSu Pitts, Guy Kibbee, and Hugh "Woo-woo" Herbert again. B&W; 90m. **DIR:** Ray Enright. **CAST:** Joan Blondell, Dick Powell, Ruby Keeler, ZaSu Pitts, Guy Kibbee, Hugh Herbert. **1934**

DAMN YANKEES ★★★½ A torrid, wiggling vamp teams with a sly, hissing devil to frame the Yankees by turning a middle-aged baseball fan into a wunderkind and planting him on the opposing team, the Washington Senators. Gwen Verdon is sensational as the temptress Lola, who gets whatever she wants. Hollywood called on her to reprise her role in the original Broadway musical hit. Lots of pep and zing in this one. 110m. **DIR:** George Abbott, Stanley Donen. **CAST:** Gwen Verdon, Ray Walston, Tab Hunter. **1958**

DAMSEL IN DISTRESS, A ★★★ By choice, Fred Astaire made this one without Ginger, who complemented him, but with Joan Fontaine—then a beginner—who could not dance. Fred's an American popular composer in stuffy London. He mistakenly thinks heiress Joan is a chorus girl. B&W; 98m. **DIR:** George Stevens. **CAST:** Fred Astaire, Joan Fontaine, Gracie Allen, George Burns, Constance Collier, Reginald Gardiner. **1937**

DANCE ★★ Mediocre story of a group of dancers, working with a high-pressure new choreographer, who are polishing their toe shoes for the National New York Ballet auditions. An interesting sound track, with IAM IAM, but the only star is black dancer, Carlton Wilborn. Not rated. 92m. **DIR:** Robin Murray. **CAST:** Johan Renvall, Ellen Troy, Carlton Wilborn. **1988**

DANCE HALL ★★ This is a minor musical about a nightclub owner (Cesar Romero) who falls in love with one of his employees (Carole Landis). Not great. The cast saves this film from being a dud. B&W; 74m. **DIR:** Irving Pichel. **CAST:** Carole Landis, Cesar Romero, William Henry, June Storey. **1941**

DANCING LADY ★★★ Joan Crawford goes from burlesque dancer to Broadway star in this backstage drama set to music. A good film, this was also one of her early money-makers. Fred Astaire made his screen debut in one dance number. B&W; 94m. **DIR:** Robert Z. Leonard. **CAST:** Joan Crawford, Clark Gable, Fred Astaire, Franchot Tone, May Robson, Grant Mitchell, Sterling Holloway, Ted Healy, The Three Stooges. **1933**

DANCING PIRATE 🦃 The kidnapping of a dancing master by pirates. 60m. **DIR:** Lloyd Corrigan. **CAST:** Steffi Duna, Charles Collins, Frank Morgan, Jack LaRue, Rita Hayworth. **1936**

DANGEROUS WHEN WET ★★ Fame and fortune await she who swims the English Channel. Esther Williams plays a corn-fed wholesome who goes for it; Fernando Lamas cheers her on. Semisour Jack Carson and high-kicking Charlotte Greenwood clown. Good music and a novel underwater Tom and Jerry cartoon sequence. 95m. **DIR:** Charles Walters. **CAST:** Esther Williams, Fernando Lamas, Jack Carson, Charlotte Greenwood, Denise Darcel. **1953**

DARLING LILI ★★★ Dismissed out of hand on original release, and a box office flop to boot, this actually is a charming WWI romance with a Mata Hari–style narrative. Johnny Mercer and Henry Mancini provide the bouncy score. The planes later turned up in Roger Corman's *Von Richthofen and Brown*. Rated G. 136m. **DIR:** Blake Edwards. **CAST:** Julie Andrews, Rock Hudson, Jeremy Kemp, Lance Percival. **1970**

DATE WITH JUDY, A ★★½ Ho-hum musical comedy about rival teenagers Jane Powell and Elizabeth Taylor fighting for the affections of Robert Stack. High point is Carmen Miranda teaching Wallace Beery to dance. 113m. **DIR:** Richard Thorpe. **CAST:** Jane Powell, Wallace Beery, Elizabeth Taylor, Carmen Miranda, Robert Stack, Xavier Cugat, Scotty Beckett, Leon Ames. **1948**

DEADMAN'S CURVE ★★★ This made-for-TV bio-pic recounts the true story of Fifties rock stars Jan and Dean. An endearing sense of humor and their engaging surf sound propels them to the top. Then a near-fatal auto accident brings their career to a screeching halt. Richard Hatch and Bruce Davison deliver strong performances as Jan Berry and Dean Torrence. The use of Jan and Dean's original hits adds spark to the film. 100m. **DIR:** Richard Compton. **CAST:** Richard Hatch, Bruce Davison, Pamela Bellwood, Susan Sullivan, Dick Clark, Wolfman Jack. **1978**

DEEP IN MY HEART ★★ Most of the films presenting the lives of great composers have been tepid and silly. This biography of Sigmund Romberg is no exception. The songs are wonderful, but the rest is pure drivel. Along the way, Gene Kelly, Tony Martin, and Ann Miller drop by for brief musical visits, and that's it. Only fair. 132m. **DIR:** Stanley Donen. **CAST:** José Ferrer, Merle Oberon, Paul Henreid, Walter Pidgeon, Helen Traubel. **1954**

DEVIL'S BROTHER, THE ★★★½ Opera star Dennis King makes a formidable lead, and Laurel and Hardy make hearty helpers with his romantic problems with Thelma Todd. Auber's operetta gets glowing treatment with its musical numbers produced with big budgets and lots of pizzazz. The original title was *Fra Diavolo*, and it confused audiences on first release, so it was anglicized for a reissue and became an instant hit. B&W; 88m. **DIR:** Charles R. Rogers. **CAST:** Stan Laurel, Oliver Hardy, Dennis King, Thelma Todd, James Finlayson, Henry Armetta. **1933**

DIMPLES ★★★ Dimpled darling Shirley Temple tries to care for her lovable rogue grandfather Frank Morgan, a street pickpocket who works the crowds she gathers with her singing and dancing. A rich patron takes her in hand, gets her off the street, and on the stage. B&W; 79m. **DIR:** William A. Seiter. **CAST:** Shirley Temple, Frank Morgan, Helen Westley, Stepin Fetchit, John Carradine. **1936**

DIPLOMANIACS ★★½ In this preposterous romp, Bert Wheeler and Robert Woolsey play Indian-reservation barbers sent to a peace convention in Switzerland. This is a musical comedy, so don't expect too much plot. Hugh Herbert is a delight. Woo-woo! B&W; 63m. **DIR:** William A. Seiter. **CAST:** Bert Wheeler, Robert Woolsey, Marjorie White, Hugh Herbert, Louis Calhern, Edgar Kennedy. **1933**

DIRTY DANCING ★★★★ A surprise hit. Jennifer Grey stars as a teenager poised at the verge of adulthood in the early Sixties. She accompanies her family on a Catskills vacation and meets up with rhythm-and-blues in the form of dancers Patrick Swayze and Cynthia Rhodes. Nothing new, but the players present the material with exuberant energy. Rated PG-13 for language and sexual themes. 97m. **DIR:** Emile Ardolino. **CAST:** Jennifer Grey, Patrick Swayze, Cynthia Rhodes, Jerry Orbach, Jack Weston. **1987**

DISORDERLIES 🦃 Ralph Bellamy and a few rap songs by The Fat Boys are all there are to recommend this embarrassingly bad film. Rated PG. 87m. **DIR:** Michael Schultz. **CAST:** The Fat Boys, Tony Plana, Ralph Bellamy, Anthony Geary. **1987**

DIXIE JAMBOREE ★★ Another B movie from lowly PRC Studios. The action takes place on the showboat *Ellabella* and the characters range from con men to various musicians and roustabouts. B&W; 80m. **DIR:** Christy Cabanne. **CAST:** Guy Kibbee, Lyle Talbot, Eddie Quillan, Frances Langford, Fifi D'Orsay, Charles Butterworth. **1945**

DR. JEKYLL AND MR. HYDE (1973) 🦃 Kirk Douglas stars in this major misfire, a made-for-television musical based on Robert Louis Stevenson's classic tale. 90m. **DIR:** David Winters. **CAST:** Kirk Douglas, Susan George, Stanley Holloway, Michael Redgrave, Donald Pleasence. **1973**

DOGS IN SPACE ★★ Michael Hutchence, the lead singer of the Australian rock group INXS, stars in this film about the pop culture in Melbourne in 1978. This is a trip through the sexually permissive commune that merely serves as a setting for the singing performances of Hutchence. This is really only for the enjoyment of his fans and not the general public. Rated R for profanity, nudity, and suggested sex. 109m. **DIR:** Richard Lowenstein. **CAST:** Michael Hutchence, Saskia Post, Chris Haywood. **1988**

DOLL FACE ★★★ "Hubba Hubba Hubba." That's the song that launched Perry Como, and it was in this movie that it was first sung. Vivian Blaine is fine as a burlesque dancer who shoots to the top with the help of her boyfriend. It's one of those nice, often overlooked movies. B&W; 80m. **DIR:** Lewis Seiler. **CAST:** Vivian Blaine, Dennis O'Keefe, Perry Como, Carmen Miranda. **1945**

DON QUIXOTE (1933) ★★★ A strange amalgam of Cervantes' novel and a quasi-operatic treatment by composer Jacques Ibert. Of interest primarily to opera purists and G. W. Pabst buffs, it is a splendid document of the great opera basso, Feodor Chaliapin. Pabst's moody visuals nicely complement the singing. In French with English subtitles. B&W; 82m. **DIR:** G. W. Pabst. **CAST:** Feodor Chaliapin. **1933**

DON QUIXOTE (1988) ★★★★★ A thrilling and gorgeous production of the tale of the old knight who dreams of chivalry and fighting windmills. Critics hailed this performance as one of the greatest large-cast ballets ever recorded. A must for a grand night at the ballet. 120m. **DIR:** Marius Petipa, Alexander Gorsky. **CAST:** Kirov Ballet. **1988**

DOORS, THE ★★★½ Writer-director Oliver Stone's screen biography of rock group The Doors is a lot like the band it portrays: outrageous, exciting, boring, insightful, silly, and awfully pretentious. Nevertheless, Val Kilmer gives an inspired, spookily accurate performance as Jim Morrison. Rated R for simulated sex, profanity, and violence. 135m. **DIR:** Oliver Stone. **CAST:** Val Kilmer, Meg Ryan, Frank Whaley, Kevin Dillon, Kyle MacLachlan, Billy Idol, Dennis Burkley, Josh Evans, Kathleen Quinlan. **1991**

DOUBLE TROUBLE (1967) ★★ Typical Elvis Presley musical. This time he plays a rock 'n' roll singer touring England. When a teenage heiress (whose life is constantly threatened) falls for him, he gets caught up in the action. 92m. **DIR:** Norman Taurog. **CAST:** Elvis Presley, Annette Day. **1967**

DOWN ARGENTINE WAY ★★★ This tuneful Technicolor extravaganza is the granddaddy of all the fruit-filled South

American musical-comedy-romances cranked out in the 1940s. The incredible production numbers feature the rubber-jointed Nicholas Brothers and the incredible Carmen Miranda. 92m. **DIR:** Irving Cummings. **CAST:** Don Ameche, Betty Grable, Carmen Miranda, Charlotte Greenwood, J. Carrol Naish, Henry Stephenson. **1940**

DU BARRY WAS A LADY ★★ A slow-moving adaptation of a popular stage hit minus most of the music that made it popular. Set in the court of Louis XIV, this musical romp gives Red Skelton a chance to mug and Gene Kelly a chance to dance. 101m. **DIR:** Roy Del Ruth. **CAST:** Red Skelton, Lucille Ball, Gene Kelly, Zero Mostel, Virginia O'Brien, Donald Meek, Louise Beavers, Tommy Dorsey. **1943**

DU-BEAT-E-O ★★ More of a pastiche than a feature movie, *du-BEAT-e-o* has the air of something thrown together by a bunch of guys goofing around in a film-editing room. The skeleton plot has underground L.A. filmmaker Dubeateo (Ray Sharkey) and his editor (Derf Scratch of the punk band Fear) trying to turn some scattered footage of rocker Joan Jett into a movie. Unrated, there is nudity and profanity. 84m. **DIR:** Alan Sacks. **CAST:** Ray Sharkey, Derf Scratch. **1984**

DUCHESS OF IDAHO ★★½ Esther Williams attempts to have businessman John Lund become interested in her friend, lovesick Paula Raymond, only leading to Esther being pursued by him and a bandleader, Van Johnson. A badly arranged appearance by 40-year-old Eleanor Powell—her swan song. 99m. **DIR:** Robert Z. Leonard. **CAST:** Esther Williams, Van Johnson, John Lund, Paula Raymond, Lena Horne, Eleanor Powell. **1950**

EARTH GIRLS ARE EASY ★★★½ A wacky but consistently funny musical comedy, *Earth Girls* is based on the bizarre premise of some extraterrestrial visitors crash-landing in the swimming pool behind Valley girl Geena Davis's house. Davis and friend Julie Brown decide to shave the hairy intruders, discover they are hunks, and acquaint the visitors with the L.A. life-style. Rated PG for mild profanity. 100m. **DIR:** Julien Temple. **CAST:** Geena Davis, Jeff Goldblum, Julie Brown, Jim Carrey, Damon Wayans, Michael McKean, Charles Rocket. **1989**

EASTER PARADE ★★★★ Judy Garland and Fred Astaire team up for this thoroughly enjoyable musical. Irving Berlin provided the songs for the story, about Astaire trying to forget ex–dance partner Ann Miller as he rises to the top with Garland. The result is an always watchable—and repeatable—treat. 104m. **DIR:** Charles Walters. **CAST:** Judy Garland, Fred Astaire, Peter Lawford, Jules Munshin, Ann Miller. **1948**

EASY COME, EASY GO ★★ For Elvis Presley fans only. Elvis sings some snappy songs, but the plot is not going to be filed under great scripts—our star is a frogman searching for treasure on behalf of the United States Navy. 95m. **DIR:** John Rich. **CAST:** Elvis Presley, Elsa Lanchester, Dodie Marshal, Pat Priest. **1967**

EASY TO LOVE ★★½ Tony Martin and Van Johnson vie for the love of mermaid Esther Williams in this most lavish of her numerous water spectacles. A toe-curling, high-speed sequence performed on water skis tops the Busby Berkeley numbers staged in lush Cypress Gardens at Winter Haven, Florida. 96m. **DIR:** Charles Walters. **CAST:** Esther Williams, Tony Martin, Van Johnson, Carroll Baker, John Bromfield. **1953**

EDDIE AND THE CRUISERS ★★★½ Long after his death, rock 'n' roll singer Eddie Wilson's (Michael Paré) songs become popular all over again. This revives interest in a long-shelved concept album. The tape for it has been stolen, and it's up to Wilson's onetime collaborator (Tom Berenger) to find them. Only other people want the tapes, too, and they may be willing to kill to get them. The songs are great! Rated PG. 92m. **DIR:** Martin Davidson. **CAST:** Tom Berenger, Michael Paré, Ellen Barkin. **1983**

EDDIE AND THE CRUISERS II: EDDIE LIVES! ★★★ Solid sequel to *Eddie and the Cruisers* finds Eddie (Michael Paré) hiding out in Montreal while his songs enjoy new popularity. This prompts him to try music again and, of course, puts him on the inevitable road back to stardom. Thoughtful, well-intentioned film. Rated PG-13 for profanity and suggested sex. 100m. **DIR:** Jean-Claude Lord. **CAST:** Michael Paré, Marini Orsini, Bernie Coulson. **1989**

ELEKTRA ★★★ This *Live from the Met* production is the Greek legend of Elektra and her obsession with revenge. Overly dramatic performances and operatic theatrics. Only opera buffs and Birgit Nilsson fans need to view this one. In German with English subtitles. 112m. **DIR:** Brian Large. **CAST:** Birgit Nilsson. **1980**

ELEPHANT PARTS ★★★½ Mike Nesmith, formerly of The Monkees, is surprisingly versatile and talented in this video record. He sings five songs; especially memorable is "Tonight Is Magic," which dramatizes the romance of a roller-skating waitress at a hamburger stand. Between songs, Nesmith presents several funny spoofs. 60m. **DIR:** William Dear. **CAST:** Mike Nesmith, Jonathan Nesmith, Bill Martin. **1981**

ELVIS AND ME 💔 Originally a TV miniseries, this film version of Priscilla Presley's biography is disturbingly one-sided. 192m. **DIR:** Larry Peerce. **CAST:** Dale Midkiff, Susan Walters, Billy Green Bush. **1988**

ELVIS: THE LOST PERFORMANCES ★★★ Only if you like Elvis would you enjoy these outtakes from two of his live-concert movies, *Elvis—That's the Way It Is* (1970) and *Elvis on Tour* (1972). Also included is footage of Elvis rehearsing at a sound studio in 1970. 60m. **DIR:** Patrick Michael Murphy. **CAST:** Elvis Presley. **1992**

EUBIE! ★★★★ Originally a Broadway tribute to legendary composer Eubie Blake, this is nonstop song, dance, and vaudeville entertainment. Gregory Hines and Maurice Hines are outstanding with their toe-stomping tap routines. About twenty of Blake's tunes are performed on this tape—including "I'm Just Wild About Harry," "I've Got the Low Down Blues," and "In Honeysuckle Time." Unrated. 85m. **DIR:** Julianne Boyd. **CAST:** Gregory Hines, Terri Burrell, Maurice Hines, Leslie Dockery. **1981**

EVERGREEN ★★★★ This superb showcase for the legendary Jessie Matthews spans two generations in its story of a British music-hall entertainer and her talented daughter (both roles played by Jessie Matthews). The captivating Rodgers and Hart score includes "Dancing on the Ceiling" and the rousing showstopper "Over My Shoulder." B&W; 85m. **DIR:** Victor Saville. **CAST:** Jessie Matthews. **1934**

EVERYBODY SING ★★ Judy Garland is the focus in this let's-put-on-a-show musical. The movie offers a rare performance by Fanny Brice singing comedy songs. The best is "Quainty, Dainty Me." Judy Garland sings swing, and Allan Jones sings love songs in this minor tunefest. B&W; 80m. **DIR:** Edwin L. Marin. **CAST:** Judy Garland, Fanny Brice, Allan Jones, Billie Burke, Monty Woolley, Reginald Gardiner, Henry Armetta. **1938**

FABULOUS DORSEYS, THE ★★ A mildly musical, plotless dual biography of the Dorsey brothers as they fight their way to the top while fighting with each other, trombone and clarinet at the ready. Janet Blair is cute, William Lundigan is personable, and Paul "Pops" Whiteman is along for the ride. B&W; 88m. **DIR:** Alfred E. Green. **CAST:** Tommy Dorsey, Jimmy Dorsey, Janet Blair, William Lundigan, Paul Whiteman. **1947**

FAME ★★★½ Today everybody wants to be a star. *Fame* addresses that contemporary dream in a most charming and lively fashion. By focusing on the aspirations, struggles, and personal lives of a group of talented and ambitious students at New York City's High School of the Performing Arts, it manages to say something about all of us and the age we live in. Rated R. 130m. **DIR:** Alan Parker. **CAST:** Irene Cara, Lee Curreri, Eddie Barth, Laura Dean, Paul McCrane, Barry Miller, Gene Anthony Ray, Maureen Teefy. **1980**

FARMER TAKES A WIFE, THE ★★ Tiresome musical remake of a 1935 Janet Gaynor–Henry Fonda drama (filmed under the same title). This depiction of life along the Erie Canal in the early nineteenth century is a mistake from word one. 81m. **DIR:** Henry Levin. **CAST:** Betty Grable, Dale Robertson, Thelma Ritter, John Carroll, Eddie Foy Jr., Merry Anders. **1953**

FAST FORWARD ★★ This is an undisguised variation on the cliché of "let's put on a show so we can make it in show biz." In it, eight high school kids from Sandusky, Ohio, journey to New York for a promised audition. *Fast Forward* is a bubbly bit of fluff that relies on sheer energy to patch up its plot and make up for the lack of an inspired score. Sometimes, it works. Rated PG. 100m. **DIR:** Sidney Poitier. **CAST:** John Scott Clough, Don Franklin. **1985**

FIDDLER ON THE ROOF ★★★★ A lavishly mounted musical, this 1971 screen adaptation of the long-running Broadway hit, based on the stories of Sholem Aleichem, works remarkably well. This is primarily thanks to Topol's immensely likable portrayal of Tevye, the proud but put-upon father clinging desperately to the old values. Rated G. 181m. **DIR:** Norman Jewison. **CAST:** Topol, Norman Crane, Leonard Frey, Molly Picon, Paul Mann, Rosalind Harris. **1971**

FIESTA ★★½ One of Esther Williams's lesser movies, this film is helped by the scenery of Mexico, the excitement of bullfighting, and the dancing skills of Cyd Charisse. Esther Williams poses as her brother in the bullring so he can slip away to compose music. Only Williams swims better than she bullfights, and there's no water in the ring. A novelty that's mildly entertaining. 104m. **DIR:** Richard Thorpe. **CAST:** Esther Williams, Ricardo Montalban, Cyd Charisse, Mary Astor, For tunio Bonanova, John Carroll. **1947**

FINIAN'S RAINBOW ★★½ Those who believe Fred Astaire can do no wrong haven't seen this little oddity. Francis Coppola's heavy direction is totally inappropriate for a musical and the story's concerns about racial progress, which were outdated when the film first appeared, are positively embarrassing now. Rated G. 145m. **DIR:** Francis Ford Coppola. **CAST:** Fred Astaire, Petula Clark, Tommy Steele, Keenan Wynn, Barbara Hancock, Don Francks. **1968**

FIREFLY, THE ★★★½ One of Jeanette MacDonald's most popular movies even though her perennial costar, Nelson Eddy, is not in it. This is the only film they made separately that clicked. Allan Jones gets to sing the film's best song, "Donkey Serenade." MacDonald gets to sing most of the others, including "Giannina Mia" and "Love Is Like a Firefly" from Rudolf Friml's 1912 operetta. B&W; 137m. **DIR:** Robert Z. Leonard. **CAST:** Jeanette MacDonald, Allan Jones, Warren William, Douglass Dumbrille, Billy Gilbert, George Zucco, Henry Daniell. **1937**

FIRST NUDIE MUSICAL, THE ★★★ A struggling young director saves the studio by producing the world's first pornographic movie musical à la Busby Berkeley. Pleasant but extremely crude little romp. Not as bad as it sounds, but definitely for the very open-minded, and that's being generous. Rated R for nudity. 100m. **DIR:** Mark Haggard. **CAST:** Bruce Kimmel, Stephen Nathan, Cindy Williams, Diana Canova. **1979**

FIVE HEARTBEATS, THE ★★★★★ Everything is just right with writer-director Robert Townsend's musical-comedy-drama about the rise and fall of a 1960s soul group. Townsend gets excellent performances from his actors (especially Michael Wright) and always manages to put an unexpected twist on the often-too-familiar show-biz story. Rated R for profanity and violence. 120m. **DIR:** Robert Townsend. **CAST:** Robert Townsend, Michael Wright, Leon, Harry J. Lennix, Tico Wells, Diahann Carroll, Harold Nicholas, Tressa Thomas, John Terrell. **1991**

FIVE PENNIES, THE ★★★ A lively biography of jazzman Red Nichols with his contemporaries playing themselves in the jam sessions. The story line is a little sticky as it deals with family tragedies as well as triumphs. But the music is great, and there are twenty-five musical numbers. Red Nichols dubbed the sound track, and that's a bonus when he and Louis Armstrong are duetting. 117m. **DIR:** Melville Shavelson. **CAST:** Danny Kaye, Barbara Bel Geddes, Tuesday Weld, Louis Armstrong, Bob Crosby, Ray Anthony, Shelley Manne, Bobby Troup, Harry Guardino. **1959**

FLASHDANCE ★★★ Director Adrian Lyne explodes images on the screen with eye-popping regularity while the spare screenplay centers on the ambitions of Alex Owens (Jennifer Beals), a welder who dreams of making the big time as a dancer. Alex finds this goal difficult to attain—until contractor Nick Hurley (Michael Nouri) decides to help. Rated R for nudity, profanity, and implied sex. 96m. **DIR:** Adrian Lyne. **CAST:** Jennifer Beals, Michael Nouri, Lilia Skala. **1983**

FLIRTATION WALK ★★½ Dull story of romantic mix-ups and misunderstandings between a West Point cadet and the commanding officer's daughter. Surprisingly few songs, all forgettable. Nominated for best picture, but, in 1934, so were eleven other movies. B&W; 98m. **DIR:** Frank Borzage. **CAST:** Dick Powell, Ruby Keeler, Pat O'Brien, Guinn Williams, Ross Alexander, John Eldredge. **1934**

FLOWER DRUM SONG ★★ Set in San Francisco's colorful Chinatown, this Rodgers and Hammerstein musical rings sour. It has its bright moments, but the score is largely second-rate. The plot is conventional: a modern son's views versus those of an old-fashioned father. Ingredients include the usual Oriental cliché of an arranged marriage. 131m. **DIR:** Henry Koster. **CAST:** Jack Soo, Nancy Kwan, Benson Fong, Miyoshi Umeki, Juanita Hall, James Shigeta. **1962**

FLYING DOWN TO RIO ★★½ We're sure the joy of watching Fred Astaire and Ginger Rogers dance is the only thing that has prevented the negatives of this embarrassing movie from being burned. The climactic dance number, in which chorus girls perform on airplane wings, is so corny it has now passed into the realm of camp. B&W; 89m. **DIR:** Thornton Freeland. **CAST:** Dolores Del Rio, Ginger Rogers, Fred Astaire. **1933**

FOLLOW THE FLEET ★★★★ In this musical Fred Astaire and Ginger Rogers are at their best, as a dance team separated by World War II. However, sailor Astaire still has time to romance Rogers while shipmate Randolph Scott gives the same treatment to her screen sister Harriet Hilliard (Mrs. Ozzie Nelson). Look for Lucille Ball in a small part. B&W; 110m. **DIR:** Mark Sandrich. **CAST:** Fred Astaire, Ginger Rogers, Randolph Scott, Harriet Nelson, Betty Grable. **1936**

FOOTLIGHT PARADE ★★★½ Brash and cocksure James Cagney is a hustling stage director bent upon continually topping himself with Busby Berkeley–type musical numbers, which, not surprisingly, are directed by Busby Berkeley. Another grand-scale musical from the early days of sound films. B&W; 100m. **DIR:** Lloyd Bacon. **CAST:** James Cagney, Ruby Keeler, Joan Blondell, Dick Powell, Guy Kibbee, Hugh Herbert, Frank McHugh. **1933**

FOOTLIGHT SERENADE ★★ Heavyweight boxing champion Victor Mature means trouble for Broadway entertainers John Payne and Betty Grable when he joins their stage show. So-so musical. One of a series Grable made to boost morale during World War II. B&W; 80m. **DIR:** Gregory Ratoff. **CAST:** John Payne, Betty Grable, Victor Mature, Jane Wyman, James Gleason, Phil Silvers. **1942**

FOOTLOOSE ★★★★ A highly entertaining film that combines the rock beat exuberance of *Flashdance* and *Risky Business* with an entertaining—and even touching—story. This features Kevin Bacon as a Chicago boy who finds himself transplanted to a small rural town where rock music and dancing are banned—until he decides to do something about it. Rated PG for slight profanity and brief violence. 107m. **DIR:** Herbert Ross. **CAST:** Kevin Bacon, Lori Singer, John Lithgow, Dianne Wiest, Christopher Penn. **1984**

FOR ME AND MY GAL ★★★ A colorful tribute to the great and grand days of vaudeville before World War I, this tuneful trip down memory lane boosted Judy Garland's stock out of sight and made a star of Gene Kelly, he of the fleet-footed and beguiling smile. Flaws aside—the predictable plot needs a shave—this is a generally warm, invigorating picture rife with the nostalgia of happy times. B&W; 104m. **DIR:** Busby Berkeley. **CAST:** Judy Garland, Gene Kelly, George Murphy, Stephen McNally, Keenan Wynn. **1942**

FOR THE BOYS ★★★½ Show-biz pseudobiography is an ambitious, larger-than-life examination of the impact on America of the last three major wars. The story is told through the experiences of two USO entertainers, the brash Dixie Leonard (Bette Midler) and the egotistical Eddie Sparks (James Caan). Not all of its ambitions are met, but this musical still succeeds as an emotional experience. Rated R for profanity and violence. 148m. **DIR:** Mark Rydell. **CAST:** Bette Midler, James Caan, George Segal, Patrick O'Neal, Christopher Rydell, Arliss Howard, Arye Gross, Norman Fell, Rosemary Murphy, Bud Yorkin. **1991**

FOR THE FIRST TIME ★★★ An opera star on tour in Europe meets and falls in love with a deaf girl. More substance than usual for a Mario Lanza movie. Sadly the last film in his short career. 97m. **DIR:** Rudolph Maté. **CAST:** Mario Lanza, Johanna Von Koszian, Kurt Kasznar, Zsa Zsa Gabor. **1959**

FORBIDDEN DANCE, THE 🦃 The Lambada, the sensuous Brazilian dance craze. Rated PG-13. 90m. **DIR:** Greydon Clark. **CAST:** Laura Herring, Jeff James, Richard Lynch. **1990**

42ND STREET ★★★★ Every understudy's dream is to get a big chance and rise to stardom. Such is the premise of *42nd Street*. This Depression-era musical of 1933 is lifted above cliché by its vitality and sincerity. B&W; 98m. **DIR:** Lloyd Bacon. **CAST:** Dick Powell, Ruby Keeler, Ginger Rogers, Warner Baxter, Una Merkel. **1933**

FOUR JACKS AND A JILL ★★ Four broke but bighearted musicians take in a young singer who manages to tangle them up with gangsters and the law. Full of tunes and silly coincidences, this typical low-budget studio B film is short on story and shorter still on credibility. B&W; 68m. **DIR:** Jack B. Hively. **CAST:** Ray Bolger, Anne Shirley, June Havoc, Desi Arnaz Sr., Eddie Foy Jr., Fritz Feld, Henry Daniell. **1942**

FRANKIE AND JOHNNY (1966) ★★★ As the song goes, Elvis, as a Mississippi riverboat singer-gambler, betrays his lady (Donna Douglas) with his roving heart. He easily captures the attention of beautiful young ladies but must suffer the consequences. Elvis fans won't be disappointed. 87m. **DIR:** Frederick de Cordova. **CAST:** Elvis Presley, Donna Douglas, Sue Ane Langdon, Harry Morgan, Nancy Kovack, Audrey Christie. **1966**

FRENCH LINE, THE ★★ This is a dull musical with forgettable songs. Ultrarich heroine Jane Russell can't find true love. She masquerades as a fashion model during a voyage, hoping her money won't show while she snags a man. Despite presenting Miss Russell in 3-D, the film was a bust. 102m. **DIR:** Lloyd Bacon. **CAST:** Jane Russell, Gilbert Roland, Mary McCarty, Craig Stevens, Steven Geray, Arthur Hunnicutt. **1954**

FUN IN ACAPULCO ★★½ Beautiful Acapulco sets the stage for this sun-filled Elvis Presley musical. This time he's a lifeguard by day and a singer by night at a fancy beachfront resort. Typical of Elvis's films. 97m. **DIR:** Richard Thorpe. **CAST:** Elvis Presley, Ursula Andress, Paul Lukas, Alejandro Rey, Elsa Cardenas. **1963**

FUNNY FACE ★★★½ One of the best of Fred Astaire's later pictures. This time he's a fashion photographer who discovers naïve Audrey Hepburn and turns her into a sensation. Typical fairy-tale plot, enlivened by Astaire's usual charm and a good score based on the works of George Gershwin. 103m. **DIR:** Stanley Donen. **CAST:** Fred Astaire, Audrey Hepburn, Kay Thompson, Michel Auclair, Ruta Lee. **1957**

FUNNY GIRL ★★★★ The early years of Ziegfeld Follies star Fanny Brice were the inspiration for a superb stage musical. Barbra Streisand re-created her Broadway triumph in as stunning a movie debut in 1968 as Hollywood ever witnessed. She sings, roller-skates, cracks jokes, and tugs at your heart in a tour-de-force performance. Rated G. 155m. **DIR:** William Wyler. **CAST:** Barbra Streisand, Omar Sharif, Walter Pidgeon, Kay Medford. **1968**

FUNNY LADY ★★★ The sequel to *Funny Girl* is not the original, but still worth seeing. We follow comedienne Fanny Brice after she became a stage luminary only to continue her misfortunes in private life. James Caan plays her second husband, producer Billy Rose, and Omar Sharif returns in his role of Fanny's first love. But Streisand's performance and a few of the musical numbers carry the day. 149m. **DIR:** Herbert Ross. **CAST:** Barbra Streisand, James Caan, Omar Sharif, Ben Vereen. **1975**

G.I. BLUES ★★★½ Juliet Prowse improves this otherwise average Elvis Presley film. The action takes place in Germany, where Elvis makes a bet with his GI buddies he can date the aloof Prowse, who plays a nightclub dancer. 104m. **DIR:** Norman Taurog. **CAST:** Elvis Presley, Juliet Prowse. **1960**

GAY DIVORCÉE, THE ★★★★ This delightful musical farce was the only Fred Astaire/Ginger Rogers film to be nominated for a best-picture Oscar. The outstanding score includes "Night and Day" and "The Continental." B&W; 107m. **DIR:** Mark Sandrich. **CAST:** Fred Astaire, Ginger Rogers, Edward Everett Horton, Alice Brady, Erik Rhodes, Eric Blore, Betty Grable. **1934**

GEORGE BALANCHINE'S THE NUTCRACKER ★★★ Despite the presence of Macaulay Culkin, this is a rather stage-bound filming of the New York City Ballet's annual production of Tchaikovsky's masterpiece. Not very cinematic, but luscious to look at and glorious to listen to. Plus, the dancing is often marvelous. Narrated by Kevin Kline. Rated G. 93m. **DIR:** Emile Ardolino. **CAST:** Macaulay Culkin, Darci Kistler, Kyra Nichols, Wendy Whelan. **1993**

GEORGE WHITE'S SCANDALS ★★ Joan Davis saves this fairly minor musical from collapsing. B&W; 95m. **DIR:** Felix Feist. **CAST:** Joan Davis, Jack Haley, Jane Greer, Philip Terry. **1945**

GIGI ★★★★ Young Leslie Caron, being groomed as a courtesan, has more serious romance (with Louis Jourdan) on her mind. This exquisite Lerner-Loewe confection won nine Oscars and was the last nugget from the Golden Age of MGM Musicals. Maurice Chevalier and Hermione Gingold lend an unforgettable touch of class. 116m. **DIR:** Vincente Minnelli. **CAST:** Leslie Caron, Louis Jourdan, Maurice Chevalier, Hermione Gingold, Jacques Bergerac, Eva Gabor. **1958**

GIRL CRAZY ★★★ Girls are driving the ever-ebullient Mickey Rooney bonkers. His family sends him to a small southwestern college, hoping the "craze" will fade, but he meets Judy Garland, and away we go into another happy kids-give-a-show musical with glorious George and Ira Gershwin tunes. B&W; 99m. **DIR:** Busby Berkeley, Norman Taurog. **CAST:** Mickey Rooney, Judy Garland, June Allyson, Rags Ragland, Guy Kibbee, Nancy Walker, Henry O'Neill. **1943**

GIRL HAPPY ★★★ This is *Where the Boys Are* in reverse, as Elvis plays chaperon to a Chicago mobster's daughter in Fort Lauderdale, Florida. While Elvis romances vixenish Mary Ann Mobley, his nerdish charge (Shelley Fabares) constantly gets into trouble with a sexy Italian. 96m. **DIR:** Boris Sagal. **CAST:** Elvis Presley, Shelley Fabares, Mary Ann Mobley. **1964**

GIRL MOST LIKELY, THE ★★★½ This musical, a remake of *Tom, Dick and Harry*, succeeds because it's light and breezy. The choreography is by the late Gower Champion and is wonderful to watch. This is a fine film for the entire family. 98m. **DIR:** Mitchell Leisen. **CAST:** Jane Powell, Cliff Robertson, Tommy Noonan, Una Merkel. **1957**

GIRL OF THE GOLDEN WEST, THE ★★½ Jeanette MacDonald is an 1850s saloon owner attracted to bold bandit Nelson Eddy in this sloppy, hitless musical version of a 1905 play (better known as a Puccini opera). B&W; 120m. **DIR:** Robert Z. Leonard. **CAST:** Jeanette MacDonald, Nelson Eddy, Walter Pidgeon, Leo Carrillo, Buddy Ebsen, Monty Woolley, H. B. Warner, Charley Grapewin. **1938**

GIRLS! GIRLS! GIRLS! ★★ In this musical-comedy, Elvis Presley is chased by an endless array of beautiful girls. Sounds like the ideal situation? Not for poor Elvis as he tries to choose just one. 105m. **DIR:** Norman Taurog. **CAST:** Elvis Presley, Stella Stevens, Benson Fong, Laurel Goodwin, Jeremy Slate. **1962**

GIVE A GIRL A BREAK ★★ This somewhat hackneyed story of three would-be's vying to replace a star when she quits a Broadway show is nice, passes the time, but lacks stature. 82m. **DIR:** Stanley Donen. **CAST:** Debbie Reynolds, Marge Champion, Gower Champion, Kurt Kasznar, Bob Fosse, Helen Wood, Lurene Tuttle. **1953**

GIVE MY REGARDS TO BROAD STREET ★★ McCartney wrote and stars in this odd, but not really offensive, combination of great rock music and a truly insipid story as a rock singer who loses the master tapes for his album and finds his future seriously threatened. Forget the story and enjoy the songs. Rated PG for mild violence. 108m. **DIR:** Peter Webb. **CAST:** Paul McCartney, Ringo Starr, Barbara Bach, Linda McCartney. **1984**

GLASS SLIPPER, THE ★★½ The supporting players steal the spotlight from the leads, throwing this musical version of *Cinderella* off balance. The ballet scenes are beautifully staged to make it worth seeing for dance enthusiasts, but others may be bored. Estelle Winwood is especially good as the fairy godmother. An unusual musical, but not a memorable one. 94m. **DIR:** Charles Walters. **CAST:** Leslie Caron, Michael Wilding, Estelle Winwood, Keenan Wynn, Elsa Lanchester, Barry Jones, Lurene Tuttle, Amanda Blake, Lisa Daniels. **1955**

GLENN MILLER STORY, THE ★★★½ Follows the life story of famous trombonist and bandleader Glenn Miller, who disappeared in a plane during World War II. Jimmy Stewart delivers a convincing portrayal of the popular bandleader whose music had all of America tapping its feet. Miller's music is the highlight of the film, with guest appearances by Louis Armstrong and Gene Krupa. 113m. **DIR:** Anthony Mann. **CAST:** James Stewart, June Allyson, Charles Drake, Harry Morgan, Frances Langford, Gene Krupa, Louis Armstrong. **1954**

GLORIANA ★★★½ Written by Benjamin Britten to celebrate the coronation of Queen Elizabeth II, this opera is the love story of Elizabeth I and the Earl of Essex. A beautiful production filmed for TV. 146m. **DIR:** Derek Bailey. **CAST:** Sarah Walker, Anthony Rolfe Johnson. **1984**

GLORIFYING THE AMERICAN GIRL ★★½ The only film produced by legendary showman Florenz Ziegfeld, this dreary backstage rags-to-riches story reeked of mothballs even in 1929. Recognizing that, Ziegfeld padded it out with Follies production numbers that provide the only reason to watch this. Highlights are an Eddie Cantor skit, a bevy of celebrity cameos, and torch singer Helen Morgan giving her all on "What I Wouldn't Do For That Man." B&W; 95m. **DIR:** Millard Webb. **CAST:** Mary Eaton, Edward Crandall, Eddie Cantor, Helen Morgan. **1929**

GO INTO YOUR DANCE ★★★ The only film to costar husband and wife Al Jolson and Ruby Keeler is a charming curiosity piece. Besides Jolson's singing and Keeler's dancing, this backstage drama has exotic Helen Morgan singing some of the torch songs she made famous. B&W; 89m. **DIR:** Archie Mayo. **CAST:** Al Jolson, Ruby Keeler, Helen Morgan, Glenda Farrell, Benny Rubin, Phil Regan, Patsy Kelly, Barton MacLane. **1935**

GO, JOHNNY, GO! Despite the presence of some great rock 'n' roll and R&B acts, this story of a boy plucked from anonymity to become a star is about as dull as they come. B&W; 75m. **DIR:** Paul Landres. **CAST:** Jimmy Clanton, Alan Freed, Sandy Stewart, Chuck Berry, Jo-Ann Campbell, Eddie Cochran, Richie Valens, The Cadillacs, Jackie Wilson, The Flamingos. **1958**

GOING HOLLYWOOD ★★★½ The music is better than the story. Marion Davies plays a hometown girl who is determined to have both Crosby and a career in that order. The best song is "Temptation" sung by Crosby in his inimitable crooning fashion. Very brisk pace; very enjoyable staging of musical numbers. B&W; 80m. **DIR:** Raoul Walsh. **CAST:** Bing Crosby, Marion Davies, Fifi D'Orsay, Patsy Kelly, Ned Sparks, Stu Erwin. **1933**

GOLD DIGGERS OF 1933 ★★★★ This typical 1930s song-and-dance musical revolves around a Broadway show. Notable tunes include: "We're in the Money," sung by Ginger Rogers; "Forgotten Man," sung by Joan Blondell; and "Shadow Waltz," by the chorus girls. Enjoyable fare if you like nostalgic musicals. B&W; 96m. **DIR:** Mervyn LeRoy. **CAST:** Joan Blondell, Ruby Keeler, Dick Powell, Aline MacMahon, Ginger Rogers, Sterling Holloway. **1933**

GOLD DIGGERS OF 1935 ★★★ Classic Busby Berkeley musical production numbers dominate this absurd story of mercenary schemers swarming around the rich at a posh resort. Though the film sags and lags, the kitsch director's staging of "Lullaby of Broadway" is a piece of cinematic brilliance. B&W; 95m. **DIR:** Busby Berkeley. **CAST:** Dick Powell, Adolphe Menjou, Winifred Shaw, Glenda Farrell. **1935**

GOLDWYN FOLLIES, THE Goldwyn's folly is a better title for this turkey. 120m. **DIR:** George Marshall. **CAST:** Adolphe Menjou, Andrea Leeds, Kenny Baker, The Ritz Brothers, Vera Zorina, Edgar Bergen. **1938**

GOOD NEWS ★★★ Football hero Peter Lawford resists the class vamp and wins the big game and the campus cutie who loves him in this quintessential musical of college life. The dialogue is painfully trite and trying, but energy and exuberance abound. 95m. **DIR:** Charles Walters. **CAST:** June Allyson, Peter Lawford, Patricia Marshall, Joan McCracken, Mel Torme. **1948**

GOODBYE, MR. CHIPS (1969) Cash in this *Chips*. Rated G. 151m. **DIR:** Herbert Ross. **CAST:** Peter O'Toole, Petula Clark, Michael Redgrave, George Baker, Sian Phillips. **1969**

GRAFFITI BRIDGE ★★ Prince's hollow fantasy sequel to *Purple Rain* is about the conflicting values (artistic integrity versus commercial success) that ignite a power struggle between two nightclub co-owners (funksters Prince and Morris Day). Rated PG-13 for profanity and sexual themes. 111m. **DIR:** Prince. **CAST:** Prince, Morris Day, Jerome Benton, Ingrid Chavez. **1990**

GREASE ★★★ After they meet and enjoy a tender summer romance, John Travolta and Olivia Newton-John tearfully part. Surprisingly, they are reunited when she becomes the new girl at his high school. Around his friends, he must play Mr. Tough Guy, and her goody-two-shoes image doesn't quite fit in. Slight, but fun. Rated PG. 110m. **DIR:** Randal Kleiser. **CAST:** John Travolta, Olivia Newton-John, Stockard Channing, Jeff Conaway, Didi Conn, Eve Arden, Sid Caesar. **1978**

GREASE 2 ★★★ A sequel to the most successful screen musical of all time, *Grease 2* takes us back to Rydell High. The result is a fun little movie that seems to work almost in spite of itself. Rated PG for suggestive gestures and lyrics. 115m. **DIR:** Patricia Birch. **CAST:** Maxwell Caulfield, Michelle Pfeiffer, Adrian Zmed, Lorna Luft, Didi Conn. **1982**

GREAT BALLS OF FIRE ★★★★ A landmark music bio. It's obvious how hard talented Dennis Quaid has worked on his piano playing (with hands, feet, head, and tail) and on his Jerry Lee Lewis hellion-touched-by-God mannerisms and he's sublime in the role. So is Alec Baldwin, playing it straight and righteous as Jerry Lee's famous cousin, Jimmy Swaggart. Some miraculous moments. Rated PG-13 for profanity and sexual themes. 110m. **DIR:** Jim McBride. **CAST:** Dennis Quaid, Winona Ryder, Alec Baldwin, Trey Wilson. **1989**

GREAT CARUSO, THE ★★★★ A number of factual liberties are taken in this lavish screen biography of the great Italian tenor, but no matter. Mario Lanza's voice is magnificent; Ann Blyth and Dorothy Kirsten sing like birds. Devotees of music will love the arias. 109m. **DIR:** Richard Thorpe. **CAST:** Mario Lanza, Ann Blyth, Dorothy Kirsten. **1950**

GREAT ROCK AND ROLL SWINDLE, THE ★★★★ Free-form pseudodocumentary about legendary punk-rock band the Sex Pistols is just an excuse for promoter Malcolm McLaren to blow his own horn, though he does that quite entertainingly. Not rated; contains profanity. 103m. **DIR:** Julien Temple. **CAST:** Malcolm McLaren, Sid Vicious, John Lydon, Paul Cook, Steve Jones. **1980**

GREAT WALTZ, THE ★★★★ This biography of Viennese waltz king Johann Strauss II may have no factual bearing whatever (and it doesn't), but it's great fun and cinematically quite stunning. Unfortunately, Oscar Hammerstein's new lyrics to the waltzes are entrusted to diva Miliza Korjus, whose weak voice and inept bel canto technique are quite awful. B&W; 103m. **DIR:** Julien Duvivier. **CAST:** Fernand Gravet, Luise Rainer, Miliza Korjus. **1938**

GREAT ZIEGFELD, THE ★★★★★ This Academy Award–winning best picture is a marvelous film biography of legendary showman Florenz Ziegfeld. William Powell is perfect in the title role and Oscar winner Luise Rainer is tremendous as the fabulous Anna Held. The sets, costumes, and production design are superb. This is Hollywood at its finest. B&W; 176m. **DIR:** Robert Z. Leonard. **CAST:** William Powell, Myrna Loy, Luise Rainer, Frank Morgan, Fanny Brice, Virginia Bruce, Reginald Owen, Dennis Morgan. **1936**

GUN IS LOADED, THE 💔 Avant-garde poet and rock performer Lydia Lunch's angst-ridden look at New York City. Not rated, but contains profanity and nudity. 65m. **DIR:** Lydia Lunch. **CAST:** Lydia Lunch. **1989**

GUYS AND DOLLS ★★★ This passable musical stars Marlon Brando and Frank Sinatra as New York gamblers with a gangster-like aura. Brando and Sinatra bet on whether or not a lovely Salvation Army soldier (Jean Simmons) is date bait. 150m. **DIR:** Joseph L. Mankiewicz. **CAST:** Marlon Brando, Frank Sinatra, Jean Simmons, Vivian Blaine, Stubby Kaye, Veda Ann Borg. **1955**

GYPSY (1962) ★★★ *Gypsy* tries to surpass its hackneyed situation with an energetic musical score and a story about real people. In this case, the characters are stripper Gypsy Rose Lee and her backstage mother supreme, Rose. The music is excellent, but the characters are weakly defined. 149m. **DIR:** Mervyn LeRoy. **CAST:** Natalie Wood, Rosalind Russell, Karl Malden. **1962**

GYPSY (1993) ★★★★ Bette Midler struts her stuff in this engaging TV adaptation of the Broadway musical. She's Mama Rose, the boisterous, driven stage mother of June Haver and Gypsy Rose Lee. It's a showstopping performance, and Midler deftly shades her hard-edged but endearing character while belting out Jule Styne's memorable tunes with élan. Made for TV. 150m. **DIR:** Emile Ardolino. **CAST:** Bette Midler, Cynthia Gibb, Peter Riegert, Edward Asner. **1993**

HAIR ★★★½ Neglected adaptation of the hit Broadway play about 1960s unrest. John Savage is the uptight Midwesterner who pals up with a group of (shudder) hippies celebrating the Age of Aquarius. Grand musical moments, due to Twyla Tharp's impressive choreography. Rated PG for nudity. 121m. **DIR:** Milos Forman. **CAST:** Treat Williams, John Savage, Beverly D'Angelo, Annie Golden, Charlotte Rae. **1979**

HALF A SIXPENCE ★★ A tuneful musical incarnation of H. G. Wells' novel, *Kipps*, as presented on Broadway with most of the original Broadway cast. The story of a British boy winning and losing a fortune, and winning, losing, and re-winning a girlfriend, is flashy and tuneful, but a mite long for one sitting. 149m. **DIR:** George Sidney. **CAST:** Tommy Steele, Julia Foster, Cyril Ritchard, Pamela Brown, James Villiers, Hilton Edwards, Penelope Horner. **1967**

HANS CHRISTIAN ANDERSEN ★★★½ Danny Kaye is superb as the famous storyteller, and Frank Loesser composed some wonderful songs for this glossy oversweet musical. Ballet great Jeanmaire is a knockout. This is top-notch family entertainment. 120m. **DIR:** Charles Vidor. **CAST:** Danny Kaye, Farley Granger, Zizi Jeanmaire, John Qualen. **1952**

HAPPY GO LOVELY ★★★ Perky Vera-Ellen is a dancing darling in this lightweight musical with a very tired plot about a producer who hires a chorus girl with the idea that her boyfriend has money to invest in his show. It's all cute, but nothing startling. 87m. **DIR:** H. Bruce Humberstone. **CAST:** David Niven, Vera-Ellen, Cesar Romero. **1951**

HAPPY LANDING ★★★½ One of Sonja Henie's most popular movies, and her co-stars get most of the credit. Two men compete for her affections between songs, dancing, and ice-skating routines. The songs are especially good, and the singers—Don Ameche, Ethel Merman, Peters Sisters, and Condos Brothers—are outstanding. B&W; 102m. **DIR:** Roy Del Ruth. **CAST:** Sonja Henie, Don Ameche, Cesar Romero, Ethel Merman, Lon Chaney Jr., Jean Hersholt, Wally Vernon, Billy Gilbert, El Brendel, Raymond Scott. **1938**

HARD DAY'S NIGHT, A ★★★★★ Put simply, this is the greatest rock 'n' roll comedy ever made. Scripted by Alan Owen as a sort of day in the life of the Beatles, it's fast-paced, funny, and full of great Lennon-McCartney songs. Even more than twenty years after its release, it continues to delight several generations of viewers. B&W; 85m. **DIR:** Richard Lester. **CAST:** The Beatles, Wilfred Brambell, Victor Spinetti, Anna Quayle. **1964**

HARD TO HOLD ★★ In this highly forgettable film, Rick Springfield plays a music superstar who has everything except the woman (Janet Eilber) he loves. The first half hour is quite good, but from there it goes downhill into soap opera. Rated PG for brief nudity and profanity. 93m. **DIR:** Larry Peerce. **CAST:** Rick Springfield, Janet Eilber, Patti Hansen, Albert Salmi. **1984**

HARDER THEY COME, THE ★★★★ Made in Jamaica by Jamaicans, this film has become an underground cult classic. In it, a rural boy comes to the big city to become a singer. There, he is forced into a life of crime. Rated R. 98m. **DIR:** Perry Henzell. **CAST:** Jimmy Cliff, Janet Barkley. **1973**

HARMONY LANE ★★ Only the music saves this halfhearted account of composer Stephen Foster's tragic life from being classed a turkey. The sets are shoddy, the camera rarely moves, most of the acting is insipid, and the screenplay is one long string of music cues. B&W; 89m. **DIR:** Joseph Santley. **CAST:** Douglass Montgomery, Evelyn Venable, Adrienne Ames, William Frawley. **1935**

HARUM SCARUM ★★★ When a swashbuckling film star (Elvis Presley) visits a primitive Arabian country, he is forced to aid assassins in their bid to destroy the king. Simultaneously, he falls in love with the king's beautiful daughter (Mary Ann Mobley). Elvis manages to belt out nine tunes, including "Shake That Tambourine" and "Harem Holiday." His fans won't be disappointed. 85m. **DIR:** Gene Nelson. **CAST:** Elvis Presley, Mary Ann Mobley, Michael Ansara, Billy Barty. **1965**

HARVEY GIRLS, THE ★★★ Rousing fun marks this big, bustling musical, which is loosely tied to the development of pioneer railroad-station restaurateur Fred Harvey's string of eateries along the Santa Fe right-of-way. Judy Garland is the innocent who goes west to grow up, Angela Lansbury is the wise bad girl, and John Hodiak is the requisite gambler. 102m. **DIR:** George Sidney. **CAST:** Judy Garland, John Hodiak, Ray Bolger, Preston Foster, Virginia O'Brien, Angela Lansbury, Marjorie Main, Chill Wills, Cyd Charisse, Kenny Baker. **1945**

HEAD (1968) ★★★ They get the funniest looks from everyone they meet. And it's no wonder. This film is truly bizarre. The Monkees were hurtled to fame in the aftershock of the Beatles' success. Their ingratiating series was accused of imitating *A Hard Day's Night*, but their innovative feature-film debut, *Head*, was ahead of its time. A free-form product of the psychedelic era. 86m. **DIR:** Bob Rafelson. **CAST:** Mickey Dolenz, David Jones, Mike Nesmith, Peter Tork, Teri Garr, Vito Scotti, Timothy Carey, Logan Ramsey. **1968**

HEART'S DESIRE ★★ Richard Tauber, a popular tenor in British operetta, stars in this ho-hum musical as a Viennese waiter who becomes a star in London. In the end, true love brings him back home. B&W; 79m. **DIR:** Paul Stein. **CAST:** Richard Tauber, Leonora Corbett. **1935**

HELLO, DOLLY! ♥ Barbra Streisand as an intrepid matchmaker. Rated G. 146m. **DIR:** Gene Kelly. **CAST:** Barbra Streisand, Walter Matthau, Michael Crawford, E. J. Peaker, Marianne McAndrew. **1969**

HELP! ★★★★ Though neither as inventive nor as charming as *A Hard Day's Night*, this second collaboration between director Richard Lester and the Fab Four has energy, fun, and memorable songs. The slim plot has a bizarre religious cult trying to retrieve a sacrificial ring from Ringo. From the reverberating opening chord of the title tune, the movie sweeps you up in its irresistibly zesty spirit. 90m. **DIR:** Richard Lester. **CAST:** The Beatles, Leo McKern, Eleanor Bron, Victor Spinetti. **1965**

HERE COME THE GIRLS ★★★ Bumbling Bob Hope is taken from the chorus and made the star of a Broadway show, unaware he is a decoy for a jealous slasher infatuated with the leading lady. Some good gags and lots of musical numbers. 78m. **DIR:** Claude Binyon. **CAST:** Bob Hope, Arlene Dahl, Tony Martin, Rosemary Clooney, Millard Mitchell, William Demarest, Fred Clark, Robert Strauss. **1953**

HERE COME THE WAVES ★★★½ Bing Crosby stars as a famous singer who enlists in the navy with best friend Sonny Tufts. A fun musical that features Betty Hutton as twins—so that both leading men get the girl. "Accentuate the Positive" was written for this film. B&W; 100m. **DIR:** Mark Sandrich. **CAST:** Bing Crosby, Betty Hutton, Sonny Tufts. **1944**

HERE COMES THE GROOM ★★★ Bing Crosby stars as a reporter returning from France with two war orphans. Jane Wyman finds herself torn between Crosby and wealthy Franchot Tone. Director Frank Capra keeps the pace brisk and adds to an otherwise familiar tale. 114m. **DIR:** Frank Capra. **CAST:** Bing Crosby, Jane Wyman, Alexis Smith, Franchot Tone. **1951**

HIGH SOCIETY ★★★½ The outstanding cast in this film is reason enough to watch this enjoyable musical remake of *The Philadelphia Story*. The film moves at a leisurely pace, helped by some nice songs by Cole Porter. 107m. **DIR:** Charles Walters. **CAST:** Bing Crosby, Frank Sinatra, Grace Kelly, Louis Armstrong. **1956**

HIGHER AND HIGHER ★★ Frank Sinatra and the entire cast do a wonderful job in this practically plotless picture about a once-rich man teaming up with his servants in his quest to be wealthy once again. This is Sinatra's first major film effort, and he does a fine job with the first-rate songs. B&W; 90m. **DIR:**

Tim Whelan. **CAST:** Frank Sinatra, Michele Morgan, Jack Haley, Leon Errol, Victor Borge, Mel Torme. **1943**

HIT THE DECK ★★½ Fancy-free sailors on shore leave meet girls, dance, sing, and cut up in this updated 1920s Vincent Youmans hit from Broadway. Good, time-filling eyewash. 112m. **DIR:** Roy Rowland. **CAST:** Jane Powell, Tony Martin, Debbie Reynolds, Vic Damone, Ann Miller, Russ Tamblyn, Walter Pidgeon, Gene Raymond. **1955**

HOLIDAY IN MEXICO ★★★½ Song-filled feast, with widowed Walter Pidgeon as the Ambassador to Mexico. He and his daughter, Jane Powell, find the loves of their lives. Powell sings the "Italian Street Song" and a moving version of "Ave Maria." Jose Iturbi plays "Polonnaise." 127m. **DIR:** George Sidney. **CAST:** Walter Pidgeon, Jose Iturbi, Roddy McDowall, Ilona Massey, Jane Powell, Xavier Cugat, Hugo Haas, Linda Christian. **1946**

HOLIDAY INN ★★★★ Irving Berlin's music and the delightful teaming of Bing Crosby and Fred Astaire are the high points of this wartime musical. The timeless renditions of "White Christmas" and "Easter Parade" more than make up for a script that at best could be called fluff. B&W; 101m. **DIR:** Mark Sandrich. **CAST:** Bing Crosby, Fred Astaire, Marjorie Reynolds, Virginia Dale. **1942**

HOLLYWOOD CANTEEN ★★★ An all-star tribute to soldiers, sailors, and Marines who frequented the famed Hollywood Canteen during World War II. Bette Davis and John Garfield founded the USO haven, and just about everybody in show business donated his and her time to make the servicemen feel at ease. The slim storyline is about the one millionth soldier to visit the Canteen. B&W; 125m. **DIR:** Delmer Daves. **CAST:** Bette Davis, John Garfield, Joan Crawford, Ida Lupino, Errol Flynn, Olivia de Havilland, Joan Leslie, Jack Benny, Roy Rogers, Robert Hutton, Dane Clark, Sydney Greenstreet, Peter Lorre, Barbara Stanwyck, Alexis Smith, Eddie Cantor, Janis Paige. **1944**

HOLLYWOOD HOTEL ★★ Saxophonist Dick Powell wins a talent contest, gets a film contract, but gets the boot because he won't cozy up to bitchy star Lola Lane, preferring her sister instead. Songs by Johnny Mercer and Richard Whiting, including "Hooray for Hollywood," help bolster this otherwise average musical mishmash. B&W; 109m. **DIR:** Busby Berkeley. **CAST:** Dick Powell, Rosemary Lane, Lola Lane, Ted Healy, Alan Mowbray, Frances Langford, Hugh Herbert, Louella Parsons, Glenda Farrell, Edgar Kennedy. **1937**

HONEYSUCKLE ROSE ★★½ For his first starring role, country singer Willie Nelson is saddled with a rather stodgy film that all but sinks in the mire of its unimaginative handling and sappy story. Rated PG. 119m. **DIR:** Jerry Schatzberg. **CAST:** Willie Nelson, Dyan Cannon, Amy Irving, Slim Pickens. **1980**

HONOLULU ★★★★ More of a comedy than a musical, this film was completely forgotten until George Burns said it was the last movie he had made before his comeback in *The Sunshine Boys* a quarter of a century later. Robert Young has the lead playing a movie star and his twin brother. They change places and cause all sorts of mix-ups. Burns and Gracie Allen fill most of the time with choice one-liners. B&W; 83m. **DIR:** Edward Buzzell. **CAST:** Eleanor Powell, George Burns, Gracie Allen, Robert Young, Rita Johnson, Sig Ruman, Ruth Hussey, Eddie "Rochester" Anderson, Ann Morris, Clarence Kolb. **1939**

HOUSE PARTY ★★★★ This delightful rap musical was one of the sleeper hits of 1990. The plot is standard let's-have-a-party-while-my-folks-are-away stuff, but with a surprisingly fresh humor and some dynamite dance numbers. The R rating (for profanity) makes it unsuitable for small children, but for mature teens and adults it's a great good time. 105m. **DIR:** Reginald Hudlin. **CAST:** Kid'n'Play (Christopher Reid, Christopher Wells), Full Force, Robin Harris. **1990**

HOUSE PARTY 2 ★★½ Inferior sequel. The film, which is dedicated to the late comedian Robin Harris (seen in flashback scenes) and features Whoopi Goldberg in a brief cameo, has some funny moments, most of which are provided by Martin Lawrence as Kid 'N' Play's out-of-control disc jockey. Otherwise, it's pretty standard fare. Rated R for profanity and violence. 90m. **DIR:** Doug McHenry, George Jackson. **CAST:** Christopher Reid, Christopher Martin, Martin Lawrence, Tisha Campbell, Georg Stanford Brown, William Schallert. **1991**

HOUSE PARTY 3 ★★ Rappers Kid 'N' Play get lost in the cluttered shuffle of their own hip-hop comedy. Kid's bachelor party and the duo's management of an all-girl group hit a few snags. Rated R for profanity. 94m. **DIR:** Eric Meza. **CAST:** Christopher Reid, Christopher Martin, Bernie Mac, Angela Means, Khandi Alexander. **1994**

HOW TO STUFF A WILD BIKINI ★★ It's no surprise to see Frankie Avalon and Annette Funicello together in this beach-party film. Dwayne Hickman (TV's Dobie Gillis) tries his hand at romancing Annette in this one. Not much plot, but lots of crazy (sometimes funny) things are going on. 90m. **DIR:** William Asher. **CAST:** Frankie Avalon, Annette Funicello, Dwayne Hickman, Mickey Rooney, Buster Keaton. **1965**

HOW TO SUCCEED IN BUSINESS WITHOUT REALLY TRYING ★★★★★ A near-perfect musical based on the Pulitzer Prize–winning Broadway show, with most of the original cast intact. Robert Morse plays the window washer who schemes, connives, and plots his way to the top of the Worldwide Wicket Company. The musical numbers are staged with inventiveness and performed with as much exuberance as most topflight Broadway shows. Maureen Arthur is a standout as the buxom beauty all the managers want in their secretarial pool. 121m. **DIR:** David Swift. **CAST:** Robert Morse, Rudy Vallee, Michele Lee, Anthony Teague, Maureen Arthur, Sammy Smith. **1967**

I COULD GO ON SINGING ★★★ In this, her last film, with a disturbing true-to-her-life plot, Judy Garland plays a successful concert singer beset by personal problems. When Judy sings, the film lives. When she doesn't, it's wistful, teary, and a bit sloppy. Strictly for Garland fanatics. 99m. **DIR:** Ronald Neame. **CAST:** Judy Garland, Dirk Bogarde, Jack Klugman, Aline MacMahon. **1963**

I DO! I DO! ★★★★ Lee Remick and Hal Linden step into the parts originally created on Broadway by Mary Martin and Robert Preston in this video of a performance taped before an audience. The play deals with the marriage of Michael to Agnes—from the night before their wedding to the day when they leave their home of forty years. Solid entertainment. 116m. **DIR:** Gower Champion. **CAST:** Lee Remick, Hal Linden. **1982**

I DOOD IT ★★½ A musical based on an old Buster Keaton silent comedy about a tailor's assistant (Red Skelton) going gaga over dancer (Eleanor Powell). Powell's tap dancing is especially noteworthy. B&W; 102m. **DIR:** Vincente Minnelli. **CAST:** Red Skelton, Eleanor Powell, Lena Horne, Hazel Scott, Butterfly McQueen, Helen O'Connell, Bob Eberly, Sam Levene, John Hodiak, Morris Ankrum, Thurston Hall. **1943**

I DREAM TOO MUCH ★★½ This picture is more of a showcase for Lily Pons's vocal abilities in the operetta form. Henry Fonda and Pons are two performers who face career obstacles. The music is okay. B&W; 95m. **DIR:** John Cromwell. **CAST:** Henry Fonda, Lily Pons, Lucille Ball, Eric Blore. **1935**

I LOVE MELVIN ★★★ Entertaining little MGM musical has Donald O'Connor pretending to be a man with connections so he can have a chance with perky Debbie Reynolds. The story is slight, but the laughs and songs are good, and O'Connor and Reynolds work well together. Entertaining and amusing. 76m. **DIR:** Don Weis. **CAST:** Debbie Reynolds, Donald O'Connor, Una Merkel, Allyn Joslyn, Noreen Corcoran, Richard Anderson, Jim Backus, Barbara Ruick. **1953**

I MARRIED AN ANGEL ★★ In this, their final film together, playboy Nelson Eddy dreams he courts and marries angel Jeanette MacDonald. *Leaden* and *bizarre* are but two of the words critics used. B&W; 84m. **DIR:** W. S. Van Dyke. **CAST:** Jeanette MacDonald, Nelson Eddy, Edward Everett Horton, Binnie Barnes, Reginald Owen. **1942**

ICELAND ★★★½ A typical Sonja Henie musical with lots of music, romancing, and slapstick comedy. Henie plays an ice skater who falls in love with an American marine. She tells her parents she is going to marry him so her younger sister can marry the man of her dreams. (In their culture, the oldest daughter always marries first.) Now she has to make good on her promise. B&W; 79m. **DIR:** H. Bruce Humberstone. **CAST:** Sonja Henie, John Payne, Jack Oakie, Felix Bressart, Osa Massen, Fritz Feld, Joan Merrill, Adeline de Walt Reynolds, Sammy Kaye. **1942**

IDOLMAKER, THE ★★★★ This superior rock 'n' roll drama stands with a handful of pictures—*The Buddy Holly Story* and *American Hot Wax* among them—as one of the few to capture the excitement of rock music while still offering something in the way of a decent plot and characterization. Ray Sharkey is excellent as a songwriter-manager who pulls, pushes, punches, and plunders his way to the top of the music world. The score, by Jeff Barry, is top-notch. Rated PG. 119m. **DIR:** Taylor Hackford. **CAST:** Ray Sharkey, Tovah Feldshuh, Peter Gallagher, Maureen McCormick. **1980**

IF YOU KNEW SUSIE ★★½ If you enjoy the comedy and musical stylings of Joan Davis and Eddie Cantor, you'll probably be pleased with this thin story of two entertainers who discover a will signed by George Washington. Dated and held together only by Cantor's sure touch and slick performance. B&W; 90m. **DIR:** Gordon Douglas. **CAST:** Eddie Cantor, Joan Davis, Allyn Joslyn. **1948**

I'LL CRY TOMORROW ★★★½ In addition to giving one of the most professional performances of her career, Susan Hayward sang (and very well) the songs in this screen biography of Lillian Roth. Her masterful portrayal, supported by a solid cast, won her a Cannes Film Festival award. B&W; 117m. **DIR:** Daniel Mann. **CAST:** Susan Hayward, Eddie Albert, Richard Conte, Jo Van Fleet, Don Taylor, Ray Danton. **1955**

I'LL SEE YOU IN MY DREAMS ★★★½ This sugarcoated biography of lyricist Gus Kahn contains a truly warm performance by Danny Thomas, coupled with fine renditions of Kahn's songs ("Pretty Baby," "It Had To Be You," "Love Me Or Leave Me," etc.) B&W; 110m. **DIR:** Michael Curtiz. **CAST:** Danny Thomas, Doris Day, Frank Lovejoy, Patrice Wymore, James Gleason, Mary Wickes, Jim Backus. **1951**

I'LL TAKE SWEDEN ★★ Bob Hope takes a job in Sweden to break up his daughter's love affair and finds romance himself. Misfires all the way. 96m. **DIR:** Frederick de Cordova. **CAST:** Bob Hope, Tuesday Weld, Frankie Avalon, Dina Merrill, John Qualen. **1965**

IN THE GOOD OLD SUMMERTIME ★★★ Despite its title, most of the action of this remake of the classic romantic comedy *The Shop Around the Corner* takes place in winter. Judy Garland and Van Johnson work in the same music store. They dislike each other, but are unknowingly secret pen pals who have much in common. Truth wins out, but by the time it does, love has struck. Buster Keaton is wasted as comic relief. 102m. **DIR:** Robert Z. Leonard. **CAST:** Judy Garland, Van Johnson, S. Z. Sakall, Buster Keaton, Spring Byington. **1949**

INDUSTRIAL SYMPHONY NO. 1 THE DREAM OF THE BROKEN HEARTED ★★★½ Bizarre glimpse into a broken love affair set against the backdrop of an industrial wasteland from the director of *Eraserhead, Twin Peaks,* and *Wild At Heart.* This surreal opera was performed at The Brooklyn Academy of Music Opera House and features an impressive score by composer Angelo Badalamenti, with lyrics by Lynch. Not rated, but contains some nudity. 50m. **DIR:** David Lynch. **CAST:** Laura Dern, Nicolas Cage, Julee Cruise. **1989**

INTERRUPTED MELODY ★★★★½ An excellent movie biography of Australian opera singer Marjorie Lawrence. She was stricken by polio but continued her career in spite of her handicap. Eleanor Parker stars as Lawrence with vocals dubbed by opera star Eileen Farrell. 106m. **DIR:** Curtis Bernhardt. **CAST:** Eleanor Parker, Glenn Ford, Roger Moore, Cecil Kellaway, Stephen Bekassy. **1955**

INVITATION TO THE DANCE ★★★ Strictly for lovers of Terpsichore, this film tells three stories entirely through dance. It sort of drags until Gene Kelly appears in a live action–cartoon sequence about "Sinbad" of Arabian Nights fame. 93m. **DIR:** Gene Kelly. **CAST:** Gene Kelly. **1957**

IT COULDN'T HAPPEN HERE 🦃 A flat and self-indulgent Pet Shop Boys vehicle consisting of loosely related scenes serving only to showcase the British music duo's all-time synth-drenched hits. Boring. Rated PG-13 for adult themes. 89m. **DIR:** Jack Bond. **CAST:** Neil Tennant, Chris Lowe, Gareth Hunt, Neil Dickson. **1992**

IT HAPPENED AT THE WORLD'S FAIR ★★½ Adorable tyke plays matchmaker for Elvis Presley and Joan O'Brien at the Seattle World's Fair. It's a breezy romantic comedy with bouncy songs. Elvis hadn't yet reached the point where he was just going through the motions. He seems to be having fun and you will, too. 105m. **DIR:** Norman Taurog. **CAST:** Elvis Presley, Joan O'Brien, Gary Lockwood, Yvonne Craig. **1963**

IT HAPPENED IN BROOKLYN ★★ A modest musical made to capitalize on the hit-parade popularity of Frank Sinatra. The story concerns several Brooklynites trying to make the big time in show business. The only energy of note is Jimmy Durante. Passable. B&W; 105m. **DIR:** Richard Whorf. **CAST:** Frank Sinatra, Kathryn Grayson, Jimmy Durante, Peter Lawford, Gloria Grahame. **1947**

IT HAPPENED IN NEW ORLEANS ★★ Bobby Breen, the male Shirley Temple, stars as a Civil War orphan forced to leave his ex-slave mammy and go to New York. There, his Yankee relatives give him a hard time until his renditions of Stephen Foster tunes and his overwhelming cuteness win them over. Also known as *Rainbow on the River.* B&W; 83m. **DIR:** Kurt Neumann. **CAST:** Bobby Breen, May Robson, Charles Butterworth, Louise Beavers, Alan Mowbray, Benita Hume, Henry O'Neill, Eddie "Rochester" Anderson. **1936**

IT'S A DATE ★★★ A teenager competes with her widowed mother for a mature man. Corny plot, but it works because of the refreshing Deanna Durbin and her crystal-clear soprano voice. Remade with Jane Powell as *Nancy Goes to Rio* with different songs and didn't work nearly as well. B&W; 103m. **DIR:** William A. Seiter. **CAST:** Deanna Durbin, Walter Pidgeon, Kay Francis, Eugene Pallette, S. Z. Sakall, Fritz Feld, Samuel S. Hinds. **1940**

IT'S A GREAT FEELING ★★★ Doris Day's third movie is more of a comedy than a musical, but she still gets to sing a half-dozen sprightly songs. Jack Carson plays an obnoxious movie star. Cameo bits by Errol Flynn, Gary Cooper, Joan Crawford, Sydney Greenstreet, Jane Wyman, Edward G. Robinson, Ronald Reagan, Eleanor Parker, Patricia Neal, and Danny Kaye. 85m. **DIR:** David Butler. **CAST:** Doris Day, Dennis Morgan, Jack Carson, Bill Goodwin. **1949**

IT'S ALWAYS FAIR WEATHER ★★★ World War II buddies Gene Kelly, Dan Dailey, and Michael Kidd meet a decade after discharge and find they actively dislike one another. Enter romance, reconciliation ploys, and attempted exploitation of their reunion on televison. Don't be surprised to realize it recalls *On the Town.* 102m. **DIR:** Gene Kelly, Stanley Donen. **CAST:** Gene Kelly, Dan Dailey, Michael Kidd, Cyd Charisse, Dolores Gray, David Burns. **1955**

JAILHOUSE ROCK ★★★★ Quite possibly Elvis Presley's best as far as musical sequences go, this 1957 film is still burdened by a sappy plot. Good-hearted Presley gets stuck in the slammer, only to hook up with a conniving manager (Mickey Shaughnessy). Forget the plot and enjoy the great rock 'n' roll songs. B&W; 96m. **DIR:** Richard Thorpe. **CAST:** Elvis Presley, Mickey Shaughnessy, Dean Jones, Judy Tyler. **1957**

JAZZ SINGER, THE (1927) ★★★½ Generally considered the first talking film, this milestone in motion-picture history is really a silent film with a musical score and a few spoken lines. Al Jolson plays the son of an orthodox cantor who wants his son to follow in his footsteps. Jolson, though touched by his father's wishes, feels he must be a jazz singer. B&W; 89m. **DIR:** Alan Crosland. **CAST:** Al Jolson, May McAvoy, Warner Oland, William Demarest, Roscoe Karns, Myrna Loy. **1927**

JAZZ SINGER, THE (1980) 🦃 Mushy mishmash that only Diamond's most devoted fans will love. Rated PG. 115m. **DIR:** Richard Fleischer. **CAST:** Neil Diamond, Laurence Olivier, Lucie Arnaz. **1980**

JESUS CHRIST, SUPERSTAR ★★★½ Believe it or not, this could be the ancestor of such rock videos as Michael Jackson's "Thriller." The movie illustrates segments of Jesus Christ's later life by staging sets and drama to go along with the soundtrack. This will not offer any religious experiences in the traditional sense, but is interesting nonetheless. Rated G. 103m. **DIR:** Norman Jewison. **CAST:** Ted Neeley, Carl Anderson, Yvonne Elliman. **1973**

JIMMY CLIFF—BONGO MAN ★★½ This little-known documentary is a tribute to reggae singer-songwriter Jimmy Cliff. The film attempts, somewhat confusingly, to portray him as a man of the people, a champion of human rights during a period of racial and political turbulence in Jamaica. Cliff's other movie vehicle, *The Harder They Come*, a crudely shot musical-drama, remains stronger than *Bongo Man*. 89m. **DIR:** Stefan Paul. **CAST:** Jimmy Cliff. **1985**

JIVE JUNCTION ★★½ Weird World War II musical about high school music students who give up playing the classics and turn to jazz in order to help the war effort! How? By opening up a canteen where soliders can dance their troubles away. Written by future novelist Irving Wallace. B&W; 62m. **DIR:** Edgar G. Ulmer. **CAST:** Dickie Moore, Tina Thayer. **1943**

JOLSON SINGS AGAIN ★★½ Larry Parks again does the great and incomparable Al Jolson to a turn; Jolson himself again sings his unforgettable standards. But the film, trumped up to cash in, hasn't the class, charm, or swagger of the original. 96m. **DIR:** Henry Levin. **CAST:** Larry Parks, Barbara Hale, William Demarest, Bill Goodwin, Ludwig Donath, Myron McCormick. **1949**

JOLSON STORY, THE ★★★★ The show-business life story of vaudeville and Broadway stage great Al Jolson gets all-stops-out treatment in this fast-paced, tuneful film. Larry Parks acts and lip-synchs the hard-driving entertainer to a T. Jolson himself dubbed the singing. 128m. **DIR:** Alfred E. Green. **CAST:** Larry Parks, William Demarest, Evelyn Keyes, Bill Goodwin, Ludwig Donath. **1946**

JOY OF LIVING ★★★ Engaging screwball musical-comedy about a playboy who will stop at nothing to win the affection of a bright singing star. Great songs by Jerome Kern. B&W; 90m. **DIR:** Tay Garnett. **CAST:** Irene Dunne, Douglas Fairbanks Jr., Lucille Ball. **1938**

JUDY GARLAND AND FRIENDS ★★★★ Back in 1963, a then 21-year-old pre-*Funny Girl* singer named Barbra Streisand got her first television exposure on this classic *Judy Garland Show*. Besides her young daughter Liza Minnelli, Garland also welcomes the grande dame of Broadway, Ethel Merman. The singing (including an eight-song medley with Streisand) is superb, and is a tribute to the talent and personality of Garland. B&W; 55m. **DIR:** Bill Hobin. **1992**

JUMBO ★★ A big-budget circus-locale musical that flopped, despite Rodgers and Hart songs, William Daniels photography, a Sidney Sheldon script from a Hecht and MacArthur story, and a cast that should have known better. 125m. **DIR:** Charles Walters. **CAST:** Doris Day, Stephen Boyd, Jimmy Durante, Martha Raye, Dean Jagger. **1962**

JUPITER'S DARLING ★★★ If you are in a lighthearted mood, this spoof of Hannibal's siege of Rome is a perfect way to pass time. Witty songs and situations coupled with a likable cast. 96m. **DIR:** George Sidney. **CAST:** Esther Williams, Howard Keel, George Sanders, Marge Champion, Gower Champion, Richard Haydn. **1955**

JUST AROUND THE CORNER ★★★ This bucket of sap has nearly too-sweet Shirley Temple ending the Depression by charming a crusty sourpussed millionaire into providing new jobs. The ridiculous becomes sublime when Shirley dances with the incomparable Bill Robinson. B&W; 70m. **DIR:** Irving Cummings. **CAST:** Shirley Temple, Joan Davis, Charles Farrell, Bill Robinson, Bert Lahr. **1938**

KID GALAHAD (1962) ★★½ Remake of a film of the same title made in 1937 starring Edward G. Robinson, Bette Davis, and Humphrey Bogart. In this version, Elvis Presley is a boxer who prefers life as a garage mechanic. Presley fans will enjoy this one, of course. 95m. **DIR:** Phil Karlson. **CAST:** Elvis Presley, Gig Young, Lola Albright, Joan Blackman, Ned Glass. **1962**

KID MILLIONS ★★ The fifth of six elaborate musicals produced with Eddie Cantor by Samuel Goldwyn. Banjo Eyes inherits a fortune and becomes the mark for a parade of con artists. Lavish Busby Berkeley musical numbers help to salvage an otherwise inane plot. B&W; 90m. **DIR:** Roy Del Ruth. **CAST:** Eddie Cantor, Ethel Merman, Ann Sothern, George Murphy, Warren Hymer. **1934**

KING AND I, THE ★★★★½ Yul Brynner and Deborah Kerr star in this superb 1956 Rodgers and Hammerstein musicalization of *Anna and the King of Siam*. Kerr is the widowed teacher who first clashes, then falls in love, with the King (Brynner). 133m. **DIR:** Walter Lang. **CAST:** Yul Brynner, Deborah Kerr, Rita Moreno. **1956**

KING CREOLE ★★★★ A surprisingly strong Elvis Presley vehicle, this musical, set in New Orleans, benefits from solid direction from Michael Curtiz and a first-rate cast. 116m. **DIR:** Michael Curtiz. **CAST:** Elvis Presley, Carolyn Jones, Dolores Hart, Dean Jagger, Walter Matthau. **1958**

KING OF JAZZ, THE ★★★ Lavish big-budget musical revue chock-full of big production numbers and great songs. Shot in early two-color Technicolor. Imaginative settings and photography make this last of the all-star extravaganzas most impressive. 93m. **DIR:** John Murray Anderson. **CAST:** Paul Whiteman, John Boles, Bing Crosby. **1930**

KISMET (1955) ★★½ The Borodin-based Arabian Nights fantasy, a hit on Broadway, is stylishly staged and ripe with "Baubles, Bangles, and Beads" and Dolores Gray's show-stopping "Bagdad." Sadly, however, the shift to film loses the snap and crackle despite great singing by Howard Keel, Vic Damone, and Ann Blyth. The earlier Ronald Colman version (1944) is more fun and half a star better. 113m. **DIR:** Vincente Minnelli. **CAST:** Howard Keel, Ann Blyth, Monty Woolley, Vic Damone, Dolores Gray. **1955**

KISS ME KATE ★★★ That which is Shakespeare's *Taming of the Shrew* in the original is deftly rendered by Cole Porter, scripter Dorothy Kingsley, and George Sidney's graceful direction, by way of some fine performances by Howard Keel and Kathryn Grayson as a married pair whose onstage and offstage lives mingle. 109m. **DIR:** George Sidney. **CAST:** Howard Keel, Kathryn Grayson, Keenan Wynn, James Whitmore, Ann Miller, Tommy Rall, Bobby Van, Bob Fosse. **1953**

KISSIN' COUSINS ★★ Would Elvis in dual roles double the fun? Divide it by two is closer to the truth. This time he is both an air force lieutenant and a *blond* hillbilly. He manages to fall in love while belting a few country tunes such as "Smokey Mountain Boy" and "Barefoot Ballad." 96m. **DIR:** Gene Nelson. **CAST:** Elvis Presley, Arthur O'Connell, Jack Albertson. **1964**

KISSING BANDIT, THE ★★★ A shy eastern-bred nerd tries to carry on the legend of his bandit father, a Casanova of the West. Made at the low point of Frank Sinatra's first career and recommended only as a curiosity piece for his fans. Ricardo Montalban, Ann Miller, and Cyd Charisse are teamed for one dance number. 102m. **DIR:** Laslo Benedek. **CAST:** Frank Sinatra, Kathryn Grayson, Mildred Natwick, J. Carrol Naish, Billy Gilbert, Ricardo Montalban, Ann Miller, Cyd Charisse. **1948**

KNICKERBOCKER HOLIDAY ★★ A plodding, lackluster rendition of the Kurt Weill/Maxwell Anderson musical about Peter Stuyvesant and Dutch New York. The best song, "September Song," was originally sung by Walter Huston. Unfortunately, he's not in the film. B&W; 85m. **DIR:** Harry Brown. **CAST:** Nelson Eddy, Charles Coburn, Shelley Winters, Chester Conklin, Constance Dowling, Percy Kilbride. **1944**

KNIGHTS OF THE CITY A New York street gang is also a pop musical group. Rated R. 89m. **DIR:** Dominic Orlando. **CAST:** Leon Isaac Kennedy, Nicholas Campbell, John Mengatti, Wendy Barry, Stoney Jackson, The Fat Boys, Michael Ansara. **1987**

KRUSH GROOVE Lame rap musical. Rated R. 95m. **DIR:** Michael Schultz. **CAST:** Blair Underwood, Sheila E., Kurtis Blow, The Fat Boys, Run-DMC. **1985**

LA BAMBA ★★★★ At the age of 17, with three huge hits under his belt, Ritchie Valens joined Buddy Holly and the Big Bopper on an ill-fated airplane ride that killed all three and left rock 'n' roll bereft of some giant talent. In this biography, *Zoot Suit* writer-director Luis Valdez achieves a fine blend of rock 'n' roll and soap opera. Rated PG-13 for language. 108m. **DIR:** Luis Valdez. **CAST:** Lou Diamond Phillips, Rosana De Soto, Esai Morales, Danielle von Zerneck, Elizabeth Peña. **1987**

LADY BE GOOD ★★★½ A lively musical version of a George Gershwin Broadway show using an entirely different plot and only part of the original score. Such Gershwin classics as "Fascinatin' Rhythm" are presented with originality. But the film's best tune, "The Last Time I Saw Paris," was written by Gershwin's competitor, Jerome Kern. Kern won an Oscar for it, and it has been associated with this musical ever since. The bland plot deals with a married couple who write songs and have marital problems between hits. B&W; 112m. **DIR:** Norman Z. McLeod. **CAST:** Ann Sothern, Robert Young, Dan Dailey, Virginia O'Brien, Red Skelton, Lionel Barrymore, Eleanor Powell, Phil Silvers. **1941**

LADY SINGS THE BLUES ★★★½ Diana Ross made a dynamic screen debut in this screen biography of another singing great, Billie Holiday, whose career was thwarted by drug addiction. Rated R. 144m. **DIR:** Sidney J. Furie. **CAST:** Diana Ross, Billy Dee Williams, Richard Pryor. **1972**

LAMBADA ★★ This attempt to exploit the sensuous dance from Brazil (do you know anyone who's actually "done" this dance?) is slightly better than *The Forbidden Dance*, which was released simultaneously—but that's not saying much. There is some nice choreography by Shabba-Doo. Rated PG. 97m. **DIR:** Joel Silberg. **CAST:** J. Eddie Peck, Melora Hardin, Dennis Burkley. **1990**

LATIN LOVERS ★★ A movie with a few musical numbers, but not enough to make it move, this is one of Lana Turner's self-indulgent romances. She plays a woman looking for true love while touring South America and not able to find it anywhere. Not until she matches wits with Ricardo Montalban. Colorful settings, but colorless acting. 104m. **DIR:** Mervyn LeRoy. **CAST:** Lana Turner, Ricardo Montalban, John Lund, Louis Calhern, Rita Moreno, Jean Hagen, Beulah Bondi, Eduard Franz. **1953**

LES GIRLS ★★★★ Gene Kelly is charming, Mitzi Gaynor is funny, Taina Elg is funnier, Kay Kendall is funniest in this tale of a libel suit over a published memoir. Three conflicting accounts of what was and wasn't emerge from the courtroom. A witty film with Cole Porter music and stylish direction by George Cukor. 114m. **DIR:** George Cukor. **CAST:** Gene Kelly, Kay Kendall, Taina Elg, Mitzi Gaynor, Jacques Bergerac. **1957**

LET FREEDOM RING ★★★ In the West of the 1880s, Nelson Eddy leads homesteaders against the selfish interests of a group of tycoons. Unadorned flag-waving written by Ben Hecht, but it works as Eddy sings many familiar American standards. B&W; 100m. **DIR:** Jack Conway. **CAST:** Nelson Eddy, Virginia Bruce, Victor McLaglen, Lionel Barrymore, Edward Arnold, Guy Kibbee, Charles Butterworth, H. B. Warner, Raymond Walburn. **1939**

LET'S DANCE ★★ A listless, disappointing musical. A miscast Betty Hutton and Fred Astaire stumble through the tired story of a song-and-dance team that splits up and reunites. 112m. **DIR:** Norman Z. McLeod. **CAST:** Betty Hutton, Fred Astaire, Roland Young, Ruth Warrick. **1950**

LET'S MAKE LOVE ★★★ A tasty soufflé filled with engaging performances. Yves Montand plays a millionaire who wants to stop a musical show because it lampoons him. When he meets cast member Marilyn Monroe, he changes his mind. He hires Milton Berle to teach him comedy, Gene Kelly to teach him dance, and Bing Crosby as a vocal coach. Monroe's "My Heart Belongs to Daddy" number is a highlight. 118m. **DIR:** George Cukor. **CAST:** Marilyn Monroe, Yves Montand, Tony Randall, Wilfrid Hyde-White. **1960**

LI'L ABNER (1959) ★★★★ A perfectly delightful combination of satire, music, and cartoonish fun based on the popular Broadway musical with most of the original cast. The highlight is the Sadie Hawkins Day race in which the women in Dogpatch get to marry the man they catch. With such songs as "Bring Them Back the Way They Was," "The Country's In the Very Best of Hands," and "I'm Past My Prime." 112m. **DIR:** Melvin Frank. **CAST:** Peter Palmer, Leslie Parrish, Julie Newmar, Stubby Kaye, Stella Stevens, Howard St. John, Billie Hayes, Robert Strauss. **1959**

LILI ★★★★ "Hi Lili, Hi Lili, Hi Low," the famous song by composer Bronislau Kaper, is just one of the delights in this musical fantasy about a French orphan who tags along with a carnival and a self-centered puppeteer. A certified pleasure to keep your spirits up. 81m. **DIR:** Charles Walters. **CAST:** Leslie Caron, Mel Ferrer, Zsa Zsa Gabor, Jean-Pierre Aumont. **1953**

LISTEN, DARLING ★★★ A clever family comedy with Judy Garland introducing "Zing Went the Strings of My Heart," one of her trademark tunes. She also sings "Nobody's Baby" while she and her teenaged brother (Freddie Bartholomew) search for the right mate for their widowed mother. An enjoyable musical. B&W; 70m. **DIR:** Edwin L. Marin. **CAST:** Judy Garland, Freddie Bartholomew, Mary Astor, Walter Pidgeon, Charley Grapewin, Scotty Beckett, Gene Lockhart. **1938**

LISZTOMANIA 🦃 Hokey screen biography of composer Franz Liszt. Rated R. 105m. **DIR:** Ken Russell. **CAST:** Roger Daltrey, Sara Kestleman, Paul Nicholas, Fiona Lewis, Ringo Starr. **1975**

LITTLE COLONEL, THE ★★★½ Grandpa Lionel Barrymore is on the outs with daughter Evelyn Venable as the South recovers from the Civil War. Adorable Shirley Temple smoothes it all over. Film's high point is her step dance with Mr. Bojangles, Bill Robinson. B&W; 80m. **DIR:** David Butler. **CAST:** Shirley Temple, Lionel Barrymore, Evelyn Venable, Bill Robinson, Sidney Blackmer. **1935**

LITTLE MISS BROADWAY ★★★ Orphan Shirley Temple is placed with the manager of a theatrical hotel whose owner, crusty Edna May Oliver, dislikes show people. When she threatens to ship Shirley back to the orphanage, nephew George Murphy sides with the actors. Along the way, Shirley dances with Murphy and clowns with hotel guest Jimmy Durante. B&W; 70m. **DIR:** Irving Cummings. **CAST:** Shirley Temple, George Murphy, Jane Darwell, Edna May Oliver, Jimmy Durante, El Brendel, Donald Meek. **1938**

LITTLE NELLIE KELLY ★★★ Charles Winninger is a stubborn Irishman who refuses to recognize the marriage of his daughter Judy Garland to George Murphy. Based on George M. Cohan's Broadway musical-comedy. Fine renditions of many old standards. B&W; 100m. **DIR:** Norman Taurog. **CAST:** Judy Garland, George Murphy, Charles Winninger, Arthur Shields. **1940**

LITTLE NIGHT MUSIC, A ★★½ Based on Ingmar Bergman's comedy about sexual liaisons at a country mansion, this musical version doesn't quite come to life. Rated PG. 124m. **DIR:** Harold Prince. **CAST:** Elizabeth Taylor, Diana Rigg, Lesley-Anne Down. **1978**

LITTLE PRINCE, THE ★★ Aviator Richard Kiley teaches an alien boy about life and love. This picture has a great cast, beautiful photography, and is based on the children's classic by Antoine de Saint-Exupéry. Unfortunately, it also has a poor musical score by Alan J. Lerner and Frederick Loewe. Rated G. 88m. **DIR:** Stanley Donen. **CAST:** Richard Kiley, Steven Warner, Bob Fosse, Gene Wilder. **1974**

LITTLE SHOP OF HORRORS (1986) ★★★★½ This totally bent musical-horror-comedy was based on director Roger Corman's bizarre horror cheapie from 1961. Rick Moranis is wonderful as the schnook who finds and cares for a man-eating plant set on conquering the world. Uproariously funny, marvelously acted, spectacularly staged, and tuneful. Rated PG-13 for violence. 94m. **DIR:** Frank Oz. **CAST:** Rick Moranis, Ellen Greene, Vincent Gardenia, Steve Martin, James Belushi, John Candy, Bill Murray, Christopher Guest. **1986**

LITTLEST REBEL, THE ★★★½ Prime Shirley Temple, in which, as the daughter of a Confederate officer during the Civil War, she thwarts a double execution by charming President Lincoln. The plot stops, of course, while she and Bojangles dance. B&W; 70m. **DIR:** David Butler. **CAST:** Shirley Temple, John Boles, Jack Holt, Bill Robinson, Karen Morley, Guinn Williams, Willie Best. **1935**

LIVE A LITTLE, LOVE A LITTLE 🦃 The interesting thing about this Elvis vehicle is that the sexual innuendos are more blatant than in his other romantic comedies. Rated PG for mild profanity. 89m. **DIR:** Norman Taurog. **CAST:** Elvis Presley, Michele Carey, Don Porter, Dick Sargent. **1968**

LIVING IN A BIG WAY ★★ A comedy-drama about a wartime marriage that goes sour, this movie uses music for all the wrong reasons. It works up to a point, mainly because Gene Kelly is such an exuberant dancer. His costar, Marie McDonald, looks a lot better than she acts. B&W; 102m. **DIR:** Gregory La Cava. **CAST:** Gene Kelly, Marie McDonald, Charles Winninger, Spring Byington, Phyllis Thaxter, Clinton Sundberg. **1947**

LOOK FOR THE SILVER LINING ★★★ This supposed biography of Marilyn Miller is a familiar vaudeville-to-Broadway story. Take it as such and enjoy the songs from that era. Ray Bolger, as Miller's mentor, has some very good numbers. 100m. **DIR:** David Butler. **CAST:** June Haver, Ray Bolger, Gordon MacRae, Charlie Ruggles, Rosemary DeCamp, S. Z. Sakall, Walter Caltett, Will Rogers Jr. **1949**

LOVE IS BETTER THAN EVER ★★½ Elizabeth Taylor is a children's dancing-school teacher out to hook a hard-boiled talent agent, Larry Parks. The songs are completely forgettable. Tom Tully, as Taylor's father, saves the movie. B&W; 81m. **DIR:** Stanley Donen. **CAST:** Elizabeth Taylor, Larry Parks, Josephine Hutchinson, Tom Tully, Ann Doran, Kathleen Freeman. **1952**

LOVE ME OR LEAVE ME ★★★★ This musical bio-pic about ambitious singer Ruth Etting and her crude and domineering racketeer husband found usually cute Doris Day and old pro James Cagney scorching the screen with strong performances. Along with biting drama, a record-setting thirteen Doris Day solos, including the title song and "Ten Cents a Dance," are served. The story won an Oscar. 122m. **DIR:** Charles Vidor. **CAST:** James Cagney, Doris Day, Cameron Mitchell, Robert Keith, Tom Tully. **1955**

LOVE ME TONIGHT ★★★★★ A romantic musical that set a pattern for many that followed. Rodgers and Hart wrote the music, and most are still being played. This is the film that introduced "Lover," "Mimi," and "Isn't It Romantic?" all sung by Maurice Chevalier with verve and style. Pure charm. B&W; 104m. **DIR:** Rouben Mamoulian. **CAST:** Jeanette MacDonald, Maurice Chevalier, Myrna Loy, Charlie Ruggles, Charles Butterworth, C. Aubrey Smith, Elizabeth Patterson. **1932**

LOVELY TO LOOK AT ★★★★ Jerome Kern's Broadway and movie hit *Roberta* gets a face-lift with a charismatic cast, Technicolor, and inventive staging. Marge and Gower Champion dance "I Won't Dance" as a ballet. All in all, a musical treat, although the story about a trio of men inheriting a dress shop strains credibility. 105m. **DIR:** Mervyn LeRoy. **CAST:** Kathryn Grayson, Howard Keel, Red Skelton, Marge Champion, Gower Champion, Ann Miller, Zsa Zsa Gabor, Kurt Kasznar. **1952**

LOVING YOU ★★★ This better-than-average Elvis Presley vehicle features him as a small-town country boy who makes good when his singing ability is discovered. It has a bit of romance but the main attraction is Elvis singing his rock 'n' roll songs, including the title tune. 101m. **DIR:** Hal Kanter. **CAST:** Elvis Presley, Lizabeth Scott, Wendell Corey, Dolores Hart. **1957**

LUCKY ME ★★ The title does not mean the viewer. Love finds an unemployed Florida chorus girl seeking work. Only the caliber of the cast keeps this matte-finished song-and-dancer from being a complete bomb. Angie Dickinson's film debut. 100m. **DIR:** Jack Donohue. **CAST:** Doris Day, Robert Cummings, Phil Silvers, Eddie Foy Jr., Nancy Walker, Martha Hyer, Angie Dickinson. **1954**

LULLABY OF BROADWAY ★★½ Musical-comedy with show girl Doris Day returning from England, believing her mother to be a Broadway star, learning she is over-the-hill, singing and boozing in a bar. Many old standards by George Gershwin, Cole Porter, Harry Warren, etc. 92m. **DIR:** David Butler.

CAST: Doris Day, Gene Nelson, Gladys George, Billy DeWolfe, S. Z. Sakall, Florence Bates. **1951**

LUXURY LINER ★★½ Jane Powell plays Cupid for her widowed sea-captain father. Forget the plot. Enjoy the music. 98m. **DIR:** Richard Whorf. **CAST:** George Brent, Jane Powell, Lauritz Melchior, Frances Gifford, Xavier Cugat, Connie Gilchrist, Richard Derr. **1948**

MACK THE KNIFE ❤ The subtle refinements of Bertolt Brecht and Kurt Weill's *Threepenny Opera* have been unceremoniously trashed in this dull-edged bore of a musical. Rated PG-13, with moderate violence and adult situations. 122m. **DIR:** Menahem Golan. **CAST:** Raul Julia, Julia Migenes-Johnson, Richard Harris, Julie Walters, Roger Daltrey. **1990**

MAGICAL MYSTERY TOUR ★★ This is a tour by bus and by mind. Unfortunately, the minds involved must have been distorted at the time that the film was made. Occasional bursts of wit and imagination come through, but sometimes this chunk of psychedelic pretension is a crashing bore. Good songs, though. 60m. **DIR:** The Beatles. **CAST:** The Beatles, Bonzo Dog Band. **1967**

MAMBO KINGS, THE ★★★★ Oscar Hijuelos's Pulitzer Prize–winning novel of Cuban immigrants, *The Mambo Kings Play Songs of Love,* has been brought to the screen with great passion, energy, style, and heart in Arne Glimcher's tuneful film. An engrossing story of brotherhood and cultural pride, and a vibrant showcase for magnificent Cuban music, it spotlights Armand Assante, a charismatic talent and hot young Spanish actor, Antonio Banderas, who charms in his first English-language role. Rated R, with profanity, violence, and nudity. 125m. **DIR:** Arne Glimcher. **CAST:** Armand Assante, Antonio Banderas, Cathy Moriarty, Maruschka Detmers, Desi Arnaz Jr., Tito Puente. **1992**

MAME ❤ You won't love Lucy in this one. Rated PG. 131m. **DIR:** Gene Saks. **CAST:** Lucille Ball, Robert Preston, Jane Connell, Bea Arthur. **1974**

MAN OF LA MANCHA ❤ For those who loved the hit Broadway musical and those who heard about how wonderful it was, this adaptation is a shameful and outrageous letdown. Rated G. 130m. **DIR:** Arthur Hiller. **CAST:** Peter O'Toole, Sophia Loren, James Coco, Harry Andrews. **1972**

MANHATTAN MERRY-GO-ROUND ★★½ Incredible lineup of popular performers is the main attraction of this catchall production about a gangster who takes over a recording company. This oddity runs the gamut from Gene Autry's country crooning to the jivin' gyrations of legendary Cab Calloway. B&W; 80m. **DIR:** Charles F. Riesner. **CAST:** Gene Autry, Phil Regan, Leo Carrillo, Ann Dvorak, Tamara Geva, Ted Lewis, Cab Calloway, Joe DiMaggio, Louis Prima, Henry Armetta, Max Terhune, Smiley Burnette, James Gleason. **1938**

MAYTIME ★★★½ A curio of the past. A penniless tenor meets and falls in love with an opera star suffering in a loveless marriage to her adoring and jealous teacher and mentor. The hands Fate deals are not pat. See if you can tell that John Barrymore is reading his lines from idiot boards off-camera. This film is one of the Eddy/MacDonald duo's best. B&W; 132m. **DIR:** Robert Z. Leonard. **CAST:** Jeanette MacDonald, Nelson Eddy, John Barrymore, Sig Ruman. **1937**

MEET ME IN LAS VEGAS ★★½ Dan Dailey romances ballerina Cyd Charisse in this inoffensive time killer. A number of star cameos (Paul Henreid, Lena Horne, Frankie Laine, Jerry Colonna) add some fun, but the film is more belly flop than big splash. 112m. **DIR:** Roy Rowland. **CAST:** Dan Dailey, Cyd Charisse, Agnes Moorehead, Lili Darvas, Jim Backus. **1956**

MEET ME IN ST. LOUIS ★★★★ Here's a fun-filled entertainment package made at the MGM studios during the heyday of their musicals. This nostalgic look at a family in St. Louis before the 1903 World's Fair dwells on the tension when the father announces an impending transfer to New York. Judy Garland's songs remain fresh and enjoyable today. 112m. **DIR:** Vincente Minnelli. **CAST:** Judy Garland, Margaret O'Brien, Tom Drake. **1944**

MEET THE NAVY ★★★ This British musical fell into obscurity because the cast contains no star names. That's because they're all from the Royal Canadian Navy revue, a troupe of drafted performers. However, there are enough talented singers, dancers, and funnymen here to make you wonder why none went on to greater success. B&W; 81m. **DIR:** Alfred Travers. **CAST:** Lionel Murton, Margaret Hurst. **1946**

MELODY CRUISE ★★½ Two millionaires enjoy cruising with a bevy of willing babes. All goes well until the bachelor (Charlie Ruggles) falls hard for a sweet little schoolmarm. This dated romp has its moments. B&W; 75m. **DIR:** Mark Sandrich. **CAST:** Charlie Ruggles, Phil Harris, Helen Mack. **1933**

MERRY WIDOW, THE ★★★ A carefully chosen cast, a witty script, an infectious score, lavish sets, and the fabled Lubitsch touch at the helm make this musical-comedy sparkle. Maurice Chevalier and Jeanette MacDonald are perfect. B&W; 99m. **DIR:** Ernst Lubitsch. **CAST:** Maurice Chevalier, Jeanette MacDonald, Una Merkel, Edward Everett Horton. **1934**

METROPOLIS (MUSICAL VERSION) ★★★★★ Fritz Lang's 1926 silent science-fiction classic has been enhanced with special individual coloring and tints, recently recovered scenes, storyboards, and stills. The rock score, supervised by Giorgio Moroder, features Pat Benatar, Bonnie Tyler, Loverboy, Billy Squier, Adam Ant, Freddie Mercury, Jon Anderson, and Cycle V. 120m. **DIR:** Fritz Lang, Giorgio Moroder. **CAST:** Brigitte Helm, Alfred Abel. **1984**

MICHAEL JACKSON MOONWALKER ★★★★½ Spectacle is what we expect of Michael Jackson, and he delivers a stunning twenty-first-century Saturday-morning special that runs the course from Disney to Claymation to sizzling sci-fi effects. But what makes it such a treat is the sensational show of humor as Jackson parodies his own treatment by the tabloids, his kooky fetishes, even his own success. 84m. **DIR:** Jerry Kramer, Collin Chivers. **CAST:** Michael Jackson, Sean Lennon. **1988**

MIKADO, THE (1939) ★★★★½ Members of the D'Oyly Carte Opera Company perform in this colorful British-made movie of the Gilbert and Sullivan operetta. Kenny Baker furnishes the American influence, but the real stars are the music, fanciful sets, and gorgeous Technicolor cinematography. As enjoyable as a professional staging. 90m. **DIR:** Victor Schertzinger. **CAST:** Kenny Baker, Martyn Green, Jean Colin. **1939**

MIKADO, THE (1987) ★★★½ Gilbert and Sullivan's delightfully amusing light opera is majestically performed at the London Coliseum by the English National Opera. Eric Idle dominates as Lord High Executioner of the town of Titipoo. Special optical effects and camera angles add to the fun. 131m. **DIR:** John Michael Phillips. **CAST:** Eric Idle, Bonaventura Bottone, Lesley Garrett. **1987**

MILLION DOLLAR MERMAID ★★ Esther Williams swims through her role as famous early distaff aquatic star Annette Kellerman, who pioneered one-piece suits and vaudeville tank acts. Victor Mature woos her in this highly fictionalized film biography. The Busby Berkeley production numbers are a highlight. 115m. **DIR:** Mervyn LeRoy. **CAST:** Esther Williams, Victor Mature, Walter Pidgeon, David Brian, Jesse White. **1952**

MISSISSIPPI ★★★½ A delightful mixture of music and personality with Bing Crosby at his best singing Rodgers and Hart's "It's Easy to Remember But So Hard to Forget." He boards a showboat run by rascally W. C. Fields. The plot comes from Booth Tarkington's novel *Magnolia*, but the personalities are pure Hollywood. B&W; 73m. **DIR:** A. Edward Sutherland. **CAST:** Bing Crosby, W. C. Fields, Joan Bennett, Gail Patrick, Queenie Smith, John Miljan, Ann Sheridan. **1935**

MR. IMPERIUM ★★ A musical that misses because there's no chemistry whatsoever between the leads. Ezio Pinza's Broadway charm isn't photogenic so it's difficult to relate to Lana Turner's attraction to him. They sing such songs as "My Love and My Mule" in a willy-nilly attempt to tug the audience's heartstrings. 87m. **DIR:** Don Hartman. **CAST:** Lana Turner, Ezio Pinza, Marjorie Main, Debbie Reynolds, Barry Sullivan, Keenan Wynn. **1951**

MR. MUSIC ★★ Bing Crosby is an easygoing songwriter living beyond his means. Nancy Olson is hired to handle his finances. Slow-moving, completely forgettable songs, and wasted guest stars. B&W; 113m. **DIR:** Richard Haydn. **CAST:** Bing Crosby, Nancy Olson, Charles Coburn, Ruth Hussey, Robert Stack, Tom Ewell, Peggy Lee, Groucho Marx, Richard Haydn. **1950**

MRS. BROWN YOU'VE GOT A LOVELY DAUGHTER ★★ England's Herman's Hermits star in this film, named after one of their hit songs. The limited plot revolves around the group acquiring a greyhound and deciding to race it. Caution: Only for hardcore Hermits fans! Rated G. 110m. **DIR:** Saul Swimmer. **CAST:** Herman's Hermits, Stanley Holloway. **1968**

MO' BETTER BLUES ★★½ Writer-director Spike Lee was trying to make a movie about a jazz musician that was free of the usual clichés—primarily in response to Clint Eastwood's *Bird*—but only Wesley Snipes's volatile performance as a sax-playing rival energizes this lackadaisical affair about a successful, slick, and attractive trumpeter (Denzel Washington). Rated R for profanity, nudity, and violence. 120m. **DIR:** Spike Lee. **CAST:** Denzel Washington, Spike Lee, Wesley Snipes, Giancarlo Esposito, Robin Harris, Joie Lee, Cynda Williams, Bill Nunn, John Turturro, Rubén Blades, Dick Anthony Williams. **1990**

MOON OVER MIAMI ★★★ Texas sisters Betty Grable and Carole Landis arrive in Miami to hunt for rich husbands. After a suitable round of romantic adventures, they snare penniless Don Ameche and millionaire Robert Cummings. A fun film that helped establish Grable. 91m. **DIR:** Walter Lang. **CAST:** Don Ameche, Robert Cummings, Betty Grable, Carole Landis, Charlotte Greenwood, Jack Haley. **1941**

MOZART STORY, THE ★★½ Though produced in Austria, this Mozart biography plays as loose with the facts as any Hollywood bio-pic. You'll only want to see it for the music, played by the Vienna Philharmonic Orchestra and Vienna State Opera. Includes excerpts from all of Mozart's best-known works. Curt Jurgens (billed as Curd Juergens) plays Emperor Joseph II. Dialogue dubbed in English. B&W; 95m. **DIR:** Carl Hartl. **CAST:** Hans Holt, Winnie Markus, Curt Jurgens. **1937**

MURDER AT THE VANITIES ★★★½ A musical whodunit, this blend of comedy and mystery finds tenacious Victor McLaglen embroiled in a murder investigation at Earl Carroll's Vanities, a popular and long-running variety show of the 1930s and 1940s. Musical numbers and novelty acts pop up between clues in this stylish oddity. Lots of fun. B&W; 89m. **DIR:** Mitchell Leisen. **CAST:** Jack Oakie, Kitty Carlisle, Victor McLaglen, Carl Brisson, Donald Meek, Gail Patrick, Jessie Ralph, Duke Ellington, Ann Sheridan. **1934**

MUSIC LOVERS, THE ★★ A tasteless movie biography of Tchaikovsky, that gets two stars for the way the music is presented, not story or acting. Director Ken Russell overdoes it with phallic symbols and homoerotic references that are embarrassing to watch. 124m. **DIR:** Ken Russell. **CAST:** Glenda Jackson, Richard Chamberlain, Christopher Gable, Max Adrian, Kenneth Colley. **1971**

MUSIC MAN, THE ★★★★½ They sure don't make musicals like this anymore, a smashing adaptation of Meredith Willson's Broadway hit. Robert Preston reprises the role of his life as a smooth-talkin' salesman who cajoles the parents of River City, Iowa, into purchasing band instruments and uniforms for their children. 151m. **DIR:** Morton Da Costa. **CAST:** Robert Preston, Shirley Jones, Buddy Hackett, Ron Howard, Paul Ford, Hermione Gingold. **1962**

MY DREAM IS YOURS ★★★ Doris Day becomes a radio star in a snappy musical-comedy based on Dick Powell's 1934 hit, *Twenty Million Sweethearts*. Day plays the role Powell played in the original, a would-be singer who makes the big time in radio. A dream sequence with Bugs Bunny is a highlight. 101m. **DIR:** Michael Curtiz. **CAST:** Doris Day, Jack Carson, Lee Bowman, Adolphe Menjou, Eve Arden, S. Z. Sakall, Edgar Kennedy, Sheldon Leonard, Franklin Pangborn. **1949**

MY FAIR LADY ★★★★½ *Pygmalion*, the timeless George Bernard Shaw play, has been a success in every form in which it has been presented. This Oscar-winning 1964 movie musical adaptation is no exception. Rex Harrison, as Professor Henry Higgins, is the perfect example of British class snobbishness. Audrey Hepburn gives a fine performance as Eliza Doolittle (with Marni Nixon supplying the singing). 170m. **DIR:** George Cukor. **CAST:** Rex Harrison, Audrey Hepburn, Stanley Holloway. **1964**

MY LUCKY STAR ★★★★ One of Sonja Henie's most entertaining films, chiefly because of its fast pace and bubbly personalities. Sonja Henie skates like a dream as a student working at a department store to pay for college. She falls for teacher Richard Greene, flirts with department-store heir Cesar Romero and performs in an "Alice in Wonderland" ice ballet to help the department store out of a jam. The most famous song in the picture is "I've Got a Date with a Dream." B&W; 81m. **DIR:** Roy Del Ruth. **CAST:** Sonja Henie, Richard Greene, Cesar Romero, Gypsy Rose Lee, Buddy Ebsen, Billy Gilbert, Arthur Treacher. **1938**

MY NAME IS BARBRA ★★★★ Barbra Streisand fans have a real treasure awaiting them in *My Name Is Barbra*. Shown in 1965, shot in black and white, and featuring no guests, it was Streisand's first television special. It's a wonderful opportunity to see this exceptional performer early in her career. Viewers will also be treated to knockout versions of "When the Sun Comes Out" and "My Man." 60m. **DIR:** Dwight Hemion. **CAST:** Barbra Streisand. **1965**

MY SISTER EILEEN ★★★★ Fast-moving musical remake of the 1940 stage play about two small-town sisters overwhelmed by New York's Greenwich Village and its inhabitants. Jack Lemmon joins Betty Garrett in a knockout rendition of "It's Bigger Than You or Me." 108m. **DIR:** Richard Quine. **CAST:** Janet Leigh, Betty Garrett, Jack Lemmon, Bob Fosse, Kurt Kasznar, Dick York, Hal March, Queenie Smith, Richard Deacon, Tommy Rall. **1955**

NANCY GOES TO RIO ★★★ Nancy (Jane Powell) wins the leading role in a musical play that her mother (Ann Sothern) has her eye on. Both old standards and original songs fill in the slight plot. 99m. **DIR:** Robert Z. Leonard. **CAST:** Ann Sothern, Jane Powell, Louis Calhern, Barry Sullivan, Carmen Miranda. **1950**

NAUGHTY MARIETTA ★★★ This warm, vibrant rehash of Victor Herbert's tuneful 1910 operetta established leads Jeanette MacDonald and Nelson Eddy as the screen's peerless singing duo. The plot's next to nothing—a French princess flees to America and falls in love with an Indian scout—but the music is stirring, charming, and corny. B&W; 106m. **DIR:** W. S. Van Dyke. **CAST:** Jeanette MacDonald, Nelson Eddy, Frank Morgan, Douglass Dumbrille, Elsa Lanchester, Akim Tamiroff. **1935**

NEPTUNE'S DAUGHTER ★★½ Big-budgeted aquatic musical from MGM studios has Esther Williams playing a (what else?) swimsuit designer on holiday in South America floating in and out of danger with Red Skelton. The plot isn't important as long as you can keep time with Xavier Cugat's mamba beat. Harmless, enjoyable nonsense. 93m. **DIR:** Edward Buzzell. **CAST:** Esther Williams, Red Skelton, Keenan Wynn, Ricardo Montalban, Betty Garrett, Mel Blanc, Mike Mazurki, Ted de Corsia, Xavier Cugat. **1949**

NEVER STEAL ANYTHING SMALL ★★½ Unbelievable musical-comedy-drama about a good-hearted union labor leader is saved by the dynamic James Cagney, who was always enough to make even the most hackneyed story worth watching. 94m. **DIR:** Charles Lederer. **CAST:** James Cagney, Shirley Jones, Roger

Smith, Cara Williams, Nehemiah Persoff, Royal Dano, Horace McMahon. **1959**

NEW FACES ★★½ This is a filmed version of the 1952 smash Broadway revue with a thin story line added. Ronny Graham is very good in a parody of *Death of a Salesman.* Eartha Kitt became a star through this vehicle and Robert Clary, Paul Lynde, and Alice Ghostley are used to good advantage. 99m. **DIR:** Harry Horner. **CAST:** Ronny Graham, Eartha Kitt, Paul Lynde, Robert Clary, Alice Ghostley, Carol Lawrence. **1954**

NEW MOON ★★★ This melodramatic romance, which takes place during the French Revolution, features Jeanette MacDonald as a spoiled aristocrat who falls for an extraordinary bondsman (Nelson Eddy). Some comic moments, and Eddy comes off looking much better than MacDonald in this one, one of eight love stories they brought to the screen. B&W; 106m. **DIR:** Robert Z. Leonard. **CAST:** Jeanette MacDonald, Nelson Eddy, Mary Boland, George Zucco. **1940**

NEW YORK, NEW YORK ★★★½ This is a difficult film to warm to, but worth it. Robert De Niro gives a splendid performance as an egomaniacal saxophonist who woos sweet-natured singer Liza Minnelli. The songs (especially the title tune) are great, and those with a taste for something different in musicals will find it rewarding. Rated PG. 163m. **DIR:** Martin Scorsese. **CAST:** Robert De Niro, Liza Minnelli, Lionel Stander, Georgie Auld, Mary Kay Place. **1977**

NEWSIES ★★★ While this Disney production may not fulfill its promise to resurrect the movie musical, it is an entertaining picture for the whole family. The songs of Academy Award-winning composer Alan Menken propel the story of the 1899 newspaper boys strike. Rated PG for violence. 120m. **DIR:** Kenny Ortega. **CAST:** Christian Bale, David Moscow, Bill Pullman, Luke Edwards, Max Casella, Michael Lerner, Ann-Margret, Robert Duvall. **1992**

NIGHT AND DAY (1946) ★★★★ There was no way Hollywood could make an accurate biography of Cole Porter in those days—it had to play footsie with his ruthless social lionizing and sexual proclivities—but the film stands out as a remarkable document of the performers and performances available to the cameras at the time. Where else can you see Mary Martin doing "My Heart Belongs to Daddy" and Monte Woolley declaiming "Miss Otis Regrets"? 132m. **DIR:** Michael Curtiz. **CAST:** Cary Grant, Alexis Smith, Alan Hale Sr., Mary Martin, Monty Woolley. **1946**

NORTHWEST OUTPOST ★★ Nelson Eddy's last movie is not up to snuff. The setting of a Russian village in nineteenth-century California is colorful, and the prospect of an Indian attack on the Russian fort is suspenseful. But the story is downright dull. So is the music, even though it was composed by Rudolf Friml. B&W; 91m. **DIR:** Allan Dwan. **CAST:** Nelson Eddy, Ilona Massey, Joseph Schildkraut, Elsa Lanchester, Hugo Haas, Lenore Ulric. **1947**

OKLAHOMA! ★★★★ This movie adaptation of Rodgers and Hammerstein's Broadway musical stars Shirley Jones as a country girl (Laurie) who is courted by Curly, a cowboy (Gordon MacRae). Rod Steiger plays a villainous Jud, who also pursues Laurie. A very entertaining musical. 140m. **DIR:** Fred Zinnemann. **CAST:** Shirley Jones, Gordon MacRae, Rod Steiger, Eddie Albert, Gloria Grahame. **1956**

OLD CURIOSITY SHOP, THE ★★★ This enjoyable British-made follow-up to *Scrooge,* the successful musical adaptation of Charles Dickens's *A Christmas Carol,* adds tunes to the author's *The Old Curiosity Shop* and casts songwriter-singer Anthony Newley as the title villain. Rated PG. 118m. **DIR:** Michael Tuchner. **CAST:** Anthony Newley, David Hemmings, David Warner, Michael Hordern, Jill Bennett. **1975**

OLIVER ★★★★★ Charles Dickens never was such fun. *Oliver Twist* has become a luxurious musical and multiple Oscar-winner (including best picture). Mark Lester is the angelic Oliver, whose adventures begin one mealtime when he pleads, "Please, sir, I want some more." Jack Wild is an impish Artful Dodger, and Ron Moody steals the show as Fagin. Oliver Reed prevents the tale from becoming *too* sugarcoated. Rated G. 153m. **DIR:** Carol Reed. **CAST:** Ron Moody, Oliver Reed, Hugh Griffith, Shani Wallis, Mark Lester, Jack Wild. **1968**

ON A CLEAR DAY, YOU CAN SEE FOREVER 🦃 A psychiatrist discovers that one of his patients has lived a former life and can recall it under hypnosis. Rated PG. 129m. **DIR:** Vincente Minnelli. **CAST:** Barbra Streisand, Yves Montand, Bob Newhart, Larry Blyden, Jack Nicholson. **1970**

ON AN ISLAND WITH YOU ★★ Lightweight story of navy flyer Peter Lawford pursuing actress Esther Williams while on location in the South Seas. Jimmy Durante's comedy and Cyd Charisse's dancing are the highlights. 117m. **DIR:** Richard Thorpe. **CAST:** Esther Williams, Peter Lawford, Ricardo Montalban, Jimmy Durante, Cyd Charisse. **1948**

ON MOONLIGHT BAY ★★★ Small-town setting, circa World War I, with tomboyish Doris Day falling for a college hero who is concerned about upcoming army service. Booth Tarkington's *Penrod* series set to music. Many fine songs of the era. 95m. **DIR:** Roy Del Ruth. **CAST:** Doris Day, Gordon MacRae, Leon Ames, Rosemary DeCamp, Billy Gray, Jack Smith, Mary Wickes, Ellen Corby. **1951**

ON THE TOWN ★★★★ This is a classic boy-meets-girl, boy-loses-girl fable set to music. Three sailors are on a twenty-four-hour leave and find themselves (for the first time) in the big city of New York. They seek romance and adventure—and find it. 98m. **DIR:** Gene Kelly, Stanley Donen. **CAST:** Gene Kelly, Frank Sinatra, Ann Miller, Vera-Ellen, Jules Munshin, Betty Garrett. **1949**

ONE FROM THE HEART ★★ This Francis Coppola film is a ballet of graceful and complex camera movements occupying magnificent sets—but the characters get lost in the process. Teri Garr and Frederic Forrest play a couple flirting with two strangers (Raul Julia and Nastassja Kinski), but they fade away in the flash and fizz. Rated R. 100m. **DIR:** Francis Ford Coppola. **CAST:** Teri Garr, Frederic Forrest, Raul Julia, Nastassja Kinski, Harry Dean Stanton, Allen Garfield, Luana Anders. **1982**

ONE HUNDRED MEN AND A GIRL ★★★★½ Story of go-getting Deanna Durbin arranging a sponsor and a guest conductor for her unemployed symphony musician father (Adolphe Menjou) and his friends is a joyful musical feast. Oscar for the music department of Charles Previn and a nomination for the original story by William A. Wellman and Robert Carson. B&W; 84m. **DIR:** Henry Koster. **CAST:** Deanna Durbin, Leopold Stokowski, Adolphe Menjou, Alice Brady, Eugene Pallette, Mischa Auer, Billy Gilbert, Frank Jenks. **1937**

ONE NIGHT OF LOVE ★★★ The prototype of the operatic film cycle of the 1930s, it bolstered the flagging fortunes of opera star Grace Moore, who had been making movies since 1930, and successfully blended classical numbers with more "popular" song stylings. Film composer Louis Silvers won an Oscar for his score. B&W; 95m. **DIR:** Victor Schertzinger. **CAST:** Grace Moore, Lyle Talbot. **1934**

ONE TRICK PONY ★★★½ This good little movie looks at life on the road with a has-been rock star. Paul Simon is surprisingly effective as the rock star who finds both his popularity slipping and his marriage falling apart. Rated R for nudity. 98m. **DIR:** Robert M. Young. **CAST:** Paul Simon, Lou Reed, Rip Torn, Blair Brown, Joan Hackett. **1980**

OPPOSITE SEX, THE ★★½ An uninspired remake of Claire Booth's *The Women*, a good satire about woman's inhumanity to woman. They diluted it by adding macho male stereotypes instead of just talking about them like the first version did. 117m. **DIR:** David Miller. **CAST:** June Allyson, Ann Sheridan, Joan Blondell, Joan Collins, Ann Miller, Charlotte Greenwood, Jim Backus, Dolores Gray, Agnes Moorehead, Leslie Nielsen, Jeff Richards. **1956**

ORCHESTRA WIVES ★★★ Taking second place to the wonderful music of Glenn Miller and his orchestra is a story about the problems of the wives of the band members, both on and off the road. Academy Award nomination for Harry Warren and Mack Gordon's "I've Got A Gal In Kalamazoo." B&W; 98m. **DIR:** Archie Mayo. **CAST:** Glenn Miller, Lynn Bari, Carole Landis, George Montgomery, Cesar Romero, Ann Rutherford. **1942**

ORPHAN BOY OF VIENNA, AN ★★ The only reason to see this hokey tearjerker about a boy who struggles to adjust to life in a German orphanage is the presence of the famous Vienna Boys' Choir, accompanied in several performances by the Vienna Philharmonic. In German with English subtitles. B&W; 90m. **DIR:** Max Neufeld. **CAST:** Ferdinand Materhofer. **1937**

OTELLO ★★★★★ As with his screen version of *La Traviata*, Franco Zeffirelli's *Otello* is a masterpiece of filmed opera. In fact, it may well be the best such motion picture ever made. Placido Domingo is brilliant in the title role, both as an actor and a singer. And he gets able support from Katia Ricciarelli as Desdemona and Justino Diaz as Iago. Rated PG for stylized violence. 122m. **DIR:** Franco Zeffirelli. **CAST:** Placido Domingo, Katia Ricciarelli, Justino Diaz, Urbano Barberini. **1987**

PAGAN LOVE SONG ★★ Watered-down love story about American schoolteacher Howard Keel who falls for native girl Esther Williams is just another excuse for singing, swimming, and a tired old plot line. 76m. **DIR:** Robert Alton. **CAST:** Esther Williams, Howard Keel, Minna Gombell, Rita Moreno. **1950**

PAINT YOUR WAGON ★★★½ Clint Eastwood and Lee Marvin play partners during the California gold rush era. They share everything, including a bride (Jean Seberg) bought from a Mormon traveler (John Mitchum), in this silly, but fun musical. Rated PG. 166m. **DIR:** Joshua Logan. **CAST:** Clint Eastwood, Lee Marvin, Jean Seberg, Harve Presnell, John Mitchum. **1969**

PAJAMA GAME, THE ★★★★ This, one of the best film versions yet made of a Broadway musical, features John Raitt (his only big-screen appearance) in his stage role as the workshop superintendent who must deal with a union demand for a 7 1/2-cent-per-hour raise. Doris Day plays the leader of the grievance committee, who fights and then falls for him. Broadway dancer Carol Haney also repeats her supporting role. 101m. **DIR:** George Abbott, Stanley Donen. **CAST:** Doris Day, John Raitt, Eddie Foy Jr., Carol Haney, Barbara Nichols, Reta Shaw. **1957**

PAL JOEY ★★★★ Frank Sinatra plays the antihero of this Rodgers and Hart classic about a hip guy who hopes to open a slick nightclub in San Francisco. With love interests Rita Hayworth and Kim Novak vying for Ol' Blue Eyes, and George Sidney's fast-paced direction, the picture is an enjoyable romp. The Rodgers and Hart score is perhaps their finest. 111m. **DIR:** George Sidney. **CAST:** Frank Sinatra, Rita Hayworth, Kim Novak, Barbara Nichols. **1957**

PANAMA HATTIE ★★ Take one hit musical play about a Panama nightclub owner, throw out all but a couple of Cole Porter tunes, refashion it for Red Skelton, then subdue him, and you have this lackluster movie that sat on the shelf for over a year before being released. Saved only by the debut of Lena Horne. B&W; 79m. **DIR:** Norman Z. McLeod. **CAST:** Red Skelton, Ann Sothern, Marsha Hunt, Virginia O'Brien, Lena Horne. **1942**

PARADISE HAWAIIAN STYLE ★★½ Elvis Presley returns to Hawaii after his 1962 film, *Blue Hawaii*. This time he plays a pilot who makes time for romance while setting up a charter service. Some laughs and lots of songs. 91m. **DIR:** Michael Moore. **CAST:** Elvis Presley, Suzanna Leigh. **1966**

PENNIES FROM HEAVEN ★★★½ Steve Martin and Bernadette Peters star in this downbeat musical. The production numbers are fabulous, but the dreary storyline—with Martin as a down-and-out song-plugger in Depression-era Chicago—may disappoint fans of the genre. Rated R for profanity and sexual situations. 107m. **DIR:** Herbert Ross. **CAST:** Steve Martin, Bernadette Peters, Jessica Harper. **1981**

PETE KELLY'S BLUES ★★½ Guys, gals, gangsters, gin, and Dixieland jazz are done to a turn in this ultrarealistic re-creation of the Roaring Twenties. 95m. **DIR:** Jack Webb. **CAST:** Jack Webb, Janet Leigh, Edmond O'Brien, Jayne Mansfield, Lee Marvin, Peggy Lee, Ella Fitzgerald, Martin Milner, Andy Devine. **1955**

PHANTOM OF THE PARADISE ★★½ Before he became obsessed with Hitchcock *hommages* and ultraviolent bloodbaths, director Brian De Palma did this odd little blend of Faust and *Phantom of the Opera*. William Finley sells his soul to Paul Williams and learns the dangers of achieving fame too quickly. Wildly erratic, with tedious dialogue alternating with droll visual bits. Rated PG—mild violence. 92m. **DIR:** Brian De Palma. **CAST:** Paul Williams, William Finley, Jessica Harper. **1974**

PIN-UP GIRL ★★★ Another in the series of happy musical comedies Betty Grable starred in during World War II, *Pin-Up Girl* logically took its title from her status with GIs. This time, a secretary falls for a sailor. To be near him, she pretends to be a Broadway star. 83m. **DIR:** H. Bruce Humberstone. **CAST:** Betty Grable, John Harvey, Martha Raye, Joe E. Brown, Eugene Pallette. **1944**

PINK FLOYD: THE WALL ★★ For all its apparent intent, this visually impressive film, which has very little dialogue but, rather, uses garish visual images to the accompaniment of the British rock band's music, ends up being more of a celebration of insanity and inhumanity than an indictment of it as intended. Rated R for violence. 99m. **DIR:** Alan Parker. **CAST:** Bob Geldof, Christine Hargreaves, Bob Hoskins. **1982**

PIRATE, THE ★★★★ This splashy, though at times narratively weak, musical features Judy Garland and Gene Kelly singing and dancing their way through a Cole Porter score. It features a terrific dance sequence titled "Be a Clown" featuring clown-pirate-acrobat Kelly and the marvelous Nicholas Brothers. Watch it for the songs and the dances. 102m. **DIR:** Vincente Minnelli. **CAST:** Judy Garland, Gene Kelly, Gladys Cooper, Reginald Owen, Walter Slezak. **1948**

PIRATE MOVIE, THE ★★ This rock 'n' roll adaptation of Gilbert and Sullivan's *The Pirates of Penzance* is passable entertainment. Expect a lot of music, a lot of swashbuckling, and a little sappy romance. This film is rated PG for slight profanity and sexual innuendo. 99m. **DIR:** Ken Annakin. **CAST:** Christopher Atkins, Kristy McNichol, Ted Hamilton, Bill Kerr. **1982**

PIRATES OF PENZANCE, THE ★★★★ Stylized sets and takeoffs of Busby Berkeley camera setups give *Pirates* a true cinematic quality. Add to that outstanding work by the principals, some nice bits of slapstick comedy, and you have an enjoyable film for the entire family. Rated G. 112m. **DIR:** Wilford Leach. **CAST:** Angela Lansbury, Kevin Kline, Linda Ronstadt, Rex Smith, George Rose. **1983**

POOR LITTLE RICH GIRL (1936) ★★★★ A strong supporting cast makes this Shirley Temple vehicle one of her finest. She plays a motherless child who gets lost. Befriended by vaudevillians Alice Faye and Jack Haley, she joins the act, wows 'em, and wins 'em. As movie musicals go this one is tops. B&W; 72m. **DIR:** Irving Cummings. **CAST:** Shirley Temple, Alice Faye, Jack Haley, Michael Whalen, Gloria Stuart, Henry Armetta, Sara Haden, Jane Darwell. **1936**

PRIVATE BUCKAROO ★★ Showcase vehicle for Patty, LaVerne, and Maxene, the Andrews Sisters, who decide to put on a show for soldiers. The Donald O'Connor/Peggy Ryan duo stands out. B&W; 68m. **DIR:** Eddie Cline. **CAST:** The Andrews Sisters, Joe E. Lewis, Dick Foran, Jennifer Holt, Donald O'Connor, Peggy Ryan, Harry James. **1942**

PURPLE RAIN ★★½ In his first movie, pop star Prince plays a struggling young musician searching for self-awareness and love while trying to break into the rock charts. The film unsuccessfully straddles the line between a concert release and a storytelling production. As it is, the music is great, but the plot leaves a lot to be desired. Rated R for nudity, suggested sex, and profanity. 113m. **DIR:** Albert Magnoli. **CAST:** Prince, Apollonia, Morris Day, Olga Karlatos. **1984**

QUADROPHENIA ★★★½ Based on The Who's rock opera, this is the story of a teenager growing up in the early 1960s and the decisions he is forced to make on the path to adulthood. Rated R because the language is rough and the violence graphic. 115m. **DIR:** Franc Roddam. **CAST:** Phil Daniels, Mark Wingett, Philip Davis, Sting. **1979**

RAPPIN' ★★ Rap songs get the *Breakin'* treatment in this uninspired formula musical. Once again, a street performer (rap singer Mario Van Peebles) takes on the baddies and still has time to make it in show biz. Rated PG for profanity. 92m. **DIR:** Joel Silberg. **CAST:** Mario Van Peebles, Tasia Valenza, Charles Flohe. **1985**

REBECCA OF SUNNYBROOK FARM (1938) ★★★½ Lightweight but engaging Shirley Temple vehicle has the 1930s superstar playing a child performer who wants to be on radio. While Temple hoofs with the likes of Jack Haley and Bill "Bojangles" Robinson, Randolph Scott, in one of his few screen appearances out of the saddle, romances Gloria Stuart. B&W; 80m. **DIR:** Allan Dwan. **CAST:** Shirley Temple, Randolph Scott, Jack Haley, Gloria Stuart, Phyllis Brooks, Helen Westley, Slim Summerville, Bill Robinson. **1938**

RED GARTERS ★★★½ A delightful and inventive spoof of Westerns with everything offbeat, from the casting to the stage-stylized sets and the original songs of Jay Livingston and Ray Evans. Oscar nomination for the truly surrealistic set decoration. 91m. **DIR:** George Marshall. **CAST:** Rosemary Clooney, Jack Carson, Guy Mitchell, Pat Crowley, Gene Barry, Cass Daley, Frank Faylen, Reginald Owen, Buddy Ebsen. **1954**

RED SHOES, THE (1948) ★★★★ Fascinating backstage look at the world of ballet manages to overcome its unoriginal, often trite, plot. A ballerina (Moira Shearer) is urged by her forceful and single-minded impresario (Anton Walbrook) to give up a romantic involvement in favor of her career, with tragic consequences. Good acting and fine camera work save this British film. 136m. **DIR:** Michael Powell, Emeric Pressburger. **CAST:** Moira Shearer, Anton Walbrook. **1948**

REET, PETITE AND GONE ★★★½ Louis Jordan, the overlooked hero of prerock days, is well captured (along with his hot backup band, the Tympany Five) in this farcical all-black musical. Jordan's sound is a blues-pop fusion known as jumpin' jive, and it gets slick film treatment in this little-known movie treasure. 67m. **DIR:** William Forest Crouch. **CAST:** Louis Jordan. **1946**

RHAPSODY IN BLUE ★★★★ Don't for a minute think this is an accurate biography of George Gershwin (played by Robert Alda), but it's a lavish, colorful, and affectionate musical film. Of special interest are the appearances by Paul Whiteman (as himself) and the dubbed-in piano work of Gershwin's friend, Oscar Levant. The "Rhapsody in Blue" and "American in Paris" numbers are standouts. 139m. **DIR:** Irving Rapper. **CAST:** Robert Alda, Alexis Smith, Joan Leslie. **1945**

RICH, YOUNG AND PRETTY ★★ A slim excuse for a movie without glossy production numbers to back up the casting of Jane Powell and Vic Damone in the leading roles. Powell plays an American-raised daughter of French Danielle Darrieux. She goes to Paris to meet her mother and gets involved in romantic dalliances. 95m. **DIR:** Norman Taurog. **CAST:** Jane Powell, Vic Damone, Danielle Darrieux, Fernando Lamas, Wendell Corey, Una Merkel, Hans Conried, Richard Anderson. **1951**

RIDE THE WILD SURF ★★ Though shot in Hawaii, this teens-on-the-beach musical contains innumerable shots of Fabian and Tab Hunter perched in front of back-projection screens of surfing footage, while someone off-camera sprays a hose at them. Jan and Dean sing the title tune. Overall, pretty feeble. 101m. **DIR:** Don Taylor. **CAST:** Fabian, Tab Hunter, Barbara Eden, Shelley Fabares. **1964**

ROBERTA ★★★½ This lighthearted story of a group of entertainers who find themselves operating a dress shop in Paris belongs to the second and third-billed Fred Astaire and Ginger Rogers. With the music of Jerome Kern and Otto Harbach, including those gems "Smoke Gets in Your Eyes" and "I Won't Dance," this carefree film is very enjoyable. Later remade as *Lovely to Look At*. B&W; 85m. **DIR:** William A. Seiter. **CAST:** Irene Dunne, Fred Astaire, Ginger Rogers, Randolph Scott, Helen Westley. **1935**

ROBIN & THE SEVEN HOODS ★★★ Musical reworking of the Robin Hood legend set in Jazz Age, gangster-ruled Chicago. Frank Sinatra and Dean Martin, et al are the Merry Men, with Bing Crosby the silver-tongued spokesman Alan A. Dale. Sometimes stretches a point to be too Runyonesque, but good tunes and actors make it pleasant. 123m. **DIR:** Gordon Douglas. **CAST:** Frank Sinatra, Dean Martin, Sammy Davis Jr., Bing Crosby, Peter Falk, Barbara Rush, Victor Buono, Edward G. Robinson. **1964**

ROCK, BABY, ROCK IT ★★ Filmed in Dallas, this obscure feature offers a threadbare let's-put-on-a-show plot as an excuse to showcase a lot of long-forgotten doo-wop and rockabilly acts. B&W; 77m. **DIR:** Murray Douglas Sporup. **CAST:** Johnny Carroll, Kay Wheeler. **1957**

ROCK, PRETTY BABY ★★ John Saxon plays Jimmy Daley, 18-year-old leader of a struggling rock 'n' roll combo whose life is complicated by his doctor father who wants him to go into the medical profession and a difficult first-love relationship with Luana Patten. So laughably awful in spots that it becomes enjoyable. B&W; 89m. **DIR:** Richard Bartlett. **CAST:** John Saxon, Sal Mineo, Rod McKuen, Luana Patten, Edward Platt, Fay Wray, Shelley Fabares. **1957**

ROCK, ROCK, ROCK ★★ If you love Tuesday Weld, Fifties rock, or entertainingly terrible movies, this nostalgic blast from the past is for you. The plot is so flimsy, Dobie Gillis would have rejected it. But watching a young Weld lip-synch to songs actually sung by Connie Francis is a wonderful treat. B&W; 83m. **DIR:** Will Price. **CAST:** Tuesday Weld, Teddy Randazzo, Alan Freed, Frankie Lymon and the Teenagers, Chuck Berry, The Flamingos, The Johnny Burnette Trio. **1956**

ROCKULA ★★½ Entertaining but ultimately silly musical-comedy about a vampire who falls in love every twenty-two years. Shot with the look and feel of a music video, this flick has some good music and some funny lines. Rated PG-13. 90m. **DIR:** Luca Bercovici. **CAST:** Dean Cameron, Susan Tyrrell, Bo Diddley, Thomas Dolby, Toni Basil. **1990**

ROCKY HORROR PICTURE SHOW, THE ★★★½ Delicious send-up of science-fiction–horror flicks, set to rock 'n' roll beat. If you're not experiencing this scintillating spoof at a midnight showing, you're missing much of the fun. Audience participation is a key, as the prologue on the video version explains. Nevertheless, this madcap musical-comedy, often clever, always outrageous, has plenty to offer, even for the solitary viewer hunched in front of a small screen. Rated R. 100m. **DIR:** Jim Sharman. **CAST:** Tim Curry, Susan Sarandon, Barry Bostwick, Richard O'Brien, Jonathan Adams, Patricia Quinn, Little Nell, Meat Loaf, Charles Gray. **1975**

ROMAN SCANDALS ★★★ Old Banjo Eyes dreams himself back to ancient Rome. Busby Berkeley staged the requisite musical numbers, including one censor-baiting stanza featuring seminude chorus girls, Goldwyn Girl Lucille Ball among them. B&W; 92m. **DIR:** Frank Tuttle. **CAST:** Eddie Cantor, Ruth Etting, Alan Mowbray, Edward Arnold. **1933**

ROMANCE ON THE HIGH SEAS ★★★ A delightful musical that introduced Doris Day to the movies. The plot is a merry mix-up about glamor gals testing their husbands' faithfulness, and Day gets third billing. Her part was originally written for Judy Garland and scaled down when Garland was unavailable. 99m. **DIR:** Michael Curtiz. **CAST:** Jack Carson, Janis Paige, Doris Day, Don DeFore, Oscar Levant, S. Z. Sakall, Franklin Pangborn, Eric Blore, Fortunio Bonanova. **1948**

ROOFTOPS ★★ What a coincidence! *West Side Story* director Robert Wise returns to make a film about streetwise teenagers in New York who dance, rumble, and struggle to survive. This time, star-crossed lovers (Jason Gedrick and Troy Beyer) combine kung fu with dirty dancing. Rated R for rampant profanity, violence, and brief nudity. 95m. **DIR:** Robert Wise. **CAST:** Jason Gedrick, Troy Beyer, Eddie Velez. **1989**

ROSALIE ★★½ From those thrilling days of yesteryear at MGM comes this gigantic musical about hero Nelson Eddy and his winning of a disguised Balkan princess (Eleanor Powell). It's big, colorful, and has a nice music score by Cole Porter. B&W; 122m. **DIR:** W. S. Van Dyke. **CAST:** Eleanor Powell, Nelson Eddy, Frank Morgan, Edna May Oliver, Ray Bolger, Ilona Massey. **1937**

ROSE, THE ★★★★ Bette Midler stars as a Janis Joplin–like rock singer who falls prey to the loneliness and temptations of superstardom. Mark Rydell directed this fine character study, which features memorable supporting performances by Alan Bates and Frederic Forrest, and a first-rate rock score. Rated R. 134m. **DIR:** Mark Rydell. **CAST:** Bette Midler, Alan Bates, Frederic Forrest, Harry Dean Stanton. **1979**

ROSE MARIE (1936) ★★½ If you enjoy MGM's perennial songbirds Nelson Eddy and Jeanette MacDonald, you might have fun with this musical romp into the Canadian Rockies. Unintentionally funny dialogue is created by the wooden way Eddy delivers it. B&W; 110m. **DIR:** W. S. Van Dyke. **CAST:** Nelson Eddy, Jeanette MacDonald, James Stewart, Alan Mowbray. **1936**

ROSE MARIE (1954) ★★ A remake that shouldn't have been. Without the chemistry of Nelson Eddy and Jeanette MacDonald, the plot is creaky and the music sounds too old-fashioned. The highlight is the subplot between raspy-voiced Marjorie Main and Bert Lahr as "The Mountie Who Never Got His Man." 115m. **DIR:** Mervyn LeRoy. **CAST:** Howard Keel, Ann Blyth, Fernando Lamas, Marjorie Main, Bert Lahr, Ray Collins, Joan Taylor. **1954**

ROSIE ★★★ Rosemary Clooney sings behind Sondra Locke's acting in this vivid, no-holds-barred rendition of the famed singer's autobiography *This for Remembrance.* Always an upfront gal, Clooney let it all hang out in telling of her rise to stardom, mental breakdown, and successful uphill fight to regain star status. Made for TV. 100m. **DIR:** Jackie Cooper. **CAST:** Sondra Locke, Tony Orlando, Katherine Helmond, Penelope Milford, Kevin McCarthy, John Karlen. **1982**

ROUND MIDNIGHT ★★★★ French director Bertrand Tavernier's ode to American jazz is a long overdue celebration of that great American music and its brilliant exponents. It tells a semifictionalized story of a friendship between a self-destructive, be-bop tenor saxophonist (Dexter Gordon) and an avid French fan (François Cluzet). Rated R. 133m. **DIR:** Bertrand Tavernier. **CAST:** Dexter Gordon, François Cluzet, Lonette McKee, Christine Pascal, Herbie Hancock. **1986**

ROUSTABOUT ★★½ Barbara Stanwyck, as the carnival owner, upgrades this typical Elvis Presley picture. In this release, Presley is a young wanderer who finds a home in the carnival as a singer. Naturally, Elvis combines romance with hard work on the midway. 101m. **DIR:** John Rich. **CAST:** Barbara Stanwyck, Elvis Presley, Leif Erickson, Sue Ane Langdon. **1964**

ROYAL WEDDING ★★★ Brother and sister Fred Astaire and Jane Powell are performing in London when Princess Elizabeth marries Philip, and manage to find their own true loves while royalty ties the knot. 92m. **DIR:** Stanley Donen. **CAST:** Fred Astaire, Jane Powell, Sarah Churchill, Peter Lawford, Keenan Wynn. **1951**

RUDE BOY ★★★½ Meandering, overlong docudrama about an unemployed British teen who gets a job as a roadie with The Clash. An interesting document of the punk era, but what makes it essential viewing for music fans are plentiful performances by The Clash. Unrated, but an R equivalent for profanity. 133m. **DIR:** Jack Hazan, David Mingay. **CAST:** Ray Gange. **1980**

RUTLES, THE (A.K.A. ALL YOU NEED IS CASH) ★★★★ Superb spoof of the Beatles has ex–Monty Python member Eric Idle in a dual role as a television reporter and one of the Rutles, whose songs include "Cheese and Onions" and "Doubleback Alley." It's great stuff for fans of the Fab Four—with cameos from rock stars (including Beatle George Harrison) and members of *Saturday Night Live*'s Not Ready for Prime-Time Players. 78m. **DIR:** Eric Idle, Gary Weis. **CAST:** Eric Idle, Neil Innes, Ricky Fataar, John Halsey, Mick Jagger, Paul Simon, George Harrison, John Belushi, Dan Aykroyd, Gilda Radner. **1978**

SALSA 🦃 The music is hot, but the rest of this movie is laughably awful. Rated PG for profanity and violence. 92m. **DIR:** Boaz Davidson. **CAST:** Robby Rosa, Rodney Harvey. **1988**

SARAFINA! ★★★★½ Both rapturous and devastating, this antiapartheid musical rockets along, alternating song and dance with the horrors of life in a South African military state. It's a film about the irreversible decision one black schoolgirl is driven to make by forces of bigotry and oppression. Whoopi Goldberg's classy, moving performance as a Soweto schoolteacher is reason enough to snatch this movie up. Rated PG-13 for violence. 101m. **DIR:** Darrell Roodt. **CAST:** Whoopi Goldberg, Leleti Khumalo, Miriam Makeba. **1992**

SATISFACTION 🦃 Justine Bateman is the leader of a rock band. Rated PG-13 for profanity and suggested sex. 95m. **DIR:** Joan Freeman. **CAST:** Justine Bateman, Liam Neeson, Trini Alvarado, Julia Roberts, Deborah Harry, Chris Nash. **1988**

SATURDAY NIGHT FEVER ★★★★ From the first notes of "Stayin' Alive" by the Bee Gees over the opening credits, it is obvious that *Saturday Night Fever* is more than just another youth exploitation film. It is *Rebel Without a Cause* for the 1970s, with realistic dialogue and effective dramatic situations. Rated R for profanity, violence, partial nudity, and simulated sex. 119m. **DIR:** John Badham. **CAST:** John Travolta, Donna Pescow, Karen Lynn Gorney. **1977**

SCROOGE (1970) ★★★ Tuneful retelling of Charles Dickens's classic *A Christmas Carol* may not be the best acted, but it's certainly the liveliest. Albert Finney paints old curmudgeon Ebeneezer Scrooge with a broad brush, but he makes his character come alive. Rated G. 118m. **DIR:** Ronald Neame. **CAST:** Albert Finney, Alec Guinness, Edith Evans, Kenneth More, Michael Medwin, Laurence Naismith, Kay Walsh. **1970**

SEASIDE SWINGERS ★★ Fans of the Sixties British invasion will want to see this comedy about a TV talent contest starring Freddie and the Dreamers. There are lots of songs by different groups. Trivia buffs may want to see costar Michael Sarne, who went on to direct *Myra Breckenridge*. 94m. **DIR:** James Hill. **CAST:** John Leyton, Michael Sarne, Freddie and the Dreamers, Ron Moody, Liz Fraser. **1965**

SECOND CHORUS ★★★ Rival trumpet players Fred Astaire and Burgess Meredith vie for the affections of Paulette Goddard, who works for Artie Shaw. The two want into Shaw's orchestra and make a comic mess of Goddard's attempts to help them. B&W; 83m. **DIR:** H. C. Potter. **CAST:** Paulette Goddard, Fred Astaire, Burgess Meredith, Charles Butterworth. **1940**

SECOND FIDDLE ★★★½ Irving Berlin's original score makes this movie work today. It's a spoof of the search for the right actress to play Scarlett O'Hara. Talent scouts seeking "A Girl of the North" go to Minnesota to interview a pretty schoolteacher who ice skates like a dream. One of Sonja Henie's most popular films with one of her best supporting casts. B&W; 86m. **DIR:** Sidney Lanfield. **CAST:** Sonja Henie, Tyrone Power, Rudy Vallee, Edna May Oliver, Mary Healy, Lyle Talbot, Alan Dinehart, King Sisters. **1939**

SENSATIONS OF 1945 ★★ Yet another one of those all-star jumbles so popular during the mid-1940s, this uninspired musical limps along, saddled with a stale story of a producer who wants to put on a show. The great W. C. Fields isn't in his best form here, but any chance to see him and Cab Calloway in action is worth something. B&W; 87m. **DIR:** Andrew L. Stone. **CAST:** Eleanor Powell, W. C. Fields, Sophie Tucker, Dennis O'Keefe, Cab Calloway, C. Aubrey Smith, Eugene Pallette. **1944**

SGT. PEPPER'S LONELY HEARTS CLUB BAND 🦃 Universally panned musical. Rated PG. 111m. **DIR:** Michael Schultz. **CAST:** The Bee Gees, Peter Frampton, Donald Pleasence, George Burns. **1978**

SEVEN BRIDES FOR SEVEN BROTHERS ★★★★★ Delightful musical. Howard Keel takes Jane Powell as his wife. The fun begins when his six younger brothers decide they want to get married, too...immediately! 103m. **DIR:** Stanley Donen. **CAST:** Howard Keel, Jane Powell, Russ Tamblyn, Julie Newmar, Marc Platt. **1954**

SEVEN HILLS OF ROME, THE ★★★ A TV star (Mario Lanza) goes to Rome to rest, finds a pretty girl, and sings his heart out. For Lanza fans, that's enough, but this isn't one of his better films. Beautiful scenery and his voice are the only selling points. 104m. **DIR:** Roy Rowland. **CAST:** Mario Lanza, Peggy Castle, Rosella Como, Marisa Allasio, Renato Rascel. **1958**

1776 ★★★★ Broadway's hit musical about the founding of the nation is brought to the screen almost intact. Original cast members William Daniels, as John Adams, and Howard da Silva, as Benjamin Franklin, shine anew in this unique piece. Rated G. 141m. **DIR:** Peter H. Hunt. **CAST:** William Daniels, Howard DaSilva, Ken Howard, Blythe Danner. **1972**

SHALL WE DANCE? ★★★★½ Fred Astaire and Ginger Rogers team up (as usual) as dance partners in this musical comedy. The only twist is they must pretend to be married in order to get the job. Great songs include "Let's Call the Whole Thing Off." B&W; 109m. **DIR:** Mark Sandrich. **CAST:** Fred Astaire, Ginger Rogers, Eric Blore, Edward Everett Horton. **1937**

SHIP AHOY ★★★ Entertaining musical, thanks to Eleanor Powell's energetic tap dancing. The World War II plot is somewhat dated, but Powell and Red Skelton are excellent. The film showcases Tommy Dorsey's orchestra when Buddy Rich was his drummer and Sinatra his soloist. Enjoyable. B&W; 95m. **DIR:** Edward Buzzell. **CAST:** Eleanor Powell, Red Skelton, Bert Lahr, Virginia O'Brien, Tommy Dorsey, Jo Stafford, Frank Sinatra, Buddy Rich. **1942**

SHOUT (1991) 🦃 This rock 'n' roll fantasy, in which a delinquent is reformed by the love of a good woman, has its heart in the right place; but its brain is dead. Rated PG-13 for violence and profanity. 89m. **DIR:** Jeffrey Hornady. **CAST:** James Walters, Heather Graham, John Travolta, Richard Jordan, Linda Fiorentino, Scott Coffey. **1991**

SHOUT: THE STORY OF JOHNNY O'KEEFE ★★★½ A slow start builds up to a satisfying send-up for the man who put Australian rock music on the international map. Terry Serio is brilliant as Johnny O'Keefe, the Boomerang Kid—a man who lets conceit and self-promotion stand in the way of his happiness and sanity. Unrated, contains profanity, violence, and drug use. 192m. **DIR:** Ted Robinson. **CAST:** Terry Serio. **1985**

SHOW BOAT (1936) ★★★★★ This, the definitive film version of America's best-loved musical, included several new Jerome Kern songs that have since become standards in other revivals. It marked the first full-sound version of the 1927 Broadway hit and featured many performers in roles they played onstage, notably Charles Winninger as Captain Andy and Helen Morgan as Julie. Paul Robeson sings "Ol' Man River" the way it is *supposed* to be sung, and the script closely follows the Edna Ferber novel. Watch for Eddie "Rochester" Anderson in a quick cameo. 113m. **DIR:** James Whale. **CAST:** Irene Dunne, Allan Jones, Helen Morgan, Charles Winninger, Hattie McDaniel, Paul Robeson. **1936**

SHOW BOAT (1951) ★★★½ This watchable musical depicts life and love on a Mississippi showboat during the early 1900s. Kathryn Grayson, Howard Keel, and Ava Gardner try but can't get any real sparks flying. 115m. **DIR:** George Sidney. **CAST:** Kathryn Grayson, Howard Keel, Ava Gardner, Joe E. Brown, Agnes Moorehead, Marge Champion, Gower Champion. **1951**

SHOW BUSINESS ★★★ Based on incidents in Eddie Cantor's entertainment career, this slick, brassy, and nostalgic picture provides fun and good music. For Cantor and Joan Davis fans, this film is a peach. B&W; 92m. **DIR:** Edwin L. Marin. **CAST:** Eddie Cantor, George Murphy, Joan Davis, Nancy Kelly, Constance Moore. **1944**

SILK STOCKINGS ★★★ In this remake, Greta Garbo's classic *Ninotchka* is given the Cole Porter musical treatment with a degree of success. Fred Astaire is a Hollywood producer who educates a Russian agent in the seductive allure of capitalism. Cyd Charisse plays the Garbo role. 117m. **DIR:** Rouben Mamoulian. **CAST:** Fred Astaire, Cyd Charisse, Janis Paige, Peter Lorre, Barrie Chase. **1957**

SING ★★★ A teen film with a commendable twist: no car chases! Actually, this is a cross between *Lady and the Tramp* and *Fame.* A tough Italian punk is forced to work with an innocent Jewish girl on the class musical. You guessed it! They fall for each other. Rated PG-13 for profanity. 99m. **DIR:** Richard

Baskin. **CAST:** Peter Dobson, Jessica Steen, Lorraine Bracco, Patti LaBelle, Louise Lasser. **1989**

SINGIN' IN THE RAIN ★★★★★ In the history of movie musicals, no single scene is more fondly remembered than Gene Kelly's song-and-dance routine to the title song of *Singin' in the Rain.* This picture has more to it than Kelly's well-choreographed splash through a wet city street. It has an interesting plot based on the panic that overran Hollywood during its conversion to sound, and it has wonderful performances. 102m. **DIR:** Gene Kelly, Stanley Donen. **CAST:** Gene Kelly, Debbie Reynolds, Donald O'Connor, Jean Hagen, Cyd Charisse, Rita Moreno. **1952**

SKIRTS AHOY! ★★ Slow-moving story of three women from different backgrounds joining the Waves, and their problems in training and the men in their lives. 109m. **DIR:** Sidney Lanfield. **CAST:** Esther Williams, Joan Evans, Vivian Blaine, Barry Sullivan. **1952**

SKY'S THE LIMIT, THE ★★★★ This rare blend of comedy and drama is more than just another Fred Astaire musical. He plays a Flying Tiger ace on leave, who meets and falls in love with magazine photographer Joan Leslie, but nixes anything permanent. Both audiences and critics misjudged this film when it debuted, seeing it as light diversion rather than incisive comment on war and its effect on people. B&W; 89m. **DIR:** Edward H. Griffith. **CAST:** Fred Astaire, Joan Leslie, Robert Benchley, Elizabeth Patterson, Clarence Kolb, Robert Ryan, Richard Davis, Peter Lawford, Eric Blore. **1943**

SMALL TOWN GIRL ★★½ Farley Granger plays a rich playboy who speeds through a small town, gets a ticket, and promptly falls in love with the judge's daughter (Jane Powell), making his fiancée (Ann Miller) so jealous she dances up a storm. Not a memorable musical, but some interesting production numbers. 93m. **DIR:** Leslie Kardos, Busby Berkeley. **CAST:** Jane Powell, Farley Granger, Ann Miller, Bobby Van, S. Z. Sakall, Billie Burke, Fay Wray, Dean Miller, William Campbell, Nat King Cole. **1953**

SMILIN' THROUGH (1941) ★★ If you can believe it, an orphaned and brave Jeanette MacDonald falls in love with the son of a murderer. Directed and played for tear value. Best thing to come out of the picture was Jeannette's marriage to Gene Raymond. 100m. **DIR:** Frank Borzage. **CAST:** Jeanette MacDonald, Gene Raymond, Brian Aherne, Ian Hunter. **1941**

SOMETHING TO SING ABOUT ★★ Even the great talents of James Cagney can't lift this low-budget musical above the level of mediocrity. In it, he plays a New York bandleader who tests his mettle in Hollywood. B&W; 93m. **DIR:** Victor Schertzinger. **CAST:** James Cagney, William Frawley, Evelyn Daw, Gene Lockhart. **1937**

SON OF DRACULA (1974) 🦃 Addle-brained vampire musical-comedy. 90m. **DIR:** Freddie Francis. **CAST:** Harry Nilsson, Ringo Starr, Freddie Jones. **1974**

SONG IS BORN, A ★★ A remake of the classic comedy *Ball of Fire*, with more music and less personality. Danny Kaye heads a team of professors studying the origin of jazz. The music is sharp but the story is flat. 115m. **DIR:** Howard Hawks. **CAST:** Danny Kaye, Virginia Mayo, Steve Cochran, Benny Goodman, Louis Armstrong, Tommy Dorsey, Lionel Hampton, Hugh Herbert, Felix Bressart. **1948**

SONG OF NORWAY 🦃 If he were not dead, Norwegian composer Edvard Grieg would expire upon seeing this insult to his life and career. Rated G. 142m. **DIR:** Andrew L. Stone. **CAST:** Florence Henderson, Torval Maurstad, Edward G. Robinson, Robert Morley. **1970**

SONG OF THE ISLANDS ★★ A Hawaiian cattle baron feuds with a planter over land while his son romances the planter's daughter. Everyone quarrels, but love wins. En route, Betty Grable sings and dances in the standard grass skirt. Mainly a slick travelogue with singing and dancing. 75m. **DIR:** Walter Lang. **CAST:** Betty Grable, Victor Mature, Jack Oakie, Thomas Mitchell. **1942**

SONG TO REMEMBER, A ★★★ The music is superb, but the plot of this Chopin biography is as frail as the composer's health is purported to have been. Cornel Wilde received an Oscar nomination as the ill-fated tubercular Chopin, and Merle Oberon is resolute but vulnerable in the role of his lover, French female novelist George Sand. 113m. **DIR:** Charles Vidor. **CAST:** Cornel Wilde, Merle Oberon, Paul Muni, George Coulouris, Nina Foch, Sig Arno. **1945**

SONG WITHOUT END ★★★ An Academy Award–winning score manages to save this bio-pic of composer Franz Lizst. As Lizst, Dirk Bogarde is not in his element, but perseveres. 141m. **DIR:** Charles Vidor, George Cukor. **CAST:** Dirk Bogarde, Capucine, Genevieve Page, Patricia Morison, Martita Hunt. **1960**

SONGWRITER ★★★★ Wonderfully wacky and entertaining wish-fulfillment by top country stars Willie Nelson and Kris Kristofferson, who play—what else?—top country stars who take on the recording industry and win. A delight. Rated R for profanity, nudity, and brief violence. 100m. **DIR:** Alan Rudolph. **CAST:** Willie Nelson, Kris Kristofferson, Lesley Ann Warren, Melinda Dillon, Rip Torn. **1984**

SOUND OF MUSIC, THE ★★★★½ Winner of the Academy Award for best picture, this musical has it all: comedy, romance, suspense. Julie Andrews plays the spunky Maria, who doesn't fit in at the convent. When she is sent to live with a large family as their governess, she falls in love with and marries her handsome boss, Baron Von Trapp (Christopher Plummer). Problems arise when the Nazi invasion of Austria forces the family to flee. 172m. **DIR:** Robert Wise. **CAST:** Julie Andrews, Christopher Plummer, Eleanor Parker. **1965**

SOUTH PACIFIC ★★★ This extremely long film, adapted from the famous Broadway play about sailors during World War II, seems dated and is slow-going for the most part. Fans of Rodgers and Hammerstein will no doubt appreciate this one more than others. 150m. **DIR:** Joshua Logan. **CAST:** Mitzi Gaynor, Rossano Brazzi, Ray Walston, John Kerr. **1958**

SPARKLE ★★★½ Largely forgotten but appealing study of a Supremes–like girl group's rise to fame in the 1960s Motown era. Lots of good musical numbers from Curtis Mayfield and the luscious Lonette McKee. Rated PG for profanity and nudity. 100m. **DIR:** Sam O'Steen. **CAST:** Irene Cara, Dorian Harewood, Lonette McKee. **1976**

SPEEDWAY ★★ Elvis Presley plays a generous stock-car driver who confronts a seemingly heartless IRS agent (Nancy Sinatra). Not surprisingly, she melts in this unremarkable musical. Rated G. 94m. **DIR:** Norman Taurog. **CAST:** Elvis Presley, Nancy Sinatra, Bill Bixby, Gale Gordon. **1968**

SPINOUT ★★ A lesser Elvis vehicle, this features a perky drummer (Deborah Walley), a spoiled heiress (Shelley Fabares), and a pushy sociologist (Diane McBain) trying to get the King to say "I do." Dated attitudes and styles don't age well. 93m. **DIR:** Norman Taurog. **CAST:** Elvis Presley, Shelley Fabares, Deborah Walley, Diane McBain, Carl Betz. **1966**

SPRING PARADE ★★★★ This lilting musical confection stars Deanna Durbin as a baker's assistant in love with an army drummer. Set in Austria. B&W; 89m. **DIR:** Henry Koster. **CAST:** Deanna Durbin, Robert Cummings, S. Z. Sakall, Henry Stephenson, Mischa Auer, Reginald Denny, Allyn Joslyn. **1940**

SPRINGTIME IN THE ROCKIES (1942) ★★★ Lake Louise and other breathtaking Canadian scenic wonders provide backgrounds for this near-plotless show-business musical. Jealous Broadway entertainers Betty Grable and John Payne fight and make up with the help of Carmen Miranda, Cesar Romero, and a bushel of songs and dances. 90m. **DIR:** Irving Cummings. **CAST:** Betty Grable, John Payne, Carmen Miranda, Cesar Romero, Edward Everett Horton, Charlotte Greenwood, Jackie Gleason, Harry James. **1942**

STAGE STRUCK (1936) ★★ A no-talent singer-dancer, Joan Blondell, makes a bid for Broadway by financing a show for herself. She hires Dick Powell to direct. They clash, fall in love, clash, and depend on good old suave Warren William to smooth it all out. Not that anyone should care too much. Below par. B&W; 86m. **DIR:** Busby Berkeley. **CAST:** Joan Blondell, Dick Powell, Warren William, Frank McHugh, Jeanne Madden, Carol Hughes, Hobart Cavanaugh, Spring Byington. **1936**

STAND BY ME (1988) ★★★ This spirited AIDS Day benefit was recorded at London's Wembley Arena April 1, 1987, and features three songs sung by George Michael, including "Everything She Wants," with his onetime Wham partner, Andrew Ridgeley. The show serves as a time capsule of the mid-80s British music scene. Not rated. 60m. **DIR:** Mike Mansfield. **CAST:** George Michael, Boy George, Meat Loaf, Elton John, John Entwistle, Andy Summers, Herbie Hancock. **1988**

STAR! ★★★½ This 1968 biopic about fabled musical-comedy star Gertrude Lawrence has been re-mastered by director Robert Wise and restored to its original length. Though star Julie Andrews is in top form, the film is overly long and uneven. Some of the many musical numbers are dazzling, but there are just as many clunkers. Plus, you never get to know Lawrence, just her performances. Not rated; contains mild profanity. 172m. **DIR:** Robert Wise. **CAST:** Julie Andrews, Richard Crenna, Daniel Massey, Michael Craig, Robert Reed. **1968**

STARS AND STRIPES FOREVER ★★★ Don't expect an in-depth biography of John Philip Sousa, the March King, and you will probably enjoy this musical tribute. Loud and stirring. Turn up the sound and we can all march around the breakfast table. Good family viewing. 89m. **DIR:** Henry Koster. **CAST:** Clifton Webb, Ruth Hussey, Debra Paget, Robert Wagner. **1952**

STARSTRUCK ★★★½ A 17-year-old (Jo Kennedy) wants to be a star and goes after it at top speed. Director Gillian Armstrong has taken the let's-put-on-a-show! plot and turned it into an affable punk-rock movie. Rated PG for nudity and profanity. 95m. **DIR:** Gillian Armstrong. **CAST:** Jo Kennedy, Ross O'Donovan, Max Cullen. **1982**

STATE FAIR (1945) ★★★ Wholesome atmosphere marks this nostalgic Middle America story of the adventures of a farm family—Pa's prize hog, Ma's spiked mincemeat, winsome daughter, and yearning son—at the Iowa State Fair. Rodgers and Hammerstein did a standout score for it, winning an Oscar with "It Might As Well Be Spring." Donald Meek's bit as a cooking judge is cameo-sharp comedy. 100m. **DIR:** Walter Lang. **CAST:** Dana Andrews, Jeanne Crain, Vivian Blaine, Dick Haymes, Fay Bainter, Charles Winninger, Donald Meek, Frank McHugh, Percy Kilbride, Harry Morgan. **1945**

STATE FAIR (1962) ★★ Lesser remake of the 1933 and 1945 films focusing on a very wholesome family's visit to the Iowa State Fair. A bit too hokey as predictable romantic situations develop. Only comic moment has Tom Ewell singing to a pig. 118m. **DIR:** José Ferrer. **CAST:** Pat Boone, Bobby Darin, Ann-Margret, Pamela Tiffin, Alice Faye, Tom Ewell. **1962**

STAY AWAY JOE 🦃 A lesser Elvis vehicle. Rated PG for countless sexual situations. 102m. **DIR:** Peter Tewksbury. **CAST:** Elvis Presley, Burgess Meredith, Joan Blondell. **1968**

STAYING ALIVE ★★ This sequel to the gutsy, effective *Saturday Night Fever* is a slick, commercial near–rip-off. Six years have passed. Tony Manero (John Travolta) now attempts to break into the competitive life of Broadway dancing. Rated PG for language and suggested sex. 96m. **DIR:** Sylvester Stallone. **CAST:** John Travolta, Cynthia Rhodes, Finola Hughes, Steve Inwood. **1983**

STEP LIVELY ★★★½ As a jazzy, bright musical remake of the Marx Brothers film *Room Service*, this film is a very enjoyable story about George Murphy's attempt to get his show produced on Broadway. It's in this film that Frank Sinatra receives his first screen kisses (from Gloria DeHaven), which caused swoons from numerous female Sinatraphiles. As the hotel manager, Walter Slezak almost steals the show. 89m. **DIR:** Tim Whelan. **CAST:** Frank Sinatra, George Murphy, Walter Slezak, Adolphe Menjou. **1944**

STEPPING OUT ★★★½ Musical-comedy fans will delight in this sweet-natured, lightweight story of a struggling dance teacher (Liza Minnelli) who decides to coach her generally inept students into a crack dance troupe. A first-rate cast, and Minnelli sparkles with enthusiasm. Rated PG for profanity. 101m. **DIR:** Lewis Gilbert. **CAST:** Liza Minnelli, Shelley Winters, Bill Irwin, Ellen Greene, Julie Walters, Jane Krakowski, Sheila McCarthy, Andrea Martin. **1991**

STORMY WEATHER ★★★★ A delightful kaleidoscope of musical numbers. Lena Horne performs the title number and Fats Waller interprets his own "Ain't Misbehavin'." Dooley Wilson of *Casablanca* fame and the Nicholas Brothers are also really great. This is an overlooked MGM classic. B&W; 77m. **DIR:** Andrew L. Stone. **CAST:** Lena Horne, Bill Robinson, Cab Calloway, Fats Waller. **1943**

STORY OF VERNON AND IRENE CASTLE, THE ★★★★ Another fine film with the flying footsies of Fred Astaire and the always lovely Ginger Rogers. B&W; 93m. **DIR:** H. C. Potter. **CAST:** Fred Astaire, Ginger Rogers, Edna May Oliver, Walter Brennan. **1939**

STOWAWAY ★★★ Tale of missionary ward Shirley Temple lost in Shanghai and befriended by American Robert Young. She holds her own against such seasoned scene snitchers as Eugene Pallette, Arthur Treacher, and J. Edward Blomberg, while bringing playboy Young and Alice Faye together romantically, singing in Chinese, and imitating Fred Astaire, Al Jolson, and Eddie Cantor. B&W; 86m. **DIR:** William A. Seiter. **CAST:** Shirley Temple, Robert Young, Alice Faye, Allan "Rocky" Lane, Eugene Pallette, Helen Westley, Arthur Treacher, J. Edward Blomberg. **1936**

STRICTLY BALLROOM ★★★★ Australian director Baz Luhrmann takes the garish visual style of cult director John Waters and gives it heart, in this offbeat *Cinderella* tale of a male dancer who breaks with the rules of ballroom dancing, and the wallflower who dreams of being his partner. While not for all tastes, this off-kilter musical has remarkable warmth. Rated PG for profanity. 94m. **DIR:** Baz Luhrmann. **CAST:** Paul Mercurio, Tara Morice, Bill Hunter, Pat Thomson, Barry Otto. **1992**

STUDENT PRINCE, THE ★★★★ A captivating, colorful, and charming rendition of Sigmund Romberg's famous operetta, and the only talkie version made from it. Mario Lanza recorded the sound track but was much too fat to play the Prince of Heidelberg who lives among the commoners and falls for a barmaid (Ann Blyth). Newcomer Edmund Purdom took his place. 107m. **DIR:** Richard Thorpe. **CAST:** Ann Blyth, Edmund Purdom, John Ericson, Louis Calhern, Edmund Gwenn. **1954**

SUMMER HOLIDAY ★★½ A musical remake of Eugene O'Neill's *Ah, Wilderness,* and the music gets in the way. It just isn't hummable and takes up time the personalities could have used to flesh out this charming coming-of-age story set in the early twentieth-century in mid-America. Walter Huston is excellent as the wise head of the house. 92m. **DIR:** Rouben Mamoulian. **CAST:** Mickey Rooney, Walter Huston, Agnes Moorehead, Marilyn Maxwell, Gloria De Haven, Frank Morgan, "Butch" Jenkins, Anne Francis. **1948**

SUMMER STOCK ★★★ An echo of the Mickey Rooney–Judy Garland talented-kids/let's-give-a-show films, this likable musical is built around a troupe of ambitious performers, led by Gene Kelly, who invade farmer Judy Garland's barn. Love blooms. Judy's "Get Happy" number, filmed long after the movie was completed and spliced in to add needed flash, is inspired. 109m. **DIR:** Charles Walters. **CAST:** Judy Garland, Gene Kelly, Eddie Bracken, Gloria De Haven, Phil Silvers, Hans Conried, Marjorie Main. **1950**

SUN VALLEY SERENADE ★★★½ John Payne agrees to care for a child refugee, who turns out to be Sonja Henie. Take it from there, but enjoy the trip. Henie is truly endearing, both on and off skates. Glenn Miller and his orchestra are on hand to help move things along. B&W; 86m. **DIR:** H. Bruce Humberstone. **CAST:** Sonja Henie, John Payne, Lynn Bari, Milton Berle, Joan Davis. **1941**

SUNDAY IN THE PARK WITH GEORGE ★★★★★ This is a taped version of a performance of one of the most honored musicals of the 1980s. A Pulitzer Prize–winner, the entire play is a fabrication of plot and characters based on the Georges Seurat painting, "Sunday Afternoon on the Island of La Grande Jatte." The painting comes to life, and each of the figures has a story to tell. Seurat is played expertly by Mandy Patinkin. 147m. **DIR:** James Lapine. **CAST:** Mandy Patinkin, Bernadette Peters, Barbara Byrne, Charles Kimbrough. **1986**

SWEENEY TODD ★★★★★ This is not a film, but rather an eight-camera video of a Broadway musical taped during a performance before an audience. And what a musical it is, this 1979 Tony Award winner! George Hearn is terrifying as Sweeney Todd, the barber who seeks revenge on the English judicial system by slashing the throats of the unfortunate who wind up in his tonsorial chair. Angela Lansbury is spooky as Mrs. Lovett, who finds a use for Todd's leftovers by baking them into meat pies. 150m. **DIR:** Harold Prince. **CAST:** Angela Lansbury, George Hearn, Sara Woods. **1982**

SWEET ADELINE ★★★★ One of the first Broadway musicals transferred to the screen with most of its original score intact, this is also the first of five Jerome Kern musicals to star Irene Dunne. She gives her all to such songs as "Why Was I Born?" The story of spies and singers may be hokey, but the music is marvelous. B&W; 87m. **DIR:** Mervyn LeRoy. **CAST:** Irene Dunne, Donald Woods, Louis Calhern, Winifred Shaw, Nydia Westman, Hugh Herbert, Ned Sparks, Phil Regan, Noah Beery Sr. **1935**

SWEET CHARITY ★★★★ This was a Broadway smash hit, and it lost nothing in transfer to the screen. Neil Simon adapted the story from Federico Fellini's *Nights of Cabiria*. Shirley MacLaine is a prostitute who falls in love with a naïve young man who is unaware of her profession. The score by Dorothy Fields and Cy Coleman is terrific. Bob Fosse, in his directorial debut, does an admirable job. Rated G. 133m. **DIR:** Bob Fosse. **CAST:** Shirley MacLaine, Chita Rivera, Paula Kelly, Ricardo Montalban, Sammy Davis Jr. **1969**

SWEET DREAMS ★★★★½ Jessica Lange is Patsy Cline, one of the greatest country-and-western singers of all time, in this film that is much more than a response to the popularity of *Coal Miner's Daughter*. Lange's performance is flawless right down to the singing, where she perfectly mouths Cline's voice. Rated PG for profanity and sex. 115m. **DIR:** Karel Reisz. **CAST:** Jessica Lange, Ed Harris, Ann Wedgeworth, David Clennon, Gary Basaraba. **1985**

SWEETHEARTS ★★★½ Good acting, splendid singing, and a bright updated script make this version of the ancient Victor Herbert operetta a winning comedy about a temperamental stage duo on a collision course set by jealousy. The Technicolor cinematography won an Oscar. 120m. **DIR:** W. S. Van Dyke. **CAST:** Jeanette MacDonald, Nelson Eddy, Frank Morgan, Ray Bolger, Mischa Auer. **1938**

SWING TIME ★★★★½ Fred Astaire is a gambler trying to save up enough money to marry the girl he left behind (Betty Furness). By the time he's saved the money, he and Ginger Rogers are madly in love with each other. B&W; 105m. **DIR:** George Stevens. **CAST:** Ginger Rogers, Fred Astaire, Betty Furness, Victor Moore, Helen Broderick. **1936**

TAKE IT BIG ★★ In the early 1940s at Paramount Pictures, a B-movie unit was formed by William H. Pine and William C. Thomas. With a good track record, they tried to produce more elaborate films. This so-so musical is one of those bigger productions. Jack Haley is at the wrong end in a horse act that inherits a dude ranch. Ozzie Nelson and his band supply the musical numbers. B&W; 75m. **DIR:** Frank McDonald. **CAST:** Jack Haley, Ozzie Nelson, Harriet Nelson. **1944**

TAKE ME OUT TO THE BALL GAME ★★★ Don't expect to see the usual Berkeley extravaganza in this one; this is just a run-of-the-mill musical. It does contain some entertaining musical numbers, such as "O'Brien to Ryan to Goldberg." 93m. **DIR:** Busby Berkeley. **CAST:** Gene Kelly, Frank Sinatra, Esther Williams, Betty Garrett, Jules Munshin. **1949**

TAKING MY TURN ★★ This is a videotape of an off-Broadway musical. Unfortunately, you had to be there to really enjoy it. Sort of *A Chorus Line* for the Geritol generation, this features aging actors lamenting the way times have changed. Their song-and-dance routines are good, but for the most part this is pretty depressing. 90m. **DIR:** Robert H. Livingston. **CAST:** Margaret Whiting, Marni Nixon, Sheila Smith, Cissy Houston. **1984**

TALES OF HOFFMAN ★★★★½ A beautifully photographed blend of opera, ballet, and cinematic effects with Jacques Offenbach's familiar score for a backdrop. Robert Rounseville stars as the tale-spinner who recalls various romantic interludes in his life. The film was a follow-up to *The Red Shoes* with the same directors, stars, and color consultants. 120m. **DIR:** Michael Powell, Emeric Pressburger. **CAST:** Moira Shearer, Robert Rounseville, Robert Helpmann, Leonide Massine, Pamela Brown. **1951**

TAP ★★★★ This *Flashdance*-style musical-drama about a gifted tap dancer (Gregory Hines) is so good, you'll want to watch it a second time—not for the silly jewel-heist story, but for the marvelous dance sequences. See it for the eye-popping choreography and a *cut* contest—featuring old pros Sammy Davis Jr., Harold Nicholas, Bunny Briggs, Sandman Sims, Steve Condos, Rico, and Arthur Duncan—that will make your jaw drop. Rated PG-13 for profanity and violence. 111m. **DIR:** Nick Castle. **CAST:** Gregory Hines, Sammy Davis Jr., Joe Morton, Dick Anthony Williams. **1989**

TEA FOR TWO ★★★ Doris Day planning to back and star in a musical play, finds she has lost her wealth in the stock market crash. To win a $25,000 bet, she must say "No" to every question for forty-eight hours, even those asked by amorous Gordon MacRae. Loosely based on *No, No, Nanette*. 98m. **DIR:** David Butler. **CAST:** Doris Day, Gordon MacRae, Gene Nelson, Eve Arden, Billy DeWolfe, S. Z. Sakall. **1950**

TELEVISION PARTS HOME COMPANION ★★★ This is more of Mike Nesmith's *Elephant Parts* style of variety-show entertainment. Again, he has hilarious skits and mock commercials, as well as choreographed stories to accompany his songs. 40m. **DIR:** William Dear, Alan Myerson. **CAST:** Mike Nesmith, Joe Allain, Bill Martin. **1984**

TEXAS CARNIVAL ★★★ When down-and-out carnival workers, Red Skelton and Esther Williams are mistaken for brother and sister cattle millionaires, they go along with the mix-up. 77m. **DIR:** Charles Walters. **CAST:** Esther Williams, Red Skelton, Howard Keel, Ann Miller, Keenan Wynn. **1951**

THANK GOD IT'S FRIDAY ★★ This film is episodic and light in mood and features a cast primarily of newcomers. Donna Summer plays an aspiring singer who pesters a disc jockey, Bobby Speed (Ray Vitte), to let her sing. Rated PG. 90m. **DIR:** Robert Klane. **CAST:** Donna Summer, The Commodores, Ray Vitte, Debra Winger, Jeff Goldblum. **1978**

THANK YOUR LUCKY STARS ★★★½ Practically nonexistent plot—involving banjo-eyed Eddie Cantor as a cabdriver and the organizer of this gala affair—takes a backseat to the wonderful array of Warner Bros. talent gathered together for the first and only time in one film. Lots of fun for film buffs. B&W; 127m. **DIR:** David Butler. **CAST:** Eddie Cantor, Dennis Morgan, Joan Leslie, Bette Davis, Olivia de Havilland, Ida Lupino, Ann Sheridan, Humphrey Bogart, Errol Flynn, John Garfield. **1943**

THAT MIDNIGHT KISS ★★★ Mario Lanza makes his film debut as an ex-GI making it as a truck driver when he gets involved with an heiress who wants to be an opera star. Slight plot, but it's the music that counts. A fine rendition of "They Won't Believe Me." 96m. **DIR:** Norman Taurog. **CAST:** Mario Lanza, Kathryn Grayson, José Iturbi, Ethel Barrymore, Keenan Wynn, J. Carrol Naish, Thomas Gomez, Marjorie Reynolds, Arthur Treacher. **1949**

THAT WAS ROCK ★★★★★ Compilation of two previous films, *The T.A.M.I. Show* and *The Big T.N.T. Show*, which were originally shot on videotape in the mid-1960s. It's black and white, but color inserts have been added, featuring Chuck Berry giving cursory introductions to each act. The video is muddy, the simulated stereo is annoying, and the audience nearly drowns out the performers, but it's one of the best collections of rock 'n' roll and R&B talent you will ever see. Unrated. 92m. **DIR:** Steve Binder, Larry Peerce. **CAST:** The Rolling Stones, Chuck Berry, Tina Turner, Marvin Gaye, The Supremes, Smokey Robinson and the Miracles, James Brown, Ray Charles, Gerry and the Pacemakers, The Ronettes. **1984**

THAT'LL BE THE DAY ★★★★ *Stardust* offers some of filmdom's most fascinating glimpses into the rock 'n' roll world. It is the sequel to *That'll Be the Day*, itself a provocative character study. Charismatic David Essex stars as a British working-class youth whose adolescent restlessness points him toward rock music. Ringo Starr contributes an engaging performance as a rough-hewn lad who eventually proves to be less morally suspect than the protagonist. 90m. **DIR:** Claude Whatham. **CAST:** David Essex, Ringo Starr, Rosemary Leach, James Booth, Billy Fury, Keith Moon. **1974**

THAT'S SINGING: THE BEST OF BROADWAY ★★½ You'll find this on the shelf with *That's Dancing* and *That's Entertainment*. It should be with *The Adventures of Ozzie and Harriet*. This is a television show where stars present an offering from Broadway musicals in which they appeared. The highlight is Jerry Orbach, singing "Try To Remember" from *The Fantasticks*. The star rating is for Broadway diehards only. 117m. **DIR:** Robert Iscove. **CAST:** Tom Bosley, Diahann Carroll, Glynis Johns, Ethel Merman, Jerry Orbach, Robert Morse, Debbie Reynolds. **1982**

THERE'S NO BUSINESS LIKE SHOW BUSINESS ★★ Even the strength of the cast can't save this marginally entertaining musical-comedy about a show-biz family. Irving Berlin's tunes and Monroe's scenes are the only redeeming qualities in this one. 117m. **DIR:** Walter Lang. **CAST:** Ethel Merman, Dan Dailey, Marilyn Monroe, Donald O'Connor, Johnnie Ray, Mitzi Gaynor, Hugh O'Brian, Frank McHugh. **1954**

THEY SHALL HAVE MUSIC ★★★ Good cast and great music increase the appeal of this attempt to make concert violinist Jascha Heifetz a film star. Simple plot has a group of poor kids convincing him to play a benefit and save Walter Brennan's music school in the slums. B&W; 101m. **DIR:** Archie Mayo. **CAST:** Jascha Heifetz, Joel McCrea, Andrea Leeds, Walter Brennan, Marjorie Main, Porter Hall. **1939**

THIN ICE ★★★★ One of Sonja Henie's most successful films. She stars as an ice-skating teacher who meets a European prince traveling in her country incognito. Naturally, they fall in love and she helps him solve his political problems. Of course, she also skates well. One of the movie's highlights is the performance of comedienne Joan Davis as an orchestra leader. B&W; 78m. **DIR:** Sidney Lanfield. **CAST:** Sonja Henie, Tyrone Power, Joan Davis, Arthur Treacher, Raymond Walburn, Alan Hale Sr., Sig Ruman, Leah Ray. **1937**

THIS IS THE ARMY ★★★ Hoofer (later U.S. senator) George Murphy portrays Ronald Reagan's father in this musical mélange penned by Irving Berlin to raise funds for Army Emergency Relief during World War II. It's a star-studded, rousing show of songs and skits from start to finish, but practically plotless. 121m. **DIR:** Michael Curtiz. **CAST:** George Murphy, Joan Leslie, Ronald Reagan, George Tobias, Alan Hale Sr., Joe Louis, Kate Smith, Irving Berlin, Frances Langford, Charles Butterworth. **1943**

THIS TIME FOR KEEPS ★★★ A typical Esther Williams swimming event with more musical variety than usual, this film pits her allure against the comedy of Jimmy Durante and the sophistication of opera-star Lauritz Melchior. On Mackinac Island Melchior's son promptly falls in love with Williams, and the movie dissolves into a series of musical numbers. More padding than plot, but the padding is classy stuff. 105m. **DIR:** Richard Thorpe. **CAST:** Esther Williams, Lauritz Melchior, Jimmy Durante, May Whitty, Johnnie Johnston, Sharon MacManus, Kenneth Tobey, Esther Dale, Ludwig Stossel, Xavier Cugat. **1947**

THOROUGHLY MODERN MILLIE ★★★ First-rate music characterizing America's Jazz Age dominates this harebrained-plotted, slapstick-punctuated spoof of the 1920s, complete with villains, a bordello, and a cooing flapper so smitten with her stuffed-shirt boss that she can't see her boyfriend for beans. It's toe-tapping entertainment, but a tad too long. 138m. **DIR:** George Roy Hill. **CAST:** Julie Andrews, Mary Tyler Moore, Carol Channing, James Fox, Beatrice Lillie, John Gavin, Noriyuki "Pat" Morita, Jack Soo. **1967**

THOSE LIPS, THOSE EYES ★★ So-so "let's put on a show" musical features Frank Langella as a would-be stage star forced to play to small towns, though he longs to appear on Broadway. Rated R for profanity and brief nudity. 106m. **DIR:** Michael Pressman. **CAST:** Frank Langella, Glynnis O'Connor, Tom Hulce, Jerry Stiller, Kevin McCarthy. **1980**

THOUSANDS CHEER ★★★ The typical story about someone putting together a talent show for some good cause who gets a major shot in the arm by the appearances of top MGM performers. 126m. **DIR:** George Sidney. **CAST:** John Boles, Kathryn Grayson, Mickey Rooney, Judy Garland, Gene Kelly, Red Skelton, Lucille Ball, Ann Sothern, Eleanor Powell, Frank Morgan, Lena Horne, Virginia O'Brien. **1943**

THREE DARING DAUGHTERS ★★★ Divorcée Jeanette MacDonald meets and weds pianist Jose Iturbi—her daughters object until they learn he can play boogie-woogie. Slight plot but wonderful music. A joke is that Iturbi plays himself. 115m. **DIR:** Fred M. Wilcox. **CAST:** Jeanette MacDonald, Jose Iturbi, Jane Powell, Edward Arnold, Harry Davenport, Elinor Donahue. **1948**

THREE LITTLE WORDS ★★½ That this is supposedly Fred Astaire's favorite among his numerous films says little for his taste. He and Red Skelton thoroughly enjoyed playing ace songwriters Bert Kalmar and Harry Ruby in this semiaccurate bio-pic, but, overall, the film lacks lustre. 102m. **DIR:** Richard Thorpe. **CAST:** Fred Astaire, Red Skelton, Vera-Ellen, Gloria De Haven, Arlene Dahl, Debbie Reynolds, Keenan Wynn. **1950**

THREE SMART GIRLS ★★★★ Starring debut of fourteen-year-old Deanna Durbin as Penny Craig, who with her two sisters, saves their easygoing father from the clutches of a gold digger. Fast-moving musical, with some fine comedy touches, particularly by Mischa Auer. B&W; 84m. **DIR:** Henry Koster. **CAST:** Deanna Durbin, Binnie Barnes, Alice Brady, Ray Milland, Charles Winninger, Mischa Auer, Nan Gray, Barbara Read, Lucile Watson. **1937**

THREE SMART GIRLS GROW UP ★★★½ Deanna Durbin returns in this sequel, this time acting as matchmaker for her two sisters and their assorted beaux. Nice mixture of light comedy and song. B&W; 90m. **DIR:** Henry Koster. **CAST:** Deanna Durbin, Charles Winninger, Nan Gray, Helen Parrish, Robert Cummings, William Lundigan. **1939**

THRILL OF A ROMANCE ★★ Esther Williams's groom deserts her on their wedding night to close a business deal. Opera star Lauritz Melchior feels she could do better with war hero Van Johnson, so he acts as cupid. 104m. **DIR:** Richard Thorpe. **CAST:** Van Johnson, Esther Williams, Lauritz Melchior, Spring Byington. **1945**

THUNDER ALLEY 💔 Midwestern teenagers form a rock band. Rated R. 102m. **DIR:** J. S. Cardone. **CAST:** Roger Wilson, Jill Schoelen, Scott McGinnis, Leif Garrett. **1985**

TICKLE ME ★★ The plot falls below that found in a standard Elvis vehicle in this unfunny comedy-musical, which has Elvis working and singing at an all-female health ranch. Mindless fluff. 90m. **DIR:** Norman Taurog. **CAST:** Elvis Presley, Jocelyn Lane, Julie Adams, Jack Mullaney, Merry Anders. **1965**

TILL THE CLOUDS ROLL BY ★★½ Biography of songwriter Jerome Kern is a barrage of MGM talent that includes Judy Garland, Frank Sinatra, Lena Horne, Dinah Shore, Kathryn Grayson, and many more in short, tuneful vignettes that tie this all-out effort together. Not too bad as musical bio-pics go, but singing talent is definitely the star in this production. 137m. **DIR:** Richard Whorf. **CAST:** Robert Walker, Van Heflin, Judy Garland, Lucille Bremer. **1946**

TIMES SQUARE 🦃 A totally unbelievable story involving two New York teens who hang out in Times Square. Rated R for profanity. 111m. **DIR:** Alan Moyle. **CAST:** Tim Curry, Robin Johnson, Trini Alvarado, Peter Coffield. **1980**

TOAST OF NEW ORLEANS ★★½ Don't look for too much plot in this colorful showcase for the considerable vocal talent of the late Mario Lanza. Aided and abetted by the engaging soprano of Kathryn Grayson, Lanza sings up a storm. "Be My Love" was the film's and record stores' big number. 97m. **DIR:** Norman Taurog. **CAST:** Kathryn Grayson, Mario Lanza, Thomas Mitchell, David Niven, J. Carrol Naish, Rita Moreno. **1950**

TOKYO POP ★★ If you want a gander at modern-day Japan and its pop-music world, *Tokyo Pop* is just the ticket. When Wendy (Carrie Hamilton) leaves her punk band in New York and flies to Tokyo, she finds herself pursued by a would-be rocker who has decided his group needs a Western girl. Despite a maudlin love story, the film is worth watching for its revealing depictions of Tokyo street life and Japanese traditions. Rated R. 101m. **DIR:** Fran Rubel Kuzui. **CAST:** Carrie Hamilton, Yutaka Tadokoro. **1988**

TOM SAWYER (1973) ★★★ This musical version of Mark Twain's classic has a few contrived moments here and there, but it is, on the whole, enjoyable. Rated G. 102m. **DIR:** Don Taylor. **CAST:** Johnny Whitaker, Celeste Holm, Jeff East, Jodie Foster, Warren Oates. **1973**

TOMMY ★★½ In bringing The Who's ground-breaking rock opera to the screen, director Ken Russell let his penchant for bad taste and garishness run wild. The result is an outrageous movie about a deaf, dumb, and blind boy who rises to prominence as a "Pinball Wizard" and then becomes the new Messiah. Rated PG. 111m. **DIR:** Ken Russell. **CAST:** Roger Daltrey, Ann-Margret, Jack Nicholson, Oliver Reed, Elton John, Tina Turner. **1975**

TONIGHT AND EVERY NIGHT ★★★ Another Forties song-and-dance extravaganza—this time in war-torn London. In spite of bomb raids and uncertainty in their private lives, a determined troupe keeps their show alive. Seems a bit dated now, but Rita Hayworth is worth watching. 92m. **DIR:** Victor Saville. **CAST:** Rita Hayworth, Lee Bowman, Janet Blair, Leslie Brooks, Marc Platt. **1945**

TOO MANY GIRLS ★★★½ Four young men are hired by prestigious Pottawatomie College in Stopgap, New Mexico, to keep an eye on carefree student Lucille Ball. This marked the debut of Eddie Bracken, Desi Arnaz, *and*, in the chorus, Van Johnson. A trivia lover's delight, this is pure fun to watch. B&W; 85m. **DIR:** George Abbott. **CAST:** Lucille Ball, Richard Carlson, Eddie Bracken, Ann Miller, Desi Arnaz Sr. **1940**

TOP HAT ★★★★★ *Top Hat* is the most delightful and enduring of the Fred Astaire–Ginger Rogers musicals of the 1930s. This movie has an agreeable wisp of a plot and amusing, if dated, comedy dialogue. B&W; 99m. **DIR:** Mark Sandrich. **CAST:** Fred Astaire, Ginger Rogers, Edward Everett Horton, Eric Blore, Helen Broderick. **1935**

TRANSATLANTIC MERRY-GO-ROUND ★★ Jack Benny is the emcee of this transatlantic showboat, the S.S. *Progress*, en route from New York to Paris. This tub is loaded with romance, blackmail, chicanery, and murder. But it's rather lightweight overall. B&W; 90m. **DIR:** Ben Stoloff. **CAST:** Gene Raymond, Nancy Carroll, Jack Benny, Mitzi Green, Boswell Sisters. **1934**

TROUBLE WITH GIRLS, THE ★★★½ First of all, forget the stupid title, which has nothing to do with this charming tale of the Chautaqua Players of 1927. It's sort of a *Music Man*–ish tale about a troupe of entertainers. Elvis is the manager of the troupe. Sheree North is the tainted woman who is ruthlessly pursued by her lecherous boss (Dabney Coleman). Refreshingly above Elvis's inane girly films. Rated G. 105m. **DIR:** Peter Tewksbury. **CAST:** Elvis Presley, Sheree North, Vincent Price, Dabney Coleman. **1969**

TWO GIRLS AND A SAILOR ★★★ June Allyson and Gloria De Haven run a canteen for servicemen, and both fall for sailor Van Johnson. Their romantic triangle is resolved, but not before guest stars perform specialty numbers to give the movie its entertainment value. The personalities are potent enough to keep the film entertaining beyond its era. 124m. **DIR:** Richard Thorpe. **CAST:** Van Johnson, June Allyson, Gloria De Haven, Tom Drake, Jimmy Durante, Jose Iturbi, Gracie Allen, Harry James, Xavier Cugat, Ben Blue. **1944**

200 MOTELS ★★½ Weird blend of comedy and music written and performed by Frank Zappa and the Mothers of Invention. This bizarre opera set against an even stranger backdrop of completely berserk gags. The film never really finds its center.

Rated R for nudity and profanity. 98m. **DIR:** Frank Zappa, Tony Palmer. **CAST:** Frank Zappa, Theodore Bikel, Ringo Starr, Keith Moon. **1971**

TWO MOON JULY ★★ The Kitchen, a New York City center for visual and performing arts, pays homage to the avant-garde with a diverse but uneven program of music, theatre, dance, and film. An adventurous but uneven endeavor. 60m. **DIR:** Tom Bowes. **CAST:** Laurie Anderson, David Byrne. **1985**

TWO SISTERS FROM BOSTON ★★★½ Turn-of-the-century fun. Kathryn Grayson comes to New York to seek an operatic career, but she and sister June Allyson end up working at a Bowery honky-tonk owned by Jimmy Durante. The whole cast shines and Durante really shows the talent that endeared him to millions. B&W; 112m. **DIR:** Henry Koster. **CAST:** Kathryn Grayson, June Allyson, Lauritz Melchior, Jimmy Durante, Peter Lawford, Ben Blue. **1946**

TWO TICKETS TO BROADWAY ★★ Clichéd let's-put-on-a-show film features Janet Leigh as a small-town ingenue who heads for New York. Ann Miller's dance routines and Tony Martin's songs are highlights. 106m. **DIR:** James V. Kern. **CAST:** Tony Martin, Janet Leigh, Gloria De Haven, Ann Miller. **1951**

TWO WEEKS WITH LOVE ★★ An old-fashioned musical set in a bygone age when corsets and long bathing suits were the norm. Debbie Reynolds and Carleton Carpenter sing "Abba Dabba Honeymoon," the novelty song that catapulted them to fame. Songs like "On Moonlight Bay" add to the romantic atmosphere. 92m. **DIR:** Roy Rowland. **CAST:** Jane Powell, Debbie Reynolds, Ricardo Montalban, Ann Harding, Louis Calhern, Carleton Carpenter. **1950**

UNSINKABLE MOLLY BROWN, THE ★★★ Noisy, big-budget version of hit Broadway musical has Debbie Reynolds at her spunkiest as the tuneful gal from Colorado who survives the sinking of the *Titanic* and lives to sing about it. High-stepping dance numbers and the performances by Reynolds and Harve Presnell make this a favorite with musicals fans, but it does drag a bit for the casual viewer. 128m. **DIR:** Charles Walters. **CAST:** Debbie Reynolds, Harve Presnell, Ed Begley Sr., Hermione Baddeley, Jack Kruschen. **1964**

VAGABOND LOVER, THE ★★★ Rudy Vallee portrays an orchestra conductor who has fallen deeply in love with the daughter (Sally Blane) of a dotty dowager (Marie Dressler). Conventional but entertaining. B&W; 69m. **DIR:** Marshall Neilan. **CAST:** Rudy Vallee, Sally Blane, Marie Dressler. **1929**

VIVA LAS VEGAS ★★ In this romantic musical, Elvis Presley plays a race-car driver who also sings. Ann-Margret is a casino dancer. Eventually Elvis and Ann-Margret get together, which is no surprise to any viewer who is awake. 86m. **DIR:** George Sidney. **CAST:** Elvis Presley, Ann-Margret, Cesare Danova, William Demarest, Jack Carter. **1964**

WAGNER ★★★ This five-hour film gives you an idea of what the greatest opera composer may have been like, but the legendary supporting cast, although credible, is not up to reputation. Not rated, but equal to an R for violence, profanity, and nudity. 300m. **DIR:** Tony Palmer. **CAST:** Richard Burton, Vanessa Redgrave, Gemma Craven, John Gielgud, Ralph Richardson, Laurence Olivier, Marthe Keller, Ronald Pickup. **1982**

WEST POINT STORY, THE ★★★ James Cagney is an athletic Broadway hoofer reluctantly becoming involved in the West Point annual cadet review, even trying out dorm life. Oscar nomination for the score by Ray Heindorf. B&W; 107m. **DIR:** Roy Del Ruth. **CAST:** James Cagney, Virginia Mayo, Doris Day, Gordon Macrae, Gene Nelson, Roland Winters, Jerome Cowan, Alan Hale Jr. **1950**

WEST SIDE STORY ★★★★★ The Romeo-and-Juliet theme (with Richard Beymer and Natalie Wood in the lead roles) is updated to 1950s New York and given an endearing music score. The story of rival white and Puerto Rican youth gangs first appeared as a hit Broadway musical. None of the brilliance of the play was lost in its transformation to the screen. It received Oscars for best picture and its supporting players, Rita Moreno and George Chakiris. (Wood's vocals were dubbed by Marni Nixon.) 151m. **DIR:** Robert Wise, Jerome Robbins. **CAST:** Natalie Wood, Richard Beymer, Rita Moreno, George Chakiris, Russ Tamblyn. **1961**

WHITE CHRISTMAS ★★★ This attempt to capitalize on the title tune is an inferior remake of 1942's *Holiday Inn* (in which the song "White Christmas" first appeared). It's another in that long line of let's-put-on-a-show stories, with the last several reels showcasing the singing, dancing, and mugging talents of the cast. 120m. **DIR:** Michael Curtiz. **CAST:** Bing Crosby, Danny Kaye, Vera-Ellen, Rosemary Clooney. **1954**

WHOOPEE ★★½ The first of six Eddie Cantor musical films of the 1930s, this one's a two-color draft of his 1928 Broadway hit of the same name. The big-eyed comic plays a superhypochondriac on an Arizona dude ranch. Cowpokes and chorines abound. Busby Berkeley production numbers make it palatable. B&W; 93m. **DIR:** Thornton Freeland. **CAST:** Eddie Cantor, Eleanor Hunt, Paul Gregory, Ethel Shutta. **1930**

WINTERTIME ★★ Sonja Henie's weakest movie and her last for a major studio. Her showy routines attract people to an old rundown hotel so the owners can afford to turn it into a profitable resort. The musical numbers are better than the dialogue and almost as good as the skating scenes. B&W; 82m. **DIR:** John Brahm. **CAST:** Sonja Henie, Cornel Wilde, Jack Oakie, Cesar Romero, Carole Landis, S. Z. Sakall, Helene Reynolds, Geary Steffen, Woody Herman. **1943**

WIZ, THE ★★ Ineffective updating of *The Wizard of Oz* with an all-black cast, including Diana Ross (who is too old for the part), Richard Pryor, and Michael Jackson. Adapted from a successful Broadway play, this picture should have been better. Rated G. 133m. **DIR:** Sidney Lumet. **CAST:** Diana Ross, Richard Pryor, Michael Jackson, Nipsey Russell, Ted Ross, Mabel King, Theresa Merritt, Thelma Carpenter, Lena Horne. **1978**

WOLF CALL ★★ Jack London's story of a dog brought from the city to join a wolf pack somehow evolves into a musical-adventure-drama in this curious film. Playboy John Carroll falls in love with Indian maiden Movita while investigating his father's radium mine. B&W; 61m. **DIR:** George Waggner. **CAST:** John Carroll, Movita. **1939**

WONDER BAR ★★ All the ingredients for a great Warner Bros.-Busby Berkeley musical, but the mixture falls flat this time. Berkeley's musical numbers are as spectacular as ever, but one, "Goin' to Heaven on a Mule" (with Al Jolson in blackface), is perhaps the most colossally tasteless number in movie history. B&W; 84m. **DIR:** Lloyd Bacon. **CAST:** Al Jolson, Kay Francis, Dolores Del Rio, Ricardo Cortez, Guy Kibbee. **1934**

WORDS AND MUSIC ★★½ Fictionalized biography of the song-writing team of Richard Rogers and Lorenz Hart, dwelling mostly on the short and tormented life of the latter. As long as there's music, song, and dance, everything is great. The rest should have been silence. 119m. **DIR:** Norman Taurog. **CAST:** Mickey Rooney, Tom Drake, June Allyson, Betty Garrett, Judy Garland, Gene Kelly, Ann Sothern, Vera-Ellen, Cyd Charisse, Allyn Ann McLerie, Mel Torme, Janet Leigh, Perry Como. **1948**

XANADU ★★½ This musical lacks inspiration and story line. It is basically a full-length video that includes some good numbers by Olivia Newton-John and Gene Kelly. See it for the musical entertainment, not for the story. Rated PG. 88m. **DIR:** Robert Greenwald. **CAST:** Olivia Newton-John, Gene Kelly, Michael Beck, James Sloyan, Sandahl Bergman. **1980**

YANKEE DOODLE DANDY ★★★★★ Magnetic James Cagney, stepping out of his gangster roles, gives a magnificent performance in the life story of dancing vaudevillian George M. Cohan. An outstanding show-business story with unassuming but effective production. B&W; 126m. **DIR:** Michael Curtiz. **CAST:** James Cagney, Joan Leslie, Walter Huston, Irene Manning, Rosemary DeCamp, Richard Whorf, Jeanne Cagney. **1942**

YENTL ★★½ Barbra Streisand, who also produced, coscripted, and directed, stars as a woman who must disguise herself as a man in order to pursue an education among Orthodox Jews in turn-of-the-century eastern Europe. The story is fine, but the songs all sound the same. Still, *Yentl* is, overall, a watchable work. Rated PG for brief nudity. 134m. **DIR:** Barbra Streisand. **CAST:** Barbra Streisand, Mandy Patinkin, Amy Irving, Nehemiah Persoff, Steven Hill. **1983**

YES, GIORGIO ★★ In this old-fashioned star vehicle, Luciano Pavarotti makes a less-than-memorable screen debut as Giorgio Fini, a macho Italian tenor who meets a pretty Boston throat specialist (Kathryn Harrold) when his voice suddenly fails him. They fall in love and the viewer falls asleep. Rated PG for adult themes. 110m. **DIR:** Franklin J. Schaffner. **CAST:** Luciano Pavarotti, Kathryn Harrold, Eddie Albert, James Hong. **1982**

YOU WERE NEVER LOVELIER ★★★★ In this interesting story, Fred Astaire goes stepping about with the most glamorous of all the stars—Rita Hayworth. This film's worth seeing twice. B&W; 97m. **DIR:** William A. Seiter. **CAST:** Fred Astaire, Rita Hayworth, Adolphe Menjou, Leslie Brooks, Adele Mara. **1942**

YOU'LL NEVER GET RICH ★★★½ This musical-comedy has play producer Fred Astaire getting drafted right before his big show. Somehow he manages to serve his country and put the show on while romancing Rita Hayworth. B&W; 88m. **DIR:** Sidney Lanfield. **CAST:** Fred Astaire, Rita Hayworth, John Hubbard, Robert Benchley, Osa Massen, Frieda Inescort, Guinn Williams. **1941**

YOUNG AT HEART ★★★½ This is a glossy remake of the Warner Bros. 1938 success *Four Daughters*. The plot presents Doris Day as a refined New England lass from a respected family who marries a down-on-his-luck musician (Frank Sinatra). 117m. **DIR:** Gordon Douglas. **CAST:** Doris Day, Frank Sinatra, Gig Young, Ethel Barrymore, Dorothy Malone. **1955**

YOUNG MAN WITH A HORN ★★★½ Interesting dramatic portrayal of a young horn player who fights to fill his need for music. Story becomes too melodramatic as Kirk Douglas becomes trapped in a romantic web between Lauren Bacall and Doris Day. Horn work by Harry James. B&W; 112m. **DIR:** Michael Curtiz. **CAST:** Kirk Douglas, Lauren Bacall, Doris Day, Hoagy Carmichael, Juano Hernandez. **1950**

YOUNG SOUL REBELS ★★★★ Two black English soul DJ's attempt to break into mainstream radio stardom during the 1977 British punk explosion. This film accurately depicts the hazy sexual boundaries of the era. Rated R for nudity and profanity. 95m.

DIR: Isaac Julien. **CAST:** Valentine Nonyela, Mo Sesau, Dorian Healy. **1991**

ZIEGFELD FOLLIES ★★★ MGM tries to imitate a Ziegfeld-style stage show. Don't get confused; this is not the Oscar-winning *The Great Ziegfeld* (with William Powell). 110m. **DIR:** Vincente Minnelli. **CAST:** Fred Astaire, Lucille Ball, William Powell, Judy Garland, Fanny Brice, Lena Horne, Red Skelton, Victor Moore, Virginia O'Brien, Cyd Charisse, Gene Kelly, Edward Arnold, Esther Williams. **1946**

ZIEGFELD GIRL ★★★ Judy Garland becomes a star, Hedy Lamarr weds rich, and poor Lana Turner hits the bottle. This all-stops-out musical-drama is jammed with show girls, lavish sets and costumes, and songs no one but trivia buffs recall. B&W; 131m. **DIR:** Robert Z. Leonard. **CAST:** Judy Garland, Hedy Lamarr, Lana Turner, Edward Everett Horton, Eve Arden, James Stewart, Jackie Cooper, Dan Dailey. **1941**

ZOOT SUIT ★★★★ Adapted from his stage drama-musical by writer-director Luis Valdez, this innovative film presents a fictionalized version of the Sleepy Lagoon murder case that took place in 1942. Rated R for profanity and violence. 104m. **DIR:** Luis Valdez. **CAST:** Edward James Olmos, Charles Aidman, John Anderson, Tyne Daly, Daniel Valdez. **1981**

ZOU ZOU ★★★ *Zou Zou* was Josephine Baker's debut in talkies and was a huge success in France. Baker's rendition of "Haiti" is the highlight. In French with English subtitles. B&W; 92m. **DIR:** Marc Allegret. **CAST:** Josephine Baker, Jean Gabin. **1934**

MYSTERY/SUSPENSE

ABDUCTION ★★ This film comes across as a cheap exploitation of the Patty Hearst kidnapping. It includes theories that may or may not be true. As in the real incident, Patty is kidnapped from the house she shares with her boyfriend. Rated R for profanity, violence, nudity, and sex. 100m. **DIR:** Joseph Zito. **CAST:** Gregory Rozakis, Leif Erickson, Dorothy Malone, Lawrence Tierney. **1975**

ABSENCE OF MALICE ★★★★ Sally Field is a Miami reporter who writes a story implicating an innocent man (Paul Newman) in the mysterious disappearance—and possible murder—of a union leader in this taut, thoughtful drama about the ethics of journalism. It's sort of *All the President's Men* turned inside out. Rated PG because of minor violence. 116m. **DIR:** Sydney Pollack. **CAST:** Paul Newman, Sally Field, Bob Balaban, Melinda Dillon, Wilford Brimley. **1982**

ACCIDENTAL MEETING ★★ In this made-for-cable movie, two women joke about having each other murder someone they don't like. However, one of the women takes it seriously. For a better version of this plot, rent Hitchcock's *Strangers on a Train.* Not rated, but contains violence and sexual situations. 95m. **DIR:** Michael Zinberg. **CAST:** Linda Gray, Linda Purl, Leigh McCloskey, Ernie Lively, David Hayward, Kent McCord. **1993**

ACTING ON IMPULSE ★★ A rather muddled thriller concerning needlessly warped horror-film star Linda Fiorentino, a conservative young salesman (C. Thomas Howell), and the obligatory assassin. The leads give better than the script deserves, and director Sam Irvin elicits stunningly awful performances from a host of cameo players. Rated R for profanity, violence, drug use, and kinky sexuality. 94m. **DIR:** Sam Irvin. **CAST:** C. Thomas Howell, Linda Fiorentino, Nancy Allen, Paul Bartel, Isaac Hayes, Adam Ant. **1993**

ADRIFT ★★ Derivative made-for-TV thriller proves those behind it saw *Dead Calm.* Kate Jackson and Kenneth Welsh are the good couple whose voyage is interrupted when they pick up bad couple Bruce Greenwood and Kelly Rowan. Predictable high-seas terror. Not rated. 92m. **DIR:** Christian Duguay. **CAST:** Kate Jackson, Kenneth Welsh, Bruce Greenwood, Kelly Rowan. **1993**

ADVENTURES OF SHERLOCK HOLMES, THE ★★★★½ The best of all the Basil Rathbone–Nigel Bruce Sherlock Holmes movies, this pits the great detective against his archnemesis, Dr. Moriarty (played by George Zucco). The period setting, atmospheric photography, and the spirited performances of the cast (which includes a young Ida Lupino as Holmes's client) make this a must-see for mystery fans. B&W; 85m. **DIR:** Alfred Werker. **CAST:** Basil Rathbone, Nigel Bruce, Ida Lupino, George Zucco. **1939**

ADVENTURES OF SHERLOCK HOLMES, THE (SERIES) ★★★★★ Jeremy Brett portrays Holmes as twitchy, arrogant, wan, humorless, and often downright rude—in short, everything Conan Doyle's hero was described to be. David Burke's Dr. Watson brings youthful dash and intelligent charm to this most famous of detectives' sidekicks. Each episode in this baker's dozen of cases is impeccably scripted and superbly acted; high points include "The Red-Headed League," "The Speckled Band," "A Scandal in Bohemia" (wherein Holmes meets Irene Adler), and "The Final Problem." Unrated, but contains frank discussions of violence and drug abuse. 52m. **DIR:** Paul Annett, John Bruce, David Carson, Ken Grieve, Alan Grint, Derek Marlowe. **CAST:** Jeremy Brett, David Burke. **1986**

ADVENTURES OF SHERLOCK HOLMES, THE (TV SERIES) ★★★ Producer-director Sheldon Reynolds generated the world's first Sherlock Holmes television series for the European market, and the 36 episodes hold up reasonably well. Ronald Howard (son of Leslie) is a bit young and overly enthusiastic as Holmes, but H. Marion Crawford makes a solid Watson. The original scripts are much lighter than Conan Doyle's stories, resulting in a finished tone that suggests the cast had a good time. Howard and Crawford bring honor to two of fiction's most enduring characters. Suitable for family viewing. B&W; 52m. **DIR:** Steve Previn, Sheldon Reynolds. **CAST:** Ronald Howard, H. Marion Crawford, Archie Duncan. **1955**

AFRAID OF THE DARK ★★ A young boy losing his eyesight seeks out a slasher who targets the blind. Scary in places, but the thrills are few and too far between. Rated R for nudity and violence. 91m. **DIR:** Mark Peploe. **CAST:** James Fox, Fanny Ardant, Paul McGaw. **1992**

AFTER DARK, MY SWEET ★★★½ Jason Patric gives a spellbinding performance as a moody, wandering ex-boxer who may or may not be as punch drunk as he seems. He meets a beguiling widow (Rachel Ward) and an ex-detective con man (Bruce Dern) and gets mixed up in a kidnap-ransom scheme that soon turns sour. Style and atmosphere dominate this gritty adaptation of Jim Thompson's hardboiled novel. Rated R for language. 114m. **DIR:** James Foley. **CAST:** Jason Patric, Rachel Ward, Bruce Dern. **1990**

AFTER DARKNESS 🦃 An odd thriller about twin brothers who share visions of their parents' deaths. 105m. **DIR:** Dominique Othenin-Girard. **CAST:** John Hurt, Julian Sands, Victoria Abril. **1985**

AFTER THE THIN MAN ★★★★½ Second of the six wonderful *Thin Man* films made with William Powell and Myrna Loy, following on the heels of 1934's *The Thin Man*. Powell, Loy, and Asta, the incorrigible terrier, trade quips and drinks in this decent murder mystery. Rising star James Stewart merely adds to the fun. The dialogue is fast-paced and quite droll, and Powell and Loy demonstrate a chemistry that explains the dozen hits they had together. Not to be missed. Followed, in 1939, by *Another Thin Man*. B&W; 113m. **DIR:** W. S. Van Dyke. **CAST:** William Powell, Myrna Loy, James Stewart, Elissa Landi, Joseph Calleia, Sam Levene. **1936**

AGAINST ALL ODDS ★★★½ A respectable remake of *Out of the Past*, a 1947 *film noir* classic, this release stars Jeff Bridges as a man hired by a wealthy gangster (James Woods) to track down his girlfriend (Rachel Ward), who allegedly tried to kill him. Bridges finds her, they fall in love, and that's when the plot's twists really begin. Rated R for nudity, suggested sex, violence, and profanity. 128m. **DIR:** Taylor Hackford. **CAST:** Jeff Bridges, Rachel Ward, Alex Karras, James Woods. **1984**

AGATHA ★★½ Supposedly based on a true event in the life of mystery author Agatha Christie (during which she disappeared for eleven days in 1926), this is a moderately effective thriller. Vanessa Redgrave is excellent in the title role, but co-star Dustin Hoffman is miscast as the American detective on her trail. Rated PG. 98m. **DIR:** Michael Apted. **CAST:** Dustin Hoffman, Vanessa Redgrave, Celia Gregory. **1979**

ALEX'S APARTMENT 🦃 When a young woman starts a new life in a coastal town, she's confronted by a maniac who kills women as "gifts" to her. Poor script. Unrated, contains violence. 79m. **DIR:** W. Mel Martins. **CAST:** Miki Welling. **1992**

ALFRED HITCHCOCK PRESENTS (TV SERIES) ★★★★ This classic anthology series features a broad range of mystery and suspense. First-rate casts adds to the fun. During breaks, Alfred Hitchcock himself drolly comments on the action. One of the four episodes on the initial video release, "Lamb to the Slaughter," stars Barbara Bel Geddes in a deliciously ironic tale of murder. Black humor and surprise endings are trademarks of the show. Hitchcock directed the episodes featured on Volume 1. 120m. **DIR:** Alfred Hitchcock. **CAST:** Barbara Bel Geddes, Tom Ewell, John Williams. **1962**

ALL-AMERICAN MURDER ★★★ This murder mystery holds a lot of surprises. Charlie Schlatter is an ex-con who is implicated in the death of a beautiful coed. Christopher Walken is the cop who has a hunch and lets him off to prove his innocence. Unfortunately for Schlatter, dead bodies keep turning up wherever he goes. Rated R for violence, profanity, and nudity. 94m. **DIR:** Anson Williams. **CAST:** Christopher Walken, Charlie Schlatter, Josie Bissett, Amy Davis, Richard Kind, Joanna Cassidy. **1991**

ALL THE KIND STRANGERS ★★ This made-for-TV thriller lacks overt terror. A family of orphans lures kind strangers to their isolated home and then forces them to act as their parents. If the strangers don't measure up, they're murdered. Interesting in an eerie way. 74m. **DIR:** Burt Kennedy. **CAST:** Stacy Keach, Samantha Eggar, John Savage, Robby Benson, Arlene Farber. **1974**

ALL THE PRESIDENT'S MEN ★★★★★ Robert Redford, who also produced, and Dustin Hoffman star in this gripping reenactment of the exposure of the Watergate conspiracy by reporters Bob Woodward and Carl Bernstein. What's so remarkable about this docudrama is, although we know how it eventually comes out, we're on the edge of our seats from beginning to end. That's inspired moviemaking. Rated PG. 136m. **DIR:** Alan J. Pakula. **CAST:** Dustin Hoffman, Robert Redford, Jason Robards Jr., Jane Alexander, Jack Warden, Martin Balsam. **1976**

ALLIGATOR EYES ★★ A group of friends pick up a hitchhiking blind woman. Nonthrilling, would-be thriller. Rated R for nudity and violence. 101m. **DIR:** John Feldman. **CAST:** Annabelle Larsen, Roger Kabler, Mary McLain. **1990**

ALPHABET MURDERS, THE ★★★ A semicomic Agatha Christie mystery with Tony Randall as Hercule Poirot and Margaret Rutherford in a cameo bit as Miss Marple. Poirot goes after a serial killer who polishes off his victims in alphabetical order. Christie fans might regard the movie as blasphemous, but Randall's fans should love it. B&W; 90m. **DIR:** Frank Tashlin. **CAST:** Tony

Randall, Robert Morley, Anita Ekberg, Margaret Rutherford, James Villiers, Guy Rolfe. 1966

AMATEUR, THE ★★★½ A CIA computer technologist (John Savage) blackmails The Company into helping him avenge the terrorist murder of his girlfriend, only to find himself abandoned—and hunted—by the CIA. Rated R because of violence. 111m. **DIR:** Charles Jarrott. **CAST:** John Savage, Christopher Plummer, Marthe Keller, John Marley. 1982

AMBITION 🦃 An unpublished author is so obsessed with a paroled slasher that he befriends the reformed psycho. Rated R for violence, language, and nudity. 100m. **DIR:** Scott Goldstein. **CAST:** Lou Diamond Phillips, Clancy Brown, Cecilia Peck, Richard Bradford, Willard E. Pugh, Grace Zabriskie. 1991

AMBULANCE, THE ★★★★ Cartoonist Eric Roberts stumbles onto what may be a weird abduction conspiracy when dream gal Janine Turner is whisked away by a mysterious ambulance and never shows up at any of the local hospitals. Campy, strange, infused with black humor and several exciting chase scenes, this is an intriguing flick. Adding to its oddball patina is James Earl Jones as a cop on the edge. Rated R for profanity and violence. 95m. **DIR:** Larry Cohen. **CAST:** Eric Roberts, Janine Turner, James Earl Jones, Eric Braeden. 1993

ANATOMY OF A MURDER ★★★★ A clever plot, realistic atmosphere, smooth direction, and sterling performances from a topflight cast make this frank and exciting small-town courtroom drama first-rate fare. For the defense, it's James Stewart at his best versus prosecuting attorney George C. Scott. Ben Gazzara plays a moody young army officer charged with killing the man who raped his wife, Lee Remick. Honest realism saturates throughout. B&W; 160m. **DIR:** Otto Preminger. **CAST:** James Stewart, Arthur O'Connell, Lee Remick, Ben Gazzara, Eve Arden, Kathryn Grant, George C. Scott, Joseph Welch, Orson Bean, Murray Hamilton. 1959

AND HOPE TO DIE ★★★½ A Frenchman who is on the run from thugs hides out with an old gangster who enlists him in a kidnap scheme. Complex, well-acted crime-drama. Rated R for nudity and violence. 95m. **DIR:** René Clement. **CAST:** Robert Ryan, Tisa Farrow, Jean-Louis Trintignant, Lea Massari, Aldo Ray. 1972

AND SOON THE DARKNESS ★★½ Two young English college girls decide to go bicycle touring through the French countryside. But when the more vivacious of the two suddenly disappears in the same spot where a young girl was killed the year before, the foundation is laid for a tale of suspense. Rated PG. 94m. **DIR:** Robert Fuest. **CAST:** Pamela Franklin, Michele Dotrice, Sandor Eles. 1970

AND THEN THERE WERE NONE ★★★★★ One of the best screen adaptations of an Agatha Christie mystery. A select group of people is invited to a lonely island and murdered one by one. René Clair's inspired visual style gives this release just the right atmosphere and tension. B&W; 98m. **DIR:** René Clair. **CAST:** Barry Fitzgerald, Walter Huston, Richard Haydn, Roland Young, Judith Anderson, Louis Hayward, June Duprez, C. Aubrey Smith. 1945

ANDERSON TAPES, THE ★★★★ Sean Connery is perfectly cast in this exciting film about an ex-con under surveillance who wants to pull off the Big Heist. Slickly done, with tight editing and direction to keep the viewer totally involved, it holds up extremely well on video. Rated PG. 98m. **DIR:** Sidney Lumet. **CAST:** Sean Connery, Dyan Cannon, Martin Balsam, Ralph Meeker, Margaret Hamilton. 1972

ANGEL HEART ★★★½ Mickey Rourke stars as a down-and-out private investigator. The elegant, dapper, and more than slightly sinister Louis Cyphre (Robert De Niro) wants a missing singer found in order to settle a vague "debt." Absolutely not for the squeamish or for children; rated R for violence, sex, and language. 113m. **DIR:** Alan Parker. **CAST:** Mickey Rourke, Lisa Bonet, Robert De Niro, Charlotte Rampling. 1987

ANIMAL INSTINCTS ★★★ Maxwell Caulfield is a cop who renews his stalled relationship with his wife when he discovers that videotaping her in bed with a parade of men and women is a real turn on. Rated R for nudity, simulated sex, and language; unrated version offers much more of the same. 94m. **DIR:** Alexander Gregory Hippolyte. **CAST:** Maxwell Caulfield, Mitch Gaylord, Delia Sheppard, David Carradine. 1992

ANOTHER THIN MAN ★★★★ Nick and Nora Charles (William Powell and Myrna Loy) contend with a gentleman who dreams about catastrophes before they take place. As usual, the plot is secondary. Follows *After the Thin Man* (1936) and precedes *Shadow of the Thin Man* (1941). Suitable for family viewing. B&W; 105m. **DIR:** W. S. Van Dyke. **CAST:** William Powell, Myrna Loy, Virginia Grey, Otto Kruger, C. Aubrey Smith, Ruth Hussey, Nat Pendleton, Tom Neal. 1939

APARTMENT ZERO ★★★★ A movie buff's delight, this is a whodunit, a twisted character study, and a creepy suspense-thriller all rolled into one tantalizing puzzle. The lead character, Adrian LeDuc (Colin Firth) is the ultimate escapist; an Argentinian who pretends to be British, he revels in movie lore and owns a run-down movie revival house. When the cinema's failure puts Adrian in a financial crunch, he decides to take in a roommate, Jack Carney (Hart Bochner), a good-looking American who knows nothing about movies and just may be a serial killer. Rated R for violence and profanity. 124m. **DIR:** Martin Donovan. **CAST:** Hart Bochner, Colin Firth. **1989**

APPOINTMENT WITH DEATH ★★ Standard Agatha Christie mystery made boring by poor editing and pedestrian direction. Peter Ustinov is Hercule Poirot again (bringing competency if not vivaciousness to the part), trying to unravel a murder at an archaeological dig. Rated PG for adult situations. 102m. **DIR:** Michael Winner. **CAST:** Peter Ustinov, Lauren Bacall, Carrie Fisher, John Gielgud, Piper Laurie, Hayley Mills, Jenny Seagrove, David Soul, Amber Bezer. **1988**

ARE YOU IN THE HOUSE ALONE? ★★½ In this substandard made-for-television treatment of Richard Peck's Edgar Award–winning mystery novel, a beautiful high school student becomes the target of a campaign of terror that eventually leads to a sexual attack and mental torture. It's been done better before, but Kathleen Beller is exceptional as the heroine. 96m. **DIR:** Walter Grauman. **CAST:** Kathleen Beller, Blythe Danner, Tony Bill, Robin Mattson, Dennis Quaid, Ellen Travolta, Tricia O'Neil. **1978**

ARE YOU LONESOME TONIGHT ★★★ A frustrated housewife (Jane Seymour) discovers her husband is tape-recording his phone-sex conversations. Her husband disappears but leaves a clue on one of the tapes. She hires a private investigator (Parker Stevenson) and together they attempt to solve the mystery. Above-average made-for-cable thriller. Rated PG-13. 91m. **DIR:** E. W. Swackhamer. **CAST:** Jane Seymour, Parker Stevenson, Beth Broderick, Joel Brooks, Robert Pine. **1991**

ART OF DYING, THE ★★★ The *film noir* detective meets the mad slasher in this atmospheric film about a filmmaker who steals scenes from famous slasher flicks to make his own private snuff films. Director-star Wings Hauser has created a moody film with a wonderful plot. Rated R for violence, profanity, and nudity. 96m. **DIR:** Wings Hauser. **CAST:** Wings Hauser, Kathleen Kinmont, Sarah Douglas, Michael J. Pollard. **1991**

ASPHALT JUNGLE, THE ★★★★½ One of the greatest crime films of all time. This realistic study of a jewel robbery that sours lets the audience in early on what the outcome will be while building tension for any unexpected surprises that might pop up. Sterling Hayden and a near-perfect cast charge the film with an electric current that never lets up and only increases in power as they scheme their way closer to their fate. John Huston broke new ground with this landmark drama. B&W; 112m. **DIR:** John Huston. **CAST:** Sterling Hayden, Sam Jaffe, Louis Calhern, Marilyn Monroe, Jean Hagen, James Whitmore, Marc Lawrence, Anthony Caruso. **1950**

AT BERTRAM'S HOTEL ★★★★½ Miss Marple (Joan Hickson) takes a London vacation, courtesy of her nephew Raymond, in this superior installment of the Agatha Christie series. Miss Marple encounters some old friends during her stay at Bertram's Hotel, where she discovers that surface appearances are just a little too good to be true. Costumes and set design are luxurious. Unrated; suitable for family viewing. 102m. **DIR:** Mary McMurray. **CAST:** Joan Hickson, Caroline Blakiston, Helena Michell, George Baker, James Cossins, Preston Lockwood, Joan Greenwood. **1986**

AT CLOSE RANGE ★★★★ A powerful thriller based on true events that occurred in Pennsylvania during the summer of 1978. A rural gang leader returns to the family he abandoned years ago. His two sons try to prove themselves worthy of joining the gang. Events beyond their control lead to a brutal showdown between father and sons. Rated R for violence and profanity. 115m. **DIR:** James Foley. **CAST:** Christopher Walken, Sean Penn, Christopher Penn. **1986**

BABY DOLL MURDERS, THE 🦃 Plodding story of a serial killer who leaves the titular toy at the scene of each crime. Rated R for violence, profanity, and sex. 90m. **DIR:** Paul Leder. **CAST:** Jeff Kober, John Saxon, Melanie Smith, Bobby DiCicco. **1993**

BACKFIRE ★★★★ Twisting thriller involves the carefully orchestrated psychological destruction of a rich, shell-shocked Vietnam vet. Who's the culprit? Excellent combination of whodunit and whydunit. Leads Karen Allen and Keith Carradine are oblique enough to keep the real truth neatly suspended. Rated R for nudity and violence. 90m. **DIR:** Gilbert Cates. **CAST:** Karen Allen, Keith Carradine, Jeff Fahey, Bernie Casey, Dean Paul Martin. **1987**

BACKSTAB 🦃 An architect who becomes embroiled in a passionate affair that leads to murder. *Fatal Attraction* wannabe. Rated R for nudity. 91m. **DIR:** James Kaufman. **CAST:** James Brolin, Meg Foster. **1990**

BAD INFLUENCE ★★ Rob Lowe stars as a demonic character who leads frustrated yuppie James Spader down the sleazy path to corruption. Disturbing amorality tale. Rated R for nudity, simulated sex, and violence. 100m. **DIR:** Curtis Hanson. **CAST:** Rob Lowe, James Spader, Lisa Zane. **1990**

BAT WHISPERS, THE ★★½ Mary Roberts Rinehart's venerable stage success featuring a caped killer, clutching hands, a spooky mansion, and plenty of scared females. Chester Morris made his screen debut in this slow-moving but stylish creaker about the mysterious "Bat" who informs his victims of the hour of their death and never fails to deliver. B&W; 82m. **DIR:** Roland West.

CAST: Spencer Charters, Una Merkel, Chester Morris. 1931

BEAR ISLAND 🦃 Pointlessly melodramatic tale mixing gold fever, murder, and other incidental intrigue. Rated PG for mild violence. 118m. DIR: Don Sharp. CAST: Donald Sutherland, Richard Widmark, Vanessa Redgrave, Christopher Lee, Lloyd Bridges. 1980

BEDROOM EYES ★★★ A young stockbroker peers into a window one evening and sees a woman so tantalizing he feels compelled to return every night. When the object of his voyeurism is murdered, the man must try to prove his innocence. A silly but undeniably erotic mystery. 90m. DIR: William Fruet. CAST: Kenneth Gilman, Dayle Haddon, Barbara Law, Christine Cattel. 1986

BEDROOM EYES II 🦃 Tawdry whodunit. Rated R for nudity, profanity, and violence. 87m. DIR: Chuck Vincent. CAST: Linda Blair, Wings Hauser. 1989

BEDROOM WINDOW, THE ★★★ Upwardly mobile architect Steve Guttenberg has it made until his boss's wife (Isabelle Huppert) sees a murder being committed—from his bedroom window. When Guttenberg goes to the police in her place, he becomes the prime suspect. This is a tense thriller that manages to stay interesting despite some wildly unbelievable plot twists. Rated R for profanity, nudity, and violence. 112m. DIR: Curtis Hanson. CAST: Steve Guttenberg, Elizabeth McGovern, Isabelle Huppert, Paul Shenar. 1987

BEGUILED, THE ★★★★ An atmospheric, daring change of pace for director Don Siegel and star Clint Eastwood, this production features the squinty-eyed actor as a wounded Yankee soldier taken in by the head (Geraldine Page) of a girls' school. He becomes the catalyst for incidents of jealousy and hatred among its inhabitants, and this leads to a startling, unpredictable conclusion. Rated R. 109m. DIR: Don Siegel. CAST: Clint Eastwood, Geraldine Page, Jo Ann Harris, Elizabeth Hartman. 1971

BELARUS FILE, THE ★★½ Telly Savalas returns as the lollipop-sucking police detective Kojak in this made-for-television movie about a maniac murdering Russian survivors of a Nazi concentration camp. For fans of the series only. 95m. DIR: Robert Markowitz. CAST: Telly Savalas, Suzanne Pleshette, Max von Sydow, Herbert Berghof, George Savalas. 1986

BELLMAN AND TRUE ★★★★ This gripping crime-drama centers around a British computer genius who is forced to aid thugs in a bank heist after his son is kidnapped. Fascinating characters and suspenseful plot twists give this film depth and realism. Rated R. 114m. DIR: Richard Loncraine. CAST: Bernard Hill, Derek Newark, Richard Hope, Ken Bones, Frances Tomelty. 1988

BELOVED ROGUE ★★★★★ Superb example of the heights in set design, camera work, and special effects achieved in the late American silent cinema. John Barrymore is poet Francois Villon—here more of a Robin Hood than a brooding aesthete. Unreservedly recommended. Silent. B&W; 100m. DIR: Alan Crosland. CAST: John Barrymore, Conrad Veidt. 1927

BENEFIT OF A DOUBT ★★★ Donald Sutherland delivers a chilling performance as a man accused of murdering his wife and sent to prison for twenty years by the testimony of his daughter. Now Dad's out of prison, and Amy Irving believes that she and her son are due for a rather unpleasant visit. Good performances and crisp direction help maintain the suspense. Rated R for violence, language, and adult situations. 92m. DIR: Jonathan Heap. CAST: Donald Sutherland, Amy Irving, Graham Greene, Christopher McDonald. 1992

BEST SELLER ★★★★ James Woods and Brian Dennehy give superb performances in this gripping character study about a ruthless hit man (Woods) who convinces a Joseph Wambaugh–type cop-turned-author (Dennehy) to help him write a book. Because the book threatens to expose the illegal empire of a wealthy industrialist, the authors soon find their lives in danger. The story by Larry Cohen is outrageous at times, but the electricity generated by the stars is undeniable. Rated R for profanity and violence. 110m. DIR: John Flynn. CAST: James Woods, Brian Dennehy, Victoria Tennant, Paul Shenar. 1987

BETRAYAL OF THE DOVE ★★★ A woman and her daughter are being spooked by someone and it looks like it is her soon-to-be ex-husband. She starts to fall in love with a doctor who used to date her best friend (Kelly LeBrock), but someone is trying to kill her. The story is interesting, but LeBrock just can't act. Not rated, but contains nudity, profanity, violence, and implied sex. 94m. DIR: Strathford Hamilton. CAST: Helen Slater, Billy Zane, Kelly LeBrock, Alan Thicke, Harvey Korman, Stuart Pankin, Heather Lind. 1992

BETRAYED (1988) ★★★½ A searing performance from Debra Winger surmounts baffling inconsistencies in Joe Eszterhas's script. She's sent by mentor John Heard to infiltrate a comfortably homespun rural American community that might conceal a nest of white supremacists. Its gut-wrenching impact is repeatedly dampened by the naïve and foolish actions taken by Winger. Focus on the message and forget the story. Rated R for violence and language. 127m. DIR: Constantin Costa-Gavras. CAST: Debra Winger, Tom Berenger, John Heard, Betsy Blair, Ted Levine. 1988

BEWARE, MY LOVELY ★★★★ Robert Ryan is terrifyingly right as an amnesiac psycho who can fly into a strangling rage one minute, then return to his simpleminded handyman guise the next. Ida Lupino is also superb as the widow who hires Ryan to clean her floors, a mistake she soon regrets. Dark suspense remains taut right up to the ending. B&W; 77m. **DIR:** Harry Horner. **CAST:** Ida Lupino, Robert Ryan, Taylor Holmes, Barbara Whiting. **1952**

BEYOND A REASONABLE DOUBT (1956) ★★★ To reveal the faults of the justice system, novelist Dana Andrews allows himself to be incriminated in a murder. The plan is to reveal his innocence at the last minute. But the one man who can exonerate him is killed. Don't expect surprise, but shock! B&W; 80m. **DIR:** Fritz Lang. **CAST:** Dana Andrews, Joan Fontaine, Sidney Blackmer, Shepperd Strudwick. **1956**

BEYOND REASONABLE DOUBT (1983) ★★★ Well-crafted mystery based on the real-life conviction for double murder of an innocent New Zealand farmer. David Hemmings turns in a polished performance as a ruthless cop who engineers Thomas's conviction. 117m. **DIR:** John Laing. **CAST:** David Hemmings, John Hargreaves. **1983**

BIG FIX, THE ★★★½ Novelist Roger Simon's laid-back detective, Moses Wine, comes to the screen in this flawed thriller. The setting—which harkens back to the revolutionary 1960s—has become dated, but a murder mystery of any stripe is still suspenseful. Rated PG. 108m. **DIR:** Jeremy Paul Kagan. **CAST:** Richard Dreyfuss, Susan Anspach, Bonnie Bedelia. **1978**

BIG SLEEP, THE (1946) ★★★★½ Raymond Chandler's fans couldn't complain about this moody, atmospheric rendition of Philip Marlowe's most bizarre case. Bogart's gritty interpretation of the tough-talking P.I. is a high point in his glorious career, and sultry Lauren Bacall throws in enough spark to ignite several city blocks. Unrated, contains adult themes and violence. B&W; 114m. **DIR:** Howard Hawks. **CAST:** Humphrey Bogart, Lauren Bacall, Martha Vickers, Bob Steele, Elisha Cook Jr., Dorothy Malone. **1946**

BIG SLEEP, THE (1978) 🦃 Remake of the classic screen detective yarn. Rated R for violence, profanity, and nudity. 100m. **DIR:** Michael Winner. **CAST:** Robert Mitchum, James Stewart, Sarah Miles, Oliver Reed, Candy Clark, Edward Fox. **1978**

BIRD WITH THE CRYSTAL PLUMAGE, THE ★★★ Stylish thriller weaves a complex adventure of an American writer who witnesses a murder and is drawn into the web of mystery and violence. Minor cult favorite, well photographed and nicely acted by resilient Tony Musante and fashion plate Suzy Kendall. Rated PG. 98m. **DIR:** Dario Argento. **CAST:** Tony Musante, Suzy Kendall, Eva Renzi, Enrico Maria Salerno. **1969**

BITTER HARVEST (1993) ★★ Strange tale about a farm boy (Stephen Baldwin) corrupted by two beautiful strangers (Patsy Kensit and Jennifer Rubin). Baldwin is good, but excessive subplots lessen the film's impact. Rated R for nudity, sex, violence, and profanity. 98m. **DIR:** Duane Clark. **CAST:** Stephen Baldwin, Patsy Kensit, Jennifer Rubin, Adam Baldwin, M. Emmet Walsh. **1993**

BLACK MAGIC (1992) ★★½ Writer-director Daniel Taplitz's overly satirical tone finally mars this quirky made-for-cable tale, which turns on whether southern seductress Rachel Ward is a witch. Although the premise and performances are engaging, the story eventually spirals out of control. Rated PG-13. 94m. **DIR:** Daniel Taplitz. **CAST:** Rachel Ward, Judge Reinhold, Brion James, Anthony LaPaglia. **1992**

BLACK MAGIC WOMAN 🦃 A dreadfully boring overworking of *Fatal Attraction*. Rated R for rubbish and erotic scenes. 91m. **DIR:** Deryn Warren. **CAST:** Mark Hamill, Amanda Wyss. **1990**

BLACK RAINBOW ★★★½ A father-daughter evangelical scam takes a twist when the girl (Rosanna Arquette) actually *does* develop precognitive talents. She then claims to have pinpointed a murderer. Old-world southern decadence permeates this nifty little thriller. Rated R for nudity, violence, and profanity. 103m. **DIR:** Mike Hodges. **CAST:** Rosanna Arquette, Jason Robards Jr., Tom Hulce. **1991**

BLACK RAVEN, THE ★★ Fogbound, poverty-row, old dark house cheapie about a murder-filled night at a country inn. Interesting mainly for its cast. B&W; 64m. **DIR:** Sam Newfield. **CAST:** George Zucco, Wanda McKay, Robert Livingston, Glenn Strange. **1943**

BLACK SUNDAY (1977) ★★★ An Arab terrorist group attempts to blow up the president at a Superbowl in Miami's Orange Bowl. Tension is maintained throughout. Rated R. 143m. **DIR:** John Frankenheimer. **CAST:** Robert Shaw, Bruce Dern, Marthe Keller, Fritz Weaver. **1977**

BLACK WIDOW ★★★★ A superb thriller from director Bob Rafelson that recalls the best of the Bette Davis–Joan Crawford "bad girl" films of earlier decades. Debra Winger stars as an inquisitive federal agent who stumbles upon an odd pattern of deaths by apparently natural causes: the victims are quite wealthy, reclusive, and leave behind a young—and very rich—widow. Rated R for nudity and adult situations. 103m. **DIR:** Bob Rafelson. **CAST:** Debra Winger, Theresa Russell, Sami Frey, Dennis Hopper, Nicol Williamson, Terry O'Quinn. **1987**

BLACK WINDMILL, THE ★★★½ Straightforward story is enhanced by Don Siegel's razor-sharp direction and Michael Caine's engrossing performance as an intelligence agent whose son has been kidnapped. The suspense builds carefully to a satisfying climax. Rated R. 106m. **DIR:** Don Siegel. **CAST:** Michael Caine, Joseph O'Conor, Donald Pleasence, John Vernon, Janet Suzman, Delphine Seyrig. **1974**

BLACKMAIL (1929) ★★★ Hitchcock's first sound film stands up well when viewed today and was responsible for pushing Great Britain into the world film market. Many bits of film business that were to become Hitchcock trademarks are evident in this film, including the first of his cameo appearances. Story of a woman who faces the legal system as well as a blackmailer for murdering an attacker in self-defense was originally shot as a silent film but partially reshot and converted into England's first sound release. B&W; 86m. **DIR:** Alfred Hitchcock. **CAST:** Anny Ondra, Sara Allgood, John Longden, Charles Paton, Donald Calthrop, Cyril Ritchard. **1929**

BLACKMAIL (1991) ★★★ This made-for-cable thriller will keep you guessing. Miguel Tejada-Flores spins a complicated yarn of greed and betrayal—adapted from a short story by Bill Crenshaw—concerning two blackmailers who set up a rich wife. Farfetched, but entertaining. 96m. **DIR:** Reuben Preuss. **CAST:** Susan Blakely, Dale Midkiff, Beth Toussaint, Mac Davis, John Saxon. **1991**

BLACKOUT (1985) ★★★½ A police detective (Richard Widmark) becomes obsessed with an unsolved murder. Six years after the incident he begins to find valuable clues. This superior made-for-HBO movie has violence and profanity. 99m. **DIR:** Douglas Hickox. **CAST:** Richard Widmark, Keith Carradine, Kathleen Quinlan, Michael Beck. **1985**

BLACKOUT (1990) 🦃 A disturbed woman returns to her childhood home after receiving a letter from her missing father. Rated R for nudity and violence. 90m. **DIR:** Doug Adams. **CAST:** Carol Lynley, Gail O'Grady, Michael Keys-Hall, Joanna Miles. **1990**

BLIND SIDE ★★★½ Just-plain-folks Ron Silver and Rebecca DeMornay accidentally hit and kill a Mexican cop on a deserted, fog-enshrouded highway. After panic propels them to flee the scene, their attempts to resume normal lives are sabotaged by the arrival of smooth-talking Rutger Hauer...who seems to know far more than he openly admits. Made-for-cable psychological thriller. Rated R for profanity, violence, nudity, and simulated sex. 98m. **DIR:** Geoff Murphy. **CAST:** Rutger Hauer, Rebecca DeMornay, Ron Silver, Jonathan Banks. **1993**

BLIND VISION ★★½ Mail clerk Lenny Von Dohlen watches the voluptuous Deborah Shelton through a telescope, admiring her from afar. Little does Von Dohlen realize that he's not alone, and when one of Shelton's boyfriends ends up dead, he becomes one of the main suspects in this intriguing made-for-cable thriller. 92m. **DIR:** Shuki Levy. **CAST:** Louise Fletcher, Lenny Von Dohlen, Ned Beatty, Deborah Shelton, Robert Vaughn. **1991**

BLINDFOLD: ACTS OF OBSESSION ★★½ Only voyeurs anxious to see television star Shannen Doherty nude will enjoy this humdrum thriller. She tries to hold onto her new husband by initiating a series of progressively kinkier sexual games, while a serial killer uses the same methods on other women. Based on this evidence, Doherty won't have much of a film career. Available in R-rated and unrated versions. 93m. **DIR:** Lawrence L. Simeone. **CAST:** Judd Nelson, Shannen Doherty, Kristian Alfonso, Drew Snyder, Michael Woods. **1994**

BLINDMAN'S BLUFF ★★★ Robert Urich successfully portrays a recently blind man whose former girlfriend is about to marry his best friend. A neighbor is murdered and Urich is the main suspect. Enjoyable made-for-cable whodunit. Rated PG-13. 86m. **DIR:** James Quinn. **CAST:** Robert Urich, Lisa Eilbacher, Patricia Clarkson, Ken Pogue, Ron Perlman. **1991**

BLINDSIDED ★★½ An ex-cop turned burglar becomes blind after being shot during a setup. He goes to the ocean to recuperate and falls in love with a mysterious woman. The plot is a bit farfetched and a little hard to follow at times. Not rated, made for cable, but contains violence and suggested sex. 95m. **DIR:** Tom Donnelly. **CAST:** Jeff Fahey, Mia Sara, Rudy Ramos, Jack Kehler, Brad Hunt, Ben Gazzara. **1992**

BLINK ★★★★ Superior suspense film benefits from director Michael Apted's flair for characterization and Madeleine Stowe's powerhouse performance as a musician whose sight is restored after years of blindness. Stowe witnesses a murder, but her brain is having trouble processing visual information, and this leads to sudden flashbacks of things she's seen hours and even days before. So the police think she's a crackpot. Rated R for profanity, violence, nudity, and simulated sex. 106m. **DIR:** Michael Apted. **CAST:** Madeleine Stowe, Aidan Quinn, James Remar, Peter Friedman, Bruce A. Young, Paul Dillon, Matt Roth, Laurie Metcalf. **1994**

BLOOD AND CONCRETE, A LOVE STORY ★★ A down-and-out con man gets tangled up in the dirty dealings of an idiotic drug lord. Limp attempt to be an avant-garde film. Rated R for violence and profanity. 97m. **DIR:** Jeffrey Reiner. **CAST:** Billy Zane, Jennifer Beals, Darren McGavin, Harry Shearer. **1990**

BLOOD GAMES 🦃 Dopey, misogynistic movie about an all-female traveling softball team. Rated R for violence and nudity. 90m.

DIR: Tanya Rosenberg. **CAST:** Gregory Cummings, Laura Albert. **1990**

BLOOD RELATIVES ★★★½ Quebec inspector Donald Sutherland, investigating the murder of a teenage girl, uncovers a conspiracy involving members of the girl's family. Not one of Claude Chabrol's best, but even a lesser effort by the French Hitchcock is better than most anything else on the mystery rack. 100m. **DIR:** Claude Chabrol. **CAST:** Donald Sutherland, Aude Landry, Lisa Langlois, Stéphane Audran, Donald Pleasence, David Hemmings. **1978**

BLOOD SIMPLE ★★★★½ A slyly suspenseful, exciting (and sometimes agonizing) edge-of-your-seat story of how a bar owner (Dan Hedaya) hires a private eye (M. Emmet Walsh) to follow his wife (Frances McDormand) to find out if she's cheating on him. *Blood Simple* is defined as a "state of confusion that follows the commission of a murder, i.e., 'He's gone blood simple.' " Rated R for suggested sex, violence, and profanity. 96m. **DIR:** Joel Coen. **CAST:** John Getz, Frances McDormand, Dan Hedaya, M. Emmet Walsh. **1984**

BLOW OUT ★★★★ John Travolta and Nancy Allen are terrific in this thriller by director Brian De Palma. The story concerns a motion picture sound man (Travolta) who becomes involved in murder when he rescues a young woman (Allen) from a car that crashes into a river. It's suspenseful, thrill-packed, adult entertainment. Rated R because of sex, nudity, profanity, and violence. 107m. **DIR:** Brian De Palma. **CAST:** John Travolta, Nancy Allen, John Lithgow, Dennis Franz. **1981**

BLOW-UP ★★★★★ Director Michelangelo Antonioni's first English-language film was this stimulating examination into what is or is not reality. On its surface, a photographer (David Hemmings) believes he has taken a snapshot of a murder taking place. Vanessa Redgrave arrives at his studio and tries to seduce him out of the photo. 108m. **DIR:** Michelangelo Antonioni. **CAST:** Vanessa Redgrave, David Hemmings, Sarah Miles. **1966**

BLOWN AWAY (1992) ★★ Pedestrian thriller has Corey Haim getting involved with young and dangerous Nicole Eggert, despite the warnings of older brother Corey Feldman. It's not until Eggert goes out of control that Haim sees her true colors. Haim spends half the film out of his clothes trying to prove that he's a big boy now. Rated R for nudity, language, and violence; unrated version contains more sex. 91m./93m. **DIR:** Brenton Spencer. **CAST:** Corey Haim, Corey Feldman, Nicole Eggert, Gary Farmer, Jean Leclerc. **1992**

BLUE CITY 🦃 Estranged son Judd Nelson returns to his hometown and learns that his father, previously the mayor, has been killed. Rated R for language and violence. 83m. **DIR:** Michelle Manning. **CAST:** Judd Nelson, Ally Sheedy, David Caruso, Paul Winfield, Scott Wilson, Anita Morris. **1986**

BLUE DESERT ★★★ Two men, one a policeman and the other a drifter, court a woman who is being terrorized in a small desert town. Solid three-person thriller that keeps the viewer intrigued with plot twists galore and solid acting. Rated R for violence. 98m. **DIR:** Bradley Battersby. **CAST:** D. B. Sweeney, Courteney Cox, Craig Sheffer. **1991**

BLUE ICE ★★★½ Michael Caine's engaging lead performance as retired-spy-turned-nightclub-owner Harry Anders (he's hoping to make a franchise of this character) rises smoothly above a derivative Ron Hutchinson script that borrows quite heavily from Len Deighton's *The Ipcress File*...which also starred Caine, as another Harry (Palmer). This particular Harry, jazz lover and chef extraordinaire, gets mixed up with Sean Young, who may be more than a consul's wife. Rated R for violence, nudity, profanity, and simulated sex. 96m. **DIR:** Russell Mulcahy. **CAST:** Michael Caine, Sean Young, Ian Holm, Bob Hoskins, Bobby Short. **1993**

BLUE SUNSHINE ★★½ Oddball mystery-thriller dealing with a series of random killings. Low-budget film is both ridiculous and terrifying at the same time. Rated PG for mild language and violence. 97m. **DIR:** Jeff Lieberman. **CAST:** Zalman King, Deborah Winters, Mark Goddard, Robert Walden, Charles Siebert. **1976**

BODILY HARM ★★ A wife tries to clear her husband's name when he's sued for malpractice. Though his career has been ruined, her help is unappreciated. This dull-edged television movie does little justice to its Hitchcockian pretensions. 100m. **DIR:** Tom Wright. **CAST:** Joe Penny, Lisa Hartman, Kathleen Quinlan. **1992**

BODY CHEMISTRY 🦃 Low-budget *Fatal Attraction* simulation. Rated R for language and nudity. 85m. **DIR:** Kristine Peterson. **CAST:** Marc Singer, Mary Crosby, Joseph Campanella. **1990**

BODY CHEMISTRY 2: VOICE OF A STRANGER ★★½ Ex-cop Gregory Harrison's tunes into talk-radio psychologist Lisa Pescia. She manages to turn him on while someone else threatens to turn him *off*...forever. Good-looking cast makes up for standard-issue thrills. Rated R for nudity and violence. 88m. **DIR:** Adam Simon. **CAST:** Gregory Harrison, Lisa Pescia, Morton Downey Jr., Robin Riker. **1991**

BODY CHEMISTRY 3: POINT OF SEDUCTION ★★ More of the same as deadly sex therapist Shari Shattuck shacks up with married television producer Andrew Stevens, who is concocting a movie based on her life. Things really get complicated when Stevens's actress wife (Morgan Fairchild) wants to star in the film. Rated R for strong sexual content, adult language, and violence. 90m. **DIR:** Jim Wynorski. **CAST:** Andrew Stevens, Morgan Fairchild, Shari Shattuck, Robert Forster. **1994**

BODY DOUBLE ★★★½ This Brian De Palma thriller is often gruesome, disgusting, and exploitative. But you can't take your eyes off the screen. Craig Wasson is first-rate as a young actor who witnesses a brutal murder, and Melanie Griffith is often hilarious as the porno star who holds the key to the crime. Rated R for nudity, suggested sex, profanity, and violence. 110m. **DIR:** Brian De Palma. **CAST:** Craig Wasson, Melanie Griffith, Gregg Henry, Deborah Shelton. **1984**

BODY HEAT ★★★★½ This is a classic piece of *film noir*; full of suspense, characterization, atmosphere, and sexuality. Lawrence Kasdan makes his directorial debut with this topflight 1940s-style entertainment about a lustful romance between an attorney (William Hurt) and a married woman (Kathleen Turner) that leads to murder. Rated R because of nudity, sex, and murder. 113m. **DIR:** Lawrence Kasdan. **CAST:** William Hurt, Kathleen Turner, Richard Crenna, Mickey Rourke, Ted Danson. **1981**

BODY IN THE LIBRARY, THE ★★★½ Agatha Christie's Miss Marple (Joan Hickson) stays close to home in this mystery when she is summoned by a good friend with the misfortune to have found a body in her library at Gossington Hall, St. Mary Mead. Careful armchair sleuths will find this one solvable, but red herrings abound. Unrated; suitable for family viewing. 153m. **DIR:** Silvio Narizzano. **CAST:** Joan Hickson, Gwen Watford, Andrew Cruickshank, Moray Watson, Valentine Dyall. **1984**

BODY LANGUAGE ★★★ Heather Locklear doesn't quite fit the role of the first woman executive at a major corporation, but Linda Purl does a great job portraying the psychotic new secretary. Above-average made-for-cable thriller. 91m. **DIR:** Arthur Allan Seidelman. **CAST:** Heather Locklear, Linda Purl, Edward Albert. **1992**

BODY OF EVIDENCE ★★½ Madonna's slut-in-distress is reasonably credible in Brad Mirman's flimsy erotic thriller, which finds our heroine (?) accused of murdering her elderly lover with a most unusual weapon: herself. Rated R for profanity and nudity. 99m. **DIR:** Uli Edel. **CAST:** Madonna, Willem Dafoe, Joe Mantegna, Anne Archer, Jurgen Prochnow. **1993**

BODY OF INFLUENCE 🦃 A Beverly Hills psychiatrist falls in love with one of his sexy patients, who then tries to murder him. Rated R for simulated sex, nudity, profanity, and violence. 96m. **DIR:** Alexander Gregory Hippolyte. **CAST:** Nick Cassavetes, Shannon Whirry, Sandahl Bergman, Don Swayze, Richard Roundtree. **1993**

BODY PUZZLE ★★ Pretty ho-hum. A serial killer collects pieces of his victims and puts them together like a puzzle. Joanna Pacula may be next on the list, or the inspiration behind the gruesome crimes. Rated R for violence, nudity, and language. 90m. **DIR:** Larry Louis. **CAST:** Joanna Pacula, Tom Aaron, Frank Quinn. **1993**

BODY SHOT ★★ Underexposed thriller finds obsessed paparazzi Robert Patrick accused of murdering a reclusive rock star he previously harassed. Halfhearted attempt at film noir. Rated R for nudity, language, and violence. 98m. **DIR:** Dimitri Logothetis. **CAST:** Robert Patrick, Michelle Johnson, Ray Wise. **1993**

BORN TO KILL ★★★½ Tough film about two bad apples whose star-crossed love brings them both nothing but grief is one of the best examples of American *film noir*. Lawrence Tierney's aggressive pursuit of his wife's sister (Claire Trevor) defies description. This hardboiled crime melodrama is an early surprise from director Robert Wise. B&W; 97m. **DIR:** Robert Wise. **CAST:** Lawrence Tierney, Claire Trevor, Walter Slezak, Elisha Cook Jr., Audrey Long, Philip Terry. **1947**

BOURNE IDENTITY, THE ★★★½ Robert Ludlum's white-knuckle bestseller makes a thrilling TV miniseries starring Richard Chamberlain as an amnesiac U.S. spy dodging assassins' bullets in Europe while trying to make sense of his situation. Jaclyn Smith complicates matters as the woman he kidnaps as protection and then falls in love with. Some slow moments, but it rallies toward the end when the truth finally begins to surface. Not rated. 185m. **DIR:** Roger Young. **CAST:** Richard Chamberlain, Jaclyn Smith, Anthony Quayle, Donald Moffat, Yorgo Voyagis, Denholm Elliott. **1988**

BOYS FROM BRAZIL, THE ★★½ In this thriller, Gregory Peck plays an evil Nazi war criminal with farfetched plans to resurrect the Third Reich. Laurence Olivier as a Jewish Nazi-hunter pursues him. Rated R. 123m. **DIR:** Franklin J. Schaffner. **CAST:** Gregory Peck, Laurence Olivier, James Mason, Lilli Palmer. **1978**

BRAINWASHED ★★½ Disquieting psychological thriller about a man who is imprisoned by Nazis during World War II. Story documents his struggle to remain rational while being brainwashed by his captors. 102m. **DIR:** Gerd Oswald. **CAST:** Curt Jurgens, Claire Bloom, Hansjor Felmy, Albert Lieven. **1961**

BRASS MONKEY, THE ★★ In this British thriller we get a not-very-effective story based on a radio program. Carole Landis is a radio singer who prevents the theft of a Buddhist religious icon. The script is weak, and Landis and the other players seem bored. B&W; 84m. **DIR:** Thornton Freeland. **CAST:** Carole Landis, Carroll Levis, Herbert Lom, Avril Angers, Ernest Thesiger. **1948**

BRIDE WORE BLACK, THE ★★★★ François Truffaut pays homage to Alfred Hitchcock in this suspenseful drama about a woman who tracks down and kills a group of men who killed her husband on their wedding day. Fine Bernard Herrmann score. 95m. **DIR:** François Truffaut. **CAST:** Jeanne Moreau, Claude Rich, Jean-Claude Brialy, Michel Bouquet, Michel Lonsdale, Charles Denner. **1968**

BROKEN TRUST 🦃 Only fans of daytime television may be able to find something to salvage in this laughable story of a woman terrorized by her sister and business rivals. Rated R for nudity. 84m. **DIR:** Ralph Portillo. **CAST:** Kimberly Foster, Kathryn Harris, Nick Cassavetes, Don Swayze, Edward Arnold. **1992**

BUREAU OF MISSING PERSONS ★★★ Pat O'Brien is the whole show as a rough, wisecracking police detective, helping fugitive Bette Davis prove she is innocent of murder. Fast-paced. B&W; 73m. **DIR:** Roy Del Ruth. **CAST:** Bette Davis, Pat O'Brien, Lewis Stone, Glenda Farrell, Allen Jenkins, Hugh Herbert. **1933**

BURIED ALIVE (1990) ★★★★ Nice guy Tim Matheson is poisoned by his greedy wife (Jennifer Jason Leigh, at her nastiest) and her lover; believed dead, Matheson is buried in a cheap casket (having fortunately bypassed technicalities such as embalming). Excellent contemporary take on Poe's "Premature Burial." Made for cable. Rated R for mild violence. 93m. **DIR:** Frank Darabont. **CAST:** Tim Matheson, Jennifer Jason Leigh, William Atherton, Hoyt Axton. **1990**

BURNDOWN ★★★ This is a murder mystery with the killer the victim of radioactivity. Peter Firth is the police chief trying to solve the murders, and Cathy Moriarty is a news reporter trying to find the far more complex problem of a nuclear leak and cover-up that could be deadly to the entire town. Rated R for violence. 87m. **DIR:** James Allen. **CAST:** Peter Firth, Cathy Moriarty. **1989**

CALL ME ★★ In this silly suspense-thriller, a New York newspaper columnist (Patricia Charbonneau) mistakenly believes an obscene phone caller to be her boyfriend and soon finds herself involved with murder and mobsters. Rated R for violence, profanity, nudity, and simulated sex. 96m. **DIR:** Sollace Mitchell. **CAST:** Patricia Charbonneau, Patti D'Arbanville, Sam Freed, Boyd Gaines, Stephen McHattie, Steve Buscemi. **1988**

CALL NORTHSIDE 777 ★★★★ A Chicago reporter digs into the 11-year-old murder of a policeman and the life sentence of a possibly innocent man. Based on fact. Outstanding on-location filming. Also released as *Calling Northside 777.* B&W; 111m. **DIR:** Henry Hathaway. **CAST:** James Stewart, Richard Conte, Lee J. Cobb, Helen Walker, Betty Garde, Howard Smith, John McIntire, Paul Harvey. **1948**

CANVAS ★★½ Artist turns to a life of crime to make good on a deal his brother had with the mob. Pedestrian but watchable. Rated R for language and violence. 94m. **DIR:** Alain Zaloum. **CAST:** Gary Busey, John Rhys-Davies, Cary Lawrence. **1992**

CAPE FEAR (1962) ★★★★ Great cast in a riveting tale of a lawyer (Gregory Peck) and his family menaced by a vengeful ex-con (Robert Mitchum), who Peck helped to send up the river eight years earlier. Now he's out, with big plans for Peck's wife and especially his daughter. B&W; 106m. **DIR:** J. Lee Thompson. **CAST:** Gregory Peck, Polly Bergen, Robert Mitchum, Lori Martin, Martin Balsam, Telly Savalas, Jack Kruschen. **1962**

CAPE FEAR (1991) ★★ A profound disappointment from Martin Scorsese, this remake of J. Lee Thompson's suspense classic seems to have everything going for it: a great cast, a story by John D. MacDonald, and even cameos by stars of the original. But somehow it all boils down to Robert De Niro doing an impression of Freddy Krueger from *A Nightmare on Elm Street.* Rated R for violence and profanity. 130m. **DIR:** Martin Scorsese. **CAST:** Robert De Niro, Nick Nolte, Jessica Lange, Joe Don Baker, Robert Mitchum, Gregory Peck, Juliette Lewis, Martin Balsam, Fred Dalton Thompson. **1991**

CARDIAC ARREST ★★ Garry Goodrow, maverick detective, investigates a series of grisly murders that has the cops puzzled and the citizens of San Francisco living in fear. Rated R for violence and adult situations. 90m. **DIR:** Murphy Mintz. **CAST:** Garry Goodrow, Mike Chan, Max Gail. **1980**

CARNAL CRIMES 🦃 When a bored housewife meets a kinky photographer, she ends up taking a walk on the wild side that threatens her life and marriage. Rated R for simulated sex, nudity, violence, and profanity. 92m. **DIR:** Alexander Gregory Hippolyte. **CAST:** Linda Carol, Martin Hewitt, Rich Crater, Paula Trickey, Alex Kubik. **1992**

CAROLINE? ★★★★ *Hallmark Hall of Fame* presentation is an excellent exercise in sustained suspense. Stephanie Zimbalist is the question mark in question, the long-lost daughter who has been presumed dead for the past fifteen years. When Caroline suddenly shows up to claim the family inheritance, her very presence raises suspicions and doubts. Pamela Reed is especially effective as the newest family member who begins to realize that things are not exactly what they seem. 100m. **DIR:** Joseph Sargent. **CAST:** Stephanie Zimbalist, Pamela Reed, George Grizzard, Patricia Neal. **1989**

CAROLINE AT MIDNIGHT ★★★★ Here's an erotic thriller that really works. Timothy Daly's a journalist who receives a phone call from a deceased girlfriend and finds himself involved with the frightened wife (Mia Sara) of a dirty cop who may have been responsible for the girlfriend's death. Travis Rink's script is logical all the way to its surprising finish, and each character behaves credibly, if not always intelligently. Rated R for nudity, rape, simulated sex, profanity, and violence. 89m. **DIR:** Scott McGinnis. **CAST:** Timothy Daly, Mia Sara, Paul LeMat, Clayton Rohner, Zach Galligan, Virginia Madsen, Judd Nelson. **1993**

CARPET OF HORROR 🦃 West German detective mystery, part of the endless series of pulp crime-thrillers turned out in imitation of Edgar Wallace's potboilers. B&W; 85m. **DIR:** Harald Reinl. **CAST:** Joachim Berger, Karin Dor, Werner Peter. **1962**

CASE FOR MURDER, A ★★½ From the beginning, it's easy to spot the murderer in this plotless suspense thriller. A lawyer in a prestigious firm is murdered, and all the evidence points to his wife, who can't remember where she was that evening. The acting is decent, but the story is boring. Rated R for violence and suggested sex. 94m. **DIR:** Duncan Gibbins. **CAST:** Jennifer Grey, Peter Berg, Belinda Bauer, Eugene Roche, Robert Do Qui. **1993**

CASE OF THE LUCKY LEGS, THE ★★★★ Best entry in the Warner Bros. series of Perry Mason pictures, this has the wisecracking lawyer (Warren William) battling a perennial hangover, doctor's orders, and pesky police officers as he tries to find the murderer of a con man. B&W; 61m. **DIR:** Archie Mayo. **CAST:** Warren William, Genevieve Tobin, Patricia Ellis, Lyle Talbot, Allen Jenkins, Barton MacLane, Porter Hall, Henry O'Neill. **1935**

CASTLE IN THE DESERT ★★★ Charlie Chan travels to the middle of the Mojave Desert as the guest of a millionaire whose wife is descended from the infamous Borgias. By some odd coincidence, people begin to die by poison, and Honolulu's answer to Sherlock Holmes must solve the mystery. Full of secret panels, mysterious shadows, and close-ups of gloved hands, this is one of the best remembered and most satisfying of the later Chans, the last in the series made by Twentieth Century Fox. B&W; 61m. **DIR:** Harry Lachman. **CAST:** Sidney Toler, Arleen Whelan, Richard Derr, Douglass Dumbrille, Henry Daniell. **1942**

CAT AND THE CANARY, THE (1927) ★★★½ This is an exceptional silent version of a mystery that has been subsequently remade several times. The entire cast is wonderful as a spooky group that spends the night in a mysterious old house. Laura LaPlante is in top form. B&W; 75m. **DIR:** Paul Leni. **CAST:** Laura LaPlante, Tully Marshall, Flora Finch, Creighton Hale. **1927**

CAT AND THE CANARY, THE (1978) ★★★½ This is a surprisingly entertaining remake of the 1927 period thriller about a group of people trapped in a British mansion and murdered one by one. Rated PG. 90m. **DIR:** Radley Metzger. **CAST:** Honor Blackman, Michael Callan, Edward Fox, Wendy Hiller, Carol Lynley, Olivia Hussey. **1978**

CAT GIRL ★★ Dreary British B movie recommended only to fans of Barbara Shelley, who plays a young girl linked by a family curse to the spirit of a murderous panther. B&W; 70m. **DIR:** Alfred Shaughnessy. **CAST:** Barbara Shelley. **1957**

CAT O'NINE TAILS ★★½ One of Italian horror maestro Dario Argento's least memorable films gets bogged down in tedious plotting. Blind Karl Malden and newspaperman James Franciscus team up to find a murderer. Dubbed in English. Rated PG. 112m. **DIR:** Dario Argento. **CAST:** Karl Malden, James Franciscus, Catherine Spaak, Carlo Alighiero. **1971**

CATAMOUNT KILLING, THE 🦃 Choppy and clichéd film about the perfect crime gone sour. 82m. **DIR:** Krzysztof Zanussi. **CAST:** Horst Buchholz, Ann Wedgeworth, Polly Holliday. **1985**

CATCH ME A SPY ★★★ This is a good suspense-thriller with, surprisingly, a few laughs. The story is built around an East-West espionage theme in which both sides trade for their captured spies. Rated PG. 93m. **DIR:** Dick Clement. **CAST:** Kirk Douglas, Marlene Jobert, Trevor Howard. **1971**

CAUGHT IN THE ACT ★★½ Gregory Harrison stars as a drama teacher in this made-for-cable original. He finds an extra $10 million in his bank account and then is arrested for murder. Unfortunately, the viewer can figure out the entire plot in the first ten minutes. Rated PG-13 for violence and suggested sex. 93m. **DIR:** Deborah Reinisch. **CAST:** Gregory Harrison, Leslie Hope, Patricia Clarkson, Kimberly Scott, Kevin Tighe. **1993**

CENTER OF THE WEB 🦃 Threadbare plot about an undercover agent for the Justice Department who's framed for the assassination of a state governor. Rated R for violence, nudity, and profanity. 90m. **DIR:** David A. Prior. **CAST:** Ted Prior, Tony Curtis, Charlene Tilton, Robert Davi, Bo Hopkins, Charles Napier. **1992**

CHARADE ★★★★½ A comedy-mystery directed in the Alfred Hitchcock suspense style, this features the ever-suave Cary Grant helping widow Audrey Hepburn find the fortune stashed by her late husband. Walter Matthau, George Kennedy, and James Coburn are first-rate in support. 114m. **DIR:** Stanley Donen. **CAST:** Cary Grant,

Audrey Hepburn, Walter Matthau, James Coburn, George Kennedy. **1963**

CHARLIE CHAN AT THE OPERA ★★★½ Charlie Chan is called in to help solve the mysterious disappearance of a mental patient. Crazed baritone Boris Karloff chews up the scenery magnificently as the odds-on killer, but sly Warner Oland as Chan and Keye Luke as his number-one son hold their own in this often confusing mystery. The thirteenth film in the Fox series, this is one of the best. B&W; 68m. **DIR:** H. Bruce Humberstone. **CAST:** Warner Oland, Boris Karloff, Charlotte Henry, Keye Luke, Thomas Beck, William Demarest. **1936**

CHARLIE CHAN AT THE WAX MUSEUM ★★★ A radio broadcast from a wax museum means murder—as Charlie Chan weaves his way through false clues, false faces, and poison darts to unravel the eerie goings-on. Spooky settings and top character actors like Marc Lawrence make this one of the best of the Sidney Toler Chans made for Twentieth Century Fox. This one is compact and tantalizing. B&W; 64m. **DIR:** Lynn Shores. **CAST:** Sidney Toler, C. Henry Gordon, Marc Lawrence, Marguerite Chapman. **1949**

CHARLIE CHAN IN PARIS ★★½ Former Fu Manchu Warner Oland drew on almost twenty years of cinematic experience playing Oriental menaces to make the character of Charlie Chan uniquely his own. This seventh entry in the series shows why he succeeded so well. The Honolulu sleuth seeks the knife-wielding killer who murdered one of his agents. Chan's oldest son Lee (Keye Luke) makes his initial appearance and aids his father. The Swedish-born Oland died in 1937 after making sixteen Chan films and will always be remembered as the definitive Charlie Chan. B&W; 72m. **DIR:** Lewis Seiler. **CAST:** Warner Oland, Mary Brian, Erik Rhodes, John Miljan, Thomas Beck, Keye Luke. **1935**

CHARLIE CHAN IN RIO ★★½ The last of the better-budgeted Charlie Chans, this film was an improvement over the previous efforts. Chan (Sidney Toler) arrives in Rio de Janeiro to bring back a murderess, only to discover that she has been killed. Chan brings the killer to bay with the aid of a psychic. B&W; 60m. **DIR:** Harry Lachman. **CAST:** Sidney Toler, Mary Beth Hughes, Cobina Wright Jr., Victor Jory, Harold Huber, Richard Derr. **1941**

CHARLIE CHAN IN THE SECRET SERVICE ★★ First of Monogram Pictures's *Charlie Chan* programmers, as the poverty-row studio picked up the series from Twentieth Century Fox. A scientist working on a new explosive is murdered, and the secret service calls upon Charlie to find his killer. For die-hard fans only. B&W; 65m. **DIR:** Phil Rosen. **CAST:** Sidney Toler, Mantan Moreland, Gwen Kenyon, Benson Fong. **1944**

CHARLIE CHAN'S SECRET ★★½ Charlie Chan travels from Honolulu to San Francisco in search of a missing heir. When the heir is murdered and then mysteriously appears during a séance, Chan nabs the culprit. Sliding panels, supernatural overtones, and plenty of red herrings highlight this tenth entry in the long-running series. B&W; 72m. **DIR:** Gordon Wiles. **CAST:** Warner Oland, Rosina Lawrence, Charles Quigley, Astrid Allwyn, Jonathan Hale. **1936**

CHEAT, THE ★★★★ A socialite gambles heavily on Wall Street, loses, and borrows money from a rich Oriental. Sensational melodrama in its time, and it holds up well today. Silent. B&W; 60m. **DIR:** Cecil B. DeMille. **CAST:** Sessue Hayakawa, Fannie Ward. **1915**

CHIEFS ★★★★ An impressive cast turns in some excellent performances in this, one of the better TV miniseries. A string of unsolved murders in 1920 in a small southern town is at the base of this engrossing suspense-drama. The story follows the various police chiefs from the time of the murders to 1962 when Billy Dee Williams, the town's first black police chief, is intrigued by the case and the spell it casts over the town and its political boss (Charlton Heston). 200m. **DIR:** Jerry London. **CAST:** Charlton Heston, Wayne Rogers, Billy Dee Williams, Brad Davis, Keith Carradine, Stephen Collins, Tess Harper, Paul Sorvino, Victoria Tennant. **1985**

CHILD IN THE NIGHT ★★½ With all the devices of a murder mystery in place, the new twist to the theme in this TV movie involves *Peter Pan's* Captain Hook. A boy swears that the pirate villain had a hand in killing his father. 93m. **DIR:** Mike Robe. **CAST:** JoBeth Williams, Tom Skerritt, Elijah Wood, Darren McGavin, Season Hubley. **1990**

CHINA LAKE MURDERS, THE ★★★ This made-for-cable TV movie centers around the killings committed by a man masquerading as a California highway patrolman. Michael Parks is the killer who befriends tormented sheriff Tom Skerritt. 89m. **DIR:** Alan Metzger. **CAST:** Tom Skerritt, Michael Parks, Lauren Tewes, Nancy Everhard. **1990**

CHINA MOON ★★★★ Hotshot Florida detective Ed Harris falls in love with femme fatale Madeleine Stowe, and finds himself a suspect when her brutal husband is murdered. It's hard-boiled detective fiction in the classic vein with terrific performances and atmospheric direction. Rated R for profanity, nudity, simulated sex, and violence. 99m. **DIR:** John Bailey. **CAST:** Ed Harris, Madeleine Stowe, Benicio Del Toro, Pruitt Taylor Vince, Roger Aaron Brown, Charles Dance. **1994**

CHINA SYNDROME, THE ★★★★★ This taut thriller, about an accident at a nuclear power plant, features strong performance and solid direction. It's superb entertainment with a timely message. Rated PG. 123m. **DIR:** James Bridges. **CAST:** Jane Fonda, Jack Lemmon, Michael Douglas, Scott Brady. **1979**

CHINATOWN ★★★★★ Robert Towne's fascinating, Oscar-winning script fuels this deliciously complicated thriller. Jack Nicholson is a seedy private investigator hired for what initially seems a simple case of spousal infidelity, but rapidly escalates into a complex affair of mistaken identity and investment schemes. Faye Dunaway is the mysterious woman who may—or may not—know more than she admits. Director Roman Polanski (who turns up in a quick cameo as a knife-wielding thug) clearly respects *film noir*, but *Chinatown* is far more than mere homage; it stands on its own. Followed by a sequel, *The Two Jakes*. Rated R for language, violence, and brief nudity. 131m. **DIR:** Roman Polanski. **CAST:** Jack Nicholson, Faye Dunaway, John Huston, Perry Lopez, Diane Ladd, John Hillerman, Burt Young. **1974**

CHINESE BOXES ★★★ Arty thriller about an innocent American caught up in murderous intrigue in West Berlin. The plot is as puzzling as the game of the title. Thoughtful, patient viewers may enjoy it. Unrated; the film has violence and profanity. 87m. **DIR:** Christopher Petit. **CAST:** Will Patton, Gottfried John, Robbie Coltrane. **1984**

CHINESE CAT, THE ★★ Second entry in the Monogram run of *Charlie Chan* mystery B features. Made just as the series was running out of energy. The red herrings drop like flies as rivals battle for possession of a statuette bearing a rare diamond. B&W; 65m. **DIR:** Phil Rosen. **CAST:** Sidney Toler, Benson Fong, Joan Woodbury, Mantan Moreland, Ian Keith. **1944**

CHOOSE ME ★★★★ A feast of fine acting and deliciously different situations, this stylish independent film works on every level and proves that inventive, nonmainstream entertainment is still a viable form. Written and directed by Alan Rudolph, *Choose Me* is a funny, quirky, suspenseful, and surprising essay on love, sex, and the wacky state of male-female relationships in the 1980s. Rated R for violence and profanity. 110m. **DIR:** Alan Rudolph. **CAST:** Lesley Ann Warren, Keith Carradine, Genevieve Bujold. **1984**

CITY GIRL ★★★ A Minnesota wheat farmer marries a waitress during a visit to Chicago and brings her back to his farm. A fragmentary, tantalizing glimpse at what was almost a Murnau masterpiece. Before the film's completion Murnau was pulled from the project, and the continuity, accordingly, is choppy. Silent. B&W; 89m. **DIR:** F. W. Murnau. **CAST:** Charles Farrell, Mary Duncan, David Torrence. **1930**

CITY IN FEAR ★★★ David Janssen is excellent in his last role, a burned-out writer goaded by a ruthless publisher (Robert Vaughn). The plot concerns a mad killer on the loose in a big city. High-quality made-for-TV feature. 150m. **DIR:** Jud Taylor. **CAST:** David Janssen, Robert Vaughn, Susan Sullivan, William Prince, Perry King, William Daniels. **1980**

CLASS ACTION ★★★½ When crusading lawyer Gene Hackman agrees to represent a group of people whose cars had the unfortunate habit of exploding on impact, he's shocked to discover his daughter (Mary Elizabeth Mastrantonio) handling the defense. The most involving aspect of this predictable movie is the subplot involving the troubled father-and-daughter relationship. Rated R for profanity and violence. 106m. **DIR:** Michael Apted. **CAST:** Gene Hackman, Mary Elizabeth Mastrantonio, Colin Friels, Joanna Merlin, Larry Fishburne, Jonathan Silverman, Jan Rubes, Matt Clark, Fred Dalton Thompson. **1991**

CLIMATE FOR KILLING, A ★★★½ Effective murder mystery about a headless and handless corpse that may be linked to a murder-suicide from sixteen years before. John Beck is the dedicated sheriff's captain and Steven Bauer is the big-city detective sent to evaluate him. Rated R for violence, profanity, and nudity. 104m. **DIR:** J. S. Cardone. **CAST:** John Beck, Steven Bauer, Mia Sara, John Diehl, Katharine Ross. **1991**

CLOAK AND DAGGER (1946) ★★½ Director Fritz Lang wanted to make *Cloak and Dagger* as a warning about the dangers of the atomic age. But Warner Bros. reedited the film into a standard spy melodrama. The story has American scientist Gary Cooper, working for the OSS, sneaking into Nazi Germany to grab an Italian scientist who is helping the Nazis build the atom bomb. B&W; 106m. **DIR:** Fritz Lang. **CAST:** Gary Cooper, Lilli Palmer, Robert Alda, James Flavin, J. Edward Bromberg, Marc Lawrence. **1946**

CLOSET LAND ★★ A writer of innocuous children's books is taken from her bed and tortured by a government representative. This bizarre suspense tale is, unfortunately, message-laden. Rated R for profanity and violence. 93m. **DIR:** Radha Bharadwaj. **CAST:** Madeleine Stowe, Alan Rickman. **1991**

CLOWN MURDERS, THE 🦃 Confusing mess about a Halloween prank. Not rated, but equivalent to an R for violence, profanity, and nudity. 94m. **DIR:** Martyn Burke. **CAST:** Stephen Young, John Candy, Lawrence Dane, Al Waxman. **1975**

CODENAME: KYRIL ★★★½ When the Kremlin discovers that someone has been leaking secrets to British intelligence, an assassin (Ian Charleson) is dispatched to England to discover the traitor's identity. Edward Woodward is the laconic agent on his trail in this splendidly acted, tautly directed spy film. Made for cable. Rated R for violence. 115m. **DIR:** Ian Sharp. **CAST:** Edward Woodward, Ian Charleson, Denholm Elliott, Joss Ackland, Richard E. Grant. **1988**

COLD COMFORT ★★ A traveling salesman is rescued from certain death only to be kept prisoner by a madman as a gift to his eighteen-year-old daughter. Rated R for profanity and nudity. 88m. **DIR:** Vic Sarin. **CAST:** Maury Chaykin, Margaret Langrick. **1988**

COLD FRONT ★★★½ Martin Sheen is an L.A. cop on assignment in Vancouver who is teamed up with Michael Ontkean to solve a murder that involves a hit man who has gone berserk. Fast-paced thriller. Unrated, with violence and strong language. 94m. **DIR:** Paul Bnarbic. **CAST:** Martin Sheen, Beverly D'Angelo, Michael Ontkean, Kim Coates. **1989**

COLLECTOR, THE ★★★★½ In this chiller, Terence Stamp plays a disturbed young man who, having no friends, collects things. Unfortunately, one of the things he collects is beautiful Samantha Eggar. He keeps her as his prisoner and waits for her to fall in love with him. Extremely interesting profile of a madman. 119m. **DIR:** William Wyler. **CAST:** Terence Stamp, Samantha Eggar, Maurice Dallimore, Mona Washbourne. **1965**

COLUMBO: MURDER BY THE BOOK ★★★½ Steven Spielberg steers a winning cast through a provoking "perfect crime" script by writer Steven Bochco (*Hill Street Blues*, *L.A. Law*). As homicide detective Columbo, Peter Falk is hard-pressed to trip up smug murderer Jack Cassidy. One of the best episodes of the long-running television series. 79m. **DIR:** Steven Spielberg. **CAST:** Peter Falk, Jack Cassidy, Martin Milner, Rosemary Forsyth. **1971**

COMA ★★★½ A doctor (Genevieve Bujold) becomes curious about several deaths at a hospital where patients have all lapsed into comas. Very original melodrama keeps the audience guessing. One of Michael Crichton's better film efforts. Rated PG for brief nudity and violence. 113m. **DIR:** Michael Crichton. **CAST:** Genevieve Bujold, Michael Douglas, Richard Widmark, Rip Torn. **1978**

COMFORT OF STRANGERS, THE ★★★ Disturbing thriller follows a British couple on vacation in Venice. Film takes its time about getting to the heart of matters, but Christopher Walken's performance is especially delicious as a crazed stranger. Rated R for nudity and violence. 117m. **DIR:** Paul Schrader. **CAST:** Christopher Walken, Natasha Richardson, Rupert Everett, Helen Mirren. **1991**

COMING OUT ALIVE ★★★ Enjoyable suspense chiller involving one mother's search for her child after he's abducted by her estranged husband. Scott Hylands is wonderful in his role as a soldier-for-hire who helps her out. 77m. **DIR:** Don McBrearty. **CAST:** Helen Shaver, Scott Hylands, Michael Ironside, Anne Ditchburn, Monica Parker. **1984**

CONFLICT ★★ Humphrey Bogart wants to get rid of his wife so he can marry his mistress in this reverse rip-off of *The Postman Always Rings Twice*. A suspense film that should have been better considering the talent involved. B&W; 86m. **DIR:** Curtis Bernhardt. **CAST:** Humphrey Bogart, Alexis Smith, Rose Hobart, Sydney Greenstreet, Charles Drake, Grant Mitchell. **1945**

CONSENTING ADULTS (1992) 💔 Almost every scene in this film is telegraphed, leaving little suspense. A name cast is wasted. Rated R for profanity, nudity, and violence. 99m. **DIR:** Alan J. Pakula. **CAST:** Kevin Kline, Mary Elizabeth Mastrantonio, Kevin Spacey, Rebecca Miller, E. G. Marshall, Forest Whitaker. **1992**

CONSPIRATOR ★★½ A bride, who comes to realize her British army officer husband is a Soviet spy, is torn between love and loyalty. Wooden performances by the stars. B&W; 85m. **DIR:** Victor Saville. **CAST:** Robert Taylor, Elizabeth Taylor, Robert Flemyng, Honor Blackman, Wilfrid Hyde-White. **1949**

CONVERSATION, THE ★★★★★ Following his box-office and artistic triumph with *The Godfather*, director Francis Ford Coppola made this absorbing character study about a bugging-device expert (Gene Hackman) who lives only for his work but finds himself developing a conscience. Although not a box-office hit when originally released, this is a fine little film. Rated PG. 113m. **DIR:** Francis Ford Coppola. **CAST:** Gene Hackman, John Cazale, Allen Garfield, Cindy Williams, Harrison Ford. **1974**

COOL SURFACE, THE ★★★ In this quirky thriller, aspiring screenwriter Robert Patrick bases his new screenplay on a neighbor, an actress played by Teri Hatcher. Things really start snowballing when Hatcher attempts to land the lead in Patrick's movie and life. Change-of-pace role for Patrick, who plays a mouse ready to roar. Rated R for nudity, violence, and language. 88m. **DIR:** Erik Anjou. **CAST:** Robert Patrick, Teri Hatcher, Matt McCoy, Ian Buchanan, Cyril O'Reilly. **1993**

COP-OUT ★★ In this ambitious but shoestring-budgeted murder mystery, a detective tries to get his incarcerated brother off the hook. The resolution of this whodunit comes as no real surprise. Not rated, though there is partial nudity, violence, and considerable profanity. 102m. **DIR:** Lawrence L. Simeone. **CAST:** David D. Buff. **1991**

CORRUPT ★★ Turtle-paced psychological thriller featuring Harvey Keitel as a corrupt narcotics officer. Not rated, but equivalent to an R for violence and profanity. 99m.

DIR: Roberto Faenza. **CAST:** Harvey Keitel, John Lydon, Sylvia Sidney, Nicole Garcia. **1984**

COVER GIRL MURDERS, THE ★★½ If you like to see beautiful women in skimpy bathing suits, you'll love this made-for-cable original—just don't expect much of a plot or great acting. During a remote-island photo shoot, the cover girls are murdered one by one. Rated PG-13 for violence and an attempted rape. 87m. **DIR:** James A. Contner. **CAST:** Lee Majors, Jennifer O'Neill, Adrian Paul, Beverly Johnson, Vanessa Angel, Arthur Taxier, Bobbie Phillips, Fawna MacLaren, Mowava Pryor. **1993**

CRACK-UP ★★½ Cast against type, Pat O'Brien does a commendable job portraying an art critic investigating a forgery ring in this taut low-budget suspense-thriller. B&W; 93m. **DIR:** Irving Reis. **CAST:** Pat O'Brien, Claire Trevor, Herbert Marshall. **1946**

CRADLE WILL FALL, THE ★★ This made-for-television suspense movie falls flat. Lauren Hutton is an attorney who gets entangled with a doctor (Ben Murphy). Along comes another doctor—straight out of Dachau, one would think—who turns things upside down. The story is silly and the direction uninspired. 100m. **DIR:** John Llewellyn Moxey. **CAST:** Lauren Hutton, Ben Murphy, James Farentino, Charlita Bauer, Carolyn Ann Clark. **1983**

CRIMINAL LAW ★★½ Gary Oldman gives a strong performance in this suspense-thriller as an attorney who successfully defends accused killer Kevin Bacon. It is only after proving his client's innocence by discrediting eyewitnesses, that Oldman discovers Bacon is guilty—and intends to kill again. At first, the film bristles with tension and intelligence, yet it goes on to become predictable and ludicrous. Rated R for violence, simulated sex, and profanity. 112m. **DIR:** Martin Campbell. **CAST:** Gary Oldman, Kevin Bacon, Karen Young, Tess Harper, Joe Don Baker. **1989**

CRISS CROSS (1948) ★★★ A less than riveting plot mars this otherwise gritty *film noir*. Burt Lancaster plays an armored-car guard who, along with his less than trustworthy wife, gets involved with a bunch of underworld thugs. B&W; 87m. **DIR:** Robert Siodmak. **CAST:** Burt Lancaster, Yvonne De Carlo, Dan Duryea, Stephen McNally, Richard Long. **1948**

CROSSFIRE (1947) ★★★½ While on leave from the army, psychopathic bigot Robert Ryan meets Sam Levene in a nightclub and later murders him during an argument. An army buddy is blamed; another is also murdered. Often billed as a *film noir*, this interesting film is more of a message indicting anti-Semitism, and it was the first major Hollywood picture to explore racial bigotry. B&W; 86m. **DIR:** Edward Dmytryk. **CAST:** Robert Ryan, Robert Mitchum, Robert Young, Sam Levene, Gloria Grahame, Paul Kelly, Steve Brodie. **1947**

CRUCIFER OF BLOOD ★★½ Charlton Heston is far from believable as Sherlock Holmes in this melodramatic, yet atmospheric cable movie about a thirty-year-old curse involving a stolen treasure. Written and directed by Heston's son, Fraser. Richard Johnson fares a bit better as Dr. Watson, while Susannah Harker steals the film as their client. 105m. **DIR:** Fraser Heston. **CAST:** Charlton Heston, Richard Johnson, Susannah Harker, John Castle, Clive Wood, Simon Callow, Edward Fox. **1991**

CRUISE INTO TERROR 🦃 Dreadful suspense flick made for the tube. 100m. **DIR:** Bruce Kessler. **CAST:** Dirk Benedict, John Forsythe, Lynda Day George, Christopher George, Stella Stevens, Ray Milland, Frank Converse, Lee Meriwether, Hugh O'Brian. **1977**

CRUISING 🦃 *Cruising* is horror in the real sense of the word. Rated R. 106m. **DIR:** William Friedkin. **CAST:** Al Pacino, Paul Sorvino, Karen Allen, Richard Cox, Don Scardino. **1980**

CRUSH, THE 🦃 Trash from the very start, a teen tart from hell becomes obsessed with the hunkish, nice-guy journalist who rents her parents' guest house. Rated R for language, sexual themes, and violence. 90m. **DIR:** Alan Shapiro. **CAST:** Alicia Silverstone, Cary Elwes, Jennifer Rubin. **1993**

CRY DANGER ★★★ Dick Powell plays a wisecracking ex-con who has been framed for a robbery. Upon his release, he sets out to take revenge on the people who set him up. Rhonda Fleming is the woman he loves. Not bad! Unrated, this contains violence. B&W; 80m. **DIR:** Robert Parrish. **CAST:** Dick Powell, Rhonda Fleming, William Conrad, Richard Erdman. **1950**

CRY IN THE NIGHT, A ★★ Based on the Mary Higgins Clark bestseller, this begins as a decent mystery-thriller and soon descends into campy melodrama. Perry King is a wealthy Canadian who falls for Carol Higgins Clark, a dead ringer for his dead mama. Apt to leave you giggling. Rated PG-13 for violence. 99m. **DIR:** Robin Spry. **CAST:** Perry King, Carol Higgins Clark. **1992**

CRY OF THE INNOCENT ★★★½ This exciting made-for-TV suspense-thriller has Rod Taylor playing the grieving husband and father who loses his wife and children when a plane crashes into their summer home in Ireland. When a Dublin detective tells Taylor the crash was no accident, Taylor is determined to find out who planted the bomb in the plane. 93m. **DIR:** Michael O'Herlihy. **CAST:** Rod Taylor, Joanna Pettet, Nigel Davenport, Cyril Cusack, Jim Norton, Alexander Knox. **1980**

CRY TERROR ★★ Disappointingly slow, but well-acted BBC teleplay about a recently paroled ex-con being hounded by a vicious gang. The gang holds his brother and the patrons of a roadside garage hostage until they get the loot from a bank job the ex-con pulled. 71m. **DIR:** Robert Tronson. **CAST:** Bob Hoskins, Susan Hampshire. **1974**

CURIOSITY KILLS ★★★ C. Thomas Howell and Rae Dawn Chong help make an improbable story fascinating. He's a photographer paying the rent by working as handyman in his inner-city warehouse-turned-apartment complex; she's a neighbor who joins him to learn why a new tenant showed up so quickly after the apparent suicide of another neighbor. Rated R for violence and gore. Made for cable. 86m. **DIR:** Colin Bucksey. **CAST:** C. Thomas Howell, Rae Dawn Chong, Courteney Cox, Paul Guilfoyle. **1990**

CURSE OF THE YELLOW SNAKE, THE ★★ An Oriental death cult is on the rampage in this lively comic-strip fantasy from the pen of the incredibly prolific pulp author Edgar Wallace, whose hundreds of yarns were the foundation for a cottage industry in West German exploitation movies from the Fifties through the Seventies. B&W; 98m. **DIR:** Franz Gottlieb. **CAST:** Joachim Fuchsberger. **1963**

CUTTER'S WAY ★★★★ *Cutter's Way* comes very close to being a masterpiece. The screenplay, by Jeffrey Alan Fiskin, adapted from the novel *Cutter and Bone* by Newton Thornburg, is a murder mystery. The three lead performances are first-rate. Rated R because of violence, nudity, and profanity. 105m. **DIR:** Ivan Passer. **CAST:** Jeff Bridges, John Heard, Lisa Eichhorn, Ann Dusenberry. **1981**

D.O.A. (1949) ★★★½ CPA Edmond O'Brien, slowly dying from radiation poisoning, seeks those responsible in this fast-paced, stylized *film noir* thriller. Most unusual is the device of having the victim play detective and hunt his killers as time runs out. Neville Brand takes honors as a psychopath who tries to turn the tables on the victim before he can inform the police. B&W; 83m. **DIR:** Rudolph Maté. **CAST:** Edmond O'Brien, Pamela Britton, Luther Adler, Lynne Baggett, Neville Brand. **1949**

D.O.A. (1988) ★★ This failed update of the 1949 *film noir* classic makes the crippling mistake of hauling its Chandleresque story line into the 1980s. Dennis Quaid is the hard-drinking college professor who wakes to find he's been fatally poisoned; with mere hours to live, he drags love-struck college student Meg Ryan along on the hunt for his killer. Rated R for language and violence. 96m. **DIR:** Rocky Morton, Annabel Jankel. **CAST:** Dennis Quaid, Meg Ryan, Charlotte Rampling, Daniel Stern, Jane Kaczmarek. **1988**

DADDY'S GONE A-HUNTING ★★★ Veteran director Mark Robson knows how to get the best out of the material he has to work with. And this is an exciting, neatly crafted psychological drama—in which Carol White gets involved with a psychotic photographer (Scott Hylands). If you get a chance to go a-hunting for this one at your local video store, you won't go unrewarded. Not rated, but with some violent content. 108m. **DIR:** Mark Robson. **CAST:** Carol White, Paul Burke, Scott Hylands, Mala Powers. **1969**

DAIN CURSE, THE 🦃 A poor, two-hour version of a just passable TV miniseries based on the Dashiell Hammett classic. 123m. **DIR:** E. W. Swackhamer. **CAST:** James Coburn, Hector Elizondo, Jason Miller, Jean Simmons. **1978**

DANCE WITH DEATH ★★½ Sordid thriller with Barbara Alyn Woods as a cop who goes undercover as a stripper to flush out a killer. Getting naked was obviously a prerequisite to getting a role. Rated R for nudity, violence, and strong language. 90m. **DIR:** Charles Philip Moore. **CAST:** Maxwell Caulfield, Martin Mull, Barbara Alyn Woods, Drew Snyder. **1991**

DANCING MAN 🦃 A gigolo gets involved with a woman *and* her daughter. B&W; 64m. **DIR:** Albert Ray. **CAST:** Reginald Denny, Judith Allen, Natalie Moorhead. **1934**

DANDY IN ASPIC, A ★★ Who's on whose side? That's the question that pops up most often in this confusing, rather flat spy thriller. Laurence Harvey plays a double agent based in Berlin who is ordered to kill himself. This was director Anthony Mann's last film; he died during production and Harvey completed the direction. 107m. **DIR:** Anthony Mann. **CAST:** Laurence Harvey, Tom Courtenay, Mia Farrow, Lionel Stander, Harry Andrews. **1968**

DANGER ★★★ Three *film noir* espisodes created for television: "The Lady on the Rock," "The System," and "Death Among the Relics." Sophisticated Alfred Hitchcock–like suspense chillers. Turn down the lights. B&W; 77m. **DIR:** Sidney Lumet. **CAST:** Don Hammer, Olive Deering, Kim Stanley, Eli Wallach. **1952**

DANGEROUS GAME ★★½ Group of adventurous kids break into a large department store, but a vengeful cop enters the picture and decides to teach the rowdy youths a lesson in blue light specials. Rated R for violence. 102m. **DIR:** Stephen Hopkins. **CAST:** Steven Grives, Marcus Graham, Miles Buchanan, Kathryn Walker. **1990**

DANGEROUS HEART 🦃 In this made-for-cable original, the widow of a cop unwittingly starts dating the drug dealer who killed her husband. He only wants the money her husband stole from him. Boring, unbelievable, badly acted, and poorly written. Not rated, but contains violence and sexual situations. 95m. **DIR:** Michael Scott. **CAST:** Timothy Daly,

Lauren Holly, Jeffrey Nordling, Alice Carter, Bill Nunn. 1993

DANGEROUS MISSION ★★ In this below-average movie, Piper Laurie witnesses a mob killing in New York City and has to flee the city because the killers are after her. The chase ends at Glacier National Park. A good cast but an overdone plot. 75m. **DIR:** Louis King. **CAST:** Victor Mature, Piper Laurie, Vincent Price, William Bendix. 1954

DANGEROUS PURSUIT ★★ A nightclub waitress sleeps with a stranger for money and then realizes he is a contract killer. Three years later, after running to the other side of the United States and getting married to a cop, she discovers the stranger in her new town and that he is going to kill again. Mediocre made-for-cable thriller. 96m. **DIR:** Sandor Stern. **CAST:** Gregory Harrison, Alexandra Powers, Brian Wimmer, Scott Valentine, Robert Prosky. 1989

DANGEROUSLY CLOSE ★★ In this disappointing modern-day vigilante film, a group of students, led by a Vietnam veteran teacher, tries to purge their school of "undesirable elements" by any means necessary—including murder. Film starts out promising enough but soon loses focus with its rambling script and stereotypical situations. Rated R for profanity, violence, and brief nudity. 95m. **DIR:** Albert Pyun. **CAST:** John Stockwell, Carey Lowell, Bradford Bancroft, Madison Mason. 1986

DARK ANGEL, THE ★★★½ This episode of the PBS series *Mystery!* is eerie, edgy, and atmospheric. Based on an 1864 Sheridan Le Fanu novel which is said to have influenced Bram Stoker, this Gothic piece explores the darker side of familial ties, focusing on vices, decay, and misplaced trust. The melodrama is made memorable by the deliciously creepy performance of Peter O'Toole. 150m. **DIR:** Peter Hammond. **CAST:** Peter O'Toole, Jane Lapotaire, Alan MacNaughton, Tim Woodward. 1992

DARK FORCES ★★★ Robert Powell plays a modern-day conjurer who gains the confidence of a family by curing their terminally ill son; or does he? The evidence stacks up against Powell as we find he may be a foreign spy and stage magician extraordinaire. While uneven, this film is decent entertainment. Rated PG for brief nudity and some violence. 96m. **DIR:** Simon Wincer. **CAST:** Robert Powell, Broderick Crawford, David Hemmings, Carmen Duncan, Alyson Best. 1984

DARK JOURNEY ★★★ Espionage with a twist. A British and a German spy fall in love in Stockholm during World War I. B&W; 82m. **DIR:** Victor Saville. **CAST:** Vivien Leigh, Conrad Veidt, Joan Gardner, Anthony Bushell. 1937

DARK MIRROR, THE ★★★½ Olivia de Havilland, who did this sort of thing extremely well, plays twin sisters—one good, one evil—enmeshed in murder. Lew Ayres is the shrink who must divine who is who. Good suspense. B&W; 85m. **DIR:** Robert Siodmak. **CAST:** Olivia de Havilland, Lew Ayres, Thomas Mitchell, Richard Long. 1946

DARK PASSAGE ★★★ This is an okay Humphrey Bogart vehicle in which the star plays an escaped convict who hides out at Lauren Bacall's apartment while undergoing a face change. The stars are watchable, but the uninspired direction (including some disconcerting subjective camera scenes) and the outlandish plot keep the movie from being a real winner. B&W; 106m. **DIR:** Delmer Daves. **CAST:** Humphrey Bogart, Lauren Bacall, Bruce Bennett, Agnes Moorehead. 1947

DARK WIND ★★★ Investigating a murder on his reservation, Navajo cop Lou Diamond Phillips finds a mystery involving rival tribes, drug smugglers, and government agents. Documentary filmmaker Errol Morris approaches his material matter-of-factly, but a capable cast maintains the suspense and intrigue. Rated R for language and violence. 111m. **DIR:** Errol Morris. **CAST:** Lou Diamond Phillips, Gary Farmer, Fred Ward, Guy Boyd. 1991

DAY OF THE JACKAL, THE ★★★★ Edward Fox is a cunning assassin roaming Europe in hopes of a crack at General Charles de Gaulle. High suspense and a marvelous performance by Fox underscore a strong story line. Rated PG. 141m. **DIR:** Fred Zinnemann. **CAST:** Edward Fox, Alan Badel, Tony Britton, Cyril Cusack. 1973

DEAD AGAIN ★★★★★ For his second film as a director, British theatre wunderkind Kenneth Branagh continues to amaze with a highly stylized suspense thriller. It's a marvelous piece of pure cinema in which a Los Angeles detective (Branagh, with a flawless accent) is hired to uncover the identity of a woman (Emma Thompson) who has lost her memory. He enlists the aid of a hypnotist (Derek Jacobi), who discovers that the woman may have led a previous life, one that may have involved the detective. Either way, someone is out to kill them both. Rated R for violence. 107m. **DIR:** Kenneth Branagh. **CAST:** Kenneth Branagh, Emma Thompson, Andy Garcia, Derek Jacobi, Hanna Schygulla, Robin Williams, Campbell Scott. 1991

DEAD CALM ★★★½ A married couple (Sam Neill and Nicole Kidman) are terrorized at sea by a maniac (Billy Zane) in this intelligent, stylish thriller from Australian director Phillip Noyce. Although impressive overall, the movie has some unnecessarily explicit scenes. A near classic. Rated R for violence, profanity, nudity, and simulated sex. 95m. **DIR:** Phillip Noyce. **CAST:** Sam Neill, Nicole Kidman, Billy Zane. **1989**

DEAD CENTER ★★ Derivative thriller finds punk Justin Lazard caught between some rock and a hard place when a drug deal turns sour. He agrees to be trained by the government as a professional assassin. The only twist here is that Lazard is being set up for a fall. Rated R for violence, language, and nudity. 90m. **DIR:** Steve Carver. **CAST:** Justin Lazard, Rachel York, Eb Lottimer. **1994**

DEAD CERTAIN ★★ A psycho killer (Brad Dourif yet again) is tracked by an equally seedy cop. Better made than average, but that doesn't help the tired plot. Not rated, but an R equivalent for violence and sexuality. 93m. **DIR:** Anders Palm. **CAST:** Francesco Quinn, Brad Dourif, Karen Russell. **1990**

DEAD CONNECTION ★★½ Pedestrian thriller fails to live up to its pedigree. Instead, this is just another shaggy-dog story about a phone-sex killer and the hard-as-nails detective (Michael Madsen) intent on catching him. Lisa Bonet is the reporter who knows a hot story when she sees one. Madsen's moody performance is a treat. Rated R for violence, nudity, and language. 93m. **DIR:** Nigel Dick. **CAST:** Michael Madsen, Lisa Bonet, Gary Stretch. **1993**

DEAD EASY ★★★½ George, Alexa, and Armstrong are three friends who anger a crime boss whose overreaction sets off a chain of events that results in every small-time hood and paid killer chasing them. Well-done contemporary crime-thriller. Rated R for nudity, violence, language. 90m. **DIR:** Bert Diling. **CAST:** Scott Burgess, Rosemary Paul, Tim McKenzie. **1978**

DEAD HEAT ON A MERRY-GO-ROUND ★★★½ This thoroughly engrossing film depicts the heist of an airport bank. Not a breezy caper flick, it unfolds a complex plot in a darkly intelligent manner. The cast is impeccable. James Coburn delivers one of his most effective performances. 104m. **DIR:** Bernard Girard. **CAST:** James Coburn, Camilla Sparv, Aldo Ray, Ross Martin, Severn Darden, Robert Webber. **1966**

DEAD IN THE WATER ★★★½ Bryan Brown energizes this droll little made-for-cable thriller, as an amoral womanizer determined to plot the perfect murder—of his wife—so he can retire in comfort with his sexy secretary. Things naturally go awry, and our poor antihero finds himself suspected in a murder he *didn't* commit. Rated PG-13. Mild violence and sexual themes. 90m. **DIR:** Bill Condon. **CAST:** Bryan Brown, Teri Hatcher, Anne De Salvo, Veronica Cartwright. **1991**

DEAD OF WINTER ★★★ When aspiring actress Mary Steenburgen steps in at the last minute to replace a performer who has walked off the set of a film in production, she is certain it is the chance of a lifetime. But once trapped in a remote mansion with the creepy filmmakers, she begins to believe it may be the last act of her lifetime. The story is a bit contrived, but one only realizes it after the film is over. Rated R for profanity and violence. 98m. **DIR:** Arthur Penn. **CAST:** Mary Steenburgen, Roddy McDowall, Jan Rubes, William Russ, Ken Pogue. **1987**

DEAD ON ★★ A woman has an affair with a man and then suggests that they kill each other's spouses. If you like all sex and no plot, you'll love this. Available in R and unrated versions, both with nudity, graphic sex, violence, and profanity. 90m. **DIR:** Ralph Hemecker. **CAST:** Matt McCoy, Tracy Scoggins, Shari Shattuck, David Ackroyd, Thomas Wagner. **1993**

DEAD ON THE MONEY ★★½ Clever made-for-cable thriller has debonair Corbin Bernsen and John Glover vying for the affections of Amanda Pays, who always wanted a man who would love her to death. Too bad one of her suitors is willing to accommodate that request. 92m. **DIR:** Mark Cullingham. **CAST:** Corbin Bernsen, Amanda Pays, John Glover, Kevin McCarthy, Eleanor Parker. **1990**

DEAD RECKONING (1990) ★★★ Cliff Robertson enlivens this cat-and-mouse thriller, as the doting husband of a younger wife (Susan Blakely) who may—or may not—be conspiring with her ex-lover (Rick Springfield) to kill him. At times faintly reminiscent of Roman Polanski's *Knife in the Water* (though nowhere as subtle), this made-for-cable tale kicks into gear once our uneasy trio is stranded in an abandoned lighthouse. Rated R for considerable violence. 95m. **DIR:** Robert Lewis. **CAST:** Cliff Robertson, Susan Blakely, Rick Springfield. **1990**

DEAD RINGER ★★★ Proof positive that nobody's as good as Bette Davis when she's bad. She plays twins—one good, one bad. The bad one gets the upper hand. Bette chews the scenery with so much relish that the movie is fun to watch in spite of its ghoulish plot. B&W; 116m. **DIR:** Paul Henreid. **CAST:** Bette Davis, Peter Lawford, Karl Malden, Jean Hagen, Estelle Winwood, George Macready, Bert Remsen. **1964**

DEAD SLEEP ★★★ Australian thriller features Linda Blair as a nurse in a rather peculiar psychiatric hospital. It seems that the head doctor (Tony Bonner) keeps patients comatose to "cure" them of their day-to-day anxieties. If this weren't bad enough, he resorts to murder on the rebellious ones. Rated R for nudity, profanity, and violence. 92m. **DIR:** Alec Mills. **CAST:** Linda Blair, Tony Bonner, Andrew Booth. **1990**

DEADBOLT ★★★ Effective thriller finds student Justine Bateman looking for a roommate to help share expenses. Enter Adam Baldwin, who seems perfect. Then his true colors start shining through, and Bateman finds herself a captive in her own apartment. Baldwin is appropriately creepy. Not rated, but contains adult language and violence. 95m. **DIR:** Douglas Jackson. **CAST:** Justine Bateman, Adam Baldwin, Chris Mulkey, Michele Scarabelli. **1992**

DEADFALL ★★★ Gimmicky tale of con artists has plenty going for it, most notably director Christopher Coppola's over-the-top approach to the material. Young con artist Michael Biehn mistakenly kills his father during a sting, then teams up with his uncle and gets involved in a series of double crosses. High-rent cast keeps this one interesting. Rated R for nudity, violence, and language. 99m. **DIR:** Christopher Coppola. **CAST:** Michael Biehn, Sarah Trigger, Nicolas Cage, James Coburn, Charlie Sheen, Peter Fonda, Talia Shire. **1993**

DEADLY ALLIANCE 🦃 Two shoestring filmmakers get caught up in the dealings of a secret cartel composed of the world's seven largest oil companies. 90m. **DIR:** Paul Salvatore Parco. **CAST:** Mike Lloyd Gentry. **1975**

DEADLY COMPANION 🦃 Slow-moving, confusing film has Michael Sarrazin trying to find his wife's killer. Unrated, but contains violence and nudity. 90m. **DIR:** George Bloomfield. **CAST:** Anthony Perkins, Michael Sarrazin, Susan Clark, Howard Duff. **1986**

DEADLY DESIRE ★★★ Greed and lust rear their ugly heads in this made-for-cable thriller, about a cop-turned-private investigator (Jack Scalia) lured into a web woven by sexpot Kathryn Harrold. Nothing new here, but the performances are strong. Rated R for violence and sex. 93m. **DIR:** Charles Correll. **CAST:** Jack Scalia, Kathryn Harrold, Will Patton, Joe Santos. **1991**

DEADLY DREAMS ★★ Run-of-the-mill suspenser about a writer who dreams that the psychotic murderer who slew his parents is coming after him. Soon his dreams spill over into reality. Rated R for violence, nudity, and language. 79m. **DIR:** Kristine Peterson. **CAST:** Mitchell Anderson. **1988**

DEADLY GAMES ★★ The central motif of this goofy slasher drama is a board game. Sam Groom is excellent as the small-town cop-protagonist. R rating. 95m. **DIR:** Scott Mansfield. **CAST:** Sam Groom, Steve Railsback, Alexandra Morgan, Colleen Camp, June Lockhart, Jo Ann Harris, Dick Butkus. **1982**

DEADLY ILLUSION 🦃 An unlicensed private detective on the trail of a murderer. Rated R for violence, nudity, and profanity. 90m. **DIR:** William Tannen, Larry Cohen. **CAST:** Billy Dee Williams, Vanity, Morgan Fairchild, John Beck, Joe Cortese. **1987**

DEADLY POSSESSION ★★ This Aussie thriller presents two college students on the trail of a masked slasher plaguing downtown Adelaide. Low-budget chiller picks up pace halfway through, and then leaves several burning questions. Not rated. 99m. **DIR:** Craig Lahiff. **CAST:** Penny Cook, Anna-Maria Winchester, Olivia Hamnett. **1987**

DEAR DETECTIVE ★★½ A lighthearted film with moments of quality about a female homicide detective involved in a series of murdered local government officials, counterpointed by an amusing love interest with a mild-mannered university professor. Unrated with mild violence. Made for TV. 92m. **DIR:** Dean Hargrove. **CAST:** Brenda Vaccaro, Arlen Dean Snyder, Ron Silver, Michael MacRae, Jack Ging, M. Emmet Walsh. **1979**

DEATH AT LOVE HOUSE ★★ Much tamer than the lurid title would suggest. Robert Wagner plays a writer who becomes obsessed with a movie queen who died years earlier. This mildly suspenseful hokum is made palatable by the engaging cast. Made for TV. 78m. **DIR:** E. W. Swackhamer. **CAST:** Robert Wagner, Kate Jackson, Sylvia Sidney, Joan Blondell, Dorothy Lamour, John Carradine, Bill Macy, Marianna Hill. **1976**

DEATH BY DIALOGUE 🦃 Teenagers find a script from an old film project that was plagued with mysterious tragic accidents. Rated R for violence, profanity, and nudity. 90m. **DIR:** Tom DeWier. **CAST:** Ken Sagoes. **1988**

DEATH KISS, THE ★★★ Entertaining movie-within-a-movie whodunit is a treat for fans of early 1930s films and a pretty well-paced mystery to boot as Bela Lugosi (in fine, hammy form) is embroiled in the investigation of a murder that took place during filming. B&W; 75m. **DIR:** Edwin L. Marin. **CAST:** Bela Lugosi, David Manners, Adrienne Ames, John Wray, Vince Barnett, Edward Van Sloan. **1933**

DEATH ON THE NILE ★★★½ The second in the series of films based on the Hercule Poirot mysteries, written by Agatha Christie, is good, but nothing special. Peter Ustinov stars as the fussy Belgian detective adrift in Africa with a set of murder suspects. Despite a better-than-average Christie plot, this film, directed by John Guillermin, tends to sag here and there. Rated PG. 140m. **DIR:** John Guillermin. **CAST:** Peter Ustinov, Bette Davis, David Niven, Mia Farrow, Angela Lansbury, George Kennedy, Jack Warden. **1978**

DEATH TRAIN ★★★★ An excellent adaptation of an Alistair MacLean story about a renegade Soviet general who terrorizes the world with two nuclear bombs. One bomb is aboard a hijacked train traveling through Europe. A blend of fine acting, editing, and suspense makes for a top-notch film. Not rated, made for cable, but contains violence. 95m. **DIR:** David S. Jackson. **CAST:** Pierce Brosnan, Patrick Stewart, Alexandra Paul, Ted Levine, Christopher Lee. **1992**

DEATHTRAP ★★★ An enjoyable mystery-comedy based on the Broadway play, this Sidney Lumet film stars Michael Caine, Christopher Reeve, and Dyan Cannon. Caine plays a once-successful playwright who decides to steal a brilliant murder mystery just written by one of his students (Reeve), murder the student, and collect the royalties. Rated PG for violence and adult themes. 116m. **DIR:** Sidney Lumet. **CAST:** Michael Caine, Christopher Reeve, Dyan Cannon, Irene Worth, Henry Jones. **1982**

DECEIVED ★★★½ In this suspense thriller, Goldie Hawn finds out what happens when Mr. Right (John Heard) turns out to be the bogeyman. Director Damian Harris keeps the screws turned tight. Rated PG-13 for violence and profanity. 104m. **DIR:** Damian Harris. **CAST:** Goldie Hawn, John Heard, Robin Bartlett, Amy Wright, Jan Rubes, Kate Reid. **1991**

DECEPTION (1993) ★★½ Postcard gorgeous but empty-headed, this exotic pseudothriller is amazingly fun because it makes so little sense. When an aviation-supply vendor is burned beyond recognition in a plane crash, his wife tries to keep their business afloat. While settling bills, she finds a packet of coded baseball cards that leads to clandestine bank accounts around the world. Rated PG-13 for profanity. 95m. **DIR:** Graeme Clifford. **CAST:** Andie MacDowell, Liam Neeson, Viggo Mortensen. **1993**

DECEPTIONS 🦃 Soggy plot about a hot babe killing her husband. Made for cable. 105m. **DIR:** Reuben Preuss. **CAST:** Harry Hamlin, Robert Davi, Nicollette Sheridan. **1989**

DEEP COVER (1980) 🦃 A Soviet spy poses as a Cambridge professor. Rated R for nudity, violence, and profanity. 81m. **DIR:** Richard Loncraine. **CAST:** Tom Conti, Donald Pleasence, Denholm Elliott. **1980**

DEEP END ★★★½ A young man working in a London bathhouse becomes obsessed with a beautiful female coworker. Offbeat drama with realistic performances by the cast. Rated R. 88m. **DIR:** Jerzy Skolimowski. **CAST:** John Moulder-Brown, Jane Asher, Diana Dors. **1970**

DEEP TROUBLE ★★ In this made-for-cable original, Robert Wagner plays a deep-sea diver who happens upon an armored car, filled with diamonds, under the waves. Now he must hide the jewels, save a beautiful woman, and avenge the death of his partner. Too unbelievable to be enjoyed. Not rated, but contains violence. 95m. **DIR:** Armand Mastroianni. **CAST:** Robert Wagner, Isabelle Pasco, Jean-Yves Berteloot, Frederic Darie, Jean-François Pages, Ben Cross. **1993**

DEFENSE OF THE REALM ★★★★ In London, two reporters (Gabriel Byrne and Denholm Elliott) become convinced that a scandal involving a government official (Ian Bannen) may be a sinister cover-up. Acting on this belief puts both their lives in danger. A tough-minded British thriller that asks some thought-provoking questions. Rated PG for suspense. 96m. **DIR:** David Drury. **CAST:** Gabriel Byrne, Greta Scacchi, Denholm Elliott, Ian Bannen, Bill Paterson, Fulton MacKay. **1986**

DEFENSELESS ★★★ A successful attorney (Barbara Hershey) becomes involved with a sleazy landlord (J. T. Walsh) who is a child pornographer. Suspenseful whodunit, with Sam Shepard as a detective who investigates the landlord's mysterious murder. Rated R for violence, profanity, and murder. 104m. **DIR:** Martin Campbell. **CAST:** Barbara Hershey, Sam Shepard, Mary Beth Hurt, J. T. Walsh. **1991**

DELUSION (1980) 🦃 A nurse relates a series of murders that occurred while she cared for an elderly invalid. Rated R for violence and gore. 83m. **DIR:** Alan Beattie. **CAST:** Patricia Pearcy, David Hayward, John Dukakis, Joseph Cotten. **1980**

DESIRE AND HELL AT SUNSET MOTEL ★★★ When hot and sultry Sherilyn Fenn checks into the Sunset Motel with her husband, Whip Hubley, they get more room service than they bargained for. She wants her husband, who thinks she's fooling around, dead, and her lover, David Johansen, is willing to oblige. Director Alien Castle's film debut is a handsome, lush stab at *film noir*. Rated PG-13 for profanity and violence. 87m. **DIR:** Alien Castle. **CAST:** Sherilyn Fenn, Whip Hubley, David Hewlett, David Johansen, Paul Bartel. **1990**

DESPERATE ★★★ Tidy little chase film finds Steve Brodie and his wife Audrey Long on the lam from the law and a gang of thieves after he witnesses a warehouse robbery that results in the death of a police officer. The story is anything but new, yet director Anthony Mann breathes some life into it and keeps the level of suspense up. B&W; 73m. **DIR:** Anthony Mann. **CAST:** Steve Brodie, Audrey Long, Raymond Burr, Douglas Fowley. **1947**

DESPERATE HOURS, THE (1955) ★★★★ Three escaped convicts terrorize a suburban Indiana family; based on Joseph Hayes's novel and play. Humphrey Bogart is too old for the part that made a star of Paul Newman on Broadway, but the similarity to the *The Petrified Forest* must have been too good to pass up. Fredric March takes top acting honors. Not rated. B&W; 112m. **DIR:** William Wyler. **CAST:** Humphrey Bogart, Fredric March, Arthur Kennedy, Martha Scott, Gig Young. **1955**

DESPERATE MOTIVE ★★★½ Creepy David Keith moves into his long-lost cousin's home with hopes of moving into his life. Chilling because it seems so plausible, although successful adman William Katt is a little too trusting. Keith's economic and intent performance foils Marg Helgenberger's edgy destructiveness. Rated R for violence and profanity. 92m. **DIR:** Andrew Lane. **CAST:** David Keith, Marg Helgenberger, Mel Harris, William Katt. **1991**

DESTRUCTORS, THE ★★ Anthony Quinn plays a narcotics agent who just can't seem to get the goods on a major drug dealer (James Mason). Dated. Unrated. 89m. **DIR:** Robert Parrish. **CAST:** Michael Caine, Anthony Quinn, James Mason. **1974**

DETECTIVE, THE (1954) ★★★½ The versatile Alec Guinness is sublime in this deft film presentation of G. K. Chesterton's priest-detective in action. Here Father Brown seeks out purloined art treasures and the culprits responsible. Joan Greenwood, of the ultrathroaty voice, and the rest of the cast fit like Savile Row tailoring. Intelligent, highly entertaining fare from Britain. B&W; 91m. **DIR:** Robert Hamer. **CAST:** Alec Guinness, Joan Greenwood, Peter Finch, Bernard Lee, Sidney James. **1954**

DETOUR ★★★ This routine story about a drifter enticed into crime is skillfully constructed, economically produced, and competently acted; it has long been considered one of the best (if not *the* best) low-budget films ever made. Ann Savage as the beguiling, destructive enchantress playing off Tom Neal's infatuation rings just as true in this bargain-basement production as it does in the highly acclaimed adult crime-dramas produced by the major studios. B&W; 69m. **DIR:** Edgar G. Ulmer. **CAST:** Tom Neal, Ann Savage, Claudia Drake, Tim Ryan. **1945**

DEVIL THUMBS A RIDE, THE ★★★½ After murdering an innocent citizen during a robbery, a cold-blooded killer hitches a ride with a tipsy, unsuspecting salesman, picks up two female riders, and continues his murderous path. Nifty noir. B&W; 62m. **DIR:** Felix Feist. **CAST:** Lawrence Tierney, Ted North, Nan Leslie. **1947**

DEVLIN ★★★ Dedicated cop Bryan Brown takes quite a pounding in scripter David Taylor's twisty adaptation of Roderick Thorp's book, which finds our hero set up as the prime suspect in a highly visible political slaying. Devlin gradually works his way into a complex scheme involving departmental corruption. Totally preposterous made-for-cable mystery, but entertaining. 110m. **DIR:** Rick Rosenthal. **CAST:** Bryan Brown, Roma Downey, Lloyd Bridges, Lisa Eichhorn, Jan Rubes. **1992**

DEVLIN CONNECTION III, THE ★★ One of the *Devlin Connection* TV episodes entitled "Love, Sex, Sin and Death at Point Dume" features Rock Hudson and Jack Scalia as a father-son duo who try to find a murderer before he kills their friend (Leigh Taylor-Young). Nothing special here, folks. 50m. **DIR:** Christian I. Nyby II. **CAST:** Rock Hudson, Jack Scalia, Leigh Taylor-Young, Tina Chen. **1982**

DIAL M FOR MURDER ★★★★ Alfred Hitchcock imbues this classic thriller with his well-known touches of sustained suspense. Ray Milland is a rather sympathetic villain whose desire to inherit his wife's fortune leads him to one conclusion: murder. His plan for pulling off the perfect crime is foiled temporarily. Undaunted, he quickly switches to Plan B, with even more entertaining results. 105m. **DIR:** Alfred Hitchcock. **CAST:** Grace Kelly, Robert Cummings, Ray Milland, John Williams. **1954**

DIAMOND FLEECE, THE ★★½ An ex-convict who is a master at security systems is hired to protect a $5 million diamond. All the actors, especially Brian Dennehy, do a wonderful job, but the plot lacks depth. Made for cable. 91m. **DIR:** Al Waxman. **CAST:** Ben Cross, Kate Nelligan, Brian Dennehy, Tony Rosato. **1992**

DIAMOND TRAP, THE ★★½ A stubborn New York detective follows the trail of a femme fatale. Touches of lighthearted comedy liven this droll made-for-TV film about a $12-million diamond heist. Otherwise, this mystery has little in the way of genuine plot twists. 93m. **DIR:** Don Taylor. **CAST:** Howard Hesseman, Brooke Shields, Ed Marinaro, Darren McGavin. **1992**

DIARY OF A HITMAN 🦃 A hired killer struggles with his conscience when asked to perform his last hit on a young wife and her baby. Laughable dialogue, Forest Whitaker's Italian accent, and Sherilyn Fenn's awful acting are just three contributing factors to this mess. Rated R for violence, profanity, and nudity. 90m. **DIR:** Roy London. **CAST:** Forest Whitaker, Sherilyn Fenn, James Belushi, Lois Chiles, Sharon Stone. **1991**

DIE WATCHING 🦃 An emotionally scarred video director lures women to fake auditions where he gives them scenes worth dying for. They should have left the lens cap on. Rated R for nudity, violence, and language. 92m. **DIR:** Charles Davis. **CAST:** Christopher Atkins, Vali Ashton, Tim Thomerson. **1993**

DIRTY WORK ★★½ A gambling, crooked bail bondsman murders a drug dealer and steals his money. He doesn't realize the money is marked by a crime boss. Rated R for violence and profanity. 88m. **DIR:** John McPherson. **CAST:** Kevin Dobson, John Ashton, Donnelly Rhodes, Jim Byrnes, Mitchell Ryan. **1992**

DISAPPEARANCE OF AIMEE, THE ★★★½ Strong performers and taut direction made this one made-for-television movie that is way above average. Faye Dunaway plays preacher Aimee Semple McPherson, whose mysterious disappearance in 1926 gave rise to all sorts of speculation. A literate script, solid supporting performances by Bette Davis and James Woods, and plenty of period flavor make this one a winner. 110m. **DIR:** Anthony Harvey. **CAST:** Faye Dunaway, Bette Davis, James Woods, Severn Darden. **1976**

DISAPPEARANCE OF CHRISTINA, THE ★★★ In this made-for-cable original, an unhappy, wealthy wife disappears during a boating trip. The police think her husband killed her, while he is sure that she's still alive and is trying to drive him crazy. Interesting plot with an unexpected ending. Rated PG-13 for violence. 92m. **DIR:** Karen Arthur. **CAST:** John Stamos, Kim Delaney, C.C.H. Pounder, Robert Carradine. **1993**

DISTURBED ★★½ At first glance this film looks quite hokey, but soon the viewer starts to wonder if sex-obsessed Sandy Ramirez (Pamela Gidley) really *is* dead, or if Dr. Russell (Malcolm McDowall) is actually just going crazy. Rated R for nudity, profanity, and violence. 96m. **DIR:** Charles Winkler. **CAST:** Malcolm McDowell, Geoffrey Lewis, Priscilla Pointer, Clint Howard, Pamela Gidley. **1990**

DR. MABUSE, THE GAMBLER (PARTS I AND II) ★★★★ This is it—the granddaddy of all criminal mastermind films. The pacing, though slow and deliberate, pays off in a spectacular climax, with the evil and elusive Mabuse gone mad in a counterfeiter's cellar. Silent. B&W; Pt. One, 120m; Pt. Two, 122m. **DIR:** Fritz Lang. **CAST:** Rudolf Klein-Rogge. **1922–1923**

DOG DAY AFTERNOON ★★★★½ *Dog Day Afternoon* is a masterpiece of contemporary commentary. Al Pacino once again proves himself to be in the front rank of America's finest actors. Director Sidney Lumet scores high with masterful pacing and real suspense. This is an offbeat drama about a gay man who's involved in bank robbing. Highly recommended. Rated R. 130m. **DIR:** Sidney Lumet. **CAST:** Al Pacino, John Cazale, Charles Durning, Carol Kane, Chris Sarandon. **1975**

$ (DOLLARS) ★★★★★ Simply one of the best heist capers ever filmed. Warren Beatty, bank employee, teams with Goldie Hawn, hooker, to duplicate critical safe deposit keys for a cool $1.5 million. Intriguing concept, deftly directed in a fashion that reveals continuous unexpected plot twists. Rated R for violence and sexual situations. 119m. **DIR:** Richard Brooks. **CAST:** Warren Beatty, Goldie Hawn, Gert Fröbe, Robert Webber. **1972**

DOMINIQUE IS DEAD ★★½ Weird film from England about a greedy man attempting to rid himself of his wife in order to get his hands on her money. Of course, things don't quite work out as planned. Mildly interesting movie, also known as *Dominique*. Rated PG. 98m. **DIR:** Michael Anderson. **CAST:** Cliff Robertson, Jean Simmons, Jenny Agutter, Flora Robson, Judy Geeson. **1978**

DOMINO PRINCIPLE, THE 💔 Assassination/double-cross/conspiracy thriller. R for violence. 100m. **DIR:** Stanley Kramer. **CAST:** Gene Hackman, Richard Widmark, Candice Bergen, Eli Wallach, Mickey Rooney. **1977**

DON'T BOTHER TO KNOCK ★★★ An early and very effective performance by Marilyn Monroe as a neurotic baby-sitter who goes over the edge. Will hold your interest. Anne Bancroft's film debut. B&W; 76m. **DIR:** Roy Ward Baker. **CAST:** Richard Widmark, Marilyn Monroe, Anne Bancroft, Elisha Cook Jr. **1952**

DON'T LOOK NOW ★★★★ Excellent psychic thriller about a married couple who, just after the accidental drowning of their young daughter, start having strange occurrences in their lives. Beautifully photographed by director Nicolas Roeg. Strong performances by Julie Christie and Donald Sutherland make this film a must-see. Rated R. 110m. **DIR:** Nicolas Roeg. **CAST:** Julie Christie, Donald Sutherland. **1973**

DOOMSDAY FLIGHT, THE ★★★ Rod Serling wrote the script for this made-for-television movie, the first to depict the hijacking of an airliner. A distraught Edmond O'Brien blackmails an airline company by planting a bomb aboard a passenger plane. May not be as provocative today. Still, good acting is on hand as the search for the bomb is carried out. 100m. **DIR:** William A. Graham. **CAST:** Jack Lord, Edmond O'Brien, Van Johnson, John Saxon, Michael Sarrazin. **1966**

DOUBLE AGENTS ★★★ A German agent tries to smuggle war secrets from England to France, while British intelligence tries to discover her identity and stop her. Intricate World War II suspense-drama. Dubbed. B&W; 81m. **DIR:** Robert Hossein. **CAST:** Marina Vlady, Robert Hossein. **1959**

DOUBLE EXPOSURE (1982) ★★★½ This psychological thriller about a photographer (Michael Callan) who has nightmares of murders that come true has some pretty ghoulish scenes. The cast puts in solid performances. Not rated, the film contains violence, profanity, nudity, and adult subject matter. 95m. **DIR:** Wiliam Byron Hillman. **CAST:** Michael Callan, Joanna Pettet, James Stacy, Pamela Hensley, Cleavon Little, Seymour Cassel, Robert Tessier. **1982**

DOUBLE EXPOSURE (1993) ★★ Abusive, obsessive husband Ian Buchanan believes his lovely wife (Jennifer Gatti) is having an affair, and hires private detective Ron Perlman to investigate. When the news comes back positive, Buchanan plots to do away with his wife. When Gatti turns up dead, the plot blows up in Buchanan's face. But did he really do it? Rated R for nudity, violence, and language. 93m. **DIR:** Claudia Hoover. **CAST:** Ron Perlman, Ian Buchanan, Jennifer Gatti, Dedee Pfeiffer, James McEachin, William R. Moses. **1993**

DOUBLE INDEMNITY ★★★★★ This is one of the finest suspense films ever made. Fred MacMurray is an insurance salesman who, with Barbara Stanwyck, concocts a scheme to murder her husband and collect the benefits. The husband's policy, however, contains a rider that states that if the husband's death is caused by a moving train the policy pays double face value. Edward G. Robinson is superb as MacMurray's suspicious boss. B&W; 106m. **DIR:** Billy Wilder. **CAST:** Fred MacMurray, Barbara Stanwyck, Edward G. Robinson, Porter Hall. **1944**

DOUBLE JEOPARDY ★★ Romantic thrillers don't come much dumber than this mess, which finds Salt Lake City schoolmaster Bruce Boxleitner the sole witness to ex-girlfriend Rachel Ward's justifiable (?) murder of her violent boyfriend. Made for cable. 100m. **DIR:** Lawrence Schiller. **CAST:** Rachel Ward, Bruce Boxleitner, Sela Ward, Sally Kirkland, Jay Patterson. **1992**

DOUBLE OBSESSION ★★ *Fatal Attraction* meets *Single White Female* as college coed Margaux Hemingway falls for roommate Maryam d'Abo. When d'Abo falls in love with someone else, the fun begins. Vindictive roommates have become a genre all their own, and this entry tries to punch the right buttons, but to no avail. Over-the-top acting erases any hope. Rated R for violence, language, and nudity. 88m. **DIR:** Eduardo Montes. **CAST:** Margaux Hemingway, Maryam D'Abo, Frederic Forrest, Scott Valentine. **1992**

DOUBLE VISION 🦃 A prudish identical twin steps into her naughty sister's shoes to retrace the last days before her death. Despite a fine supporting cast, sexy Kim Cattrall can't wade through this murky murder mystery. Unrated, but contains profanity. 92m. **DIR:** Robert Knights. **CAST:** Kim Cattrall, Gale Hansen, Christopher Lee, Macha Meril. **1992**

DRAUGHTMAN'S CONTRACT, THE ★★★½ Set in 1964 in the English countryside, this stylish British production is about a rich lady (Janet Suzman) who hires an artist to make detailed drawings of her house. Then strange things begin to happen—a murder not being the least. Rated R for nudity, profanity, and violence. 103m. **DIR:** Peter Greenaway. **CAST:** Anthony Higgins, Janet Suzman. **1982**

DREAM LOVER (1986) 🦃 A struggling musician suffers bloodcurdling nightmares. Rated R for violence. 104m. **DIR:** Alan J. Pakula. **CAST:** Kristy McNichol, Ben Masters, Paul Shenar, Justin Deas, John McMartin, Gayle Hunnicutt. **1986**

DREAM LOVER (1994) ★★½ Rebounding from a divorce, Ray (James Spader) marries Lena (Madchen Amick), who seems to be the woman of his dreams. Then he finds out that her name isn't really Lena—and that's just the beginning. This psychological thriller is rather coldly calculated, but slickly made and unpredictable—it will certainly hold your interest, though you may hate yourself in the morning. Rated R for profanity and nudity. 103m. **DIR:** Nicholas Kazan. **CAST:** James Spader, Madchen Amick, Bess Armstrong, Fredric Lehne, Larry Miller, Clyde Kusatsu. **1994**

DRESSED TO KILL (1946) ★★★ Final entry in Universal's popular Rathbone/Bruce Sherlock Holmes series. This one involves counterfeiting, specifically a Bank of England plate hidden in one of three music boxes. After filming was completed, Rathbone—fearing typecasting—had had enough; his concerns clearly were genuine, as he did not work again for nearly nine years. Unrated—suitable for family viewing. B&W; 72m. **DIR:** Roy William Neill. **CAST:** Basil Rathbone, Nigel Bruce, Patricia Morison, Edmund Breon, Frederic Worlock, Harry Cording. **1946**

DRESSED TO KILL (1980) ★★★½ Director Brian De Palma again borrows heavily from Alfred Hitchcock in this story of sexual frustration, madness, and murder set in New York City. Angie Dickinson plays a sexually active housewife whose affairs lead to an unexpected conclusion. Rated R for violence, strong language, nudity, and simulated sex. 105m. **DIR:** Brian De Palma. **CAST:** Michael Caine, Angie Dickinson, Nancy Allen, Keith Gordon. **1980**

DROP DEAD GORGEOUS 🦃 Sally Kellerman's career remains in the toilet with this disaster. Made for cable. 88m. **DIR:** Paul Lynch. **CAST:** Jennifer Rubin, Peter Outerbridge, Stephen Shellen, Sally Kellerman, Michael Ironside. **1991**

DROWNING POOL, THE ★★½ Disappointing follow-up to *Harper*, with Paul Newman re-creating the title role. Director Stuart Rosenberg doesn't come up with anything fresh in this stale entry into the detective genre. Rated PG—violence. 108m. **DIR:** Stuart Rosenberg. **CAST:** Paul Newman, Joanne Woodward, Anthony Franciosa, Richard Jaeckel, Murray Hamilton, Melanie Griffith, Gail Strickland, Linda Haynes. **1976**

DUEL ★★★★★ *Duel*, an early Spielberg film, was originally a 73-minute ABC made-for-TV movie, but this full-length version was released theatrically overseas. The story is a simple one: a mild-mannered businessman (Dennis Weaver) alone on a desolate stretch of highway suddenly finds himself the unwitting prey of the maniacal driver of a big, greasy oil tanker. 91m. **DIR:** Steven Spielberg. **CAST:** Dennis Weaver, Eddie Firestone. **1971**

DUPLICATES ★★★½ Surprisingly good made-for-cable movie. A hospital in upstate New York is really a government research facility for altering criminal minds. Good acting by all—and a well-written script. 91m. **DIR:** Sandor Stern. **CAST:** Gregory Harrison, Kim Greist, Cicely Tyson, Lane Smith, Bill Lucking, Kevin McCarthy. **1992**

DYING TO REMEMBER ★★★ A fashion designer dreams about a former life in which she was murdered. She goes to San Francisco looking for answers and finds the man who may have killed her. The movie has a good suspenseful plot and is also well-acted. Rated PG-13 for violence. 87m. **DIR:** Arthur Allan Seidelman. **CAST:** Melissa Gilbert, Ted Shackelford, Scott Plank, Christopher Stone, Jay Robinson. **1993**

DYNASTY OF FEAR ★★ A slow-paced British murder mystery. An emotionally disturbed young lady is set up with psychological traps to take the blame for murder by a devious and greedy pair of lovers. Rated PG for relatively mild violence. 93m. **DIR:** Jimmy Sangster. **CAST:** Joan Collins, Peter Cushing, Judy Geeson, Ralph Bates. **1985**

EDGE OF DARKNESS (1986) ★★★★½ A complex mystery produced as a miniseries for British television. The story revolves around a nuclear processing plant and its covert government relations. Bob Peck offers an intense portrayal of a British police detective who, step-by-step, uncovers the truth as he investigates the murder of his daughter. 307m. **DIR:** Martin Campbell. **CAST:** Bob Peck, Joe Don Baker, Jack Woodson, John Woodvine, Joanne Whalley. **1986**

8 MILLION WAYS TO DIE ★★ An alcoholic ex-cop, Jeff Bridges, attempts to help a high-priced L.A. prostitute get away from her crazed Colombian coke-dealer boyfriend, Andy Garcia. Considering the talent involved, this one should have been a real killer, but there are holes in the script and dead spots throughout. Rated R for violence, nudity, and language. 115m. **DIR:** Hal Ashby. **CAST:** Jeff Bridges, Rosanna Arquette, Alexandra Paul, Andy Garcia. **1986**

11 HARROWHOUSE ★★½ Confused heist caper vacillates wildly between straight drama and dark comedy. Diamond salesman Charles Grodin is talked into stealing valuable gems. Too farfetched to be taken seriously. An excellent cast goes to waste. Rated PG—mild sexual overtones. 95m. **DIR:** Aram Avakian. **CAST:** Charles Grodin, Candice Bergen, James Mason, John Gielgud. **1974**

EMINENT DOMAIN ★★½ Unsettling political thriller with Donald Sutherland as a high-ranking official in Poland who is stripped of his power, only to get stonewalled when he attempts to find out the reason. Plenty of suspense. Rated PG-13 for profanity. 102m. **DIR:** John Irvin. **CAST:** Donald Sutherland, Anne Archer, Jodhi May, Paul Freeman. **1991**

ENDLESS NIGHT 💔 Routine suspense from the pen of Agatha Christie. Not rated; contains slight nudity and some violence. 95m. **DIR:** Sidney Gilliat. **CAST:** Hayley Mills, Hywel Bennett, Britt Ekland, George Sanders. **1972**

ENTANGLED ★★ Judd Nelson overacts his way through this thriller about a jealous American novelist involved in a romantic triangle and murder. Pierce Brosnan's charismatic performance deserves better than this amazingly transparent plot. Rated R for profanity, nudity, and violence. 98m. **DIR:** Max Fischer. **CAST:** Judd Nelson, Pierce Brosnan, Laurence Treil. **1992**

EQUUS ★★★★ Peter Firth plays a stable boy whose mysterious fascination with horses results in an act of meaningless cruelty and violence. Richard Burton plays the psychiatrist brought in to uncover Firth's hidden hostilities. The expanding of Peter Shaffer's play leaves the film somewhat unfocused but the scenes between Burton and Firth are intense, riveting, and beautifully acted. This was Burton's last quality film role; he was nominated for best actor. Rated R for profanity and nudity. 137m. **DIR:** Sidney Lumet. **CAST:** Richard Burton, Peter Firth, Colin Blakely, Joan Plowright, Harry Andrews, Eileen Atkins, Jenny Agutter. **1977**

EVERY BREATH ★★ Weak thriller runs out of breath well before the race is over. Judd Nelson stars as a young man who is seduced by a couple's looks, money, and kinky games. As he plays, he finds out that his hosts have some very weird ideas. What might have been decadent is merely docile. Rated R for nudity, adult situations, and language. 89m. **DIR:** Steve Bing. **CAST:** Judd Nelson, Joanna Pacula, Patrick Bauchau. **1993**

EVERYBODY WINS ★★½ Private eye Nick Nolte meets woman of mystery Debra Winger and finds himself drawn into her efforts to clear a man convicted of murder. The script by playwright Arthur Miller (his first since *The Misfits* in 1960) has a clever enough plot, but the dialogue is stiff, and director Karel Reisz paces the film at a reckless gallop. Rated R. 94m. **DIR:** Karel Reisz. **CAST:** Nick Nolte, Debra Winger, Will Patton, Judith Ivey, Kathleen Wilhoite, Jack Warden. **1990**

EVIL UNDER THE SUN ★★★★ This highly entertaining mystery, starring Peter Ustinov as Agatha Christie's Belgian detective Hercule Poirot, is set on a remote island in the Adriatic Sea where a privileged group gathers at a luxury hotel. Of course, someone is murdered and Poirot cracks the case.

Rated PG because of a scene involving a dead rabbit. 102m. **DIR:** Guy Hamilton. **CAST:** Peter Ustinov, Jane Birkin, Colin Blakely, James Mason, Roddy McDowall, Diana Rigg, Maggie Smith, Nicholas Clay. **1982**

EX-MRS. BRADFORD, THE ★★★★ Appealing story about physician William Powell and ex-wife Jean Arthur "keeping company" again is fast and funny. Arthur has a taste for murder mysteries and wants to write them, and Powell is attempting to help the police solve a series of murders. The pace is quick and the dialogue sparkles in this vintage gem. B&W; 80m. **DIR:** Stephen Roberts. **CAST:** William Powell, Jean Arthur, James Gleason, Eric Blore, Robert Armstrong, Lila Lee, Grant Mitchell. **1936**

EXECUTION, THE ★★ Five women survivors of the Holocaust, now living in Los Angeles, have a chance meeting with a former Nazi doctor from their camp. They plot to seduce and then kill him. There is some suspense in this made-for-TV movie, but it is too melodramatic to be believable. 100m. **DIR:** Paul Wendkos. **CAST:** Jessica Walter, Barbara Barrie, Sandy Dennis, Valerie Harper, Michael Lerner, Robert Hooks. **1985**

EXECUTIONER, THE ★★ This British spy picture features George Peppard as an intelligence agent who believes he is being compromised by fellow spy Keith Michell. Joan Collins is the love interest. Average. Rated PG. 107m. **DIR:** Sam Wanamaker. **CAST:** George Peppard, Joan Collins, Judy Geeson, Oscar Homolka, Keith Michell, Nigel Patrick. **1970**

EXPERIMENT IN TERROR ★★★½ A sadistic killer (Ross Martin) kidnaps the teenage sister (Stefanie Powers) of a bank teller (Lee Remick). An FBI agent is hot on the trail, fighting the clock. The film crackles with suspense. The acting is uniformly excellent. Martin paints an unnerving portrait of evil. B&W; 123m. **DIR:** Blake Edwards. **CAST:** Glenn Ford, Lee Remick, Stefanie Powers, Ross Martin, Ned Glass. **1962**

EXPRESS TO TERROR ★★ This mystery set on a supertrain will come in handy for those times when you're missing those old NBC *Wednesday Night at the Movies* flicks. 120m. **DIR:** Dan Curtis. **CAST:** George Hamilton, Steve Lawrence, Stella Stevens, Don Meredith, Fred Williamson, Don Stroud. **1979**

EYE OF THE NEEDLE ★★★½ In this adaptation of Ken Follett's novel, Donald Sutherland stars as the deadly Nazi agent who discovers a ruse by the Allies during World War II. Plenty of suspense and thrills for those new to the story. Rated R because of nudity, sex, and violence. 112m. **DIR:** Richard Marquand. **CAST:** Donald Sutherland, Ian Bannen, Kate Nelligan, Christopher Cazenove. **1981**

EYE OF THE STORM ★★ After witnessing his parents' brutal murder, a boy is blinded by the trauma. Raised by his older brother, the two run a Bates-type hotel. The latest unlucky boarders are an abusive drunk (Dennis Hopper) and his glitzy wife (Lara Flynn Boyle). Rated R for profanity and violence. 98m. **DIR:** Yuri Zeltser. **CAST:** Craig Sheffer, Lara Flynn Boyle, Bradley Gregg, Leon Rippy, Dennis Hopper. **1991**

EYES OF LAURA MARS, THE ★★ Laura Mars (Faye Dunaway) is a kinky commercial photographer whose photographs, which are composed of violent scenes, somehow become the blueprints for a series of actual killings. It soon becomes apparent the maniac is really after her. Although well acted and suspenseful, *The Eyes of Laura Mars* is an unrelentingly cold and gruesome movie. Rated R. 103m. **DIR:** Irvin Kershner. **CAST:** Faye Dunaway, Tommy Lee Jones, Brad Dourif, René Auberjonois. **1978**

EYES OF THE BEHOLDER ★★ Okay thriller about a doctor who performs a new radical surgery on disturbed Lenny Von Dohlen, who escapes and wreaks havoc. Pretty pedestrian, but an interesting cast keeps things merrily rolling along. Rated R for violence. 89m. **DIR:** Lawrence L. Simeone. **CAST:** Joanna Pacula, Matt McCoy, George Lazenby, Charles Napier, Lenny Von Dohlen. **1992**

EYEWITNESS ★★★★ A humdinger of a movie. William Hurt plays a janitor who, after discovering a murder victim, meets the glamorous television reporter (Sigourney Weaver) he has admired from afar. In order to prolong their relationship, he pretends to know the killer's identity—and puts both their lives in danger. Rated R for violence and profanity. 102m. **DIR:** Peter Yates. **CAST:** William Hurt, Sigourney Weaver, Christopher Plummer, James Woods. **1981**

FADE TO BLACK (1993) ★★ A professor of social anthropology videotapes a murder from his window, but the police won't believe him. He decides he must play detective with the help of his wheelchair-bound friend. A bad attempt at remaking Alfred Hitchcock's brilliant *Rear Window*. Not rated, made for cable, but contains violence. 95m. **DIR:** John McPherson. **CAST:** Timothy Busfield, Heather Locklear, Michael Beck, Louis Giambalvo, David Byron, Cloris Leachman. **1993**

FAIL-SAFE ★★★★ In this gripping film, a United States aircraft is mistakenly assigned to drop the big one on Russia, and the leaders of the two countries grapple for some kind of solution as time runs out. B&W; 111m. **DIR:** Sidney Lumet. **CAST:** Henry Fonda, Walter Matthau, Fritz Weaver, Larry Hagman, Dom DeLuise, Frank Overton. **1964**

FAIR GAME 💔 A jilted, tyrannical technowizard plans to get even with his wife. Rated R for profanity and nudity. 81m. **DIR:** Mario Orfini. **CAST:** Trudie Styler, Gregg Henry. **1990**

FALCON IN MEXICO, THE ★★ The ninth film in the long-running series finds the suave sleuth south of the border as he tries to recover a woman's portrait. The owner of the gallery where the painting was displayed has been murdered and the artist responsible for the painting was reportedly killed fifteen years earlier, but Tom Conway as the smooth Falcon untangles the mystery. B&W; 70m. **DIR:** William Berke. **CAST:** Tom Conway, Mona Maris, Nestor Paiva, Bryant Washburn. **1944**

FALCON TAKES OVER, THE ★★★ Early entry in the popular *Falcon* mystery-film series sets star George Sanders in a search for a missing woman. He encounters a good many of Hollywood's favorite character actors and actresses as well as much of the plot from Raymond Chandler's *Farewell My Lovely*, of which this is the first filmed version. B&W; 63m. **DIR:** Irving Reis. **CAST:** George Sanders, James Gleason, Ward Bond, Hans Conried, Lynn Bari. **1942**

FALCON'S BROTHER, THE ★★★ The sophisticated Falcon (played by former Saint, George Sanders) races against time to prevent the assassination of a South American diplomat. Aided by his brother (in fact Sanders's real-life brother, Tom Conway), the Falcon realizes his goal but pays with his life at the end. Brother Tom vows to continue the work his martyred sibling has left undone. This well-made, nicely acted little detective film is a true oddity. B&W; 63m. **DIR:** Stanley Logan. **CAST:** George Sanders, Tom Conway, Don Barclay, Jane Randolph, Amanda Varela. **1942**

FALSE IDENTITY ★★★ Stacy Keach returns to his home after seventeen years in prison and cannot remember many prior events. A clumsy finale is the one shortcoming of this otherwise interesting suspense-drama. Rated PG-13. 97m. **DIR:** James Keach. **CAST:** Stacy Keach, Genevieve Bujold, Veronica Cartwright. **1990**

FAMILY PLOT ★★★★ Alfred Hitchcock's last film proved to be a winner. He interjects this story with more humor than his other latter-day films. A seedy medium and her ne'er-do-well boyfriend (Barbara Harris and Bruce Dern) encounter a sinister couple (Karen Black and William Devane) while searching for a missing heir. They all become involved in diamond theft and attempted murder. Rated PG. 120m. **DIR:** Alfred Hitchcock. **CAST:** Karen Black, Bruce Dern, Barbara Harris, William Devane, Ed Lauter, Cathleen Nesbitt, Katherine Helmond. **1976**

FAN, THE ★★★½ In this fast-moving suspense yarn, a young fan is obsessed with a famous actress (Lauren Bacall). When his love letters to her are ignored, he embarks on a murder spree. *The Fan* is an absorbing thriller. The acting is first-rate and the camera work breathtaking. Rated R. 95m. **DIR:** Edward Bianchi. **CAST:** Lauren Bacall, James Garner, Maureen Stapleton, Michael Biehn. **1981**

FANTASIST, THE 🦃 A psychotic killer in Dublin sets up his victims with provocative phone calls, then kills them. Rated R for violence and nudity. 98m. **DIR:** Robin Hardy. **CAST:** Christopher Cazenove, Timothy Bottoms. **1986**

FAR FROM HOME ★★★ On vacation, pubescent Drew Barrymore and divorced dad Matt Frewer make the mistake of stopping at a trailer camp where a mad killer is at work. Off-kilter thriller with some interesting twists. Rated R for violence and nudity. 86m. **DIR:** Meiert Avis. **CAST:** Matt Frewer, Drew Barrymore, Richard Masur, Karen Austin, Susan Tyrrell, Jennifer Tilly, Dick Miller. **1988**

FAREWELL MY LOVELY ★★★★½ This superb film adaptation of Raymond Chandler's celebrated mystery novel stands as a tribute to the talents of actor Robert Mitchum. In director Dick Richards's brooding classic *film noir*, Mitchum makes a perfect, world-weary Philip Marlowe, private eye. The detective's search for the long-lost love of gangster Moose Malloy takes us into the netherworld of pre–World War II Los Angeles for a fast-paced, fascinating period piece. Rated R. 97m. **DIR:** Dick Richards. **CAST:** Robert Mitchum, Charlotte Rampling, John Ireland, Sylvia Miles, Harry Dean Stanton. **1975**

FATAL ATTRACTION (1985) ★★★½ In this suspenseful film, two people get caught up in sexual fantasy games so intense that they begin to act them out—in public. *Fatal Attraction* would receive a higher rating if it had a smoother transition from the innocent flirting to the heavy-duty sexual activity that leads to the film's thrilling and ironic close. Rated R for nudity, violence, and profanity. 90m. **DIR:** Michael Grant. **CAST:** Sally Kellerman, Stephen Lack, Lawrence Dane, John Huston. **1985**

FATAL ATTRACTION (1987) ★★★★ This adult shocker works beautifully as a nail-biting update of *Play Misty for Me*. It's the married man's ultimate nightmare. Glenn Close chews up the screen as Michael Douglas's one-night stand; when he (very married, to Anne Archer, an underappreciated talent) backs away and tries to resume his ordinary routine, Close becomes progressively more dangerous. Rated R for nudity and language. 119m. **DIR:** Adrian Lyne. **CAST:** Glenn Close, Michael Douglas, Anne Archer. **1987**

FATAL BOND 🦃 Linda Blair doesn't turn any heads in this fatally flawed thriller about a woman who suspects her lover is a serial killer. Rated R for nudity, violence, and language. 89m. **DIR:** Phil Avalon. **CAST:** Linda Blair, Jerome Elhers, Stephen Leeder, Joe Bugner, Donal Gibson. **1991**

FATAL CHARM ★★½ Did he...or didn't he? Teenaged Amanda Peterson initiates a relationship-by-mail with beguiling Christopher Atkins, sentenced and jailed—protesting his innocence all the way—for the brutal murders of numerous young women. Although Nicolas Niciphor's script tosses in a few clever twists, the ho-hum execution (director Fritz Kiersch, hiding behind a pseudonym perhaps because of studio tampering) turns this made-for-cable production into a standard, paint-by-numbers thriller. 89m. **DIR:** Alan Smithee. **CAST:** Christopher Atkins, Amanda Peterson, Mary Frann, James Remar, Andrew Robinson, Peggy Lipton. **1992**

FATAL IMAGE, THE ★★★ Watchable made-for-TV film features a Philadelphia mother-daughter team (Michele Lee and Justine Bateman) as they find romance, murder, and each other on a Parisian vacation. Bateman's obsession with her camcorder enables her to inadvertently film a murder. Now the murderer and her henchman want the videotape and are willing to kill the American tourists to get it. 96m. **DIR:** Thomas Wright. **CAST:** Michele Lee, Justine Bateman, François Dunoyer. **1990**

FATAL INSTINCT (1992) ★★½ Sexy thriller is ready-made for video, throwing sex and violence into a sordid tale of a private detective who jeopardizes everything in his life to prove the woman he loves isn't guilty. Rated R for nudity, language, and violence; unrated version contains more sexual content. 95m. **DIR:** John Dirlam. **CAST:** Michael Madsen, Laura Johnson, Tony Hamilton. **1992**

FEAR (1988) ★★★ Vicious, brutal story of four escaped convicts who go on a rampage of murder and kidnapping. Cliff De Young and Kay Lenz star as a married couple whose vacation is terrifyingly interrupted when the cons take them hostage. A surprisingly fine performance by Frank Stallone highlights this impressive study in terror. Rated R for violence and profanity. 96m. **DIR:** A. Ferretti. **CAST:** Cliff De Young, Kay Lenz, Frank Stallone. **1988**

FEAR (1990) ★★★½ Until a rather rushed climax, which culminates in a *Lady From Shanghai*-styled maze of mirrors, writer-director Rockne S. O'Bannon's deft made-for-cable thriller makes a slick showcase for star Ally Sheedy. As a psychic who "tunes in" to the thoughts of serial killers, she lives well by assisting skeptical police and then penning bestsellers based on her exploits...until she encounters a deranged killer who's *also* a psychic. Rated R for violence and nudity. 98m. **DIR:** Rockne S. O'Bannon. **CAST:** Ally Sheedy, Lauren Hutton, Michael O'Keefe, Stan Shaw. **1990**

FEAR INSIDE, THE ★★★ Christine Lahti's gripping performance lends credibility to this otherwise routine made-for-cable shocker. She plays a frantic agoraphobiac (fear of open spaces) unable to flee her home after it's invaded by a pair of nasty psychopaths. The cat-and-mouse games wear thin after a while, but Lahti definitely puts us in her corner. 105m. **DIR:** Leon Ichaso. **CAST:** Christine Lahti, Dylan McDermott, Jennifer Rubin. **1992**

FEATHERED SERPENT, THE 🦃 Charlie Chan mystery—with Roland Winters the least convincing of the movie Chans—is unwatchable. B&W; 61m. **DIR:** William Beaudine. **CAST:** Roland Winters, Keye Luke, Victor Sen Yung. **1948**

FEMME FATALE ★★ Colin Firth plays a newlywed who travels to Los Angeles to track down his runaway bride. A sordid look at L.A. nightlife is the main attraction in this otherwise routine suspense film. Rated R for nudity and violence. 96m. **DIR:** Andre Guttfreund. **CAST:** Colin Firth, Lisa Zane, Billy Zane, Scott Wilson. **1990**

FER-DE-LANCE ★★ Made-for-TV suspense film is mildly entertaining as a cargo of poisonous snakes escape aboard a crippled submarine at the bottom of the sea, making life unpleasant for all concerned. 100m. **DIR:** Russ Mayberry. **CAST:** David Janssen, Hope Lange, Jason (Herb) Evers, Ivan Dixon. **1974**

FEW GOOD MEN, A ★★★★ Calling this film the best Perry Mason movie ever made may sound like a put-down, but it isn't. Director Rob Reiner keeps the viewer guessing throughout this courtroom-based drama, which features Tom Cruise as a wisecracking navy defense lawyer whose clients have been accused of murder. The acting is first-rate—especially Jack Nicholson at his growling, maniacal best. Rated R for violence and profanity. 134m. **DIR:** Rob Reiner. **CAST:** Tom Cruise, Jack Nicholson, Demi Moore, Kevin Bacon, Kiefer Sutherland, Kevin Pollak, James Marshall, J. T. Walsh, Christopher Guest, Matt Craven, Wolfgang Bodison, Cuba Gooding Jr. **1992**

52 PICK-UP ★½ Generally unentertaining tale of money, blackmail, and pornography, as adapted from Elmore Leonard's story. Roy Scheider's secret fling with Kelly Preston leads to big-time blackmail and murder. It's more cards than Scheider could ever pick up, and a more mean and nasty movie than most people will want to watch. Rated R for nudity, profanity, simulated sex, and violence. 111m. **DIR:** John Frankenheimer. **CAST:** Roy Scheider, Ann-Margret, Vanity, John Glover, Clarence Williams III, Kelly Preston. **1986**

FINAL ANALYSIS ★★ Hitchcock meets Ken and Barbie in this silly suspense movie about a psychiatrist who becomes a murder suspect. Too serious to be funny and too campy to be believable. Rated R for violence, profanity, and nudity. 122m. **DIR:** Phil Joanou. **CAST:** Richard Gere, Kim Basinger, Uma Thurman, Eric Roberts, Paul Guilfoyle, Keith David. 1992

FINAL EMBRACE ★★½ Video director Oley Sassone treads on familiar turf, a seamy tale of murder in the music video business. Attractive cast, but there's more plot and energy in a music video. Rated R for nudity, violence, and adult language. 88m. **DIR:** Oley Sassone. **CAST:** Robert Rusler, Nancy Valen, Dick Van Patten, Linda Dona. 1992

FINAL EXTRA, THE ★★ After a star reporter is shot by an arch-criminal known as The Shadow, the case is taken over by his sister and an eager cub reporter. Obscure silent mystery will appeal only to nostalgia buffs. B&W; 75m. **DIR:** James Hogan. **CAST:** Marguerite de la Motte, Grant Withers. 1927

FINAL JUDGMENT 🦃 Brad Dourif stars as a Hollywood priest whose shady past catches up with him when he becomes the prime suspect in the murder of a stripper. Rated R for violence, nudity, and profanity. 90m. **DIR:** Louis Morneau. **CAST:** Brad Dourif, Isaac Hayes, Karen Black, Maria Ford, Orson Bean, David Ledingham. 1992

FINAL NOTICE 🦃 Failed TV pilot with Gil Gerard as a romantic private eye who has help from a stuffy yet sexy librarian (Melody Anderson). Boring made-for-cable fodder. 91m. **DIR:** Steven H. Stern. **CAST:** Gil Gerard, Melody Anderson, Jackie Burroughs, Kevin Hicks, Louise Fletcher, David Ogden Stiers, Steve Landesberg. 1989

FINAL OPTION, THE ★★★★ Judy Davis stars in this first-rate British-made suspense-thriller as the leader of a fanatical antinuclear group that takes a group of U.S. and British officials hostage and demands that a nuclear missile be launched at a U.S. base in Scotland. If not, the hostages will die. And it's up to Special Air Services undercover agent Peter Skellen (Lewis Collins) to save their lives. Rated R for violence and profanity. 125m. **DIR:** Ian Sharp. **CAST:** Judy Davis, Lewis Collins, Richard Widmark, Robert Webber, Edward Woodward. 1982

FINISHING TOUCH, THE ★★½ Soon-to-be-divorced husband-and-wife detectives are assigned to the same case, a psychotic killer who sells the videotapes of the murders. The viewer knows exactly what will happen in the unimaginative plot. Rated R for nudity, profanity, and graphic sex. 82m. **DIR:** Fred Gallo. **CAST:** Michael Nader, Shelley Hack, Arnold Vosloo, Art Evans. 1991

FIRM, THE ★★★★ Director Sydney Pollack takes the old-style Hollywood approach in this adaptation of John Grisham's bestselling suspense thriller by surrounding star Tom Cruise with a top-flight cast of supporting actors—and it works. Cruise plays an ambitious young lawyer who joins a law firm in Memphis only to find that his high salary and impressive perks come with a price: either go along with the company's corrupt dealings or become its next victim. Gripping. Rated R for profanity, violence, and suggested sex. 154m. **DIR:** Sydney Pollack. **CAST:** Tom Cruise, Gene Hackman, Jeanne Tripplehorn, Ed Harris, Holly Hunter, Hal Holbrook, David Strathairn, Wilford Brimley, Gary Busey. 1993

FIRST DEADLY SIN, THE ★★ Lawrence Sanders's excellent mystery is turned into a so-so cop flick with Frank Sinatra looking bored as aging Detective Edward X. Delaney, on the trail of a murdering maniac (David Dukes). Costar Faye Dunaway spends the entire picture flat on her back in a hospital bed. Rated R. 112m. **DIR:** Brian G. Hutton. **CAST:** Frank Sinatra, Faye Dunaway, James Whitmore, David Dukes, Brenda Vaccaro, Martin Gabel, Anthony Zerbe. 1980

FIVE FINGERS ★★★★½ James Mason, the trusted valet to the British ambassador in World War II Ankara, sells government secrets to the Germans. He gets rich but does no harm as the Germans mistakenly think he is a double agent and take no action on the material he gives them. It seems far-fetched, but it's based on fact. Wonderful suspense. Also released as *Five Fingers (Operation Cicero)*. B&W; 108m. **DIR:** Joseph L. Mankiewicz. **CAST:** James Mason, Danielle Darrieux, Michael Rennie, Walter Hampden. 1952

FLASH OF GREEN, A ★★★½ This is a compelling adaptation of John D. MacDonald's novel about a small-town Florida reporter (Ed Harris) whose boredom, lust, and curiosity lead him into helping an ambitious, amoral county official (Richard Jordan) win approval for a controversial housing project. The acting is superb. 118m. **DIR:** Victor Nunez. **CAST:** Ed Harris, Blair Brown, Richard Jordan, George Coe, Isa Thomas, William Mooney, Joan Goodfellow, Helen Stenborg, John Glover. 1984

FLASHPOINT ★★★½ Kris Kristofferson and Treat Williams star in this taut, suspenseful, and action-filled thriller as two Texas-border officers who accidentally uncover an abandoned jeep containing a skeleton, a rifle, and $800,000 in cash—a discovery that puts their lives in danger. Rated PG-13 for profanity and violence. 95m. **DIR:** William Tannen. **CAST:** Kris Kristofferson, Treat Williams, Rip Torn, Kevin Conway, Tess Harper. 1984

FLATLINERS ★★★ In this morbid but compelling thriller a group of medical students experiment with death. They kill each other one by one and then are brought back to life. But things don't work out as they expect. Rated R. 111m. **DIR:** Joel Schumacher. **CAST:** Kiefer Sutherland, Julia Roberts, Kevin Bacon, William Baldwin, Oliver Platt. 1990

FLETCH ★★★★ Chevy Chase is first-rate as Gregory McDonald's wisecracking reporter, I. M. "Fletch" Fletcher, who starts out doing what seems to be a fairly simple exposé of drug dealing in Los Angeles and ends up taking on a corrupt cop (Joe Don Baker), a tough managing editor (Richard Libertini), and a powerful millionaire (Tim Matheson) who wants Fletch to kill him. The laughs are plenty and the action almost nonstop. Rated PG for violence and profanity. 96m. **DIR:** Michael Ritchie. **CAST:** Chevy Chase, Joe Don Baker, Tim Matheson, Dana Wheeler-Nicholson, Richard Libertini, M. Emmet Walsh. **1985**

FLETCH LIVES ★★★½ Chevy Chase returns to the role of I. M. Fletcher and scores another triumph. In this one, Fletch finds himself heir to a southern plantation and quits his newspaper job—only to become both a murder suspect and a target for unscrupulous villains. If you enjoyed the original *Fletch*, this sequel is guaranteed to satisfy. Rated PG. 98m. **DIR:** Michael Ritchie. **CAST:** Chevy Chase, Cleavon Little, Hal Holbrook, Julianne Phillips, Richard Libertini, Randall "Tex" Cobb, George Wyner. **1989**

FLOWERS IN THE ATTIC ★★½ After the death of their father, four children are taken (by their mother) to live with their religious-zealot grandmother and dying grandfather. The kids are locked into the attic of the family mansion because of some dark family secrets. Louise Fletcher chews up the scenery as the domineering grandmother in this adaptation of V. C. Andrews's gothic horror novel. Rated PG-13. 92m. **DIR:** Jeffrey Bloom. **CAST:** Louise Fletcher, Victoria Tennant, Kristy Swanson, Jeb Adams. **1987**

FOG ISLAND ★★ This *Old Dark House* rip-off from poverty row's Monogram Pictures never takes off, but mystery and suspense buffs should enjoy its rare teaming of genre veterans George Zucco and Lionel Atwill. B&W; 72m. **DIR:** Terry Morse. **CAST:** George Zucco, Veda Ann Borg, Lionel Atwill, Jerome Cowan. **1945**

FOLLOW ME QUIETLY ★★★ Low-budget thriller about a deranged killer who strangles people when it rains. Tight, fast-moving detective drama with standout performances. B&W; 60m. **DIR:** Richard Fleischer. **CAST:** William Lundigan, Dorothy Patrick, Jeff Corey. **1949**

FOOL KILLER, THE ★★ Set in the 1800s, this is a tale of a mischievous young runaway who learns about a legendary killer—who may well be his new traveling companion. A shivery variation on *Huckleberry Finn*. Unrated. B&W; 100m. **DIR:** Servando Gonzalez. **CAST:** Anthony Perkins, Edward Albert, Dana Elcar, Salome Jens, Henry Hull. **1967**

FOREIGN CORRESPONDENT ★★★★★ Classic Alfred Hitchcock thriller still stands as one of his most complex and satisfying films. Joel McCrea stars as an American reporter in Europe during the war, caught up in all sorts of intrigue, romance, etc., in his dealings with Nazi spies, hired killers, and the like as he attempts to get the truth to the American public. B&W; 120m. **DIR:** Alfred Hitchcock. **CAST:** Joel McCrea, Laraine Day, Herbert Marshall, George Sanders, Edmund Gwenn. **1940**

FORGOTTEN ONE, THE ★★½ Unusual romantic triangle, in which novelist Terry O'Quinn moves into a house haunted by a ghost from his past life. The ghost attempts to have O'Quinn kill himself, so that they may be together in the afterlife. Kristy McNichol contributes a fine performance. Rated R for nudity and profanity. 89m. **DIR:** Phillip Badger. **CAST:** Terry O'Quinn, Kristy McNichol. **1989**

FORMULA, THE ★★ Take a plot to conceal a method of producing enough synthetic fuel to take care of the current oil shortage and add two superstars like George C. Scott and Marlon Brando. Sounds like the formula for a real blockbuster, doesn't it? Unfortunately, it turns out to be the formula for a major disappointment. Rated R. 117m. **DIR:** John G. Avildsen. **CAST:** George C. Scott, Marlon Brando, Marthe Keller, John Gielgud, G. D. Spradlin. **1980**

FOURTH PROTOCOL, THE ★★★ Michael Caine is the best component of this stiff screen version of Frederick Forsyth's thriller. Caine is a British agent who suspects "something big" is being smuggled into England; his guess is accurate, and he discovers an atomic-bomb delivery is being supervised by ultracool Russian agent Pierce Brosnan. Rated R for violence, nudity, and language. 119m. **DIR:** John Mackenzie. **CAST:** Michael Caine, Pierce Brosnan, Joanna Cassidy, Ned Beatty. **1987**

FOURTH STORY ★★★ Mark Harmon's amiable private detective lands a most intriguing case when a puzzled woman (Mimi Rogers) hires him to find her husband...who simply vanished after breakfast one morning. Although the finale is somewhat clumsy in this made-for-cable thriller, getting there is quite fun. Rated PG-13 for brief nudity. 91m. **DIR:** Ivan Passer. **CAST:** Mark Harmon, Mimi Rogers, Paul Gleason, Michael Patrick Boatman, Cliff De Young, M. Emmet Walsh. **1991**

FRANTIC (1988) ★★★½ Director Roman Polanski bounces back with this clever and often darkly funny Hitchcockian thriller, which makes Harrison Ford a stranger in the very strange underbelly of Paris. He's a surgeon visiting the city to lecture at a medical conference; when his wife (Betty Buckley) vanishes from their hotel room, he confronts indifference through official channels before trying to puzzle things out on his own. Inexplicably rated R for minimal violence. 120m. **DIR:** Roman Polanski. **CAST:** Harrison Ford, Emmanuelle Seigner, Betty Buckley, John Mahoney, David Huddleston. **1988**

FRENZY ★★★★½ *Frenzy* marks a grand return to one of Hitchcock's favorite themes: that of a man accused of a murder he did not commit and all but trapped by the circumstantial evidence. Rated R. 116m. **DIR:** Alfred Hitchcock. **CAST:** Jon Finch, Barry Foster, Barbara Leigh-Hunt, Anna Massey, Alec McCowen. **1972**

FROM HOLLYWOOD TO DEADWOOD ★★★ Two loser detectives need to score a case or give it up. Finding a missing starlet leaving a trail of blackmail and murder may be too much for them. Offbeat mystery. Rated R for violence and language. 96m. **DIR:** Rex Pickett. **CAST:** Scott Paulin, Jim Haynie, Barbara Schock. **1989**

FUNERAL IN BERLIN ★★★½ Second in Michael Caine's series of three "Harry Palmer" films, following *The Ipcress File* and preceding *The Billion-Dollar Brain*. This time, working-class spy Palmer assists in the possible defection of a top Russian security chief (Oscar Homolka). As usual, Caine can do no wrong; his brittle performance and the authentic footage of the Berlin Wall add considerably to the film's bleak tone. Unrated; suitable for family viewing. 102m. **DIR:** Guy Hamilton. **CAST:** Michael Caine, Oscar Homolka, Eva Renzi, Paul Hubschmid, Guy Doleman. **1967**

F/X ★★★½ In this fast-paced, well-acted suspense-thriller, Bryan Brown plays special-effects wizard Rollie Tyler, who accepts thirty thousand dollars from the Justice Department's Witness Relocation Program to stage the fake assassination of a mob figure who has agreed to name names. After he successfully fulfills his assignment, Tyler is double-crossed and must use his wits and movie magic to survive. Rated R for profanity, suggested sex, and violence. 110m. **DIR:** Robert Mandel. **CAST:** Bryan Brown, Brian Dennehy, Diane Venora, Cliff De Young, Mason Adams, Jerry Orbach. **1986**

F/X 2: THE DEADLY ART OF ILLUSION ★★★ Special-effects expert Bryan Brown gets himself into trouble again when he agrees to help a police officer catch a serial killer. With the help of ex-cop Brian Dennehy and some of his own movie magic, Brown outwits the bad guys in this fast-paced, enjoyable, and never-believable-for-a-minute sequel. Rated PG-13 for violence, nudity, and profanity. 104m. **DIR:** Richard Franklin. **CAST:** Bryan Brown, Brian Dennehy, Rachel Ticotin, Joanna Gleason, Philip Bosco, Kevin J. O'Connor, Tom Mason. **1991**

GANGSTER STORY ★★★ Walter Matthau ventured behind the camera for the first and only time to make this B movie about a smooth operator who gets in over his head with a treacherous mobster. Just as you'd expect from Matthau, this quirky *noir* exercise has a strong vein of dry humor (beginning with the theme song, "The Itch for Scratch"). B&W; 66m. **DIR:** Walter Matthau. **CAST:** Walter Matthau, Carol Grace. **1960**

GASLIGHT (1940) ★★★★ The first version of Patrick Hamilton's play is much tighter and more suspenseful than the version starring Ingrid Bergman. Diana Wynyard isn't as good as Bergman, but Anton Walbrook is much more sinister than Charles Boyer as the scheming husband trying to drive his wife insane. This British-made version was supposedly destroyed so as not to compete with the Hollywood version. Bits and pieces of surviving prints were edited together and a new negative made. B&W; 84m. **DIR:** Thorold Dickinson. **CAST:** Anton Walbrook, Diana Wynyard, Robert Newton. **1940**

GASLIGHT (1944) ★★★★ Ingrid Bergman won her first Academy Award as the innocent young bride who, unfortunately, marries Charles Boyer. Boyer is trying to persuade her she is going insane. Many consider this the definitive psychological thriller. B&W; 114m. **DIR:** George Cukor. **CAST:** Ingrid Bergman, Joseph Cotten, Charles Boyer, Angela Lansbury. **1944**

GENUINE RISK ★★★½ Losers caught in a love triangle tangle in this neat homage to Forties crime-boss pictures. The film is ragged, but it's also erotic and occasionally funny. Rated R for profanity, nudity, and violence. 86m. **DIR:** Kurt Voss. **CAST:** Terence Stamp, Michelle Johnson. **1990**

GEORGIA ★★★½ Intense psychological drama. Judy Davis stars in dual roles as a successful attorney investigating her own mother's accidental drowning and as the mother, a photographer. While attempting to find out more, she runs into some deadly roadblocks. Davis is powerfully mesmerizing as both a professional woman and a free spirit whose acquaintances are at the core of this mystery. Unrated, but contains violence and adult situations. 90m. **DIR:** Ben Lewin. **CAST:** Judy Davis, John Bach, Julia Blake, Alex Menglet, Marshall Naper. **1987**

GIRL HUNTERS, THE ★★½ Mickey Spillane plays his creation Mike Hammer in this unusual detective film about a private eye who pulls himself together after a seven-year binge, when he discovers that the woman he thought he sent to her death might still be alive. Lloyd Nolan and Shirley Eaton are the only real actors in this uneven production—the rest of the cast are Spillane's cronies, and many of his favorite bars and hangouts are carefully re-created in this British-made film. 103m. **DIR:** Roy Rowland. **CAST:** Mickey Spillane, Shirley Eaton, Lloyd Nolan, Hy Gardner, Scott Peters. **1963**

GIRL ON A SWING, THE ★★★½ In this atmospheric, and sensual suspense-thriller, a young executive travels to Amsterdam, where he falls in love with a woman who may be a murderer. Rated R for nudity, profanity, and violence. 119m. **DIR:** Gordon Hessler. **CAST:** Meg Tilly, Rupert Frazer. **1989**

GIRL TO KILL FOR, A A sociopathic heiress manipulates a naïve college student into killing her strict guardian. Rated R for nudity, profanity, and violence. 89m. **DIR:** Richard Oliver. **CAST:** Karen Medak, Sasha Jeason, Karen Austin, Alex Cord, Rod McCary. **1990**

GLASS KEY, THE ★★★★ Solid version of Dashiell Hammett's excellent novel has Alan Ladd as the bodyguard to politician Brian Donlevy, who is accused of murder. It's up to Ladd to get him off, and he has to take on vicious gangsters to get the job done. Fine work by everyone involved makes this a cinematic gem. B&W; 85m. **DIR:** Stuart Heisler. **CAST:** Brian Donlevy, Alan Ladd, Veronica Lake, William Bendix. **1942**

GLITTER DOME, THE ★★½ Made-for-HBO cable version of Joseph Wambaugh's depressingly downbeat story concerning two police detectives in Los Angeles, James Garner and John Lithgow, out to solve a murder. Both cops appear on the edge of losing control. 90m. **DIR:** Stuart Margolin. **CAST:** James Garner, Margot Kidder, John Lithgow, Colleen Dewhurst, John Marley. **1985**

GLITZ Drearily botched TV adaptation of excellent Elmore Leonard crime novel, with Jimmy Smits ineffective as Miami Beach detective. 96m. **DIR:** Sandor Stern. **CAST:** Jimmy Smits, Markie Post, John Diehl. **1988**

GOOD SON, THE ★★★ Against-the-grain casting makes this updated *Bad Seed* a kinky hoot. Cutie-pie Macaulay Culkin stars in his first R-rated movie as a wicked, psychotic child whose cousin temporarily moves in after his mother dies. This psychological thriller delivers some creepy chills as Culkin escorts his new pal to the edge of hell. Going *Home Alone* again will never be the same. Rated R for profanity and violence. 87m. **DIR:** Joseph Ruben. **CAST:** Macaulay Culkin, Elijah Wood, Quinn Culkin, Wendy Crewson. **1993**

GOOSE WOMAN, THE ★★★ Unusual drama, based on a novel by Rex Beach: a famous opera star, after giving birth to an illegitimate son, loses her standing and is reduced to poverty and drink. A contrived ending mars an otherwise sensitive outing for Louise Dresser and then-young director Clarence Brown. Silent. B&W; 90m. **DIR:** Clarence Brown. **CAST:** Louise Dresser, Jack Pickford, Constance Bennett. **1925**

GORKY PARK ★★½ In this maddeningly uninvolving screen version of Martin Cruz Smith's bestselling mystery novel, three mutilated bodies are found in the Moscow park, and it's up to Russian policeman Arkady Renko (a miscast William Hurt) to find the maniacal killer. Lee Marvin is quite good as a suave bad guy, as are Joanna Pacula and Brian Dennehy. Rated R for nudity, sex, violence, and profanity. 128m. **DIR:** Michael Apted. **CAST:** William Hurt, Lee Marvin, Joanna Pacula, Brian Dennehy, Ian Bannen, Alexander Knox. **1983**

GOTCHA! ★★★★ In this entertaining mixture of coming-of-age comedy and suspense-thriller, a college boy (Anthony Edwards) goes to Paris in search of romance and adventure. He gets both when he meets a beautiful, mysterious woman (Linda Fiorentino) who puts both of their lives in danger. Rated PG-13 for slight nudity, suggested sex, profanity, and violence. 97m. **DIR:** Jeff Kanew. **CAST:** Anthony Edwards, Linda Fiorentino, Alex Rocco, Nick Corri, Marla Adams, Klaus Lowitsch. **1985**

GOTHAM ★★ A *film noir* thriller that's confusing, slow, and tediously melodramatic. Tommy Lee Jones is a Marlowesque detective hired as a go-between for a well-to-do husband and his murdered wife (Virginia Madsen). Romantically atmospheric and beautifully photographed, the film is marred by terrible dialogue and anemic acting. Rated R for nudity, simulated sex, violence, and profanity. 92m. **DIR:** Lloyd Fonvielle. **CAST:** Tommy Lee Jones, Virginia Madsen, Frederic Forrest. **1988**

GRANDMA'S HOUSE ★★★½ Two orphaned teens sent to live with their grandparents suspect that this seemingly kindly old couple have a few skeletons in the closet. Cleverly written thriller has more than its share of surprises. Unrated, but violence makes this unsuitable for kids. 89m. **DIR:** Peter Rader. **CAST:** Eric Foster, Kim Valentine, Brinke Stevens. **1989**

GRAVE SECRETS: THE LEGACY OF HILLTOP DRIVE ★★ The paranormal goings-on in this made-for-TV movie are pretty mild. Too much of a resemblance to the ghost story classic *Poltergeist*. 94m. **DIR:** John Patterson. **CAST:** Patty Duke, David Soul, David Selby, Keirsten Warren, Kimberly Cullum. **1992**

GREAT RIVIERA BANK ROBBERY, THE ★★★½ In 1976, a group of French right-wing terrorists called "The Chain," with the assistance of a gang of thieves, pulled off one of the largest heists in history. The step-by-step illustration of this bold operation proves to be interesting, and the fact that this incident really happened makes this film all the more enjoyable. 98m. **DIR:** Francis Megahy. **CAST:** Ian McShane, Warren Clarke, Stephen Greif, Christopher Malcolm. **1979**

GREAT TRAIN ROBBERY, THE ★★★★ Based on a true incident, this suspense-filled caper has plenty of hooks to keep you interested. Sean Connery is dashing and convincing as mastermind Edward Pierce. Lesley-Anne Down is stunning as his mistress, accomplice, and disguise expert. Add a pinch of Donald Sutherland as a boastful pickpocket and cracksman, and you have a trio of crooks that can steal your heart. Rated PG. 111m. **DIR:** Michael Crichton. **CAST:** Sean Connery, Lesley-Anne Down, Donald Sutherland, Alan Webb. **1979**

GREEN ARCHER ★★ Detective Spike Holland tries to unravel the mystery of Garr Castle after he is called in to investigate the disappearance of Valerie Howett's sister, Elaine. Lots of sliding panels and silhouettes of the phantom bowman in this slow-moving chapterplay. B&W; 15 chapters. **DIR:** James W. Horne. **CAST:** Victor Jory, Iris Meredith, James Craven, Robert Fiske. **1940**

GREEN ICE ★★ Unconvincing tale of an emerald theft in Colombia. Ryan O'Neal engineers the robbery. Rated PG. 115m. **DIR:** Ernest Day. **CAST:** Ryan O'Neal, Anne Archer, Omar Sharif. **1981**

GREEN MAN, THE ★★★½ Albert Finney chews up the scenery in great style as an alcoholic innkeeper who tantalizes guests by suggesting that his bed-and-breakfast is haunted...and then discovers, with shock, that his unlikely yarns may have come true. A darkly comic novel by Kingsley Amis is the inspiration for this made-for-TV tale. Definitely not for the prudish. 150m. **DIR:** Elijah Moshinsky. **CAST:** Albert Finney, Michael Hordern, Sarah Berger, Linda Marlowe. **1991**

GROUND ZERO ★★½ Political thriller that lacks the strike capability to give it a complete victory. While a cameraman investigates his father's death, he stumbles onto a cover-up by the British and Australian governments involving nuclear testing in the Fifties. Aborigines, political influence, corruption, murder, and genocide are just some of the fallout from his investigation. Just enough to keep you interested, but ultimately misses the target. Rated PG-13 for violence and profanity. 100m. **DIR:** Michael Pattinson, Bruce Myles. **CAST:** Colin Friels, Jack Thompson, Donald Pleasence. **1988**

GUN CRAZY (1950) ★★★½ Young man obsessed by guns teams up with a carnival sharpshooter who leads him into a life of robbery and murder. This odd little cult classic is fast and lean. MacKinlay Kantor wrote the original story and cowrote the screenplay. B&W; 86m. **DIR:** Joseph H. Lewis. **CAST:** Peggy Cummins, John Dall, Morris Carnovsky. **1950**

HALF-MOON STREET ★★ Half-baked adaptation of Paul Theroux's *Doctor Slaughter*, which was equally flawed as a novel. Sigourney Weaver stars as an American abroad who decides to supplement her academic (but low-paid) government position by moonlighting as a sophisticated "escort." Rated R for nudity and sexual themes. 90m. **DIR:** Bob Swaim. **CAST:** Sigourney Weaver, Michael Caine, Patrick Kavanagh. **1986**

HAMMETT ★★ A disappointing homage to mystery writer Dashiell Hammett, this Wim Wenders–directed and Francis Ford Coppola–meddled production was two years in the making and hardly seems worth it. The plot is nearly incomprehensible, something that could never be said of the real-life Hammett's works (*The Maltese Falcon*, *The Thin Man*, etc.). Rated PG. 97m. **DIR:** Wim Wenders. **CAST:** Frederic Forrest, Peter Boyle, Marilu Henner, Elisha Cook Jr., R. G. Armstrong. **1982**

HAND THAT ROCKS THE CRADLE, THE ★★★½ Once you get past the utterly disgusting first ten minutes, this becomes an effective little suspense tale of a woman who gets revenge for her husband's death by posing as a nanny. Rebecca DeMornay is chilling as the menacing cradle rocker. Rated R for violence, profanity, and nudity. 110m. **DIR:** Curtis Hanson. **CAST:** Annabella Sciorra, Rebecca DeMornay, Matt McCoy, Ernie Hudson, John de Lancie. **1992**

HANDS OF A STRANGER ★★ Mediocre remake of *The Hands of Orlac*, the old chestnut about a pianist who receives the hands of a murderer after his own are mangled in an accident. The preposterously purple dialogue is a hoot. B&W; 86m. **DIR:** Newt Arnold. **CAST:** Paul Lukather, Joan Harvey, Irish McCalla, Barry Gordon. **1962**

HARDCORE ★★ This film stars George C. Scott as Jake Van Dorn, whose family leads a church-oriented life in their home in Grand Rapids, Michigan. When the church sponsors a youth trip to California, Van Dorn's daughter Kristen (Ilah Davis) is allowed to go. She disappears, so Van Dorn goes to Los Angeles and learns she's now making porno flicks. *Hardcore* is rated R, but is closer to an X. 108m. **DIR:** Paul Schrader. **CAST:** George C. Scott, Peter Boyle, Season Hubley, Dick Sargent. **1979**

HARPER ★★★★½ Ross MacDonald's detective, Lew Archer, undergoes a name change but still survives as a memorable screen character in the capable hands of Paul Newman. This one ranks right up there with *The Maltese Falcon*, *The Big Sleep* (the Humphrey Bogart version), *Farewell My Lovely*, and *The Long Goodbye* as one of the best of its type. 121m. **DIR:** Jack Smight. **CAST:** Paul Newman, Lauren Bacall, Shelley Winters, Arthur Hill, Julie Harris, Janet Leigh, Robert Wagner. **1966**

HARVEST, THE ★★½ While in Mexico investigating a series of killings, screenwriter Miguel Ferrer is abducted and drugged. When he awakens he finds out that one of his kidneys has been removed. Now black-market organ dealers want his second kidney. Interesting idea gets only a modicum of suspense from writer-director David Marconi, while familiar faces do their best to flesh out the background. Rated R for violence and language. 97m. **DIR:** David Marconi. **CAST:** Miguel Ferrer, Harvey Fierstein, Leilani Sarelle, Anthony Denison, Tim Thomerson, Henry Silva. **1992**

HATBOX MYSTERY, THE ★★ In a scant 44 minutes private detective Tom Neal saves his secretary from prison, brings the guilty party to bay, and still has time to explain just what happened. Not great but a real curio, perhaps the shortest detective film ever sold as a feature. B&W; 44m. **DIR:** Lambert Hillyer. **CAST:** Tom Neal, Pamela Blake, Allen Jenkins, Virginia Sale. **1947**

HAUNTING OF SARAH HARDY, THE ★★★ A suspense story of a recently married heiress who returns to her estate after a fifteen-year absence. Fairly standard TV film. 92m. **DIR:** Jerry London. **CAST:** Sela Ward, Michael Woods, Roscoe Born, Morgan Fairchild, Polly Bergen. **1989**

HAWK, THE ★★★ A wife who was once institutionalized starts to think her husband is a serial killer. Is she going crazy again, or is she right? The plot has a few good twists, but it's too easy to figure out. Rated R for profanity and violence. 84m. **DIR:** David Hayman. **CAST:** Helen Mirren, George Costigan, Rosemary Leach, Owen Teale, Melanie Hill. **1992**

HE WALKED BY NIGHT ★★★★½ Richard Basehart is superb in this documentary-style drama as a killer stalked by methodical policemen. A little-known cinematic gem, it's first-rate in every department and reportedly inspired Jack Webb to create *Dragnet*. B&W; 79m. **DIR:** Alfred Werker, Anthony Mann. **CAST:** Richard Basehart, Scott Brady, Jack Webb, Roy Roberts, Whit Bissell. **1948**

HEAR NO EVIL ★★★½ A deaf athletic trainer finds herself living a nightmare after a client plants a rare coin on her. Restaurant owner D. B. Sweeney tries to help while becoming sensitized to her handicap. The deaf angle gives this thriller a decent edge, but it's too predictable to be totally gripping. Rated R for violence and profanity. 98m. **DIR:** Robert Greenwald. **CAST:** Marlee Matlin, D. B. Sweeney, Martin Sheen. **1993**

HEART OF MIDNIGHT ★★★ What begins as a disturbing haunted-house movie becomes a chilling whodunit. Jennifer Jason Leigh inherits a dilapidated ballroom with a steamy past. Grippingly weird. Rated R. 95m. **DIR:** Matthew Chapman. **CAST:** Jennifer Jason Leigh, Peter Coyote, Frank Stallone, Brenda Vaccaro. **1989**

HENNESSY ★★★ After his family is killed by a bomb, an Irishman plots to assassinate the Queen of England in revenge. Fairly suspenseful thriller with a sympathetic performance by Rod Steiger, though the fact that we know the queen is still alive tends to ruin the suspense. Rated PG. 103m. **DIR:** Don Sharp. **CAST:** Rod Steiger, Lee Remick, Richard Johnson, Trevor Howard, Eric Porter. **1975**

HIDDEN OBSESSION ★★ A news anchorwoman, stalked by an obsessive fan, falls for the likable deputy next door, but is he really what he seems? Slow. Rated R for nudity, violence, and simulated sex. 92m. **DIR:** John Stewart. **CAST:** Jan-Michael Vincent, Heather Thomas, Nicholas Celozzi. **1993**

HIDER IN THE HOUSE ★★ Unfortunately Gary Busey's wonderful portrayal of an ex-convict who builds a secret room in a stranger's house is not enough to save this poorly written film. Good cast, but just too unbelievable. Rated R for violence. 109m. **DIR:** Matthew Patrick. **CAST:** Gary Busey, Mimi Rogers, Michael McKean, Elizabeth Ruscio, Bruce Glover. **1989**

HILLSIDE STRANGLERS, THE ★★★ A video release of a made-for-television flick concerning two of California's most wanted criminals. Richard Crenna is the hard-nosed detective. Dennis Farina and Billy Zane are the cousins holding Los Angeles in a stranglehold of fear. 95m. **DIR:** Steven Gethers. **CAST:** Richard Crenna, Dennis Farina, Billy Zane, Tony Plana. **1989**

HIT LIST (1988) ★★ The Mafia hires a hit man (Lance Henriksen) to stifle a key witness. The hit man gets the address wrong and ends up kidnapping Jan-Michael Vincent's son. Some familiar faces pop up in the supporting cast of this not-so-bad suspense-drama. Rated R for violence and profanity. 87m. **DIR:** William Lustig. **CAST:** Jan-Michael Vincent, Rip Torn, Lance Henriksen, Leo Rossi. **1988**

HIT LIST, THE (1992) ★★★★ High marks to this twisty thriller from scripter Reed Steiner. Jeff Fahey stars as an implacable assassin whose professional routine goes awry after meeting client Yancy Butler. Post-dubbing is inexplicably awful for an American-made film. Rated R for extreme violence, profanity, simulated sex, and nudity. 97m. **DIR:** William Webb. **CAST:** Jeff Fahey, Yancy Butler, James Coburn, Michael Beach, Jeff Kober. **1992**

HOLCROFT COVENANT, THE ★★ In the closing days of World War II, three infamous Nazi officers deposit a large sum of money into a Swiss bank account to be withdrawn years later by their children. This slow but intriguing film, based on the novel by Robert Ludlum, will undoubtedly please spy-film enthusiasts, although others may find it tedious and contrived. Rated R for adult situations. 105m. **DIR:** John Frankenheimer. **CAST:** Michael

Caine, Anthony Andrews, Victoria Tennant, Mario Adorf, Lilli Palmer. **1985**

HOLLYWOOD BOULEVARD II 💔 Sleazoid trash takes place on a movie set. Rated R for nudity, profanity, and violence. 82m. **DIR:** Steve Barnett. **CAST:** Ginger Lynn Allen, Kelly Monteith, Eddie Deezen. **1989**

HOLLYWOOD DETECTIVE, THE ★★½ This chatty thriller bears all the earmarks of a failed television pilot, with Telly Savalas starring as a has-been TV actor rather improbably hired by jittery flake Helene Udy to find her missing boyfriend. Christopher Crowe's script is cute but nothing special; his few topical references to Malathion and Medflies do not a *Chinatown* make. 93m. **DIR:** Kevin Connor. **CAST:** Telly Savalas, Helene Udy, George Coe, Joe Dallesandro. **1991**

HOME FOR THE HOLIDAYS ★★★ This TV movie focuses on a family that gathers for Christmas, only to learn they're being stalked by a psycho with a pitchfork. A chilling whodunit. 90m. **DIR:** John Llewellyn Moxey. **CAST:** Sally Field, Jessica Walter, Eleanor Parker, Julie Harris, Jill Haworth, Walter Brennan. **1972**

HOMICIDAL IMPULSE ★★½ Derivative thriller stars Scott Valentine as an assistant district attorney who gets involved with scheming intern Vanessa Angel, who's willing to do anything to rise to the top, including murder. Rated R for nudity and violence. 86m. **DIR:** David Tausik. **CAST:** Scott Valentine, Vanessa Angel, Charles Napier. **1992**

HOMICIDE ★★★½ A detective is assigned against his will to investigate the murder of an older Jewish woman killed at her shop in a predominantly black neighborhood. Crackling dialogue and a suspenseful atmosphere make up for a plot twist that doesn't quite ring true in this Chinese puzzle of a movie. Rated R for profanity and violence. 102m. **DIR:** David Mamet. **CAST:** Joe Mantegna, William H. Macy, Natalija Nogulich, Ving Rhames. **1991**

HONEYMOON KILLERS, THE ★★★ Grim story of a smooth-talking Lothario and his obese lover who befriend and murder vulnerable older women for their money is based on the infamous "lonely hearts killers" of the 1940s and 1950s. Not for the squeamish, but a solid entry in the growing file of true-crime films. 108m. **DIR:** Leonard Kastle. **CAST:** Tony Lo Bianco, Shirley Stoler, Mary Jane Higby. **1970**

HOPSCOTCH ★★★★ Walter Matthau is wonderful in this fast-paced and funny film as a spy who decides to extract a little revenge on the pompous supervisor (Ned Beatty) who demoted him. Glenda Jackson has a nice bit as Matthau's romantic interest. Rated R. 104m. **DIR:** Ronald Neame. **CAST:** Walter Matthau, Ned Beatty, Glenda Jackson. **1980**

HORSEPLAYER ★★ Strange tale, unremarkably told, of two takers (M. K. Harris and Sammi Davis) who use a disturbed man (Brad Dourif) for their own ends. Rated R for violence and profanity. 89m. **DIR:** Kurt Voss. **CAST:** Brad Dourif, Sammi Davis, M. K. Harris, Vic Tayback. **1990**

HOT ROCK, THE ★★★★ A neatly planned jewelry heist goes awry and the fun begins. Peter Yates's direction is razor sharp. The cast is absolutely perfect. This movie is a crowd-pleasing blend of action, humor, and suspense. Rated PG. 105m. **DIR:** Peter Yates. **CAST:** Robert Redford, George Segal, Ron Leibman, Paul Sand, Zero Mostel, Moses Gunn, William Redfield, Charlotte Rae. **1972**

HOTEL ROOM ★★★★ One hotel room, three weird stories. David Lynch directed the two most effective tales. In one, Harry Dean Stanton is a cantankerous drunk with an eerie past. In the other, Crispin Glover embarks on an unsettling psychological journey with his unstable wife. Chelsea Field is fighting mad at shallow boyfriend Griffin Dunne in a slighter, more comic story. Not rated; contains adult themes, sexual situations, and violence. 96m. **DIR:** David Lynch, James Signorelli. **CAST:** Harry Dean Stanton, Glenne Headly, Griffin Dunne, Chelsea Field, Crispin Glover. **1992**

HOUND OF THE BASKERVILLES, THE (1939) ★★★★ The second best of the Basil Rathbone–Nigel Bruce Sherlock Holmes movies, this 1939 release marked the stars' debut in the roles for which they would forever be known. While *The Adventures of Sherlock Holmes*, which was made the same year, featured the on-screen detective team at its peak, this Twentieth Century Fox–produced adaptation can be called a classic. For those unfamiliar with the story, Holmes and Watson are called upon by Henry Baskerville (Richard Greene) to save him from a curse—in the form of a hound from hell—that has plagued his family for centuries. B&W; 84m. **DIR:** Sidney Lanfield. **CAST:** Basil Rathbone, Nigel Bruce, John Carradine, Lionel Atwill, Mary Gordon, E. E. Clive, Richard Greene. **1939**

HOUND OF THE BASKERVILLES, THE (1959) ★★★★ One of the better adaptations of A. Conan Doyle's moody novel, and particularly enjoyable for its presentation of Peter Cushing (as Sherlock Holmes) and Christopher Lee together in nonhorror roles. This British entry (from the Hammer House of Horror) caught more of the murky atmosphere than any other version of any other Holmes tale. Intelligent scripting, compelling acting, and spooky cinematography. 84m. **DIR:** Terence Fisher. **CAST:** Peter Cushing, Christopher Lee, Andre Morell, Marla Landi, Miles Malleson. **1959**

HOUND OF THE BASKERVILLES, THE (1983) ★★★½ Ian Richardson makes a fine Sherlock Holmes in this enjoyable version of Sir Arthur Conan Doyle's oft-filmed tale. While we prefer the Basil Rathbone and Peter Cushing vehicles, there's certainly nothing wrong with this suspenseful, well-mounted and atmospheric thriller. 101m. **DIR:** Douglas Hickox. **CAST:** Ian Richardson, Donald Churchill, Denholm Elliot, Martin Shaw, Brian Blessed, Ronald Lacey, Eleanor Bron, Edward Judd, Glynis Barber. **1983**

HOUSE BY THE RIVER ★★★ Fritz Lang explores one of his favorite themes: obsession. A moody chamber work about a man who kills his maid out of passionate rage, then implicates his own brother to relieve his guilt. Full of fascinating psychological touches that manage to create a disturbing atmosphere. B&W; 88m. **DIR:** Fritz Lang. **CAST:** Louis Hayward, Jane Wyatt, Lee Bowman, Ann Shoemaker, Kathleen Freeman. **1950**

HOUSE IN THE HILLS, A ★★½ While house-sitting, an aspiring actress is taken hostage and falls in love with her captor. Very bizarre love story with an even more bizarre ending. Rated R for nudity, simulated sex, and profanity. 89m. **DIR:** Ken Wiederhorn. **CAST:** Michael Madsen, Helen Slater, James Laurenson, Elyssa Davalos, Jeffrey Tambor. **1993**

HOUSE OF FEAR ★★★★ The last of the high-quality entries in the Universal Sherlock Holmes series has Holmes (Basil Rathbone) and Watson (Nigel Bruce) attempting to solve a series of murders among the guests at a Scottish mansion. It was based on Conan Doyle's "The Adventure of the Five Orange Pips" and combines atmosphere, pacing, fine acting, and sure direction. B&W; 69m. **DIR:** Roy William Neill. **CAST:** Basil Rathbone, Nigel Bruce, Aubrey Mather, Dennis Hoey. **1945**

HOUSE OF GAMES ★★★★½ Pulitzer Prize–winning playwright David Mamet makes an impressive directorial debut with this suspense-thriller. Lindsay Crouse, the writer-director's wife, gives an effective performance as a psychiatrist who attempts to intercede with a con man (Joe Mantegna) on behalf of one of her patients, a compulsive gambler who owes him several thousand dollars. She is sucked into a world of mirrors where nothing is what it seems. Rated R for profanity and violence. 102m. **DIR:** David Mamet. **CAST:** Lindsay Crouse, Joe Mantegna, Lilia Skala. **1987**

HOUSE OF TERROR [turkey] A private nurse and her ex-con boyfriend try to bilk a millionaire out of his riches. Rated PG for violence. 90m. **DIR:** Sergei Goncharff. **CAST:** Jennifer Bishop, Arell Blanton, Mitchell Gregg. **1987**

HOUSE ON CARROLL STREET, THE ★★★ Commendable suspense film about a young accused communist (Kelly McGillis) who becomes involved in a Nazi smuggling ring in 1951 Washington, D.C. Jeff Daniels is one of the investigating FBI men who falls for McGillis. A good costume piece, and McGillis and Daniels turn in solid performances, along with Jessica Tandy as McGillis's crusty employer. Rated PG for language, violence, and slight nudity. 111m. **DIR:** Peter Yates. **CAST:** Kelly McGillis, Jeff Daniels, Jessica Tandy, Mandy Patinkin. **1988**

HUNT FOR RED OCTOBER, THE ★★★★½ In this edge-of-your-seat winner adapted from Tom Clancy's best-selling suspense novel, the ever-watchable Sean Connery plays a Soviet submarine captain who uses Russia's ultimate underwater weapon as a means to defect to the West. A superb supporting cast enlivens this crackerjack thriller, directed with great skill by John McTiernan. Rated PG for brief violence. 132m. **DIR:** John McTiernan. **CAST:** Sean Connery, Alec Baldwin, Scott Glenn, James Earl Jones, Sam Neill, Richard Jordan, Tim Curry, Jeffrey Jones, Peter Firth, Joss Ackland. **1990**

HUNT THE MAN DOWN ★★½ A public defender has the difficult chore of defending a man who has been a fugitive from a murder charge for twelve years. In attempting to follow an ice-cold trail and prove his defendant innocent, Gig Young fights an uphill battle. B&W; 68m. **DIR:** George Archainbaud. **CAST:** Gig Young, Lynne Roberts (Mary Hart), Mary Anderson, Willard Parker, Carla Balenda, Gerald Mohr, James Anderson, Harry Shannon, Cleo Moore. **1950**

HUSH LITTLE BABY ★★½ In this made-for-cable movie, an adopted woman is located by her biological mother. They become friends, but she doesn't know that her mother tried to kill her when she was a child. This so-so film's story has been done much better before. Not rated, but contains violence. 95m. **DIR:** Jorge Montesi. **CAST:** Diane Ladd, Wendel Meldrum, Geraint Wyn Davies, Illya Woloshyn, Ingrid Veninger. **1993**

HYSTERIA ★★½ After their success in remaking old Universal horror movies, the folks at England's Hammer Films decided to try their luck with Hitchcockian suspense. This film is one of the results. Robert Webber plays an American amnesia victim in England. This unrated film contains some mild violence. B&W; 85m. **DIR:** Freddie Francis. **CAST:** Robert Webber, Lelia Goldoni, Maurice Denham, Jennifer Jayne. **1964**

I CONFESS ★★★ In spite of shortcomings, this is the film that best reflects many of Hitch's puritanical ethics. Clift stars as a priest who takes confession from a man who—coincidentally—killed a blackmailer who knew of Clift's prevows relationship with Baxter. (Whew!) Moody and atmospheric. B&W; 95m. **DIR:** Alfred Hitchcock.

CAST: Montgomery Clift, Karl Malden, Anne Baxter, Brian Aherne. **1953**

I, THE JURY 🦃 Armand Assante is a passable Mike Hammer in this sleazy hybrid of James Bond and *Death Wish II*. Rated R. 111m. **DIR:** Richard T. Heffron. **CAST:** Armand Assante, Barbara Carrera, Alan King. **1982**

I WAKE UP SCREAMING ★★★ Laird Cregar's performance as a menacing and sinister detective bent on convicting an innocent Victor Mature for the murder of Carole Landis dominates this suspense-filled *film noir.* Betty Grable is surprisingly effective in her first nonmusical role as the victim's sister, who finds herself attracted to the chief suspect. A classy whodunit. B&W; 82m. **DIR:** H. Bruce Humberstone. **CAST:** Betty Grable, Victor Mature, Carole Landis, Laird Cregar, William Gargan. **1941**

IF LOOKS COULD KILL (1986) ★★ A photographer is hired to videotape a woman's apartment to gather evidence against her. Suspense and duplicity follow. But the dialogue is poor and the direction is mediocre. Rated R for violence, profanity, nudity, and sex. 90m. **DIR:** Chuck Vincent. **CAST:** Kim Lambert, Tim Gail. **1986**

ILLICIT BEHAVIOR ★★ Mediocre film with a twisted plot involving good and bad cops. Jack Scalia spends most of the movie either roughing up or killing people he dislikes, only to find out that he has severely tangled himself up in a conspiracy. Rated R for violence, nudity, and language. 101m. **DIR:** Worth Keeter. **CAST:** Robert Davi, Joan Severance, Jack Scalia, James Russo, Kent McCord, Jenilee Harrison. **1992**

ILLUSIONS ★★ Mediocre story in which a former mental patient (Heather Locklear) believes her sister-in-law is trying to drive her insane. Narration distracts the viewer and only exists to fill gaps in the plot. Not rated, but contains nudity. 90m. **DIR:** Victor Kulle. **CAST:** Robert Carradine, Heather Locklear, Emma Samms, Ned Beatty, Paul Mantee, Susannah York. **1992**

IMPACT ★★ Shades of *Double Indemnity*! Unfaithful wife and lover plot to kill rich husband, but lover gets bumped instead. Interesting, but don't believe the title. B&W; 111m. **DIR:** Arthur Lubin. **CAST:** Brian Donlevy, Helen Walker, Tony Barrett, Ella Raines, Charles Coburn, Anna May Wong. **1948**

IMPOSSIBLE SPY, THE ★★★★ This video is based on the true exploits of Elie Cohen, a spy for Israel's Mossad. Cohen, played by John Shea, is recruited by the Mossad in 1959 and sent to Argentina, where he works his way into the good graces of a group that is plotting to overthrow the Syrian government. He participates while sending information to Israel. The results of his work affect not only his family but the future of Israel. Made for British television, this is unrated. 96m. **DIR:** Jim Goddard. **CAST:** John Shea, Eli Wallach, Sasson Gabay. **1987**

IMPULSE (1974) 🦃 William Shatner plays an emotionally disturbed ex-mental patient with a penchant for murder. Not rated, but with several unconvincing murders and lots of phony blood. 85m. **DIR:** William Grefe. **CAST:** William Shatner, Ruth Roman, Harold Sakata. **1974**

IMPULSE (1984) ★★ This mildly interesting thriller takes place in a town where the inhabitants find they have increasing difficulties in controlling their urges. A hasty, unconvincing final ten minutes. Rated R for profanity and violence. 91m. **DIR:** Graham Baker. **CAST:** Tim Matheson, Meg Tilly, Hume Cronyn. **1984**

IMPULSE (1990) ★★★ Honest cop Theresa Russell yields to temptation while working undercover as a hooker, then tries to extricate herself from the ensuing investigation. Director Sondra Locke keeps the action tense through some pretty implausible plot twists. Rated R for violence and language. 109m. **DIR:** Sondra Locke. **CAST:** Theresa Russell, Jeff Fahey, George Dzundza. **1990**

IN A LONELY PLACE ★★★★ Humphrey Bogart gives one of his finest performances in this taut psychological thriller. He plays a hard-drinking, fiercely opinionated screenwriter whose violent temper has more than once landed him in trouble. He has an affair with a sexy neighbor (Gloria Grahame) who begins to fear for her life when Bogart becomes the prime suspect in a murder case. B&W; 91m. **DIR:** Nicholas Ray. **CAST:** Humphrey Bogart, Gloria Grahame, Frank Lovejoy, Robert Warwick. **1950**

IN A STRANGER'S HANDS ★★★ Robert Urich is the private investigator tracking down a missing girl. The deeper he digs, the more complex the case gets, until he comes face-to-face with the kidnapper. Tough, gritty, and socially relevant, this made-for-cable thriller works, although some of the subject matter is grim. 93m. **DIR:** David Greene. **CAST:** Robert Urich, Megan Gallagher, Brett Cullen, Isabella Hoffmann. **1991**

IN COLD BLOOD ★★★★★ A chilling documentarylike re-creation of the senseless murder of a Kansas farm family. This stark black-and-white drama follows two ex-convicts (Robert Blake and Scott Wilson) from the point at which they hatch their plan until their eventual capture and execution. This is an emotionally powerful film that is not for the faint of heart. B&W; 134m. **DIR:** Richard Brooks. **CAST:** Robert Blake, Scott Wilson, John Forsythe, Jeff Corey. **1967**

IN LOVE AND WAR ★★★ James Woods portrays navy pilot Jim Stockdale who is shot down over enemy territory and suffers POW camp tortures for nearly eight years of war in Vietnam. This emotionally compelling story pays tribute to America's fighting men and the parts their resolute wives play in the politics of bringing their husbands home. Rated R for mature subject matter. 96m. **DIR:** Paul Aaron. **CAST:** James Woods, Jane Alexander, Haing S. Ngor. **1991**

IN THE COLD OF THE NIGHT 🦃 Jeff Lester is a man plagued by a nightmare in which he attempts to kill a mysterious woman. Rated R for nudity and violence. 112m. **DIR:** Nico Mastorakis. **CAST:** Jeff Lester, Adrienne Sachs, David Soul, Tippi Hedren. **1990**

IN THE HEAT OF PASSION ★★½ In this case, the end doesn't justify the means as Sally Kirkland leads Nick Corri on a wild sleazefest. She appears to be a bored but fabulously wealthy wife out to have forbidden pleasure with a younger man. Comes in both R and an unrated version, both containing violence, nudity, and profanity. 93m. **DIR:** Rodman Flender. **CAST:** Sally Kirkland, Nick Corri, Jack Carter. **1991**

IN THE HEAT OF THE NIGHT ★★★★ This film is a rousing murder mystery elevated by the excellent acting of Rod Steiger and Sidney Poitier. Racial tension is created when a rural southern sheriff (Steiger) and a black northern detective reluctantly join forces to solve the crime. The picture received Oscars for best picture and Steiger's performance. 109m. **DIR:** Norman Jewison. **CAST:** Sidney Poitier, Rod Steiger, Warren Oates, Lee Grant. **1967**

INDECENCY ★★★ A suspenseful whodunit about the murder of an ad agency owner. Was it the soon-to-be ex-husband, the partner who was sleeping with the husband, or the drug dealer? Good plot and good acting make this an enjoyable film. Rated PG for sensuality and profanity. 88m. **DIR:** Marisa Silver. **CAST:** Jennifer Beals, Sammi Davis, James Remar, Barbara Williams, Christopher John Fields. **1992**

INNER SANCTUM ★★½ Wheelchair-bound wife Valerie Wildman suspects her husband and new nurse are plotting to drive her insane. The plot's not hot, but the sex in the unrated version is pretty steamy. Available in both a tamer R version and a soft-core unrated version. 90m. **DIR:** Fred Olen Ray. **CAST:** Joseph Bottoms, Margaux Hemingway, Tanya Roberts, Valerie Wildman, William Butler, Brett Clark. **1991**

INNOCENT VICTIM ★★★ Lauren Bacall stars as a woman recovering from a nervous breakdown visiting her daughter (Helen Shaver) in England. When Shaver's son dies suddenly, Bacall makes a fateful decision. Fine performances by Bacall and Shaver highlight this quirky little thriller, based on Ruth Rendell's *Tree of Hands*. Rated R for violence and profanity. 100m. **DIR:** Giles Foster. **CAST:** Lauren Bacall, Helen Shaver, Peter Firth. **1990**

INSPECTOR MORSE (TV SERIES) ★★★★½ Colin Dexter's introspective and moody Chief Inspector Morse (John Thaw) and his amiable assistant, Detective-Sergeant Lewis (Kevin Whately), are perfectly rendered in this British mystery series. Morse, an opera lover who enjoys his pints of bitter, is a lonely bachelor who never finds the right woman, but solves his murder cases with zeal and intelligence. Lewis is an affable family man who makes an excellent counterpart to his demanding boss. A well-paced set of stories concerning crime and passion in Oxford. per episode. 52m. **DIR:** Peter Hammond, Brian Parker, Alastair Reid. **CAST:** John Thaw, Kevin Whately, Peter Woodthorpe, Norman Jones. **1987–1988**

INTERNECINE PROJECT, THE ★★★ James Coburn plays an ambitious business tycoon who finds he has to kill four associates to meet a business agreement. The fashion in which he does this proves to be interesting. Worth a look for the trick ending. Rated PG. 89m. **DIR:** Ken Hughes. **CAST:** James Coburn, Lee Grant, Harry Andrews, Ian Hendry, Michael Jayston, Keenan Wynn. **1974**

INTIMATE OBSESSION 🦃 Bored wife meets dangerous stranger in this cheap "erotic mystery" that's as generic as its title. Rated R for nudity and sexual situations. 80m. **DIR:** Lawrence Unger. **CAST:** Jodie Fisher, James Quarter. **1992**

INTIMATE STRANGER ★★ Deborah Harry takes a part-time job on a sex phone line and meets up with the ultimate psycho. Now she must find him before he gets her. Rated R for profanity, nudity, and violence. 96m. **DIR:** Allan Holzman. **CAST:** Deborah Harry, James Russo, Tim Thomerson, Grace Zabriskie. **1991**

INTRIGUE ★★ Robert Loggia plays a former CIA agent who has defected to the KGB. Realizing that he's terminally ill, he wants to return to the United States. Slow start, decent middle, and just okay ending sum up the quality of this made-for-TV spy flick. Rated PG for violence. 96m. **DIR:** David Drury. **CAST:** Scott Glenn, Robert Loggia, William Atherton. **1988**

INVASION OF PRIVACY ★★ A worn-out story line about a psychotic ex-convict who goes to work for the journalist that he idolizes. Robby Benson still can't act, and Jennifer O'Neill doesn't do much better. Made for cable. 95m. **DIR:** Kevin Meyer. **CAST:** Robby Benson, Jennifer O'Neill, Ian Ogilvy. **1992**

IPCRESS FILE, THE ★★★★ First and by far the best of Michael Caine's three "Harry Palmer" films, this one introduces Len Deighton's reluctant thief-turned-secret agent. Caine, relentlessly serious behind owl-like spectacles, investigates the mystery of specialists kidnapped behind the Iron Curtain. John Barry's moody jazz score superbly counterpoints the action, and Sidney J. Furie's direction is taut and suspenseful. Unrated, suitable for family viewing. 108m. **DIR:** Sidney J. Furie. **CAST:** Michael Caine, Nigel Green, Guy Doleman, Gordon Jackson, Sue Lloyd. **1965**

IRON MAZE ★★ Japanese tycoon buys a shutdown steel plant in an economically depressed American town. Sparks fly when his impulsive American wife has an affair with a former employee of the plant. Meandering maze of cinematic clichés. Rated R for profanity, violence, and nudity. 102m. **DIR:** Hiroaki Yoshida. **CAST:** Jeff Fahey, Bridget Fonda, J. T. Walsh. **1991**

JACK THE RIPPER (1979) ★★ Klaus Kinski plays Jack the Ripper, and Josephine Chaplin is Cynthia, the Scotland Yard inspector's girlfriend. Jack the Ripper is terrorizing London by killing women and disposing of their bodies in the Thames River. Rated R for violence and nudity. 82m. **DIR:** Jess (Jesus) Franco. **CAST:** Klaus Kinski, Josephine Chaplin. **1979**

JACK'S BACK ★★★ Not a splatter film, but a fairly thoughtful suspense melodrama. James Spader portrays twin brothers in this tale of a Jack-the-Ripper copycat killer operating in modern-day Los Angeles. Rated R for gore. 90m. **DIR:** Rowdy Herrington. **CAST:** James Spader, Cynthia Gibb, Robert Picardo, Rod Loomis, Chris Mulkey. **1988**

JADE MASK, THE ★★ *Charlie Chan* programmer from cheapie Monogram period. Charlie seeks an inventor's murderer. Routine. B&W; 66m. **DIR:** Phil Rosen. **CAST:** Sidney Toler, Mantan Moreland, Edwin Luke, Janet Warren, Frank Reicher. **1945**

JANUARY MAN, THE ★★ Whew! We've seen some weird movies in our time, but this one deserves a special place in some museum. John Patrick Shanley (*Moonstruck*) wrote this goofy mystery about a former police detective (Kevin Kline) who is drafted back into service when a serial killer begins to terrorize New York City. Rated R for profanity and violence. 110m. **DIR:** Pat O'Connor. **CAST:** Kevin Kline, Susan Sarandon, Mary Elizabeth Mastrantonio, Harvey Keitel, Danny Aiello, Alan Rickman, Rod Steiger. **1989**

JENNIFER 8 ★★★½ A solid, inventive ending and crisp dialogue help this sometimes contrived thriller, in which burned-out L.A. cop Andy Garcia joins former partner Lance Henriksen on a small-town police force only to find himself on the trail of a serial killer. Rated R for violence, profanity, and nudity. 127m. **DIR:** Bruce Robinson. **CAST:** Andy Garcia, Uma Thurman, John Malkovich, Lance Henriksen, Kathy Baker, Graham Beckel, Kevin Conway, Perry Lang, Lenny Von Dohlen. **1992**

JEZEBEL'S KISS ★★ Steamy, sleazy thriller about a beautiful young woman who seeks revenge for the death of her grandfather. Inept. Rated R for nudity, violence, and profanity. 95m. **DIR:** Harvey Keith. **CAST:** Katherine Barrese, Malcolm McDowell, Everett McGill, Meredith Baxter-Birney, Meg Foster, Bert Remsen. **1990**

JIGSAW MAN, THE ★★★★ In this suspense film, Michael Caine plays a British secret agent who has defected, under orders, to Russia. Before leaving, he discovered a list of Soviet spies operating in England and hid it. After forty years, he returns to England in order to get the list with spies from both countries hot on his trail. This is a wonderfully entertaining puzzle of a movie. Rated PG for violence and profanity. 90m. **DIR:** Freddie Francis. **CAST:** Michael Caine, Laurence Olivier, Susan George, Robert Powell, Charles Gray. **1984**

JIGSAW MURDERS, THE 🦃 A psycho killer leaves body parts around L.A. 98m. **DIR:** Jag Mundhra. **CAST:** Chad Everett, Yaphet Kotto, Michelle Johnson, Michael Sabatino. **1988**

JOURNEY INTO FEAR (1942) ★★★★ A sometimes confusing but always suspenseful World War II tale of an American ordnance expert (Joseph Cotten) targeted for assassination in Istanbul. Like *The Magnificent Ambersons*, this faulted classic was started by Orson Welles but was taken over by RKO. Uncredited Welles partly directed and, with Cotten, adapted this Eric Ambler mystery for the screen. Remade in 1975. B&W; 69m. **DIR:** Norman Foster, Orson Welles. **CAST:** Joseph Cotten, Orson Welles, Dolores Del Rio, Ruth Warrick, Agnes Moorehead, Everett Sloane, Edgar Barrier, Hans Conried. **1942**

JOURNEY INTO FEAR (1975) ★★ This Canadian remake of Orson Welles's 1942 spy drama is occasionally intriguing but ultimately ambiguous and lacking in dramatic punch. Sam Waterston's portrayal of a research geologist, and wide-ranging European locations, help sustain interest. Rated PG. 103m. **DIR:** Daniel Mann. **CAST:** Sam Waterston, Zero Mostel, Yvette Mimieux, Scott Marlowe, Ian McShane, Joseph Wiseman, Shelley Winters, Stanley Holloway, Donald Pleasence, Vincent Price. **1975**

JUGGERNAUT (1936) ★★½ In this low-budget mystery-drama filmed in England, Boris Karloff plays Dr. Sartorius, a brilliant (but cracked) specialist on the verge of perfecting a cure for paralysis. He makes a deal with a patient to murder her husband. B&W; 64m. **DIR:** Henry Edwards. **CAST:** Boris Karloff. **1936**

JUGGERNAUT (1974) ★★★★½ Here's a first-rate, suspenseful thriller about demolitions expert Richard Harris attempting to deactivate a bomb aboard a luxury liner. Richard Lester elevates the familiar plot line with inspired direction, and Lester regular Roy Kinnear is on hand to add some deft bits of comedy. Rated PG. 109m. **DIR:** Richard Lester. **CAST:** Richard Harris, Omar Sharif, David Hemmings, Anthony Hopkins, Shirley Knight, Ian Holm, Roy Kinnear. **1974**

KAFKA ★★★½ Director Steven Soderbergh's follow-up to *sex, lies and videotape* is a deliciously odd, tongue-in-cheek thriller that will delight some viewers and annoy others. About an insurance claims clerk in Prague, circa 1919, it's a study in paranoia, with the title character (Jeremy Irons at his twitching best) being thrust into a world of plots and counterplots. It has little to do with the life and writings of Franz Kafka. Much better than Woody Allen's similarly themed *Shadows and Fog*. Rated PG-13 for violence. 98m. **DIR:** Steven Soderbergh. **CAST:** Jeremy Irons, Theresa Russell, Joel Grey, Ian Holm, Jeroen Krabbé, Armin Mueller-Stahl, Alec Guinness, Brian Glover, Keith Allen, Robert Flemyng. **1992**

KANSAS CITY CONFIDENTIAL ★★★ Four masked men pull a split-second-timed bank heist and get away while innocent ex-con John Payne gets the third degree. After the police lose interest in him, Payne follows the robbers to Guatemala. Good photography and atmosphere, but overlong. B&W; 98m. **DIR:** Phil Karlson. **CAST:** John Payne, Coleen Gray, Preston Foster, Lee Van Cleef, Neville Brand, Jack Elam. **1952**

KENNEL MURDER CASE, THE ★★★★ A classic detective thriller, this features William Powell as the dapper Philo Vance solving a locked-door murder. The supporting players complement his suave characterization perfectly. Dated, but good. B&W; 73m. **DIR:** Michael Curtiz. **CAST:** William Powell, Mary Astor, Eugene Pallette, Ralph Morgan, Jack LaRue. **1933**

KEY LARGO ★★★★ Humphrey Bogart is one of a group of dissimilar individuals held in a run-down Florida Keys hotel by a band of hoodlums on the lam. Lauren Bacall looks to him as her white knight, but as a disillusioned war vet he has had enough violence. That is, until a crime kingpin (Edward G. Robinson) pushes things a little too far. B&W; 101m. **DIR:** John Huston. **CAST:** Humphrey Bogart, Lauren Bacall, Edward G. Robinson, Claire Trevor, Lionel Barrymore. **1948**

KIDNAPPING OF THE PRESIDENT, THE ★★★★ As the title implies, terrorists kidnap the president and hold him hostage in this excellent action-thriller. The acting is excellent, the suspense taut, and the direction tightly paced. 120m. **DIR:** George Mendeluk. **CAST:** William Shatner, Hal Holbrook, Van Johnson, Ava Gardner. **1979**

KILL, THE ★★ Richard Jaeckel plays a world-weary, womanizing private eye in this overly familiar story of a hunt for stolen money in the byways of the Orient. The locale is Macao, famed gambling haven across the bay from Hong Kong. No rating, but contains violence and nudity. 81m. **DIR:** Rolf Bamer. **CAST:** Richard Jaeckel. **1973**

KILL ME AGAIN ★★ A fairly suspenseful thriller about a private eye who gets caught up in plot twist after plot twist after a woman asks him to fake her death. Predictable, but there are worse ways to spend an hour and a half. Rated R for violence. 94m. **DIR:** John Dahl. **CAST:** Val Kilmer, Joanne Whalley, Michael Madsen, Jonathan Gries, Michael Greene, Bibi Besch. **1990**

KILLER IMAGE 🦃 Confusing film with a complete lack of continuity starts with the murder of a photographer who just happens to capture a murderer on film. Now his brother is pursued by the psycho. Rated R for violence and profanity. 97m. **DIR:** David Winning. **CAST:** Michael Ironside, M. Emmet Walsh, John Pyper-Ferguson, Krista Erickson. **1992**

KILLER INSIDE ME, THE ★★★ Stacy Keach plays a schizophrenic sheriff in a small town. A tightly woven plot offers the viewer plenty of surprises. Rated R for violence and profanity. 99m. **DIR:** Burt Kennedy. **CAST:** Stacy Keach, Susan Tyrrell, Tisha Sterling, Keenan Wynn, Charles McGraw, John Dehner, Pepe Serna, Royal Dano, John Carradine, Don Stroud. **1975**

KILLING, THE ★★★★ Strong noir thriller from Stanley Kubrick has Sterling Hayden leading a group of criminals in an intricately timed heist at a racetrack. Excellent performances and atmospheric handling of the subject matter mark Kubrick, even at this early stage of his career, as a filmmaker to watch. B&W; 83m. **DIR:** Stanley Kubrick. **CAST:** Sterling Hayden, Coleen Gray, Jay C. Flippen, Marie Windsor, Timothy Carey, Vince Edwards, Elisha Cook Jr. **1956**

KILLING AFFAIR, A ★★★ Exceptional psychological drama about a young woman (Kathy Baker) who befriends a stranger (Peter Weller). As it turns out, he killed her husband to avenge the death of his own wife and family. The relationship between the two intensifies to an unexpected, terrifying conclusion. Rated R for nudity and violence. 100m. **DIR:** David Saperstein. **CAST:** Peter Weller, Kathy Baker, John Glover, Bill Smitrovich. **1988**

KILLING HOUR, THE ★★ Elizabeth Kemp plays a clairvoyant art student who, through her drawings, becomes involved in a series of murders. The story is a rip-off of *The Eyes of Laura Mars*. With that said, suspense is achieved during the last fifteen minutes of the film. Rated R for violence, nudity, and profanity. 97m. **DIR:** Armand Mastroianni.

CAST: Perry King, Elizabeth Kemp, Norman Parker, Kenneth McMillan. 1984

KILLING MIND, THE A young girl witnesses a murder and grows up to become a homicide investigator so that she can reopen the case. This murder-mystery plot is so old and tired it would be a bigger mystery why anyone would have trouble figuring it out in this made-for-cable film. 96m. **DIR:** Michael Ray Rhodes. **CAST:** Stephanie Zimbalist, Daniel Roebuck, Tony Bill. 1991

KISS BEFORE DYING, A ★★½ Psychotic Matt Dillon stalks Sean Young in this all-too-familiar tale—derived from Ira Levin's novel. Still, the leads are fine, especially Young in a dual role as sisters. The 1956 adaptation is better. Rated R for violence, nudity, and profanity. 93m. **DIR:** James Dearden. **CAST:** Matt Dillon, Sean Young, Max von Sydow, Diane Ladd, James Russo. 1991

KISS DADDY GOOD NIGHT ★★ Uma Thurman stars as a struggling model who survives by picking up wealthy men in bars, then drugging and robbing them. She finds the situation reversed when an obsessive suitor decides that he wants her all to himself. Moody, ultimately incomprehensible thriller. Rated R for nudity and violence. 89m. **DIR:** Peter Ily Huemer. **CAST:** Uma Thurman, Paul Dillon, Paul Richards. 1988

KISS ME A KILLER A young wife and a drifter plot to eliminate her older husband. This is the Hispanic version of *The Postman Always Rings Twice*. The final irony this time out isn't nearly as satisfying. Rated R for nudity and profanity. 91m. **DIR:** Marcus De Leon. **CAST:** Julie Carmen, Robert Beltran, Guy Boyd, Ramon Franco, Charles Boswell. 1991

KISS ME DEADLY ★★★½ Robert Aldrich's adaptation of Mickey Spillane's Mike Hammer novel was hailed by French new wave film critics in the 1960s as a masterpiece. Brutal and surrealistic, it has Hammer attempting to protect a woman (Cloris Leachman) from the men who want to kill her. B&W; 105m. **DIR:** Robert Aldrich. **CAST:** Ralph Meeker, Albert Dekker, Cloris Leachman, Paul Stewart. 1955

KISSING PLACE, THE ★★★★ An absolutely chilling performance by Meredith Baxter-Birney sparks this made-for-TV thriller. She's a woman who has kidnapped a boy to replace her dead child. All goes well for nearly eight years until unsettling dreams force the boy to question his identity. 88m. **DIR:** Tony Wharmby. **CAST:** Meredith Baxter-Birney, David Ogden Stiers, Nathaniel Moreau, Victoria Snow. 1989

KLUTE ★★★★ Jane Fonda dominates every frame in this study of a worldly call girl. Her Oscar-winning performance looks into the hidden sides of a prostitute's lifestyle; the dreams, fears, shame, and loneliness of Klute's world are graphically illustrated. Donald Sutherland costars as an out-of-town cop looking for a missing friend. He feels Fonda holds the key to his whereabouts. Rated R. 114m. **DIR:** Alan J. Pakula. **CAST:** Jane Fonda, Donald Sutherland, Roy Scheider. 1971

KNIGHT MOVES ★★ At an international chess tournament in the Pacific Northwest one of the top touring masters becomes the prime suspect in a macabre, ritual murder. This atmospheric thriller makes less sense the more one thinks about it, but it certainly isn't dull. Rated R for violence and language. 110m. **DIR:** Carl Schenkel. **CAST:** Christopher Lambert, Diane Lane, Tom Skerritt, Daniel Baldwin. 1993

LADY BEWARE ★★ Decent but unriveting film along the lines of *Fatal Attraction*, with a psychotic pursuing pretty window dresser Diane Lane. The rest of the cast and situations are stereotypical and fairly mundane. Rated R for nudity and violence. 108m. **DIR:** Karen Arthur. **CAST:** Diane Lane, Michael Woods, Cotter Smith. 1987

LADY FROM SHANGHAI ★★★½ Orson Welles and Rita Hayworth were husband and wife when they made this taut, surprising thriller about a beautiful, amoral woman, her crippled, repulsive lawyer husband, his partner, and a somewhat naïve Irish sailor made cat's-paw in a murder scheme. Under Welles's inventive direction, Everett Sloane and the camera steal the show with a climactic scene in the hall of mirrors at San Francisco's old oceanfront Playland. B&W; 87m. **DIR:** Orson Welles. **CAST:** Rita Hayworth, Orson Welles, Everett Sloane, Glenn Anders, Erskine Sanford, Ted de Corsia. 1948

LADY ICE ★★ Donald Sutherland is an investigator for an insurance firm and Jennifer O'Neill is his romantic interest. The catch is that her father is a crook who sells stolen gems. Rated PG. 93m. **DIR:** Tom Gries. **CAST:** Donald Sutherland, Robert Duvall, Jennifer O'Neill, Patrick Magee. 1973

LADY IN A CAGE ★★★★ Superb shocker may finally get the recognition it deserves, thanks to home video. Olivia de Havilland is terrorized by a gang of punks when she becomes trapped in an elevator in her home. Good acting, especially by a young James Caan, and excellent photography help make this film really something special. Very violent at times. B&W; 93m. **DIR:** Walter Grauman. **CAST:** Olivia de Havilland, James Caan, Ann Sothern. 1964

LADY IN CEMENT ★★ Sequel to *Tony Rome* misses the mark. Once again private eye Frank Sinatra is immersed into the underbelly of Miami, this time with rather undistinguished results. 93m. **DIR:** Gordon Douglas. **CAST:** Frank Sinatra, Raquel Welch,

Richard Conte, Dan Blocker, Lainie Kazan, Martin Gabel. 1968

LADY IN THE LAKE ★★★ Director-star Robert Montgomery's adaptation of Raymond Chandler's mystery is a failed attempt at screen innovation. Montgomery uses a subjective camera to substitute for detective Philip Marlowe's first-person narrative of his efforts to find a missing wife. A clever but ineffectual whodunit. B&W; 103m. **DIR:** Robert Montgomery. **CAST:** Robert Montgomery, Audrey Totter, Lloyd Nolan, Jayne Meadows, Tom Tully, Leon Ames. 1946

LADY IN WHITE ★★★★ A high-grade suspenser. A grade schoolboy (Lukas Haas) is locked in his classroom closet. While there, he sees the ghost of one of ten children who've been molested and killed in the past ten years. He also sees (but not clearly) the murderer, who then begins pursuing him. Now the question: Who did it? Well worth a watch! Rated PG-13 for violence and obscenities. 112m. **DIR:** Frank LaLoggia. **CAST:** Lukas Haas, Len Cariou, Alex Rocco, Katherine Helmond. 1988

LADY KILLERS 🦃 Lady Killers, a male strip joint, attracts police attention when one of the performers is murdered. A good-looking officer goes undercover as a stripper to solve the crime. Unbelievably bad! Unrated, contains nudity and violence. 93m. **DIR:** Robert Lewis. **CAST:** Marilu Henner, Susan Blakely, Lesley-Anne Down, Thomas Calabro. 1988

LADY VANISHES, THE (1938) ★★★★★ Along with *The Thirty-nine Steps,* this is the most admired film from Alfred Hitchcock's early directorial career. The comedy-suspense-thriller centers around a group of British types on a train trip from England to central Europe. A young woman (Margaret Lockwood) seeks the aid of a fellow passenger (Michael Redgrave) in an attempt to locate a charming old lady (May Whitty) she had met earlier on the train and who now is apparently missing. B&W; 97m. **DIR:** Alfred Hitchcock. **CAST:** Margaret Lockwood, Michael Redgrave, May Whitty. 1938

LADY VANISHES, THE (1979) 🦃 A better title for this remake might be *The Plot Vanishes.* Rated PG. 95m. **DIR:** Anthony Page. **CAST:** Elliott Gould, Cybill Shepherd, Angela Lansbury, Herbert Lom, Arthur Lowe, Ian Carmichael. 1979

LADYKILLER ★★★½ An ex-police detective turned evidence photographer (Mimi Rogers) becomes obsessed with a murder case. She joins a computer dating service, only to be matched with the prime murder suspect. Good acting all around. Made for cable. 91m. **DIR:** Michael Scott. **CAST:** Mimi Rogers, John Shea, Tom Irwin, Alice Krige, Bob Gunton, Bert Remsen. 1992

LAGUNA HEAT ★★★½ This well-written script was made for HBO cable. Harry Hamlin is an ex–L.A. cop who lives with his father in Laguna Beach. He soon gets involved in a murder investigation. Director Simon Langton keeps the action moving and the plot twisting. 110m. **DIR:** Simon Langton. **CAST:** Harry Hamlin, Jason Robards Jr., Rip Torn, Catharine Hicks, Anne Francis, James Gammon. 1987

LANDSLIDE ★★★ Intriguing mystery follows young geologist Anthony Edwards's trek back to a small town he left years ago. Several of the locals try to figure out if he's the mysterious stranger who disappeared after a fatal car crash that killed the town leader and his family. Director Jean-Claude Lord guides his attractive cast through their paces with a tight reign. Rated PG-13 for violence. 95m. **DIR:** Jean-Claude Lord. **CAST:** Anthony Edwards, Tom Burlinson, Joanna Cassidy, Melody Anderson, Lloyd Bochner. 1992

LASER MOON ★★ Former adult star Traci Lords gets down and dirty again as an undercover policewoman using herself as bait to trap a killer. Of note, the killer uses a laser on his victims, and then indulges his fantasies. Unrated, contains nudity, violence, and adult language. 90m. **DIR:** Douglas K. Grimm. **CAST:** Traci Lords, Crystal Shaw, Harrison Leduke, Bruce Carter. 1992

LAST DANCE 🦃 Silly slasher film features sexy dancers being murdered one by one. Insipid. Unrated, contains nudity, violence, and profanity. 86m. **DIR:** Anthony Markes. **CAST:** Cynthia Bassinet, Elaine Hendrix, Kurt T. Williams. 1991

LAST EMBRACE, THE ★★★½ A CIA agent must track down an obsessed, methodical killer. A complex, intelligent thriller in the Hitchcock style with skilled performances, a lush music score, and a cliff-hanging climax at Niagara Falls. Rated R for nudity and violence. 102m. **DIR:** Jonathan Demme. **CAST:** Roy Scheider, Janet Margolin, Sam Levene, Marcia Rodd, Christopher Walken, John Glover, Charles Napier. 1979

LAST HIT, THE ★★★ A government assassin wants to retire, but is told he must first kill one more person. He falls in love with the woman he purchased his house from, and then realizes his target is her father. A few good twists and good acting will keep you watching. Not rated, made for cable, but contains violence. 95m. **DIR:** Jan Egleson. **CAST:** Bryan Brown, Brooke Adams, Daniel Von Bargen, Sally Kemp, Rider Strong, Harris Yulin. 1993

LAST INNOCENT MAN, THE ★★★★ When a talented young district attorney meets a mysterious and beautiful woman in a bar, their ensuing affair entangles him in a web of deceit. This suspenseful courtroom drama provides a number of intriguing plot twists and makes for a delicious combination of action and suspense. Produced by Home Box Office; has brief nudity and sexual situations. 114m. **DIR:** Roger Spottiswoode. **CAST:** Ed Harris, Roxanne Hart, David Suchet, Bruce McGill. **1987**

LAST OF PHILIP BANTER, THE ★★½ Scott Paulin gives a stunning performance in this lurid psychodrama. He's a self-destructive alcoholic whose life degenerates into madness after the discovery of some mysterious manuscripts. Rated R; contains profanity and violence. 100m. **DIR:** Herve Hachuel. **CAST:** Scott Paulin, Irene Miracle, Gregg Henry, Kate Vernon, Tony Curtis. **1986**

LAST OF SHEILA, THE ★★★★ A cleverly planned, very watchable whodunit. Because of some unusual camera angles and subtle dialogue, the audience is drawn into active participation in the mystery. A sundry collection of Hollywood types are invited on a yachting cruise by James Coburn. It seems one of them has been involved in the murder of Coburn's wife. Rated PG. 120m. **DIR:** Herbert Ross. **CAST:** James Coburn, Dyan Cannon, James Mason, Raquel Welch, Richard Benjamin. **1973**

LAST RIDE, THE ★★½ Recently paroled ex-convict innocently accepts a ride from a psychotic truck driver, only to have it turn into the ride of his life. Doesn't put the pedal to the metal, but grabs your interest. 84m. **DIR:** Karl Krogstad. **CAST:** Dan Ranger. **1991**

LAST WAVE, THE ★★★½ In this suspenseful, fascinating film, Richard Chamberlain plays a lawyer defending a group of aborigines on trial for murder. His investigation into the incident leads to a frightening series of apocalyptic visions. Rated PG. 106m. **DIR:** Peter Weir. **CAST:** Richard Chamberlain, Olivia Hamnett. **1977**

LATE SHOW, THE ★★★★½ Just prior to directing *Kramer vs. Kramer*, Robert Benton created this little gem. It stars Art Carney as an aging private eye out to avenge the death of his partner (Howard Duff) with the unwanted help of wacky Lily Tomlin. Loosely lifted from Sam Peckinpah's *Ride the High Country* and John Huston's *The Maltese Falcon*, this detective story is a bittersweet, sometimes tragic, takeoff on the genre. That it works so well is a credit to all involved. Rated PG. 94m. **DIR:** Robert Benton. **CAST:** Art Carney, Howard Duff, Lily Tomlin, Bill Macy, John Considine. **1977**

LAUGHING POLICEMAN, THE ★★★½ Little-known police thriller that deserved far better than it got at the box office. Walter Matthau and Bruce Dern are a pair of cops seeking a mass murderer who preys on bus passengers. Taut drama, taken from the superb thriller by Maj Sjowall and Per Wahloo. Rated R for violence. 111m. **DIR:** Stuart Rosenberg. **CAST:** Walter Matthau, Bruce Dern, Lou Gossett Jr., Albert Paulsen, Cathy Lee Crosby, Anthony Zerbe. **1974**

LAURA ★★★★★ A lovely socialite (Gene Tierney) is apparently murdered, and the police detective (Dana Andrews) assigned to the case is up to his neck in likely suspects. To compound matters, he has developed a strange attraction for the deceased woman through her portrait. So starts one of the most original mysteries ever to come from Hollywood. B&W; 88m. **DIR:** Otto Preminger. **CAST:** Gene Tierney, Dana Andrews, Vincent Price, Judith Anderson, Clifton Webb. **1944**

LEGACY FOR LEONETTE ★★ Romance Theatre tries a murder mystery but devotes too much time to the love angle. A young woman goes to England to investigate her father's mysterious death but is distracted by her handsome lawyer. Episodic and mildly entertaining. Unrated; contains no objectionable material. 99m. **DIR:** Jim Drake. **CAST:** Loyita Chapel, Michael Anderson Jr., Dinah Anne Rogers, Shane McCamey. **1982**

LEGAL EAGLES ★★★½ This droll comedy-mystery succeeds due to the engaging presence of Robert Redford as an assistant district attorney and Debra Winger as a defense attorney. The two become uneasy partners in a complex case involving art theft and a loopy performance artist, played by Daryl Hannah. The story doesn't bear close examination, but Redford and Winger keep things moving with energy and charisma. Rated PG for mild adult situations. 114m. **DIR:** Ivan Reitman. **CAST:** Robert Redford, Debra Winger, Daryl Hannah, Brian Dennehy, Terence Stamp, Steven Hill, Jennie Dundas, Roscoe Lee Browne. **1986**

LENA'S HOLIDAY ★★½ Decent romantic thriller. A newly freed East German on vacation in Los Angeles becomes inadvertently involved with diamond thieves and must run for her life. Rated PG-13. 97m. **DIR:** Michael Keusch. **CAST:** Felicity Waterman, Chris Lemmon, Michael Sarrazin, Nick Mancuso. **1990**

LEOPARD MAN, THE ★★★½ This Val Lewton–produced thriller depicts the havoc and killing that begin when a leopard escapes and terrorizes a New Mexico village. B&W; 59m. **DIR:** Jacques Tourneur. **CAST:** Dennis O'Keefe, Isabel Jewell. **1943**

LETTER, THE ★★★★ Bette Davis stars in this screen adaptation of Somerset Maugham's play as the coldly calculating wife of a rubber plantation owner (Herbert Marshall) in Malaya. In a fit of pique, she shoots her lover and concocts elaborate lies to protect herself. With tension mounting all the way, we wonder if her evil ways will eventually lead to her downfall. B&W; 95m. **DIR:** William Wyler. **CAST:** Bette Davis, Herbert Marshall, James Stephenson. **1940**

LIARS' CLUB, THE ★★½ Somewhat interesting tale about a group of high-school friends who try to cover up a rape and end up involved in a murder. The more they try to conceal their crimes, the deeper they sink. Rated R for nudity and language. 91m. **DIR:** Jeffrey Porter. **CAST:** Wil Wheaton, Brian Krause, Michael Cudutz, Bruce Weitz. **1993**

LIAR'S EDGE 🦃 Writer-director Ron Oliver's tawdry psychological thriller, a reprehensible waste of celluloid, concerns a psychologically damaged teen terrorized by his mother's new husband and brother-in-law. Moronic. Rated R for profanity and violence. 98m. **DIR:** Ron Oliver. **CAST:** David Keith, Shannon Tweed, Joseph Bottoms, Nicholas Shields, Christopher Plummer. **1992**

LIEBESTRAUM ★★★ A strange tale comparable to the stylings of director David Lynch. Here a young architect is enmeshed in an ill-fated love triangle when he becomes obsessed with an old office building. Rated R for sexual situations and violence. 105m. **DIR:** Mike Figgis. **CAST:** Kevin Anderson, Pamela Gidley, Kim Novak, Bill Pullman. **1991**

LIES OF THE TWINS ★★½ Aidan Quinn has a field day playing identical twin psychiatrists (or *are* they actually two different people?), the gentler of whom falls in love with fashion model Isabella Rossellini. Things keep us guessing; alas, concluding events are just plain silly. Made for cable. 93m. **DIR:** Tim Hunter. **CAST:** Aidan Quinn, Isabella Rossellini, Iman, Hurd Hatfield. **1991**

LIFEBOAT ★★★½ A microcosm of American society, survivors of a World War II torpedoing, adrift in a lifeboat, nearly come a cropper when they take a Nazi aboard. Dumbly dismissed as an artistic failure by most critics, it has some ridiculous flaws, but is nonetheless an interesting and engrossing film. Tunnel-voiced Tallulah Bankhead is tops in this seagoing *Grand Hotel*. Look for Hitchcock's pictorial trademark in a newspaper. B&W; 96m. **DIR:** Alfred Hitchcock. **CAST:** Tallulah Bankhead, John Hodiak, William Bendix, Walter Slezak, Henry Hull, Canada Lee, Hume Cronyn, Heather Angel. **1944**

LINDA ★★★★ In this made-for-cable movie based on a John D. MacDonald novella, two neighborhood couples become good friends and go on vacation together. Tensions build and one wife shoots the other couple. Thus starts one very twisted plot. Good acting and a suspenseful plot keep the viewer watching. Rated PG-13 for violence. 88m. **DIR:** Nathaniel Gutman. **CAST:** Virginia Madsen, Richard Thomas, Ted McGinley, Laura Harrington, T. E. Russell. **1993**

LIPSTICK 🦃 Model is sexually molested by a composer. Rated R. 89m. **DIR:** Lamont Johnson. **CAST:** Margaux Hemingway, Mariel Hemingway, Anne Bancroft, Perry King, Chris Sarandon. **1976**

LIPSTICK CAMERA ★★ An aspiring television newscaster uses a miniature camera to get a scoop and impress her idol. But after novice reporter Ele Keats has the film developed, someone makes every attempt to silence her and retrieve the film. Pedestrian and underexposed. Rated R for nudity, adult situations, and violence. 93m. **DIR:** Mike Bonifer. **CAST:** Brian Wimmer, Ele Keats, Terry O'Quinn, Sandahl Bergman, Charlotte Lewis, Corey Feldman. **1993**

LISA ★★ A teenage girl plays flirtatious sex games on the telephone, unaware that her latest "partner" is a vicious serial killer. Implausible plot, cheap thrills. Rated PG-13. 95m. **DIR:** Gary A. Sherman. **CAST:** Cheryl Ladd, D. W. Moffett, Stacy Keenan. **1990**

LIST OF ADRIAN MESSENGER, THE ★★★★½ Excellent suspenser has a mysterious stranger visiting an English estate and the puzzling series of murders that coincide with his arrival. Crisp acting, coupled with John Huston's taut direction, make this crackerjack entertainment. With cameo appearances by Kirk Douglas, Tony Curtis, Burt Lancaster, Robert Mitchum, Frank Sinatra. B&W; 98m. **DIR:** John Huston. **CAST:** George C. Scott, Dana Wynter, Clive Brook, Herbert Marshall. **1963**

LITTLE DRUMMER GIRL, THE ★★½ Director George Roy Hill did everything he could to make this adaptation of John Le Carré's bestseller a fast-paced, involving political thriller. However, his work is thwarted by an unconvincing lead performance by Diane Keaton, who plays an actress recruited by an Israeli general (Klaus Kinski) to help trap a terrorist. Rated R for violence, profanity, suggested sex, and nudity. 130m. **DIR:** George Roy Hill. **CAST:** Diane Keaton, Yorgo Voyagis, Klaus Kinski. **1984**

LITTLE GIRL WHO LIVES DOWN THE LANE, THE ★★★½ *The Little Girl Who Lives Down the Lane* is a remarkably subdued film from a genre that has existed primarily on gore, violence, and audience manipulation. Jodie Foster gives an absorbingly realistic performance in the title role. Martin Sheen is the child molester who menaces her. It's a well-acted chiller. Rated PG. 94m. **DIR:** Nicolas Gessner. **CAST:** Jodie Foster, Martin Sheen, Alexis Smith. **1976**

LITTLE NIKITA ★★★½ Well-crafted, old-fashioned espionage story about the awakening of "sleeper" agents (planted by the Soviets twenty years earlier in San Diego). Sidney Poitier is the FBI agent tracking the situation, and River Phoenix plays a teenager caught in the middle. Richard Bradford is great as a manipulative but likable KGB agent. Rated PG for language and violence. 98m. **DIR:** Richard Benjamin. **CAST:** Sidney Poitier, River Phoenix, Richard Jenkins, Caroline

Kava, Richard Bradford, Richard Lynch, Loretta Devine, Lucy Deakins. 1988

LIVING TO DIE ★★ Private eye Nick Carpenter is called upon to stop an embezzling scheme that involves a Las Vegas luminary. The Vegas backdrop enlivens what is essentially a dreary story. Rated R for nudity and violence. 92m. **DIR:** Wings Hauser. **CAST:** Wings Hauser, Darcy Demiss. 1990

LOCK AND LOAD ★★ Members of the Eighty-second Airborne Special Forces group are stealing large sums of cash and jewels and killing themselves. One such member, haunted by dreams, wants to know why. Interesting premise. Rated R for violence. 89m. **DIR:** David A. Prior. **CAST:** Jack Vogel. 1990

LODGER, THE ★★★★ Alfred Hitchock's first signature thriller remains a timeless piece of wonder, showcasing the unique visual and stylistic tricks that would mark Hitchcock's work for years to come. Ivor Novello stars as a man who checks into a boardinghouse and becomes the object of scrutiny when a series of murders plague the area. Silent. B&W; 75m. **DIR:** Alfred Hitchcock. **CAST:** Ivor Novello, Malcolm Keen, Marie Ault. 1926

LONG GOODBYE, THE ★★★★ Elliott Gould gives one of his best performances in director Robert Altman's revisionist, haunting telling of the Raymond Chandler detective novel. "It's okay with me" is the easygoing credo of private eye Philip Marlowe (Gould) as he drifts among the rich and nasty. Multilayered movie adapted by Leigh Brackett, who also worked with Howard Hawks on *The Big Sleep*. Not for all tastes, but a must-see in our book. Rated R for violence and profanity. 112m. **DIR:** Robert Altman. **CAST:** Elliott Gould, Nina Van Pallandt, Sterling Hayden, Henry Gibson, Mark Rydell, Jim Bouton, David Carradine, David Arkin, Warren Berlinger. 1973

LOOKALIKE, THE ★★★½ Kate Wilhelm's thoughtful story becomes an absorbing made-for-cable thriller. Melissa Gilbert stars as a young woman not entirely convinced of her sanity, following the death of her young daughter. It all builds to a stylish climax, with a few well-hidden surprises. Brief violence. Rated PG-13. 88m. **DIR:** Gary Nelson. **CAST:** Melissa Gilbert, Diane Ladd, Thaao Penghlis, Frances Lee McCain. 1990

LOOKING FOR MR. GOODBAR ★★ A strong performance by star Diane Keaton almost saves this dismal character study about a woman drawn to sleazy sex and lowlifes. Rated R. 135m. **DIR:** Richard Brooks. **CAST:** Diane Keaton, Tuesday Weld, Richard Gere, Richard Kiley, Tom Berenger. 1977

LOOKING GLASS WAR, THE ★★ This plodding adaptation of John Le Carré's espionage novel about a Pole sent to get the scam on a rocket in East Berlin. Never gets off the ground. Most of the acting is as wooden as bleacher seating. Where's Smiley when we need him? Rated PG. 106m. **DIR:** Frank Pierson. **CAST:** Christopher Jones, Pia Degermark, Ralph Richardson, Anthony Hopkins. 1970

LOOPHOLE ★★½ In yet another heist film, unemployed architect Albert Finney concocts an ambitious plan to break into a highly guarded and impenetrable London bank. There is a bit of snap in the scenario and dialogue, but ultimately *Loophole* loses its freshness. Susannah York gives a fine performance. Not rated. 105m. **DIR:** John Quested. **CAST:** Albert Finney, Martin Sheen, Susannah York, Colin Blakely. 1980

LOVE AND MURDER ★★½ Decent low-budget thriller features a struggling photographer suddenly involved in a girl's questionable suicide. Rated R for violence and profanity. 87m. **DIR:** Steven H. Stern. **CAST:** Todd Waring. 1988

LOVE, CHEAT & STEAL ★★★½ Financial-wizard John Lithgow returns to his small-town roots to help save his father's bank and uncovers a drug-tinged money-laundering scheme. As if that weren't bad enough, he gets a visit from the "brother" of his attractive new wife...whom we know is actually her dangerously vengeful first husband (Eric Roberts, properly sinister). Thanks to dedicated performances, this complex yarn of double and triple crosses is quite fun. Rated R for profanity, violence, and nudity. 95m. **DIR:** William Curran. **CAST:** John Lithgow, Eric Roberts, Madchen Amick, Richard Edson, Donald Moffat, David Ackroyd. 1993

LOVE CRIMES ★★ For most of its brief running time, this movie, about the capture of a clever con man–rapist, is a gripping thriller with erotic overtones—then it ends abruptly, leaving the viewer wondering exactly what happened. This is because the studio nixed director Lizzie Borden's original ending and a quick fix was substituted. Rated R for nudity, violence, and profanity. 85m. **DIR:** Lizzie Borden. **CAST:** Sean Young, Patrick Bergin, Arnetia Walker, James Read, Ron Orbach. 1992

LOVE FROM A STRANGER ★★★ Just-married woman suspects her new husband is a murderer and that she will be his next victim in this suspense-thriller in the vein of *Suspicion*. B&W; 81m. **DIR:** Richard Whorf. **CAST:** Sylvia Sidney, John Hodiak, John Howard, Isobel Elsom, Ernest Cossart. 1947

LOVE KILLS ★★ Increasingly chaotic plot twists muddy this otherwise tedious made-for-cable thriller, which features Virginia Madsen as a professional photographer led to believe that her criminal psychologist husband has hired a maniac to kill her. Madsen sighs and pouts a lot, but she really doesn't make us care. Rated PG-13 for mild profanity and sexual themes. 92m. **DIR:** Brian Grant. **CAST:** Virginia Madsen, Lenny Von Dohlen, Erich Anderson, Jim Metzler. **1991**

LOVE, LIES AND MURDER ★★★ Made as a TV miniseries, this violent thriller is based on a 1985 murder. It appears at first to be clear-cut. However, there were actually two murderers and one Manson-like manipulator behind the ugly scenes. Talk about dysfunctional families! 200m. **DIR:** Robert Markowitz. **CAST:** Clancy Brown, Sheryl Lee, Moira Kelly, John Ashton. **1991**

LOVELY BUT DEADLY 🦃 A teenage boy dies by drowning while under the influence of illegal drugs. Rated PG. 88m. **DIR:** David Sheldon. **CAST:** Lucinda Dooling, John Randolph, Marie Windsor, Mark Holden. **1981**

LOWER LEVEL ★★★ A psychotic security guard manipulates elevators, doors, and alarms to set up the perfect date with his object of obsession. Surprisingly watchable. Rated R for nudity, violence, and gore. 85m. **DIR:** Kristine Peterson. **CAST:** David Bradley, Elizabeth Gracen, Jeff Yagher. **1990**

MACKINTOSH MAN, THE ★★★ A cold war spy thriller with all the edge-of-seat trimmings: car chases, beatings, escapes, and captures. Trouble is, it has been done before, before, and before. Paul Newman is the agent; wily and wonderful James Mason is the communist spy he must catch. Rated PG. 98m. **DIR:** John Huston. **CAST:** Paul Newman, James Mason, Dominique Sanda, Ian Bannen, Nigel Patrick. **1973**

MAD BOMBER, THE 🦃 Bert I. Gordon wrote, produced, and directed this mess. It's not even up to his usual low standards. Rated R for violence. 91m. **DIR:** Bert I. Gordon. **CAST:** Vince Edwards, Chuck Connors, Neville Brand. **1973**

MAD EXECUTIONERS, THE ★★½ After *Dark Eyes of London*, this is probably the quintessential Edgar Wallace–style chiller from West Germany (albeit based on a story by his son, Bryan). A vigilante court is executing elusive criminals, while in an unrelated subplot, a mad scientist is beheading women! Ignore the dubbing and concentrate on the pulpy thrills and creepy set design. B&W; 94m. **DIR:** Edward Willeg. **CAST:** Wolfgang Preiss, Harry Riebauer, Chris Howland. **1963**

MADONNA 🦃 Not the singer, but an unimaginative twist on *Fatal Attraction*. Rated R for nudity. 92m. **DIR:** Alain Zaloum. **CAST:** Deborah Mansy. **1990**

MAGIC ★★★½ *Magic* will make your skin crawl. The slow descent into madness of the main character, Corky (Anthony Hopkins), a ventriloquist-magician, is the most disturbing study in terror to hit the screens since *Psycho*. Rated R. 106m. **DIR:** Richard Attenborough. **CAST:** Anthony Hopkins, Burgess Meredith, Ed Lauter, Ann-Margret. **1978**

MAKE HASTE TO LIVE ★★★ A mobster framed for killing his wife, is finally released. Now he wants revenge from the one woman who escaped his grasp by outsmarting him. Compact, chilling thriller. B&W; 90m. **DIR:** William A. Seiter. **CAST:** Dorothy McGuire, Stephen McNally, Edgar Buchanan. **1954**

MALE AND FEMALE ★★★ Cecil B. DeMille yarn from his best period of exotic erotic fables. Loosely derived from James M. Barrie's play, *The Admirable Crichton*. For DeMille fans, it's quintessential fun. Silent. B&W; 100m. **DIR:** Cecil B. DeMille. **CAST:** Gloria Swanson, Thomas Meighan, Lila Lee. **1919**

MALICE ★★★ When a serial killer begins murdering female students in a New England college town, the institution's mild-mannered dean becomes involved in the investigation because he fears his wife, a former student, may be next. This thriller starts off extremely well, recalling the demented delights of Jonathan Demme's *Something Wild* but then settles into television-style drama. Even so, it never gets boring—thanks primarily to the high-powered performances. Rated R for profanity, violence, and simulated sex. 106m. **DIR:** Harold Becker. **CAST:** Alec Baldwin, Nicole Kidman, Bill Pullman, Bebe Neuwirth, George C. Scott, Anne Bancroft, Peter Gallagher, Josef Sommer. **1993**

MALTESE FALCON, THE ★★★★★ One of the all-time great movies, John Huston's first effort as a director is the definitive screen version of Dashiell Hammett's crime story. In a maze of double crosses and back stabbing, Humphrey Bogart, as Sam Spade, fights to get hold of a black bird, "the stuff that dreams are made of." B&W; 100m. **DIR:** John Huston. **CAST:** Humphrey Bogart, Mary Astor, Sydney Greenstreet, Peter Lorre, Elisha Cook Jr., Ward Bond. **1941**

MAN, A WOMAN AND A BANK, A ★★ An odd little caper flick that never quite gets off the ground. A couple of guys decide to rob a bank via computer, and—of course—things don't work out as planned. Rated PG. 100m. **DIR:** Noel Black. **CAST:** Donald Sutherland, Brooke Adams, Paul Mazursky. **1979**

MAN HUNT (1941) ★★★★ Based on *Rogue Male*, Geoffrey Household's crackerjack suspense novel about a British big-game hunter who wants to see if it's possible to assassinate Hitler, this is one of Fritz Lang's tensest American films. Dudley Nichols's script and Walter Pidgeon's performance lend authority and conviction, and the only shortcoming is a sentimental subplot with Joan Bennett. B&W; 105m. **DIR:** Fritz Lang. **CAST:** Walter Pidgeon, George Sanders, Joan Bennett. **1941**

MAN IN THE EIFFEL TOWER, THE ★★★★ A rarely seen little gem of suspense: an intriguing plot, a crafty police inspector (Charles Laughton), an equally crafty murderer (Franchot Tone), and an exciting conclusion. Well acted. 97m. **DIR:** Burgess Meredith. **CAST:** Charles Laughton, Franchot Tone, Burgess Meredith, Robert Hutton, Jean Wallace. **1949**

MAN WHO HAUNTED HIMSELF, THE ★★★½ Freaky melodrama about a car crash with unexpected side effects. Recovering from the wreck, a man (Roger Moore) begins to question his sanity when it appears that his exact double has assumed his position in the world. Imaginative film keeps the viewer involved from start to finish. Rated PG. 94m. **DIR:** Basil Dearden. **CAST:** Roger Moore, Hildegard Neil. **1970**

MAN WHO KNEW TOO MUCH, THE (1934) ★★★★★ The remake with James Stewart can't hold a candle to this superb suspense film about a man (Leslie Banks) who stumbles onto a conspiracy and then is forced into action when his child is kidnapped to ensure his silence. This is Hitchcock at his best, with Peter Lorre in fine fettle as the sneering villain. B&W; 83m. **DIR:** Alfred Hitchcock. **CAST:** Leslie Banks, Peter Lorre, Edna Best, Nova Pilbeam. **1934**

MAN WHO KNEW TOO MUCH, THE (1955) ★★★ James Stewart and Doris Day star in this fairly entertaining Hitchcock thriller as a married couple who take a vacation trip to Africa and become involved in international intrigue when they happen on the scene of a murder. It's no match for the original, but the director's fans no doubt will enjoy it. 120m. **DIR:** Alfred Hitchcock. **CAST:** James Stewart, Doris Day, Carolyn Jones. **1955**

MAN WITH BOGART'S FACE, THE ★★½ A modern-day Humphrey Bogart–type mystery. Film has fun with the genre while avoiding outright parody. A warmhearted homage. Enjoyable, but of no great importance. Rated PG. 106m. **DIR:** Robert Day. **CAST:** Robert Sacchi, Michelle Phillips, Olivia Hussey, Franco Nero, Misty Rowe, Victor Buono, Herbert Lom, Sybil Danning, George Raft, Mike Mazurki. **1980**

MANCHURIAN CANDIDATE, THE ★★★★½ This cold-war black comedy is still topical, chilling, and hilarious. Frank Sinatra gives a superbly controlled performance as a Korean War veteran who begins to believe that the honored heroics of a former member of his squad (Laurence Harvey) may be the product of brainwashing by an enemy with even more sinister designs. A delicate balance between hilarity and horror. Unrated, the film has violence. B&W; 126m. **DIR:** John Frankenheimer. **CAST:** Frank Sinatra, Laurence Harvey, Janet Leigh, Angela Lansbury, James Gregory, Leslie Parrish. **1962**

MANHATTAN PROJECT, THE ★★★ This contemporary comedy-adventure-thriller concerns a high school youth (Christopher Collet) who, with the aid of his idealistic girlfriend (Cynthia Nixon), steals some plutonium and makes his own nuclear bomb. There's a pleasing balance of humor and suspense. Rated PG for violence. 115m. **DIR:** Marshall Brickman. **CAST:** John Lithgow, Christopher Collet, Cynthia Nixon, Jill Eikenberry. **1986**

MANHUNTER ★★★★½ Thoroughly engrossing tale of an FBI man (William Petersen) following a trail of blood through the southeast left by a ruthless, calculating psychopath known only as "The Tooth Fairy," for reasons made shockingly clear. Rated R for violence and various adult contents. 118m. **DIR:** Michael Mann. **CAST:** William L. Petersen, Kim Greist, Brian Cox, Dennis Farina, Joan Allen. **1986**

MANIAC (1962) ★★★ Spooky mystery film about a madman on the loose in France, with Kerwin Mathews perfect as an American artist whose vacation there turns out to be anything but. Chilling atmosphere. B&W; 86m. **DIR:** Michael Carreras. **CAST:** Kerwin Mathews, Nadia Gray, Donald Houston. **1962**

MANTRAP ★★★ Although the plot about a New York bachelor lawyer who is vamped during a camping trip by a bored Clara Bow is pretty silly, the picture benefits from some outstanding location woodland photography by James Wong Howe. Silent. B&W; 68m. **DIR:** Victor Fleming. **CAST:** Clara Bow, Ernest Torrence, Eugene Pallette. **1926**

MARLOWE ★★★½ In this adaptation of Raymond Chandler's *The Little Sister*, James Garner makes a spiffy Philip Marlowe. This time, the noble detective is hired to find a missing man, and Bruce Lee, in an early but sparkling film appearance, is one of several interested parties who wants our hero to drop the case. 95m. **DIR:** Paul Bogart. **CAST:** James Garner, Gayle Hunnicutt, Carroll O'Connor, Rita Moreno, Sharon Farrell, William Daniels, Jackie Coogan, Bruce Lee. **1969**

MARNIE ★★★½ Unsung Alfred Hitchcock film about a strange young woman (Tippi Hedren) who isn't at all what she appears to be, and Sean Connery as the man determined to find out what makes her tick. Compelling, if overlong, but in the best Hitchcock tradition. 129m. **DIR:** Alfred Hitchcock. **CAST:** Sean Connery, Tippi Hedren, Diane Baker, Martin Gabel, Bruce Dern. **1964**

MASQUERADE (1988) ★★½ Overblown variation on Hitchcock's *Suspicion* with Rob Lowe playing the devious but attractive husband who may be after heiress Meg Tilly's money. Some new plot twists are introduced, but unfortunately these don't save *Masquerade* from playing a lot like *Dallas*. Rated R for language, nudity, simulated sex, and violence. 98m. **DIR:** Bob Swaim. **CAST:** Rob Lowe, Meg Tilly, Kim Cattrall, Doug Savant, John Glover, Dana Delany. **1988**

MCGUFFIN, THE ★★★ This British suspense-drama begins like Alfred Hitchcock's *Rear Window*, which is well and good, considering its title is taken from a phrase coined by Hitchcock himself! Charles Dance offers an excellent portrayal of a movie critic who becomes embroiled in a government cover-up. Brief nudity and sexual situations. 104m. **DIR:** Colin Bucksey. **CAST:** Charles Dance, Brian Glover, Ritza Brown, Francis Matthews, Phyllis Logan, Jerry Stiller. **1985**

MEAN SEASON, THE ★★★½ Miami crime reporter Kurt Russell finds himself the unwilling confidant of a maniacal killer in this exciting thriller. The film occasionally relies on stock shocks. Still, it is fast-paced and inventive enough to overcome the clichés. Rated R for violence. 109m. **DIR:** Phillip Borsos. **CAST:** Kurt Russell, Richard Jordan, Mariel Hemingway, Richard Masur. **1985**

MEETING AT MIDNIGHT Flat, dark, dreary *Charlie Chan* programmer from the Monogram Pictures period. Charlie investigates fortune tellers and mediums. A bore. B&W; 67m. **DIR:** Phil Rosen. **CAST:** Sidney Toler, Mantan Moreland, Frances Chan. **1944**

MEMORIES OF MURDER ★★ A wealthy Seattle socialite wakes up one morning to find she has been leading an alternate life for two years. 94m. **DIR:** Robert Lewis. **CAST:** Nancy Allen, Vanity, Robin Thomas, Olivia Brown, Donald Davis. **1990**

MERRY-GO-ROUND, THE ★★ A mismatched love affair between a count and a hurdy-gurdy operator with the backdrop of World War I. Silent. B&W; 115m. **DIR:** Rupert Julian. **CAST:** Norman Kerry, Mary Philbin. **1923**

MESMERIZED ★★½ In this modern take-off on *Svengali*, Jodie Foster plays a young orphan whose marriage to an older man (John Lithgow) proves stifling. Her imagination turns to murder, with the lovely New Zealand landscape in perfect contrast to her dreary thoughts. Unrated, contains mild profanity and sexual innuendo. 90m. **DIR:** Michael Laughlin. **CAST:** Jodie Foster, John Lithgow, Michael Murphy, Dan Shor. **1984**

MIDNIGHT (1989) ★★½ A sultry hostess who introduces horror movies is pursued by a struggling actor and fan. On the sound track: some listenable original songs and a nice version of "Low Spark of High-Heeled Boys," sung by Jim Capaldi. Rated R for language. 90m. **DIR:** Norman Thaddeus Vane. **CAST:** Lynn Redgrave, Tony Curtis, Frank Gorshin, Wolfman Jack. **1989**

MIDNIGHT COP ★★ The investigation of a drug-related murder leads a detective into a dangerous world of drug and prostitution rings. Rated R for profanity and nudity. 100m. **DIR:** Peter Patzack. **CAST:** Morgan Fairchild, Michael York. **1989**

MIDNIGHT WITNESS ★★ After a fight with his live-in girlfriend, Paul can't sleep, so he decides to play with his new video camera. Shooting out his window, he videotapes the police beating up a suspect. Now he and his girlfriend must run for their lives. Try not to fall asleep due to the bad plot and poor acting. Not rated, but contains violence, nudity, and simulated sex. 90m. **DIR:** Peter Foldy. **CAST:** Paul Johansson, Maxwell Caulfield, Karen Moncrieff, Jan-Michael Vincent, Mick Murray, Mark Pellegrino, Virginia Mayo. **1992**

MINDGAMES ★★★ Taut thriller features Maxwell Caulfield as a psychotic hitchhiker who attaches himself to an unhappy couple and their son. What follows is a series of violent and unnerving mind games. Rated R for violence. 93m. **DIR:** Bob Yari. **CAST:** Maxwell Caulfield, Edward Albert, Shawn Weatherly. **1989**

MIRACLE MILE ★★★★ A fascinatingly frightful study of mass hysteria centered on a spreading rumor that a nuclear holocaust is imminent. Anthony Edwards accidentally overhears a phone conversation that "the button has been pushed." He learns that Los Angeles is seventy minutes from destruction and must scramble about, trying to discover the truth and possibly save himself and others. Superb. Rated R. 87m. **DIR:** Steve DeJarnett. **CAST:** Anthony Edwards, Mare Winningham, John Agar. **1989**

MIRROR CRACK'D, THE ★★ Elizabeth Taylor, Kim Novak, and Tony Curtis seem to be vying to see who can turn in the worst performance in this tepid adaptation of the Agatha Christie murder mystery. Angela Lansbury makes an excellent Miss Marple, and Edward Fox is top-notch as her Scotland Yard inspector nephew. Rated PG. 105m. **DIR:** Guy Hamilton. **CAST:** Elizabeth Taylor, Kim Novak, Tony Curtis, Angela Lansbury, Edward Fox, Rock Hudson. **1980**

MIRROR IMAGES *Penthouse* pet Delia Sheppard plays twin sisters, one a stripper, the other a bored housewife. When the housewife steps into her sister's stiletto shoes, they take her face-to-face with a psychotic madman. Unrated, but contains enough nudity to make it equivalent to soft porn. 92m. **DIR:** Alexander Gregory Hippolyte. **CAST:** Delia Sheppard, Jeff Conaway, John O'Hurley, Nels Van Patten. **1991**

MIRROR IMAGES II In spite of its pretensions as an erotic thriller, the only element separating this pathetic, would-be drama from hard-core sex films is the absence of gynecological close-ups. Available in R-rated and unrated versions, both with incessant nudity, profanity, and simulated sex. 92m. **DIR:** Alexander Gregory Hippolyte. **CAST:**

Shannon Whirry, Luca Bercovici, Tom Reilly. **1993**

MR. FROST ★★★½ After being arrested for 125 murders by an English detective (Alan Bates), the mysterious Mr. Frost (Jeff Goldblum) refuses to speak for three years until a psychiatrist (Kathy Baker) attempts to reach him. That's when Frost begins claiming he is Satan. Intriguing blend of suspense and black comedy. Rated R for violence and profanity. 92m. **DIR:** Philip Setbon. **CAST:** Jeff Goldblum, Alan Bates, Kathy Baker. **1990**

MR. MOTO'S LAST WARNING ★★★ One of the last in the low-budget series that produced eight films in less than three years. This time out, the detective gets involved with terrorist spies intent on blowing up the French fleet in the Suez Canal. Enjoyable, quaint entertainment with a good supporting cast. B&W; 71m. **DIR:** Norman Foster. **CAST:** Peter Lorre, Ricardo Cortez, Virginia Field, John Carradine, George Sanders. **1939**

MR. WONG, DETECTIVE ★★★ First of five Mr. Wong films starring Boris Karloff as Hugh Wiley's black-suited sleuth is a notch above most of Mascot Pictures programmers. Mr. Wong attempts to solve the deaths of three industrialists, which have baffled the authorities and have the government and media in an uproar. Fun for mystery and detective fans. B&W; 69m. **DIR:** William Nigh. **CAST:** Boris Karloff, Grant Withers, Evelyn Brent, Maxine Jennings, Lucien Prival. **1938**

MR. WONG IN CHINATOWN ★★ A Chinese princess and her bodyguards are killed while she is trying to buy defense planes for her homeland, and Mr. Wong steps in to find the culprits. Tepid entry to a tolerable series. B&W; 70m. **DIR:** William Nigh. **CAST:** Boris Karloff, Grant Withers, Marjorie Reynolds. **1939**

MONA LISA ★★★★½ Bob Hoskins is Britain's answer to Humphrey Bogart and James Cagney. In this crime-thriller, Hoskins plays a simple but moral man whose less than honest endeavors have landed him in prison. Upon his release, he goes to his former boss (Michael Caine) in search of a job. Unrated; the film has profanity, suggested sex, and violence. 100m. **DIR:** Neil Jordan. **CAST:** Bob Hoskins, Cathy Tyson, Michael Caine, Clark Peters. **1986**

MOONLIGHTING (1985) ★★★★ This is the pilot film for the delightfully offbeat ABC series. Maddie, a supersuccessful model, suddenly finds herself facing poverty, thanks to an embezzler. She decides to sell off all her assets, including a money-losing detective agency. David, a fast-talking, irresistible eccentric, tries to talk her into making a career of sleuthing instead. Bruce Willis is dazzling as David. And the chemistry beween Willis and Cybill Shepherd heats up to just the right temperature. 97m. **DIR:** Robert Butler. **CAST:** Cybill Shepherd, Bruce Willis, Allyce Beasley. **1985**

MORAN OF THE LADY LETTY ★★★ A shanghaied socialite meets and falls in love with a tough seafarer, who turns out to be a woman in disguise. Dandy location photography around Catalina. A change of pace for Valentino purists. Silent. B&W; 70m. **DIR:** George Melford. **CAST:** Rudolph Valentino. **1922**

MORNING AFTER, THE ★★★½ An alcoholic ex-movie star (Jane Fonda) wakes up one morning in bed next to a dead man and is unable to remember what happened the night before. Fonda is terrific as the heroine-victim, and Jeff Bridges gives a solid performance as the ex-cop who comes to her aid. The result is an enjoyable thriller in the style of *Jagged Edge*. Rated R for profanity. 103m. **DIR:** Sidney Lumet. **CAST:** Jane Fonda, Jeff Bridges, Raul Julia, Diane Salinger, Richard Foronjy. **1986**

MORTAL PASSIONS 🦃 A slut plots to murder her wealthy husband with the help of her sheepish boyfriend. Rated R for violence, nudity, and profanity. 96m. **DIR:** Andrew Lane. **CAST:** Zach Galligan, Krista Erickson, Luca Bercovici, Michael Bowen. **1990**

MORTAL SINS (1990) ★★½ Private eye Brian Benben becomes embroiled in a series of murders that lead to television ministries and the mysterious daughter of a powerful television evangelist. (Alternate title: *Dangerous Obsession.*) Rated R for violence and nudity. 85m. **DIR:** Yuri Sivo. **CAST:** Debrah Farentino, Brian Benben, Anthony LaPaglia, James Harper. **1990**

MORTAL SINS (1992) ★★★ It appears that a priest is murdering young women, then giving them last rites. Father Thomas (Christopher Reeve) hears the confession of the murderer and starts to play detective. A few good twists keep the viewer guessing. Not rated, made for cable, but contains violence. 95m. **DIR:** Bradford May. **CAST:** Christopher Reeve, Roxann Biggs, Francis Guinan, Weston McMillan, Phillip R. Allen, Lisa Vultaggio, George Touliatos, Mavor Moore, Karen Kondazian. **1992**

MORTAL THOUGHTS ★★★ Demi Moore and Glenne Headly give strong performances in this relentlessly downbeat and disturbing drama. Director Alan Rudolph and screenwriters William Reilly and Claude Kerven explore the possible murder of an abusive, foulmouthed, drug-addicted husband (Bruce Willis) by his wife (Headly) and her best friend (Moore). Rated R for violence and profanity. 104m. **DIR:** Alan Rudolph. **CAST:** Demi Moore, Glenne Headly, Bruce Willis, John Pankow, Harvey Keitel, Billie Neal, Frank Vincent. **1991**

MOST DANGEROUS GAME, THE ★★★½ This sister production to *King Kong* utilizes the same sets, same technical staff, and most of the same cast to tell the story of Count Zaroff, the insane ruler of a secret island who spends his time hunting the victims of the ships that he wrecks. Filmed many times since and used as a theme for countless television plots, this original is still the standard to measure all the others by. Nonstop action for sixty-three tight minutes. B&W; 63m. **DIR:** Ernest B. Schoedsack, Irving Pichel. **CAST:** Joel McCrea, Fay Wray, Leslie Banks, Robert Armstrong. **1932**

MOTHER'S BOYS ★★½ A mentally unbalanced woman is willing to go to terrible lengths to get back the husband and three sons she abandoned years before. Everything-but-the-kitchen-sink thriller is stylish and effective, but has a nasty edge that keeps the supense from being pleasurable. Rated R for violence. 96m. **DIR:** Yves Simoneau. **CAST:** Jamie Lee Curtis, Peter Gallagher, Joanne Whalley, Vanessa Redgrave, Joss Ackland. **1994**

MOVING FINGER, THE ★★★½ The sleepy village of Lymston loses its serenity when residents begin receiving nasty anonymous letters; the situation so upsets the vicar's wife that she summons her good friend Miss Marple (Joan Hickson). This tale is highlighted by its engaging characters. Unrated; suitable for family viewing. 102m. **DIR:** Roy Boulting. **CAST:** Joan Hickson, Michael Culver, Sandra Payne, Richard Pearson, Andrew Bicknell. **1984**

MURDER ★★★ An early Alfred Hitchcock thriller, and a good one, although it shows its age. Herbert Marshall, a producer-director, is selected to serve on a murder-trial jury. He believes the accused, an aspiring actress, is innocent of the crime and takes it upon himself to apprehend the real killer. B&W; 92m. **DIR:** Alfred Hitchcock. **CAST:** Herbert Marshall, Norah Baring. **1930**

MURDER AHOY ★★½ Threadbare mystery has Miss Marple (Margaret Rutherford) investigating murder aboard ship. This was the last film in the British series, although it was released in America before the superior *Murder Most Foul.* Despite her considerable talents, Rutherford could not raise this sinking ship above the level of mediocrity. B&W; 74m. **DIR:** George Pollock. **CAST:** Margaret Rutherford, Lionel Jeffries, Stringer Davis, Charles Tingwell. **1964**

MURDER AT THE GALLOP ★★★★ Margaret Rutherford has her best Miss Marple outing in this adaptation of Agatha Christie's Hercule Poirot mystery, *After the Funeral.* She and Robert Morley play off each other beautifully in this comedy-laced tale, which has Marple insinuating herself into a murder investigation. Her assistant, Mr. Stringer, is played by Rutherford's real-life husband, Stringer Davis. B&W; 81m. **DIR:** George Pollock. **CAST:** Margaret Rutherford, Robert Morley, Flora Robson, Stringer Davis, Charles Tingwell. **1963**

MURDER BY DECREE ★★★½ Excellent cast stylishly serves up this Sherlock Holmes mystery. Christopher Plummer and James Mason are well suited to the roles of Holmes and Dr. Watson. The murky story deals with Jack the Ripper. Rated R for violence and gore. 121m. **DIR:** Bob Clark. **CAST:** Christopher Plummer, James Mason, Donald Sutherland, Genevieve Bujold, Susan Clark, David Hemmings, John Gielgud, Anthony Quayle. **1979**

MURDER BY NUMBERS (turkey) A dud. Rated PG-13. 91m. **DIR:** Paul Leder. **CAST:** Sam Behrens, Shari Belafonte-Harper, Dick Sargent, Cleavon Little, Jayne Meadows, Ronee Blakley. **1989**

MURDER BY PHONE ★★★ In this okay shocker, Richard Chamberlain is cast as an environmentalist whose lecture engagement in New York City turns out to be an opportunity to investigate the gruesome death of one of his students. Rated R. 79m. **DIR:** Michael Anderson. **CAST:** Richard Chamberlain, John Houseman. **1980**

MURDER BY TELEVISION ★★ Bela Lugosi plays an inventor in this low-budget murder mystery. Television was still something out of *Science and Invention* back in 1935, so it was fair game as a contrivance used to commit the crime. B&W; 60m. **DIR:** Clifford Sanforth. **CAST:** Bela Lugosi, June Collyer, George Meeker, Hattie McDaniel. **1935**

MURDER IN TEXAS ★★★★ Absorbing TV docudrama based on a true story. Sam Elliott is Dr. John Hill, a prominent plastic surgeon accused of murdering his socialite wife. A gripping study of psychopathic behavior. Good performances all around, including Farrah Fawcett and Andy Griffith, who reaped an Emmy nomination. 200m. **DIR:** William Hale. **CAST:** Farrah Fawcett, Sam Elliott, Katharine Ross, Andy Griffith, Bill Dana. **1983**

MURDER IS ANNOUNCED, A ★★★½ The sedate personals column of Chipping Cleghorn's *North Benham Gazette,* usually filled with pleas regarding lost dogs and bicycles for sale, is enlivened by a classified announcing a murder, which then takes place, as scheduled. Miss Marple (Joan Hickson) is summoned by the village constabulary. This is one of Agatha Christie's more convoluted stories. Unrated; suitable for family viewing. 153m. **DIR:** David Giles. **CAST:** Joan Hickson, Ursula Howells, Renée Asherson, John Castle, Sylvia Syms, Joan Sims. **1984**

MURDER MOST FOUL ★★★½ Like *Murder at the Gallop,* this is another Miss Marple adventure fashioned out of a Hercule Poirot mystery (*Mrs. McGinty's Dead*). The plot is only a framework for Margaret Rutherford's delightful antics. This time, she is the only dissenting member of a jury in a murder case. B&W; 91m. **DIR:** George Pollock. **CAST:** Margaret Rutherford, Ron Moody, Charles Tingwell, Stringer Davis, Francesca Annis, Dennis Price. **1964**

MURDER MY SWEET ★★★★ In the mid-1940s, Dick Powell decided to change his clean-cut crooner image by playing Raymond Chandler's hardboiled detective, Philip Marlowe. It worked marvelously, with Powell making a fine white knight in tarnished armor on the trail of killers and blackmailers. B&W; 95m. **DIR:** Edward Dmytryk. **CAST:** Dick Powell, Claire Trevor, Anne Shirley. **1944**

MURDER ON THE ORIENT EXPRESS ★★★★½ Belgian detective Hercule Poirot solves a murder on a train in this stylish prestige picture based on the Agatha Christie mystery. Albert Finney is terrific as the detective and is supported by an all-star cast. Rated PG. 127m. **DIR:** Sidney Lumet. **CAST:** Albert Finney, Ingrid Bergman, Lauren Bacall, Sean Connery, Vanessa Redgrave, Michael York, Jacqueline Bisset. **1974**

MURDER 101 ★★★★ Pierce Brosnan's considerable charm works perfectly in this cable-TV mystery by writer-director Bill Condon. Brosnan stars as a college writing instructor teaching his students the fundamentals of suspense fiction; naturally, somebody adopts his lesson plan and makes the poor professor Suspect Number One in a deft murder. Rated PG-13. 93m. **DIR:** Bill Condon. **CAST:** Pierce Brosnan, Dey Young, Raphael Sbarge, Kim Thomson. **1991**

MURDER OVER NEW YORK ★★ The world's most famous Oriental detective, Charlie Chan (Sidney Toler), goes after a gang of saboteurs plaguing the airways after a Scotland Yard inspector is felled by poisonous gas. Although cast with plenty of top-flight character actors, this one falls a little flat. The formula was wearing pretty thin after twenty-four films. B&W; 64m. **DIR:** Harry Lachman. **CAST:** Sidney Toler, Marjorie Weaver, Robert Lowery, Ricardo Cortez, Donald MacBride, Melville Cooper, Kane Richmond, Clarence Muse, John Sutton. **1940**

MURDER SHE SAID ★★★★ Now that Joan Hickson has brought Agatha Christie's Miss Marple to life in the superb BBC series, it has become common for mystery buffs to denigrate the four films starring Margaret Rutherford as Marple. We beg to differ. Rutherford makes a delightful screen sleuth, and this adaptation of *4:50 to Paddington* is quite enjoyable. The first entry in the series, it has Marple witnessing a murder on a train. B&W; 87m. **DIR:** George Pollock. **CAST:** Margaret Rutherford, Arthur Kennedy, Charles Tingwell, Muriel Pavlow, James Robertson Justice, Thorley Walters, Joan Hickson. **1961**

MURDER STORY ★★★½ In this little-known gem, an aspiring mystery writer (Bruce Boa) involves his mentor-hero (Christopher Lee) in a real-life killing. The story is a trifle contrived but generally enjoyable. Lee gets a rare chance to play a heroic character and makes the most of it. A must-see for fans of the genre. Rated PG. 90m. **DIR:** Eddie Arno, Markus Innocenti. **CAST:** Christopher Lee, Bruce Boa. **1989**

MURDER WITH MIRRORS ★★★ Inspired casting saves an otherwise pedestrian TV adaptation of Agatha Christie. Helen Hayes (never the best Miss Marple) comes to the aid of an old friend (Bette Davis), whose ancestral home is threatened. Although noteworthy as the only time Hayes and Davis appeared in the same project, George Eckstein's script is pretty ho-hum. 100m. **DIR:** Dick Lowry. **CAST:** Helen Hayes, Bette Davis, John Mills, Leo McKern. **1985**

MURDEROUS VISION ★★½ A missing-persons investigator (Bruce Boxleitner) teams with a reluctant psychic (Laura Johnson) to track down a psychotic killer with a penchant for severed heads. Writer Paul Joseph Gulino borrows pretty heavily from Thomas Harris's *Silence of the Lambs* for this chaotic made-for-cable thriller. Rated R for violence and language. 93m. **DIR:** Gary A. Sherman. **CAST:** Bruce Boxleitner, Laura Johnson, Robert Culp. **1991**

MURDERS IN THE RUE MORGUE (1986) ★★★ Here again: the Poe tale of a grisly double murder in nineteenth-century Paris. Solid performances by a top-notch cast, along with fine atmospheric cinematography by Bruno de Keyzer, give this made-for-television production a lift. Rated PG. 100m. **DIR:** Jeannot Szwarc. **CAST:** George C. Scott, Rebecca DeMornay, Ian McShane, Neil Dickson. **1986**

MUSIC BOX, THE ★★★½ An American lawyer is called upon to defend her Hungarian immigrant father when he is accused of having committed heinous war crimes during World War II in Nazi-occupied Hungary. Jessica Lange is excellent in this mystery with a message. Rated PG-13 for profanity. 123m. **DIR:** Constantin Costa-Gavras. **CAST:** Jessica Lange, Armin Mueller-Stahl, Frederic Forrest, Lukas Haas. **1989**

MY DAUGHTER'S KEEPER ★★½ British entry into *The Hand That Rocks the Cradle* subgenre features (surprise) a psychotic nanny who takes over the household, her charge, and finally the husband. Some chilling moments, but it all seems derivative at this point in the game. Not rated, but contains violence, nudity, and adult language. 109m. **DIR:** Heinrich Dahms. **CAST:** Nicholas Guest, Ana Padrao, Jocelyn Broderick, Kelly Westhof. **1993**

MYSTERY OF THE MARIE CELESTE, THE ★★★ On December 4, 1872, the brigantine *Marie Celeste*, said to have been jinxed by death, fire, and collision since its launching in 1861, was found moving smoothly under half-sail, completely deserted, east of the Azores. No trace of the crew was ever found. To this day, what happened remains a true mystery of the sea. This account offers one explanation. Also released as *The Phantom Ship*. B&W; 64m. **DIR:** Dension Clift. **CAST:** Bela Lugosi, Shirley Grey. **1937**

NAKED CITY, THE ★★★★½ Detailed story of a police investigation into the murder of a model takes the backseat to the star of this movie—New York City. Pace-setting location filming helps this interesting crime-drama that was the basis for the superior and long-running TV series. Producer-narrator Mark Hellinger died shortly before the premier showing. B&W; 96m. **DIR:** Jules Dassin. **CAST:** Barry Fitzgerald, Howard Duff, Dorothy Hart, Don Taylor, Ted de Corsia, House Jameson, James Gregory, Paul Ford. **1948**

NAKED EDGE, THE ★★★ Familiar, slow-moving story of a wife who suspects her husband is a murderer. Lots of red herrings. Gary Cooper's last film. B&W; 97m. **DIR:** Michael Anderson. **CAST:** Gary Cooper, Deborah Kerr, Eric Portman, Diane Cilento, Hermione Gingold, Peter Cushing, Michael Wilding. **1961**

NAKED FACE, THE ★★★ A psychiatrist (Roger Moore) finds himself the target of murder in this enjoyable suspense film. The police think he's the killer, as the first attempt on his life results in the death of a patient who had borrowed his raincoat. Rated R for violence and profanity. 98m. **DIR:** Bryan Forbes. **CAST:** Roger Moore, Rod Steiger, Elliott Gould, Art Carney, Anne Archer. **1984**

NAKED KISS, THE ★★★½ An ex-hooker makes a break and winds up in a small town only to discover more evil and trouble. Constance Towers as the girl who begins to find herself is a standout; the cast includes former veteran star Patsy Kelly and the silent screen's *Peter Pan*, Betty Bronson. Gritty *film noir* mystery. B&W; 90m. **DIR:** Samuel Fuller. **CAST:** Constance Towers, Anthony Eisley, Michael Dante, Virginia Grey, Patsy Kelly, Betty Bronson. **1965**

NAKED OBSESSION ★★ When a councilman samples his city's red-light district, he's framed for murder. This sexually explicit film plays faintly as a dark comic buddy picture. Unrated, but with considerable nudity and profanity. 85m. **DIR:** Dan Golden. **CAST:** William Katt, Maria Ford, Rick Dean, Roger Craig, Elena Sahagun. **1990**

NEIGHBOR, THE ★★★ Earnest performances give Kurt Wimmer's predictable script far more power than it deserves. Linda Kozlowski is properly sympathetic as a pregnant woman who fears next-door neighbor Rod Steiger might be more than a beloved, small-town obstetrician. Naturally, hubby Ron Lea dismisses her concerns as second-trimester hysteria. Steiger, for once subdued, delivers his best work in years. Rated PG for intensity and mild violence. 93m. **DIR:** Rodney Gibbons. **CAST:** Linda Kozlowski, Ron Lea, Rod Steiger. **1993**

NEMESIS (1986) ★★★½ Joan Hickson's Miss Marple beomes the "unbeatable rival no man may escape" in this adaptation of Agatha Christie's last novel. The English countryside forms the backdrop for this clever story. Unrated; suitable for family viewing. 102m. **DIR:** David Tucker. **CAST:** Joan Hickson, Margaret Tyzack, Anna Cropper, Valerie Lush, Peter Tilbury, Bruce Payne, Helen Cherry. **1986**

NEW ADVENTURES OF CHARLIE CHAN, THE (TV SERIES) ★★★ What do you get when you have an Irish actor (J. Carrol Naish) playing a retired Chinese detective? Unintentional but nonetheless delightful camp. Each of the three volumes released thus far contains three episodes of this British TV mystery series. B&W; 90m. **DIR:** Charles Haas. **CAST:** J. Carrol Naish, James Hong. **1957**

NIAGARA ★★★½ A sexy, slightly sleazy, and sinister Marilyn Monroe plots the murder of husband Joseph Cotten in this twisted tale of infidelity and greed, shot against the pulsing scenic grandeur of Niagara Falls. But plans go awry and the falls redeem a killer. Excellent location camera work adds to the thrills. 89m. **DIR:** Henry Hathaway. **CAST:** Marilyn Monroe, Joseph Cotten, Jean Peters. **1953**

NIGHT EYES 🦃 Andrew Stevens as a security guard/voyeur. Unrated version contains nudity, profanity, and violence. 95m. **DIR:** Jag Mundhra. **CAST:** Andrew Stevens, Tanya Roberts, Cooper Huckabee. **1990**

NIGHT EYES 2 ★★ Like watching a train wreck. Sleazy, yet oddly compelling, story of a private security guard who has an affair with the wife of a diplomat he was hired to protect. Not rated, but contains violence, profanity, and nudity. (An R-rated version is also available.) 97m. **DIR:** Rodney McDonald. **CAST:** Andrew Stevens, Shannon Tweed, Tim Ross. **1991**

NIGHT EYES 3 🦃 More of the same in the popular direct-to-video series about private security guard Andrew Stevens, who's always getting involved with his clients. Rated R for nudity; unrated version contains more. 97m./101m. **DIR:** Andrew Stevens. **CAST:** Andrew Stevens, Shannon Tweed, Tracy Tweed. **1993**

NIGHT GAME ★★½ Familiar story of a police officer (Roy Scheider) attempting to track down a serial killer before he can claim another female victim. The predictable ending is a bummer. Good performances, though. Rated R for violence and profanity. 95m. **DIR:** Peter Masterson. **CAST:** Roy Scheider, Karen Young, Richard Bradford, Paul Gleason, Carlin Glynn. **1989**

NIGHT GAMES ★★★ This film, which was originally made for television, led to the *Petrocelli* TV series for Barry Newman. He plays a lawyer who defends Stefanie Powers when she's accused of her husband's murder. There's enough intrigue and suspense in this film to capture most viewers' attention. Rated R. 78m. **DIR:** Don Taylor. **CAST:** Barry Newman, Susan Howard, Albert Salmi, Luke Askew, Ralph Meeker, Stefanie Powers. **1974**

NIGHT HAS EYES, THE ★★★½ This suspense film from war-weary Great Britain focuses on a schoolmarm who searches for a colleague who is missing on a mist-shrouded moor. Joyce Howard is excellent as the teacher-sleuth and the young James Mason does a credible job as a disturbed composer. B&W; 79m. **DIR:** Leslie Arliss. **CAST:** James Mason, Joyce Howard, Wilfrid Lawson. **1942**

NIGHT MOVES ★★★★ A dark and disturbing detective study with Gene Hackman superb as the private eye trying to solve a baffling mystery. This release was unfairly overlooked when in theatres—but you don't have to miss it now. Rated R. 95m. **DIR:** Arthur Penn. **CAST:** Gene Hackman, Susan Clark, Melanie Griffith. **1975**

NIGHT OF THE CYCLONE 🦃 Chicago detective stumbles onto a murder when he travels to the Caribbean. Rated R for profanity, nudity, and violence. 90m. **DIR:** David Irving. **CAST:** Kris Kristofferson, Jeff Meek, Marisa Berenson. **1989**

NIGHT OF THE FOLLOWING DAY, THE ★★★ Three men and a woman abduct an heiress as she returns home to France. Marlon Brando plays the compassionate Bud, who is tired of being a criminal. His coconspirators include a drug addict, an old washed-up criminal, and a sadist. The story line moves slowly but becomes very suspenseful near the end. Rated R for violence and nudity. 93m. **DIR:** Hubert Cornfield. **CAST:** Marlon Brando, Richard Boone, Rita Moreno, Pamela Franklin, Jess Hahn. **1968**

NIGHT OF THE HUNTER ★★★★½ Absolutely the finest film from star Robert Mitchum, who is cast as a suave, smooth-talking—and absolutely evil—preacher determined to catch and kill his stepchildren. The entire film is eerie, exquisitely beautiful, and occasionally surreal; watch for the graceful, haunting shot of the children's freshly killed mother. B&W; 93m. **DIR:** Charles Laughton. **CAST:** Robert Mitchum, Shelley Winters, Lillian Gish, James Gleason. **1955**

NIGHT RHYTHMS 🦃 Radio talk-show host Martin Hewitt awakes from one of his little after-hours liaisons, and finds his companion dead and himself framed for murder. Dull soft-core porn. Rated R for nudity, language, and violence; unrated version contains more of the same. 99m. **DIR:** Alexander Gregory Hippolyte. **CAST:** Martin Hewitt, Sam Jones, Deborah Driggs, Tracy Reed, David Carradine. **1992**

NIGHT SCHOOL 🦃 Students are (literally) losing their heads with worry over their grades. Rated R for graphic, but sloppy, violence. 88m. **DIR:** Ken Hughes. **CAST:** Leonard Mann, Rachel Ward, Drew Snyder, Joseph R. Sicari. **1981**

NIGHT TERROR ★★ Tepid made-for-TV suspense with Valerie Harper as terrified motorist pursued by madman Richard Romanus. Strictly by-the-numbers. 78m. **DIR:** E. W. Swackhamer. **CAST:** Valerie Harper, Richard Romanus, Nicholas Pryor. **1977**

NIGHT VISITOR (1989) ★★ When a compulsive liar (Derek Rydall) witnesses a Satanic murder committed by his history teacher, no one believes him. Rydall's childish whining is inconsistent with his role. Rated R for nudity, violence, and profanity. 93m. **DIR:** Rupert Hitzig. **CAST:** Derek Rydall, Allen Garfield, Michael J. Pollard, Shannon Tweed, Elliott Gould, Richard Roundtree. **1989**

NIGHT WALKER, THE ★★★½ Robert Bloch's intriguing script is the chief attraction of this moody little thriller, definitely among the best of director-producer William Castle's gimmick horror films. Wealthy Barbara Stanwyck can't stop dreaming about her dead husband, and the recurring nightmares prove to have an unusual cause. 86m. **DIR:** William Castle. **CAST:** Barbara Stanwyck, Robert Taylor, Lloyd Bochner. **1964**

NIGHTKILL ★★★ Largely unreleased in theatres, this is a tidy little cat-and-mouse thriller with former Charlie's Angel Jaclyn Smith as a conniving widow and Robert Mitchum as the world-weary investigator who gets caught up in her scheme. Despite some inept direction, the last half hour is a nail biter, particularly scenes in a bathroom shower. Rated R for violence, nudity, and profanity. 97m. **DIR:** Ted Post. **CAST:** Jaclyn Smith, Robert Mitchum, James Franciscus. **1983**

NIGHTMAN, THE ★★★ Steamy southern romantic thriller. A woman suspects she's being stalked by a former lover who spent eighteen years in prison for the murder of her mother. In flashbacks, she recalls the events and the passion that led to a bitter love triangle and the killing. Rated R for simulated sex, nudity, violence, and profanity. 96m. **DIR:** Charles Haid. **CAST:** Joanna Kerns, Jenny Robertson, Latanya Richardson, Lou Walker. **1993**

NIGHTMARE AT BITTERCREEK ★★ Nazi survivalists stalk a group of women camping in the mountains. The mediocre script offers a few chills and a modicum of suspense, but overall leaves one feeling unsatisfied. Made for TV. 92m. **DIR:** Tim Burstall. **CAST:** Lindsay Wagner, Tom Skerritt, Constance McCashin, Joanna Cassidy. **1990**

NO SECRETS 🖤 Silly teen fantasy features three wealthy girls vacationing at a remote ranch. When a psychotic drifter joins them, each girl finds his antisocial behavior irresistible. Senseless time waster. Rated R for profanity, violence, and sexual situations. 92m. **DIR:** Dezso Magyar. **CAST:** Adam Coleman Howard, Amy Locane. **1990**

NO WAY OUT ★★★½ In this gripping, sexy, and surprising suspense thriller, Kevin Costner stars as a morally upright naval hero who accepts a position with the secretary of defense (Gene Hackman) and his somewhat overzealous assistant (Will Patton, who walks away with the film). Things become a bit sticky when the secretary becomes involved in murder. Rated R for nudity, sexual situations, language, and violence. 116m. **DIR:** Roger Donaldson. **CAST:** Kevin Costner, Gene Hackman, Sean Young, Will Patton, Howard Duff, Iman. **1987**

NO WAY TO TREAT A LADY ★★★★ Excellent thriller with a tour-de-force performance by Rod Steiger, who dons various disguises and personas to strangle women and imprint them with red lipstick lips. Superb script, adapted from William Goldman's novel, and a skilled supporting cast: George Segal as a mothered cop, Eileen Heckart as his delightfully pick-pick-picking mother, and Lee Remick as the attractive love interest. Rated PG for violence. 108m. **DIR:** Jack Smight. **CAST:** Rod Steiger, George Segal, Lee Remick, Eileen Heckart, Michael Dunn, Murray Hamilton. **1968**

NOCTURNE ★★★ Somewhat deliberate but involving mystery yarn has police detective George Raft risking his career to prove that a composer's apparent suicide was actually murder. Colorful characters and good dialogue. B&W; 88m. **DIR:** Edwin L. Marin. **CAST:** George Raft, Lynn Bari, Virginia Huston, Joseph Pevney. **1946**

NORTH BY NORTHWEST ★★★★★ Cary Grant and Eva Marie Saint star in this classic thriller by the master himself, Alfred Hitchcock, who plays (or preys) on the senses and keeps the action at a feverish pitch. The story is typical Hitchcock fare—a matter of mistaken identity embroils a man in espionage and murder. 136m. **DIR:** Alfred Hitchcock. **CAST:** Cary Grant, Eva Marie Saint, James Mason, Martin Landau. **1959**

NOT A PENNY MORE, NOT A PENNY LESS ★★★½ Merciless business tycoon Edward Asner fleeces four investors residing in England, one of whom is a transplanted American college instructor (Ed Begley Jr.). Refusing to remain a victim, the professor gathers the other three and proposes they regain all their losses—not a penny more, nor a penny less—by whatever means necessary. Solid TV adaptation of the Jeffrey Archer novel. 180m. **DIR:** Clive Donner. **CAST:** Ed Begley Jr., Edward Asner, François-Eric Gendron, Brian Protheroe, Nicholas Jones, Maryam D'Abo, Jenny Agutter. **1990**

NOTHING UNDERNEATH 🖤 A ranger from Yellowstone goes to Italy, to investigate the disappearance of his kid sister. Not rated, but contains violence and nudity. 96m. **DIR:** Carlo Vanzina. **CAST:** Tom Schanley, Renée Simonson, Donald Pleasence. **1987**

NOTORIOUS ★★★★½ *Notorious* is among the finest Alfred Hitchcock romantic thrillers. Cary Grant, as an American agent, and Ingrid Bergman, as the "notorious" daughter of a convicted traitor, join forces to seek out Nazis in postwar Rio. Claude Rains gives one of his greatest performances. B&W; 101m. **DIR:** Alfred Hitchcock. **CAST:** Cary Grant, Ingrid Bergman, Claude Rains, Louis Calhern. **1946**

NUMBER 17 ★★½ Seldom-seen thriller from Alfred Hitchcock is a humorous departure from his later more obsessive films, but it still maintains his wry touches and unusual characters. Once again an unsuspecting innocent (in this case, a hobo) comes across something that places him in jeopardy (a gang of jewel thieves). B&W; 83m. **DIR:** Alfred Hitchcock. **CAST:** Leon M. Lion, Anne Grey, Donald Calthrop, Barry Jones. **1932**

NUTS ★★★★ Star-producer Barbra Streisand chaperoned Tom Topor's deft play to the big screen and gave herself a meaty starring role in the process. She's a high-toned prostitute facing a murder charge who may not get her day in court, because her mother and stepfather would rather bury her in an insane asylum. Rated R for language and sexual themes. 116m. **DIR:** Martin Ritt. **CAST:** Barbra Streisand, Richard Dreyfuss, Maureen Stapleton, Eli Wallach, Robert Webber, James Whitmore, Karl Malden. **1987**

OBSESSION ★★★★ This is director Brian De Palma's tour de force. Bernard Hermann scores again, his music as effective as that in *Taxi Driver*. The script, about a widower who meets his former wife's exact double, was written by Paul Schrader (in collaboration with De Palma). Critics enthusiastically compare this with prime Hitchcock, and it more than qualifies. Rated PG. 98m. **DIR:** Brian De Palma. **CAST:** Cliff Robertson, Genevieve Bujold, John Lithgow. **1976**

OBSESSIVE LOVE ★★½ *Fatal Attraction*-like made-for-TV thriller has soap-opera star Simon MacCorkindale fending off fan Yvette Mimieux. Handsome leads and topical story make up for an overly familiar plot. Unrated, but contains adult language and situations. 97m. **DIR:** Steven H. Stern. **CAST:** Yvette Mimieux, Simon MacCorkindale, Constance McCashin, Lainie Kazan, Kin Shriner. **1984**

ODD MAN OUT ★★★★ Carol Reed directed this suspenseful drama about a wounded IRA gunman (James Mason) on the run in Belfast and the people who help and hinder his escape. One of the hallmarks of postwar British cinema. B&W; 113m. **DIR:** Carol Reed. **CAST:** James Mason, Robert Newton, Kathleen Ryan, Dan O'Herlihy. **1946**

ODESSA FILE, THE ★★ Frederick Forsyth wrote the bestselling novel, but little of the zip remains in this weary film adaptation. German journalist Jon Voight learns of a secret file that may expose some former Nazis. Rated PG for violence. 128m. **DIR:** Ronald Neame. **CAST:** Jon Voight, Maximilian Schell, Derek Jacobi, Maria Schell. **1974**

ON DANGEROUS GROUND ★★½ Robert Ryan does a credible job as a crime-weary patrol cop who takes out his frustrations on the men he arrests and winds up transferred after bloodying one too many suspects. B&W; 82m. **DIR:** Nicholas Ray. **CAST:** Robert Ryan, Ida Lupino, Ward Bond, Ed Begley Sr., Cleo Moore, Olive Carey. **1951**

ON THE BLOCK ★★½ Baltimore strip joints threatened by a greedy land developer. This low-budget film would have been better if they had cut back on the dance acts. Rated R for nudity, profanity, and violence. 96m. **DIR:** Steve Yeager. **CAST:** Marilyn Jones, Michael Gabel, Howard Rollins Jr. **1991**

ONE BODY TOO MANY ★★½ Snappy dialogue and a memorable cast make this fast-paced whodunit worth a watch. Wisecracking Jack Haley is mistaken for a private investigator and finds himself in the thick of murder and intrigue. Bela Lugosi is again typecast as a menace. Nothing special, but not too bad for a low-budget programmer. B&W; 75m. **DIR:** Frank McDonald. **CAST:** Bela Lugosi, Jack Haley, Jean Parker, Blanche Yurka, Lyle Talbot, Douglas Fowley. **1944**

ONE FRIGHTENED NIGHT ★★ A stormy night, a spooky mansion, an eccentric millionaire, and a group of people stranded together was about all it used to take to make a scary movie. A good cast and some witty dialogue help, but there's only so much that can be done with this kind of mystery. B&W; 69m. **DIR:** Christy Cabanne. **CAST:** Wallace Ford, Mary Carlisle, Hedda Hopper, Charley Grapewin. **1935**

ONE SHOE MAKES IT MURDER ★★½ In this made-for-television movie, reminiscent in plot of *Out of the Past*, Robert Mitchum plays a world-weary detective who is hired by a crime boss (Mel Ferrer) to find his wayward wife (Angie Dickinson). Mitchum is watchable, but the story and direction never achieve a level of intensity. 97m. **DIR:** William Hale. **CAST:** Robert Mitchum, Angie Dickinson, Mel Ferrer, Jose Perez, John Harkins, Howard Hesseman. **1982**

ORDEAL BY INNOCENCE ★★ In this production of yet another Agatha Christie novel, the cast may be stellar, but the performances are almost all phoned in. Donald Sutherland plays a man who is certain that justice has been ill served in a small British community. Rated PG-13 for language and nudity. 91m. **DIR:** Desmond Davis. **CAST:** Donald Sutherland, Sarah Miles, Christopher Plummer, Ian McShane, Diana Quick, Faye Dunaway. **1984**

OTHER WOMAN, THE ★★ In this silly story about political corruption, an investigative reporter thinks her husband is having an affair with a hooker and later finds herself sexually attracted to the woman. Sam Jones is a corrupt politician with a punk hairdo. Rated R for nudity. 92m. **DIR:** Jag Mundhra. **CAST:** Sam Jones, Adrian Zmed, Lee Anne Beaman. **1992**

OUT OF SIGHT OUT OF MIND 🦃 Confusing tale involving a serial killer. A real waste of time. Rated R for violence. 94m. **DIR:** Greydon Clark. **CAST:** Susan Blakely, Edward Albert, Lynn-Holly Johnson, Wings Hauser. **1991**

OUT OF THE DARKNESS ★★★ Fine reenactment of the New York police chase of the serial killer known as Son of Sam. Martin Sheen plays the man responsible for his capture. Made for TV. 96m. **DIR:** Jud Taylor. **CAST:** Martin Sheen, Hector Elizondo, Matt Clark. **1985**

OUT OF THE PAST ★★★★½ This film, which stars Robert Mitchum, is perhaps the quintessential example of *film noir*. A private eye (Mitchum, in a role intended for Bogart) allows himself to be duped by the beautiful but two-faced mistress (Jane Greer) of a big-time gangster (Kirk Douglas). It's a forgotten masterwork. B&W; 97m. **DIR:** Jacques Tourneur. **CAST:** Robert Mitchum, Jane Greer, Kirk Douglas, Richard Webb, Rhonda Fleming, Dickie Moore, Steve Brodie. **1947**

OUT OF THE RAIN ★★ A drifter returns home to find his brother murdered and too many questions regarding his death. Although the movie offers a few surprises, it tries too hard to be a taut suspense-thriller, rarely delivering. Not rated, but contains violence, profanity, and brief nudity. 91m. **DIR:** Gary Winick. **CAST:** Bridget Fonda, Michael O'Keefe, John E. O'Keefe, John Seitz. **1990**

PACIFIC HEIGHTS ★★★★ When a yuppie couple (Melanie Griffith, Matthew Modine) purchases a Victorian apartment house in San Francisco, they figure they've found the home of their dreams. But it quickly turns into a nightmare when a secretive tenant moves in without permission and begins slowly destroying their property. An intelligent thriller that holds you right up to the edge-of-your-seat climax. Rated R for profanity and violence. 107m. **DIR:** John Schlesinger. **CAST:** Melanie Griffith, Matthew Modine, Michael Keaton, Beverly D'Angelo, Nobu McCarthy, Laurie Metcalf, Carl Lumbly, Dorian Harewood, Luca Bercovici, Tippi Hedren. **1990**

PACKAGE, THE ★★★★ In this taut thriller, skillfully directed by Andrew Davis, Gene Hackman gives one of his best performances as a soldier assigned to take a prisoner (Tommy Lee Jones) from Berlin to Washington, D.C. When his prisoner escapes, Hackman finds himself in the middle of a conspiracy whose masterminds want him out of the way. Rated R for violence and profanity. 109m. **DIR:** Andrew Davis. **CAST:** Gene Hackman, Tommy Lee Jones, Joanna Cassidy, John Heard, Dennis Franz, Pam Grier. **1989**

PAINT JOB, THE ★★½ Margaret has a problem. She's in love with two men. One is her husband. One is a painter who also happens to be her neighbor. Her husband also happens to be the neighbor's boss. Torn between two lovers, she could be torn apart when she finds out that one of them is a serial killer. Interesting cast makes this confusing thriller click. Rated R for violence, language, and adult situations. 90m. **DIR:** Michael Taav. **CAST:** Will Patton, Bebe Neuwirth, Robert Pastorelli. **1992**

PALERMO CONNECTION, THE ★★★ Political intrigue surrounds New York's mayoral candidate after he proposes drug legalization. On his honeymoon, he's framed by the mob. Now he must choose between accepting the status quo and challenging the Sicilian Mafia. Unrated, contains violence, profanity, and nudity. 100m. **DIR:** Francesco Rosi. **CAST:** James Belushi, Mimi Rogers, Joss Ackland, Vittorio Gassman. **1989**

PAMELA PRINCIPLE, THE 🦃 A dress designer attempts to have an affair with one of his customers, an act that eventually threatens his life. Rated R for simulated sex, nudity, profanity, and violence. 94m. **DIR:** Toby Phillips. **CAST:** J. K. Dumont, Veronica Cash, Shelby Lane, Troy Donahue, Frank Pesce. **1992**

PANIC IN THE STREETS ★★★★ Oscar-winning story focuses on a New Orleans criminal who is unknowingly the carrier of a deadly virus. The police attempt to capture him before he can infect others. Taut thriller. B&W; 93m. **DIR:** Elia Kazan. **CAST:** Richard Widmark, Jack Palance, Paul Douglas, Barbara Bel Geddes, Zero Mostel. **1950**

PAPER MASK ★★★ Intriguing British thriller features Paul McGann as an ambitious young man who poses as an emergency room doctor. His lack of training has a deadly effect on a female patient (Barbara Leigh-Hunt). The nurse on duty (Amanda Donohoe) may cover up for or expose him. Rated R for nudity and violence. 105m. **DIR:** Christopher Morahan. **CAST:** Paul McGann, Amanda Donohoe, Frederick Treves, Tom Wilkinson, Barbara Leigh-Hunt. **1989**

PARADINE CASE, THE ★★ Even the Master of Suspense can't win 'em all. Obviously chafing under the rein of mentor David O. Selznick, Alfred Hitchcock produced one of his few failures—a boring, talky courtroom drama that stalls long before its conclusion. Unrated; suitable for family viewing. B&W; 112m. **DIR:** Alfred Hitchcock. **CAST:** Gregory Peck, Ann Todd, Charles Laughton, Ethel Barrymore, Charles Coburn, Louis Jourdan, Alida Valli, Leo G. Carroll, John Williams. **1947**

PARALLAX VIEW, THE ★★★★ This fine film offers a fascinating study of a reporter, played by Warren Beatty, trying to penetrate the cover-up of an assassination in which the hunter becomes the hunted. Rated R. 102m. **DIR:** Alan J. Pakula. **CAST:** Warren Beatty, Paula Prentiss, William Daniels. **1974**

PARANOIA 🦃 American widow makes the mistake of taking an evil young couple into her isolated villa. Originally rated X for nudity and sexual situations, but a tame R equivalent now. 91m. **DIR:** Umberto Lenzi. **CAST:** Carroll Baker, Lou Castel, Colette Descombes. **1969**

PARTNERS IN CRIME (TV SERIES) ★★★½ Agatha Christie's high-society private detectives, Tommy and Tuppence (James Warwick and Francesca Annis), are introduced in the feature-length World War I–era tale, *The Secret Adversary*, lacking personal finances or steady jobs after having left war service, they band together and advertise their services as amateur sleuths. Series highlights include "Finessing the King," where sharp-eyed viewers will find all the clues necessary to match wits with the detectives; "The Affair of the Pink Pearl," in which Tommy and Tuppence's "guaranteed twenty-four-hour-service" is truly put to the test; and "The Case of the Missing Lady," where Tuppence's attempts to work undercover become particularly amusing. The authentic re-creations—from Tommy's antique cars to Tuppence's stylish hats—truly do justice to these classic Christie mysteries. 51m. **DIR:** Paul Annett, Christopher Hodson, Tony Wharmby. **CAST:** Francesca Annis, James Warwick, Reece Dinsdale. **1982–1983**

PASSENGER, THE ★★ Billed as a suspense-drama, *The Passenger* is a very slow-moving tale about a disillusioned TV reporter (Jack Nicholson) working in Africa. He becomes involved with arms smugglers. Rated R. 119m. **DIR:** Michelangelo Antonioni. **CAST:** Jack Nicholson, Maria Schneider, Jenny Runacre, Ian Hendry. **1975**

PEARL OF DEATH, THE ★★★★ Director Roy William Neill fashions Arthur Conan Doyle's "The Six Napoleons" into a rip-snorting screen adventure for Holmes (Basil

Rathbone) and Watson (Nigel Bruce). They're tracking a trio of criminals: Giles Conover (Miles Mander), Naomi (Evelyn Ankers), and the Creeper (Rondo Hatton). Good stuff. B&W; 69m. **DIR:** Roy William Neill. **CAST:** Basil Rathbone, Nigel Bruce, Evelyn Ankers, Miles Mander, Dennis Hoey, Mary Gordon, Ian Wolfe, Rondo Hatton. **1944**

PEEPING TOM ★★★½ Carl Boehm gives a chilling performance as a lethal psychopath who photographs his victims as they are dying. This film outraged both critics and viewers alike when it was first released, and rarely has been revived since. Not for all tastes, to be sure, but if you're adventurous, give this one a try. Rated R. 109m. **DIR:** Michael Powell. **CAST:** Carl Boehm, Moira Shearer, Anna Massey. **1960**

PELICAN BRIEF, THE ★★★½ Overlong but generally entertaining and suspenseful adaptation of the bestselling novel by John Grisham casts Julia Roberts as a student who accidently stumbles onto the truth behind the killings of two Supreme Court justices, a discovery that puts her life in danger. Roberts gets solid support, especially from the equally charismatic Denzel Washington as the investigative reporter who comes to her aid. Rated R for violence and profanity. 141m. **DIR:** Alan J. Pakula. **CAST:** Julia Roberts, Denzel Washington, Sam Shepard, John Heard, John Lithgow, Hume Cronyn, Tony Goldwyn, James B. Sikking, William Atherton, Robert Culp, Stanley Tucci. **1993**

PENDULUM ★★ In this rather confusing mystery, police captain George Peppard must acquit himself of a murder charge and catch the real culprit. A good cast perks things up some, but the story is too full of holes to be taken seriously. Some violence and adult situations. Rated PG. 106m. **DIR:** George Schaefer. **CAST:** George Peppard, Richard Kiley, Jean Seberg, Charles McGraw. **1969**

PENTHOUSE, THE 🦃 Oh, boy, another woman-in-jeopardy thriller. This one has Robin Givens trapped in her high rise with a fanatical ex-boyfriend. 93m. **DIR:** David Greene. **CAST:** Robin Givens, David Hewlett, Robert Guillaume, Cedric Smith. **1993**

PERFECT FAMILY ★★ A young, widowed mother hires a housekeeper who moves in along with her brother; incidentally, his family died in a mysterious accident. The story is ruined in the middle, and there's really no reason to finish watching. Not rated, made for cable, but contains violence. 95m. **DIR:** E. W. Swackhamer. **CAST:** Bruce Boxleitner, Jennifer O'Neill, Juliana Hansen, Shiri Appleby, Joanna Cassidy. **1992**

PERFECT STRANGERS ★★½ A hired assassin loses his cool when he discovers that an infant boy witnessed his last contract. An uneven but gritty suspense film with many nice touches and effective use of grungy Manhattan locations. Rated R for violence. 90m. **DIR:** Larry Cohen. **CAST:** Anne Carlisle, Brad Rijn, Stephen Lack. **1984**

PERFORMANCE ★★★★ Mick Jagger, the leader of the Rolling Stones rock group, stars in this bizarre film as Turner, a rock singer who decides to switch identities with a hunted hit man (James Fox). Codirected by Nicolas Roeg and Donald Cammell, *Performance* is a chilling, profoundly disturbing cinematic nightmare about the dark side of man's consciousness. Rated R for profanity, nudity, and violence. 105m. **DIR:** Nicolas Roeg, Donald Cammell. **CAST:** Mick Jagger, James Fox, Anita Pallenberg. **1970**

PHANTOM BROADCAST, THE ★★★ The murder of a popular radio crooner reveals he was little more than the handsome lip-synching front for the real offstage singer, a twisted hunchback with a velvet voice. Cleverly plotted drama. B&W; 68m. **DIR:** Phil Rosen. **CAST:** Ralph Forbes, Gail Patrick, Guinn Williams, George "Gabby" Hayes. **1933**

PHILBY, BURGESS AND MACLEAN: SPY SCANDAL OF THE CENTURY ★★★★ Yes, you can have an exciting spy story without James Bond chases and gimmicks. This riveting film spins the quiet, chilling tale of three of Britain's most notorious spies. They attended college together, were recruited by the Russians, and held high government security posts for thirty years before their discovery. Unrated. 83m. **DIR:** Gordon Flemyng. **CAST:** Anthony Bate, Derek Jacobi, Michael Culver, Ingrid Hafner, Elizabeth Seal. **1986**

PHILIP MARLOWE, PRIVATE EYE: FINGER MAN ★★★★ Another installment in the HBO series featuring Powers Boothe's delicious interpretation of Raymond Chandler's square-jawed detective. This time out, Philip Marlowe has his own life to worry about, as the sole witness to the killing of a government investigator who was poking into mob activities. Chandler would have been pleased. Unrated; brief violence. 55m. **DIR:** Sidney Hayers. **CAST:** Powers Boothe, William Kearns, Gayle Hunnicutt, Ed Bishop, William Hootkins. **1983**

PHILIP MARLOWE, PRIVATE EYE: THE PENCIL ★★★★ First in the series of absolutely gorgeous made-for-cable adaptations of Raymond Chandler's famed detective. Production values are superb, from the meticulous attention paid to period authenticity, to the mournful wail of John Cameron's music. Powers Boothe is perfect as the cynical, world-weary, hardboiled dick. In this episode, Marlowe is hired to protect a stoolie who's been sent a pencil by the mob (signaling their intention to kill him). 55m. **DIR:** Peter R. Hunt. **CAST:** Powers Boothe, William Kearns, Kathryn Leigh Scott, David Healy, Stephen Davies. **1983**

PHOBIA 💔 An almost-unwatchable nonthrilling thriller that combines psychobabble with murder. Rated R. 90m. **DIR:** John Huston. **CAST:** Paul Michael Glaser, Susan Hogan, John Colicos, Patricia Collins. **1980**

PHYSICAL EVIDENCE ★★½ Polished performances by Theresa Russell and Burt Reynolds are wasted in this convoluted police thriller. Russell is a public defender assigned to defend Reynolds, a cop accused of murder. A threadbare, erratic plot and haphazard direction by Michael Crichton ruin what could have been a first-rate film. Rated R for adult situations, violence, and profanity. 100m. **DIR:** Michael Crichton. **CAST:** Burt Reynolds, Theresa Russell, Ned Beatty, Kay Lenz. **1989**

PICKUP ON SOUTH STREET ★★★★ Samuel Fuller's lean and mean thriller about a pickpocket (Richard Widmark) who accidentally lifts a roll of top-secret microfilm and becomes a target for espionage agents. It's prime Fuller: suspenseful, tough, and violent. B&W; 80m. **DIR:** Samuel Fuller. **CAST:** Richard Widmark, Jean Peters, Thelma Ritter. **1953**

PICNIC AT HANGING ROCK ★★★★½ Surreal, hypnotic suspense story revolves around the mysterious disappearance of a group of students from an all-girls' school at the turn of the century in Australia. Director Peter Weir fashions a truly unsettling motion picture. His fans will rank it among his best. 110m. **DIR:** Peter Weir. **CAST:** Rachel Roberts, Dominic Guard, Helen Morse, Jacki Weaver. **1975**

PLAY MISTY FOR ME ★★★★ A suspenseful shocker in which director-star Clint Eastwood, playing a disc jockey, is stalked by a crazed fan (Jessica Walter). It puts goose bumps on your goose bumps and marked an auspicious directorial debut for the squinty-eyed star. Rated R. 102m. **DIR:** Clint Eastwood. **CAST:** Clint Eastwood, Jessica Walter, Donna Mills, John Larch, Irene Hervey. **1971**

PLAY NICE ★★ A game of cat and mouse is played by an angry cop and a brutal serial killer. Predictable thriller. Rated R for violence and language. 89m. **DIR:** Terri Treas. **CAST:** Ed O'Ross. **1992**

PLUMBER, THE ★★★½ A slightly unhinged plumber completely destroys a young couple's bathroom and begins to terrorize the woman of the house during his visits to make the repairs. A very black comedy-horror-film from the director of *Witness*. Originally made for Australian television. No rating; contains some strong language. 76m. **DIR:** Peter Weir. **CAST:** Ivar Kants, Judy Morris, Robert Coleby. **1980**

POCKETFUL OF RYE, A ★★½ Agatha Christie's Miss Marple (Joan Hickson) arrives late in this mystery, which concerns a murder that is somehow connected with a nursery rhyme. Unrated, suitable for family viewing. 102m. **DIR:** Guy Slater. **CAST:** Joan Hickson, Peter Davison, Fabia Drake, Timothy West, Tom Wilkinson, Clive Merrison. **1984**

POIROT (SERIES) ★★★★★ Agatha Christie's endearing and eccentric private detective, Hercule Poirot—a Belgian policeman who fled to England in 1914 as a refugee—is perfectly portrayed by David Suchet (down to the natty wardrobe and impeccably groomed mustache) in this engaging series of mysteries faithfully dramatized by Clive Exton. Poirot—joined by his faithful companion Captain Hastings (Hugh Fraser) and loyal and efficient secretary Miss Lemon (Pauline Moran)—solves a variety of murder mysteries with panache. Highlights include "Murder in the Mews," in which Poirot and his friend, Inspector Japp of Scotland Yard (Philip Jackson), work together to solve a murder; "Triangle at Rhodes," filmed on location in the beautiful Greek islands, with a wonderfully tricky plot and an intriguing cast of characters; and "Problem at Sea," where Poirot and Hastings's Mediterranean cruise soon turns into a busman's holiday. each tape. 52m. **DIR:** Edward Bennett, Renny Rye. **CAST:** David Suchet, Hugh Fraser, Philip Jackson, Pauline Moran. **1989**

POISON IVY (1992) ★★★½ Drew Barrymore makes a heck of an impact in a very adult role as Ivy, a sleazy teen who is taken in by a wealthy family. Ivy likes what she sees, especially dad (Tom Skerritt), whom she slowly seduces as she works to make the family her own. Rated R for profanity and suggested sex. 92m. **DIR:** Katt Shea Ruben. **CAST:** Drew Barrymore, Sara Gilbert, Tom Skerritt, Cheryl Ladd. **1992**

POSITIVE I.D. ★★½ Slow-developing story about a suburban housewife (Stephanie Rascoe) who, after being raped, assumes another identity to escape her past life. Rascoe makes a remarkable transformation from plain housewife to knockout, and the twist ending is ample reward for those patient enough to sit through the first hour of the film. Rated R for language and nudity. 93m. **DIR:** Andy Anderson. **CAST:** Stephanie Rascoe, John Davies, Steve Fromholz. **1988**

POSSESSED BY THE NIGHT ★★½ A sizzling thriller about a strange talisman that unleashes a writer's most erotic and dangerous desires. While in a tender relationship with wife Sandahl Bergman, Ted Prior tests the limits of his control by bedding sensual Shannon Tweed. When he becomes uncontrollable, the fireworks really begin to explode. Rated R for nudity, language, and violence; unrated version contains more sex. 87m. **DIR:** Fred Olen Ray. **CAST:** Ted Prior, Shannon Tweed, Sandahl Bergman, Chad McQueen, Henry Silva. **1993**

POSTMAN ALWAYS RINGS TWICE, THE (1946) ★★★★ If you wondered what went wrong in the sometimes steamily sexy and all too often soggy 1981 screen version of James M. Cain's celebrated novel, you need only watch this 1946 adaptation. John Garfield and Lana Turner play the lovers who murder the husband who stands in the way of their lust and suffer the consequences. B&W; 113m. **DIR:** Tay Garnett. **CAST:** John Garfield, Lana Turner, Cecil Kellaway, Hume Cronyn. **1946**

POSTMAN ALWAYS RINGS TWICE, THE (1981) ★★★ Jack Nicholson plays the drifter whose lust for a married woman (Jessica Lange) leads to murder in this disappointing remake based on James M. Cain's hardboiled novel of sex and violence. After an electric first hour, it begins to ramble and ends abruptly, leaving the viewer dissatisfied. Rated R for graphic sex and violence. 123m. **DIR:** Bob Rafelson. **CAST:** Jessica Lange, Jack Nicholson, John Colicos, Michael Lerner, John P. Ryan, Anjelica Huston. **1981**

PRAYER FOR THE DYING, A ★★ An overwrought adaptation of Jack Higgins's exciting thriller which sounds preachy even when trying to be suspenseful. Mickey Rourke is an IRA assassin who finds his conscience after unintentionally killing some schoolchildren; he flees to London and engages natty Alan Bates to help him out of the country. Rated R for language and violence. 107m. **DIR:** Mike Hodges. **CAST:** Mickey Rourke, Bob Hoskins, Alan Bates, Sammi Davis. **1987**

PRAYING MANTIS ★★★ In this made-for-cable original, a woman (Jane Seymour) who was abused as a child by her father kills her husbands on their wedding nights. Now she has fallen in love with a bookstore owner (Barry Bostwick), whose son and sister-in-law (Frances Fisher) don't trust her. Very good acting by Bostwick and Fisher, but the plot is on the predictable side. Rated PG-13 for violence. 90m. **DIR:** James Keach. **CAST:** Jane Seymour, Barry Bostwick, Chad Allen, Frances Fisher. **1993**

PRESIDENT'S PLANE IS MISSING, THE ★★★ Crisis after crisis occurs when *Air Force One* disappears with the president on board. This story of indecision and desire for control against a background of international crisis is an engaging suspense yarn. A very good story is helped by a veteran cast. 100m. **DIR:** Daryl Duke. **CAST:** Buddy Ebsen, Peter Graves, Arthur Kennedy, Raymond Massey, Mercedes McCambridge, Rip Torn, Dabney Coleman. **1971**

PRESUMED INNOCENT ★★★★½ Director Alan J. Pakula's superb version of Scott Turow's critically acclaimed best-seller features Harrison Ford as a prosecuting attorney who finds himself under suspicion when his mistress is murdered. Ford is supported by a terrific cast, with character actor John Spencer giving a standout performance. Even if you've read the novel, you'll want to watch this gripping thriller. Rated R for violence, profanity, and nudity. 124m. **DIR:** Alan J. Pakula. **CAST:** Harrison Ford, Brian Dennehy, Bonnie Bedelia, Greta Scacchi, Raul Julia, Paul Winfield, John Spencer. **1990**

PRETTY KILL 💔 A madam involved with a police detective hires a hooker who just happens to have a multiple-personality disorder. Rated R for violence and nudity. 95m. **DIR:** George Kaczender. **CAST:** David Birney, Season Hubley, Yaphet Kotto. **1987**

PREY OF THE CHAMELEON ★★★ Escaped mental patient Daphne Zuniga adopts the identity and personality of each woman she meets and kills, much to the frustration of pursuing FBI agents. Good ol' boy James Wilder, making a mess of his reconciliation with girlfriend Alexandra Paul (nicely credible as a small-town deputy sheriff), unwittingly gives a ride to the wrong hitchhiker. Made-for-cable mystery. 91m. **DIR:** Fleming B. Fuller. **CAST:** Daphne Zuniga, James Wilder, Alexandra Paul, Don Harvey. **1992**

PRIDE OF THE CLAN, THE ★★★★ Picturesque, crisply photographed saga of the Scottish Highlands. To those viewers who know Mary Pickford's later costume pictures in the 1920s, the spunky character and the action pacing will be a welcome surprise. Silent. B&W; 70m. **DIR:** Maurice Tourneur **CAST:** Mary Pickford, Matt Moore. **1917**

PRIME SUSPECT 1 ★★★★★ Gritty crime-dramas don't get better than this contemporary murder mystery, which introduces author Lynda La Plante's outspoken Detective Chief Inspector Jane Tennison (Helen Mirren). Determined to make her mark in the mostly all-boys club of the British police force, Tennison inherits a baffling murder case after another detective suffers a heart attack. While coping with her often-hostile colleagues, she comes across a connected second murder. The story ranks among the best police procedurals, but Mirren herself brings this miniseries to life—although often arrogant and unlikable, Tennison always fascinates. 240m. **DIR:** Chris Menaul. **CAST:** Helen Mirren, Tom Bell, John Benfield, John Bowe, Zoe Wanamaker. **1990**

PRIME SUSPECT 2 ★★★★ Helen Mirren, returning as Detective Chief Inspector Jane Tennison, tries to integrate her squad with the team's first black inspector. The remains of a young girl are found beneath an apartment patio in a primarily Afro-Caribbean neighborhood, and race relations are strained past the breaking point by an opportunistic politician. While at times overly melodramatic, this miniseries suffers only when compared to its predecessor—by most standards, it's a corker. 240m. **DIR:** John

Strickland. **CAST:** Helen Mirren, Colin Salmon, John Benfield, Jack Ellis, Claire Benedict, George Harris. **1992**

PRIME SUSPECT 3 ★★★★ Helen Mirren's gutsy, caustic Detective Chief Inspector Jane Tennison is back, this time after having been demoted from homicide to Soho's Vice Squad, where she must again endure the sexist derision of a colleague she thought she had left behind (back in *Prime Suspect 1*). Personal antagonisms are shuttled aside, however, when the burned body of a 15-year-old male prostitute is found in the apartment of a cross-dressing cabaret entertainer. Creator Lynda La Plante weaves a particularly complex mystery involving cover-ups, departmental spying, and homophobia. 240m. **DIR:** David Drury. **CAST:** Helen Mirren, Tom Bell, Peter Capaldi, David Thewlis, Michael J. Shannon, Mark Strong. **1993**

PRIVATE LIFE OF SHERLOCK HOLMES, THE ★★★★½ Director Billy Wilder's affectionately satirical pastiche of the Conan Doyle stories reveals the "secrets" allegedly shared by Sherlock Holmes (Robert Stephens) and Dr. John H. Watson (Colin Blakely). It does so with wit, humor, taste, and even suspense. Rated PG. 125m. **DIR:** Billy Wilder. **CAST:** Robert Stephens, Colin Blakely, Genevieve Page, Christopher Lee, Irene Handl, Clive Revill, Stanley Holloway. **1970**

PSYCHIC ★★ A serial killer is on the loose with a deadly belt buckle. A psychic (Zach Galligan) dreams the deaths of various females, including the professor (Catherine Mary Stewart) that he has fallen in love with. Poor writing and acting strangle this film. Made for cable. 91m. **DIR:** George Mihalka. **CAST:** Zach Galligan, Catherine Mary Stewart, Michael Nouri. **1992**

PUBLIC EYE, THE ★★★½ Writer-director Howard Franklin's fascinating *film noir* homage concerns a scrappy 1940s tabloid photographer (Joe Pesci) whose reputation for quality makes him the shutterbug of choice when major criminals get booked. Our hero gets involved in a twisty case involving a nightclub owner. Rated R for violence and profanity. 98m. **DIR:** Howard Franklin. **CAST:** Joe Pesci, Barbara Hershey, Jared Harris, Stanley Tucci. **1992**

PURSUIT TO ALGIERS ★★★ Basil Rathbone's Holmes and Nigel Bruce's Watson become bodyguards accompanying the young heir to a royal throne on a hazardous sea voyage. Their client disguises himself as Watson's nephew, which makes for some droll dialogue. One of the few Rathbone/Bruce films that borrows nothing from the canon. Unrated—suitable for family viewing. B&W; 65m. **DIR:** Roy William Neill. **CAST:** Basil Rathbone, Nigel Bruce, John Abbott, Marjorie Riordan, Martin Kosleck, Rosalind Ivan. **1945**

PYX, THE 🦃 A dead prostitute and the police investigation mounted to uncover her killer. Rated R for violence. 111m. **DIR:** Harvey Hart. **CAST:** Karen Black, Christopher Plummer, Donald Pilon. **1973**

Q & A ★★★★ Nick Nolte gives a compelling performance as a much-decorated police detective whose brutal killing of a Puerto Rican drug dealer brings about an investigation, which novice assistant district attorney Timothy Hutton is drafted into conducting. Rated R for brutal violence, profanity, and nudity. 134m. **DIR:** Sidney Lumet. **CAST:** Nick Nolte, Timothy Hutton, Armand Assante, Patrick O'Neal. **1990**

QUAKE ★★ The good news is that lovely Erika Anderson has survived a ravaging San Francisco earthquake. The bad news is that Steve Railsback, obsessed with Anderson, kidnaps her amidst all the confusion. The psychological aftershocks between the two barely keep this slight effort from slipping into the cracks. Rated R for language and violence. 89m. **DIR:** Louis Morneau. **CAST:** Steve Railsback, Erika Anderson, Eb Lottimer, Burton Gilliam, Dick Miller. **1992**

QUICKSAND: NO ESCAPE ★★½ An honest family man (Tim Matheson) gets mixed up in deceit, bribery, and murder. Donald Sutherland is great at portraying the nemesis: a slimy private detective. The twists in this made-for-cable chiller seem interesting at first, but then they just become unbelievable. 96m. **DIR:** Michael Pressman. **CAST:** Donald Sutherland, Tim Matheson, Jay Acovone, Timothy Carhart. **1991**

RAGGEDY MAN ★★★½ Sissy Spacek gives another outstanding performance as a World War II divorcée trying to raise two sons and improve their lives in a small Texas Gulf Coast town. *Raggedy Man* is a curious mixture of styles. It begins as a character study and ends like a horror film. But it works. Rated PG for violence. 94m. **DIR:** Jack Fisk. **CAST:** Sissy Spacek, Eric Roberts, William Sanderson, Tracey Walter, Sam Shepard, Henry Thomas. **1981**

RAIN KILLER, THE ★★★ Good suspense film, in which the police try to track down a homicidal maniac, who only kills women during rainstorms. Many impressive plot twists, as well as interesting sets and lighting. Rated R for violence, nudity, and profanity. 94m. **DIR:** Ken Stein. **CAST:** Ray Sharkey, David Beecroft, Michael Chiklis, Tania Coleridge, Woody Brown. **1990**

RAINBOW WARRIOR ★★½ Direct-to-video mystery is based on the real-life bombing of the Greenpeace vessel *Rainbow Warrior*, which resulted in the death of a crew member. Sam Neill and Jon Voight play men on opposite sides of the law who team up to solve the crime. Less preachy than one might expect, it makes a statement while remaining entertaining. Rated PG for violence. 93m. **DIR:** Michael Tuchner. **CAST:** Sam Neill, Jon Voight, Bruno Lawrence, Kerry Fox, John Callen. **1994**

RAMPAGE ★★ Based on the "vampire killings" committed by Richard Trenton Chase in Sacramento, California, in the late 1970s, writer-director William Friedkin's *Rampage* sat on the shelf for more than five years—and probably should have stayed there. Rated R for violence and profanity. 97m. **DIR:** William Friedkin. **CAST:** Michael Biehn, Alex McArthur, Nicholas Campbell, Deborah Van Valkenburgh, John Harkins, Art La Fleur. **1992**

RANSOM ★★½ When a psycho begins killing people in a small town and refuses to stop until he receives a $4 million ransom, Stuart Whitman (the richest man in town) hires a mercenary (Oliver Reed) to kill the extortionist. There are some slow moments, but worse than these are the unanswered questions about why the murderer dresses like an American Indian and what his motive really is. Rated PG for violence. 90m. **DIR:** Richard Compton. **CAST:** Oliver Reed, Stuart Whitman, Deborah Raffin, John Ireland, Jim Mitchum, Paul Koslo. **1977**

REAL MCCOY, THE ★★ Kim Basinger plays an ace safecracker, trying to go straight, who is blackmailed into one last heist by her former boss. Except for the gender switch on the protagonist, the premise is old hat. Still, with the actors on hand, it could have been better if there had been a few surprises in the script or any suspense in the direction. Rated PG-13 for violence and profanity. 104m. **DIR:** Russell Mulcahy. **CAST:** Kim Basinger, Val Kilmer, Terence Stamp, Gailard Sartain. **1993**

REAR WINDOW ★★★★★ James Stewart plays a magazine photographer who, confined to a wheelchair because of a broken leg, seeks diversion in watching his neighbors, often with a telephoto lens. He soon becomes convinced that one neighbor (Raymond Burr) has murdered his spouse and dismembered the body. One of the director's best. 112m. **DIR:** Alfred Hitchcock. **CAST:** James Stewart, Raymond Burr, Grace Kelly, Wendell Corey, Thelma Ritter, Judith Evelyn. **1954**

REBECCA ★★★★★ *Rebecca* won an Oscar for best picture and nominations for its stars, Laurence Olivier and Joan Fontaine. The popular Daphne du Maurier novel was transferred to the screen without losing any of its gothic blend of romance and mystery. Judith Anderson as the sinister housekeeper is one of the most compelling figures in film history. B&W; 130m. **DIR:** Alfred Hitchcock. **CAST:** Laurence Olivier, Joan Fontaine, George Sanders, Nigel Bruce, Reginald Denny, Judith Anderson. **1940**

RED HEAT (1985) ★★ Linda Blair is mistakenly arrested as a spy and sentenced to prison. Lurid and excessively violent. 104m. **DIR:** Robert Collector. **CAST:** Linda Blair, Sylvia Kristel, William Ostrander, Sue Kiel. **1985**

RED HOUSE, THE ★★★½ A gripping suspense melodrama enhanced by a musical score by Miklos Rozsa. Edward G. Robinson employs Rory Calhoun to keep the curious away from a decaying old house deep in the woods. But his niece and a young hired hand *must* learn the secret. B&W; 100m. **DIR:** Delmer Daves. **CAST:** Edward G. Robinson, Lon McCallister, Allene Roberts, Julie London, Judith Anderson, Rory Calhoun, Ona Munson. **1947**

RED ROCK WEST ★★★½ Try as he might, mostly honest drifter Nicolas Cage can't leave the small town of Red Rock West...and he gets in more trouble each time he returns. John and Rick Dahl's twisty script involves a corrupt sheriff (J. T. Walsh) arranging the murder of his scheming wife (Lara Flynn Boyle), and the impertinent killer (Dennis Hopper) hired for the job. The seriocomic tone properly emphasizes Cage's plight, and the plot will definitely keep you guessing. Rated R for profanity and violence. 98m. **DIR:** John Dahl. **CAST:** Nicolas Cage, Dennis Hopper, Lara Flynn Boyle, Timothy Carhart, J. T. Walsh. **1993**

RED WIND [turkey] Moronic psychosexual made-for-cable thriller. Rated R for violence and gore. 93m. **DIR:** Alan Metzger. **CAST:** Lisa Hartman, Philip Casnoff, Antoni Corone, Deanna Lund. **1991**

REFLECTION OF FEAR ★★½ Confusing, uninspired story of a beautiful young girl who becomes the central figure in a cobweb of crime and murder. Should have been better, considering the cast. Rated R. 102m. **DIR:** William Fraker. **CAST:** Robert Shaw, Mary Ure, Sally Kellerman, Signe Hasso, Sondra Locke. **1973**

REFLECTIONS OF MURDER ★★★ A wife and a mistress set out to kill their abusive mate. They set up a foolproof trap to lure him to his death. The "accident" that kills him leads to more terror and horror than either woman expected. A TV-movie version of the French classic *Diabolique*. 98m. **DIR:** John Badham. **CAST:** Tuesday Weld, Joan Hackett, Sam Waterston. **1987**

REHEARSAL FOR MURDER ★★★½ Richard Levinson and William Link, those clever fellows behind the creation of *Columbo*, occasionally stray into the realm of made-for-television movies; this is one of the best. Robert Preston leads his stage friends through the reading of a play designed to ferret out the killer of star Lynn Redgrave. The excellent cast does a fine job with the witty material, and Levinson and Link deliver another of their surprise conclusions. 100m. **DIR:** David Greene. **CAST:** Robert Preston, Lynn

Redgrave, Jeff Goldblum, Patrick Macnee, William Daniels, Lawrence Pressman. 1982

RELENTLESS ★★★ Catch this modest police procedural as the vehicle to boost minor player Leo Rossi's career. He's cast as a transplanted New York cop itching, in the wake of a string of murders committed by a so-called Sunset Killer, to show new Los Angeles partner Robert Loggia a thing or two. The deft and sympathetic screenplay, although credited to one Jack T. D. Robinson, is actually the work of Phil Alden Robinson. Rated R for violence and brief nudity. 92m. **DIR:** William Lustig. **CAST:** Judd Nelson, Robert Loggia, Leo Rossi, Meg Foster. 1989

RELENTLESS 3 ★★ Ex–New York cop Sam Dietz, played by series-star Leo Rossi, finds himself drawn into the case of a Los Angeles serial killer who carves up his victims and mails the evidence to the police. His interest in the case is heightened when he learns that his past connection to the killer could endanger his girlfriend. Familiar territory for Rossi, but William Forsythe has some good, creepy moments as the killer. Rated R for nudity, violence, and language. 84m. **DIR:** James Lemmo. **CAST:** Leo Rossi, William Forsythe, Signy Coleman, Robert Costanzo. 1992

REMINGTON STEELE (TV SERIES) ★★★ Early episodes feature dashing Pierce Brosnan as a front man for Laura Holt's (Stephanie Zimbalist) savvy detective. Steele provides comic relief as he and another partner (played by James Read) vie for Holt's attentions. Very watchable, the first two volumes are entitled "Steele Crazy after All These Years" and "In the Steele of the Night." Each volume 50m. **DIR:** Don Weis, Burt Brinckerhoff. **CAST:** Stephanie Zimbalist, Pierce Brosnan, James Read. 1982–83

RETURN OF FRANK CANNON, THE ★★½ When an ex-CIA agent is murdered, portly detective Frank Cannon (William Conrad) comes out of retirement. Made for television. 96m. **DIR:** Corey Allen. **CAST:** William Conrad, Arthur Hill, Diana Muldaur, Ed Nelson. 1980

RETURNING, THE 🦃 A woman copes with the death of her son and the apparent madness of her husband. 86m. **DIR:** Joel Bender. **CAST:** Gabriel Walsh, Susan Strasberg. 1990

REVENGE (1971) ★★ Made for television, this has Shelley Winters out for—you guessed it—revenge for her daughter's rape. Not as bad as it could have been. 78m. **DIR:** Jud Taylor. **CAST:** Shelley Winters, Stuart Whitman, Bradford Dillman, Roger Perry. 1971

REVENGE (1971) ★★ When a little girl is abducted and murdered, her family kidnaps the man they believe responsible, torturing and finally killing him. Interesting suspense film, but it lacks the intensity it should have. Not rated. 85m. **DIR:** Sidney Hayers. **CAST:** Joan Collins, James Booth, Sinead Cusack. 1971

RIDER ON THE RAIN ★★★★ Charles Bronson gives one of his finest screen performances in this gripping, Hitchcock-style thriller made in France. The story deals with the plight of a woman (Marlene Jobert) who kills an unhinged rapist and dumps his body into the sea. She is soon pursued by a mysterious American (Bronson). Thus begins a fascinating game of cat and mouse. Rated R for violence. 115m. **DIR:** René Clement. **CAST:** Charles Bronson, Marlene Jobert, Jill Ireland. 1970

RIFIFI ★★★★ A milestone that begat a continuing breed of films hinging on the big, carefully planned robbery that falls apart—usually just as the criminals and the audience are convinced of success. This one is sure to have you pumping adrenaline from start to finish, especially during the brilliant twenty-minute silent robbery sequence that is its selling point, and the falling out of thieves that follows. B&W; 115m. **DIR:** Jules Dassin. **CAST:** Jean Servais, Carl Mohner, Perlo Vita, Robert Manuel, Magali Noel. 1955

RISING SUN ★★★½ In attempting to tone down the alleged Japan-bashing in Michael Crichton's novel, director Phil Kaufman delivers a somewhat confusing thriller that succeeds primarily because of the performances. Sean Connery and Wesley Snipes are terrific in what is best viewed as another in the long line of cop/buddy flicks. As such it's a cut above the competition. Rated R for violence, nudity, simulated sex, and profanity. 130m. **DIR:** Phil Kaufman. **CAST:** Sean Connery, Wesley Snipes, Harvey Keitel, Cary-Hiroyuki Tagawa, Kevin Anderson, Mako, Ray Wise, Stan Egi, Stan Shaw, Tia Carrere, Steve Buscemi. 1993

RITUALS ★★ Several middle-aged men head up to the wilds on a camping trip, only to be stalked by a relentless killer. This cheap rip-off of *Deliverance* offers little in the way of entertainment. Rated R for violence and profanity. 100m. **DIR:** Peter Carter. **CAST:** Hal Holbrook, Lawrence Dane, Robin Gammell. 1981

ROAD GAMES ★★ An elusive latter-day Jack the Ripper is loose in Australia. Even though director Richard Franklin (*Psycho II*) actually studied under Alfred Hitchcock, he doesn't show any of his mentor's ability here. Rated PG. 100m. **DIR:** Richard Franklin. **CAST:** Stacy Keach, Jamie Lee Curtis, Marion Howard, Grant Page. 1981

ROAD HOUSE (1948) ★★★½ Nifty little *film noir* about nightclub singer Ida Lupino and the two men competing for her. Gritty and well acted. B&W; 95m. **DIR:** Jean Negulesco. **CAST:** Ida Lupino, Cornel Wilde, Richard Widmark, Celeste Holm. 1948

ROBBERY ★★★½ Suspenseful crime-drama about the complex heist of the British Royal Mail. Solid direction and excellent performances surpass the predictable script. 114m. **DIR:** Peter Yates. **CAST:** Stanley Baker, Joanna Pettet, James Booth. **1967**

ROLLERCOASTER ★★★★½ Fast-paced suspense film about an extortionist (Timothy Bottoms) blowing up rides in some of the nation's most famous amusement parks, and the efforts of a county safety inspector (George Segal) and an FBI agent (Richard Widmark) to nab him. Very well-done, this much-maligned film has great action, crisp dialogue, and a brilliant, nail-biting climax. Rated PG for language and violence. 119m. **DIR:** James Goldstone. **CAST:** George Segal, Richard Widmark, Timothy Bottoms, Susan Strasberg, Henry Fonda. **1977**

ROLLOVER ★★★½ Jane Fonda plays an ex–film star who inherits a multimillion-dollar empire when her husband is mysteriously murdered in this gripping, but not great, film. Kris Kristofferson is the financial troubleshooter who joins forces with her to save the company. Soon both their lives are in danger. Rated R because of profanity. 118m. **DIR:** Alan J. Pakula. **CAST:** Jane Fonda, Kris Kristofferson, Hume Cronyn, Josef Sommer, Bob Gunton. **1981**

ROPE ★★★★½ This recently resurrected Alfred Hitchcock film is based in part on the famous Leopold-Loeb thrill-murder case in Chicago in the 1920s. In it, the two killers divulge clues to their horrific escapade at a dinner party, to the growing suspicion of the other guests. It's one of Hitchcock's best. 80m. **DIR:** Alfred Hitchcock. **CAST:** James Stewart, John Dall, Farley Granger, Cedric Hardwicke. **1948**

ROSARY MURDERS, THE ★★★ Donald Sutherland is a priest who hears the confession of a killer who is murdering nuns and priests. An interesting film, thanks to strong performances by Sutherland and Charles Durning as the bishop. Slow pacing by director Fred Walton and a needlessly murky denouement keep this murder mystery from being top rank. Rated R for violence and nudity. 107m. **DIR:** Fred Walton. **CAST:** Donald Sutherland, Charles Durning, Belinda Bauer, Josef Sommer, James Murtaugh. **1987**

ROUGH CUT ★★★ The screenplay, by Francis Burns, is a welcome return to the stylish romantic comedies of the 1930s and 1940s with the accent on witty dialogue, action, and suspense. Burt Reynolds and Lesley-Anne Down are a perfect screen combination. As two sophisticated jewel thieves who plot to steal $30 million in uncut diamonds, they exchange quips, become romantically entwined, and are delightful. Rated R. 112m. **DIR:** Don Siegel. **CAST:** Burt Reynolds, Lesley-Anne Down, David Niven, Patrick Magee. **1980**

RUBDOWN ★★ In this made-for-cable original, an ex–baseball player who is now a masseuse is paid to seduce a man's wife so the man can get a divorce. Instead, the husband winds up dead. Weak story line and mediocre acting. Unrated for violence and suggested sex. 88m. **DIR:** Stuart Cooper. **CAST:** Michelle Phillips, Jack Coleman, Kent Williams, Alan Thicke, Catherine Oxenberg, William Devane. **1993**

RUMPOLE OF THE BAILEY (TV SERIES) ★★★★★ John Mortimer's charming and witty *Rumpole of the Bailey* is faithfully adapted in this British TV mystery series concerning a lovable old barrister who defends his clients with originality and flamboyance. Leo McKern's Horace Rumpole brings the English criminal justice system to life with the help (or hindrance) of fellow Chambers members Claude Erskine-Brown (Julian Curry), Phyllida Trant (Patricia Hodge), and Guthrie Featherstone (Peter Bowles). Rumpole's wife, Hilda—also known as "She who must be obeyed"—is wonderfully portrayed by Marion Mathie. Although the entire series is superb, take particular note of "Rumpole and the Alternative Society," a poignant tale of love and loyalty, and "Rumpole and the Blind Tasting," where our hero's lack of expertise in wine does not prevent him from solving the case. each episode. 52m. **DIR:** Roger Bamford, Rodney Bennett, Martyn Friend. **CAST:** Leo McKern, Marion Mathie, Julian Curry, Patricia Hodge, Peter Bowles. **1979–1981**

RUTANGA TAPES, THE ★★½ A frighteningly current movie dealing with the use of chemical weapons by a government on its own people. David Dukes is the spy-economic adviser sent to the African nation with the purpose of uncovering the details. Rated R for violence. 88m. **DIR:** David Lister. **CAST:** David Dukes, Susan Anspach. **1990**

SABOTAGE ★★★ One of the first of Alfred Hitchcock's characteristic thrillers. London's being terrorized by an unknown bomber, and movie theatre cashier Sylvia Sidney begins to fear that her husband (Oscar Homolka) is behind it all. Hitch was still experimenting, and his use of shadows and sound effects betrays the influence of German silent films. B&W; 76m. **DIR:** Alfred Hitchcock. **CAST:** Sylvia Sidney, Oscar Homolka, John Loder. **1936**

SABOTEUR ★★★★½ Outstanding Alfred Hitchcock film about a World War II factory worker (Robert Cummings) turned fugitive after he's unjustly accused of sabotage. The briskly paced story follows his efforts to elude police while he tries to unmask the real culprit. A humdinger of a climax. B&W; 108m. **DIR:** Alfred Hitchcock. **CAST:** Robert

Cummings, Priscilla Lane, Norman Lloyd, Otto Kruger. **1942**

SAINT, THE (TV SERIES) ★★ Before essaying the role of James Bond, Roger Moore honed his suavity in the series *The Saint*. He sparkled as international adventurer Simon Templar, a connoisseur of fine wine and women. The devilishly daring troubleshooter continually aided the police, who considered him a foe. Made in England, the production could usually be relied on to provide intriguing mysteries, witty dialogue, and solid action. Two episodes per tape. each. 100m. **DIR:** Roy Ward Baker, Leslie Norman. **CAST:** Roger Moore, Winsley Pithey, Norman Pitt, Ivor Dean, Percy Herbert, Ronald Radd, Lois Maxwell. **1963–1969**

SAINT IN LONDON, THE ★★★ George Sanders as The Saint is up to his halo in spies, murder, and intrigue in this entertaining series entry, the second to star Sanders as Simon Templar. Entrusted to protect a foreign ambassador from hired killers, The Saint fails and feels honor-bound to track down the culprits. This handsome programmer is fun to watch. B&W; 72m. **DIR:** John Paddy Carstairs. **CAST:** George Sanders, Sally Gray, David Burns, Ralph Truman. **1939**

SAINT IN NEW YORK, THE ★★★ The first of Leslie Charteris's popular crime novels to hit the screen, this smooth adventure features Louis Hayward as The Saint, gentleman crime fighter, and his efforts to put an end to six gangsters who have been plaguing their metropolis. Hayward is fine in the title role. B&W; 71m. **DIR:** Ben Holmes. **CAST:** Louis Hayward, Kay Sutton, Jonathan Hale, Jack Carson, Sig Ruman. **1938**

SAINT STRIKES BACK, THE ★★★ A good cast, a good story, and a charming performance by George Sanders as Simon Templar, debonair crime fighter, make this one of the best of a very pleasant series. Sanders, in his first appearance as the suave adventurer, pulls out all the stops in his efforts to clear the name of a dead policeman and straighten out his wayward daughter. B&W; 67m. **DIR:** John Farrow. **CAST:** George Sanders, Wendy Barrie, Jonathan Hale, Jerome Cowan, Neil Hamilton, Barry Fitzgerald. **1939**

SAINT'S VACATION, THE ★★ Simon Templar finds mystery and adventure instead of peace and quiet when he encounters intrigue on his vacation attempt. Hugh Sinclair plays the sophisticated Saint for the first time. Passable, but not up to the earlier entries in the series. B&W; 60m. **DIR:** Leslie Fenton. **CAST:** Hugh Sinclair, Sally Gray, Arthur Macrae, Cecil Parker, Gordon McLeod. **1941**

SANCTUARY OF FEAR ★★ Barnard Hughes does a fine job of bringing G. K. Chesterton's crime-busting priest, Father Brown, to life. Unfortunately, the rest of the cast seems detached from the action. This TV movie contains violence. 98m. **DIR:** John Llewellyn Moxey. **CAST:** Barnard Hughes, Kay Lenz, Michael McGuire, George Hearn. **1979**

SAPPHIRE ★★★ This mystery about Scotland Yard detectives searching for the murderer of a young black woman was judged a failure at the time because of the reticent way it addressed then current racial tensions. Now it can be enjoyed as a solid police procedural. 92m. **DIR:** Basil Dearden. **CAST:** Nigel Patrick, Yvonne Mitchell, Michael Craig, Paul Massie, Bernard Miles. **1959**

SATAN MET A LADY ★★ A pale shadow of *The Maltese Falcon*, using the same plot with different character names and a ram's horn instead of a statuette of a falcon. Bette Davis often ridiculed it as one of her worst pictures. B&W; 77m. **DIR:** William Dieterle. **CAST:** Bette Davis, Warren William, Alison Skipworth, Arthur Treacher, Marie Wilson, Winifred Shaw, Porter Hall. **1936**

SAVAGE ATTRACTION ★★★★ A psychotic German becomes sadistically obsessed with a lovely Australian girl in this bizarre but true tale. He uses both mental and physical cruelty to keep her with him. The suspense is never lacking. Rated R for sadism, nudity, and violence. 93m. **DIR:** Frank Shields. **CAST:** Kerry Mack, Ralph Schicha. **1983**

SAVE ME ★★½ Harry Hamlin strips down for some steamy sex with a mystery woman (Lysette Anthony). Hamlin finds plenty of diversion with Anthony, whom he believes he is saving from an abusive husband, but then someone tries to kill him. Thanks to his latest tryst, the list of suspects keeps growing. R-rated and unrated versions available; both contain sex, nudity, adult language, and violence. 90m. **DIR:** Alan Roberts. **CAST:** Harry Hamlin, Lysette Anthony, Steve Railsback, Olivia Hussey, Michael Ironside. **1993**

SCAM ★★½ Sultry Lorraine Bracco, who picks up rich men only to drug and rob them, reluctantly agrees to help FBI agent Christopher Walken execute a similar sting on a specific target. Sadly, Craig Smith's twisty mystery eventually gets too convoluted for its own good, resulting in a double-reverse climax which makes no sense in view of what has taken place earlier. Rated R for profanity and violence. 102m. **DIR:** John Flynn. **CAST:** Christopher Walken, Lorraine Bracco, Miguel Ferrer, Martin Donovan. **1993**

SCANDALOUS (1988) 🦃 A penniless playboy is hired to find a secretary who has witnessed the murder of a renowned author. 90m. **DIR:** Robert W. Young. **CAST:** Lauren Hutton, Albert Fortell, Capucine. **1988**

SCARLET CLAW, THE ★★★★ Stunningly atmospheric entry in the Universal series of Sherlock Holmes mysteries has the detective journeying to Canada to find the culprit in a bizarre series of murders. This is a true whodunit, which keeps you guessing right to the end. B&W; 74m. **DIR:** Roy William Neill. **CAST:** Basil Rathbone, Nigel Bruce, Gerald Hamer, Paul Cavanagh, Arthur Hohl, Miles Mander, Ian Wolfe. **1944**

SCARLET CLUE, THE ★★ Standard, workmanlike *Charlie Chan* entry in the latter-day Monogram Pictures cycle, from its most prolific hack director. A suspect is killed as Charlie investigates a plot to purloin government radar plans. Some atmosphere on a grade-C scale, but no tension. B&W; 64m. **DIR:** Phil Rosen. **CAST:** Sidney Toler, Benson Fong, Mantan Moreland, I. Stanford Jolley. **1945**

SCENE OF THE CRIME (1985) ★★ A cross between a game show and a murder mystery, this film is cut into three episodes, narrated by Orson Welles, that ask the viewers to try to solve the murder at the end of each. Originally made for network TV. 74m. **DIR:** Walter Grauman, Harry Falk. **CAST:** Orson Welles, Markie Post, Alan Thicke, Ben Piazza. **1985**

SCISSORS ★★½ Scissors are the weapon of choice in this intense psychological thriller. Sharon Stone believes she's going insane—or is someone driving her to the edge? Rated R for violence. 105m. **DIR:** Frank DeFelitta. **CAST:** Sharon Stone, Steve Railsback, Michelle Phillips, Ronny Cox. **1990**

SCREAM OF FEAR ★★★★ In this overlooked crackerjack thriller, Susan Strasberg plays an invalid who visits her father's Riviera mansion, only to be followed by the corpse of her away-on-business daddy. Well-crafted tale will have you second-guessing yourself to the very end. B&W; 81m. **DIR:** Seth Holt. **CAST:** Susan Strasberg, Ronald Lewis, Ann Todd, Christopher Lee. **1961**

SEA OF LOVE ★★★★ Al Pacino made an explosive comeback in this sexy thriller as a New York police detective in the midst of a middle-age crisis. To forget his woes, Pacino throws himself into an investigation of some serial killings, which seems to have something to do with the lonely hearts listings in the newspaper personals columns. Rated R for violence, profanity, and simulated sex. 110m. **DIR:** Harold Becker. **CAST:** Al Pacino, Ellen Barkin, John Goodman. **1989**

SEANCE ON A WET AFTERNOON ★★★★½ This is an absolutely fabulous movie. An unbalanced medium (Kim Stanley) involves her meek husband (Richard Attenborough) in a kidnapping scheme that brings about their downfall. Brilliant acting by all, working from a superb script. No rating, but some intense sequences. B&W; 115m. **DIR:** Bryan Forbes. **CAST:** Kim Stanley, Richard Attenborough, Patrick Magee, Nanette Newman. **1964**

SEASON OF FEAR ★★ Upon locating his estranged inventor father, a young man discovers Dad's latest wife to be the victim of extreme mental and physical cruelty at the homestead. Or is she? Fetid thriller has overtones of *Body Heat*. Rated R for nudity. 89m. **DIR:** Doug Campbell. **CAST:** Michael Bowen, Ray Wise, Clancy Brown, Clare Wren, Michael J. Pollard. **1989**

SECRET AGENT, THE ★★★ Offbeat espionage film by the master of suspense contains many typical Alfred Hitchcock touches, but lacks the pacing and characterizations that set his best efforts apart from those of his contemporaries. Alternately grim and humorous, this uneven film (based on a novel by Somerset Maugham) is still watchable and comparable with many of the best films in the genre. B&W; 93m. **DIR:** Alfred Hitchcock. **CAST:** John Gielgud, Madeleine Carroll, Robert Young, Peter Lorre, Percy Marmont, Lilli Palmer. **1936**

SECRET PASSION OF ROBERT CLAYTON, THE ★★★ Who really killed the stripper? If you like good court scenes, you'll enjoy this twisted plot of love, death, family, and the law. Made for cable. 91m. **DIR:** E. W. Swackhamer. **CAST:** John Mahoney, Scott Valentine, Eve Gordon, Kevin Conroy. **1992**

SEDUCED ★★ The supporting cast attracts most of the attention in made-for-TV tale about an up-and-coming young politician who falls for the wife of an influential businessman. The wife gets murdered, and the politico is forced to become a sleuth. 100m. **DIR:** Jerrold Freedman. **CAST:** Gregory Harrison, Cybill Shepherd, Adrienne Barbeau, Mel Ferrer, José Ferrer. **1985**

SET-UP, THE ★★★★ Taut *film noir* boxing flick takes the simple story of an over-the-hill boxer who refuses to disregard his principles and throw the big fight and elevates it to true tragedy. Robert Ryan as the has-been fighter gives another of the finely drawn and fiercely independent portrayals that marked his illustrious career as one of Hollywood's finest character actors. B&W; 72m. **DIR:** Robert Wise. **CAST:** Robert Ryan, Audrey Totter, George Tobias, Alan Baxter, James Edwards, Wallace Ford. **1949**

SEVEN DIALS MYSTERY, THE ★★★★ This lighthearted Agatha Christie whodunit concerns a group of friends who spend the weekend at The Chimneys, the ancestral home of one Lady Eileen Brent (affectionately known as Bundle). A misfired practical joke leads to an unexpectedly tragic conclusion, which somehow involves a secret society known as the Seven Dials Club. Made for TV. 110m. **DIR:** Tony Wharmby. **CAST:** Cheryl Campbell, Harry Andrews, James Warwick, John Gielgud. **1981**

SEVEN-PER-CENT SOLUTION, THE ★★★★ Sherlock Holmes (Nicol Williamson) attempts to get rid of his cocaine addiction by getting treatment from Sigmund

Freud (Alan Arkin). This is a fast-paced adventure with touches of humor. Robert Duvall's portrayal of Dr. Watson nearly steals the show. Great fun. Rated PG; okay for everyone. 113m. **DIR:** Herbert Ross. **CAST:** Nicol Williamson, Alan Arkin, Robert Duvall, Laurence Olivier, Vanessa Redgrave, Joel Grey. **1976**

SEX, LOVE, AND COLD HARD CASH ★★★½ High marks to this clever mystery from writer-director Harry S. Longstreet. Ex-con Anthony Denison teams up with call-girl JoBeth Williams to find a mob accountant who skipped with millions. Pleasant chemistry between the two leads, and Longstreet's tale moves in genuinely unexpected directions. Rated PG-13 for violence and mild sensuality. 86m. **DIR:** Harry S. Longstreet. **CAST:** JoBeth Williams, Anthony Denison, Robert Forster, Eric Pierpont. **1993**

SEXTON BLAKE AND THE HOODED TERROR ★★½ One of a series of British mysteries featuring Sexton Blake, a detective in the Sherlock Holmes tradition. He's on the trail of an international gang known as the Hooded Terror, led by a millionaire (Tod Slaughter). Slaughter, Britain's king of Grand Guignol, is the best reason to see this, even though he's relatively restrained in a supporting role. B&W; 69m. **DIR:** George King. **CAST:** George Curzon, Tod Slaughter, Greta Gynt. **1938**

SEXUAL INTENT ★★ Libidinous lothario wines, dines, and rips off women for a living, but he's about to face a career crisis. Based on a true story, with Gary Hudson as the Sweetheart Scammer, who took over forty women for a ride. Now they're in the driver's seat, and what they've got planned for Mr. Romance is a vigilante feminist's dream come true. Rated R for nudity, language, and adult situations. 88m. **DIR:** Kurt Mac Carley. **CAST:** Gary Hudson, Michele Brin, Sarah Hill. **1993**

SEXUAL RESPONSE ★★ Radio sex psychologist Shannon Tweed sets into motion a series of events that lead to betrayal, lust, and eventually murder. Another made-for-video entry with lots of flesh and simulated sex. 90m. **DIR:** Yaky Yosha. **CAST:** Shannon Tweed, Catherine Oxenberg, Vernon Wells. **1992**

SHADOW DANCING ★★★ Surprisingly entertaining suspense-thriller about an aspiring dancer who desperately wants to become a member of a dance ensemble. Her obsession is the perfect target for the resurrection of a former star, who died fifty years earlier in the same theatre. Rated R for violence. 95m. **DIR:** Lewis Furey. **CAST:** Nadine Van Der Velde, John Colicos, Christopher Plummer. **1989**

SHADOW OF A DOUBT ★★★★½ This disturbing suburban drama, regarded by Alfred Hitchcock as the personal favorite among his films, probes the hidden facets of a family with a secret. Teenager Charlie (Teresa Wright) adores the uncle (Joseph Cotten) after whom she was named and is delighted when he comes to stay for an indefinite period. Her love grows tainted, however, as she begins to suspect that "dear Uncle Charlie" may be the killer wanted by the police for having sent several widows to their premature reward. Unrated; a bit intense for younger viewers. B&W; 108m. **DIR:** Alfred Hitchcock. **CAST:** Joseph Cotten, Teresa Wright, Macdonald Carey, Henry Travers, Hume Cronyn. **1943**

SHADOW OF THE THIN MAN ★★★★ Fourth in the series, with sleuths Nick and Nora Charles (William Powell and Myrna Loy) dividing their time between mysteries, Asta the wonder dog, and a stroller-bound Nick Jr. (who arrived in the previous film). Barry Nelson and Donna Reed are among the innocents this time around, and the story concerns dire deeds at the local race track. Another sumptuous serving of sophisticated fun. B&W; 97m. **DIR:** W. S. Van Dyke. **CAST:** William Powell, Myrna Loy, Sam Levene, Donna Reed, Barry Nelson. **1941**

SHADOW STRIKES, THE ★★ Loosely based on *The Ghost of the Manor*, one of hundreds of stories featuring the mysterious Shadow, this effort finds Rod La Rocque on the trail of a gang of crooks who have murdered his father, a prominent attorney. B&W; 61m. **DIR:** Lynn Shores. **CAST:** Rod La Rocque, Lynn Anders, Norman Ainsley. **1937**

SHAMUS ★★½ An okay detective thriller, with Burt playing Burt. Nothing new, but lots of action keeps things moving along in this story of a private eye investigating a weapons-smuggling ring. Rated PG. 106m. **DIR:** Buzz Kulik. **CAST:** Burt Reynolds, Dyan Cannon, John P. Ryan. **1973**

SHANGHAI COBRA, THE ★★ Routine poverty-row *Charlie Chan* programmer, from Monogram Pictures. A murderer stages his killings to make them resemble snake attacks. B&W; 64m. **DIR:** Phil Karlson. **CAST:** Sidney Toler, Benson Fong, Mantan Moreland, Joan Barclay. **1945**

SHATTERED (1991) ★★½ Director Wolfgang Petersen's adaptation of Richard Neely's novel is a well-acted and fairly suspenseful flick about a man who wakes up in a hospital remembering nothing of his past. Even though his wife has pictures of them together, our hero has a feeling that something isn't quite right. Rated R for violence, nudity, and profanity. 106m. **DIR:** Wolfgang Petersen. **CAST:** Tom Berenger, Bob Hoskins, Greta Scacchi, Joanne Whalley, Corbin Bernsen, Theodore Bikel. **1991**

SHATTERED IMAGE ★★ The FBI tries to locate the criminals who kidnapped the owner of a modeling agency. This made-for-cable movie is quite confusing and contains too many twists—it feels as if even the writer really didn't know what was going on. Not rated, but contains violence and sex. 95m. **DIR:** Fritz Kiersch. **CAST:** Jack Scalia, Bo Derek, John Savage, Dorian Harewood, Ramon Franco, Michael Harris, Carol Lawrence. **1993**

SHERLOCK HOLMES AND THE DEADLY NECKLACE ★★★ Director Terence Fisher made one of the best versions of Sir Conan Doyle's *Hound of the Baskervilles* for Hammer Films in 1959, yet only three years later he foundered with this loose, German-made (dubbed) adaptation of *The Valley of Fear.* Curt Siodmak's screenplay is sometimes silly and a bit too skewed to the tastes of German audiences. B&W; 85m. **DIR:** Terence Fisher, Frank Winterstein. **CAST:** Christopher Lee, Thorley Walters, Senta Berger. **1962**

SHERLOCK HOLMES AND THE INCIDENT AT VICTORIA FALLS ★★★½ A request from King George (Joss Ackland) to safeguard the Star of Africa diamond on its journey from South Africa to England brings Sherlock Holmes (Christopher Lee) and Dr. Watson (Patrick Macnee) out of retirement. First of a series. Unrated; the film has violence. 120m. **DIR:** Bill Corcoran. **CAST:** Christopher Lee, Patrick Macnee, Jenny Seagrove, Claude Akins, Richard Todd, Joss Ackland. **1991**

SHERLOCK HOLMES AND THE LEADING LADY ★★ Edited down from a miniseries that ran over three hours (sans commercials), this romantic mystery of Sherlock Holmes and Dr. Watson in retirement emerges as a fitfully coherent, highlights-only digest version. But Christopher Lee and Patrick Macnee are splendid as Holmes and Watson. 100m. **DIR:** Peter Sasdy. **CAST:** Christopher Lee, Patrick Macnee, Morgan Fairchild. **1992**

SHERLOCK HOLMES AND THE SECRET WEAPON ★★★ Although the contemporary (1940s) setting makes the Baker Street sleuth seem oddly out of place, Basil Rathbone remains one of the definitive Holmeses. In this case, he once again faces the ruthless Professor Moriarty (Lionel Atwill). A code that appears in this film is borrowed from *The Adventure of the Dancing Man.* This also is the first Rathbone Holmes to be rereleased in color, a dubious distinction that won't improve it a bit; these films were made for the shadowy world of black and white. 68m. **DIR:** Roy William Neill. **CAST:** Basil Rathbone, Nigel Bruce, Lionel Atwill, Kaaren Verne, Dennis Hoey, Mary Gordon. **1942**

SHERLOCK HOLMES AND THE SPIDER WOMAN ★★★½ Originally released under the abridged title *Spider Woman,* this Sherlockian adventure is one of the better modernized versions of the Conan Doyle stories. In this one, the villain is the fiendishly evil Adrea Spedding (Gale Sondergaard), a woman who drives gambling men to suicide in order to increase her personal fortune. It's full of sexual attitudes that are now archaic, but it has tension and fine performances. B&W; 62m. **DIR:** Roy William Neill. **CAST:** Basil Rathbone, Nigel Bruce, Gale Sondergaard, Dennis Hoey. **1944**

SHERLOCK HOLMES AND THE VOICE OF TERROR ★★★ After starring in the classics *The Hound of the Baskervilles* and *The Adventures of Sherlock Holmes* at Twentieth Century Fox, Basil Rathbone and Nigel Bruce moved to Universal to continue in the roles of Holmes and Watson. This first entry in the series is enjoyable. Set during World War II, it has our heroes going after spies who are using radio broadcasts to sabotage Allied efforts. A strong cast helps. B&W; 65m. **DIR:** John Rawlins. **CAST:** Basil Rathbone, Nigel Bruce, Evelyn Ankers, Henry Daniell, Montagu Love, Thomas Gomez, Hillary Brooke, Mary Gordon. **1942**

SHERLOCK HOLMES FACES DEATH ★★★ Holmes (Basil Rathbone) and Watson (Nigel Bruce) find themselves back in the shadows and fog—albeit in modern times—as they attempt to solve a murder. Based on Conan Doyle's "The Musgrave Ritual," this is a good entry in the series. B&W; 68m. **DIR:** Roy William Neill. **CAST:** Basil Rathbone, Nigel Bruce, Dennis Hoey, Hillary Brooke. **1943**

SHERLOCK HOLMES IN WASHINGTON ★★½ Cornball wartime propaganda has Sherlock Holmes (Basil Rathbone) and Dr. Watson (Nigel Bruce) chasing after spies in Washington, D.C. Strong villainy from George Zucco and Henry Daniell helps, and the stars are as watchable as ever. B&W; 71m. **DIR:** Roy William Neill. **CAST:** Basil Rathbone, Nigel Bruce, Marjorie Lord, Henry Daniell, George Zucco. **1943**

SHOCK CORRIDOR ★★½ Newspaper reporter Peter Breck poses as insane to learn who committed a murder inside a state asylum, and we watch as he goes bonkers himself. Brilliant action sequences interspersed with tedium. B&W; 101m. **DIR:** Samuel Fuller. **CAST:** Peter Breck, Constance Towers, Gene Evans. **1963**

SHOCK TO THE SYSTEM, A ★★★★ In this deliciously wicked black comedy, Michael Caine plays a middle-aged executive waiting impatiently for a big promotion, which goes instead to younger man Peter Riegert. So, Caine does what any man in that position would do: he plots murder. Screenwriter Andrew Klavan's loose adaptation of Simon Brett's novel makes an uncommonly satisfying thriller. Rated R for violence and profanity. 91m. **DIR:** Jan Egleson. **CAST:** Michael Caine, Peter Riegert, Elizabeth McGovern, Swoosie Kurtz, Will Patton, John McMartin. **1990**

SHOW OF FORCE, A ★★ This engaging but occasionally unconvincing conspiracy thriller is loosely based on an infamous Puerto Rican scandal involving the fatal shooting of two pro-independence activists. Amy Irving stars as a television journalist who finds that the incident may have been a politically motivated murder. Rated R for language and violence. 93m. **DIR:** Bruno Barreto. **CAST:** Amy Irving, Lou Diamond Phillips, Robert Duvall, Andy Garcia. **1990**

SHRIEK IN THE NIGHT, A ★★★ Ginger Rogers and Lyle Talbot play two fast-talking reporters competing for a juicy scoop on a murder case in this entertaining low-budget whodunit. This tidy thriller makes up for its lack of production quality by the spunky, enthusiastic performances by the two leads. B&W; 66m. **DIR:** Albert Ray. **CAST:** Ginger Rogers, Lyle Talbot, Arthur Hoyt, Purnell Pratt. **1933**

SIESTA ★★★½ Oddly fascinating and sexually intense drama. Ellen Barkin plays a stuntwoman in love with a former trainer (Gabriel Byrne), a man who loved her but married someone else. *Siesta* plays with time, reality, and consciousness, turning them into something suspenseful. Rated R for language and sex. 90m. **DIR:** Mary Lambert. **CAST:** Ellen Barkin, Gabriel Byrne, Julian Sands, Jodie Foster, Martin Sheen, Isabella Rossellini, Grace Jones. **1987**

SIGN OF FOUR, THE ★★★½ Ian Richardson makes a fine Sherlock Holmes in this film produced for British television and fairly faithful adaptation from the story by Sir Arthur Conan Doyle. A cache of jewels brings nothing but avarice and danger to whoever possesses it, and it's up to Holmes and Dr. John H. Watson (well played by David Healy) to bring to justice a couple of creepy killers out to claim the treasure. 103m. **DIR:** Desmond Davis. **CAST:** Ian Richardson, David Healy, Cherie Lunghi, Terrence Rigby, Thorley Walters. **1983**

SILENCE OF THE LAMBS ★★★★★ In this shock-filled powerhouse, an FBI cadet (Jodie Foster) is assigned by her superior (Scott Glenn) to interview an imprisoned, cannibalistic psychopath (Anthony Hopkins) in the hopes of getting his help in capturing a crazed serial killer (Ted Levine). Superb performances by Foster and Hopkins. From the novel by Thomas Harris, whose *Red Dragon* was adapted by Michael Mann for *Manhunter,* a "prequel" of sorts to this first-rate chiller. Rated R for violence, gore, nudity, and profanity. 118m. **DIR:** Jonathan Demme. **CAST:** Jodie Foster, Anthony Hopkins, Scott Glenn, Ted Levine, Tracey Walter, Charles Napier, Roger Corman. **1991**

SILENT MOTIVE ★★★ Scandalous screenwriter Patricia Wettig gets a taste of her own medicine when a copycat killer uses her scripts as a blueprint for murder. Detective Mike Farrell must prove she didn't do it, or did she? Right! Standard made-for-TV thriller gets a boost from familiar, durable cast. 90m. **DIR:** Lee Philips. **CAST:** Patricia Wettig, Edward Asner, Mike Farrell, Rick Springfield, David Packer. **1991**

SILENT PARTNER, THE ★★★★½ This suspense-thriller is what they call a sleeper. It's an absolutely riveting tale about a bank teller (Elliott Gould) who, knowing of a robbery in advance, pulls a switch on a psychotic criminal (Christopher Plummer) and might not live to regret it. *Silent Partner* is a real find for movie buffs. But be forewarned; it has a couple of truly unsettling scenes of violence. Rated R. 103m. **DIR:** Daryl Duke. **CAST:** Elliott Gould, Christopher Plummer, Susannah York, John Candy. **1978**

SILENT SHERLOCK HOLMES, THE ★★ A compilation of two rare Sherlock Holmes silent films. Supposedly Sir Arthur Conan Doyle himself supervised *The Copper Beeches* (1912); while *The Man with the Twisted Lip* (1922) presents a welcome opportunity to see the esteemed Eille Norwood in one of his early efforts. The first example is absurdly melodramatic while the second may be too tame for all but the most avid buffs. Silent. B&W; 68m. **CAST:** Ellie Norwood.

SILHOUETTE 🦃 Cosmopolitan Faye Dunaway witnesses a murder in this insipid made-for-cable whodunit. 95m. **DIR:** Carl Schenkel. **CAST:** Faye Dunaway, David Rasche, John Terry. **1990**

SILVER BLAZE ★★★ Beginning with *Sherlock Holmes's Fatal Hour,* in 1931, Arthur Wontner starred as Holmes in five handsome but low-budget films, of which *Silver Blaze* was the last. Ironically, this movie was not released in America until after the 1939 *Hound of the Baskervilles* introduced Basil Rathbone as the screen's most famous detective. So impressive was Rathbone's debut as Holmes, the American distributor retitled *Silver Blaze* as *Murder at the Baskervilles.* Indeed, Sir Henry Baskerville himself pops up in this loose adaptation of the original story about the disappearance of a prized racehorse. In a further variation, Professor Moriarty (Lyn Harding) and Colonel Moran (Arthur Goulet) are behind the nefarious goings-on. It may not be faithful, but *Silver Blaze* is fun for mystery fans. B&W; 60m. **DIR:** Thomas Bentley. **CAST:** Arthur Wontner, Ian Fleming, Lyn Harding, John Turnbull, Robert Horton, Arthur Goulet. **1937**

SINGLE WHITE FEMALE ★★★ This entry in the stranger from hell subgenre gets a good start when cultivated career woman Bridget Fonda, recovering from the betrayal of an unfaithful boyfriend, accepts mousy Jennifer Jason Leigh as her new roommate. Alas, things go to pot in the third act. Rated R for language, violence, and nudity. 107m. **DIR:** Barbet Schroeder. **CAST:** Bridget Fonda, Jennifer Jason Leigh, Steven Weber, Peter Friedman. **1992**

SINS OF DESIRE ★★ Tanya Roberts infiltrates a sex-therapy institute to find evidence against her sisters' corrupt therapist (Jay Richardson). Overdose of sleaze detracts from what could have been a believable suspense-thriller. Unrated, contains violence, profanity, and rampant nudity and sex. 90m. **DIR:** Jim Wynorski. **CAST:** Tanya Roberts, Jay Richardson, Delia Sheppard, Nick Cassavetes, Jan-Michael Vincent. **1992**

SINS OF THE NIGHT ★★ Another in the long line of sizzling thrillers made directly for video, this one delivers plenty of sweaty flesh but nothing else. Nick Cassavetes is an insurance investigator who becomes personally involved with his latest case—a beautiful but dangerous exotic dancer. Rated R for nudity, sex, language, and violence; unrated version contains more flesh. 90m. **DIR:** Alexander Gregory Hippolyte. **CAST:** Nick Cassavetes, Deborah Shelton, Miles O'Keeffe, Richard Roundtree. **1993**

SISTERS (1973) ★★★★½ A terrifying tale of twin sisters (Margot Kidder). One is normal; the other is a dangerous psychopath. It's an extremely effective thriller on all levels. Charles Durning and Jennifer Salt give the standout performances in this Brian De Palma release. Rated R for violence, nudity, and language. 93m. **DIR:** Brian De Palma. **CAST:** Margot Kidder, Charles Durning, Jennifer Salt, Barnard Hughes. **1973**

SKETCH ARTIST ★★½ This sexy made-for-cable thriller benefits from writer Michael Angeli's intriguing premise. Jeff Fahey is a police sketch artist whose rendition of a murder suspect—concocted from a description given by a briefly seen Drew Barrymore—turns out to be the spitting image of his wife (Sean Young). Alas, he then turns total fool, and plot cohesion goes right out the window. 88m. **DIR:** Phedon Papamichael. **CAST:** Jeff Fahey, Sean Young, Frank McRae, Drew Barrymore. **1992**

SKETCHES OF A STRANGLER 🦃 Allen Garfield, in the days when he was billing himself as Allan Goorwitz, stars as a painter with a fixation on his dead mother. 91m. **DIR:** Paul Leder. **CAST:** Allen Garfield, Meredith MacRae. **1978**

SKULL AND CROWN ★★½ A border patrolman and his faithful guard dog combine talents to break up a band of smugglers. Lassie fans will love this one. B&W; 55m. **DIR:** Elmer Clifton. **CAST:** Rin Tin Tin Jr., Regis Toomey, Jack Mulhall. **1935**

SLAM DANCE ★★½ An L.A. artist (Tom Hulce) becomes embroiled in two murders of high-priced call girls in this Hitchcockian thriller. The standard situations involving an innocent man trying to clear himself are given some fresh approaches, but there are several holes in the plot, and some events make little sense. Rated R. 99m. **DIR:** Wayne Wang. **CAST:** Tom Hulce, Mary Elizabeth Mastrantonio, Virginia Madsen, Harry Dean Stanton, Adam Ant, Don Opper. **1987**

SLAUGHTER OF THE INNOCENTS ★★★½ Thanks to a morbidly fascinating tone that is borrowed from *Silence of the Lambs*, you'll probably forgive writer-director James Glickenhaus's effort to make his grade-school son a star. The youthful Glickenhaus plays an overly precocious boy forever sharing insights overlooked by his father, F.B.I. investigator Scott Glenn...whose effective performance establishes more credibility than this story deserves. Rated R for graphic violence and profanity. 103m. **DIR:** James Glickenhaus. **CAST:** Scott Glenn, Jesse Cameron-Glickenhaus, Sheila Tousey, Zitto Kazann, Darlanne Fluegel, Zakes Mokae. **1993**

SLAYGROUND ★★ Based on the hard-boiled Parker series of crime novels, *Slayground* will disappoint fans of the books. The character of Parker, a tough, no-nonsense professional criminal who shoots first and walks away, has been softened into a whiny thief named Stone (Peter Coyote). Rated R. 89m. **DIR:** Terry Bedford. **CAST:** Peter Coyote, Billie Whitelaw, Philip Sayer, Bill Luhr. **1984**

SLEEPING MURDER ★★★★ Two newlyweds fall in love with a strange old house in an English seaside town. Into this well-established mood of foreboding comes Miss Marple (Joan Hickson), who helps the young couple decipher the events behind an unsolved murder. Unrated, but suitable for family viewing. 102m. **DIR:** John Davies. **CAST:** Joan Hickson, Geraldine Alexander, John Moulder-Brown, Frederick Treves, Jack Watson. **1986**

SLEEPING WITH THE ENEMY ★★★½ Battered wife Julia Roberts manages to escape from her sadistic husband (Patrick Bergin) and create a new life—but only for a short time until hubby discovers the ruse and comes for revenge. Recalls director Joseph Rubin's *The Stepfather* so much that it might have been called *The Husband*. Rated R for violence and profanity. 99m. **DIR:** Joseph Ruben. **CAST:** Julia Roberts, Patrick Bergin, Kevin Anderson. **1991**

SLEEPWALKER ★★★ Bilingual computer operator translates an ancient Chinese manuscript as a free-lance job, only to find the content manifesting itself in her daily existence. Offbeat low-budget suspenser has genuine intrigue and fine values. Rated R. 78m. **DIR:** Sara Driver. **CAST:** Suzanne Fletcher, Ann Magnuson, Dexter Lee. **1987**

SLEUTH ★★★★★ Michael Caine and Laurence Olivier engage in a heavyweight acting *bataille royal* in this stimulating mystery. Both actors are brilliant as the characters engage in the struggle of one-upmanship and social game-playing. Without giving away the movie's twists and turns, we can let on that the ultimate game is being played on its audience. Rated PG. 138m. **DIR:** Joseph L. Mankiewicz. **CAST:** Michael Caine, Laurence Olivier. **1972**

SLIVER ★★½ Sharon Stone moves into a high-rise, Manhattan apartment building—a sliver—and ends up becoming romantically involved with Tom Berenger and William Baldwin. After a while, Stone gets the feeling she's being watched, and that's when her new life becomes a nightmare. An involving but trashy movie. Rated R for nudity, simulated sex, profanity, and violence. 115m. **DIR:** Phillip Noyce. **CAST:** Sharon Stone, Tom Berenger, William Baldwin, Martin Landau, Colleen Camp, Polly Walker, C.C.H. Pounder, Nina Foch. **1993**

SLOW BURN ★★ Newspaper reporter Eric Roberts is hired as a private investigator to find the son of a Palm Springs artist. Beverly D'Angelo plays the lost son's mother who may or may not know what happened to him. A muddled plot and apprentice-like direction. This made-for-cable movie is equivalent to a PG-13 for violence and profanity. 88m. **DIR:** Matthew Chapman. **CAST:** Eric Roberts, Beverly D'Angelo, Dennis Lipscomb. **1986**

SMASHING THE RACKETS ★★ Chester Morris plays an easily recognizable facsimile of racket-busting Thomas E. Dewey in this cardboard melodrama about an assistant district attorney who becomes a special prosecutor and the scourge of crooks everywhere. Strictly routine. B&W; 68m. **DIR:** Lew Landers. **CAST:** Chester Morris, Frances Mercer, Bruce Cabot, Rita Johnson. **1938**

SMOOTH TALKER ★★½ Cop Joe Guzaldo is at the end of his rope: his attorney wife just walked out and unless he can come up with a lead on a killer of 976-Phone Girls, he's about to hit the pavement, sans badge. Things heat up when the only suspect in the case winds up being prosecuted by his ex-wife. Rated R for language and violence. 89m. **DIR:** Tom E. Milo. **CAST:** Joe Guzaldo, Burt Ward, Stuart Whitman. **1991**

SNAPDRAGON ★★ A detective (Chelsea Field), investigating a case involving serial murders, requests the assistance of a police psychologist (Steve Bauer). A young amnesic woman may know something about the murders or the identity of the killer. Predictable but watchable thriller. Rated R for nudity, profanity, and violence. 96m. **DIR:** Worth Keeter. **CAST:** Steven Bauer, Chelsea Field, Pamela Anderson. **1993**

SNEAKERS ★★★★ In this slick, enjoyable piece of escapism, Robert Redford gives a star-quality performance as a former computer trickster plying his trade as a security expert—until government agents use his shady past to force him into a battle of wits with a former colleague. Fine acting and sly bits of humor add to the fun. Rated PG-13 for profanity and violence. 126m. **DIR:** Phil Alden Robinson. **CAST:** Robert Redford, Dan Aykroyd, Ben Kingsley, Mary McDonnell, River Phoenix, Sidney Poitier, David Strathairn, Timothy Busfield, George Hearn. **1992**

SOLDIER'S STORY, A ★★★★★ A murder mystery, a character study, and a deeply affecting drama rolled into one, *A Soldier's Story*, based on Charles Fuller's 1981 Pulitzer Prize–winning play, is an unforgettable viewing experience. This riveting movie examines man's inhumanity to man in one of its most venal forms: racial hatred. Rated PG for violence and profanity. 102m. **DIR:** Norman Jewison. **CAST:** Howard Rollins Jr., Adolph Caesar. **1984**

SOMEONE BEHIND THE DOOR ★★½ A brain surgeon takes an amnesiac into his home and, during the course of his treatment, conditions him to murder his wife. Intense suspense-drama with a decent cast. The story contains too many plot twists though. Not rated, but contains violence. 93m. **DIR:** Nicolas Gessner. **CAST:** Charles Bronson, Anthony Perkins, Jill Ireland, Henri Garcin. **1971**

SOMEONE TO WATCH OVER ME ★★★★ This first-rate thriller benefits from director Ridley Scott's visual dynamics and an intelligent script. Ultrarich lady Mimi Rogers witnesses a horrible murder and barely escapes with her life; Tom Berenger is the down-home cop from the Bronx assigned to protect her. Rated R for language, nudity, and violence. 106m. **DIR:** Ridley Scott. **CAST:** Tom Berenger, Mimi Rogers, Lorraine Bracco, Andreas Katsulas. **1987**

SONG OF THE THIN MAN ★★★½ Sixth and final entry in the series, a cut above the previous one because of its involvement in jazz music circles. Nick and Nora Charles (William Powell and Myrna Loy) match wits with a murderer this time out, and the setting helps their dialogue regain its crisp sparkle. All in all, a worthy effort with which to conclude things. B&W; 86m. **DIR:** Edward Buzzell. **CAST:** William Powell, Myrna Loy, Keenan Wynn, Dean Stockwell, Gloria Grahame, Patricia Morison. **1947**

SORCEROR ★★★★ Rejected by filmgoers in 1977 because the title seemed to suggest a follow-up to director William Friedkin's megahit, *The Exorcist*, this remake of Henri Couzot's classic, *Wages of Fear*, is now a cult favorite. Roy Scheider is top-notch as an American criminal who has fled to Latin America to escape prosecution but finds life there to be a living hell. He takes a job transporting nitroglycerine as a way of getting out and finds terror at every turn. A superb score by Tangerine Dream enhances this atmospheric thriller. Rated R for violence and profanity. 122m. **DIR:** William Friedkin. **CAST:**

Roy Scheider, Bruno Cremer, Francisco Rabal, Souad Amidou, Ramon Bieri. 1977

SORRY, WRONG NUMBER (1948) ★★★★ Slick cinema adaptation, by the author herself, of Lucille Fletcher's famed radio drama. Barbara Stanwyck is superb—and received an Oscar nomination—as an invalid who, due to those "crossed wires" so beloved in fiction, overhears two men plotting the murder of a woman. Gradually Stanwyck realizes that she is the target. B&W; 89m. **DIR:** Anatole Litvak. **CAST:** Barbara Stanwyck, Burt Lancaster, Wendell Corey, Ed Begley Sr., Ann Richards. 1948

SORRY, WRONG NUMBER (1989) ★★ A made-for-TV update of the suspenseful story of an invalid who learns that her husband plans to have her killed. But it doesn't hold a candle to the Barbara Stanwyck version. Loni Anderson looks better than she acts, and that's not all bad in this case. 100m. **DIR:** Tony Wharmby. **CAST:** Loni Anderson, Patrick Macnee, Carl Weintraub, Hal Holbrook. 1989

SOUTH BEACH 🦃 Has-been, ex-football players Gary Busey and Fred Williamson are wanna-be Miami private eyes, who become embroiled with mystery-woman Vanity. This slice of Miami could have used more vice. Rated R for violence and adult situations. 93m. **DIR:** Fred Williamson. **CAST:** Fred Williamson, Peter Fonda, Gary Busey, Vanity, Robert Forster. 1992

SPECIAL BULLETIN ★★★ A group of antinuclear scientists on a tugboat in Charleston, South Carolina, take a TV crew hostage then demand network airtime. They have a nuclear bomb and threaten to detonate it. Realistically effective made-for-television movie. 103m. **DIR:** Edward Zwick. **CAST:** Ed Flanders, Kathryn Walker, Roxanne Hart, Christopher Allport, David Clennon, David Rasche, Rosalind Cash. 1983

SPECKLED BAND, THE ★★★ In his motion-picture debut, Raymond Massey makes a sturdy Sherlock Holmes, who must bring to justice the evil villain, Dr. Grimesby Roylott (Lyn Harding). Harding, who later played Professor Moriarty in the Arthur Wontner series of Holmes mysteries, is a superb villain, and the sets are decidedly gothic. Time has not been kind to the overall production, but *The Speckled Band* has much to offer fans of the canon. B&W; 48m. **DIR:** Jack Raymond. **CAST:** Raymond Massey, Lyn Harding. 1931

SPECTER OF THE ROSE, THE ★★★★ Surreal thriller written and directed by Ben Hecht about a young ballerina who discovers that her new husband is going insane. Unique, stylish filmmaking that is reminiscent of the work of Jean Cocteau. B&W; 90m. **DIR:** Ben Hecht. **CAST:** Judith Anderson, Michael Chekhov, Lionel Stander. 1946

SPELLBOUND ★★★★ Hitchcock said in his usual, understated manner that *Spellbound* "is just another manhunt story wrapped up in pseudo-psychoanalysis." The story is more than just another manhunt story; of that we can assure you. We can divulge that Ingrid Bergman plays the psychiatrist, Gregory Peck is the patient, and Salvador Dalí provides the nightmare sequences. B&W; 111m. **DIR:** Alfred Hitchcock. **CAST:** Ingrid Bergman, Gregory Peck, Leo G. Carroll, John Emery, Wallace Ford, Rhonda Fleming, Bill Goodwin. 1945

SPHINX, THE (1933) ★★½ Horror-film great Lionel Atwill plays a dual role in this effective low-budget murder mystery with overtones of the supernatural. The Sphinx of the title refers to Atwill's twin brother, who is a deaf-mute. B&W; 63m. **DIR:** Phil Rosen. **CAST:** Lionel Atwill, Sheila Terry, Paul Fix. 1933

SPIRAL STAIRCASE, THE (1946) ★★★★ Dorothy McGuire gives what some call the performance of her career as a mute servant in a hackle-raising household harboring a killer. Watch this one late at night, but not alone. B&W; 83m. **DIR:** Robert Siodmak. **CAST:** George Brent, Dorothy McGuire, Ethel Barrymore, Kent Smith, Elsa Lanchester, Sara Allgood. 1946

SPIRAL STAIRCASE, THE (1975) 🦃 Sad remake. Not rated, but contains mild violence. 89m. **DIR:** Peter Collinson. **CAST:** Jacqueline Bisset, Christopher Plummer, Sam Wanamaker, Gayle Hunnicutt. 1975

SPY ★★½ A mediocre spy thriller involving a retired spy turned artist, who goes into hiding when his former colleagues decide he must die. Made for cable. 91m. **DIR:** Philip F. Messina. **CAST:** Bruce Greenwood, Jameson Parker, Tim Choate, Catharine Hicks, Ned Beatty, Michael Tucker. 1989

STAGE FRIGHT ★★★ Another winner from Alfred Hitchcock. Drama student Jane Wyman spies on actress Marlene Dietrich to prove she murdered her husband. Alastair Sim steals his moments as Wyman's protective parent, but most of the other moments go to the hypnotic Dietrich. B&W; 110m. **DIR:** Alfred Hitchcock. **CAST:** Marlene Dietrich, Jane Wyman, Michael Wilding, Alastair Sim, Richard Todd, Kay Walsh, Patricia Hitchcock. 1950

STAR CHAMBER, THE ★★★★ A model group of superior court judges lose faith in the constitutional bylaws that they have sworn to uphold and decide to take the law into their own hands. Michael Douglas plays the idealistic young judge who uncovers the organization. Rated R for violence and profanity. 109m. **DIR:** Peter Hyams. **CAST:** Michael Douglas, Hal Holbrook, Yaphet Kotto, Sharon Gless, Jack Kehoe. 1983

STAR OF MIDNIGHT ★★½ William Powell, in a role cloned from his *Thin Man* series, is a debonair, urbane lawyer accused of murder. Abetted by Ginger Rogers, he sallies forth, repartee in mouth, to catch the real culprit. The police and gangsters alike make it difficult. Not bad. B&W; 90m. **DIR:** Stephen Roberts. **CAST:** William Powell, Ginger Rogers, Paul Kelly, Gene Lockhart, Ralph Morgan. **1935**

STELLA MARIS ★★★★★ Arguably Mary Pickford's masterpiece, although it stands in stark contrast to the sweetness-and-light qualities of many other popular vehicles. Some amazing double-exposure photography allows her to play *two* roles, a beautiful invalid and an ugly drab who plays an important part in the invalid's life. Silent. B&W; 70m. **DIR:** Marshall Neilan. **CAST:** Mary Pickford, Conway Tearle. **1918**

STEPFATHER, THE ★★★★ Jerry Blake (Terry O'Quinn) is so relentlessly cheerful that his stepdaughter, Stephanie Maine (Jill Schoelen), complains to a friend, "It's just like living with Ward Cleaver." Little does she know that the accent should be on the cleaver. Jerry, you see, is a raving maniac. A thriller of a chiller. Rated R for violence, profanity, and brief nudity. 90m. **DIR:** Joseph Ruben. **CAST:** Terry O'Quinn, Shelley Hack, Jill Schoelen, Charles Lanyer, Stephen Shellen. **1987**

STILL OF THE NIGHT ★★★½ In this well-crafted thriller by writer-director Robert Benton a psychiatrist (Roy Scheider) falls in love with an art curator (Meryl Streep) who may have killed one of his patients and may be after him next. If you like being scared out of your wits, you won't want to miss it. Rated PG for violence and adult themes. 91m. **DIR:** Robert Benton. **CAST:** Roy Scheider, Meryl Streep, Jessica Tandy, Joe Grifasi, Sara Botsford. **1982**

STONE COLD DEAD ★★ This fair film, based on the novel *Sin Sniper* by Hugh Garner, centers on the investigation by Sergeant Boyd (Richard Crenna) into a bizarre series of prostitute killings. Rated R. 97m. **DIR:** George Mendeluk. **CAST:** Richard Crenna, Belinda Montgomery, Paul Williams, Linda Sorenson. **1980**

STORM ★★★ Thieves return years after the crime to dig up their buried cache. Suspenseful low-budget film. Rated PG-13 for violence. 100m. **DIR:** David Winning. **CAST:** David Palfy. **1987**

STORMY MONDAY ★★★★ In this stylish British thriller, Melanie Griffith and Sean Bean play unlikely lovers who attempt to stop ruthless American businessman Tommy Lee Jones from taking over a jazz nightclub owned by Sting. The generally strong performances, inventive filmmaking techniques, and offbeat sensibilities of *Stormy Monday* make it worth watching. Rated R for violence. 93m. **DIR:** Mike Figgis. **CAST:** Melanie Griffith, Tommy Lee Jones, Sting, Sean Bean. **1988**

STRANGE ILLUSION ★★ Following the mysterious disappearance of his father, a teenager on a fishing holiday with the family physician is disturbed by a strange dream concerning his mother. Trite. B&W; 80m. **DIR:** Edgar G. Ulmer. **CAST:** Jimmy Lydon, Sally Eilers, Regis Toomey. **1945**

STRANGER, THE (1947) ★★★★ Nazi war criminal (Orson Welles) assumes a new identity in a midwestern town following World War II, unaware that a government agent (Edward G. Robinson) is tailing him. Extremely well-done film, holds the viewer's interest from start to finish. B&W; 95m. **DIR:** Orson Welles. **CAST:** Orson Welles, Edward G. Robinson, Loretta Young, Richard Long. **1946**

STRANGER, THE (1986) ★★★★ Taut psychological thriller that keeps you on the edge of your seat. Bonnie Bedelia plays a woman with amnesia trying to put the pieces together after a car accident. She thinks she may or may not have witnessed a murder. Peter Riegert is her psychiatrist who may or may not be trying to help her. This unique sleeper is fast-paced and suspenseful. Rated R for brief nudity and violence. 93m. **DIR:** Adolfo Aristarian. **CAST:** Bonnie Bedelia, Peter Riegert. **1986**

STRANGER AMONG US, A ★★★½ Melanie Griffith becomes a tough-talkin' New York cop in this fish-out-of-water thriller. She penetrates New York's Hasidic Jewish community after a jeweler turns up dead and his sizable inventory is missing. Rated PG-13 for violence and profanity. 111m. **DIR:** Sidney Lumet. **CAST:** Melanie Griffith, Eric Thal, John Pankow, Tracy Pollan, Lee Richardson, Mia Sara, Jamey Sheridan. **1992**

STRANGER ON THE THIRD FLOOR ★★★★ Peter Lorre gives yet another singular performance as a disinterested murderer, a character truly alien yet strangely sympathetic. A great hallucination sequence and good performances all the way around make this a compelling treat. B&W; 64m. **DIR:** Boris Ingster. **CAST:** Peter Lorre, John McGuire, Elisha Cook Jr., Margaret Tallichet. **1940**

STRANGERS ON A TRAIN ★★★★★ One of the most discussed and analyzed of all of Alfred Hitchcock's films. *Strangers on a Train* was made during the height of Hitchcock's most creative period, the early 1950s. When you add a marvelous performance by Robert Walker as the stranger, you have one of the most satisfying thrillers ever. B&W; 101m. **DIR:** Alfred Hitchcock. **CAST:** Farley Granger, Robert Walker, Ruth Roman, Leo G. Carroll, Patricia Hitchcock, Marion Lorne. **1951**

STRANGLER, THE ★★½ Victor Buono gives a good performance as corpulent, mother-fixated maniac who murders nurses and throws Chicago into a state of alarm. This low-budget thriller didn't get a lot of play dates as a result of the real-life horrors of Boston strangler Albert De Salvo and the senseless murder of eight nurses by Richard Speck. Not rated, but violent and gruesome. Also available at 80 minutes. B&W; 89m. **DIR:** Burt Topper. **CAST:** Victor Buono, David McLean, Ellen Corby, Jeanne Bates. **1964**

STRAW DOGS ★★★★ An American intellectual mathematician (played brilliantly by Dustin Hoffman) takes a wife (Susan George) and returns to her ancestral village on the coast of England. She taunts her former boyfriends with her wealth and power, and soon she is viciously raped. This violent, controversial shocker by Sam Peckinpah is rated R. 113m. **DIR:** Sam Peckinpah. **CAST:** Dustin Hoffman, Susan George, Peter Vaughan, T. P. McKenna, Peter Arne, David Warner. **1971**

STREET WITH NO NAME ★★★½ Semi-documentary about the FBI's infiltration of a gang of young hoodlums is hard-hitting and grimly realistic. Richard Widmark is at his best as the gang leader who rules his young thugs with military precision, and Mark Stevens plays the agent who poses as a tough in order to get the goods on the hoods. B&W; 94m. **DIR:** William Keighley. **CAST:** Mark Stevens, Richard Widmark, Lloyd Nolan, Barbara Lawrence, Ed Begley Sr., John McIntire. **1948**

STUDY IN SCARLET, A ★★ Bearing absolutely no resemblance to the first of Arthur Conan Doyle's Sherlock Holmes stories, this low-budget entry is perhaps the most lackluster of all the sound Holmes films. B&W; 70m. **DIR:** Edwin L. Marin. **CAST:** Reginald Owen, Anna May Wong, Alan Dinehart, June Clyde, Alan Mowbray. **1933**

STUDY IN TERROR, A ★★★★ This superior Sherlock Holmes adventure pits "the original caped crusader," as the ads called him, against Jack the Ripper. John Neville is an excellent Holmes. And Donald Houston is perhaps the screen's finest Dr. John Watson. 94m. **DIR:** James Hill. **CAST:** John Neville, Donald Houston, Georgia Brown, John Fraser, Anthony Quayle, Barbara Windsor, Robert Morley, Cecil Parker. **1965**

SUBSTITUTE, THE ★★★ In this made-for-cable original, a college professor kills her husband and his lover, then resurfaces as a substitute high-school teacher. She falls in love with the father of one of her students, but people are getting suspicious, so she must kill again. Pretty predictable story line, but the acting is good. Rated R for violence and suggested sex. 86m. **DIR:** Martin Donovan. **CAST:** Amanda Donohoe, Dalton James, Natasha Gregson Wagner, Eugene Glazer, Marky Mark. **1993**

SUDDENLY ★★★★ Here's top-notch entertainment with Frank Sinatra perfectly cast as a leader of a gang of assassins out to kill the president of the United States. *Suddenly* has gone largely unnoticed over the last few years, but thanks to home video, we can all enjoy this gem of a picture. B&W; 77m. **DIR:** Lewis Allen. **CAST:** Frank Sinatra, Sterling Hayden, James Gleason, Nancy Gates. **1954**

SUICIDE CLUB, THE ★★ This uneven, contrived shocker features Mariel Hemingway as a bored heiress involved with a group of self-indulgent aristocrats who engage in bizarre ritualistic games. Hemingway turns in a compelling performance in this otherwise disappointing thriller. Rated R; contains nudity and violence. 90m. **DIR:** James Bruce. **CAST:** Mariel Hemingway, Robert Joy, Madeleine Potter, Michael O'Donoghue. **1988**

SUNBURN 🦃 Farrah Fawcett pretends to be the wife of insurance investigator Charles Grodin to get the real scoop on a suicide case in Acapulco. Rated PG. 94m. **DIR:** Richard C. Sarafian. **CAST:** Farrah Fawcett, Charles Grodin, Art Carney, William Daniels, Joan Collins. **1979**

SUNSET ★★★½ Writer-director Blake Edwards begins this charming little *soufflé* with an intriguing notion: what if legendary lawman Wyatt Earp (James Garner) had met silent-screen cowboy Tom Mix (Bruce Willis) and the two had become fast friends? The boys get involved in a seamy murder case. Rated R for language and violence. 107m. **DIR:** Blake Edwards. **CAST:** James Garner, Bruce Willis, Malcolm McDowell, Mariel Hemingway, Kathleen Quinlan, Jennifer Edwards, Patricia Hodge, M. Emmet Walsh, Joe Dallesandro. **1988**

SUNSET GRILL ★★½ Passable private-investigator mystery features Peter Weller as a down-and-out detective trying to find his wife's assassin. Weller elevates an otherwise low-budget effort by creating a quirky, mesmerizing character. Unrated; contains nudity, sex, violence, and profanity. 105m. **DIR:** Kevin Connor. **CAST:** Peter Weller, Lori Singer, Stacy Keach, Alexandra Paul, John Rhys-Davies. **1992**

SUNSTROKE 🦃 Bad accents, poor acting, and a horrible plot ruin this tale about a woman trying to locate her daughter. Rated R for violence and profanity. 91m. **DIR:** James Keach. **CAST:** Jane Seymour, Stephen Meadows, Steve Railsback, Ray Wise, Don Ameche. **1992**

SURVIVE THE NIGHT ★★★½ Surprisingly believable film in which three women end up fighting for their lives in a part of New York where the police don't like to go. Stefanie Powers does a fine job portraying the mother who will do anything to protect her daughter. Not rated, made for cable, but contains violence. 95m. **DIR:** Bill Corcoran. **CAST:** Stefanie Powers, Helen Shaver, Kathleen

Robertson, Lawrence Gilliard Jr., Currie Graham. 1992

SUSPECT ★★☆½ Cher is just fine as a public defender assigned to prove a deaf and mute street bum (Liam Neeson) innocent of the murder of a Washington, D.C., secretary. One of the jurors, lobbyist Dennis Quaid, takes a liking to Cher and begins helping her with the seemingly impossible case, thus putting her career and their lives in danger. Rated R for violence and profanity. 128m. **DIR:** Peter Yates. **CAST:** Cher, Dennis Quaid, Joe Mantegna, Liam Neeson, Philip Bosco, John Mahoney, Fred Melamed. 1987

SUSPICION (1941) ★★★★ A timid woman is gradually unnerved by apprehension. Bits of evidence lead her to believe that her charming husband is a killer and that she is the intended victim. Joan Fontaine played a similar role in *Rebecca* and eventually won a best-actress Oscar for her performance in *Suspicion*. Cary Grant is excellent, too. B&W; 99m. **DIR:** Alfred Hitchcock. **CAST:** Joan Fontaine, Cary Grant, Cedric Hardwicke, Nigel Bruce, May Whitty, Isabel Jeans. 1941

SUSPICION (1987) ★★ A plain country Jane (Curtin) grows suspicious of her hubby's intentions after piecing together the plot for a murder that would benefit her penniless mate. This Alfred Hitchcock remake lacks the subtle suspense of the original. Rated PG. 97m. **DIR:** Andrew Grieve. **CAST:** Jane Curtin, Anthony Andrews, Betsy Blair, Michael Hordern, Vivian Pickles, Jonathan Lynn. 1987

SVENGALI (1931) ★★★★ This film is adapted from the George Du Maurier novel that put Svengali into the language as one who controls another. John Barrymore plays Svengali, a demonic artist obsessed with Trilby, a young artist's model. Under his hypnotic influence, she becomes a singer who obeys his every command. Bizarre sets and arresting visual effects make this a surrealistic delight. B&W; 76m. **DIR:** Archie Mayo. **CAST:** John Barrymore, Marian Marsh, Donald Crisp, Carmel Myers, Bramwell Fletcher. 1931

SWEET KILLING 🦃 A strong cast is wasted in this imbecilic mess. A bored husband kills his wife and concocts a fictitious murderer, then meets a man claiming to be that very murderer. Rated R for profanity, nudity, and simulated sex. 87m. **DIR:** Eddy Matalon. **CAST:** Anthony Higgins, F. Murray Abraham, Leslie Hope, Andrea Ferreol, Michael Ironside. 1993

SWEET MURDER 🦃 Attractive Helene Udy allows Embeth Davidtz to move into her apartment, although Davidtz looks amazingly like the ax murderer she is. Could become infamous as the worst impersonation plot on film. Rated R for violence, profanity, and nudity. 101m. **DIR:** Percival Rubens. **CAST:** Helene Udy, Embeth Davidtz, Russell Todd. 1993

SWISS CONSPIRACY, THE ★★½ Swiss banker Ray Milland hires ex-Fed David Janssen to thwart a sophisticated blackmail scheme involving supposedly secret numbered accounts. Sexy Senta Berger and John Saxon, as a Chicago gangster double-crossing his friends, are among those being threatened with exposure and death. Rated PG. 92m. **DIR:** Jack Arnold. **CAST:** David Janssen, Senta Berger, Ray Milland, Elke Sommer, John Ireland, John Saxon. 1977

TAINTED BLOOD ★★★½ A nationally known writer is doing research on children who inherit killer tendencies. She goes in search of a girl whose mother killed her parents and whose twin brother killed his adoptive parents. The viewer meets two families who each have an adopted daughter. At every turn, the very twisted plot keeps the viewer unsure which girl has the tainted blood. Not rated, made for cable, but contains violence. 95m. **DIR:** Matthew Patrick. **CAST:** Raquel Welch, Alley Mills, Kerri Green, Natasha Gregson Wagner, Joan Van Ark. 1993

TAKING OF PELHAM ONE TWO THREE, THE ★★★★ Walter Matthau is at his growling, grumbling, gum-chewing best in this edge-of-your-seat movie. He plays the chief detective of security on the New York subway who must deal with the unthinkable: the hijacking of a commuter train by four men (with a fine Robert Shaw as their leader) and a demand by them for a $1 million ransom to prevent their killing the passengers one by one. Rated PG. 104m. **DIR:** Joseph Sargent. **CAST:** Walter Matthau, Robert Shaw, Martin Balsam, Tony Roberts. 1974

TALES OF THE UNEXPECTED ★★½ Four half-hour made-for-television shows are included in this compilation. The best is the third, "Skeleton in the Cupboard," starring Charles Dance as a man who mistakes a young woman's intentions about his past and in turn ruins his future. Other titles include: "People Don't Do Such Things" with Don Johnson as a womanizing author; "Youth From Vienna" starring Dick Smothers who gets revenge on an ex-flame; and "Bird of Prey" wherein a mutant parrot gives away a wife's infidelities. Unfortunately, the story lines are more expected than unexpected. 101m. **DIR:** Gordon Hessler, Norman Lloyd, Paul Annett, Ray Danton. **CAST:** Don Johnson, Arthur Hill, Samantha Eggar, Sharon Gless, Dick Smothers, James Carroll Jordan, Charles Dance, Zoe Wanamaker, Sondra Locke, Frank Converse, Charles Hallahan. 1981–1987

TARGETS ★★★★★ The stunning filmmaking debut of critic-turned-director Peter Bogdanovich juxtaposes real-life terror, in the form of an unhinged mass murderer (Tim O'Kelly), with its comparatively subdued and safe screen counterpart, as represented by the scare films of Byron Orlock (Boris Karloff in a brilliant final bow). Rated PG. 90m. **DIR:** Peter Bogdanovich. **CAST:** Tim O'Kelly, Boris Karloff, Nancy Hsueh, Peter Bogdanovich. **1968**

TAXI DRIVER ★★★★★ Robert De Niro plays an alienated Vietnam-era vet thrust into the nighttime urban sprawl of New York City. In his despair after a romantic rejection by an attractive political campaign aide, he focuses on "freeing" a 12-year-old prostitute by unleashing violent retribution on her pimp. It's unnerving and realistic. Rated R for violence and profanity. 113m. **DIR:** Martin Scorsese. **CAST:** Robert De Niro, Harvey Keitel, Cybill Shepherd, Jodie Foster, Peter Boyle. **1976**

TELEFON ★★★ In this good suspense film, Charles Bronson is a KGB agent who, with the help of the CIA's Lee Remick, is out to stop some preprogrammed Soviet spies from blowing up the United States. Rated PG. 102m. **DIR:** Don Siegel. **CAST:** Charles Bronson, Lee Remick, Donald Pleasence, John Mitchum, Patrick Magee. **1977**

TEN DAYS WONDER ★★★★ One of Claude Chabrol's superb *hommages* to the American detective thriller. Originally titled *La Decade Prodigieuse*, it is based on one of Ellery Queen's finest psychological studies of a serial murderer. Typically, Chabrol is more interested in characterization and mood than in pacing and graphic violence. 100m. **DIR:** Claude Chabrol. **CAST:** Orson Welles, Marlene Jobert, Anthony Perkins, Michel Piccoli. **1972**

TEN LITTLE INDIANS (1966) ★★★½ A good retelling of the Agatha Christie classic with ten complete strangers trapped in an Alpine chateau, one among them having murder in mind. B&W; 92m. **DIR:** George Pollock. **CAST:** Hugh O'Brian, Shirley Eaton, Fabian, Leo Genn, Stanley Holloway, Marianne Hoppe, Wilfrid Hyde-White, Daliah Lavi, Dennis Price, Mario Adorf. **1966**

TEN LITTLE INDIANS (1975) 🦃 Absolutely dismal third version of the Agatha Christie classic. This one completely mucks up the plot, switching from an isolated island mansion to a hotel deep in the Iranian desert(!). Rated PG—mild violence. 98m. **DIR:** Peter Collinson. **CAST:** Oliver Reed, Richard Attenborough, Elke Sommer, Herbert Lom, Gert Fröbe. **1975**

TEN LITTLE INDIANS (1989) ★★ Agatha Christie's suspenseful whodunit loses much of its flair in this slow-moving, poorly acted rendition. A group of ten is systematically picked off at an isolated African campsite. Rated PG. 99m. **DIR:** Alan Birkinshaw. **CAST:** Donald Pleasence, Frank Stallone, Brenda Vaccaro. **1989**

TENANT, THE ★★★ Roman Polanski is superb in this cryptic thriller about a bumbling Polish expatriate in France who leases an apartment owned previously by a young woman who committed suicide. Increasingly, Polanski believes the apartment's tenants conspired demonically to destroy the woman and are attempting to do the same to him. Rated R. 125m. **DIR:** Roman Polanski. **CAST:** Roman Polanski, Melvyn Douglas, Shelley Winters. **1976**

TERROR BY NIGHT ★★★ Penultimate entry in the Rathbone/Bruce Sherlock Holmes series, with the master sleuth and his loyal companion up against a series of murders on a train bound from London to Edinburgh. The culprit ultimately turns out to be Col. Sebastian Moran, but you'll have to watch the film to discover which of the passengers he impersonates! B&W; 69m. **DIR:** Roy William Neill. **CAST:** Basil Rathbone, Nigel Bruce, Alan Mowbray, Renee Godfrey, Billy Bevan, Dennis Hoey. **1946**

TERROR ON ALCATRAZ 🦃 A group of teenagers split off from a tour of a former prison and end up locked in overnight. Not rated, but contains violence. 96m. **DIR:** Philip Marcus. **CAST:** Aldo Ray. **1987**

TERROR ON THE 40TH FLOOR ★★ A typical disaster film, this deals with a skyscraper fire. Unrated. 100m. **DIR:** Jerry Jameson. **CAST:** John Forsythe, Joseph Campanella, Don Meredith. **1974**

TERRORISTS, THE ★★★★ Solid suspense-thriller has Sean Connery as the bullheaded commander of Norway's national security force, which is galvanized into action when a group of English terrorists takes over the British embassy. Rated PG for violence. 100m. **DIR:** Caspar Wrede. **CAST:** Sean Connery, Ian McShane, James Maxwell, Isabel Dean, Jeffrey Wickham, John Quentin, Robert Harris. **1975**

TESTAMENT OF DR. MABUSE ★★★½ In this sequel to *Dr. Mabuse the Gambler* by Thea Von Harboll and the director Fritz Lang, the infamous criminal mastermind dies in an asylum, and his assistant takes over his identity. It's a fast-moving picture, said by Lang to be a diatribe against Adolf Hitler. Whatever it is, it rates as slick entertainment. B&W; 122m. **DIR:** Fritz Lang. **CAST:** Rudolf Klein-Rogge, Otto Wernicke. **1933**

THEY MIGHT BE GIANTS ★★★★ Stylish and engaging study of a retired judge (George C. Scott) who imagines himself to be Sherlock Holmes. With visions of dollar signs floating before his eyes, the judge's brother hopes to have this ersatz detective committed; to this end, the brother brings in a female psychiatrist whose name happens to be—you guessed it—Watson. Rated PG. 88m. **DIR:** Anthony Harvey. **CAST:** George C. Scott, Joanne Woodward, Jack Gilford. **1971**

THEY ONLY KILL THEIR MASTERS ★★★ Pretty solid whodunit (if a bit TV-ish), with James Garner terrific as always, playing a small-town Californian sheriff. He solves a pregnant woman's murder. The title refers to a deadly Doberman pinscher. Rated PG. 97m. **DIR:** James Goldstone. **CAST:** James Garner, Katharine Ross, Hal Holbrook, Harry Guardino, June Allyson, Peter Lawford, Edmond O'Brien, Arthur O'Connell, Christopher Connelly, Tom Ewell, Ann Rutherford. 1972

THIEF, THE (1952) ★★½ A scientist for the Atomic Energy Commission tries to flee the country when the FBI discovers he's been selling information to enemy spies. Filmed entirely without dialogue, this noir thriller has strong visuals and an intense performance by Ray Milland, but the silence becomes a burdensome gimmick before long. B&W; 87m. **DIR:** Russell Rouse. **CAST:** Ray Milland, Martin Gabel, Rita Gam. 1952

THIN MAN, THE ★★★★½ Viewers and critics alike were captivated by William Powell and Myrna Loy in this first (and best) of a series based on Dashiell Hammett's mystery novel about his "other" detective and wife, Nick and Nora Charles. The thin man is a murder victim. But never mind. The delight of this fun film is the banter between its stars. You'll like their little dog, too. B&W; 89m. **DIR:** W. S. Van Dyke. **CAST:** William Powell, Myrna Loy, Edward Brophy, Porter Hall, Maureen O'Sullivan. 1934

THIN MAN GOES HOME, THE ★★½ Fifth and weakest entry in the series. Nick Charles (William Powell) returns to his old hometown, accompanied by Nora (Myrna Loy) and young Nick Jr. Still entertaining, but a lesser effort. B&W; 101m. **DIR:** Richard Thorpe. **CAST:** William Powell, Myrna Loy, Lucile Watson, Gloria De Haven, Anne Revere, Helen Vinson, Harry Davenport, Leon Ames, Donald Meek, Edward Brophy. 1944

THIRD DEGREE BURN ★★★ Debt-ridden ex-cop reluctantly accepts a domestic investigation, only to fall headlong for the blonde subject. (Virginia Madsen is the perfect Monroe-like sex bomb.) Steamy mystery twists like a snake. Made for HBO. 97m. **DIR:** Roger Spottiswoode. **CAST:** Treat Williams, Virginia Madsen, C.C.H. Pounder, Richard Masur. 1989

THIRD MAN, THE ★★★★★ Considered by many to be the greatest suspense film of all time, this classic inevitably turns up on every best-film list. It rivals any Hitchcock thriller as being the ultimate masterpiece of film suspense. A writer (Joseph Cotten) discovers an old friend he thought dead to be the head of a vicious European black market organization. Unfortunately for him, that information makes him a marked man. B&W; 104m. **DIR:** Carol Reed. **CAST:** Joseph Cotten, Orson Welles, Alida Valli, Trevor Howard. 1949

13 AT DINNER ★★★½ Above-average made-for-TV Agatha Christie mystery, with Peter Ustinov reprising his big-screen role as fastidious Belgian sleuth Hercule Poirot. This time out, the dapper detective contends with a murdered British lord and his thespian widow (Faye Dunaway). Notable for the presence of David Suchet as Scotland Yard's Inspector Japp, a few years before Suchet took over the role of Poirot himself. 100m. **DIR:** Lou Antonio. **CAST:** Peter Ustinov, Faye Dunaway, David Suchet, Lee Horsley, Amanda Pays. 1985

THIRTEENTH GUEST, THE ★★★ A gathering of relatives in a spooky old mansion invites murder in this superior thriller. While a storm rages outside, the reading of a strange will is interrupted by a mysterious figure, and when the lights come on there's a corpse. B&W; 65m. **DIR:** Albert Ray. **CAST:** Ginger Rogers, Lyle Talbot, J. Farrell MacDonald. 1932

THIRTY-NINE STEPS, THE (1935) ★★★★★ Alfred Hitchcock was assigned to direct what was intended to be a simple, low-budget spy-chase thriller. Using the style and technique that were to make him famous, he gained immediate audience sympathy for the plight of his central character, an innocent Canadian (Robert Donat) who while visiting England is implicated in the theft of national secrets and murder. The result was a big hit. B&W; 87m. **DIR:** Alfred Hitchcock. **CAST:** Robert Donat, Madeleine Carroll, Lucie Mannheim. 1935

THIRTY-NINE STEPS, THE (1959) ★★½ Inferior remake of Alfred Hitchcock's suspense classic has Kenneth More as the hapless fellow who innocently becomes involved in a murder plot. The 1978 version with Robert Powell also has it beat. 93m. **DIR:** Ralph Thomas. **CAST:** Kenneth More, Taina Elg, Brenda de Banzie, Barry Jones, Sidney James. 1959

THIRTY-NINE STEPS, THE (1978) ★★★½ An innocent man stumbles onto a spy plot in pre–World War I London. Hunted by enemy agents who think he has intercepted an important communiqué, and civil authorities who believe he is a murderer, the man has nowhere to turn. The best of several Hitchcock remakes in the 1970s. It can't compete with the original, of course, but the cast is good. The script is witty, and the climax atop Big Ben is exciting. Rated PG. 102m. **DIR:** Don Sharp. **CAST:** Robert Powell, David Warner, Eric Porter, Karen Dotrice, John Mills. 1978

THREAT, THE ★★★½ This underrated suspense feature packs every minute with tension as vengeance-minded Charles McGraw escapes from jail and kidnaps the police detective and district attorney as well as snatches a singer he thinks may have told on him for good measure. The police put the pressure on the kidnapper, and he puts the squeeze on his captives. B&W; 65m. **DIR:** Felix Feist. **CAST:** Charles McGraw, Michael O'Shea, Frank Conroy, Virginia Grey, Julie Bishop, Robert Shayne, Anthony Caruso, Don McGuire. **1949**

THREE DAYS OF THE CONDOR ★★★★ Robert Redford is a CIA information researcher who is forced to flee for his life when his New York cover operation is blown and all of his coworkers brutally murdered. What seems at first to be a standard man-on-the-run drama gradually deepens into an engrossing mystery as to who is chasing him and why. Faye Dunaway expertly handles a vignette as the stranger Redford uses to avoid capture. Rated R. 117m. **DIR:** Sydney Pollack. **CAST:** Robert Redford, Cliff Robertson, Max von Sydow, Faye Dunaway, John Houseman. **1975**

THRILLED TO DEATH ★★ An unsuspecting couple is framed for murder and drug running. The dupes are so incredibly naïve that you'll find yourself yelling at them to wake up. Rated R for nudity and violence. 93m. **DIR:** Chuck Vincent. **CAST:** Blake Bahner. **1988**

THRILLKILL 🦃 Woman has a falling-out with her partners after stealing $3 million via computer. Not rated, but contains some violence and frank language. 88m. **DIR:** Anthony Kramreither, Anthony D'Andrea. **CAST:** Robin Ward, Gina Massey. **1986**

THUNDERHEART ★★★★½ FBI agent Val Kilmer is assigned to help veteran agent Sam Shepard investigate the murder of an Oglala Sioux on a reservation in the badlands of South Dakota. Michael Apted's richest and most compelling movie since *Coal Miner's Daughter*. Rated R for violence and profanity. 127m. **DIR:** Michael Apted. **CAST:** Val Kilmer, Sam Shepard, Graham Greene, Fred Ward, Fred Dalton Thompson. **1992**

TIGHTROPE ★★★★★ A terrific, taut suspense-thriller, this ranks with the best films in the genre. Written and directed by Richard Tuggle, *Tightrope* casts Clint Eastwood as Wes Block, homicide inspector for the New Orleans Police Department. His latest assignment is to track down a Jack the Ripper–style sex murderer. This case hits disturbingly close to home in more ways than one. Rated R for violence. 115m. **DIR:** Richard Tuggle. **CAST:** Clint Eastwood, Genevieve Bujold, Dan Hedaya, Alison Eastwood. **1984**

TIME BOMB ★★ Michael Biehn plays an amnesiac who suddenly finds himself a target for assassination. Patsy Kensit costars as a psychiatrist who Biehn first abducts and persuades to restore his memory. Rated R for violence, profanity, and simulated sex. 96m. **DIR:** Avi Nesher. **CAST:** Michael Biehn, Patsy Kensit, Tracy Scoggins, Robert Culp, Richard Jordan. **1991**

TIME TO DIE, A (1990) 🦃 The only mystery in this tale of a female photographer (former porn star Traci Lords) who catches a cop in a compromising position, is why anyone would want to watch it in the first place. Rated R for violence and profanity. 90m. **DIR:** Charles Kanganis. **CAST:** Traci Lords, Richard Roundtree, Jeff Conaway. **1991**

TO CATCH A KILLER ★★★ Much-edited, former miniseries chronicles the mounting evidence against—and eventual arrest of—serial killer John Wayne Gacy. Brian Dennehy is truly frightening as Gacy, the man responsible for the deaths of thirty-two teenage boys. Michael Riley is also convincing as the dedicated lieutenant who would stop at nothing to halt Gacy's reign of terror. 95m. **DIR:** Eric Till. **CAST:** Brian Dennehy, Michael Riley, Margot Kidder, David Eisner. **1991**

TO CATCH A KING ★★ Made-for-cable spy thriller that fails to live up to its promising premise. In 1940, cunning Nazis plot to kidnap the Duke and Duchess of Windsor during the romantic couple's respite in Lisbon. Robert Wagner plays a café owner, a more debonair version of *Casablanca*'s Rick. Teri Garr is a nightclub singer. The film is neither convincing nor exciting. 113m. **DIR:** Clive Donner. **CAST:** Robert Wagner, Teri Garr, Horst Janson, Barbara Parkins. **1984**

TO CATCH A THIEF ★★★★ John Robie (Cary Grant) is a retired cat burglar living in France in peaceful seclusion. When a sudden rash of jewel thefts hits the Riviera, he is naturally blamed. He sets out to clear himself, and the fun begins. This is certainly one of director Alfred Hitchcock's most amusing films. 103m. **DIR:** Alfred Hitchcock. **CAST:** Cary Grant, Grace Kelly, John Williams, Jessie Royce Landis. **1955**

TO KILL A CLOWN 🦃 A husband and wife move from the big city to a remote island in an effort to save their marriage. Rated R for violence. 82m. **DIR:** George Bloomfield. **CAST:** Alan Alda, Blythe Danner. **1983**

TONY ROME ★★★ Pretty good private eye film has detective Frank Sinatra looking for clues into the disappearance of a wealthy man's daughter. Good atmosphere and a fine cast lend support as well. 110m. **DIR:** Gordon Douglas. **CAST:** Frank Sinatra, Jill St. John, Sue Lyon, Richard Conte, Simon Oakland, Gena Rowlands. **1967**

TOO SCARED TO SCREAM 🦃 Pathetic "demented killer" movie features Mike Connors as a grizzled New York detective on the trail of a psychopath. Rated R for nudity and gore. 104m. **DIR:** Tony Lo Bianco. **CAST:** Mike Connors, Anne Archer, Leon Isaac Kennedy, Ian McShane. **1982**

TOOLBOX MURDERS, THE 🦃 What can you say about a film whose sole purpose is to show someone using screwdrivers, pliers, and hammers on another human being? Not Cameron Mitchell's shining hour. 93m. **DIR:** Dennis Donnelly. **CAST:** Cameron Mitchell, Pamelyn Ferdin, Wesley Eure, Aneta Corseaut, Tim Donnelly. **1978**

TOPAZ ★★★ Medium-to-rare Hitchcock suspense-thriller about cloak-and-dagger intrigue concerning Russian involvement in Cuba and infiltration of the French government. Constant shift of scene keeps viewers on their toes. Rated PG. 127m. **DIR:** Alfred Hitchcock. **CAST:** John Forsythe, Frederick Stafford, Dany Robin, John Vernon. **1969**

TOPKAPI ★★★★★ This is one of the finest and funniest of the "big heist" genre. Director Jules Dassin assembled a highly talented international cast. They are members of a charming group of jewel thieves whose target is a priceless jeweled dagger in a Turkish museum. The execution of their clever plan is both humorous and exciting. 120m. **DIR:** Jules Dassin. **CAST:** Peter Ustinov, Melina Mercouri, Maximilian Schell. **1964**

TORMENT ★★ This low-budget slasher film starts off slow and, if it weren't for one interesting plot twist halfway through, would be an exercise in boredom. The story revolves around a man who becomes a psychotic killer when he is rejected by a younger woman. R for violence and gore. 90m. **DIR:** Samson Aslanian, John Hopkins. **CAST:** Taylor Gilbert. **1986**

TORN CURTAIN ★★★ This just-okay film was directed by Alfred Hitchcock in 1966. Paul Newman plays an American scientist posing as a defector, with Julie Andrews as his secretary-lover. Somehow we aren't moved by the action or the characters. 128m. **DIR:** Alfred Hitchcock. **CAST:** Paul Newman, Julie Andrews, Lila Kedrova, David Opatoshu. **1966**

TOTAL EXPOSURE ★★★ When fashion photographer Season Hubley is framed for murdering a model, she turns to private eye Michael Nouri to clear her name. Nouri begins to suspect that his client might actually be guilty. Watch this one to see what develops. Rated R for nudity, strong language, and violence. 96m. **DIR:** John Quinn. **CAST:** Michael Nouri, Season Hubley, Christian Bocher, Jeff Conaway, Robert Prentiss. **1990**

TOUCH AND DIE 🦃 Martin Sheen stars as an American journalist in Rome assigned to cover the murders of three people. His investigation reveals a conspiracy. Warning: title tells it all. Rated R for violence, profanity, and nudity. 108m. **DIR:** Piernico Solinas. **CAST:** Martin Sheen, René Estevez, David Birney, Franco Nero. **1991**

TOUCH OF EVIL ★★★★½ In 1958, director-actor Orson Welles proved that he was still a filmmaking genius, with this dark and disturbing masterpiece about crime and corruption in a border town. B&W; 108m. **DIR:** Orson Welles. **CAST:** Orson Welles, Charlton Heston, Marlene Dietrich, Janet Leigh, Zsa Zsa Gabor. **1958**

TOURIST TRAP 🦃 Another psycho-hack film. Rated R for violence, gore, nudity, and profanity. 83m. **DIR:** David Schmoeller. **CAST:** Chuck Connors, Jon Van Ness, Jocelyn Jones, Tanya Roberts. **1979**

TOWN THAT DREADED SUNDOWN, THE ★★★½ The fact that *The Town that Dreaded Sundown* is based on actual events makes this effective little film all the more chilling. The story takes place in the year 1946 in the small border town of Texarkana. It begins in documentary style, with a narrator describing the post–World War II atmosphere, but soon gets to the unsettling business of the Phantom, a killer who terrorized the locals. Rated R for violence. 90m. **DIR:** Charles B. Pierce. **CAST:** Ben Johnson, Andrew Prine, Dawn Wells. **1977**

TRACES OF RED ★★ This half-baked erotic thriller—narrated by the fresh corpse of a homicide detective—features a Palm Beach serial killer who slashes women with a letter opener, smears their faces with Yves Saint Laurent lipstick, steals their clothes, and mails out lousy poetry that warns of further mayhem. Rated R for language, nudity, simulated sex, and violence. 104m. **DIR:** Andy Wolk. **CAST:** James Belushi, Lorraine Bracco, Tony Goldwyn, William Russ. **1993**

TRACK 29 ★★ British director Nicolas Roeg continues his downhill creative slide with this psycho-silly story of a bored, alcoholic housewife (Theresa Russell) who takes up with a strange hitchhiker (Gary Oldman) who may or may not be her son. Rated R for violence and gore. 90m. **DIR:** Nicolas Roeg. **CAST:** Theresa Russell, Gary Oldman, Christopher Lloyd, Colleen Camp, Sandra Bernhard, Seymour Cassel. **1988**

TRADE SECRETS ★★ Picture-postcard locations set the tone for this sophisticated but uninvolving French whodunit, as ex-Interpol policeman Sam Waterston probes the suspicious demise of a Bordeaux-wine heiress. Rated R for nudity and adult situations. 91m. **DIR:** Claude Feraldo. **CAST:** Sam Waterston, Marisa Berenson, Bernard Pierre Donnadieu, Lauren Hutton, Arielle Dombasle. **1986**

TRAP, THE ★★★½ Fast pace and taut suspense mark this thriller about as fine a gaggle of fleeing gangsters as ever menaced the innocent inhabitants of a small California desert town. This is edge-of-chair stuff. It was in films such as this that Richard Widmark made his name praisingly hissable. 84m. **DIR:** Norman Panama. **CAST:** Richard Widmark, Lee J. Cobb, Earl Holliman, Tina Louise, Lorne Greene. 1958

TRAPPED ★★½ Kathleen Quinlan's resourceful businesswoman saves this low-rent stuck-in-a-deserted-building-with-a-maniac programmer from complete turkeydom, but there's little to admire in Fred Walton's inane script or hackneyed direction. Made for cable. 88m. **DIR:** Fred Walton. **CAST:** Kathleen Quinlan, Bruce Abbott, Katy Boyer. 1989

TREACHEROUS CROSSING ★★★½ Lindsay Wagner is a newlywed who goes on a honeymoon cruise with her new husband, only to have him disappear right after boarding. Wagner portrays the unstable character quite convincingly, and the story is twisted enough, so that one does not know who to believe. Made for cable. 95m. **DIR:** Tony Wharmby. **CAST:** Lindsay Wagner, Angie Dickinson, Grant Show, Joseph Bottoms, Karen Medak, Charles Napier, Jeffrey DeMunn. 1992

TRIAL & ERROR ★★★ A prosecutor who sent a man to death row starts to have doubts about the man's guilt right before his execution. Tim Matheson does a fine job portraying the prosecutor. Not rated, made for cable, but contains violence. 95m. **DIR:** Mark Sobel. **CAST:** Tim Matheson, Helen Shaver, Sean McCann, Page Fletcher, Michael J. Reynolds, Ian D. Clark, Eugene A. Clark. 1992

TRIUMPH OF SHERLOCK HOLMES, THE ★★★½ A candle is the clue that unlocks the secret of a murder in this superior Sherlock Holmes film featuring Arthur Wontner and Ian Fleming as the infallible consulting detective and his friend and assistant Dr. John Watson. Made by an independent production company on a limited budget, this rendering of Conan Doyle's "Valley of Fear" retains much of the story's original dialogue. B&W; 75m. **DIR:** Leslie S. Hiscott. **CAST:** Arthur Wontner, Ian Fleming, Lyn Harding, Leslie Perrins. 1935

TROPICAL HEAT ★★½ Exotic locales enhance this sultry mystery, as insurance-investigator Rick Rossovich travels to India to track down the widow of a maharaja killed on a hunting safari. What starts off as a job becomes an infatuation as dangerous as the woman he has fallen for. Sexual content in unrated version really turns up the *Tropical Heat*. Rated R for sex, nudity, adult situations, and violence; unrated version contains more of the same. 86m./88m. **DIR:** Jag Mundhra. **CAST:** Rick Rossovich, Maryam D'Abo, Lee Anne Beaman, Asha Siewkumar. 1993

TROUBLE BOUND ★★ Michael Madsen is a luckless gambler who wins a car with a body in the trunk. Then he hooks up with sexy waitress Patricia Arquette, who turns out to be the granddaughter of a Mafia kingpin. Decent performances, but a thriller should never be wacky. Rated R for profanity and violence. 90m. **DIR:** Jeffrey Reiner. **CAST:** Michael Madsen, Patricia Arquette. 1992

TRUE BELIEVER ★★★★ James Woods gives a powerhouse performance in this gripping thriller, tautly directed by Joseph Ruben. Woods plays a maverick lawyer who takes on the case of a convicted killer, only to find himself bucking the powers-that-be in New York City. Robert Downey Jr. gives an effective performance as Woods's assistant. Rated R for violence and profanity. 103m. **DIR:** Joseph Ruben. **CAST:** James Woods, Robert Downey Jr., Margaret Colin, Kurtwood Smith. 1989

TRUE CONFESSIONS ★★★★½ This is the thoughtful, powerful story of two brothers (Robert De Niro and Robert Duvall)—one a priest, the other a jaded detective—caught in the sordid world of power politics in post–World War II Los Angeles. It's a brilliant and disturbing film. Rated R. 108m. **DIR:** Ulu Grosbard. **CAST:** Robert De Niro, Robert Duvall, Charles Durning, Burgess Meredith. 1981

TWICE DEAD ★★★ An all-American family moves into an old mansion inhabited by a street gang. The gang, furious about losing their clubhouse, starts terrorizing the family. This movie is highlighted by good performances, above-average effects, and a sharp wit. Rated R for violence and nudity. 90m. **DIR:** Bert L. Dragin. **CAST:** Tom Breznahan, Jill Whitlow, Todd Bridges. 1988

TWIN PEAKS (MOVIE) ★★★ The television pilot that was expected to be the mystery-soap opera for thinking persons, where "Who killed Laura Palmer?" would rival "Who shot J. R.?" But the series went off in too many directions, confusing the most die-hard fans. This still is a fascinating opening, where the logging town of Twin Peaks is stunned when two teenage girls have been kidnapped, tortured, and raped—with one murdered, the other found in shock. Contains added footage to wrap up the crime, but much of this is in conflict with what was shown in the limited series that followed. 113m. **DIR:** David Lynch. **CAST:** Kyle MacLachlan, Michael Ontkean, Joan Chen, Richard Beymer, Peggy Lipton, Jack Nance, Piper Laurie, Russ Tamblyn. 1989

TWIN PEAKS (TV SERIES) ★★ These seven episodes, following one of the most talked-about television pilot movies in years, became the shaggiest of all dogs when writers David Lynch and Mark Frost tried to attack our senses from too many directions, losing focus on an intriguing mystery. Those not familiar with the pilot will find these episodes valueless; those initially hooked may want to reflect on what might have been. each. 48m. **DIR:** Various. **CAST:** Kyle MacLachlan, Michael Ontkean, Joan Chen, Richard Beymer, Peggy Lipton, Jack Nance, Piper Laurie, Russ Tamblyn. 1990

TWIN PEAKS: FIRE WALK WITH ME ★★★ Fans of David Lynch's self-indulgent television series will no doubt be thrilled with this prequel; the rest of America is advised to steer clear. Aside from the obligatory references to dwarfs, coffee, and the phenomenal deductive skill of FBI Agent Cooper (Kyle MacLachlan), there's little to recommend this slightly spicier, big-screen soap opera (although Angelo Badalamenti's main theme still brings a chill). Given Laura Palmer's incessantly nasty and self-destructive behavior, most viewers will wish for her demise long before the conclusion of this chaotic exercise in oblique symbolism. Rated R for nudity and language. 135m. **DIR:** David Lynch. **CAST:** Kyle MacLachlan, Sheryl Lee, Moira Kelly, David Bowie, Chris Isaak, Harry Dean Stanton, Ray Wise, Kiefer Sutherland, Peggy Lipton. **1992**

TWINSANITY ★★★ Twins (Judy Geeson and Martin Potter) who still play games together are lured into London's underbelly. Sleazy sexual encounters lead the twins to concoct a game of murder. Though dated by its music and costuming, this film (originally released as *Goodbye Gemini*) does include some fine acting and a complex story line. Rated R for violence. 91m. **DIR:** Alan Gibson. **CAST:** Judy Geeson, Martin Potter, Alexis Kanner, Michael Redgrave, Mike Pratt, Freddie Jones, Peter Jeffrey. **1970**

TWISTED ★★½ Early Christian Slater thriller has the budding star playing a troubled teen who torments the new baby-sitter. Unrated, contains strong language and violence. 87m. **DIR:** Adam Holender. **CAST:** Christian Slater, Lois Smith, Tandy Cronyn, Dina Merrill, Noelle Parker. **1985**

TWO JAKES, THE ★★★½ Okay, so this sequel is not as good as its predecessor, *Chinatown,* but how many movies are? We loved the performances in this detective thriller set in 1948, when private eye Jake Gittes (Jack Nicholson, who also directed) is hired by another Jake (Harvey Keitel) to follow his wife. A convoluted, but noble effort. Rated R for violence and profanity. 133m. **DIR:** Jack Nicholson. **CAST:** Jack Nicholson, Harvey Keitel, Meg Tilly, Madeleine Stowe, Eli Wallach, Rubén Blades, Frederic Forrest, David Keith, Richard Farnsworth, Perry Lopez. **1990**

TWO-MINUTE WARNING ★★★ An all-star disaster film about a sniper loose in a crowded football stadium that is more exciting on video than it was on the big screen. The main reason is the lingering close-ups of the crowd and individual reactions are more impressive on a smaller screen. Rated R for violence, but the violence is tame by today's movie standards. 112m. **DIR:** Larry Peerce. **CAST:** John Cassavetes, Charlton Heston, Beau Bridges, Gena Rowlands, Marilyn Hassett, Martin Balsam, David Janssen, Walter Pidgeon, Jack Klugman, Brock Peters, Merv Griffin. **1976**

TWO MRS. CARROLLS, THE ★★½ It won't take you as long as it takes Barbara Stanwyck to realize that the moody artist she has married is a self-made repeat widower. No real suspense, just hysteria galore. B&W; 99m. **DIR:** Peter Godfrey. **CAST:** Humphrey Bogart, Barbara Stanwyck, Alexis Smith, Nigel Bruce. **1947**

TWO OF A KIND (1951) ★★ Average suspense-drama concerning a con-artist team who attempt to steal the inheritance of two elderly people. Both the cast and script are okay, but that's just the problem. B&W; 75m. **DIR:** Henry Levin. **CAST:** Edmond O'Brien, Lizabeth Scott, Terry Moore, Alexander Knox. **1951**

ULTIMATE DESIRES 🦃 A public defender poses as a prostitute to solve a murder mystery. Low-budget time waster with an overdose of sleaze. Rated R for drug use, violence, nudity, and profanity. 90m. **DIR:** Lloyd A. Simandl. **CAST:** Tracy Scoggins, Marc Singer, Brion James. **1991**

UNCAGED 🦃 Thankfully short sleazefest features a psychotic pimp on a bloody rampage after being set up by his number one girl. Rated R for nudity, violence, gore, and profanity. 78m. **DIR:** William Duprey. **CAST:** Leslie Bega. **1991**

UNDER CAPRICORN ★★★ This film is about a nineteenth-century Australian household that is hiding some dark secrets. Michael Wilding is drawn into solving the family's mystery because of his attraction to the lady of the house, Ingrid Bergman. This is not a typical Alfred Hitchcock movie. It lacks his customary suspense, and its pace could be called leisurely at best. 117m. **DIR:** Alfred Hitchcock. **CAST:** Michael Wilding, Ingrid Bergman, Joseph Cotten. **1949**

UNDER INVESTIGATION ★★ Harry Hamlin stars as a grungy L.A. detective in this sordid murder mystery. His main suspect is the wife of a famous murdered artist who stands to inherit a small fortune. Lustful looks, heavy breathing, and panting are substituted for plot and dialogue. Rated R for nudity, simulated sex, violence, and profanity. 99m. **DIR:** Kevin Meyer. **CAST:** Harry Hamlin, Joanna Pacula, Ed Lauter, Richard Beymer, John Mese, Lydie Denier. **1993**

UNDER SUSPICION ★★★ Womanizing private investigator Liam Neeson's wife and client are murdered, he becomes the prime suspect. Multiple plot twists and an edge-of-your-seat climax that border on the unbelievable. Rated R for nudity, violence, and profanity. 100m. **DIR:** Simon Moore. **CAST:** Liam Neeson, Laura San Giacomo, Kenneth Cranham, Maggie O'Neill. **1991**

UNDERGROUND (1990) 🦃 A young woman takes a job as a waitress in a sleazy strip joint where she falls in love with a disc jockey searching for his missing sister, last seen in the bar. Unrated, with violence and nudity. 87m. **DIR:** Bret Carr. **CAST:** Rachel Carr, Clement von Franckenstein, Sean Rankin. **1990**

UNDERWORLD STORY ★★½ Hard-boiled story of a mercenary reporter who exposes a ruthless publisher who is attempting to frame an innocent man for murder. The story is full of holes, and the portrait of journalism is about as sordid as anything done on the subject before or since. B&W; 90m. **DIR:** Cy Endfield. **CAST:** Dan Duryea, Herbert Marshall, Gale Storm, Howard DaSilva, Michael O'Shea, Mary Anderson, Melville Cooper, Gar Moore, Frieda Inescort, Art Baker. **1950**

UNHOLY THREE ★★★½ With his last film and first talkie, Lon Chaney became the man of a thousand voices. If he hadn't, in an ironic twist, died of cancer of the throat, Chaney would have starred in *Dracula* and maybe even *Frankenstein*. As it is, we have this early sound remake of Tod Browning's 1925 silent thriller, in which Chaney's carnival ventriloquist teams up with a midget and a strong man to commit crimes. B&W; 73m. **DIR:** Jack Conway. **CAST:** Lon Chaney Sr., Lila Lee, Elliott Nugent, Harry Earles. **1930**

UNINVITED, THE (1944) ★★★★★ Probably the greatest ghost-haunted house film ever made, all the terror being in the unseen, with a particularly satisfying and logical conclusion to the mystery. When brother and sister Ray Milland and Ruth Hussey buy a house on the English coast, a moody girl from the nearby village finds herself being drawn to it, although she has not lived there since she was a small child. Don't see this alone. B&W; 98m. **DIR:** Lewis Allen. **CAST:** Ray Milland, Ruth Hussey, Gail Russell, Donald Crisp, Cornelia Otis Skinner, Alan Napier. **1944**

UNION CITY ★★★ Called the "punk rock *film noir*," *Union City* is a quietly disturbing tale of murder and paranoia circa 1953. Deborah Harry (of the rock group Blondie) stars as a bored housewife; Dennis Lipscomb is her high-strung, paranoid husband. The mood, tone, and feel of the film are spooky, though it may be too oblique for some. Rated PG for adult themes and violence. 87m. **DIR:** Mark Reichert. **CAST:** Deborah Harry, Dennis Lipscomb, Pat Benatar. **1980**

UNION STATION ★★★ A big, bustling railroad terminal is the backdrop of this suspense-thriller centering on the manhunt that ensues following the kidnapping of a blind girl for ransom. William Holden is the hero, Lyle Bettger is the villain, Allene Roberts is the victim. The plot's tired, but ace cinematographer-turned-director Rudolph Maté keeps everything moving fast and frantic. B&W; 80m. **DIR:** Rudolph Maté. **CAST:** William Holden, Nancy Olson, Allene Roberts, Barry Fitzgerald, Lyle Bettger, Jan Sterling. **1950**

UNLAWFUL ENTRY ★★★½ After finding an intruder in their home, upscale L.A. suburbanites Kurt Russell and Madeleine Stowe are grateful for the arrival of police officers Ray Liotta and Roger E. Mosley. But when Liotta becomes fixated on Stowe being his "perfect woman," he turns into the cop from hell. Suspense-flick fans will get a good fix from this formula thriller. Rated R for violence, profanity, and nudity. 111m. **DIR:** Jonathan Kaplan. **CAST:** Kurt Russell, Ray Liotta, Madeleine Stowe, Roger E. Mosley. **1992**

UNNATURAL ★★½ Gothic fantasy about a scientist who creates a beautiful femme fatale through artificial insemination. This German production is laced with impressive cinematography, giving the film an impressionistic look reminiscent of the early silent-film period. Unfortunately, it suffers from a weak script. B&W; 90m. **DIR:** Arthur Maria Rabenalt. **CAST:** Erich Von Stroheim, Hildegarde Neff, Carl Boehm. **1952**

V. I. WARSHAWSKI ★★★½ The mystery novels by Sara Paretsky are better, but we enjoyed this *Thin Man*-ish movie romp with Kathleen Turner as the wisecracking, two-fisted female detective of the title. In what, sadly, may be her only on-screen adventure because of a poor showing at the box office, V. I. Warshawski is hired by the daughter of a murdered pro hockey player to find his killer. Rated R for violence and profanity. 95m. **DIR:** Jeff Kanew. **CAST:** Kathleen Turner, Jay O. Sanders, Charles Durning, Angela Goethals, Frederick Coffin. **1991**

VAMPING ★★ Dreary attempt to update *film noir*, with Patrick Duffy as a down-and-out musician persuaded to break into the home of a dead man. Once there, he falls in love with a photo of the man's widow. Overlong. Rated R for profanity. 110m. **DIR:** Frederick King Keller. **CAST:** Patrick Duffy, Catherine Hyland, Rod Arrants. **1984**

VANISHING, THE (1993) ★★★½ Director George Sluizer's Americanized remake of his superb, 1988 Dutch thriller suffers from an imbalance caused by an overemphasis on the sociopathic killer played by Jeff Bridges. The acting is fine, however, with Kiefer Sutherland as a young man obsessed with finding out what happened to his girlfriend after she disappeared at a roadside gas station. Rated R for profanity and violence. 120m. **DIR:** George Sluizer. **CAST:** Jeff Bridges, Kiefer Sutherland, Nancy Travis, Sandra Bullock, Park Overall, Maggie Linderman, Lisa Eichhorn. **1993**

VERTIGO ★★★★ The first hour of this production is slow, gimmicky, and artificial. However, the rest of this suspense picture takes off at high speed. James Stewart stars as a San Francisco detective who has a fear of heights and is hired to shadow an old friend's wife (Kim Novak). He finds himself falling in love with her—then tragedy strikes. 128m. **DIR:** Alfred Hitchcock. **CAST:** James Stewart, Kim Novak, Barbara Bel Geddes. **1958**

VICTIM OF BEAUTY 🦃 Beautiful schoolteacher becomes instant success as a model, and then the men in her life begin dying. The suspense is not successfully sustained. Unrated, contains nudity, sex, and violence. 90m. **DIR:** Paul Lynch. **CAST:** Peter Outerbridge, Jennifer Rubin, Sally Kellerman. **1991**

VICTIM OF LOVE ★★½ Psychologist JoBeth Williams finds herself in a quandary when she falls for professor Pierce Brosnan, who is having an affair with her patient Virginia Madsen. Director Jerry London keeps this made-for-television thriller on its toes, and additional footage added to the video adds just the right risqué touch. 92m. **DIR:** Jerry London. **CAST:** Pierce Brosnan, JoBeth Williams, Virginia Madsen. **1991**

VICTIMLESS CRIMES ★★½ Conspiracy and betrayal in the art world. Everyone from the gallery owner to the insurance company are making a buck off stolen paintings, until the artist decides that he's about to make a killing, too! Rated R for violence. 85m. **DIR:** Peter Hawley. **CAST:** Debra Sandlund, Craig Bierko. **1990**

VOYAGE ★★★ A middle-aged couple, trying to find the love they once felt, takes a world trip on their yacht in this made-for-cable original. They pick up another couple along the way. Now starts the voyage from hell. Good acting all around, but the story doesn't move quickly enough. Not rated, but contains implied sex. 95m. **DIR:** John Mackenzie. **CAST:** Rutger Hauer, Eric Roberts, Karen Allen, Connie Nielsen. **1993**

W ★★★½ Someone is trying to kill the Lewises, Katy (Twiggy) and Ben (Michael Witney). Each gets into a car and finds too late that it has been tampered with and nearly is killed in a headlong, high-speed crash. On each vehicle, the letter *W* is scrawled in the dust. Who could be after them? This is a highly involving, Hitchcockian thriller that will keep mystery lovers captivated. Rated PG. 95m. **DIR:** Richard Quine. **CAST:** Twiggy, Michael Witney, Eugene Roche, John Vernon, Dirk Benedict. **1974**

WAIT UNTIL DARK ★★★★ Suspense abounds in this chiller about a blind housewife (Audrey Hepburn) who is being pursued by a gang of criminals. She has inadvertently gotten hold of a doll filled with heroin. Alan Arkin is especially frightening as the psychotic gang's mastermind who alternates between moments of deceptive charm and sudden violence in his attempt to separate Hepburn from the doll. 108m. **DIR:** Terence Young. **CAST:** Audrey Hepburn, Alan Arkin, Richard Crenna, Efrem Zimbalist Jr. **1967**

WALK SOFTLY, STRANGER ★★½ Joseph Cotten plays a calculating predator who falls for crippled victim Alida Valli and decides to call the swindle off. The plot thickens when a tough gambler Cotten had robbed in the past shows up to cut himself in and put our hero out—permanently. B&W; 81m. **DIR:** Robert Stevenson. **CAST:** Joseph Cotten, Alida Valli, Spring Byington, Paul Stewart, Jack Paar, Jeff Donnell, John McIntire. **1950**

WARNING SHADOWS (1933) ★★ Bela Lugosi hams it to the hilt as the curator of the House of Mystery. He's the tainted genius behind the lifelike wax figures that move and speak like human creatures. But is he the mysterious Whispering Shadow who jams the airwaves and can eavesdrop and even murder people by remote-control radio and television? This Mascot serial, though stilted and creaky, is worth a watch. B&W; 12 chapters. **DIR:** Albert Herman, Colbert Clark. **CAST:** Bela Lugosi, Henry B. Walthall, Karl Dane, Roy D'Arcy, Bob Kortman, Tom London, Lafe McKee, Ethel Clayton. **1933**

WEB OF DECEIT ★★½ West Coast lawyer Linda Purl gets summoned back to the aristocratic Atlanta of her youth, to defend a young man (Paul de Souza) accused of rape and murder. Writer-director Sandor Stern's by-the-numbers mystery is redeemed by the performances. Rated PG-13 for violence. 93m. **DIR:** Sandor Stern. **CAST:** Linda Purl, James Read, Paul de Souza, Larry Black, Barbara Rush. **1990**

WEEP NO MORE MY LADY ★★½ Agreeable adaptation of Mary Higgins Clark's bestselling mystery about the murder of a popular actress, with a French chateau full of suspects. Made-for-Canadian-cable effort maintains its level of suspense thanks to a tight script and a strong leading performance by Daniel J. Travanti. Rated PG-13 for violence and drug content. 92m. **DIR:** Michel Andrieu. **CAST:** Daniel J. Travanti, Shelley Winters, Kristin Scott-Thomas, Francesca Annis. **1992**

WEST OF ZANZIBAR ★★★ Over-the-top melodrama casts Lon Chaney Sr. as a crippled magician in a jungle village plotting revenge against the man who caused his injuries. The plot is corny, but thanks to Chaney and director Tod Browning (*Freaks*) this is one intense film. Silent. B&W; 63m. **DIR:** Tod Browning. **CAST:** Lon Chaney Sr., Lionel Barrymore, Warner Baxter. **1928**

WHEN A STRANGER CALLS ★★★ A *Psycho II*–style atmosphere pervades this film when the murderer of two children returns after seven years to complete his crime. Rated R. 97m. **DIR:** Fred Walton. **CAST:** Carol Kane, Charles Durning, Colleen Dewhurst, Tony Beckley, Rachel Roberts, Ron O'Neal. **1979**

WHEN A STRANGER CALLS BACK ★★★ Writer-director Fred Walton's sequel to the 1979 chiller begins superbly, with Jill Schoelen just right as a cautious baby-sitter being taunted by someone. Sadly, the momentum flags once the girl makes contact with psychologist Jill Johnson (Carol Kane) and investigator John Clifford (Charles Durning), who see parallels to the events they survived years earlier. Rated R for violence and nudity. 94m. **DIR:** Fred Walton. **CAST:** Carol Kane, Charles Durning, Jill Schoelen, Gene Lythgow. 1993

WHEN TIME RAN OUT! 🦃 Time never seems to run out as we wait and wait for a volcano to erupt and put the all-star cast out of its misery. Rated PG. 121m. **DIR:** James Goldstone. **CAST:** Paul Newman, Jacqueline Bisset, William Holden, James Franciscus, Edward Albert, Red Buttons, Ernest Borgnine, Burgess Meredith, Valentina Cortese, Alex Karras, Barbara Carrera. 1980

WHERE ARE THE CHILDREN? ★★★ On the ninth anniversary of the murder of her previous children, a mother's children from her new marriage disappear. Jill Clayburgh is very good as the mother attempting to piece together the reason for this second occurrence. This film has a crackerjack surprise ending. Rated R. 97m. **DIR:** Bruce Malmuth. **CAST:** Jill Clayburgh, Max Gail, Clifton James, Elizabeth Wilson, Barnard Hughes, Frederic Forrest. 1986

WHERE SLEEPING DOGS LIE ★★★ Investigating a brutal murder, writer Dylan McDermott moves into the house where it took place. He gets more than he bargained for when a mysterious stranger, chillingly played by Tom Sizemore, arrives, offering information that only the killer could know. Respectful attempt at *film noir* costars Sharon Stone as McDermott's sultry editor. Rated R for violence, language, and adult situations. 92m. **DIR:** Charles Finch. **CAST:** Dylan McDermott, Tom Sizemore, Sharon Stone. 1991

WHISPERS ★★ A woman is repeatedly attacked by a man with the perfect alibi, prompting the police to disbelieve her. Mediocre. Rated R for violence and nudity. 96m. **DIR:** Douglas Jackson. **CAST:** Victoria Tennant, Jean Leclerc, Chris Sarandon. 1990

WHISPERS IN THE DARK ★★ Psychiatrist Annabella Sciorra finds herself drawn into a murder investigation, during which she enlists the aid of mentors Jill Clayburgh and Alan Alda. Over-the-top, campy, contrived suspense. Rated R for violence and profanity. 112m. **DIR:** Christopher Crowe. **CAST:** Annabella Sciorra, Jamey Sheridan, Anthony LaPaglia, Jill Clayburgh, Alan Alda, John Leguizamo, Deborah Unger. 1992

WHISTLE BLOWER, THE ★★★★ This taut suspense-thriller from England combines the elements of a murder mystery with real-life human drama. Michael Caine, in one of his finest performances, stars as a stoic British subject whose tidy life is disrupted when his son (Nigel Havers) discovers what he believes are immoral acts on the part of the government. Rated PG for suspense. 100m. **DIR:** Simon Langton. **CAST:** Michael Caine, Nigel Havers, James Fox, Felicity Dean, John Gielgud, Kenneth Colley, Gordon Jackson, Barry Foster. 1987

WHITE GOLD ★★★★ Remarkable drama about a woman condemned to a boring life on a sheep ranch. She is caught between a resentful father-in-law and a timid husband; and when she commits murder to fend off a would-be rapist, everyone can only believe the worst of her. Silent. B&W; 70m. **DIR:** William K. Howard. **CAST:** Jetta Goudal, Kenneth Thompson, George Bancroft. 1927

WHITE HOT: THE MYSTERIOUS MURDER OF THELMA TODD ★★ Melodramatic staging and dialogue mar what could have been compelling in this made-for-TV speculation on the death of Thirties starlet Thelma Todd. Loni Anderson is ever so glamorous in the title role of the siren who captivated men even after her death. 90m. **DIR:** Paul Wendkos. **CAST:** Loni Anderson, Robert Davi, Scott Paulin, Robin Strasser, Paul Dooley. 1991

WHITE OF THE EYE ★★½ Tense film deals with a serial killer on the loose in Arizona. David Keith plays a commercial-stereo whiz who becomes a suspect in a series of bizarre and brutal murders of affluent women. Director Donald Cammell avoids the usual slasher pitfalls, although this one is saddled with a truly abysmal finale. Rated R. 113m. **DIR:** Donald Cammell. **CAST:** David Keith, Cathy Moriarty, Art Evans. 1988

WHO IS THE BLACK DAHLIA? ★★★★ An above-average semidocumentary crime-drama based on one of the Los Angeles Police Department's most famous unsolved cases: the 1947 murder and gruesome dissection of a mysterious young woman whose life-style and mode of dress earned her the nickname of Black Dahlia. An excellent cast performs a first-rate script in this gripping telemovie. 100m. **DIR:** Joseph Pevney. **CAST:** Lucie Arnaz, Efrem Zimbalist Jr., Ronny Cox, Macdonald Carey, Gloria De Haven, Tom Bosley, Mercedes McCambridge, Donna Mills, June Lockhart. 1975

WHO KILLED MARY WHAT'S 'ER NAME? ★★½ Gritty detective melodrama about an ex-boxer who solves the murder of a prostitute when no one else seems to care. Above-average low-budget thriller. Rated PG. 90m. **DIR:** Ernest Pintoff. **CAST:** Red Buttons, Sylvia Miles, Conrad Bain, David Doyle, Ron Carey, Alice Playten, Sam Waterston. 1971

WHODUNIT? 🦃 Low-budget murder mystery in which characters are being systematically eliminated at a place called Creep Island. Rated R for violence and profanity. 82m. **DIR:** Bill Naud. **CAST:** Rick Bean, Gary Phillips. **1982**

WHY DIDN'T THEY ASK EVANS? ★★★★ A famous explorer's dying question sends amateur sleuths Lady Derwent and Bobby Jones (Francesca Annis and James Warwick, who later teamed up for the popular *Partners in Crime* series) on the trail in this entertaining Agatha Christie TV yarn. That cryptic query, an attempt on Bobby's life, and an apparent suicide are just a few of the mysteries tackled by the energetic duo. The 1930s setting is re-created faithfully, and the costume design is excellent. Suitable for family viewing. 180m. **DIR:** John Davies, Tony Wharmby. **CAST:** Francesca Annis, James Warwick, Eric Porter, John Gielgud, Joan Hickson. **1980**

WILD CARD ★★★ A former preacher is asked to investigate the mysterious death of a Texas landowner. Made for cable. 95m. **DIR:** Mel Damski. **CAST:** Powers Boothe, Cindy Pickett, Terry O'Quinn, René Auberjonois, M. Emmet Walsh. **1992**

WIND, THE (1986) ★★½ There's some solid suspense in this tale of a mystery novelist on a secluded Mediterranean island who is terrorized by a psychopath. Director Nico Mastorakis makes good use of the Greek locations. Unfortunately, he lets his two stars overact. 92m. **DIR:** Nico Mastorakis. **CAST:** Meg Foster, Wings Hauser, Robert Morley. **1986**

WINDOW, THE ★★★½ This chilling drama about a young boy who witnesses a murder and finds himself unable to convince any authority figures of what he has seen is one of the classic nightmare films of the postwar period. Bobby Driscoll (who earned a special Academy Award for this film) is kidnapped by the murderers and the film becomes one taut encounter after another. B&W; 73m. **DIR:** Ted Tetzlaff. **CAST:** Bobby Driscoll, Arthur Kennedy, Barbara Hale, Paul Stewart, Ruth Roman. **1949**

WITHOUT A TRACE ★★★ A drama about a boy who vanishes and his mother's unrelenting faith that he will return, this is yet another entry in the family-in-trouble movie genre. Well-acted but sometimes overwrought and predictable. Rated PG for mature content. 120m. **DIR:** Stanley Jaffe. **CAST:** Kate Nelligan, Judd Hirsch, David Dukes, Stockard Channing, Jacqueline Brooks, Kathleen Widdoes. **1983**

WITNESS ★★★★½ This is three terrific movies in one: an exciting cop thriller, a touching romance, and a fascinating screen study of a modern-day clash of cultures. Harrison Ford is superb as a detective who must protect an 8-year-old Amish boy, the only witness to a drug-related murder. Rated R for violence, profanity, and nudity. 112m. **DIR:** Peter Weir. **CAST:** Harrison Ford, Kelly McGillis, Josef Sommer, Lukas Haas, Alexander Godunov, Danny Glover. **1985**

WITNESS FOR THE PROSECUTION (1957) ★★★★★ Superb performances help make this gripping courtroom drama an enduring favorite of film buffs. The screenplay was adapted from a play by Agatha Christie and features Laughton as an aging lawyer called upon to defend an alleged murderer (Power). It is Dietrich, in one of her greatest screen performances, who nearly steals the show. B&W; 114m. **DIR:** Billy Wilder. **CAST:** Tyrone Power, Charles Laughton, Marlene Dietrich, Elsa Lanchester, John Williams, Henry Daniell, Una O'Connor. **1957**

WITNESS FOR THE PROSECUTION (1982) ★★★ An enjoyable made-for-television remake of Agatha Christie's courtroom drama. Ralph Richardson and Deborah Kerr are adequate as the wily yet ailing barrister and his continually frustrated nurse. Unfortunately, they lack the rich humor brought to the roles by Charles Laughton and Elsa Lanchester in the original. Beau Bridges is particularly outstanding as the defendant. 100m. **DIR:** Alan Gibson. **CAST:** Ralph Richardson, Beau Bridges, Diana Rigg, Deborah Kerr. **1982**

WOMAN IN GREEN, THE ★★★ This is a grisly little entry in the Rathbone/Bruce Sherlock Holmes series, with the master sleuth investigating a series of severed fingers sent to Scotland Yard. The culprit is, once again, Professor Moriarty (Henry Daniell). Careful viewers will detect moments from *The Adventure of the Empty House*. B&W; 68m. **DIR:** Roy William Neill. **CAST:** Basil Rathbone, Nigel Bruce, Hillary Brooke, Henry Daniell, Paul Cavanagh. **1945**

WOMAN OBSESSED, A ★★ When a mentally unstable woman who had been forced to give up her son for adoption meets him as an adult, she goes crazy and kidnaps him, thinking he is her dead husband. Lurid melodrama takes too long to get going, though the later scenes are suspenseful. Rated R for violence and sexual situations. 103m. **DIR:** Chuck Vincent. **CAST:** Ruth Raymond, Gregory Patrick, Troy Donahue, Linda Blair. **1989**

WOMAN OF DESIRE ★★ The South African scenery and Robert Mitchum's shrewd defense attorney are the sole attractions in this relentlessly silly erotic thriller. It's impossible to determine who did what to whom, except that Bo Derek—who still acts with her fingers in her mouth—does it with nearly everybody. Rated R for profanity, nudity, and simulated sex. 97m. **DIR:** Robert Ginty. **CAST:** Jeff Fahey, Bo Derek, Steven Bauer, Robert Mitchum. **1993**

WOMAN'S SECRET, A ★★ Confusing story about a once-popular singer who confesses to the shooting of her protégé; done with flashbacks and testimonials. Second-rate whodunit. B&W; 85m. **DIR:** Nicholas Ray. **CAST:** Maureen O'Hara, Melvyn Douglas, Gloria Grahame, Victor Jory, Bill Williams, Jay C. Flippen, Ellen Corby. 1949

WRITE TO KILL ★★½ Routine vendetta thriller has writer Scott Valentine tracking down the gang of counterfeiters who killed his brother. Rated R for violence and profanity. 94m. **DIR:** Reuben Preuss. **CAST:** Scott Valentine, Joan Severance, Chris Mulkey, G. W. Bailey. 1990

WRITER'S BLOCK 🦃 They don't come much dumber than this made-for-cable groaner. Laughably miscast, Morgan Fairchild plays a bestselling novelist whose fictitious creation comes to life (!) and starts killing people...or is she merely imagining the whole thing? Do we care? Rated R for violence and profanity. 90m. **DIR:** Charles Correll. **CAST:** Morgan Fairchild, Michael Praed, Joe Regalbuto. 1991

WRONG MAN, THE (1956) ★★★★ In this frightening true-life tale, Henry Fonda plays a man falsely accused of robbery. Vera Miles is his wife, who can't handle the changes wrought in their lives by this gross injustice. Fonda is excellent. B&W; 105m. **DIR:** Alfred Hitchcock. **CAST:** Henry Fonda, Vera Miles, Anthony Quayle, Harold J. Stone, Nehemiah Persoff. 1956

YEAR OF THE GUN ★★★ An American novelist (Andrew McCarthy) returns to terrorist-plagued Italy in 1978, hoping to free a married woman (Valeria Golino) from her abusive, politically powerful husband. A chance meeting with a photojournalist (Sharon Stone) puts our hero's life in danger, and a series of crosses and double crosses leads him to the truth. Rated R for violence, nudity, and profanity. 111m. **DIR:** John Frankenheimer. **CAST:** Andrew McCarthy, Valeria Golino, Sharon Stone, John Pankow. 1991

YIN AND YANG OF MR. GO, THE ★★ Jeff Bridges would probably like to forget that he made his debut in this confusing comic thriller about a Hong Kong weapons dealer who becomes a good guy due to the intervention of Buddha. Rated PG; contains brief nudity and violence. 89m. **DIR:** Burgess Meredith. **CAST:** James Mason, Jeff Bridges, Peter Lind Hayes, Burgess Meredith, Broderick Crawford. 1970

YOUNG AND INNOCENT ★★★ Reputedly director Alfred Hitchcock's favorite of the films he made in Great Britain, this film employs one of his favorite devices, that of an innocent man avoiding the police while attempting to catch the real criminal and prove his innocence. Not as well-known as many of his other films, this seldom-seen movie is vintage Hitchcock and on a par with much of his best work. B&W; 80m. **DIR:** Alfred Hitchcock. **CAST:** Derrek de Marney, Nova Pilbeam, Percy Marmont, Edward Rigby, Mary Clare, Basil Radford. 1937

YOUNG SAVAGES, THE ★★★½ Members of an Italian-American gang are charged with the murder of a seemingly innocent blind Puerto Rican boy, and DA Burt Lancaster begins to wonder if everything is as it seems. Good adaptation of Evan Hunter's novel, *A Matter of Conviction*. B&W; 110m. **DIR:** John Frankenheimer. **CAST:** Burt Lancaster, Shelley Winters, Edward Andrews, Vivian Nathan, Larry Gates, Telly Savalas. 1961

ZIPPERFACE 🦃 Beautiful cop must go undercover to catch a serial killer who preys on prostitutes. Been there, done that. Not rated, but contains nudity, violence, and language. 90m. **DIR:** Mansour Pourmand. **CAST:** Dona Adams, David Clover, Jonathan Mandell. 1992

SCIENCE-FICTION FANTASY

ABRAXAS GUARDIAN OF THE UNIVERSE ★★ A renegade alien peace officer flees to Earth and impregnates a young woman, only to be caught and sent to prison. Five years later he escapes and returns to earth to engage in countless, violent chase scenes. Not rated, but contains violence. 87m. **DIR:** Damien Lee. **CAST:** Jesse Ventura, Marjorie Bransfield, Sven-Ole Thorsen. **1992**

ABYSS, THE ★★★★ After suffering the deep-sea disappointments in *Leviathan* and *Deepstar Six,* viewers are likely to be a little cautious of getting back into the water with this thriller-adventure-fantasy film. They shouldn't be. The third time's the charm with the underwater plot, thanks to the inventiveness of director James Cameron (*The Terminator, Aliens*). Rated PG-13. 110m. **DIR:** James Cameron. **CAST:** Ed Harris, Mary Elizabeth Mastrantonio, Michael Biehn. **1989**

ADVENTURES OF A GNOME NAMED GNORM, THE 🦃 A buffoonish young cop and a hairy, stubby creature from a mystic underworld team up to nab a jewel thief in this overly violent fantasy-caper. Rated PG for language and violence. 86m. **DIR:** Stan Winston. **CAST:** Anthony Michael Hall, Claudia Christian, Jerry Orbach. **1993**

ADVENTURES OF BARON MÜNCHAUSEN, THE ★★★★ Terry Gilliam, that inspired madman of the movies, completes the fantasy trilogy—which began with *Time Bandits* and *Brazil*—with this eye-popping phantasmagoria about the celebrated eighteenth-century liar. The film begins in the Age of Reason when a small theatrical troupe attempts to put on a play about Münchausen, only to have an old soldier (John Neville) turn up claiming to be the real thing. He goes on to prove his identity with a series of wild tales. Rated PG for violence. 126m. **DIR:** Terry Gilliam. **CAST:** John Neville, Robin Williams, Eric Idle, Oliver Reed, Uma Thurman, Sarah Polley. **1989**

ADVENTURES OF BUCKAROO BANZAI, THE ★★★★ Peter Weller plays Buckaroo Banzai, a skilled neurosurgeon and physicist who becomes bored with his scientific and medical work and embarks on a career as a rock star and two-fisted defender of justice. This offbeat genre film is a silly movie for smart people. Rated PG. 103m. **DIR:** W. D. Richter. **CAST:** Peter Weller, John Lithgow, Ellen Barkin, Jeff Goldblum. **1984**

ADVENTURES OF HERCULES, THE 🦃 This is the sequel to *Hercules,* the 1983 bomb with Lou "the Hulk" Ferrigno. The first Ferrigno folly was a laughfest. This tiresome piece of junk would only benefit insomniacs. Rated PG for violence (yes, even *that* can be boring). 89m. **DIR:** Lewis Coates. **CAST:** Lou Ferrigno, Milly Carlucci. **1984**

AFTER THE FALL OF NEW YORK 🦃 Michael Sopkiw as a two-fisted, post-apocalypse hero. Rated R for violence and profanity. 91m. **DIR:** Martin Dolman. **CAST:** Michael Sopkiw, Valentine Monnier, Anna Kanakis. **1983**

AFTERMATH, THE ★★½ Two astronauts return to Earth after a nuclear war and battle the crazies who survived. Low-budget sci-fi flick strives to go above the subject matter. Not rated, but contains violence. 94m. **DIR:** Steve Barkett. **CAST:** Steve Barkett, Lynne Margulies, Sid Haig. **1981**

AKIRA ★★★★ Based by writer-director Katsuhiro Otomo on his popular comic book, this is a spectacular film set in twenty-first-century post–World War III Japan, where a member of a motorcycle gang becomes an unwilling guinea pig in a scientific experiment that backfires. Unrated, the film has oodles of violence. 124m. **DIR:** Katsuhiro Otomo. **1990**

ALICE (1988) ★★★★ Outstanding adaptation of Lewis Carroll's story by Jan Svankmajer, one of the world's leading figures in animation. The film brilliantly captures the surreal world of little Alice with bizarre erotic overtones. Not rated. 85m. **DIR:** Jan Svankmajer. **CAST:** Kristyna Kohoutova. **1988**

ALIEN ★★★★½ A superb cinematic combination of science fiction and horror, this is a heart-pounding, visually astounding shocker. The players are all excellent as the crew of a futuristic cargo ship that picks up an unwanted passenger: an alien that lives on human flesh and continually changes form. Rated R. 116m. **DIR:** Ridley Scott. **CAST:** Tom Skerritt, Sigourney Weaver, John Hurt, Ian Holm, Harry Dean Stanton, Yaphet Kotto, Veronica Cartwright. **1979**

ALIEN CONTAMINATION 🦃 A malevolent monster from outer space tries to conquer

Earth with the aid of slime-spurting alien eggs that cause people to blow up. Rated R. 90m. **DIR:** Lewis Coates. **CAST:** Ian McCulloch, Marino Masé. 1982

ALIEN DEAD 🦃 Low-grade, alien-loose-on-Earth drivel. Rated R. 87m. **DIR:** Fred Olen Ray. **CAST:** Buster Crabbe, Linda Lewis. 1980

ALIEN FACTOR, THE ★★★ As an amateur film, this is pretty decent. The cast and production crew are one and the same. There are four aliens on the planet Earth. Only one alien is good, and the Earthlings have a hard time figuring out which one is on their side. Rated PG. 82m. **DIR:** Don Dohler. **CAST:** Don Leifert, Tom Griffith. 1977

ALIEN INTRUDER ★★½ An alien virus disguises itself as a femme fatale to lure space warriors to their doom. This low-budgeter rips off so many sci-fi hits that it sustains interest. Rated R for violence and profanity. 94m. **DIR:** Ricardo Jacques Gale. **CAST:** Billy Dee Williams, Maxwell Caulfield, Tracy Scoggins, Jeff Conaway. 1992

ALIEN NATION ★★★ There are some slow moments in *Alien Nation,* but just sit back and enjoy the ride through familiar territory in this cop-buddy movie with a sci-fi slant. James Caan plays a detective in Los Angeles of the future. Mandy Patinkin is the "newcomer," as the aliens are called, who is teamed with Caan to ferret out the perpetrators of a series of mysterious murders among the aliens. Rated R for profanity, violence, and nudity. 96m. **DIR:** Graham Baker. **CAST:** James Caan, Mandy Patinkin, Terence Stamp. 1988

ALIEN P.I. ★★ A new twist to the old private eye theme. This time the private investigator is from the planet Styx. He's just vacationing on our planet when he stumbles onto an intergalactic crime involving an ancient Egyptian disc. Rated R for violence and nudity. 90m. **DIR:** Viktor. **CAST:** Nikki Fastinetti, John Alexander. 1987

ALIEN PREDATORS 🦃 Three young American adventurers stumble into an alien invasion. Rated R for violence and gore. 92m. **DIR:** Deran Sarafian. **CAST:** Dennis Christopher, Martin Hewitt, Lynn-Holly Johnson. 1986

ALIEN SEED 🦃 What seems like the fifty-seventh movie about an alien plot to use Earth women for breeding proves that some things don't get better with practice. Not rated; contains adult themes and violence. 88m. **DIR:** Bob James. **CAST:** Erik Estrada, Heidi Payne. 1989

ALIEN SPACE AVENGER 🦃 Low-budget reworking of *The Hidden*, detailing the plight of four alien convicts being stalked by an alien bounty hunter through the streets of New York. In true sci-fi fashion, they get around by hiding inside poor New Yorkers. All this time we thought they were just rude. Unrated, but contains violence. 88m. **DIR:** Richard W. Haines. **CAST:** Robert Prichard. 1991

ALIEN 3 ★★★ Ripley (Sigourney Weaver) crash-lands on an all-but-deserted penal colony for madmen and rapists. The acid-spitting, flesh-eating space creature has, unfortunately for them all, hitched a ride with our heroine, and the battle rages once again. More like *Alien* than *Aliens*, this visually stunning, atmospheric thriller, by first-time filmmaker David Fincher, disintegrates into an outer space version of Agatha Christie's *And Then There Were None.* Rated R for profanity and violence. 115m. **DIR:** David Fincher. **CAST:** Sigourney Weaver, Charles S. Dutton, Charles Dance, Paul McGann, Brian Glover. 1992

ALIEN WARRIOR 🦃 In this unwatchable film, a father on another planet sends his son to Earth to confront the ultimate evil—a pimp. Rated R for nudity, violence, and profanity. 100m. **DIR:** Edward Hunt. **CAST:** Brett Clark, Pamela Saunders. 1985

ALIENATOR 🦃 Lame *Terminator* clone. Rated R for violence. 93m. **DIR:** Fred Olen Ray. **CAST:** Jan-Michael Vincent, John Phillip Law, P. J. Soles. 1989

ALIENS ★★★★½ Fifty-seven years have passed during Warrant Officer Ripley's (Sigourney Weaver) deep-space sleep; when she wakes, the planet LV-425—where the crew of the ill-fated *Nostromo* first encountered the nasty extraterrestrial—has been colonized. Then, to everybody's surprise except Ripley's, contact is lost with the colonists. Equal to, although different from, the original. Rated R for considerable violence and profanity. 137m. **DIR:** James Cameron. **CAST:** Sigourney Weaver, Carrie Henn, Michael Biehn, Paul Reiser, Lance Henriksen, Jenette Goldstein. 1986

ALPHA INCIDENT, THE ★★ A deadly organism from Mars, an attempted government cover-up, a radiation leak, panic, and havoc. Okay, if you like this sort of now-tired thing. Rated PG. 84m. **DIR:** Bill Rebane. **CAST:** Ralph Meeker. 1977

ALTERED STATES ★★★½ At times in *Altered States*, you can't help but be swept along...and almost overwhelmed. William Hurt, Blair Brown, Bob Balaban, and Charles Haid star in this suspenseful film as scientists involved in the potentially dangerous exploration of the mind. Rated R for nudity, profanity, and violence. 102m. **DIR:** Ken Russell. **CAST:** William Hurt, Blair Brown, Bob Balaban, Charles Haid, Drew Barrymore. 1980

AMAZING COLOSSAL MAN, THE ★★ Exposed to a nuclear blast, an army colonel grows as big as a house...and keeps on growing, as scientists and his understandably worried fiancée search for a cure. Basically a C-budget rip-off of one of Jack Arnold's stylish Universal International chillers of the Fifties. Best scene: the struggle with a king-size syringe. B&W; 80m. **DIR:** Bert I. Gordon. **CAST:** Glenn Langan, Cathy Downs, William Hudson, James Seay, Larry Thor. **1957**

AMAZING STORIES (TV SERIES) ★★★½ Steven Spielberg's *Amazing Stories* produced very few noteworthy episodes, but the best (possibly faint praise) have been paired up for video release. "Book Two" is by far the strongest, highlighted by director Robert Zemeckis's "Go to the Head of the Class," definitely one of his fastest and funniest features. This tape also includes Tim Burton's manic "Family Dog," an animated short that beat *The Simpsons* by several years and features voices by Stan Freberg, Annie Potts, and Mercedes McCambridge. "Book One" includes Spielberg's overlong segment, "The Mission," in which Kevin Costner's World War II bomber takes enemy fire and seems doomed, until rescue arrives from a most unlikely source. Danny DeVito rounds out that tape by directing and starring in the occasionally uproarious "The Wedding Ring" with real-life wife Rhea Perlman. 70–71m. **DIR:** Steven Spielberg, Robert Zemeckis, Danny DeVito, Brad Bird. **CAST:** Kevin Costner, Kiefer Sutherland, Christopher Lloyd, Mary Stuart Masterson, Casey Siemaszko, Danny DeVito, Rhea Perlman, Scott Coffey. **1985–1986**

AMAZING TRANSPARENT MAN, THE ★★ This zero-budget thriller from cult director Edgar Ulmer has gotten a bad rap over the years, while the talky sci-fi film shot back-to-back with it, *Beyond the Time Barrier*, has been overpraised. The admittedly lame premise has a refugee scientist blackmailed into turning an escaped convict invisible so he can commit bank robberies—but Ulmer provides some thrills, including an exciting, sadistic climax. B&W; 58m. **DIR:** Edgar G. Ulmer. **CAST:** Douglas Kennedy, Marguerite Chapman, James Griffith. **1960**

AMERICAN TIGER ★★ A sexy and insipid tale of the return of a stolen statue to a Chinese princess who is scorned by her suitor. Set in Miami. Rated R for hot sex scenes and violence. 93m. **DIR:** Martin Dolman. **CAST:** Donald Pleasence. **1989**

ANDROID ★★★★ A highly enjoyable tongue-in-cheek sci-fi adventure, this takes place on a space station where a mad scientist, Dr. Daniel (played by a surprisingly subdued and effective Klaus Kinski), is trying to create the perfect android. As a group of criminal castaways arrives at the station, the doctor's current robot assistant, Max 404 (Don Opper), decides it is time to rebel. Rated PG for nudity, violence, and profanity. 80m. **DIR:** Aaron Lipstadt. **CAST:** Klaus Kinski, Don Opper, Brie Howard, Norbert Weiser. **1982**

ANDROMEDA STRAIN, THE ★★★★ A tense science-fiction thriller, this film focuses on a team of scientists attempting to isolate a deadly virus while racing against time and the possibility of nuclear war. Though not as flashy as other entries in the genre, it's highly effective. Rated G. 130m. **DIR:** Robert Wise. **CAST:** Arthur Hill, David Wayne, James Olson, Kate Reid, Paula Kelly. **1971**

ANGRY RED PLANET, THE ★★½ Entertaining (if unoriginal) science-fiction tale of an expedition to Mars running into all sorts of alien terrors, most notable of which is a terrifying kind of giant mouse/spider hybrid. A fun film, though it takes forever to get to the action. 83m. **DIR:** Ib Melchior. **CAST:** Gerald Mohr, Nora Hayden, Les Tremayne, Jack Kruschen. **1959**

ANNA TO THE INFINITE POWER ★★★★ Is individuality determined purely by genetic code, or by some other factor beyond the control of science? This film explores the dimensions of that question via the struggles of a brilliant, troubled child—who is also the unwitting subject of a scientific experiment to establish her own identity. Brilliant. 107m. **DIR:** Robert Wiemer. **CAST:** Martha Byrne, Dina Merrill, Mark Patton, Loretta Devine, Jack Gilford. **1982**

APEX ★★★½ Time paradoxes have always been great sci-fi fodder, and this film is full of them. In the year 2073, a probe is sent back in time, but its interference causes a paradox that changes the future into a dying wasteland. When scientist Mitchell Cox returns from the past in an attempt to fix the future, he finds himself at war with robots bent on destroying the rest of humanity. Great special effects and a tricky screenplay. Rated R for violence. 103m. **DIR:** Phillip Roth. **CAST:** Mitchell Cox, Lisa Ann Russell, Marcus Aurelius, Adam Lawson. **1993**

ARCADE ★★★ Computer animation enhances this tale of a virtual-reality arcade game that actually makes players engage in mortal combat. The local teens just can't stop playing, and when they start disappearing, Megan Ward must enter the game and pull its plug. Interesting update on the *Tron* theme. Rated R for violence. 85m. **DIR:** Albert Pyun. **CAST:** Megan Ward, Peter Billingsley, John de Lancie, Sharon Farrell, Norbert Weiser. **1994**

ARCHER: FUGITIVE FROM THE EMPIRE ★★ This uninspired sword-and-sorcery movie was the pilot for a television series. Lane Caudell is the young warrior of the title who must overcome numerous challenges in his quest to gain a throne. 99m. **DIR:** Nick Corea. **CAST:** Lane Caudell, George Kennedy, Belinda Bauer. **1981**

ARENA ★★ Dopey sci-fi version of *Rocky* features a human who must take on extraterrestrials from around the galaxy in the famed Arena. Rated PG-13 for violence. 97m. **DIR:** Peter Manoogian. **CAST:** Claudia Christian, Hamilton Camp, Marc Alaimo. **1989**

ART COM VIDEO (VOL. 1–3) ★★★ Excellent three-volume tape collection of conceptual video art and computer animation from around the world. Not rated, but contains nudity and profanity. 201m. **DIR:** Karl Druner, Max Almy, Marikka Hakola, Vibke Vogel, Ulrik al Brask, Ane Mette Ruge, Ko Nakajima, Shinsuke Ina, Yoshiomi. **1979–1989**

ASSASSIN ★★½ Now-familiar tale of a killer cyborg running loose and out of control. Robert Conrad, retired from the Agency, is brought in from the cold to hunt and destroy the robot with the symbolic name of Golem. Originally a television movie, but released on cassette with an R rating for violence. 94m. **DIR:** Sandor Stern. **CAST:** Robert Conrad, Karen Austin, Richard Young, Robert Webber. **1986**

ASTROBOY—VOLS. 1–10 ★★ This Japanese animated television series about a diminutive robotic superhero shaped a generation of animators with tales of action and adventure. B&W; Each 50m. **DIR:** Fred Ladd. **1964**

AT THE EARTH'S CORE ★★½ *At the Earth's Core*, an Edgar Rice Burroughs adaptation, benefits enormously from an inspired performance by Peter Cushing. He even manages to make Doug McClure look good occasionally. It's mostly for the kiddies, but we found ourselves clutching the arm of the chair a couple of times at the height of suspense. Rated PG. 90m. **DIR:** Kevin Connor. **CAST:** Doug McClure, Peter Cushing, Caroline Munro, Godfrey James. **1976**

ATOMIC SUBMARINE, THE ★★★ Solid little thriller about U.S. atomic submarine and its encounter with an alien flying saucer in the Arctic suffers from budgetary limitations but benefits from a decent script, good direction, and an effective and thoroughly believable cast of fine character actors. B&W; 72m. **DIR:** Spencer Gordon Bennet. **CAST:** Arthur Franz, Dick Foran, Brett Halsey, Tom Conway, Bob Steele, Joi Lansing. **1959**

ATOR: THE FIGHTING EAGLE 🦃 A low-budget stupid sword-and-sorcery flick. Rated PG for violence and nudity. 98m. **DIR:** David Hills. **CAST:** Miles O'Keeffe, Sabrina Siani, Warren Hillman. **1983**

ATTACK OF THE 50-FOOT WOMAN (1993) ★★½ The effects look good, but everything else is pretty ho-hum in this arch remake of one of cinema's all-time turkeys. Scripter Joseph Dougherty's attempt to inject politically correct feminism is simply laughable, and it's hard to decide whether title character Daryl Hannah is less interesting before or after her transformation. Rated PG-13 for profanity and brief nudity. 90m. **DIR:** Christopher Guest. **CAST:** Daryl Hannah, Daniel Baldwin, William Windom, Christi Conaway, Frances Fisher. **1993**

AURORA ENCOUNTER ★★★½ Here's one that can be enjoyed by the whole family. Jack Elam is outstanding in a story about a small Texas town visited by aliens in the late 1800s. Rated PG. 90m. **DIR:** Jim McCullough. **CAST:** Jack Elam, Peter Brown, Carol Bagdasarian, Dottie West. **1985**

BABY...SECRET OF THE LOST LEGEND ★★½ Set on the Ivory Coast of West Africa, this Disney story offers more than a cute fable about the discovery of a family of brontosauri. Violence and a hint of sex represent Disney's attempt to appeal to a wider audience. The special effects of the ancient critters make the show worth watching. Rated PG. 90m. **DIR:** B.W.L. Norton. **CAST:** William Katt, Sean Young, Patrick McGoohan. **1985**

BACK TO THE FUTURE ★★★★½ Michael J. Fox as a teenager who is zapped back in time by mad scientist Christopher Lloyd. Once there, Fox meets his parents as teenagers, an act that could result in disaster. The first fifteen minutes of this film are pretty bad, but once Fox gets back to where he doesn't belong, it's terrific entertainment. Rated PG. 116m. **DIR:** Robert Zemeckis. **CAST:** Michael J. Fox, Christopher Lloyd, Lea Thompson, Crispin Glover, Thomas F. Wilson. **1985**

BACK TO THE FUTURE II ★★★ This futuristic sequel is so fast-paced and gimmick-laden that one only realizes after seeing it how essentially empty it is. The story jumps from 1985 to 2015 to 1985 to 1955, as Marty McFly attempts to save the future from the consequences of his tampering with the past. Convoluted, but it's an agreeable enough time passer. Rated PG for light violence and profanity. 105m. **DIR:** Robert Zemeckis. **CAST:** Michael J. Fox, Christopher Lloyd, Lea Thompson, Thomas F. Wilson, Elisabeth Shue, Charles Fleischer. **1989**

BACK TO THE FUTURE III ★★★★½ Director Robert Zemeckis and screenwriter Bob Gale make up for the excesses and inadequacies of *Back to the Future II* with this rip-roaring conclusion, which has Marty McFly in the Old West attempting to get back to 1985. Rated PG for light violence. 118m. **DIR:** Robert Zemeckis. **CAST:** Michael J. Fox, Christopher Lloyd, Mary Steenburgen, Lea Thompson, Thomas F. Wilson, Elisabeth Shue, Matt Clark, Richard Dysart. **1990**

BAD CHANNELS ★★½ At KDUL Radio, the music, is, well, *dull!* That is, until a new DJ enters the scene. Unfortunately, he happens to be an alien, who has come to Earth to pick up chicks, shrink them, and imprison them in small bottles for the trip back home. There's plenty of off-the-wall fun when the townsfolk, including ex-MTV veejay Martha Quinn, decide to pull this guy's plug. Rated R for violence. 88m. **DIR:** Ted Nicolaou. **CAST:**

Paul Hipp, Martha Quinn, Aaron Lustig, Ian Patrick Williams. 1992

BAD TASTE ★★★★ One of the grossest, yet most hysterically funny movies ever made. Aliens have come to Earth to harvest the new fast-food sensation of the universe—human flesh! It's up to the highly trained, if not totally adept, Alien Invasion Defense Service to save the world. Not rated, but contains profanity and gore. 90m. **DIR:** Peter Jackson. **CAST:** Pete O'Herne. 1987

BAMBOO SAUCER (A.K.A. COLLISION COURSE) ★★½ America and the USSR compete with each other as they investigate reports of a UFO crash in the People's Republic of China. More concerned with plot and substance than special effects, this low-budget effort is thought-provoking and succeeds where a more gimmicky, less suspenseful approach would have failed. 100m. **DIR:** Frank Telford. **CAST:** Dan Duryea, John Ericson, Lois Nettleton, Nan Leslie. 1968

BARBARELLA ★★½ Futuristic fantasy has Jane Fonda in the title role of a space beauty being drooled over by various male creatures on a strange planet. Drags at times, but Jane's fans won't want to miss it. Rated PG for partial nudity-sexual content. 98m. **DIR:** Roger Vadim. **CAST:** Jane Fonda, John Phillip Law, Anita Pallenberg, Milo O'Shea. 1968

BARBARIAN QUEEN 🦃 Another one of those lame fantasy flicks à la *Yor*, the *Conan* films, and Lou Ferrigno's *Hercules* films. Although not rated, *Barbarian Queen* has lots of nudity and violence. 75m. **DIR:** Hector Olivera. **CAST:** Lana Clarkson, Katt Shea, Frank Zagarino, Dawn Dunlap. 1985

BARBARIAN QUEEN II: EMPRESS STRIKES BACK 🦃 More sword and sorcery from buxom babe Lana Clarkson, whom you might remember from the first *Barbarian Queen*, but then again: maybe not. Rated R. 87m. **DIR:** Joe Finley. **CAST:** Lana Clarkson, Greg Wrangler. 1989

BARBARIANS, THE 🦃 Unconvincing fantasy film casts David and Peter Paul (wrestling's Barbarian Brothers) as twins trying to save the queen of their people. Not rated. 88m. **DIR:** Ruggero Deodato. **CAST:** Peter Paul, David Paul, Richard Lynch, Michael Berryman. 1987

BARON MÜENCHHAUSEN ★★★ This lavish epic was intended to be a cinematic jewel in the crown of Hitler's Third Reich, a big-budget masterpiece designed to prove that Germany could compete with Hollywood. While the outlandish adventures of Baron Hieronymus Müenchhausen are at times amusing and quite clever, the incredible visual spectacle—huge and chaotic sets, overly ornate costumes—often overwhelms the story. Very brief nudity; otherwise suitable for family viewing. 110m. **DIR:** Josef von Baky. **CAST:** Hans Albers, Brigitte Horney, Leo Slezak. 1943

BARRACUDA 🦃 Made-in-Florida bore about chemical waste and its predictable effect on fish. Rated R. 90m. **DIR:** Harry Kerwin. **CAST:** Wayne Crawford, Jason (Herb) Evers, Bert Freed. 1978

BATTLE BEYOND THE STARS ★★★★ Here's something different: a space fantasy-comedy. Richard Thomas stars in this funny and often exciting movie as an emissary from a peaceful planet desperately searching for champions to save it from an evil warlord. It's *Star Wars* meets *The Magnificent Seven*, with fine tongue-in-cheek performances. Rated PG. 104m. **DIR:** Jimmy T. Murakami. **CAST:** Richard Thomas, John Saxon, Robert Vaughn, George Peppard. 1980

BATTLE FOR THE PLANET OF THE APES ★★ Events come full circle in this final *Apes* film, with simian Roddy McDowall attempting peaceful coexistence with conquered humanity. Naturally, not everybody plays along with such a plan, and an impending nuclear threat adds little tension to a story whose outcome is known. Rated PG for violence. 92m. **DIR:** J. Lee Thompson. **CAST:** Roddy McDowall, Severn Darden, John Huston, Claude Akins, Paul Williams. 1973

BATTLESTAR GALACTICA 🦃 This film, adapted from the television series, is a seventh-rate *Star Wars*. Rated PG. 125m. **DIR:** Richard A. Colla. **CAST:** Lorne Greene, Richard Hatch, Dirk Benedict, Lew Ayres, Jane Seymour. 1978

BEACH BABES FROM BEYOND 🦃 The title says it all. Not worth watching even to see celebrity relatives embarrass their families. Rated R for profanity and nudity. 78m. **DIR:** Ellen Cabot. **CAST:** Joe Estevez, Don Swayze, Joey Travolta, Burt Ward, Jacqueline Stallone, Linnea Quigley, Sara Bellomo, Tamara Landry, Nicole Posey. 1993

BEAST FROM 20,000 FATHOMS, THE ★★★ An experimental atom bomb blast in the Arctic thaws a million-year-old giant rhedosaurus that seeks its home in the Atlantic depths off the New York coast. Based on Ray Bradbury's *Saturday Evening Post* story. B&W; 80m. **DIR:** Eugene Lourie. **CAST:** Paul Christian, Paula Raymond, Cecil Kellaway, Donald Woods, Kenneth Tobey, Lee Van Cleef. 1953

BEASTMASTER, THE ★★★½ A young medieval warrior (Marc Singer) who possesses the ability to communicate psychically with animals takes revenge—with the help of a slave (Tanya Roberts) and a master warrior (John Amos)—on the evil sorcerer (Rip Torn). It's fun for kids of all ages. Rated PG for violence and brief nudity. 118m. **DIR:** Don Coscarelli. **CAST:** Marc Singer, Tanya

Roberts, Rip Torn, John Amos, Rod Loomis. 1982

BEASTMASTER 2: THROUGH THE PORTAL OF TIME ★★★½ The Beastmaster (Marc Singer) travels through a hole in time to present-day Los Angeles in order to chase down his evil nemesis. More than just another stranger-in-a-strange-land tale, this film will please fans of the genre as well as those who just like a good laugh. Rated PG-13 for violence. 107m. **DIR:** Sylvio Tabet. **CAST:** Marc Singer, Wings Hauser, Kari Wuhrer, Sarah Douglas. 1991

BEAUTY AND THE BEAST (TV SERIES) ★★★½ The classic legend received an updated facelift with this popular cult television series, which teamed Linda Hamilton's crusading district attorney with Ron Perlman's underworld dweller. Some admire the Renaissance surroundings and unusually literate scripts; others simply yearn for the sort of deep, platonic love shared by the two central characters. This much is certain: You'll either roll with the poetic dialogue or find it outrageously melodramatic. Unrated; suitable for family viewing. 100m. **DIR:** Richard Franklin, Victor Lobl. **CAST:** Ron Perlman, Linda Hamilton, Roy Dotrice, Jay Acovone. 1987

BENEATH THE PLANET OF THE APES ★★½ Charlton Heston let himself get sucked into this sequel to *Planet of the Apes*. Astronaut James Franciscus—sent to find out what happened to the first team sent to the planet—has more than simians to contend with; he also discovers a race of u-g-l-y mutants that worships an atomic bomb, since it made them what they are.... Some of the original's energy remains. Rated PG for violence. 95m. **DIR:** Ted Post. **CAST:** Charlton Heston, James Franciscus, Maurice Evans, Kim Hunter, Linda Harrison, James Gregory. 1970

BEYOND THE RISING MOON ★★ In the twenty-first century, a genetically created troubleshooter rebels. The same theme was handled much better in *Blade Runner*, though here the plot is secondary to the mediocre special effects and outer-space shoot-outs. 93m. **DIR:** Philip Cook. **CAST:** Tracy Davis, Hans Bachmann. 1988

BEYOND THE STARS ★★★ Troubled teen Christian Slater, spending the summer with divorced father Robert Foxworth, runs into reclusive ex-astronaut Martin Sheen, who opens up and takes the kid under his wing. They eventually form a trust that allows Sheen to introduce Slater to a secret he discovered on the moon. Rated PG. 94m. **DIR:** David Saperstein. **CAST:** Martin Sheen, Christian Slater, Robert Foxworth, Sharon Stone, Olivia D'Abo, F. Murray Abraham. 1989

BEYOND TOMORROW ★★½ Sudden success goes to singer Richard Carlson's head. He switches his affections from fiancée Jean Parker to captivating stage star Helen Vinson. To see that right is done, three ghosts return from the grave and change his troubled mind. An interesting premise on paper, the film fails to live up to its possibilities. B&W; 84m. **DIR:** A. Edward Sutherland. **CAST:** Jean Parker, Richard Carlson, Helen Vinson, Charles Winninger, Harry Carey, C. Aubrey Smith, Maria Ouspenskaya, Rod La Rocque. 1940

BIGGLES—ADVENTURES IN TIME ★★★★ Delightful fantasy film focuses on the adventures of a New York frozen-food merchandiser, Jim Ferguson (Neil Dickson), who discovers he has a time twin—a World War I British fighter ace named Biggles (Alex Hyde-White). Every time Biggles is in danger, Ferguson finds himself bouncing back through time to come to his twin's rescue. Rated PG for profanity and violence. 100m. **DIR:** John Hough. **CAST:** Neil Dickson, Alex Hyde-White, Peter Cushing, Fiona Hutchison, William Hootkins. 1985

BILL VIOLA: SELECTED WORKS ★★½ Four major works by conceptual video artist Bill Viola are a study in visual poetry, while cleverly exploiting the medium of video technology. Unfortunately these four pieces suffer from tedium. Not rated. 54m. **DIR:** Bill Viola. 1981

BIONIC WOMAN, THE ★★ What we have here is the female equivalent of TV's *The Six Million Dollar Man*. Lindsay Wagner is the superwoman who annihilates the bad guys. 96m. **DIR:** Richard Moder. **CAST:** Lindsay Wagner, Lee Majors, Richard Anderson. 1975

BLACK HOLE, THE 🦃 Space movie clichés. Rated PG. 97m. **DIR:** Gary Nelson. **CAST:** Maximilian Schell, Anthony Perkins, Robert Forster, Joseph Bottoms, Yvette Mimieux, Ernest Borgnine. 1979

BLACK MAGIC M-66 ★★★½ Japanese animation. Another from screenwriter-director Masamune Shirow, the Walter Hill of animation and creative force behind *Appleseed* and *Dominion*. *Black Magic* is a streamlined tale of android destruction as two military prototypes are accidentally unleashed. Typical of Shirow's other works, this feature has all the fast-paced action and more suspense than most Hollywood blockbusters. Unrated; contains nudity and violence. 48m. **DIR:** Takayuki Sawaura. 1987

BLADE RUNNER ★★★★½ This Ridley Scott (*Alien*) production is thought-provoking and visually impressive. Harrison Ford stars as a futuristic Philip Marlowe trying to find and kill the world's remaining rebel androids in 2019 Los Angeles. *Blade Runner* may not be for everyone, but those who appreciate something of substance will find it worthwhile. Rated R for brief nudity and violence. 118m. **DIR:** Ridley Scott. **CAST:** Harrison Ford, Rutger Hauer, Sean Young, Daryl Hannah,

Joanna Cassidy, Edward James Olmos, M. Emmet Walsh. 1982

BLAKE'S 7 (TV SERIES) ★★★ In a post-nuclear future, Earth and other populated planets are strictly controlled by "the Federation." Blake's 7, a group of escaped criminals and rebels, wanders the galaxy seeking to undercut the Federation's omnipotence. This British TV series, a cult favorite in the United States, is less campy than *Dr. Who* but not as intellectual as *The Prisoner*. Each tape includes two episodes. 105m. **DIR:** Various. **CAST:** Gareth Thomas, Sally Knyvette, Paul Darrow. 1978–1981

BODY SNATCHERS, THE (1993) ★★★½ Third screen version of Jack Finney's science-fiction tale is distinctive in its own way, although we still prefer Don Siegel's 1956 version. This time the invasion takes place on a military base, with director Abel Ferrara's stark storytelling enhanced by the atmospheric cinematography of Bojan Bazelli. Rated R for violence, nudity, and profanity. 87m. **DIR:** Abel Ferrara. **CAST:** Gabrielle Anwar, Terry Kinney, Meg Tilly, Forest Whitaker, Christine Elise, R. Lee Ermey, Reilly Murphy. 1993

BORROWER, THE ★★ The director of *Henry: Portrait of a Serial Killer* brings us this gory tale of an alien killer sentenced to life without parole on planet Earth. Better-than-average effects help to ease us through the film's weak plot. Rated R for profanity and violence. 97m. **DIR:** John McNaughton. **CAST:** Rae Dawn Chong, Don Gordon, Antonio Fargas. 1991

BOY AND HIS DOG, A ★★★★½ Looking for intelligence and biting humor in a science-fiction satire? Try this Hugo Award–winning screen adaptation of Harlan Ellison's novel, which focuses on the adventures of a young scavenger (Don Johnson) and his telepathic dog as they roam the Earth circa 2024 after a nuclear holocaust. Rated R for violence, sexual references, and nudity. 87m. **DIR:** L. Q. Jones. **CAST:** Don Johnson, Suzanne Benton, Jason Robards Jr. 1976

BRAIN, THE (1965) ★★ Adequate remake of the oft-filmed *Donovan's Brain*, a little short on thrills and originality, but atmospheric fun nevertheless. A German-British coproduction. B&W; 85m. **DIR:** Freddie Francis. **CAST:** Peter Van Eyck, Anne Heywood, Bernard Lee, Jack MacGowran. 1965

BRAIN DEAD ★★★ A research doctor (Bill Pullman) is pressured by his corporate sponsor to use his research on brain patterns to open a chain of attitude adjustment centers. Something snaps, and the mild-mannered doctor soon becomes the apparent victim of severe paranoia. Rated R for profanity, violence, and nudity. 85m. **DIR:** Adam Simon. **CAST:** Bill Pullman, Bud Cort, George Kennedy, Bill Paxton. 1989

BRAIN EATERS, THE ★★ Robert Heinlein's *The Puppet Masters* is the unacknowledged source for this grade-C sci-fi melodrama in the *Invasion of the Body Snatchers* tradition. It's too brief to overstay its welcome, and has earned a cult following. B&W; 60m. **DIR:** Bruno VeSota. **CAST:** Joanna Lee, Jody Fair, Ed Nelson, Leonard Nimoy. 1958

BRAIN FROM PLANET AROUS, THE ★★★ Great little film is much better than the plot or title would suggest. Giant brain from outer space takes over John Agar's body in an attempt to conquer the world. Not far behind is another brain that inhabits the body of Agar's dog and tries to prevent it. Good stuff. B&W; 70m. **DIR:** Nathan Juran. **CAST:** John Agar, Joyce Meadows, Robert Fuller. 1958

BRAIN THAT WOULDN'T DIE, THE 🦃 A doctor experiments with human limbs. B&W; 81m. **DIR:** Joseph Green. **CAST:** Jason (Herb) Evers, Virginia Leith, Adele Lamont. 1963

BRAINSTORM ★★★½ Christopher Walken and Natalie Wood star in this sci-fi thriller about an invention that can read and record physical, emotional, and intellectual sensations as they are experienced by an individual and allow them to be reexperienced by another human being. But what happens if it's used for evil? Rated PG for nudity and profanity. 106m. **DIR:** Douglas Trumbull. **CAST:** Christopher Walken, Natalie Wood, Louise Fletcher. 1983

BRONX EXECUTIONER, THE 🦃 A group of humans battle for their lives against cyborgs bent on their destruction. Not rated, but contains violence. 88m. **DIR:** Bob Collins. **CAST:** Margie Newton, Chuck Valenti, Woody Strode. 1989

BROTHER FROM ANOTHER PLANET, THE ★★★★ In this thoughtful comic fantasy, a dark-skinned extraterrestrial (Joe Morton) on the lam from alien cops crash-lands his spaceship in New York harbor, staggers ashore on Ellis Island, then makes his way to Harlem. Unrated; the film has profanity and violence. 110m. **DIR:** John Sayles. **CAST:** Joe Morton, Darryl Edwards, Steve James. 1984

BUCK ROGERS: DESTINATION SATURN (A.K.A. PLANET OUTLAWS) ★★½ Edited-down version of the popular serial loses much of the continuity of the twelve-episode chapterplay, but still proves to be great fun as ideal hero Buster Crabbe enthusiastically goes after the vile Killer Kan. B&W; 91m. **DIR:** Ford Beebe, Saul Goodkind. **CAST:** Buster Crabbe, Constance Moore, Jackie Moran, Jack Mulhall, Anthony Warde, C. Montague Shaw, Philip Ahn. 1939

BUCK ROGERS IN THE 25TH CENTURY ★★ Updating of the Buck Rogers legend finds Buck (Gil Gerard), after years of suspended animation, awakened in a future society under attack by the power-mad Princess Ardala (Pamela Hensley). Substandard space fare was originally made as a TV pilot. Rated PG. 89m. **DIR:** Daniel Haller. **CAST:** Gil Gerard, Erin Gray, Pamela Hensley, Tim O'Connor, Henry Silva. **1979**

CALLER, THE 🦃 Sci-fi thriller about a man and a woman playing a cat-and-mouse game of mind trips. Rated R for violence and profanity. 97m. **DIR:** Arthur Allan Seidelman. **CAST:** Malcolm McDowell, Madolyn Smith. **1987**

CAPRICORN ONE ★★★★ In this suspenseful release, the government stages a mock flight to Mars in a television studio, with astronauts James Brolin, Sam Waterston, and O. J. Simpson pretending to be in outer space and landing on the planet. Then the news is released by the Pentagon that the ship crashed upon reentry and all aboard were killed, which puts the lives of the astronauts in danger. Rated PG. 124m. **DIR:** Peter Hyams. **CAST:** Elliott Gould, James Brolin, Hal Holbrook, Sam Waterston, Karen Black, O. J. Simpson, Telly Savalas. **1978**

CAPTIVE PLANET 🦃 Earth is once again besieged by alien invaders in this very missable movie. 105m. **DIR:** Al Bradley. **CAST:** Sharon Baker, Chris Avran. **1986**

CAST A DEADLY SPELL ★★★½ Scriptwriter Joseph Dougherty's premise is hard to resist: that, in a slightly altered Los Angeles of 1948, *everybody* would use magic as a means to get ahead...except one lone private detective named H. Phillip Lovecraft (Fred Ward), last of the truly honest men. This made-for-cable noir fantasy is often wry and always entertaining. Rated R for violence and profanity. 93m. **DIR:** Martin Campbell. **CAST:** Fred Ward, David Warner, Julianne Moore, Clancy Brown. **1991**

CAT WOMEN OF THE MOON 🦃 Another ludicrous entry in the travel-to-a-planet-of-barely-dressed-women subgenre. 64m. **DIR:** Arthur Hilton. **CAST:** Sonny Tufts, Marie Windsor, Victor Jory. **1954**

CAVE GIRL 🦃 A high school student gets lost in a cave during a field trip and pops up in prehistoric times. Rated R for nudity and profanity. 85m. **DIR:** David Oliver. **CAST:** Daniel Roebuck, Cindy Ann Thompson. **1985**

CHARLY ★★★★ Cliff Robertson won the best-actor Oscar for his role in this excellent science-fiction film as a retarded man turned into a genius through scientific experiments. Claire Bloom is also excellent as the caseworker who becomes his friend. Rated PG. 103m. **DIR:** Ralph Nelson. **CAST:** Cliff Robertson, Claire Bloom, Lilia Skala, Dick Van Patten. **1968**

CHERRY 2000 ★★½ Made before she graduated to better roles in *Stormy Monday* and *Working Girl*, Melanie Griffith starred in this barely released movie as a sort of female Mad Max. Set in the year 2017, this semi-parody casts Griffith as a mercenary who guides yuppie David Andrews through the deserts of the Southwest, now the domain of psychotic terrorists, in search of a robot warehouse. Rated PG-13. 93m. **DIR:** Steve DeJarnett. **CAST:** Melanie Griffith, David Andrews, Ben Johnson, Tim Thomerson, Brion James, Harry Carey Jr., Michael C. Gwynne. **1988**

CIRCUITRY MAN ★★★ Kinky tale of a futuristic world where computer chips simulate drugs and sex. A beautiful bodyguard must smuggle the chips across the country through an elaborate underground maze. Dennis Christopher steals the show as a scummy subterranean dweller who helps her get there. Rated R for violence and profanity. 85m. **DIR:** Steven Lovy. **CAST:** Dana Wheeler-Nicholson, Jim Metzler, Lu Leonard, Dennis Christopher, Vernon Wells. **1989**

CITY LIMITS 🦃 Another in the endless parade of life-after-the-apocalypse, *Mad Max* rip-off films. Rated PG-13 for brief nudity, violence, and language. 85m. **DIR:** Aaron Lipstadt. **CAST:** Darrell Larson, John Stockwell, Kim Cattrall, Rae Dawn Chong, Robby Benson, James Earl Jones. **1984**

CLAN OF THE CAVE BEAR 🦃 In this dreadfully dumb adaptation of Jean M. Auel's bestselling fantasy novel, a Cro-Magnon child is grudgingly adopted by a tribe of Neanderthals. Rated R. 100m. **DIR:** Michael Chapman. **CAST:** Daryl Hannah, Pamela Reed, Thomas Waites. **1986**

CLASH OF THE TITANS ★★½ Perseus (Harry Hamlin), the son of Zeus (Laurence Olivier), mounts his flying horse, Pegasus, and fights for the hand of Andromeda (Judi Bowker). Plagued by corny situations and stilted dialogue, only the visual wonders by special-effects wizard Ray Harryhausen make this movie worth seeing. Rated PG for violence and gore. 118m. **DIR:** Desmond Davis. **CAST:** Laurence Olivier, Harry Hamlin, Judi Bowker, Burgess Meredith, Maggie Smith. **1981**

CLASS OF 1999 ★★½ Exciting sequel to *Class of 1984*. High school has become a battleground in 1999, forcing the administration to rely on android faculty to teach the kids. When the new teachers malfunction, they initiate a killer curriculum. Rated R for violence. 96m. **DIR:** Mark L. Lester. **CAST:** Bradley Gregg, Traci Lin, John P. Ryan, Pam Grier, Stacy Keach, Malcolm McDowell. **1989**

CLASS OF 1999 II: THE SUBSTITUTE ★★½ Agreeable sequel finds rogue android soldier Sasha Mitchell posing as a high-school teacher to rid the school of human vermin. He's programmed to kill and finds plenty of prey among the thugs and gangs that rule the halls, but a mysterious stranger is out to force Mitchell to do his dirty work. Rated R for violence, language, and nudity. 90m. **DIR:** Spiro Razatos. **CAST:** Sasha Mitchell, Nick Cassavetes, Caitlin Dulany, Jack Knight. **1993**

CLOCKWORK ORANGE, A ★★★★ Not for every taste, this is a stylized, "ultraviolent" black comedy. Malcolm McDowell stars as the number-one "malchick," Alex, who leads his "droogs" through "a bit of the old ultraviolence" for a real "horror show." Rated R. 137m. **DIR:** Stanley Kubrick. **CAST:** Malcolm McDowell, Patrick Magee, Adrienne Corri. **1971**

CLONES, THE ★★½ In a sinister plot to control the weather, several government scientists are duplicated and placed in strategic meteorological stations. Basically silly film is made watchable by the believable performances of Michael Greene and Gregory Sierra, and there's a terrific roller-coaster–chase finale. Rated PG for language and violence. 86m. **DIR:** Paul Hunt, Lamar Card. **CAST:** Michael Greene, Bruce Bennett, Gregory Sierra, John Drew Barrymore. **1973**

CLONUS HORROR, THE ★★½ Government scientists are hard at work creating a master race of superhumans in a laboratory. One of them breaks free to warn the world. Not a bad time waster for science-fiction fans. Also known as *Parts: The Clonus Horror*. Rated R. 90m. **DIR:** Robert S. Fiveson. **CAST:** Tim Donnelly, Dick Sargent, Peter Graves, Keenan Wynn, Lurene Tuttle. **1979**

CLOSE ENCOUNTERS OF THE THIRD KIND ★★★★ This is director Steven Spielberg's enchanting, pre-*E.T.* vision of an extraterrestrial visit to Earth. The movie goes against many long-nurtured conceptions about space aliens. The humans, such as Richard Dreyfuss, act more bizarre than the nonthreatening childlike visitors. Spielberg never surrenders his role as storyteller to the distractions of special effects. Rated PG. 132m. **DIR:** Steven Spielberg. **CAST:** Richard Dreyfuss, François Truffaut, Teri Garr, Melinda Dillon. **1977**

CLUB EXTINCTION 🦃 A grim, depressing movie—ostensibly set in twenty-first-century Berlin—that fails on all levels. The plot revolves around apparent suicides that one cop believes are murders. Rated R for violence and gore. 112m. **DIR:** Claude Chabrol. **CAST:** Alan Bates, Jennifer Beals, Andrew McCarthy, Jan Niklas. **1990**

COCOON ★★★★★ *Cocoon* is a splendid entertainment about a group of people in a retirement home who find what they believe is the fountain of youth. Only trouble is the magic place belongs to a group of extraterrestrials, who may or may not be friendly. Rated PG-13 for suggested sex, brief nudity, and light profanity. 118m. **DIR:** Ron Howard. **CAST:** Don Ameche, Wilford Brimley, Hume Cronyn, Brian Dennehy, Jack Gilford, Steve Guttenberg, Barret Oliver, Maureen Stapleton, Jessica Tandy, Gwen Verdon, Tahnee Welch. **1985**

COCOON: THE RETURN ★★★½ Daniel Petrie pulls off something of a minor miracle in this sequel, which has the elderly Earthlings returning home to help their alien friends rescue some cocoons that have been endangered by an earthquake. Petrie keeps our interest by concentrating on the characters and getting uniformly splendid performances. Rated PG for slight profanity. 112m. **DIR:** Daniel Petrie. **CAST:** Don Ameche, Wilford Brimley, Courteney Cox, Hume Cronyn, Brian Dennehy, Jack Gilford, Steve Guttenberg, Maureen Stapleton, Jessica Tandy, Gwen Verdon, Tahnee Welch. **1988**

COLOSSUS: THE FORBIN PROJECT ★★★½ Low-key thriller about a supercomputer designed for defense that becomes too big for its bytes. Colossus launches its own plan for world domination. This intelligent production is disturbing and very well made. Lack of stars and a downbeat story kept it from becoming the box-office hit it deserved. Rated PG. 100m. **DIR:** Joseph Sargent. **CAST:** Eric Braeden, Susan Clark, William Schallert. **1969**

COMMUNION ★★★½ Science-fiction author Whitley Strieber based this remarkable movie on his alleged real-life close encounters of the third kind. Unlike Steven Spielberg's fantasy-like film about the first mass-human contact with aliens, Strieber's story, directed by his longtime friend Phillippe Mora, is an often terrifying movie. And it's all the more powerful because of Strieber's insistence that the events depicted are true. Rated R for profanity. 100m. **DIR:** Philippe Mora. **CAST:** Christopher Walken, Lindsay Crouse, Frances Sternhagen, Andreas Katsulas. **1989**

COMPANY OF WOLVES, THE ★★★½ Neither a horror film nor a fantasy for the kiddies, this dark, psychologically oriented rendering of the "Little Red Riding Hood" story is for thinking viewers only. Angela Lansbury stars as Grandmother, who turns the dreams of her granddaughter (Sarah Patterson) into tales of spooky terror. Rated R for violence and gore. 95m. **DIR:** Neil Jordan. **CAST:** Angela Lansbury, David Warner, Sarah Patterson. **1985**

CONAN THE BARBARIAN ★★★½ Featuring Arnold Schwarzenegger in the title role, this $19 million sword-and-sorcery epic is just as corny, raunchy, sexist, and unbelievably brutal as the original tales by Robert E. Howard. Therefore, it seems likely Conan fans will be delighted. Rated R for nudity, profanity, and violence. 129m. **DIR:** John Milius. **CAST:** Arnold Schwarzenegger, Sandahl Bergman, James Earl Jones, Mako. **1982**

NAN THE DESTROYER ★★★ In this htweight, violent sequel, Conan (Arnold hwarzenegger) bests beasts and blood-irsty battlers at every turn with the help of s sidekick (Tracey Walter), a wizard Iako), a staff-wielding thief (androgynous race Jones), and a giant warrior (Wilt hamberlain) as they go on a perilous mis-on to find a sacred stone. Rated PG for vio-nce. 103m. **DIR:** Richard Fleischer. **CAST:** Ar-ld Schwarzenegger, Grace Jones, Wilt amberlain, Tracey Walter. **1984**

NQUEST OF THE PLANET OF THE APES ★ Having been rescued by Ricardo Mon-lban at the end of his previous film adven-re, simian Roddy McDowall matures and ads his fellow apes—now domesticated— a freedom revolt that sets the stage for the ents in the very first film. Very melodra-atic and formulaic, with few clichés left un-ed. Rated PG for violence. 87m. **DIR:** J. Lee ompson. **CAST:** Roddy McDowall, Ricardo ontalban, Don Murray, Severn Darden. **1972**

OOL WORLD ★★ Cartoonist Gabriel yrne is lured by his sexy creation Kim Bas-ger into a bizarre animated world that me from his imagination. Brad Pitt is the tective who attempts to bring Byrne back. ke no feature-length cartoon you've ever en before. Rated PG-13 for sexual content. 3m. **DIR:** Ralph Bakshi. **CAST:** Kim Basinger, abriel Byrne, Brad Pitt. **1992**

OSMIC MAN, THE 🦃 An invisible alien omes to this planet in a giant levitating Ping-ong ball. B&W; 72m. **DIR:** Herbert Greene. **AST:** John Carradine, Bruce Bennett, Angela reene. **1959**

RASH AND BURN ★★½ Futuristic tale f a rebel television station infiltrated by an droid from the corporation that now runs e world. Fast-paced, with above-par special ffects, this film is directed with uncommon race by B-movie king Charles Band. Rated for violence and profanity. 85m. **DIR:** Char-s Band. **CAST:** Paul Ganus, Megan Ward, Ralph aite. **1990**

REATION OF THE HUMANOIDS ★★ In is futuristic parable, Don Megowan plays cop who is paranoid about the develop-ent of near-perfect androids. This low-udget vision of the future is long on talk, hort on action, and hard to take seriously. 5m. **DIR:** Wesley E. Barry. **CAST:** Don Me-owan. **1962**

REATURE 🦃 The reawakening of hu-an-devouring life on one of Jupiter's oons. Rated R for violence. 97m. **DIR:** Wil-am Malone. **CAST:** Stan Ivar, Wendy Schaal, laus Kinski, Marie Laurin, Lyman Ward. **1985**

REATURE FROM THE HAUNTED SEA, THE 🦃 A muddled horror-comedy about a ogart-type crook planning to steal a treas-re with the help of a mythical sea monster. B&W; 60m. **DIR:** Roger Corman. **CAST:** Anthony Carbone, Betsy Jones-Moreland. **1960**

CREATURES THE WORLD FORGOT 🦃 Migrating cavemen battle for superiority of the tribe. Rated PG, but contains some nudity. 95m. **DIR:** Don Chaffey. **CAST:** Julie Ege, Tony Bonner. **1970**

CREEPING TERROR, THE ★★ A so-bad-it's-good classic. Lake Tahoe is terrorized by a pair of outer-space monsters, played by extras dressed in old carpets. One of the cheapest movies you'd ever want to see. B&W; 75m. **DIR:** Art J. Nelson. **CAST:** Vic Savage, Shannon O'Neill. **1964**

CREMATORS, THE 🦃 Semipro effort by the coscenarist for *It Came from Outer Space,* with a nearly identical premise. Not rated. 90m. **DIR:** Harry Essex. **CAST:** Maria Di Aragon, Marvin Howard. **1972**

CRIME ZONE 🦃 A young couple struggles to escape a futuristic society turned police state. Rated R for nudity and profanity. 96m. **DIR:** Luis Llosa. **CAST:** David Carradine, Peter Nelson, Sherilyn Fenn. **1988**

CYBERNATOR 🦃 In the near future, a police detective (Lonnie Schuyler) has his hands full battling a group of evil cyborg assassins developed by the military. Rated R for violence and nudity. 84m. **DIR:** Robert Rundle. **CAST:** Lonnie Schuyler, Christina Peralta, James K. Williams, William Smith. **1991**

CYBORG 🦃 A study in bad. Bad script. Bad acting. Bad directing. Bad special effects. A soldier of the future (Jean-Claude Van Damme) seeks vengeance against the savage gang that killed his family. Rated R for violence. 90m. **DIR:** Albert Pyun. **CAST:** Jean-Claude Van Damme, Deborah Richter, Dayle Haddon. **1989**

CYBORG 2 🦃 This turgid sequel-in-name-only steals profusely from *Blade Runner* and *Max Headroom.* A martial-arts instructor (Elias Koteas) does the unthinkable by falling in love with a pouting cyborg (Angelina Jolie). Rated R for violence, profanity, nudity, and simulated sex. 99m. **DIR:** Michael Schroeder. **CAST:** Elias Koteas, Angelina Jolie, Allen Garfield, Billy Drago, Jack Palance. **1993**

CYBORG COP ★★ Convoluted concoction borrows from several different genres, but can't come to grips with its own identity. A former DEA agent locates his brother on a Caribbean island, but learns that his sibling has become a cyborg in a cruel experiment. John Rhys-Davies is cheerfully villainous, while the rest of the cast must grin and bear tiresome clichés. Rated R for violence and language. 94m. **DIR:** Sam Firstenberg. **CAST:** David Bradley, Todd Jensen, Alonna Shaw, John Rhys-Davies. **1993**

CYBORG: THE SIX-MILLION DOLLAR MAN ★★★ Pilot for the long-running ABC series is more serious and subdued than the episodes to follow. Col. Steve Austin (Lee Majors), after flying an experimental jet that crashes, is turned into a superman with powerful robotic limbs. Very good. 73m. **DIR:** Richard Irving. **CAST:** Lee Majors, Darren McGavin, Martin Balsam. **1973**

D.A.R.Y.L. ★★★★ In this delightful science-fiction film, Barret Oliver stars as a boy adopted by Mary Beth Hurt and Michael McKean. He turns out to be a perfect little fellow...maybe a little too perfect. *D.A.R.Y.L.* is a film the whole family can enjoy. Rated PG for violence and light profanity. 99m. **DIR:** Simon Wincer. **CAST:** Barret Oliver, Mary Beth Hurt, Michael McKean, Josef Sommer. **1985**

DAGORA, THE SPACE MONSTER 🦃 A cache of gems stolen by Japanese gangsters is ripped off by a giant, flying, diamond-eating jellyfish. Probably a true story. 80m. **DIR:** Inoshiro Honda. **CAST:** Yosuke Natsuki. **1964**

DALEKS—INVASION EARTH 2150 A.D. ★★★ The always watchable Peter Cushing revives his distinctive interpretation of the ever-popular Dr. Who in this honorable sequel to *Dr. Who and the Daleks.* This time, the title creatures are attempting to take over Earth. 84m. **DIR:** Gordon Flemyng. **CAST:** Peter Cushing, Bernard Cribbins, Andrew Keir, Ray Brooks. **1966**

DAMNATION ALLEY ★★ The nuclear holocaust movie, which disappeared after its heyday in the 1950s, was revived by *Damnation Alley*, complete with giant mutations and roaming survivors. While it's not a bad movie, it's not particularly good, either. The laser effects are awful. Rated PG. 91m. **DIR:** Jack Smight. **CAST:** Jan-Michael Vincent, George Peppard, Dominique Sanda, Jackie Earle Haley, Paul Winfield. **1977**

DANGER: DIABOLIK ★★★ Director Mario Bava departed from the horror genre he normally specialized in, and staged this pop-art fantasy, based on an Italian comic strip of the time. Master criminal Diabolik outwits the police and government agents assigned to catch him in a garishly colored, playful spoof that sometimes is worthy of silent serial master Louis Feuillade. 105m. **DIR:** Mario Bava. **CAST:** John Phillip Law, Marisa Mell, Michel Piccoli, Terry-Thomas, Adolfo Celi. **1967**

DARK CRYSTAL, THE ★★★★ Jim Henson of "The Muppets" fame created this lavish fantasy tale in the style of J .R.R. Tolkien (*The Lord of the Rings*), using the movie magic that brought E.T. and Yoda (*The Empire Strikes Back*) to life. It's a delight for children of all ages. Rated PG. 93m. **DIR:** Jim Henson, Frank Oz. **CAST:** Animated. **1983**

DARK SIDE OF THE MOON, THE 🦃 A lunar mission crew sheds some light on the moon's shaded half and its relationship to the Bermuda Triangle. Rated R. 96m. **DIR:** D. J. Webster. **CAST:** Will Bledsoe, Alan Blumenfeld, John Diehl, Robert Sampson. **1989**

DARK STAR ★★★½ This is one of the strangest sci-fi films you are likely to run across. Four astronauts have been in space entirely too long as they seek and destroy unstable planets. Director John Carpenter's first film is very funny in spurts and always crazy. Rated PG because of language. 83m. **DIR:** John Carpenter. **CAST:** Dan O'Bannon, Brian Narelle. **1974**

DARKMAN ★★★★ Sam Raimi's *Darkman* borrows elements from *The Invisible Man, The Phantom of the Opera,* and the Marvel Comics line of brooding superheroes. Liam Neeson is just right as the horribly disfigured scientist who becomes a crime fighter. Some of the sequences in this ultraviolent but inventive movie are so outrageous, they'll make your jaw drop. Rated R for violence and profanity. 96m. **DIR:** Sam Raimi. **CAST:** Liam Neeson, Frances McDormand, Colin Friels, Larry Drake. **1990**

DAY AFTER, THE ★★★★ This excellent made-for-TV movie special received much advance publicity because of its timely topic: the effects of a nuclear war. Jason Robards Jr. plays a hospital doctor who treats many of the victims after the nuclear attack. 126m. **DIR:** Nicholas Meyer. **CAST:** Jason Robards Jr., JoBeth Williams, Steve Guttenberg, John Cullum, John Lithgow. **1983**

DAY OF THE DOLPHIN, THE ★★★ Fine film centering on a research scientist (George C. Scott) who teaches a pair of dolphins to speak, and how they're kidnapped and used in an assassination attempt. Rated PG for language. 104m. **DIR:** Mike Nichols. **CAST:** George C. Scott, Trish Van Devere, Paul Sorvino, Fritz Weaver. **1973**

DAY OF THE TRIFFIDS, THE ★★★½ This British film has triffids—alien plants—arriving on Earth during a meteor shower. The shower blinds most of the Earth's people. Then the plants grow, begin walking, and eat humans. This one will grow on you. 95m. **DIR:** Steve Sekely. **CAST:** Howard Keel, Nicole Maurey, Janette Scott, Kieron Moore, Mervyn Johns. **1963**

DAY THE EARTH CAUGHT FIRE, THE ★★★★ Veteran director Val Guest helmed this near-classic film concerning the fate of the Earth following simultaneous nuclear explosions at both poles, sending the planet on a collision course with the sun. Incredibly realistic production is unsettling, with Edward Judd perfectly cast as an Everyman caught up in the mass panic and hysteria. B&W; 99m. **DIR:** Val Guest. **CAST:** Edward Judd, Janet Munro, Leo McKern. **1962**

DAY THE EARTH STOOD STILL, THE ★★★★ *The Day the Earth Stood Still* is one f the better science-fiction films. Even ıough some of the space gimmicks are ımpy and not up to today's standards of ›ecial effects, the film holds up well be-ıuse of a good adult script and credible per-rmances by Michael Rennie and Patricia eal. B&W; 92m. **DIR:** Robert Wise. **CAST:** Mi-ıael Rennie, Patricia Neal, Hugh Marlowe, Sam ıffe, Billy Gray. **1951**

AY THE WORLD ENDED, THE ★★ After nuclear holocaust, a handful of survivors attle each other and the local mutant mon-:er. Minor melodrama featuring one of oger Corman's cheaper monster suits. &W; 82m. **DIR:** Roger Corman. **CAST:** Richard ənning, Lori Nelson, Mike Connors. **1956**

AY TIME ENDED, THE 🦃 Grade-Z sci-fi unker, about nature gone wild. 79m. **DIR:** ɔhn "Bud" Cardos. **CAST:** Jim Davis, Dorothy lalone, Chris Mitchum. **1980**

AYBREAK (1993) ★★★★ Writer-direc-ɔr Stephen Tolkin's cautionary drama, ased on Alan Bowne's play *Beirut*, takes lace in a decrepit New York City of the near ıture, controlled by a fascistic government ıat has made social outcasts of those tricken with an AIDS-like plague. One oung woman (Moira Kelly), dismayed by ıe Orwellian youth patrols, contacts under-round rebels who spirit diseased victims to afer quarters. Rated R for nudity, simulated ex, profanity, and violence. 91m. **DIR:** tephen Tolkin. **CAST:** Cuba Gooding Jr., Moira elly, Omar Epps, Alice Drummond, Martha limpton, John Savage. **1993**

EAD END DRIVE-IN ★★ It's the year 990. After widespread economic collapse, ıe world is in chaos. The Dead-End Drive-In ; a relocation camp for the undesirable ele-ıent. Rated R for language, violence, and nu-ity. 92m. **DIR:** Brian Trenchard-Smith. **CAST:** ed Manning, Natalie McCurry. **1986**

EAD MAN WALKING ★★★ Surpris-ıgly well-done low-budget science fiction in vhich a disease has divided the world's opulation into the haves and the have-nots. young man (Jeffrey Combs) hires a dare-levil mercenary (Wings Hauser) to rescue ıis girlfriend (Pamela Ludwig) from the lague zone. Rated R for violence. 90m. **DIR:** regory Brown. **CAST:** Wings Hauser, Brion ames, Jeffrey Combs, Pamela Ludwig. **1987**

EAD SPACE 🦃 A galactic lawman an-wers a distress signal from a space lab. Eve-yone associated with this film exhibits dead pace from the shoulders up. Rated R for vio-ence and nudity. 72m. **DIR:** Fred Gallo. **CAST:** larc Singer, Laura Tate, Bryan Cranston, Judith hapman. **1990**

EADLOCK ★★★★ High marks to this igh-tech update of *The Defiant Ones*, which airs Rutger Hauer and Mimi Rogers (both uperb) as convicts linked by futuristic collars necessitating their remaining in close mutual proximity...at the risk of impromptu decapitations. Broderick Miler's clever script blends perfectly with Lewis Teague's wry direction. Rated R for violence and sexual content. 95m. **DIR:** Lewis Teague. **CAST:** Rutger Hauer, Mimi Rogers, Joan Chen, James Remar. **1991**

DEADLY HARVEST 🦃 Mankind's unrelenting industrialization of arable land and subsequent cold winters (and summers!) wreak havoc with America's ecological system. Rated PG. 86m. **DIR:** Timothy Bond. **CAST:** Clint Walker, Nehemiah Persoff, Kim Cattrall, David Brown. **1976**

DEADLY MANTIS, THE ★★½ Can heroic scientists head off a mammoth praying mantis winging its way from the North Pole to New York City? Okay special effects, though even at 78 minutes it seems too long. B&W; 78m. **DIR:** Nathan Juran. **CAST:** Craig Stevens, William Hopper. **1957**

DEATH BECOMES HER ★★★½ Meryl Streep and Goldie Hawn seem to have a ball clowning around in this marvelously entertaining, special-effects-laden fantasy about the secret of eternal life and the war between two women. There are scenes in this very, very twisted comedy guaranteed to make your jaw drop, and it is most definitely not for children. That said, open-minded adults and older teenagers will get a real kick out of it. Rated PG-13 for profanity, nudity, and violence. 104m. **DIR:** Robert Zemeckis. **CAST:** Meryl Streep, Goldie Hawn, Bruce Willis, Isabella Rossellini, Ian Ogilvy. **1992**

DEATH OF THE INCREDIBLE HULK, THE ★★★ Supposedly dead David Banner (Bill Bixby) works as a janitor at a laboratory where a world-renowned scientist is creating a formula that could free Banner from the monster within him. Unfortunately, an international spy ring also wants the formula. Made for TV. 96m. **DIR:** Bill Bixby. **CAST:** Bill Bixby, Lou Ferrigno, Philip Sterling, Andreas Katsulas. **1990**

DEATH RACE 2000 ★★★ Futuristic look at what has become our national sport: road racing where points are accumulated for killing people with the race cars. David Carradine and Sylvester Stallone star in this tongue-in-cheek sci-fi action film. Stallone is a howl as one of the competitors. Rated R—violence, nudity, and language. 78m. **DIR:** Paul Bartel. **CAST:** David Carradine, Sylvester Stallone, Louisa Moritz, Mary Woronov, Joyce Jameson, Fred Grandy. **1975**

DEATH WATCH ★★★★ A thought-provoking look at the power and the misuse of the media in a future society. Harvey Keitel has a camera implanted in his brain. A television producer (Harry Dean Stanton) uses Keitel to film a documentary of a terminally ill woman (Romy Schneider) without her knowledge. Suspenseful science-fiction drama. Rated R for profanity and suggested sex. 117m. **DIR:** Bertrand Tavernier. **CAST:** Romy Schneider, Harvey Keitel, Harry Dean Stanton, Max von Sydow. **1980**

DEATHSPORT ★★ Not really a sequel to *Death Race 2000*, but cut from the same cloth. Both are low-budget action films centered around futuristic no-holds-barred road races. The first film, though, was a lot more fun. Rated R for violence and nudity. 82m. **DIR:** Henry Suso, Allan Arkush. **CAST:** David Carradine, Claudia Jennings, Richard Lynch. **1978**

DEATHSTALKER 💔 This film has a muscle-bound warrior attempting to save a beautiful princess (Barbi Benton) from an evil wizard. Rated R for nudity, profanity, simulated rape, and violence. 80m. **DIR:** John Watson. **CAST:** Robert Hill, Barbi Benton, Lana Clarkson. **1984**

DEATHSTALKER II: DUEL OF THE TITANS ★★½ Deathstalker and a feisty deposed princess battle the evil magician who has taken over her kingdom. Lowbrow fun is too busy making fun of itself to be taken seriously. The R rating is for nudity and violence. 85m. **DIR:** Jim Wynorski. **CAST:** John Terlesky, Monique Gabrielle. **1987**

DEATHSTALKER III—THE WARRIORS FROM HELL ★★½ Tongue-in-cheek sword-and-sorcery tale about the search for three magical stones that will lead to the riches of the world. You have so much fun with this one, you forget how hokey it really is. Rated R for nudity and violence. 85m. **DIR:** Alfonso Corona. **CAST:** John Allen Nelson, Carla Herd, Thom Christopher, Terri Treas. **1988**

DEATHSTALKER IV: MATCH OF THE TITANS 💔 Unbelievably bad sword-and-sorcery flick finds all the greatest warriors gathered for a tournament. Acting is nonexistent and fight scenes are poorly staged. Rated R for nudity and violence. 85m. **DIR:** Howard R. Cohen. **CAST:** Richard Hill, Maria Ford, Michelle Moffett, Brett Clark. **1992**

DECEIT ★★★ Alien sex fiends sent to destroy Earth find a little time to sample its women. When one of them chooses a street-smart prostitute she proves to be more than a match for them. Original, offbeat story is amusing as well as thought-provoking, if somewhat erratic. Rated R for nudity, profanity, and violence. 92m. **DIR:** Albert Pyun. **CAST:** Norbert Weisser, Samantha Phillips, Diane DeFoe, Christian Andrews, Scott Paulin. **1993**

DEEP RED (1994) ★★★★ Recalling *Blade Runner*, this well-made thriller casts Michael Biehn as a private investigator in the near future who agrees to track down a missing husband. When the man, a scientist working on a top-secret project called "Deep Red," is killed just as Biehn finds him, our hero realizes he's being used—but for what and by whom? Odd flashback style is disconcerting at first, but the acting and intriguing premise hold the viewer's interest. Made for cable. 86m. **DIR:** Craig R. Baxley. **CAST:** Michael Biehn, Joanna Pacula, Lisa Collins, John De Lancie, Tobin Bell, John Kapelos, Steven Williams, Michael Des Barres. **1994**

DEEP SPACE 💔 A creature created by the air force runs amok, and two rebel policemen track it down. Rated R for violence and language. 90m. **DIR:** Fred Olen Ray. **CAST:** Charles Napier, Ann Turkel, Ron Glass, Julie Newmar, James Booth, Anthony Eisley, Bo Svenson. **1988**

DEF-CON 4 ★★½ The first half of this film contains special effects the equal of any in modern science fiction, an intelligent script, and excellent acting. The second half is one postholocaust yawn. The overall impression is that perhaps the filmmakers ran out of time or money or both. Rated R for language and violence. 85m. **DIR:** Paul Donovan. **CAST:** Maury Chaykin, Kate Lynch, Tim Choate, Lenore Zann. **1985**

DELUGE ★★ The destruction of much of New York by earthquakes and a tidal wave. B&W; 70m. **DIR:** Felix Feist. **CAST:** Peggy Shannon, Sidney Blackmer, Lois Wilson, Matt Moore, Edward Van Sloan, Fred Kohler Sr., Samuel S. Hinds. **1933**

DEMOLITION MAN ★★½ High-concept action-thrillers just don't get much dumber than this, which attempts to argue that society is much better with heapin' helpings of exaggerated violence. Renegade cop Sylvester Stallone goes into the deep freeze for several decades, and then wakes in an insipid future civilization which cannot handle the mayhem of crazed psychotic Wesley Snipes. Stallone has said it himself—he just can't play comedy. Rated R for profanity and violence. 114m. **DIR:** Marco Brambilla. **CAST:** Sylvester Stallone, Wesley Snipes, Sandra Bullock, Nigel Hawthorne. **1993**

DEMON (GOD TOLD ME TO) ★★★½ A minor masterpiece, this movie opens with several mass murders. The only thing that connects these incidents is they are committed by pleasant, smiling people who explain their acts by saying, "God told me to." Rated R for nudity, profanity, and violence. 95m. **DIR:** Larry Cohen. **CAST:** Tony Lo Bianco, Sandy Dennis, Sylvia Sidney, Deborah Raffin, Sam Levene, Mike Kellin. **1977**

DEMON SEED ★★★ Good, but not great, science-fiction film about a superintelligent computer designed by scientist Fritz Weaver to solve problems beyond the scope of man. The computer, however, has other ideas. Weaver's wife (Julie Christie) becomes its unwilling guinea pig and, eventually, mate. Rated R. 94m. **DIR:** Donald Cammell. **CAST:** Julie Christie, Fritz Weaver, Gerrit Graham. **1977**

DESERT WARRIOR 🦃 After World War III, two warring factions fight for dominance. Rated PG-13 for violence and nudity. 89m. **DIR:** Jim Goldman. **CAST:** Lou Ferrigno, Shari Shattuck. **1988**

DESTINATION MOON ★★★½ This story involves the first American spaceship to land on the moon. Even though the sets are dated today, they were what scientists expected to find when people did land on the moon. This film boasts the classic pointed spaceship and bubble helmets on the space travelers, but it is still great fun for fans of the genre. Rated PG-13. 99m. **DIR:** Irving Pichel. **CAST:** Warner Anderson, John Archer, Tom Powers, Dick Wesson. **1950**

DINOSAUR ISLAND 🦃 Extremely low-budget effort uses rubber prehistoric beasts to get women out of their clothes. Absolutely horrid. Rated R for nudity and violence. 85m. **DIR:** Jim Wynorski, Fred Olen Ray. **CAST:** Ross Hagen, Richard Gabi, Antonia Dorian, Toni Naples. **1994**

DOC SAVAGE...THE MAN OF BRONZE ★★★ Perfectly acceptable—although campy—first appearance by the famed hero of pulp novels, Doc Savage. Ron Ely makes a suitable Savage, complete with torn shirt and deadpan delivery. Special effects and set design are minimal, a true shame since this is the last film produced by science-fiction pioneer George Pal. Rated PG—some violence. 100m. **DIR:** Michael Anderson. **CAST:** Ron Ely, Pamela Hensley, Darrell Zwerling, Michael Miller, Paul Gleason. **1975**

DOCTOR MORDRID ★★★½ Jeffrey Combs is Doctor Mordrid, a sorcerer biding his time in a New York brownstone. He keeps watch over the portal to another dimension, a dimension that is reigned over by his mortal enemy. Fanciful special effects. Rated R for violence and nudity. 102m. **DIR:** Albert Band, Charles Band. **CAST:** Jeffrey Combs, Yvette Nipar, Brian Thompson, Jay Acovone. **1992**

DR. STRANGE ★★ Another Marvel Comics superhero comes to life. Dr. Strange is chosen by the guardian of the spirit world to protect Earth from the evil villainess who is set on invading. The adventures of our hero are high on magic and sorcery for a fair rendition of the comic-book hero. 94m. **DIR:** Philip DeGuere. **CAST:** Peter Hooten, Clyde Kusatsu, Jessica Walter, Eddie Benton, John Mills. **1978**

DR. WHO AND THE DALEKS ★★★ In this feature film derived from—but not faithful to—the long-running BBC television series, an eccentric old scientist (Peter Cushing) takes his friends on a trip through space and time. They end up on a planet that has been devastated by nuclear war and must help a peace-loving people fight the Daleks, a race of war-mongering mutants who have encased their fragile bodies in robot shells. This juvenile science-fiction adventure should please youngsters. Rated G. 83m. **DIR:** Gordon Flemyng. **CAST:** Peter Cushing, Roy Castle, Jennie Linden, Barrie Ingham. **1965**

DR. WHO: REVENGE OF THE CYBERMEN ★★★ This is the first video from the popular British TV series and stars the fourth Dr. Who, Tom Baker. In this film, the evil Cybermen attempt to destroy the planet Voga, which is made of solid gold, the only item that can kill them. A good introduction to *Dr. Who*, the longest-running science-fiction TV series. 92m. **DIR:** Michael E. Briant. **CAST:** Tom Baker, Elizabeth Sladen. **1986**

DOG SOLDIER: SHADOWS OF THE PAST ★★ Japanese animation. A troubled ex-Green Beret and his buddy are enlisted by the government to take on a supervillain who has stolen a virus with a potential for biological warfare. Only for die-hard animation fans. In Japanese with English subtitles. Unrated; contains violence. 45m. **DIR:** Hiroyuki Ebata. **1989**

DOG STAR MAN ★★★★ An abstract vision of the creation of the universe—an epic work consisting of a prelude and four parts, making brilliant use of superimpositions, painting on film, distorting lenses, and rhythmic montage. This feature makes for hypnotic experimenting in silent filmmaking. 78m. **DIR:** Stan Brakhage. **1964**

DOLLMAN ★★½ Futuristic cop chases a suspect through a time warp, crash landing on present-day Earth, where the bigger-than-life hero finds himself only thirteen inches tall—but with an attitude. The carnage that permeates this film is vicious. Rated R for violence. 87m. **DIR:** Albert Pyun. **CAST:** Tim Thomerson, Jackie Earle Haley, Nicholas Guest. **1991**

DOLLMAN VS. DEMONIC TOYS ★★ In this high-concept, low-budget jumble, several drive-in regulars meet for one final, lackluster showdown. Dollman (Tim Thomerson) teams up with Tracy Scoggins and shrunken nurse Melissa Behr (so reduced in *Bad Channels*) to fight possessed toys. Rated R for violence, language, and brief nudity. 84m. **DIR:** Charles Band. **CAST:** Tim Thomerson, Tracy Scoggins, Melissa Behr, Phil Brock, Phil Fondacaro. **1993**

DONOVAN'S BRAIN ★★★ After his death in a plane crash, a powerful business magnate has his brain removed by a research scientist (Lew Ayres) who hopes to communicate with the organ by feeding it electricity. Before you know it, the brain is in control, forcing the doctor to obey its ever-increasing demands. Credible acting and tight pacing. B&W; 83m. **DIR:** Felix Feist. **CAST:** Lew Ayres, Nancy Davis, Gene Evans, Steve Brodie. **1953**

DOOMWATCH ★★½ Sci-fi for the *Masterpiece Theatre* crowd, with plenty of British reserve. A scientist aids the army in investigating an island where pollution has turned the population into mutants. Thoughtful, though not very scary. Based on a BBC miniseries. Unrated. 92m. **DIR:** Peter Sasdy. **CAST:** George Sanders, Ian Bannen, Judy Geeson. **1972**

DRAGONSLAYER ★★½ Peter MacNicol plays a sorcerer's apprentice who, to save a damsel in distress, must face a fearsome fire-breathing dragon. While the special effects are spectacular, the rest of the film doesn't quite live up to them. It's slow, and often too corny for older viewers. Rated PG for violence. 110m. **DIR:** Matthew Robbins. **CAST:** Peter MacNicol, Caitlin Clarke, Ralph Richardson. **1981**

DREAMCHILD ★★★★ Some of those familiar with *Alice's Adventures in Wonderland* may be surprised to learn that there was a real Alice. Author Lewis Carroll first told his fanciful stories to 10-year-old Alice Liddel on a summer boat ride down the River Isis on July 1, 1862. In 1932, at the age of 80, Alice went to New York City to participate in a Columbia University tribute to Carroll. From these facts, director Gavin Millar and writer Dennis Potter have fashioned this rich and thought-provoking film. Rated PG. 94m. **DIR:** Gavin Millar. **CAST:** Coral Browne, Peter Gallagher, Ian Holm, Jane Asher, Nicola Cowper. **1986**

DREAMS COME TRUE 🦃 A restless young factory worker meets a young woman with whom he shares an unusual power, the ability to control and live in their dreams. Rated R. 95m. **DIR:** Max Kalmanowicz. **CAST:** Michael Sanville, Stephanie Shuford. **1984**

DREAMSCAPE ★★★★ If you can go along with its intriguing but farfetched premise—that trained psychics can enter other people's nightmares and put an end to them—this film will reward you with top-flight special effects, thrills, chills, and surprises. Rated PG-13 for suggested sex, violence, and profanity. 99m. **DIR:** Joseph Ruben. **CAST:** Dennis Quaid, Max von Sydow, Christopher Plummer, Eddie Albert, Kate Capshaw. **1984**

DUNE 🦃 The only good thing about the movie version of *Dune* is it makes one want to read (or reread) the book. Otherwise, it's a $47 million mess. Rated PG-13 for gore, suggested sex, and violence. 145m. **DIR:** David Lynch. **CAST:** Sting, Kyle MacLachlan, Max von Sydow, Jurgen Prochnow, Sean Young, Kenneth McMillan, Richard Jordan. **1984**

DUNGEONMASTER, THE 🦃 It's corny, it's bad, it's simplistic. Rated PG-13 for mild violence. 73m. **DIR:** Rosemarie Turko, John Carl Buechler, Charles Band, David Allen, Steve Ford, Peter Manoogian, Ted Nic. **CAST:** Jeffrey Byron, Richard Moll. **1985**

E.T.—THE EXTRA-TERRESTRIAL ★★★★★ The most entertaining science-fiction film of all time, this is Steven Spielberg's gentle fairy tale about what happens when a young boy meets up with a very special fellow from outer space. Sheer wonder is joined with warmth and humor in this movie classic. Rated PG. 115m. **DIR:** Steven Spielberg. **CAST:** Dee Wallace, Henry Thomas, Peter Coyote, Robert MacNaughton, Drew Barrymore. **1982**

EARTH VS. THE FLYING SAUCERS ★★★★ Stunning special effects by Ray Harryhausen enhance this familiar 1950s plot about an invasion from outer space. After misinterpreting a message for peace from the initially easygoing aliens, the military opens fire—and then all hell breaks loose! B&W; 83m. **DIR:** Fred F. Sears. **CAST:** Hugh Marlowe, Joan Taylor, Donald Curtis, Morris Ankrum. **1956**

EARTH VS. THE SPIDER ★★ A giant spider invades a mountain community in this American-International rip-off of Jack Arnold's *Tarantula*. Special effects are so-so; one of Bert I. Gordon's more tolerable time wasters. B&W; 72m. **DIR:** Bert I. Gordon. **CAST:** Ed Kemmer, June Kenney, Gene Roth. **1958**

EAT AND RUN 🦃 This science-fiction spoof is about a four-hundred pound alien named Murry Creature. Rated R for nudity. 85m. **DIR:** Christopher Hunt. **CAST:** Ron Silver, R. L. Ryan. **1986**

EDWARD SCISSORHANDS ★★★ A mean-spirited, violent ending irrevocably mars what might have been a charming fantasy. Through the character of Edward Scissorhands (Johnny Depp), a sweet-natured android whose exposure to civilization is anything but pleasant, cowriter-director Tim Burton seems to be exorcising the pain of his own adolescence. Rated PG-13 for violence and profanity. 89m. **DIR:** Tim Burton. **CAST:** Johnny Depp, Winona Ryder, Dianne Wiest, Anthony Michael Hall, Alan Arkin, Vincent Price, Kathy Baker, Conchata Ferrell. **1990**

ELECTRIC GRANDMOTHER, THE ★★★★ Heartwarming TV adaptation of Ray Bradbury's "Sing the Body Electric" features Maureen Stapleton as a loving grandmother hired to raise three motherless children. She has some rather magical powers and only one drawback: she must be plugged in each night in order to recharge. 35m. **DIR:** Noel Black. **CAST:** Maureen Stapleton, Edward Herrmann. **1981**

ELIMINATORS, THE 🦃 A mad scientist creates the perfect weapon, the "Mandroid". Rated PG. 95m. **DIR:** Peter Manoogian. **CAST:** Andrew Prine, Denise Crosby, Patrick Reynolds, Roy Dotrice. **1986**

EMBRYO ★★½ Rock Hudson plays a scientist who succeeds in developing a fetus into a full-grown woman in record time. But something isn't quite right. Adequate thriller with a good ending. Rated PG. 104m. **DIR:** Ralph Nelson. **CAST:** Rock Hudson, Barbara Carrera, Diane Ladd. 1976

EMPIRE OF THE ANTS 🦃 H. G. Wells must somersault in his grave every time somebody watches this insulting adaptation of one of his more intriguing sci-fi stories. Rated PG for violence. 90m. **DIR:** Bert I. Gordon. **CAST:** Joan Collins, Robert Lansing, Albert Salmi, Robert Pine. 1977

EMPIRE STRIKES BACK, THE ★★★★★ In George Lucas's follow-up to *Star Wars*, Billy Dee Williams joins Mark Hamill (Luke Skywalker), Harrison Ford (Han Solo), Carrie Fisher (Princess Leia), and the gang in their fight against the forces of the Empire led by Darth Vader. It's more action-packed fun in that faraway galaxy a long time ago. Rated PG. 124m. **DIR:** Irvin Kershner. **CAST:** Billy Dee Williams, Harrison Ford, Carrie Fisher, Mark Hamill, Anthony Daniels, Dave Prowse, James Earl Jones (voice). 1980

ENCOUNTER AT RAVEN'S GATE ★★★½ A small Australian town is stricken by unusual occurrences: electrical faults, violent and psychotic human behavior. Solid acting, vivid characterizations, a refreshing atmosphere of alternative cinema, and a sedately haunting sound track make this one worth a watch. Rated R for violence. 85m. **DIR:** Rolf Deheer. **CAST:** Ritchie Singer, Steven Vidler, Vincent Gil, Saturday Rosenberg. 1988

ENCOUNTER WITH THE UNKNOWN ★★★½ Rod Serling narrates a series of true events in psychic phenomena. The episodes are based on studies made by Dr. Jonathan Rankin between 1949 and 1970. Each deals with a person's encounter with the unknown or supernatural. Rated PG. 90m. **DIR:** Harry Thomason. **CAST:** Rod Serling, Rosie Holotik, Gene Ross. 1973

END OF THE WORLD 🦃 Aliens plot to destroy the Earth while disguised as religious figures. Rated PG. 87m. **DIR:** John Hayes. **CAST:** Christopher Lee, Sue Lyon, Lew Ayres, Dean Jagger, Macdonald Carey. 1977

ENDANGERED SPECIES ★★★½ Everything about this nifty science-fiction suspense-thriller is well-done. The story deals with bizarre incidents involving cattle mutilation and is based on fact. In it, a country sheriff (JoBeth Williams) and a hard-boiled New York detective (Robert Urich) join forces to find out who or what is responsible. Rated R for discreetly handled nudity, violence, and profanity. 97m. **DIR:** Alan Rudolph. **CAST:** Robert Urich, JoBeth Williams, Paul Dooley, Hoyt Axton. 1982

ENDGAME 🦃 Mutants communicate via telepathy. Equivalent of a PG-13 for violence and partial nudity. 98m. **DIR:** Steven Benson. **CAST:** Al Cliver, Moira Chen, George Eastman, Gordon Mitchell. 1985

ENEMY FROM SPACE ★★★★ Brian Donlevy makes his second appearance as Professor Quatermass, a scientist hero who discovers that aliens are slowly taking over the governments of Earth—starting with Britain. It's an uncommonly powerful film. The first entry in the theatrical trilogy was *The Creeping Unknown* and the last was *Five Million Years to Earth*. B&W; 85m. **DIR:** Val Guest. **CAST:** Brian Donlevy, William Franklyn. 1957

ENEMY MINE ★★ A would-be outer-space epic. Two futuristic foes, an Earthman (Dennis Quaid) and a reptilian alien (Louis Gossett Jr.), are stranded on a hostile planet and forced to rely on each other for survival. Rated PG-13 for violence and profanity. 108m. **DIR:** Wolfgang Petersen. **CAST:** Dennis Quaid, Lou Gossett Jr., Brion James, Richard Marcus, Lance Kerwin. 1985

ERIK THE VIKING ★★★ The first half hour of this account of the exploits of Erik the Red is so awful, one is tempted to hit the reject button. However, perseverance pays off in this movie from ex-Monty Python crazy Terry Jones. It actually gets to be fun. Rated PG-13 for profanity and suggested sex. 106m. **DIR:** Terry Jones. **CAST:** Tim Robbins, Mickey Rooney, Eartha Kitt, Terry Jones, Imogen Stubbs, John Cleese, Antony Sher. 1989

ESCAPE FROM SAFEHAVEN 🦃 Futuristic film about a family that is terrorized by a ruthless government. Rated R. 87m. **DIR:** Brian Thomas Jones, James McCalmont. **CAST:** Rick Gianasi. 1988

ESCAPE FROM THE PLANET OF THE APES ★★★ Escaping the nuclear destruction of their own world and time, intelligent simians Roddy McDowall and Kim Hunter arrive on ours. This third *Apes* entry makes wonderful use of the *Strangers in a Strange Land* theme, which turns ugly all too quickly as humanity decides to destroy the apes. Rated PG for violence. 98m. **DIR:** Don Taylor. **CAST:** Roddy McDowall, Kim Hunter, Eric Braeden, Bradford Dillman, William Windom, Ricardo Montalban. 1971

ESCAPE 2000 🦃 A nauseating science-fiction film from Britain, this consists of a series of close-ups of people in the throes of death. Rated R. 92m. **DIR:** Brian Trenchard-Smith. **CAST:** Steve Railsback, Olivia Hussey, Michael Craig, Carmen Duncan, Roger Ward. 1981

ESCAPES ★★★ Low-budget anthology in the *Twilight Zone* vein, featuring six stories of the bizarre and done with great style by director David Steensland. Top honors go to "A Little Fishy," a grimly funny tale, and "Who's There?" a neat yarn about an escaped laboratory experiment and a Sunday jogger. 71m. **DIR:** David Steensland. **CAST:** Vincent Price, Michael Patton-Hall, John Mitchum, Todd Fulton, Jerry Grisham, Ken Thorley. **1985**

EVE OF DESTRUCTION 🦃 Gregory Hines is a counterinsurgency expert battling a state-of-the-art female robot. Rated R for violence, nudity, and profanity. 90m. **DIR:** Duncan Gibbins. **CAST:** Gregory Hines, Renee Soutendijk, Michael Greene. **1991**

EXCALIBUR ★★★★ Swords cross and magic abounds in this spectacular, highly enjoyable version of the Arthurian legend. A gritty, realistic view of the rise to power of King Arthur, the forbidden love of Queen Guinevere and Sir Lancelot and the quest of the Knights of the Round Table for the Holy Grail. *Excalibur* is highlighted by lush photography and fine performances. Rated R. 140m. **DIR:** John Boorman. **CAST:** Nicol Williamson, Nigel Terry, Helen Mirren, Nicholas Clay, Cherie Lunghi, Corin Redgrave, Paul Geoffrey. **1981**

EXPERIMENTAL FILMS OF MAYA DEREN VOL. I ★★★★★ From the early 1940s until her death in 1961 Maya Deren exemplified the American avant-garde film movement. This compilation of her fantasy film shorts, considered to be some of the finest examples of independent moviemaking, is reminiscent of other great film surrealists such as Luis Buñuel, Jean Cocteau, and René Clair. This collection contains *Meshes of the Afternoon, At Land, A Study in Choreography for Camera, Ritual in Transfigured Time, Meditation on Violence,* and *The Very Eye of Night.* Not rated. B&W; 76m. **DIR:** Maya Deren. **CAST:** None Credited.

EXPLORERS ★★★½ The young and the young at heart are certain to have a grand time watching *Explorers.* It's a just-for-fun fantasy about three kids (Ethan Hawke, River Phoenix, and Jason Presson) taking off on the greatest adventure of all: a journey through outer space. Rated PG for minor violence and light profanity. 109m. **DIR:** Joe Dante. **CAST:** Ethan Hawke, River Phoenix, Jason Presson, Dick Miller, Robert Picardo. **1985**

EXTERMINATORS OF THE YEAR 3000 🦃 This one rips off George Miller's *The Road Warrior* almost to the letter. Rated R for violence and profanity. 101m. **DIR:** Jules Harrison. **CAST:** Robert Jannucci, Alicia Moro, Alan Collins, Fred Harris, Beryl Cunningham, Luca Venantini. **1983**

EYES BEHIND THE STARS 🦃 A reporter and a UFO specialist investigate reports that extraterrestrial beings have landed on Earth. Unrated. 95m. **DIR:** Roy Garrett. **CAST:** Robert Hoffman, Nathalie Delon, Martin Balsam. **1972**

FAHRENHEIT 451 ★★★★ Still the best adaptation of a Ray Bradbury book to hit the screen (big or small). Oskar Werner is properly troubled as a futuristic "fireman" responsible for the destruction of books, who begins to wonder about the necessity of his work. This is director François Truffaut's first English-language film, and he treats the subject of language and literature with a dignity not found in most American films. Unrated—family fare. 111m. **DIR:** François Truffaut. **CAST:** Oskar Werner, Julie Christie, Cyril Cusack, Anton Diffring. **1967**

FANTASTIC PLANET ★★★ This French-Czechoslovakian production is an animated metaphor concerning the class struggles—and, eventually, war—between two races on an alien planet. Lovely animation and a non-preachy approach to the story combine to produce a fine little film that makes its points and sticks in the memory. Short, but sincere and effective. Voices of Barry Bostwick, Nora Heflin. Rated PG—intense subject matter and some violence. 71m. **DIR:** René Laloux. **CAST:** Animated. **1973**

FANTASTIC VOYAGE ★★★ Scientists journey into inner space—the human body—by being shrunk to microscopic size. They then are threatened by the system's natural defenses. This Richard Fleischer film still packs an unusually potent punch. 100m. **DIR:** Richard Fleischer. **CAST:** Stephen Boyd, Raquel Welch, Edmond O'Brien, Donald Pleasence, Arthur O'Connell, William Redfield, Arthur Kennedy. **1966**

FANTASY ISLAND ★★½ Dreams and fantasies come true and then some on a mysterious millionaire's island paradise in this sub-average TV-er that spawned the hit series. Yawn. 100m. **DIR:** Richard Lang. **CAST:** Ricardo Montalban, Bill Bixby, Sandra Dee, Peter Lawford, Carol Lynley, Hugh O'Brian. **1977**

FIELD OF DREAMS ★★★★★ A must-see motion picture, this spirit-lifting work stars Kevin Costner as an Iowa farmer who hears a voice telling him to build a baseball diamond in the middle of his cornfield. Against all common sense, he does so and sets in motion a chain of wonderful events. Costner gets strong support from Amy Madigan, Burt Lancaster, James Earl Jones, and Ray Liotta in this all-ages delight adapted from the novel, *Shoeless Joe,* by W. P. Kinsella. Rated PG for brief profanity. 106m. **DIR:** Phil Alden Robinson. **CAST:** Kevin Costner, Amy Madigan, James Earl Jones, Burt Lancaster, Ray Liotta, Timothy Busfield. **1989**

FILMS OF JAMES BROUGHTON, THE ★★★★ The collected works of celebrated poet-filmmaker James Broughton can be best described as a celebration of life where eroticism and mysticism embrace in the garden of earthly delights. Featuring his 1968 masterpiece *The Bed* and the comic fantasy *The Pleasure Garden,* which won a prize for poetic fantasy at the Cannes Film Festival in 1954. A five-volume tape set. Not rated, but contains nudity and simulated sex.

B&W/color; 246m. **DIR:** James Broughton. **CAST:** James Broughton. **1950–1979**

FINAL APPROACH ★★ Confusing, muddled sci-fi entry has test pilot James B. Sikking trying to recall the moments before a fateful crash. Virtual reality effects are film's only saving grace, which attempts to surprise viewers with a twist ending, but one that comes too little, too late. Rated PG-13. 101m. **DIR:** Eric Steven Stahl. **CAST:** James B. Sikking, Hector Elizondo, Madolyn Smith, Kevin McCarthy. **1992**

FINAL COUNTDOWN, THE ★★½ Farfetched but passable story about an aircraft carrier traveling backward in time to just before the start of World War II. The crew must then decide whether or not to change the course of history. Some good special effects and performances by the leads manage to keep this one afloat. Rated PG. 104m. **DIR:** Don Taylor. **CAST:** Kirk Douglas, Martin Sheen, Katharine Ross. **1980**

FINAL EXECUTIONER, THE 🦃 Following a nuclear holocaust, a small undamaged elite hunt down the contaminated human leftovers. Not rated, but contains violence and sex. 95m. **DIR:** Romolo Guerrieri. **CAST:** William Mang, Marina Costa, Harrison Muller, Woody Strode. **1983**

FIRE AND ICE (1983) ★★★★ This animated film is geared more to adults than children. Sword-and-sorcery fantasy keeps the action moving. The plot begins with evil sorcerer Nekron planning world domination. It thickens when he kidnaps the princess, Teegra, to force her father to turn his kingdom over to him as his daughter's ransom. Rated PG. 81m. **DIR:** Ralph Bakshi. **1983**

FIRE AND SWORD 🦃 Tristan and Isolde. Not rated, but contains violence and nudity. 84m. **DIR:** Vieth von Furstenburg. **CAST:** Christopher Waltz, Antonia Presser, Peter Firth, Leigh Lawson. **1985**

FIRE IN THE SKY ★★ UFO buffs might get a lift out of this dramatization of the alleged abduction of Travis Walton (D. B. Sweeney) in 1975, but most viewers will be disappointed. Rated PG-13 for profanity and nudity. 110m. **DIR:** Robert Lieberman. **CAST:** D. B. Sweeney, Robert Patrick, James Garner, Craig Sheffer, Peter Berg, Henry Thomas, Noble Willingham, Kathleen Wilhoite. **1993**

FIRE NEXT TIME, THE ★★★ Preachy futuristic disaster film repeatedly delivers a heavy-handed environmental message. Due to global warming, coastal towns are flooding while plains dry up. Amidst this, Craig T. Nelson tries to reunite his estranged family. Unbelievable plot twists and occasional lectures weaken the film's effectiveness. Unrated; contains profanity and suggestive comments. 180m. **DIR:** Tom McLoughlin. **CAST:** Craig T. Nelson, Bonnie Bedelia, Richard Farnsworth, Jurgen Prochnow. **1992**

FIREBIRD 2015 AD 🦃 In the near future, gas is so scarce that the government outlaws private ownership of automobiles and sets up an agency to destroy them. Rated PG. 97m. **DIR:** David Robertson. **CAST:** Darren McGavin, Doug McClure, George Touliatos. **1981**

FIRST MAN INTO SPACE, THE ★★½ An arrogant test pilot is mutated, by cosmic rays, into a blood-hungry monster. Although it's dated and scientifically incorrect, this sci-fi chiller still has some B-film fun. Not rated, but suitable for all viewers. B&W; 78m. **DIR:** Robert Day. **CAST:** Marshall Thompson. **1958**

FIRST MEN *IN* THE MOON ★★★½ This whimsical adaptation of an H. G. Wells novel benefits greatly from the imaginative genius of Ray Harryhausen, who concocts the critters—stop-motion and otherwise—which menace some turn-of-the-century lunar explorers who arrive via a Victorian-era spaceship. Although the tone is initially tongue-in-cheek, this adventurous plot eventually develops some rather chilling teeth. Great fun for the entire family. 103m. **DIR:** Nathan Juran. **CAST:** Edward Judd, Martha Hyer, Lionel Jeffries, Peter Finch. **1964**

FIRST SPACESHIP ON VENUS 🦃 Low-budget, lackluster German science fiction plants an international crew of astronauts on Venus. 78m. **DIR:** Kurt Maetzig. **CAST:** Yoko Tani. **1960**

FISHER KING, THE ★★★★½ Jeff Bridges is Jack Lucas, a radio talk host whose irreverent manner indirectly causes a tragedy and remorse that plunges him into an alcoholic haze. Enter a street person named Parry (Robin Williams), who involves Jack in a quest for the Holy Grail in New York City. That madman of the movies, Terry Gilliam, has created another adult-oriented fairy tale that will win the hearts of those who haven't lost their sense of wonder. Rated R for profanity, nudity, and violence. 137m. **DIR:** Terry Gilliam. **CAST:** Robin Williams, Jeff Bridges, Mercedes Ruehl, Amanda Plummer, Michael Jeter. **1991**

FIST OF THE NORTH STAR ★★½ Japanese animation. Extreme violence is the main plot ingredient in this animated post-apocalyptic kung fu epic wherein a trio of brothers vie for the title of "Fist of the North Star." Released in some U.S. theatrical markets, probably because of the unrivaled spectacle of animated carnage. 110m. **DIR:** Toyoo Ashida. **1986**

FLASH, THE ★★★★ When police scientist Barry Allen is doused in chemicals during a freak thunderstorm, he's transformed into the fastest man alive. And just in time to avenge his brother's murder and save Central City from a bloodthirsty gang of bikers, called the Dark Riders. This TV movie is one of the few times a comic book has translated well to film. 94m. **DIR:** Robert Iscove. **CAST:** John Wesley Shipp, Amanda Pays, Michael Nader, Tim Thomerson. **1990**

FLASH GORDON ★★★½ If you don't take it seriously, this campy film based on the classic Alex Raymond comic strip of the 1930s is a real hoot. Sam Jones, as Flash, and Melody Anderson, as Dale Arden, race through the intentionally hokey special effects to do battle with Max von Sydow, who makes an excellent Ming the Merciless. Rated PG. 110m. **DIR:** Mike Hodges. **CAST:** Sam Jones, Topol, Max von Sydow, Melody Anderson, Timothy Dalton. **1980**

FLASH GORDON CONQUERS THE UNIVERSE ★★★ The third and last of Universal's landmark Flash Gordon serials finds the Earth in jeopardy again as Ming the Merciless spreads an epidemic known as the Plague of the Purple Death in yet another attempt to rule the universe. Not as ingenious or spectacular as the original, this serial was still a strong competitor in that great period from 1937 to 1945 when the chapterplay market was important. B&W; 12 chapters. **DIR:** Ford Beebe, Ray Taylor. **CAST:** Buster Crabbe, Carol Hughes, Charles Middleton, Frank Shannon, Lee Powell. **1940**

FLASH GORDON: MARS ATTACKS THE WORLD (A.K.A. TRIP TO MARS; DEADLY RAY FROM MARS, THE) ★★½ In this edited version of the second Flash Gordon serial, Buster Crabbe and the gang head out to Mars to put a halt to a ray that is drawing nitrogen away from the Earth. Of course, Ming the Merciless is behind it all. Hokey but fun, even trimmed of almost half its running time, this space romp from simpler times is worth a watch just for the character acting, including Charles Middleton as the greatest of all serial scoundrels. B&W; 99m. **DIR:** Ford Beebe, Robert Hill. **CAST:** Buster Crabbe, Jean Rogers, Charles Middleton, Frank Shannon. **1938**

FLASH GORDON: ROCKETSHIP (A.K.A. SPACESHIP TO THE UNKNOWN; PERILS FROM PLANET MONGO) ★★★ This original feature version of the first *Flash Gordon* serial is one of the best reedited chapterplays ever released. Boyish Buster Crabbe is the perfect Flash Gordon; Jean Rogers is one of the loveliest of all serial queens; and classic character heavy Charles Middleton becomes the embodiment of malevolent villainy as the infamous Ming the Merciless. B&W; 97m. **DIR:** Frederick Stephani. **CAST:** Buster Crabbe, Jean Rogers, Frank Shannon, Charles Middleton, Priscilla Lawson. **1936**

FLESH GORDON ★★½ Porno version of the famed serial *Flash Gordon*, this fitfully amusing parody's main point of interest is the often excellent miniature work and dimensional animation by Jim Danforth and other special-effects pros. The story, about a sex ray aimed at Earth by Emperor Wang of the planet Porno, is obvious and amateurish. Rated X for nudity, language, and overall content. 70m. **DIR:** Howard Ziehm, Michael Benveniste. **CAST:** Jason Williams, Suzanne Fields, John Hoyt. **1974**

FLESH GORDON 2: FLESH GORDON MEETS THE COSMIC CHEERLEADERS ★★★ Believe it or not, imaginative and surprisingly good set design make this overtly tasteless sequel entertaining. Flesh is kidnapped by a group of cosmic cheerleaders and taken to their home planet where an evil villain has sapped the collective libido of the male population. Filled with gratuitous nudity and bad jokes, this one is not for everybody. Two versions are available, an R-rated and an unrated, both with nudity and sexual situations. 101m. **DIR:** Howard Ziehm. **CAST:** Vince Murdocco, Robyn Kelly, Tony Travis, Morgan Fox. **1993**

FLIGHT OF THE NAVIGATOR ★★★ This all-ages Disney delight concerns a youngster (Joey Kramer) who has the unique ability to communicate with machines and uses this to help a UFO find its way home. Kids will love its crazy creatures, special effects, and action-packed conclusion, while parents will appreciate its nice balance of sense and nonsense. Rated PG for mild cussing. 90m. **DIR:** Randal Kleiser. **CAST:** Joey Kramer, Veronica Cartwright, Cliff De Young, Sarah Jessica Parker, Howard Hesseman, Matt Adler. **1986**

FLIGHT TO MARS ★★½ Scientists and newsmen crash on Mars during a space voyage and discover a race of humans living beneath the surface of the planet. Although slow, a fairly effective plea for international and intergalactic harmony. 72m. **DIR:** Lesley Selander. **CAST:** Cameron Mitchell, Arthur Franz, Marguerite Chapman, Morris Ankrum, John Litel, Virginia Huston. **1951**

FLYING SAUCER, THE 🦃 American agent sent to Alaska to investigate a report of an unidentified flying object. B&W; 69m. **DIR:** Mikel Conrad. **CAST:** Mikel Conrad, Denver Pyle, Russell Hicks. **1950**

FOOD OF THE GODS 🦃 H. G. Wells's story is thrashed in this Bert I. Gordon bomb. After ingesting an unknown substance, various animals become giant and threaten the occupants of a remote mountain cabin. Rated PG. 88m. **DIR:** Bert I. Gordon. **CAST:** Marjoe Gortner, Ida Lupino, Pamela Franklin, Ralph Meeker. **1976**

FOOD OF THE GODS PART II 🦃 Disgusting sequel. Rated R for violence, profanity, and nudity. 90m. **DIR:** Damien Lee. **CAST:** Paul Coufos. **1989**

FORBIDDEN PLANET ★★★★½ This is the most highly regarded sci-fi film of the

1950s. Its special-effects breakthroughs are rather tame today, but its story remains interesting. As a space mission from Earth lands on the Planet Altair-4 in the year 2200, they encounter a doctor (Walter Pidgeon) and his daughter (Anne Francis) who are all that remain from a previous colonization attempt. It soon becomes apparent that some unseen force on the planet does not bid them welcome. 98m. **DIR:** Fred M. Wilcox. **CAST:** Walter Pidgeon, Anne Francis, Leslie Nielsen, Jack Kelly. **1956**

FORBIDDEN ZONE 💔 Absurd, would-be "cult" film has Herve Villechaize as the ruler of a bizarre kingdom located in the "Sixth Dimension." A sort-of comedy, this should be avoided by all means. Rated R for nudity and adult content. B&W; 76m. **DIR:** Richard Elfman. **CAST:** Herve Villechaize, Susan Tyrrell, Marie-Pascale Elfman, Viva. **1980**

FOREVER YOUNG (1992) ★★★ In a charming performance, Mel Gibson plays a test pilot who has himself cryogenically frozen in 1939 only to wake up in 1992—alone. Gibson and his costars give this piece of fluff a buoyancy. Rated PG for profanity. 104m. **DIR:** Steve Miner. **CAST:** Mel Gibson, Jamie Lee Curtis, Elijah Wood, Isabel Glasser, Joe Morton, David Marshall Grant. **1993**

FORTRESS (1993) ★★½ Grim science-fiction thriller about a married couple thrown into a monstrous, underground prison for having a second child. Inmates are controlled by small explosive devices that are blasted into the digestive system via the throat. The couple must escape before their baby is delivered and turned into a "kidbot" that is half human and half gadgetry. Another cultish, ghoulish, deadpan joke from the maker of *Re-Animator*. Rated R for violence and profanity. 92m. **DIR:** Stuart Gordon. **CAST:** Christopher Lambert, Loryn Locklin, Kurtwood Smith. **1993**

4D MAN ★★★ A scientist (Robert Lansing) learns of a method of moving through objects (walls, doors, bank vaults, etc.), without realizing the terrible consequences, which eventually lead to madness and murder. Eerie sci-fi film hampered only by often brash music. From the director of *The Blob*. 85m. **DIR:** Irvin S. Yeaworth Jr. **CAST:** Robert Lansing, Lee Meriwether, James Congdon, Robert Strauss, Patty Duke. **1959**

FREEJACK ★★★ Technology in the year 2009, when the haves have more and the have-nots are destitute, has made it possible for the ultrarich to extend their lives—by finding a donor from the past. Emilio Estevez is the race-car driver who, after a spectacular crash, wakes up to find himself eighteen years in the future and runnng from those who want to erase his mind. It's not great, but not bad. Rated R for violence and profanity. 101m. **DIR:** Geoff Murphy. **CAST:** Emilio Estevez, Mick Jagger, René Russo, Anthony Hopkins, Jonathan Banks, David Johansen. **1992**

FROM THE EARTH TO THE MOON ★★★ Entertaining tale based on Jules Verne's story of a turn-of-the-century trip to the Moon led by Joseph Cotten and sabotaged by George Sanders. 100m. **DIR:** Byron Haskin. **CAST:** Joseph Cotten, George Sanders, Debra Paget, Don Dubbins. **1958**

FUTURE SHOCK ★★ In this hit-or-miss episodic thriller, three patients face their worst fears when doctor Martin Kove subjects them to virtual-reality therapy. The best bit features Bill Paxton as a roommate from hell. Rated PG-13 for violence and sexual situations. 93m. **DIR:** Eric Parkinson. **CAST:** Vivian Schilling, Martin Kove, Scott Thompson, Brion James, Bill Paxton. **1993**

FUTUREKICK 💔 A kung fu kick-boxing mystery set in a bleak futuristic technocratic society. Low-budget rip-off. Rated R for nudity, profanity, and violence. 80m. **DIR:** Damian Klaus. **CAST:** Meg Foster, Christopher Penn, Eb Lottimer. **1991**

FUTUREWORLD ★★★ An amusement park of the future caters to any adult fantasy. Lifelike androids carry out your every whim. A fun place, right? Not so, as reporter Peter Fonda finds out in this sequel to *Westworld*. This is okay escapist fare. Rated PG. 104m. **DIR:** Richard T. Heffron. **CAST:** Peter Fonda, Blythe Danner, Arthur Hill, Yul Brynner, Stuart Margolin, John P. Ryan. **1976**

GALAXINA ★★ See Captain Cornelius Butt (Avery Schreiber), of the spaceship *Infinity*, consume a raw egg and regurgitate a rubbery creature that later calls him "Mommy." Visit an intergalactic saloon that serves humans (they're on the menu, not the guest list). Low-budget space spoof. Rated R. 95m. **DIR:** William Sachs. **CAST:** Avery Schreiber, Dorothy Stratten, Stephen Macht. **1980**

GALAXY OF TERROR ★★½ In this movie, which was also known as *Planet of Horrors*, the crew of a spaceship sent to rescue a crash survivor finds itself facing one horror after another on a barren planet. This chiller wastes no time in getting to the thrills. Rated R because of profanity, nudity, and violence. 82m. **DIR:** B. D. Clark. **CAST:** Erin Moran, Edward Albert, Ray Walston. **1981**

GAMERA THE INVINCIBLE ★★ Typical cheesy Japanese giant-monster movie starring a prehistoric fire-breathing turtle. (It flies, too.) Neither as silly nor as campy as its sequels, this features clumsily spliced-in footage of Albert Dekker and Brian Donlevy that was added for the U.S. market. B&W; 86m. **DIR:** Noriyaki Yuasa. **CAST:** Albert Dekker, Brian Donlevy. **1965**

GAMERA VERSUS BARUGON ★★ In this first sequel, the giant flying turtle becomes a good guy, as he was to remain for the rest of the series. The bad guy, Barugon, is a giant dinosaur. Of course, several Japanese cities are leveled as the two battle, but no problem—civilization was reconstructed in time for the next sequel. 101m. **DIR:** Shigeo Tanaka. **CAST:** Kojiro Hongo. **1966**

GAMERA VERSUS GAOS ★★ Ever the friend of little children, Gamera does his giant flaming Frisbee impression once again to save his little pals from Gaos, another giant monster. Opinion differs as to whether Gaos more closely resembles a bat or a fox, as if it mattered at all to the poor stuntman sweating it out inside that rubber suit. 87m. **DIR:** Noriyaki Yuasa. **CAST:** Kojiro Hongo. **1967**

GAMERA VERSUS GUIRON ★★ Flame on! The twirling turtle battles spearheaded Guiron, an evil giant (of course) monster from outer space. Does Japan have a Ministry of Giant Monsters responsible for naming all these behemoths? 82m. **DIR:** Noriyaki Yuasa. **1969**

GAMERA VERSUS ZIGRA 🦃 Fans of this kind of stuff will be disappointed to note that, in the last of the Gamera movies, the titanic turtle battles a silly Transformer-style swordfish. Some film student should do a paper comparing this with *Godzilla vs. the Smog Monster.* 87m. **DIR:** Noriyaki Yuasa. **CAST:** Reiko Kasahara. **1971**

GAMMA PEOPLE, THE 🦃 Weak science-fiction tale about children being transformed into homicidal monsters or geniuses. B&W; 79m. **DIR:** John Gilling. **CAST:** Paul Douglas, Eva Bartok, Leslie Phillips, Walter Rilla. **1956**

GAS-S-S-S 🦃 A gas accidentally escapes from a chemical company doing military work and everyone in the world over the age of thirty dies, creating a society that is a twisted parody of certain aspects of the destroyed civilization. Rated PG for language and sexual situations. 78m. **DIR:** Roger Corman. **CAST:** Robert Corff, Elaine Giftos, Bud Cort, Ben Vereen, Cindy Williams, Country Joe and the Fish. **1970**

GENESIS SURVIVOR GAIARTH: STAGE 1 ★★★★ Japanese animation. A young man is raised in the wilderness by a "war-roid": an aging, sentient robotic warrior that has been hiding for a hundred years. When his surrogate father is destroyed by a marauder, the boy makes his way to a city where people have forgotten how to defend themselves. In Japanese with English subtitles. Unrated; contains violence and nudity. 51m. **DIR:** Kitazume Hiroyuki, Aramaki Shinji. **1992**

GIANT OF METROPOLIS, THE ★★½ This above-average sword-and-sandal adventure has nothing to do with Fritz Lang's silent classic, *Metropolis*, despite title similarities. Set in 10,000 B.C., it's about a mythical strongman (Gordon Mitchell) who emerges from the desert to battle a sadistic despot. 82m. **DIR:** Umberto Scarpelli. **CAST:** Gordon Mitchell. **1962**

GLEN AND RANDA ★★★ As with all cult films, *Glen and Randa* will not appeal to everyone. The film, at times thought-provoking, is both depressing and satirical. Two young people, Glen (Steve Curry) and Randa (Shelley Plimpton), set out on a search for knowledge across postholocaust America. Rated R for nudity and violence. 94m. **DIR:** Jim McBride. **CAST:** Steven Curry, Shelley Plimpton, Woodrow Chambliss, Garry Goodrow. **1986**

GODZILLA VERSUS BIOLLANTE ★★½ Resurrected after more than a decade and given an A-movie budget, Godzilla is still just a big lug in a green monster suit. This time he battles a giant slime mold. Well-made but overlong. Rated PG for (and we quote the MPAA) "traditional Godzilla violence." 104m. **DIR:** Kazuki Omori. **1989**

GODZILLA VS. THE SMOG MONSTER 🦃 In this ecology-minded disaster flick, the big guy takes on an amorphous, pollution-belching monstrosity spawned by the excesses of industrial waste. 87m. **DIR:** Yoshimitu Banno. **CAST:** Akira Yamauchi. **1972**

GOLDEN VOYAGE OF SINBAD, THE ★★★★ This first-rate Arabian Nights adventure pits Captain Sinbad (John Phillip Law) against the evil Prince Koura (Tom Baker) for possession of a magical amulet with amazing powers. This is a superb fantasy, with some truly incredible effects by master animator Ray Harryhausen. Rated G. 105m. **DIR:** Gordon Hessler. **CAST:** John Phillip Law, Tom Baker, Caroline Munro, Gregoire Aslan, John Garfield Jr. **1974**

GOLDENGIRL 🦃 This modern retread of *Frankenstein* fails on all counts. Rated PG. 104m. **DIR:** Joseph Sargent. **CAST:** Susan Anton, James Coburn, Curt Jurgens, Robert Culp, Leslie Caron, Jessica Walter. **1979**

GOR ★★ A mild-mannered college professor is thrust through time and space to help a simple tribe recover its magical stone in this Conan-inspired sword-and-sorcery flick. Elaborate costumes and sets don't make up for the second-rate story. Rated PG for violence. 95m. **DIR:** Fritz Kiersch. **CAST:** Urbano Barberini, Rebecca Ferratti, Jack Palance, Paul Smith, Oliver Reed. **1987**

GRAND TOUR: DISASTER IN TIME ★★★ Lawrence O'Donnell and C. L. Moore's classic science-fiction novella, *The Vintage Season*, is the basis of this intriguing made-for-cable drama, which finds innkeeper Jeff Daniels rather puzzled over the strange behavior of some new tourists . . . who, for example, clearly don't understand the principle behind tying shoes. Unfortunately, writer-director

David N. Twohy ruins a good thing with his needlessly upbeat conclusion. Rated PG-13. 99m. **DIR:** David N. Twohy. **CAST:** Jeff Daniels, Ariana Richards, Emilia Crow, Jim Haynie. **1992**

GREEN SLIME, THE 🦃 A bit of alien green gluck makes its way onto a space station, multiplies itself into ookie monsters. Laughable, with such poor special effects that no one asked to be listed in the credits. Unrated, but it won't scare the kids. 88m. **DIR:** Kinji Fukasaku. **CAST:** Robert Horton, Richard Jaeckel, Luciana Paluzzi. **1969**

GREMLINS ★★★★ This "Steven Spielberg Presentation" is highly wacky. It's one part *E.T.—The Extra-Terrestrial*, one part scary-funny horror film, one part Muppet movie, and one part Bugs Bunny–Warner Bros. cartoon. Sound strange? You got it. In the story, Billy Peltzer (Zach Galligan) gets a cute little pet from his inventor-father (Hoyt Axton) for Christmas. But there's a catch. Rated PG for profanity and stylized violence. 111m. **DIR:** Joe Dante. **CAST:** Zach Galligan, Phoebe Cates, Hoyt Axton, Frances Lee McCain, Polly Holliday, Glynn Turman, Dick Miller, Keye Luke, Scott Brady. **1984**

GREMLINS 2: THE NEW BATCH ★★★★ Those mischievous mutating creatures are back. This time they invade a futuristic New York office complex run by a Donald Trump–like billionaire. Playful, energetic, and much like the first movie in its use of visual gags, social satire, cartoonish mayhem, surprise in-jokes for film fans. Rated PG-13 for cartoon violence. 114m. **DIR:** Joe Dante. **CAST:** Zach Galligan, Phoebe Cates, John Glover, Robert Prosky, Robert Picardo, Christopher Lee, Dick Miller, Jackie Joseph. **1990**

GROUNDSTAR CONSPIRACY, THE ★★★½ This nifty thriller has gone unrecognized for years. George Peppard stars as a government investigator sent to uncover the security leak that led to the destruction of a vital—and secret—space laboratory, and the amnesia-stricken Michael Sarrazin is his only lead. The clever plot and excellent character interactions build to a surprising climax. Rated PG. 103m. **DIR:** Lamont Johnson. **CAST:** George Peppard, Michael Sarrazin, Christine Belford. **1972**

GUYVER, THE ★★★½ Japanese comic-book superhero jumps to the big screen in a film that's truly comic book in look and style. Jack Armstrong is a college student who stumbles across a helmet that transforms him into a superhero. Hot on his tail are a gang of mutants and CIA agent Mark Hamill, trying to make sense of it all. Outrageous special effects combine with tongue-in-cheek humor to make an adventure film worthy of continuation. Rated PG-13 for violence. 92m. **DIR:** Screaming Mad George, Steve Wang. **CAST:** Mark Hamill, David Gale, Michael Berryman, Jack Armstrong. **1992**

GUYVER, THE, VOLS. 1–4 ★★½ Japanese animation. This tale about a reluctant superhero has plenty of villains and monsters. Unrated, but contains violence. 60m. **DIR:** Koichi Ishiguro. **1989**

HANDMAID'S TALE, THE ★★★★ Margaret Atwood's chilling cautionary novel gets first-cabin treatment from director Volker Schlondörff and scripter Harold Pinter, who faithfully retain the often gut-churning impact of this feminist horror story. Natasha Richardson stars as one of the few remaining fertile women (thanks to a nasty chemical accident) in a futuristic United States—renamed the Republic of Gilead—where ultraconservatives rule and mandate that all such women must "serve" to provide children for carefully selected members of the upper crust. Rated R for language and explicit sexual themes. 109m. **DIR:** Volker Schlondörff. **CAST:** Natasha Richardson, Robert Duvall, Faye Dunaway, Aidan Quinn, Elizabeth McGovern, Victoria Tennant. **1990**

HANDS OF STEEL 🦃 A cyborg assassin goes wrong and is pursued by police and baddies. Rated R for language and violence. 94m. **DIR:** Martin Dolman. **CAST:** Daniel Greene, Janet Agren, Claudio Cassinelli, George Eastman, John Saxon. **1986**

HANGAR 18 🦃 The story revolves around an alien spaceship that is accidentally disabled by a U.S. satellite. Rated PG. 93m. **DIR:** James L. Conway. **CAST:** Darren McGavin, Robert Vaughn, Gary Collins, Joseph Campanella, James Hampton. **1980**

HARDWARE 🦃 A post-apocalypse salvage expert gives the remains of a robot to his lady friend unaware that the mechanical creature was programmed to kill humans. Rated R for violence, gore, nudity, and profanity. 95m. **DIR:** Richard Stanley. **CAST:** Dylan McDermott, Stacey Travis, John Lynch, Iggy Pop. **1990**

HARRY AND THE HENDERSONS ★★★ A shaggy *E.T.* story, this focuses on the plight of a family (headed by John Lithgow and Melinda Dillon) that just happens to run into Bigfoot one day. It's silly, outrageously sentimental, and a gentle poke in the ribs of Steven Spielberg, whose Amblin Productions financed the film. Rated PG for profanity and violence. 110m. **DIR:** William Dear. **CAST:** John Lithgow, Melinda Dillon, Don Ameche, Lainie Kazan, David Suchet. **1987**

HAUNTING PASSION, THE ★★ An uneven made-for-TV supernatural romance in which a ghost seduces housewife Jane Seymour. There are a few chills, but more often than not, it falls short of the mark. 98m. **DIR:** John Korty. **CAST:** Jane Seymour, Gerald McRaney, Millie Perkins, Ruth Nelson. **1983**

HAUNTS OF THE VERY RICH ★★ This TV movie brings together a handful of people who have had close calls with death. It's sort of a low-quality *Twilight Zone* version of *Fantasy Island*. 72m. **DIR:** Paul Wendkos. **CAST:** Lloyd Bridges, Donna Mills, Edward Asner, Cloris Leachman, Anne Francis, Tony Bill, Robert Reed, Moses Gunn. **1972**

HEADLESS HORSEMAN, THE ★★½ The time-honored (but worn) story of lanky Yankee schoolmaster Ichabod Crane's rube-ish efforts to wed wealthy Katrina Van Tassel. Will Rogers looks the part of the homespun Crane and gives a fair impression of the character. Silent. B&W; 52m. **DIR:** Edward Venturini. **CAST:** Will Rogers, Lois Meredith. **1922**

HEART AND SOULS ★★★½ Sentimental fantasy follows the misadventures of Robert Downey Jr., who, at the moment of his birth, is "adopted" by a quartet of ghosts. The spirits cut off all communication with him when he's ten, breaking the boy's heart. So he's not exactly happy to see them again when he's an adult and they reappear asking for help. If you enjoyed *Field of Dreams*, you'll like this movie. Rated PG-13 for brief profanity, one sexy scene, and light violence. 104m. **DIR:** Ron Underwood. **CAST:** Robert Downey Jr., Charles Grodin, Alfre Woodard, Kyra Sedgwick, Elisabeth Shue, Tom Sizemore, David Paymer. **1993**

HEAVEN, EARTH AND MAGIC ★★★★ Harry Smith, one of the truly original forces in film animation, has created a hypnotic, graphic description of spiritual evolution through alchemy, using cut-up techniques to animate collages of images. A mesmerizing piece of work of epic proportions. B&W; 66m. **DIR:** Harry Smith. **1957–1962**

HELL COMES TO FROGTOWN 🦃 This laughable poverty-row quickie is set in one of those post-apocalyptic futures that allow a minimum of set design. Rated R for nudity, language, and violence. 88m. **DIR:** R. J. Kizer, Donald G. Jackson. **CAST:** Roddy Piper, Sandahl Bergman, Rory Calhoun. **1987**

HERCULES (1959) ★★½ The first and still the best of the Italian-made epics based on the mythical superhero. Steve Reeves looks perfect in the part as Hercules out to win over his true love, the ravishing Sylva Koscina. Some nice action scenes. 107m. **DIR:** Pietro Francisci. **CAST:** Steve Reeves, Sylva Koscina, Ivo Garrani. **1959**

HERCULES (1983) 🦃 Lou Ferrigno as the most famous muscle man of them all. Rated PG for violence. 98m. **DIR:** Lewis Coates. **CAST:** Lou Ferrigno, Sybil Danning, Brad Harris, Rossana Podesta. **1983**

HERCULES AGAINST THE MOON MEN 🦃 One of the cheesiest entries in the sword-and-sandal genre. 88m. **DIR:** Giacomo Gentilomo. **CAST:** Alan Steel, Jany Clair. **1964**

HERCULES AND THE CAPTIVE WOMEN ★★½ Hercules, his stowaway son, the King of Thebes, and a midget sail toward the lost city of Atlantis searching for the answers to a string of mysterious occurrences. Cornball, campy, and a good deal of fun. An Italian and French production, but dubbed in English. Not rated. 95m. **DIR:** Vittorio Cottafari. **CAST:** Reg Park, Fay Spain. **1963**

HERCULES UNCHAINED ★★ When the god of muscles sets his little mind on something, don't get in his way! In this one, he's out to rescue his lady fair. It's a silly but diverting adventure. Steve Reeves is still the best Hercules on film, dubbed voice and all. 101m. **DIR:** Pietro Francisci. **CAST:** Steve Reeves, Sylva Koscina, Primo Carnera, Sylvia Lopez. **1960**

HIDDEN, THE ★★★½ When a bizarre series of crimes wreaks havoc in Los Angeles, police detective Michael Nouri finds himself paired with an FBI agent (Kyle MacLachlan) whose behavior becomes increasingly strange as they pursue what may be an alien intruder. This hybrid science-fiction–adventure will delight those who like their entertainment upredictable. Rated R for violence, nudity, and profanity. 97m. **DIR:** Jack Sholder. **CAST:** Michael Nouri, Kyle MacLachlan, Ed O'Ross, Clu Gulager, Claudia Christian, Clarence Felder. **1987**

HIGHLANDER ★★ A sixteenth-century Scottish clansman discovers he is one of a small group of immortals destined to fight each other through the centuries. The movie is a treat for the eyes, but you'll owe your brain an apology. Rated R for violence. 110m. **DIR:** Russell Mulcahy. **CAST:** Christopher Lambert, Clancy Brown, Sean Connery. **1986**

HIGHLANDER 2: THE QUICKENING ★★½ Christopher Lambert and Sean Connery reprise their roles as the Highlander and his mentor Ramirez who have been banished to Earth. Great special effects can't keep one from thinking that something is missing from the film—like a cohesive plot. Rated R for violence. 91m. **DIR:** Russell Mulcahy. **CAST:** Christopher Lambert, Virginia Madsen, Michael Ironside, Sean Connery, John C. McGinley. **1991**

HIGHLANDER: THE GATHERING ★★ This is a combination of two episodes from the TV series, which is why the plot seems disjointed. Duncan and Connor must battle the evil immortals. Mind-numbing. Rated PG-13 for nudity and violence. 98m. **DIR:** Thomas J. Wright, Ray Austin. **CAST:** Adrian Paul, Alexandra Vandernoot, Stan Kirsch, Christopher Lambert, Richard Moll, Vanity. **1992**

HITCHHIKER'S GUIDE TO THE GALAXY, THE ★★★★ While perhaps the least successful adaptation (behind the book and LP) of Douglas Adam's now-classic BBC radio series, this television incarnation nonetheless succeeds quite well. Simon Jones is perfect as bathrobe-garbed Arthur Dent, an insignificant ordinary citizen thrown into the adventure of his life after narrowly escaping the Earth's destruction by aliens annoyed at how our planet blocked their proposed spatial thoroughfare. 194m. **DIR:** Alan Bell. **CAST:** Peter Jones, Simon Jones, David Dixon, Joe Melia, Martin Benson. **1985**

HOMEWRECKER ★★★½ Scientist Robby Benson suffers a breakdown after accidentally killing a family during a military defense test. When he privately rebuilds his computer, he adds human traits, and the computer (voiced by Kate Jackson) takes on a very human, and jealous, persona. An imaginative plot, tight editing, and Benson's performance overcome the low budget. Rated PG-13 for profanity. 88m. **DIR:** Fred Walton. **CAST:** Robby Benson, Sydney Walsh, Sarah Rose Karr. **1992**

HORROR OF THE BLOOD MONSTERS 🦃 Astronauts land on mystery planet and find it inhabited by stock footage from Filipino monster movies. Rated R. 85m. **DIR:** Al Adamson. **CAST:** John Carradine, Robert Dix, Vicki Volante. **1970**

HOWARD THE DUCK 🦃 An extremely rotten egg. Unwisely rated PG, considering some smarmy sex scenes and frightening monster makeup. 111m. **DIR:** Willard Huyck. **CAST:** Lea Thompson, Jeffrey Jones, Tim Robbins, Ed Gale. **1986**

HUMAN VAPOR, THE ★★ Essentially reworking the premise of the more interesting Honda film, *The H-Man*, this tells of a scientist transformed by a misbegotten experiment into a hideous, gaseous killer. Film dispenses with the draggy subplots of its forerunner, but still manages to outlast its welcome. 79m. **DIR:** Inoshiro Honda. **CAST:** Yoshio Tsuchiya. **1964**

HUMANOID DEFENDER 🦃 This movie is actually two episodes from a TV series that never made it, sort of a mix of *The Six Million Dollar Man* and *The Fugitive*. 94m. **DIR:** Ron Satlof. **CAST:** Terence Knox, Gary Kasper, Aimee Eccles, Marie Windsor. **1985**

HYPER SAPIAN: PEOPLE FROM ANOTHER STAR ★★ Two youngsters from another star system escape their elders to visit Wyoming. Predictable, bland nonsense. Rated PG for violence. 95m. **DIR:** Peter R. Hunt. **CAST:** Ricky Paul Goldin, Sydney Penny, Keenan Wynn, Gail Strickland, Peter Jason. **1986**

I COME IN PEACE ★★ Ridiculous subplot involving a preppie gang mars the first half of this sci-fi adventure. Dolph Lundgren must stop an alien's murderous rampage. The alien's method of sucking the endorphins of his victims' brains is pretty disgusting. Rated R for violence and gore. 90m. **DIR:** Craig R. Baxley. **CAST:** Dolph Lundgren, Brian Benben, Betsy Brantley. **1990**

I MARRIED A MONSTER FROM OUTER SPACE ★★★ This riveting story is about aliens who duplicate their bodies in the form of Earth men in hopes of repopulating their planet. One earthwoman who unknowingly marries one of the aliens discovers the secret, but can't get anyone to believe her. B&W; 78m. **DIR:** Gene Fowler Jr. **CAST:** Tom Tryon, Gloria Talbott, Ken Lynch, Maxie Rosenbloom. **1958**

I MARRIED A WITCH ★★★½ The whimsy of humorist Thorne Smith (the author of *Topper*) shows its age, but watching Veronica Lake and Fredric March perform together is a treat in this very pre-*Bewitched* farce. Look for Susan Hayward in a small role. B&W; 76m. **DIR:** René Clair. **CAST:** Veronica Lake, Fredric March, Cecil Kellaway, Robert Benchley. **1942**

I WAS A ZOMBIE FOR THE FBI ★★ Intentionally (and sometimes winningly) campy satire about alien invaders who pollute the world's soft drink industry while seeking a top-secret cola formula. Contains a hokey, claymation monster and granite-jaw acting. B&W; 105m. **DIR:** Marius Penczner. **CAST:** James Raspberry, Larry Raspberry. **1982**

ICE PIRATES ★★★½ This entertaining and often funny sci-fi film takes place countless years from now, when the universe has run out of water. Rated PG for violence, profanity, scatological humor, and suggested sex. 91m. **DIR:** Stewart Raffill. **CAST:** Robert Urich, Mary Crosby, John Matuszak, Anjelica Huston, John Carradine. **1984**

ICEMAN ★★★½ Timothy Hutton stars in this often gripping and always watchable movie as an anthropologist who is part of an arctic exploration team that discovers the body of a prehistoric man (John Lone), who is still alive. Hutton finds himself defending the creature from those who want to poke, prod, and even dissect their terrified subject. Rated PG for violence and profanity. 99m. **DIR:** Fred Schepisi. **CAST:** Timothy Hutton, Lindsay Crouse, John Lone, Josef Sommer. **1984**

ICZER-ONE, VOLS. 1–4 ★★½ Japanese animation. Unusual-looking blend of horror and sci-fi action. The mysterious Iczer-One makes life particularly difficult for a young schoolgirl whom she chooses as her partner to help defeat evil space invaders threatening the Earth. Unrated, but contains violence and nudity. 48m.–60m. **DIR:** Toshihiro Hirano. **1985–1987**

IDAHO TRANSFER 🦃 Young scientists invent a time-travel machine. No rating. 90m. **DIR:** Peter Fonda. **CAST:** Keith Carradine, Kelly Bohannon. **1973**

ILLUSTRATED MAN, THE 🦃 Ponderous, dull, and overly talkie adaptation of the work of Ray Bradbury. Rated PG for violence and partial nudity. 103m. **DIR:** Jack Smight. **CAST:** Rod Steiger, Claire Bloom, Robert Drivas. **1969**

IN THE AFTERMATH: ANGELS NEVER SLEEP ★★ Uneasy mixture of animation and live-action in this sci-fi story concerning an angel sent to assist an Earthman after the nuclear holocaust. The animation and the live action are good, but the two don't gel. A decent attempt to add life to an overworked genre, though. Contains rough language and violence. 85m. **DIR:** Carl Colpaert. **CAST:** Tony Markes, Rainbow Dolan. **1987**

IN THE SHADOW OF THE SUN ★★½ Interesting but overlong experimental film by Derek Jarman. This multilayered, hypnotic, nonlinear film was shot in Super-8 at the cost of $200 and features a dizzying sound track with the music of Throbbing Gristle and Chris Carter. Not rated. 54m. **DIR:** Derek Jarman. **1974**

IN THE TIME OF BARBARIANS 🦃 Doran, the good barbarian king of Armana, faces danger as he pursues an evil marauder across his lands and into present-day Los Angeles. Rated R for violence and nudity. 96m. **DIR:** Joseph L. Barmettler. **CAST:** Deron Michael McBee, Jo Ann Ayres. **1990**

IN THE TIME OF BARBARIANS II ★★ Wandering swordsman Galen finds service with the good guys as two sisters battle for the throne of a magical land. Falling in love with a beautiful princess, he soon finds that his employer is not as pure as he once thought. Rated R for violence and nudity. 85m. **DIR:** Ricardo Jacques Gale. **CAST:** Diana Frank, Lenore Andriel, Tom Schultz. **1992**

INCREDIBLE HULK, THE ★★½ Bill Bixby is sincere in the role of Dr. David Banner, a scientist whose experiments with gamma rays result in his being transformed into a huge green creature (Lou Ferrigno) whenever something angers him. Pilot for the series is a lot of fun, with better production values than most TV efforts. Based on the Marvel Comics character. 100m. **DIR:** Kenneth Johnson. **CAST:** Bill Bixby, Susan Sullivan, Lou Ferrigno, Jack Colvin, Charles Siebert. **1977**

INCREDIBLE MELTING MAN, THE ★★ Superb makeup by Rick Baker highlights this story of an astronaut (Alex Rebar) who contracts a strange ailment that results in his turning into a gooey, melting mess upon his return to Earth. Wild stuff. Rated R for terminal grossness. 86m. **DIR:** William Sachs. **CAST:** Alex Rebar, Burr DeBenning, Myron Healey, Ann Sweeney. **1978**

INCREDIBLE PETRIFIED WORLD, THE 🦃 Stupefying concoction, set almost entirely in a diving bell. B&W; 78m. **DIR:** Jerry Warren. **CAST:** John Carradine, Phyllis Coates. **1958**

INCREDIBLE SHRINKING MAN, THE ★★★★ Good special effects as a man (Grant Williams), exposed to a strange radioactive mist, finds himself becoming smaller...and smaller...and smaller. Well-mounted thriller from Universal with many memorable scenes, including the classic showdown with an ordinary house spider. B&W; 81m. **DIR:** Jack Arnold. **CAST:** Grant Williams, Randy Stuart, Paul Langton, April Kent. **1957**

INDIANA JONES AND THE LAST CRUSADE ★★★★½ Creator-producer George Lucas and director Steven Spielberg end their big-budget, Saturday-matinee cliff-hanger series in style with this sublimely entertaining movie, in which Indiana Jones (Harrison Ford) embarks on a quest for the Holy Grail when his father (Sean Connery) disappears while on the same mission. Father and son, with the help of *Raiders of the Lost Ark* returnees Denholm Elliott and John Rhys-Davies, are soon slugging it out with some nasty Nazis in this all-ages delight. Ford and Connery work beautifully together. Rated PG-13 for violence and profanity. 127m. **DIR:** Steven Spielberg. **CAST:** Harrison Ford, Sean Connery, Denholm Elliott, John Rhys-Davies, River Phoenix. **1989**

INDIANA JONES AND THE TEMPLE OF DOOM ★★★★ This sequel is almost as good as the original, *Raiders of the Lost Ark*. The story takes place before the events of *Raiders* with its two-fisted, whip-wielding hero, Dr. Indiana Jones (Harrison Ford) performing feats of derring-do in Singapore and India circa 1935. Parents may want to see this fast-paced and sometimes scary film before allowing their kids to watch it. Rated PG for profanity and violence. 118m. **DIR:** Steven Spielberg. **CAST:** Harrison Ford, Kate Capshaw. **1984**

INFRA-MAN ★★½ Mainly for kids, this *Ultraman* rip-off, about a giant superhero protecting the Earth from a bunch of crazy-looking monsters, still manages to succeed, despite the lame acting and hokey special effects. Ridiculous but enjoyable. Rated PG. 92m. **DIR:** Hua-Shan. **CAST:** Wang Hsieh. **1976**

INNERSPACE ★★★★ Get this story line: Dennis Quaid is a rebel astronaut who is miniaturized in order to be injected into the body of a rabbit. By accident the syringe carrying Quaid ends up being injected into the body of hypochondriac Martin Short. Sound weird? It is. Sound funny? We thought so. Rated PG for profanity and violence. 130m. **DIR:** Joe Dante. **CAST:** Dennis Quaid, Martin Short, Meg Ryan, Kevin McCarthy, Fiona Lewis, Henry Gibson. **1987**

INSIDE OUT (1992) ★★★ Nine vignettes—ranging from the pure sci-fi of "The Leda" to the borderline pornography of "My Secret Moments"—populate this strange tape from Playboy Video. Despite some overly erotic content, this is an entertaining, sometimes comic slice of *Twilight Zone*-style storytelling. Not rated, but contains violence, profanity, nudity, and simulated sex. 90m. **DIR:** Tony Randel, Richard Shepard, Jeffrey Reiner, Alexander Payne, Linda Hassani, Lizzie Borden, Adam Friedman. **CAST:** William Bumiller, Barbara Alyn Woods, Joseph Malone, Joe Dallesandro. **1992**

INSIDE OUT 2 ★★½ Nine more vignettes ranging from the absurd "The Hitchhiker" to the very funny "I've Got a Crush on You." Although not as sex-soaked as the first in the series, there are numerous soft-core encounters, the most notable of which is "The Right Number," wherein a couple become lovers over a phone sex line and then find they can't make love unless they are holding phones. Not rated; the film contains profanity and nudity. 90m. **DIR:** Nicholas Brandt, John Wentworth, Tony Randel, Nigel Dick, Linda Hassani, Yuri Sivo, Martin Donovan, Paul Rachman. **CAST:** Bruce Glover, Michael Griffin, Page Moseley, George (Buck) Flower. **1992**

INTRUDER WITHIN, THE 🦃 Cheesy *Alien*. Action takes place on an ocean oil-drilling rig instead of commercial spacecraft. 100m. **DIR:** Peter Carter. **CAST:** Chad Everett, Joseph Bottoms, Jennifer Warren. **1981**

INTRUDERS ★★★★ Two sisters, through hypnotic regression, convince a psychologist that they've been repeatedly abducted, since childhood, by aliens. The story moves suspensefully, exploring government conspiracies and theories why extraterrestrials are kidnapping humans. Made for TV, yet still effectively creepy. 163m. **DIR:** Dan Curtis. **CAST:** Richard Crenna, Mare Winningham, Susan Blakely, Daphne Ashbrook. **1992**

INVADER ★★ A reporter for a trashy tabloid discovers government officials and scientists working on a new computerized weapons system from an abandoned UFO. But no one will believe him, until the megacomputer tries to take control of military bases and personnel. Rated R for violence and profanity. 95m. **DIR:** Philip Cook. **CAST:** Hans Bachmann, A. Thomas Smith, Rick Foucheux, John Cooke, Ally Sheedy. **1993**

INVADERS FROM MARS (1953) ★★★★ Everybody remembers this one. Kid sees a flying saucer land in a nearby field, only nobody will believe him. Some really weird visuals throughout this minor sci-fi classic. 78m. **DIR:** William Cameron Menzies. **CAST:** Helena Carter, Jimmy Hunt, Leif Erickson, Arthur Franz. **1953**

INVADERS FROM MARS (1986) ★★★ Director Tobe Hooper maintains the tone of the original; this *Invaders from Mars* feels like a 1950s movie made with 1980s production values. Rated PG-13 for rather intense situations and ugly beasties. 94m. **DIR:** Tobe Hooper. **CAST:** Karen Black, Hunter Carson, Timothy Bottoms, Laraine Newman, James Karen, Louise Fletcher, Bud Cort. **1986**

INVASION OF THE ANIMAL PEOPLE 🦃 Extraterrestrial visitors assume various forms. B&W; 73m. **DIR:** Virgil Vogel, Jerry Warren. **CAST:** Robert Burton, Barbara Wilson, John Carradine (narrator). **1962**

INVASION OF THE BEE GIRLS ★★★ Enjoyable film about strange female invaders doing weird things to the male population of a small town in California. Plot is not too important in this wacky sci-fi spoof. Not for kids. Rated PG. 85m. **DIR:** Denis Sanders. **CAST:** Victoria Vetri, William Smith, Cliff Osmond, Anitra Ford. **1973**

INVASION OF THE BODY SNATCHERS (1956) ★★★★★ Quite possibly the most frightening film ever made, this stars Kevin McCarthy as a small-town doctor who discovers his patients, family, and friends are being taken over by cold, emotionless, human-duplicating pods from outer space. Not many films can be considered truly disturbing, but this one more than qualifies. Coming from the B-movie science-fiction boom of the 1950s, it has emerged as a cinema classic. B&W; 80m. **DIR:** Don Siegel. **CAST:** Kevin McCarthy, Dana Wynter, Carolyn Jones, King Donovan. **1956**

INVASION OF THE BODY SNATCHERS (1978) ★★★★ Excellent semisequel to Don Siegel's 1956 classic of the same name, with Donald Sutherland fine in the role originally created by Kevin McCarthy (who has a cameo here). This time the story takes place in San Francisco, with mysterious "seeds" from outer space duplicating—then destroying—San Francisco Bay Area residents at an alarming rate. Rated PG. 115m. **DIR:** Phil Kaufman. **CAST:** Donald Sutherland, Brooke Adams, Leonard Nimoy, Jeff Goldblum, Veronica Cartwright. **1978**

INVASION OF THE SAUCER MEN ★★★ Goofy-looking aliens with alcohol for blood battle hot-rodding teens. A minor camp classic that doesn't take itself seriously for a moment. B&W; 69m. **DIR:** Edward L. Cahn. **CAST:** Steve Terrell, Gloria Castillo, Frank Gorshin. **1957**

INVASION UFO ★★ Strictly for fans of the short-lived science-fiction TV series, whose title explains all. 97m. **DIR:** Gerry Anderson, David Lane, David Tomblin. **CAST:** Ed Bishop, George Sewell, Michael Billington. **1980**

INVISIBLE AGENT ★★★ Universal Pictures recycles H. G. Wells's *The Invisible Man* again, this time as a World War II spy thriller. The result is above-average—crisply plotted and atmospheric. Jon Hall plays the dashing title character, but John P. Fulton's special effects are the real star. B&W; 81m. **DIR:** Edwin L. Marin. **CAST:** Ilona Massey, Jon Hall, Cedric Hardwicke, Peter Lorre. **1942**

INVISIBLE BOY, THE ★★ Sci-fi parable about a computer's scheme to rule the world. The special effects are okay, and

Robby the Robot has a supporting role, but it was too dull even in the 1950s. B&W; 85m. **DIR:** Herman Hoffman. **CAST:** Richard Eyer, Diane Brewster, Philip Abbott. 1957

INVISIBLE KID, THE ★★ Geared for preteens, this sci-fi comedy about a boy who accidentally discovers an invisibility potion might be a little too juvenile for all audiences. Rated PG for language and nudity. 96m. **DIR:** Avery Crounse. **CAST:** Jay Underwood, Wally Ward, Mike Genovese, Karen Black. 1988

INVISIBLE MANIAC ★★ Tacky Fifties-style sci-fi pastiche has voyeuristic physics professor perfecting an invisibility potion for the purpose of ogling the high school cheerleading team. Titillating silliness has its camp moments. Rated R. 85m. **DIR:** Rif Coogan. **CAST:** Noel Peters. 1990

INVISIBLE: THE CHRONICLES OF BENJAMIN KNIGHT 🦃 Dreadful foray into the *Invisible Man* genre presents nothing new, but borrows heavily from other films. Produced as a sequel to *Mandroid.* Rated R for violence, language, and nudity. 80m. **DIR:** Jack Ersgard. **CAST:** Brian Cousins, Jennifer Nash, Alan Oppenheimer, Aharon Ipale. 1994

IRON WARRIOR 🦃 *Conan*-type action flick with plenty of sabers, smoke, and skin. Rated R for violence and nudity. 82m. **DIR:** Al Bradley. **CAST:** Miles O'Keeffe, Savina Gersak, Tim Lane. 1987

ISLAND AT THE TOP OF THE WORLD, THE ★★★ A rich man ventures into the Arctic in search of his son. Unbelievably, he finds a Viking kingdom. Rated G. 93m. **DIR:** Robert Stevenson. **CAST:** David Hartman, Mako, Donald Sinden. 1974

ISLAND OF DR. MOREAU, THE ★★ Remake of 1933's *Island of Lost Souls* isn't nearly as good. Burt Lancaster develops process of turning animals into half-humans on a desolate tropical island. Watchable only for Burt's sturdy performance and Richard Basehart's portrayal of one of the beasts. Rated PG. 104m. **DIR:** William Witney. **CAST:** Burt Lancaster, Michael York, Barbara Carrera, Richard Basehart. 1977

IT CAME FROM OUTER SPACE ★★★★ Science-fiction author Ray Bradbury wrote the screenplay for this surprisingly effective 3-D chiller from the 1950s about creatures from outer space taking over the bodies of Earthlings. It was the first film to use this theme and still holds up today. B&W; 81m. **DIR:** Jack Arnold. **CAST:** Richard Carlson, Barbara Rush, Charles Drake. 1953

IT CONQUERED THE WORLD ★★ Paul Blaisdell's five-foot-high monster, which resembles an angry, upended cucumber that comes to a point at the top, looks better in the stills printed in monster magazines of the Sixties than in the movie itself—an above-average variation on *Invasion of the Body Snatchers.* A campy, frantic B movie. B&W; 68m. **DIR:** Roger Corman. **CAST:** Peter Graves, Beverly Garland, Lee Van Cleef. 1956

IT! THE TERROR FROM BEYOND SPACE 🦃 Supposedly the inspiration for *Alien*, this is a dull tale of a spaceship returning from Mars in 1973, carrying a hitchhiking scaly being that disposes of the crew, one by one. B&W; 69m. **DIR:** Edward L. Cahn. **CAST:** Marshall Thompson, Ann Doran. 1958

JACOB'S LADDER ★★★ *Ghost* screenwriter Bruce Joel Rubin takes us on another trip into the spiritual plane with this tale of a Vietnam veteran (Tim Robbins) who is plagued by strange nightmares and, after awhile, daymares. Is it the aftereffects of a drug tested on soldiers? Is a parallel universe of demons invading our own? Is Mr. Rubin getting a little carried away with all this "other-side" stuff? You decide for yourself. Rated R for violence, nudity, and profanity. 115m. **DIR:** Adrian Lyne. **CAST:** Tim Robbins, Elizabeth Peña, Danny Aiello, Matt Craven, Jason Alexander, Macaulay Culkin. 1990

JASON AND THE ARGONAUTS ★★★★ The captivating special effects by master Ray Harryhausen are the actual stars of this movie. This is the telling of the famous myth of Jason (Todd Armstrong), his crew of derring-doers, and their search for the Golden Fleece. 104m. **DIR:** Don Chaffey. **CAST:** Todd Armstrong, Gary Raymond, Honor Blackman. 1963

JOURNEY TO THE CENTER OF TIME ★★½ A group of scientists working on a time-travel device are accidentally propelled five thousand years into the future following an equipment malfunction. Once there, they discover an alien civilization (headed by a young Lyle Waggoner) attempting to take over the world. Low-budget film features passable special effects, but the dialogue and acting are subpar. 82m. **DIR:** David L. Hewitt. **CAST:** Scott Brady, Gigi Perreau, Anthony Eisley, Abraham Sofaer, Lyle Waggoner. 1967

JOURNEY TO THE CENTER OF THE EARTH (1959) ★★★ This Jules Verne story was impressive when first released, but it looks pretty silly these days. However, James Mason is always fascinating to watch, production values are high, and kids should enjoy its innocent fun. 132m. **DIR:** Henry Levin. **CAST:** James Mason, Pat Boone, Arlene Dahl, Diane Baker. 1959

JOURNEY TO THE CENTER OF THE EARTH (1987) 🦃 There's little Jules Verne in this hopelessly muddled adventure, notable only for some impressive sets. Rated PG. 79m. **DIR:** Rusty Lemorande. **CAST:** Nicola Cowper, Ilan Mitchell-Smith, Paul Carafotes, Kathy Ireland, Emo Philips. 1987

JOURNEY TO THE FAR SIDE OF THE SUN ★★★½ This extremely clever sci-fi thriller concerns the discovery of a planet rotating in Earth's orbit, but always hidden from view on the other side of the Sun. Thoughtful, literate, and fascinating, this effort is marred only by a needlessly oblique and frustrating conclusion. Unrated; suitable for family viewing. 99m. **DIR:** Robert Parrish. **CAST:** Roy Thinnes, Lynn Loring, Herbert Lom, Patrick Wymark, Ian Hendry. **1969**

JUBILEE ★★ Avant-garde filmmaker Derek Jarman's surreal fantasy about a futuristic England, a postpunk-Thatcherian wasteland where civilization is in anarchaic terrorism. Highly uneven. Not rated, but contains nudity and graphic violence. 105m. **DIR:** Derek Jarman. **CAST:** Jenny Runacre, Jordan, Little Nell, Richard O'Brien, Adam Ant. **1978**

JULIA AND JULIA 🦃 This dreary Italian-made, English-language movie is an uninspired rehash of the parallel-worlds plot from the old science-fiction pulp magazines. Rated R for profanity, nudity, and violence. 95m. **DIR:** Peter Del Monte. **CAST:** Kathleen Turner, Gabriel Byrne, Sting, Gabriele Ferzetti. **1988**

JURASSIC PARK ★★★★ Adapted from the novel by Michael Crichton, this is director Steven Spielberg's triumphant return to his filmmaking roots, *à la Duel* and *Jaws*. Dinosaurs are genetically re-created to populate the ultimate theme park, and a special few—scientists and children—are allowed a sneak preview. Awe and wonder soon turns to terror as the creatures break out of their confines and go on a rampage. It's *King Kong* to the max. Rated PG-13 for violence. 120m. **DIR:** Steven Spielberg. **CAST:** Sam Neill, Laura Dern, Jeff Goldblum, Richard Attenborough, Bob Peck, Martin Ferrero, B. D. Wong, Samuel L. Jackson, Wayne Knight, Joseph Mazzello, Ariana Richards. **1993**

KILLERS FROM SPACE 🦃 Bug-eyed men from outer space. B&W; 68m. **DIR:** W. Lee Wilder. **CAST:** Peter Graves, James Seay. **1954**

KILLING EDGE, THE ★★ Fairly decent low-budget account of one man's search through a nuclear wasteland for his wife and son. The acting is good and the writing is solid, but the film occasionally gets bogged down in repetition. Not rated, contains violence and language. 90m. **DIR:** Lindsay Shonteff. **CAST:** Bill French, Marv Spencer. **1986**

KNIGHTS ★★★ Vampiric cyborgs in futuristic Taos see people as a handy source of fuel. Hoping to save humankind, robot Kris Kristofferson teaches kick-boxing champ Kathy Long all the right moves. Aside from the weak ending and a laughable battle scene (featuring a dismembered Kristofferson), this sword-and-sorcery cheapo isn't bad. Rated R for violence and profanity. 89m. **DIR:** Albert Pyun. **CAST:** Kris Kristofferson, Lance Henriksen, Kathy Long. **1992**

KRONOS ★★★ In this alien invasion film, a giant, featureless robot is sent to Earth. The robot absorbs all forms of energy and grows as it feeds. The scientists must find a way to destroy the giant before it reaches the high-population areas of southern California. Although the special effects are nothing by today's filmmaking standards, this picture is one of the best from a decade dominated by giant monsters and alien invaders. B&W; 78m. **DIR:** Kurt Neumann. **CAST:** Jeff Morrow, Barbara Lawrence. **1957**

KRULL 🦃 In this poor sci-fi–sword-and-sorcery film, a young man is called upon to do battle with a master of evil to save a beautiful princess. Rated PG for violence. 117m. **DIR:** Peter Yates. **CAST:** Ken Marshall, Freddie Jones, Lysette Anthony. **1983**

KURT VONNEGUT'S MONKEY HOUSE ★★★ Three Kurt Vonnegut short stories receive first-class treatment in this made-for-cable production. Sociological debate and brutal danger make "All the King's Men" the strongest tale: A U.S. ambassador (Len Cariou) is forced to use his family and military advisers in a human chess game against a communist rebel leader (Miguel Fernandes) with an ax to grind and nothing to lose. Other tales: "Next Door" and "The Euphio Question." Mild violence, but otherwise suitable for family viewing. 90m. **DIR:** Allan Winton King, Paul Shapiro, Gilbert Shilton. **CAST:** Len Cariou, Miguel Fernandes, Gordon Clapp, Donnelly Rhodes. **1991**

LABYRINTH ★★★ A charming fantasy that combines live actors with another impressive collection of Jim Henson's Muppets. Jennifer Connelly wishes for the Goblin King (David Bowie) to kidnap her baby brother; when that idle desire is granted, she must journey to an enchanted land and solve a giant maze in order to rescue her little brother. Rated PG for mild violence. 101m. **DIR:** Jim Henson. **CAST:** David Bowie, Jennifer Connelly, Toby Froud. **1986**

LAND THAT TIME FORGOT, THE ★★ Poor Edgar Rice Burroughs, his wonderful adventure books for kids rarely got the right screen treatment. This British production tries hard, but the cheesy special effects eventually do it in. A sequel, *The People That Time Forgot*, fared no better. Rated PG. 90m. **DIR:** Kevin Connor. **CAST:** Doug McClure, Susan Penhaligon, John McEnery. **1975**

LAND UNKNOWN, THE ★★ A navy helicopter forced down in the Antarctic lands in a warm-water region where prehistoric animals still live. The production is better than the average B movie, but the dinosaurs are cheesy. B&W; 79m. **DIR:** Virgil Vogel. **CAST:** Jock Mahoney, Shawn Smith, William Reynolds. **1957**

LASERBLAST ★★ Dreadful low-budget film with some excellent special effects by David Allen. Story concerns a young man who accidentally lays his hands on an alien ray gun. Rated PG. 90m. **DIR:** Michael Raye. **CAST:** Kim Milford, Cheryl Smith, Roddy McDowall, Keenan Wynn. **1978**

LAST ACTION HERO, THE ★★½ An 11-year-old movie buff (Austin O'Brien) gets a magic ticket and suddenly finds himself thrust into the big-screen adventures of his hero, Jack Slater (Arnold Schwarzenegger). Although not the total turkey its detractors claim, this bloated movie-within-a-movie does have some serious flaws. The last half is plagued by lapses in logic and sappy sentimentality. Rated PG-13 for violence and brief profanity. 130m. **DIR:** John McTiernan. **CAST:** Arnold Schwarzenegger, F. Murray Abraham, Art Carney, Charles Dance, Frank McRae, Tom Noonan, Robert Prosky, Anthony Quinn, Mercedes Ruehl, Joan Plowright, Austin O'Brien. **1993**

LAST CHASE, THE ★★½ Made at the end of the OPEC oil crisis, this film assumes the crisis only got worse until there was a civil war in America and the eastern states banned all cars and planes. Lee Majors plays an aged race-car driver who flees New York to California with a runaway (Chris Makepeace). Confusing at times, and the Orwellian touches have been done so often that all the scare has left them. Not rated. 106m. **DIR:** Martyn Burke. **CAST:** Lee Majors, Chris Makepeace, Burgess Meredith. **1980**

LAST DAYS OF MAN ON EARTH, THE ★★★½ Kinetic adaptation of Michael Moorcock's weird little novel, *The Final Programme*, the first of his adventures featuring Jerry Cornelius. Jon Finch plays Jerry as a smart-assed James Bond, and the prize he fights for is a microfilm containing the secret to self-replicating beings...highly useful in case of nuclear war. Finch encounters a variety of oddball characters, none stranger than Jenny Runacre, an enigmatic adversary who absorbs her lovers. Rated R for violence and sex. 73m. **DIR:** Robert Fuest. **CAST:** Jon Finch, Sterling Hayden, Patrick Magee, Jenny Runacre, Hugh Griffith. **1973**

LAST MAN ON EARTH, THE ★★★ In this nightmarish tale, a scientist (Vincent Price) is a bit late in developing a serum to stem the tide of a plague epidemic. He becomes the last man on Earth and lives in fear of the walking dead, who crave his blood. This paranoid horror film (based on Richard Matheson's *I Am Legend*) is more chilling than its higher-budget remake, *The Omega Man*. B&W; 86m. **DIR:** Sidney Salkow. **CAST:** Vincent Price, Franca Bettoia, Emma Danieli, Giacomo Rossi-Stuart. **1964**

LAST OF THE WARRIORS Ridiculous futuristic dud is a mishmash of leather-clad bad guys, cult religious leaders, and near-normal rebels. A real time waster. Unrated, but contains violence, nudity, and profanity. 98m. **DIR:** Lloyd A. Simandl, Michael Mazo. **CAST:** Melanie Kilgour, William Smith, Ken Farmer. **1989**

LAST STARFIGHTER, THE ★★★★ In this enjoyable comedy–science-fiction film, a young man (Lance Guest) beats a video game called the Starfighter and soon finds himself recruited by an alien (Robert Preston) to do battle in outer space. Thanks to its witty dialogue and hilarious situations, this hybrid is a viewing delight. Rated PG for violence and profanity. 100m. **DIR:** Nick Castle. **CAST:** Lance Guest, Robert Preston, Dan O'Herlihy, Catherine Mary Stewart, Barbara Bosson. **1984**

LATE FOR DINNER ★★★★ In what is sort of a cross between *Back to the Future* and *Of Mice and Men*, Brian Wimmer and Peter Berg drive from Santa Fe, New Mexico, to Pomona, California, in 1962 only to wake up twenty-nine years later in 1991 with no idea what happened. What begins as a wacky, offbeat romp becomes a profoundly moving story about loss and reconciliation. Rated PG for violence. 106m. **DIR:** W. D. Richter. **CAST:** Brian Wimmer, Peter Berg, Marcia Gay Harden, Colleen Flynn, Kyle Secor, Michael Beach, Peter Gallagher. **1991**

LAWLESS LAND Just another grade-Z turkey about survival in a post-apocalypse civilization. Rated R for violence and nudity. 81m. **DIR:** Jon Hess. **CAST:** Nick Corri, Amanda Peterson. **1988**

LAWNMOWER MAN, THE ★★★½ The mind-blowing special effects of this film lose a little in the translation to the small screen. But they still are the highlight of this story about a scientist (Pierce Brosnan) who uses computer "virtual reality" to turn a simple-minded gardener (Jeff Fahey) into a psychopathic genius. Some of the most outstanding computer animation since Disney's *Tron*. Rated R for violence, profanity, and nudity. 148m. **DIR:** Brett Leonard. **CAST:** Jeff Fahey, Pierce Brosnan, Jenny Wright, Geoffrey Lewis. **1992**

LEGEND Tom Cruise simply looks embarrassed as a forest-living lad who joins a quest to save a unicorn, keeper of his world's Light. Rated PG for mild violence. 89m. **DIR:** Ridley Scott. **CAST:** Tom Cruise, Tim Curry, Mia Sara, David Bennent, Billy Barty. **1986**

LENSMAN ★★ A poorly animated Japanese sci-fi flick about a young man who gains a mystical power and must use it to defeat the enemies of the universe. *Star Wars* told the same story much better and with considerably more flair. Unrated; the film contains violence and profanity. 107m. **DIR:** Yoshiaki Kawajiri, Kazuyuki Hirokawa. **1990**

LIFEFORCE ★★ In this disappointing and disjointed science-fiction–horror film by director Tobe Hooper (*Poltergeist*), ancient vampires from outer space return to Earth via Halley's Comet to feed on human souls. Rated R for violence, gore, nudity, profanity, and suggested sex. 96m. **DIR:** Tobe Hooper. **CAST:** Steve Railsback, Peter Firth, Mathilda May, Frank Finlay, Michael Gothard. 1985

LIFEFORCE EXPERIMENT, THE ★★★½ Scientist Donald Sutherland is working on a top-secret project, and the CIA sends agent Mimi Kuzyk to investigate. She finds he is conducting an experiment with psychic energy, which will have its final test when a young man dies of cancer and Sutherland attempts to capture his "lifeforce." Appalled, Kuzyk wants her bosses to stop the experiment, but they have other plans. Good, but not great made-for-cable adaptation of the Daphne du Maurier story. 96m. **DIR:** Piers Haggard. **CAST:** Donald Sutherland, Mimi Kuzyk, Vlasta Vrana, Corin Nemec, Hayley Reynolds, Miguel Fernandes, Michael Rudder, Michael J. Reynolds. 1994

LIFEPOD ★★★ It's Alfred Hitchcock's *Lifeboat* in outer space as eight people are trapped in a crippled escape pod after an intergalactic passenger ship is blown up en route. Supplies are short and communications down, plus one of the survivors seems intent on killing off the others. Good special effects and performances help make this film involving, though unexceptional. Made for TV. 90m. **DIR:** Ron Silver. **CAST:** Robert Loggia, Ron Silver, Jessica Tuck, Stan Shaw, Adam Storke, Kelli Williams, Ed Gale, C.C.H. Pounder. 1993

LIFESPAN 🦃 A young scientist tries to discover the secret of a long-life formula that belonged to a dead colleague. Unrated; it does have nudity and simulated sex. 85m. **DIR:** Alexander Whitelaw. **CAST:** Klaus Kinski, Hiram Keller, Tina Aumont, Fons Rademakers. 1974

LIGHT YEARS ★★½ Imaginative and daring sci-fi–fantasy cartoon written by Issac Asimov and produced by René Laloux. Sylvain, a young warrior, seeks out the evil that is destroying his world and embarks on an adventure into the future. Strong story, but rather simplistic animation and poor characterization. Rated PG for nudity. 79m. **DIR:** René Laloux. 1988

LIQUID SKY ★★★½ An alien spaceship lands on Earth in search of chemicals produced in the body during sex. One of the aliens enters the life of a new wave fashion model and feeds off her lovers, most of whom she's more than happy to see dead. *Liquid Sky* alternately shocks and amuses us with this unusual, stark, and ugly—but somehow fitting—look at an American subculture. Rated R for profanity, violence, rape, and suggested sex. 112m. **DIR:** Slava Tsukerman. **CAST:** Anne Carlisle, Paula E. Sheppard. 1983

LITTLE MONSTERS 🦃 Irritating, ugly monsters living in a dark, chaotic netherworld pop out from under unsuspecting children's beds at night. Rated PG, but it's definitely not Disney fare. 103m. **DIR:** Richard Alan Greenburg. **CAST:** Fred Savage, Howie Mandel, Daniel Stern, Frank Whaley, Margaret Whitton, Ben Savage. 1989

LOGAN'S RUN ★★★ Popular but overlong sci-fi film concerning a futuristic society where people are only allowed to live to the age of 30, and a policeman nearing the limit who searches desperately for a way to avoid mandatory extermination. Nice production is enhanced immeasurably by outlandish sets and beautiful, imaginative miniatures. Rated PG. 120m. **DIR:** Michael Anderson. **CAST:** Michael York, Jenny Agutter, Peter Ustinov, Richard Jordan. 1976

LOOKER ★★ Writer-director Michael Crichton describes this movie as "a thriller about television commercials," but it's really a fairly simpleminded suspense film. Plastic surgeon Albert Finney discovers a plot by evil mastermind James Coburn to clone models for television commercials. This is fiction? Rated PG because of nudity and violence. 94m. **DIR:** Michael Crichton. **CAST:** Albert Finney, James Coburn, Susan Dey, Leigh Taylor-Young. 1981

LORD OF THE RINGS, THE 🦃 J.R.R. Tolkien's beloved epic fantasy is trashed in this animated film. Rated PG. 133m. **DIR:** Ralph Bakshi. 1978

LORDS OF THE DEEP 🦃 Poverty-row quickie, designed solely to cash in on the underwater menace subgenre spearheaded by *The Abyss*. Inexplicably rated PG-13. 79m. **DIR:** Mary Ann Fisher. **CAST:** Bradford Dillman, Priscilla Barnes. 1989

LOST CITY, THE ★★ Incredibly bad serial becomes an incredible feature as crazy Zolok, maniacal ruler of a lost African city, uses a kidnapped scientist to wreak havoc on the rest of the world. Laughable thriller. B&W; 74m. **DIR:** Harry Revier. **CAST:** William "Stage" Boyd, Kane Richmond, George "Gabby" Hayes. 1935

LOST CONTINENT, THE ★★ Air force pilot Cesar Romero teams up with scientist John Hoyt to find a rocket ship that crash-landed on an uncharted island. They discover death and dinosaurs instead. Mild adventure-fantasy. B&W; 83m. **DIR:** Sam Newfield. **CAST:** Cesar Romero, Hillary Brooke, Chick Chandler, John Hoyt, Acquanetta, Sid Melton, Whit Bissell, Hugh Beaumont. 1951

LOST IN SPACE (TV SERIES) ★★★ The Robinson family volunteers to help Earth solve its overpopulation problem by exploring space. That incessantly fussy saboteur, Colonel Zachary Smith, thwarts their mission. The crew vows to continue to search for the welcoming climes of the star Alpha Centauri, while cowardly Smith connives to return to Earth. Terrifically tacky special effects and loads of campy humor earned the show a cult following. The robot proved to be the most endearing personality on board. 60m. **DIR:** Leo Penn, Alexander Singer, Tony Leader. **CAST:** Guy Williams, June Lockhart, Mark Goddard, Jonathan Harris, Marta Kristen, Angela Cartwright, Billy Mumy. **1965–1968**

LOST PLANET, THE ★★ Interplanetary nonsense for the grammar-school set is the order of the day as reporters Judd Holdren and Vivian Mason lock electrons with an evil scientist and his allies from the planet Ergro. Suitably silly serial. B&W; 15 chapters. **DIR:** Spencer Gordon Bennet. **CAST:** Judd Heldren, Vivian Mason. **1953**

LOST WORLD, THE (1925) ★★★★ Silent version of Arthur Conan Doyle's classic story of Professor Challenger and his expedition to a desolate plateau roaming with prehistoric beasts. The movie climaxes with a brontosaurus running amok in London. An ambitious production, interesting as film history and quite entertaining, considering its age. B&W; 60m. Also available in a restored 102m. version. **DIR:** Harry Hoyt. **CAST:** Bessie Love, Lewis Stone, Wallace Beery. **1925**

MAC AND ME 🖤 Imagine the most product-friendly film ever made and you have (Big) *Mac and Me*. To be fair, *Mac and Me* stars the courageous Jade Calegory, a paraplegic wheelchair-bound since birth, and a share of the producer's net profits will be donated to Ronald McDonald's Children's Charities. But the plot rips off everything in sight. Rated PG. 101m. **DIR:** Stewart Raffill. **CAST:** Jade Calegory, Christine Ebersole, Jonathan Ward. **1988**

MACROSS II, VOLS. 1–4 ★★ Japanese animation. Very standard entry in the field, *Macross II* is unlikely to appeal to any but avid Japanese animation fans. No surprises or twists, just more of the same. 55m. **DIR:** Kenichi Yatagai. **1992**

MAD MAX ★★★½ The most successful Australian film of all time ($100 million in worldwide rentals), this exciting sci-fi adventure features Mel Gibson as a fast-driving cop who has to take on a gang of crazies in the dangerous world of the future. Rated R. 93m. **DIR:** George Miller. **CAST:** Mel Gibson, Joanne Samuel, Hugh Keays-Byrne, Tim Burns, Roger Ward. **1979**

MAD MAX BEYOND THUNDERDOME ★★★½ Mad Max is back—and he's angrier than ever. Those who enjoyed *Road Warrior* will find more of the same in director George Miller's third post-apocalypse, action-packed adventure film. This time the resourceful futuristic warrior (Mel Gibson) confronts evil ruler Tina Turner. Rated PG-13 for violence and profanity. 109m. **DIR:** George Miller, George Ogilvie. **CAST:** Mel Gibson, Tina Turner, Helen Buday, Frank Thring, Bruce Spence. **1985**

MADE IN HEAVEN (1987) 🖤 Timothy Hutton stars as a lad who dies heroically, winds up in Heaven, and falls in love with unborn spirit Kelly McGillis. Rated PG for brief nudity. 103m. **DIR:** Alan Rudolph. **CAST:** Timothy Hutton, Kelly McGillis, Maureen Stapleton, Mare Winningham, Ellen Barkin, Debra Winger. **1987**

MAKING CONTACT ★★ After his father dies, a little boy begins to exhibit telekinetic powers and begins giving life to his favorite toys. Obviously aimed at children, this film is quite imaginative. 82m. **DIR:** Roland Emmerich. **CAST:** Joshua Morell, Eve Kryll. **1985**

MAN CALLED RAGE, A 🖤 Rage, a Mad Max–type of character, leads a team to find uranium deposits that are vital to the survival of the human race. Rated PG for violence. 90m. **DIR:** Anthony Richmond. **CAST:** Conrad Nichols. **1987**

MAN FROM ATLANTIS, THE ★★½ The pilot for the 1977 TV sci-fi series. Patrick Duffy plays the man from beneath the waves, recruited by the navy to retrieve a top-secret submarine. Belinda Montgomery is the marine biologist who holds Duffy's reins. 60m. **DIR:** Lee H. Katzin. **CAST:** Patrick Duffy, Belinda Montgomery, Victor Buono, Art Lund, Lawrence Pressman. **1977**

MAN FROM BEYOND, THE ★★★ Legendary escape artist Harry Houdini wrote and starred in this timeless story of a man encased in a block of ice for one hundred years who is discovered, thawed out, and thrust into twentieth-century life. While the special effects lack sophistication and the acting seems pretty broad, this is one of the few existing examples of Houdini's film work. Silent. B&W; 50m. **DIR:** Burton King. **CAST:** Harry Houdini. **1921**

MAN WHO COULD WORK MIRACLES, THE ★★★½ A timid department store clerk suddenly finds he possesses the power to do whatever he desires. Roland Young is matchless as the clerk, and is supported by a first-rate cast in this captivating fantasy. B&W; 82m. **DIR:** Lothar Mendes. **CAST:** Roland Young, Ralph Richardson, Joan Gardner, George Zucco. **1937**

MAN WHO FELL TO EARTH, THE ★★★★ A moody, cerebral science-fiction thriller about an alien (David Bowie) who becomes trapped on our planet. Its occasional ambiguities are overpowered by sheer mind-tugging bizarreness and directorial brilliance. Rated R. 140m. **DIR:** Nicolas Roeg. **CAST:** David Bowie, Rip Torn, Candy Clark, Buck Henry. **1976**

MANDROID ★★★ Scientists and the CIA struggle for control of a powerful, man-made element with both curative and destructive powers—depending on who has it. Covers every sci-fi detail from invisibility to a mad doctor in an iron mask! Just don't ponder the details. Rated R for violence, profanity, and brief nudity. 81m. **DIR:** Jack Ersgard. **CAST:** Brian Cousins, Janette Allyson Caldwell, Michael DellaFemina, Curt Lowens, Patrick Ersgard. **1993**

MAROONED 🦃 Tale of three astronauts unable to return to Earth and the ensuing rescue attempt. Rated PG. 134m. **DIR:** John Sturges. **CAST:** Gregory Peck, Richard Crenna, David Janssen, Gene Hackman, James Franciscus, Lee Grant. **1969**

MARS NEEDS WOMEN 🦃 Laughable science-fiction yarn featuring Tommy Kirk as a Martian who invades Earth in search of female mates. Ridiculous costumes and special effects only add to the campy effect. Not rated. 80m. **DIR:** Larry Buchanan. **CAST:** Tommy Kirk. **1966**

MARTIAN CHRONICLES, PARTS I-III, THE ★★★ Mankind colonizes Mars in this adaptation of the Ray Bradbury classic. As this was originally a TV miniseries, the budget was low and it shows in the cheap sets and poor special effects. The acting is very good, however. 314m. **DIR:** Michael Anderson. **CAST:** Rock Hudson, Darren McGavin, Gayle Hunnicutt, Bernadette Peters, Nicholas Hammond, Roddy McDowall. **1979**

MASTER OF THE WORLD ★★★ Jules Verne's tale brought excitingly to the screen. Vincent Price plays a self-proclaimed god trying to end all war by flying around the world in a giant airship, blowing ships from the water, etc. Lots of fun. 104m. **DIR:** William Witney. **CAST:** Vincent Price, Charles Bronson, Henry Hull. **1961**

MAX HEADROOM ★★★½ The original British production, later remade as a short-lived American TV series. Post-apocalypse newsman discovers an insidious form of advertising that causes viewers to explode. After being murdered by network executives, he's reborn as a computer-generated figure named Max Headroom. A sly parody of ratings-hungry television, the film is visually superb. 60m. **DIR:** Rocky Morton, Annabel Jankel. **CAST:** Matt Frewer, Nickolas Grace, Hilary Tindall, Morgan Shepherd, Amanda Pays. **1986**

MEGAFORCE 🦃 This dull sci-fi adventure is about a rapid-deployment defense unit that galvanizes into action whenever freedom is threatened. PG for no discernible reason. 99m. **DIR:** Hal Needham. **CAST:** Barry Bostwick, Michael Beck, Persis Khambatta, Henry Silva. **1982**

MEGAVILLE ★★ In the world of the future, intimacy is reviled, openness is frowned upon, and commercial TV is a capital offense. Enter Megaville, a television-free zone that the government must send an experimental supersoldier to eliminate. An overblown plot. Rated R for violence, profanity, and nudity. 96m. **DIR:** Peter Lehner. **CAST:** Billy Zane, J. C. Quinn, Grace Zabriskie, Daniel J. Travanti. **1991**

MEMOIRS OF AN INVISIBLE MAN ★★★★ Terrific special effects and inventive comedy combine to make this adaptation of the book by H. F. Saint much more than just another Chevy Chase vehicle. Chase plays an executive who turns invisible as the result of a freak accident, and finds himself pursued by a ruthless spy (Sam Neill). Thanks to top-notch direction by John Carpenter, plenty of suspense and excitement. Rated PG-13, for violence and nudity. 99m. **DIR:** John Carpenter. **CAST:** Chevy Chase, Daryl Hannah, Sam Neill, Michael McKean, Stephen Tobolowsky. **1992**

MERLIN ★★ Reporter Christy Lake (Nadia Cameron) learns that she's the reincarnated daughter of legendary magician Merlin, and she must guard a powerful sword from an evil wizard who is chasing her through time. This confusing film relies too heavily on gimmicks and mediocre special effects. Rated PG-13 for violence and adult situations. 112m. **DIR:** Paul Hunt. **CAST:** Nadia Cameron, Richard Lynch, Peter Phelps, James Hong. **1992**

MERLIN & THE SWORD 🦃 Retelling of the King Arthur legend. Not rated, contains mild sex and violence. 94m. **DIR:** Clive Donner. **CAST:** Malcolm McDowell, Candice Bergen, Edward Woodward, Dyan Cannon, Rupert Everett. **1982**

METALSTORM: THE DESTRUCTION OF JARED-SYN 🦃 An outer-space ranger takes on the powerful villain of the title. Rated PG for violence. 84m. **DIR:** Charles Band. **CAST:** Jeffrey Byron, Mike Preston, Tim Thomerson, Kelly Preston. **1983**

METAMORPHOSIS: THE ALIEN FACTOR ★★ Splashy special effects highlight this pedestrian science-fiction entry about a lab scientist who begins to mutate after being bitten by a frog injected with a mysterious serum from outer space. Will his co-workers cure him before they become lunch? Rated R for gore, nudity, language, and violence. 92m. **DIR:** Glen Takakjian. **CAST:** George Gerard, Tony Gigante, Katherine Romaine. **1993**

METEOR 🦃 A comet strikes an asteroid, and sends a huge chunk of rock hurtling on a collision course with Earth. Rated PG. 103m. **DIR:** Ronald Neame. **CAST:** Sean Connery, Natalie Wood, Karl Malden, Brian Keith, Henry Fonda. **1979**

METROPOLIS (1926) ★★★★★ Fritz Lang's 1926 creation embodies the fine difference between classic and masterpiece. Using some of the most innovative camera work in film of any time, it's also an uncannily accurate projection of futuristic society. It is a silent-screen triumph. B&W; 120m. **DIR:** Fritz Lang. **CAST:** Brigitte Helm, Alfred Abel. 1926

MIAMI HORROR 🦃 Poorly dubbed Italian thriller about scientists who believe that Earth life originated from bacteria on meteorites from outer space. 88m. **DIR:** Martin Herbert. **CAST:** David Warbeck, Laura Trotter, John Ireland. 1985

MIDSUMMER NIGHT'S DREAM, A (1935) ★★★★ Warner Bros. rolled out many of its big-name contract stars during the studio's heyday for this engrossing rendition of Shakespeare's classic comedy. Enchantment is the key element in this fairy-tale story of the misadventures of a group of mythical mischief makers. B&W; 117m. **DIR:** Max Reinhardt. **CAST:** James Cagney, Olivia de Havilland, Dick Powell, Mickey Rooney. 1935

MIGHTY JOE YOUNG ★★★½ In this timeless fantasy from the creator of *King Kong* (Willis O'Brien with his young apprentice, Ray Harryhausen), the story follows the discovery of a twelve-foot gorilla in Africa by a fast-talking, money-hungry nightclub owner (Robert Armstrong), who schemes to bring the animal back to Hollywood. B&W; 94m. **DIR:** Ernest B. Schoedsack. **CAST:** Terry Moore, Ben Johnson, Robert Armstrong, Frank McHugh. 1949

MILLENNIUM 🦃 Terrible time-travel story has Kris Kristofferson as an air-disaster troubleshooter, who meets a mysterious woman from the future. Rated PG-13 for violence and suggested sex. 110m. **DIR:** Michael Anderson. **CAST:** Kris Kristofferson, Cheryl Ladd, Daniel J. Travanti, Robert Joy. 1989

MINDWARP ★★★½ After a nuclear war, randomly chosen individuals dwell in underground bunkers, living their lives out in computer-generated fantasies. But when one girl rebels, she is exiled to the surface. Low-budget, but fun gross-out action-thriller. Rated R for nudity, profanity, and violence. 91m. **DIR:** Steve Barnett. **CAST:** Bruce Campbell, Angus Scrimm, Elizabeth Kent. 1991

MISFITS OF SCIENCE ★★½ Dean Paul Martin stars as the ringleader of a group of individuals possessing unique abilities. He rallies them together to combine their powers. No rating. This was the first installment in the failed television series. 96m. **DIR:** James D. Parriott. **CAST:** Dean Paul Martin, Kevin Peter Hall, Mark Thomas Miller, Courteney Cox. 1986

MISSILE TO THE MOON 🦃 Silly story of renegade expedition to the Moon. B&W; 78m. **DIR:** Richard Cunha. **CAST:** Richard Travis, Cathy Downes, K. T. Stevens, Michael Whalen, Tommy Cook, Gary Clarke. 1958

MISSION GALACTICA: THE CYLON ATTACK ★★½ Feature-length reediting of episodes from TV's *Battlestar Galactica* finds crew of this extremely simplistic, juvenile space opera under attack from their mortal enemy, the Cylons. 108m. **DIR:** Vince Edwards. **CAST:** Lorne Greene, Dirk Benedict. 1979

MISSION MARS 🦃 Danger-in-outer-space adventure has a trio of astronauts coping with mysterious forces while on the way to Mars. 95m. **DIR:** Nicholas Webster. **CAST:** Darren McGavin, Nick Adams. 1968

MISSION STARDUST ★★ Only diehard fans of Italian space operas are likely to seek out this adaptation of one of the Perry Rhodan pulp novels. And that's a shame, because, given its meager budget and indifferent dubbing, this is still one of the more imaginative European sci-fi adventures. 90m. **DIR:** Primo Zeglio. **CAST:** Essy Persson, Gianni Rizzo. 1965

MR. CORBETT'S GHOST ★★★ New Year's Eve, 1767, somewhere in England and young Ben Partridge has a choice to make: desire or duty. His decision on which road to pursue forms the basis of this fine atmospheric ghost story, produced for TV. 75m. **DIR:** Danny Huston. **CAST:** John Huston, Paul Scofield, Burgess Meredith, Mark Farmer. 1986

MOLE PEOPLE, THE ★★ Explorers discover a lost civilization of albino Sumerians living under a mountain. For fright-night nostalgists only. B&W; 78m. **DIR:** Virgil Vogel. **CAST:** John Agar, Hugh Beaumont, Alan Napier. 1956

MONOLITH ★★ Two cops who dislike each other discover a government secret—an alien being that grows more powerful every day. Extremely bad acting and not much of a plot. Rated R for profanity and violence. 96m. **DIR:** John Eyres. **CAST:** Bill Paxton, Lindsay Frost, John Hurt, Lou Gossett Jr. 1993

MONSTER FROM A PREHISTORIC PLANET ★★ A bit of added humanity makes this more than just another Japanese big-rubber-monster movie. Parents of a captive baby monster smash across the countryside trying to find him. Plenty of smashed models and bad dialogue make this a must for fans of this genre. Rated PG. 90m. **DIR:** Haruyasu Noguchi. **CAST:** Tarrin. 1967

MONSTER THAT CHALLENGED THE WORLD, THE ★★ This late-1950s sci-fi programmer is set apart by only one thing: the giant monster, which is life-size (not a miniature) and given plenty of screen time. Hero Tim Holt is ludicrous as a navy commander battling huge, caterpillarlike creatures and romancing a young widow. B&W; 83m. **DIR:** Arnold Laven. **CAST:** Tim Holt, Audrey Dalton, Hans Conried. 1957

MOON 44 ★★½ Michael Paré is an internal affairs cop for a large corporation investigating the theft of giant outer-space mining rigs in this passable sci-fi adventure. Good flying effects. Rated R for violence and profanity. 102m. **DIR:** Roland Emmerich. **CAST:** Michael Paré, Lisa Eichhorn, Malcolm McDowell, Stephen Geoffreys, Roscoe Lee Browne. 1990

MOON TRAP 🦃 Two astronauts find a race of resourceful mechanical aliens on the lunar surface. Rated R for language and nudity. 92m. **DIR:** Robert Dyke. **CAST:** Walter Koenig, Bruce Campbell. 1989

MOTHRA ★★★ Two six-inch-tall princesses are taken from their island home to perform in a Tokyo nightclub. A native tribe prays for the return of the princesses, and their prayers hatch a giant egg, releasing a giant caterpillar. The caterpillar goes to Tokyo searching for the princesses and turns into a giant moth while wrecking the city. Although the story may sound corny, this is one of the best of the giant-monster movies to come out of Japan. 100m. **DIR:** Inoshiro Honda. **CAST:** Lee Kresel, Franky Sakai, Hiroshi Koizumi. 1962

MURDER BY MOONLIGHT 🦃 Detective thriller set in a colony on the Moon, circa 2105. NASA agent Brigitte Nielsen joins Russian counterpart Julian Sands to solve a murder in this low-budget effort. Rated PG-13 for violence. 100m. **DIR:** Michael Lindsay-Hogg. **CAST:** Julian Sands, Brigitte Nielsen, Brian Cox, Gerald McRaney. 1989

MURDER IN SPACE ★★ As you watch this made-for-TV whodunit, you must immediately look for clues. If not, you'll get bored and the long-awaited solution won't make sense to you. Wilford Brimley as the head of Mission Control tries to put the pieces together. 95m. **DIR:** Steven H. Stern. **CAST:** Wilford Brimley, Michael Ironside, Martin Balsam, Arthur Hill. 1985

MY SCIENCE PROJECT ★★ John Stockwell finds some UFO debris abandoned (!) by the military in 1959. The doohickey quickly rages out of control sending Stockwell and chums to battle dinosaurs and futuristic soldiers. Rated PG for profanity. 94m. **DIR:** Jonathan Betuel. **CAST:** John Stockwell, Danielle von Zerneck, Fisher Stevens, Dennis Hopper, Richard Masur. 1985

MYSTERIANS, THE ★★½ An alien civilization attempts takeover of Earth after its home planet is destroyed. Massive destruction from the director of *Godzilla*. Quaint Japanese-style special effects look pretty silly these days, but the film can be fun if seen in the right spirit. 85m. **DIR:** Inoshiro Honda. **CAST:** Kenji Sahara. 1959

MYSTERIOUS ISLAND ★★★★ Fantasy-adventure based on Jules Verne's novel about a group of Civil War prisoners who escape by balloon and land on an uncharted island in the Pacific, where they must fight to stay alive against incredible odds. With fantastic effects work by Ray Harryhausen and a breathtaking Bernard Herrmann score. 101m. **DIR:** Cy Endfield. **CAST:** Michael Craig, Joan Greenwood, Michael Callan, Gary Merrill, Herbert Lom. 1961

NAKED LUNCH ★★★ A nightmare brought to life with sometimes nauseating intensity, director David Cronenberg's adaptation of William S. Burroughs's novel weds incidents from the author's life into the fantastical, drug-induced hallucinations that comprised the book. Peter Weller is the exterminator who, through the encouragement of wife Judy Davis, becomes addicted to bug powder and ends up in Interzone, where he writes reports dictated by his slimy, roach-like typewriter. Utterly bizarre and not for all tastes. Rated R for profanity, violence, and nudity. 115m. **DIR:** David Cronenberg. **CAST:** Peter Weller, Judy Davis, Ian Holm, Julian Sands, Roy Scheider. 1992

NAVIGATOR: A MEDIEVAL ODYSSEY, THE ★★★★½ A visionary film from New Zealand that involves a medieval quest through time. The film opens in Cumbria in 1348, in the midst of the terrifying Black Plague. A village of miners tries to appease what they view as a vengeful God by vowing to travel a great distance to fulfill a child's vision. The adventurers travel through the center of the Earth—and surface in a modern-day New Zealand town. Astonishingly original. In B&W and color. 91m. **DIR:** Vincent Ward. **CAST:** Bruce Lyons, Chris Haywood. 1989

NEGATIVES ★★★ Quirky satire of a married couple (Glenda Jackson and Peter McEnery) whose fantasy world of playacting and charades is interrupted by the intrusive overtures of a third person. Peter Medak's direction is sharp, and the fantasy sequences are pungently imaginative. 99m. **DIR:** Peter Medak. **CAST:** Glenda Jackson, Peter McEnery. 1968

NEMESIS (1992) ★★ In the year 2027, an ex-L.A.P.D. detective must determine whether the humans or the cyborgs are his enemy. He has three days to complete his mission or else the bomb in his heart will explode. Rated R for violence and profanity. 92m. **DIR:** Albert Pyun. **CAST:** Olivier Gruner, Tim Thomerson, Cary-Hiroyuki Tagawa, Merle Kennedy, Yuji Okumoto, Marjorie Monaghan, Brion James, Deborah Shelton. 1993

NEON CITY ★★½ In order to get to the fabled Neon City, a group of travelers must cross a barren wasteland where they are in constant danger of solar flares and attacks by mutant bandits. Some great stunt work helps this futuristic adventure. Rated R for violence and profanity. 107m. **DIR:** Monte Markham. **CAST:** Michael Ironside, Vanity, Lyle Alzado, Richard Sanders. **1991**

NEPTUNE FACTOR, THE ★★ Ben Gazzara stars as the commander of an experimental deep-sea submarine. He is called in to rescue an aquatic research team trapped in the remains of their lab on the ocean floor. Why they built it in the middle of a quake zone is the first in a series of dumb plot ideas. Rated G. 94m. **DIR:** Daniel Petrie. **CAST:** Ben Gazzara, Yvette Mimieux, Walter Pidgeon, Ernest Borgnine. **1973**

NEVERENDING STORY, THE ★★★★½ This is a superb fantasy about a sensitive 10-year-old boy named Bastian (Barrett Oliver) who takes refuge in a fairy tale. In reading it, he's swept off to a land of startlingly strange creatures and heroic adventures where a young warrior, Atreyu (Noah Hathaway), does battle with the Nothing, a force that threatens to obliterate the land of mankind's hope and dreams—and only Bastian has the power to save the day. Rated PG for slight profanity. 92m. **DIR:** Wolfgang Petersen. **CAST:** Barret Oliver, Noah Hathaway. **1984**

NEVERENDING STORY II, THE ★★½ Disappointing sequel to director Wolfgang Petersen's original has a new actor (Jonathan Brandis) as Bastion, the young reader/hero who is once again called upon to save the magical world of Fantasia. Rated PG for scary stuff. 90m. **DIR:** George Miller. **CAST:** Jonathan Brandis, Kenny Morrison, Clarissa Burt, John Wesley Shipp. **1991**

NEW GLADIATORS, THE 🦃 Italian fantasy about Rome in the twenty-first century. Not rated, but has violence. 90m. **DIR:** Lucio Fulci. **CAST:** Jared Martin, Fred Williamson, Claudio Cassinelli. **1987**

NEXT ONE, THE 🦃 A prophet from the future suddenly appears on the beach of a Greek island. Not rated. 105m. **DIR:** Nico Mastorakis. **CAST:** Keir Dullea, Adrienne Barbeau, Jeremy Licht, Peter Hobbs. **1981**

NIGHT CALLER FROM OUTER SPACE ★★½ Here's another one of those perennial sci-fi plots: outer space alien from a dying world comes to Earth looking for human women to serve as breeding stock. (With a planet named Ganymede, it's no wonder they're dying out!) A little British reserve keeps this in check; not bad of its type. B&W; 84m. **DIR:** John Gilling. **CAST:** John Saxon, Maurice Denham, Patricia Haines, Alfred Burke. **1965**

NIGHT OF THE COMET ★★★½ The passage of the comet wipes out all but a few people on our planet. The survivors, mostly young adults, are hunted by a pair of baddies, played by Geoffrey Lewis and Mary Woronov. It all adds up to a zesty low-budget spoof of science-fiction movies. Rated PG-13. 94m. **DIR:** Thom Eberhardt. **CAST:** Geoffrey Lewis, Mary Woronov, Catherine Mary Stewart. **1984**

NIGHTFALL 🦃 David Birney is the ruler of a land that has never known night. Rated PG-13, but contains abundant nudity and violence. 83m. **DIR:** Paul Mayersberg. **CAST:** David Birney, Sarah Douglas. **1988**

NIGHTFLYERS ★★★ A motley crew of space explorers search for an ancient and mysterious entity. Their ship is controlled by a computer, programmed from the brain patterns of an abused, jealous, and telepathic woman. This film's only weaknesses are inconsistent special effects and an ending that leaves you hanging. Sci-fi fans should find this entertaining. Rated R for violence and language. 90m. **DIR:** T. C. Blake. **CAST:** Catherine Mary Stewart, Michael Praed, John Standing, Lisa Blount, Michael Des Barres. **1987**

NIGHTMARE BEFORE CHRISTMAS, THE ★★★★ Literally years in the making, Tim Burton's warped holiday fantasy is a true stunner. Employing a blend of conventional stop-motion and replacement animation (the latter rarely seen beyond George Pal's efforts), Burton and scripter Caroline Thompson spin a wonderfully weird tale about Halloweentown-hero Jack Skellington's efforts to redefine Christmas. Longtime Burton collaborator Danny Elfman provides a suitably baroque score, but his operatic songs are too simplistic and repetitious. While not for average tastes, this is one of those rare films with "sense of wonder" to spare. Rated G. 75m. **DIR:** Henry Selick. **1993**

NIGHTWISH ★★ A team of graduate student dream researchers explores supernatural phenomena in a house haunted by a sinister alien presence. There are some good effects, and a fairly imaginative ending given the confused story line. Not rated, but with partial nudity and profanity. 96m. **DIR:** Bruce R. Cook. **CAST:** Clayton Rohner, Jack Starrett, Robert Tessier, Brian Thompson. **1990**

1984 (1955) ★★ Workmanlike adaptation of George Orwell's famous novel that, in spite of a good stab at Winston Smith by Edmond O'Brien, just doesn't capture the misery and desolation of the book. Frankly, this plays more like a postwar polemic than a drama, and great liberties have been taken with the story line. This movie is currently out of circulation. B&W; 91m. **DIR:** Michael Anderson. **CAST:** Edmond O'Brien, Jan Sterling, Michael Redgrave, Donald Pleasence. **1955**

1984 (1984) ★★★★½ A stunning adaptation of George Orwell's novel, which captures every mote of bleak despair found within those pages. John Hurt looks positively emaciated as the forlorn Winston Smith, the tragic figure who dares to fall in love in a totalitarian society where emotions are outlawed. Richard Burton, in his last film role, makes a grand interrogator. Rated R for nudity and adult themes. 123m. DIR: Michael Radford. CAST: John Hurt, Richard Burton, Suzanna Hamilton, Cyril Cusack. 1984

1990: THE BRONX WARRIORS 🦃 Near the end of the 1980s, the Bronx becomes a kind of no-man's-land ruled by motorcycle gangs. Rated R for violence and language. 89m. DIR: Enzo G. Castellari. CAST: Vic Morrow, Christopher Connelly, Mark Gregory. 1983

NO ESCAPE ★★★ In the year 2022, decorated soldier Ray Liotta is sent to prison for shooting his commanding officer. When he fails to follow the rules, Liotta is dropped on a prison island where a tribe of grungy killers called the "Outsiders" do battle with the more civilized "Insiders." It's diverting and action-packed, but little more. Rated R for violence and gore. 118m. DIR: Martin Campbell. CAST: Ray Liotta, Lance Henriksen, Stuart Wilson, Kevin Dillon, Ernie Hudson, Michael Lerner, Kevin J. O'Connor. 1994

NUDES ON THE MOON 🦃 Laughable, cheapo production about a couple of airhead scientists who blast off for the moon. Not rated, but contains nudity. 76m. DIR: Anthony Brooks. CAST: Marietta, William Mayer. 1963

OFFICIAL DENIAL ★★★½ Parker Stevenson believes he's been abducted and examined by extraterrestrials, but no one will believe him, including wife Erin Gray. Then a spacecraft crashes near his home, leaving an alien stranded, and the military decides to let Stevenson attempt to communicate with it. A well-acted and thought-provoking science-fiction thriller. Made for cable. 96m. DIR: Brian Trenchard-Smith. CAST: Parker Stevenson, Erin Gray, Dirk Benedict, Chad Everett. 1993

OMEGA MAN, THE ★★★½ Charlton Heston does a last-man-on-Earth number in this free adaptation of Richard Matheson's *I Am Legend.* The novel's vampirism has been toned down, but Chuck still is holed up in his high-rise mansion by night, and killing robed (and sleeping) zombies by day. Although this is no more faithful to Matheson's work than 1964's *The Last Man on Earth, The Omega Man* has enough throat-grabbing suspense to keep it moving. Rated PG—considerable violence. 98m. DIR: Boris Sagal. CAST: Charlton Heston, Anthony Zerbe, Rosalind Cash. 1971

ON THE BEACH ★★★★ The effect of a nuclear holocaust on a group of people in Australia makes for engrossing drama in this film. Gregory Peck is a submarine commander who ups anchor and goes looking for survivors as a radioactive cloud slowly descends upon this apparently last human enclave. Director Stanley Kramer is a bit heavy-handed in his moralizing and the romance between Peck and Ava Gardner is distracting, yet the film remains a powerful antiwar statement. B&W; 133m. DIR: Stanley Kramer. CAST: Gregory Peck, Ava Gardner, Fred Astaire, Anthony Perkins. 1959

ONE MILLION B.C. ★★ D. W. Griffith reportedly directed parts of this prehistoric-age picture before producer Hal Roach and his son took over. Victor Mature, Carole Landis, and Lon Chaney Jr. try hard—and there are some good moments—but the result is a pretty dumb fantasy film. B&W; 80m. DIR: Hal Roach, Hal Roach Jr. CAST: Victor Mature, Carole Landis, Lon Chaney Jr. 1940

ORGUSS, VOLS. 1–4 ★★ Japanese animation. Mediocre series involving a young soldier who is transplanted suddenly from his own world into a parallel dimension. Standard television-series entry. Unrated, with brief nudity. 55m.–80m. DIR: Noboru Ishiguro, Yasuyoshi Mikamoto. 1983

OUTER LIMITS, THE (TV SERIES) ★★★½ This well-remembered television classic of science fiction produced some fine morality plays. Assisted by the control voice which promised "there is nothing wrong with your television set," viewers experienced compelling *film noir* science fiction. With literate and absorbing scripts, the episodes hold up quite well today. The best is Harlan Ellison's "Demon with a Glass Hand," starring Robert Culp. Other noteworthy episodes include "The Sixth Finger," in which Welsh coal miner David McCallum takes a trip into his own biologic future, and "The Man Who Was Never Born," which sends Martin Landau back in time (to *our* present). Suitable for family viewing, although a bit intense for small fry. B&W; 52m. per tape. DIR: Laslo Benedek, John Erman, James Goldstone, Charles Haas, Byron Haskin, Leonard Horn, Gerd Oswald. CAST: Robert Culp, Bruce Dern, Robert Duvall, Cedric Hardwicke, Shirley Knight, Martin Landau, David McCallum, Vera Miles, Edward Mulhare, Donald Pleasence, Cliff Robertson, Martin Sheen, Robert Webber. 1964

OUTLAND ★★★★ Sean Connery stars as the two-fisted marshal in this thoroughly enjoyable outer-space remake of *High Noon* directed by Peter Hyams. Much of the credit for that goes to Connery. As he has proved in many pictures, he is one of the few actors today who can play a fully credible adventure hero. Rated R. 109m. DIR: Peter Hyams. CAST: Sean Connery, Peter Boyle, Frances Sternhagen. 1981

OUTLAW OF GOR 🦃 Boring follow-up to the Conan-style original, *Gor.* Rated PG-13 for violence. 90m. DIR: John "Bud" Cardos. CAST: Urbano Barberini, Rebecca Ferratti, Jack Palance. 1987

PEACEMAKER ★★½ An interplanetary serial killer is hunted down on Earth by a policeman from back home—but which one is which? Limp effects and dull direction may weaken your concern. Rated R. 90m. **DIR:** Kevin S. Tenney. **CAST:** Robert Forster, Lance Edwards, Robert Davi. **1990**

PEOPLE, THE ★★ This TV movie is a fair interpretation of the science-fiction stories of Zenna Henderson about psychically talented aliens whose home world has been destroyed and who must survive on Earth. The script gives Henderson's subtle themes a heavy-handed and unbalanced treatment. 74m. **DIR:** John Korty. **CAST:** William Shatner, Dan O'Herlihy, Diane Varsi, Kim Darby. **1971**

PEOPLE THAT TIME FORGOT, THE ★★ Edgar Rice Burroughs probably would have been outraged by this and its companion piece, *The Land That Time Forgot.* Doug McClure gets rescued by friend Patrick Wayne from a fate worse than death on a strange island circa 1919. Laughable rubber-suited monsters mix it up with ludicrous wire-controlled beasties. Rated PG. 90m. **DIR:** Kevin Connor. **CAST:** Doug McClure, Patrick Wayne, Sarah Douglas, Thorley Walters. **1977**

PHANTOM FROM SPACE 🖤 Drab sci-fi about an invisible alien trapped in L.A. B&W; 72m. **DIR:** W. Lee Wilder. **CAST:** Ted Cooper, Rudolph Anders, Noreen Nash. **1953**

PHASE IV ★★★½ An interesting sci-fi mood piece from 1973 about scientists (Nigel Davenport, Michael Murphy) attempting to outwit superintelligent mutant ants. Good effects and fine acting. Rated PG. 86m. **DIR:** Saul Bass. **CAST:** Nigel Davenport, Michael Murphy, Lynne Frederick. **1974**

PHILADELPHIA EXPERIMENT, THE ★★★½ Reportedly based on a true incident during World War II involving an antiradar experiment that caused a naval battleship to disappear in Virginia, this entertaining science-fiction film stars Michael Paré as a sailor on that ship. But instead of ending up in Virginia, he finds himself in the modern world of 1984. Rated PG for violence and profanity. 102m. **DIR:** Stewart Raffill. **CAST:** Michael Paré, Nancy Allen, Bobby DiCicco, Eric Christmas. **1984**

PHILADELPHIA EXPERIMENT 2, THE ★★★ Although it bears little relation to its predecessor, Kevin Rock and Nick Paine have scripted an engaging time-travel thriller that explores the consequences of a stealth bomber unexpectedly landing in Nazi hands during World War II. Brad Johnson makes a suitably wholesome hero, and Gerrit Graham is amusing as a reckless scientist. Rated PG-13 for violence. 98m. **DIR:** Stephen Cornwell. **CAST:** Brad Johnson, Marjean Holden, Gerrit Graham, John Christian Graas. **1993**

PHOENIX THE WARRIOR 🖤 In the distant future germ warfare has killed all the men, and women have become warriors. Not rated, but contains violence. 90m. **DIR:** Robert Hayes. **CAST:** Persis Khambatta. **1987**

PLAGUE DOGS, THE ★★★★½ This animated film is definitely *not* for children. It is a powerfully disturbing film which makes an unforgettable statement about animal rights. In it, two dogs escape from an experimental veterinary lab in which they had both been subjected to cruel and senseless operations and tests. Once free, they are hunted by both the "white coats" (lab doctors) and the nearby sheep owners. Rated PG. 99m. **DIR:** Martin Rosen. **1984**

PLAN 9 FROM OUTER SPACE ★★★ Ever seen a movie that was so bad it was funny? Well, this low-budget 1950s program is considered to be the very worst picture ever made, and it's hilarious. Written and directed by Edward D. Wood, it's a ponderous science-fiction cheapie that attempts to deliver an antiwar message as well as thrills and chills. It does neither. The acting is atrocious, the sets are made of cardboard (and often bumped into by the stars), the dialogue moronic, and the filmmaking technique execrable. Even worse, Bela Lugosi is top-billed even though he died months before the film was made. Undaunted, Wood used silent home-movie footage of the once-great horror film star. Get the idea? B&W; 79m. **DIR:** Edward D. Wood Jr. **CAST:** Bela Lugosi, Gregory Walcott, Tom Keene, Duke Moore, Mona McKinnon. **1959**

PLANET BUSTERS ★★ Japanese animation. While the artwork is more than passable, this entry suffers heavily from a free adaptation by the director of the Americanized version. The seemingly endless chase sequences and the gonzo philosophy destroy any comedic pacing. 80m. **DIR:** Shinya Sadamitsu. **1986**

PLANET EARTH ★★ After the original *Star Trek* went off the air but before it was revived on the big screen, creator Gene Roddenberry experimented with several failed television series pilots. *Planet Earth*, essentially Woody Allen's *Sleeper* as straight drama, was one of the silliest. Lead hunk John Saxon goes under in 1979 and awakens in 2133, only to discover that a "great catastrophe" has fragmented people into a series of iconoclastic colonies. 74m. **DIR:** Marc Daniels. **CAST:** John Saxon, Janet Margolin, Ted Cassidy, Diana Muldaur. **1974**

PLANET OF BLOOD ★★ Curtis Harrington's two-week wonder is the best of a handful of space operas cobbled together using footage from the late Fifties Soviet sci-fi epic, *Planet of Storms*. An expedition rescues a strange, mute alien, not realizing she's the vampire who wiped out a previous ship from Earth! Slow-paced but oddly fascinating. Original theatrical title: *Queen of Blood.* 81m. **DIR:** Curtis Harrington. **CAST:** John Saxon, Basil Rathbone, Judi Meredith, Dennis Hopper, Florence Marly. **1966**

PLANET OF THE APES ★★★★ Here is the first and best of the *Planet of the Ape* sci-fi series. Four American astronauts crash on a far-off planet and discover a culture where evolution has gone awry. The dominant form of primates are apes and gorillas. Man is reduced to a beast of burden. Much of the social comment is cutesy and forced, but this remains an enjoyable fantasy. Rated PG for violence. 112m. **DIR:** Franklin J. Schaffner. **CAST:** Charlton Heston, Kim Hunter, Roddy McDowall, Maurice Evans. **1968**

PLANET OF THE DINOSAURS ★★ A spacecraft crash-lands on a planet inhabited by dinosaurs. Juvenile time killer with decent animation effects. Rated PG. 85m. **DIR:** James K. Shea. **CAST:** James Whitworth. **1978**

PLANET ON THE PROWL 🦃 A runaway planet. Originally released as *War Between the Planets*. 80m. **DIR:** Anthony M. Dawson. **CAST:** Giacomo Rossi-Stuart. **1965**

PLANTS ARE WATCHING, THE ★★½ Originally titled *The Kirlian Witness*, this low-budget melodrama is a well-intentioned fantasy about a clairvoyant woman who taps into the "minds" of plants. She uses the gift to learn the identity of the murderer of her sister. Clever and original, if unexciting. Not rated. 100m. **DIR:** Jonathan Sarno. **CAST:** Nancy Snyder, Joel Colodner, Nancy Boykin. **1978**

POLAR BEAR KING, THE ★★★ In this slow-moving fairy tale, a prince is turned into a polar bear by a wicked witch. He travels north and encounters a young woman. They fall in love and battle the evil crone together. Rated PG. 87m. **DIR:** Ola Solum. **CAST:** Maria Bonnevie, Jack Fieldstad, Tobias Hoesl, Anna-Lotta Larsson, Jon Laxdal, Monica Nordquist. **1992**

PREDATOR ★★★★½ Sort of an earthbound *Alien*, *Predator* stars Arnold Schwarzenegger as a commando out to terminate a kill-crazy creature in a Latin American jungle. Although it sounds derivative, this film delivers a pulse-pounding tale. Rated R for profanity and violence. 107m. **DIR:** John McTiernan. **CAST:** Arnold Schwarzenegger, Carl Weathers, Elpidia Carrillo, Bill Duke, Sonny Landham, Richard Chaves, R. G. Armstrong, Kevin Peter Hall. **1987**

PREDATOR 2 🦃 This sequel lacks the creativity. Rated R for violence, profanity, nudity, and gore. 108m. **DIR:** Stephen Hopkins. **CAST:** Danny Glover, Gary Busey, Rubén Blades, Maria Conchita Alonso, Bill Paxton, Robert Davi, Adam Baldwin, Kent McCord, Morton Downey Jr. **1990**

PREHISTORIC WOMEN (1950) 🦃 A tribe of female bimbos runs into a tribe of male bimbos. 74m. **DIR:** Gregg Tallas. **CAST:** Laurette Luez, Allan Nixon, Joan Shawlee. **1950**

PRIMAL SCREAM ★★ A futuristic psychological thriller that's heavy on psychology and weak on script and acting, but with some pretty neat special effects. Rated R for profanity, violence, and some nudity. 95m. **DIR:** William Murray. **CAST:** Kenneth McGregor. **1987**

PRINCESS BRIDE, THE ★★★★½ This grand adaptation of William Goldman's cult novel owes its success to director Rob Reiner's understanding of gentle whimsy. In a land long ago and far away, Cary Elwes battles horrible monsters and makes unusual friends while fighting to save his beloved Buttercup (Robin Wright) from the clutches of the smarmy Prince Humperdinck (Chris Sarandon). The cast is uniformly excellent, with Mandy Patinkin a standout as the swordsman determined to find the man who killed his father. A wonderful fantasy for all ages. Rated PG for modest violence and language. 98m. **DIR:** Rob Reiner. **CAST:** Cary Elwes, Robin Wright, Mandy Patinkin, Andre the Giant, Chris Sarandon, Wallace Shawn, Billy Crystal, Carol Kane, Peter Falk. **1987**

PRINCESS WARRIOR 🦃 Fleeing to Earth from her home planet (where men are the weaker sex), the good Princess Ovule is pursued by her evil sister and her minions. Rated R for violence and nudity. 84m. **DIR:** Lindsay Norgard. **CAST:** Sharon Lee Jones, Mark Pacific. **1990**

PRISON PLANET 🦃 More *Mad Max*-inspired silliness about futuristic warriors beating each other senseless for an hour and a half. Rated R for violence. 90m. **DIR:** Armand Gazarian. **CAST:** James Phillips, Michael M. Foley, Deborah Thompson. **1992**

PRISONER, THE (TV SERIES) ★★★★ Probably the finest science-fiction series ever created for television, this was the brainchild of star Patrick McGoohan, who intended it to be an oblique follow-up to his successful *Danger Man* and *Secret Agent* series. The main character (McGoohan), whose name never is given—although he is believed to be *Secret Agent*'s John Drake—abruptly resigns from a sensitive intelligence position without explanation. He is abducted and awakens one morning in a mysterious community known only as The Village. Now he is called Number Six—every resident is known only by a number, never by a name. McGoohan conceived the show as a limited series of seventeen episodes; it therefore was the *first* television miniseries. Superior episodes are "The Arrival," wherein the Prisoner is abducted and learns about his new surroundings; "The Chimes of Big Ben," which details his first complicated escape scheme; "Schizoid Man," wherein the Prisoner is brainwashed into a new identity and confronts another person claiming to be Number Six; "Many Happy Returns," wherein the Prisoner wakes one morning to find The Village completely deserted; "Living in Harmony," an episode never shown on American television, which finds the Prisoner replaying a weird parody of his life in a Western setting; and "Once Upon a Time" and "Fallout," the two-parter that brings the story to a close. Each 52m. **DIR:** Patrick McGoohan, David Tomblin, Don Chaffey, Pat Jackson. **CAST:** Patrick McGoohan, Angelo Muscat, Leo McKern, Peter Bowles, Nigel Stock, Peter Wyngarde. **1968**

PRISONER VIDEO COMPANION, THE ★★ This badly organized overview of *The Prisoner* is less than an ideal viewer's guide. The whole point of star-cocreator Patrick McGoohan's groundbreaking series was its ambiguity. Instead of simply introducing characters, events, and locales, the writer and director of this study (who, perhaps wisely, retreat behind anonymity) offer half-baked answers and forced explanations. 55m. **CAST:** Patrick McGoohan, Angelo Muscat, Leo McKern. **1990**

PRISONERS OF THE LOST UNIVERSE ★★ A low-budget science-fantasy adventure about three people transported to a parallel universe. Once there, they must use modern technology and archaic weaponry to battle an evil warlord. Although riddled with poor special effects, the film is actually a lot of good-natured fun. Made for Showtime cable network; contains some profanity and mild violence. 94m. **DIR:** Terry Marcel. **CAST:** Richard Hatch, Kay Lenz, John Saxon. **1983**

PROGRAMMED TO KILL ★★ Sandahl Bergman plays a terrorist who is killed only to be brought back to life as a computer-controlled antiterrorist weapon for the United States. The plan backfires. Acting is poor and so is the script. Rated R for violence, profanity, and nudity. 91m. **DIR:** Allan Holzman. **CAST:** Robert Ginty, Sandahl Bergman, James Booth. **1987**

PROJECT: ALIEN 💔 Confusing sci-fi dud surrounds an explosion and shower of flaming objects over Norway. Rated R for language. 92m. **DIR:** Frank Shields. **CAST:** Michael Nouri, Darlanne Fluegel, Maxwell Caulfield, Charles Durning. **1992**

PROJECT MOON BASE ★★ Futuristic story (set in far-off 1970!) chronicles the fate of an expedition that leaves a space station orbiting Earth and heads for the Moon. Made by independent producer Robert Lippert, this dull space story was co-authored by the esteemed Robert E. Heinlein, but it doesn't reflect his touch. B&W; 53m. **DIR:** Richard Talmadge. **CAST:** Ross Ford, Donna Martell, James Craven. **1953**

PROJECT X ★★ A misguided attempt to turn a serious issue—the abuse of research animals—into a mainstream comedy-drama. Matthew Broderick is an air force misfit who winds up assigned to a secret project involving chimpanzees and air-flight simulators. Rated PG for intensity of theme. 108m. **DIR:** Jonathan Kaplan. **CAST:** Matthew Broderick, Helen Hunt, Bill Sadler, Jonathan Stark, Robin Gammell, Stephen Lang. **1987**

PROTOTYPE ★★★ Christopher Plummer heads a government research team that has perfected an android. Contrary to his wishes, the Pentagon reprograms the android for their own sinister reasons. Nothing original, but entertaining nonetheless. Made for TV. 97m. **DIR:** David Greene. **CAST:** Christopher Plummer, David Morse, Stephen Elliott, Frances Sternhagen, Arthur Hill. **1983**

PROTOTYPE X29A ★★½ In a postnuclear-war future, cyborg hunter killers seek out mutants. This is basically a cross between *Robocop* and *Terminator*, with none of the originality that made those two films smash hits. Rated R for violence, profanity, and nudity. 98m. **DIR:** Phillip Roth. **CAST:** Lane Lenhart. **1992**

QUANTUM LEAP (TV SERIES) ★★★★ When scientist Dr. Sam Beckett (Scott Bakula) gets lost during a time-travel experiment, he's bounced from time to time, leaping into troubled individuals and helping them overcome their problems. His only companion is a holographic image of another scientist (Dean Stockwell). Television series tackles important issues in a sensitive yet entertaining way. Available episodes include "The Pilot Episode," "The Color of Truth," "Camikazi Kid," "What Price Gloria?" and "Catch a Falling Star." Pilot episode 93m; other episodes 48m. **DIR:** David Hemmings, Mike Vejar, Alan J. Levi, Donald P. Bellisario. **CAST:** Scott Bakula, Dean Stockwell, Jennifer Runyon, Jason Priestley, John Cullum, Janine Turner. **1989**

QUARANTINE ★★★ A power-mad politician quarantines victims of an unknown disease, leading to two societies, one rated at risk and the other that rates them. Rated R for violence and profanity. 92m. **DIR:** Charles Wilkinson. **CAST:** Beatrice Boepple. **1989**

QUATERMASS AND THE PIT ★★★ Nigel Kneale's inscrutable, indefatigable Prof. Quatermass—who launched rockets from Britain to deep space, locked horns with authority figures and became one of the most popular British TV heroes of the Fifties—is played here by Andre Morell in a full-length BBC telecast. It's technically primitive and rather talky, but as the talk is by top fantasy scripter Kneale, who's complaining? B&W; 180m. **DIR:** Rudolph Cartier. **CAST:** Andre Morell, Cec Linder, Anthony Bushell, Michael Ripper. **1958**

QUATERMASS CONCLUSION, THE ★★ It's sad to see a great premise destroyed by bad editing and sloppy script continuity. Of course, the fact that this film is an edited-down version of a British miniseries may be the cause. In the strange future world of the story, society seems to be suffering a terrible case of inertia. The world's teen population is committing mass suicide, and only Dr. Quatermass (John Mills), genius scientist, can save them. 105m. **DIR:** Piers Haggard. **CAST:** John Mills, Simon MacCorkindale, Barbara Kellerman, Margaret Tyzack. **1979**

QUATERMASS EXPERIMENT, THE ★★★ The first Hammer horror film is a splendid, low-budget exercise in British suspense, science fiction, and futuristic horror. When an experimental spacecraft returns to Britain, its crew has mysteriously vanished—all save one member, who is comatose and covered in a thin layer of slime, which subtly begins to change him. An enormous success internationally, this film launched the world horror and sci-fi revival that otherwise was dominated by dreadful teen horror flicks. Also titled (in U.S. only): *The Creeping Unknown*. B&W; 78m. **DIR:** Val Guest. **CAST:** Brian Donlevy, Jack Warner, Richard Wordsworth. **1956**

QUAY BROTHERS, THE: VOLUME I&II ★★★★★ Impressive animation collection from the American twins who reside in London. Their universe of puppet animation, inspired by Czech animator Jan Svankmajer, strikes at the heart of the human subconscious where decaying dolls and primitive machinery interact. Not rated, but recommended for adult viewers. 90m. **DIR:** Stephen Quay, Timothy Quay. **1990**

QUEEN OF OUTER SPACE ★★★ Earthmen venture to Venus to find an all-female civilization led by Zsa Zsa Gabor. So bad, it's hysterical. A must for all B-film fanatics. 80m. **DIR:** Edward L. Bernds. **CAST:** Zsa Zsa Gabor, Eric Fleming, Paul Birch. **1958**

QUEST FOR FIRE ★★★★½ In this movie, about the attempt to learn the secret of making fire by a tribe of primitive men, director Jean-Jacques Annaud (*Black and White in Color*) and screenwriter Gerard Brach (*Tess*) have achieved what once seemed to be impossible: a first-rate, compelling film about the dawn of man. Rated R for violence, gore, nudity, and semi-explicit sex. 97m. **DIR:** Jean-Jacques Annaud. **CAST:** Everett McGill, Rae Dawn Chong, Ron Perlman. **1981**

QUEST FOR THE MIGHTY SWORD 🦃 Latest, and hopefully last, of the *Ator* sword-'n'-sorcery sagas. None of these films were any good, but this one's the pits. Rated PG-13 for violence. 94m. **DIR:** David Hills. **CAST:** Eric Allen Kramer, Margaret Lenzey, Donal O'Brian, Laura Gemser. **1989**

QUEST OF THE DELTA KNIGHTS ★★★ In this enchanting, funny medieval story about good and evil, a young slave finds he's the key to the treasures of Archimedes and ventures on a dangerous journey. Good fight scenes. Rated PG. 97m. **DIR:** James Dodson. **CAST:** David Warner, Olivia Hussey, Corbin Allred, Brigid Conley Walsh, David Kind, Sarah Douglas. **1993**

QUIET EARTH, THE ★★★★ First-rate science-fiction thriller from New Zealand. A scientific researcher (Bruno Lawrence) wakes one morning and discovers that all living beings—people and animals—have vanished. Fearful that the world-encircling energy grid on which he'd been working may have been responsible, he sets out to find other people. Intelligent and absorbing adaptation of the book by Craig Harrison. Rated R for nudity and sexual situations. 91m. **DIR:** Geoff Murphy. **CAST:** Bruno Lawrence, Alison Routledge. **1985**

QUINTET ★★ This is about as pessimistic a view of the future as one is likely to see. Director Robert Altman has fashioned a murky, hard-to-follow film, concerning the ultimate game of death, set against the background of a frozen postnuclear wasteland. An intriguing idea, but Altman doesn't pull this one off. Rated R. 110m. **DIR:** Robert Altman. **CAST:** Paul Newman, Fernando Rey, Bibi Andersson. **1979**

R.O.T.O.R. 🦃 Abysmal variation on the *Robocop* theme has a part-man, part-machine police officer going berserk. Rated R for violence and profanity. 91m. **DIR:** Cullen Blaine. **CAST:** Richard Gesswein. **1988**

RADIOACTIVE DREAMS ★★★ This one has a little bit of everything: action, adventure, science fiction, fantasy, and an excellent score. Essentially a spoof, the story begins in a post-apocalypse fallout shelter where two boys have lived most of their lives. They end up in the middle of a gang war with a mutant surfer, hippie cannibals, and biker women. Rated R for nudity and violence. 94m. **DIR:** Albert Pyun. **CAST:** John Stockwell, Michael Dudikoff, George Kennedy, Don Murray, Michelle Little, Norbert Weiser, Lisa Blount. **1984**

RAIDERS OF THE LOST ARK ★★★★★ For sheer spirit-lifting entertainment, you can't do better than this film, by director Steven Spielberg and writer-producer George Lucas. Harrison Ford stars as Indiana Jones, the roughest, toughest, and most unpredictable hero to grace the silver screen, who risks life and limb against a set of the nastiest villains you've ever seen. It's all to save the world—what else? Rated PG for violence and gore. 115m. **DIR:** Steven Spielberg. **CAST:** Harrison Ford, Karen Allen, Wolf Kahler, Paul Freeman, Ronald Lacey, John Rhys-Davies, Denholm Elliott. **1981**

RAY BRADBURY'S CHRONICLES: THE MARTIAN EPISODES ★★★½ Although clearly produced with minimal budgets, these five installments of TV's *Ray Bradbury Theater* are infinitely superior to the network-television miniseries containing the same stories. Credit Bradbury himself, whose adaptations retain the pathos and poetic impact that have made his tales classics. "Mars Is Heaven" remains the best known, with its unsettling image of Mars as Smalltown, U.S.A., but "The Martian" is by far the best piece, featuring an alien willing to kill itself to please the strangers who've settled its native planet. The tape also includes "The Concrete Mixer," "And the Moon Be Still as Bright," and "The Earthmen." 112m. **DIR:** Various. **CAST:** Hal Linden, Ben Cross, John Vernon, Sheila Moore, David Carradine, David Birney. **1989–1990**

REBEL STORM ★★½ Mildly diverting futuristic thriller about a group of freedom fighters attempting to overthrow a suppressive government. 99m. **DIR:** Franky Schaeffer. **CAST:** Zach Galligan, Wayne Crawford, June Chadwick, John Rhys-Davies. **1990**

RED PLANET MARS Anti-commie sci-fi from the 1950s, as mysterious coded transmissions from Mars turn out to be God telling Earth that communists can't be trusted! Talky, uneventful, and visually flat. B&W; 87m. **DIR:** Harry Horner. **CAST:** Peter Graves, Andrea King, Marvin Miller. **1952**

RESURRECTION OF ZACHARY WHEELER, THE ★★ Disappointing science-fiction–mystery has a well-known senator (Bradford Dillman) taken to a bizarre out-of-the-way treatment center in New Mexico after a serious car accident. Confusing movie. Rated G. 100m. **DIR:** Bob Wynn. **CAST:** Bradford Dillman, Angie Dickinson, Leslie Nielsen. **1971**

RETURN, THE Terminally boring flick about a close encounter. Rated PG. 91m. **DIR:** Greydon Clark. **CAST:** Jan-Michael Vincent, Cybill Shepherd, Martin Landau, Raymond Burr, Neville Brand. **1980**

RETURN OF THE JEDI ★★★★★ This third film in the *Star Wars* series more than fulfills the viewer's expectations. The story centers on the all-out attempt by the Rebel forces—led by Luke Skywalker (Mark Hamill), Han Solo (Harrison Ford), Princess Leia (Carrie Fisher), and Lando Calrissian (Billy Dee Williams)—to turn back the tidal wave of interplanetary domination by the evil Galactic Empire and its forces, led by Darth Vader (Dave Prowse—with the voice of James Earl Jones). Rated PG. 133m. **DIR:** Richard Marquand. **CAST:** Mark Hamill, Harrison Ford, Carrie Fisher, Billy Dee Williams, Dave Prowse, Peter Mayhew, Anthony Daniels, James Earl Jones. **1983**

RETURN TO FANTASY ISLAND ★★ If you liked the television series *Fantasy Island*, you'll like this made-for-TV movie. Ricardo Montalban is the suave operator of a wish-fulfillment island, assisted by his tiny friend Tattoo (Herve Villechaize). It's pure hokum, but it does offer a chance to watch some fine actors. 100m. **DIR:** George McCowan. **CAST:** Ricardo Montalban, Joseph Campanella, Joseph Cotten, Adrienne Barbeau, Laraine Day, Herve Villechaize, Cameron Mitchell, Karen Valentine, France Nuyen, George Chakiris, Horst Buchholz, George Maharis. **1977**

RETURN TO FROGTOWN Unbelievably bad sequel to *Hell Comes to Frogtown*. When a flying Texas ranger (Lou Ferrigno) is captured by a crazed amphibian, a sexy doctor and her reluctant partner try to rescue him. Grade-Z sets, story, and dialogue. Rated PG-13 for violence. 90m. **DIR:** Donald G. Jackson. **CAST:** Lou Ferrigno, Charles Napier, Robert Z'dar, Denice Duff, Don Stroud. **1992**

RETURN TO THE LOST WORLD ★★½ Continuation of British remake is actually more exciting than the first try, although the dinosaurs are still laughable. A group of scientists and tagalongs returns to the mysterious plateau, now threatened by a greedy oil prospector and a volcano. Modest but engaging. Rated PG for violence. 99m. **DIR:** Timothy Bond. **CAST:** John Rhys-Davies, David Warner, Eric McCormack, Tamara Gorski, Nathania Stanford. **1992**

RIDING WITH DEATH ★★ Compilation of two hour-long shows from *The Gemini Man* television series, edited together by some mysterious and unconvincing process. Ben Murphy plays a man who, through a scientific accident, can render himself invisible for short bursts of time. Real comic-book stuff. 97m. **DIR:** Alan J. Levi, Don McDougall. **CAST:** Ben Murphy, Katherine Crawford, Richard Dysart, William Sylvester, Andrew Prine, Alan Oppenheimer, Don Galloway. **1976.**

ROAD WARRIOR, THE ★★★★ A sequel to *Mad Max*, the most successful Australian film of all time ($100 million in worldwide rentals), this exciting adventure features Mel Gibson as a fast-driving, cynical Robin Hood in the desolate post-apocalypse world of the future. Good fun! Rated R for violence, nudity, and profanity. 94m. **DIR:** George Miller. **CAST:** Mel Gibson, Bruce Spence, Vernon Wells, Mike Preston. **1981**

ROBO C.H.I.C. Female crime fighter made in a lab has all of the right parts as played by former *Playboy* Playmate Kathy Shower, but film is long in the tooth and light in the budget department. Send this one back to the factory unopened. Unrated, but contains violence and nudity. 101m. **DIR:** Ed Hansen, Jeff Mandel. **CAST:** Kathy Shower, Jack Carter, Burt Ward, Philip Proctor. **1990**

ROBOCOP ★★★★ *RoboCop* is the ultimate superhero movie. A stylish and stylized cop thriller set in the far future, it concerns a mortally wounded policeman (Peter Weller) who is melded with a machine to become the ultimate defender of justice, RoboCop. One word of warning: this is an extremely violent motion picture. Rated R. 103m. **DIR:** Paul Verhoeven. **CAST:** Peter Weller, Nancy Allen, Dan O'Herlihy, Ronny Cox, Kurtwood Smith, Miguel Ferrer. **1987**

ROBOCOP 2 ★★ Inferior, overly gory sequel pits RoboCop (Peter Weller) against a wily gang of drug dealers and the title creature, a supposedly improved version of himself that has gone berserk. Some interesting character angles but these are all too quickly abandoned in favor of mind-numbing violence. Rated R. 110m. **DIR:** Irvin Kershner. **CAST:** Peter Weller, Nancy Allen, Dan O'Herlihy, Felton Perry, Belinda Bauer. **1990**

ROBOCOP 3 ★★ Completed in 1991 and unreleased for two years, this second sequel to the 1987 hit was hardly worth waiting for, although it is a slight improvement over *RoboCop 2*. The mayhem is a little more under control, but the story is thin and the Japanese villains are straight off a World War II recruiting poster. Rated PG-13 for violence. 104m. **DIR:** Fred Dekker. **CAST:** Robert Burke, Nancy Allen, Rip Torn, Mako, C.C.H. Pounder. **1993**

ROBOT CARNIVAL ★★★ Splendid collection of nine short films representing a variety of styles from some of the finest Japanese animators. 90m. **DIR:** Atsuko Fukushima, Katsuhiro Otomo, Kouji Morimoto, Hiroyuki Kitazume, Hideotoshi Ohmori, Mao Lamdo, Yasuomi Umetsu. **1987**

ROBOT JOX ★★ Transformers-style gladiator adventure aimed at preteen boys, this futuristic tale of battles for world territorial possession will play better on home video than on the big screen. Rated PG for violence and mild profanity. 85m. **DIR:** Stuart Gordon. **CAST:** Gary Graham, Anne-Marie Johnson, Paul Koslo, Robert Sampson, Hilary Mason. **1990**

ROBOT WARS 🦃 Albert Band has a go at remaking his son Charles's film *Robot Jox*, about post-apocalyptic humanity battling it out in giant machines, and fails more miserably. Unrated, but with profanity and violence. 106m. **DIR:** Albert Band. **CAST:** Don Michael Paul, Barbara Crampton, James Staley, Yuji Okumoto, Danny Kamekona. **1993**

ROCK AND RULE ★★½ Muddled fantasy of an aging rock star looking for the secret to immortality. The backgrounds are strong but the animation is static, and while the score boasts names like Lou Reed, Iggy Pop, Cheap Trick, and Blondie, the songs they contribute are mostly throwaways. Rated PG. 85m. **DIR:** Clive Smith. **1983**

ROCKET ATTACK USA 🦃 American spies attempt to steal the plans for Sputnik from the Russians. B&W; 71m. **DIR:** Barry Mahon. **CAST:** John McKay. **1958**

ROCKETSHIP X-M ★★½ A rocket heading for the moon is knocked off course by a meteor storm and is forced to land on Mars. The crewmen find Mars to be very inhospitable, as it has been devastated by atomic war and has mutated creatures inhabiting the planet. While the story is weak and the acting only passable, this is one of the first of the science-fiction films that dominated the 1950s. B&W; 77m. **DIR:** Kurt Neumann. **CAST:** Lloyd Bridges, Hugh O'Brian, Noah Beery Jr., Osa Massen, John Emery. **1950**

RODAN ★★★½ This minor classic was Japan's answer to the nuclear "big bug" films of the decade. Murderous insects are just a prelude to the main event featuring not one but *two* supersonic-speed giant pterodactyls. Released in the United States with a stock-footage preface concerning the danger of radioactive experiments, this well-constructed thriller boasts special effects by Eiji Tsuburaya that are superior to many of its American counterparts. 72m. **DIR:** Inoshiro Honda. **CAST:** Kenji Sahara. **1956**

ROLLERBALL ★★★★ Vastly underappreciated science-fiction film envisions a world controlled by business corporations; with no wars or other aggressive activities, the public gets its release in rollerball, a violent combination of basketball, ice hockey, and roller derby. James Caan is a top rollerball champ who refuses to quit the game in spite of threats from industrialist John Houseman, who fears that Caan may turn into a public folk hero. Rated R for violence. 128m. **DIR:** Norman Jewison. **CAST:** James Caan, John Houseman, Maud Adams, Ralph Richardson, John Beck. **1975**

ROLLERBLADE 🦃 *Mad Max* meets *Kansas City Bomber* and *Red Sonja*. 88m. **DIR:** Donald G. Jackson. **CAST:** Suzanne Solari, Jeff Hutchinson. **1986**

RUNAWAY ★★★ Tom Selleck is a futuristic cop trying to track down a bunch of killer robots controlled by the evil villain (Gene Simmons, from the rock band KISS). It's a cinematic comic book and, although meant to be a thriller, never really gets the viewer involved in the story. Rated PG-13 for violence. 99m. **DIR:** Michael Crichton. **CAST:** Tom Selleck, Cynthia Rhodes, Gene Simmons, Kirstie Alley. **1984**

RUNNING AGAINST TIME ★★½ Historian Robert Hays employs physicist Sam Wanamaker's time-travel machine in an effort to prevent Kennedy's assassination but things go horribly awry. Those accustomed to the carefully plotted intricacies of *Back to the Future* will be dismayed by this sloppy made-for-cable time-travel tale, adapted rather freely from Stanley Shapiro's *A Time to Remember*. Rated PG. 93m. **DIR:** Bruce Seth Green. **CAST:** Robert Hays, Catharine Hicks, Sam Wanamaker. **1990**

RUNNING MAN, THE ★★★½ In this silly but exciting outing, Arnold Schwarzenegger is an honest cop who is framed for a crime he didn't commit and forced to fight for his life on a bizarre twenty-first-century game show. Another successful variation on the big guy's standard film formula. Rated R for profanity and violence. 101m. **DIR:** Paul Michael Glaser. **CAST:** Arnold Schwarzenegger, Maria Conchita Alonso, Richard Dawson, Yaphet Kotto, Jim Brown. **1987**

SAMSON 🦃 Samson uses his strength to restore peace in his kingdom. This dubbed film is a yawner. 99m. **DIR:** Gianfranco Parolini. **CAST:** Brad Harris, Bridgette Corey. **1960**

SANTA CLAUS CONQUERS THE MARTIANS 🦃 About a bunch of aliens abducting St. Nick because they don't have one of their own. 80m. **DIR:** Nicholas Webster. **CAST:** John Call, Leonard Hicks. **1964**

SATURN 3 ★★ Although this space shocker is endowed with a fair amount of chills and surprises, there's very little else to it. The story takes place in the distant future on the Eden-like space station Titan, which is happily inhabited by two chemists (Kirk Douglas and Farrah Fawcett). A strangely hostile newcomer (Harvey Keitel) unleashes a terror that threatens to destroy them all. Rated R. 88m. **DIR:** Stanley Donen. **CAST:** Kirk Douglas, Farrah Fawcett, Harvey Keitel. **1980**

SEARCH AND DESTROY (1988) ★★ There's no shortage of action, but little else noteworthy in this science-fiction action yarn about the capturing of a secret biological warfare research station. Rated R, primarily for violence. 90m. **DIR:** J. Christian Ingvordsen. **CAST:** Stuart Garrison Day. **1988**

SEARCH FOR THE GODS ★★ This fairly involving but failed TV-pilot about three adventurers in search of missing pieces to an ancient puzzle makes for an unfinished picture. 90m. **DIR:** Jud Taylor. **CAST:** Kurt Russell, Stephen McHattie, Victoria Racimo, Raymond St. Jacques, Albert Paulsen, Ralph Bellamy. **1975**

SEEDPEOPLE ★★½ Obviously the creators have seen *Invasion of the Body Snatchers*, because they snatch the plot from that classic almost verbatim. Intergalactic pod-people invade a small community in a film that's so awful, it's actually quite entertaining on that level. Overall, fails to take root. Rated R for violence. 87m. **DIR:** Peter Manoogian. **CAST:** Sam Hennings. **1992**

7 FACES OF DR. LAO ★★★★ A first-rate fantasy taken from Charles Finney's classic story, "The Circus of Dr. Lao." Tony Randall plays multiple roles as a mysterious Chinese gentleman and his many strange circus sideshow creatures. Fabulous makeup and special effects, surrounded by a heartwarming story. Perfect for all ages, one of the few films to capture the wonder and sinister overtones of a traveling circus. 100m. **DIR:** George Pal. **CAST:** Tony Randall, Barbara Eden, Arthur O'Connell. **1964**

7TH VOYAGE OF SINBAD, THE ★★★★ Sinbad battles an evil magician who has reduced the princess, who is also Sinbad's fiancée, to six inches in height. Our hero must battle a sword-wielding skeleton, a roc (giant bird), and other dangers to restore his bride-to-be to her normal size. This film contains some of the best stop-motion animation ever created by the master in that craft, Ray Harryhausen. 87m. **DIR:** Nathan Juran. **CAST:** Kerwin Mathews, Kathryn Grant, Torin Thatcher. **1958**

SHE (1925) ★★½ Statuesque vamp Betty Blythe portrays the ageless Queen Ayesha (She) to perfection in this seventh and final silent version of adventure novelist H. Rider Haggard's fantasy about a lost tribe and a flame of eternal life in darkest Africa. Filmed in London and Berlin. Silent, with background music. B&W; 77m. **DIR:** G. B. Samuelson. **CAST:** Betty Blythe, Carlyle Blackwell, Mary Odette. **1925**

SHE (1983) 🦃 Sandahl Bergman is She, the leader of a post-apocalyptic nation that looks upon men as second-class citizens. Not rated, but would be an R for violence and nudity. 90m. **DIR:** Avi Nesher. **CAST:** Sandahl Bergman, Quin Kessler, Harrison Muller, Gordon Mitchell. **1983**

SHORT ANIMATIONS BY LARRY JORDAN ★★★ Filmmaker Larry Jordan uses familiar images of the past and present in these interesting animated short subjects, creating a stunning collage using the cutout method. Titles include "Patricia Gives Birth to a Dream," "Our Lady of the Sphere," "Orb," and "Once Upon a Time." Absorbing and meditative. 42m. **DIR:** Larry Jordan. **1989**

SHORT CIRCUIT ★★★★ In this enjoyable sci-fi comedy-adventure, a sophisticated robot, Number Five, is zapped by lightning during a storm and comes alive (à la Frankenstein's monster) to the shock of his creator (Steve Guttenberg). Created as the ultimate war weapon, the mechanical man learns the value of life from an animal lover (Ally Sheedy) and sets off on his own—with the military in hot pursuit. Rated PG for profanity and violence. 95m. **DIR:** John Badham. **CAST:** Ally Sheedy, Steve Guttenberg, Fisher Stevens, Austin Pendleton, G. W. Bailey. **1986**

SHORT CIRCUIT 2 ★★ If it weren't filled with profanity, *Short Circuit 2* might have been a good film for the kiddies. Indian inventor Fisher Stevens goes into the toy business with streetwise hustler Michael McKean and that lovable robot, Number Five. Rated PG for profanity and violence. 110m. **DIR:** Kenneth Johnson. **CAST:** Fisher Stevens, Michael McKean, Cynthia Gibb, Jack Weston. **1988**

SILENT RUNNING ★★★★ True science fiction is most entertaining when it is not just glittering special effects and is, instead, accompanied by a well-developed plot and worthwhile message. This is such a picture. Bruce Dern is in charge of a futuristic space station that is entrusted with the last living remnants of Earth's botanical heritage. His efforts to preserve those trees and plants in spite of an order to destroy them makes for thoughtful moviemaking. Rated G. 89m. **DIR:** Douglas Trumbull. **CAST:** Bruce Dern, Cliff Potts, Ron Rifkin. **1971**

SINBAD AND THE EYE OF THE TIGER ★★½ The story has Sinbad (Patrick Wayne) seeking the hand of Princess Farah (Jane Seymour) and permission from her brother, Prince Kassim (Damian Thomas), who has been turned into a baboon. Sinbad must sail to a distant isle to find Melanthius (Patrick Troughton), the only wizard capable of breaking the spell. Not a terrible movie (children will love it), but all the movie tricks in the world cannot disguise a bad story. Rated G. 113m. **DIR:** Sam Wanamaker. **CAST:** Patrick Wayne, Jane Seymour, Damien Thomas, Margaret Whiting, Patrick Troughton, Taryn Power. **1977**

SISTERHOOD, THE ★★½ Futuristic tale set in a post-apocalyptic society, where a secret society of female superwarriors battle the male establishment. Filipino-made movie is okay for fans of the genre. Rated R. 76m. **DIR:** Cirio H. Santiago. **CAST:** Rebecca Holden, Chuck Wagner, Lynn-Holly Johnson. **1988**

SLAUGHTERHOUSE FIVE ★★★★ This film, based on Kurt Vonnegut's novel, centers around the activities of Billy Pilgrim, who has become unstuck in time. This enables, or forces, him to jump back and forth among different periods in his life and even experience two separate time-space incidents simultaneously. Well done. Rated R. 104m. **DIR:** George Roy Hill. **CAST:** Michael Sacks, Valerie Perrine, Eugene Roche, John Dehner, Holly Near. **1972**

SLIME PEOPLE, THE 🦃 Hideous monsters burrow up from deep inside Earth and invade Los Angeles. Grade Z. B&W; 76m. **DIR:** Robert Hutton. **CAST:** Robert Hutton, Les Tremayne, Susan Hart. **1962**

SLIPSTREAM ★★½ With its high production values and sweeping Elmer Bernstein score, this movie about a futuristic world raises high hopes. Unfortunately, the story becomes mired down in its sluggishness. Oscar-winners Ben Kingsley and F. Murray Abraham have far too brief cameos late in the film. Rated PG-13 for violence. 92m. **DIR:** Steven Lisberger. **CAST:** Bob Peck, Bill Paxton, Kitty Aldridge, Mark Hamill, Eleanor David, Ben Kingsley, F. Murray Abraham. **1989**

SOLAR CRISIS ★★ The sun is the only thing that flares up in this minor effort. A solar flare-up threatens to destroy life on Earth unless a group of scientists can shoot an antimatter bomb into the sun. The direction reduces everything to bargain-basement clichés. Rated PG-13 for violence. 111m. **DIR:** Alan Smithee. **CAST:** Tim Matheson, Charlton Heston, Peter Boyle, Corin Nemec, Jack Palance, Annabel Schofield. **1992**

SOLARBABIES 🦃 In the far future, a group of sports teens joins forces with a mystical force. Rated PG-13 for violence. 94m. **DIR:** Alan Johnson. **CAST:** Richard Jordan, Jami Gertz, Jason Patric, Charles Durning, Lukas Haas. **1986**

SOMETHING WICKED THIS WAY COMES ★★★ Ray Bradbury's classic fantasy novel has been fashioned into a good, but not great, movie by the Walt Disney Studios. Jason Robards Jr. stars as the town librarian whose task it is to save his family and friends from the evil temptations of Mr. Dark (Jonathan Pryce) and his Pandemonium Carnival. It's an old-fashioned, even gentle tale of the supernatural; a gothic *Wizard of Oz* that seems likely to be best appreciated by preteens. Rated PG. 94m. **DIR:** Jack Clayton. **CAST:** Jason Robards Jr., Jonathan Pryce, Pam Grier, Shawn Carson. **1983**

SOMEWHERE IN TIME ★★★ This gentle, old-fashioned film directed by Jeannot Szwarc celebrates tender passions with great style and atmosphere. The story by Richard Matheson does have a bit of a twist to it—instead of the lovers having to overcome such mundane obstacles as dissenting parents, terminal illness, or other tragedies, they must overcome time itself. Rated PG. 103m. **DIR:** Jeannot Szwarc. **CAST:** Christopher Reeve, Jane Seymour, Christopher Plummer, Bill Erwin, Teresa Wright. **1980**

SORCERESS (1982) 🦃 Twin girls are bestowed with the power of sorcery. Rated R for nudity and simulated sex. 83m. **DIR:** Brian Stuart. **CAST:** Leigh and Lynette Harris. **1982**

SOYLENT GREEN ★★★ In this watchable science-fiction flick, the year is 2022, and New York City is grossly overcrowded. Food is so scarce the government creates a product, Soylent Green, for people to eat. Heston plays the policeman who discovers what it's made of. There is some violence. Rated PG. 97m. **DIR:** Richard Fleischer. **CAST:** Charlton Heston, Edward G. Robinson, Joseph Cotten, Chuck Connors. **1973**

SPACE 1999 (TV SERIES) ★★ An atomic explosion occurs on the Moon, throwing it out of orbit and forcing the occupants of Moon Base Alpha to wander the stars aimlessly. Low production values on this TV series hold back the occasionally original stories. This show still has a small cult following, and the producers have managed to compile some of the better episodes. Not rated. 92m. **DIR:** Ray Austin, Lee H. Katzin. **CAST:** Martin Landau, Barbara Bain, Barry Morse. **1974**

SPACE PATROL (TV SERIES) ★★ Exploits of a twenty-first-century security force responsible for protecting The United Planets (Earth, Venus, Mars, Jupiter, and Mercury) from nasty beings, evil deeds, and intergalactic threats. Early science-fiction series ran for five years. Needless to say, the scripts were simplistic, the effects were cheap, and the performances were far from subtle. B&W; 60m. **DIR:** Dick Darley. **CAST:** Ed Kemmer, Lyn Osborn, Virginia Hewitt, Nina Bara, Rudolph Anders. **1950–1955**

SPACE RAGE 🦃 Richard Farnsworth as a retired twenty-first-century cop living on a prison planet. Rated R for violence galore. 78m. **DIR:** Conrad E. Palmisano. **CAST:** Richard Farnsworth, Michael Paré, John Laughlin, Lee Purcell, William Windom. **1986**

SPACE RAIDERS ★★★½ In this low-budget sci-fi flick from B-movie king Roger Corman, a 10-year-old boy (David Mendenhall) is kidnapped by a group of space pirates led by Vince Edwards, who becomes his mentor. It's an entertaining adventure film which not-too-young youngsters will enjoy. Rated PG for profanity and violence. 82m. **DIR:** Howard R. Cohen. **CAST:** Vince Edwards, David Mendenhall. **1983**

SPACECAMP ★★★ Kate Capshaw is a reluctant instructor at the U.S. Space Camp in Alabama. She and her independent charges—four teens and a younger child—board a real space shuttle and are accidentally launched on a perilous journey. With an attractive cast, impressive special effects, and a noble heart, the movie should inspire the astronauts of the future. Rated PG for suspense. 104m. **DIR:** Harry Winer. **CAST:** Kate Capshaw, Lea Thompson, Tom Skerritt, Kelly Preston, Tate Donovan, Leaf Phoenix. **1986**

SPACEHUNTER: ADVENTURES IN THE FORBIDDEN ZONE 🦃 A futuristic hero takes on an army of militant humanoids on a plague-infested planet. Rated PG for violence. 90m. **DIR:** Lamont Johnson. **CAST:** Peter Strauss, Molly Ringwald, Ernie Hudson, Andrea Marcovicci, Michael Ironside, Beeson Carroll. **1983**

SPLIT SECOND (1992) 🦃 This murky sci-fi thriller—about a cop searching for the inhuman killer of his partner in twenty-first-century London—is a poor rip-off of the visuals of *Blade Runner* and the story line of *Predator*. Rated R for violence, profanity, and nudity. 90m. **DIR:** Tony Maylam. **CAST:** Rutger Hauer, Kim Cattrall, Pete Postlethwaite, Michael J. Pollard. **1992**

STAR CRASH 🦃 A vapid science-fiction space opera with but one redeeming quality: the scanty costumes worn by Caroline Munro as heroine Stella Star. Rated PG—some violence. 92m. **DIR:** Lewis Coates. **CAST:** Caroline Munro, Christopher Plummer, Joe Spinell, Marjoe Gortner, David Hasselhoff. **1979**

STAR CRYSTAL 🦃 Two astronauts encounter a rock containing a monster that feeds on and destroys humans. Rated R for nudity and violence. 93m. **DIR:** Lance Lindsay. **CAST:** Juston Campbell. **1986**

STAR KNIGHT 🦃 Medieval knights meet a visitor from outer space in a film that depicts the period with authenticity, but is pure hokum. Rated R for nudity and violence. 92m. **DIR:** Fernando Colombo. **CAST:** Klaus Kinski, Harvey Keitel, Fernando Rey. **1991**

STAR TREK (TV SERIES) ★★★½ These are the voyages of the Starship *Enterprise*. Her original five-year mission was given short shrift by television executives who pulled the plug after a mere three years from late 1966 to mid-1969, and then watched in horror as fans turned it into the single most popular television series ever made. Paramount has reissued the original shows on tapes made from 35-mm masters, and the *Enterprise* and her crew never have looked lovelier. Superior episodes are "The City on the Edge of Forever," scripted by fantasist Harlan Ellison, "The Trouble with Tribbles," "Court Martial," "Shore Leave," scripted by science-fiction writer Theodore Sturgeon, "A Piece of the Action," "Amok Time," also scripted by Sturgeon; "Menagerie," a two-parter that incorporates the program's original pilot, "Space Seed," which introduces the evil Khan (Ricardo Montalban) and sets up the events later resolved in the second big-screen film; "Wolf in the Fold," scripted by horror writer Robert Bloch, which postulates that Jack the Ripper was a malevolent force that never died; and "Where No Man Has Gone Before," wherein two members of the *Enterprise* crew suddenly acquire incredible mental abilities at the expense of their humanity. Each tape 50m. **DIR:** Marc Daniels, Joseph Pevney, James Goldstone, Gerd Oswald, Vincent McEveety. **CAST:** William Shatner, Leonard Nimoy, DeForest Kelley, George Takei, Walter Koenig, Nichelle Nichols, Majel Barrett, Grace Lee Whitney, James Doohan. **1966–1969**

STAR TREK: THE CAGE ★★★★ This is the first pilot episode of the *Star Trek* television series, initially rejected by NBC for being "too cerebral" and "too good for TV." This is the only recorded story of Captain Christopher Pike (Jeffrey Hunter) and his quite different *Enterprise* crew. The plot concerns a planet of aliens who entrap various forms of animal life in their interplanetary "zoo." Unrated; suitable for family viewing. 65m. **DIR:** Robert Butler. **CAST:** Jeffrey Hunter, Leonard Nimoy, Majel Barrett, John Hoyt, Susan Oliver. **1964**

STAR TREK: THE MENAGERIE ★★★★ Combining the original *Star Trek* pilot, which starred Jeffrey Hunter as the captain, with footage featuring the show's eventual stars, it tells a fascinating story of how Spock brings comfort to his former commander on a planet capable of fulfilling any fantasy. It's science-fiction entertainment of the first order. 100m. **DIR:** Marc Daniels. **CAST:** William Shatner, Leonard Nimoy, Jeffrey Hunter, Susan Oliver, DeForest Kelley, James Doohan, Nichelle Nichols, George Takei. **1967**

STAR TREK—THE MOTION PICTURE ★★½ Even though it reunites the cast of the popular television series and was directed by Robert Wise, who made one of the best science-fiction films of all time (*The Day the Earth Stood Still*), this $35 million film is a real hit-and-miss affair. Fans of the series may find much to love, but others will be bewildered—and sometimes bored—by the overemphasis on special effects and the underemphasis on characterization. Rated G. 132m. **DIR:** Robert Wise. **CAST:** William Shatner, Leonard Nimoy, DeForest Kelley, James Doohan, Nichelle Nichols, George Takei, Walter Koenig. **1979**

STAR TREK: THE NEXT GENERATION (TV SERIES) ★★★★ The second crew of the Starship *Enterprise* "to boldly go" on a series of intergalactic adventures boasts an ensemble of fine actors, including Shakespearean-trained Patrick Stewart as Captain Jean-Luc Picard. This second series by Gene Roddenberry is a lavishly produced, well-written program that, in our opinion, outclasses its predecessor in nearly every respect. The first episode is a feature-length story in which the *Enterprise* crew is sent to examine Far Point, in the outer reaches of the galaxy, to determine whether or not it would be suitable for a Federation star base. 96m. **DIR:** Paul Lynch. **CAST:** Patrick Stewart, Jonathan Frakes, Brent Spiner, Marina Sirtis, Gates McFadden, LeVar Burton, Denise Crosby, Michael Dorn, Wil Wheaton, DeForest Kelley. **1987**

STAR TREK II: THE WRATH OF KHAN ★★★★ James T. Kirk (William Shatner), Mr. Spock (Leonard Nimoy), Doc "Bones" McCoy (DeForest Kelley), and the entire crew of the Starship *Enterprise* once more "boldly go where no man has gone before". It's no *Gone With the Wind*—or even *Raiders of the Lost Ark*. But it is fun to watch, and Trekkies are sure to love it. As Khan, Ricardo Montalban reprises his supervillain role from the 1967 "Space Seed" episode. Rated PG for violence and gore. 113m. **DIR:** Nicholas Meyer. **CAST:** William Shatner, Leonard Nimoy, DeForest Kelley, Ricardo Montalban, James Doohan, George Takei, Nichelle Nichols, Walter Koenig, Kirstie Alley. **1982**

STAR TREK III: THE SEARCH FOR SPOCK ★★★★½ In this thrill-packed release, the crew of the U.S.S. *Enterprise* goes looking for Spock, who appeared to give his life to save his friends—at the end of *Star Trek II: The Wrath of Khan*. But is he dead? Finding out may be one of the most entertaining things you ever do in front of a TV set. Rated PG. 105m. **DIR:** Leonard Nimoy. **CAST:** Leonard Nimoy, William Shatner, DeForest Kelley, James Doohan, George Takei, Nichelle Nichols, Walter Koenig, Christopher Lloyd. **1984**

STAR TREK IV: THE VOYAGE HOME ★★★★½ Our stalwart heroes journey back to Earth in their "borrowed" enemy spacecraft just in time to witness a new tragedy in the making: an alien deep-space probe is disrupting our planet's atmosphere by broadcasting a message that nobody understands. When Spock identifies the "language" as that of the humpback whale, extinct in the twenty-third century, Kirk leads his crew back to the twentieth century in an attempt to locate two of the great mammals and utilize them for translation duty. Charming and lighthearted, though rated PG for somewhat intense themes. 119m. **DIR:** Leonard Nimoy. **CAST:** William Shatner, Leonard Nimoy, DeForest Kelley, James Doohan, George Takei, Walter Koenig, Nichelle Nichols, Catharine Hicks. **1986**

STAR TREK V: THE FINAL FRONTIER ★★½ In this entry of the big-screen series, a Vulcan (Laurence Luckinbill) takes control of the *Enterprise* to pursue his personal quest for spiritual enlightenment. Luckinbill delivers a strong performance, and the script features a number of witty exchanges between the stars. However, its ambitious, metaphysical premise is diluted by a weak, unsatisfying ending. Rated PG for profanity. 110m. **DIR:** William Shatner. **CAST:** William Shatner, Leonard Nimoy, DeForest Kelley, James Doohan, Walter Koenig, Nichelle Nichols, George Takei, David Warner, Laurence Luckinbill. **1989**

STAR TREK VI: THE UNDISCOVERED COUNTRY ★★★★ In this enjoyable piece of entertainment, the crew of the original Starship *Enterprise* becomes involved in a detective tale. After a Klingon ambassador (David Warner) attempts to open peace negotiations with the Federation, he is murdered and Capt. Kirk and Dr. McCoy find themselves on trial for murder. Rated PG for violence. 101m. **DIR:** Nicholas Meyer. **CAST:** William Shatner, Leonard Nimoy, DeForest Kelley, George Takei, James Doohan, Nichelle Nichols, Walter Koenig, Kim Cattrall, David Warner, Christopher Plummer, Michael Dorn, Kurtwood Smith, Brock Peters, Iman. **1991**

STAR WARS ★★★★★ May the Force be with you! Writer-director George Lucas blended the best of vintage pulp science fiction, old-fashioned cliff-hangers, comic books, and classic fantasy to come up with the ultimate adventure "a long time ago in a galaxy far, far away." Rated PG. 121m. **DIR:** George Lucas. **CAST:** Mark Hamill, Harrison Ford, Carrie Fisher, Alec Guinness, Peter Cushing, Anthony Daniels. **1977**

STARFLIGHT ONE 🦃 Airport '82? 115m. **DIR:** Jerry Jameson. **CAST:** Lee Majors, Hal Linden, Lauren Hutton, Ray Milland, Gail Strickland,

George DiCenzo, Tess Harper, Terry Kiser, Robert Webber. 1982

STARMAN ★★★★ Jeff Bridges stars as an alien who falls in love with Earthling Karen Allen. *Starman* is best described as a fairy tale for adults, but the kiddies undoubtedly will enjoy it, too. Rated PG-13 for suggested sex, violence, and profanity. 115m. **DIR:** John Carpenter. **CAST:** Jeff Bridges, Karen Allen, Charles Martin Smith, Richard Jaeckel. 1984

STARSHIP 🦃 Rebels on a mining planet strive to overcome the evil rulers, who want to replace the workers with robots. Rated PG. 98m. **DIR:** Roger Christian. **CAST:** John Tarrant. 1985

STARSHIP INVASIONS 🦃 How did these wily Canadians get such a top cast for such a dreadful movie? By lying to them about how cheesy it would be, assert Robert Vaughn and Chris Lee. Imagine an amalgam of the worst liabilities of Monogram's early Fifties sci-fi stiffs (e.g., *Flight to Mars*) and Sunn Classics's mid-Seventies UFO schlockumentaries. Rated PG. 87m. **DIR:** Edward Hunt. **CAST:** Robert Vaughn, Christopher Lee, Helen Shaver. 1977

STEEL AND LACE ★★ A rather depressingly brutal sci-fi thriller involving a classical pianist's brutal gang rape. Her brother, an ex-NASA scientist, plots to reap revenge on her attackers. Rated R for language and violence. 92m. **DIR:** Ernest Farino. **CAST:** Bruce Davison, David Naughton, Clare Wren, Stacy Naiduk, Michael Cerveris, David L. Lander, Brian Backer, John J. York. 1991

STEEL DAWN 🦃 Brainless bore set in the post-apocalyptic future has martial arts warrior joining in to help widow protect a colony of peaceful settlers. Rated R for violence. 100m. **DIR:** Lance Hool. **CAST:** Patrick Swayze, Lisa Niemi, Christopher Neame, Brion James, Anthony Zerbe. 1987

STEPHEN KING'S GOLDEN YEARS (TV SERIES) ★★★ Seven-episode TV miniseries about an elderly janitor who is exposed to a mysterious form of radiation during a lab accident at a secret government research facility. Soon the old man finds himself slowly growing younger and developing unexplained powers, while being pursued by a shadowy intelligence organization. Quirky, funny, and suspenseful. Alas, the show was canceled before the story could be completed and a quickly shot, 10-minute wrap-up of the story added to tape seven doesn't do the series justice. Not rated, but contains violence and adult situations. 232m. **DIR:** Josef Anderson. **CAST:** Keith Szarabajka, Felicity Huffman, Frances Sternhagen, Ed Lauter. 1991

STEPMONSTER ★★★★ A Tropopkin, a comic-book monster who can assume a human form, becomes engaged to a man. His son, who's an avid comic-book reader, realizes what is happening, but no one believes him. Enjoyable for all ages, with good acting all around. Rated PG-13 for profanity and violence. 87m. **DIR:** Jeremy Stanford. **CAST:** Alan Thicke, Robin Riker, George Gaynes, Ami Dolenz, Edie McClurg, John Astin, Corey Feldman, Billy Corben, Molly Cheek. 1992

STORMQUEST 🦃 Amazon women battling a band of renegade men from a neighboring tribe. Not rated. 90m. **DIR:** Alex Sessa. **CAST:** Brent Huff. 1987

STRANDED ★★★ A story of bigotry and intolerance centered around aliens escaping from another world and landing in a small town. Cameron Dye is the young man who tries to help them escape from the local sheriff, a gang of good ol' boys, and an assassin from outer space. More character development and pacing than usual for a science-fiction film. Rated PG-13 for profanity and violence. 80m. **DIR:** Tex Fuller. **CAST:** Ione Skye, Joe Morton, Cameron Dye, Brendan Hughes, Maureen O'Sullivan. 1987

STRANGE INVADERS ★★★★ A splendid parody of 1950s science-fiction movies, this film begins in 1958, with bug-like aliens taking over a farm town called Centerville, Illinois. The story then jumps to New York City, twenty-five years later, where a college professor (Paul LeMat) is suddenly running off to Illinois after his ex-wife (Diana Scarwid), who has disappeared during a visit to Centerville. Rated PG for violence. 94m. **DIR:** Michael Laughlin. **CAST:** Paul LeMat, Diana Scarwid, Nancy Allen, Louise Fletcher, Michael Lerner, Kenneth Tobey, June Lockhart. 1983

STRANGE NEW WORLD ★★½ After spending almost two centuries in suspended animation, three astronauts return to Earth to discover a *Strange New World* in this made-for-television entry. Through the miracle of cloning, Earth's inhabitants face eternal life, but with a price. 78m. **DIR:** Robert Butler. **CAST:** John Saxon, Keene Curtis, Martine Beswick, James Olson, Kathleen Miller. 1975

STRANGE TALES: RAY BRADBURY THEATER ★★★★ These three initial episodes from cable's *Ray Bradbury Theater* are noteworthy for strong casting and Bradbury's faithful adaptations of his own short stories. The most disturbing entry is "The Town Where No One Got Off," with Jeff Goldblum as a rail commuter who gets involved in a perfect murder scheme. Young Drew Barrymore hears subdued cries for help in "The Screaming Woman." Finally, Charles Martin Smith stands in as Bradbury's surrogate in "The Banshee," which fictitiously explores the relationship between the writer and rogue director John Huston. Superior production values. 86m. **DIR:** Don McBrearty, Bruce Pittman, Douglas Jackson. **CAST:** Peter O'Toole, Charles

Martin Smith, Drew Barrymore, Jeff Goldblum, Ed McNamara, Cec Linder. 1986

STRANGER FROM VENUS 🦃 The same plot and the same star (Patricia Neal) as the classic *The Day the Earth Stood Still* does not guarantee the same quality. A visitor from Venus attempts to warn Earth of the dangers of nuclear weapons but meets with suspicion and hatred. B&W; 78m. **DIR:** Burt Balaban. **CAST:** Patricia Neal, Helmut Dantine, Derek Bond. 1954

STRYKER 🦃 A soldier of fortune attempting to wrest a group of warrior women from the clutches of an evil tribe. Rated R. 86m. **DIR:** Cirio H. Santiago. **CAST:** Steve Sandor, Andria Savio. 1983

SUPER FORCE 🦃 Despite an engaging early cameo by Patrick Macnee, this TV pilot is far from super; Ken Olandt is terminally bland as an astronaut-turned-cop who dons an ersatz RoboCop suit to battle crime in the year 2020. Although not rated, the squeaky-clean material could pass for G. 92m. **DIR:** Richard Compton. **CAST:** Ken Olandt, Larry B. Scott, Patrick Macnee, G. Gordon Liddy. 1993

SUPER FUZZ ★★½ For adults, this is a silly, mindless film...but it's great fun for the kids. Terence Hill stars as Dave Speed, a police officer with supernatural powers. Rated PG. 94m. **DIR:** Sergio Corbucci. **CAST:** Terence Hill, Ernest Borgnine, Joanne Dru, Marc Lawrence. 1981

SUPERGIRL ★★½ Helen Slater makes a respectable film debut as Superman's cousin in this screen comic book, which should delight the kiddies and occasionally tickle the adults. The stellar supporting cast doesn't seem to take it seriously, so why should we? Rated PG. 105m. **DIR:** Jeannot Szwarc. **CAST:** Faye Dunaway, Peter O'Toole, Helen Slater, Mia Farrow, Brenda Vaccaro, Simon Ward, Peter Cook, Hart Bochner. 1984

SUPERMAN ★★★½ After a somewhat overblown introduction, which encompasses the end of Krypton and Clark Kent's adolescence in Smallville, this film takes off to provide some great moments as Superman swings into action. The action is complemented by fine tongue-in-cheek comedy. Rated PG. 143m. **DIR:** Richard Donner. **CAST:** Christopher Reeve, Margot Kidder, Jackie Cooper, Marc McClure, Marlon Brando, Glenn Ford. 1978

SUPERMAN II ★★★★ Even better than the original, this terrific adventure of the Man of Steel includes a full-fledged—and beautifully handled—romance between Lois Lane (Margot Kidder) and Superman (Christopher Reeve) and a spectacular battle that pits our hero against three supervillains (during which the city of Metropolis is almost completely destroyed). Rated PG. 127m. **DIR:** Richard Lester. **CAST:** Margot Kidder, Christopher Reeve, Gene Hackman, Ned Beatty, Jackie Cooper, Terence Stamp. 1980

SUPERMAN III ★★½ If it weren't for Christopher Reeve's excellent performance in the title role, *Superman III* would be a total disappointment. The story features a subdued Richard Pryor as a computer whiz who is hired by bad guy Robert Vaughn to do dastardly deeds with his magic programming. Rated PG. 125m. **DIR:** Richard Lester. **CAST:** Christopher Reeve, Richard Pryor, Robert Vaughn, Annette O'Toole, Jackie Cooper, Marc McClure, Pamela Stephenson. 1983

SUPERMAN IV: THE QUEST FOR PEACE ★★ A well-intentioned plot about Superman (Christopher Reeve) attempting to rid the Earth of nuclear weapons cannot save this overlong, overwrought, confusing, and sometimes downright dull third sequel. Rated PG for violence. 90m. **DIR:** Sidney J. Furie. **CAST:** Christopher Reeve, Gene Hackman, Margot Kidder, Jackie Cooper, Mariel Hemingway, Jon Cryer, Marc McClure, Sam Wanamaker. 1987

SUPERMAN AND THE MOLE MEN ★★½ George Reeves dons the tights and cape that he was to be identified with for the rest of his life. This story concerns a huge oil well that drills too far and yields fuzzy midgets from inside the Earth. This film led to the famous television series and was subsequently shown as a two-part episode. B&W; 67m. **DIR:** Lee Sholem. **CAST:** George Reeves, Phyllis Coates, Jeff Corey, Walter Reed. 1951

SUPERMAN—THE SERIAL ★★½ The first live-action Superman serial was one of the highest grossing of all chapterplays ever made, as well as Columbia's most prestigious effort in that field. As Superman, wavy-haired serial and B-movie hero Kirk Alyn manfully strove to bring life to a story that centered around a female crime czar known as the Spider Lady. The film relies on inept flying sequences and the by-now classic relationship between Clark Kent and Lois Lane for the bulk of its action. B&W; **DIR:** Spencer Gordon Bennet, Thomas Carr. **CAST:** Kirk Alyn, Noel Neill, Tommy Bond, Carol Forman, Pierre Watkin, George Meeker, Charles King, Charles Quigley, Herbert Rawlinson. 1948

SURVIVAL ZONE 🦃 Nuclear-holocaust survivors battling evil. Not rated, contains violence and nudity. 90m. **DIR:** Percival Rubens. **CAST:** Gary Lockwood, Morgan Stevens, Camilla Sparv. 1983

SURVIVOR ★★ While on a space mission, an astronaut witnesses a full-scale nuclear war. Upon return to Earth, he finds total destruction. Richard Moll, of TV's *Night Court*, plays a fine villain in this otherwise routine and violent science-fiction story. 92m. **DIR:** Michael Shackleton. **CAST:** Chris

Mayer, Richard Moll, Sue Kiel, Richard Haines. **1987**

SWORD AND THE SORCERER, THE ★★ But for the derring-do and bits of comedy provided by star Lee Horsley, this film would be a complete waste of time and talent. A soldier of fortune (Horsley) rescues a damsel in distress (Kathleen Beller) and her brother (Simon MacCorkindale) from an evil king and his powerful wizard. Rated R because of nudity, violence, gore, and sexual references. 100m. **DIR:** Albert Pyun. **CAST:** Lee Horsley, Kathleen Beller, Simon MacCorkindale, George Maharis, Richard Lynch, Richard Moll. **1982**

TALES OF TOMORROW (VOLS. I - III) ★★½ All of the several volumes of this admittedly primitive—but compulsively watchable—early-Fifties sci-fi TV series are well worth a look. Each single-volume tape contains four half-hour shows, minus commercials. One tape is highlighted by an early performance by James Dean and another contains a *Frankenstein* adaptation in which Lon Chaney, as the monster, stumbles drunkenly about, thinking it's only a dress rehearsal! B&W; 120m. **CAST:** Lon Chaney Jr., Rod Steiger, James Dean, Boris Karloff. **1953**

TC 2000 🦃 In the year 2020, the atmosphere is gone, so the worthy inhabitants of the Earth live underground. A female cop is killed, turned into a powerful evil android, and sent to destroy all the surface people. Extremely bad acting. Rated R for violence and profanity. 92m. **DIR:** T. J. Scott. **CAST:** Bolo Yeung, Jalal Merhi, Billy Banks, Bobbie Phillips, Matthias Hues. **1993**

TENTH VICTIM, THE ★★★½ A weird little science-fiction film that has achieved minor cult status, thanks to droll performances from Marcello Mastroianni and Ursula Andress and an intriguing plot taken from the novel by Robert Sheckley. The setting is the near future, and pop culture has embraced an assassination game that is played for keeps: ten participants start the hunt against one another, and the sequential elimination of opponents results in one winner. Unrated, contains sexual situations. 92m. **DIR:** Elio Petri. **CAST:** Marcello Mastroianni, Ursula Andress, Elsa Martinelli, Massimo Serato. **1965**

TERMINAL ENTRY ★★ This *War Games* clone is only moderately entertaining. Three teenage couples tap into a computer game called Terminal Entry. It turns out that the game is real and they're caught in the middle of a U.S. antiterrorist strike force and foreign invaders. Rated R for nudity and violence. 95m. **DIR:** John Kincade. **CAST:** Edward Albert, Paul Smith, Yaphet Kotto, Patrick Laborteaux. **1986**

TERMINATOR, THE ★★★½ In this science-fiction–time-travel adventure, Arnold Schwarzenegger stars as a cyborg (part man, part machine) sent from the future to present-day Los Angeles to murder a woman (Linda Hamilton). Her offspring will play an important part in the world from which the killer came. Michael Biehn is the rebel soldier sent to thwart Schwarzenegger's plans. Rated R for nudity, simulated sex, violence, and profanity. 108m. **DIR:** James Cameron. **CAST:** Arnold Schwarzenegger, Linda Hamilton, Michael Biehn. **1984**

TERMINATOR 2: JUDGMENT DAY ★★★★★ A rip-roaring juggernaut of a thriller that far surpasses the original *Terminator*. What elevates *Terminator 2* are elements you may not expect: a fascinating continuation of the original time-travel plot and an engrossing human story about the conflict between man and machine. There's even an important moral agenda, a thought-provoking statement about the increasing dangers of turning over our battles and our lives to computerized machinery. Rated R, with strong violence and profanity. 135m. **DIR:** James Cameron. **CAST:** Arnold Schwarzenegger, Linda Hamilton, Robert Patrick, Joe Morton, Edward Furlong. **1991**

TERROR FROM THE YEAR 5,000 ★★ Not-bad cheapjack sci-fi about contemporary scientists who bring a woman from A.D. 5,000 to their own time and soon regret it. Fast-paced. B&W; 74m. **DIR:** Robert Gurney Jr. **CAST:** Ward Costello, Joyce Holden, Salome Jens. **1958**

TERROR VISION ★★★ An imaginative spoof of sci-fi films, with a hip slant. A family of swinging yuppies accidentally beam down a hostile alien through their satellite dish. Horror fans will be delighted. Rated R for violence and adult situations. 84m. **DIR:** Ted Nicolaou. **CAST:** Diane Franklin, Gerrit Graham, Mary Woronov, Chad Allen. **1986**

TERRORNAUTS, THE ★★ A British scientist succeeds in contacting an alien civilization. They beam the entire building in which he works to their galaxy. British science fiction tends to be talky, and this is no exception. 75m. **DIR:** Montgomery Tully. **CAST:** Simon Oates, Zena Marshall, Charles Hawtrey, Max Adrian. **1967**

TESTAMENT ★★★★★ In its own quiet, unspectacular way, this film tells a simple story about what happens to one family when World War III begins and ends in a matter of minutes. Jane Alexander is superb as the mother attempting to cope with the unthinkable, and this fine movie is one you won't soon forget. Rated PG. 90m. **DIR:** Lynne Littman. **CAST:** Jane Alexander, William Devane, Ross Harris, Roxana Zal, Lukas Haas, Lila Kedrova, Leon Ames. **1983**

TESTAMENT OF DR. CORDELIER, THE ★★★½ This is the great Jean Renoir's exploration of the Jekyll/Hyde theme, and of interest primarily for that unique departure.

Made for French TV but released to theatres, it has a certain flatness that belies its director's talent. The transformation scenes, however, have an almost transcendent energy. B&W; 74m. **DIR:** Jean Renoir. **CAST:** Jean-Louis Barrault. **1959**

THEM! ★★★★ Classic 1950s sci-fi about colossal mutant ants, at large in a New Mexico desert, threatening to take over the world. Frightening special effects and lightning pace make this a supercharged entertainment, with Edmund Gwenn delivering a standout performance as the scientist who foretells the danger. Great. B&W; 94m. **DIR:** Gordon Douglas. **CAST:** Edmund Gwenn, James Arness, James Whitmore, Fess Parker. **1954**

THEY CAME FROM BEYOND SPACE ★★★ Enjoyable tale of formless aliens landing in Cornwall and taking over the minds and bodies of a group of scientists in an effort to preserve their dissipating race. Robert Hutton plays the one man who can't be controlled because of a metal plate in his skull. Based on *The Gods Hate Kansas* by Joseph Millard. 86m. **DIR:** Freddie Francis. **CAST:** Robert Hutton, Jennifer Jayne, Zia Mohyeddin, Bernard Kay, Michael Gough. **1967**

THIEF OF BAGDAD, THE (1924) ★★★½ The first of four spectacular versions of this classic Arabian Nights–ish fantasy-adventure of derring-do with magically flying carpets, giant genies, and crafty evil sorcery. The now-fabled Douglas Fairbanks Sr. is the thief, Julanne Johnson the beautiful princess he carries away on an airborne rug. Of all silent epics, this one is rated the most imaginative. The sets rival everything filmed before and since. Silent. B&W; 140m. **DIR:** Raoul Walsh. **CAST:** Douglas Fairbanks Sr., Julanne Johnson, Anna May Wong, Sojin. **1924**

THIEF OF BAGDAD, THE (1940) ★★★★★ With its flying carpets, giant genies, magic spells, and evil wizards, *Thief of Bagdad* ranks as one of the finest fantasy films of all time. John Justin plays a young king, Ahmad, who is duped by his Grand Vizier, Jaffar, and loses his throne. With the aid of a colossal genie (excellently played by Rex Ingram) and other magical devices, Ahmad must do battle with Jaffar in a rousing fairy tale of good versus evil. 106m. **DIR:** Ludwig Berger, Tim Whelan, Michael Powell. **CAST:** Sabu, John Justin, June Duprez, Rex Ingram, Conrad Veidt. **1940**

THING (FROM ANOTHER WORLD), THE (1951) ★★★★★ A highly entertaining film, this was based on John W. Campbell's story "Who Goes There?" about a hostile visitor from space at large at an army radar station in the Arctic. Considered by many to be a classic, this relies on the unseen rather than the seen for its power, and as such it is almost unbearably suspenseful. Tight direction, deliberate pacing—not to mention exceptional performances by the entire cast—make this a viewing must. James Arness, in an early role, plays the monster. B&W; 87m. **DIR:** Christian Nyby. **CAST:** Kenneth Tobey, Margaret Sheridan, James Arness. **1951**

THING, THE (1982) ★★★★ The modern master of fright, John Carpenter, has created a movie so terrifying, it'll crawl right up your leg. Rather than a remake, this updated version of Howard Hawks's 1951 science-fiction–horror classic is closer to a sequel, with Kurt Russell and his crew arriving at the Antarctic encampment after the chameleon-like creature from outer space has finished off its inhabitants. It's good ol' "tell me a scary story" fun. Rated R for profanity and gore. 108m. **DIR:** John Carpenter. **CAST:** Kurt Russell, Wilford Brimley, Richard Dysart. **1982**

THINGS TO COME ★★★★ The world of the future as viewed from the perspective of the 1930s, this is an interesting screen curio based on the book by H. G. Wells. Special effects have come a long way since then, but sci-fi fans will still enjoy the spectacular sets in this honorable, thoughtful production. B&W; 92m. **DIR:** William Cameron Menzies. **CAST:** Raymond Massey, Cedric Hardwicke, Ralph Richardson. **1936**

THIS ISLAND EARTH ★★★ A fine 1950s sci-fi flick about scientists kidnapped by aliens to help them save their planet, this has good makeup and effects for the era. 86m. **DIR:** Joseph M. Newman. **CAST:** Jeff Morrow, Rex Reason, Faith Domergue. **1955**

THOUSAND EYES OF DR. MABUSE, THE ★★½ Famed suspense *auteur* Fritz Lang's return to Germany and his attempt to revive Dr. Mabuse, his notorious master criminal, is a middling success. But a Lang near miss is better than a triumph by almost anyone else, so this intricately plotted mystery should delight film buffs. Ignore the dopey romantic subplot. Also titled: *Eyes of Evil*, *The Secret of Dr. Mabuse* and *The Diabolical Dr. Mabuse*. B&W; 103m. **DIR:** Fritz Lang. **CAST:** Dawn Addams, Peter Van Eyck, Gert Fröbe, Wolfgang Preiss. **1960**

THREE WORLDS OF GULLIVER, THE ★★★ Following a violent storm at sea, Dr. Lemuel Gulliver (Kerwin Mathews) finds himself ashore on Lilliput, an island with miniature people. A biting satire on human nature, featuring seamless special effects by Ray Harryhausen and an ear-filling Bernard Herrmann score. Based on the classic by Jonathan Swift. Great fun. 100m. **DIR:** Jack Sher. **CAST:** Kerwin Mathews, June Thorburn, Jo Morrow, Gregoire Aslan. **1960**

THRESHOLD ★★ Donald Sutherland stars in this film about the first artificial-heart transplant. Rated PG. 106m. **DIR:** Richard Pearce. **CAST:** Donald Sutherland, John Marley, Jeff Goldblum, Michael Lerner. **1981**

THX 1138 ★★★½ Science-fiction and movie buffs may want to rent this moody, atmospheric picture, starring Robert Duvall and Donald Pleasence, to see an example of the type of work director George Lucas was doing pre–*Star Wars*. It was the fabulously successful filmmaker's first. Interesting. Rated PG. 88m. **DIR:** George Lucas. **CAST:** Robert Duvall, Donald Pleasence, Maggie McOmie. **1971**

TIME AFTER TIME ★★★★ H. G. Wells (Malcolm McDowell) pursues Jack the Ripper (David Warner) into modern-day San Francisco via a time machine. It's an enjoyable pastiche that has quite a few nice moments. Rated PG. 112m. **DIR:** Nicholas Meyer. **CAST:** Malcolm McDowell, David Warner, Mary Steenburgen. **1979**

TIME BANDITS ★★★★ Anyone with a sense of adventure will find a lot to like about this delightful tale of a boy and six dwarves—no, this isn't *Snow White*—who travel back in time through holes in the fabric of the universe. Rated PG for violence and adult themes. 110m. **DIR:** Terry Gilliam. **CAST:** Sean Connery, Shelley Duvall, Ralph Richardson, Ian Holm, David Warner, John Cleese, Michael Palin. **1981**

TIME GUARDIAN, THE 🖤 Enemies of the future—man and metallic man—go back in time to prepare to do battle. Rated PG for violence. 80m. **DIR:** Brian Hannant. **CAST:** Carrie Fisher, Tom Burlinson, Dean Stockwell. **1987**

TIME MACHINE, THE ★★★★ Rod Taylor plays a scientist in the early 1900s who invents a device that can transport him within the dimensions of time. He goes forward past three world wars and into the year 802,701, where he encounters a world very different from the one he left. This movie has all the elements that make up a classic in science fiction. 103m. **DIR:** George Pal. **CAST:** Rod Taylor, Yvette Mimieux, Alan Young, Sebastian Cabot. **1960**

TIME RUNNER ★★ This story alternates between the year 2022, when Earth is at war with aliens, and 1992, when a man from 2022 has arrived on Earth. Of course his actions during 1992 will determine the outcome of the future war. Predictable. Rated R for profanity and violence. 90m. **DIR:** Michael Mazo. **CAST:** Mark Hamill, Brion James, Marc Baur, Gordon Tipple, Rae Dawn Chong. **1992**

TIME STALKERS ★★★ A mildly entertaining made-for-TV movie about a modern-day Old West buff who helps a scientist from the future track a villain into the past. An exciting conclusion. Not rated, but contains mild violence. 96m. **DIR:** Michael Schultz. **CAST:** William Devane, Lauren Hutton, John Ratzenberger, Forrest Tucker, Klaus Kinski. **1986**

TIME TRACKERS ★★ Scientists from the future chase one of their own through time in an effort to stop him from changing the course of history. Great medieval costumes, but the production is too amateurish to soar very high. Rated PG. 86m. **DIR:** Howard R. Cohen. **CAST:** Wil Shriner, Ned Beatty, Kathleen Beller, Bridget Hoffman, Lee Bergere, Alex Hyde-White. **1989**

TIME TRAVELERS, THE ★★★½ Imaginative story of scientists who plunge into a time corridor to rescue a colleague and find themselves stuck in the wreckage of the Earth of the future. Similar in many respects to other survival-after-nuclear-holocaust films, this entertaining film boasts vicious mutants, intelligent survivors who live under the surface of Earth, and a trick ending that is unique and intriguing. 82m. **DIR:** Ib Melchior. **CAST:** Preston Foster, Philip Carey, Merry Anders, Steve Franken, John Hoyt, Joan Woodbury. **1964**

TOBOR THE GREAT ★★ Kids foil commie plot to steal secret robot plans. Terrific-looking robot is only saving grace. B&W; 77m. **DIR:** Lee Sholem. **CAST:** Charles Drake, Karin Booth, Billy Chapin. **1954**

TOMCAT: DANGEROUS DESIRES ★★ Richard Grieco is purr-fectly cast as a handsome loner whose rare blood disease leads him to scientist Maryam D'Ado. After being injected with a new serum, he develops unusual catlike tendencies. The good news is that he's an animal in bed. The bad news is that he uses people who discover his secret as a scratching post. Made-for-cable erotic sci-fi thriller just manages to keep its paws out of the litter box. Rated R for nudity and violence. 96m. **DIR:** Paul Donovan. **CAST:** Richard Grieco, Maryam D'Abo, Natalie Radford. **1993**

TOMMYKNOCKERS, THE ★★½ This network-television miniseries suffers from the same flaws that plagued Stephen King's novel: second-rate characters you don't give a damn about and a slow, rambling narrative. Scripter Lawrence D. Cohen had quite a task, condensing this tale of a small town taken over by long-dormant aliens. Sadly, his screenplay will annoy everybody, particularly King fans destined to howl over the altered conclusion. Rated R for violence, profanity, and sensuality. 120m. **DIR:** John Power. **CAST:** Jimmy Smits, Marg Helgenberger, John Ashton, Allyce Beasley, Robert Carradine, Joanna Cassidy, Traci Lords, E. G. Marshall. **1993**

TOTAL RECALL ★★★★½ Arnold Schwarzenegger flexes plenty of action-movie muscle in this terrific sci-fi adventure. The film has impressive bloodlines: it's adapted from a short story by Philip K. Dick (who also inspired *Blade Runner*), with a screenplay from the *Alien* creators, and direction by the creator of *RoboCop*. A thrill-a-minute futuristic tale. Rated R, with strong violence and profanity. 109m. **DIR:** Paul Verhoeven. **CAST:** Arnold Schwarzenegger, Rachel Ticotin, Sharon Stone, Ronny Cox, Michael Ironside. 1990

TRANCERS ★★ Tim Thomerson is Jack Death, a police officer in the 2280s who is sent to bring back a violent cult leader who escaped into the twentieth century. Rated PG-13 for profanity and lots of violence. 76m. **DIR:** Charles Band. **CAST:** Tim Thomerson, Helen Hunt, Michael Stefani, Art Le Fleur, Telma Hopkins, Richard Herd, Anne Seymour. 1985

TRANCERS II (THE RETURN OF JACK DEATH) 🦃 Jack Death returns to Los Angeles to battle zombielike creatures in this technically abysmal production. Rated R for nudity and violence. 86m. **DIR:** Charles Band. **CAST:** Tim Thomerson, Helen Hunt. 1991

TRANCERS III: DEATH LIVES ★★★ In this third installment, Trancer tracker Jack Death, played with aplomb by Tim Thomerson, is back to hunt down some new Trancers in town, and this time they're rougher and tougher. This series from Full Moon Productions is one of their highlights, and is entertaining in a brutal, self-mocking sort of way. Rated R for violence and language. 83m. **DIR:** C. Courtney Joyner. **CAST:** Tim Thomerson, Melanie Smith, Andrew Robinson, Helen Hunt, Megan Ward. 1992

TRANCERS 4: JACK OF SWORDS ★★½ In his fourth outing as Trancer hunter Jack Deth, Tim Thomerson is transported to another dimension where the locals are being bred as food. Trapped in a medieval world, Deth must utilize knowledge from his time to end the Trancers' reign of terror. New setting and swordplay breathe life into the series. Rated R for violence, nudity, and adult situations. 74m. **DIR:** David Nutter. **CAST:** Tim Thomerson, Stacie Randall, Ty Miller, Stephen Macht, Alan Oppenheimer. 1993

TRANSATLANTIC TUNNEL ★★½ A truly splendid cast still manages to get bogged down a bit in this heavy-handed account of the building of a passageway under the Atlantic Ocean. Richard Dix plays the stalwart engineer who can get the job done and Walter Huston plays the president of the United States. B&W; 90m. **DIR:** Maurice Elvey. **CAST:** Richard Dix, Leslie Banks, Madge Evans, C. Aubrey Smith, George Arliss, Walter Huston, Helen Vinson. 1935

TREASURES OF THE TWILIGHT ZONE ★★★★★ Television historians and fans of Rod Serling's crowning TV achievement won't find better than this two-tape package, which features four of the best *Zones* ever aired (including the series premiere, "Where is Everybody," and Charles Beaumont's most famous story, "The Howling Man"), two episodes never released into syndication (the most notorious of which, "The Encounter," was vociferously protested by the Japanese-American community and never re-aired after its debut), and televised promotional material (notably a 1959 interview with Serling and a youthful Mike Wallace). 175m. **DIR:** Douglas Heyes, Ida Lupino, Robert Stevens, Robert Butler, Robert Enrico. **CAST:** Earl Holliman, Neville Brand, George Takei, Donna Douglas, John Carradine, Robert Keith. 1959–1964

TRIAL OF THE INCREDIBLE HULK ★★★ The green goliath hits New York City, only to be jailed on murder charges. Defending him is blind attorney, Matt Murdock, whose alter ego is the swashbuckling superhero, Daredevil. Together they team up to bring down the city's biggest crime lord, The Kingpin. Made for TV. 93m. **DIR:** Bill Bixby. **CAST:** Bill Bixby, Lou Ferrigno, Rex Smith. 1989

TRIPODS ★★½ Though a bit hard to follow because it is a compilation of episodes from the middle of a BBC science-fiction TV series, *Tripods* is an interesting release about a young man's attempts to escape alien conquerors of Earth in the far future. Once free, our hero decides to join the rebel forces. 150m. **DIR:** Groham Theakston, Christopher Barry. **CAST:** John Shackley, Jim Baker, Ceri Seel, Richard Wordsworth. 1984

TROLL 🦃 A family besieged by evil little creatures. Rated PG-13 for profanity, violence, and gore. 95m. **DIR:** John Carl Buechler. **CAST:** Noah Hathaway, Michael Moriarty, Shelley Hack, Jenny Beck, June Lockhart, Anne Lockhart, Sonny Bono, Brad Hall. 1986

TRON ★★★ An enjoyable, if somewhat light-headed, piece of escapism, this science-fiction adventure concerns a computer genius (Jeff Bridges) who suspects evil doings by a corporate executive (David Warner). During his investigation, Bridges is zapped into another dimension and finds himself a player in a gladiatorial video game. Rated PG. 96m. **DIR:** Steven Lisberger. **CAST:** Jeff Bridges, David Warner, Bruce Boxleitner, Cindy Morgan, Barnard Hughes. 1982

TROUBLE WITH DICK, THE 🦃 Study of frustrated author's peculiar work habits becomes self-consciously banal after the first five minutes. 86m. **DIR:** Gary Walkow. **CAST:** Tom Villard, Susan Dey, Elaine Giftos, Elizabeth Gorcey. 1986

TV CLASSICS: FLASH GORDON AND THE PLANET OF DEATH ★★ Silly by today's standards, this tape, part of a series of Fifties TV classics, is fun for those interested in early television. Bad acting and makeshift special effects may bore some; for others it's a bit of old-time TV fun. Not rated. 30m. **DIR:** Gunther Von Fristch. **CAST:** Steve Holland, Irene Champlin, Joe Nash. 1955

TV'S BEST ADVENTURES OF SUPERMAN ★★★½ Excellent series of tapes combines two episodes of the TV series from the

1950s, one color and one black-and-white, with a Superman cartoon from the Max Fleischer Studios. This series is highly collectible for fans. In general, the black-and-white episodes of the TV series were the best, but you'll be surprised at how entertaining they all are. George Reeves makes a fine Superman–Clark Kent, and Phyllis Coates and Noel Neill do fine jobs in their particular series as Lois Lane. B&W; Each 60m. **DIR:** Thomas Carr, George Reeves, Harry Gerstad, Dave Fleischer. **CAST:** George Reeves, Noel Neill, Phyllis Coates, Jack Larson, John Hamilton. **1950**

12:01 ★★★★ Surprisingly effective science-fiction thriller has accountant Jonathan Silverman trapped in time when an electrical shock "saves" him when the Earth is destroyed by a controversial experiment. Like Bill Murray in *Groundhog Day*, Silverman is fated to live the same day over and over again—unless he can change the course of history. Made for TV. 96m. **DIR:** Jack Sholder. **CAST:** Jonathan Silverman, Helen Slater, Martin Landau, Nicolas Surovy, Robin Bartlett, Jeremy Piven. **1993**

20 MILLION MILES TO EARTH ★★★★ An egg from outer space grows into a giant monster that terrorizes Rome. Ray Harryhausen's stop-motion special effects are still impressive as the gargantuan Ymir battles an elephant and meets its fate in the ruins of the Colosseum. B&W; 84m. **DIR:** Nathan Juran. **CAST:** William Hopper, Joan Taylor. **1957**

20,000 LEAGUES UNDER THE SEA (1916) ★★½ Confusing blend of three tales (Jules Verne's *Mysterious Island* and *20,000 Leagues Under the Sea* as well as the creation of an original past for Captain Nemo) forces viewers to jump back and forth trying to get a handle on what's actually happening. Further, the director's fascination with underwater photography reduces this to a lesser entry of a Jacques Cousteau documentary. Silent. B&W; 105m. **DIR:** Stuart Paton. **CAST:** Allan Holubar. **1916**

TWILIGHT OF THE COCKROACHES ★★★ Japanese animation and live action. Allegorical story told from the viewpoint of a large clan of cockroaches living in the home of a divorced man who is "at peace" with them. Roaming their world in safety, the roaches with the knowledge of how others of their species in bordering lands do not fare as well. Interesting commentary on the nature of war, peace, and survival. 102m. **DIR:** Hiroaki Yoshida. **1987**

TWILIGHT ZONE, THE (TV SERIES) ★★★★½ Writer-producer Rod Serling's precedent-shattering anthology series, which ruled television during the early 1960s, earned its place in history thanks to a deft blend of credible human emotions amid *in*credible situations. Although Serling handled the lion's share of scripting chores, this program also showcased the early work of Richard Matheson, Charles Beaumont, and George Clayton Johnson; indeed, two of Matheson's stories are among the best remembered: the mute Agnes Moorehead stalked in her isolated house by "The Invaders" and William Shatner's panic-stricken battle with an airplane gremlin during his "Nightmare at 20,000 Feet." Both are among the episodes released to video; other must-sees include "Nothing in the Dark" (with Gladys Cooper helping a mysterious young stranger, played by Robert Redford) and "Time Enough at Last" (with Burgess Meredith as a bookworm *desperate* for more reading time). Each video includes two episodes; Volume One—with "The Invaders" and "Nothing in the Dark"—is by far the strongest. 55m. **DIR:** Richard Donner, Douglas Heyes, Lamont Johnson, Buzz Kulik. **CAST:** Robert Redford, Agnes Moorehead, Lee Marvin, Burgess Meredith, Jack Klugman, Gladys Cooper, William Shatner. **1959**

2001: A SPACE ODYSSEY ★★★★★ There's no denying the visual magnificence of Stanley Kubrick's science-fiction epic. Ponderous, ambiguous, and arty, it's nevertheless considered a classic of the genre by many film buffs. The set design, costumes, cinematography, and Oscar-winning special effects combine to create unforgettable imagery. Rated G. 139m. **DIR:** Stanley Kubrick. **CAST:** Keir Dullea, William Sylvester, Gary Lockwood. **1968**

2010 ★★★★ The exciting sequel stars Roy Scheider, John Lithgow, Helen Mirren, and Bob Balaban as participants in a joint American-Russian space mission. We finally find out what really happened to astronaut Dave Bowman (Keir Dullea); the computer, HAL 9000; and the spaceship, *Discovery*, near the planet Jupiter. Rated PG. 116m. **DIR:** Peter Hyams. **CAST:** Roy Scheider, John Lithgow, Helen Mirren, Bob Balaban, Keir Dullea. **1984**

2020 TEXAS GLADIATORS 🦃 Alternately hilarious and just plain boring *Road Warrior* clone. Rated R for sex and gore, but turns up in censored version on Saturday-afternoon TV. 91m. **DIR:** Kevin Mancuso (Joe d'Amato). **CAST:** Harrison Muller. **1984**

TWO WORLDS OF JENNIE LOGAN, THE 🦃 A young woman is magically transported one hundred years into the past. Made for TV. 99m. **DIR:** Frank DeFelitta. **CAST:** Lindsay Wagner, Marc Singer, Linda Gray, Alan Feinstein, Irene Tedrow, Henry Wilcoxon. **1979**

UFO—VOLUMES I AND II ★★½ Four episodes of the sci-fi soap opera from England concerning SHADO, an organization set up to protect Earth from invading aliens. The first, "Exposed," has the top fighter pilot at SHADO convinced his craft was destroyed by a UFO, while the government tries to argue him out of it. In the second installment, the Earth is threatened by lethal flying saucers. "Conflict" has Earth ships being sabotaged by aliens. "A Dalotek Affair" deals with a mysterious communications lapse between SHADO-Earth and its moon colony. The stories are not as good as *Star Trek*, but sci-fi buffs may want to see more. 102m. **DIR:** David Lane, Ken Turner. **CAST:** Ed Bishop, George Sewell, Michael Billington, Jean Marsh. **1979**

ULTIMATE WARRIOR, THE ★★½ The payoff doesn't match the promise of the premise in this less-than-thrilling science-fiction thriller. In the not-so-distant future, ragged residents of devastated New York City battle vicious gangs. Initially intriguing, the film stumbles to a ludicrous conclusion. Rated R. 94m. **DIR:** Robert Clouse. **CAST:** Yul Brynner, Max von Sydow, Joanna Miles, William Smith, Stephen McHattie. **1975**

UNDERSEA KINGDOM ★★½ "Crash" Corrigan plays himself in this science-fiction serial of the 1930s as he attempts to thwart the evil plans of Sharad and his followers, who live under the ocean in the ancient city of Atlantis. Filled with gadgetry, robots, and futuristic machines, this cliff-hanger was extremely popular with young audiences, and it's still a lot of fun today. B&W; 12 chapters. **DIR:** B. Reeves "Breezy" Eason, Joseph Kane. **CAST:** Ray "Crash" Corrigan, Lois Wilde, Monte Blue, William Farnum, Lee Van Atta, Smiley Burnette, Lon Chaney Jr. **1936**

UNKNOWN WORLD ★★ Low-budget science-fiction story about an inventor who builds a drill capable of exploring inner Earth seems to borrow from Edgar Rice Burroughs's *Pellucidar* series, but it is actually closer to the nuclear-holocaust films of the postwar period. Short on thrills, this effort uses extensive footage of Carlsbad Caverns to simulate the interior of our planet. B&W; 74m. **DIR:** Terrel O. Morse. **CAST:** Victor Kilian, Bruce Kellogg, Marilyn Nash. **1950**

UNTIL THE END OF THE WORLD ★★ Futuristic folly follows a good-time girl as she pursues a fugitive (William Hurt). Bounty hunters, bank robbers, her boyfriend, and a private eye become entangled in her cross-continental chase. New wave sound track and directionless plot make this nearly impossible to enjoy. Rated R for violence, nudity, and profanity. 158m. **DIR:** Wim Wenders. **CAST:** William Hurt, Solveig Dommartin, Sam Neill, Max von Sydow, Jeanne Moreau. **1991**

VALLEY OF GWANGI ★★★ Prehistoric reptiles are found in Mexico in the early 1900s; attempts are made to capture them alive to be put on display. A cross between *King Kong* and *Hatari!*, with a Western flavor. Fine special effects by Ray Harryhausen. Rated PG. 95m. **DIR:** Jim O'Connolly. **CAST:** James Franciscus, Richard Carlson, Gila Golan. **1969**

VIBES ★★ This sad misfire should have been much better, given the track record of scripters Lowell Ganz and Babaloo Mandel, but the talented parts simply don't make an impressive whole. Cyndi Lauper and Jeff Goldblum play psychic hotshots hired by shifty Peter Falk, but everything plods along to a foolish finale. Rated PG. 99m. **DIR:** Ken Kwapis. **CAST:** Cyndi Lauper, Jeff Goldblum, Julian Sands, Peter Falk. **1988**

VINDICATOR, THE ★★ A comic-bookish story about a scientist who is blown up by his evil employers and put back together using Cybornetic systems and a nearly indestructible futuristic space suit. Overall, it's a pretty typical story with some thrills and a fair amount of action and graphic violence. Rated R for violence, adult language, and brief nudity. 92m. **DIR:** Jean-Claude Lord. **CAST:** Teri Austin, Richard Cox, Pam Grier, Maury Chaykin. **1984**

VIRUS ★★★ Japan goes Hollywood. *Virus* provides some moments of high drama and decent special effects, not to mention panoramic location shots in Antarctica. The story concerns a polar expedition that becomes the last vestige of humanity when a plague and nuclear war decimate the population. Rated PG. 155m. **DIR:** Kinji Fukasaku. **CAST:** George Kennedy, Chuck Connors, Glenn Ford, Sonny Chiba, Olivia Hussey, Henry Silva. **1980**

VISITANTS, THE 🦃 Two aliens move into a house in an American suburb. Not rated. 93m. **DIR:** Rick Sloane. **CAST:** Marcus Vaughter, Johanna Grika, Nicole Rio. **1987**

VISITOR, THE ★★ An 8-year-old girl, gifted with incredible powers, uses her abilities maliciously. As she formulates a plan that could lead the world toward destruction, an ancient alien mystic comes to Earth to stop her evil scheme. Great premise, flawed execution. Rated R for violence. 96m. **DIR:** Michael J. Paradise. **CAST:** Mel Ferrer, John Huston, Glenn Ford, Shelley Winters. **1979**

VOYAGE TO THE BOTTOM OF THE SEA ★★★ An atomic submarine rushes to save Earth from destruction by a burning radiation belt. Intrigue, adventure, and hokey fun, with a low-level all-star cast. Much better than the subsequent television show. Unrated, the film has mild violence. 105m. **DIR:** Irwin Allen. **CAST:** Walter Pidgeon, Joan Fontaine, Robert Sterling, Barbara Eden, Michael Ansara, Peter Lorre, Frankie Avalon, Henry Daniell. **1961**

VOYAGE TO THE PREHISTORIC PLANET 🦃 Wisely hiding behind a pseudonym, director Curtis Harrington cobbled together this deadly dull space opera by mixing footage from a Soviet sci-fi movie (*Planet of Storms*) with a few talky scenes involving Basil Rathbone and Faith Domergue. Released directly to TV. 80m. **DIR:** Jonathan Sebastian. **CAST:** Basil Rathbone, Faith Domergue. 1965

WAR OF THE COLOSSAL BEAST ★★½ This sequel to *The Amazing Colossal Man* actually restores the long missing color ending, in which our oversize friend (now looking like the title character of *The Cyclops*, after being mutilated in the climax to the previous film) stumbles into high-tension electrical wires. That lends this American-International cheapie some stature as a video keeper. B&W and co; 68m. **DIR:** Bert I. Gordon. **CAST:** Sally Fraser, Roger Pace, Russ Bender. 1958

WAR OF THE GARGANTUAS ★★ Giant, furry monsters—one good, one evil—slug it out in mountainous and eventually urban Japan. Eye-filling, brain-dead Toho Films sci fi. 93m. **DIR:** Inoshiro Honda. **CAST:** Russ Tamblyn, Kumi Mizuno, Kipp Hamilton. 1966

WAR OF THE WORLDS, THE ★★★★ This science-fiction film stars Gene Barry as a scientist who is among the first Earthlings to witness the Martian invasion of Earth. The film is an updated version of H. G. Wells's classic story, with the action heightened by excellent special effects. 85m. **DIR:** Byron Haskin. **CAST:** Gene Barry, Les Tremayne, Ann Robinson. 1953

WARGAMES ★★★★½ A young computer whiz (Matthew Broderick) who thinks he's hooking into a game manufacturer's computer accidentally starts World War III when he decides to "play" a selection titled "Global Thermonuclear Warfare." Though the movie contains almost no violence or any other sensationalistic content (apart from a wee bit of vulgar language), it still grips the viewer. Rated PG. 114m. **DIR:** John Badham. **CAST:** Matthew Broderick, Dabney Coleman, Ally Sheedy, John Wood, Barry Corbin. 1983

WARLORDS OF THE 21ST CENTURY 🦃 A cold-blooded killer leads his band of roving outlaws in a siege against a peaceful community. Rated R for violence. 91m. **DIR:** Harley Cokliss. **CAST:** James Wainwright, Annie McEnroe, Michael Beck. 1982

WARRIOR AND THE SORCERESS, THE 🦃 Sword-and-sorcery version of *A Fistful of Dollars*. Rated R for gore and nudity. 81m. **DIR:** John Broderick. **CAST:** David Carradine, Luke Askew, Maria Socas. 1984

WARRIOR OF THE LOST WORLD 🦃 A lone warrior is convinced to help find a woman's father who has been kidnapped by their enemy in a post-apocalyptic world. Not rated, but contains violence. 90m. **DIR:** David Worth. **CAST:** Robert Ginty, Persis Khambatta, Donald Pleasence, Fred Williamson. 1988

WARRIORS OF THE APOCALYPSE ★★ Another low-rent post-apocalyptic adventure. Fifty years after war has killed most of the Earth's population, a band of nomads search for a mountain that is said to hold the secret of survival. Rated R for violence and brief nudity. 96m. **DIR:** Bobby A. Suarez. **CAST:** Michael James, Deborah Moore. 1985

WARRIORS OF THE WASTELAND 🦃 Cheap Italian copy of *Road Warrior*, with nuclear-holocaust survivors battling the evil Templars. Not rated, contains violence and slight nudity. 92m. **DIR:** Enzo G. Castellari. **CAST:** Fred Williamson, Timothy Brent, George Eastman, Anna Kanakis, Thomas Moore. 1983

WARRIORS OF THE WIND ★★★★ This movie-length Japanese animated feature easily ranks with the best of American animated films. The characters are believable, the action is convincing, and the plot delivers the positive message that not everything good is beautiful and that ugliness, like true beauty, may take more than looking to be seen. Definitely not for the kiddies only. 95m. **DIR:** Tokuma Shoten Pub. Co. Ltd. 1984

WATCHERS ★★★½ Based on the novel by Dean R. Koontz, *Watchers* is a refreshing sci-fi–horror film. About a boy (Corey Haim) who finds a superintelligent dog and becomes the target of a scientifically created monster, it plays fair with the viewer throughout. Director Jon Hess even leaves quite a bit to the imagination, building the kind of suspense so seldom seen in this age of gore-infested hack-'em-ups. Rated R for violence and profanity. 91m. **DIR:** Jon Hess. **CAST:** Corey Haim, Barbara Williams, Michael Ironside. 1988

WATERSHIP DOWN ★★★★ Although it's a full-length cartoon about the adventures of a group of rabbits, you'll find no cutesy, Disney-styled Thumpers à la *Bambi*. About the odyssey that a small group of rabbits undertakes after one of them has a vision of evil things coming to destroy their homes. Their arduous journey is full of surprises and rewards. Rated PG. 92m. **DIR:** Martin Rosen. **CAST:** Animated. 1978

WAVELENGTH ★★★★ You've seen it all many times before in science-fiction movies of wide-ranging quality: the innocent visitors from outer space, the callous government officials who see them as guinea pigs instead of guests, the handful of compassionate Earthlings, even the race to the mother ship. But rarely has the plot been used so effectively. Rated PG. 87m. **DIR:** Mike Gray. **CAST:** Robert Carradine, Cherie Currie, Keenan Wynn. 1983

WAX ★★½ Bizarre, hallucinatory film about a NASA weapons-guidance programmer and beekeeper. He enters an alternative reality after his bees drill a hole in his head and install a mirrored crystal that sends strange images to his brain. Shot on videotape, with film spliced in, plus some nifty computer simulated graphics. This film can either fascinate or disconcert, depending on the viewer's taste. Not rated. 85m. **DIR:** David Blair. **CAST:** David Blair, Meg Savlov, William S. Burroughs. **1993**

WESTWORLD ★★★★ This is another science-fiction yarn from the author (Michael Crichton) of *The Andromeda Strain*. The film concerns an expensive world for well-to-do vacationers. They can live out their fantasies in the Old West or King Arthur's Court with the aid of programmed robots repaired nightly by scientists so they can be "killed" the next day by tourists. Richard Benjamin and James Brolin are tourists who come up against a rebellious robot (Yul Brynner). Rated PG. 88m. **DIR:** Michael Crichton. **CAST:** Yul Brynner, Richard Benjamin, James Brolin. **1973**

WHEN DINOSAURS RULED THE EARTH ★★★ British novelist and fantasy author J. G. Ballard (*Empire of the Sun*) wrote the treatment for this unusually ambitious Hammer Films epic, shot in the Canary Islands. Director Val Guest (one of Hammer's top talents) and effects wizard Jim Danforth succeed, possibly for the first time, in integrating the stop-motion dinosaur sequences seamlessly into the narrative—they aren't mere "stop-the-show" set pieces. Rated G. 96m. **DIR:** Val Guest. **CAST:** Victoria Vetri, Robin Hawdon, Patrick Allen. **1969**

WHEN THE WIND BLOWS ★★★ Ironic full-length British cartoon that chronicles the preparations of a retired English couple for the coming nuclear holocaust. Their ignorance of the facts and innocent faith in the "powers that be" make *When the Wind Blows* a touching and moving statement about the nuclear Armageddon. 80m. **DIR:** Jimmy T. Murakami. **1988**

WHEN WORLDS COLLIDE ★★ Interesting end-of-the-world sci-fi fable from George Pal has dated badly since its original release in 1951. Final scene of Earth pilgrims landing on the planet and walking into an obvious superimposed painting is laughable today, but many of the other Oscar-winning effects are still quite convincing. 81m. **DIR:** Rudolph Maté. **CAST:** Richard Derr, Barbara Rush, Peter Hanson, Larry Keating, John Hoyt. **1951**

WHERE THE RIVER RUNS BLACK ★★★½ A primitive child is snatched from his home in the Amazon rain forest and brought into the modern world of corruption and violence. Sumptuous images, courtesy of Juan Ruiz-Anchia's superb cinematography, fill the screen as its eerie, fanciful, and finally suspenseful tale is told. Rated PG for violence and suggested sex. 105m. **DIR:** Christopher Cain. **CAST:** Charles Durning, Peter Horton, Ajay Naidu, Conchata Ferrell. **1986**

WHITE LIGHT ★★½ When cop Martin Kove bites the bullet, he meets the woman of his dreams on the other side. Weird fantasy directed by Kove's *Cagney and Lacey* costar, Al Waxman. Rated R for profanity and violence. 96m. **DIR:** Al Waxman. **CAST:** Martin Kove, Martha Henry. **1990**

WILD IN THE STREETS ★★ Ridiculous what-if? film about future America when youth runs the show, the voting age is lowered to 14, and a rock singer involved in drug selling sits as president in the White House. This dated daydream of the 1960s was considered lame at the time of its release, but has gathered a following over the years. Rated PG. 97m. **DIR:** Barry Shear. **CAST:** Christopher Jones, Shelley Winters, Hal Holbrook, Diane Varsi, Ed Begley Sr., Millie Perkins, Richard Pryor, Bert Freed. **1968**

WILD PALMS ★★★½ James Belushi is a lawyer-turned-television-executive whose life becomes a nightmarish power struggle involving mind control. Twenty-five years in the future, a pseudoreligious government tries to alter reality through drugs and television. Eerie because it is so plausible, this made-for-TV miniseries looks great, but it's too dense and too slow. Not rated, but contains violence. Two 150m. episodes. **DIR:** Paul Hewitt, Keith Gordon, Kathryn Bigelow, Phil Joanou. **CAST:** James Belushi, Dana Delany, Robert Loggia, Kim Cattrall, Angie Dickinson. **1993**

WILD WOMEN OF WONGO 🦃 This early sex-exploitation adventure pits two primitive tribes against each other. 72m. **DIR:** James L. Wolcott. **CAST:** Jean Hawkshaw, Johnny Walsh, Ed Fury, Pat Crowley. **1958**

WILD WORLD OF BATWOMAN, THE 🦃 Execrable James Bond spoof. Alternate title: *She Was a Hippy Vampire*. B&W; 70m. **DIR:** Jerry Warren. **CAST:** Katherine Victor, George Andre, Steve Brodie. **1966**

WILLOW ★★★ A formulaic but entertaining fantasy epic, this focuses on the quest of an apprentice sorcerer, Willow (Warwick Davis), to keep a magicial child safe from the minions of the wicked queen (Jean Marsh) she is destined to destroy. The first half tends to drag as the characters and situations are somewhat laboriously introduced. However, things pick up midway. Rated PG for violence. 120m. **DIR:** Ron Howard. **CAST:** Val Kilmer, Joanne Whalley, Jean Marsh, Warwick Davis, Patricia Hayes, Billy Barty. **1988**

WIRED TO KILL 🦃 The year is 1998, and 120 million Americans are dead from a killer plague. Rated R for violence and raw language. 90m. **DIR:** Franky Schaeffer. **CAST:** Emily Longstreth, Devon Holescher, Merritt Buttrick. **1986**

WITCHES, THE ★★★★ Do not rent this British film for younger children. They'll have nightmares for weeks. However, everyone over the age of eight will be fascinated by this spooky tale of a 9-year-old boy who attempts to thwart the evil designs of the Grand High Witch (Anjelica Huston in top form) as she embarks on a campaign to turn all children into mice. The special effects and makeup by producer Jim Henson's talented staff are marvelous. Wonderfully spooky adaptation of a story by Roald Dahl. Rated PG for scary stuff. 90m. **DIR:** Nicolas Roeg. **CAST:** Anjelica Huston, Mai Zetterling, Jasen Fisher. **1990**

WITHOUT WARNING Hollywood veterans battle with an intergalactic alien hunter (a rubber-faced leftover from the *Outer Limits* television series) and his hungry pets. 89m. **DIR:** Greydon Clark. **CAST:** Jack Palance, Martin Landau, Cameron Mitchell, Larry Storch, Sue Ane Langdon. **1980**

WIZARD OF MARS, THE ★★ Low-budget interplanetary version of *The Wizard of Oz* finds a rocketship full of Earthlings on the planet Mars where magic and fantasy are the prevalent forces. Written, directed, and produced by David Hewitt, with technical assistance from famed science-fiction–fantasy expert Forrest J. Ackerman, this doesn't really compare to major science-fiction or fantasy films. 81m. **DIR:** David L. Hewitt. **CAST:** John Carradine, Vic McGee, Roger Gentry. **1964**

WIZARD OF THE LOST KINGDOM Bo Svenson as a master swordsman who comes to the aid of a sorcerer's son. Rated PG for violence. 76m. **DIR:** Hector Olivera. **CAST:** Bo Svenson, Vidal Peterson, Thom Christopher. **1985**

WIZARD OF THE LOST KINGDOM II In medieval times, a boy wizard is sent on a quest to bring freedom to three kingdoms. Rated PG. 80m. **DIR:** Charles B. Griffith. **CAST:** David Carradine, Bobby Jacoby, Mel Wells. **1989**

WIZARDS ★★★ Director-animator Ralph Bakshi's cost-cutting corners, which had not been that evident in his *Fritz the Cat* films, become a bit too noticeable in this charming little tale of ultimate good versus ultimate evil. Our hero is an aged wizard who relies on magic; his evil doppelgänger resorts to the horrors of technology. The conflict builds well until its climax, which (sadly) negates the premise of the entire battle. Rated PG for occasionally graphic violence. 81m. **DIR:** Ralph Bakshi. **1977**

WOMEN OF THE PREHISTORIC PLANET Not only is this outer-space saga incredibly cheap, it's also misleadingly titled. There is only one woman, and she's not from the prehistoric planet. 92m. **DIR:** Arthur C. Pierce. **CAST:** Wendell Corey, John Agar, Keith Larsen, Merry Anders, Paul Gilbert, Adam Roarke, Stuart Margolin, Gavin MacLeod, Lyle Waggoner. **1966**

WONDERFUL WORLD OF THE BROTHERS GRIMM, THE ★★★★ Excellent adaptations of the Grimm tales, featuring brilliant animation by Puppetoon master George Pal and Oscar-winning costumes by Mary Willis. One of the standout sequences has Buddy Hackett battling a fire-breathing dragon in a toy shop. Originally shown in Cinerama. 129m. **DIR:** Henry Levin, George Pal. **CAST:** Laurence Harvey, Claire Bloom, Karlheinz Böhm, Oscar Homolka, Barbara Eden, Russ Tamblyn, Buddy Hackett, Terry-Thomas. **1962**

WORLD GONE WILD On Earth after the nuclear holocaust, a group of flower children live in Lost Wells, a desert oasis. Rated R for violence, profanity, and nudity. 84m. **DIR:** Lee H. Katzin. **CAST:** Bruce Dern, Michael Paré, Catherine Mary Stewart, Adam Ant. **1988**

X (THE MAN WITH THE X-RAY EYES) ★★★ Intriguing, offbeat tale of a scientist (Ray Milland) who discovers a drug that gives him the power to see through objects. He has a great time at first, but soon becomes addicted and begins seeing more and more, until.... This production is highly enjoyable, with a surprisingly effective role by comedian Don Rickles as a carnival barker. 80m. **DIR:** Roger Corman. **CAST:** Ray Milland, Diana Van Der Vlis, Harold J. Stone, John Hoyt, Don Rickles. **1963**

X FROM OUTER SPACE, THE ★★½ A mission to Mars returns with an alien spore that grows into Guilala, a huge, energy-absorbing monster that looks like a giant chicken with scales. Abundant destruction of model cities and planes highlight this none-too-professional entry in the Japanese big-rubber-monster movie category. Rated PG. 88m. **DIR:** Kazui Nihonmatzu. **CAST:** Toshiya Wazaki, Peggy Neal. **1967**

XTRO II ★★★ If you saw the original *Xtro*, forget all about it. *Xtro II* has a whole new exciting plot that doesn't even follow the original. The Nexus computer program transports three scientists to a parallel universe, only to have one return with a hideous creature inside of it. The few remaining scientists inside the project attempt to kill off the beast. Rated R for violence. 92m. **DIR:** Harry Davenport. **CAST:** Jan-Michael Vincent, Paul Koslo, Tara Buckman. **1991**

YESTERDAY MACHINE, THE Nazi scientist has invented a time machine that can move people to the past and the future. 85m. **DIR:** Russ Marker. **CAST:** Tim Holt, Jack Herman. **1962**

YONGARY—MONSTER FROM THE DEEP ★★ A Korean entry in the big-rubber-monster movie genre. An earthquake-causing monster (a dead ringer for Godzilla) rises to wage a destructive path across the country. Bad miniatures and a poor script make this more funny than scary. Rated PG. 79m. **DIR:** Kim Ki-duk. **CAST:** Oh Young Il. **1969**

YOR: THE HUNTER FROM THE FUTURE 🦃 A mighty warrior attempts to discover his true identity on a planet trapped in a time warp. Rated PG for violence and profanity. 88m. **DIR:** Anthony M. Dawson. **CAST:** Reb Brown, Corinne Clery, John Steiner, Carole André, Alan Collins. **1983**

Z.P.G. (ZERO POPULATION GROWTH) 🦃 In the pre–*Star Wars* 1970s, science fiction languished, and dreary films like this were a dime a dozen. Overpopulation imposes severe restrictions on life in the future. We guarantee no moviegoer will want to suffer through it. Rated PG. 95m. **DIR:** Michael Campus. **CAST:** Oliver Reed, Geraldine Chaplin, Don Gordon, Diane Cilento. **1972**

ZARDOZ ★★½ Cult sci-fi about a strange society of the future and Sean Connery's attempts to free the people from the evil rulers. Murky plot is hard to follow, but it is amusing to watch Connery running around in a diaper for two hours. Rated R. 105m. **DIR:** John Boorman. **CAST:** Sean Connery, Charlotte Rampling. **1974**

ZONE TROOPERS ★★ This is a dumb comic-book tale about an American troop in World War II lost behind German lines. Eventually, soldiers encounter space aliens who have crash-landed in the woods. Rated PG for mild violence. 86m. **DIR:** Danny Bilson. **CAST:** Tim Thomerson, Timothy Van Patten. **1985**

WESTERN

ABILENE TOWN ★★★ Cattlemen and homesteaders are at loggerheads in the 1870s in this fast-paced shoot-'em-up. Randolph Scott is the trusty tall man with the star. Edgar Buchanan is sly, as always. B&W; 89m. **DIR:** Edwin L. Marin. **CAST:** Randolph Scott, Ann Dvorak, Rhonda Fleming, Lloyd Bridges, Edgar Buchanan. **1946**

ACE HIGH ★★ In this violent spaghetti Western written and directed by Giuseppe Colizzi, a condemned outlaw is offered a chance to save himself from the hangman's noose. Having just completed the entertaining *The Good, The Bad, and The Ugly*, Eli Wallach is wasted. There is some humor, but the dialogue and dubbing are simply terrible. 123m. **DIR:** Giuseppe Colizzi. **CAST:** Eli Wallach, Brock Peters, Terence Hill, Kevin McCarthy, Bud Spencer. **1969**

ACES AND EIGHTS ★★½ Although lacking in action, this Tim McCoy Western nevertheless has its moments. McCoy comes to the aid of a young Mexican unfairly accused of murder. B&W; 62m. **DIR:** Sam Newfield. **CAST:** Tim McCoy, Luana Walters. **1936**

ACROSS THE RIO GRANDE ★★★½ Jimmy Wakely straightens out a young lawyer involved with border silver-ore smugglers and captures the killer of the lawyer's father. Noteworthy as the first film appearance of Polly Bergen. B&W; 55m. **DIR:** Oliver Drake. **CAST:** Jimmy Wakely, Dub Taylor, Polly Bergen. **1949**

ACROSS THE WIDE MISSOURI ★★½ Scenery is the big and only plus in this plotless pedestrian tale of fortune seekers led by a Kentucky trapper seeking wealth in Indian-held virgin beaver territory. 78m. **DIR:** William Wellman. **CAST:** Clark Gable, Ricardo Montalban, Adolphe Menjou, John Hodiak, J. Carrol Naish, Alan Napier, Jack Holt. **1951**

ADIOS AMIGO ★★★ Writer-director-actor-producer Fred Williamson's whimsical parody of the Hollywood Western is about the misadventures of a cowboy (Williamson) and his sly, con-man partner (hilariously performed by Richard Pryor). Rated PG for profanity, but not much violence. 87m. **DIR:** Fred Williamson. **CAST:** Fred Williamson, Richard Pryor, Thalmus Rasulala, James Brown, Mike Henry. **1975**

ADIOS, HOMBRE ★★ Tiny, a sleazy outlaw, and his gang try to rob a bank but find it empty, so they decide to take the town hostage until the next gold shipment arrives. Enter a falsely accused escaped convict, Will Flagherty, out to prove his innocence and a one-man war is unleashed against the outlaw gang. Good action and an over-the-top performance by Eduardo Fajardo as Tiny. Unrated, but contains violence. 90m. **DIR:** Mario Caiano. **CAST:** Craig Hill, Giulia Rubini, Piero Lulli, Eduardo Fajardo, Nazzareno Zemperla, Jacques Herlin, Nello Pazzafini, Roberto Camardiel. **1966**

ADVENTURES OF FRANK AND JESSE JAMES ★★½ Frank and Jesse James go into the gold-mining business in an effort to raise enough money to pay back what they stole in their wilder days. This serial boasts a solid cast and fine action sequences by stunt master Yakima Canutt. B&W; 13 chapters. **DIR:** Fred Brannon, Yakima Canutt. **CAST:** Clayton Moore, Steve Darrell, Noel Neill, George J. Lewis, Tom Steele. **1948**

ADVENTURES OF RED RYDER ★★★★½ Action-packed serial as Red Ryder thwarts at every turn a banker's attempts to defraud ranchers whose land is wanted for a coming railroad. B&W; 12 chapters. **DIR:** William Witney, John English. **CAST:** Don Barry, Tommy Cook, Noah Beery Sr. **1940**

ADVENTURES OF REX AND RINTY ★★★½ A trio of unscrupulous Americans steal the God-Horse, Rex, from the island of Sujan and sell it to a greedy United States ranch owner. Rex escapes, meets Rinty, and the animals team up to avoid capture by the thieves. B&W; 12 chapters **DIR:** Ford Beebe, B. Reeves "Breezy" Eason. **CAST:** Rin Tin Tin Jr., Kane Richmond, Norma Taylor, Smiley Burnette, Harry Woods. **1935**

AGAINST A CROOKED SKY ★★ Nothing new in this familiar tale of a boy searching for his sister, who has been kidnapped by Indians. Another inferior reworking of John Ford's classic Western *The Searchers*. For fans who watch anything with a horse and a saddle. Rated PG for violence. 89m. **DIR:** Earl Bellamy. **CAST:** Richard Boone, Clint Ritchie, Henry Wilcoxon, Stewart Peterson. **1975**

ALAMO, THE ★★★½ This Western, directed by and starring John Wayne, may have seemed overlong when originally released. But today it's the answer to a Duke-deprived fan's dream. Of course, there's the expected mushy flag-waving here and there. However, once Davy Crockett (Wayne), Jim Bowie (Richard Widmark), Will Travis (Laurence Harvey), and their respective followers team up to take on Santa Ana's forces, it's a humdinger of a period war movie. 161m. **DIR:** John Wayne. **CAST:** John Wayne, Richard Widmark, Laurence Harvey, Frankie Avalon, Richard Boone, Chill Wills. **1960**

ALAMO, THE: THIRTEEN DAYS TO GLORY 🦃 Jim Bowie, Davy Crockett, Col. William Travis and their men defend the Texas fort to the death, in this made-for-TV movie. The two-part film suffers from inaccuracies, and the significance of the siege is trivialized by focusing on bickering between Travis and Bowie. 168m. **DIR:** Burt Kennedy. **CAST:** James Arness, Brian Keith, Alec Baldwin, David Ogden Stiers, Raul Julia, Lorne Greene. **1987**

ALLEGHENY UPRISING ★★★ John Wayne and Claire Trevor were reteamed the same year of their costarring triumph in 1939's *Stagecoach* for this potboiler set in the pre-Revolutionary American colonies, but the results were hardly as auspicious. Still, it's a decent time passer and features Brian Donlevy in one of his better villain roles. B&W; 81m. **DIR:** William A. Seiter. **CAST:** John Wayne, Claire Trevor, George Sanders, Chill Wills, Brian Donlevy. **1939**

ALONG CAME JONES ★★★★ Highly watchable comic Western with Gary Cooper as an innocent cowboy who's mistaken for an infamous outlaw. Both lawmen and the real outlaw (Dan Duryea) pursue him. B&W; 90m. **DIR:** Stuart Heisler. **CAST:** Gary Cooper, Loretta Young, Dan Duryea. **1945**

ALONG THE GREAT DIVIDE ★★½ With his usual determination and grit, lawman Kirk Douglas fights a sandstorm to capture an escaped criminal. The pace is slow, but the scenery is grand. B&W; 88m. **DIR:** Raoul Walsh. **CAST:** Kirk Douglas, John Agar, Walter Brennan, Virginia Mayo. **1951**

ALONG THE NAVAJO TRAIL ★★★ Deputy Marshal Roy Rogers investigates the disappearance of another government agent on Dale Evans's ranch and discovers land grabbers. Standard fare, exciting climax. B&W; 70m. **DIR:** Frank McDonald. **CAST:** Roy Rogers, George "Gabby" Hayes, Dale Evans, Douglas Fowley, Estelita Rodriguez. **1945**

ALVAREZ KELLY ★★ Edward Dymtryk unimaginatively directed this plodding Western starring William Holden as a cattle driver supplying beef to the Yankees. Confederate officer Richard Widmark wants him to steal that much-needed food for the South. Dull. 116m. **DIR:** Edward Dmytryk. **CAST:** William Holden, Richard Widmark, Janice Rule, Patrick O'Neal, Victoria Shaw. **1966**

AMBUSH VALLEY ★★ Paradise Valley is turned into Ambush Valley when a rancher's son murders a nester's son. It's up to Marshal Bob Custer to restore peace and prevent a range war. Routine. B&W; 57m. **DIR:** Raymond Samuels. **CAST:** Bob Custer, John Elliott. **1936**

AMERICAN EMPIRE ★★★ A formula film featuring the now-standard grand opening, dramatic problem-posing center, and slam-bang breathtaking climax, but a good, entertaining Western nonetheless. Richard Dix and Preston Foster team to found a cattle empire in Texas. Villain Leo Carrillo makes most of the trouble the pair encounters. Fans of the genre will love it. B&W; 82m. **DIR:** William McGann. **CAST:** Richard Dix, Frances Gifford, Preston Foster, Leo Carrillo, Guinn Williams. **1942**

AMERICANO, THE ★★½ Texas cowboy Glenn Ford gets embroiled with a bunch of Brazilian bad guys in this way-south-of-the-border Western. A change of scenery is commendable, but a familiar plot makes this film all but pedestrian. 85m. **DIR:** William Castle. **CAST:** Glenn Ford, Cesar Romero, Frank Lovejoy, Abbe Lane. **1954**

AND GOD SAID TO CAIN 🦃 Gary Hamilton is released from prison, and he seeks to kill the men who framed him. The climax of the film looks like it was filmed in a coal mine at midnight. Even a full-length appearance by Klaus Kinski can't save this mess. Unrated, contains violence. 99m. **DIR:** Anthony M. Dawson. **CAST:** Klaus Kinski, Peter Carsten, Calla Michelangeli, Lee Burton, Alan Collins. **1969**

ANGEL AND THE BADMAN ★★★★ A fine low-budget Western with John Wayne as a gunman who sees the light through the love of Quaker girl Gail Russell. Harry Carey and Bruce Cabot also are memorable in this thoughtful action film directed by longtime Wayne screenwriter James Edward Grant. B&W; 100m. **DIR:** James Edward Grant. **CAST:** John Wayne, Gail Russell, Harry Carey, Irene Rich, Bruce Cabot. **1947**

ANIMAL CALLED MAN, AN 🦃 Based on a *They Call Me Trinity*-type character, this comic spaghetti Western fails on all counts. A rogue enters a sharp-shooting contest and beats the local gunman. The next thing he knows, the gunman is after him. Surprise, surprise! Unrated, contains some violence. 83m. **DIR:** Roberto Mauri. **CAST:** Vassilli Karis, Craig Hill, Omero Capanna, Gillian Bray. **1973**

ANNIE OAKLEY (1935) ★★★ Highly atmospheric, action-packed, flavorful bio-pic of the famed rodeo performer, nicely played by Barbara Stanwyck. Preston Foster plays her partner and occasional love interest. B&W; 88m. **DIR:** George Stevens. **CAST:** Barbara Stanwyck, Preston Foster, Melvyn Douglas, Andy Clyde. **1935**

ANNIE OAKLEY (TV SERIES) ★★★ Annie Oakley, woman rancher and expert sharpshooter, helps Sheriff Lofty Craig maintain law and order in the 1860s town of Diablo. Two nostalgia-packed episodes on one cassette: "Trouble Shooters" and "Twisted Trails." B&W; 50m. **CAST:** Gail Davis, Brad Johnson, Jimmy Hawkins. **1953**

ANOTHER MAN, ANOTHER CHANCE ★★ In 1977, director Claude Lelouch, inexplicably, decided to remake his charming film *A Man and a Woman* and set it in the American West of the late 1800s. Widow Genevieve Bujold and widower James Caan fall in love. It's light on romance and heavy on tedium. 128m. **DIR:** Claude Lelouch. **CAST:** James Caan, Genevieve Bujold, Francis Huster, Jennifer Warren, Susan Tyrrell. **1977**

ANOTHER PAIR OF ACES ★★★½ Texas Ranger Rip Metcalf (Kris Kristofferson) enlists the aid of streetwise gambler Billy Roy Barker (Willie Nelson) in tracking down the vigilante killer of a crime lord. Engaging performances help elevate this modern-day Western/detective story, which was made for TV. 93m. **DIR:** Bill Bixby. **CAST:** Willie Nelson, Kris Kristofferson, Joan Severance, Rip Torn. **1991**

APACHE ★★ Moralistic message Western features a hammy Burt Lancaster as an idealistic warrior who resents yet understands the encroachment of the whites and refuses to live on government reservations. Strangely typical of early-to-mid-1950s Hollywood Westerns, this entry is long on conscience and short on action. 91m. **DIR:** Robert Aldrich. **CAST:** Burt Lancaster, Jean Peters, Charles Bronson, John Dehner, Monte Blue. **1954**

APACHE ROSE ★★½ Roy's an oil-well engineer, Dale's the skipper of a tugboat, and the fellow that's causing all the trouble runs a gambling ship. But it's still a Western because Trigger and the Sons of the Pioneers are close at hand. This is the first of the popular series to be shot in color. 75m. **DIR:** William Witney. **CAST:** Roy Rogers, Dale Evans, Bob Nolan and the Sons of the Pioneers, George Meeker, Minerva Urecal, LeRoy Mason. **1947**

APACHE WOMAN 🦃 Dull, awkwardly acted and directed story of an Indian affairs agent, Lloyd Bridges, investigating stagecoach holdups blamed on reservation Apaches. Released theatrically in color. B&W; 83m. **DIR:** Roger Corman. **CAST:** Lloyd Bridges, Joan Taylor, Lance Fuller, Paul Birch, Dick Miller, Chester Conklin. **1955**

APPALOOSA, THE ★★ This slight, often boring Western follows Marlon Brando's attempts to recover an Appaloosa horse stolen by a Mexican bandit. Brando's brooding, Method-acting approach to the character only makes things worse in an already slow-moving film. 98m. **DIR:** Sidney J. Furie. **CAST:** Marlon Brando, John Saxon, Anjanette Comer, Frank Silvera. **1966**

ARIZONA ★★★½ The cowgirl reigns supreme in a Western that was ahead of its time. Jean Arthur stars as an independent woman coping with male bullies and barely taking time for romance with William Holden. The black-and-white scenery is gorgeous, and the verbal battles and fistfights are spiced up with Indian attacks. B&W; 125m. **DIR:** Wesley Ruggles. **CAST:** Jean Arthur, William Holden, Warren William, Edgar Buchanan, Porter Hall, Regis Toomey, George Chandler, Byron Foulger. **1940**

ARIZONA BOUND ★★★ The first of the Rough Riders movies, this entry keeps secret the fact that Buck Roberts (Buck Jones), Tim McCall (Tim McCoy), and Sandy Hopkins (Raymond Hatton) are Texas Rangers who work together—but fans of classic Westerns will be familiar with the best cowboy-trio series of them all. In this case, they're called upon to save a stagecoach line from crooks operating in Mesa City. B&W; 57m. **DIR:** Spencer Gordon Bennet. **CAST:** Buck Jones, Tim McCoy, Raymond Hatton, Dennis Moore, Luana Walters, Slim Whitaker. **1941**

ARIZONA BUSHWHACKERS 🦃 Howard Keel, looking as if he might break into a chorus of "Old Man River" at any moment, leads a weary cast through this dreary, formulaic Western. 86m. **DIR:** Lesley Selander. **CAST:** Howard Keel, Yvonne De Carlo, John Ireland, Marilyn Maxwell, Scott Brady, Brian Donlevy, Roy Rogers Jr. **1968**

ARIZONA COWBOY ★★½ Rex Allen's first in a series of nineteen Westerns, giving him the distinction of being the last of the singing cowboys. Ex-GI turned rodeo star, Rex is framed for a robbery by bad guys. B&W; 67m. **DIR:** R. G. Springsteen. **CAST:** Rex Allen, Gordon Jones, Roy Barcroft. **1950**

ARIZONA DAYS ★★ Entertaining shoot-'em-up as somber-voiced Tex Ritter exposes the villain while shyly wooing the girl of his dreams. Ritter's films usually contained a tune or three and healthy doses of knockdown, drag-out fighting and this early entry is no exception. B&W; 57m. **DIR:** John English. **CAST:** Tex Ritter, Eleanor Stewart, Syd Saylor, William Faversham, Snub Pollard, Forrest Taylor, Glenn Strange, William Desmond, Earl Dwire, Budd Buster. **1937**

ARIZONA GUNFIGHTER ★★★½ Fast-draw Bob Steele takes the law into his own hands to avenge the killing of his father. To do so he becomes part of an outlaw gang. An unusual spin on the typical Bob Steele revenge motif. B&W; 57m. **DIR:** Sam Newfield. **CAST:** Bob Steele, Jean Carmen, Ted Adams, Ernie Adams. **1937**

ARIZONA KID ★★★½ Roy Rogers tracks down an outlaw guerrilla bandleader in the halcyon days before the outbreak of the Civil War. B&W; 54m. **DIR:** Joseph Kane. **CAST:** Roy Rogers, George "Gabby" Hayes. **1939**

ARIZONA LEGION ★★★★ In this energetic entry in his superior Western series for RKO Pictures, George O'Brien is a Texas Ranger who goes undercover to bring a bunch of baddies to bay. Chill Wills, as his sidekick, provides comic relief that is honestly funny. Fresh and enjoyable. B&W; 58m. **DIR:** David Howard. **CAST:** George O'Brien, Laraine Day, Chill Wills. **1939**

ARIZONA RAIDERS ★★★½ Two reformed Quantrill Raiders help Buster Crabbe's Arizona Rangers track down former comrades turned outlaws. Historical accuracies aside—The Arizona Rangers weren't formed until 1902—plenty of action keeps this one moving. 88m. **DIR:** William Witney. **CAST:** Audie Murphy, Ben Cooper, Buster Crabbe, Gloria Talbott. **1950**

ARIZONA RANGER ★★★½ The only Tim Holt Western to costar his father, onetime Western star Jack Holt, is one of Tim's best. Discharged from the Rough Riders, Tim joins the Arizona Rangers and tracks down a wife-beating outlaw. B&W; 63m. **DIR:** John Rawlins. **CAST:** Tim Holt, Jack Holt, Richard Martin, Nan Leslie, Steve Brodie. **1948**

ARIZONA ROUNDUP ★★½ Federal agent Tom Keene goes undercover selling wild horses to bust up an outlaw combine. B&W; 56m. **DIR:** Robert Emmett Tansey. **CAST:** Tom Keene, I. Stanford Jolley. **1942**

ARIZONA STAGECOACH ★★★ A girl whose brother has been taken in by highwaymen is helped by the Range Busters when they pose as heavies themselves. Last film with the original Range Busters trio. B&W; 58m. **DIR:** S. Roy Luby. **CAST:** Ray "Crash" Corrigan, John King, Max Terhune, Nell O'Day, Charles King. **1942**

ARROWHEAD ★★★ Charlton Heston is pitted against Jack Palance in this one-sided view of the Apache conflicts. Intense, action-packed Western. Weak script is overcome by powerful acting. B&W; 105m. **DIR:** Charles Marquis Warren. **CAST:** Charlton Heston, Jack Palance, Brian Keith. **1953**

AT GUNPOINT ★★★ Fred MacMurray plays a mild-mannered storekeeper who accidentally foils a bank robbery. The grateful town makes him sheriff, then turns to him when the outlaws return. The story is a clever reworking of *High Noon* to match MacMurray's unique screen personality, and the supporting cast is uniformly fine. Not rated, but may be too violent for young children. 81m. **DIR:** Alfred Werker. **CAST:** Fred MacMurray, Dorothy Malone, Walter Brennan, Tommy Rettig, John Qualen, Skip Homeier. **1955**

AVENGING, THE ★★ Michael Horse's half-Native American ancestry alienates him from his two brothers when he returns from college to take over the family ranch. Slow-moving tale of betrayal and revenge. Rated PG for violence. 100m. **DIR:** Lyman Dayton. **CAST:** Michael Horse, Efrem Zimbalist Jr., Sherry Hursey, Taylor Larcher, Joseph Running Fox. **1992**

BAD COMPANY ★★★★ This is a much underrated Civil War–era Western. The cultured Barry Brown and the streetwise Jeff Bridges team up as robbers. Charming performances by the leads and an intriguing, intelligent script by Robert Benton and David Newman make this well worth watching. Rated R. 94m. **DIR:** Robert Benton. **CAST:** Jeff Bridges, Barry Brown, Jim Davis, David Huddleston, John Savage, Jerry Houser, Geoffrey Lewis. **1972**

BAD GIRLS (1994) ★★★½ Action-packed tale of four saloon gals who must elude Pinkerton bounty hunters and sadistic outlaws after one of them kills a prominent citizen in self-defense. First-rate performances by the quartet of top-billed stars and fast-paced direction by Jonathan Kaplan make this a winner. Rated R for violence and suggested sex. 81m. **DIR:** Jonathan Kaplan. **CAST:** Madeleine Stowe, Andie MacDowell, Mary Stuart Masterson, Drew Barrymore, Dermot Mulroney, James Russo, Robert Loggia, James LeGros. **1994**

BAD JIM 🦃 When an innocent man buys Billy the Kid's horse, the man, the horse, and this never-theatrically released movie all turn bad. 90m. **DIR:** Clyde Ware. **CAST:** James Brolin, Richard Roundtree, John Clark Gable, Rory Calhoun, Ty Hardin. **1989**

BAD LANDS ★★½ A posse chasing rapist-killer Apache Jack finds more trouble than they bargained for when their quarry reaches his friends and shifts the balance of power. Western version of RKO's own *Lost Patrol* is a somber, downbeat adventure. B&W; 70m. **DIR:** Lew Landers. **CAST:** Robert Barrat, Noah Beery Jr., Robert Coote, Guinn Williams, Andy Clyde, Francis Ford, Addison Richards, Francis McDonald. **1939**

BAD MAN OF DEADWOOD ★★★★ One of the best Roy Rogers films of this era. Trying to get away from an unlawful past, sharpshooter Roy Rogers joins a medicine show and becomes allied with a citizens group opposing a crooked conglomeration of businessmen. B&W; 54m. **DIR:** Joseph Kane. **CAST:** Roy Rogers, George "Gabby" Hayes, Sally Payne, Carol Adams, Henry Brandon. **1941**

BAD MAN'S RIVER ★★ A humorous Western about the "dreaded" King gang, which robs banks along the Texas and Mexican borders. A Mexican revolutionary offers them a million dollars to blow up the arsenal used by the Mexican army, which the gang does, only to find that they have been double-crossed. 96m. **DIR:** Gene Martin. **CAST:** Lee Van Cleef, Gina Lollobrigida, James Mason. **1959**

BADLANDERS, THE ★★★ Alan Ladd is a geologist, Ernest Borgnine a rancher. Both are robbed of a gold mine, so they join forces to recover their loss from an evil businessman. Mild suspense and action, but sincere performances. 83m. **DIR:** Delmer Daves. **CAST:** Alan Ladd, Ernest Borgnine, Katy Jurado, Kent Smith, Nehemiah Persoff. **1958**

BADLANDS DRIFTER ★★ An ex-priest gets caught in a range war and tries to make things right. He ends up in a battle of power, revenge, greed, and love. Exceptional performances by the entire cast make this a better-than-average spaghetti Western, with a good story to match the action and violence. Rated R for violence. 90m. **DIR:** Leon Klimovsky. **CAST:** John Ireland, Robert Woods, Daniela Giordana, Annabella Incontrera, Roberto Camardiel. **1969**

BADMAN'S TERRITORY ★★★ Staunch and true marshal combats saddle scum when they flee across the border into territory beyond the government's reach. Good watching. B&W; 97m. **DIR:** Tim Whelan. **CAST:** Randolph Scott, Ann Richards, George "Gabby" Hayes, Ray Collins, Chief Thundercloud. **1946**

BADMEN OF THE BORDER ★★ U.S. Marshal Kirby Grant, masquerading as a bandit, joins forces with a lady Mexican government agent to break up a counterfeiting gang below the border. Grant's first Western in a series of only seven for Universal is the slowest of the batch. B&W; 56m. **DIR:** Wallace Fox. **CAST:** Kirby Grant, Armida, Fuzzy Knight. **1945**

BADMEN OF THE HILLS ★★★ A crooked sheriff tries to stop Charles Starrett's investigation into the murder of a U.S. marshal. Action-packed. B&W; 58m. **DIR:** William Berke. **CAST:** Charles Starrett, Russell Hayden, Cliff Edwards, Alan Bridge, Luana Walters. **1942**

BALLAD OF A GUNFIGHTER ★★ Marty Robbins is a rough-and-ready rebel who robs stages and gives to the poor. He ends up battling guys even worse than himself. Stilted dialogue and acting interlaced with a couple of good old songs. Unrated and inoffensive. 84m. **DIR:** Bill Ward. **CAST:** Marty Robbins, Joyce Redd, Bob Barron, Nestor Paiva, Laurette Luez. **1964**

BALLAD OF CABLE HOGUE, THE ★★★★½ Jason Robards has one of his finest roles as Hogue, a loner who discovers water in the desert and becomes a successful entrepreneur by opening a stagecoach stopover. Director Sam Peckinpah's deft eye for period detail and outstanding acting by all involved make this one a winner. Rated R. 121m. **DIR:** Sam Peckinpah. **CAST:** Jason Robards Jr., Stella Stevens, Strother Martin, L. Q. Jones, David Warner. **1970**

BALLAD OF GREGORIO CORTEZ, THE ★★★★½ This superb independent production tells the powerful story of one man's courage, pain, tragedy, and heartbreak—all of which come as the result of a simple misunderstanding. Edward James Olmos (*Miami Vice*) gives a haunting portrayal of the title character, who becomes a fugitive through no fault of his own. Rated PG for violence. 99m. **DIR:** Robert M. Young. **CAST:** Edward James Olmos, James Gammon, Tom Bower, Alan Vint, Timothy Scott, Barry Corbin. **1982**

BALLAD OF LITTLE JO, THE ★★★½ Revisionist Western stars Suzy Amis as a woman who feels trapped in a man's world, so she disguises herself as a man to get a fair shake. Amis delivers a stunning performance as she attempts to fit into a world designed for men. The usual complications arise, but Amis and a terrific supporting cast make them new and invigorating. Rated R for violence, language, and nudity. 124m. **DIR:** Maggie Greenwald. **CAST:** Suzy Amis, Bo Hopkins, David Chung, René Auberjonois, Carrie Snodgress, Ian McKellen. **1993**

BANDITS (1967) 🦃 A boring horse opera about three outlaws rescued from the hangman's noose. Not rated, but equivalent to PG-13 for violence. 89m. **DIR:** Robert Conrad, Alfredo Zacharias. **CAST:** Robert Conrad, Jan-Michael Vincent, Roy Jensen, Pedro Armendariz Jr. **1967**

BANDITS OF DARK CANYON ★★★½ Texas Ranger Rocky Lane helps escaped convict Bob Steele clear his name on a phony murder charge. The apparent victim is alive and working with Steele's best friend to cheat him out of his fortune. Above-average Lane Western—and they were all good. B&W; 59m. **DIR:** Phillip Ford. **CAST:** Allan "Rocky" Lane, Bob Steele, Eddy Waller, Roy Barcroft, Linda Johnson. **1947**

BANDOLERO! ★★★ Escape south of the border with outlaw brothers James Stewart and Dean Martin (if you can buy this), who ride just a few furlongs ahead of the law (George Kennedy), taking Raquel Welch along as hostage. 106m. **DIR:** Andrew V. McLaglen. **CAST:** James Stewart, Dean Martin, Raquel Welch, Will Geer, George Kennedy, Andrew Prine. **1968**

BAR 20 ★★★ Hopalong Cassidy sets out to buy cattle but ends up riding into a plot to steal from a young couple about to be wed. Hoppy is set up to look like a murderer and must save himself and his pals from the noose. B&W; 54m. **DIR:** Lesley Selander. **CAST:**

William Boyd, Andy Clyde, George Reeves, Robert Mitchum, Douglas Fowley. 1943

BARBAROSA ★★★★ This action-packed Western stars Willie Nelson and Gary Busey as a pair of outcasts on the run. Australian director Fred Schepisi has created an exciting, funny movie that combines the scenic majesty of the great John Ford Westerns with the light touch of George Roy Hill's *Butch Cassidy and the Sundance Kid.* Rated PG for violence. 90m. **DIR:** Fred Schepisi. **CAST:** Willie Nelson, Gary Busey, Isela Vega, Gilbert Roland, Danny De La Paz, George Voskovec. 1982

BARON OF ARIZONA, THE ★★½ Vincent Price hams it up as a smooth con man who nearly succeeds in claiming most of the Arizona Territory as his own. This early directorial effort by Samuel Fuller lacks the edge he gave his best films, but it's well played by a good cast. Based on a real incident. B&W; 90m. **DIR:** Samuel Fuller. **CAST:** Vincent Price, Ellen Drew, Beulah Bondi, Vladimir Sokoloff, Reed Hadley, Robert Barrat. 1950

BATTLE OF ELDERBUSH GULCH, THE/THE MUSKETEERS OF PIG ALLEY ★★★ Two of pioneer director D. W. Griffith's finest early works, a gripping Western and the first important gangster film. In the first, a baby gets caught in the crossfire between greenhorn settlers who have provoked an attack by Indians. In the second, clearly an ancestor of *Little Caesar* and *The Godfather*, the wife of a struggling musician finds herself the helpless object of a gangster's attention. Silent. B&W; 50m. **DIR:** D. W. Griffith. **CAST:** Lillian Gish, Mae Marsh, Robert Harron, Dorothy Gish, Walter Miller. 1914

BATTLING MARSHAL 🦃 Hackneyed plot about marshals investigating attempts on the life of a rancher. B&W; 55m. **DIR:** Oliver Drake. **CAST:** Sunset Carson, Lee Roberts. 1950

BELLS OF CORONADO ★★½ Grant Withers heads an evil gang of foreign agents out to smuggle uranium to unfriendly powers. Roy Rogers plays a modern-day heroic insurance agent who is able to thwart the heavies. Comic-book story is full of fast riding and action. 67m. **DIR:** William Witney. **CAST:** Roy Rogers, Dale Evans, Pat Brady, Grant Withers. 1950

BELLS OF ROSARITA ★★½ Movie cowboy Roy Rogers enlists the aid of Republic Studios' top Western stars in order to save Gabby Hayes's and Dale Evans's circus. A fun Western. B&W; 54m. **DIR:** Frank McDonald. **CAST:** Roy Rogers, Dale Evans, George "Gabby" Hayes, Bob Nolan and the Sons of the Pioneers, Don Barry, Allan "Rocky" Lane, Sunset Carson, William Elliott, Robert Livingston. 1945

BELLS OF SAN ANGELO ★★★½ This is a sharp and unusually violent Roy Rogers film. Roy portrays a lawman who attempts to capture a bunch of smugglers. With the help of Dale Evans and Andy Devine, he succeeds. B&W; 78m. **DIR:** William Witney. **CAST:** Roy Rogers, Dale Evans, Andy Devine, John McGuire. 1947

BELOW THE BORDER ★★★ Energetic Rough Riders adventure has Buck Roberts (Buck Jones) going underground as a bandit while Tim McCall (Tim McCoy) poses as a cattle buyer. It's all to trap evil Roy Barcroft and put an end to his cattle rustling. B&W; 57m. **DIR:** Howard Bretherton. **CAST:** Buck Jones, Tim McCoy, Raymond Hatton, Linda Brent, Roy Barcroft, Charles King. 1942

BEND OF THE RIVER ★★★★ James Stewart and director Anthony Mann teamed up during the early 1950s to make a series of exceptional Westerns that helped the genre return to popularity. This one deals with Stewart leading a wagon train across the country and his dealings with ex-friend Arthur Kennedy, who hijacks their supplies. Superior Western fare in every sense. 91m. **DIR:** Anthony Mann. **CAST:** James Stewart, Arthur Kennedy, Rock Hudson, Julie Adams. 1952

BEST OF THE BADMEN ★★★½ Another of those all-star outlaw roundups with the James Boys, Younger Brothers, Sundance Kid, and Ringo Kid—all being forced into outlawry by crooked banking and railroad interests. 84m. **DIR:** William D. Russell. **CAST:** Robert Ryan, Claire Trevor, Jack Buetel, Robert Preston, Walter Brennan, Bruce Cabot. 1951

BETWEEN GOD, THE DEVIL AND A WINCHESTER 🦃 A treasure is stolen from a church in Texas and a band of outlaws and a holy man go on the trail to find it. 98m. **DIR:** Dario Silvester. **CAST:** Richard Harrison, Gilbert Roland. 1972

BETWEEN MEN ★★★ Johnny Mack Brown heads west to find the rejected granddaughter of the man who raised him after his own father (William Farnum) fled, mistakenly thinking he was responsible for his son's death. Complicated plot line, good performances, and competent production. Above the norm. B&W; 59m. **DIR:** Robert N. Bradbury. **CAST:** Johnny Mack Brown, William Farnum, Beth Marion. 1935

BEYOND THE LAW 🦃 A spaghetti Western, with Lee Van Cleef as a bad guy turned good. Unrated; contains adult language and some gratuitous, badly staged violence. 90m. **DIR:** Giorgio Stegani. **CAST:** Lee Van Cleef, Antonio Sabato, Lionel Stander, Bud Spencer. 1968

BEYOND THE PURPLE HILLS ★★★ Sheriff Gene Autry finds an old lawman friend murdered and arrests the victim's son, soon to be TV's Wyatt Earp, Hugh O'Brian, in his film debut. Autry realizes he can't be guilty and sets out to bring in the real killer. This film treats us to not only Autry's horse, Champion, but Little Champ as well, strutting his stuff. B&W; 70m. **DIR:**

John English. **CAST:** Gene Autry, Pat Buttram, Hugh O'Brian, James Millican, Don Beddoe. **1950**

BIG COUNTRY, THE ★★★ Big-budget Western pits Gregory Peck and Charlton Heston as adversaries in an ongoing feud between rival cowmen Burl Ives and Charles Bickford. This would-be epic looks good but lacks the punch and plot of the best and most famous Westerns. 163m. **DIR:** William Wyler. **CAST:** Gregory Peck, Jean Simmons, Charlton Heston, Carroll Baker, Burl Ives, Charles Bickford. **1958**

BIG HAND FOR THE LITTLE LADY, A ★★★½ A compulsive gambler (Henry Fonda) talks his way into a high-stakes poker game, bets everything he owns, then promptly keels over, leaving his wife (Joanne Woodward) to play out his hand. Nifty Western-comedy is a bit too padded (it was originally a one-hour TV play, *Big Deal in Laredo*), but the expert cast puts it over. 95m. **DIR:** Fielder Cook. **CAST:** Henry Fonda, Joanne Woodward, Jason Robards Jr., Charles Bickford, Burgess Meredith, Paul Ford, John Qualen, Robert Middleton. **1966**

BIG JAKE ★★★ Big John Wayne takes up the trail of a gang of no-goods who kidnapped his grandson and shot up Maureen O'Hara's homestead and hired hands. One wishes there had been more scenes with Wayne and O'Hara together in this film, their last together. 110m. **DIR:** George Sherman. **CAST:** John Wayne, Richard Boone, Maureen O'Hara, Patrick Wayne, Chris Mitchum, Bobby Vinton, Bruce Cabot. **1971**

BIG RIP-OFF, THE 🦃 In the closing days of the Civil War, an outlaw stumbles across a dying Confederate soldier who tells him of hidden gold in the home of his blind father. Unbelievably, the outlaw passes himself off to the blind father as his son. Before he can find the gold, the blind man is killed by a gang of outlaws and our hero(?) goes after the gang. Rated R for violence. 90m. **DIR:** Franco Rossetti. **CAST:** Chip Corman, Rosemarie Dexter, Piero Lulli, Dana Ghia, Aldo Berti. **1967**

BIG SHOW, THE ★★ Big-budget Gene Autry series film benefits from location shooting and the musical talent that appears on the show, including young Leonard Slye (soon to be known as Roy Rogers), with the Sons of the Pioneers. Autry plays a double role as a spoiled movie cowboy and the look-alike stuntman. B&W; 70m. **DIR:** Mack V. Wright. **CAST:** Gene Autry, Smiley Burnette, Kay Hughes, Sally Payne, William Newell, Max Terhune. **1936**

BIG SKY, THE ★★ Even the normally reliable director Howard Hawks can't enliven this average tale of early-day fur trappers on an expedition up the Missouri River. Action was Hawks's forte, and there just isn't enough to sustain the viewer's interest. Plenty of beautiful scenery, but that's about it. B&W; 122m. **DIR:** Howard Hawks. **CAST:** Kirk Douglas, Arthur Hunnicutt, Dewey Martin. **1952**

BIG SOMBRERO, THE ★★½ An impoverished Gene Autry comes to the aid of Elena Verdugo and saves her from land swindlers as well as a money-grubbing fiancé in this south-of-the-border tale. This is more of a musical than a horse opera. 77m. **DIR:** Frank McDonald. **CAST:** Gene Autry, Elena Verdugo, Stephen Dunne, George J. Lewis, Martin Garralaga, Gene Roth. **1949**

BIG STAMPEDE, THE ★★★½ In one of John Wayne's best B Westerns for Warner Bros., our hero is a deputy sheriff who goes undercover to bring a corrupt cattle baron to justice. Noah Beery Sr. is in fine form as the bad guy (black hat and all), who builds up his stock by rustling steers and killing anyone who stands in his way. Good action and suspense for the genre, with Wayne (allowed more than one take per scene) more convincing than he would be in the series of low-budget Westerns that followed. B&W; 54m. **DIR:** Tenny Wright. **CAST:** John Wayne, Noah Beery Sr., Paul Hurst, Mae Madison, Luis Alberni, Berton Churchill, Lafe McKee. **1932**

BIG TRAIL, THE ★★★½ John Wayne made his starring debut in this exciting, although somewhat dated epic. Contrary to Hollywood legend, the Duke acquits himself well enough as a revenge-minded scout leading a wagon train across the wilderness. His allegedly stiff acting was long thought to be the reason for the film's box-office failure. In truth, the film was shot in wide-screen 55mm and cinema owners were unwilling to invest in the projection equipment needed to show the film in Fox Grandeur, as it was called, and Wayne found himself grinding out B Westerns for the next nine years—until John Ford picked him to play the Ringo Kid in *Stagecoach*. B&W; 110m. **DIR:** Raoul Walsh. **CAST:** John Wayne, Marguerite Churchill, El Brendel, Ian Keith, Tyrone Power Sr. **1930**

BIG VALLEY, THE (TV SERIES) ★★★ Set in Stockton, California, circa 1878, this is the TV-born saga of the Barkleys, a family of cattle ranchers. Victoria (Barbara Stanwyck) is the iron-willed widow who heads the clan. Jarrod (Richard Long), her oldest son, is a suave attorney. His brother Nick (Peter Breck) is a rugged cowpoke. Their half-brother is Heath (Lee Majors), whose illegitimacy has bred a rebellious streak. All three are protective of Audra (Linda Evans), their gorgeous, haughty sister. A pair of two-part episodes are available on tape: "Legend of a General" and "Explosion." Each tape 90m. **DIR:** Virgil Vogel. **CAST:** Barbara Stanwyck, Richard Long, Peter Breck, Lee Majors, Linda Evans. **1965–1969**

BILLY THE KID ★★★½ The legendary outlaw is romanticized, but the highlights of his life and death are straight from the history books. Predictable but fascinating, chiefly because the studio used top stars and photographed lush surroundings. Pat Garrett is missing, though. The sheriff who tangles with the Kid is completely fictional. 95m. **DIR:** David Miller. **CAST:** Robert Taylor, Brian Donlevy, Chill Wills, Ethel Griffies, Mary Howard, Gene Lockhart, Ian Hunter, Guinn Williams. **1941**

BILLY THE KID RETURNS ★★½ Rogers plays a look-alike to the dead Billy the Kid and restores the tranquillity of Lincoln County after subduing the criminal element. Fun for fans. B&W; 58m. **DIR:** Joseph Kane. **CAST:** Roy Rogers, Smiley Burnette, Lynne Roberts (Mary Hart), Morgan Wallace, Fred Kohler Sr., Trigger. **1938**

BITE THE BULLET ★★★★½ A six-hundred-mile horse race is the subject of this magnificent adventure, an epic in every sense of the word. A real sleeper, hardly noticed during its theatrical release. Rated PG. 131m. **DIR:** Richard Brooks. **CAST:** Gene Hackman, James Coburn, Candice Bergen, Ben Johnson, Jan-Michael Vincent, Dabney Coleman, Ian Bannen. **1975**

BLACK LASH ★★ Lash LaRue poses as an outlaw to catch a band of outlaws in this routine oater. Comprised mostly of stock footage from Lash's 1948 *Frontier Revenge*. For devotees only. B&W; 57m. **DIR:** Ron Ormond. **CAST:** Lash LaRue, Al St. John, Peggy Stewart. **1952**

BLACK MARKET RUSTLERS ★★½ The Range Busters break up a gang of rustlers that are supplying beef for the World War II black market. B&W; 54m. **DIR:** S. Roy Luby. **CAST:** Ray "Crash" Corrigan, Dennis Moore, Max Terhune, Glenn Strange. **1946**

BLADE RIDER ★★ Several *Branded* TV episodes with cavalry and Indian themes loosely patched together to make up a video feature. Released to TV under the title *Ride to Glory*. Sadly, even the famous *Branded* opening theme is edited out. 102m. **DIR:** Various. **CAST:** Chuck Connors, Burt Reynolds, Lee Van Cleef, Robert Lansing, David Brian. **1966**

BLOOD ON THE MOON ★★★½ Robert Mitchum is in top form in this atmospheric Western concerning cattle ranchers trying to terminate homesteaders. B&W; 88m. **DIR:** Robert Wise. **CAST:** Robert Mitchum, Barbara Bel Geddes, Robert Preston. **1948**

BLOODY TRAIL 💔 This Western has no plot, just an ex-Union soldier wandering through the recently defeated South. Rated R for nudity, profanity, and violence. 91m. **DIR:** Richard Robinson. **CAST:** Paul Harper, Rance Howard, John Mitchum. **1972**

BLUE (1968) 💔 God-awful, pretentious Western with Terence Stamp as a monosyllabic gunman. 113m. **DIR:** Silvio Narizzano. **CAST:** Terence Stamp, Joanna Pettet, Karl Malden, Ricardo Montalban, Sally Kirkland. **1968**

BLUE AND THE GRAY, THE ★★★½ Star-studded saga dramatizes many viewpoints of the only war in history pitting American against American. Seen mostly through the eyes of an artist-correspondent, this TV miniseries is a polished, if occasionally sanitized, version of the bloodiest conflict in U.S. history. 295m. **DIR:** Andrew V. McLaglen. **CAST:** Stacy Keach, John Hammond, Lloyd Bridges, Rory Calhoun, Colleen Dewhurst, Warren Oates, Geraldine Page, Rip Torn, Robert Vaughn, Sterling Hayden, Paul Winfield, Gregory Peck. **1982**

BLUE CANADIAN ROCKIES 💔 Processed stock footage of Canada forms the backdrop for this weak story about a young girl's ambitions. B&W; 58m. **DIR:** George Archainbaud. **CAST:** Gene Autry, Pat Buttram, Gail Davis, Ross Ford, Tom London, John Merton, Don Beddoe, Gene Roth. **1952**

BLUE MONTANA SKIES ★★★½ The fur flies when Gene Autry and Smiley "Frog" Burnette discover the murder of their partner, which leads them on the trail of Canadian border pelt smugglers. Unusual snow-country Western action. B&W; 54m. **DIR:** B. Reeves "Breezy" Eason. **CAST:** Gene Autry, Smiley Burnette, June Storey, Harry Woods, Dorothy Granger. **1939**

BLUE STEEL (1934) ★★★ Fun but undistinguished B Western with a very young John Wayne as a cowpoke who saves a town from extinction when he reveals there's gold in them thar hills. B&W; 60m. **DIR:** Robert N. Bradbury. **CAST:** John Wayne, Eleanor Hunt, George "Gabby" Hayes, Ed Peil, Yakima Canutt, George Cleveland. **1934**

BOLD CABALLERO, THE ★★½ This little-known color film is the first sound Zorro movie and an early effort from Republic Studios, better known for their action-filled serials. Robert Livingston plays the masked avenger who sweeps tyranny out of his part of California, while clearing himself of a murder charge. 69m. **DIR:** Wells Root. **CAST:** Robert Livingston, Heather Angel, Sig Ruman, Robert Warwick, Charles Stevens, Slim Whitaker. **1936**

BOLDEST JOB IN THE WEST, THE ★★ A bloodless bank robbery leads to the slaughter of a small western town and one of the gang members escaping with all the loot. Is this a comedy, a parody, or a serious action film? Veteran Spanish character-actor Fernando Sancho saves this clichéd Western from the trash can. Rated PG for violence. 100m. **DIR:** Joseph Loman (Jose Antonio De La Loma). **CAST:** Mark Edwards, Fernando Sancho, Carmen Seville. **1969**

BONANZA (TV SERIES) ★★★ This Western series dominated the Sunday-night ratings for over a decade. It's the story of patriarch Ben Cartwright (Lorne Greene) and his three sons, all from different mothers. Adam (Pernell Roberts) is suave and mature. Hoss (Dan Blocker) is a big man with a bigger heart. Little Joe (Michael Landon) is earnest and hot-tempered. Together they make the Ponderosa the most prosperous ranch in the Comstock Lode country. The Cartwrights, noble gents that they were, used their position, their money, their fists, and their guns to help those in distress. Volume I includes the pilot episode, "A Rose for Lotta," as well as "The Underdog," guest-starring Charles Bronson. Volume II features James Coburn in "The Dark Gate" and DeForest Kelley in "Honor of Cochise." 120m. **DIR:** Edward Ludwig, William F. Claxton, Robert Gordon, Don McDougall. **CAST:** Lorne Greene, Pernell Roberts, Dan Blocker, Michael Landon, Victor Sen Yung. **1959–1973**

BONANZA: THE RETURN ★★ Nepotism on the range as Cartwright offspring attempt to save the Ponderosa from an unscrupulous land developer. Michael Landon Jr. plays little Joe's son Benj, while Dirk Blocker plays a newspaper reporter. Likable cast features a plethora of familiar faces, including Dean Stockwell as the hissable villain. Made-for-TV movie lacks the warmth of the original series, but it tries. 96m. **DIR:** Jerry Jameson. **CAST:** Michael Landon Jr., Richard Roundtree, Linda Gray, Dirk Blocker, Ben Johnson, Dean Stockwell. **1993**

BOOT HILL ★★ Once again, Terence Hill and Bud Spencer are teamed in a spaghetti Western. This one pits them against bad guy Victor Buono. It's violent, bloody, and far from good. Rated PG. 87m. **DIR:** Giuseppe Colizzi. **CAST:** Terence Hill, Bud Spencer, Woody Strode, Lionel Stander, Victor Buono. **1969**

BOOTHILL BANDITS ★★★ Top-notch Range Busters Western, as they rout Wells Fargo bandits. Glenn Strange is a standout as a lumbering, moronic killer. B&W; 58m. **DIR:** S. Roy Luby. **CAST:** Ray "Crash" Corrigan, John King, Max Terhune, Glenn Strange, John Merton, Jean Brooks. **1942**

BOOTS AND SADDLES ★★ An English tenderfoot learns his lessons in the "code of the West" from no-nonsense Gene Autry and his not-so-subtle sidekick Smiley Burnette in this standard story of a foreigner who inherits a working ranch. B&W; 59m. **DIR:** Joseph Kane. **CAST:** Gene Autry, Smiley Burnette, Judith Allen, William Elliott. **1937**

BOOTS MALONE ★★½ Workmanlike Western, nothing special, but with a typically solid William Holden performance in the title role of a tough guy who trains a boy to be a jockey. B&W; 103m. **DIR:** William Dieterle. **CAST:** William Holden, Johnny Stewart, Ed Begley Sr., Harry Morgan, Whit Bissell. **1952**

BORDER FEUD ★★½ The Cheyenne Kid (Lash LaRue) comes to the aid of his pal to settle a blazing feud over a mine. Second in the ever-popular La Rue's string of twenty Westerns. B&W; 54m. **DIR:** Ray Taylor. **CAST:** Lash LaRue, Al St. John, Bob Duncan. **1947**

BORDER PATROL ★★★ In this Hopalong Cassidy entry, Hoppy must put a stop to the criminal atrocities committed by the owner of a silver mine who is using Mexicans as virtual slaves. Robert Mitchum makes his film debut as one of the bad guys. Not the best of the series, but still good, with plenty of action. B&W; 66m. **DIR:** Lesley Selander. **CAST:** William Boyd, Andy Clyde, Russell Simpson, Duncan Renaldo, Robert Mitchum. **1943**

BORDER PHANTOM ★★½ Although *Border Phantom*, like all B Westerns, looks pretty creaky today, it's entertaining, thanks to Bob Steele's energetic performance and an intriguing premise, which involves mysterious murders and slavery. B&W; 59m. **DIR:** S. Roy Luby. **CAST:** Bob Steele, Harley Wood, Don Barclay, Karl Hackett. **1937**

BORDER ROUNDUP ★★ The Lone Rider (George Houston) comes to the aid of a friend who has been framed for murder by outlaws attempting to steal his gold mine. Houston was an opera singer who did a better job in his Westerns than some critics give him credit for. B&W; 57m. **DIR:** Sam Newfield. **CAST:** George Houston, Al St. John, Dennis Moore, Charles King, I. Stanford Jolley. **1942**

BORDER SHOOTOUT ★★★½ Fine actioner from an Elmore Leonard story features an honest farmer (Cody Glenn) who is suddenly appointed deputy in a corrupt town that is at the mercy of a spoiled, violent brat (Jeff Kaake). Glenn Ford portrays his usual tough-but-cool character as the sheriff out transporting a prisoner when all hell breaks loose back home. 110m. **DIR:** C. T. McIntyre. **CAST:** Cody Glenn, Glenn Ford, Jeff Kaake, Charlene Tilton, Michael Ansara. **1989**

BORDERLAND ★★★½ Hopalong Cassidy, an outlaw! Well, sort of. In this B oater, Hoppy must pretend to be a bad guy to save the day. The characterizations are strong. The script is literate, and Morris Ankrum is great as the main outlaw. Good fun for all. B&W; 82m. **DIR:** Nate Watt. **CAST:** William Boyd, James Ellison, George "Gabby" Hayes. **1937**

BORROWED TROUBLE ★★ Hopalong Cassidy and his pals get bogged down in this comedy-drama about a town gone to seed and the outspoken (and obnoxious) schoolteacher who wants to run the bad element out. Cutesy at times and light on the action, this one is perked up occasionally by the dialogue. B&W; 58m. **DIR:** George Archainbaud. **CAST:** William Boyd, Andy Clyde, Rand Brooks, Elaine Riley. **1948**

BOSS ★★½ In the Old West, bounty hunter Fred Williamson and his sidekick D'Urville Martin ride into a town and set themselves up as the law. It's part of their plan to capture a bad guy with a hefty price on his head. Familiar but entertaining oater. Original title: *Boss Nigger*. Not rated. 87m. **DIR:** Jack Arnold. **CAST:** Fred Williamson, D'Urville Martin, R. G. Armstrong, William Smith, Barbara Leigh. **1975**

BOUNTY MAN, THE ★★★½ Made-for-television Western is dark, complex, and quite good. Bounty hunter Clint Walker follows a murderer into a town but is set upon by a group of outlaws. Richard Basehart is particularly good as the outlaw leader. 73m. **DIR:** John Llewellyn Moxey. **CAST:** Clint Walker, Richard Basehart, Margot Kidder, John Ericson, Arthur Hunnicutt, Gene Evans. **1972**

BRANDED ★★½ Farfetched sagebrush melodrama finds Alan Ladd and his shady sidekick hatching a plot to fleece an old rancher and his wife—as Ladd impersonates their long-missing son. Pretty creaky, but a good cast, some exciting chase scenes, and fine outdoor Technicolor photography make this worth watching. 103m. **DIR:** Rudolph Maté. **CAST:** Alan Ladd, Mona Freeman, Charles Bickford, Robert Keith, Joseph Calleia, Peter Hanson, Tom Tully, Milburn Stone. **1951**

BRANDED A COWARD ★★ A minuscule budget and uninspired handling sabotage a potentially top-notch series Western. Johnny Mack Brown is a brave man who cannot bring himself to shoot others—even villains who taunt him—after witnessing the massacre of his family as a child. B&W; 57m. **DIR:** Sam Newfield. **CAST:** Johnny Mack Brown, Billie Seward, Yakima Canutt. **1935**

BRAVADOS, THE ★★★½ In this revenge Western, Gregory Peck tracks down the four men who raped and killed his wife. Directors Budd Boetticher and Anthony Mann handled this theme more involvingly in their films with Randolph Scott and James Stewart, respectively, but this is nonetheless a serviceable Western. 98m. **DIR:** Henry King. **CAST:** Gregory Peck, Joan Collins, Stephen Boyd, Henry Silva, Lee Van Cleef. **1958**

BREAKHEART PASS ★★★ Charles Bronson is a government agent on the trail of gunrunners in the Old West. Most of the action of this modest Western takes place aboard a train, so the excited pitch needed to fully sustain viewers' interest is never reached. Rated PG—some violence and rough language. 95m. **DIR:** Tom Gries. **CAST:** Charles Bronson, Ben Johnson, Ed Lauter, Richard Crenna, Charles Durning, Jill Ireland, John Mitchum. **1976**

BRIMSTONE ★★★★ Undercover lawman Rod Cameron breaks up a cattle-rustling family headed by Walter Brennan. Solid performances and direction make this one of Cameron's best Westerns. 90m. **DIR:** Joseph Kane. **CAST:** Rod Cameron, Walter Brennan, Forrest Tucker, Jack Holt, Adrian Booth, Jim Davis. **1949**

BROADWAY TO CHEYENNE ★★½ A New York mob moves west to set up a cattlemen's protection association, but a New York cop on vacation breaks up their racket. This was Rex Bell's first Western, and it set the formula for many of his pictures. B&W; 60m. **DIR:** Harry Fraser. **CAST:** Rex Bell, George "Gabby" Hayes, Marceline Day. **1932**

BROKEN ARROW ★★★ Jeff Chandler is the Apache chief Cochise and James Stewart is a cavalry scout in this sympathetic look at Indians and white settlers struggling to coexist on the Western frontier in the 1870s. The film was the first to treat the Indian with respect and understanding. 93m. **DIR:** Delmer Daves. **CAST:** James Stewart, Jeff Chandler, Debra Paget, Will Geer, Arthur Hunnicutt, Basil Ruysdael, Jay Silverheels. **1950**

BROKEN LANCE ★★★★ Spencer Tracy's superb performance as a cattle baron at odds with his Indian wife and bickering sons is but one of the pleasures in this first-rate adult Western. The screenplay, based on 1949's *House of Strangers*, won an Oscar, and Jurado was nominated for best supporting actress. 97m. **DIR:** Edward Dmytryk. **CAST:** Spencer Tracy, Richard Widmark, Jean Peters, Robert Wagner, Katy Jurado, Earl Holliman, Hugh O'Brian. **1954**

BRONCO (TV SERIES) ★★★½ Originally tapped to take over the role of *Cheyenne* when Clint Walker walked out during a salary dispute, Ty Hardin became *Bronco* in a series that drew many of its stories from historic events. In "Shadow of Jesse James," Bronco must arrest the famed outlaw (James Coburn). In "Death of an Outlaw," Bronco Layne finds himself involved in the Lincoln County Wars alongside Billy the Kid and Pat Garrett. Each 49m. **DIR:** Leslie Goodwins, Robert L. Strock. **CAST:** Ty Hardin, James Coburn, Allan "Rocky" Lane, Rhodes Reason. **1958–1962**

BROTHERS IN THE SADDLE ★★★ Steve Brodie is the ne'er-do-well brother of straight shooter Tim Holt in this above-average Western. Uncommonly hard-edged for a series Western of the late 1940s, when interest in the genre was flagging and most cowboy movies were lifeless remakes. B&W; 60m. **DIR:** Lesley Selander. **CAST:** Tim Holt, Richard Martin, Steve Brodie. **1949**

BROTHERS OF THE WEST ★★½ Standard plot in which the hero (Tom Tyler) must clear his framed brother. B&W; 58m. **DIR:** Sam Katzman. **CAST:** Tom Tyler, Lois Wilde. **1937**

BUCK AND THE PREACHER ★★½ Harry Belafonte and director Sidney Poitier play two escaped slaves heading west. On the way, they meet up with "bad guy" Cameron Mitchell and lovely Ruby Dee. So-so Western. Rated PG. 102m. **DIR:** Sidney Poitier. **CAST:** Sidney Poitier, Harry Belafonte, Ruby Dee, Cameron Mitchell. **1972**

BUCKEYE AND BLUE ★★ Disappointing *Bonnie and Clyde*–style Western featuring Robin Lively and Jeff Osterhage as a couple of desperadoes who engage in a crime spree after the Civil War. No new twists on this tired theme. Rated PG. 94m. **DIR:** J. C. Compton. **CAST:** Robyn Lively, Jeff Osterhage, Rick Gibbs, Will Hannah. **1988**

BUCKSKIN ★★½ Trite, overwritten, A. C. Lyles-produced Western featuring a score of familiar-face, long-in-the-tooth actors—which is the best feature of this film about a heroic marshal battling a domineering cattle baron. 97m. **DIR:** Michael Moore. **CAST:** Barry Sullivan, Wendell Corey, Joan Caulfield, Bill Williams, John Russell, Barbara Hale, Lon Chaney Jr., Barton MacLane. **1968**

BUCKSKIN FRONTIER ★★★ Railroad representative Richard Dix and freight-line owner Lee J. Cobb fight over business and a crucial mountain pass in this big-budget, fast-action Western. B&W; 82m. **DIR:** Lesley Selander. **CAST:** Richard Dix, Jane Wyatt, Lee J. Cobb, Albert Dekker, Joe Sawyer, Victor Jory, Lola Lane. **1943**

BUFFALO BILL ★★★½ The famed frontiersman William Cody gets the Hollywood biography treatment in this slick, but sometimes bland motion picture. Star Joel McCrea brings his usual dignity to the role. 90m. **DIR:** William Wellman. **CAST:** Joel McCrea, Maureen O'Hara, Linda Darnell, Thomas Mitchell, Anthony Quinn, Edgar Buchanan. **1944**

BUFFALO BILL AND THE INDIANS ★★½ In this offbeat Western, Paul Newman, Burt Lancaster, Harvey Keitel, Geraldine Chaplin, Joel Grey, Kevin McCarthy, and Will Sampson are fun to watch as they interact like jazz musicians jamming on the theme of distorted history and the delusion of celebrity. Rated PG. 120m. **DIR:** Robert Altman. **CAST:** Paul Newman, Joel Grey, Kevin McCarthy, Burt Lancaster, Harvey Keitel, Geraldine Chaplin, Will Sampson. **1976**

BUFFALO STAMPEDE ★★★ Zane Grey story has buffalo hunter Randolph Scott in love with the daughter of an outlaw stirring up Indian trouble. B&W; 59m. **DIR:** Henry Hathaway. **CAST:** Randolph Scott, Harry Carey, Buster Crabbe, Noah Beery Sr. **1933**

BUGLES IN THE AFTERNOON ★★½ In this modest Western a young army officer is made a victim by a jealous rival. Set in the time of Custer's last stand, it has fairly good scenery and cinematography. 85m. **DIR:** Roy Rowland. **CAST:** Ray Milland, Hugh Marlowe, Helena Carter, Forrest Tucker, Barton MacLane, George Reeves. **1952**

BULLDOG COURAGE ★★½ Tim McCoy is excellent in the dual role of father and son in this slow-paced series Western. When Slim Braddock (McCoy) is killed, it's up to his son, Tim (McCoy), to avenge his death after a period of several years. This was one of McCoy's last starring films. B&W; 66m. **DIR:** Sam Newfield. **CAST:** Tim McCoy, Joan Woodbury, Paul Fix, Eddie Buzzard. **1935**

BULLET FOR SANDOVAL, A ★★½ A gritty story of Warner, a rebel soldier who deserts to be with his fiancée at childbirth. When he arrives at the Sandoval hacienda he finds her dead and her father blames him for his daughter's death. Warner is given his baby son and thrown out. He assembles a band of renegades to seek vengeance on Sandoval. Good acting from Ernest Borgnine and George Hilton. Rated PG. 96m. **DIR:** Julio Buchs. **CAST:** Ernest Borgnine, George Hilton, Annabella Incontrera, Alberto De Mendoza, Leo Anchoriz. **1969**

BULLET FOR THE GENERAL, A ★★★ A spaghetti Western with a social conscience. Gian Maria Volonté hams it up as a Mexican revolutionary explaining his cause to Lou Castel, who unbeknownst to him is really an American mercenary hired to assassinate him. Dubbed in English. 95m. **DIR:** Damiano Damiani. **CAST:** Gian Maria Volonté, Lou Castel, Martine Beswick, Klaus Kinski. **1967**

BULLET FROM GOD, A 🦃 When the town priest is gunned down in broad daylight, his young friend goes to the priest's retired gunfighter-brother Louis. When Louis finds out about his brother's death, he straps on his gun and takes on the entire gang. Terrible dubbing wastes a veteran cast. You won't believe Richard Boone's dubbed voice. Filmed in Israel. Rated R for violence and brief nudity. 90m. **DIR:** Frank Kramer. **CAST:** Lee Van Cleef, Jack Palance, Richard Boone, Sybil Danning, Leif Garrett, Robert Lipton. **1976**

BULLWHIP ★★½ In this agreeable movie, Guy Madison avoids the hangin' tree by agreeing to marry a fiery half-breed (Rhonda Fleming). If the plot sounds familiar, it should. Jack Nicholson used a similar one in *Goin' South*. 80m. **DIR:** Harmon Jones. **CAST:** Rhonda Fleming, Guy Madison, James Griffith, Don Beddoe. **1958**

BUSHWHACKERS ★★★ Ex-Confederate John Ireland tries to hang up his guns, but a ruthless land baron forces him to buckle 'em on again. Routine range-war tale saved by a better-than-competent cast. B&W; 70m. **DIR:** Rod Amateau. **CAST:** John Ireland, Dorothy Malone, Wayne Morris, Lawrence Tierney, Lon Chaney Jr. **1951**

BUTCH AND SUNDANCE: THE EARLY DAYS ★★ Director Richard Lester has made better films (see *A Hard Day's Night* and *Superman II*), and because his usual film is a comedy, this outing is especially disappointing. Nearly all of the jokes fall flat despite a screenplay that hints at the original film with Paul Newman and Robert Redford. Rated PG for some mildly crude language and (very little) violence. 111m. **DIR:** Richard Lester. **CAST:** William Katt, Tom Berenger, Brian Dennehy, John Schuck, Jeff Corey. **1979**

BUTCH CASSIDY AND THE SUNDANCE KID ★★★★½ George Roy Hill directed this gentle Western spoof featuring personal-best performances by Paul Newman, Robert Redford, and Katharine Ross. A spectacular box-office success, and deservedly so, the release deftly combines action with comedy. Rated PG. 112m. **DIR:** George Roy Hill. **CAST:** Paul Newman, Robert Redford, Katharine Ross. **1969**

CAHILL—US MARSHAL ★★½ John Wayne was still making B Westerns in the 1970s—to the disappointment of those who (rightly) expected better. Although still enjoyable, this film about a lawman (Wayne) whose son (Gary Grimes) becomes a bank robber is routine at best. Still, the performances by the Duke and George Kennedy (as the chief baddie) do bring pleasure. Rated PG. 103m. **DIR:** Andrew V. McLaglen. **CAST:** John Wayne, George Kennedy, Gary Grimes, Neville Brand. **1973**

CALAMITY JANE (1984) ★★★★ Director James Goldstone provides more than just the story of Calamity Jane, which is fascinating in itself as a tale of one of America's first feminists. His unglamorous production and straightforward storytelling give a true feeling of the Old West. Jane Alexander, in an Emmy-nominated performance, shows the many sides of this spirited lady. A made-for-TV movie. 100m. **DIR:** James Goldstone. **CAST:** Jane Alexander, Frederic Forrest, David Hemmings, Ken Kercheval, Talia Balsam. **1984**

CALIFORNIA FRONTIER ★★ Army Captain Buck Jones brings to justice bandits stealing land from Mexicans in a routine California land-grab plot. B&W; 54m. **DIR:** Elmer Clifton. **CAST:** Buck Jones, Milburn Stone, Glenn Strange. **1938**

CALIFORNIA GOLD RUSH ★★ The writer Bret Harte (Robert Hays) is in the right place at the right time to chronicle the gold rush days of California from Sutter's Fort. Rated PG. 100m. **DIR:** Jack B. Hively. **CAST:** Robert Hays, John Dehner, Ken Curtis, Henry Jones, Dan Haggerty. **1985**

CALL OF THE CANYON ★★ Even-tempered Gene Autry sides with the local cattlemen in their struggle against an unscrupulous meat-packing company tycoon in this enjoyable Republic Studios Western. B&W; 71m. **DIR:** Joseph Santley. **CAST:** Gene Autry, Smiley Burnette, Ruth Terry, Thurston Hall, Pat Brady, Marc Lawrence, Budd Buster, Bob Nolan and the Sons of the Pioneers, Bob Burns. **1942**

CALL OF THE COYOTE 🦃 A Mexican Robin Hood. B&W; 40m. **DIR:** Patrick Carlyle. **CAST:** Kenneth Thompson, Charles Stevens. **1934**

CALLING WILD BILL ELLIOTT ★★½ In his first assignment in an A picture for Republic Studios, Wild Bill Elliott pals up with Gabby Hayes to fight off evil robbers harassing the lovely Anne Jeffreys. Gabby Hayes is supposed to be a funny sidekick, but here he is more of an anvil around the neck. Average. B&W; 78m. **DIR:** Spencer Gordon Bennet. **CAST:** William Elliott, Anne Jeffreys, George "Gabby" Hayes. **1943**

CAPTAIN APACHE ★★ Muddled Western has Lee Van Cleef in title role gunning down dozens of one-dimensional characters who cross his path or appear likely to. Rated PG for violence. 94m. **DIR:** Alexander Singer. **CAST:** Lee Van Cleef, Stuart Whitman, Carroll Baker, Percy Herbert. **1971**

CARAVAN TRAIL ★★★★ The leader (Eddie Dean) of a wagon train of settlers takes the job of marshal to restore homesteaders' land being stolen by outlaws. He enlists the aid of some not-so-bad outlaws to stop the land grabbers. Lash LaRue (in his second supporting role to Dean) steals the picture. LaRue went on to star in his own series of well-received Bs. 57m. **DIR:** Robert Emmett Tansey. **CAST:** Eddie Dean, Lash LaRue, Charles King. **1946**

CARIBOO TRAIL ★★★★ Cattleman Randolph Scott finds gold in Canada but has to fight off Victor Jory's claim jumpers. Gorgeous Colorado scenery stands in for the Canadian wilderness. 81m. **DIR:** Edwin L. Marin. **CAST:** Randolph Scott, George "Gabby" Hayes, Bill Williams, Victor Jory, Douglas Kennedy, Dale Robertson, Jim Davis. **1950**

CARSON CITY CYCLONE ★★★★ Donald "Red" Barry plays a cocky young defense attorney framed for the murder of his father (a judge and banker). Intricate plot that proves how good B Westerns can be. B&W; 55m. **DIR:** Howard Bretherton. **CAST:** Don Barry, Noah Beery Sr., Roy Barcroft. **1943**

CARSON CITY KID ★★★★ Top-notch Roy Rogers period Western dominated by Bob Steele in an offbeat villainous role. Roy Rogers, in the title role, pursues a cunning gambler who murdered his brother. B&W; 54m. **DIR:** Joseph Kane. **CAST:** Roy Rogers, George "Gabby" Hayes, Bob Steele, Noah Beery Jr., Pauline Moore. **1940**

CAT BALLOU ★★★ In this offbeat, uneven but fun comedy-Western, Jane Fonda plays Cat, a former schoolteacher out to avenge her father's death. Michael Callan is her main romantic interest. Lee Marvin outshines all with his Oscar-winning performance in the dual roles of the drunken hired gun and his evil look-alike. 96m. **DIR:** Elliot Silverstein. **CAST:** Jane Fonda, Lee Marvin, Michael Callan, Jay C. Flippen. **1965**

CATLOW ★★ A Louis L'Amour yarn is the basis for this minor Western about a gold robbery. Typical effort by formerly blacklisted Sam Wanamaker. Rated PG. 103m. **DIR:** Sam Wanamaker. **CAST:** Yul Brynner, Richard Crenna, Leonard Nimoy, Daliah Lavi, Jeff Corey, Jo Ann Pflug. **1971**

CATTLE QUEEN OF MONTANA ★★ Barbara Stanwyck gives a strong performance in this otherwise routine Western. Plot revolves around Stanwyck trying to protect her farm from land grabbers, who also murdered her father. Meanwhile, the Indians are out to wipe out everybody. 88m. **DIR:** Allan Dwan. **CAST:** Barbara Stanwyck, Ronald Reagan, Gene Evans, Jack Elam. **1954**

CHARRO! ★★ Nonmusical Western was intended to introduce Elvis Presley, serious actor. However, the only thing this misfire proved was that its star could go without shaving. Try Don Siegel's *Flaming Star* instead. 98m. **DIR:** Charles Marquis Warren. **CAST:** Elvis Presley, Ina Balin, Victor French. **1969**

CHATO'S LAND ★★½ Unjustly accused of murdering a lawman, a half-breed Apache (the top-billed, but seldom seen Charles Bronson) must fight off a posse bent on killing him. Overly violent Western substitutes types for characters and bloodshed for story structure. Rated PG. 110m. **DIR:** Michael Winner. **CAST:** Charles Bronson, Jack Palance, Jill Ireland, Richard Basehart, James Whitmore, Simon Oakland, Richard Jordan. **1972**

CHEROKEE FLASH ★★★ Old-time outlaw Roy Barcroft tries to go straight, but his old henchmen don't intend to allow him to do so. Barcroft's foster son, Sunset Carson, comes to his rescue. B&W; 58m. **DIR:** Thomas Carr. **CAST:** Sunset Carson, Roy Barcroft, Linda Stirling, Tom London, John Merton. **1945**

CHEROKEE STRIP ★★ The Oklahoma land rush is the basis for this routine story of a bunch of land grabbers. Dick Foran is good as the hero who puts the crimp in their plan. B&W; 55m. **DIR:** Noel Smith. **CAST:** Dick Foran, Jane Bryan, David Carlyle, Glenn Strange. **1937**

CHEYENNE (TV SERIES) ★★★★ Warner Bros. Television's first entry into the Western series boom of the Fifties ranks with *Gunsmoke*, *Rawhide*, and *Maverick* as one of the very best of its kind. Big Clint Walker (six-foot-six-inches tall) plays the laconic Cheyenne Bodie, who roams the West in episodes that explore every possible theme in the genre. In "White Warrior," one of two shows released so far on video, a pre-*Bonanza* Michael Landon plays a white man raised by Indians who causes problems for wagon master Cheyenne. In "The Iron Trail," Cheyenne must stop outlaw Dennis Hopper, who is out to kidnap President Ulysses S. Grant. B&W; Each 49m. **DIR:** Leslie Martinson, Lee Sholem. **CAST:** Clint Walker, Michael Landon, Dennis Hopper. **1955–1962**

CHEYENNE AUTUMN ★★★½ John Ford strays away from his traditional glorification of Western mythology to bring us this story of the mistreatment of the American Indian. His standard heroes, the U.S. cavalry, are placed in the role of the villains as they try to stop a group of desperate Cheyenne Indians from migrating back to their Wyoming homeland from a barren reservation in Oklahoma. This movie is uniformly well acted, and as with any John Ford Western, the scenery is breathtaking. 160m. **DIR:** John Ford. **CAST:** Richard Widmark, Karl Malden, Carroll Baker, James Stewart, Edward G. Robinson, Ricardo Montalban, Sal Mineo. **1964**

CHEYENNE SOCIAL CLUB, THE ★★★ This Western-comedy has a number of pleasing moments. James Stewart, an itinerant cowhand, and his low-key cohort Henry Fonda inherit some property in Cheyenne—which turns out to be a bordello. The premise is good, but at times director Gene Kelly doesn't have a firm grip on the script or on these hugely talented actors. Rated PG. 103m. **DIR:** Gene Kelly. **CAST:** James Stewart, Henry Fonda, Shirley Jones, Sue Ane Langdon. **1970**

CHEYENNE TAKES OVER ★★★ Lash LaRue's long-needed vacation at the Lobos ranch is anything but restful as he discovers it's been taken over by an impersonator who claims birthright to the land. B&W; 58m. **DIR:** Ray Taylor. **CAST:** Lash LaRue, Al St. John, Nancy Gates. **1947**

CHINO ★★ A surprisingly low-key Charles Bronson Western about a horse breeder who attempts to live a peaceful life. An above-average performance by Bronson and an adequate one by his wife, Jill Ireland, as Chino's love interest. Rated PG. 98m. **DIR:** John Sturges. **CAST:** Charles Bronson, Jill Ireland, Vincent Van Patten. **1973**

CHISHOLMS, THE ★★★ This made-for-TV oater is a vast saga of a family's trek west from Virginia to California. A bit talky, but worth a viewing. 300m. **DIR:** Mel Stuart. **CAST:** Robert Preston, Rosemary Harris, Ben Murphy, Brian Kerwin. **1979**

CHISUM ★★★½ The best of the John Wayne Westerns directed by Andrew V. McLaglen, this sprawling epic centers around the revenge sought by Billy the Kid (Geoffrey Duel) after his mentor (Patric Knowles) is murdered by the corrupt, land-grabbing bad guys. Rated G. 111m. **DIR:** Andrew V. McLaglen. **CAST:** John Wayne, Forrest Tucker, Christopher George, Ben Johnson, Patric Knowles, Bruce Cabot, Glenn Corbett. **1970**

CHRISTMAS KID, THE ★★ A woman dies on Christmas Eve while giving birth to a son who is christened "The Christmas Kid" and raised by the town. He becomes a gunman and is hired by the town boss but switches sides when his girlfriend is killed. He becomes the sheriff and cleans up the lawlessness. A good story and acting. Filmed in Spain. Rated G. 87m. **DIR:** Sidney Pink. **CAST:** Jeffrey Hunter, Louis Hayward, Gustavo Rojo, Perla Cristal, Luis Prendes, Jack Taylor. **1966**

CHUKA ★★ A hard-bitten gunfighter and a disgraced cavalry officer try to keep marauding Indians from getting to the voluptuous Italian beauty who happened to end up in the Southwest in full makeup. Ho hum. 105m. **DIR:** Gordon Douglas. **CAST:** Rod Taylor, John Mills, Ernest Borgnine, Luciana Paluzzi, James Whitmore, Louis Hayward. **1967**

CIMARRON (1931) ★★★ One of the panoramic, expensive early sound films, this Western based on Edna Ferber's novel presents the story of a pioneer family bent on building an empire out of the primitiveness of early Oklahoma. It won the Academy Award for best picture, but some scenes now seem dated. B&W; 124m. **DIR:** Wesley Ruggles. **CAST:** Richard Dix, Irene Dunne, Estelle Taylor, William Collier Jr., Roscoe Ates. **1931**

CIMARRON (1960) ★★★ This overlong Western opens with a spectacular re-creation of the 1889 Oklahoma land rush, but bogs down into a familiar building-of-the-West tale. Tries for epic status but misses the mark. 147m. **DIR:** Anthony Mann. **CAST:** Glenn Ford, Maria Schell, Anne Baxter, Arthur O'Connell, Mercedes McCambridge, Russ Tamblyn, Vic Morrow, Robert Keith, Aline MacMahon, Harry Morgan, Charles McGraw, Royal Dano, Edgar Buchanan. **1960**

CISCO KID, THE ★★★ The Cisco Kid and his faithful companion, Pancho, battle the French Occupation Army and American gunners in Mexico. Enjoyable, lighthearted Western is spiced with humor and enthusiastic performances by Jimmy Smits and Richard "Cheech" Marin. Made for TV. 95m. **DIR:** Luis Valdez. **CAST:** Jimmy Smits, Richard "Cheech" Marin, Sadie Frost, Ron Perlman, Bruce Payne. **1994**

CISCO KID (TV SERIES) ★★★ The Cisco Kid, O'Henry's Robin Hood of the Old West, and his English language mangling sidekick Pancho, rode the TV range for 176 episodes. The only series of its type filmed entirely in color. Volume one features two of the best episodes: "Quarter Horse" and "Postmaster." 50m. **DIR:** Eddie Davis. **CAST:** Duncan Renaldo, Leo Carillo. **1951**

COLORADO ★★ Roy Rogers and Gabby Hayes settle comfortably into what became a profitable and highly successful series in this routine shoot-'em-up about the riders who clean up the territory for decent folk. Not too imaginative, but enjoyable. B&W; 54m. **DIR:** Joseph Kane. **CAST:** Roy Rogers, George "Gabby" Hayes, Milburn Stone. **1940**

COLORADO SERENADE ★★★ Eddie Dean and stuntman extraordinaire Dave Sharpe help a crusading judge clean out a nest of outlaws. More trouble arises when the judge learns his long lost son is the leader of the gang. 68m. **DIR:** Robert Emmett Tansey. **CAST:** Eddie Dean, Roscoe Ates, David Sharpe, Forrest Taylor, Dennis Moore. **1946**

COLORADO SUNSET ★★★ A phony protective association causes a milk war among ranchers until they vote Gene Autry in as sheriff. B&W; 61m. **DIR:** George Sherman. **CAST:** Gene Autry, Smiley Burnette, June Storey, Buster Crabbe. **1939**

COLT COMRADES ★★ Hopalong Cassidy and pals catch a crook and decide to settle down with the reward money. B&W; 67m. **DIR:** Lesley Selander. **CAST:** William Boyd, Andy Clyde, Victor Jory, Herbert Rawlinson, Robert Mitchum, George Reeves. **1943**

COMANCHEROS, THE ★★★★ Big John Wayne is the laconic Texas Ranger assigned to bring in dandy gambler Stuart Whitman for murder. Along the way, Wayne bests bad guy Lee Marvin, and Whitman proves himself a hero by helping the big guy take on the ruthless gun- and liquor-running villains of the title, led by Nehemiah Persoff. It's a fine Western with lots of nice moments. 107m. **DIR:** Michael Curtiz. **CAST:** John Wayne, Stuart Whitman, Lee Marvin, Ina Balin, Bruce Cabot, Nehemiah Persoff, Bob Steele. **1961**

COME ON TARZAN ★★★★ Wild horses are being sold for dog food. Ken Maynard and steed Tarzan must stop it. Top-notch. B&W; 61m. **DIR:** Alan James. **CAST:** Ken Maynard, Kate Campbell, Roy Stewart. **1932**

COMES A HORSEMAN ★★★★ Dark, somber, but haunting Western set in the 1940s about the efforts of a would-be land baron (Jason Robards Jr.) to cheat his long-suffering neighbor (Jane Fonda) out of her land. She fights back with the help of a World War II veteran (James Caan) and a crusty old-timer (Richard Farnsworth). Rated PG for violence. 118m. **DIR:** Alan J. Pakula. **CAST:** Jane Fonda, James Caan, Jason Robards Jr., George Grizzard, Richard Farnsworth, Jim Davis. **1978**

CONAGHER ★★★½ Katharine Ross is a lonely widow with two children running a stagecoach way station and Sam Elliott is a cowhand she's attracted to, in this made-for-cable Western. Elliott seems to have been born to play cowboys. A welcome addition to a fading genre. 118m. **DIR:** Reynaldo Villalobos. **CAST:** Sam Elliott, Katharine Ross, Barry Corbin, Billy Green Bush, Ken Curtis, Paul Koslo, Gavan O'Herlihy, Pepe Serna, Dub Taylor. **1991**

CONQUEST OF CHEYENNE ★★ Red Ryder aids a lady rancher fending off a ruthless banker trying to get her land because of vast oil deposits. B&W; 54m. **DIR:** R. G. Springsteen. **CAST:** William Elliott, Robert Blake, Peggy Stewart, Jay Kirby. **1946**

CONQUEST OF COCHISE Historically inaccurate story of Apache leader Cochise. 70m. **DIR:** William Castle. **CAST:** Robert Stack, John Hodiak. **1953**

COPPER CANYON ★★ A gunslinger helps homesteaders stake their claims after the Civil War. This would have been a more believable picture with a different cast. Milland's British accent and Lamarr's Austrian one are completely out of place in the American Southwest. 83m. **DIR:** John Farrow. **CAST:** Ray Milland, Hedy Lamarr, Macdonald Carey, Mona Freeman, Harry Carey Jr., Frank Faylen, Hope Emerson, Ian Wolfe, Peggy Knudsen. **1950**

CORONER CREEK ★★★★ Solid Western marks the first film in the series produced by the company set up by Randolph Scott and Harry Brown. Their collaboration culminated in the superb series directed by Budd Boetticher *(Ride Lonesome, The Tall T)*. Even so, this film is no slouch, with Scott attempting to track down the man responsible for the murder of his fiancée. 90m. **DIR:** Ray Enright. **CAST:** Randolph Scott, Marguerite Chapman, George Macready, Forrest Tucker, Edgar Buchanan. **1948**

COVERED WAGON, THE ★★★½ Touted as "the biggest thing the screen has had since *The Birth of A Nation*," this epic pioneer saga broke audience attendance records all over the world and remained in circulation for many years. Love, adventure, humor, danger, and despair overlap each other in this somewhat dated but still exciting blockbuster. A landmark Western. Silent. B&W; 83m. **DIR:** James Cruze. **CAST:** J. Warren Kerrigan, Lois Wilson, Alan Hale Sr., Ernest Torrence, Tully Marshall. **1923**

COVERED WAGON DAYS ★★½ The Three Mesquiteers have until sunset to prove a friend innocent of a murder actually committed by silver smugglers. B&W; 54m. **DIR:** George Sherman. **CAST:** Robert Livingston, Duncan Renaldo, Raymond Hatton. **1940**

COW TOWN ★★½ Action and stunts as well as a good crew of familiar faces make this, Gene Autry's seventy-second film as himself, better than many of his earlier efforts. Grazing rights, stampedes, gunplay, and a song or two (or three) are packed into the film. B&W; 70m. **DIR:** John English. **CAST:** Gene Autry, Gail Davis, Harry Shannon, Jock Mahoney. **1950**

COWBOY AND THE BANDIT ★★ An outlaw comes to the aid of a lone cowboy in busting up a gang of gamblers and killers. The diminutive Lease was better suited to character roles and, in fact, became a working Western character actor clear into the heyday of TV Westerns in the early Sixties. B&W; 57m. **DIR:** Albert Herman. **CAST:** Rex Lease, Bobby Nelson, William Desmond, Franklyn Farnum. **1935**

COWBOY AND THE SENORITA ★★ In the first of her twenty-seven costarring Westerns with Roy Rogers, Dale Evans is a headstrong young lady out to protect her vulnerable younger sister from outlaws. Although this one set the tone for nearly all their costarring vehicles, it was done much better later on. B&W; 54m. **DIR:** Joseph Kane. **CAST:** Roy Rogers, Dale Evans, Mary Lee, Bob Nolan and the Sons of the Pioneers, Guinn Williams, Fuzzy Knight. **1944**

COWBOY MILLIONAIRE ★★★ The accent is on humor in this series Western, which has two-fisted George O'Brien and sidekick Edgar Kennedy acting as "colorful cowboy types" at a hotel out west. It's just a way to raise money to finance their mining operation. B&W; 65m. **DIR:** Eddie Cline. **CAST:** George O'Brien, Edgar Kennedy. **1935**

COWBOYS, THE ★★★★½ Along with Don Siegel's *The Shootist*, this is the best of John Wayne's latter-day Westerns. The Duke plays a rancher whose wranglers get gold fever. He's forced to recruit a bunch of green kids in order to take his cattle to market. Bruce Dern is on hand as the outlaw leader who fights our hero in one of the genre's most memorable (and violent) scenes. Rated PG. 128m. **DIR:** Mark Rydell. **CAST:** John Wayne, Roscoe Lee Browne, Bruce Dern, Colleen Dewhurst, Slim Pickens. **1972**

CROSSFIRE (1986) Outlaws are saved from execution by a gang of Mexican freedom fighters. 82m. **DIR:** Robert Conrad, Alfredo Zacharias. **CAST:** Robert Conrad, Jan-Michael Vincent, Manuel Ochoa Lopez. **1986**

CRY BLOOD, APACHE ★★½ Joel McCrea, in a cameo appearance as a favor to his son, tells in flashback how he and a bunch of prospectors slaughtered a band of Indians. A girl, the lone survivor of the massacre, promises to lead them to a secret gold mine. 85m. **DIR:** Jack Starrett. **CAST:** Jody McCrea, Dan Kemp, Jack Starrett, Joel McCrea. **1970**

CULPEPPER CATTLE CO., THE ★★★½ A strong supporting cast makes this coming-of-age story set in the Old West into a real treat for fans of shoot-'em-ups. Gary Grimes is a 16-year-old farm boy who dreams of becoming a cowboy. Rated R for violence. 92m. **DIR:** Dick Richards. **CAST:** Gary Grimes, Billy Green Bush, Luke Askew, Bo Hopkins, Geoffrey Lewis, Royal Dano. **1972**

CUT THROATS NINE 🖤 More slasher movie than Western, this brutal film tells the story of a cavalry officer and his daughter who accompany a wagon load of convicts. The wagon overturns and the guards are killed, and a gruesome tale of violence, rape, and murder follows. Only for the strong of stomach. Rated R for violence and nudity. 90m. **DIR:** Joaquin Romero Marchent. **CAST:** Robert Hundar, Emma Cohen, Manuel Tejada, Alberto Dalbes, Antonio Itanzo. **1973**

CYCLONE IN THE SADDLE 🖤 Absolute bottom-of-the-barrel wagon train oater. B&W; 52m. **DIR:** Elmer Clifton. **CAST:** Rex Lease, Bobby Nelson, William Desmond, Yakima Canutt. **1935**

CYCLONE RANGER ★★ A blind woman mistakes Bill Cody for her outlaw son who was killed by a posse. Remake of Jack Hoxie's *Gun Law*. B&W; 60m. **DIR:** Bob Hill. **CAST:** Bill Cody, Earle Hodgins. **1935**

DAKOTA (1945) ★★½ Any Western with John Wayne, Walter Brennan, and Ward Bond has to be a winner, right? Wrong. This substandard film may be interesting to see for their performances, but you also have to put up with the incredibly untalented Vera Ralston (she was the wife of Republic Studio head Herbert Yates). It's almost worth it. B&W; 82m. **DIR:** Joseph Kane. **CAST:** John Wayne, Vera Hruba Ralston, Walter Brennan, Ward Bond. **1945**

DAKOTA INCIDENT ★★½ It's a fight to the finish in this fairly good Western as the Indians attack a stagecoach rolling through Dakota Territory in those thrilling days of yesteryear. 88m. **DIR:** Lewis R. Foster. **CAST:** Dale Robertson, Linda Darnell, John Lund. **1956**

DANCES WITH WOLVES ★★★★★ Heartfelt, thoroughly involving saga of a disillusioned Union soldier's flight from the Civil War, and his eventual finding of inner peace in harmony with nature and the Lakota Sioux. A brilliant filmmaking debut from director-star Kevin Costner, this epic reestablished the Western's viability at the box office. In English and Lakota Sioux with subtitles. Rated PG-13 for violence and brief nudity. 185m. **DIR:** Kevin Costner. **CAST:** Kevin Costner, Mary McDonnell, Graham Greene, Rodney A. Grant. **1990**

DANGEROUS VENTURE ★★½ This better-than-average Hopalong Cassidy adventure finds our heroes searching for Aztec ruins in the Southwest. B&W; 55m. **DIR:** George Archainbaud. **CAST:** William Boyd, Andy Clyde, Rand Brooks. **1947**

DANIEL BOONE ★★★★ Action-packed story of the early American frontier features rugged outdoor star George O'Brien in the title role and evil John Carradine as a renegade who aids the Indians. This rousing film is great schoolboy adventure stuff. B&W; 77m. **DIR:** David Howard. **CAST:** George O'Brien, Heather Angel, John Carradine. **1936**

DANIEL BOONE, TRAIL BLAZER ★★½ This is a slightly better-than-average Western that has Daniel Boone (Bruce Bennett) not only pathfinding for settlers but fighting off what seems to be the entire population of Native Americans. Good performances and lots of action save it from being mundane. 76m. **DIR:** Albert C. Gannaway. **CAST:** Bruce Bennett, Lon Chaney Jr., Faron Young. **1956**

DARK COMMAND ★★★★½ Raoul Walsh, who directed John Wayne's first big Western, *The Big Trail*, was reunited with the star after the latter's triumph in *Stagecoach* for this dynamic shoot-'em-up. Walter Pidgeon is Quantrill, a once-honest man who goes renegade and forms Quantrill's Raiders. It's up to the Duke, with help from his *Stagecoach* costar Claire Trevor, Roy Rogers, and Gabby Hayes, to set things right. B&W; 94m. **DIR:** Raoul Walsh. **CAST:** John Wayne, Claire Trevor, Walter Pidgeon, Roy Rogers, George "Gabby" Hayes. **1940**

DAWN ON THE GREAT DIVIDE ★★★ With a bigger budget than usual and a story with more plot twists than the average B Western, the result is a good shoot-'em-up in the series vein. Buck Jones, of course, dominates as the two-fisted leader of a wagon train who takes on Indians, bad guys, and corrupt officials with equal aplomb. It was the last movie made by Jones, who died heroically trying to save lives during a fire at Boston's Coconut Grove on November 28, 1942. B&W; 63m. **DIR:** Howard Bretherton. **CAST:** Buck Jones, Raymond Hatton, Rex Bell, Mona Barrie. **1942**

DAWN RIDER ★★ John Wayne is out for revenge in this formula B Western. His loving father is killed during a robbery, and it's up to a gangly, slightly stilted Wayne to get the bad guys. B&W; 56m. **DIR:** Robert N. Bradbury. **CAST:** John Wayne, Marion Burns, Yakima Canutt, Reed Howes. **1935**

DAYS OF JESSE JAMES ★★ In this B Western, Roy Rogers sets out to prove that Jesse James, as played by Don Barry, didn't stage the famous Northfield, Minnesota, bank robbery. Yep! It was those corrupt bankers who set it up. A confusing plot line doesn't help. B&W; 63m. **DIR:** Joseph Kane. **CAST:** Roy Rogers, George "Gabby" Hayes, Don Barry, Harry Woods. **1939**

DAYS OF OLD CHEYENNE ★★★★ Don Barry accepts the job of town marshal from Big Bill Harmon (William Haade) in the belief Harmon is interested in maintaining law and order. Above-average oater. B&W; 56m. **DIR:** Elmer Clifton. **CAST:** Don Barry, Emmet Lynn, Lynn Merrick, William Haade. **1943**

DAYS OF WRATH ★★★ One of the best non-Leone spaghetti Westerns. A veteran gunfighter teaches the town bastard how to use a gun. He gains his self-respect and the fear of the townspeople. All goes well until the gunfighter kills his student's only friend, the town sheriff. The student turns on the teacher, putting to use all that he's been taught. A strong performance by veteran Hollywood heavy Lee Van Cleef. Rated PG. 97m. **DIR:** Tonino Valerii. **CAST:** Lee Van Cleef, Giuliano Gemma, Walter Rilla, Crista Linder, Piero Lulli, Andrea Bosic. **1967**

DEAD AIM (1973) 🖤 An orphaned infant is raised by an undertaker until he becomes an adult and leaves the old man for a married woman with disastrous results. Filmed in Mexico with spaghetti Western overtones. Rated R for violence and sex. 90m. **DIR:** Jose Antonio Bolanos. **CAST:** Glen Lee, James Westerfield, Virgil Frye, Venetia Vianello, Tony Monaco, Billy Joe Roucke. **1973**

DEAD DON'T DREAM, THE ★★ Hopalong Cassidy's partner "Lucky" finally decides to tie the knot, but his wedding plans are dashed when his fiancée's father is murdered before the ceremony. Hoppy tries to get to the bottom of this mystery. Originally released at 62 minutes. B&W; 55m. **DIR:** George Archainbaud. **CAST:** William Boyd, Andy Clyde, Rand Brooks, John Parrish. **1948**

DEAD FOR A DOLLAR ★★ Three double-crossing gunmen try to hunt down a $200,000 bank-robbery cache, but a woman outsmarts them all. A good performance by John Ireland is all that holds the film together. Unrated, but contains violence. 92m. **DIR:** Osvaldo Civirani. **CAST:** George Hilton, John Ireland, Sandra Milo, Piero Vida. **1968**

DEAD MAN'S GULCH ★★★ Story of two former pony express riders. One becomes an outlaw, the other a lawman. B&W; 56m. **DIR:** John English. **CAST:** Don Barry, Lynn Merrick. **1943**

DEADLY COMPANIONS, THE ★★½ When gunfighter Brian Keith accidentally kills the son of dance-hall hostess Maureen O'Hara, he attempts to make amends by escorting her through hostile Indian Territory. A less than grade-A Western made notable because it was director Sam Peckinpah's first feature. 90m. **DIR:** Sam Peckinpah. **CAST:** Brian Keith, Maureen O'Hara, Chill Wills, Steve Cochran. **1961**

DEADLY TRACKERS, THE ★★½ Extremely violent Western follows sheriff Richard Harris's attempt to track down the outlaw gang responsible for killing his family during a bank robbery. Film starts out well, but quickly becomes a standard revenge tale and is far too long. Be warned: There are some truly brutal scenes throughout. Rated R. 110m. **DIR:** Barry Shear. **CAST:** Richard Harris, Rod Taylor, Neville Brand, William Smith, Al Lettieri, Isela Vega. **1973**

DEATH OF A GUNFIGHTER ★★★ Any time you see the name Allen Smithee in the directorial slot, that means the real director had his name taken off the credits. In this case, Don Siegel and Robert Totten were alternately at the helm of what still emerges as a sturdy Western. Richard Widmark is very good as the sheriff who has outlived his usefulness to the town but refuses to change, thus setting the stage for tragic results. Rated PG. 100m. **DIR:** Alan Smithee. **CAST:** Richard Widmark, Lena Horne, Carroll O'Connor, John Saxon, Kent Smith. **1969**

DEATH RIDES A HORSE 🖤 Needlessly tedious spaghetti Western about a young boy who witnesses the butchery of his family and then grows up to take his revenge. Rated PG for violence. 114m. **DIR:** Giulio Petroni. **CAST:** Lee Van Cleef, John Phillip Law, Mario Brega, Anthony Dawson. **1969**

DEATH RIDES THE PLAINS ★★★ The Lone Rider must stop a rancher who sells his land and then kills the multiple buyers. Offbeat land-grab plot. A class act. B&W; 56m. **DIR:** Sam Newfield. **CAST:** Robert Livingston, Al St. John, I. Stanford Jolley. **1943**

DEATH VALLEY MANHUNT ★★★ Wild Bill Elliott routs the efforts of swindlers to take over Gabby Hayes and the homesteaders' oil well. Ingenue Anne Jeffreys later gained fame on TV's *Topper*. B&W; 55m. **DIR:** John English. **CAST:** William Elliott, George "Gabby" Hayes, Anne Jeffreys. **1943**

DECISION AT SUNDOWN ★★★★ Full of hate, Randolph Scott arrives in town to avenge himself and kill the man responsible for his wife's death. Many surprises in the brooding script. A class act. 77m. **DIR:** Budd Boetticher. **CAST:** Randolph Scott, John Carroll, Karen Steele, Noah Beery Jr., Bob Steele. **1957**

DEEP IN THE HEART OF TEXAS ★★★½ This is a well-directed, finely photographed film about post–Civil War land snatching. It's the first in a series of seven films to co-star the two great Western stars, Johnny Mack Brown and Tex Ritter. This one has lots of black hats, a few white hats, and plenty of action. B&W; 74m. **DIR:** Elmer Clifton. **CAST:** Johnny Mack Brown, Tex Ritter. **1942**

DEERSLAYER, THE ★★½ Made-for-TV movie, based on James Fenimore Cooper's classic, *The Deerslayer*, is a film of adventure in early America. The heroes, Hawkeye (Steve Forrest) and Chingachgook (Ned Romero), attempt to save a Mahican princess and avenge the death of Chingachgook's son. 98m. **DIR:** Dick Friedenberg. **CAST:** Steve Forrest, John Anderson, Ned Romero, Joan Prather. **1978**

DENVER AND RIO GRANDE, THE ★★½ A fairly routine Western about railroad men and their rivalries. Enlivened by a spectacular train crash staged by outdoor specialist

Byron Haskin. 89m. **DIR:** Byron Haskin. **CAST:** Edmond O'Brien, Sterling Hayden, Dean Jagger, ZaSu Pitts, J. Carrol Naish. **1952**

DENVER KID ★★★ Border patrolman Rocky Lane joins an outlaw gang to solve a brutal massacre. B&W; 60m. **DIR:** Phillip Ford. **CAST:** Allan "Rocky" Lane, Eddy Waller, William Henry, Douglas Fowley. **1948**

DESERT TRAIL ★★ Rodeo fans might like this standard B Western about a big-time bronc rider (John Wayne) who fights on the side of justice, but others may want to ride in the opposite direction. B&W; 54m. **DIR:** Robert N. Bradbury. **CAST:** John Wayne, Mary Kornman, Paul Fix, Edward Chandler. **1935**

DESERTER, THE 🦃 Arid, interminable spaghetti Western (a U.S.-Italian-Yugoslavian coproduction) with an absolute stiff for a leading man, and a bewildered supporting cast. Rated PG. 99m. **DIR:** Burt Kennedy. **CAST:** Bekim Fehmiu, John Huston, Richard Crenna, Chuck Connors, Ricardo Montalban, Woody Strode, Slim Pickens, Ian Bannen, Brandon de Wilde, Patrick Wayne. **1971**

DESPERADOS, THE ★★ After the Civil War, a paranoid parson heads a gang of cutthroats and outlaws, including his three sons, in a violent crime spree. Roughly made (in Spain) and quite savage. Rated PG. 90m. **DIR:** Henry Levin. **CAST:** Vince Edwards, Jack Palance, Neville Brand, George Maharis, Sylvia Syms, Christian Roberts. **1969**

DESPERATE WOMEN ★★ Three convicted women crossing a desert on their way to prison meet up with an ol' softy (Dan Haggerty) who takes them under his wing. 98m. **DIR:** Earl Bellamy. **CAST:** Dan Haggerty, Susan Saint James, Ronee Blakley, Ann Dusenberry. **1978**

DESTRY RIDES AGAIN ★★★★ *Destry's* plot may seem a trifle clichéd, but it is the classic Western that copycats imitate. The story of a mild-mannered citizen who finds himself grudgingly forced to stand up against the bad guys may seem familiar, especially with Jimmy Stewart in the lead. But this is the original. B&W; 95m. **DIR:** George Marshall. **CAST:** James Stewart, Marlene Dietrich, Brian Donlevy, Mischa Auer, Una Merkel. **1939**

DETOUR TO DANGER 🦃 Modern-day Western as two pals on a fishing trip encounter damsels in distress and payroll bandits. 56m. **DIR:** Richard Talmadge. **CAST:** John Day, Britt Wood. **1945**

DEVIL HORSE, THE ★★★ One of the best Mascot serials and a real audience favorite, this top-notch adventure features Harry Carey as a man tracking his brother's killer, evil Noah Beery. Codirector Richard Talmadge was one of the most famous and popular of silent stuntmen, and his apt hand as well as a fine cast, good photography, and exciting stunts make this a memorable serial. B&W; 12 chapters. **DIR:** Otto Brower, Richard Talmadge. **CAST:** Harry Carey, Noah Beery Sr., Frankie Darro, Greta Granstedt, Barrie O'Daniels, Yakima Canutt, Lane Chandler. **1932**

DEVIL'S CANYON ★★ Essentially a prison-break movie dressed up in cowboy clothes. Lawman Dale Robertson is railroaded into the Arizona State Pen at the turn of the century after killing two men in self-defense. Static, claustrophobic, set-bound—originally made in 3-D. 92m. **DIR:** Alfred Werker. **CAST:** Dale Robertson, Virginia Mayo, Stephen McNally, Arthur Hunnicutt. **1953**

DEVIL'S PLAYGROUND ★★ This so-so entry in the long-running Hopalong Cassidy series concerns crooked politicians, rumors of gold, and strange goings-on in the adjoining valley. B&W; 65m. **DIR:** George Archainbaud. **CAST:** William Boyd, Andy Clyde, Rand Brooks, Elaine Riley. **1946**

DJANGO ★★ This spaghetti Western lacks convincing performances. A border town is about to explode, and the stranger, Django (Franco Nero), lights the fuse. 90m. **DIR:** Sergio Corbucci. **CAST:** Franco Nero. **1965**

DJANGO SHOOTS FIRST ★★★ One of the better comic spaghetti Westerns. Django's son inherits half a town. The only problem is he must share it with his old man's crooked partner. Good performances by Glenn Saxon and veteran European character actor Fernando Sancho highlight this funny, entertaining film. Unrated. 96m. **DIR:** Alberto De Martino. **CAST:** Glenn Saxon, Fernando Sancho, Evelyn Stewart, Erica Blanc, Alberto Lupo. **1966**

DODGE CITY ★★★★ Swashbuckler Errol Flynn sets aside his sword for a pair of six-guns to clean up the wild, untamed frontier city of the title. The best of Flynn's Westerns, this release is beautifully photographed in color with an all-star supporting cast. 105m. **DIR:** Michael Curtiz. **CAST:** Errol Flynn, Olivia de Havilland, Ann Sheridan, Bruce Cabot, Alan Hale Sr., Ward Bond. **1939**

DON DAREDEVIL RIDES AGAIN ★★ Racketeers and crooked politicians are trying to steal those old Spanish land grants again, and a masked avenger by the name of Don Daredevil rides in to right the wrongs. New footage was blended with action scenes from previous *Zorro* and similar films to send a surefire product to a new and receptive audience. B&W; 12 chapters. **DIR:** Fred Bannon. **CAST:** Ken Curtis, Aline Towne, Roy Barcroft, Lane Bradford. **1951**

DONNER PASS: THE ROAD TO SURVIVAL ★★ This fair made-for-TV retelling of the true story of the Donner party is based on historical accounts and tells of the snowstorm that traps the party and the physical hardship and starvation that lead to the infamous conclusion. Made for TV. 98m. **DIR:** James L. Conway. **CAST:** Robert Fuller, Diane McBain, Andrew Prine, John Anderson, Michael Callan. **1978**

DON'T FENCE ME IN ★★★★½ Outstanding Roy Rogers film. Fans rate it one of his five best. Reporter Dale Evans comes west seeking legendary gunslinger Wildcat Kelly, who turns out to be Gabby Hayes. Hayes steals the film, which includes the Sons of the Pioneers' classic "Tumbling Tumbleweeds" as well as the Cole Porter title song. B&W; 71m. **DIR:** John English. **CAST:** Roy Rogers, George "Gabby" Hayes, Dale Evans, Robert Livingston, Marc Lawrence, Bob Nolan and the Sons of the Pioneers. **1945**

DOOLINS OF OKLAHOMA ★★★★½ Oklahoma outlaw Bill Doolin attempts to go straight when he meets the right girl, only to be hounded by his own gang and an unrelenting marshal. Historically inaccurate, but well staged and action packed. B&W; 90m. **DIR:** Gordon Douglas. **CAST:** Randolph Scott, Louise Allbritton, George Macready, John Ireland, Noah Beery Jr. **1949**

DOWN DAKOTA WAY ★★½ Roy Rogers takes a harder line with the bad guys in this exciting B Western, tracking down the no-goods responsible for the death of his friend, a veterinarian who could finger the man responsible for flooding the market with diseased meat. 67m. **DIR:** William Witney. **CAST:** Roy Rogers, Dale Evans, Pat Brady, Monte Montana, Roy Barcroft. **1949**

DOWN TEXAS WAY ★★½ An agreeable if undistinguished entry in the Rough Riders series, this feature has Rangers Buck Jones and Tim McCoy coming to the aid of their pal, Raymond Hatton, when he is accused of murder. B&W; 57m. **DIR:** Howard Bretherton. **CAST:** Buck Jones, Tim McCoy, Raymond Hatton, Luana Walters, Harry Woods, Glenn Strange. **1942**

DRAW ★★½ Kirk Douglas and James Coburn play outlaw and lawman respectively. Both appear on a collision course for a gunfight but, alas, what we are treated to is a trick ending. Lots of missed chances in this one. Made for HBO cable television. 98m. **DIR:** Steven H. Stern. **CAST:** James Coburn, Kirk Douglas. **1984**

DRIFTIN' KID ★★½ It seems every B-Western star was required to make at least one oater wherein he played a dual role. Tom Keene does it here—but it's all been done better elsewhere. Outlaws after government grazing contracts. B&W; 57m. **DIR:** Robert Emmett Tansey. **CAST:** Tom Keene, Betty Miles, Frank Yaconelli, Stanley Price. **1941**

DRUM BEAT ★★½ Indian fighter Alan Ladd is detailed to ensure peace with marauding Modocs on the California-Oregon border in 1869. His chief adversary, in beads and buckskins, is Charles Bronson. As usual, white man speaks with forked tongue, but everything ends well. 111m. **DIR:** Delmer Daves. **CAST:** Alan Ladd, Audrey Dalton, Marisa Pavan, Robert Keith, Anthony Caruso, Warner Anderson, Elisha Cook Jr., Charles Bronson. **1954**

DRUM TAPS ★★★ Ken Maynard and the Boy Scouts drive land grabbers from the range. Only time Kermit Maynard (who had his own Western series) ever appears in one of his brother's Westerns. B&W; 61m. **DIR:** J. P. McGowan. **CAST:** Ken Maynard, Frank Coghlan Jr., Kermit Maynard. **1933**

DRUMS IN THE DEEP SOUTH ★★½ Two friends, both in love with the same girl, find themselves on opposite sides in the Civil War. 87m. **DIR:** William Cameron Menzies. **CAST:** James Craig, Guy Madison, Barbara Payton, Craig Stevens. **1951**

DUCHESS AND THE DIRTWATER FOX, THE 🦃 This Western-comedy romp never clicks. Rated PG. 103m. **DIR:** Melvin Frank. **CAST:** George Segal, Goldie Hawn, Conrad Janis, Thayer David. **1976**

DUDE RANGER ★★★★ In this sturdy, well-played, and skillfully directed adaptation of the Zane Grey story, George O'Brien is a city boy who heads west to claim his inheritance: a ranch he fully intends to sell the first chance he gets. As it turns out, rustlers have been depleting his stock, and O'Brien stays on to find the culprits. B&W; 65m. **DIR:** Eddie Cline. **CAST:** George O'Brien, Irene Hervey. **1934**

DUEL AT DIABLO ★★½ This overly complicated Western stars James Garner as a revenge-minded scout helping a cavalry troop transport guns and ammunition through Indian Territory. Subplots abound in this well-meant but unnecessarily dreary indictment of racism. The performances are good, however. 103m. **DIR:** Ralph Nelson. **CAST:** James Garner, Sidney Poitier, Bibi Andersson, Dennis Weaver, Bill Travers, John Hoyt. **1966**

DUEL IN THE SUN ★★★ This sprawling, brawling Western has land baron Lionel Barrymore's sons, unbroken, short-fused Gregory Peck, and solid-citizen Joseph Cotten vying for the hand of hot-blooded, half-breed Jennifer Jones. Peck and Jones take a lusty love-hate relationship to the max in the steaming desert. A near epic with a great musical score. 130m. **DIR:** King Vidor. **CAST:** Jennifer Jones, Gregory Peck, Joseph Cotten, Lionel Barrymore, Walter Huston, Lillian Gish, Harry Carey. **1946**

DYNAMITE AND GOLD ★★½ Passable made-for-television effort teams Willie Nelson and Delta Burke as two fortune seekers looking for buried cache of gold. Also known as *Where The Hell's That Gold?* 91m. **DIR:** Burt Kennedy. **CAST:** Willie Nelson, Delta Burke, Jack Elam, Gerald McRaney. **1990**

DYNAMITE CANYON ★★½ Tom Keene infiltrates an outlaw gang that is attempting to grab Evelyn Finley's ranch for its copper deposits. It's a bit slower than other Keene oaters. B&W; 58m. **DIR:** Robert Emmett Tansey. **CAST:** Tom Keene, Evelyn Finley, Kenne Duncan. **1941**

DYNAMITE PASS ★★½ Unconventional shoot-'em-up hae cowpoke Tim Holt and sidekick Richard Martin helping a construction engineer battle a tyrannical toll-road operator and his hired guns. All of the principals and supporting players give it their best shot, and this modest little oater has a nice edge to it. B&W; 61m. **DIR:** Lew Landers. **CAST:** Tim Holt, Richard Martin, Regis Toomey, Lynne Roberts (Mary Hart), John Dehner, Robert Shayne, Cleo Moore, Denver Pyle, Ross Elliott. **1950**

EAGLE'S WING ★★ When an Indian brave steals a magnificent white stallion from a fur trapper, a struggle of wits, courage, and endurance begins for the horse. Magnificent scenery highlights this British production. Rated PG. 100m. **DIR:** Anthony Harvey. **CAST:** Martin Sheen, Sam Waterston, Harvey Keitel, Stéphane Audran, Caroline Langrishe. **1980**

EL CONDOR ★★ A disappointing Western, this features cardboard performances by Jim Brown and Lee Van Cleef as two adventurers determined to take a fortress of gold called El Condor. Not rated, but equivalent to an R for nudity and violence. 102m. **DIR:** John Guillermin. **CAST:** Jim Brown, Lee Van Cleef, Patrick O'Neal. **1970**

EL DIABLO ★★★½ When one of his students is kidnapped by outlaws, schoolteacher Anthony Edwards joins forces with gunfighter Lou Gossett to bring her back. This cable-produced Western adds offbeat plot twists and oddball bits of comedy to the shoot-'em-up formula. It's entertaining, if not particularly believable. 115m. **DIR:** Peter Markle. **CAST:** Anthony Edwards, Lou Gossett Jr., John Glover, M. C. Gainey, Sarah Trigger, Robert Beltran, Joe Pantoliano. **1990**

EL DORADO ★★★★½ Few stars could match John Wayne's ability to dominate a scene—and one of those few, Robert Mitchum, costars in this tale of a land war between bad, bad Edward Asner and family man R. G. Armstrong. Mitchum plays the drunk in this takeoff on *Rio Bravo*, and Wayne is the gunfighter with whom he forms an uneasy alliance. It's basically an upscale B Western with some of the best scenes ever to be found in a cowboy movie. 126m. **DIR:** Howard Hawks. **CAST:** John Wayne, Robert Mitchum, James Caan, Arthur Hunnicutt, Edward Asner, Michele Carey, Christopher George, Charlene Holt, Jim Davis, Paul Fix, R. G. Armstrong, Johnny Crawford. **1967**

EL PASO KID ★★★ Ex-outlaw Sunset Carson becomes a lawman through a series of coincidences, eventually redeeming himself for his past. B&W; 54m. **DIR:** Thomas Carr. **CAST:** Sunset Carson, Hank Patterson. **1946**

ELFEGO BACA: SIX GUN LAW ★★½ Two-fisted lawyer Elfego Baca is charismatically portrayed by top actor Robert Loggia in this compilation of episodes from *Walt Disney Presents* originally aired from 1958 to 1962. Defending justice in Tombstone, Arizona, Elfego Baca fights for the lives of an Englishman framed for murder and a rancher charged with bank robbery. 77m. **DIR:** Christian Nyby. **CAST:** Robert Loggia, James Dunn, Lynn Bari, James Drury, Jay C. Flippen, Kenneth Tobey, Annette Funicello, Patric Knowles, Audrey Dalton. **1962**

EMPTY HOLSTERS ★★★ Cowboy crooner Dick Foran is framed for murder and sent up the river. Once out of prison, Foran is forced to prove his innocence and defend the townsfolk without the aid of his six-shooters. Veteran heavy Glenn Strange, in a nice twist, is a good-guy sidekick. B&W; 58m. **DIR:** B. Reeves "Breezy" Eason. **CAST:** Dick Foran, Glenn Strange. **1937**

END OF THE TRAIL ★★★★ The great Western star Colonel Tim McCoy was a lifelong champion of the American Indian. *End of the Trail* is his magnum opus, a movie sympathetic to Native Americans made nearly twenty years before *Broken Arrow*. It's an ambitious, somewhat dated story of a cavalry officer (McCoy) falsely accused of treason and forced to prove his innocence by uncovering the true villain. B&W; 62m. **DIR:** D. Ross Lederman. **CAST:** Tim McCoy, Luana Walters, Wheeler Oakman. **1932**

ENEMY OF THE LAW ★★★★ The Texas Rangers track down an outlaw gang who, years before, robbed a safe and hid the money. There are some hilarious escapades in this well-above-average oater. Tex Ritter's songs are always good. B&W; 59m. **DIR:** Harry Fraser. **CAST:** Tex Ritter, Dave O'Brien, Guy Wilferson, Charles King. **1945**

ESCAPE FROM FORT BRAVO ★★★½ Union-officer William Holden is in charge of a wilderness outpost holding Confederate prisoners. He must keep them in while trying to keep out marauding Indians. Good suspense and action scenes. B&W; 98m. **DIR:** John Sturges. **CAST:** William Holden, Eleanor Parker, John Forsythe, William Demarest, William Campbell, John Lupton, Richard Anderson, Polly Bergen. **1953**

EYES OF TEXAS ★★★★½ Villainess Nana Bryant out to acquire valuable ranch land at any cost, including using vicious killer dogs to discourage prospective landowners. Director William Witney brought much-needed action and a harder, often brutal, edge to the Rogers films in the late 1940s after they had stagnated into overblown musicals in the mid-1940s. B&W; 70m. **DIR:** William Witney. **CAST:** Roy Rogers, Andy Devine, Nana Bryant, Lynne Roberts (Mary Hart), Roy Barcroft, Bob Nolan and the Sons of the Pioneers. **1948**

FABULOUS TEXAN, THE ★★★ Upon returning from the Civil War, Confederate officers Wild Bill Elliott and John Carroll find their part of Texas to be under the dictatorial rule of carpetbagger Albert Dekker. While not directed with much inspiration, this benefits from earnest performances. B&W; 95m. **DIR:** Edward Ludwig. **CAST:** William Elliott, John Carroll, Albert Dekker, Catherine McLeod, Andy Devine, Jim Davis. **1947**

FALSE COLORS ★★½ Typical entry in the Hopalong Cassidy series places Hoppy on the side of the innocent people who are being terrorized and murdered by ace heavy Douglas Dumbrille, who wants their property and water rights. B&W; 65m. **DIR:** George Archainbaud. **CAST:** William Boyd, Andy Clyde, Jimmy Rogers, Claudia Drake, Douglass Dumbrille, Robert Mitchum. **1943**

FALSE PARADISE ★★ Straight-shooting Hopalong Cassidy comes to the aid of a girl in peril and finds crooked ranch owners and false mining claims. B&W; 59m. **DIR:** George Archainbaud. **CAST:** William Boyd, Andy Clyde, Rand Brooks, Joel Friedkin. **1948**

FAR COUNTRY, THE ★★★½ James Stewart is a tough-minded cattleman intent on establishing himself in Alaska during the Klondike gold rush of 1896. The result is fine Western fare. 97m. **DIR:** Anthony Mann. **CAST:** James Stewart, Ruth Roman, Walter Brennan, Corinne Calvet, John McIntire, Jay C. Flippen, Steve Brodie, Harry Morgan. **1955**

FAR FRONTIER ★★★★ Top-of-the-line, hard-edged, later Roy Rogers oater as desperadoes smuggle deported owl hoots back into the U.S. in oil drums. Border patrolman Rogers makes the vicious scheme a losing venture. Action-packed. B&W; 67m. **DIR:** William Witney. **CAST:** Roy Rogers, Gail Davis, Andy Devine, Roy Barcroft, Clayton Moore, Riders of the Purple Sage. **1948**

FARGO EXPRESS ★★ When Helen Mack's brother (Paul Fix) is accused of a crime he didn't commit, Ken Maynard attempts to clear his name by impersonating him at another robbery. Strange plot, dumb Western. B&W; 61m. **DIR:** Alan James. **CAST:** Ken Maynard, Helen Mack, Paul Fix. **1933**

FASTEST GUITAR ALIVE, THE ★★ Weak action yarn about Confederate spies who steal a fortune. Worth a viewing, mainly for Roy Orbison's appearance. 87m. **DIR:** Michael Moore. **CAST:** Roy Orbison, Sammy Jackson, Maggie Pierce, Joan Freeman. **1968**

FASTEST GUN ALIVE, THE ★★★ Serviceable Western casts Glenn Ford as a mild-mannered storekeeper who gets unwanted fame as a fast draw. After beating a string of cowpokes seeking a reputation, Ford must face a miscast Broderick Crawford, a badman who doesn't relish the idea of being thought of as second best. 92m. **DIR:** Russell Rouse. **CAST:** Glenn Ford, Broderick Crawford, Jeanne Crain, Leif Erickson, Russ Tamblyn, Rhys Williams, Noah Beery Jr., Chubby Johnson, J. M. Kerrigan, Allyn Joslyn. **1956**

FEUD OF THE TRAIL ★★ Tom Tyler, working as a Cattleman's Association agent, looks like and is mistaken for the son of a rancher. This puts him square in the middle of the age-old land-grab Western plot. Every B-Western star did at least one dead-ringer script, and this is Tyler's. No better, no worse than the rest. B&W; 56m. **DIR:** Robert Hill. **CAST:** Tom Tyler, Lafe McKee. **1937**

FIDDLIN' BUCKAROO ★★★ Secret service agent Ken Maynard, on the trail of outlaw Fred Kohler, is mistakenly arrested for a crime Kohler's gang committed. One of several Maynard Westerns he directed himself, this one is heavy on the music end. B&W; 65m. **DIR:** Ken Maynard. **CAST:** Ken Maynard, Fred Kohler Sr., Frank Rice. **1933**

FIGHTING CARAVANS ★★★½ Despite the title, this is a Zane Grey Western—and a good one, full of intrigue, action, and, for leavening, a smattering of comedy. Lanky, taciturn Gary Cooper, wanted by the law, avoids arrest by conning a wagon-train girl to pose as his wife. Romance blooms as the train treks west, into the sights of hostile forces. B&W; 80m. **DIR:** Otto Brower, David Burton. **CAST:** Gary Cooper, Lily Damita, Ernest Torrence, Eugene Pallette, Charles Winninger. **1931**

FIGHTING CODE ★★½ Buck Jones impersonates a girl's dead brother in order to solve a murder and save the ranch from a scheming lawyer. A young Ward Bond shows why he later became such a star and fine actor. B&W; 65m. **DIR:** Lambert Hillyer. **CAST:** Buck Jones, Ward Bond. **1933**

FIGHTING DEPUTY ★★ Deputy Sheriff Fred Scott is forced to pursue the outlaw brother of the girl he loves when the outlaw kills Fred's father. Not one of the best from Scott, who was a minor-league singing cowboy. B&W; 54m. **DIR:** Sam Newfield. **CAST:** Fred Scott, Charles King, Al St. John, Lafe McKee. **1937**

FIGHTING KENTUCKIAN, THE ★★★ Worth seeing if only for the rare and wonderful on-screen combination of John Wayne and Oliver Hardy, this period adventure casts the duo as frontiersmen who come to the aid of the homesteading Napoleonic French. If only Vera Hruba Ralston weren't the Duke's love interest, this could have been a real winner. B&W; 100m. **DIR:** George

Waggner. **CAST:** John Wayne, Vera Hruba Ralston, Philip Dorn, Oliver Hardy. **1940**

FIGHTING RANGER, THE ★★★ This entertaining but predictable piece has Buck Jones and sidekick Frank Rice chasing down a killer. Good cast and production values. B&W; 60m. **DIR:** George B. Seitz. **CAST:** Buck Jones, Frank Rice, Ward Bond, Frank La Rue. **1934**

FIGHTING SHADOWS ★★★ Royal Canadian Mountie Tim O'Farrell (Tim McCoy) returns to his former home to find out who is terrorizing fur trappers there. Standard fare is made watchable by the stars. B&W; 57m. **DIR:** David Selman. **CAST:** Tim McCoy, Ward Bond. **1935**

FIGHTING WESTERNER, THE ★★★ Rugged mining engineer Randolph Scott works undercover to learn who is responsible for murders at a radium mine. Tense mystery-Western. B&W; 54m. **DIR:** Charles Barton. **CAST:** Randolph Scott, Kathleen Burke, Ann Sheridan, Chic Sale. **1935**

FIGHTING WITH KIT CARSON ★★ Western scout Kit Carson is the only survivor of a deadly attack by the Mystery Riders. So-so serial. B&W; 12 chapters. **DIR:** Armand Schaefer, Colbert Clark. **CAST:** Johnny Mack Brown, Betsy King Ross, Noah Beery Sr., Noah Beery Jr., Robert Warwick. **1933**

FINAL DEFEAT, THE ★★ After the Civil War, Guy Madison leads a group of ex-Confederate rebels on a rampage through the West. He unknowingly takes on a government undercover agent who tricks him into believing that he knows the whereabouts of a buried treasure. A good score and the presence of Madison make this a nice film. Rated PG. 90m. **DIR:** E. G. Rowland. **CAST:** Guy Madison, Edd Byrnes, Louise Barrett, Enio Girolami, Pedro Sanchez. **1968**

FINGER ON THE TRIGGER ★★ Ex-Union and ex-Confederate soldiers band together to defeat a party of Indians on the warpath. They must make bullets out of the only source available, a stash of golden horseshoes. This B Western filmed in Spain is Rory Calhoun's only European Western. Unrated; contains violence. 89m. **DIR:** Sidney Pink. **CAST:** Rory Calhoun, James Philbrook, Todd Martin, Leo Anchoriz, Silvia Solar. **1965**

FISTFUL OF DOLLARS, A ★★★ Clint Eastwood parlayed his multi-year stint on television's *Rawhide* into international fame with this film, a slick remake of Akira Kurosawa's *Yojimbo*. Eastwood's laconic "Man With No Name" blows into a town nearly blown apart by two feuding families; after considerable manipulation by all concerned, he moves on down the road. 96m. **DIR:** Sergio Leone. **CAST:** Clint Eastwood, Mario Brega, Gian Maria Volonté. **1964**

FISTFUL OF DYNAMITE, A ★★★ After his success with Clint Eastwood's "Man with No Name" Westerns, Sergio Leone made this sprawling, excessive film set during the Mexican revolution. A thief, played by Rod Steiger, is drawn into the revolution by Irish mercenary James Coburn. Soon both are blowing up everything in sight and single-handedly winning the war. 121m. **DIR:** Sergio Leone. **CAST:** Rod Steiger, James Coburn, Maria Monti, Romolo Valli. **1972**

FIVE BLOODY GRAVES ★★ Somewhat imaginative as Death narrates the tale of an odd mix of travelers pursued across the desert by a savage band of Indians. Extreme violence. Also titled: *Gun Riders* and *Lonely Man*. 81m. **DIR:** Al Adamson. **CAST:** Robert Dix, Scott Brady, Jim Davis, John Carradine. **1969**

FIVE CARD STUD ★★½ Muddled Western with a whodunit motif. Gambler-gunfighter Dean Martin attempts to discover who is systematically murdering the members of a lynching party. Robert Mitchum adds some memorable moments as a gun-toting preacher, but most of the performances are lifeless, with Roddy McDowall's gunslinger the most ludicrous of all. This is far from top-notch Henry Hathaway. 103m. **DIR:** Henry Hathaway. **CAST:** Dean Martin, Robert Mitchum, Inger Stevens, Roddy McDowall, Katherine Justice, Yaphet Kotto, Denver Pyle. **1968**

FLAMING FRONTIERS ★★ Former football favorite Johnny Mack Brown rides into a long career as a Western star in this pretty standard serial. He plays Tex Houston, famous Indian scout. B&W; 15 chapters. **DIR:** Ray Taylor, Alan James. **CAST:** Johnny Mack Brown, Eleanor Hansen, Ralph Bowman, Charles Middleton. **1938**

FLAMING STAR ★★★★ A solid Western directed by Don Siegel (*Dirty Harry*), this features Elvis Presley in a remarkably effective performance as a half-breed Indian who must choose sides when his mother's people go on the warpath. 92m. **DIR:** Don Siegel. **CAST:** Elvis Presley, Barbara Eden, Steve Forrest, Dolores Del Rio, John McIntire. **1960**

FOR A FEW DOLLARS MORE ★★½ Plot-heavy and overlong sequel to *A Fistful of Dollars* finds Clint Eastwood's "Man With No Name" partnered with shifty Lee Van Cleef, with both in pursuit of bad guy Gian Maria Volonté. Eastwood has his hands full, but the story contains few surprises. 130m. **DIR:** Sergio Leone. **CAST:** Clint Eastwood, Lee Van Cleef, Gian Maria Volonté, Klaus Kinski. **1965**

FORBIDDEN TRAIL ★★★½ In this superior series Western, one of several Buck Jones made for Columbia Pictures in the 1930s, the star and Al Smith play a couple of happy-go-lucky cowboys who find themselves in the middle of a range war. Jones, usually the stalwart, square-jawed defender of justice, takes a comedic approach to his part, and the results are quite pleasing. B&W; 71m. **DIR:** Lambert Hillyer. **CAST:** Buck Jones, Barbara Weeks, Mary Carr, Al Smith. **1932**

FORBIDDEN TRAILS ★★ In this, the least interesting of the Rough Riders Westerns, a pair of hardened criminals (Charles King and Bud Osborne) force a youngster (Dave O'Brien) to take part in their evil schemes. Robert N. Bradbury's direction lacks the energy brought to the series by Howard Bretherton, but the stars are as watchable as ever. B&W; 55m. **DIR:** Robert N. Bradbury. **CAST:** Buck Jones, Tim McCoy, Raymond Hatton, Dave O'Brien, Tristram Coffin, Charles King. **1941**

FORLORN RIVER ★★★ Exciting Zane Grey story has horse thieves trying to buy army mounts with six-guns. Good photography, literate script. B&W; 56m. **DIR:** Charles Barton. **CAST:** Buster Crabbe, June Martel, Harvey Stephens. **1937**

FORT APACHE ★★★★½ The first entry in director John Ford's celebrated cavalry trilogy stars Henry Fonda as a post commandant who decides to make a name for himself by starting a war with the Apaches, against the advice of an experienced soldier (John Wayne). Great film. B&W; 127m. **DIR:** John Ford. **CAST:** John Wayne, Henry Fonda, Shirley Temple, Ward Bond, John Agar, George O'Brien. **1948**

FORT OSAGE ★★★ Nefarious businessmen cause an Indian uprising while taking money from settlers. Compact oater is better than one would expect. B&W; 72m. **DIR:** Lesley Selander. **CAST:** Rod Cameron, Jane Nigh, Morris Ankrum, Douglas Kennedy. **1951**

FORTY THIEVES ★★★ An ex-convict comes to town paroled into the custody of Sheriff Hopalong Cassidy. Unhappy about Hoppy's control, he rounds up his old gang, the Forty Thieves. B&W; 61m. **DIR:** Lesley Selander. **CAST:** William Boyd, Andy Clyde, Jimmy Rogers, Louise Currie. **1944**

FOUR EYES AND SIX GUNS ★★½ Fairly amusing comedy-Western about an optometrist who goes west to run a store and ends up helping Wyatt Earp clean up Tombstone. Made for TV. 92m. **DIR:** Peter Markle. **CAST:** Judge Reinhold, Patricia Clarkson, Fred Ward, Dan Hedaya, M. Emmet Walsh, Dennis Burkley, John Schuck, Jonathan Gries, Austin Pendleton. **1992**

FOUR FACES WEST ★★★ A small-scale Western that tends to be overlooked, it uses a standard formula (an outlaw is pursued by a determined sheriff). But the writing, acting, and direction find those nuances that can make a story fresh. B&W; 90m. **DIR:** Alfred E. Green. **CAST:** Joel McCrea, Frances Dee, Charles Bickford, Joseph Calleia. **1948**

FOUR FOR TEXAS ★★ Nonsensical story about tough-guy Frank Sinatra teaming up with fast-shooting Dean Martin to operate a floating gambling casino. Long and pretty silly. 124m. **DIR:** Robert Aldrich. **CAST:** Frank Sinatra, Dean Martin, Anita Ekberg, Ursula Andress, Victor Buono, Charles Bronson, Mike Mazurki, Richard Jaeckel. **1963**

FOUR RODE OUT 🦃 U.S. marshall in pursuit of a Mexican bank robber. 90m. **DIR:** John Peyser. **CAST:** Pernell Roberts, Sue Lyon, Julian Mateos, Leslie Nielsen. **1968**

FRISCO KID, THE ★★★ Gene Wilder and Harrison Ford make a surprisingly effective and funny team as a rabbi and outlaw, respectively, making their way to San Francisco. Good fun. Rated PG. 122m. **DIR:** Robert Aldrich. **CAST:** Gene Wilder, Harrison Ford, William Smith, Ramon Bieri, Penny Peyser. **1979**

FRONTIER HORIZON ★★★ In this modern-day Western, the Three Mesquiteers ride to the rescue when a group of ranchers battle unscrupulous land grabbers. Jennifer Jones makes an early screen appearance here under the name Phyllis Isley. B&W; 56m. **DIR:** George Sherman. **CAST:** John Wayne, Ray "Crash" Corrigan, Raymond Hatton, Jennifer Jones. **1939**

FRONTIER PONY EXPRESS ★★½ Good action-packed Western finds Roy Rogers (in one of his early starring roles) coming to the aid of pony express riders who have been preyed on by robbers. B&W; 54m. **DIR:** Joseph Kane. **CAST:** Roy Rogers, Lynne Roberts (Mary Hart), Raymond Hatton, Edward Keane. **1939**

FRONTIERSMAN, THE ★★ Hopalong Cassidy (William Boyd) and his pals (George "Gabby" Hayes and Russell Hayden) take a break from upholding the law to help a schoolteacher (Evelyn Venable). B&W; 58m. **DIR:** Lesley Selander. **CAST:** William Boyd, George "Gabby" Hayes, Russell Hayden, Evelyn Venable. **1938**

FUGITIVE VALLEY ★★★ An outlaw gang led by "The Whip" terrorizes the West until the Range Busters infiltrate the outlaws and uncover several surprises, including a lady Robin Hood. B&W; 61m. **DIR:** S. Roy Luby. **CAST:** Ray "Crash" Corrigan, John King, Max Terhune, Julie Duncan, Glenn Strange. **1941**

GAMBLER, THE (1980) ★★★ Bringing his late 1970s hit record to life, Kenny Rogers teams with Bruce Boxleitner in this story of a drifting cardplayer, his lost son, a shady railroad magnate, and the usual bunch of black-hatted villains. This made-for-TV movie spawned two equally entertaining sequels. 95m. **DIR:** Dick Lowry. **CAST:** Kenny Rogers, Bruce Boxleitner, Christine Belford, Harold Gould, Clu Gulager. **1980**

GAMBLER, PART II—THE ADVENTURE CONTINUES, THE ★★★ Reprising his role as gambler Brady Hawks, Kenny Rogers ambles his way farther west with sidekick Bruce Boxleitner—toward the poker game to end all poker games in San Francisco. Fans loved how to fold 'em the first time around, so here it is again. Made for TV. 190m. **DIR:** Dick Lowry. **CAST:** Kenny Rogers, Bruce Boxleitner, Linda Evans, Johnny Crawford, Cameron Mitchell, Mitchell Ryan, Harold Gould, Gregory Sierra, Ken Swofford. **1983**

GAMBLER, PART III—THE LEGEND CONTINUES, THE ★★★ Again playing gambler Brady Hawks, Kenny Rogers nearly comes a cropper on the end of a rope when he's hung by a zealous Mexican army officer. Made for TV. 185m. **DIR:** Dick Lowry. **CAST:** Kenny Rogers, Bruce Boxleitner, Melanie Chartoff, Matt Clark, George Kennedy, Charles Durning, Jeffrey Jones. **1987**

GAMBLER RETURNS, THE: LUCK OF THE DRAW ★★½ A high-stakes, winner-take-all poker game is held in San Francisco, but the main draw in Kenny Rogers's fourth outing as gambler Brady Hawks is cameo appearances by the stars of classic TV-Western series such as *Cheyenne, Maverick, The Life and Legend of Wyatt Earp, The Rifleman, The Virginan, Rawhide,* and *Bat Masterson.* Overlong, but fun for fans. Made for TV. 180m. **DIR:** Dick Lowry. **CAST:** Kenny Rogers, Rick Rossovich, Reba McEntire, Claude Akins, Gene Barry, Paul Brinegar, David Carradine, Chuck Connors, Johnny Crawford, James Drury, Linda Evans, Brian Keith, Jack Kelly, Patrick Macnee, Doug McClure, Hugh O'Brian, Park Overall, Mickey Rooney, Dub Taylor, Clint Walker. **1991**

GANGS OF SONORA ★★★ The Three Mesquiteers aid a lady newspaper editor opposing a corrupt official trying to prevent Wyoming's entrance into the Union. B&W; 56m. **DIR:** John English. **CAST:** Robert Livingston, Bob Steele, Rufe Davis, Robert Frazer. **1941**

GENTLE SAVAGE ★★★½ In this well-paced Western, William Smith portrays an American Indian framed for the rape and beating of a white girl in a small town. The girl's stepfather, who actually committed the crime, incites the townsmen to go after the innocent man. When the townsmen kill the hapless fellow's brother, the American Indian community retaliates. Rated R for violence. 85m. **DIR:** Sean MacGregor. **CAST:** William Smith, Gene Evans, Barbara Luna, Joe Flynn. **1978**

GENTLEMAN FROM CALIFORNIA ★★½ Ricardo Cortez returns from Spain to find his California homeland being robbed and plundered by unscrupulous newcomers. He soon becomes the Robin Hood of the Californians. B&W; 58m. **DIR:** Gus Meins. **CAST:** Ricardo Cortez, Marjorie Weaver, Katherine DeMille, Helen Holmes. **1937**

GENTLEMAN KILLER ★★ The brother of a murdered army officer takes revenge on the outlaws who have taken over a small border town. A better than average Western with a surprise ending with good performances by Anthony Steffen and Eduardo Fajardo. Unrated; contains violence. 97m. **DIR:** George Finley. **CAST:** Anthony Steffen, Eduardo Fajardo, Silvia Solar, Mariano Vidal Molina. **1969**

GERONIMO ★★½ This superficial account of the great Apache leader tries to cover too much ground within its limited time frame. Not to be confused with the theatrical film *Geronimo: An American Legend.* Made for cable television. 92m. **DIR:** Roger Young. **CAST:** Joseph Running Fox, Ryan Black, Jimmy Herman, Nick Ramus, Michelle St. John. **1993**

GERONIMO: AN AMERICAN LEGEND ★★★½ Strong performances by Robert Duvall and Gene Hackman, along with a thought-provoking screenplay by John Milius and Larry Gross, add grit to director Walter Hill's powerhouse Western about the Apache warrior (the charismatic Wes Studi). Told through the eyes of an idealistic officer, this near epic is a collection of what Howard Hawks called "good scenes" that will please fans of the genre. Rated PG-13 for profanity and violence. 110m. **DIR:** Walter Hill. **CAST:** Jason Patric, Gene Hackman, Robert Duvall, Wes Studi, Mark Damon, Rodney A. Grant, Kevin Tighe, Steve Reevis, Scott Wilson, Carlos Palomino. **1994**

GHOST TOWN LAW ★★★ Atmospheric B Western has the Rough Riders on the trail of a gang that murdered two of their colleagues. The gang, in a nice touch, hides out in a ghost town, where there might be more than just outlaws for our heroes to contend with. B&W; 62m. **DIR:** Howard Bretherton. **CAST:** Buck Jones, Tim McCoy, Raymond Hatton, Charles King. **1942**

GHOST TOWN RENEGADES ★★★ Outlaws try to take over an abandoned mining town from its rightful owners. Lash's bullwhip dispenses its usual fast justice. B&W; 57m. **DIR:** Ray Taylor. **CAST:** Lash LaRue, Jack Ingram, Terry Frost. **1947**

GIT ALONG, LITTLE DOGIES ★★ Typical of Gene Autry's prewar films, this thin story of a spoiled, willful girl who is eventually tamed and socialized by the silver-voiced cowboy is heavy on the music and singing stars. B&W; 60m. **DIR:** Joseph Kane. **CAST:** Gene Autry, Smiley Burnette, Judith Allen, William Farnum. **1937**

GO KILL AND COME BACK ★★ Unique opening, but routine viewing, as a bounty hunter tracks a notorious bandit hoping to locate a treasure of buried gold. Only the always-fine acting of veteran Gilbert Roland and a great musical score by Francesco De Masi make this worthwhile. Rated PG; contains violence. 98m. **DIR:** Enzo G. Castellari. **CAST:** George Hilton, Gilbert Roland, Edd Byrnes, Kareen O'Hara, Gerard Herter, Pedro Sanchez. **1968**

GOD'S GUN 🦃 Lee Van Cleef plays a dual role as a murdered priest and his vengeful brother. This film has to be in contention for the worst dubbing in film history. You won't believe the voices used for Van Cleef and Richard Boone. Rated R for nudity and violence. 90m. **DIR:** Frank Kramer. **CAST:** Lee Van Cleef, Jack Palance, Leif Garrett, Richard Boone, Sybil Danning. **1976**

GOIN' SOUTH ★★★ Star Jack Nicholson also directed this odd little Western tale of an outlaw (Nicholson) saved from the gallows by a spinster (Mary Steenburgen). The catch is he must marry her and work on her farm. Lots of attempts at comedy, but only a few work. Look for John Belushi in a small role as a Mexican cowboy. Rated PG, contains some violence and language. 109m. **DIR:** Jack Nicholson. **CAST:** Jack Nicholson, Mary Steenburgen, John Belushi. **1978**

GOLDEN STALLION, THE ★★½ This offbeat entry to the Roy Rogers series places the emphasis on Trigger and his efforts to save a cute palomino mare from a life of crime. Absolute hooey, but fun to watch, for kids and animal lovers. 67m. **DIR:** William Witney. **CAST:** Roy Rogers, Dale Evans, Estelita Rodriguez, Pat Brady. **1949**

GONE TO TEXAS ★★★ Sam Elliott plays frontier hero Sam Houston in this sprawling, action-packed, but overlong biography. 144m. **DIR:** Peter Levin. **CAST:** Sam Elliott, Michael Beck, James Stephens, Devon Ericson. **1986**

GONE WITH THE WEST ★★ With this excellent cast, one would expect more, but this is a confusing and vague tale about an Old West ex-con on the vengeance trail. 92m. **DIR:** Bernard Gerard. **CAST:** James Caan, Stefanie Powers, Aldo Ray, Barbara Werle, Robert Walker Jr., Sammy Davis Jr., Michael Conrad. **1972**

GOOD THE BAD AND THE UGLY, THE ★★★★ The best of Italian director Sergio Leone's spaghetti Westerns with Clint Eastwood, this release features the latter in the dubiously "good" role, with Lee Van Cleef as "the bad" and Eli Wallach as "the ugly." All three are after a cache of gold hidden in a Confederate army graveyard. For Leone fans, it's full of what made his movies so memorable. Others might find it a bit long, but no one can deny its sense of style. 161m. **DIR:** Sergio Leone. **CAST:** Clint Eastwood, Eli Wallach, Lee Van Cleef. **1966**

GORE VIDAL'S BILLY THE KID ★★ Uninspired retelling of the last years of Billy the Kid. Fine location cinematography enhance the realism, but the script and direction all but sink this TV movie. 92m. **DIR:** William A. Graham. **CAST:** Val Kilmer, Wilford Brimley. **1989**

GRAND CANYON TRAIL ★★ Roy Rogers is saddled with what he thinks is a useless mine, and former serial hero Robert Livingston just about succeeds in swindling him out of what is actually a bonanza in silver. Fast-paced and almost tongue-in-cheek. B&W; 67m. **DIR:** William Witney. **CAST:** Roy Rogers, Jane Frazee, Andy Devine, Robert Livingston. **1948**

GRAYEAGLE ★★ Disappointing reworking of John Wayne's *The Searchers*, with Alex Cord as the Cheyenne warrior Grayeagle, who kidnaps Lana Wood and is pursued by the girl's father, Ben Johnson. Rated PG for violence and mild nudity. 104m. **DIR:** Charles B. Pierce. **CAST:** Ben Johnson, Iron Eyes Cody, Lana Wood, Alex Cord, Jack Elam, Paul Fix. **1977**

GREAT ADVENTURE, THE ★★ Spin-off of *Call of the Wild* has an orphan boy, his dog, and a dance-hall queen take on a Yukon bully in gold-rush Dawson. Good family story with veterans Jack Palance and Joan Collins in prime form. Rated PG. 90m. **DIR:** Paul Elliotts. **CAST:** Joan Collins, Jack Palance, Fred Romer, Elisabetta Virgili. **1976**

GREAT GUNDOWN 🦃 Filmed in New Mexico in the mid-Seventies and released sporadically under varying titles: *El Salvejo (The Savage), Savage Red, Outlaw White,* and finally *Great Gundown*. 98m. **DIR:** Paul Hunt. **CAST:** Robert Padilla, Richard Rust. **1976**

GREAT MISSOURI RAID, THE ★★ Another depiction of Frank and Jesse James and their pals the Younger brothers. This picture is good for a late-night view or while you're microwaving your dinner. Passable, but better accounts of the James boys are available. 83m. **DIR:** Gordon Douglas. **CAST:** Wendell Corey, Macdonald Carey, Ellen Drew, Ward Bond. **1950**

GREAT NORTHFIELD MINNESOTA RAID, THE ★★★ A strong cast of character actors propels this offbeat Western, which chronicles the exploits of the James-Younger gang. Cliff Robertson is an effectively world-weary and witty Cole Younger, and Robert Duvall sets off sparks as a crafty, calculating Jesse James. The film never quite satisfies as a whole though there are some terrific moments. Rated R for violence and profanity. 91m. **DIR:** Phil Kaufman. **CAST:** Cliff Robertson, Robert Duvall, Luke Askew, R. G. Armstrong, Dana Elcar, Donald Moffat, Jack Pearce, Matt Clark, Elisha Cook Jr. **1972**

GREAT SCOUT AND CATHOUSE THURSDAY, THE ★★★ Eccentric Western-comedy involving a variety of get-rich-quick schemes concocted by an amusing band of rogues. Oliver Reed steals the show as a wacky American Indian whose double-crosses usually backfire. Not much plot and considerable silliness, but fun nonetheless. Rated PG for sexual situations. 102m. **DIR:** Don Taylor. **CAST:** Lee Marvin, Oliver Reed, Elizabeth Ashley, Robert Culp, Strother Martin, Kay Lenz. **1976**

GREY FOX, THE ★★★★★ Richard Farnsworth (*Comes a Horseman*) stars in this marvelously entertaining Canadian feature as the gentleman bandit Bill Miner who, as the movie poster proclaimed, "on June 17, 1901, after thirty-three years in San Quentin Prison for robbing stagecoaches, was released into the twentieth century." Rated PG for brief violence. 92m. **DIR:** Phillip Borsos. **CAST:** Richard Farnsworth, Jackie Burroughs, Ken Pogue, Timothy Webber. **1982**

GUN CODE ★★★ When the residents of Miller's Flats find themselves being coerced into paying protection money, Tim Haines (Tim McCoy) rides to the rescue, guns ablazing. Even the minuscule budgets of Producers Releasing Corporation couldn't stop McCoy from turning out above-average Westerns. B&W; 52m. **DIR:** Peter Stewart. **CAST:** Tim McCoy, Dave O'Brien. **1940**

GUN FURY ★★★ Donna Reed is kidnapped. Rock Hudson chases the bad men and saves her from a fate worse than death in Arizona's mesmerizing Red Rock country. Villainy abounds. 83m. **DIR:** Raoul Walsh. **CAST:** Rock Hudson, Donna Reed, Lee Marvin, Philip Carey, Neville Brand. **1953**

GUN RIDERS, THE ★★ Genre fans may enjoy this violent adult Western, though others will find it nihilistic and sleazy. A sadistic gunman, nicknamed the Messenger of Death, is the center of a story pitting Indians, gunrunners, and settlers against each other. Photographed by Vilmos Zsigmond. Rated PG. 88m. **DIR:** Al Adamson. **CAST:** Robert Dix, Scott Brady, Jim Davis, John Carradine, Paula Raymond. **1969**

GUN SMUGGLERS ★★★½ When an entire shipment of Gatling guns is stolen, Tim Holt must act fast. B&W; 61m. **DIR:** Frank McDonald. **CAST:** Tim Holt, Richard Martin, Martha Hyer, Paul Hurst, Gary Gray, Douglas Fowley. **1948**

GUNDOWN AT SANDOVAL ★★★ Texas John Slaughter faces overwhelming odds when he vows to avenge a friend's death and goes against the inhabitants of Sandoval, an infamous outlaw hideout. Featuring lots of hard riding and gunplay, this Disney television show was originally shown in Europe as a feature film. 72m. **DIR:** Harry Keller. **CAST:** Tom Tryon, Dan Duryea, Beverly Garland, Lyle Bettger, Harry Carey Jr. **1959**

GUNFIGHT, A ★★ This lifeless Western features the acting debut of country singer Johnny Cash. He is teamed with Kirk Douglas in a story of two long-in-the-tooth gunslingers. 90m. **DIR:** Lamont Johnson. **CAST:** Kirk Douglas, Johnny Cash, Jane Alexander, Karen Black, Raf Vallone. **1971**

GUNFIGHT AT THE O.K. CORRAL ★★★★ The Wyatt Earp–Doc Holliday legend got another going-over in this rather good Western. Burt Lancaster and Kirk Douglas portray these larger-than-life gunfighters, who shoot it out with the nefarious Clanton family in 1881 Tombstone. The movie effectively builds up its tension until the climactic gunfight. 122m. **DIR:** John Sturges. **CAST:** Burt Lancaster, Kirk Douglas, Rhonda Fleming, Jo Van Fleet, John Ireland, Lee Van Cleef, Frank Faylen. **1957**

GUNFIGHTER, THE ★★★★★ A notorious gunslinger (Gregory Peck) tries to settle down, but his reputation dogs him wherever he goes. Peck (though almost too young for his role) gives one of his best performances in this neglected classic. There's not much action, but it's an engrossing character study. B&W; 84m. **DIR:** Henry King. **CAST:** Gregory Peck, Helen Westcott, Millard Mitchell, Skip Homeier, Jean Parker, Karl Malden. **1950**

GUNFIGHTERS, THE ★★ The Everett Boys (Art Hindle, Reiner Schoene, and Tony Addabbo) are forced to become outlaws when a powerful rancher sets his sights on their land. The Western suffers from erratic storytelling and so-so acting. 96m. **DIR:** Clay Borris. **CAST:** Art Hindle, Reiner Schoene, Tony Addabbo, George Kennedy. **1987**

GUNFIRE ★★★ More story than action in this tale of an outlaw who is pardoned on the condition he kill a rancher whose land the railroad wants. Problems set in when the gunfighter sympathizes with the rancher and falls in love with his wife. Convincing performances by Warren Oates, Fabio Testi, and Jenny Agutter make this better than average. Unrated; contains violence. 90m. **DIR:** Monte Hellman. **CAST:** Warren Oates, Jenny Agutter, Fabio Testi, Carlos Bravo, Sam Peckinpah. **1978**

GUNMAN FROM BODIE ★★★½ The best of the many trio series Westerns of the 1930s and 40s, "The Rough Riders" teamed two of the genre's most charismatic stars, Buck Jones and Tim McCoy, with one of the best sidekicks in the business, Raymond Hatton. The second film in the series, *Gunman from Bodie* is considered by most aficionados to be the best, and we agree. The plot, about a trio of marshals who set out to capture a gang of cattle thieves, may be old and worn-out, but the sheer star power and personality of Jones, McCoy, and Hatton make this first-rate. B&W; 60m. **DIR:** Spencer Gordon Bennet. **CAST:** Buck Jones, Tim McCoy, Raymond Hatton, Dave O'Brien. **1941**

GUNS FOR DOLLARS ★★ Every gimmick is used in this comedy-spaghetti Western about a bounty hunter hired by Mexican revolutionaries, a Russian spy, and a female

American spy disguised as a nun seeking the missing jewels of Emperor Maximilian. Plenty of action and humor are weaved throughout the plot. Unrated; contains violence. 94m. **DIR:** Anthony Ascot. **CAST:** George Hilton, Charles Southwood, Agata Flory, Roberto Camardiel, Paolo Gozlino, Rick Boyd. **1971**

GUNS OF DIABLO ★★★ Wagon train guide Charles Bronson, accompanied by young Kurt Russell, rides into a strange town where he unexpectantly rekindles an old romance and is ambushed by ruthless outlaws. Edited from two episodes of the TV series *Travels of Jamie McPheeters.* 91m. **DIR:** Boris Ingster. **CAST:** Charles Bronson, Kurt Russell, Susan Oliver, Jan Merlin. **1964**

GUNS OF FORT PETTICOAT ★★★½ Cavalry officer Audie Murphy trains a group of women to defend their settlement against marauding Indians. Unusual twist on a tired plot. 82m. **DIR:** George Marshall. **CAST:** Audie Murphy, Kathryn Grant, Hope Emerson, Jeff Donnell, James Griffith. **1957**

GUNS OF HATE ★★★ When a prospector finds the fabled Lost Dutchman mine, outlaws try to steal it from him and his daughter. Tim Holt to the rescue in one of his best RKO outings. B&W; 62m. **DIR:** Lesley Selander. **CAST:** Tim Holt, Richard Martin, Steve Brodie, Nan Leslie, Myrna Dell. **1948**

GUNS OF THE MAGNIFICENT SEVEN ★★★ George Kennedy, fresh from his success with *Cool Hand Luke,* steps in for Yul Brynner as Chris, a well-meaning gunfighter who has a bad habit of getting his friends killed while defending the downtrodden. This second sequel has some fine performances—particularly by Kennedy and James Whitmore—and some rousing action scenes, but the original *Seven* has yet to be equaled. Rated PG. 106m. **DIR:** Paul Wendkos. **CAST:** George Kennedy, Monte Markham, James Whitmore, Bernie Casey, Joe Don Baker, Michael Ansara. **1969**

GUNSLINGER ★★★ Outlaw John Ireland is hired by land-grabbing saloon boss Allison Hayes to kill female sheriff, Beverly Garland. An early one from director Roger Corman, who has become somewhat of a cult figure. 83m. **DIR:** Roger Corman. **CAST:** John Ireland, Beverly Garland, Allison Hayes, Chris Alcaide, Dick Miller. **1956**

GUNSMOKE: RETURN TO DODGE ★★★ When Matt Dillon (James Arness), now retired from the job of town marshal, is badly wounded in a fight, Miss Kitty (Amanda Blake) leaves her new home in New Orleans to be at his side in Dodge, where an old enemy of theirs is also headed to exact revenge. Buoyed by a series of flashbacks from the series' twenty years of episodes. 96m. **DIR:** Vincent McEveety. **CAST:** James Arness, Amanda Blake, Buck Taylor, Steve Forrest, Earl Holliman. **1987**

GUNSMOKE (TV SERIES) ★★★★ Television's finest Western series benefited from excellent scripts from Charles Marquis Warren, John Meston, and Sam Peckinpah, among others. The show's most important asset was the exquisite ensemble playing of the cast: James Arness as Marshal Matt Dillon, Amanda Blake as Kitty the saloon keeper, Dennis Weaver and Ken Curtis as well-meaning deputies, and Milburn Stone as the irascible Doc Adams. The best episodes are the half hours, which feature some of the tightest, most evocative storytelling ever to be presented. 60m. per tape. **DIR:** Various. **CAST:** James Arness, Milburn Stone, Amanda Blake, Dennis Weaver, Ken Curtis, Burt Reynolds, Glenn Strange, Buck Taylor. **1955–1975**

HALF-BREED, THE ★★½ Predictable oater about a saloon owner determined to drive Apaches off their land so he can mine the gold he's sure is there. 81m. **DIR:** Stuart Gilmore. **CAST:** Robert Young, Janis Carter, Jack Buetel, Reed Hadley, Barton MacLane. **1952**

HALLELUJAH TRAIL, THE ★★★ Those who fondly remember television's *F Troop* should adore this cavalry comedy, which finds Burt Lancaster and Jim Hutton leading a wagon-train load of liquor through Indian territory. Temperance leader Lee Remick wants it all destroyed. Overlong, but fun nonetheless. 167m. **DIR:** John Sturges. **CAST:** Burt Lancaster, Lee Remick, Jim Hutton, Brian Keith, Martin Landau, Donald Pleasence. **1965**

HANDS ACROSS THE BORDER ★★ One of Roy Rogers's weakest films with a plot about a cavalry horse breeding contract subordinate to the overabundance of musical numbers. B&W; 54m. **DIR:** Joseph Kane. **CAST:** Roy Rogers, Ruth Terry, Guinn Williams, Sons of the Pioneers. **1944**

HANG 'EM HIGH ★★★ Clint Eastwood's first stateside spaghetti Western is a good one, with the star out to get the vigilantes who tried to hang him for a murder he didn't commit. Pat Hingle is the hangin' judge who gives Clint his license to hunt, and Ben Johnson is the marshal who saves his life. Ed Begley Sr. is memorable as the leader of the vigilantes. Rated PG. 114m. **DIR:** Ted Post. **CAST:** Clint Eastwood, Inger Stevens, Ed Begley Sr., Pat Hingle, Arlene Golonka, Ben Johnson. **1968**

HANGING TREE, THE ★★★★ A strange, haunting tale, with Gary Cooper as a withdrawn and secretive doctor in a mining town. When he cares for a blinded traveler (Maria Schell), the jealousy of the miners brings about violence and tragedy. All but ignored when released, this is worth a look. George C. Scott's movie debut. 106m. **DIR:** Delmer Daves. **CAST:** Gary Cooper, Maria Schell, Karl Malden, George C. Scott, Ben Piazza, Virginia regg, Guy Wilkerson, Karl Swensen, King onovan, John Dierkes. 1956

ANGMAN'S KNOT ★★★½ Randolph cott as a Confederate officer who hijacks a nion gold shipment and then learns the ivil War is over. While deciding what to do ith their bounty, outlaws attack them at an olated way station. 81m. **DIR:** Roy Huggins. **AST:** Randolph Scott, Donna Reed, Lee Marvin, ichard Denning, Claude Jarman Jr. 1952

ANNIE CAULDER ★★½ Revenge Westrn has Raquel Welch learning to be a gunlinger with the help of laid-back Robert ulp, so that she can hunt down and kill the aree maniacs (Ernest Borgnine, Jack Elam, nd Strother Martin) who murdered her usband. Rated R for violence. 85m. **DIR:** urt Kennedy. **CAST:** Raquel Welch, Robert Culp, rnest Borgnine, Jack Elam, Strother Martin, hristopher Lee. 1972

ARLEM RIDES THE RANGE ★★½ Stale lot about stolen mine rights (to a radium nine this time) is secondary to the limited ction and uniqueness of seeing an all-black ast in what had traditionally been the terriory of white actors and actresses. B&W; 8m. **DIR:** Richard Kahn. **CAST:** Herbert Jeffrey Jeffries), Lucius Brooks. 1939

ARRY TRACY ★★★½ Bruce Dern lays the title role in this surprisingly amible little Western, with the star as the last f a gentlemanly outlaw breed. Although e's a crafty character, Harry always seems o get caught. His mind is all too often on ther things—in particular, a well-to-do voman (Helen Shaver). Rated PG. 100m. **IR:** William A. Graham. **CAST:** Bruce Dern, lelen Shaver, Michael C. Gwynne, Gordon Lightoot. 1982

ATFIELDS AND THE MCCOYS, THE ★★½ The great American legend of backwoods euding long celebrated in song and story. ack Palance and Steve Forrest make the nost of portraying the clan patriarchs. The eud was reason enough to leave the hills nd head west in the 1880s. Made for TV. 4m. **DIR:** Clyde Ware. **CAST:** Jack Palance, Steve Forrest, Richard Hatch, Joan Caulfield. 1975

HAUNTED GOLD ★★★½ John Wayne gives one of his best early performances in his enjoyable Warner Bros. B Western, in which a gold mine is haunted by a mysterious figure known as "The Phantom." Wayne and his saddle pal, Blue Washington, ride to he rescue of Sheila Terry, who is threatened by both the spooky villain and a gang of outlaws led by veteran heavy Harry Woods. An effective mix of genres. B&W; 58m. **DIR:** Mack V. Wright. **CAST:** John Wayne, Sheila Terry, Harry Woods, Erville Anderson, Otto Hoffman, Martha Mattox, Blue Washington, Slim Whitaker. 1932

HAVE A NICE FUNERAL ★★★ Is Sartana a ghost or a magician? Whatever, he's an avenging angel who goes after an evil banker and his devious daughter. An over-the-top performance by John Garko makes this one of the best of the Sartana series. Unrated; contains violence. 90m. **DIR:** Anthony Ascot. **CAST:** John Garko, Antonio Vilar, Daniela Giordana, George Wang, Frank Ressel, Franco Pesce. 1971

HEART OF THE GOLDEN WEST ★★½ This modern-day adventure pits Roy Rogers and his fellow ranchers against cheating city slickers intent on defrauding the cowboys and putting them out of business. Enjoyable Western hokum. B&W; 65m. **DIR:** Joseph Kane. **CAST:** Roy Rogers, Smiley Burnette, George "Gabby" Hayes, Ruth Terry. 1942

HEART OF THE RIO GRANDE ★★ Gene Autry and the gang sing some sense into a snooty, spoiled-rich-girl and manage to bring her and her too busy father back together again. Standard. B&W; 70m. **DIR:** William Morgan. **CAST:** Gene Autry, Smiley Burnette, Fay McKenzie. 1942

HEART OF THE ROCKIES ★★★★ Possibly the best of the Three Mesquiteers series as the trio find a vicious mountain family behind cattle rustling and the illegal trapping of game. B&W; 56m. **DIR:** Joseph Kane. **CAST:** Robert Livingston, Ray "Crash" Corrigan, Max Terhune, Yakima Canutt, Lynne Roberts (Mary Hart). 1937

HEARTLAND ★★★★ This is an excellent and deceptively simple story, of a widow (Conchata Ferrell) who settled, with her daughter and a homesteader (Rip Torn), in turn-of-the-century Wyoming. The film deals with the complex problems of surviving in nature and society. It's well worth watching. Rated PG. 96m. **DIR:** Richard Pearce. **CAST:** Conchata Ferrell, Rip Torn, Lilia Skala, Megan Folsom. 1979

HEAVEN'S GATE ★★½ Written and directed by Michael Cimino (*The Deer Hunter*), this $36 million epic Western about the land wars in Wyoming between the cattle barons and immigrant farmers, is awkward and overlong but at least makes sense in the complete video version. Rated R for nudity, sex, and violence. 219m. **DIR:** Michael Cimino. **CAST:** Kris Kristofferson, Christopher Walken, Isabelle Huppert, John Hurt, Sam Waterston, Brad Dourif, Jeff Bridges, Joseph Cotten. 1980

HELL HOUNDS OF ALASKA ★★ Action tale taking place in Alaska during the gold rush. Outlaws ambush and murder a miner and kidnap his son. When the deed is discovered, a friend of the slain man tries to rescue the boy. Beautiful scenery and direction make this a fine family film. Rated G. 90m. **DIR:** Harald Reinl. **CAST:** Doug McClure, Harold Leipnitz, Angelica Ott, Roberto Blanco. 1973

HELL TOWN ★★★½ Here's a real find for fans of John Wayne, a pre-*Stagecoach* Western of good quality. Stepping up from his low-budget programmers for Republic and Monogram, the Duke was cast in this, the last of Paramount's series of films based on the stories of Zane Grey. He plays a happy-go-lucky cowhand who falls in with rustlers much to the chagrin of lawman Johnny Mack Brown. Also known as *Born to the West*. B&W; 50m. **DIR:** Charles Barton. **CAST:** John Wayne, Marsha Hunt, Johnny Mack Brown, Alan Ladd, James Craig, Monte Blue, Lucien Littlefield. **1938**

HELLBENDERS, THE 🦃 Story of a washed-out Confederate and his band of sons. 92m. **DIR:** Sergio Corbucci. **CAST:** Joseph Cotten, Norma Bengell, Julian Mateos, Angel Aranda. **1967**

HELLDORADO (1946) ★★ Roy and the boys exercise their fists and tonsils while breaking up a gang of black-market racketeers in postwar Las Vegas. The popular rodeo forms the backdrop as Roy, Dale, and Gabby entertain the likes of singer Eddie Acuff and future Lone Ranger Clayton Moore. B&W; 70m. **DIR:** William Witney. **CAST:** Roy Rogers, George "Gabby" Hayes, Dale Evans, Bob Nolan and the Sons of the Pioneers, LeRoy Mason, Paul Harvey, Rex Lease, Eddie Acuff, Clayton Moore. **1946**

HELLER IN PINK TIGHTS ★★½ Legendary nineteenth-century actress and love goddess Adah Issacs Menken inspired this odd film about a ragtag theatrical troupe wandering the West in the 1880s. Colorful but air-filled, it offers a busty blonde Sophia Loren with lusty Tony Quinn. 100m. **DIR:** George Cukor. **CAST:** Sophia Loren, Anthony Quinn, Margaret O'Brien, Edmund Lowe, Steve Forrest, Eileen Heckart, Ramon Novarro. **1960**

HELLFIRE ★★★½ Solid, offbeat Western in which a ne'er-do-well gambler, William ("Wild Bill") Elliott, is shoved onto the path of righteousness when a preacher saves his life. A bit preachy at times, *Hellfire* still packs a solid wallop of entertainment. 79m. **DIR:** R. G. Springsteen. **CAST:** William Elliott, Marie Windsor, Forrest Tucker, Jim Davis, Grant Withers, Paul Fix, Denver Pyle. **1949**

HELL'S HINGES ★★★ William S. Hart's trademark character, the good-bad man, loses his heart to the new minister's sister when she arrives in Hell's Hinges. The minister is corrupted and the church burned down, causing Hart to seek revenge. This grim story is perhaps Hart's best film, and certainly his most imitated. Silent. B&W; 65m. **DIR:** William S. Hart, Charles Swickard. **CAST:** William S. Hart, Clara Williams, Robert McKim. **1916**

HERITAGE OF THE DESERT ★★★ Donald Woods comes West to claim an inheritance and is soon mixed up with outlaws. Best of three screen versions based on th[e] Zane Grey novel. B&W; 74m. **DIR:** Lesley Se[lander]. **CAST:** Donald Woods, Russell Hayden, Evelyn Venable, Sidney Toler. **1939**

HEROES OF THE SADDLE ★★ Th[e] Three Mesquiteers help an orphaned gi[rl] and discover the orphanage where she ha[s] been placed is siphoning off cash from th[e] institution to run a criminal empire. Routin[e] Mesquiteer outing. B&W; 54m. **DIR:** Willian[m] Witney. **CAST:** Robert Livingston, Duncan Renaldo, Raymond Hatton. **1940**

HIDDEN GOLD ★★★ Hopalong Cassidy takes the job of ranch foreman for a girl t[o] stop a crook who wants to steal a gold mine. B&W; 61m. **DIR:** Lesley Selander. **CAST:** William Boyd, Russell Hayden, Britt Wood, Roy Barcroft, Ruth Rogers. **1940**

HIDDEN VALLEY OUTLAWS ★★★★ Marshall Bill Elliott is duped by an outlaw leader—but only for a while—as he searches for the Whistler, an unemotional killer who whistles while he robs and plunders. B&W; 54m. **DIR:** Howard Bretherton. **CAST:** William Elliott, George "Gabby" Hayes, Anne Jeffreys, Roy Barcroft, LeRoy Mason. **1944**

HIGH NOON ★★★★★ Gary Cooper won his second Oscar for his role of the abandoned lawman in this classic Western. It's the sheriff's wedding day, and the head of an outlaw band, who has sworn vengeance against him, is due to arrive in town at high noon. When Cooper turns to his fellow townspeople for help, no one comes forward. The suspense of this movie keeps snowballing as the clock ticks ever closer to noon. B&W; 84m. **DIR:** Fred Zinnemann. **CAST:** Gary Cooper, Grace Kelly, Lloyd Bridges, Thomas Mitchell, Katy Jurado, Otto Kruger, Lon Chaney Jr. **1952**

HIGH NOON, PART TWO 🦃 This is a poor attempt at a sequel. 100m. **DIR:** Jerry Jameson. **CAST:** Lee Majors, David Carradine, J. A. Preston, Pernell Roberts, M. Emmet Walsh. **1980**

HIGH PLAINS DRIFTER ★★★ Star-director Clint Eastwood tried to revive the soggy spaghetti Western genre one more time, with watchable results. Eastwood comes to a frontier town just in time to make sure its sleazy citizens are all but wiped out by a trio of revenge-seeking outlaws. Although atmospheric, it's also confusing and sometimes just downright nasty. Rated R for violence, profanity, and suggested sex. 105m. **DIR:** Clint Eastwood. **CAST:** Clint Eastwood, Verna Bloom, Marianna Hill, Mitchell Ryan, Jack Ging, Geoffrey Lewis, John Mitchum. **1973**

HILLS OF UTAH, THE ★★½ Harking back to a classic theme, Gene returns to the town where his father was killed and manages to settle a local feud as well as uncover the truth about his father's murder. Even ith Pat Buttram, this is somber for a Gene utry film. B&W; 70m. **DIR:** John English. **ST:** Gene Autry, Pat Buttram, Elaine Riley, nslow Stevens, Donna Martell. **1951**

IRED HAND, THE ★★★½ This low-key estern follows two drifters, Peter Fonda d Warren Oates, as they return to Fonda's rm and the wife, Verna Bloom, he deserted ven years earlier. While working on the rm, Fonda and Bloom begin to rekindle eir relationship. Beautiful cinematography d fine performances, especially by Oates, ld greatly to this worthy entry in the genre. ated R. 93m. **DIR:** Peter Fonda. **CAST:** Peter onda, Warren Oates, Verna Bloom, Severn Dar- en. **1971**

IS BROTHER'S GHOST ★★★½ Sturdy ntry in the Billy Carson series has Buster rabbe as a two-fisted rancher bent on cap- uring the gang that killed his best friend. It's uch better than it sounds, one of the best rabbe made in the series, which originally arred Bob Steele as a whitewashed Billy e Kid. B&W; 54m. **DIR:** Sam Newfield. **CAST:** uster Crabbe, Al St. John, Charles King, Karl ackett. **1945**

IS FIGHTING BLOOD ★★ Kermit May- ard goes to jail for his outlaw brother. Upon elease he is cleared, becomes a Mountie, nd tracks down the real outlaws. B&W; 0m. **DIR:** John English. **CAST:** Kermit Maynard, olly Ann Young, Ted Adams, Paul Fix. **1935**

IS NAME WAS KING ★★ Spaghetti Vestern about a bounty hunter named King Richard Harrison) who tracks down a ring f gunrunners near the Mexican border. Not ated, but equal to a PG. 90m. **DIR:** Don eynolds. **CAST:** Richard Harrison, Klaus Kinski. **983**

IT THE SADDLE ★★★ A gold digging andango dancer (Rita Hayworth, née ansino) comes between two of the Three Mesquiteers while they battle a sinister out- aw gang. B&W; 54m. **DIR:** Mack V. Wright. **AST:** Robert Livingston, Ray "Crash" Corrigan, Max Terhune, Rita Hayworth. **1937**

IOMBRE ★★★★ Paul Newman gives a uperb performance as a white man raised y Indians who is enticed into helping a tagecoach full of settlers make its way cross treacherous country. Richard Boone s the baddie who makes this chore difficult, ut the racism Newman encounters in this Martin Ritt film provides the real—and hought-provoking—thrust. 111m. **DIR:** Mar- in Ritt. **CAST:** Paul Newman, Fredric March, Richard Boone, Diane Cilento, Cameron Mitchell, Barbara Rush, Martin Balsam. **1967**

IOME IN OKLAHOMA ★★ Roy Rogers nd Dale Evans play a newspaper editor and reporter who question the "accidental" leath of a millionaire ranch owner. Adhering o the tried-and-true formula of all series films, Roy and his cohort risk their reputa- tions and lives for the rancher's niece (Carol Hughes). An enjoyable example of what kids watched before television. B&W; 72m. **DIR:** William Witney. **CAST:** Roy Rogers, George "Gabby" Hayes, Dale Evans, Carol Hughes, Bob Nolan and the Sons of the Pioneers, George Meeker, Frank Reicher. **1946**

HONDO ★★★★ One of John Wayne's best films and performances, this 3-D West- ern overcomes the gimmicky process with excellent performances, plenty of action, and an uncommonly strong screenplay from frequent Wayne collaborator James Edward Grant. The Duke plays an army scout who adopts a widowed frontierswoman (Gerald- ine Page in her Oscar-nominated film debut) and her son. 84m. **DIR:** John Farrow. **CAST:** John Wayne, Geraldine Page, Ward Bond, Lee Aaker, James Arness, Michael Pate, Leo Gordon, Paul Fix. **1953**

HONDO AND THE APACHES ★★★ Based on the John Wayne film. Ralph Taeger is Indian scout, Hondo Lane. Three episodes of the *Hondo* TV series edited into feature form. 85m. **DIR:** Lee H. Katzin. **CAST:** Ralph Taeger, Robert Taylor, Noah Beery Jr., Michael Rennie, John Smith, Kathie Browne. **1967**

HONKY TONK ★★★ A gambler fleeing tar and feathers meets a Boston beauty and her con man father on the train going to a new frontier town. He grows rich from graft and marries the beauty. Clark Gable and Lana Turner clicked as a team in this lively, lusty oater. B&W; 105m. **DIR:** Jack Conway. **CAST:** Clark Gable, Lana Turner, Frank Morgan, Claire Trevor, Marjorie Main, Albert Dekker, Henry O'Neill, Chill Wills, Veda Ann Borg. **1941**

HOPALONG CASSIDY ENTERS ★★★½ Solid series Western marked the debut of William Boyd as novelist Clarence E. Mul- ford's fictional hero, who was considerably changed by the time he reached the screen. Boyd gives a strong performance as Cassidy, who, in his initial movie, is possessed of a hair-trigger temper. James Ellison is the hot- headed but basically decent kid whom Cas- sidy turns around. B&W; 62m. **DIR:** Howard Bretherton. **CAST:** William Boyd, James Ellison, George "Gabby" Hayes, Charles Middleton. **1935**

HOPPY SERVES A WRIT ★★½ Hopalong Cassidy in Oklahoma Territory. Strictly a for- mula series Western, but well mounted, breezy, and moves along at a fast clip with a good cast. B&W; 67m. **DIR:** George Archain- baud. **CAST:** William Boyd, Andy Clyde, Victor Jory, George Reeves, Robert Mitchum, Byron Foulger. **1943**

HOPPY'S HOLIDAY ★★ A weak entry in the last of twelve Hopalong Cassidy films pits Hoppy and the Bar-20 cowboys against mechanized bank robbers. B&W; 60m. **DIR:** George Archainbaud. **CAST:** William Boyd, Andy Clyde, Rand Brooks, Jeff Corey. **1947**

HORSE SOLDIERS, THE ★★★★ Based on a true incident during the Civil War, this is a minor, but enjoyable, John Ford cavalry outing. John Wayne and William Holden play well-matched adversaries. 119m. **DIR:** John Ford. **CAST:** John Wayne, William Holden, Constance Towers, Hoot Gibson. **1959**

HOSTILE COUNTRY ★★ James Ellison and his pal Russell Hayden come to a new territory to take over half interest in Ellison's stepfather's ranch, but outlaws are holding the old man prisoner and have brought in a ringer. B&W; 61m. **DIR:** Thomas Carr. **CAST:** James Ellison, Russell Hayden, Julie Adams, Fuzzy Knight, Raymond Hatton. **1950**

HOSTILE GUNS ★★ Incredible cast of veteran B-movie Western actors is the main attraction in this routine drama of two peace officers who transport an unsavory group of criminals to prison. 91m. **DIR:** R. G. Springsteen. **CAST:** George Montgomery, Tab Hunter, Yvonne De Carlo, Brian Donlevy, John Russell, Leo Gordon, Richard Arlen, Don Barry, Emile Meyer. **1967**

HOT LEAD ★★★ Tim Holt must team up with an ex-con in order to stop a murderous gang of train robbers. B&W; 60m. **DIR:** Stuart Gilmore. **CAST:** Tim Holt, Richard Martin, John Dehner, Joan Dixon, Ross Elliott. **1951**

HOW THE WEST WAS WON ★★★½ Any Western with this cast is at least worth a glimpse. Sadly, this 1962 epic doesn't hold up that well on video because it was released on the three-screen Cinerama process. Much of the grandeur of the original version is lost. But shoot-'em-up fans won't want to miss a chance to see many of the genre's greats in one motion picture. For a taste of its original grandeur, check out the letter-boxed Laserdisc version, where the clear, sharp picture and excellent stereo sound do the film justice. 155m. **DIR:** Henry Hathaway, George Marshall, John Ford. **CAST:** Gregory Peck, Henry Fonda, James Stewart, John Wayne, Debbie Reynolds, Walter Brennan, Karl Malden, Richard Widmark, Robert Preston, George Peppard, Carolyn Jones, Carroll Baker. **1963**

I SHOT BILLY THE KID ★★ Pat Garrett (Robert Lowery) tells this sympathetic tale of a good young man who went bad. A standard but watchable rehash of familiar material. B&W; 59m. **DIR:** William Berke. **CAST:** Don Barry, Robert Lowery, Tom Neal, John Morton, Jack Perrin. **1950**

I WILL FIGHT NO MORE FOREVER ★★★½ Effective and affecting story of how the Nez Percé Indian tribe, under Chief Joseph, were driven to war with U.S. government in 1877. The Nez Percé tied up five thousand troops for more than eight months, even though fighting with only a hundred able-bodied warriors. Ned Romero is superb as the proud but wise Chief Joseph, and James Whitmore turns in a fine performance as the craggy General Howard. Made for T 106m. **DIR:** Richard T. Heffron. **CAST:** Ne Romero, James Whitmore, Sam Elliott, Linc Redfern. **1975**

IDAHO ★★ The king of the Cowboys ta gles with the local evil influences as he help put an end to bad-girl Ona Munson's vic dens. Gene Autry was in the air force i 1943, so Roy found himself in the numbe one spot with a bigger budget and ex-Autr sidekick Smiley Burnette. B&W; 70m. **DI** Joseph Kane. **CAST:** Roy Rogers, Smile Burnette, Bob Nolan and the Sons of the Pio neers, Virginia Grey, Harry Shannon, Ona Mun son, Dick Purcell, Onslow Stevens, Ha Taliaferro, Rex Lease, Tom London, Jack Ingran **1943**

IN EARLY ARIZONA ★★★½ In this big budget B, Wild Bill Elliott tames the town o Tombstone by getting rid of the evil Harr Woods. A fine example of this type of Wes ern lore. Plenty of action and energy. B&W 53m. **DIR:** Joseph Levering. **CAST:** William E liott, Harry Woods, Charles King. **1938**

IN OLD AMARILLO ★★★½ A sever range drought that threatens ranchers i compounded by a vicious ranch foreman who plans to profit from the disaster. An other in the ahead-of-their-time environ mental Roy Rogers contemporary Westerns B&W; 67m. **DIR:** William Witney. **CAST:** Ro Rogers, Estelita Rodriguez, Penny Edwards Pinky Lee, Roy Barcroft. **1951**

IN OLD ARIZONA ★★ The first Wester talkie and the first sound film made outdoor is also the first movie to spawn a series Warner Baxter (in his Oscar-winning role) plays O. Henry's Mexican bandido, the Cisco Kid, changing the concept to suit his personality. The Cisco Kid was originally a parody on Billy the Kid. Baxter gave him an accent, an eagerness to enjoy life, and a girl friend. The movie is slow by today's stand ards, so it is mostly a curiosity piece. B&W 63m. **DIR:** Raoul Walsh, Irving Cummings **CAST:** Warner Baxter, Dorothy Burgess, Edmunc Lowe, J. Farrell MacDonald. **1929**

IN OLD CALIENTE ★★★★ The coming of the Americans to California provides the story to one of Roy Rogers's finest musical Westerns from the early years. Classic Rogers-Gabby Hayes duet, "We're Not Comin Out Tonight." B&W; 54m. **DIR:** Joseph Kane. **CAST:** Roy Rogers, Mary Hart, George "Gabby" Hayes, Jack LaRue, Katherine DeMille. **1939**

IN OLD CALIFORNIA ★★★ In one of his numerous B-plus pictures for Republic Studios, John Wayne plays a mild-mannered pharmacist who is forced to take up arms when he settles down in a Western town run by the corrupt Albert Dekker. Director William McGann keeps things moving at a sprightly pace, which is more than one can say of the other films in the series. B&W;

lm. **DIR:** William McGann. **CAST:** John Wayne, nnie Barnes, Albert Dekker, Helen Parrish, tsy Kelly, Edgar Kennedy. **1942**

OLD CHEYENNE ★★ Forgotten low-idget star Rex Lease takes a backseat to a nart stallion. Predictable old creaker. &W; 60m. **DIR:** Stuart Paton. **CAST:** Rex ase, Dorothy Gulliver, Harry Woods, Jay Hunt. **31**

OLD MEXICO ★★★ In this suspense-estern, a sequel to *Borderland,* Hopalong assidy solves a murder while working in lexico. A good script plus fine direction and cting make this a sure-bet B Western. &W; 62m. **DIR:** Edward Venturini. **CAST:** Wil-m Boyd, George "Gabby" Hayes, Russell Hay-n, Jan Clayton, Glenn Strange. **1938**

OLD SANTA FE ★★★ As this film roves, Gene Autry was not the first singing owboy no matter what he claims. Ken May-ard sings here as he'd done a few times be-re. Introductory Autry film has Gene and niley Burnette performing at a dance while laynard stops the villain. B&W; 64m. **DIR:** avid Howard. **CAST:** Ken Maynard, George abby" Hayes, Evalyn Knapp, Gene Autry, niley Burnette. **1934**

IDIAN UPRISING ★★ The surrender f Apache Indian Chief, Geronimo—here, ighly fictionalized to involve mercenary hite men and heroic cavalry men. Al-ough the cassette box lists 74 minutes, this a severely edited print of an original color lm. B&W; 60m. **DIR:** Ray Nazarro. **CAST:** eorge Montgomery, Audrey Long, Carl Benton eid, Joe Sawyer. **1952**

ITO THE BADLANDS ★★ This trio of eird made-for-cable Western tales ranges om tepid to terrible. Rod Serling might ave penned the first, with Helen Hunt and ylan McDermott sharing a damned ro-ance, on a bad day; the other two make ab-olutely no sense. Only Dern's engaging nar-ation saves this mess from turkeydom. 93m. **IR:** Sam Pillsbury. **CAST:** Bruce Dern, Mariel emingway, Helen Hunt, Dylan McDermott, Lisa elikan, Andrew Robinson. **1991**

IVITATION TO A GUNFIGHTER ★★ Stu-io-slick Western is short on action and long n dialogue as a hired professional killer omes to town and changes the balance of ower. Everybody gets a chance to emote in is gabfest. 92m. **DIR:** Richard Wilson. **CAST:** ul Brynner, George Segal, Janice Rule, Pat Hin-le. **1964**

AYHAWKERS, THE ★★★ A routine Vestern story line enhanced by strong per-onalities in leading roles. Jeff Chandler and ess Parker come to blows in a power strug-le, and French actress Nicole Maurey is aught in the middle. 100m. **DIR:** Melvin rank. **CAST:** Jeff Chandler, Fess Parker, Nicole laurey, Henry Silva, Herbert Rudley. **1959**

JEREMIAH JOHNSON ★★★★ Robert Redford plays Johnson, a simple man who has no taste for cities. We see him as he grows from his first feeble attempts at survival to a hunter who has quickened his senses with wild meat and vegetation—a man who is a part of the wildlife of the mountains. *Jeremiah Johnson* gives a sense of humanness to a genre that had, up until its release, spent time reworking the same myths. Rated PG. 107m. **DIR:** Sydney Pollack. **CAST:** Robert Redford, Will Geer, Charles Tyner, Stefan Gierasch, Allyn Ann McLerie. **1972**

JESSE JAMES ★★★½ Tyrone Power is Jesse, and Henry Fonda is Frank in this legend-gilding account of the life and misdeeds of Missouri's most famous outlaw. Bending history, the film paints Jesse as a peaceful man driven to a life of crime by heartless big business in the form of a railroad, and a loving husband and father murdered for profit by a coward. 105m. **DIR:** Henry King. **CAST:** Tyrone Power, Henry Fonda, Nancy Kelly, Randolph Scott, Henry Hull, Jane Darwell, Brian Donlevy, Donald Meek, John Carradine, Slim Summerville, J. Edward Bromberg. **1939**

JESSE JAMES AT BAY ★★½ Roy Rogers is a fictionalized Jesse James who rides not against the railroads, but against one evil bunch misrepresenting the railroad and stealing the land of poor, honest farmers. A top contender for *the* most farfetched, fallacious frontier foolishness ever filmed. B&W; 56m. **DIR:** Joseph Kane. **CAST:** Roy Rogers, George "Gabby" Hayes, Sally Payne. **1941**

JESSE JAMES RIDES AGAIN ★★½ The first of Clayton Moore's two Jesse James serials finds our misunderstood hero trying to go straight, as he leaves his home territory and goes to Tennessee to lead an anonymous life. He runs afoul of hooded terrorists who threaten his newfound friends. B&W; 13 chapters. **DIR:** Fred Brannon, Thomas Carr. **CAST:** Clayton Moore, Linda Stirling, Roy Barcroft, Tristram Coffin. **1947**

JOE KIDD ★★★½ While not exactly a thrill-a-minute movie, this Western has a number of memorable moments. Director John Sturges has been better, but Clint Eastwood and Robert Duvall are at the peak of their forms in this story of a gunman (Eastwood) hired by a cattle baron (Duvall) to track down some Mexican-Americans who are fighting back because they've been cheated out of their land. Rated PG. 88m. **DIR:** John Sturges. **CAST:** Clint Eastwood, Robert Duvall, John Saxon, Don Stroud. **1972**

JOHNNY GUITAR ★★★½ A positively weird Western, this Nicholas Ray film features the ultimate role reversal. Bar owner Joan Crawford and landowner Mercedes McCambridge shoot it out while their gun-toting boyfriends (Sterling Hayden and Scott Brady) look on. 110m. **DIR:** Nicholas Ray.

CAST: Joan Crawford, Mercedes McCambridge, Sterling Hayden, Scott Brady, Ward Bond, Ernest Borgnine, John Carradine. **1954**

JOHNNY RENO ★★ Another in producer A. C. Lyles's anachronistic, mid-Sixties Paramount Westerns featuring old-time sagebrush stars in an old-fashioned oater. Relentlessly corny, but watchable. 83m. **DIR:** R. G. Springsteen. **CAST:** Dana Andrews, Jane Russell, Lon Chaney Jr., John Agar, Lyle Bettger, Tom Drake, Richard Arlen, Robert Lowery. **1966**

JORY ★★★ A surprisingly sensitive film for the genre finds Robby Benson, in his first film role, as a 15-year-old boy who must learn to go it alone in the Wild West after his father is senselessly murdered. While remaining exciting and suspenseful, the film takes time to make commentary about manhood and machismo in an adult, thoughtful manner. Rated PG. 97m. **DIR:** Jorge Fons. **CAST:** Robby Benson, John Marley, B. J. Thomas, Linda Purl. **1972**

JUBAL ★★★½ Adult Western finds drifter Jubal Troop (Glenn Ford) enmeshed in just about everybody's problems when he signs on with rancher Ernest Borgnine. Beautifully photographed and well acted, this tale of jealousy and revenge is standout entertainment. 101m. **DIR:** Delmer Daves. **CAST:** Glenn Ford, Ernest Borgnine, Valerie French, Rod Steiger, Charles Bronson, Noah Beery Jr., Felicia Farr. **1956**

JUBILEE TRAIL ★★ Tired romantic triangle in old California is short on action and long on melodrama as a young woman has to choose among the rough-hewn men who court her. This fine cast can't drag the film out of the syrupy mire it settles into. Director Joseph Kane had a lot more luck with Gene Autry and Roy Rogers programmers. 103m. **DIR:** Joseph Kane. **CAST:** Forrest Tucker, Vera Hruba Ralston, Joan Leslie, John Russell, Jim Davis, Pat O'Brien, Barton MacLane, Ray Middleton, Buddy Baer, Jack Elam. **1953**

JUNIOR BONNER ★★★ A rodeo has-been, Steve McQueen, returns home for one last rousing performance in front of the home folks. McQueen is quite good as the soft-spoken cowboy who tries to make peace with his family. Robert Preston is a real scene stealer as his hard-drinking carouser of a father. Rated PG. 103m. **DIR:** Sam Peckinpah. **CAST:** Steve McQueen, Robert Preston, Ida Lupino, Ben Johnson, Joe Don Baker. **1972**

KANSAN, THE ★★★ Tough, two-fisted Richard Dix sets his jaw and routs the baddies in a wide-open prairie town but must then contend with a corrupt official in this enjoyable Western, the third to pair him with Jane Wyatt and heavies Victor Jory and Albert Dekker. B&W; 79m. **DIR:** George Archainbaud. **CAST:** Richard Dix, Jane Wyatt, Victor Jory, Albert Dekker, Eugene Pallette, Robert Armstrong. **1943**

KANSAS CYCLONE ★★★ A crooke mine owner is holding up gold ore shi ments from other mines and running the o back through his dummy mine. Don Barr an undercover marshal, poses as a geologi to catch the bandits. The action, under th capable hands of Yakima Canutt, and a co ple of interesting subplots from screenwrite Oliver Drake lift this one above the averag B&W; 58m. **DIR:** George Sherman. **CAST:** Do Barry, Lynn Merrick. **1941**

KANSAS PACIFIC ★★½ Railroad dram set in pre–Civil War days has rangy Sterlin Hayden romancing Eve Miller and battlin pro-Confederate saboteurs. 73m. **DIR:** Ra Nazarro. **CAST:** Sterling Hayden, Eve Miller, Ba ton MacLane, Douglas Fowley, Myron Heale Clayton Moore, Reed Hadley. **1953**

KANSAS TERRORS ★★★ The Thre Mesquiteers must recover gold paid the for selling a herd of horses. They encounte a tyrant who rules an island in the Carib bean. B&W; 57m. **DIR:** George Sherma **CAST:** Robert Livingston, Duncan Renaldo, Ra mond Hatton, Jacqueline Wells, Howard Hick man. **1939**

KEEP THE CHANGE ★★★½ An unin spired artist (William L. Petersen) realize he needs to return to his family's ranch i Montana to get back to his roots. Not rated but contains implied sex. 95m. **DIR:** And Tennant. **CAST:** William L. Petersen, Lolita Davi dovich, Rachel Ticotin, Jack Palance, Buc Henry, Fred Dalton Thompson, Jeff Kober, Loi Smith. **1992**

KENTUCKIAN, THE ★★★ Pushing wes in the 1820s, Burt Lancaster bucks all odds to reach Texas and begin a new life. A goo mix of history, adventure, romance, an comedy make this one worth a family watch ing. 104m. **DIR:** Burt Lancaster. **CAST:** Burt Lancaster, Diana Lynn, Dianne Foster, Walter Matthau, John Carradine, Una Merkel. **1955**

KENTUCKY RIFLE ★★½ Pioneers going west are stranded in Comanche country They must barter the Kentucky long rifles i their wagons for safe passage. Passable oater. 80m. **DIR:** Carl K. Hittleman. **CAST:** Chil Wills, Jeanne Cagney, Cathy Downes, Lance Fuller, Sterling Holloway. **1955**

KID RANGER ★★★ Trouble begins when a ranger shoots a man he wrongly believes to be part of an outlaw gang. Two-fisted hero Bob Steele must track down the real gang. B&W; 56m. **DIR:** Robert N. Bradbury. **CAST:** Bob Steele, Joan Barclay, William Farnum, Charles King. **1936**

KID VENGEANCE 🦃 A boy witnesses the death of his parents at the hands of an outlaw gang. He goes in pursuit with the aid of another victim of the gang, and eliminates the band one by one until only he and the bandit leader remain. This vehicle for teen-idol Leif

;arrett wastes the talents of Jim Brown and ee Van Cleef. Filmed in Israel. Rated R for iolence and brief nudity. 90m. **DIR:** Joseph /landuke. **CAST:** Leif Garrett, Jim Brown, Lee 'an Cleef, Glynnis O'Connor, Matt Clark, Timothy icott, John Marley. **1976**

ING AND FOUR QUEENS, THE ★★★½ his blend of mystery, comedy, and romance akes place in a western ghost town where tagecoach robbery gold is hidden. Desper-do Clark Gable plays up to four women in opes of finding the money. B&W; 86m. **DIR:** aoul Walsh. **CAST:** Clark Gable, Eleanor Parker, o Van Fleet, Jean Willes, Barbara Nichols, Sara hane, Roy Roberts, Jay C. Flippen, Arthur hields. **1956**

ING OF THE BULLWHIP ★★½ Looking very bit like Humphrey Bogart's twin rother in a black hat, Lash LaRue was the hip-wielding westerner in a series of low-udget shoot-'em-ups in the 1950s. This, his rst for a major distributor, was one of his etter efforts. Lash and his sidekick Al St. ohn must go undercover when a bandit pre-ends to be our hero while robbing a bank. 0m. **DIR:** Ron Ormond. **CAST:** Lash LaRue, Al t. John, Jack Holt, Dennis Moore, Tom Neal, nne Gwynne. **1951**

ING OF THE COWBOYS ★★★★ Roy ogers at his best as a government agent orking undercover as a rodeo performer nfiltrating a ring of WWII saboteurs. B&W; 4m. **DIR:** Joseph Kane. **CAST:** Roy Rogers, miley Burnette, Peggy Moran, Sons of the Pio-eers, Gerald Mohr. **1943**

ING OF THE PECOS ★★★ John Wayne ses his law school training and a profi-iency with firearms to exact revenge on the and robber who killed our hero's father. tandard B Western plot is enhanced by lenty of action, and Wayne's increasing skill n front of the camera. B&W; 54m. **DIR:** oseph Kane. **CAST:** John Wayne, Muriel Evans, y Kendall, Jack Clifford, Yakima Canutt. **1936**

ING OF THE TEXAS RANGERS ★★½ tandard Republic Studios cliff-hanger serial as some truly bizarre qualities. The lead, lingin' Sammy Baugh, was a famous foot-all star in the 1940s. Baugh plays Tom King, football player who gives up a successful areer in the sport to avenge the death of his ather, a Texas Ranger who was killed by ifth columnists. Yes, this is a modern-day Vestern with cars, phones, Nazis, and even zeppelin(!). B&W; 12 chapters. **DIR:** William Vitney, John English. **CAST:** Sammy Baugh, Neil lamilton, Pauline Moore, Duncan Renaldo. **1941**

IT CARSON ★★★½ This lively Western bout the two-fisted frontiersman gave Jon Iall one of his best roles. Good action cenes. B&W; 97m. **DIR:** George B. Seitz. **AST:** Jon Hall, Dana Andrews, Lynn Bari. **1940**

LADY FROM LOUISIANA ★★ John Wayne is a crusading lawyer in this middling Republic period piece. B&W; 82m. **DIR:** Bernard Vorhaus. **CAST:** John Wayne, Ray Middleton, Ona Munson. **1941**

LADY TAKES A CHANCE, A ★★★ John Wayne is a rough-'n'-ready, not-the-marrying kind, rodeo star. Jean Arthur is an innocent girl from New York City out west. He falls off a horse into her lap, she falls for him, and the chase is on. *It Happened One Night* with spurs. B&W; 86m. **DIR:** William A. Seiter. **CAST:** Jean Arthur, John Wayne, Phil Silvers, Charles Winninger, Grady Sutton, Hans Conried, Grant Withers, Mary Field. **1943**

LAND OF THE OPEN RANGE ★★½ Sheriff Tim Holt has his hands full of ex-cons when a local no-good dies and leaves his ranch open to a land rush. However, to qualify for a homestead, each man must have served two years or more in prison. A different twist on the standard B land grab plot, and one of Holt's better prewar efforts. B&W; 60m. **DIR:** Edward Killy. **CAST:** Tim Holt, Ray Whitley, Roy Barcroft. **1942**

LAND RAIDERS Spanish-made violent oater with Telly Savalas as the Indian-hating town boss. 101m. **DIR:** Nathan Juran. **CAST:** Telly Savalas, George Maharis, Arlene Dahl. **1970**

LAST COMMAND, THE (1955) ★★½ This is a watchable Western about the famed last stand at the Alamo during Texas's fight for independence from Mexico. Jim Bowie (Sterling Hayden), Davy Crockett (Arthur Hunnicutt), and Colonel Travis (Richard Carlson) are portrayed in a more realistic manner than they were in John Wayne's *The Alamo*, but the story is still mostly hokum. 110m. **DIR:** Frank Lloyd. **CAST:** Sterling Hayden, Richard Carlson, Anna Maria Alberghetti, Ernest Borgnine, Arthur Hunnicutt, Jim Davis, J. Carrol Naish. **1955**

LAST DAYS OF FRANK AND JESSE JAMES ★★★ Once you get past the country-western motif, this is an honorable biography of the notorious Wild West hoodlums. Kris Kristofferson and Johnny Cash are convincingly brotherly, and director William A. Graham adds just enough grittiness to make them a little less than heroic. 97m. **DIR:** William A. Graham. **CAST:** Kris Kristofferson, Johnny Cash, Willie Nelson. **1986**

LAST FRONTIER, THE ★★½ Another serial set in the Old West. The mysterious Black Ghost helps newspaper editor Tom Kirby (Lon Chaney Jr.) fight a band of ruffians who are intent on provoking Indians to attack the settlers and drive them from their homes. As usual, there's gold at the bottom of all the trouble. B&W; 12 chapters. **DIR:** Spencer Gordon Bennet, Thomas L. Story. **CAST:** Lon Chaney Jr., Dorothy Gulliver, Mary Jo Desmond, Francis X. Bushman, Yakima Canutt, LeRoy Mason, William Desmond. **1932**

LAST GUN, THE ★★ In this Italian Western dubbed into English, a gunfighter tired of killing hangs up his pistols and settles down in a small town. The story is classic. The acting and directing are not. 98m. **DIR:** Serge Bergone. **CAST:** Cameron Mitchell, Frank Wolff, Carl Mohner. **1964**

LAST HUNT, THE ★★½ A downer disguised as an upper. This outdoor drama has more talk than action, as buffalo try to escape from crafty white men. Stewart Granger makes a weak hero, but Robert Taylor is pretty good as the villain. 108m. **DIR:** Richard Brooks. **CAST:** Robert Taylor, Stewart Granger, Constance Ford, Debra Paget, Lloyd Nolan, Joe De Santis, Russ Tamblyn. **1955**

LAST OF THE COMANCHES ★★ Tough cavalry sergeant has to lead a stagecoach load of passengers to safety across the desert following an Indian raid. Broderick Crawford was woefully miscast in the handful of Westerns he did. B&W; 85m. **DIR:** André de Toth. **CAST:** Broderick Crawford, Barbara Hale, Lloyd Bridges. **1953**

LAST OF THE MOHICANS (1932) ★★ Plenty of liberties are taken with the famous James Fenimore Cooper novel of Hawkeye in colonial America. Principally a chase back and forth as Hurons capture an English colonel's two daughters. B&W; 12 chapters. **DIR:** Ford Beebe, B. Reeves "Breezy" Eason. **CAST:** Harry Carey, Edwina Booth. **1932**

LAST OF THE MOHICANS, THE (1936) ★★★★ Blood, thunder, and interracial romance during the French and Indian War are brought to life from James Fenimore Cooper's novel. Randolph Scott is the intrepid Hawkeye; Robert Barrat is the noble Chingachgook; Binnie Barnes is Alice Monroe. The star-crossed lovers are Phillip Reed, as Uncas, the title character, and Heather Angel, as Cora Monroe. B&W; 100m. **DIR:** George B. Seitz. **CAST:** Randolph Scott, Binnie Barnes, Heather Angel, Robert Barrat, Phillip Reed, Henry Wilcoxon, Bruce Cabot. **1936**

LAST OF THE MOHICANS (1985) ★★½ In this TV film based on James Fenimore Cooper's classic, a small party headed for a fort is deserted by their guide and must turn to Hawkeye and Chingachgook to bring them to safety. When two of the party are captured, our heroes must rescue them and battle the leader of the Indians. 97m. **DIR:** James L. Conway. **CAST:** Steve Forrest, Ned Romero, Andrew Prine, Robert Tessier. **1985**

LAST OF THE MOHICANS, THE (1992) ★★★★★ A classy romance angle and director Michael Mann's sweeping vision highlight this retelling of James Fenimore Cooper's novel of colonial America. A first-class production all the way, this historic tale never feels dated and the action scenes are state-of-the-art. Rated R for violence. 120m. **DIR:** Michael Mann. **CAST:** Daniel Day-Lewis, Madeleine Stowe, Russell Means, Eric Schweig, Jodhi May, Steven Waddington, Maurice Roeves, Patrice Chereau. **1992**

LAST OF THE PONY RIDERS ★★★ Gene Autry's last feature film concerns the old West transition period from pony express to stagecoach and telegraph. Action-packed ending to Autry's twenty years of B-Western films. B&W; 59m. **DIR:** George Archainbaud. **CAST:** Gene Autry, Smiley Burnette, Dick Jones, Kathleen Case. **1953**

LAST OF THE REDMEN ★★★ Low-budget remake of James Fenimore Cooper's immortal *Last of the Mohicans* story with Michael O'Shea sorely miscast as an Irish Hawkeye. The French-Indian wars rage in gorgeous Cinecolor as Hawkeye and Rick Vallin as Uncas, the last of the Mohicans, brave danger to rescue two sisters from warring Iroquois Indians. 79m. **DIR:** George Sherman. **CAST:** Jon Hall, Michael O'Shea, Buster Crabbe, Evelyn Ankers, Julie Bishop, Rick Vallin. **1947**

LAST OUTLAW, THE (1936) ★★★★ Possibly Harry Carey's best film as a star, this is a delightful remake of a John Ford story of the silent era. Carey is a former outlaw released from prison, only to find that the West he knew is gone. Hoot Gibson is Carey's old saddle pal, and they soon take on a group of modern-day outlaws. B&W; 62m. **DIR:** Christy Cabanne. **CAST:** Harry Carey, Hoot Gibson, Henry B. Walthall, Tom Tyler. **1936**

LAST OUTLAW, THE (1993) ★★½ After a prologue stolen from *The Wild Bunch*, this laughably macho revenge saga becomes an exercise in sadistic gore...no surprise, considering the involvement of scripter Eric Red (*The Hitcher*). Betrayed by his own gang, outlaw Mickey Rourke joins the posse hunting his former associates...just so he can kill them, one by one. Rated R for profanity and extreme violence. 90m. **DIR:** Geoff Murphy. **CAST:** Mickey Rourke, Dermot Mulroney, Ted Levine, John C. McGinley. **1993**

LAST RIDE OF THE DALTON GANG, THE ★★½ When two former Dalton Gang train robbers are reunited in Hollywood in 1934, they relive the early days as they share a bottle of whiskey. 146m. **DIR:** Dan Curtis. **CAST:** Jack Palance, Larry Wilcox, Dale Robertson, Bo Hopkins, Cliff Potts. **1979**

LAST ROUND-UP ★★★★ Gene Autry's first for his own production company at Columbia Pictures is his personal favorite. Set in the modern West, Gene must relocate a tribe of Indians when their homeland is marked for an aqueduct project. B&W; 77m. **DIR:** John English. **CAST:** Gene Autry, Bobby Blake, Jean Heather, Ralph Morgan. **1947**

LAST TRAIN FROM GUN HILL ★★★½ In this hybird suspense-Western, a marshal (Kirk Douglas) is searching for the man who raped and murdered his wife. When the culprit (Earl Holliman) turns out to be the son of a wealthy rancher (Anthony Quinn), our hero holes up in a hotel room and takes on all comers until the next train arrives. A minor classic. 94m. **DIR:** John Sturges. **CAST:** Kirk Douglas, Anthony Quinn, Carolyn Jones, Earl Holliman, Brad Dexter. **1959**

LAW AND JAKE WADE, THE ★★½ A robust Western with Richard Widmark chewing the scenery as the bad guy looking for buried treasure and conning good guy Robert Taylor into helping him. *Star Trek's* DeForest Kelley has an important supporting role. 86m. **DIR:** John Sturges. **CAST:** Robert Taylor, Richard Widmark, Patricia Owens, Robert Middleton, DeForest Kelley, Henry Silva. **1958**

LAW AND ORDER ★★★★ In a story coscripted by John Huston, Walter Huston gets one of the best roles of his career as a Wyatt Earp–style lawman. Harry Carey and Raymond Hatton are superb as his ready-for-anything sidekicks in an excellent Western that still seems fresh and innovative today. B&W; 70m. **DIR:** Edward L. Cahn. **CAST:** Walter Huston, Harry Carey, Raymond Hatton, Andy Devine. **1932**

LAW OF THE LASH ★★ Lash LaRue establishes law and order in an outlaw-ridden town in the first film of his own series, which would hit its stride about two pictures later. B&W; 53m. **DIR:** Ray Taylor. **CAST:** Lash LaRue, Al St. John, Lee Roberts, Charles King. **1947**

LAW OF THE PAMPAS ★★★ South-of-the-border action. This is a good Hopalong Cassidy with all the right elements and an exotic locale to boot. B&W; 74m. **DIR:** Nate Watt. **CAST:** William Boyd, Russell Hayden, Sidney Blackmer, Sidney Toler, Pedro De Cordoba, Glenn Strange. **1939**

LAW RIDES AGAIN, THE 🦃 Dismal low-budget entry in the "Trail Blazers" series. B&W; 58m. **DIR:** Alan James. **CAST:** Ken Maynard, Hoot Gibson, Betty Miles, Jack LaRue, Kenneth Harlan, Chief Thundercloud. **1943**

LAW WEST OF TOMBSTONE ★★★½ Enjoyable, folksy Western has the marvelous Harry Carey starring as a con artist who becomes the law in Tombstone. Tim Holt, in a strong film debut, is the young hothead he befriends and reforms. Look for Allan "Rocky" Lane in a brief bit at the beginning as Holt's saddle pal. B&W; 72m. **DIR:** Glenn Tryon. **CAST:** Harry Carey, Tim Holt, Evelyn Brent, Ward Bond, Allan "Rocky" Lane. **1938**

LAWLESS FRONTIER ★★½ A Mexican bandit (Earl Dwire) manages to evade the blame for a series of crimes he's committed because the sheriff is sure that John Wayne is the culprit. The Duke, of course, traps the bad guy and clears his good name in this predictable B Western. B&W; 59m. **DIR:** Robert N. Bradbury. **CAST:** John Wayne, Sheila Terry, George "Gabby" Hayes, Earl Dwire. **1935**

LAWLESS NINETIES, THE ★★★ When outlaws use underhanded tactics to keep the citizens of Wyoming from voting for statehood, it's up to government agent John Wayne and his men to put a stop to it. Gabby Hayes has an uncharacteristic role as a Southern gentleman. It's predictable, but a notch above many oaters. B&W; 55m. **DIR:** Joseph Kane. **CAST:** John Wayne, Ann Rutherford, Lane Chandler, Harry Woods, George "Gabby" Hayes, Snowflake, Charles King. **1936**

LAWLESS RANGE ★★ In this low, low-budget early John Wayne Western, a banker attempts to drive out the local ranchers and get his hands on some rich gold mines. Wayne, sent by the governor, soon sets things aright. B&W; 59m. **DIR:** Robert N. Bradbury. **CAST:** John Wayne, Sheila Manners, Earl Dwire. **1935**

LAWLESS STREET, A ★★★ Randolph Scott portrays a no-nonsense marshal in Medicine Bend until the arrival of an old flame (Angela Lansbury) and the evil plottings of a power-hungry citizen (Warner Anderson) threaten to cost him his job—and maybe his life. Some amusing quips from Scott and the involving climax make this one worth watching. 78m. **DIR:** Joseph H. Lewis. **CAST:** Randolph Scott, Angela Lansbury, Warner Anderson, Jean Parker, Wallace Ford, John Emery, Michael Pate, Don Megowan. **1955**

LAWLESS VALLEY ★★★★ Prison parolee George O'Brien returns home to clear his name and put the true guilty parties behind bars in this solid series Western. In a nice touch, Fred Kohler Sr. and Fred Kohler Jr. play father-and-son heavies. B&W; 59m. **DIR:** Bert Gilroy. **CAST:** George O'Brien, Kay Sutton, Walter Miller, Fred Kohler Sr., Fred Kohler Jr., Chill Wills. **1938**

LAWMAN ★★ There's no fire in Burt Lancaster this time around. He plays a marshal who is determined to bring in the bad guys, despite the protestations of an entire town. The story has promise, but doesn't deliver. Robert Ryan is worth watching, cast against type as a meek sheriff. Rated PG. 98m. **DIR:** Michael Winner. **CAST:** Burt Lancaster, Robert Ryan, Lee J. Cobb, Robert Duvall, Sheree North, Richard Jordan, Ralph Waite, John Hillerman, J. D. Cannon, Albert Salmi. **1971**

LAWMAN IS BORN, A ★★½ Former football star Johnny Mack Brown is a two-fisted good guy who foils the nefarious plans of an outlaw gang. This time, the baddies are after land (as opposed to the alternate formulas of cattle, money, gold, or horses). It's fun for fans. B&W; 58m. **DIR:** Sam Newfield. **CAST:** Johnny Mack Brown, Iris Meredith, Al St. John. **1937**

LEATHER BURNERS, THE ★★½ In this oddball series Western, Hopalong Cassidy (William Boyd) and his sidekick, California (Andy Clyde), are framed for murder by a calculating cattle rustler (Victor Jory). It's up to a junior detective (Bobby Larson) to prove our heroes' innocence in time to allow them to participate in the final showdown. B&W; 58m. **DIR:** Joseph E. Henabery. **CAST:** William Boyd, Andy Clyde, Victor Jory, Bobby Larson, Robert Mitchum. **1943**

LEFT HANDED GUN, THE (1958) ★★★½ Effective Western follows the exploits of Billy the Kid from the Lincoln County cattle wars until his death at the hands of Pat Garrett. One of the best of several Westerns to deal with the legend of Billy the Kid. B&W; 102m. **DIR:** Arthur Penn. **CAST:** Paul Newman, John Dehner, James Best, Hurd Hatfield, Lita Milan. **1958**

LEGEND OF FRENCHIE KING, THE 🦃 This muddled Western about a gang of female outlaws falls flat. Rated R for profanity, violence, and adult situations. 97m. **DIR:** Christian Jaque. **CAST:** Brigitte Bardot, Claudia Cardinale, Guy Casaril, Michael J. Pollard. **1971**

LEGEND OF THE LONE RANGER, THE 🦃 While kids may slightly enjoy this often corny, slow-paced Western—adults will probably be falling asleep. Rated PG. 98m. **DIR:** William Fraker. **CAST:** Klinton Spilsbury, Michael Horse, Jason Robards Jr. **1981**

LEGEND OF WALKS FAR WOMAN, THE 🦃 Badly miscast Raquel Welch portrays an Indian heroine facing the perils of the Indian versus white man's culture clash. 150m. **DIR:** Mel Damski. **CAST:** Raquel Welch, Bradford Dillman, George Clutsei, Nick Mancuso, Nick Ramos. **1982**

LIFE AND TIMES OF JUDGE ROY BEAN, THE ★★★ Weird Western with Paul Newman as the fabled hanging judge. It has some interesting set pieces among the strangeness. Stacy Keach is outstanding as Bad Bob. Rated PG. 120m. **DIR:** John Huston. **CAST:** Paul Newman, Stacy Keach, Victoria Principal, Jacqueline Bisset, Ava Gardner. **1972**

LIGHTNIN' CRANDALL ★★★★ Bob Steele buys a ranch that is sandwiched between two feuding cattle ranches. Terrific action and stunt work make this one a cavalcade of fast thrills, and one of Steele's best. B&W; 60m. **DIR:** Sam Newfield. **CAST:** Bob Steele, Lois January, Dave O'Brien, Charles King. **1937**

LIGHTNING CARSON RIDES AGAIN ★★ Captain Bill Carson (Tim McCoy) of the U.S. Justice Department rides to the rescue when his nephew is accused of robbery and murder. Made on a minuscule budget by the penny-pinching producer Sam Katzman, this is one of the least of McCoy's Westerns. B&W; 58m. **DIR:** Sam Newfield. **CAST:** Tim McCoy, Joan Barclay, Ted Adams, Forrest Taylor. **1938**

LIGHTNING JACK ★★★ Easygoing outlaw Paul Hogan justs wants to be wanted—by the law—but his attempts at infamy are continually thwarted. It's the mild, mild West, with Cuba Gooding Jr. supplying most of the laughs as Hogan's mute sidekick in a pleasant movie that should please the star's fans. Rated PG-13 for suggested sex and light violence. 98m. **DIR:** Simon Wincer. **CAST:** Paul Hogan, Cuba Gooding Jr., Beverly D'Angelo, Kamala Dawson, Pat Hingle, Richard Riehle, L. Q. Jones, Frank McRae. **1994**

LIGHTNING TRIGGERS ★★ A lawman joins an outlaw gang to bring them to justice—only to find his father is the leader. Reb Russell was an ex-football player who made a string of low-budget Westerns in the 1930s. B&W; 50m. **DIR:** S. Roy Luby. **CAST:** Reb Russel, Fred Kohler Sr. **1935**

LIGHTS OF OLD SANTA FE ★★★ A sneaky rival rodeo owner has his eyes on Dale Evans's show, and her, too! Roy Rogers and sidekick Gabby Hayes to the rescue. No dramatic climax, just a big rodeo finale weakens this one. B&W; 78m. **DIR:** Frank McDonald. **CAST:** Roy Rogers, George "Gabby" Hayes, Dale Evans, Tom Keene, Lloyd Corrigan. **1944**

LITTLE BIG HORN ★★★★ A small patrol of cavalry men attempt to get through hostile Indian Territory to warn Custer's Seventh Cavalry of the impending Sioux-Cheyenne ambush. Highly suspenseful. B&W; 86m. **DIR:** Charles Marquis Warren. **CAST:** Lloyd Bridges, John Ireland, Marie Windsor, Reed Hadley, Hugh O'Brian, Jim Davis. **1951**

LITTLE BIG MAN ★★★★ Dustin Hoffman gives a bravura performance as Jack Crabbe, a 121-year-old survivor of Custer's last stand. An offbeat Western-comedy, this film chronicles, in flashback, Crabbe's numerous adventures in the Old West. It's a remarkable film in more ways than one. Rated PG. 150m. **DIR:** Arthur Penn. **CAST:** Dustin Hoffman, Chief Dan George, Faye Dunaway, Martin Balsam, Jeff Corey, Richard Mulligan. **1970**

LITTLE MOON & JUD MCGRAW 🦃 Comedy-Western that has James Caan as a falsely accused man hunting for the real crook. Rated R, contains nudity and violence. 92m. **DIR:** Bernard Girard. **CAST:** James Caan, Stefanie Powers, Sammy Davis Jr., Aldo Ray, Barbara Werle, Robert Walker Jr. **1978**

LOADED PISTOLS ★★★★ Well-handled, typical B-Western plot finds Gene Autry safeguarding young cowpoke Russell Arms (of TV's "Your Hit Parade") wrongly accused of murder. B&W; 77m. **DIR:** John English. **CAST:** Gene Autry, Barbara Britton, Jack Holt, Russell Arms, Chill Wills, Robert Shayne. **1948**

LONE JUSTICE ★★ So much for truth in packaging. This is only the first portion of the *Ned Blessing* television miniseries. Soon after star Daniel Baldwin arrives on screen to play the Western gunfighter as an adult, the tape screeches to a halt without resolving any plot elements. Don't be suckered by this one. Rated PG-13 for violence and profanity. 94m. **DIR:** Peter Werner. **CAST:** Daniel Baldwin, Luis Avalos, Chris Cooper, Julia Campbell, René Auberjonois, Jeff Kober. **1993**

LONE RANGER, THE (1938) ★★★½ One of America's most popular heroes rode out of the radio and onto the screen in one of the best and most fondly remembered serials of all time. The ballyhoo that accompanied the release of this exciting chapterplay made it an overwhelming hit at the box office. Thought to be lost until recently, most versions of this serial feature two chapters in French, the only copy available. B&W; 15 chapters. **DIR:** William Witney, John English. **CAST:** Lee Powell, Chief Thundercloud, Bruce Bennett, Lynne Roberts (Mary Hart), William Farnum, Lane Chandler, George Montgomery, Hal Taliaferro, George Cleveland. **1938**

LONE RANGER, THE (1956) ★★★½ The first color feature film based on the legend of the Lone Ranger is a treat for the kids and not too tough for the adults to sit through. Clayton Moore and Jay Silverheels reprise their television roles and find themselves battling white settlers, led by an evil Lyle Bettger, and the much put-upon Indians, riled up by a surly Michael Ansara. 86m. **DIR:** Stuart Heisler. **CAST:** Clayton Moore, Jay Silverheels, Lyle Bettger, Bonita Granville. **1956**

LONE RANGER, THE (TV SERIES) ★★★½ Emerging from a cloud of dust, with a hearty "Hi-yo Silver!" the Lone Ranger (Clayton Moore), with his faithful Indian companion, Tonto (Jay Silverheels), leads the fight for law and order in the Old West. Wearing a black mask fashioned from the vest of his murdered brother, the former Texas Ranger used silver bullets to remind him of the value of human life. He sought justice, not vengeance. His simplistic, moralistic adventures made him a hero to millions of youngsters. Now, these two-episode videocassettes enable you to return to those thrilling days of yesteryear, as the Lone Ranger rides again! A bonus is the Lone Ranger trivia segments presented by Clayton Moore. Each tape 55m. **DIR:** Various. **CAST:** Clayton Moore, Jay Silverheels. **1949–1965**

LONE RANGER AND THE LOST CITY OF GOLD, THE ★★½ The Lone Ranger and Tonto, as immortalized by Clayton Moore and Jay Silverheels, expose the murderers who hold a clue to a fabulously wealthy lost city's location. 80m. **DIR:** Lesley Selander. **CAST:** Clayton Moore, Jay Silverheels, Douglas Kennedy, Noreen Nash, John Miljan. **1958**

LONE STAR ★★★ This rip-roaring Western disguised as a historical document works as both. Lionel Barrymore steals every scene he's in as the aging Andrew Jackson. He sends no-nonsense cattleman (Clark Gable) to keep Sam Houston from establishing Texas as a republic. Good action and lots of glamour from the stars. B&W; 94m. **DIR:** Vincent Sherman. **CAST:** Clark Gable, Ava Gardner, Broderick Crawford, Lionel Barrymore, Beulah Bondi, Ed Begley Sr. **1952**

LONE STAR RAIDERS ★★ The Three Mesquiteers try to save an old lady's ranch from bankruptcy by selling a herd of wild horses. Weak Mesquiteers entry burdened by too much stock footage. B&W; 54m. **DIR:** George Sherman. **CAST:** Robert Livingston, Bob Steele, Rufe Davis, Sarah Padden. **1940**

LONE STAR TRAIL ★★★½ In this entertaining oater, Johnny Mack Brown is framed in a robbery case. Obviously upset, he hits the trail to find the real perpetrators. In the process, he meets up with outlaw Robert Mitchum, and one of the great fistfights in movie history is the result. Certainly worth a view. B&W; 77m. **DIR:** Ray Taylor. **CAST:** Johnny Mack Brown, Tex Ritter, Fuzzy Knight, Robert Mitchum. **1943**

LONELY ARE THE BRAVE ★★★★ A "little" Hollywood Western set in modern times has a lot to offer those who can endure its heavy-handed message. Kirk Douglas is just right as the cowboy out of step with his times. His attempts to escape from jail on horseback in contrast to the mechanized attempts to catch him by a modern police force are handled well. B&W; 107m. **DIR:** David Miller. **CAST:** Kirk Douglas, Walter Matthau, Gena Rowlands. **1962**

LONELY MAN, THE ★★★ Interesting, but not exciting, this tautly directed oater is about a gunfighter, bent on reforming, who returns to his family after a seventeen-year hiatus. A brooding Jack Palance is the gunfighter. He is not warmly welcomed home by his deserted son, brooding Anthony Perkins. B&W; 87m. **DIR:** Henry Levin. **CAST:** Jack Palance, Anthony Perkins, Neville Brand, Robert Middleton, Elisha Cook Jr., Lee Van Cleef. **1957**

LONELY TRAIL, THE ★★★ When former Yankee soldier John Wayne returns to his Texas ranch after the Civil War, he is greeted with suspicion and open hostility by his neighbors, whose sympathies were on the side of the Confederacy. Solid sagebrush saga. B&W; 58m. **DIR:** Joseph Kane. **CAST:** John Wayne, Ann Rutherford, Cy Kendall, Snowflake, Bob Kortman, Dennis Moore, Yakima Canutt. **1936**

LONESOME DOVE ★★★★★ Superb miniseries adapted from the sprawling novel by Larry McMurtry and originally written as a screenplay for John Wayne, Jimmy Stewart, and Henry Fonda. This is truly one of the great Westerns. Robert Duvall and Tommy Lee Jones give what are arguably the finest performances of their careers as a pair of aging Texas Rangers who go on one last adventure: a treacherous cattle drive to Montana. 384m. **DIR:** Simon Wincer. **CAST:** Robert Duvall, Tommy Lee Jones, Danny Glover, Diane Lane, Robert Urich, Frederic Forrest, D. B. Sweeney, Rick Schroder, Anjelica Huston, Chris Cooper, Timothy Scott, Glenne Headly, Barry Corbin, William Sanderson. **1989**

LONG LIVE YOUR DEATH ★★ A fake prince, a fake Mexican revolutionary hero, and a journalist try to locate a hidden treasure. A comedy-spaghetti Western set in Mexico with some good sight gags and dialogue. Eli Wallach is at his best. Unrated; contains violence. 98m. **DIR:** Duccio Tessari. **CAST:** Franco Nero, Eli Wallach, Lynn Redgrave, Marilu Tolo, Eduardo Fajardo. **1974**

LONG LONG TRAIL ★★★ Hooter is the Ramblin' Kid in a typical, but above-average, lighthearted Gibson Western. This one's a racehorse story. Love interest Sally Eilers became the real Mrs. Gibson a few months later. B&W; 60m. **DIR:** Arthur Rosson. **CAST:** Hoot Gibson, Sally Eilers, Walter Brennan. **1929**

LONG RIDERS, THE ★★★½ This film about the James-Younger Gang has a few deficiencies. Character development and plot complexity are ignored in favor of lots of action. This is partly offset by the casting of real-life brothers. While it sounds like a gimmick, it actually adds a much-needed dimension of character to the picture. Rated R for violence. 100m. **DIR:** Walter Hill. **CAST:** David Carradine, Keith Carradine, Robert Carradine, Stacy Keach, James Keach, Nicholas Guest, Christopher Guest, Dennis Quaid, Randy Quaid. **1980**

LONGEST DRIVE, THE ★★½ Culled from the 1976 television series, *The Quest*, this passable Western features Kurt Russell and Tim Matheson as two young brothers who help save an Irish rancher's herd, land, and fiery reputation. 92m. **DIR:** Bernard McEveety. **CAST:** Kurt Russell, Tim Matheson, Dan O'Herlihy, Keenan Wynn, Woody Strode, Erik Estrada. **1976**

LONGEST HUNT, THE ★★ A legendary gunfighter named Stark is hired by a wealthy Mexican landowner to bring back his rebellious son who has joined a gang of American bandits. Stark succeeds but a surprise awaits when he finds out the boy is not the landowner's son. A good story twist makes this an enjoyable film. Unrated; contains violence. 89m. **DIR:** Frank B. Corlish. **CAST:** Brian Kelly, Keenan Wynn, Erica Blanc, Fred Munroe, Virginia Field, Duane Rowland. **1968**

LONGHORN ★★★★ Rancher Bill Elliott tries to drive Herefords backward on the Oregon Trail to mate with Texas longhorns and form a tough new breed of cattle. Along the way he battles Indians, discontent cowhands, and a treacherous partner. The first, and possibly best, of Elliott's later Allied Artists films after leaving Republic where he'd starred in 34 Westerns over an eight-year period. B&W; 70m. **DIR:** Lewis D. Collins. **CAST:** William Elliott, Phyllis Coates, Myron Healey, John Hart. **1951**

LOVE ME TENDER ★★★ This Western drama takes place in Texas after the Civil War, with Elvis and his brother fighting over Debra Paget. The most distinguishing characteristic of this movie is the fact that it was Elvis's first film. Elvis fans will, of course, enjoy his singing the ballad "Love Me Tender." B&W; 89m. **DIR:** Robert D. Webb. **CAST:** Elvis Presley, Debra Paget, Richard Egan. **1956**

LUCKY BOOTS ★★ A map to a hidden treasure is concealed in Guinn "Big Boys" Williams's boot heel and everyone's after it. Low-budget independent starring Williams, who fared better as a sidekick. B&W; 59m. **DIR:** Albert Herman. **CAST:** Guinn Williams, Marion Shilling, Tom London. **1935**

LUCKY TEXAN ★★★ Gold miners John Wayne and Gabby Hayes strike it rich. But before they can cash in their claim, Hayes is falsely accused of robbery and murder. Of course, the Duke rides to his aid. Creaky, but fun for fans. B&W; 56m. **DIR:** Robert N. Bradbury. **CAST:** John Wayne, Barbara Sheldon, George "Gabby" Hayes. **1934**

LUST FOR GOLD ★★★½ Based on the true story of the Lost Dutchman mine, told in flashbacks and recounting the double dealings of Glenn Ford, Ida Lupino, and husband Gig Young as they plot against one another. B&W; 90m. **DIR:** S. Sylvan Simon. **CAST:** Glenn Ford, Ida Lupino, Edgar Buchanan, Will Geer, Gig Young. **1949**

LUSTY MEN, THE ★★★★ The world of rodeo cowboys is explored in this well-made film directed by cult favorite Nicholas Ray. Robert Mitchum has one of his best roles as a broken-down ex–rodeo star who gets a second chance at the big money by tutoring an egotistical newcomer on the circuit, well played by Arthur Kennedy. B&W; 113m. **DIR:** Nicholas Ray. **CAST:** Robert Mitchum, Susan Hayward, Arthur Kennedy, Arthur Hunnicutt. **1952**

MACHINE GUN KILLERS ★★ A falsely accused Union officer is given thirty days to prove that he was not the thief of a machine gun that ended up in Confederate hands. Tight direction and acting place this spaghetti Western a cut above. Rated PG. 98m. **DIR:** Paolo Bianchini. **CAST:** Robert Woods, John Ireland, Evelyn Stewart, Claudie Lange, Gerard Herter, Roberto Camardiel. **1968**

MACHO CALLAHAN ★★★ David Janssen convincingly portrays Macho Callahan, a man hardened by his confinement in a horrid Confederate prison camp. When he kills a man (David Carradine) over a bottle of champagne, the man's bride (Jean Seberg) seeks revenge. Rated R for violence and gore. 99m. **DIR:** Bernard Kowalski. **CAST:** David Janssen, Jean Seberg, Lee J. Cobb, James Booth, David Carradine, Bo Hopkins. **1970**

MACKENNA'S GOLD ★★ Disappointing "big" Western follows search for gold. Impressive cast cannot overcome a poor script and uninspired direction. 128m. **DIR:** J. Lee Thompson. **CAST:** Gregory Peck, Omar Sharif, Telly Savalas, Julie Newmar, Lee J. Cobb. **1969**

MADRON ★★½ You've heard of the spaghetti Western. Well here's an Israeli Western. The story involves a nun and a gunslinger who, after a typical wagon-train massacre, are chased by a band of Apaches. The actors are good, but the story is pedestrian. Rated PG. 93m. **DIR:** Jerry Hopper. **CAST:** Richard Boone, Leslie Caron, Paul Smith, Gabi Amrani. **1970**

MAGNIFICENT SEVEN, THE ★★★★ Japanese director Akira Kurosawa's *The Seven Samurai* served as the inspiration for this enjoyable Western, directed by John Sturges (*The Great Escape*). It's the rousing tale of how a group of American gunfighters come to the aid of a village of Mexican farmers plagued by bandits. 126m. **DIR:** John Sturges. **CAST:** Yul Brynner, Steve McQueen, Charles Bronson, James Coburn, Eli Wallach, Robert Vaughn. **1960**

MAJOR DUNDEE ★★★ This is a flawed but watchable Western directed with typical verve by Sam Peckinpah. The plot follows a group of Confederate prisoners who volunteer to go into Mexico and track down a band of rampaging Apache Indians. 124m. **DIR:** Sam Peckinpah. **CAST:** Charlton Heston, Richard Harris, James Coburn, Jim Hutton, Warren Oates, Ben Johnson. **1965**

MAN ALONE, A ★★★ Ray Milland's first directorial effort finds him hiding from a lynch mob in a small Western town. And who is he hiding with? The sheriff's daughter! Not too bad, as Westerns go. 96m. **DIR:** Ray Milland. **CAST:** Ray Milland, Mary Murphy, Ward Bond, Raymond Burr, Lee Van Cleef. **1955**

MAN AND BOY ★★½ Bill Cosby and his family try to make a go of it by homesteading on the prairie. The story provides ample opportunity for some Cosbyesque explanations about the black experience of that period. Rated G. 98m. **DIR:** E. W. Swackhamer. **CAST:** Bill Cosby, Gloria Foster, George Spell, Leif Erickson, Yaphet Kotto, Douglas Turner Ward, John Anderson, Henry Silva, Dub Taylor. **1971**

MAN CALLED HORSE, A ★★★ Richard Harris (in one of his best roles) portrays an English aristocrat who's enslaved and treated like a pack animal by Sioux Indians in the Dakotas. He loses his veneer of sophistication and finds the core of his manhood. This strong film offers an unusually realistic depiction of American Indian life. Rated PG. 114m. **DIR:** Elliot Silverstein. **CAST:** Richard Harris, Judith Anderson, Jean Gascon, Corinna Tsopei, Dub Taylor. **1970**

MAN CALLED NOON, THE ★★★★ The Louis L'Amour classic remains faithful to the book. A bounty hunter and a female rancher help Jubal Noon, a gunfighter with amnesia, unravel his identity while seeking vengeance for the deaths of his wife and child. Great photography, direction, and score make this one of the best. Rated R for violence. 90m. **DIR:** Peter Collinson. **CAST:** Richard Crenna, Stephen Boyd, Farley Granger, Rosanna Schiaffino, Patty Shepard. **1974**

MAN FROM COLORADO, THE ★★★ A great cast and solid performances elevate this post–Civil War psychological Western about a former northern colonel (Glenn Ford) who becomes a federal judge in Colorado. William Holden plays his friend. 99m. **DIR:** Henry Levin. **CAST:** Glenn Ford, William Holden, Ellen Drew, Ray Collins, Edgar Buchanan, Jerome Courtland, Denver Pyle. **1948**

MAN FROM LARAMIE, THE ★★★★½ Magnificent Western has James Stewart as a stranger who finds himself at odds with a powerful ranching family. The patriarch (Donald Crisp) is going blind, so the running of the ranch is left to his psychotic son (Alex Nicol) and longtime ranch foreman (Arthur Kennedy). Possibly the summit of director Anthony Mann's career; certainly Stewart's finest Western performance. 101m. **DIR:** Anthony Mann. **CAST:** James Stewart, Arthur Kennedy, Donald Crisp, Alex Nicol, Cathy O'Donnell, Jack Elam. **1955**

MAN FROM MONTEREY, THE ★★★ Swashbuckling action mixes with gunplay in this enjoyable Warner Bros. B Western set in Old California. American army officer John Wayne rides to the rescue of a Spanish aristocrat, while silent-screen veteran Francis Ford (brother of director John) adds class as the chief heavy. Luis Alberni provides a few chuckles in comic support. B&W; 57m. **DIR:** Mack V. Wright. **CAST:** John Wayne, Ruth Hall, Francis Ford, Donald Reed, Lafe McKee, Luis Alberni, Slim Whitaker. **1933**

MAN FROM MUSIC MOUNTAIN ★★★ Gene Autry thwarts unscrupulous land developers attempting to sell worthless mining stock. Routine. B&W; 54m. **DIR:** Joseph Kane. **CAST:** Gene Autry, Smiley Burnette, Carol Hughes, Sally Payne, Earl Dwire. **1938**

MAN FROM SNOWY RIVER, THE ★★★★ If you've been looking for an adventure film for the whole family, this Australian Western about the coming-of-age of a mountain man (Tom Burlinson) is it. Rated PG, the film has no objectionable material. 115m. **DIR:** George

Miller. **CAST:** Tom Burlinson, Kirk Douglas, Jack Thompson, Bruce Kerr. **1982**

MAN FROM THE ALAMO, THE ★★★½ This is an exciting, well-acted story of a soldier (Glenn Ford) who escapes from the doomed Alamo in an effort to warn others about Santa Ana's invasion of Texas. After the Alamo falls, he is branded a traitor and deserter and must prove his mettle to the Texicans. Historically inaccurate, but exciting and fun. 79m. **DIR:** Budd Boetticher. **CAST:** Glenn Ford, Julie Adams, Victor Jory, Chill Wills, Hugh O'Brian, Neville Brand. **1953**

MAN FROM UTAH, THE ★★ Low, low-budget Western with a very young John Wayne as a lawman going undercover to catch some crooks using a rodeo to bilk unsuspecting cowboys. The rodeo footage was used over and over again by the film company, Monogram Pictures, in similar films. B&W; 57m. **DIR:** Robert N. Bradbury. **CAST:** John Wayne, Polly Ann Young, George "Gabby" Hayes, Yakima Canutt, George Cleveland. **1934**

MAN IN THE SADDLE ★★★★ Insanely jealous Alexander Knox tries to run Randolph Scott off the range after Scott's former girl, Joan Leslie, decides to marry Knox. One of director André de Toth's best Westerns. Memorable for its prolonged well-staged fight between Scott and John Russell. 87m. **DIR:** André de Toth. **CAST:** Randolph Scott, Joan Leslie, John Russell, Alexander Knox, Ellen Drew, Cameron Mitchell. **1951**

MAN IN THE WILDERNESS ★★★½ Exciting outdoor adventure film follows the exploits of a trapper left for dead by his fellow hunters after a bear attack. Gritty film is beautifully filmed and acted. Rated R for violence. 105m. **DIR:** Richard C. Sarafian. **CAST:** Richard Harris, John Huston, John Bindon, Prunella Ransome, Henry Wilcoxon. **1971**

MAN OF ACTION ★★ Slow-going as Ranger Tim McCoy ferrets out a mysterious bank robber. B&W; 57m. **DIR:** George Melford. **CAST:** Tim McCoy, Wheeler Oakman, Walter Brennan. **1933**

MAN OF THE FOREST ★★★★ This is one of two very good Westerns made by Randolph Scott in a year that produced many fine films. Based on Zane Grey's novel, Scott plays a cowboy who kidnaps a young woman to keep her from the clutches of a bad guy. Zesty and action-packed. B&W; 62m. **DIR:** Henry Hathaway. **CAST:** Randolph Scott, Harry Carey, Buster Crabbe, Noah Beery Sr., Guinn Williams. **1933**

MAN OF THE FRONTIER (RED RIVER VALLEY) ★★½ This early entry in the Gene Autry series features Gene as an undercover agent out to stop a gang bent on sabotaging construction of a much-needed dam. Very enjoyable, and a nice example of the kind of film Autry could make but didn't have to after a while. B&W; 60m. **DIR:** B. Reeves "Breezy" Eason. **CAST:** Gene Autry, Smiley Burnette, Frances Grant. **1936**

MAN OF THE WEST ★★★★ Reformed outlaw Gary Cooper reluctantly falls in with former boss Lee J. Cobb to save innocent hostages from Cobb's gang. This tense, claustrophobic Western takes place almost entirely indoors. A minor classic. 100m. **DIR:** Anthony Mann. **CAST:** Gary Cooper, Lee J. Cobb, Julie London, Arthur O'Connell, Jack Lord, John Dehner. **1958**

MAN WHO LOVED CAT DANCING, THE [turkey] Burt Reynolds is wasted in this tale of a train robber. Rated PG. 114m. **DIR:** Richard C. Sarafian. **CAST:** Burt Reynolds, Sarah Miles, George Hamilton, Lee J. Cobb, Jack Warden. **1973**

MAN WHO SHOT LIBERTY VALANCE, THE ★★★★★ This release was director John Ford's bittersweet farewell to the Western. John Wayne reprises his role of the western man of action, this time with a twist. James Stewart's part could well be called *Mr. Smith Goes to Shinbone*, it draws so much on his most famous image. Combined with Ford's visual sense and belief in sparse dialogue, as well as fine ensemble playing in supporting roles, it adds up to a highly satisfying film. B&W; 119m. **DIR:** John Ford. **CAST:** John Wayne, James Stewart, Vera Miles, Lee Marvin, Edmond O'Brien, Woody Strode, Andy Devine, Strother Martin, Lee Van Cleef. **1962**

MAN WITHOUT A STAR ★★★ With charm, fists, and guns, foreman Kirk Douglas swaggers through this stock story of rival ranchers. Jeanne Crain is his beautiful boss; Claire Trevor is, as usual, a big-hearted saloon hostess. 89m. **DIR:** King Vidor. **CAST:** Kirk Douglas, Jeanne Crain, Claire Trevor, Richard Boone, Jack Elam, Mara Corday. **1955**

MARAUDERS ★★ Hopalong Cassidy and his two sidekicks take refuge in an abandoned church one rainy night and find a battle between a pious clergyman and mean-spirited Harry Cording. This later effort by William Boyd still packs the good-natured humor and action of the earlier entries, but the story is predictable. B&W; 63m. **DIR:** George Archainbaud. **CAST:** William Boyd, Andy Clyde, Rand Brooks, Ian Wolfe, Harry Cording, Earle Hodgins. **1947**

MARSHAL OF CEDAR ROCK ★★★ Marshal Rocky Lane lets a young man escape from prison in order to lead him to money the man apparently stole in a bank robbery. Instead, the trail leads him straight into a railroad land-grab swindle. B&W; 54m. **DIR:** Harry Keller. **CAST:** Allan "Rocky" Lane, Phyllis Coates, Roy Barcroft, William Henry, Robert Shayne, Eddy Waller. **1953**

MARSHAL OF CRIPPLE CREEK ★★★★ Last of the Republic Red Ryder series is one of the fastest-paced, most action-packed of the twenty-three they produced. The discovery of gold in Cripple Creek causes the boomtown to be overrun by a lawless element. B&W; 54m. **DIR:** R. G. Springsteen. **CAST:** Allan "Rocky" Lane, Robert Blake, Gene Roth, Trevor Bardette. **1947**

MARSHAL OF MESA CITY ★★★★ Outstanding series Western features George O'Brien as a retired lawman who rides into a town ruled by a corrupt sheriff (Leon Ames) and stays on to end his reign of terror. Excellent character development and plot twists. B&W; 62m. **DIR:** David Howard. **CAST:** George O'Brien, Virginia Vale, Leon Ames, Henry Brandon. **1939**

MASSACRE AT FORT HOLMAN (REASON TO LIVE...A REASON TO DIE, A) ★½ Spaghetti Western of marginal interest. Eight condemned men led by James Coburn get a chance to redeem themselves by overtaking a rebel fort. Plenty of action can't help the worn-out plot or Western clichés. Rated PG for violence and profanity. 90m. **DIR:** Tonino Valerii. **CAST:** James Coburn, Telly Savalas, Bud Spencer. **1984**

MAVERICK (TV SERIES) ★★★★ One of the best TV Western series, this tongue-in-cheek show starred James Garner and Jack Kelly as the Maverick brothers, Bret and Bart, and after Garner left, Roger Moore as British cousin Beau. The first two episodes to be released on video are classics. The superb "Shady Deal at Sunny Acres" preceded the similar *The Sting* by fifteen years, and has Bret and Bart outwitting corrupt banker John Dehner with the help of most of the series' semiregular shady characters (Efrem Zimbalist Jr., Richard Long, Diane Brewster, Leo Gordon, and Arlene Howell). "Duel at Sundown" features a young Clint Eastwood as a trigger-happy character who presages his Rowdy Yates from *Rawhide*. B&W; each. 49m. **DIR:** Leslie Martinson, Arthur Lubin. **CAST:** James Garner, Jack Kelly, Roger Moore, Clint Eastwood, Efrem Zimbalist Jr., Richard Long, Diane Brewster, John Dehner, Leo Gordon, Edgar Buchanan, Abby Dalton. **1958–1962**

MAVERICK ★★★★½ This hilarious and action-packed big-screen adaptation of the TV series features Mel Gibson as gambler and reluctant hero Bret Maverick. In an inspired casting move, James Garner, the first and most popular actor to play the title character, costars as a lawman who anticipates Maverick's every move. Sexy grafter Jodie Foster keeps our hero preoccupied in other ways, as this unlikely trio heads for a high stakes poker competition. It's great fun for Western fans, since a number of TV and movie cowboys make cameo appearances. Rated PG for violence. 129m. **DIR:** Richard Donner. **CAST:** Mel Gibson, Jodie Foster, James Garner, James Coburn, Graham Greene, Alfred Molina, Max Perlich, Leo Gordon, Danny Glover, Margot Kidder, Robert Fuller, Denver Pyle, Dennis Kimple, Bert Ramson, Doug McClure, Will Hutchins, Waylon Jennings. **1994**

MAVERICK QUEEN, THE ★★★ Sparks erupt when a Pinkerton detective works undercover at a Wyoming gambling hotel that is a hangout for an outlaw gang. Barbara Stanwyck is cast aptly as the beauty who owns the hotel and is caught between her jealous lover and the lawman. 90m. **DIR:** Joseph Kane. **CAST:** Barbara Stanwyck, Barry Sullivan, Scott Brady, Mary Murphy, Wallace Ford. **1955**

MCCABE AND MRS. MILLER ★★★★ Life in the turn-of-the-century Northwest is given a first-class treatment in director Robert Altman's visually perfect comedy-drama. Sparkling performances by Warren Beatty, as a small-town wheeler-dealer, and Julie Christie, as a whore with a heart that beats to the jingle of gold. Rated R. 121m. **DIR:** Robert Altman. **CAST:** Warren Beatty, Julie Christie, Shelley Duvall, Keith Carradine. **1971**

MCLINTOCK! ★★★½ This broad Western-comedy stars John Wayne as a prosperous rancher who attempts to keep the peace between settlers and landowners while fighting a war of his own with headstrong wife Maureen O'Hara. A bit overlong, the film still features some priceless scenes, including a classic confrontation between Wayne and a pushy Leo Gordon, and a hilarious, climactic battle of the sexes. 127m. **DIR:** Andrew V. McLaglen. **CAST:** John Wayne, Maureen O'Hara, Yvonne De Carlo, Patrick Wayne, Stefanie Powers, Jack Kruschen, Chill Wills, Jerry Van Dyke, Edgar Buchanan, Bruce Cabot, Perry Lopez, Michael Pate, Strother Martin, Leo Gordon, Robert Lowery, Hank Worden. **1963**

MEANEST MEN IN THE WEST, THE 🦃 Two episodes of the 1960s television series *The Virginian* edited together. 92m. **DIR:** Samuel Fuller, Charles S. Dubin. **CAST:** Charles Bronson, Lee Marvin, Lee J. Cobb, James Drury, Albert Salmi, Charles Grodin. **1962**

MELODY RANCH ★★½ The creative forces at Republic Studios decided to team Gene Autry with Jimmy Durante and Ann Miller, replace Smiley Burnette with Gabby Hayes, and pretend nothing was different. Venerable heavy Barton MacLane provides the menace as a local gangster intent on running honorary sheriff Gene Autry out of town, but there isn't enough action. B&W; 80m. **DIR:** Joseph Santley. **CAST:** Gene Autry, Jimmy Durante, Ann Miller, Barton MacLane, George "Gabby" Hayes. **1940**

MELODY TRAIL ★★½ The fifth Gene Autry–Smiley Burnette film is a pleasant story about a rodeo rider who loses his winnings and is forced to work for a rancher with a romantic daughter. B&W; 60m. **DIR:** Joseph Kane. **CAST:** Gene Autry, Smiley Burnette, Ann Rutherford. **1935**

MEXICALI ROSE ★★★★ Radio singer Gene Autry discovers the oil company sponsoring his radio show is involved in a stock promotion fraud. Among their victims is an orphanage run by a girl. One of Autry's best. B&W; 60m. **DIR:** George Sherman. **CAST:** Gene Autry, Smiley Burnette, Noah Beery Sr., William Farnum, Luana Walters. **1939**

MINUTE TO PRAY, A SECOND TO DIE, A ★★ This is a routine Western with Alex Cord as an outlaw trying to turn himself in when amnesty is declared by the governor of New Mexico (played by Robert Ryan). Arthur Kennedy, as the marshal, has other plans. Rated R for violence. 99m. **DIR:** Franco Giraldi. **CAST:** Alex Cord, Arthur Kennedy, Robert Ryan, Nicoletta Machiavelli. **1967**

MIRACLE RIDER, THE ★★½ Tom Mix plays a Texas Ranger and friend of the Indian in this sometimes slow but enjoyable pseudoscience-fiction serial. Charles Middleton plays Zaroff, leader of a gang who preys on the superstitions of the Indians in order to scare them off their reservation. After this, Mix retired from the screen. B&W; 12 chapters. **DIR:** Armand Schaefer, B. Reeves "Breezy" Eason. **CAST:** Tom Mix, Jean Gale, Charles Middleton, Jason Robards Sr., Edward Hearn. **1935**

MISSOURI BREAKS, THE ★★ For all its potential, this Western really lets you down. Jack Nicholson is acceptable as the outlaw trying to ply his trade. Marlon Brando, on the other hand, is inconsistent as a relentless bounty hunter. Rated PG. 126m. **DIR:** Arthur Penn. **CAST:** Marlon Brando, Jack Nicholson, Kathleen Lloyd, Harry Dean Stanton. **1976**

MISSOURIANS, THE ★★★★ A band of vicious killers, known as the Missourians, attempt to hide out in a town where the leader's Polish immigrant mother and brother live; only complicating matters for them as the town already holds malice against foreigners. Strong story line and good action make this one of Monte Hale's best. B&W; 60m. **DIR:** George Blair. **CAST:** Monte Hale, Paul Hurst, Roy Barcroft. **1950**

MR. HORN ★★★ *Mr. Horn* is a bittersweet, near-melancholy chronicle of the exploits of Horn (David Carradine), who is shown first as an idealistic young man helping an old-timer (Richard Widmark) track down Geronimo and later as a cynical gunman hired to eliminate some rustlers. 200m. **DIR:** Jack Starrett. **CAST:** David Carradine, Richard Widmark, Karen Black, Richard Masur, Jeremy Slate, Pat McCormick, Jack Starrett. **1979**

MOHAWK ★½ Cornball story about love between settler Scott Brady and Indian Rita Gam must have been inspired by access to footage from John Ford's classic *Drums Along the Mohawk*. 79m. **DIR:** Kurt Neumann. **CAST:** Scott Brady, Rita Gam, Neville Brand, Lori Nelson, Allison Hayes, Ted de Corsia. **1956**

MOJAVE FIREBRAND ★★★ Wild Bill Elliott helps old pal Gabby Hayes protect his silver mine from a lawless element. B&W; 56m. **DIR:** Spencer Gordon Bennet. **CAST:** William Elliott, George "Gabby" Hayes, Anne Jeffreys, LeRoy Mason. **1944**

MONTANA BELLE ★★½ Jane Russell plays notorious Belle Starr, the female bandit who rode with the Dalton Gang. As Western programmers go, this is not bad, but Jane in a blonde wig just doesn't cut it! Originally filmed in color, but video copies are in black and white. B&W; 81m. **DIR:** Allan Dwan. **CAST:** Jane Russell, George Brent, Scott Brady, Forrest Tucker. **1951**

MONTE WALSH ★★★½ Sad but satisfying Western about a couple of saddle pals (Lee Marvin, Jack Palance) attempting to make the transition to a new age and century. Cinematographer William Fraker made an impressive directorial debut with this fine film. Rated R for violence. 106m. **DIR:** William Fraker. **CAST:** Lee Marvin, Jack Palance, Jeanne Moreau, Mitchell Ryan, Jim Davis. **1970**

MORE WILD WILD WEST ★★½ This TV movie is a pale reminder of the irresistible original series. The Old West's most invincible secret service agents, James West and Artemus Gordon, again come out of retirement, this time to rescue the world from an invisibility plot. Jonathan Winters hams it up as the villainous Albert Paradine II. There's too much silly comedy, not enough excitement. 94m. **DIR:** Burt Kennedy. **CAST:** Robert Conrad, Ross Martin, Jonathan Winters, Harry Morgan, René Auberjonois, Liz Torres, Victor Buono, Dr. Joyce Brothers, Emma Samms. **1980**

MOUNTAIN MEN, THE 🦃 A buddy movie about two bickering fur trappers who get involved in Indian uprisings. Rated R. 102m. **DIR:** Richard Lang. **CAST:** Charlton Heston, Brian Keith, Victoria Racimo, Stephen Macht. **1980**

MULE TRAIN ★★½ Gene Autry helps a pal keep a valuable cement claim from crooked businessman, Bob Livingston. Classic song incorporated into a so-so plot with an actionless windup. Sidekick Pat Buttram and Shelia Ryan were real-life man and wife. B&W; 70m. **DIR:** John English. **CAST:** Gene Autry, Pat Buttram, Sheila Ryan, Robert Livingston, Gregg Barton. **1950**

MY DARLING CLEMENTINE ★★★★½ The epic struggle between good and evil is wrapped up in this classic retelling of the shoot-out at the O.K. Corral; between the Earps and the lawless Clanton family. Henry Fonda gives his Wyatt Earp a feeling of believability, perfectly matched by Walter Brennan's riveting portrayal of villainy as the head of the Clanton gang. B&W; 97m. **DIR:** John Ford. **CAST:** Henry Fonda, Victor Mature,

Walter Brennan, Linda Darnell, Ward Bond, Tim Holt. **1946**

MY HEROES HAVE ALWAYS BEEN COWBOYS ★★★★ The themes explored in Sam Peckinpah's *Junior Bonner* get a reworking in this surprisingly effective film about a rodeo bull rider (Scott Glenn) who comes home to heal his injuries and ends up rescuing his father (Ben Johnson) from a retirement home. Wonderful performances and strong character development even make up for the expected *Rocky*-style ending. Rated PG for brief profanity and violence. 106m. **DIR:** Stuart Rosenberg. **CAST:** Scott Glenn, Kate Capshaw, Ben Johnson, Tess Harper, Gary Busey, Mickey Rooney, Balthazar Getty, Clarence Williams III, Dub Taylor, Clu Gulager. **1991**

MY NAME IS NOBODY ★★★½ This is a delightful spoof of the Clint Eastwood spaghetti Westerns. Terence Hill is a gunfighter who worships old-timer Henry Fonda, who merely wishes to go away and retire. Rated PG. 115m. **DIR:** Tonino Valerii. **CAST:** Henry Fonda, Terence Hill, Leo Gordon, Geoffrey Lewis. **1974**

MY PAL, THE KING ★★★ Cowboy Tom Mix befriends boy king Mickey Rooney and teaches him the ways of the West. Mix's Wild West Show takes center stage for some entertaining passages, and cliff-hanger action keeps the story moving along. B&W; 74m. **DIR:** Kurt Neumann. **CAST:** Tom Mix, Mickey Rooney. **1932**

MY PAL TRIGGER ★★★½ One of the most fondly remembered and perhaps the best of all the Roy Rogers movies, this gentle story centers on Roy's attempts to mate his mare with a superb golden stallion. Villain Jack Holt is responsible for the death of the mare, and Roy is blamed and incarcerated. B&W; 79m. **DIR:** Frank McDonald. **CAST:** Roy Rogers, George "Gabby" Hayes, Dale Evans, Jack Holt. **1946**

MYSTERIOUS DESPERADO ★★★ Tim Holt's sidekick is heir to a large estate. Ruthless land grabbers have other plans for the property and frame Chito's cousin on a murder charge. B&W; 60m. **DIR:** Lesley Selander. **CAST:** Tim Holt, Richard Martin, Edward Norris, Robert Livingston. **1949**

MYSTERY MAN ★★★ Hopalong Cassidy and his pals foil an outlaw gang's attempt to rob a bank. For revenge, the gang steals Hoppy's cattle and turns him over to the sheriff as the real outlaw leader. The most action-packed of all the Cassidy series. B&W; 60m. **DIR:** George Archainbaud. **CAST:** William Boyd, Andy Clyde, Jimmy Rogers, Eleanor Stewart. **1944**

MYSTERY MOUNTAIN ★★ Cowboy great Ken Maynard stars in his only serial, the story of the mysterious master of disguise known as the "Rattler," who lives to wreck trains. Gene Autry and his silly sidekick Smiley Burnette make their second screen appearance in this chapterplay. B&W; 12 chapters. **DIR:** Otto Brewer, B. Reeves "Breezy" Eason. **CAST:** Ken Maynard, Verna Hillie, Syd Saylor, Gene Autry, Smiley Burnette. **1934**

MYSTERY OF THE HOODED HORSEMEN ★★½ One of Tex Ritter's most popular oaters. A group of night riders in dark hoods and cloaks add just a touch of the supernatural to an otherwise standard story of land greed and cattle conniving. B&W; 60m. **DIR:** Ray Taylor. **CAST:** Tex Ritter, Iris Meredith, Charles King, Forrest Taylor, Earl Dwire, Lafe McKee, Hank Worden, Joe Girard. **1937**

NAKED IN THE SUN ★★½ Osceola (James Craig), war chief of the Seminole Indians, must battle unscrupulous whites, the United States government, and his own tribe to live in dignity. This is well-acted and effective in evoking audience sympathy. 79m. **DIR:** R. John Hugh. **CAST:** James Craig, Barton MacLane, Lita Milan, Tony Hunter. **1957**

NAKED SPUR, THE ★★★★½ Superb Western finds bounty hunter James Stewart chasing bad guy Robert Ryan through the Rockies. Once captured, Ryan attempts to cause trouble between Stewart and his sidekicks. 91m. **DIR:** Anthony Mann. **CAST:** James Stewart, Janet Leigh, Robert Ryan, Ralph Meeker, Millard Mitchell. **1953**

NARROW TRAIL, THE ★★★ "Better a painted pony than a painted woman" was the slogan selling this above-average Western about a cowboy's love for his horse. One of early-Western star William S. Hart's many pictures, this one was something of a paean to his great horse, Fritz. Like all Hart films, this one is marked by his scrupulous attention to authenticity of setting, scenery, and costume. Silent. B&W; 56m. **DIR:** Lambert Hillyer. **CAST:** William S. Hart. **1917**

'NEATH ARIZONA SKIES ★★½ Formula B Western has John Wayne as the protector of the heir to rich oil lands, a little Indian girl. Of course, the baddies try to kidnap her and the Duke rides to the rescue. Low-budget and predictable. B&W; 57m. **DIR:** Henry Frazer. **CAST:** John Wayne, Sheila Terry, Yakima Canutt, George "Gabby" Hayes. **1934**

NEVADA SMITH ★★★ Steve McQueen, in the title role, is butcher's-freezer–cold, calculating, and merciless in this hard-hitting, gripping Western. The focus is on a senseless, vicious double murder and the revenge taken by the son of the innocent victims. Story and characters are excerpted from a section of Harold Robbins's sensational novel *The Carpetbaggers* not used in the 1964 film. 135m. **DIR:** Henry Hathaway. **CAST:** Steve McQueen, Karl Malden, Brian Keith, Arthur Kennedy, Suzanne Pleshette, Raf Vallone, Pat Hingle, Howard DaSilva, Martin Landau. **1966**

NEVADAN, THE ★★★½ Government agent Randolph Scott works undercover with outlaw Forrest Tucker to retrieve stolen gold. Originally filmed in color, only B&W prints seem to exist today. B&W; 81m. **DIR:** Gordon Douglas. **CAST:** Randolph Scott, Dorothy Malone, Forrest Tucker, George Macready, Jock Mahoney. **1950**

NEW FRONTIER ★★½ In a familiar plot, John Wayne is the son of a murdered sheriff out to find the baddies who did the dirty deed. Creaky but fun for fans. B&W; 59m. **DIR:** Carl Pierson. **CAST:** John Wayne, Muriel Evans, Mary McLaren, Murdock McQuarrie, Warner Richmond, Sam Flint, Earl Dwire. **1935**

NIGHT OF THE GRIZZLY, THE ★★★★ In order to maintain a peaceful standing in the rugged Old West, big Clint Walker must fight all the local bad guys (who should have known better) as well as a giant grizzly bear who moves in and out of camera range on a wheeled dolly. Nice outdoor sets and some good characterization help this no-frills family story. 102m. **DIR:** Joseph Pevney. **CAST:** Clint Walker, Martha Hyer, Ron Ely, Jack Elam. **1966**

NIGHT RIDERS, THE ★★½ The Three Mesquiteers (John Wayne, Ray Corrigan, and Max Terhune) make like Zorro by donning capes and masks to foil a villain's attempt to enforce a phony Spanish land grant. Good formula Western fun. B&W; 58m. **DIR:** George Sherman. **CAST:** John Wayne, Ray "Crash" Corrigan, Max Terhune, Doreen McKay, Ruth Rogers, Tom Tyler, Kermit Maynard. **1939**

NIGHT STAGE TO GALVESTON ★★ Old-fashioned actioner set in post–Civil War South finds Gene Autry and his buddy Pat Buttram working for a crusading newspaperman. This routine story is easy to watch and not too hard to forget. B&W; 61m. **DIR:** George Archainbaud. **CAST:** Gene Autry, Pat Buttram, Virginia Huston, Robert Livingston. **1952**

NIGHTTIME IN NEVADA ★★★ Remorse-ridden killer Grant Withers, to cover up a murder he committed sixteen years ago, plans to steal Roy Rogers's cattle to pay off and make amends to the dead man's daughter. B Western badman logic. B&W; 67m. **DIR:** William Witney. **CAST:** Roy Rogers, Andy Devine, Adele Mara, Grant Withers, Bob Nolan and the Sons of the Pioneers. **1948**

NINE LIVES OF ELFEGO BACA, THE ★★★ Robert Loggia, as the long-lived hero of the Old West, faces one of his most harrowing perils as he confronts scores of gunmen. Lots of action and fun for the whole family. Rated G. 78m. **DIR:** Norman Foster. **CAST:** Robert Loggia, Robert F. Simon, Lisa Montell, Nestor Paiva. **1958**

NORTH OF THE GREAT DIVIDE ★½ No-good Roy Barcroft is a greedy salmon cannery owner who overfishes the waters and forces the local Indians to go hungry or turn to a life of crime. Roy Rogers lacks the familiar support of Dale Evans, Gabby Hayes, or even Pat Brady. 67m. **DIR:** William Witney. **CAST:** Roy Rogers, Penny Edwards, Gordon Jones, Roy Barcroft. **1950**

NORTH TO ALASKA ★★★★ Rather than a typical John Wayne Western, this is a John Wayne Northern. It's a rough-and-tumble romantic comedy. Delightfully tongue-in-cheek, it presents the Duke at his two-fisted best. 122m. **DIR:** Henry Hathaway. **CAST:** John Wayne, Stewart Granger, Capucine, Fabian, Ernie Kovacs. **1960**

NORTHWEST TRAIL ★★★ Mountie Bob Steele uncovers a plot to rob the Canadian government by taking gold from an old mine and flying it across the border. 62m. **DIR:** Derwin Abrahams. **CAST:** Bob Steele, Joan Woodbury, John Litel. **1945**

OH! SUSANNA! ★★★ Gene Autry is mistaken for a bad man and must clear his name. B&W; 59m. **DIR:** Joseph Kane. **CAST:** Gene Autry, Smiley Burnette, Frances Grant. **1936**

OKLAHOMA KID, THE ★★★ Definitely one of the oddest of all major sagebrush sagas, this film, about a feared gunman (James Cagney) taking revenge on the men who hanged his innocent father, boasts a great cast of familiar characters as well as a musical interlude with Cagney singing "I Don't Want to Play in Your Yard" to the accompaniment of a honky-tonk piano and pair of six-shooters. A competent curio. B&W; 85m. **DIR:** Lloyd Bacon. **CAST:** James Cagney, Humphrey Bogart, Rosemary Lane, Donald Crisp, Charles Middleton, Ward Bond, Harvey Stephens. **1939**

OKLAHOMAN, THE ★★ Run-of-the-trail Western with Joel McCrea riding point to protect the rights of an outcast Indian against white-eyed crooks. 80m. **DIR:** Francis D. Lyon. **CAST:** Joel McCrea, Barbara Hale, Brad Dexter, Douglas Dick, Verna Felton. **1957**

OLD BARN DANCE, THE ★★ Typical Gene Autry hooey features the former railroad telegrapher as—what else?—a singing cowboy. He croons over the radio for a tractor company that's putting horse-dependent farmers and ranchers out of business. B&W; 60m. **DIR:** Joseph Kane. **CAST:** Gene Autry, Smiley Burnette, Helen Valkis, Sammy McKim, Ivan Miller, Roy Rogers. **1938**

OLD CORRAL ★★★ Sheriff Gene Autry pursues a group of singing bandits, the Sons of the Pioneers, and battles tommy gun-wielding gangsters in order to save a runaway lounge singer who witnessed a murder. Noteworthy as the B Western where Autry fights Roy Rogers and forces Rogers to yodel. B&W; 54m. **DIR:** Joseph Kane. **CAST:** Gene Autry, Smiley Burnette, Roy Rogers, Bob Nolan and the Sons of the Pioneers, Hope Manning, Lon Chaney Jr. **1936**

ON THE OLD SPANISH TRAIL ★★ This odd collaboration of Republic Studios contract players finds Roy Rogers sharing the screen with Tito Guizar and Estelita Rodriguez as they take on villainous Charles McGraw and his cohorts. 75m. **DIR:** William Witney. **CAST:** Roy Rogers, Tito Guizar, Jane Frazee, Andy Devine, Estelita Rodriguez, Charles McGraw. **1947**

ON TOP OF OLD SMOKY ★★ Gene Autry is reunited with old saddle pal Smiley Burnette in this familiar story of a singing cowpoke (Autry) who is mistaken for a Texas Ranger. B&W; 59m. **DIR:** George Archainbaud. **CAST:** Gene Autry, Smiley Burnette, Gail Davis, Sheila Ryan. **1953**

ONCE UPON A TIME IN THE WEST ★★★★★ This superb film is the only spaghetti Western that can be called a classic. A mythic tale about the coming of the railroad and the exacting of revenge with larger-than-life characters, it is a work on a par with the best by great American Western film directors. Like *The Wild Bunch*, it has a fervent—and well-deserved—cult following in America. Rated PG. 165m. **DIR:** Sergio Leone. **CAST:** Claudia Cardinale, Henry Fonda, Charles Bronson, Jason Robards Jr., Jack Elam, Woody Strode, Lionel Stander. **1969**

ONE-EYED JACKS ★★★★ Star Marlon Brando took over the reins of directing this Western from Stanley Kubrick midway through production, and the result is a terrific entry in the genre. Superb supporting performances help this beautifully photographed film about an outlaw seeking revenge on a double-dealing former partner. 141m. **DIR:** Marlon Brando. **CAST:** Marlon Brando, Karl Malden, Katy Jurado, Ben Johnson, Slim Pickens, Elisha Cook Jr. **1961**

100 RIFLES ★★ The picture stirred controversy over Raquel Welch's interracial love scene with Jim Brown. But at this point, who cares? We're left with a so-so Western yarn. Rated R. 110m. **DIR:** Tom Gries. **CAST:** Burt Reynolds, Raquel Welch, Jim Brown, Fernando Lamas, Dan O'Herlihy. **1969**

ONLY THE VALIANT ★★½ Cavalry captain Gregory Peck is saddled not only with problems with Native Americans but irritability among his own troops. Produced by Cagney Productions, this Western is predictable but entertaining. B&W; 105m. **DIR:** Gordon Douglas. **CAST:** Gregory Peck, Ward Bond, Barbara Payton, Gig Young. **1951**

OUT CALIFORNIA WAY ★★½ Monte Hale, a cowboy looking for work in Hollywood, comes to the attention of a movie producer. Hale's debut film. Guest Stars: Allan "Rocky" Lane, Roy Rogers, Dale Evans, Don Barry. 67m. **DIR:** Lesley Selander. **CAST:** Monte Hale, Adrian Booth, Robert Blake, John Dehner. **1946**

OUTCAST, THE ★★ Before he became disenchanted with acting and turned to still photography, John Derek made a number of mostly mediocre films, this one among them. In this standard Western, he fights to win his rightful inheritance. Justice prevails, of course, but you know that going in. B&W; 90m. **DIR:** William Witney. **CAST:** John Derek, Joan Evans, Jim Davis. **1954**

OUTLAW, THE ★★ This once-notorious Western now seems almost laughable. Jane Russell keeps her best attributes forward, but one wonders what Walter Huston and Thomas Mitchell are doing in this film. Only for those who want to know what all the fuss was about. 103m. **DIR:** Howard Hughes, Howard Hawks. **CAST:** Jane Russell, Walter Huston, Thomas Mitchell, Jack Buetel. **1943**

OUTLAW EXPRESS ★★ California Spanish land grants are being stolen from pony express riders. Bob Baker is a post office investigator sent to rout the raiders. B&W; 58m. **DIR:** George Waggner. **CAST:** Bob Baker, Don Barclay, LeRoy Mason, Carleton Young. **1938**

OUTLAW JOSEY WALES, THE ★★★★½ This Western, a masterpiece of characterization and action, is Clint Eastwood's best film as both an actor and director. Josey Wales (Eastwood) is a farmer whose family is murdered by Red Legs, a band of cutthroats who have allied themselves with the Union Army. Wales joins the Confederacy to avenge their deaths. After the war, everyone in his troop surrenders to the victorious Union except Wales. Rated PG. 135m. **DIR:** Clint Eastwood. **CAST:** Clint Eastwood, Sondra Locke, Chief Dan George, Bill McKinney, John Vernon, John Mitchum, John Russell. **1976**

OUTLAWS OF SONORA ★★½ A vicious outlaw captures his exact double: Bob Livingston of the Three Mesquiteers. When the outlaw leader then robs a bank and murders the banker, the other Mesquiteers believe their pal has turned killer. B&W; 56m. **DIR:** George Sherman. **CAST:** Robert Livingston, Ray "Crash" Corrigan, Max Terhune, Jack Mulhall. **1938**

OVERLAND STAGE RAIDERS ★★½ Louise Brooks made her last big-screen appearance in this series Western, which has the Three Mesquiteers investing in an airport used by gold miners to ship ore. Of course, our heroes must battle a group of crooks attempting to rob the shipments. B&W; 55m. **DIR:** George Sherman. **CAST:** John Wayne, Louise Brooks, Ray "Crash" Corrigan, Max Terhune. **1938**

OX-BOW INCIDENT, THE ★★★★½ One of the finest Westerns ever made, this thought-provoking drama stars Henry

Fonda and Harry Morgan as a pair of drifters who try to stop the lynching of three men (Dana Andrews, Anthony Quinn, and Francis Ford) who may be innocent. Seldom has the terror of mob rule been so effectively portrayed. B&W; 75m. **DIR:** William Wellman. **CAST:** Henry Fonda, Dana Andrews, Mary Beth Hughes, Anthony Quinn, William Eythe, Harry Morgan, Jane Darwell, Frank Conroy, Harry Davenport. **1943**

PAINTED DESERT, THE ★★½ The future Hopalong Cassidy, William Boyd, plays a foundling who grows up on the other side of the range from his ladylove and must decide between the family feud and the cattle or Helen Twelvetrees and the cattle. A young Clark Gable plays the dark cloud that is menacing the future of these two nice kids. B&W; 75m. **DIR:** Howard Higgin. **CAST:** William Boyd, Helen Twelvetrees, William Farnum, J. Farrell MacDonald, Clark Gable. **1931**

PAINTED STALLION, THE ★★ This history-bending serial finds Kit Carson, Davy Crockett, and Jim Bowie coming to the aid of Hoot Gibson as he leads a wagon train to Santa Fe. Lots of action and plot reversals. B&W; 12 chapters. **DIR:** William Witney, Ray Taylor. **CAST:** Ray "Crash" Corrigan, Hoot Gibson, Sammy McKim, Jack Perrin, Hal Taliaferro, Duncan Renaldo, LeRoy Mason, Yakima Canutt. **1937**

PALE RIDER ★★★½ Star-producer-director Clint Eastwood donned six-guns and a Stetson for the first time since the classic *The Outlaw Josey Wales* (1976) for this enjoyable Western. The star is a mysterious avenger who comes to the aid of embattled gold prospectors in the Old West. Rated R for violence and profanity. 113m. **DIR:** Clint Eastwood. **CAST:** Clint Eastwood, Michael Moriarty, Carrie Snodgress, Christopher Penn, Richard Dysart, Richard Kiel, John Russell. **1985**

PALS OF THE SADDLE ★★½ The Three Mesquiteers (John Wayne, Ray Corrigan, and Max Terhune) help a woman government agent (Doreen McKay) trap a munitions ring in this enjoyable B Western series entry. B&W; 60m. **DIR:** George Sherman. **CAST:** John Wayne, Ray "Crash" Corrigan, Max Terhune, Doreen McKay, Frank Milan, Jack Kirk. **1938**

PANCHO VILLA ★★ Telly Savalas plays the famous bandit to the hilt and beyond. Clint Walker runs guns for him. Chuck Connors postures as a stiff and stuffy military type. You'll soon see why the title role forever belongs to Wallace Beery. It all builds to a rousing head-on train wreck. Rated R. 92m. **DIR:** Eugenio Martin. **CAST:** Telly Savalas, Clint Walker, Chuck Connors, Anne Francis. **1972**

PARADISE CANYON ★★ A very young and sometimes awkward John Wayne stars in this low, low-budget Western as an undercover agent on the trail of counterfeiters (led by Yakima Canutt). For staunch Wayne and Western fans only. B&W; 59m. **DIR:** Carl Pierson. **CAST:** John Wayne, Marion Burns, Yakima Canutt, Reed Howes. **1935**

PAT GARRETT AND BILLY THE KID ★★★★½ Sam Peckinpah's last masterpiece—in this "Restored Director's Cut"—begins with a stunning, never-before-seen ten-minute credit sequence that finally puts the film in focus. Other restored sequences make sense of what happens later between the main characters, Pat Garrett (James Coburn) and Billy (Kris Kristofferson), and feature a who's who of character actors doing what they do best. You may have to buy this film from a mail-order house just to watch it, but it's well worth the cost. Rated R for violence, nudity, and profanity. 122m. **DIR:** Sam Peckinpah. **CAST:** James Coburn, Kris Kristofferson, Bob Dylan, Jason Robards Jr., Barry Sullivan, John Beck, Chill Wills, Slim Pickens, Katy Jurado, Harry Dean Stanton, Jack Elam, Luke Askew, Richard Bright, R. G. Armstrong, Matt Clark, Elisha Cook Jr., Dub Taylor. **1973**

PHANTOM OF THE PLAINS ★★★ A pompous, polished crook whose specialty is marrying wealthy women is about to dupe the duchess until Red Ryder steps in to expose his con game. B&W; 56m. **DIR:** Lesley Selander. **CAST:** William Elliott, Robert Blake, Alice Fleming, Ian Keith, Virginia Christine. **1945**

PHANTOM OF THE WEST ★★ This early sound serial featured a whole gallery of suspects to be the mysterious Phantom. Tom Tyler is looking for his father's murderer as well as disproving rumors that he is the hooded villain. Primitive but virile. B&W; 10 chapters. **DIR:** D. Ross Lederman. **CAST:** Tom Tyler, William Desmond, Tom Santschi. **1931**

PHANTOM RIDER ★★★ A doctor becomes the mysterious masked phantom rider to bring about justice for the Indians who are being threatened by outlaws. B&W; 12 chapters **DIR:** Spencer Gordon Bennet, Fred Brannon. **CAST:** Robert Kent, Peggy Stewart, LeRoy Mason, George J. Lewis. **1946**

PHANTOM THUNDERBOLT ★★½ The Thunderbolt Kid is hired by a town's citizens to round up a lawless gang. B&W; 63m. **DIR:** Alan James. **CAST:** Ken Maynard, Frances Dade, Bob Kortman. **1933**

PIONEER WOMAN ★★½ In this passable made-for-television movie, the trials and tribulations of homesteading in Wyoming during the 1860s are told through the point of view of a wife and mother. After her husband is killed, she must make the difficult decision about staying on or going back east. 78m. **DIR:** Buzz Kulik. **CAST:** Joanna Pettet, William Shatner, David Janssen, Lance LeGault, Helen Hunt. **1973**

PIRATES OF THE PRAIRIE ★★★ Deputy marshal Tim Holt is assigned to go undercover as a gunsmith and find out why vigilantes have been terrorizing the citizens of East Spencerville. Solid effort from director Howard Bretherton in a series that managed to maintain an impressive standard of quality for its entire run. B&W; 57m. **DIR:** Howard Bretherton. **CAST:** Tim Holt, Cliff Edwards, Roy Barcroft. **1942**

PLACE CALLED TRINITY, A 🦃 A gunfighting gambler and his brother, a Mormon preacher, have different ideas on how to spend their sizable inheritance, but first they have to find the bandits who stole it. This idiotic comedy-Western filmed in Spain shows why spaghetti Westerns got their undeserved reputation. Only for the easily entertained. Unrated. 97m. **DIR:** James London. **CAST:** Richard Harrison, Donal O'Brien, Anna Zinneman, Rick Boyd. **1972**

PLAINSMAN, THE ★★★ If you can imagine a scenario uniting George Custer, Wild Bill Hickok, Calamity Jane, and Abraham Lincoln and you're willing to suspend historical disbelief, you should enjoy this stylish Cecil B. DeMille shoot-'em-up. Gary Cooper as Wild Bill Hickok does his best to keep Charles Bickford from selling guns to the Indians. B&W; 113m. **DIR:** Cecil B. DeMille. **CAST:** Gary Cooper, Jean Arthur, Charles Bickford, George "Gabby" Hayes. **1936**

POKER ALICE ★★½ A nifty supporting cast outclasses Elizabeth Taylor in this poky TV movie. Liz seems bored playing a New Orleans gambler who travels to the Old West and wins a bordello in a poker game. 109m. **DIR:** Arthur Allan Seidelman. **CAST:** Elizabeth Taylor, Tom Skerritt, George Hamilton, Susan Tyrrell, Richard Mulligan, David Wayne. **1987**

PONY EXPRESS ★★★ Bigger than they were in life, Western legends Buffalo Bill Cody and Wild Bill Hickok battle stagecoach station owners and Cheyenne Indians to establish the short-lived but glamorous pony express mail route in the early 1860s. Rousing good action for the historical Western fan who doesn't check every fact. 101m. **DIR:** Jerry Hopper. **CAST:** Charlton Heston, Rhonda Fleming, Jan Sterling, Forrest Tucker. **1953**

PONY EXPRESS RIDER ★★★★ A young man joins the pony express to find those responsible for the murder of his father. Solid performances from a host of veteran Western character actors. 100m. **DIR:** Hal Harrison Jr. **CAST:** Stewart Peterson, Henry Wilcoxon, Buck Taylor, Joan Caulfield, Maureen McCormick, Ken Curtis, Slim Pickens, Dub Taylor, Jack Elam. **1976**

POSSE (1975) ★★ Sheriff Kirk Douglas uses his pursuit of bandit Burce Dern to boost his career. This disappointing message Western juxtaposes the evil of political ambition against the basic honesty of traditional law-breaking. 94m. **DIR:** Kirk Douglas. **CAST:** Kirk Douglas, Bruce Dern, James Stacy, Bo Hopkins, Luke Askew, David Canary, Alfonso Arau, Katherine Woodville, Mark Roberts. **1975**

POSSE (1993) ★★★★ A rip-snortin' Western with a twist. Black infantrymen desert their unit after the Spanish-American War, and their sadistic commanding officer goes after them. Mario Van Peebles and his men ride into town, and the tight-knit group finds itself headed for a showdown. Fine acting by an unusual cast and plenty of action (including a steamy love scene that caused rating problems) add up to a highly charged adventure. Rated R for violence, profanity, nudity, and simulated sex. 107m. **DIR:** Mario Van Peebles. **CAST:** Mario Van Peebles, Stephen Baldwin, Charles Lane, Tiny Lister Jr., Tone Loc, Big Daddy Kane, Billy Zane, Salli Richardson, Melvin Van Peebles, Richard Jordan, Blair Underwood, Pam Grier, Richard E. Grant, Isaac Hayes, Reginald Vel Johnson, Woody Strode. **1993**

POWDERKEG ★★ Mildly entertaining Western about two barnstorming adventurers (Rod Taylor and Dennis Cole) hired by a railroad owner to liberate a train taken hostage by a Mexican bandit. This was the pilot for the mid-Seventies TV series *The Bearcats.* 88m. **DIR:** Douglas Heyes. **CAST:** Rod Taylor, Dennis Cole, Fernando Lamas, Michael Ansara, Tisha Sterling, Luciana Paluzzi. **1976**

POWDERSMOKE RANGE ★★½ Despite its impressive all-star cast of Western players, *Powdersmoke Range* is just an average B Western. Its significance lies in it being the first film to feature William Colt MacDonald's Three Mesquiteers. 71m. **DIR:** Wallace Fox. **CAST:** Harry Carey, Hoot Gibson, Bob Steele, Tom Tyler, Guinn Williams, William Farnum, William Desmond. **1935**

PRAIRIE MOON ★★ Well-worn story about a promise to a dying man is shifted to Gene Autry's west and puts him in a position to care for a gangster's three children on his ranch. The kids are city-tough and cause no end of trouble, but by the end they have reformed (naturally) and help Gene and Smiley bring in a gang of rustlers. B&W; 58m. **DIR:** Ralph Straub. **CAST:** Gene Autry, Smiley Burnette, Shirley Deane, Tommy Ryan, David Gorcey. **1938**

PRAIRIE RUSTLERS ★★★ Buster Crabbe is accused of his outlaw cousin's crimes because of their dead-ringer resemblance. B&W; 56m. **DIR:** Sam Newfield. **CAST:** Buster Crabbe, Al St. John, Evelyn Finley, Karl Hackett. **1945**

PROUD AND THE DAMNED, THE ★★ Standard Western plot with a Latin accent results in a below-par account. The cast does a poor job, but the South American locales save this film from a lower rating. 94m. **DIR:**

Ferde Grofe Jr. **CAST:** Chuck Connors, Jose Greco, Cesar Romero, Aron Kincaid. **1973**

PROUD MEN ★★½ Routine father-and-son conflicts are given conviction by a strong cast, led by Charlton Heston and Peter Strauss in this made-for-cable Western. 94m. **DIR:** William A. Graham. **CAST:** Charlton Heston, Peter Strauss, Belinda Balaski. **1987**

PROUD REBEL, THE ★★★½ A post–Civil War sentimental drama about a Confederate veteran searching for a doctor who can cure his mute son. The principals in this one are excellent, the chemistry great. Well worth the watching, this was the ill-fated Alan Ladd's last "class" film. 103m. **DIR:** Michael Curtiz. **CAST:** Alan Ladd, Olivia de Havilland, David Ladd, Dean Jagger, Henry Hull. **1958**

PUBLIC COWBOY #1 ★★½ Singing cowboy Gene Autry battles modern-day rustlers who utilize airplanes. B&W; 59m. **DIR:** Joseph Kane. **CAST:** Gene Autry, Smiley Burnette, Ann Rutherford, William Farnum. **1937**

PURSUED ★★★ A cowboy, Robert Mitchum, searches for the murderer of his father in this taut, atmospheric Western. The entire cast is very good, and famed action director Raoul Walsh keeps things moving along at a brisk pace. B&W; 101m. **DIR:** Raoul Walsh. **CAST:** Robert Mitchum, Teresa Wright, Judith Anderson, Dean Jagger, Harry Carey Jr., Alan Hale Sr. **1947**

QUICK AND THE DEAD, THE ★★★★ This made-for-HBO Western is the third in a trilogy of high-class shoot-'em-ups adapted from the stories by Louis L'Amour for star Sam Elliott. He is marvelous as a grizzled frontiersman who comes to the aid of a family (headed by Tom Conti and Kate Capshaw) making its way across the American wilderness. 90m. **DIR:** Robert Day. **CAST:** Sam Elliott, Kate Capshaw, Tom Conti, Matt Clark, Kenny Morrison. **1987**

QUIGLEY DOWN UNDER ★★★★ In this rip-snorting adventure movie, Tom Selleck plays a sharpshooting American cowboy who travels to Australia in the 1860s to work for British rancher Alan Rickman. Old-fashioned Western that just as easily might have starred John Wayne or, in one of his mellower moods, Clint Eastwood. Fans of the genre should love it. Rated PG for light violence and nudity. 106m. **DIR:** Simon Wincer. **CAST:** Tom Selleck, Laura San Giacomo, Alan Rickman. **1990**

RACHEL AND THE STRANGER ★★★½ The leisurely paced Western is made easier to watch by a fine cast. William Holden's love for his wife Loretta Young finally comes to full blossom only after she is wooed by stranger Robert Mitchum. A nice story done with charm and class. B&W; 93m. **DIR:** Norman Foster. **CAST:** William Holden, Loretta Young, Robert Mitchum. **1948**

RADIO RANCH (MEN WITH STEEL FACES & PHANTOM EMPIRE) ★★½ Condensed version of popular science-fiction serial *Phantom Empire*, this sketchily tells the story of Gene Autry and his fight against scientists who want his Radio Ranch for the precious ore it contains, and his strange adventures in the underground city of Murania. Running about one-third the length of the original serial, this version takes less time to view but doesn't make quite as much sense as the 12-chapter serial. B&W; 80m. **DIR:** Otto Brewer, B. Reeves "Breezy" Eason. **CAST:** Gene Autry, Frankie Darro, Betsy King Ross, Dorothy Christy, Smiley Burnette. **1940**

RAGE AT DAWN ★★★★ Solid Western has granite-jawed Randolph Scott as an undercover agent out to trap the infamous Reno brothers (played with zest by Forrest Tucker, J. Carrol Naish, and Myron Healey). Scott takes time out to romance their pretty sister (Mala Powers) before bringing the boys to justice. 87m. **DIR:** Tim Whelan. **CAST:** Randolph Scott, Forrest Tucker, Mala Powers, J. Carrol Naish, Myron Healey, Edgar Buchanan. **1955**

RAINBOW VALLEY ★★★ A young John Wayne goes undercover to round up the outlaws who have been blocking the building of a road into the mining town of Rainbow Valley. In this breezy outing, Wayne works especially well with Gabby Hayes. B&W; 52m. **DIR:** Robert N. Bradbury. **CAST:** John Wayne, Lucille Brown, LeRoy Mason, George "Gabby" Hayes, Buffalo Bill Jr. **1935**

RAMROD ★★½ It's sheep versus cattle again in the Old West. Joel McCrea fights off Preston Foster's murderous cowhands and the increasingly amorous Veronica Lake. B&W; 94m. **DIR:** André de Toth. **CAST:** Veronica Lake, Joel McCrea, Ian McDonald, Charlie Ruggles, Preston Foster, Arleen Whelan, Lloyd Bridges, Donald Crisp. **1947**

RANCHO DELUXE ★★★ Two small-time cattle rustlers (Jeff Bridges, Sam Waterston) run afoul of lawmen almost as incompetent as they are. Raunchy but good-natured Western-comedy with slow stretches; look for country singer Jimmy Buffett in a small role. Rated R for nudity and profanity. 93m. **DIR:** Frank Perry. **CAST:** Jeff Bridges, Sam Waterston, Elizabeth Ashley, Clifton James, Slim Pickens, Harry Dean Stanton, Patti D'Arbanville. **1975**

RANCHO NOTORIOUS ★★★½ Brooding revenge Western is a curio of the 1950s, one of those films that appears to mean something more than what the action implies. This film, while not a great Western, is fun to watch and a treat for Marlene Dietrich fans. 89m. **DIR:** Fritz Lang. **CAST:** Marlene Dietrich, Arthur Kennedy, Mel Ferrer, Lloyd Gough, William Frawley, Gloria Henry, Jack Elam, George Reeves. **1952**

RANDY RIDES ALONE ★★★ John Wayne stars in this enjoyable B Western as a lawman who goes undercover to catch a gang that has been robbing an express office. The opening is particularly good. B&W; 60m. **DIR:** Henry Frazer. **CAST:** John Wayne, Alberta Vaughan, George "Gabby" Hayes, Earl Dwire, Yakima Canutt. **1934**

RANGE DEFENDERS ★★★ Cattlemen try to rid the range of sheep at all costs. The Three Mesquiteers settle the feud. Certainly nothing new, but well-done. B&W; 54m. **DIR:** Mack V. Wright. **CAST:** Robert Livingston, Ray "Crash" Corrigan, Max Terhune, Eleanor Stewart, Harry Woods. **1937**

RANGE FEUD ★★★★ It's *Romeo and Juliet* on the range as lawman Buck Jones tries to keep the peace between two feuding ranchers whose offspring have fallen in love. A gangly John Wayne does just fine as the youthful hero in another better-than-B Western from the great Buck Jones. B&W; 64m. **DIR:** D. Ross Lederman. **CAST:** Buck Jones, John Wayne, Susan Fleming, Harry Woods, Glenn Strange. **1931**

RANGE WAR ★★½ Hopalong Cassidy (William Boyd) rounds up a gang that is trying to stop construction on the railroad. Lesser entry in the Cassidy series. Britt Wood is no replacement for George "Gabby" Hayes or Andy Clyde, who was yet to come. B&W; 64m. **DIR:** Lesley Selander. **CAST:** William Boyd, Russell Hayden, Britt Wood. **1939**

RANGER AND THE LADY, THE ★★½ Buckskin-clad Roy Rogers is a Texas Ranger trying to clear up some trouble on the old Santa Fe Trail in the days before the Civil War. Fetching Jacqueline Wells plays the lady leading a wagon train to Texas. B&W; 59m. **DIR:** Joseph Kane. **CAST:** Roy Rogers, George "Gabby" Hayes, Jacqueline Wells, Harry Woods, Henry Brandon, Noble Johnson, Yakima Canutt, Art Dillard. **1940**

RARE BREED, THE (1966) ★★★ This is a generally rewarding Western. Jimmy Stewart is a Texas cattle rancher who grudgingly assists an Englishwoman's (Maureen O'Hara) attempts to introduce a new line of short-horned cattle to the Texan range. The story is quite original and holds one's interest throughout. 108m. **DIR:** Andrew V. McLaglen. **CAST:** James Stewart, Maureen O'Hara, Brian Keith, Juliet Mills, Jack Elam, Ben Johnson. **1966**

RATTLER KID 🦃 An unjustly accused army officer escapes prison and turns to a life of crime. Believing his own press clippings, he thinks of himself as a legendary outlaw. An unbelievable story line makes this one of the worst of the spaghetti Westerns. Unrated; contains violence. 87m. **DIR:** Leon Klimovsky. **CAST:** Richard Wyler, Brad Harris, Femi Benussi, William Spolt. **1968**

RAWHIDE (1938) ★★ Lou Gehrig in a Western? Yes, the Pride of the Yankees made one sagebrush adventure in support of former bandleader Smith Ballew. Gehrig plays a rancher at constant odds with the badmen and Ballew plays the two-fisted young lawyer who helps to organize the honest folk. Ballew is a rather bland lead, but the presence of Gehrig makes this one worth a watch. B&W; 58m. **DIR:** Ray Taylor. **CAST:** Smith Ballew, Lou Gehrig, Lafe McKee, Evalyn Knapp. **1938**

RAWHIDE (1951) ★★★ Sturdy Western concerns an outlaw gang holding hostages at a remote stagecoach station. Veteran director Henry Hathaway knows how to keep things clicking right along; the final shootout is electrifying. A good cast keeps this one on target. 86m. **DIR:** Henry Hathaway. **CAST:** Tyrone Power, Susan Hayward, Dean Jagger, Hugh Marlowe, Jack Elam, Edgar Buchanan, Jeff Corey, George Tobias. **1951**

RAWHIDE (TV SERIES) ★★★★ One of TV's best written and directed Western series. The theme of the show was the long cattle drive from Texas to Kansas, but it was the wide variety of people that trail boss Gil Favor and his drovers encountered along the way that gave the series its momentum. B&W; Several volumes; two one-hour episodes **DIR:** Charles Marquis Warren. **CAST:** Eric Fleming, Clint Eastwood, Sheb Wooley, Paul Brinegar. **1959–1966**

RED-HEADED STRANGER, THE ★★★ Willie Nelson's country "opera" served as the basis for this little-seen Western which most fans of the genre will enjoy. Nelson plays a right-thinking preacher who takes on an evil family (headed by Royal Dano) that is terrorizing the townspeople of this new parish. Rated R for violence and profanity. 105m. **DIR:** William Witliff. **CAST:** Willie Nelson, R. G. Armstrong, Morgan Fairchild, Royal Dano, Katharine Ross. **1986**

RED RIVER ★★★★★ After seeing this Western, directed by Howard Hawks, John Ford remarked, "I didn't know the big lug could act." The "big lug" he was referring to was the picture's star, John Wayne, whom Ford had brought to stardom in 1939's *Stagecoach.* This shoot-'em-up adaptation of *Mutiny on the Bounty* definitely features Wayne at his best in the role of a tough rancher making a historic cattle drive. B&W; 133m. **DIR:** Howard Hawks. **CAST:** John Wayne, Montgomery Clift, Walter Brennan, Joanne Dru, John Ireland, Noah Beery Jr., Paul Fix, Coleen Gray, Harry Carey, Harry Carey Jr. **1948**

RED RIVER RANGE ★★½ When entire herds of cattle begin disappearing from the Red River range, the Three Mesquiteers are called in to solve the mystery. John Wayne's presence makes it worth watching for fans. B&W; 59m. **DIR:** George Sherman. **CAST:** John

Wayne, Ray "Crash" Corrigan, Max Terhune, Polly Moran, Kirby Grant. **1938**

RED RIVER RENEGADES ★★★½ Postal inspector Sunset Carson sets out to stop a series of mail robberies on the Red River stage line. He is helped and hindered by a female Pinkerton agent. B&W; 55m. **DIR:** Thomas Carr. **CAST:** Sunset Carson, Peggy Stewart, Tom London. **1946**

RED RIVER SHORE ★★★½ Marshall Rex Allen is forced to kill a crooked businessman but vows to keep the man's guilt a secret. When the man's son arrives, trouble develops over the dead man's bogus oil-drilling operation. B&W; 54m. **DIR:** Harry Keller. **CAST:** Rex Allen, Slim Pickens, Douglas Fowley, Bill Phipps. **1953**

RED SUN ★★½ All-star, fitfully entertaining Western has an interesting premise—samurai vs. cowboys—but ultimately wastes the considerable talents of the great Japanese actor Toshiro Mifune. Charles Bronson has another of those offbeat-character parts that he underplays into a leading role. Rated PG. 112m. **DIR:** Terence Young. **CAST:** Charles Bronson, Alain Delon, Toshiro Mifune, Ursula Andress, Capucine. **1972**

RENEGADE GIRL ★★½ Ann Savage plays a free-thinking, vixen leader of a band of Confederate raiders. She tragically falls in love with the Union soldier stalking her. B&W; 65m. **DIR:** William Berke. **CAST:** Ann Savage, Alan Curtis, Russell Wade, Jack Holt, Ray "Crash" Corrigan, John King. **1946**

RENEGADE RANGER ★★★★ Star George O'Brien and director David Howard made some of the finest series Westerns in the Thirties and Forties. O'Brien, a member of director John Ford's stock company since starring in the classic *Iron Horse*, is in top form as a Texas Ranger who is assigned to bring in a female bandit (Rita Hayworth) accused of murder. B&W; 60m. **DIR:** David Howard. **CAST:** George O'Brien, Rita Hayworth, Tim Holt, Ray Whitley. **1938**

RENEGADE TRAIL ★★★ Hopalong Cassidy helps a woman and her son save the day when their cattle are the target of the woman's outlaw ex-husband and the boy's father whom he thinks died a hero. Bit slower than most of the Hoppy series. B&W; 61m. **DIR:** Lesley Selander. **CAST:** William Boyd, George "Gabby" Hayes, Russell Hayden, Roy Barcroft, Sonny Bupp. **1939**

RESTLESS BREED, THE 🦃 B Western murdered-father/son-takes-revenge plot. 86m. **DIR:** Allan Dwan. **CAST:** Scott Brady, Anne Bancroft, Jay C. Flippen, Jim Davis. **1957**

RETURN OF A MAN CALLED HORSE, THE ★★★ *The Return of a Man Called Horse* is every bit as good as its predecessor, *A Man Called Horse*. Both films present an honest, and sometimes shocking, glimpse at the culture of the American Indian. The new film picks up with a bored and unhappy Morgan deciding to return to America. Rated PG for violence. 129m. **DIR:** Irvin Kershner. **CAST:** Richard Harris, Gale Sondergaard, Geoffrey Lewis, Bill Lucking, Jorge Luke, Enrique Lucero. **1976**

RETURN OF FRANK JAMES, THE ★★★ Gene Tierney made her film debut in this inevitable sequel to *Jesse James* (1939). Henry Fonda reprises his role as brother Frank and attempts to avenge Jesse's death at the hands of "dirty little coward" Bob Ford, played by John Carradine. Thanks to Fonda's fine acting and Fritz Lang's sensitive direction, what could have been a pale rip-off is an enjoyable Western. 92m. **DIR:** Fritz Lang. **CAST:** Henry Fonda, Gene Tierney, Donald Meek, John Carradine, Jackie Cooper, J. Edward Bromberg, Henry Hull. **1940**

RETURN OF JESSE JAMES, THE ★★½ In this low-budget oater, John Ireland portrays a small-time outlaw who bears a striking resemblance to Jesse James. Taking advantage of this rumor, he sets out to prove to everyone that Jesse James, shot and killed by fellow gang member Bob Ford, did not die and is still in business. Plodding, but fairly well acted. B&W; 75m. **DIR:** Arthur Hilton. **CAST:** John Ireland, Ann Dvorak, Hugh O'Brian, Henry Hull. **1950**

RETURN OF JOSEY WALES ★★ The name is the only similarity between Clint Eastwood's *The Outlaw Josey Wales* and this mediocre Western. Wanted man Wales stands up to a crooked Mexican sheriff. Rated R for a rape scene and violence. 90m. **DIR:** Michael Parks. **CAST:** Michael Parks. **1986**

RETURN OF THE BADMEN ★★★ Randolph Scott has his hands full in this routine Western. No sooner does he settle down in Oklahoma than he must slap leather with Billy the Kid, the Dalton gang, the Younger brothers, and the Sundance Kid. As the latter, Robert Ryan shore ain't the appealing gun hand who rode with Butch Cassidy. B&W; 90m. **DIR:** Ray Enright. **CAST:** Randolph Scott, Anne Jeffreys, Robert Ryan, George "Gabby" Hayes, Lex Barker. **1948**

RETURN OF THE LASH ★★ Stop us if you've seen this one before: two marshals step into a range war caused by outlaws who want the land because a railroad is coming through. B&W; 55m. **DIR:** Ray Taylor. **CAST:** Lash LaRue, Al St. John. **1947**

RETURN OF THE SEVEN ★★½ This drab, inferior sequel to *The Magnificent Seven* follows Yul Brynner doing what he does best, getting six Yankee gunfighters fool enough to take on scores of Mexican bandits for no pay at all. 96m. **DIR:** Burt Kennedy. **CAST:** Yul Brynner, Robert Fuller, Warren Oates, Claude Akins, Emilio Fernandez, Jordan Christopher. **1966**

RETURN TO LONESOME DOVE ★★★★ Sequel to the milestone miniseries lacks the quirky, bawdy qualities of its predecessor—the pigs and the "pokes," for example—but there is much for Western fans to enjoy in this sprawling epic. Captain Call (Jon Voight) and his son Newt (Rick Schroder) become involved in a range war. Unrelated to author Larry McMurtry's own continuation of the story, *Streets of Laredo*. 330m. **DIR:** Mike Robe. **CAST:** Jon Voight, Barbara Hershey, Rick Schroder, Lou Gossett Jr., William L. Petersen, Oliver Reed, Dennis Haysbert, Reese Witherspoon, Timothy Scott, Chris Cooper, C.C.H. Pounder, Nia Peeples, William Sanderson. **1993**

RETURN TO SNOWY RIVER, PART II ★★★★½ In this spectacular sequel to *The Man from Snowy River*, Tom Burlinson returns to right wrongs and romance Sigrid Thornton in rugged, Old West-style Australia. Director Geoff Burrowes, who produced the first film, outdoes the original at every turn. A movie the whole family can love. Rated PG for some violence. 100m. **DIR:** Geoff Burrowes. **CAST:** Tom Burlinson, Sigrid Thornton, Brian Dennehy, Nicholas Eadie, Bryan Marshall. **1988**

RIDE BEYOND VENGEANCE ★★ A buffalo hunter, branded by three badmen, sets out for revenge. A great cast, savage brutality, and sexual innuendo aren't able to save this adult Western from being a waste of time. 100m. **DIR:** Bernard McEveety. **CAST:** Chuck Connors, Michael Rennie, Kathryn Hays, Gary Merrill, Claude Akins, Gloria Grahame, Bill Bixby, Joan Blondell, James MacArthur, Ruth Warrick, Arthur O'Connell. **1966**

RIDE 'EM COWGIRL ★★ Singing cowgirl Dorothy Page and her horse Snowy battle the bad guys who bilked her father out of $5,000. The concept seems designed to prove that a woman can rope, ride, and yodel as well as any cowboy. Well, in this case, they were wrong. 52m. **DIR:** Samuel Diege. **CAST:** Dorothy Page, Milton Frome, Vince Barnett. **1939**

RIDE HIM COWBOY ★★½ Thanks to the unfunny antics of would-be comic relief Harry Gribbon and the belief-stretching feats of Duke, the miracle horse, John Wayne's first B Western for Warner Bros. has much less to recommend it than his later outings. Even the plot, in which a town is terrorized by a masked rider and his gang, is more melodramatic and simplistic than usual. B&W; 56m. **DIR:** Fred Allen. **CAST:** John Wayne, Ruth Hall, Henry B. Walthall, Otis Harlan, Harry Gribbon, Frank Hagney, Lafe McKee. **1932**

RIDE IN THE WHIRLWIND 🦃 Throwaway Western with good cast goes nowhere in the muddled story of three riders wrongfully pursued by an unrelenting posse. 83m. **DIR:** Monte Hellman. **CAST:** Jack Nicholson, Cameron Mitchell, Millie Perkins, Harry Dean Stanton, Rupert Crosse. **1965**

RIDE LONESOME ★★★★½ Lawman Randolph Scott competes with two bounty hunters for possession of outlaw James Best. Well written by Burt Kennedy; superbly acted under the able direction of Budd Boetticher, who directed Scott in some of the best Westerns made in the 1950s. 73m. **DIR:** Budd Boetticher. **CAST:** Randolph Scott, Pernell Roberts, Karen Steele, Lee Van Cleef, James Coburn, James Best. **1959**

RIDE, RANGER, RIDE ★★½ Texas Ranger Gene Autry works undercover to stop Comanches from looting ammunition-laden wagon trains. Film debut of Max Terhune, who soon starred in Three Mesquiteer Westerns. B&W; 54m. **DIR:** Joseph Kane. **CAST:** Gene Autry, Smiley Burnette, Kay Hughes, Monte Blue, Max Terhune. **1936**

RIDE THE HIGH COUNTRY ★★★★½ Joel McCrea and Randolph Scott play two old-time gunslingers who team up to guard a gold shipment. McCrea just wants to do a good job so he can "enter (his) house justified." Scott, on the other hand, cares nothing for noble purpose and tries to steal the gold. From that point on, they are friends no longer. The result is a picture so good that McCrea and Scott decided to retire after making it—both wanted to go out with a winner. 94m. **DIR:** Sam Peckinpah. **CAST:** Joel McCrea, Randolph Scott, Warren Oates, R. G. Armstrong, Mariette Hartley, John Anderson, James Drury, L. Q. Jones, Edgar Buchanan. **1962**

RIDE THE MAN DOWN ★★ A Western shot in the traditional manner. A ranch manager fights to keep the property out of the greedy hands of land grabbers. 90m. **DIR:** Joseph Kane. **CAST:** Brian Donlevy, Rod Cameron, Ella Raines, Chill Wills, Jack LaRue. **1952**

RIDER FROM TUCSON ★★★ Tim Holt is a rodeo star who aids an old friend whose gold strike is the target of claim jumpers. B&W; 60m. **DIR:** Lesley Selander. **CAST:** Tim Holt, Richard Martin, Elaine Riley, Douglas Fowley, Veda Ann Borg, Robert Shayne. **1950**

RIDERS FOR JUSTICE ★★★ Late-in-the-run Three Mesquiteers entry benefits from no-nonsense direction from John English, a relatively straightforward story, and the charisma of Western-film veterans Tom Tyler and Bob Steele. This time, our heroes are out to foil a gang of bank robbers who are implicating innocent men. Retitled from *Westward Ho* to *Riders for Justice* for release to television so as not to conflict with the John Wayne Western of the same name. B&W; 56m. **DIR:** John English. **CAST:** Tom Tyler, Bob Steele, Rufe Davis, Evelyn Brent, Donald Curtis, Kenne Duncan. **1942**

RIDERS OF DEATH VALLEY ★★★½ Dick Foran and his pals Buck Jones and Leo Carrillo head a group of men organized to police the mining districts and to fight it out with the thieves and murderers that flocked to the gold claims. A fine serial. B&W; 15 chapters. **DIR:** Ford Beebe, Ray Taylor. **CAST:** Dick Foran, Buck Jones, Leo Carrillo, Charles Bickford, Lon Chaney Jr., Noah Beery Jr., Guinn Williams, Monte Blue, Glenn Strange. **1941**

RIDERS OF DESTINY ★★★ The earliest low, low-budget John Wayne B Western available on tape, this casts an extremely young-looking Duke as Singin' Sandy, an undercover agent out to help ranchers regain their water rights. Fun for fans of the star. B&W; 50m. **DIR:** Robert N. Bradbury. **CAST:** John Wayne, Cecilia Parker, George "Gabby" Hayes, Forrest Taylor, Al St. John, Heinie Conklin, Earl Dwire. **1933**

RIDERS OF THE BLACK HILLS ★★★ Just before the richest horse race of the year, an illustrious Thoroughbred is kidnapped in a daring train robbery. The Three Mesquiteers ride to the rescue. B&W; 54m. **DIR:** George Sherman. **CAST:** Robert Livingston, Ray "Crash" Corrigan, Max Terhune. **1938**

RIDERS OF THE DEADLINE ★★ Hopalong Cassidy pretends to befriend a smuggler in order to smoke out the real boss of the bad guys, who turns out to be the local banker. Routine stuff, but better than the later films in the series and superior to many programmers of the time. B&W; 70m. **DIR:** Lesley Selander. **CAST:** William Boyd, Andy Clyde, Jimmy Rogers, Richard Crane, Robert Mitchum. **1943**

RIDERS OF THE RIO GRANDE ★★★★ The last in an eight-year string of Three Mesquiteers Westerns is one of the best. Involved plot line has the Mesquiteers mistaken for the Cherokee Boys, a trio of outlaws. Plenty of action and a tongue-in-cheek story that often spoofs the genre without belittling it. B&W; 55m. **DIR:** Howard Bretherton. **CAST:** Bob Steele, Tom Tyler, Jimmie Dodd, Edward Van Sloan, Rick Vallin, Roy Barcroft, Charles King. **1943**

RIDERS OF THE ROCKIES ★★½ Entertaining Tex Ritter Western finds the two-fisted singer joining a gang of rustlers in order to get the goods on them. Silent comedian Snub Pollard plays his comic sidekick. One of Ritter's best Westerns. B&W; 56m. **DIR:** Robert N. Bradbury. **CAST:** Tex Ritter, Louise Stanley, Charles King, Snub Pollard, Yakima Canutt. **1937**

RIDERS OF THE WHISTLING PINES ★★★½ Framed as a timberland killer and cattle poisoner, Gene Autry fights to prove his innocence and save the woodlands for the Forestry Department. B&W; 70m. **DIR:** John English. **CAST:** Gene Autry, Patricia White, Jimmy Lloyd, Clayton Moore. **1949**

RIDERS OF THE WHISTLING SKULL ★★★ The Three Mesquiteers gallop into one of their best adventures. They brave Indians and ghostly goings-on to find a fabled lost city and its fabulous treasure. An eerie story, and the easy camaraderie of the three saddle pals makes this outdoor adventure one of the most popular in the series. B&W; 58m. **DIR:** Mack V. Wright. **CAST:** Robert Livingston, Ray "Crash" Corrigan, Max Terhune, Mary Russell, Yakima Canutt, C. Montague Shaw, Chief Thundercloud. **1937**

RIDIN' DOWN THE TRAIL ★★ Crooked cattle buyers fool the townspeople—yet again! It takes Jimmy Wakely to smoke out the culprits. Less music, more plot than usual for a Wakely Western. B&W; 53m. **DIR:** Howard Bretherton. **CAST:** Jimmy Wakely, Dub Taylor, Douglas Fowley. **1947**

RIDIN' ON A RAINBOW ★★ Investigation of a bank robbery leads Gene Autry to a showboat where teenaged Mary Lee's father is implicated in the holdup. Features Oscar-nominated song, "Be Honest With Me." B&W; 79m. **DIR:** Lew Landers. **CAST:** Gene Autry, Smiley Burnette, Mary Lee, Carol Adams, Byron Foulger. **1941**

RIDING TORNADO, THE ★★★ A strong series entry for Tim McCoy. He's a wandering cowboy hired by rancher Shirley Grey, whose cattle are being systematically stolen. Of course, our hero sets things right. B&W; 64m. **DIR:** D. Ross Lederman. **CAST:** Tim McCoy, Shirley Grey. **1932**

RIFLEMAN, THE (TV SERIES) ★★★½ Created by Sam Peckinpah, this sometimes brutal, sometimes touching Western series starred brawny Chuck Connors as the rifle-toting rancher, Lucas McCain. A widower, McCain raises his young son, Mark (Johnny Crawford), as best he can, while frequently being called upon by Marshal Micah Torrance (Paul Fix) to help keep the peace in the town of Northfork, New Mexico. The early episodes are the best. B&W; 30m. **DIR:** Various. **CAST:** Chuck Connors, Johnny Crawford, Paul Fix, Joan Taylor, Patricia Blair. **1958–1963**

RIM OF THE CANYON ★★★½ Gene Autry in a dual role as a marshal who corrals a gang of stagecoach bandits and as his son who faces the same gang twenty years later in a ghost town showdown. Supernatural overtones give this one a different twist. B&W; 70m. **DIR:** John English. **CAST:** Gene Autry, Nan Leslie, Jock Mahoney, Alan Hale Jr., Thurston Hall. **1949**

RIMFIRE ★★★ Better-than-average B Western has federal agent James Millican looking for stolen gold. He's aided in his search by the ghost of a gambler who was unjustly hanged for cheating! 64m. **DIR:** B. Reeves "Breezy" Eason. **CAST:** James Millican, Mary Beth Hughes, Reed Hadley, Henry Hull, Fuzzy Knight, Jason Robards Sr., Glenn Strange. **1949**

RIO BRAVO ★★★★½ A super-Western, with John Wayne, Walter Brennan, Ward Bond, Ricky Nelson (aping Montgomery Clift's performance in *Red River*), and the scene-stealing Dean Martin taking on cattle baron John Russell, who's out to get his kill-crazy brother (Claude Akins) out of jail. 141m. **DIR:** Howard Hawks. **CAST:** John Wayne, Walter Brennan, Ward Bond, Ricky Nelson, Dean Martin, John Russell, Claude Akins, Angie Dickinson, Bob Steele. **1959**

RIO CONCHOS ★★★ Rip-roaring Western action ignites this briskly paced yarn set in post–Civil War Texas. Richard Boone and his pals go undercover to get the goods on outlaws responsible for stealing a shipment of rifles. Boone gives a wry performance. 107m. **DIR:** Gordon Douglas. **CAST:** Richard Boone, Stuart Whitman, Anthony Franciosa, Edmond O'Brien, Jim Brown. **1964**

RIO DIABLO ★★½ Country singers ride the TV-movie West again in this middling tale of a hard-boiled bounty hunter reluctantly helping a young man track down the outlaws who kidnapped his bride. 97m. **DIR:** Rod Hardy. **CAST:** Kenny Rogers, Travis Tritt, Naomi Judd, Stacy Keach, Brion James, Bruce Greenwood, Laura Harring, Michael G. Hagerty. **1993**

RIO GRANDE ★★★★ The last entry in director John Ford's celebrated cavalry trilogy (which also includes *Fort Apache* and *She Wore a Yellow Ribbon*), this stars John Wayne as a company commander coping with renegade Indians and a willful wife (Maureen O'Hara), who wants to take their soldier son (Claude Jarman Jr.) home. B&W; 105m. **DIR:** John Ford. **CAST:** John Wayne, Maureen O'Hara, Claude Jarman Jr., Ben Johnson, Harry Carey Jr., Victor McLaglen, Chill Wills, J. Carrol Naish. **1950**

RIO LOBO ★★★ Neither star John Wayne nor director Howard Hawks was exactly at the peak of his powers when this second reworking of *Rio Bravo* (the first being *El Dorado*) was released. If one adjusts the normally high expectations he or she would have for a Western made by these two giants, *Rio Lobo* is a fun show. Jack Elam is terrific in a delightful supporting role. Rated G. 114m. **DIR:** Howard Hawks. **CAST:** John Wayne, Jack Elam, Jorge Rivero, Jennifer O'Neill, Chris Mitchum, Mike Henry. **1970**

RIVER OF NO RETURN ★★★ Rory Calhoun has deserted Marilyn Monroe, believe it or not. She hires Robert Mitchum to track him down. The story line is predictable and sometimes plodding, under Otto Preminger's heavy directorial hand. Nevertheless, Mitchum's quirky strength and the gorgeous color shots of Monroe and western vistas make the film sufficiently entertaining. 91m. **DIR:** Otto Preminger. **CAST:** Robert Mitchum, Marilyn Monroe, Rory Calhoun, Tommy Rettig. **1954**

ROAD AGENT ★★★½ Tim Holt and his sidekick Chito pose as masked riders to overcome a tyrannical land boss. B&W; 60m. **DIR:** Lesley Selander. **CAST:** Tim Holt, Richard Martin, Dorothy Patrick, Tom Tyler. **1952**

ROAMIN' WILD ★★★ Undercover marshal (Tom Tyler) goes after a gang of outlaws operating in the goldfields trying to take over a woman's stage line. Fast-moving, with plenty of excitement. B&W; 56m. **DIR:** Bernard B. Ray. **CAST:** Tom Tyler, Carol Wyndham, Al Ferguson, George Chesebro. **1936**

ROARING GUNS ★★★ A ruthless cattle baron attempts to drive out the independent ranchers. It's up to steely-eyed Tim McCoy to set things aright in this low-budget but enjoyable series Western. B&W; 66m. **DIR:** Sam Newfield. **CAST:** Tim McCoy, Rosalinda Price, Wheeler Oakman. **1936**

ROBIN HOOD OF TEXAS ★★★ More of a detective story than a formula Western, Gene Autry's last film for Republic Studios finds him accused of bank robbery and keeping one step ahead of the law in order to clear his name. Better than many of his films with a nicely turned story and more action and fisticuffs than most of Autry's productions, B&W; 71m. **DIR:** Lesley Selander. **CAST:** Gene Autry, Lynne Roberts (Mary Hart), Sterling Holloway, Adele Mara. **1947**

ROBIN HOOD OF THE PECOS ★★★ Roy Rogers and Gabby Hayes fight for law, order, and honest government in this history-based post–Civil War Western-drama. B&W; 50m. **DIR:** Joseph Kane. **CAST:** Roy Rogers, George "Gabby" Hayes, Marjorie Reynolds, Jay Novello, Roscoe Ates. **1941**

ROCKY MOUNTAIN RANGERS ★★★ The Three Mesquiteers impersonate outlaws in order to avenge the murder of a young Texas Ranger comrade. Then the real outlaws show up. Bob Livingston has a meaty dual role. B&W; 54m. **DIR:** George Sherman. **CAST:** Robert Livingston, Duncan Renaldo, Raymond Hatton, Sammy McKim, LeRoy Mason. **1940**

RODEO KING AND THE SENORITA ★★★ In this remake of Roy Rogers' *My Pal Trigger*, rodeo rider Rex Allen exposes the crook who's trying to bankrupt a traveling wild West show. B&W; 67m. **DIR:** Phillip Ford. **CAST:** Rex Allen, Buddy Ebsen, Mary Ellen Kay, Roy Barcroft, Tristram Coffin. **1951**

ROLL ON TEXAS MOON ★★★½ Gabby Hayes's standout role in Roy Rogers's Westerns as the owner of a cattle ranch at odds with encroaching sheep herders led by Dale Evans. Outlaws play the two sides against each other. First of the "new era" William Witney–directed, less-songs-more-action Rogers B Westerns. B&W; 67m. **DIR:** William

Witney. **CAST:** Roy Rogers, George "Gabby" Hayes, Dale Evans, Elisabeth Risdon, Bob Nolan and the Sons of the Pioneers. **1946**

ROOSTER COGBURN ★★★½ Okay, so this sequel to *True Grit* is only *The African Queen* reworked, with John Wayne playing the Humphrey Bogart part opposite the incomparable Katharine Hepburn, but we like—no, love—it. Watching these two professionals playing off each other is what movie watching is all about. The plot? Well, it's not much, but the scenes with Wayne and Hepburn are, as indicated, priceless. Rated PG. 107m. **DIR:** Stuart Millar. **CAST:** John Wayne, Katharine Hepburn, Richard Jordan, Anthony Zerbe, Strother Martin, John McIntire. **1975**

ROOTIN' TOOTIN' RHYTHM ★★ Gene Autry and Smiley "Frog" Burnette assume identities of presumably dead outlaws to capture cattle rustlers. B&W; 54m. **DIR:** Mack V. Wright. **CAST:** Gene Autry, Smiley Burnette, Armida, Monte Blue, Charles King. **1937**

ROUGH JUSTICE 🦃 Spaghetti Western, with Kinski as a sex-crazed outlaw. Not rated, but contains violence. 95m. **DIR:** Mario Costa. **CAST:** Klaus Kinski, Steven Tedd. **1987**

ROUGH NIGHT IN JERICHO ★★½ Former marshal George Peppard doesn't want to get involved when Jean Simmons finds her stagecoach line threatened with a takeover. Power-hungry town boss Dean Martin's brutal tactics make Peppard change his mind. Violent Western has its moments, both good and not so good. 104m. **DIR:** Arnold Laven. **CAST:** Dean Martin, Jean Simmons, George Peppard, John McIntire, Slim Pickens, Don Galloway. **1967**

ROUGH RIDERS' ROUNDUP ★★½ The accent is more on action than music in this early Roy Rogers Western about the Rough Riders reuniting to rid the range of an outlaw gang. In all, it's better than most of the Rogers vehicles that followed. B&W; 58m. **DIR:** Joseph Kane. **CAST:** Roy Rogers, Lynne Roberts (Mary Hart), Raymond Hatton, Eddie Acuff. **1939**

ROUNDERS, THE ★★½ Burt Kennedy, a solid scriptwriter of Fifties Westerns turned director in the Sixties—with hit-and-miss results. He had one of his stronger casts in this comic saga of two reluctant ranch-hand cronies. 85m. **DIR:** Burt Kennedy. **CAST:** Glenn Ford, Henry Fonda, Sue Ane Langdon, Hope Holiday, Edgar Buchanan, Chill Wills, Kathleen Freeman. **1965**

ROUND-UP TIME IN TEXAS ★★ Gene Autry brings his usual air of contained energy to this fairly early entry in the long-running series. Typical Autry programmer. B&W; 58m. **DIR:** Joseph Kane. **CAST:** Gene Autry, Smiley Burnette, Maxine Doyle. **1937**

ROY ROGERS SHOW, THE (TV SERIES) ★★★ These six tapes contain two episodes each of the 1954–56 TV series. All the memories come back as Roy, Dale, Pat, Trigger, Bulle, and Nellybelle keep the West a safe place to live. Good fun for all. B&W; 46m. **CAST:** Roy Rogers, Dale Evans, Pat Brady. **1954–56**

RUN OF THE ARROW ★★★ One of the strangest of all adult Westerns of the 1950s, this film tells the story of a man who joins the Sioux tribe after the Civil War rather than accept the reality of the South's defeat. Rod Steiger does a good job in a difficult role. While not entirely successful, this thought-provoking film is worth watching. 85m. **DIR:** Samuel Fuller. **CAST:** Rod Steiger, Brian Keith, Ralph Meeker, Sarita Montiel, Tim McCoy, Jay C. Flippen, Charles Bronson. **1957**

RUSTLERS, THE ★★★★ Clever, sprightly paced Western has Tim Holt and his saddle pal, the ever-amorous Richard "Chito" Martin, tracking down Steve Brodie and his gang of rustlers. A winner. B&W; 61m. **DIR:** Lesley Selander. **CAST:** Tim Holt, Martha Hyer, Richard Martin, Steve Brodie, Addison Richards. **1949**

RUSTLER'S VALLEY ★★ William Boyd as Hopalong Cassidy helps a rancher save his range while putting a stop to a villainous lawyer who is squeezing the locals dry with his thieving and legal shenanigans. B&W; 60m. **DIR:** Nate Watt. **CAST:** William Boyd, George "Gabby" Hayes, Russell Hayden, Lee J. Cobb. **1937**

RUTHLESS FOUR, THE ★★ This spaghetti Western could have been a lot worse, but that's no reason to watch it. Van Heflin plays a prospector who strikes gold, only to have to split the fortune with three other men less honest than he. 96m. **DIR:** Giorgio Capitani. **CAST:** Van Heflin, Gilbert Roland, Klaus Kinski, George Hilton. **1969**

SACKETTS, THE ★★★★ Fine made-for-TV Western adapted from two novels by Louis L'Amour, *The Daybreakers* and *The Sacketts*. Sam Elliott, Tom Selleck, Glenn Ford, and Ben Johnson are terrific in the lead roles, and there's plenty of action. 200m. **DIR:** Robert Totten. **CAST:** Sam Elliott, Tom Selleck, Glenn Ford, Ben Johnson, Ruth Roman, Gilbert Roland, Slim Pickens, Jack Elam, Gene Evans. **1979**

SACRED GROUND ★★★½ Interracial marriage between a white mountain man and an Apache woman is further complicated when they have their child on the burial grounds of another Indian tribe. The trials they endure should hold viewer interest. Rated PG. 100m. **DIR:** Charles B. Pierce. **CAST:** Tim McIntire, Jack Elam, Serene Hedin. **1983**

SADDLE MOUNTAIN ROUNDUP ★★★ The Range Busters set out to find the killer of a grouchy old rancher. B&W; 55m. **DIR:** S. Roy Luby. **CAST:** Ray "Crash" Corrigan, John

King, Max Terhune, Jack Mulhall, George Chesebro. 1941

SADDLE TRAMPS ★★ A Casanova named Coburn (Bud Spencer) seduces Mary, the sister of a gunfighter named Sonny (Jack Palance), and Sonny pursues Coburn all over the West. Good performance by Spencer, in a role where he's not his usual brutish clown, makes this a fine parody Western. Rated PG. 90m. **DIR:** Maurizio Lucidi. **CAST:** Bud Spencer, Jack Palance, Francisco Rabal, Renato Cestie. 1971

SAGA OF DEATH VALLEY ★★½ Early Roy Rogers film finds him fighting a gang of outlaws led by a desperado who turns out to be his own brother! This well-produced Western isn't lacking in action and excitement. B&W; 56m. **DIR:** Joseph Kane. **CAST:** Roy Rogers, George "Gabby" Hayes, Don Barry. 1939

SAGEBRUSH TRAIL ★★★ Big John Wayne, almost before he was shaving, is sent to prison for a murder he didn't commit. Naturally, our hero breaks out of the big house to clear his name. In a nice twist, he becomes friends—unknowingly—with the killer, who dies bravely in a climactic shoot-out. Good B Western. B&W; 58m. **DIR:** Armand Schaefer. **CAST:** John Wayne, Nancy Shubert, Lane Chandler, Yakima Canutt. 1933

SAGINAW TRAIL 🦃 Similar in plot to a half dozen or more previous Gene Autry films, the only thing that's as tired as the story is Smiley Burnette, resurrected to co-star in the last six titles in the series. Overall, this is a pretty tame ending to a pretty lame run of ninety-three movies. B&W; 56m. **DIR:** George Archainbaud. **CAST:** Gene Autry, Connie Marshall, Smiley Burnette. 1953

SAN ANTONIO ★★★ Sturdy Warner Bros. Western pits Errol Flynn against villain Victor Francen, with Alexis Smith in the middle. Nothing new, just solid action and production values. Final shoot-out at the Alamo is pretty good. 111m. **DIR:** David Butler. **CAST:** Errol Flynn, Alexis Smith, Victor Francen, S. Z. Sakall, Paul Kelly, Florence Bates. 1945

SAN ANTONIO KID ★★★½ Outlaws use violence and vandalism to scare ranchers off oil-rich rangeland until Red Ryder and Little Beaver intervene with blazing guns. B&W; 59m. **DIR:** Howard Bretherton. **CAST:** William Elliot, Robert Blake, Alice Fleming, Linda Stirling, Glenn Strange, Duncan Renaldo. 1944

SAN FERNANDO VALLEY ★★½ Cowgirls replace cowboys on a large cattle ranch. Nevertheless, Roy Rogers is brought in to rid the valley of the lawless element. Roy got his first screen kiss, from Jean Porter, in this leisurely paced oater, which was the year's number one box-office Western. B&W; 54m. **DIR:** John English. **CAST:** Roy Rogers, Dale Evans, Bob Nolan and the Sons of the Pioneers, Jean Porter. 1944

SANTA FE MARSHAL ★★½ Hopalong Cassidy goes undercover with a medicine show. B&W; 54m. **DIR:** Lesley Selander. **CAST:** William Boyd, Russell Hayden. 1940

SANTA FE SADDLEMATES ★★★★½ Government investigator Sunset Carson sets out to bust up a diamond-smuggling ring along the U.S.-Mexican border. Top-notch action makes this the best of Carson's fifteen Republic Westerns. B&W; 56m. **DIR:** Thomas Carr. **CAST:** Sunset Carson, Linda Stirling, Olin Howlin, Roy Barcroft. 1945

SANTA FE STAMPEDE ★★½ The Three Mesquiteers (John Wayne, Ray Corrigan, and Max Terhune) ride to the rescue of an old friend (William Farnum) who strikes it rich with a gold mine. A villain (LeRoy Mason) is trying to steal his claim. Lightweight Western with plenty of action. B&W; 58m. **DIR:** George Sherman. **CAST:** John Wayne, Ray "Crash" Corrigan, Max Terhune, William Farnum, LeRoy Mason. 1938

SANTA FE TRAIL ★★★½ Errol Flynn, Alan Hale, and Olivia de Havilland save this muddled Western, with Ronald Reagan as one of Flynn's soldier buddies who go after John Brown (Raymond Massey). B&W; 110m. **DIR:** Michael Curtiz. **CAST:** Errol Flynn, Alan Hale Sr., Olivia de Havilland, Ronald Reagan, Raymond Massey, Ward Bond, Van Heflin. 1940

SANTA FE UPRISING ★★★★ Allan Lane takes over the role of Red Ryder for this first of seven films. Outlaws kidnap Little Beaver to stop the duchess from taking over a toll road she has inherited. B&W; 55m. **DIR:** R. G. Springsteen. **CAST:** Allan "Rocky" Lane, Robert Blake, Barton MacLane, Jack LaRue, Dick Curtis. 1946

SANTEE ★★½ Bounty hunter with a heart (Glenn Ford) loses his son and adopts the son of an outlaw he kills. A fine variety of old Western hands add zip to this otherwise average oater. As usual, Ford turns in a solid performance. PG. 93m. **DIR:** Gary Nelson. **CAST:** Glenn Ford, Dana Wynter, Michael Burns, Robert Donner, Jay Silverheels, Harry Townes, John Larch. 1973

SAVAGE GUNS ★★ Revenge story has an outlaw destroy a saloon to prevent the owner from testifying against him. Only a gunfighter is wounded and his brother killed in the attack. The gunfighter recuperates and goes after the outlaw. Exciting action but weak story. Unrated; contains violence. 85m. **DIR:** Miles Deem. **CAST:** Robert Woods, Dean Stratford, Dennis Colt, Simone Blondell. 1971

SAVAGE JOURNEY 🦃 Simplistic, white-washed account of the formation of the Mormon Church. Not rated, contains some violence. 96m. **DIR:** Tom McGowan. **CAST:** Maurice Grandmaison, Charles Moll. **1983**

SCALPHUNTERS, THE ★★★½ Fine, old-fashioned Western finds fur-trapper Burt Lancaster and runaway slave Ossie Davis pitted against Telly Savalas and his gang of cutthroats. Frequent bits of comedy make this a solid genre entry. 102m. **DIR:** Sydney Pollack. **CAST:** Burt Lancaster, Shelley Winters, Telly Savalas, Ossie Davis, Dabney Coleman, Nick Cravat. **1968**

SCARLET RIVER ★★★ Unique movie within a movie, as Western screen star Tom Keene comes to Scarlet River ranch to shoot his next movie and ends up in a series of real shoot-outs with badmen plotting to take over the ranch. Cameo appearances by Joel McCrea and Myrna Loy as themselves. B&W; 54m. **DIR:** Otto Brower. **CAST:** Tom Keene, Lon Chaney Jr., Edgar Kennedy. **1933**

SEA OF GRASS, THE ★★½ This is more soap than horse opera, where ruthless cattle baron Spencer Tracy drives his eastern-bred wife, Katharine Hepburn, into the arms of lawyer Melvyn Douglas. Disappointing. B&W; 123m. **DIR:** Elia Kazan. **CAST:** Spencer Tracy, Katharine Hepburn, Melvyn Douglas, Robert Walker, Harry Carey. **1946**

SEARCHERS, THE ★★★★★ John Ford is without a doubt the most celebrated director of Westerns, and *The Searchers* is considered by many to be his masterpiece. In it, he and his favorite actor, John Wayne, reached the peak of their long and successful screen collaboration. This thoughtful film follows Ethan Edwards (Wayne), an embittered Indian-hating, ex–Confederate soldier as he leads the search for his niece (Natalie Wood), who was kidnapped years earlier by Indians. As time goes on, we begin to wonder whether Edwards is out to save the girl or kill her. 119m. **DIR:** John Ford. **CAST:** John Wayne, Natalie Wood, Jeffrey Hunter, Ward Bond, Vera Miles, Harry Carey Jr., Ken Curtis, Lana Wood, Patrick Wayne. **1956**

SEPTEMBER GUN ★★ A good cast can't save this overly talky TV Western about an aged good-hearted gunfighter reluctantly becoming the protector of a nun and some orphaned Apache children. 100m. **DIR:** Don Taylor. **CAST:** Robert Preston, Patty Duke, Christopher Lloyd, Sally Kellerman. **1983**

SERGEANT PRESTON OF THE YUKON (TV SERIES) ★★½ This syndicated adventure series, set in the 1890s, stars Richard Simmons as the Northwest Mounted Policeman. No, it's not *that* Richard Simmons; this character gets most of his exercise from chasing bad guys. In the wild, gold-rush days of Alaska, there were plenty of villains around. Preston could always count on the assistance of his husky, Yukon King. B&W; 55m. **DIR:** Various. **CAST:** Richard Simmons, Yukon King. **1955**

SERGEANT RUTLEDGE ★★★½ Underrated and somewhat forgotten Western tells the story of a black cavalry officer on trial for rape and murder. The film's main focus is on the characters. Very good use of flashbacks to show events leading up to court-martial. B&W; 118m. **DIR:** John Ford. **CAST:** Woody Strode, Jeffrey Hunter, Constance Towers, Billie Burke. **1960**

7TH CAVALRY ★★ Randolph Scott as a cavalry officer accused of cowardice for being on leave during the battle of the Little Big Horn. Talkie and slow-moving. 75m. **DIR:** Joseph H. Lewis. **CAST:** Randolph Scott, Barbara Hale, Donald Curtis, Jay C. Flippen. **1956**

SHADOW RIDERS, THE ★★★½ The stars of the superb made-for-television Western *The Sacketts* reunite for another adventure inspired by a Louis L'Amour tale. This time, brothers Tom Selleck, Sam Elliott, and Jeffrey Osterhage take on a white slaver. Good, old-fashioned cowboy fun. 96m. **DIR:** Andrew V. McLaglen. **CAST:** Sam Elliott, Tom Selleck, Ben Johnson, Katharine Ross, Geoffrey Lewis, Jeff Osterhage, Gene Evans, Harry Carey Jr., Jane Greer. **1982**

SHALAKO ★★ Odd British Western about European immigrants Sean Connery, Brigitte Bardot, Stephen Boyd, Jack Hawkins, and Honor Blackman menaced by Apaches in the Old West. 113m. **DIR:** Edward Dmytryk. **CAST:** Sean Connery, Brigitte Bardot, Stephen Boyd, Jack Hawkins, Honor Blackman, Woody Strode. **1968**

SHANE ★★★★★ *Shane* is surely among the best Westerns ever made. Alan Ladd plays the title role, the mysterious stranger who helps a group of homesteaders in their struggle against the cattlemen. 118m. **DIR:** George Stevens. **CAST:** Alan Ladd, Jean Arthur, Jack Palance, Van Heflin, Ben Johnson, Elisha Cook Jr., Brandon de Wilde. **1953**

SHANGAI JOE ★★ One of the last spaghetti Westerns to incorporate martial arts. A young Chinese laborer wants to become a cowboy, but he is faced with racial prejudice. He uses his brain and kung-fu skills to fight back, and in the meantime, uncovers an illegal-alien smuggling ring. Lots of kung-fu action. Rated R for violence. 97m. **DIR:** Mario Caiano. **CAST:** Chen Lee, Carla Romanelli, Klaus Kinski, Giacomo Rossi-Stuart, Gordon Mitchell. **1973**

SHE WORE A YELLOW RIBBON ★★★★★ Lest we forget, John Wayne was one of the screen's greatest actors. The Duke gave what was arguably his greatest performance in this gorgeous color Western made by John Ford. As the aging Captain Nathan Brittles, Wayne plays a man set to retire but unwilling to leave his command at a time of impending war with the Apaches. This is one of the great Westerns. 103m. **DIR:** John Ford. **CAST:** John Wayne, Ben

Johnson, Victor McLaglen, Harry Carey Jr., George O'Brien. 1949

SHENANDOAH ★★★★ James Stewart gives a superb performance in this, director Andrew V. McLaglen's best Western. Stewart plays a patriarch determined to keep his family out of the Civil War. He ultimately fails and is forced into action to save his children from the ravages of war. It's an emotionally moving, powerful tale. 105m. **DIR:** Andrew V. McLaglen. **CAST:** James Stewart, Doug McClure, Glenn Corbett, Patrick Wayne, Katharine Ross, George Kennedy, Strother Martin. 1965

SHERIFF OF LAS VEGAS ★★★ Red Ryder steps in to clear a young man framed for the murder of his father. B&W; 54m. **DIR:** Lesley Selander. **CAST:** William Elliott, Robert Blake, Peggy Stewart, Jay Kirby. 1944

SHINE ON HARVEST MOON ★★ Roy Rogers rides to the rescue once again as he brings a gang of robbers to justice while clearing an old man's name. B&W; 60m. **DIR:** Joseph Kane. **CAST:** Roy Rogers, Lynne Roberts (Mary Hart). 1938

SHOOT THE LIVING...PRAY FOR THE DEAD ♥ Overlong and nothing-new story line makes this film a waste of time. A gang hires a guide to lead them to Mexico after a bank robbery, but the guide plans to kill the gang himself for killing his family. Unrated; contains violence. 94m. **DIR:** Joseph Warren. **CAST:** Klaus Kinski, Victoria Zinni, Paul Sullivan, Dean Stratford. 1971

SHOOTING, THE ★★★ This early Jack Nicholson vehicle, directed by cult figure Monte Hellman, is a moody Western about revenge and murder. An interesting entry into the genre, it may not be everyone's cup of tea. No rating; contains some violence. 82m. **DIR:** Monte Hellman. **CAST:** Warren Oates, Millie Perkins, Will Hutchins, Jack Nicholson. 1967

SHOOTIST, THE ★★★★½ *The Shootist* is a special film in many ways. Historically, it is John Wayne's final film. Cinematically, it stands on its own as an intelligent tribute to the passing of the era known as the "wild West." Wayne's masterful performance is touching and bitterly ironic as well. He plays a famous gunfighter dying of cancer and seeking a place to die in peace, only to become a victim of his own reputation. Rated PG. 99m. **DIR:** Don Siegel. **CAST:** John Wayne, Lauren Bacall, James Stewart, Ron Howard, Richard Boone, Hugh O'Brian, John Carradine, Harry Morgan, Scatman Crothers. 1976

SHORT GRASS ★★★★ Returning home after several years, Rod Cameron is pushed off his land by larger ranchers. Intricate script, from his own novel, by Tom Blackburn. B&W; 82m. **DIR:** Lesley Selander. **CAST:** Rod Cameron, Johnny Mack Brown, Cathy Downs, Alan Hale Jr. 1950

SHOTGUN ★★★ Violent melodramatic track-down story has Marshal Sterling Hayden pursuing the gunrunning shotgun killer of a town sheriff. Along the way he encounters a saloon girl and a bounty hunter. 80m. **DIR:** Lesley Selander. **CAST:** Sterling Hayden, Zachary Scott, Yvonne De Carlo. 1955

SHOWDOWN (1940) ★★ Hopalong Cassidy and partner Lucky tangle with some sinister characters disguised as European horse buyers. Leading lady Jan Clayton later gained fame as Tommy Rettig's mother on the *Lassie* TV series. B&W; 65m. **DIR:** Howard Bretherton. **CAST:** William Boyd, Russell Hayden, Britt Wood, Morris Ankrum, Jan Clayton. 1940

SHOWDOWN, THE (1950) ★★★★ "Wild" Bill Elliott's last Western for Republic Pictures is one of his best, a revenge story enlivened by a top-flight cast and a powerful performance by its star. Elliott is a former lawman on the trail of the man who murdered his brother, a trail that leads to a cattle drive. B&W; 86m. **DIR:** Darrell McGowan, Stuart McGowan. **CAST:** William Elliott, Walter Brennan, Marie Windsor, Harry Morgan, Jim Davis, Rhys Williams, Leif Erickson, Yakima Canutt. 1950

SHOWDOWN (1973) ★★★★ Starting with the familiar tale of childhood friends who end up on opposite sides of the law (à la *Manhattan Melodrama* and *Angels with Dirty Faces*), director George Seaton and his screenwriters mix inventive plot twists and sharply drawn characterizations for a compelling tale that plays especially well on the small screen. The three top-billed stars add an easygoing charm and genuine warmth to Seaton's last film. Rated PG for violence. 100m. **DIR:** George Seaton. **CAST:** Rock Hudson, Dean Martin, Susan Clark, Donald Moffat, John McLiam, Ed Begley Jr. 1973

SHOWDOWN AT BOOT HILL ★★½ Stone-faced Charles Bronson does some impressive work as a lawman who finds that the criminal he has killed in the line of duty is actually a respected citizen in another community. B&W; 71m. **DIR:** Gene Fowler Jr. **CAST:** Charles Bronson, Robert Hutton, John Carradine. 1958

SHOWDOWN AT WILLIAMS CREEK ★★★½ A British soldier, John Brown (Tom Burlinson), leaves Ireland for America in hopes of making his fortune and "coming back a gentleman." But the rugged, dangerous life in the frontier, with its treacherous schemers, teaches Brown what it means to be a survivor—and on trial for murder. Donnelly Rhodes gives a superb supporting turn. Fascinating, hard-edged Western was based on true events. Rated R for violence, nudity, and profanity. 97m. **DIR:** Allan Kroeker. **CAST:**

Tom Burlinson, Donnelly Rhodes, Raymond Burr. **1991**

SILENT CONFLICT ★★ A traveling charlatan hypnotizes and drugs Lucky into stealing money and trying to kill Hoppy and California. A fair series Western. B&W; 61m. **DIR:** George Archainbaud. **CAST:** William Boyd, Andy Clyde, Rand Brooks, Virginia Belmont. **1948**

SILVER QUEEN ★★ Young and devoted daughter Priscilla Lane is determined to uphold her family's honor and pay her father's debts by gambling in San Francisco, where she develops a reputation as a real sharpie. B&W; 81m. **DIR:** Lloyd Bacon. **CAST:** George Brent, Priscilla Lane, Bruce Cabot, Lynne Overman, Eugene Pallette, Guinn Williams. **1942**

SILVER RIVER ★★½ Promising Western starts out well enough but becomes bogged down. A good cast of veterans manage to make things interesting, but film could have been much better. B&W; 110m. **DIR:** Raoul Walsh. **CAST:** Errol Flynn, Ann Sheridan, Thomas Mitchell, Bruce Bennett, Barton MacLane. **1948**

SILVER SPURS ★★★½ Better-than-average cast and strong screenplay raise the routine plot to make this one of Roy Rogers's better middle-era Westerns. Nefarious John Carradine tries to fleece Rogers's boss out of oil-rich land. B&W; 54m. **DIR:** Joseph Kane. **CAST:** Roy Rogers, Smiley Burnette, John Carradine, Phyllis Brooks, Sons of the Pioneers, Jerome Cowan. **1943**

SILVERADO ★★★★½ Scott Glenn, Kevin Kline, Kevin Costner, and Danny Glover ride side by side to clean up the town of Silverado. Excitement, laughs, thrills, and chills abound in this marvelous movie. Even those who don't ordinarily like Westerns are sure to enjoy it. Rated PG-13 for violence and profanity. 133m. **DIR:** Lawrence Kasdan. **CAST:** Kevin Kline, Scott Glenn, Kevin Costner, Danny Glover, Rosanna Arquette, John Cleese, Brian Dennehy, Linda Hunt, Jeff Goldblum. **1985**

SING, COWBOY, SING ★★★★ Wagontrain raiders are thwarted by Tex Ritter and his pards masquerading as entertainers. They needn't masquerade—this one entertains with the best of the B Westerns. Look for ex–Mack Sennett clowns Snub Pollard, Chester Conklin, and Al St. John. B&W; 59m. **DIR:** Robert N. Bradbury. **CAST:** Tex Ritter, Louise Stanley, Al St. John, Karl Hackett, Charles King, Snub Pollard, Chester Conklin. **1937**

SINGING BUCKAROO ★★ Lesser-known Western hero Fred Scott yodels the range in this hard-ridin' horse opera about a frontier knight who pounds the prairie to help an innocent girl. Nothing special, but full of action interrupted by a few tunes. B&W; 50m. **DIR:** Tom Gibson. **CAST:** Fred Scott, William Faversham, Victoria Vinton. **1937**

SINISTER JOURNEY ★★ Coming to the aid of an old friend, Hoppy and his saddle pals find themselves involved in a mystery on a westbound railroad. Standard Hopalong Cassidy film doesn't have the punch of the earlier ones. B&W; 58m. **DIR:** George Archainbaud. **CAST:** William Boyd, Andy Clyde, Rand Brooks, Elaine Riley. **1948**

SIOUX CITY SUE ★★ Gene Autry's first film after World War II finds him in Hollywood, where he tries his luck in the movie business. Originally intended as the voice of an animated donkey, Autry wins the leading role in the picture when the big shots hear him stretch his tonsils. Rampaging rustlers throw a monkey wrench into the proceedings and provide Gene with an opportunity to show his stuff on the ground and on horseback. B&W; 69m. **DIR:** Frank McDonald. **CAST:** Gene Autry, Lynne Roberts (Mary Hart), Sterling Holloway. **1946**

SIX GUN SERENADE ★★ Framed as a rustler, Jimmy Wakely eventually routs out the real culprits. A bit slow-paced. B&W; 54m. **DIR:** Ford Beebe. **CAST:** Jimmy Wakely, Pierce Lyden. **1947**

SIX-SHOOTIN' SHERIFF ★★ Ken Maynard, a reformed outlaw, personifies this movie's title as he cleans up the town, saves the payroll, sets his young brother straight, roughs up the outlaws, and gets the girl. Look for a young Marjorie Reynolds, who later gained fame as Peg on TV's *Life of Riley.* B&W; 59m. **DIR:** Harry Fraser. **CAST:** Ken Maynard, Marjorie Reynolds, Walter Long. **1938**

SKIN GAME ★★★★ Perceptive social comedy-drama set during the slave era. James Garner and Louis Gossett Jr. are con artists; Garner "sells" Gossett to unsuspecting slave owners and later helps break him free. The fleecing continues until they meet up with evil Edward Asner, who catches on to the act...then the story takes a chilling turn toward realism. Excellent on all levels. Rated PG for light violence. 102m. **DIR:** Paul Bogart. **CAST:** James Garner, Lou Gossett Jr., Susan Clark, Edward Asner, Andrew Duggan. **1971**

SLAUGHTER TRAIL 🦃 Good actors trapped in a clichéd story with outlaws, Indians, and cavalry. One of the hokiest sound track songs ever recorded. 78m. **DIR:** Irving Allen. **CAST:** Brian Donlevy, Virginia Grey, Gig Young, Andy Devine. **1951**

SMITH! ★★★ A fine cast and sensitive screenplay distinguish this story of a strongman's efforts to secure a fair trial for an Indian accused of murder. Glenn Ford is believably rugged and righteous, and Chief Dan George is highly effective as the stoic focal point of the territory's rage. Good fare for the whole family. Rated G. 101m. **DIR:** Michael O'Herlihy. **CAST:** Glenn Ford, Nancy Olson,

Dean Jagger, Keenan Wynn, Warren Oates, Chief Dan George. **1969**

SMOKEY TRAILS ★★★ Once again Bob Steele is after the killer of his father—chasing him right into Lost Canyon, an outlaw den that he cleans out with plenty of fisticuffs and blazing six-shooters. Above average. B&W; 57m. **DIR:** Bernard B. Ray. **CAST:** Bob Steele, Jimmy Aubrey, Ted Adams, Carleton Young. **1939**

SOLDIER BLUE ★★½ An extremely violent film that looks at the mistreatment of Indians at the hands of the U.S. Cavalry. This familiar subject has fared much better in films such as *Little Big Man*. Final attack is an exercise in excessive gore and violence. Rated R. 112m. **DIR:** Ralph Nelson. **CAST:** Candice Bergen, Peter Strauss, John Anderson, Donald Pleasence. **1970**

SOMEWHERE IN SONORA ★★★ John Wayne, wrongly accused of cheating during a rodeo race, redeems himself by joining an outlaw gang to foil their plans. This was the first of many films to team Wayne with character actor Paul Fix, who wrote the screenplay for *Tall in the Saddle*, and played the wise old lawman on TV's *The Rifleman*. B&W; 57m. **DIR:** Mack V. Wright. **CAST:** John Wayne, Henry B. Walthall, Shirley Palmer, J. P. Macgowan, Ann Fay, Frank Rice, Paul Fix, Ralph Lewis, Billy Franey. **1933**

SON OF THE MORNING STAR ★★★★½ Impressively mounted, acted, and directed TV miniseries was based on the bestseller by Evan S. Connell *(Mr. Bridge, Mrs. Bridge)* and chronicles the life and times of Gen. George Armstrong Custer (Gary Cole), culminating in the Battle of the Little Bighorn. Outstanding. 183m. **DIR:** Mike Robe. **CAST:** Gary Cole, Rosanna Arquette, Dean Stockwell, Rodney A. Grant, David Strathairn, Terry O'Quinn. **1990**

SONG OF NEVADA ★★½ Roy, Dale, and the boys at the ranch come to the aid of an innocent girl who has become prey of a crook and his henchmen. This tuneful, hard-riding horse opera is chock-full of former cowboys and familiar faces. It's typical of Roy's mid-1940s movies. B&W; 75m. **DIR:** Joseph Kane. **CAST:** Roy Rogers, Dale Evans, Mary Lee, Bob Nolan and the Sons of the Pioneers, Lloyd Corrigan, Thurston Hall, John Eldredge, Forrest Taylor, George Meeker, LeRoy Mason, Kenne Duncan. **1944**

SONG OF TEXAS ★★½ Most of the action comes at the end of this songfest as Roy competes in a chuck-wagon race in order to win back yet another stolen ranch. Roy and the boys squeeze ten songs into this programmer. B&W; 69m. **DIR:** Joseph Kane. **CAST:** Roy Rogers, Sheila Ryan, Barton MacLane, Harry Shannon, Pat Brady, Arline Judge, Eve March, Hal Taliaferro, Bob Nolan and the Sons of the Pioneers, Tom London. **1943**

SONG OF THE GRINGO ★★ Tex Ritter's first Western for Grand National is a low-budget shoot-'em-up with the singing cowboy as a deputy sheriff bent on cleaning out a gang of ruthless claim-jumpers. Ritter's films for Grand National lack the pacing and budget that other studios added to their product. B&W; 62m. **DIR:** John P. McCarthy. **CAST:** Tex Ritter, Monte Blue, Fuzzy Knight, Joan Woodbury. **1936**

SONNY AND JED 🦃 A naive young girl seeks adventure by following a noted outlaw hunted by a determined lawman. This Western approach to the Bonnie and Clyde story doesn't work. An irritating performance by Tomas Milian. Even an effective musical score by the master Ennio Morricone can't help this film. Rated PG. 85m. **DIR:** Sergio Corbucci. **CAST:** Tomas Milian, Susan George, Telly Savalas, Eduardo Fajardo, Rosanna Yanni. **1973**

SONS OF KATIE ELDER, THE ★★★ John Wayne stars in this entertaining film about four brothers reunited after the death of their mother and forced to fight to get back their land. Although this Western rarely goes beyond the predictable, there's plenty of action and roughhouse comedy. 122m. **DIR:** Henry Hathaway. **CAST:** John Wayne, Dean Martin, Earl Holliman, Michael Anderson Jr., James Gregory, George Kennedy, Martha Hyer, Jeremy Slate, Paul Fix. **1965**

SONS OF THE PIONEERS ★★★½ Roy Rogers plays a scientist who returns to his hometown after numerous ranches have been sabotaged. Using his scientific savvy and an occasional yodel, he saves the day. B&W; 53m. **DIR:** Joseph Kane. **CAST:** Roy Rogers, George "Gabby" Hayes, Maris Wrixon, Forrest Taylor, Pat Brady. **1942**

SOUTH OF ST. LOUIS ★★★★ Joel McCrea, Zachary Scott, and Douglas Kennedy seek revenge for the burning of their respective spreads. Dorothy Malone and Alexis Smith provide the love interest. If you like dusty, exciting ranch epics, this film should be high on your list. 88m. **DIR:** Ray Enright. **CAST:** Joel McCrea, Zachary Scott, Douglas Kennedy, Dorothy Malone, Alexis Smith. **1949**

SOUTH OF THE BORDER ★★½ Gene and Smiley mosey on down to Mexico as government operatives in order to quell a rebellion engineered by foreign powers who wish to control that country's oil resources. This patriotic film contains some good action scenes. B&W; 71m. **DIR:** George Sherman. **CAST:** Gene Autry, Smiley Burnette, Duncan Renaldo, June Storey. **1939**

SOUTH OF THE RIO GRANDE ★★ Viewers who fondly remember the *Cisco Kid* television series might get a mild kick out of seeing series star Duncan Renaldo in one of his first appearances as the Robin Hood of Mexico. Otherwise, this is a dreary effort. B&W; 62m. **DIR:** Lambert Hillyer. **CAST:** Duncan Renaldo, Martin Garralaga. 1945

SPAGHETTI WESTERN ★★★ Typical of the genre: some big-name American actors trek to Italy for large bucks to film the kind of grade-B Western that made Clint Eastwood a household word. It's hard to tell, at times, if this is a literal send-up of the genre, but it succeeds on several levels anyway. Unrated, with violence. 90m. **DIR:** Uncredited. **CAST:** Franco Nero, Martin Balsam, Sterling Hayden. 1969

SPIRIT OF THE WEST ★★ This entertaining but primitive Western employs a tired old gimmick that Hoot Gibson had used in previous films—that of a tough hombre who masquerades as a silly fool in order to help the gal in distress and bring the greedy, land-grabbing varmints to justice. B&W; 60m. **DIR:** Otto Brower. **CAST:** Hoot Gibson, Doris Hill, Lafe McKee, Hooper Atchley. 1932

SPOILERS, THE ★★★★ John Wayne is a miner who strikes gold in Nome, Alaska. An unscrupulous gold commissioner (Randolph Scott) and his cronies plot to steal the rich claim. But the Duke, his partner (Harry Carey), and their backer (Marlene Dietrich) have other ideas. This was the fourth of five screen versions of Rex Beach's novel. B&W; 87m. **DIR:** Ray Enright. **CAST:** Marlene Dietrich, Randolph Scott, John Wayne, Harry Carey, Russell Simpson, George Cleveland. 1942

SPRINGTIME IN THE ROCKIES (1937) ★★ Foreman Gene Autry has all he can handle as a young girl arrives at his cattle ranch with a herd of sheep. Pretty tame. B&W; 54m. **DIR:** Joseph Kane. **CAST:** Gene Autry, Smiley Burnette, Polly Rowles. 1937

SPRINGTIME IN THE SIERRAS ★★ Beady-eyed Roy Rogers sets his sights on stopping evil Stephanie Bachelor and her hulking henchman Roy Barcroft from shooting game animals out of season. There's more action than story in this fast-paced series entry. 75m. **DIR:** William Witney. **CAST:** Roy Rogers, Jane Frazee, Andy Devine, Stephanie Bachelor. 1947

STAGE TO CHINO ★★★½ In this first-rate B Western, George O'Brien is a postal inspector who goes undercover to investigate a gold-shipping scam. The always reliable Roy Barcroft is the leader of the baddies, and Virginia Vale is the not-so-helpless principal victim. O'Brien's Westerns were always marked by fine acting, lots of action, and snappy dialogue, and this is a good example. B&W; 58m. **DIR:** Edward Killy. **CAST:** George O'Brien, Virginia Vale, Roy Barcroft, Hobart Cavanaugh, Carl Stockdale, William Haade, Glenn Strange. 1940

STAGE TO MESA CITY ★★★ Lash LaRue and sidekick Fuzzy Q. Jones set out to nail bandits who are robbing stagecoaches. B&W; 56m. **DIR:** Ray Taylor. **CAST:** Lash LaRue, Al St. John, Jennifer Holt. 1947

STAGE TO TUCSON ★★★★ After several stagecoaches are stolen, two government agents are sent to lead an investigation. Well scripted, action-packed. B&W; 82m. **DIR:** Ralph Moody. **CAST:** Rod Cameron, Wayne Morris, Kay Buckley, Carl Benton Reid. 1951

STAGECOACH (1939) ★★★★★ John Ford utilized the *Grand Hotel* formula of placing a group of unrelated characters together. A stagecoach trip across the Old West provides the common setting and plenty of shared danger. Riding together with the mysterious Ringo Kid (John Wayne) is a grand assortment of some of Hollywood's best character actors. B&W; 99m. **DIR:** John Ford. **CAST:** John Wayne, Claire Trevor, Thomas Mitchell, John Carradine, Donald Meek, Andy Devine, George Bancroft, Tim Holt. 1939

STAGECOACH (1986) ★★★ This made-for-television remake of John Ford's classic 1939 Western bears little resemblance to its predecessor, but the cast of country stars seems to be enjoying itself so much you can't help but join in. Certain conceits, such as Willie Nelson substituting the character of Doc Holliday for the less glamorous original character, seem out of place, but it's enjoyable. 98m. **DIR:** Ted Post. **CAST:** Willie Nelson, Kris Kristofferson, Johnny Cash, Waylon Jennings, John Schneider, Elizabeth Ashley, Anthony Franciosa, Anthony Newley, Mary Crosby, Lash LaRue. 1986

STAGECOACH TO DENVER ★★★½ A supposedly good citizen resorts to murder and kidnapping in an all-out effort to get a woman's property. Red Ryder and Little Beaver put the owl hoots in their place. Action-packed. B&W; 54m. **DIR:** R. G. Springsteen. **CAST:** Allan "Rocky" Lane, Bobby Blake, Peggy Stewart, Roy Barcroft. 1946

STAGECOACH WAR ★★★½ Hopalong Cassidy finds himself in the middle of a contract war between rival stage lines. B&W; 63m. **DIR:** Lesley Selander. **CAST:** William Boyd, Russell Hayden, J. Farrell MacDonald. 1940

STALKING MOON, THE ★★★ Gregory Peck is an army scout who takes in a white woman (Eva Marie Saint) and the child she bore while a captive of the Apaches. The Apache father kidnaps the child and starts a chase that lasts through most of the movie. Familiar, but captivating and with exceptional performances. 109m. **DIR:** Robert Mulligan. **CAST:** Gregory Peck, Eva Marie Saint, Robert Forster, Frank Silvera, Lou Frizell. 1969

STAMPEDE ★★★★ Rod Cameron and his brother fight to hold on to their cattle empire against encroaching settlers. B&W;

78m. **DIR:** Lesley Selander. **CAST:** Rod Cameron, Don Castle, Gale Storm, Johnny Mack Brown. **1949**

STANDING TALL ★★½ During the Depression, the struggling owner of a small cattle ranch refuses to sell out to a competitor and finds himself under attack. The always-watchable Robert Forster is the only reason to see this standard made-for-TV Western. 100m. **DIR:** Harvey Hart. **CAST:** Robert Forster, Will Sampson, L. Q. Jones, Buck Taylor, Linda Evans, Chuck Connors. **1978**

STAR PACKER, THE ★★★ The Shadow and his band of outlaws have a group of ranchers cowed until John Wayne rides into town and turns the tables on the baddies. A good B Western that will be best appreciated by Wayne fans. B&W; 60m. **DIR:** Robert N. Bradbury. **CAST:** John Wayne, Verna Hillie, George "Gabby" Hayes, Yakima Canutt. **1934**

STARS IN MY CROWN ★★★★ Joel McCrea plays a frontier minister with quiet strength in a warm, gentle tale of pioneer families in the nineteenth century. A strong cast gives the story dignity as well as charm. B&W; 89m. **DIR:** Jacques Tourneur. **CAST:** Joel McCrea, Amanda Blake, James Arness, Ellen Drew, Dean Stockwell, Ed Begley Sr., Alan Hale Sr. **1950**

STATION WEST ★★★ An army undercover agent (Dick Powell) attempts to find out who is responsible for a rash of gold robberies, eventually falling in love with the ringleader (Jane Greer). This sturdy Western boasts a fine supporting cast, good location cinematography, and nice action scenes. 92m. **DIR:** Sidney Lanfield. **CAST:** Dick Powell, Jane Greer, Tom Powers, Raymond Burr, Agnes Moorehead, Burl Ives, Regis Toomey, Steve Brodie, Guinn Williams. **1948**

STONE OF SILVER CREEK ★★★★ Another of producer-star Buck Jones's superior Westerns for Universal, this offbeat, often funny movie casts Jones as a straight-shooting saloon owner who fights off a pair of persistent baddies, gives the town preacher an education in manliness, and weighs in as an all-around champion of justice. B&W; 62m. **DIR:** Nick Grindé. **CAST:** Buck Jones, Noel Francis. **1935**

STRAIGHT SHOOTING ★★★ John Ford's first major film holds up remarkably well today. Everything about it seems a prototype for his great Westerns to come: the authoritative presence of the solitary cowboy, Harry Carey; the striking location photography; and the rousing action scenes. Silent. B&W; 57m. **DIR:** John Ford. **CAST:** Harry Carey. **1917**

STRAIGHT TO HELL 🦃 Self-indulgent Western spoof with bank robbers and thugs shooting at each other in a desert town. 86m. **DIR:** Alex Cox. **CAST:** Sy Richardson, Joe Strummer, Dennis Hopper, Elvis Costello. **1987**

STRANGE GAMBLE ★★ The crooked "boss" of a small town steals valuable mining rights from a drunken customer and leaves his sick sister without any money or a place to stay. Hoppy and his pals attempt to return to the victim her rightful fortune. Last of the Hopalong Cassidy series. B&W; 61m. **DIR:** George Archainbaud. **CAST:** William Boyd, Andy Clyde, Rand Brooks, Elaine Riley. **1948**

STRANGER AND THE GUNFIGHTER, THE ★★½ The world may never be ready for this improbable mix, a tongue-in-cheek spaghetti Western by way of a standard kung fu chop-chop flick. Lee Van Cleef, as another of his weary gunslingers, teams with martial arts master Lo Lieh. A classic this isn't, but the fast action and camp humor make it watchable. Rated PG for violence. 107m. **DIR:** Anthony M. Dawson. **CAST:** Lee Van Cleef, Lo Lieh, Patty Shepard. **1976**

STRANGER WORE A GUN, THE ★★½ Randolph Scott joins forces with evil George Macready in a plot to steal government gold shipments. Scott has a change of heart, and they end up as enemies. Initially released in 3-D; the action scenes were obviously devised for that medium. 83m. **DIR:** André de Toth. **CAST:** Randolph Scott, Claire Trevor, George Macready, Lee Marvin, Ernest Borgnine. **1953**

SUNDOWN RIDER, THE ★★★★ Solid, brooding Western has Buck Jones as an easygoing cowpoke who happens upon a band of rustlers. The baddies leave Jones to "guard" their camp, where he is caught and brutally branded by revenge-minded lawmen despite his protests of innocence. So Jones swears revenge. Rewarding shoot-'em-up. B&W; 66m. **DIR:** Lambert Hillyer. **CAST:** Buck Jones, Barbara Weeks, Wheeler Oakman, Ward Bond. **1933**

SUNDOWN RIDERS ★★★ First of a proposed trio series (Russell Wade, Jay Kirby, Andy Clyde) that never materialized. Too bad, because it has plenty of action. Good chance to see famed stuntman Henry Wills in an acting role. B&W; 56m. **DIR:** Lambert Hillyer. **CAST:** Russell Wade, Jay Kirby, Andy Clyde, Evelyn Finley, Jack Ingram, Marshall Reed. **1948**

SUNDOWNERS, THE (1950) ★★★ Robert Preston is the good brother and Robert Sterling is the bad one in this tolerable Western. The siblings face each other in a climactic showdown. 83m. **DIR:** George Templeton. **CAST:** Robert Preston, Cathy Downes, Robert Sterling, John Drew Barrymore, Jack Elam. **1950**

SUNSET CARSON RIDES AGAIN ★★ Sunset Carson's partner is actually behind a gang trying to cheat folks out of money raised for a new school. Pretty low scheme even for B Western badmen, but production values are just as low. Color is the only saving grace for this oater made several years after Carson's starring days at Republic ended. 63m. **DIR:** Oliver Drake. **CAST:** Sunset Carson, Pat Starling, John Cason. **1948**

SUNSET ON THE DESERT ★★ Roy's strong resemblance to a notorious crook gives him a chance to infiltrate the gang, but the usual complications arise when the lookalike desperado returns. The cast is better than the story in this series entry. B&W; 63m. **DIR:** Joseph Kane. **CAST:** Roy Rogers, George "Gabby" Hayes, Lynne Garver, Frank M. Thomas, Bob Nolan and the Sons of the Pioneers, Beryl Wallace, Glenn Strange, Douglas Fowley, Roy Barcroft, Pat Brady. **1942**

SUNSET SERENADE ★★½ Beady-eyed Roy Rogers and his ornery sidekick Gabby Hayes thwart the plans of a couple of no-goods who aim to murder the heir to a ranch and take it over for themselves. Enjoyable enough and not too demanding. B&W; 58m. **DIR:** Joseph Kane. **CAST:** Roy Rogers, George "Gabby" Hayes, Helen Parrish, Onslow Stevens, Joan Woodbury. **1942**

SUPPORT YOUR LOCAL GUNFIGHTER ★★★½ Although not quite as fresh or genuinely rib tickling as predecessor *Support Your Local Sheriff*, this charming Western spoof nonetheless gives James Garner another chance to modify the charming hustler honed to perfection during all those years on television's *Maverick*. This time out he's a con artist "selling" drifter Jack Elam as a professional gunfighter. Rated PG for minimal violence. 92m. **DIR:** Burt Kennedy. **CAST:** James Garner, Suzanne Pleshette, Jack Elam, Harry Morgan, John Dehner, Joan Blondell, Chuck Connors. **1971**

SUPPORT YOUR LOCAL SHERIFF! ★★★★½ The time-honored backbone of the industry, the Western, takes a real ribbing in this all-stops-out send-up. If it can be parodied, it is—in spades. James Garner is great as a gambler "just passing through" who gets roped into being sheriff and tames a lawless mining town against all odds, including an inept deputy, a fem-lib mayor's daughter, and a snide gunman. A very funny picture. Rated G. 93m. **DIR:** Burt Kennedy. **CAST:** James Garner, Joan Hackett, Walter Brennan, Harry Morgan, Jack Elam, Bruce Dern, Henry Jones. **1969**

SUSANNA PASS ★★ Another variation on the crooked newspaper-publisher theme, this minor effort again teams Roy Rogers and Dale Evans, the "King and Queen of the Westerns," with "Cuban Fireball" Estelita Rodriguez. 67m. **DIR:** William Witney. **CAST:** Roy Rogers, Dale Evans, Estelita Rodriguez, Martin Garralaga. **1949**

TAKE A HARD RIDE ★★½ When his friend and partner (Dana Andrews) dies, big Jim Brown is charged with taking the proceeds from a cattle sale to their homestead in Sonora, Mexico. On the way, a ruthless bounty hunter (Lee Van Cleef) attempts to take the money. A good cast falls prey to the shortcomings of this spaghetti Western, but there is some enjoyable action and humor. Rated R. 103m. **DIR:** Anthony M. Dawson. **CAST:** Jim Brown, Lee Van Cleef, Fred Williamson, Catherine Spaak, Dana Andrews, Barry Sullivan, Jim Kelly, Harry Carey Jr. **1975**

TAKE ME BACK TO OKLAHOMA ★★★★★ This belongs among the top 50 B Westerns ever made as Tex Ritter comes to the aid of a female owner of a stage line being harassed by unscrupulous competitors. This is the first Western to feature Bob Wills's fabulous Western swing music and as such contains many of his classics as well as a terrific rendition of Jimmy Davis's "You Are My Sunshine." Contains possibly the most exciting stagecoach race on film. B&W; 67m. **DIR:** Albert Herman. **CAST:** Tex Ritter, Bob Wills and the Texas Playboys, Arkansas Slim Andrews, Terry Walker, Karl Hackett. **1940**

TALION ★★ Two bounty hunters (Robert Lansing and Patrick Wayne) go on the vengeance trail against a turncoat (Slim Pickens). The twist is that in an early gun battle, Wayne is blinded and Lansing's gun hand is crippled. Lansing looks vaguely uncomfortable in a cowboy hat, and the writing is sometimes ridiculous. 92m. **DIR:** Michael Moore. **CAST:** Robert Lansing, Patrick Wayne, Slim Pickens, Gloria Talbott, Paul Fix, Strother Martin, Clint Howard. **1966**

TALL IN THE SADDLE ★★★★ A first-rate B Western that combines mystery with shoot-'em-up action. John Wayne is wrongly accused of murder and must find the real culprit. Helping him is Gabby Hayes, and hindering is Ward Bond. B&W; 87m. **DIR:** Edwin L. Marin. **CAST:** John Wayne, George "Gabby" Hayes, Ward Bond, Ella Raines. **1944**

TALL MEN, THE ★★ Confederate army veterans Clark Gable and Cameron Mitchell join cattle baron Robert Ryan to drive his herd to market through Indian country. All three fancy Jane Russell. 122m. **DIR:** Raoul Walsh. **CAST:** Clark Gable, Jane Russell, Robert Ryan, Cameron Mitchell, Mae Marsh. **1955**

TALL T, THE ★★★★★ Rancher Randolph Scott and several stagecoach passengers are captured and held by outlaws. Top-notch Burt Kennedy script from an Elmore Leonard story. Fine performances from all concerned. This is a little-known classic. 78m. **DIR:** Budd Boetticher. **CAST:** Randolph Scott, Richard Boone, Maureen O'Sullivan, Henry Silva, Skip Homeier. **1957**

TELEGRAPH TRAIL, THE ★★★½ Before moving on to Hollywood's poverty row, John

Wayne made a series of quality B Westerns for Warner Bros.—this film about the stringing of telegraph lines is one of the best. Character actor Frank McHugh's easygoing acting style seems to inspire Wayne to relax and enjoy his role, while the romantic subplot benefits from nice touches of humor. The scenes featuring Wayne's "miracle horse," Duke, do strain credibility, however. B&W; 54m. **DIR:** Tenny Wright. **CAST:** John Wayne, Marceline Day, Frank McHugh, Otis Harlan, Albert J. Smith, Yakima Canutt, Lafe McKee. **1933**

TELL THEM WILLIE BOY IS HERE ★★★ Robert Redford is a southwestern sheriff in the early days of this country. He is pursuing an Indian (Robert Blake) who is fleeing to avoid arrest. The story is elevated from a standard Western chase by the dignity and concern shown to the Indian's viewpoint. Rated PG. 96m. **DIR:** Abraham Polonsky. **CAST:** Robert Redford, Robert Blake, Katharine Ross. **1969**

TEN WANTED MEN ★★★½ Small Arizona landowner Richard Boone attempts to wrest control of the territory by framing cattle baron Randolph Scott's nephew. 80m. **DIR:** H. Bruce Humberstone. **CAST:** Randolph Scott, Richard Boone, Dennis Weaver, Lee Van Cleef, Skip Homeier, Leo Gordon. **1955**

TENNESSEE'S PARTNER ★★½ Allan Dwan directed this minor Western featuring Ronald Reagan as a stranger who steps into the middle of a fight between gamblers and ends up befriending one (John Payne). This is one of Payne's better roles. Good little drama; better than the title suggests. 87m. **DIR:** Allan Dwan. **CAST:** John Payne, Ronald Reagan, Rhonda Fleming, Coleen Gray. **1955**

TERROR OF TINY TOWN, THE 🦃 The definitive all-midget Western, with action, gunplay, romance, and a happy ending to boot. B&W; 63m. **DIR:** Sam Newfield. **CAST:** Billy Curtis, Yvonne Moray, Little Billy. **1938**

TEX AND THE LORD OF THE DEEP ★★ Based on the Italian cartoon-character Tex Willer. Tex fights an Indian uprising spurred on by a medicine man who has discovered a glowing green rock that turns people into instant mummies. Good performances by spaghetti Western veterans Giuliano Gemma and William Berger are not enough to overcome the concept. Unrated, contains violence. 90m. **DIR:** Duccio Tessari. **CAST:** Giuliano Gemma, William Berger, Carlo Mucari, Isabel Russinova, Aldo Sambrell. **1985**

TEXAS ★★★ Friends William Holden and Glenn Ford are rivals for the affections of Claire Trevor in this lively, action-jammed Western pitting cattleman against cattle rustler. It might have been an epic, but a cost-conscious producer kept a tight rein. Good, though! B&W; 93m. **DIR:** George Marshall. **CAST:** William Holden, Glenn Ford, Claire Trevor, George Bancroft, Edgar Buchanan, Raymond Hatton. **1941**

TEXAS ACROSS THE RIVER ★★½ Lowbrow Western comedy has the dubious distinction of being the only movie to feature Joey Bishop as an Indian. That said, the film was a sizable hit and has its fans, despite inept postproduction work that is glaringly obvious on the small screen. Alain Delon is a Spanish nobleman fleeing revenge-minded army officers Peter Graves and Andrew Prine as he attempts to rejoin fiancée Rosemary Forsyth in Texas, where con-man Dean Martin enlists his aid in saving a small settlement from an inept Comanche tribe. 101m. **DIR:** Michael Gordon. **CAST:** Dean Martin, Alain Delon, Rosemary Forsyth, Joey Bishop, Tina Marquand, Peter Graves, Michael Ansara, Andrew Prine, Roy Barcroft. **1966**

TEXAS CYCLONE ★★★★ An easygoing cowpoke (Tim McCoy) is mistaken for a straight-shooting rancher and sticks around to help the rancher's wife (Shirley Grey) fight off cattle rustlers. A top-notch McCoy gets some solid support from a couple of newcomers, John Wayne and Walter Brennan. B&W; 63m. **DIR:** D. Ross Lederman. **CAST:** Tim McCoy, Shirley Grey, John Wayne, Walter Brennan, Wheeler Oakman, Mary Gordon. **1932**

TEXAS GUNS ★★★ Enjoyable romp from veteran Western helmer Burt Kennedy, who lassos a bevy of old stable hands to tell the tale of a group of aging train robbers whose efforts are thwarted by a senior citizen posse and a young upstart played by Shaun Cassidy. Made-for-television film also known as *Once Upon a Texas Train*. 100m. **DIR:** Burt Kennedy. **CAST:** Willie Nelson, Richard Widmark, Shaun Cassidy, Angie Dickinson, Chuck Connors, Stuart Whitman. **1988**

TEXAS JOHN SLAUGHTER: GERONIMO'S REVENGE ★★½ Peace-loving Texan John Slaughter is forced to take up arms against his Apache friends when renegade Geronimo goes on the warpath. Full of action and filmed in authentic-looking locations, this feature is composed of episodes originally broadcast on the popular television show *Walt Disney Presents*. 77m. **DIR:** James Neilson. **CAST:** Tom Tryon, Darryl Hickman, Betty Lynn, Brian Corcoran, Adeline Harris. **1960**

TEXAS JOHN SLAUGHTER: STAMPEDE AT BITTER CREEK ★★½ Former Texas Ranger John Slaughter is falsely accused of rustling as he attempts to drive his cattle into New Mexico despite threats from a rival rancher and his hired gun. Tom Tryon is ruggedly heroic in this Disney adventure Western culled from episodes originally featured on *Walt Disney Presents* from 1958 to 1962. 52m. **DIR:** Harry Keller. **CAST:** Tom Tryon,

Harry Carey Jr., Adeline Harris, Annette Gorman, Betty Lynn. 1962

TEXAS JOHN SLAUGHTER: WILD TIMES ★★½ This film is a compilation of episodes from the popular series starring future best-selling author Tom Tryon as the lawman-turned-rancher. Handsomely photographed and well acted. 77m. **DIR:** Harry Keller. **CAST:** Tom Tryon, Harry Carey Jr., Adeline Harris, Annette Gorman, Betty Lynn, Brian Corcoran, Robert Middleton. 1962

TEXAS LADY ★★ An out-of-her-element Claudette Colbert is a crusading newspaper editor in the Old West. If you're a Western fan, you'll like it. 86m. **DIR:** Tim Whelan. **CAST:** Claudette Colbert, Barry Sullivan, John Litel. 1955

TEXAS MASQUERADE ★★★★ Hopalong Cassidy masquerades as an eastern Milquetoast to get the goods on badmen in this slam-bang Western that is one of the best of the series. B&W; 59m. **DIR:** George Archainbaud. **CAST:** William Boyd, Andy Clyde, Jimmy Rogers, Don Costello. 1944

TEXAS RANGERS, THE ★★★★ George Montgomery and the Texas Rangers vs. Sam Bass, the Sundance Kid and their band of outlaws. Superior B filmmaking. 74m. **DIR:** Phil Karlson. **CAST:** George Montgomery, Gale Storm, Jerome Courtland, William Bishop, John Dehner, Douglas Kennedy, Noah Beery Jr. 1951

TEXAS TERROR ★★½ John Wayne hangs up his guns (for a while) in this Lone Star Western about a lawman falsely accused of the death of his friend. Wayne finds the real culprits and gets a chance to do some hard ridin' and fancy sluggin'. B&W; 58m. **DIR:** Robert N. Bradbury. **CAST:** John Wayne, Lucille Brown, LeRoy Mason, George "Gabby" Hayes, Yakima Canutt. 1935

TEXAS TO BATAAN ★★ A trio of Texas cowboys, the Range Busters, join the U.S. Army, take a herd of cavalry horses to the Philippines, and find a spy in the kitchen—as the Japanese advance. A real Western cheapie. B&W; 56m. **DIR:** Robert Emmett Tansey. **CAST:** John King, David Sharpe, Max Terhune, Marjorie Manners. 1942

THERE WAS A CROOKED MAN ★★★½ Crooked-as-they-come Kirk Douglas bides and does his time harried by holier-than-thou Arizona prison warden Henry Fonda, who has more than redemption on his mind. A good plot and clever casting make this oater well worth the watching. And, yes, rattlesnakes do make good watchdogs. Rated R. 123m. **DIR:** Joseph L. Mankiewicz. **CAST:** Kirk Douglas, Henry Fonda, Hume Cronyn, Warren Oates, Burgess Meredith, Arthur O'Connell. 1970

THEY CALL ME TRINITY ★★½ This Western-comedy can be best described as an Italian *Blazing Saddles*. Terence Hill and Bud Spencer team up as half brothers trying to protect a colony from cattle rustlers and a shady sheriff. Rated G. 109m. **DIR:** E. B. Clucher. **CAST:** Terence Hill, Bud Spencer, Farley Granger. 1971

THEY DIED WITH THEIR BOOTS ON ★★★★ Errol Flynn gives a first-rate performance as General George Custer in this Warner Bros. classic directed by Raoul Walsh. The superb supporting cast adds to this Western epic. B&W; 138m. **DIR:** Raoul Walsh. **CAST:** Errol Flynn, Olivia de Havilland, Arthur Kennedy, Gene Lockhart, Anthony Quinn, Sydney Greenstreet. 1941

THIS MAN CAN'T DIE ★★★ Yet another "revenge for a slaughtered family" sadistic spaghetti Western with Guy Madison as a government agent avenger on the trail of an outlaw who murdered his parents. 90m. **DIR:** Gianfranco Baldanello. **CAST:** Guy Madison, Lucienne Bridou, Rik Battaglia. 1968

THOUSAND PIECES OF GOLD ★★★★ Ah, the joys of independent cinema: no formulas, no studio-policy compromises, no catering to star's images—just solid storytelling and committed filmmaking. Encompassing a story that begins in China and settles in Idaho's gold country in 1880, this wonderful movie about a woman who goes from slavery to fierce independence, offers a fresh perspective on the Old West. Unrated; the film has profanity and suggested sex. 105m. **DIR:** Nancy Kelly. **CAST:** Rosalind Chao, Chris Cooper, Dennis Dun. 1991

THREE BULLETS FOR A LONG GUN 🦃 A gunfighter and a Mexican bandit join forces to find a hidden Confederate treasure, but there isn't enough for both of them. Boring story line and bad acting. Unrated; contains violence. 89m. **DIR:** Peter Henkel. **CAST:** Beau Brummel, Keith Van Der Wat, Don McCorkindale, Janis Reinhardt. 1970

THREE GODFATHERS, THE ★★★½ Director John Ford's second version of Peter B. Kyne's biblically oriented Western features John Wayne, Harry Carey Jr., and Pedro Armendariz as three good-hearted outlaws who discover a baby in the desert and dedicate themselves to saving its life. The three leads work well together, and Ford's stock company—Ward Bond in particular—adds grit to the sentimental story. 103m. **DIR:** John Ford. **CAST:** John Wayne, Harry Carey Jr., Pedro Armendariz, Ward Bond, Mae Marsh, Jane Darwell, Ben Johnson. 1949

THREE IN THE SADDLE ★★ Standard B Western land-grab fare with the Texas Rangers coming to the aid of a girl whose ranch is being sought by outlaws. B&W; 60m. **DIR:** Harry Fraser. **CAST:** Tex Ritter, Dave O'Brien, Charles King, Guy Wilkerson. 1945

THREE MEN FROM TEXAS ★★★★★ A likely contender for the best Hopalong Cassidy film made. This one breaks every rule in the book as the romantic interest is killed off. Sidekick Andy Clyde is a reformed outlaw as he and Hoppy bust up Morris Ankrum's plot to gain control of the Mexican border territory. B&W; 75m. **DIR:** Lesley Selander. **CAST:** William Boyd, Russell Hayden, Andy Clyde, Morris Ankrum, Dick Curtis. **1940**

3:10 TO YUMA ★★★★ This first-rate adult Western draws its riveting drama and power from the interaction of well-drawn characters rather than gun-blazing action. A farmer (Van Heflin) captures a notorious gunman (Glenn Ford) and, while waiting for the train to take them to Yuma prison, must hole up in a hotel and overcome the killer's numerous ploys to gain his freedom. B&W; 92m. **DIR:** Delmer Daves. **CAST:** Glenn Ford, Van Heflin, Felicia Farr, Leora Dana, Henry Jones, Richard Jaeckel, Robert Emhardt. **1957**

THREE TEXAS STEERS ★★★ The Three Mesquiteers ride to the rescue of Carole Landis when bad guys try to force her to sell her ranch. Their solution is to enter her horse into a trotting race, which produces some amusing footage of John Wayne spitting the horse's tail out of his mouth while being pursued by the baddies. Max Terhune's last appearance as a Mesquiteer. B&W; 59m. **DIR:** George Sherman. **CAST:** John Wayne, Ray "Crash" Corrigan, Max Terhune, Carole Landis, Ralph Graves, Roscoe Ates, Billy Curtis, David Sharpe. **1939**

THREE VIOLENT PEOPLE ★★★ Charlton Heston returns to Texas after the Civil War with his bride and finds himself fighting land grabbers. Should have been better but Elaine Stritch is colorful as a saloon hostess. 100m. **DIR:** Rudolph Maté. **CAST:** Charlton Heston, Anne Baxter, Gilbert Roland, Tom Tryon, Forrest Tucker, Bruce Bennett, Elaine Stritch, Barton MacLane. **1956**

THREE-WORD BRAND, THE ★★★ Indians murder a homesteader, thus orphaning his twin sons. The brothers become separated—going their own ways—until circumstances reunite them many years later. William S. Hart deftly portrays the father and the sons in this silent sagebrush drama. B&W; 75m. **DIR:** Lambert Hillyer. **CAST:** William S. Hart, Jane Novak. **1921**

THRILL HUNTER ★★ Roaming cowboy Buck Jones tells some real whoppers about his past exploits to a movie production company and gets a job as their new star. When he is forced to drive a race car and fly a plane, his lies catch up with him. One of Jones's lighter movies that shows off his comedic style. B&W; 61m. **DIR:** George B. Seitz. **CAST:** Buck Jones, Dorothy Revier. **1933**

THUNDER PASS ★★ A good cast wasted as cavalry captain Dane Clark leads settlers out of Indian Territory. B&W; 80m. **DIR:** Frank McDonald. **CAST:** Dane Clark, Dorothy Patrick, Raymond Burr, Andy Devine, John Carradine, Mary Ellen Kay. **1954**

THUNDER TRAIL ★★½ Gilbert Roland and James Craig, two brothers, are separated as youngsters by outlaws. Years later they are on opposite sides of the law. An A cast fails to lift this Zane Grey story out of a B-movie mold. B&W; 58m. **DIR:** Charles Barton. **CAST:** Gilbert Roland, Charles Bickford, Marsha Hunt, J. Carrol Naish, James Craig. **1937**

THUNDERING HERD ★★ Lash LaRue is assigned to protect the new territorial governor from a threatening outlaw gang. Mostly stock footage from previous LaRue Westerns. B&W; 53m. **DIR:** Ron Ormond. **CAST:** Lash LaRue, Al St. John, Ray Bennett. **1951**

TIN STAR, THE ★★★★ Solid Anthony Mann–directed adult Western has Anthony Perkins as the inexperienced sheriff of a wild-and-woolly town seeking the help of hardened gunfighter Henry Fonda. Although it contains some unconvincing moments, *The Tin Star* succeeds overall thanks to the skilled playing of its cast. B&W; 93m. **DIR:** Anthony Mann. **CAST:** Henry Fonda, Anthony Perkins, Betsy Palmer, John McIntire, Michel Ray, Neville Brand, Lee Van Cleef. **1957**

TO THE LAST MAN ★★★★ Feudin' and fussin' in the Old West, Zane Grey style. Based on an actual clan clash that took place in Arizona during the 1880s, this is a top-quality oater from Paramount Pictures' series of films based on Grey's novels. Randolph Scott was directed in several of these by Henry Hathaway, and they made a potent team. Look for Shirley Temple in one of her earliest roles. B&W; 61m. **DIR:** Henry Hathaway. **CAST:** Randolph Scott, Richard Dix, Esther Ralston, Noah Beery Sr., Buster Crabbe, Jack LaRue. **1933**

TOM HORN ★★½ Steve McQueen doesn't give a great performance in his next-to-last motion picture, about the last days of a real-life Wyoming bounty hunter, nor does director William Wiard craft a memorable Western. Rated R. 98m. **DIR:** William Wiard. **CAST:** Steve McQueen, Richard Farnsworth, Billy Green Bush, Slim Pickens, Elisha Cook Jr. **1980**

TOMBSTONE ★★★★ After cleaning up Dodge City, the Earp brothers—Wyatt (Kurt Russell), Virgil (Sam Elliott), and Morgan (Bill Paxton)—attempt to settle down with their wives in Tombstone, but a marauding outlaw gang forces them to put their guns back on. Russell makes a fine Earp, Elliott is top-notch as always, and Val Kilmer may well be the screen's best Doc Holliday. Rated R for violence and profanity. 130m. **DIR:** George Pan Cosmatos. **CAST:** Kurt Russell, Val Kilmer, Michael Biehn, Powers Boothe, Robert Burke, Dana Delany, Sam Elliott, Stephen Lang, Terry O'Quinn, Jason Priestley, Joanna Pacula, Dana

Wheeler-Nicholson, Harry Carey Jr., Billy Zane. 1993

TRACKER, THE ★★★ In this generally effective made-for-HBO Western, Kris Kristofferson stars as famed tracker Noble Adams. He hunts down a bloodthirsty religious zealot–turned-outlaw (Scott Wilson) wanted for multiple murders and the kidnapping of a teenage girl. The film is sometimes slow and a bit too talky, but it's sporadically inventive. 90m. **DIR:** John Guillermin. **CAST:** Kris Kristofferson, Scott Wilson, Mark Moses, David Huddleston, Karen Kopins. 1988

TRACKERS, THE ★★ Ernest Borgnine plays a vengeful rancher out to get the men who killed his son and kidnapped his daughter. He reluctantly enlists the aid of a black professional tracker (Sammy Davis Jr.). It's a mildly entertaining Western made for TV. 73m. **DIR:** Earl Bellamy. **CAST:** Sammy Davis Jr., Ernest Borgnine. 1971

TRAIL BEYOND, THE ★★½ Once again, John Wayne rides to the rescue in a low-budget Western from the 1930s. It's pretty typical stuff as the Duke fights outlaws who are attempting to steal a gold mine. But this B Western has lots of action and a rare appearance of father and son actors Noah Beery Sr. and Noah Beery Jr. B&W; 55m. **DIR:** Robert N. Bradbury. **CAST:** John Wayne, Verna Hillie, Noah Beery Sr., Noah Beery Jr. 1934

TRAIL BLAZERS ★★★ The Three Mesquiteers stop a bandit gang run by a newspaper editor trying to halt the westward development of the telegraph. B&W; 54m. **DIR:** George Sherman. **CAST:** Robert Livingston, Bob Steele, Rufe Davis, Pauline Moore. 1940

TRAIL DRIVE ★★★★ Cattleman Ken Maynard brings to justice an unscrupulous rancher on a thrill packed cattle drive. B&W; 60m. **DIR:** Alan James. **CAST:** Ken Maynard, Cecilia Parker, Bob Kortman. 1933

TRAIL OF ROBIN HOOD ★★★ This star-studded oddity finds Roy Rogers and a handful of contemporary Western heroes aiding screen great Jack Holt (playing himself) in his effort to provide Christmas trees to needy families in time for the holidays. Enjoyable film for all ages and a special treat for fans of the genre. 67m. **DIR:** William Witney. **CAST:** Roy Rogers, Penny Edwards, Gordon Jones, Jack Holt, Emory Parnell, Clifton Young, Rex Allen, Allan "Rocky" Lane, Monte Hale, Kermit Maynard, Tom Keene, Ray "Crash" Corrigan, William Farnum. 1950

TRAIL OF THE SILVER SPURS ★★★ The Range Busters investigate hidden passages, salted mines, and a mysterious ghost-town killer known as the Jingler. B&W; 58m. **DIR:** S. Roy Luby. **CAST:** Ray "Crash" Corrigan, John King, Max Terhune, Dorothy Short, I. Stanford Jolley. 1941

TRAIL STREET ★★★ Randolph Scott plays Bat Masterson in this well-acted story of conflicting western philosophies as Robert Ryan defends the farmers against gambler Steve Brodie and the cattle-rancher faction. Gabby Hayes lends some levity to this otherwise dramatic adult Western. Skillful repackaging of a familiar story. B&W; 84m. **DIR:** Ray Enright. **CAST:** Randolph Scott, Robert Ryan, Anne Jeffreys, George "Gabby" Hayes, Steve Brodie. 1947

TRAILIN' NORTH ★★ Texas Ranger Bob Steele heads to Canada where he works with the Mounties to bring back a prisoner. Every B-Western cliché in the book. B&W; 57m. **DIR:** John P. McCarthy. **CAST:** Bob Steele, Doris Hill, George "Gabby" Hayes. 1933

TRAILING TROUBLE ★★ Cowboy great Ken Maynard is past his prime in this oater, but there's still enough vitality left to please genre fans. Straight-shootin' Ken clears a cloud over his name and rights the local wrongs. B&W; 57m. **DIR:** Arthur Rosson. **CAST:** Ken Maynard, Lona Andre, Vince Barnett, Roger Wiliams. 1937

TRAIN ROBBERS, THE ★★½ John Wayne and Ben Johnson join Ann-Margret in a search for a lost train and gold. Some nice moments but generally unsatisfying. For hard-core Wayne fans only. Rated PG for violence, but nothing extreme. 92m. **DIR:** Burt Kennedy. **CAST:** John Wayne, Ben Johnson, Ann-Margret, Rod Taylor, Ricardo Montalban. 1973

TRAITOR, THE ★★½ Marshal Tim McCoy goes undercover to catch a gang of cutthroats. He succeeds in his plan of joining the outlaws, but his life is in constant danger. A game performance by McCoy, but the story is too typical and the direction is plodding. B&W; 56m. **DIR:** Sam Newfield. **CAST:** Tim McCoy, Frances Grant, Wally Wales, Karl Hackett. 1936

TRAMPLERS, THE ★★ Gordon Scott returns from the Civil War to find his father (Joseph Cotten) trying to preserve the prewar South by burning out settlers and starting mass lynchings. Scott and his younger brother (Jim Mitchum) join up with their father's enemies. 105m. **DIR:** Albert Band. **CAST:** Gordon Scott, Joseph Cotten, Jim Mitchum, Franco Nero. 1966

TREASURE OF PANCHO VILLA, THE ★★½ Rory Calhoun and Gilbert Roland pull off a gold robbery with the intention of giving the loot to the Mexican revolutionary forces. However, Calhoun begins to think the money would be better in his pocket. Complications ensue. Calhoun carries a great machine gun in this watchable Western, and Roland is fascinating as always. Good action scenes. 96m. **DIR:** George Sherman. **CAST:** Rory Calhoun, Shelley Winters, Gilbert Roland, Joseph Calleia. 1955

TRIBUTE TO A BAD MAN ★★★★ A mean-spirited Western that works because of the personalities. James Cagney chews the scenery as a ruthless land baron who defies everyone to take advantage of him and his holdings. Cagney treats the role as if it were written for him, even though it was meant for Spencer Tracy, who passed on the project. 95m. **DIR:** Robert Wise. **CAST:** James Cagney, Irene Papas, Lee Van Cleef, Vic Morrow, Don Dubbins, Royal Dano, Stephen McNally. **1956**

TRIGGER, JR. ★★★ This Trucolor Roy Rogers film has everything going for it in the form of plot, songs, character actors, and hard ridin'. Roy, Dale, and the gang battle an unscrupulous gang of blackmailers as well as teach a young boy to overcome his fear of horses. 68m. **DIR:** William Witney. **CAST:** Roy Rogers, Dale Evans, Pat Brady, Gordon Jones, Grant Withers. **1950**

TRINITY IS STILL MY NAME ★★ In this comedy sequel to *They Call Me Trinity*, Bud Spencer and Terence Hill again team up as the unlikely heroes of an Italian Western. Rated G. 117m. **DIR:** E. B. Clucher. **CAST:** Bud Spencer, Terence Hill, Harry Carey Jr. **1972**

TRIPLE JUSTICE ★★★½ Once again, star George O'Brien and director David Howard take a standard B Western plot and infuse it with intelligence, character, and excitement. O'Brien is a peaceable cowpoke who innocently joins a gang of bank robbers. Silly, but surprisingly effective. B&W; 65m. **DIR:** David Howard. **CAST:** George O'Brien, Virginia Vale, Paul Fix, Glenn Strange. **1940**

TRIUMPHS OF A MAN CALLED HORSE 🦃 Richard Harris only makes a brief appearance in the title role as John Morgan, an English nobleman who was captured by the Sioux in 1825. Instead, the story focuses on his bland warrior son. Rated PG for violence and implied sex. 86m. **DIR:** John Hough. **CAST:** Richard Harris, Michael Beck, Ana De Sade. **1983**

TROUBLE IN TEXAS ★★½ Two-fisted singing rodeo cowboy Tex Ritter investigates crooked rodeo contests and seeks the men responsible for the death of his brother. Future glamour girl Rita Hayworth appears on-screen for the last time under her real name (Cansino). This enjoyable oater boasts a wild chase on a dynamite-laden wagon for a finale. B&W; 53m. **DIR:** Robert N. Bradbury. **CAST:** Tex Ritter, Rita Hayworth, Earl Dwire, Yakima Canutt. **1937**

TRUE GRIT ★★★★ John Wayne finally won his best-actor Oscar for his 1969 portrayal of a boozy marshal helping a tough-minded girl (Kim Darby) track down her father's killers. Well-directed by Henry Hathaway, it's still not one of the Duke's classics—although it does have many good scenes, the best of which is the final shoot-out between Wayne's Rooster Cogburn and chief baddie, Ned Pepper (Robert Duvall). Rated G. 128m. **DIR:** Henry Hathaway. **CAST:** John Wayne, Kim Darby, Robert Duvall, Glen Campbell. **1969**

TULSA KID ★★★½ Don Barry deserts his gunfighter heritage to aid defenseless pioneers threatened by a ruthless racketeer and his hired gunman—who turns out to be Barry's foster father. B&W; 57m. **DIR:** George Sherman. **CAST:** Don Barry, Noah Beery Sr., Luana Walters. **1940**

TUMBLEWEEDS ★★★½ One of silent films' greatest action sequences, the Oklahoma Land Rush along the Cherokee Strip, highlights this prestigious Western, famed cowboy star William S. Hart's final film. He retired to write novels. This version, which was introduced with a prologue spoken by Hart—his only venture into sound film—was released in 1939. Silent, with musical score. B&W; 114m. **DIR:** William S. Hart, King Baggott. **CAST:** William S. Hart, Barbara Bedford, Lucien Littlefield, Lillian Leighton. **1925**

TV CLASSICS: ANNIE OAKLEY ★★★ One episode from the TV series of the 1950s, this tale has Annie helping a Dutch gunsmith protect his special rifle from bad guys. Fun nostalgia. 30m. **DIR:** Not Credited. **CAST:** Gail Davis, Brad Johnson, Jimmy Hawkins. **1955**

TWICE A JUDAS 🦃 Another case of amnesia on the prairie. Luke, suffering from amnesia, is set upon by a local swindler who, after murdering Luke's family, passes himself off as Luke's brother. An unbelievable story and lack of action make this a dull film, even with Klaus Kinski in a leading role. Unrated; contains violence. 96m. **DIR:** Nando Cicero. **CAST:** Klaus Kinski, Antonio Sabato, Cristina Galbo, Pepe Calvo. **1968**

TWILIGHT IN THE SIERRAS ★★ Roy Rogers and his sweetheart Dale Evans are weighed down by Estelita Rodriguez and moronic comedy relief Pat Brady in this story about state parole officer Roy and his two-fisted battles with a group of counterfeiters. Not as good as most. Filmed in Trucolor. 67m. **DIR:** William Witney. **CAST:** Roy Rogers, Dale Evans, Estelita Rodriguez, Pat Brady, George Meeker, Fred Kohler Jr., House Peters Jr., Edward Keane, Bob Burns, Foy Willing and the Riders of the Purple Sage. **1950**

TWO-FISTED LAW ★★★★ A couple of young whippersnappers, John Wayne and Walter Brennan, add zest to this tale of a rancher (Tim McCoy in top form) out to get the goods on the crooks who cheated him out of his ranch. The screenplay by Three Mesquiteers creator William Colt MacDonald makes this one of McCoy's best; an outstanding B-plus Western. B&W; 64m. **DIR:** D. Ross Lederman. **CAST:** Tim McCoy, Wheeler Oakman, Tully Marshall, John Wayne, Walter Brennan. **1932**

TWO MULES FOR SISTER SARA ★★★ Clint Eastwood returns in his role of the "Man With No Name" (originated in Sergio Leone's Italian spaghetti Westerns) and Shirley MacLaine is an unlikely nun in this entertaining comedy-Western. Rated PG. 105m. **DIR:** Don Siegel. **CAST:** Clint Eastwood, Shirley MacLaine. **1970**

TWO RODE TOGETHER ★★★ In this variation of *The Searchers*, director John Ford explores the anguish of settlers over the children they have lost to Indian raiding parties and the racial prejudice that arises when one boy, now a full-blown warrior, is returned to his "people." It is not a fully effective film, but it does have its moments. 109m. **DIR:** John Ford. **CAST:** James Stewart, Richard Widmark, Shirley Jones, John McIntire, Woody Strode, Linda Cristal, Andy Devine. **1961**

ULZANA'S RAID ★★★★ A tense and absorbing film. Burt Lancaster and an expert cast and director take a fine screenplay penned by Alan Short and create a cavalry-Indians tale that is far from ordinary. Burt Lancaster plays an Indian scout who helps an inexperienced cavalry officer try to roust renegade Apache Ulzana and his tribe. Rated R. 103m. **DIR:** Robert Aldrich. **CAST:** Burt Lancaster, Bruce Davison, Jorge Luke, Richard Jaeckel, Lloyd Bochner. **1972**

UNDEFEATED, THE ★★ Lumbering large-scale Western has Yankee colonel John Wayne forming an uneasy alliance with Confederate colonel Rock Hudson to sell wild horses in Mexico. This film has little to recommend it—even to die-hard Wayne fans. Even the action is minimal. Rated PG. 119m. **DIR:** Andrew V. McLaglen. **CAST:** John Wayne, Rock Hudson, Bruce Cabot, Ben Johnson, Antonio Aguilar, Harry Carey Jr., Lee Meriwether, Jan-Michael Vincent. **1969**

UNDER CALIFORNIA STARS ★★½ Trigger, the "Smartest Horse in the Movies," is the victim of a horse-napping plot in this enjoyable Roy Rogers oater. 71m. **DIR:** William Witney. **CAST:** Roy Rogers, Jane Frazee, Andy Devine, Michael Chapin. **1948**

UNDER MEXICALI STARS ★★★ Modern-day Western involves counterfeiters and gold smugglers using helicopters to transport their contraband. B&W; 67m. **DIR:** George Blair. **CAST:** Rex Allen, Buddy Ebsen, Dorothy Patrick, Roy Barcroft. **1950**

UNDER TEXAS SKIES ★★★ Bob Steele's first with the Three Mesquiteers finds him suspected of killing a sheriff. B&W; 54m. **DIR:** George Sherman. **CAST:** Robert Livingston, Bob Steele, Rufe Davis, Henry Brandon. **1940**

UNDER WESTERN STARS ★★★½ Roy Rogers, in his first feature, plays a young congressman trying to obtain waterpower for the Dust Bowl area. Academy Award nomination for the song "Dust." B&W; 54m. **DIR:** Joseph Kane. **CAST:** Roy Rogers, Smiley Burnette, Carol Hughes. **1938**

UNEXPECTED GUEST ★★ Hopalong Cassidy comes to the aid of his saddle pal and comic relief California (Andy Clyde) after they discover that someone is trying to murder the cantankerous old cuss and all of his relatives. B&W; 59m. **DIR:** George Archainbaud. **CAST:** William Boyd, Andy Clyde, Rand Brooks, Una O'Connor. **1947**

UNFORGIVEN, THE (1960) ★★★½ This tough Texas saga is filled with pride, prejudice, and passion. Audrey Hepburn, as a troubled Indian girl raised by whites, is at the center of the turmoil. In addition to some intriguing relationships, the movie provides plenty of thrills with intense cowboy-versus-Indian action scenes. The cast is uniformly excellent. 125m. **DIR:** John Huston. **CAST:** Burt Lancaster, Audrey Hepburn, Audie Murphy, John Saxon, Charles Bickford, Lillian Gish, Doug McClure, Joseph Wiseman, Albert Salmi. **1960**

UNFORGIVEN (1992) ★★★★ A former outlaw promises his wife to change his ways, but, after she dies, he returns to violence in order to bring down a corrupt sheriff in the troubled town of Big Whiskey. Actor-director Clint Eastwood returns to the Western genre in high style by going up against a strong adversary in the always reliable Gene Hackman (as the corrupt lawman) and ensuring solid character support from Morgan Freeman and Richard Harris. Rated R for violence and profanity. 127m. **DIR:** Clint Eastwood. **CAST:** Clint Eastwood, Gene Hackman, Morgan Freeman, Richard Harris. **1992**

UNINVITED, THE (1993) 🦃 Embarrassingly bad Western finds a ragtag group of prospectors looking for gold on sacred Indian burial ground. Top-billed Jack Elam disappears before the opening credits are over. Unrated, but contains violence and adult situations. 90m. **DIR:** Michael Bohusz. **CAST:** Jack Elam, Christopher Boyer, Erin Noble. **1993**

UNION PACIFIC ★★★½ Lots of action in this fast-moving tale of the building of the transcontinental railroad, with a stellar cast playing the heroes and villains. With Cecil B. DeMille at the helm, you know it is an epic, in every sense, for the entire family. B&W; 135m. **DIR:** Cecil B. DeMille. **CAST:** Barbara Stanwyck, Joel McCrea, Brian Donlevy, Robert Preston, Akim Tamiroff, Anthony Quinn. **1939**

UTAH ★★★ Roy Rogers tries to prevent eastern show girl Dale Evans from selling her western ranch to raise money to back a Broadway musical. Short on action. B&W; 78m. **DIR:** John English. **CAST:** Roy Rogers, George "Gabby" Hayes, Dale Evans, Peggy Stewart, Grant Withers. **1945**

VALDEZ IS COMING ★★★½ Burt Lancaster is superb as Valdez, an aging town constable who takes it upon himself to collect $100 from a ruthless rancher after the senseless killing of an innocent black man leaves a pregnant Apache woman alone and destitute. Not everything in this Western works; however, Lancaster's towering performance as the Hispanic hero is a wonder to watch. Rated R for violence, profanity, and simulated sex. 90m. **DIR:** Edwin Sherin. **CAST:** Burt Lancaster, Susan Clark, Richard Jordan, Jon Cypher, Barton Heyman, Frank Silvera, Maria Montez, Nick Cravat, Hector Elizondo. **1971**

VALLEY OF FIRE ★★ After dispersing or recruiting the bad elements in town, Gene Autry plays matchmaker and delivers a flock of females just dying to marry up with smelly prospectors and settle down in greasy tents. Pretty good fun. B&W; 63m. **DIR:** John English. **CAST:** Gene Autry, Pat Buttram, Gail Davis, Russell Hayden. **1951**

VALLEY OF THE SUN ★★★ A discredited army scout runs into conflict with an unscrupulous government agent responsible for the maltreatment of Indians in the Arizona Territory in the 1800s. A Western that mixes in comedy. B&W; 84m. **DIR:** George Marshall. **CAST:** Lucille Ball, Cedric Hardwicke, Dean Jagger, James Craig. **1942**

VANISHING AMERICAN, THE ★★★½ One of the few major studio releases of the silent era to treat the American Indian with compassion and dignity, this is a beautifully photographed silent gem from Paramount. Based on Zane Grey's popular melodramatic adventure, this landmark film is still historically important as well as being a fine job by director George Seitz. Silent. B&W; 114m. **DIR:** George B. Seitz. **CAST:** Richard Dix, Lois Wilson, Noah Beery Sr., Charles Stevens. **1925**

VENGEANCE VALLEY ★★ Slow-moving story of no-good cattle heir Robert Walker and his protective foster brother Burt Lancaster lacks suspense and doesn't have enough action. 83m. **DIR:** Richard Thorpe. **CAST:** Burt Lancaster, Robert Walker, Joanne Dru, Ray Collins, John Ireland, Sally Forrest. **1951**

VERA CRUZ ★★★ Two American soldiers of fortune find themselves in different camps during one of the many Mexican revolutions of the 1800s. Gary Cooper is the good guy, but Burt Lancaster steals every scene as the smiling, black-dressed baddie. The plot is pretty basic but holds your interest until the traditional climactic gunfight. 94m. **DIR:** Robert Aldrich. **CAST:** Gary Cooper, Burt Lancaster, Denise Darcel, Ernest Borgnine. **1954**

VIGILANTES ARE COMING! ★★½ This early Republic serial features Robert Livingston in a story suspiciously similar to the Zorro legend: A young man returns to 1840s California and finds that an evil despot has taken his family's lands so he dons a mask and robe and finds the oppressor under the name of The Eagle. Action-packed and with impressive stunts. B&W; 12 chapters. **DIR:** Mack V. Wright, Ray Taylor. **CAST:** Robert Livingston, Kay Hughes, Guinn Williams, Raymond Hatton, Fred Kohler Sr., William Farnum, Bob Kortman, Ray "Crash" Corrigan, Yakima Canutt. **1936**

VIGILANTES OF BOOMTOWN ★★★½ Factions oppose the sanctioning of the heavyweight boxing bout between James Corbett and Bob Fitzsimmons in 1897 Carson City, Nevada. It takes Red Ryder to keep peace between the two pugilists as well as rout bank robbers and foil a kidnapping. B&W; 54m. **DIR:** R. G. Springsteen. **CAST:** Allan "Rocky" Lane, Bobby Blake, Peggy Stewart, Roy Barcroft, George Chesebro. **1947**

VILLA RIDES ★★ Uneven rehash of the Pancho Villa legend ignores the wealth of the real story and becomes yet another comic-book adventure. Good cast, but this ill-fated production doesn't deliver what it should. 125m. **DIR:** Buzz Kulik. **CAST:** Yul Brynner, Robert Mitchum, Charles Bronson, Herbert Lom, Jill Ireland, Alexander Knox, Fernando Rey. **1968**

VIOLENT MEN, THE ★★★ Edward G. Robinson is a crippled cattle baron, manipulated by his greedy wife and brother into a range war with a peace-loving rancher and valley settlers. Good action sequences. 96m. **DIR:** Rudolph Maté. **CAST:** Glenn Ford, Barbara Stanwyck, Edward G. Robinson, Brian Keith, Richard Jaeckel. **1954**

VIRGINIA CITY ★★★½ Errol Flynn's second big-budget Western for Warner Bros. is a hit-and-miss affair about three groups vying for a shipment of gold during the Civil War. Confederate officer Randolph Scott and southern-belle-turned-spy Miriam Hopkins hope to revive the South with it, Union officer Flynn must stop it at all costs, and Mexican bandit (!) Humphrey Bogart simply wants it for himself. B&W; 121m. **DIR:** Michael Curtiz. **CAST:** Errol Flynn, Miriam Hopkins, Randolph Scott, Humphrey Bogart, Alan Hale Sr., Guinn Williams, Frank McHugh, Douglass Dumbrille, John Litel, Ward Bond, Charles Middleton, Paul Fix, Russell Simpson. **1940**

VIRGINIAN, THE (1923) ★★ Lackluster version of Owen Wister's classic Western play and novel features good photography and some nice panoramas of the wide-open spaces, but the leads are stiff and the action is lacking. Kenneth Harlan doesn't cut it as the Virginian, and he brings the film down with him. Silent. B&W; 73m. **DIR:** Tom Forman. **CAST:** Kenneth Harlan, Florence Vidor, Russell Simpson, Pat O'Malley, Raymond Hatton. **1923**

VIRGINIAN, THE (1929) ★★★★ "If you want to call me that—smile!" Although a bit slow in parts, this early Western still impresses today. Gary Cooper (with a drawl helped along by coach Randolph Scott) is terrific in the title role as a fun-loving but tough ranch foreman who has to face the worst task of his life when a friend (Richard Arlen) falls in with an outlaw (Walter Huston). Huston, in his first film, plays the role of Trampas with an air of easygoing menace. B&W; 90m. **DIR:** Victor Fleming. **CAST:** Gary Cooper, Walter Huston, Mary Brian, Richard Arlen, Eugene Pallette, Chester Conklin. **1929**

VIVA VILLA! ★★★★ Even though he left the project before completion, director Howard Hawks's breezy style is still in evidence throughout this, Wallace Beery's best starring vehicle. A whitewashed account of Pancho Villa's activities from 1910 to 1916, it allows Beery to do some hard riding, fast shooting, and a whole lot of mugging as he leads his *bandido* revolutionaries against the Federales. Hawks, who shot all the outdoor scenes, was taken off the picture after trying to stop studio head Louis B. Mayer from firing original costar Lee Tracy (who was replaced by Stu Erwin). B&W; 115m. **DIR:** Jack Conway, Howard Hawks. **CAST:** Wallace Beery, Leo Carrillo, Fay Wray, Donald Cook, Stu Erwin, George E. Stone, Joseph Schildkraut, Katherine DeMille, Henry B. Walthall, Arthur Treacher. **1934**

WAGON TRAIN (TV SERIES) ★★★½ John Ford's *Wagonmaster* inspired the creation of this Western series, which starred Ward Bond as Major Seth Adams, the no-nonsense leader of a wagon train headed West, and Robert Horton, a scout Flint McCullough. In the premiere episode of this anthology-oriented show, Ernest Borgnine plays a former soldier from Adams's command. B&W; 60m. **DIR:** Herschel Daugherty. **CAST:** Ward Bond, Robert Horton, Ernest Borgnine, Marjorie Lord, Andrew Duggan, Beverly Washburn, Frank McGrath, Terry Wilson. **1957**

WAGON WHEELS ★★★ Scout Randolph Scott guides a wagon train to Oregon against all the Westward trek odds—the worst of which is a half-breed inciting the Indians into an uprising. Remake of *Fighting Caravans* (with Gary Cooper), including much stock footage. B&W; 56m. **DIR:** Charles Barton. **CAST:** Randolph Scott, Gail Patrick, Raymond Hatton, Monte Blue. **1934**

WAGON WHEELS WESTWARD ★★★ Red Ryder leads a wagon train of settlers into a seemingly deserted town, only to find it is inhabited by a gang of vicious outlaws. B&W; 56m. **DIR:** R. G. Springsteen. **CAST:** William Elliott, Robert Blake, Linda Stirling, Roy Barcroft. **1945**

WAGONMASTER ★★★★½ John Ford was unquestionably the greatest director of Westerns. This release ranks with the best of Ford's work. Ward Bond, who plays the elder in this story of a Mormon congregation migrating west, became a star, thanks to the popular television series it inspired: *Wagon Train*. And Ben Johnson, who won the best-supporting-actor Oscar in 1971 for *The Last Picture Show*, is excellent in his first starring role. B&W; 86m. **DIR:** John Ford. **CAST:** Ben Johnson, Ward Bond, Harry Carey Jr., Joanne Dru, James Arness. **1950**

WALL STREET COWBOY ★★★ Roy Rogers takes to the concrete canyons when a trial requires his presence in New York in his first contemporary Western of many to come. Often good-naturedly pokes fun at Roy's image. B&W; 54m. **DIR:** Joseph Kane. **CAST:** Roy Rogers, George "Gabby" Hayes, Raymond Hatton, Ann Baldwin. **1939**

WANTED: DEAD OR ALIVE (TV SERIES) ★★★½ The public was first captivated by Steve McQueen's cool, tough, intense persona with this top-notch Western series. McQueen plays dedicated bounty hunter Josh Randall, who travels the country searching for outlaws. The first video releases feature "Reunion for Revenge" with James Coburn and Ralph Meeker and "Medicine Man" with J. Pat O'Malley and Cloris Leachman. 30m. **DIR:** Thomas Carr, Richard Donner. **CAST:** Steve McQueen, Wright King. **1958–1961**

WAR OF THE WILDCATS ★★★ Big John Wayne takes on bad guy Albert Dekker in this story of oil drillers at the turn of the century. Gabby Hayes adds a vintage touch to this standard-formula Republic feature. B&W; 102m. **DIR:** Albert S. Rogell. **CAST:** John Wayne, Martha Scott, Albert Dekker, George "Gabby" Hayes, Sidney Blackmer, Dale Evans. **1943**

WAR WAGON, THE ★★★ While not John Wayne at his best, this Western, costarring Kirk Douglas and directed by Burt Kennedy, does have plenty of laughs and action. It's guaranteed to keep fans of the Duke pleasantly entertained. 101m. **DIR:** Burt Kennedy. **CAST:** John Wayne, Kirk Douglas, Howard Keel, Keenan Wynn. **1967**

WARLOCK (1959) ★★★ Even a high-voltage cast cannot energize this slow-paced "adult" Western. Lack of action hurts this film, which concentrates on psychological homosexual aspects of the relationship between gunfighter Henry Fonda and gambler Anthony Quinn. Richard Widmark is all but lost in the background as the town sheriff. 121m. **DIR:** Edward Dmytryk. **CAST:** Henry Fonda, Richard Widmark, Anthony Quinn, Dorothy Malone. **1959**

WATER RUSTLERS ★★ Standard land-grab plot failed to do much to establish Dorothy Page as a singing cowgirl star. After three attempts, she gave up and disappeared from the screen. B&W; 54m. **DIR:** Samuel Diege. **CAST:** Dorothy Page, Dave O'Brien. **1939**

WATERHOLE #3 ★★★ This amusing Western-comedy follows the misadventures of three outlaws, led by James Coburn, who rob the Union Army of a fortune in gold. 95m. **DIR:** William A. Graham. **CAST:** James Coburn, Carroll O'Connor, Margaret Blye, Bruce Dern, Claude Akins, Joan Blondell, James Whitmore. **1967**

WAY WEST, THE ★★ A strong cast cannot buoy this bloated Western about a wagon train inching its way along the Oregon Trail in 1843. Director Andrew McLaglen is obviously trying to make an epic in the style of his mentor, John Ford, but he fails miserably. 122m. **DIR:** Andrew V. McLaglen. **CAST:** Robert Mitchum, Kirk Douglas, Richard Widmark, Sally Field, Lola Albright, Stubby Kaye, John Mitchum. **1967**

WE ARE NO ANGELS ★★ Another *Trinity* wannabe. In 1910 a race is set to determine which company will obtain a transport concession. Of course the villains try to stop our heroes Rafael and Angel, but they invent hanggliders and win the race. A good cast makes this enjoyable. Rated PG. 90m. **DIR:** Frank Kramer. **CAST:** John Ireland, Woody Strode, Michael Coby, Paul Smith. **1976.**

WEST OF TEXAS ★★ Two Texas Rangers sent to organize a New Mexico Rangers outfit run smack into the standard railroad land-grab plot. B&W; 54m. **DIR:** Oliver Drake. **CAST:** James Newill, Dave O'Brien, Jack Ingram. **1943**

WEST OF THE DIVIDE ★★★ John Wayne is on the trail of his father's murderer (again) in this standard B Western, which has the slight twist of having the Duke also searching for his younger brother, who has been missing since dear old Dad took the fatal bullet. Looks as if it was made in a day—and probably was. Good stunt work, though. B&W; 54m. **DIR:** Robert N. Bradbury. **CAST:** John Wayne, Virginia Brown Faire, George "Gabby" Hayes, Yakima Canutt, Earl Dwire. **1934**

WEST OF THE LAW ★★★ The last of the Rough Riders Westerns, this entry takes the series out in style. The heroes help the townspeople defeat a band of rustlers. Jones handles most of the horseback heroics while McCoy instills fear in the bad guys with his steelie-eyed stare. B&W; 60m. **DIR:** Howard Bretherton. **CAST:** Buck Jones, Tim McCoy, Raymond Hatton, Evelyn Cooke, Harry Woods, Jack Daley, Roy Barcroft. **1942**

WESTERN UNION ★★★½ Randolph Scott's strong performance as an outlaw trying to go straight elevates this somewhat predictable Western epic about the coming of telegraph lines to the Wild West. 94m. **DIR:** Fritz Lang. **CAST:** Randolph Scott, Robert Young, Dean Jagger, Virginia Gilmore, John Carradine, Slim Summerville, Chill Wills, Barton MacLane. **1941**

WESTERNER, THE ★★★★ The plot revolves around earnest settlers being run off their land. But the heart of this classic yarn rests in the complex relationship that entwines Judge Roy Bean (Walter Brennan) and a lanky stranger (Gary Cooper). Bean is a fascinating character, burdened with a strange sense of morality and an obsession for actress Lily Langtree. Brennan won an Oscar for his portrayal. Cooper is at his laconic best. B&W; 100m. **DIR:** William Wyler. **CAST:** Gary Cooper, Walter Brennan, Forrest Tucker, Chill Wills, Dana Andrews, Tom Tyler, Fred Stone. **1940**

WESTWARD HO ★★★ The incorporation of Monogram Pictures and Lone Star Productions in a new mini-major studio called Republic Pictures brought bigger budgets and better production values to John Wayne's B Westerns, beginning with this enjoyable outing in which the star is once again seeking revenge on the outlaws who killed his parents and (in an extra twist) kidnapped his brother. B&W; 60m. **DIR:** Robert N. Bradbury. **CAST:** John Wayne, Sheila Manners, Frank McGlynn Jr., Jack Curtis, Yakima Canutt, Dickie Jones. **1935**

WESTWARD THE WOMEN ★★★★½ A rousing Western that emphasizes the problems of women on the frontier. Indian attacks, cat fights among the women, and accidental deaths can't keep these strong women from finding lonesome cowpokes and populating the frontier. 118m. **DIR:** William Wellman. **CAST:** Robert Taylor, Denise Darcel, Hope Emerson, Julie Bishop, John McIntire, Marilyn Erskine. **1951**

WHEN A MAN RIDES ALONE ★★ Whenever John Wayne needed a formidable screen opponent, Tom Tyler was a good choice. But mostly, Tyler was a star of B Westerns like this none-too-original entry about a Robin Hood–style good guy thwarting a crooked mine owner. B&W; 60m. **DIR:** J. P. McGowan. **CAST:** Tom Tyler, Alan Bridge. **1933**

WHEN A MAN SEES RED ★★★★ Writer-director Alan James gives producer-star Buck Jones a marvelous story line, and Jones gives a breezy, authoritative performance. Peggy Campbell plays the spoiled rich girl who is heir to the California ranch that Jones oversees, and he is charged with looking after her interests. B&W; 60m. **DIR:** Alan James. **CAST:** Buck Jones, Peggy Campbell, LeRoy Mason. **1934**

WHEN THE LEGENDS DIE ★★★½ A young Ute Indian is taken from his home in the Colorado Rockies after his parents die. In the modern white world he is taught the "new ways." His extraordinary riding abilities make him a target for exploitation as Red Dillon (Richard Widmark) trains him as a rodeo bronco rider, then proceeds to cash in on his protégé's success. A touching story that finds Widmark in one of his better roles and introduces a young Frederic Forrest. Rated PG for some mild profanity. 105m. **DIR:** Stuart Millar. **CAST:** Richard Widmark, Frederic Forrest. **1972**

WHERE TRAILS END ★★½ World War II is in full swing. Aided by his wonder horse Prince, U.S. Marshal Tom Keene, in glaring white from hat to boots, protects ranchers from ruthless outlaws working for Nazis. B&W; 58m. **DIR:** Robert Emmett Tansey. **CAST:** Tom Keene, Joan Curtis, Charles King. **1942**

WHITE BUFFALO 🦃 All-star cast wallows in weird *Jaws*-inspired Western, which has Wild Bill Hickok (Charles Bronson) on the trail of a mythical beast. Myth thith one. Rated R for violence. 97m. **DIR:** J. Lee Thompson. **CAST:** Charles Bronson, Kim Novak, Clint Walker, Jack Warden, Will Sampson, Stuart Whitman, Slim Pickens, John Carradine. **1977**

WHITE COMANCHE ★★ Twin sons of an Indian mother and a white settler fight amongst themselves. One, Notah, leads a band of renegade Comanches while the other, Johnny Moon, lives among the whites. William Shatner plays dual roles and is aided by Joseph Cotten as the sheriff. Unrated; contains violence. 90m. **DIR:** Gilbert Kay. **CAST:** William Shatner, Joseph Cotten, Rossana Yani, Perla Cristal. **1967**

WILD BUNCH, THE ★★★★½ *The Wild Bunch*, a classic Western, was brilliantly directed by Sam Peckinpah. He created a whole new approach to violence in this landmark film about men making a last stand. It is without a doubt Peckinpah's greatest film and is bursting with action, vibrant characters, and memorable dialogue. Good acting, too, by a first-rate cast. Rated R. 145m. **DIR:** Sam Peckinpah. **CAST:** William Holden, Ernest Borgnine, Robert Ryan, Ben Johnson, Edmond O'Brien, Warren Oates, Strother Martin, L. Q. Jones, Emilio Fernandez. **1969**

WILD FRONTIER ★★★★ Sheriff Rocky Lane goes after the outlaws responsible for his father's death, led by the town's dishonest saddle shop owner. First in the Rocky Lane series. B&W; 59m. **DIR:** Phillip Ford. **CAST:** Allan "Rocky" Lane, Jack Holt, Eddy Waller, Roy Barcroft. **1947**

WILD ROVERS, THE ★★★★ Sadly overlooked Western tells the story of two cowboys running from the law after robbing a bank. Holden is perfect as the older and not so wiser of the two, and O'Neal gives one of his best performances as the young partner. Rich in texture and smoothly directed by Blake Edwards. Rated PG. 109m. **DIR:** Blake Edwards. **CAST:** William Holden, Ryan O'Neal, Karl Malden, Tom Skerritt, Lynn Carlin, Joe Don Baker, Moses Gunn. **1971**

WILD TIMES ★★★ A two-cassette Western originally made for television. Sam Elliott plays sharpshooter High Cardiff, whose life is anything but easy as he makes his way across the Old West. This could have been helped by some trimming. 200m. **DIR:** Richard Compton. **CAST:** Sam Elliott, Ben Johnson, Timothy Scott, Harry Carey Jr., Bruce Boxleitner, Penny Peyser, Dennis Hopper. **1980**

WILD WEST (1946) ★★★★½ Eddie Dean and his pals string the Western telegraph against all odds including Indians and outlaws. The absolute best of Eddie Dean's Westerns with plenty of great action and good songs. 70m. **DIR:** Robert Emmett Tansey. **CAST:** Eddie Dean, Lash LaRue, Roscoe Ates, Buzz Henry, Louise Currie. **1946**

WILD, WILD WEST, THE (TV SERIES) ★★★★ The mid-60s spy craze produced a lot of TV shows, none more inventive than this Civil War–era adventure series starring Robert Conrad as James T. West, an undercover agent for President Ulysses Grant. Operating out of a gadget-laden railroad car and paired with Ross Martin's often-disguised Artemus Gordon, West tackled numerous foes bent on creating havoc or fomenting rebellion in the still-youthful United States. Look for the black-and-white first-season episodes, vastly superior to those that followed during the full-color remainder of the show's five-year run. 52m. each. **DIR:** Various. **CAST:** Robert Conrad, Ross Martin, Michael Dunn. **1965–70**

WILD WILD WEST REVISITED, THE ★★★ That diminutive genius, Miguelito Loveless, has a new plan for world domination. He's cloning heads of state. It's worked in England, Spain, and Russia. The United States and President Cleveland could be next. Those legendary agents James West and Artemus Gordon are called out of retirement to save the day. This revival of the Sixties series is breezily entertaining. 95m. **DIR:** Burt Kennedy. **CAST:** Robert Conrad, Ross Martin, Paul Williams, Harry Morgan, René Auberjonois, Robert Shields, Lorene Yarnell. **1979**

WILDFIRE (1945) ★★★ Bob Steele—in color—protecting the rights of wild horses. 57m. **DIR:** Robert Emmett Tansey. **CAST:** Bob Steele, Sterling Holloway, William Farnum, Eddie Dean. **1945**

WILL PENNY ★★★★½ Charlton Heston gives the finest performance of his distinguished career in this gritty, unsentimental look at the life of an illiterate cowboy in the American West. Director Tom Gries's screenplay leans a bit too heavily on George Stevens's *Shane* and Henry Hathaway's *Rawhide*, but his film can stand the comparison, which is high praise, indeed. Lucien Ballard's fine cinematography is another plus. Equivalent to a PG-13. 108m. **DIR:** Tom Gries. **CAST:** Charlton Heston, Joan Hackett, Donald

Pleasence, Lee Majors, Bruce Dern, Anthony Zerbe, Clifton James, Ben Johnson, Slim Pickens. 1968

WINCHESTER '73 ★★★ Cowboy James Stewart acquires the latest iron from the East, a Winchester '73 rifle, loses it to a thief, and pursues the prized weapon as it passes from hand to hand. Simple, brisk-paced, direct, action-packed, tongue-in-cheek, mean, sweaty, suspenseful, and entirely entertaining. B&W; 82m. **DIR:** Anthony Mann. **CAST:** James Stewart, Shelley Winters, Dan Duryea, Stephen McNally, Will Geer, Rock Hudson, Tony Curtis, John McIntire. 1950

WINDS OF THE WASTELAND ★★★ Big John Wayne is the head of a stagecoach company that competes for a government mail contract in the days after the pony express. Better than most B Westerns made by the Duke, because he was beginning to show more polish and confidence, but still no classic. B&W; 57m. **DIR:** Mack V. Wright. **CAST:** John Wayne, Phyllis Fraser, Yakima Canutt, Lane Chandler. 1936

WINDWALKER ★★★★ Trevor Howard plays the title role in this superb film which spans three generations of a Cheyenne Indian family. It refutes the unwritten rule that family entertainment has to be bland and predictable and is proof that films don't need to include sensationalism to hold the attention of modern filmgoers. Rated PG. 108m. **DIR:** Kieth Merrill. **CAST:** Trevor Howard, Nick Ramus, James Remar, Serene Hedin. 1980

WINNERS OF THE WEST ★★★ The white hats of the railroad fight it out with the black hats of the unscrupulous land baron in this classic thirteen-part oater jammed with gunplay, burning work trains, dynamited bridges, and a kidnapped heroine. B&W; 234m. **DIR:** Ford Beebe, Ray Taylor. **CAST:** Dick Foran, James Craig, Anne Nagel, Harry Woods. 1940

WINNING OF THE WEST ★★ Same old stuff about a brave newspaper publisher who enlists the aid of no-nonsense Gene Autry and all-nonsense Smiley Burnette. B&W; 57m. **DIR:** George Archainbaud. **CAST:** Gene Autry, Smiley Burnette, Gail Davis, Robert Livingston. 1953

WOLFHEART'S REVENGE ★★½ Wolfheart, a Rin-Tin-Tin look-alike, helps Guinn "Big Boy" Williams bring a killer to justice and win the girl in this silent oater. Silent. B&W; 64m. **DIR:** Fritz Lang. **CAST:** Guinn Williams, Helen Walton. 1925

WOMAN OF THE TOWN ★★½ Albert Dekker, as famed sheriff Bat Masterson, is forced to choose between his job and his love for saloon girl Claire Trevor. Good supporting cast can't save the slow pace of this Western soap opera. B&W; 87m. **DIR:** George Archainbaud. **CAST:** Albert Dekker, Claire Trevor, Barry Sullivan, Henry Hull. 1943

WYOMING OUTLAW ★★★½ With no-nonsense sidekick Raymond Hatton joining John Wayne and Ray "Crash" Corrigan as the Three Mesquiteers, the most popular of all the cowboy trio series marks one of its best episodes. *Wyoming Outlaw* made a star of Don Barry, in the title role as a hot-tempered youngster who turns cattle rustler. Silent-era *Tarzan* Elmo Lincoln, in a rare return to the screen, appears as a marshal. Call this one a B-plus Western. B&W; 62m. **DIR:** George Sherman. **CAST:** John Wayne, Ray "Crash" Corrigan, Raymond Hatton, Pamela Blake, Don Barry, LeRoy Mason, Yakima Canutt, Charles Middleton, Elmo Lincoln, David Sharpe. 1939

YELLOW HAIR AND THE FORTRESS OF GOLD ★★ Made to look like a 1940s serial, this film is more like a female *Indiana Jones*. Yellow Hair is a famed female Indian warrior, who is sent to find a lost treasure. Along the way she fights arrows, avalanches, and greedy gringos. Cameo appearances by spaghetti Western character actors make this a fun film. Rated R for violence. 102m. **DIR:** Matt Cimber. **CAST:** Laurene Landon, Ken Roberson, Luis Lorenzo, Aldo Sambrell, Claudia Gravy, Frank Brana, Eduardo Fajardo. 1984

YELLOW ROSE OF TEXAS ★★ Roy Rogers plays an undercover insurance agent out to clear the name of an old man who has been accused of aiding a stage robbery. B&W; 55m. **DIR:** Joseph Kane. **CAST:** Roy Rogers, Dale Evans, George Cleveland, Harry Shannon, Grant Withers, Bob Nolan and the Sons of the Pioneers, Tom London, Rex Lease. 1944

YODELIN' KID FROM PINE RIDGE ★★★ Plot is reminiscent of his first film, *Tumbling Tumbleweeds*, as Gene Autry is banished by his father only to return to his Georgia hometown with a Wild West show five years later to find his father murdered. B&W; 54m. **DIR:** Joseph Kane. **CAST:** Gene Autry, Smiley Burnette, Betty Bronson, Charles Middleton. 1937

YOUNG BILL HICKOK ★★½ Highly fictionalized tale of Wild Bill Hickok takes place after the Civil War when Roy Rogers (as Hickok) goes after foreign agents trying to gain control of California land. Muddled. B&W; 54m. **DIR:** Joseph Kane. **CAST:** Roy Rogers, George "Gabby" Hayes, Julie Bishop, Sally Payne. 1940

YOUNG GUNS ★★ The Brat Pack attempts to ape the Wild Bunch in this disappointing Western. Emilio Estevez seems to be having a great time playing Billy the Kid, while his brother Charlie Sheen makes a more convincing cowboy. But it's all for naught because the story lacks any authenticity. The only bright moments are provided by genre veterans Jack Palance, Brian Keith, and Patrick Wayne in all-too-brief supporting roles. Rated R for violence and profanity. 102m. **DIR:** Christopher Cain. **CAST:** Emilio Estevez, Kiefer Sutherland, Charlie Sheen, Lou Diamond Phillips, Dermot Mulroney, Casey Siemaszko, Jack Palance, Brian Keith, Patrick Wayne. **1988**

YOUNG GUNS II ★★ More pop Western nonsense. This time Billy the Kid and his gang find themselves pursued by an old saddle pal, Pat Garrett. *Lonesome Dove* it ain't. Rated PG-13 for violence and profanity. 109m. **DIR:** Geoff Murphy. **CAST:** Emilio Estevez, Kiefer Sutherland, Lou Diamond Phillips, William L. Petersen, Christian Slater, James Coburn, Alan Ruck, Balthazar Getty. **1990**

YOU'RE JINXED FRIEND, YOU JUST MET SACRAMENTO ★★ A peaceful cowboy and his children are forced into a showdown with a spiteful town boss. Unimaginative, mindless spaghetti oater with Ty Hardin, made after his successful Warner Bros. *Bronco* TV series ended. 90m. **DIR:** Giorgio Cristallini. **CAST:** Ty Hardin, Christian Hay, Jenny Atkins. **1970**

YUMA ★★½ Big Clint Walker fights most of the rowdy elements of a tough town and has to expose a plan to undermine his authority as a lawman in this enjoyable made-for-television Western. 73m. **DIR:** Ted Post. **CAST:** Clint Walker, Barry Sullivan, Edgar Buchanan, Kathryn Hays, Peter Mark Richman, Morgan Woodward. **1970**

ZACHARIAH ★★½ Forget the story line in this midnight movie Western and sit back and enjoy the music and the images. Television performers, a variety of musicians and actors, (including a youthful Don Johnson), populate this minor cult favorite and take every opportunity to be cool and break into song. There are tunes for most tastes and the fast-moving nature of the film makes it a good choice for company or a party. 93m. **DIR:** George Englund. **CAST:** John Rubinstein, Pat Quinn, Don Johnson, Country Joe and the Fish, Doug Kershaw. **1971**

ZANDY'S BRIDE ★★½ Gene Hackman takes Liv Ullmann as a mail-order bride, uses (and abuses) her as chattel until shared hardships bring about respect and devotion. Also released as *For Better, For Worse*. Rated PG. 116m. **DIR:** Jan Troell. **CAST:** Gene Hackman, Liv Ullmann, Eileen Heckart, Harry Dean Stanton, Susan Tyrrell, Sam Bottoms, Joe Santos. **1974**

ZORRO RIDES AGAIN ★★★ A modern-day Zorro, played by John Carroll, lends his hand to a railway under siege by ruthless Noah Beery Sr., one of the cinema's greatest heavies. Constant harassment keeps Zorro on his toes. A great cast keeps this serial moving at a rapid clip. B&W; 12 chapters. **DIR:** William Witney, John English. **CAST:** John Carroll, Helen Christian, Reed Howes, Duncan Renaldo, Noah Beery Sr., Nigel de Brulier, Bob Kortman, Tom London. **1937**

ZORRO'S BLACK WHIP ★★ Zorro never makes an appearance in this serial, but lovely-yet-lethal action star Linda Stirling dons a black outfit and becomes the Black Whip, riding in the hoofprints of her crusading brother. After several setbacks, the lovely heroine and her boyfriend (George J. Lewis) help the good people of Idaho thwart the greedy plans of a meanie who stands in the way of statehood for the territory. B&W; 12 chapters. **DIR:** Spencer Gordon Bennet, Wallace Grissell. **CAST:** George J. Lewis, Linda Stirling, Lucien Littlefield, John Merton, Tom London, Jack Kirk. **1944**

ZORRO'S FIGHTING LEGION ★★★ Quality serial places Reed Hadley (as Zorro) at the helm of a determined band of patriotic ranchers eager to ensure safe passage of the gold shipments needed to continue Juarez's rule. B&W; 12 chapters. **DIR:** William Witney, John English. **CAST:** Reed Hadley, Sheila Darcy, C. Montague Shaw, Budd Buster, Carleton Young, Charles King. **1939**

CAST INDEX

Aadland, Beverly: Assault of the Rebel Girls, *7*
Aaker, Lee: Hondo, *1121*
Aames, Angela: Basic Training, *232;* Lost Empire, The, *79*
Aames, Willie: Cut and Run, *493;* Frankenstein (1973), *842;* Paradise (1982), *97;* Zapped!, *416*
Aaron, Tom: Body Puzzle, *958*
Abatantuono, Diego: Mediterraneo, *766*
Abbott, Bruce: Bad Dreams, *811;* Bride of Re-Animator, *819;* Re-Animator, *879;* Summer Heat (1987), *672;* Tag—The Assassination Game, *124;* Trapped, *1027*
Abbott, Bud: Abbott and Costello in Hollywood, *221;* Abbott and Costello Meet Captain Kidd, *221;* Abbott and Costello Meet Dr. Jekyll and Mr. Hyde, *221;* Abbott and Costello Meet Frankenstein, *221;* Abbott and Costello Meet the Invisible Man, *221;* Abbott and Costello Meet the Killer, Boris Karloff, *221;* Abbott and Costello Meet the Mummy, *221;* Abbott and Costello Show, The (TV Series), *221;* Africa Screams, *223;* Buck Privates, *246;* Buck Privates Come Home, *246;* Here Come the Co-Eds, *296;* Hey Abbott!, *296;* Hit the Ice, *298;* Hold That Ghost, *298;* In Society, *306;* Little Giant, *319;* Lost in a Harem, *321;* Lost in Alaska, *321;* Mexican Hayride, *331;* MGM's The Big Parade of Comedy, *331;* Naughty Nineties, The, *342;* Noose Hangs High, The, *346;* One Night in the Tropics, *350;* Pardon My Sarong, *354;* Ride 'em Cowboy, *368;* Rio Rita, *368;* Time of Their Lives, The, *396;* Who Done It?, *410;* Wistful Widow of Wagon Gap, The, *412;* World of Abbott and Costello, The, *414*
Abbott, Diahnne: Jo Jo Dancer, Your Life Is Calling, *558;* Love Streams, *582*
Abbott, John: Pursuit to Algiers, *1008*
Abbott, Philip: Invisible Boy, The, *1059*
Abdul-Jabbar, Kareem: Airplane!, *224;* Game of Death, *54;* Jake Spanner Private Eye, *68*
Abel, Alan: Putney Swope, *363*
Abel, Alfred: Metropolis (1926), *1065;* Metropolis (musical version), *930*
Abel, Walter: Fury, *524;* Island in the Sky, *554;* Mirage, *595;* Mr. Skeffington, *597;* Quick, Let's Get Married, *363;* Raintree County, *634;* 13 Rue Madeleine, *127;* Three Musketeers, The (1935), *128;* Wake Island, *136*
Abele, Jim: Wimps, *412*
Abella, Helena: Final Justice, *48*
Abercrombie, Ian: Army of Darkness, *810;* Curse IV: The Ultimate Sacrifice, *828;* Puppet Master III: Toulon's Revenge, *878*
Abercrombie, Jabee: Fugitive Girls, *53*
Abraham, F. Murray: Amadeus, *906;* Beyond the Stars, *1039;* Innocent Man, An, *66;* Intimate Power, *553;* Last Action Hero, The, *1062;* Mobsters, *86;* Name of the Rose, The, *89;* Ritz, The, *368;* Season of Giants, A, *650;* Slipstream, *1077;* Surviving the Game, *123;* Sweet Killing, *1022;* Third Solution, The, *794*
Abraham, Ken: Creepozoids, *826;* Deadly Embrace, *34*
Abrams, Michael: Summer Camp, *388*
Abril, Victoria: After Darkness, *951;* Caged Heart, The (L'Addition), *721;* High Heels (1992), *744;* Jimmy Hollywood, *310;* Kika, *751;* Lovers (1992), *762;* Moon in the Gutter, The, *768;* On the Line, *94;* Tie Me Up! Tie Me Down!, *795*
Ackerman, Forrest J.: Hard to Die, *848*
Ackerman, Leslie: Blame It on the Night, *463*
Ackland, Joss: Bill and Ted's Bogus Journey, *239;* Codename: Kyril, *962;* Ghost Ship, *846;* Hunt for Red October, The, *984;* Lethal Weapon 2, *76;* Mighty Ducks, The, *187;* Mind Snatchers, The, *865;* Mother's Boys, *998;* Nowhere to Run (1993), *92;* Palermo Connection, The, *1004;* Project: Shadowchaser, *101;* Saint Jack, *646;* Sherlock Holmes and the Incident at Victoria Falls, *1015;* Sicilian, The, *115;* Spymaker: The Secret Life of Ian Fleming, *119;* S*P*Y*S, *385;* To Kill a Priest, *684;* White Mischief, *700;* Zed and Two Noughts, A, *709*
Ackridge, Bill: Signal 7, *657*
Ackroyd, David: And I Alone Survived, *447;* Children of Times Square, The, *481;* Cocaine: One Man's Seduction, *485;* Dark Secret of Harvest Home, The, *829;* Dead On, *967;* Gun in the House, A, *534;* Love, Cheat & Steal, *993;* When Your Lover Leaves, *699*
Acosta, Rodolfo: Littlest Outlaw, The, *184*
Acovone, Jay: Beauty and the Beast (TV Series), *1039;* Born To Run, *18;* Doctor Mordrid, *1047;* Quicksand: No Escape, *1008*
Acquanetta: Lost Continent, The, *1063*
Acuff, Eddie: G-Men Never Forget, *54;* Helldorado (1946), *1120;* Rough Riders' Roundup, *1146*
Adair, Deborah: Endless Descent, *838*
Adair, Dick: Blind Rage, *15*
Adair, Jean: Arsenic and Old Lace, *228*
Adames, John: Gloria, *56*
Adams, Beverly: Ambushers, The, *4;* Torture Garden, *896*
Adams, Brandon: People Under the Stairs, The, *873*
Adams, Brooke: Almost You, *225;* Cuba, *31;* Days of Heaven, *496;* Dead Zone, The, *831;* Gas, Food, Lodging, *525;* Invasion of the Body Snatchers (1978), *1059;* James Dean—A Legend in His Own Time, *556;* Key Exchange, *563;* Last Hit, The, *990;* Lion of Africa, The, *77;* Man, a Woman and a Bank, A, *994;* Man on Fire, *81;* Murder on Flight 502, *87;* Paul Reiser Out on a Whim, *355;* Shock Waves (Death Corps), *885;* Sometimes They Come Back, *888;* Tell Me a Riddle, *678;* Unborn, The, *898;* Utilities, *404*
Adams, Carol: Bad Man of Deadwood, *1095;* Ridin' on a Rainbow, *1144*
Adams, Casey: Bus Stop, *248;* Indestructible Man, *856*
Adams, Don: Don Rickles: Buy This Tape You Hockey Puck, *267;* Get Smart Again, *285;* Nude Bomb, The, *347;* Two Top Bananas, *402*
Adams, Dona: Zipperface, *1033*
Adams, Edie: Adventures Beyond Belief, *222;* Apartment, The, *228;* Best Man, The, *459;* Boxoffice, *467;* Call Me Bwana, *249;* Cry for Love, A, *492;* Ernie Kovacs: Television's Original Genius, *272;* Happy Hooker Goes Hollywood, The, *293;* Honey Pot, The, *300;* It's a Mad Mad Mad Mad World, *308;* Jake Spanner Private Eye, *68;* Love with the Proper Stranger, *582;* Lover Come Back, *323;* Seekers, The, *651;* Up in Smoke, *403*
Adams, Ernie: Arizona Gunfighter, *1094*
Adams, Jane: Batman and Robin, *9;* Brute Man, The, *820;* House of Dracula, *852;* Light Sleeper, *575;* Lost City of the Jungle, *79*
Adams, Jason: Ollie Hopnoodle's Haven of Bliss, *192;* Puppet Master Four, *878*

Adams, Jeb: Flowers in the Attic, *978*
Adams, Jill: Brothers in Law, *246*
Adams, Jonathan: Rocky Horror Picture Show, The, *937*
Adams, Julie: Away all Boats, *8;* Bend of the River, *1097;* Creature from the Black Lagoon, *826;* Francis Joins the Wacs, *280;* Hostile Country, *1122;* Last Movie, The, *570;* Man from the Alamo, The, *1132;* Psychic Killer, *877;* Tickle Me, *945*
Adams, Kathryn: Fifth Avenue Girl, *276*
Adams, Lynn: Carpenter, The, *821*
Adams, Lynne: Blood Relations, *816*
Adams, Maria: Gotcha!, *980*
Adams, Mason: Assault at West Point, *451;* Final Conflict, The, *841;* F/X, *979;* Kid with the Broken Halo, The, *313;* Night They Saved Christmas, The, *191;* Revenge of the Stepford Wives, *881;* Shining Season, A, *656*
Adams, Maud: Deadly Intent, *34;* Girl in Blue, The, *527;* Hostage Tower, The, *64;* Intimate Power, *553;* Jane and the Lost City, *309;* Killer Force, *71;* Man of Passion, A, *587;* Man with the Golden Gun, The, *81;* Nairobi Affair, *603;* Octopussy, *93;* Playing for Time, *623;* Rollerball, *1075;* Silent Night, Deadly Night 4—Initiation, *886;* Target Eagle, *125;* Tattoo, *677;* Women's Club, The, *413*
Adams, Nick: Die, Monster, Die!, *834;* FBI Story, The, *515;* Godzilla vs. Monster Zero, *846;* Hell Is for Heroes, *60;* Interns, The, *553;* Mission Mars, *1066;* No Time for Sergeants, *345;* Picnic, *622;* Rebel without a Cause, *636;* Teacher's Pet, *392*
Adams, Ted: Arizona Gunfighter, *1094;* His Fighting Blood, *1121;* Holt of the Secret Service, *63;* Lightning Carson Rides Again, *1128;* Smokey Trails, *1151*
Adams, Tom: Fighting Prince of Donegal, The, *167*
Adamson, Dave: City in Panic, *824*
Adamson, George: Christian the Lion, *158*
Addabbo, Tony: Gunfighters, The, *1117*
Addams, Dawn: King in New York, A, *313;* Liars, The, *760;* Moon Is Blue, The, *336;* Robe, The, *642;* Silent Enemy, The, *116;* Thousand Eyes of Dr. Mabuse, The, *1083;* Vampire Lovers, The, *900;* Vault of Horror, *900;* Voulez Vous Danser avec Moi? (Will You Dance with Me?), *801*
Addison, Nancy: Somewhere, Tomorrow, *206*
Addy, Wesley: Bostonians, The, *467;* Europeans, The, *511*
Adele, Jan: High Tide, *541*
Adix, Vern: Teen Alien, *892*
Adjani, Isabelle: Camille Claudel, *721;* Driver, The, *42;* Ishtar, *307;* Next Year If All Goes Well, *771;* One Deadly Summer, *773;* Possession, *876;* Quartet (1981), *631;* Story of Adele H, The, *789;* Subway, *790*
Adler, Jerry: Manhattan Murder Mystery, *328*
Adler, Luther: Brotherhood, The, *471;* Cornered, *29;* Crashout, *30;* D.O.A. (1949), *965;* Desert Fox, The, *37;* Hoodlum Empire, *64;* House of Strangers, *545;* Kiss Tomorrow Goodbye, *73;* Last Angry Man, The, *568;* Loves of Carmen, The, *582;* Murph the Surf, *87;* Von Ryan's Express, *136;* Wake of the Red Witch, *136*
Adler, Matt: Diving In, *502;* Flight of the Navigator, *1052;* North Shore, *609;* White Water Summer, *139*
Adler, Stella: My Girl Tisa, *602*
Adolphson, Edvin: Only One Night, *773*
Adorée, Renée: Big Parade, The, *460;* Buster Keaton Festival: Vol. 3, *248;* Buster Keaton: The Golden Years, *248*
Adorf, Mario: Holcroft Covenant, The, *982;* Invitation au Voyage, *748;* King, Queen and Knave, *565;* Lola (1982), *761;* Manhunt (1973), *81;* Ten Little Indians (1966), *1023;* Tin Drum, The, *795*
Adrian, Iris: Blue Hawaii, *909;* Bluebeard (1944), *817;* Lady of Burlesque, *74;* Road to Zanzibar, *369*
Adrian, Max: Boy Friend, The, *909;* Devils, The, *500;* Music Lovers, The, *932;* Terronauts, The, *1082*
Adrian, Patricia: I'm the One You're Looking For, *747*
Adu, Robinson Frank: Heart, *537*
Adu, Sade: Absolute Beginners, *906*
Aerosmith: Wayne's World 2, *406*
Affleck, Neil: My Bloody Valentine, *867*
Agar, John: Along the Great Divide, *1093;* Brain from Planet Arous, The, *1040;* Daughter of Dr. Jekyll, *829;* Fort Apache, *1114;* Jet Attack, *68;* Johnny Reno, *1124;* Miracle Mile, *996;* Mole People, The, *1066;* Perfect Bride, The, *873;* Revenge of the Creature, *881;* Sands of Iwo Jima, *111;* Tarantula, *892;* Women of the Prehistoric Planet, *1090*
Agbayani, Tetchie: Deathfight, *36;* Gymkata, *58*
Agostino, Pierre: Hollywood Strangler Meets the Skid Row Slasher, *851*
Agren, Janet: Aladdin (1987), *144;* Emerald Jungle, *838;* Gates of Hell, *845;* Hands of Steel, *1055;* Lobster for Breakfast, *761*
Agterberg, Toon: Spetters, *788*
Aguilar, Antonio: Undefeated, The, *1160*
Agutter, Jenny: American Werewolf in London, An, *808;* Amy, *146;* Child's Play 2, *823;* Dark Tower, *829;* Dominique Is Dead, *971;* Equus, *973;* Gunfire, *1117;* King of the Wind, *180;* Logan's Run, *1063;* Man in the Iron Mask, The (1977), *81;* Not a Penny More, Not a Penny Less, *1002;* Othello (1982), *615;* Railway Children, The, *198;* Riddle of the Sands, *106;* Silas Marner, *657;* Sweet William, *389*
Aherne, Brian: Beloved Enemy, *458;* Forever and a Day, *520;* I Confess, *984;* I Live My Life, *547;* Juarez, *560;* Lady in Question, *568;* Night to Remember, A (1943), *345;* Prince Valiant, *100;* Smilin' Through (1941), *940;* Swan, The (1956), *674;* Sword of Lancelot, *124;* Sylvia Scarlett, *676;* Waltz King, The, *215*
Aherne, Michael: Commitments, The, *912*
Ahlstedt, Borje: Emma's Shadow, *734;* I Am Curious Blue, *746;* I Am Curious Yellow, *746*
Ahn, Philip: Battle Circus, *456;* Betrayal from the East, *11;* Buck Rogers: Destination Saturn (a.k.a. Planet Outlaws), *1040;* Halls of Montezuma, *59;* His Majesty O'Keefe, *62;* Kung Fu, *73;* They Got Me Covered, *393*
Aidman, Charles: Countdown, *489;* House of the Dead, *853;* King Lear (1982), *564;* Kotch, *314;* Menace on the Mountain, *593;* Prime Suspect, *627;* Zoot Suit, *949*
Aiello, Danny: Alone in the Neon Jungle, *445;* Cemetery Club, The, *478;* Closer, The, *484;* Defiance, *36;* Do the Right Thing, *502;* Harlem Nights, *59;* Hudson Hawk, *64;* Jacob's Ladder, *1060;* January Man, The, *987;* Key Exchange, *563;* Man on Fire, *81;* Me and the Kid, *83;* Mistress (1992), *597;* Moonstruck, *336;* Old Enough, *611;* Once Around, *349;* Pickle, The, *357;* Preppie Murder, The, *626;* Protector, The, *101;* Purple Rose of Cairo, The, *363;* Question of Honor, A, *632;* Ruby (1991), *644;* Stuff, The, *891;* Third Solution, The, *794;* 29th Street, *401;* White Hot, *138*
Aiello, Rick: Me and the Kid, *83*
Aimée, Anouk: Dr. Bethune, *502;* 8½, *733;* Head Against the Wall, *743;* Justine, *561;* La Dolce Vita, *753;* Lola (1960), *761;* Man and a Woman, A, *764;* Man and a Woman, A: 20 Years Later, *764;* Paris Express, The, *97;* Success Is the Best Revenge, *672;* Tragedy of a Ridiculous Man, *796*
Ainsley, Norman: Shadow Strikes, The, *1014*
Aird, Holly: Overindulgence, *617*
Aitchison, Suzy: Bloody New Year, *817*
Aitken, Spottiswoode: Eagle, The, *269;* Home, Sweet Home, *543*
Ajaye, Franklin: Car Wash, *250;* Get Crazy, *284;* Wrong Guys, The, *414*
Akemay: Army Brats, *228*
Akili, Ali Mohammed El: Wedding in Galilee, A, *802*
Akin, Tarik: Yol, *806*
Akins, Claude: Battle for the Planet of the Apes, *1038;* Curse, The, *827;* Death Squad, The, *35;* Devil's Brigade, The, *37;* Eric, *510;* Falling from Grace, *513;* Gambler Returns, the: Luck of the Draw, *1115;* Inherit the Wind, *552;* Manhunt for Claude Dallas, *81;* Monster in the Closet, *866;* Night Stalker, The (1971), *870;* Onionhead, *350;* Pecos Bill, King of the Cowboys, *194;* Return of the Seven, *1142;* Ride Beyond Vengeance, *1143;* Rio Bravo, *1145;* Sea Chase, The, *112;* Sherlock Holmes and the Incident at Victoria Falls, *1015;* Tarantulas—The Deadly Cargo, *892;* Waterhole #3, *1163*

utagawa, Hiroshi: Mistress, The (1953), *768*
aimo, Marc: Arena, *1036;* Avenging Force, *8*
eimo, Steve: Stanley, *890*
an, Craig: Game, The, *54*
an-Lee, Jeff: Beniker Gang, The, *149*
ard, Nelly: Eating, *507;* Venica/Venice, *693*
askey, Joe: Gross Jokes, *291;* Lucky Stiff, *324;* ramount Comedy Theatre, Vol. 2: Decent Exposures, *354*
ba, Maria: Mr. Robinson Crusoe, *86;* Return of Chandu he Magician), *105*
bano, Lou: Body Slam, *17;* It's a Complex World, *308*
basiny, John: Kipperbang, *566*
bee, Josh: Tom Sawyer (1973), *213*
berghetti, Anna Maria: Cinderfella, *912;* Last Command, e (1955), *1125*
berni, Luis: Big Stampede, The, *1098;* Madame X (1937), *34;* Man from Monterey, The, *1131;* Road to Zanzibar, *369*
beroni, Sherry: Nightmare Circus, *871*
bers, Hans: Baron Müenchhausen, *1038*
bert, Annie: Tomb of Torture, *896*
bert, Eddie: Act, The, *441;* Actors and Sin, *441;* Airport 9: The Concorde, *443;* Beulah Land, *459;* Birch Interval, The, *50;* Bombardier, *17;* Captain Newman, M.D., *474;* Carrie 952), *476;* Crash of Flight 401, *490;* Devil's Rain, The, *834;* reamscape, *1048;* Dress Gray, *505;* Escape to Witch ountain, *165;* Foolin' Around, *278;* Fuller Brush Girl, The, *82;* Goliath Awaits, *56;* Head Office, *294;* Heartbreak Kid, he, *295;* Hustle, *65;* I'll Cry Tomorrow, *924;* Longest Yard, he, *78;* McQ, *83;* Miracle of the White Stallions, *187;* Moving olation, *87;* Oklahoma!, *933;* Our Mr. Sun, *193;* Perfect arriage, *356;* Roman Holiday, *642;* Smash-Up: The Story of Woman, *661;* Stitches, *386;* Take This Job and Shove It, *90;* Teahouse of the August Moon, The, *392;* Whiffs, *410;* ho's Got the Action?, *411;* Yes, Giorgio, *948*
lbert, Edward: Body Language, *958;* Butterflies Are Free, *73;* Demon Keeper, *832;* Distortions, *834;* Exiled in America, *5;* Fist Fighter, *49;* Fool Killer, The, *978;* Forty Carats, *279;* alaxy of Terror, *1053;* Getting Even, *55;* Greek Tycoon, The, *33;* Guarding Tess, *291;* House Where Evil Dwells, The, *853;* e Runner, *65;* Midway, *84;* Mindgames, *996;* Out of Sight ut of Mind, *1003;* Purple Taxi, The, *631;* Rescue, The, *105;* hootfighter, *115;* Silent Victory: The Kitty O'Neil Story, *658;* erminal Entry, *1082;* Time to Die, A (1983), *130;* When Time an Out!, *1031*
lbert, Laura: Blood Games, *956*
lbert, Maxine: Home Remedy, *300*
lbertazzi, Giorgio: Last Year at Marienbad, *756*
lberti, Lima: Clowns, The, *725*
lbertson, Frank: Ah, Wilderness, *223;* Alice Adams, *444;* achelor Mother, *230;* Connecticut Yankee, A, *258;* Dr. hristian Meets the Women, *502;* Doubting Thomas, *268;* nemy Below, The, *44;* Hucksters, The, *545;* Louisiana urchase, *322;* Navy Blue and Gold, *342;* Psycho, *877;* hining Hour, The, *656*
lbertson, Jack: Big Business Girl, *460;* Dead and Buried, *330;* Don't Go Near the Water, *267;* Flim-Flam Man, The, *518;* ow to Murder your Wife, *303;* Justine, *561;* Kissin' Cousins, *27;* Lover Come Back, *323;* Period of Adjustment, *356;* abbit Run, *632;* Subject Was Roses, The, *671;* Teacher's Pet, *92;* Willy Wonka and the Chocolate Factory, *217*
lbrecht, Marcy: Hollywood High, *299*
lbright, Hardie: Scarlet Letter, The (1934), *649;* Silver treak (1934), *658*
lbright, Lola: Impossible Years, The, *305;* Joy House, *559;* id Galahad (1962), *926;* Lord Love a Duck, *321;* Monolith onsters, The, *865;* Peter Gunn (TV Series), *98;* Tender Trap, he, *392;* Way West, The, *1163;* Where Were You When the ights Went Out?, *409*
lcaide, Chris: Gunslinger, *1118*
lcroft, Jamie: Million Dollar Mystery, *332*
lda, Alan: And the Band Played on, *447;* Betsy's Wedding, *236;* California Suite, *249;* Crimes and Misdemeanors, *490;* Four Seasons, The, *521;* Glass House, The, *528;* Lily Tomlin Special—Vol. I, The, *319;* M*A*S*H* (TV Series), *325;* M*A*S*H: Goodbye, Farewell, Amen, *325;* Manhattan Murder Mystery, *328;* Mephisto Waltz, The, *864;* New Life, A, *343;* Paper Lion, *618;* Playmates, *358;* Purlie Victorious, *363;* Same Time Next Year, *372;* Seduction of Joe Tynan, The, *651;* Sweet Liberty, *389;* To Kill a Clown, *1025;* Whispers in the Dark, *1031*
Alda, Antony: Hot Child in the City, *64*
Alda, Beatrice: New Life, A, *343*
Alda, Robert: Beast with Five Fingers, The, *812;* Bittersweet Love, *462;* Cloak and Dagger (1946), *962;* Devil in the House of Exorcism, The, *833;* House of Exorcism, The, *852;* I Will, I Will…for Now, *304;* Imitation of Life, *549;* Man I Love, The, *586;* Rhapsody in Blue, *936*
Alda, Rutanya: Amityville II: The Possession, *809;* Apprentice to Murder, *810;* Dark Half, The, *829;* Racing with the Moon, *633*
Alden, Ginger: Lady Grey, *568*
Alden, Matt: Doin' Time on Planet Earth, *267*
Alden, Norman: Red Line 7000, *104*
Alden, Priscilla: Crazy Fat Ethel II, *826;* Criminally Insane, *826;* Death Nurse, *831*
Alden, Terry: Last Game, The, *569*
Alderman, John: Boob Tube, The, *243*
Aldon, Mari: Distant Drums, *40*
Aldredge, Tom: Man That Corrupted Hadleyburg, The, *327;* O Pioneers!, *610;* Rain People, The, *634;* Seize the Day, *651*
Aldrich, John: Wild Beasts, The, *903*
Aldridge, Kitty: African Dream, An, *442;* American Roulette, *4;* Slipstream, *1077*
Aldridge, Michael: Bullshot, *247*
Aldrige, Kay: Nyoka and the Tiger Men (Perils of Nyoka), *92*
Aldrin, Buzz: Boy in the Plastic Bubble, The, *468*
Aleandro, Norma: Cousins, *260;* Gaby, a True Story, *524;* Official Story, The, *772;* One Man's War, *613*
Aleman, Julio: Green Wall, The, *742*
Alentova, Vera: Moscow Does Not Believe in Tears, *768*
Aleong, Aki: Braddock: Missing in Action III, *18*
Alerme, Andre: Carnival in Flanders, *722*
Alexander, Alphonso: Bustin' Loose, *248*
Alexander, Barbara Lee: Illegal Entry, *66*
Alexander, Ben: Dragnet (1954), *41;* Hearts of the World, *538*
Alexander, Denise: Lindbergh Kidnapping Case, The, *575*
Alexander, Geraldine: Sleeping Murder, *1017*
Alexander, Jane: All the President's Men, *951;* Betsy, The, *459;* Brubaker, *471;* Calamity Jane (1984), *1103;* City Heat, *255;* Great White Hope, The, *533;* Gunfight, A, *1117;* In Love and War, *985;* Kramer vs. Kramer, *567;* Love and War, *581;* New Centurions, The, *605;* Night Crossing, *90;* Playing for Time, *623;* Rumor Mill, The, *645;* Square Dance, *665;* Sweet Country, *674;* Testament, *1082*
Alexander, Jason: Coneheads, *258;* I Don't Buy Kisses Anymore, *303;* Jacob's Ladder, *1060;* Paper, The, *617;* White Palace, *700*
Alexander, John: Alien P.I., *1035;* Horn Blows at Midnight, The, *301*
Alexander, Katharine: Great Man Votes, The, *289;* Operator 13, *614*
Alexander, Khandi: House Party 3, *923*
Alexander, Liz: Killing of Angel Street, The, *564*
Alexander, Ross: Captain Blood, *22;* Flirtation Walk, *917*
Alexander, Spike: Brain Donors, *245*
Alexander, Terence: Frankenstein (1984), *842*
Alexander, Terry: Day of the Dead, *830*
Alexander, Tiana: Catch the Heat, *24*
Alexandridis, Helene: Therese, *793*
Alexandrov, Grigori: Strike, *790*
Alexiadis, Anna: Fantasies, *514*
Alexio, Dennis: Kickboxer, *70*

Alfonso, Kristian: Blindfold: Acts of Obsession, *956*
Alford, Philip: To Kill a Mockingbird, *684*
Alfredson, Hans: Adventures of Picasso, The, *222*
Algeria: Ramparts of Clay, *779*
Ali, Muhammad: Greatest, The, *533*
Alice, Mary: Laurel Avenue, *571;* To Sleep with Anger, *685*
Alicia, Ana: Coward of the County, *490;* Romero, *643*
Aliff, Lisa: Playroom, *875*
Alighiero, Carlo: Cat O'Nine Tails, *960*
Alison, Dorothy: Amazing Mr. Blunden, The, *146;* See No Evil, *884*
Allain, Joe: Television Parts Home Companion, *944*
Allan, Andrea: House That Vanished, The, *853*
Allan, Elizabeth: Ace of Aces, *1;* Camille, *474;* Haunted Strangler, The, *849;* Java Head, *557;* Mark of the Vampire, *863;* Tale of Two Cities, A (1935), *676;* Woman Rebels, A, *705*
Allasio, Marisa: Seven Hills of Rome, The, *939*
Allaylis, Toni: Fast Talking, *166*
Allbritton, Louise: Doolins of Oklahoma, *1110;* Egg and I, The, *270;* Pittsburgh, *622;* Son of Dracula (1943), *888;* Who Done It?, *410*
Allen, Bill: Rad, *102*
Allen, Chad: Murder in New Hampshire, *600;* Praying Mantis, *1007;* Terror Vision, *1082*
Allen, Corey: Rebel without a Cause, *636*
Allen, Debbie: Blank Check, *151;* Jo Jo Dancer, Your Life Is Calling, *558*
Allen, Elizabeth: Donovan's Reef, *267;* From the Terrace, *523*
Allen, Fred: It's in the Bag, *308;* We're Not Married, *408*
Allen, Ginger Lynn: Bound and Gagged: A Love Story, *18;* Hollywood Boulevard II, *983;* Leather Jackets, *76;* Vice Academy, *404;* Vice Academy 2, *404;* Vice Academy III, *404*
Allen, Gracie: College Swing, *912;* Damsel in Distress, A, *913;* George Burns and Gracie Allen Show, The (TV Series), *284;* Honolulu, *923;* International House, *307;* Two Girls and a Sailor, *946*
Allen, India: Wild Cactus, *139*
Allen, Jay: Night of the Demon, *869*
Allen, Jeffrey: 2,000 Maniacs, *898*
Allen, Joan: All My Sons, *444;* Ethan Frome, *511;* In Country, *550;* Josh and S.A.M., *69;* Manhunter, *995;* Peggy Sue Got Married, *355;* Searching for Bobby Fischer, *202;* Tucker: A Man and His Dream, *689;* Without Warning: The James Brady Story, *704*
Allen, Judith: Boots and Saddles, *1100;* Bright Eyes, *152;* Dancing Man, *965;* Git Along, Little Dogies, *1115*
Allen, Karen: Animal Behavior, *227;* Animal House, *227;* Backfire, *953;* Cruising, *964;* Ghost in the Machine, *845;* Glass Menagerie, The, *528;* King of the Hill, *565;* Raiders of the Lost Ark, *1073;* Sandlot, The, *201;* Scrooged, *374;* Secret Weapon, *651;* Shoot the Moon, *656;* Small Circle of Friends, A, *660;* Split Image, *664;* Starman, *1080;* Sweet Talker, *389;* Until September, *692;* Voyage, *1030;* Wanderers, The, *695*
Allen, Keith: Kafka, *988*
Allen, Nancy: Acting on Impulse, *950;* Blow Out, *957;* Buddy System, The, *471;* Carrie (1976), *821;* Dressed to Kill (1980), *972;* Forced Entry, *842;* Gladiator, The, *55;* Home Movies, *299;* I Wanna Hold Your Hand, *304;* Last Detail, The, *569;* Limit Up, *319;* Memories of Murder, *996;* 1941, *345;* Not for Publication, *347;* Philadelphia Experiment, The, *1070;* Poltergeist III, *876;* RoboCop, *1074;* RoboCop 2, *1075;* RoboCop 3, *1075;* Strange Invaders, *1080;* Sweet Revenge (1987), *123;* Terror in the Aisles, *893*
Allen, Patrick: Diamonds on Wheels, *162;* Long Haul, *578;* When Dinosaurs Ruled the Earth, *1089*
Allen, Phillip R.: Honeyboy, *63;* Mortal Sins (1992), *997*
Allen, Rae: Where's Poppa?, *409*
Allen, Randi: Cathy's Curse, *822*
Allen, Rex: Arizona Cowboy, *1094;* Charlie, the Lonesome Cougar, *158;* Red River Shore, *1142;* Rodeo King and the Senorita, *1145;* Tomboy and the Champ, *213;* Trail of Robin Hood, *1158;* Under Mexicali Stars, *1160*
Allen, Robert: Black Room, The (1935), *814;* Perils of Pauline, The (1933), *98*
Allen, Ronald: Eat the Rich, *270*
Allen, Rosalind: Children of the Corn II: The Final Sacrifice, *823;* Infested, *856;* Ticks, *895;* To Die For 2: Son of Darkness *896*
Allen, Seth: Futz, *524*
Allen, Shaun: Pink Nights, *357*
Allen, Sheila: Alice in Wonderland (1985), *145;* Alice Through the Looking Glass (1985), *145*
Allen, Sian Barbara: Eric, *510;* Lindbergh Kidnapping Case, The, *575*
Allen, Steve: Alice Through the Looking Glass (1985), *145;* Amazon Women on the Moon, *225;* Benny Goodman Story, The, *458;* Best of Comic Relief, The, *235;* Ernie Kovacs: Television's Original Genius, *272;* Hey Abbott!, *296;* Richard Lewis—"I'm Exhausted", *367;* Where Were You When the Lights Went Out?, *409*
Allen, Todd: Brothers in Arms, *819;* Storm and Sorrow, *120* Witchboard, *903*
Allen, Woody: Annie Hall, *228;* Bananas, *232;* Broadway Danny Rose, *246;* Casino Royale (1967), *252;* Crimes and Misdemeanors, *490;* Everything You Always Wanted to Know About Sex but Were Afraid to Ask, *273;* Front, The, *523;* Hannah and Her Sisters, *293;* Husbands and Wives, *546;* Love and Death, *322;* Manhattan, *328;* Manhattan Murder Mystery, *328;* Midsummer Night's Sex Comedy, A, *332;* New York Stories, *343;* Play It Again, Sam, *358;* Scenes from a Mall, *373;* Shadows and Fog, *654;* Sleeper, *381;* Stardust Memories, *385;* Take the Money and Run, *390;* What's New, Pussycat?, *408;* What's Up, Tiger Lily?, *408;* Zelig, *416*
Alley, Kirstie: Blind Date (1984), *463;* Bunny's Tale, A, *472;* Look Who's Talking, *320;* Look Who's Talking Too, *321;* Look Who's Talking Now, *321;* Loverboy, *323;* Madhouse (1990), *326;* North and South, *608;* Prince of Bel Air, *627;* Runaway, *1075;* Shoot to Kill, *115;* Sibling Rivalry, *378;* Star Trek II: The Wrath of Khan, *1079;* Summer School, *388*
Allgood, Sara: Blackmail (1929), *956;* Challenge to Lassie, *157;* City without Men, *483;* Dr. Jekyll and Mr. Hyde (1941), *835;* Jane Eyre (1944), *557;* Juno and the Paycock, *561;* Spiral Staircase, The (1946), *1019;* Storm in a Teacup, *387;* Strange Affair of Uncle Harry, The, *669*
Alliotto, Annette: Escapade in Florence, *165*
Allman, Daniel: Close to Home, *484*
Allman, Gregg: Rush, *645;* Rush Week, *882*
Allport, Christopher: Savage Weekend, *883;* Special Bulletin, *1019*
Allred, Corbin: Quest of the Delta Knights, *1073*
Allred, Sammy: Fast Money, *46*
Allwin, Pernilla: Fanny and Alexander, *736*
Allwyn, Astrid: Charlie Chan's Secret, *961*
Allyson, June: Battle Circus, *456;* Best Foot Forward, *908;* Blackout (1978), *14;* Curse of the Black Widow, *828;* Executive Suite, *512;* Girl Crazy, *919;* Glenn Miller Story, The, *919;* Good News, *920;* Kid with the Broken Halo, The, *313;* Little Women (1949), *577;* McConnell Story, The, *591;* My Man Godfrey (1957), *340;* Opposite Sex, The, *934;* Strategic Air Command, *670;* Stratton Story, The, *670;* That's Entertainment! III, *436;* They Only Kill Their Masters, *1024;* Three Musketeers, The (1948), *128;* Two Girls and a Sailor, *946;* Two Sisters from Boston, *947;* Words and Music, *948*
Almendros, Nestor: Visions of Light: The Art of Cinematography, *438*
Almgren, Susan: Deadly Surveillance, *35;* Shades of Love: Lilac Dream, *654*
Alonso, Chelo: Goliath and the Barbarians, *56*
Alonso, Ernesto: Criminal Life of Archibaldo de la Cruz, The, *727*
Alonso, Maria Conchita: Colors, *485;* Extreme Prejudice, *45;* Fine Mess, A, *277;* House of the Spirits, The, *545;* McBain, *83;* Moscow on the Hudson, *337;* Predator 2, *1071;*

nning Man, The, *1075;* Teamster Boss: The Jackie Presser ry, *678;* Touch and Go, *398;* Vampire's Kiss, *900*
onso, Rafael: Mr. Superinvisible, *188*
ic, Catherine: Associate, The, *714*
ter, Pamela: Sgt. Kabukiman N.Y.P.D., *114*
, Carol: Beyond Justice, *11;* Bye Bye, Baby, *473;* Family tter, A, *514;* Millions, *594;* My Wonderful Life, *603;* rtfolio, *624;* Ring of Steel, *106;* Thunder in Paradise, *129*
erio, Hector: Basileus Quartet, *715;* Camila, *721;* Nest, (1981), *771;* Official Story, The, *772*
haus, Urs: Warbus, *137*
man, Bruce: Rookie of the Year, *200*
man, Jeff: American Hot Wax, *906;* Doin' Time, *266;* In ve with an Older Woman, *550;* Rodney Dangerfield: "It's Not sy Being Me", *370;* Wacko, *405*
man, Steve: Transylvania Twist, *399*
varado, Angela: Shadow Hunter, *654*
varado, Trini: American Blue Note, *446;* American Friends, *6;* Babe, The, *452;* Chair, The, *822;* Mrs. Soffel, *598;* Nitti: e Enforcer, *91;* Rich Kids, *640;* Satisfaction, *938;* Stella 990), *667;* Sweet Lorraine, *674;* Times Square, *946*
yn, Kirk: Atom Man vs. Superman, *7;* Scalps, *883;* perman—The Serial, *1081*
zado, Lyle: Club Fed, *256;* Comrades in Arms, *28;* stroyer, *833;* Double McGuffin, The, *163;* Ernest Goes to mp, *272;* Neon City, *1067;* Oceans of Fire, *93;* Tapeheads, *1;* Zapped Again, *416*
nachi, Shigero: Zatoichi: The Blind Swordsman's ngeance, *806*
nano, Sayoko: Tokyo Decadence, *795*
nar, Leonora: Captain Scarlett, *23*
nastutz, Roland: Eyes of the Birds, *735*
neche, Don: Alexander's Ragtime Band, *906;* Cocoon, *42;* Cocoon: The Return, *1042;* Down Argentine Way, *914;* lks, *278;* Guest Wife, *291;* Happy Landing, *921;* Harry and Hendersons, *1055;* Heaven Can Wait (1943), *295;* In Old icago, *550;* It's in the Bag, *308;* Moon Over Miami, *931;* dball Hall, *348;* One in a Million, *350;* Oscar (1991), *351;* ls, *353;* Picture Mommy Dead, *874;* Sunstroke, *1021;* ppose They Gave a War and Nobody Came?, *388;* Things ange, *394;* Three Musketeers, The (1939), *396;* Trading aces, *398;* Wing and a Prayer, A, *140*
nendola, Claudio: Forever Mary, *737*
nerica, Paul: Ciao! Manhattan, *482*
nes, Adrienne: Death Kiss, The, *968;* Harmony Lane, *922*
nes, Leon: Any Number Can Play, *450;* Big Hangover, The, *8;* By the Light of the Silvery Moon, *910;* Date with Judy, A, *3;* Deadly Encounter (1975), *498;* From the Terrace, *523;* on Major, The, *554;* Jake Speed, *68;* Lady in the Lake, *990;* arshal of Mesa City, *1133;* Merton of the Movies, *331;* isadventures of Merlin Jones, The, *188;* Monkey's Uncle, e, *188;* Murders in the Rue Morgue (1932), *867;* On oonlight Bay, *933;* Peggy Sue Got Married, *355;* Peyton ace, *621;* Show-Off, The, *378;* Son of Lassie, *206;* stament, *1082;* Thin Man Goes Home, The, *1024;* Velvet ouch, The, *693;* Yolanda and the Thief, *708*
nes, Ramsay: G-Men Never Forget, *54;* Mummy's Ghost, e, *867*
nes, Rosemary: Our Little Girl, *193*
nick, Madchen: Don't Tell Her It's Me, *267;* Dream Lover 994), *972;* I'm Dangerous Tonight, *855;* Love, Cheat & eal, *993;* Stephen King's Sleepwalkers, *890*
nidou, Souad: Petit Con, *777;* Sorceror, *1018*
nis, Suzy: Ballad of Little Jo, The, *1096;* Big Town, The, *61;* Blown Away (1994), *16;* Plain Clothes, *358;* Rich in ve, *640;* Rocket Gibraltar, *642;* Twister, *401;* Watch It, *696*
mmelrooy, Willeke Van: On Top of the Whale, *773*
mos, John: American Flyers, *446;* Beastmaster, The, *1038;* oming to America, *258;* Die Hard 2: Die Harder, *39;* Jungle eat, *69;* Let's Do It Again, *318;* Lock Up, *78;* Mac, *583;* ardi Gras for the Devil, *863;* Sweet Sweetback's Baadasssss Song, *123;* Touched by Love, *686;* Two Evil Eyes, *898;* Willa, *703;* World's Greatest Athlete, The, *218*
Amphlett, Christina: Monkey Grip, *598*
Amplas, John: Martin, *863;* Midnight (1980), *864*
Amrani, Gabi: Lupo, *324;* Madron, *1131*
Amsterdam, Morey: Beach Party, *908;* Gay Purr-ee, *168;* Machine-Gun Kelly, *80;* Muscle Beach Party, *338;* Sooner or Later, *663*
Anchoriz, Leo: Bullet for Sandoval, A, *1102;* Finger on the Trigger, *1113*
Anconina, Richard: Love Songs (Paroles et Musique), *762;* Police, *778;* Tchao Pantin, *793*
Anders, Donna: Count Yorga, Vampire, *825*
Anders, Glenn: Lady from Shanghai, *989*
Anders, Luana: Border Radio, *466;* Dementia 13, *832;* Easy Rider, *506;* Greaser's Palace, *532;* Manipulator, The, *588;* One from the Heart, *934;* Pit and the Pendulum, The (1961), *875;* Sex and the College Girl, *653;* That Cold Day in the Park, *680;* Trip, The, *688*
Anders, Lynn: Shadow Strikes, The, *1014*
Anders, Merry: Farmer Takes a Wife, The, *916;* Tickle Me, *945;* Time Travelers, The, *1084;* Women of the Prehistoric Planet, *1090*
Anders, Rudolph: Phantom from Space, *1070;* Space Patrol (TV Series), *1077*
Andersen, Dana: Ginger Ale Afternoon, *286*
Andersen, Elga: Global Affair, A, *287*
Andersen, Isa: Night Angel, *868*
Andersen, Suzy: Black Sabbath, *814;* Gangster's Law, *525*
Anderson, Adisa: Daughters of the Dust, *496*
Anderson, Bridgette: Fever Pitch, *516;* Hansel and Gretel, *173;* Savannah Smiles, *201*
Anderson, Bruce: Thinkin' Big, *394*
Anderson, Carl: Jesus Christ, Superstar, *926*
Anderson, Daphne: Hobson's Choice (1954), *298*
Anderson, Dave: No Dead Heroes, *91*
Anderson, Eddie "Rochester": Brewster's Millions (1945), *245;* Buck Benny Rides Again, *246;* Cabin in the Sky, *473;* Green Pastures, *533;* Honolulu, *923;* It Happened in New Orleans, *925;* Jack Benny Program, The (TV Series), *309;* Meanest Man in the World, The, *330;* Show-Off, The, *378;* Three Men on a Horse, *395;* Topper Returns, *398;* You Can't Cheat an Honest Man, *415*
Anderson, Erich: Love Kills, *993*
Anderson, Erika: Quake, *1008;* Zandalee, *709*
Anderson, Ernest: Well, The, *698*
Anderson, Erville: Haunted Gold, *1119*
Anderson, Harry: Best of the Big Laff Off, The, *236;* Happy Birthday Bugs: 50 Looney Years, *173;* It (1991), *857;* Mother Goose Rock N' Roll Rhyme, *189;* Rich Hall's Vanishing America, *367;* Spies, Lies, and Naked Thighs, *384;* Your Favorite Laughs from an Evening at the Improv, *416*
Anderson, Haskell V.: Brotherhood of Death, *20*
Anderson, Herbert: Benny Goodman Story, The, *458;* I Bury the Living, *855*
Anderson, James: Hunt the Man Down, *984*
Anderson, Jean: Back Home, *147*
Anderson, John: Deerslayer, The, *1108;* Donner Pass: The Road to Survival, *1109;* Executive Action, *512;* Firehouse (1987), *277;* In Search of Historic Jesus, *550;* Man and Boy, *1131;* Medicine Hat Stallion, The, *186;* Namu, the Killer Whale, *190;* Psycho, *877;* Ride the High Country, *1143;* Smile, Jenny, You're Dead, *661;* Soldier Blue, *1151;* Zoot Suit, *949*
Anderson, Judith: All Through the Night, *3;* And Then There Were None, *952;* Blood Money (1933), *464;* Edge of Darkness (1943), *43;* King's Row, *565;* Lady Scarface, *74;* Laura, *991;* Macbeth (1961), *583;* Man Called Horse, A, *1131;* Pursued, *1140;* Rebecca, *1009;* Red House, The, *1009;* Salome (1953), *647;* Specter of the Rose, The, *1019;* Strange Love of Martha Ivers, The, *669;* Tycoon, *133*

Anderson, Kevin: Hoffa, *542;* In Country, *550;* Liebestraum, *992;* Miles from Home, *594;* Night We Never Met, The, *345;* Orphans, *615;* Orpheus Descending, *615;* Pink Nights, *357;* Rising Sun, *1010;* Sleeping with the Enemy, *1017;* Wrong Man, The (1993), *707*

Anderson, Laurie: Heavy Petting, *426;* Two Moon July, *947*

Anderson, Lindsay: O Lucky Man!, *610;* Prisoner of Honor, *628*

Anderson, Loni: Jayne Mansfield Story, The, *557;* Munchie, *867;* My Mother's Secret Life, *602;* Sizzle, *659;* Sorry, Wrong Number (1989), *1019;* Stroker Ace, *387;* Whisper Kills, A, *902;* White Hot: The Mysterious Murder of Thelma Todd, *1031*

Anderson, Louie: Louie Anderson: Mom! Louie's Looking at Me Again!, *322;* Ratboy, *635;* Wrong Guys, The, *414*

Anderson, Mary: Hunt the Man Down, *984;* Underworld Story, *1029*

Anderson, Melissa Sue: Chattanooga Choo Choo, *254;* Dead Men Don't Die, *262;* Equalizer, The: "Memories of Manon", *44;* First Affair, *517;* Happy Birthday to Me, *848;* Little House on the Prairie (TV Series), *181*

Anderson, Melody: Dead and Buried, *830;* Elvis—The Movie, *509;* Final Notice, *977;* Firewalker, *49;* Flash Gordon, *1052;* Hitler's Daughter, *542;* Landslide, *990;* Marilyn & Bobby: Her Final Affair, *588*

Anderson, Michael J.: Great Land of Small, The, *171*

Anderson Jr., Michael: In Search of the Castaways, *176;* Legacy for Leonette, *991;* Sons of Katie Elder, The, *1151*

Anderson, Mitchell: Back to Hannibal: The Return of Tom Sawyer and Huckleberry Finn, *454;* Deadly Dreams, *968;* Goodbye, Miss 4th of July, *171*

Anderson, Pamela: Snapdragon, *1018*

Anderson, Pat: Summer School Teachers, *673;* TNT Jackson, *130*

Anderson, Richard: Bionic Woman, The, *1039;* Escape from Fort Bravo, *1111;* Gettysburg, *526;* I Love Melvin, *924;* It's a Dog's Life, *177;* Magnificent Yankee, The, *585;* Rich, Young and Pretty, *936*

Anderson, Richard Dean: Ordinary Heroes, *614*

Anderson, Warner: Armored Command, *6;* Destination Moon, *1047;* Destination Tokyo, *37;* Drum Beat, *1110;* Go for Broke!, *528;* Lawless Street, A, *1127;* Objective, Burma!, *93;* Star, The, *665*

Andersson, Bibi: All These Women, *712;* Babette's Feast, *714;* Brink of Life, *720;* Devil's Eye, The, *730;* Duel at Diablo, *1110;* I Never Promised You a Rose Garden, *547;* Magician, The, *764;* Passion of Anna, The, *776;* Persona, *777;* Quintet, *1073;* Scenes from a Marriage, *784;* Seventh Seal, The, *785;* Wild Strawberries, *804*

Andersson, Harriet: Cries and Whispers, *726;* Dreams, *732;* Lesson in Love, A, *760;* Monika, *768;* Sawdust and Tinsel, *784;* Smiles of a Summer Night, *787;* Through a Glass Darkly, *795*

Andes, Keith: Away all Boats, *8;* Blackbeard the Pirate, *14;* Clash by Night, *483;* Farmer's Daughter, The, *274*

Ando: Paper Tiger, *97*

Ando, Eiko: Barbarian and the Geisha, The, *455*

André, Carole: One Russian Summer, *613;* Violent Breed, The, *136;* Yor: The Hunter from the Future, *1091*

André, Gaby: Cosmic Monsters, The, *825;* East of Kilimanjaro, *43;* Goliath and the Dragon, *56*

Andre, George: Wild World of Batwoman, The, *1089*

Andre, Lona: Trailing Trouble, *1158*

Andre the Giant: Princess Bride, The, *1071*

Andreasi, Felice: Story of Boys and Girls, *789*

Andrei, Frederic: Diva, *731*

Andress, Ursula: Blue Max, The, *16;* Casino Royale (1967), *252;* Chinatown Murders, The: Man Against the Mob, *25;* Dr. No, *40;* Fifth Musketeer, The, *47;* Four for Texas, *1114;* Fun in Acapulco, *918;* Loaded Guns, *78;* Loves and Times of Scaramouche, The, *324;* Red Sun, *1142;* Sensuous Nurse, The, *784;* Slave of the Cannibal God, *117;* Stateline Motel, *789;* Tenth Victim, The, *1082;* What's New, Pussycat?, *408*

Andreu, Simon: Blood Spattered Bride, The, *816*

Andrews, Anthony: Brideshead Revisited, *469;* Hanna's War, *536;* Holcroft Covenant, The, *982;* Ivanhoe (1982), *68;* Scarlet Pimpernel, The (1982), *112;* Strange Case of Dr. Jekyll and Mr. Hyde, The (1989), *890;* Suspicion (1987), *1022;* Under the Volcano, *691*

Andrews, Arkansas Slim: Take Me Back to Oklahoma, *1154*

Andrews, Barry: Blood on Satan's Claw, *815;* Dracula Has Risen from the Grave, *837*

Andrews, Carl: Lion of Africa, The, *77*

Andrews, Carol: Bullfighters, The, *247*

Andrews, Christian: Deceit, *1046*

Andrews, Dana: Ball of Fire, *231;* Battle of the Bulge, *10;* Best Years of Our Lives, The, *459;* Beyond a Reasonable Doubt (1956), *955;* Born Again, *466;* Cobra, The (1967), *27;* Crash Dive, *30;* Curse of the Demon, *828;* Devil's Brigade, The, *37;* Elephant Walk, *508;* Enchanted Island, *44;* Good Guys Wear Black, *56;* In Harm's Way, *66;* Johnny Reno, *1124;* Kit Carson, *1125;* Last Tycoon, The, *571;* Laura, *991;* North Star, The, *92;* Ox-Bow Incident, The, *1137;* Pilot, The, *622;* Purple Heart, The, *630;* State Fair (1945), *941;* Take a Hard Ride, *1154;* Up in Arms, *403;* Walk in the Sun, A, *136;* Westerner, The, *1163;* While the City Sleeps, *138;* Wing and a Prayer, A, *140*

Andrews, David: Cherry 2000, *1041;* Stephen King's Graveyard Shift, *890*

Andrews, Edward: Avanti!, *230;* Kisses for My President, *314;* Send Me No Flowers, *375;* Seniors, The, *375;* Sixteen Candles, *380;* Summertime, *673;* Tea and Sympathy, *678;* Thrill of It All, The, *396;* Wilbur and Orville: The First to Fly, *217;* Young Savages, The, *1033*

Andrews, Harry: Agony and the Ecstasy, The, *443;* Battle of Britain, *9;* Charge of the Light Brigade, The (1968), *24;* Curse of King Tut's Tomb, The, *828;* Dandy in Aspic, A, *965;* Devil's Disciple, The, *264;* Entertaining Mr. Sloane, *271;* Equus, *973;* Four Feathers, The (1978), *52;* Hill, The, *541;* Horrors of Burke and Hare, *852;* I Want What I Want, *548;* Internecine Project, The, *986;* Man of La Mancha, *930;* Medusa Touch, The, *864;* Nice Girl Like Me, A, *344;* Nightcomers, The, *870;* Ruling Class, The, *371;* Saint Joan, *646;* Seven Dials Mystery, The, *1013;* 633 Squadron, *116;* Story of Jacob and Joseph, The, *207;* Wuthering Heights (1971), *707*

Andrews, Julie: Americanization of Emily, The, *226;* Darling Lili, *913;* Duet for One, *505;* Fine Romance, A, *277;* Hawaii, *537;* Little Miss Marker (1980), *182;* Man Who Loved Women, The (1983), *328;* Mary Poppins, *185;* S.O.B., *372;* Sound of Music, The, *940;* Star!, *941;* Tamarind Seed, The, *124;* 10, *392;* That's Life, *393;* Thoroughly Modern Millie, *945;* Torn Curtain, *1026;* Victor/Victoria, *405*

Andrews, Naveen: Wild West (1993), *411*

Andrews, Robert: Geek Maggot Bingo, *283*

Andrews, Sarah Hollis: Secret Garden, The (1984), *202*

Andrews Sisters, The: Private Buckaroo, *935;* Road to Rio, *369*

Andrews, Susan: Angel of Death, *5*

Andrews, Tige: Gypsy Angels, *535;* Mod Squad, The (TV Series), *86*

Andrews, Todd Eric: Zapped Again, *416*

Andriel, Lenore: In the Time of Barbarians II, *1058*

Andros, Spiro: Matter of Time, A, *590*

Anemone: Le Grand Chemin (The Grand Highway), *757;* Peril, *777*

Ange, Julie: Girl on a Chain Gang, *55*

Angel, Heather: Arrest Bulldog Drummond, *6;* Bold Caballero, The, *1099;* Bulldog Drummond Escapes, *20;* Bulldog Drummond in Africa, *20;* Bulldog Drummond's Bride, *20;* Bulldog Drummond's Secret Police, *21;* Daniel Boone, *1107;* Informer, The, *552;* Last of the Mohicans, The (1936), *1126;* Lifeboat, *992;* Premature Burial, The, *876;* Three Musketeers, The (1935), *128*

gel, Vanessa: Cover Girl Murders, The, *964;* Homicidal
pulse, *983*
geli, Pier: Octaman, *872;* One Step to Hell, *95;* Silver
alice, The, *658;* Sodom and Gomorrah, *661;* Somebody Up
ere Likes Me, *662*
gelis, Michael: No Surrender, *345*
gelou, Maya: Poetic Justice, *624*
gelus, Muriel: Great McGinty, The, *290*
ger, Kenneth: Kenneth Anger—Volume One, *562;*
nneth Anger—Volume Two, *562*
gers, Avril: Brass Monkey, The, *958*
glade, Jean-Hugues: Betty Blue, *717;* La Femme Nikita,
3; L'Homme Blessé (The Wounded Man), *760*
glim, Philip: Deadly Currents, *34;* Elephant Man, The
982), *508;* Haunted Summer, *537;* Thornbirds, The, *682*
gus, David: Hours and Times, *544*
gustain, Ira: Can You Hear the Laughter? The Story of
eddie Prinze, *474*
imals, The: Monterey Pop, *431*
iston, Jennifer: Leprechaun, *860*
ka, Paul: Captain Ron, *250;* Girls Town, *55;* Jerry Lee
wis—I Am What I Am, *428;* Ordinary Magic, *614*
kers, Evelyn: Black Beauty (1946), *150;* Last of the
admen, *1126;* Pearl of Death, The, *1004;* Sherlock Holmes
d the Voice of Terror, *1015;* Son of Dracula (1943), *888;*
olf Man, The, *904*
krum, Morris: Chain Lightning, *478;* Earth vs. the Flying
aucers, *1048;* Flight to Mars, *1052;* Fort Osage, *1114;* Half
uman, *848;* I Dood It, *924;* Showdown (1940), *1149;* Three
en from Texas, *1157*
n-Margret: Bye Bye Birdie, *910;* C.C. & Company, *21;*
arnal Knowledge, *475;* Cheap Detective, The, *254;* Cincinnati
d, The, *26;* 52 Pick-Up, *976;* Grumpy Old Men, *291;* I Ought
Be in Pictures, *304;* Joseph Andrews, *311;* Last Remake of
eau Geste, The, *316;* Lookin' to Get Out, *321;* Magic, *994;*
iddle-Age Crazy, *332;* Murderers' Row, *87;* New Life, A,
43; Newsies, *933;* Nobody's Children, *608;* Pocketful of
iracles, *359;* R.P.M. (Revolutions Per Minute), *632;* Return
the Soldier, The, *638;* State Fair (1962), *941;* Tiger and The
assycat, The, *795;* Tiger's Tale, A, *396;* Tommy, *946;* Train
obbers, The, *1158;* Twice in a Lifetime, *690;* Viva Las Vegas,
47
nnabella: Dinner at the Ritz, *39;* Le Million, *758;* Quatorze
uliet, *779;* 13 Rue Madeleine, *127*
nnen, Glory: Spaced Out, *384*
nnese, Frank: House of the Rising Sun, *64*
nniballi, Francesco: Down and Dirty, *732*
nnis, Francesca: Coming Out of the Ice, *486;* Flipper's
ew Adventure, *167;* Lillie, *575;* Macbeth (1971), *584;*
urder Most Foul, *998;* Onassis: The Richest Man in the
orld, *612;* Partners in Crime (TV Series), *1004;* Under the
herry Moon, *691;* Weep No More My Lady, *1030;* Why
idn't They Ask Evans?, *1032*
nsara, Michael: Access Code, *1;* Action in Arabia, *2;*
ssassination, *7;* Bayou Romance, *456;* Border Shootout,
100; Daring Game, *32;* Day of the Animals, *830;* Dear Dead
elilah, *831;* Guns of the Magnificent Seven, *1118;* Harum
carum, *922;* It's Alive!, *857;* Knights of the City, *927;*
anitou, The, *863;* Message, The (Mohammad, Messenger of
od), *593;* Mission to Glory, *596;* Powderkeg, *1139;* Quick,
et's Get Married, *363;* Texas Across the River, *1155;* Voyage
the Bottom of the Sea, *1087*
nsley, Zachary: Princes in Exile, *627*
nspach, Susan: Back to Back, *8;* Big Fix, The, *955;* Blue
onkey, *817;* Blume in Love, *465;* Deadly Encounter (1972),
4; Devil and Max Devlin, The, *264;* Five Easy Pieces, *517;*
as, *283;* Gone Are the Days, *288;* Hitchhiker (Series), The,
50; Into the Fire, *67;* Mad Bull, *584;* Montenegro, *599;* Play
Again, Sam, *358;* Rutanga Tapes, The, *1011*
nt, Adam: Acting on Impulse, *950;* Cold Steel, *28;* Jubilee,
061; Nomads, *872;* Slam Dance, *1017;* Spellcaster, *889;*
unset Heat, *122;* Trust Me, *400;* World Gone Wild, *1090*
Anthony, Gerald: To Die Standing, *130*
Anthony, Lysette: Face the Music, *273;* Ghost in Monte Carlo, A, *527;* Krull, *1061;* Save Me, *1012;* Without a Clue, *413*
Anthony, Ray: Five Pennies, The, *917;* Girl Can't Help It, The, *286;* Girls Town, *55*
Anthony, Scott: Savage Messiah, *648*
Anthony, Tony: Treasure of the Four Crowns, *132*
Antin, Steve: Accused, The, *441;* Inside Monkey Zetterland, *306;* Last American Virgin, The, *315;* Penitentiary III, *98*
Anton, Susan: Goldengirl, *1054;* Spring Fever, *385*
Antonelli, Laura: Collector's Item, *485;* Divine Nymph, The, *731;* High Heels (1972), *744;* How Funny Can Sex Be?, *745;* Innocent, The, *748;* Malicious, *764;* Passion of Love, *776;* Swashbuckler, The (1984), *123;* Till Marriage Do Us Part, *795;* Wifemistress, *804*
Antonio, Jim: Annihilators, The, *5;* Pigs, *875*
Antonio, Lou: Cool Hand Luke, *29*
Antonov, Alexander: Battleship Potemkin, The, *716;* Strike, *790*
Antonutti, Omero: Basileus Quartet, *715;* Kaos, *751;* Night of the Shooting Stars, *771;* Padre Padrone, *774*
Anulka: Vampyres, *900*
Anwar, Gabrielle: Body Snatchers, The (1993), *1040;* For Love or Money, *279;* Scent of a Woman, *649;* Three Musketeers, The (1993), *129;* Wild Hearts Can't Be Broken, *217*
Anzaldo, Jon: Little Ninjas, *183*
Apicella, Tina: Bellissima, *716*
Apollonia: Back to Back, *8;* Purple Rain, *935*
Appleby, Shiri: Perfect Family, *1005*
Applegate, Christina: Dance 'Til Dawn, *262;* Don't Tell Mom the Babysitter's Dead, *267;* It's a Bundyful Life, *308;* Streets, *121*
Applegate, Royce D.: Million Dollar Mystery, *332*
Aprea, John: Savage Beach, *111*
Aquino, Amy: Alan and Naomi, *443*
Aragon, Frank: Angel Town, *5*
Aragon, Raul: Sloane, *117*
Arakawa, Jane: Street Trash, *891*
Arana, Tomas: Church, The, *824*
Aranda, Angel: Hellbenders, The, *1120;* Last Days of Pompeii (1960), *75;* Planet of the Vampires, *875*
Aranguiz, Manuel: Paper Wedding, *618*
Aratama, Michiyo: Human Condition, The, Part One: No Greater Love, *745;* Kwaidan, *752*
Arau, Alfonso: Posse (1975), *1139;* Romancing the Stone, *108;* Scandalous John, *202;* Three Amigos, *395*
Araya, Zenda: Hearts and Armour, *59*
Arbatt, Alexandre: Dangerous Moves, *728*
Arbuckle, Roscoe "Fatty": Buster Keaton: The Great Stone Face, *248;* Fatty and His Funny Friends, *275;* Fatty and Mabel Adrift/Mabel, Fatty and the Law, *275;* Fatty Arbuckle Comedy Collection, Vol. 1, *275;* Fatty's Tin-Type Tangle/Our Congressman, *275;* Keystone Comedies, Vol. 1, *312;* Keystone Comedies, Vol. 2, *312;* Keystone Comedies, Vol. 3, *312;* Keystone Comedies, Vol. 4, *312;* Keystone Comedies, Vol. 5, *313;* Lizzies of Mack Sennett, The, *320;* Lost and Found Chaplin: Keystone, *321;* Mabel and Fatty, *325;* Mack Sennett Comedies, Vol. 2, *325*
Arbus, Allan: Coffy, *27;* Greaser's Palace, *532*
Arcand, Denys: Jesus of Montreal, *749*
Archer, Anne: Body of Evidence, *958;* Cancel My Reservation, *250;* Check Is in the Mail, The, *254;* Eminent Domain, *973;* Family Prayers, *514;* Fatal Attraction (1987), *975;* Good Guys Wear Black, *56;* Green Ice, *981;* Hero at Large, *296;* Last of His Tribe, The, *570;* Lifeguard, *574;* Love at Large, *322;* Nails, *88;* Naked Face, The, *1000;* Narrow Margin (1990), *89;* Patriot Games, *97;* Question of Faith, *632;* Raise the Titanic, *103;* Short Cuts, *657;* Too Scared to Scream, *1025*

Archer, John: Big Trees, The, *13;* Bowery at Midnight, *818;* Destination Moon, *1047;* Gangs, Inc., *54;* King of the Zombies, *859*

Ardant, Fanny: Afraid of the Dark, *950;* Confidentially Yours, *725;* Family, The (1987), *735;* Melo, *766;* Next Summer, *771;* Swann in Love, *791;* Woman Next Door, The, *805*

Arden, Eve: Anatomy of a Murder, *952;* At the Circus, *229;* Cinderella (1985), *159;* Comrade X, *258;* Cover Girl, *912;* Doughgirls, The, *268;* Eternally Yours, *511;* Grease, *920;* Guide for the Married Woman, A, *291;* Having a Wonderful Time, *294;* Kid from Brooklyn, The, *313;* Letter of Introduction, *573;* Mildred Pierce, *594;* My Dream Is Yours, *932;* Our Miss Brooks (TV Series), *351;* Slightly Honorable, *381;* Stage Door, *385;* Tea for Two, *944;* That Uncertain Feeling, *393;* Under the Rainbow, *402;* We're Not Married, *408;* Whistling in the Dark, *410;* Ziegfeld Girl, *949*

Arditi, Pierre: Melo, *766*

Arenas, Rosita: Curse of the Crying Woman, The, *828;* Witch's Mirror, The, *904*

Aresco, Joey: Circle of Fear, *26;* Primary Target, *627*

Arestrup, Neils: Meeting Venus, *591;* Sincerely Charlotte, *786*

Argento, Asia: Palombella Rossa, *775;* Trauma, *897*

Argo, Victor: Bad Lieutenant, *454;* Florida Straits, *51;* King of New York, *72;* Monkey Trouble, *188*

Argue, David: Backlash, *8;* BMX Bandits, *17;* Gallipoli, *524*

Arhondis, Tina: Test of Love, A, *679*

Ariane: Skin Art, *659;* Year of the Dragon, *141*

Arias, Imanol: Camila, *721;* Demons in the Garden, *729;* Labyrinth of Passion, *755*

Arias, Joey: Mondo New York, *598*

Ariffin, Nora: Skin Art, *659*

Arkin, Adam: Doctor, The, *502;* Fourth Wise Man, The, *521;* Necessary Parties, *604;* Tom Edison—The Boy Who Lit Up the World, *213*

Arkin, Alan: Bad Medicine, *231;* Big Trouble, *239;* Catch-22, *252;* Chu Chu and the Philly Flash, *255;* Cooperstown, *488;* Coupe De Ville, *260;* Edward Scissorhands, *1048;* Emperor's New Clothes, The (1984), *164;* Escape from Sobibor, *45;* Fourth Wise Man, The, *521;* Freebie and the Bean, *281;* Glengarry Glen Ross, *528;* Havana, *537;* Heart Is a Lonely Hunter, The, *538;* Hearts of the West, *295;* Improper Channels, *305;* In-Laws, The, *305;* Indian Summer, *306;* Joshua Then and Now, *311;* Last of the Red Hot Lovers, *315;* Little Murders, *319;* Magician of Lublin, The, *585;* Matter of Principle, A, *330;* Necessary Parties, *604;* Popi, *360;* Rafferty and the Gold Dust Twins, *364;* Return of Captain Invincible, The, *366;* Rocketeer, The, *108;* Russians Are Coming, the Russians Are Coming, The, *371;* Seven-Per-Cent Solution, The, *1013;* Simon, *379;* So I Married an Axe Murderer, *382;* Taking the Heat, *676;* Wait Until Dark, *1030;* Woman Times Seven, *705*

Arkin, David: Long Goodbye, The, *993;* Three in the Cellar, *395*

Arkin, Tony: Matter of Principle, A, *330*

Arkins, Robert: Commitments, The, *912*

Arlen, Harold: Wonderful Wizard of Oz, The: The Making of a Movie Classic, *438*

Arlen, Richard: Feel My Pulse, *276;* Flying Blind, *51;* Helldorado (1934), *60;* Hostile Guns, *1122;* Human Duplicators, The, *854;* Island of Lost Souls, *857;* Johnny Reno, *1124;* Mountain, The, *600;* Sex and the College Girl, *653;* Virginian, The (1929), *1161;* Wings, *140*

Arletty: Children of Paradise, The, *723;* Le Jour Se Leve (Daybreak) (1939), *757;* Les Visiteurs Du Soir, *759;* Pearls of the Crown, The, *776*

Arling, Charles: Keystone Comedies, Vol. 5, *313*

Arliss, Florence: Disraeli, *502*

Arliss, George: Disraeli, *502;* Dr. Syn, *40;* Iron Duke, The, *554;* Transatlantic Tunnel, *1085*

Armendariz, Pedro: Captain Sinbad, *156;* Conqueror, The, *29;* El Bruto (The Brute), *733;* Flor Sylvestre, *737;* Fugitive, The (1947), *523;* Littlest Outlaw, The, *184;* Pearl, The, *620;* Three Godfathers, The, *1156;* Tulsa, *689*

Armendariz Jr., Pedro: Bandits (1967), *1096;* Don't Be Afraid of the Dark, *836;* Le Chêvre (The Goat), *757*

Armetta, Henry: Devil's Brother, The, *914;* Everybody Sing, *916;* Make a Wish, *586;* Manhattan Merry-Go-Round, *930;* Poor Little Rich Girl (1936), *935;* Speak Easily, *384*

Armida: Badmen of the Border, *1096;* Rootin' Tootin' Rhythm, *1146*

Arms, Russell: By the Light of the Silvery Moon, *910;* Loaded Pistols, *1128*

Armstrong, Bess: Dream Lover (1994), *972;* High Road to China, *62;* Jaws 3, *858;* Jekyll & Hyde—Together Again, *310;* Nothing in Common, *609;* Second Sight, *374*

Armstrong, Curtis: Adventures of Huck Finn, The (1993), *143;* Bad Medicine, *231;* One Crazy Summer, *349;* Revenge of the Nerds, *367;* Revenge of the Nerds II: Nerds in Paradise, *367;* Revenge of the Nerds III: The Next Generation, *367;* Risky Business, *368*

Armstrong, Jack: Guyver, The, *1055*

Armstrong, Kerry: Hunting, *546*

Armstrong, Louis: Cabin in the Sky, *473;* Every Day's a Holiday, *273;* Five Pennies, The, *917;* Glenn Miller Story, The, *919;* High Society, *922;* Jazz on a Summer's Day, *427;* Man Called Adam, A, *586;* Paris Blues, *618;* Song Is Born, A, *940*

Armstrong, Perry: Solo, *661*

Armstrong, R. G.: Angels Die Hard, *5;* Best of Times, The, *236;* Boss, *1101;* Bulletproof, *21;* Children of the Corn, *823;* Dick Tracy (1990), *38;* Dixie Dynamite, *40;* El Dorado, *1111;* Evilspeak, *839;* Great Northfield Minnesota Raid, The, *1116;* Hammett, *981;* Lone Wolf McQuade, *78;* Pack, The, *873;* Pat Garrett and Billy the Kid, *1138;* Predator, *1071;* Pursuit of D. B. Cooper, *363;* Red-Headed Stranger, The, *1141;* Ride the High Country, *1143;* Stay Hungry, *667;* Steel, *120;* Where the Buffalo Roam, *409*

Armstrong, Robert: Action in Arabia, *2;* Adventures of the Flying Cadets, *2;* Big News, *238;* Blood on the Sun, *15;* Danger Lights, *494;* Dive Bomber, *502;* Ex-Mrs. Bradford, The, *974;* Fugitive, The (1947), *523;* G-Men, *54;* Hold 'em Jail, *298;* Kansan, The, *1124;* King Kong (1933), *859;* Lost Squadron, *79;* Mighty Joe Young, *1066;* Mr. Winkle Goes to War, *334;* Most Dangerous Game, The, *997;* Paleface, The, *353;* Palooka, *617;* Racketeer, *102;* Son of Kong, The, *888*

Armstrong, Todd: Jason and the Argonauts, *1060*

Arnaz Jr., Desi: Fakeout, *513;* House of the Long Shadows, *853;* Joyride, *560;* Mambo Kings, The, *930;* Paul Reiser Out on a Whim, *355;* Wedding, A, *407*

Arnaz Sr., Desi: Bataan, *9;* Escape Artist, The, *165;* Forever Darling, *279;* Four Jacks and a Jill, *918;* I Love Lucy (TV Series), *303;* Long, Long Trailer, The, *320;* Too Many Girls, *946*

Arnaz, Lucie: Jazz Singer, The (1980), *926;* Mating Season, The, *330;* Who Is the Black Dahlia?, *1031*

Arndt, Jurgen: Celeste, *722*

Arne, Peter: Return of the Pink Panther, The, *366;* Straw Dogs, *1021*

Arness, James: Alamo, The: Thirteen Days to Glory, *1093;* Big Jim McLain, *460;* Farmer's Daughter, The, *274;* Gunsmoke: Return to Dodge, *1118;* Gunsmoke (TV Series), *1118;* Hondo, *1121;* Island in the Sky, *554;* Sea Chase, The, *112;* Stars in My Crown, *1153;* Them!, *1083;* Thing (From Another World), The (1951), *1083;* Two Lost Worlds, *133;* Wagonmaster, *1162*

Arnez, Eva: Ferocious Female Freedom Fighters, *276*

Arngrim, Stephan: Fear No Evil, *840*

Arno, Alice: Erotikill, *838*

Arno, Sig: Melody Master, *592;* Palm Beach Story, The, *353;* Song to Remember, A, *940*

Arnold, Edward: Ambassador's Daughter, The, *226;* Annie Get Your Gun, *907;* Broken Trust, *959;* City That Never Sleeps, *483;* Come and Get It, *28;* Command Decision, *487;* Crime and Punishment (1935), *490;* Dear Wife, *263;* Devil and Daniel Webster, The, *500;* Hucksters, The, *545;* Idiot's Delight, *548;*

I'm No Angel, *305;* Johnny Apollo, *559;* Johnny Eager, *559;* Kismet (1944), *566;* Let Freedom Ring, *928;* Mrs. Parkington, *598;* Roman Scandals, *937;* Sadie McKee, *646;* Slightly Honorable, *381;* Three Daring Daughters, *945;* Three on a Match, *683;* Toast of New York, The, *685;* Weekend at the Waldorf, *697;* Yellow Cab Man, The, *415;* You Can't Take it with You (1938), *415;* Ziegfeld Follies, *949*

Arnold, Roseanne: Backfield in Motion, *230;* Even Cowgirls Get the Blues, *272;* Rodney Dangerfield: "It's Not Easy Being Me", *370;* Roseanne Barr Show, The, *370;* She-Devil, *377*

Arnold, Tom: Backfield in Motion, *230;* Hero, *296*

Arnott, David: Crisscross (1992), *491*

Arnott, Mark: Return of the Secaucus 7, *366*

Arnoul, Françoise: Jacko and Lise, *749;* Little Theatre of Jean Renoir, The, *760*

Aronson, Judie: American Ninja, *4;* Desert Kickboxer, *37*

Arp, Philip: Last Five Days, The, *755*

Arquette, Alexis: Jumpin' at the Boneyard, *561*

Arquette, David: Webber's World, *406*

Arquette, Patricia: Ethan Frome, *511;* Far North, *274;* Holy Matrimony, *299;* Indian Runner, The, *551;* Inside Monkey Zetterland, *306;* Nightmare on Elm Street 3, A: The Dream Warriors, *871;* Prayer of the Rollerboys, *100;* Pretty Smart, *361;* Trouble Bound, *1027;* True Romance, *133;* Wild Flower, *702*

Arquette, Rosanna: After Hours, *223;* ...Almost, *225;* Amazon Women on the Moon, *225;* Aviator, The, *452;* Baby, It's You, *453;* Big Blue, The, *12;* Black Rainbow, *955;* Dark Secret of Harvest Home, The, *829;* Desperately Seeking Susan, *264;* 8 Million Ways to Die, *973;* Executioner's Song, The, *512;* Fathers & Sons, *515;* Flight of the Intruder, The, *50;* Gorp, *289;* Linguini Incident, The, *319;* More American Graffiti, *599;* New York Stories, *343;* Nobody's Fool, *346;* Nowhere to Run (1993), *92;* Off the Wall, *348;* One Cooks, the Other Doesn't, *349;* Promised a Miracle, *629;* S.O.B., *372;* Silverado, *1150;* Son of the Morning Star, *1151;* Sweet Revenge (1990), *389;* Wrong Man, The (1993), *707*

Arrants, Rod: Vamping, *1029*

Arrindell, Lisa: Livin' Large, *320*

Arrington, James: Petronella, *195*

Artaud, Antonin: Napoleon (1927), *770;* Passion of Joan of Arc, The, *776*

Arthur, Bea: Lovers and Other Strangers, *323;* Mame, *930*

Arthur, Carol: Sunshine Boys, The, *388*

Arthur, Jean: Arizona, *1094;* Danger Lights, *494;* Devil and Miss Jones, The, *264;* Ex-Mrs. Bradford, The, *974;* History Is Made at Night, *542;* Lady Takes a Chance, A, *1125;* Mr. Deeds Goes to Town, *333;* Mr. Smith Goes to Washington, *597;* More the Merrier, The, *337;* Only Angels Have Wings, *95;* Plainsman, The, *1139;* Shane, *1148;* Talk of the Town, The, *390;* You Can't Take it with You (1938), *415*

Arthur, Johnny: Masked Marvel, The, *83;* Road to Singapore, *369*

Arthur, Maureen: How to Succeed in Business without Really Trying, *923*

Arthur, Robert: September Affair, *652*

Ashbrook, Dan: Return of the Living Dead Part II, *880*

Ashbrook, Dana: Girlfriend from Hell, *287*

Ashbrook, Daphne: Gimme an "F", *286;* Intruders, *1059;* Quiet Cool, *102;* Sunset Heat, *122*

Ashby, Linden: Night Angel, *868;* Perfect Bride, The, *873*

Ashcroft, Peggy: Hullabaloo over George and Bonnie's Pictures, *303;* Jewel in the Crown, The, *557;* Joseph Andrews, *311;* Madame Sousatzka, *584;* Nun's Story, The, *609;* Passage to India, A, *619;* Rhodes of Africa, *639;* Secret Ceremony, *650;* Sunday, Bloody Sunday, *673*

Asher, Jane: Deep End, *969;* Dreamchild, *1048;* Masque of the Red Death, The (1964), *863;* Success Is the Best Revenge, *672;* Voyage 'Round My Father, A, *695*

Asher, Joel: Merry Wives of Windsor, The, *331*

Asherson, Renée: Henry V (1944), *540;* Murder Is Announced, A, *998*

Ashley, Edward: Dick Tracy Meets Gruesome, *38*

Ashley, Elizabeth: Dragnet (1987), *268;* Great Scout and Cathouse Thursday, The, *1116;* Man of Passion, A, *587;* 92 in the Shade, *345;* Paternity, *355;* Rancho Deluxe, *1140;* Ship of Fools, *656;* Stagecoach (1986), *1152;* Svengali (1983), *674;* Vampire's Kiss, *900*

Ashley, John: Beach Blanket Bingo, *908;* Beach Party, *908;* Beast of the Yellow Night, *812;* Beyond Atlantis, *11;* Brides of the Beast, *819;* Dragstrip Girl, *42;* Frankenstein's Daughter, *843;* High School Caesar, *62;* Mad Doctor of Blood Island, The, *861;* Motorcycle Gang, *87;* Muscle Beach Party, *338;* Suicide Battalion, *122;* Twilight People, *898;* Woman Hunt, The, *140*

Ashton, John: Beverly Hills Cop, *11;* Beverly Hills Cop II, *11;* Deliberate Stranger, The, *499;* Dirty Work, *970;* King Kong Lives, *859;* Last Resort, *316;* Love, Lies and Murder, *994;* Midnight Run, *84;* Psychopath, The, *877;* Some Kind of Wonderful, *382;* Tommyknockers, The, *1084*

Ashton, Laura: America, *226*

Ashton, Vali: Die Watching, *970*

Ashworth, Ernest: Farmer's Other Daughter, The, *274*

Askew, Luke: Bulletproof, *21;* Culpepper Cattle Co., The, *1106;* Dune Warriors, *42;* Great Northfield Minnesota Raid, The, *1116;* Kung Fu—The Movie, *73;* Legend of the White Horse, *76;* Night Games, *1001;* Pat Garrett and Billy the Kid, *1138;* Posse (1975), *1139;* Rolling Thunder, *108;* Walking Tall Part II, *136;* Warrior and the Sorceress, The, *1088*

Askwith, Robin: Hans Brinker, *173;* Horror Hospital, *851*

Aslan, Gregoire: Concrete Jungle, The (1962) (a.k.a. The Criminal), *487;* Golden Voyage of Sinbad, The, *1054;* Paris When It Sizzles, *354;* Three Worlds of Gulliver, The, *1083;* Windom's Way, *703*

Asner, Edward: Case of Libel, A, *476;* Change of Habit, *479;* Daniel, *495;* El Dorado, *1111;* Fort Apache—The Bronx, *520;* Gathering, The, *525;* Gus, *172;* Gypsy (1993), *921;* Haunts of the Very Rich, *1055;* Heads, *294;* Hey, I'm Alive!, *541;* JFK, *558;* Life and Assassination of the Kingfish, The, *574;* Not a Penny More, Not a Penny Less, *1002;* O'Hara's Wife, *611;* Pinocchio and the Emperor of the Night, *195;* Roots, *644;* Silent Motive, *1016;* Skin Game, *1150;* Slender Thread, The, *660;* Small Killing, A, *660;* Switched at Birth, *675;* Todd Killings, The, *685*

Assa, Rene: 976-EVIL II: The Astral Factor, *872*

Assante, Armand: Animal Behavior, *227;* Belizaire the Cajun, *458;* Eternity, *511;* Fatal Instinct (1993), *274;* Fever, *47;* 1492: The Conquest of Paradise, *52;* Hoffa, *542;* I, the Jury, *985;* Lady of the House, *568;* Little Darlings, *319;* Mambo Kings, The, *930;* Marrying Man, The, *329;* Napoleon and Josephine: A Love Story, *603;* Paradise Alley, *618;* Penitent, The, *620;* Private Benjamin, *361;* Prophecy, *877;* Q & A, *1008;* Rage of Angels, *633;* Unfaithfully Yours (1984), *403*

Ast, Pat: Heat (1972), *539;* Reform School Girls, *105*

Astaire, Fred: Amazing Dobermans, *146;* American Film Institute Life Achievement Awards, The, *418;* Band Wagon, The, *908;* Barkleys of Broadway, The, *908;* Belle of New York, The, *908;* Broadway Melody of 1940, *910;* Carefree, *911;* Daddy Long Legs, *913;* Damsel in Distress, A, *913;* Dancing Lady, *913;* Easter Parade, *915;* Family Upside Down, A, *514;* Finian's Rainbow, *916;* Flying Down to Rio, *917;* Follow the Fleet, *917;* Funny Face, *918;* Gay Divorcée, The, *918;* Ghost Story, *846;* Holiday Inn, *923;* It Takes a Thief (TV Series), *68;* Let's Dance, *928;* Man in the Santa Claus Suit, The, *185;* On the Beach, *1069;* Purple Taxi, The, *631;* Roberta, *936;* Royal Wedding, *938;* Second Chorus, *938;* Shall We Dance?, *939;* Silk Stockings, *939;* Sky's the Limit, The, *940;* Story of Vernon and Irene Castle, The, *942;* Swing Time, *943;* That's Entertainment, *436;* That's Entertainment Part II, *436;* Three Little Words, *945;* Top Hat, *946;* Towering Inferno, The, *131;* Yolanda and the Thief, *708;* You Were Never Lovelier, *948;* You'll Never Get Rich, *948;* Ziegfeld Follies, *949*

Asther, Nils: Bitter Tea of General Yen, The, *462;* Bluebeard (1944), *817;* Our Dancing Daughters, *616;* Single Standard, The, *659;* Son of Lassie, *206;* Wild Orchids, *702*

Asti, Adriana: Before the Revolution, *716;* Zorro, *142*
Astin, John: Addams Family, The (TV Series), *222;* Adventures Beyond Belief, *222;* Freaky Friday, *168;* Get to Know Your Rabbit, *285;* Killer Tomatoes Eat France, *313;* Killer Tomatoes Strike Back, *313;* National Lampoon's European Vacation, *342;* Night Life, *869;* Return of the Killer Tomatoes, *366;* Stepmonster, *1080;* Teen Wolf, Too, *892;* That Touch of Mink, *393;* Wheeler Dealers, The, *409*
Astin, Mackenzie: Garbage Pail Kids Movie, The, *168;* Iron Will, *67*
Astin, Sean: Encino Man, *271;* Goonies, The, *56;* Like Father, Like Son, *318;* Memphis Belle (1990), *592;* Rudy, *200;* Staying Together, *667;* Toy Soldiers (1991), *131;* War of the Roses, The, *406;* Where the Day Takes You, *699;* White Water Summer, *139;* Willies, The, *903*
Astor, Mary: Across the Pacific, *1;* Any Number Can Play, *450;* Beau Brummell (1924), *457;* Cass Timberlane, *476;* Dodsworth, *503;* Don Juan, *503;* Don Q, Son of Zorro, *41;* Fiesta, *916;* Great Lie, The, *532;* Hurricane, The (1937), *546;* Hush...Hush, Sweet Charlotte, *854;* Kennel Murder Case, The, *988;* Listen, Darling, *928;* Little Women (1949), *577;* Lost Squadron, *79;* Maltese Falcon, The, *994;* Palm Beach Story, The, *353;* Prisoner of Zenda, The (1937), *100;* Red Dust, *636;* Return to Peyton Place, *639;* This Happy Feeling, *394*
Astor, Patti: Film Musicals, *277*
Atchley, Hooper: Spirit of the West, *1152*
Ates, Roscoe: Captain Caution, *23;* Cimarron (1931), *1105;* Colorado Serenade, *1105;* Freaks, *843;* Robin Hood of the Pecos, *1145;* Three Texas Steers, *1157;* What! No Beer?, *408;* Wild West (1946), *1164*
Atherton, William: Buried Alive (1990), *959;* Chrome Soldiers, *26;* Class of '44, *483;* Day of the Locust, The, *496;* Die Hard, *38;* Die Hard 2: Die Harder, *39;* Ghostbusters, *285;* Grim Prairie Tales, *847;* Hindenburg, The, *541;* Intrigue, *986;* No Mercy, *91;* Oscar (1991), *351;* Pelican Brief, The, *1005;* Real Genius, *365;* Sugarland Express, The, *672;* Tomorrow's Child, *686*
Atkin, Harvey: Meatballs, *330*
Atkine, Feodor: Pauline at the Beach, *776*
Atkins, Christopher: Beaks the Movie, *812;* Blue Lagoon, The, *465;* Child Bride of Short Creek, *480;* Die Watching, *970;* Dracula Rising, *837;* Fatal Charm, *976;* Mortuary Academy, *337;* Night in Heaven, A, *606;* Pirate Movie, The, *935;* Shoot (1991), *378;* Wet and Wild Summer, *408*
Atkins, David: Squizzy Taylor, *119*
Atkins, Eileen: Devil within Her, The, *833;* Equus, *973;* Lost Language of Cranes, The, *580*
Atkins, Jenny: You're Jinxed Friend, You Just Met Sacramento, *1166*
Atkins, Tom: Halloween III: Season of the Witch, *848;* Lethal Weapon, *76;* Maniac Cop, *862;* Night of the Creeps, *869;* Ninth Configuration, The, *608;* Skeezer, *659;* Striking Distance, *121*
Atkinson, Don: Down Under, *41*
Atkinson, Jayne: Blank Check, *151;* Free Willy, *168*
Atkinson, Rowan: Bernard and the Genie, *234;* Black Adder III (TV Series), *240;* Four Weddings and a Funeral, *280;* Tall Guy, The, *391*
Atsuta, Yuharu: Tokyo-Ga, *796*
Attenborough, Richard: Bliss of Mrs. Blossom, The, *241;* Brannigan, *18;* Brothers In Law, *246;* Doctor Dolittle, *162;* Flight of the Phoenix, The, *51;* Glory at Sea, *56;* Great Escape, The, *57;* Jurassic Park, *1061;* League of Gentlemen, The, *317;* Loot, *321;* Magic Christian, The, *326;* Only Two Can Play, *350;* Sand Pebbles, The, *111;* Seance on a Wet Afternoon, *1013;* Ten Little Indians (1975), *1023;* 10 Rillington Place, *678*
Atterbury, Malcolm: How to Make a Monster, *853*
Atwill, Lionel: Balalaika, *907;* Boom Town, *466;* Captain America (1944), *22;* Captain Blood, *22;* Doctor X, *836;* Fog Island, *978;* Ghost of Frankenstein, *845;* Gorilla, The, *289;* High Command, The, *61;* Hound of the Baskervilles, The (1939), *983;* House of Dracula, *852;* House of Frankenstein, *852;* Johnny Apollo, *559;* Lost City of the Jungle, *79;* Mark of the Vampire, *863;* Murders in the Zoo, *867;* Mystery of the Wax Museum, *868;* Pardon My Sarong, *354;* Sherlock Holmes and the Secret Weapon, *1015;* Son of Frankenstein, *888;* Sphinx, The (1933), *1019;* Three Comrades, *682;* Three Musketeers, The (1939), *396;* Vampire Bat, The, *899*
Atzorn, Robert: From the Lives of the Marionettes, *739*
Auberjonois, René: Ballad of Little Jo, The, *1096;* Eyes of Laura Mars, The, *974;* Feud, The, *276;* Lone Justice, *1129;* Lost Language of Cranes, The, *580;* More Wild Wild West, *1134;* My Best Friend Is a Vampire, *339;* Once Upon a Midnight Scary, *192;* Police Academy 5—Assignment: Miami Beach, *359;* Tale of the Frog Prince, *209;* 3:15—The Moment of Truth, *128;* Walker, *695;* Where the Buffalo Roam, *409;* Wild Card, *1032;* Wild Wild West Revisited, The, *1164*
Aubert, Lenore: Abbott and Costello Meet the Killer, Boris Karloff, *221;* They Got Me Covered, *393*
Aubrey, Cecile: Manon, *765*
Aubrey, James: Forever Young (1983), *520;* Lord of the Flies (1963), *579*
Aubrey, Jimmy: Smokey Trails, *1151*
Aubry, Danielle: Operation C.I.A., *95*
Auclair, Michel: Funny Face, *918;* Manon, *765;* Story of a Love Story, *668;* Swashbuckler, The (1984), *123*
Audran, Stéphane: Babette's Feast, *714;* Bad Girls (1969), *715;* Black Bird, The, *240;* Blood of Others, The, *464;* Blood Relatives, *957;* Brideshead Revisited, *469;* Clean Slate (Coup de Torchon), *724;* Discreet Charm of the Bourgeoisie, The, *730;* Eagle's Wing, *1111;* La Cage aux Folles III, The Wedding, *753;* Le Boucher (The Butcher), *756;* Les Biches, *759;* Mistral's Daughter, *597;* Silver Bears, *379;* Six in Paris (Paris Vue par . . .), *786;* Turn of the Screw (1992), *898;* Vincent, François, Paul and the Others, *801;* Wedding in Blood, *802*
Audrey, Brigitte: President's Target, *100*
Auer, Mischa: Around the World, *907;* Brewster's Millions (1945), *245;* Destry Rides Again, *1109;* Mr. Arkadin (a.k.a. Confidential Report), *596;* Monster Walks, The, *866;* One Hundred Men and a Girl, *934;* One Rainy Afternoon, *350;* Rage of Paris, The, *364;* Seven Sinners, *113;* Spring Parade, *941;* Sputnik, *788;* Sweethearts, *943;* Three Smart Girls, *945;* Winterset, *704;* You Can't Take it with You (1938), *415*
Auffay, Patrick: 400 Blows, The, *738*
Auger, Claudine: Associate, The, *714;* Lobster for Breakfast, *761;* Summertime Killer, The, *122;* Thunderball, *129;* Twitch of the Death Nerve, *898*
Augger, Florrie: Bugsy Malone, *155*
August, Pernilla: Best Intentions, The, *717*
August, Robert: Endless Summer, The, *44*
Auld, Georgie: New York, New York, *933*
Aulin, Ewa: Blood Castle (1972), *815*
Ault, Marie: Lodger, The, *993*
Aumont, Jean-Pierre: Bizarre, Bizarre, *718;* Blackout (1978), *14;* Blood of Others, The, *464;* Cat and Mouse, *722;* Catherine & Co., *722;* Cauldron of Blood, *822;* Devil at 4 O'Clock, The, *500;* Happy Hooker, The, *293;* Horse Without a Head, The, *175;* Lili, *928;* Seven Deadly Sins, The, *785;* Something Short of Paradise, *383;* Sweet Country, *674;* Tale of Two Cities, A (1991), *677*
Aumont, Michel: La Vie Continue, *755;* Sunday in the Country, A, *791*
Aumont, Tina: Lifespan, *1063;* Malicious, *764;* Partner, *775;* Torso, *896*
Aurelius, Marcus: Apex, *1036;* Full Contact, *53*
Austin, Al: Pay or Die, *620*
Austin, Albert: Charlie Chaplin Cavalcade, *253;* Charlie Chaplin Festival, *253;* Charlie Chaplin—The Early Years, Vol. 1, *253;* Charlie Chaplin—The Early Years, Vol. 2, *253;* Charlie Chaplin—The Early Years, Vol. 4, *254*
Austin, Charlotte: Bride and the Beast, The, *19*
Austin, Jerry: Adventures of Don Juan, The, *2*
Austin, Karen: Assassin, *1037;* Far from Home, *975;* Girl to Kill For, A, *980;* Ladies Club, *74;* Summer Rental, *388;*

Taming of the Shrew (1982), *391;* When the Time Comes, *699*

Austin, Patty Duke: Miracle Worker, The (1979), *595*

Austin, Teri: Vindicator, The, *1087*

Austin, William: It (1927), *307*

Auteuil, Daniel: Elegant Criminal, The, *734;* Jean De Florette, *749;* Mama, There's a Man in Your Bed, *764;* Manon of the Spring, *765;* Un Coeur En Hiver, *798*

Autry, Alan: Great Los Angeles Earthquake, The, *532;* Roadhouse 66, *107*

Autry, Gene: Beyond the Purple Hills, *1097;* Big Show, The, *1098;* Big Sombrero, The, *1098;* Blue Canadian Rockies, *1099;* Blue Montana Skies, *1099;* Boots and Saddles, *1100;* Call of the Canyon, *1103;* Colorado Sunset, *1105;* Cow Town, *1106;* Git Along, Little Dogies, *1115;* Heart of the Rio Grande, *1119;* Hills of Utah, The, *1120;* In Old Santa Fe, *1123;* Last of the Pony Riders, *1126;* Last Round-Up, *1126;* Loaded Pistols, *1128;* Man from Music Mountain, *1131;* Man of the Frontier (Red River Valley), *1132;* Manhattan Merry-Go-Round, *930;* Melody Ranch, *1133;* Melody Trail, *1133;* Mexicali Rose, *1134;* Mule Train, *1134;* Mystery Mountain, *1135;* Night Stage to Galveston, *1136;* Oh! Susanna!, *1136;* Old Barn Dance, The, *1136;* Old Corral, *1136;* On Top of Old Smoky, *1137;* Phantom Empire (1935), *98;* Prairie Moon, *1139;* Public Cowboy #1, *1140;* Radio Ranch (Men with Steel Faces & Phantom Empire), *1140;* Ride, Ranger, Ride, *1143;* Riders of the Whistling Pines, *1144;* Ridin' on a Rainbow, *1144;* Rim of the Canyon, *1144;* Robin Hood of Texas, *1145;* Rootin' Tootin' Rhythm, *1146;* Round-Up Time in Texas, *1146;* Saginaw Trail, *1147;* Sioux City Sue, *1150;* South of the Border, *1151;* Springtime in the Rockies (1937), *1152;* Valley of Fire, *1161;* Winning of the West, *1165;* Yodelin' Kid from Pine Ridge, *1165*

Avalon, Frankie: Alamo, The, *1092;* Back to the Beach, *907;* Beach Blanket Bingo, *908;* Beach Party, *908;* Bikini Beach, *909;* How to Stuff a Wild Bikini, *923;* I'll Take Sweden, *924;* Muscle Beach Party, *338;* Pee-Wee's Playhouse Christmas Special, *194;* Voyage to the Bottom of the Sea, *1087*

Avalon, Phil: Summer City, *122*

Avalos, Luis: Fires Within, *517;* Ghost Fever, *285;* Lone Justice, *1129*

Avedon, Loreen: No Retreat, No Surrender II, *92;* No Retreat, No Surrender 3: Blood Brothers, *92*

Avellano, Jose Mari: Deathfight, *36*

Avery, Linda: Hitchhikers, *850*

Avery, Margaret: Blueberry Hill, *465;* Color Purple, The, *485;* For Us the Living: The Medgar Evers Story, *519;* Heat Wave, *539;* Hell Up in Harlem, *60;* Jacksons: An American Dream, The, *556;* Mardi Gras for the Devil, *863;* Return of Superfly, The, *105;* Sky Is Gray, The, *660;* Which Way Is Up?, *410*

Avery, Val: Black Caesar, *13;* Dream of Kings, A, *504;* Firehouse (1972), *49;* Heroes, *540*

Aviles, Rick: Mondo New York, *598;* Saint of Fort Washington, The, *646*

Avran, Chris: Captive Planet, *1041;* Twitch of the Death Nerve, *898*

Awashima, Chikage: Human Condition, The, Part One: No Greater Love, *745*

Axelrod, Nina: Cross Country, *491;* Motel Hell, *866;* Time Walker, *895;* Trading Hearts, *398*

Axman, Hanne: Red Menace, The, *636*

Axton, Hoyt: Act of Vengeance, *441;* Black Stallion, The, *151;* Buried Alive (1990), *959;* Disorganized Crime, *40;* Dixie Lanes, *265;* Endangered Species, *1049;* Goldilocks and the Three Bears, *171;* Gremlins, *1055;* Heart Like a Wheel, *538;* Liar's Moon, *574;* Retribution, *879;* We're No Angels (1989), *408;* Woody Guthrie—Hard Travelin', *439*

Aykroyd, Dan: Best of Chevy Chase, The, *235;* Best of Dan Aykroyd, The, *235;* Best of Gilda Radner, The, *235;* Best of John Belushi, The, *235;* Blues Brothers, The, *242;* Caddyshack II, *249;* Chaplin, *479;* Coneheads, *258;* Couch Trip, The, *259;* Doctor Detroit, *266;* Dragnet (1987), *268;* Driving Miss Daisy, *505;* Ghostbusters, *285;* Ghostbusters II, *285;* Great Outdoors, The, *290;* Into the Night, *553;* It Came from Hollywood, *307;* Loose Cannons, *321;* Love at First Sight, *322;* Mr. Mike's Mondo Video, *334;* My Girl, *190;* My Girl 2, *190;* My Stepmother Is an Alien, *341;* Neighbors, *343;* 1941, *345;* Nothing But Trouble (1991), *347;* Rutles, The (a.k.a. All You Need Is Cash), *938;* Saturday Night Live, *372;* Sneakers, *1018;* Spies Like Us, *384;* Things We Did Last Summer, *394;* This Is My Life, *394;* Trading Places, *398;* Twilight Zone—The Movie, *898*

Aykroyd, Peter: Gas, *283*

Aylmer, Felix: As You Like It, *229;* Citadel, The, *482;* From the Terrace, *523;* Ghosts of Berkeley Square, *285;* Hamlet (1948), *535;* Henry V (1944), *540;* Iron Duke, The, *554;* Knights of the Round Table, *73;* Nine Days a Queen, *607;* Quo Vadis (1951), *632;* Saint Joan, *646*

Aymerie, Catherine: Rabid Grannies, *878*

Ayres, Agnes: Sheik, The, *655*

Ayres, Jo Ann: In the Time of Barbarians, *1058*

Ayres, Leah: Bloodsport, *16;* Burning, The, *820;* Eddie Macon's Run, *43;* Hot Child in the City, *64*

Ayres, Lew: Advise and Consent, *442;* All Quiet on the Western Front (1930), *3;* Battlestar Galactica, *1038;* Broadway Serenade, *910;* Carpetbaggers, The, *475;* Cast the First Stone, *476;* Damien: Omen II, *829;* Dark Mirror, The, *966;* Dr. Kildare's Strange Case, *40;* Donovan's Brain, *1047;* End of the World, *1049;* Francis Gary Powers: The True Story of the U-2 Spy Incident, *522;* Holiday, *298;* Johnny Belinda, *559;* Of Mice and Men (1981), *610;* She Waits, *885*

Ayres, Robert: Battle Beneath the Earth, *9*

Azema, Sabine: Life and Nothing But, *760;* Melo, *766;* Sunday in the Country, A, *791*

Azito, Tony: Private Resort, *362*

Aznavour, Charles: Blockhouse, The, *464;* Head Against the Wall, *743;* Shoot the Piano Player, *785*

Azzara, Candy: Doin' Time on Planet Earth, *267;* Easy Money, *269;* Fatso, *275;* Pandemonium, *353*

Baal, Karin: Dead Eyes of London, *830*

Babatunde, Obba: Undercover Blues, *403*

Babcock, Barbara: Christmas Coal Mine Miracle, The, *159;* Far and Away, *514;* News at Eleven, *605;* Quarterback Princess, *631;* That Was Then...This Is Now, *680*

Baby Rose Marie: International House, *307*

Bacall, Lauren: All I Want for Christmas, *145;* Appointment with Death, *953;* Big Sleep, The (1946), *955;* Blood Alley, *15;* Dark Passage, *966;* Designing Woman, *263;* Dinner at Eight (1990), *265;* Fan, The, *975;* Flame over India, *50;* Harper, *981;* How to Marry a Millionaire, *303;* Innocent Victim, *986;* Key Largo, *988;* Misery, *865;* Mr. North, *334;* Murder on the Orient Express, *999;* Portrait, The, *625;* Sex and the Single Girl, *376;* Shootist, The, *1149;* To Have and Have Not, *130;* Written on the Wind, *707;* Young Man with a Horn, *948*

Baccaloni: Fanny (1961), *514*

Bach, Barbara: Caveman, *252;* Force Ten from Navarone, *51;* Give My Regards to Broad Street, *919;* Great Alligator, The, *847;* Princess Daisy, *627;* Spy Who Loved Me, The, *119;* Stateline Motel, *789;* Unseen, The, *899;* Up the Academy, *403*

Bach, Catherine: Masters of Menace, *329;* Rage and Honor, *102;* Street Justice, *121*

Bach, John: Georgia, *979;* Lost Tribe, The, *861*

Bachelor, Stephanie: I've Always Loved You, *555;* Springtime in the Sierras, *1152*

Bachmann, Hans: Beyond the Rising Moon, *1039;* Invader, *1059*

Backer, Brian: Burning, The, *820;* Fast Times at Ridgemont High, *274;* Steel and Lace, *1080*

Backus, Jim: Above and Beyond, *1;* Androcles and the Lion, *227;* Ask Any Girl, *229;* Billie, *150;* C.H.O.M.P.S., *155;* Crazy Mama, *30;* Critic's Choice, *261;* Francis in the Navy, *280;* Good Guys Wear Black, *56;* Great Lover, The, *289;* His Kind of Woman, *62;* Horizontal Lieutenant, The, *301;* I Love Melvin, *924;* Ice Palace, *548;* I'll See You in My Dreams, *924;* Man of a Thousand Faces, *587;* Meet Me in Las Vegas, *930;* Now You

See Him, Now You Don't, *191;* Opposite Sex, The, *934;* Pete's Dragon, *195;* Rebel without a Cause, *636;* Wheeler Dealers, The, *409;* Where Were You When the Lights Went Out?, *409;* Zotzl, *417*
Backus, Richard: Deathdream, *832;* Soldier's Home, *661*
Baclanova, Olga: Docks of New York, The, *502;* Freaks, *843*
Bacon, Irving: Blondie Has Trouble, *241;* Blondie Takes a Vacation, *242;* Caught in the Draft, *252;* Dreaming Out Loud, *269;* Guest Wife, *291;* Howards of Virginia, The, *545;* It's a Great Life, *308;* Two Weeks to Live, *402*
Bacon, Kevin: Air Up There, The, *223;* Big Picture, The, *238;* Criminal Law, *964;* Diner, *265;* End of the Line, *509;* Few Good Men, A, *976;* Flatliners, *977;* Footloose, *917;* Friday the 13th, *843;* He Said, She Said, *294;* JFK, *558;* Pyrates, *363;* Queens Logic, *363;* Quicksilver, *632;* She's Having a Baby, *377;* Tremors, *897;* White Water Summer, *139*
Bacon, Lloyd: Charlie Chaplin Carnival, *253;* Charlie Chaplin Cavalcade, *253;* Charlie Chaplin...Our Hero, *253;* Charlie Chaplin—The Early Years, Vol. 4, *254*
Bad, Steven: Evil Laugh, *839*
Badal, Tom: Out on Bail, *96*
Badalucco, Michael: Mac, *583*
Baddeley, Hermione: Adventures of Bullwhip Griffin, The, *143;* Belles of St. Trinian's, The, *234;* Mary Poppins, *185;* Passport to Pimlico, *355;* Pickwick Papers, The, *357;* Quartet (1948), *631;* Room at the Top, *643;* Tom Brown's Schooldays (1950), *685;* Unsinkable Molly Brown, The, *947*
Badel, Alan: Arabesque, *6;* Children of the Damned, *823;* Day of the Jackal, The, *966*
Badema: Close to Eden, *725*
Bader, Diedrich: Beverly Hillbillies, The, *237*
Badford, Basil: Quartet (1948), *631*
Badham, Mary: To Kill a Mockingbird, *684*
Baer, Buddy: Jubilee Trail, *1124;* Quo Vadis (1951), *632;* Snow White and the Three Stooges, *205*
Baer, Harry: Fox and His Friends, *738*
Baer, Max: Africa Screams, *223;* Beverly Hillbillies, The (TV Series), *237;* Beverly Hillbillies Go Hollywood, The, *237;* Harder They Fall, The, *536*
Baer Jr., Max: Macon County Line, *80*
Baer, Meredith: Chicken Chronicles, The, *254*
Baer, Parley: Ugly Dachshund, The, *214;* White Dog, *700*
Baerwitz, Jerry: Varan, the Unbelievable, *900*
Baez, Joan: Don't Look Back, *423;* Woody Guthrie—Hard Travelin', *439*
Baff, Regina: Below the Belt, *458*
Bagdasarian, Carol: Aurora Encounter, *1037*
Baggett, Lynne: D.O.A. (1949), *965*
Baggetta, Vincent: Man Who Wasn't There, The, *328*
Baggi, Angiola: Story of Boys and Girls, *789*
Bahner, Blake: Blackbelt 2: Fatal Force, *14;* Sensations, *651;* Thrilled to Death, *1025*
Bai, Xue: Yellow Earth, *806*
Baijley, John: Visions of Light: The Art of Cinematography, *438*
Bail, Chuck: Stunt Man, The, *671*
Bailey, Bill: On the Edge, *612*
Bailey, G. W.: Burglar (1987), *247;* Capture of Grizzly Adams, The, *156;* Doublecrossed, *504;* Mannequin (1987), *328;* Police Academy 4: Citizens on Patrol, *359;* Police Academy 6: City Under Siege, *359;* Rustler's Rhapsody, *371;* Short Circuit, *1076;* Warning Sign, *901;* Write to Kill, *1033*
Bailey, Jim: Penitentiary III, *98;* Surrogate, The, *674*
Bailey, Kathleen: Witchtrap, *904*
Bailey, Mark: Unbelievable Truth, The, *691*
Bailey, Pearl: Carmen Jones, *911;* Norman...Is That You?, *346*
Bailey, Raymond: Beverly Hillbillies, The (TV Series), *237;* Beverly Hillbillies Go Hollywood, The, *237*
Bailey, Richard: Manhunt of Mystery Island, *82*
Bailey, Robin: See No Evil, *884*
Baily, Joel: King Lear (1982), *564*
Bain, Barbara: Skinheads, *116;* Space 1999 (TV Series), *1077;* Spirit of '76, The, *384;* Trust Me, *400*
Bain, Conrad: C.H.O.M.P.S., *155;* Child Bride of Short Creek, *480;* Last Summer, *570;* Postcards from the Edge, *360;* Who Killed Mary What's 'Er Name?, *1031*
Bain, Cynthia: Spontaneous Combustion, *889;* Vietnam War Story—Part Two, *694*
Bain, Ron: Experience Preferred...But Not Essential, *273*
Bainter, Fay: Babes on Broadway, *907;* Children's Hour, The, *481;* Dark Waters, *496;* Human Comedy, The, *546;* Journey for Margaret, *559;* June Bride, *311;* Our Town (1940), *616;* Presenting Lily Mars, *626;* Shining Hour, The, *656;* State Fair (1945), *941;* Woman of the Year, *413;* Young Tom Edison, *708*
Baio, Jimmy: Brass, *468;* Playing for Keeps, *358*
Baio, Scott: Alice in Wonderland (1985), *145;* Bugsy Malone, *155;* Foxes, *521;* I Love N. Y., *547;* Zapped!, *416*
Baird, Harry: Story of a Three Day Pass, The, *668*
Baird, Roxanne: Blackbelt 2: Fatal Force, *14*
Bairstow, Scott: White Fang 2: Myth of the White Wolf, *217*
Baisho, Mitsuko: Eijanaika (Why Not?), *733*
Bakalyan, Dick: Blame It on the Night, *463;* Paratroop Command, *97*
Baker, Art: Underworld Story, *1029*
Baker, Blanche: Cold Feet (1984), *257;* French Postcards, *281;* Livin' Large, *320;* Mary and Joseph: A Story of Faith, *589;* Romeo and Juliet (1983), *643;* Shakedown, *114;* Sixteen Candles, *380*
Baker, Bob: Outlaw Express, *1137*
Baker, Carroll: Andy Warhol's Bad, *447;* Baby Doll, *453;* Big Country, The, *1098;* But Not For Me, *472;* Captain Apache, *1103;* Carpetbaggers, The, *475;* Cheyenne Autumn, *1104;* Easy to Love, *915;* Giant, *527;* Greatest Story Ever Told, The, *533;* Harlow, *536;* How the West Was Won, *1122;* Ironweed, *554;* Kindergarten Cop, *313;* Miracle, The (1959), *594;* Native Son, *604;* Paranoia, *1004;* Secret Diary of Sigmund Freud, The, *374;* Star 80, *666;* Watcher in the Woods, The, *901;* World Is Full of Married Men, The, *707*
Baker, Chet: Let's Get Lost, *429*
Baker, Diane: Baker's Hawk, *148;* Closer, The, *484;* Horse in the Gray Flannel Suit, The, *175;* Journey to the Center of the Earth (1959), *1060;* Marnie, *995;* Mirage, *595;* Pilot, The, *622;* Prize, The, *629;* Stolen Hours, *668;* Strait-Jacket, *890*
Baker, Dylan: Delirious, *263;* Long Walk Home, The, *579*
Baker, Fay: Chain Lightning, *478;* Double Deal, *41*
Baker, Frank: New Adventures of Tarzan, *90;* Tarzan and the Green Goddess, *125*
Baker, George: At Bertram's Hotel, *953;* For Queen and Country, *519;* Goodbye, Mr. Chips (1969), *920;* Robin Hood: Herne's Son, *107;* Sword of Lancelot, *124*
Baker, Jay: April Fool's Day, *810*
Baker, Jim: Tripods, *1085*
Baker, Joby: Last Angry Man, The, *568;* Wackiest Ship in the Army, The, *405*
Baker, Joe Don: Adam at 6 A.M., *441;* Cape Fear (1991), *959;* Charley Varrick, *25;* Citizen Cohn, *482;* Criminal Law, *964;* Distinguished Gentleman, The, *265;* Edge of Darkness (1986), *973;* Final Justice, *48;* Fletch, *978;* Framed (1975), *52;* Getting Even, *55;* Guns of the Magnificent Seven, *1118;* Joy Sticks, *311;* Junior Bonner, *1124;* Killing Time, The, *72;* Leonard Part 6, *317;* Living Daylights, The, *78;* Natural, The, *604;* Pack, The, *873;* Ring of Steel, *106;* Wacko, *405;* Walking Tall, *136;* Wild Rovers, The, *1164*
Baker, Josephine: French Way, The, *738;* Princess Tam Tam, *778;* Zou Zou, *949*
Baker, Kathy: Article 99, *451;* Clean and Sober, *484;* Dad, *493;* Edward Scissorhands, *1048;* Image, The, *549;* Jackknife, *556;* Jennifer 8, *987;* Killing Affair, A, *988;* Mad Dog and Glory, *584;* Mr. Frost, *997;* Street Smart, *670*

Baker, Kenny: At the Circus, *229;* Cannon Movie Tales: Sleeping Beauty, *155;* Goldwyn Follies, The, *920;* Harvey Girls, The, *922;* Mikado, The (1939), *931*

Baker, Kirsten: Gas Pump Girls, *283*

Baker, Lee Anne: Necropolis, *868*

Baker, Lenny: Next Stop, Greenwich Village, *605*

Baker, Nellie Bly: Red Kimono, The, *636*

Baker, Pamela: Bloody Wednesday, *817*

Baker, Ray: Hexed, *296;* Masters of Menace, *329;* Stacking, *665*

Baker, Renee: Delirious, *263*

Baker, Sharon: Captive Planet, *1041*

Baker, Stanley: Accident, *440;* Concrete Jungle, The (1962) (a.k.a. The Criminal), *487;* Cruel Sea, The, *492;* Dingaka, *501;* Guns of Navarone, The, *58;* Knights of the Round Table, *73;* Robbery, *1011;* Sodom and Gomorrah, *661;* Zorro, *142;* Zulu, *142*

Baker, Tom: Angels Die Hard, *5;* Canterbury Tales, The, *722;* Curse of King Tut's Tomb, The, *828;* Dr. Who: Revenge of the Cybermen, *1047;* Freakmaker, *843;* Golden Voyage of Sinbad, The, *1054;* Nicholas and Alexandra, *605;* Vault of Horror, *900*

Bakewell, Gary: BackBeat, *907*

Bakke, Brenda: Death Spa, *831;* Hot Shots Part Deux, *301;* Scavengers, *373*

Bako, Brigitte: Dark Tide, *495;* Red Shoe Diaries, *637*

Bakri, Muhamad: Beyond the Walls, *717;* Double Edge, *504*

Bakula, Scott: Last Fling, The, *315;* Necessary Roughness, *342;* Quantum Leap (TV Series), *1072;* Sibling Rivalry, *378*

Balaban, Bob: Absence of Malice, *950;* Altered States, *1035;* Dead-Bang, *33;* End of the Line, *509;* For Love or Money, *279;* Greedy, *290;* Strawberry Statement, The, *670;* 2010, *1086;* Whose Life Is It, Anyway?, *701*

Balaboe, Bob: City Slickers II, *256*

Balaski, Belinda: Bobbie Jo and the Outlaw, *17;* Cannonball, *22;* Proud Men, *1140*

Balasko, Josiane: Too Beautiful for You, *796*

Balasz, Samu: Cat's Play, *722*

Balding, Rebecca: Gathering, Part II, The, *525;* Silent Scream, *886*

Baldwin, Adam: Bad Guys, *8;* Bitter Harvest (1993), *955;* Chocolate War, The, *481;* Cohen and Tate, *485;* Cold Sweat (1993), *28;* D.C. Cab, *261;* Deadbolt, *968;* 800 Leagues Down the Amazon, *43;* Full Metal Jacket, *523;* Hadley's Rebellion, *173;* My Bodyguard, *601;* Next of Kin (1989), *90;* Poison Ivy (1985), *359;* Predator 2, *1071;* Radio Flyer, *633;* Reckless (1984), *636;* 3:15—The Moment of Truth, *128;* Where the Day Takes You, *699*

Baldwin, Alec: Alamo, The: Thirteen Days to Glory, *1093;* Alice (1990), *224;* Beetlejuice, *233;* Dress Gray, *505;* Forever Lulu, *279;* Getaway, The (1994), *55;* Glengarry Glen Ross, *528;* Great Balls of Fire, *920;* Hunt for Red October, The, *984;* Malice, *994;* Marrying Man, The, *329;* Miami Blues, *84;* Prelude to a Kiss, *360;* Talk Radio, *677;* Working Girl, *414*

Baldwin, Ann: Wall Street Cowboy, *1162*

Baldwin, Daniel: Attack of the 50-Foot Woman (1993), *1037;* Heroes of Desert Storm, *61;* Knight Moves, *989;* Lone Justice, *1129*

Baldwin, Michael: Phantasm, *874*

Baldwin, Peter: Ghost, The (1963), *845*

Baldwin, Robert: Courageous Dr. Christian, The, *489;* Meet Dr. Christian, *591;* They Meet Again, *681*

Baldwin, Stephen: Bitter Harvest (1993), *955;* Crossing the Bridge, *492;* 8 Seconds, *43;* Posse (1993), *1139;* Threesome, *396*

Baldwin, William: Backdraft, *8;* Flatliners, *977;* Internal Affairs, *67;* Preppie Murder, The, *626;* Sliver, *1018;* Three of Hearts, *683*

Bale, Christian: Empire of the Sun, *509;* Newsies, *933;* Swing Kids, *675;* Treasure Island (1990), *214*

Balenda, Carla: Hunt the Man Down, *984*

Balfour, Betty: Champagne, *479*

Balin, Ina: Black Orchid, The, *463;* Charro!, *1104;* Children of An Lac, The, *480;* Comancheros, The, *1105;* From the Terrace, *523;* Patsy, The, *355;* Projectionist, The, *362*

Balin, Mireille: Pepe Le Moko, *777*

Balint, Andras: Father, *736*

Balint, Eszter: Bail Jumper, *455;* Linguini Incident, The, *319;* Stranger Than Paradise, *387*

Balk, Fairuza: Gas, Food, Lodging, *525;* Outside Chance of Maximilian Glick, The, *193;* Return to Oz, *199;* Worst Witch, The, *219*

Balkin, Karen: Our Time, *616*

Ball, Angeline: Commitments, The, *912*

Ball, Lucille: Affairs of Annabel, The, *223;* Annabel Takes a Tour, *227;* Beauty for the Asking, *457;* Best Foot Forward, *908;* Big Street, The, *460;* Broadway Bill, *470;* Critic's Choice, *261;* Dance, Girl, Dance, *261;* Dark Corner, The, *495;* Du Barry Was a Lady, *915;* Easy Living, *506;* Fancy Pants, *274;* Five Came Back, *517;* Forever Darling, *279;* Fuller Brush Girl, The, *282;* Girl, a Guy and a Gob, A, *286;* Guide for the Married Man, A, *291;* Having a Wonderful Time, *294;* I Dream Too Much, *924;* I Love Lucy (TV Series), *303;* Joy of Living, *926;* Long, Long Trailer, The, *320;* Look Who's Laughing, *320;* Mame, *930;* Miss Grant Takes Richmond, *333;* Next Time I Marry, *344;* Panama Lady, *353;* Room Service, *370;* Seven Day's Leave, *376;* Sorrowful Jones, *383;* Stage Door, *385;* Thousands Cheer, *945;* Too Many Girls, *946;* Valley of the Sun, *1161;* Without Love, *413;* You Can't Fool Your Wife, *415;* Yours, Mine and Ours, *416;* Ziegfeld Follies, *949*

Ball, Nicholas: Claudia, *484;* House That Bled to Death, The, *853*

Ball, Vincent: Blood of the Vampire, *815*

Ballantine, Carl: Revenge of the Cheerleaders, *367;* World's Greatest Lover, The, *414;* Young at Heart Comedians, The, *415*

Ballard, Kaye: Fate, *274;* Freaky Friday, *168;* Ritz, The, *368;* Which Way to the Front?, *410*

Ballesteros, Carlos: Night of the Walking Dead, *870*

Ballew, Smith: Rawhide (1938), *1141*

Ballhaus, Michael: Visions of Light: The Art of Cinematography, *438*

Balme, Timothy: Dead Alive, *830*

Balmer, Jean-François: Madame Bovary (1991), *763*

Balpetre, Antoine: Devil's Commandment, The, *834*

Balsam, Martin: After the Fox, *223;* Al Capone, *3;* All the President's Men, *951;* Anderson Tapes, The, *952;* Bedford Incident, The, *457;* Breakfast at Tiffany's, *468;* Cape Fear (1962), *959;* Cape Fear (1991), *959;* Carpetbaggers, The, *475;* Catch-22, *252;* Confessions of a Police Captain, *487;* Cyborg: The Six-Million Dollar Man, *1043;* Death Wish III, *36;* Delta Force, The, *36;* Eyes Behind the Stars, *1050;* Goodbye People, The, *530;* Grown-ups, *534;* Harlow, *536;* Hombre, *1121;* House on Garibaldi Street, *545;* Lindbergh Kidnapping Case, The, *575;* Little Big Man, *1128;* Little Gloria...Happy at Last, *576;* Middle of the Night, *593;* Murder in Space, *1067;* People vs. Jean Harris, *620;* Psycho, *877;* Queenie, *632;* Raid on Entebbe, *633;* St. Elmo's Fire, *646;* Salamander, The, *111;* Sentinel, The, *884;* Seven Days in May, *653;* Silver Bears, *379;* Spaghetti Western, *1152;* Stone Killer, The, *120;* Summer Wishes, Winter Dreams, *673;* Taking of Pelham One Two Three, The, *1022;* Thousand Clowns, A, *395;* Tora! Tora! Tora!, *131;* 12 Angry Men, *690;* Two-Minute Warning, *1028;* Warning, The, *137*

Balsam, Talia: Calamity Jane (1984), *1103;* Consenting Adults (1985), *488;* Crawlspace, *825;* In the Mood, *306;* Kent State, *563;* Private Investigations, *101;* Supernaturals, The, *891;* Trust Me, *400*

Baltz, Kirk: On the Make, *612;* Skin Art, *659*

Bamber, George: Brothers of the Wilderness, *471*

Bana[illegible]k, Lynn: Fatal Games, *840*

Bancroft, Anne: Agnes of God, *443;* Bert Rigby, You're a Fool, *908;* Demetrius and the Gladiators, *499;* Don't Bother to Knock, *971;* 84 Charing Cross Road, *508;* Elephant Man, The (1980), *508;* Fatso, *275;* Garbo Talks, *283;* Graduate, The,

531; Hindenburg, The, 541; Honeymoon in Vegas, 300; Jesus of Nazareth, 557; Lipstick, 992; Love Potion #9, 323; Malice, 994; Miracle Worker, The (1962), 595; 'Night, Mother, 606; Point of No Return, 99; Prisoner of Second Avenue, The, 361; Restless Breed, The, 1142; Silent Movie, 379; Slender Thread, The, 660; To Be or Not to Be (1983), 397; Torch Song Trilogy, 686; Turning Point, The, 689; Young Winston, 709

Bancroft, Bradford: Dangerously Close, 966

Bancroft, Cameron: Just One of the Girls, 312

Bancroft, George: Angels with Dirty Faces, 5; Blood Money (1933), 464; Docks of New York, The, 502; Each Dawn I Die, 42; Little Men (1940), 576; Mr. Deeds Goes to Town, 333; Old Ironsides, 93; Stagecoach (1939), 1152; Texas, 1155; Underworld (1927), 691; Whistling in Dixie, 410; White Gold, 1031; Young Tom Edison, 708

Band, The: Last Waltz, The, 428

Banderas, Antonio: House of the Spirits, The, 545; Labyrinth of Passion, 755; Law of Desire, 756; Mambo Kings, The, 930; Matador, 766; Philadelphia, 621; Stilts, The (Los Zancos), 789; Tie Me Up! Tie Me Down!, 795; Women on the Verge of a Nervous Breakdown, 805

Banducci, Enrico: Hungry I Reunion, 303

Banerjee, Victor: Foreign Body, 279; Home and the World, 744; Hullabaloo over George and Bonnie's Pictures, 303; Passage to India, A, 619

Banerji, Karuna: Pather Panchali, 776

Banerji, Subir: Pather Panchali, 776

Banes, Lisa: Look Back in Anger (1980), 579

Bang, Joy: Night of the Cobra Woman, 869

Banionis, Donatas: Solaris, 787

Banjac, Mira: Do You Remember Dolly Bell?, 731

Bankee, Isaach De: Heart of Darkness, 538

Bankhead, Tallulah: Daydreamer, The, 161; Die! Die! My Darling!, 834; Lifeboat, 992; Main Street to Broadway, 326

Banks, Billy: TC 2000, 1082

Banks, Jonathan: Armed and Dangerous, 228; Blind Side, 956; Boiling Point, 17; Cold Steel, 28; Freejack, 1053; Honeymoon Academy, 300; Marilyn & Bobby: Her Final Affair, 588

Banks, Laura: Demon of Paradise, 832; Wheels of Fire, 138

Banks, Leslie: Henry V (1944), 540; Jamaica Inn, 556; Man Who Knew Too Much, The (1934), 995; Most Dangerous Game, The, 997; Sanders of the River, 111; Ships with Wings, 115; Sons of the Sea, 663; Transatlantic Tunnel, 1085

Banky, Vilma: Eagle, The, 269; Son of the Sheik, 118

Bannen, Ian: Bite the Bullet, 1099; Crossing the Line (1991), 492; Damage, 493; Defense of the Realm, 969; Deserter, The, 1109; Doomwatch, 1048; Driver's Seat, The, 505; Eye of the Needle, 974; Flight of the Phoenix, The, 51; From Beyond the Grave, 844; Gathering Storm, 525; George's Island, 169; Gorky Park, 980; Hope and Glory, 544; Mackintosh Man, The, 994; Night Crossing, 90; Offence, The, 611

Banner, John: Once Upon a Honeymoon, 349

Bannerjee, Chandana: Two Daughters, 797

Bannister, Reggie: Phantasm, 874; Phantasm II, 874

Bannon, Jack: Miracle of the Heart, 595

Baotian, Li: Ju Dou, 750

Baquet, Maurice: Voyage en Ballon (Stowaway to the Stars), 801

Bara, Nina: Space Patrol (TV Series), 1077

Barak, Ari: Jericho Fever, 68

Barak, Michael: Cause of Death, 24

Baranski, Christine: Ref, The, 365; To Dance with the White Dog, 684

Barasch, Cassie: Little Sweetheart, 577

Barash, Olivia: Child of Glass, 158

Barathy, Richie: Caged Fury, 21

Barbareschi, Luca: Bye Bye, Baby, 473; Cannibal Holocaust, 821

Barbeau, Adrienne: Back to School, 230; Cannibal Women in the Avocado Jungle of Death, 22; Crash of Flight 401, 490; Creepshow, 826; Doublecrossed, 504; Escape from New York, 45; Father Hood, 47; Fog, The, 842; Next One, The, 1068; Open House, 872; Red Alert, 104; Return to Fantasy Island, 1074; Seduced, 1013; Swamp Thing, 891; Terror at London Bridge, 893; Two Evil Eyes, 898

Barber, Frances: Sammy and Rosie Get Laid, 372; Secret Friends, 651; We Think the World of You, 406; Zed and Two Noughts, A, 709

Barber, Glynis: Edge of Sanity, 838; Hound of the Baskervilles, The (1983), 984; Wicked Lady, The (1983), 139

Barberi, Katie: Garbage Pail Kids Movie, The, 168; Not Quite Human 2, 347

Barberini, Urbano: Demons, 833; Gor, 1054; Otello, 934; Outlaw of Gor, 1069; Torrents of Spring, 686

Barbier, George: Tarzan's Revenge, 126

Barbour, John: Ernie Kovacs: Television's Original Genius, 272

Barclay, Don: Border Phantom, 1100; Falcon's Brother, The, 975; Outlaw Express, 1137

Barclay, Joan: Black Dragons, 814; Blake of Scotland Yard, 15; Kid Ranger, 1124; Lightning Carson Rides Again, 1128; Shanghai Cobra, The, 1014

Barcroft, Roy: Arizona Cowboy, 1094; Bandits of Dark Canyon, 1096; Below the Border, 1097; Carson City Cyclone, 1103; Cherokee Flash, 1104; Don Daredevil Rides Again, 1109; Down Dakota Way, 1110; Eyes of Texas, 1111; Far Frontier, 1112; G-Men Never Forget, 54; Hidden Gold, 1120; Hidden Valley Outlaws, 1120; In Old Amarillo, 1122; Jesse James Rides Again, 1123; Land of the Open Range, 1125; Manhunt of Mystery Island, 82; Marshal of Cedar Rock, 1132; Missourians, The, 1134; North of the Great Divide, 1136; Pirates of the Prairie, 1139; Purple Monster Strikes, The, 101; Radar Men from the Moon, 102; Renegade Trail, 1142; Riders of the Rio Grande, 1144; Rodeo King and the Senorita, 1145; Santa Fe Saddlemates, 1147; Son of Zorro, 118; Stage to Chino, 1152; Stagecoach to Denver, 1152; Sunset on the Desert, 1154; Texas Across the River, 1155; Under Mexicali Stars, 1160; Vigilantes of Boomtown, 1161; Wagon Wheels Westward, 1162; West of the Law, 1163; Wild Frontier, 1164

Bardeem, Javier: Jamon, Jamon, 749

Bardette, Trevor: Marshal of Cripple Creek, 1132

Bardot, Brigitte: A Coeur Joie (Head Over Heels), 710; And God Created Woman (1957), 712; Contempt, 726; Crazy For Love, 726; Dear Brigitte, 263; Doctor at Sea, 266; Le Repos du Guerrier (Warrior's Rest), 758; Legend of Frenchie King, The, 1128; Mademoiselle Striptease, 763; Ravishing Idiot, The, 364; Shalako, 1148; Very Private Affair, A, 800; Viva Maria!, 801; Voulez Vous Danser avec Moi? (Will You Dance with Me?), 801

Barenholtz, Ben: Time Stands Still, 795

Barger, Sonny: Hell's Angels '69, 60

Bari, Lynn: Amazing Mr. X, 445; Bridge of San Luis Rey, The, 469; Elfego Baca: Six Gun Law, 1111; Falcon Takes Over, The, 975; Francis Joins the Wacs, 280; Kit Carson, 1125; Nocturne, 1002; Orchestra Wives, 934; Shock (1946), 885; Sun Valley Serenade, 942

Barilli, Francesco: Before the Revolution, 716

Baring, Norah: Murder, 998

Barjac, Sophie: Alice (1981), 906; Holiday Hotel, 744

Barkan, Yuda: Lupo, 324

Barker, Lex: Away all Boats, 8; Farmer's Daughter, The, 274; Mission in Morocco, 85; Return of the Badmen, 1142; Torture Chamber of Dr. Sadism, The, 896; Velvet Touch, The, 693

Barkett, Steve: Aftermath, The, 1034; Empire of the Dark, 838

Barkin, Ellen: Act of Vengeance, 441; Adventures of Buckaroo Banzai, The, 1034; Big Easy, The, 12; Clinton and Nadine, 26; Desert Bloom, 499; Diner, 265; Down by Law, 268; Eddie and the Cruisers, 915; Harry and Son, 537; Into the West, 177; Johnny Handsome, 69; Mac, 583; Made in Heaven (1987), 1064; Man Trouble, 327; Princess Who Had Never Laughed, The, 197; Sea of Love, 1013; Siesta, 1016; Switch, 390; Tender Mercies, 679; Terminal Choice, 893; This Boy's Life, 682

Barkley, Janet: Harder They Come, The, *922*
Barkworth, Peter: Littlest Horse Thieves, The, *184*
Barl, Gail: Real Men, *365*
Barnes, Binnie: Broadway Melody of 1938, *910;* Call Out the Marines, *249;* Decameron Nights, *263;* Divorce of Lady X, The, *265;* Holiday, *298;* I Married an Angel, *924;* In Old California, *1122;* It's in the Bag, *308;* Last of the Mohicans, The (1936), *1126;* Melody Master, *592;* Private Life of Don Juan, The, *628;* Private Life of Henry the Eighth, The, *628;* Three Musketeers, The (1939), *396;* Three Smart Girls, *945;* Time of Their Lives, The, *396*
Barnes, Christopher Daniel: Murder Without Motive, *601*
Barnes, Jake: Drive-In Massacre, *838;* Summer Camp, *388*
Barnes, Joanna: Parent Trap, The, *193*
Barnes, Priscilla: Delta Fox, *37;* Last Married Couple in America, The, *315;* Lords of the Deep, *1063;* Scruples, *650;* Seniors, The, *375;* Stepfather III: Father's Day, *890;* Talons of the Eagle, *124;* Traxx, *132*
Barnes, Roosevelt: Mississippi Blues, *430*
Barnes, Walter: Escape from the KGB, *45;* Smokey Bites the Dust, *382*
Barnett, Charlie: Mondo New York, *598*
Barnett, Vince: Death Kiss, The, *968;* Gangs, Inc., *54;* Ride 'em Cowgirl, *1143;* Trailing Trouble, *1158;* We're in the Legion Now, *137*
Baron, Lita: Jungle Jim, *69*
Baron, Sandy: Birdy, *462;* Broadway Danny Rose, *246;* If It's Tuesday, This Must Be Belgium, *305;* Out of Towners, The, *352;* Vamp, *899*
Barondes, Elizabeth: Oscar (1991), *351*
Baroub, Pierre: Man and a Woman, A, *764*
Barr, Douglas: Spaced Invaders, *206*
Barr, Gabriel: Luggage of the Gods, *324*
Barr, Jean-Marc: Big Blue, The, *12;* Hope and Glory, *544;* Plague, The, *623;* Zentropa, *807*
Barr, Patrick: House of Whipcord, *853*
Barrat, Robert: Bad Lands, *1095;* Baron of Arizona, The, *1097;* Captain Caution, *23;* Distant Drums, *40;* Last of the Mohicans, The (1936), *1126;* Strangler of the Swamp, *891;* Time of Their Lives, The, *396*
Barrault, Jean-Louis: Children of Paradise, The, *723;* La Nuit de Varennes, *754;* Testament of Dr. Cordelier, The, *1082*
Barrault, Marie-Christine: Cousin, Cousine, *726;* Daydreamer, The (Le Distrait), *728;* L'Etat Sauvage (The Savage State), *756;* Love in Germany, A, *762;* My Night at Maud's, *770;* Stardust Memories, *385;* Swann in Love, *791*
Barrese, Katherine: Jezebel's Kiss, *987*
Barrett, Adrienne: Daughter of Horror, *829*
Barrett, Claudia: Robot Monster, *881*
Barrett, Jamie: House of the Rising Sun, *64*
Barrett, John: American Kickboxer, *4*
Barrett, Laurinda: Heart Is a Lonely Hunter, The, *538*
Barrett, Louise: Final Defeat, The, *1113*
Barrett, Majel: Star Trek (TV Series), *1078;* Star Trek: The Cage, *1078*
Barrett, Nitchie: Preppies, *360*
Barrett, Raina: Oh! Calcutta!, *348*
Barrett, Ray: Frenchman's Farm, *843;* Rebel (1985), *636;* Where the Green Ants Dream, *803*
Barrett, Tony: Impact, *985*
Barrett, Victoria: Three Kinds of Heat, *128*
Barrie, Amanda: Carry on Cleo, *251;* Koroshi, *73*
Barrie, Barbara: Bell Jar, The, *458;* Breaking Away, *245;* Child of Glass, *158;* End of the Line, *509;* Execution, The, *974;* Real Men, *365;* Two of a Kind (1982), *690*
Barrie, Chris: Red Dwarf (TV Series), *365*
Barrie, John: Victim, *693*
Barrie, Mona: Dawn on the Great Divide, *1107;* Here Comes Trouble, *296*
Barrie, Wendy: Five Came Back, *517;* I Am the Law, *547;* If I Were Rich, *305;* Saint Strikes Back, The, *1012;* Wedding Rehearsal, *407*
Barrier, Edgar: Arabian Nights (1942), *6;* Journey Into Fear (1942), *987;* Macbeth (1948), *583;* Phantom of the Opera (1943), *874;* Snow White and the Three Stooges, *205*
Barrile, Anthony: Hamburger Hill, *535*
Barringer, Pat: Orgy of the Dead, *873*
Barrington, Rebecca: Dance or Die, *32*
Barrish, Seth: Home Remedy, *300*
Barron, Bob: Ballad of a Gunfighter, *1096*
Barron, Dana: Death Wish IV: The Crackdown, *36;* National Lampoon's Vacation, *342*
Barron, John: Whoops Apocalypse, *411*
Barron, Robert: Sea Hound, The, *112*
Barros, Esmeralda: King of Kong Island, *859*
Barry, Don: Adventures of Red Ryder, *1092;* Bells of Rosarita, *1097;* Carson City Cyclone, *1103;* Days of Jesse James, *1107;* Days of Old Cheyenne, *1107;* Dead Man's Gulch, *1108;* Frankenstein 1970, *843;* Hostile Guns, *1122;* I Shot Billy the Kid, *1122;* Kansas Cyclone, *1124;* Saga of Death Valley, *1147;* Shakiest Gun in the West, The, *377;* Sinners in Paradise, *659;* Tulsa Kid, *1159;* Wyoming Outlaw, *1165*
Barry, Gene: Adventures of Nellie Bly, The, *442;* China Gate, *481;* Cry for Love, A, *492;* Gambler Returns, the: Luck of the Draw, *1115;* Maroc 7, *82;* Red Garters, *936;* Soldier of Fortune, *118;* Thunder Road, *129;* War of the Worlds, The, *1088*
Barry, Joan: Rich and Strange, *639*
Barry, Lynda: Comic Book Confidential, *421*
Barry, Neill: Heat (1987), *60;* O.C. & Stiggs, *348;* Old Enough, *611;* Slipping into Darkness, *117*
Barry, Patricia: Bogie, *466;* Sammy, the Way-Out Seal, *201*
Barry, Raymond J.: Born on the Fourth of July, *467;* Cop, *29;* K2, *70;* Out of Bounds, *96;* Rapid Fire, *103;* Ref, The, *365*
Barry, Sarah: Evil Dead 2, *839*
Barry, Tony: Archer's Adventure, *147;* Quest, The, *878;* Shame (1987), *114;* We of the Never Never, *137*
Barry, Wendy: Knights of the City, *927*
Barrymore, Drew: Altered States, *1035;* Amy Fisher Story, The, *447;* Babes in Toyland (1986), *147;* Bad Girls (1994), *1095;* Cat's Eye, *822;* Doppelganger: The Evil Within, *836;* E.T.—The Extra-Terrestrial, *1048;* Far from Home, *975;* Firestarter, *841;* Guncrazy (1992), *535;* Irreconcilable Differences, *554;* Motorama, *337;* No Place To Hide, *91;* Poison Ivy (1992), *1006;* See You in the Morning, *651;* Sketch Artist, *1017;* Strange Tales: Ray Bradbury Theater, *1080*
Barrymore, Ethel: Deadline USA, *497;* Farmer's Daughter, The, *274;* It's a Big Country, *308;* Moonrise, *599;* None But the Lonely Heart, *608;* Paradine Case, The, *1004;* Pinky, *622;* Portrait of Jennie, *625;* Rasputin and the Empress, *635;* Spiral Staircase, The (1946), *1019;* That Midnight Kiss, *944;* Young at Heart, *948*
Barrymore, John: Beau Brummell (1924), *457;* Beloved Rogue, *954;* Bill of Divorcement, A, *461;* Bulldog Drummond Comes Back, *20;* Bulldog Drummond's Peril, *20;* Bulldog Drummond's Revenge, *21;* Dinner at Eight (1933), *265;* Dr. Jekyll and Mr. Hyde (1920), *835;* Don Juan, *503;* Grand Hotel, *531;* Great Man Votes, The, *289;* Invisible Woman, The, *307;* Marie Antoinette, *588;* Maytime, *930;* Rasputin and the Empress, *635;* Romeo and Juliet (1936), *643;* State's Attorney, *666;* Svengali (1931), *1022;* Tempest (1928), *678;* Topaze (1933), *397;* Twentieth Century, *401*
Barrymore, John Blythe: Americana, *446;* Smokey Bites the Dust, *382*
Barrymore, John Drew: Clones, The, *1042;* High School Confidential!, *541;* Never Love a Stranger, *604;* Sundowners, The (1950), *1153;* While the City Sleeps, *138*
Barrymore, Lionel: Ah, Wilderness, *223;* Camille, *474;* Captains Courageous, *474;* David Copperfield, *496;* Devil Doll, The (1936), *833;* Dr. Kildare's Strange Case, *40;* Duel in the

Sun, *1110;* Free Soul, A, *522;* Girl from Missouri, The, *286;* Gorgeous Hussy, The, *531;* Grand Hotel, *531;* Guy Named Joe, A, *535;* It's a Wonderful Life, *555;* Key Largo, *988;* Lady Be Good, *927;* Let Freedom Ring, *928;* Little Colonel, The, *928;* Lone Star, *1129;* Mark of the Vampire, *863;* Mata Hari (1931), *590;* Navy Blue and Gold, *342;* On Borrowed Time, *612;* Rasputin and the Empress, *635;* Return of Peter Grimm, The, *638;* Sadie Thompson, *646;* Saratoga, *372;* Since You Went Away, *658;* Test Pilot, *679;* Treasure Island (1934), *213;* West of Zanzibar, *1030;* You Can't Take it with You (1938), *415*

Barsky, Vladimir: Battleship Potemkin, The, *716*

Bartel, Paul: Acting on Impulse, *950;* Desire and Hell at Sunset Motel, *969;* Eating Raoul, *270;* Hollywood Boulevard, *299;* Out of the Dark, *873;* Pope Must Diet, The, *360;* Pucker Up and Bark Like a Dog, *363;* White Dog, *700*

Barth, Eddie: Fame, *916*

Barthelmess, Richard: Broken Blossoms, *470;* Cabin in the Cotton, *473;* Heroes for Sale, *540;* Idol Dancer, The, *548;* Only Angels Have Wings, *95;* Spy of Napoleon, *664;* Tol'able David, *685;* Way Down East, *697*

Bartholomew, Freddie: Anna Karenina (1935), *449;* Captains Courageous, *474;* David Copperfield, *496;* Listen, Darling, *928;* Little Lord Fauntleroy (1936), *576;* St. Benny the Dip, *646;* Tom Brown's School Days (1940), *685*

Bartlett, Nicola: Contagion, *825*

Bartlett, Robin: Deceived, *969;* If Looks Could Kill (1991), *66;* 12:01, *1086*

Barto, Robyn: Blue Skies Again, *465*

Bartok, Eva: Blood and Black Lace, *814;* Crimson Pirate, The, *30;* Gamma People, The, *1054;* Operation Amsterdam, *95*

Barton, Gregg: Mule Train, *1134*

Barton, Joe: Slaughterhouse, *887*

Barton, Peter: Friday the 13th—The Final Chapter, *843;* Hell Night, *849*

Barty, Billy: Best of Spike Jones, Volumes 1 & 2, The, *236;* Cannon Movie Tales: Snow White, *155;* Harum Scarum, *922;* Legend, *1062;* Lobster Man from Mars, *320;* Night Patrol, *344;* Rumpelstiltskin (1987), *200;* UHF, *402;* Willow, *1089;* Wishful Thinking, *412*

Baryshnikov, Mikhail: Company Business, *28;* Dancers, *494;* That's Dancing, *436;* Turning Point, The, *689;* White Nights (1985), *700*

Basaraba, Gary: No Mercy, *91;* One Magic Christmas, *613;* Sweet Dreams, *943*

Basehart, Richard: Andersonville Trial, The, *447;* Bounty Man, The, *1101;* Brothers Karamazov, The, *471;* Chato's Land, *1104;* Flood!, *51;* Great Bank Hoax, The, *289;* Hans Brinker, *173;* He Walked by Night, *982;* Hitler, *542;* Il Bidone, *747;* Island of Dr. Moreau, The, *1060;* La Strada, *754;* Mark Twain's Connecticut Yankee in King Arthur's Court, *185;* Moby Dick, *86;* Rage (1972), *633*

Basham, Tom: Psychopath, The, *877*

Basie, Count: Stage Door Canteen, *665*

Basil, Toni: Rockula, *937*

Basinger, Kim: Batman (1989), *9;* Blind Date (1987), *241;* Cool World, *1043;* Final Analysis, *976;* Fool for Love, *518;* From Here to Eternity (1979), *523;* Getaway, The (1994), *55;* Hard Country, *293;* Man Who Loved Women, The (1983), *328;* Marrying Man, The, *329;* Mother Lode, *87;* My Stepmother Is an Alien, *341;* Nadine, *341;* Natural, The, *604;* Never Say Never Again, *89;* 9½ Weeks, *607;* No Mercy, *91;* Real McCoy, The, *1009;* Wayne's World 2, *406*

Baskin, Elya: Name of the Rose, The, *89*

Baskin, Jim: Slow Bullet, *660*

Basler, Marianne: Overseas, *774;* Soldier's Tale, A, *661*

Bass, Alfie: Carry on Admiral, *251;* Fearless Vampire Killers, or, Pardon Me, But Your Teeth Are in My Neck, The, *840;* Lavender Hill Mob, The, *317*

Basserman, Albert: Escape Me Never, *510;* Madame Curie, *584;* Melody Master, *592;* Moon and Sixpence, The, *599;* Once Upon a Honeymoon, *349;* Private Affairs of Bel Ami, The, *628;* Shanghai Gesture, The, *655;* Woman's Face, A, *705*

Bassett, Angela: City of Hope, *483;* Critters 4, *827;* Heroes of Desert Storm, *61;* Jacksons: An American Dream, The, *556;* Malcolm X, *586;* Passion Fish, *619;* What's Love Got to Do with It?, *698*

Bassett, Carling: Spring Fever, *385*

Bassett, Linda: Waiting for the Moon, *695*

Bassett, Steve: Spring Break, *385*

Bassett, William H.: Tempest, The (1983), *678*

Bassinet, Cynthia: Last Dance, *990*

Bassis, Paul: Ganjasaurus Rex, *845*

Bastedo, Alexandra: Blood Spattered Bride, The, *816;* Find the Lady, *277;* Kashmiri Run, The, *70*

Bastien, Fanny: Wolf at the Door, *804*

Bataille, Sylvia: Day in the Country, A, *728*

Batalov, Alexei: Cranes are Flying, The, *726;* Lady With the Dog, The, *755*

Batalov, Nikolai: Bed and Sofa, *716*

Bate, Anthony: Philby, Burgess and Maclean: Spy Scandal of the Century, *1005*

Bateman, Charles: Brotherhood of Satan, *819*

Bateman, Jason: Breaking the Rules, *469;* Necessary Roughness, *342;* Poison Ivy (1985), *359;* Taste for Killing, A, *126;* Teen Wolf, Too, *892*

Bateman, Justine: Closer, The, *484;* Deadbolt, *968;* Fatal Image, The, *976;* Night We Never Met, The, *345;* Primary Motive, *627;* Satisfaction, *938*

Bates, Alan: Club Extinction, *1042;* Collection, The, *485;* Day in the Death of Joe Egg, A, *262;* Duet for One, *505;* Englishman Abroad, An, *510;* Entertainer, The, *510;* Far from the Madding Crowd, *514;* Fixer, The, *517;* Georgy Girl, *284;* Hamlet (1990), *535;* Kind of Loving, A, *564;* King of Hearts, *752;* Mr. Frost, *997;* Nijinsky, *607;* Prayer for the Dying, A, *1007;* Quartet (1981), *631;* Return of the Soldier, The, *638;* Rose, The, *937;* Secret Friends, *651;* Separate Tables, *652;* Shout, The (1979), *886;* Story of a Love Story, *668;* Unmarried Woman, An, *691;* Voyage 'Round My Father, A, *695;* We Think the World of You, *406;* Whistle Down the Wind, *216;* Wicked Lady, The (1983), *139;* Women in Love, *706;* Zorba the Greek, *709*

Bates, Florence: Chocolate Soldier, The, *911;* Heaven Can Wait (1943), *295;* Judge Steps Out, The, *560;* Kismet (1944), *566;* Love Crazy, *322;* Lullaby of Broadway, *929;* Moon and Sixpence, The, *599;* San Antonio, *1147;* Secret Life of Walter Mitty, The, *374;* Son of Monte Cristo, The, *118;* Tuttles of Tahiti, The, *400;* Winter Meeting, *704*

Bates, Jeanne: Eraserhead, *838;* Mom, *865;* Strangler, The, *1020*

Bates, Kathy: At Play in the Fields of the Lord, *451;* Come Back to the Five and Dime, Jimmy Dean, Jimmy Dean, *486;* Fried Green Tomatoes, *522;* Home of our Own, A, *542;* Hostages, *544;* Men Don't Leave, *331;* Misery, *865;* Prelude to a Kiss, *360;* Road to Mecca, The, *641;* Roe vs. Wade, *642;* Shadows and Fog, *654;* Summer Heat (1987), *672;* Used People, *404;* White Palace, *700*

Bates, Ralph: Devil within Her, The, *833;* Dr. Jekyll and Sister Hyde, *835;* Dynasty of Fear, *973;* Fear in the Night (Dynasty of Fear), *840;* Horror of Frankenstein, *851;* Lust for a Vampire, *861;* Persecution, *621;* Taste the Blood of Dracula, *892*

Bates, William: Orgy of the Dead, *873*

Batinkoff, Randall: For Keeps, *519*

Batista, Lloyd: Last Plane Out, *75*

Battaglia, Rik: Call of the Wild (1972), *22;* This Man Can't Die, *1156*

Battisti, Carlo: Umberto D, *798*

Bauchau, Patrick: Blood Ties (1993), *816;* Every Breath, *973;* Rapture, The, *635;* State of Things, The, *789*

Bauer, Belinda: Act of Piracy, *1;* Archer: Fugitive from the Empire, *1036;* Case for Murder, A, *960;* Game of Love, The, *524;* Paul Reiser Out on a Whim, *355;* RoboCop 2, *1075;* Rosary Murders, The, *1011;* Samson and Delilah (1984), *648;*

Servants of Twilight, *884;* Sins of Dorian Gray, The, *886;* Timerider, *130;* Winter Kills, *704*

Bauer, Cathleen: Music School, The, *601*

Bauer, Charlita: Cradle Will Fall, The, *964*

Bauer, Michelle: Lady Avenger, *74*

Bauer, Richard: Sicilian, The, *115*

Bauer, Steven: Beast, The, *10;* Climate for Killing, A, *962;* Drive Like Lightning, *42;* False Arrest, *513;* Gleaming the Cube, *55;* Raising Cain, *878;* Red Shoe Diaries II: Double Dare, *637;* Running Scared (1986), *110;* Scarface (1983), *112;* Snapdragon, *1018;* Sweet Poison, *123;* Sword of Gideon, *123;* Thief of Hearts, *681;* Wildfire (1988), *703;* Woman of Desire, *1032*

Baugh, Sammy: King of the Texas Rangers, *1125*

Bauman, Andy: Night of the Kickfighters, *90*

Baur, Harry: Abel Gance's Beethoven, *710;* Crime and Punishment (1935), *726;* Golgotha, *741;* I Stand Condemned, *548;* Volpone, *801*

Baur, Marc: Time Runner, *1084*

Bausch, Pina: Seduction, The: Cruel Woman, *784*

Bavier, Frances: Andy Griffith Show, The (TV Series), *227;* Benji, *149*

Baxley, Barbara: Come Along with Me, *257*

Baxter, Alan: Set-Up, The, *1013*

Baxter, Anne: All About Eve, *444;* Angel on My Shoulder (1946), *448;* Carnival Story, *475;* Cimarron (1960), *1105;* Crash Dive, *30;* East of Eden (1982), *506;* Fighting Sullivans, The, *516;* Guest in the House, *534;* Homecoming (1948), *543;* I Confess, *984;* Jane Austen in Manhattan, *309;* Masks of Death, *83;* North Star, The, *92;* Razor's Edge, The (1946), *635;* Ten Commandments, The (1956), *678;* Three Violent People, *1157;* Walk on the Wild Side, *695*

Baxter, Dr. Frank: Alphabet Conspiracy, The, *146;* Gateway to the Mind, *168;* Our Mr. Sun, *193;* Strange Case of the Cosmic Rays, The, *207*

Baxter, Keith: Ash Wednesday, *451;* Chimes at Midnight, *481*

Baxter, Warner: Adam Had Four Sons, *441;* Broadway Bill, *470;* 42nd Street, *918;* In Old Arizona, *1122;* Stand Up and Cheer, *206;* West of Zanzibar, *1030*

Baxter-Birney, Meredith: Beulah Land, *459;* Bittersweet Love, *462;* Jezebel's Kiss, *987;* Kissing Place, The, *989*

Bay, Sara: Devil's Wedding Night, The, *834*

Bayaertu: Close to Eden, *725*

Baye, Nathalie: Beethoven's Nephew, *457;* Green Room, The, *742;* Honeymoon, *851;* La Balance, *753;* Man Inside, The (1990), *587;* Man Who Loved Women, The (1977), *765;* Return of Martin Guerre, The, *781*

Bayer, Gary: Will, G. Gordon Liddy, *703*

Baylor, Hal: Island in the Sky, *554*

Bazlen, Brigid: Honeymoon Machine, The, *300*

Beach Boys, The: Beach Boys, The: An American Band, *419*

Beach, Michael: Cadence, *473;* Hit List, The (1992), *982;* In a Shallow Grave, *550;* Late for Dinner, *1062;* One False Move, *94;* Weekend War, *697*

Beach, Scott: Out, *96*

Beacham, Stephanie: And Now the Screaming Starts, *809;* Foreign Affairs, *520;* Napoleon and Josephine: A Love Story, *603;* Nightcomers, The, *870*

Beal, Cindy: Slave Girls from Beyond Infinity, *381*

Beal, John: Break of Hearts, *468;* Double Wedding, *268;* Edge of Darkness (1943), *43;* I Am the Law, *547;* Little Minister, The, *576;* Madame X (1937), *584;* Ten Who Dared, *210*

Beals, Jennifer: Blood and Concrete, A Love Story, *956;* Bride, The, *819;* Cinderella (1985), *159;* Club Extinction, *1042;* Day of Atonement, *33;* Flashdance, *917;* Gamble, The, *54;* In the Soup, *306;* Indecency, *986;* Split Decisions, *664;* Terror Stalks the Class Reunion, *894;* Vampire's Kiss, *900*

Beaman, Lee Anne: Other Woman, The, *1003;* Tropical Heat, *1027*

Bean, Orson: Anatomy of a Murder, *952;* Final Judgment, *977*

Bean, Rick: Whodunit?, *1031*

Bean, Robert: Wild Ride, The, *702*

Bean, Sean: Caravaggio, *475;* Field, The, *516;* Lorna Doone, *580;* Patriot Games, *97;* Stormy Monday, *1020*

Beard, Stymie: Broken Strings, *470*

Bearse, Amanda: First Affair, *517;* Fright Night, *844;* It's a Bundyful Life, *308*

Beart, Emmanuelle: Date with an Angel, *262;* La Belle Noiseuse, *753;* Manon of the Spring, *765;* Un Coeur En Hiver, *798*

Beasley, Allyce: Moonlighting (1985), *997;* Silent Night, Deadly Night 4—Initiation, *886;* Tommyknockers, The, *1084*

Beastie Boys, The: Tougher Than Leather, *131*

Beatles, The: Compleat Beatles, The, *421;* Hard Day's Night, A, *921;* Help!, *922;* Let It Be, *429;* Magical Mystery Tour, *930*

Beatty, Clyde: Africa Screams, *223;* Darkest Africa, *33;* Lost Jungle, The, *79*

Beatty, Ned: All God's Children, *444;* Back to Hannibal: The Return of Tom Sawyer and Huckleberry Finn, *454;* Back to School, *230;* Big Bad John, *12;* Big Bus, The, *238;* Big Easy, The, *12;* Blind Vision, *956;* Captain America (1990), *22;* Chattahoochee, *480;* Cry in the Wild, A, *31;* Deliverance, *36;* Ed & His Dead Mother, *270;* Execution of Private Slovik, The, *512;* Fourth Protocol, The, *978;* Friendly Fire, *522;* Going Under, *288;* Gray Lady Down, *57;* Great Bank Hoax, The, *289;* Hear My Song, *295;* Hopscotch, *983;* Illusions, *985;* Incredible Shrinking Woman, The, *306;* Last American Hero, The, *75;* Last Train Home, *181;* Midnight Crossing, *84;* Mikey and Nicky, *332;* Ministry of Vengeance, *85;* Nashville, *603;* Network, *604;* 1941, *345;* Our Town (1980), *616;* Physical Evidence, *1006;* Pray TV (1982), *626;* Prelude to a Kiss, *360;* Promises in the Dark, *629;* Purple People Eater, *198;* Repossessed, *366;* Restless Natives, *366;* Rolling Vengeance, *108;* Rudy, *200;* Rumpelstiltskin (1980), *200;* Shadows in the Storm, *654;* Silver Streak (1976), *379;* Spy, *1019;* Stroker Ace, *387;* Superman II, *1081;* Switching Channels, *390;* TBone N Weasel, *391;* Thief Who Came to Dinner, The, *393;* Time Trackers, *1084;* Touched, *686;* Toy, The, *398;* Tragedy of Flight 103: The Inside Story, The, *687;* Trouble with Spies, The, *399;* Unholy, The, *899;* White Lightning, *139;* Wise Blood, *704*

Beatty, Robert: Captain Horatio Hornblower, *23;* Where Eagles Dare, *138*

Beatty, Warren: All Fall Down, *444;* Bonnie and Clyde, *17;* Bugsy, *471;* Dick Tracy (1990), *38;* $ (Dollars), *971;* Heaven Can Wait (1978), *295;* Ishtar, *307;* Lilith, *575;* McCabe and Mrs. Miller, *1133;* Parallax View, The, *1004;* Promise Her Anything, *362;* Reds, *637;* Roman Spring of Mrs. Stone, The, *643;* Shampoo, *655;* Splendor in the Grass, *664;* Truth or Dare, *437*

Beauchamp, Carolyn: Troma's War, *132*

Beaumont, Chris: Wilbur and Orville: The First to Fly, *217*

Beaumont, Hugh: Human Duplicators, The, *854;* Lost Continent, The, *1063;* Mole People, The, *1066;* Objective, Burma!, *93;* Phone Call from a Stranger, *622;* Railroaded, *633;* Seventh Victim, The, *885*

Beaumont, Richard: Can It Be Love, *249*

Beaver, Terry: Impure Thoughts, *305*

Beavers, Louise: Big Street, The, *460;* Coquette, *488;* Du Barry Was a Lady, *915;* General Spanky, *169;* Goodbye, My Lady, *171;* It Happened in New Orleans, *925;* Jackie Robinson Story, The, *556;* Never Wave at a WAC, *343;* She Done Him Wrong, *377;* Tammy and the Bachelor, *677;* Tell It to the Judge, *392*

Beccaria, Mario: Le Boucher (The Butcher), *756*

Becher, John C.: Below the Belt, *458*

Beck, Jeff: Secret Policeman's Other Ball, The, *375*

Beck, Jenny: Troll, *1085*

Beck, John: Audrey Rose, *811;* Big Bus, The, *238;* Climate for Killing, A, *962;* Deadly Illusion, *968;* Other Side of

Midnight, The, *615;* Pat Garrett and Billy the Kid, *1138;* Rollerball, *1075;* Sleeper, *381*
Beck, Julian: Oedipus Rex (1967), *772*
Beck, Kimberly: Friday the 13th—The Final Chapter, *843;* Massacre at Central High, *864;* Private War, *629*
Beck, Michael: Blackout (1985), *956;* Celebrity, *477;* Chiller, *823;* Deadly Game, *34;* Fade to Black (1993), *974;* Gone to Texas, *1116;* Megaforce, *1065;* Triumphs of a Man Called Horse, *1159;* Warlords of the 21st Century, *1088;* Warriors, The (1979), *137;* Xanadu, *948*
Beck, Thomas: Charlie Chan at the Opera, *961;* Charlie Chan in Paris, *961*
Beckel, Graham: Jennifer 8, *987;* Lost Angels, *580;* Rising Son, *641*
Becker, Gretchen: Firehead, *49;* Maniac Cop 3: Badge of Silence, *863*
Becker, Tony: Vietnam War Story, *694*
Beckett, Scotty: Ali Baba and the Forty Thieves, *3;* Date with Judy, A, *913;* Listen, Darling, *928*
Beckinsale, Kate: Much Ado About Nothing, *338*
Beckley, Tony: When a Stranger Calls, *1030*
Beckman, Henry: Man Upstairs, The, *327*
Beckwith, Reginald: Men of Sherwood Forest, *84*
Beckwith, William: Prime Evil, *876*
Beddoe, Don: Beyond the Purple Hills, *1097;* Blue Canadian Rockies, *1099;* Buck Privates Come Home, *246;* Bullwhip, *1102;* Impossible Years, The, *305;* Talk of the Town, The, *390;* They Won't Believe Me, *681*
Bedelia, Bonnie: Big Fix, The, *955;* Boy Who Could Fly, The, *468;* Die Hard, *38;* Die Hard 2: Die Harder, *39;* Fallen Angels, *513;* Fat Man and Little Boy, *515;* Fire Next Time, The, *1051;* Heart Like a Wheel, *538;* Lady from Yesterday, The, *567;* Lovers and Other Strangers, *323;* Memorial Day, *592;* Needful Things, *868;* Presumed Innocent, *1007;* Prince of Pennsylvania, *361;* Somebody Has to Shoot the Picture, *662;* Stranger, The (1986), *1020;* Switched at Birth, *675;* Violets Are Blue, *694;* When the Time Comes, *699*
Bedford, Barbara: Last of the Mohicans, The (1920), *75;* Mockery, *598;* Tumbleweeds, *1159*
Bedford, Brian: Grand Prix, *531*
Bedi, Kabir: Beyond Justice, *11*
Bednarz, Wendy: There's Nothing Out There, *894*
Bedos, Guy: Pardon Mon Affaire, *775;* Pardon Mon Affaire, Too!, *775*
Bee Gees, The: Sgt. Pepper's Lonely Hearts Club Band, *939*
Bee, Molly: Hillbillys in a Haunted House, *297*
Beecroft, David: Rain Killer, The, *1008;* Shadowzone, *885*
Beery Jr., Noah: Ace Drummond, *1;* Bad Lands, *1095;* Capture of Grizzly Adams, The, *156;* Carson City Kid, *1103;* Decision at Sundown, *1108;* Doolins of Oklahoma, *1110;* Fastest Gun Alive, The, *1112;* Fighting with Kit Carson, *1113;* Francis Gary Powers: The True Story of the U-2 Spy Incident, *522;* Gung Ho! (1943), *58;* Hondo and the Apaches, *1121;* Jubal, *1124;* Only Angels Have Wings, *95;* Red River, *1141;* Riders of Death Valley, *1143;* Rocketship X-M, *1075;* Savages (1974), *883;* Sergeant York, *113;* Texas Rangers, The, *1156;* Three Musketeers, The (1933), *128;* Trail Beyond, The, *1158;* Walking Tall, *136;* Walking Tall Part II, *136*
Beery Sr., Noah: Adventures of Red Ryder, *1092;* Big Stampede, The, *1098;* Buffalo Stampede, *1102;* Carson City Cyclone, *1103;* Cockeyed Cavaliers, *257;* Devil Horse, The, *1109;* Fighting with Kit Carson, *1113;* Laughing at Life, *571;* Man of the Forest, *1132;* Mark of Zorro, The (1920), *82;* Mexicali Rose, *1134;* Noah's Ark, *608;* She Done Him Wrong, *377;* Sweet Adeline, *943;* To the Last Man, *1157;* Trail Beyond, The, *1158;* Tulsa Kid, *1159;* Vanishing American, The, *1161;* Zorro Rides Again, *1166*
Beery, Wallace: Ah, Wilderness, *223;* Champ, The (1931), *478;* China Seas, *25;* Date with Judy, A, *913;* Dinner at Eight (1933), *265;* Grand Hotel, *531;* Last of the Mohicans, The (1920), *75;* Lost World, The (1925), *1064;* Min and Bill, *594;* Old Ironsides, *93;* Robin Hood (1923), *107;* Three Ages, The, *395;* Treasure Island (1934), *213;* Viva Villa!, *1162*
Bega, Leslie: Uncaged, *1028*
Beghe, Jason: Full Eclipse, *844;* Monkey Shines: An Experiment in Fear, *865*
Begley Jr., Ed: Accidental Tourist, The, *440;* Amazon Women on the Moon, *225;* Cat People (1982), *822;* Citizen's Band, *255;* Cooperstown, *488;* Dark Horse, *161;* Dead of Night (1977), *831;* Doctor Duck's Super Secret All-Purpose Sauce, *266;* Elvis—The Movie, *509;* Even Cowgirls Get the Blues, *272;* Get Crazy, *284;* Great Los Angeles Earthquake, The, *532;* Greedy, *290;* Meet the Applegates, *331;* Not a Penny More, Not a Penny Less, *1002;* Rip Van Winkle, *199;* Running Mates (1992), *371;* Scenes from the Class Struggle in Beverly Hills, *373;* She-Devil, *377;* Shining Season, A, *656;* Showdown (1973), *1149;* Spies, Lies, and Naked Thighs, *384;* Transylvania 6-5000, *399*
Begley Sr., Ed: Boots Malone, *1100;* Dark City, *495;* Dunwich Horror, The, *838;* Hang 'em High, *1118;* It Happens Every Spring, *307;* Lone Star, *1129;* On Dangerous Ground, *1003;* Patterns, *619;* Sorry, Wrong Number (1948), *1019;* Stars in My Crown, *1153;* Street with No Name, *1021;* Sweet Bird of Youth (1962), *674;* Tulsa, *689;* 12 Angry Men, *690;* Unsinkable Molly Brown, The, *947;* Wild in the Streets, *1089*
Behar, Joy: Manhattan Murder Mystery, *328*
Behets, Briony: Long Weekend, *861*
Behling, Robert: Northern Lights, *609*
Behr, Melissa: Dollman vs. Demonic Toys, *1047*
Behr, Roger: Can I Do It 'Til I Need Glasses?, *249*
Behrens, Sam: Murder by Numbers, *998*
Bekassy, Stephen: Interrupted Melody, *925*
Bekes, Rita: 25, Firemen's Street, *797*
Bekins, Richard: George Washington: The Forging of a Nation, *526*
Bel Geddes, Barbara: Alfred Hitchcock Presents (TV Series), *951;* Blood on the Moon, *1099;* Caught, *477;* I Remember Mama, *548;* Panic in the Streets, *1004;* Todd Killings, The, *685;* Vertigo, *1029*
Bel, Roger Le: Night Zoo, *607*
Belack, Doris: Hearst and Davies Affair, The, *537*
Belafonte, Harry: Buck and the Preacher, *1102;* Carmen Jones, *911;* Uptown Saturday Night, *404*
Belafonte-Harper, Shari: Fire, Ice & Dynamite, *49;* If You Could See What I Hear, *548;* Midnight Hour, *864;* Murder by Numbers, *998;* Time Walker, *895*
Belford, Christine: Christine, *824;* Gambler, The (1980), *1114;* Groundstar Conspiracy, The, *1055;* Ladies Club, *74;* Pocket Money, *359*
Belgrave, Richard: Riff-Raff (1992), *640*
Belita: Gangster, The, *525;* Never Let Me Go, *89*
Bell, Christopher: Sarah, Plain and Tall, *648;* Skylark, *660*
Bell, E. E.: 800 Leagues Down the Amazon, *43*
Bell, James: My Friend Flicka, *190*
Bell, Jeanne: TNT Jackson, *130*
Bell, Marie: Phedre, *777*
Bell, Marshall: Heroes of Desert Storm, *61;* Wildfire (1988), *703*
Bell, Rex: Broadway to Cheyenne, *1101;* Dawn on the Great Divide, *1107*
Bell, Sonny: Demon Lover, The, *832*
Bell, Tobin: Deep Red (1994), *1046;* Ruby (1991), *644*
Bell, Tom: Holocaust, *542;* Prime Suspect 1, *1007;* Prime Suspect 3, *1008;* Red King, White Knight, *636;* Wish You Were Here, *412*
Belladonna, Joey: Pledge Night, *875*
Bellamy, Madge: White Zombie, *903*
Bellamy, Ralph: Ace of Aces, *1;* Amazon Women on the Moon, *225;* Awful Truth, The, *230;* Boy in the Plastic Bubble, The, *468;* Boy Meets Girl, *244;* Brother Orchid, *20;* Cancel My Reservation, *250;* Carefree, *911;* Court-martial of Billy Mitchell, The, *489;* Disorderlies, *914;* Dive Bomber, *502;* Fourth Wise Man, The, *521;* Ghost of Frankenstein, *845;* Good Mother, The, *530;* Guest in the House, *534;* Helldorado (1934), *60;* His Girl Friday, *297;* Missiles of October, The,

596; Murder on Flight 502, *87;* Oh, God!, *349;* Pretty Woman, *361;* Professionals, The, *101;* Rosemary's Baby, *881;* Search for the Gods, *1076;* Spitfire, *664;* Sunrise at Campobello, *673;* Trading Places, *398;* Wolf Man, The, *904*

Beller, Kathleen: Are You in the House Alone?, *953;* Cloud Waltzing, *484;* Fort Apache—The Bronx, *520;* Movie Movie, *338;* Promises in the Dark, *629;* Rappaccini's Daughter, *635;* Surfacing, *123;* Sword and the Sorcerer, The, *1082;* Time Trackers, *1084;* Touched, *686*

Belli, Agostina: Blood Castle (1970), *815;* Blood in the Streets, *15;* Holocaust 2000, *851;* Night of the Devils, *869;* Purple Taxi, The, *631;* Seduction of Mimi, The, *784*

Belli, Melvin: Gimme Shelter, *424*

Bellin, Olga: Tomorrow, *685*

Bellman, Gina: Secret Friends, *651*

Bellomo, Sara: Beach Babes from Beyond, *1038*

Bellwood, Pamela: Cocaine: One Man's Seduction, *485;* Deadman's Curve, *913;* Double Standard, *504;* Incredible Shrinking Woman, The, *306*

Belmondo, Jean-Paul: Borsalino, *18;* Breathless (1959), *720;* Cartouche, *722;* Casino Royale (1967), *252;* High Heels (1972), *744;* Is Paris Burning?, *554;* Le Doulos, *757;* Le Magnifique, *758;* Love and the Frenchwoman, *762;* Mississippi Mermaid, *768;* Pierrot Le Fou, *777;* Sois Belle Et Tais-Toi (Just Another Pretty Face), *787;* Stavisky, *789;* Swashbuckler, The (1984), *123;* That Man From Rio, *793;* Two Women, *797;* Un Singe en Hiver (A Monkey in Winter), *798;* Woman Is a Woman, A, *805*

Belmont, Virginia: Silent Conflict, *1150*

Beltran, Robert: Eating Raoul, *270;* El Diablo, *1111;* Gaby, a True Story, *524;* Kiss Me a Killer, *989;* Latino, *571;* Scenes from the Class Struggle in Beverly Hills, *373;* Shadow Hunter, *654;* Streethawk, *121;* To Die Standing, *130*

Belushi, James: About Last Night, *440;* Best Legs in the 8th Grade, The, *235;* Birthday Boy, The, *240;* Curly Sue, *261;* Diary of a Hitman, *970;* Homer and Eddie, *543;* Jumpin' Jack Flash, *311;* K-9, *312;* Little Shop of Horrors (1986), *929;* Man with One Red Shoe, The, *328;* Mr. Destiny, *334;* Once Upon a Crime, *349;* Only the Lonely, *350;* Palermo Connection, The, *1004;* Pinocchio (1983), *195;* Principal, The, *628;* Real Men, *365;* Red Heat (1988), *104;* Royce, *109;* Salvador, *647;* Taking Care of Business, *390;* Thief (1981), *127;* Traces of Red, *1026;* Wild Palms, *1089;* Working Stiffs, *414*

Belushi, John: Animal House, *227;* Best of Chevy Chase, The, *235;* Best of Dan Aykroyd, The, *235;* Best of Gilda Radner, The, *235;* Best of John Belushi, The, *235;* Blues Brothers, The, *242;* Continental Divide, *259;* Goin' South, *1116;* Neighbors, *343;* 1941, *345;* Old Boyfriends, *611;* Rutles, The (a.k.a. All You Need Is Cash), *938;* Saturday Night Live, *372;* Things We Did Last Summer, *394*

Belvaux, Rémy: Man Bites Dog, *764*

Belzer, Richard: America, *226;* Flicks, *278;* Freeway, *52;* Groove Tube, The, *291;* Tommy Chong Roast, The, *397;* Wrong Guys, The, *414*

Ben Salem, El Hedi: Ali: Fear Eats the Soul, *711*

Benaderet, Bea: George Burns and Gracie Allen Show, The (TV Series), *284*

Benatar, Pat: Union City, *1029*

Benben, Brian: Gangster Wars, *54;* I Come in Peace, *1057;* Mortal Sins (1990), *997*

Benchley, Robert: I Married a Witch, *1057;* It's in the Bag, *308;* Road to Utopia, *369;* Sky's the Limit, The, *940;* Weekend at the Waldorf, *697;* You'll Never Get Rich, *948;* Young and Willing, *708*

Bender, Russ: Suicide Battalion, *122;* War of the Colossal Beast, *1088*

Bendetti, Michael: Netherworld, *868*

Bendix, William: Babe Ruth Story, The, *453;* Big Steal, The, *13;* Blackbeard the Pirate, *14;* Boys' Night Out, *244;* Connecticut Yankee in King Arthur's Court, A (1948), *258;* Crashout, *30;* Dangerous Mission, *966;* Dark Corner, The, *495;* Girl in Every Port, A, *286;* Glass Key, The, *980;* Guadalcanal Diary, *58;* Hairy Ape, The, *535;* It's in the Bag, *308;* Lifeboat, *992;* Macao, *80;* Wake Island, *136;* Who Done It?, *410;* Woman of the Year, *413*

Bendova, Jitka: Closely Watched Trains, *725*

Bendsen, Rikke: Memories of a Marriage, *766*

Benedetti, Nelly: Soft Skin, The, *787*

Benedict, Claire: Prime Suspect 2, *1007*

Benedict, Dirk: Battlestar Galactica, *1038;* Blue Tornado, *16;* Body Slam, *17;* Cruise into Terror, *964;* Demon Keeper, *832;* Follow That Car, *51;* Georgia, Georgia, *526;* Mission Galactica: The Cylon Attack, *1066;* Official Denial, *1069;* Ruckus, *109;* Scruples, *650;* Underground Aces, *403;* W, *1030*

Benedict, Nick: Pistol, The: The Birth of a Legend, *195*

Benedict, Paul: Arthur 2: On the Rocks, *229;* Chair, The, *822;* Desperate Moves, *264;* Man with Two Brains, The, *328;* Sibling Rivalry, *378*

Benedict, William: Adventures of Captain Marvel, The, *2;* Adventures of the Flying Cadets, *2;* Blues Busters, *242;* Bowery Boys, The (Series), *244;* Nyoka and the Tiger Men (Perils of Nyoka), *92*

Beneyton, Yves: By The Blood Of Others, *721;* Lacemaker, The, *755;* Letters to an Unknown Lover, *573*

Benfield, John: Prime Suspect 1, *1007;* Prime Suspect 2, *1007*

Bengell, Norma: Hellbenders, The, *1120;* Planet of the Vampires, *875*

Benigni, Roberto: Down by Law, *268;* Johnny Stecchino, *750;* Night on Earth, *606;* Son of the Pink Panther, *383*

Bening, Annette: Bugsy, *471;* Grifters, The, *534;* Guilty by Suspicion, *534;* Postcards from the Edge, *360;* Regarding Henry, *637;* Valmont, *693*

Benjamin, Paul: Education of Sonny Carson, The, *507;* Mr. Inside/Mr. Outside, *85*

Benjamin, Richard: Catch-22, *252;* Diary of a Mad Housewife, *501;* First Family, *277;* Goodbye Columbus, *288;* House Calls, *302;* How to Beat the High Co$t of Living, *302;* Last of Sheila, The, *991;* Love at First Bite, *322;* Packin' It In, *193;* Portnoy's Complaint, *624;* Saturday the 14th, *882;* Scavenger Hunt, *373;* Steagle, The, *386;* Sunshine Boys, The, *388;* Westworld, *1089;* Witches' Brew, *412*

Benji: Benji the Hunted, *150;* For the Love of Benji, *167;* Oh, Heavenly Dog!, *192*

Bennent, David: Legend, *1062;* Tin Drum, The, *795*

Bennent, Heinz: From the Lives of the Marionettes, *739;* Possession, *876*

Bennett, Bill: Keystone Comedies, Vol. 5, *313*

Bennett, Bruce: Before I Hang, *812;* Clones, The, *1042;* Cosmic Man, The, *1043;* Daniel Boone, Trail Blazer, *1107;* Daredevils of the Red Circle, *32;* Dark Passage, *966;* Fighting Devil Dogs, The, *48;* Lone Ranger, The (1938), *1129;* Man I Love, The, *586;* Mildred Pierce, *594;* New Adventures of Tarzan, *90;* Sahara (1943), *110;* Silver River, *1150;* Stolen Life, A, *668;* Strategic Air Command, *670;* Tarzan and the Green Goddess, *125;* Three Violent People, *1157;* Treasure of the Sierra Madre, *132*

Bennett, Constance: Common Law, The, *487;* Goose Woman, The, *980;* Madame X (1966), *584;* Topper, *397;* Topper Takes a Trip, *398;* Two-Faced Woman, *401;* What Price Hollywood?, *698*

Bennett, Earl: Best of Spike Jones, Volumes 1 & 2, The, *236*

Bennett, Enid: Robin Hood (1923), *107*

Bennett, Helen: Lost City of the Jungle, *79*

Bennett, Hywel: Deadline (1987), *497;* Endless Night, *973;* Loot, *321;* Murder Elite, *600;* Virgin Soldiers, The, *694*

Bennett, Jill: Charge of the Light Brigade, The (1968), *24;* Concrete Jungle, The (1962) (a.k.a. The Criminal), *487;* I Want What I Want, *548;* Lady Jane, *568;* Old Curiosity Shop, The, *933;* Sheltering Sky, The, *655;* Skull, The, *887*

Bennett, Joan: Best of Dark Shadows, The, *813;* Bulldog Drummond, *20;* Colonel Effingham's Raid, *257;* Dark Shadows (TV Series), *829;* Disraeli, *502;* Father of the Bride (1950), *275;* Father's Little Dividend, *275;* House Across the Bay, The, *545;* House of Dark Shadows, *852;* Little Women

(1933), *577;* Man Hunt (1941), *994;* Man in the Iron Mask, The (1939), *81;* Mississippi, *931;* Scar, The, *649;* Scarlet Street, *649;* Secret Beyond the Door, *650;* Son of Monte Cristo, The, *118;* Suspiria, *891;* We're No Angels (1955), *407*

Bennett, Julie: Hey There, It's Yogi Bear, *174*

Bennett, Marion: Lantern Hill, *180*

Bennett, Ray: Lovers' Lovers, *582;* Thundering Herd, *1157*

Bennett, Richard: Arrowsmith, *451;* If I Had a Million, *304*

Bennett, Tony: Oscar, The (1966), *615*

Bennett, Zachary: Looking for Miracles, *579;* Tales From Avonlea (TV series), *209*

Benny, Jack: Broadway Melody of 1936, *910;* Buck Benny Rides Again, *246;* George Washington Slept Here, *284;* Guide for the Married Man, A, *291;* Hollywood Canteen, *923;* Horn Blows at Midnight, The, *301;* It's in the Bag, *308;* Jack Benny Program, The (TV Series), *309;* Meanest Man in the World, The, *330;* Red Skelton: A Career of Laughter, *433;* To Be or Not to Be (1942), *397;* Transatlantic Merry-Go-Round, *946*

Benrath, Martin: White Rose, The (1983), *803*

Benrubi, Abraham: Program, The, *629*

Benson, Deborah: Mutant on the Bounty, *338;* September 30, 1955, *652*

Benson, Lucille: Private Parts, *876*

Benson, Martin: Battle Beneath the Earth, *9;* Gorgo, *847;* Hitchhiker's Guide to the Galaxy, The, *1056*

Benson, Robby: All the Kind Strangers, *951;* Chosen, The, *481;* City Limits, *1041;* Die Laughing, *264;* End, The, *271;* Harry and Son, *537;* Homewrecker, *1057;* Ice Castles, *548;* Invasion of Privacy, *986;* Jory, *1124;* Last of Mrs. Lincoln, The, *570;* Modern Love, *335;* Ode to Billy Joe, *610;* One on One, *613;* Our Town (1980), *616;* Rent-a-Cop, *105;* Running Brave, *645;* Tribute, *688;* Two of a Kind (1982), *690;* Webber's World, *406;* White Hot, *138*

Bentine, Michael: Down Among the "Z" Men, *268*

Bentley, John: Chair, The, *822;* Flight from Vienna, *518*

Bentley, Ray: Scarlet Spear, The, *112*

Benton, Barbi: Deathstalker, *1046;* For the Love of It, *279;* Hospital Massacre, *852*

Benton, Eddie: Dr. Strange, *1047*

Benton, Helen: Bloodbeat, *816*

Benton, Jerome: Graffiti Bridge, *920;* Under the Cherry Moon, *691*

Benton, Kevin: No Escape, No Return, *91*

Benton, Suzanne: Boy and His Dog, A, *1040;* That Cold Day in the Park, *680*

Benussi, Femi: Rattler Kid, *1141*

Beradino, John: Moon of the Wolf, *866*

Beraud, Luc: Sincerely Charlotte, *786*

Bercovici, Luca: Frightmare, *844;* K2, *70;* Mirror Images II, *996;* Mission of Justice, *85;* Mortal Passions, *997;* Pacific Heights, *1003;* Parasite, *873*

Berenger, Eric: Monsieur Hire, *768*

Berenger, Tom: At Play in the Fields of the Lord, *451;* Betrayed (1988), *954;* Beyond Obsession, *717;* Big Chill, The, *460;* Born on the Fourth of July, *467;* Butch and Sundance: The Early Days, *1103;* Chasers, *254;* Dogs of War, The, *40;* Eddie and the Cruisers, *915;* Fear City, *47;* Field, The, *516;* Gettysburg, *526;* In Praise of Older Women, *550;* Last Rites, *75;* Looking for Mr. Goodbar, *993;* Love at Large, *322;* Major League, *326;* Major League II, *326;* Platoon, *623;* Rustler's Rhapsody, *371;* Shattered (1991), *1014;* Shoot to Kill, *115;* Sliver, *1018;* Sniper, *117;* Someone to Watch Over Me, *1018*

Berenson, Marisa: Barry Lyndon, *456;* Death in Venice, *498;* Killer Fish, *71;* Night of the Cyclone, *1001;* Secret Diary of Sigmund Freud, The, *374;* Sex on the Run, *376;* Trade Secrets, *1026;* White Hunter Black Heart, *700*

Berfield, Lorne: Double Blast, *41*

Berg, Joanna: Visitors, The, *901*

Berg, Peter: Aspen Extreme, *451;* Case for Murder, A, *960;* Crooked Hearts, *491;* Fire in the Sky, *1051;* Late for Dinner, *1062;* Midnight Clear, A, *593;* Never on Tuesday, *604;* Race for Glory, *102*

Berge, Colette: Les Abysses, *759*

Berge, Francine: Judex, *750;* Les Abysses, *759;* Mr. Klein, *768*

Bergen, Candice: Best of Chevy Chase, The, *235;* Best of Gilda Radner, The, *235;* Bite the Bullet, *1099;* Carnal Knowledge, *475;* Domino Principle, The, *971;* 11 Harrowhouse, *973;* Gandhi, *524;* Getting Straight, *526;* Mayflower Madam, *591;* Merlin & the Sword, *1065;* Night Full of Rain, A, *605;* Oliver's Story, *612;* Rich and Famous, *639;* Sand Pebbles, The, *111;* Soldier Blue, *1151;* Starting Over, *385;* Stick, *120;* Wind and the Lion, The, *140*

Bergen, Edgar: Fun and Fancy Free, *168;* Goldwyn Follies, The, *920;* Letter of Introduction, *573;* Look Who's Laughing, *320;* Muppet Movie, The, *189;* Stage Door Canteen, *665;* You Can't Cheat an Honest Man, *415*

Bergen, Frances: Eating, *507*

Bergen, Polly: Across the Rio Grande, *1092;* At War with the Army, *229;* Cape Fear (1962), *959;* Cry-Baby, *912;* Escape from Fort Bravo, *1111;* Haunting of Sarah Hardy, The, *982;* Kisses for My President, *314;* Lightning Incident, The, *860;* Making Mr. Right, *327;* Murder on Flight 502, *87;* War and Remembrance, *696;* Winds of War, The, *703*

Bergen, Tushka: Wrangler, *141*

Berger, Helmut: Ash Wednesday, *451;* Battle Force, *9;* Code Name: Emerald, *27;* Conversation Piece, *726;* Damned, The, *727;* Dorian Gray, *837;* Garden of the Finzi-Continis, The, *740;* Godfather, Part III, The, *529;* Romantic Englishwoman, The, *643*

Berger, Joachim: Carpet of Horror, *960*

Berger, Nicole: Shoot the Piano Player, *785;* Story of a Three Day Pass, The, *668*

Berger, Sarah: Green Man, The, *981*

Berger, Senta: Ambushers, The, *4;* Cast a Giant Shadow, *23;* Diabolically Yours, *730;* Full Hearts and Empty Pockets, *739;* Killing Cars, *563;* Quiller Memorandum, The, *102;* Scarlet Letter (1973), *784;* Sherlock Holmes and the Deadly Necklace, *1015;* Swiss Conspiracy, The, *1022;* Waltz King, The, *215;* When Women Had Tails, *409;* When Women Lost Their Tails, *409*

Berger, Sidney: Carnival of Souls, *821*

Berger, William: Tex and the Lord of the Deep, *1155*

Bergerac, Jacques: Gigi, *919;* Les Girls, *928;* Unkissed Bride, *403*

Bergere, Lee: Time Trackers, *1084*

Berggren, Thommy: Elvira Madigan, *734;* Sunday's Children, *791*

Berghof, Herbert: Belarus File, The, *954;* Target, *125;* Voices, *694*

Bergin, Patrick: Frankenstein (1992), *842;* Highway to Hell, *850;* Love Crimes, *993;* Map of the Human Heart, *588;* Mountains of the Moon, *87;* Patriot Games, *97;* Robin Hood (1991), *107;* Sleeping with the Enemy, *1017;* They, *894*

Bergman, Henry: Charlie Chaplin Cavalcade, *253;* Charlie Chaplin Festival, *253;* Charlie Chaplin—The Early Years, Vol. 3, *254;* Circus, The/A Day's Pleasure, *255;* Woman of Paris, A, *705*

Bergman, Ingrid: Adam Had Four Sons, *441;* Anastasia, *447;* Arch of Triumph, *450;* Autumn Sonata, *714;* Bells of St. Mary's, The, *458;* Cactus Flower, *248;* Casablanca, *476;* Dr. Jekyll and Mr. Hyde (1941), *835;* Dollar, *731;* Elena and Her Men, *734;* Fear (1955), *515;* Gaslight (1944), *979;* Goodbye Again, *530;* Hideaways, The, *174;* Indiscreet (1958), *306;* Inn of the Sixth Happiness, The, *552;* Intermezzo (1936), *748;* Intermezzo (1939), *553;* Joan of Arc, *558;* June Night, *751;* Matter of Time, A, *590;* Murder on the Orient Express, *999;* Notorious, *1002;* Only One Night, *773;* Spellbound, *1019;* Stromboli, *790;* Under Capricorn, *1028;* Voyage in Italy, *801;* Walk in the Spring Rain, A, *695;* Woman Called Golda, A, *705*

Bergman, Peter: Firesign Theatre's Hot Shorts, *277;* J-Men Forever, *310;* Phantom of the Ritz, *874*

Bergman, Sandahl: Body of Influence, *958;* Conan the Barbarian, *1042;* Getting Physical, *526;* Hell Comes to Frogtown, *1056;* Kandyland, *562;* Lipstick Camera, *992;*

Possessed by the Night, *1006;* Programmed to Kill, *1072;* Raw Nerve, *103;* Red Sonja, *104;* She (1983), *1076;* Stewardess School, *386;* Xanadu, *948*
Bergner, Elisabeth: As You Like It, *229;* Catherine the Great, *477;* Cry of the Banshee, *827*
Bergryd, Ulla: Bible, The, *460*
Bergstrom, Helena: House of Angels, *745*
Berkeley, Keith: Visitors, The, *901*
Berkeley, Xander: Candyman (1992), *820*
Berkoff, Steven: Barry Lyndon, *456;* Rambo: First Blood II, *103;* Season of Giants, A, *650;* Transmutations, *897;* Under the Cherry Moon, *691*
Berland, Terri: Pink Motel, *357;* Strangeness, The, *890*
Berle, Milton: Broadway Danny Rose, *246;* Cracking Up, *260;* Happy Birthday Bugs: 50 Looney Years, *173;* It's a Mad Mad Mad Mad World, *308;* Legend of Valentino, *572;* Lepke, *76;* Loved One, The, *323;* More Milton Berle's Mad World of Comedy, *431;* Muppet Movie, The, *189;* Sun Valley Serenade, *942;* TV Classics: Milton Berle, *401;* Who's Minding the Mint?, *411*
Berlin Comic Opera Ballet: Cinderella (1987), *912*
Berlin, Irving: This Is the Army, *945*
Berlin, Jeannie: Baby Maker, The, *453;* Heartbreak Kid, The, *295;* Housewife, *545;* In the Spirit, *306;* Portnoy's Complaint, *624*
Berlinger, Warren: Billie, *150;* Four Deuces, The, *52;* Free Ride, *281;* I Will, I Will...for Now, *304;* Lepke, *76;* Long Goodbye, The, *993;* Magician of Lublin, The, *585;* Outlaw Force, *96;* Wackiest Ship in the Army, The, *405*
Berman, Shelley: Best Man, The, *459;* Son of Blob (Beware! The Blob), *888;* Teen Witch, *392;* Young at Heart Comedians, The, *415*
Berman, Susan: Smithereens, *661*
Bernard, Crystal: Slumber Party Massacre II, *887*
Bernard, Jason: Wilma, *703*
Bernard, Juan: Faster Pussycat! Kill! Kill!, *46*
Bernard, Maurice: Lucy and Desi: Before the Laughter, *583*
Bernard, Paul: Pattes Blanches (White Paws), *776*
Bernard, Thelonious: Little Romance, A, *319*
Bernardi, Herschel: Irma La Douce, *307;* Love with the Proper Stranger, *582;* No Deposit, No Return, *191;* Peter Gunn (TV Series), *98;* Story of Jacob and Joseph, The, *207*
Bernhard, Joachim: Last Five Days, The, *755*
Bernhard, Sandra: Best of the Big Laff Off, The, *236;* Heavy Petting, *426;* Hudson Hawk, *64;* Inside Monkey Zetterland, *306;* King of Comedy, The, *565;* Sesame Street Presents Follow That Bird, *203;* Track 29, *1026;* Truth or Dare, *437;* Without You I'm Nothing, *413;* Your Favorite Laughs from an Evening at the Improv, *416*
Bernhardt, Kevin: Beauty School, *233;* Hellraiser 3: Hell On Earth, *850;* Kick or Die, *70*
Bernhardt, Sarah: Queen Elizabeth, *631*
Bernsen, Collin: Puppet Master II, *878*
Bernsen, Corbin: Bert Rigby, You're a Fool, *908;* Breaking Point, *469;* Dead Aim (1987), *33;* Dead on the Money, *967;* Disorganized Crime, *40;* Frozen Assets, *282;* Hello Again, *296;* L.A. Law, *567;* Major League, *326;* Major League II, *326;* Shattered (1991), *1014*
Bernstein, Sheryl: Gross Jokes, *291*
Berri, Claude: Le Sex Shop, *758;* Seven Deadly Sins, The, *785*
Berridge, Elizabeth: Amadeus, *906;* Funhouse, The, *845;* Montana, *599;* Smooth Talk, *661;* When the Party's Over, *699*
Berry, Amanda: Palm Beach, *617*
Berry, Bill: High Country, The, *61*
Berry, Chuck: American Hot Wax, *906;* Chuck Berry Hail! Hail! Rock 'n' Roll, *421;* Go, Johnny, Go!, *920;* Jazz on a Summer's Day, *427;* Rock, Rock, Rock, *937;* That Was Rock, *944*
Berry, Halle: Boomerang, *244;* Father Hood, *47;* Flintstones, The, *167;* Program, The, *629;* Strictly Business, *387*
Berry, John: Man in Love, A, *587;* Window Shopping, *804*
Berry, Jules: Crime of Monsieur Lange, The, *727;* Le Jour Se Leve (Daybreak) (1939), *757;* Les Visiteurs Du Soir, *759*
Berry, Ken: Cat from Outer Space, The, *157;* Herbie Rides Again, *174*
Berry, Richard: Caged Heart, The (L'Addition), *721;* Day of Atonement, *33;* Honeymoon, *851;* La Balance, *753;* Man and a Woman, A: 20 Years Later, *764*
Berryman, Dorothee: Decline of the American Empire, The, *729;* Paper Wedding, *618*
Berryman, Michael: Auntie Lee's Meat Pies, *811;* Barbarians, The, *1038;* Cut and Run, *493;* Guyver, The, *1055;* Hills Have Eyes, The: Part Two, *850*
Berteloot, Jean-Yves: Deep Trouble, *969*
Berti, Aldo: Big Rip-off, The, *1098*
Bertin, Roland: Hairdresser's Husband, The, *742;* L'Homme Blessé (The Wounded Man), *760*
Bertinelli, Valerie: Aladdin and His Wonderful Lamp, *145;* C.H.O.M.P.S., *155;* Number One with a Bullet, *92;* Ordinary Heroes, *614;* Pancho Barnes, *617;* Shattered Vows, *655;* Taken Away, *676;* Young Love, First Love, *708*
Bertish, Suzanne: Venice/Venice, *693*
Berto, Juliet: Le Gai Savior (The Joy of Knowledge), *757;* Le Sex Shop, *758;* Mr. Klein, *768*
Bertrand, Janette: Big Red, *150*
Bervoets, Gene: Vanishing, The (1988), *800*
Berz, Michael: Hot Resort, *301*
Besch, Bibi: Beast Within, The, *812;* Betrayal (1978), *459;* Kill Me Again, *988;* Lonely Lady, The, *577;* Medicine Hat Stallion, The, *186*
Besnehard, Dominique: A Nos Amours, *710*
Besse, Ariel: Beau Pere, *716*
Bessell, Ted: Billie, *150;* Breaking Up Is Hard to Do, *469;* Don't Drink the Water, *267*
Besser, Joe: Abbott and Costello Show, The (TV Series), *221;* Hey Abbott!, *296*
Best, Alyson: Dark Forces, *966;* Man of Flowers, *327*
Best, Edna: Ghost and Mrs. Muir, The, *285;* Man Who Knew Too Much, The (1934), *995*
Best, James: Left Handed Gun, The (1958), *1128;* Ride Lonesome, *1143;* Rolling Thunder, *108;* Savages (1974), *883;* Sounder, *663*
Best, Kevin: South Central, *663*
Best, Willie: Littlest Rebel, The, *929;* Monster Walks, The, *866;* Vivacious Lady, *405*
Beswick, Martine: Bullet for the General, A, *1102;* Cyclone, *31;* Dr. Jekyll and Sister Hyde, *835;* Happy Hooker Goes Hollywood, The, *293;* Prehistoric Women (1967), *100;* Seizure, *884;* Strange New World, *1080*
Bethune, Zina: Who's That Knocking at My Door?, *701*
Bett, John: Gregory's Girl, *290;* Tess, *679*
Bettger, Lyle: Gundown at Sandoval, *1117;* Johnny Reno, *1124;* Lone Ranger, The (1956), *1129;* Sea Chase, The, *112;* Union Station, *1029*
Betti, Laura: Canterbury Tales, The, *722;* Hatchet for the Honeymoon, *848;* Lovers and Liars, *323;* Twitch of the Death Nerve, *898*
Bettina: Journey to Spirit Island, *179*
Bettis, Paul: Urinal, *692*
Bettles, Robert: Fourth Wish, The, *521*
Bettoia, Franca: Last Man on Earth, The, *1062*
Betz, Carl: Deadly Encounter (1975), *498;* Spinout, *941*
Bevan, Billy: Caution: Funny Men at Work, *420;* Cavalcade, *477;* High Voltage, *62;* Li'l Abner (1940), *318;* Lost Patrol, The, *79;* Terror by Night, *1023*
Bevans, Clem: Of Human Hearts, *610;* Young Tom Edison, *708*
Bever, Carol: Waitress, *405*
Bey, Turhan: Ali Baba and the Forty Thieves, *3;* Amazing Mr. X, *445;* Arabian Nights (1942), *6;* Background to Danger, *8;* Dragon Seed, *504;* Mummy's Tomb, The, *867;* Out of the Blue, *352*

Beyer, Troy: Rooftops, *937;* Weekend at Bernie's II, *407*
Beymer, Richard: Blackbelt, *14;* Cross Country, *491;* Indiscretion of an American Wife, *551;* Johnny Tremain, *179;* State of Emergency, *666;* Stripper, The (1963), *671;* Twin Peaks (Movie), *1027;* Twin Peaks (TV Series), *1027;* Under Investigation, *1028;* West Side Story, *947*
Bezace, Didier: Little Thief, The, *760*
Bezer, Amber: Appointment with Death, *953*
Bhasker: Dragon Chow, *732*
Biagin, Isabella: Loaded Guns, *78*
Biagli, Claudio: Mediterraneo, *766*
Bianchi, Daniela: From Russia with Love, *53*
Bianco, Tony Lo: Story of Jacob and Joseph, The, *207*
Biao, Yuen: Eastern Condors, *733;* Mr. Vampire (Vol. 1–4), *768*
Bibby, Charles K.: Order of the Black Eagle, *95*
Biberman, Abner: Betrayal from the East, *11;* Panama Lady, *353*
Bickford, Charles: Anna Christie (1930), *449;* Babe Ruth Story, The, *453;* Big Country, The, *1098;* Big Hand for the Little Lady, A, *1098;* Branded, *1101;* Command Decision, *487;* Court-martial of Billy Mitchell, The, *489;* Days of Wine and Roses, *496;* East of Borneo, *43;* Farmer's Daughter, The, *274;* Four Faces West, *1114;* Jim Thorpe—All American, *558;* Johnny Belinda, *559;* Little Miss Marker (1934), *182;* Not as a Stranger, *609;* Plainsman, The, *1139;* Reap the Wild Wind, *104;* Riders of Death Valley, *1143;* Song of Bernadette, The, *662;* Star Is Born, A (1954), *666;* Tarzan's New York Adventure, *126;* Thunder Trail, *1157;* Unforgiven, The (1960), *1160;* Wing and a Prayer, A, *140*
Bickley, Tony: Swimmer, The, *675*
Bicknell, Andrew: Moving Finger, The, *998*
Bicknell, Gene: Gypsy Angels, *535*
Bideau, Jean-Luc: Jonah Who Will Be 25 in the Year 2000, *750*
Bidonde, Hector: Funny Dirty Little War (No Habra Mas Penas ni Olvido), *739*
Biehn, Michael: Abyss, The, *1034;* Aliens, *1035;* Coach, *484;* Deadfall, *968;* Deep Red (1994), *1046;* Fan, The, *975;* In a Shallow Grave, *550;* K2, *70;* Navy Seals, *89;* Rampage, *1009;* Seventh Sign, The, *885;* Strapped, *670;* Taste for Killing, A, *126;* Terminator, The, *1082;* Time Bomb, *1025;* Tombstone, *1157*
Bierbichler, Josef: Heart of Glass, *743*
Bieri, Ramon: Badlands, *454;* Christmas without Snow, A, *482;* Frisco Kid, The, *1114;* Grandview, U.S.A., *531;* It's Good to Be Alive, *555;* Sicilian, The, *115;* Sorceror, *1018*
Bierko, Craig: Victimless Crimes, *1030*
Biggs, Roxann: Broken Angel, *470;* Mortal Sins (1992), *997*
Bignamini, Nino: All Screwed Up, *712*
Bikel, Theodore: African Queen, The, *442;* Assassination Game, The, *7;* Colditz Story, The, *485;* Dark Tower, *829;* Defiant Ones, The, *499;* Dog of Flanders, A, *163;* Enemy Below, The, *44;* Flight from Vienna, *518;* I Bury the Living, *855;* I Want to Live!, *548;* Murder on Flight 502, *87;* My Side of the Mountain, *190;* Never Let Me Go, *89;* Pride and the Passion, The, *626;* Russians Are Coming, the Russians Are Coming, The, *371;* Shattered (1991), *1014;* 200 Motels, *946*
Bill, Tony: Are You in the House Alone?, *953;* Come Blow Your Horn, *257;* Haunts of the Very Rich, *1055;* Ice Station Zebra, *65;* Initiation of Sarah, The, *856;* Killing Mind, The, *989;* Less Than Zero, *573;* None But the Brave, *92;* Soldier in the Rain, *661;* You're a Big Boy Now, *416*
Billingsley, Barbara: Eye of the Demon, *840*
Billingsley, Jennifer: C.C. & Company, *21;* Thirsty Dead, The, *895;* White Lightning, *139*
Billingsley, Peter: Arcade, *1036;* Beverly Hills Brats, *237;* Christmas Story, A, *159;* Dirt Bike Kid, The, *162;* Russkies, *371*
Billington, Francis: Blind Husbands, *464*
Billington, Michael: Invasion UFO, *1059;* UFO—Volumes I and II, *1086*
Billy Vera and The Beaters: Father Guido Sarducci Goes to College, *275*
Bindon, John: Man in the Wilderness, *1132*
Bing, Herman: Bitter Sweet, *909;* Guardsman, The, *291*
Binkley, Lane: Bernice Bobs Her Hair, *234;* Soldier's Home, *661*
Binns, Edward: Hunter (1971), *65;* Oliver's Story, *612;* Pilot, The, *622;* 12 Angry Men, *690*
Binoche, Juliette: Blue (1993), *719;* Damage, *493;* Lovers on the Bridge, *762;* Rendez-Vous, *780;* Unbearable Lightness of Being, The, *691;* Women & Men 2, *706*
Birch, Paul: Apache Woman, *1094;* Queen of Outer Space, *1073*
Birch, Thora: All I Want for Christmas, *145;* Hocus Pocus, *175;* Monkey Trouble, *188;* Paradise (1991), *618*
Bird, Billie: End of Innocence, The, *509;* Ernest Saves Christmas, *165;* Sixteen Candles, *380*
Bird, John: 30 Is a Dangerous Age, Cynthia, *394*
Bird, Norman: Whistle Down the Wind, *216*
Birdsall, Jesse: Getting It Right, *285;* Wish You Were Here, *412*
Birdsong, Lori: Blood Salvage, *816*
Birell, Tala: Purple Heart, The, *630;* White Legion, *700*
Birkin, Jane: Beethoven's Nephew, *457;* Catherine & Co., *722;* Daddy Nostalgia, *727;* Dark Places, *829;* Dust, *506;* Evil under the Sun, *973;* La Belle Noiseuse, *753;* Le Petit Amour, *758;* Make Room For Tomorrow, *764;* Swimming Pool, The, *792;* Wonderwall, *805*
Birkin, Ned: Cement Garden, The, *478*
Birman, Len: Captain America (1979), *22;* Captain America II: Death Too Soon, *22;* Man Inside, The (1984), *81;* Undergrads, The, *214*
Birney, David: Caravan to Vaccares, *23;* King Richard II, *565;* Night of the Fox, *90;* Nightfall, *1068;* Oh, God! Book II, *349;* Only with Married Men, *350;* Pretty Kill, *1007;* Ray Bradbury's Chronicles: The Martian Episodes, *1073;* Touch and Die, *1026*
Birney, Reed: Greatest Man in the World, The, *290*
Bishop, Debby: Blue Money, *242*
Bishop, Ed: Invasion UFO, *1059;* Philip Marlowe, Private Eye: Finger Man, *1005;* UFO—Volumes I and II, *1086*
Bishop, Jennifer: House of Terror, *984;* Jaws of Death, The, *858*
Bishop, Joey: Betsy's Wedding, *236;* Delta Force, The, *36;* Guide for the Married Man, A, *291;* Naked and the Dead, The, *88;* Onionhead, *350;* Texas Across the River, *1155;* Who's Minding the Mint?, *411*
Bishop, Julie: Action in the North Atlantic, *2;* Hard Way, The (1942), *536;* High and the Mighty, The, *541;* Last of the Redmen, *1126;* Northern Pursuit, *92;* Threat, The, *1024;* Westward the Women, *1163;* Young Bill Hickok, *1165*
Bishop, Kirsten: Shades of Love: Champagne for Two, *653*
Bishop, Pat: Don's Party, *267*
Bishop, William: Texas Rangers, The, *1156*
Bishopric, Thor: Breaking All the Rules, *245*
Bisio, Claudio: Mediterraneo, *766*
Bisley, Steve: Chain Reaction, *24;* Fast Talking, *166;* Summer City, *122*
Bissell, Whit: Atomic Kid, The, *229;* Boots Malone, *1100;* Creature from the Black Lagoon, *826;* He Walked by Night, *982;* I Was a Teenage Frankenstein, *855;* I Was a Teenage Werewolf, *855;* Lost Continent, The, *1063;* Shack-Out on 101, *653;* Spencer's Mountain, *664*
Bisset, Jacqueline: Airport, *443;* Anna Karenina (1985), *449;* Bullitt, *21;* Class, *256;* Cul-de-Sac, *492;* Day for Night, *728;* Deep, The, *36;* Detective, The (1968), *500;* Forbidden, *519;* Greek Tycoon, The, *533;* High Season, *297;* Le Magnifique, *758;* Life and Times of Judge Roy Bean, The, *1128;* Maid, The, *326;* Mephisto Waltz, The, *864;* Murder on the Orient Express, *999;* Napoleon and Josephine: A Love Story, *603;* Rich and Famous, *639;* St. Ives, *110;* Scenes from the Class Struggle in Beverly Hills, *373;* Secrets, *651;* Spiral

Staircase, The (1975), *1019;* Thief Who Came to Dinner, The, *393;* Two for the Road, *401;* Under the Volcano, *691;* When Time Ran Out!, *1031;* Who Is Killing the Great Chefs of Europe?, *410;* Wild Orchid, *702*

Bissett, Josie: All-American Murder, *951;* Mikey, *865*

Bisson, Yannick: Toby McTeague, *212*

Biswas, Chhabi: Devi (The Goddess), *729*

Bixby, Bill: Apple Dumpling Gang, The, *147;* Clambake, *912;* Death of the Incredible Hulk, The, *1045;* Fantasy Island, *1050;* Incredible Hulk, The, *1058;* Kentucky Fried Movie, *312;* Ride Beyond Vengeance, *1143;* Speedway, *941;* Trial of the Incredible Hulk, *1085*

Bixler, Denise: Assassination Game, The, *7*

Bizot, Philippe: Marquis, *765*

Bjork, Anita: Miss Julie, *767;* Secrets of Women (Waiting Women), *784*

Björnstrand, Gunnar: Devil's Eye, The, *730;* Dreams, *732;* Lesson in Love, A, *760;* Magician, The, *764;* Persona, *777;* Secrets of Women (Waiting Women), *784;* Seventh Seal, The, *785;* Smiles of a Summer Night, *787;* Through a Glass Darkly, *795;* Wild Strawberries, *804;* Winter Light, *804*

Black, Jennifer: Gospel According to Vic, The, *289*

Black, Karen: Airport 1975, *443;* Auntie Lee's Meat Pies, *811;* Bad Manners, *231;* Born to Win, *467;* Bound and Gagged: A Love Story, *18;* Burnt Offerings, *820;* Caged Fear, *21;* Can She Bake a Cherry Pie?, *250;* Capricorn One, *1041;* Chanel Solitaire, *479;* Children of the Night, *823;* Club Fed, *256;* Come Back to the Five and Dime, Jimmy Dean, Jimmy Dean, *486;* Crime & Passion, *260;* Cut and Run, *493;* Day of the Locust, The, *496;* Dixie Lanes, *265;* Double-O Kid, The, *41;* Easy Rider, *506;* Evil Spirits, *839;* Family Plot, *975;* Final Judgment, *977;* Five Easy Pieces, *517;* Great Gatsby, The, *532;* Gunfight, A, *1117;* Haunting Fear, *849;* Hitchhiker (Series), The, *850;* Homer and Eddie, *543;* Hostage (1987), *64;* In Praise of Older Women, *550;* Invaders from Mars (1986), *1059;* Invisible Kid, The, *1060;* It's Alive III: Island of the Alive, *857;* Killer Fish, *71;* Killing Heat, *563;* Last Word, The, *571;* Little Laura and Big John, *77;* Little Mermaid, The (1984), *182;* Martin's Day, *185;* Mirror Mirror, *865;* Miss Right, *333;* Mr. Horn, *1134;* Nashville, *603;* Night Angel, *868;* Out of the Dark, *873;* Overexposed, *873;* Portnoy's Complaint, *624;* Pyx, The, *1008;* Quiet Fire, *102;* Rubin & Ed, *371;* Savage Dawn, *111;* Trilogy of Terror, *898;* You're a Big Boy Now, *416*

Black, Larry: Web of Deceit, *1030*

Black, Ryan: Geronimo, *1115*

Blackburn, Diana: French Lessons, *281*

Blackman, Honor: Cat and the Canary, The (1978), *960;* Conspirator, *963;* Goldfinger, *56;* Jason and the Argonauts, *1060;* Night to Remember, A (1958), *606;* Shalako, *1148;* To the Devil, a Daughter, *896;* Virgin and the Gypsy, The, *694*

Blackman, Joan: Blue Hawaii, *909;* Career, *475;* Daring Game, *32;* Kid Galahad (1962), *926*

Blackmer, Sidney: Beyond a Reasonable Doubt (1956), *955;* Cheers for Miss Bishop, *480;* Count of Monte Cristo, The (1934), *30;* Deluge, *1046;* High and the Mighty, The, *541;* How to Murder your Wife, *303;* In Old Chicago, *550;* Law of the Pampas, *1127;* Little Colonel, The, *928;* Love Crazy, *322;* People Will Talk, *356;* Tammy and the Bachelor, *677;* War of the Wildcats, *1162*

Blackwell, Carlyle: She (1925), *1076*

Blacque, Taurean: Deepstar Six, *832*

Blade, Richard: Spellcaster, *889*

Blades, Rubén: Crazy from the Heart, *490;* Critical Condition, *260;* Crossover Dreams, *912;* Dead Man Out, *497;* Disorganized Crime, *40;* Fatal Beauty, *46;* Josephine Baker Story, The, *559;* Lemon Sisters, The, *317;* Milagro Beanfield War, The, *594;* Million to Juan, A, *332;* Mo' Better Blues, *931;* One Man's War, *613;* Predator 2, *1071;* Super, The, *388;* Two Jakes, The, *1028*

Blain, Gerard: American Friend, The, *712;* Le Beau Serge, *756;* Les Cousins, *759*

Blaine, Vivian: Cracker Factory, *490;* Dark, The, *829;* Doll Face, *914;* Guys and Dolls, *921;* Parasite, *873;* Skirts Ahoy!, *940;* State Fair (1945), *941*

Blair, Betsy: Betrayed (1988), *954;* Il Grido, *747;* Marty, *589;* Snake Pit, The, *661;* Suspicion (1987), *1022*

Blair, David: Wax, *1088*

Blair, Isla: Taste the Blood of Dracula, *892*

Blair, Janet: Black Arrow, The (1948), *13;* Boys' Night Out, *244;* Fabulous Dorseys, The, *916;* Fuller Brush Man, The, *282;* Tonight and Every Night, *946*

Blair, Kevin: Bloodlust: Subspecies III, *816*

Blair, Linda: Bad Blood, *811;* Bail Out, *8;* Bedroom Eyes II, *954;* Born Innocent, *466;* Chained Heat, *24;* Chilling, The, *823;* Dead Sleep, *967;* Double Blast, *41;* Exorcist, The, *839;* Exorcist II: The Heretic, *840;* Fatal Bond, *975;* Grotesque, *847;* Hell Night, *849;* Moving Target, *87;* Night Patrol, *344;* Nightforce, *91;* Red Heat (1985), *1009;* Repossessed, *366;* Ruckus, *109;* Savage Streets, *111;* Silent Assassins, *116;* Summer of Fear, *891;* Sweet Hostage, *674;* Up Your Alley, *403;* Wild Horse Hank, *217;* Witchery, *903;* Woman Obsessed, A, *1032;* Zapped Again, *416*

Blair, Patricia: Rifleman, The (TV Series), *1144*

Blair, Tom: Last Chants for a Slow Dance, *568;* Sure Fire, *674*

Blaisdell, Deborah: Wimps, *412*

Blaise, Jean: Wanderer, The, *802*

Blaise, Peter: Pied Piper of Hamelin, The, *195*

Blake, Amanda: Glass Slipper, The, *919;* Gunsmoke: Return to Dodge, *1118;* Gunsmoke (TV Series), *1118;* Stars in My Crown, *1153*

Blake, Andre: Who's the Man?, *411*

Blake, Bobby: Last Round-Up, *1126;* Stagecoach to Denver, *1152;* Vigilantes of Boomtown, *1161*

Blake, Geoffrey: Fatal Exposure, *46;* Marilyn & Bobby: Her Final Affair, *588*

Blake, Jeremy: McVicar, *591*

Blake, Jon: Lighthorsemen, The, *77*

Blake, Julia: Georgia, *979;* Lonely Hearts (1981), *577;* Travelling North, *687*

Blake, Pamela: Hatbox Mystery, The, *982;* Sea Hound, The, *112;* Wyoming Outlaw, *1165*

Blake, Peter: Murder on Line One, *867*

Blake, Robert: Coast to Coast, *256;* Conquest of Cheyenne, *1106;* Electra Glide in Blue, *43;* Heart of a Champion: The Ray Mancini Story, *538;* In Cold Blood, *985;* Marshal of Cripple Creek, *1132;* Of Mice and Men (1981), *610;* Out California Way, *1137;* Phantom of the Plains, *1138;* PT 109, *630;* San Antonio Kid, *1147;* Santa Fe Uprising, *1147;* Sheriff of Las Vegas, *1149;* Tell Them Willie Boy Is Here, *1155;* This Property Is Condemned, *682;* Wagon Wheels Westward, *1162*

Blake, Stephen: Mad at the Moon, *861*

Blake, Teresa: Payback, *98*

Blake, Valerie: Blastfighter, *15*

Blakely, Colin: Dogs of War, The, *40;* Equus, *973;* Evil under the Sun, *973;* Little Lord Fauntleroy (1980), *182;* Loophole, *993;* Pink Panther Strikes Again, The, *357;* Private Life of Sherlock Holmes, The, *1008;* Shattered (1972), *655;* This Sporting Life, *682*

Blakely, Donald: Strike Force, *121*

Blakely, Susan: Airport '79: The Concorde, *443;* Blackmail (1991), *956;* Broken Angel, *470;* Cry for Love, A, *492;* Dead Reckoning (1990), *967;* Dreamer, *505;* Incident, The (1989), *551;* Intruders, *1059;* Lady Killers, *990;* Lords of Flatbush, The, *579;* Make Me an Offer, *586;* My Mom's a Werewolf, *341;* Out of Sight Out of Mind, *1003;* Over the Top, *617;* Report to the Commissioner, *638;* Survivalist, The, *123;* Wild Flower, *702*

Blakiston, Caroline: At Bertram's Hotel, *953*

Blakley, Ronee: Baltimore Bullet, The, *231;* Desperate Women, *1109;* Driver, The, *42;* Murder by Numbers, *998;* Nashville, *603;* Nightmare on Elm Street, A, *871;* Private Files of J. Edgar Hoover, The, *100;* Student Confidential, *387*

Blanc, Erica: Django Shoots First, *1109;* Longest Hunt, The, *1130;* Mark of the Devil, Part 2, *863*
Blanc, Mel: Gay Purr-ee, *168;* Hey There, It's Yogi Bear, *174;* Jack Benny Program, The (TV Series), *309;* Neptune's Daughter, *932*
Blanc, Michel: Favor, the Watch and the Very Big Fish, The, *275;* Ménage, *767;* Merci La Vie, *767;* Monsieur Hire, *768;* Prospero's Books, *629;* Uranus, *798*
Blanchar, Pierre: Crime and Punishment (1935), *726;* Man from Nowhere, The, *765*
Blanchard, Alan: Slithis, *887*
Blanchard, Felix "Doc": Spirit of West Point, The, *664*
Blanchard, Mari: Twice-Told Tales, *898*
Blanck, Gerry: Full Contact, *53*
Blanco, Roberto: Hell Hounds of Alaska, *1119*
Bland, Peter: Came a Hot Friday, *22*
Blandick, Clara: Can't Help Singing, *911;* Girl from Missouri, The, *286;* Wizard of Oz, The, *218*
Blane, Sally: Phantom Express, *99;* Silver Streak (1934), *658;* Vagabond Lover, The, *947*
Blankfield, Mark: Frankenstein General Hospital, *280;* Incredible Shrinking Woman, The, *306;* Jack and the Beanstalk, *178;* Jekyll & Hyde—Together Again, *310;* Rip Van Winkle, *199;* Robin Hood: Men in Tights, *369*
Blanks, Billy: Talons of the Eagle, *124*
Blanton, Arell: House of Terror, *984*
Blassie, Fred: My Breakfast with Blassie, *339*
Blatchford, Ed: Birthday Boy, The, *240*
Blavette, Charles: Toni, *796*
Blech, Hans-Christian: Scarlet Letter (1973), *784*
Bledsoe, Tempestt: Dance 'Til Dawn, *262;* Dream Date, *269*
Bledsoe, Will: Dark Side of the Moon, The, *1044*
Blee, Debra: Beach Girls, The, *233;* Malibu Bikini Shop, The, *327;* Sloane, *117*
Blessed, Brian: High Road to China, *62;* Hound of the Baskervilles, The (1983), *984;* I, Claudius, *547;* King Arthur, The Young Warlord, *72;* Much Ado About Nothing, *338;* Prisoner of Honor, *628;* Return to Treasure Island, *199;* Robin Hood: Prince of Thieves, *108;* Story of David, The, *207*
Blessing, Jack: Game of Love, The, *524;* Last of His Tribe, The, *570*
Blethyn, Brenda: River Runs Through It, A, *641*
Blier, Bernard: Buffet Froid (Cold Cuts), *720;* By The Blood Of Others, *721;* Daydreamer, The (Le Distrait), *728;* Dedee D'Anvers, *729;* Jenny Lamour, *749;* L'Ecole Buissonniere, *758;* Les Miserables (1957), *759;* Passion For Life, *776;* Passion of Love, *776;* Tall Blond Man with One Black Shoe, The, *792*
Block, Larry: Dead Man Out, *497*
Block, Lars: Heroes in Hell, *61*
Blocker, Dan: Bonanza (TV Series), *1100;* Come Blow Your Horn, *257;* Lady in Cement, *989*
Blocker, Dirk: Bonanza: The Return, *1100*
Blodgett, Michael: Velvet Vampire, The, *900*
Blomberg, J. Edward: Stowaway, *942*
Blondell, Joan: Adventure, *441;* Battered, *456;* Big Business Girl, *460;* Blonde Crazy, *241;* Bullets or Ballots, *21;* Dames, *913;* Dead Don't Die, The, *830;* Death at Love House, *968;* Desk Set, *263;* Footlight Parade, *917;* Gold Diggers of 1933, *920;* Illicit, *549;* Lady for a Night, *567;* Night Nurse, *606;* Opening Night, *614;* Opposite Sex, The, *934;* Rebels, The, *636;* Ride Beyond Vengeance, *1143;* Stage Struck (1936), *941;* Stand-In, *385;* Stay Away Joe, *942;* Support Your Local Gunfighter, *1154;* This Could Be the Night, *394;* Three Broadway Girls, *395;* Three Men on a Horse, *395;* Three on a Match, *683;* Topper Returns, *398;* Tree Grows in Brooklyn, A, *687;* Waterhole #3, *1163*
Blondell, Simone: Jungle Master, The, *69;* Savage Guns, *1147*
Bloom, Anne: Best of Not Necessarily the News, The, *236;* Dirt Bike Kid, The, *162*
Bloom, Brian: Webber's World, *406*
Bloom, Claire: Alexander the Great, *443;* Brainwashed, *958;* Brideshead Revisited, *469;* Brothers Karamazov, The, *471;* Buccaneer, The, *20;* Charly, *1041;* Deja Vu, *499;* Doll's House, A (1989), *503;* Haunting, The, *849;* Illustrated Man, The, *1057;* Intimate Contact, *553;* Islands in the Stream, *555;* Limelight, *319;* Look Back in Anger (1958), *579;* Queenie, *632;* Richard III, *640;* Sammy and Rosie Get Laid, *372;* Separate Tables, *652;* Spy Who Came in from the Cold, The, *664;* Wonderful World of the Brothers Grimm, The, *1090*
Bloom, John: Brain of Blood, *818*
Bloom, Michael Allan: Screen Test, *374*
Bloom, Verna: After Hours, *223;* Badge 373, *8;* Blue Knight, The (1975), *465;* High Plains Drifter, *1120;* Hired Hand, The, *1121;* Last Temptation of Christ, The, *570;* Medium Cool, *591*
Bloomfield, Don: Lost Angels, *580*
Bloomfield, George: And Then You Die, *5*
Blore, Eric: Ex-Mrs. Bradford, The, *974;* Gay Divorcée, The, *918;* I Dream Too Much, *924;* Lady Scarface, *74;* Moon and Sixpence, The, *599;* Quality Street, *631;* Road to Zanzibar, *369;* Romance on the High Seas, *937;* Shall We Dance?, *939;* Shanghai Gesture, The, *655;* Sky's the Limit, The, *940;* Sullivan's Travels, *388;* Swiss Miss, *390;* Top Hat, *946*
Blossom, Roberts: American Clock, The, *446;* Christine, *824;* Citizen's Band, *255;* Escape from Alcatraz, *45;* Home Alone, *299;* Resurrection, *638;* Reuben, Reuben, *367*
Blouin, Michael: Great Land of Small, The, *171*
Blount, Lisa: Blind Fury, *15;* Cease Fire, *477;* Cut and Run, *493;* Nightflyers, *1068;* Prince of Darkness, *876;* Radioactive Dreams, *1073;* September 30, 1955, *652;* South of Reno, *663;* Swap, The, *674;* What Waits Below, *902*
Blow, Kurtis: Krush Groove, *927*
Blue, Ben: Broadway Rhythm, *910;* College Swing, *912;* Two Girls and a Sailor, *946;* Two Sisters from Boston, *947;* Where Were You When the Lights Went Out?, *409*
Blue, Monte: Apache, *1094;* Hell Town, *1120;* Intolerance, *553;* Lives of a Bengal Lancer, The, *78;* Marriage Circle, The, *329;* Orphans of the Storm, *615;* Ride, Ranger, Ride, *1143;* Riders of Death Valley, *1143;* Rootin' Tootin' Rhythm, *1146;* So This Is Paris, *382;* Song of the Gringo, *1151;* Undersea Kingdom, *1087;* Wagon Wheels, *1162;* White Shadows in the South Seas, *700*
Bluestone, Abby: Night of the Juggler, *90*
Bluestone, Ed: Comedy Tonight, *257*
Blum, Mark: Blind Date (1987), *241;* "Crocodile" Dundee, *261;* Desperately Seeking Susan, *264;* Just Between Friends, *561;* Presidio, The, *100;* Worth Winning, *414*
Blumenfeld, Alan: Dark Side of the Moon, The, *1044;* Instant Karma, *306;* Night Life, *869*
Blundell, John: Scum, *650*
Bluteau, Lothaire: Black Robe, *463;* Jesus of Montreal, *749*
Blyden, Larry: On a Clear Day, You Can See Forever, *933*
Blye, Margaret: Ash Wednesday, *451;* Final Chapter—Walking Tall, *48;* Melvin Purvis: G-Man, *83;* Sporting Club, The, *664;* Waterhole #3, *1163*
Blyth, Ann: Great Caruso, The, *920;* Kismet (1955), *927;* Mildred Pierce, *594;* Mr. Peabody and the Mermaid, *334;* One Minute to Zero, *94;* Rose Marie (1954), *937;* Student Prince, The, *942*
Blythe, Betty: Gangster's Boy, *525;* She (1925), *1076*
Blythe, John: Alfred Hitchcock's Bon Voyage and Aventure Malgache, *711*
Blythe, Robert: Experience Preferred...But Not Essential, *273*
Blythe, Robin: Deathrow Gameshow, *263*
Boa, Bruce: Murder Story, *999*
Boardman, Eleanor: Crowd, The, *492;* She Goes to War, *377*
Boatman, Michael Patrick: China Beach (TV Series), *481;* Fourth Story, *978;* Hamburger Hill, *535*
Bob Wills and the Texas Playboys: Take Me Back to Oklahoma, *1154*
Bobochkin, Boris: Chapayev, *723*

Boccardo, Delia: Assisi Underground, The, *7*
Bocher, Christian: Total Exposure, *1026*
Bochner, Hart: Apartment Zero, *952;* Die Hard, *38;* Fellow Traveler, *515;* Having It All, *294;* Islands in the Stream, *555;* Mad at the Moon, *861;* Making Mr. Right, *327;* Mr. Destiny, *334;* Rich and Famous, *639;* Supergirl, *1081;* Terror Train, *894;* War and Remembrance, *696*
Bochner, Lloyd: Crystal Heart, *492;* Good Idea, *288;* Horse in the Gray Flannel Suit, The, *175;* Landslide, *990;* Lonely Lady, The, *577;* Mary and Joseph: A Story of Faith, *589;* Mazes and Monsters, *864;* Morning Glory (1992), *599;* Night Walker, The, *1001;* Point Blank, *624;* Ulzana's Raid, *1160*
Bodison, Wolfgang: Few Good Men, A, *976*
Boehm, Carl: Peeping Tom, *1005;* Unnatural, *1029*
Boensh III, Paul: This Is Elvis, *436*
Boepple, Beatrice: Quarantine, *1072*
Boer, Nikki De: Prom Night IV—Deliver Us from Evil, *877*
Bogarde, Dirk: Accident, *440;* Bridge Too Far, A, *19;* Daddy Nostalgia, *727;* Damn the Defiant!, *31;* Damned, The, *727;* Darling, *496;* Death in Venice, *498;* Despair, *729;* Doctor at Large, *265;* Doctor at Sea, *266;* Doctor in Distress, *266;* Doctor in the House, *266;* Fixer, The, *517;* I Could Go On Singing, *924;* Ill Met by Moonlight, *548;* Justine, *561;* Night Ambush, *90;* Night Flight from Moscow, *90;* Night Porter, The, *606;* Permission to Kill, *98;* Providence, *630;* Quartet (1948), *631;* Sea Shall Not Have Them, The, *113;* Servant, The, *652;* Simba, *658;* Sleeping Tiger, The, *660;* Song without End, *940;* Tale of Two Cities (1967), *676;* To See Such Fun, *397;* Victim, *693*
Bogart, Humphrey: Across the Pacific, *1;* Action in the North Atlantic, *2;* African Queen, The, *442;* All Through the Night, *3;* Angels with Dirty Faces, *5;* Barefoot Contessa, The, *455;* Battle Circus, *456;* Beat the Devil, *233;* Big Sleep, The (1946), *955;* Brother Orchid, *20;* Bullets or Ballots, *21;* Caine Mutiny, The, *473;* Casablanca, *476;* Chain Lightning, *478;* Conflict, *963;* Dark Passage, *966;* Dark Victory, *495;* Dead End, *497;* Dead Reckoning (1947), *34;* Deadline USA, *497;* Desperate Hours, The (1955), *969;* Enforcer, The (1951), *44;* Harder They Fall, The, *536;* High Sierra, *62;* Hollywood Outtakes, *299;* In a Lonely Place, *985;* Key Largo, *988;* Kid Galahad (1937), *563;* Knock on Any Door, *566;* Left Hand of God, The, *76;* Maltese Falcon, The, *994;* Marked Woman, *82;* Midnight (1934), *593;* Oklahoma Kid, The, *1136;* Passage to Marseilles, *97;* Petrified Forest, The, *621;* Roaring Twenties, The, *107;* Sabrina, *372;* Sahara (1943), *110;* Sirocco, *116;* Stand-In, *385;* Thank Your Lucky Stars, *944;* They Drive by Night, *127;* Three on a Match, *683;* To Have and Have Not, *130;* Tokyo Joe, *130;* Treasure of the Sierra Madre, *132;* Two Mrs. Carrolls, The, *1028;* Virginia City, *1161;* We're No Angels (1955), *407*
Bogdanovich, Peter: Saint Jack, *646;* Targets, *1022;* Trip, The, *688*
Bogosian, Eric: Arena Brains, *450;* Caine Mutiny Court Martial, The, *473;* Eric Bogosian—Funhouse, *272;* New Wave Comedy, *343;* Sex, Drugs, Rock & Roll, *653;* Special Effects, *889;* Talk Radio, *677*
Bohannon, Kelly: Idaho Transfer, *1057*
Böhm, Karlheinz: Fox and His Friends, *738;* Wonderful World of the Brothers Grimm, The, *1090*
Bohnen, Roman: Hard Way, The (1942), *536*
Bohrer, Corinne: Dead Solid Perfect, *497;* Surf 2, *389*
Bohringer, Richard: Accompanist, The, *710;* Barjo, *715;* Bolero (1982), *720;* Caged Heart, The (L'Addition), *721;* Cook, the Thief, His Wife & Her Lover, The, *259;* Le Grand Chemin (The Grand Highway), *757;* Peril, *777;* Subway, *790*
Bohringer, Romane: Accompanist, The, *710;* Savage Nights, *783*
Bois, Curt: Caught, *477;* Tovaritch, *398;* Tuttles of Tahiti, The, *400;* Wings of Desire, *804*
Bois, Elaine: Legacy of Horror, *860*
Boisson, Christine: Sorceress, The (1988), *788*
Bok, Sarel: Far Off Place, A, *166*
Bolam, James: Crucible of Terror, *827*
Boland, Mary: If I Had a Million, *304;* Julia Misbehaves, *311;* New Moon, *933;* Nothing But Trouble (1944), *347;* Ruggles of Red Gap, *371*
Bolder, Cal: Jesse James Meets Frankenstein's Daughter, *858*
Boles, John: Craig's Wife, *490;* Curly Top, *912;* Frankenstein (1931), *842;* King of Jazz, The, *927;* Littlest Rebel, The, *929;* Sinners in Paradise, *659;* Stella Dallas, *667;* Thousands Cheer, *945*
Bolger, John: Parting Glances, *618*
Bolger, Ray: April in Paris, *907;* Babes in Toyland (1961), *147;* Daydreamer, The, *161;* Four Jacks and a Jill, *918;* Harvey Girls, The, *922;* Just You and Me, Kid, *312;* Look For The Silver Lining, *929;* Rosalie, *937;* Sweethearts, *943;* That's Dancing, *436;* Wizard of Oz, The, *218;* Wonderful Wizard of Oz, The: The Making of a Movie Classic, *438*
Bolkan, Florinda: Aqua E Sapone, *713;* Collector's Item, *485;* Day that Shook the World, The, *496;* Some Girls, *382*
Bolling, Tiffany: Bonnie's Kids, *17;* Centerfold Girls, *478;* Kingdom of the Spiders, *859;* Open House, *872*
Bologna, Joseph: Alligator II, *808;* Big Bus, The, *238;* Blame It on Rio, *240;* Chapter Two, *479;* Citizen Cohn, *482;* Cops and Robbers, *29;* Deadly Rivals, *35;* Honor Thy Father, *543;* Jersey Girl, *310;* Joe Piscopo Video, The, *310;* My Favorite Year, *340;* Not Quite Human, *347;* One Cooks, the Other Doesn't, *349;* Rags to Riches, *364;* Torn Between Two Lovers, *686;* Transylvania 6-5000, *399;* Woman in Red, The, *413*
Bolshoi Ballet: Anna Karenina (1974), *907*
Bolton, Michael: Simply Mad About the Mouse, *204*
Bom, Dor Zweigen: Late Summer Blues, *756*
Bonacelli, Paolo: Johnny Stecchino, *750;* Salo: 120 Days of Sodom, *783*
Bonaduce, Danny: H.O.T.S., *292*
Bonanno, Louie: Sex Appeal, *376;* Wimps, *412*
Bonanova, Fortunio: Ali Baba and the Forty Thieves, *3;* Fiesta, *916;* Romance on the High Seas, *937*
Bond, Derek: Nicholas Nickleby, *605;* Scott of the Antarctic, *650;* Stranger from Venus, *1081*
Bond, Graham: Fast Lane Fever, *46*
Bond III, James: Def by Temptation, *832;* Sky Is Gray, The, *660*
Bond, Rene: Fugitive Girls, *53*
Bond, Steve: Magdalene, *585;* Prey, The, *876;* To Die For, *896;* To Die For 2: Son of Darkness, *896*
Bond, Sudie: Come Back to the Five and Dime, Jimmy Dean, Jimmy Dean, *486;* Greatest Man in the World, The, *290;* Silkwood, *658;* Swing Shift, *675;* Tomorrow, *685;* Where the Lilies Bloom, *216*
Bond, Tommy: Atom Man vs. Superman, *7;* Superman—The Serial, *1081*
Bond, Ward: Blowing Wild, *16;* Bride Walks Out, The, *245;* Broadway Bill, *470;* Dakota (1945), *1107;* Devil Dogs of the Air, *37;* Dodge City, *1109;* Drums Along the Mohawk, *42;* Falcon Takes Over, The, *975;* Fighting Code, *1112;* Fighting Ranger, The, *1113;* Fighting Shadows, *1113;* Fighting Sullivans, The, *516;* Fort Apache, *1114;* Fugitive, The (1947), *523;* Great Missouri Raid, The, *1116;* Guy Named Joe, A, *535;* Gypsy Colt, *173;* Hitler—Dead or Alive, *542;* Hondo, *1121;* It Happened One Night, *307;* It's a Wonderful Life, *555;* Joan of Arc, *558;* Johnny Guitar, *1123;* Kiss Tomorrow Goodbye, *73;* Law West of Tombstone, *1127;* Long Grey Line, The, *578;* Maltese Falcon, The, *994;* Man Alone, A, *1131;* Mr. Roberts, *334;* Mortal Storm, The, *600;* My Darling Clementine, *1134;* Oklahoma Kid, The, *1136;* On Dangerous Ground, *1003;* Only the Valiant, *1137;* Operation Pacific, *614;* Quiet Man, The, *364;* Rio Bravo, *1145;* Santa Fe Trail, *1147;* Searchers, The, *1148;* Sergeant York, *113;* Sundown Rider, The, *1153;* Tall in the Saddle, *1154;* They Made Me a Criminal, *681;* They Were Expendable, *127;* Three Godfathers, The, *1156;* Time of Your Life, The, *684;* Virginia City, *1161;* Wagon Train (TV Series), *1162;* Wagonmaster, *1162;* Wheel of Fortune, *409;* Wings of

Eagles, The, *703;* You Only Live Once, *708;* Young Mr. Lincoln, *708*
Bondarchuk, Natalya: Solaris, *787*
Bondarchuk, Sergei: War and Peace (1968), *802*
Bondi, Beulah: Arrowsmith, *451;* Back to Bataan, *8;* Baron of Arizona, The, *1097;* Breakfast in Hollywood, *245;* Latin Lovers, *928;* Lone Star, *1129;* Of Human Hearts, *610;* On Borrowed Time, *612;* Painted Veil, The, *617;* Rain, *634;* She Waits, *885;* Sister Kenny, *659;* Sisters, The (1938), *659;* Snake Pit, The, *661;* So Dear to My Heart, *205;* Street Scene, *670;* Summer Place, A, *672;* Tammy and the Doctor, *677;* Vivacious Lady, *405*
Bondy, Christopher: Deadly Surveillance, *35*
Bonerz, Peter: Medium Cool, *591*
Bones, Ken: Bellman and True, *954*
Bonet, Lisa: Angel Heart, *952;* Bank Robber, *232;* Dead Connection, *967*
Bonet, Nai: Nocturna, *346;* Soul Hustler, *118*
Bonifant, Evan: Three Ninjas Kick Back, *211*
Bonilla, Hector: Mary My Dearest, *766*
Bonnaffe, Jacques: First Name: Carmen, *737*
Bonnaire, Sandrine: A Nos Amours, *710;* La Puritaine, *754;* Monsieur Hire, *768;* Plague, The, *623;* Police, *778;* Under the Sun of Satan, *798;* Vagabond, *799*
Bonner, Frank: You Can't Hurry Love, *415*
Bonner, Priscilla: Red Kimono, The, *636;* Strong Man, The, *387*
Bonner, Tony: Creatures the World Forgot, *1043;* Dead Sleep, *967;* Hurricane Smith, *65;* Lighthorsemen, The, *77*
Bonnevie, Maria: Polar Bear King, The, *1071*
Bono, Sonny: Dirty Laundry, *265;* Escape to Athena, *45;* Hairspray, *292;* Murder on Flight 502, *87;* Troll, *1085;* Under the Boardwalk, *691*
Bonsall, Brian: Blank Check, *151;* Father Hood, *47;* Mikey, *865*
Bonzo Dog Band: Magical Mystery Tour, *930*
Booke, Sorrell: Amazing Howard Hughes, The, *445;* Black Like Me, *462;* Joy House, *559;* Purlie Victorious, *363*
Booker T. and the MGs: Monterey Pop, *431*
Bookwalter, DeVeren: Othello (1982), *615*
Boone, Libby: Final Chapter—Walking Tall, *48*
Boone, Pat: Journey to the Center of the Earth (1959), *1060;* State Fair (1962), *941*
Boone, Richard: Against a Crooked Sky, *1092;* Alamo, The, *1092;* Arrangement, The, *450;* Away all Boats, *8;* Beneath the 12-Mile Reef, *10;* Big Jake, *1098;* Bullet from God, A, *1102;* Bushido Blade, *21;* Dragnet (1954), *41;* God's Gun, *1116;* Hombre, *1121;* I Bury the Living, *855;* Madron, *1131;* Man without a Star, *1132;* Night of the Following Day, The, *1001;* Rio Conchos, *1145;* Robe, The, *642;* Shootist, The, *1149;* Tall T, The, *1154;* Ten Wanted Men, *1155;* War Lord, The, *137;* Winter Kills, *704*
Boorman, Charley: Emerald Forest, The, *44*
Boosler, Elayne: Elayne Boosler—Broadway Baby, *270;* Live at Harrah's, *320;* Your Favorite Laughs from an Evening at the Improv, *416*
Booth, Adrian: Brimstone, *1101;* Out California Way, *1137*
Booth, Andrew: Dead Sleep, *967*
Booth, Connie: American Friends, *226;* Fawlty Towers, *276;* How to Irritate People, *302;* Little Lord Fauntleroy (1980), *182;* Romance with a Double Bass, *370*
Booth, Edwina: Last of the Mohicans (1932), *1126*
Booth, James: American Ninja IV: The Annihilation, *4;* Avenging Force, *8;* Bliss of Mrs. Blossom, The, *241;* Deep Space, *1046;* Macho Callahan, *1130;* Man Who Had Power Over Women, The, *587;* Programmed to Kill, *1072;* Revenge (1971), *1010;* Robbery, *1011;* That'll Be the Day, *944*
Booth, Karin: Tobor the Great, *1084*
Booth, Shirley: Come Back, Little Sheba, *486;* Hot Spell, *544;* Matchmaker, The, *329*
Boothe, Powers: Breed Apart, A, *19;* By Dawn's Early Light, *473;* Cry for Love, A, *492;* Emerald Forest, The, *44;* Extreme Prejudice, *45;* Into the Homeland, *67;* Philip Marlowe, Private Eye: Finger Man, *1005;* Philip Marlowe, Private Eye: The Pencil, *1005;* Rapid Fire, *103;* Red Dawn, *104;* Southern Comfort, *119;* Tombstone, *1157;* Wild Card, *1032*
Borchers, Cornell: Big Lift, The, *460*
Bordeaux, Joe: Keystone Comedies, Vol. 1, *312;* Keystone Comedies, Vol. 2, *312;* Keystone Comedies, Vol. 5, *313*
Borelli, Carla: Asylum of Satan, *810*
Borg, Veda Ann: Big Jim McLain, *460;* Bitter Sweet, *909;* Dr. Christian Meets the Women, *502;* Fog Island, *978;* Guys and Dolls, *921;* Honky Tonk, *1121;* Julia Misbehaves, *311;* Kid Galahad (1937), *563;* Revenge of the Zombies, *881;* Rider from Tucson, *1143*
Borgard, Christopher: 84 Charlie Mopic, *43*
Borge, Victor: Daydreamer, The, *161;* Higher and Higher, *922*
Borgese, Sal: Flight of the Innocent, *737*
Borgnine, Ernest: Alice Through the Looking Glass (1985), *145;* All Quiet on the Western Front (1979), *444;* Any Man's Death, *450;* Bad Day at Black Rock, *454;* Badlanders, The, *1096;* Barabbas, *455;* Black Hole, The, *1039;* Bullet for Sandoval, A, *1102;* Catered Affair, The, *477;* Chuka, *1105;* Code Name: Wild Geese, *27;* Convoy (1978), *29;* Deadly Blessing, *831;* Demetrius and the Gladiators, *499;* Devil's Rain, The, *834;* Dirty Dozen, The, *39;* Dirty Dozen, The: The Next Mission, *39;* Dirty Dozen, The: The Deadly Mission, *39;* Dirty Dozen, The: The Fatal Mission, *39;* Double McGuffin, The, *163;* Escape from New York, *45;* Fire!, *48;* Flight of the Phoenix, The, *51;* From Here to Eternity (1953), *523;* Greatest, The, *533;* Hannie Caulder, *1119;* High Risk, *61;* Hustle, *65;* Ice Station Zebra, *65;* Jake Spanner Private Eye, *68;* Johnny Guitar, *1123;* Jubal, *1124;* Laser Mission, *75;* Last Command, The (1955), *1125;* Marty, *589;* Mistress (1992), *597;* Moving Target, *87;* Neptune Factor, The, *1068;* Opponent, The, *95;* Oscar, The (1966), *615;* Pay or Die, *620;* Poseidon Adventure, The, *99;* Shoot (1976), *115;* Spike of Bensonhurst, *384;* Stranger Wore a Gun, The, *1153;* Super Fuzz, *1081;* Suppose They Gave a War and Nobody Came?, *388;* Torpedo Run, *131;* Trackers, The, *1158;* Vengeance Is Mine (1976), *135;* Vera Cruz, *1161;* Vikings, The, *135;* Wagon Train (TV Series), *1162;* When Time Ran Out!, *1031;* Wild Bunch, The, *1164;* Willard, *903;* Young Warriors, The, *141*
Boris, Nicoletta: Desperate Crimes, *37*
Borizans, Pierre: Blue Jeans, *719*
Borland, Carol: Mark of the Vampire, *863;* Scalps, *883*
Borland, Scott: Heroes Die Young, *61*
Born, Roscoe: Haunting of Sarah Hardy, The, *982;* Lady Mobster, *74*
Borowitz, Katherine: Mac, *583;* Men of Respect, *592*
Borrego, Jessie: Bound by Honor, *467*
Borris, Clay: Alligator Shoes, *445*
Borris, Gary: Alligator Shoes, *445*
Bory, Jean-Marc: Le Repos du Guerrier (Warrior's Rest), *758;* Lovers, The (1958), *762*
Boschi, Giula: Sicilian, The, *115*
Bosco, Philip: Angie, *448;* Children of a Lesser God, *480;* F/X 2: The Deadly Art of Illusion, *979;* Money Pit, The, *335;* Shadows and Fog, *654;* Straight Talk, *387;* Suspect, *1022;* Walls of Glass, *695*
Bose, Lucia: Blood Castle (1972), *815;* Lumiere, *763*
Bosé, Miguel: High Heels (1992), *744*
Bosic, Andrea: Days of Wrath, *1107*
Bosley, Tom: Bang Bang Kid, The, *232;* Bastard, The, *456;* For the Love of It, *279;* Jessie Owens Story, The, *557;* Love with the Proper Stranger, *582;* Million Dollar Mystery, *332;* O'Hara's Wife, *611;* Pinocchio and the Emperor of the Night, *195;* That's Singing: The Best of Broadway, *944;* Who Is the Black Dahlia?, *1031;* Wicked Stepmother, The, *903;* Yours, Mine and Ours, *416*
Bosson, Barbara: Last Starfighter, The, *1062;* Little Sweetheart, *577*
Bostwick, Barry: 800 Leagues Down the Amazon, *43;* George Washington, *526;* George Washington: The Forging of

a Nation, *526;* Hitchhiker (Series), The, *850;* Megaforce, *1065;* Movie Movie, *338;* Praying Mantis, *1007;* Red Flag: The Ultimate Game, *104;* Rocky Horror Picture Show, The, *937;* Weekend at Bernie's II, *407;* Woman of Substance, A, *705*
Boswell, Charles: Kiss Me a Killer, *989*
Boswell Sisters: Transatlantic Merry-Go-Round, *946*
Bosworth, Brian: Stone Cold, *120*
Bosworth, Hobart: Abraham Lincoln, *440;* Big Parade, The, *460;* General Spanky, *169;* My Best Girl, *339;* Phantom Express, *99;* Sea Lion, The, *650;* Woman of Affairs, A, *705*
Botsford, Sara: By Design, *473;* Deadly Eyes, *831;* Gunrunner, The, *58;* Still of the Night, *1020*
Bottoms, John: Blue Hotel, *465*
Bottoms, Joseph: Black Hole, The, *1039;* Blind Date (1984), *463;* Born to Race, *17;* Celebrity, *477;* Cloud Dancer, *27;* Crime & Passion, *260;* High Rolling, *62;* Inner Sanctum, *986;* Intruder Within, The, *1059;* King of the Mountain, *565;* Liar's Edge, *992;* Open House, *872;* Side by Side: The True Story of the Osmond Family, *203;* Sins of Dorian Gray, The, *886;* Surfacing, *123;* Treacherous Crossing, *1027*
Bottoms, Sam: Bronco Billy, *246;* Dolly Dearest, *836;* Gardens of Stone, *525;* Hunter's Blood, *546;* Prime Risk, *100;* Savages (1974), *883;* Up from the Depths, *899;* Zandy's Bride, *1166*
Bottoms, Timothy: Drifter, The, *837;* East of Eden (1982), *506;* Fantasist, The, *975;* Gift of Love, The, *527;* Hambone and Hillie, *535;* High Country, The, *61;* In the Shadow of Kilimanjaro, *855;* Invaders from Mars (1986), *1059;* Istanbul: Keep Your Eyes Open, *555;* Johnny Got His Gun, *559;* Land of Faraway, The, *180;* Last Picture Show, The, *570;* Love Leads the Way, *581;* Other Side of the Mountain, Part II, The, *615;* Paper Chase, The, *617;* Rollercoaster, *1011;* Shining Season, A, *656;* Small Town in Texas, A, *117;* Story of David, The, *207;* Texasville, *680;* Tin Man, *684;* What Waits Below, *902;* White Dawn, The, *138*
Bottone, Bonaventura: Mikado, The (1987), *931*
Bouchet, Barbara: Sex with a Smile, *376*
Bouchey, Willis: Bridges at Toko-Ri, The, *19*
Bouchitey, Patrick: Great, My Parents Are Divorcing, *742*
Bouise, Jean: Final Combat, The, *48;* Mr. Klein, *768*
Bouix, Evelyne: Edith and Marcel, *733;* Jacko and Lise, *749*
Boujenah, Michel: Three Men and a Cradle, *794*
Boulting, Ingrid: Last Tycoon, The, *571*
Boundin, Bo: Great Waldo Pepper, The, *57*
Bouquet, Carole: For Your Eyes Only, *51;* That Obscure Object of Desire, *793;* Too Beautiful for You, *796*
Bouquet, Michel: Beyond Fear, *717;* Borsalino, *18;* Bride Wore Black, The, *959;* Le Complot (The Conspiracy), *757;* Mississippi Mermaid, *768;* This Special Friendship, *794;* Toto the Hero, *796*
Bourgnine, Elisabeth: Un Coeur En Hiver, *798*
Bourseiller, Antoine: Cleo from 5 to 7, *725*
Bourvil: Crazy For Love, *726;* Four Bags Full, *738;* Les Grandes Gueules (Jailbirds' Vacation), *759;* Les Miserables (1957), *759;* When Wolves Cry, *699*
Bouton, Jim: Long Goodbye, The, *993*
Boutsikaris, Dennis: Dream Team, The, *269*
Bouvier, Jean Pierre: Goodbye Emmanuelle, *741*
Bovasso, Julie: Gentleman Bandit, The, *525;* Moonstruck, *336*
Bovo, Brunella: White Sheik, The, *803*
Bow, Clara: Dancing Mothers, *262;* Down to the Sea in Ships, *504;* It (1927), *307;* Mantrap, *995;* Wild Party, The (1929), *702;* Wings, *140*
Bow, Simmy: Doberman Gang, The, *40*
Bowe, David: UHF, *402*
Bowe, John: Prime Suspect 1, *1007*
Bowe, Rosemarie: Big Bluff, The, *460*
Bowen, Dennis: Gas Pump Girls, *283*
Bowen, Lori: Pumping Iron II: The Women, *630*
Bowen, Michael: Check Is in the Mail, The, *254;* Echo Park, *507;* Less Than Zero, *573;* Mortal Passions, *997;* Season of Fear, *1013;* Taking of Beverly Hills, The, *124*
Bowen, Roger: Playmates, *358*
Bowen, Sean: Troma's War, *132*
Bowens, Malick: Out of Africa, *616*
Bower, David: Four Weddings and a Funeral, *280*
Bower, Tom: Ballad of Gregorio Cortez, The, *1096;* River's Edge, *641;* Talent for the Game, *677;* Wild Rose, *702*
Bowie, David: Absolute Beginners, *906;* Hunger, The (1983), *854;* Into the Night, *553;* Just a Gigolo, *561;* Labyrinth, *1061;* Last Temptation of Christ, The, *570;* Linguini Incident, The, *319;* Man Who Fell to Earth, The, *1064;* Merry Christmas, Mr. Lawrence, *593;* Twin Peaks: Fire Walk with Me, *1028;* Ziggy Stardust and the Spiders from Mars, *439*
Bowie, Trixxie: Fraternity Demon, *280*
Bowker, Judi: Brother Sun, Sister Moon, *470;* Clash of the Titans, *1041;* East of Elephant Rock, *506*
Bowles, Peter: Day in the Death of Joe Egg, A, *262;* Prisoner, The (TV Series), *1071;* Rumpole of the Bailey (TV Series), *1011*
Bowman, Don: Hillbillys in a Haunted House, *297*
Bowman, Jessica: Remote, *198*
Bowman, Lee: Buck Privates, *246;* Having a Wonderful Time, *294;* House by the River, *984;* My Dream Is Yours, *932;* Next Time I Marry, *344;* Smash-Up: The Story of a Woman, *661;* Tonight and Every Night, *946*
Bowman, Loretta Leigh: Offerings, *872*
Bowman, Ralph: Flaming Frontiers, *1113*
Boxleitner, Bruce: Babe, The, *452;* Baltimore Bullet, The, *231;* Diplomatic Immunity, *39;* Double Jeopardy, *972;* East of Eden (1982), *506;* From the Dead of Night, *844;* Gambler, The (1980), *1114;* Gambler, Part II—The Adventure Continues, The, *1115;* Gambler, Part III—The Legend Continues, The, *1115;* Kuffs, *73;* Murderous Vision, *999;* Passion Flower, *619;* Perfect Family, *1005;* Secret, The, *650;* Tron, *1085;* Wild Times, *1164*
Boy George: Stand by Me (1988), *941*
Boyar, Sully: Car Wash, *250*
Boyce, Alan: Permanent Record, *621*
Boyd, Guy: Dark Wind, *966;* Doctor Quinn Medicine Woman, *502;* Ewok Adventure, The, *165;* Eyes of Fire, *840;* Kiss Me a Killer, *989;* Past Midnight, *619;* Pride of Jesse Hallman, The, *626*
Boyd, Jan Gan: Assassination, *7;* Chorus Line, A, *911*
Boyd, Janette: Stripper (1985), *435*
Boyd, Rick: Guns for Dollars, *1117;* Place Called Trinity, A, *1139*
Boyd, Sarah: Old Enough, *611*
Boyd, Stephen: Ben-Hur (1959), *10;* Bravados, The, *1101;* Caper of the Golden Bulls, The, *22;* Fall of the Roman Empire, The, *513;* Fantastic Voyage, *1050;* Jumbo, *926;* Man Called Noon, The, *1131;* Man Who Never Was, The, *81;* Oscar, The (1966), *615;* Shalako, *1148;* Squeeze, The (1977), *665*
Boyd, William: Bar 20, *1096;* Border Patrol, *1100;* Borderland, *1100;* Borrowed Trouble, *1100;* Colt Comrades, *1105;* Dangerous Venture, *1107;* Dead Don't Dream, The, *1108;* Devil's Playground, *1109;* False Colors, *1112;* False Paradise, *1112;* Flying Fool, The, *51;* Forty Thieves, *1114;* Frontiersman, The, *1114;* Hidden Gold, *1120;* High Voltage, *62;* Hopalong Cassidy Enters, *1121;* Hoppy Serves a Writ, *1121;* Hoppy's Holiday, *1121;* In Old Mexico, *1123;* King of Kings, The (1927), *565;* Law of the Pampas, *1127;* Leather Burners, The, *1128;* Marauders, *1132;* Mystery Man, *1135;* Painted Desert, The, *1138;* Range War, *1141;* Renegade Trail, *1142;* Riders of the Deadline, *1144;* Road to Yesterday, The, *641;* Rustler's Valley, *1146;* Santa Fe Marshal, *1147;* Showdown (1940), *1149;* Silent Conflict, *1150;* Sinister Journey, *1150;* Stagecoach War, *1152;* Strange Gamble, *1153;* Texas Masquerade, *1156;* Three Men from Texas, *1157;* Unexpected Guest, *1160;* Yankee Clipper, *141*

Boyd, William "Stage": Lost City, The, *1063;* Oliver Twist (1933), *612;* State's Attorney, *666*

Boyer, Charles: Adorable Julia, *710;* All This and Heaven Too, *445;* April Fools, The, *228;* Arch of Triumph, *450;* Barefoot in the Park, *232;* Break of Hearts, *468;* Buccaneer, The, *20;* Casino Royale (1967), *252;* Conquest, *487;* Earrings of Madame De..., The, *732;* Fanny (1961), *514;* Four Horsemen of the Apocalypse, *52;* Garden of Allah, The, *525;* Gaslight (1944), *979;* History Is Made at Night, *542;* Is Paris Burning?, *554;* Madwoman of Chaillot, The, *585;* Matter of Time, A, *590;* Mayerling, *766;* Nana, *770;* Stavisky, *789;* Tovaritch, *398*

Boyer, Christopher: Uninvited, The (1993), *1160*

Boyer, Katy: Trapped, *1027*

Boyer, Marie-France: Le Bonheur, *756*

Boyer, Myriam: Jonah Who Will Be 25 in the Year 2000, *750;* Un Coeur En Hiver, *798;* Window Shopping, *804*

Boyer, Tom: Massive Retaliation, *83*

Boykin, Nancy: Plants Are Watching, The, *1071*

Boyle, Lara Flynn: Dark Backward, The, *262;* Equinox (1993), *510;* Eye of the Storm, *974;* May Wine, *330;* Preppie Murder, The, *626;* Red Rock West, *1009;* Temp, The, *893;* Threesome, *396;* Wayne's World, *406;* Where the Day Takes You, *699*

Boyle, Peter: Beyond the Poseidon Adventure, *11;* Brinks Job, The, *246;* Candidate, The, *474;* Dream Team, The, *269;* Echoes in the Darkness, *507;* F.I.S.T., *512;* Ghost in the Noonday Sun, *285;* Hammett, *981;* Hardcore, *981;* Honeymoon in Vegas, *300;* Joe, *558;* Kickboxer 2: The Road Back, *70;* Men of Respect, *592;* Nervous Ticks, *343;* Outland, *1069;* Red Heat (1988), *104;* Royce, *109;* Slither, *381;* Solar Crisis, *1077;* Speed Zone, *119;* Steelyard Blues, *386;* Surrender, *389;* Swashbuckler (1976), *123;* Taking the Heat, *676;* Taxi Driver, *1023;* Tragedy of Flight 103: The Inside Story, The, *687;* Turk 182, *689;* Walker, *695;* Where the Buffalo Roam, *409;* Yellowbeard, *415;* Young Frankenstein, *416*

Bozo: Life and Times of Grizzly Adams, The, *181*

Bozyk, Reizl: Crossing Delancey, *491*

Bozzuffi, Marcel: Caravan to Vaccares, *23*

Bracco, Lorraine: Being Human, *458;* Dream Team, The, *269;* Even Cowgirls Get the Blues, *272;* Goodfellas, *531;* Medicine Man, *591;* Radio Flyer, *633;* Scam, *1012;* Sing, *939;* Someone to Watch Over Me, *1018;* Switch, *390;* Talent for the Game, *677;* Traces of Red, *1026*

Bracken, Eddie: American Clock, The, *446;* Caught in the Draft, *252;* Hail the Conquering Hero, *292;* Home Alone 2: Lost in New York, *175;* Miracle of Morgan's Creek, The, *332;* Oscar (1991), *351;* Rookie of the Year, *200;* Summer Stock, *942;* Too Many Girls, *946;* We're Not Married, *408;* Young and Willing, *708*

Braconnier, Liza: Dirty Dishes, *730*

Bradbury, Ray: Fantasy Film Worlds of George Pal, The, *424*

Bradford, Greg: Lovelines, *323;* Zapped!, *416*

Bradford, Jesse: King of the Hill, *565*

Bradford, Lane: Don Daredevil Rides Again, *1109;* Satan's Satellites, *111;* Zombies of the Stratosphere (Satan's Satellites), *141*

Bradford, Richard: Ambition, *952;* Chinatown Murders, The: Man Against the Mob, *25;* Cold Heaven, *485;* Dr. Giggles, *835;* Little Nikita, *992;* Milagro Beanfield War, The, *594;* Night Game, *1000;* Permanent Record, *621;* Servants of Twilight, *884;* Trip to Bountiful, The, *688;* Untouchables, The, *134*

Bradley, Chris: Killer Instinct, *71*

Bradley, David: American Ninja III, *4;* American Ninja IV: The Annihilation, *4;* Cyborg Cop, *1043;* Lower Level, *994*

Bradley, Doug: Hellraiser 3: Hell On Earth, *850*

Bradna, Olympe: South of Pago Pago, *119*

Bradshaw, Booker: Coffy, *27*

Bradshaw, Cathryn: Bert Rigby, You're a Fool, *908*

Bradshaw, Terry: Magic Christmas Tree, The, *184*

Brady, Alice: Gay Divorcée, The, *918;* Go West, Young Man, *287;* In Old Chicago, *550;* My Man Godfrey (1936), *340;* One Hundred Men and a Girl, *934;* Three Smart Girls, *945;* Young Mr. Lincoln, *708*

Brady, Janelle: Allnighter, The, *225;* Class of Nuke 'em High, *824*

Brady, Pat: Bells of Coronado, *1097;* Call of the Canyon, *1103;* Down Dakota Way, *1110;* Golden Stallion, The, *1116;* Roy Rogers Show, The (TV Series), *1146;* Song of Texas, *1151;* Sons of the Pioneers, *1151;* Sunset on the Desert, *1154;* Trigger, Jr., *1159;* Twilight in the Sierras, *1159*

Brady, Ruth: Caught, *477*

Brady, Scott: Arizona Bushwhackers, *1094;* Bonnie's Kids, *17;* Castle of Evil, *821;* China Syndrome, The, *961;* Five Bloody Graves, *1113;* Gremlins, *1055;* Gun Riders, The, *1117;* He Walked by Night, *982;* Johnny Guitar, *1123;* Journey to the Center of Time, *1060;* Kansas City Massacre, The, *70;* Maverick Queen, The, *1133;* Mohawk, *1134;* Montana Belle, *1134;* Nightmare in Wax (Crimes in the Wax Museum), *871;* Port of New York, *624;* Restless Breed, The, *1142*

Braeden, Eric: Adultress, The, *441;* Ambulance, The, *952;* Colossus: The Forbin Project, *1042;* Escape from the Planet of the Apes, *1049;* Herbie Goes to Monte Carlo, *174*

Braekman, Caroline: Rabid Grannies, *878*

Braga, Sonia: Dona Flor and Her Two Husbands, *731;* Gabriela, *739;* I Love You (Eu Te Amo), *746;* Kiss of the Spider Woman, *566;* Lady on the Bus, *755;* Last Prostitute, The, *570;* Man Who Broke 1000 Chains, The, *587;* Milagro Beanfield War, The, *594;* Moon Over Parador, *336;* Rookie, The, *109*

Brambell, Wilfred: Adventures of Picasso, The, *222;* Hard Day's Night, A, *921*

Bramley, Flora: College, *257*

Brana, Frank: Street Warriors, *670;* Yellow Hair and the Fortress of Gold, *1165*

Brana, Jonathon von: Legends, *429*

Branagh, Kenneth: Dead Again, *966;* Fortunes of War, *520;* Henry V (1989), *540;* High Season, *297;* Look Back In Anger (1989), *579;* Month in the Country, A, *599;* Much Ado About Nothing, *338;* Peter's Friends, *621;* Swing Kids, *675*

Brancato, Lillio: Bronx Tale, A, *470*

Brand, Neville: Adventures of Huckleberry Finn, The (1960), *144;* Cahill—US Marshal, *1103;* D.O.A. (1949), *965;* Deadly Trackers, The, *1108;* Desperados, The, *1109;* Eaten Alive, *838;* Evils of the Night, *839;* Fire!, *48;* Gun Fury, *1117;* Kansas City Confidential, *988;* Kiss Tomorrow Goodbye, *73;* Lonely Man, The, *1129;* Mad Bomber, The, *994;* Man from the Alamo, The, *1132;* Mohawk, *1134;* Ninth Configuration, The, *608;* Prince Valiant, *100;* Prodigal, The, *629;* Psychic Killer, *877;* Return, The, *1074;* Riot in Cell Block Eleven, *107;* That Darn Cat, *210;* Tin Star, The, *1157;* Treasures of the Twilight Zone, *1085;* Untouchables, The: Scarface Mob (TV), *134*

Brandauer, Klaus Maria: Becoming Colette, *457;* Burning Secret, *472;* Colonel Redl, *725;* Hanussen, *743;* Lightship, The, *575;* Mephisto, *767;* Never Say Never Again, *89;* Out of Africa, *616;* Quo Vadis? (1985), *632;* Russia House, The, *646;* Salzburg Connection, The, *111;* Streets of Gold, *671;* White Fang, *217*

Brander, Leslie: Sizzle Beach, U.S.A., *380*

Brandi, Walter: Slaughter of the Vampires, *887;* Terror Creatures from the Grave, *893*

Brandis, Jonathan: Ladybugs, *315;* NeverEnding Story II, The, *1068;* Sidekicks, *203;* Stepfather II, *890*

Brando, Jocelyn: Big Heat, The, *12;* Dark Night of the Scarecrow, *829;* Ugly American, The, *690*

Brando, Marlon: Apocalypse Now, *6;* Appaloosa, The, *1094;* Bedtime Story, *233;* Burn!, *472;* Chase, The (1966), *479;* Christopher Columbus: The Discovery, *26;* Desirée, *500;* Dry White Season, A, *505;* Formula, The, *978;* Freshman, The, *281;* Fugitive Kind, The, *523;* Godfather, The, *529;* Godfather Epic, The, *529;* Guys and Dolls, *921;* Julius Caesar (1953), *561;* Last Tango in Paris, *570;* Men, The, *592;* Missouri

Breaks, The, *1134;* Moriturl, *87;* Mutiny on the Bounty (1962), *88;* Night of the Following Day, The, *1001;* Nightcomers, The, *870;* On the Waterfront, *612;* One-Eyed Jacks, *1137;* Reflections in a Golden Eye, *637;* Roots: The Next Generation, *644;* Sayonara, *648;* Streetcar Named Desire, A, *671;* Superman, *1081;* Teahouse of the August Moon, The, *392;* Ugly American, The, *690;* Viva Zapata!, *694;* Wild One, The, *139;* Young Lions, The, *708*

Brando, Rikki: Bikini Carwash Company 2, *239;* Buford's Beach Bunnies, *247*

Brando, Yasusuka: Mishima: A Life in Four Chapters, *595*

Brandon, David: Beyond Darkness, *813*

Brandon, Henry: Bad Man of Deadwood, *1095;* Captain Sinbad, *156;* Drums of Fu Manchu, *42;* Marshal of Mesa City, *1133;* Okefenokee, *93;* Ranger and the Lady, The, *1141;* Under Texas Skies, *1160*

Brandon, Michael: Change of Seasons, A, *253;* FM, *278;* James Dean—A Legend in His Own Time, *556;* Lovers and Other Strangers, *323;* Promises in the Dark, *629;* Queen of the Stardust Ballroom, *632;* Red Alert, *104;* Rich and Famous, *639*

Brandstader, Ron: Field of Honor (1986), *47*

Brandt, Carolyn: Hollywood Strangler Meets the Skid Row Slasher, *851;* Incredibly Strange Creatures Who Stopped Living and Became Mixed-Up Zombies, The, *856;* Rat Pfink a Boo Boo, *364;* Thrill Killers, The, *895*

Branham, Craig: One Last Run, *613*

Branigan, Laura: Mugsy's Girls, *338*

Bransfield, Marjorie: Abraxas Guardian of the Universe, *1034*

Branski, David: 9½ Weeks, *607*

Brantley, Betsy: Five Days One Summer, *517;* I Come in Peace, *1057*

Braoude, Patrick: Great, My Parents Are Divorcing, *742*

Braschi, Nicoletta: Johnny Stecchino, *750*

Brascia, Dominick: Evil Laugh, *839*

Brasselle, Keefe: It's a Big Country, *308;* Place in the Sun, A, *622;* Railroaded, *633*

Brasseur, Claude: Act of Aggression, *710;* Band of Outsiders, *715;* Elusive Corporal, The, *734;* Josepha, *750;* La Boum, *753;* Liars, The, *760;* Pardon Mon Affaire, *775;* Pardon Mon Affaire, Too!, *775;* Seven Deadly Sins, The, *785;* Simple Story, A, *786*

Brasseur, Pierre: Candide, *722;* Children of Paradise, The, *723;* Eyes without a Face, *735;* Head Against the Wall, *743;* Le Schpountz, *758*

Bratt, Benjamin: Bound by Honor, *467*

Braugher, Andre: Court-Martial of Jackie Robinson, The, *489;* Striking Distance, *121*

Braun, John: S. S. Hell Camp, *882*

Brauner, Asher: American Eagle, *4;* Boss' Son, The, *467*

Brauss, Arthur: Goalie's Anxiety at the Penalty Kick, *741*

Braverman, Bart: Alligator, *808;* Gladiator, The, *55;* Hit and Run, *63*

Bravo, Carlos: Gunfire, *1117*

Bray, Gillian: Animal Called Man, An, *1093*

Bray, Thomas: Lady Mobster, *74*

Brazzi, Rossano: Barefoot Contessa, The, *455;* Bobo, The, *243;* Dr. Frankenstein's Castle of Freaks, *835;* Far Pavilions, The, *514;* Fear City, *47;* Final Conflict, The, *841;* Italian Job, The, *308;* Legend of the Lost, *572;* One Step to Hell, *95;* Rome Adventure, *643;* South Pacific, *941;* Summertime, *673;* We the Living, *802;* Woman Times Seven, *705*

Breaks, Sebastian: Big Switch, The, *13*

Breck, Peter: Benji, *149;* Big Valley, The (TV Series), *1098;* Crawling Hand, The, *825;* Shock Corridor, *1015;* Unnamable II, The, *899*

Breeding, Larry: Street Music, *670*

Breen, Bobby: Breaking the Ice, *909;* It Happened in New Orleans, *925;* Make a Wish, *586*

Breen, Danny: Avery Schreiber—Live From the Second City, *230;* Best of Not Necessarily the News, The, *236*

Breen, Patrick: For Love or Money, *279*

Brega, Mario: Death Rides a Horse, *1108;* Fistful of Dollars, A, *1113*

Bregman, Tracy: Concrete Jungle, The (1982), *28*

Brejchova, Hana: Baron Munchausen, *148;* Loves of a Blonde, *762*

Brel, Jacques: Assassins de L'Ordre, Les (Law Breakers), *714;* Franz, *738;* Pain in the A—, A, *774*

Bremer, Lucille: Till the Clouds Roll By, *946;* Yolanda and the Thief, *708*

Brendel, El: Big Trail, The, *1098;* Captain Caution, *23;* Happy Landing, *921;* Little Miss Broadway, *928;* Wings, *140*

Breneman, Tom: Breakfast in Hollywood, *245*

Brennan, Brid: Four Days in July, *521*

Brennan, Claire: She Freak, The, *885*

Brennan, Eileen: Babes in Toyland (1986), *147;* Blood Vows: The Story of a Mafia Wife, *464;* Cheap Detective, The, *254;* Clue, *256;* Daisy Miller, *493;* FM, *278;* Fourth Wise Man, The, *521;* Great Smokey Roadblock, The, *57;* History of White People in America, The (Volume II), *298;* I Don't Buy Kisses Anymore, *303;* Murder So Sweet, *601;* My Old Man, *602;* New Adventures of Pippi Longstocking, The, *191;* Playmates, *358;* Private Benjamin, *361;* Rented Lips, *366;* Scarecrow, *649;* Sticky Fingers, *386;* Sting, The, *120;* Texasville, *680;* White Palace, *700*

Brennan, Kerry: Party Camp, *354;* Terror Squad, *127*

Brennan, Stephen: Eat the Peach, *270*

Brennan, Tom: Gore Vidal's Lincoln, *531*

Brennan, Walter: Adventures of Tom Sawyer, The, *144;* Along the Great Divide, *1093;* At Gunpoint, *1095;* Bad Day at Black Rock, *454;* Barbary Coast, The, *455;* Best of the Badmen, *1097;* Brimstone, *1101;* Come and Get It, *28;* Cowboy and the Lady, The, *260;* Dakota (1945), *1107;* Far Country, The, *1112;* Fury, *524;* Gnome-Mobile, The, *169;* Goodbye, My Lady, *171;* Green Promise, The, *533;* Hangmen Also Die, *536;* Home for the Holidays, *983;* How the West Was Won, *1122;* Long Long Trail, *1130;* Man of Action, *1132;* Meet John Doe, *591;* My Darling Clementine, *1134;* Northwest Passage, *92;* One and Only, Genuine, Original Family Band, The, *192;* Pride of the Yankees, The, *627;* Princess and the Pirate, The, *361;* Red River, *1141;* Rio Bravo, *1145;* Sergeant York, *113;* Showdown, The (1950), *1149;* Stolen Life, A, *668;* Story of Vernon and Irene Castle, The, *942;* Support Your Local Sheriff!, *1154;* Tammy and the Bachelor, *677;* Task Force, *677;* Texas Cyclone, *1155;* They Shall Have Music, *944;* To Have and Have Not, *130;* Two-Fisted Law, *1159;* Westerner, The, *1163;* Who's Minding the Mint?, *411*

Brenner, Barry: Surf Nazis Must Die, *123*

Brenner, David: Worth Winning, *414;* Young at Heart Comedians, The, *415*

Brenner, Dori: Summer Wishes, Winter Dreams, *673*

Brent, Evelyn: Framed (1930), *521;* Holt of the Secret Service, *63;* Last Command, The (1928), *568;* Law West of Tombstone, *1127;* Mr. Wong, Detective, *997;* Panama Lady, *353;* Riders for Justice, *1143;* Seventh Victim, The, *885;* Tarzan and the Trappers, *125;* Underworld (1927), *691;* World Gone Mad, The, *707*

Brent, George: Baby Face, *453;* Dark Victory, *495;* Female, *276;* Fighting 69th, The, *48;* Great Lie, The, *532;* In Person, *305;* In This Our Life, *550;* Jezebel, *557;* Luxury Liner, *930;* Montana Belle, *1134;* Old Maid, The, *611;* Out of the Blue, *352;* Painted Veil, The, *617;* Purchase Price, The, *630;* Rains Came, The, *634;* Silver Queen, *1150;* Spiral Staircase, The (1946), *1019;* They Call It Sin, *680;* Tomorrow Is Forever, *685*

Brent, Linda: Below the Border, *1097*

Brent, Romney: Adventures of Don Juan, The, *2;* Dinner at the Ritz, *39*

Brent, Timothy: Warriors of the Wasteland, *1088*

Brentano, Amy: Blood Sisters, *816*

Brenton, Gilbert: Class of Nuke 'em High, *824*

Breon, Edmund: Dressed to Kill (1946), *972*

Bresee, Bobbie: Evil Spawn, *839;* Mausoleum, *864*

Breslin, Jimmy: If Ever I See You Again, *548*

Bressart, Felix: Bitter Sweet, *909;* Comrade X, *258;* Iceland, *924;* I've Always Loved You, *555;* Seventh Cross, The, *653;* Song Is Born, A, *940;* Without Love, *413*

Brett, Jeremy: Adventures of Sherlock Holmes, The (Series), *950;* Macbeth (1981), *584*

Breuer, Jacques: Berlin Tunnel 21, *10*

Brewer, Jerry: Offerings, *872*

Brewster, Diane: Fugitive, The: The Last Episode (TV Series), *53;* Invisible Boy, The, *1059;* Maverick (TV Series), *1133;* Torpedo Run, *131*

Brewton, Maia: Adventures in Babysitting, *222*

Breznahan, Tom: Brain, The (1988), *818;* Diplomatic Immunity, *39;* Ski School, *380;* Twice Dead, *1027*

Brialy, Jean-Claude: Bride Wore Black, The, *959;* Burning Court, The, *721;* Catherine & Co., *722;* Circle of Love, *482;* Claire's Knee, *724;* Judge and the Assassin, The, *750;* Le Beau Serge, *756;* Les Cousins, *759;* Paris Belongs to Us, *775;* Phantom of Liberty, The, *777;* Robert et Robert, *782;* Seven Deadly Sins, The, *785;* Tonio Kroger, *796;* Woman Is a Woman, A, *805*

Brian, David: Beyond the Forest, *460;* Blade Rider, *1099;* Castle of Evil, *821;* Flamingo Road, *518;* High and the Mighty, The, *541;* Intruder in the Dust, *553;* Million Dollar Mermaid, *931*

Brian, Mary: Amazing Adventure, *225;* Blessed Event, *241;* Charlie Chan in Paris, *961;* Dragnet (1947), *41;* Front Page, The (1931), *281;* Running Wild (1927), *371;* Virginian, The (1929), *1161;* World Gone Mad, The, *707*

Briant, Shane: Captain Kronos: Vampire Hunter, *821;* Cassandra, *821;* Frankenstein and the Monster from Hell, *842;* Grievous Bodily Harm, *533;* Shaker Run, *114*

Brice, Fanny: Everybody Sing, *916;* Great Ziegfeld, The, *921;* Ziegfeld Follies, *949*

Brice, Pierre: Mill of the Stone Women, *865*

Bridge, Alan: Badmen of the Hills, *1096;* When a Man Rides Alone, *1163*

Bridges, Beau: Alice Through the Looking Glass (1985), *145;* Daddy's Dyin' and Who's Got the Will, *261;* Dangerous Company, *494;* Fabulous Baker Boys, The, *512;* Fifth Musketeer, The, *47;* For Love of Ivy, *279;* Four Feathers, The (1978), *52;* Greased Lightning, *57;* Hammersmith Is Out, *292;* Heart Like a Wheel, *538;* Honky Tonk Freeway, *300;* Hotel New Hampshire, The, *544;* Incident, The (1967), *551;* Iron Triangle, The, *554;* Killing Time, The, *72;* Love Child, *581;* Married to It, *589;* Night Crossing, *90;* Norma Rae, *608;* Other Side of the Mountain, The, *615;* Outrage!, *616;* Positively True Adventures of the Alleged Texas Cheerleader-Murdering Mom, The, *360;* Red Light Sting, The, *636;* Runner Stumbles, The, *645;* Seven Hours to Judgment, *113;* Sidekicks, *203;* Signs of Life, *657;* Silver Dream Racer, *658;* Swashbuckler (1976), *123;* Two-Minute Warning, *1028;* Village of the Giants, *900;* Wild Flower, *702;* Wild Pair, The, *140;* Without Warning: The James Brady Story, *704;* Witness for the Prosecution (1982), *1032;* Wizard, The, *218;* Women & Men: Stories of Seduction, *706*

Bridges, Jeff: Against All Odds, *951;* American Heart, *446;* Bad Company, *1095;* Blown Away (1994), *16;* Cutter's Way, *965;* 8 Million Ways to Die, *973;* Fabulous Baker Boys, The, *512;* Fat City, *515;* Fearless (1993), *515;* Fisher King, The, *1051;* Hearts of the West, *295;* Heaven's Gate, *1119;* Jagged Edge, *556;* King Kong (1976), *859;* Kiss Me Goodbye, *313;* Last American Hero, The, *75;* Last Picture Show, The, *570;* Morning After, The, *997;* Nadine, *341;* Rancho Deluxe, *1140;* Rapunzel, *198;* See You in the Morning, *651;* Starman, *1080;* Stay Hungry, *667;* Texasville, *680;* Thunderbolt and Lightfoot, *129;* Tron, *1085;* Tucker: A Man and His Dream, *689;* Vanishing, The (1993), *1029;* Winter Kills, *704;* Yin and Yang of Mr. Go, The, *1033*

Bridges, Lloyd: Abilene Town, *1092;* Airplane!, *224;* Alice Through the Looking Glass (1985), *145;* Apache Woman, *1094;* Around the World Under the Sea, *6;* Bear Island, *954;* Blown Away (1994), *16;* Blue and the Gray, The, *1099;* Cousins, *260;* Daring Game, *32;* Devlin, *970;* Dress Gray, *505;* East of Eden (1982), *506;* Fifth Musketeer, The, *47;* George Washington, *526;* Goddess, The, *528;* Great Wallendas, The, *533;* Haunts of the Very Rich, *1055;* Heat's On, The, *295;* High Noon, *1120;* Honey, I Blew Up the Kid, *175;* Hot Shots, *301;* Hot Shots Part Deux, *301;* Joe Versus the Volcano, *310;* Last of the Comanches, *1126;* Little Big Horn, *1128;* Master Race, The, *590;* Moonrise, *599;* Rainmaker, The, *634;* Ramrod, *1140;* Rocketship X-M, *1075;* Roots, *644;* Sahara (1943), *110;* Silent Night, Lonely Night, *658;* Try and Get Me, *133;* Tucker: A Man and His Dream, *689;* Weekend Warriors, *407;* White Tower, The, *701;* Wild Pair, The, *140;* Winter People, *704*

Bridges, Todd: Homeboys, *543;* Twice Dead, *1027*

Bridou, Lucienne: This Man Can't Die, *1156*

Briers, Richard: Norman Conquests, The, Episode 1: Table Manners, *346;* Norman Conquests, The, Episode 2: Living Together, *346;* Norman Conquests, The, Episode 3: Round and Round the Garden, *346*

Brieux, Bernard: Petit Con, *777;* Rascals, The, *779*

Briggs, Donald: Panama Lady, *353*

Briggs, Joe Bob: Joe Bob Briggs—Dead in Concert, *310*

Bright, Richard: Cut and Run, *493;* Godfather, Part III, The, *529;* On the Yard, *94;* Pat Garrett and Billy the Kid, *1138;* Red Heat (1988), *104;* Ref, The, *365*

Brignoli, Omar: Tree of the Wooden Clogs, The, *797*

Brill, Fran: Look Back in Anger (1980), *579*

Brill, Jason: Hell High, *849*

Brill, Robert: Look Back in Anger (1980), *579*

Brilli, Nancy: Demons 2, *833*

Brillinger, Brian: Brighton Beach Memoirs, *246*

Brimhall, Cynthia: Fit to Kill, *49*

Brimley, Wilford: Absence of Malice, *950;* Act of Vengeance, *441;* American Justice, *4;* Borderline, *17;* Cocoon, *1042;* Cocoon: The Return, *1042;* Country, *489;* Death Valley, *831;* End of the Line, *509;* Eternity, *511;* Ewoks: The Battle for Endor, *165;* Firm, The, *977;* Gore Vidal's Billy The Kid, *1116;* Hard Target, *59;* Harry and Son, *537;* High Road to China, *62;* Murder in Space, *1067;* Natural, The, *604;* Remo Williams: The Adventure Begins, *105;* Rodeo Girl, *642;* Stone Boy, The, *668;* Thing, The (1982), *1083;* Thompson's Last Run, *128;* Tough Enough, *131*

Brin, Michele: Secret Games, *651;* Sexual Intent, *1014*

Brinegar, Paul: Gambler Returns, the: Luck of the Draw, *1115;* How to Make a Monster, *853;* Rawhide (TV Series), *1141*

Brink, Irvin: On Deadly Ground, *93*

Brinkley, Christie: National Lampoon's Vacation, *342*

Brinkley, Ritch: Cabin Boy, *248*

Brion, Françoise: French Lessons, *281*

Brisco, Gwen: Getting Over, *526*

Brisebois, Danielle: Big Bad Mama II, *12;* Premonition, The, *876*

Brisson, Carl: Manxman, The, *588;* Murder at the Vanities, *931;* Ring, The, *640*

Bristow, Michael: Karate Cop, *70*

Britt, May: Secrets of Women (Waiting Women), *784;* Summer Interlude, *791;* Young Lions, The, *708*

Brittany, Morgan: In Search of Historic Jesus, *550;* Initiation of Sarah, The, *856;* LBJ: The Early Years, *571;* Sundown (1990), *891*

Britton, Barbara: Captain Kidd, *23;* Champagne for Caesar, *252;* Loaded Pistols, *1128;* Young and Willing, *708*

Britton, Pamela: D.O.A. (1949), *965;* If It's Tuesday, This Must Be Belgium, *305;* Key to the City, *312*

Britton, Tony: Day of the Jackal, The, *966;* Dr. Syn, Alias the Scarecrow, *163;* Horsemasters, *176;* Night Watch, *870;* Operation Amsterdam, *95;* There's a Girl in My Soup, *393*

Broadbent, Jim: Crying Game, The, *492;* Enchanted April, *271;* Good Father, The, *530;* Life Is Sweet, *574*

Broaderup, Bernd: Taxi Zum Klo (Taxi to the Toilet), *793*

Broadhurst, Kent: Dark Half, The, *829*

Broadnax, David: Zombie Island Massacre, *905*

Broberg, Lily: Famous Five Get into Trouble, The, *166*

Brochet, Anne: Barjo, *715;* Cyrano De Bergerac (1990), *727;* Tous les Matins du Monde, *796*

Brock, Alan: Shriek of the Mutilated, *886*

Brock, Phil: Dollman vs. Demonic Toys, *1047*

Brockius, Lawrence: Deadmate, *831*

Brockman, Jay: Penpal Murders, *873*

Brockwell, Gladys: Oliver Twist (1922), *611*

Broderick, Beth: Are You Lonesome Tonight, *953*

Broderick, Chris: Legacy of Horror, *860*

Broderick, Helen: Bride Walks Out, The, *245;* My Love for Yours, *340;* Rage of Paris, The, *364;* Swing Time, *943;* Top Hat, *946*

Broderick, James: Alice's Restaurant, *444;* Group, The, *534;* Shadow Box, The, *654;* Todd Killings, The, *685*

Broderick, Jocelyn: My Daughter's Keeper, *999*

Broderick, Matthew: Biloxi Blues, *240;* Cinderella (1985), *159;* Family Business, *514;* Ferris Bueller's Day Off, *276;* Freshman, The, *281;* Glory, *528;* Ladyhawke, *74;* Life in the Theater, A, *574;* Master Harold and the Boys, *590;* Night We Never Met, The, *345;* 1918, *607;* On Valentine's Day, *612;* Out on a Limb (1992), *352;* Project X, *1072;* Torch Song Trilogy, *686;* Wargames, *1088*

Brodie, Steve: Arizona Ranger, *1095;* Brothers in the Saddle, *1101;* Crossfire (1947), *964;* Desperate, *969;* Donovan's Brain, *1047;* Far Country, The, *1112;* Frankenstein Island, *842;* Guns of Hate, *1118;* Home of the Brave, *543;* Kiss Tomorrow Goodbye, *73;* Out of the Past, *1003;* Rustlers, The, *1146;* Station West, *1153;* Steel Helmet, The, *120;* Trail Street, *1158;* Wild World of Batwoman, The, *1089*

Brody, Michael: Forest, The, *842*

Brogi, Giulio: Spider's Stratagem, The, *788*

Brokop, Lisa: Harmony Cats, *536*

Brolin, James: Ambush Murders, The, *446;* Amityville Horror, The, *809;* Backstab, *953;* Bad Jim, *1095;* Capricorn One, *1041;* Cheatin' Hearts, *480;* Finish Line, *516;* Gas, Food, Lodging, *525;* High Risk, *61;* Hold the Dream, *542;* Mae West, *585;* Night of the Juggler, *90;* Nightmare on the 13th Floor, *871;* Ted & Venus, *392;* Von Ryan's Express, *136;* Westworld, *1089*

Brolin, Josh: Finish Line, *516;* Goonies, The, *56;* Prison for Children, *628;* Thrashin', *128*

Bromberg, J. Edward: Cloak and Dagger (1946), *962;* Jesse James, *1123;* Lady of Burlesque, *74;* Mark of Zorro, The (1940), *82;* Return of Frank James, The, *1142;* Son of Dracula (1943), *888;* Strange Cargo, *669*

Bromfield, John: Big Bluff, The, *460;* Easy to Love, *915;* Manfish, *862;* Revenge of the Creature, *881*

Bromfield, Lois: Doctor Duck's Super Secret All-Purpose Sauce, *266*

Bromfield, Valri: Home Is Where the Hart Is, *299*

Bron, Eleanor: Attic: The Hiding of Anne Frank, *452;* Bedazzled, *233;* Help!, *922;* Hound of the Baskervilles, The (1983), *984;* Turtle Diary, *400;* Women in Love, *706*

Bronsky, Brick: Class of Nuke 'em High 2: Subhumanoid Meltdown, *824;* Sgt. Kabukiman N.Y.P.D., *114*

Bronson, Betty: Are Parents People?, *228;* Ben-Hur (1926), *458;* Naked Kiss, The, *1000;* Yodelin' Kid from Pine Ridge, *1165*

Bronson, Charles: Act of Vengeance, *441;* Apache, *1094;* Assassination, *7;* Battle of the Bulge, *10;* Borderline, *17;* Breakheart Pass, *1101;* Breakout, *19;* Cabo Blanco, *21;* Chato's Land, *1104;* Chino, *1104;* Cold Sweat (1970), *28;* Death Hunt, *35;* Death Wish, *35;* Death Wish II, *36;* Death Wish III, *36;* Death Wish IV: The Crackdown, *36;* Death Wish V: The Face of Death, *36;* Dirty Dozen, The, *39;* Drum Beat, *1110;* Evil That Men Do, The, *45;* Family, The (1970), *46;* Four for Texas, *1114;* Great Escape, The, *57;* Guns of Diablo, *1118;* Hard Times, *59;* Honor Among Thieves, *63;* Indian Runner, The, *551;* Jubal, *1124;* Kinjite (Forbidden Subjects), *73;* Love and Bullets, *79;* Machine-Gun Kelly, *80;* Magnificent Seven, The, *1131;* Master of the World, *1065;* Meanest Men in the West, The, *1133;* Mechanic, The, *83;* Messenger of Death, *84;* Mr. Majestyk, *86;* Murphy's Law, *87;* Never So Few, *89;* Once Upon a Time in the West, *1137;* Raid on Entebbe, *633;* Red Sun, *1142;* Rider on the Rain, *1010;* Run of the Arrow, *1146;* St. Ives, *110;* Sandpiper, The, *648;* Sea Wolf, The (1993), *113;* Showdown at Boot Hill, *1149;* Someone Behind the Door, *1018;* Stone Killer, The, *120;* Telefon, *1023;* Ten to Midnight, *126;* This Property Is Condemned, *682;* Villa Rides, *1161;* White Buffalo, *1164*

Brook, Claudio: Cronos, *727;* Dr. Tarr's Torture Dungeon, *836;* Foxtrot, *521;* Interval, *553;* Simon of the Desert, *786*

Brook, Clive: Cavalcade, *477;* Convoy (1940), *488;* List of Adrian Messenger, The, *992;* On Approval, *349;* Shanghai Express, *655*

Brook, Faith: After Julius, *442*

Brook, Irina: Captive, *475;* Girl in the Picture, The, *286*

Brooke, Hillary: Abbott and Costello Meet Captain Kidd, *221;* Abbott and Costello Show, The (TV Series), *221;* Africa Screams, *223;* Enchanted Cottage, The, *509;* Lost Continent, The, *1063;* Monsieur Beaucaire, *336;* Road to Utopia, *369;* Sherlock Holmes and the Voice of Terror, *1015;* Sherlock Holmes Faces Death, *1015;* Strange Woman, The, *669;* Woman in Green, The, *1032*

Brooke, Walter: Green Hornet, The (TV Series), *58*

Brooke-Taylor, Tim: How to Irritate People, *302*

Brooks, Albert: Broadcast News, *246;* Defending Your Life, *263;* I'll Do Anything, *305;* Lost in America, *321;* Modern Romance, *335;* Real Life, *365;* Twilight Zone—The Movie, *898;* Unfaithfully Yours (1984), *403*

Brooks, Avery: Ernest Green Story, The, *165;* Roots—The Gift, *644*

Brooks, Christopher: Almos' a Man, *445*

Brooks, Claude: Hiding Out, *61*

Brooks, David: Scream for Help, *884*

Brooks, David Allen: Kindred, The, *859*

Brooks, Foster: Oddballs, *348*

Brooks, Geraldine: Challenge to Lassie, *157;* Johnny Tiger, *559;* Possessed (1947), *625*

Brooks, Hazel: Body and Soul (1947), *466*

Brooks, Jacqueline: Entity, The, *838;* Gambler, The (1974), *524;* Rodeo Girl, *642;* Without a Trace, *1032*

Brooks, Jay: Laurel Avenue, *571*

Brooks, Jean: Boothill Bandits, *1100;* Seventh Victim, The, *885*

Brooks, Jeremy: Torture Dungeon, *896*

Brooks, Joe: If Ever I See You Again, *548*

Brooks, Joel: Are You Lonesome Tonight, *953;* Dinner at Eight (1990), *265;* Mating Season, The, *330;* Skin Deep, *380*

Brooks, Leslie: Blonde Ice, *464;* Scar, The, *649;* Tonight and Every Night, *946;* You Were Never Lovelier, *948*

Brooks, Louise: Diary of a Lost Girl, *730;* Overland Stage Raiders, *1137;* Pandora's Box, *775;* Prix De Beaute (Beauty Prize), *778*

Brooks, Lucius: Harlem Rides the Range, *1119*

Brooks, Mel: Audience with Mel Brooks, An, *229;* Blazing Saddles, *241;* High Anxiety, *297;* History of the World, Part One, The, *298;* Life Stinks, *318;* Muppet Movie, The, *189;* Putney Swope, *363;* Robin Hood: Men in Tights, *369;* Silent Movie, *379;* Spaceballs, *384;* To Be or Not to Be (1983), *397;* Twelve Chairs, The, *401*

Brooks, Pauline: Make a Million, *327*

Brooks, Phyllis: Dangerous Passage, *32;* In Old Chicago, *550;* Rebecca of Sunnybrook Farm (1938), *936;* Silver Spurs, *1150;* Slightly Honorable, *381*

Brooks, Rand: Borrowed Trouble, *1100;* Dangerous Venture, *1107;* Dead Don't Dream, The, *1108;* Devil's Playground, *1109;* False Paradise, *1112;* Hoppy's Holiday, *1121;* Ladies of the Chorus, *567;* Marauders, *1132;* Silent Conflict, *1150;* Sinister Journey, *1150;* Strange Gamble, *1153;* Unexpected Guest, *1160*

Brooks, Randi: Cop, *29;* Hamburger—The Motion Picture, *292*
Brooks, Randy: Assassination, *7;* Colors, *485;* Reservoir Dogs, *105*
Brooks, Ray: Daleks—Invasion Earth 2150 A.D., *1044;* Flesh and Blood Show, The, *841;* House of Whipcord, *853;* Knack...and How To Get It, The, *314;* Office Romances, *611*
Brooks, Richard: 84 Charlie Mopic, *43;* Memphis, *592;* To Sleep with Anger, *685*
Brooks, Van: Trespasses, *687*
Brophy, Brian: Skinheads, *116*
Brophy, Edward: All Through the Night, *3;* Cameraman, The, *249;* Doughboys, *268;* Evelyn Prentice, *511;* Great Guy, *532;* Last Hurrah, The, *569;* Mad Love, *861;* Parlor, Bedroom and Bath, *354;* Show Them No Mercy, *657;* Speak Easily, *384;* Thin Man, The, *1024;* Thin Man Goes Home, The, *1024;* What! No Beer?, *408;* Wonder Man, *413*
Brophy, Kevin: Delos Adventure, The, *36;* Time Walker, *895*
Brosnan, Pierce: Broken Chain, The, *20;* Death Train, *968;* Deceivers, The, *36;* Entangled, *973;* Fourth Protocol, The, *978;* Happy Birthday Bugs: 50 Looney Years, *173;* Heist, The, *540;* Lawnmower Man, The, *1062;* Live Wire, *78;* Long Good Friday, The, *78;* Manions of America, The, *588;* Mister Johnson, *597;* Mrs. Doubtfire, *334;* Murder 101, *999;* Nomads, *872;* Remington Steele (TV series), *1010;* Taffin, *124;* Victim of Love, *1030*
Brosse, Simon de la: Strike It Rich, *387*
Brothers, Dr. Joyce: For Love of Angela, *519;* Lonely Guy, The, *320;* More Wild Wild West, *1134*
Broughton, James: Films of James Broughton, The, *1050*
Brown, Andre: Bronx War, The, *20*
Brown, Barry: Bad Company, *1095;* Daisy Miller, *493*
Brown, Blair: Altered States, *1035;* And I Alone Survived, *447;* Choirboys, The, *481;* Continental Divide, *259;* Flash of Green, A, *977;* Kennedy (TV Miniseries), *562;* One Trick Pony, *934;* Passed Away, *355;* Stealing Home, *667;* Strapless, *670*
Brown, Bobby: Mother Goose Rock N' Roll Rhyme, *189*
Brown, Bryan: Blame It on the Bellboy, *240;* Breaker Morant, *19;* Cocktail, *485;* Dead in the Water, *967;* Devlin, *970;* F/X, *979;* F/X 2: The Deadly Art of Illusion, *979;* Good Wife, The, *530;* Gorillas in the Mist, *531;* Last Hit, The, *990;* Odd Angry Shot, The, *610;* Palm Beach, *617;* Prisoners of the Sun, *628;* Rebel (1985), *636;* Sweet Talker, *389;* Tai-Pan, *124;* Thornbirds, The, *682;* Town Like Alice, A, *686;* Winter of Our Dreams, *704*
Brown, Carlos: Dangerous Company, *494*
Brown, Charles: Old Swimmin' Hole, The, *611*
Brown, Clancy: Ambition, *952;* Blue Steel (1990), *16;* Bride, The, *819;* Cast a Deadly Spell, *1041;* Extreme Prejudice, *45;* Highlander, *1056;* Last Light, *569;* Love, Lies and Murder, *994;* Past Midnight, *619;* Pet Sematary Two, *874;* Season of Fear, *1013;* Shoot to Kill, *115;* Waiting for the Light, *695*
Brown, D. W.: Mischief, *333;* Weekend Pass, *407*
Brown, David: Chasing Dreams, *480;* Deadly Harvest, *1045*
Brown, Dwier: Cutting Edge, The, *493;* Guardian, The (1990), *848*
Brown, Dyann: Lone Wolf, *861*
Brown, Eleanora: Two Women, *797*
Brown, Eric: Private Lessons, *361;* They're Playing with Fire, *681*
Brown, Georg Stanford: Dayton's Devils, *33;* House Party 2, *923;* Jessie Owens Story, The, *557;* Kid with the Broken Halo, The, *313;* Night the City Screamed, The, *606;* Roots: The Next Generation, *644;* Stir Crazy, *386*
Brown, Georgia: Bawdy Adventures of Tom Jones, The, *233;* Devil's Undead, The, *834;* Fixer, The, *517;* Long Ago Tomorrow, *578;* Study in Terror, A, *1021*
Brown, Gibran: Marvin and Tige, *589*
Brown, Henry: Stepfather II, *890*
Brown, James: Adios Amigo, *1092;* Chain Lightning, *478;* Objective, Burma!, *93;* That Was Rock, *944*
Brown, Jim: Crack House, *30;* Dark of the Sun, *32;* Dirty Dozen, The, *39;* Divine Enforcer, *40;* El Condor, *1111;* Fingers, *516;* Ice Station Zebra, *65;* I'm Gonna Git You Sucka!, *305;* Kid Vengeance, *1124;* One Down, Two to Go, *94;* 100 Rifles, *1137;* Pacific Inferno, *96;* Rio Conchos, *1145;* Riot, *106;* Running Man, The, *1075;* Slaughter, *117;* Slaughter's Big Rip-Off, *117;* Take a Hard Ride, *1154;* Three the Hard Way, *129;* Tick ... Tick ... Tick ..., *129*
Brown, Joe E.: Beware of Spooks, *237;* Daring Young Man, The, *262;* Earthworm Tractors, *269;* Pin-Up Girl, *935;* Riding on Air, *368;* Show Boat (1951), *939;* Some Like It Hot, *382;* Tender Years, The, *679;* When's Your Birthday?, *409*
Brown, Johnny Mack: Belle of the Nineties, *234;* Between Men, *1097;* Branded a Coward, *1101;* Coquette, *488;* Deep in the Heart of Texas, *1108;* Female, *276;* Fighting with Kit Carson, *1113;* Flaming Frontiers, *1113;* Hell Town, *1120;* Lawman Is Born, A, *1127;* Lone Star Trail, *1129;* Our Dancing Daughters, *616;* Ride 'em Cowboy, *368;* Short Grass, *1149;* Single Standard, The, *659;* Stampede, *1152;* Woman of Affairs, A, *705*
Brown, Juanita: Caged Heat, *22*
Brown, Julie: Earth Girls Are Easy, *915;* Medusa: Dare to be Truthful, *331;* Nervous Ticks, *343;* Opposite Sex (And How to Live with Them), The, *351;* Shakes the Clown, *377;* Spirit of '76, The, *384*
Brown, Kale: Bloodfist IV—Die Trying, *16*
Brown, Ken: Palm Beach, *617*
Brown, Lou: Alison's Birthday, *808;* Irishman, The, *554*
Brown, Lowell: High School Caesar, *62*
Brown, Lucille: Mystery Squadron, *88;* Rainbow Valley, *1140;* Texas Terror, *1156*
Brown, Murray: Vampyres, *900*
Brown, Olivia: Memories of Murder, *996;* Miami Vice, *84;* Miami Vice: "The Prodigal Son", *84*
Brown, Pamela: Becket, *457;* Cleopatra (1963), *484;* Dracula (1973), *837;* Half a Sixpence, *921;* Lust for Life, *583;* One of Our Aircraft Is Missing, *94;* Secret Ceremony, *650;* Tales of Hoffman, *943*
Brown, Peter: Aurora Encounter, *1037;* Commies Are Coming, the Commies Are Coming, The, *258;* Concrete Jungle, The (1982), *28;* Foxy Brown, *52;* Summer Magic, *208;* Tiger Walks, A, *211*
Brown, Phil: Without Reservations, *413*
Brown, Ralph: Crying Game, The, *492*
Brown, Reb: Cage, *21;* Captain America (1979), *22;* Captain America II: Death Too Soon, *22;* Death of a Soldier, *498;* Fast Break, *274;* Firing Line, The, *49;* Howling II...Your Sister Is a Werewolf, *854;* Last Flight to Hell, *75;* Mercenary Fighters, *84;* Street Hunter, *121;* Strike Commando, *121;* That's Action, *127;* Uncommon Valor, *134;* White Ghost, *138;* Yor: The Hunter from the Future, *1091*
Brown, Ritza: McGuffin, The, *996*
Brown, Roger: Paper Lion, *618*
Brown, Roger Aaron: China Moon, *961*
Brown, Ron: Charlie, the Lonesome Cougar, *158*
Brown, Terry: Bloodbeat, *816*
Brown, Tim: Pacific Inferno, *96*
Brown, Tom: Anne of Green Gables (1934), *146;* Buck Privates Come Home, *246;* In Old Chicago, *550;* Judge Priest, *560;* Navy Blue and Gold, *342*
Brown, Vanessa: Bless the Beasts and Children, *463;* Heiress, The, *539;* I've Always Loved You, *555*
Brown, Violet: Firehouse (1987), *277*
Brown, Wally: Girl Rush, *286;* High and the Mighty, The, *541;* Zombies on Broadway, *416*
Brown, Wendell: Up the Academy, *403*
Brown, Woody: Accused, The, *441;* Rain Killer, The, *1008*
Browne, Coral: Auntie Mame, *229;* Courtney Affair, The, *489;* Dreamchild, *1048;* Eleanor: First Lady of the World, *508;* Englishman Abroad, An, *510;* Killing of Sister George, The, *564;* Ruling Class, The, *371*
Browne, Jackson: No Nukes, *432*

Browne, Kathie: Hondo and the Apaches, *1121*
Browne, Leslie: Dancers, *494;* Nijinsky, *607;* Turning Point, The, *689*
Browne, Roscoe Lee: Black Like Me, *462;* Connection, The (1961), *487;* Cowboys, The, *1106;* For Us the Living: The Medgar Evers Story, *519;* Jumpin' Jack Flash, *311;* King, *564;* Legal Eagles, *991;* Liberation of L. B. Jones, The, *574;* Mark Twain's Connecticut Yankee in King Arthur's Court, *185;* Moon 44, *1067;* Nothing Personal, *347;* Superfly T.N.T., *122;* World's Greatest Athlete, The, *218*
Browne, Suzanne: Bikini Carwash Company 2, *239*
Browning, Rod: Double McGuffin, The, *163*
Browning, Tod: Intolerance, *553*
Bruce, Angela: Charlie Boy, *823*
Bruce, Brenda: Back Home, *147;* Steaming, *667*
Bruce, Cheryl Lynn: Daughters of the Dust, *496*
Bruce, David: Cannibal Attack, *22;* Can't Help Singing, *911;* Gung Ho! (1943), *58;* Salome, Where She Danced, *647;* Sea Wolf, The (1941), *113*
Bruce, Lenny: Dance Hall Racket, *494;* Lenny Bruce Performance Film, The, *317*
Bruce, Nigel: Adventures of Sherlock Holmes, The, *950;* Becky Sharp, *457;* Blue Bird, The, *151;* Chocolate Soldier, The, *911;* Corn Is Green, The (1945), *488;* Dressed to Kill (1946), *972;* Hound of the Baskervilles, The (1939), *983;* House of Fear, *984;* Journey for Margaret, *559;* Julia Misbehaves, *311;* Lassie Come Home, *180;* Last of Mrs. Cheney, The, *315;* Limelight, *319;* Pearl of Death, The, *1004;* Pursuit to Algiers, *1008;* Rains Camé, The, *634;* Rebecca, *1009;* Scarlet Claw, The, *1012;* Scarlet Pimpernel, The (1934), *112;* Sherlock Holmes and the Secret Weapon, *1015;* Sherlock Holmes and the Spider Woman, *1015;* Sherlock Holmes and the Voice of Terror, *1015;* Sherlock Holmes Faces Death, *1015;* Sherlock Holmes in Washington, *1015;* Son of Lassie, *206;* Susan and God, *674;* Suspicion (1941), *1022;* Terror by Night, *1023;* Thunder in the City, *683;* Two Mrs. Carrolls, The, *1028;* Woman in Green, The, *1032*
Bruce, Virginia: Action in Arabia, *2;* Born to Dance, *909;* Great Ziegfeld, The, *921;* Invisible Woman, The, *307;* Jane Eyre (1934), *557;* Let Freedom Ring, *928;* Pardon My Sarong, *354;* Strangers When We Meet, *670*
Brudin, Bo: Russian Roulette, *110*
Bruel, Patrick: Bandits (1987), *715;* Secret Obsessions, *651*
Bruhl, Heidi: Captain Sinbad, *156*
Brulier, Nigel de: Three Musketeers, The (1935), *128*
Brummel, Beau: Three Bullets for a Long Gun, *1156*
Brunkhorst, Natja: Christiane F., *724*
Bruno, Nando: Pardon My Trunk, *775*
Bruns, Phil: Mr. Inside/Mr. Outside, *85;* Opposite Sex (And How to Live with Them), The, *351*
Brush, Peter: Separate Peace, A, *652*
Bryan, Dora: Great St. Trinian's Train Robbery, The, *290;* Taste of Honey, A, *677*
Bryan, Jane: Cherokee Strip, *1104;* Each Dawn I Die, *42;* Kid Galahad (1937), *563;* Sisters, The (1938), *659*
Bryant, Lee: Deathmask, *36*
Bryant, Michael: Girly, *846;* Sakharov, *647*
Bryant, Nana: Bathing Beauty, *908;* Eyes of Texas, *1111;* Return of October, The, *366*
Bryant, Pamela: Lunch Wagon, *324;* Private Lessons, *361*
Bryant, William: Hell Squad (1985), *60*
Bryceland, Yvonne: Road to Mecca, The, *641*
Bryne, Michael: Overindulgence, *617*
Brynner, Yul: Anastasia, *447;* Brothers Karamazov, The, *471;* Buccaneer, The, *20;* Catlow, *1104;* Futureworld, *1053;* Fuzz, *282;* Invitation to a Gunfighter, *1123;* King and I, The, *926;* Light at the End of the World, The, *77;* Madwoman of Chaillot, The, *585;* Magic Christian, The, *326;* Magnificent Seven, The, *1131;* Morituri, *87;* Night Flight from Moscow, *90;* Poppy Is Also a Flower, The, *99;* Port of New York, *624;* Return of the Seven, *1142;* Solomon and Sheba, *661;* Surprise Package, *389;* Taras Bulba, *125;* Ten Commandments, The (1956), *678;* Ultimate Warrior, The, *1087;* Villa Rides, *1161;* Westworld, *1089*
Bucci, Flavio: Suspiria, *891*
Buchanan, Barry: Loch Ness Horror, The, *861*
Buchanan, Claude: Running Wild (1927), *371*
Buchanan, Edgar: Abilene Town, *1092;* Any Number Can Play, *450;* Arizona, *1094;* Benji, *149;* Big Hangover, The, *238;* Big Trees, The, *13;* Black Arrow, The (1948), *13;* Buffalo Bill, *1102;* Cimarron (1960), *1105;* Coroner Creek, *1106;* Human Desire, *546;* It Started With a Kiss, *308;* Lust for Gold, *1130;* Make Haste to Live, *994;* Man from Colorado, The, *1131;* Maverick (TV Series), *1133;* McLintock!, *1133;* Penny Serenade, *620;* Rage at Dawn, *1140;* Rawhide (1951), *1141;* Ride the High Country, *1143;* Rounders, The, *1146;* She Couldn't Say No, *377;* Talk of the Town, The, *390;* Texas, *1155;* Yuma, *1166*
Buchanan, Ian: Cool Surface, The, *963;* Double Exposure (1993), *971;* Marilyn & Bobby: Her Final Affair, *588*
Buchanan, Jack: Band Wagon, The, *908*
Buchanan, Miles: Dangerous Game, *965*
Buchanan, Robert: That Sinking Feeling, *392*
Buchanan, Simone: Run, Rebecca, Run, *201;* Shame (1987), *114*
Buchegger, Christine: From the Lives of the Marionettes, *739*
Buchholz, Horst: Aces: Iron Eagle III, *1;* Aphrodite, *713;* Berlin Tunnel 21, *10;* Catamount Killing, The, *960;* Code Name: Emerald, *27;* Empty Canvas, The, *509;* Fanny (1961), *514;* Faraway, So Close, *736;* From Hell to Victory, *53;* One, Two, Three, *350;* Raid on Entebbe, *633;* Return to Fantasy Island, *1074;* Sahara (1984), *110;* Savage Bees, The, *882;* Tiger Bay, *683*
Buck, Frank: Africa Screams, *223*
Buckley, Betty: Baby Cakes, *453;* Frantic (1988), *978;* Rain without Thunder, *634;* Wild Thing, *702*
Buckley, Kay: Stage to Tucson, *1152*
Buckman, Tara: Xtro II, *1090*
Buckner, Susan: Deadly Blessing, *831*
Buday, Helen: For Love Alone, *519;* Mad Max Beyond Thunderdome, *1064*
Budin, Gilles: Blue Jeans, *719*
Buechler, Nancy: Thinkin' Big, *394*
Buetel, Jack: Best of the Badmen, *1097;* Half-Breed, The, *1118;* Outlaw, The, *1137*
Buff, David D.: Cop-Out, *963*
Buffalo Bill Jr.: Rainbow Valley, *1140*
Buffett, Jimmy: Doctor Duck's Super Secret All-Purpose Sauce, *266*
Bugner, Joe: Fatal Bond, *975*
Buhagiar, Valerie: Highway 61, *297*
Buick, Denise: Angel Fist, *5;* Full Contact, *53*
Bujold, Genevieve: Anne of the Thousand Days, *449;* Another Man, Another Chance, *1094;* Choose Me, *962;* Coma, *963;* Dead Ringers, *831;* Earthquake, *43;* False Identity, *975;* King of Hearts, *752;* Last Flight of Noah's Ark, *180;* Moderns, The, *335;* Monsignor, *598;* Murder by Decree, *998;* Obsession, *1002;* Oh, What a Night, *611;* Paper Wedding, *618;* Swashbuckler (1976), *123;* Tightrope, *1025;* Trojan Women, The, *688;* Trouble in Mind, *688*
Buktenica, Raymond: Adventures of Nellie Bly, The, *442*
Bull, Peter: African Queen, The, *442;* Beau Brummell (1954), *457;* Goodbye Again, *530*
Bull, Richard: Secret Life of an American Wife, The, *374*
Bullock, Burl: Bus Is Coming, The, *472*
Bullock, Sandra: Demolition Man, *1046;* Love Potion #9, *323;* Thing Called Love, The, *681;* Vanishing, The (1993), *1029;* When the Party's Over, *699;* Who Shot Pat?, *701;* Wrestling Ernest Hemingway, *707*
Bumiller, William: Death Spa, *831;* Inside Out (1992), *1058*
Bumpass, Rodger: National Lampoon's Class of '86, *342*
Bunce, Alan: Sunrise at Campobello, *673*

Bundy, Brooke: Francis Gary Powers: The True Story of the U-2 Spy Incident, *522*
Bundy, Robert: Screen Test, *374*
Bunnage, Avis: No Surrender, *345*
Bunster, Carmen: Alsino and the Condor, *712*
Buono, Victor: Arnold, *810;* Better Late than Never, *237;* Boot Hill, *1100;* Evil, The, *839;* Four for Texas, *1114;* Man from Atlantis, The, *1064;* Man with Bogart's Face, The, *995;* More Wild Wild West, *1134;* Northeast of Seoul, *92;* Robin & the Seven Hoods, *936;* Strangler, The, *1020;* What Ever Happened to Baby Jane?, *902;* Who's Minding the Mint?, *411*
Bupp, Sonny: Renegade Trail, *1142*
Burchill, Andrea: Housekeeping, *545*
Burdon, Eric: Comeback, *912*
Burfield, Kim: Hero, The, *540*
Burgess, Dorothy: Hold Your Man, *542;* In Old Arizona, *1122*
Burgess, Scott: Dead Easy, *967*
Burghoff, Gary: Casino, *476;* M*A*S*H, *324;* M*A*S*H* (TV Series), *325;* Man in the Santa Claus Suit, The, *185*
Burke, Alfred: Children of the Damned, *823;* Glory Boys, The, *56;* Night Caller from Outer Space, *1068;* One Day in the Life of Ivan Denisovich, *613*
Burke, Billie: Becky Sharp, *457;* Bill of Divorcement, A, *461;* Bride Wore Red, The, *469;* Christopher Strong, *482;* Craig's Wife, *490;* Dinner at Eight (1933), *265;* Doubting Thomas, *268;* Eternally Yours, *511;* Everybody Sing, *916;* Father of the Bride (1950), *275;* Father's Little Dividend, *275;* Finishing School, *516;* Forsaking All Others, *279;* In This Our Life, *550;* Man Who Came to Dinner, The, *328;* Navy Blue and Gold, *342;* Sergeant Rutledge, *1148;* Small Town Girl, *940;* Topper, *397;* Topper Takes a Trip, *398;* Wizard of Oz, The, *218;* Young in Heart, The, *416;* Young Philadelphians, The, *708*
Burke, Charlotte: Paperhouse, *873*
Burke, David: Adventures of Sherlock Holmes, The (Series), *950*
Burke, Delta: Bunny's Tale, A, *472;* Dynamite and Gold, *1110;* First and Ten, *277;* Seekers, The, *651*
Burke, Edmund: She Goes to War, *377*
Burke, Kathleen: Fighting Westerner, The, *1113;* Island of Lost Souls, *857;* Lives of a Bengal Lancer, The, *78;* Murders in the Zoo, *867*
Burke, Matt: Anna Christie (1922), *449*
Burke, Michelle: Coneheads, *258;* Dazed and Confused, *497*
Burke, Mildred: Below the Belt, *458*
Burke, Paul: Daddy's Gone A-Hunting, *965;* Francis in the Navy, *280;* Killing at Hell's Gate, *71;* Little Ladies of the Night, *576;* Psychic Killer, *877;* Red Light Sting, The, *636;* Thomas Crown Affair, The, *128;* Valley of the Dolls, *693*
Burke, Robert: Dust Devil, *838;* RoboCop 3, *1075;* Simple Men, *379;* Tombstone, *1157;* Unbelievable Truth, The, *691*
Burke, Sam: Five for Hell, *50*
Burke, Simon: Irishman, The, *554;* Slate, Wyn, and Me, *660*
Burkett, Laura: Daddy's Boys, *31;* Overkill, *96*
Burkholder, Scott: House IV, *852*
Burkley, Dennis: Doors, The, *914;* Four Eyes and Six Guns, *1114;* Lambada, *927;* Pass the Ammo, *355;* Stop! Or My Mom Will Shoot, *386*
Burks, Rick: Blood Diner, *815*
Burlaiev, Kolya: My Name Is Ivan, *770*
Burlinson, Tom: Flesh and Blood, *50;* Landslide, *990;* Man from Snowy River, The, *1131;* Phar Lap, *621;* Return to Snowy River, Part II, *1143;* Showdown at Williams Creek, *1149;* Time Guardian, The, *1084;* Windrider, *140*
Burner, Oscar: Tombs of the Blind Dead, *896*
Burnett, Carol: Annie, *907;* Between Friends, *459;* Carol Burnett's My Personal Best, *251;* Chu Chu and the Philly Flash, *255;* Four Seasons, The, *521;* Friendly Fire, *522;* Front Page, The (1974), *281;* Grass Is Always Greener Over the Septic Tank, The, *289;* Noises Off, *346;* Pete 'n' Tillie, *357;* Tenth Month, The, *679;* Wedding, A, *407*
Burnett, Olivia: Final Verdict, *516*
Burnette, Billy: Saturday Night Special, *111*
Burnette, Smiley: Adventures of Rex and Rinty, *1092;* Big Show, The, *1098;* Billy the Kid Returns, *1099;* Blue Montana Skies, *1099;* Boots and Saddles, *1100;* Call of the Canyon, *1103;* Colorado Sunset, *1105;* Dick Tracy (1937), *38;* Git Along, Little Dogies, *1115;* Heart of the Golden West, *1119;* Heart of the Rio Grande, *1119;* Idaho, *1122;* In Old Santa Fe, *1123;* King of the Cowboys, *1125;* Last of the Pony Riders, *1126;* Man from Music Mountain, *1131;* Man of the Frontier (Red River Valley), *1132;* Manhattan Merry-Go-Round, *930;* Melody Trail, *1133;* Mexicali Rose, *1134;* Mystery Mountain, *1135;* Oh! Susanna!, *1136;* Old Barn Dance, The, *1136;* Old Corral, *1136;* On Top of Old Smoky, *1137;* Phantom Empire (1935), *98;* Prairie Moon, *1139;* Public Cowboy #1, *1140;* Radio Ranch (Men with Steel Faces & Phantom Empire), *1140;* Ride, Ranger, Ride, *1143;* Ridin' on a Rainbow, *1144;* Rootin' Tootin' Rhythm, *1146;* Round-Up Time in Texas, *1146;* Saginaw Trail, *1147;* Silver Spurs, *1150;* South of the Border, *1151;* Springtime in the Rockies (1937), *1152;* Under Western Stars, *1160;* Undersea Kingdom, *1087;* Winning of the West, *1165;* Yodelin' Kid from Pine Ridge, *1165*
Burnette Trio, The Johnny: Rock, Rock, Rock, *937*
Burns, Bob: Call of the Canyon, *1103;* Twilight in the Sierras, *1159*
Burns, Carol: Dusty, *164*
Burns, Cathy: Last Summer, *570*
Burns, David: It's Always Fair Weather, *925;* Saint in London, The, *1012*
Burns, George: College Swing, *912;* Damsel in Distress, A, *913;* 18 Again, *270;* George Burns and Gracie Allen Show, The (TV Series), *284;* George Burns—His Wit and Wisdom, *284;* George Burns in Concert, *284;* Going in Style, *288;* Honolulu, *923;* International House, *307;* Just You and Me, Kid, *312;* Oh, God!, *349;* Oh, God! Book II, *349;* Oh, God, You Devil!, *349;* Sgt. Pepper's Lonely Hearts Club Band, *939;* Sunshine Boys, The, *388;* Two of a Kind (1982), *690*
Burns, Jere: Greedy, *290*
Burns, Marilyn: Eaten Alive, *838;* Future-Kill, *845;* Helter Skelter, *540;* Texas Chainsaw Massacre, The, *894*
Burns, Marion: Dawn Rider, *1107;* Paradise Canyon, *1138*
Burns, Mark: Death in Venice, *498;* Virgin and the Gypsy, The, *694*
Burns, Michael: Santee, *1147;* That Cold Day in the Park, *680*
Burns, Paul E.: Double Deal, *41*
Burns, Robert A.: Confessions of a Serial Killer, *825*
Burns, Ronnie: George Burns and Gracie Allen Show, The (TV Series), *284*
Burns, Stephan W.: Herbie Goes Bananas, *174*
Burns, Tim: Mad Max, *1064*
Burr, Raymond: Black Magic (1949), *462;* Bride of the Gorilla, *819;* Casanova's Big Night, *252;* Crime of Passion, *490;* Curse of King Tut's Tomb, The, *828;* Delirious, *263;* Desperate, *969;* Godzilla, King of the Monsters, *846;* Godzilla 1985, *846;* His Kind of Woman, *62;* Key to the City, *312;* Love Happy, *322;* Love's Savage Fury, *582;* Man Alone, A, *1131;* Night the City Screamed, The, *606;* Passion (1954), *97;* Pitfall, *622;* Place in the Sun, A, *622;* Rear Window, *1009;* Return, The, *1074;* Showdown at Williams Creek, *1149;* Station West, *1153;* Thunder Pass, *1157;* Tomorrow Never Comes, *686*
Burrell, Maryedith: Say Yes, *373*
Burrell, Terri: Eubie!, *916*
Burroughs, Jackie: Final Notice, *977;* Grey Fox, The, *1117;* Housekeeper, The, *853;* John and the Missus, *558;* Tales From Avonlea (TV series), *209;* Undergrads, The, *214*
Burroughs, William S.: Drugstore Cowboy, *505;* Heavy Petting, *426;* Wax, *1088*
Burrows, Darren E.: Northern Exposure (TV Series), *609*
Burstyn, Ellen: Act of Vengeance, *441;* Alex in Wonderland, *224;* Alice Doesn't Live Here Anymore, *444;* Ambassador, The, *445;* Cemetery Club, The, *478;* Dream of Passion, A, *504;* Dying Young, *506;* Exorcist, The, *839;* Grand Isle, *531;*

Hanna's War, *536;* Harry and Tonto, *537;* King of Marvin Gardens, The, *565;* People vs. Jean Harris, *620;* Providence, *630;* Resurrection, *638;* Same Time Next Year, *372;* Silence of the North, *657;* Thursday's Game, *683;* Tropic of Cancer, *688;* Twice in a Lifetime, *690*

Burszteln, David: La Belle Noiseuse, *753*

Burt, Andrew: Gulliver in Lilliput, *291*

Burt, Clarissa: NeverEnding Story II, The, *1068*

Burton, Kate: Big Trouble in Little China, *13;* Love Matters, *581*

Burton, Lee: And God Said to Cain, *1093*

Burton, LeVar: Almos' a Man, *445;* Battered, *456;* Hunter, The (1980), *65;* Jessie Owens Story, The, *557;* Midnight Hour, *864;* Roots, *644;* Roots—The Gift, *644;* Star Trek: The Next Generation (TV Series), *1079;* Supernaturals, The, *891*

Burton, Mark: Apprentice to Murder, *810*

Burton, Normann: Bloodsport, *16;* Gumball Rally, The, *58;* Scorchy, *112*

Burton, Richard: Absolution, *440;* Alexander the Great, *443;* Anne of the Thousand Days, *449;* Assassination of Trotsky, The, *451;* Becket, *457;* Bluebeard (1972), *817;* Bramble Bush, The, *468;* Breakthrough, *19;* Brief Encounter (1974), *470;* Circle of Two, *482;* Cleopatra (1963), *484;* Comedians, The, *486;* Desert Rats, The, *500;* Divorce His: Divorce Hers, *502;* Dr. Faustus, *502;* Ellis Island, *508;* Equus, *973;* Exorcist II: The Heretic, *840;* Gathering Storm, *525;* Hammersmith Is Out, *292;* Ice Palace, *548;* Klansman, The, *566;* Longest Day, The, *78;* Look Back in Anger (1958), *579;* Love Spell, *79;* Massacre in Rome, *590;* Medusa Touch, The, *864;* Night of the Iguana, The, *606;* 1984 (1984), *1068;* Raid on Rommel, *103;* Robe, The, *642;* Sandpiper, The, *648;* Spy Who Came in from the Cold, The, *664;* Taming of the Shrew, The (1966), *391;* Under Milk Wood, *691;* V.I.P.s, The, *693;* Wagner, *947;* Where Eagles Dare, *138;* Who's Afraid of Virginia Woolf?, *701;* Wild Geese, The, *139*

Burton, Robert: I Was a Teenage Frankenstein, *855;* Invasion of the Animal People, *1059;* Trilogy of Terror, *898*

Burton, Tony: Assault on Precinct 13, *7;* Inside Moves, *552;* Oceans of Fire, *93;* Rocky IV, *642*

Burton, Tony C.: Crystal Force, *827*

Burton, Wendell: Fortune and Men's Eyes, *520;* Sterile Cuckoo, The, *667*

Bus Boys, The: Eddie Murphy—Delirious, *270*

Buscemi, Steve: Airheads, *906;* Billy Bathgate, *461;* Call Me, *959;* Crisscross (1992), *491;* Ed & His Dead Mother, *270;* Heart, *537;* In the Soup, *306;* Parting Glances, *618;* Reservoir Dogs, *105;* Rising Sun, *1010;* Twenty Bucks, *401*

Busch, Ernest: Kameradschaft, *751*

Busch, Mae: Clutching Hand, The, *27;* Foolish Wives, *518;* Keystone Comedies, Vol. 4, *312;* Laurel and Hardy Classics, Volume 3, *316;* Laurel and Hardy Classics, Volume 4, *316;* Laurel and Hardy Classics, Volume 6, *316;* Laurel and Hardy Classics, Volume 9, *316;* Laurel and Hardy on the Lam, *317*

Busey, Gary: Act of Piracy, *1;* Angels Hard as They Come, *5;* Barbarosa, *1097;* Big Wednesday, *461;* Buddy Holly Story, The, *910;* Bulletproof, *21;* Canvas, *959;* Carny, *475;* Chasers, *254;* Chrome Soldiers, *26;* D.C. Cab, *261;* Dangerous Life, A, *494;* Execution of Private Slovik, The, *512;* Eye of the Tiger, *46;* Fallen Angels, *513;* Firm, The, *977;* Foolin' Around, *278;* Gumball Rally, The, *58;* Hider in the House, *982;* Hitchhiker (Series), The, *850;* Insignificance, *553;* Last American Hero, The, *75;* Lethal Weapon, *76;* Let's Get Harry, *573;* My Heroes Have Always Been Cowboys, *1135;* Neon Empire, The, *89;* Point Break, *99;* Predator 2, *1071;* Rookie of the Year, *200;* Shrieking, The, *886;* Silver Bullet, *886;* South Beach, *1019;* Star Is Born, A (1976), *666;* Straight Time, *668;* Surviving the Game, *123;* Thunderbolt and Lightfoot, *129;* Under Siege, *134*

Busfield, Timothy: Fade to Black (1993), *974;* Field of Dreams, *1050;* Revenge of the Nerds, *367;* Revenge of the Nerds II: Nerds in Paradise, *367;* Sneakers, *1018;* Strays, *891;* Striking Distance, *121*

Bush, Billy Green: Alice Doesn't Live Here Anymore, *444;* Conagher, *1105;* Culpepper Cattle Co., The, *1106;* Electra Glide in Blue, *43;* Elvis and Me, *915;* Five Easy Pieces, *517;* Jericho Mile, The, *557;* Tom Horn, *1157*

Bush, Chuck: Fandango, *274*

Bush, Jovila: Cheerleaders, *254*

Bush, Rebeccah: Hunk, *303*

Bush, Sam: High Lonesome—The Story of Bluegrass Music, *426*

Bushell, Anthony: Dark Journey, *966;* Disraeli, *502;* Quatermass and the Pit, *1072;* Vanity Fair, *693*

Bushey, Trent: American Shaolin: King of the Kickboxers II, *5*

Bushman, Francis X.: Ben-Hur (1926), *458;* Dick Tracy (1937), *38;* Last Frontier, The, *1125;* Three Musketeers, The (1933), *128;* When Lightning Strikes, *138*

Bushman, Ralph: Our Hospitality, *351*

Busia, Akosua: Color Purple, The, *485;* George McKenna Story, The, *526;* Low Blow, *79;* Native Son, *604*

Busia, Marion: Gone in 60 Seconds, *56*

Busker, Ricky: Big Shots, *238*

Buster, Budd: Arizona Days, *1094;* Call of the Canyon, *1103;* Zorro's Fighting Legion, *1166*

Butkus, Dick: Cracking Up, *260;* Deadly Games, *968;* Hamburger—The Motion Picture, *292;* Spontaneous Combustion, *889*

Butler, Calvin: Drying Up the Streets, *505*

Butler, Cindy: Boggy Creek II, *818*

Butler, Daws: Hey There, It's Yogi Bear, *174*

Butler, Dean: Desert Hearts, *499;* Kid with the 200 I.Q., The, *180;* Little House on the Prairie (TV Series), *181*

Butler, Paul: Crime Story, *30;* To Sleep with Anger, *685*

Butler, William: Inner Sanctum, *986;* Leatherface—the Texas Chainsaw Massacre III, *860*

Butler, Yancy: Hard Target, *59;* Hit List, The (1992), *982*

Butrick, Merritt: Death Spa, *831;* Head Office, *294;* Shy People, *657*

Butterworth, Charles: Cat and the Fiddle, The, *911;* Dixie Jamboree, *914;* Every Day's a Holiday, *273;* Forsaking All Others, *279;* Illicit, *549;* It Happened in New Orleans, *925;* Let Freedom Ring, *928;* Love Me Tonight, *929;* Second Chorus, *938;* Swing High, Swing Low, *390;* This Is the Army, *945*

Butterworth, Donna: Family Jewels, The, *273*

Butterworth, Peter: Carry on Doctor, *251;* Carry on Emmanuelle, *251;* Follow That Camel, *278*

Butterworth, Tyler: Consuming Passions, *259*

Buttons, Red: Alice in Wonderland (1985), *145;* Alice Through the Looking Glass (1985), *145;* C.H.O.M.P.S., *155;* 18 Again, *270;* Five Weeks in a Balloon, *50;* Gay Purr-ee, *168;* Harlow, *536;* Hatari!, *59;* Leave 'em Laughing, *572;* Movie Movie, *338;* One, Two, Three, *350;* Pete's Dragon, *195;* Poseidon Adventure, The, *99;* Sayonara, *648;* Side Show, *886;* Users, The, *692;* When Time Ran Out!, *1031;* Who Killed Mary What's 'Er Name?, *1031*

Buttram, Pat: Beyond the Purple Hills, *1097;* Blue Canadian Rockies, *1099;* Hills of Utah, The, *1120;* More Milton Berle's Mad World of Comedy, *431;* Mule Train, *1134;* Night Stage to Galveston, *1136;* Valley of Fire, *1161*

Buttrick, Merritt: Wired to Kill, *1089*

Buxton, Sarah: Welcome to Spring Break, *902*

Buy, Margherita: Station, The, *789*

Buzby, Zane: Americathon, *226;* Cracking Up, *260;* National Lampoon's Class Reunion, *342*

Buzzanca, Lando: Playing the Field, *358;* When Women Had Tails, *409;* When Women Lost Their Tails, *409*

Buzzard, Eddie: Bulldog Courage, *1102*

Buzzi, Ruth: Apple Dumpling Gang Rides Again, The, *147;* Bad Guys, *8;* Being, The, *812;* Chu Chu and the Philly Flash, *255;* Dixie Lanes, *265;* Freaky Friday, *168;* My Mom's a Werewolf, *341;* Surf 2, *389;* Up Your Alley, *403;* Wishful Thinking, *412*

Byington, Spring: Big Wheel, The, *461;* Blue Bird, The, *151;* Devil and Miss Jones, The, *264;* Dodsworth, *503;* Enchanted Cottage, The, *509;* Heaven Can Wait (1943), *295;* In the Good

Old Summertime, *925;* Jezebel, *557;* Little Women (1933), *577;* Living In A Big Way, *929;* Lucky Partners, *324;* Meet John Doe, *591;* Please Don't Eat the Daisies, *358;* Presenting Lily Mars, *626;* Stage Struck (1936), *941;* Thrill of a Romance, *945;* Walk Softly, Stranger, *1030;* Werewolf of London, *902;* When Ladies Meet, *698;* You Can't Take it with You (1938), *415*

Bykov, Rolan: Overcoat, The, *774*

Byner, John: Great Smokey Roadblock, The, *57;* Man in the Santa Claus Suit, The, *185;* Mouse and the Motorcycle, The, *189;* Transylvania 6-5000, *399*

Byrd, Ralph: Blake of Scotland Yard, *15;* Dick Tracy (1937), *38;* Dick Tracy Meets Gruesome, *38;* Dick Tracy Returns, *38;* Dick Tracy vs. Crime Inc., *38;* Dick Tracy's Dilemma, *38;* Dick Tracy's G-Men, *38;* Son of Monte Cristo, The, *118;* SOS Coast Guard, *118*

Byrd, Tom: Wet Gold, *138*

Byrd-Nethery, Miriam: Civil War Diary, *483*

Byrne, Barbara: Sunday in the Park with George, *943*

Byrne, Catherine: Eat the Peach, *270*

Byrne, David: Heavy Petting, *426;* True Stories, *400;* Two Moon July, *947*

Byrne, Debbie: Rebel (1985), *636*

Byrne, Eddie: Jack the Ripper (1959), *858*

Byrne, Gabriel: Christopher Columbus (1985), *25;* Cool World, *1043;* Dangerous Woman, A, *494;* Dark Obsession, *495;* Defense of the Realm, *969;* Gothic, *847;* Hanna K., *743;* Hello Again, *296;* Into the West, *177;* Julia and Julia, *1061;* Lionheart, *181;* Miller's Crossing, *594;* Point of No Return, *99;* Shipwrecked, *203;* Siesta, *1016;* Soldier's Tale, A, *661*

Byrne, Martha: Anna to the Infinite Power, *1036;* Eyes of the Amaryllis, *165*

Byrne, Niall: Miracle, The (1990), *595*

Byrnes, Edd: Final Defeat, The, *1113;* Go Kill and Come Back, *1115;* Mankillers, *82;* Reform School Girl, *104*

Byrnes, Jim: Dirty Work, *970;* Harmony Cats, *536*

Byrnes, Josephine: Frauds, *281*

Byron, Bruce: Kenneth Anger—Volume Three, *563*

Byron, David: Based on an Untrue Story, *232;* Fade to Black (1993), *974*

Byron, Jeffrey: Dungeonmaster, The, *1048;* Metalstorm: The Destruction of Jared-Syn, *1065;* Seniors, The, *375*

Byron, Kathleen: Gambler and the Lady, The, *524*

Byron, Marion: Steamboat Bill Jr., *386*

Byrska, Irene: Man of Iron, *765*

Byun, Susan: Sgt. Kabukiman N.Y.P.D., *114*

Caan, James: Alien Nation, *1035;* Another Man, Another Chance, *1094;* Bolero (1982), *720;* Brian's Song, *469;* Bridge Too Far, A, *19;* Chapter Two, *479;* Cinderella Liberty, *482;* Comes a Horseman, *1105;* Countdown, *489;* Dark Backward, The, *262;* Dick Tracy (1990), *38;* Don Rickles: Buy This Tape You Hockey Puck, *267;* El Dorado, *1111;* Flesh and Bone, *518;* For the Boys, *918;* Freebie and the Bean, *281;* Funny Lady, *918;* Gambler, The (1974), *524;* Gardens of Stone, *525;* Godfather, The, *529;* Godfather Epic, The, *529;* Gone with the West, *1116;* Harry and Walter Go to New York, *294;* Hide in Plain Sight, *541;* Honeymoon in Vegas, *300;* Killer Elite, The, *71;* Kiss Me Goodbye, *313;* Lady in a Cage, *989;* Little Moon & Jud McGraw, *1128;* Misery, *865;* Program, The, *629;* Rabbit Run, *632;* Rain People, The, *634;* Red Line 7000, *104;* Rollerball, *1075;* Silent Movie, *379;* Slither, *381;* Thief (1981), *127*

Cabot, Bruce: Angel and the Badman, *1093;* Ann Vickers, *448;* Best of the Badmen, *1097;* Big Jake, *1098;* Captain Caution, *23;* Chisum, *1104;* Comancheros, The, *1105;* Diamonds Are Forever, *38;* Dodge City, *1109;* Fancy Pants, *274;* Finishing School, *516;* Fury, *524;* Goliath and the Barbarians, *56;* Green Berets, The, *57;* Hellfighters, *60;* King Kong (1933), *859;* Last of the Mohicans, The (1936), *1126;* McLintock!, *1133;* Show Them No Mercy, *657;* Silver Queen, *1150;* Sinners in Paradise, *659;* Smashing the Rackets, *1018;* Sorrowful Jones, *383;* Sundown (1941), *673;* Undefeated, The, *1160*

Cabot, Sebastian: Family Jewels, The, *273;* Ivanhoe (1952), *68;* Johnny Tremain, *179;* Omar Khayyam, *93;* Seven Thieves, *653;* Time Machine, The, *1084;* Twice-Told Tales, *898;* Westward Ho, the Wagons, *216*

Cabot, Susan: Carnival Rock, *911;* Machine-Gun Kelly, *80;* Saga of the Viking Women and their Voyage to the Waters of the Great Sea Serpent, The, *110;* Son of Ali Baba, *118;* Sorority Girl, *118;* Wasp Woman, *901*

Cadeau, Lally: Tales From Avonlea (TV series), *209*

Cadenat, Garry: Sugarcane Alley, *791*

Cadillacs, The: Go, Johnny, Go!, *920*

Cadorette, Mary: Stewardess School, *386*

Caesar, Adolph: Club Paradise, *256;* Color Purple, The, *485;* Fortune Dane, *52;* Soldier's Story, A, *1018*

Caesar, Shirley: Gospel, *425*

Caesar, Sid: Airport 1975, *443;* Alice in Wonderland (1985), *145;* Barnaby and Me, *232;* Best of Comic Relief, The, *235;* Cannon Movie Tales: The Emperor's New Clothes, *155;* Cheap Detective, The, *254;* Fiendish Plot of Dr. Fu Manchu, The, *276;* Grease, *920;* Guide for the Married Man, A, *291;* It's a Mad Mad Mad Mad World, *308;* Munsters' Revenge, The, *338;* Over the Brooklyn Bridge, *352;* Silent Movie, *379;* Stoogemania, *386;* 10 from Your Show of Shows, *392*

Caffaro, Cheri: Place Called Today, A, *622*

Caffrey, Stephen: Tour of Duty, *131*

Cage, Nicolas: Amos & Andrew, *226;* Birdy, *462;* Boy in Blue, The, *467;* Deadfall, *968;* Fire Birds, *49;* Guarding Tess, *291;* Honeymoon in Vegas, *300;* Industrial Symphony No. 1 The Dream of the Broken Hearted, *925;* Moonstruck, *336;* Peggy Sue Got Married, *355;* Racing with the Moon, *633;* Raising Arizona, *364;* Red Rock West, *1009;* Time to Kill, *684;* Valley Girl, *404;* Vampire's Kiss, *900;* Wild at Heart, *702;* Zandalee, *709*

Cagen, Andrea: Hot Box, The, *64*

Cagney, James: American Film Institute Life Achievement Awards, The, *418;* Angels with Dirty Faces, *5;* Blonde Crazy, *241;* Blood on the Sun, *15;* Boy Meets Girl, *244;* Bride Came C.O.D., The, *245;* Captains of the Clouds, *23;* Ceiling Zero, *24;* City for Conquest, *482;* Devil Dogs of the Air, *37;* Each Dawn I Die, *42;* Fighting 69th, The, *48;* Footlight Parade, *917;* G-Men, *54;* Gallant Hours, The, *524;* Great Guy, *532;* Hollywood Outtakes, *299;* Johnny Come Lately, *311;* Kiss Tomorrow Goodbye, *73;* Lady Killer, *74;* Lion in the Streets, A, *575;* Love Me or Leave Me, *929;* Man of a Thousand Faces, *587;* Midsummer Night's Dream, A (1935), *1066;* Mr. Roberts, *334;* Never Steal Anything Small, *932;* Oklahoma Kid, The, *1136;* One, Two, Three, *350;* Public Enemy, *101;* Ragtime, *633;* Roaring Twenties, The, *107;* Seven Little Foys, The, *376;* Shake Hands with the Devil, *114;* Something to Sing About, *940;* Strawberry Blonde, The, *670;* 13 Rue Madeleine, *127;* Time of Your Life, The, *684;* Tribute to a Bad Man, *1159;* West Point Story, The, *947;* What Price Glory, *408;* White Heat, *138;* Yankee Doodle Dandy, *948*

Cagney, Jeanne: Kentucky Rifle, *1124;* Lion in the Streets, A, *575;* Man of a Thousand Faces, *587;* Time of Your Life, The, *684;* Yankee Doodle Dandy, *948*

Cagney, William: Palooka, *617*

Caine, Michael: Alfie, *224;* Ashanti, *7;* Battle of Britain, *9;* Beyond the Limit, *460;* Beyond the Poseidon Adventure, *11;* Black Windmill, The, *956;* Blame It on Rio, *240;* Blue Ice, *957;* Bridge Too Far, A, *19;* Bullseye, *247;* Deathtrap, *969;* Destructors, The, *970;* Dirty Rotten Scoundrels, *265;* Don Rickles: Buy This Tape You Hockey Puck, *267;* Dressed to Kill (1980), *972;* Eagle Has Landed, The, *42;* Educating Rita, *270;* Fourth Protocol, The, *978;* Funeral in Berlin, *979;* Gambit, *283;* Half-Moon Street, *981;* Hand, The, *848;* Hannah and Her Sisters, *293;* Harry and Walter Go to New York, *294;* Holcroft Covenant, The, *982;* Ipcress File, The, *986;* Island, The, *857;* Italian Job, The, *308;* Jaws: The Revenge, *858;* Jigsaw Man, The, *987;* Last Valley, The, *75;* Man Who Would Be King, The, *81;* Mr. Destiny, *334;* Mona Lisa, *997;* Muppet Christmas Carol, The, *189;* Noises Off, *346;* On Deadly Ground, *93;* Pulp, *363;* Romantic Englishwoman, The, *643;* Shock to the

System, A, *1015;* Silver Bears, *379;* Sleuth, *1017;* Surrender, *389;* Swarm, The, *891;* Sweet Liberty, *389;* Too Late the Hero, *131;* Victory, *135;* Water, *406;* Whistle Blower, The, *1031;* Wilby Conspiracy, The, *701;* Without a Clue, *413;* Woman Times Seven, *705;* Wrong Box, The, *414;* X, Y and Zee, *707;* Zulu, *142*

Caire, Audrey: They Saved Hitler's Brain, *895*

Calabro, Thomas: Lady Killers, *990*

Calamai, Clara: Ossessione, *774*

Calder-Marshall, Anna: King Lear (1984), *564;* Wuthering Heights (1971), *707*

Calderon, Paul: Bad Lieutenant, *454*

Caldwell, Janette Allyson: Mandroid, *1065;* Night Screams, *870*

Caldwell, Zoe: Lantern Hill, *180*

Cale, John: Velvet Underground, The: Velvet Redux—Live MCMXCIII, *437*

Calegory, Jade: Mac and Me, *1064*

Calfa, Don: Bank Shot, *232;* Blue Movies, *242;* Chopper Chicks in Zombietown, *823;* Greaser's Palace, *532;* Me, Myself & I, *330;* Return of the Living Dead, The, *880*

Calfan, Nicole: Permission to Kill, *98*

Calhern, Louis: Annie Get Your Gun, *907;* Arch of Triumph, *450;* Asphalt Jungle, The, *953;* Athena, *907;* Betrayed (1954), *11;* Blonde Crazy, *241;* Bridge of San Luis Rey, The, *469;* Count of Monte Cristo, The (1934), *30;* Diplomaniacs, *914;* Duck Soup, *269;* Executive Suite, *512;* Forever Darling, *279;* Heaven Can Wait (1943), *295;* Julius Caesar (1953), *561;* Last Days of Pompeii, The (1935), *569;* Latin Lovers, *928;* Life of Emile Zola, The, *574;* Life of Her Own, A, *574;* Magnificent Yankee, The, *585;* Men of the Fighting Lady, *84;* Nancy Goes to Rio, *932;* Night after Night, *344;* Notorious, *1002;* Prisoner of Zenda, The (1952), *100;* Prodigal, The, *629;* Red Pony, The, *198;* Rhapsody, *639;* Student Prince, The, *942;* Sweet Adeline, *943;* They Call It Sin, *680;* Two Weeks with Love, *947;* We're Not Married, *408;* World Gone Mad, The, *707*

Calhoun, Rory: Avenging Angel, *8;* Bad Jim, *1095;* Blue and the Gray, The, *1099;* Dayton's Devils, *33;* Finger on the Trigger, *1113;* Flatbed Annie and Sweetie Pie: Lady Truckers, *50;* Hell Comes to Frogtown, *1056;* How to Marry a Millionaire, *303;* Mission to Glory, *596;* Motel Hell, *866;* Pure Country, *630;* Red House, The, *1009;* River of No Return, *1145;* Treasure of Pancho Villa, The, *1158*

Call, Brandon: Blind Fury, *15*

Call, John: Santa Claus Conquers the Martians, *1076*

Callahan, James: Outlaw Blues, *352;* Tropic of Cancer, *688*

Callan, K.: Unborn, The, *898*

Callan, Michael: Bon Voyage!, *151;* Cat and the Canary, The (1978), *960;* Cat Ballou, *1103;* Donner Pass: The Road to Survival, *1109;* Double Exposure (1982), *971;* Frasier the Lovable Lion (Frasier the Sensuous Lion), *168;* Freeway, *52;* Gidget Goes Hawaiian, *286;* Interns, The, *553;* Lepke, *76;* Mysterious Island, *1067;* Tom Edison—The Boy Who Lit Up the World, *213*

Callard, Rebecca: Borrowers, The, *152*

Callas, Maria: Medea, *766*

Calleia, Joseph: After the Thin Man, *951;* Branded, *1101;* Five Came Back, *517;* Four Faces West, *1114;* Gilda, *527;* Jungle Book (1942), *179;* Littlest Outlaw, The, *184;* My Little Chickadee, *340;* Noose Hangs High, The, *346;* RiffRaff (1936), *640;* Sundown (1941), *673;* Treasure of Pancho Villa, The, *1158*

Callen, John: Rainbow Warrior, *1008*

Callow, Simon: Crucifer of Blood, *964;* Four Weddings and a Funeral, *280;* Good Father, The, *530;* Manifesto, *328;* Mr. and Mrs. Bridge, *596;* Room with a View, A, *644*

Calloway, Cab: International House, *307;* Manhattan Merry-Go-Round, *930;* Sensations of 1945, *938;* Stormy Weather, *942*

Caltett, Walter: Look For The Silver Lining, *929*

Calthrop, Donald: Blackmail (1929), *956;* Number 17, *1002;* Scrooge (1935), *650*

Calton, Darren: Montana, *599*

Calvert, Bill: Bodywaves, *243*

Calvert, Phyllis: Man in Grey, The, *587*

Calvert, Steve: Bride and the Beast, The, *19*

Calvet, Corinne: Dr. Heckyl and Mr. Hype, *266;* Far Country, The, *1112;* She's Dressed to Kill, *656;* What Price Glory, *408*

Calvin, Henry: Sign of Zorro, The, *204;* Toby Tyler, *212*

Calvin, John: Foolin' Around, *278;* Ghost Warrior, *55;* Primary Target, *627*

Calvo, Armando: Witch's Mirror, The, *904*

Calvo, Pepe: Twice a Judas, *1159*

Camara, Gloria: Kashmiri Run, The, *70*

Camardiel, Roberto: Adios, Hombre, *1092;* Badlands Drifter, *1096;* Guns for Dollars, *1117;* Machine Gun Killers, *1130*

Cambridge, Godfrey: Friday Foster, *53;* President's Analyst, The, *360;* Purlie Victorious, *363;* Son of Blob (Beware! The Blob), *888;* Watermelon Man, *406*

Cameron, Dean: Men at Work, *592;* Miracle Beach, *332;* Rockula, *937;* Ski School, *380*

Cameron, Jane: Unborn, The, *898*

Cameron, Kirk: Like Father, Like Son, *318;* Listen to Me, *576*

Cameron, Marjorie: Kenneth Anger—Volume Two, *562*

Cameron, Nadia: Merlin, *1065*

Cameron, Rod: Brimstone, *1101;* Evel Knievel, *45;* Fort Osage, *1114;* G-Men vs. The Black Dragon, *54;* Manhunt in the African Jungle (Secret Service in Darkest Africa), *81;* Mrs. Parkington, *598;* Ride the Man Down, *1143;* Salome, Where She Danced, *647;* Short Grass, *1149;* Stage to Tucson, *1152;* Stampede, *1152*

Cameron, Trent: Kid Who Loved Christmas, The, *180*

Cameron-Glickenhaus, Jesse: Slaughter of the Innocents, *1017*

Camilleri, Terry: Cars That Eat People (The Cars That Ate Paris), *821*

Cammell, Donald: Kenneth Anger—Volume Four, *563*

Camp, Colleen: Backfield in Motion, *230;* Cloud Dancer, *27;* Deadly Games, *968;* Doin' Time, *266;* Game of Death, *54;* Greedy, *290;* Illegally Yours, *548;* Police Academy II: Their First Assignment, *359;* Rosebud Beach Hotel, The, *370;* Screwball Academy, *374;* Seducers, The, *651;* Sliver, *1018;* Smile, *381;* Track 29, *1026;* Valley Girl, *404;* Wayne's World, *406*

Camp, Hamilton: Arena, *1036;* Casey at the Bat, *156;* It Came Upon a Midnight Clear, *177;* Rosebud Beach Hotel, The, *370*

Campa, Jo: Beretta's Island, *10*

Campanella, Frank: Chesty Anderson, U.S. Navy (a.k.a. Anderson's Angels), *25;* Free Ride, *281*

Campanella, Joseph: Body Chemistry, *957;* Club Fed, *256;* Down the Drain, *41;* Game, The, *54;* Hangar 18, *1055;* Hit Lady, *63;* Last Call, *568;* No Retreat, No Surrender 3: Blood Brothers, *92;* Return to Fantasy Island, *1074;* St. Valentine's Day Massacre, The, *111;* Sky Heist, *117;* Steele Justice, *120;* Terror on the 40th Floor, *1023*

Campbell, Beatrice: Last Holiday, *569;* Master of Ballantrae, The, *83*

Campbell, Bill: Checkered Flag, *480;* Crime Story, *30;* Rocketeer, The, *108*

Campbell, Bruce: Army of Darkness, *810;* Crimewave, *260;* Evil Dead, The, *839;* Evil Dead 2, *839;* Hudsucker Proxy, The, *303;* Lunatics: A Love Story, *324;* Maniac Cop, *862;* Maniac Cop 2, *863;* Mindwarp, *1066;* Moon Trap, *1067;* Sundown (1990), *891;* Waxwork II: Lost in Time, *902*

Campbell, Cheryl: Greystoke: The Legend of Tarzan, Lord of the Apes, *58;* Seven Dials Mystery, The, *1013;* Shooting Party, The, *656*

Campbell, Colin: Leather Boys, The, *572*

Campbell, Douglas: If You Could See What I Hear, *548;* Oedipus Rex (1957), *610*

Campbell, Elizabeth: Rock 'n' Roll Wrestling Women vs. the Aztec Ape, *108*
Campbell, Eric: Charlie Chaplin Carnival, *253;* Charlie Chaplin Cavalcade, *253;* Charlie Chaplin Festival, *253;* Charlie Chaplin—The Early Years, Vol. 1, *253;* Charlie Chaplin—The Early Years, Vol. 2, *253;* Charlie Chaplin—The Early Years, Vol. 3, *254;* Charlie Chaplin—The Early Years, Vol. 4, *254*
Campbell, Glen: True Grit, *1159;* Uphill All the Way, *404*
Campbell, Graeme: And Then You Die, *5*
Campbell, Jo-Ann: Go, Johnny, Go!, *920*
Campbell, Judy: Convoy (1940), *488*
Campbell, Julia: Livin' Large, *320;* Lone Justice, *1129;* Opportunity Knocks, *351*
Campbell, Juston: Star Crystal, *1078*
Campbell, Kate: Come on Tarzan, *1105*
Campbell, Louise: Bulldog Drummond Comes Back, *20;* Bulldog Drummond's Peril, *20;* Bulldog Drummond's Revenge, *21*
Campbell, Mrs. Patrick: Crime and Punishment (1935), *490;* Riptide, *640*
Campbell, Nicholas: Big Slice, The, *12;* Certain Fury, *24;* Dirty Tricks, *265;* Knights of the City, *927;* Rampage, *1009;* Shades of Love: Champagne for Two, *653;* Terminal Choice, *893*
Campbell, Paul: Lunatic, The, *324*
Campbell, Peggy: When a Man Sees Red, *1163*
Campbell, Stuart: Gallagher's Travels, *54*
Campbell, Tisha: House Party 2, *923;* Rags to Riches, *364;* School Daze, *373*
Campbell, Torquil: Golden Seal, The, *170*
Campbell, William: Battle Circus, *456;* Dementia 13, *832;* Escape from Fort Bravo, *1111;* Operation Pacific, *614;* Running Wild (1955), *645;* Small Town Girl, *940*
Campeau, Frank: Man from Painted Post, The, *327*
Campell, Bill: Bram Stoker's Dracula, *819*
Campion, Cris: Beyond Therapy, *237;* Field of Honor (1988), *736;* Pirates, *358*
Campisi, Tony: Home of our Own, A, *542*
Campo, Wally: Hell Squad (1958), *60*
Campos, Rafael: Astro-Zombies, *810;* Where the Buffalo Roam, *409*
Canada, Robert: Danger Zone, The, *32*
Canale, Gianna Maria: Devil's Commandment, The, *834;* Goliath and the Vampires, *847*
Canalito, Lee: Paradise Alley, *618*
Canary, David: Posse (1975), *1139*
Candy, John: Armed and Dangerous, *228;* Best of John Candy, The, *236;* Big City Comedy, *238;* Blues Brothers, The, *242;* Brewster's Millions (1985), *245;* Career Opportunities, *251;* Clown Murders, The, *962;* Cool Runnings, *259;* Delirious, *263;* Find the Lady, *277;* Going Berserk, *287;* Good Idea, *288;* Great Outdoors, The, *290;* Home Alone, *299;* It Came from Hollywood, *307;* JFK, *558;* Last Polka, The, *315;* Little Shop of Horrors (1986), *929;* National Lampoon's Vacation, *342;* 1941, *345;* Nothing But Trouble (1991), *347;* Once Upon a Crime, *349;* Only the Lonely, *350;* Planes, Trains and Automobiles, *358;* Really Weird Tales, *365;* Second City Comedy Show, The, *374;* Sesame Street Presents Follow That Bird, *203;* Silent Partner, The, *1016;* Spaceballs, *384;* Speed Zone, *119;* Splash, *384;* Stripes, *387;* Summer Rental, *388;* Uncle Buck, *402;* Volunteers, *405;* Who's Harry Crumb?, *411*
Cane, Charles: Dead Reckoning (1947), *34*
Cann, Sheila: Mark of the Beast, The, *863*
Canning, James: Boys in Company C, The, *18*
Cannon, Dyan: Anderson Tapes, The, *952;* Author! Author!, *230;* Based on an Untrue Story, *232;* Bob & Carol & Ted & Alice, *243;* Caddyshack II, *249;* Christmas in Connecticut (1992), *255;* Coast to Coast, *256;* Deathtrap, *969;* Doctors' Wives, *503;* End of Innocence, The, *509;* Having It All, *294;* Heaven Can Wait (1978), *295;* Honeysuckle Rose, *923;* Jenny's War, *68;* Lady of the House, *568;* Last of Sheila, The, *991;* Love Machine, The, *581;* Merlin & the Sword, *1065;* Pickle, The, *357;* Revenge of the Pink Panther, The, *367;* Rise and Fall of Legs Diamond, The, *107;* Shamus, *1014*
Cannon, J. D.: Adventures of Nellie Bly, The, *442;* Cool Hand Luke, *29;* Death Wish II, *36;* Ike: The War Years, *548;* Lawman, *1127;* Pleasure Palace, *623;* Raise the Titanic, *103*
Cannon, Katherine: Will, G. Gordon Liddy, *703*
Canova, Diana: First Nudie Musical, The, *917*
Canova, Judy: Adventures of Huckleberry Finn, The (1960), *144;* Oklahoma Annie, *349*
Canovas, Anne: Revenge of the Dead, *881*
Cantafora, Antonio: Gabriela, *739*
Cantinflas: Around the World in 80 Days (1956), *228*
Cantor, Eddie: Glorifying the American Girl, *919;* Hollywood Canteen, *923;* If You Knew Susie, *924;* Kid Millions, *926;* Roman Scandals, *937;* Show Business, *939;* Thank Your Lucky Stars, *944;* Whoopee, *947*
Canutt, Yakima: Blue Steel (1934), *1099;* Branded a Coward, *1101;* Clutching Hand, The, *27;* Cyclone in the Saddle, *1107;* Dawn Rider, *1107;* Devil Horse, The, *1109;* Heart of the Rockies, *1119;* King of the Pecos, *1125;* Last Frontier, The, *1125;* Lonely Trail, The, *1129;* Man from Utah, The, *1132;* 'Neath Arizona Skies, *1135;* Painted Stallion, The, *1138;* Paradise Canyon, *1138;* Randy Rides Alone, *1141;* Ranger and the Lady, The, *1141;* Riders of the Rockies, *1144;* Riders of the Whistling Skull, *1144;* Sagebrush Trail, *1147;* Shadow of the Eagle, *[illegible];* Showdown, The (1950), *1149;* Star Packer, The, *1153;* Telegraph Trail, The, *1154;* Texas Terror, *1156;* Trouble in Texas, *1159;* Vigilantes Are Coming!, *1161;* West of the Divide, *1163;* Westward Ho, *1163;* Winds of the Wasteland, *1165;* Wyoming Outlaw, *1165*
Capaldi, Peter: John & Yoko: A Love Story, *559;* Lair of the White Worm, *859;* Prime Suspect 3, *1008*
Capanna, Omero: Animal Called Man, An, *1093*
Capelja, Jad: Puberty Blues, *630*
Capers, Hedge: Legend of Hillbilly John, The, *181*
Capers, Virginia: North Avenue Irregulars, The, *191;* Off the Mark, *348;* White Mama, *700*
Capobianco, Carmine: Galactic Gigolo, *282;* Psychos in Love, *877*
Capolicchio, Lino: Garden of the Finzi-Continis, The, *740*
Capotoro, Carl: Mac, *583*
Capra, Francis: Bronx Tale, A, *470*
Capri, Ahna: Brotherhood of Satan, *819;* Enter the Dragon, *44;* Payday, *620*
Capri, Alaina: Good Morning...and Goodbye!, *530*
Caprio, Antonio: Overkill, *96*
Capshaw, Kate: Best Defense, *234;* Black Rain (1989), *14;* Code Name: Dancer, *27;* Dreamscape, *1048;* Indiana Jones and the Temple of Doom, *1058;* Little Sex, A, *319;* Love at Large, *322;* My Heroes Have Always Been Cowboys, *1135;* Power (1986), *625;* Private Affairs, *361;* Quick and the Dead, The, *1140;* SpaceCamp, *1078;* Windy City, *703*
Capucine: Aphrodite, *713;* Con Artists, The, *487;* Fellini Satyricon, *736;* From Hell to Victory, *53;* Honey Pot, The, *300;* North to Alaska, *1136;* Pink Panther, The, *357;* Red Sun, *1142;* Scandalous (1988), *1012;* Song without End, *940;* Trail of the Pink Panther, The, *398;* Walk on the Wild Side, *695;* What's New, Pussycat?, *408*
Cara, Irene: Aaron Loves Angela, *440;* Busted Up, *472;* Certain Fury, *24;* City Heat, *255;* Fame, *916;* For Us the Living: The Medgar Evers Story, *519;* Killing 'Em Softly, *563;* Sparkle, *941*
Carafotes, Paul: Journey to the Center of the Earth (1987), *1060*
Carberry, Joseph: 10 Million Dollar Getaway, The, *678*
Carbone, Anthony: Bucket of Blood, A, *820;* Creature from the Haunted Sea, The, *1043;* Pit and the Pendulum, The (1961), *875*
Cardella, Richard: Crater Lake Monster, The, *825*
Cardenas, Elsa: Brave One, The, *152;* Fun in Acapulco, *918*
Cardille, Lori: Day of the Dead, *830*
Cardin, Ann: Buried Alive (1984), *820*

Cardinal, Tantoo: Lightning Incident, The, *860;* Loyalties, *582*

Cardinale, Claudia: Battle of Austerlitz, The, *9;* Big Deal on Madonna Street, *717;* Burden of Dreams, *420;* Cartouche, *722;* Circus World, *482;* Conversation Piece, *726;* Corleone, *29;* 8½, *733;* Escape to Athena, *45;* Fitzcarraldo, *737;* Gift, The, *740;* Henry IV, *743;* Immortal Bachelor, The, *747;* Legend of Frenchie King, The, *1128;* Leopard, The, *572;* Lost Command, *79;* Man in Love, A, *587;* Next Summer, *771;* Once Upon a Time in the West, *1137;* One Russian Summer, *613;* Pink Panther, The, *357;* Princess Daisy, *627;* Professionals, The, *101;* Red Tent, The, *637;* Rocco & His Brothers, *782;* Salamander, The, *111;* Son of the Pink Panther, *383*

Cardona, Annette: Latino, *571*

Careil, Lianella: Bicycle Thief, The, *717*

Carette, Bruno: May Fools, *766*

Carette, Julien: Grand Illusion, *742;* La Bête Humaine, *753;* La Marseillaise, *754;* Sylvia and the Phantom, *792*

Carey, Harry: Air Force, *3;* Angel and the Badman, *1093;* Beyond Tomorrow, *1039;* Buffalo Stampede, *1102;* Devil Horse, The, *1109;* Duel in the Sun, *1110;* Great Moment, The, *290;* Kid Galahad (1937), *563;* Last of the Mohicans (1932), *1126;* Last Outlaw, The (1936), *1126;* Law and Order, *1127;* Law West of Tombstone, *1127;* Man of the Forest, *1132;* Powdersmoke Range, *1139;* Red River, *1141;* Sea of Grass, The, *1148;* So Dear to My Heart, *205;* Spoilers, The, *1152;* Straight Shooting, *1153;* Sundown (1941), *673;* They Knew What They Wanted, *681*

Carey Jr., Harry: Billy the Kid vs. Dracula, *813;* Breaking In, *245;* Challenge to White Fang, *24;* Cherry 2000, *1041;* Copper Canyon, *1106;* Crossroads, *912;* Gundown at Sandoval, *1117;* Island in the Sky, *554;* Pursued, *1140;* Red River, *1141;* Rio Grande, *1145;* Searchers, The, *1148;* Shadow Riders, The, *1148;* She Wore a Yellow Ribbon, *1148;* Take a Hard Ride, *1154;* Texas John Slaughter: Stampede at Bitter Creek, *1155;* Texas John Slaughter: Wild Times, *1156;* Three Godfathers, The, *1156;* Tombstone, *1157;* Trinity Is Still My Name, *1159;* Uforia, *402;* Undefeated, The, *1160;* Wagonmaster, *1162;* Whales of August, The, *698;* Wild Times, *1164*

Carey, Joyce: Brief Encounter (1945), *470;* Cry, the Beloved Country, *492*

Carey, Macdonald: Access Code, *1;* Copper Canyon, *1106;* End of the World, *1049;* Great Missouri Raid, The, *1116;* Let's Make It Legal, *318;* Shadow of a Doubt, *1014;* Summer of Fear, *891;* Tammy and the Doctor, *677;* Wake Island, *136;* Who Is the Black Dahlia?, *1031*

Carey, Michele: El Dorado, *1111;* In the Shadow of Kilimanjaro, *855;* Live a Little, Love a Little, *929;* Scandalous John, *202*

Carey, Olive: On Dangerous Ground, *1003*

Carey, Pauline: Urinal, *692*

Carey, Philip: Calamity Jane (1953), *910;* Fighting Mad, *516;* Gun Fury, *1117;* Operation Pacific, *614;* Time Travelers, The, *1084;* Tonka, *213*

Carey, Ron: Fatso, *275;* High Anxiety, *297;* Silent Movie, *379;* Who Killed Mary What's 'Er Name?, *1031*

Carey, Timothy: Finger Man, *48;* Head (1968), *922;* Killing, The, *988;* Killing of a Chinese Bookie, *564;* Paths of Glory, *619;* Poor White Trash, *624*

Cargol, Jean-Pierre: Wild Child, The (L'Enfant Sauvage), *804*

Carhart, Timothy: Beverly Hills Cop 3, *11;* Quicksand: No Escape, *1008;* Red Rock West, *1009*

Carides, Gia: Backlash, *8*

Carides, Zoe: Stones of Death, *890*

Carillo, Leo: Cisco Kid (TV Series), *1105*

Cariou, Len: Drying Up the Streets, *505;* Four Seasons, The, *521;* Kurt Vonnegut's Monkey House, *1061;* Lady in White, *990*

Carlin, Deborah: Fraternity Demon, *280*

Carlin, George: Best of Comic Relief, The, *235;* Bill and Ted's Bogus Journey, *239;* Bill and Ted's Excellent Adventure, *239;* Carlin at Carnegie, *251;* Carlin on Campus, *251;* George Carlin: Doin' It Again, *284;* George Carlin: Jammin' in New York, *284;* George Carlin Live! What Am I Doing in New Jersey?, *284;* George Carlin—Playin' with Your Head, *284;* Outrageous Fortune, *352;* Prince of Tides, The, *627;* Saturday Night Live, *372*

Carlin, Leka: Night Stalker, The (1986), *870*

Carlin, Lynn: Baxter, *456;* Deathdream, *832;* Tick ... Tick ... Tick ..., *129;* Wild Rovers, The, *1164*

Carlisle, Anne: Liquid Sky, *1063;* Perfect Strangers, *1005*

Carlisle, Kitty: Murder at the Vanities, *931;* Night at the Opera, A, *344*

Carlisle, Mary: Beware of Spooks, *237;* Dead Men Walk, *830;* Kentucky Kernels, *312;* One Frightened Night, *1003;* Palooka, *617*

Carlson, June: Delinquent Daughters, *499*

Carlson, Karen: Brotherly Love, *819;* Dangerous Company, *494;* Fleshburn, *841;* In Love with an Older Woman, *550;* Octagon, The, *93;* Student Nurses, The, *671;* Teen Vamp, *392*

Carlson, Moose: Can I Do It 'Til I Need Glasses?, *249*

Carlson, Richard: Beyond Tomorrow, *1039;* Creature from the Black Lagoon, *826;* Flat Top, *50;* Ghost Breakers, *285;* Hold That Ghost, *298;* Howards of Virginia, The, *545;* It Came from Outer Space, *1060;* Last Command, The (1955), *1125;* Little Foxes, The, *576;* Presenting Lily Mars, *626;* Retreat Hell, *105;* Too Many Girls, *946;* Try and Get Me, *133;* Valley of Gwangi, *1087;* White Cargo, *699*

Carlson, Veronica: Dracula Has Risen from the Grave, *837;* Horror of Frankenstein, *851*

Carlton, Hope Marie: Hard Ticket to Hawaii, *59;* Savage Beach, *111*

Carlucci, Milly: Adventures of Hercules, The, *1034*

Carlyle, David: Cherokee Strip, *1104*

Carlyle, Robert: Riff-Raff (1992), *640*

Carmel, Roger C.: Hardly Working, *293;* Thunder and Lightning, *129*

Carmen, Jean: Arizona Gunfighter, *1094*

Carmen, Jewel: American Aristocracy, An, *226*

Carmen, Julie: Can You Hear the Laughter? The Story of Freddie Prinze, *474;* Deadly Currents, *34;* Fright Night II, *844;* Gloria, *56;* Kiss Me a Killer, *989;* Last Plane Out, *75;* Milagro Beanfield War, The, *594;* Neon Empire, The, *89;* Paint It Black, *97;* Penitent, The, *620*

Carmet, Jean: Black and White in Color, *718;* Buffet Froid (Cold Cuts), *720;* Dog Day, *40;* Investigation, *748;* Little Theatre of Jean Renoir, The, *760;* Secret Obsessions, *651;* Sorceress, The (1988), *788*

Carmichael, Hoagy: Johnny Angel, *69;* Las Vegas Story, The, *568;* Young Man with a Horn, *948*

Carmichael, Ian: Betrayed (1954), *11;* Brothers In Law, *246;* Colditz Story, The, *485;* Dark Obsession, *495;* I'm All Right Jack, *305;* Lady Vanishes, The (1979), *990;* Lucky Jim, *324*

Carminati, Tullio: London Melody, *577*

Carmine, Michael: Band of the Hand, *9*

Carne, Judy: Americanization of Emily, The, *226;* Only with Married Men, *350*

Carnera, Primo: Hercules Unchained, *1056*

Carney, Alan: Zombies on Broadway, *416*

Carney, Art: Bitter Harvest (1981), *462;* Blue Yonder, The, *151;* Defiance, *36;* Emperor's New Clothes, The (1984), *164;* Going in Style, *288;* Guide for the Married Man, A, *291;* Harry and Tonto, *537;* Honeymooners, The (TV Series), *300;* Honeymooners, The: Lost Episodes (TV Series), *300;* House Calls, *302;* Izzy & Moe, *309;* Jackie Gleason's Honeybloopers, *309;* Katherine, *562;* Last Action Hero, The, *1062;* Late Show, The, *991;* Miracle of the Heart, *595;* Movie Movie, *338;* Muppets Take Manhattan, The, *189;* Naked Face, The, *1000;* Night Friend, *90;* Night They Saved Christmas, The, *191;* St. Helens, *646;* Steel, *120;* Sunburn, *1021;* Take This Job and Shove It, *390;* Undergrads, The, *214*

Carnovsky, Morris: Cornered, 29; Dead Reckoning (1947), 34; Edge of Darkness (1943), 43; Gambler, The (1974), 524; Gun Crazy (1950), 981

Carol, Cindy: Dear Brigitte, 263; Gidget Goes to Rome, 286

Carol, Linda: Carnal Crimes, 959; Reform School Girls, 105

Carol, Martine: Lola Montes, 761; Nana, 770

Carol, Sue: Check and Double Check, 254

Caron, Glenn Gordon: Wilder Napalm, 411

Caron, Leslie: American in Paris, An, 906; Battle of Austerlitz, The, 9; Contract, 726; Courage Mountain, 160; Daddy Long Legs, 913; Damage, 493; Dangerous Moves, 728; Fanny (1961), 514; Father Goose, 274; Gigi, 919; Glass Slipper, The, 919; Goldengirl, 1054; Is Paris Burning?, 554; Lili, 928; Madron, 1131; Man Who Loved Women, The (1977), 765; Promise Her Anything, 362; QB VII, 631; Unapproachable, The, 691; Valentino, 693

Carpendale, Howard: No One Cries Forever, 608

Carpenter, Carleton: Two Weeks with Love, 947; Up Periscope, 134

Carpenter, David: Crimes of the Heart, 260; Warlock (1988), 901

Carpenter, Horace: Maniac (1934), 862

Carpenter, Peter: Blood Mania, 815

Carpenter, Thelma: Wiz, The, 948

Carr, Carol: Down Among the "Z" Men, 268

Carr, Hayley: Back Home, 147

Carr, Jane: Something for Everyone, 662

Carr, Marian: Indestructible Man, 856

Carr, Mary: Forbidden Trail, 1113; Red Kimono, The, 636

Carr, Paul: Severed Arm, The, 885

Carr, Rachel: Underground (1990), 1029

Carr, Sarah Rose: Beethoven's 2nd, 149

Carradine, Bruce: Americana, 446

Carradine, David: Americana, 446; Animal Instincts, 952; Armed Response, 6; Bird on a Wire, 13; Bound for Glory, 467; Boxcar Bertha, 18; Cannonball, 22; Circle of Iron, 26; Cloud Dancer, 27; Crime Zone, 1043; Deadly Surveillance, 35; Death Race 2000, 1045; Deathsport, 1046; Dune Warriors, 42; Evil Toons, 273; Field of Fire, 47; Future Zone, 54; Gambler Returns, the: Luck of the Draw, 1115; Gray Lady Down, 57; High Noon, Part Two, 1120; Karate Cop, 70; Kill Zone, 71; Kung Fu, 73; Kung Fu—The Movie, 73; Lone Wolf McQuade, 78; Long Goodbye, The, 993; Long Riders, The, 1130; Macho Callahan, 1130; Martial Law, 82; Mean Streets, 591; Misfit Brigade, The, 85; Mr. Horn, 1134; Night Rhythms, 1001; North and South, 608; Nowhere to Run (1989), 609; Oceans of Fire, 93; On the Line, 94; P.O.W.: The Escape, 96; Project: Eliminator, 101; Q, 878; Ray Bradbury's Chronicles: The Martian Episodes, 1073; Roadside Prophets, 641; Serpent's Egg, The, 652; Sonny Boy, 889; Sundown (1990), 891; That's Action, 127; Think Big, 394; Thunder and Lightning, 129; Trick or Treat (1982), 897; Tropical Snow, 132; Warlords, 901; Warrior and the Sorceress, The, 1088; Wizard of the Lost Kingdom II, 1090

Carradine, John: Adventures of Huckleberry Finn, The (1960), 144; Adventures of Mark Twain, The (1944), 442; Antony and Cleopatra (1981), 450; Astro-Zombies, 810; Bees, The, 812; Big Foot, 813; Billy the Kid vs. Dracula, 813; Blood and Sand (1941), 464; Blood of Dracula's Castle, 815; Bloodsuckers, The, 816; Bluebeard (1944), 817; Boogeyman, The, 818; Boxcar Bertha, 18; Captain Kidd, 23; Casanova's Big Night, 252; Christmas Coal Mine Miracle, The, 159; Cosmic Man, The, 1043; Daniel Boone, 1107; Death at Love House, 968; Dimples, 914; Drums Along the Mohawk, 42; Everything You Always Wanted to Know About Sex but Were Afraid to Ask, 273; Evil Spawn, 839; Evils of the Night, 839; Female Jungle, 516; Five Bloody Graves, 1113; Five Came Back, 517; Frankenstein Island, 842; Garden of Allah, The, 525; Goliath Awaits, 56; Grapes of Wrath, The, 531; Gun Riders, The, 1117; Half Human, 848; Hell Ship Mutiny, 60; Hillbillys in a Haunted House, 297; Horror of the Blood Monsters, 1057; Hound of the Baskervilles, The (1939), 983; House of Dracula, 852; House of Frankenstein, 852; House of Seven Corpses, The, 853; House of the Long Shadows, 853; Howling, The, 853; Ice Pirates, 1057; Incredible Petrified World, The, 105[illegible] Invasion of the Animal People, 1059; Jesse James, 1123; Johnny Guitar, 1123; Kentuckian, The, 1124; Killer Inside M[illegible] The, 988; Last Hurrah, The, 569; Last Tycoon, The, 571; Mary, Mary, Bloody Mary, 863; Mary of Scotland, 589; Mr. Moto's Last Warning, 997; Monster Club, The, 865; Monste[illegible] in the Closet, 866; Mummy and the Curse of the Jackals, The 867; Mummy's Ghost, The, 867; Myra Breckenridge, 341; Nesting, The, 868; Nocturna, 346; Of Human Hearts, 610; Patsy, The, 355; Peggy Sue Got Married, 355; Private Affairs of Bel Ami, The, 628; Return of Frank James, The, 1142; Return of the Ape Man, 880; Reunion in France, 639; Reveng[illegible] of the Zombies, 881; Satan's Cheerleaders, 882; Secret of Nimh, The, 202; Seekers, The, 651; Sentinel, The, 884; Seve[illegible] Minutes, The, 653; Shock Waves (Death Corps), 885; Shootist, The, 1149; Showdown at Boot Hill, 1149; Silent Night, Bloody Night, 886; Silver Spurs, 1150; Stagecoach (1939), 1152; Terror in the Wax Museum, 894; Thunder Pas[illegible] 1157; Tomb, The, 896; Treasures of the Twilight Zone, 108[illegible] Unearthly, The, 899; Vampire Hookers, 900; Waterfront, 69[illegible] Western Union, 1163; White Buffalo, 1164; Winterset, 704; Wizard of Mars, The, 1090

Carradine, Keith: All Quiet on the Western Front (1979), 444; Almost Perfect Affair, An, 225; Annie Oakley (1992), 147; Bachelor, The, 453; Backfire, 953; Ballad of the Sad Cafe, The, 455; Blackout (1985), 956; Capone, 22; Chiefs, 961; Choose Me, 962; Cold Feet (1989), 257; Crisscross (1992), 491; Daddy's Dyin' and Who's Got the Will, 261; Duellists, The, 42; Eye on the Sparrow, 512; Forgotten, The, 520; Idaho Transfer, 1057; Inquiry, The, 552; Judgment, 56[illegible] Kung Fu, 73; Long Riders, The, 1130; Lumiere, 763; Man on[illegible] String, 81; Maria's Lovers, 588; McCabe and Mrs. Miller, 1133; Moderns, The, 335; Nashville, 603; Old Boyfriends, 611; Payoff, 98; Pretty Baby, 626; Rumor of War, A, 109; Shrieking, The, 886; Southern Comfort, 119; Thieves Like Us 681; Trouble in Mind, 688; Welcome to L.A., 698

Carradine, Robert: Aladdin and His Wonderful Lamp, 145; All's Fair, 225; As Is, 451; Big Red One, The, 12; Blackout (1978), 14; Buy and Cell, 248; Cannonball, 22; Clarence, 256 Coming Home, 486; Conspiracy: The Trial of the Chicago 8, 488; Disappearance of Christina, The, 971; Doublecrossed, 504; Heartaches, 538; Illusions, 985; Incident, The (1989), 551; Jackson County Jail, 68; John Carpenter Presents: Body Bags, 858; Joyride, 560; Long Riders, The, 1130; Massacre a[illegible] Central High, 864; Mean Streets, 591; Number One with a Bullet, 92; Orca, 873; Revenge of the Nerds, 367; Revenge of the Nerds II: Nerds in Paradise, 367; Revenge of the Nerds III: The Next Generation, 367; Rude Awakening (1989), 371; Somebody Has to Shoot the Picture, 662; Tag—The Assassination Game, 124; Tommyknockers, The, 1084; Wavelength, 1088

Carrara, Chris: Remote, 198

Carrera, Barbara: Condorman, 159; Embryo, 1048; I, the Jury, 985; Island of Dr. Moreau, The, 1060; Lone Wolf McQuade, 78; Love at Stake, 322; Loverboy, 323; Masada, 590; Never Say Never Again, 89; Point of Impact, 99; When Time Ran Out!, 1031; Wicked Stepmother, The, 903; Wild Geese II, 139

Carrere, Tia: Aloha Summer, 445; Fatal Mission, 46; Quick, 102; Rising Sun, 1010; Showdown in Little Tokyo, 115; Wayne's World, 406; Wayne's World 2, 406; Zombie Nightmare, 905

Carrey, Jim: Ace Ventura: Pet Detective, 221; Earth Girls Are Easy, 915; Once Bitten, 349

Carrico, Monica: Running Hot, 645

Carriere, Mathieu: Beethoven's Nephew, 457; Bilitis, 717; Coup De Grace, 726; Woman in Flames, A, 804

Carrillo, Elpidia: Beyond the Limit, 460; Border, The, 17; Lightning Incident, The, 860; Predator, 1071; Salvador, 647

Carrillo, Leo: American Empire, 1093; Captain Caution, 23; Fugitive, The (1947), 523; Girl of the Golden West, The, 919; History Is Made at Night, 542; Manhattan Melodrama, 81; Manhattan Merry-Go-Round, 930; One Night in the Tropics,

350; Riders of Death Valley, *1143;* Too Hot to Handle, *130;* Viva Villa!, *1162*

Carrol, Brandon: Hell Squad (1958), *60*

Carroll, Barbara: Last Days of Pompeii (1960), *75*

Carroll, Beeson: Spacehunter: Adventures in the Forbidden Zone, *1078*

Carroll, Diahann: Carmen Jones, *911;* Five Heartbeats, The, *917;* From the Dead of Night, *844;* Goodbye Again, *530;* I Know Why the Caged Bird Sings, *547;* Paris Blues, *618;* That's Singing: The Best of Broadway, *944*

Carroll, Helena: Man Upstairs, The, *327*

Carroll, Janet: Talent for the Game, *677*

Carroll, Jill: Vals, The, *404*

Carroll, John: Decision at Sundown, *1108;* Fabulous Texan, The, *1112;* Farmer Takes a Wife, The, *916;* Fiesta, *916;* Flying Tigers, The, *51;* Go West, *287;* Only Angels Have Wings, *95;* Rio Rita, *368;* Susan and God, *674;* Wolf Call, *948;* Zorro Rides Again, *1166*

Carroll, Johnny: Rock, Baby, Rock It, *936*

Carroll, Lane: Crazies, The, *825*

Carroll, Leo G.: Adventures of Topper, The, *223;* Bulldog Drummond's Secret Police, *21;* Christmas Carol, A (1938), *158;* Father of the Bride (1950), *275;* Forever Amber, *520;* Man from U.N.C.L.E., The (TV Series), *80;* Paradine Case, The, *1004;* Prize, The, *629;* Sadie McKee, *646;* Snows of Kilimanjaro, The, *118;* Song of Love, *662;* Spellbound, *1019;* Strangers on a Train, *1020;* Swan, The (1956), *674;* Tarantula, *892;* Tower of London (1939), *897;* We're No Angels (1955), *407*

Carroll, Lisa Hart: Midnight Cabaret, *864*

Carroll, Madeleine: General Died at Dawn, The, *55;* My Favorite Blonde, *340;* My Love for Yours, *340;* Prisoner of Zenda, The (1937), *100;* School for Scandal, *373;* Secret Agent, The, *1013;* Thirty-Nine Steps, The (1935), *1024*

Carroll, Matthew: Dance with a Stranger, *494*

Carroll, Nancy: Scarlet Dawn, *649;* Transatlantic Merry-Go-Round, *946*

Carroll, Regina: Brain of Blood, *818*

Carroll, Susan: Stanley, *890*

Carson, Charles: Cry, the Beloved Country, *492*

Carson, Crystal: Cartel, *23*

Carson, Hunter: Invaders from Mars (1986), *1059;* Paris, Texas, *618;* Rip Van Winkle, *199*

Carson, Jack: Arsenic and Old Lace, *228;* Bride Came C.O.D., The, *245;* Carefree, *911;* Cat on a Hot Tin Roof (1958), *477;* Dangerous When Wet, *913;* Doughgirls, The, *268;* Gentleman Jim, *525;* Hard Way, The (1942), *536;* Having a Wonderful Time, *294;* It's a Great Feeling, *925;* King of the Roaring Twenties, *565;* Love Crazy, *322;* Lucky Partners, *324;* Mildred Pierce, *594;* Mr. and Mrs. Smith, *333;* My Dream Is Yours, *932;* Red Garters, *936;* Romance on the High Seas, *937;* Saint in New York, The, *1012;* Sammy, the Way-Out Seal, *201;* Stand-In, *385;* Star Is Born, A (1954), *666;* Strawberry Blonde, The, *670;* Vivacious Lady, *405*

Carson, John: After Julius, *442;* Taste the Blood of Dracula, *892*

Carson, John David: Captain Kronos: Vampire Hunter, *821;* Creature from Black Lake, *826;* Savage Is Loose, The, *648*

Carson, Johnny: Garry Shandling Show, The, *283*

Carson, Shawn: Something Wicked This Way Comes, *1077*

Carson, Sunset: Battling Marshal, *1097;* Bells of Rosarita, *1097;* Cherokee Flash, *1104;* El Paso Kid, *1111;* Red River Renegades, *1142;* Santa Fe Saddlemates, *1147;* Sunset Carson Rides Again, *1153*

Carson, Terrence "T. C.": Firehawk, *49;* Livin' Large, *320*

Carsten, Peter: And God Said to Cain, *1093;* Dark of the Sun, *32;* Mr. Superinvisible, *188;* Zeppelin, *709*

Carstensen, Margit: Bitter Tears of Petra Von Kant, The, *718;* Chinese Roulette, *723;* Mother Kusters Goes to Heaven, *769*

Cartaxo, Marcelia: Hour of the Star, *745*

Cartel, Michael: Runaway Nightmare, *109*

Carter, Alice: Dangerous Heart, *965*

Carter, Bruce: Laser Moon, *990*

Carter, Dixie: Killing of Randy Webster, The, *564*

Carter, Finn: Sweet Justice, *123;* Tremors, *897*

Carter, Helena: Bugles in the Afternoon, *1102;* Invaders from Mars (1953), *1059*

Carter, Helena Bonham: Getting It Right, *285;* Hamlet (1990), *535;* Howards End, *545;* Lady Jane, *568;* Room with a View, A, *644;* Where Angels Fear to Tread, *699*

Carter, Jack: Alligator, *808;* Amazing Dobermans, *146;* Deadly Embrace, *34;* Happy Hooker Goes to Washington, The, *293;* Horizontal Lieutenant, The, *301;* Hustle, *65;* In the Heat of Passion, *986;* Octagon, The, *93;* Opposite Sex (And How to Live with Them), The, *351;* Red Nights, *637;* Robo C.H.I.C., *1074;* Viva Las Vegas, *947*

Carter, Janis: Half-Breed, The, *1118;* Miss Grant Takes Richmond, *333;* My Forbidden Past, *602;* Woman of Distinction, A, *413*

Carter, Judy: Paramount Comedy Theatre, Vol. 1: Well Developed, *353*

Carter, Karen: Big Bust Out, The, *12*

Carter, Lynda: Bobbie Jo and the Outlaw, *17;* I Posed for Playboy, *548;* Rita Hayworth: The Love Goddess, *641*

Carter, T. K.: Doctor Detroit, *266;* He's My Girl, *296;* Runaway Train, *110*

Carter, Terry: Foxy Brown, *52*

Carteris, Gabrielle: Beverly Hills 90210, *460*

Cartledge, Miranda: Save the Lady, *201*

Cartlidge, Katrin: Naked, *603*

Cartwright, Angela: High School, USA, *297;* Lost in Space (TV Series), *1063*

Cartwright, Veronica: Alien, *1034;* Bernice Bobs Her Hair, *234;* Birds, The, *813;* Children's Hour, The, *481;* Dead in the Water, *967;* False Identity, *975;* Flight of the Navigator, *1052;* Hitler's Daughter, *542;* Inserts, *552;* Invasion of the Body Snatchers (1978), *1059;* Man Trouble, *327;* My Man Adam, *340;* One Man's Way, *613;* Prime Suspect, *627;* Right Stuff, The, *640;* Valentino Returns, *693;* Wisdom, *140;* Witches of Eastwick, The, *412*

Caruso, Anthony: Asphalt Jungle, The, *953;* Drum Beat, *1110;* Objective, Burma!, *93;* Threat, The, *1024;* When Gangland Strikes, *138*

Caruso, David: Blue City, *957;* China Girl, *25;* First Blood, *49;* King of New York, *72;* Mad Dog and Glory, *584;* Rainbow Drive, *103*

Carver, Brent: Cross Country, *491;* Love and Hate, *581;* One-Night Stand, *613*

Carver, Lynn: Adventures of Huckleberry Finn, The (1939), *143*

Carver, Lynne: Madame X (1937), *584*

Carvey, Dana: Clean Slate (1994), *256;* Moving, *338;* Opportunity Knocks, *351;* Tough Guys, *398;* Wayne's World, *406;* Wayne's World 2, *406*

Casanovas, Alex: Kika, *751*

Casares, Maria: Children of Paradise, The, *723;* La Lectrice (The Reader), *754;* Orpheus, *774*

Casaril, Guy: Legend of Frenchie King, The, *1128*

Cascio, Salvatore: Cinema Paradiso, *724*

Cascone, Nicholas: Vietnam War Story, *694*

Case, Katherine: Running Wild (1955), *645*

Case, Kathleen: Last of the Pony Riders, *1126*

Casella, Max: Newsies, *933*

Casey, Bernie: Backfire, *953;* Boxcar Bertha, *18;* Cemetery Club, The, *478;* Chains of Gold, *478;* Cleopatra Jones, *26;* Cornbread, Earl and Me, *488;* Dr. Black and Mr. Hyde, *835;* Guns of the Magnificent Seven, *1118;* I'm Gonna Git You Sucka!, *305;* Never Say Never Again, *89;* Rent-a-Cop, *105;* Revenge of the Nerds, *367;* Sharky's Machine, *115;* Sophisticated Gents, The, *663;* Spies Like Us, *384;* Steele Justice, *120*

Cash, Johnny: Gunfight, A, *1117;* Jerry Lee Lewis—I Am What I Am, *428;* Last Days of Frank and Jesse James, *1125;*

Murder in Coweta County, *600;* Pride of Jesse Hallman, The, *626;* Stagecoach (1986), *1152*

Cash, Rosalind: Cornbread, Earl and Me, *488;* Death Drug, *498;* Death Spa, *831;* Dr. Black and Mr. Hyde, *835;* Omega Man, The, *1069;* Special Bulletin, *1019;* Wrong Is Right, *414*

Cash, Roseanne: Doctor Duck's Super Secret All-Purpose Sauce, *266*

Cash, Veronica: Pamela Principle, The, *1004*

Casilio, Maria Pia: Umberto D, *798*

Casini, Stefania: Suspiria, *891*

Casnoff, Philip: Gorp, *289;* Ironclads, *554;* Red Wind, *1009*

Cason, John: Sunset Carson Rides Again, *1153*

Caspary, Katrina: My Mom's a Werewolf, *341*

Caspary, Tina: Can't Buy Me Love, *250*

Cass, Peggy: Gidget Goes Hawaiian, *286;* If It's Tuesday, This Must Be Belgium, *305;* Paddy, *353*

Cassavetes, John: Brass Target, *19;* Dirty Dozen, The, *39;* Fury, The, *845;* Incubus, The, *856;* Killers, The, *71;* Love Streams, *582;* Marvin and Tige, *589;* Mikey and Nicky, *332;* Rosemary's Baby, *881;* Tempest (1982), *678;* Two-Minute Warning, *1028;* Whose Life Is It, Anyway?, *701*

Cassavetes, Nick: Backstreet Dreams, *454;* Body of Influence, *958;* Broken Trust, *959;* Class of 1999 II: The Substitute, *1041;* Delta Force 3, *37;* Quiet Cool, *102;* Sins of Desire, *1017;* Sins of the Night, *1017*

Cassel, Jean-Pierre: Alice (1981), *906;* Baxter, *456;* Candide, *722;* Discreet Charm of the Bourgeoisie, The, *730;* Elusive Corporal, The, *734;* Favor, the Watch and the Very Big Fish, The, *275;* Is Paris Burning?, *554;* La Vie Continue, *755;* Les Rendez-Vous D'Anna, *759;* Maid, The, *326;* Return of the Musketeers, *106;* Who Is Killing the Great Chefs of Europe?, *410*

Cassel, Sandra: Last House on the Left, *860*

Cassel, Seymour: Adventures in Spying, *2;* Boiling Point, *17;* California Dreaming, *474;* Double Exposure (1982), *971;* Eye of the Tiger, *46;* In the Soup, *306;* Indecent Proposal, *551;* Johnny Be Good, *311;* Killing of a Chinese Bookie, *564;* Love Streams, *582;* Plain Clothes, *358;* Seducers, The, *651;* Survival Game, *123;* Track 29, *1026;* Valentino, *693;* White Fang, *217*

Cassell, Alan: Squizzy Taylor, *119*

Cassidy, David: Instant Karma, *306;* Night the City Screamed, The, *606;* Spirit of '76, The, *384*

Cassidy, Jack: Andersonville Trial, The, *447;* Columbo: Murder by the Book, *963;* Eiger Sanction, The, *43*

Cassidy, Joanna: All-American Murder, *951;* Bank Shot, *232;* Barbarians at the Gate, *455;* Blade Runner, *1039;* Children of Times Square, The, *481;* Club Paradise, *256;* Don't Tell Mom the Babysitter's Dead, *267;* Father's Revenge, A, *515;* Fourth Protocol, The, *978;* Invitation to Hell, *857;* Landslide, *990;* Live! From Death Row, *577;* Lonely Hearts (1991), *577;* May Wine, *330;* Nightmare at Bittercreek, *1002;* 1969, *607;* Package, The, *1004;* Perfect Family, *1005;* Tommyknockers, The, *1084;* Under Fire, *134;* Wheels of Terror, *138;* Where the Heart Is, *699;* Who Framed Roger Rabbit, *410*

Cassidy, Patrick: Hitler's Daughter, *542;* Longtime Companion, *579;* Love at Stake, *322;* Off the Wall, *348*

Cassidy, Shaun: Roots—The Gift, *644;* Texas Guns, *1155*

Cassidy, Susan: Torture Dungeon, *896*

Cassidy, Ted: Addams Family, The (TV Series), *222;* Planet Earth, *1070*

Cassinelli, Claudio: Great Alligator, The, *847;* Hands of Steel, *1055;* New Gladiators, The, *1068;* Screamers, *884*

Cassisi, John: Bugsy Malone, *155*

Castaldi, Jean-Pierre: French Connection II, The, *53*

Castel, Lou: Bullet for the General, A, *1102;* Eyes, the Mouth, The, *735;* Paranoia, *1004;* Rorret, *782;* Scarlet Letter (1973), *784*

Castellano, Richard: Godfather, The, *529;* Lovers and Other Strangers, *323;* Night of the Juggler, *90*

Castelli, Paulo: Happily Ever After, *743*

Castellitto, Sergio: Alberto Express, *711*

Castello, Willy: Confessions of a Vice Baron, *487*

Castelnuovo, Nino: Escapade in Florence, *165;* Umbrellas of Cherbourg, The, *798*

Castille, Christopher: Beethoven's 2nd, *149*

Castillo, Gloria: Invasion of the Saucer Men, *1059;* Meteor Monster, *864;* Reform School Girl, *104*

Castle, DeShonn: Zebrahead, *709*

Castle, Don: Stampede, *1152*

Castle, John: Antony and Cleopatra (1973), *450;* Crucifer of Blood, *964;* Lion in Winter, The, *576;* Murder Is Announced, A, *998*

Castle, Peggie: Finger Man, *48*

Castle, Peggy: Seven Hills of Rome, The, *939*

Castle, Roy: Alice Through the Looking Glass (1966), *906;* Dr. Terror's House of Horrors, *836;* Dr. Who and the Daleks, *1047*

Castro, Analia: Official Story, The, *772*

Castrodad, Eddie: Night Train to Katmandu, *607*

Cat: Sign o' the Times, *434*

Cataldo, Giusi: Flight of the Innocent, *737*

Catalifo, Patrick: Sand and Blood, *783*

Cates, Helen: Taste for Killing, A, *126*

Cates, Phoebe: Bodies, Rest & Motion, *465;* Bright Lights, Big City, *470;* Date with an Angel, *262;* Drop Dead Fred, *269;* Fast Times at Ridgemont High, *274;* Gremlins, *1055;* Gremlins 2: The New Batch, *1055;* Heart of Dixie, The, *538;* Paradise (1982), *97;* Private School, *362;* Shag, the Movie, *654*

Catillon, Brigitte: Un Coeur En Hiver, *798*

Catlett, Walter: Every Day's a Holiday, *273;* Rain, *634*

Cato, Hil: Skin Art, *659*

Caton, Juliette: Courage Mountain, *160*

Cattand, Gabriel: Blue Jeans, *719*

Cattel, Christine: Bedroom Eyes, *954*

Cattrall, Kim: Bastard, The, *456;* Big Trouble in Little China, *13;* City Limits, *1041;* Deadly Harvest, *1045;* Double Vision, *972;* Good Night, Michelangelo, *288;* Honeymoon Academy, *300;* Mannequin (1987), *328;* Masquerade (1988), *995;* Midnight Crossing, *84;* Miracle in the Wilderness, *595;* Palais Royale, *97;* Police Academy, *359;* Porky's, *360;* Return of the Musketeers, *106;* Running Delilah, *110;* Smokescreen, *661;* Split Second (1992), *1078;* Star Trek VI: The Undiscovered Country, *1079;* Ticket to Heaven, *683;* Turk 182, *689;* Wild Palms, *1089*

Caubère, Philippe: My Father's Glory, *769;* My Mother's Castle, *770*

Cauchy, Daniel: Bob le Flambeur, *719*

Caudell, Lane: Archer: Fugitive from the Empire, *1036;* Hanging on a Star, *536*

Caulfield, Joan: Buckskin, *1102;* Daring Dobermans, The, *32;* Dear Wife, *263;* Hatfields and the McCoys, The, *1119;* Monsieur Beaucaire, *336;* Pony Express Rider, *1139*

Caulfield, Maxwell: Alien Intruder, *1035;* Animal Instincts, *952;* Beverly Hills 90210, *460;* Boys Next Door, The, *468;* Dance with Death, *965;* Exiled in America, *45;* Gettysburg, *526;* Grease 2, *920;* In a Moment of Passion, *549;* Midnight Witness, *996;* Mindgames, *996;* No Escape, No Return, *91;* Project: Alien, *1072;* Sundown (1990), *891;* Supernaturals, The, *891*

Causey, Mathew: Party Animal, *354*

Cavagnaro, Gary: Drive-In, *269*

Cavallo, Victor: Tragedy of a Ridiculous Man, *796*

Cavanagh, Paul: Bill of Divorcement, A, *461;* Bride of the Gorilla, *819;* Goin' to Town, *287;* Scarlet Claw, The, *1012;* Tarzan and His Mate, *125;* Woman in Green, The, *1032*

Cavanaugh, Hobart: Kismet (1944), *566;* Stage Struck (1936), *941;* Stage to Chino, *1152*

Cavanaugh, Megan: League of Their Own, A, *571;* Robin Hood: Men in Tights, *369*

Cavanaugh, Michael: Forced Vengeance, *51;* Full Fathom Five, *53;* Two to Tango, *133*

Cavazos, Lumi: Like Water for Chocolate, *760*

Cave, Des: Paddy, *353*
Cave, Nick: Johnny Suede, *311*
Caven, Ingrid: Malou, *764;* Mother Kusters Goes to Heaven, *769*
Cavender, Glen: General, The, *283;* Keystone Comedies, Vol. 4, *312*
Cavett, Dick: Doctor Duck's Super Secret All-Purpose Sauce, *266;* Jimi Hendrix, *428*
Cayton, Elizabeth: Necromancer, *868;* Silent Night, Deadly Night Part 2, *886*
Cazale, John: Conversation, The, *963;* Deer Hunter, The, *499;* Dog Day Afternoon, *971;* Godfather, The, *529;* Godfather, Part II, The, *529;* Godfather Epic, The, *529*
Cazenove, Christopher: Aces: Iron Eagle III, *1;* Children of the Full Moon, *823;* Eye of the Needle, *974;* Fantasist, The, *975;* Heat and Dust, *539;* Jenny's War, *68;* Mata Hari (1985), *83;* Three Men and a Little Lady, *395;* Until September, *692*
Ceccaldi, Daniel: Holiday Hotel, *744;* Stolen Kisses, *789*
Cedema, Giuseppi: Mediterraneo, *766*
Celarie, Clementine: Great, My Parents Are Divorcing, *742*
Celedonio, Maria: You Must Remember This, *708*
Celi, Adolfo: Cafe Express, *721;* Danger: Diabolik, *1044;* Grand Prix, *531;* Hitler, the Last Ten Days, *542;* Manhunt (1973), *81;* Murders in the Rue Morgue (1971), *867;* Phantom of Liberty, The, *777;* That Man From Rio, *793;* Thunderball, *129*
Celli, Teresa: Black Hand, The, *462*
Cellier, Antoinette: River of Unrest, *641*
Cellier, Caroline: L'Année des Meduses, *752;* Petit Con, *777;* This Man Must Die, *794*
Celozzi, Nicholas: Hidden Obsession, *982;* Slaughterhouse Rock, *887*
Celulari, Edson: Opera do Malandro, *774*
Cerdan Jr., Marcel: Edith and Marcel, *733*
Cerusico, Enzo: Zorro, *142*
Cervenka, Exene: Salvation, *647*
Cervera Jr, Jorge: Wrong Man, The (1993), *707*
Cerveris, Michael: Steel and Lace, *1080*
Cervi, Gino: Full Hearts and Empty Pockets, *739;* Indiscretion of an American Wife, *551;* Little World of Don Camillo, The, *761;* Naked Maja, The, *603*
Cesak, Brian: Fandango, *274*
Cestie, Renato: Saddle Tramps, *1147*
Chabrol, Claude: Six in Paris (Paris Vue par . . .), *786*
Chabrol, Thomas: Rascals, The, *779*
Chadwick, June: Distortions, *834;* Forbidden World, *842;* Quiet Thunder, *102;* Rebel Storm, *1074*
Chadwick, Justin: London Kills Me, *577*
Chaffee, Suzy: Fire and Ice (1987), *49*
Chaing, David: Seven Brothers Meet Dracula, The, *884*
Chakiris, George: Diamond Head, *500;* Pale Blood, *873;* Return to Fantasy Island, *1074;* 633 Squadron, *116;* West Side Story, *947*
Challa, George: Kameradschaft, *751*
Chaliapin, Feodor: Church, The, *824;* Curse IV: The Ultimate Sacrifice, *828;* Don Quixote (1933), *914;* King's Whore, The, *566;* Moonstruck, *336;* Name of the Rose, The, *89;* Stanley and Iris, *665*
Chamberlain, Margaret: Tuck Everlasting, *214*
Chamberlain, Richard: Allan Quartermain and the Lost City of Gold, *4;* Bourne Identity, The, *958;* Casanova (1987), *252;* Count of Monte Cristo, The (1975), *30;* Four Musketeers, The, *52;* Julius Caesar (1970), *561;* King Solomon's Mines (1985), *73;* Lady Caroline Lamb, *567;* Last Wave, The, *991;* Madwoman of Chaillot, The, *585;* Man in the Iron Mask, The (1977), *81;* Murder by Phone, *998;* Music Lovers, The, *932;* Petulia, *621;* Return of the Musketeers, *106;* Shogun (Full-Length Version), *115;* Swarm, The, *891;* Thornbirds, The, *682;* Three Musketeers, The (1973), *128;* Towering Inferno, The, *131*
Chamberlain, Wilt: Conan the Destroyer, *1043;* Rich Hall's Vanishing America, *367*
Chambers, Carrie: Divine Enforcer, *40;* Karate Cop, *70*
Chambers, Marilyn: Angel of H.E.A.T., *5;* Party Girls (Party Inc.), *355;* Rabid, *878*
Chambers, Michael: Breakin', *909;* Breakin' 2 Electric Boogaloo, *909*
Chambliss, Woodrow: Glen and Randa, *1054*
Champion, Beth: One Crazy Night, *349*
Champion, Gower: Give a Girl a Break, *919;* Jupiter's Darling, *926;* Lovely to Look At, *929;* Show Boat (1951), *939*
Champion, Marge: Give a Girl a Break, *919;* Jupiter's Darling, *926;* Lovely to Look At, *929;* Party, The, *354;* Show Boat (1951), *939;* Swimmer, The, *675*
Champion, Michael: Swordsman, The, *124*
Champlin, Irene: TV Classics: Flash Gordon and the Planet of Death, *1085*
Chan, Dennis: Kickboxer, *70;* Kickboxer 2: The Road Back, *70;* Kickboxer Three—Art of War, *71*
Chan, Frances: Meeting at Midnight, *996*
Chan, Jackie: Armour Of God, *713;* Big Brawl, The, *12;* Dragons Forever, *732;* Jackie Chan's Police Force, *309;* Police Story III—Super Cop, *778;* Project A (Part I), *778;* Project A (Part II), *779;* Protector, The, *101;* World of Suzie Wong, The, *707*
Chan, Kim: American Shaolin: King of the Kickboxers II, *5*
Chan, Mike: Cardiac Arrest, *959*
Chan, Spencer: Sea Hound, The, *112*
Chance, Naomi: Gambler and the Lady, The, *524*
Chancellor, Anna: Four Weddings and a Funeral, *280*
Chandler, Andrew: La Petite Bande, *754*
Chandler, Chick: Blood Money (1933), *464;* Dangerous Charter, *32;* Lost Continent, The, *1063*
Chandler, Edward: Desert Trail, *1109*
Chandler, George: Arizona, *1094;* Dead Reckoning (1947), *34;* Fatal Glass of Beer, A/Pool Sharks, *274;* Flask of Fields, A, *278;* High and the Mighty, The, *541;* Island in the Sky, *554*
Chandler, Helen: Christopher Strong, *482;* Dracula (1931), *837*
Chandler, Jeff: Away all Boats, *8;* Broken Arrow, *1101;* Jayhawkers, The, *1123;* Return to Peyton Place, *639*
Chandler, Lane: Devil Horse, The, *1109;* Lawless Nineties, The, *1127;* Lone Ranger, The (1938), *1129;* Sagebrush Trail, *1147;* Winds of the Wasteland, *1165*
Chandler, Simon: Who's Who, *411*
Chanel, Helene: Maciste in Hell, *861*
Chaney Jr., Lon: Abbott and Costello Meet Frankenstein, *221;* Ace Drummond, *1;* Bird of Paradise, *13;* Bloodsuckers, The, *816;* Bride of the Gorilla, *819;* Buckskin, *1102;* Bushwhackers, *1102;* Casanova's Big Night, *252;* Cyclops, The, *829;* Daniel Boone, Trail Blazer, *1107;* Defiant Ones, The, *499;* Devil's Messenger, The, *834;* Dracula vs. Frankenstein, *837;* Frankenstein Meets the Wolf Man, *843;* Ghost of Frankenstein, *845;* Happy Landing, *921;* Haunted Palace, The, *849;* Here Come the Co-Eds, *296;* High Noon, *1120;* Hillbillys in a Haunted House, *297;* House of Dracula, *852;* House of Frankenstein, *852;* I Died a Thousand Times, *65;* Indestructible Man, *856;* Johnny Reno, *1124;* Last Frontier, The, *1125;* Lion in the Streets, A, *575;* Manfish, *862;* Mummy's Curse, The, *867;* Mummy's Ghost, The, *867;* Mummy's Tomb, The, *867;* My Favorite Brunette, *340;* Not as a Stranger, *609;* Old Corral, *1136;* One Million B.C., *1069;* Passion (1954), *97;* Riders of Death Valley, *1143;* Scarlet River, *1148;* 16 Fathoms Deep, *116;* Son of Dracula (1943), *888;* Spider Baby, *889;* Tales of Tomorrow (Vols. I - III), *1082;* Three Musketeers, The (1933), *128;* Undersea Kingdom, *1087;* Wolf Man, The, *904*
Chaney Sr., Lon: Hunchback of Notre Dame, The (1923), *854;* Mockery, *598;* Monster, The, *865;* Oliver Twist (1922), *611;* Outside the Law, *616;* Phantom of the Opera (1925), *874;* Shadows, *654;* Shock, The (1923), *656;* Unholy Three, *1029;* West of Zanzibar, *1030;* Where East Is East, *138*
Chang, Billy: American Shaolin: King of the Kickboxers II, *5*
Chang, Sari: China Girl, *25*

Chang, Shwu Sen: Song of the Exile, *787*

Chang, Sylvia: Aces Go Places (1–3) (Aka Mad Mission 1–3), *710*

Channing, Carol: Alice Through the Looking Glass (1985), *145;* Thoroughly Modern Millie, *945;* TV Classics: Milton Berle, *401*

Channing, Stockard: Big Bus, The, *238;* Cheap Detective, The, *254;* Echoes in the Darkness, *507;* Fish That Saved Pittsburgh, The, *278;* Grease, *920;* Heartburn, *295;* Married to It, *589;* Meet the Applegates, *331;* Men's Club, The, *593;* Not My Kid, *609;* Perfect Witness, *620;* Silent Victory: The Kitty O'Neil Story, *658;* Six Degrees of Separation, *659;* Staying Together, *667;* Tidy Endings, *683;* Time of Destiny, A, *684;* Without a Trace, *1032*

Chao, Rosalind: Joy Luck Club, The, *559;* Terry Fox Story, The, *679;* Thousand Pieces of Gold, *1156;* White Ghost, *138*

Chao, Winston: Wedding Banquet, The, *407*

Chapa, Damian: Bound by Honor, *467*

Chapel, Loyita: Legacy for Leonette, *991*

Chapin, Billy: Tobor the Great, *1084*

Chapin, Jonathan: Prison for Children, *628*

Chapin, Michael: Under California Stars, *1160*

Chapin, Miles: Bless the Beasts and Children, *463;* French Postcards, *281;* Funhouse, The, *845;* Get Crazy, *284;* Pandemonium, *353*

Chapin, Richard: Ring of Steel, *106*

Chapin, Tom: Lord of the Flies (1963), *579*

Chaplin, Charlie: Burlesque of Carmen, *247;* Chaplin Revue, The, *253;* Charlie Chaplin Carnival, *253;* Charlie Chaplin Cavalcade, *253;* Charlie Chaplin Festival, *253;* Charlie Chaplin...Our Hero, *253;* Charlie Chaplin—The Early Years, Vol. 1, *253;* Charlie Chaplin—The Early Years, Vol. 2, *253;* Charlie Chaplin—The Early Years, Vol. 3, *254;* Charlie Chaplin—The Early Years, Vol. 4, *254;* Circus, The/A Day's Pleasure, *255;* City Lights, *255;* Days of Thrills and Laughter, *262;* Gold Rush, The, *288;* Great Dictator, The, *289;* Kid, The/The Idle Class, *313;* King in New York, A, *313;* Limelight, *319;* Lost and Found Chaplin: Keystone, *321;* Modern Times, *335;* Monsieur Verdoux, *336;* Rare Chaplin, *364;* Three Charlies and a Phoney!, *395;* When Comedy Was King, *409*

Chaplin, Geraldine: Age of Innocence, The, *443;* Bolero (1982), *720;* Buffalo Bill and the Indians, *1102;* Chaplin, *479;* Dr. Zhivago, *503;* Duel of Hearts, *505;* I Killed Rasputin, *746;* Mama Turns 100, *764;* Moderns, The, *335;* Return of the Musketeers, *106;* Roseland, *644;* Wedding, A, *407;* Welcome to L.A., *698;* Z.P.G. (Zero Population Growth), *1091*

Chaplin, Josephine: Canterbury Tales, The, *722;* Escape to the Sun, *511;* Jack the Ripper (1979), *987;* L'Odeur Des Fauves (Scandal Man), *761*

Chaplin, Michael: King in New York, A, *313*

Chaplin, Sydney: Abdulla the Great, *221;* Chaplin Revue, The, *253;* Land of the Pharaohs, *568;* Limelight, *319;* Three Charlies and a Phoney!, *395*

Chapman, Edward: Convoy (1940), *488;* Juno and the Paycock, *561*

Chapman, Graham: And Now for Something Completely Different, *226;* How to Irritate People, *302;* Life of Brian, *318;* Monty Python and the Holy Grail, *336;* Monty Python Live at the Hollywood Bowl, *336;* Monty Python's Flying Circus (TV Series), *336;* Monty Python's the Meaning of Life, *336;* Odd Job, The, *348;* Secret Policemen's Other Ball, The, *375;* Secret Policeman's Private Parts, The, *375;* Yellowbeard, *415*

Chapman, Judith: Dead Space, *1045;* Scalpel, *883*

Chapman, Lonny: Baby Doll, *453;* Bad News Bears Go to Japan, The, *231;* King, *564;* Moving Violation, *87;* Running Scared (1980), *110;* Terror Out of the Sky, *894;* Where the Red Fern Grows, *216*

Chapman, Marguerite: Amazing Transparent Man, The, *1036;* Charlie Chan at the Wax Museum, *961;* Coroner Creek, *1106;* Daring Young Man, The, *262;* Flight to Mars, *1052;* Green Promise, The, *533;* Spy Smasher, *119*

Chappel, Dawn: Evil Spirits in the House, *839*

Chappell, Anna: Mountaintop Motel Massacre, *866*

Chappelle, Dave: Robin Hood: Men in Tights, *369*

Charbonneau, Patricia: Call Me, *959;* Desert Hearts, *499;* K2, *70;* Shakedown, *114*

Charisse, Cyd: Band Wagon, The, *908;* Black Tights, *909;* Brigadoon, *909;* East Side, West Side, *506;* Fiesta, *916;* Five Golden Hours, *278;* Harvey Girls, The, *922;* It's Always Fair Weather, *925;* Kissing Bandit, The, *927;* Maroc 7, *82;* Meet Me in Las Vegas, *930;* On an Island with You, *933;* Party Girl, *618;* Silk Stockings, *939;* Singin' in the Rain, *940;* Swimsuit, *390;* That's Entertainment! III, *436;* Two Weeks in Another Town, *690;* Words and Music, *948;* Ziegfeld Follies, *949*

Charkravarty, Alok: World of Apu, The, *805*

Charles, Craig: Red Dwarf (TV Series), *365*

Charles, David: Julia Has Two Lovers, *560*

Charles, Emile: Wonderland, *706*

Charles, Josh: Cooperstown, *488;* Crossing the Bridge, *492;* Don't Tell Mom the Babysitter's Dead, *267;* Threesome, *396*

Charles, Leon: Merry Wives of Windsor, The, *331*

Charles, Ray: Saturday Night Live, *372;* That Was Rock, *944*

Charleson, Ian: Chariots of Fire, *479;* Codename: Kyril, *962;* Louisiana, *580;* Terror at the Opera, *893*

Charlie Daniels Band: Urban Cowboy, *692*

Charney, Jordan: Imposter, The, *549*

Charon, Jacques: Le Bourgeois Gentilhomme, *756*

Charpin: Le Schpountz, *758;* Well-Digger's Daughter, The, *803*

Charters, Spencer: Bat Whispers, The, *953;* Three Faces West, *683*

Chartoff, Melanie: Doin' Time, *266;* Gambler, Part III—The Legend Continues, The, *1115;* Having It All, *294;* Stoogemania, *386*

Chase, Barrie: Silk Stockings, *939*

Chase, Charlie: Keystone Comedies, Vol. 5, *313;* Laurel and Hardy's Laughing 20s, *317;* Sons of the Desert, *383*

Chase, Chevy: Best of Chevy Chase, The, *235;* Best of Dan Aykroyd, The, *235;* Best of Gilda Radner, The, *235;* Best of John Belushi, The, *235;* Caddyshack, *249;* Caddyshack II, *249;* Cops and Robbersons, *259;* Deal of the Century, *263;* Ernie Kovacs: Television's Original Genius, *272;* Fletch, *978;* Fletch Lives, *978;* Foul Play, *280;* Funny Farm, *282;* Groove Tube, The, *291;* Here's Looking at You, Warner Brothers, *426;* Hero, *296;* Memoirs of an Invisible Man, *1065;* Modern Problems, *335;* National Lampoon's Christmas Vacation, *342;* National Lampoon's European Vacation, *342;* National Lampoon's Vacation, *342;* Nothing But Trouble (1991), *347;* Oh, Heavenly Dog!, *192;* Saturday Night Live, *372;* Seems Like Old Times, *375;* Sesame Street Presents Follow That Bird, *203;* Spies Like Us, *384;* Three Amigos, *395;* Tunnelvision, *400;* Under the Rainbow, *402*

Chase, Ilka: Animal Kingdom, The, *448*

Chase, Karen: Vendetta, *135*

Chase, Steve: Eden (TV Series), *507*

Chatel, Peter: Fox and His Friends, *738*

Chatterjee, Anil: Two Daughters, *797*

Chatterjee, Dhritiman: Adversary, The, *711*

Chatterjee, Soumitra: Devi (The Goddess), *729;* Distant Thunder (1974), *730;* Home and the World, *744;* Two Daughters, *797;* World of Apu, The, *805*

Chatterton, Ruth: Dodsworth, *503;* Female, *276*

Chatterton, Tom: Drums of Fu Manchu, *42*

Chaulet, Emmanuelle: Boyfriends and Girlfriends, *720*

Chauvin, Lilyan: Silent Night, Deadly Night, *886*

Chaveau, Zoe: Longshot (1981), *579*

Chaves, Richard: Cease Fire, *477;* Predator, *1071*

Chavez, Ingrid: Graffiti Bridge, *920*

Chavez, Oscar: Break of Dawn, *468*

Chaykin, Maury: Adjuster, The, *441;* Cold Comfort, *963;* Def-Con 4, *1046;* George's Island, *169;* Money for Nothing, *335;* My Cousin Vinny, *339;* Stars and Bars, *385;* Vindicator, The, *1087*

Cheadle, Don: Colors, *485;* Hamburger Hill, *535*

Checci, Andrea: Black Sunday (1961), *814*

Cheech and Chong: Cheech and Chong's Next Movie, *254;* Corsican Brothers, The (1984), *259;* Get Out of My Room, *284;* It Came from Hollywood, *307;* Nice Dreams, *344;* Still Smokin', *386;* Things Are Tough All Over, *393;* Up in Smoke, *403;* Yellowbeard, *415*
Cheek, Molly: Stepmonster, *1080*
Cheirel, Micheline: Carnival in Flanders, *722;* Cornered, *29*
Chekhov, Michael: Rhapsody, *639;* Specter of the Rose, The, *1019*
Chelton, Tsilla: Tatie Danielle, *792*
Chemel, David: Taming of the Shrew (1982), *391*
Chen, Joan: Blood of Heroes, *15;* Deadlock, *1045;* Heaven and Earth (1993), *539;* Last Emperor, The, *569;* On Deadly Ground, *93;* Strangers, *669;* Tai-Pan, *124;* Turtle Beach, *690;* Twin Peaks (Movie), *1027;* Twin Peaks (TV Series), *1027*
Chen, Moira: Endgame, *1049*
Chen, Tina: Alice's Restaurant, *444;* Devlin Connection III, The, *970;* Lady from Yesterday, The, *567*
Chenier, Clifton: Hot Pepper, *426*
Chepil, Bill: Street Trash, *891*
Cher: Come Back to the Five and Dime, Jimmy Dean, Jimmy Dean, *486;* Mask (1985), *590;* Mermaids, *331;* Moonstruck, *336;* Silkwood, *658;* Suspect, *1022;* Witches of Eastwick, The, *412*
Chereau, Patrice: Danton, *728;* Last of the Mohicans, The (1992), *1126*
Cherkassov, Nikolai: Alexander Nevsky, *711;* Ivan the Terrible—Part I & Part II, *749*
Cherrill, Virginia: City Lights, *255*
Cherry, Byron: Fix, The, *50*
Cherry, Helen: Nemesis (1986), *1000*
Cheryl, Karen: Here Comes Santa Claus, *174*
Chesebro, George: Roamin' Wild, *1145;* Saddle Mountain Roundup, *1146;* Vigilantes of Boomtown, *1161*
Chesnais, Patrick: La Lectrice (The Reader), *754*
Chester, Craig: Swoon, *675*
Chestnut, Morris: Boyz N the Hood, *468;* Ernest Green Story, The, *165*
Cheung, Leslie: Better Tomorrow, A, *717;* Better Tomorrow 2, A, *717;* Chinese Ghost Story, A, *723;* Farewell My Concubine, *736*
Cheung, Maggie: Paper Marriage (1988), *775;* Police Story III—Super Cop, *778;* Project A (Part II), *779;* Song of the Exile, *787*
Chevalia, Kevin: Homeward Bound: The Incredible Journey, *175*
Chevalier, Anna: Tabu, *676*
Chevalier, Maurice: Breath of Scandal, A, *245;* Can-Can, *911;* Fanny (1961), *514;* Gigi, *919;* Hollywood on Parade, *299;* In Search of the Castaways, *176;* Love in the Afternoon, *323;* Love Me Tonight, *929;* Merry Widow, The, *930;* Monkeys Go Home, *188;* New Kind of Love, A, *343;* Panic Button, *353*
Chew, Kim: Dim Sum: A Little Bit of Heart, *501*
Chew, Laureen: Dim Sum: A Little Bit of Heart, *501*
Chi-Vy, Sam: China, My Sorrow, *723*
Chiaki, Minoru: Hidden Fortress, The, *744;* Throne of Blood, *794*
Chiao, Roy: Protector, The, *101*
Chiari, Walter: Bellissima, *716;* Chimes at Midnight, *481*
Chiaureli, Sofico: Color of Pomegranates, The, *725*
Chiba, Sachiko: Wife! Be Like a Rose!, *803*
Chiba, Sonny: Aces: Iron Eagle III, *1;* Legend of the Eight Samurai, *758;* Street Fighter, *121;* Virus, *1087*
Chibas, Marissa: Cold Feet (1984), *257*
Chicot, Etienne: 36 Fillette, *794*
Chief Thundercloud: Lone Ranger, The (1938), *1129;* Riders of the Whistling Skull, *1144*
Chiklis, Michael: Rain Killer, The, *1008;* Wired, *704*
Childress, Alvin: Amos and Andy (TV Series), *226*
Chiles, Linden: Forbidden World, *842*
Chiles, Lois: Creepshow 2, *826;* Diary of a Hitman, *970;* Moonraker, *86;* Raw Courage, *103;* Sweet Liberty, *389;* Twister, *401;* Way We Were, The, *697*
Chin, Joey: China Girl, *25*
Chin, May: Wedding Banquet, The, *407*
Chin, Tsai: Joy Luck Club, The, *559*
Ching, William: Pat and Mike, *355;* Wistful Widow of Wagon Gap, The, *412*
Chinh, Kieu: Joy Luck Club, The, *559;* Operation C.I.A., *95*
Chinn, Jade: Girl Who Spelled Freedom, The, *169*
Chirizzi, Gian Luigi: Burial Ground, *820*
Chlumsky, Anna: My Girl, *190;* My Girl 2, *190*
Choate, Tim: Def-Con 4, *1046;* Europeans, The, *511;* First Time, The, *277;* Jane Austen in Manhattan, *309;* Spy, *1019*
Chong, Jun: Silent Assassins, *116;* Street Soldiers, *121*
Chong, Rae Dawn: Amazon, *4;* American Flyers, *446;* Beat Street, *908;* Borrower, The, *1040;* City Limits, *1041;* Color Purple, The, *485;* Commando, *28;* Common Bonds, *487;* Curiosity Kills, *965;* Dangerous Relations, *494;* Denial, *499;* Far Out Man, *274;* Fear City, *47;* Principal, The, *628;* Prison Stories: Women on the Inside, *628;* Quest for Fire, *1073;* Soul Man, *383;* Squeeze, The (1987), *385;* Time Runner, *1084;* When the Party's Over, *699*
Chong, Tommy: After Hours, *223;* Far Out Man, *274;* Spirit of '76, The, *384;* Tommy Chong Roast, The, *397*
Choudhury, Sarita: House of the Spirits, The, *545;* Mississippi Masala, *596;* Wild West (1993), *411*
Chow, Yun Fat: City on Fire, *724*
Chowdhry, Navin: King of the Wind, *180;* Madame Sousatzka, *584;* Seventh Coin, The, *203*
Chowdhry, Ranjit: Lonely in America, *320*
Christensen, Stacy: Virgin Queen of St. Francis High, The, *405*
Christensen, Ute: Berlin Tunnel 21, *10*
Christian, Claudia: Adventures of a Gnome Named Gnorm, The, *1034;* Arena, *1036;* Hexed, *296;* Hidden, The, *1056;* Mad About You, *325;* Maniac Cop 2, *863;* Never on Tuesday, *604;* Strays, *891;* Think Big, *394*
Christian, Helen: Zorro Rides Again, *1166*
Christian, Keely: Slumber Party Massacre 3, *887*
Christian, Leigh: Beyond Atlantis, *11*
Christian, Linda: Athena, *907;* Casino Royale (1954), *23;* Full Hearts and Empty Pockets, *739;* Holiday in Mexico, *923*
Christian, Paul: Beast From 20,000 Fathoms, The, *1038*
Christian, Robert: Bustin' Loose, *248;* Roll of Thunder, Hear My Cry, *642*
Christians, Mady: Letter from an Unknown Woman, *573*
Christians, Rudolph: Foolish Wives, *518*
Christie, Audrey: Frankie and Johnny (1966), *918;* Splendor in the Grass, *664;* Streets of L.A., The, *671*
Christie, Julie: Billy Liar, *461;* Darling, *496;* Demon Seed, *1046;* Dr. Zhivago, *503;* Don't Look Now, *971;* Fahrenheit 451, *1050;* Far from the Madding Crowd, *514;* Fools of Fortune, *518;* Heat and Dust, *539;* Heaven Can Wait (1978), *295;* McCabe and Mrs. Miller, *1133;* Miss Mary, *767;* Petulia, *621;* Power (1986), *625;* Railway Station Man, The, *633;* Return of the Soldier, The, *638;* Secret Obsessions, *651;* Separate Tables, *652;* Shampoo, *655*
Christine, Virginia: Billy the Kid vs. Dracula, *813;* Guess Who's Coming to Dinner, *534;* Mummy's Curse, The, *867;* Not as a Stranger, *609;* One Man's Way, *613;* Phantom of the Plains, *1138;* Prize, The, *629*
Christmas, Eric: Home Is Where the Hart Is, *299;* Philadelphia Experiment, The, *1070*
Christophe, Françoise: Walk into Hell, *136*
Christopher, Dennis: Alien Predators, *1035;* Bernice Bobs Her Hair, *234;* Breaking Away, *245;* California Dreaming, *474;* Chariots of Fire, *479;* Circuitry Man, *1041;* Don't Cry, It's Only Thunder, *503;* Fade to Black (1980), *840;* It (1991), *857;* Jack and the Beanstalk, *178;* Jake Speed, *68;* Last Word, The, *571;* September 30, 1955, *652;* Sinful Life, A, *379;* Young Graduates, *708*

Christopher, Jean: Playgirl Killer, The, *875*
Christopher, Jordan: Return of the Seven, *1142*
Christopher, Kay: Dick Tracy's Dilemma, *38*
Christopher, Thom: Deathstalker III—The Warriors from Hell, *1046;* Wizard of the Lost Kingdom, *1090*
Christy, Dorothy: Big Business Girl, *460;* Parlor, Bedroom and Bath, *354;* Radio Ranch (Men with Steel Faces & Phantom Empire), *1140*
Christy, Vic: Challenge to Be Free, *157*
Chuckles, The: Girl Can't Help It, The, *286*
Chuckster, Simon: Sweet Sweetback's Baadasssss Song, *123*
Chung, Cherie: Peking Opera Blues, *776*
Chung, David: Ballad of Little Jo, The, *1096*
Church, Sandra: Ugly American, The, *690*
Churchill, Berton: Big Stampede, The, *1098*
Churchill, Donald: Hound of the Baskervilles, The (1983), *984*
Churchill, Marguerite: Ambassador Bill, *225;* Big Trail, The, *1098;* Dracula's Daughter, *837*
Churchill, Sarah: Royal Wedding, *938*
Chuvelov, Ivan: End of St. Petersburg, The, *734*
Ciampa, Jo: Salome (1985), *647*
Ciannelli, Eduardo: Adventures of the Flying Cadets, *2;* Bulldog Drummond's Bride, *20;* Creeper, The, *826;* Dillinger (1945), *39;* Gunga Din, *58;* Kitty Foyle, *566;* Lost Moment, The, *580;* Marked Woman, *82;* Monster from Green Hell, *866;* Mummy's Hand, The, *867;* Mysterious Dr. Satan, *88;* Strange Cargo, *669;* They Got Me Covered, *393;* They Met in Bombay, *127;* Winterset, *704*
Ciardi, Francesca: Cannibal Holocaust, *821*
Ciesar, Jennifer: Lovers' Lovers, *582*
Cilento, Diane: Agony and the Ecstasy, The, *443;* Hitler, the Last Ten Days, *542;* Hombre, *1121;* Naked Edge, The, *1000;* Rattle of a Simple Man, *635;* Truth About Women, The, *689;* Wicker Man, The, *903;* Z.P.G. (Zero Population Growth), *1091*
Cimino, Leonardo: Rappaccini's Daughter, *635*
Cinnante, Kelly: Christmas in Connecticut (1992), *255*
Cioffi, Charles: Don Is Dead, The, *40;* Lucky Luciano, *79;* Remo Williams: The Adventure Begins, *105;* Shaft, *114;* Thief Who Came to Dinner, The, *393*
Citera, Tom: Up the Academy, *403*
Citti, Franco: Accattone, *710;* Arabian Nights (1974), *713;* Decameron, The, *729;* Oedipus Rex (1967), *772;* Pigsty, *777*
Clair, Jany: Hercules Against the Moon Men, *1056*
Claire, Cyrielle: Code Name: Emerald, *27;* Sword of Gideon, *123*
Claire, Ina: Three Broadway Girls, *395*
Claire, Jennifer: Right Hand Man, The, *640*
Claire, Marion: Make a Wish, *586*
Clairiond, Aimée: Monsieur Vincent, *768*
Clanton, Jimmy: Go, Johnny, Go!, *920*
Clanton, Rony: Education of Sonny Carson, The, *507*
Clapp, Gordon: Kurt Vonnegut's Monkey House, *1061;* Return of the Secaucus 7, *366;* Small Sacrifices, *660;* Termini Station, *679*
Clapton, Eric: Chuck Berry Hail! Hail! Rock 'n' Roll, *421;* Jimi Hendrix, *428;* Last Waltz, The, *428;* Secret Policemen's Other Ball, The, *375*
Clare, Mary: Citadel, The, *482;* Evil Mind, The (a.k.a. The Clairvoyant), *839;* Young and Innocent, *1033*
Clark, Alexander: No Time for Sergeants (Television), *608*
Clark, Andrew: Anzacs, *450*
Clark, Anthony: Dogfight, *503*
Clark, Bobby: Clark and McCullough: Inspired Madness, *256*
Clark, Brett: Alien Warrior, *1035;* Deathstalker IV: Match of the Titans, *1046;* Eye of the Eagle, *46;* Inner Sanctum, *986;* Malibu Express, *327*
Clark, Bryan: Without Warning: The James Brady Story, *704*
Clark, Candy: American Graffiti, *226;* Amityville III: The Demon, *809;* Big Sleep, The (1978), *955;* Blob, The (1988), *814;* Blue Thunder, *16;* Cat's Eye, *822;* Citizen's Band, *255;* Cool As Ice, *488;* Fat City, *515;* Hambone and Hillie, *535;* James Dean—A Legend in His Own Time, *556;* Man Who Fell to Earth, The, *1064;* More American Graffiti, *599;* Original Intent, *614;* Q, *878;* Rodeo Girl, *642;* Tale of the Frog Prince, *209*
Clark, Carol Higgins: Cry in the Night, A, *964*
Clark, Carolyn Ann: Cradle Will Fall, The, *964*
Clark, Dane: Action in the North Atlantic, *2;* Destination Tokyo, *37;* Gambler and the Lady, The, *524;* Hollywood Canteen, *923;* Moonrise, *599;* Murder on Flight 502, *87;* Stolen Life, A, *668;* Thunder Pass, *1157*
Clark, Dick: Deadman's Curve, *913*
Clark, Doran: Black Eagle, *13*
Clark, Eugene A.: Trial & Error, *1027*
Clark, Fred: Auntie Mame, *229;* Bells Are Ringing, *908;* Boys' Night Out, *244;* Caddy, The, *249;* Don't Go Near the Water, *267;* George Burns and Gracie Allen Show, The (TV Series), *284;* Here Come the Girls, *922;* Horse in the Gray Flannel Suit, The, *175;* It Started With a Kiss, *308;* Laugh for Joy, *756;* Lemon Drop Kid, The, *317;* Mating Game, The, *330;* Passionate Thief, The (1961), *776;* Sunset Boulevard, *673;* Three for Bedroom C, *395*
Clark, Harry: No Time for Sergeants (Television), *608*
Clark, Ian D.: Trial & Error, *1027*
Clark, Jameson: Battle of the Sexes, The, *233*
Clark, Ken: Attack of the Giant Leeches, *810*
Clark, Liddy: Blue Fin, *151;* Kitty and the Bagman, *73*
Clark, Mamo: Robinson Crusoe of Clipper Island, *108*
Clark, Marlene: Night of the Cobra Woman, *869*
Clark, Matt: Back to the Future III, *1037;* Class Action, *962;* Country, *489;* Driver, The, *42;* Gambler, Part III—The Legend Continues, The, *1115;* Great Northfield Minnesota Raid, The, *1116;* Kid Vengeance, *1124;* Out of the Darkness, *1003;* Pat Garrett and Billy the Kid, *1138;* Quick and the Dead, The, *1140;* Return to Oz, *199;* Ruckus, *109;* White Lightning, *139*
Clark, Michael: Prospero's Books, *629*
Clark, Oliver: Ernest Saves Christmas, *165;* One Cooks, the Other Doesn't, *349;* Star Is Born, A (1976), *666*
Clark, Petula: Finian's Rainbow, *916;* Goodbye, Mr. Chips (1969), *920;* Made in Heaven (1948), *326;* Promoter, The, *362*
Clark, Robin: Boxoffice, *467*
Clark, Roy: Matilda, *330;* Uphill All the Way, *404*
Clark Sisters: Gospel, *425*
Clark, Susan: Apple Dumpling Gang, The, *147;* Choice, The, *481;* Colossus: The Forbin Project, *1042;* Coogan's Bluff, *29;* Deadly Companion, *968;* Murder by Decree, *998;* Night Moves, *1001;* Nobody's Perfekt, *346;* North Avenue Irregulars, The, *191;* Promises in the Dark, *629;* Showdown (1973), *1149;* Skin Game, *1150;* Valdez Is Coming, *1160*
Clarke, Alex: Learning Tree, The, *572*
Clarke, Brian Patrick: Sleepaway Camp II: Unhappy Campers, *887*
Clarke, Caitlin: Dragonslayer, *1048;* Penn & Teller Get Killed, *356*
Clarke, Gary: How to Make a Monster, *853;* Missile to the Moon, *1066*
Clarke, Mae: Flying Tigers, The, *51;* Frankenstein (1931), *842;* Great Guy, *532;* King of the Rocketmen, *72;* Lady Killer, *74;* Public Enemy, *101*
Clarke, Margi: Letter to Brezhnev, *318*
Clarke, Melinda: Return to Two-Moon Junction, *639*
Clarke, Mindy: Return of the Living Dead 3, *880*
Clarke, Robert: Frankenstein Island, *842;* Hideous Sun Demon, The, *850;* Midnight Movie Massacre, *332*
Clarke, Warren: Cold Room, The, *485;* Firefox, *49;* Great Riviera Bank Robbery, The, *980;* Mandela, *588*
Clarke, Zelah: Jane Eyre (1983), *557*
Clarkson, Lana: Barbarian Queen, *1038;* Barbarian Queen II: Empress Strikes Back, *1038;* Deathstalker, *1046*

Clarkson, Patricia: Blindman's Bluff, *956;* Caught in the Act, *960;* Dead Pool, The, *33;* Four Eyes and Six Guns, *1114;* Legacy of Lies, *572*
Clarkson, Robert: Save the Lady, *201*
Clary, Robert: New Faces, *933*
Clay, Andrew Dice: Adventures of Ford Fairlane, The, *2;* Brain Smasher...A Love Story, *18;* Dice Rules, *264;* One Night with Dice, *350*
Clay, Jennifer: Suburbia, *672*
Clay, Nicholas: Cannon Movie Tales: Sleeping Beauty, *155;* Evil under the Sun, *973;* Excalibur, *1050;* Lady Chatterley's Lover (1981), *567;* Love Spell, *79*
Clayburgh, Jill: Day of Atonement, *33;* First Monday in October, *517;* Griffin and Phoenix: A Love Story, *533;* Hanna K., *743;* Hustling, *547;* I'm Dancing As Fast As I Can, *549;* It's My Turn, *555;* Miles to Go, *594;* Portnoy's Complaint, *624;* Rich in Love, *640;* Semi-Tough, *375;* Shy People, *657;* Silver Streak (1976), *379;* Starting Over, *385;* Terminal Man, The, *893;* Thief Who Came to Dinner, The, *393;* Unmarried Woman, An, *691;* Unspeakable Acts, *692;* Wedding Party, The, *407;* Where Are the Children?, *1031;* Whispers in the Dark, *1031*
Claypool, Les: Adventures of the Kung Fu Rascals, The, *223*
Clayton, Ethel: Warning Shadows (1933), *1030*
Clayton, Jan: In Old Mexico, *1123;* Showdown (1940), *1149*
Clayton, John: High Rolling, *62*
Clayworth, June: Dick Tracy Meets Gruesome, *38*
Cleef, Lee Van: Beast From 20,000 Fathoms, The, *1038;* Blade Rider, *1099;* Days of Wrath, *1107;* Gypsy Colt, *173;* Kid Vengeance, *1124;* Tribute to a Bad Man, *1159*
Cleese, John: And Now for Something Completely Different, *226;* Clockwise, *256;* Erik the Viking, *1049;* Fawlty Towers, *276;* Fish Called Wanda, A, *277;* How to Irritate People, *302;* Life of Brian, *318;* Monty Python and the Holy Grail, *336;* Monty Python Live at the Hollywood Bowl, *336;* Monty Python's Flying Circus (TV Series), *336;* Monty Python's the Meaning of Life, *336;* Privates on Parade, *362;* Romance with a Double Bass, *370;* Secret Policemen's Other Ball, The, *375;* Secret Policeman's Private Parts, The, *375;* Silverado, *1150;* Splitting Heirs, *384;* Statue, The, *385;* Time Bandits, *1084;* Whoops Apocalypse, *411;* Yellowbeard, *415*
Clemens, Paul: Beast Within, The, *812;* Promises in the Dark, *629*
Clement, Aurore: Eighties, The, *733;* Invitation au Voyage, *748;* Les Rendez-Vous D'Anna, *759;* Paris, Texas, *618;* Toute Une Nuit, *796*
Clementi, Pierre: Conformist, The, *725;* Partner, *775;* Pigsty, *777;* Steppenwolf, *667;* Sweet Movie, *792*
Clements, Edward: Metropolitan, *593*
Clements, John: Convoy (1940), *488;* Four Feathers, The (1939), *52;* Ships with Wings, *115;* Silent Enemy, The, *116*
Clements, Stanley: Babe Ruth Story, The, *453;* Bowery Boys, The (Series), *244*
Clemmons, Clarence: Fatal Instinct (1993), *274*
Clennon, David: Couch Trip, The, *259;* Hanna K., *743;* Light Sleeper, *575;* Man Trouble, *327;* Missing, *596;* Special Bulletin, *1019;* Sweet Dreams, *943*
Clery, Corinne: Story of O, The, *668;* Yor: The Hunter from the Future, *1091*
Cleveland, George: Angel on My Shoulder (1946), *448;* Blue Steel (1934), *1099;* Courage of Lassie, *160;* Drums of Fu Manchu, *42;* Lone Ranger, The (1938), *1129;* Man from Utah, The, *1132;* Revolt of the Zombies, *881;* Spoilers, The, *1152;* Wistful Widow of Wagon Gap, The, *412;* Yellow Rose of Texas, *1165*
Cleveland, Rev. James: Gospel, *425*
Clevot, Philippe: Eyes of the Birds, *735*
Cliff, Jimmy: Club Paradise, *256;* Harder They Come, The, *922;* Jimmy Cliff—Bongo Man, *926*
Clifford, Jack: King of the Pecos, *1125*
Clifford, Kim: Save the Lady, *201*
Clift, Montgomery: Big Lift, The, *460;* From Here to Eternity (1953), *523;* Heiress, The, *539;* I Confess, *984;* Indiscretion of an American Wife, *551;* Judgment at Nuremberg, *560;* Lonelyhearts, *578;* Misfits, The, *595;* Place in the Sun, A, *622;* Raintree County, *634;* Red River, *1141;* Search, The, *650;* Suddenly, Last Summer, *672;* Young Lions, The, *708*
Climo, Brett: Archer's Adventure, *147*
Cline, Eddie: Buster Keaton Festival: Vol. 1, *248;* Buster Keaton Festival: Vol. 2, *248;* Buster Keaton Scrapbook, Vol. I, *248*
Clinger, Debra: Midnight Madness, *332*
Clive, Colin: Bride of Frankenstein, *819;* Christopher Strong, *482;* Frankenstein (1931), *842;* History Is Made at Night, *542;* Jane Eyre (1934), *557;* Mad Love, *861*
Clive, E. E.: Arrest Bulldog Drummond, *6;* Bulldog Drummond Comes Back, *20;* Bulldog Drummond Escapes, *20;* Bulldog Drummond's Revenge, *21;* Hound of the Baskervilles, The (1939), *983;* Invisible Man, The, *856;* Night Must Fall, *606;* Personal Property, *356;* Tarzan Escapes, *125*
Cliver, Al: Endgame, *1049*
Clooney, George: Red Surf, *104;* Return of the Killer Tomatoes, *366*
Clooney, Rosemary: Here Come the Girls, *922;* Red Garters, *936;* White Christmas, *947*
Close, Glenn: Big Chill, The, *460;* Dangerous Liaisons, *494;* Fatal Attraction (1987), *975;* Hamlet (1990), *535;* Hook, *175;* House of the Spirits, The, *545;* Immediate Family, *549;* Jagged Edge, *556;* Maxie, *330;* Meeting Venus, *591;* Natural, The, *604;* Orphan Train, *615;* Paper, The, *617;* Reversal of Fortune, *639;* Sarah, Plain and Tall, *648;* Skylark, *660;* Stone Boy, The, *668;* World According to Garp, The, *706*
Clough, John Scott: Fast Forward, *916*
Cloutier, Suzanne: Othello (1952), *615*
Clouzot, Vera: Diabolique, *730;* Wages of Fear, The, *801*
Clover, David: Zipperface, *1033*
Clushenko, Yevgenia: Unfinished Piece for the Player Piano, An, *798*
Clute, Sidney: Cry of Battle, *31*
Clutsei, George: Legend of Walks Far Woman, The, *1128*
Cluzet, François: Horse of Pride, The, *744;* One Deadly Summer, *773;* Round Midnight, *937;* Story of Women, The, *790*
Clyde (the ape): Every Which Way but Loose, *273*
Clyde, Andy: Annie Oakley (1935), *1093;* Bad Lands, *1095;* Bar 20, *1096;* Border Patrol, *1100;* Borrowed Trouble, *1100;* Caution: Funny Men at Work, *420;* Colt Comrades, *1105;* Dangerous Venture, *1107;* Dead Don't Dream, The, *1108;* Devil's Playground, *1109;* False Colors, *1112;* False Paradise, *1112;* Forty Thieves, *1114;* Hoppy Serves a Writ, *1121;* Hoppy's Holiday, *1121;* Leather Burners, The, *1128;* Little Minister, The, *576;* Lizzies of Mack Sennett, The, *320;* Marauders, *1132;* Mystery Man, *1135;* Riders of the Deadline, *1144;* Silent Conflict, *1150;* Sinister Journey, *1150;* Strange Gamble, *1153;* Sundown Riders, *1153;* Texas Masquerade, *1156;* Three Men from Texas, *1157;* Unexpected Guest, *1160*
Clyde, June: Study in Scarlet, A, *1021*
Coates, Kim: Amityville Curse, The, *809;* Club, The (1993), *824;* Cold Front, *963;* Harmony Cats, *536;* Model by Day, *86;* Red-Blooded American Girl, *879;* Smokescreen, *661*
Coates, Phyllis: Blues Busters, *242;* I Was a Teenage Frankenstein, *855;* Incredible Petrified World, The, *1058;* Longhorn, *1130;* Marshal of Cedar Rock, *1132;* Panther Girl of the Congo, *97;* Superman and the Mole Men, *1081;* TV's Best Adventures of Superman, *1085*
Cobanoglu, Necmettin: Journey of Hope, *750*
Cobb, Lee J.: Anna and the King of Siam, *449;* Brothers Karamazov, The, *471;* Buckskin Frontier, *1102;* But Not For Me, *472;* Call Northside 777, *959;* Come Blow Your Horn, *257;* Coogan's Bluff, *29;* Dark Past, The, *495;* Exodus, *512;* Exorcist, The, *839;* Four Horsemen of the Apocalypse, *52;* Golden Boy, *529;* In Like Flint, *66;* Lawman, *1127;* Left Hand of God, The, *76;* Liberation of L. B. Jones, The, *574;* Macho Callahan, *1130;* Mackenna's Gold, *1131;* Man in the Gray

Flannel Suit, The, *587;* Man of the West, *1132;* Man Who Loved Cat Dancing, The, *1132;* Meanest Men in the West, The, *1133;* Men of Boys Town, *592;* Miracle of the Bells, The, *595;* On the Waterfront, *612;* Our Man Flint, *96;* Party Girl, *618;* Racers, The, *632;* Rustler's Valley, *1146;* Sirocco, *116;* Song of Bernadette, The, *662;* That Lucky Touch, *392;* Three Faces of Eve, The, *682;* Trap, The, *1026;* 12 Angry Men, *690*

Cobb, Randall "Tex": Blind Fury, *15;* Buy and Cell, *248;* Collision Course, *257;* Critical Condition, *260;* Diggstown, *264;* Dirty Dozen, The: The Deadly Mission, *39;* Ernest Goes to Jail, *272;* Fletch Lives, *978;* Golden Child, The, *56;* Raising Arizona, *364;* Uncommon Valor, *134*

Cobbs, Bill: Bodyguard, The, *466;* Decoration Day, *498;* Hudsucker Proxy, The, *303*

Cobo, Roberto: Los Olvidados, *761*

Coburn, Charles: Bachelor Mother, *230;* Colonel Effingham's Raid, *257;* Devil and Miss Jones, The, *264;* Edison, The Man, *507;* Gentlemen Prefer Blondes, *284;* George Washington Slept Here, *284;* Heaven Can Wait (1943), *295;* Idiot's Delight, *548;* Impact, *985;* In Name Only, *550;* In This Our Life, *550;* King's Row, *565;* Knickerbocker Holiday, *927;* Lady Eve, The, *315;* Made for Each Other, *325;* Mr. Music, *931;* Monkey Business (1952), *336;* More the Merrier, The, *337;* Of Human Hearts, *610;* Paradine Case, The, *1004;* Road to Singapore, *369;* Three Faces West, *683;* Trouble Along the Way, *688;* Vivacious Lady, *405;* Wilson, *703*

Coburn, David: Born American, *17*

Coburn, James: Americanization of Emily, The, *226;* Baltimore Bullet, The, *231;* Bite the Bullet, *1099;* Bronco (TV Series), *1101;* Bruce Lee: Curse of the Dragon, *420;* Charade, *960;* Cross of Iron, *31;* Dain Curse, The, *965;* Dead Heat on a Merry-Go-Round, *967;* Deadfall, *968;* Death of a Soldier, *498;* Draw, *1110;* Firepower, *49;* Fistful of Dynamite, A, *1113;* Goldengirl, *1054;* Great Escape, The, *57;* Hard Times, *59;* Hell Is for Heroes, *60;* High Risk, *61;* Hit List, The (1992), *982;* Hudson Hawk, *64;* In Like Flint, *66;* Internecine Project, The, *986;* Last of Sheila, The, *991;* Looker, *1063;* Loved One, The, *323;* Loving Couples, *324;* Magnificent Seven, The, *1131;* Major Dundee, *1131;* Martin's Day, *185;* Massacre at Fort Holman (Reason to Live...A Reason to Die, A), *1133;* Maverick, *1133;* Muppet Movie, The, *189;* Our Man Flint, *96;* Pat Garrett and Billy the Kid, *1138;* Pinocchio (1983), *195;* President's Analyst, The, *360;* Ride Lonesome, *1143;* Sister Act 2: Back in the Habit, *380;* Waterhole #3, *1163;* Young Guns II, *1166*

Coburn Jr., James: Tuxedo Warrior, *133*

Coby, Michael: Bitch, The, *462;* We Are No Angels, *1163*

Coca, Imogene: Alice in Wonderland (1985), *145;* 10 from Your Show of Shows, *392*

Coca, Richard: Hitz, *63;* Only the Strong, *95*

Cochran, Eddie: Girl Can't Help It, The, *286;* Go, Johnny, Go!, *920*

Cochran, Robert: I Stand Condemned, *548;* Sanders of the River, *111;* Scrooge (1935), *650*

Cochran, Steve: Carnival Story, *475;* Chase, The (1946), *479;* Copacabana, *259;* Deadly Companions, The, *1108;* I, Mobster, *65;* Il Grido, *747;* Jim Thorpe—All American, *558;* Kid from Brooklyn, The, *313;* Private Hell 36, *628;* Song Is Born, A, *940;* White Heat, *138*

Cochrane, Rory: Dazed and Confused, *497;* Fathers & Sons, *515*

Cocker, Joe: Mad Dogs and Englishmen, *429*

Coco, James: Chair, The, *822;* Cheap Detective, The, *254;* Generation, *283;* Hunk, *303;* Littlest Angel, The, *184;* Man of La Mancha, *930;* Murder by Death, *338;* New Leaf, A, *343;* Only When I Laugh, *614;* Scavenger Hunt, *373;* That's Adequate, *393;* Wholly Moses!, *410;* Wild Party, The (1975), *702*

Cocteau, Jean: Blood of a Poet, *719;* Testament of Orpheus, The, *793*

Codrescu, Andrei: Road Scholar, *434*

Cody, Bill: Cyclone Ranger, *1107*

Cody, Iron Eyes: Ernest Goes to Camp, *272;* Grayeagle, *1116;* Son of Paleface, *383*

Cody, Lew: Dishonored, *501*

Coe, Barry: But Not For Me, *472;* Cat, The, *157;* Dr. Death: Seeker of Souls, *835;* Peyton Place, *621*

Coe, George: Blind Date (1987), *241;* End of Innocence, The, *509;* Flash of Green, A, *977;* Hollywood Detective, The, *983;* Listen to Your Heart, *319;* Red Flag: The Ultimate Game, *104;* Remo Williams: The Adventure Begins, *105*

Coe, Peter: Mummy's Curse, The, *867;* Okefenokee, *93*

Coffey, Scott: Amazing Stories (TV Series), *1036;* Montana, *599;* Shag, the Movie, *654;* Shout (1991), *939*

Coffield, Peter: Times Square, *946*

Coffin, Frederick: V. I. Warshawski, *1029*

Coffin, Tristram: Corpse Vanishes, The, *825;* Forbidden Trails, *1114;* Holt of the Secret Service, *63;* Jesse James Rides Again, *1123;* King of the Rocketmen, *72;* Ma Barker's Killer Brood, *80;* Pirates of the High Seas, *99;* Rodeo King and the Senorita, *1145;* Spy Smasher, *119*

Coggio, Roger: Immortal Story, *549*

Coghill, Nikki: Dark Age, *32*

Coghlan Jr., Frank: Adventures of Captain Marvel, The, *2;* Drum Taps, *1110;* Hell's House, *61;* Yankee Clipper, *141*

Cogley, Nick: Keystone Comedies, Vol. 5, *313*

Cohen, Alain: Two of Us, The, *797*

Cohen, Emma: Cut Throats Nine, *1107;* Horror Rises from the Tomb, *852;* Night of the Walking Dead, *870*

Cohen, Jacques: In Trouble, *550*

Cohen, Jeff: Goonies, The, *56*

Cohen, Matthew Roy: Trained to Fight, *132*

Cohen, Mitchell: Toxic Avenger, The, *897*

Cohn, Mindy: Boy Who Could Fly, The, *468*

Coinman, John: Laughing Horse, *571*

Colegrande, Stefano: Misunderstood (1988), *598*

Colao, Manuel: Flight of the Innocent, *737*

Colasanto, Nicholas: Fat City, *515;* Mad Bull, *584;* Raging Bull, *633*

Colbert, Claudette: Cleopatra (1934), *484;* Drums Along the Mohawk, *42;* Egg and I, The, *270;* Guest Wife, *291;* I Cover the Waterfront, *65;* It Happened One Night, *307;* Let's Make It Legal, *318;* Palm Beach Story, The, *353;* Parrish, *618;* Since You Went Away, *658;* Texas Lady, *1156;* Three Came Home, *682;* Tomorrow Is Forever, *685;* Tovaritch, *398;* Without Reservations, *413*

Colbert, Ray: RSVP, *371*

Colbourne, Maurice: Littlest Horse Thieves, The, *184*

Cole, Alexandra: Dr. Butcher, M.D. (Medical Deviate), *835*

Cole, Dennis: Connection (1973), *487;* Death House, *35;* Powderkeg, *1139;* Pretty Smart, *361*

Cole, Gary: Echoes in the Darkness, *507;* Fatal Vision, *515;* In the Line of Fire, *66;* Son of the Morning Star, *1151*

Cole, George: Adventures of Sadie, *223;* Belles of St. Trinian's, The, *234;* Dr. Syn, Alias the Scarecrow, *163;* Gone in 60 Seconds, *56;* Vampire Lovers, The, *900*

Cole, Henry: Shaka Zulu, *654*

Cole, Michael: Mod Squad, The (TV Series), *86*

Cole, Nat King: China Gate, *481;* Small Town Girl, *940*

Cole, Olivia: Sky Is Gray, The, *660;* Some Kind of Hero, *382*

Cole, Skyler: Adventures Beyond Belief, *222*

Coleby, Robert: Archer's Adventure, *147;* Great Expectations—The Untold Story, *532;* Now and Forever, *609;* Plumber, The, *1006*

Coleman, Charlotte: Four Weddings and a Funeral, *280*

Coleman, Dabney: Amos & Andrew, *226;* Bad Ronald, *811;* Beverly Hillbillies, The, *237;* Bite the Bullet, *1099;* Callie and Son, *474;* Clifford, *256;* Cloak and Dagger (1984), *27;* Dragnet (1987), *268;* Hot to Trot, *302;* How to Beat the High Co$t of Living, *302;* I Love My Wife, *304;* Man with One Red Shoe, The, *328;* Meet the Applegates, *331;* Muppets Take Manhattan, The, *189;* Murrow, *601;* Never Forget, *604;* Nine to Five, *345;* Nothing Personal, *347;* Pray TV (1980), *360;*

President's Plane Is Missing, The, *1007;* Rolling Thunder, *108;* Scalphunters, The, *1148;* Short Time, *378;* Slender Thread, The, *660;* There Goes the Neighborhood, *393;* Tootsie, *397;* Trouble with Girls, The, *946;* Wargames, *1088;* Where the Heart Is, *699;* Young Doctors in Love, *415*

Coleman, Frank J.: Charlie Chaplin Cavalcade, *253*

Coleman, Gary: Jimmy the Kid, *178;* Kid from Left Field, The, *180;* Kid with the Broken Halo, The, *313;* Kid with the 200 I.Q., The, *180;* On the Right Track, *192*

Coleman, Jack: Rubdown, *1011*

Coleman, Jimmy: Riff-Raff (1992), *640*

Coleman, John: President's Target, *100*

Coleman, Nancy: Edge of Darkness (1943), *43*

Coleman, Ornette: Ornette—Made in America, *432*

Coleman, Signy: Relentless 3, *1010*

Coleridge, Tania: Rain Killer, The, *1008*

Coles, Michael: I Want What I Want, *548*

Coley, Thomas: Dr. Cyclops, *835*

Colga, Eileen: Quackser Fortune Has a Cousin in the Bronx, *631*

Colicos, John: Drum, *505;* King Solomon's Treasure, *73;* Nowhere to Hide, *92;* Phobia, *1006;* Postman Always Rings Twice, The (1981), *1007;* Raid on Rommel, *103;* Shadow Dancing, *1014*

Colin Jr., David: Beyond the Door, *813;* Beyond the Door 2, *813*

Colin, Gregoire: Olivier, Olivier, *773*

Colin, Jean: Mikado, The (1939), *931*

Colin, Margaret: Amos & Andrew, *226;* Butcher's Wife, The, *248;* Like Father, Like Son, *318;* Martians Go Home, *329;* Something Wild, *383;* Three Men and a Baby, *395;* Traveling Man, *687;* True Believer, *1027*

Coll, Melanie: Lust for Freedom, *80*

Collard, Cyril: Savage Nights, *783*

Collet, Christopher: Manhattan Project, The, *995;* Prayer of the Rollerboys, *100*

Collette, Toni: Efficiency Expert, The, *508*

Colley, Kenneth: And Nothing But the Truth, *447;* Music Lovers, The, *932;* Return to Treasure Island, *199;* Summer Story, A, *673;* Whistle Blower, The, *1031*

Collier, Constance: Damsel in Distress, A, *913;* Monsieur Beaucaire, *336;* Perils of Pauline, The (1947), *356;* Wee Willie Winkie, *216*

Collier, Lois: Naughty Nineties, The, *342;* Night in Casablanca, A, *344*

Collier Jr., William: Cimarron (1931), *1105;* Phantom Express, *99;* Street Scene, *670*

Collin, Maxime: Leolo, *759*

Collins, Alan: And God Said to Cain, *1093;* Ark of the Sun God...Temple of Hell, The, *6;* Exterminators of the Year 3000, *1050;* Yor: The Hunter from the Future, *1091*

Collins, Charles: Dancing Pirate, *913*

Collins, Gary: Hangar 18, *1055;* Kid from Left Field, The, *180*

Collins, Jackie: Richard Lewis—"I'm Exhausted", *367*

Collins, Joan: Adventures of Sadie, *223;* Bawdy Adventures of Tom Jones, The, *233;* Bitch, The, *462;* Bravados, The, *1101;* Cartier Affair, The, *252;* Dark Places, *829;* Decameron Nights, *263;* Devil within Her, The, *833;* Dynasty of Fear, *973;* Empire of the Ants, *1049;* Executioner, The, *974;* Fear in the Night (Dynasty of Fear), *840;* Fearless (1978), *736;* Game for Vultures, *54;* Great Adventure, The, *1116;* Hansel and Gretel, *173;* Homework, *543;* Land of the Pharaohs, *568;* Monte Carlo, *599;* Oh, Alfie, *611;* Opposite Sex, The, *934;* Playing the Field, *358;* Revenge (1971), *1010;* Road to Hong Kong, The, *368;* Seven Thieves, *653;* Stopover Tokyo, *120;* Stud, The, *671;* Sunburn, *1021;* Tales from the Crypt, *892;* Tales that Witness Madness, *892;* Three in the Cellar, *395;* Virgin Queen, The, *694*

Collins, Judy: Woody Guthrie—Hard Travelin', *439*

Collins, Kevin: Garden, The, *525*

Collins, Lewis: Code Name: Wild Geese, *27;* Final Option, The, *977*

Collins, Lisa: Deep Red (1994), *1046*

Collins, Matt: World's Greatest Lover, The, *414*

Collins, Patricia: Phobia, *1006*

Collins, Patrick: Dirt Bike Kid, The, *162*

Collins, Pauline: City of Joy, *483;* Shirley Valentine, *378;* Upstairs, Downstairs, *692*

Collins, Phil: And the Band Played on, *447;* Buster, *472;* Frauds, *281;* Hook, *175;* Secret Policeman's Private Parts, The, *375*

Collins, Ray: Badman's Territory, *1096;* Big Street, The, *460;* Can't Help Singing, *911;* Citizen Kane, *482;* Commandos Strike at Dawn, *28;* Double Life, A, *504;* Francis, the Talking Mule, *280;* Heiress, The, *539;* Homecoming (1948), *543;* Human Comedy, The, *546;* It Happens Every Spring, *307;* Man from Colorado, The, *1131;* Racket, The, *633;* Rose Marie (1954), *937;* Seventh Cross, The, *653;* Vengeance Valley, *1161;* Whistling in Brooklyn, *410*

Collins, Roberta: Hardbodies, *293;* Unholy Rollers, *691;* Vendetta, *135*

Collins, Russell: Enemy Below, The, *44;* Matchmaker, The, *329*

Collins, Ruth: Doom Asylum, *836;* Galactic Gigolo, *282*

Collins, Stephen: Between the Lines, *237;* Brewster's Millions (1985), *245;* Chiefs, *961;* Choke Canyon, *25;* Hold the Dream, *542;* Jumpin' Jack Flash, *311;* Loving Couples, *324;* My New Gun, *341;* Promise, The, *629;* Stella (1990), *667;* Weekend War, *697*

Collins, Steve: Hitchhiker (Series), The, *850*

Collinson, Madeleine: Twins of Evil, *898*

Collinson, Mary: Twins of Evil, *898*

Collyer, June: Murder by Television, *998*

Colman, Ronald: Arrowsmith, *451;* Bulldog Drummond, *20;* Champagne for Caesar, *252;* Double Life, A, *504;* Kismet (1944), *566;* Lady Windermere's Fan, *568;* Lost Horizon, *580;* Lucky Partners, *324;* Prisoner of Zenda, The (1937), *100;* Random Harvest, *635;* Tale of Two Cities, A (1935), *676;* Talk of the Town, The, *390;* White Sister, The, *700*

Colodner, Joel: Plants Are Watching, The, *1071*

Colomby, Scott: Porky's, *360;* Porky's II: The Next Day, *360;* Porky's Revenge, *360*

Colonna, Jerry: College Swing, *912;* Road to Rio, *369;* Road to Singapore, *369*

Colston, Karen: Sweetie, *675*

Colt, Dennis: Savage Guns, *1147*

Colt, Marshall: Beverly Hills Madam, *460;* To Heal a Nation, *684*

Coltrane, Robbie: Adventures of Huck Finn, The (1993), *143;* Bert Rigby, You're a Fool, *908;* Chinese Boxes, *962;* Nuns on the Run, *347;* Oh, What a Night, *611;* Perfectly Normal, *356;* Pope Must Diet, The, *360;* Wonderland, *706*

Coluche: My Best Friend's Girl, *769;* Tchao Pantin, *793*

Columbu, Franco: Beretta's Island, *10;* Desperate Crimes, *37;* Last Man Standing, *569*

Colvin, Jack: Incredible Hulk, The, *1058*

Combes, Norman: Kill or Be Killed, *71*

Combs, Holly Marie: Dr. Giggles, *835*

Combs, Jeffrey: Bride of Re-Animator, *819;* Cyclone, *31;* Dead Man Walking, *1045;* Doctor Mordrid, *1047;* From Beyond, *844;* Phantom Empire, The (1986), *99;* Pit and the Pendulum, The (1991), *875;* Re-Animator, *879*

Comer, Anjanette: Appaloosa, The, *1094;* Baby, The, *811;* Lepke, *76;* Loved One, The, *323;* Netherworld, *868;* Rabbit Run, *632*

Commodores, The: Thank God It's Friday, *944*

Como, Perry: Doll Face, *914;* Words and Music, *948*

Como, Rosella: Seven Hills of Rome, The, *939*

Compson, Betty: Docks of New York, The, *502;* Great Gabbo, The, *532;* Invisible Ghost, *856;* These Girls Won't Talk, *393*

Compton, Fay: Haunting, The, *849;* Othello (1952), *615*

Compton, Joyce: Balalaika, *907;* Country Gentlemen, *260;* Scared to Death, *883*
Comyn, Charles: Place of Weeping, *623*
Conant, Oliver: Summer of '42, *672*
Conaway, Christi: Attack of the 50-Foot Woman (1993), *1037*
Conaway, Jeff: Alien Intruder, *1035;* Almost Pregnant, *225;* Breaking Up Is Hard to Do, *469;* Dirty Dozen, The: The Fatal Mission, *39;* Elvira, Mistress of the Dark, *271;* For the Love of It, *279;* Grease, *920;* L.A. Goddess, *314;* Mirror Images, *996;* Patriot, *97;* Sleeping Car, The, *887;* Sunset Strip, *674;* Time to Die, A (1990), *1025;* Total Exposure, *1026*
Conelle, Patricia: Naked Venus, *603*
Congdon, James: 4D Man, *1053*
Congie, Terry: Sizzle Beach, U.S.A., *380*
Conklin, Chester: Apache Woman, *1094;* Charlie Chaplin...Our Hero, *253;* Every Day's a Holiday, *273;* Knickerbocker Holiday, *927;* Li'l Abner (1940), *318;* Lizzies of Mack Sennett, The, *320;* Sing, Cowboy, Sing, *1150;* Virginian, The (1929), *1161*
Conklin, Heinie: Riders of Destiny, *1144*
Conlin, Jimmy: Great Moment, The, *290;* Mad Wednesday, *325;* Miracle of Morgan's Creek, The, *332;* Palm Beach Story, The, *353;* Sin of Harold Diddlebock (a.k.a. Mad Wednesday), *379;* Sullivan's Travels, *388;* Whistle Stop, *138*
Conlon, Tom: Prom Night III—Last Kiss, *877*
Conn, Didi: Grease, *920;* Grease 2, *920;* You Light Up My Life, *708*
Connell, Edward: Equinox (The Beast), *838*
Connell, Jane: Mame, *930*
Connelly, Christopher: Foxtrap, *52;* Hawmps!, *294;* Incredible Rocky Mountain Race, The, *306;* Jungle Raiders, *69;* Liar's Moon, *574;* Manhattan Baby, *862;* Mines of Kilimanjaro, *85;* Night of the Sharks, *90;* 1990: The Bronx Warriors, *1069;* Operation 'Nam, *95;* Strike Commando, *121;* They Only Kill Their Masters, *1024*
Connelly, Jennifer: Career Opportunities, *251;* Creepers, *826;* Heart of Justice, *538;* Hot Spot, *544;* Labyrinth, *1061;* Rocketeer, The, *108;* Seven Minutes in Heaven, *376;* Some Girls, *382*
Connelly, Marc: Spirit of St. Louis, The, *664;* Tall Story, *391*
Connery, Jason: Bye Bye, Baby, *473;* Robin Hood: Herne's Son, *107;* Spymaker: The Secret Life of Ian Fleming, *119*
Connery, Sean: Anderson Tapes, The, *952;* Another Time, Another Place (1958), *449;* Bridge Too Far, A, *19;* Cuba, *31;* Darby O'Gill and the Little People, *161;* Diamonds Are Forever, *38;* Dr. No, *40;* Family Business, *514;* Fine Madness, A, *277;* Five Days One Summer, *517;* From Russia with Love, *53;* Goldfinger, *56;* Great Train Robbery, The, *980;* Happy Anniversary 007: 25 Years of James Bond, *425;* Highlander, *1056;* Highlander 2: The Quickening, *1056;* Hill, The, *541;* Hunt for Red October, The, *984;* Indiana Jones and the Last Crusade, *1058;* Longest Day, The, *78;* Man Who Would Be King, The, *81;* Marnie, *995;* Medicine Man, *591;* Meteor, *1065;* Molly Maguires, The, *598;* Murder on the Orient Express, *999;* Name of the Rose, The, *89;* Never Say Never Again, *89;* Offence, The, *611;* Outland, *1069;* Presidio, The, *100;* Red Tent, The, *637;* Rising Sun, *1010;* Robin and Marian, *107;* Robin Hood: Prince of Thieves, *108;* Russia House, The, *646;* Shalako, *1148;* Sword of the Valiant, *208;* Terrorists, The, *1023;* Thunderball, *129;* Time Bandits, *1084;* Untouchables, The, *134;* Wind and the Lion, The, *140;* Wrong Is Right, *414;* You Only Live Twice, *141;* Zardoz, *1091*
Connick Jr., Harry: Little Man Tate, *182;* Memphis Belle (1990), *592;* Simply Mad About the Mouse, *204*
Connolly, Billy: Absolution, *440;* Blue Money, *242;* Crossing the Line (1991), *492*
Connolly, Kevin: Alan and Naomi, *443*
Connolly, Walter: Adventures of Huckleberry Finn, The (1939), *143;* Bitter Tea of General Yen, The, *462;* Broadway Bill, *470;* Fifth Avenue Girl, *276;* Good Earth, The, *530;* Lady by Choice, *567;* Lady for a Day, *567;* Nothing Sacred, *347;* Twentieth Century, *401*
Connor, Kenneth: Carry on Cleo, *251;* Carry on Cruising, *251;* Carry on Emmanuelle, *251;* Carry on Nurse, *251*
Connors, Chuck: Balboa, *455;* Blade Rider, *1099;* Capture of Grizzly Adams, The, *156;* Day of the Assassin, *33;* Deserter, The, *1109;* Designing Woman, *263;* Flipper, *167;* Gambler Returns, the: Luck of the Draw, *1115;* High Desert Kill, *850;* Last Flight to Hell, *75;* Mad Bomber, The, *994;* 99 and 44/100 Percent Dead, *91;* Old Yeller, *192;* One Last Run, *613;* Pancho Villa, *1138;* Proud and the Damned, The, *1139;* Ride Beyond Vengeance, *1143;* Rifleman, The (TV Series), *1144;* Roots, *644;* Skinheads, *116;* Soylent Green, *1077;* Standing Tall, *1153;* Summer Camp Nightmare, *672;* Support Your Local Gunfighter, *1154;* Target Eagle, *125;* Terror Squad, *127;* Texas Guns, *1155;* Three Days to a Kill, *128;* Tourist Trap, *1026;* Trouble Along the Way, *688;* Virus, *1087*
Connors, Michael: Where Love Has Gone, *699*
Connors, Mike: Casino, *476;* Day the World Ended, The, *1045;* Fist Fighter, *49;* Harlow, *536;* Island in the Sky, *554;* Panic Button, *353;* Suicide Battalion, *122;* Too Scared to Scream, *1025;* Voodoo Woman, *901*
Conrad, Chris: Airborne, *224*
Conrad, Michael: Gone with the West, *1116;* Longest Yard, The, *78;* Scream, Blacula, Scream, *884*
Conrad, Mikel: Flying Saucer, The, *1052*
Conrad, Robert: Assassin, *1037;* Bandits (1967), *1096;* Breaking Up Is Hard to Do, *469;* Commies Are Coming, the Commies Are Coming, The, *258;* Crossfire (1986), *1106;* Lady in Red, *74;* More Wild Wild West, *1134;* Murph the Surf, *87;* Palm Springs Weekend, *353;* Wild, Wild West, The (TV series), *1164;* Wild Wild West Revisited, The, *1164;* Will, G. Gordon Liddy, *703;* Wrong Is Right, *414*
Conrad, William: Any Number Can Play, *450;* Body and Soul (1947), *466;* Cry Danger, *964;* Killing Cars, *563;* Moonshine County Express, *86;* Naked Jungle, The, *88;* Return of Frank Cannon, The, *1010*
Conried, Hans: Affairs of Dobie Gillis, The, *906;* Alphabet Conspiracy, The, *146;* Big Jim McLain, *460;* Big Street, The, *460;* Blondie's Blessed Event, *242;* Davy Crockett, King of the Wild Frontier, *161;* Falcon Takes Over, The, *975;* Five Thousand Fingers of Dr. T, The, *167;* Journey Into Fear (1942), *987;* Lady Takes a Chance, A, *1125;* Monster That Challenged the World, The, *1066;* My Friend Irma, *340;* Rich, Young and Pretty, *936;* Senator Was Indiscreet, The, *375;* Summer Stock, *942;* Three for Bedroom C, *395*
Conroy, Frank: Ox-Bow Incident, The, *1137;* Threat, The, *1024*
Conroy, Kevin: Secret Passion of Robert Clayton, The, *1013;* Tour of Duty, *131*
Conroy, Rory: Into the West, *177*
Considine, John: Dixie Changing Habits, *265;* Dr. Death: Seeker of Souls, *835;* Forbidden Love, *519;* Late Show, The, *991;* Opposing Force, *95;* Rita Hayworth: The Love Goddess, *641;* Shadow Box, The, *654;* Thirsty Dead, The, *895;* Wedding, A, *407*
Considine, Tim: Clown, The, *484;* Daring Dobermans, The, *32;* Patton, *619*
Constable, Barbara Anne: Lady Terminator, *74*
Constanduros, Mabel: Salute John Citizen!, *647*
Constantin, Michel: Very Curious Girl, A, *800*
Constantine, Eddie: Alphaville, *712;* Boxoffice, *467;* Room 43, *644;* Seven Deadly Sins, The, *785;* Zentropa, *807*
Constantine, Michael: Beyond Fear, *717;* Cold Sweat (1970), *28;* Don't Drink the Water, *267;* Family, The (1970), *46;* If It's Tuesday, This Must Be Belgium, *305;* In the Mood, *306;* Justine, *561;* My Life, *602;* North Avenue Irregulars, The, *191;* Prancer, *197;* Question of Faith, *632;* Reivers, The, *365;* Say Goodbye, Maggie Cole, *648;* Silent Rebellion, *658;* Summer of My German Soldier, *672*
Conte, Richard: Assault on a Queen, *7;* Big Combo, The, *12;* Call Northside 777, *959;* Circus World, *482;* Godfather, The, *529;* Guadalcanal Diary, *58;* Hotel, *544;* House of Strangers, *545;* I'll Cry Tomorrow, *924;* Lady in Cement, *989;* Purple

Heart, The, *630;* They Came to Cordura, *681;* 13 Rue Madeleine, *127;* Tony Rome, *1025;* Walk in the Sun, A, *136*

Conti, Tom: American Dreamer, *226;* Beyond Therapy, *237;* Deep Cover (1980), *969;* Duellists, The, *42;* Dumb Waiter, The, *506;* Gospel According to Vic, The, *289;* Haunting of Julia, The, *537;* Merry Christmas, Mr. Lawrence, *593;* Miracles, *332;* Norman Conquests, The, Episode 1: Table Manners, *346;* Norman Conquests, The, Episode 2: Living Together, *346;* Norman Conquests, The, Episode 3: Round and Round the Garden, *346;* Princess and the Pea, The, *197;* Quick and the Dead, The, *1140;* Reuben, Reuben, *367;* Saving Grace, *373;* Shirley Valentine, *378;* That Summer of White Roses, *680*

Contino, Dick: Daddy-O, *31*

Contouri, Chantal: Goodbye, Miss 4th of July, *171;* Thirst, *895*

Converse, Frank: Bushido Blade, *21;* Cruise into Terror, *964;* Pilot, The, *622;* Spring Fever, *385;* Tales of the Unexpected, *1022*

Converse-Roberts, William: Courtship, *490;* 1918, *607;* On Valentine's Day, *612*

Convy, Bert: Hero at Large, *296;* Jennifer, *858;* Man in the Santa Claus Suit, The, *185;* Semi-Tough, *375*

Conway, Deborah: Fast Lane Fever, *46*

Conway, Gary: American Ninja II, *4;* How to Make a Monster, *853;* I Was a Teenage Frankenstein, *855*

Conway, Kevin: Elephant Man, The (1982), *508;* Flashpoint, *977;* Gettysburg, *526;* Homeboy, *543;* Jennifer 8, *987;* One Good Cop, *613;* Rage of Angels, *633;* Rambling Rose, *634*

Conway, Morgan: Brother Orchid, *20;* Dick Tracy, Detective, *38;* Dick Tracy versus Cueball, *38*

Conway, Pat: Brighty of the Grand Canyon, *152*

Conway, Russ: Interval, *553*

Conway, Tim: Apple Dumpling Gang, The, *147;* Apple Dumpling Gang Rides Again, The, *147;* Billion Dollar Hobo, The, *150;* Carol Burnett's My Personal Best, *251;* Dorf and the First Games of Mount Olympus, *267;* Dorf Goes Auto Racing, *267;* Dorf on Golf, *267;* Longshot, The (1985), *320;* Private Eyes, The, *361;* Prizefighter, The, *197;* Rip Van Winkle, *199;* Shaggy D.A., The, *203;* They Went That-A-Way and That-A-Way, *210;* World's Greatest Athlete, The, *218*

Conway Jr., Tim: Beverly Hills Vamp, *237*

Conway, Tom: Atomic Submarine, The, *1037;* Bride of the Gorilla, *819;* Cat People (1942), *822;* Death of a Scoundrel, *498;* Falcon in Mexico, The, *975;* Falcon's Brother, The, *975;* I Walked with a Zombie, *855;* Prince Valiant, *100;* Rio Rita, *368;* Seventh Victim, The, *885;* She Creature, The, *885;* Tarzan's Secret Treasure, *126;* Voodoo Woman, *901;* Whistle Stop, *138*

Coogan, Jackie: Addams Family, The (TV Series), *222;* Dr. Heckyl and Mr. Hype, *266;* Kid, The/The Idle Class, *313;* Lonelyhearts, *578;* Marlowe, *995;* Oliver Twist (1922), *611;* Peck's Bad Boy, *194;* Prey, The, *876;* Shakiest Gun in the West, The, *377*

Coogan, Keith: Adventures in Babysitting, *222;* Book of Love, *243;* Cheetah, *158;* Cousins, *260;* Don't Tell Mom the Babysitter's Dead, *267;* Hiding Out, *61;* Toy Soldiers (1991), *131;* Under the Boardwalk, *691*

Cook, Barbara: Killing 'Em Softly, *563*

Cook, Carole: Grandview, U.S.A., *531;* Incredible Mr. Limpet, The, *306;* Summer Lovers, *672*

Cook, Dale "Apollo": Double Blast, *41;* Triple Impact, *132*

Cook, Donald: Baby Face, *453;* Viva Villa!, *1162*

Cook Jr., Elisha: Big Sleep, The (1946), *955;* Born to Kill, *958;* Dark Waters, *496;* Dillinger (1945), *39;* Don't Bother to Knock, *971;* Drum Beat, *1110;* Electra Glide in Blue, *43;* Gangster, The, *525;* Great Northfield Minnesota Raid, The, *1116;* Hammett, *981;* Harry's War, *294;* Haunted Palace, The, *849;* House on Haunted Hill, *853;* Killing, The, *988;* Leave 'em Laughing, *572;* Lonely Man, The, *1129;* Mad Bull, *584;* Maltese Falcon, The, *994;* One-Eyed Jacks, *1137;* Papa's Delicate Condition, *617;* Pat Garrett and Billy the Kid, *1138;* Rosemary's Baby, *881;* St. Ives, *110;* Salem's Lot, *882;* Shane, *1148;* Stranger on the Third Floor, *1020;* Tom Horn, *1157*

Cook, Gwendoline: Warbus, *137*

Cook, Paul: Great Rock and Roll Swindle, The, *921*

Cook, Penny: Deadly Possession, *968*

Cook, Peter: Bedazzled, *233;* Find the Lady, *277;* Getting It Right, *285;* Hound of the Baskervilles, The (1977), *302;* Secret Policemen's Other Ball, The, *375;* Secret Policeman's Private Parts, The, *375;* Supergirl, *1081;* Those Daring Young Men in Their Jaunty Jalopies, *394;* Without a Clue, *413;* Wrong Box, The, *414;* Yellowbeard, *415*

Cook, Roger: Garden, The, *525*

Cook, Tommy: Adventures of Red Ryder, *1092;* Missile to the Moon, *1066*

Cooke, Christopher: Unbelievable Truth, The, *691*

Cooke, Evelyn: West of the Law, *1163*

Cooke, Gregory: Gore Vidal's Lincoln, *531*

Cooke, Jennifer: Friday the 13th, Part VI: Jason Lives, *844;* Gimme an "F", *286*

Cooke, John: Invader, *1059*

Cookie: Street Hitz, *121*

Coolidge, Rita: Mad Dogs and Englishmen, *429*

Cooney, Kevin: Full Moon in Blue Water, *282*

Cooper, Alice: Decline of Western Civilization, Part II—The Metal Years, *422;* Monster Dog, *865;* Prince of Darkness, *876;* Wayne's World, *406*

Cooper, Barrett: Buford's Beach Bunnies, *247*

Cooper, Ben: Arizona Raiders, *1095;* Rose Tattoo, The, *644*

Cooper, Chris: Lone Justice, *1129;* Lonesome Dove, *1129;* Matewan, *590;* Return to Lonesome Dove, *1143;* This Boy's Life, *682;* Thousand Pieces of Gold, *1156*

Cooper, Clancy: Distant Drums, *40*

Cooper, Gary: Along Came Jones, *1093;* Ball of Fire, *231;* Beau Geste, *10;* Blowing Wild, *16;* Casanova Brown, *252;* Cloak and Dagger (1946), *962;* Court-martial of Billy Mitchell, The, *489;* Cowboy and the Lady, The, *260;* Distant Drums, *40;* Farewell to Arms, A, *514;* Fighting Caravans, *1112;* Fountainhead, The, *520;* Friendly Persuasion, *522;* General Died at Dawn, The, *55;* Good Sam, *288;* Hanging Tree, The, *1118;* High Noon, *1120;* If I Had a Million, *304;* It (1927), *307;* It's a Big Country, *308;* Lives of a Bengal Lancer, The, *78;* Love in the Afternoon, *323;* Man of the West, *1132;* Meet John Doe, *591;* Mr. Deeds Goes to Town, *333;* Morocco, *599;* Naked Edge, The, *1000;* Operator 13, *614;* Plainsman, The, *1139;* Pride of the Yankees, The, *627;* Real Glory, The, *103;* Return to Paradise, *106;* Sergeant York, *113;* Task Force, *677;* They Came to Cordura, *681;* Today We Live, *685;* Vera Cruz, *1161;* Virginian, The (1929), *1161;* Westerner, The, *1163;* Wings, *140;* Wreck of the Mary Deare, The, *141*

Cooper, Gladys: At Sword's Point, *7;* Happiest Millionaire, The, *173;* Homecoming (1948), *543;* Iron Duke, The, *554;* Kitty Foyle, *566;* Mrs. Parkington, *598;* Nice Girl Like Me, A, *344;* Pirate, The, *935;* Secret Garden, The (1949), *202;* Song of Bernadette, The, *662;* Twilight Zone, The (TV Series), *1086*

Cooper, Jackie: Champ, The (1931), *478;* Gangster's Boy, *525;* Hollywood on Parade, *299;* Little Rascals, The, *183;* Love Machine, The, *581;* Return of Frank James, The, *1142;* Superman, *1081;* Superman II, *1081;* Superman III, *1081;* Superman IV: The Quest for Peace, *1081;* Surrender, *389;* Treasure Island (1934), *213;* Ziegfeld Girl, *949*

Cooper, Jean: Commies Are Coming, the Commies Are Coming, The, *258*

Cooper, Jeanne: Intruder, The (1961), *553;* Plunder Road, *99*

Cooper, Jeff: Circle of Iron, *26;* Impossible Years, The, *305*

Cooper, Jeremy: Reflecting Skin, The, *637*

Cooper, Joe: Mississippi Blues, *430*

Cooper, Maggie: And Baby Makes Six, *447;* Eye for an Eye, *46*

Cooper, Melville: Dawn Patrol, The, *33;* Immortal Sergeant, The, *549;* Murder Over New York, *999;* Private Life of Don

Juan, The, *628;* 13 Rue Madeleine, *127;* Tovaritch, *388;* Underworld Story, *1029*

Cooper, Miriam: Birth of a Nation, The, *462;* Home, Sweet Home, *543*

Cooper, Ted: Phantom from Space, *1070*

Cooper, Terence: Heart of the Stag, *538*

Coote, Robert: Alice Through the Looking Glass (1966), *906;* Bad Lands, *1095;* Berlin Express, *10;* Nurse Edith Cavell, *610;* Othello (1952), *615;* Swan, The (1956), *674;* You Can't Fool Your Wife, *415*

Copeland, Joan: Middle of the Night, *593*

Copley, Peter: Knack...and How To Get It, The, *314*

Copley, Teri: Down the Drain, *41;* I Married a Centerfold, *547;* Masters of Menace, *329;* Transylvania Twist, *399*

Copperfield, David: Terror Train, *894*

Coppola, Sofia: Godfather, Part III, The, *529;* Inside Monkey Zetterland, *306*

Coq, Bernard Le: Van Gogh, *800*

Corben, Billy: Stepmonster, *1080*

Corbett, Glenn: Chisum, *1104;* Shenandoah, *1149;* Violent Years, The, *136*

Corbett, Gretchen: Jaws of Satan, *858*

Corbett, Harry H.: Adventures of a Private Eye, *222;* Crooks and Coronets (Sophie's Place), *261;* Rattle of a Simple Man, *635;* Silver Dream Racer, *658*

Corbett, Jeff: Talent for the Game, *677*

Corbett, John: Northern Exposure (TV Series), *609*

Corbett, Leonora: Heart's Desire, *922*

Corbin, Barry: Ballad of Gregorio Cortez, The, *1096;* Career Opportunities, *251;* Conagher, *1105;* Critters 2: The Main Course, *827;* Hard Traveling, *536;* Hot Spot, *544;* Lonesome Dove, *1129;* Man Who Loved Women, The (1983), *328;* Northern Exposure (TV Series), *609;* Nothing in Common, *609;* Off the Mark, *348;* Prime Suspect, *627;* Red King, White Knight, *636;* Short Time, *378;* Six Pack, *380;* Undercover, *134;* Wargames, *1088;* What Comes Around, *698;* Who's Harry Crumb?, *411*

Corby, Ellen: I Remember Mama, *548;* Monsoon, *599;* On Moonlight Bay, *933;* Strangler, The, *1020;* Thanksgiving Story, The, *210;* Woman's Secret, A, *1032*

Corcoran, Brian: Texas John Slaughter: Geronimo's Revenge, *1155;* Texas John Slaughter: Wild Times, *1156*

Corcoran, Donna: Gypsy Colt, *173*

Corcoran, Kevin: Bon Voyage!, *151;* Johnny Shiloh, *179;* Mooncussers, *189;* Savage Sam, *201;* Tiger Walks, A, *211;* Toby Tyler, *212*

Corcoran, Noreen: I Love Melvin, *924*

Cord, Alex: Brotherhood, The, *471;* CIA Codename Alexa, *26;* Dirty Dozen, The: The Fatal Mission, *39;* Fire!, *48;* Girl to Kill For, A, *980;* Grayeagle, *1116;* Jungle Warriors, *69;* Minute to Pray, A Second to Die, A, *1134;* Roots of Evil, *109;* Sidewinder 1, *115;* Stiletto, *120;* Street Asylum, *121;* Uninvited, The (1987), *899*

Corday, Mara: Man without a Star, *1132;* Tarantula, *892*

Corday, Paula: Because You're Mine, *908*

Corday, Rita: Dick Tracy versus Cueball, *38*

Cordell, Chase: Track of the Moon Beast, *897*

Cording, Harry: Dressed to Kill (1946), *972;* Marauders, *1132*

Cordy, Raymond: A Nous la Liberte, *710*

Corey, Bridgette: Fury of Hercules, The, *54;* Old Testament, The, *772;* Samson, *1076*

Corey, Isabel: Bob le Flambeur, *719*

Corey, Jeff: Boston Strangler, The, *818;* Boy Who Left Home to Find Out About the Shivers, The, *152;* Butch and Sundance: The Early Days, *1103;* Catlow, *1104;* Follow Me Quietly, *978;* Getting Straight, *526;* Home of the Brave, *543;* Hoppy's Holiday, *1121;* In Cold Blood, *985;* Little Big Man, *1128;* Messenger of Death, *84;* My Friend Flicka, *190;* Next Voice You Hear, The, *605;* Premonition, The, *876;* Rawhide (1951), *1141;* Rose and the Jackal, The, *644;* Superman and the Mole Man, *1081*

Corey, Joseph: Greenstone, The, *172*

Corey, Professor Irwin: Hungry I Reunion, *303;* Stuck on You, *387*

Corey, Wendell: Any Number Can Play, *450;* Astro-Zombies, *810;* Buckskin, *1102;* Great Missouri Raid, The, *1116;* Holiday Affair, *542;* Light in the Forest, The, *181;* Loving You, *929;* Rainmaker, The, *634;* Rear Window, *1009;* Rich, Young and Pretty, *936;* Search, The, *650;* Sorry, Wrong Number (1948), *1019;* Women of the Prehistoric Planet, *1090*

Corff, Robert: Gas-s-s-s, *1054*

Corlan, Anthony: Something for Everyone, *662*

Corley, Al: Torchlight, *686*

Corman, Chip: Big Rip-off, The, *1098*

Corman, Maddie: Seven Minutes in Heaven, *376*

Corman, Roger: Silence of the Lambs, *1016;* State of Things, The, *789*

Cornaly, Anne: Occurrence at Owl Creek Bridge, An, *772*

Cornelison, Michael: Stephen King's Night Shift Collection, *890*

Cornell, Ellie: Chips, the War Dog, *158;* Halloween IV: The Return of Michael Myers, *848;* Halloween V: The Revenge of Michael Myers, *848*

Cornthwaite, Robert: Matinee, *330*

Cornu, Aurora: Claire's Knee, *724*

Cornwall, Anne: College, *257*

Cornwell, Judy: Santa Claus—The Movie, *201*

Corona, Antoni: Red Wind, *1009*

Corraface, George: Christopher Columbus: The Discovery, *26*

Correll, Charles: Check and Double Check, *254*

Corri, Adrienne: Clockwork Orange, A, *1042;* Corridors of Blood, *825;* Hellfire Club, The, *60;* Madhouse (1972), *862;* Tell-Tale Heart, The, *893*

Corri, Nick: Gotcha!, *980;* In the Heat of Passion, *986;* Lawless Land, *1062;* Tropical Snow, *132*

Corrieri, Sergio: Memories of Underdevelopment, *766*

Corrigan, Lloyd: Blondie Hits the Jackpot, *241;* It (1927), *307;* Lady in Question, *568;* Lights of Old Santa Fe, *1128;* Song of Nevada, *1151*

Corrigan, Ray "Crash": Arizona Stagecoach, *1095;* Black Market Rustlers, *1099;* Boothill Bandits, *1100;* Frontier Horizon, *1114;* Fugitive Valley, *1114;* Heart of the Rockies, *1119;* Hit the Saddle, *1121;* Night Riders, The, *1136;* Outlaws of Sonora, *1137;* Overland Stage Raiders, *1137;* Painted Stallion, The, *1138;* Pals of the Saddle, *1138;* Range Defenders, *1141;* Red River Range, *1141;* Renegade Girl, *1142;* Riders of the Black Hills, *1144;* Riders of the Whistling Skull, *1144;* Saddle Mountain Roundup, *1146;* Santa Fe Stampede, *1147;* Three Texas Steers, *1157;* Trail of Robin Hood, *1158;* Trail of the Silver Spurs, *1158;* Undersea Kingdom, *1087;* Vigilantes Are Coming!, *1161;* Wyoming Outlaw, *1165*

Corseaut, Aneta: Blob, The (1958), *814;* Return to Mayberry, *366;* Toolbox Murders, The, *1026*

Corsia, Ted de: Naked City, The, *1000*

Cort, Bud: Bernice Bobs Her Hair, *234;* Brain Dead, *1040;* Brewster McCloud, *245;* Chocolate War, The, *481;* Die Laughing, *264;* Electric Dreams, *271;* Gas-s-s-s, *1054;* Going Under, *288;* Harold and Maude, *294;* Hysterical, *303;* Invaders from Mars (1986), *1059;* Love at Stake, *322;* Love Letters, *581;* M*A*S*H, *324;* Maria's Lovers, *588;* Nightingale, The, *191;* Out of the Dark, *873;* Rumpelstiltskin (1980), *200;* Secret Diary of Sigmund Freud, The, *374;* Ted & Venus, *392;* Why Shoot the Teacher?, *701*

Cortese, Joe: Born To Run, *18;* Closer, The, *484;* Deadly Illusion, *968;* Evilspeak, *839;* Ruby (1991), *644;* To Protect and Serve, *130*

Cortese, Valentina: Juliet of the Spirits, *750;* Kidnap Syndicate, The, *751;* When Time Ran Out!, *1031*

Cortez, Ricardo: Big Business Girl, *460;* Gentleman from California, *1115;* Illicit, *549;* Mr. Moto's Last Warning, *997;*

Mockery, 598; Murder Over New York, 999; Sorrows of Satan, The, 663; Swan, The (1925), 389; Wonder Bar, 948

Cortne, Carole: Boxoffice, 467

Cosby, Bill: Bill Cosby: 49, 239; Bill Cosby—Himself, 239; California Suite, 249; Devil and Max Devlin, The, 264; Ghost Dad, 285; Happy Birthday Bugs: 50 Looney Years, 173; I Spy (TV Series), 65; Leonard Part 6, 317; Let's Do It Again, 318; Live at Harrah's, 320; Man and Boy, 1131; Meteor Man, 186; Mother, Jugs, and Speed, 337; Piece of the Action, A, 357; To All My Friends on Shore, 684; Uptown Saturday Night, 404

Cosell, Howard: Bananas, 232; Casey at the Bat, 156

Cosola, John: Beach House, 233

Cossart, Ernest: Kitty Foyle, 566; Letter of Introduction, 573; Love from a Stranger, 993

Cossins, James: At Bertram's Hotel, 953

Cosso, Pierre: My Wonderful Life, 603

Costa, Cosie: Missing in Action 2: The Beginning, 85; Ten to Midnight, 126

Costa, Marina: Final Executioner, The, 1051; Jungle Raiders, 69

Costa, Sara: Stripper (1985), 435

Costanzo, Robert: Delusion (1991), 499; Relentless 3, 1010; Triplecross, 399

Coste, Pierre: L'Ecole Buissonniere, 758

Costello, Dolores: Breaking the Ice, 909; Little Lord Fauntleroy (1936), 576; Noah's Ark, 608

Costello, Don: Texas Masquerade, 1156

Costello, Elvis: No Surrender, 345; Straight to Hell, 1153

Costello, Lou: Abbott and Costello in Hollywood, 221; Abbott and Costello Meet Captain Kidd, 221; Abbott and Costello Meet Dr. Jekyll and Mr. Hyde, 221; Abbott and Costello Meet Frankenstein, 221; Abbott and Costello Meet the Invisible Man, 221; Abbott and Costello Meet the Killer, Boris Karloff, 221; Abbott and Costello Meet the Mummy, 221; Abbott and Costello Show, The (TV Series), 221; Africa Screams, 223; Buck Privates, 246; Buck Privates Come Home, 246; Here Come the Co-Eds, 296; Hey Abbott!, 296; Hit the Ice, 298; Hold That Ghost, 298; In Society, 306; Little Giant, 319; Lost in a Harem, 321; Lost in Alaska, 321; Mexican Hayride, 331; MGM's The Big Parade of Comedy, 331; Naughty Nineties, The, 342; Noose Hangs High, The, 346; One Night in the Tropics, 350; Pardon My Sarong, 354; Ride 'em Cowboy, 368; Rio Rita, 368; 30 Foot Bride of Candy Rock, The, 394; Time of Their Lives, The, 396; Who Done It?, 410; Wistful Widow of Wagon Gap, The, 412; World of Abbott and Costello, The, 414

Costello, Mariclare: Coward of the County, 490; Execution of Private Slovik, The, 512; Heart of a Champion: The Ray Mancini Story, 538; Skeezer, 659

Costello, Ward: Gallant Hours, The, 524; Terror from the Year 5,000, 1082

Coster, Nicolas: Big Business, 238; Electric Horseman, The, 508; M.A.D.D.: Mothers Against Drunk Driving, 583; Sporting Club, The, 664

Costigan, George: Hawk, The, 982; Rita, Sue and Bob Too, 368

Costner, Kevin: Amazing Stories (TV Series), 1036; American Flyers, 446; Bodyguard, The, 466; Bull Durham, 247; Chasing Dreams, 480; Dances with Wolves, 1107; Fandango, 274; Field of Dreams, 1050; Gunrunner, The, 58; JFK, 558; No Way Out, 1002; Perfect World, A, 621; Revenge (1990), 106; Robin Hood: Prince of Thieves, 108; Silverado, 1150; Sizzle Beach, U.S.A., 380; Stacy's Knights, 665; Truth or Dare, 437; Untouchables, The, 134

Coteas, Elias: Full Moon in Blue Water, 282

Cotten, Joseph: Abominable Dr. Phibes, The, 808; Beyond the Forest, 460; Brighty of the Grand Canyon, 152; Caravans, 475; Casino, 476; Citizen Kane, 482; Delusion (1980), 969; Duel in the Sun, 1110; Farmer's Daughter, The, 274; From the Earth to the Moon, 1053; Gaslight (1944), 979; Hearse, The, 849; Heaven's Gate, 1119; Hellbenders, The, 1120; Hush...Hush, Sweet Charlotte, 854; Journey into Fear (1942), 987; Lady Frankenstein, 859; Lindbergh Kidnapping Case, The, 575; Lydia, 583; Magnificent Ambersons, The, 585; Niagara, 1000; Oscar, The (1966), 615; Petulia, 621; Portrait of Jennie, 625; Return to Fantasy Island, 1074; Screamers, 884; September Affair, 652; Shadow of a Doubt, 1014; Since You Went Away, 658; Soylent Green, 1077; Third Man, The, 1024; Tora! Tora! Tora!, 131; Torture Chamber of Baron Blood, The, 896; Tramplers, The, 1158; Twilight's Last Gleaming, 133; Under Capricorn, 1028; Walk Softly, Stranger, 1030; White Comanche, 1164

Cottençon, Fanny: Window Shopping, 804

Cotton, Oliver: Hiding Out, 61; Robin Hood: Herne's Son, 107

Coufos, Paul: Busted Up, 472; City of Shadows, 26; Dragon Fight, 42; Food of the Gods Part II, 1052; Lost Empire, The, 79

Coulouris, George: Arabesque, 6; Citizen Kane, 482; King of Kings (1961), 565; Lady in Question, 568; Master Race, The, 590; Mr. Skeffington, 597; Song to Remember, A, 940; Surprise Package, 389

Coulson, Bernie: Accused, The, 441; Adventures in Spying, 2; Eddie and the Cruisers II: Eddie Lives!, 915

Coulthard, Alice: Cement Garden, The, 478

Country Joe and the Fish: Gas-s-s-s, 1054; Monterey Pop, 431; Woodstock, 438; Zachariah, 1166

Courcel, Nicole: Le Cas du Dr. Laurent, 757

Courdi, Camille: King Ralph, 313

Court, Hazel: Devil Girl from Mars, 833; Ghost Ship, 846; Masque of the Red Death, The (1964), 863; Premature Burial, The, 876; Raven, The (1963), 879

Courtenay, Tom: Billy Liar, 461; Dandy in Aspic, A, 965; Dr. Zhivago, 503; Dresser, The, 505; Happy New Year, 293; I Heard the Owl Call My Name, 547; King Rat, 565; Leonard Part 6, 317; Let Him Have It, 573; Night of the Generals, 90; One Day in the Life of Ivan Denisovich, 613; Operation Crossbow, 95

Courtland, Jerome: Man from Colorado, The, 1131; Texas Rangers, The, 1156; Tharus, Son of Attila, 127; Tonka, 213

Courtney, Alex: Enter the Ninja, 44

Courtney, Bob: Dingaka, 501

Courtney, Chuck: Billy the Kid vs. Dracula, 813

Courtney, James: Freeway Maniac, 843

Courtot, Marguerite: Down to the Sea in Ships, 504

Cousineau, Maggie: Return of the Secaucus 7, 366

Cousins, Brian: Invisible: The Chronicles of Benjamin Knight, 1060; Mandroid, 1065

Cousins, Christopher: Critters 3, 827; Hell High, 849

Cousins, Joseph: Critters 3, 827

Coutu, Jean: Nikki, Wild Dog of the North, 191

Covaire, Jastereo: L.A. Vice, 74

Cowan, Jerome: Blondie Hits the Jackpot, 241; Blondie Knows Best, 241; City for Conquest, 482; Critic's Choice, 261; Deadline at Dawn, 34; Fog Island, 978; Fuller Brush Girl, The, 282; Great Lie, The, 532; Guest in the House, 534; June Bride, 311; Mr. Ace, 85; Mr. Skeffington, 597; Perfect Marriage, 356; RiffRaff (1947), 106; Saint Strikes Back, The, 1012; Silver Spurs, 1150; West Point Story, The, 947; Who Done It?, 410; You Only Live Once, 708

Cowan, Nicolas: Surf Ninjas, 208

Coward, Denise: Sudden Death, 122

Coward, Noel: In Which We Serve, 550; Italian Job, The, 308; Paris When It Sizzles, 354; Scoundrel, The, 374; Surprise Package, 389

Cowling, Bruce: Painted Hills, The, 193

Cowper, Nicola: Dreamchild, 1048; Journey to the Center of the Earth (1987), 1060; Lionheart, 181; Transmutations, 897

Cox, Alan: Young Sherlock Holmes, 141

Cox, Billy: Jimi Hendrix, 428

Cox, Brian: Hidden Agenda, 541; Iron Will, 67; Lost Language of Cranes, The, 580; Manhunter, 995; Murder by Moonlight, 1067; Pope John Paul II, 624

Cox, Courteney: Ace Ventura: Pet Detective, 221; Blue Desert, 957; Cocoon: The Return, 1042; Curiosity Kills, 965;

Masters of the Universe, *186;* Misfits of Science, *1066;* Opposite Sex (And How to Live with Them), The, *351;* Prize Pulitzer, The: The Roxanne Pulitzer Story, *629;* Shaking the Tree, *655*

Cox, David: Last Season, The, *75*

Cox, Elizabeth: Intruder (1988), *856*

Cox, Mitchell: Apex, *1036*

Cox, Richard: Between the Lines, *237;* Cruising, *964;* King of the Mountain, *565;* Vindicator, The, *1087;* Zombie High, *904*

Cox, Ronny: Beast Within, The, *812;* Beverly Hills Cop II, *11;* Bound for Glory, *467;* Captain America (1990), *22;* Connection (1973), *487;* Deliverance, *36;* Fallen Angel, *513;* FBI Murders, The, *47;* Gray Lady Down, *57;* Harper Valley P.T.A., *294;* Hollywood Vice Squad, *63;* Kavik the Wolf Dog, *179;* Loose Cannons, *321;* Mind Snatchers, The, *865;* One-Man Force, *94;* Onion Field, The, *613;* Our Town (1980), *616;* Raw Courage, *103;* RoboCop, *1074;* Scandal in a Small Town, *649;* Scissors, *1013;* Some Kind of Hero, *382;* Steele Justice, *120;* Taps, *677;* Target: Favorite Son, *677;* Total Recall, *1084;* Two of a Kind (1982), *690;* Vision Quest, *694;* Who Is the Black Dahlia?, *1031*

Cox, Veanne: National Lampoon's Class of '86, *342*

Cox, Wally: Barefoot Executive, The, *148;* Bedford Incident, The, *457;* Morituri, *87;* Spencer's Mountain, *664*

Coyne, Bill: Suburbia, *672*

Coyote, Peter: Baja Oklahoma, *455;* Best Kept Secrets, *11;* Bitter Moon, *462;* Blue Yonder, The, *151;* Crooked Hearts, *491;* Cross Creek, *491;* E.T.—The Extra-Terrestrial, *1048;* Echoes in the Darkness, *507;* Exposure, *45;* Heart of Midnight, *982;* Heartbreakers, *538;* Hitchhiker (Series), The, *850;* Jagged Edge, *556;* Keeper of the City, *562;* Kika, *751;* Legend of Billie Jean, The, *76;* Man in Love, A, *587;* Man Inside, The (1990), *587;* Out, *96;* Outrageous Fortune, *352;* People vs. Jean Harris, *620;* Slayground, *1017;* Stacking, *665;* Strangers Kiss, *669;* Timerider, *130*

Crabbe, Buster: Alien Dead, *1035;* Arizona Raiders, *1095;* Buck Rogers: Destination Saturn (a.k.a. Planet Outlaws), *1040;* Buffalo Stampede, *1102;* Captain Gallant—Foreign Legion, *23;* Colorado Sunset, *1105;* Flash Gordon Conquers the Universe, *1052;* Flash Gordon: Mars Attacks the World (a.k.a. Trip to Mars; Deadly Ray From Mars, The), *1052;* Flash Gordon: Rocketship (a.k.a. Spaceship to the Unknown; Perils from Planet Mongo), *1052;* Forlorn River, *1114;* His Brother's Ghost, *1121;* King of the Congo, *72;* Last of the Redmen, *1126;* Man of the Forest, *1132;* Pirates of the High Seas, *99;* Prairie Rustlers, *1139;* Red Barry, *104;* Sea Hound, The, *112;* Tarzan the Fearless, *125;* To the Last Man, *1157*

Crabbe, Cullen "Cuffy": Captain Gallant—Foreign Legion, *23*

Cracknell, Ruth: Alice to Nowhere, *3;* Island Trader, *67*

Craig, Carolyn: House on Haunted Hill, *853;* Studs Lonigan, *671*

Craig, Charmaine: White Fang 2: Myth of the White Wolf, *217*

Craig, Daimon: Claire of the Moon, *483*

Craig, Daniel: Power of One, The, *625*

Craig, James: Cyclops, The, *829;* Devil and Daniel Webster, The, *500;* Drums in the Deep South, *1110;* Hell Town, *1120;* Human Comedy, The, *546;* Kismet (1944), *566;* Kitty Foyle, *566;* Naked in the Sun, *1135;* Our Vines Have Tender Grapes, *193;* Thunder Trail, *1157;* Valley of the Sun, *1161;* Winners of the West, *1165*

Craig, Michael: Escape 2000, *1049;* Irishman, The, *554;* Mysterious Island, *1067;* Ride a Wild Pony, *199;* Robin Hood: Herne's Son, *107;* Sapphire, *1012;* Star!, *941;* Stolen Hours, *668;* Vault of Horror, *900*

Craig, Roger: Naked Obsession, *1000*

Craig, Wendy: Joseph Andrews, *311*

Craig, Yvonne: Gene Krupa Story, The, *525;* It Happened at the World's Fair, *925*

Craigie, Ingrid: Dead, The, *497*

Crain, Jeanne: Fastest Gun Alive, The, *1112;* Letter to Three Wives, A, *573;* Man without a Star, *1132;* People Will Talk, *356;* Pinky, *622;* State Fair (1945), *941*

Cramer, Grant: Hardbodies, *293;* Killer Klowns from Outer Space, *859*

Cramer, Joey: Stone Fox, The, *207*

Crampton, Barbara: From Beyond, *844;* Kidnapped (1988), *71;* Re-Animator, *879;* Robot Wars, *1075*

Crandall, Edward: Glorifying the American Girl, *919*

Crane, Bob: Return to Peyton Place, *639;* Superdad, *208*

Crane, Norman: Fiddler on the Roof, *916*

Crane, Richard: Riders of the Deadline, *1144;* Wing and a Prayer, A, *140*

Cranham, Kenneth: Hellbound: Hellraiser II, *849;* Tale of a Vampire, *891;* Under Suspicion, *1028*

Cranston, Bryan: Dead Space, *1045*

Crater, Rich: Carnal Crimes, *959*

Crauchet, Paul: King's Whore, The, *566*

Cravat, Nick: Crimson Pirate, The, *30;* Flame and the Arrow, The, *50;* Scalphunters, The, *1148;* Valdez Is Coming, *1160*

Craven, Frank: Barbary Coast, The, *455;* City for Conquest, *482;* Dreaming Out Loud, *269;* In This Our Life, *550;* Jack London, *556;* Our Town (1940), *616;* Pittsburgh, *622;* Son of Dracula (1943), *888*

Craven, Gemma: Wagner, *947*

Craven, James: Green Archer, *981;* Project Moon Base, *1072*

Craven, Matt: Agent on Ice, *3;* Few Good Men, A, *976;* Happy Birthday to Me, *848;* Indian Summer, *306;* Jacob's Ladder, *1060;* K2, *70;* Palais Royale, *97;* Smokescreen, *661*

Crawford, Broderick: All the King's Men, *444;* Beau Geste, *10;* Between Heaven and Hell, *459;* Born Yesterday (1950), *244;* Dark Forces, *966;* Eternally Yours, *511;* Fastest Gun Alive, The, *1112;* Goliath and the Dragon, *56;* Human Desire, *546;* Il Bidone, *747;* Last of the Comanches, *1126;* Little Romance, A, *319;* Lone Star, *1129;* Not as a Stranger, *609;* Private Files of J. Edgar Hoover, The, *100;* Real Glory, The, *103;* Seven Sinners, *113;* Slightly Honorable, *381;* Terror in the Wax Museum, *894;* Time of Your Life, The, *684;* Yin and Yang of Mr. Go, The, *1033*

Crawford, Ellen: Ulterior Motives, *133*

Crawford, H. Marion: Adventures of Sherlock Holmes, The (TV Series), *950*

Crawford, Joan: Above Suspicion, *1;* Autumn Leaves, *452;* Berserk, *812;* Bride Wore Red, The, *469;* Chained, *478;* Dance, Fools, Dance, *493;* Dancing Lady, *913;* Flamingo Road, *518;* Forsaking All Others, *279;* Gorgeous Hussy, The, *531;* Grand Hotel, *531;* Hollywood Canteen, *923;* Humoresque, *546;* I Live My Life, *547;* Johnny Guitar, *1123;* Last of Mrs. Cheney, The, *315;* Laughing Sinners, *571;* Love on the Run (1936), *323;* Mannequin (1937), *588;* Mildred Pierce, *594;* Night Gallery, *869;* Our Dancing Daughters, *616;* Our Modern Maidens, *616;* Possessed (1931), *625;* Possessed (1947), *625;* Rain, *634;* Reunion in France, *639;* Sadie McKee, *646;* Shining Hour, The, *656;* Strait-Jacket, *890;* Strange Cargo, *669;* Susan and God, *674;* Today We Live, *685;* Torch Song, *686;* What Ever Happened to Baby Jane?, *902;* When Ladies Meet, *698;* Woman's Face, A, *705;* Women, The, *413*

Crawford, John: Devil's Messenger, The, *834;* Grave Secrets, *847;* Satan's Satellites, *111*

Crawford, Johnny: El Dorado, *1111;* Gambler, Part II—The Adventure Continues, The, *1115;* Gambler Returns, the: Luck of the Draw, *1115;* Great Texas Dynamite Chase, The, *57;* Macbeth (1981), *584;* Rifleman, The (TV Series), *1144;* Village of the Giants, *900*

Crawford, Katherine: Riding with Death, *1074;* Walk in the Spring Rain, A, *695*

Crawford, Michael: Barnum (1986), *908;* Condorman, *159;* Funny Thing Happened on the Way to the Forum, A, *282;* Hello, Dolly!, *922;* How I Won the War, *302;* Knack...and How To Get It, The, *314*

Crawford, Wayne: Barracuda, *1038;* Crime Lords, *30;* Jake Speed, *68;* Quiet Thunder, *102;* Rebel Storm, *1074;* White Ghost, *138*
Creer, Erica: Circle of Iron, *26*
Cregar, Laird: Heaven Can Wait (1943), *295;* I Wake Up Screaming, *985;* Joan of Paris, *558*
Creley, Jack: Reincarnate, The, *879*
Cremer, Bruno: Josepha, *750;* Ménage, *767;* Simple Story, A, *786;* Sorceror, *1018;* 317th Platoon, The, *794*
Crenna, Richard: Body Heat, *958;* Breakheart Pass, *1101;* Case of Deadly Force, A, *476;* Catlow, *1104;* Deathship, *832;* Deserter, The, *1109;* Devil Dog: The Hound of Hell, *833;* Doctors' Wives, *503;* Evil, The, *839;* First Blood, *49;* Flamingo Kid, The, *278;* Hillside Stranglers, The, *982;* Hot Shots Part Deux, *301;* Intruders, *1059;* Leviathan, *860;* Man Called Noon, The, *1131;* Marooned, *1065;* Montana, *599;* On Wings of Eagles, *94;* Our Miss Brooks (TV Series), *351;* Pride of St. Louis, The, *627;* Rambo: First Blood II, *103;* Rambo III, *103;* Sand Pebbles, The, *111;* Star!, *941;* Stone Cold Dead, *1020;* Summer Rental, *388;* Table for Five, *676;* Wait Until Dark, *1030;* Wild Horse Hank, *217*
Crew, Carl: Blood Diner, *815;* Secret Life of Jeffrey Dahmer, The, *651*
Crew, Eddie: Queen Victoria and the Zombies, *878*
Crew, Robin: Mark of Cain, *863*
Crews, Laura Hope: Camille, *474;* Idiot's Delight, *548*
Crewson, Wendy: Buffalo Jump, *471;* Doctor, The, *502;* Folks, *278;* Good Son, The, *980;* Mark of Cain, *863;* Mazes and Monsters, *864;* Skullduggery, *887;* Spies, Lies, and Naked Thighs, *384*
Cribbins, Bernard: Adventures of Picasso, The, *222;* Daleks—Invasion Earth 2150 A.D., *1044;* Don't Raise the Bridge, Lower the River, *267;* Railway Children, The, *198;* Two-Way Stretch, *402;* Water Babies, The, *216;* Wrong Arm of the Law, The, *414*
Crick, Ed: Eye of the Eagle, *46*
Crisa, Erno: Lady Chatterley's Lover (1959), *567*
Crisp, Donald: Adventures of Mark Twain, The (1944), *442;* Black Pirate, The, *14;* Broken Blossoms, *470;* Brother Orchid, *20;* Challenge to Lassie, *157;* Charge of the Light Brigade, The (1936), *24;* City for Conquest, *482;* Dawn Patrol, The, *33;* Dr. Jekyll and Mr. Hyde (1941), *835;* Dog of Flanders, A, *163;* Don Q, Son of Zorro, *41;* Greyfriars Bobby, *172;* Hills of Home, *174;* Home, Sweet Home, *543;* How Green Was My Valley, *545;* Knute Rockne—All American, *567;* Lassie Come Home, *180;* Last Hurrah, The, *569;* Life of Emile Zola, The, *574;* Little Minister, The, *576;* Long Grey Line, The, *578;* Man from Laramie, The, *1131;* Mutiny on the Bounty (1935), *88;* National Velvet, *190;* Oklahoma Kid, The, *1136;* Old Maid, The, *611;* Prince Valiant, *100;* Private Lives of Elizabeth and Essex, The, *629;* Ramrod, *1140;* Red Dust, *636;* Sea Hawk, The, *112;* Sisters, The (1938), *659;* Son of Lassie, *206;* Spencer's Mountain, *664;* Svengali (1931), *1022;* That Certain Woman, *680;* Uninvited, The (1944), *1029;* Woman Rebels, A, *705*
Crisp, Quentin: Orlando, *614*
Criss, Peter: Kiss Meets the Phantom of the Park, *859*
Cristal, Linda: Dead Don't Die, The, *830;* Mr. Majestyk, *86;* Perfect Furlough, *356;* Two Rode Together, *1160*
Cristal, Perla: Christmas Kid, The, *1105;* White Comanche, *1164*
Cristiani, Antoinette: Mudhoney, *600*
Cristofer, Michael: Last of Mrs. Lincoln, The, *570*
Criswell: Night of the Ghouls, *869;* Orgy of the Dead, *873*
Crnkovich, Thomas: Sgt. Kabukiman N.Y.P.D., *114*
Croce, Gerard: Blue Jeans, *719*
Crocker, Barry: Barry McKenzie Holds His Own, *232*
Crocker, Harry: Circus, The/A Day's Pleasure, *255*
Crockett, Karlene: Massive Retaliation, *83;* Return, *638*
Crohem, Daniel: Paris Belongs to Us, *775*
Crombie, Jonathan: Bullies, *820;* Cafe Romeo, *249*
Cromwell, James: Christmas without Snow, A, *482;* Revenge of the Nerds, *367*
Cromwell, Richard: Lives of a Bengal Lancer, The, *78;* Strange Love of Molly Louvain, The, *669;* Villain Still Pursued Her, The, *135;* Young Mr. Lincoln, *708*
Cron, Claudia: Hit and Run, *63*
Cronenberg, David: Night Breed, *869*
Cronyn, Hume: Age-Old Friends, *443;* Batteries Not Included, *148;* Brewster's Millions (1985), *245;* Cocoon, *1042;* Cocoon: The Return, *1042;* Conrack, *488;* FoxFire, *521;* Gin Game, The, *527;* Impulse (1984), *985;* Lifeboat, *992;* Pelican Brief, The, *1005;* People Will Talk, *356;* Phantom of the Opera (1943), *874;* Postman Always Rings Twice, The (1946), *1007;* Rollover, *1011;* Seventh Cross, The, *653;* Shadow of a Doubt, *1014;* Sunrise at Campobello, *673;* There Was a Crooked Man, *1156;* To Dance with the White Dog, *684;* World According to Garp, The, *706*
Cronyn, Tandy: Age-Old Friends, *443;* Twisted, *1028;* Twisted: A Step Beyond Insanity, *690*
Cropper, Anna: Nemesis (1986), *1000*
Crosbie, Annette: Chernobyl: The Final Warning, *480;* Six Wives of Henry VIII, The (TV Series), *659*
Crosby, Bing: Bells of St. Mary's, The, *458;* Connecticut Yankee in King Arthur's Court, A (1948), *258;* Country Girl, The (1954), *489;* Going Hollywood, *920;* Going My Way, *529;* Here Come the Waves, *922;* Here Comes the Groom, *922;* High Society, *922;* Holiday Inn, *923;* King of Jazz, The, *927;* Little Boy Lost, *576;* Mississippi, *931;* Mr. Music, *931;* Red Skelton: A Career of Laughter, *433;* Road to Bali, *368;* Road to Hong Kong, The, *368;* Road to Rio, *369;* Road to Singapore, *369;* Road to Utopia, *369;* Road to Zanzibar, *369;* Robin & the Seven Hoods, *936;* White Christmas, *947*
Crosby, Bob: Five Pennies, The, *917;* Presenting Lily Mars, *626*
Crosby, Cathy: Girls Town, *55*
Crosby, Cathy Lee: Coach, *484;* Dark, The, *829;* Laughing Policeman, The, *991;* Roughnecks, *109;* World War III, *141*
Crosby, David: Hook, *175*
Crosby, Denise: Arizona Heat, *6;* Desperate Crimes, *37;* Dolly Dearest, *836;* Eliminators, The, *1048;* Pet Sematary, *874;* Red Shoe Diaries II: Double Dare, *637;* Star Trek: The Next Generation (TV Series), *1079*
Crosby, Gary: Justin Morgan Had a Horse, *179;* Which Way to the Front?, *410*
Crosby, Harry: Friday the 13th, *843*
Crosby, Kathryn: Initiation of Sarah, The, *856*
Crosby, Lucinda: Blue Movies, *242;* Naked Cage, The, *88*
Crosby, Mary: Berlin Conspiracy, The, *10;* Body Chemistry, *957;* Corporate Affairs, *259;* Eating, *507;* Ice Pirates, *1057;* Quicker Than the Eye, *102;* Stagecoach (1986), *1152;* Tapeheads, *391*
Crosby, Norm: Young at Heart Comedians, The, *415*
Crosby Stills and Nash: No Nukes, *432*
Cross, Ben: Assisi Underground, The, *7;* Chariots of Fire, *479;* Cold Sweat (1993), *28;* Coming Out of the Ice, *486;* Deep Trouble, *969;* Diamond Fleece, The, *970;* Far Pavilions, The, *514;* Live Wire, *78;* Nightlife, *870;* Paperhouse, *873;* Ray Bradbury's Chronicles: The Martian Episodes, *1073;* Steal the Sky, *667;* Unholy, The, *899*
Cross, Harley: Cohen and Tate, *485;* Stanley and Iris, *665*
Cross, Rebecca: Wet and Wild Summer, *408*
Crosse, Rupert: Reivers, The, *365;* Ride in the Whirlwind, *1143*
Crossley, Laura: Secret Garden, The (1993), *202*
Crothers, Scatman: Between Heaven and Hell, *459;* Black Belt Jones, *13;* Bronco Billy, *246;* Chesty Anderson, U.S. Navy (a.k.a. Anderson's Angels), *25;* Deadly Eyes, *831;* Detroit 9000 (Detroit Heat), *37;* Journey of Natty Gann, The, *179;* King of Marvin Gardens, The, *565;* One Flew Over the Cuckoo's Nest, *613;* Scavenger Hunt, *373;* Shining, The, *885;* Shootist, The, *1149;* Streetfight, *671;* Truck Turner, *132;* Twilight Zone—The Movie, *898;* Zapped!, *416*
Crouse, Lindsay: Being Human, *458;* Between the Lines, *237;* Chantilly Lace, *479;* Communion, *1042;* Daniel, *495;*

Desperate Hours (1990), *37;* House of Games, *984;* Iceman, *1057;* Paul's Case, *620;* Places in the Heart, *623;* Slap Shot, *380*
Crovato, Luciano: Evil Clutch, *839*
Crow, Ashley: Final Verdict, *516*
Crow, Emilia: Grand Tour: Disaster in Time, *1054;* Hitz, *63*
Crowden, Graham: Britannia Hospital, *246;* Romance with a Double Bass, *370*
Crowder, Jessie: Blind Rage, *15*
Crowe, Russell: Crossing, The, *491;* Proof, *629;* Romper Stomper, *109*
Crowe, Tonya: Dark Night of the Scarecrow, *829*
Crowell, Frank: Attack of the Swamp Creature, *810*
Crowley, Kathleen: Female Jungle, *516;* Westward Ho, the Wagons, *216*
Crowley, Pat: Hollywood or Bust, *299;* Menace on the Mountain, *593;* Red Garters, *936;* Untouchables, The: Scarface Mob (TV), *134;* Wild Women of Wongo, *1089*
Crowley, Suzan: Born of Fire, *467*
Croxton, Dee: Stephen King's Night Shift Collection, *890*
Cruickshank, Andrew: Body in the Library, The, *958*
Cruickshank, Laura: Buying Time, *21*
Cruise, Julee: Industrial Symphony No. 1 The Dream of the Broken Hearted, *925*
Cruise, Tom: All the Right Moves, *444;* Born on the Fourth of July, *467;* Cocktail, *485;* Color of Money, The, *485;* Days of Thunder, *33;* Far and Away, *514;* Few Good Men, A, *976;* Firm, The, *977;* Legend, *1062;* Losin' It, *321;* Outsiders, The, *616;* Rain Man, *634;* Risky Business, *368;* Taps, *677;* Top Gun, *131*
Crumb, Robert: Comic Book Confidential, *421*
Crumpacker, Amy: Revenge of the Teenage Vixens from Outer Space, *881*
Cruttwell, Greg: Naked, *603*
Cruz, Charmain: Bronx War, The, *20*
Cruz, Penelope: Belle Epoque, *716;* Jamon, Jamon, *749*
Cryer, Jon: Dudes, *505;* Heads, *294;* Hiding Out, *61;* Hot Shots, *301;* Morgan Stewart's Coming Home, *337;* No Small Affair, *345;* Noon Wine, *608;* O.C. & Stiggs, *348;* Pretty in Pink, *626;* Rap Master Ronnie—A Report Card, *364;* Superman IV: The Quest for Peace, *1081*
Crystal, Billy: All-Star Toast to the Improv, An, *224;* Best of Comic Relief, The, *235;* Big City Comedy, *238;* Billy Crystal: A Comic's Line, *239;* Billy Crystal: Don't Get Me Started, *239;* Billy Crystal: Midnight Train to Moscow, *240;* Breaking Up Is Hard to Do, *469;* City Slickers, *255;* City Slickers II, *256;* Comic Relief 2, *258;* Enola Gay: The Men, the Mission, the Atomic Bomb, *510;* Memories of Me, *331;* Mr. Saturday Night, *334;* Princess Bride, The, *1071;* Rabbit Test, *364;* Richard Lewis—"I'm in Pain Concert", *367;* Running Scared (1986), *110;* Three Little Pigs, The, *211;* Throw Momma from the Train, *396;* When Harry Met Sally, *409;* Your Favorite Laughs from an Evening at the Improv, *416*
Cube, Ice: Boyz N the Hood, *468*
Cucciolla, Riccardo: Sacco and Vanzetti, *782*
Cudutz, Michael: Liars' Club, The, *992*
Cuervo, Frank: Indigo 2: The Revolt, *66*
Cuff, John Haslett: Psycho Girls, *877*
Cugat, Xavier: Date with Judy, A, *913;* Heat's On, The, *295;* Holiday in Mexico, *923;* Luxury Liner, *930;* Neptune's Daughter, *932;* This Time For Keeps, *945;* Two Girls and a Sailor, *946*
Cuka, Frances: Attic: The Hiding of Anne Frank, *452*
Culkin, Kiernan: Nowhere to Run (1993), *92*
Culkin, Macaulay: George Balanchine's The Nutcracker, *919;* Getting Even with Dad, *285;* Good Son, The, *980;* Home Alone, *299;* Home Alone 2: Lost in New York, *175;* Jacob's Ladder, *1060;* My Girl, *190;* Only the Lonely, *350*
Culkin, Michael: Candyman (1992), *820*
Culkin, Quinn: Good Son, The, *980*
Cullen, Brett: In a Stranger's Hands, *985;* Prehysteria, *197;* Stewardess School, *386*
Cullen, Max: Fast Lane Fever, *46;* Starstruck, *941;* Sunday Too Far Away, *673*
Cullum, John: Day After, The, *1044;* Northern Exposure (TV Series), *609;* Quantum Leap (TV Series), *1072;* Sweet Country, *674*
Cullum, Kimberly: Grave Secrets: The Legacy of Hilltop Drive, *980;* Rapture, The, *635*
Culp, Jason: Skinheads, *116*
Culp, Nancy: Beverly Hillbillies Go Hollywood, The, *237*
Culp, Robert: Big Bad Mama II, *12;* Blue Lighting, The, *16;* Bob & Carol & Ted & Alice, *243;* Castaway Cowboy, The, *157;* Flood!, *51;* Gladiator, The, *55;* Goldengirl, *1054;* Great Scout and Cathouse Thursday, The, *1116;* Hannie Caulder, *1119;* I Spy (TV Series), *65;* Inside Out (1975), *66;* Key to Rebecca, The, *70;* Murderous Vision, *999;* Night the City Screamed, The, *606;* Outer Limits, The (TV Series), *1069;* Pelican Brief, The, *1005;* PT 109, *630;* Pucker Up and Bark Like a Dog, *363;* Sammy, the Way-Out Seal, *201;* That's Action, *127;* Time Bomb, *1025;* Turk 182, *689;* Voyage of Terror: The Achille Lauro Affair, *694*
Culp, Stephen: Gore Vidal's Lincoln, *531*
Culp, Steven: Jason Goes to Hell: The Final Friday, *858*
Culver, Michael: Moving Finger, The, *998;* Philby, Burgess and Maclean: Spy Scandal of the Century, *1005*
Culver, Roland: Betrayed (1954), *11;* Encore, *509;* Great Lover, The, *289;* On Approval, *349*
Cumbuka, Ji-Tu: Bound for Glory, *467*
Cumming, Dorothy: Dancing Mothers, *262*
Cummings, Burton: Melanie, *591*
Cummings, Constance: Battle of the Sexes, The, *233;* Night after Night, *344*
Cummings, Gregory: Blood Games, *956*
Cummings, Quinn: Babysitter, The, *811;* Goodbye Girl, The, *288*
Cummings Jr., Richard: Beverly Hills 90210, *460*
Cummings, Robert: Beach Party, *908;* Carpetbaggers, The, *475;* Chase, The (1946), *479;* College Swing, *912;* Devil and Miss Jones, The, *264;* Dial M for Murder, *970;* Everything Happens at Night, *273;* Five Golden Dragons, *50;* Forever and a Day, *520;* King's Row, *565;* Lost Moment, The, *580;* Lucky Me, *929;* Moon Over Miami, *931;* My Geisha, *340;* One Night in the Tropics, *350;* Promise Her Anything, *362;* Saboteur, *1011;* Spring Parade, *941;* Tell It to the Judge, *392;* Three Smart Girls Grow Up, *945*
Cummins, Peggy: Captain's Table, *250;* Carry on Admiral, *251;* Curse of the Demon, *828;* Gun Crazy (1950), *981;* Salute John Citizen!, *647*
Cummins, Peter: Blue Fire Lady, *151*
Cumo, Brett: Wicked, The, *903*
Cunningham, Beryl: Exterminators of the Year 3000, *1050*
Cunningham, Margo: Sailor Who Fell from Grace with the Sea, The, *646*
Cuny, Alain: Camille Claudel, *721;* Christ Stopped at Eboli, *724;* Emmanuelle, *734;* Les Visiteurs Du Soir, *759;* Lovers, The (1958), *762;* Milky Way, The (1970), *767*
Curcio, E. J.: Hard Rock Zombies, *848*
Curran, Lynette: Bliss, *241*
Curreri, Lee: Crystal Heart, *492;* Fame, *916*
Currie, Cherie: Foxes, *521;* Wavelength, *1088*
Currie, Finlay: Billy Liar, *461;* 49th Parallel, The, *520;* Great Expectations (1946), *532;* People Will Talk, *356;* Quo Vadis (1951), *632;* Rob Roy, the Highland Rogue, *200*
Currie, Gordon: Puppet Master Four, *878*
Currie, Louise: Adventures of Captain Marvel, The, *2;* Ape Man, The, *809;* Forty Thieves, *1114;* Masked Marvel, The, *83;* Wild West (1946), *1164*
Curry, Christopher: C.H.U.D., *820;* Return of Superfly, The, *105*
Curry, Julian: Rumpole of the Bailey (TV Series), *1011*
Curry, Steven: Glen and Randa, *1054*
Curry, Tim: Blue Money, *242;* Clue, *256;* Home Alone 2: Lost in New York, *175;* Hunt for Red October, The, *984;* It (1991),

857; Legend, 1062; National Lampoon's Loaded Weapon 1, 342; Oscar (1991), 351; Pass the Ammo, 355; Passed Away, 355; Ploughman's Lunch, The, 623; Rocky Horror Picture Show, The, 937; Shout, The (1979), 886; Three Musketeers, The (1993), 129; Times Square, 946; Worst Witch, The, 219

Curtin, Jane: Best of Chevy Chase, The, 235; Best of Dan Aykroyd, The, 235; Best of Gilda Radner, The, 235; Best of John Belushi, The, 235; Bob & Ray, Jane, Laraine & Gilda, 243; Coneheads, 258; How to Beat the High Co$t of Living, 302; Mr. Mike's Mondo Video, 334; O.C. & Stiggs, 348; Saturday Night Live, 372; Suspicion (1987), 1022

Curtin, Valerie: Big Trouble, 239; Christmas without Snow, A, 482; Different Story, A, 501; Maxie, 330

Curtis, Alan: Buck Privates, 246; Gung Ho! (1943), 58; High Sierra, 62; Mannequin (1937), 588; Melody Master, 592; Naughty Nineties, The, 342; Renegade Girl, 1142; Shopworn Angel, The, 656

Curtis, Billy: Terror of Tiny Town, The, 1155; Three Texas Steers, 1157

Curtis, Dick: Government Agents vs. Phantom Legion, 57; Santa Fe Uprising, 1147; Three Men from Texas, 1157

Curtis, Donald: Earth vs. the Flying Saucers, 1048; It Came from Beneath the Sea, 857; Riders for Justice, 1143; 7th Cavalry, 1148; Son of Lassie, 206

Curtis, Jack: Westward Ho, 1163

Curtis, Jamie Lee: Amazing Grace and Chuck, 445; Annie Oakley (1985), 146; As Summers Die, 451; Blue Steel (1990), 16; Coming Soon, 824; Death of a Centerfold, 498; Dominick and Eugene, 503; Fish Called Wanda, A, 277; Fog, The, 842; Forever Young (1992), 1053; Grandview, U.S.A., 531; Halloween, 848; Halloween II, 848; Love Letters, 581; Man in Love, A, 587; Mother's Boys, 998; My Girl, 190; My Girl 2, 190; Perfect, 620; Prom Night, 876; Queens Logic, 363; Road Games, 1010; She's in the Army Now, 656; Terror Train, 894; Trading Places, 398

Curtis, Joan: Where Trails End, 1164

Curtis, Keene: Blade, 14; Strange New World, 1080

Curtis, Ken: California Gold Rush, 1103; Conagher, 1105; Don Daredevil Rides Again, 1109; Gunsmoke (TV Series), 1118; Pony Express Rider, 1139; Searchers, The, 1148; Wings of Eagles, The, 703

Curtis, Liane: Critters 2: The Main Course, 827; Girlfriend from Hell, 287

Curtis, Robin: Unborn II, The, 898

Curtis, Susan: Octavia, 610

Curtis, Tony: Bad News Bears Go to Japan, The, 231; Balboa, 455; Boeing, Boeing, 243; Boston Strangler, The, 818; Brainwaves, 818; Captain Newman, M.D., 474; Center of the Web, 960; Chamber of Horrors, 822; Christmas in Connecticut (1992), 255; Club Life, 27; Count of Monte Cristo, The (1975), 30; Defiant Ones, The, 499; Francis, the Talking Mule, 280; Great Impostor, The, 532; Great Race, The, 290; Houdini, 544; Insignificance, 553; It Rained All Night the Day I Left, 555; Kings Go Forth, 565; Last of Philip Banter, The, 991; Last Tycoon, The, 571; Lepke, 76; Little Miss Marker (1980), 182; Lobster Man from Mars, 320; Mafia Princess, 585; Manitou, The, 863; Midnight (1989), 996; Mirror Crack'd, The, 996; Operation Petticoat, 351; Perfect Furlough, 356; Persuaders, The (TV Series), 98; Portrait of a Showgirl, 625; Prime Target, 100; Sex and the Single Girl, 376; Sex on the Run, 376; Sextette, 376; Some Like It Hot, 382; Son of Ali Baba, 118; Spartacus, 119; Suppose They Gave a War and Nobody Came?, 388; Sweet Smell of Success, 675; Taras Bulba, 125; Those Daring Young Men in Their Jaunty Jalopies, 394; Trapeze, 687; Users, The, 692; Vega$, 135; Vikings, The, 135; Winchester '73, 1165

Curtis-Hall, Vondie: Passion Fish, 619

Curzi, Pierre: Blind Trust (Pouvoir Intime), 719

Curzon, George: Sexton Blake and the Hooded Terror, 1014

Cusack, Cyril: Children of Rage, 481; Cry of the Innocent, 964; Day of the Jackal, The, 966; Elusive Pimpernel, The, 509; Fahrenheit 451, 1050; Harold and Maude, 294; Homecoming, The (1973), 543; Ill Met by Moonlight, 548; King Lear (1971), 564; Les Miserables (1978), 573; Love Spell, 79; Manhunt (1973), 81; My Left Foot, 602; Night Ambush, 90; 1984 (1984), 1068; Sacco and Vanzetti, 782; Shake Hands with the Devil, 114; Taming of the Shrew, The (1966), 391; Tenth Man, The, 679

Cusack, Joan: Addams Family Values, 222; Allnighter, The, 225; Broadcast News, 246; Hero, 296; Men Don't Leave, 331; My Blue Heaven, 339; Stars and Bars, 385; Toys, 398; Working Girl, 414

Cusack, John: Better Off Dead, 237; Eight Men Out, 508; Elvis Stories, 271; Fat Man and Little Boy, 515; Grifters, The, 534; Hot Pursuit, 301; Journey of Natty Gann, The, 179; Map of the Human Heart, 588; Money for Nothing, 335; One Crazy Summer, 349; Roadside Prophets, 641; Say Anything, 373; Shadows and Fog, 654; Stand by Me (1986), 665; Sure Thing, The, 389; Tapeheads, 391; True Colors, 688

Cusack, Sinead: Bad Behaviour, 231; Cement Garden, The, 478; Revenge (1971), 1010; Waterland, 697

Cushing, Peter: And Now the Screaming Starts, 809; Asylum, 810; At the Earth's Core, 1037; Beast Must Die, The, 812; Biggles—Adventures in Time, 1039; Blood Beast Terror, The, 815; Brides of Dracula, 819; Creeping Flesh, The, 826; Curse of Frankenstein, The, 828; Daleks—Invasion Earth 2150 A.D., 1044; Devil's Undead, The, 834; Dr. Phibes Rises Again, 836; Dr. Terror's House of Horrors, 836; Dr. Who and the Daleks, 1047; Dynasty of Fear, 973; Evil of Frankenstein, The, 839; Fear in the Night (Dynasty of Fear), 840; Frankenstein and the Monster from Hell, 842; From Beyond the Grave, 844; Ghoul, The (1975), 846; Gorgon, The, 847; Hamlet (1948), 535; Hellfire Club, The, 60; Horror Express, 851; Horror of Dracula, 851; Hound of the Baskervilles, The (1959), 983; House of the Long Shadows, 853; House That Dripped Blood, The, 853; Island of Terror, 857; Land of the Minotaur, 859; Legend of the Werewolf, 860; Madhouse (1972), 862; Mania, 862; Masks of Death, 83; Moulin Rouge, 600; Mummy, The (1959), 866; Naked Edge, The, 1000; Satanic Rites of Dracula, The, 882; Scream and Scream Again, 883; Seven Brothers Meet Dracula, The, 884; Shock Waves (Death Corps), 885; Skull, The, 887; Star Wars, 1079; Tale of Two Cities, A (1980), 677; Tales from the Crypt, 892; Top Secret, 397; Torture Garden, 896; Twins of Evil, 898; Uncanny, The, 899; Vampire Lovers, The, 900

Custer, Bob: Ambush Valley, 1093

Cuthbertson, Allan: Tunes of Glory, 689

Cuthbertson, Ian: Railway Children, The, 198

Cutler, Brian: Wilderness Family, Part 2, The, 217

Cutler, Wendy: Nick Danger in the Case of the Missing Yolk, 344

Cutt, Michael: Night of the Demon, 869

Cwiklinska, M.: Border Street, 720

Cybulski, Zbigniew: Ashes and Diamonds, 714

Cypher, Jon: Blade, 14; Off the Mark, 348; Spontaneous Combustion, 889; Strictly Business, 387; Valdez Is Coming, 1160

Cyphers, Charles: Halloween, 848; Halloween II, 848

Cyton, Elizabeth: Slave Girls from Beyond Infinity, 381

Czar, Nancy: Wild Guitar, 702

Czyzewska, Elzbieta: Misplaced, 595

D, Deezer: CB4, 252

D'Abo, Maryam: Double Obsession, 972; Immortal Sins, 855; Living Daylights, The, 78; Nightlife, 870; Not a Penny More, Not a Penny Less, 1002; Red Shoe Diaries 3: Another Woman's Lipstick, 637; Shootfighter, 115; Tomcat: Dangerous Desires, 1084; Tropical Heat, 1027; Xtro, 904

D'Abo, Olivia: Bank Robber, 232; Beyond the Stars, 1039; Bolero (1984), 466; Bullies, 820; Dream to Believe, 504; Greedy, 290; Into the Fire, 67; Midnight's Child, 865; Point of No Return, 99; Really Weird Tales, 365; Spirit of '76, The, 384; Wayne's World 2, 406

d'Amboise, Charlotte: American Blue Note, 446

d'Amboise, Jacques: Carousel, 911

D'Angelo, Beverly: Big Trouble, 239; Coal Miner's Daughter, 912; Cold Front, 963; Daddy's Dyin' and Who's Got the Will, *261;* Finders Keepers, *277;* First Love, *517;* Hair, *921;* High Spirits, *297;* Highpoint, *62;* Honky Tonk Freeway, *300;* In the Mood, *306;* Lightning Jack, *1128;* Lonely Hearts (1991), *577;* Maid to Order, *326;* Man Trouble, *327;* Miracle, The (1990), *595;* National Lampoon's Christmas Vacation, *342;* National Lampoon's European Vacation, *342;* National Lampoon's Vacation, *342;* Pacific Heights, *1003;* Paternity, *355;* Pope Must Diet, The, *360;* Sleeping Beauty (1983), *205;* Slow Burn, *1018;* Trading Hearts, *398*

D'Arbanville, Patti: Big Wednesday, *461;* Bilitis, *717;* Boys Next Door, The, *468;* Call Me, *959;* Fifth Floor, The, *841;* Flesh, *518;* Fresh Horses, *522;* Modern Problems, *335;* Rancho Deluxe, *1140;* Snow Kill, *118;* Wired, *704*

D'Arcy, Alex: Blood of Dracula's Castle, *815;* Soldier of Fortune, *118*

D'Arcy, Jake: Gregory's Girl, *290;* Sense of Freedom, A, *652*

D'Arcy, Roy: Revolt of the Zombies, *881;* Warning Shadows (1933), *1030*

d'Hondt, Danica: Unkissed Bride, *403*

D'Obici, Valeria: Passion of Love, *776*

D'Onofrio, Vincent: Adventures in Babysitting, *222;* Being Human, *458;* Crooked Hearts, *491;* Desire, *500;* Dying Young, *506;* Fires Within, *517;* Full Metal Jacket, *523;* Mr. Wonderful, *597;* Mystic Pizza, *603;* Naked Tango, *603;* Player, The, *358;* Signs of Life, *657*

D'Orsay, Fifi: Delinquent Daughters, *499;* Dixie Jamboree, *914;* Going Hollywood, *920*

D., Chris: Border Radio, *466*

Da Silva, Fernando Ramos: Pixote, *778*

Dabney, Augusta: Violets Are Blue, *694*

Dacqumine, Jacques: Phedre, *777*

Daddo, Andrew: Body Melt, *817*

Dade, Frances: Phantom Thunderbolt, *1138*

Dafoe, Willem: Body of Evidence, *958;* Born on the Fourth of July, *467;* Cry-Baby, *912;* Faraway, So Close, *736;* Flight of the Intruder, The, *50;* Hitchhiker (Series), The, *850;* Last Temptation of Christ, The, *570;* Light Sleeper, *575;* Loveless, The, *582;* Mississippi Burning, *596;* Off Limits (1988), *93;* Platoon, *623;* Roadhouse 66, *107;* Streets of Fire, *121;* To Live and Die in L.A., *130;* Triumph of the Spirit, *688;* White Sands, *700;* Wild at Heart, *702*

Dagermark, Pia: Vampire Happening, *900*

Daggett, Jensen: Friday the 13th, Part VIII: Jason Takes Manhattan, *844*

Dagover, Lil: Cabinet of Doctor Caligari, The, *721;* Destiny, *729;* Spiders, The, *119*

Dahl, Arlene: Here Come the Girls, *922;* Journey to the Center of the Earth (1959), *1060;* Kisses for My President, *314;* Land Raiders, *1125;* Night of the Warrior, *90;* Slightly Scarlet, *660;* Southern Yankee, A, *383;* Three Little Words, *945;* Watch the Birdie, *406*

Dahl, Lisbet: Topsy Turvy, *796*

Dahlbeck, Eva: Brink of Life, *720;* Counterfeit Traitor, The, *30;* Dreams, *732;* Lesson in Love, A, *760;* Secrets of Women (Waiting Women), *784;* Smiles of a Summer Night, *787*

Dailey, Dan: It's Always Fair Weather, *925;* Lady Be Good, *927;* Meet Me in Las Vegas, *930;* Mortal Storm, The, *600;* Pride of St. Louis, The, *627;* Private Files of J. Edgar Hoover, The, *100;* There's No Business Like Show Business, *944;* What Price Glory, *408;* Wings of Eagles, The, *703;* Ziegfeld Girl, *949*

Dailey, Irene: Grissom Gang, The, *534*

Daily, Elizabeth: One Dark Night, *872;* Pee-Wee's Big Adventure, *355;* Street Music, *670*

Daimon, Masaaki: Godzilla vs. Mechagodzilla, *846*

Dainaro, Neil: Dawson Patrol, The, *33*

Dalban, Max: Boudu Saved from Drowning, *720;* Toni, *796*

Dalbes, Alberto: Cut Throats Nine, *1107*

Dale, Colin: Diamond's Edge, *162*

Dale, Cynthia: Boy in Blue, The, *467;* Heavenly Bodies, *296*

Dale, Esther: Blondie Has Trouble, *241;* This Time For Keeps, *945*

Dale, Jennifer: Of Unknown Origin, *872;* Separate Vacations, *375*

Dale, Jim: American Clock, The, *446;* Carry on Cleo, *251;* Carry on Cowboy, *251;* Carry on Doctor, *251;* Follow That Camel, *278;* Hot Lead and Cold Feet, *176;* Joseph Andrews, *311;* Pete's Dragon, *195;* Scandalous (1983), *373;* Unidentified Flying Oddball, *214*

Dale, Tony: Fix, The, *50*

Dale, Virginia: Buck Benny Rides Again, *246;* Dragnet (1947), *41;* Holiday Inn, *923*

Daley, Cass: Red Garters, *936*

Daley, Jack: West of the Law, *1163*

Dall, Tracy: Virgin High, *405*

Dalio, Marcel: Black Jack, *14;* Cartouche, *722;* Grand Illusion, *742;* Lady L, *568;* Pepe Le Moko, *777;* Rules of the Game, The, *782*

Dall, John: Corn Is Green, The (1945), *488;* Gun Crazy (1950), *981;* Rope, *1011*

Dalle, Beatrice: Betty Blue, *717*

Dallesandro, Joe: Andy Warhol's Dracula, *809;* Andy Warhol's Frankenstein, *809;* Critical Condition, *260;* Cry-Baby, *912;* Double Revenge, *504;* Flesh, *518;* Guncrazy (1992), *535;* Heat (1972), *539;* Hollywood Detective, The, *983;* Inside Out (1992), *1058;* Private War, *629;* Sunset, *1021;* Trash, *687*

Dallimore, Maurice: Collector, The, *963*

Dalton, Abby: Maverick (TV Series), *1133;* Saga of the Viking Women and their Voyage to the Waters of the Great Sea Serpent, The, *110*

Dalton, Audrey: Çasanova's Big Night, *252;* Drum Beat, *1110;* Elfego Baca: Six Gun Law, *1111;* Monster That Challenged the World, The, *1066*

Dalton, Timothy: Antony and Cleopatra (1981), *450;* Brenda Starr, *19;* Chanel Solitaire, *479;* Cromwell, *491;* Doctor and the Devils, The, *835;* Emperor's New Clothes, The (1984), *164;* Flash Gordon, *1052;* Happy Anniversary 007: 25 Years of James Bond, *425;* Hawks, *537;* Jane Eyre (1983), *557;* King's Whore, The, *566;* License to Kill, *77;* Lion in Winter, The, *576;* Living Daylights, The, *78;* Mistral's Daughter, *597;* Permission to Kill, *98;* Rocketeer, The, *108;* Sextette, *376;* Wuthering Heights (1971), *707*

Daltrey, Roger: Buddy's Song, *471;* Cold Justice, *28;* Forgotten Prisoners, *520;* If Looks Could Kill (1991), *66;* Legacy, The, *860;* Lisztomania, *928;* Mack the Knife, *930;* McVicar, *591;* Tommy, *946*

Daly, Timothy: Caroline at Midnight, *960;* Dangerous Heart, *965;* I Married a Centerfold, *547;* In the Line of Duty: Ambush in Waco, *66;* Love or Money?, *323;* Spellbinder, *889;* Year of the Comet, *415*

Daly, Tyne: Adultress, The, *441;* Aviator, The, *452;* Better Late than Never, *237;* Enforcer, The (1976), *44;* Intimate Strangers, *553;* Movers and Shakers, *337;* Zoot Suit, *949*

Damien, Leo: Ghosts Can't Do It, *285*

Damita, Lily: Fighting Caravans, *1112*

Damme, Jean-Claude Van: Universal Soldier, *134*

Dammett, Blackie: Nine Deaths of the Ninja, *91*

Damon, Mark: Anzio, *6;* Black Sabbath, *814;* Crypt of the Living Dead, *827;* Devil's Wedding Night, The, *834;* Fall of the House of Usher, The (1960), *840;* Geronimo: An American Legend, *1115;* Scalawag Bunch, The, *111*

Damon, Matt: Rising Son, *641*

Damon, Stuart: Cinderella (1964), *911*

Damone, Vic: Athena, *907;* Hell to Eternity, *540;* Hit the Deck, *923;* Kismet (1955), *927;* Rich, Young and Pretty, *936*

Dana, Barbara: Matter of Principle, A, *330;* Necessary Parties, *604*

Dana, Bill: Murder in Texas, *998*

Dana, Leora: Kings Go Forth, *565;* 3:10 to Yuma, *1157*

Dana, Viola: That Certain Thing, *392*

Dance, Charles: Alien 3, *1035;* China Moon, *961;* Golden Child, The, *56;* Good Morning, Babylon, *530;* Jewel in the Crown, The, *557;* Last Action Hero, The, *1062;* McGuffin, The,

996; Out on a Limb (1986), 616; Pascali's Island, 619; Plenty, 623; Tales of the Unexpected, 1022; White Mischief, 700

Dandridge, Dorothy: Carmen Jones, 911

Dane, Karl: Scarlet Letter, The (1926), 649; Son of the Sheik, 118; Warning Shadows (1933), 1030

Dane, Lawrence: Case of Libel, A, 476; Clown Murders, The, 962; Fatal Attraction (1985), 975; Find the Lady, 277; Good Fight, The, 530; Good Idea, 288; Nothing Personal, 347; Of Unknown Origin, 872; Rituals, 1010; Rolling Vengeance, 108; Scanners, 883

Dane, Patricia: Johnny Eager, 559; Somewhere I'll Find You, 662

Dangerfield, Rodney: Back to School, 230; Caddyshack, 249; Easy Money, 269; Ladybugs, 315; Moving, 338; Projectionist, The, 362; Rodney Dangerfield: "It's Not Easy Being Me", 370; Rodney Dangerfield—Nothin' Goes Right, 370; Saturday Night Live, 372

Daniel, Trudik: Castle, The, 476

Danieli, Emma: Last Man on Earth, The, 1062

Daniell, Henry: All This and Heaven Too, 445; Body Snatcher, The, 817; Camille, 474; Castle in the Desert, 960; Diane, 500; Firefly, The, 916; Five Weeks in a Balloon, 50; Four Jacks and a Jill, 918; Holiday, 298; Jane Eyre (1944), 557; Madame X (1937), 584; Private Lives of Elizabeth and Essex, The, 629; Sea Hawk, The, 112; Sherlock Holmes and the Voice of Terror, 1015; Sherlock Holmes in Washington, 1015; Song of Love, 662; Voyage to the Bottom of the Sea, 1087; Witness for the Prosecution (1957), 1032; Woman in Green, The, 1032; Woman's Face, A, 705

Danielle, Suzanne: Carpathian Eagle, 821; Carry on Emmanuelle, 251

Daniels, Alex: Meridian, 864

Daniels, Anthony: Empire Strikes Back, The, 1049; Return of the Jedi, 1074; Star Wars, 1079

Daniels, Bebe: Feel My Pulse, 276; Harold Lloyd's Comedy Classics, 294; Reaching for the Moon (1931), 365

Daniels, Danny D.: Outing, The, 873

Daniels, Jeff: Arachnophobia, 810; Butcher's Wife, The, 248; Caine Mutiny Court Martial, The, 473; Checking Out, 254; Gettysburg, 526; Grand Tour: Disaster in Time, 1054; Heartburn, 295; House on Carroll Street, The, 984; Love Hurts, 323; Marie, 588; Purple Rose of Cairo, The, 363; Rain without Thunder, 634; Something Wild, 383; Sweethearts' Dance, 675; Teamster Boss: The Jackie Presser Story, 678; Terms of Endearment, 679; There Goes the Neighborhood, 393; Welcome Home, Roxy Carmichael, 407

Daniels, John: Bare Knuckles, 9; Getting Over, 526

Daniels, Lisa: Glass Slipper, The, 919

Daniels, Phil: Bad Behaviour, 231; Breaking Glass, 909; Quadrophenia, 936; Scum, 650

Daniels, William: Blind Date (1987), 241; Blue Lagoon, The, 465; City in Fear, 962; Francis Gary Powers: The True Story of the U-2 Spy Incident, 522; Her Alibi, 296; Marlowe, 995; One and Only, The, 613; Parallax View, The, 1004; Rehearsal for Murder, 1009; 1776, 939; Sunburn, 1021; Thousand Clowns, A, 395

Danielson, Lynn: Mortuary Academy, 337

Danner, Blythe: Alice (1990), 224; Another Woman, 450; Are You in the House Alone?, 953; Brighton Beach Memoirs, 246; Futureworld, 1053; Great Santini, The, 533; Hearts of the West, 295; Inside the Third Reich, 552; Judgment, 560; Man, Woman and Child, 587; Mr. and Mrs. Bridge, 596; Never Forget, 604; Prince of Tides, The, 627; 1776, 939; To Kill a Clown, 1025

Danning, Sybil: Albino, 808; Amazon Women on the Moon, 225; Bullet from God, A, 1102; Chained Heat, 24; God's Gun, 1116; Hercules (1983), 1056; Hitchhiker (Series), The, 850; Howling II...Your Sister Is a Werewolf, 854; Jungle Warriors, 69; Kill Castro, 71; L.A. Bounty, 73; Malibu Express, 327; Man with Bogart's Face, The, 995; Phantom Empire, The (1986), 99; Reform School Girls, 105; Salamander, The, 111; Seven Magnificent Gladiators, The, 113; Swap, The, 674; Talking Walls, 391; They're Playing with Fire, 681; Warrior Queen, 137

Dannis, Ray: Undertaker and His Pals, The, 899

Dano, Royal: Adventures of Huckleberry Finn, The (1960), 144; Cimarron (1960), 1105; Cocaine Wars, 27; Crime of Passion, 490; Culpepper Cattle Co., The, 1106; Electra Glide in Blue, 43; Ghoulies II, 846; House II: The Second Story, 852; Huckleberry Finn (1975), 176; Killer Inside Me, The, 988; Killer Klowns from Outer Space, 859; King of Kings (1961), 565; Never Steal Anything Small, 932; Red Badge of Courage, The, 636; Red-Headed Stranger, The, 1141; Spaced Invaders, 206; Strangers: The Story of a Mother and a Daughter, 669; Tribute to a Bad Man, 1159

Danova, Cesare: Chamber of Horrors, 822; Scorchy, 112; Tentacles, 893; Viva Las Vegas, 947

Danson, Ted: Body Heat, 958; Chinese Web, The, 25; Cousins, 260; Dad, 493; Fine Mess, A, 277; Getting Even with Dad, 285; Just Between Friends, 561; Little Treasure, 77; Made in America, 325; Onion Field, The, 613; Our Family Business, 616; Three Men and a Baby, 395; Three Men and a Little Lady, 395; We Are the Children, 697

Dante, Michael: Beyond Evil, 813; Big Score, The, 12; Cage, 21; Naked Kiss, The, 1000; Seven Thieves, 653

Dantine, Helmut: Bring Me the Head of Alfredo Garcia, 20; Edge of Darkness (1943), 43; Operation Crossbow, 95; Stranger from Venus, 1081

Danton, Ray: Centerfold Girls, 478; I'll Cry Tomorrow, 924; Majority of One, A, 326; Onionhead, 350; Rise and Fall of Legs Diamond, The, 107

Danuta: Big Gag, The, 238

Danza, Tony: Going Ape!, 287; She's Out of Control, 378; Single Bars, Single Women, 658; Truth or Die, 689

Dao-Lin, Sun: Go-Masters, The, 741

Darby, Kim: Better Off Dead, 237; Capture of Grizzly Adams, The, 156; Don't Be Afraid of the Dark, 836; Enola Gay: The Men, the Mission, the Atomic Bomb, 510; Flatbed Annie and Sweetie Pie: Lady Truckers, 50; Generation, 283; Grissom Gang, The, 534; One and Only, The, 613; People, The, 1070; Strawberry Statement, The, 670; Teen Wolf, Too, 892; True Grit, 1159

Darc, Mireille: Return of the Tall Blond Man with One Black Shoe, The, 781; Tall Blond Man with One Black Shoe, The, 792; Weekend, 803

Darc, Mirelle: Icy Breasts, 746

Darcel, Denise: Battleground, 456; Dangerous When Wet, 913; Vera Cruz, 1161; Westward the Women, 1163

Darcy, Sheila: Zorro's Fighting Legion, 1166

Darden, Severn: Back to School, 230; Battle for the Planet of the Apes, 1038; Conquest of the Planet of the Apes, 1043; Dead Heat on a Merry-Go-Round, 967; Disappearance of Aimee, The, 970; Hired Hand, The, 1121; Justine, 561; Legend of Hillbilly John, The, 181; Luv, 324; Once Upon a Midnight Scary, 192; Playmates, 358; Telephone, The, 392

Dare, Debra: Hard to Die, 848

Darel, Florence: Tale of Springtime, A, 792

Darie, Frederic: Deep Trouble, 969

Darin, Bobby: Captain Newman, M.D., 474; Hell Is for Heroes, 60; Pressure Point, 626; Run Stranger Run, 882; State Fair (1962), 941

Darlene, Gigi: Bad Girls Go to Hell, 454

Darling, Candy: Flesh, 518

Darmon, Gerard: Obsession: A Taste for Fear, 93

Darnell, Linda: Anna and the King of Siam, 449; Blackbeard the Pirate, 14; Blood and Sand (1941), 464; Buffalo Bill, 1102; City without Men, 483; Dakota Incident, 1107; Forever Amber, 520; Island of Desire, 555; Letter to Three Wives, A, 573; Mark of Zorro, The (1940), 82; My Darling Clementine, 1134; Second Chance, 113; Unfaithfully Yours (1948), 403

Darnoux, George: Day in the Country, A, 728

Darrell, Steve: Adventures of Frank and Jesse James, 1092

Darren, James: Boss' Son, The, 467; Diamond Head, 500; Gene Krupa Story, The, 525; Gidget, 286; Gidget Goes

Hawaiian, *286;* Gidget Goes to Rome, *286;* Guns of Navarone, The, *58;* Scruples, *650;* Venus in Furs, *135*

Darrieux, Danielle: Alexander the Great, *443;* Bluebeard (1963), *719;* Club des Femmes, *725;* Earrings of Madame De..., The, *732;* Five Fingers, *977;* La Ronde, *754;* Lady Chatterley's Lover (1959), *567;* Le Plaisir, *758;* Mayerling, *766;* Rage of Paris, The, *364;* Rich, Young and Pretty, *936;* Scene of the Crime (1987), *784*

Darro, Frankie: Broadway Bill, *470;* Devil Horse, The, *1109;* Little Men (1935), *182;* Phantom Empire (1935), *98;* Radio Ranch (Men with Steel Faces & Phantom Empire), *1140;* Way Back Home, *406*

Darrough, Al: Fraternity Demon, *280*

Darrow, Henry: Attica, *452;* Badge 373, *8;* In Dangerous Company, *550;* L.A. Bounty, *73;* Last of the Finest, The, *75*

Darrow, Oliver: Spirits, *889*

Darrow, Paul: Blake's 7 (TV Series), *1040*

Dartez, Gail: Out, *96*

Darvas, Lili: Love, *761;* Meet Me in Las Vegas, *930*

Darvi, Bella: Racers, The, *632*

Darwell, Jane: Aggie Appleby, Maker of Men, *223;* All Through the Night, *3;* Bigamist, The, *461;* Captain January, *155;* Craig's Wife, *490;* Curly Top, *912;* Devil and Daniel Webster, The, *500;* Grapes of Wrath, The, *531;* Jesse James, *1123;* Last Hurrah, The, *569;* Lemon Drop Kid, The, *317;* Little Miss Broadway, *928;* Mary Poppins, *185;* Ox-Bow Incident, The, *1137;* Poor Little Rich Girl (1936), *935;* Rains Came, The, *634;* Scarlet Empress, The, *649;* Three Godfathers, The, *1156*

Dascasos, Mark: Only the Strong, *95*

Dash, Stacey: Mo' Money, *335*

DaSilva, Howard: David and Lisa, *496;* Garbo Talks, *283;* Greatest Man in the World, The, *290;* Keeper of the Flame, *562;* Lost Weekend, The, *580;* Missiles of October, The, *596;* Nevada Smith, *1135;* Sea Wolf, The (1941), *113;* 1776, *939;* Smile, Jenny, You're Dead, *661;* They Live By Night, *681;* Underworld Story, *1029*

Dassin, Jules: Never on Sunday, *604*

Dassule, Helene: La Petite Bande, *754*

Dasté, Jean: Boudu Saved from Drowning, *720;* Green Room, The, *742;* L'Atalante, *753;* Zero for Conduct, *807*

Dauden, Marlene: Combat Killers, *28*

Daughton, James: Blind Date (1984), *463;* Girlfriend from Hell, *287;* House of the Rising Sun, *64*

Daugirda, Jerry: Gone in 60 Seconds, *56*

Dauphin, Claude: April in Paris, *907;* Is Paris Burning?, *554;* Lady L, *568;* Les Miserables (1978), *573;* Little Boy Lost, *576;* Madame Rosa, *763*

Davalos, Dominique: Salvation, *647*

Davalos, Elyssa: House in the Hills, A, *984;* Jericho Fever, *68*

Davalos, Richard: Snatched, *117*

Davao, Charlie: Blind Rage, *15*

Davazac, Emilie: Undefeatable, *134*

Davenport, Alice: Keystone Comedies, Vol. 2, *312;* Keystone Comedies, Vol. 3, *312;* Keystone Comedies, Vol. 4, *312*

Davenport, Harry: Adventure, *441;* All This and Heaven Too, *445;* Courage of Lassie, *160;* Cowboy and the Lady, The, *260;* December 7th: The Movie, *422;* Enchanted Forest, The, *165;* Jack London, *556;* Kismet (1944), *566;* Lucky Partners, *324;* Made for Each Other, *325;* Ox-Bow Incident, The, *1137;* Rage of Paris, The, *364;* That Forsyte Woman, *680;* Thin Man Goes Home, The, *1024;* Three Daring Daughters, *945*

Davenport, Nigel: Chariots of Fire, *479;* Cry of the Innocent, *964;* Dracula (1973), *837;* Living Free, *184;* Phase IV, *1070;* Virgin Soldiers, The, *694;* Without a Clue, *413;* Zulu Dawn, *142*

Davi, Robert: Amazon, *4;* Center of the Web, *960;* Christopher Columbus: The Discovery, *26;* Cops and Robbersons, *259;* Deceptions, *969;* Illicit Behavior, *985;* Legal Tender, *76;* License to Kill, *77;* Maniac Cop 2, *863;* Maniac Cop 3: Badge of Silence, *863;* Mardi Gras for the Devil, *863;* Peacemaker, *1069;* Predator 2, *1071;* Quick, *102;* Raw Deal, *103;* Son of the Pink Panther, *383;* Traxx, *132;* White Hot: The Mysterious Murder of Thelma Todd, *1031;* Wild Orchid 2: Two Shades of Blue, *702;* Wild Thing, *702*

David, Angel: Mixed Blood, *86*

David, Clifford: Agent on Ice, *3;* Resurrection, *638*

David, Eleanor: Comfort and Joy, *258;* King's Whore, The, *566;* Scarlet Pimpernel, The (1982), *112;* Slipstream, *1077;* Sylvia, *676*

David, Elizabeth: Gruesome Twosome, *848*

David, Keith: Bird, *909;* Final Analysis, *976;* Marked for Death, *82;* Men at Work, *592;* Nails, *88;* Stars and Bars, *385;* They Live, *895*

David, Thayer: Duchess and the Dirtwater Fox, The, *1110;* Eiger Sanction, The, *43;* Savages (1973), *373;* Save the Tiger, *648*

Davidovich, Lolita: Blaze, *463;* Boiling Point, *17;* Inner Circle, The, *552;* Intersection, *553;* Keep the Change, *1124;* Leap of Faith, *572;* Prison Stories: Women on the Inside, *628;* Raising Cain, *878*

Davidson, Eileen: Easy Wheels, *270;* Eternity, *511;* House on Sorority Row, *853*

Davidson, Jaye: Crying Game, The, *492*

Davidson, John: Captain America (1944), *22;* Dick Tracy vs. Crime Inc., *38;* Happiest Millionaire, The, *173;* One and Only, Genuine, Original Family Band, The, *192;* Perils of Pauline, The (1933), *98*

Davidson, Tommy: Strictly Business, *387*

Davidtz, Embeth: Army of Darkness, *810;* Schindler's List, *649;* Sweet Murder, *1022*

Davies, Geraint Wyn: Hush Little Baby, *984;* Terror Stalks the Class Reunion, *894*

Davies, John: Positive I.D., *1006*

Davies, John Howard: Oliver Twist (1948), *612;* Rocking Horse Winner, The, *642;* Tom Brown's Schooldays (1950), *685*

Davies, Kate Emma: Queenie, *632*

Davies, Lane: Funland, *282;* Impure Thoughts, *305;* Magic of Lassie, The, *185*

Davies, Lindy: Malcolm, *327*

Davies, Marion: Going Hollywood, *920;* MGM's The Big Parade of Comedy, *331;* Operator 13, *614;* Show People, *378*

Davies, Ray: Absolute Beginners, *906*

Davies, Rudi: Object of Beauty, The, *348*

Davies, Rupert: Dracula Has Risen from the Grave, *837;* Five Golden Dragons, *50;* Night Visitor, The (1970), *607;* Oblong Box, The, *872*

Davies, Sian Leisa: Heaven on Earth, *539*

Davies, Stephen: Berlin Conspiracy, The, *10;* Nest, The (1988), *868;* Philip Marlowe, Private Eye: The Pencil, *1005*

Davis, Amy: All-American Murder, *951*

Davis, Ann B.: Lover Come Back, *323;* Very Brady Christmas, A, *215*

Davis, Bette: All About Eve, *444;* All This and Heaven Too, *445;* American Film Institute Life Achievement Awards, The, *418;* As Summers Die, *451;* Beyond the Forest, *460;* Bride Came C.O.D., The, *245;* Bureau of Missing Persons, *959;* Burnt Offerings, *820;* Cabin in the Cotton, *473;* Catered Affair, The, *477;* Corn Is Green, The (1945), *488;* Dangerous, *494;* Dark Secret of Harvest Home, The, *829;* Dark Victory, *495;* Dead Ringer, *967;* Death on the Nile, *968;* Deception (1946), *498;* Disappearance of Aimee, The, *970;* Empty Canvas, The, *509;* Ex-Lady, *512;* Great Lie, The, *532;* Hell's House, *61;* Hollywood Canteen, *923;* Hollywood Outtakes, *299;* Hush...Hush, Sweet Charlotte, *854;* In This Our Life, *550;* Jezebel, *557;* Juarez, *560;* June Bride, *311;* Kid Galahad (1937), *563;* Letter, The, *991;* Little Foxes, The, *576;* Little Gloria...Happy at Last, *576;* Madame Sin, *80;* Man Who Came to Dinner, The, *328;* Marked Woman, *82;* Mr. Skeffington, *597;* Murder with Mirrors, *999;* Now, Voyager, *609;* Of Human Bondage (1934), *610;* Old Maid, The, *611;* Petrified Forest, The, *621;* Phone Call from a Stranger, *622;* Piano for

Mrs. Cimino, A, *622;* Pocketful of Miracles, *359;* Private Lives of Elizabeth and Essex, The, *629;* Return from Witch Mountain, *199;* Right of Way, *640;* Satan Met a Lady, *1012;* Sisters, The (1938), *659;* Star, The, *665;* Stolen Life, A, *668;* Strangers: The Story of a Mother and a Daughter, *669;* Thank Your Lucky Stars, *944;* That Certain Woman, *680;* Three on a Match, *683;* Virgin Queen, The, *694;* Watch on the Rhine, *696;* Watcher in the Woods, The, *901;* Way Back Home, *406;* Whales of August, The, *698;* What Ever Happened to Baby Jane?, *902;* Where Love Has Gone, *699;* White Mama, *700;* Wicked Stepmother, The, *903;* Winter Meeting, *704*

Davis, Brad: Blood Ties (1987), *464;* Caine Mutiny Court Martial, The, *473;* Campus Corpse, The, *820;* Chariots of Fire, *479;* Chiefs, *961;* Child of Darkness, Child of Light, *823;* Cold Steel, *28;* Greatest Man in the World, The, *290;* Heart, *537;* Midnight Express, *594;* Querelle, *779;* Rosalie Goes Shopping, *370;* Rumor of War, A, *109;* Small Circle of Friends, A, *660;* Unspeakable Acts, *692;* When the Time Comes, *699*

Davis, Clifton: Dream Date, *269;* Night the City Screamed, The, *606*

Davis, Cynthia: Cooley High, *259*

Davis, Daniel: Glen or Glenda, *528*

Davis, Donald: Man Inside, The (1984), *81;* Memories of Murder, *996*

Davis, Drew: Hollywood High, Part II, *299*

Davis, Duane: Program, The, *629*

Davis, Frances: Devil's Wedding Night, The, *834*

Davis, Gail: Annie Oakley (TV Series), *1094;* Blue Canadian Rockies, *1099;* Cow Town, *1106;* Far Frontier, *1112;* On Top of Old Smoky, *1137;* TV Classics: Annie Oakley, *1159;* Valley of Fire, *1161;* Winning of the West, *1165*

Davis, Geena: Accidental Tourist, The, *440;* Angie, *448;* Beetlejuice, *233;* Earth Girls Are Easy, *915;* Fly, The (1986), *841;* Hero, *296;* League of Their Own, A, *571;* Quick Change, *363;* Secret Weapons, *113;* Thelma & Louise, *127*

Davis, George: Circus, The/A Day's Pleasure, *255*

Davis, Guy: Beat Street, *908*

Davis, Jim: Bad Company, *1095;* Brimstone, *1101;* Cariboo Trail, *1103;* Comes a Horseman, *1105;* Day Time Ended, The, *1045;* Dracula vs. Frankenstein, *837;* El Dorado, *1111;* Fabulous Texan, The, *1112;* Five Bloody Graves, *1113;* Gun Riders, The, *1117;* Hellfire, *1120;* Jesse James Meets Frankenstein's Daughter, *858;* Jubilee Trail, *1124;* Last Command, The (1955), *1125;* Little Big Horn, *1128;* Monster from Green Hell, *866;* Monte Walsh, *1134;* Outcast, The, *1137;* Restless Breed, The, *1142;* Showdown, The (1950), *1149;* Winter Meeting, *704;* Zebra in the Kitchen, *220*

Davis, Joan: Around the World, *907;* George White's Scandals, *919;* Hold That Ghost, *298;* If You Knew Susie, *924;* Just Around the Corner, *926;* Show Business, *939;* Sun Valley Serenade, *942;* Thin Ice, *945*

Davis, Judy: Alice (1990), *224;* Barton Fink, *232;* Final Option, The, *977;* Georgia, *979;* Heatwave, *539;* High Rolling, *62;* High Tide, *541;* Husbands and Wives, *546;* Impromptu, *549;* Kangaroo, *562;* My Brilliant Career, *601;* Naked Lunch, *1067;* One Against the Wind, *613;* Passage to India, A, *619;* Ref, The, *365;* Where Angels Fear to Tread, *699;* Winter of Our Dreams, *704;* Woman Called Golda, A, *705*

Davis, Mac: Blackmail (1991), *956;* Cheaper to Keep Her, *254;* North Dallas Forty, *609;* Sting II, The, *120*

Davis, Mike: Best of the Big Laff Off, The, *236*

Davis, Mildred: His Royal Slyness/Haunted Spooks, *298*

Davis, Nancy: Donovan's Brain, *1047;* East Side, West Side, *506;* Hellcats of the Navy, *60;* It's a Big Country, *308;* Next Voice You Hear, The, *605*

Davis, Nathan: Code of Silence, *27*

Davis, Ossie: All God's Children, *444;* Avenging Angel, *8;* Do the Right Thing, *502;* Gladiator, *528;* Grumpy Old Men, *291;* Harry and Son, *537;* Hill, The, *541;* Hot Stuff, *301;* Joe Versus the Volcano, *310;* Jungle Fever, *561;* King, *564;* Man Called Adam, A, *586;* Purlie Victorious, *363;* Roots: The Next Generation, *644;* Scalphunters, The, *1148;* School Daze, *373*

Davis, Philip: High Hopes, *297;* Howling V—The Rebirth, *854;* Quadrophenia, *936;* Who's Who, *411*

Davis, Phyllis: Guns, *58;* Sizzle, *659;* Terminal Island, *126*

Davis, Richard: Sky's the Limit, The, *940*

Davis, Robert: Taking of Beverly Hills, The, *124*

Davis, Roger: Flash and the Firecat, *50;* Ruby (1977), *881*

Davis, Rufe: Gangs of Sonora, *1115;* Lone Star Raiders, *1129;* Riders for Justice, *1143;* Trail Blazers, *1158;* Under Texas Skies, *1160*

Davis, Sammi: Chernobyl: The Final Warning, *480;* Consuming Passions, *259;* Hope and Glory, *544;* Horseplayer, *983;* Indecency, *986;* Lair of the White Worm, *859;* Perfect Bride, The, *873;* Prayer for the Dying, A, *1007;* Rainbow, The, *634;* Shadow of China, *654*

Davis Jr., Sammy: Alice in Wonderland (1985), *145;* Bloopers from Star Trek and Laugh-In, *242;* Cannonball Run, *250;* Cannonball Run II, *250;* Carol Burnett's My Personal Best, *251;* Gone with the West, *1116;* Kid Who Loved Christmas, The, *180;* Little Moon & Jud McGraw, *1128;* Man Called Adam, A, *586;* Ocean's Eleven, *93;* Robin & the Seven Hoods, *936;* Sweet Charity, *943;* Tap, *944;* That's Dancing, *436;* Trackers, The, *1158*

Davis, Sonny: Last Night at the Alamo, *315*

Davis, Sonny Carl: Fast Money, *46;* Verne Miller, *135*

Davis, Stringer: Murder Ahoy, *998;* Murder at the Gallop, *998;* Murder Most Foul, *998*

Davis, Tom: Franken and Davis at Stockton State, *280;* One More Saturday Night, *350*

Davis, Tracy: Beyond the Rising Moon, *1039*

Davis, Viveka: Dangerous Woman, A, *494;* End of Innocence, The, *509;* Man Trouble, *327;* Morgan Stewart's Coming Home, *337*

Davis, Warwick: Ewok Adventure, The, *165;* Ewoks: The Battle for Endor, *165;* Leprechaun, *860;* Willow, *1089*

Davison, Bruce: Affair, The, *442;* Brass Target, *19;* Deadman's Curve, *913;* French Quarter, *522;* High Risk, *61;* Last Summer, *570;* Lies, *574;* Live! From Death Row, *577;* Longtime Companion, *579;* Misfit Brigade, The, *85;* Poor Little Rich Girl: The Barbara Hutton Story, *624;* Short Cuts, *657;* Short Eyes, *657;* Six Degrees of Separation, *659;* Spies Like Us, *384;* Steel and Lace, *1080;* Strawberry Statement, The, *670;* Summer Heat (1983), *672;* Summer of My German Soldier, *672;* Taming of the Shrew (1982), *391;* Tomorrow's Child, *686;* Ulzana's Raid, *1160;* Willard, *903*

Davison, Peter: All Creatures Great and Small, *145;* Pocketful of Rye, A, *1006*

Daw, Evelyn: Something to Sing About, *940*

Dawber, Pam: Little Mermaid, The (1984), *182;* Stay Tuned, *385;* Through Naked Eyes, *129;* Wedding, A, *407*

Dawn, Marpessa: Black Orpheus, *718*

Dawn, Michelle: Yum-Yum Girls, The, *709*

Dawson, Anthony: Curse of the Werewolf, The, *828;* Death Rides a Horse, *1108;* Haunted Strangler, The, *849;* Tiger Bay, *683*

Dawson, Kamala: Lightning Jack, *1128*

Dawson, Richard: Running Man, The, *1075*

Day, Annette: Double Trouble (1967), *914*

Day, Cora Lee: Daughters of the Dust, *496*

Day, Dennis: Buck Benny Rides Again, *246;* Jack Benny Program, The (TV Series), *309*

Day, Doris: April in Paris, *907;* By the Light of the Silvery Moon, *910;* Calamity Jane (1953), *910;* Glass Bottom Boat, The, *287;* I'll See You in My Dreams, *924;* It's a Great Feeling, *925;* Jumbo, *926;* Love Me or Leave Me, *929;* Lover Come Back, *323;* Lucky Me, *929;* Lullaby of Broadway, *929;* Man Who Knew Too Much, The (1955), *995;* Midnight Lace, *84;* My Dream Is Yours, *932;* On Moonlight Bay, *933;* Pajama Game, The, *934;* Pillow Talk, *357;* Please Don't Eat the Daisies, *358;* Romance on the High Seas, *937;* Send Me No Flowers, *375;* Tea for Two, *944;* Teacher's Pet, *392;* That Touch of Mink, *393;* Thrill of It All, The, *396;* Tunnel of Love, The, *400;* West Point Story, The, *947;* Where Were You When the Lights Went Out?, *409;* Winning Team, The, *704;* With Six You Get Eggroll, *412;* Young at Heart, *948;* Young Man with a Horn, *948*

Day, John: Detour to Danger, *1109*

Day, Josette: Beauty and the Beast (1946), *716*

Day, Laraine: Arizona Legion, *1095;* Dr. Kildare's Strange Case, *40;* Foreign Correspondent, *978;* High and the Mighty, The, *541;* Journey for Margaret, *559;* Mr. Lucky, *86;* Murder on Flight 502, *87;* My Dear Secretary, *339;* Return to Fantasy Island, *1074;* Tarzan Finds a Son, *125;* Those Endearing Young Charms, *394;* Tycoon, *133*

Day, Marceline: Broadway to Cheyenne, *1101;* Cameraman, The, *249;* Telegraph Trail, The, *1154*

Day, Morris: Graffiti Bridge, *920;* Purple Rain, *935*

Day, Stuart Garrison: Search and Destroy (1988), *1076*

Day, Vera: Up the Creek (1958), *403*

Day-Lewis, Daniel: Age of Innocence, The, *443;* Eversmile New Jersey, *511;* In the Name of the Father, *550;* Last of the Mohicans, The (1992), *1126;* My Beautiful Laundrette, *601;* My Left Foot, *602;* Room with a View, A, *644;* Stars and Bars, *385;* Unbearable Lightness of Being, The, *691*

Dayan, Assaf: Operation Thunderbolt, *95*

Dayka, Margit: Cat's Play, *722*

Dayrit, Dina: Infested, *856*

Dayton, Danny: Mad Bull, *584*

de Almeida, Joaquim: Good Morning, Babylon, *530*

De Aragon, Maria: Blood Mania, *815*

De Baer, Jean: Tidy Endings, *683*

de Banzie, Brenda: Doctor at Sea, *266;* Entertainer, The, *510;* Hobson's Choice (1954), *298;* Thirty-Nine Steps, The (1959), *1024*

De Bartolli, Moreno: When Father Was Away on Business, *803*

de Brulier, Nigel: Iron Mask, The, *67;* Zorro Rides Again, *1166*

De Carlo, Yvonne: American Gothic, *808;* Arizona Bushwhackers, *1094;* Captain's Paradise, The, *250;* Cellar Dweller, *822;* Criss Cross (1948), *964;* Death of a Scoundrel, *498;* Global Affair, A, *287;* Good Idea, *288;* Hostile Guns, *1122;* Liar's Moon, *574;* McLintock!, *1133;* Mirror Mirror, *865;* Munsters' Revenge, The, *338;* Nocturna, *346;* Oscar (1991), *351;* Passion (1954), *97;* Salome, Where She Danced, *647;* Satan's Cheerleaders, *882;* Seven Minutes, The, *653;* Shotgun, *1149;* Silent Scream, *886;* Vultures, *901*

De Coff, Linda: Hurry Up or I'll Be 30, *303*

De Cordoba, Pedro: Before I Hang, *812;* Law of the Pampas, *1127;* Mexican Hayride, *331*

De Cordova, Arturo: El (This Strange Passion), *733*

de Corsia, Ted: Buccaneer, The, *20;* Enforcer, The (1951), *44;* It Happens Every Spring, *307;* Lady from Shanghai, *989;* Mohawk, *1134;* Neptune's Daughter, *932;* Three Secrets, *683*

De Filippo, Peppino: Variety Lights, *800*

de Funes, Louis: Candide, *722;* Delusions of Grandeur, *729;* Four Bags Full, *738*

de Grasse, Sam: Blind Husbands, *464*

de Grazia, Julio: Deadly Revenge, *35*

De Haven, Gloria: Best Foot Forward, *908;* Bog, *818;* Broadway Rhythm, *910;* Summer Holiday, *942;* Summer Stock, *942;* Susan and God, *674;* Thin Man Goes Home, The, *1024;* Three Little Words, *945;* Two Girls and a Sailor, *946;* Two Tickets to Broadway, *947;* Who Is the Black Dahlia?, *1031;* Yellow Cab Man, The, *415*

de Havilland, Olivia: Adventures of Robin Hood, The, *2;* Ambassador's Daughter, The, *226;* Anastasia: The Mystery of Anna, *447;* Anthony Adverse, *450;* Captain Blood, *22;* Charge of the Light Brigade, The (1936), *24;* Dark Mirror, The, *966;* Dodge City, *1109;* Fifth Musketeer, The, *47;* Gone with the Wind, *530;* Heiress, The, *539;* Hollywood Canteen, *923;* Hush...Hush, Sweet Charlotte, *854;* In This Our Life, *550;* Lady in a Cage, *989;* Midsummer Night's Dream, A (1935), *1066;* Not as a Stranger, *609;* Private Lives of Elizabeth and Essex, The, *629;* Proud Rebel, The, *1140;* Roots: The Next Generation, *644;* Santa Fe Trail, *1147;* Snake Pit, The, *661;* Strawberry Blonde, The, *670;* Swarm, The, *891;* Thank Your Lucky Stars, *944*

de Hoyos, Jaime: El Mariachi, *733*

de Jonge, Marc: Rambo III, *103*

De Keyser, David: Valentino, *693*

de Koff, Ton: Rembrandt—1669, *780*

De La Croix, Raven: Lost Empire, The, *79*

de la Motte, Marguerite: Final Extra, The, *977;* Iron Mask, The, *67;* Mark of Zorro, The (1920), *82;* Shadows, *654*

De La Paz, Danny: American Me, *446;* Barbarosa, *1097;* Boulevard Nights, *467;* Wild Pair, The, *140*

de La Pena, George: Brain Donors, *245;* Nijinsky, *607*

de Lancie, John: Arcade, *1036;* Fearless (1993), *515;* Hand That Rocks the Cradle, The, *981*

de Lint, Derek: Assault, The, *714;* Mascara, *82;* Stealing Heaven, *667;* Unbearable Lightness of Being, The, *691*

De Longis, Anthony: Final Round, *48*

de Marney, Derrek: Dangerous Moonlight (a.k.a. Suicide Squadron), *32;* Young and Innocent, *1033*

de Medeiros, Maria: Henry & June, *540*

De Meio, Carlo: Other Hell, The, *873*

De Mendoza, Alberto: Bullet for Sandoval, A, *1102*

De Niro, Robert: Angel Heart, *952;* Awakenings, *452;* Backdraft, *8;* Bang the Drum Slowly, *455;* Bloody Mama, *16;* Born to Win, *467;* Brazil, *245;* Cape Fear (1991), *959;* Deer Hunter, The, *499;* Falling in Love, *513;* Godfather, Part II, The, *529;* Godfather Epic, The, *529;* Goodfellas, *531;* Greetings, *290;* Guilty by Suspicion, *534;* Hi Mom, *297;* Jackknife, *556;* King of Comedy, The, *565;* Last Tycoon, The, *571;* Mad Dog and Glory, *584;* Mean Streets, *591;* Midnight Run, *84;* Mission, The, *596;* Mistress (1992), *597;* New York, New York, *933;* Night and the City (1992), *605;* 1900, *607;* Once Upon a Time in America (Long Version), *94;* Raging Bull, *633;* Stanley and Iris, *665;* Swap, The, *674;* Taxi Driver, *1023;* This Boy's Life, *682;* True Confessions, *1027;* Untouchables, The, *134;* Wedding Party, The, *407;* We're No Angels (1989), *408*

de Oliveira, Lourdes: Black Orpheus, *718*

De Palma, Rossy: Kika, *751*

de Putti, Lya: Othello (1922), *615;* Sorrows of Satan, The, *663;* Variety, *800*

de Roche, Charles: Ten Commandments, The (1923), *678*

de Rossi, Barbara: Blood Ties (1987), *464;* Hearts and Armour, *59;* Mussolini and I, *601*

De Sade, Ana: Triumphs of a Man Called Horse, *1159*

De Salvo, Anne: Bad Manners, *231;* Compromising Positions, *258;* Dead in the Water, *967*

De Santis, Joe: Dino, *501;* Last Hunt, The, *1126*

de Shields, Andre: Prison, *876*

De Sica, Christian: Detective School Dropouts, *264*

De Sica, Vittorio: Andy Warhol's Dracula, *809;* Battle of Austerlitz, The, *9;* Earrings of Madame De..., The, *732;* General Della Rovere, *740;* Gold of Naples, The, *529;* It Started in Naples, *308;* L'Odeur Des Fauves (Scandal Man), *761;* Pardon My Trunk, *775;* Shoes of the Fisherman, *656*

De Soto, Rosana: La Bamba, *927;* Stand and Deliver, *665*

de Souza, Paul: Web of Deceit, *1030*

de Toth, Nicolas: Welcome to Spring Break, *902*

de Villalonga, Jose Luis: Darling, *496*

de Vogy, Carl: Spiders, The, *119*

De Vos, Ingrid: Istanbul, *749*

De Vries, Jon: Act of Passion, *441;* Lianna, *573;* Sarah, Plain and Tall, *648;* Truth or Die, *689*

de Wilde, Brandon: All Fall Down, *444;* Deserter, The, *1109;* Goodbye, My Lady, *171;* Hud, *546;* In Harm's Way, *66;* Member of the Wedding, The, *592;* Shane, *1148;* Those Calloways, *211*

De Young, Cliff: Annie Oakley (1985), *146;* Code Name: Dancer, *27;* Dr. Giggles, *835;* Fear (1988), *976;* Flashback, *50;* Flight of the Navigator, *1052;* Forbidden Sun, *519;* Fourth Story, *978;* F/X, *979;* Hunger, The (1983), *854;* Immortal Sins, *855;* In Dangerous Company, *550;* Independence Day,

551; King, 564; Lindbergh Kidnapping Case, The, 575; Nails, 88; Protocol, 363; Pulse, 877; Reckless (1984), 636; Revenge of the Red Baron, 881; Rude Awakening (1989), 371; Secret Admirer, 374; Shock Treatment, 378; Survivalist, The, 123; To Die Standing, 130
Dea, Marie: Les Visiteurs Du Soir, 759
Deacon, Brian: Jesus, 557; Vampyres, 900; Zed and Two Noughts, A, 709
Deacon, Eric: Zed and Two Noughts, A, 709
Deacon, Richard: Abbott and Costello Meet the Mummy, 221; Awakening of Cassie, The, 452; Happy Hooker Goes Hollywood, The, 293; My Sister Eileen, 932
Dead End Kids, The: They Made Me a Criminal, 681
Deakins, Lucy: Boy Who Could Fly, The, 468; Cheetah, 158; Little Nikita, 992
Dean, Allison: Ruby in Paradise, 645
Dean, Bill: Family Life, 514
Dean, Eddie: Caravan Trail, 1103; Colorado Serenade, 1105; Wild West (1946), 1164; Wildfire (1945), 1164
Dean, Fabian: Single Room Furnished, 659
Dean, Felicity: Steaming, 667; Whistle Blower, The, 1031
Dean, Isabel: Terrorists, The, 1023
Dean, Ivor: Saint, The (TV Series), 1012
Dean, James: East of Eden (1955), 506; Giant, 527; Rebel without a Cause, 636; Tales of Tomorrow (Vols. I - III), 1082
Dean, Jimmy: Big Bad John, 12
Dean, Laura: Fame, 916
Dean, Loren: American Clock, The, 446; Billy Bathgate, 461; 1492: The Conquest of Paradise, 52; JFK: Reckless Youth, 558
Dean, Priscilla: Outside the Law, 616
Dean, Rick: Naked Obsession, 1000; One Man Army, 94; Saturday Night Special, 111
Dean, Ron: Birthday Boy, The, 240; Cold Justice, 28
DeAnda, Rodolfo: Toy Soldiers (1983), 131
Deane, Lezlie: To Protect and Serve, 130
Deane, Shirley: Prairie Moon, 1139
DeAngelo, Paul: Sleepaway Camp, 887
Deas, Justin: Dream Lover (1986), 972; Montana, 599
DeBell, Kristine: Big Brawl, The, 12
DeBenning, Burr: Incredible Melting Man, The, 1058
Debucourt, Jean: Monsieur Vincent, 768
DeCamp, Rosemary: Big Hangover, The, 238; By the Light of the Silvery Moon, 910; Look For The Silver Lining, 929; Main Street to Broadway, 326; On Moonlight Bay, 933; Saturday the 14th, 882; Story of Seabiscuit, The, 207; Strategic Air Command, 670; 13 Ghosts, 895; Tom Edison—The Boy Who Lit Up the World, 213; Yankee Doodle Dandy, 948
Deckert, Blue: Taste for Killing, A, 126
Decomble, Guy: Jour de Fête, 750
Dee, Catherine: Stuff Stephanie in the Incinerator, 388
Dee, Frances: Becky Sharp, 457; Blood Money (1933), 464; Finishing School, 516; Four Faces West, 1114; Gypsy Colt, 173; I Walked with a Zombie, 855; If I Had a Million, 304; Little Women (1933), 577; Of Human Bondage (1934), 610; Private Affairs of Bel Ami, The, 628; So Ends Our Night, 661; Wheel of Fortune, 409
Dee, Gloria: King of the Congo, 72
Dee, Ruby: All God's Children, 444; Buck and the Preacher, 1102; Cat People (1982), 822; Cop and a Half, 160; Court-Martial of Jackie Robinson, The, 489; Decoration Day, 498; Do the Right Thing, 502; Ernest Green Story, The, 165; Gore Vidal's Lincoln, 531; I Know Why the Caged Bird Sings, 547; Incident, The (1967), 551; It's Good to Be Alive, 555; Jackie Robinson Story, The, 556; Jungle Fever, 561; Purlie Victorious, 363; Raisin in the Sun, A (1961), 634; Windmills of the Gods, 703
Dee, Sandra: Dunwich Horror, The, 838; Fantasy Island, 1050; Gidget, 286; Imitation of Life, 549; Reluctant Debutante, The, 365; Summer Place, A, 672; Tammy and the Doctor, 677; Until They Sail, 692
Deering, Olive: Danger, 965
Dees, Kevin: Jet Benny Show, The, 310
Deezen, Eddie: Beverly Hills Vamp, 237; Desperate Moves, 264; Dorf Goes Auto Racing, 267; Hollywood Boulevard II, 983; I Wanna Hold Your Hand, 304; Midnight Madness, 332; Million Dollar Mystery, 332; Mob Boss, 335; Mugsy's Girls, 338; Polish Vampire in Burbank, A, 359; Rosebud Beach Hotel, The, 370; Surf 2, 389; Whoopee Boys, The, 411
DeFoe, Diane: Deceit, 1046
DeFore, Don: Adventures of Ozzie and Harriet, The (TV Series), 222; Dark City, 495; Girl in Every Port, A, 286; Jumping Jacks, 311; My Friend Irma, 340; Rare Breed, A (1981), 198; Romance on the High Seas, 937; Time to Love and a Time to Die, A, 684; Without Reservations, 413
Degermark, Pia: Elvira Madigan, 734; Looking Glass War, The, 993
Deguy, Marie-Armelle: Elegant Criminal, The, 734
Dehner, John: Apache, 1094; California Gold Rush, 1103; Creator, 490; Dynamite Pass, 1111; Golden Earrings, 56; Hot Lead, 1122; Killer Inside Me, The, 988; Left Handed Gun, The (1958), 1128; Man of the West, 1132; Maverick (TV Series), 1133; Nothing Personal, 347; Out California Way, 1137; Slaughterhouse Five, 1077; Support Your Local Gunfighter, 1154; Texas Rangers, The, 1156
DeJong, Geert: Army Brats, 228
Dekker, Albert: Beau Geste, 10; Buckskin Frontier, 1102; Cass Timberlane, 476; Dr. Cyclops, 835; Fabulous Texan, The, 1112; Gamera the Invincible, 1053; Gentlemen's Agreement, 526; Honky Tonk, 1121; In Old California, 1122; Kansan, The, 1124; Kiss Me Deadly, 989; Once Upon a Honeymoon, 349; Salome, Where She Danced, 647; Seven Sinners, 113; Strange Cargo, 669; Wake Island, 136; War of the Wildcats, 1162; Woman of the Town, 1165
Del Poggio, Carla: Variety Lights, 800
Del Prete, Duilio: Sensuous Nurse, The, 784
Del Rio, Dolores: Bird of Paradise, 13; Children of Sanchez, The, 481; Flaming Star, 1113; Flor Sylvestre, 737; Flying Down to Rio, 917; Fugitive, The (1947), 523; Journey Into Fear (1942), 987; Wonder Bar, 948
Del Sol, Laura: El Amor Brujo, 733; Hit, The, 63; Stilts, The (Los Zancos), 789
Del Toro, Benicio: China Moon, 961; Fearless (1993), 515
Del Toro, Guadalupe: Donna Herlinda and Her Son, 731
Delair, Suzy: Fernandel the Dressmaker, 736; Gervaise, 740; Jenny Lamour, 749; Pattes Blanches (White Paws), 776
Delaney, Joan: Don't Drink the Water, 267
Delaney, Kim: Body Parts, 817; Campus Man, 249; Disappearance of Christina, The, 971; Drifter, The, 837; First Affair, 517; Hunter's Blood, 546; That Was Then...This Is Now, 680
Delany, Dana: China Beach (TV Series), 481; Housesitter, 302; Light Sleeper, 575; Masquerade (1988), 995; Tombstone, 1157; Wild Palms, 1089
Delgado, Camilo: Strangers in the City, 669
Delger, Jeff: On the Line, 94
Dell, Claudia: Ghost Patrol, 55
Dell, Dorothy: Little Miss Marker (1934), 182
Dell, Gabriel: Blues Busters, 242; Bowery Boys, The (Series), 244; Framed (1975), 52; Junior G-Men, 69; Little Tough Guys, 319
Dell, Myrna: Guns of Hate, 1118
DellaFemina, Michael: Mandroid, 1065
Delmar, Kenny: It's a Joke, Son!, 308
Delon, Alain: Airport '79: The Concorde, 443; Assassination of Trotsky, The, 451; Borsalino, 18; Diabolically Yours, 730; Eclipse, The, 733; Honor Among Thieves, 63; Icy Breasts, 746; Is Paris Burning?, 554; Joy House, 559; Leopard, The, 572; Lost Command, 79; Melodie en Sous-Sol (The Big Grab), 766; Mr. Klein, 768; Red Sun, 1142; Rocco & His Brothers, 782; Sois Belle Et Tais-Toi (Just Another Pretty Face), 787; Swann in Love, 791; Swimming Pool, The, 792; Texas Across the River, 1155; Widow Couderc, 803; Zorro, 142

Delon, Nathalie: Eyes Behind the Stars, *1050;* Game of Seduction, *739*
Delora, Jennifer: Deranged, *833*
DeLorenzo, Michael: Judgment Night, *69*
Delorme, Daniele: Les Miserables (1957), *759;* Pardon Mon Affaire, Too!, *775*
Delpy, Julie: Beatrice, *716;* Three Musketeers, The (1993), *129;* Voyager, *695*
Deluc, Xavier: Tale of Two Cities, A (1991), *677*
DeLuise, Dom: Adventure of Sherlock Holmes' Smarter Brother, The, *223;* Almost Pregnant, *225;* American Tail, An, *146;* Best Little Whorehouse in Texas, The, *908;* Cannonball Run, *250;* Cannonball Run II, *250;* Cheap Detective, The, *254;* Diary of a Young Comic, *264;* Driving Me Crazy, *269;* End, The, *271;* Fail-Safe, *974;* Fatso, *275;* Glass Bottom Boat, The, *287;* Going Bananas, *169;* Haunted Honeymoon, *294;* History of the World, Part One, The, *298;* Hot Stuff, *301;* Last Married Couple in America, The, *315;* Loose Cannons, *321;* Muppet Movie, The, *189;* Only with Married Men, *350;* Robin Hood: Men in Tights, *369;* Secret of Nimh, The, *202;* Sextette, *376;* Silent Movie, *379;* Smokey and the Bandit II, *381;* Twelve Chairs, The, *401;* Wholly Moses!, *410;* World's Greatest Lover, The, *414*
DeLuise, Michael: Encino Man, *271;* Man without a Face, The, *587*
DeLuise, Peter: Children of the Night, *823;* Free Ride, *281;* Rescue Me, *105*
Delys, Max: Gangster's Law, *525*
Demarest, William: All Through the Night, *3;* Charlie Chan at the Opera, *961;* Christmas in July, *255;* Devil and Miss Jones, The, *264;* Don't Be Afraid of the Dark, *836;* Escape from Fort Bravo, *1111;* Great Moment, The, *290;* Hail the Conquering Hero, *292;* Hell on Frisco Bay, *60;* Here Come the Girls, *922;* It's a Mad Mad Mad Mad World, *308;* Jazz Singer, The (1927), *925;* Jolson Sings Again, *926;* Jolson Story, The, *926;* Lady Eve, The, *315;* Little Men (1940), *576;* Love on the Run (1936), *323;* Miracle of Morgan's Creek, The, *332;* Mountain, The, *600;* Palm Beach Story, The, *353;* Pardon My Sarong, *354;* Perils of Pauline, The (1947), *356;* Sincerely Yours, *658;* Son of Flubber, *206;* Sorrowful Jones, *383;* Sullivan's Travels, *388;* That Darn Cat, *210;* Viva Las Vegas, *947;* What Price Glory, *408*
Demazis, Orane: Angele, *713;* César, *723;* Fanny (1932), *736;* Harvest, *743;* Le Schpountz, *758;* Marius, *765*
Demetral, Chris: Blank Check, *151*
DeMille, Katherine: Black Room, The (1935), *814;* Gentleman from California, *1115;* In Old Caliente, *1122;* Viva Villa!, *1162*
Demiss, Darcy: Living to Die, *993*
Demongeot, Catherine: Zazie dans le Metro, *807*
Demongeot, Mylene: Bonjour Tristesse, *466;* Rape of the Sabines, *103;* Sois Belle Et Tais-Toi (Just Another Pretty Face), *787*
DeMornay, Rebecca: And God Created Woman (1987), *447;* Backdraft, *8;* Blind Side, *956;* By Dawn's Early Light, *473;* Dealers, *498;* Feds, *276;* Guilty as Sin, *534;* Hand That Rocks the Cradle, The, *981;* Inconvenient Woman, An, *551;* Murders in the Rue Morgue (1986), *999;* Pecos Bill, King of the Cowboys, *194;* Risky Business, *368;* Runaway Train, *110;* Slugger's Wife, The, *381;* Three Musketeers, The (1993), *129;* Trip to Bountiful, The, *688*
DeMoss, Darcy: Eden (TV Series), *507*
Dempsey, Chris: Virgin High, *405*
Dempsey, Mark: Oh! Calcutta!, *348*
Dempsey, Patrick: Bank Robber, *232;* Bugsy Malone, *155;* Can't Buy Me Love, *250;* Coupe De Ville, *260;* Face the Music, *273;* For Better and for Worse, *279;* Happy Together, *293;* In a Shallow Grave, *550;* In the Mood, *306;* JFK: Reckless Youth, *558;* Loverboy, *323;* Meatballs III, *330;* Mobsters, *86;* Run, *109;* Some Girls, *382;* With Honors, *412*
Dempster, Carol: Dream Street, *504;* Sally of the Sawdust, *647;* Sorrows of Satan, The, *663;* True Heart Susie, *688;* White Rose, The (1923), *700*
DeMunn, Jeffrey: Blob, The (1988), *814;* By Dawn's Early Light, *473;* Christmas Evil, *824;* Frances, *521;* Hitcher, The, *850;* Sessions, *652;* Treacherous Crossing, *1027;* Warning Sign, *901;* Windy City, *703*
Demy, Mathieu: Le Petit Amour, *758*
DeNatale, Don: Roseland, *644*
Dench, Judi: 84 Charing Cross Road, *508;* Henry V (1989), *540;* Luther, *583;* Midsummer Night's Dream, A (1968), *332;* Room with a View, A, *644;* Wetherby, *698*
Deneuve, Catherine: Act of Aggression, *710;* April Fools, The, *228;* Choice of Arms, A, *724;* Donkey Skin (Peau D'Âne), *731;* Hunger, The (1983), *854;* Hustle, *65;* Indochine, *747;* Je Vous Aime (I Love You All), *749;* La Grande Bourgeoise, *754;* Last Metro, The, *755;* Love Songs (Paroles et Musique), *762;* March or Die, *82;* Mississippi Mermaid, *768;* Repulsion, *879;* Scene of the Crime (1987), *784;* Slightly Pregnant Man, A, *787;* Tales of Paris, *792;* Tristana, *797;* Umbrellas of Cherbourg, The, *798*
Deng, Xiaotuang: Girl from Hunan, *740*
Dengel, Jake: Bloodsucking Pharaohs in Pittsburgh, *816*
Denham, Maurice: Carrington, V. C., *476;* Curse of the Demon, *828;* Damn the Defiant!, *31;* 84 Charing Cross Road, *508;* Hysteria, *984;* Luther, *583;* Mr. Love, *597;* Night Caller from Outer Space, *1068;* Sunday, Bloody Sunday, *673;* Torture Garden, *896;* Very Edge, The, *693;* Virgin and the Gypsy, The, *694*
Denicourt, Marianne: La Belle Noiseuse, *753*
Denier, Lydie: Mardi Gras for the Devil, *863;* Red-Blooded American Girl, *879;* Satan's Princess, *882;* Under Investigation, *1028*
Denis, Jacques: Jonah Who Will Be 25 in the Year 2000, *750*
Denison, Anthony: Amy Fisher Story, The, *447;* Child of Darkness, Child of Light, *823;* City of Hope, *483;* Crime Story, *30;* Full Eclipse, *844;* Full Exposure, *523;* Harvest, The, *981;* Little Vegas, *319;* Sex, Love, and Cold Hard Cash, *1014*
Denison, Leslie: Snow Creature, The, *888*
Denison, Michael: Importance of Being Earnest, The, *305;* Shadowlands, *654*
Dennehy, Brian: Acceptable Risks, *440;* Annie Oakley (1985), *146;* Ants!, *809;* Belly of an Architect, The, *458;* Best Seller, *954;* Butch and Sundance: The Early Days, *1103;* Check Is in the Mail, The, *254;* Cocoon, *1042;* Cocoon: The Return, *1042;* Day One, *496;* Diamond Fleece, The, *970;* Father's Revenge, A, *515;* First Blood, *49;* Foreign Affairs, *520;* F/X, *979;* F/X 2: The Deadly Art of Illusion, *979;* Gladiator, *528;* Gorky Park, *980;* Indigo, *66;* Jericho Mile, The, *557;* Killing in a Small Town, *564;* Last of the Finest, The, *75;* Legal Eagles, *991;* Lion of Africa, The, *77;* Little Mermaid, The (1984), *182;* Never Cry Wolf, *89;* Perfect Witness, *620;* Presumed Innocent, *1007;* Real American Hero, The, *635;* Return to Snowy River, Part II, *1143;* Rising Son, *641;* River Rat, The, *641;* Silent Victory: The Kitty O'Neil Story, *658;* Silverado, *1150;* Skokie, *660;* Teamster Boss: The Jackie Presser Story, *678;* To Catch a Killer, *1025;* Twice in a Lifetime, *690*
Denner, Charles: And Now, My Love, *712;* Assassins de L'Ordre, Les (Law Breakers), *714;* Bluebeard (1963), *719;* Bride Wore Black, The, *959;* Holes, The, *744;* Mado, *763;* Man Who Loved Women, The (1977), *765;* Robert et Robert, *782;* Sleeping Car Murders, The, *786;* Window Shopping, *804;* Z, *806*
Denner, Joyce: Behind Locked Doors, *812*
Denning, Richard: Affair to Remember, An, *442;* Alice Through the Looking Glass (1966), *906;* Black Beauty (1946), *150;* Creature from the Black Lagoon, *826;* Day the World Ended, The, *1045;* Double Deal, *41;* Hangman's Knot, *1119*
Dennis, Sandy: Another Woman, *450;* Come Back to the Five and Dime, Jimmy Dean, Jimmy Dean, *486;* Demon (God Told Me To), *1046;* Execution, The, *974;* Four Seasons, The, *521;* Indian Runner, The, *551;* Mr. Sycamore, *334;* Nasty Habits, *342;* 976-EVIL, *871;* Out of Towners, The, *352;*

Parents, *354;* That Cold Day in the Park, *680;* Up the Down Staircase, *403;* Who's Afraid of Virginia Woolf?, *701*
Denniston, Leslie: Blue Heaven, *465*
Denny, Reginald: Anna Karenina (1935), *449;* Arrest Bulldog Drummond, *6;* Bulldog Drummond Comes Back, *20;* Bulldog Drummond Escapes, *20;* Bulldog Drummond's Bride, *20;* Bulldog Drummond's Peril, *20;* Bulldog Drummond's Revenge, *21;* Bulldog Drummond's Secret Police, *21;* Dancing Man, *965;* Escape Me Never, *510;* Lost Patrol, The, *79;* Madame Satan, *584;* Parlor, Bedroom and Bath, *354;* Private Lives, *362;* Rebecca, *1009;* Romeo and Juliet (1936), *643;* Secret Life of Walter Mitty, The, *374;* Spring Parade, *941;* We're in the Legion Now, *137*
Denton, Chris: Bound and Gagged: A Love Story, *18*
Denton, Christa: Scandal in a Small Town, *649*
Denver, Bob: TV's Greatest Bits, *401*
Denver, John: FoxFire, *521;* Oh, God!, *349*
Depardieu, Elisabeth: Manon of the Spring, *765*
Depardieu, Gérard: Buffet Froid (Cold Cuts), *720;* Camille Claudel, *721;* Choice of Arms, A, *724;* Cyrano De Bergerac (1990), *727;* Danton, *728;* 1492: The Conquest of Paradise, *52;* Get Out Your Handkerchiefs, *740;* Going Places, *741;* Green Card, *290;* Holes, The, *744;* Jean De Florette, *749;* Last Metro, The, *755;* Le Chêvre (The Goat), *757;* Les Comperes, *759;* Loulou, *761;* Maitresse, *764;* Ménage, *767;* Merci La Vie, *767;* Mon Oncle d'Amerique, *768;* Moon in the Gutter, The, *768;* My Father, the Hero, *339;* 1900, *607;* One Woman or Two, *773;* Police, *778;* Return of Martin Guerre, The, *781;* Stavisky, *789;* Too Beautiful for You, *796;* Tous les Matins du Monde, *796;* Under the Sun of Satan, *798;* Uranus, *798;* Vincent, François, Paul and the Others, *801;* Woman Next Door, The, *805*
Depardieu, Guillaume: Tous les Matins du Monde, *796*
Depp, Johnny: Benny & Joon, *234;* Cry-Baby, *912;* Edward Scissorhands, *1048;* Private Resort, *362;* What's Eating Gilbert Grape?, *408*
Depuay, Theo: Gore-Met, Zombie Chef from Hell, *847*
Derek, Bo: Bolero (1984), *466;* Change of Seasons, A, *253;* Fantasies, *514;* Ghosts Can't Do It, *285;* Hot Chocolate, *301;* Orca, *873;* Shattered Image, *1014;* Tarzan the Ape Man (1981), *125;* 10, *392;* Woman of Desire, *1032*
Derek, John: All the King's Men, *444;* Annapolis Story, An, *449;* Knock on Any Door, *566;* Omar Khayyam, *93;* Outcast, The, *1137;* Ten Commandments, The (1956), *678*
Dern, Bruce: After Dark, My Sweet, *951;* Big Town, The, *461;* Black Sunday (1977), *955;* Bloody Mama, *16;* 'Burbs, The, *247;* Carolina Skeletons, *475;* Coming Home, *486;* Court-Martial of Jackie Robinson, The, *489;* Cowboys, The, *1106;* Diggstown, *264;* Driver, The, *42;* Family Plot, *975;* Great Gatsby, The, *532;* Harry Tracy, *1119;* Hush…Hush, Sweet Charlotte, *854;* Incredible Two-Headed Transplant, The, *855;* Into the Badlands, *1123;* King of Marvin Gardens, The, *565;* Laughing Policeman, The, *991;* Marnie, *995;* Middle-Age Crazy, *332;* 1969, *607;* On the Edge, *612;* Outer Limits, The (TV Series), *1069;* Posse (1975), *1139;* Psych-Out, *630;* Rebel Rousers, *104;* St. Valentine's Day Massacre, The, *111;* Silent Running, *1076;* Smile, *381;* Support Your Local Sheriff!, *1154;* Tattoo, *677;* That Championship Season, *680;* Trip, The, *688;* Waterhole #3, *1163;* Wild Angels, The, *139;* Will Penny, *1164;* World Gone Wild, *1090*
Dern, Laura: Afterburn, *442;* Blue Velvet, *817;* Fallen Angels, *513;* Fat Man and Little Boy, *515;* Haunted Summer, *537;* Industrial Symphony No. 1 The Dream of the Broken Hearted, *925;* Jurassic Park, *1061;* Mask (1985), *590;* Perfect World, A, *621;* Rambling Rose, *634;* Smooth Talk, *661;* Strange Case of Dr. Jekyll and Mr. Hyde, The (1989), *890;* Wild at Heart, *702*
Derr, Richard: Castle in the Desert, *960;* Charlie Chan in Rio, *961;* Luxury Liner, *930;* When Worlds Collide, *1089*
Derricks, Cleavant: Moscow on the Hudson, *337;* Off Beat, *348;* Slugger's Wife, The, *381*
Derricks-Carroll, Clinton: Sky Is Gray, The, *660*
Derrig, Joe: Occultist, The, *93*
Deruddere, Dominique: Istanbul, *749*
Des Barres, Michael: Deep Red (1994), *1046;* Midnight Cabaret, *864;* Nightflyers, *1068*
Desailly, Jean: Soft Skin, The, *787*
Descombes, Colette: Paranoia, *1004*
DeSelle, Loraiane: Make Them Die Slowly, *862*
Desmond, Mary Jo: Last Frontier, The, *1125*
Desmond, William: Arizona Days, *1094;* Cowboy and the Bandit, *1106;* Cyclone in the Saddle, *1107;* Last Frontier, The, *1125;* Phantom of the West, *1138;* Powdersmoke Range, *1139*
Desmouceaux, Geary: Small Change, *787*
Desny, Ivan: Escapade in Florence, *165;* Escape from the KGB, *45;* I Killed Rasputin, *746;* Marriage of Maria Braun, The, *765*
Detmers, Maruschka: Devil in the Flesh (1987), *730;* First Name: Carmen, *737;* Hanna's War, *536;* Mambo Kings, The, *930*
Devane, William: Bad News Bears in Breaking Training, The, *231;* Chips, the War Dog, *158;* Dark, The, *829;* Family Plot, *975;* From Here to Eternity (1979), *523;* Hadley's Rebellion, *173;* Honky Tonk Freeway, *300;* Jane Doe, *556;* Marathon Man, *82;* Missiles of October, The, *596;* My Old Man's Place, *602;* Pursuit of Happiness, The, *631;* Red Alert, *104;* Report to the Commissioner, *638;* Rolling Thunder, *108;* Rubdown, *1011;* Testament, *1082;* Time Stalkers, *1084;* Urge to Kill, *692;* Yanks, *707*
DeVasquez, Devin: Society, *888*
Deveau, Alan: Recruits, *365*
Devere, Trish Van: Deadly Currents, *34*
Devine, Andy: Adventures of Huckleberry Finn, The (1960), *144;* Ali Baba and the Forty Thieves, *3;* Bells of San Angelo, *1097;* Buck Benny Rides Again, *246;* Eyes of Texas, *1111;* Fabulous Texan, The, *1112;* Far Frontier, *1112;* Grand Canyon Trail, *1116;* Great American West, *425;* In Old Chicago, *550;* Island in the Sky, *554;* It's a Mad Mad Mad Mad World, *308;* Law and Order, *1127;* Man Who Shot Liberty Valance, The, *1132;* Nighttime in Nevada, *1136;* On the Old Spanish Trail, *1137;* Pete Kelly's Blues, *935;* Romeo and Juliet (1936), *643;* Slaughter Trail, *1150;* Smoke, *205;* Springtime in the Sierras, *1152;* Stagecoach (1939), *1152;* Thunder Pass, *1157;* Two Rode Together, *1160;* Under California Stars, *1160;* Zebra in the Kitchen, *220*
Devine, Loretta: Anna to the Infinite Power, *1036;* Little Nikita, *992*
DeVito, Danny: Amazing Stories (TV Series), *1036;* Batman Returns, *9;* Going Ape!, *287;* Head Office, *294;* Hoffa, *542;* Hurry Up or I'll Be 30, *303;* Jack the Bear, *556;* Jewel of the Nile, The, *68;* My Little Pony: The Movie, *190;* One Flew Over the Cuckoo's Nest, *613;* Other People's Money, *351;* Ratings Game, The, *364;* Romancing the Stone, *108;* Ruthless People, *371;* Terms of Endearment, *679;* Throw Momma from the Train, *396;* Tin Men, *396;* Twins, *401;* Van, The, *404;* War of the Roses, The, *406;* Wise Guys, *412*
DeVito, Karla: Modern Love, *335*
DeVitt, Faith: Claire of the Moon, *483*
Devlin, Alan: Playboys, The, *623*
Devlin, J. G.: Caper of the Golden Bulls, The, *22*
Devon, Laura: Red Line 7000, *104*
Dewaere, Patrick: Beau Pere, *716;* Catherine & Co., *722;* French Detective, The, *738;* Get Out Your Handkerchiefs, *740;* Going Places, *741;* Heat of Desire, *743;* Hot Head, *745*
Dewhurst, Colleen: And Baby Makes Six, *447;* Anne of Avonlea, *449;* Anne of Green Gables (1985), *449;* As Is, *451;* Bed and Breakfast, *457;* Between Two Women, *459;* Blue and the Gray, The, *1099;* Boy Who Could Fly, The, *468;* Cowboys, The, *1106;* Dying Young, *506;* Glitter Dome, The, *980;* Ice Castles, *548;* Lantern Hill, *180;* Mary and Joseph: A Story of Faith, *589;* McQ, *83;* Nun's Story, The, *609;* Obsessed, *610;* Silent Victory: The Kitty O'Neil Story, *658;* Story of Jacob and Joseph, The, *207;* Sword of Gideon, *123;* Termini Station, *679;* Tribute, *688;* When a Stranger Calls, *1030;* You Can't Take it with You (1984), *415*

DeWolfe, Billy: Billie, *150;* Dear Wife, *263;* Lullaby of Broadway, *929;* Perils of Pauline, The (1947), *356;* Tea for Two, *944*

Dexter, Anthony: Married Too Young, *589*

Dexter, Brad: Between Heaven and Hell, *459;* Las Vegas Story, The, *568;* Last Train from Gun Hill, *1126;* None But the Brave, *92;* Oklahoman, The, *1136*

Dexter, Rosemarie: Big Rip-off, The, *1098*

Dey, Deepankar: Stranger, The (1992), *790*

Dey, Susan: Comeback Kid, The, *486;* Echo Park, *507;* First Love, *517;* L.A. Law, *567;* Looker, *1063;* Love Leads the Way, *581;* Sunset Limousine, *388;* Trouble with Dick, The, *1085*

Dezina, Kate: Sure Fire, *674*

Di Aragon, Maria: Cremators, The, *1043*

Di Lazzaro, Dalila: Creepers, *826*

Diabo, Alice: Strangers in Good Company, *669*

Diamantidou, Despo: Dream of Passion, A, *504*

Diamond, Barry: Gross Jokes, *291*

Diamond, Neil: Jazz Singer, The (1980), *926;* Last Waltz, The, *428*

Diamond, Reed Edward: Blind Spot, *464;* Ironclads, *554*

Diaz, Justino: Otello, *934*

Diaz, Vic: Pacific Inferno, *96*

DiBenedetto, Tony: Exterminator, The, *45*

Diberti, Luigi: All Screwed Up, *712*

DiCaprio, Leonardo: This Boy's Life, *682;* What's Eating Gilbert Grape?, *408*

DiCenzo, George: About Last Night, *440;* Helter Skelter, *540;* Killing at Hell's Gate, *71;* Las Vegas Lady, *74;* Ninth Configuration, The, *608;* Omega Syndrome, *93;* Starflight One, *1079*

DiCicco, Bobby: Baby Doll Murders, The, *953;* Big Red One, The, *12;* Frame Up, *52;* I Wanna Hold Your Hand, *304;* Last Hour, The, *75;* Philadelphia Experiment, The, *1070*

Dick, Douglas: Home of the Brave, *543;* Oklahoman, The, *1136;* Red Badge of Courage, The, *636*

Dicken, Dieter: Virus Knows No Morals, A, *801*

Dickerson, Ernest: Visions of Light: The Art of Cinematography, *438*

Dickerson, George: Death Warrant, *35;* Death Wish IV: The Crackdown, *36*

Dickey, James: Deliverance, *36*

Dickey, Lucinda: Breakin', *909;* Breakin' 2 Electric Boogaloo, *909;* Cheerleader Camp, *823;* Ninja III: The Domination, *91*

Dickinson, Angie: Big Bad Mama, *12;* Big Bad Mama II, *12;* Bramble Bush, The, *468;* Captain Newman, M.D., *474;* Cast a Giant Shadow, *23;* Charlie Chan and the Curse of the Dragon Queen, *253;* Chase, The (1966), *479;* China Gate, *481;* Death Hunt, *35;* Dressed to Kill (1980), *972;* Even Cowgirls Get the Blues, *272;* Killers, The, *71;* Lucky Me, *929;* Ocean's Eleven, *93;* One Shoe Makes it Murder, *1003;* Point Blank, *624;* Poppy Is Also a Flower, The, *99;* Pray for the Wildcats, *100;* Resurrection of Zachary Wheeler, The, *1074;* Rio Bravo, *1145;* Rome Adventure, *643;* Texas Guns, *1155;* Treacherous Crossing, *1027;* Wild Palms, *1089*

Dickinson, Ron: Zoo Radio, *416*

Dickson, Gloria: They Made Me a Criminal, *681*

Dickson, Neil: Biggles—Adventures in Time, *1039;* It Couldn't Happen Here, *925;* Murders in the Rue Morgue (1986), *999*

Diddley, Bo: Chuck Berry Hail! Hail! Rock 'n' Roll, *421;* Rockula, *937*

Diego, Juan: Cabeza de Vaca, *721*

Diehl, John: Climate for Killing, A, *962;* Dark Side of the Moon, The, *1044;* Gettysburg, *526;* Glitz, *980;* Kickboxer 2: The Road Back, *70;* Madhouse (1990), *326;* Miami Vice, *84;* Mikey, *865;* Mo' Money, *335;* Remote, *198*

Dienstag, Christopher: Moneytree, The, *598*

Dierkes, John: Daughter of Dr. Jekyll, *829;* Hanging Tree, The, *1118*

Dierkop, Charles: Angels Hard as They Come, *5;* Fix, The, *50;* Grotesque, *847;* Hot Box, The, *64;* Roots of Evil, *109*

Diessl, Gustav: Westfront 1918, *803*

Dieterle, William: Backstairs, *714;* Waxworks, *802*

Dietrich, Marlene: Around the World in 80 Days (1956), *228;* Blonde Venus, *464;* Blue Angel, The, *719;* Destry Rides Again, *1109;* Dishonored, *501;* Evening with Marlene Dietrich, An, *423;* Garden of Allah, The, *525;* Golden Earrings, *56;* Judgment at Nuremberg, *560;* Just a Gigolo, *561;* Kismet (1944), *566;* Knight Without Armour, *566;* Lady Is Willing, The, *315;* Marlene, *589;* Morocco, *599;* Paris When It Sizzles, *354;* Pittsburgh, *622;* Rancho Notorious, *1140;* Scarlet Empress, The, *649;* Seven Sinners, *113;* Shanghai Express, *655;* Spoilers, The, *1152;* Stage Fright, *1019;* Touch of Evil, *1026;* Witness for the Prosecution (1957), *1032*

Dieudonné, Albert: Napoleon (1927), *770*

Diffring, Anton: Beast Must Die, The, *812;* Circus of Horrors, *824;* Colditz Story, The, *485;* Fahrenheit 451, *1050;* Mark of the Devil, Part 2, *863;* Where Eagles Dare, *138;* Zeppelin, *709*

Digges, Dudley: Emperor Jones, The, *509;* General Died at Dawn, The, *55;* Mutiny on the Bounty (1935), *88*

Dignam, Arthur: Everlasting Secret Family, The, *511;* Right Hand Man, The, *640;* Strange Behavior, *890;* We of the Never Never, *137;* Wild Duck, The, *702*

Dignam, Mark: Hamlet (1969), *535*

Dilian, Irasema: Wuthering Heights (1953), *805*

Dillard, Art: Ranger and the Lady, The, *1141*

Dillard, Victoria: Deep Cover (1992), *36*

Dillaway, Denise: Cheerleaders, *254*

Diller, Phyllis: Boneyard, The, *818;* Boy, Did I Get a Wrong Number!, *244;* Mad Monster Party, *184;* Pink Motel, *357;* Pucker Up and Bark Like a Dog, *363*

Dillion, Kevin: When He's Not a Stranger, *698*

Dillman, Bradford: Amsterdam Kill, The, *5;* Bridge at Remagen, The, *469;* Brother John, *470;* Bug, *820;* Compulsion, *487;* Enforcer, The (1976), *44;* Escape from the Planet of the Apes, *1049;* Force Five, *51;* Heart of Justice, *538;* Heroes Stand Alone, *61;* Legend of Walks Far Woman, The, *1128;* Lords of the Deep, *1063;* Love and Bullets, *79;* Mastermind, *329;* Moon of the Wolf, *866;* 99 and 44/100 Percent Dead, *91;* Piranha, *875;* Resurrection of Zachary Wheeler, The, *1074;* Revenge (1971), *1010;* Running Scared (1980), *110;* Sergeant Ryker, *652;* Sudden Impact, *122;* Suppose They Gave a War and Nobody Came?, *388;* Treasure of the Amazon, *132;* Way We Were, The, *697*

Dillon, Kevin: Blob, The (1988), *814;* Doors, The, *914;* Heaven Help Us, *295;* Immediate Family, *549;* Midnight Clear, A, *593;* No Big Deal, *608;* No Escape, *1069;* Remote Control, *879;* Rescue, The, *105;* War Party, *137*

Dillon, Matt: Big Town, The, *461;* Bloodhounds of Broadway, *242;* Drugstore Cowboy, *505;* Flamingo Kid, The, *278;* Kansas, *562;* Kiss Before Dying, A, *989;* Liar's Moon, *574;* Little Darlings, *319;* Mr. Wonderful, *597;* My Bodyguard, *601;* Native Son, *604;* Outsiders, The, *616;* Over the Edge, *616;* Rebel (1985), *636;* Rumble Fish, *645;* Saint of Fort Washington, The, *646;* Singles, *379;* Target, *125;* Tex, *680;* Women & Men 2, *706*

Dillon, Melinda: Absence of Malice, *950;* Bound for Glory, *467;* Captain America (1990), *22;* Christmas Story, A, *159;* Close Encounters of the Third Kind, *1042;* F.I.S.T., *512;* Fallen Angel, *513;* Harry and the Hendersons, *1055;* Prince of Tides, The, *627;* Right of Way, *640;* Shadow Box, The, *654;* Shattered Spirits, *655;* Slap Shot, *380;* Songwriter, *940;* Spontaneous Combustion, *889;* State of Emergency, *666;* Staying Together, *667*

Dillon, Mia: Lots of Luck, *322*

Dillon, Paul: Blink, *956;* Kiss Daddy Good Night, *989*

DiMaggio, Joe: Manhattan Merry-Go-Round, *930*

Dimambro, Joseph: Concrete Angels, *487*

DiMattia, Victor: Dennis the Menace: Dinosaur Hunter, *162*

Dimitri, Richard: When Things Were Rotten (TV Series), *409*

Dimitrijevic, Mikica: Meetings with Remarkable Men, *591*

Din, Ayub Khan: Sammy and Rosie Get Laid, *372*

Dinehart, Alan: Everything Happens at Night, *273;* It's a Great Life, *308;* Second Fiddle, *938;* Study in Scarlet, A, *1021*
Dingham, Arthur: Between Wars, *459*
Dingle, Charles: Guest Wife, *291;* Sister Kenny, *659;* Somewhere I'll Find You, *662;* Talk of the Town, The, *390*
Dingo, Ernie: Waltz Through the Hills, *216*
Dingwall, Kelly: Custodian, The, *31*
Dinome, Jerry: Tomboy, *130*
Dinsdale, Reece: Partners in Crime (TV Series), *1004;* Threads, *682;* Young Catherine, *708*
Dishy, Bob: Brighton Beach Memoirs, *246;* Critical Condition, *260;* First Family, *277;* Last Married Couple in America, The, *315;* Used People, *404*
Disney, Roy: Fantasy Film Worlds of George Pal, The, *424*
DiSue, Joe: Blackenstein, *814*
Ditchburn, Anne: Coming Out Alive, *963;* Curtains, *828*
Divine: Divine, *265;* Female Trouble, *276;* Hairspray, *292;* Lust in the Dust, *324;* Mondo Trasho, *335;* Multiple Maniacs, *866;* Out of the Dark, *873;* Pink Flamingos, *357;* Polyester, *359;* Trouble in Mind, *688*
Divoff, Andrew: Back in the U.S.S.R., *8;* Interceptor, *67;* Running Cool, *110;* Stephen King's Graveyard Shift, *890*
Dix, Richard: Ace of Aces, *1;* American Empire, *1093;* Buckskin Frontier, *1102;* Cimarron (1931), *1105;* Kansan, The, *1124;* Lost Squadron, *79;* Ten Commandments, The (1923), *678;* To the Last Man, *1157;* Transatlantic Tunnel, *1085;* Vanishing American, The, *1161*
Dix, Robert: Blood of Dracula's Castle, *815;* Five Bloody Graves, *1113;* Gun Riders, The, *1117;* Horror of the Blood Monsters, *1057*
Dix, Tommy: Best Foot Forward, *908*
Dixon, David: Hitchhiker's Guide to the Galaxy, The, *1056*
Dixon, Donna: Beverly Hills Madam, *460;* Couch Trip, The, *259;* Lucky Stiff, *324;* Speed Zone, *119;* Spies Like Us, *384;* Wayne's World, *406*
Dixon, Ivan: Car Wash, *250;* Fer-de-Lance, *976;* Patch of Blue, A, *619;* Raisin in the Sun, A (1961), *634;* Suppose They Gave a War and Nobody Came?, *388*
Dixon, James: It's Alive III: Island of the Alive, *857;* Q, *878*
Dixon, Jill: Night to Remember, A (1958), *606*
Dixon, Joan: Hot Lead, *1122*
Dixon, MacIntyre: Comedy Tonight, *257;* Funny Farm, *282*
Dixon, Pamela: L.A. Crackdown, *73;* L.A. Crackdown II, *74*
Dixon, Steve: Carrier, *821*
Dixon, Willie: Rich Girl, *640*
Djola, Badja: Who's the Man?, *411*
Dobos, Bruce: Hollywood High, Part II, *299*
Dobrowolska, Gosia: Custodian, The, *31*
Dobson, Kevin: Dirty Work, *970;* Hardhat and Legs, *536;* Orphan Train, *615*
Dobson, Peter: Last Exit to Brooklyn, *569;* Marrying Man, The, *329;* Sing, *939;* Where the Day Takes You, *699*
Dobson, Tamara: Chained Heat, *24;* Cleopatra Jones, *26;* Cleopatra Jones and the Casino of Gold, *26*
Dockery, Leslie: Eubie!, *916*
Dodd, Jimmie: Private Snuffy Smith, *362;* Riders of the Rio Grande, *1144*
Doe, John: Pure Country, *630;* Roadside Prophets, *641*
Doerr, James: Savage Weekend, *883*
Dogileva, Tatyana: Forgotten Tune for the Flute, A, *738*
Doherty, Matt: So I Married an Axe Murderer, *382*
Doherty, Shannen: Beverly Hills 90210, *460;* Blindfold: Acts of Obsession, *956;* Freeze Frame, *168*
Dohlen, Lenny Von: Blind Vision, *956*
Dolan, Michael: Hamburger Hill, *535*
Dolan, Rainbow: In the Aftermath: Angels Never Sleep, *1058*
Dolby, Thomas: Rockula, *937*
Doleman, Guy: Funeral in Berlin, *979;* Ipcress File, The, *986*
Dolenz, Ami: Can't Buy Me Love, *250;* Children of the Night, *823;* Infested, *856;* Miracle Beach, *332;* Rescue Me, *105;* She's Out of Control, *378;* Stepmonster, *1080;* Ticks, *895;* White Wolves: A Cry in the Wild II, *139;* Witchboard 2, *903*
Dolenz, Mickey: Head (1968), *922*
Doll, Dora: Black and White in Color, *718*
Dollaghan, Patrick: Circle of Fear, *26*
Dolsky, Neige: Tatie Danielle, *792*
Domasin, Larry: Island of the Blue Dolphins, *555*
Dombasle, Arielle: Boss' Wife, The, *244;* Le Beau Mariage, *756;* Pauline at the Beach, *776;* Trade Secrets, *1026*
Domergue, Faith: Cult of the Cobra, *827;* House of Seven Corpses, The, *853;* It Came from Beneath the Sea, *857;* Psycho Sisters, *877;* This Island Earth, *1083;* Voyage to the Prehistoric Planet, *1087*
Domingo, Placido: Bizet's Carmen, *718;* La Traviata, *754;* Otello, *934*
Domino, Fats: Girl Can't Help It, The, *286*
Dommartin, Solveig: Faraway, So Close, *736;* Until the End of the World, *1087;* Wings of Desire, *804*
Domrose, Angelica: Scorpion Woman, The, *784*
Dona, Linda: Delta Heat, *37;* Final Embrace, *977*
Donahue, Elinor: Girls Town, *55;* Three Daring Daughters, *945*
Donahue, Troy: Chilling, The, *823;* Cockfighter, *27;* Cry-Baby, *912;* Cyclone, *31;* Deadly Prey, *34;* Deadly Spygames, *35;* Dr. Alien, *834;* Grandview, U.S.A., *531;* Hollywood Cop, *63;* Imitation of Life, *549;* Low Blow, *79;* Monster on the Campus, *866;* Nudity Required, *347;* Omega Cop, *93;* Palm Springs Weekend, *353;* Pamela Principle, The, *1004;* Parrish, *618;* Perfect Furlough, *356;* Rome Adventure, *643;* Seizure, *884;* Shock'em Dead, *885;* Summer Place, A, *672;* This Happy Feeling, *394;* Tin Man, *684;* Woman Obsessed, A, *1032*
Donald, James: Beau Brummell (1954), *457;* Bridge on the River Kwai, The, *19;* Glory at Sea, *56;* Immortal Battalion, The (a.k.a. The Way Ahead), *549;* Lust for Life, *583;* Pickwick Papers, The, *357*
Donat, Peter: Babe, The, *452;* Different Story, A, *501;* Highpoint, *62;* Honeymoon, *851;* Lindbergh Kidnapping Case, The, *575;* Massive Retaliation, *83;* Mazes and Monsters, *864;* Russian Roulette, *110;* School Ties, *649;* War of the Roses, The, *406*
Donat, Richard: My American Cousin, *339*
Donat, Robert: Adventures of Tartu, *2;* Citadel, The, *482;* Count of Monte Cristo, The (1934), *30;* Ghost Goes West, The, *285;* Goodbye, Mr. Chips (1939), *530;* If I Were Rich, *305;* Inn of the Sixth Happiness, The, *552;* Knight Without Armour, *566;* Private Life of Henry the Eighth, The, *628;* Thirty-Nine Steps, The (1935), *1024;* Winslow Boy, The, *704*
Donath, Ludwig: Jolson Sings Again, *926;* Jolson Story, The, *926*
Donlevy, Brian: Allegheny Uprising, *1093;* Arizona Bushwhackers, *1094;* Barbary Coast, The, *455;* Beau Geste, *10;* Billy the Kid, *1099;* Command Decision, *487;* Destry Rides Again, *1109;* Enemy from Space, *1049;* Errand Boy, The, *272;* Five Golden Dragons, *50;* Gamera the Invincible, *1053;* Glass Key, The, *980;* Great McGinty, The, *290;* Hangmen Also Die, *536;* Hoodlum Empire, *64;* Hostile Guns, *1122;* Impact, *985;* In Old Chicago, *550;* Jesse James, *1123;* Kiss of Death, *566;* Miracle of Morgan's Creek, The, *332;* Never So Few, *89;* Quatermass Experiment, The, *1073;* Ride the Man Down, *1143;* Slaughter Trail, *1150;* Southern Yankee, A, *383;* Union Pacific, *1160;* Wake Island, *136*
Donley, Robert: Rockford Files, The (TV Series), *108*
Donmyer, Steve: Glitch!, *287*
Donnadieu, Bernard Pierre: Beatrice, *716;* Trade Secrets, *1026;* Vanishing, The (1988), *800*
Donnell, Jeff: Because You're Mine, *908;* Gidget Goes to Rome, *286;* Guns of Fort Petticoat, *1118;* My Man Godfrey (1957), *340;* Night to Remember, A (1943), *345;* Walk Softly, Stranger, *1030*
Donnellan, Jill: Order of the Black Eagle, *95*
Donnelly, Donal: Dead, The, *497;* Knack...and How To Get It, The, *314*

Donnelly, Patrice: Personal Best, *621*

Donnelly, Ruth: Affairs of Annabel, The, *223;* Annabel Takes a Tour, *227;* Bells of St. Mary's, The, *458;* Female, *276;* Snake Pit, The, *661*

Donnelly, Tim: Clonus Horror, The, *1042;* Toolbox Murders, The, *1026*

Donner, Robert: Allan Quartermain and the Lost City of Gold, *4;* Bad Golf Made Easier, *231;* Hysterical, *303;* Santee, *1147*

Donohoe, Amanda: Castaway, *476;* Dark Obsession, *495;* Foreign Body, *279;* Lair of the White Worm, *859;* Paper Mask, *1004;* Rainbow, The, *634;* Substitute, The, *1021*

Donovan: Don't Look Back, *423;* Secret Policeman's Private Parts, The, *375*

Donovan, King: Hanging Tree, The, *1118;* Invasion of the Body Snatchers (1956), *1059*

Donovan, Martin: Hard Choices, *536;* Quick, *102;* Scam, *1012;* Surviving Desire, *389;* Trust, *689*

Donovan, Tate: Case of Deadly Force, A, *476;* Dangerous Curves, *262;* Holy Matrimony, *299;* Inside Monkey Zetterland, *306;* Little Noises, *576;* Love Potion #9, *323;* Memphis Belle (1990), *592;* Not My Kid, *609;* SpaceCamp, *1078*

Donovan, Terence: Winds of Jarrah, The, *703*

Doobie Brothers, The: No Nukes, *432*

Doody, Alison: Duel of Hearts, *505;* Taffin, *124*

Doohan, James: Star Trek (TV Series), *1078;* Star Trek: The Menagerie, *1078;* Star Trek—The Motion Picture, *1079;* Star Trek II: The Wrath of Khan, *1079;* Star Trek III: The Search for Spock, *1079;* Star Trek IV: The Voyage Home, *1079;* Star Trek V: The Final Frontier, *1079;* Star Trek VI: The Undiscovered Country, *1079*

Dooley, Paul: Big Trouble, *239;* Breaking Away, *245;* Court-Martial of Jackie Robinson, The, *489;* Dangerous Woman, A, *494;* Endangered Species, *1049;* Flashback, *50;* Hansel and Gretel, *173;* Last Rites, *75;* Lip Service, *576;* Murder of Mary Phagan, The, *600;* My Boyfriend's Back, *339;* O.C. & Stiggs, *348;* Popeye, *196;* Rich Kids, *640;* Shakes the Clown, *377;* Sixteen Candles, *380;* State of Emergency, *666;* Strange Brew, *387;* Wedding, A, *407;* White Hot: The Mysterious Murder of Thelma Todd, *1031*

Dooling, Lucinda: Alchemist, The, *808;* Lovely But Deadly, *994*

Doors, The: Dance on Fire, *422;* Doors, The: A Tribute to Jim Morrison, *423;* Soft Parade, The, *435*

DoQui, Robert: Almos' a Man, *445;* Coffy, *27;* Mercenary Fighters, *84;* Original Intent, *614*

Dor, Karin: Carpet of Horror, *960;* Torture Chamber of Dr. Sadism, The, *896;* You Only Live Twice, *141*

Doran, Ann: Blondie, *241;* High and the Mighty, The, *541;* It! The Terror from Beyond Space, *1060;* Love is Better Than Ever, *929;* Painted Hills, The, *193;* Perfect Marriage, *356;* Pitfall, *622;* Rebel without a Cause, *636*

Doran, Jesse: Heart, *537*

Doran, Johnny: Hideaways, The, *174*

Doran, Mary: Strange Love of Molly Louvain, The, *669*

Dore, Charlie: Ploughman's Lunch, The, *623*

Doren, Mamie Van: Francis Joins the Wacs, *280*

Dorff, Stephen: BackBeat, *907;* Gate, The, *845;* Judgment Night, *69;* Power of One, The, *625;* Rescue Me, *105*

Dorian, Antonia: Dinosaur Island, *1047*

Dorleac, Françoise: Cul-de-Sac, *492;* Soft Skin, The, *787;* That Man From Rio, *793*

Dorn, Dolores: Tell Me a Riddle, *678;* Underworld U.S.A., *691*

Dorn, Michael: Star Trek: The Next Generation (TV Series), *1079;* Star Trek VI: The Undiscovered Country, *1079*

Dorn, Philip: Fighting Kentuckian, The, *1112;* I Remember Mama, *548;* I've Always Loved You, *555;* Random Harvest, *635;* Reunion in France, *639;* Tarzan's Secret Treasure, *126*

Dorne, Sandra: Eat the Rich, *270*

Doroff, Sarah Rowland: Three Fugitives, *395*

Dors, Diana: Adventures of a Private Eye, *222;* Amazing Mr. Blunden, The, *146;* Berserk, *812;* Children of the Full Moon, *823;* Deep End, *969;* Devil's Undead, The, *834;* From Beyond the Grave, *844;* I Married a Woman, *304;* King of the Roaring Twenties, *565;* Long Haul, *578;* Room 43, *644;* Steaming, *667;* There's a Girl in My Soup, *393;* Unicorn, The, *214*

Dorsett, Tony: Kill Zone, *71*

Dorsey, Jimmy: Fabulous Dorseys, The, *916*

Dorsey, Louise: Last Season, The, *75*

Dorsey, Thomas A.: Say Amen, Somebody, *434*

Dorsey, Tommy: Broadway Rhythm, *910;* Du Barry Was a Lady, *915;* Fabulous Dorseys, The, *916;* Presenting Lily Mars, *626;* Ship Ahoy, *939;* Song Is Born, A, *940*

Dossett, John: Longtime Companion, *579*

Dotrice, Karen: Gnome-Mobile, The, *169;* Mary Poppins, *185;* Thirty-Nine Steps, The (1978), *1024;* Three Lives of Thomasina, The, *211*

Dotrice, Michele: And Soon the Darkness, *952*

Dotrice, Roy: Beauty and the Beast (TV Series), *1039;* Carmilla, *821;* Corsican Brothers, The (1984), *259;* Cutting Edge, The, *493;* Dancing Princesses, The, *161;* Eliminators, The, *1048;* Shaka Zulu, *654*

Doucette, John: Fighting Mad, *516*

Douds, Betsy: Ruby in Paradise, *645*

Doug, Doug E.: Class Act, *256;* Cool Runnings, *259;* Hangin' with the Homeboys, *292*

Douglas, Angela: Carry on Cowboy, *251*

Douglas, Ann: Lone Wolf, *861*

Douglas, Brandon: Chips, the War Dog, *158;* Journey to Spirit Island, *179*

Douglas, Diana: Monsoon, *599*

Douglas, Don: Great Gabbo, The, *532*

Douglas, Donna: Beverly Hillbillies, The (TV Series), *237;* Beverly Hillbillies Go Hollywood, The, *237;* Frankie and Johnny (1966), *918;* Treasures of the Twilight Zone, *1085*

Douglas, Eric: Delta Force 3, *37;* Student Confidential, *387*

Douglas, James B.: Dawson Patrol, The, *33*

Douglas, John: Hell's Brigade, *61*

Douglas, Kirk: Along the Great Divide, *1093;* Arrangement, The, *450;* Bad and the Beautiful, The, *454;* Big Sky, The, *1098;* Big Trees, The, *13;* Brotherhood, The, *471;* Cast a Giant Shadow, *23;* Catch Me a Spy, *960;* Champion, *479;* Devil's Disciple, The, *264;* Dr. Jekyll and Mr. Hyde (1973), *914;* Draw, *1110;* Eddie Macon's Run, *43;* Final Countdown, The, *1051;* Fury, The, *845;* Greedy, *290;* Gunfight, A, *1117;* Gunfight at the O.K. Corral, *1117;* Holocaust 2000, *851;* Home Movies, *299;* In Harm's Way, *66;* Is Paris Burning?, *554;* Last Train from Gun Hill, *1126;* Letter to Three Wives, A, *573;* Light at the End of the World, The, *77;* Lonely Are the Brave, *1129;* Lust for Life, *583;* Man from Snowy River, The, *1131;* Man without a Star, *1132;* My Dear Secretary, *339;* Once Is Not Enough, *613;* Oscar (1991), *351;* Out of the Past, *1003;* Paths of Glory, *619;* Posse (1975), *1139;* Queenie, *632;* Racers, The, *632;* Saturn 3, *1076;* Secret, The, *650;* Seven Days in May, *653;* Spartacus, *119;* Strange Love of Martha Ivers, The, *669;* Strangers When We Meet, *670;* There Was a Crooked Man, *1156;* Tough Guys, *398;* 20,000 Leagues Under the Sea (1954), *133;* Two Weeks in Another Town, *690;* Ulysses, *133;* Vikings, The, *135;* War Wagon, The, *1162;* Way West, The, *1163;* Young Man with a Horn, *948*

Douglas, Melvyn: Americanization of Emily, The, *226;* Annie Oakley (1935), *1093;* As You Desire Me, *451;* Being There, *234;* Captains Courageous, *474;* Changeling, The, *822;* Death Squad, The, *35;* Ghost Story, *846;* Gorgeous Hussy, The, *531;* Hotel, *544;* Hud, *546;* I Never Sang for My Father, *547;* Intimate Strangers, *553;* Mr. Blandings Builds His Dream House, *333;* My Forbidden Past, *602;* Ninotchka, *345;* Sea of Grass, The, *1148;* Seduction of Joe Tynan, The, *651;* Shining Hour, The, *656;* Tell Me a Riddle, *678;* Tenant, The, *1023;* That Uncertain Feeling, *393;* Twilight's Last Gleaming, *133;* Two-Faced Woman, *401;* Vampire Bat, The, *899;* Woman's Face, A, *705;* Woman's Secret, A, *1032*

Douglas, Michael: Adam at 6 A.M., *441;* Basic Instinct, *456;* Black Rain (1989), *14;* China Syndrome, The, *961;* Chorus Line, A, *911;* Coma, *963;* Falling Down, *513;* Fatal

Attraction (1987), *975;* Hail, Hero!, *535;* It's My Turn, *555;* Jewel of the Nile, The, *68;* Napoleon and Samantha, *190;* Romancing the Stone, *108;* Shining Through, *656;* Star Chamber, The, *1019;* Wall Street, *695;* War of the Roses, The, *406*

Douglas, Mike: Gator, *54;* Incredible Shrinking Woman, The, *306*

Douglas, Paul: Big Lift, The, *460;* Clash by Night, *483;* Executive Suite, *512;* Gamma People, The, *1054;* It Happens Every Spring, *307;* Letter to Three Wives, A, *573;* Mating Game, The, *330;* Never Wave at a WAC, *343;* Panic in the Streets, *1004;* This Could Be the Night, *394;* We're Not Married, *408*

Douglas, Robert: Adventures of Don Juan, The, *2;* At Sword's Point, *7;* Fountainhead, The, *520*

Douglas, Sarah: Art of Dying, The, *953;* Beastmaster 2: Through the Portal of Time, *1039;* Meatballs 4, *330;* Nightfall, *1068;* People That Time Forgot, The, *1070;* Puppet Master III: Toulon's Revenge, *878;* Quest of the Delta Knights, *1073;* Return of the Living Dead 3, *880;* Steele Justice, *120*

Douglas, Suzzanne: Inkwell, The, *552*

Douglass, Robyn: Freeze Frame, *168;* Lonely Guy, The, *320;* Romantic Comedy, *370*

Dougnac, France: Hot Head, *745*

Dougnac, Marie-Laure: Delicatessen, *729*

Dourif, Brad: Amos & Andrew, *226;* Body Parts, *817;* Child's Play, *823;* Child's Play 2, *823;* Child's Play 3, *823;* Common Bonds, *487;* Critters 4, *827;* Dead Certain, *967;* Exorcist III: Legion, *840;* Eyes of Laura Mars, The, *974;* Fatal Beauty, *46;* Final Judgment, *977;* Grim Prairie Tales, *847;* Heaven's Gate, *1119;* Hidden Agenda, *541;* Horseplayer, *983;* Impure Thoughts, *305;* Istanbul, *749;* Jungle Fever, *561;* London Kills Me, *577;* Mississippi Burning, *596;* One Flew Over the Cuckoo's Nest, *613;* Ragtime, *633;* Sonny Boy, *889;* Spontaneous Combustion, *889;* Stephen King's Graveyard Shift, *890;* Trauma, *897;* Wise Blood, *704*

Dove, Billie: Black Pirate, The, *14*

Dow, Peggy: Harvey, *294*

Dowhen, Garrick: Appointment with Fear, *6*

Dowie, Freda: Distant Voices/Still Lives, *502*

Dowling, Constance: Knickerbocker Holiday, *927;* Up in Arms, *403*

Dowling, Doris: Bitter Rice, *718*

Down, Lesley-Anne: Betsy, The, *459;* Death Wish V: The Face of Death, *36;* From Beyond the Grave, *844;* Great Train Robbery, The, *980;* Hanover Street, *536;* Hunchback, *854;* Lady Killers, *990;* Little Night Music, A, *928;* Mardi Gras for the Devil, *863;* Nomads, *872;* North and South, *608;* Pink Panther Strikes Again, The, *357;* Rough Cut, *1011;* Scenes from the Goldmine, *649;* Sphinx (1981), *889;* Upstairs, Downstairs, *692*

Downes, Cathy: Kentucky Rifle, *1124;* Missile to the Moon, *1066;* Noose Hangs High, The, *346;* Sundowners, The (1950), *1153;* Winter of Our Dreams, *704*

Downey Jr., Morton: Body Chemistry 2: Voice of a Stranger, *957;* Legal Tender, *76;* Predator 2, *1071;* Revenge of the Nerds III: The Next Generation, *367*

Downey Jr., Robert: Air America, *3;* Back to School, *230;* Chances Are, *253;* Chaplin, *479;* Hail Caesar, *292;* Heart and Souls, *1056;* Johnny Be Good, *311;* Less Than Zero, *573;* 1969, *607;* Pick-Up Artist, The, *357;* Rented Lips, *366;* Short Cuts, *657;* Soapdish, *382;* Too Much Sun, *397;* True Believer, *1027*

Downey Sr., Robert: Johnny Be Good, *311*

Downey, Roma: Devlin, *970*

Downing, David: Gordon's War, *57*

Downs, Cathy: Amazing Colossal Man, The, *1035;* Short Grass, *1149*

Downs, Johnny: Adventures of the Flying Cadets, *2;* Mad Monster, *862*

Doyle, David: Love or Money?, *323;* Murphy's Laws of Golf, *338;* My Boys Are Good Boys, *601;* Paper Lion, *618;* Pursuit of Happiness, The, *631;* Stranger Within, The, *891;* Who Killed Mary What's 'Er Name?, *1031*

Doyle, John: Contagion, *825;* Wicked, The, *903*

Doyle, Maria: Commitments, The, *912*

Doyle, Maxine: Round-Up Time in Texas, *1146*

Doyle, Tony: Secret Friends, *651*

Doyle-Murray, Brian: Cabin Boy, *248;* JFK, *558;* Razor's Edge, The (1984), *635;* Wayne's World, *406*

Drach, Michel: Les Violons du Bal, *759*

Drago, Billy: China White, *25;* Cyborg 2, *1043;* Death Ring, *35;* Delta Force 2, *36;* Diplomatic Immunity, *39;* In Self Defense, *550;* Lady Dragon 2, *74;* Martial Law Two—Undercover, *82;* Outfit, The, *96;* Secret Games, *651;* Untouchables, The, *134*

Dragonette, Jessica: Gulliver's Travels (1939), *172*

Drainie, John: Incredible Journey, The, *177*

Drake, Betsy: Clarence, the Cross-Eyed Lion, *159;* Every Girl Should Be Married, *273;* Second Woman, The, *650*

Drake, Carol: Waitress, *405*

Drake, Charles: Air Force, *3;* Conflict, *963;* Glenn Miller Story, The, *919;* Harvey, *294;* It Came from Outer Space, *1060;* Night in Casablanca, A, *344;* Tender Years, The, *679;* To Hell and Back, *130;* Tobor the Great, *1084;* Until They Sail, *692;* Whistle Stop, *138*

Drake, Claudia: Detour, *970;* False Colors, *1112*

Drake, Dennis: Preppies, *360*

Drake, Dona: Louisiana Purchase, *322*

Drake, Fabia: Pocketful of Rye, A, *1006;* Valmont, *693*

Drake, Frances: Invisible Ray, The, *857;* Mad Love, *861*

Drake, Larry: Darkman, *1044;* Dr. Giggles, *835;* Murder in New Hampshire, *600;* Tales from the Crypt (Series), *892;* Taming of the Shrew (1982), *391*

Drake, Paul: Midnight Cabaret, *864*

Drake, Peggy: Tuttles of Tahiti, The, *400*

Drake, Tom: Bramble Bush, The, *468;* Cass Timberlane, *476;* Courage of Lassie, *160;* Hills of Home, *174;* Johnny Reno, *1124;* Meet Me in St. Louis, *930;* Mrs. Parkington, *598;* Mortal Storm, The, *600;* Two Girls and a Sailor, *946;* Words and Music, *948*

Draper, Polly: Million to Juan, A, *332*

Dravic, Milena: WR: Mysteries of the Organism, *805*

Dre, Doctor: Who's the Man?, *411*

Dreamers, Freddie and the: Seaside Swingers, *938*

Drescher, Fran: American Hot Wax, *906;* Cadillac Man, *249;* Car 54, Where Are You?, *250;* We're Talking Serious Money, *408*

Dresden, John: Final Mission, *48;* No Dead Heroes, *91*

Dresser, Louise: Eagle, The, *269;* Goose Woman, The, *980;* Scarlet Empress, The, *649*

Dressler, Lieux: Truckstop Women, *132*

Dressler, Marie: Anna Christie (1930), *449;* Dinner at Eight (1933), *265;* Min and Bill, *594;* Vagabond Lover, The, *947*

Drew, Ellen: Baron of Arizona, The, *1097;* Buck Benny Rides Again, *246;* China Sky, *25;* Christmas in July, *255;* Great Missouri Raid, The, *1116;* Isle of the Dead, *857;* Man from Colorado, The, *1131;* Man in the Saddle, *1132;* Stars in My Crown, *1153*

Dreyfus, Jean Claude: Delicatessen, *729*

Dreyfuss, Lorin: Detective School Dropouts, *264*

Dreyfuss, Richard: Always (1989), *445;* American Graffiti, *226;* Another Stakeout, *6;* Apprenticeship of Duddy Kravitz, The, *450;* Big Fix, The, *955;* Buddy System, The, *471;* Close Encounters of the Third Kind, *1042;* Competition, The, *487;* Dillinger (1973), *39;* Down and Out in Beverly Hills, *268;* Goodbye Girl, The, *288;* Inserts, *552;* Jaws, *858;* Let It Ride, *317;* Lost in Yonkers, *580;* Moon Over Parador, *336;* Nuts, *1002;* Once Around, *349;* Postcards from the Edge, *360;* Prisoner of Honor, *628;* Rosencrantz and Guildenstern Are Dead, *370;* Stakeout, *119;* Stand by Me (1986), *665;* Tin Men, *396;* What About Bob?, *408;* Whose Life Is It, Anyway?, *701*

Driggs, Deborah: Night Rhythms, *1001*

Driscoll, Bobby: Fighting Sullivans, The, *516;* So Dear to My Heart, *205;* Treasure Island (1950), *214;* Window, The, *1032*
Driscoll, Martha: Li'l Abner (1940), *318*
Driscoll, Patricia: TV Classics: Adventures of Robin Hood, The—TV Series, *133*
Drivas, Robert: Cool Hand Luke, *29;* Illustrated Man, The, *1057*
Dru, Joanne: All the King's Men, *444;* Hell on Frisco Bay, *60;* Light in the Forest, The, *181;* Pride of St. Louis, The, *627;* Red River, *1141;* Sincerely Yours, *658;* Super Fuzz, *1081;* Thunder Bay, *129;* Vengeance Valley, *1161;* Wagonmaster, *1162;* Warriors, The (1955), *137*
Drummond, Alice: Daybreak (1993), *1045*
Druon, Claire: Le Bonheur, *756*
Druon, Jean-Claude: Le Bonheur, *756*
Drouot, Jean-Claude: Light at the End of the World, The, *77*
Drury, James: Elfego Baca: Six Gun Law, *1111;* Gambler Returns, the: Luck of the Draw, *1115;* Meanest Men in the West, The, *1133;* Ride the High Country, *1143;* Ten Who Dared, *210;* Toby Tyler, *212*
Dryden, Mack: Million Dollar Mystery, *332*
Drye, Jenny: Man Bites Dog, *764*
Dryer, Fred: Death Before Dishonor, *35*
Dryer, Robert: Savage Streets, *111*
Du Bois, Marta: Boulevard Nights, *467*
Du Maurier, Gerald: Catherine the Great, *477*
Duane, Michael: City without Men, *483*
Duarte, Regina: Happily Ever After, *743*
Dubarry, Denise: Monster in the Closet, *866*
Dubbins, Don: D.I., The, *493;* Enchanted Island, *44;* Fix, The, *50;* From the Earth to the Moon, *1053;* Prize, The, *629;* Tribute to a Bad Man, *1159*
Dubois, Marie: Les Grandes Gueules (Jailbirds' Vacation), *759;* Shoot the Piano Player, *785;* Vincent, François, Paul and the Others, *801*
Dubost, Paulette: May Fools, *766;* Viva Maria!, *801*
Dubov, Paul: Ma Barker's Killer Brood, *80*
Ducasse, Cecile: Chocolat, *723*
Ducati, Kristi: Bikini Carwash Company 2, *239*
Ducaux, Annie: Abel Gance's Beethoven, *710*
Duce, Sharon: Buddy's Song, *471*
Duchamp, Marcel: Avant Garde Program #2, *714*
Duchaussoy, Michel: May Fools, *766;* Road to Ruin (1991), *369;* This Man Must Die, *794*
Duchesne, Roger: Bob le Flambeur, *719*
Duchovny, David: Beethoven (1992), *149;* Julia Has Two Lovers, *560;* Kalifornia, *561;* Red Shoe Diaries, *637;* Red Shoe Diaries II: Double Dare, *637;* Red Shoe Diaries 4: Auto Erotica, *637;* Ruby (1991), *644;* Venice/Venice, *693*
Ducommun, Rick: Blank Check, *151;* 'Burbs, The, *247*
Ducreux, Louis: Sunday in the Country, A, *791*
Dudikoff, Michael: American Ninja, *4;* American Ninja II, *4;* American Ninja IV: The Annihilation, *4;* Avenging Force, *8;* Human Shield, The, *64;* Platoon Leader, *99;* Radioactive Dreams, *1073;* Rescue Me, *105;* River of Death, *107*
Dudley, Doris: Moon and Sixpence, The, *599*
Duel, Peter: Generation, *283*
Duering, Carl: Arabesque, *6*
Duff, Debbie: Helter-Skelter Murders, The, *540*
Duff, Denice: Bloodfist V: Human Target, *16;* Bloodlust: Subspecies III, *816;* Bloodstone: Subspecies II, *816;* Return to Frogtown, *1074*
Duff, Howard: Battered, *456;* Boys' Night Out, *244;* Deadly Companion, *968;* East of Eden (1982), *506;* Kramer vs. Kramer, *567;* Late Show, The, *991;* Naked City, The, *1000;* No Way Out, *1002;* Oh, God! Book II, *349;* Private Hell 36, *628;* Snatched, *117;* Too Much Sun, *397;* Wedding, A, *407;* While the City Sleeps, *138*
Duffey, Todd: Civil War Diary, *483*
Duffy, Dee: Hellcats, The, *60*
Duffy, Karen: Blank Check, *151*
Duffy, Patrick: Alice Through the Looking Glass (1985), *145;* Enola Gay: The Men, the Mission, the Atomic Bomb, *510;* Last of Mrs. Lincoln, The, *570;* Man from Atlantis, The, *1064;* Vamping, *1029*
Dufilho, Jacques: Black and White in Color, *718;* Horse of Pride, The, *744*
Dugan, Dennis: Can't Buy Me Love, *250;* Howling, The, *853;* New Adventures of Pippi Longstocking, The, *191;* Norman...Is That You?, *346;* Unidentified Flying Oddball, *214*
Duggan, Andrew: Commies Are Coming, the Commies Are Coming, The, *258;* Firehouse (1972), *49;* Frankenstein Island, *842;* Housewife, *545;* In Like Flint, *66;* Incredible Journey of Dr. Meg Laurel, The, *551;* Incredible Mr. Limpet, The, *306;* It Lives Again, *857;* It's Alive!, *857;* Palm Springs Weekend, *353;* Return to Salem's Lot, A, *880;* Secret War of Harry Frigg, The, *375;* Skin Game, *1150;* Wagon Train (TV Series), *1162*
Duggan, Tom: Frankenstein 1970, *843*
Dujmovic, Davor: Time of the Gypsies, *795*
Dukakis, John: Delusion (1980), *969*
Dukakis, Olympia: Cemetery Club, The, *478;* Dad, *493;* In the Spirit, *306;* Look Who's Talking, *320;* Look Who's Talking Too, *321;* Moonstruck, *336;* Over the Hill, *352;* Steel Magnolias, *667;* Walls of Glass, *695*
Duke, Bill: Action Jackson, *2;* Bird on a Wire, *13;* Menace II Society, *593;* No Man's Land, *91;* Predator, *1071*
Duke, Patty: Amityville 4: The Evil Escapes, *809;* Babysitter, The, *811;* Best Kept Secrets, *11;* Billie, *150;* By Design, *473;* Curse of the Black Widow, *828;* Daydreamer, The, *161;* Family Upside Down, A, *514;* 4D Man, *1053;* George Washington, *526;* George Washington: The Forging of a Nation, *526;* Grave Secrets: The Legacy of Hilltop Drive, *980;* Miracle Worker, The (1962), *595;* My Sweet Charlie, *602;* Prelude to a Kiss, *360;* September Gun, *1148;* She Waits, *885;* Something Special, *383;* Valley of the Dolls, *693*
Duke, Robin: Blue Monkey, *817*
Dukes, David: Cat on a Hot Tin Roof (1985), *477;* Catch the Heat, *24;* Date with an Angel, *262;* First Deadly Sin, The, *977;* George Washington, *526;* Josephine Baker Story, The, *559;* Little Romance, A, *319;* Me and the Kid, *83;* Men's Club, The, *593;* Rawhead Rex, *879;* Rutanga Tapes, The, *1011;* See You in the Morning, *651;* Snow Kill, *118;* Strange Interlude (1988), *669;* Wild Party, The (1975), *702;* Without a Trace, *1032*
Dulany, Caitlin: Class of 1999 II: The Substitute, *1041;* Maniac Cop 3: Badge of Silence, *863*
Dullea, Keir: Black Christmas, *814;* Blind Date (1984), *463;* Brainwaves, *818;* David and Lisa, *496;* Haunting of Julia, The, *537;* Hoodlum Priest, The, *543;* Leopard in the Snow, *572;* Next One, The, *1068;* Oh, What a Night, *611;* 2001: A Space Odyssey, *1086;* 2010, *1086*
Dumbrille, Douglas: Son of Paleface, *383*
Dumbrille, Douglass: Baby Face, *453;* Big Store, The, *238;* Broadway Bill, *470;* Buccaneer, The, *20;* Castle in the Desert, *960;* Dragnet (1947), *41;* False Colors, *1112;* Female, *276;* Firefly, The, *916;* It's a Joke, Son!, *308;* Lady Killer, *74;* Lost in a Harem, *321;* Mr. Deeds Goes to Town, *333;* Naughty Marietta, *932;* Operator 13, *614;* Ride 'em Cowboy, *368;* Road to Utopia, *369;* Road to Zanzibar, *369;* Virginia City, *1161*
Dumont, J. K.: Pamela Principle, The, *1004*
Dumont, Margaret: Animal Crackers, *227;* At the Circus, *229;* Bathing Beauty, *908;* Big Store, The, *238;* Cocoanuts, *257;* Day at the Races, A, *262;* Duck Soup, *269;* Horn Blows at Midnight, The, *301;* Marx Brothers in a Nutshell, The, *430;* Night at the Opera, A, *344;* Three for Bedroom C, *395*
Dun, Dennis: Big Trouble in Little China, *13;* Last Emperor, The, *569;* Prince of Darkness, *876;* Thousand Pieces of Gold, *1156*
Duna, Steffi: Dancing Pirate, *913*
Dunarie, Malcolm: Heaven Help Us, *295*
Dunaway, Faye: Arrangement, The, *450;* Barfly, *455;* Beverly Hills Madam, *460;* Bonnie and Clyde, *17;* Burning Secret, *472;* Casanova (1987), *252;* Champ, The (1979), *479;* Chinatown, *962;* Christopher Columbus (1985), *25;* Cold Sassy Tree, *485;* Country Girl, The (1982), *489;*

Disappearance of Aimee, The, *970;* Double Edge, *504;* Ellis Island, *508;* Eyes of Laura Mars, The, *974;* First Deadly Sin, The, *977;* Four Musketeers, The, *52;* Gamble, The, *54;* Handmaid's Tale, The, *1055;* Little Big Man, *1128;* Midnight Crossing, *84;* Mommie Dearest, *598;* Network, *604;* Ordeal by Innocence, *1003;* Scorchers, *650;* Silhouette, *1016;* Supergirl, *1081;* Temp, The, *893;* 13 at Dinner, *1024;* Thomas Crown Affair, The, *128;* Three Days of the Condor, *1025;* Three Musketeers, The (1973), *128;* Towering Inferno, The, *131;* Voyage of the Damned, *694;* Wait Until Spring, Bandini, *695;* Wicked Lady, The (1983), *139*

Dunbar, Adrian: Crying Game, The, *492;* Hear My Song, *295*

Dunbar, Dixie: Alexander's Ragtime Band, *906;* One in a Million, *350*

Duncan, Andrew: Gig, The, *286*

Duncan, Archie: Adventures of Sherlock Holmes, The (TV Series), *950;* TV Classics: Adventures of Robin Hood, The—TV Series, *133*

Duncan, Bob: Border Feud, *1100*

Duncan, Bud: Private Snuffy Smith, *362*

Duncan, Carmen: Dark Forces, *966;* Escape 2000, *1049;* Now and Forever, *609*

Duncan, Jayson: Mystery Island, *190*

Duncan, John: Batman and Robin, *9*

Duncan, Julie: Fugitive Valley, *1114*

Duncan, Kenne: Crimson Ghost, The, *30;* Dynamite Canyon, *1111;* Night of the Ghouls, *869;* Riders for Justice, *1143;* Sinister Urge, The, *116;* Song of Nevada, *1151*

Duncan, Lindsay: Body Parts, *817;* Loose Connections, *321;* Manifesto, *328;* Reflecting Skin, The, *637;* Year in Provence, A, *414*

Duncan, Mary: City Girl, *962*

Duncan, Nancy: Little Match Girl, The (1983), *182*

Duncan, Pamela: Attack of the Crab Monsters, *810*

Duncan, Sandy: Cat from Outer Space, The, *157;* Million Dollar Duck, The, *187;* Roots, *644*

Dundas, Jennie: Beniker Gang, The, *149;* Legal Eagles, *991*

Dungan, Sebastian: Man, Woman and Child, *587*

Dunlap, Carla: Pumping Iron II: The Women, *630*

Dunlap, Dawn: Barbarian Queen, *1038;* Forbidden World, *842*

Dunlop, Donn: Down Under, *41*

Dunn, Carolyn: Breaking All the Rules, *245*

Dunn, Emma: Dr. Kildare's Strange Case, *40;* Hell's House, *61;* Madame X (1937), *584;* Talk of the Town, The, *390*

Dunn, James: Baby Take a Bow, *147;* Bramble Bush, The, *468;* Bright Eyes, *152;* Elfego Baca: Six Gun Law, *1111;* Stand Up and Cheer, *206;* Tree Grows in Brooklyn, A, *687*

Dunn, Kevin: Beethoven's 2nd, *149;* Chaplin, *479;* Dave, *262;* 1492: The Conquest of Paradise, *52;* Hit Woman: The Double Edge, *63;* Hot Shots, *301;* Only the Lonely, *350;* Taken Away, *676*

Dunn, Michael: Dr. Frankenstein's Castle of Freaks, *835;* Freakmaker, *843;* Madigan, *80;* Murders in the Rue Morgue (1971), *867;* No Way to Treat a Lady, *1002;* Ship of Fools, *656;* Werewolf of Washington, *902;* Wild, Wild West, The (TV series), *1164;* You're a Big Boy Now, *416*

Dunn, Nora: Born Yesterday (1993), *244;* Miami Blues, *84*

Dunne, Dominique: Diary of a Teenage Hitchhiker, *501;* Poltergeist, *875*

Dunne, Elizabeth: Blondie Takes a Vacation, *242*

Dunne, Griffin: After Hours, *223;* Almost You, *225;* Amazon Women on the Moon, *225;* American Werewolf in London, An, *808;* Big Blue, The, *12;* Big Girls Don't Cry...They Get Even, *238;* Cold Feet (1984), *257;* Hotel Room, *983;* Lip Service, *576;* Love Matters, *581;* Me and Him, *330;* My Girl, *190;* Secret Weapon, *651;* Straight Talk, *387;* Who's That Girl, *411*

Dunne, Irene: Ann Vickers, *448;* Anna and the King of Siam, *449;* Awful Truth, The, *230;* Bachelor Apartment, *230;* Cimarron (1931), *1105;* Consolation Marriage, *488;* Guy Named Joe, A, *535;* I Remember Mama, *548;* Joy of Living, *926;* Life with Father, *318;* My Favorite Wife, *340;* Penny Serenade, *620;* Roberta, *936;* Show Boat (1936), *939;* Sweet Adeline, *943;* White Cliffs of Dover, The, *699*

Dunne, Murphy: Bad Manners, *231*

Dunne, Stephen: Big Sombrero, The, *1098*

Dunnock, Mildred: And Baby Makes Six, *447;* Baby Doll, *453;* Butterfield 8, *472;* Corn Is Green, The (1945), *488;* Nun's Story, The, *609;* Peyton Place, *621;* Sweet Bird of Youth (1962), *674;* Whatever Happened to Aunt Alice?, *902*

Dunoyer, François: Fatal Image, The, *976*

Dunsmore, Rosemary: Blades of Courage, *463;* Dancing in the Dark, *494*

Duperey, Anny: Blood Rose, *816;* Pardon Mon Affaire, *775;* Stavisky, *789*

Dupois, Starletta: Hollywood Shuffle, *299;* Raisin in the Sun, A (1988), *634*

Duport, Catherine Isabelle: Le Départ, *757;* Masculine Feminine, *766*

Duprez, June: And Then There Were None, *952;* Brighton Strangler, The, *819;* Four Feathers, The (1939), *52;* None But the Lonely Heart, *608;* Spy in Black, The, *664;* Thief of Bagdad, The (1940), *1083*

Dupus, Roy: Being at Home with Claude, *716*

Durante, Jimmy: Alice Through the Looking Glass (1966), *906;* Hollywood Party, *299;* It Happened in Brooklyn, *925;* It's a Mad Mad Mad Mad World, *308;* Jumbo, *926;* Little Miss Broadway, *928;* Man Who Came to Dinner, The, *328;* Melody Ranch, *1133;* On an Island with You, *933;* Palooka, *617;* Speak Easily, *384;* This Time For Keeps, *945;* TV Classics: Jimmy Durante, *400;* Two Girls and a Sailor, *946;* Two Sisters from Boston, *947;* What! No Beer?, *408*

Durbin, Deanna: Can't Help Singing, *911;* It's a Date, *925;* One Hundred Men and a Girl, *934;* Spring Parade, *941;* Three Smart Girls, *945;* Three Smart Girls Grow Up, *945*

Durfee, Minta: Fatty Arbuckle Comedy Collection, Vol. 1, *275;* Keystone Comedies, Vol. 1, *312;* Keystone Comedies, Vol. 2, *312;* Keystone Comedies, Vol. 3, *312;* Keystone Comedies, Vol. 5, *313;* Lizzies of Mack Sennett, The, *320;* Lost and Found Chaplin: Keystone, *321;* Mack Sennett Comedies, Vol. 2, *325*

Durham, Geoffrey: Wish You Were Here, *412*

Durham, Steve: Born American, *17*

Durkin, James: Perils of Pauline, The (1933), *98*

Durkin, Junior: Hell's House, *61;* Little Men (1935), *182*

Durning, Charles: Attica, *452;* Best Little Girl in the World, The, *459;* Best Little Whorehouse in Texas, The, *908;* Big Trouble, *239;* Breakheart Pass, *1101;* Cat Chaser, *24;* Choirboys, The, *481;* Connection (1973), *487;* Cop, *29;* Crisis at Central High, *491;* Dark Night of the Scarecrow, *829;* Death of a Salesman, *498;* Dick Tracy (1990), *38;* Die Laughing, *264;* Dinner at Eight (1990), *265;* Dog Day Afternoon, *971;* Far North, *274;* Front Page, The (1974), *281;* Fury, The, *845;* Gambler, Part III—The Legend Continues, The, *1115;* Greek Tycoon, The, *533;* Hadley's Rebellion, *173;* Happy New Year, *293;* Harry and Walter Go to New York, *294;* Hindenburg, The, *541;* Hudsucker Proxy, The, *303;* Man Who Broke 1000 Chains, The, *587;* Man with One Red Shoe, The, *328;* Mass Appeal, *590;* Music of Chance, The, *601;* Project: Alien, *1072;* Pursuit of Happiness, The, *631;* Queen of the Stardust Ballroom, *632;* Rosary Murders, The, *1011;* Sharky's Machine, *115;* Sisters (1973), *1017;* Solarbabies, *1077;* Starting Over, *385;* Stick, *120;* Sting, The, *120;* Tiger's Tale, A, *396;* Tilt, *396;* To Be or Not to Be (1983), *397;* Tough Guys, *398;* True Confessions, *1027;* Twilight's Last Gleaming, *133;* Two of a Kind (1983), *402;* V. I. Warshawski, *1029;* Water Engine, The, *696;* When a Stranger Calls, *1030;* When a Stranger Calls Back, *1031;* Where the River Runs Black, *1089*

Durock, Dick: Return of the Swamp Thing, *880*

Durrell, Alexandra: Unnamable, The, *899*

Duryea, Dan: Along Came Jones, *1093;* Bamboo Saucer (a.k.a. Collision Course), *1038;* Criss Cross (1948), *964;* Five Golden Dragons, *50;* Flight of the Phoenix, The, *51;* Great Flamarion, The, *532;* Gundown at Sandoval, *1117;* Little Foxes, The, *576;* Mrs. Parkington, *598;* None But the Lonely

Heart, *608;* Platinum High School, *623;* Pride of the Yankees, The, *627;* Sahara (1943), *110;* Scarlet Street, *649;* Thunder Bay, *129;* Underworld Story, *1029;* Winchester '73, *1165*
Dusenberry, Ann: Basic Training, *232;* Cutter's Way, *965;* Desperate Women, *1109;* Heart Beat, *537;* Lies, *574;* Possessed, The (1977), *876*
Dushku, Eliza: That Night, *680*
Dusic, Joe: Bikini Carwash Company, The, *239*
Dussolier, André: And Now, My Love, *712;* Le Beau Mariage, *756;* Melo, *766;* Three Men and a Cradle, *794;* Un Coeur En Hiver, *798*
Dutronc, Jacques: L'Etat Sauvage (The Savage State), *756;* Les Tricheurs, *759;* Van Gogh, *800*
Dutt, Utpal: Stranger, The (1992), *790*
Dutton, Charles S.: Alien 3, *1035;* "Crocodile" Dundee II, *261;* Distinguished Gentleman, The, *265;* Menace II Society, *593;* Mississippi Masala, *596;* Rudy, *200;* Surviving the Game, *123*
Dutton, Simon: Lion and the Hawk, The, *77*
Duvall, Robert: Apocalypse Now, *6;* Badge 373, *8;* Betsy, The, *459;* Breakout, *19;* Chase, The (1966), *479;* Colors, *485;* Countdown, *489;* Days of Thunder, *33;* Detective, The (1968), *500;* Eagle Has Landed, The, *42;* Falling Down, *513;* Geronimo: An American Legend, *1115;* Godfather, The, *529;* Godfather, Part II, The, *529;* Godfather Epic, The, *529;* Great Northfield Minnesota Raid, The, *1116;* Great Santini, The, *533;* Greatest, The, *533;* Handmaid's Tale, The, *1055;* Hotel Colonial, *64;* Ike: The War Years, *548;* Joe Kidd, *1123;* Killer Elite, The, *71;* Lady Ice, *989;* Lawman, *1127;* Let's Get Harry, *573;* Lightship, The, *575;* Lonesome Dove, *1129;* M*A*S*H, *324;* Natural, The, *604;* Network, *604;* Newsies, *933;* Outer Limits, The (TV Series), *1069;* Paper, The, *617;* Plague, The, *623;* Pursuit of D. B. Cooper, *363;* Rain People, The, *634;* Rambling Rose, *634;* Seven-Per-Cent Solution, The, *1013;* Show of Force, A, *1015;* Stalin, *665;* Stone Boy, The, *668;* Tender Mercies, *679;* Terry Fox Story, The, *679;* THX 1138, *1084;* Tomorrow, *685;* True Confessions, *1027;* True Grit, *1159;* Wrestling Ernest Hemingway, *707*
Duvall, Shelley: Annie Hall, *228;* Bernice Bobs Her Hair, *234;* Best of Dan Aykroyd, The, *235;* Frankenweenie, *280;* Frog, *168;* McCabe and Mrs. Miller, *1133;* Mother Goose Rock N' Roll Rhyme, *189;* Popeye, *196;* Rapunzel, *198;* Roxanne, *370;* Rumpelstiltskin (1980), *200;* Shining, The, *885;* Suburban Commando, *388;* Thieves Like Us, *681;* Time Bandits, *1084*
Dux, Pierre: La Vie Continue, *755*
Dvorak, Ann: Abilene Town, *1092;* Flame of the Barbary Coast, *50;* G-Men, *54;* Life of Her Own, A, *574;* Manhattan Merry-Go-Round, *930;* Out of the Blue, *352;* Private Affairs of Bel Ami, The, *628;* Return of Jesse James, The, *1142;* Scarface (1932), *112;* Strange Love of Molly Louvain, The, *669;* Three on a Match, *683*
Dwire, Earl: Arizona Days, *1094;* Assassin of Youth (a.k.a. Marijuana), *451;* Lawless Frontier, *1127;* Lawless Range, *1127;* Man from Music Mountain, *1131;* Mystery of the Hooded Horseman, *1135;* New Frontier, *1136;* Randy Rides Alone, *1141;* Riders of Destiny, *1144;* Trouble in Texas, *1159;* West of the Divide, *1163*
Dwyer, Hilary: Conqueror Worm, The, *825*
Dyall, Franklyn: Easy Virtue, *507*
Dyall, Valentine: Body in the Library, The, *958*
Dye, Cameron: Body Rock, *909;* Fraternity Vacation, *280;* Heated Vengeance, *60;* Joy of Sex, The, *311;* Out of the Dark, *873;* Scenes from the Goldmine, *649;* Stranded, *1080*
Dye, Dale: Relentless II: Dead On, *879*
Dye, John: Campus Man, *249*
Dylan, Bob: Backtrack, *454;* Don't Look Back, *423;* Hearts of Fire, *538;* Last Waltz, The, *428;* Pat Garrett and Billy the Kid, *1138*
Dylan, Justin: Unexpected Encounters, *691*
Dyneley, Peter: Manster, The, *863;* Romeo and Juliet (1988), *643*
Dysart, Richard: Autobiography of Miss Jane Pittman, The, *452;* Back to the Future III, *1037;* Bitter Harvest (1981), *462;* Day One, *496;* Falcon and the Snowman, The, *513;* L.A. Law, *567;* Last Days of Patton, The, *569;* Marilyn & Bobby: Her Final Affair, *588;* Ordeal of Dr. Mudd, The, *614;* Pale Rider, *1138;* People vs. Jean Harris, *620;* Prophecy, *877;* Riding with Death, *1074;* Rumor Mill, The, *645;* Sporting Club, The, *664;* Thing, The (1982), *1083;* Warning Sign, *901*
Dytri, Mike: Living End, The, *577*
Dzundza, George: Act of Passion, *441;* Basic Instinct, *456;* Beast, The, *10;* Best Defense, *234;* Brotherly Love, *819;* Butcher's Wife, The, *248;* Glory Years, *287;* Impulse (1990), *985;* No Mercy, *91;* White Hunter Black Heart, *700*
Eadie, Nicholas: Return to Snowy River, Part II, *1143*
Eagle, Jeff: Slammer Girls, *380*
Earles, Harry: Unholy Three, *1029*
Easley, Richert: Outrageous, *352*
East, Jeff: Campus Corpse, The, *820;* Deadly Blessing, *831;* Huckleberry Finn (1974), *176;* Mary and Joseph: A Story of Faith, *589;* Pumpkinhead, *878;* Summer of Fear, *891;* Tom Sawyer (1973), *946*
East Side Kids, The: Ghosts on the Loose, *286;* Spooks Run Wild, *385*
Easterbrook, Leslie: Police Academy III: Back in Training, *359;* Police Academy 5—Assignment: Miami Beach, *359*
Eastland, Todd: Pledge Night, *875*
Eastman, George: Blastfighter, *15;* Detective School Dropouts, *264;* Endgame, *1049;* Hands of Steel, *1055;* Warriors of the Wasteland, *1088*
Easton, Sheena: John Carpenter Presents: Body Bags, *858*
Eastwood, Alison: Tightrope, *1025*
Eastwood, Clint: Any Which Way You Can, *228;* Beguiled, The, *954;* Bronco Billy, *246;* City Heat, *255;* Coogan's Bluff, *29;* Dead Pool, The, *33;* Dirty Harry, *39;* Eiger Sanction, The, *43;* Enforcer, The (1976), *44;* Escape from Alcatraz, *45;* Every Which Way but Loose, *273;* Firefox, *49;* Fistful of Dollars, A, *1113;* For a Few Dollars More, *1113;* Francis in the Navy, *280;* Gauntlet, The, *55;* Good the Bad and the Ugly, The, *1116;* Hang 'em High, *1118;* Heartbreak Ridge, *59;* Here's Looking at You, Warner Brothers, *426;* High Plains Drifter, *1120;* Honkytonk Man, *543;* In the Line of Fire, *66;* Joe Kidd, *1123;* Kelly's Heroes, *70;* Magnum Force, *80;* Maverick (TV Series), *1133;* Outlaw Josey Wales, The, *1137;* Paint Your Wagon, *934;* Pale Rider, *1138;* Perfect World, A, *621;* Pink Cadillac, *99;* Play Misty for Me, *1006;* Rawhide (TV Series), *1141;* Revenge of the Creature, *881;* Rookie, The, *109;* Sudden Impact, *122;* Tarantula, *892;* Thunderbolt and Lightfoot, *129;* Tightrope, *1025;* Two Mules for Sister Sara, *1160;* Unforgiven (1992), *1160;* Where Eagles Dare, *138;* White Hunter Black Heart, *700*
Eastwood, Jayne: Hostile Take Over, *544*
Eastwood, Kyle: Honkytonk Man, *543*
Eaton, Mary: Glorifying the American Girl, *919*
Eaton, Shirley: Against All Odds (Kiss and Kill, Blood of Fu Manchu), *808;* Around the World Under the Sea, *6;* Doctor at Large, *265;* Girl Hunters, The, *979;* Naked Truth, *342;* Ten Little Indians (1966), *1023*
Eaves, John: Fire and Ice (1987), *49*
Eberhardt, Norma: Return of Dracula, *880*
Eberly, Bob: I Dood It, *924*
Ebersole, Christine: Acceptable Risks, *440;* Folks, *278;* Mac and Me, *1064*
Ebon, Al: White Pongo (a.k.a. Blond Gorilla), *902*
Ebsen, Buddy: Andersonville Trial, The, *447;* Between Heaven and Hell, *459;* Beverly Hillbillies, The, *237;* Beverly Hillbillies, The (TV Series), *237;* Beverly Hillbillies Go Hollywood, The, *237;* Born to Dance, *909;* Breakfast at Tiffany's, *468;* Broadway Melody of 1936, *910;* Broadway Melody of 1938, *910;* Captain January, *155;* Davy Crockett and the River Pirates, *161;* Davy Crockett, King of the Wild Frontier, *161;* Girl of the Golden West, The, *919;* Interns, The, *553;* My Lucky Star, *932;* One and Only, Genuine, Original Family Band, The, *192;* President's Plane Is Missing, The,

1007; Red Garters, 936; Rodeo King and the Senorita, 1145; Stone Fox, The, 207; Tom Sawyer (1973), 213; Under Mexicali Stars, 1160
Eburne, Maude: Guardsman, The, 291; Vampire Bat, The, 899
Eccles, Aimee: Humanoid Defender, 1057
Eccles, Teddy: My Side of the Mountain, 190
Eccleston, Chris: Let Him Have It, 573
Eckhardt, Fritz: Almost Angels, 146; Waltz King, The, 215
Eckhouse, James: Blue Heaven, 465
Eckstine, Billy: Jo Jo Dancer, Your Life Is Calling, 558
Eddy, Helen Jerome: Helldorado (1934), 60; Klondike Annie, 314; Rebecca of Sunnybrook Farm (1917), 635
Eddy, Nelson: Balalaika, 907; Bitter Sweet, 909; Chocolate Soldier, The, 911; Girl of the Golden West, The, 919; I Married an Angel, 924; Knickerbocker Holiday, 927; Let Freedom Ring, 928; Maytime, 930; Naughty Marietta, 932; New Moon, 933; Northwest Outpost, 933; Phantom of the Opera (1943), 874; Rosalie, 937; Rose Marie (1936), 937; Sweethearts, 943
Edel, Alfred: My Father Is Coming, 339
Edelman, Herb: Barefoot in the Park, 232; Cracking Up, 260; Front Page, The (1974), 281; Marathon, 329; Odd Couple, The, 348; Yakuza, The, 141
Eden, Barbara: Amazing Dobermans, 146; Chattanooga Choo Choo, 254; Five Weeks in a Balloon, 50; Flaming Star, 1113; From the Terrace, 523; Harper Valley P.T.A., 294; How to Break Up a Happy Divorce, 302; Lethal Charm, 573; Quick, Let's Get Married, 363; Ride the Wild Surf, 936; 7 Faces of Dr. Lao, 1076; Stranger Within, The, 891; Voyage to the Bottom of the Sea, 1087; Wonderful World of the Brothers Grimm, The, 1090
Eden, Elana: Story of Ruth, The, 668
Edgerton, Earle: Carnival of Blood, 821
Edmond, J. Trevor: Return of the Living Dead 3, 880
Edmonds, Elizabeth: Experience Preferred...But Not Essential, 273; Scrubbers, 650
Edmondson, Adrian: Supergrass, The, 388; Young Ones, The, 416
Edson, Richard: Crossing the Bridge, 492; Do the Right Thing, 502; Joey Breaker, 558; Love, Cheat & Steal, 993; Platoon, 623; Stranger Than Paradise, 387; Super Mario Brothers, The, 208
Edwall, Allan: Brothers Lionheart, The, 152; Sacrifice, The, 782
Edwards, Anthony: Delta Heat, 37; Downtown, 41; El Diablo, 1111; Gotcha!, 980; Hawks, 537; Hometown Boy Makes Good, 300; How I Got into College, 302; Landslide, 990; Miracle Mile, 996; Mr. North, 334; Pet Sematary Two, 874; Revenge of the Nerds, 367; Revenge of the Nerds II: Nerds in Paradise, 367; Summer Heat (1987), 672; Sure Thing, The, 389; Top Gun, 131
Edwards, Blake: Strangler of the Swamp, 891
Edwards, Cassandra: Vasectomy, 404
Edwards, Cliff: Badmen of the Hills, 1096; Dance, Fools, Dance, 493; Doughboys, 268; Laughing Sinners, 571; Parlor, Bedroom and Bath, 354; Pirates of the Prairie, 1139; Sidewalks of New York, 378
Edwards, Darryl: Brother from Another Planet, The, 1040
Edwards, Edward: Tempest, The (1983), 678
Edwards, Elizabeth: Pink Chiquitas, The, 357
Edwards, Hilton: Half a Sixpence, 921
Edwards, Hugh: Lord of the Flies (1963), 579
Edwards, James: Home of the Brave, 543; Joe Louis Story, The, 558; Pork Chop Hill, 624; Set-Up, The, 1013; Steel Helmet, The, 120
Edwards, Jennifer: All's Fair, 225; Fine Mess, A, 277; Overexposed, 873; Perfect Match, The, 356; Son of the Pink Panther, 383; Sunset, 1021; That's Life, 393
Edwards, Lance: Peacemaker, 1069; Woman Her Men and Her Futon, A, 705
Edwards, Luke: Newsies, 933; Wizard, The, 218
Edwards, Mark: Boldest Job in the West, The, 1099
Edwards, Meredith: Run for Your Money, A, 371
Edwards, Paul: Combat Killers, 28
Edwards, Penny: In Old Amarillo, 1122; North of the Great Divide, 1136; Trail of Robin Hood, 1158
Edwards, Rick: Hearts and Armour, 59
Edwards, Sam: Gang Busters, 54
Edwards, Sebastian Rice: Hope and Glory, 544
Edwards, Stacy: Dinner at Eight (1990), 265
Edwards, Vince: Cellar Dweller, 822; Deal of the Century, 263; Desperados, The, 1109; Devil's Brigade, The, 37; Dirty Dozen, The: The Deadly Mission, 39; Firehouse (1972), 49; Fix, The, 50; Gumshoe Kid, The, 292; Killing, The, 988; Mad Bomber, The, 994; Original Intent, 614; Return to Horror High, 880; Seduction, The, 884; Sno-Line, 117; Space Raiders, 1078; Three Faces of Eve, The, 682
Efron, Marshall: Blade, 14
Egan, Eddie: Badge 373, 8; French Connection, The, 53
Egan, Michael: Rappaccini's Daughter, 635
Egan, Peter: Lillie, 575; Reilly: The Ace of Spies, 637
Egan, Richard: Amsterdam Kill, The, 5; Demetrius and the Gladiators, 499; Love Me Tender, 1130; Mission to Glory, 596; One Minute to Zero, 94; Seven Cities of Gold, 653; Split Second (1953), 664; Summer Place, A, 672; Underwater!, 134
Egan, Will: Glitch!, 287
Ege, Julie: Creatures the World Forgot, 1043; Seven Brothers Meet Dracula, The, 884
Eggar, Samantha: All the Kind Strangers, 951; Battle Force, 9; Brood, The, 819; Collector, The, 963; Curtains, 828; Dark Horse, 161; Demonoid, 833; Doctor Dolittle, 162; Doctor in Distress, 266; Exterminator, The, 45; Ghost in Monte Carlo, A, 527; Light at the End of the World, The, 77; Molly Maguires, The, 598; Round Numbers, 370; Tales of the Unexpected, 1022; Uncanny, The, 899; Walk, Don't Run, 405; Why Shoot the Teacher?, 701
Eggert, Nicole: Blown Away (1992), 957; Double-O Kid, The, 41; Haunting of Morella, The, 849; Just One of the Girls, 312
Eggerth, Marta: Presenting Lily Mars, 626
Egi, Stan: Rising Sun, 1010
Ehl, Jennifer: BackBeat, 907
Eichhorn, Lisa: Cutter's Way, 965; Devlin, 970; Europeans, The, 511; Grim Prairie Tales, 847; King of the Hill, 565; Moon 44, 1067; Opposing Force, 95; Vanishing, The (1993), 1029; Wild Rose, 702; Yanks, 707
Eiding, Paul: Personals, The, 357
Eigeman, Christopher: Metropolitan, 593
Eikenberry, Jill: Assault & Matrimony, 229; Between the Lines, 237; Cast the First Stone, 476; Chantilly Lace, 479; Hide in Plain Sight, 541; Inconvenient Woman, An, 551; L.A. Law, 567; Manhattan Project, The, 995; Night Full of Rain, A, 605; Orphan Train, 615; Sessions, 652
Eilbacher, Lisa: Amazing Spiderman, The, 4; Beverly Hills Cop, 11; Blindman's Bluff, 956; Deadly Intent, 34; Hunt for the Night Stalker, 546; Leviathan, 860; Live Wire, 78; Ten to Midnight, 126
Eilber, Janet: Hard to Hold, 922; Romantic Comedy, 370; Whose Life Is It, Anyway?, 701
Eilers, Sally: Long Long Trail, 1130; Parlor, Bedroom and Bath, 354; Strange Illusion, 1020
Eisenberg, Aron: Playroom, 875
Eisenberg, Avner: Jewel of the Nile, The, 68
Eisenberg, Ned: Hiding Out, 61
Eisenmann, Ike: Escape to Witch Mountain, 165; Return from Witch Mountain, 199; Terror Out of the Sky, 894
Eisley, Anthony: Deep Space, 1046; Journey to the Center of Time, 1060; Mummy and the Curse of the Jackals, The, 867; Naked Kiss, The, 1000; Navy vs. the Night Monsters, The, 868; Wasp Woman, 901
Eisner, David: To Catch a Killer, 1025
Eisner, Will: Comic Book Confidential, 421
Ek, Anders: Sawdust and Tinsel, 784

Ekberg, Anita: Alphabet Murders, The, *951;* Artists and Models, *229;* Back from Eternity, *453;* Boccaccio 70, *719;* Call Me Bwana, *249;* Cobra, The (1967), *27;* Four for Texas, *1114;* Hollywood or Bust, *299;* La Dolce Vita, *753;* Northeast of Seoul, *92;* Paris Holiday, *354;* S.H.E., *110;* Woman Times Seven, *705*

Ekland, Britt: After the Fox, *223;* Baxter, *456;* Beverly Hills Vamp, *237;* Bobo, The, *243;* Cold Heat, *28;* Endless Night, *973;* Great Wallendas, The, *533;* High Velocity, *62;* King Solomon's Treasure, *73;* Man with the Golden Gun, The, *81;* Monster Club, The, *865;* Moon in Scorpio, *599;* Night They Raided Minsky's, The, *345;* Sex on the Run, *376;* Slavers, *117;* Stiletto, *120;* Wicker Man, The, *903*

Eklund, Bengt: Port of Call, *778*

Ekman, Gosta: Adventures of Picasso, The, *222;* Faust, *736;* Inside Man, The, *66;* Intermezzo (1936), *748*

Elam, Jack: Apple Dumpling Gang Rides Again, The, *147;* Appointment in Honduras, *6;* Aurora Encounter, *1037;* Big Bad John, *12;* Cattle Queen of Montana, *1104;* Creature from Black Lake, *826;* Dynamite and Gold, *1110;* Grayeagle, *1116;* Hannie Caulder, *1119;* Hawmps!, *294;* Hot Lead and Cold Feet, *176;* Huckleberry Finn (1975), *176;* Jubilee Trail, *1124;* Kansas City Confidential, *988;* Man from Laramie, The, *1131;* Man without a Star, *1132;* Night of the Grizzly, The, *1136;* Once Upon a Time in the West, *1137;* Pat Garrett and Billy the Kid, *1138;* Pocketful of Miracles, *359;* Pony Express Rider, *1139;* Rancho Notorious, *1140;* Rare Breed, The (1966), *1141;* Rawhide (1951), *1141;* Rio Lobo, *1145;* Sacketts, The, *1146;* Sacred Ground, *1146;* Suburban Commando, *388;* Sundowners, The (1950), *1153;* Support Your Local Gunfighter, *1154;* Support Your Local Sheriff!, *1154;* Uninvited, The (1993), *1160*

Elcar, Dana: Blue Skies Again, *465;* Fool Killer, The, *978;* Great Northfield Minnesota Raid, The, *1116;* Inside Out (1986), *552;* Jungle Warriors, *69;* Learning Tree, The, *572;* Nude Bomb, The, *347;* Quarterback Princess, *631;* St. Ives, *110;* Shaming, The, *655;* Sting, The, *120*

Eldard, Ron: Drop Dead Fred, *269;* True Love, *400*

Eldbert, Jim: Warbirds, *137*

Eldor, Gabi: Boy Takes Girl, *152*

Eldredge, John: Dangerous, *494;* Flirtation Walk, *917;* Lost City of the Jungle, *79;* Song of Nevada, *1151*

Eldridge, Florence: Divorcee, The, *502;* Les Miserables (1935), *573*

Elenlac, Erika: Under Siege, *134*

Eleniak, Erika: Beverly Hillbillies, The, *237;* Chasers, *254*

Eles, Sandor: And Soon the Darkness, *952*

Elfman, Marie-Pascale: Forbidden Zone, *1053*

Elg, Taina: Diane, *500;* Great Wallendas, The, *533;* Les Girls, *928;* Prodigal, The, *629;* Thirty-Nine Steps, The (1959), *1024*

Elhers, Jerome: Fatal Bond, *975*

Elian, Yona: Last Winter, The, *571*

Elias, Alix: Citizen's Band, *255;* Munchies, *867*

Elise, Christine: Body Snatchers, The (1993), *1040;* Boiling Point, *17;* Child's Play 2, *823*

Elizondo, Hector: American Gigolo, *446;* Backstreet Justice, *8;* Being Human, *458;* Beverly Hills Cop 3, *11;* Born to Win, *467;* Chains of Gold, *478;* Cuba, *31;* Dain Curse, The, *965;* Final Approach, *1051;* Flamingo Kid, The, *278;* Forgotten Prisoners, *520;* Frankie and Johnny (1991), *522;* Getting Even with Dad, *285;* Honeyboy, *63;* Leviathan, *860;* Necessary Roughness, *342;* Nothing in Common, *609;* Out of the Darkness, *1003;* Power, Passion, and Murder, *625;* Private Resort, *362;* Report to the Commissioner, *638;* Samantha, *372;* There Goes the Neighborhood, *393;* Valdez Is Coming, *1160;* Young Doctors in Love, *415*

Elkin, Karen: Great Land of Small, The, *171*

Ellenstein, Peter: Weekend Pass, *407*

Ellers, Sally: Doughboys, *268*

Elliman, Yvonne: Jesus Christ, Superstar, *926*

Ellington, Duke: Belle of the Nineties, *234;* Murder at the Vanities, *931*

Ellington, Harry: Saint of Fort Washington, The, *646*

Elliot, Denholm: Hound of the Baskervilles, The (1983), *984;* Trading Places, *398*

Elliot, Jane: Change of Habit, *479*

Elliot, Laura: Two Lost Worlds, *133*

Elliot, Shawn: Crossover Dreams, *912*

Elliot, Tim: UTU, *134*

Elliot, William: San Antonio Kid, *1147*

Elliott, Alison: Monkey Trouble, *188*

Elliott, Bob: Bob & Ray, Jane, Laraine & Gilda, *243*

Elliott, Chris: Cabin Boy, *248;* CB4, *252;* Groundhog Day, *291*

Elliott, Denholm: Apprenticeship of Duddy Kravitz, The, *450;* Bleak House, *463;* Bourne Identity, The, *958;* Brimstone and Treacle, *819;* Child's Christmas in Wales, A, *158;* Codename: Kyril, *962;* Cuba, *31;* Deep Cover (1980), *969;* Defense of the Realm, *969;* Doll's House, A (1989), *503;* Hound of the Baskervilles, The (1977), *302;* House That Dripped Blood, The, *853;* Indiana Jones and the Last Crusade, *1058;* Madame Sin, *80;* Maurice, *590;* Missionary, The, *333;* Noises Off, *346;* Overindulgence, *617;* Private Function, A, *361;* Raiders of the Lost Ark, *1073;* Robin and Marian, *107;* Room with a View, A, *644;* Rude Awakening (1982), *881;* Russian Roulette, *110;* Saint Jack, *646;* Scorchers, *650;* September, *652;* Stealing Heaven, *667;* Strange Case of Dr. Jekyll and Mr. Hyde, The (1968), *890;* To the Devil, a Daughter, *896;* Toy Soldiers (1991), *131;* Transmutations, *897;* Vault of Horror, *900;* Whoopee Boys, The, *411;* Wicked Lady, The (1983), *139*

Elliott, John: Ambush Valley, *1093*

Elliott, Patricia: Natural Enemies, *604*

Elliott, Peter: Missing Link, *85*

Elliott, Ross: Dynamite Pass, *1111;* Hot Lead, *1122;* Indestructible Man, *856*

Elliott, Sam: Blue Knight, The (1973), *465;* Blue Lighting, The, *16;* Conagher, *1105;* Fatal Beauty, *46;* Frogs, *844;* Gettysburg, *526;* Gone to Texas, *1116;* I Will Fight No More Forever, *1122;* Legacy, The, *860;* Lifeguard, *574;* Mask (1985), *590;* Murder in Texas, *998;* Prancer, *197;* Quick and the Dead, The, *1140;* Road House (1989), *107;* Rush, *645;* Sacketts, The, *1146;* Shadow Riders, The, *1148;* Shakedown, *114;* Sibling Rivalry, *378;* Tombstone, *1157;* Wild Times, *1164*

Elliott, Stephen: Arthur, *229;* Arthur 2: On the Rocks, *229;* Assassination, *7;* Golden Honeymoon, The, *529;* Prototype, *1072;* Roadhouse 66, *107*

Elliott, William: Bells of Rosarita, *1097;* Boots and Saddles, *1100;* Calling Wild Bill Elliott, *1103;* Conquest of Cheyenne, *1106;* Death Valley Manhunt, *1108;* Fabulous Texan, The, *1112;* Hellfire, *1120;* Hidden Valley Outlaws, *1120;* In Early Arizona, *1122;* Longhorn, *1130;* Mojave Firebrand, *1134;* Phantom of the Plains, *1138;* Sheriff of Las Vegas, *1149;* Showdown, The (1950), *1149;* Wagon Wheels Westward, *1162*

Ellis, Diane: High Voltage, *62*

Ellis, Edward: Fury, *524;* Return of Peter Grimm, The, *638*

Ellis, Jack: Prime Suspect 2, *1007*

Ellis, James: No Surrender, *345*

Ellis, Patricia: Block-Heads, *241;* Case of the Lucky Legs, The, *960*

Ellis, Robin: Curse of King Tut's Tomb, The, *828;* Europeans, The, *511*

Ellison, Gwen: Luggage of the Gods, *324*

Ellison, James: Borderland, *1100;* Fifth Avenue Girl, *276;* Hopalong Cassidy Enters, *1121;* Hostile Country, *1122;* I Walked with a Zombie, *855;* Next Time I Marry, *344;* Vivacious Lady, *405;* You Can't Fool Your Wife, *415*

Elmendorf, Raymond: Bloody Wednesday, *817*

Elphick, Michael: Arthur's Hallowed Ground, *451;* Buddy's Song, *471;* Element of Crime, The, *508;* Lion and the Hawk, The, *77;* Privates on Parade, *362*

Elsom, Isobel: Desirée, *500;* Escape Me Never, *510;* Love from a Stranger, *993;* Love is a Many-Splendored Thing, *581;* Monsieur Verdoux, *336*
Elvira (Cassandra Peterson): Elvira, Mistress of the Dark, *271;* Get Out of My Room, *284*
Elwes, Cary: Another Country, *449;* Bram Stoker's Dracula, *819;* Chase, The (1994), *25;* Crush, The, *964;* Days of Thunder, *33;* Glory, *528;* Hot Shots, *301;* Lady Jane, *568;* Leather Jackets, *76;* Princess Bride, The, *1071;* Robin Hood: Men in Tights, *369*
Ely, Ron: Doc Savage...The Man of Bronze, *1047;* Night of the Grizzly, The, *1136;* Slavers, *117*
Emberg, Kelly: Portfolio, *624*
Emerson, Faye: Hard Way, The (1942), *536*
Emerson, Hope: All Mine to Give, *444;* Casanova's Big Night, *252;* Copper Canyon, *1106;* Guns of Fort Petticoat, *1118;* Peter Gunn (TV Series), *98;* Westward the Women, *1163*
Emerson, Karrie: Evils of the Night, *839*
Emerton, Roy: Dr. Syn, *40*
Emery, John: Lawless Street, A, *1127;* Mademoiselle Fifi, *585;* Rocketship X-M, *1075;* Spellbound, *1019*
Emge, David: Dawn of the Dead, *830;* Hellmaster, *849*
Emhardt, Robert: Mooncussers, *189;* No Time for Sergeants (Television), *608;* 3:10 to Yuma, *1157*
Emil, Michael: Adventures in Spying, *2;* Can She Bake a Cherry Pie?, *250;* Insignificance, *553;* Sitting Ducks, *380;* Someone to Love, *662;* Tracks, *687*
Emmanuel, Alphonsia: Peter's Friends, *621*
Emmanuel, Takis: Caddie, *473;* Kostas, *567*
Emney, Fred: Adventures of a Private Eye, *222*
Emo, Maria: Hitler, *542*
Endre, Lena: Sunday's Children, *791;* Visitors, The, *901*
Engel, Georgia: Care Bears Movie, The, *156*
Engel, Tina: Boat Is Full, The, *719*
Engel, Tobias: 38 Vienna Before the Fall, *794*
Engler, Lori-Nan: Head Office, *294*
English, Alex: Amazing Grace and Chuck, *445*
English, Maria: She Creature, The, *885;* Voodoo Woman, *901*
Englund, Robert: Adventures of Ford Fairlane, The, *2;* Danse Macabre, *829;* Eaten Alive, *838;* Freddy's Dead: The Final Nightmare, *843;* Hobson's Choice (1983), *175;* Nightmare on Elm Street, A, *871;* Nightmare on Elm Street 3, A: The Dream Warriors, *871;* Nightmare on Elm Street 4, A: The Dream Master, *871;* Nightmare on Elm Street 5: The Dream Child, *871;* Phantom of the Opera (1989), *874*
Ennis, Ethel: Mad Monster Party, *184*
Enoki, Takaaki: Heaven and Earth (1991), *743*
Enriquez, Rene: Bulletproof, *21*
Entwistle, John: Stand by Me (1988), *941*
Epps, Omar: Daybreak (1993), *1045;* Juice, *560;* Major League II, *326;* Program, The, *629*
Epstein, Alvin: Truth or Die, *689*
Erbe, Kathryn: D2: The Mighty Ducks, *160;* Rich in Love, *640*
Erdman, Richard: Cry Danger, *964;* Namu, the Killer Whale, *190;* Objective, Burma!, *93*
Erickson, Krista: First Time, The, *277;* Jekyll & Hyde—Together Again, *310;* Killer Image, *988;* Mortal Passions, *997*
Erickson, Leif: Abbott and Costello Meet Captain Kidd, *221;* Abduction, *950;* Arabian Nights (1942), *6;* Conquest, *487;* Fastest Gun Alive, The, *1112;* Gangster, The, *525;* Invaders from Mars (1953), *1059;* Man and Boy, *1131;* Mirage, *595;* Roustabout, *938;* Showdown, The (1950), *1149;* Snake Pit, The, *661;* Stella (1950), *667;* Strait-Jacket, *890;* Tea and Sympathy, *678;* Three Secrets, *683;* Trouble Along the Way, *688*
Erickson, Lisa: Power, The (1980), *876*
Ericson, Devon: Gone to Texas, *1116*
Ericson, John: Bamboo Saucer (a.k.a. Collision Course), *1038;* Bounty Man, The, *1101;* House of the Dead, *853;* Rhapsody, *639;* Student Prince, The, *942*
Erin, Tami: New Adventures of Pippi Longstocking, The, *191*
Erkal, Genco: Horse, The, *744*
Ermey, R. Lee: Body Snatchers, The (1993), *1040;* Demonstone, *833;* Endless Descent, *838;* Full Metal Jacket, *523;* I'm Dangerous Tonight, *855;* Kid, *71;* Mississippi Burning, *596;* On Deadly Ground, *93;* Siege of Firebase Gloria, The, *116;* Take, The, *124;* Terror Within 2, The, *894;* Toy Soldiers (1991), *131*
Ernest, Harry: New Adventures of Tarzan, *90*
Ernsberger, Duke: Ernest Rides Again, *272*
Ernst, Laura: Too Much Sun, *397*
Ernst, Max: Age of Gold, *711*
Ernst, Robert: Sure Fire, *674*
Errol, Leon: Flustered Comedy of Leon Errol, The, *278;* Higher and Higher, *922;* Make a Wish, *586;* Mexican Spitfire, *331;* Never Give a Sucker an Even Break, *343;* Noose Hangs High, The, *346;* Two-Reelers: Comedy Classics #2, *402*
Ersgard, Patrick: Mandroid, *1065;* Visitors, The, *901*
Erskine, Eileen: Hills of Home, *174*
Erskine, Marilyn: Westward the Women, *1163*
Erving, Julius: Fish That Saved Pittsburgh, The, *278*
Erwin, Bill: Silent Assassins, *116;* Somewhere in Time, *1077*
Erwin, Stu: Backdoor to Heaven, *454;* Ceiling Zero, *24;* Chained, *478;* Going Hollywood, *920;* Hold Your Man, *542;* International House, *307;* Misadventures of Merlin Jones, The, *188;* Palooka, *617;* Viva Villa!, *1162*
Esmond, Carl: Smash-Up: The Story of a Woman, *661*
Esmond, Jill: Casanova Brown, *252*
Espiritu, Johnnie Saiko: Adventures of the Kung Fu Rascals, The, *223*
Esposito, Giancarlo: Amos & Andrew, *226;* Bob Roberts, *243;* Do the Right Thing, *502;* Harley Davidson and the Marlboro Man, *59;* Mo' Better Blues, *931;* Night on Earth, *606;* School Daze, *373;* Sweet Lorraine, *674*
Esposito, Gianni: Les Miserables (1957), *759*
Esposti, Piera Degli: Joke of Destiny, *750*
Esquivel, Alan: Alsino and the Condor, *712*
Essary, Lisa: Soldier's Home, *661*
Essex, David: Silver Dream Racer, *658;* That'll Be the Day, *944*
Essman, Jefferey: New Wave Comedy, *343*
Estelita: Jesse James Meets Frankenstein's Daughter, *858*
Estes, Rob: Checkered Flag, *480;* Phantom of the Mall—Eric's Revenge, *874;* Trapper County War, *132*
Estevez, Emilio: Another Stakeout, *6;* Breakfast Club, The, *245;* D2: The Mighty Ducks, *160;* Freejack, *1053;* Judgment Night, *69;* Maximum Overdrive, *864;* Men at Work, *592;* Mighty Ducks, The, *187;* National Lampoon's Loaded Weapon 1, *342;* Nightbreaker, *607;* Nightmares, *871;* Outsiders, The, *616;* Repo Man, *366;* St. Elmo's Fire, *646;* Stakeout, *119;* Tex, *680;* That Was Then...This Is Now, *680;* Wisdom, *140;* Young Guns, *1165;* Young Guns II, *1166*
Estevez, Joe: Beach Babes from Beyond, *1038;* Blood on the Badge, *15;* Dark Rider, *33;* Double Blast, *41;* L.A. Goddess, *314;* Soultaker, *889*
Estevez, Ramon: Cadence, *473*
Estevez, René: Forbidden Sun, *519;* Intruder (1988), *856;* Sleepaway Camp II: Unhappy Campers, *887;* Touch and Die, *1026*
Estrada, Erik: Alien Seed, *1035;* Caged Fury, *21;* Dirty Dozen, The: The Fatal Mission, *39;* Divine Enforcer, *40;* Do or Die, *40;* Fire!, *48;* Guns, *58;* Honeyboy, *63;* Hour of the Assassin, *64;* Last Riders, The, *75;* Longest Drive, The, *1130;* New Centurions, The, *605;* Night of the Wilding, *606;* Spirits, *889*
Estrinn, Patricia: Dennis the Menace: Dinosaur Hunter, *162*
Etting, Ruth: Hips, Hips, Hooray, *297;* Roman Scandals, *937*

Eubank, Shari: Chesty Anderson, U.S. Navy (a.k.a. Anderson's Angels), *25;* Supervixens, *123*
Eubanks, Corey Michael: Payback, *98*
Eure, Wesley: C.H.O.M.P.S., *155;* Jennifer, *858;* Toolbox Murders, The, *1026*
Evans, Angelo: Angelo, My Love, *448*
Evans, Art: CB4, *252;* Die Hard 2: Die Harder, *39;* Finishing Touch, The, *977;* Jo Jo Dancer, Your Life Is Calling, *558;* Mom, *865;* Native Son, *604;* Trespass, *132;* White of the Eye, *1031*
Evans, Barry: Die Screaming, Marianne, *834*
Evans, Clifford: Courageous Mr. Penn, *489;* Curse of the Werewolf, The, *828;* Love on the Dole, *581;* River of Unrest, *641*
Evans, Dale: Along the Navajo Trail, *1093;* Apache Rose, *1094;* Bells of Coronado, *1097;* Bells of Rosarita, *1097;* Bells of San Angelo, *1097;* Cowboy and the Senorita, *1106;* Don't Fence Me In, *1110;* Down Dakota Way, *1110;* Golden Stallion, The, *1116;* Helldorado (1946), *1120;* Home in Oklahoma, *1121;* Lights of Old Santa Fe, *1128;* My Pal Trigger, *1135;* Roll on Texas Moon, *1145;* Roy Rogers Show, The (TV Series), *1146;* San Fernando Valley, *1147;* Song of Nevada, *1151;* Susanna Pass, *1154;* Trigger, Jr., *1159;* Twilight in the Sierras, *1159;* Utah, *1160;* War of the Wildcats, *1162;* Yellow Rose of Texas, *1165*
Evans, Edith: Chalk Garden, The, *478;* Crooks and Coronets (Sophie's Place), *261;* Importance of Being Earnest, The, *305;* Madwoman of Chaillot, The, *585;* Nasty Habits, *342;* Nun's Story, The, *609;* Scrooge (1970), *938;* Tom Jones, *397*
Evans, Estelle: Learning Tree, The, *572*
Evans, Evans: Story of a Love Story, *668*
Evans, Gene: Bounty Man, The, *1101;* Casino, *476;* Cattle Queen of Montana, *1104;* Donovan's Brain, *1047;* Fire!, *48;* Gentle Savage, *1115;* Magic of Lassie, The, *185;* Operation Petticoat, *351;* Sacketts, The, *1146;* Shadow Riders, The, *1148;* Shock Corridor, *1015;* Steel Helmet, The, *120*
Evans, Joan: Outcast, The, *1137;* Skirts Ahoy!, *940*
Evans, Josh: Doors, The, *914;* Ricochet, *106*
Evans, Linda: Beach Blanket Bingo, *908;* Big Valley, The (TV Series), *1098;* Gambler, Part II—The Adventure Continues, The, *1115;* Gambler Returns, the: Luck of the Draw, *1115;* Klansman, The, *566;* Standing Tall, *1153;* Those Calloways, *211*
Evans, Madge: Helldorado (1934), *60;* Sinners in Paradise, *659;* Stand Up and Cheer, *206;* Three Broadway Girls, *395;* Transatlantic Tunnel, *1085*
Evans, Mary Beth: Lovelines, *323*
Evans, Maurice: Androcles and the Lion, *227;* Beneath the Planet of the Apes, *1039;* Macbeth (1961), *583;* Planet of the Apes, *1071;* Rosemary's Baby, *881;* Scrooge (1935), *650;* Terror in the Wax Museum, *894;* War Lord, The, *137;* Wedding Rehearsal, *407*
Evans, Michael: Angelo, My Love, *448*
Evans, Mike: House on Skull Mountain, *853*
Evans, Muriel: King of the Pecos, *1125;* New Frontier, *1136*
Evans, Rex: Matchmaker, The, *329*
Evans, Robert: Man of a Thousand Faces, *587*
Evans, Robin: One Dark Night, *872;* Rage of Honor, *103*
Evans, Terry: Mongrel, *865*
Evelyn, Judith: Rear Window, *1009*
Evenson, Kim: Big Bet, The, *238;* Kandyland, *562;* Kidnapped (1988), *71*
Everett, Chad: Fever Pitch, *516;* Heroes Stand Alone, *61;* Impossible Years, The, *305;* Intruder Within, The, *1059;* Jigsaw Murders, The, *987;* Johnny Tiger, *559;* Official Denial, *1069;* Rome Adventure, *643;* Rousters, The, *109;* Singing Nun, The, *204*
Everett, Kenny: Bloodbath at the House of Death, *242*
Everett, Rupert: Another Country, *449;* Comfort of Strangers, The, *963;* Dance with a Stranger, *494;* Duet for One, *505;* Hearts of Fire, *538;* Inside Monkey Zetterland, *306;* Merlin & the Sword, *1065;* Princess Daisy, *627;* Right Hand Man, The, *640*
Everhard, Nancy: China Lake Murders, The, *961;* Deepstar Six, *832;* Demonstone, *833;* Double Revenge, *504;* This Gun for Hire (1991), *128*
Everhart, Rex: Blue Hotel, *465*
Everly, Trish: Madhouse (1987), *862*
Evers, Jason (Herb): Barracuda, *1038;* Brain That Wouldn't Die, The, *1040;* Fer-de-Lance, *976*
Evigan, Greg: Deepstar Six, *832;* Lies Before Kisses, *574;* Stripped to Kill, *122*
Ewart, John: Island Trader, *67;* Quest, The, *878;* Sunday Too Far Away, *673*
Ewell, Tom: Adam's Rib, *222;* Alfred Hitchcock Presents (TV Series), *951;* Girl Can't Help It, The, *286;* Life of Her Own, A, *574;* Lost in Alaska, *321;* Mr. Music, *931;* Seven Year Itch, The, *376;* State Fair (1962), *941;* Suppose They Gave a War and Nobody Came?, *388;* They Only Kill Their Masters, *1024*
Ewing, Carlos: Heroes in Hell, *61*
Excell, Matthew: Save the Lady, *201*
Excoffier, Stephane: Pointsman, The, *624*
Eyer, Richard: Friendly Persuasion, *522;* Invisible Boy, The, *1059;* Sincerely Yours, *658*
Eyre, Peter: Hedda, *539;* Orlando, *614*
Eythe, William: Colonel Effingham's Raid, *257;* Ox-Bow Incident, The, *1137;* Song of Bernadette, The, *662;* Wilson, *703;* Wing and a Prayer, A, *140*
Ezlashi, Maynard: Mister Johnson, *597*
Fabares, Shelley: Brian's Song, *469;* Clambake, *912;* Girl Happy, *919;* Love or Money?, *323;* Memorial Day, *592;* Ride the Wild Surf, *936;* Rock, Pretty Baby, *936;* Sky Heist, *117;* Spinout, *941*
Faber, Juliette: L'Ecole Buissonniere, *758;* Passion For Life, *776*
Faber, Peter: Army Brats, *228;* Soldier of Orange, *787*
Fabian: Dear Brigitte, *263;* Five Weeks in a Balloon, *50;* Get Crazy, *284;* Little Laura and Big John, *77;* Mr. Hobbs Takes a Vacation, *334;* North to Alaska, *1136;* Ride the Wild Surf, *936;* Soul Hustler, *118;* Ten Little Indians (1966), *1023*
Fabian, Françoise: Chloe in the Afternoon, *723;* Fernandel the Dressmaker, *736;* French Woman, The, *522;* Happy New Year (La Bonne Année), *743;* My Night at Maud's, *770;* Salut L'Artiste, *783*
Fabian, Janis: Invasion Earth: The Aliens Are Here, *856*
Fabiani, Joel: Reuben, Reuben, *367*
Fabray, Nanette: Alice Through the Looking Glass (1966), *906;* Amy, *146;* Band Wagon, The, *908;* Harper Valley P.T.A., *294;* Man in the Santa Claus Suit, The, *185;* Private Lives of Elizabeth and Essex, The, *629*
Fabrizi, Aldo: Open City, *773*
Fabrizi, Franco: Duel of Champions, *42;* Ginger and Fred, *740;* I Vitelloni, *746;* Il Bidone, *747*
Fahey, Jeff: Backfire, *953;* Blindsided, *956;* Body Parts, *817;* Freefall, *52;* Hit List, The (1992), *982;* Impulse (1990), *985;* In Search of the Serpent of Death, *66;* Iran Days of Crisis, *554;* Iron Maze, *987;* Last of the Finest, The, *75;* Lawnmower Man, The, *1062;* Psycho III, *877;* Quick, *102;* Sketch Artist, *1017;* Split Decisions, *664;* Trueblood, *689;* White Hunter Black Heart, *700;* Woman of Desire, *1032;* Wrangler, *141*
Fahey, Myrna: Fall of the House of Usher, The (1960), *840*
Fai, Leung Ka: Prison on Fire, *778*
Fails, J. W.: No Retreat, No Surrender, *92*
Fair, Elinor: Yankee Clipper, *141*
Fair, Jody: Brain Eaters, The, *1040*
Fairbairn, Bruce: Nightstick, *91*
Fairbanks Jr., Douglas: Angels Over Broadway, *448;* Catherine the Great, *477;* Corsican Brothers, The (1941), *29;* Ghost Story, *846;* Gunga Din, *58;* Having a Wonderful Time, *294;* Hostage Tower, The, *64;* Joy of Living, *926;* Little Caesar, *77;* Morning Glory (1933), *599;* Our Modern Maidens, *616;* Prisoner of Zenda, The (1937), *100;* Rage of Paris, The,

364; Scarlet Dawn, 649; Sinbad the Sailor, 116; Woman of Affairs, A, 705; Young in Heart, The, 416

Fairbanks Sr., Douglas: American Aristocracy, An, 226; Black Pirate, The, 14; Days of Thrills and Laughter, 262; Don Q, Son of Zorro, 41; Down to Earth, 268; Great Chase, The, 57; His Picture in the Papers, 297; Iron Mask, The, 67; Man from Painted Post, The, 327; Mark of Zorro, The (1920), 82; Mr. Robinson Crusoe, 86; Mystery of the Leaping Fish/Chess Fever, 341; Private Life of Don Juan, The, 628; Reaching for the Moon (1917), 365; Reaching for the Moon (1931), 365; Robin Hood (1923), 107; Taming of the Shrew, The (1929), 391; Thief of Bagdad, The (1924), 1083; When the Clouds Roll By, 409

Fairchild, Margaret: For Love of Angela, 519

Fairchild, Morgan: Based on an Untrue Story, 232; Body Chemistry 3: Point of Seduction, 957; Campus Man, 249; Cannon Movie Tales: Sleeping Beauty, 155; Deadly Illusion, 968; Haunting of Sarah Hardy, The, 982; Honeyboy, 63; Midnight Cop, 996; Mob Boss, 335; Phantom of the Mall—Eric's Revenge, 874; Red-Headed Stranger, The, 1141; Seduction, The, 884; Sherlock Holmes and the Leading Lady, 1015; Writer's Block, 1033; Zany Adventures of Robin Hood, The, 416

Faire, Virginia Brown: West of the Divide, 1163

Fairman, Michael: Glory Years, 287

Falsco, Frankie: Exterminator 2, The, 45

Faith, Adam: McVicar, 591; Yesterday's Hero, 708

Faithfull, Marianne: Assault on Agathon, 7; Hamlet (1969), 535; Kenneth Anger—Volume Four, 563; Turn of the Screw (1992), 898

Fajardo, Eduardo: Adios, Hombre, 1092; Gentleman Killer, 1115; Long Live Your Death, 1130; Oasis of the Zombies, 872; Sonny and Jed, 1151; Yellow Hair and the Fortress of Gold, 1165

Falana, Lola: Klansman, The, 566; Liberation of L. B. Jones, The, 574; Man Called Adam, A, 586

Falcao, Luzia: Luzia, 763

Falco, Edie: Laws of Gravity, 76

Falconetti, Maria: Passion of Joan of Arc, The, 776

Faldaas, Morten: Heart of Darkness, 538

Falk, Peter: All the Marbles, 225; Anzio, 6; Balcony, The, 455; Big Trouble, 239; Brinks Job, The, 246; Cheap Detective, The, 254; Columbo: Murder by the Book, 963; Cookie, 259; Faraway, So Close, 736; Great Muppet Caper, The, 171; Great Race, The, 290; Griffin and Phoenix: A Love Story, 533; Happy New Year, 293; In-Laws, The, 305; In the Spirit, 306; It's a Mad Mad Mad Mad World, 308; Luv, 324; Mikey and Nicky, 332; Murder by Death, 338; Pocketful of Miracles, 359; Pressure Point, 626; Princess Bride, The, 1071; Robin & the Seven Hoods, 936; Tune in Tomorrow, 400; Vibes, 1087; Wings of Desire, 804; Woman Under the Influence, A, 705

Fallender, Deborah: Jabberwocky, 309

Fancher, Hampton: Rome Adventure, 643

Fancy, Richard: Nick Knight, 868

Fantoni, Sergio: Prize, The, 629

Faracy, Stephanie: Great Outdoors, The, 290

Faraldo, Daniel: Above the Law, 1; Trenchcoat, 399

Farber, Arlene: All the Kind Strangers, 951

Farentino, Debrah: Capone, 22; Mortal Sins (1990), 997

Farentino, James: Cradle Will Fall, The, 964; Dead and Buried, 830; Possessed, The (1977), 876; Silent Victory: The Kitty O'Neil Story, 658; Summer to Remember, A, 673; War Lord, The, 137

Fargas, Antonio: Ambush Murders, The, 446; Borrower, The, 1040; Florida Straits, 51; Howling VI: The Freaks, 854; Huckleberry Finn (1975), 176; I'm Gonna Git You Sucka!, 305; Night of the Sharks, 90; Pretty Baby, 626; Putney Swope, 363; Shakedown, 114; Streetwalkin', 671; Whore, 701

Faria, Betty: Bye Bye Brazil, 721; Story of Fausta, The, 789

Farina, Carolyn: Age of Innocence, The, 443; Metropolitan, 593

Farina, Dennis: Another Stakeout, 6; Birthday Boy, The, 240; Code of Silence, 27; Crime Story, 30; Hillside Stranglers, The, 982; Manhunter, 995; Men of Respect, 592; Midnight Run, 84; Romeo is Bleeding, 108; Street Crimes, 121; Striking Distance, 121; Triplecross, 399; We're Talking Serious Money, 408

Farley, Chris: Coneheads, 258; Wayne's World 2, 406

Farley, Jim: General, The, 283

Farmer, Donald: No Justice, 91

Farmer, Frances: Come and Get It, 28; South of Pago Pago, 119; Toast of New York, The, 685

Farmer, Gary: Blown Away (1992), 957; Dark Wind, 966; Powwow Highway, 360

Farmer, Ken: Last of the Warriors, 1062

Farmer, Mark: Mr. Corbett's Ghost, 1066

Farmer, Mimsy: Autopsy, 811; Black Cat, The (1981), 813; Code Name: Wild Geese, 27; More, 768

Farmer, Suzan: Die, Monster, Die!, 834

Farnsworth, Richard: Anne of Green Gables (1985), 449; Comes a Horseman, 1105; Fire Next Time, The, 1051; Getaway, The (1994), 55; Grey Fox, The, 1117; Highway to Hell, 850; Independence Day, 551; Into the Night, 553; Misery, 865; Natural, The, 604; Resurrection, 638; Rhinestone, 367; Ruckus, 109; Space Rage, 1078; Sylvester, 675; Tom Horn, 1157; Two Jakes, The, 1028

Farnum, Franklyn: Clutching Hand, The, 27; Cowboy and the Bandit, 1106

Farnum, William: Between Men, 1097; Clutching Hand, The, 27; Connecticut Yankee, A, 258; Git Along, Little Dogies, 1115; Kid Ranger, 1124; Law of the Sea, 571; Lone Ranger, The (1938), 1129; Mexicali Rose, 1134; Mr. Robinson Crusoe, 86; Painted Desert, The, 1138; Powdersmoke Range, 1139; Public Cowboy #1, 1140; Santa Fe Stampede, 1147; Silver Streak (1934), 658; Trail of Robin Hood, 1158; Undersea Kingdom, 1087; Vigilantes Are Coming!, 1161; Wildfire (1945), 1164

Farr, Felicia: Charley Varrick, 25; Jubal, 1124; Kiss Me, Stupid, 314; Kotch, 314; Onionhead, 350; 3:10 to Yuma, 1157

Farr, Jamie: Blue Knight, The (1973), 465; Curse II—The Bite, 827; Fearless Tiger, 47; Happy Hour, 293; M*A*S*H: Goodbye, Farewell, Amen, 325; Speed Zone, 119; Who's Minding the Mint?, 411

Farrar, David: Black Narcissus, 463; Escape to Burma, 510; Pearl of the South Pacific, 620; Sea Chase, The, 112

Farrell, Charles: Aggie Appleby, Maker of Men, 223; City Girl, 962; Convoy (1940), 488; Just Around the Corner, 926; Old Ironsides, 93

Farrell, Glenda: Bureau of Missing Persons, 959; City without Men, 483; Disorderly Orderly, The, 265; Go Into Your Dance, 920; Gold Diggers of 1935, 920; Hollywood Hotel, 923; I Am a Fugitive from a Chain Gang, 547; Johnny Eager, 559; Lady for a Day, 567; Middle of the Night, 593; Mystery of the Wax Museum, 868; Rage of Paris, The, 364; Susan Slept Here, 389; Talk of the Town, The, 390; Three on a Match, 683

Farrell, Kenneth: It's a Joke, Son!, 308

Farrell, Mike: Battered, 456; Dark River: A Father's Revenge, 495; Incident at Dark River, 551; Memorial Day, 592; Prime Suspect, 627; Silent Motive, 1016; Vanishing Act, 693

Farrell, Nicolas: Berlin Tunnel 21, 10; Chariots of Fire, 479

Farrell, Sharon: Arcade, 1036; Can't Buy Me Love, 250; Fifth Floor, The, 841; It's Alive!, 857; Marlowe, 995; Premonition, The, 876; Rage (1980), 633; Reivers, The, 365

Farrell, Terry: Beverly Hills Madam, 460; Off the Mark, 348

Farrell, Timothy: Glen or Glenda, 528; Jail Bait (1954), 68

Farrell, Tommy: Pirates of the High Seas, 99

Farrington, Debbie: Black Panther, The, 463

Farrington, Hugh: Arizona Heat, 6

Farrow, Mia: Alice (1990), 224; Another Woman, 450; Avalanche, 7; Broadway Danny Rose, 246; Crimes and Misdemeanors, 490; Dandy in Aspic, A, 965; Death on the

Nile, *968;* Great Gatsby, The, *532;* Hannah and Her Sisters, *293;* Haunting of Julia, The, *537;* High Heels (1972), *744;* Hurricane (1979), *65;* Husbands and Wives, *546;* Midsummer Night's Sex Comedy, A, *332;* New York Stories, *343;* Purple Rose of Cairo, The, *363;* Radio Days, *364;* Rosemary's Baby, *881;* Secret Ceremony, *650;* See No Evil, *884;* September, *652;* Shadows and Fog, *654;* Supergirl, *1081;* Zelig, *416*

Farrow, Tisa: And Hope to Die, *952;* Fingers, *516;* Grim Reaper, The (1980), *847;* Search and Destroy (1981), *113;* Some Call It Loving, *662;* Strange Shadows in an Empty Room, *121;* Zombie, *904*

Farugia, Lena: Gods Must Be Crazy II, The, *287*

Fassbinder, Rainer Werner: Ali: Fear Eats the Soul, *711;* American Soldier, The, *712;* Fox and His Friends, *738;* Kamikaze 89, *751;* Querelle, *779*

Fastinetti, Nikki: Alien P.I., *1035*

Fat Boys, The: Disorderlies, *914;* Knights of the City, *927;* Krush Groove, *927*

Fataar, Ricky: Rutles, The (a.k.a. All You Need Is Cash), *938*

Faulkner, Graham: Brother Sun, Sister Moon, *470*

Faulkner, James: Albino, *808;* Maid, The, *326*

Faulkner, Sally: Alien Prey, *808*

Faulkner, Stephanie: Bus Is Coming, The, *472*

Faustino, David: It's a Bundyful Life, *308;* Perfect Harmony, *194*

Faustino, Michael: Blank Check, *151;* Judgment, *560*

Faversham, William: Arizona Days, *1094;* Singing Buckaroo, *1150*

Fawcett, Allen: Blindside, *15*

Fawcett, Farrah: Between Two Women, *459;* Burning Bed, The, *472;* Cannonball Run, *250;* Double Exposure (1989), *504;* Extremities, *512;* Murder in Texas, *998;* Murder on Flight 502, *87;* Myra Breckenridge, *341;* Poor Little Rich Girl: The Barbara Hutton Story, *624;* Red Light Sting, The, *636;* Saturn 3, *1076;* See You in the Morning, *651;* Small Sacrifices, *660;* Sunburn, *1021*

Fawcett, George: Son of the Sheik, *118;* Tempest (1928), *678;* True Heart Susie, *688;* Wedding March, The, *697*

Fay, Ann: Somewhere in Sonora, *1151*

Fay, Frank: Love Nest, *323*

Fay, Hugh: Little Annie Rooney, *576*

Faye, Alice: Alexander's Ragtime Band, *906;* In Old Chicago, *550;* Magic of Lassie, The, *185;* Poor Little Rich Girl (1936), *935;* State Fair (1962), *941;* Stowaway, *942*

Faye, Frances: Pretty Baby, *626*

Faye, Herbie: Sgt. Bilko (TV Series), *376*

Faylen, Frank: Copper Canyon, *1106;* Flustered Comedy of Leon Errol, The, *278;* Gunfight at the O.K. Corral, *1117;* Kid Galahad (1937), *563;* Lost Weekend, The, *580;* McConnell Story, The, *591;* Monkey's Uncle, The, *188;* Perils of Pauline, The (1947), *356;* Red Garters, *936;* Riot in Cell Block Eleven, *107;* Road to Rio, *369*

Fazenda, Louise: Keystone Comedies, Vol. 1, *312;* Mack Sennett Comedies, Vol. 2, *325;* Noah's Ark, *608*

Fazio, Ron: Toxic Avenger Part II, The, *897;* Toxic Avenger Part III: The Last Temptation of Toxie, The, *897*

Federman, Wayne: New Wave Comedy, *343*

Fehmiu, Bekim: Deserter, The, *1109;* Permission to Kill, *98*

Feig, Paul: Paramount Comedy Theatre, Vol. 2: Decent Exposures, *354*

Feig, Peter: Zoo Radio, *416*

Feinstein, Alan: Two Worlds of Jennie Logan, The, *1086*

Fejto, Raphael: Au Revoir, Les Enfants, *714*

Feld, Fritz: Affairs of Annabel, The, *223;* Everything Happens at Night, *273;* Four Jacks and a Jill, *918;* Iceland, *924;* It's a Date, *925;* I've Always Loved You, *555;* Mexican Hayride, *331;* Noose Hangs High, The, *346;* Promises, Promises, *362;* World's Greatest Lover, The, *414*

Felder, Clarence: Hidden, The, *1056;* Killing Floor, The, *563*

Feldman, Andrea: Heat (1972), *539*

Feldman, Corey: Blown Away (1992), *957;* 'Burbs, The, *247;* Dream a Little Dream, *269;* Edge of Honor, *43;* Friday the 13th—The Final Chapter, *843;* Goonies, The, *56;* License to Drive, *318;* Lipstick Camera, *992;* Lost Boys, The, *861;* Meatballs 4, *330;* National Lampoon's Last Resort, *342;* Rock 'n' Roll High School Forever, *369;* Round Trip to Heaven, *370;* Stand by Me (1986), *665;* Stepmonster, *1080;* Willa, *703*

Feldman, Marty: Adventure of Sherlock Holmes' Smarter Brother, The, *223;* Last Remake of Beau Geste, The, *316;* Sex with a Smile, *376;* Silent Movie, *379;* Slapstick of Another Kind, *380;* To See Such Fun, *397;* Yellowbeard, *415;* Young Frankenstein, *416*

Feldon, Barbara: Get Smart Again, *285;* No Deposit, No Return, *191;* Playmates, *358;* Smile, *381;* Sooner or Later, *663*

Feldshuh, Tovah: Amazing Howard Hughes, The, *445;* Blue Iguana, *242;* Brewster's Millions (1985), *245;* Cheaper to Keep Her, *254;* Day in October, A, *496;* Holocaust, *542;* Idolmaker, The, *924;* Terror Out of the Sky, *894*

Fell, Norman: Boatniks, The, *151;* Boneyard, The, *818;* Bullitt, *21;* C.H.U.D. II (Bud the C.H.U.D.), *820;* Cleopatra Jones and the Casino of Gold, *26;* For the Boys, *918;* For the Love of It, *279;* Hexed, *296;* If It's Tuesday, This Must Be Belgium, *305;* On the Right Track, *192;* Paternity, *355;* Stone Killer, The, *120;* Stripped to Kill, *122*

Fellini, Federico: Alex in Wonderland, *224;* Ciao Federico!, *724;* Fellini's Roma, *736*

Felmy, Hansjor: Brainwashed, *958*

Felt, Asbestos: Killing Spree, *859*

Felton, Verna: Oklahoman, The, *1136*

Fenech, Edwige: Phantom of Death, *874;* Sex with a Smile, *376*

Fengyi, Zhang: Farewell My Concubine, *736*

Fenn, Sherilyn: Backstreet Dreams, *454;* Boxing Helena, *818;* Crime Zone, *1043;* Desire and Hell at Sunset Motel, *969;* Diary of a Hitman, *970;* Fatal Instinct (1993), *274;* Meridian, *864;* Of Mice and Men (1992), *611;* Ruby (1991), *644;* Three of Hearts, *683;* Two Moon Junction, *690*

Fenneman, George: You Bet Your Life (TV Series), *415*

Fenton, Frank: Clay Pigeon, The, *26*

Fenton, Leslie: Strange Love of Molly Louvain, The, *669*

Fenton, Simon: Matinee, *330*

Feore, Colm: Beautiful Dreamers, *457;* Blades of Courage, *463;* Dr. Bethune, *502;* Thirty-Two Short Films About Glenn Gould, *682*

Feraco, Scott: Nasty Hero, *89*

Ferdin, Pamelyn: Toolbox Murders, The, *1026*

Ferency, Adam: Interrogation, *748*

Ferguson, Al: Roamin' Wild, *1145;* Tarzan the Mighty, *125;* Tarzan the Tiger, *126*

Ferguson, Andrew: Miracle Down Under, *187*

Ferguson, Frank: Caught, *477;* They Won't Believe Me, *681*

Ferguson, Jane: Mystery Mansion, *190*

Fergusson, Karen: Angel at My Table, An, *447*

Fernán-Gomez, Fernando: Half of Heaven, *743*

Fernandel: Angele, *713;* Fernandel the Dressmaker, *736;* Harvest, *743;* Le Schpountz, *758;* Little World of Don Camillo, The, *761;* Nais, *770;* Pantaloons, *775;* Paris Holiday, *354;* Sheep Has Five Legs, *785;* Topaze (1951), *796;* Well-Digger's Daughter, The, *803*

Fernandes, Miguel: Kurt Vonnegut's Monkey House, *1061;* Lifeforce Experiment, The, *1063*

Fernandez, Abel: Untouchables, The: Scarface Mob (TV), *134*

Fernandez, Emilio: Bring Me the Head of Alfredo Garcia, *20;* Flor Sylvestre, *737;* Return of the Seven, *1142;* Wild Bunch, The, *1164*

Fernandez, Evelina: American Me, *446*

Fernandez, Juan: Amazing Transplant, The, *445;* "Crocodile" Dundee II, *261*

Fernandez, Wilhemenia Wiggins: Diva, *731*

Ferrare, Cristina: Impossible Years, The, *305;* Mary, Mary, Bloody Mary, *863*

Ferrari, Doug: Paramount Comedy Theatre, Vol. 2: Decent Exposures, *354*

Ferratti, Rebecca: Gor, *1054;* Outlaw of Gor, *1069*

Ferrell, Conchata: Backfield in Motion, *230;* Deadly Hero, *34;* Edward Scissorhands, *1048;* Eye on the Sparrow, *512;* For Keeps, *519;* Heartland, *1119;* Rape And Marriage: The Rideout Case, *635;* Runaway Ralph, *201;* True Romance, *138;* Where the River Runs Black, *1089*

Ferrell, Terry: Hellraiser 3: Hell On Earth, *850*

Ferrell, Tyra: Boyz N the Hood, *468;* Poetic Justice, *624;* White Men Can't Jump, *410*

Ferreol, Andrea: Infernal Trio, The, *748;* Louisiana, *580;* Mysteries, *770;* Sleazy Uncle, The, *786;* Stroke of Midnight, *387;* Sweet Killing, *1022;* Zed and Two Noughts, A, *709*

Ferrer, José: Being, The, *812;* Berlin Tunnel 21, *10;* Big Brawl, The, *12;* Big Bus, The, *238;* Bloodtide, *817;* Bloody Birthday, *817;* Caine Mutiny, The, *473;* Christopher Columbus (1985), *25;* Cyrano De Bergerac (1950), *493;* Deep in My Heart, *913;* Don Rickles: Buy This Tape You Hockey Puck, *267;* Enter Laughing, *271;* Evil That Men Do, The, *45;* Fedora, *515;* Fifth Musketeer, The, *47;* George Washington, *526;* Gideon's Trumpet, *527;* Greatest Story Ever Told, The, *533;* Hired to Kill, *62;* Joan of Arc, *558;* Midsummer Night's Sex Comedy, A, *332;* Miss Sadie Thompson, *596;* Moulin Rouge, *600;* Natural Enemies, *604;* Old Explorers, *192;* Pleasure Palace, *623;* Private Files of J. Edgar Hoover, The, *100;* Samson and Delilah (1984), *648;* Seduced, *1013;* Sentinel, The, *884;* Ship of Fools, *656;* Strange Interlude (1988), *669;* Zoltan—Hound of Dracula, *904*

Ferrer, Mel: Blood and Roses, *814;* Born to Be Bad, *467;* Brannigan, *18;* City of the Walking Dead, *824;* Eaten Alive, *838;* Elena and Her Men, *734;* Emerald Jungle, *838;* Fall of the Roman Empire, The, *513;* Fifth Floor, The, *841;* Great Alligator, The, *847;* Knights of the Round Table, *73;* Lili, *928;* Lili Marleen, *760;* Norseman, The, *92;* One Shoe Makes it Murder, *1003;* Rancho Notorious, *1140;* Scaramouche, *111;* Seduced, *1013;* Sex and the Single Girl, *376;* Tempter, The, *893;* Visitor, The, *1087;* War and Peace (1956), *695*

Ferrer, Miguel: Another Stakeout, *6;* Blank Check, *151;* Deepstar Six, *832;* Harvest, The, *981;* Point of No Return, *99;* RoboCop, *1074;* Royce, *109;* Scam, *1012*

Ferrer, Tony: Blind Rage, *15*

Ferrero, Martin: Jurassic Park, *1061;* Miami Vice, *84;* Oscar (1991), *351;* Planes, Trains and Automobiles, *358;* Stop! Or My Mom Will Shoot, *386*

Ferreux, Benoit: Murmur of the Heart, *769*

Ferrier, Noel: Great Expectations—The Untold Story, *532;* Year of Living Dangerously, The, *141*

Ferrigno, Lou: Adventures of Hercules, The, *1034;* All's Fair, *225;* Cage, *21;* Death of the Incredible Hulk, The, *1045;* Desert Warrior, *1047;* Hercules (1983), *1056;* Incredible Hulk, The, *1058;* Liberty and Bash, *77;* Pumping Iron, *630;* Return to Frogtown, *1074;* Seven Magnificent Gladiators, The, *113;* Sinbad of the Seven Seas, *116;* Trial of the Incredible Hulk, *1085*

Ferrigno, Matty and Victoria: Pumping Iron, *630*

Ferris, Barbara: Children of the Damned, *823;* Nice Girl Like Me, A, *344*

Ferro, Turi: Malicious, *764*

Ferry, David: High-Ballin', *61*

Ferzetti, Gabriele: Cold Sweat (1970), *28;* Divorce His: Divorce Hers, *502;* Julia and Julia, *1061;* L'Aventura, *753;* Night Porter, The, *606*

Fetchit, Stepin: Dimples, *914;* Judge Priest, *560;* Stand Up and Cheer, *206*

Feuer, Debra: Homeboy, *543;* Night Angel, *868;* To Live and Die in L.A., *130*

Fiedler, John: Odd Couple, The, *348;* Raisin in the Sun, A (1961), *634;* Seize the Day, *651;* 12 Angry Men, *690*

Field, Arabella: Laws of Gravity, *76*

Field, Betty: Bus Stop, *248;* Butterfield 8, *472;* Coogan's Bluff, *29;* Great Moment, The, *290;* King's Row, *565;* Peyton Place, *621;* Southerner, The, *663*

Field, Chelsea: Birds II, The: Land's End, *813;* Dust Devil, *838;* Extreme Justice, *512;* Harley Davidson and the Marlboro Man, *59;* Hotel Room, *983;* Last Boy Scout, The, *75;* Prison, *876;* Royce, *109;* Snapdragon, *1018*

Field, Karin: Cave of the Living Dead, *822*

Field, Mary: Lady Takes a Chance, A, *1125*

Field, Sally: Absence of Malice, *950;* Back Roads, *453;* Beyond the Poseidon Adventure, *11;* End, The, *271;* Heroes, *540;* Home for the Holidays, *983;* Hooper, *300;* Kiss Me Goodbye, *313;* Mrs. Doubtfire, *334;* Murphy's Romance, *601;* Norma Rae, *608;* Not without My Daughter, *609;* Places in the Heart, *623;* Punchline, *630;* Smokey and the Bandit, *381;* Soapdish, *382;* Stay Hungry, *667;* Steel Magnolias, *667;* Surrender, *389;* Sybil, *675;* Way West, The, *1163*

Field, Shirley Anne: Alfie, *224;* Hear My Song, *295;* My Beautiful Laundrette, *601;* War Lover, The, *696*

Field, Todd: Eye of the Eagle 2, *46;* Ruby in Paradise, *645*

Field, Virginia: Longest Hunt, The, *1130;* Mr. Moto's Last Warning, *997;* Perfect Marriage, *356*

Fielding, Gerald: Dracula's Last Rites (1980), *837*

Fields, Charles: Beniker Gang, The, *149;* Fish Hawk, *517*

Fields, Christopher John: Indecency, *986*

Fields, Maurie: Death of a Soldier, *498*

Fields, Robert: Anna, *448;* Sporting Club, The, *664*

Fields, Sidney: Abbott and Costello Show, The (TV Series), *221*

Fields, Stanley: Island of Lost Souls, *857*

Fields, Suzanne: Flesh Gordon, *1052*

Fields, W. C.: Bank Dick, The, *232;* Bill Fields and Will Rogers, *239;* David Copperfield, *496;* Fatal Glass of Beer, A/Pool Sharks, *274;* Flask of Fields, A, *278;* If I Had a Million, *304;* International House, *307;* It's a Gift, *308;* Mississippi, *931;* Mrs. Wiggs of the Cabbage Patch, *598;* My Little Chickadee, *340;* Never Give a Sucker an Even Break, *343;* Running Wild (1927), *371;* Sally of the Sawdust, *647;* Sensations of 1945, *938;* You Can't Cheat an Honest Man, *415*

Fieldstad, Jack: Polar Bear King, The, *1071*

Fiennes, Ralph: Schindler's List, *649*

Fierstein, Harvey: Harvest, The, *981;* Mrs. Doubtfire, *334;* Tidy Endings, *683;* Torch Song Trilogy, *686*

Fil, Aye: Rembrandt—1669, *780*

Filho, Brandao: Story of Fausta, The, *789*

Filho, Daniel: Story of Fausta, The, *789*

Filkins, Jennifer: Evil Spirits in the House, *839*

Fimple, Dennis: Creature from Black Lake, *826*

Finch, Flora: Cat and the Canary, The (1927), *960*

Finch, Jon: And Nothing But the Truth, *447;* Breaking Glass, *909;* Frenzy, *979;* Game of Seduction, *739;* Lady Caroline Lamb, *567;* Last Days of Man on Earth, The, *1062;* Macbeth (1971), *584;* Witching Time, *904*

Finch, Peter: Detective, The (1954), *970;* Elephant Walk, *508;* Far from the Madding Crowd, *514;* First Men *in* the Moon, *1051;* Flight of the Phoenix, The, *51;* Kidnapped (1960), *180;* Miniver Story, The, *594;* Network, *604;* No Love for Johnnie, *608;* Nun's Story, The, *609;* Operation Amsterdam, *95;* Pursuit of the Graf Spee, *101;* Raid on Entebbe, *633;* Red Tent, The, *637;* Shattered (1972), *655;* Story of Robin Hood, The, *207;* Sunday, Bloody Sunday, *673;* Warriors, The (1955), *137;* Windom's Way, *703;* Wooden Horse, The, *706*

Fine, Larry: Lost Stooges, The, *322;* Stoogemania, *386;* Three Stooges, The (Volumes 1–10), *396*

Finetti, Anthony: Prime Time Murder, *100*

Finlay, Frank: Cromwell, *491;* Cthulhu Mansion, *827;* Death of Adolf Hitler, The, *498;* Enigma, *44;* Four Musketeers, The, *52;* Gumshoe, *291;* Lifeforce, *1063;* Molly Maguires, The, *598;* Ploughman's Lunch, The, *623;* Return of the Musketeers, *106;* Return of the Soldier, The, *638;* Wild Geese, The, *139*

Finlayson, James: All Over Town, *224;* Block-Heads, *241;* Bonnie Scotland, *243;* Chump at Oxford, A, *255;* Clark and McCullough: Inspired Madness, *256;* Devil's Brother, The,

914; Laurel and Hardy Classics, Volume 4, *316;* Laurel and Hardy Classics, Volume 7, *316;* Laurel and Hardy Classics, Volume 9, *316;* Laurel and Hardy on the Lam, *317;* Our Relations, *351;* Two-Reelers: Comedy Classics #2, *402*

Finley, Evelyn: Dynamite Canyon, *1111;* Prairie Rustlers, *1139;* Sundown Riders, *1153*

Finley, William: Eaten Alive, *838;* Phantom of the Paradise, *935;* Simon, *379*

Finn, John: Cover-Up (1990), *30*

Finnegan, Dave: Commitments, The, *912*

Finneran, Siobhan: Rita, Sue and Bob Too, *368*

Finnerty, Warren: Brig, The, *470;* Connection, The (1961), *487*

Finney, Albert: Annie, *907;* Dresser, The, *505;* Duellists, The, *42;* Endless Game, The, *510;* Entertainer, The, *510;* Green Man, The, *981;* Gumshoe, *291;* Image, The, *549;* Looker, *1063;* Loophole, *993;* Miller's Crossing, *594;* Murder on the Orient Express, *999;* Orphans, *615;* Playboys, The, *623;* Pope John Paul II, *624;* Rich in Love, *640;* Scrooge (1970), *938;* Shoot the Moon, *656;* Tom Jones, *397;* Two for the Road, *401;* Under the Volcano, *691;* Wolfen, *904*

Finney, Shirley Jo: Echo Park, *507;* Wilma, *703*

Finocciaro, Angela: Volere Volare, *801*

Fiona: Hearts of Fire, *538*

Fiorentino, Linda: Acting on Impulse, *950;* After Hours, *223;* Chain of Desire, *478;* Gotcha!, *980;* Moderns, The, *335;* Neon Empire, The, *89;* Queens Logic, *363;* Shout (1991), *939;* Strangers, *669;* Vision Quest, *694;* Wildfire (1988), *703*

Firbank, Ann: Flame to the Phoenix, A, *50*

Firesign Theatre Players: Eat or Be Eaten, *270;* Nick Danger in the Case of the Missing Yolk, *344*

Firestone, Eddie: Duel, *972*

Firth, Colin: Another Country, *449;* Apartment Zero, *952;* Dutch Girls, *506;* Femme Fatale, *976;* Hostages, *544;* Month in the Country, A, *599;* Valmont, *693;* Wings of Fame, *412*

Firth, Peter: Born of Fire, *467;* Burndown, *959;* Diamonds on Wheels, *162;* Equus, *973;* Fire and Sword, *1051;* Hunt for Red October, The, *984;* Incident, The (1989), *551;* Innocent Victim, *986;* Joseph Andrews, *311;* King Arthur, The Young Warlord, *72;* Letter to Brezhnev, *318;* Lifeforce, *1063;* Prisoner of Honor, *628;* Shadowlands, *654;* Tess, *679*

Fischer, Kate: Sirens, *379*

Fishburne, Larry: Boyz N the Hood, *468;* Cadence, *473;* Class Action, *962;* Decoration Day, *498;* Deep Cover (1992), *36;* King of New York, *72;* Quicksilver, *632;* Red Heat (1988), *104;* School Daze, *373;* Searching for Bobby Fischer, *202;* What's Love Got to Do with It?, *698*

Fisher, Brad: Cthulhu Mansion, *827*

Fisher, Carrie: Amazon Women on the Moon, *225;* Appointment with Death, *953;* Blues Brothers, The, *242;* 'Burbs, The, *247;* Drop Dead Fred, *269;* Empire Strikes Back, The, *1049;* Frankenstein (1984), *842;* Garbo Talks, *283;* Hannah and Her Sisters, *293;* Hollywood Vice Squad, *63;* Loverboy, *323;* Man with One Red Shoe, The, *328;* Mr. Mike's Mondo Video, *334;* Paul Reiser Out on a Whim, *355;* Return of the Jedi, *1074;* Shampoo, *655;* She's Back, *377;* Sibling Rivalry, *378;* Soapdish, *382;* Star Wars, *1079;* Sweet Revenge (1990), *389;* This Is My Life, *394;* Thumbelina (1983), *211;* Time Guardian, The, *1084;* Under the Rainbow, *402;* When Harry Met Sally, *409*

Fisher, Cindy: Liar's Moon, *574*

Fisher, Eddie: Bundle of Joy, *247;* Butterfield 8, *472*

Fisher, Frances: Attack of the 50-Foot Woman (1993), *1037;* Cold Sassy Tree, *485;* Frame Up, *52;* Heart, *537;* Lucy and Desi: Before the Laughter, *583;* Patty Hearst, *620;* Praying Mantis, *1007;* Sudie & Simpson, *672;* Tough Guys Don't Dance, *686*

Fisher, Gail: Mankillers, *82*

Fisher, Gregor: Girl in the Picture, The, *286;* Silent Mouse, *204*

Fisher, Jasen: Witches, The, *1089*

Fisher, Jodie: Intimate Obsession, *986*

Fisher, Tricia Leigh: Pretty Smart, *361*

Fishman, Jeff: Hot Moves, *301*

Fiske, Robert: Green Archer, *981*

Fitts, Rick: Platoon Leader, *99*

Fitzgerald, Barry: And Then There Were None, *952;* Catered Affair, The, *477;* Dawn Patrol, The, *33;* Fighting Father Dunne, *516;* Going My Way, *529;* How Green Was My Valley, *545;* Long Voyage Home, The, *578;* Naked City, The, *1000;* None But the Lonely Heart, *608;* Quiet Man, The, *364;* Saint Strikes Back, The, *1012;* Sea Wolf, The (1941), *113;* Story of Seabiscuit, The, *207;* Tarzan's Secret Treasure, *126;* Union Station, *1029*

Fitzgerald, Ciaran: Into the West, *177*

Fitzgerald, Ella: Pete Kelly's Blues, *935*

Fitzgerald, Geraldine: Arthur 2: On the Rocks, *229;* Dark Victory, *495;* Easy Money, *269;* Harry and Tonto, *537;* Jilting of Granny Weatherall, The, *558;* Kennedy (TV Miniseries), *562;* Last American Hero, The, *75;* Mill on the Floss, The, *594;* Pawnbroker, The, *620;* Poltergeist II: The Other Side, *875;* Strange Affair of Uncle Harry, The, *669;* Watch on the Rhine, *696;* Wilson, *703*

Fitzgerald, Tara: Hear My Song, *295;* Sirens, *379*

Fitzpatrick, Colleen: Hairspray, *292*

Fix, Paul: Blood Alley, *15;* Bulldog Courage, *1102;* Desert Trail, *1109;* El Dorado, *1111;* Fargo Express, *1112;* Grayeagle, *1116;* Hellfire, *1120;* High and the Mighty, The, *541;* His Fighting Blood, *1121;* Hitler—Dead or Alive, *542;* Hondo, *1121;* Island in the Sky, *554;* Last Mile, The, *570;* Pittsburgh, *622;* Red River, *1141;* Rifleman, The (TV Series), *1144;* Somewhere in Sonora, *1151;* Sons of Katie Elder, The, *1151;* Sphinx, The (1933), *1019;* Talion, *1154;* Triple Justice, *1159;* Virginia City, *1161*

Flagg, Cash: Incredibly Strange Creatures Who Stopped Living and Became Mixed-Up Zombies, The, *856;* Thrill Killers, The, *895;* Wild Guitar, *702*

Flagg, Fannie: Five Easy Pieces, *517;* My Best Friend Is a Vampire, *339*

Flaherty, Joe: Best of John Candy, The, *236;* Blue Monkey, *817;* Going Berserk, *287;* Looking for Miracles, *579;* One Crazy Summer, *349;* Really Weird Tales, *365;* Sesame Street Presents Follow That Bird, *203;* Speed Zone, *119*

Flamingos, The: Go, Johnny, Go!, *920;* Rock, Rock, Rock, *937*

Flanagan, Fionnula: Death Dreams, *831;* Ewok Adventure, The, *165;* James Joyce's Women, *556;* Mad at the Moon, *861;* Youngblood, *709*

Flanders, Ed: Amazing Howard Hughes, The, *445;* Citizen Cohn, *482;* Exorcist III: Legion, *840;* MacArthur, *583;* Ninth Configuration, The, *608;* Pursuit of D. B. Cooper, *363;* Salem's Lot, *882;* Special Bulletin, *1019;* Tomorrow's Child, *686;* Trial of the Cantonsville Nine, The, *687*

Flanders, Michael: Long Ago Tomorrow, *578*

Flannigan, Maureen: Teenage Bonnie and Klepto Clyde, *126*

Flatley, Nigel: I Want What I Want, *548*

Flavin, James: Abbott and Costello Meet the Killer, Boris Karloff, *221;* Cloak and Dagger (1946), *962*

Flea: Dudes, *505;* Motorama, *337*

Fleet, James: Four Weddings and a Funeral, *280*

Fleet, Jo Van: King and Four Queens, The, *1125*

Fleetwood, Susan: Heat and Dust, *539;* Krays, The, *567;* Sacrifice, The, *782*

Fleischer, Charles: Back to the Future II, *1037;* Straight Talk, *387*

Fleiss, Jane: Kent State, *563*

Fleiss, Noah: Josh and S.A.M., *69*

Fleming, Alice: Phantom of the Plains, *1138;* San Antonio Kid, *1147*

Fleming, Craig: Dead Silence, *262*

Fleming, Cynthia: Invasion of the Blood Farmers, *856*

Fleming, Eric: Queen of Outer Space, *1073;* Rawhide (TV Series), *1141*

Fleming, Ian: School for Scandal, *373;* Silver Blaze, *1016;* Triumph of Sherlock Holmes, The, *1027*

Fleming, Rhonda: Abilene Town, *1092;* Bullwhip, *1102;* Connecticut Yankee in King Arthur's Court, A (1948), *258;* Cry Danger, *964;* Great Lover, The, *289;* Gunfight at the O.K. Corral, *1117;* Nude Bomb, The, *347;* Out of the Past, *1003;* Pony Express, *1139;* Slightly Scarlet, *660;* Spellbound, *1019;* Tennessee's Partner, *1155;* While the City Sleeps, *138*

Fleming, Robert Barry: Adventures in Wonderland, *143*

Fleming, Susan: Range Feud, *1141*

Flemyng, Robert: Blood Beast Terror, The, *815;* Conspirator, *963;* Horrible Dr. Hichcock, The, *851;* Kafka, *988;* Man Who Never Was, The, *81;* Windom's Way, *703;* Young Winston, *709*

Fletcher, Bramwell: Bill of Divorcement, A, *461;* Svengali (1931), *1022*

Fletcher, Dexter: Lionheart, *181;* Rachel Papers, *364;* Raggedy Rawney, The, *633;* Twisted Obsession, *690*

Fletcher, Jack: Rumpelstiltskin (1980), *200*

Fletcher, Jay: Born to Win, *467*

Fletcher, Louise: Blind Vision, *956;* Blue Steel (1990), *16;* Brainstorm, *1040;* Cheap Detective, The, *254;* Exorcist II: The Heretic, *840;* Final Notice, *977;* Flowers in the Attic, *978;* Invaders from Mars (1986), *1059;* Lady in Red, *74;* Magician of Lublin, The, *585;* Mamma Dracula, *862;* Natural Enemies, *604;* Nightmare on the 13th Floor, *871;* Nobody's Fool, *346;* One Flew Over the Cuckoo's Nest, *613;* Return to Two-Moon Junction, *639;* Russian Roulette, *110;* Shadowzone, *885;* Strange Behavior, *890;* Strange Invaders, *1080;* Summer to Remember, A, *673;* Thieves Like Us, *681;* Two Moon Junction, *690*

Fletcher, Page: Buying Time, *21;* Friends, Lovers & Lunatics, *281;* Hitchhiker (Series), The, *850;* Trial & Error, *1027*

Fletcher, Suzanne: Sleepwalker, *1017*

Flint, Sam: Monster Maker, The, *866;* New Frontier, *1136;* Spy Smasher, *119*

Flippen, Jay C.: Carnival Story, *475;* Cat Ballou, *1103;* Elfego Baca: Six Gun Law, *1111;* Far Country, The, *1112;* Flying Leathernecks, *51;* Killing, The, *988;* King and Four Queens, The, *1125;* Las Vegas Story, The, *568;* Lemon Drop Kid, The, *317;* Restless Breed, The, *1142;* Run of the Arrow, *1146;* Seven Minutes, The, *653;* 7th Cavalry, *1148;* Studs Lonigan, *671;* They Live By Night, *681;* Thunder Bay, *129;* Wild One, The, *139;* Woman's Secret, A, *1032;* Yellow Cab Man, The, *415*

Flippin, Lucy Lee: Summer School, *388*

Flohe, Charles: Rappin', *936*

Flon, Suzanne: Moulin Rouge, *600;* One Deadly Summer, *773;* Un Singe en Hiver (A Monkey in Winter), *798*

Flood, Joe: Blue Yonder, The, *151;* Student Bodies, *891*

Flood, Michael: Crazy Fat Ethel II, *826;* Death Nurse, *831*

Florance, Sheila: Woman's Tale, A, *705*

Floria, Holly: Bikini Island, *813*

Flory, Agata: Guns for Dollars, *1117*

Flower, George (Buck): Across the Great Divide, *143;* Adventures of the Wilderness Family, *144;* Inside Out 2, *1059;* Wilderness Family, Part 2, The, *217*

Flowers, Bess: One in a Million, *350*

Floyd, Charles R.: P.O.W.: The Escape, *96*

Fluegel, Darlanne: Border Heat, *17;* Bulletproof, *21;* Crime Story, *30;* Deadly Stranger, *35;* Freeway, *52;* Lock Up, *78;* Project: Alien, *1072;* Running Scared (1986), *110;* Slaughter of the Innocents, *1017;* To Live and Die in L.A., *130;* Tough Guys, *398*

Flynn, Colleen: Late for Dinner, *1062*

Flynn, Errol: Adventures of Captain Fabian, *2;* Adventures of Don Juan, The, *2;* Adventures of Robin Hood, The, *2;* Against All Flags, *3;* Assault of the Rebel Girls, *7;* Captain Blood, *22;* Charge of the Light Brigade, The (1936), *24;* Dawn Patrol, The, *33;* Desperate Journey, *500;* Dive Bomber, *502;* Dodge City, *1109;* Edge of Darkness (1943), *43;* Escape Me Never, *510;* Gentleman Jim, *525;* Hollywood Canteen, *923;* Hollywood Outtakes, *299;* Kim, *72;* Master of Ballantrae, The, *83;* Northern Pursuit, *92;* Objective, Burma!, *93;* Prince and the Pauper, The (1937), *197;* Private Lives of Elizabeth and Essex, The, *629;* San Antonio, *1147;* Santa Fe Trail, *1147;* Sea Hawk, The, *112;* Silver River, *1150;* Sisters, The (1938), *659;* Thank Your Lucky Stars, *944;* That Forsyte Woman, *680;* They Died with Their Boots On, *1156;* Virginia City, *1161;* Warriors, The (1955), *137*

Flynn, Joe: Barefoot Executive, The, *148;* Computer Wore Tennis Shoes, The, *159;* Gentle Savage, *1115;* Love Bug, The, *184;* Lover Come Back, *323;* Million Dollar Duck, The, *187;* Now You See Him, Now You Don't, *191;* Superdad, *208*

Flynn, Miriam: 18 Again, *270;* For Keeps, *519*

Flynn, Sean: Son of Captain Blood, *118*

Flynn, Steven: Without Warning: The James Brady Story, *704*

Foch, Nina: American in Paris, An, *906;* Cash McCall, *252;* Child of Glass, *158;* Dark Past, The, *495;* Executive Suite, *512;* Jennifer, *858;* Morning Glory (1992), *599;* Return of the Vampire, The, *880;* St. Benny the Dip, *646;* Skin Deep, *380;* Sliver, *1018;* Song to Remember, A, *940*

Fogel, Vladimir: Bed and Sofa, *716;* By the Law, *721;* Girl with the Hatbox, The, *741*

Foley, Dave: Best of the Kids in the Hall, The, *236*

Foley, David: High Stakes (1986), *297*

Foley, Jake: Octavia, *610*

Foley, Michael: Divine Enforcer, *40*

Foley, Michael M.: Prison Planet, *1071*

Folk, Abel: All Tied Up, *225*

Follows, Megan: Anne of Avonlea, *449;* Anne of Green Gables (1985), *449;* Back to Hannibal: The Return of Tom Sawyer and Huckleberry Finn, *454;* Cry in the Wind, *492;* Silver Bullet, *886;* Stacking, *665;* Termini Station, *679*

Folsom, Megan: Heartland, *1119*

Fonda, Bridget: Aria, *907;* Bodies, Rest & Motion, *465;* Doc Hollywood, *265;* Frankenstein Unbound, *843;* Iron Maze, *987;* Jacob I Have Loved, *556;* Leather Jackets, *76;* Out of the Rain, *1003;* Point of No Return, *99;* Scandal, *648;* Shag, the Movie, *654;* Single White Female, *1016;* Singles, *379;* Strapless, *670;* You Can't Hurry Love, *415*

Fonda, Henry: Advise and Consent, *442;* American Film Institute Life Achievement Awards, The, *418;* Ash Wednesday, *451;* Battle Force, *9;* Battle of the Bulge, *10;* Best Man, The, *459;* Big Hand for the Little Lady, A, *1098;* Big Street, The, *460;* Boston Strangler, The, *818;* Cheyenne Social Club, The, *1104;* Clarence Darrow, *483;* Drums Along the Mohawk, *42;* Fail-Safe, *974;* Fort Apache, *1114;* Fugitive, The (1947), *523;* Gideon's Trumpet, *527;* Grapes of Wrath, The, *531;* Great American West, *425;* Great Smokey Roadblock, The, *57;* How the West Was Won, *1122;* I Dream Too Much, *924;* Immortal Sergeant, The, *549;* In Harm's Way, *66;* Jesse James, *1123;* Jezebel, *557;* Lady Eve, The, *315;* Longest Day, The, *78;* Mad Miss Manton, The, *325;* Madigan, *80;* Meteor, *1065;* Midway, *84;* Mr. Roberts, *334;* My Darling Clementine, *1134;* My Name Is Nobody, *1135;* Night Flight from Moscow, *90;* Oldest Living Graduate, The, *611;* On Golden Pond, *612;* Once Upon a Time in the West, *1137;* Ox-Bow Incident, The, *1137;* Return of Frank James, The, *1142;* Rollercoaster, *1011;* Roots: The Next Generation, *644;* Rounders, The, *1146;* Sex and the Single Girl, *376;* Sometimes a Great Notion, *662;* Spencer's Mountain, *664;* Stage Struck (1958), *665;* Swarm, The, *891;* Tentacles, *893;* That Certain Woman, *680;* There Was a Crooked Man, *1156;* Tin Star, The, *1157;* Too Late the Hero, *131;* 12 Angry Men, *690;* War and Peace (1956), *695;* Warlock (1959), *1162;* Wrong Man, The (1956), *1033;* You Only Live Once, *708;* Young Mr. Lincoln, *708;* Yours, Mine and Ours, *416*

Fonda, Jane: Agnes of God, *443;* Any Wednesday, *228;* Barbarella, *1038;* Barefoot in the Park, *232;* California Suite, *249;* Cat Ballou, *1103;* Chase, The (1966), *479;* China Syndrome, The, *961;* Circle of Love, *482;* Comes a Horseman, *1105;* Coming Home, *486;* Dollmaker, The, *503;* Doll's House,

A (1973), *503;* Electric Horseman, The, *508;* Fun with Dick and Jane, *282;* Game Is Over, The, *739;* Joy House, *559;* Julia, *560;* Klute, *989;* Morning After, The, *997;* Nine to Five, *345;* Old Gringo, The, *611;* On Golden Pond, *612;* Period of Adjustment, *356;* Rollover, *1011;* Stanley and Iris, *665;* Steelyard Blues, *386;* Tall Story, *391;* They Shoot Horses, Don't They?, *681;* Walk on the Wild Side, *695*

Fonda, Peter: Certain Fury, *24;* Deadfall, *968;* Dirty Mary, Crazy Larry, *39;* Easy Rider, *506;* Fatal Mission, *46;* Fighting Mad, *516;* Futureworld, *1053;* High-Ballin', *61;* Hired Hand, The, *1121;* Hostage Tower, The, *64;* Jungle Heat, *69;* Killer Force, *71;* Last Movie, The, *570;* Lilith, *575;* Mercenary Fighters, *84;* Montana, *599;* 92 in the Shade, *345;* Outlaw Blues, *352;* Race with the Devil, *878;* Rose Garden, The, *644;* South Beach, *1019;* Spasms, *889;* Split Image, *664;* Tammy and the Doctor, *677;* Trip, The, *688;* Wanda Nevada, *136;* Wild Angels, The, *139*

Fondacaro, Phil: Dollman vs. Demonic Toys, *1047*

Fondue, Stephanie: Cheerleaders, *254*

Fong, Benson: Charlie Chan in the Secret Service, *961;* Chinese Cat, The, *962;* Chinese Web, The, *25;* First Yank into Tokyo, *49;* Flower Drum Song, *917;* Girls! Girls! Girls!, *919;* Jinxed, *310;* Kung Fu—The Movie, *73;* Scarlet Clue, The, *1013;* Shanghai Cobra, The, *1014*

Fong, Leo: Blind Rage, *15;* Kill Point, *71;* Low Blow, *79*

Fontaine, Frank: Stella (1950), *667*

Fontaine, Jean: Sinister Urge, The, *116*

Fontaine, Joan: Beyond a Reasonable Doubt (1956), *955;* Bigamist, The, *461;* Born to Be Bad, *467;* Casanova's Big Night, *252;* Damsel in Distress, A, *913;* Decameron Nights, *263;* Gunga Din, *58;* Ivanhoe (1952), *68;* Jane Eyre (1944), *557;* Letter from an Unknown Woman, *573;* Maid's Night Out, The, *326;* Quality Street, *631;* Rebecca, *1009;* September Affair, *652;* Suspicion (1941), *1022;* Until They Sail, *692;* Users, The, *692;* Voyage to the Bottom of the Sea, *1087;* Women, The, *413*

Fontanel, Genevieve: Grain of Sand, The, *741*

Fontanne, Lynn: Guardsman, The, *291*

Fontes, Guilherme: Subway to the Stars, *791*

Foody, Ralph: Code of Silence, *27*

Foote, Hallie: Courtship, *490;* 1918, *607;* On Valentine's Day, *612*

Foran, Dick: Atomic Submarine, The, *1037;* Boy Meets Girl, *244;* Brighty of the Grand Canyon, *152;* Cherokee Strip, *1104;* Dangerous, *494;* Earthworm Tractors, *269;* Empty Holsters, *1111;* Fighting 69th, The, *48;* Guest Wife, *291;* House of the Seven Gables, The, *545;* Mummy's Hand, The, *867;* My Little Chickadee, *340;* Petrified Forest, The, *621;* Private Buckaroo, *935;* Ride 'em Cowboy, *368;* Riders of Death Valley, *1143;* Sisters, The (1938), *659;* Studs Lonigan, *671;* Winners of the West, *1165*

Forbes, Brenda: Man Upstairs, The, *327*

Forbes, Bryan: Colditz Story, The, *485;* League of Gentlemen, The, *317*

Forbes, Francine: Splatter University, *889*

Forbes, Gary: Wiz Kid, The, *413*

Forbes, Martin: Wiz Kid, The, *413*

Forbes, Mary: You Can't Cheat an Honest Man, *415*

Forbes, Michelle: Kalifornia, *561*

Forbes, Ralph: Lilies of the Field (1930), *575;* Phantom Broadcast, The, *1005;* Riptide, *640;* Three Musketeers, The (1935), *128*

Forbes, Scott: Operation Pacific, *614*

Force, John: Visitors, The, *901*

Ford, Anitra: Big Bird Cage, The, *12;* Invasion of the Bee Girls, *1059*

Ford, Constance: Last Hunt, The, *1126;* Rome Adventure, *643;* Summer Place, A, *672*

Ford, Faith: Murder So Sweet, *601;* You Talkin' to Me, *141*

Ford, Francis: Bad Lands, *1095;* Man from Monterey, The, *1131*

Ford, Glenn: Affair in Trinidad, *442;* Americano, The, *1098;* Appointment in Honduras, *6;* Big Heat, The, *12;* Blackboard Jungle, The, *463;* Border Shootout, *1100;* Cimarron (1960), *1105;* Courtship of Eddie's Father, The, *260;* Day of the Assassin, *33;* Don't Go Near the Water, *267;* Experiment in Terror, *974;* Fastest Gun Alive, The, *1112;* Final Verdict, *516;* Four Horsemen of the Apocalypse, *52;* Gazebo, The, *283;* Gilda, *527;* Happy Birthday to Me, *848;* Human Desire, *546;* Interrupted Melody, *925;* Is Paris Burning?, *554;* It Started With a Kiss, *308;* Jubal, *1124;* Lady in Question, *568;* Loves of Carmen, The, *582;* Lust for Gold, *1130;* Man from Colorado, The, *1131;* Man from the Alamo, The, *1132;* Pocketful of Miracles, *359;* Raw Nerve, *103;* Return of October, The, *366;* Rounders, The, *1146;* Sacketts, The, *1146;* Santee, *1147;* Smith!, *1150;* So Ends Our Night, *661;* Stolen Life, A, *668;* Superman, *1081;* Teahouse of the August Moon, The, *392;* Texas, *1155;* 3:10 to Yuma, *1157;* Torpedo Run, *131;* Violent Men, The, *1161;* Virus, *1087;* Visitor, The, *1087;* White Tower, The, *701*

Ford, Harrison: American Graffiti, *226;* Apocalypse Now, *6;* Blade Runner, *1039;* Conversation, The, *963;* Empire Strikes Back, The, *1049;* Force Ten from Navarone, *51;* Frantic (1988), *978;* Frisco Kid, The, *1114;* Fugitive, The (1993), *53;* Hanover Street, *536;* Heroes, *540;* Indiana Jones and the Last Crusade, *1058;* Indiana Jones and the Temple of Doom, *1058;* More American Graffiti, *599;* Mosquito Coast, The, *600;* Patriot Games, *97;* Possessed, The (1977), *876;* Presumed Innocent, *1007;* Raiders of the Lost Ark, *1073;* Regarding Henry, *637;* Return of the Jedi, *1074;* Star Wars, *1079;* Witness, *1032;* Working Girl, *414*

Ford, Harrison: Shadows, *654*

Ford, John: American Film Institute Life Achievement Awards, The, *418;* Great American West, *425*

Ford, Maria: Deathstalker IV: Match of the Titans, *1046;* Final Judgment, *977;* Naked Obsession, *1000;* Saturday Night Special, *111;* Stripped to Kill II, *891*

Ford, Marshall: Fast Money, *46*

Ford, Mick: Scum, *650*

Ford, Paul: Advise and Consent, *442;* Big Hand for the Little Lady, A, *1098;* Comedians, The, *486;* Matchmaker, The, *329;* Music Man, The, *932;* Naked City, The, *1000;* Russians Are Coming, the Russians Are Coming, The, *371;* Sgt. Bilko (TV Series), *376;* Spy with a Cold Nose, The, *385;* Teahouse of the August Moon, The, *392;* Who's Got the Action?, *411*

Ford, Ross: Blue Canadian Rockies, *1099;* Jungle Patrol, *69;* Project Moon Base, *1072;* Reform School Girl, *104*

Ford, Ruth: Eyes of the Amaryllis, *165*

Ford, Terrence: Escape from Survival Zone, *45*

Ford, Val: Dead Man Out, *497*

Ford, Wallace: All Through the Night, *3;* Ape Man, The, *809;* Backdoor to Heaven, *454;* Blood on the Sun, *15;* Dead Reckoning (1947), *34;* Employees' Entrance, *271;* Freaks, *843;* Jericho, *557;* Last Hurrah, The, *569;* Lawless Street, A, *1127;* Lost Patrol, The, *79;* Matchmaker, The, *329;* Maverick Queen, The, *1133;* Mummy's Hand, The, *867;* Mysterious Mr. Wong, The, *88;* One Frightened Night, *1003;* Patch of Blue, A, *619;* Possessed (1931), *625;* Rainmaker, The, *634;* Set-Up, The, *1013;* Spellbound, *1019;* Swing It, Sailor, *390;* T-Men, *676*

Forde, Jessica: Four Adventures of Reinette and Mirabelle, *738*

Foree, Ken: Dawn of the Dead, *830;* From Beyond, *844;* Leatherface—the Texas Chainsaw Massacre III, *860*

Foreman, Deborah: April Fool's Day, *810;* Destroyer, *833;* Experts, The, *273;* Friends, Lovers & Lunatics, *281;* Lobster Man from Mars, *320;* Love in the Present Tense, *581;* Lunatics: A Love Story, *324;* My Chauffeur, *339;* 3:15—The Moment of Truth, *128;* Valley Girl, *404;* Waxwork, *902*

Foreman, Michelle: Sunset Strip, *674*

Forest, Andy J.: Bridge to Hell, *19*

Forest, Delphine: Europa, Europa, *735*

Forest, Mark: Goliath and the Dragon, *56*

Forest, Michael: Atlas, *7*

Forman, Carol: Superman—The Serial, *1081*
Forman, Joey: Nude Bomb, The, *347*
Forman, Milos: Heartburn, *295;* New Year's Day, *605*
Foronjy, Richard: Carlito's Way, *23;* Morning After, The, *997;* Prince of the City, *627*
Forque, Veronica: Kika, *751*
Forrest, Frederic: Against the Wall, *442;* Best Kept Secrets, *11;* Calamity Jane (1984), *1103;* Cat Chaser, *24;* Citizen Cohn, *482;* Deliberate Stranger, The, *499;* Don Is Dead, The, *40;* Double Exposure (1989), *504;* Double Obsession, *972;* Falling Down, *513;* Gotham, *980;* Hammett, *981;* It Lives Again, *857;* Lonesome Dove, *1129;* Music Box, The, *999;* One from the Heart, *934;* Permission to Kill, *98;* Quo Vadis? (1985), *632;* Rain without Thunder, *634;* Return, *638;* Rose, The, *937;* Stacking, *665;* Stone Boy, The, *668;* Tucker: A Man and His Dream, *689;* Two Jakes, The, *1028;* Valentino Returns, *693;* Valley Girl, *404;* When the Legends Die, *1163;* Where Are the Children?, *1031*
Forrest, Frederick: Trauma, *897*
Forrest, Mike: Shark Hunter, The, *114*
Forrest, Sally: Vengeance Valley, *1161*
Forrest, Steve: Battle Circus, *456;* Captain America (1979), *22;* Deerslayer, The, *1108;* Flaming Star, *1113;* Gunsmoke: Return to Dodge, *1118;* Hatfields and the McCoys, The, *1119;* Heller in Pink Tights, *1120;* Last of the Mohicans (1985), *1126;* Mommie Dearest, *598;* Roughnecks, *109;* Spies Like Us, *384*
Forrest, William: Masked Marvel, The, *83*
Forster, Kathrine: Hollywood Harry, *299*
Forster, Robert: Alligator, *808;* Avalanche, *7;* Black Hole, The, *1039;* Body Chemistry 3: Point of Seduction, *957;* Committed, *824;* Counterforce, *30;* Death Squad, The, *35;* Delta Force, The, *36;* Diplomatic Immunity, *39;* Don Is Dead, The, *40;* Goliath Awaits, *56;* Hollywood Harry, *299;* Justine, *561;* Lady in Red, *74;* Medium Cool, *591;* Once a Hero, *94;* Peacemaker, *1069;* Reflections in a Golden Eye, *637;* Satan's Princess, *882;* Sex, Love, and Cold Hard Cash, *1014;* South Beach, *1019;* Stalking Moon, The, *1152;* Standing Tall, *1153;* 29th Street, *401*
Forster, Rudolph: Threepenny Opera, The, *794*
Forsyth, Rosemary: Columbo: Murder by the Book, *963;* Gladiator, The, *55;* Gray Lady Down, *57;* Texas Across the River, *1155;* War Lord, The, *137;* Whatever Happened to Aunt Alice?, *902*
Forsyth, Tony: Wonderland, *706*
Forsythe, Drew: Test of Love, A, *679*
Forsythe, Henderson: Crisis at Central High, *491*
Forsythe, John: Ambassador's Daughter, The, *226;* And Justice for All, *447;* Cruise into Terror, *964;* Escape from Fort Bravo, *1111;* In Cold Blood, *985;* Madame X (1966), *584;* Scrooged, *374;* Sizzle, *659;* Terror on the 40th Floor, *1023;* Topaz, *1026;* Trouble with Harry, The, *399*
Forsythe, Stephen: Hatchet for the Honeymoon, *848*
Forsythe, William: American Me, *446;* Career Opportunities, *251;* Dead-Bang, *33;* Dick Tracy (1990), *38;* Extreme Prejudice, *45;* Gun in Betty Lou's Handbag, The, *292;* Out for Justice, *96;* Patty Hearst, *620;* Raising Arizona, *364;* Relentless 3, *1010;* Savage Dawn, *111;* Smokey Bites the Dust, *382;* Stone Cold, *120;* Torrents of Spring, *686;* Waterdance, The, *696;* Weeds, *697*
Fortell, Albert: Scandalous (1988), *1012*
Fortescue, Gregory: Carrier, *821*
Forth, Jane: Trash, *687*
Fortune, John: Bloodbath at the House of Death, *242*
Foschi, Massimo: Cannibal, *820*
Fosse, Bob: Affairs of Dobie Gillis, The, *906;* Give a Girl a Break, *919;* Kiss Me Kate, *927;* Little Prince, The, *929;* My Sister Eileen, *932*
Fossey, Brigitte: Blue Country, *719;* Chanel Solitaire, *479;* Enigma, *44;* Forbidden Games, *737;* Going Places, *741;* Honor Among Thieves, *63;* La Boum, *753;* Man Who Loved Women, The (1977), *765;* Wanderer, The, *802*
Foster, Barry: Divorce His: Divorce Hers, *502;* Frenzy, *979;* Quiet Day in Belfast, A, *632;* Three Kinds of Heat, *128;* Whistle Blower, The, *1031*
Foster, Dianne: Kentuckian, The, *1124;* King of the Roaring Twenties, *565;* Last Hurrah, The, *569*
Foster, Eric: Grandma's House, *980*
Foster, Frances: Enemy Territory, *44*
Foster, Gloria: Man and Boy, *1131;* To All My Friends on Shore, *684*
Foster, Helen: Road to Ruin, The (1928), *641*
Foster, Jodie: Accused, The, *441;* Alice Doesn't Live Here Anymore, *444;* Backtrack, *454;* Blood of Others, The, *464;* Bugsy Malone, *155;* Candleshoe, *155;* Carny, *475;* Five Corners, *517;* Foxes, *521;* Freaky Friday, *168;* Hotel New Hampshire, The, *544;* Little Girl Who Lives Down the Lane, The, *992;* Little Man Tate, *182;* Maverick, *1133;* Mesmerized, *996;* Napoleon and Samantha, *190;* O'Hara's Wife, *611;* Shadows and Fog, *654;* Siesta, *1016;* Silence of the Lambs, *1016;* Smile, Jenny, You're Dead, *661;* Sommersby, *662;* Stealing Home, *667;* Svengali (1983), *674;* Taxi Driver, *1023;* Tom Sawyer (1973), *946*
Foster, Julia: Alfie, *224;* Half a Sixpence, *921*
Foster, Kimberly: Broken Trust, *959;* It Takes Two, *308*
Foster, Lisa: Blade Master, The, *15*
Foster, Meg: Backstab, *953;* Best Kept Secrets, *11;* Best of the Best 2, *11;* Carny, *475;* Different Story, A, *501;* Diplomatic Immunity, *39;* Emerald Forest, The, *44;* Futurekick, *1053;* James Dean—A Legend in His Own Time, *556;* Jezebel's Kiss, *987;* Leviathan, *860;* Masters of the Universe, *186;* Osterman Weekend, The, *96;* Project: Shadowchaser, *101;* Relentless, *1010;* Relentless II: Dead On, *879;* Stepfather II, *890;* They Live, *895;* Ticket to Heaven, *683;* Wind, The (1986), *1032*
Foster, Preston: American Empire, *1093;* Annie Oakley (1935), *1093;* Big Cat, The, *12;* Doctor X, *836;* Guadalcanal Diary, *58;* Harvey Girls, The, *922;* I Am a Fugitive from a Chain Gang, *547;* Informer, The, *552;* Kansas City Confidential, *988;* Ladies They Talk About, *567;* Last Days of Pompeii, The (1935), *569;* Last Mile, The, *570;* My Friend Flicka, *190;* Ramrod, *1140;* Sea Devils, *112;* Time Travelers, The, *1084*
Foster, Susanna: Phantom of the Opera (1943), *874*
Foucheux, Rick: Invader, *1059*
Foulger, Byron: Arizona, *1094;* Hoppy Serves a Writ, *1121;* Ridin' on a Rainbow, *1144*
Foures, Alain: Rape of Love (L'Amour Violé), *779*
Fowlds, Derek: Over the Hill, *352*
Fowle, Susannah: Getting of Wisdom, The, *526*
Fowley, Douglas: Along the Navajo Trail, *1093;* Bar 20, *1096;* Denver Kid, *1109;* Desperate, *969;* Gun Smugglers, *1117;* High and the Mighty, The, *541;* Homebodies, *851;* Hucksters, The, *545;* Kansas Pacific, *1124;* Naked Jungle, The, *88;* One Body Too Many, *1003;* Poor White Trash, *624;* Red River Shore, *1142;* Rider from Tucson, *1143;* Ridin' Down the Trail, *1144;* Scared to Death, *883;* Sunset on the Desert, *1154*
Fox, Bernard: House of the Dead, *853;* Private Eyes, The, *361*
Fox, David: Ordinary Magic, *614*
Fox, Earle: Scarlet Dawn, *649*
Fox, Edward: Anastasia: The Mystery of Anna, *447;* Battle of Britain, *9;* Big Sleep, The (1978), *955;* Bounty, The, *18;* Cat and the Canary, The (1978), *960;* Crucifer of Blood, *964;* Day of the Jackal, The, *966;* Dresser, The, *505;* Duellists, The, *42;* Edward and Mrs. Simpson, *507;* Force Ten from Navarone, *51;* Gandhi, *524;* Mirror Crack'd, The, *996;* Never Say Never Again, *89;* Robin Hood (1991), *107;* Shaka Zulu, *654;* Shooting Party, The, *656;* Squeeze, The (1977), *665;* Wild Geese II, *139*
Fox, Huckleberry: Blue Yonder, The, *151;* Misunderstood (1984), *598*
Fox, James: Absolute Beginners, *906;* Afraid of the Dark, *950;* Chase, The (1966), *479;* Farewell to the King, *46;* Greystoke: The Legend of Tarzan, Lord of the Apes, *58;* Heart of Darkness, *538;* High Season, *297;* Hostage (1992), *64;*

Isadora (1969), *554;* King Rat, *565;* Mighty Quinn, The, *85;* Patriot Games, *97;* Performance, *1005;* Remains of the Day, *637;* Russia House, The, *646;* Servant, The, *652;* Thoroughly Modern Millie, *945;* Whistle Blower, The, *1031*

Fox, John: Truly Tasteless Jokes, *400*

Fox, Kerry: Angel at My Table, An, *447;* Last Days of Chez Nous, The, *569;* Rainbow Warrior, *1008*

Fox, Linda: Big Bust Out, The, *12*

Fox, Michael J.: Back to the Future, *1037;* Back to the Future II, *1037;* Back to the Future III, *1037;* Bright Lights, Big City, *470;* Casualties of War, *477;* Doc Hollywood, *265;* For Love or Money, *279;* Greedy, *290;* Hard Way, The (1991), *293;* High School, USA, *297;* Life with Mikey, *318;* Light of Day, *575;* Poison Ivy (1985), *359;* Secret of My Success, The, *375;* Teen Wolf, *892*

Fox, Morgan: Flesh Gordon 2: Flesh Gordon meets the Cosmic Cheerleaders, *1052*

Fox, Peter: Minor Miracle, A, *187*

Fox, Samantha: Night to Dismember, A, *870*

Fox, Sidney: Midnight (1934), *593;* Murders in the Rue Morgue (1932), *867*

Fox, Virginia: Blacksmith, The/Cops, *240;* Buster Keaton Festival: Vol. 1, *248;* Buster Keaton Festival: Vol. 2, *248;* Buster Keaton Festival: Vol. 3, *248;* Buster Keaton: The Golden Years, *248*

Foxworth, Robert: Ants!, *809;* Beyond the Stars, *1039;* Black Marble, The, *463;* Deathmoon, *832;* Double Standard, *504;* Frankenstein (1973), *842;* Invisible Strangler, *857;* Prophecy, *877*

Foxx, Elizabeth: School Spirit, *374*

Foxx, Redd: Harlem Nights, *59;* Norman...Is That You?, *346*

Foy Jr., Eddie: Bells Are Ringing, *908;* Farmer Takes a Wife, The, *916;* Four Jacks and a Jill, *918;* Gidget Goes Hawaiian, *286;* Lucky Me, *929;* Pajama Game, The, *934;* 30 Is a Dangerous Age, Cynthia, *394*

Foy Willing and the Riders of the Purple Sage: Twilight in the Sierras, *1159*

Frailey, David: Love Street, *582*

Frakes, Jonathan: Star Trek: The Next Generation (TV Series), *1079*

Frampton, Peter: Sgt. Pepper's Lonely Hearts Club Band, *939*

Francen, Victor: J'Accuse, *749;* Madame Curie, *584;* San Antonio, *1147;* Tuttles of Tahiti, The, *400*

Francescatto, Paula: Rock 'n' Roll Nightmare, *881*

Francine, Anne: Savages (1973), *373*

Franciosa, Anthony: Across 110th Street, *1;* Assault on a Queen, *7;* Backstreet Dreams, *454;* Career, *475;* Cricket, The, *726;* Curse of the Black Widow, *828;* Death House, *35;* Death Wish II, *36;* Double Threat, *504;* Drowning Pool, The, *972;* Face in the Crowd, A, *512;* Firepower, *49;* Ghost in the Noonday Sun, *285;* Long Hot Summer, The (1958), *578;* Naked Maja, The, *603;* Period of Adjustment, *356;* Rio Conchos, *1145;* Side Show, *886;* Stagecoach (1986), *1152;* Summer Heat (1983), *672;* This Could Be the Night, *394;* Unsane, *899;* World Is Full of Married Men, The, *707*

Francis, Anne: Bad Day at Black Rock, *454;* Battle Cry, *9;* Blackboard Jungle, The, *463;* Born Again, *466;* Don't Go Near the Water, *267;* Double-O Kid, The, *41;* Forbidden Planet, *1052;* Haunts of the Very Rich, *1055;* Laguna Heat, *990;* Lion in the Streets, A, *575;* Little Vegas, *319;* Pancho Villa, *1138;* Return, *638;* Summer Holiday, *942;* Susan Slept Here, *389*

Francis, Arlene: Murders in the Rue Morgue (1932), *867;* One, Two, Three, *350;* Thrill of It All, The, *396*

Francis, Bev: Pumping Iron II: The Women, *630*

Francis, Carol Ann: Shades of Love: Champagne for Two, *653*

Francis, Connie: Where the Boys Are, *409*

Francis, Jan: Champions, *479;* Dracula (1979), *837*

Francis, Kay: Cocoanuts, *257;* In Name Only, *550;* It's a Date, *925;* Little Men (1940), *576;* Wonder Bar, *948*

Francis, Noel: Stone of Silver Creek, *1153*

Francis, Robert: Caine Mutiny, The, *473;* Long Grey Line, The, *578*

Franciscus, James: Amazing Dobermans, *146;* Beneath the Planet of the Apes, *1039;* Cat O'Nine Tails, *960;* Good Guys Wear Black, *56;* Greek Tycoon, The, *533;* Killer Fish, *71;* Man Inside, The (1984), *81;* Marooned, *1065;* Miracle of the White Stallions, *187;* Nightkill, *1001;* Secret Weapons, *113;* Valley of Gwangi, *1087;* When Time Ran Out!, *1031*

Francks, Don: Christmas Wife, The, *482;* Drying Up the Streets, *505;* Finian's Rainbow, *916;* Fish Hawk, *517;* Terminal Choice, *893*

Franco, Angel Fernandez: Street Warriors II, *671*

Franco, Jess: Demoniac, *832;* Ilsa, the Wicked Warden, *855*

Franco, Margarita: Three Ninjas Kick Back, *211*

Franco, Ramon: Kiss Me a Killer, *989;* Shattered Image, *1014*

François, Jacques: Too Shy to Try, *796*

Francois Montagut: Strangers, *669*

Franey, Billy: Somewhere in Sonora, *1151*

Frank, Ben: Hollywood Zap, *299*

Frank, Charles: Guide for the Married Woman, A, *291;* LBJ: The Early Years, *571;* Russkies, *371;* Tarantulas—The Deadly Cargo, *892*

Frank, Diana: In the Time of Barbarians II, *1058*

Frank, Evelyn: World of Strangers, A, *805*

Frank, Gary: Enemy Territory, *44;* Enola Gay: The Men, the Mission, the Atomic Bomb, *510*

Frank, Horst: Head, The (1959), *849*

Frank, Joanna: Always (1984), *225*

Frankel, Mark: Season of Giants, A, *650;* Young Catherine, *708*

Franken, Al: Franken and Davis at Stockton State, *280;* One More Saturday Night, *350*

Franken, Steve: Can't Buy Me Love, *250;* Hardly Working, *293;* Sky Heist, *117;* Terror Out of the Sky, *894;* Time Travelers, The, *1084;* Transylvania Twist, *399*

Frankeur, Paul: Jour de Fête, *750;* Le Gentleman D'Espom (Duke of the Derby), *757;* Milky Way, The (1970), *767;* Un Singe en Hiver (A Monkey in Winter), *798*

Frankham, David: Return of the Fly, The, *880*

Franklin, Carl: Eye of the Eagle 3, *46*

Franklin, Diane: Better Off Dead, *237;* Last American Virgin, The, *315;* Terror Vision, *1082*

Franklin, Don: Fast Forward, *916*

Franklin, Gloria: Drums of Fu Manchu, *42*

Franklin, John: Children of the Corn, *823*

Franklin, Pamela: And Soon the Darkness, *952;* Flipper's New Adventure, *167;* Food of the Gods, *1052;* Horse Without a Head, The, *175;* Legend of Hell House, The, *860;* Night of the Following Day, The, *1001;* Prime of Miss Jean Brodie, The, *361;* Satan's School for Girls, *882;* Tiger Walks, A, *211;* Witching, The (Necromancy), *904*

Franklyn, Sabina: Worst Witch, The, *219*

Franklyn, William: Enemy from Space, *1049*

Franks, Chloe: Littlest Horse Thieves, The, *184;* Who Slew Auntie Roo?, *903*

Frann, Mary: Fatal Charm, *976*

Franz, Arthur: Abbott and Costello Meet the Invisible Man, *221;* Amazing Howard Hughes, The, *445;* Atomic Submarine, The, *1037;* Flight to Mars, *1052;* Hellcats of the Navy, *60;* Invaders from Mars (1953), *1059;* Jungle Patrol, *69;* Member of the Wedding, The, *592;* Monster on the Campus, *866;* Sands of Iwo Jima, *111;* Young Lions, The, *708*

Franz, Dennis: Blow Out, *957;* Die Hard 2: Die Harder, *39;* Kiss Shot, *566;* Package, The, *1004;* Psycho II, *877*

Franz, Eduard: Latin Lovers, *928;* Magnificent Yankee, The, *585;* Scar, The, *649*

Fraser, Bill: Captain's Paradise, The, *250;* Corn Is Green, The (1979), *488*

Fraser, Brendan: Airheads, *906;* Encino Man, *271;* School Ties, *649;* Twenty Bucks, *401;* With Honors, *412*

Fraser, Duncan: Call of the Wild (1992), *474*

Fraser, Elisabeth: Sammy, the Way-Out Seal, *201;* Sgt. Bilko (TV Series), *376;* Two for the Seesaw, *690*
Fraser, Hugh: Poirot (Series), *1006*
Fraser, John: Repulsion, *879;* Study in Terror, A, *1021;* Tunes of Glory, *689*
Fraser, Liz: Adventures of a Private Eye, *222;* Carry on Cruising, *251;* Chicago Joe and the Showgirl, *480;* Seaside Swingers, *938*
Fraser, Phyllis: Winds of the Wasteland, *1165*
Fraser, Richard: Bedlam, *812;* White Pongo (a.k.a. Blond Gorilla), *902*
Fraser, Ronald: Flight of the Phoenix, The, *51*
Fraser, Sally: Dangerous Charter, *32;* It's a Dog's Life, *177;* War of the Colossal Beast, *1088*
Fratkin, Stuart: Remote, *198*
Frawley, William: Abbott and Costello Meet the Invisible Man, *221;* Adventures of Huckleberry Finn, The (1939), *143;* Babe Ruth Story, The, *453;* Blondie in Society, *241;* Fighting Seabees, The, *48;* Flame of the Barbary Coast, *50;* Harmony Lane, *922;* I Love Lucy (TV Series), *303;* Lemon Drop Kid, The, *317;* Monsieur Verdoux, *336;* Rancho Notorious, *1140;* Something to Sing About, *940;* Whistling in Brooklyn, *410*
Frazee, Jane: Buck Privates, *246;* Grand Canyon Trail, *1116;* On the Old Spanish Trail, *1137;* Springtime in the Sierras, *1152;* Under California Stars, *1160*
Frazer, Robert: Clutching Hand, The, *27;* Gangs of Sonora, *1115;* White Zombie, *903*
Frazer, Rupert: Back Home, *147;* Girl on a Swing, The, *980*
Frazier, Ron: Dead Ahead: The Exxon Valdez Disaster, *497;* Head Office, *294*
Frazier, Sheila: Firehouse (1972), *49;* Lazarus Syndrome, The, *571;* Superfly, *122;* Superfly T.N.T., *122;* Three the Hard Way, *129*
Frechette, Mark: Zabriskie Point, *709*
Frederick, Lynne: Amazing Mr. Blunden, The, *146;* Phase IV, *1070;* Prisoner of Zenda, The (1979), *361;* Schizo, *883*
Frederick, Vicki: All the Marbles, *225;* Body Rock, *909;* Chopper Chicks in Zombietown, *823;* Stewardess School, *386*
Fredro: Strapped, *670*
Freed, Alan: Go, Johnny, Go!, *920;* Rock, Rock, Rock, *937*
Freed, Bert: Barracuda, *1038;* Billy Jack, *13;* Gazebo, The, *283;* Wild in the Streets, *1089*
Freed, Sam: Call Me, *959*
Freeman Jr., Al: Detective, The (1968), *500;* Malcolm X, *586;* My Sweet Charlie, *602;* Seven Hours to Judgment, *113*
Freeman, Eric: Silent Night, Deadly Night Part 2, *886*
Freeman, J. E.: Hard Traveling, *536;* Memphis, *592*
Freeman, Joan: Fastest Guitar Alive, The, *1112;* Friday the 13th—The Final Chapter, *843;* Mooncussers, *189;* Tower of London (1962), *897*
Freeman, Kathleen: Adventures of Topper, The, *223;* Disorderly Orderly, The, *265;* Dragnet (1987), *268;* House by the River, *984;* In the Mood, *306;* Ladies' Man, The, *314;* Love is Better Than Ever, *929;* Nutty Professor, The, *348;* Reckless Kelly, *365;* Rounders, The, *1146;* Willies, The, *903;* Wrong Guys, The, *414*
Freeman, Mona: Black Beauty (1946), *150;* Branded, *1101;* Copper Canyon, *1106;* Dear Wife, *263;* Heiress, The, *539;* Jumping Jacks, *311*
Freeman, Morgan: Bonfire of the Vanities, *466;* Clean and Sober, *484;* Clinton and Nadine, *26;* Death of a Prophet, *498;* Driving Miss Daisy, *505;* Glory, *528;* Johnny Handsome, *69;* Lean on Me, *571;* Power of One, The, *625;* Robin Hood: Prince of Thieves, *108;* Roll of Thunder, Hear My Cry, *642;* Street Smart, *670;* That Was Then...This Is Now, *680;* Unforgiven (1992), *1160*
Freeman, Paul: Aces: Iron Eagle III, *1;* Eminent Domain, *973;* Hit Woman: The Double Edge, *63;* May Wine, *330;* Raiders of the Lost Ark, *1073;* Sakharov, *647;* Sender, The, *884;* Shanghai Surprise, *377;* Whose Child Am I?, *701;* Without a Clue, *413*
Frehley, Ace: Kiss Meets the Phantom of the Park, *859*
Freiss, Stephane: Does This Mean We're Married?, *266;* King's Whore, The, *566*
French, Bill: Killing Edge, The, *1061*
French, Bruce: Pipe Dreams, *622*
French, George: Tarzan of the Apes, *125*
French, Leigh: White Line Fever, *139*
French, Valerie: Jubal, *1124*
French, Victor: Charro!, *1104;* House on Skull Mountain, *853;* Little House on the Prairie (TV Series), *181*
Fresh, Dave: Ganjasaurus Rex, *845*
Fresnay, Pierre: César, *723;* Fanny (1932), *736;* Grand Illusion, *742;* Le Corbeau, *757;* Marius, *765;* Monsieur Vincent, *768*
Fresson, Bernard: French Connection II, The, *53;* Hiroshima, Mon Amour, *744;* Voyage of Terror: The Achille Lauro Affair, *694*
Frewer, Matt: Far from Home, *975;* Honey, I Shrunk the Kids, *175;* Max Headroom, *1065;* Positively True Adventures of the Alleged Texas Cheerleader-Murdering Mom, The, *360;* Short Time, *378;* Taking of Beverly Hills, The, *124*
Frey, Glenn: Let's Get Harry, *573*
Frey, Leonard: Boys in the Band, The, *468;* Fiddler on the Roof, *916;* Where the Buffalo Roam, *409*
Frey, Sami: Band of Outsiders, *715;* Black Widow, *955;* César and Rosalie, *723;* Nea (A Young Emmanuelle), *771;* Sand and Blood, *783;* Seven Deadly Sins, The, *785;* Sweet Movie, *792*
Freyd, Bernard: Alexina, *711*
Fricker, Brenda: Field, The, *516;* Home Alone 2: Lost in New York, *175;* My Left Foot, *602;* So I Married an Axe Murderer, *382;* Utz, *693*
Frid, Jonathan: Best of Dark Shadows, The, *813;* Dark Shadows (TV Series), *829;* House of Dark Shadows, *852;* Seizure, *884*
Fridell, Squire: Pink Motel, *357*
Friedkin, Joel: False Paradise, *1112*
Friedman, Budd: Gross Jokes, *291*
Friedman, Peter: Blink, *956;* Single White Female, *1016*
Friedrich, John: Final Terror, The, *841;* Small Circle of Friends, A, *660;* Thornbirds, The, *682;* Wanderers, The, *695*
Friell, Vincent: Restless Natives, *366*
Friels, Colin: Class Action, *962;* Darkman, *1044;* Grievous Bodily Harm, *533;* Ground Zero, *981;* High Tide, *541;* Kangaroo, *562;* Malcolm, *327;* Monkey Grip, *598;* Warm Nights on a Slow Moving Train, *696*
Friend, Philip: Pimpernel Smith, *99*
Frijda, Nelly: Question of Silence, A, *779*
Fritsch, Thomas: Full Hearts and Empty Pockets, *739*
Fritsch, Willy: Spies (1928), *788;* Woman in the Moon (a.k.a. Girl in the Moon; By Rocket to the Moon), *805*
Frizell, Lou: Stalking Moon, The, *1152;* Summer of '42, *672*
Gert, Gert Fröbe*$Frobe,*: $ (Dollars), *971;* Goldfinger, *56;* I Killed Rasputin, *746;* Is Paris Burning?, *554;* Serpent's Egg, The, *652;* Ten Little Indians (1975), *1023;* Those Daring Young Men in Their Jaunty Jalopies, *394;* Those Magnificent Men in Their Flying Machines, *394;* Thousand Eyes of Dr. Mabuse, The, *1083;* Tonio Kroger, *796*
Froler, Samuel: Best Intentions, The, *717*
Frome, Milton: Ride 'em Cowgirl, *1143*
Fromholz, Steve: Positive I.D., *1006*
Fromin, Troy: Adventures of the Kung Fu Rascals, The, *223*
Frost, Lindsay: Dead Heat, *830;* Monolith, *1066*
Frost, Sadie: Bram Stoker's Dracula, *819;* Cisco Kid, The, *1105;* Splitting Heirs, *384*
Frost, Terry: Atom Man vs. Superman, *7;* Ghost Town Renegades, *1115;* Waterfront, *697*
Froud, Toby: Labyrinth, *1061*
Fry, Stephen: Jeeves and Wooster (TV Series), *309*
Fry, Steven: Peter's Friends, *621*
Frye, Brittain: Hide and Go Shriek, *850*

Frye, Dwight: Bride of Frankenstein, *819;* Crime of Dr. Crespi, The, *826;* Dead-Men Walk, *830;* Dracula (1931), *837;* Drums of Fu Manchu, *42;* Invisible Man, The, *856;* Vampire Bat, The, *899*
Frye, Virgil: Dead Aim (1973), *1108;* Running Hot, *645;* Up from the Depths, *899*
Fryer, Eric: Terry Fox Story, The, *679*
Fuchsberger, Joachim: Curse of the Yellow Snake, The, *965*
Fudge, Alan: Children of An Lac, The, *480;* My Demon Lover, *339*
Fugard, Athol: Meetings with Remarkable Men, *591;* Road to Mecca, The, *641*
Fuizat, Allen: For the Love of Benji, *167*
Fuji, Tatsuya: In the Realm of Passion, *747;* In the Realm of the Senses, *747*
Fujioka, Hiroshi: Ghost Warrior, *55;* K2, *70*
Fujiwara, Kei: Tetsuo: The Iron Man, *793*
Fujuita, Susumu: Sanshiro Sugata, *783*
Full Force: House Party, *923*
Fuller, Barbara: Red Menace, The, *636*
Fuller, Brook: When Wolves Cry, *699*
Fuller, Dolores: Glen or Glenda, *528;* Jail Bait (1954), *68*
Fuller, Jonathan: Pit and the Pendulum, The (1991), *875*
Fuller, Lance: Apache Woman, *1094;* Bride and the Beast, The, *19;* Kentucky Rifle, *1124*
Fuller, Penny: Cat on a Hot Tin Roof (1985), *477;* Elephant Man, The (1982), *508;* George Washington: The Forging of a Nation, *526;* Lois Gibbs and the Love Canal, *577;* Miss Rose White, *596;* Piano for Mrs. Cimino, A, *622*
Fuller, Robert: Brain from Planet Arous, The, *1040;* Donner Pass: The Road to Survival, *1109;* Maverick, *1133;* Return of the Seven, *1142;* Whatever Happened to Aunt Alice?, *902*
Fuller, Samuel: Last Movie, The, *570;* Pierrot Le Fou, *777;* Return to Salem's Lot, A, *880;* State of Things, The, *789*
Fullerton, Fiona: Alice's Adventures in Wonderland, *145;* Ghost in Monte Carlo, A, *527;* Shaka Zulu, *654*
Fulton, Christina: Red Shoe Diaries 3: Another Woman's Lipstick, *637*
Fulton, Rikki: Girl in the Picture, The, *286*
Fulton, Todd: Escapes, *1049*
Funakoshi, Eiji: Fires on the Plain, *737*
Funicello, Annette: Babes in Toyland (1961), *147;* Back to the Beach, *907;* Beach Blanket Bingo, *908;* Beach Party, *908;* Bikini Beach, *909;* Elfego Baca: Six Gun Law, *1111;* Horsemasters, *176;* How to Stuff a Wild Bikini, *923;* Lots of Luck, *322;* Misadventures of Merlin Jones, The, *188;* Monkey's Uncle, The, *188;* Muscle Beach Party, *338;* Pee-Wee's Playhouse Christmas Special, *194;* Shaggy Dog, The, *203*
Funt, Allen: Best of Candid Camera, The, *235;* What Do You Say to a Naked Lady?, *408*
Furey, John: Friday the 13th, Part II, *843;* Mutant on the Bounty, *338*
Furlong, Edward: American Heart, *446;* Brainscan, *818;* Home of our Own, A, *542;* Pet Sematary Two, *874;* Terminator 2: Judgment Day, *1082*
Furman, Roger: Georgia, Georgia, *526*
Furneaux, Yvonne: Master of Ballantrae, The, *83;* Mummy, The (1959), *866;* Repulsion, *879;* Warriors, The (1955), *137*
Furness, Betty: Aggie Appleby, Maker of Men, *223;* Swing Time, *943*
Furness, Deborra-Lee: Shame (1987), *114;* Waiting, *695*
Furst, Stephen: Dream Team, The, *269;* Midnight Madness, *332;* National Lampoon's Class Reunion, *342;* Silent Rage, *116;* Take Down, *390;* Unseen, The, *899;* Up the Creek (1984), *403*
Furuya, Fumio: Sgt. Kabukiman N.Y.P.D., *114*
Fury, Billy: That'll Be the Day, *944*
Fury, Ed: Wild Women of Wongo, *1089*
Fyodora, Victoria: Target, *125*
Gabai, Richard: Hot Under the Collar, *302*
Gabay, Sasson: Impossible Spy, The, *985*
Gabel, Martin: First Deadly Sin, The, *977;* Lady in Cement, *989;* Lord Love a Duck, *321;* Mamie, *995;* Smile, Jenny, You're Dead, *661;* Thief, The (1952), *1024*
Gabel, Michael: On the Block, *1003*
Gabel, Scilla: Mill of the Stone Women, *865*
Gabela, Glen: Warriors From Hell, *137*
Gabl, Richard: Dinosaur Island, *1047*
Gabin, Jean: Cat, The (Le Chat), *722;* Four Bags Full, *738;* French Can Can, *738;* Golgotha, *741;* Grand Illusion, *742;* La Bête Humaine, *753;* Le Cas du Dr. Laurent, *757;* Le Gentleman D'Esporn (Duke of the Derby), *757;* Le Jour Se Leve (Daybreak) (1939), *757;* Le Plaisir, *758;* Les Miserables (1957), *759;* Lower Depths (1936), *762;* Melodie en Sous-Sol (The Big Grab), *766;* Pepe Le Moko, *777;* Stormy Waters, *789;* Un Singe en Hiver (A Monkey in Winter), *798;* Zou Zou, *949*
Gable, Christopher: Boy Friend, The, *909;* Music Lovers, The, *932;* Rainbow, The, *634*
Gable, Clark: Across the Wide Missouri, *1092;* Adventure, *441;* Any Number Can Play, *450;* Betrayed (1954), *11;* Boom Town, *466;* But Not For Me, *472;* Chained, *478;* China Seas, *25;* Command Decision, *487;* Comrade X, *258;* Dance, Fools, Dance, *493;* Dancing Lady, *913;* Forsaking All Others, *279;* Free Soul, A, *522;* Gone with the Wind, *530;* Hold Your Man, *542;* Homecoming (1948), *543;* Honky Tonk, *1121;* Hucksters, The, *545;* Idiot's Delight, *548;* It Happened One Night, *307;* It Started in Naples, *308;* Key to the City, *312;* King and Four Queens, The, *1125;* Laughing Sinners, *571;* Lone Star, *1129;* Love on the Run (1936), *323;* Manhattan Melodrama, *81;* Misfits, The, *595;* Mogambo, *86;* Mutiny on the Bounty (1935), *88;* Never Let Me Go, *89;* Night Nurse, *606;* No Man of Her Own, *345;* Painted Desert, The, *1138;* Possessed (1931), *625;* Red Dust, *636;* Run Silent, Run Deep, *109;* San Francisco, *648;* Saratoga, *372;* Soldier of Fortune, *118;* Somewhere I'll Find You, *662;* Strange Cargo, *669;* Strange Interlude (1932), *669;* Susan Lenox: Her Fall and Rise, *674;* Tall Men, The, *1154;* Teacher's Pet, *392;* Test Pilot, *679;* They Met in Bombay, *127;* To Please a Lady, *130;* Too Hot to Handle, *130;* Wife Vs. Secretary, *701*
Gable, John Clark: Bad Jim, *1095*
Gabor, Eva: Artists and Models, *229;* Don't Go Near the Water, *267;* Gigi, *919;* It Started With a Kiss, *308;* Last Time I Saw Paris, The, *570;* My Man Godfrey (1957), *340;* New Kind of Love, A, *343;* Princess Academy, The, *361;* Truth About Women, The, *689*
Gabor, Miklos: Father, *736*
Gabor, Zsa Zsa: Beverly Hillbillies, The, *237;* Boys' Night Out, *244;* Death of a Scoundrel, *498;* For the First Time, *918;* Lili, *928;* Lovely to Look At, *929;* Moulin Rouge, *600;* Pee-Wee's Playhouse Christmas Special, *194;* Picture Mommy Dead, *874;* Queen of Outer Space, *1073;* Touch of Evil, *1026;* We're Not Married, *408*
Gabriel, John: Sex and the College Girl, *653*
Gabrielle, Monique: Deathstalker II: Duel of the Titans, *1046;* Silk 2, *116*
Gabrio, Gabriel: Harvest, *743*
Gades, Antonio: Blood Wedding, *719;* El Amor Brujo, *733*
Gadsden, Jacqueline: It (1927), *307*
Gael, Anna: Therese and Isabelle, *794*
Gage, Patricia: Rabid, *878*
Gagnon, Jacques: Mon Oncle Antoine, *768*
Gaigalas, Regina: Body Melt, *817*
Gail, Max: Cardiac Arrest, *959;* D.C. Cab, *261;* Game of Love, The, *524;* Heartbreakers, *538;* Judgment in Berlin, *560;* Street Crimes, *121;* Where Are the Children?, *1031*
Gail, Tim: If Looks Could Kill (1986), *985*
Gaines, Boyd: Call Me, *959;* Sure Thing, The, *389*
Gaines, William M.: Comic Book Confidential, *421*
Gainey, M. C.: El Diablo, *1111;* Leap of Faith, *572;* Ulterior Motives, *133*

Gains, Courtney: Can't Buy Me Love, *250;* Memphis Belle (1990), *592*
Gainsbourg, Charlotte: Cement Garden, The, *478;* Le Petit Amour, *758;* Little Thief, The, *760;* Merci La Vie, *767*
Gainsbourg, Serge: Je Vous Aime (I Love You All), *749*
Galabru, Michel: Choice of Arms, A, *724;* Holes, The, *744;* Judge and the Assassin, The, *750;* Uranus, *798*
Galati, Tony: Dark Side, The, *829;* Darkside, The, *33*
Galbo, Cristina: Twice a Judas, *1159*
Gale, David: Brain, The (1988), *818;* Bride of Re-Animator, *819;* Guyver, The, *1055;* Re-Animator, *879*
Gale, Ed: Chopper Chicks in Zombietown, *823;* Howard the Duck, *1057;* Lifepod, *1063*
Gale, Jean: Miracle Rider, The, *1134*
Galiena, Anna: Being Human, *458;* Hairdresser's Husband, The, *742;* Jamon, Jamon, *749;* Rorret, *782*
Gallagher: Comedy Tonight, *257;* Gallagher—Melon Crazy, *282;* Gallagher—Over Your Head, *282;* Gallagher—Stuck in the 60s, *283;* Gallagher—The Bookkeeper, *283;* Gallagher—The Maddest, *283*
Gallagher, Bronagh: Commitments, The, *912*
Gallagher, Helen: Strangers When We Meet, *670*
Gallagher, Megan: In a Stranger's Hands, *985*
Gallagher, Peter: Caine Mutiny Court Martial, The, *473;* Dreamchild, *1048;* Fallen Angels, *513;* Idolmaker, The, *924;* Inconvenient Woman, An, *551;* Late for Dinner, *1062;* Long Day's Journey into Night (1987), *578;* Malice, *994;* Mother's Boys, *998;* Murder of Mary Phagan, The, *600;* Player, The, *358;* Sex, Lies and Videotape, *653;* Short Cuts, *657;* Skag, *659;* Summer Lovers, *672;* Watch It, *696*
Gallagher, Skeets: Bird of Paradise, *13;* Riptide, *640*
Galland, Philippe: Overseas, *774*
Gallardo, Carlos: El Mariachi, *733*
Galle, Matthew: Simple Justice, *658*
Gallego, Gina: My Demon Lover, *339*
Galligan, Zach: Caroline at Midnight, *960;* Gremlins, *1055;* Gremlins 2: The New Batch, *1055;* Lawrenceville Stories, The, *317;* Mortal Passions, *997;* Psychic, *1008;* Rebel Storm, *1074;* Round Trip to Heaven, *370;* Waxwork, *902;* Waxwork II: Lost in Time, *902*
Gallo, Mario: Revenge of the Ninja, *106*
Gallo, William: Night of the Demons, *869*
Galloway, Don: Riding with Death, *1074;* Rough Night in Jericho, *1146*
Gam, Rita: Distortions, *834;* King of Kings (1961), *565;* Mohawk, *1134;* Thief, The (1952), *1024*
Gamble, Mason: Dennis the Menace, *161*
Gambon, Michael: Clean Slate (1994), *256;* Cook, the Thief, His Wife & Her Lover, The, *259;* Missing Link, *85;* Toys, *398;* Turtle Diary, *400*
Gammell, Robin: Circle of Two, *482;* Project X, *1072;* Rituals, *1010*
Gammon, James: Adventures of Huck Finn, The (1993), *143;* Ballad of Gregorio Cortez, The, *1096;* Cabin Boy, *248;* Crisscross (1992), *491;* Deadly Encounter (1972), *34;* I Love You to Death, *304;* Laguna Heat, *990;* Leaving Normal, *572;* Major League, *326;* Major League II, *326;* Milagro Beanfield War, The, *594;* Roe vs. Wade, *642;* Running Cool, *110;* Silver Bullet, *886*
Gampu, Ken: Act of Piracy, *1;* African Rage, *3;* American Ninja IV: The Annihilation, *4;* Dingaka, *501;* King Solomon's Mines (1985), *73;* Naked Prey, The, *88;* Scavengers, *373*
Gandolfini, James: Angie, *448*
Gange, Ray: Rude Boy, *938*
Ganios, Tony: Porky's Revenge, *360;* Wanderers, The, *695*
Ganoung, Richard: Parting Glances, *618*
Gant, Richard: CB4, *252*
Ganus, Paul: Crash and Burn, *1043;* Silencer, The, *116*
Ganz, Bruno: American Friend, The, *712;* Children of Nature, *723;* Faraway, So Close, *736;* In the White City, *747;* Last Days of Chez Nous, The, *569;* Lumiere, *763;* Strapless, *670;* Wings of Desire, *804*
Gaon, Yehoram: Operation Thunderbolt, *95*
Garas, Kaz: Devastator, The, *37;* Final Mission, *48;* Last Safari, *570;* Naked Vengeance, *88*
Garbani, Ivo: Morgan the Pirate, *86*
Garber, Matthew: Gnome-Mobile, The, *169;* Mary Poppins, *185*
Garber, Victor: Light Sleeper, *575;* Sleepless in Seattle, *381*
Garbo, Greta: Anna Christie (1930), *449;* Anna Karenina (1935), *449;* As You Desire Me, *451;* Camille, *474;* Conquest, *487;* Flesh and the Devil, *518;* Grand Hotel, *531;* Inspiration, *553;* Joyless Street, *560;* Kiss, The (1929), *566;* Mata Hari (1931), *590;* Mysterious Lady, The, *603;* Ninotchka, *345;* Painted Veil, The, *617;* Queen Christina, *631;* Romance, *643;* Single Standard, The, *659;* Susan Lenox: Her Fall and Rise, *674;* Two-Faced Woman, *401;* Wild Orchids, *702;* Woman of Affairs, A, *705*
Garcia, Allan: Circus, The/A Day's Pleasure, *255*
Garcia, Andres: Dance of Death, *829;* Day of the Assassin, *33*
Garcia, Andy: American Roulette, *4;* Black Rain (1989), *14;* Clinton and Nadine, *26;* Dead Again, *966;* 8 Million Ways to Die, *973;* Godfather, Part III, The, *529;* Hero, *296;* Internal Affairs, *67;* Jennifer 8, *987;* Show of Force, A, *1015;* Stand and Deliver, *665;* Untouchables, The, *134;* When a Man Loves a Woman, *698*
Garcia, Darnell: Blind Rage, *15*
Garcia, Eddie: Beast of the Yellow Night, *812*
Garcia, Lea: Black Orpheus, *718*
Garcia, Nicole: Beau Pere, *716;* Bolero (1982), *720;* Corrupt, *963;* Mon Oncle d'Amerique, *768;* Overseas, *774;* Peril, *777*
Garcin, Ginette: Blue Country, *719*
Garcin, Henri: Someone Behind the Door, *1018;* Woman Next Door, The, *805*
Garde, Betty: Call Northside 777, *959*
Gardenia, Vincent: Age-Old Friends, *443;* Bang the Drum Slowly, *455;* Cold Turkey, *257;* Death Wish, *35;* Death Wish II, *36;* Firepower, *49;* Front Page, The (1974), *281;* Heaven Can Wait (1978), *295;* Home Movies, *299;* Kennedy (TV Miniseries), *562;* Last Flight of Noah's Ark, *180;* Little Murders, *319;* Little Shop of Horrors (1986), *929;* Lucky Luciano, *79;* Marciano, *588;* Moonstruck, *336;* Movers and Shakers, *337;* Skin Deep, *380;* Super, The, *388;* Tragedy of Flight 103: The Inside Story, The, *687;* Where's Poppa?, *409*
Gardiner, Reginald: Androcles and the Lion, *227;* Born to Dance, *909;* Christmas in Connecticut (1945), *255;* Damsel in Distress, A, *913;* Doctor Takes a Wife, The, *266;* Everybody Sing, *916;* Halls of Montezuma, *59;* Horn Blows at Midnight, The, *301;* Immortal Sergeant, The, *549;* Man Who Came to Dinner, The, *328;* Marie Antoinette, *588;* Sundown (1941), *673;* Yank in the RAF, A, *707*
Gardner, Arthur: Assassin of Youth (a.k.a. Marijuana), *451*
Gardner, Ava: Barefoot Contessa, The, *455;* Bhowani Junction, *12;* Bible, The, *460;* Cassandra Crossing, The, *476;* Earthquake, *43;* East Side, West Side, *506;* 55 Days at Peking, *516;* Ghosts on the Loose, *286;* Hucksters, The, *545;* Kidnapping of the President, The, *988;* Knights of the Round Table, *73;* Life and Times of Judge Roy Bean, The, *1128;* Lone Star, *1129;* Long Hot Summer, The (1985), *578;* Mogambo, *86;* My Forbidden Past, *602;* Naked Maja, The, *603;* Night of the Iguana, The, *606;* On the Beach, *1069;* One Touch of Venus, *350;* Permission to Kill, *98;* Priest of Love, *627;* Regina, *780;* Sentinel, The, *884;* Seven Days in May, *653;* Show Boat (1951), *939;* Snows of Kilimanjaro, The, *118;* Whistle Stop, *138*
Gardner, Daniel: How U Like Me Now, *303*
Gardner, David: Bethune, *459*
Gardner, Hy: Girl Hunters, The, *979*
Gardner, Joan: Catherine the Great, *477;* Dark Journey, *966;* Man Who Could Work Miracles, The, *1064;* Private Life of Don Juan, The, *628*
Gardner, Kenny: Hoppity Goes to Town, *175*

Garfield, Allen: Beverly Hills Cop II, *11;* Black Stallion Returns, The, *151;* Brinks Job, The, *246;* Candidate, The, *474;* Club Fed, *256;* Continental Divide, *259;* Conversation, The, *963;* Cry Uncle!, *261;* Cyborg 2, *1043;* Desert Bloom, *499;* Family Prayers, *514;* Front Page, The (1974), *281;* Get Crazy, *284;* Greetings, *290;* Hi Mom, *297;* Let It Ride, *317;* Night Visitor (1989), *1001;* One from the Heart, *934;* Putney Swope, *363;* Sketches of a Strangler, *1017;* State of Things, The, *789;* Stunt Man, The, *671*

Garfield, Frank: Night of the Zombies, *870*

Garfield, John: Air Force, *3;* Body and Soul (1947), *466;* Destination Tokyo, *37;* Fallen Sparrow, The, *513;* Force of Evil, *519;* Four Daughters, *520;* Gentlemen's Agreement, *526;* Hollywood Canteen, *923;* Humoresque, *546;* Juarez, *560;* Postman Always Rings Twice, The (1946), *1007;* Sea Wolf, The (1941), *113;* Thank Your Lucky Stars, *944;* They Made Me a Criminal, *681;* Tortilla Flat, *686*

Garfield, John David: Savage Intruder, The, *883*

Garfield Jr., John: Golden Voyage of Sinbad, The, *1054;* That Cold Day in the Park, *680*

Garfield, Michael: Slugs, the Movie, *887*

Garfunkel, Art: Boxing Helena, *818;* Carnal Knowledge, *475;* Catch-22, *252;* Mother Goose Rock N' Roll Rhyme, *189;* Short Fuse, *115*

Gargan, William: Aggie Appleby, Maker of Men, *223;* Animal Kingdom, The, *448;* Black Fury, *462;* Broadway Serenade, *910;* Canterville Ghost, The (1944), *155;* Cheers for Miss Bishop, *480;* Devil's Party, The, *500;* I Wake Up Screaming, *985;* Miss Annie Rooney, *188;* Rain, *634;* They Knew What They Wanted, *681;* Who Done It?, *410;* You Only Live Once, *708*

Gario, Gabriel: Pepe Le Moko, *777*

Garko, Gianni: Night of the Devils, *869*

Garko, John: Five for Hell, *50;* Have a Nice Funeral, *1119*

Garland, Beverly: Gamble on Love, *524;* Gundown at Sandoval, *1117;* Gunslinger, *1118;* It Conquered the World, *1060;* It's My Turn, *555;* Pretty Poison, *626;* Say Goodbye, Maggie Cole, *648;* Twice-Told Tales, *898;* Where the Red Fern Grows, *216*

Garland, Judy: Andy Hardy Meets a Debutante, *227;* Babes in Arms, *907;* Babes on Broadway, *907;* Broadway Melody of 1938, *910;* Child is Waiting, A, *480;* Clock, The, *484;* Easter Parade, *915;* Everybody Sing, *916;* For Me and My Gal, *917;* Gay Purr-ee, *168;* Girl Crazy, *919;* Harvey Girls, The, *922;* Hollywood Outtakes, *299;* I Could Go On Singing, *924;* In the Good Old Summertime, *925;* Judgment at Nuremberg, *560;* Life Begins for Andy Hardy, *318;* Listen, Darling, *928;* Little Nellie Kelly, *928;* Love Finds Andy Hardy, *322;* Meet Me in St. Louis, *930;* Pirate, The, *935;* Presenting Lily Mars, *626;* Star Is Born, A (1954), *666;* Strike Up the Band, *387;* Summer Stock, *942;* That's Entertainment, *436;* Thoroughbreds Don't Cry, *210;* Thousands Cheer, *945;* Till the Clouds Roll By, *946;* Wizard of Oz, The, *218;* Wonderful Wizard of Oz, The: The Making of a Movie Classic, *438;* Words and Music, *948;* Ziegfeld Follies, *949;* Ziegfeld Girl, *949*

Garland, Richard: Attack of the Crab Monsters, *810*

Garlick, Sean: Fortress (1985), *520*

Garlicki, Piotr: Camouflage, *722*

Garlington, Mary: Polyester, *359*

Garneau, Constance: Strangers in Good Company, *669*

Garner, James: Americanization of Emily, The, *226;* Barbarians at the Gate, *455;* Boys' Night Out, *244;* Breathing Lessons, *469;* Cash McCall, *252;* Castaway Cowboy, The, *157;* Children's Hour, The, *481;* Decoration Day, *498;* Distinguished Gentleman, The, *265;* Duel at Diablo, *1110;* Fan, The, *975;* Fire in the Sky, *1051;* Glitter Dome, The, *980;* Grand Prix, *531;* Great Escape, The, *57;* Marlowe, *995;* Maverick (TV Series), *1133;* Maverick, *1133;* Murphy's Romance, *601;* Rockford Files, The (TV Series), *108;* Sayonara, *648;* Skin Game, *1150;* Sunset, *1021;* Support Your Local Gunfighter, *1154;* Support Your Local Sheriff!, *1154;* Tank, *124;* They Only Kill Their Masters, *1024;* 36 Hours, *681;* Thrill of It All, The, *396;* Up Periscope, *134;* Victor/Victoria, *405;* Wheeler Dealers, The, *409*

Garner, Peggy Ann: Betrayal (1978), *459;* Cat, The, *157;* In Name Only, *550;* Jane Eyre (1944), *557;* Tree Grows in Brooklyn, A, *687*

Garnett, Gale: Children, The, *823;* Mad Monster Party, *184*

Garofalo, Janeane: Reality Bites, *635*

Garr, Teri: After Hours, *223;* Black Stallion, The, *151;* Black Stallion Returns, The, *151;* Close Encounters of the Third Kind, *1042;* Escape Artist, The, *165;* Firstborn, *517;* Full Moon in Blue Water, *282;* Head (1968), *922;* Honky Tonk Freeway, *300;* Let It Ride, *317;* Miracles, *332;* Mr. Mike's Mondo Video, *334;* Mr. Mom, *334;* Mom and Dad Save the World, *188;* Mother Goose Rock N' Roll Rhyme, *189;* Oh, God!, *349;* One from the Heart, *934;* Out Cold, *351;* Paul Reiser Out on a Whim, *355;* Perfect Little Murder, A, *356;* Prime Suspect, *627;* Short Time, *378;* Steve Martin Live, *386;* Sting II, The, *120;* Tale of the Frog Prince, *209;* To Catch a King, *1025;* Tootsie, *397;* Waiting for the Light, *695;* Witches' Brew, *412;* Young Frankenstein, *416*

Garralaga, Martin: Big Sombrero, The, *1098;* South of the Rio Grande, *1151;* Susanna Pass, *1154*

Garrani, Ivo: Black Sunday (1961), *814;* Hercules (1959), *1056*

Garrel, Maurice: Un Coeur En Hiver, *798*

Garrett, Betty: My Sister Eileen, *932;* Neptune's Daughter, *932;* On the Town, *934;* Take Me Out to the Ball Game, *943;* Words and Music, *948*

Garrett, Hank: Blood Frenzy, *815;* Boys Next Door, The, *468;* Rosebud Beach Hotel, The, *370*

Garrett, Leif: Bullet from God, A, *1102;* Cheerleader Camp, *823;* God's Gun, *1116;* Kid Vengeance, *1124;* Longshot (1981), *579;* Medicine Hat Stallion, The, *186;* Outsiders, The, *616;* Party Line, *97;* Shaker Run, *114;* Spirit of '76, The, *384;* Thunder Alley, *945*

Garrett, Lesley: Mikado, The (1987), *931*

Garrett, Patsy: Benji, *149;* Dennis the Menace: Dinosaur Hunter, *162;* For the Love of Benji, *167*

Garrick, Barbara: Sleepless in Seattle, *381*

Garrison, David: Homeboys, *543*

Garron, David: It's a Bundyful Life, *308*

Garrone, Riccardo: Bang Bang Kid, The, *232*

Garson, Greer: Adventure, *441;* Goodbye, Mr. Chips (1939), *530;* Happiest Millionaire, The, *173;* Julia Misbehaves, *311;* Julius Caesar (1953), *561;* Madame Curie, *584;* Miniver Story, The, *594;* Mrs. Miniver, *597;* Mrs. Parkington, *598;* Pride and Prejudice (1940), *626;* Random Harvest, *635;* Singing Nun, The, *204;* Sunrise at Campobello, *673;* That Forsyte Woman, *680;* When Ladies Meet, *698*

Garth, Daniel: Behind Locked Doors, *812*

Garth, Jennie: Beverly Hills 90210, *460*

Gartin, Christopher: Matters of the Heart, *590;* No Big Deal, *608*

Garver, Lynne: Sunset on the Desert, *1154*

Garvie, Elizabeth: Pride and Prejudice (1985), *626*

Garvin, Anita: Chump at Oxford, A, *255;* Laurel and Hardy Classics, Volume 5, *316*

Garwood, John: Hell's Angels on Wheels, *60*

Gary, Lorraine: Jaws, *858;* Jaws 2, *858;* Jaws: The Revenge, *858;* Just You and Me, Kid, *312;* Pray for the Wildcats, *100*

Gascon, Jean: Man Called Horse, A, *1131*

Gassman, Alessandro: Sacrilege, *782*

Gassman, Vittorio: Big Deal on Madonna Street, *717;* Bitter Rice, *718;* Catch As Catch Can, *252;* Family, The (1987), *735;* Immortal Bachelor, The, *747;* Mambo, *586;* Miracle, The (1959), *594;* Nude Bomb, The, *347;* Palermo Connection, The, *1004;* Rhapsody, *639;* Sharky's Machine, *115;* Sleazy Uncle, The, *786;* Tempest (1982), *678;* Tiger and The Pussycat, The, *795;* We All Loved Each Other So Much, *802;* Wedding, A, *407;* Woman Times Seven, *705*

Gastoni, Lisa: Tharus, Son of Attila, *127*

Gates, Anthony: L.A. Crackdown II, *74*
Gates, B. J.: Midnight Kiss, *864*
Gates, Larry: Hoodlum Priest, The, *543;* Toys in the Attic, *687;* Young Savages, The, *1033*
Gates, Nancy: Cheyenne Takes Over, *1104;* Death of a Scoundrel, *498;* Suddenly, *1021*
Gateson, Marjorie: Goin' to Town, *287*
Gatti, Jennifer: Double Exposure (1993), *971*
Gaup, Mikkel: Pathfinder, *776*
Gautier, Dick: Glitch!, *287;* Marathon, *329;* When Things Were Rotten (TV Series), *409*
Gautreaux, David: Hearse, The, *849*
Gavin, Erica: Caged Heat, *22;* Vixen, *405*
Gavin, John: Back Street, *453;* Breath of Scandal, A, *245;* Imitation of Life, *549;* Jennifer, *858;* Madwoman of Chaillot, The, *585;* Midnight Lace, *84;* Psycho, *877;* Sophia Loren: Her Own Story, *663;* Thoroughly Modern Millie, *945;* Time to Love and a Time to Die, A, *684*
Gavioca, Cassandra: Black Room, The (1985), *814*
Gawthorne, Peter: Amazing Adventure, *225*
Gaxton, William: Best Foot Forward, *908;* Heat's On, The, *295*
Gaye, Lisa: Class of Nuke 'em High 2: Subhumanoid Meltdown, *824;* Sign of Zorro, The, *204;* Toxic Avenger Part II, The, *897;* Toxic Avenger Part III: The Last Temptation of Toxie, The, *897*
Gaye, Marvin: That Was Rock, *944*
Gayle, Jackie: Bert Rigby, You're a Fool, *908;* Young at Heart Comedians, The, *415*
Gaylord, Mitch: American Anthem, *446;* Animal Instincts, *952*
Gaynes, George: Dead Men Don't Wear Plaid, *262;* It Came Upon a Midnight Clear, *177;* Micki & Maude, *331;* Police Academy, *359;* Police Academy II: Their First Assignment, *359;* Police Academy III: Back in Training, *359;* Police Academy 6: City Under Siege, *359;* Stepmonster, *1080;* Tootsie, *397*
Gaynor, Gloria: Second City Comedy Show, The, *374*
Gaynor, Janet: Star Is Born, A (1937), *666;* Sunrise, *673;* Young in Heart, The, *416*
Gaynor, Mitzi: Birds and the Bees, The, *240;* Les Girls, *928;* South Pacific, *941;* Surprise Package, *389;* There's No Business Like Show Business, *944;* We're Not Married, *408*
Gazelle, Wendy: Hot Pursuit, *301;* Understudy, The: Graveyard Shift II, *899*
Gazzara, Ben: Anatomy of a Murder, *952;* Blindsided, *956;* Bloodline, *464;* Bridge at Remagen, The, *469;* Early Frost, An, *506;* High Velocity, *62;* Killing of a Chinese Bookie, *564;* Laugh for Joy, *756;* Lies Before Kisses, *574;* Neptune Factor, The, *1068;* Opening Night, *614;* Passionate Thief, The (1961), *776;* QB VII, *631;* Question of Honor, A, *632;* Quicker Than the Eye, *102;* Road House (1989), *107;* Saint Jack, *646;* Secret Obsessions, *651;* Tales of Ordinary Madness, *677;* They All Laughed, *393*
Gazzo, Michael: Alligator, *808;* Blood Ties (1987), *464;* Cookie, *259;* Fingers, *516;* Godfather, Part II, The, *529;* Kill Castro, *71*
Geary, Anthony: Antony and Cleopatra (1981), *450;* Crack House, *30;* Dangerous Love, *32;* Disorderlies, *914;* High Desert Kill, *850;* Imposter, The, *549;* Johnny Got His Gun, *559;* Night Life, *869;* Night of the Warrior, *90;* Penitentiary III, *98;* Scorchers, *650;* UHF, *402;* You Can't Hurry Love, *415*
Geary, Cynthia: 8 Seconds, *43;* Northern Exposure (TV Series), *609*
Gecks, Nicholas: Forever Young (1983), *520*
Geddes, Barbara Bel: Five Pennies, The, *917*
Gedrick, Jason: Crossing the Bridge, *492;* Heavenly Kid, The, *296;* Iron Eagle, *67;* Massive Retaliation, *83;* Promised Land, *629;* Rooftops, *937;* Stacking, *665;* Zoo Gang, The, *416*
Gee, Prunella: Witching Time, *904*
Geer, Ellen: Hard Traveling, *536;* Harold and Maude, *294;* On the Nickel, *612*
Geer, Will: Bandolero!, *1096;* Billion Dollar Hobo, The, *150;* Black Like Me, *462;* Broken Arrow, *1101;* Brother John, *470;* Bunco, *21;* Dear Dead Delilah, *831;* Executive Action, *512;* Intruder in the Dust, *553;* Jeremiah Johnson, *1123;* Lust for Gold, *1130;* Moving Violation, *87;* My Sister, My Love, *867;* Napoleon and Samantha, *190;* President's Analyst, The, *360;* Reivers, The, *365;* Salt of the Earth, *647;* Thanksgiving Story, The, *210;* To Please a Lady, *130;* Winchester '73, *1165;* Woman Called Moses, A, *705*
Geeson, Judy: Berserk, *812;* Brannigan, *18;* Dominique Is Dead, *971;* Doomwatch, *1048;* Dynasty of Fear, *973;* Executioner, The, *974;* Fear in the Night (Dynasty of Fear), *840;* 10 Rillington Place, *678;* To Sir with Love, *685;* Twinsanity, *1028*
Geeson, Sally: Oblong Box, The, *872*
Gefner, Deborah: Exterminator 2, The, *45*
Gegauff, Danielle: Une Partie De Plaisir, *798*
Gegauff, Paul: Une Partie De Plaisir, *798*
Gehrig, Lou: Rawhide (1938), *1141*
Gehring, Ted: Gypsy Warriors, The, *58*
Geldof, Bob: Pink Floyd: The Wall, *935;* Secret Policeman's Private Parts, The, *375*
Gélin, Daniel: Iran Days of Crisis, *554;* Is Paris Burning?, *554;* Killing Cars, *563;* La Ronde, *754;* Mademoiselle Striptease, *763;* Murmur of the Heart, *769*
Gelin, Manuel: Oasis of the Zombies, *872;* One Deadly Summer, *773*
Gemma, Giuliano: Corleone, *29;* Days of Wrath, *1107;* Tex and the Lord of the Deep, *1155;* Unsane, *899;* Warning, The, *137;* When Women Had Tails, *409*
Gemser, Laura: Caged Women, *22;* Quest for the Mighty Sword, *1073;* Trap Them and Kill Them, *897*
Gendron, François-Eric: Boyfriends and Girlfriends, *720;* Cloud Waltzing, *484;* Not a Penny More, Not a Penny Less, *1002*
Gene't, Sabyn: Illegal Entry, *66*
Genest, Emile: Big Red, *150;* Incredible Journey, The, *177;* Nikki, Wild Dog of the North, *191*
Genn, Leo: Henry V (1944), *540;* Immortal Battalion, The (a.k.a. The Way Ahead), *549;* Lady Chatterley's Lover (1959), *567;* Miniver Story, The, *594;* Moby Dick, *86;* Quo Vadis (1951), *632;* Snake Pit, The, *661;* Strange Case of Dr. Jekyll and Mr. Hyde, The (1968), *890;* Ten Little Indians (1966), *1023;* Velvet Touch, The, *693;* Wooden Horse, The, *706*
Genovese, Mike: Code of Silence, *27;* Invisible Kid, The, *1060;* Triplecross, *399*
Gentile, Denise: Netherworld, *868*
Gentile, Robert: Strangers in the City, *669*
Gentry, Don: Breaker! Breaker!, *19*
Gentry, Mike Lloyd: Deadly Alliance, *968*
Gentry, Minnie: Georgia, Georgia, *526*
Gentry, Roger: Wizard of Mars, The, *1090*
Geoffrey, Paul: Excalibur, *1050*
Geoffreys, Stephen: Chair, The, *822;* Fraternity Vacation, *280;* Fright Night, *844;* Heaven Help Us, *295;* Moon 44, *1067;* 976-EVIL, *871*
George, Anthony: Untouchables, The: Scarface Mob (TV), *134*
George, Chief Dan: Americathon, *226;* Cancel My Reservation, *250;* Dan Candy's Law, *32;* Harry and Tonto, *537;* Little Big Man, *1128;* Outlaw Josey Wales, The, *1137;* Smith!, *1150*
George, Christopher: Angkor: Cambodia Express, *5;* Chisum, *1104;* Cruise into Terror, *964;* Day of the Animals, *830;* Dixie Dynamite, *40;* El Dorado, *1111;* Exterminator, The, *45;* Gates of Hell, *845;* Graduation Day, *847;* Grizzly, *847;* Man on a String, *81;* Mortuary, *866;* Pieces, *875*
George, Gladys: Flamingo Road, *518;* Hard Way, The (1942), *536;* House Across the Bay, The, *545;* Lullaby of Broadway, *929;* Madame X (1937), *584;* Marie Antoinette, *588;* Roaring Twenties, The, *107*
George, Grace: Johnny Come Lately, *311*

George, Lynda Day: Ants!, *809;* Beyond Evil, *813;* Casino, *476;* Cruise into Terror, *964;* Day of the Animals, *830;* Junkman, The, *70;* Mortuary, *866;* Pieces, *875;* Young Warriors, The, *141*

George, Rita: Hollywood Boulevard, *299*

George, Susan: Die Screaming, Marianne, *834;* Dirty Mary, Crazy Larry, *39;* Dr. Jekyll and Mr. Hyde (1973), *914;* Enter the Ninja, *44;* House Where Evil Dwells, The, *853;* Jigsaw Man, The, *987;* Lightning, the White Stallion, *181;* Mandingo, *588;* Out of Season, *616;* Small Town in Texas, A, *117;* Sonny and Jed, *1151;* Straw Dogs, *1021;* Summer Heat (1983), *672;* That Summer of White Roses, *680;* Tintorera, *895;* Tomorrow Never Comes, *686;* Venom, *900*

Georges-Picot, Olga: Children of Rage, *481*

Georgeson, Tom: Fish Called Wanda, A, *277;* No Surrender, *345*

Gerard, Charles: Bandits (1987), *715;* Happy New Year (La Bonne Année), *743*

Gerard, Danny: Robot in the Family, *200*

Gerard, George: Metamorphosis: The Alien Factor, *1065*

Gerard, Gil: Buck Rogers in the 25th Century, *1040;* Final Notice, *977;* Soldier's Fortune, *118*

Geray, Steven: French Line, The, *918;* Gilda, *527;* Seventh Cross, The, *653*

Gerber, Jay: Cartier Affair, The, *252*

Gere, Richard: American Gigolo, *446;* And the Band Played on, *447;* Beyond the Limit, *460;* Bloodbrothers, *464;* Breathless (1983), *469;* Cotton Club, The, *29;* Days of Heaven, *496;* Final Analysis, *976;* Internal Affairs, *67;* Intersection, *553;* King David, *564;* Looking for Mr. Goodbar, *993;* Miles from Home, *594;* Mr. Jones, *597;* No Mercy, *91;* Officer and a Gentleman, An, *611;* Power (1986), *625;* Pretty Woman, *361;* Report to the Commissioner, *638;* Rhapsody in August, *781;* Sommersby, *662;* Strike Force, *121;* Yanks, *707*

Geret, Georges: Diary of a Chambermaid (1964), *730;* Very Curious Girl, A, *800*

German, Gretchen: Man Called Sarge, A, *327*

Gerroll, Daniel: Big Business, *238*

Gerron, Kurt: Blue Angel, The, *719*

Gerry, Alex: Bellboy, The, *234*

Gerry and the Pacemakers: That Was Rock, *944*

Gersak, Savina: Iron Warrior, *1060;* Lone Runner, *78*

Gershon, Gina: Joey Breaker, *558;* Love Matters, *581;* Red Heat (1988), *104;* Voodoo Dawn, *901*

Gerson, Betty Lou: Red Menace, The, *636*

Gerstle, Frank: Gang Busters, *54*

Gert, Valeska: Diary of a Lost Girl, *730*

Gertz, Jami: Crossroads, *912;* Don't Tell Her It's Me, *267;* Jersey Girl, *310;* Less Than Zero, *573;* Listen to Me, *576;* Lost Boys, The, *861;* Quicksilver, *632;* Renegades, *105;* Sibling Rivalry, *378;* Silence Like Glass, *657;* Solarbabies, *1077*

Gesswein, Richard: R.O.T.O.R., *1073*

Getty, Balthazar: December, *498;* Lord of the Flies (1989), *579;* My Heroes Have Always Been Cowboys, *1135;* Pope Must Diet, The, *360;* Turn of the Screw, The (1989), *898;* Where the Day Takes You, *699;* Young Guns II, *1166*

Getty, Estelle: Mannequin (1987), *328;* Stop! Or My Mom Will Shoot, *386*

Getty III, Paul: State of Things, The, *789*

Getz, John: Blood Simple, *957;* Curly Sue, *261;* Don't Tell Mom the Babysitter's Dead, *267;* Fly, The (1986), *841;* Fly II, The, *842;* Kent State, *563;* Men at Work, *592;* Tattoo, *677*

Getz, Stuart: Van, The, *404*

Geva, Tamara: Manhattan Merry-Go-Round, *930*

Ghia, Dana: Big Rip-off, The, *1098*

Gholson, Julie: Where the Lilies Bloom, *216*

Ghosal, Smaran: Aparajito, *713*

Ghostley, Alice: Gator, *54;* New Faces, *933;* Wrong Guys, The, *414*

Giachetti, Fosco: We the Living, *802*

Giacomo, Laura San: Once Around, *349;* Quigley Down Under, *1140*

Giambalva, Joe: Mother Goose Video Treasury Vol. I–IV, *189*

Giambalvo, Louis: Fade to Black (1993), *974;* Question of Faith, *632;* Ratings Game, The, *364*

Gian, Joe: Mad About You, *325;* Night Stalker, The (1986), *870*

Gianasi, Rick: Escape from Safehaven, *1049;* Occultist, The, *93;* Sgt. Kabukiman N.Y.P.D., *114*

Giannini, Giancarlo: American Dreamer, *226;* Blood Feud, *719;* Blood Red, *464;* Fever Pitch, *516;* How Funny Can Sex Be?, *745;* Immortal Bachelor, The, *747;* Innocent, The, *748;* La Grande Bourgeoise, *754;* Lili Marleen, *760;* Love and Anarchy, *762;* Lovers and Liars, *323;* New York Stories, *343;* Night Full of Rain, A, *605;* Once Upon a Crime, *349;* Saving Grace, *373;* Seduction of Mimi, The, *784;* Sensual Man, The, *375;* Seven Beauties, *785;* Sleazy Uncle, The, *786;* Swept Away, *792;* Where's Piccone?, *803*

Gibb, Cynthia: Death Warrant, *35;* Drive Like Lightning, *42;* Gypsy (1993), *921;* Jack's Back, *987;* Malone, *80;* Modern Girls, *335;* Salvador, *647;* Short Circuit 2, *1076;* Youngblood, *709*

Gibb, Donald: Bloodsport, *16*

Gibbs, Marla: Meteor Man, *186;* Up Against the Wall, *692*

Gibbs, Rick: Buckeye and Blue, *1102*

Gibbs, Timothy: Witchboard 2, *903*

Gibel, Michel: Blue Jeans, *719*

Gibney, Rebecca: I Live With Me Dad, *547*

Gibson, Donal: Fatal Bond, *975*

Gibson, Henry: 'Burbs, The, *247;* For the Love of It, *279;* Incredible Shrinking Woman, The, *306;* Innerspace, *1058;* Long Gone, *578;* Long Goodbye, The, *993;* Monster in the Closet, *866;* Nashville, *603;* Switching Channels, *390;* Tulips, *400*

Gibson, Hoot: Horse Soldiers, The, *1122;* Last Outlaw, The (1936), *1126;* Law Rides Again, The, *1127;* Long Long Trail, *1130;* Painted Stallion, The, *1138;* Powdersmoke Range, *1139;* Spirit of the West, *1152*

Gibson, Mel: Air America, *3;* Attack Force Z, *7;* Bird on a Wire, *13;* Bounty, The, *18;* Forever Young (1992), *1053;* Gallipoli, *524;* Hamlet (1990), *535;* Lethal Weapon, *76;* Lethal Weapon 2, *76;* Lethal Weapon 3, *77;* Mad Max, *1064;* Mad Max Beyond Thunderdome, *1064;* Man without a Face, The, *587;* Maverick, *1133;* Mrs. Soffel, *598;* River, The (1984), *641;* Road Warrior, The, *1074;* Summer City, *122;* Tequila Sunrise, *126;* Tim, *684;* Year of Living Dangerously, The, *141*

Gibson, Paulette: Getting Over, *526*

Gibson, Thomas: Far and Away, *514*

Gibson, Virginia: Athena, *907*

Gibson, Wynne: Aggie Appleby, Maker of Men, *223;* Night after Night, *344*

Gidley, Pamela: Cheatin' Hearts, *480;* Disturbed, *971;* Freefall, *52;* Liebestraum, *992*

Gielgud, John: Appointment with Death, *953;* Arthur, *229;* Arthur 2: On the Rocks, *229;* Brideshead Revisited, *469;* Canterville Ghost, The (1986), *155;* Charge of the Light Brigade, The (1968), *24;* Chariots of Fire, *479;* Chimes at Midnight, *481;* 11 Harrowhouse, *973;* Formula, The, *978;* Frankenstein (1984), *842;* Gandhi, *524;* Getting It Right, *285;* Hunchback, *854;* Inside the Third Reich, *552;* Invitation to the Wedding, *307;* Joseph Andrews, *311;* Julius Caesar (1953), *561;* Julius Caesar (1970), *561;* Les Miserables (1978), *573;* Loved One, The, *323;* Murder by Decree, *998;* Plenty, *623;* Portrait of the Artist as a Young Man, A, *625;* Power of One, The, *625;* Priest of Love, *627;* Prospero's Books, *629;* Providence, *630;* Richard III, *640;* Romance on the Orient Express, *643;* Saint Joan, *646;* Scandalous (1983), *373;* Scarlet and the Black, The, *112;* Secret Agent, The, *1013;* Seven Dials Mystery, The, *1013;* Shining Through, *656;* Shoes of the Fisherman, *656;* Shooting Party, The, *656;* Sphinx (1981), *889;* Strike It Rich, *387;* Wagner, *947;* Whistle Blower, The, *1031;* Why Didn't They Ask Evans?, *1032;* Wicked Lady, The (1983), *139*

Gierasch, Stefan: Jack the Bear, *556;* Jeremiah Johnson, *1123*

Gifford, Frances: American Empire, *1093;* Luxury Liner, *930;* Our Vines Have Tender Grapes, *193*

Giftos, Elaine: Gas-s-s-s, *1054;* Student Nurses, The, *671;* Trouble with Dick, The, *1085*

Gigante, Tony: Metamorphosis: The Alien Factor, *1065*

Gil, Ariadna: Belle Epoque, *716*

Gil, Vincent: Encounter at Raven's Gate, *1049;* Solo, *661*

Gilbert, Billy: Arabian Nights (1942), *6;* Block-Heads, *241;* Breaking the Ice, *909;* Bride Walks Out, The, *245;* Broadway Melody of 1938, *910;* Firefly, The, *916;* Five Weeks in a Balloon, *50;* Happy Landing, *921;* Kissing Bandit, The, *927;* Laurel and Hardy Classics, Volume 1, *316;* Laurel and Hardy Classics, Volume 8, *316;* Laurel and Hardy on the Lam, *317;* Love on the Run (1936), *323;* Melody Master, *592;* My Lucky Star, *932;* One Hundred Men and a Girl, *934;* Peck's Bad Boy with the Circus, *194;* Toast of New York, The, *685;* Two-Reelers: Comedy Classics #2, *402;* Villain Still Pursued Her, The, *135*

Gilbert, John: Big Parade, The, *460;* Flesh and the Devil, *518;* Queen Christina, *631;* Woman of Affairs, A, *705*

Gilbert, Lou: Great White Hope, The, *533*

Gilbert, Marcus: Army of Darkness, *810*

Gilbert, Melissa: Blood Vows: The Story of a Mafia Wife, *464;* Christmas Coal Mine Miracle, The, *159;* Dying to Remember, *973;* Little House on the Prairie (TV Series), *181;* Lookalike, The, *993;* Miracle Worker, The (1979), *595;* Snow Queen, *205;* Sylvester, *675*

Gilbert, Paul: Three Nuts in Search of a Bolt, *396;* Women of the Prehistoric Planet, *1090*

Gilbert, Ronnie: Wasn't That a Time!, *438*

Gilbert, Sara: Poison Ivy (1992), *1006;* Runaway Ralph, *201;* Sudie & Simpson, *672*

Gilbert, Taylor: Torment, *1026*

Gilchrist, Connie: Long John Silver, *78;* Luxury Liner, *930;* Presenting Lily Mars, *626*

Gilden, Richard: Black Klansman, The, *14*

Giles, Sandra: Daddy-O, *31*

Gilford, Jack: Anna to the Infinite Power, *1036;* Cocoon, *1042;* Cocoon: The Return, *1042;* Daydreamer, The, *161;* Enter Laughing, *271;* Funny Thing Happened on the Way to the Forum, A, *282;* Save the Tiger, *648;* They Might Be Giants, *1023;* Wholly Moses!, *410*

Gill, Basil: School for Scandal, *373*

Gille, André: Voyage en Ballon (Stowaway to the Stars), *801*

Gillen, Jeffrey: Children Shouldn't Play with Dead Things, *823*

Gillette, Anita: Marathon, *329*

Gilley, Mickey: Jerry Lee Lewis—I Am What I Am, *428;* Off the Wall, *348*

Gilliam, Burton: Convicted, *488;* Foxfire Light, *521;* Getaway, The (1994), *55;* Quake, *1008;* Terror Within 2, The, *894*

Gilliam, Seth: Assault at West Point, *451*

Gilliam, Terry: And Now for Something Completely Different, *226;* Life of Brian, *318;* Monty Python and the Holy Grail, *336;* Monty Python Live at the Hollywood Bowl, *336;* Monty Python's Flying Circus (TV Series), *336;* Monty Python's the Meaning of Life, *336;* Secret Policeman's Private Parts, The, *375*

Gilliard Jr., Lawrence: Straight out of Brooklyn, *668;* Survive the Night, *1021*

Gillies, Fiona: Frankenstein (1992), *842*

Gilliland, Richard: Bug, *820;* Challenge of a Lifetime, *478;* Happy Hour, *293;* Killing in a Small Town, *564*

Gillin, Hugh: Psycho II, *877;* Psycho III, *877*

Gillin, Linda: Terror at the Red Wolf Inn, *893*

Gilling, Rebecca: Blue Lighting, The, *16;* Dangerous Life, A, *494;* Heaven Tonight, *539;* Naked Country, The, *603;* Return to Eden, *639*

Gillis, Ann: Adventures of Tom Sawyer, The, *144;* Little Men (1940), *576;* Peck's Bad Boy with the Circus, *194*

Gillis, Jamie: Deranged, *833*

Gilman, Kenneth: Bedroom Eyes, *954;* Nights in White Satin, *607;* Scavengers, *373*

Gilman, Sam: Gator Bait, *55*

Gilmore, Craig: Living End, The, *577*

Gilmore, Margalo: Peter Pan (1960), *194*

Gilmore, Virginia: Western Union, *1163*

Gilmour, Ian: Dangerous Summer, A, *494*

Gilroy, Dan: Mother Goose Rock N' Roll Rhyme, *189*

Gilyard Jr., Clarence: One Riot, One Ranger, *95*

Ging, Jack: Dear Detective, *968;* High Plains Drifter, *1120;* Where the Red Fern Grows, *216*

Gingold, Hermione: Adventures of Sadie, *223;* Garbo Talks, *283;* Gay Purr-ee, *168;* Gigi, *919;* Music Man, The, *932;* Naked Edge, The, *1000*

Ginsberg, Allen: Heavy Petting, *426*

Ginty, Robert: Act, The, *441;* Alchemist, The, *808;* Bounty Hunter, *18;* Coming Home, *486;* Exterminator, The, *45;* Exterminator 2, The, *45;* Harley Davidson and the Marlboro Man, *59;* Loverboy, *323;* Madhouse (1990), *326;* Out on Bail, *96;* Programmed to Kill, *1072;* That's Action, *127;* Three Kinds of Heat, *128;* Vietnam, Texas, *135;* Warrior of the Lost World, *1088*

Giordana, Daniela: Badlands Drifter, *1096;* Have a Nice Funeral, *1119*

Giorgi, Eleonora: Beyond Obsession, *717;* Inferno, *856;* Nudo di Donna (Portrait of a Woman, Nude), *772;* To Forget Venice, *795*

Giorgiade, Nick: Untouchables, The: Scarface Mob (TV), *134*

Giradot, Hippolyte: Barjo, *715*

Girard, Joe: Mystery of the Hooded Horseman, *1135*

Girardot, Annie: Jacko and Lise, *749;* Jupiter's Thigh, *751;* La Vie Continue, *755;* Le Cavaleur, *757;* Love and the Frenchwoman, *762;* Mussolini and I, *601;* Rocco & His Brothers, *782*

Girardot, Hippolyte: Love without Pity, *762*

Giraud, Claude: Phedre, *777*

Giraud, Roland: Three Men and a Cradle, *794*

Giraudeau, Bernard: Bilitis, *717;* L'Année des Meduses, *752;* Passion of Love, *776*

Girolami, Enio: Final Defeat, The, *1113*

Giron, Ali: Dead Man Out, *497*

Girotti, Massimo: Ossessione, *774;* Passion of Love, *776;* Red Tent, The, *637;* Stateline Motel, *789;* Teorema, *793;* Torture Chamber of Baron Blood, The, *896;* Wanton Contessa, The, *802*

Gish, Annabeth: Desert Bloom, *499;* Hiding Out, *61;* Mystic Pizza, *603;* Shag, the Movie, *654;* When He's Not a Stranger, *698*

Gish, Dorothy: Battle of Elderbush Gulch, The/The Musketeers of Pig Alley, *1097;* Hearts of the World, *538;* Home, Sweet Home, *543;* Judith of Bethulia, *560;* Orphans of the Storm, *615*

Gish, Lillian: American Film Institute Life Achievement Awards, The, *418;* Battle of Elderbush Gulch, The/The Musketeers of Pig Alley, *1097;* Birth of a Nation, The, *462;* Broken Blossoms, *470;* Comedians, The, *486;* Commandos Strike at Dawn, *28;* D. W. Griffith Triple Feature, *493;* Duel in the Sun, *1110;* Follow Me, Boys!, *167;* Great Chase, The, *57;* Hambone and Hillie, *535;* Hearts of the World, *538;* His Double Life, *297;* Hobson's Choice (1983), *175;* Home, Sweet Home, *543;* Intolerance, *553;* Judith of Bethulia, *560;* Night of the Hunter, *1001;* Orphans of the Storm, *615;* Portrait of Jennie, *625;* Scarlet Letter, The (1926), *649;* Sweet Liberty, *389;* True Heart Susie, *688;* Unforgiven, The (1960), *1160;* Way Down East, *697;* Wedding, A, *407;* Whales of August, The, *698;* White Sister, The, *700;* Wind, The (1928), *703*

Givens, Robin: Beverly Hills Madam, *460;* Boomerang, *244;* Penthouse, The, *1005;* Rage in Harlem, A, *103;* Woman of Brewster Place, The, *706*
Gladstone, Dana: Presidio, The, *100*
Glanzelius, Anton: My Life as a Dog, *769*
Glas, Uschi: Tower of Screaming Virgins, The, *897*
Glaser, Étienne: Mozart Brothers, The, *769*
Glaser, Paul Michael: Phobia, *1006;* Princess Daisy, *627;* Single Bars, Single Women, *658*
Glass, Ned: Dick Tracy Returns, *38;* Experiment in Terror, *974;* Kid Galahad (1962), *926;* Requiem for a Heavyweight (Television), *638;* Street Music, *670*
Glass, Ron: Deep Space, *1046*
Glasser, Isabel: Forever Young (1992), *1053;* Pure Country, *630*
Glasser, Phillip: American Tail, An, *146*
Glaudini, Robert: Parasite, *873*
Glazer, Eugene: Substitute, The, *1021*
Gleason, Jackie: All Through the Night, *3;* Don't Drink the Water, *267;* Honeymooners, The (TV Series), *300;* Honeymooners, The: Lost Episodes (TV Series), *300;* Hustler, The, *547;* Izzy & Moe, *309;* Jackie Gleason's Honeybloopers, *309;* Mr. Billion, *85;* Mr. Halpern and Mr. Johnson, *597;* Nothing in Common, *609;* Papa's Delicate Condition, *617;* Requiem for a Heavyweight, *638;* Return of October, The, *366;* Smokey and the Bandit, *381;* Smokey and the Bandit II, *381;* Smokey and the Bandit III, *382;* Soldier in the Rain, *661;* Springtime in the Rockies (1942), *941;* Sting II, The, *120;* Toy, The, *398*
Gleason, James: Arsenic and Old Lace, *228;* Bishop's Wife, The, *240;* Clock, The, *484;* Crash Dive, *30;* Ex-Mrs. Bradford, The, *974;* Falcon Takes Over, The, *975;* Flying Fool, The, *51;* Footlight Serenade, *917;* Free Soul, A, *522;* Guy Named Joe, A, *535;* Helldorado (1934), *60;* Here Comes Mr. Jordan, *296;* I'll See You in My Dreams, *924;* Key to the City, *312;* Last Hurrah, The, *569;* Manhattan Merry-Go-Round, *930;* Miss Grant Takes Richmond, *333;* Night of the Hunter, *1001;* Return of October, The, *366;* Suddenly, *1021;* Tree Grows in Brooklyn, A, *687;* Tycoon, *133;* What Price Glory, *408;* Yellow Cab Man, The, *415*
Gleason, Joanna: For Richer, for Poorer, *279;* F/X 2: The Deadly Art of Illusion, *979*
Gleason, Paul: Breakfast Club, The, *245;* Challenge of a Lifetime, *478;* Die Hard, *38;* Doc Savage...The Man of Bronze, *1047;* Ewoks: The Battle for Endor, *165;* Forever Lulu, *279;* Fourth Story, *978;* Ghost Chase, *845;* Johnny Be Good, *311;* Morgan Stewart's Coming Home, *337;* Night Game, *1000;* Pursuit of D. B. Cooper, *363;* Rich Girl, *640;* Running Cool, *110;* Supercarrier, *122*
Gleason, Russell: Flying Fool, The, *51*
Gledhill, Nicholas: Careful He Might Hear You, *475*
Glen, Iain: Fools of Fortune, *518;* Mountains of the Moon, *87*
Glenn, Cody: Border Shootout, *1100*
Glenn, Roy: Carmen Jones, *911*
Glenn, Scott: Angels Hard as They Come, *5;* As Summers Die, *451;* Baby Maker, The, *453;* Backdraft, *8;* Challenge, The, *24;* Extreme Justice, *512;* Fighting Mad, *516;* Hunt for Red October, The, *984;* Intrigue, *986;* Keep, The, *859;* Man on Fire, *81;* Miss Firecracker, *333;* More American Graffiti, *599;* My Heroes Have Always Been Cowboys, *1135;* Off Limits (1988), *93;* Personal Best, *621;* Right Stuff, The, *640;* River, The (1984), *641;* Shadow Hunter, *654;* Shrieking, The, *886;* Silence of the Lambs, *1016;* Silverado, *1150;* Slaughter of the Innocents, *1017;* Urban Cowboy, *692;* Verne Miller, *135;* Wild Geese II, *139;* Women & Men 2, *706*
Gless, Sharon: Hardhat and Legs, *536;* Hobson's Choice (1983), *175;* Revenge of the Stepford Wives, *881;* Star Chamber, The, *1019;* Tales of the Unexpected, *1022*
Glick, Stacey: Brighton Beach Memoirs, *246*
Glover, Brian: Alien 3, *1035;* Kafka, *988;* McGuffin, The, *996*
Glover, Bruce: Big Bad Mama II, *12;* Ghost Town, *846;* Hider in the House, *982;* Inside Out 2, *1059*
Glover, Crispin: Back to the Future, *1037;* Chasers, *254;* Even Cowgirls Get the Blues, *272;* Hotel Room, *983;* Little Noises, *576;* River's Edge, *641;* Rubin & Ed, *371;* Twister, *401;* What's Eating Gilbert Grape?, *408;* Wild at Heart, *702*
Glover, Danny: Bat 21, *9;* Color Purple, The, *485;* Dead Man Out, *497;* Flight of the Intruder, The, *50;* Grand Canyon, *531;* Lethal Weapon, *76;* Lethal Weapon 2, *76;* Lethal Weapon 3, *77;* Lonesome Dove, *1129;* Mandela, *588;* Maverick, *1133;* Memorial Day, *592;* Out, *96;* Places in the Heart, *623;* Predator 2, *1071;* Pure Luck, *363;* Rage in Harlem, A, *103;* Raisin in the Sun, A (1988), *634;* Saint of Fort Washington, The, *646;* Silverado, *1150;* To Sleep with Anger, *685;* Witness, *1032*
Glover, John: Apology, *809;* Assault at West Point, *451;* Breaking Point, *469;* Chocolate War, The, *481;* Dead on the Money, *967;* Early Frost, An, *506;* Ed & His Dead Mother, *270;* El Diablo, *1111;* 52 Pick-Up, *976;* Flash of Green, A, *977;* Gremlins 2: The New Batch, *1055;* Killing Affair, A, *988;* Last Embrace, The, *990;* Masquerade (1988), *995;* Meet the Hollowheads, *331;* Rocket Gibraltar, *642;* Scrooged, *374;* Season of Giants, A, *650;* Something Special, *383;* Traveling Man, *687*
Glover, Julian: Hearts of Fire, *538;* Heat and Dust, *539;* Mandela, *588;* Mastermind (TV Series), *186;* Story of Jacob and Joseph, The, *207;* Theatre of Death, *894;* Treasure Island (1990), *214;* Tusks, *133*
Glover, Kara: Caribe, *23*
Glynn, Carlin: Continental Divide, *259;* Night Game, *1000;* Trip to Bountiful, The, *688*
Go, Hiromi: Gonza the Spearman, *741*
Gobel, George: Alice Through the Looking Glass (1985), *145;* Better Late than Never, *237;* Birds and the Bees, The, *240;* History of White People in America, The (Volume II), *298;* I Married a Woman, *304;* Young at Heart Comedians, The, *415*
Godard, Jean-Luc: Contempt, *726;* First Name: Carmen, *737*
Goddard, John: Naked Youth, *89*
Goddard, Mark: Blue Sunshine, *957;* Lost in Space (TV Series), *1063*
Goddard, Paulette: Diary of a Chambermaid (1946), *730;* Ghost Breakers, *285;* Great Dictator, The, *289;* Modern Times, *335;* Pot O' Gold, *625;* Reap the Wild Wind, *104;* Second Chorus, *938;* Women, The, *413;* Young in Heart, The, *416*
Godfrey, Arthur: Don Rickles: Buy This Tape You Hockey Puck, *267;* Flatbed Annie and Sweetie Pie: Lady Truckers, *50;* Glass Bottom Boat, The, *287;* Great Bank Hoax, The, *289*
Godfrey, Renee: Terror by Night, *1023*
Godin, Jacques: Being at Home with Claude, *716;* Man Inside, The (1984), *81*
Godunov, Alexander: Die Hard, *38;* Money Pit, The, *335;* Runestone, *882;* Waxwork II: Lost in Time, *902;* Witness, *1032*
Goethals, Angela: V. I. Warshawski, *1029*
Goetz, Peter Michael: Beer, *233;* Jumpin' Jack Flash, *311;* King Kong Lives, *859;* Tagget, *124*
Goetz, Scot: Living End, The, *577*
Goetzke, Bernhard: Destiny, *729;* Kriemhilde's Revenge, *752;* Siegfried, *786*
Goff, Norris: Dreaming Out Loud, *269;* So This Is Washington, *382;* Two Weeks to Live, *402*
Golan, Gila: Catch As Catch Can, *252;* Our Man Flint, *96;* Valley of Gwangi, *1087*
Gold, Tracey: Dance 'Til Dawn, *262;* Lots of Luck, *322;* Shoot the Moon, *656*
Goldberg, Adam: Dazed and Confused, *497*
Goldberg, Jakub: Two Men and a Wardrobe, *797*
Goldberg, Whoopi: Best of Comic Relief, The, *235;* Burglar (1987), *247;* Clara's Heart, *483;* Color Purple, The, *485;* Comic Relief 2, *258;* Doctor Duck's Super Secret All-Purpose Sauce, *266;* Fatal Beauty, *46;* Ghost (1990), *527;* Homer and Eddie, *543;* Jumpin' Jack Flash, *311;* Kiss Shot, *566;* Long Walk Home, The, *579;* Made in America, *325;* National

Lampoon's Loaded Weapon 1, *342;* Pee-Wee's Playhouse Christmas Special, *194;* Player, The, *358;* Sarafinal, *938;* Sister Act, *379;* Sister Act 2: Back in the Habit, *380;* Soapdish, *382;* Telephone, The, *392*

Goldblum, Jeff: Adventures of Buckaroo Banzai, The, *1034;* Between the Lines, *237;* Beyond Therapy, *237;* Big Chill, The, *460;* Death Wish, *35;* Deep Cover (1992), *36;* Earth Girls Are Easy, *915;* Fathers & Sons, *515;* Favor, the Watch and the Very Big Fish, The, *275;* Fly, The (1986), *841;* Framed (1990), *280;* Into the Night, *553;* Invasion of the Body Snatchers (1978), *1059;* Jurassic Park, *1061;* Mr. Frost, *997;* Next Stop, Greenwich Village, *605;* Rehearsal for Murder, *1009;* Right Stuff, The, *640;* Shooting Elizabeth, *378;* Silverado, *1150;* Strange Tales: Ray Bradbury Theater, *1080;* Tall Guy, The, *391;* Thank God It's Friday, *944;* Three Little Pigs, The, *211;* Threshold, *1083;* Transylvania 6-5000, *399;* Twisted Obsession, *690;* Vibes, *1087*

Golden, Annie: Forever Lulu, *279;* Hair, *921;* National Lampoon's Class of '86, *342*

Golden II, Norman D.: Cop and a Half, *160*

Golden, Rachel: I Married a Vampire, *855*

Goldin, Ricky Paul: Hyper Sapian: People from Another Star, *1057*

Goldman, Philippe: Small Change, *787*

Goldoni, Lelia: Hysteria, *984;* Theatre of Death, *894*

Goldsby, Matthew: Student Bodies, *891*

Goldsmith, Clio: Cricket, The, *726;* Gift, The, *740;* Heat of Desire, *743;* Miss Right, *333*

Goldsmith, Jonathan: Phantom of the Mall—Eric's Revenge, *874*

Goldstein, Jenette: Aliens, *1035;* Near Dark, *868*

Goldthwait, Bob: Burglar (1987), *247;* Doctor Duck's Super Secret All-Purpose Sauce, *266;* Evening with Bob Goldthwait, An: Share the Warmth, *272;* Freaked, *281;* Hot to Trot, *302;* Medusa: Dare to be Truthful, *331;* One Crazy Summer, *349;* Police Academy III: Back in Training, *359;* Police Academy 4: Citizens on Patrol, *359;* Scrooged, *374;* Shakes the Clown, *377*

Goldwyn, Tony: Ghost (1990), *527;* Iran Days of Crisis, *554;* Kuffs, *73;* Love Matters, *581;* Pelican Brief, The, *1005;* Taking the Heat, *676;* Traces of Red, *1026*

Goleen, Frank Rozelaar: Goodnight, God Bless, *847*

Golino, Valeria: Big Top Pee-Wee, *239;* Clean Slate (1994), *256;* Detective School Dropouts, *264;* Hot Shots, *301;* Hot Shots Part Deux, *301;* Indian Runner, The, *551;* King's Whore, The, *566;* Rain Man, *634;* Torrents of Spring, *686;* Year of the Gun, *1033*

Golisano, Francesco: Miracle in Milan, *767*

Golonka, Arlene: Dr. Alien, *834;* Foxtrap, *52;* Hang 'em High, *1118;* Last Married Couple in America, The, *315;* Survival Game, *123*

Golovine, Marina: Olivier, Olivier, *773*

Golub, David: From Mao to Mozart, *424*

Gombell, Minna: Block-Heads, *241;* Pagan Love Song, *934*

Gomez, Consuelo: El Mariachi, *733*

Gomez, Fernando Fernan: Belle Epoque, *716;* Spirit of the Beehive, The, *788;* Stilts, The (Los Zancos), *789*

Gomez, Jamie: Silencer, The, *116*

Gomez, Jose Luis: Roads to the South, *781*

Gomez, Paloma: Valentina, *799*

Gomez, Panchito: Run for the Roses, *201*

Gomez, Thomas: But Not For Me, *472;* Force of Evil, *519;* Kim, *72;* Macao, *80;* Pittsburgh, *622;* Sherlock Holmes and the Voice of Terror, *1015;* Sorrowful Jones, *383;* That Midnight Kiss, *944;* Trapeze, *687;* Who Done It?, *410*

Gong, Li: Raise the Red Lantern, *779;* Story of Qiu Ju, The, *789*

Gonzales, Peter: Fellini's Roma, *736*

Goodall, Caroline: Ring of Scorpio, *640;* Schindler's List, *649;* Webber's World, *406*

Goodfellow, Joan: Buster and Billie, *472;* Flash of Green, A, *977*

Gooding Jr., Cuba: Boyz N the Hood, *468;* Daybreak (1993), *1045;* Few Good Men, A, *976;* Gladiator, *528;* Judgment Night, *69;* Lightning Jack, *1128*

Goodliffe, Michael: One That Got Away, The, *95*

Goodman, Benny: Song Is Born, A, *940*

Goodman, Dody: Cool As Ice, *488;* Private Resort, *362;* Splash, *384*

Goodman, John: Always (1989), *445;* Arachnophobia, *810;* Babe, The, *452;* Barton Fink, *232;* Big Easy, The, *12;* Born Yesterday (1993), *244;* Everybody's All-American, *511;* Flintstones, The, *167;* King Ralph, *313;* Matinee, *330;* Punchline, *630;* Raising Arizona, *364;* Sea of Love, *1013;* Stella (1990), *667;* True Stories, *400;* Wrong Guys, The, *414*

Goodrich, Deborah: Remote Control, *879;* Survival Game, *123*

Goodrow, Garry: Almos' a Man, *445;* Cardiac Arrest, *959;* Connection, The (1961), *487;* Glen and Randa, *1054;* Steelyard Blues, *386*

Goodwin, Bill: Bathing Beauty, *908;* It's a Great Feeling, *925;* Jolson Sings Again, *926;* Jolson Story, The, *926;* Spellbound, *1019*

Goodwin, Kia Joy: Strapped, *670*

Goodwin, Laurel: Girls! Girls! Girls!, *919;* Papa's Delicate Condition, *617*

Goodwin, Michael: Sizzle, *659*

Gora, Claudio: Catch As Catch Can, *252*

Gorbe, Janos: Round-Up, The, *782*

Gorcey, Bernard: Blues Busters, *242;* Bowery Boys, The (Series), *244*

Gorcey, David: Bowery Boys, The (Series), *244;* Little Tough Guys, *319;* Prairie Moon, *1139;* Pride of the Bowery, *627*

Gorcey, Elizabeth: Trouble with Dick, The, *1085*

Gorcey, Leo: Blues Busters, *242;* Bowery Boys, The (Series), *244;* Boys of the City, *18;* Pride of the Bowery, *627;* Road to Zanzibar, *369*

Gordon, Barry: Body Slam, *17;* Girl Can't Help It, The, *286;* Hands of a Stranger, *981;* Thousand Clowns, A, *395*

Gordon, Ben: Goof Balls, *289*

Gordon, Bobby: Big Business Girl, *460*

Gordon, Bruce: Elephant Boy, *44;* Untouchables, The: Scarface Mob (TV), *134*

Gordon, C. Henry: Charlie Chan at the Wax Museum, *961;* Gabriel over the White House, *524;* Tarzan's Revenge, *126*

Gordon, Colin: One That Got Away, The, *95*

Gordon, Dexter: Round Midnight, *937*

Gordon, Don: Beast Within, The, *812;* Borrower, The, *1040;* Bullitt, *21;* Education of Sonny Carson, The, *507;* Final Conflict, The, *841;* Mack, The, *584;* Papillon, *97;* Skin Deep, *380;* Slaughter, *117;* Warbus, *137;* Z.P.G. (Zero Population Growth), *1091*

Gordon, Eve: Paradise (1991), *618;* Secret Passion of Robert Clayton, The, *1013;* Switched at Birth, *675*

Gordon, Gale: All in a Night's Work, *224;* Our Miss Brooks (TV Series), *351;* Speedway, *941;* 30 Foot Bride of Candy Rock, The, *394*

Gordon, Gavin: Bitter Tea of General Yen, The, *462;* Matchmaker, The, *329;* Romance, *643;* Scarlet Empress, The, *649*

Gordon, Gerald: Force Five, *51*

Gordon, Hannah: Oh, Alfie, *611*

Gordon, Joyce: Killing 'Em Softly, *563*

Gordon, Julius: D.P., *493*

Gordon, Keith: Back to School, *230;* Christine, *824;* Dressed to Kill (1980), *972;* Home Movies, *299;* Kent State, *563;* Legend of Billie Jean, The, *76;* Silent Rebellion, *658;* Single Bars, Single Women, *658;* Static, *666*

Gordon, Leo: Haunted Palace, The, *849;* Hondo, *1121;* Hostile Guns, *1122;* Intruder, The (1961), *553;* Maverick (TV Series), *1133;* Maverick, *1133;* McLintock!, *1133;* My Name Is Nobody, *1135;* Rage (1980), *633;* Riot in Cell Block Eleven, *107;* Ten Wanted Men, *1155*

Gordon, Mary: Double Wedding, *268;* Hound of the Baskervilles, The (1939), *983;* Pearl of Death, The, *1004;* Pot O' Gold, *625;* Sherlock Holmes and the Secret Weapon, *1015;* Sherlock Holmes and the Voice of Terror, *1015;* Texas Cyclone, *1155*

Gordon, Philip: Bridge to Nowhere, *469;* Came a Hot Friday, *22*

Gordon, Robert: Loveless, The, *582*

Gordon, Ruth: Abe Lincoln in Illinois, *440;* Action in the North Atlantic, *2;* Any Which Way You Can, *228;* Big Bus, The, *238;* Don't Go to Sleep, *836;* Every Which Way but Loose, *273;* Harold and Maude, *294;* Inside Daisy Clover, *552;* Lord Love a Duck, *321;* Maxie, *330;* Mugsy's Girls, *338;* My Bodyguard, *601;* North Star, The, *92;* Prince of Central Park, The, *197;* Rosemary's Baby, *881;* Scavenger Hunt, *373;* Trouble with Spies, The, *399;* Two-Faced Woman, *401;* Whatever Happened to Aunt Alice?, *902;* Where's Poppa?, *409*

Gordon, Serena: Tale of Two Cities, A (1991), *677*

Gordon, Stuart: Age of Innocence, The, *443*

Gordon, Susan: Picture Mommy Dead, *874*

Gordon-Levitt, Joseph: Holy Matrimony, *299*

Gorg, Galyn: Living the Blues, *577*

Gorg, Gwyn: Living the Blues, *577*

Goring, Marius: Barefoot Contessa, The, *455;* Ill Met by Moonlight, *548;* Night Ambush, *90;* Paris Express, The, *97;* Spy in Black, The, *664;* Zeppelin, *709*

Gorman, Annette: Texas John Slaughter: Stampede at Bitter Creek, *1155;* Texas John Slaughter: Wild Times, *1156*

Gorman, Cliff: Angel, *5;* Boys in the Band, The, *468;* Cops and Robbers, *29;* Hoffa, *542;* Justine, *561;* Night and the City (1992), *605;* Night of the Juggler, *90;* Strike Force, *121*

Gorme, Eydie: Alice Through the Looking Glass (1985), *145*

Gormley, Felim: Commitments, The, *912*

Gorney, Karen Lynn: Saturday Night Fever, *938*

Gorshin, Frank: Batman (1966), *148;* Beverly Hills Bodysnatchers, *237;* Dragstrip Girl, *42;* Goliath Awaits, *56;* Hail Caesar, *292;* Hollywood Vice Squad, *63;* Hot Resort, *301;* Invasion of the Saucer Men, *1059;* Meteor Man, *186;* Midnight (1989), *996;* Sky Heist, *117;* Studs Lonigan, *671;* Sweet Justice, *123;* That Darn Cat, *210;* Underground Aces, *403*

Gorski, Tamara: Lost World, The (1992), *79;* Return to the Lost World, *1074*

Gortner, Marjoe: American Ninja III, *4;* Bobbie Jo and the Outlaw, *17;* Food of the Gods, *1052;* Hellhole, *849;* Jungle Warriors, *69;* Marjoe, *588;* Mausoleum, *864;* Pray for the Wildcats, *100;* Sidewinder 1, *115;* Star Crash, *1078;* Survivalist, The, *123;* Viva Knievel, *136*

Gosch, Christopher: Last Season, The, *75*

Gosden, Freeman: Check and Double Check, *254*

Gosfield, Maurice: Sgt. Bilko (TV Series), *376*

Goss, David: Hollywood Cop, *63*

Gosselaar, Mark Paul: Necessary Parties, *604*

Gossett Jr., Lou: Aces: Iron Eagle III, *1;* Carolina Skeletons, *475;* Choirboys, The, *481;* Cover-Up (1990), *30;* Dangerous Relations, *494;* Deep, The, *36;* Diggstown, *264;* El Diablo, *1111;* Enemy Mine, *1049;* Finders Keepers, *277;* Firewalker, *49;* Goodbye, Miss 4th of July, *171;* Guardian, The (1984), *534;* Iron Eagle, *67;* Iron Eagle II, *67;* It Rained All Night the Day I Left, *555;* It's Good to Be Alive, *555;* J.D.'s Revenge, *858;* Jaws 3, *858;* Josephine Baker Story, The, *559;* Keeper of the City, *562;* Laughing Policeman, The, *991;* Lazarus Syndrome, The, *571;* Little Ladies of the Night, *576;* Monolith, *1066;* Murder on the Bayou, *600;* Officer and a Gentleman, An, *611;* Principal, The, *628;* Punisher, The, *101;* Raisin in the Sun, A (1961), *634;* Return to Lonesome Dove, *1143;* Roots, *644;* Roots—The Gift, *644;* Sadat, *646;* Skin Game, *1150;* Sudie & Simpson, *672;* Toy Soldiers (1991), *131;* Travels with My Aunt, *399;* White Dawn, The, *138*

Gostukhin, Vladimir: Close to Eden, *725*

Gotell, Walter: Basic Training, *232*

Gotestam, Staffan: Brothers Lionheart, The, *152*

Gothard, Michael: King Arthur, The Young Warlord, *72;* Lifeforce, *1063;* Scream and Scream Again, *883;* Valley, The, *799*

Gottfried, Gilbert: Problem Child, *362*

Gottlieb, Carl: Cannonball, *22*

Gottschalk, Thomas: Driving Me Crazy, *269*

Goudal, Jetta: White Gold, *1031*

Gough, Lloyd: Green Hornet, The (TV Series), *58;* It's Good to Be Alive, *555;* Rancho Notorious, *1140*

Gough, Michael: Age of Innocence, The, *443;* Anna Karenina (1947), *449;* Batman (1989), *9;* Batman Returns, *9;* Berserk, *812;* Caravaggio, *475;* Crucible of Horror, *827;* Horror Hospital, *851;* Horror of Dracula, *851;* Horse's Mouth, The, *301;* Out of Africa, *616;* Phantom of the Opera (1962), *874;* Rob Roy, the Highland Rogue, *200;* Savage Messiah, *648;* Sword and the Rose, The (1953), *208;* They Came from Beyond Space, *1083*

Gould, Elliott: Best of John Belushi, The, *235;* Beyond Justice, *11;* Bob & Carol & Ted & Alice, *243;* Bugsy, *471;* Capricorn One, *1041;* Casey at the Bat, *156;* Conspiracy: The Trial of the Chicago 8, *488;* Dangerous Love, *32;* Dead Men Don't Die, *262;* Devil and Max Devlin, The, *264;* Dirty Tricks, *265;* Don Rickles: Buy This Tape You Hockey Puck, *267;* Escape to Athena, *45;* Falling in Love Again, *273;* Frog, *168;* Getting Straight, *526;* Harry and Walter Go to New York, *294;* Hitz, *63;* I Love My Wife, *304;* I Will, I Will...for Now, *304;* Inside Out (1986), *552;* Jack and the Beanstalk, *178;* Lady Vanishes, The (1979), *990;* Last Flight of Noah's Ark, *180;* Lemon Sisters, The, *317;* Lethal Obsession, *76;* Little Murders, *319;* Long Goodbye, The, *993;* M*A*S*H, *324;* Matilda, *330;* Mean Johnny Barrows, *83;* Muppet Movie, The, *189;* Muppets Take Manhattan, The, *189;* My Wonderful Life, *603;* Naked Face, The, *1000;* Night They Raided Minsky's, The, *345;* Night Visitor (1989), *1001;* Over the Brooklyn Bridge, *352;* Paul Reiser Out on a Whim, *355;* Quick, Let's Get Married, *363;* Silent Partner, The, *1016;* S*P*Y*S, *385;* Telephone, The, *392;* Vanishing Act, *693;* Wet and Wild Summer, *408;* Whiffs, *410*

Gould, Harold: Better Late than Never, *237;* Big Bus, The, *238;* Fourth Wise Man, The, *521;* Front Page, The (1974), *281;* Gambler, The (1980), *1114;* Gambler, Part II—The Adventure Continues, The, *1115;* How to Break Up a Happy Divorce, *302;* Love and Death, *322;* Man in the Santa Claus Suit, The, *185;* One and Only, The, *613;* Playing for Keeps, *358;* Red Light Sting, The, *636;* Romero, *643;* Seems Like Old Times, *375;* Sting, The, *120*

Gould, Jason: Prince of Tides, The, *627*

Goulding, Ray: Bob & Ray, Jane, Laraine & Gilda, *243*

Goulet, Arthur: Silver Blaze, *1016*

Goulet, Robert: Based on an Untrue Story, *232;* Gay Purr-ee, *168;* Naked Gun 2 1/2, The, *341*

Gower, Andre: Monster Squad, The, *866*

Gowland, Gibson: Blind Husbands, *464;* Greed, *533*

Goya, Chantal: Masculine Feminine, *766*

Gozlino, Paolo: Guns for Dollars, *1117*

Gozzi, Patricia: Sundays and Cybèle, *791*

Graas, John Christian: Philadelphia Experiment 2, The, *1070*

Grable, Betty: Beautiful Blonde from Bashful Bend, The, *233;* College Swing, *912;* Down Argentine Way, *914;* Farmer Takes a Wife, The, *916;* Follow the Fleet, *917;* Footlight Serenade, *917;* Gay Divorcée, The, *918;* Hold 'em Jail, *298;* How to Marry a Millionaire, *303;* I Wake Up Screaming, *985;* Moon Over Miami, *931;* Pin-Up Girl, *935;* Song of the Islands, *940;* Springtime in the Rockies (1942), *941;* Three Broadway Girls, *395;* Yank in the RAF, A, *707*

Grace, Carol: Gangster Story, *979*

Grace, Nickolas: Max Headroom, *1065;* Robin Hood and the Sorcerer, *107;* Robin Hood: Herne's Son, *107;* Robin Hood: The Swords of Wayland, *108;* Salome's Last Dance, *647*

Gracen, Elizabeth: Lower Level, *994*

Grady, Ed L.: Last Game, The, *569*

Graf, David: Police Academy II: Their First Assignment, *359;* Police Academy III: Back in Training, *359;* Police Academy 4: Citizens on Patrol, *359;* Police Academy 5—Assignment: Miami Beach, *359;* Police Academy 6: City Under Siege, *359*
Graff, Ilene: Ladybugs, *315*
Graff, Todd: Framed (1990), *280;* Opportunity Knocks, *351*
Graham, Bill: Bugsy, *471*
Graham, Currie: Survive the Night, *1021*
Graham, Gary: Arrogant, The, *450;* Dirty Dozen, The: The Deadly Mission, *39;* Last Warrior, The, *76;* Robot Jox, *1075*
Graham, Gerrit: Annihilators, The, *5;* Bobbie Jo and the Outlaw, *17;* C.H.U.D. II (Bud the C.H.U.D.), *820;* Cannonball, *22;* Child's Play 2, *823;* Demon Seed, *1046;* Game of Love, The, *524;* Greetings, *290;* Home Movies, *299;* It's Alive III: Island of the Alive, *857;* Love Matters, *581;* National Lampoon's Class Reunion, *342;* Philadelphia Experiment 2, The, *1070;* Ratboy, *635;* Ratings Game, The, *364;* Son of Blob (Beware! The Blob), *888;* Spaceship, *384;* Terror Vision, *1082;* Used Cars, *404*
Graham, Heather: Diggstown, *264;* Guilty as Charged, *291;* License to Drive, *318;* O Pioneers!, *610;* Shout (1991), *939;* Six Degrees of Separation, *659*
Graham, Marcus: Dangerous Game, *965*
Graham, Ronny: New Faces, *933;* Ratings Game, The, *364;* World's Greatest Lover, The, *414*
Graham, Sheilah: Girls Town, *55*
Graham, William: Just William's Luck, *179*
Grahame, Gloria: Bad and the Beautiful, The, *454;* Big Heat, The, *12;* Chilly Scenes of Winter, *481;* Crossfire (1947), *964;* Greatest Show on Earth, The, *533;* Human Desire, *546;* In a Lonely Place, *985;* It Happened in Brooklyn, *925;* Macao, *80;* Man Who Never Was, The, *81;* Merry Wives of Windsor, The, *331;* Merton of the Movies, *331;* Nesting, The, *868;* Not as a Stranger, *609;* Oklahoma!, *933;* Ride Beyond Vengeance, *1143;* Song of the Thin Man, *1018;* Todd Killings, The, *685;* Woman's Secret, A, *1032*
Grahame, Margot: Three Musketeers, The (1935), *128*
Grammer, Kelsey: Dance 'Til Dawn, *262*
Grana, Sam: 90 Days, *345*
Granados, Daisy: Portrait of Teresa, *778;* Very Old Man with Enormous Wings, A, *800*
Granados, Rosario: Woman without Love, A, *805*
Grandmaison, Maurice: Savage Journey, *1147*
Grandy, Fred: Death Race 2000, *1045*
Grange, Harold "Red": Galloping Ghost, The, *54*
Granger, Dorothy: Blue Montana Skies, *1099*
Granger, Farley: Arnold, *810;* Deathmask, *36;* Hans Christian Andersen, *921;* Imagemaker, The, *549;* Man Called Noon, The, *1131;* Night Flight from Moscow, *90;* Purple Heart, The, *630;* Rope, *1011;* Slasher, *887;* Small Town Girl, *940;* Strangers on a Train, *1020;* They Call Me Trinity, *1156;* They Live By Night, *681;* Wanton Contessa, The, *802*
Granger, Stewart: Beau Brummell (1954), *457;* Bhowani Junction, *12;* Caesar and Cleopatra, *473;* King Solomon's Mines (1950), *72;* Last Hunt, The, *1126;* Last Safari, *570;* Man in Grey, The, *587;* North to Alaska, *1136;* Prisoner of Zenda, The (1952), *100;* Salome (1953), *647;* Scaramouche, *111;* Sodom and Gomorrah, *661;* Wild Geese, The, *139*
Granstedt, Greta: Devil Horse, The, *1109*
Grant, Barra: Daughters of Satan, *830*
Grant, Beth: Dark Half, The, *829*
Grant, Cary: Affair to Remember, An, *442;* Amazing Adventure, *225;* Arsenic and Old Lace, *228;* Awful Truth, The, *230;* Bachelor and the Bobby-Soxer, The, *230;* Bishop's Wife, The, *240;* Blonde Venus, *464;* Bringing Up Baby, *246;* Charade, *960;* Destination Tokyo, *37;* Every Girl Should Be Married, *273;* Father Goose, *274;* Grass Is Greener, The, *289;* Gunga Din, *58;* His Girl Friday, *297;* Holiday, *298;* Houseboat, *302;* Howards of Virginia, The, *545;* I Was a Male War Bride, *304;* I'm No Angel, *305;* In Name Only, *550;* Indiscreet (1958), *306;* Mr. Blandings Builds His Dream House, *333;* Mr. Lucky, *86;* Monkey Business (1952), *336;* My Favorite Wife, *340;* Night and Day (1946), *933;* None But the Lonely Heart, *608;* North by Northwest, *1002;* Notorious, *1002;* Once Upon a Honeymoon, *349;* Only Angels Have Wings, *95;* Operation Petticoat, *351;* Penny Serenade, *620;* People Will Talk, *356;* Philadelphia Story, The, *357;* Pride and the Passion, The, *626;* She Done Him Wrong, *377;* Suspicion (1941), *1022;* Suzy, *674;* Sylvia Scarlett, *676;* Talk of the Town, The, *390;* That Touch of Mink, *393;* To Catch a Thief, *1025;* Toast of New York, The, *685;* Topper, *397;* Walk, Don't Run, *405*
Grant, David Marshall: American Flyers, *446;* Bat 21, *9;* Breaking Point, *469;* Forever Young (1992), *1053;* French Postcards, *281;* Happy Birthday, Gemini, *293;* Strictly Business, *387*
Grant, Donald: Monster in the Closet, *866*
Grant, Faye: Omen IV: The Awakening, *872*
Grant, Frances: Man of the Frontier (Red River Valley), *1132;* Oh! Susanna!, *1136;* Traitor, The, *1158*
Grant, Hugh: Bitter Moon, *462;* Crossing the Line (1991), *492;* Four Weddings and a Funeral, *280;* Impromptu, *549;* Jenny's War, *68;* Lair of the White Worm, *859;* Maurice, *590;* Remains of the Day, *637;* Sirens, *379*
Grant, Kathryn: Anatomy of a Murder, *952;* Guns of Fort Petticoat, *1118;* 7th Voyage of Sinbad, The, *1076*
Grant, Kirby: Badmen of the Border, *1096;* In Society, *306;* Red River Range, *1141*
Grant, Lee: Airport '77, *443;* Balcony, The, *455;* Big Town, The, *461;* Billion for Boris, A, *239;* Buono Sera, Mrs. Campbell, *247;* Charlie Chan and the Curse of the Dragon Queen, *253;* Citizen Cohn, *482;* Damien: Omen II, *829;* Defending Your Life, *263;* For Ladies Only, *519;* In the Heat of the Night, *986;* Internecine Project, The, *986;* Little Miss Marker (1980), *182;* Marooned, *1065;* Middle of the Night, *593;* My Sister, My Love, *867;* Plaza Suite, *358;* Portnoy's Complaint, *624;* Shampoo, *655;* Valley of the Dolls, *693;* Visiting Hours, *901;* Voyage of the Damned, *694*
Grant, Leon W.: Playing for Keeps, *358*
Grant, Micah: High Desert Kill, *850*
Grant, Peter: Song Remains the Same, The, *435*
Grant, Richard E.: Age of Innocence, The, *443;* Bram Stoker's Dracula, *819;* Codename: Kyril, *962;* Henry & June, *540;* How to Get Ahead in Advertising, *302;* Hudson Hawk, *64;* L.A. Story, *314;* Player, The, *358;* Posse (1993), *1139;* Warlock (1988), *901;* Withnail and I, *412*
Grant, Rodney A.: Dances with Wolves, *1107;* Geronimo: An American Legend, *1115;* Son of the Morning Star, *1151*
Grantham, Lucy: Last House on the Left, *860*
Granval, Charles: Boudu Saved from Drowning, *720*
Granville, Bonita: Ah, Wilderness, *223;* Breakfast in Hollywood, *245;* Cavalcade, *477;* Hitler's Children, *63;* Lone Ranger, The (1956), *1129;* Love Laughs at Andy Hardy, *323;* Mortal Storm, The, *600;* These Three, *680*
Grapewin, Charley: Alice Adams, *444;* Anne of Green Gables (1934), *146;* Girl of the Golden West, The, *919;* Grapes of Wrath, The, *531;* Hell's House, *61;* Johnny Apollo, *559;* Listen, Darling, *928;* Of Human Hearts, *610;* One Frightened Night, *1003;* Three Comrades, *682;* Wizard of Oz, The, *218*
Grassle, Karen: Battered, *456;* Best Christmas Pageant Ever, The, *150;* Cocaine: One Man's Seduction, *485;* Harry's War, *294;* Little House on the Prairie (TV Series), *181*
Grateful Dead: Grateful Dead Movie, The, *425;* So Far, *434*
Grauman, Walter: Pleasure Palace, *623*
Gravel, Jacques Robert: Blind Trust (Pouvoir Intime), *719*
Graver, Chris: Trick or Treat (1982), *897*
Graves, Leslie: Piranha Part Two: The Spawning, *875*
Graves, Peter: Addams Family Values, *222;* Airplane!, *224;* Airplane II: The Sequel, *224;* Clonus Horror, The, *1042;* Court-martial of Billy Mitchell, The, *489;* Encore, *509;* It Conquered the World, *1060;* Killers from Space, *1061;* Number One with a Bullet, *92;* Poor White Trash, *624;* President's Plane Is Missing, The, *1007;* Red Planet Mars, *1074;* Savannah Smiles, *201;* Sergeant Ryker, *652;* Stalag 17, *119;* Texas Across the River, *1155*

Graves, Ralph: Batman and Robin, *9;* Dream Street, *504;* Extra Girl, The, *273;* Ladies of Leisure, *567;* That Certain Thing, *392;* Three Texas Steers, *1157*
Graves, Rupert: Damage, *493;* Fortunes of War, *520;* Handful of Dust, A, *535;* Maurice, *590;* Room with a View, A, *644;* Where Angels Fear to Tread, *699*
Graves, Teresa: Get Christie Love!, *55*
Gravet, Fernand: Great Waltz, The, *921*
Gravina, Carla: Tempter, The, *893*
Gravy, Claudia: Yellow Hair and the Fortress of Gold, *1165*
Gray, Billy: By the Light of the Silvery Moon, *910;* Day the Earth Stood Still, The, *1044;* On Moonlight Bay, *933;* Seven Little Foys, The, *376;* Werewolves on Wheels, *902*
Gray, Carole: Island of Terror, *857*
Gray, Charles: Beast Must Die, The, *812;* Diamonds Are Forever, *38;* Englishman Abroad, An, *510;* Jigsaw Man, The, *987;* Rocky Horror Picture Show, The, *937*
Gray, Coleen: Death of a Scoundrel, *498;* Kansas City Confidential, *988;* Killing, The, *988;* Kiss of Death, *566;* Leech Woman, The, *860;* Red River, *1141;* Tennessee's Partner, *1155*
Gray, David Barry: Cops and Robbersons, *259;* Mr. Wonderful, *597*
Gray, Dolores: Designing Woman, *263;* It's Always Fair Weather, *925;* Kismet (1955), *927;* Opposite Sex, The, *934*
Gray, Donald: Flight from Vienna, *518;* Island of Desire, *555*
Gray, Dulcie: Mine Own Executioner, *594*
Gray, Erin: Breaking Home Ties, *469;* Buck Rogers in the 25th Century, *1040;* Jason Goes to Hell: The Final Friday, *858;* Official Denial, *1069;* Six Pack, *380*
Gray, Gary: Captain Midnight—Vols. 1–2, *155;* Gun Smugglers, *1117;* Painted Hills, The, *193*
Gray, Gordon: Kenneth Anger—Volume One, *562*
Gray, Linda: Accidental Meeting, *950;* Bonanza: The Return, *1100;* Grass Is Always Greener Over the Septic Tank, The, *289;* Oscar (1991), *351;* Two Worlds of Jennie Logan, The, *1086*
Gray, Lorna: Captain America (1944), *22;* Man They Could Not Hang, The, *862;* Nyoka and the Tiger Men (Perils of Nyoka), *92*
Gray, Nadia: Captain's Table, *250;* La Dolce Vita, *753;* Maniac (1962), *995*
Gray, Nan: Three Smart Girls, *945;* Three Smart Girls Grow Up, *945*
Gray, Rhonda: Twisted Nightmare, *898*
Gray, Sally: Dangerous Moonlight (a.k.a. Suicide Squadron), *32;* Keeper, The, *859;* Saint in London, The, *1012;* Saint's Vacation, The, *1012*
Gray, Sam: Heart, *537*
Gray, Spalding: Beaches, *457;* Clara's Heart, *483;* Hard Choices, *536;* Heavy Petting, *426;* King of the Hill, *565;* Monster in a Box, *336;* Paper, The, *617;* Spalding Gray: Terrors of Pleasure, *384;* Stars and Bars, *385;* Straight Talk, *387;* Swimming to Cambodia, *390;* True Stories, *400;* Zelda, *709*
Gray, Vernon: To Paris with Love, *397*
Grayson, Kathryn: Anchors Aweigh, *906;* Andy Hardy's Private Secretary, *227;* It Happened in Brooklyn, *925;* Kiss Me Kate, *927;* Kissing Bandit, The, *927;* Lovely to Look At, *929;* Rio Rita, *368;* Show Boat (1951), *939;* That Midnight Kiss, *944;* Thousands Cheer, *945;* Toast of New Orleans, *946;* Two Sisters from Boston, *947*
Greco, Jose: Proud and the Damned, The, *1139*
Greco, Juliette: Elena and Her Men, *734*
Green, Abel: Copacabana, *259*
Green, Adolph: Lily in Love, *318*
Green, Brian Austin: American Summer, An, *5;* Kid, *71*
Green, Gilbert: Executive Action, *512*
Green, Janet Laine: Bullies, *820;* Primo Baby, *197*
Green, Kerri: Goonies, The, *56;* Lucas, *583;* Summer Rental, *388;* Tainted Blood, *1022;* Three for the Road, *395*
Green, Leif: Joy Sticks, *311*
Green, Marika: Emmanuelle, *734*
Green, Martyn: Mikado, The (1939), *931*
Green, Mitzi: Little Orphan Annie, *183;* Lost in Alaska, *321;* Transatlantic Merry-Go-Round, *946*
Green, Nigel: Corridors of Blood, *825;* Ipcress File, The, *986;* Skull, The, *887;* Tobruk, *130;* Zulu, *142*
Green, Seth: Airborne, *224;* Can't Buy Me Love, *250;* Infested, *856;* Radio Days, *364;* Something Special, *383;* Ticks, *895*
Greenberg, Esther: Lupo, *324*
Greenbush, Lindsay and Sidney: Little House on the Prairie (TV Series), *181*
Greene, Angela: At War with the Army, *229;* Cosmic Man, The, *1043*
Greene, Daniel: Elvira, Mistress of the Dark, *271;* Hands of Steel, *1055;* Opponent, The, *95*
Greene, Elizabeth: Offerings, *872*
Greene, Ellen: Dinner at Eight (1990), *265;* Glory! Glory!, *287;* Little Shop of Horrors (1986), *929;* Me and Him, *330;* Next Stop, Greenwich Village, *605;* Pump Up the Volume, *630;* Stepping Out, *942;* Talk Radio, *677*
Greene, Graham: Benefit of a Doubt, *954;* Broken Chain, The, *20;* Clearcut, *26;* Cooperstown, *488;* Dances with Wolves, *1107;* Last of His Tribe, The, *570;* Maverick, *1133;* Rain without Thunder, *634;* Thunderheart, *1025*
Greene, Lorne: Alamo, The: Thirteen Days to Glory, *1093;* Autumn Leaves, *452;* Battlestar Galactica, *1038;* Bonanza (TV Series), *1100;* Buccaneer, The, *20;* Earthquake, *43;* Mission Galactica: The Cylon Attack, *1066;* Peyton Place, *621;* Roots, *644;* Silver Chalice, The, *658;* Trap, The, *1026;* Vasectomy, *404*
Greene, Michael: Americana, *446;* Clones, The, *1042;* Eve of Destruction, *1050;* Johnny Be Good, *311;* Kill Me Again, *988;* Rubin & Ed, *371*
Greene, Michele: Double Standard, *504;* I Posed for Playboy, *548;* Nightmare on the 13th Floor, *871;* Silent Victim, *658;* Unborn II, The, *898*
Greene, Peter: Judgment Night, *69;* Laws of Gravity, *76*
Greene, Richard: Against All Odds (Kiss and Kill, Blood of Fu Manchu), *808;* Captain Scarlett, *23;* Castle of Fu Manchu, *822;* Forever Amber, *520;* Hound of the Baskervilles, The (1939), *983;* Island of the Lost, *857;* Little Princess, The, *183;* My Lucky Star, *932;* Stanley and Livingstone, *665;* TV Classics: Adventures of Robin Hood, The—TV Series, *133*
Greene, Shecky: Love Machine, The, *581*
Greenleaf, Raymond: When Gangland Strikes, *138*
Greenlee, David: Slumber Party Massacre 3, *887*
Greenless, Billy: That Sinking Feeling, *392*
Greenquist, Brad: Mutants in Paradise, *338*
Greenstreet, Sydney: Across the Pacific, *1;* Background to Danger, *8;* Casablanca, *476;* Christmas in Connecticut (1945), *255;* Conflict, *963;* Flamingo Road, *518;* Hollywood Canteen, *923;* Hucksters, The, *545;* Maltese Falcon, The, *994;* Passage to Marseilles, *97;* They Died with Their Boots On, *1156;* Velvet Touch, The, *693*
Greenwood, Bruce: Adrift, *950;* Another Chance, *228;* Climb, The, *26;* FBI Murders, The, *47;* Malibu Bikini Shop, The, *327;* Passenger 57, *97;* Rio Diablo, *1145;* Servants of Twilight, *884;* Spy, *1019;* Striker's Mountain, *121*
Greenwood, Charlotte: Dangerous When Wet, *913;* Down Argentine Way, *914;* Great Dan Patch, The, *532;* Moon Over Miami, *931;* Opposite Sex, The, *934;* Parlor, Bedroom and Bath, *354;* Springtime in the Rockies (1942), *941*
Greenwood, Joan: At Bertram's Hotel, *953;* Detective, The (1954), *970;* Hound of the Baskervilles, The (1977), *302;* Importance of Being Earnest, The, *305;* Little Dorrit, *576;* Man in the White Suit, The, *327;* Moonspinners, The, *189;* Mysterious Island, *1067;* Stage Struck (1958), *665;* Tight Little Island, *396;* Uncanny, The, *899;* Water Babies, The, *216*
Greer, Gregory A.: Midnight Kiss, *864*
Greer, Jane: Big Steal, The, *13;* Billie, *150;* Clown, The, *484;* Dick Tracy, Detective, *38;* George White's Scandals, *919;* Man

of a Thousand Faces, *587;* Out of the Past, *1003;* Prisoner of Zenda, The (1952), *100;* Run for the Sun, *109;* Shadow Riders, The, *1148;* Sinbad the Sailor, *116;* Station West, *1153;* They Won't Believe Me, *681;* Where Love Has Gone, *699*

Greer, Michael: Fortune and Men's Eyes, *520*

Greeson, Timothy: Disturbance, The, *834*

Gregg, Bradley: Class of 1999, *1041;* Eye of the Storm, *974*

Gregg, Julie: From Hell to Borneo, *53*

Gregg, Mitchell: House of Terror, *984*

Gregg, Virginia: D.I., The, *493;* Hanging Tree, The, *1118;* Spencer's Mountain, *664*

Greggory, Pascal: Pauline at the Beach, *776*

Gregor, Nora: Rules of the Game, The, *782*

Gregory, Andre: Last Temptation of Christ, The, *570;* Linguini Incident, The, *319;* Mosquito Coast, The, *600;* My Dinner with Andre, *602;* Street Smart, *670*

Gregory, Celia: Agatha, *951;* Children of the Full Moon, *823;* Inside Man, The, *66*

Gregory, David: Deadmate, *831*

Gregory, Dick: Sweet Love, Bitter, *675*

Gregory, James: Al Capone, *3;* Ambushers, The, *4;* Beneath the Planet of the Apes, *1039;* Clambake, *912;* Comeback Kid, The, *486;* Francis Gary Powers: The True Story of the U-2 Spy Incident, *522;* Manchurian Candidate, The, *995;* Murderers' Row, *87;* Naked City, The, *1000;* Onionhead, *350;* PT 109, *630;* Secret War of Harry Frigg, The, *375;* Sons of Katie Elder, The, *1151;* Two Weeks in Another Town, *690*

Gregory, Lola: Coming Up Roses, *725*

Gregory, Mark: 1990: The Bronx Warriors, *1069;* Thunder Warrior, *129;* Thunder Warrior II, *129*

Gregory, Natalie: Alice in Wonderland (1985), *145;* Alice Through the Looking Glass (1985), *145*

Gregory, Paul: Whoopee, *947*

Gregson, John: Captain's Table, *250;* Genevieve, *283;* Hans Brinker, *173;* Pursuit of the Graf Spee, *101*

Greif, Stephen: Great Riviera Bank Robbery, The, *980*

Greist, Kim: Duplicates, *973;* Homeward Bound: The Incredible Journey, *175;* Manhunter, *995;* Payoff, *98;* Throw Momma from the Train, *396;* Why Me?, *139*

Grellier, Michel: Holiday Hotel, *744*

Grenfell, Joyce: Americanization of Emily, The, *226;* Belles of St. Trinian's, The, *234;* Old Dark House, The, *872;* Pickwick Papers, The, *357*

Grevill, Laurent: Camille Claudel, *721*

Grey, Anne: Number 17, *1002*

Grey, Denise: Devil in the Flesh (1946), *730;* Sputnik, *788*

Grey, Jennifer: Bloodhounds of Broadway, *242;* Case for Murder, A, *960;* Criminal Justice, *491;* Dirty Dancing, *914;* Ferris Bueller's Day Off, *276;* Stroke of Midnight, *387;* Wind (1992), *140*

Grey, Joel: Buffalo Bill and the Indians, *1102;* Cabaret, *910;* Kafka, *988;* Man on a String, *81;* Music of Chance, The, *601;* Queenie, *632;* Remo Williams: The Adventure Begins, *105;* Seven-Per-Cent Solution, The, *1013*

Grey, Nan: House of the Seven Gables, The, *545;* Invisible Man Returns, *856;* Tower of London (1939), *897*

Grey, Reatha: Soul Vengeance, *118*

Grey, Shirley: Hurricane Express, *65;* Mystery of the Marie Celeste, The, *1000;* Riding Tornado, The, *1144;* Texas Cyclone, *1155;* Uptown New York, *692*

Grey, Virginia: Another Thin Man, *952;* Big Store, The, *238;* Broadway Serenade, *910;* Idaho, *1122;* Idiot's Delight, *548;* Jungle Jim, *69;* Love Has Many Faces, *581;* Mexican Hayride, *331;* Naked Kiss, The, *1000;* Rose Tattoo, The, *644;* Slaughter Trail, *1150;* Tarzan's New York Adventure, *126;* Threat, The, *1024;* Whistling in the Dark, *410*

Greyn, Clinton: Raid on Rommel, *103*

Gribbon, Harry: Ride Him Cowboy, *1143*

Grieco, Richard: Born To Run, *18;* If Looks Could Kill (1991), *66;* Mobsters, *86;* Tomcat: Dangerous Desires, *1084*

Griem, Helmut: Cabaret, *910;* Children of Rage, *481;* Damned, The, *727;* Les Rendez-Vous D'Anna, *759;* Malou, *764*

Grier, David Alan: Bear, *233;* Boomerang, *244*

Grier, Pam: Above the Law, *1;* Big Bird Cage, The, *12;* Bill and Ted's Bogus Journey, *239;* Bucktown, *20;* Class of 1999, *1041;* Coffy, *27;* Drum, *505;* Foxy Brown, *52;* Friday Foster, *53;* Greased Lightning, *57;* Miami Vice: "The Prodigal Son", *84;* On the Edge, *612;* Package, The, *1004;* Posse (1993), *1139;* Scream, Blacula, Scream, *884;* Sheba Baby, *115;* Something Wicked This Way Comes, *1077;* Tough Enough, *131;* Twilight People, *898;* Vindicator, The, *1087*

Grier, Rosey: Sophisticated Gents, The, *663*

Gries, Jonathan: Four Eyes and Six Guns, *1114;* Fright Night II, *844;* Kill Me Again, *988;* Pucker Up and Bark Like a Dog, *363;* Running Scared (1986), *110*

Grieve, Russ: Hills Have Eyes, The, *850*

Grifasi, Joe: Bad Medicine, *231;* Benny & Joon, *234;* Feud, The, *276;* Gentleman Bandit, The, *525;* Hide in Plain Sight, *541;* On the Yard, *94;* Still of the Night, *1020*

Griffeth, Simone: Hot Target, *64;* Patriot, *97*

Griffies, Ethel: Billy Liar, *461;* Billy the Kid, *1099;* Birds, The, *813*

Griffin, Eddie: Meteor Man, *186*

Griffin, Lynne: Strange Brew, *387*

Griffin, Merv: Alice Through the Looking Glass (1985), *145;* Lonely Guy, The, *320;* Two-Minute Warning, *1028*

Griffin, Michael: Inside Out 2, *1059*

Griffin, Tod: She Demons, *885*

Griffith, Andy: Andy Griffith Show, The (TV Series), *227;* Face in the Crowd, A, *512;* Fatal Vision, *515;* Hearts of the West, *295;* Murder in Coweta County, *600;* Murder in Texas, *998;* No Time for Sergeants, *345;* No Time for Sergeants (Television), *608;* Onionhead, *350;* Pray for the Wildcats, *100;* Return to Mayberry, *366;* Rustler's Rhapsody, *371;* Savages (1974), *883*

Griffith, Corinne: Lilies of the Field (1930), *575*

Griffith, Geraldine: Experience Preferred...But Not Essential, *273*

Griffith, Hugh: Abominable Dr. Phibes, The, *808;* Canterbury Tales, The, *722;* Counterfeit Traitor, The, *30;* Cry of the Banshee, *827;* Diary of Forbidden Dreams, *501;* Dr. Phibes Rises Again, *836;* Fixer, The, *517;* Hound of the Baskervilles, The (1977), *302;* Joseph Andrews, *311;* Last Days of Man on Earth, The, *1062;* Legend of the Werewolf, *860;* Lucky Jim, *324;* Luther, *583;* Mutiny on the Bounty (1962), *88;* Oliver, *933;* Run for Your Money, A, *371;* Start the Revolution without Me, *385;* Tom Jones, *397;* Who Slew Auntie Roo?, *903;* Wuthering Heights (1971), *707*

Griffith, James: Amazing Transparent Man, The, *1036;* Blonde Ice, *464;* Bullwhip, *1102;* Double Deal, *41;* Dynamo, *42;* Guns of Fort Petticoat, *1118;* Tom Edison—The Boy Who Lit Up the World, *213*

Griffith, Katharine: Pollyanna (1920), *196*

Griffith, Kenneth: Koroshi, *73*

Griffith, Kristin: Europeans, The, *511*

Griffith, Melanie: Body Double, *958;* Bonfire of the Vanities, *466;* Born Yesterday (1993), *244;* Cherry 2000, *1041;* Drowning Pool, The, *972;* Fear City, *47;* In the Spirit, *306;* Joyride, *560;* Milagro Beanfield War, The, *594;* Night Moves, *1001;* Pacific Heights, *1003;* Paradise (1991), *618;* She's in the Army Now, *656;* Shining Through, *656;* Smile, *381;* Something Wild, *383;* Stormy Monday, *1020;* Stranger Among Us, A, *1020;* Underground Aces, *403;* Women & Men: Stories of Seduction, *706;* Working Girl, *414*

Griffith, Raymond: Hands Up!, *292*

Griffith, Thomas Ian: Excessive Force, *45;* Ulterior Motives, *133*

Griffith, Tom: Alien Factor, The, *1035*

Griffith, Tracy: All Tied Up, *225;* Finest Hour, The, *48;* First Power, The, *841;* Skeeter, *887*

Griffiths, Linda: Lianna, *573;* Reno and the Doc, *638;* Sword of Gideon, *123*
Griffiths, Richard: Blame It on the Bellboy, *240;* Guarding Tess, *291;* King Ralph, *313;* Private Function, A, *361;* Shanghai Surprise, *377;* Whoops Apocalypse, *411;* Withnail and I, *412*
Griffiths, Susan: Legends, *429*
Griggs, Camilla: Forced Vengeance, *51*
Grika, Johanna: Visitants, The, *1087*
Grimaldi, Dan: Don't Go in the House, *836*
Grimes, Frank: Crystalstone, *160;* Dive, The, *40*
Grimes, Gary: Cahill—US Marshal, *1103;* Class of '44, *483;* Culpepper Cattle Co., The, *1106;* Gus, *172;* Summer of '42, *672*
Grimes, Scott: Critters, *827;* Critters 2: The Main Course, *827;* Frog, *168;* It Came Upon a Midnight Clear, *177;* Night Life, *869*
Grimes, Tammy: America, *226;* Can't Stop the Music, *911;* No Big Deal, *608*
Grimm, Dick: Night of the Bloody Transplant, *869*
Grinberg, Anouk: Merci La Vie, *767*
Grisham, Jerry: Escapes, *1049*
Grives, Steven: Dangerous Game, *965*
Grizzard, George: Attica, *452;* Bachelor Party, *230;* Caroline?, *959;* Comes a Horseman, *1105;* Deliberate Stranger, The, *499;* From the Terrace, *523;* Iran Days of Crisis, *554;* Oldest Living Graduate, The, *611;* Stranger Within, The, *891;* Wrong Is Right, *414*
Grodin, Charles: Beethoven (1992), *149;* Beethoven's 2nd, *149;* Clifford, *256;* Couch Trip, The, *259;* Dave, *262;* 11 Harrowhouse, *973;* Grass Is Always Greener Over the Septic Tank, The, *289;* Great Muppet Caper, The, *171;* Grown-ups, *534;* Heart and Souls, *1056;* Heartbreak Kid, The, *295;* Heaven Can Wait (1978), *295;* Incredible Shrinking Woman, The, *306;* Ishtar, *307;* It's My Turn, *555;* King Kong (1976), *859;* Last Resort, *316;* Lonely Guy, The, *320;* Meanest Men in the West, The, *1133;* Midnight Run, *84;* Movers and Shakers, *337;* Real Life, *365;* Seems Like Old Times, *375;* Sex and the College Girl, *653;* So I Married an Axe Murderer, *382;* Sunburn, *1021;* Taking Care of Business, *390;* Woman in Red, The, *413*
Grody, Kathryn: Lemon Sisters, The, *317*
Grogan, C. P.: Comfort and Joy, *258*
Grogan, Clare: Gregory's Girl, *290*
Groh, David: King Lear (1982), *564;* Return of Superfly, The, *105*
Gronemeyer, Herbert: Das Boot (The Boat), *728;* Spring Symphony, *788*
Groom, Sam: Baby Maker, The, *453;* Deadly Eyes, *831;* Deadly Games, *968;* Run for the Roses, *201*
Gross, Arye: Couch Trip, The, *259;* Coupe De Ville, *260;* Experts, The, *273;* For the Boys, *918;* Hexed, *296;* House II: The Second Story, *852;* Matter of Degrees, A, *590;* Midnight Clear, A, *593;* Opposite Sex (And How to Live with Them), The, *351;* Shaking the Tree, *655;* Soul Man, *383*
Gross, Edan: And You Thought Your Parents Were Weird, *227*
Gross, Mary: Avery Schreiber—Live From the Second City, *230;* Casual Sex?, *252;* Couch Trip, The, *259;* Feds, *276;* Hot to Trot, *302;* Troop Beverly Hills, *399*
Gross, Michael: Alan and Naomi, *443;* Big Business, *238;* Cool As Ice, *488;* FBI Murders, The, *47;* Little Gloria...Happy at Last, *576;* Tremors, *897*
Gross, Paul: Aspen Extreme, *451;* Buffalo Jump, *471;* Northern Extremes, *346*
Gross, Sonny: French Connection, The, *53*
Grossmith, George: Wedding Rehearsal, *407*
Grove, Richard: Army of Darkness, *810*
Grovenor, Linda: Die Laughing, *264;* Wheels of Fire, *138*
Grover, Edward: Strike Force, *121*
Groves, Robin: Nesting, The, *868;* Silver Bullet, *886*
Grubb, Robert: Gallipoli, *524*
Grubbs, Gary: Ernest Green Story, The, *165;* Fatal Vision, *515;* JFK, *558*
Grunberg, Klaus: More, *768*
Grundgens, Gustav: M, *763*
Gruner, Olivier: Angel Town, *5;* Nemesis (1992), *1067*
Gryglaszewska, Halina: Double Life of Veronique, The, *731*
Guard, Christopher: Return to Treasure Island, *199*
Guard, Dominic: Absolution, *440;* Picnic at Hanging Rock, *1006*
Guardino, Harry: Adventures of Bullwhip Griffin, The, *143;* Dirty Harry, *39;* Enforcer, The (1976), *44;* Five Pennies, The, *917;* Get Christie Love!, *55;* Hell Is for Heroes, *60;* Houseboat, *302;* Lovers and Other Strangers, *323;* Madigan, *80;* Matilda, *330;* Neon Empire, The, *89;* Pork Chop Hill, *624;* St. Ives, *110;* They Only Kill Their Masters, *1024;* Whiffs, *410*
Guarnica, Lupe: Gloria, *56*
Guedj, Vanessa: Le Grand Chemin (The Grand Highway), *757*
Guerra, Blanca: Danzon, *728*
Guerra, Danny: Plutonium Baby, *875*
Guerra, Ruy: Aguirre: Wrath of God, *711*
Guerrero, Evelyn: Cheech and Chong's Next Movie, *254;* Nice Dreams, *344*
Guerrero, Franco: Deathfight, *36*
Guest, Christopher: Beyond Therapy, *237;* Billy Crystal: Don't Get Me Started, *239;* Few Good Men, A, *976;* Girlfriends, *528;* Last Word, The, *571;* Little Shop of Horrors (1986), *929;* Long Riders, The, *1130;* Piano for Mrs. Cimino, A, *622;* Return of Spinal Tap, The, *366;* Sticky Fingers, *386;* This Is Spinal Tap, *394*
Guest, Lance: Halloween II, *848;* Jaws: The Revenge, *858;* Last Starfighter, The, *1062*
Guest, Nicholas: Brain Smasher...A Love Story, *18;* Chrome Soldiers, *26;* Dollman, *1047;* Long Riders, The, *1130;* My Daughter's Keeper, *999;* Strange Case of Dr. Jekyll and Mr. Hyde, The (1989), *890*
Guetary, Francois: Running Delilah, *110*
Guevara, Nacha: Miss Mary, *767*
Guffey, Cary: Mutant, *867*
Gugino, Carla: Murder Without Motive, *601;* Son-in-Law, *383*
Guier, Adam: Pistol, The: The Birth of a Legend, *195*
Guild, Nancy: Abbott and Costello Meet the Invisible Man, *221;* Black Magic (1949), *462*
Guilfoyle, James: Two Lost Worlds, *133*
Guilfoyle, Paul: Brother Orchid, *20;* Crime of Dr. Crespi, The, *826;* Curiosity Kills, *965;* Final Analysis, *976;* Hoffa, *542;* Wintarset, *704*
Guillaume, Robert: Death Warrant, *35;* Kid with the Broken Halo, The, *313;* Kid with the 200 I.Q., The, *180;* Lean on Me, *571;* Meteor Man, *186;* North and South, *608;* Penthouse, The, *1005;* Seems Like Old Times, *375;* Superfly T.N.T., *122;* Wanted: Dead or Alive, *136;* You Must Remember This, *708*
Guillen, Fernando: Women on the Verge of a Nervous Breakdown, *805*
Guinan, Francis: Mortal Sins (1992), *997*
Guinee, Tim: Chain of Desire, *478;* Tai-Pan, *124;* Vietnam War Story—Part Two, *694*
Guinness, Alec: Bridge on the River Kwai, The, *19;* Brother Sun, Sister Moon, *470;* Captain's Paradise, The, *250;* Comedians, The, *486;* Cromwell, *491;* Damn the Defiant!, *31;* Detective, The (1954), *970;* Dr. Zhivago, *503;* Fall of the Roman Empire, The, *513;* Great Expectations (1946), *532;* Handful of Dust, A, *535;* Hitler, the Last Ten Days, *542;* Horse's Mouth, The, *301;* Hotel Paradiso, *302;* Kafka, *988;* Kind Hearts and Coronets, *313;* Ladykillers, The, *315;* Last Holiday, *569;* Lavender Hill Mob, The, *317;* Lawrence of Arabia, *76;* Little Dorrit, *576;* Little Lord Fauntleroy (1980), *182;* Lovesick, *324;* Majority of One, A, *326;* Malta Story, The, *586;* Man in the White Suit, The, *327;* Monsignor Quixote, *599;* Murder by Death, *338;* Oliver Twist (1948), *612;* Passage to India, A, *619;* Prisoner, The, *628;* Promoter, The,

362; Quiller Memorandum, The, *102;* Raise the Titanic, *103;* Run for Your Money, A, *371;* Scrooge (1970), *938;* Star Wars, *1079;* Swan, The (1956), *674;* To Paris with Love, *397;* To See Such Fun, *397;* Tunes of Glory, *689*

Guiomar, Julien: Leolo, *759;* Swashbuckler, The (1984), *123*

Guiry, Tom: Sandlot, The, *201*

Guitry, Sacha: Pearls of the Crown, The, *776*

Guizar, Tito: On the Old Spanish Trail, *1137*

Gulager, Clu: Gambler, The (1980), *1114;* Glass House, The, *528;* Hidden, The, *1056;* Hit Lady, *63;* Hunter's Blood, *546;* I'm Gonna Git You Sucka!, *305;* Initiation, The, *856;* Lies, *574;* Living Proof: The Hank Williams, Jr., Story, *577;* McQ, *83;* My Heroes Have Always Been Cowboys, *1135;* Nightmare on Elm Street 2, A: Freddy's Revenge, *871;* Offspring, The, *872;* Other Side of Midnight, The, *615;* Prime Risk, *100;* Return of the Living Dead, The, *880;* Smile, Jenny, You're Dead, *661;* Summer Heat (1987), *672;* Teen Vamp, *392;* Touched by Love, *686;* Uninvited, The (1987), *899;* Willa, *703*

Gulliver, Dorothy: Galloping Ghost, The, *54;* In Old Cheyenne, *1123;* Last Frontier, The, *1125;* Shadow of the Eagle, *114*

Gulpilil, David: "Crocodile" Dundee, *261;* Mad Dog Morgan, *80*

Gunn, Moses: Aaron Loves Angela, *440;* Amityville II: The Possession, *809;* Certain Fury, *24;* Cornbread, Earl and Me, *488;* Dixie Lanes, *265;* Haunts of the Very Rich, *1055;* Heartbreak Ridge, *59;* Hot Rock, The, *983;* Killing Floor, The, *563;* Leonard Part 6, *317;* Memphis, *592;* Ninth Configuration, The, *608;* Perfect Harmony, *194;* Shaft, *114;* Shaft's Big Score!, *114;* Wild Rovers, The, *1164*

Gunning, Paul: Hollywood Hot Tubs, *299*

Gunton, Bob: Father Hood, *47;* Ladykiller, *990;* Lois Gibbs and the Love Canal, *577;* Rollover, *1011;* Static, *666*

Gupta, Kamlesh: Crystalstone, *160*

Gurie, Sigrid: Three Faces West, *683*

Gurney, Rachel: Upstairs, Downstairs, *692*

Gurry, Eric: Bad Boys, *454;* Something Special, *383;* Zoo Gang, The, *416*

Gurwitch, Annabelle: Pizza Man, *358*

Guthrie, Arlo: Alice's Restaurant, *444;* Roadside Prophets, *641;* Wasn't That a Time!, *438;* Woody Guthrie—Hard Travelin', *439*

Guthrie, Tyrone: Beachcomber, The, *457;* Sidewalks of London, *657*

Gutierrez, Zaide Silvia: El Norte, *733*

Guttenberg, Steve: Amazon Women on the Moon, *225;* Bad Medicine, *231;* Bedroom Window, The, *954;* Can't Stop the Music, *911;* Chicken Chronicles, The, *254;* Cocoon, *1042;* Cocoon: The Return, *1042;* Day After, The, *1044;* Diner, *265;* Don't Tell Her It's Me, *267;* High Spirits, *297;* Man Who Wasn't There, The, *328;* Miracle on Ice, *595;* Pecos Bill, King of the Cowboys, *194;* Police Academy, *359;* Police Academy II: Their First Assignment, *359;* Police Academy III: Back in Training, *359;* Police Academy 4: Citizens on Patrol, *359;* Short Circuit, *1076;* Surrender, *389;* Three Men and a Baby, *395;* Three Men and a Little Lady, *395*

Gutteridge, Lucy: Little Gloria...Happy at Last, *576;* Top Secret, *397;* Trouble with Spies, The, *399;* Tusks, *133*

Guve, Bertil: Fanny and Alexander, *736*

Guy, Frank: Comic Cabby, *258*

Guzaldo, Joe: Smooth Talker, *1018*

Guzman, Luis: Carlito's Way, *23;* Jumpin' at the Boneyard, *561;* Mr. Wonderful, *597*

Gwenn, Edmund: Anthony Adverse, *450;* Bigamist, The, *461;* Challenge to Lassie, *157;* Cheers for Miss Bishop, *480;* Doctor Takes a Wife, The, *266;* Foreign Correspondent, *978;* Green Dolphin Street, *533;* Hills of Home, *174;* If I Were Rich, *305;* It's a Dog's Life, *177;* Java Head, *557;* Lassie Come Home, *180;* Life with Father, *318;* Meanest Man in the World, The, *330;* Miracle on 34th Street, *187;* Student Prince, The, *942;* Sylvia Scarlett, *676;* Them!, *1083;* Trouble with Harry, The, *399;* Undercurrent, *691;* Waltzes from Vienna, *406;* Woman of Distinction, A, *413*

Gwynne, Anne: Arson Inc., *7;* Dick Tracy Meets Gruesome, *38;* House of Frankenstein, *852;* King of the Bullwhip, *1125;* Meteor Monster, *864;* Ride 'em Cowboy, *368*

Gwynne, Fred: Any Friend of Nicholas Nickleby Is a Friend of Mine, *147;* Boy Who Could Fly, The, *468;* Car 54 Where Are You? (TV Series), *250;* Disorganized Crime, *40;* Ironweed, *554;* Littlest Angel, The, *184;* Man That Corrupted Hadleyburg, The, *327;* Munsters' Revenge, The, *338;* My Cousin Vinny, *339;* Mysterious Stranger, The, *190;* Pet Sematary, *874;* Secret of My Success, The, *375;* Shadows and Fog, *654;* Simon, *379;* So Fine, *382;* Vanishing Act, *693;* Water, *406*

Gwynne, Michael C.: Cherry 2000, *1041;* Deadly Encounter (1972), *34;* Harry Tracy, *1119;* Last of the Finest, The, *75;* Payday, *620;* Streets of L.A., The, *671;* Village of the Damned, *900*

Gyngell, Kim: Boulevard of Broken Dreams, *467;* Heaven Tonight, *539;* Wacky World of Wills and Burke, The, *405*

Gynt, Greta: Human Monster, The (Dark Eyes of London), *854;* Sexton Blake and the Hooded Terror, *1014*

Haade, William: Days of Old Cheyenne, *1107;* Kid Galahad (1937), *563;* Stage to Chino, *1152*

Haas, Hubo: Merton of the Movies, *331*

Haas, Hugo: Holiday in Mexico, *923;* King Solomon's Mines (1950), *72;* Northwest Outpost, *933;* Private Affairs of Bel Ami, The, *628*

Haas, Lukas: Alan and Naomi, *443;* Lady in White, *990;* Leap of Faith, *572;* Music Box, The, *999;* Rambling Rose, *634;* See You in the Morning, *651;* Shattered Spirits, *655;* Solarbabies, *1077;* Testament, *1082;* Witness, *1032;* Wizard of Loneliness, The, *704*

Habbema, Cox: Question of Silence, A, *779*

Habich, Matthias: Coup De Grace, *726;* Straight for the Heart, *790*

Hack, Shelley: Finishing Touch, The, *977;* If Ever I See You Again, *548;* Me, Myself & I, *330;* Single Bars, Single Women, *658;* Stepfather, The, *1020;* Troll, *1085*

Hacker, George: Manhattan Baby, *862*

Hackett, Buddy: Bud and Lou, *471;* God's Little Acre, *529;* It's a Mad Mad Mad Mad World, *308;* Loose Shoes, *321;* Love Bug, The, *184;* Muscle Beach Party, *338;* Music Man, The, *932;* Wonderful World of the Brothers Grimm, The, *1090*

Hackett, Joan: Escape Artist, The, *165;* Flicks, *278;* Group, The, *534;* One Trick Pony, *934;* Only When I Laugh, *614;* Possessed, The (1977), *876;* Reflections of Murder, *1009;* Support Your Local Sheriff!, *1154;* Terminal Man, The, *893;* Will Penny, *1164*

Hackett, John: Dead of Night (1977), *831*

Hackett, Karl: Border Phantom, *1100;* His Brother's Ghost, *1121;* Prairie Rustlers, *1139;* Sing, Cowboy, Sing, *1150;* Take Me Back to Oklahoma, *1154;* Traitor, The, *1158*

Hackett, Sandy: Hamburger—The Motion Picture, *292*

Hackl, Karl Heinz: Assisi Underground, The, *7*

Hackman, Gene: All Night Long, *224;* Another Woman, *450;* Bat 21, *9;* Bite the Bullet, *1099;* Bonnie and Clyde, *17;* Class Action, *962;* Company Business, *28;* Conversation, The, *963;* Doctors' Wives, *503;* Domino Principle, The, *971;* Downhill Racer, *504;* Eureka, *511;* Firm, The, *977;* French Connection, The, *53;* French Connection II, The, *53;* Full Moon in Blue Water, *282;* Geronimo: An American Legend, *1115;* Hawaii, *537;* Hoosiers, *543;* I Never Sang for My Father, *547;* Lilith, *575;* Loose Cannons, *321;* March or Die, *82;* Marooned, *1065;* Mississippi Burning, *596;* Misunderstood (1984), *598;* Narrow Margin (1990), *89;* Night Moves, *1001;* No Way Out, *1002;* Package, The, *1004;* Poseidon Adventure, The, *99;* Postcards from the Edge, *360;* Power (1986), *625;* Prime Cut, *100;* Reds, *637;* Riot, *106;* Scarecrow, *649;* Split Decisions, *664;* Superman II, *1081;* Superman IV: The Quest for Peace, *1081;* Target, *125;* Twice in a Lifetime, *690;* Uncommon Valor, *134;* Under Fire, *134;* Unforgiven (1992), *1160;* Young Frankenstein, *416;* Zandy's Bride, *1166*

Hadary, Jonathan: As Is, *451*

Haddon, Dayle: Bedroom Eyes, *954;* Cheaters, The, *723;* Cyborg, *1043;* French Woman, The, *522;* North Dallas Forty, *609;* Sex with a Smile, *376*

Haden, Sara: Anne of Green Gables (1934), *146;* Life Begins for Andy Hardy, *318;* Life of Her Own, A, *574;* Love Laughs at Andy Hardy, *323;* Mad Love, *861;* Mr. Ace, *85;* Our Vines Have Tender Grapes, *193;* Poor Little Rich Girl (1936), *935;* Spitfire, *664*

Hadley, Reed: Baron of Arizona, The, *1097;* Half-Breed, The, *1118;* Kansas Pacific, *1124;* Little Big Horn, *1128;* Rimfire, *1144;* Shock (1946), *885;* Whistling in the Dark, *410;* Zorro's Fighting Legion, *1166*

Hafner, Ingrid: Philby, Burgess and Maclean: Spy Scandal of the Century, *1005*

Hagalin, Sigridur: Children of Nature, *723*

Hagan, Jennifer: Gallagher's Travels, *54*

Hagar, Ivan: Behind Locked Doors, *812*

Hagen, Jean: Asphalt Jungle, The, *953;* Dead Ringer, *967;* Latin Lovers, *928;* Life of Her Own, A, *574;* Shaggy Dog, The, *203;* Singin' in the Rain, *940*

Hagen, Ross: Armed Response, *6;* B.O.R.N., *811;* Commando Squad, *28;* Dinosaur Island, *1047;* Hellcats, The, *60;* Night Creature, *869;* Phantom Empire, The (1986), *99;* Warlords, *901*

Hagen, Uta: Other, The, *873;* Reversal of Fortune, *639*

Hager, Kristi: Sure Fire, *674*

Hagerty, Julie: Airplane!, *224;* Airplane II: The Sequel, *224;* Bad Medicine, *231;* Beyond Therapy, *237;* Bloodhounds of Broadway, *242;* Goodbye New York, *289;* Lost in America, *321;* Midsummer Night's Sex Comedy, A, *332;* Necessary Parties, *604;* Noises Off, *346;* Rude Awakening (1989), *371;* What About Bob?, *408*

Hagerty, Michael G.: Rio Diablo, *1145*

Haggard, Merle: Hillbillys in a Haunted House, *297;* Huckleberry Finn (1975), *176*

Haggerty, Dan: Abducted, *1;* Angels Die Hard, *5;* California Gold Rush, *1103;* Capture of Grizzly Adams, The, *156;* Chilling, The, *823;* Desperate Women, *1109;* Elves, *838;* Life and Times of Grizzly Adams, The, *181;* Soldier's Fortune, *118;* Spirit of the Eagle, *119;* Terror Out of the Sky, *894*

Haggerty, H. B.: Four Deuces, The, *52*

Haggiag, Brahim: Battle of Algiers, *716*

Hagler, Marvin: Indigo 2: The Revolt, *66*

Hagman, Larry: Big Bus, The, *238;* Deadly Encounter (1972), *34;* Ensign Pulver, *271;* Fail-Safe, *974;* Group, The, *534;* Harry and Tonto, *537;* Intimate Strangers, *553;* Mother, Jugs, and Speed, *337;* S.O.B., *372;* Son of Blob (Beware! The Blob), *888;* Three in the Cellar, *395*

Hagney, Frank: Ride Him Cowboy, *1143*

Hahn, Archie: Bad Golf Made Easier, *231;* Glory Years, *287;* Pray TV (1980), *360*

Hahn, Jess: Mamma Dracula, *862;* Night of the Following Day, The, *1001*

Haid, Charles: Altered States, *1035;* Capone, *22;* Chinatown Murders, The: Man Against the Mob, *25;* Cop, *29;* Deathmoon, *832;* Execution of Private Slovik, The, *512;* Freeze Frame, *168;* Great Escape II, The, *57;* Night Breed, *869;* Rescue, The, *105;* Weekend War, *697*

Haig, Sid: Aftermath, The, *1034;* Beyond Atlantis, *11;* Big Bird Cage, The, *12;* C.C. & Company, *21;* Coffy, *27;* Commando Squad, *28;* Warlords, *901;* Woman Hunt, The, *140*

Haig, Terry: Shades of Love: Champagne for Two, *653*

Haigh, Kenneth: Bitch, The, *462;* Robin and Marian, *107*

Haim, Corey: Blown Away (1992), *957;* Double-O Kid, The, *41;* Dream Machine, *269;* Fast Getaway, *274;* Just One of the Girls, *312;* License to Drive, *318;* Lost Boys, The, *861;* Lucas, *583;* Murphy's Romance, *601;* National Lampoon's Last Resort, *342;* Oh, What a Night, *611;* Prayer of the Rollerboys, *100;* Silver Bullet, *886;* Watchers, *1088*

Haines, Donald: Boys of the City, *18;* Pride of the Bowery, *627*

Haines, Patricia: Night Caller from Outer Space, *1068*

Haines, Richard: Survivor, *1081*

Haines, William: Show People, *378*

Haji: Faster Pussycat! Kill! Kill!, *46;* Motor Psycho, *87*

Hakim, Omar: Bring on the Night, *419*

Haldane, Don: Nikki, Wild Dog of the North, *191*

Hale Jr., Alan: At Sword's Point, *7;* Big Trees, The, *13;* Fifth Musketeer, The, *47;* It Happens Every Spring, *307;* Rim of the Canyon, *1144;* Short Grass, *1149;* To the Shores of Tripoli, *130;* West Point Story, The, *947*

Hale Sr., Alan: Action in the North Atlantic, *2;* Adventures of Don Juan, The, *2;* Adventures of Mark Twain, The (1944), *442;* Adventures of Robin Hood, The, *2;* Broadway Bill, *470;* Captains of the Clouds, *23;* Covered Wagon, The, *1106;* Desperate Journey, *500;* Destination Tokyo, *37;* Dodge City, *1109;* Fighting 69th, The, *48;* Gentleman Jim, *525;* Last Days of Pompeii, The (1935), *569;* Lost Patrol, The, *79;* Man I Love, The, *586;* Man in the Iron Mask, The (1939), *81;* My Girl Tisa, *602;* Night and Day (1946), *933;* Of Human Bondage (1934), *610;* Our Relations, *351;* Prince and the Pauper, The (1937), *197;* Private Lives of Elizabeth and Essex, The, *629;* Pursued, *1140;* Robin Hood (1923), *107;* Santa Fe Trail, *1147;* Sea Hawk, The, *112;* Sisters, The (1938), *659;* Spirit of West Point, The, *664;* Stella Dallas, *667;* Strawberry Blonde, The, *670;* Susan Lenox: Her Fall and Rise, *674;* Thin Ice, *945;* This Is the Army, *945;* Up Periscope, *134;* Virginia City, *1161*

Hale, Barbara: Boy With Green Hair, The, *468;* Buckskin, *1102;* Clay Pigeon, The, *26;* First Yank into Tokyo, *49;* Jolson Sings Again, *926;* Last of the Comanches, *1126;* Lion in the Streets, A, *575;* Oklahoman, The, *1136;* 7th Cavalry, *1148;* Seventh Victim, The, *885;* Window, The, *1032*

Hale, Creighton: Cat and the Canary, The (1927), *960;* Idol Dancer, The, *548;* Orphans of the Storm, *615*

Hale, Diana: My Friend Flicka, *190*

Hale, Georgia: Gold Rush, The, *288*

Hale, Georgina: Mahler, *585*

Hale, Jean: In Like Flint, *66;* St. Valentine's Day Massacre, The, *111*

Hale, Jonathan: Blondie, *241;* Blondie Has Trouble, *241;* Blondie in Society, *241;* Blondie Knows Best, *241;* Charlie Chan's Secret, *961;* Saint in New York, The, *1012;* Saint Strikes Back, The, *1012*

Hale, Louise Closser: Shanghai Express, *655;* Today We Live, *685*

Hale, Michael: Devil Bat's Daughter, *833*

Hale, Monte: Missourians, The, *1134;* Out California Way, *1137;* Trail of Robin Hood, *1158*

Hale Sr, Alan: Stars in My Crown, *1153*

Haley, Jack: Alexander's Ragtime Band, *906;* George White's Scandals, *919;* Higher and Higher, *922;* Moon Over Miami, *931;* Movie Struck (a.k.a. Pick a Star), *338;* One Body Too Many, *1003;* People Are Funny, *356;* Poor Little Rich Girl (1936), *935;* Rebecca of Sunnybrook Farm (1938), *936;* Take It Big, *943;* Wizard of Oz, The, *218;* Wonderful Wizard of Oz, The: The Making of a Movie Classic, *438*

Haley, Jackie Earle: Bad News Bears, The, *231;* Bad News Bears Go to Japan, The, *231;* Bad News Bears in Breaking Training, The, *231;* Breaking Away, *245;* Damnation Alley, *1044;* Dollman, *1047;* Losin' It, *321;* Maniac Cop 3: Badge of Silence, *863*

Halicki, H. B.: Gone in 60 Seconds, *56*

Hall, Albert: Malcolm X, *586;* Rookie of the Year, *200*

Hall, Anthony Michael: Adventures of a Gnome Named Gnorm, The, *1034;* Breakfast Club, The, *245;* Edward Scissorhands, *1048;* Hail Caesar, *292;* Into the Sun, *67;* Johnny Be Good, *311;* National Lampoon's Vacation, *342;* Out of Bounds, *96;* Six Degrees of Separation, *659;* Sixteen Candles, *380;* Weird Science, *407*

Hall Jr., Arch: Eegah!, *838;* Nasty Rabbit, *342;* Sadist, The, *882;* Wild Guitar, *702*

Hall, Arsenio: Amazon Women on the Moon, *225;* Coming to America, *258;* Harlem Nights, *59*

Hall, Brad: Limit Up, *319;* Troll, *1085*
Hall, Carol E.: Love Your Mama, *582*
Hall, Charlie: Laurel and Hardy Classics, Volume 1, *316;* Laurel and Hardy Classics, Volume 2, *316;* Laurel and Hardy Classics, Volume 3, *316;* Laurel and Hardy Classics, Volume 4, *316;* Laurel and Hardy Classics, Volume 6, *316;* Laurel and Hardy Classics, Volume 7, *316;* Laurel and Hardy Classics, Volume 9, *316*
Hall, Cleve: Twisted Nightmare, *898*
Hall, Delores: Leap of Faith, *572*
Hall, Grayson: Adam at 6 A.M., *441;* House of Dark Shadows, *852;* Night of Dark Shadows, *869*
Hall, Huntz: Auntie Lee's Meat Pies, *811;* Blues Busters, *242;* Bowery Boys, The (Series), *244;* Cyclone, *31;* Gas Pump Girls, *283;* Junior G-Men, *69;* Little Tough Guys, *319;* Ratings Game, The, *364;* Valentino, *693*
Hall, John: No Nukes, *432*
Hall, Jon: Ali Baba and the Forty Thieves, *3;* Arabian Nights (1942), *6;* Hell Ship Mutiny, *60;* Hurricane, The (1937), *546;* Invisible Agent, *1059;* Kit Carson, *1125;* Last of the Redmen, *1126;* South of Pago Pago, *119;* Tuttles of Tahiti, The, *400*
Hall, Juanita: Flower Drum Song, *917*
Hall, Kevin Peter: Misfits of Science, *1066;* Predator, *1071*
Hall, Lois: Pirates of the High Seas, *99*
Hall, Mark Edward: Across the Great Divide, *143*
Hall, Nathaniel: Livin' Large, *320*
Hall, Peter: Pedestrian, The, *620*
Hall, Philip Baker: Secret Honor, *651;* Three O'Clock High, *396*
Hall, Porter: Arizona, *1094;* Beautiful Blonde from Bashful Bend, The, *233;* Bulldog Drummond Escapes, *20;* Case of the Lucky Legs, The, *960;* Double Indemnity, *972;* General Died at Dawn, The, *55;* Great Moment, The, *290;* Intruder in the Dust, *553;* Miracle of Morgan's Creek, The, *332;* Satan Met a Lady, *1012;* Story of Louis Pasteur, The, *668;* Sullivan's Travels, *388;* They Shall Have Music, *944;* Thin Man, The, *1024*
Hall, Rich: Best of Not Necessarily the News, The, *236;* Million Dollar Mystery, *332;* Rich Hall's Vanishing America, *367;* Your Favorite Laughs from an Evening at the Improv, *416*
Hall, Ron: Triple Impact, *132*
Hall, Ruth: Man from Monterey, The, *1131;* Monkey Business (1931), *335;* Ride Him Cowboy, *1143;* Three Musketeers, The (1933), *128*
Hall, Shana: Boogeyman 2, The, *818*
Hall, Thurston: Adventures of Topper, The, *223;* Affairs of Annabel, The, *223;* Black Room, The (1935), *814;* Call of the Canyon, *1103;* Great Moment, The, *290;* I Dood It, *924;* Rim of the Canyon, *1144;* Secret Life of Walter Mitty, The, *374;* Song of Nevada, *1151;* Without Reservations, *413;* You Can't Cheat an Honest Man, *415*
Hall, Zooey: Fortune and Men's Eyes, *520;* I Dismember Mama, *855*
Hall-Davies, Lillian: Ring, The, *640*
Hallahan, Charles: Going in Style, *288;* Tales of the Unexpected, *1022*
Hallam, John: Murphy's War, *87*
Halldorsson, Gisli: Children of Nature, *723*
Hallick, Tom: Rare Breed, A (1981), *198*
Halliday, Bryant: Devil Doll (1963), *833*
Halliday, John: Bird of Paradise, *13;* Consolation Marriage, *488;* Finishing School, *516*
Hallier, Lori: Blindside, *15;* My Bloody Valentine, *867*
Halloran, Jane: Lianna, *573*
Hallyday, David: He's My Girl, *296*
Hallyday, Johnny: Iron Triangle, The, *554;* Tales of Paris, *792*
Halop, Billy: Junior G-Men, *69;* Little Tough Guys, *319;* Tom Brown's School Days (1940), *685*
Halpin, Luke: Flipper, *167;* Flipper's New Adventure, *167;* Flipper's Odyssey, *167;* Island of the Lost, *857*
Halprin, Daria: Zabriskie Point, *709*
Halsey, Brett: Atomic Submarine, The, *1037;* Return of the Fly, The, *880;* Return to Peyton Place, *639;* Twice-Told Tales, *898*
Halsey, John: Rutles, The (a.k.a. All You Need Is Cash), *938*
Halsted, Christopher: Haunting of Morella, The, *849*
Halton, Charles: Dr. Cyclops, *835*
Hama, Mie: You Only Live Twice, *141*
Hamamura, Jun: Zatoichi: The Blind Swordsman's Vengeance, *806*
Hamblen, Stuart: King of the Forest Rangers, *72*
Hamblin, John: Who Killed Baby Azaria?, *701*
Hamel, Veronica: Cannonball, *22;* New Life, A, *343;* Sessions, *652*
Hamer, Gerald: Scarlet Claw, The, *1012*
Hamill, John: Beast in the Cellar, The, *812*
Hamill, Mark: Big Red One, The, *12;* Black Magic Woman, *955;* Corvette Summer, *29;* Empire Strikes Back, The, *1049;* Eric, *510;* Guyver, The, *1055;* John Carpenter Presents: Body Bags, *858;* Night the Lights Went Out in Georgia, The, *606;* Return of the Jedi, *1074;* Slipstream, *1077;* Star Wars, *1079;* Time Runner, *1084*
Hamilton, Alexa: Death Spa, *831*
Hamilton, Antony: Howling IV, *854;* Samson and Delilah (1984), *648*
Hamilton, Bernie: Bucktown, *20;* Losers, The, *79*
Hamilton, Carrie: Checkered Flag, *480;* Tokyo Pop, *946*
Hamilton, Chico: Jazz on a Summer's Day, *427*
Hamilton, Dan: Romeo and Juliet (1983), *643*
Hamilton, Dean: Rush Week, *882*
Hamilton, Gay: Barry Lyndon, *456*
Hamilton, George: Dead Don't Die, The, *830;* Doc Hollywood, *265;* Evel Knievel, *45;* Express to Terror, *974;* From Hell to Victory, *53;* Godfather, Part III, The, *529;* Happy Hooker Goes to Washington, The, *293;* Home from the Hill, *542;* Love at First Bite, *322;* Man Who Loved Cat Dancing, The, *1132;* Monte Carlo, *599;* Once Is Not Enough, *613;* Once Upon a Crime, *349;* Poker Alice, *1139;* Seekers, The, *651;* Sextette, *376;* Two Weeks in Another Town, *690;* Viva Maria!, *801;* Where the Boys Are, *409;* Zorro, the Gay Blade, *417*
Hamilton, Jane: Beauty School, *233;* Cleo/Leo, *256;* Deranged, *833;* Slammer Girls, *380;* Wimps, *412*
Hamilton, John: Captain Midnight—Vols. 1–2, *155;* TV's Best Adventures of Superman, *1085*
Hamilton, Josh: Alive, *444;* With Honors, *412*
Hamilton, Kipp: War of the Gargantuas, *1088*
Hamilton, Linda: Beauty and the Beast (TV Series), *1039;* Black Moon Rising, *14;* Children of the Corn, *823;* Club Med, *484;* King Kong Lives, *859;* Mr. Destiny, *334;* Rape And Marriage: The Rideout Case, *635;* Secret Weapons, *113;* Tag—The Assassination Game, *124;* Terminator, The, *1082;* Terminator 2: Judgment Day, *1082*
Hamilton, Lois: Armed Response, *6*
Hamilton, Margaret: Anderson Tapes, The, *952;* Babes in Arms, *907;* Beautiful Blonde from Bashful Bend, The, *233;* Breaking the Ice, *909;* Broadway Bill, *470;* City without Men, *483;* Daydreamer, The, *161;* Invisible Woman, The, *307;* People Will Talk, *356;* Red Pony, The, *198;* Sin of Harold Diddlebock (a.k.a. Mad Wednesday), *379;* Sun Comes Up, The, *208;* 13 Ghosts, *895;* Villain Still Pursued Her, The, *135;* When's Your Birthday?, *409;* Wizard of Oz, The, *218;* Wonderful Wizard of Oz, The: The Making of a Movie Classic, *438;* You Only Live Once, *708*
Hamilton, Murray: Anatomy of a Murder, *952;* Boston Strangler, The, *818;* Brotherhood, The, *471;* Brubaker, *471;* Casey's Shadow, *157;* Drowning Pool, The, *972;* FBI Story, The, *515;* Hustler, The, *547;* Hysterical, *303;* If It's Tuesday, This Must Be Belgium, *305;* Jaws, *858;* Jaws 2, *858;* Last Days of Patton, The, *569;* 1941, *345;* No Time for Sergeants, *345;* No Way to Treat a Lady, *1002;* Papa's Delicate Condition, *617;* Sergeant Ryker, *652;* Spirit of St. Louis, The, *664;* Tall Story, *391*

Hamilton, Neil: Animal Kingdom, The, *448;* King of the Texas Rangers, *1125;* Laughing Sinners, *571;* Saint Strikes Back, The, *1012;* Sin of Madelon Claudet, The, *658;* Tarzan and His Mate, *125;* Tarzan the Ape Man (1932), *125;* They Meet Again, *681;* What Price Hollywood?, *698;* World Gone Mad, The, *707*

Hamilton, Paula: Four Days in July, *521*

Hamilton, Richard: In Country, *550;* On Deadly Ground, *93*

Hamilton, Rusty: Rock 'n' Roll Nightmare, *881*

Hamilton, Suzanna: Brimstone and Treacle, *819;* 1984 (1984), *1068;* Out of Africa, *616;* Tale of a Vampire, *891*

Hamilton, Ted: Pirate Movie, The, *935*

Hamilton, Tony: Fatal Instinct (1992), *976*

Hamlin, Harry: Blue Skies Again, *465;* Clash of the Titans, *1041;* Deceptions, *969;* Dinner at Eight (1990), *265;* Hitchhiker (Series), The, *850;* King of the Mountain, *565;* L.A. Law, *567;* Laguna Heat, *990;* Making Love, *586;* Movie Movie, *338;* Murder So Sweet, *601;* Save Me, *1012;* Target: Favorite Son, *677;* Under Investigation, *1028*

Hamlin, Marilyn: Savage Weekend, *883*

Hammel, Fritz: Scorpion Woman, The, *784*

Hammer, Don: Danger, *965*

Hammond, John: Blue and the Gray, The, *1099*

Hammond, Kay: Abraham Lincoln, *440;* Five Golden Hours, *278*

Hammond, Nicholas: Amazing Spiderman, The, *4;* Chinese Web, The, *25;* King Richard II, *565;* Martian Chronicles, Parts I-III, The, *1065;* Tempest, The (1983), *678;* Trouble in Paradise, *399*

Hammond, Patricia Lee: Dracula's Last Rites (1980), *837*

Hamnett, Olivia: Deadly Possession, *968;* Earthling, The, *164;* Last Wave, The, *991*

Hampden, Walter: Five Fingers, *977*

Hampen, Walter: Adventures of Mark Twain, The (1944), *442*

Hampshire, Susan: Cry Terror, *964;* Fighting Prince of Donegal, The, *167;* Living Free, *184;* Those Daring Young Men in Their Jaunty Jalopies, *394;* Three Lives of Thomasina, The, *211*

Hampton, James: Bunco, *21;* Condorman, *159;* Hangar 18, *1055;* Hawmps!, *294;* Pump Up the Volume, *630;* Teen Wolf, *892;* Teen Wolf, Too, *892*

Hampton, Lionel: Song Is Born, A, *940*

Hampton, Paul: Hit!, *62;* Never Forget, *604;* They Came from Within, *895*

Han, Mary: Dynamo, *42*

Hana, Miya: What's Up, Tiger Lily?, *408*

Hancock, Barbara: Finian's Rainbow, *916*

Hancock, Herbie: Round Midnight, *937;* Stand by Me (1988), *941*

Hancock, John: Catch the Heat, *24;* Collision Course, *257;* Traxx, *132*

Hancock, Sheila: Buster, *472*

Hancock, Tony: Wrong Box, The, *414*

Handl, Irene: Adventures of a Private Eye, *222;* Morgan, *337;* Private Life of Sherlock Holmes, The, *1008;* Wonderwall, *805*

Handy, James: Dangerous Life, A, *494;* False Arrest, *513*

Haney, Anne: Mrs. Doubtfire, *334*

Haney, Carol: Pajama Game, The, *934*

Haney, Daryl: Daddy's Boys, *31*

Hanin, Roger: Day of Atonement, *33;* My Other Husband, *770*

Hankerson, Barry L.: Pipe Dreams, *622*

Hankin, Larry: Out on a Limb (1992), *352;* TBone N Weasel, *391*

Hanks, Jim: Buford's Beach Bunnies, *247*

Hanks, Steve: Island Claws, *857*

Hanks, Tom: Bachelor Party, *230;* Big, *237;* Bonfire of the Vanities, *466;* 'Burbs, The, *247;* Dragnet (1987), *268;* Every Time We Say Goodbye, *511;* Fallen Angels, *513;* He Knows You're Alone, *849;* Joe Versus the Volcano, *310;* League of Their Own, A, *571;* Man with One Red Shoe, The, *328;* Mazes and Monsters, *864;* Money Pit, The, *335;* Nothing in Common, *609;* Philadelphia, *621;* Punchline, *630;* Radio Flyer, *633;* Sleepless in Seattle, *381;* Splash, *384;* Turner and Hooch, *400;* Volunteers, *405*

Hanlon, Julie: I Was a Teenage TV Terrorist, *304*

Hann-Byrd, Adam: Little Man Tate, *182*

Hannah, Daryl: At Play in the Fields of the Lord, *451;* Attack of the 50-Foot Woman (1993), *1037;* Blade Runner, *1039;* Clan of the Cave Bear, *1041;* Crazy People, *260;* Final Terror, The, *841;* Grumpy Old Men, *291;* Hard Country, *293;* High Spirits, *297;* Legal Eagles, *991;* Memoirs of an Invisible Man, *1065;* Pope of Greenwich Village, The, *624;* Reckless (1984), *636;* Roxanne, *370;* Splash, *384;* Steel Magnolias, *667;* Summer Lovers, *672;* Wall Street, *695*

Hannah, John: Four Weddings and a Funeral, *280*

Hannah, Page: My Man Adam, *340;* Shag, the Movie, *654*

Hannah, Will: Buckeye and Blue, *1102*

Hannigan, Alison: My Stepmother Is an Alien, *341*

Hansard, Glen: Commitments, The, *912*

Hansen, Eleanor: Flaming Frontiers, *1113*

Hansen, Gale: Double Vision, *972;* Finest Hour, The, *48;* Shaking the Tree, *655*

Hansen, Gunnar: Demon Lover, The, *832;* Hollywood Chainsaw Hookers, *850;* Scream of the Demon Lover (1976), *884;* Texas Chainsaw Massacre, The, *894*

Hansen, Juliana: Perfect Family, *1005*

Hansen, Patti: Hard to Hold, *922*

Hanson, Lars: Scarlet Letter, The (1926), *649;* Wind, The (1928), *703*

Hanson, Peter: Branded, *1101;* When Worlds Collide, *1089*

Hara, Setsuko: Early Summer, *732;* Idiot, The, *746;* Late Spring, *756;* No Regrets for Our Youth, *772*

Harada, Kiwako: Days of Hell, *33*

Haralde, Ralf: Framed (1930), *521*

Hardaway, Anfernee: Blue Chips, *465*

Harden, Ernest: White Mama, *700*

Harden, Marcia Gay: Fever, *47;* Late for Dinner, *1062;* Miller's Crossing, *594;* Used People, *404*

Hardester, Crofton: Devastator, The, *37*

Hardie, Raymond: Look Back in Anger (1980), *579*

Hardie, Russell: Operator 13, *614*

Hardin, Jerry: Hot Spot, *544*

Hardin, Melora: Lambada, *927;* Reckless Kelly, *365*

Hardin, Sherry: Hollywood High, *299*

Hardin, Ty: Bad Jim, *1095;* Berserk, *812;* Born Killer, *17;* Bronco (TV Series), *1101;* Fire!, *48;* One Step to Hell, *95;* Palm Springs Weekend, *353;* PT 109, *630;* You're Jinxed Friend, You Just Met Sacramento, *1166*

Harding, Ann: Animal Kingdom, The, *448;* Devotion, *500;* Magnificent Yankee, The, *585;* Those Endearing Young Charms, *394;* Two Weeks with Love, *947*

Harding, June: Trouble with Angels, The, *399*

Harding, Lyn: Silver Blaze, *1016;* Speckled Band, The, *1019;* Triumph of Sherlock Holmes, The, *1027*

Hardison, Kadeem: Def by Temptation, *832;* Dream Date, *269;* Gunmen, *58*

Hardwick, Derek: Among the Cinders, *446*

Hardwicke, Cedric: Becky Sharp, *457;* Commandos Strike at Dawn, *28;* Connecticut Yankee in King Arthur's Court, A (1948), *258;* Desert Fox, The, *37;* Diane, *500;* Five Weeks in a Balloon, *50;* Ghost of Frankenstein, *845;* Ghoul, The (1933), *846;* Howards of Virginia, The, *545;* Hunchback of Notre Dame, The (1939), *854;* Invisible Agent, *1059;* Invisible Man Returns, *856;* King Solomon's Mines (1937), *72;* Les Miserables (1935), *573;* Nicholas Nickleby, *605;* Nine Days a Queen, *607;* On Borrowed Time, *612;* Outer Limits, The (TV Series), *1069;* Rope, *1011;* Salome (1953), *647;* Stanley and Livingstone, *665;* Sundown (1941), *673;* Suspicion (1941), *1022;* Ten Commandments, The (1956), *678;* Things to Come, *1083;* Tom Brown's School Days (1940), *685;* Tycoon,

133; Valley of the Sun, 1161; White Tower, The, 701; Wilson, 703; Wing and a Prayer, A, 140; Winslow Boy, The, 704
Hardwicke, Edward: Shadowlands, 654
Hardy, Oliver: Air Raid Wardens, 223; Atoll K (Utopia), 229; Block-Heads, 241; Bohemian Girl, The, 243; Bonnie Scotland, 243; Bullfighters, The, 247; Chump at Oxford, A, 255; Days of Thrills and Laughter, 262; Devil's Brother, The, 914; Fighting Kentuckian, The, 1112; Flying Deuces, 278; Golden Age of Comedy, The, 288; Great Guns, 289; Hollywood Party, 299; Laurel and Hardy: At Work, 316; Laurel and Hardy Classics, Volume 1, 316; Laurel and Hardy Classics, Volume 2, 316; Laurel and Hardy Classics, Volume 3, 316; Laurel and Hardy Classics, Volume 4, 316; Laurel and Hardy Classics, Volume 5, 316; Laurel and Hardy Classics, Volume 6, 316; Laurel and Hardy Classics, Volume 7, 316; Laurel and Hardy Classics, Volume 8, 316; Laurel and Hardy Classics, Volume 9, 316; Laurel and Hardy on the Lam, 317; Laurel and Hardy's Laughing 20s, 317; Little Rascals, The, 183; March of the Wooden Soldiers, 329; MGM's The Big Parade of Comedy, 331; Movie Struck (a.k.a. Pick a Star), 338; Nothing But Trouble (1944), 347; Our Relations, 351; Pack Up Your Troubles, 352; Pardon Us, 354; Saps at Sea, 372; Sons of the Desert, 383; Swiss Miss, 390; Three Ages, The, 395; TV Classics: Laurel & Hardy, 401; Way Out West, 406; When Comedy Was King, 409
Hardy, Robert: All Creatures Great and Small, 145; Dark Places, 829; Gathering Storm, 525; Jenny's War, 68; Shooting Party, The, 656
Harelik, Mark: Barbarians at the Gate, 455
Harewood, Dorian: Ambush Murders, The, 446; American Christmas Carol, An, 146; Full Metal Jacket, 523; God Bless the Child, 528; Jessie Owens Story, The, 557; Kiss Shot, 566; Pacific Heights, 1003; Roots: The Next Generation, 644; Shattered Image, 1014; Sparkle, 941
Hargitay, Mariska: Finish Line, 516; Jocks, 310; Welcome to 18, 407
Hargitay, Mickey: Bloody Pit of Horror, 817; Lady Frankenstein, 859; Promises, Promises, 362
Hargrave, Doris: Fast Money, 46
Hargrave, T. J.: Prince of Central Park, The, 197
Hargreaves, Amy: Brainscan, 818
Hargreaves, Christine: Pink Floyd: The Wall, 935
Hargreaves, John: Beyond Reasonable Doubt (1983), 955; Careful He Might Hear You, 475; Don's Party, 267; Killing of Angel Street, The, 564; Long Weekend, 861; Malcolm, 327; My First Wife, 602; Odd Angry Shot, The, 610; Sky Pirates, 117
Harker, Gordon: Champagne, 479
Harker, Susannah: Crucifer of Blood, 964
Harkins, John: Birdy, 462; One Shoe Makes It Murder, 1003; Rampage, 1009; Right of Way, 640; This Gun for Hire (1991), 128
Harlan, Kenneth: Law Rides Again, The, 1127; Shadow of the Eagle, 114; Virginian, The (1923), 1161
Harlan, Otis: Ride Him Cowboy, 1143; Telegraph Trail, The, 1154
Harlan, Robin: Party Animal, 354
Harlow, Jean: Bombshell, 243; China Seas, 25; Dinner at Eight (1933), 265; Girl from Missouri, The, 286; Hold Your Man, 542; Hollywood on Parade, 299; Laurel and Hardy Classics, Volume 9, 316; Libeled Lady, 318; Personal Property, 356; Platinum Blonde, 623; Public Enemy, 101; Reckless (1935), 636; Red Dust, 636; Red-Headed Woman, 636; RiffRaff (1936), 640; Saratoga, 372; Suzy, 674; Wife Vs. Secretary, 701
Harmon, Deborah: Used Cars, 404
Harmon, Mark: After the Promise, 442; Cold Heaven, 485; Deliberate Stranger, The, 499; Fourth Story, 978; Goliath Awaits, 56; Let's Get Harry, 573; Presidio, The, 100; Prince of Bel Air, 627; Stealing Home, 667; Summer School, 388; Sweet Bird of Youth (1989), 674; Till There Was You, 684; Worth Winning, 414
Harmon, Tom: Spirit of West Point, The, 664
Harnois, Elisabeth: Adventures in Wonderland, 143
Harnos, Kristina: Rescue, The, 105
Haroide, Ralf: I'm No Angel, 305
Harper, James: Mortal Sins (1990), 997
Harper, Jessica: Blue Iguana, 242; Evictors, The, 839; Imagemaker, The, 549; Inserts, 552; Mr. Wonderful, 597; Pennies from Heaven, 935; Phantom of the Paradise, 935; Shock Treatment, 378; Stardust Memories, 385; Suspiria, 891
Harper, Marjory: Life and Times of Grizzly Adams, The, 181
Harper, Paul: Bloody Trail, 1099
Harper, Robert: Nick Knight, 868; Not Quite Human, 347; Payoff, 98
Harper, Samantha: Oh! Calcutta!, 348
Harper, Tess: Amityville III: The Demon, 809; Chiefs, 961; Crimes of the Heart, 260; Criminal Law, 964; Daddy's Dyin' and Who's Got the Will, 261; Dark River: A Father's Revenge, 495; Far North, 274; Flashpoint, 977; Her Alibi, 296; Incident at Dark River, 551; Ishtar, 307; Man in the Moon, The, 587; My Heroes Have Always Been Cowboys, 1135; My New Gun, 341; Starflight One, 1079; Tender Mercies, 679
Harper, Valerie: Blame It on Rio, 240; Chapter Two, 479; Don't Go to Sleep, 836; Execution, The, 974; Freebie and the Bean, 281; Last Married Couple in America, The, 315; Night Terror, 1001; Shadow Box, The, 654; Thursday's Game, 683
Harrelson, Woody: Cool Blue, 488; Doc Hollywood, 265; Eye of the Demon, 840; Indecent Proposal, 551; Ted & Venus, 392; White Men Can't Jump, 410; Wildcats, 411
Harring, Laura: Rio Diablo, 1145
Harrington, Al: White Fang 2: Myth of the White Wolf, 217
Harrington, Kate: Rachel, Rachel, 632
Harrington, Laura: Linda, 992; Maximum Overdrive, 864; Midnight Cabaret, 864; Perfect Witness, 620
Harrington, Linda: Secret, The, 650
Harrington, Pat: Affair, The, 442; President's Analyst, The, 360
Harris, Adeline: Texas John Slaughter: Geronimo's Revenge, 1155; Texas John Slaughter: Stampede at Bitter Creek, 1155; Texas John Slaughter: Wild Times, 1156
Harris, Anita: Follow That Camel, 278; Martians Go Home, 329
Harris, Barbara: Dirty Rotten Scoundrels, 265; Family Plot, 975; Freaky Friday, 168; Movie Movie, 338; Nice Girls Don't Explode, 344; North Avenue Irregulars, The, 191; Oh Dad, Poor Dad—Mama's Hung You in the Closet and I'm Feeling So Sad, 348; Peggy Sue Got Married, 355; Plaza Suite, 358; Seduction of Joe Tynan, The, 651; Thousand Clowns, A, 395
Harris, Brad: Fury of Hercules, The, 54; Hercules (1983), 1056; King of Kong Island, 859; Old Testament, The, 772; Rattler Kid, 1141; Samson, 1076; Seven Magnificent Gladiators, The, 113
Harris, Bud: Moon Over Harlem, 599
Harris, Cynthia: Edward and Mrs. Simpson, 507; Izzy & Moe, 309; Pancho Barnes, 617; Reuben, Reuben, 367
Harris, Danielle: Halloween IV: The Return of Michael Myers, 848; Halloween V: The Revenge of Michael Myers, 848
Harris, David: Badge of the Assassin, 454; Dangerous Relations, 494; Undercover, 134
Harris, Ed: Abyss, The, 1034; Alamo Bay, 443; Borderline, 17; China Moon, 961; Code Name: Emerald, 27; Firm, The, 977; Flash of Green, A, 977; Glengarry Glen Ross, 528; Jackknife, 556; Knightriders, 73; Last Innocent Man, The, 990; Needful Things, 868; Paris Trout, 618; Places in the Heart, 623; Right Stuff, The, 640; Running Mates (1992), 371; Seekers, The, 651; State of Grace, 666; Sweet Dreams, 943; Swing Shift, 675; To Kill a Priest, 684; Under Fire, 134; Walker, 695
Harris, Fred: Exterminators of the Year 3000, 1050
Harris, George: Prime Suspect 2, 1007
Harris, Jared: Public Eye, The, 1008
Harris, Jim: Squeeze Play, 385; Waitress, 405
Harris, Jo Ann: Beguiled, The, 954; Deadly Games, 968

Harris, Jonathan: Lost in Space (TV Series), *1063*
Harris Jr, Wendell B.: Chameleon Street, *478*
Harris, Julie: Bell Jar, The, *458;* Christmas Wife, The, *482;* Dark Half, The, *829;* East of Eden (1955), *506;* Gorillas in the Mist, *531;* Harper, *981;* Haunting, The, *849;* Hiding Place, The, *541;* Home for the Holidays, *983;* Housesitter, *302;* I Am a Camera, *547;* Last of Mrs. Lincoln, The, *570;* Member of the Wedding, The, *592;* Reflections in a Golden Eye, *637;* Requiem for a Heavyweight, *638;* Truth About Women, The, *689;* Voyage of the Damned, *694;* You're a Big Boy Now, *416*
Harris, Julius W.: Black Caesar, *13;* Friday Foster, *53;* Harley Davidson and the Marlboro Man, *59;* Hell Up in Harlem, *60;* Islands in the Stream, *555;* Superfly, *122;* To Sleep with Anger, *685*
Harris, Kathryn: Broken Trust, *959*
Harris, Lara: All Tied Up, *225;* No Man's Land, *91*
Harris, Leigh and Lynette: Sorceress (1982), *1077*
Harris, M. K.: Horseplayer, *983;* Slumber Party Massacre 3, *887*
Harris, Mel: Cameron's Closet, *820;* Desperate Motive, *970;* K-9, *312;* Wanted: Dead or Alive, *136*
Harris, Michael: Shattered Image, *1014*
Harris, Moira: One More Saturday Night, *350*
Harris, Neil Patrick: Clara's Heart, *483;* Cold Sassy Tree, *485;* Purple People Eater, *198*
Harris, Phil: Buck Benny Rides Again, *246;* Dreaming Out Loud, *269;* Goodbye, My Lady, *171;* High and the Mighty, The, *541;* Melody Cruise, *930;* Wheeler Dealers, The, *409*
Harris, Priscilla: Nights in White Satin, *607*
Harris, Richard: Bible, The, *460;* Camelot, *911;* Cassandra Crossing, The, *476;* Cromwell, *491;* Deadly Trackers, The, *1108;* Field, The, *516;* Game for Vultures, *54;* Gulliver's Travels (1977), *172;* Hawaii, *537;* Hero, The, *540;* Highpoint, *62;* Juggernaut (1974), *987;* King of the Wind, *180;* Last Word, The, *571;* Mack the Knife, *830;* Major Dundee, *1131;* Man Called Horse, A, *1131;* Man in the Wilderness, *1132;* Martin's Day, *185;* Molly Maguires, The, *598;* Mutiny on the Bounty (1962), *88;* 99 and 44/100 Percent Dead, *91;* Orca, *873;* Patriot Games, *97;* Red Desert, *780;* Return of a Man Called Horse, The, *1142;* Robin and Marian, *107;* Shake Hands with the Devil, *114;* Tarzan the Ape Man (1981), *125;* This Sporting Life, *682;* Triumphs of a Man Called Horse, *1159;* Unforgiven (1992), *1160;* Wild Geese, The, *139;* Wreck of the Mary Deare, The, *141;* Wrestling Ernest Hemingway, *707*
Harris, Robert: Terrorists, The, *1023*
Harris, Robert H.: How to Make a Monster, *853*
Harris, Robin: House Party, *923;* Mo' Better Blues, *931;* Sorority House Massacre 2, *889*
Harris, Robyn: Hard to Die, *848*
Harris, Rolf: Toby and the Koala Bear, *212*
Harris, Rosalind: Fiddler on the Roof, *916*
Harris, Rosemary: Beau Brummell (1954), *457;* Chisholms, The, *1104;* Heartbreak House, *295;* Ploughman's Lunch, The, *623*
Harris, Ross: Nightmare House, *871;* Testament, *1082*
Harris, Steve: Street Hunter, *121*
Harris, Zelda: Crooklyn, *261*
Harrison, Andrew: Littlest Horse Thieves, The, *184*
Harrison, Catherine: Blue Fire Lady, *151;* Empire State, *44*
Harrison, George: Imagine: John Lennon, *427;* Rutles, The (a.k.a. All You Need Is Cash), *938*
Harrison, Gregory: Bare Essentials, *232;* Body Chemistry 2: Voice of a Stranger, *957;* Caught in the Act, *960;* Dangerous Pursuit, *966;* Duplicates, *973;* Enola Gay: The Men, the Mission, the Atomic Bomb, *510;* For Ladies Only, *519;* Hasty Heart, *537;* North Shore, *609;* Oceans of Fire, *93;* Razorback, *879;* Seduced, *1013*
Harrison, Jenilee: Curse III: Blood Sacrifice, *827;* Illicit Behavior, *985;* Prime Target, *100*
Harrison, Kathleen: Christmas Carol, A (1951), *159;* Ghoul, The (1933), *846;* Night Must Fall, *606*
Harrison, Linda: Beneath the Planet of the Apes, *1039*
Harrison, Rex: Agony and the Ecstasy, The, *443;* Anastasia: The Mystery of Anna, *447;* Anna and the King of Siam, *449;* Ashanti, *7;* Citadel, The, *482;* Cleopatra (1963), *484;* Doctor Dolittle, *162;* Fifth Musketeer, The, *47;* Ghost and Mrs. Muir, The, *285;* Heartbreak House, *295;* Honey Pot, The, *300;* Major Barbara, *326;* Midnight Lace, *84;* My Fair Lady, *932;* Night Train to Munich, *91;* Prince and the Pauper, The (1978), *197;* Reluctant Debutante, The, *365;* Sidewalks of London, *657;* Storm in a Teacup, *387;* Time to Die, A (1983), *130;* Unfaithfully Yours (1948), *403*
Harrison, Richard: Between God, the Devil and a Winchester, *1097;* Empire of the Dark, *838;* His Name Was King, *1121;* Place Called Trinity, A, *1139;* Rescue Force, *105*
Harrison, Sandra: Blood of Dracula, *815*
Harrison, Susan: Sweet Smell of Success, *675*
Harrod, David: Blood on the Badge, *15*
Harrold, Kathryn: Best Legs in the 8th Grade, The, *235;* Bogie, *466;* Dead Solid Perfect, *497;* Deadly Desire, *968;* Heartbreakers, *538;* Hunter, The (1980), *65;* Into the Night, *553;* Modern Romance, *335;* Nightwing, *871;* Pursuit of D. B. Cooper, *363;* Rainbow Drive, *103;* Raw Deal, *103;* Sender, The, *884;* Yes, Giorgio, *948*
Harron, Dan: Really Weird Tales, *365*
Harron, Robert: Avenging Conscience, The, *811;* Battle of Elderbush Gulch, The/The Musketeers of Pig Alley, *1097;* Hearts of the World, *538;* Home, Sweet Home, *543;* Intolerance, *553;* Judith of Bethulia, *560;* Mother and the Law, The, *600*
Harrow, Lisa: Final Conflict, The, *841;* Last Days of Chez Nous, The, *569;* Shaker Run, *114*
Harry, Deborah: Forever Lulu, *279;* Hairspray, *292;* Intimate Stranger, *986;* John Carpenter Presents: Body Bags, *858;* Mr. Mike's Mondo Video, *334;* Satisfaction, *938;* Tales from the Darkside, The Movie, *892;* Union City, *1029;* Videodrome, *900*
Harryhausen, Ray: Fantasy Film Worlds of George Pal, The, *424*
Hart, Christopher: Addams Family Values, *222*
Hart, Christopher J.: Lady Terminator, *74*
Hart, Dolores: King Creole, *927;* Lonelyhearts, *578;* Loving You, *929;* Where the Boys Are, *409*.
Hart, Dorothy: Naked City, The, *1000*
Hart, Ian: BackBeat, *907;* Hours and Times, *544*
Hart, John: Blackenstein, *814;* Longhorn, *1130*
Hart, Kevin: Lone Wolf, *861*
Hart, Mary: In Old Caliente, *1122*
Hart, Richard: Green Dolphin Street, *533*
Hart, Roxanne: Last Innocent Man, The, *990;* Oh, God, You Devil!, *349;* Pulse, *877;* Samaritan: The Mitch Snyder Story, *647;* Special Bulletin, *1019;* Tagget, *124*
Hart, Susan: Slime People, The, *1077*
Hart, Veronica: RSVP, *371;* Stocks and Blondes, *668*
Hart, William S.: Hell's Hinges, *1120;* Narrow Trail, The, *1135;* Three-Word Brand, The, *1157;* Tumbleweeds, *1159*
Hartford, Glen: Hell Squad (1985), *60*
Hartley, Mariette: Encino Man, *271;* Improper Channels, *305;* M.A.D.D.: Mothers Against Drunk Driving, *583;* 1969, *607;* O'Hara's Wife, *611;* Ride the High Country, *1143*
Hartman, David: Island at the Top of the World, The, *1060*
Hartman, Elizabeth: Beguiled, The, *954;* Fixer, The, *517;* Group, The, *534;* Patch of Blue, A, *619;* Walking Tall, *136;* You're a Big Boy Now, *416*
Hartman, Lawrence: Zentropa, *807*
Hartman, Lisa: Bare Essentials, *232;* Bodily Harm, *957;* Full Exposure, *523;* Red Wind, *1009;* Take, The, *124;* Where the Boys Are '84, *409*
Hartman, Phil: Blind Date (1987), *241;* CB4, *252;* Coneheads, *258;* Greedy, *290;* Pee-Wee Herman Show, The, *355;* So I Married an Axe Murderer, *382*
Hartmann, Paul: Haunted Castle, *849*
Hartnell, William: Battle Hell, *9*

rvest, Rainbow: Mirror Mirror, *865;* Old Enough, *611*
rvey, Don: American Heart, *446;* Casualties of War, *477;* y of the Chameleon, *1007*
rvey, Don: Atom Man vs. Superman, *7;* Batman and bin, *9;* Gang Busters, *54*
rvey, Forrester: Chump at Oxford, A, *255*
rvey, Jean: Hands of a Stranger, *981*
rvey, John: Pin-Up Girl, *935*
rvey, Laurence: Alamo, The, *1092;* Butterfield 8, *472;* ndy in Aspic, A, *965;* Darling, *496;* Escape to the Sun, *511;* n a Camera, *547;* Manchurian Candidate, The, *995;* Night tch, *870;* Of Human Bondage (1964), *610;* Room at the , *643;* Silent Enemy, The, *116;* Spy with a Cold Nose, The, 5; Summer and Smoke, *672;* Truth About Women, The, 9; Walk on the Wild Side, *695;* Wonderful World of the thers Grimm, The, *1090*
rvey, Paul: Call Northside 777, *959;* Helldorado (1946), 20; Meet Dr. Christian, *591*
rvey, Rodney: Guncrazy (1992), *535;* Mixed Blood, *86;* sa, *938*
rvey, Tom: And Then You Die, *5*
segawa, Kazuo: Chikamatsu Monogatari, *723*
sgawa, Machiko: Zatoichi: Masseur Ichi and a Chest of d, *806*
skell, Peter: Christina, *25;* Cracker Factory, *490;* Riding Edge, *106*
ss, Dolly: Spy of Napoleon, *664*
sse, O. E.: Betrayed (1954), *11;* Big Lift, The, *460;* State Siege, *788*
sselhoff, David: Bail Out, *8;* Cartier Affair, The, *252;* Final ance, *48;* Revenge of the Cheerleaders, *367;* Star Crash, 78; Terror at London Bridge, *893;* Witchery, *903*
ssett, Marilyn: Bell Jar, The, *458;* Body Count, *817;* osy Angels, *535;* Massive Retaliation, *83;* Messenger of ath, *84;* Other Side of the Mountain, The, *615;* Other Side of Mountain, Part II, The, *615;* Two-Minute Warning, *1028*
sso, Signe: Heaven Can Wait (1943), *295;* Johnny Angel, ; Picture Mommy Dead, *874;* Reflection of Fear, *1009;* venth Cross, The, *653*
sson, Ann: Romeo and Juliet (1988), *643*
tch, Richard: Battlestar Galactica, *1038;* Charlie Chan and Curse of the Dragon Queen, *253;* Deadman's Curve, *913;* lta Force, Commando Two, *37;* Hatfields and the McCoys, e, *1119;* Heated Vengeance, *60;* Party Line, *97;* Prisoners the Lost Universe, *1072*
tcher, Teri: All Tied Up, *225;* Brain Smasher...A Love ory, *18;* Cool Surface, The, *963;* Dead in the Water, *967;* apdish, *382;* Straight Talk, *387*
tfield, Hurd: Boston Strangler, The, *818;* Crimes of the art, *260;* Dragon Seed, *504;* El Cid, *43;* Her Alibi, *296;* King Kings (1961), *565;* Left Handed Gun, The (1958), *1128;* s of the Twins, *992;* Picture of Dorian Gray, The, *875*
thaway, Noah: NeverEnding Story, The, *1068;* Troll, 85
tton, Raymond: Arizona Bound, *1094;* Below the Border, 97; Covered Wagon Days, *1106;* Dawn on the Great Divide, 07; Down Texas Way, *1110;* Forbidden Trails, *1114;* ontier Horizon, *1114;* Frontier Pony Express, *1114;* G-Men, ; Ghost Town Law, *1115;* Gunman from Bodie, *1117;* roes of the Saddle, *1120;* Hostile Country, *1122;* Kansas rrors, *1124;* Lady Killer, *74;* Law and Order, *1127;* Peck's d Boy, *194;* Rocky Mountain Rangers, *1145;* Rough Riders' undup, *1146;* Texas, *1155;* Three Musketeers, The (1933), 28; Vigilantes Are Coming!, *1161;* Virginian, The (1923), 61; Wagon Wheels, *1162;* Wall Street Cowboy, *1162;* West the Law, *1163;* Wyoming Outlaw, *1165*
tton, Rondo: Brute Man, The, *820;* In Old Chicago, *550;* arl of Death, The, *1004*
auber, W. C.: Keystone Comedies, Vol. 5, *313*
audepin, Didier: Assassins de L'Ordre, Les (Law Breakers), 4; This Special Friendship, *794*
Hauer, Rutger: Beyond Justice, *11;* Blade Runner, *1039;* Blind Fury, *15;* Blind Side, *956;* Blood of Heroes, *15;* Bloodhounds of Broadway, *242;* Breed Apart, A, *19;* Buffy, The Vampire Slayer, *247;* Chanel Solitaire, *479;* Dandelions, *727;* Deadlock, *1045;* Escape from Sobibor, *45;* Eureka, *511;* Flesh and Blood, *50;* Hitcher, The, *850;* Inside the Third Reich, *552;* Katie's Passion, *751;* Ladyhawke, *74;* Mysteries, *770;* Nighthawks, *91;* Osterman Weekend, The, *96;* Past Midnight, *619;* Soldier of Orange, *787;* Split Second (1992), *1078;* Surviving the Game, *123;* Turkish Delight, *797;* Voyage, *1030;* Wanted: Dead or Alive, *136*
Hauff, Thomas: Climb, The, *26*
Hauser, Fay: Christmas Lilies of the Field, *159;* Jimmy the Kid, *178;* Jo Jo Dancer, Your Life Is Calling, *558;* Marvin and Tige, *589*
Hauser, Patrick: Weekend Pass, *407*
Hauser, Wings: Art of Dying, The, *953;* Beastmaster 2: Through the Portal of Time, *1039;* Bedroom Eyes II, *954;* Carpenter, The, *821;* Dead Man Walking, *1045;* Deadly Force, *34;* Exiled in America, *45;* Frame Up, *52;* Homework, *543;* Hostage (1987), *64;* Jo Jo Dancer, Your Life Is Calling, *558;* L.A. Bounty, *73;* Living to Die, *993;* Long Hot Summer, The (1985), *578;* Mutant, *867;* Nightmare at Noon, *870;* No Safe Haven, *92;* Out of Sight Out of Mind, *1003;* Pale Blood, *873;* Reason to Die, *879;* Siege of Firebase Gloria, The, *116;* Street Asylum, *121;* 3:15—The Moment of Truth, *128;* Tough Guys Don't Dance, *686;* Vice Squad, *135;* Wilding, The Children of Violence, *140;* Wind, The (1986), *1032*
Haustein, Thomas: Christiane F., *724*
Havens, Richie: Greased Lightning, *57*
Haver, June: Look For The Silver Lining, *929;* Love Nest, *323*
Haver, Phyllis: Balloonatic, The/One Week, *231;* Buster Keaton Festival: Vol. 3, *248;* Buster Keaton: The Great Stone Face, *248*
Havers, Nigel: Burke and Wills, *472;* Chariots of Fire, *479;* Empire of the Sun, *509;* Farewell to the King, *46;* Little Princess, A, *183;* Whistle Blower, The, *1031*
Haverstock, Thom: Skullduggery, *887*
Havoc, June: Brewster's Millions (1945), *245;* Can't Stop the Music, *911;* Four Jacks and a Jill, *918;* Gentlemen's Agreement, *526*
Hawdon, Robin: When Dinosaurs Ruled the Earth, *1089*
Hawke, Ethan: Alive, *444;* Dad, *493;* Dead Poets Society, *497;* Explorers, *1050;* Midnight Clear, A, *593;* Mystery Date, *341;* Reality Bites, *635;* Rich in Love, *640;* Waterland, *697;* White Fang, *217;* White Fang 2: Myth of the White Wolf, *217*
Hawkes, Chesney: Buddy's Song, *471*
Hawkes, Steve: Blood Freak, *815*
Hawkins and the Hawkins Family, Walter: Gospel, *425*
Hawkins, Jack: Ben-Hur (1959), *10;* Bridge on the River Kwai, The, *19;* Cruel Sea, The, *492;* Elusive Pimpernel, The, *509;* Escape to the Sun, *511;* Fallen Idol, The, *513;* Land of the Pharaohs, *568;* League of Gentlemen, The, *317;* Malta Story, The, *586;* Prisoner, The, *628;* Shalako, *1148;* Tales that Witness Madness, *892;* Waterloo, *697;* Young Winston, *709;* Zulu, *142*
Hawkins, Jimmy: Annie Oakley (TV Series), *1094;* TV Classics: Annie Oakley, *1159*
Hawkins, Screamin' Jay: Mystery Train, *603*
Hawkshaw, Jean: Wild Women of Wongo, *1089*
Hawn, Goldie: Best Friends, *235;* Bird on a Wire, *13;* Butterflies Are Free, *473;* Cactus Flower, *248;* Crisscross (1992), *491;* Death Becomes Her, *1045;* Deceived, *969;* $ (Dollars), *971;* Duchess and the Dirtwater Fox, The, *1110;* Foul Play, *280;* Girl from Petrovka, The, *527;* Here's Looking at You, Warner Brothers, *426;* Housesitter, *302;* Lovers and Liars, *323;* One and Only, Genuine, Original Family Band, The, *192;* Overboard, *352;* Private Benjamin, *361;* Protocol, *363;* Seems Like Old Times, *375;* Shampoo, *655;* Sugarland Express, The, *672;* Swing Shift, *675;* There's a Girl in My Soup, *393;* Wildcats, *411*

Haworth, Jill: Exodus, 512; Home for the Holidays, 983; In Harm's Way, 66
Haworth, Vinton: Riding on Air, 368
Hawthorne, Nigel: Demolition Man, 1046; Pope John Paul II, 624; Tartuffe, 677
Hawtrey, Charles: Carry on at Your Convenience, 251; Carry on Cleo, 251; Carry on Doctor, 251; Carry on Nurse, 251; Follow That Camel, 278; Terrornauts, The, 1082
Hay, Christian: You're Jinxed Friend, You Just Met Sacramento, 1166
Hay, Colin: Wacky World of Wills and Burke, The, 405
Hayakawa, Sessue: Bridge on the River Kwai, The, 19; Cheat, The, 961; Hell to Eternity, 540; Swiss Family Robinson, The, 208; Three Came Home, 682; Tokyo Joe, 130
Hayashi, Chizu: Zatoichi: The Blind Swordsman and the Chess Expert, 806
Hayashi, Marc: Chan Is Missing, 253; Laser Man, The, 315
Hayden, Dennis: One Man Army, 94
Hayden, Linda: Blood on Satan's Claw, 815; Madhouse (1972), 862; Shattered (1972), 655; Taste the Blood of Dracula, 892
Hayden, Nora: Angry Red Planet, The, 1036
Hayden, Russell: Badmen of the Hills, 1096; Frontiersman, The, 1114; Heritage of the Desert, 1120; Hidden Gold, 1120; Hostile Country, 1122; In Old Mexico, 1123; Law of the Pampas, 1127; Lost City of the Jungle, 79; Range War, 1141; Renegade Trail, 1142; Rustler's Valley, 1146; Santa Fe Marshal, 1147; Showdown (1940), 1149; Stagecoach War, 1152; Three Men from Texas, 1157; Valley of Fire, 1161
Hayden, Sterling: Asphalt Jungle, The, 953; Blue and the Gray, The, 1099; Crime of Passion, 490; Denver and Rio Grande, The, 1108; Dr. Strangelove or How I Learned to Stop Worrying and Love the Bomb, 266; Fighter Attack, 47; Flat Top, 50; Gas, 283; Godfather, The, 529; Johnny Guitar, 1123; Kansas Pacific, 1124; Killing, The, 988; King of the Gypsies, 565; Last Command, The (1955), 1125; Last Days of Man on Earth, The, 1062; Long Goodbye, The, 993; Prince Valiant, 100; Shotgun, 1149; Spaghetti Western, 1152; Star, The, 665; Suddenly, 1021; Venom, 900; Winter Kills, 704
Haydn, Richard: Adventures of Bullwhip Griffin, The, 143; And Then There Were None, 952; Ball of Fire, 231; Clarence, the Cross-Eyed Lion, 159; Five Weeks in a Balloon, 50; Forever Amber, 520; Jupiter's Darling, 926; Mr. Music, 931; Mutiny on the Bounty (1962), 88; Never Let Me Go, 89; Please Don't Eat the Daisies, 358; Young Frankenstein, 416
Haydon, Julie: Scoundrel, The, 374
Hayenga, Jeff: Unborn, The, 898
Hayes, Allan: Neon Maniacs, 868
Hayes, Allison: Attack of the 50-Foot Woman (1958), 810; Gunslinger, 1118; Mohawk, 1134; Unearthly, The, 899; Zombies of Mora Tav, 905
Hayes, Billie: Li'l Abner (1959), 928
Hayes, Carey: RSVP, 371
Hayes, Frank: Fatty and Mabel Adrift/Mabel, Fatty and the Law, 275
Hayes, George "Gabby": Along the Navajo Trail, 1093; Arizona Kid, 1095; Bad Man of Deadwood, 1095; Badman's Territory, 1096; Bells of Rosarita, 1097; Blue Steel (1934), 1099; Borderland, 1100; Broadway to Cheyenne, 1101; Calling Wild Bill Elliott, 1103; Cariboo Trail, 1103; Carson City Kid, 1103; Colorado, 1105; Dark Command, 1107; Days of Jesse James, 1107; Death Valley Manhunt, 1108; Don't Fence Me In, 1110; Frontiersman, The, 1114; Heart of the Golden West, 1119; Helldorado (1946), 1120; Hidden Valley Outlaws, 1120; Home in Oklahoma, 1121; Hopalong Cassidy Enters, 1121; In Old Caliente, 1122; In Old Mexico, 1123; In Old Santa Fe, 1123; Jesse James at Bay, 1123; Lawless Frontier, 1127; Lawless Nineties, The, 1127; Lights of Old Santa Fe, 1128; Lost City, The, 1063; Lucky Texan, 1130; Man from Utah, The, 1132; Melody Ranch, 1133; Mojave Firebrand, 1134; My Pal Trigger, 1135; 'Neath Arizona Skies, 1135; Phantom Broadcast, The, 1005; Plainsman, The, 1139; Rainbow Valley, 1140; Randy Rides Alone, 1141; Ranger and the Lady, The, 1141; Renegade Trail, 1142; Return of the Badmen, 1142; Riders of Destiny, 1144; Robin Hood of the Pecos, 1145; Roll on Texas Moon, 1145; Rustler's Valley, 1146; Saga of Death Valley, 1147; Sons of the Pioneers, 1151; Star Packer, The, 1153; Sunset on the Desert, 1154; Sunset Serenade, 1154; Tall in the Saddle, 1154; Texas Terror, 1156; Trail Street, 1158; Trailin' North, 1158; Utah, 1160; Wall Street Cowboy, 1162; War of the Wildcats, 116 West of the Divide, 1163; Young Bill Hickok, 1165
Hayes, Helen: Airport, 443; Anastasia, 447; Arrowsmith, 451; Candleshoe, 155; Family Upside Down, A, 514; Farew to Arms, A, 514; Herbie Rides Again, 174; Murder with Mirrors, 999; One of Our Dinosaurs Is Missing, 192; Sin of Madelon Claudet, The, 658; Stage Door Canteen, 665
Hayes, Isaac: Acting on Impulse, 950; Counterforce, 30; Dead Aim (1987), 33; Final Judgment, 977; Good Idea, 288 Guilty as Charged, 291; I'm Gonna Git You Sucka!, 305; Po (1993), 1139; Prime Target, 100; Robin Hood: Men in Tight 369; Truck Turner, 132
Hayes, Jerri: Black Sister's Revenge, 463
Hayes, Maggie: Girls Town, 55
Hayes, Patricia: Corn Is Green, The (1979), 488; Fish Call Wanda, A, 277; Willow, 1089
Hayes, Peter Lind: Five Thousand Fingers of Dr. T, The, 167; Senator Was Indiscreet, The, 375; Yin and Yang of Mr. Go, The, 1033
Hayes, Susan Seaforth: Dream Machine, 269
Hayman, Cyd: After Julius, 442; Godsend, The, 846
Hayman, David: Gospel According to Vic, The, 289; Hope and Glory, 544; Sense of Freedom, A, 652; Sid and Nancy, 657
Haymer, John: Four Deuces, The, 52
Haymes, Dick: St. Benny the Dip, 646; State Fair (1945), 941
Hayner, Daniel: Hallelujah!, 535
Haynes, Linda: Drowning Pool, The, 972; Human Experiments, 64; Rolling Thunder, 108
Haynes, Lloyd: Good Guys Wear Black, 56
Haynes, Roberta: Hell Ship Mutiny, 60; Return to Paradise 106
Haynie, Jim: From Hollywood to Deadwood, 979; Grand Tour: Disaster in Time, 1054; On the Edge, 612; Out, 96; Staying Together, 667; Stephen King's Sleepwalkers, 890; T Much Sun, 397
Hays, Dan: Little Match Girl, The (1983), 182
Hays, Kathryn: Ride Beyond Vengeance, 1143; Yuma, 116
Hays, Lee: Wasn't That a Time!, 438
Hays, Robert: Airplane!, 224; Airplane II: The Sequel, 224; California Gold Rush, 1103; Cat's Eye, 822; Fall of the House of Usher, The (1979), 840; Fifty/Fifty, 47; Homeward Bound: The Incredible Journey, 175; Honeymoon Academy, 300; Ho Chocolate, 301; Running Against Time, 1075; Scandalous (1983), 373; Take This Job and Shove It, 390; Touched, 686 Trenchcoat, 399; Utilities, 404
Haysbert, Dennis: Love Field, 581; Mr. Baseball, 333; Return to Lonesome Dove, 1143
Hayshi, Henry: Pushed to the Limit, 101
Hayter, James: Pickwick Papers, The, 357; Story of Robin Hood, The, 207; Tom Brown's Schooldays (1950), 685
Hayward, Chad: Killing Game, The, 71
Hayward, Chris: In Search of Anna, 550
Hayward, David: Accidental Meeting, 950; Delusion (1980) 969; Fallen Angel, 513; Red Alert, 104
Hayward, Louis: And Then There Were None, 952; Anthony Adverse, 450; Black Arrow, The (1948), 13; Christmas Kid, The, 1105; Chuka, 1105; Dance, Girl, Dance, 261; House by the River, 984; Man in the Iron Mask, The (1939), 81; Rage o Paris, The, 364; Saint in New York, The, 1012; Search for Bridey Murphy, The, 650; Son of Monte Cristo, The, 118; Strange Woman, The, 669; Terror in the Wax Museum, 894
Hayward, Susan: Adam Had Four Sons, 441; Back Street, 453; Beau Geste, 10; Conqueror, The, 29; David and

thsheba, *496;* Deadline at Dawn, *34;* Demetrius and the diators, *499;* Fighting Seabees, The, *48;* Hairy Ape, The, 5; Honey Pot, The, *300;* House of Strangers, *545;* I Want to e!, *548;* I'll Cry Tomorrow, *924;* Jack London, *556;* Lost ment, The, *580;* Lusty Men, The, *1130;* Rawhide (1951), 41; Reap the Wild Wind, *104;* Say Goodbye, Maggie Cole, 8; Smash-Up: The Story of a Woman, *661;* Snows of imanjaro, The, *118;* Soldier of Fortune, *118;* Stolen Hours, 8; They Won't Believe Me, *681;* Tulsa, *689;* Valley of the lls, *693;* Where Love Has Gone, *699;* Young and Willing, 8

ywood, Chris: Attack Force Z, *7;* Dogs in Space, *914;* atwave, *539;* Malcolm, *327;* Man of Flowers, *327;* vigator: A Medieval Odyssey, The, *1067;* Sweet Talker, *389;* e of Ruby Rose, The, *676*

yworth, Rita: Affair in Trinidad, *442;* Angels Over oadway, *448;* Blood and Sand (1941), *464;* Circus World, 2; Cover Girl, *912;* Dancing Pirate, *913;* Fire Down Below, 7; Gilda, *527;* Hit the Saddle, *1121;* Lady from Shanghai, 9; Lady in Question, *568;* Loves of Carmen, The, *582;* Miss die Thompson, *596;* Only Angels Have Wings, *95;* Pal Joey, 4; Poppy Is Also a Flower, The, *99;* Renegade Ranger, 42; Salome (1953), *647;* Strawberry Blonde, The, *670;* san and God, *674;* They Came to Cordura, *681;* Tonight and ery Night, *946;* Trouble in Texas, *1159;* You Were Never velier, *948;* You'll Never Get Rich, *948*

aze, Jonathan: Little Shop of Horrors, The (1960), *861;* oor White Trash, *624*

azeldine, James: Business As Usual, *472*

azlehurst, Noni: Monkey Grip, *598*

ead, Murray: French Woman, The, *522;* Sunday, Bloody unday, *673*

eadey, Lena: Summer House, The, *388*

eadley, Lena: Waterland, *697*

eadly, Glenne: Dick Tracy (1990), *38;* Dirty Rotten coundrels, *265;* Getting Even with Dad, *285;* Grand Isle, 31; Hotel Room, *983;* Lonesome Dove, *1129;* Making Mr. ght, *327;* Mortal Thoughts, *997;* Nadine, *341;* Ordinary agic, *614;* Paperhouse, *873;* Seize the Day, *651*

ealey, Myron: Gang Busters, *54;* Incredible Melting Man, e, *1058;* Kansas Pacific, *1124;* Longhorn, *1130;* Monsoon, 99; Panther Girl of the Congo, *97;* Rage at Dawn, *1140;* nearthly, The, *899;* Varan, the Unbelievable, *900*

ealy, David: Philip Marlowe, Private Eye: The Pencil, *1005;* gn of Four, The, *1016*

ealy, Dorian: Young Soul Rebels, *948*

ealy, Katherine: Six Weeks, *659*

ealy, Mary: Five Thousand Fingers of Dr. T, The, *167;* econd Fiddle, *938*

ealy, Patricia: Sweet Poison, *123;* Ultraviolet, *133*

ealy, Ted: Dancing Lady, *913;* Hollywood Hotel, *923;* Lost tooges, The, *322;* Mad Love, *861;* Operator 13, *614*

eard, John: After Hours, *223;* Awakenings, *452;* Beaches, 57; Best Revenge, *11;* Betrayed (1988), *954;* Between the ines, *237;* Big, *237;* C.H.U.D., *820;* Cat People (1982), *822;* hilly Scenes of Winter, *481;* Cutter's Way, *965;* Dead Ahead: he Exxon Valdez Disaster, *497;* Deceived, *969;* End of nnocence, The, *509;* First Love, *517;* Gladiator, *528;* Heart eat, *537;* Heaven Help Us, *295;* Home Alone, *299;* Home lone 2: Lost in New York, *175;* Milagro Beanfield War, The, 94; Mindwalk, *430;* On the Yard, *94;* Out on a Limb (1986), 16; Package, The, *1004;* Pelican Brief, The, *1005;* Radio lyer, *633;* Rambling Rose, *634;* Seventh Sign, The, *885;* elephone, The, *392;* Trip to Bountiful, The, *688;* Violated, 36; Waterland, *697*

earn, Ann: Dollmaker, The, *503*

earn, Edward: Miracle Rider, The, *1134*

earn, George: Piano for Mrs. Cimino, A, *622;* Sanctuary of ear, *1012;* Sneakers, *1018;* Sweeney Todd, *943*

earst, Patty: Cry-Baby, *912*

earst, Rick: Crossing the Line (1990), *492*

eather, Jean: Last Round-Up, *1126*

Heatherton, Joey: Bluebeard (1972), *817;* Cry-Baby, *912;* Happy Hooker Goes to Washington, The, *293;* Where Love Has Gone, *699*

Heavener, David: L.A. Goddess, *314;* Outlaw Force, *96;* Prime Target, *100*

Heche, Anne: Adventures of Huck Finn, The (1993), *143;* O Pioneers!, *610*

Hecht, Donatella: Flesh Eating Mothers, *841*

Hecht, Ted: Lost City of the Jungle, *79*

Heckart, Eileen: Bad Seed, The, *454;* Burnt Offerings, *820;* Butterflies Are Free, *473;* Heller in Pink Tights, *1120;* Hiding Place, The, *541;* Hot Spell, *544;* No Way to Treat a Lady, *1002;* Somebody Up There Likes Me, *662;* Up the Down Staircase, *403;* White Mama, *700;* Zandy's Bride, *1166*

Hedaya, Dan: Addams Family, The, *222;* Based on an Untrue Story, *232;* Benny & Joon, *234;* Blood Simple, *957;* Boiling Point, *17;* Commando, *28;* For Love or Money, *279;* Four Eyes and Six Guns, *1114;* Joe Versus the Volcano, *310;* Mr. Wonderful, *597;* Reckless (1984), *636;* Rookie of the Year, *200;* Running Scared (1986), *110;* Searching for Bobby Fischer, *202;* Smoky Mountain Christmas, *205;* Tightrope, *1025;* Wise Guys, *412*

Hedin, Serene: Sacred Ground, *1146;* Windwalker, *1165*

Hedison, David: Awakening of Cassie, The, *452;* Enemy Below, The, *44;* ffolkes, *47;* Fly, The (1958), *841*

Hedley, Jack: New York Ripper, The, *868;* Very Edge, The, *693*

Hedren, Tippi: Birds, The, *813;* Birds II, The: Land's End, *813;* Deadly Spygames, *35;* Foxfire Light, *521;* Harrad Experiment, The, *537;* In the Cold of the Night, *986;* Marnie, *995;* Pacific Heights, *1003*

Hedwall, Deborah: Alone in the Dark, *808*

Heffner, Kyle T.: Runaway Train, *110*

Heflin, Marta: Come Back to the Five and Dime, Jimmy Dean, Jimmy Dean, *486*

Heflin, Van: Airport, *443;* Backdoor to Heaven, *454;* Battle Cry, *9;* Cry of Battle, *31;* East Side, West Side, *506;* Greatest Story Ever Told, The, *533;* Green Dolphin Street, *533;* Johnny Eager, *559;* Madame Bovary (1949), *584;* Patterns, *619;* Possessed (1947), *625;* Presenting Lily Mars, *626;* Ruthless Four, The, *1146;* Santa Fe Trail, *1147;* Shane, *1148;* Strange Love of Martha Ivers, The, *669;* They Came to Cordura, *681;* Three Musketeers, The (1948), *128;* 3:10 to Yuma, *1157;* Till the Clouds Roll By, *946;* Woman Rebels, A, *705*

Heggie, O. P.: Anne of Green Gables (1934), *146;* Count of Monte Cristo, The (1934), *30;* Devotion, *500;* Midnight (1934), *593;* Smilin' Through (1932), *661*

Hegyes, Robert: Underground Aces, *403*

Hehn, Sasha: Melody in Love, *592*

Heidt, Horace: Pot O' Gold, *625*

Heifetz, Jascha: They Shall Have Music, *944*

Heigl, Katherine: My Father, the Hero, *339*

Heilbron, Lorna: Creeping Flesh, The, *826*

Heilveil, Elayne: Birds of Prey, *13;* Payday, *620*

Heinz, Werner: Tonio Kroger, *796*

Heiss, Carol: Snow White and the Three Stooges, *205*

Heit, Michael: Bare Knuckles, *9*

Heldren, Judd: Lost Planet, The, *1064*

Helgenberger, Marg: After Midnight, *808;* Blind Vengeance, *15;* Crooked Hearts, *491;* Death Dreams, *831;* Desperate Motive, *970;* Tommyknockers, The, *1084*

Helger, Annemarie: Ladies on the Rocks, *755*

Hell, Richard: Geek Maggot Bingo, *283;* Smithereens, *661*

Heller, Randee: Can You Hear the Laughter? The Story of Freddie Prinze, *474*

Hellerman, Fred: Wasn't That a Time!, *438*

Hellstrom, Gunnar: Return to Peyton Place, *639*

Helm, Anne: Follow That Dream, *278;* Magic Sword, The, *185;* Nightmare in Wax (Crimes in the Wax Museum), *871;* Unkissed Bride, *403*

Helm, Brigitta: Love of Jeanne Ney, *762;* Metropolis (1926), *1065;* Metropolis (musical version), *930*

Helm, Fay: Blondie Has Trouble, *241*
Helm, Levon: Best Revenge, *11;* Coal Miner's Daughter, *912;* Dollmaker, The, *503;* End of the Line, *509;* Right Stuff, The, *640;* Smooth Talk, *661;* Staying Together, *667*
Helmer, Heidi: Beachballs, *233*
Helmond, Katherine: Brazil, *245;* Diary of a Teenage Hitchhiker, *501;* Family Plot, *975;* Inside Monkey Zetterland, *306;* Jack and the Beanstalk, *178;* Lady in White, *990;* Overboard, *352;* Rosie, *937;* Shadey, *377;* World War III, *141*
Helmore, Tom: Flipper's New Adventure, *167*
Helmuth, Frits: Memories of a Marriage, *766*
Helpmann, Robert: Patrick, *873;* Quiller Memorandum, The, *102;* Tales of Hoffman, *943*
Helpmann, Sheila: Getting of Wisdom, The, *526*
Hemblen, David: Family Viewing, *514*
Hemingway, Margaux: Deadly Rivals, *35;* Double Obsession, *972;* Inner Sanctum, *986;* Killer Fish, *71;* Lipstick, *992;* Over the Brooklyn Bridge, *352;* They Call Me Bruce?, *393*
Hemingway, Mariel: Creator, *490;* Delirious, *263;* Falling from Grace, *513;* Into the Badlands, *1123;* Lipstick, *992;* Manhattan, *328;* Mean Season, The, *996;* Personal Best, *621;* Star 80, *666;* Steal the Sky, *667;* Suicide Club, The, *1021;* Sunset, *1021;* Superman IV: The Quest for Peace, *1081*
Hemingway, Susan: Women in Cell Block 9, *140*
Hemmings, David: Beyond Reasonable Doubt (1983), *955;* Blood Relatives, *957;* Blow-Up, *957;* Calamity Jane (1984), *1103;* Camelot, *911;* Charge of the Light Brigade, The (1968), *24;* Dark Forces, *966;* Deep Red (1975), *832;* Disappearance, The, *39;* Islands in the Stream, *555;* Juggernaut (1974), *987;* Just a Gigolo, *561;* Key to Rebecca, The, *70;* Love Machine, The, *581;* Murder by Decree, *998;* Old Curiosity Shop, The, *933;* Rainbow, The, *634;* Snow Queen, *205;* Squeeze, The (1977), *665;* Thirst, *895;* Thumbelina (1983), *211;* Turn of the Screw, The (1989), *898*
Hemsley, Sherman: Alice in Wonderland (1985), *145;* Club Fed, *256;* Ghost Fever, *285;* Mr. Nanny, *188*
Henderson, Bill: Get Crazy, *284*
Henderson, Florence: Shakes the Clown, *377;* Song of Norway, *940;* Very Brady Christmas, A, *215*
Henderson, Jo: Lianna, *573*
Hendricks, Gorman: On the Bowery, *612*
Hendrickson, Nancy: Mother's Day, *866*
Hendrix, Elaine: Last Dance, *990*
Hendrix, Jimi: Jimi Hendrix, *428;* Monterey Pop, *431;* Woodstock, *438*
Hendrix, Wanda: Admiral Was a Lady, The, *222*
Hendry, Gloria: Bare Knuckles, *9;* Black Belt Jones, *13;* Black Caesar, *13;* Hell Up in Harlem, *60*
Hendry, Ian: Children of the Damned, *823;* Hill, The, *541;* Internecine Project, The, *986;* Journey to the Far Side of the Sun, *1060;* Passenger, The, *1004;* Repulsion, *879*
Henie, Sonja: Everything Happens at Night, *273;* Happy Landing, *921;* Iceland, *924;* My Lucky Star, *932;* One in a Million, *350;* Second Fiddle, *938;* Sun Valley Serenade, *942;* Thin Ice, *945;* Wintertime, *947*
Henn, Carrie: Aliens, *1035*
Henner, Marilu: Between the Lines, *237;* Bloodbrothers, *464;* Cannonball Run II, *250;* Chains of Gold, *478;* Chasers, *254;* Grand Larceny, *289;* Grown-ups, *534;* Hammett, *981;* Johnny Dangerously, *311;* L.A. Story, *314;* Lady Killers, *990;* Love with a Perfect Stranger, *582;* Man Who Loved Women, The (1983), *328;* Noises Off, *346;* Perfect, *620;* Rustler's Rhapsody, *371;* Stark, *119*
Hennessy, Mark: Double Exposure (1987), *268*
Henning, Eva: Three Strange Loves, *794*
Hennings, Sam: Seedpeople, *1076*
Henreid, Paul: Battle Shock, *812;* Casablanca, *476;* Deception (1946), *498;* Deep in My Heart, *913;* Four Horsemen of the Apocalypse, *52;* Joan of Paris, *558;* Madwoman of Chaillot, The, *585;* Never So Few, *89;* Night Train to Munich, *91;* Now, Voyager, *609;* Operation Crossbow, *95;* Scar, The, *649;* Song of Love, *662;* Stolen Face, *890*
Henrey, Bobby: Fallen Idol, The, *513*
Henriksen, Lance: Aliens, *1035;* Choke Canyon, *25;* Comrades in Arms, *28;* Deadly Intent, *34;* Delta Heat, *37;* Excessive Force, *45;* Hard Target, *59;* Hit List (1988), *982;* Horror Show, The, *852;* Jennifer 8, *987;* Johnny Handsome, *69;* Knights, *1061;* Man's Best Friend (1993), *863;* Near Dark, *868;* Nightmares, *871;* No Escape, *1069;* Outfit, The, *96;* Piranha Part Two: The Spawning, *875;* Pit and the Pendulum, The (1991), *875;* Pumpkinhead, *878;* Savage Dawn, *111;* Stone Cold, *120;* Survival Quest, *123*
Henry, Buck: Aria, *907;* Best of Gilda Radner, The, *235;* Best of John Belushi, The, *235;* Defending Your Life, *263;* Even Cowgirls Get the Blues, *272;* Gloria, *56;* Grumpy Old Men, *291;* Heaven Can Wait (1978), *295;* Keep the Change, *1124;* Linguini Incident, The, *319;* Man Who Fell to Earth, The, *106*[illegible] Old Boyfriends, *611;* Rude Awakening (1989), *371;* Short Cuts, *657;* Steve Martin Live, *386*
Henry, Buzz: Wild West (1946), *1164*
Henry, Charlotte: Charlie Chan at the Opera, *961;* March of the Wooden Soldiers, *329*
Henry, Gloria: Rancho Notorious, *1140*
Henry, Gregg: Body Double, *958;* Fair Game, *974;* Last of Philip Banter, The, *991;* Patriot, *97;* Positively True Adventures of the Alleged Texas Cheerleader-Murdering Mom, The, *360;* White Lie, *700*
Henry, Justin: Martin's Day, *185;* Sweethearts' Dance, *675;* Tiger Town, *211*
Henry, Laura: Heavenly Bodies, *296*
Henry, Lenny: Bernard and the Genie, *234;* True Identity, *399*
Henry, Martha: Dancing in the Dark, *494;* White Light, *108*[illegible]
Henry, Mike: Adios Amigo, *1092;* Rio Lobo, *1145;* Smokey and the Bandit, *381;* Smokey and the Bandit II, *381*
Henry, Tim: Dawson Patrol, The, *33*
Henry, Tom: Lone Wolf, *861*
Henry, William: Dance Hall, *913;* Denver Kid, *1109;* Fury of the Congo, *54;* Marshal of Cedar Rock, *1132;* Tarzan Escapes, *125*
Hensley, Lisa: Thirteenth Floor, The, *895*
Hensley, Pamela: Buck Rogers in the 25th Century, *1040;* Doc Savage...The Man of Bronze, *1047;* Double Exposure (1982), *971*
Henson, Brad: Warlords of Hell, *137*
Henson, Nicky: Bawdy Adventures of Tom Jones, The, *233;* Number One of the Secret Service, *347;* Psychomania, *877*
Henteloff, Alex: Red Light Sting, The, *636*
Hentenryck, Kevin Van: Basket Case 3: The Progeny, *811*
Hepburn, Audrey: Always (1989), *445;* Bloodline, *464;* Breakfast at Tiffany's, *468;* Charade, *960;* Children's Hour, The, *481;* Funny Face, *918;* Love in the Afternoon, *323;* My Fair Lady, *932;* Nun's Story, The, *609;* Paris When It Sizzles, *354;* Robin and Marian, *107;* Roman Holiday, *642;* Sabrina, *372;* They All Laughed, *393;* Two for the Road, *401;* Unforgiven, The (1960), *1160;* Wait Until Dark, *1030;* War and Peace (1956), *695*
Hepburn, Dee: Gregory's Girl, *290*
Hepburn, Doreen: Da, *493*
Hepburn, Katharine: Adam's Rib, *222;* African Queen, The, *442;* Alice Adams, *444;* Bill of Divorcement, A, *461;* Break of Hearts, *468;* Bringing Up Baby, *246;* Christopher Strong, *482*[illegible] Corn Is Green, The (1979), *488;* Desk Set, *263;* Dragon Seed, *504;* Grace Quigley, *289;* Guess Who's Coming to Dinner, *534;* Holiday, *298;* Keeper of the Flame, *562;* Lion in Winter, The, *576;* Little Minister, The, *576;* Little Women (1933), *577*[illegible] Long Day's Journey into Night (1962), *578;* Love Among the Ruins, *322;* Madwoman of Chaillot, The, *585;* Man Upstairs, The, *327;* Mary of Scotland, *589;* Morning Glory (1933), *599;* On Golden Pond, *612;* Pat and Mike, *355;* Philadelphia Story, The, *357;* Quality Street, *631;* Rainmaker, The, *634;* Rooster Cogburn, *1146;* Sea of Grass, The, *1148;* Song of Love, *662;* Spitfire, *664;* Stage Door, *385;* Stage Door Canteen, *665;*

State of the Union, *666;* Suddenly, Last Summer, *672;* Summertime, *673;* Sylvia Scarlett, *676;* Trojan Women, The, *688;* Undercurrent, *691;* Without Love, *413;* Woman of the Year, *413;* Woman Rebels, A, *705*
Herbert, Charles: 13 Ghosts, *895*
Herbert, Chris: Check Is in the Mail, The, *254*
Herbert, Dorothy: Mysterious Dr. Satan, *88*
Herbert, Hugh: Beautiful Blonde from Bashful Bend, The, *233;* Bureau of Missing Persons, *959;* Dames, *913;* Danger Lights, *494;* Diplomaniacs, *914;* Eternally Yours, *511;* Footlight Parade, *917;* Hollywood Hotel, *923;* Hook, Line and Sinker, *300;* It's a Great Life, *308;* Kismet (1944), *566;* One Rainy Afternoon, *350;* Song Is Born, A, *940;* Sweet Adeline, *943;* Villain Still Pursued Her, The, *135*
Herbert, Percy: Captain Apache, *1103;* Saint, The (TV Series), *1012*
Herbert, Sidney: Orphans of the Storm, *615*
Herbst, Rich: Brain Damage, *818*
Herd, Carla: Deathstalker III—The Warriors from Hell, *1046*
Herd, Richard: Gleaming the Cube, *55;* Marciano, *588;* Trancers, *1085*
Herder, Andreas: Blue Hour, The, *719*
Heredia, Lisa: Summer, *791*
Herlie, Eileen: Hamlet (1948), *535*
Herlihy, James Leo: Four Friends, *521*
Herlin, Jacques: Adios, Hombre, *1092*
Herman, Jack: Yesterday Machine, The, *1090*
Herman, Jimmy: Geronimo, *1115*
Herman, Pee-Wee: Big Top Pee-Wee, *239;* Nice Dreams, *344;* Pee-Wee Herman Show, The, *355;* Pee-Wee's Big Adventure, *355;* Pee-Wee's Playhouse Christmas Special, *194;* Pinocchio (1983), *195*
Herman, Woody: Wintertime, *947*
Hermann, Irm: Last Five Days, The, *755;* Merchant of Four Seasons, The, *767*
Hermine, Pepi: Putney Swope, *363*
Hermine, Ruth: Putney Swope, *363*
Hermits, Herman's: Mrs. Brown You've Got a Lovely Daughter, *931*
Hermosa, Leila: Blind Rage, *15*
Hernandez, Felicia: Ruby in Paradise, *645*
Hernandez, Juano: Intruder in the Dust, *553;* Mark of the Hawk, The, *589;* Something of Value, *118;* Young Man with a Horn, *948*
Herrier, Mark: Porky's, *360;* Porky's II: The Next Day, *360;* Porky's Revenge, *360*
Herring, Laura: Forbidden Dance, The, *918*
Herrmann, Edward: Annie, *907;* Big Business, *238;* Born Yesterday (1993), *244;* Compromising Positions, *258;* Electric Grandmother, The, *1048;* Harry's War, *294;* Lawrenceville Stories, The, *317;* Little Sex, A, *319;* Lost Boys, The, *861;* Man with One Red Shoe, The, *328;* Memorial Day, *592;* Mrs. Soffel, *598;* Murrow, *601;* My Boyfriend's Back, *339;* North Avenue Irregulars, The, *191;* Overboard, *352;* Portrait of a Stripper, *625;* Purple Rose of Cairo, The, *363;* Reds, *637;* Sweet Poison, *123;* Take Down, *390*
Herron, Robert: True Heart Susie, *688*
Herschberger, Gary: Free Ride, *281;* Paradise Motel, *353*
Hershey, Barbara: Americana, *446;* Angel on My Shoulder (1980), *448;* Baby Maker, The, *453;* Beaches, *457;* Boxcar Bertha, *18;* Dangerous Woman, A, *494;* Defenseless, *969;* Diamonds, *38;* Entity, The, *838;* Falling Down, *513;* Flood!, *51;* Hannah and Her Sisters, *293;* Hoosiers, *543;* Killing in a Small Town, *564;* Last Summer, *570;* Last Temptation of Christ, The, *570;* Liberation of L. B. Jones, The, *574;* My Wicked, Wicked Ways, *602;* Nightingale, The, *191;* Paris Trout, *618;* Passion Flower, *619;* Public Eye, The, *1008;* Pursuit of Happiness, The, *631;* Return to Lonesome Dove, *1143;* Right Stuff, The, *640;* Shy People, *657;* Splitting Heirs, *384;* Stunt Man, The, *671;* Swing Kids, *675;* Take This Job and Shove It, *390;* Tin Men, *396;* Tune in Tomorrow, *400;* With Six You Get Eggroll, *412;* World Apart, A, *706*
Hersholt, Jean: Cat and the Fiddle, The, *911;* Courageous Dr. Christian, The, *489;* Dr. Christian Meets the Women, *502;* Greed, *533;* Happy Landing, *921;* Heidi (1937), *173;* Mask of Fu Manchu, The, *82;* Meet Dr. Christian, *591;* Melody for Three, *592;* One in a Million, *350;* Painted Veil, The, *617;* Remedy for Riches, *638;* Sin of Madelon Claudet, The, *658;* Skyscraper Souls, *660;* Student Prince in Old Heidelberg, The, *671;* Susan Lenox: Her Fall and Rise, *674;* They Meet Again, *681*
Herter, Gerard: Go Kill and Come Back, *1115;* Machine Gun Killers, *1130*
Hervey, Irene: Count of Monte Cristo, The (1934), *30;* Dude Ranger, *1110;* Mr. Peabody and the Mermaid, *334;* Play Misty for Me, *1006*
Herzog, Werner: Burden of Dreams, *420;* Man of Flowers, *327;* Tokyo-Ga, *796*
Hess, David: Last House on the Left, *860;* Let It Rock, *573;* Swamp Thing, *891*
Hess, Joe: Master Blaster, *83*
Hess, Michelle: Taxi Dancers, *678*
Hess, Susan: Dress Gray, *505*
Hesseman, Howard: Amazon Women on the Moon, *225;* Big Bus, The, *238;* Diamond Trap, The, *970;* Doctor Detroit, *266;* Flight of the Navigator, *1052;* Heat (1987), *60;* Hot Chocolate, *301;* Inside Out (1986), *552;* Little Miss Millions, *182;* Loose Shoes, *321;* Murder in New Hampshire, *600;* My Chauffeur, *339;* One Shoe Makes it Murder, *1003;* Police Academy II: Their First Assignment, *359;* Princess Who Had Never Laughed, The, *197;* Private Lessons, *361;* Rubin & Ed, *371;* Sunshine Boys, The, *388;* Tarantulas—The Deadly Cargo, *892;* Tunnelvision, *400*
Heston, Charlton: Agony and the Ecstasy, The, *443;* Airport 1975, *443;* Antony and Cleopatra (1973), *450;* Arrowhead, *1095;* Awakening, The, *811;* Ben-Hur (1959), *10;* Beneath the Planet of the Apes, *1039;* Big Country, The, *1098;* Buccaneer, The, *20;* Call of the Wild (1972), *22;* Chiefs, *961;* Crucifer of Blood, *964;* Dark City, *495;* Diamond Head, *500;* Earthquake, *43;* El Cid, *43;* Fantasy Film Worlds of George Pal, The, *424;* 55 Days at Peking, *516;* Four Musketeers, The, *52;* Gray Lady Down, *57;* Greatest Show on Earth, The, *533;* Greatest Story Ever Told, The, *533;* Julius Caesar (1970), *561;* Khartoum, *70;* Major Dundee, *1131;* Midway, *84;* Mother Lode, *87;* Mountain Men, The, *1134;* Nairobi Affair, *603;* Naked Jungle, The, *88;* Omega Man, The, *1069;* Planet of the Apes, *1071;* Pony Express, *1139;* Prince and the Pauper, The (1978), *197;* Proud Men, *1140;* Ruby Gentry, *644;* Solar Crisis, *1077;* Soylent Green, *1077;* Ten Commandments, The (1956), *678;* Three Musketeers, The (1973), *128;* Three Violent People, *1157;* Touch of Evil, *1026;* Treasure Island (1990), *214;* Two-Minute Warning, *1028;* War Lord, The, *137;* Will Penny, *1164;* Wreck of the Mary Deare, The, *141*
Hewett, Christopher: Producers, The, *362;* Ratboy, *635*
Hewitt, Alan: Barefoot Executive, The, *148;* Misadventures of Merlin Jones, The, *188*
Hewitt, Barbara: Equinox (The Beast), *838*
Hewitt, Love: Little Miss Millions, *182*
Hewitt, Martin: Alien Predators, *1035;* Carnal Crimes, *959;* Crime Lords, *30;* Endless Love, *510;* Night Rhythms, *1001;* Out of Control, *352;* Private War, *629;* Secret Games, *651;* White Ghost, *138*
Hewitt, Virginia: Space Patrol (TV Series), *1077*
Hewlett, David: Desire and Hell at Sunset Motel, *969;* Penthouse, The, *1005;* Pin, *875;* Scanners 2: The New Order, *883*
Hey, Virginia: Obsession: A Taste for Fear, *93*
Heydt, Louis Jean: Great McGinty, The, *290;* Great Moment, The, *290;* Test Pilot, *679;* They Were Expendable, *127*
Heyl, John: Separate Peace, A, *652*
Heyman, Barton: Billy Galvin, *461;* Let's Scare Jessica to Death, *860;* Trial of the Cantonsville Nine, The, *687;* Valdez Is Coming, *1160*

Heywood, Anne: Brain, The (1965), *1040;* I Want What I Want, *548;* Sadat, *646;* Scenes from a Murder, *112;* Shaming, The, *655;* Very Edge, The, *693;* What Waits Below, *902*

Heywood, Colin: Bloody New Year, *817*

Heywood, Pat: Girly, *846;* Rude Awakening (1982), *881;* Wish You Were Here, *412*

Hezelhurst, Noni: Waiting, *695*

Hickey, Barry: Las Vegas Weekend, *315*

Hickey, Brendan: I Married a Vampire, *855*

Hickey, William: Any Man's Death, *450;* Bright Lights, Big City, *470;* Da, *493;* Mob Boss, *335;* Name of the Rose, The, *89;* Pink Cadillac, *99;* Prizzi's Honor, *362;* Puppet Master, The, *878;* Runestone, *882;* Tales from the Darkside, The Movie, *892;* Walls of Glass, *695*

Hickland, Catherine: Ghost Town, *846;* Witchery, *903*

Hickman, Darryl: Any Number Can Play, *450;* Fighting Father Dunne, *516;* Human Comedy, The, *546;* Island in the Sky, *554;* Johnny Shiloh, *179;* Keeper of the Flame, *562;* King Lear (1982), *564;* Men of Boys Town, *592;* Strange Love of Martha Ivers, The, *669;* Tea and Sympathy, *678;* Texas John Slaughter: Geronimo's Revenge, *1155*

Hickman, Dwayne: High School, USA, *297;* How to Stuff a Wild Bikini, *923*

Hickman, Howard: Civilization, *483;* Kansas Terrors, *1124*

Hicks, Catharine: Child's Play, *823;* Death Valley, *831;* Fever Pitch, *516;* Laguna Heat, *990;* Like Father, Like Son, *318;* Peggy Sue Got Married, *355;* Razor's Edge, The (1984), *635;* Running Against Time, *1075;* She's Out of Control, *378;* Souvenir, *663;* Spy, *1019;* Star Trek IV: The Voyage Home, *1079*

Hicks, Danny: Intruder (1988), *856*

Hicks, Greg: Deadline (1988), *34*

Hicks, Hilly: Amazing Spiderman, The, *4;* Cartier Affair, The, *252*

Hicks, Kevin: Blood Relations, *816;* Final Notice, *977*

Hicks, Leonard: Santa Claus Conquers the Martians, *1076*

Hicks, Redmond: She's Gotta Have It, *377*

Hicks, Russell: Captain America (1944), *22;* Devil Dogs of the Air, *37;* Flying Saucer, The, *1052;* Junior G-Men, *69*

Hicks, Seymour: Scrooge (1935), *650*

Hicks, Taral: Bronx Tale, A, *470*

Hicks, William T.: Day of Judgment, A, *830;* Order of the Black Eagle, *95*

Hickson, Joan: At Bertram's Hotel, *953;* Body in the Library, The, *958;* Clockwise, *256;* Great Expectations (1988), *532;* Moving Finger, The, *998;* Murder Is Announced, A, *998;* Murder She Said, *999;* Nemesis (1986), *1000;* Pocketful of Rye, A, *1006;* Sleeping Murder, *1017;* Why Didn't They Ask Evans?, *1032*

Hidalgo-Gato, Raymundo: El Super, *734*

Hidari, Sachiko: Insect Woman, *748*

Higashiyama, Chiyeko: Tokyo Story, *796*

Higby, Mary Jane: Honeymoon Killers, The, *983*

Higby, Wilbur: True Heart Susie, *688*

Higgins, Anthony: Bride, The, *819;* Cold Room, The, *485;* Draughtman's Contract, The, *972;* For Love or Money, *279;* Quartet (1981), *631;* Sweet Killing, *1022;* Taste the Blood of Dracula, *892;* Young Sherlock Holmes, *141*

Higgins, Clare: Hellbound: Hellraiser II, *849;* Hellraiser, *850*

Higgins, Joel: First Affair, *517;* Killing at Hell's Gate, *71*

Higgins, John Michael: National Lampoon's Class of '86, *342*

Higgins, Michael: Courtship, *490;* 1918, *607;* On Valentine's Day, *612;* Paul's Case, *620*

Higginson, Jane: Silent Night, Deadly Night 5: The Toy Maker, *886*

Hilboldt, Lise: George Washington: The Forging of a Nation, *526;* Married Man, A, *589;* Noon Wine, *608;* Pudd'nhead Wilson, *630;* Sweet Liberty, *389*

Hildebrandt, Charles George: Return of the Alien's Deadly Spawn, The, *880*

Hill, Arthur: Andromeda Strain, The, *1036;* Dirty Tricks, 2 Futureworld, *1053;* Guardian, The (1984), *534;* Harper, *981* Killer Elite, The, *71;* Love Leads the Way, *581;* Murder in Space, *1067;* One Magic Christmas, *613;* Ordeal of Dr. Mud The, *614;* Petulia, *621;* Prototype, *1072;* Pursuit of Happiness, The, *631;* Return of Frank Cannon, The, *1010;* Revenge of the Stepford Wives, *881;* Tales of the Unexpecte *1022;* Tomorrow's Child, *686;* Ugly American, The, *690*

Hill, Benny: Best of Benny Hill, The, *235;* Chitty Chitty Ban Bang, *158;* Italian Job, The, *308;* To See Such Fun, *397*

Hill, Bernard: Bellman and True, *954;* No Surrender, *345;* Shirley Valentine, *378*

Hill, Bonnie: Buster Keaton Festival: Vol. 2, *248*

Hill, Charles: Rebel Love, *636*

Hill, Craig: Adios, Hombre, *1092;* Animal Called Man, An, *1093*

Hill, Dana: Boy Who Left Home to Find Out About the Shivers, The, *152;* Cross Creek, *491;* Fallen Angel, *513;* National Lampoon's European Vacation, *342;* Shoot the Moo *656*

Hill, Dennis: Confessions of a Serial Killer, *825*

Hill, Doris: Spirit of the West, *1152;* Trailin' North, *1158*

Hill, Jean: Desperate Living, *264*

Hill, Julie: Fix, The, *50*

Hill, Karyn: Lethal Ninja, *76*

Hill, Marianna: Baby, The, *811;* Blood Beach, *814;* Death a Love House, *968;* High Plains Drifter, *1120;* Red Line 7000, *104;* Schizoid, *883*

Hill, Melanie: Hawk, The, *982*

Hill, Richard: Deathstalker IV: Match of the Titans, *1046;* Devastator, The, *37;* Mark of the Beast, The, *863;* Warrior Queen, *137*

Hill, Rick: Dune Warriors, *42*

Hill, Robert: Deathstalker, *1046*

Hill, Sarah: Sexual Intent, *1014*

Hill, Steven: Between Two Women, *459;* Billy Bathgate, *461;* Boost, The, *466;* Child is Waiting, A, *480;* Goddess, Th *528;* Legal Eagles, *991;* On Valentine's Day, *612;* Raw Deal, *103;* Rich and Famous, *639;* Slender Thread, The, *660;* Whit Palace, *700;* Yentl, *948*

Hill, Terence: Ace High, *1092;* Boot Hill, *1100;* March or Die, *82;* Miami Supercops, *331;* Mr. Billion, *85;* My Name Is Nobody, *1135;* Super Fuzz, *1081;* They Call Me Trinity, *1156* Trinity Is Still My Name, *1159*

Hill, Teresa: Puppet Master Four, *878*

Hillaire, Marcel: Take the Money and Run, *390*

Hiller, Wendy: Anne of Avonlea, *449;* Cat and the Canary, The (1978), *960;* Elephant Man, The (1980), *508;* Lonely Passion of Judith Hearne, The, *577;* Major Barbara, *326;* Man for All Seasons, A, *586;* Pygmalion, *363;* Something of Value *118;* Toys in the Attic, *687*

Hillerman, John: Assault & Matrimony, *229;* Chinatown, *962;* Guide for the Married Woman, A, *291;* Lawman, *1127;* Marathon, *329;* Paper Moon, *353;* Up the Creek (1984), *403*

Hillie, Verna: Mystery Mountain, *1135;* Star Packer, The, *1153;* Trail Beyond, The, *1158*

Hilligoss, Candace: Carnival of Souls, *821*

Hillman, Warren: Ator: The Fighting Eagle, *1037*

Hills, Beverly: Brides of the Beast, *819;* Knights and Emeralds, *314*

Hills, Gillian: Demons of the Mind, *833*

Hilton, Daisy: Chained for Life, *478*

Hilton, George: Battle of El Alamein, The, *10;* Bullet for Sandoval, A, *1102;* Dead for a Dollar, *1108;* Go Kill and Come Back, *1115;* Guns for Dollars, *1117;* Ruthless Four, The, *114*

Hilton, Violet: Chained for Life, *478*

Hilton-Jacobs, Lawrence: Annihilators, The, *5;* Cooley High, *259;* Indecent Behavior, *551;* Jacksons: An American Dream, The, *556;* L.A. Vice, *74;* Paramedics, *353;* Quiet Fire, *102*

Himes, Frank: Deathshot, *36*

Hindle, Art: Brood, The, *819;* Dixie Lanes, *265;* Gunfighters, The, *1117;* Into the Fire, *67;* Man Who Wasn't There, The, *328;* Raw Courage, *103;* Say Yes, *373;* Small Town in Texas, A, *117;* Surrogate, The, *674*
Hindman, Earl: Murder in Coweta County, *600*
Hinds, Ciaran: Hostages, *544*
Hinds, Samuel S.: Deluge, *1046;* Dr. Kildare's Strange Case, *40;* Egg and I, The, *270;* Gabriel over the White House, *524;* In Person, *305;* It's a Date, *925;* Navy Blue and Gold, *342;* Pardon My Sarong, *354;* Rage of Paris, The, *364;* Raven, The (1935), *878;* Return of October, The, *366;* Ride 'em Cowboy, *368;* Strange Affair of Uncle Harry, The, *669;* Wives Under Suspicion, *704*
Hines, Dennis: To All My Friends on Shore, *684*
Hines, Gregory: Cotton Club, The, *29;* Deal of the Century, *263;* Eubie!, *916;* Eve of Destruction, *1050;* History of the World, Part One, The, *298;* Off Limits (1988), *93;* Puss in Boots, *198;* Rage in Harlem, A, *103;* Running Scared (1986), *110;* Tap, *944;* TBone N Weasel, *391;* White Lie, *700;* White Nights (1985), *700;* Wolfen, *904*
Hines, Maurice: Eubie!, *916*
Hingle, Pat: Act, The, *441;* Baby Boom, *230;* Batman (1989), *9;* Batman Returns, *9;* Bloody Mama, *16;* Brewster's Millions (1985), *245;* Citizen Cohn, *482;* Elvis—The Movie, *509;* Falcon and the Snowman, The, *513;* Gauntlet, The, *55;* Going Berserk, *287;* Grifters, The, *534;* Hang 'em High, *1118;* Invitation to a Gunfighter, *1123;* Lady from Yesterday, The, *567;* LBJ: The Early Years, *571;* Lightning Jack, *1128;* Maximum Overdrive, *864;* Nevada Smith, *1135;* Noon Wine, *608;* Norma Rae, *608;* Of Mice and Men (1981), *610;* Running Brave, *645;* Running Scared (1980), *110;* Splendor in the Grass, *664;* Sudden Impact, *122;* Ugly American, The, *690*
Hinkley, Tommy: Human Shield, The, *64;* Silent Night, Deadly Night 4—Initiation, *886*
Hinton, Darby: Malibu Express, *327*
Hipp, Paul: Bad Channels, *1037*
Hird, Thora: Consuming Passions, *259;* Kind of Loving, A, *564;* Nightcomers, The, *870*
Hirsch, Casey: Order of the Eagle, *96*
Hirsch, Daniel: Lady Avenger, *74;* Zero Boys, The, *904*
Hirsch, Judd: Brotherly Love, *819;* Goodbye People, The, *530;* Great Escape II, The, *57;* Legend of Valentino, *572;* Ordinary People, *614;* Running on Empty, *645;* Sooner or Later, *663;* Teachers, *391;* Without a Trace, *1032*
Hirsch, Robert: Mademoiselle Striptease, *763*
Hirschmuller, Hans: Last Five Days, The, *755*
Hirt, Al: Rome Adventure, *643*
Hirt, Christianne: Blades of Courage, *463*
Hitchcock, Alfred: American Film Institute Life Achievement Awards, The, *418*
Hitchcock, Patricia: Psycho, *877;* Stage Fright, *1019;* Strangers on a Train, *1020*
Hoa, Nguyen Anh: Scent of Green Papaya, The, *784*
Hoag, Judith: Matter of Degrees, A, *590;* Teenage Mutant Ninja Turtles, *209*
Hobart, Rose: Brighton Strangler, The, *819;* Conflict, *963;* Dr. Jekyll and Mr. Hyde (1932), *835;* East of Borneo, *43*
Hobbs, Peter: Next One, The, *1068;* Steagle, The, *386*
Hobbs, Valerie: Magic Christmas Tree, The, *184*
Hobson, Valerie: Adventures of Tartu, *2;* Bride of Frankenstein, *819;* Clouds Over Europe, *484;* Drums, *42;* Great Expectations (1946), *532;* Kind Hearts and Coronets, *313;* Promoter, The, *362;* Rocking Horse Winner, The, *642;* Spy in Black, The, *664;* Werewolf of London, *902*
Hodder, Kane: Jason Goes to Hell: The Final Friday, *858*
Hoddy, Steve: Their Only Chance, *210*
Hodge, Charlie: Elvis—The Movie, *509*
Hodge, Douglas: Dark Obsession, *495;* Salome's Last Dance, *647*
Hodge, Patricia: Betrayal (1983), *459;* Diamond's Edge, *162;* Naked Civil Servant, The, *603;* Rumpole of the Bailey (TV Series), *1011;* Spymaker: The Secret Life of Ian Fleming, *119;* Sunset, *1021*
Hodges, Eddie: Adventures of Huckleberry Finn, The (1960), *144;* Hole in the Head, A, *298;* Summer Magic, *208*
Hodges, Ralph: Sea Hound, The, *112*
Hodges, Tom: Excessive Force, *45*
Hodgins, Earle: Cyclone Ranger, *1107;* Marauders, *1132*
Hodiak, John: Across the Wide Missouri, *1092;* Battleground, *456;* Command Decision, *487;* Conquest of Cochise, *1106;* Harvey Girls, The, *922;* Homecoming (1948), *543;* I Dood It, *924;* Lifeboat, *992;* Love from a Stranger, *993;* Miniver Story, The, *594*
Hodson, Donal: Lone Runner, *78*
Hoesl, Tobias: Mines of Kilimanjaro, *85;* Polar Bear King, The, *1071*
Hoey, Dennis: Golden Earrings, *56;* House of Fear, *984;* Pearl of Death, The, *1004;* Sherlock Holmes and the Secret Weapon, *1015;* Sherlock Holmes and the Spider Woman, *1015;* Sherlock Holmes Faces Death, *1015;* Terror by Night, *1023*
Hoffman, Basil: Double-O Kid, The, *41;* Ice Runner, *65*
Hoffman, Bridget: Time Trackers, *1084*
Hoffman, Dustin: Agatha, *951;* All the President's Men, *951;* Billy Bathgate, *461;* Death of a Salesman, *498;* Dick Tracy (1990), *38;* Family Business, *514;* Graduate, The, *531;* Hero, *296;* Hook, *175;* Ishtar, *307;* Kramer vs. Kramer, *567;* Lenny, *572;* Little Big Man, *1128;* Madigan's Millions, *326;* Marathon Man, *82;* Midnight Cowboy, *593;* Papillon, *97;* Private Conversations: On the Set of Death of a Salesman, *433;* Rain Man, *634;* Straight Time, *668;* Straw Dogs, *1021;* Tootsie, *397*
Hoffman, Elizabeth: Fear No Evil, *840*
Hoffman, Erika: Last Days of Patton, The, *569*
Hoffman, Gaby: Man without a Face, The, *587;* Sleepless in Seattle, *381;* This Is My Life, *394*
Hoffman, Gertrude: Ape, The, *809*
Hoffman, Isabella: Tripwire, *132*
Hoffman, Jane: Up the Sandbox, *403*
Hoffman, John Robert: Adventures in Wonderland, *143*
Hoffman, Otto: Haunted Gold, *1119*
Hoffman, Philip Seymour: Leap of Faith, *572*
Hoffman, Robert: Black Veil for Lisa, A, *14;* Eyes Behind the Stars, *1050*
Hoffman, Shawn: Adventures in Dinosaur City, *143*
Hoffman, Thom: Lily Was Here, *575;* Orlando, *614*
Hoffman, Tracey: Forever Evil, *842*
Hoffmann, Isabella: In a Stranger's Hands, *985*
Hoffs, Susanna: Allnighter, The, *225*
Hogan, Bosco: Portrait of the Artist as a Young Man, A, *625*
Hogan, Hulk: Mr. Nanny, *188;* No Holds Barred, *91;* Suburban Commando, *388;* Thunder in Paradise, *129*
Hogan, Michael: Clearcut, *26;* Lost!, *580*
Hogan, Paul: Almost an Angel, *225;* Anzacs, *450;* "Crocodile" Dundee, *261;* "Crocodile" Dundee II, *261;* Lightning Jack, *1128*
Hogan, Robert: Gone Are the Days, *288;* Lady in Red, *74*
Hogan, Susan: Phobia, *1006;* White Fang, *217*
Hohl, Arthur: Lady by Choice, *567;* Scarlet Claw, The, *1012*
Holbrook, Hal: Capricorn One, *1041;* Creepshow, *826;* Dress Gray, *505;* Firm, The, *977;* Fletch Lives, *978;* Fog, The, *842;* George Washington, *526;* Girl from Petrovka, The, *527;* Great White Hope, The, *533;* Group, The, *534;* Kidnapping of the President, The, *988;* Killing of Randy Webster, The, *564;* Magnum Force, *80;* Midway, *84;* Natural Enemies, *604;* North and South, *608;* Our Town (1980), *616;* Rituals, *1010;* Sorry, Wrong Number (1989), *1019;* Star Chamber, The, *1019;* They Only Kill Their Masters, *1024;* Unholy, The, *899;* Wall Street, *695;* Wild in the Streets, *1089*
Holden, Bob: Deadly Vengeance, *35*
Holden, Fay: Andy Hardy Gets Spring Fever, *227;* Andy Hardy Meets a Debutante, *227;* Andy Hardy's Double Life, *227;* Andy Hardy's Private Secretary, *227;* Big Hangover, The,

238; Bulldog Drummond Escapes, *20;* Life Begins for Andy Hardy, *318;* Love Finds Andy Hardy, *322;* Love Laughs at Andy Hardy, *323*

Holden, Gloria: Dracula's Daughter, *837;* Having a Wonderful Crime, *294;* Life of Emile Zola, The, *574;* Miss Annie Rooney, *188*

Holden, Joyce: Terror from the Year 5,000, *1082*

Holden, Marjean: Philadelphia Experiment 2, The, *1070*

Holden, Mark: Blue Fire Lady, *151;* Lovely But Deadly, *994*

Holden, Peter: Great Man Votes, The, *289*

Holden, Rebecca: Sisterhood, The, *1077*

Holden, Tommy: What's Up Front, *408*

Holden, William: Alvarez Kelly, *1093;* Arizona, *1094;* Ashanti, *7;* Blue Knight, The (1973), *465;* Boots Malone, *1100;* Born Yesterday (1950), *244;* Bridge on the River Kwai, The, *19;* Bridges at Toko-Ri, The, *19;* Casino Royale (1967), *252;* Counterfeit Traitor, The, *30;* Country Girl, The (1954), *489;* Damien: Omen II, *829;* Dark Past, The, *495;* Dear Wife, *263;* Devil's Brigade, The, *37;* Earthling, The, *164;* Escape from Fort Bravo, *1111;* Executive Suite, *512;* Fedora, *515;* Golden Boy, *529;* Horse Soldiers, The, *1122;* Key, The, *563;* Love is a Many-Splendored Thing, *581;* Man from Colorado, The, *1131;* Miss Grant Takes Richmond, *333;* Moon Is Blue, The, *336;* Network, *604;* Our Town (1940), *616;* Paris When It Sizzles, *354;* Picnic, *622;* Rachel and the Stranger, *1140;* S.O.B., *372;* Sabrina, *372;* Stalag 17, *119;* Sunset Boulevard, *673;* Texas, *1155;* Towering Inferno, The, *131;* Union Station, *1029;* When Time Ran Out!, *1031;* When Wolves Cry, *699;* Wild Bunch, The, *1164;* Wild Rovers, The, *1164;* World of Suzie Wong, The, *707;* Young and Willing, *708*

Holder, Geoffrey: Boomerang, *244;* Live and Let Die, *78;* Swashbuckler (1976), *123*

Holdren, Judd: Satan's Satellites, *111;* Zombies of the Stratosphere (Satan's Satellites), *141*

Holescher, Devon: Wired to Kill, *1089*

Holiday, Billie: Ladies Sing the Blues, The, *428*

Holiday, Billy: Terror in the Swamp, *893*

Holiday, Hope: Kill Point, *71;* Ladies' Man, The, *314;* Rounders, The, *1146*

Holiday, Kene: Dangerous Company, *494;* Josephine Baker Story, The, *559*

Holland, Agnieszka: Interrogation, *748*

Holland, Betty Lou: Goddess, The, *528*

Holland, John: Blonde Ice, *464;* She Goes to War, *377;* They Saved Hitler's Brain, *895*

Holland, Nicholas: Dusty, *164*

Holland, Pamela: Dorm that Dripped Blood, The, *837*

Holland, Reece: Adventures in Wonderland, *143*

Holland, Steve: TV Classics: Flash Gordon and the Planet of Death, *1085*

Hollander, David: Call to Glory, *474*

Holliday, David: Cannon Movie Tales: Sleeping Beauty, *155*

Holliday, Judy: Adam's Rib, *222;* Bells Are Ringing, *908;* Born Yesterday (1950), *244;* It Should Happen to You, *308*

Holliday, Polly: Bernice Bobs Her Hair, *234;* Catamount Killing, The, *960;* Gremlins, *1055;* Lots of Luck, *322;* Mrs. Doubtfire, *334;* Moon Over Parador, *336*

Holliman, Earl: Anzio, *6;* Bridges at Toko-Ri, The, *19;* Broken Lance, *1101;* Don't Go Near the Water, *267;* Gunsmoke: Return to Dodge, *1118;* Hot Spell, *544;* I Died a Thousand Times, *65;* Last Train from Gun Hill, *1126;* Rainmaker, The, *634;* Smoke, *205;* Sons of Katie Elder, The, *1151;* Trap, The, *1026;* Treasures of the Twilight Zone, *1085;* Tribes, *688*

Holloway, Stanley: Brief Encounter (1945), *470;* Dr. Jekyll and Mr. Hyde (1973), *914;* Hamlet (1948), *535;* Immortal Battalion, The (a.k.a. The Way Ahead), *549;* In Harm's Way, *66;* Journey into Fear (1975), *987;* Lavender Hill Mob, The, *317;* Mrs. Brown You've Got a Lovely Daughter, *931;* My Fair Lady, *932;* No Love for Johnnie, *608;* Passport to Pimlico, *355;* Private Life of Sherlock Holmes, The, *1008;* Salute John Citizen!, *647;* Ten Little Indians (1966), *1023;* This Happy Breed, *682*

Holloway, Sterling: Adventures of Huckleberry Finn, The (1960), *144;* Beautiful Blonde from Bashful Bend, The, *233;* Cheers for Miss Bishop, *480;* Dancing Lady, *913;* Doubting Thomas, *268;* Gold Diggers of 1933, *920;* International House *307;* Kentucky Rifle, *1124;* Little Men (1940), *576;* Melody Master, *592;* Robin Hood of Texas, *1145;* Sioux City Sue, *1150;* Thunder and Lightning, *129;* Walk in the Sun, A, *136;* Wildfire (1945), *1164*

Holloway, W. E.: Elephant Boy, *44*

Holly, Lauren: Band of the Hand, *9;* Dangerous Heart, *965;* Dragon: The Bruce Lee Story, *42*

Holm, Astrid: Master of the House (Du Skal Aere Din Hustru), *766*

Holm, Celeste: All About Eve, *444;* Bittersweet Love, *462;* Champagne for Caesar, *252;* Cinderella (1964), *911;* Gentlemen's Agreement, *526;* Private Files of J. Edgar Hoover, The, *100;* Road House (1948), *1010;* Snake Pit, The, *661;* Tender Trap, The, *392;* Tom Sawyer (1973), *946*

Holm, Eleanor: Tarzan's Revenge, *126*

Holm, Ian: Alien, *1034;* All Quiet on the Western Front (1979), *444;* Another Woman, *450;* Blue Ice, *957;* Borrowers, The, *152;* Brazil, *245;* Chariots of Fire, *479;* Dance with a Stranger, *494;* Dreamchild, *1048;* Fixer, The, *517;* Greystoke: The Legend of Tarzan, Lord of the Apes, *58;* Hamlet (1990), *535;* Henry V (1989), *540;* Homecoming, The (1973), *543;* Inside the Third Reich, *552;* Juggernaut (1974), *987;* Kafka, *988;* Midsummer Night's Dream, A (1968), *332;* Naked Lunch *1067;* Return of the Soldier, The, *638;* Robin and Marian, *107;* Season of Giants, A, *650;* Shout at the Devil, *115;* Singleton's Pluck, *379;* Thief of Baghdad (1978), *127;* Time Bandits, *1084;* Wetherby, *698*

Holmes, Helen: Gentleman from California, *1115*

Holmes, Hollye: Adventures of the Wilderness Family, *144*

Holmes, Michelle: Rita, Sue and Bob Too, *368*

Holmes, Phillips: Criminal Code, The, *491;* General Spanky, *169*

Holmes, Taylor: Beware, My Lovely, *955;* Double Deal, *41;* Hoodlum Empire, *64*

Holotik, Rosie: Encounter with the Unknown, *1049*

Holschneider, Marco: Europa, Europa, *735*

Holt, Charlene: El Dorado, *1111;* Man's Favorite Sport?, *328;* Red Line 7000, *104*

Holt, Hans: Almost Angels, *146;* Mozart Story, The, *931*

Holt, Jack: Across the Wide Missouri, *1092;* Arizona Ranger, *1095;* Brimstone, *1101;* Holt of the Secret Service, *63;* King of the Bullwhip, *1125;* Littlest Rebel, The, *929;* Loaded Pistols, *1128;* My Pal Trigger, *1135;* Renegade Girl, *1142;* Task Force, *677;* They Were Expendable, *127;* Trail of Robin Hood, *1158;* Wild Frontier, *1164*

Holt, Jennifer: Private Buckaroo, *935;* Stage to Mesa City, *1152*

Holt, Patrick: Psychomania, *877*

Holt, Sandrine: Black Robe, *463*

Holt, Steven: Preppies, *360*

Holt, Tim: Arizona Ranger, *1095;* Brothers in the Saddle, *1101;* Dynamite Pass, *1111;* Fifth Avenue Girl, *276;* Gun Smugglers, *1117;* Guns of Hate, *1118;* His Kind of Woman, *62;* Hitler's Children, *63;* Hot Lead, *1122;* Land of the Open Range, *1125;* Law West of Tombstone, *1127;* Magnificent Ambersons, The, *585;* Monster That Challenged the World, The, *1066;* My Darling Clementine, *1134;* Mysterious Desperado, *1135;* Pirates of the Prairie, *1139;* Renegade Ranger, *1142;* Rider from Tucson, *1143;* Road Agent, *1145;* Rustlers, The, *1146;* Stagecoach (1939), *1152;* Stella Dallas, *667;* Treasure of the Sierra Madre, *132;* Yesterday Machine, The, *1090*

Holt, Ula: New Adventures of Tarzan, *90;* Tarzan and the Green Goddess, *125*

Holton, Mark: Leprechaun, *860;* Pee-Wee's Big Adventure, *355*

Holtzman, Thomas: Qui Etes-Vous, Mr. Sorge? (Soviet Spy), *779*
Holubar, Allan: 20,000 Leagues Under the Sea (1916), *1086*
Holvoe, Maria: Worth Winning, *414*
Holyfield, Evander: Blood Salvage, *816*
Holzer, Baby Jane: Ciao! Manhattan, *482*
Homeier, Skip: At Gunpoint, *1095;* Between Heaven and Hell, *459;* Cry Vengeance, *492;* Gunfighter, The, *1117;* Johnny Shiloh, *179;* Tall T, The, *1154;* Ten Wanted Men, *1155*
Homolka, Oscar: Ball of Fire, *231;* Boys' Night Out, *244;* Comrade X, *258;* Executioner, The, *974;* Funeral in Berlin, *979;* I Remember Mama, *548;* Invisible Woman, The, *307;* Key, The, *563;* Madwoman of Chaillot, The, *585;* Mooncussers, *189;* Rhodes of Africa, *639;* Sabotage, *1011;* Seven Year Itch, The, *376;* Strange Case of Dr. Jekyll and Mr. Hyde, The (1968), *890;* White Tower, The, *701;* Wonderful World of the Brothers Grimm, The, *1090*
Hong, James: Bethune, *459;* Big Trouble in Little China, *13;* China Girl, *25;* Framed (1990), *280;* Golden Child, The, *56;* Merlin, *1065;* Missing in Action, *85;* New Adventures of Charlie Chan, The (TV Series), *1000;* Shadowzone, *885;* Talons of the Eagle, *124;* Tango and Cash, *124;* Wayne's World 2, *406;* Yes, Giorgio, *948*
Hongo, Kojiro: Gamera Versus Barugon, *1054;* Gamera Versus Gaos, *1054*
Hood, Darla: Little Rascals, The, *183*
Hooks, Jan: Coneheads, *258;* Dangerous Woman, A, *494;* Funland, *282;* Joe Piscopo Video, The, *310*
Hooks, Kevin: Aaron Loves Angela, *440;* Can You Hear the Laughter? The Story of Freddie Prinze, *474;* Sounder, *663;* Take Down, *390*
Hooks, Robert: Aaron Loves Angela, *440;* Execution, The, *974;* Fast-Walking, *515;* Passenger 57, *97;* Sophisticated Gents, The, *663;* Supercarrier, *122;* Sweet Love, Bitter, *675;* Woman Called Moses, A, *705*
Hooten, Peter: Dr. Strange, *1047;* Fantasies, *514*
Hootkins, William: Biggles—Adventures in Time, *1039;* Hear My Song, *295;* Philip Marlowe, Private Eye: Finger Man, *1005*
Hoover, Phil: Black Gestapo, The, *13*
Hope, Bob: Bachelor in Paradise, *230;* Boy, Did I Get a Wrong Number!, *244;* Call Me Bwana, *249;* Cancel My Reservation, *250;* Casanova's Big Night, *252;* Caught in the Draft, *252;* College Swing, *912;* Critic's Choice, *261;* Fancy Pants, *274;* Ghost Breakers, *285;* Global Affair, A, *287;* Great Lover, The, *289;* Here Come the Girls, *922;* I'll Take Sweden, *924;* Lemon Drop Kid, The, *317;* Louisiana Purchase, *322;* Monsieur Beaucaire, *336;* Muppet Movie, The, *189;* My Favorite Blonde, *340;* My Favorite Brunette, *340;* Off Limits (1953), *348;* Paleface, The, *353;* Paris Holiday, *354;* Princess and the Pirate, The, *361;* Road to Bali, *368;* Road to Hong Kong, The, *368;* Road to Rio, *369;* Road to Singapore, *369;* Road to Utopia, *369;* Road to Zanzibar, *369;* Seven Little Foys, The, *376;* Son of Paleface, *383;* Sorrowful Jones, *383;* They Got Me Covered, *393*
Hope, Leslie: Big Slice, The, *12;* Caught in the Act, *960;* Kansas, *562;* Men at Work, *592;* Prep School, *360;* Sweet Killing, *1022;* Sword of Gideon, *123*
Hope, Richard: Bellman and True, *954*
Hopely, Jason: War Boy, The, *137*
Hopkins, Anthony: Audrey Rose, *811;* Bounty, The, *18;* Bram Stoker's Dracula, *819;* Change of Seasons, A, *253;* Chaplin, *479;* Chorus of Disapproval, A, *254;* Dawning, The, *496;* Desperate Hours (1990), *37;* Doll's House, A (1989), *503;* Efficiency Expert, The, *508;* 84 Charing Cross Road, *508;* Elephant Man, The (1980), *508;* Freejack, *1053;* Girl from Petrovka, The, *527;* Good Father, The, *530;* Great Expectations (1989), *171;* Hamlet (1969), *535;* Howards End, *545;* Hunchback, *854;* International Velvet, *177;* Juggernaut (1974), *987;* Lindbergh Kidnapping Case, The, *575;* Lion in Winter, The, *576;* Looking Glass War, The, *993;* Magic, *994;* Married Man, A, *589;* Mussolini and I, *601;* One Man's War, *613;* QB VII, *631;* Remains of the Day, *637;* Shadowlands, *654;* Silence of the Lambs, *1016;* Tenth Man, The, *679*
Hopkins, Barrett: Firehouse (1987), *277*
Hopkins, Bo: American Graffiti, *226;* Ballad of Little Jo, The, *1096;* Big Bad John, *12;* Blood Ties (1993), *816;* Bounty Hunter, *18;* Center of the Web, *960;* Culpepper Cattle Co., The, *1106;* Day of the Locust, The, *496;* Fifth Floor, The, *841;* Final Alliance, *48;* Inside Monkey Zetterland, *306;* Kansas City Massacre, The, *70;* Killer Elite, The, *71;* Last Ride of the Dalton Gang, The, *1126;* Macho Callahan, *1130;* Mark of the Beast, The, *863;* More American Graffiti, *599;* Mutant, *867;* Nightmare at Noon, *870;* Posse (1975), *1139;* President's Target, *100;* Rodeo Girl, *642;* Small Town in Texas, A, *117;* Smoky Mountain Christmas, *205;* Sweet Sixteen, *123;* Tentacles, *893;* Trapper County War, *132;* What Comes Around, *698;* White Lightning, *139*
Hopkins, Harold: Club, The (1985), *484;* Sara Dane, *648;* Winds of Jarrah, The, *703*
Hopkins, Jermaine: Juice, *560*
Hopkins, Miriam: Barbary Coast, The, *455;* Becky Sharp, *457;* Carrie (1952), *476;* Chase, The (1966), *479;* Children's Hour, The, *481;* Dr. Jekyll and Mr. Hyde (1932), *835;* Fanny Hill: Memoirs of a Woman of Pleasure, *514;* Heiress, The, *539;* Old Maid, The, *611;* Savage Intruder, The, *883;* These Three, *680;* Virginia City, *1161*
Hopkins, Telma: Kid with the Broken Halo, The, *313;* Trancers, *1085*
Hoppe, Marianne: Ten Little Indians (1966), *1023*
Hopper, Dennis: American Friend, The, *712;* Backtrack, *454;* Black Widow, *955;* Blood Red, *464;* Blue Velvet, *817;* Boiling Point, *17;* Chasers, *254;* Chattahoochee, *480;* Cheyenne (TV Series), *1104;* Doublecrossed, *504;* Easy Rider, *506;* Eye of the Storm, *974;* Flashback, *50;* Giant, *527;* Glory Stompers, The, *56;* Heart of Justice, *538;* Hoosiers, *543;* Inside Man, The, *66;* King of the Mountain, *565;* Last Movie, The, *570;* Let It Rock, *573;* Mad Dog Morgan, *80;* My Science Project, *1067;* Nails, *88;* Night Tide, *606;* O.C. & Stiggs, *348;* Osterman Weekend, The, *96;* Paris Trout, *618;* Pick-Up Artist, The, *357;* Planet of Blood, *1070;* Rebel without a Cause, *636;* Red Rock West, *1009;* Riders of the Storm, *368;* River's Edge, *641;* Rumble Fish, *645;* Stark, *119;* Straight to Hell, *1153;* Sunset Heat, *122;* Super Mario Brothers, The, *208;* Texas Chainsaw Massacre 2, The, *894;* Tracks, *687;* Trip, The, *688;* True Romance, *133;* Wild Times, *1164*
Hopper, Hal: Mudhoney, *600*
Hopper, Hedda: Alice Adams, *444;* As You Desire Me, *451;* Common Law, The, *487;* Maid's Night Out, The, *326;* One Frightened Night, *1003;* Racketeer, *102;* Skyscraper Souls, *660;* Speak Easily, *384;* Sunset Boulevard, *673;* Tarzan's Revenge, *126*
Hopper, William: Bad Seed, The, *454;* Deadly Mantis, The, *1045;* Goodbye, My Lady, *171;* 20 Million Miles to Earth, *1086*
Hopton, Russell: G-Men, *54;* Lady Killer, *74*
Horan, Barbara: Bayou Romance, *456;* Malibu Bikini Shop, The, *327;* Triplecross, *399*
Horan, Gerard: Look Back In Anger (1989), *579*
Horan, James: Image of Passion, *549*
Hordern, Michael: Christmas Carol, A (1951), *159;* Dark Obsession, *495;* Green Man, The, *981;* How I Won the War, *302;* Joseph Andrews, *311;* Lady Jane, *568;* Man Who Never Was, The, *81;* Missionary, The, *333;* Old Curiosity Shop, The, *933;* Secret Garden, The (1987), *202;* Sink the Bismarck, *116;* Story of Robin Hood, The, *207;* Suspicion (1987), *1022;* Trouble with Spies, The, *399;* Warriors, The (1955), *137;* Where Eagles Dare, *138;* Windom's Way, *703*
Horino, Tad: Pacific Inferno, *96*
Horn, Camilla: Faust, *736;* Tempest (1928), *678*
Horne, Lena: Broadway Rhythm, *910;* Cabin in the Sky, *473;* Death of a Gunfighter, *1108;* Duchess of Idaho, *915;* I Dood It, *924;* Ladies Sing the Blues, The, *428;* Panama Hattie, *935;* Stormy Weather, *942;* That's Entertainment! III, *436;* Thousands Cheer, *945;* Wiz, The, *948;* Ziegfeld Follies, *949*

Horner, Penelope: Half a Sixpence, *921*
Horney, Brigitte: Baron Müenchhausen, *1038*
Horovitz, Adam: Lost Angels, *580;* Roadside Prophets, *641*
Horrocks, Jane: Dressmaker, The, *505;* Getting It Right, *285;* Life Is Sweet, *574*
Horse, Michael: Avenging, The, *1095;* House of Cards, *545;* Legend of the Lone Ranger, The, *1128;* Passenger 57, *97*
Horsford, Anna Maria: Murder Without Motive, *601*
Horsley, Lee: Sword and the Sorcerer, The, *1082;* 13 at Dinner, *1024*
Horton, Edward Everett: Cold Turkey, *257;* Front Page, The (1931), *281;* Gay Divorcée, The, *918;* Here Comes Mr. Jordan, *296;* Holiday, *298;* I Married an Angel, *924;* Lost Horizon, *580;* Merry Widow, The, *930;* Pocketful of Miracles, *359;* Reaching for the Moon (1931), *365;* Sex and the Single Girl, *376;* Shall We Dance?, *939;* Springtime in the Rockies (1942), *941;* Top Hat, *946;* Ziegfeld Girl, *949*
Horton, Peter: Children of the Corn, *823;* Side Out, *657;* Where the River Runs Black, *1089*
Horton, Robert: Green Slime, The, *1055;* Men of the Fighting Lady, *84;* Silver Blaze, *1016;* Wagon Train (TV Series), *1162*
Hoshi, Yuriko: Ghidrah, the Three-Headed Monster, *845;* Godzilla vs. Mothra, *846;* Kojiro, *752*
Hoskins, Bob: Beyond the Limit, *460;* Blue Ice, *957;* Brazil, *245;* Cry Terror, *964;* Dunera Boys, The, *506;* Favor, the Watch and the Very Big Fish, The, *275;* Heart Condition, *295;* Hook, *175;* Inner Circle, The, *552;* Inserts, *552;* Lassiter, *75;* Lonely Passion of Judith Hearne, The, *577;* Long Good Friday, The, *78;* Mermaids, *331;* Mona Lisa, *997;* Mussolini and I, *601;* Passed Away, *355;* Pink Floyd: The Wall, *935;* Prayer for the Dying, A, *1007;* Raggedy Rawney, The, *633;* Shattered (1991), *1014;* Super Mario Brothers, The, *208;* Sweet Liberty, *389;* Who Framed Roger Rabbit, *410*
Hossein, Robert: Battle of El Alamein, The, *10;* Bolero (1982), *720;* Double Agents, *971;* Le Repos du Guerrier (Warrior's Rest), *758*
Hotaru, Yukijiro: Zeram, *807*
Hotchkis, Joan: Last Game, The, *569;* Ode to Billy Joe, *610*
Hotton, Donald: Hearse, The, *849*
Houdini, Harry: Man from Beyond, The, *1064*
Houghton, Barrie: Mastermind (TV Series), *186*
Houghton, Katharine: Ethan Frome, *511;* Guess Who's Coming to Dinner, *534;* Night We Never Met, The, *345*
House, Billy: People Will Talk, *356*
House, Ron: Bullshot, *247*
Houseman, John: Another Woman, *450;* Babysitter, The, *811;* Bright Lights, Big City, *470;* Cheap Detective, The, *254;* Christmas without Snow, A, *482;* Displaced Person, The, *501;* Fog, The, *842;* Ghost Story, *846;* Gideon's Trumpet, *527;* Merry Wives of Windsor, The, *331;* Murder by Phone, *998;* Old Boyfriends, *611;* Our Town (1980), *616;* Paper Chase, The, *617;* Rollerball, *1075;* St. Ives, *110;* Three Days of the Condor, *1025;* Wholly Moses!, *410;* Winds of War, The, *703*
Houser, Jerry: Bad Company, *1095;* Class of '44, *483;* Summer of '42, *672*
Houser, Patrick: Hot Dog...The Movie, *301*
Houston, Cissy: Taking My Turn, *943*
Houston, Donald: Battle Hell, *9;* Doctor in the House, *266;* Maniac (1962), *995;* Run for Your Money, A, *371;* 633 Squadron, *116;* Study in Terror, A, *1021;* Where Eagles Dare, *138*
Houston, George: Border Roundup, *1100*
Houston, Renee: Horse's Mouth, The, *301*
Houston, Robert: Hills Have Eyes, The, *850*
Houston, Whitney: Bodyguard, The, *466*
Hove, Anders: Bloodlust: Subspecies III, *816;* Bloodstone: Subspecies II, *816*
Hoven, Adrian: Castle of the Creeping Flesh, *822;* Cave of the Living Dead, *822*
Hovey, Helen: Sadist, The, *882*
Hovey, Natasha: Aqua E Sapone, *713*
Howard, Adam Coleman: No Secrets, *1002;* Quiet Cool, *102*
Howard, Alan: Cook, the Thief, His Wife & Her Lover, The, *259;* Return of the Musketeers, *106*
Howard, Andrea: Nude Bomb, The, *347*
Howard, Arliss: Crisscross (1992), *491;* Door to Door, *267;* For the Boys, *918;* Full Metal Jacket, *523;* Iran Days of Crisis, *554;* Men Don't Leave, *331;* Plain Clothes, *358;* Ruby (1991), *644;* Sandlot, The, *201;* Somebody Has to Shoot the Picture, *662;* Till Death Do Us Part, *683;* Wilder Napalm, *411*
Howard, Arthur: Paradisio, *353*
Howard, Barbara: Running Mates (1985), *645*
Howard, Brie: Android, *1036;* Running Kind, The, *371*
Howard, Clint: Carnosaur, *821;* Disturbed, *971;* Evilspeak, *839;* Gentle Giant, *169;* Gung Ho (1985), *292;* Infested, *856;* Paper, The, *617;* Rock 'n' Roll High School, *369;* Silent Night, Deadly Night 4—Initiation, *886;* Talion, *1154;* Wraith, The, *904*
Howard, Curly: Lost Stooges, The, *322;* Stoogemania, *386;* Three Stooges, The (Volumes 1–10), *396*
Howard, Frances: Swan, The (1925), *389*
Howard, John: Arrest Bulldog Drummond, *6;* Bulldog Drummond Comes Back, *20;* Bulldog Drummond in Africa, *20;* Bulldog Drummond's Bride, *20;* Bulldog Drummond's Peril, *20;* Bulldog Drummond's Revenge, *21;* Bulldog Drummond's Secret Police, *21;* Club, The (1985), *484;* High and the Mighty, The, *541;* Highest Honor, The, *62;* Invisible Woman, The, *307;* Lost Horizon, *580;* Love from a Stranger, *993;* Philadelphia Story, The, *357*
Howard, Joyce: Night Has Eyes, The, *1001*
Howard, Kathleen: It's a Gift, *308*
Howard, Ken: Country Girl, The (1982), *489;* Murder in New Hampshire, *600;* Pudd'nhead Wilson, *630;* Rage of Angels, *633;* Real American Hero, The, *635;* 1776, *939;* Strange Interlude (1988), *669;* Ulterior Motives, *133*
Howard, Leslie: Animal Kingdom, The, *448;* Devotion, *500;* 49th Parallel, The, *520;* Free Soul, A, *522;* Gone with the Wind, *530;* Intermezzo (1939), *553;* Of Human Bondage (1934), *610;* Petrified Forest, The, *621;* Pimpernel Smith, *99;* Pygmalion, *363;* Romeo and Juliet (1936), *643;* Scarlet Pimpernel, The (1934), *112;* Smilin' Through (1932), *661;* Stand-In, *385*
Howard, Lisa: Rolling Vengeance, *108*
Howard, Marion: Road Games, *1010*
Howard, Marvin: Cremators, The, *1043*
Howard, Mary: Abe Lincoln in Illinois, *440;* All Over Town, *224;* Billy the Kid, *1099;* Nurse Edith Cavell, *610*
Howard, Mel: Hester Street, *541*
Howard, Moe: Lost Stooges, The, *322;* Stoogemania, *386;* Three Stooges, The (Volumes 1–10), *396*
Howard, Rance: Bloody Trail, *1099*
Howard, Ron: American Graffiti, *226;* Andy Griffith Show, The (TV Series), *227;* Bitter Harvest (1981), *462;* Courtship of Eddie's Father, The, *260;* Eat My Dust, *43;* Fugitive, The (TV Series), *523;* Grand Theft Auto, *57;* Huckleberry Finn (1975), *176;* I'm a Fool, *549;* More American Graffiti, *599;* Music Man, The, *932;* Return to Mayberry, *366;* Run Stranger Run, *882;* Shootist, The, *1149;* Smoke, *205;* Village of the Giants, *900*
Howard, Ronald: Adventures of Sherlock Holmes, The (TV Series), *950;* Browning Version, The, *471;* Koroshi, *73*
Howard, Shemp: Africa Screams, *223;* Arabian Nights (1942), *6;* Bank Dick, The, *232;* Blondie Knows Best, *241;* Pittsburgh, *622;* Stoogemania, *386*
Howard, Susan: Moonshine County Express, *86;* Night Games, *1001;* Sidewinder 1, *115*
Howard, Trevor: Albino, *808;* Battle of Britain, *9;* Bawdy Adventures of Tom Jones, The, *233;* Brief Encounter (1945), *470;* Catch Me a Spy, *960;* Catholics, *477;* Charge of the Light Brigade, The (1968), *24;* Dawning, The, *496;* Doll's House, A (1973), *503;* Dust, *506;* Foreign Body, *279;* Gandhi, *524;* George Washington, *526;* Glory at Sea, *56;* Hennessy, *982;*

Hurricane (1979), *65;* I See a Dark Stranger, *65;* Immortal Battalion, The (a.k.a. The Way Ahead), *549;* Inside the Third Reich, *552;* Key, The, *563;* Last Remake of Beau Geste, The, *316;* Missionary, The, *333;* Morituri, *87;* Mutiny on the Bounty (1962), *88;* Night Visitor, The (1970), *607;* Offence, The, *611;* Operation Crossbow, *95;* Persecution, *621;* Poppy Is Also a Flower, The, *99;* Run for the Sun, *109;* Ryan's Daughter, *646;* Sea Wolves, The, *113;* Shaka Zulu, *654;* Slavers, *117;* Stevie, *668;* Sword of the Valiant, *208;* Third Man, The, *1024;* Unholy, The, *899;* Von Ryan's Express, *136;* Windwalker, *1165*

Howard, Vanessa: Girly, *846*

Howard, Willie: Broadway Melody of 1938, *910*

Howat, Clark: Billy Jack, *13*

Howe, Wallace: His Royal Slyness/Haunted Spooks, *298*

Howell, C. Thomas: Acting on Impulse, *950;* All Tied Up, *225;* Breaking the Rules, *469;* Curiosity Kills, *965;* Far Out Man, *274;* Gettysburg, *526;* Grandview, U.S.A., *531;* Hitcher, The, *850;* Into the Homeland, *67;* Jailbait (1992), *68;* Kid, *71;* Nickel & Dime, *344;* Outsiders, The, *616;* Red Dawn, *104;* Return of the Musketeers, *106;* Secret Admirer, *374;* Side Out, *657;* Soul Man, *383;* Tank, *124;* Tattle Tale, *391;* That Night, *680;* Tiger's Tale, A, *396;* To Protect and Serve, *130*

Howell, Hoke: B.O.R.N., *811*

Howell, Jeff: Cemetery Club, The, *478*

Howell, Kenneth: Junior G-Men, *69;* Pride of the Bowery, *627*

Howells, Ursula: Girly, *846;* Murder Is Announced, A, *998*

Howerd, Frankie: Carry on Doctor, *251;* Great St. Trinian's Train Robbery, The, *290*

Howes, Reed: Clutching Hand, The, *27;* Dawn Rider, *1107;* Paradise Canyon, *1138;* Zorro Rides Again, *1166*

Howes, Sally Ann: Anna Karenina (1947), *449;* Chitty Chitty Bang Bang, *158;* Dead of Night (1945), *830;* Deathship, *832;* Nicholas Nickleby, *605*

Howland, Chris: Mad Executioners, The, *994*

Howlin, Olin: Blob, The (1958), *814;* Santa Fe Saddlemates, *1147*

Hoyos, Cristina: Blood Wedding, *719;* El Amor Brujo, *733*

Hoyos, Rodolfo: Brave One, The, *152*

Hoyt, Arthur: Great McGinty, The, *290;* Shriek in the Night, A, *1016;* They Meet Again, *681*

Hoyt, John: Androcles and the Lion, *227;* Casanova's Big Night, *252;* Death of a Scoundrel, *498;* Desirée, *500;* Duel at Diablo, *1110;* Flesh Gordon, *1052;* In Search of Historic Jesus, *550;* Lost Continent, The, *1063;* My Favorite Brunette, *340;* Operation C.I.A., *95;* Star Trek: The Cage, *1078;* Time Travelers, The, *1084;* When Worlds Collide, *1089;* Winter Meeting, *704;* X (The Man with the X-Ray Eyes), *1090*

Hsia, Lin Ching: Peking Opera Blues, *776*

Hsieh, Wang: Infra-Man, *1058*

Hsio, Miao Ker: Chinese Connection, The, *25*

Hsueh, Nancy: Targets, *1022*

Hubbard, John: Mexican Hayride, *331;* Mummy's Tomb, The, *867;* You'll Never Get Rich, *948*

Hubbard, Tom: ~~Two Lost~~ Worlds, *133*

Huber, Harold: Charlie Chan in Rio, *961;* G-Men, *54;* Klondike Annie, *314*

Hubert, Antoine: Le Grand Chemin (The Grand Highway), *757*

Hubley, Season: Child in the Night, *961;* Elvis—The Movie, *509;* Hardcore, *981;* Key to Rebecca, The, *70;* Pretty Kill, *1007;* Stepfather III: Father's Day, *890;* Total Exposure, *1026;* Unspeakable Acts, *692;* Vice Squad, *135*

Hubley, Whip: Desire and Hell at Sunset Motel, *969;* Russkies, *371;* Top Gun, *131*

Hubschmid, Paul: Funeral in Berlin, *979*

Huckabee, Cooper: Funhouse, The, *845;* Night Eyes, *1000*

Hudd, Walter: Elephant Boy, *44*

Huddleston, David: Bad Company, *1095;* Double Exposure (1989), *504;* Frantic (1988), *978;* Gorp, *289;* M.A.D.D.: Mothers Against Drunk Driving, *583;* Santa Claus—The Movie, *201;* Tracker, The, *1158*

Huddleston, Michael: Woman in Red, The, *413;* World's Greatest Lover, The, *414*

Hudson, Brett: Hysterical, *303*

Hudson, Elain: Who Killed Baby Azaria?, *701*

Hudson, Ernie: Collision Course, *257;* Crow, The, *827;* Dirty Dozen, The: The Fatal Mission, *39;* Ghostbusters, *285;* Ghostbusters II, *285;* Hand That Rocks the Cradle, The, *981;* Leviathan, *860;* No Escape, *1069;* Penitentiary II, *98;* Spacehunter: Adventures in the Forbidden Zone, *1078;* Sugar Hill, *122;* Trapper County War, *132;* Weeds, *697;* Wrong Guys, The, *414*

Hudson, Gary: Indecent Behavior, *551;* Lights, Camera, Action, Love, *575;* Martial Outlaw, *82;* Sexual Intent, *1014;* Wild Cactus, *139*

Hudson, John: Screaming Skull, The, *884;* When Gangland Strikes, *138*

Hudson, Mark: Hysterical, *303*

Hudson, Rochelle: Curly Top, *912;* Mr. Skitch, *334;* She Done Him Wrong, *377;* Show Them No Mercy, *657*

Hudson, Rock: Ambassador, The, *445;* Avalanche, *7;* Bend of the River, *1097;* Darling Lili, *913;* Devlin Connection III, The, *970;* Embryo, *1048;* Giant, *527;* Gun Fury, *1117;* Hornet's Nest, *64;* Ice Station Zebra, *65;* Lover Come Back, *323;* Magnificent Obsession, *585;* Man's Favorite Sport?, *328;* Martian Chronicles, Parts I-III, The, *1065;* Mirror Crack'd, The, *996;* Pillow Talk, *357;* Send Me No Flowers, *375;* Showdown (1973), *1149;* Something of Value, *118;* Tobruk, *130;* Undefeated, The, *1160;* Winchester '73, *1165;* World War III, *141;* Written on the Wind, *707*

Hudson, Toni: Just One of the Guys, *312;* Prime Risk, *100;* Uninvited, The (1987), *899*

Hudson, William: Amazing Colossal Man, The, *1035;* Attack of the 50-Foot Woman (1958), *810;* Hysterical, *303*

Hues, Matthias: Blackbelt, *14;* Bounty Tracker, *18;* Mission of Justice, *85;* TC 2000, *1082*

Huff, Brent: Armed Response, *6;* Nine Deaths of the Ninja, *91;* Perils of Gwendoline, The, *98;* Stormquest, *1080*

Huffman, David: F.I.S.T., *512;* Firefox, *49;* Jane Doe, *556;* St. Helens, *646;* Tom Edison—The Boy Who Lit Up the World, *213;* Winds of Kitty Hawk, The, *703;* Witchcraft V: Dance with the Devil, *903*

Huffman, Felicity: Stephen King's Golden Years (TV Series), *1080*

Hufsey, Billy: Off the Wall, *348*

Hugeny, Sharon: Majority of One, A, *326*

Huggins, Leslie: Kenneth Anger—Volume Four, *563*

Hugh-Kelly, Daniel: Cujo, *827;* Nowhere to Hide, *92*

Hughes, Barnard: Cold Turkey, *257;* Da, *493;* First Monday in October, *517;* Hospital, The, *301;* Incident, The (1989), *551;* Lost Boys, The, *861;* Maxie, *330;* Midnight Cowboy, *593;* Pursuit of Happiness, The, *631;* Rage (1972), *633;* Sanctuary of Fear, *1012;* Sister Act 2: Back in the Habit, *380;* Sisters (1973), *1017;* Tron, *1085;* Under the Biltmore Clock, *691;* Where Are the Children?, *1031;* Where's Poppa?, *409*

Hughes, Brendan: Howling VI: The Freaks, *854;* Return to Horror High, *880;* Stranded, *1080;* To Die For, *896*

Hughes, Carol: Flash Gordon Conquers the Universe, *1052;* Home in Oklahoma, *1121;* Man from Music Mountain, *1131;* Stage Struck (1936), *941;* Three Men on a Horse, *395;* Under Western Stars, *1160*

Hughes, Catherine: Radio Patrol, *102*

Hughes, Finola: Aspen Extreme, *451;* Staying Alive, *942*

Hughes, Helen: Incubus, The, *856;* Peanut Butter Solution, The, *194*

Hughes, John: That Sinking Feeling, *392*

Hughes, Kathleen: Cult of the Cobra, *827*

Hughes, Kay: Big Show, The, *1098;* Dick Tracy (1937), *38;* Ride, Ranger, Ride, *1143;* Vigilantes Are Coming!, *1161*

Hughes, Kristen: Jane and the Lost City, *309*

Hughes, Lloyd: Blake of Scotland Yard, *15;* Ella Cinders, *271;* Where East Is East, *138*

Hughes, Mary Beth: Charlie Chan in Rio, *961;* Great Flamarion, The, *532;* Ox-Bow Incident, The, *1137;* Rimfire, *1144*

Hughes, Miko: Cops and Robbersons, *259;* Jack the Bear, *556*

Hughes, Rhetta: Sweet Sweetback's Baadasssss Song, *123*

Hughes, Robin: Sometimes Aunt Martha Does Dreadful Things, *888*

Hughes, Stuart: Blades of Courage, *463*

Hughes, Wendy: Careful He Might Hear You, *475;* Dangerous Summer, A, *494;* Happy New Year, *293;* Heist, The, *540;* Indecent Obsession, An, *551;* Kostas, *567;* Lonely Hearts (1981), *577;* My Brilliant Career, *601;* My First Wife, *602;* Newsfront, *605;* Return to Eden, *639;* Warm Nights on a Slow Moving Train, *696;* Wild Orchid 2: Two Shades of Blue, *702*

Hughs, Sandy: High Rolling, *62*

Hui, Ricky: Mr. Vampire (Vol. 1–4), *768*

Hui, Samuel: Aces Go Places (1–3) (Aka Mad Mission 1–3), *710*

Hulce, Tom: Amadeus, *906;* Animal House, *227;* Black Rainbow, *955;* Dominick and Eugene, *503;* Echo Park, *507;* Fearless (1993), *515;* Inner Circle, The, *552;* Parenthood, *354;* September 30, 1955, *652;* Slam Dance, *1017;* Those Lips, Those Eyes, *945*

Hulette, Gladys: Tol'able David, *685*

Hull, Dianne: Aloha, Bobby and Rose, *4;* Fifth Floor, The, *841;* New Adventures of Pippi Longstocking, The, *191;* Onion Field, The, *613*

Hull, Henry: Babes in Arms, *907;* Boys' Town, *468;* Fool Killer, The, *978;* High Sierra, *62;* Jesse James, *1123;* Lifeboat, *992;* Master of the World, *1065;* Midnight (1934), *593;* Objective, Burma!, *93;* Portrait of Jennie, *625;* Proud Rebel, The, *1140;* Return of Frank James, The, *1142;* Return of Jesse James, The, *1142;* Rimfire, *1144;* Werewolf of London, *902;* Woman of the Town, *1165*

Hull, Josephine: Arsenic and Old Lace, *228;* Harvey, *294*

Hulswit, Mart: Island of the Lost, *857*

Humbert, George: I Cover the Waterfront, *65*

Hume, Benita: It Happened in New Orleans, *925;* Last of Mrs. Cheney, The, *315;* Peck's Bad Boy with the Circus, *194;* Private Life of Don Juan, The, *628;* Suzy, *674;* Tarzan Escapes, *125*

Humphrey, Mark: Iron Eagle II, *67*

Humphrey, Renee: Jailbait (1992), *68*

Humphries, Barry: Barry McKenzie Holds His Own, *232;* Les Patterson Saves the World, *317*

Humphries, Tessa: Cassandra, *821*

Hundar, Robert: Cut Throats Nine, *1107*

Hung, Samo: Eastern Condors, *733;* Painted Faces, *774;* Paper Marriage (1988), *775;* Project A (Part I), *778*

Hunnicutt, Arthur: Big Sky, The, *1098;* Bounty Man, The, *1101;* Broken Arrow, *1101;* Devil's Canyon, *1109;* Distant Drums, *40;* El Dorado, *1111;* French Line, The, *918;* Harry and Tonto, *537;* Last Command, The (1955), *1125;* Lusty Men, The, *1130;* Pinky, *622;* Red Badge of Courage, The, *636;* She Couldn't Say No, *377*

Hunnicutt, Gayle: Dream Lover (1986), *972;* Legend of Hell House, The, *860;* Marlowe, *995;* Martian Chronicles, Parts I-III, The, *1065;* Once in Paris, *612;* Philip Marlowe, Private Eye: Finger Man, *1005;* Return of the Man from U.N.C.L.E., The, *105;* Sell-Out, The, *113;* Silence Like Glass, *657;* Spiral Staircase, The (1975), *1019;* Target, *125;* Wild Angels, The, *139*

Hunt, Bonnie: Beethoven (1992), *149;* Beethoven's 2nd, *149*

Hunt, Brad: Blindsided, *956*

Hunt, Eleanor: Blue Steel (1934), *1099;* Whoopee, *947*

Hunt, Gareth: Bloodbath at the House of Death, *242;* It Couldn't Happen Here, *925*

Hunt, Helen: Bill: On His Own, *461;* Dark River: A Father's Revenge, *495;* Incident at Dark River, *551;* Into the Badlands, *1123;* Mr. Saturday Night, *334;* Murder in New Hampshire, *600;* Next of Kin (1989), *90;* Only You, *351;* Pioneer Woman, *1138;* Project X, *1072;* Quarterback Princess, *631;* Trancers, *1085;* Trancers II (The Return of Jack Death), *1085;* Trancers III: Death Lives, *1085;* Waterdance, The, *696*

Hunt, Jay: In Old Cheyenne, *1123*

Hunt, Jimmy: Invaders from Mars (1953), *1059*

Hunt, Linda: Bostonians, The, *467;* Eleni, *508;* If Looks Could Kill (1991), *66;* Kindergarten Cop, *313;* Rain without Thunder, *634;* She-Devil, *377;* Silverado, *1150;* Twenty Bucks, *401;* Waiting for the Moon, *695;* Year of Living Dangerously, The, *141*

Hunt, Marsha: Actors and Sin, *441;* Hell Town, *1120;* Human Comedy, The, *546;* Johnny Got His Gun, *559;* Panama Hattie, *935;* Pride and Prejudice (1940), *626;* Smash-Up: The Story of a Woman, *661;* Thunder Trail, *1157*

Hunt, Martita: Becket, *457;* Brides of Dracula, *819;* Great Expectations (1946), *532;* Man in Grey, The, *587;* Song without End, *940;* Wicked Lady, The (1945), *701*

Hunter, Bill: Custodian, The, *31;* Death of a Soldier, *498;* Heatwave, *539;* Hit, The, *63;* In Search of Anna, *550;* Last Days of Chez Nous, The, *569;* Newsfront, *605;* Rebel (1985), *636;* Strictly Ballroom, *942*

Hunter, Debra: Nightmare Weekend, *871*

Hunter, Holly: Always (1989), *445;* Animal Behavior, *227;* Broadcast News, *246;* Crazy in Love, *490;* End of the Line, *509;* Firm, The, *977;* Miss Firecracker, *333;* Murder on the Bayou, *600;* Once Around, *349;* Piano, The, *622;* Positively True Adventures of the Alleged Texas Cheerleader-Murdering Mom, The, *360;* Raising Arizona, *364;* Roe vs. Wade, *642;* Svengali (1983), *674;* Urge to Kill, *692*

Hunter, Ian: Adventures of Robin Hood, The, *2;* Andy Hardy's Private Secretary, *227;* Billy the Kid, *1099;* Bitter Sweet, *909;* Broadway Melody of 1940, *910;* Broadway Serenade, *910;* Easy Virtue, *507;* Flame over India, *50;* Little Princess, The, *183;* Order of the Black Eagle, *95;* Pursuit of the Graf Spee, *101;* Ring, The, *640;* Smilin' Through (1941), *940;* Strange Cargo, *669;* Tarzan Finds a Son, *125;* That Certain Woman, *680;* Tower of London (1939), *897*

Hunter, Jeffrey: Christmas Kid, The, *1105;* Great Locomotive Chase, The, *171;* Guide for the Married Man, A, *291;* Hell to Eternity, *540;* King of Kings (1961), *565;* Last Hurrah, The, *569;* Searchers, The, *1148;* Sergeant Rutledge, *1148;* Seven Cities of Gold, *653;* Star Trek: The Cage, *1078;* Star Trek: The Menagerie, *1078*

Hunter, Kaki: Just the Way You Are, *561;* Porky's II: The Next Day, *360;* Porky's Revenge, *360;* Whose Life Is It, Anyway?, *701*

Hunter, Kim: Bad Ronald, *811;* Beneath the Planet of the Apes, *1039;* Born Innocent, *466;* Comedian, The, *486;* Deadline USA, *497;* Escape from the Planet of the Apes, *1049;* Kindred, The, *859;* Lilith, *575;* Planet of the Apes, *1071;* Requiem for a Heavyweight (Television), *638;* Seventh Victim, The, *885;* Skokie, *660;* Streetcar Named Desire, A, *671;* Swimmer, The, *675;* Three Sovereigns for Sarah, *683*

Hunter, Matthew: Tearaway, *678*

Hunter, Ron: Rage of Angels, *633*

Hunter, Ronald: Lazarus Syndrome, The, *571;* Three Sovereigns for Sarah, *683*

Hunter, Tab: Battle Cry, *9;* Cameron's Closet, *820;* Damn Yankees, *913;* Dark Horse, *161;* Grotesque, *847;* Hostile Guns, *1122;* Island of Desire, *555;* Kid from Left Field, The, *180;* Loved One, The, *323;* Lust in the Dust, *324;* Pandemonium, *353;* Polyester, *359;* Ride the Wild Surf, *936;* Sea Chase, The, *112;* They Came to Cordura, *681*

Hunter, Thomas: Battle of the Commandos, *10;* Escape from the KGB, *45;* Vampire Happening, *900*

Hunter, Tony: Naked in the Sun, *1135*

Huntley, Raymond: I See a Dark Stranger, *65;* Immortal Battalion, The (a.k.a. The Way Ahead), *549;* Upstairs, Downstairs, *692*

Huppert, Isabelle: Bedroom Window, The, *954;* Cactus, *473;* Clean Slate (Coup de Torchon), *724;* Entre Nous (Between Us), *734;* Going Places, *741;* Heaven's Gate, *1119;* Judge and the Assassin, The, *750;* La Truite (The Trout), *755;* Lacemaker, The, *755;* Loulou, *761;* Madame Bovary (1991), *763;* My Best Friend's Girl, *769;* Sincerely Charlotte, *786;* Story of Women, The, *790*

Hurdle, James: Climb, The, *26*

Hurkos, Peter: Boxoffice, *467*

Hurley, Elizabeth: Kill Cruise, *563*

Hursey, Sherry: Avenging, The, *1095*

Hurst, Margaret: Meet the Navy, *930*

Hurst, Michael: Death Warmed Up, *831*

Hurst, Paul: Big Stampede, The, *1098;* Gun Smugglers, *1117;* Missourians, The, *1134;* Racketeer, *102*

Hurt, John: After Darkness, *951;* Alien, *1034;* Aria, *907;* Champions, *479;* Deadline (1988), *34;* Disappearance, The, *39;* East of Elephant Rock, *506;* Elephant Man, The (1980), *508;* Even Cowgirls Get the Blues, *272;* Field, The, *516;* Frankenstein Unbound, *843;* From the Hip, *281;* Ghoul, The (1975), *846;* Heaven's Gate, *1119;* Hit, The, *63;* I, Claudius, *547;* Jake Speed, *68;* King Lear (1984), *564;* King Ralph, *313;* Little Sweetheart, *577;* Midnight Express, *594;* Monolith, *1066;* Naked Civil Servant, The, *603;* Night Crossing, *90;* 1984 (1984), *1068;* Osterman Weekend, The, *96;* Partners, *354;* Scandal, *648;* Shout, The (1979), *886;* Success Is the Best Revenge, *672;* 10 Rillington Place, *678;* White Mischief, *700*

Hurt, Mary Beth: Age of Innocence, The, *443;* Baby Girl Scott, *453;* Chilly Scenes of Winter, *481;* Compromising Positions, *258;* D.A.R.Y.L., *1044;* Defenseless, *969;* Light Sleeper, *575;* My Boyfriend's Back, *339;* Parents, *354;* Six Degrees of Separation, *659;* Slaves of New York, *381;* World According to Garp, The, *706*

Hurt, Wesley Ivan: Popeye, *196*

Hurt, William: Accidental Tourist, The, *440;* Alice (1990), *224;* Altered States, *1035;* Big Chill, The, *460;* Body Heat, *958;* Broadcast News, *246;* Children of a Lesser God, *480;* Doctor, The, *502;* Eyewitness, *974;* Gorky Park, *980;* I Love You to Death, *304;* Kiss of the Spider Woman, *566;* Mr. Wonderful, *597;* Plague, The, *623;* Time of Destiny, A, *684;* Until the End of the World, *1087*

Husky, Ferlin: Hillbillys in a Haunted House, *297;* Las Vegas Hillbillys, *315*

Hussey, Olivia: Bastard, The, *456;* Black Christmas, *814;* Cat and the Canary, The (1978), *960;* Distortions, *834;* Escape 2000, *1049;* H-Bomb, *58;* Ivanhoe (1982), *68;* Jesus of Nazareth, *557;* Man with Bogart's Face, The, *995;* Psycho 4: The Beginning, *877;* Quest of the Delta Knights, *1073;* Romeo and Juliet (1968), *643;* Save Me, *1012;* Summertime Killer, The, *122;* Virus, *1087*

Hussey, Ruth: Another Thin Man, *952;* Honolulu, *923;* Madame X (1937), *584;* Marine Raiders, *82;* Mr. Music, *931;* Northwest Passage, *92;* Philadelphia Story, The, *357;* Stars and Stripes Forever, *941;* Susan and God, *674;* Tender Comrade, *679;* Uninvited, The (1944), *1029*

Huster, Francis: Another Man, Another Chance, *1094;* Edith and Marcel, *733*

Huston, Anjelica: Addams Family, The, *222;* Addams Family Values, *222;* And the Band Played on, *447;* Cowboy and the Ballerina, The, *490;* Crimes and Misdemeanors, *490;* Dead, The, *497;* Enemies—A Love Story, *510;* Gardens of Stone, *525;* Grifters, The, *534;* Handful of Dust, A, *535;* Ice Pirates, *1057;* Lonesome Dove, *1129;* Manhattan Murder Mystery, *328;* Mr. North, *334;* Postman Always Rings Twice, The (1981), *1007;* Prizzi's Honor, *362;* Swashbuckler (1976), *123;* Witches, The, *1089*

Huston, James: Outing, The, *873*

Huston, John: American Film Institute Life Achievement Awards, The, *418;* Angela, *448;* Battle for the Planet of the Apes, *1038;* Battle Force, *9;* Bible, The, *460;* Breakout, *19;* Cardinal, The, *475;* Casino Royale (1967), *252;* Chinatown, *962;* Deserter, The, *1109;* Fatal Attraction (1985), *975;* Lovesick, *324;* Man in the Wilderness, *1132;* Minor Miracle, A, *187;* Mr. Corbett's Ghost, *1066;* Myra Breckenridge, *341;* Tentacles, *893;* Visitor, The, *1087;* Wind and the Lion, The, *140;* Winter Kills, *704;* Word, The, *706*

Huston, Virginia: Flight to Mars, *1052;* Night Stage to Galveston, *1136;* Nocturne, *1002*

Huston, Walter: Abraham Lincoln, *440;* And Then There Were None, *952;* Ann Vickers, *448;* Criminal Code, The, *491;* December 7th: The Movie, *422;* Devil and Daniel Webster, The, *500;* Dodsworth, *503;* Dragon Seed, *504;* Duel in the Sun, *1110;* Edge of Darkness (1943), *43;* Gabriel over the White House, *524;* Law and Order, *1127;* North Star, The, *92;* Of Human Hearts, *610;* Outlaw, The, *1137;* Rain, *634;* Rhodes of Africa, *639;* Shanghai Gesture, The, *655;* Summer Holiday, *942;* Transatlantic Tunnel, *1085;* Treasure of the Sierra Madre, *132;* Virginian, The (1929), *1161;* Yankee Doodle Dandy, *948*

Hutchence, Michael: Dogs in Space, *914*

Hutchins, Will: Clambake, *912;* Maverick, *1133;* Shooting, The, *1149*

Hutchinson, Jeff: Rollerblade, *1075*

Hutchinson, Josephine: Adventures of Huckleberry Finn, The (1960), *144;* Love is Better Than Ever, *929;* Son of Frankenstein, *888;* Story of Louis Pasteur, The, *668;* Tender Years, The, *679;* Tom Brown's School Days (1940), *685*

Hutchison, Fiona: Biggles—Adventures in Time, *1039*

Hutton, Betty: Annie Get Your Gun, *907;* Greatest Show on Earth, The, *533;* Here Come the Waves, *922;* Let's Dance, *928;* Miracle of Morgan's Creek, The, *332;* Perils of Pauline, The (1947), *356*

Hutton, Brian: Carnival Rock, *911*

Hutton, Jim: Bachelor in Paradise, *230;* Don't Be Afraid of the Dark, *836;* Green Berets, The, *57;* Hallelujah Trail, The, *1118;* Hellfighters, *60;* Honeymoon Machine, The, *300;* Horizontal Lieutenant, The, *301;* Major Dundee, *1131;* Period of Adjustment, *356;* Psychic Killer, *877;* Time to Love and a Time to Die, A, *684;* Walk, Don't Run, *405;* Where the Boys Are, *409;* Who's Minding the Mint?, *411*

Hutton, Lauren: American Gigolo, *446;* Cradle Will Fall, The, *964;* Fear (1990), *976;* Forbidden Sun, *519;* Gambler, The (1974), *524;* Gator, *54;* Guilty as Charged, *291;* Lassiter, *75;* Malone, *80;* Millions, *594;* Monte Carlo, *599;* Once Bitten, *349;* Paper Lion, *618;* Paternity, *355;* Scandalous (1988), *1012;* Snow Queen, *205;* Starflight One, *1079;* Time Stalkers, *1084;* Trade Secrets, *1026;* Viva Knievel, *136;* Wedding, A, *407;* Welcome to L.A., *698;* Zorro, the Gay Blade, *417*

Hutton, Marion: In Society, *306*

Hutton, Robert: Big Bluff, The, *460;* Casanova's Big Night, *252;* Hollywood Canteen, *923;* Man in the Eiffel Tower, The, *995;* Naked Youth, *89;* Racket, The, *633;* Showdown at Boot Hill, *1149;* Slime People, The, *1077;* Steel Helmet, The, *120;* They Came from Beyond Space, *1083;* Torture Garden, *896*

Hutton, Timothy: And Baby Makes Six, *447;* Daniel, *495;* Dark Half, The, *829;* Everybody's All-American, *511;* Falcon and the Snowman, The, *513;* Friendly Fire, *522;* Iceman, *1057;* Made in Heaven (1987), *1064;* Oldest Living Graduate, The, *611;* Ordinary People, *614;* Q & A, *1008;* Strangers, *669;* Taps, *677;* Temp, The, *893;* Time of Destiny, A, *684;* Torrents of Spring, *686;* Turk 182, *689;* Young Love, First Love, *708;* Zelda, *709*

Huy-Quan, Ke: Goonies, The, *56*

Hvenegaard, Pelle: Pelle the Conqueror, *776*

Hyams, Leila: Freaks, *843;* Island of Lost Souls, *857;* Red-Headed Woman, *636;* Ruggles of Red Gap, *371*

Hyde, Tracy: Melody, *186*

Hyde-White, Alex: Biggles—Adventures in Time, *1039;* Ironclads, *554;* Phantom of the Opera (1989), *874;* Romeo and Juliet (1983), *643;* Silent Victim, *658;* Time Trackers, *1084*

Hyde-White, Wilfrid: Betrayed (1954), *11;* Browning Version, The, *471;* Chamber of Horrors, *822;* Conspirator, *963;* Flame over India, *50;* Ghosts of Berkeley Square, *285;* In Search of the Castaways, *176;* Last Holiday, *569;* Let's Make Love, *928;* Ten Little Indians (1966), *1023;* Trio, *688;* Truth

About Women, The, *689;* Two-Way Stretch, *402;* Up the Creek (1958), *403;* Winslow Boy, The, *704*
Hyer, Martha: Catch As Catch Can, *252;* Chase, The (1966), *479;* Clay Pigeon, The, *26;* Cry Vengeance, *492;* Delicate Delinquent, The, *263;* First Men in the Moon, *1051;* Francis in the Navy, *280;* Gun Smugglers, *1117;* House of 1,000 Dolls, *64;* Houseboat, *302;* Ice Palace, *548;* Lucky Me, *929;* My Man Godfrey (1957), *340;* Night of the Grizzly, The, *1136;* Paris Holiday, *354;* Picture Mommy Dead, *874;* Rustlers, The, *1146;* Scarlet Spear, The, *112;* Some Came Running, *662;* Sons of Katie Elder, The, *1151*
Hyland, Catherine: Vamping, *1029*
Hyland, Diana: Boy in the Plastic Bubble, The, *468;* One Man's Way, *613*
Hylands, Scott: Coming Out Alive, *963;* Daddy's Gone A-Hunting, *965;* Fools, *518*
Hylton, Jane: Manster, The, *863*
Hyman, Flo: Order of the Black Eagle, *95*
Hymer, Warren: Hitler—Dead or Alive, *542;* Kid Millions, *926*
Hynson, Mike: Endless Summer, The, *44*
Hyry, David: Northville Cemetery Massacre, The, *92*
Hyser, Joyce: Greedy, *290;* Just One of the Guys, *312*
Hytten, Olaf: Drums of Fu Manchu, *42*
Hywel, Dafydd: Coming Up Roses, *725*
Iandoli, Dean: Monster High, *336*
Ice Cube: Trespass, *132*
Ice T: New Jack City, *90;* Ricochet, *106;* Surviving the Game, *123;* Trespass, *132*
Ice, Vanilla: Cool As Ice, *488*
Ichikawa, Raizo: Shin Heinke Monogatari, *785*
Ida, Kunihiko: Zeram, *807*
Idle, Eric: Adventures of Baron Münchausen, The, *1034;* And Now for Something Completely Different, *226;* Life of Brian, *318;* Mikado, The (1987), *931;* Mom and Dad Save the World, *188;* Monty Python Live at the Hollywood Bowl, *336;* Monty Python's Flying Circus (TV Series), *336;* Monty Python's the Meaning of Life, *336;* National Lampoon's European Vacation, *342;* Nuns on the Run, *347;* Pied Piper of Hamelin, The, *195;* Rutles, The (a.k.a. All You Need Is Cash), *938;* Splitting Heirs, *384;* To See Such Fun, *397;* Too Much Sun, *397;* Yellowbeard, *415*
Idol, Billy: Doors, The, *914*
Ieracitano, Guiseppe: Il Ladro Di Bambini (Stolen Children), *747*
Igawa, Hisashi: Rhapsody in August, *781*
Igraju: Time of the Gypsies, *795*
Ihnat, Steve: Hunter (1971), *65;* Madigan, *80*
Ikebe, Ryo: Snow Country, *787*
Illery, Pola: Under the Roofs of Paris, *798*
Iman: Heart of Darkness, *538;* Lies of the Twins, *992;* No Way Out, *1002;* Star Trek VI: The Undiscovered Country, *1079*
Imhoff, Gary: Seniors, The, *375*
Incontrera, Annabella: Badlands Drifter, *1096;* Bullet for Sandoval, A, *1102*
Inescort, Frieda: Beauty for the Asking, *457;* Casanova's Big Night, *252;* Judge Steps Out, The, *560;* Return of the Vampire, The, *880;* Tarzan Finds a Son, *125;* Underworld Story, *1029;* You'll Never Get Rich, *948*
Ingalls, Joyce: Deadly Force, *34*
Ingels, Marty: Horizontal Lieutenant, The, *301;* If It's Tuesday, This Must Be Belgium, *305*
Ingerman, Randi: Desperate Crimes, *37*
Ingersoll, Amy: Knightriders, *73*
Ingham, Barrie: Antony and Cleopatra (1981), *450;* Dr. Who and the Daleks, *1047*
Ingram, Jack: Atom Man vs. Superman, *7;* Ghost Town Renegades, *1115;* Idaho, *1122;* Sea Hound, The, *112;* Sundown Riders, *1153;* West of Texas, *1163*
Ingram, Rex: Adventures of Huckleberry Finn, The (1939), *143;* Cabin in the Sky, *473;* Dark Waters, *496;* Green Pastures, *533;* Talk of the Town, The, *390;* Thief of Bagdad, The (1940), *1083*
Inkizhinov, Valeri: Storm over Asia, *789*
Innes, Neil: Rutles, The (a.k.a. All You Need Is Cash), *938*
Innocent, Harold: Canterville Ghost, The (1986), *155*
Inosanto, Danny: Game of Death, *54*
Interlenghi, Franco: I Vitelloni, *746;* Little World of Don Camillo, The, *761;* Shoeshine, *785*
Inwood, Steve: Human Shield, The, *64;* Staying Alive, *942*
Iorio, Jeffrey R.: Deadly Obsession, *831*
Ipale, Aharon: Invisible: The Chronicles of Benjamin Knight, *1060*
Irazoque, Enrique: Gospel According to Saint Matthew, The, *741*
Ireland, Jill: Assassination, *7;* Breakheart Pass, *1101;* Breakout, *19;* Chato's Land, *1104;* Chino, *1104;* Cold Sweat (1970), *28;* Death Wish II, *36;* Family, The (1970), *46;* Hard Times, *59;* Love and Bullets, *79;* Mechanic, The, *83;* Rider on the Rain, *1010;* Someone Behind the Door, *1018;* Villa Rides, *1161*
Ireland, John: All the King's Men, *444;* Arizona Bushwhackers, *1094;* Badlands Drifter, *1096;* Bushwhackers, *1102;* Dead for a Dollar, *1108;* Delta Fox, *37;* Doolins of Oklahoma, *1110;* Escape to the Sun, *511;* Fall of the Roman Empire, The, *513;* Farewell My Lovely, *975;* 55 Days at Peking, *516;* Gangster, The, *525;* Gunfight at the O.K. Corral, *1117;* Gunslinger, *1118;* House of Seven Corpses, The, *853;* Incubus, The, *856;* Kavik the Wolf Dog, *179;* Little Big Horn, *1128;* Machine Gun Killers, *1130;* Martin's Day, *185;* Messenger of Death, *84;* Miami Horror, *1066;* Northeast of Seoul, *92;* Party Girl, *618;* Railroaded, *633;* Ransom, *1009;* Red River, *1141;* Return of Jesse James, The, *1142;* Satan's Cheerleaders, *882;* Southern Yankee, A, *383;* Sundown (1990), *891;* Swiss Conspiracy, The, *1022;* Thunder Run, *129;* Tomorrow Never Comes, *686;* Treasure of the Amazon, *132;* Vengeance Valley, *1161;* Walk in the Sun, A, *136;* We Are No Angels, *1163;* Wild in the Country, *702*
Ireland, Kathy: Alien From L.A., *3;* Journey to the Center of the Earth (1987), *1060;* National Lampoon's Loaded Weapon 1, *342;* Necessary Roughness, *342*
Irlen, Steve: On the Make, *612*
Irons, Jeremy: Betrayal (1983), *459;* Brideshead Revisited, *469;* Chorus of Disapproval, A, *254;* Damage, *493;* Dead Ringers, *831;* French Lieutenant's Woman, The, *522;* House of the Spirits, The, *545;* Kafka, *988;* M. Butterfly, *583;* Mission, The, *596;* Moonlighting (1983), *768;* Nijinsky, *607;* Reversal of Fortune, *639;* Swann in Love, *791;* Waterland, *697;* Wild Duck, The, *702*
Ironside, Michael: Black Ice, *14;* Coming Out Alive, *963;* Common Bonds, *487;* Cross Country, *491;* Deadly Surveillance, *35;* Destiny to Order, *264;* Drop Dead Gorgeous, *972;* Extreme Prejudice, *45;* Father Hood, *47;* Ford: The Man & the Machine, *519;* Free Willy, *168;* Guncrazy (1992), *535;* Hello, Mary Lou: Prom Night II, *850;* Highlander 2: The Quickening, *1056;* Hostile Take Over, *544;* Jo Jo Dancer, Your Life Is Calling, *558;* Killer Image, *988;* Mardi Gras for the Devil, *863;* McBain, *83;* Mind Field, *85;* Murder in Space, *1067;* Neon City, *1067;* Nowhere to Hide, *92;* Payback, *98;* Point of Impact, *99;* Save Me, *1012;* Sins of Dorian Gray, The, *886;* Spacehunter: Adventures in the Forbidden Zone, *1078;* Surrogate, The, *674;* Sweet Killing, *1022;* Top Gun, *131;* Total Recall, *1084;* Vagrant, The, *404;* Visiting Hours, *901;* Watchers, *1088*
Irvine, Kathleen: Greenstone, The, *172*
Irving, Amy: Anastasia: The Mystery of Anna, *447;* Benefit of a Doubt, *954;* Carrie (1976), *821;* Competition, The, *487;* Crossing Delancey, *491;* Far Pavilions, The, *514;* Fury, The, *845;* Heartbreak House, *295;* Honeysuckle Rose, *923;* I'm a Fool, *549;* James Dean—A Legend in His Own Time, *556;* Micki & Maude, *331;* Rumpelstiltskin (1987), *200;* Show of Force, A, *1015;* Turn of the Screw, The (1989), *898;* Voices, *694;* Yentl, *948*
Irving, Christopher: Dedicated Man, A, *499*

Irving, George S.: Deadly Hero, *34*
Irwin, Bill: Bette Midler's Mondo Beyondo, *236;* My Blue Heaven, *339;* Scenes from a Mall, *373;* Stepping Out, *942*
Irwin, Tom: Ladykiller, *990*
Isaac, Brad: Shock! Shock! Shock!, *885*
Isaak, Chris: Twin Peaks: Fire Walk with Me, *1028*
Isacksen, Peter: Rich Hall's Vanishing America, *367*
Ishikawa, Hiroshi: Godzilla vs. Gigan, *846*
Isunza, Agustin: Illusion Travels by Streetcar, *747*
Itami, Juzo: Family Game, The, *735*
Itanzo, Antonio: Cut Throats Nine, *1107*
Iturbi, Jose: Holiday in Mexico, *923;* That Midnight Kiss, *944;* Three Daring Daughters, *945;* Two Girls and a Sailor, *946*
Ivan, Daniel: Slaughter in San Francisco, *117*
Ivan, Rosalind: Pursuit to Algiers, *1008;* Scarlet Street, *649*
Ivanek, Zeljko: Mass Appeal, *590;* School Ties, *649;* Sender, The, *884*
Ivar, Stan: Creature, *1043*
Ivashov, Vladimir: Ballad of a Soldier, *715*
Ivernel, Daniel: Diary of a Chambermaid (1964), *730*
Ives, Burl: Baker's Hawk, *148;* Big Country, The, *1098;* Cat on a Hot Tin Roof (1958), *477;* Daydreamer, The, *161;* Desire under the Elms, *500;* East of Eden (1955), *506;* Ensign Pulver, *271;* Just You and Me, Kid, *312;* Roots, *644;* So Dear to My Heart, *205;* Station West, *1153;* Summer Magic, *208;* Two Moon Junction, *690;* White Dog, *700*
Ivey, Dana: Addams Family Values, *222;* Adventures of Huck Finn, The (1993), *143;* Sleepless in Seattle, *381*
Ivey, Judith: Brighton Beach Memoirs, *246;* Compromising Positions, *258;* Decoration Day, *498;* Everybody Wins, *973;* Hello Again, *296;* In Country, *550;* Long Hot Summer, The (1985), *578;* Love Hurts, *323;* Sister, Sister, *886;* There Goes the Neighborhood, *393;* We Are the Children, *697;* Woman in Red, The, *413*
Ivgi, Moshe: Cup Final, *727*
Iwai, Sharon: Great Wall, A, *290*
Iwasaski, Kaneko: Zatoichi: The Blind Swordsman and the Chess Expert, *806*
Iwashita, Shima: Autumn Afternoon, An, *714;* Double Suicide, *731;* Red Lion, *780*
Izewska, Teresa: Kanal, *751*
Izumiya, Shigeru: Eijanaika (Why Not?), *733*
Jackée: Ladybugs, *315;* Women of Brewster Place, The, *706*
Jackson, Anne: Bell Jar, The, *458;* Folks, *278;* Funny About Love, *282;* Leave 'em Laughing, *572;* Lovers and Other Strangers, *323;* Out on a Limb (1986), *616;* Sam's Son, *647;* Secret Life of an American Wife, The, *374;* Tall Story, *391*
Jackson, Barry: Mr. Love, *597*
Jackson, Carson: Northville Cemetery Massacre, The, *92*
Jackson, Eddie: TV Classics: Jimmy Durante, *400*
Jackson, Ernestine: Aaron Loves Angela, *440*
Jackson, Freda: Brides of Dracula, *819*
Jackson, Glenda: And Nothing But the Truth, *447;* Beyond Therapy, *237;* Boy Friend, The, *909;* Business As Usual, *472;* Class of Miss MacMichael, The, *483;* Hedda, *539;* Hopscotch, *983;* House Calls, *302;* Incredible Sarah, The, *551;* King of the Wind, *180;* Lost and Found, *321;* Marat/Sade, *588;* Music Lovers, The, *932;* Nasty Habits, *342;* Negatives, *1067;* Rainbow, The, *634;* Return of the Soldier, The, *638;* Romantic Englishwoman, The, *643;* Sakharov, *647;* Salome's Last Dance, *647;* Stevie, *668;* Strange Interlude (1988), *669;* Sunday, Bloody Sunday, *673;* Touch of Class, A, *398;* Turtle Diary, *400;* Women in Love, *706*
Jackson, Gordon: Fighting Prince of Donegal, The, *167;* Hamlet (1969), *535;* Ipcress File, The, *986;* Madame Sin, *80;* Medusa Touch, The, *864;* Mutiny on the Bounty (1962), *88;* Prime of Miss Jean Brodie, The, *361;* Russian Roulette, *110;* Shaka Zulu, *654;* Shooting Party, The, *656;* Tight Little Island, *396;* Town Like Alice, A, *686;* Tunes of Glory, *689;* Upstairs, Downstairs, *692;* Whistle Blower, The, *1031*
Jackson, Ivan: World of Strangers, A, *805*
Jackson, Janet: Poetic Justice, *624*
Jackson, John: Sudie & Simpson, *672*
Jackson, John M.: Ginger Ale Afternoon, *286*
Jackson, Kate: Adrift, *950;* Best of Dark Shadows, The, *813;* Death at Love House, *968;* Dirty Tricks, *265;* Listen to Your Heart, *319;* Loverboy, *323;* Making Love, *586;* Night of Dark Shadows, *869;* Satan's School for Girls, *882;* Thunder and Lightning, *129*
Jackson, Lamont: Class Act, *256*
Jackson, Mahalia: Jazz on a Summer's Day, *427*
Jackson, Mallie: Hollywood Harry, *299*
Jackson, Marlon: Student Confidential, *387*
Jackson, Mary: Terror at the Red Wolf Inn, *893*
Jackson, Michael: Michael Jackson Moonwalker, *931;* Wiz, The, *948*
Jackson, Philip: Bad Behaviour, *231;* Poirot (Series), *1006*
Jackson, Sammy: Fastest Guitar Alive, The, *1112*
Jackson, Samuel L.: Against the Wall, *442;* Amos & Andrew, *226;* Assault at West Point, *451;* Dead Man Out, *497;* Hail Caesar, *292;* Jumpin' at the Boneyard, *561;* Jurassic Park, *1061;* Menace II Society, *593;* National Lampoon's Loaded Weapon 1, *342;* True Romance, *133;* White Sands, *700*
Jackson, Sherry: Bare Knuckles, *9;* Miracle of Our Lady of Fatima, The, *595;* Stingray, *120;* Trouble Along the Way, *688*
Jackson, Stoney: Knights of the City, *927;* Up Against the Wall, *692*
Jackson, Victoria: Based on an Untrue Story, *232;* Casual Sex?, *252;* I Love You to Death, *304;* UHF, *402*
Jacob, Catherine: Tatie Danielle, *792*
Jacob, Irène: Double Life of Veronique, The, *731*
Jacobi, Derek: Dead Again, *966;* Enigma, *44;* Henry V (1989), *540;* Hunchback, *854;* I, Claudius, *547;* Inside the Third Reich, *552;* Little Dorrit, *576;* Odessa File, The, *1003;* Philby, Burgess and Maclean: Spy Scandal of the Century, *1005;* Secret Garden, The (1987), *202;* Tenth Man, The, *679*
Jacobi, Lou: Avalon, *452;* Better Late than Never, *237;* Everything You Always Wanted to Know About Sex but Were Afraid to Ask, *273;* I Don't Buy Kisses Anymore, *303;* Irma La Douce, *307;* Little Murders, *319;* Magician of Lublin, The, *585;* Next Stop, Greenwich Village, *605;* Roseland, *644*
Jacobs, André: Curse of the Crystal Eye, *31;* Prey for the Hunter, *100*
Jacobs, Christian: History of White People in America, The (Volume II), *298*
Jacobs, Emma: Murder on Line One, *867*
Jacobs, Mark: Blood Hook, *815*
Jacobs, Steve: Alice to Nowhere, *3*
Jacobsson, Ulla: Smiles of a Summer Night, *787*
Jacoby, Billy: Dr. Alien, *834;* Just One of the Guys, *312*
Jacoby, Bobby: Meet the Applegates, *331;* Wizard of the Lost Kingdom II, *1090*
Jacoby, Scott: Bad Ronald, *811;* Baxter, *456;* Return to Horror High, *880;* To Die For, *896;* To Die For 2: Son of Darkness, *896*
Jacques, Hattie: Adventures of Sadie, *223;* Carry on Doctor, *251*
Jacquet, Roger: Occurrence at Owl Creek Bridge, An, *772*
Jade, Claude: Love on the Run (1979), *762;* Stolen Kisses, *789*
Jaeckel, Richard: Black Moon Rising, *14;* Cold River, *159;* Come Back, Little Sheba, *486;* Dark, The, *829;* Day of the Animals, *830;* Delta Force 2, *36;* Delta Fox, *37;* Devil's Brigade, The, *37;* Dirty Dozen, The: The Next Mission, *39;* Drowning Pool, The, *972;* Firehouse (1972), *49;* Fix, The, *50;* Four for Texas, *1114;* Gallant Hours, The, *524;* Green Slime, The, *1055;* Grizzly, *847;* Guadalcanal Diary, *58;* Hoodlum Empire, *64;* Jaws of Death, The, *858;* Jungle Patrol, *69;* Kill, The, *988;* King of the Kickboxers, The, *72;* Martial Outlaw, *82;* Pacific Inferno, *96;* Sands of Iwo Jima, *111;* Sometimes a Great Notion, *662;* Starman, *1080;* Supercarrier, *122;* 3:10 to Yuma, *1157;* Ulzana's Raid, *1160;* Violent Men, The, *1161;* Walking Tall Part II, *136;* Wing and a Prayer, A, *140*

Jaenicke, Hannes: Tigress, The, *130*
Jaffe, Chapelle: Confidential, *28;* One-Night Stand, *613*
Jaffe, Sam: Asphalt Jungle, The, *953;* Barbarian and the Geisha, The, *455;* Ben-Hur (1959), *10;* Day the Earth Stood Still, The, *1044;* Dunwich Horror, The, *838;* Gentlemen's Agreement, *526;* Guide for the Married Man, A, *291;* Gunga Din, *58;* Lost Horizon, *580;* On the Line, *94;* Scarlet Empress, The, *649;* 13 Rue Madeleine, *127*
Jaffrey, Madhur: Autobiography of a Princess, *452;* Shakespeare Wallah, *655*
Jaffrey, Saeed: Courtesans of Bombay, *489;* Deceivers, The, *36;* Diamond's Edge, *162;* Gandhi, *524;* Hullabaloo over George and Bonnie's Pictures, *303;* Masala, *329;* My Beautiful Laundrette, *601*
Jagger, Bianca: C.H.U.D. II (Bud the C.H.U.D.), *820*
Jagger, Dean: Alligator, *808;* Cash McCall, *252;* Dark City, *495;* Denver and Rio Grande, The, *1108;* Elmer Gantry, *509;* End of the World, *1049;* Evil Town, *839;* Executive Suite, *512;* Game of Death, *54;* Glass House, The, *528;* Honeymoon Machine, The, *300;* I Heard the Owl Call My Name, *547;* It's a Dog's Life, *177;* Jumbo, *926;* King Creole, *927;* Lindbergh Kidnapping Case, The, *575;* Nun's Story, The, *609;* Parrish, *618;* Private Hell 36, *628;* Proud Rebel, The, *1140;* Pursued, *1140;* Rawhide (1951), *1141;* Revolt of the Zombies, *881;* Robe, The, *642;* Sister Kenny, *659;* Smith!, *1150;* Twelve O'Clock High, *133;* Valley of the Sun, *1161;* Vanishing Point, *135;* Western Union, *1163*
Jagger, Mick: Burden of Dreams, *420;* Freejack, *1053;* Nightingale, The, *191;* Performance, *1005;* Rutles, The (a.k.a. All You Need Is Cash), *938*
Jaglom, Henry: Always (1984), *225;* New Year's Day, *605;* Someone to Love, *662;* Venice/Venice, *693*
Jakobson, Maggie: New Year's Day, *605*
Jakub, Lisa: Matinee, *330;* Mrs. Doubtfire, *334*
James, Billy T.: Came a Hot Friday, *22*
James, Brion: Another 48 Hrs., *5;* Armed and Dangerous, *228;* Black Magic (1992), *955;* Brain Smasher...A Love Story, *18;* Cabin Boy, *248;* Cherry 2000, *1041;* Crimewave, *260;* Dead Man Walking, *1045;* Enemy Mine, *1049;* Future Shock, *1053;* Horror Show, The, *852;* Killing at Hell's Gate, *71;* Nemesis (1992), *1067;* Nightmare at Noon, *870;* Player, The, *358;* Rio Diablo, *1145;* Southern Comfort, *119;* Steel Dawn, *1080;* Street Asylum, *121;* Tango and Cash, *124;* Time Runner, *1084;* Ultimate Desires, *1028;* Wrong Guys, The, *414*
James, Cheryl: Who's the Man?, *411*
James, Clifton: Bad News Bears in Breaking Training, The, *231;* Buster and Billie, *472;* David and Lisa, *496;* Eight Men Out, *508;* Rancho Deluxe, *1140;* Tick ... Tick ... Tick ..., *129;* Werewolf of Washington, *902;* Where Are the Children?, *1031;* Will Penny, *1164*
James, Dalton: My Father, the Hero, *339;* Substitute, The, *1021*
James, Don: Hamburger Hill, *535*
James, Elizabeth: Born Losers, *17*
James, Gennie: Secret Garden, The (1987), *202*
James, Geraldine: Jewel in the Crown, The, *557*
James, Godfrey: At the Earth's Core, *1037*
James, Harry: Bathing Beauty, *908;* Private Buckaroo, *935;* Springtime in the Rockies (1942), *941;* Two Girls and a Sailor, *946*
James, Jeff: Forbidden Dance, The, *918*
James, Michael: Warriors of the Apocalypse, *1088*
James, Olga: Carmen Jones, *911*
James, Ron K.: Ernest Rides Again, *272*
James, Sidney: Another Time, Another Place (1958), *449;* Carry on at Your Convenience, *251;* Carry on Behind, *251;* Carry on Cleo, *251;* Carry on Cowboy, *251;* Carry on Cruising, *251;* Carry on Doctor, *251;* Detective, The (1954), *970;* Lavender Hill Mob, The, *317;* Thirty-Nine Steps, The (1959), *1024*
James, Sonny: Hillbillys in a Haunted House, *297;* Las Vegas Hillbillys, *315*
James, Steve: American Ninja, *4;* American Ninja II, *4;* American Ninja III, *4;* Avenging Force, *8;* Bloodfist V: Human Target, *16;* Brother from Another Planet, The, *1040;* Exterminator, The, *45;* Hero and the Terror, *61;* I'm Gonna Git You Sucka!, *305;* Johnny Be Good, *311;* P.O.W.: The Escape, *96;* Weekend at Bernie's II, *407*
Jameson, House: Naked City, The, *1000*
Jameson, Joyce: Death Race 2000, *1045;* Pray TV (1980), *360;* Scorchy, *112*
Jamieson, Malcolm: Meridian, *864*
Jamison-Olsen, Mikki: Sea Gypsies, The, *202*
Janda, Krystyna: Interrogation, *748;* Man of Iron, *765;* Man of Marble, *765;* Mephisto, *767;* Suspended, *791*
Jandl, Ivan: Search, The, *650*
Janezar, Tadeusz: Generation, A, *740*
Janis, Conrad: Duchess and the Dirtwater Fox, The, *1110;* Red Light Sting, The, *636*
Jankovskij, Oleg: My 20th Century, *770*
Janney, William: Bonnie Scotland, *243*
Jannings, Emil: Blue Angel, The, *719;* Faust, *736;* Fortune's Fool, *738;* Last Command, The (1928), *568;* Last Laugh, The, *755;* Othello (1922), *615;* Passion (1919), *775;* Variety, *800;* Waxworks, *802*
Jannucci, Robert: Exterminators of the Year 3000, *1050*
Jansen, Andre: Waltz Through the Hills, *216*
Jansen, James W.: Dennis the Menace: Dinosaur Hunter, *162*
Janson, Horst: Captain Kronos: Vampire Hunter, *821;* Murphy's War, *87;* To Catch a King, *1025*
Janssen, David: Birds of Prey, *13;* City in Fear, *962;* Fer-de-Lance, *976;* Francis in the Navy, *280;* Fugitive, The (TV Series), *523;* Fugitive, The: The Last Episode (TV Series), *53;* Generation, *283;* Green Berets, The, *57;* Hell to Eternity, *540;* King of the Roaring Twenties, *565;* Macho Callahan, *1130;* Marooned, *1065;* Moon of the Wolf, *866;* Once Is Not Enough, *613;* Pioneer Woman, *1138;* S.O.S. Titanic, *646;* Shoes of the Fisherman, *656;* Smile, Jenny, You're Dead, *661;* Swiss Conspiracy, The, *1022;* To Hell and Back, *130;* Two-Minute Warning, *1028;* Word, The, *706*
Janssen, Famke: Model by Day, *86*
Janssen, Walter: Destiny, *729*
January, Lois: Cocaine Fiends, *485;* Lightnin' Crandall, *1128*
Jardine, Al: Beach Boys, The: An American Band, *419*
Jarman Jr., Claude: Hangman's Knot, *1119;* Intruder in the Dust, *553;* Rio Grande, *1145;* Sun Comes Up, The, *208;* Yearling, The, *219*
Jarmusch, Jim: In the Soup, *306*
Jarratt, John: Dark Age, *32;* Next of Kin (1987), *868*
Jarret, Gabe: Real Genius, *365*
Jarvis, Graham: Doin' Time, *266;* Mary Hartman, Mary Hartman (TV Series), *329;* Middle-Age Crazy, *332;* TBone N Weasel, *391;* Vanishing Act, *693;* Weekend Warriors, *407*
Jason, David: Odd Job, The, *348*
Jason, Donna: Honor and Glory, *64;* Undefeatable, *134*
Jason, Peter: Hyper Sapian: People from Another Star, *1057;* Party Camp, *354;* Trick or Treat (1982), *897*
Jason, Rick: Color Me Dead, *485*
Jasper, Star: Jersey Girl, *310*
Jayne, Jennifer: Hysteria, *984;* They Came from Beyond Space, *1083*
Jayston, Michael: Homecoming, The (1973), *543;* Internecine Project, The, *986;* Nicholas and Alexandra, *605*
Jean, Gloria: Never Give a Sucker an Even Break, *343*
Jean, Lorin: Rest in Pieces, *879*
Jeanmaire, Zizi: Black Tights, *909;* Hans Christian Andersen, *921*
Jeanneret, Anais: Desire, *500*
Jeans, Isabel: Easy Virtue, *507;* Heavens Above, *296;* Suspicion (1941), *1022;* Tovaritch, *398*
Jeans, Ursula: Cavalcade, *477;* Dam Busters, The, *31*
Jeason, Sasha: Girl to Kill For, A, *980*

Jedrusik, Kalina: Double Life of Veronique, The, *731*
Jedwab, Rusty: Young Magician, The, *219*
Jefferson Airplane: Monterey Pop, *431;* Woodstock, *438*
Jefferson, Paris: Escape from Survival Zone, *45*
Jefferson, Roy: Brotherhood of Death, *20*
Jefford, Barbara: And the Ship Sails On, *712;* Lust for a Vampire, *861;* Shoes of the Fisherman, *656*
Jeffrey, Herbert (Jeffries): Harlem Rides the Range, *1119*
Jeffrey, Peter: Dr. Phibes Rises Again, *836;* Horsemen, The, *64;* Romeo and Juliet (1988), *643;* Twinsanity, *1028*
Jeffreys, Anne: Adventures of Topper, The, *223;* Boys' Night Out, *244;* Calling Wild Bill Elliott, *1103;* Death Valley Manhunt, *1108;* Dick Tracy, Detective, *38;* Dick Tracy versus Cueball, *38;* Dillinger (1945), *39;* Hidden Valley Outlaws, *1120;* Mojave Firebrand, *1134;* Return of the Badmen, *1142;* RiffRaff (1947), *106;* Those Endearing Young Charms, *394;* Trail Street, *1158;* Zombies on Broadway, *416*
Jeffreys, Chuck: Deathfight, *36;* Honor and Glory, *64*
Jeffries, Lang: Junkman, The, *70*
Jeffries, Lionel: Bananas Boat, The, *232;* Bhowani Junction, *12;* Call Me Bwana, *249;* Camelot, *911;* Chitty Chitty Bang Bang, *158;* Colditz Story, The, *485;* Fanny (1961), *514;* First Men in the Moon, *1051;* Murder Ahoy, *998;* Oh Dad, Poor Dad—Mama's Hung You in the Closet and I'm Feeling So Sad, *348;* Prisoner of Zenda, The (1979), *361;* Spy with a Cold Nose, The, *385;* Two-Way Stretch, *402;* Up the Creek (1958), *403;* Who Slew Auntie Roo?, *903;* Wrong Arm of the Law, The, *414*
Jeffs, Deanne: Midnight Dancer, *594*
Jei, Li Lin: Shaolin Temple, *785*
Jemison, Anna: Heatwave, *539;* Smash Palace, *660*
Jemma, Dorothee: Hot Head, *745*
Jendly, Roger: Jonah Who Will Be 25 in the Year 2000, *750*
Jenkin, Devon: Slammer Girls, *380*
Jenkins, "Butch": Human Comedy, The, *546;* Our Vines Have Tender Grapes, *193;* Summer Holiday, *942*
Jenkins, Allen: Ball of Fire, *231;* Big Wheel, The, *461;* Brother Orchid, *20;* Bureau of Missing Persons, *959;* Case of the Lucky Legs, The, *960;* Employees' Entrance, *271;* Five Came Back, *517;* Hatbox Mystery, The, *982;* Marked Woman, *82;* Oklahoma Annie, *349;* Three Men on a Horse, *395;* Tomorrow at Seven, *685;* Wonder Man, *413*
Jenkins, Anthony: Blood Spell, *816*
Jenkins, Carol Mayo: Hollywood Heartbreak, *542*
Jenkins, Daniel H.: Florida Straits, *51;* O.C. & Stiggs, *348;* Tanner '88, *391*
Jenkins, John: Patti Rocks, *619*
Jenkins, Ken: Edge of Honor, *43*
Jenkins, Rebecca: Till Death Do Us Part, *683*
Jenkins, Richard: Doublecrossed, *504;* Little Nikita, *992;* Witches of Eastwick, The, *412*
Jenkins, Sam: Ed & His Dead Mother, *270*
Jenks, Frank: Corregidor, *489;* One Hundred Men and a Girl, *934*
Jenner, Bruce: Can't Stop the Music, *911*
Jenney, Lucinda: American Heart, *446;* Verne Miller, *135;* Whoopee Boys, The, *411*
Jennings, Brent: Live Wire, *78;* Nervous Ticks, *343*
Jennings, Claudia: Deathsport, *1046;* Gator Bait, *55;* Great Texas Dynamite Chase, The, *57;* Truckstop Women, *132;* Unholy Rollers, *691*
Jennings, DeWitt: Arrowsmith, *451*
Jennings, Joseph: Rock House, *108*
Jennings, Juanita: Laurel Avenue, *571*
Jennings, Maxine: Mr. Wong, Detective, *997*
Jennings, Tom: Stones of Death, *890*
Jennings, Waylon: Maverick, *1133;* Sesame Street Presents Follow That Bird, *203;* Stagecoach (1986), *1152*
Jenrette, Rita: Zombie Island Massacre, *905*
Jens, Salome: Fool Killer, The, *978;* Harry's War, *294;* Jolly Corner, The, *559;* Savages (1973), *373;* Terror from the Year 5,000, *1082;* Tomorrow's Child, *686*
Jensen, David: Petronella, *195*
Jensen, Maren: Deadly Blessing, *831*
Jensen, Roy: Bandits (1967), *1096*
Jensen, Todd: Cyborg Cop, *1043;* Prey for the Hunter, *100*
Jenson, Sasha: Dazed and Confused, *497*
Jergens, Adele: Abbott and Costello Meet the Invisible Man, *221;* Blues Busters, *242;* Dark Past, The, *495;* Fuller Brush Man, The, *282;* Ladies of the Chorus, *567*
Jergens, Diane: FBI Story, The, *515*
Jesse, Dan: Angel of H.E.A.T., *5*
Jessel, George: Diary of a Young Comic, *264*
Jeter, Michael: Bank Robber, *232;* Fisher King, The, *1051;* Sister Act 2: Back in the Habit, *380*
Jett, Joan: Light of Day, *575*
Jett, Roger: Smithereens, *661*
Jewel, Jimmy: Arthur's Hallowed Ground, *451*
Jewell, Isabel: Ceiling Zero, *24;* Ciao! Manhattan, *482;* Evelyn Prentice, *511;* Go West, Young Man, *287;* Leopard Man, The, *991;* Little Men (1940), *576;* Lost Horizon, *580;* Manhattan Melodrama, *81;* Marked Woman, *82;* Seventh Victim, The, *885;* Swing It, Sailor, *390*
Ji, Liu: Red Sorghum, *780*
Jillette, Penn: Miami Vice: "The Prodigal Son", *84;* Penn & Teller Get Killed, *356;* Penn & Teller's Cruel Tricks for Dear Friends, *356*
Jillian, Ann: Alice Through the Looking Glass (1985), *145;* Ellis Island, *508;* Little White Lies, *320;* Mae West, *585;* Mr. Mom, *334;* Sammy, the Way-Out Seal, *201*
Jittlov, Mike: Wizard of Speed and Time, The, *413*
Jobert, Marlene: Catch Me a Spy, *960;* Le Secret, *758;* Masculine Feminine, *766;* Rider on the Rain, *1010;* Swashbuckler, The (1984), *123;* Ten Days Wonder, *1023*
Jodorowsky, Axel: Santa Sangre, *882*
Joel, Billy: Simply Mad About the Mouse, *204*
Joh, Kenzaburo: Zatoichi: Masseur Ichi and a Chest of Gold, *806*
Johann, Zita: Mummy, The (1932), *866*
Johansen, David: Candy Mountain, *474;* Car 54, Where Are You?, *250;* Desire and Hell at Sunset Motel, *969;* Freejack, *1053;* Let It Ride, *317;* Mr. Nanny, *188;* Tales from the Darkside, The Movie, *892*
Johansson, Paul: Midnight Witness, *996*
Johar, I. S.: Flame over India, *50;* Maya, *186*
John, Dr.: Candy Mountain, *474*
John, Elton: Stand by Me (1988), *941;* Tommy, *946*
John, Gottfried: Chinese Boxes, *962*
John-Jules, Danny: Red Dwarf (TV Series), *365*
Johnes, Alexandra: Zelly and Me, *709*
Johns, Glynis: Adventures of Tartu, *2;* All Mine to Give, *444;* Another Time, Another Place (1958), *449;* Court Jester, The, *260;* Dear Brigitte, *263;* Encore, *509;* 49th Parallel, The, *520;* Little Gloria...Happy at Last, *576;* Mary Poppins, *185;* Nukie, *191;* Papa's Delicate Condition, *617;* Promoter, The, *362;* Ref, The, *365;* Rob Roy, the Highland Rogue, *200;* Shake Hands with the Devil, *114;* Sundowners, The (1960), *673;* Sword and the Rose, The (1953), *208;* That's Singing: The Best of Broadway, *944;* Under Milk Wood, *691;* Vault of Horror, *900;* Zelly and Me, *709*
Johns, Mervyn: Day of the Triffids, The, *1044;* Dead of Night (1945), *830;* Jamaica Inn, *556;* Never Let Go, *604;* Old Dark House, The, *872;* Quartet (1948), *631*
Johns, Stratford: Great Expectations (1988), *532;* Salome's Last Dance, *647;* Splitting Heirs, *384;* Wild Geese II, *139*
Johns, Tracy Camilla: She's Gotta Have It, *377*
Johnson, Anne-Marie: Dream Date, *269;* Hollywood Shuffle, *299;* Robot Jox, *1075;* Strictly Business, *387;* True Identity, *399*
Johnson, Anthony Rolfe: Gloriana, *919*

Johnson, Arch: Deathmask, *36;* Napoleon and Samantha, *190*
Johnson, Ariyan: Just Another Girl on the I.R.T, *561*
Johnson, Arte: Alice in Wonderland (1985), *145;* Alice Through the Looking Glass (1985), *145;* Bud and Lou, *471;* Bunco, *21;* Evil Spirits, *839;* Evil Toons, *273;* Love at First Bite, *322;* Munchie, *867;* What Comes Around, *698*
Johnson, Ben: Back to Back, *8;* Bite the Bullet, *1099;* Bonanza: The Return, *1100;* Breakheart Pass, *1101;* Champions, *479;* Cherry 2000, *1041;* Chisum, *1104;* Dillinger (1973), *39;* Getaway, The (1972), *55;* Grayeagle, *1116;* Hang 'em High, *1118;* Hunter, The (1980), *65;* Hustle, *65;* Junior Bonner, *1124;* Last Picture Show, The, *570;* Major Dundee, *1131;* Mighty Joe Young, *1066;* My Heroes Have Always Been Cowboys, *1135;* One-Eyed Jacks, *1137;* Radio Flyer, *633;* Rare Breed, The (1966), *1141;* Red Dawn, *104;* Rio Grande, *1145;* Ruckus, *109;* Sacketts, The, *1146;* Savage Bees, The, *882;* Shadow Riders, The, *1148;* Shane, *1148;* She Wore a Yellow Ribbon, *1148;* Sugarland Express, The, *672;* Terror Train, *894;* Tex, *680;* Three Godfathers, The, *1156;* Tomboy and the Champ, *213;* Town That Dreaded Sundown, The, *1026;* Train Robbers, The, *1158;* Trespasses, *687;* Undefeated, The, *1160;* Wagonmaster, *1162;* Wild Bunch, The, *1164;* Wild Times, *1164;* Will Penny, *1164*
Johnson, Beverly: Ashanti, *7;* Cover Girl Murders, The, *964*
Johnson, Bobby: Demon Wind, *832*
Johnson, Brad: Always (1989), *445;* Annie Oakley (TV Series), *1094;* Birds II, The: Land's End, *813;* Flight of the Intruder, The, *50;* Philadelphia Experiment 2, The, *1070;* TV Classics: Annie Oakley, *1159*
Johnson, Celia: Brief Encounter (1945), *470;* Captain's Paradise, The, *250;* Prime of Miss Jean Brodie, The, *361;* This Happy Breed, *682;* Unicorn, The, *214*
Johnson, Chic: All Over Town, *224;* Country Gentlemen, *260*
Johnson, Chubby: Fastest Gun Alive, The, *1112*
Johnson, Clark: Model by Day, *86*
Johnson, Don: Beulah Land, *459;* Born Yesterday (1993), *244;* Boy and His Dog, A, *1040;* Cease Fire, *477;* Dead-Bang, *33;* Guilty as Sin, *534;* Harley Davidson and the Marlboro Man, *59;* Harrad Experiment, The, *537;* Hot Spot, *544;* Long Hot Summer, The (1985), *578;* Melanie, *591;* Miami Vice, *84;* Miami Vice: "The Prodigal Son", *84;* Paradise (1991), *618;* Rebels, The, *636;* Return to Macon County, *106;* Revenge of the Stepford Wives, *881;* Sweethearts' Dance, *675;* Tales of the Unexpected, *1022;* Zachariah, *1166*
Johnson, Georgann: Front, The, *523*
Johnson, Jim: Birthday Boy, The, *240*
Johnson, Johnnie: Chuck Berry Hail! Hail! Rock 'n' Roll, *421*
Johnson, Joseph Alan: Berserker, *813*
Johnson, Julanne: Thief of Bagdad, The (1924), *1083*
Johnson, Kathryn: Taming of the Shrew (1982), *391*
Johnson, Kay: Madame Satan, *584*
Johnson, Kelly: UTU, *134*
Johnson, Kurt: Sole Survivor, *888*
Johnson, Kyle: Learning Tree, The, *572*
Johnson, Laura: Chiller, *823;* Fatal Instinct (1992), *976;* Lights, Camera, Action, Love, *575;* Murderous Vision, *999;* Nick Knight, *868;* Red Shoe Diaries II: Double Dare, *637*
Johnson, Linda: Bandits of Dark Canyon, *1096*
Johnson, Lynn-Holly: Alien Predators, *1035;* For Your Eyes Only, *51;* Ice Castles, *548;* Out of Sight Out of Mind, *1003;* Sisterhood, The, *1077;* Watcher in the Woods, The, *901;* Where the Boys Are '84, *409*
Johnson, Mary: Treasure of Arne, *797*
Johnson, Michael: Lust for a Vampire, *861*
Johnson, Michelle: Beaks the Movie, *812;* Blame It on Rio, *240;* Blood Ties (1993), *816;* Body Shot, *958;* Driving Me Crazy, *269;* Far and Away, *514;* Genuine Risk, *979;* Jigsaw Murders, The, *987;* Slipping into Darkness, *117;* Waxwork, *902;* Wishful Thinking, *412*
Johnson, Noble: East of Borneo, *43;* King Kong (1933), *859;* Murders in the Rue Morgue (1932), *867;* Ranger and the Lady, The, *1141;* Ten Commandments, The (1923), *678*
Johnson, Penny: Imposter, The, *549*
Johnson, Raymond: Escape from Survival Zone, *45*
Johnson, Richard: Amorous Adventures of Moll Flanders, The, *226;* Beyond the Door, *813;* Crucifer of Blood, *964;* Duel of Hearts, *505;* Haunting, The, *849;* Hennessy, *982;* Khartoum, *70;* Never So Few, *89;* Operation Crossbow, *95;* Restless, *638;* Screamers, *884;* Spymaker: The Secret Life of Ian Fleming, *119;* Treasure Island (1990), *214;* Turtle Diary, *400;* What Waits Below, *902;* Zombie, *904*
Johnson, Rita: Broadway Serenade, *910;* Edison, The Man, *507;* Here Comes Mr. Jordan, *296;* Honolulu, *923;* Letter of Introduction, *573;* My Friend Flicka, *190;* Naughty Nineties, The, *342;* Perfect Marriage, *356;* Smashing the Rackets, *1018;* They Won't Believe Me, *681*
Johnson, Robin: Times Square, *946*
Johnson, Russell: Attack of the Crab Monsters, *810*
Johnson, Stephen: Angel of H.E.A.T., *5*
Johnson, Sunny: Dr. Heckyl and Mr. Hype, *266*
Johnson, Tor: Bride of the Monster, *819;* Meanest Man in the World, The, *330*
Johnson, Van: Battleground, *456;* Big Hangover, The, *238;* Brigadoon, *909;* Caine Mutiny, The, *473;* Command Decision, *487;* Delta Force, Commando Two, *37;* Doomsday Flight, The, *971;* Duchess of Idaho, *915;* Easy to Love, *915;* Go for Broke!, *528;* Guy Named Joe, A, *535;* Human Comedy, The, *546;* In the Good Old Summertime, *925;* It's a Big Country, *308;* Kidnapping of the President, The, *988;* Last Time I Saw Paris, The, *570;* Madame Curie, *584;* Men of the Fighting Lady, *84;* State of the Union, *666;* Thirty Seconds Over Tokyo, *127;* Three Days to a Kill, *128;* Thrill of a Romance, *945;* Two Girls and a Sailor, *946;* Weekend at the Waldorf, *697;* White Cliffs of Dover, The, *699;* Yours, Mine and Ours, *416*
Johnston, Bobby: Maximum Breakout, *83*
Johnston, Bruce: Beach Boys, The: An American Band, *419*
Johnston, Denny: Truly Tasteless Jokes, *400*
Johnston, Grace: God Bless the Child, *528*
Johnston, John Dennis: Miracle in the Wilderness, *595;* Pink Cadillac, *99*
Johnston, Johnnie: This Time For Keeps, *945*
Johnstone, Jane Anne: Dixie Dynamite, *40*
Jokovic, Mirjana: Eversmile New Jersey, *511*
Jolie, Angelina: Cyborg 2, *1043*
Jolivet, Pierre: Final Combat, The, *48*
Jolley, I. Stanford: Arizona Roundup, *1095;* Border Roundup, *1100;* Crimson Ghost, The, *30;* Death Rides the Plains, *1108;* Scarlet Clue, The, *1013;* Trail of the Silver Spurs, *1158;* Violent Years, The, *136*
Jolly, Mike: Bad Guys, *8*
Jolson, Al: Go Into Your Dance, *920;* Jazz Singer, The (1927), *925;* Wonder Bar, *948*
Jones & His City Slickers, Spike: Best of Spike Jones, Volumes 1 & 2, The, *236*
Jones, Allan: Day at the Races, A, *262;* Everybody Sing, *916;* Firefly, The, *916;* My Love for Yours, *340;* Night at the Opera, A, *344;* One Night in the Tropics, *350;* Show Boat (1936), *939*
Jones, Andras: Sorority Babes in the Slimeball Bowl-O-Rama, *383*
Jones, Barbara: Desire, *500*
Jones, Barry: Brigadoon, *909;* Glass Slipper, The, *919;* Number 17, *1002;* Return to Paradise, *106;* Thirty-Nine Steps, The (1959), *1024*
Jones, Buck: Arizona Bound, *1094;* Below the Border, *1097;* California Frontier, *1103;* Dawn on the Great Divide, *1107;* Down Texas Way, *1110;* Fighting Code, *1112;* Fighting Ranger, The, *1113;* Forbidden Trail, *1113;* Forbidden Trails, *1114;* Ghost Town Law, *1115;* Gunman from Bodie, *1117;* Range Feud, *1141;* Riders of Death Valley, *1143;* Stone of

Silver Creek, *1153;* Sundown Rider, The, *1153;* Thrill Hunter, *1157;* West of the Law, *1163;* When a Man Sees Red, *1163*

Jones, Carolyn: Addams Family, The (TV Series), *222;* Big Heat, The, *12;* Career, *475;* Color Me Dead, *485;* Eaten Alive, *838;* Hole in the Head, A, *298;* House of Wax, *853;* How the West Was Won, *1122;* Ice Palace, *548;* Invasion of the Body Snatchers (1956), *1059;* King Creole, *927;* Last Train from Gun Hill, *1126;* Little Ladies of the Night, *576;* Man Who Knew Too Much, The (1955), *995;* Marjorie Morningstar, *589;* Seven Year Itch, The, *376;* Shaming, The, *655;* Tender Trap, The, *392*

Jones, Catherine Zeta: Splitting Heirs, *384*

Jones, Christopher: Looking Glass War, The, *993;* Ryan's Daughter, *646;* Three in the Attic, *395;* Wild in the Streets, *1089*

Jones, Claude Earl: Bride of Re-Animator, *819;* Evilspeak, *839*

Jones, Darryl: Bring on the Night, *419*

Jones, David: Head (1968), *922*

Jones, Dean: Any Wednesday, *228;* Beethoven (1992), *149;* Blackbeard's Ghost, *151;* Born Again, *466;* Herbie Goes to Monte Carlo, *174;* Horse in the Gray Flannel Suit, The, *175;* Jailhouse Rock, *925;* Love Bug, The, *184;* Million Dollar Duck, The, *187;* Mr. Superinvisible, *188;* Monkeys Go Home, *188;* Never So Few, *89;* Other People's Money, *351;* Shaggy D.A., The, *203;* Snowball Express, *205;* Tea and Sympathy, *678;* That Darn Cat, *210;* Torpedo Run, *131;* Ugly Dachshund, The, *214;* Until They Sail, *692*

Jones, Desmond: Romance with a Double Bass, *370*

Jones, Dick: Last of the Pony Riders, *1126*

Jones, Dickie: Blake of Scotland Yard, *15;* Westward Ho, *1163*

Jones, Duane: Night of the Living Dead (1968), *870;* To Die For, *896*

Jones, Eddie: Apprentice to Murder, *810*

Jones, Freddie: And the Ship Sails On, *712;* Consuming Passions, *259;* Elephant Man, The (1980), *508;* Firefox, *49;* Krull, *1061;* Romance with a Double Bass, *370;* Satanic Rites of Dracula, The, *882;* Son of Dracula (1974), *940;* Twinsanity, *1028;* Young Sherlock Holmes, *141*

Jones, Gemma: Devils, The, *500*

Jones, Geraldine: Tall Guy, The, *391*

Jones, Gordon: Arizona Cowboy, *1094;* Flying Tigers, The, *51;* North of the Great Divide, *1136;* Trail of Robin Hood, *1158;* Trigger, Jr., *1159;* Wistful Widow of Wagon Gap, The, *412*

Jones, Grace: Boomerang, *244;* Conan the Destroyer, *1043;* Pee-Wee's Playhouse Christmas Special, *194;* Siesta, *1016;* Vamp, *899;* View to a Kill, A, *135*

Jones, Griff Rhys: Misadventures of Mr. Wilt, The, *333;* Morons from Outer Space, *337*

Jones, Helen: Bliss, *241*

Jones, Henry: Bad Seed, The, *454;* Bramble Bush, The, *468;* California Gold Rush, *1103;* Cash McCall, *252;* Deathtrap, *969;* Girl Can't Help It, The, *286;* Grifters, The, *534;* Napoleon and Samantha, *190;* Nowhere to Run (1989), *609;* Rabbit Run, *632;* Support Your Local Sheriff!, *1154;* 3:10 to Yuma, *1157*

Jones, James Earl: Aladdin and His Wonderful Lamp, *145;* Allan Quartermain and the Lost City of Gold, *4;* Ambulance, The, *952;* Best of the Best, *11;* Bingo Long Traveling All-Stars and Motor Kings, The, *240;* Bloodtide, *817;* Bushido Blade, *21;* By Dawn's Early Light, *473;* City Limits, *1041;* Clean Slate (1994), *256;* Comedians, The, *486;* Coming to America, *258;* Conan the Barbarian, *1042;* Deadly Hero, *34;* Dr. Strangelove or How I Learned to Stop Worrying and Love the Bomb, *266;* Empire Strikes Back, The, *1049;* End of the Road, *510;* Excessive Force, *45;* Exorcist II: The Heretic, *840;* Field of Dreams, *1050;* Gardens of Stone, *525;* Great White Hope, The, *533;* Greatest, The, *533;* Grim Prairie Tales, *847;* Heat Wave, *539;* Hunt for Red October, The, *984;* Ivory Hunters, *555;* Matewan, *590;* Meteor Man, *186;* My Little Girl, *602;* Patriot Games, *97;* Piece of the Action, A, *357;* Pinocchio and the Emperor of the Night, *195;* Return of the Jedi, *1074;* Roots: The Next Generation, *644;* Sandlot, The, *201;* Scorchers, *650;* Sommersby, *662;* Soul Man, *383;* Swashbuckler (1976), *123;* Three Fugitives, *395*

Jones, Janet: American Anthem, *446;* Flamingo Kid, The, *278;* Police Academy 5—Assignment: Miami Beach, *359*

Jones, Jeffrey: Beetlejuice, *233;* Ferris Bueller's Day Off, *276;* Gambler, Part III—The Legend Continues, The, *1115;* George Washington: The Forging of a Nation, *526;* Hanoi Hilton, The, *536;* Howard the Duck, *1057;* Hunt for Red October, The, *984;* Mom and Dad Save the World, *188;* Out on a Limb (1992), *352;* Over Her Dead Body, *352;* Stay Tuned, *385;* Transylvania 6-5000, *399;* Valmont, *693;* Who's Harry Crumb?, *411;* Without a Clue, *413*

Jones, Jennifer: Beat the Devil, *233;* Carrie (1952), *476;* Dick Tracy's G-Men, *38;* Duel in the Sun, *1110;* Frontier Horizon, *1114;* Indiscretion of an American Wife, *551;* Love is a Many-Splendored Thing, *581;* Madame Bovary (1949), *584;* Man in the Gray Flannel Suit, The, *587;* Portrait of Jennie, *625;* Ruby Gentry, *644;* Since You Went Away, *658;* Song of Bernadette, The, *662*

Jones, Jerry: Dolemite, *267*

Jones, Jocelyn: Great Texas Dynamite Chase, The, *57;* Tourist Trap, *1026*

Jones, Josephine Jacqueline: Black Venus, *718;* Warrior Queen, *137*

Jones, Ken: Melody, *186*

Jones, L. Q.: Ballad of Cable Hogue, The, *1096;* Brotherhood of Satan, *819;* Bulletproof, *21;* Lightning Jack, *1128;* Lone Wolf McQuade, *78;* Ride the High Country, *1143;* River of Death, *107;* Standing Tall, *1153;* Timerider, *130;* White Line Fever, *139;* Wild Bunch, The, *1164*

Jones, Lisa: Life and Times of Grizzly Adams, The, *181*

Jones, Lucinda: Wild Duck, The, *702*

Jones, Marcia Mae: Meet Dr. Christian, *591;* Misadventures of Buster Keaton, The, *332;* Old Swimmin' Hole, The, *611;* These Three, *680*

Jones, Marilyn: On the Block, *1003*

Jones, Nicholas: Not a Penny More, Not a Penny Less, *1002*

Jones, Norman: Inspector Morse (TV Series), *986*

Jones, Paul: Demons of the Mind, *833*

Jones, Peter: Hitchhiker's Guide to the Galaxy, The, *1056;* Whoops Apocalypse, *411*

Jones, Robert: Slaughter in San Francisco, *117*

Jones, Robert Earl: Displaced Person, The, *501*

Jones, Ronalda: Alligator Shoes, *445*

Jones, Rosie: Alice to Nowhere, *3;* Ganjasaurus Rex, *845*

Jones, Sam: Davinci's War, *33;* Flash Gordon, *1052;* In Gold We Trust, *66;* Jane and the Lost City, *309;* Lady Dragon 2, *74;* Maximum Force, *83;* My Chauffeur, *339;* Night Rhythms, *1001;* Other Woman, The, *1003;* Silent Assassins, *116;* Thunder in Paradise, *129;* Under the Gun, *691*

Jones, Samantha: Get to Know Your Rabbit, *285*

Jones, Sharon Lee: Princess Warrior, *1071*

Jones, Shirley: Bedtime Story, *233;* Carousel, *911;* Cheyenne Social Club, The, *1104;* Children of An Lac, The, *480;* Courtship of Eddie's Father, The, *260;* Elmer Gantry, *509;* Girls of Huntington House, *528;* Music Man, The, *932;* Never Steal Anything Small, *932;* Oklahoma!, *933;* Silent Night, Lonely Night, *658;* Tank, *124;* Two Rode Together, *1160*

Jones, Simon: Brideshead Revisited, *469;* For Love or Money, *279;* Hitchhiker's Guide to the Galaxy, The, *1056;* Privates on Parade, *362*

Jones, Steve: Great Rock and Roll Swindle, The, *921*

Jones, Terry: And Now for Something Completely Different, *226;* Erik the Viking, *1049;* Life of Brian, *318;* Monty Python and the Holy Grail, *336;* Monty Python Live at the Hollywood Bowl, *336;* Monty Python's Flying Circus (TV Series), *336;* Monty Python's the Meaning of Life, *336;* Secret Policemen's

Other Ball, The, *375;* Secret Policeman's Private Parts, The, *375*

Jones, Tim: Gross Jokes, *291*

Jones, Tommy Lee: Amazing Howard Hughes, The, *445;* Back Roads, *453;* Barn Burning, *456;* Betsy, The, *459;* Big Town, The, *461;* Black Moon Rising, *14;* Blown Away (1994), *16;* Cat on a Hot Tin Roof (1985), *477;* Coal Miner's Daughter, *912;* Executioner's Song, The, *512;* Eyes of Laura Mars, The, *974;* Fire Birds, *49;* Fugitive, The (1993), *53;* Gotham, *980;* Heaven and Earth (1993), *539;* House of Cards, *545;* Jackson County Jail, *68;* JFK, *558;* Lonesome Dove, *1129;* Nate and Hayes, *89;* Package, The, *1004;* Park Is Mine, The, *618;* River Rat, The, *641;* Rolling Thunder, *108;* Stormy Monday, *1020;* Under Siege, *134;* Yuri Nosenko, KGB, *709*

Jones-Moreland, Betsy: Creature from the Haunted Sea, The, *1043*

Jonsson, Nine-Christine: Port of Call, *778*

Joplin, Janis: Monterey Pop, *431*

Jordan: Jubilee, *1061*

Jordan, Bobby: Adventures of the Flying Cadets, *2;* Angels with Dirty Faces, *5;* Bowery Boys, The (Series), *244;* Boys of the City, *18;* Pride of the Bowery, *627*

Jordan, Dorothy: Cabin in the Cotton, *473;* Lost Squadron, *79;* Min and Bill, *594;* Taming of the Shrew, The (1929), *391*

Jordan, James Carroll: Diary of a Teenage Hitchhiker, *501;* Dirty Dozen, The: The Fatal Mission, *39;* Tales of the Unexpected, *1022;* Wilbur and Orville: The First to Fly, *217*

Jordan, Jim: Look Who's Laughing, *320*

Jordan, Louis: Reet, Petite and Gone, *936*

Jordan, Marion: Look Who's Laughing, *320*

Jordan, Nick: Five for Hell, *50*

Jordan, Richard: Chato's Land, *1104;* Dune, *1048;* Flash of Green, A, *977;* Gettysburg, *526;* Heaven Is a Playground, *539;* Hunt for Red October, The, *984;* Hunt for the Night Stalker, *546;* Interiors, *553;* Lawman, *1127;* Les Miserables (1978), *573;* Logan's Run, *1063;* Mean Season, The, *996;* Men's Club, The, *593;* Murder of Mary Phagan, The, *600;* Old Boyfriends, *611;* Posse (1993), *1139;* Primary Motive, *627;* Raise the Titanic, *103;* Romero, *643;* Rooster Cogburn, *1146;* Secret of My Success, The, *375;* Shout (1991), *939;* Sky Heist, *117;* Solarbabies, *1077;* Time Bomb, *1025;* Trial of the Cantonsville Nine, The, *687;* Valdez Is Coming, *1160;* Yakuza, The, *141*

Jordan, Will: I Wanna Hold Your Hand, *304*

Jordano, Daniel: Playing for Keeps, *358*

Jory, Victor: Adventures of Tom Sawyer, The, *144;* Buckskin Frontier, *1102;* Cariboo Trail, *1103;* Cat Women of the Moon, *1041;* Charlie Chan in Rio, *961;* Colt Comrades, *1105;* Death of a Scoundrel, *498;* Devil Dog: The Hound of Hell, *833;* Fugitive Kind, The, *523;* Green Archer, *981;* Hoppy Serves a Writ, *1121;* Kansan, The, *1124;* Leather Burners, The, *1128;* Loves of Carmen, The, *582;* Man from the Alamo, The, *1132;* Manfish, *862;* Papillon, *97;* Son of Ali Baba, *118;* Woman's Secret, A, *1032*

Joseph, Don: Color Me Blood Red, *824*

Joseph, Jackie: Gremlins 2: The New Batch, *1055;* Little Shop of Horrors, The (1960), *861*

Josephs, Tony: Lady Avenger, *74*

Josephson, Erland: After the Rehearsal, *711;* Brink of Life, *720;* Hanussen, *743;* Passion of Anna, The, *776;* Sacrifice, The, *782;* Saving Grace, *373;* Scenes from a Marriage, *784;* Sofie, *787;* To Forget Venice, *795;* Unbearable Lightness of Being, The, *691*

Joshua, Larry: Sugar Hill, *122;* Svengali (1983), *674*

Joslyn, Allyn: Colonel Effingham's Raid, *257;* Fastest Gun Alive, The, *1112;* Heaven Can Wait (1943), *295;* Horn Blows at Midnight, The, *301;* I Love Melvin, *924;* If You Knew Susie, *924;* Immortal Sergeant, The, *549;* Island in the Sky, *554;* Only Angels Have Wings, *95;* Shining Hour, The, *656;* Spring Parade, *941*

Joslyn, Don: Hoodlum Priest, The, *543*

Joston, Darwin: Assault on Precinct 13, *7*

Jouanneau, Jacques: Judex, *750*

Jourdan, Jimi: Chains, *24*

Jourdan, Louis: Beverly Hills Madam, *460;* Can-Can, *911;* Count of Monte Cristo, The (1975), *30;* Counterforce, *30;* Decameron Nights, *263;* Gigi, *919;* Grand Larceny, *289;* Letter from an Unknown Woman, *573;* Madame Bovary (1949), *584;* Man in the Iron Mask, The (1977), *81;* Octopussy, *93;* Paradine Case, The, *1004;* Return of the Swamp Thing, *880;* Silver Bears, *379;* Swamp Thing, *891;* Swan, The (1956), *674;* V.I.P.s, The, *693;* Year of the Comet, *415*

Jourdan, Raymond: Rise of Louis XIV, The, *781*

Jouvet, Louis: Bizarre, Bizarre, *718;* Carnival in Flanders, *722;* Jenny Lamour, *749;* La Marseillaise, *754;* Lower Depths (1936), *762;* Volpone, *801*

Jovovich, Milla: Chaplin, *479;* Dazed and Confused, *497;* Kuffs, *73;* Return to the Blue Lagoon, *639*

Joy, Leatrice: Old Swimmin' Hole, The, *611;* Ten Commandments, The (1923), *678*

Joy, Robert: Amityville III: The Demon, *809;* Big Shots, *238;* Dark Half, The, *829;* Death Wish V: The Face of Death, *36;* Desperately Seeking Susan, *264;* Judgment, *560;* Lawrenceville Stories, The, *317;* Millennium, *1066;* Shadows and Fog, *654;* She's Back, *377;* Suicide Club, The, *1021;* Sword of Gideon, *123;* Terminal Choice, *893*

Joyce, Alice: Dancing Mothers, *262*

Joyce, Brenda: Enchanted Forest, The, *165;* Little Giant, *319;* Rains Came, The, *634*

Joyce, Elaine: Guide for the Married Woman, A, *291;* Motel Hell, *866;* Trick or Treat (1986), *897*

Joyce, Luis: Heroes in Hell, *61*

Joyce, Peggy Hopkins: International House, *307*

Joyeux, Odette: Sylvia and the Phantom, *792*

Joyner, Mario: Hangin' with the Homeboys, *292*

Juarez, Ruben: Tango Bar, *792*

Judd, Ashley: Ruby in Paradise, *645*

Judd, Edward: Concrete Jungle, The (1962) (a.k.a. The Criminal), *487;* Day the Earth Caught Fire, The, *1044;* First Men *in* the Moon, *1051;* Hound of the Baskervilles, The (1983), *984;* Island of Terror, *857;* Stolen Hours, *668;* Vault of Horror, *900;* Whose Child Am I?, *701*

Judd, John: Scum, *650*

Judd, Naomi: Rio Diablo, *1145*

Judge, Arline: Here Comes Trouble, *296;* Lady Is Willing, The, *315;* Mad Wednesday, *325;* Mysterious Mr. Wong, The, *88;* One in a Million, *350;* Sin of Harold Diddlebock (a.k.a. Mad Wednesday), *379;* Song of Texas, *1151*

Juhlin, Niklas: Mystery Island, *190*

Julia, Raul: Addams Family, The, *222;* Addams Family Values, *222;* Alamo, The: Thirteen Days to Glory, *1093;* Compromising Positions, *258;* Escape Artist, The, *165;* Florida Straits, *51;* Frankenstein Unbound, *843;* Gumball Rally, The, *58;* Havana, *537;* Kiss of the Spider Woman, *566;* Mack the Knife, *930;* Moon Over Parador, *336;* Morning After, The, *997;* Onassis: The Richest Man in the World, *612;* One from the Heart, *934;* Organization, The, *96;* Penitent, The, *620;* Plague, The, *623;* Presumed Innocent, *1007;* Romero, *643;* Rookie, The, *109;* Tango Bar, *792;* Tequila Sunrise, *126;* Trading Hearts, *398*

Julian, Janet: Choke Canyon, *25;* Ghost Warrior, *55;* Humongous, *854;* King of New York, *72*

Julien, Max: Getting Straight, *526;* Mack, The, *584*

Jurado, Katy: Badlanders, The, *1096;* Barabbas, *455;* Broken Lance, *1101;* Bullfighter and the Lady, The, *21;* El Bruto (The Brute), *733;* High Noon, *1120;* One-Eyed Jacks, *1137;* Pat Garrett and Billy the Kid, *1138;* Racers, The, *632;* Trapeze, *687*

Jurgens, Curt: And God Created Woman (1957), *712;* Battle of Britain, *9;* Battle of the Commandos, *10;* Brainwashed, *958;* Breakthrough, *19;* Enemy Below, The, *44;* Goldengirl, *1054;* Inn of the Sixth Happiness, The, *552;* Just a Gigolo, *561;* Mephisto Waltz, The, *864;* Miracle of the White Stallions, *187;* Mozart Story, The, *931;* Spy Who Loved Me, The, *119;* This Happy Feeling, *394;* Vault of Horror, *900*

Jurgens, Deana: Tin Man, *684*
Jurisic, Melita: Tale of Ruby Rose, The, *676*
Justice, James Robertson: Captain Horatio Hornblower, *23;* Doctor at Large, *265;* Doctor at Sea, *266;* Doctor in Distress, *266;* Doctor in the House, *266;* Land of the Pharaohs, *568;* Le Repos du Guerrier (Warrior's Rest), *758;* Murder She Said, *999;* Rob Roy, the Highland Rogue, *200;* Story of Robin Hood, The, *207;* Sword and the Rose, The (1953), *208;* Tight Little Island, *396*
Justice, Katherine: Five Card Stud, *1113;* Frasier the Lovable Lion (Frasier the Sensuous Lion), *168*
Justin, John: Savage Messiah, *648;* Thief of Bagdad, The (1940), *1083*
Justin, Larry: Hollywood Meatcleaver Massacre, *850*
Justine, William: Bride and the Beast, The, *19*
Jutra, Claude: Mon Oncle Antoine, *768*
Ka'ne, Dayton: Hurricane (1979), *65*
Kaake, Jeff: Border Shootout, *1100*
Kaaren, Suzanne: Devil Bat, The, *833*
Kaatz, Christy: Nick Danger in the Case of the Missing Yolk, *344*
Kabler, Roger: Alligator Eyes, *951*
Kabo, Olga: Ice Runner, *65*
Kaczmarek, Jane: All's Fair, *225;* D.O.A. (1988), *965;* Door to Door, *267;* Heavenly Kid, The, *296;* Vice Versa, *404*
Kadler, Karen: Devil's Messenger, The, *834*
Kadochnikova, Larisa: Shadows of Forgotten Ancestors, *785*
Kagan, Diane: Barn Burning, *456*
Kagawa, Kyoko: Chikamatsu Monogatari, *723*
Kahan, Judy: Lily Tomlin Special—Vol. I, The, *319*
Kahan, Saul: Schlock, *373*
Kahler, Wolf: Dirty Dozen, The: The Deadly Mission, *39;* Raiders of the Lost Ark, *1073*
Kahn, Madeline: Adventure of Sherlock Holmes' Smarter Brother, The, *223;* American Tail, An, *146;* Best of Dan Aykroyd, The, *235;* Best of Gilda Radner, The, *235;* Betsy's Wedding, *236;* Blazing Saddles, *241;* Cheap Detective, The, *254;* City Heat, *255;* Clue, *256;* First Family, *277;* For Richer, for Poorer, *279;* Happy Birthday, Gemini, *293;* Hideaways, The, *174;* High Anxiety, *297;* History of the World, Part One, The, *298;* Muppet Movie, The, *189;* My Little Pony: The Movie, *190;* Paper Moon, *353;* Simon, *379;* Slapstick of Another Kind, *380;* Wholly Moses!, *410;* Yellowbeard, *415;* Young Frankenstein, *416*
Kaidanovsky, Alexander: Stalker, *788*
Kain, Khalil: Juice, *560*
Kaitan, Elizabeth: Desperate Crimes, *37*
Kalem, Toni: Billy Galvin, *461*
Kalfon, Jean-Pierre: Confidentially Yours, *725;* Valley, The, *799*
Kalipha, Stefan: Born of Fire, *467*
Kallo, John: My Samurai, *88*
Kaloper, Jagoda: WR: Mysteries of the Organism, *805*
Kalyagin, Alexandar: Slave of Love, A, *786*
Kalyagin, Alexander: Unfinished Piece for the Player Piano, An, *798*
Kam-bo: Painted Faces, *774*
Kamamoto, Gayo: Zatoichi: The Blind Swordsman and the Chess Expert, *806*
Kaman, Bob: Bloodfist, *15*
Kamekona, Danny: Robot Wars, *1075*
Kaminska, Ida: Shop on Main Street, The, *786*
Kamm, Kris: Heroes of Desert Storm, *61;* When the Party's Over, *699*
Kanakis, Anna: After the Fall of New York, *1034;* Warriors of the Wasteland, *1088*
Kanaly, Steve: Balboa, *455;* Dillinger (1973), *39;* Double Trouble (1991), *268;* Eye of the Eagle 3, *46;* Fleshburn, *841;* Wind and the Lion, The, *140*
Kanan, Sean: Rich Girl, *640*
Kane, Alden: Prom Night IV—Deliver Us from Evil, *877*
Kane, Big Daddy: Posse (1993), *1139*
Kane, Bridget: Who's Who, *411*
Kane, Carol: Addams Family Values, *222;* Annie Hall, *228;* Baby on Board, *8;* Casey at the Bat, *156;* Dog Day Afternoon, *971;* Even Cowgirls Get the Blues, *272;* Flashback, *50;* Games of Countess Dolingen of Gratz, The, *739;* Greatest Man in the World, The, *290;* Hester Street, *541;* In the Soup, *306;* Ishtar, *307;* Jumpin' Jack Flash, *311;* Lemon Sisters, The, *317;* License to Drive, *318;* Muppet Movie, The, *189;* My Blue Heaven, *339;* My Sister, My Love, *867;* Norman Loves Rose, *346;* Over the Brooklyn Bridge, *352;* Pandemonium, *353;* Paul Reiser Out on a Whim, *355;* Princess Bride, The, *1071;* Racing with the Moon, *633;* Rap Master Ronnie—A Report Card, *364;* Scrooged, *374;* Secret Diary of Sigmund Freud, The, *374;* Sticky Fingers, *386;* Ted & Venus, *392;* Transylvania 6-5000, *399;* Valentino, *693;* Wedding in White, *697;* When a Stranger Calls, *1030;* When a Stranger Calls Back, *1031;* World's Greatest Lover, The, *414*
Kane, Irene: Killer's Kiss, *71*
Kane, Jimmy: Challenge to Be Free, *157*
Kaner, Iris: Soldier of the Night, *787*
Kani, John: African Dream, An, *442;* Killing Heat, *563;* Master Harold and the Boys, *590;* Options, *351;* Saturday Night at the Palace, *648*
Kanner, Alexis: Kings and Desperate Men: A Hostage Incident, *73;* Twinsanity, *1028*
Kanter, Jennifer: Occultist, The, *93*
Kanter, Marin: Loveless, The, *582*
Kants, Ivar: Gallagher's Travels, *54;* Plumber, The, *1006*
Kapelos, John: Deep Red (1994), *1046;* Nick Knight, *868*
Kaplan, Gabe: Fast Break, *274;* Gabe Kaplan as Groucho, *282;* Nobody's Perfekt, *346;* Tulips, *400*
Kaplan, Marvin: New Kind of Love, A, *343;* Severed Arm, The, *885*
Kapoor, Shashi: Bombay Talkie, *720;* Deceivers, The, *36;* Heat and Dust, *539;* Householder, The, *745;* Sammy and Rosie Get Laid, *372;* Shakespeare Wallah, *655*
Kaprisky, Valerie: Aphrodite, *713;* Breathless (1983), *469;* Iran Days of Crisis, *554;* L'Année des Meduses, *752*
Karabatsos, Ron: Hollywood Heartbreak, *542;* Rich Girl, *640*
Karasun, May: Lake Consequence, *568*
Karen, James: Frankenstein Meets the Space Monster, *842;* Hardbodies 2, *293;* Invaders from Mars (1986), *1059;* Return of the Living Dead, The, *880;* Return of the Living Dead Part II, *880;* Unborn, The, *898;* Willies, The, *903*
Karina, Anna: Alphaville, *712;* Band of Outsiders, *715;* Chinese Roulette, *723;* Circle of Love, *482;* Justine, *561;* My Life to Live, *769;* Nun, The (La Religieuse), *772;* Oldest Profession, The, *773;* Pierrot Le Fou, *777;* Regina, *780;* Salzburg Connection, The, *111;* Woman Is a Woman, A, *805*
Karis, Vassilli: Animal Called Man, An, *1093*
Karlatos, Olga: Purple Rain, *935;* Sins of Dorian Gray, The, *886*
Karlen, John: Baby Cakes, *453;* Dark Shadows (TV Series), *829;* Daughters of Darkness, *830;* Gimme an "F", *286;* Nightmare on the 13th Floor, *871;* Racing with the Moon, *633;* Rosie, *937;* Trilogy of Terror, *898*
Karloff, Boris: Abbott and Costello Meet Dr. Jekyll and Mr. Hyde, *221;* Abbott and Costello Meet the Killer, Boris Karloff, *221;* Ape, The, *809;* Bedlam, *812;* Before I Hang, *812;* Black Cat, The (1934), *813;* Black Room, The (1935), *814;* Black Sabbath, *814;* Body Snatcher, The, *817;* Bride of Frankenstein, *819;* Cauldron of Blood, *822;* Chamber of Fear, *822;* Charlie Chan at the Opera, *961;* Corridors of Blood, *825;* Criminal Code, The, *491;* Dance of Death, *829;* Daydreamer, The, *161;* Dick Tracy Meets Gruesome, *38;* Die, Monster, Die!, *834;* Doomed to Die, *41;* Fatal Hour, The, *46;* Frankenstein (1931), *842;* Frankenstein 1970, *843;* Ghoul, The (1933), *846;* Haunted Strangler, The, *849;* House of Frankenstein, *852;* Invisible Ray, The, *857;* Isle of the Dead, *857;* Juggernaut (1936), *987;* King of the Kongo, *72;* Lost Patrol, The, *79;*

Macabre Serenade, *861;* Mad Monster Party, *184;* Man They Could Not Hang, The, *862;* Man Who Lived Again, The, *862;* Mask of Fu Manchu, The, *82;* Mr. Wong, Detective, *997;* Mr. Wong in Chinatown, *997;* Monster of the Island, The, *86;* Mummy, The (1932), *866;* Old Ironsides, *93;* Raven, The (1935), *878;* Raven, The (1963), *879;* Scarface (1932), *112;* Secret Life of Walter Mitty, The, *374;* Sinister Invasion, *886;* Snake People, *888;* Son of Frankenstein, *888;* Tales of Tomorrow (Vols. I - III), *1082;* Targets, *1022;* Terror, The, *893;* Tower of London (1939), *897;* You'll Find Out, *415*

Karns, Roscoe: Jazz Singer, The (1927), *925;* Laughing Sinners, *571;* Man's Favorite Sport?, *328;* Onionhead, *350;* Today We Live, *685;* Twentieth Century, *401*

Karr, Marcia: Night of the Kickfighters, *90*

Karr, Sarah Rose: Homewrecker, *1057*

Karras, Alex: Against All Odds, *951;* FM, *278;* Goldilocks and the Three Bears, *171;* Jacob Two-Two Meets the Hooded Fang, *178;* Mad Bull, *584;* Nobody's Perfekt, *346;* Paper Lion, *618;* When Time Ran Out!, *1031;* Win, Place or Steal, *412*

Karras, Athan: Crime Killer, The, *30*

Kartalian, Buck: Please Don't Eat My Mother!, *358*

Karvan, Claudia: High Tide, *541*

Karyo, Tcheky: Bear, The, *149;* Exposure, *45;* 1492: The Conquest of Paradise, *52;* Full Moon in Paris, *739;* Husbands and Lovers, *546;* La Femme Nikita, *753;* Sorceress, The (1988), *788;* Toute Une Nuit, *796*

Kasahara, Reiko: Gamera Versus Zigra, *1054*

Kasdorf, Lenore: Missing in Action, *85;* Mr. Bill's Real Life Adventures, *333*

Kasem, Casey: Glory Stompers, The, *56;* Incredible Two-Headed Transplant, The, *855*

Kash, Linda: Ernest Rides Again, *272*

Kasper, Gary: Humanoid Defender, *1057;* Ring of Steel, *106*

Kassir, John: New Wave Comedy, *343*

Kastner, Daphna: Julia Has Two Lovers, *560;* Venice/Venice, *693*

Kastner, Peter: You're a Big Boy Now, *416*

Kastner, Shelley: My Father Is Coming, *339*

Kasznar, Kurt: Ambushers, The, *4;* For the First Time, *918;* Give a Girl a Break, *919;* Legend of the Lost, *572;* Lovely to Look At, *929;* My Sister Eileen, *932*

Katch, Kurt: Ali Baba and the Forty Thieves, *3*

Katsu, Shintaro: Zatoichi: Masseur Ichi and a Chest of Gold, *806;* Zatoichi: The Blind Swordsman and the Chess Expert, *806;* Zatoichi: The Blind Swordsman's Vengeance, *806;* Zatoichi vs. Yojimbo, *806*

Katsulas, Andreas: Blame It on the Bellboy, *240;* Communion, *1042;* Death of the Incredible Hulk, The, *1045;* Fugitive, The (1993), *53;* Sicilian, The, *115;* Someone to Watch Over Me, *1018;* True Identity, *399*

Katt, William: Baby...Secret of the Lost Legend, *1037;* Big Wednesday, *461;* Butch and Sundance: The Early Days, *1103;* Desperate Motive, *970;* First Love, *517;* House, *852;* House IV, *852;* Last Call, *568;* Naked Obsession, *1000;* Swimsuit, *390;* Thumbelina (1983), *211;* White Ghost, *138*

Katz, Allan: Big Man on Campus, *238*

Katz, Mike: Pumping Iron, *630*

Katz, Omri: Adventures in Dinosaur City, *143;* Hocus Pocus, *175;* Matinee, *330*

Katzur, Yftach: Baby Love, *230;* Private Popsicle, *362;* Soldier of the Night, *787;* Up Your Anchor, *404*

Kaudoh, Youki: Mystery Train, *603*

Kaufman, Andy: Andy Kaufman Special, The, *227;* Comedy Tonight, *257;* Heartbeeps, *173;* My Breakfast with Blassie, *339*

Kaufman, David: Last Prostitute, The, *570*

Kaufman, Kendrick: Curse of the House Surgeon, The, *828;* Queen Victoria and the Zombies, *878*

Kaufmann, Christine: Last Days of Pompeii (1960), *75;* Murders in the Rue Morgue (1971), *867*

Kaufmann, Gunther: Kamikaze 89, *751*

Kava, Caroline: Little Nikita, *992*

Kavanagh, Patrick: Half-Moon Street, *981*

Kavner, Julie: Alice (1990), *224;* Awakenings, *452;* Bad Medicine, *231;* I'll Do Anything, *305;* Katherine, *562;* New York Stories, *343;* Radio Days, *364;* Shadows and Fog, *654;* Surrender, *389;* This Is My Life, *394*

Kawaguchi, Saeda: Violence at Noon, *801*

Kawarsaki, Chojuro: Forty Seven Ronin, *738*

Kawazu, Yusuke: Cruel Story of Youth, *727*

Kay, Bernard: They Came from Beyond Space, *1083*

Kay, Dianne: Portrait of a Showgirl, *625*

Kay, Fiona: Vigil, *800*

Kay, Mary Ellen: Government Agents vs. Phantom Legion, *57;* Rodeo King and the Senorita, *1145;* Thunder Pass, *1157*

Kaye, Caren: Kill Castro, *71;* My Tutor, *341;* Poison Ivy (1985), *359;* Satan's Princess, *882*

Kaye, Celia: Final Comedown, The, *48;* Island of the Blue Dolphins, *555*

Kaye, Danny: Court Jester, The, *260;* Five Pennies, The, *917* Hans Christian Andersen, *921;* Inspector General, The, *306;* Kid from Brooklyn, The, *313;* Madwoman of Chaillot, The, *585;* Secret Life of Walter Mitty, The, *374;* Skokie, *660;* Song Is Born, A, *940;* Up in Arms, *403;* White Christmas, *947;* Wonder Man, *413*

Kaye, Davy: Wrong Arm of the Law, The, *414*

Kaye, Lila: Canterville Ghost, The (1986), *155*

Kaye, Norman: Cactus, *473;* Frenchman's Farm, *843;* Lonely Hearts (1981), *577;* Man of Flowers, *327;* Turtle Beach, *690;* Warm Nights on a Slow Moving Train, *696;* Where the Green Ants Dream, *803;* Woman's Tale, A, *705*

Kaye, Richard: Wizard of Speed and Time, The, *413*

Kaye, Sammy: Iceland, *924*

Kaye, Stubby: Guys and Dolls, *921;* Li'l Abner (1959), *928;* Sex and the Single Girl, *376;* Way West, The, *1163;* Who Framed Roger Rabbit, *410*

Kaz, Fred: Birthday Boy, The, *240*

Kazan, Elia: City for Conquest, *482*

Kazan, Lainie: Cemetery Club, The, *478;* Cry for Love, A, *492;* Dayton's Devils, *33;* Delta Force, The, *36;* Harry and the Hendersons, *1055;* I Don't Buy Kisses Anymore, *303;* Journey of Natty Gann, The, *179;* Lady in Cement, *989;* Lust in the Dust, *324;* My Favorite Year, *340;* Obsessive Love, *1002;* Pinocchio (1983), *195;* Sunset Limousine, *388;* 29th Street, *401*

Kazann, Zitto: Slaughter of the Innocents, *1017*

Kazurinsky, Tim: Avery Schreiber—Live From the Second City, *230;* Big City Comedy, *238;* Billion for Boris, A, *239;* Dinner at Eight (1990), *265;* Neighbors, *343;* Police Academy III: Back in Training, *359;* Police Academy 4: Citizens on Patrol, *359;* Princess and the Pea, The, *197;* Second City Comedy Show, The, *374*

Keach, James: Blue Hotel, *465;* Evil Town, *839;* Experts, The, *273;* FM, *278;* Long Riders, The, *1130;* Love Letters, *581;* Man Who Broke 1000 Chains, The, *587;* Moving Violations, *338;* Razor's Edge, The (1984), *635;* Wildcats, *411*

Keach, Stacy: All the Kind Strangers, *951;* Battle Force, *9;* Blue and the Gray, The, *1099;* Butterfly, *473;* Class of 1999, *1041;* Diary of a Young Comic, *264;* End of the Road, *510;* False Identity, *975;* Fat City, *515;* Forgotten, The, *520;* Gray Lady Down, *57;* Heart Is a Lonely Hunter, The, *538;* John Carpenter Presents: Body Bags, *858;* Killer Inside Me, The, *988;* Life and Times of Judge Roy Bean, The, *1128;* Long Riders, The, *1130;* Luther, *583;* Mission of the Shark, *596;* Mistral's Daughter, *597;* New Centurions, The, *605;* Nice Dreams, *344;* Ninth Configuration, The, *608;* Princess Daisy, *627;* Rio Diablo, *1145;* Road Games, *1010;* Rumor of War, A, *109;* Slave of the Cannibal God, *117;* Squeeze, The (1977), *665;* Street People, *121;* Sunset Grill, *1021;* That Championship Season, *680;* Up in Smoke, *403;* Watched!, *137*

Kean, Marie: Danny Boy (1982), *495;* Dead, The, *497;* Lonely Passion of Judith Hearne, The, *577*

Keane, Edward: Frontier Pony Express, *1114;* Twilight in the Sierras, *1159*

Keane, James: Life on the Mississippi, *574*

Keane, Kerrie: Incubus, The, *856;* Kung Fu—The Movie, *73;* Malarek, *586;* Mistress (1987), *597;* Nightstick, *91;* Obsessed, *610;* Spasms, *889*

Kearns, William: Philip Marlowe, Private Eye: Finger Man, *1005;* Philip Marlowe, Private Eye: The Pencil, *1005*

Kearny, Stephen: Rikki and Pete, *368*

Keating, Larry: Above and Beyond, *1;* Francis Goes to the Races, *280;* George Burns and Gracie Allen Show, The (TV Series), *284;* Gypsy Colt, *173;* Incredible Mr. Limpet, The, *306;* Monkey Business (1952), *336;* When Worlds Collide, *1089*

Keaton, Buster: Adventures of Huckleberry Finn, The (1960), *144;* Balloonatic, The/One Week, *231;* Beach Blanket Bingo, *908;* Blacksmith, The/Cops, *240;* Boom in the Moon, *243;* Buster Keaton Festival: Vol. 1, *248;* Buster Keaton Festival: Vol. 2, *248;* Buster Keaton Festival: Vol. 3, *248;* Buster Keaton Rides Again, *420;* Buster Keaton Scrapbook, Vol. I, *248;* Buster Keaton: The Golden Years, *248;* Buster Keaton: The Great Stone Face, *248;* Cameraman, The, *249;* College, *257;* Days of Thrills and Laughter, *262;* Doughboys, *268;* Forever and a Day, *520;* Free and Easy, *281;* Fuller Brush Man, The, *282;* Funny Thing Happened on the Way to the Forum, A, *282;* General, The, *283;* Great Chase, The, *57;* How to Stuff a Wild Bikini, *923;* In the Good Old Summertime, *925;* It's a Mad Mad Mad Mad World, *308;* Keaton Rides Again/Railroader, *312;* Li'l Abner (1940), *318;* Limelight, *319;* Misadventures of Buster Keaton, The, *332;* Old Spanish Custom, An, *349;* Our Hospitality, *351;* Parlor, Bedroom and Bath, *354;* Sherlock Jr., *377;* Sidewalks of New York, *378;* Speak Easily, *384;* Spite Marriage, *384;* Steamboat Bill Jr., *386;* Sunset Boulevard, *673;* Three Ages, The, *395;* Two Houses of Keaton, *402;* Villain Still Pursued Her, The, *135;* What! No Beer?, *408;* When Comedy Was King, *409*

Keaton Jr., Buster: Our Hospitality, *351*

Keaton, Camille: I Spit on Your Grave, *855*

Keaton, Diane: Annie Hall, *228;* Baby Boom, *230;* Crimes of the Heart, *260;* Father of the Bride (1991), *275;* Godfather, The, *529;* Godfather, Part II, The, *529;* Godfather, Part III, The, *529;* Godfather Epic, The, *529;* Good Mother, The, *530;* Harry and Walter Go to New York, *294;* I Will, I Will…for Now, *304;* Interiors, *553;* Lemon Sisters, The, *317;* Little Drummer Girl, The, *992;* Looking for Mr. Goodbar, *993;* Love and Death, *322;* Lovers and Other Strangers, *323;* Manhattan, *328;* Manhattan Murder Mystery, *328;* Mrs. Soffel, *598;* Play It Again, Sam, *358;* Reds, *637;* Running Mates (1992), *371;* Shoot the Moon, *656;* Sleeper, *381*

Keaton, Joseph: Buster Keaton Festival: Vol. 2, *248;* Buster Keaton: The Great Stone Face, *248;* General, The, *283*

Keaton, Louise: Buster Keaton Festival: Vol. 2, *248*

Keaton, Michael: Batman (1989), *9;* Batman Returns, *9;* Beetlejuice, *233;* Clean and Sober, *484;* Dream Team, The, *269;* Gung Ho (1985), *292;* Johnny Dangerously, *311;* Mr. Mom, *334;* Much Ado About Nothing, *338;* My Life, *602;* Night Shift, *344;* One Good Cop, *613;* Pacific Heights, *1003;* Paper, The, *617;* Squeeze, The (1987), *385;* Touch and Go, *398;* Working Stiffs, *414;* Your Favorite Laughs from an Evening at the Improv, *416*

Keaton, Michael: Our Hospitality, *351*

Keaton, Myra: Buster Keaton Festival: Vol. 2, *248*

Keats, Ele: Lipstick Camera, *992*

Keats, Steven: Hester Street, *541;* In Dangerous Company, *550*

Keays-Byrne, Hugh: Blue Fin, *151;* Kangaroo, *562;* Mad Max, *1064*

Kedrova, Lila: Bloodtide, *817;* Some Girls, *382;* Tell Me a Riddle, *678;* Testament, *1082;* Torn Curtain, *1026;* Zorba the Greek, *709*

Keegan, Kari: Jason Goes to Hell: The Final Friday, *858*

Keehne, Virginya: Infested, *856*

Keel, Howard: Annie Get Your Gun, *907;* Arizona Bushwhackers, *1094;* Armored Command, *6;* Calamity Jane (1953), *910;* Day of the Triffids, The, *1044;* Jupiter's Darling, *926;* Kismet (1955), *927;* Kiss Me Kate, *927;* Lovely to Look At, *929;* Pagan Love Song, *934;* Rose Marie (1954), *937;* Seven Brides for Seven Brothers, *939;* Show Boat (1951), *939;* Texas Carnival, *944;* That's Entertainment! III, *436;* War Wagon, The, *1162*

Keeler, Ruby: Dames, *913;* Flirtation Walk, *917;* Footlight Parade, *917;* 42nd Street, *918;* Go Into Your Dance, *920;* Gold Diggers of 1933, *920*

Keen, Geoffrey: Born Free, *152;* Cry, the Beloved Country, *492;* Dr. Syn, Alias the Scarecrow, *163;* Living Free, *184;* Number One of the Secret Service, *347;* Sink the Bismarck, *116;* Taste the Blood of Dracula, *892*

Keen, Malcolm: Lodger, The, *993;* Manxman, The, *588*

Keenan, Stacy: Lisa, *992*

Keene, Tom: Arizona Roundup, *1095;* Driftin' Kid, *1110;* Dynamite Canyon, *1111;* Lights of Old Santa Fe, *1128;* Our Daily Bread, *615;* Plan 9 from Outer Space, *1070;* Scarlet River, *1148;* Trail of Robin Hood, *1158;* Where Trails End, *1164*

Keener, Catherine: Johnny Suede, *311*

Kehler, Jack: Blindsided, *956*

Kehoe, Jack: On the Nickel, *612;* Paper, The, *617;* Serpico, *652;* Servants of Twilight, *884;* Star Chamber, The, *1019*

Keir, Andrew: Absolution, *440;* Catholics, *477;* Daleks—Invasion Earth 2150 A.D., *1044*

Keitel, Harvey: Alice Doesn't Live Here Anymore, *444;* Bad Lieutenant, *454;* Blindside, *15;* Blue Collar, *465;* Border, The, *17;* Buffalo Bill and the Indians, *1102;* Bugsy, *471;* Camorra, *722;* Corrupt, *963;* Death Watch, *1045;* Duellists, The, *42;* Eagle's Wing, *1111;* Exposed, *840;* Falling in Love, *513;* Fingers, *516;* Inquiry, The, *552;* January Man, The, *987;* La Nuit de Varennes, *754;* Last Temptation of Christ, The, *570;* Mean Streets, *591;* Men's Club, The, *593;* Monkey Trouble, *188;* Mortal Thoughts, *997;* Mother, Jugs, and Speed, *337;* Off Beat, *348;* Piano, The, *622;* Pick-Up Artist, The, *357;* Point of No Return, *99;* Reservoir Dogs, *105;* Rising Sun, *1010;* Saturn 3, *1076;* Sister Act, *379;* Star Knight, *1078;* Taxi Driver, *1023;* Thelma & Louise, *127;* Two Evil Eyes, *898;* Two Jakes, The, *1028;* Welcome to L.A., *698;* Who's That Knocking at My Door?, *701;* Wise Guys, *412*

Keith, Brian: Alamo, The: Thirteen Days to Glory, *1093;* Arrowhead, *1095;* Deadly Companions, The, *1108;* Death Before Dishonor, *35;* Dino, *501;* Gambler Returns, the: Luck of the Draw, *1115;* Hallelujah Trail, The, *1118;* Hooper, *300;* Johnny Shiloh, *179;* Meteor, *1065;* Moon Pilot, *189;* Mountain Men, The, *1134;* Nevada Smith, *1135;* Parent Trap, The, *193;* Rare Breed, The (1966), *1141;* Reflections in a Golden Eye, *637;* Run of the Arrow, *1146;* Russians Are Coming, the Russians Are Coming, The, *371;* Savage Sam, *201;* Scandalous John, *202;* Seekers, The, *651;* Sharky's Machine, *115;* Suppose They Gave a War and Nobody Came?, *388;* Ten Who Dared, *210;* Those Calloways, *211;* Tiger Walks, A, *211;* Violent Men, The, *1161;* Welcome Home, *698;* Wind and the Lion, The, *140;* With Six You Get Eggroll, *412;* World War III, *141;* Yakuza, The, *141;* Young Guns, *1165;* Young Philadelphians, The, *708*

Keith, Clete: Dead Silence, *262*

Keith, David: Back Roads, *453;* Caged Fear, *21;* Desperate Motive, *970;* Firestarter, *841;* Further Adventures of Tennessee Buck, The, *53;* Gulag, *534;* Heartbreak Hotel, *538;* Independence Day, *551;* Liar's Edge, *992;* Lords of Discipline, The, *579;* Major League II, *326;* Officer and a Gentleman, An, *611;* Two Jakes, The, *1028;* White of the Eye, *1031*

Keith, Ian: Abraham Lincoln, *440;* Big Trail, The, *1098;* Chinese Cat, The, *962;* Corregidor, *489;* Dick Tracy's Dilemma, *38;* It Came from Beneath the Sea, *857;* Phantom of the Plains, *1138;* Strange Woman, The, *669;* Three Musketeers, The (1935), *128;* White Legion, *700*

Keith, Michael: King Kong vs. Godzilla, *859*

Keith, Penelope: Norman Conquests, The, Episode 1: Table Manners, *346;* Norman Conquests, The, Episode 2: Living Together, *346;* Norman Conquests, The, Episode 3: Round and Round the Garden, *346;* Priest of Love, *627*

Keith, Robert: Battle Circus, *456;* Branded, *1101;* Cimarron (1960), *1105;* Drum Beat, *1110;* Duel of Champions, *42;* Love Me or Leave Me, *929;* My Man Godfrey (1957), *340;* Treasures of the Twilight Zone, *1085;* Wild One, The, *139;* Written on the Wind, *707*

Keleghan, Peter: Screwballs, *374*

Kellard, Robert: Drums of Fu Manchu, *42*

Kellaway, Cecil: Adventures of Bullwhip Griffin, The, *143;* Beast From 20,000 Fathoms, The, *1038;* Brother Orchid, *20;* Francis Goes to the Races, *280;* Guess Who's Coming to Dinner, *534;* Harvey, *294;* Hush…Hush, Sweet Charlotte, *854;* I Married a Witch, *1057;* Intermezzo (1939), *553;* Interrupted Melody, *925;* Invisible Man Returns, *856;* Kim, *72;* Maid's Night Out, The, *326;* Mrs. Parkington, *598;* Monsieur Beaucaire, *336;* Postman Always Rings Twice, The (1946), *1007;* Prodigal, The, *629*

Kelleghar, Tina: Snapper, The, *382*

Kellen, Mike: King Lear (1982), *564*

Keller, Dorothy: Single Room Furnished, *659*

Keller, Flint: Fresh Kill, *53*

Keller, Fred A.: Tuck Everlasting, *214*

Keller, Hiram: Ciao Federico!, *724;* Countryman, *489;* Fellini Satyricon, *736;* Lifespan, *1063*

Keller, Marthe: Amateur, The, *952;* And Now, My Love, *712;* Black Sunday (1977), *955;* Bobby Deerfield, *465;* Dark Eyes, *728;* Fedora, *515;* Formula, The, *978;* Marathon Man, *82;* Nightmare Years, The, *607;* Red Kiss (Rouge Baiser), *780;* Wagner, *947;* Young Catherine, *708*

Keller, Mary Page: Scared Stiff, *883;* Ulterior Motives, *133*

Kellerman, Barbara: Quatermass Conclusion, The, *1072;* Sea Wolves, The, *113*

Kellerman, Sally: All's Fair, *225;* April Fools, The, *228;* Back to School, *230;* Big Bus, The, *238;* Boris and Natasha, *244;* Boston Strangler, The, *818;* Brewster McCloud, *245;* Dempsey, *499;* Drop Dead Gorgeous, *972;* Fatal Attraction (1985), *975;* Foxes, *521;* It Rained All Night the Day I Left, *555;* Last of the Red Hot Lovers, *315;* Little Romance, A, *319;* M*A*S*H, *324;* Meatballs III, *330;* Moving Violations, *338;* Ponce de Leon and the Fountain of Youth, *196;* Rafferty and the Gold Dust Twins, *364;* Reflection of Fear, *1009;* Reform School Girl, *104;* Secret Weapons, *113;* September Gun, *1148;* Sleeping Beauty (1983), *205;* Slither, *381;* Someone to Love, *662;* That's Life, *393;* Three for the Road, *395;* Victim of Beauty, *1030;* Welcome to L.A., *698*

Kellerman, Susan: Elvira, Mistress of the Dark, *271*

Kelley, Barry: Well, The, *698*

Kelley, DeForest: Bloopers from Star Trek and Laugh-In, *242;* Law and Jake Wade, The, *1127;* Star Trek (TV Series), *1078;* Star Trek: The Menagerie, *1078;* Star Trek—The Motion Picture, *1079;* Star Trek: The Next Generation (TV Series), *1079;* Star Trek II: The Wrath of Khan, *1079;* Star Trek III: The Search for Spock, *1079;* Star Trek IV: The Voyage Home, *1079;* Star Trek V: The Final Frontier, *1079;* Star Trek VI: The Undiscovered Country, *1079*

Kelley, Sheila: Pure Luck, *363;* Singles, *379*

Kellin, Mike: At War with the Army, *229;* Boston Strangler, The, *818;* Demon (God Told Me To), *1046;* Hell Is for Heroes, *60;* Lonelyhearts, *578;* On the Yard, *94;* Riot, *106;* Sleepaway Camp, *887;* So Fine, *382*

Kellogg, Bruce: Unknown World, *1087*

Kellogg, John: Jacob I Have Loved, *556*

Kelly, Andrew: For a Lost Soldier, *737*

Kelly, Brian: Around the World Under the Sea, *6;* Flipper's New Adventure, *167;* Flipper's Odyssey, *167;* Longest Hunt, The, *1130*

Kelly, David: Into the West, *177*

Kelly, David Patrick: Cheap Shots, *254;* Crooklyn, *261;* Crow, The, *827;* 48 Hrs., *279;* Misfit Brigade, The, *85;* Penn & Teller Get Killed, *356*

Kelly, Desmond: Smash Palace, *660*

Kelly, Gene: American Film Institute Life Achievement Awards, The, *418;* American in Paris, An, *906;* Anchors Aweigh, *906;* Black Hand, The, *462;* Brigadoon, *909;* Cover Girl, *912;* Du Barry Was a Lady, *915;* For Me and My Gal, *917;* Forty Carats, *279;* Inherit the Wind, *552;* Invitation to the Dance, *925;* It's a Big Country, *308;* It's Always Fair Weather, *925;* Les Girls, *928;* Living In A Big Way, *929;* Marjorie Morningstar, *589;* North and South, *608;* On the Town, *934;* Pirate, The, *935;* Singin' in the Rain, *940;* Summer Stock, *942;* Take Me Out to the Ball Game, *943;* That's Dancing, *436;* That's Entertainment, *436;* That's Entertainment Part II, *436;* That's Entertainment! III, *436;* Thousands Cheer, *945;* Three Musketeers, The (1948), *128;* Viva Knievel, *136;* Words and Music, *948;* Xanadu, *948;* Ziegfeld Follies, *949*

Kelly, Grace: Bridges at Toko-Ri, The, *19;* Country Girl, The (1954), *489;* Dial M for Murder, *970;* High Noon, *1120;* High Society, *922;* Mogambo, *86;* Poppy Is Also a Flower, The, *99;* Rear Window, *1009;* Swan, The (1956), *674;* To Catch a Thief, *1025*

Kelly, Jack: Commandos, *28;* Commies Are Coming, the Commies Are Coming, The, *258;* Cult of the Cobra, *827;* Forbidden Planet, *1052;* Gambler Returns, the: Luck of the Draw, *1115;* Maverick (TV Series), *1133;* To Hell and Back, *130*

Kelly, James F.: Marilyn & Bobby: Her Final Affair, *588*

Kelly, James T.: Charlie Chaplin—The Early Years, Vol. 4, *254*

Kelly, Jean: Uncle Buck, *402*

Kelly, Jim: Black Belt Jones, *13;* Enter the Dragon, *44;* One Down, Two to Go, *94;* Take a Hard Ride, *1154;* Tattoo Connection, *126;* Three the Hard Way, *129*

Kelly, Lesley: Home for Christmas, *542*

Kelly, Moira: Chaplin, *479;* Cutting Edge, The, *493;* Daybreak (1993), *1045;* Love, Lies and Murder, *994;* Twin Peaks: Fire Walk with Me, *1028;* With Honors, *412*

Kelly, Monika: Corpse Grinders, The, *825*

Kelly, Nancy: Bad Seed, The, *454;* Betrayal from the East, *11;* Jesse James, *1123;* One Night in the Tropics, *350;* Show Business, *939;* Stanley and Livingstone, *665;* To the Shores of Tripoli, *130*

Kelly, Patsy: Cowboy and the Lady, The, *260;* Girl from Missouri, The, *286;* Go Into Your Dance, *920;* Going Hollywood, *920;* In Old California, *1122;* Movie Struck (a.k.a. Pick a Star), *338;* Naked Kiss, The, *1000;* North Avenue Irregulars, The, *191;* Please Don't Eat the Daisies, *358;* Rosemary's Baby, *881*

Kelly, Paul: Call Out the Marines, *249;* Crossfire (1947), *964;* Devil's Party, The, *500;* Here Comes Trouble, *296;* High and the Mighty, The, *541;* Howards of Virginia, The, *545;* Navy Blue and Gold, *342;* Painted Hills, The, *193;* San Antonio, *1147;* Split Second (1953), *664;* Star of Midnight, *1020;* Tarzan's New York Adventure, *126*

Kelly, Paula: Andromeda Strain, The, *1036;* Jo Jo Dancer, Your Life Is Calling, *558;* Sweet Charity, *943*

Kelly, Rachel: Scream for Help, *884*

Kelly, Robyn: Flesh Gordon 2: Flesh Gordon meets the Cosmic Cheerleaders, *1052*

Kelly, Roz: New Year's Evil, *868*

Kelly, Sam: Who's Who, *411*

Kelly, Tommy: Adventures of Tom Sawyer, The, *144;* Peck's Bad Boy with the Circus, *194*

Kelman, Paul: My Bloody Valentine, *867*

Kelso, Bobby: Jack Knife Man, The, *556*

Kelton, Pert: Comic, The (1969), *486*

Kemmer, Ed: Earth vs. the Spider, *1048;* Space Patrol (TV Series), *1077*

Kemmerling, Warren: Eat My Dust, *43*

Kemp, Dan: Cry Blood, Apache, *1106*

Kemp, Elizabeth: He Knows You're Alone, *849;* Killing Hour, The, *988*

Kemp, Gary: Bodyguard, The, *466;* Krays, The, *567;* Paper Marriage (1992), *618*
Kemp, Jeremy: Belstone Fox, The, *149;* Blockhouse, The, *464;* Blue Max, The, *16;* Caravans, *475;* Darling Lili, *913;* East of Elephant Rock, *506;* George Washington, *526;* Leopard in the Snow, *572;* Operation Crossbow, *95;* Prisoner of Honor, *628;* Return of the Soldier, The, *638;* Sadat, *646;* When the Whales Came, *699*
Kemp, Lindsay: Savage Messiah, *648*
Kemp, Martin: Krays, The, *567*
Kemp, Sally: Last Hit, The, *990*
Kemp, Tina: Waltz Through the Hills, *216*
Kempe, Will: Hit the Dutchman, *63;* Pledge Night, *875*
Kemper, Charles: Intruder in the Dust, *553*
Kempson, Rachel: Captive Heart, *475*
Kendal, Felicity: Shakespeare Wallah, *655;* Valentino, *693*
Kendal, Jennifer: Bombay Talkie, *720*
Kendall, Cy: Junior G-Men, *69;* King of the Pecos, *1125;* Lonely Trail, The, *1129*
Kendall, Geoffrey: Shakespeare Wallah, *655*
Kendall, Henry: Amazing Adventure, *225;* Rich and Strange, *639*
Kendall, Kay: Abdulla the Great, *221;* Doctor in the House, *266;* Genevieve, *283;* Les Girls, *928;* Reluctant Debutante, The, *365*
Kendall, Suzy: Adventures of a Private Eye, *222;* Bird with the Crystal Plumage, The, *955;* Circus of Fear, *824;* Tales that Witness Madness, *892;* 30 Is a Dangerous Age, Cynthia, *394;* To Sir with Love, *685;* Torso, *896*
Kendall, Tony: When the Screaming Stops, *902*
Kenin, Alexa: Piano for Mrs. Cimino, A, *622*
Kennard, Malcolm: One Crazy Night, *349*
Kennedy, Angela: Wicked, The, *903*
Kennedy, Arthur: Air Force, *3;* Anzio, *6;* Bend of the River, *1097;* Champion, *479;* City for Conquest, *482;* Crashout, *30;* Desperate Hours, The (1955), *969;* Desperate Journey, *500;* Elmer Gantry, *509;* Fantastic Voyage, *1050;* Hail, Hero!, *535;* High Sierra, *62;* Lawrence of Arabia, *76;* Lusty Men, The, *1130;* Man from Laramie, The, *1131;* Minute to Pray, A Second to Die, A, *1134;* Murder She Said, *999;* My Old Man's Place, *602;* Nevada Smith, *1135;* Peyton Place, *621;* President's Plane Is Missing, The, *1007;* Rancho Notorious, *1140;* Sentinel, The, *884;* Shark! (a.k.a. Maneaters!), *114;* Signs of Life, *657;* Some Came Running, *662;* Summer Place, A, *672;* Tempter, The, *893;* They Died with Their Boots On, *1156;* Window, The, *1032*
Kennedy, Betty: Cheech and Chong's Next Movie, *254;* Flicks, *278*
Kennedy, Bill: Two Lost Worlds, *133*
Kennedy, Douglas: Adventures of Don Juan, The, *2;* Amazing Transparent Man, The, *1036;* Cariboo Trail, *1103;* Cry Vengeance, *492;* Fort Osage, *1114;* Lone Ranger and the Lost City of Gold, The, *1129;* South of St. Louis, *1151;* Texas Rangers, The, *1156*
Kennedy, Edgar: Air Raid Wardens, *223;* Cowboy Millionaire, *1106;* Diplomaniacs, *914;* Dr. Christian Meets the Women, *502;* Double Wedding, *268;* Duck Soup, *269;* Fatty and His Funny Friends, *275;* Hold 'em Jail, *298;* Hollywood Hotel, *923;* In Old California, *1122;* In Person, *305;* Keystone Comedies, Vol. 1, *312;* Keystone Comedies, Vol. 4, *312;* Keystone Comedies, Vol. 5, *313;* Laurel and Hardy Classics, Volume 5, *316;* Laurel and Hardy's Laughing 20s, *317;* Li'l Abner (1940), *318;* Little Orphan Annie, *183;* Mack Sennett Comedies, Vol. 2, *325;* Mad Wednesday, *325;* My Dream Is Yours, *932;* Peck's Bad Boy with the Circus, *194;* Private Snuffy Smith, *362;* Remedy for Riches, *638;* Scarlet River, *1148;* Sin of Harold Diddlebock (a.k.a. Mad Wednesday), *379;* Three Men on a Horse, *395;* Twentieth Century, *401;* Two-Reelers: Comedy Classics #1, *402;* Two-Reelers: Comedy Classics #2, *402;* When's Your Birthday?, *409*
Kennedy, George: Airport, *443;* Airport 1975, *443;* Airport '77, *443;* Airport '79: The Concorde, *443;* Archer: Fugitive from the Empire, *1036;* Bandolero!, *1096;* Blue Knight, The (1975), *465;* Bolero (1984), *466;* Born to Race, *17;* Boston Strangler, The, *818;* Brain Dead, *1040;* Brass Target, *19;* Cahill—US Marshal, *1103;* Charade, *960;* Chattanooga Choo Choo, *254;* Cool Hand Luke, *29;* Counterforce, *30;* Creepshow 2, *826;* Death on the Nile, *968;* Deathship, *832;* Delta Force, The, *36;* Double McGuffin, The, *163;* Driving Me Crazy, *269;* Earthquake, *43;* Eiger Sanction, The, *43;* Flight of the Phoenix, The, *51;* Gambler, Part III—The Legend Continues, The, *1115;* Gunfighters, The, *1117;* Guns of the Magnificent Seven, *1118;* Hired to Kill, *62;* Island of the Blue Dolphins, *555;* Jessie Owens Story, The, *557;* Ministry of Vengeance, *85;* Mirage, *595;* Naked Gun, The, *341;* Naked Gun 2 1/2, The, *341;* Naked Gun 33 1/3, The—The Final Insult, *341;* Nightmare at Noon, *870;* Radioactive Dreams, *1073;* Rare Breed, A (1981), *198;* Savage Dawn, *111;* Search and Destroy (1981), *113;* Shenandoah, *1149;* Sons of Katie Elder, The, *1151;* Steel, *120;* Strait-Jacket, *890;* Terror Within, The, *894;* Thunderbolt and Lightfoot, *129;* Tick ... Tick ... Tick ..., *129;* Uninvited, The (1987), *899;* Virus, *1087;* Wacko, *405*
Kennedy, Gerald: Newsfront, *605*
Kennedy, Gerard: Body Melt, *817*
Kennedy, Graham: Club, The (1985), *484;* Don's Party, *267;* Odd Angry Shot, The, *610*
Kennedy, Jayne: Body and Soul (1981), *466*
Kennedy, Jo: Starstruck, *941*
Kennedy, Leon Isaac: Body and Soul (1981), *466;* Hollywood Vice Squad, *63;* Knights of the City, *927;* Penitentiary, *98;* Penitentiary II, *98;* Penitentiary III, *98;* Too Scared to Scream, *1025*
Kennedy, Marklen: Witchcraft V: Dance with the Devil, *903*
Kennedy, Merle: Nemesis (1992), *1067*
Kennedy, Merna: Circus, The/A Day's Pleasure, *255*
Kennedy, Patricia: Getting of Wisdom, The, *526*
Kenney, Don: Tonight for Sure, *397*
Kenney, James: Battle Hell, *9*
Kenney, June: Earth vs. the Spider, *1048;* Sorority Girl, *118*
Kenney, Sean: Corpse Grinders, The, *825*
Kensit, Patsy: Absolute Beginners, *906;* Bitter Harvest (1993), *955;* Blame It on the Bellboy, *240;* Blue Tornado, *16;* Chicago Joe and the Showgirl, *480;* Does This Mean We're Married?, *266;* Full Eclipse, *844;* Kill Cruise, *563;* Lethal Weapon 2, *76;* Silas Marner, *657;* Time Bomb, *1025;* Turn of the Screw (1992), *898;* Twenty-One, *690*
Kent, April: Incredible Shrinking Man, The, *1058*
Kent, Barbara: Oliver Twist (1933), *612;* Vanity Fair, *693*
Kent, Chantellese: Home for Christmas, *542*
Kent, Elizabeth: Mindwarp, *1066*
Kent, Jean: Browning Version, The, *471*
Kent, Marjorie: Blondie Hits the Jackpot, *241;* Blondie Knows Best, *241*
Kent, Robert: Phantom Rider, *1138*
Kenyon, Gwen: Charlie Chan in the Secret Service, *961*
Kenyon, Sandy: Loch Ness Horror, The, *861*
Keogh, Alexia: Angel at My Table, An, *447*
Kepler, Shell: Homework, *543*
Keraga, Kelvin: Deadmate, *831*
Kercheval, Ken: Beretta's Island, *10;* Calamity Jane (1984), *1103;* Corporate Affairs, *259;* Devil Dog: The Hound of Hell, *833*
Kérien, Jean-Pierre: Muriel, *769*
Kerin, Jackie: Next of Kin (1987), *868*
Kerman, Robert: Cannibal Holocaust, *821;* Emerald Jungle, *838*
Kern, Roger: Delos Adventure, The, *36*
Kerns, Joanna: American Summer, An, *5;* Bunny's Tale, A, *472;* Cross My Heart (1987), *261;* Great Los Angeles Earthquake, The, *532;* Mistress (1987), *597;* Nightman, The, *1001;* Preppie Murder, The, *626;* Street Justice, *121*
Kerr, Bill: Coca Cola Kid, The, *257;* Dusty, *164;* Lighthorsemen, The, *77;* Miracle Down Under, *187;* Pirate Movie, The, *935;* Sweet Talker, *389;* Vigil, *800;* Year of Living Dangerously, The, *141*

Kerr, Bruce: Man from Snowy River, The, *1131*
Kerr, Deborah: Affair to Remember, An, *442;* Arrangement, The, *450;* Black Narcissus, *463;* Bonjour Tristesse, *466;* Casino Royale (1967), *252;* Chalk Garden, The, *478;* Courageous Mr. Penn, *489;* From Here to Eternity (1953), *523;* Grass Is Greener, The, *289;* Hold the Dream, *542;* Hucksters, The, *545;* I See a Dark Stranger, *65;* Julius Caesar (1953), *561;* King and I, The, *926;* King Solomon's Mines (1950), *72;* Life and Death of Colonel Blimp, The, *574;* Love on the Dole, *581;* Major Barbara, *326;* Naked Edge, The, *1000;* Night of the Iguana, The, *606;* Prisoner of Zenda, The (1952), *100;* Quo Vadis (1951), *632;* Sundowners, The (1960), *673;* Tea and Sympathy, *678;* Witness for the Prosecution (1982), *1032;* Woman of Substance, A, *705*
Kerr, E. Katherine: Reuben, Reuben, *367*
Kerr Jr., J. Herbert: Place Called Today, A, *622*
Kerr, John: Pit and the Pendulum, The (1961), *875;* South Pacific, *941;* Tea and Sympathy, *678*
Kerr, Ken: Beneath the Valley of the Ultra-Vixens, *234*
Kerr, Michael: Living the Blues, *577*
Kerridge, Linda: Alien From L.A., *3;* Down Twisted, *41;* Fade to Black (1980), *840;* Mixed Blood, *86;* Surf 2, *389*
Kerrigan, J. M.: Black Beauty (1946), *150;* Fastest Gun Alive, The, *1112;* Lost Patrol, The, *79*
Kerrigan, J. Warren: Covered Wagon, The, *1106*
Kerry, Norman: Bachelor Apartment, *230;* Merry-Go-Round, The, *996;* Phantom of the Opera (1925), *874*
Kershaw, Doug: Zachariah, *1166*
Kerwin, Brian: Antony and Cleopatra (1981), *450;* Chisholms, The, *1104;* Code Name: Chaos, *257;* Hard Promises, *536;* King Kong Lives, *859;* Love Field, *581;* Murphy's Romance, *601;* Power, Passion, and Murder, *625;* Real American Hero, The, *635;* Switched at Birth, *675;* Torch Song Trilogy, *686;* Wet Gold, *138*
Kerwin, Lance: Enemy Mine, *1049;* Fourth Wise Man, The, *521;* Mysterious Stranger, The, *190;* Salem's Lot, *882;* Side Show, *886;* Snow Queen, *205*
Kessler, Quin: She (1983), *1076*
Kessler, Robert: Lonely in America, *320*
Kessler, Wulf: White Rose, The (1983), *803*
Kestleman, Sara: Lady Jane, *568;* Lisztomania, *928*
Kestner, Boyd: Lethal Lolita—Amy Fisher: My Story, *573*
Ketchum, Orville: Hard to Die, *848*
Kettle, Ross: Lethal Ninja, *76*
Keyes, Evelyn: Before I Hang, *812;* Here Comes Mr. Jordan, *296;* Jolson Story, The, *926;* Lady in Question, *568;* Return to Salem's Lot, A, *880;* Slightly Honorable, *381*
Keyloun, Mark: Gimme an "F", *286;* Mike's Murder, *594;* Separate Vacations, *375*
Keys-Hall, Michael: Blackout (1990), *956*
Keystone Kops: Days of Thrills and Laughter, *262;* Dough and Dynamite/Knockout, The, *268*
Khambatta, Persis: Megaforce, *1065;* Phoenix the Warrior, *1070;* Warrior of the Lost World, *1088*
Khanjian, Arsinée: Adjuster, The, *441;* Speaking Parts, *664*
Khokhlova, Alexandra: By the Law, *721*
Khouth, Gabe: Just One of the Girls, *312*
Khumalo, Leleti: Sarafina!, *938*
Kibbee, Guy: Babes in Arms, *907;* Blonde Crazy, *241;* Captain Blood, *22;* Captain January, *155;* Dames, *913;* Dixie Jamboree, *914;* Earthworm Tractors, *269;* Footlight Parade, *917;* Girl Crazy, *919;* Hold Your Man, *542;* Horn Blows at Midnight, The, *301;* Lady for a Day, *567;* Laughing Sinners, *571;* Let Freedom Ring, *928;* Little Lord Fauntleroy (1936), *576;* Miss Annie Rooney, *188;* Of Human Hearts, *610;* Rain, *634;* Riding on Air, *368;* Strange Love of Molly Louvain, The, *669;* Three Comrades, *682;* Three Men on a Horse, *395;* Whistling in Dixie, *410;* Wonder Bar, *948*
Kidd, Chris: Cry from the Mountain, *160*
Kidd, Michael: It's Always Fair Weather, *925;* Smile, *381*
Kidder, Margot: Amityville Horror, The, *809;* Best of Dan Aykroyd, The, *235;* Black Christmas, *814;* Bounty Man, The, *1101;* Glitter Dome, The, *980;* Heartaches, *538;* Hitchhiker (Series), The, *850;* Keeping Track, *70;* Little Treasure, *77;* Louisiana, *580;* Maverick, *1133;* Miss Right, *333;* Mr. Mike's Mondo Video, *334;* Mob Story, *335;* 92 in the Shade, *345;* Quackser Fortune Has a Cousin in the Bronx, *631;* Quiet Day in Belfast, A, *632;* Reincarnation of Peter Proud, The, *879;* Sisters (1973), *1017;* Some Kind of Hero, *382;* Superman, *1081;* Superman II, *1081;* Superman IV: The Quest for Peace, *1081;* To Catch a Killer, *1025;* Trenchcoat, *399;* Vanishing Act, *693;* Willie and Phil, *412*
Kidman, Nicole: Billy Bathgate, *461;* BMX Bandits, *17;* Days of Thunder, *33;* Dead Calm, *966;* Far and Away, *514;* Flirting, *518;* Malice, *994;* My Life, *602;* Wacky World of Wills and Burke, The, *405*
Kieffer, Ray: Dance or Die, *32*
Kiel, Richard: Eegah!, *838;* Flash and the Firecat, *50;* Force Ten from Navarone, *51;* Human Duplicators, The, *854;* Hysterical, *303;* Las Vegas Hillbillys, *315;* Nasty Rabbit, *342;* Pale Rider, *1138;* Silver Streak (1976), *379;* So Fine, *382;* Spy Who Loved Me, The, *119;* They Went That-A-Way and That-A-Way, *210;* Think Big, *394*
Kiel, Sue: Red Heat (1985), *1009;* Survivor, *1081*
Kier, Udo: Andy Warhol's Dracula, *809;* Andy Warhol's Frankenstein, *809;* Even Cowgirls Get the Blues, *272;* For Love or Money, *279;* Mark of the Devil, *863;* Salzburg Connection, The, *111;* Story of O, The, *668;* Suspiria, *891;* Zentropa, *807*
Kiger, Susan: H.O.T.S., *292*
Kilbride, Percy: Adventures of Mark Twain, The (1944), *442;* Egg and I, The, *270;* George Washington Slept Here, *284;* Keeper of the Flame, *562;* Knickerbocker Holiday, *927;* RiffRaff (1947), *106;* State Fair (1945), *941;* Sun Comes Up, The, *208*
Kilburn, Terry: Black Beauty (1946), *150;* Christmas Carol, A (1938), *158;* Fiend without a Face, *841*
Kiley, Richard: Angel on My Shoulder (1980), *448;* George Washington, *526;* Little Prince, The, *929;* Looking for Mr. Goodbar, *993;* Night Gallery, *869;* Pendulum, *1005;* Pray TV (1982), *626;* Separate But Equal, *652;* Thornbirds, The, *682*
Kilgour, Melanie: Last of the Warriors, *1062*
Kilian, Victor: Dangerous Passage, *32;* Dr. Cyclops, *835;* Mary Hartman, Mary Hartman (TV Series), *329;* Unknown World, *1087*
Killion, Cynthia: Killing Game, The, *71*
Kilmer, Val: Doors, The, *914;* Gore Vidal's Billy The Kid, *1116;* Kill Me Again, *988;* Man Who Broke 1000 Chains, The, *587;* Real Genius, *365;* Real McCoy, The, *1009;* Thunderheart, *1025;* Tombstone, *1157;* Top Gun, *131;* Top Secret, *397;* True Romance, *133;* Willow, *1089*
Kilpatrick, Lincoln: Hollywood Cop, *63;* Prison, *876*
Kilpatrick, Patrick: Cellar, The, *822*
Kim, Daniel Dae: American Shaolin: King of the Kickboxers II, *5*
Kim, Evan: Dead Pool, The, *33;* Kentucky Fried Movie, *312*
Kim, Hang Yip: Undefeatable, *134*
Kim, Miki: Primary Target, *627*
Kimball, Anne: Monster from the Ocean Floor, The, *866*
Kimbrough, Charles: Seduction of Joe Tynan, The, *651;* Sunday in the Park with George, *943*
Kimmel, Bruce: First Nudie Musical, The, *917;* Spaceship, *384*
Kimmel, Dana: Friday the 13th, Part III, *843*
Kimple, Dennis: Maverick, *1133*
Kincaid, Aron: Proud and the Damned, The, *1139*
Kinchev, Konstantin: Burglar (1987), *721*
Kind, David: Quest of the Delta Knights, *1073*
Kind, Richard: All-American Murder, *951*
King, Adrienne: Friday the 13th, *843;* Friday the 13th, Part II, *843*
King, Alan: Author! Author!, *230;* Cat's Eye, *822;* Enemies—A Love Story, *510;* I, the Jury, *985;* Just Tell Me What You Want, *312;* Memories of Me, *331;* Night and the City (1992), *605;* Steve Martin Live, *386*

King, Andrea: Beast with Five Fingers, The, *812;* Lemon Drop Kid, The, *317;* Man I Love, The, *586;* Red Planet Mars, *1074*
King, Atlas: Incredibly Strange Creatures Who Stopped Living and Became Mixed-Up Zombies, The, *856;* Thrill Killers, The, *895*
King, B. B.: Amazon Women on the Moon, *225*
King, Bernard: Fast Break, *274*
King, Brenda: Dawn of the Mummy, *830*
King, Caroline Junko: Three Ninjas Kick Back, *211*
King, Charles: Arizona Stagecoach, *1095;* Below the Border, *1097;* Border Roundup, *1100;* Broadway Melody, The, *910;* Caravan Trail, *1103;* Enemy of the Law, *1111;* Fighting Deputy, *1112;* Forbidden Trails, *1114;* Ghost Town Law, *1115;* His Brother's Ghost, *1121;* In Early Arizona, *1122;* Kid Ranger, *1124;* Law of the Lash, *1127;* Lawless Nineties, The, *1127;* Lightnin' Crandall, *1128;* Mystery of the Hooded Horsemen, *1135;* Riders of the Rio Grande, *1144;* Riders of the Rockies, *1144;* Rootin' Tootin' Rhythm, *1146;* Sing, Cowboy, Sing, *1150;* Superman—The Serial, *1081;* Three in the Saddle, *1156;* Unnamable, The, *899;* Where Trails End, *1164;* Zorro's Fighting Legion, *1166*
King, Dennis: Devil's Brother, The, *914;* Miracle, The (1959), *594*
King, Erik: Joey Breaker, *558*
King, John: Ace Drummond, *1;* Arizona Stagecoach, *1095;* Boothill Bandits, *1100;* Fugitive Valley, *1114;* Renegade Girl, *1142;* Saddle Mountain Roundup, *1146;* Texas to Bataan, *1156;* Trail of the Silver Spurs, *1158*
King, Larry: Richard Lewis—"I'm Exhausted", *367*
King, Loretta: Bride of the Monster, *819*
King, Mabel: Dead Men Don't Die, *262;* Wiz, The, *948*
King, Manuel: Darkest Africa, *33*
King, Meegan: Sweater Girls, *389*
King, Perry: Andy Warhol's Bad, *447;* Choirboys, The, *481;* City in Fear, *962;* Class of 1984, *824;* Cracker Factory, *490;* Cry in the Night, A, *964;* Different Story, A, *501;* Hasty Heart, *537;* Jericho Fever, *68;* Killing Hour, The, *988;* Lipstick, *992;* Lords of Flatbush, The, *579;* Love's Savage Fury, *582;* Mandingo, *588;* Prize Pulitzer, The: The Roxanne Pulitzer Story, *629;* Search and Destroy (1981), *113;* Switch, *390;* Wild Party, The (1975), *702*
King, Regina: Poetic Justice, *624*
King, Sammy: Live at Harrah's, *320*
King, Scott: Double Exposure (1987), *268*
King, Stephen: Creepshow, *826*
King, Tony: Bucktown, *20;* Gordon's War, *57;* Report to the Commissioner, *638*
King, Walter Woolf: Go West, *287;* Swiss Miss, *390*
King, Wright: Wanted: Dead or Alive (TV Series), *1162*
King, Yolanda: Death of a Prophet, *498*
King, Zalman: Blue Sunshine, *957;* Smile, Jenny, You're Dead, *661;* Some Call It Loving, *662;* Tell Me a Riddle, *678*
Kingsley, Ben: Betrayal (1983), *459;* Bugsy, *471;* Dave, *262;* Fifth Monkey, The, *516;* Gandhi, *524;* Harem, *536;* Murderers Among Us: The Simon Wiesenthal Story, *601;* Pascali's Island, *619;* Schindler's List, *649;* Searching for Bobby Fischer, *202;* Silas Marner, *657;* Slipstream, *1077;* Sneakers, *1018;* Turtle Diary, *400;* Without a Clue, *413*
Kingsley, Danitza: Amazons, *4*
Kingsley, Susan: Dollmaker, The, *503*
Kingston, Mark: Intimate Contact, *553*
Kingston, Natalie: Tarzan the Mighty, *125;* Tarzan the Tiger, *126*
Kingston Trio, The: Hungry I Reunion, *303*
Kinmont, Kathleen: Art of Dying, The, *953;* CIA Codename Alexa, *26;* Final Impact, *48;* Final Round, *48;* Night of the Warrior, *90;* Sweet Justice, *123*
Kinnaman, Melanie: Friday the 13th, Part V—A New Beginning, *844*
Kinnear, Roy: Diamond's Edge, *162;* Herbie Goes to Monte Carlo, *174;* Hound of the Baskervilles, The (1977), *302;* Juggernaut (1974), *987;* Madame Sin, *80;* Melody, *186;* Pirates, *358;* Return of the Musketeers, *106;* Taste the Blood of Dracula, *892;* Willy Wonka and the Chocolate Factory, *217*
Kinney, Kathy: Parting Glances, *618*
Kinney, Terry: Body Snatchers, The (1993), *1040;* JFK: Reckless Youth, *558;* No Mercy, *91;* Talent for the Game, *677*
Kinnison, Sam: It's a Bundyful Life, *308;* Rodney Dangerfield: "It's Not Easy Being Me", *370;* Sam Kinnison Live!, *372*
Kinoshita, Keisuke: Twenty-four Eyes, *797*
Kinsella, Neil: Octavia, *610*
Kinsey, Lance: Club Fed, *256*
Kinskey, Leonid: Can't Help Singing, *911;* Everything Happens at Night, *273*
Kinski, Klaus: Aguirre: Wrath of God, *711;* And God Said to Cain, *1093;* Android, *1036;* Beauty and the Beast (1983), *149;* Buddy, Buddy, *247;* Bullet for the General, A, *1102;* Burden of Dreams, *420;* Circus of Fear, *824;* Code Name: Wild Geese, *27;* Count Dracula, *825;* Counterfeit Traitor, The, *30;* Crawlspace, *825;* Creature, *1043;* Dead Eyes of London, *830;* Deadly Sanctuary, *831;* Fitzcarraldo, *737;* Five for Hell, *50;* For a Few Dollars More, *1113;* French Woman, The, *522;* Gangster's Law, *525;* Heroes in Hell, *61;* His Name Was King, *1121;* Jack the Ripper (1979), *987;* Lifespan, *1063;* Little Drummer Girl, The, *992;* Operation Thunderbolt, *95;* Rough Justice, *1146;* Ruthless Four, The, *1146;* Schizoid, *883;* Secret Diary of Sigmund Freud, The, *374;* Shangai Joe, *1148;* Shoot the Living...Pray for the Dead, *1149;* Soldier, The, *118;* Star Knight, *1078;* Time Stalkers, *1084;* Time to Love and a Time to Die, A, *684;* Twice a Judas, *1159;* Venom, *900;* Venus in Furs, *135;* Woyzeck, *805*
Kinski, Nastassja: Boarding School, *243;* Cat People (1982), *822;* Exposed, *840;* Faraway, So Close, *736;* For Your Love Only, *519;* Harem, *536;* Hotel New Hampshire, The, *544;* Magdalene, *585;* Maria's Lovers, *588;* Moon in the Gutter, The, *768;* One from the Heart, *934;* Paris, Texas, *618;* Revolution, *639;* Spring Symphony, *788;* Stay as You Are, *666;* Tess, *679;* To the Devil, a Daughter, *896;* Torrents of Spring, *686;* Unfaithfully Yours (1984), *403;* Wrong Move, The, *805*
Kirby, Bruce: Mr. Wonderful, *597*
Kirby, Bruno: Between the Lines, *237;* Birdy, *462;* Borderline, *17;* City Slickers, *255;* Fallen Angels, *513;* Freshman, The, *281;* Good Morning, Vietnam, *530;* Harrad Experiment, The, *537;* Modern Romance, *335;* Nitti: The Enforcer, *91;* We're No Angels (1989), *408;* When Harry Met Sally, *409;* Where the Buffalo Roam, *409*
Kirby, George: Puss in Boots, *198*
Kirby, Jack: Comic Book Confidential, *421*
Kirby, Jay: Conquest of Cheyenne, *1106;* Sheriff of Las Vegas, *1149;* Sundown Riders, *1153*
Kirby, Michael: Swoon, *675*
Kirchenbauer, Bill: Gallagher—Melon Crazy, *282*
Kirk, Jack: Pals of the Saddle, *1138;* Zorro's Black Whip, *1166*
Kirk, Phyllis: Back from Eternity, *453;* House of Wax, *853;* Life of Her Own, A, *574;* Sad Sack, The, *372*
Kirk, Tommy: Absent-Minded Professor, The, *143;* Babes in Toyland (1961), *147;* Bon Voyage!, *151;* Escapade in Florence, *165;* Horsemasters, *176;* Mars Needs Women, *1065;* Misadventures of Merlin Jones, The, *188;* Monkey's Uncle, The, *188;* Old Yeller, *192;* Savage Sam, *201;* Shaggy Dog, The, *203;* Son of Flubber, *206;* Swiss Family Robinson, The, *208;* Unkissed Bride, *403;* Village of the Giants, *900*
Kirkland, Kenny: Bring on the Night, *419*
Kirkland, Sally: Anna, *448;* Best of the Best, *11;* Blue (1968), *1099;* Bullseye, *247;* Cheatin' Hearts, *480;* Cold Feet (1989), *257;* Double Jeopardy, *972;* Double Threat, *504;* Fatal Games, *840;* Futz, *524;* Gunmen, *58;* High Stakes (1989), *62;* Hit the Dutchman, *63;* In the Heat of Passion, *986;* JFK, *558;* Paint It Black, *97;* Primary Motive, *627;* Prime Time Murder, *100;* Revenge (1990), *106;* Talking Walls, *391;* Young Nurses, The, *708*

Kirkwood, Gene: Night and the City (1992), *605*
Kirov Ballet: Don Quixote (1988), *914*
Kirsch, Stan: Highlander: The Gathering, *1056*
Kirsten, Dorothy: Great Caruso, The, *920*
Kirtley, Virginia: Lost and Found Chaplin: Keystone, *321*
Kirwin, William: Playgirl Killer, The, *875*
Kiser, Terry: Friday the 13th, Part VII: The New Blood, *844;* Into the Sun, *67;* Mannequin Two: On the Move, *328;* Offspring, The, *872;* Rich Kids, *640;* Starflight One, *1079;* Steel, *120;* Weekend at Bernie's, *407;* Weekend at Bernie's II, *407*
Kishi, Keiko: Kwaidan, *752;* Qui Etes-Vous, Mr. Sorge? (Soviet Spy), *779*
Kissinger, Charles: Asylum of Satan, *810;* Three on a Meathook, *895*
Kissmuller, Johnny: Jungle Master, The, *69*
Kistler, Darci: George Balanchine's The Nutcracker, *919*
Kitaen, Tawny: Bachelor Party, *230;* Crystal Heart, *492;* Glory Years, *287;* Happy Hour, *293;* Instant Justice, *67;* Perils of Gwendoline, The, *98;* White Hot, *138;* Witchboard, *903*
Kitaoji, Kinya: Himatsuri, *744*
Kitchen, Michael: Enchanted April, *271;* Fools of Fortune, *518;* Out of Africa, *616;* Russia House, The, *646*
Kitt, Eartha: Boomerang, *244;* Erik the Viking, *1049;* Ernest Scared Stupid, *272;* Fatal Instinct (1993), *274;* Friday Foster, *53;* Mark of the Hawk, The, *589;* New Faces, *933;* Pink Chiquitas, The, *357*
Kitzmiller, John: Cave of the Living Dead, *822*
Kivette, Charles: Brothers of the Wilderness, *471*
Klar, Norman: Hitchhikers, *850*
Klausmeyer, Charles: Can It Be Love, *249*
Klein, Gerald: Honor and Glory, *64;* Undefeatable, *134*
Klein, Nita: Muriel, *769*
Klein, Robert: All-Star Toast to the Improv, An, *224;* Bell Jar, The, *458;* Best of John Belushi, The, *235;* Dangerous Curves, *262;* Nobody's Perfekt, *346;* Owl and the Pussycat, The, *352;* Poison Ivy (1985), *359;* Pursuit of Happiness, The, *631*
Klein-Rogge, Rudolf: Destiny, *729;* Dr. Mabuse, the Gambler (Parts I and II), *971;* Kriemhilde's Revenge, *752;* Spies (1928), *788;* Testament of Dr. Mabuse, *1023*
Kleiner, Towje: Train Killer, The, *687*
Klenck, Margaret: Hard Choices, *536*
Kline, Kevin: Big Chill, The, *460;* Chaplin, *479;* Consenting Adults (1992), *963;* Cry Freedom, *492;* Dave, *262;* Fish Called Wanda, A, *277;* Grand Canyon, *531;* I Love You to Death, *304;* January Man, The, *987;* Pirates of Penzance, The, *935;* Silverado, *1150;* Soapdish, *382;* Sophie's Choice, *663;* Violets Are Blue, *694*
Kline, Val: Beach Girls, The, *233*
Kling, Heidi: Mighty Ducks, The, *187;* Out on a Limb (1992), *352*
Klisser, Evan J.: Hellgate, *849*
Klopfer, Eugen: Street, The, *790*
Klos, Elmar: Shop on Main Street, The, *786*
Klose, Debra: Can I Do It 'Til I Need Glasses?, *249*
Kluga, Henlyk: Two Men and a Wardrobe, *797*
Klugman, Jack: Days of Wine and Roses, *496;* Detective, The (1968), *500;* Don Rickles: Buy This Tape You Hockey Puck, *267;* Goodbye Columbus, *288;* I Could Go On Singing, *924;* 12 Angry Men, *690;* Twilight Zone, The (TV Series), *1086;* Two-Minute Warning, *1028*
Klusak, Jan: Report on the Party and the Guests, A, *781*
Knapp, Dave: Honeymoon Murders, *851*
Knapp, Evalyn: In Old Santa Fe, *1123;* Perils of Pauline, The (1933), *98;* Rawhide (1938), *1141*
Knell, David: Life on the Mississippi, *574;* Spring Break, *385*
Knepper, Rob: Red Shoe Diaries II: Double Dare, *637;* Wild Thing, *702;* Zelda, *709*
Knievel, Evel: Viva Knievel, *136*
Knight, Christopher: Studs Lonigan, *671*
Knight, David: Demons 2, *833;* Who Shot Pat?, *701*
Knight, Esmond: Element of Crime, The, *508;* Waltzes from Vienna, *406*
Knight, Fuzzy: Adventures of Gallant Bess, *442;* Badmen of the Border, *1096;* Captain Gallant—Foreign Legion, *23;* Cowboy and the Senorita, *1106;* Egg and I, The, *270;* Hostile Country, *1122;* Lone Star Trail, *1129;* Operator 13, *614;* Rimfire, *1144;* Song of the Gringo, *1151*
Knight, Gladys: Pipe Dreams, *622*
Knight, Jack: Class of 1999 II: The Substitute, *1041*
Knight, Michael E.: Date with an Angel, *262;* Hexed, *296*
Knight, Sandra: Frankenstein's Daughter, *843;* Terror, The, *893*
Knight, Shirley: Endless Love, *510;* Group, The, *534;* Juggernaut (1974), *987;* Outer Limits, The (TV Series), *1069;* Petulia, *621;* Playing for Time, *623;* Rain People, The, *634;* Secrets, *651;* Sender, The, *884;* Sweet Bird of Youth (1962), *674*
Knight, Stephen: Black Room, The (1985), *814*
Knight, Ted: Caddyshack, *249*
Knight, Wayne: Jurassic Park, *1061*
Knight, Wyatt: Porky's, *360;* Porky's II: The Next Day, *360;* Porky's Revenge, *360*
Knott, Andrew: Secret Garden, The (1993), *202*
Knotts, Don: Andy Griffith Show, The (TV Series), *227;* Apple Dumpling Gang, The, *147;* Apple Dumpling Gang Rides Again, The, *147;* Gus, *172;* Herbie Goes to Monte Carlo, *174;* Hot Lead and Cold Feet, *176;* Incredible Mr. Limpet, The, *306;* No Deposit, No Return, *191;* No Time for Sergeants, *345;* Pinocchio and the Emperor of the Night, *195;* Private Eyes, The, *361;* Prizefighter, The, *197;* Return to Mayberry, *366;* Shakiest Gun in the West, The, *377*
Knowles, Patric: Beauty for the Asking, *457;* Big Steal, The, *13;* Charge of the Light Brigade, The (1936), *24;* Chisum, *1104;* Elfego Baca: Six Gun Law, *1111;* Five Came Back, *517;* Frankenstein Meets the Wolf Man, *843;* Hit the Ice, *298;* Monsieur Beaucaire, *336;* Terror in the Wax Museum, *894;* Three Came Home, *682;* Who Done It?, *410;* Wolf Man, The, *904*
Knox, Alexander: Commandos Strike at Dawn, *28;* Cry of the Innocent, *964;* Gorky Park, *980;* Judge Steps Out, The, *560;* Khartoum, *70;* Man in the Saddle, *1132;* Operation Amsterdam, *95;* Puppet on a Chain, *101;* Sea Wolf, The (1941), *113;* Sister Kenny, *659;* Sleeping Tiger, The, *660;* Tokyo Joe, *130;* Two of a Kind (1951), *1028;* Villa Rides, *1161;* Wilson, *703;* Wreck of the Mary Deare, The, *141*
Knox, Elyse: Don Winslow of the Coast Guard, *41;* Hit the Ice, *298;* Mummy's Tomb, The, *867*
Knox, Terence: Children of the Corn II: The Final Sacrifice, *823;* Distortions, *834;* Humanoid Defender, *1057;* Lies, *574;* Murder So Sweet, *601;* Rebel Love, *636;* Snow Kill, *118;* Tour of Duty, *131;* Tripwire, *132*
Knudsen, Peggy: Copper Canyon, *1106*
Knyvette, Sally: Blake's 7 (TV Series), *1040*
Kobayashi, Keiji: Godzilla 1985, *846*
Kobayashi, Tsuruko: Varan, the Unbelievable, *900*
Kober, Jeff: Baby Doll Murders, The, *953;* First Power, The, *841;* Hit List, The (1992), *982;* Keep the Change, *1124;* Lone Justice, *1129;* Lucky Stiff, *324;* Out of Bounds, *96;* Viper, *136*
Koenig, Tommy: National Lampoon's Class of '86, *342*
Koenig, Walter: Antony and Cleopatra (1981), *450;* Moon Trap, *1067;* Star Trek (TV Series), *1078;* Star Trek—The Motion Picture, *1079;* Star Trek II: The Wrath of Khan, *1079;* Star Trek III: The Search for Spock, *1079;* Star Trek IV: The Voyage Home, *1079;* Star Trek V: The Final Frontier, *1079;* Star Trek VI: The Undiscovered Country, *1079*
Kogure, Michiyo: Geisha, A, *740*
Kohler Jr., Fred: Lawless Valley, *1127;* Twilight in the Sierras, *1159*
Kohler Sr., Fred: Billy the Kid Returns, *1099;* Deluge, *1046;* Fiddlin' Buckaroo, *1112;* Lawless Valley, *1127;* Lightning Triggers, *1128;* Old Ironsides, *93;* Vigilantes Are Coming!, *1161*

Kohner, Susan: Dino, *501;* Gene Krupa Story, The, *525;* Imitation of Life, *549;* To Hell and Back, *130*
Kohnert, Mary: Beyond the Door 3, *813*
Kohoutova, Kristyna: Alice (1988), *1034*
Koizumi, Hiroshi: Ghidrah, the Three-Headed Monster, *845;* Godzilla vs. Mothra, *846;* Mothra, *1067*
Kolb, Clarence: Beware of Spooks, *237;* Honolulu, *923;* Sky's the Limit, The, *940;* Toast of New York, The, *685*
Kollek, Amos: Double Edge, *504;* Goodbye New York, *289*
Komarov, Sergei: By the Law, *721*
Komorowska, Liliana: Scanners 3: The Takeover, *883*
Komorowska, Maja: Contract, *726;* Year of the Quiet Sun, *805*
Kondazian, Karen: Mortal Sins (1992), *997*
Koo, Josephine: Police Story III—Super Cop, *778*
Koock, Guich: American Ninja, *4;* Square Dance, *665*
Kopecky, Milos: Baron Munchausen, *148*
Kopell, Bernie: When Things Were Rotten (TV Series), *409*
Kopins, Karen: Jake Speed, *68;* Once Bitten, *349;* Tracker, The, *1158*
Korjus, Miliza: Great Waltz, The, *921*
Korkes, Jon: Between the Lines, *237;* Jaws of Satan, *858*
Korman, Harvey: Alice Through the Looking Glass (1985), *145;* Americathon, *226;* Based on an Untrue Story, *232;* Betrayal of the Dove, *954;* Blazing Saddles, *241;* Bud and Lou, *471;* Carol Burnett's My Personal Best, *251;* Curse of the Pink Panther, The, *261;* First Family, *277;* Gone Are the Days, *288;* Herbie Goes Bananas, *174;* High Anxiety, *297;* History of the World, Part One, The, *298;* Huckleberry Finn (1974), *176;* Longshot, The (1985), *320;* Lord Love a Duck, *321;* Munchies, *867;* Your Favorite Laughs from an Evening at the Improv, *416*
Kornman, Mary: Desert Trail, *1109*
Korsmo, Charlie: Doctor, The, *502;* Hook, *175;* What About Bob?, *408*
Kortman, Bob: Lonely Trail, The, *1129;* Phantom Thunderbolt, *1138;* Trail Drive, *1158;* Vigilantes Are Coming!, *1161;* Warning Shadows (1933), *1030;* Zorro Rides Again, *1166*
Kortner, Fritz: Pandora's Box, *775;* Warning Shadows (1923), *696*
Korvin, Charles: Berlin Express, *10;* Ship of Fools, *656*
Koscina, Sylva: Deadly Sanctuary, *831;* Hercules (1959), *1056;* Hercules Unchained, *1056;* Hornet's Nest, *64;* Juliet of the Spirits, *750;* Manhunt (1973), *81;* Secret War of Harry Frigg, The, *375*
Kosinski, Jerzy: Reds, *637*
Kosleck, Martin: All Through the Night, *3;* Flesh Eaters, The, *841;* Mummy's Curse, The, *867;* Nurse Edith Cavell, *610;* Pursuit to Algiers, *1008*
Koslo, Paul: Conagher, *1105;* Drive Like Lightning, *42;* Loose Cannons, *321;* Mr. Majestyk, *86;* Project: Shadowchaser, *101;* Ransom, *1009;* Robot Jox, *1075;* Tomorrow Never Comes, *686;* Xtro II, *1090*
Kossof, David: Unicorn, The, *214*
Kosti, Maria: Night of the Death Cult, *869*
Kosugi, Sho: Black Eagle, *13;* Enter the Ninja, *44;* Journey of Honor, *69;* Nine Deaths of the Ninja, *91;* Ninja III: The Domination, *91;* Rage of Honor, *103;* Revenge of the Ninja, *106*
Koteas, Elias: Adjuster, The, *441;* Almost an Angel, *225;* Backstreet Dreams, *454;* Chain of Desire, *478;* Cyborg 2, *1043;* Desperate Hours (1990), *37;* Look Who's Talking Too, *321;* Malarek, *586;* Teenage Mutant Ninja Turtles, *209;* Teenage Mutant Ninja Turtles III, *209*
Kotero, Apollonia: Ministry of Vengeance, *85*
Kotto, Yaphet: Across 110th Street, *1;* After the Shock, *442;* Alien, *1034;* American Clock, The, *446;* Badge of the Assassin, *454;* Blue Collar, *465;* Brubaker, *471;* Chrome Soldiers, *26;* Drum, *505;* Extreme Justice, *512;* Eye of the Tiger, *46;* Fighting Back, *47;* Five Card Stud, *1113;* Freddy's Dead: The Final Nightmare, *843;* Friday Foster, *53;* Housewife, *545;* In Self Defense, *550;* Jigsaw Murders, The, *987;* Live and Let Die, *78;* Man and Boy, *1131;* Midnight Run, *84;* Ministry of Vengeance, *85;* Park Is Mine, The, *618;* Pretty Kill, *1007;* Rage (1980), *633;* Raid on Entebbe, *633;* Report to the Commissioner, *638;* Running Man, The, *1075;* Shark's Treasure, *115;* Star Chamber, The, *1019;* Terminal Entry, *1082;* Tripwire, *132;* Truck Turner, *132;* Warning Sign, *901*
Kovack, Nancy: Diary of a Madman, *834;* Enter Laughing, *271;* Frankie and Johnny (1966), *918*
Kovacs, Ernie: Bell, Book and Candle, *234;* Ernie Kovacs: Television's Original Genius, *272;* Five Golden Hours, *278;* Kovacs, *314;* North to Alaska, *1136;* Strangers When We Meet, *670*
Kovacs, Geza: Baby on Board, *8*
Kove, Martin: Firehawk, *49;* Four Deuces, The, *52;* Future Shock, *1053;* Karate Kid Part II, The, *562;* Karate Kid Part III, The, *562;* Outfit, The, *96;* President's Target, *100;* Project: Shadowchaser, *101;* Rambo: First Blood II, *103;* Shootfighter, *115;* Steele Justice, *120;* White Light, *1089*
Koyama, Akiko: Violence at Noon, *801*
Kozak, Andreas: Red and the White, The, *780*
Kozak, Harley Jane: All I Want for Christmas, *145;* Amy Fisher Story, The, *447;* Arachnophobia, *810;* Favor, The, *275;* Necessary Roughness, *342;* Taking of Beverly Hills, The, *124*
Kozlowski, Linda: Almost an Angel, *225;* Backstreet Justice, *8;* "Crocodile" Dundee, *261;* "Crocodile" Dundee II, *261;* Neighbor, The, *1000;* Pass the Ammo, *355;* Target: Favorite Son, *677*
Krabbé, Jeroen: Code Name: Dancer, *27;* Crossing Delancey, *491;* For a Lost Soldier, *737;* Fourth Man, The, *738;* Fugitive, The (1993), *53;* Jumpin' Jack Flash, *311;* Kafka, *988;* King of the Hill, *565;* Living Daylights, The, *78;* No Mercy, *91;* Prince of Tides, The, *627;* Punisher, The, *101;* Robin Hood (1991), *107;* Secret Weapon, *651;* Soldier of Orange, *787;* Stalin, *665;* Till There Was You, *684;* Turtle Diary, *400;* World War III, *141*
Krakowski, Jane: Stepping Out, *942*
Kramer, Eric Allen: Quest for the Mighty Sword, *1073*
Kramer, Jeffrey: Halloween II, *848;* Hero and the Terror, *61;* Hollywood Boulevard, *299;* Jaws 2, *858*
Kramer, Joey: Flight of the Navigator, *1052*
Kramer, Michael: Over the Edge, *616*
Kramer, Stepfanie: Terror at London Bridge, *893*
Kramer, Sylvia: Watch Me When I Kill, *901*
Krantz, Robert: Paradise Motel, *353;* Winners Take All, *140*
Kratka, Paul: Friday the 13th, Part III, *843*
Kraus, Peter: Waltz King, The, *215*
Krause, Brian: December, *498;* Liars' Club, The, *992;* Return to the Blue Lagoon, *639;* Stephen King's Sleepwalkers, *890*
Krauss, Alison: High Lonesome—The Story of Bluegrass Music, *426*
Krauss, Werner: Cabinet of Doctor Caligari, The, *721;* Jud Suss, *750;* Othello (1922), *615;* Secrets of a Soul, *784;* Student of Prague, *790;* Waxworks, *802*
Kravchenko, Alexei: Come and See, *725*
Kresadlova, Vera: Larks on a String, *755*
Kresel, Lee: Mothra, *1067*
Kreuger, Kurt: Dark Corner, The, *495;* Enemy Below, The, *44;* Fear (1955), *515;* Mademoiselle Fifi, *585;* Unfaithfully Yours (1948), *403*
Kreuzer, Lisa: Alice in the City, *711;* American Friend, The, *712;* Birgit Haas Must Be Killed, *718;* Kings of the Road, *752;* L'Homme Blessé (The Wounded Man), *760;* Man Like Eva, A, *765*
Kriegman, Michael: My Neighborhood, *341*
Kriel, Anneline: Kill and Kill Again, *71*
Kriener, Ulrike: Men..., *767*
Krige, Alice: Barfly, *455;* Chariots of Fire, *479;* Code Name: Chaos, *257;* Ghost Story, *846;* Haunted Summer, *537;* Iran Days of Crisis, *554;* King David, *564;* Ladykiller, *990;* Max and Helen, *590;* See You in the Morning, *651;* Stephen King's Sleepwalkers, *890;* Tale of Two Cities, A (1980), *677*

Krishna, Srinivas: Masala, *329*
Kristel, Sylvia: Arrogant, The, *450;* Beauty School, *233;* Big Bet, The, *238;* Casanova (1987), *252;* Dracula's Widow, *837;* Emmanuelle, *734;* Fifth Musketeer, The, *47;* Game of Seduction, *739;* Goodbye Emmanuelle, *741;* Lady Chatterley's Lover (1981), *567;* Mata Hari (1985), *83;* Mysteries, *770;* Nude Bomb, The, *347;* Private Lessons, *361;* Private School, *362;* Red Heat (1985), *1009*
Kristen, Marta: Beach Blanket Bingo, *908;* Lost in Space (TV Series), *1063;* Savage Sam, *201;* Terminal Island, *126*
Kristoff, Rom: Warbus, *137*
Kristofferson, Kris: Act of Passion, *441;* Alice Doesn't Live Here Anymore, *444;* Another Pair of Aces, *1094;* Big Top Pee-Wee, *239;* Blume in Love, *465;* Bring Me the Head of Alfredo Garcia, *20;* Cheatin' Hearts, *480;* Christmas in Connecticut (1992), *255;* Convoy (1978), *29;* Flashpoint, *977;* Heaven's Gate, *1119;* Knights, *1061;* Last Days of Frank and Jesse James, *1125;* Last Movie, The, *570;* Millennium, *1066;* Miracle in the Wilderness, *595;* Night of the Cyclone, *1001;* No Place To Hide, *91;* Original Intent, *614;* Pat Garrett and Billy the Kid, *1138;* Rollover, *1011;* Sailor Who Fell from Grace with the Sea, The, *646;* Semi-Tough, *375;* Songwriter, *940;* Stagecoach (1986), *1152;* Star Is Born, A (1976), *666;* Tracker, The, *1158;* Trouble in Mind, *688;* Welcome Home, *698*
Krix, Cristof: Blue Hour, The, *719*
Kroegen, Chris: Magic Christmas Tree, The, *184*
Kroeger, Gary: Man Called Sarge, A, *327*
Kroner, Josef: Shop on Main Street, The, *786*
Krook, Margaretha: Adventures of Picasso, The, *222*
Kruger, Alma: Craig's Wife, *490*
Krüger, Hardy: Barry Lyndon, *456;* Blue Fin, *151;* Flight of the Phoenix, The, *51;* Hatari!, *59;* Inside Man, The, *66;* One That Got Away, The, *95;* Paper Tiger, *97;* Red Tent, The, *637;* Sundays and Cybèle, *791;* Wild Geese, The, *139;* Wrong Is Right, *414*
Kruger, Otto: Another Thin Man, *952;* Chained, *478;* Corregidor, *489;* Dracula's Daughter, *837;* High Noon, *1120;* Hitler's Children, *63;* I Am the Law, *547;* Magnificent Obsession, *585;* Saboteur, *1011;* Young Philadelphians, The, *708*
Krumholtz, David: Addams Family Values, *222*
Krupa, Gene: Benny Goodman Story, The, *458;* Glenn Miller Story, The, *919*
Krupa, Olek: Mac, *583*
Kruschen, Jack: Angry Red Planet, The, *1036;* Apartment, The, *228;* Cape Fear (1962), *959;* Follow That Dream, *278;* Incredible Rocky Mountain Race, The, *306;* Lover Come Back, *323;* McLintock!, *1133;* Satan's Cheerleaders, *882;* Unsinkable Molly Brown, The, *947*
Kruse, Line: Emma's Shadow, *734*
Kryll, Eve: Making Contact, *1064*
Kubik, Alex: Carnal Crimes, *959*
Kuhlman, Richard: Adventures in Wonderland, *143*
Kuhlman, Ron: Omega Syndrome, *93;* Shadow Play, *885*
Kuhn, Robert: Trespasses, *687*
Kulky, Henry: Five Thousand Fingers of Dr. T, The, *167*
Kulle, Jarl: Babette's Feast, *714;* Devil's Eye, The, *730;* Secrets of Women (Waiting Women), *784;* Smiles of a Summer Night, *787*
Kulp, Nancy: Beverly Hillbillies, The (TV Series), *237*
Kunen, James: Strawberry Statement, The, *670*
Kurnitzov, Alexander: Ice Runner, *65*
Kurtiz, Tuncel: Wall, The, *802*
Kurts, Alwyn: Earthling, The, *164;* Tim, *684*
Kurtz, Swoosie: Baja Oklahoma, *455;* Bright Lights, Big City, *470;* Dangerous Liaisons, *494;* Image, The, *549;* Mating Season, The, *330;* Positively True Adventures of the Alleged Texas Cheerleader-Murdering Mom, The, *360;* Shock to the System, A, *1015;* Stanley and Iris, *665;* True Stories, *400;* Vice Versa, *404;* Wildcats, *411;* World According to Garp, The, *706*
Kurtzman, Katy: Child of Glass, *158;* Diary of a Teenage Hitchhiker, *501*
Kurz, Eva: Virus Knows No Morals, A, *801*
Kusatsu, Clyde: Dr. Strange, *1047;* Dream Lover (1994), *972*
Kuter, Kay E.: Tempest, The (1983), *678*
Kutner, Rima: Black Klansman, The, *14*
Kuwano, Miyuji: Cruel Story of Youth, *727*
Kuzyk, Mimi: Lifeforce Experiment, The, *1063;* Miles to Go, *594;* Striker's Mountain, *121*
Kwan, Nancy: Angkor: Cambodia Express, *5;* Corrupt Ones, The, *29;* Dragon: The Bruce Lee Story, *42;* Flower Drum Song, *917;* Lt. Robin Crusoe, U.S.N., *181;* Night Creature, *869;* World of Suzie Wong, The, *707*
Kwan, Rosamund: Armour Of God, *713*
Kwan, Teddy Robin: Banana Cop, *715*
Kwouk, Burt: Pink Panther Strikes Again, The, *357;* Return of the Pink Panther, The, *366;* Revenge of the Pink Panther, The, *367;* Shooting Elizabeth, *378;* Shot in the Dark, A, *378;* Son of the Pink Panther, *383*
Kyo, Machiko: Drifting Weeds, *732;* Gate of Hell, *740;* Odd Obsession, *772;* Princess Yang Kwei Fei, *778;* Rashomon, *780;* Street of Shame, *790;* Teahouse of the August Moon, The, *392;* Ugetsu, *798*
Kyser, Kay: Around the World, *907;* You'll Find Out, *415*
L. L. Cool J: Simply Mad About the Mouse, *204*
La Fleur, Art: Jack the Bear, *556;* Live! From Death Row, *577;* Rampage, *1009*
La Motta, Jake: Hangmen, *59;* Mob War, *86*
La Mura, Mark: Soldier's Home, *661*
La Placa, Alison: Madhouse (1990), *326*
La Place, Victor: Letters from the Park, *760*
La Planche, Rosemary: Devil Bat's Daughter, *833;* Strangler of the Swamp, *891*
La Rocque, Rod: Beyond Tomorrow, *1039;* Dr. Christian Meets the Women, *502;* Our Modern Maidens, *616;* Shadow Strikes, The, *1014;* Ten Commandments, The (1923), *678*
La Rue, Frank: Fighting Ranger, The, *1113*
La Salle, Eriq: Vietnam War Story, *694*
la Vollette, Juliette: White Sister, The, *700*
Laage, Barbara: Therese and Isabelle, *794*
Labarthe, Samuel: Accompanist, The, *710*
LaBelle, Patti: Sing, *939;* Unnatural Causes, *692*
Laborteaux, Matthew: Deadly Friend, *831;* Little House on the Prairie (TV Series), *181;* Shattered Spirits, *655*
Laborteaux, Patrick: Ski School, *380;* Terminal Entry, *1082*
Labourier, Dominique: Jonah Who Will Be 25 in the Year 2000, *750*
Lacey, Ronald: Disciple of Death, *834;* Firefox, *49;* Flesh and Blood, *50;* Hound of the Baskervilles, The (1983), *984;* Lone Runner, *78;* Of Human Bondage (1964), *610;* Raiders of the Lost Ark, *1073;* Sky Bandits, *116*
Lachapelle, Julie: In Trouble, *550*
Lack, Stephen: Dead Ringers, *831;* Fatal Attraction (1985), *975;* Perfect Strangers, *1005;* Scanners, *883*
Lacombrade, Francis: This Special Friendship, *794*
Lacoste, Philippe: Hail Mary, *742*
Lacoste, Thierry: Hail Mary, *742*
Lacy, Jerry: Play It Again, Sam, *358*
Ladd, Alan: Badlanders, The, *1096;* Botany Bay, *18;* Branded, *1101;* Carpetbaggers, The, *475;* Drum Beat, *1110;* Duel of Champions, *42;* Gangs, Inc., *54;* Glass Key, The, *980;* Hell on Frisco Bay, *60;* Hell Town, *1120;* Joan of Paris, *558;* McConnell Story, The, *591;* Proud Rebel, The, *1140;* Shane, *1148;* This Gun for Hire (1942), *128*
Ladd, Cheryl: Fulfillment, *523;* Hasty Heart, *537;* Lisa, *992;* Millennium, *1066;* Now and Forever, *609;* Poison Ivy (1992), *1006;* Purple Hearts, *631;* Romance on the Orient Express, *643;* Satan's School for Girls, *882*
Ladd, David: Dog of Flanders, A, *163;* Misty, *188;* Proud Rebel, The, *1140*

Ladd, Diane: Alice Doesn't Live Here Anymore, *444;* Carnosaur, *821;* Cemetery Club, The, *478;* Chinatown, *962;* Code Name: Chaos, *257;* Doctor Quinn Medicine Woman, *502;* Embryo, *1048;* Father Hood, *47;* Hold Me, Thrill Me, Kiss Me, *298;* Hush Little Baby, *984;* I Married a Centerfold, *547;* Kiss Before Dying, A, *989;* Lookalike, The, *993;* National Lampoon's Christmas Vacation, *342;* Rambling Rose, *634;* Rebel Rousers, *104;* White Lightning, *139;* Wild Angels, The, *139;* Wild at Heart, *702;* Willa, *703*

Ladengast, Walter: Every Man for Himself and God Against All, *735*

Ladham, Sonny: Taxi Dancers, *678*

Ladmiral, Nicole: Diary of a Country Priest, *730*

Laffan, Pat: Snapper, The, *382*

Laffan, Patricia: Devil Girl from Mars, *833;* Quo Vadis (1951), *632*

Lafont, Bernadette: Le Beau Serge, *756;* Very Curious Girl, A, *800;* Waiting for the Moon, *695*

Lafont, Jean-Philippe: Babette's Feast, *714*

Lagrange, Valerie: Cat and Mouse, *722;* Man and a Woman, A, *764;* Morgan the Pirate, *86*

Lahr, Bert: Just Around the Corner, *926;* Rose Marie (1954), *937;* Ship Ahoy, *939;* Wizard of Oz, The, *218*

Lahti, Christine: Crazy from the Heart, *490;* Doctor, The, *502;* Executioner's Song, The, *512;* Fear Inside, The, *976;* Funny About Love, *282;* Good Fight, The, *530;* Gross Anatomy, *534;* Housekeeping, *545;* Just Between Friends, *561;* Leaving Normal, *572;* Running on Empty, *645;* Single Bars, Single Women, *658;* Stacking, *665;* Swing Shift, *675;* Whose Life Is It, Anyway?, *701*

Lai, Me Me: Cannibal, *820*

Lai, Vuong Han: China, My Sorrow, *723*

Laine, Jimmy: Driller Killer, The, *838*

Laird, Marvin: Beyond Reason, *460*

Lake, Arthur: Blondie, *241;* Blondie Has Trouble, *241;* Blondie Hits the Jackpot, *241;* Blondie in Society, *241;* Blondie Knows Best, *241;* Blondie Takes a Vacation, *242;* Blondie's Blessed Event, *242;* Indiscreet (1931), *306;* It's a Great Life, *308;* Silver Streak (1934), *658*

Lake, Ricki: Baby Cakes, *453;* Based on an Untrue Story, *232;* Cry-Baby, *912;* Hairspray, *292;* Inside Monkey Zetterland, *306;* Last Exit to Brooklyn, *569;* Serial Mom, *376*

Lake, Veronica: Flesh Feast, *841;* Glass Key, The, *980;* I Married a Witch, *1057;* Ramrod, *1140;* Sullivan's Travels, *388;* This Gun for Hire (1942), *128*

Lakeman, Elaine: Death Target, *35*

Lam, George: Banana Cop, *715*

Lamarr, Hedy: Boom Town, *466;* Comrade X, *258;* Copper Canyon, *1106;* Dishonored Lady, *39;* Ecstasy, *733;* Loves of Three Queens, *762;* Samson and Delilah (1949), *648;* Strange Woman, The, *669;* Tortilla Flat, *686;* White Cargo, *699;* Ziegfeld Girl, *949*

Lamas, Fernando: Cheap Detective, The, *254;* Dangerous When Wet, *913;* Girl Who Had Everything, The, *527;* Murder on Flight 502, *87;* 100 Rifles, *1137;* Powderkeg, *1139;* Rich, Young and Pretty, *936;* Rose Marie (1954), *937*

Lamas, Lorenzo: Body Rock, *909;* Bounty Tracker, *18;* CIA Codename Alexa, *26;* Final Impact, *48;* Final Round, *48;* Killing Streets, *72;* Night of the Warrior, *90;* Snake Eater, *117;* Snake Eater 2, the Drug Buster, *117;* Snake Eater III: His Law, *117;* Swordsman, The, *124;* Take Down, *390*

Lamatsch, Andrea: Sudden Thunder, *122*

Lamb, Larry: Transmutations, *897*

Lambert, Christopher: Fortress (1993), *1053;* Greystoke: The Legend of Tarzan, Lord of the Apes, *58;* Gunmen, *58;* Highlander, *1056;* Highlander 2: The Quickening, *1056;* Highlander: The Gathering, *1056;* Knight Moves, *989;* Love Songs (Paroles et Musique), *762;* Priceless Beauty, *626;* Sicilian, The, *115;* Subway, *790;* To Kill a Priest, *684;* Why Me?, *139*

Lambert, Jack: Dick Tracy's Dilemma, *38*

Lambert, Kim: If Looks Could Kill (1986), *985*

Lambert, Martine: Love and the Frenchwoman, *762*

Lamer, Susan: Hills Have Eyes, The, *850*

Lamont, Adele: Brain That Wouldn't Die, The, *1040*

Lamont, Duncan: Evil of Frankenstein, The, *839*

Lamont, Molly: Awful Truth, The, *230;* Devil Bat's Daughter, *833*

Lamorisse, Pascal: Red Balloon, The, *198;* Voyage en Ballon (Stowaway to the Stars), *801*

Lamos, Mark: Longtime Companion, *579*

Lamour, Dorothy: Caught in the Draft, *252;* Creepshow 2, *826;* Death at Love House, *968;* Donovan's Reef, *267;* Greatest Show on Earth, The, *533;* Hurricane, The (1937), *546;* Johnny Apollo, *559;* My Favorite Brunette, *340;* Road to Bali, *368;* Road to Hong Kong, The, *368;* Road to Rio, *369;* Road to Singapore, *369;* Road to Utopia, *369;* Road to Zanzibar, *369;* Swing High, Swing Low, *390;* They Got Me Covered, *393*

Lampert, Zohra: Alan and Naomi, *443;* Alphabet City, *445;* Connection (1973), *487;* Izzy & Moe, *309;* Lady of the House, *568;* Let's Scare Jessica to Death, *860;* Opening Night, *614;* Pay or Die, *620*

Lamprecht, Gunter: Berlin Alexanderplatz, *716;* Red Kiss (Rouge Baiser), *780*

Lancaster, Burt: Airport, *443;* Apache, *1094;* Atlantic City, *452;* Barnum (1987), *456;* Bird Man of Alcatraz, *462;* Buffalo Bill and the Indians, *1102;* Cassandra Crossing, The, *476;* Child is Waiting, A, *480;* Come Back, Little Sheba, *486;* Conversation Piece, *726;* Crimson Pirate, The, *30;* Criss Cross (1948), *964;* Devil's Disciple, The, *264;* Elmer Gantry, *509;* Executive Action, *512;* Field of Dreams, *1050;* Flame and the Arrow, The, *50;* From Here to Eternity (1953), *523;* Go Tell the Spartans, *56;* Gunfight at the O.K. Corral, *1117;* Hallelujah Trail, The, *1118;* His Majesty O'Keefe, *62;* Island of Dr. Moreau, The, *1060;* Jim Thorpe—All American, *558;* Judgment at Nuremberg, *560;* Kentuckian, The, *1124;* Lawman, *1127;* Leopard, The, *572;* Little Treasure, *77;* Local Hero, *320;* Moses, *600;* 1900, *607;* On Wings of Eagles, *94;* Osterman Weekend, The, *96;* Professionals, The, *101;* Rainmaker, The, *634;* Rocket Gibraltar, *642;* Rose Tattoo, The, *644;* Run Silent, Run Deep, *109;* Scalphunters, The, *1148;* Separate But Equal, *652;* Seven Days in May, *653;* Sorry, Wrong Number (1948), *1019;* Sweet Smell of Success, *675;* Swimmer, The, *675;* Tough Guys, *398;* Train, The, *131;* Trapeze, *687;* Twilight's Last Gleaming, *133;* Ulzana's Raid, *1160;* Unforgiven, The (1960), *1160;* Valdez Is Coming, *1160;* Vengeance Valley, *1161;* Vera Cruz, *1161;* Voyage of Terror: The Achille Lauro Affair, *694;* Young Savages, The, *1033;* Zulu Dawn, *142*

Lancaster, Stuart: Good Morning...and Goodbye!, *530*

Lancaster, William: Moses, *600*

Lanchester, Elsa: Androcles and the Lion, *227;* Arnold, *810;* Beachcomber, The, *457;* Blackbeard's Ghost, *151;* Bride of Frankenstein, *819;* Easy Come, Easy Go, *915;* Forever and a Day, *520;* Glass Slipper, The, *919;* Inspector General, The, *306;* Lassie Come Home, *180;* Naughty Marietta, *932;* Northwest Outpost, *933;* Private Life of Henry the Eighth, The, *628;* Razor's Edge, The (1946), *635;* Rembrandt, *638;* Secret Garden, The (1949), *202;* Spiral Staircase, The (1946), *1019;* Terror in the Wax Museum, *894;* That Darn Cat, *210;* Witness for the Prosecution (1957), *1032*

Lancie, John De: Deep Red (1994), *1046*

Lanctot, Micheline: Apprenticeship of Duddy Kravitz, The, *450*

Land, Paul: Spring Break, *385*

Landa, Alfredo: Holy Innocents, *744*

Landau, David: Horse Feathers, *301;* Purchase Price, The, *630;* Street Scene, *670*

Landau, Martin: Access Code, *1;* Alone in the Dark, *808;* Being, The, *812;* By Dawn's Early Light, *473;* Crimes and Misdemeanors, *490;* Cyclone, *31;* Empire State, *44;* Fall of the House of Usher, The (1979), *840;* Firehead, *49;* Gazebo, The, *283;* Hallelujah Trail, The, *1118;* Intersection, *553;* Last Word, The, *571;* Legacy of Lies, *572;* Max and Helen, *590;* Mistress

(1992), *597;* Neon Empire, The, *89;* Nevada Smith, *1135;* No Place To Hide, *91;* North by Northwest, *1002;* Outer Limits, The (TV Series), *1069;* Paint It Black, *97;* Return, The, *1074;* Run if You Can, *645;* Sliver, *1018;* Space 1999 (TV Series), *1077;* Strange Shadows in an Empty Room, *121;* Sweet Revenge (1987), *123;* They Call Me Mister Tibbs, *127;* Tucker: A Man and His Dream, *689;* 12:01, *1086;* Without Warning, *1090*

Landen, Dindsdale: Morons from Outer Space, *337*

Lander, David L.: Funland, *282;* Masters of Menace, *329;* Steel and Lace, *1080;* Wholly Moses!, *410*

Landers, Audrey: California Casanova, *249;* Chorus Line, A, *911;* Deadly Twins, *35;* Getting Even, *55;* Tennessee Stallion, *126;* Underground Aces, *403*

Landers, Judy: Club Fed, *256;* Deadly Twins, *35;* Dr. Alien, *834;* Doin' Time, *266;* Hellhole, *849;* Stewardess School, *386;* Tennessee Stallion, *126;* Vega$, *135;* Yum-Yum Girls, The, *709*

Landes, Michael: American Summer, An, *5*

Landesberg, Steve: Blade, *14;* Final Notice, *977;* Leader of the Band, *317;* Little Miss Millions, *182*

Landgard, Janet: Swimmer, The, *675*

Landgrebe, Gudrun: Berlin Affair, The, *459;* Woman in Flames, A, *804*

Landgren, Karl: Urban Warriors, *134*

Landham, Sonny: Fleshburn, *841;* Predator, *1071;* Three Days to a Kill, *128*

Landi, Elissa: After the Thin Man, *951;* Corregidor, *489;* Count of Monte Cristo, The (1934), *30*

Landi, Maria: Hound of the Baskervilles, The (1959), *983*

Landi, Sal: Savage Streets, *111*

Landis, Carole: Brass Monkey, The, *958;* Dance Hall, *913;* Daredevils of the Red Circle, *32;* Having a Wonderful Crime, *294;* I Wake Up Screaming, *985;* Moon Over Miami, *931;* One Million B.C., *1069;* Orchestra Wives, *934;* Out of the Blue, *352;* Three Texas Steers, *1157;* Topper Returns, *398;* Wintertime, *947*

Landis, Jessie Royce: Boys' Night Out, *244;* Gidget Goes to Rome, *286;* Goodbye Again, *530;* I Married a Woman, *304;* It Happens Every Spring, *307;* My Man Godfrey (1957), *340;* Swan, The (1956), *674;* To Catch a Thief, *1025*

Landis, John: Schlock, *373*

Landis, Nina: Rikki and Pete, *368*

Landiss, Brent: Visitors, The, *901*

Lando, Joe: Doctor Quinn Medicine Woman, *502*

Landon, Laurene: All the Marbles, *225;* Armed Response, *6;* Yellow Hair and the Fortress of Gold, *1165*

Landon, Michael: Bonanza (TV Series), *1100;* Cheyenne (TV Series), *1104;* I Was a Teenage Werewolf, *855;* Little House on the Prairie (TV Series), *181*

Landon Jr., Michael: Bonanza: The Return, *1100*

Landry, Aude: Blood Relatives, *957*

Landry, Karen: Patti Rocks, *619;* Personals, The, *357*

Landry, Tamara: Beach Babes from Beyond, *1038*

Landsberg, David: Detective School Dropouts, *264*

Lane, Abbe: Americano, The, *1093*

Lane, Allan "Rocky": Bandits of Dark Canyon, *1096;* Bells of Rosarita, *1097;* Bronco (TV Series), *1101;* Denver Kid, *1109;* Law West of Tombstone, *1127;* Maid's Night Out, The, *326;* Marshal of Cedar Rock, *1132;* Marshal of Cripple Creek, *1132;* Panama Lady, *353;* Perils of the Darkest Jungle, *98;* Santa Fe Uprising, *1147;* Stagecoach to Denver, *1152;* Stowaway, *942;* Trail of Robin Hood, *1158;* Vigilantes of Boomtown, *1161;* Wild Frontier, *1164*

Lane, Charles: But Not For Me, *472;* Dr. Jekyll and Mr. Hyde (1920), *835;* Papa's Delicate Condition, *617;* Posse (1993), *1139;* 30 Foot Bride of Candy Rock, The, *394;* True Identity, *399;* White Sister, The, *700*

Lane, Diane: Big Town, The, *461;* Chaplin, *479;* Child Bride of Short Creek, *480;* Cotton Club, The, *29;* Descending Angel, *499;* Indian Summer, *306;* Knight Moves, *989;* Lady Beware, *989;* Little Romance, A, *319;* Lonesome Dove, *1129;* My New Gun, *341;* Priceless Beauty, *626;* Six Pack, *380;* Streets of Fire, *121;* Touched by Love, *686;* Vital Signs, *694*

Lane, Jocelyn: Tickle Me, *945*

Lane, Lola: Buckskin Frontier, *1102;* Deadline at Dawn, *34;* Four Daughters, *520;* Hollywood Hotel, *923;* Marked Woman, *82*

Lane, Michael: Gypsy Warriors, The, *58*

Lane, Mike: Curse of the Crystal Eye, *31;* Demon Keeper, *832;* Harder They Fall, The, *536*

Lane, Nathan: Addams Family Values, *222;* Frankie and Johnny (1991), *522;* He Said, She Said, *294;* Life with Mikey, *318*

Lane, Priscilla: Arsenic and Old Lace, *228;* Four Daughters, *520;* Meanest Man in the World, The, *330;* Roaring Twenties, The, *107;* Saboteur, *1011;* Silver Queen, *1150*

Lane, Ray: Season of the Witch, *884*

Lane, Richard: Arabian Nights (1942), *6;* Bullfighters, The, *247;* Mr. Winkle Goes to War, *334*

Lane, Rosemary: Four Daughters, *520;* Hollywood Hotel, *923;* Oklahoma Kid, The, *1136*

Lane, Shelby: Pamela Principle, The, *1004*

Lane, Tim: Iron Warrior, *1060*

Lang, Charley: First Affair, *517;* Kent State, *563*

Lang, Fritz: Contempt, *726*

Lang, June (Vlasek): Bonnie Scotland, *243*

Lang, Melvin: Doomed to Die, *41*

Lang, Perry: Alligator, *808;* Body and Soul (1981), *466;* Jennifer 8, *987;* Jocks, *310;* Little Vegas, *319;* Mortuary Academy, *337;* Spring Break, *385*

Lang, Robert: Night Watch, *870*

Lang, Stephen: Another You, *228;* Band of the Hand, *9;* Crime Story, *30;* Death of a Salesman, *498;* Gettysburg, *526;* Guilty as Sin, *534;* Hard Way, The (1991), *293;* Last Exit to Brooklyn, *569;* Project X, *1072;* Tombstone, *1157*

Langan, Glenn: Amazing Colossal Man, The, *1035;* Forever Amber, *520;* Snake Pit, The, *661;* Wing and a Prayer, A, *140*

Langdon, Harry: Golden Age of Comedy, The, *288;* Strong Man, The, *387*

Langdon, Sue Ane: Cheyenne Social Club, The, *1104;* Frankie and Johnny (1966), *918;* Guide for the Married Man, A, *291;* Rounders, The, *1146;* Roustabout, *938;* Without Warning, *1090*

Lange, Claudie: Machine Gun Killers, *1130*

Lange, Hope: Beulah Land, *459;* Cooperstown, *488;* Death Wish, *35;* Fer-de-Lance, *976;* Ford: The Man & the Machine, *519;* I Am the Cheese, *547;* Nightmare on Elm Street 2, A: Freddy's Revenge, *871;* Peyton Place, *621;* Pleasure Palace, *623;* Pocketful of Miracles, *359;* Wild in the Country, *702;* Young Lions, The, *708*

Lange, Jessica: All That Jazz, *906;* Cape Fear (1991), *959;* Cat on a Hot Tin Roof (1985), *477;* Country, *489;* Crimes of the Heart, *260;* Everybody's All-American, *511;* Far North, *274;* Frances, *521;* How to Beat the High Co$t of Living, *302;* King Kong (1976), *859;* Men Don't Leave, *331;* Music Box, The, *999;* Night and the City (1992), *605;* O Pioneers!, *610;* Postman Always Rings Twice, The (1981), *1007;* Sweet Dreams, *943;* Tootsie, *397*

Lange, Ted: Blade, *14;* Glitch!, *287*

Langella, Frank: And God Created Woman (1987), *447;* Brainscan, *818;* Dave, *262;* Diary of a Mad Housewife, *501;* Dracula (1979), *837;* 1492: The Conquest of Paradise, *52;* Masters of the Universe, *186;* Men's Club, The, *593;* Sphinx (1981), *889;* Those Lips, Those Eyes, *945;* True Identity, *399;* Twelve Chairs, The, *401*

Langenfeld, Sarah: Act, The, *441*

Langenkamp, Heather: Nightmare on Elm Street, A, *871;* Nightmare on Elm Street 3, A: The Dream Warriors, *871*

Langford, Caroline: Big Gag, The, *238*

Langford, Frances: Born to Dance, *909;* Dixie Jamboree, *914;* Dreaming Out Loud, *269;* Girl Rush, *286;* Glenn Miller Story, The, *919;* Hollywood Hotel, *923;* People Are Funny, *356;* This Is the Army, *945*

Langlet, Amanda: Pauline at the Beach, *776*
Langley, Angel: Curse of the House Surgeon, The, *828*
Langlois, Lisa: Blood Relatives, *957;* Joy of Sex, The, *311;* Man Who Wasn't There, The, *328;* Mind Field, *85;* Nest, The (1988), *868;* Truth or Die, *689*
Langmann, Thomas: Night and Day (1991), *771*
Langrick, Margaret: American Boyfriends, *446;* Cold Comfort, *963;* My American Cousin, *339*
Langrishe, Caroline: Eagle's Wing, *1111*
Langston, Murray: Night Patrol, *344;* Two Top Bananas, *402;* Up Your Alley, *403;* Wishful Thinking, *412*
Langton, Jeff: Final Impact, *48*
Langton, Paul: Incredible Shrinking Man, The, *1058;* Snow Creature, The, *888*
Langton-Lloyd, Robert: Mahabharata, The, *585*
Lanko, Vivian: Rejuvenator, The, *879*
Lanoux, Victor: Cousin, Cousine, *726;* Dog Day, *40;* French Detective, The, *738;* Investigation, *748;* Louisiana, *580;* Make Room For Tomorrow, *764;* National Lampoon's European Vacation, *342;* One Wild Moment, *773;* Pardon Mon Affaire, *775;* Pardon Mon Affaire, Too!, *775;* Scene of the Crime (1987), *784;* Shameless Old Lady, The, *785*
Lansbury, Angela: All Fall Down, *444;* Amorous Adventures of Moll Flanders, The, *226;* Bedknobs and Broomsticks, *149;* Blue Hawaii, *909;* Breath of Scandal, A, *245;* Company of Wolves, The, *1042;* Court Jester, The, *260;* Death on the Nile, *968;* Gaslight (1944), *979;* Greatest Story Ever Told, The, *533;* Harlow, *536;* Harvey Girls, The, *922;* Lady Vanishes, The (1979), *990;* Lawless Street, A, *1127;* Little Gloria...Happy at Last, *576;* Long Hot Summer, The (1958), *578;* Manchurian Candidate, The, *995;* Mirror Crack'd, The, *996;* National Velvet, *190;* Picture of Dorian Gray, The, *875;* Pirates of Penzance, The, *935;* Private Affairs of Bel Ami, The, *628;* Reluctant Debutante, The, *365;* Samson and Delilah (1949), *648;* Something for Everyone, *662;* State of the Union, *666;* Sweeney Todd, *943;* Three Musketeers, The (1948), *128;* World of Henry Orient, The, *414*
Lansing, Joi: Atomic Submarine, The, *1037;* Big Foot, *813;* Brave One, The, *152;* Hillbillys in a Haunted House, *297;* Hole in the Head, A, *298*
Lansing, Robert: Bittersweet Love, *462;* Blade Rider, *1099;* Empire of the Ants, *1049;* Equalizer, The: "Memories of Manon", *44;* 4D Man, *1053;* Grissom Gang, The, *534;* Island Claws, *857;* Life on the Mississippi, *574;* Namu, the Killer Whale, *190;* Nest, The (1988), *868;* S.H.E., *110;* Scalpel, *883;* Talion, *1154*
Lantz, Walter: Fantasy Film Worlds of George Pal, The, *424*
Lanvin, Gerard: Choice of Arms, A, *724*
Lanyer, Charles: Stepfather, The, *1020*
Lanza, Mario: Because You're Mine, *908;* For the First Time, *918;* Great Caruso, The, *920;* Seven Hills of Rome, The, *939;* That Midnight Kiss, *944;* Toast of New Orleans, *946*
LaPaglia, Anthony: Betsy's Wedding, *236;* Black Magic (1992), *955;* Criminal Justice, *491;* Custodian, The, *31;* He Said, She Said, *294;* Innocent Blood, *856;* Keeper of the City, *562;* Mortal Sins (1990), *997;* Nitti: The Enforcer, *91;* One Good Cop, *613;* So I Married an Axe Murderer, *382;* 29th Street, *401;* Whispers in the Dark, *1031*
Lapensee, Francine: Demon Wind, *832*
LaPlante, Laura: Cat and the Canary, The (1927), *960*
Lapotaire, Jane: Dark Angel, The, *966;* Eureka, *511;* Lady Jane, *568;* Spirit of the Dead, *889*
Larch, John: Miracle of the White Stallions, *187;* Play Misty for Me, *1006;* Santee, *1147*
Larcher, Taylor: Avenging, The, *1095*
Largo, Diana: Battle of the Commandos, *10*
Lario, Veronica: Sotto Sotto, *788*
Larive, Leon: Children of Paradise, The, *723*
Larkin, Mary: Psychomania, *877*
LaRosa, Julius: Mr. Mike's Mondo Video, *334*
Larquey, Pierre: Le Corbeau, *757*
Larroquette, John: Blind Date (1987), *241;* Convicted, *488;* Madhouse (1990), *326;* Second Sight, *374;* Stripes, *387*
Larsen, Annabelle: Alligator Eyes, *951*
Larsen, Ham: Adventures of the Wilderness Family, *144;* Mountain Family Robinson, *189;* Wilderness Family, Part 2, The, *217*
Larsen, Keith: Flat Top, *50;* Whitewater Sam, *217;* Women of the Prehistoric Planet, *1090*
Larson, Bobby: Leather Burners, The, *1128*
Larson, Christine: Well, The, *698*
Larson, Darrell: City Limits, *1041;* Danielle Steele's "Fine Things", *495;* Little Red Riding Hood, *183;* Mike's Murder, *594;* Miracle of the Heart, *595;* Uforia, *402*
Larson, Eric: Demon Wind, *832;* '68, *659*
Larson, Jack: TV's Best Adventures of Superman, *1085*
Larsson, Anna-Lotta: Polar Bear King, The, *1071*
Larsson, Dana: Music School, The, *601*
LaRue, Jack: Christopher Strong, *482;* Dancing Pirate, *913;* Dangerous Passage, *32;* Farewell to Arms, A, *514;* Gangs, Inc., *54;* Go West, Young Man, *287;* In Old Caliente, *1122;* Kennel Murder Case, The, *988;* Law Rides Again, The, *1127;* Ride the Man Down, *1143;* Road to Utopia, *369;* Santa Fe Uprising, *1147;* To the Last Man, *1157*
LaRue, Lash: Black Lash, *1099;* Border Feud, *1100;* Caravan Trail, *1103;* Cheyenne Takes Over, *1104;* Dark Power, The, *829;* Ghost Town Renegades, *1115;* King of the Bullwhip, *1125;* Law of the Lash, *1127;* Return of the Lash, *1142;* Stage to Mesa City, *1152;* Stagecoach (1986), *1152;* Thundering Herd, *1157;* Wild West (1946), *1164*
Laser, Dieter: Man Inside, The (1990), *587*
Laskey, Kathleen: Lethal Lolita—Amy Fisher: My Story, *573*
Laskin, Michael: Personals, The, *357*
Lass, Barbara: Werewolf in a Girl's Dormitory, *902*
Lassander, Dagmar: Dandelions, *727;* Hatchet for the Honeymoon, *848*
Lasser, Louise: Bananas, *232;* Blood Rage, *815;* Crimewave, *260;* Everything You Always Wanted to Know About Sex but Were Afraid to Ask, *273;* For Ladies Only, *519;* Frankenhooker, *842;* Mary Hartman, Mary Hartman (TV Series), *329;* Night We Never Met, The, *345;* Rude Awakening (1989), *371;* Sing, *939;* Slither, *381*
Lassick, Sidney: Cool As Ice, *488;* Deep Cover (1992), *36;* Further Adventures of Tennessee Buck, The, *53;* Out on Bail, *96;* Silent Madness, *886;* Sonny Boy, *889;* Unseen, The, *899*
Lassie: Magic of Lassie, The, *185*
Laster, Debbie: Nightmare Weekend, *871*
Latell, Lyle: Dick Tracy versus Cueball, *38;* Dick Tracy's Dilemma, *38*
Latham, Louise: Crazy from the Heart, *490;* Love Field, *581;* Mass Appeal, *590;* Paradise (1991), *618;* Pray TV (1982), *626;* White Lightning, *139;* Wilbur and Orville: The First to Fly, *217*
Latimore, Frank: Black Magic (1949), *462;* Shock (1946), *885;* 13 Rue Madeleine, *127*
Lattanzi, Matt: Blueberry Hill, *465;* Catch Me if You Can, *24;* Diving In, *502;* My Tutor, *341;* Rich and Famous, *639*
Lauck, Charles: So This Is Washington, *382*
Lauck, Chester: Dreaming Out Loud, *269;* Two Weeks to Live, *402*
Lauer, Andrew: Never on Tuesday, *604*
Laughlin, John: Crimes of Passion, *491;* Hills Have Eyes, The: Part Two, *850;* Midnight Crossing, *84;* Space Rage, *1078*
Laughlin, Tom: Billy Jack, *13;* Born Losers, *17;* Tall Story, *391*
Laughton, Charles: Abbott and Costello Meet Captain Kidd, *221;* Advise and Consent, *442;* Arch of Triumph, *450;* Barretts of Wimpole Street, The, *456;* Beachcomber, The, *457;* Canterville Ghost, The (1944), *155;* Captain Kidd, *23;* Epic That Never Was, The, *423;* Forever and a Day, *520;* Hobson's Choice (1954), *298;* Hunchback of Notre Dame, The (1939), *854;* If I Had a Million, *304;* Island of Lost Souls, *857;* Jamaica Inn, *556;* Les Miserables (1935), *573;* Man in the

Eiffel Tower, The, *995;* Mutiny on the Bounty (1935), *88;* Paradine Case, The, *1004;* Private Life of Henry the Eighth, The, *628;* Rembrandt, *638;* Ruggles of Red Gap, *371;* Salome (1953), *647;* Sidewalks of London, *657;* Spartacus, *119;* They Knew What They Wanted, *681;* This Land Is Mine, *682;* Tuttles of Tahiti, The, *400;* Witness for the Prosecution (1957), *1032*

Lauper, Cyndi: Life with Mikey, *318;* Vibes, *1087*

Laurance, Mitchell: Best of Not Necessarily the News, The, *236;* Stepfather II, *890*

Laure, Carole: Get Out Your Handkerchiefs, *740;* Surrogate, The, *674;* Sweet Country, *674;* Sweet Movie, *792*

Laure, Odette: Daddy Nostalgia, *727*

Laurel, Stan: Air Raid Wardens, *223;* Atoll K (Utopia), *229;* Block-Heads, *241;* Bohemian Girl, The, *243;* Bonnie Scotland, *243;* Bullfighters, The, *247;* Chump at Oxford, A, *255;* Days of Thrills and Laughter, *262;* Devil's Brother, The, *914;* Flying Deuces, *278;* Golden Age of Comedy, The, *288;* Great Guns, *289;* Hollywood Party, *299;* Laurel and Hardy: At Work, *316;* Laurel and Hardy Classics, Volume 1, *316;* Laurel and Hardy Classics, Volume 2, *316;* Laurel and Hardy Classics, Volume 3, *316;* Laurel and Hardy Classics, Volume 4, *316;* Laurel and Hardy Classics, Volume 5, *316;* Laurel and Hardy Classics, Volume 6, *316;* Laurel and Hardy Classics, Volume 7, *316;* Laurel and Hardy Classics, Volume 8, *316;* Laurel and Hardy Classics, Volume 9, *316;* Laurel and Hardy on the Lam, *317;* Laurel and Hardy's Laughing 20s, *317;* March of the Wooden Soldiers, *329;* MGM's The Big Parade of Comedy, *331;* Movie Struck (a.k.a. Pick a Star), *338;* Nothing But Trouble (1944), *347;* Our Relations, *351;* Pack Up Your Troubles, *352;* Pardon Us, *354;* Saps at Sea, *372;* Sons of the Desert, *383;* Swiss Miss, *390;* TV Classics: Laurel & Hardy, *401;* Way Out West, *406;* When Comedy Was King, *409*

Lauren, Dixie: 10 Violent Women, *126*

Lauren, Rod: Crawling Hand, The, *825*

Lauren, Veronica: Homeward Bound: The Incredible Journey, *175*

Laurence, Ashley: Hellbound: Hellraiser II, *849;* Hellraiser, *850;* Hellraiser 3: Hell On Earth, *850;* One Last Run, *613*

Laurenson, James: House in the Hills, A, *984;* Rude Awakening (1982), *881*

Laurent, Jacqueline: Le Jour Se Leve (Daybreak) (1939), *757*

Laurette, Charles: Fraternity Demon, *280*

Lauria, Dan: Great Los Angeles Earthquake, The, *532;* In the Line of Duty: Ambush in Waco, *66;* Stakeout, *119*

Laurie, Hugh: Black Adder III (TV Series), *240;* Jeeves and Wooster (TV Series), *309;* Peter's Friends, *621*

Laurie, Piper: Appointment with Death, *953;* Boss' Son, The, *467;* Carrie (1976), *821;* Children of a Lesser God, *480;* Dangerous Mission, *966;* Days of Wine and Roses, The (Television), *497;* Distortions, *834;* Dream a Little Dream, *269;* Francis Goes to the Races, *280;* Hustler, The, *547;* Macbeth (1981), *584;* Mae West, *585;* Other People's Money, *351;* Return to Oz, *199;* Rich in Love, *640;* Rising Son, *641;* Ruby (1977), *881;* Skag, *659;* Son of Ali Baba, *118;* Tiger Warsaw, *683;* Tim, *684;* Trauma, *897;* Twin Peaks (Movie), *1027;* Twin Peaks (TV Series), *1027;* Until They Sail, *692;* Wrestling Ernest Hemingway, *707*

Laurin, Marie: Creature, *1043;* Talking Walls, *391*

Lauter, Ed: Big Score, The, *12;* Breakheart Pass, *1101;* Chicken Chronicles, The, *254;* Death Hunt, *35;* Death Wish III, *36;* Eureka, *511;* Extreme Justice, *512;* Family Plot, *975;* Gleaming the Cube, *55;* Jericho Mile, The, *557;* Last American Hero, The, *75;* Last Days of Patton, The, *569;* Longest Yard, The, *78;* Magic, *994;* Murder So Sweet, *601;* Raw Deal, *103;* Real Genius, *365;* Revenge of the Nerds II: Nerds in Paradise, *367;* Rocketeer, The, *108;* Stephen King's Golden Years (TV Series), *1080;* 3:15—The Moment of Truth, *128;* Timerider, *130;* Under Investigation, *1028;* Youngblood, *709;* Yuri Nosenko, KGB, *709*

Lauter, Harry: Hellcats of the Navy, *60;* Jungle Patrol, *69;* Trader Tom of the China Seas, *131*

Lauterbach, Heiner: Men..., *767;* Wiz Kid, The, *413*

Lavant, Denis: Lovers on the Bridge, *762*

Lavender, Ian: Adventures of a Private Eye, *222*

Laverick, June: Mania, *862*

Lavi, Daliah: Candide, *722;* Catlow, *1104;* Spy with a Cold Nose, The, *385;* Ten Little Indians (1966), *1023;* Two Weeks in Another Town, *690*

Lavia, Gabriele: Deep Red (1975), *832;* Inferno, *856;* Revenge of the Dead, *881*

Lavin, Linda: See You in the Morning, *651*

Law, Barbara: Bedroom Eyes, *954*

Law, John Phillip: African Rage, *3;* Alienator, *1035;* Attack Force Z, *7;* Barbarella, *1038;* Cold Heat, *28;* Danger: Diabolik, *1044;* Death Rides a Horse, *1108;* Golden Voyage of Sinbad, The, *1054;* Last Movie, The, *570;* Love Machine, The, *581;* Moon in Scorpio, *599;* Night Train to Terror, *870;* Tarzan the Ape Man (1981), *125;* Tin Man, *684*

Law, Phyllida: Much Ado About Nothing, *338;* Peter's Friends, *621*

Law, Tom: Shallow Grave, *114*

Lawford, Christopher: Run, *109*

Lawford, Peter: Advise and Consent, *442;* April Fools, The, *228;* Buono Sera, Mrs. Campbell, *247;* Dead Ringer, *967;* Easter Parade, *915;* Exodus, *512;* Fantasy Island, *1050;* Good News, *920;* Harlow, *536;* It Happened in Brooklyn, *925;* It Should Happen to You, *308;* Julia Misbehaves, *311;* Little Women (1949), *577;* Man Called Adam, A, *586;* Mrs. Parkington, *598;* Never So Few, *89;* Ocean's Eleven, *93;* On an Island with You, *933;* Picture of Dorian Gray, The, *875;* Royal Wedding, *938;* Sky's the Limit, The, *940;* Son of Lassie, *206;* They Only Kill Their Masters, *1024;* TV Classics: Milton Berle, *401;* Two Sisters from Boston, *947*

Lawrence, Adam: Drive-In Massacre, *838*

Lawrence, Barbara: Kronos, *1061;* Letter to Three Wives, A, *573;* Star, The, *665;* Street with No Name, *1021;* Unfaithfully Yours (1948), *403*

Lawrence, Bruno: Bridge to Nowhere, *469;* Efficiency Expert, The, *508;* Grievous Bodily Harm, *533;* Heart of the Stag, *538;* Quiet Earth, The, *1073;* Rainbow Warrior, *1008;* Rikki and Pete, *368;* Smash Palace, *660;* Treasure of the Yankee Zephyr, *132;* UTU, *134*

Lawrence, Carol: New Faces, *933;* Shattered Image, *1014;* Summer of Fear, *891*

Lawrence, Cary: Canvas, *959*

Lawrence, Gail: Maniac (1980), *862*

Lawrence, Gertrude: Rembrandt, *638*

Lawrence, Jim: High Country, The, *61*

Lawrence, Joey: Chains of Gold, *478;* Pulse, *877*

Lawrence, Josie: Enchanted April, *271*

Lawrence, Marc: Asphalt Jungle, The, *953;* Call of the Canyon, *1103;* Charlie Chan at the Wax Museum, *961;* Cloak and Dagger (1946), *962;* Dillinger (1945), *39;* Don't Fence Me In, *1110;* I Am the Law, *547;* King of Kong Island, *859;* Lady Scarface, *74;* Night Train to Terror, *870;* Pigs, *875;* Revenge of the Pink Panther, The, *367;* Ruby (1991), *644;* Sundown (1941), *673;* Super Fuzz, *1081*

Lawrence, Martin: Boomerang, *244;* House Party 2, *923;* Talkin' Dirty After Dark, *391*

Lawrence, Matthew: Mrs. Doubtfire, *334;* Pulse, *877*

Lawrence, Michael: Came a Hot Friday, *22*

Lawrence, Ronald William: Blackbelt 2: Fatal Force, *14*

Lawrence, Rosina: Charlie Chan's Secret, *961;* General Spanky, *169*

Lawrence, Scott: Laurel Avenue, *571;* Sometimes Aunt Martha Does Dreadful Things, *888*

Lawrence, Steve: Alice Through the Looking Glass (1985), *145;* Express to Terror, *974*

Lawrence, Vicki: Carol Burnett's My Personal Best, *251*

Laws, Barry: Shadow Play, *885*

Lawson, Adam: Apex, *1036*

Lawson, Charles: Four Days in July, *521*

Lawson, Leigh: Charlie Boy, *823;* Fire and Sword, *1051;* Love Among the Ruins, *322*
Lawson, Linda: Night Tide, *606*
Lawson, Priscilla: Flash Gordon: Rocketship (a.k.a. Spaceship to the Unknown; Perils from Planet Mongo), *1052*
Lawson, Wilfrid: Danny Boy (1941), *495;* Night Has Eyes, The, *1001;* Pygmalion, *363;* Wrong Box, The, *414*
Lawton, Frank: Cavalcade, *477;* David Copperfield, *496;* Devil Doll, The (1936), *833;* Invisible Ray, The, *857;* Night to Remember, A (1958), *606;* Winslow Boy, The, *704*
Laxdal, Jon: Polar Bear King, The, *1071*
Laydu, Claude: Diary of a Country Priest, *730*
Layng, Lissa: Say Yes, *373*
Layton, Marcia: Cthulhu Mansion, *827*
Lazard, Justin: Dead Center, *967*
Lazarev, Eugene: Ice Runner, *65*
Lazenby, George: Eyes of the Beholder, *974;* Gettysburg, *526;* Happy Anniversary 007: 25 Years of James Bond, *425;* Never Too Young to Die, *90;* On Her Majesty's Secret Service, *94;* Return of the Man from U.N.C.L.E., The, *105;* Saint Jack, *646*
Lazure, Gabrielle: Joshua Then and Now, *311*
Le Brock, Gene: Fortress of Amerikkka, *51;* Metamorphosis, *864*
Le Fleur, Art: Trancers, *1085*
Le, Hiep Thi: Heaven and Earth (1993), *539*
Le Mesurier, John: Brideshead Revisited, *469;* Brothers In Law, *246;* Married Man, A, *589*
Le Roy, Eddie: No Time for Sergeants (Television), *608*
le Vigan, Robert: Golgotha, *741*
Lea, Ron: Neighbor, The, *1000*
Leach, Rosemary: D.P., *493;* Hawk, The, *982;* Room with a View, A, *644;* That'll Be the Day, *944;* Turtle Diary, *400*
Leachman, Cloris: Beverly Hillbillies, The, *237;* Charley and the Angel, *157;* Crazy Mama, *30;* Daisy Miller, *493;* Danielle Steele's "Fine Things", *495;* Dillinger (1973), *39;* Dixie Changing Habits, *265;* Fade to Black (1993), *974;* Foolin' Around, *278;* Haunts of the Very Rich, *1055;* Herbie Goes Bananas, *174;* High Anxiety, *297;* History of the World, Part One, The, *298;* Kiss Me Deadly, *989;* Last Picture Show, The, *570;* Love Hurts, *323;* Lovers and Other Strangers, *323;* Muppet Movie, The, *189;* My Boyfriend's Back, *339;* My Little Pony: The Movie, *190;* North Avenue Irregulars, The, *191;* Oldest Living Graduate, The, *611;* Prancer, *197;* Run Stranger Run, *882;* S.O.S. Titanic, *646;* Scavenger Hunt, *373;* Shadow Play, *885;* Someone I Touched, *662;* Steagle, The, *386;* Texasville, *680;* Thursday's Game, *683;* Walk Like a Man, *405;* Willa, *703;* Young Frankenstein, *416*
Leah, Leslie: Fix, The, *50*
Leake, Damien: Killing Floor, The, *563*
Learned, Michael: All My Sons, *444;* Dragon: The Bruce Lee Story, *42;* Roots—The Gift, *644;* Thanksgiving Story, The, *210;* Touched by Love, *686*
Leary, Denis: Gunmen, *58;* Judgment Night, *69;* Ref, The, *365;* Sandlot, The, *201;* Who's the Man?, *411*
Leary, Timothy: Hold Me, Thrill Me, Kiss Me, *298;* Roadside Prophets, *641*
Lease, Rex: Clutching Hand, The, *27;* Cowboy and the Bandit, *1106;* Cyclone in the Saddle, *1107;* Helldorado (1946), *1120;* Idaho, *1122;* In Old Cheyenne, *1123;* Monster Walks, The, *866;* Yellow Rose of Texas, *1165*
Léaud, Jean-Pierre: Day for Night, *728;* 400 Blows, The, *738;* Last Tango in Paris, *570;* Le Départ, *757;* Le Gai Savior (The Joy of Knowledge), *757;* Love on the Run (1979), *762;* Masculine Feminine, *766;* Oldest Profession, The, *773;* Pierrot Le Fou, *777;* Pigsty, *777;* Stolen Kisses, *789;* Two English Girls, *797;* Weekend, *803*
Lebedeff, Ivan: Goin' to Town, *287*
LeBrock, Kelly: Betrayal of the Dove, *954;* Hard to Kill, *59;* Weird Science, *407;* Woman in Red, The, *413*
Leclerc, Ginette: Baker's Wife, The (1938), *715;* Man from Nowhere, The, *765*
Leclerc, Jean: Blown Away (1992), *957;* Whispers, *1031*
Led Zeppelin: Song Remains the Same, The, *435*
Lederer, Francis: Bridge of San Luis Rey, The, *469;* Lisbon, *77;* One Rainy Afternoon, *350;* Return of Dracula, *880;* Romance in Manhattan, *643;* Woman of Distinction, A, *413*
Ledingham, David: Final Judgment, *977*
Ledoux, Fernand: La Bête Humaine, *753;* Stormy Waters, *789*
Leduc, Richard: Nous N'Irons Plus Au Bois, *772*
Leduke, Harrison: Laser Moon, *990*
Lee, Anna: Bedlam, *812;* Commandos Strike at Dawn, *28;* Ghost and Mrs. Muir, The, *285;* Hangmen Also Die, *536;* King Solomon's Mines (1937), *72;* Man Who Lived Again, The, *862;* Prize, The, *629;* Seven Sinners, *113*
Lee, Bernard: Brain, The (1965), *1040;* Detective, The (1954), *970;* Dr. No, *40;* Fallen Idol, The, *513;* Frankenstein and the Monster from Hell, *842;* Key, The, *563;* Last Holiday, *569;* Long Ago Tomorrow, *578;* Man with the Golden Gun, The, *81;* Pursuit of the Graf Spee, *101;* Rhodes of Africa, *639;* Spy Who Came in from the Cold, The, *664;* Spy Who Loved Me, The, *119;* Whistle Down the Wind, *216;* You Only Live Twice, *141*
Lee, Brandon: Bruce Lee: Curse of the Dragon, *420;* Crow, The, *827;* Kung Fu—The Movie, *73;* Laser Mission, *75;* Rapid Fire, *103;* Showdown in Little Tokyo, *115*
Lee, Britton: Ironheart, *67*
Lee, Bruce: Bruce Lee: Curse of the Dragon, *420;* Chinese Connection, The, *25;* Enter the Dragon, *44;* Fists of Fury, *49;* Game of Death, *54;* Green Hornet, The (TV Series), *58;* Marlowe, *995;* Return of the Dragon, *105*
Lee, Canada: Cry, the Beloved Country, *492;* Lifeboat, *992*
Lee, Carl: Gordon's War, *57;* Superfly, *122*
Lee, Chen: Shangai Joe, *1148*
Lee, Christian: Invasion Earth: The Aliens Are Here, *856*
Lee, Christopher: Against All Odds (Kiss and Kill, Blood of Fu Manchu), *808;* Airport '77, *443;* Albino, *808;* Bear Island, *954;* Boy Who Left Home to Find Out About the Shivers, The, *152;* Captain America II: Death Too Soon, *22;* Caravans, *475;* Castle of Fu Manchu, *822;* Castle of the Living Dead, *822;* Circle of Iron, *26;* Circus of Fear, *824;* Corridors of Blood, *825;* Count Dracula, *825;* Creeping Flesh, The, *826;* Crimson Pirate, The, *30;* Curse III: Blood Sacrifice, *827;* Curse of Frankenstein, The, *828;* Dark Places, *829;* Death Train, *968;* Desperate Moves, *264;* Devil's Undead, The, *834;* Dr. Terror's House of Horrors, *836;* Double Vision, *972;* Dracula and Son, *837;* Dracula Has Risen from the Grave, *837;* End of the World, *1049;* Eye for an Eye, *46;* Far Pavilions, The, *514;* Five Golden Dragons, *50;* Four Musketeers, The, *52;* Girl, The, *527;* Goliath Awaits, *56;* Gorgon, The, *847;* Gremlins 2: The New Batch, *1055;* Hannie Caulder, *1119;* Hercules in the Haunted World, *61;* Hollywood Meatcleaver Massacre, *850;* Horror Express, *851;* Horror Hotel, *851;* Horror of Dracula, *851;* Hound of the Baskervilles, The (1959), *983;* House of the Long Shadows, *853;* House That Dripped Blood, The, *853;* Howling II...Your Sister Is a Werewolf, *854;* Jocks, *310;* Journey of Honor, *69;* Julius Caesar (1970), *561;* Keeper, The, *859;* Killer Force, *71;* Land of Faraway, The, *180;* Magic Christian, The, *326;* Man with the Golden Gun, The, *81;* Moulin Rouge, *600;* Mummy, The (1959), *866;* Murder Story, *999;* 1941, *345;* Oblong Box, The, *872;* Private Life of Sherlock Holmes, The, *1008;* Pursuit of the Graf Spee, *101;* Return from Witch Mountain, *199;* Return of Captain Invincible, The, *366;* Return of the Musketeers, *106;* Rosebud Beach Hotel, The, *370;* Salamander, The, *111;* Satanic Rites of Dracula, The, *882;* Scars of Dracula, *883;* Scott of the Antarctic, *650;* Scream and Scream Again, *883;* Scream of Fear, *1013;* Serial, *376;* Shaka Zulu, *654;* Sherlock Holmes and the Deadly Necklace, *1015;* Sherlock Holmes and the Incident at Victoria Falls, *1015;* Sherlock Holmes and the Leading Lady, *1015;* Skull, The, *887;* Starship Invasions, *1080;* Tale of Two Cities (1967), *676;* Taste the Blood of Dracula, *892;* Terror of the Tongs, The, *126;* Theatre of Death, *894;* To the Devil, a Daughter, *896;*

Torture Chamber of Dr. Sadism, The, *896;* Treasure Island (1990), *214;* Virgin of Nuremberg, *901;* Wicker Man, The, *903*
Lee, Danny: City War, *724;* Killer, The, *751*
Lee, Dexter: Sleepwalker, *1017*
Lee, Dorothy: Half-Shot at Sunrise, *292;* Hips, Hips, Hooray, *297;* Hook, Line and Sinker, *300*
Lee, Elizabeth: Something Weird, *888*
Lee, Glen: Dead Aim (1973), *1108*
Lee, Gypsy Rose: My Lucky Star, *932;* Stripper, The (1963), *671*
Lee, Hey Young: Field of Honor (1986), *47*
Lee, Janis: Blink of an Eye, *15*
Lee, Jason Scott: Dragon: The Bruce Lee Story, *42;* Map of the Human Heart, *588*
Lee, Joanna: Brain Eaters, The, *1040*
Lee, Joie: Fathers & Sons, *515;* Mo' Better Blues, *931*
Lee, Jonna: Making the Grade, *327*
Lee, Julian: My Samurai, *88*
Lee, Kaaren: Roadhouse 66, *107*
Lee, Kaiulani: Zelly and Me, *709*
Lee, Lila: Blood and Sand (1922), *464;* Country Gentlemen, *260;* Ex-Mrs. Bradford, The, *974;* Male and Female, *994;* Unholy Three, *1029*
Lee, Linda Emery: Bruce Lee: Curse of the Dragon, *420*
Lee, Margaret: Five for Hell, *50;* Five Golden Dragons, *50*
Lee, Mark: Everlasting Secret Family, The, *511;* Gallipoli, *524*
Lee, Mary: Cowboy and the Senorita, *1106;* Ridin' on a Rainbow, *1144;* Song of Nevada, *1151*
Lee, Melanie: Queen Victoria and the Zombies, *878*
Lee, Michele: Bud and Lou, *471;* Comic, The (1969), *486;* Don Rickles: Buy This Tape You Hockey Puck, *267;* Fatal Image, The, *976;* How to Succeed in Business without Really Trying, *923;* Love Bug, The, *184;* Only with Married Men, *350*
Lee, Peggy: Ladies Sing the Blues, The, *428;* Mr. Music, *931;* Pete Kelly's Blues, *935*
Lee, Pinky: In Old Amarillo, *1122;* Lady of Burlesque, *74*
Lee, Porky: Little Rascals, The, *183*
Lee, Ruta: First and Ten, *277;* Funny Face, *918*
Lee, Sheryl: BackBeat, *907;* Love, Lies and Murder, *994;* Red Shoe Diaries 4: Auto Erotica, *637;* Twin Peaks: Fire Walk with Me, *1028*
Lee, Sondra: Peter Pan (1960), *194*
Lee, Spike: Do the Right Thing, *502;* Jungle Fever, *561;* Malcolm X, *586;* Mo' Better Blues, *931;* School Daze, *373;* She's Gotta Have It, *377*
Lee, Stan: Comic Book Confidential, *421*
Lee, Stephen: Dolls, *836*
Leeder, Stephen: Fatal Bond, *975*
Leeds, Andrea: Goldwyn Follies, The, *920;* Letter of Introduction, *573;* Real Glory, The, *103;* They Shall Have Music, *944*
Leeds, Elissa: Lights, Camera, Action, Love, *575*
Leeds, Lila: Show-Off, The, *378*
Leeds, Marcie: Wheels of Terror, *138*
Leegant, Dan: Signal 7, *657*
Leeman, Jacolyn: Lady Avenger, *74*
LeFevre, Adam: Mr. Wonderful, *597;* Ref, The, *365;* Return of the Secaucus 7, *366*
Lefévre, René: Crime of Monsieur Lange, The, *727;* Le Million, *758;* Sois Belle Et Tais-Toi (Just Another Pretty Face), *787*
Lefkowitz, John: Hurry Up or I'll Be 30, *303*
LeGallienne, Eva: Devil's Disciple, The, *264;* Resurrection, *638*
LeGault, Lance: Kidnapped (1988), *71;* Pioneer Woman, *1138*
Legendary Wid, The: Truly Tasteless Jokes, *400*
Legitimus, Darling: Sugarcane Alley, *791*
Legrand, Michel: Cleo from 5 to 7, *725*
LeGros, James: Bad Girls (1994), *1095;* Guncrazy (1992), *535;* My New Gun, *341;* Nervous Ticks, *343;* Phantasm II, *874*
Leguizamo, John: Carlito's Way, *23;* Hangin' with the Homeboys, *292;* Super Mario Brothers, The, *208;* Whispers in the Dark, *1031*
Lehman, Lillian: Mardi Gras for the Devil, *863*
Lehman, Manfred: Operation 'Nam, *95*
Lehmann, Beatrix: Candles at Nine, *820*
Lehne, Frederic: Coward of the County, *490;* Romeo and Juliet (1983), *643;* This Gun for Hire (1991), *128*
Lehne, Fredric: Dream Lover (1994), *972*
Lehne, John: American Hot Wax, *906;* Bound for Glory, *467*
Lehoczky, Bela: Hold Me, Thrill Me, Kiss Me, *298*
Lehr, Wendy: Marvelous Land of Oz, The, *185*
Lei, Huang: Life on a String, *760*
Lei, Lao Sheng: Story of Qiu Ju, The, *789*
Leibman, Ron: Door to Door, *267;* Hot Rock, The, *983;* Norma Rae, *608;* Phar Lap, *621;* Rhinestone, *367;* Romantic Comedy, *370;* Seven Hours to Judgment, *113;* Up the Academy, *403;* Where's Poppa?, *409;* Zorro, the Gay Blade, *417*
Leifert, Don: Alien Factor, The, *1035;* Fiend, *841*
Leigh, Barbara: Boss, *1101;* Student Nurses, The, *671*
Leigh, Janet: Bye Bye Birdie, *910;* Fog, The, *842;* Harper, *981;* Hills of Home, *174;* Holiday Affair, *542;* Houdini, *544;* It's a Big Country, *308;* Little Women (1949), *577;* Manchurian Candidate, The, *995;* My Sister Eileen, *932;* Naked Spur, The, *1135;* Perfect Furlough, *356;* Pete Kelly's Blues, *935;* Prince Valiant, *100;* Psycho, *877;* Scaramouche, *111;* That Forsyte Woman, *680;* Touch of Evil, *1026;* Two Tickets to Broadway, *947;* Vikings, The, *135;* Words and Music, *948*
Leigh, Jennifer Jason: Angel City, *448;* Backdraft, *8;* Best Little Girl in the World, The, *459;* Big Picture, The, *238;* Buried Alive (1990), *959;* Crooked Hearts, *491;* Eyes of a Stranger, *840;* Fast Times at Ridgemont High, *274;* Flesh and Blood, *50;* Grandview, U.S.A., *531;* Heart of Midnight, *982;* Hitcher, The, *850;* Hudsucker Proxy, The, *303;* Killing of Randy Webster, The, *564;* Last Exit to Brooklyn, *569;* Men's Club, The, *593;* Miami Blues, *84;* Rush, *645;* Short Cuts, *657;* Single White Female, *1016;* Sister, Sister, *886;* Undercover, *134*
Leigh, Spencer: Caravaggio, *475;* Last of England, The, *570*
Leigh, Steven Vincent: China White, *25;* Deadly Bet, *34*
Leigh, Suzanna: Lust for a Vampire, *861;* Paradise Hawaiian Style, *935*
Leigh, Tara: On the Make, *612*
Leigh, Vivien: Anna Karenina (1947), *449;* Caesar and Cleopatra, *473;* Dark Journey, *966;* Fire over England, *49;* Gone with the Wind, *530;* Roman Spring of Mrs. Stone, The, *643;* Ship of Fools, *656;* Sidewalks of London, *657;* Storm in a Teacup, *387;* Streetcar Named Desire, A, *671;* That Hamilton Woman, *680;* Waterloo Bridge, *697*
Leigh-Hunt, Barbara: Frenzy, *979;* Paper Mask, *1004*
Leighton, Lillian: Peck's Bad Boy, *194;* Tumbleweeds, *1159*
Leighton, Margaret: Best Man, The, *459;* Carrington, V. C., *476;* Elusive Pimpernel, The, *509;* From Beyond the Grave, *844;* Lady Caroline Lamb, *567;* Madwoman of Chaillot, The, *585;* Waltz of the Toreadors, *405;* Winslow Boy, The, *704;* X, Y and Zee, *707*
Leipnitz, Harold: Hell Hounds of Alaska, *1119*
Leipzig, Dina: Blue Hour, The, *719*
Leisure, David: You Can't Hurry Love, *415*
Leitch, David: Death Warmed Up, *831*
Leitch, Donovan: And God Created Woman (1987), *447;* Blob, The (1988), *814;* Cutting Class, *828;* Dark Horse, *161*
Leith, Shayne: Warriors From Hell, *137*
Leith, Virginia: Brain That Wouldn't Die, The, *1040*
Lelouch, Marie-Sophie: Bandits (1987), *715*
Lemaire, Philippe: Blood Rose, *816;* Cartouche, *722*
LeMat, Paul: Aloha, Bobby and Rose, *4;* American Graffiti, *226;* Burning Bed, The, *472;* Caroline at Midnight, *960;* Citizen's Band, *255;* Death Valley, *831;* Easy Wheels, *270;*

irehouse (1972), *49;* Grave Secrets, *847;* Hanoi Hilton, The, *536;* Into the Homeland, *67;* Jimmy the Kid, *178;* Melvin and Ioward, *331;* More American Graffiti, *599;* Night They Saved Christmas, The, *191;* On Wings of Eagles, *94;* P.K. & the Kid, *517;* Private Investigations, *101;* Puppet Master, The, *878;* Strange Invaders, *1080;* Woman with a Past, *705*

emay, Jeannine: Don't Mess with My Sister, *504*

eMay, John D.: Jason Goes to Hell: The Final Friday, *858*

embeck, Harvey: Beach Blanket Bingo, *908;* Beach Party, *908;* Sgt. Bilko (TV Series), *376*

embeck, Michael: Gorp, *289;* In-Laws, The, *305;* On the Right Track, *192*

emmon, Chris: Corporate Affairs, *259;* Firehead, *49;* Going Undercover, *288;* Happy Hooker Goes Hollywood, The, *293;* ena's Holiday, *991;* That's Life, *393;* Thunder in Paradise, *129;* Weekend Warriors, *407*

emmon, Jack: Airport '77, *443;* American Film Institute Life Achievement Awards, The, *418;* Apartment, The, *228;* April Fools, The, *228;* Avanti!, *230;* Bell, Book and Candle, *234;* Buddy, Buddy, *247;* China Syndrome, The, *961;* Dad, *493;* Days of Wine and Roses, *496;* Ernie Kovacs: Television's Original Genius, *272;* Fire Down Below, *517;* For Richer, for Poorer, *279;* Fortune Cookie, The, *279;* Front Page, The (1974), *281;* Glengarry Glen Ross, *528;* Good Neighbor Sam, *288;* Great Race, The, *290;* Grumpy Old Men, *291;* How to Murder your Wife, *303;* Irma La Douce, *307;* It Should Happen to You, *308;* JFK, *558;* Life in the Theater, A, *574;* Long Day's Journey into Night (1987), *578;* Luv, *324;* Macaroni, *325;* Mass Appeal, *590;* Missing, *596;* Mr. Roberts, *334;* Murder of Mary Phagan, The, *600;* My Sister Eileen, *932;* Odd Couple, The, *348;* Out of Towners, The, *352;* Prisoner of Second Avenue, The, *361;* Save the Tiger, *648;* Short Cuts, *657;* Some Like It Hot, *382;* That's Life, *393;* Tribute, *688;* Wackiest Ship in the Army, The, *405*

emmons, Kasi: Candyman (1992), *820;* Hard Target, *59*

emole, Lisa: Drive-In, *269*

emon, Genevieve: Sweetie, *675*

enderman, Cliff: American Shaolin: King of the Kickboxers I, *5*

enhart, Lane: Prototype X29A, *1072*

ennix, Harry J.: Five Heartbeats, The, *917;* Guarding Tess, *291*

ennon, John: How I Won the War, *302;* Imagine: John ennon, *427*

ennon, Sean: Michael Jackson Moonwalker, *931*

eno, Jay: American Hot Wax, *906;* Collision Course, *257;* Dave, *262;* Doctor Duck's Super Secret All-Purpose Sauce, *266;* Jay Leno's American Dream, *309*

enoir, Jack: Once in Paris, *612*

enska, Rula: Oh, Alfie, *611;* Robin Hood: The Swords of Wayland, *108*

enya, Lotte: From Russia with Love, *53;* Roman Spring of Mrs. Stone, The, *643;* Semi-Tough, *375;* Threepenny Opera, The, *794*

enz, Kay: Death Wish IV: The Crackdown, *36;* Falling from Grace, *513;* Fast-Walking, *515;* Fear (1988), *976;* Great Scout and Cathouse Thursday, The, *1116;* Hitler's Daughter, *542;* House, *852;* Initiation of Sarah, The, *856;* Moving Violation, *87;* Physical Evidence, *1006;* Prisoners of the Lost Universe, *1072;* Sanctuary of Fear, *1012;* Stripped to Kill, *122;* White ine Fever, *139*

enz, Rick: Scandalous John, *202*

enzey, Margaret: Quest for the Mighty Sword, *1073*

eo, Melissa: Always (1984), *225;* Streetwalkin', *671;* Time of Destiny, A, *684*

eon: Above the Rim, *440;* Cool Runnings, *259;* Five Heartbeats, The, *917*

eonard, Jack E.: Disorderly Orderly, The, *265*

Lu: Blank Check, *151;* Circuitry Man, *1041*

eonard, Queenie: Narrow Margin, The (1952), *89*

eonard, Robert Sean: Age of Innocence, The, *443;* Dead Poets Society, *497;* Married to It, *589;* Mr. and Mrs. Bridge, *596;* Much Ado About Nothing, *338;* My Best Friend Is a Vampire, *339;* Swing Kids, *675*

Leonard, Sheldon: Abbott and Costello Meet the Invisible Man, *221;* Captain Kidd, *23;* Gangster, The, *525;* My Dream Is Yours, *932;* Sinbad the Sailor, *116;* Tortilla Flat, *686*

Leonardi, Marco: Cinema Paradiso, *724;* Like Water for Chocolate, *760*

Leong, Page: White Phantom, *139*

Léotard, Philippe: La Balance, *753;* Tchao Pantin, *793*

Lepage, Gaston: Being at Home with Claude, *716*

Lerner, Michael: Amos & Andrew, *226;* Anguish, *809;* Barton Fink, *232;* Blank Check, *151;* Coast to Coast, *256;* Comrades of Summer, The, *258;* Eight Men Out, *508;* Execution, The, *974;* Framed (1990), *280;* Harlem Nights, *59;* Maniac Cop 2, *863;* National Lampoon's Class Reunion, *342;* Newsies, *933;* No Escape, *1069;* Omen IV: The Awakening, *872;* Outlaw Blues, *352;* Postman Always Rings Twice, The (1981), *1007;* Rita Hayworth: The Love Goddess, *641;* Strange Invaders, *1080;* Threshold, *1083*

LeRoy, Baby: It's a Gift, *308*

Leroy, Philippe: Castle of the Living Dead, *822;* Married Woman, A, *765;* Night Porter, The, *606*

Lesache, Bernadette: Horse of Pride, The, *744*

Leslie, Bethel: Long Day's Journey into Night (1987), *578*

Leslie, Charlotte: Queen Victoria and the Zombies, *878*

Leslie, Joan: Born to Be Bad, *467;* Hard Way, The (1942), *536;* High Sierra, *62;* Hollywood Canteen, *923;* Jubilee Trail, *1124;* Man in the Saddle, *1132;* Rhapsody in Blue, *936;* Sergeant York, *113;* Sky's the Limit, The, *940;* Thank Your Lucky Stars, *944;* This Is the Army, *945;* Yankee Doodle Dandy, *948*

Leslie, Nan: Arizona Ranger, *1095;* Bamboo Saucer (a.k.a. Collision Course), *1038;* Devil Thumbs a Ride, The, *970;* Guns of Hate, *1118;* Rim of the Canyon, *1144*

Lesniak, Emilia: Nine Deaths of the Ninja, *91*

Lesseos, Mimi: Pushed to the Limit, *101*

Lessig, Clarissa: Home of our Own, A, *542*

Lester, Andrea Virginia: Painted Hills, The, *193*

Lester, Bruce: Golden Earrings, *56*

Lester, Jeff: In the Cold of the Night, *986;* Once a Hero, *94*

Lester, Mark: Black Beauty (1971), *151;* Melody, *186;* Oliver, *933;* Prince and the Pauper, The (1978), *197;* Redneck, *104;* Who Slew Auntie Roo?, *903*

Lester, Noble Lee: Sgt. Kabukiman N.Y.P.D., *114*

Lester, Tiny: No Holds Barred, *91*

Lether, Shelli: Born To Run, *18*

Lethin, Lori: Bloody Birthday, *817;* Brotherly Love, *819;* Prey, The, *876;* Return to Horror High, *880*

Letterman, David: Steve Martin Live, *386*

Lettieri, Al: Deadly Trackers, The, *1108;* Don Is Dead, The, *40;* Godfather, The, *529;* McQ, *83;* Mr. Majestyk, *86;* Pulp, *363*

Leung, Tony: Better Tomorrow 3, A: Love And Death In Saigon, *717;* Laser Man, The, *315;* Lover, The, *582;* People's Hero, *777*

Lev, Martin: Bugsy Malone, *155*

Levant, Oscar: American in Paris, An, *906;* Band Wagon, The, *908;* Barkleys of Broadway, The, *908;* Humoresque, *546;* Romance on the High Seas, *937*

Levels, Calvin: Johnny Suede, *311*

Levene, Sam: Action in the North Atlantic, *2;* After the Thin Man, *951;* Babe Ruth Story, The, *453;* Big Street, The, *460;* Crossfire (1947), *964;* Demon (God Told Me To), *1046;* Designing Woman, *263;* Dream of Kings, A, *504;* Gung Ho! (1943), *58;* I Dood It, *924;* Last Embrace, The, *990;* Mad Miss Manton, The, *325;* Purple Heart, The, *630;* Shadow of the Thin Man, *1014;* Shopworn Angel, The, *656;* Sweet Smell of Success, *675;* Three Men on a Horse, *395;* Whistling in Brooklyn, *410*

Leverington, Shelby: Christmas Coal Mine Miracle, The, *159;* Cloak and Dagger (1984), *27*

Levin, Rachel: Gaby, a True Story, *524*

Levine, Anna: Warlock (1988), *901*
Levine, Jean: L.A. Vice, *74*
Levine, Robert: Dominick and Eugene, *503*
Levine, Ted: Betrayed (1988), *954;* Death Train, *968;* Fulfillment, *523;* Last Outlaw, The (1993), *1126;* Love at Large, *322;* Nowhere to Run (1993), *92;* Silence of the Lambs, *1016*
Levis, Carroll: Brass Monkey, The, *958*
Levitt, Steve: Blue Movies, *242;* Hunk, *303*
Levy, Eugene: Armed and Dangerous, *228;* Best of John Candy, The, *236;* Billy Crystal: Don't Get Me Started, *239;* Club Paradise, *256;* Going Berserk, *287;* Last Polka, The, *315;* Speed Zone, *119;* Splash, *384;* Stay Tuned, *385*
Levy, Jeremy: Rich Kids, *640*
Lewis, Al: Car 54, Where Are You?, *250;* Car 54 Where Are You? (TV Series), *250;* Comic Cabby, *258;* Munsters' Revenge, The, *338;* My Grandpa Is a Vampire, *340*
Lewis, Alun: Experience Preferred...But Not Essential, *273*
Lewis, Charlotte: Bare Essentials, *232;* Excessive Force, *45;* Golden Child, The, *56;* Lipstick Camera, *992;* Pirates, *358*
Lewis, Diana: Go West, *287*
Lewis, Fiona: Dr. Phibes Rises Again, *836;* Dracula (1973), *837;* Fury, The, *845;* Innerspace, *1058;* Lisztomania, *928;* Strange Behavior, *890;* Tintorera, *895;* Wanda Nevada, *136*
Lewis, Forrest: Monster of Piedras Blancas, The, *866*
Lewis, Geoffrey: Any Which Way You Can, *228;* Bad Company, *1095;* Bronco Billy, *246;* Catch Me if You Can, *24;* Culpepper Cattle Co., The, *1106;* Dillinger (1973), *39;* Disturbed, *971;* Double Impact, *41;* Every Which Way but Loose, *273;* High Plains Drifter, *1120;* Human Experiments, *64;* Lawnmower Man, The, *1062;* Lust in the Dust, *324;* Macon County Line, *80;* Man without a Face, The, *587;* Matters of the Heart, *590;* My Name Is Nobody, *1135;* National Lampoon's Last Resort, *342;* Night of the Comet, *1068;* Only the Strong, *95;* Pancho Barnes, *617;* Pink Cadillac, *99;* Point of No Return, *99;* Return of a Man Called Horse, The, *1142;* Return of the Man from U.N.C.L.E., The, *105;* Shadow Riders, The, *1148;* Smile, *381;* Stitches, *386;* Tango and Cash, *124;* Thunderbolt and Lightfoot, *129;* Tilt, *396;* White Fang 2: Myth of the White Wolf, *217;* Wind and the Lion, The, *140*
Lewis, George J.: Adventures of Frank and Jesse James, *1092;* Big Sombrero, The, *1098;* G-Men vs. The Black Dragon, *54;* Phantom Rider, *1138;* Sign of Zorro, The, *204;* Zorro's Black Whip, *1166*
Lewis, Gilbert: Gordon's War, *57;* Kid Who Loved Christmas, The, *180;* Touched, *686*
Lewis, Huey: Short Cuts, *657*
Lewis, Jarma: It's a Dog's Life, *177*
Lewis, Jenny: Runaway Father, *645;* Trading Hearts, *398;* Wizard, The, *218*
Lewis, Jerry: Artists and Models, *229;* At War with the Army, *229;* Bellboy, The, *234;* Big Mouth, The, *238;* Boeing, Boeing, *243;* Caddy, The, *249;* Cinderfella, *912;* Cookie, *259;* Cracking Up, *260;* Delicate Delinquent, The, *263;* Disorderly Orderly, The, *265;* Don't Raise the Bridge, Lower the River, *267;* Errand Boy, The, *272;* Family Jewels, The, *273;* Hardly Working, *293;* Hollywood or Bust, *299;* Jerry Lewis Live, *310;* Jumping Jacks, *311;* King of Comedy, The, *565;* Ladies' Man, The, *314;* My Friend Irma, *340;* Nutty Professor, The, *348;* Patsy, The, *355;* Sad Sack, The, *372;* Slapstick of Another Kind, *380;* Which Way to the Front?, *410*
Lewis, Jerry Lee: American Hot Wax, *906;* Jerry Lee Lewis—I Am What I Am, *428*
Lewis, Joe E.: Private Buckaroo, *935*
Lewis, Juliette: Cape Fear (1991), *959;* Crooked Hearts, *491;* Husbands and Wives, *546;* Kalifornia, *561;* Romeo is Bleeding, *108;* That Night, *680;* What's Eating Gilbert Grape?, *408*
Lewis, Justin: Big Slice, The, *12*
Lewis, Linda: Alien Dead, *1035*
Lewis, Lori: Nightmare Weekend, *871*
Lewis, Mitchell: Docks of New York, The, *502*
Lewis, Monica: Boxoffice, *467;* D.I., The, *493*
Lewis, Ralph: Avenging Conscience, The, *811;* Flying Serpent, The, *842;* Lost City of the Jungle, *79;* Outside the Law, *616;* Somewhere in Sonora, *1151*
Lewis, Rawle D.: Cool Runnings, *259*
Lewis, Richard: All-Star Toast to the Improv, An, *224;* Diary of a Young Comic, *264;* Once Upon a Crime, *349;* Richard Lewis—"I'm Exhausted", *367;* Richard Lewis—"I'm in Pain Concert", *367;* Robin Hood: Men in Tights, *369;* That's Adequate, *393;* Wrong Guys, The, *414*
Lewis, Robert Q.: Affair to Remember, An, *442*
Lewis, Ronald: Scream of Fear, *1013*
Lewis, Sheldon: Monster Walks, The, *866;* Orphans of the Storm, *615*
Lewis, Sybil: Broken Strings, *470*
Lewis, Ted: Manhattan Merry-Go-Round, *930*
Ley, John: BMX Bandits, *17*
Leyrado, Juan: Times to Come, *795*
Leysen, Johan: Egg, *733*
Leyton, John: Schizo, *883;* Seaside Swingers, *938*
Lhermitte, Thierry: My Best Friend's Girl, *769;* My New Partner, *770;* Next Year If All Goes Well, *771;* Until September, *692*
Lhotsky, Tina: Film Musicals, *277*
Li, Bruce: Dynamo, *42*
Li, Gong: Farewell My Concubine, *736;* Ju Dou, *750;* Red Sorghum, *780*
Liang-Yi, Guo: China, My Sorrow, *723*
Liapis, Peter: Ghoulies, *846*
Libby, Brion: Stephen King's Night Shift Collection, *890*
Liberace: Loved One, The, *323;* Sincerely Yours, *658*
Libert, Anne: Virgin Among the Living Dead, A, *901*
Libertini, Richard: All of Me, *224;* Big Trouble, *239;* Comedy Tonight, *257;* Don't Drink the Water, *267;* Fletch, *978;* Fletch Lives, *978;* Fourth Wise Man, The, *521;* Going Berserk, *287;* Popeye, *196*
Liberty, Richard: Crazies, The, *825;* Day of the Dead, *830*
Licht, Jeremy: Comeback Kid, The, *486;* Next One, The, *1068*
Lichtenstein, Mitchell: Streamers, *670;* Wedding Banquet, The, *407*
Liddell, Laura: Shakespeare Wallah, *655*
Liddy, G. Gordon: Adventures in Spying, *2;* Street Asylum, *121;* Super Force, *1081*
Liebeneiner, Wolfgang: Liebelei, *760*
Lieh, Lo: Stranger and the Gunfighter, The, *1153*
Lieven, Albert: Brainwashed, *958;* Convoy (1940), *488;* Seventh Veil, The, *653*
Lifford, Tina: Ernest Green Story, The, *165*
Light, John: I'm a Fool, *549*
Lightfoot, Gordon: Harry Tracy, *1119*
Lightstone, Marilyn: Spasms, *889;* Surrogate, The, *674*
Ligon, Tom: Joyride, *560*
Lillard, Matthew: Serial Mom, *376*
Lillie, Beatrice: On Approval, *349;* Thoroughly Modern Millie, *945*
Lime, Yvonne: I Was a Teenage Werewolf, *855*
Limeliters, The: Hungry I Reunion, *303*
Limon, Dina: Boy Takes Girl, *152*
Lin, Brigitte: Jackie Chan's Police Force, *309*
Lin, Traci: Class of 1999, *1041*
Linaker, Kay: Two Weeks to Live, *402*
Lincoln, Abbey: For Love of Ivy, *279*
Lincoln, Elmo: Adventures of Tarzan, The, *2;* Intolerance, *553;* Tarzan of the Apes, *125;* Wyoming Outlaw, *1165*
Lincoln, Lar Park: Friday the 13th, Part VII: The New Blood, *844;* Princess Academy, The, *361*
Lincoln, Richard: Manny's Orphans, *185*
Lincoln, Warren: Power, The (1980), *876*

Lind, Della: Swiss Miss, *390*
Lind, Greta: Rudy, *200*
Lind, Heather: Betrayal of the Dove, *954*
Lind, Traci: Model by Day, *86;* My Boyfriend's Back, *339*
Linda, Boguslaw: Masquerade (1986), *766;* Poisonous Plants, *778*
Lindblom, Gunnel: Hunger (1966), *746;* Silence, The, *786;* Virgin Spring, The, *801;* Winter Light, *804*
Linden, Doris: Private Snuffy Smith, *362*
Linden, Eric: Ah, Wilderness, *223*
Linden, Hal: How to Break Up a Happy Divorce, *302;* I Do! I Do!, *924;* Mr. Inside/Mr. Outside, *85;* My Wicked, Wicked Ways, *602;* New Life, A, *343;* Ray Bradbury's Chronicles: The Martian Episodes, *1073;* Starflight One, *1079*
Linden, Jennie: Dr. Who and the Daleks, *1047;* Women in Love, *706*
Linder, Cec: Quatermass and the Pit, *1072;* Strange Tales: Ray Bradbury Theater, *1080*
Linder, Crista: Days of Wrath, *1107*
Linder, Max: Seven Years' Bad Luck, *376*
Linderman, Maggie: Vanishing, The (1993), *1029*
Lindfors, Viveca: Adventures of Don Juan, The, *2;* Cauldron of Blood, *822;* Dark City, *495;* Exiled in America, *45;* Four in a Jeep, *521;* Girlfriends, *528;* King of Kings (1961), *565;* Misplaced, *595;* Natural Enemies, *604;* Playing for Time, *623;* Rachel River, *682;* Silent Madness, *886;* Story of Ruth, The, *668;* Voices, *694;* Way We Were, The, *697;* Zandalee, *709*
Lindley, Audra: Cannery Row, *250;* Desert Hearts, *499;* Heartbreak Kid, The, *295;* Revenge of the Stepford Wives, *881;* Spellbinder, *889*
Lindo, Delroy: Crooklyn, *261;* Malcolm X, *586*
Lindsay, Margaret: Baby Face, *453;* Cavalcade, *477;* Dangerous, *494;* Devil Dogs of the Air, *37;* G-Men, *54;* House of the Seven Gables, The, *545;* Lady Killer, *74;* Please Don't Eat the Daisies, *358;* Scarlet Street, *649;* Tammy and the Doctor, *677*
Lindsay, Robert: Bert Rigby, You're a Fool, *908;* King Lear (1984), *564;* Strike It Rich, *387*
Lindsey, George: Andy Griffith Show, The (TV Series), *227;* Return to Mayberry, *366*
Lindsey, Joseph: Amongst Friends, *447*
Lindt, Rosemary: Heroes in Hell, *61*
Line, Helga: Nightmare Castle, *871;* When the Screaming Stops, *902*
Lineback, Richard: Woman with a Past, *705*
Ling, Suzanne: Kiss of the Tarantula, *859*
Linh, Dan Pham: Indochine, *747*
Linke, Paul: Motel Hell, *866;* Time Flies When You're Alive, *684*
Linkletter, Art: Champagne for Caesar, *252;* People Are Funny, *356*
Linn-Baker, Mark: Bare Essentials, *232;* Me and Him, *330;* My Favorite Year, *340;* Noises Off, *346*
Linney, Laura: Blind Spot, *464*
Linnros, Henrik: Sunday's Children, *791*
Linville, Larry: Blue Movies, *242;* Bodywaves, *243;* M*A*S*H* (TV Series), *325;* Rock 'n' Roll High School Forever, *369;* School Spirit, *374*
Lion, Leon M.: Amazing Adventure, *225;* Number 17, *1002*
Liotard, Thérèse: My Father's Glory, *769;* My Mother's Castle, *770;* One Sings, the Other Doesn't, *773*
Liotta, Ray: Arena Brains, *450;* Article 99, *451;* Dominick and Eugene, *503;* Field of Dreams, *1050;* Goodfellas, *531;* No Escape, *1069;* Something Wild, *383;* Unlawful Entry, *1029;* Women & Men 2, *706*
Lipinski, Eugene: Moonlighting (1983), *768;* Riders of the Storm, *368*
Lipman, Maureen: Little Princess, A, *183*
Lipscomb, Dennis: Amazing Grace and Chuck, *445;* Blue Yonder, The, *151;* Crossroads, *912;* Eyes of Fire, *840;* First Power, The, *841;* Retribution, *879;* Sister, Sister, *886;* Slow Burn, *1018;* Union City, *1029*
Lipton, Peggy: Fatal Charm, *976;* Kinjite (Forbidden Subjects), *73;* Mod Squad, The (TV Series), *86;* Purple People Eater, *198;* True Identity, *399;* Twin Peaks (Movie), *1027;* Twin Peaks (TV Series), *1027;* Twin Peaks: Fire Walk with Me, *1028*
Lipton, Robert: Bullet from God, A, *1102;* Death Spa, *831;* Lethal Woman, *77;* Silent Night, Lonely Night, *658;* Woman Her Men and Her Futon, A, *705*
Lisi, Virna: Assault on a Queen, *7;* Challenge to White Fang, *24;* Christopher Columbus (1985), *25;* How to Murder your Wife, *303;* Miss Right, *333;* Night Flight from Moscow, *90;* Statue, The, *385;* When Wolves Cry, *699*
Lissek, Leon: Bloodmoon, *816*
Lister, Moira: Run for Your Money, A, *371*
Lister Jr., Tiny: Posse (1993), *1139*
Litel, John: Don Winslow of the Navy, *41;* Enchanted Forest, The, *165;* Flight to Mars, *1052;* Northwest Trail, *1136;* Pitfall, *622;* Sister Kenny, *659;* Texas Lady, *1156;* Virginia City, *1161*
Lithgow, John: Adventures of Buckaroo Banzai, The, *1034;* At Play in the Fields of the Lord, *451;* Baby Girl Scott, *453;* Blow Out, *957;* Cliffhanger, *26;* Day After, The, *1044;* Distant Thunder (1988), *502;* Footloose, *917;* Glitter Dome, The, *980;* Goldilocks and the Three Bears, *171;* Harry and the Hendersons, *1055;* Ivory Hunters, *555;* Love, Cheat & Steal, *993;* Manhattan Project, The, *995;* Memphis Belle (1990), *592;* Mesmerized, *996;* Obsession, *1002;* Out Cold, *351;* Pelican Brief, The, *1005;* Raising Cain, *878;* Rich Kids, *640;* Ricochet, *106;* Santa Claus—The Movie, *201;* Traveling Man, *687;* Twilight Zone—The Movie, *898;* 2010, *1086;* World According to Garp, The, *706;* Wrong Man, The (1993), *707*
Little Billy: Terror of Tiny Town, The, *1155*
Little, Cleavon: Blazing Saddles, *241;* Double Exposure (1982), *971;* Fletch Lives, *978;* FM, *278;* Gig, The, *286;* Greased Lightning, *57;* High Risk, *61;* Jimmy the Kid, *178;* Murder by Numbers, *998;* Once Bitten, *349;* Salamander, The, *111;* Scavenger Hunt, *373;* Separate But Equal, *652;* Sky Is Gray, The, *660;* Surf 2, *389;* Toy Soldiers (1983), *131;* Vanishing Point, *135*
Little, Michelle: Appointment with Fear, *6;* My Demon Lover, *339;* Radioactive Dreams, *1073*
Little, Rich: Dirty Tricks, *265;* Happy Hour, *293;* Rich Little—One's a Crowd, *367;* Rich Little's Little Scams on Golf, *367*
Little Richard: Chuck Berry Hail! Hail! Rock 'n' Roll, *421;* Down and Out in Beverly Hills, *268;* Girl Can't Help It, The, *286;* Happy Birthday Bugs: 50 Looney Years, *173;* Jimi Hendrix, *428;* Pee-Wee's Playhouse Christmas Special, *194*
Littlefield, Lucien: Bitter Tea of General Yen, The, *462;* Hell Town, *1120;* My Best Girl, *339;* Sheik, The, *655;* Tumbleweeds, *1159;* Zorro's Black Whip, *1166*
Liu, Pei Qi: Story of Qiu Ju, The, *789*
Liu, Qing: Girl from Hunan, *740*
Lively, Ernie: Accidental Meeting, *950*
Lively, Jason: Ghost Chase, *845;* Maximum Force, *83;* National Lampoon's European Vacation, *342;* Night of the Creeps, *869*
Lively, Robyn: Buckeye and Blue, *1102;* Not Quite Human, *347;* Not Quite Human 2, *347;* Teen Witch, *392*
Livesey, Roger: Drums, *42;* Entertainer, The, *510;* League of Gentlemen, The, *317;* Life and Death of Colonel Blimp, The, *574;* Master of Ballantrae, The, *83;* Of Human Bondage (1964), *610*
Livingston, Barry: Easy Wheels, *270*
Livingston, Margaret: Sunrise, *673*
Livingston, Robert: Bells of Rosarita, *1097;* Black Raven, The, *955;* Bold Caballero, The, *1099;* Covered Wagon Days, *1106;* Death Rides the Plains, *1108;* Don't Fence Me In, *1110;* Gangs of Sonora, *1115;* Grand Canyon Trail, *1116;* Heart of the Rockies, *1119;* Heroes of the Saddle, *1120;* Hit the Saddle, *1121;* Kansas Terrors, *1124;* Lone Star Raiders, *1129;* Mule Train, *1134;* Mysterious Desperado, *1135;* Night Stage to Galveston, *1136;* Outlaws of Sonora, *1137;* Range

Defenders, *1141;* Riders of the Black Hills, *1144;* Riders of the Whistling Skull, *1144;* Rocky Mountain Rangers, *1145;* Trail Blazers, *1158;* Under Texas Skies, *1160;* Vigilantes Are Coming!, *1161;* Winning of the West, *1165*
Livingstone, Mary: Jack Benny Program, The (TV Series), *309*
Lizer, Kari: Hit Woman: The Double Edge, *63*
Llewellyn, Desmond: Living Daylights, The, *78;* Spy Who Loved Me, The, *119;* You Only Live Twice, *141*
Llewellyn, Robert: Red Dwarf (TV Series), *365*
Lloyd, Christopher: Addams Family, The, *222;* Addams Family Values, *222;* Amazing Stories (TV Series), *1036;* Back to the Future, *1037;* Back to the Future II, *1037;* Back to the Future III, *1037;* Clue, *256;* Cowboy and the Ballerina, The, *490;* Dead Ahead: The Exxon Valdez Disaster, *497;* Dennis the Menace, *161;* Dream Team, The, *269;* Eight Men Out, *508;* Legend of the White Horse, *76;* Miracles, *332;* One Flew Over the Cuckoo's Nest, *613;* Schizoid, *883;* September Gun, *1148;* Star Trek III: The Search for Spock, *1079;* Streethawk, *121;* Suburban Commando, *388;* TBone N Weasel, *391;* Track 29, *1026;* Twenty Bucks, *401;* Walk Like a Man, *405;* Who Framed Roger Rabbit, *410;* Why Me?, *139*
Lloyd, Emily: Chicago Joe and the Showgirl, *480;* Cookie, *259;* In Country, *550;* River Runs Through It, A, *641;* Scorchers, *650;* Wish You Were Here, *412*
Lloyd, Gaylord: His Royal Slyness/Haunted Spooks, *298*
Lloyd, Harold: Days of Thrills and Laughter, *262;* Fatty and His Funny Friends, *275;* Harold Lloyd's Comedy Classics, *294;* His Royal Slyness/Haunted Spooks, *298;* Keystone Comedies, Vol. 5, *313;* Mad Wednesday, *325;* Milky Way, The (1936), *332;* Sin of Harold Diddlebock (a.k.a. Mad Wednesday), *379*
Lloyd Jr., Harold: Frankenstein's Daughter, *843;* Married Too Young, *589*
Lloyd, Jeremy: Bawdy Adventures of Tom Jones, The, *233*
Lloyd, Jimmy: Riders of the Whistling Pines, *1144;* Sea Hound, The, *112*
Lloyd, John Bedford: Sweet Lorraine, *674;* Waiting for the Light, *695*
Lloyd, Kathleen: It Lives Again, *857;* Jayne Mansfield Story, The, *557;* Missouri Breaks, The, *1134;* Take Down, *390*
Lloyd, Norman: Age of Innocence, The, *443;* Amityville 4: The Evil Escapes, *809;* Dead Poets Society, *497;* FM, *278;* Journey of Honor, *69;* Nude Bomb, The, *347;* Saboteur, *1011*
Lloyd, Sabrina: Father Hood, *47*
Lloyd, Sue: Ipcress File, The, *986;* Number One of the Secret Service, *347*
Lo Bianco, Tony: Blood Ties (1987), *464;* Bloodbrothers, *464;* Boiling Point, *17;* City Heat, *255;* City of Hope, *483;* Demon (God Told Me To), *1046;* F.I.S.T., *512;* Honeymoon Killers, The, *983;* Marciano, *588;* Mr. Inside/Mr. Outside, *85;* Seven-Ups, The, *114;* 10 Million Dollar Getaway, The, *678*
Lo Verso, Enrico: Il Ladro Di Bambini (Stolen Children), *747*
Lobel, Bruni: Almost Angels, *146*
Loc, Tone: Ace Ventura: Pet Detective, *221;* Blank Check, *151;* Posse (1993), *1139;* Surf Ninjas, *208*
Loc, Truong Thi: Scent of Green Papaya, The, *784*
Locane, Amy: Cry-Baby, *912;* Lost Angels, *580;* No Secrets, *1002;* School Ties, *649*
Lochary, David: Female Trouble, *276;* Mondo Trasho, *335;* Multiple Maniacs, *866;* Pink Flamingos, *357*
Locke, Nancy: Hostage (1987), *64*
Locke, Robert: '68, *659*
Locke, Sondra: Any Which Way You Can, *228;* Bronco Billy, *246;* Every Which Way but Loose, *273;* Gauntlet, The, *55;* Heart Is a Lonely Hunter, The, *538;* Outlaw Josey Wales, The, *1137;* Ratboy, *635;* Reflection of Fear, *1009;* Rosie, *937;* Seducers, The, *651;* Sudden Impact, *122;* Tales of the Unexpected, *1022;* Willard, *903*
Locke, Terrence: Goodbye, Norma Jean, *530*
Lockhart, Anne: Dark Tower, *829;* Joyride, *560;* Troll, *1085;* Young Warriors, The, *141*
Lockhart, Calvin: Beast Must Die, The, *812;* Dark of the Sun, *32;* Let's Do It Again, *318*
Lockhart, Gene: Abe Lincoln in Illinois, *440;* Action in Arabia, *2;* Androcles and the Lion, *227;* Big Hangover, The, *238;* Billy the Kid, *1099;* Blondie, *241;* Carousel, *911;* Christmas Carol, A (1938), *158;* Devil and Daniel Webster, The, *500;* Earthworm Tractors, *269;* Edison, The Man, *507;* Girl in Every Port, A, *286;* Going My Way, *529;* Hangmen Also Die, *536;* His Girl Friday, *297;* Hoodlum Empire, *64;* Listen, Darling, *928;* Man in the Gray Flannel Suit, The, *587;* Of Human Hearts, *610;* Sea Wolf, The (1941), *113;* Sinners in Paradise, *659;* Something to Sing About, *940;* South of Pago Pago, *119;* Star of Midnight, *1020;* Strange Woman, The, *669;* They Died with Their Boots On, *1156*
Lockhart, June: All This and Heaven Too, *445;* C.H.U.D. II (Bud the C.H.U.D.), *820;* Capture of Grizzly Adams, The, *156;* Deadly Games, *968;* Gift of Love, The, *527;* It's a Joke, Son!, *308;* Lost in Space (TV Series), *1063;* Night They Saved Christmas, The, *191;* Rented Lips, *366;* Sergeant York, *113;* Son of Lassie, *206;* Strange Invaders, *1080;* T-Men, *676;* Troll, *1085;* Whisper Kills, A, *902;* Who Is the Black Dahlia?, *1031*
Lockhart, Kathleen: Blondie, *241;* Christmas Carol, A (1938), *158*
Locklear, Heather: Big Slice, The, *12;* Body Language, *958;* Fade to Black (1993), *974;* Illusions, *985;* Lethal Charm, *573;* Return of the Swamp Thing, *880*
Locklin, Loryn: Fortress (1993), *1053*
Lockwood, Gary: Incredible Journey of Dr. Meg Laurel, The, *551;* It Happened at the World's Fair, *925;* Magic Sword, The, *185;* R.P.M. (Revolutions Per Minute), *632;* Survival Zone, *1081;* Tall Story, *391;* Terror in Paradise, *126;* 2001: A Space Odyssey, *1086;* Wild Pair, The, *140*
Lockwood, Margaret: Dr. Syn, *40;* Lady Vanishes, The (1938), *990;* Man in Grey, The, *587;* Night Train to Munich, *91;* Stars Look Down, The, *666;* Susannah of the Mounties, *208;* Trouble in the Glen, *399;* Wicked Lady, The (1945), *701*
Lockwood, Paul: Finders Keepers, Lovers Weepers, *516*
Lockwood, Preston: At Bertram's Hotel, *953*
Loder, John: Brighton Strangler, The, *819;* Dishonored Lady, *39;* Dr. Syn, *40;* Hairy Ape, The, *535;* How Green Was My Valley, *545;* Java Head, *557;* King Solomon's Mines (1937), *72;* Man Who Lived Again, The, *862;* Racketeer, *102;* River of Unrest, *641;* Sabotage, *1011;* Wedding Rehearsal, *407*
Lodge, David: Edge of Sanity, *838;* Two-Way Stretch, *402*
Lodge, John: Murders in the Zoo, *867;* River of Unrest, *641;* Scarlet Empress, The, *649*
Lodolo, Massimo: Flight of the Innocent, *737*
Loft, Arthur: My Friend Flicka, *190*
Logan, Jacqueline: King of Kings, The (1927), *565;* King of the Kongo, *72*
Logan, Janice: Dr. Cyclops, *835*
Logan, Phyllis: Another Time, Another Place (1984), *450;* Doctor and the Devils, The, *835;* Inquiry, The, *552;* Kitchen Toto, The, *566;* McGuffin, The, *996*
Logan, Robert: Across the Great Divide, *143;* Adventures of the Wilderness Family, *144;* Born to Race, *17;* Mountain Family Robinson, *189;* Night in Heaven, A, *606;* Sea Gypsies, The, *202;* Snowbeast, *888;* Wilderness Family, Part 2, The, *217*
Loggia, Robert: Afterburn, *442;* Armed and Dangerous, *228;* Bad Girls (1994), *1095;* Believers, The, *812;* Big, *237;* Code Name: Chaos, *257;* Conspiracy: The Trial of the Chicago 8, *488;* Echoes in the Darkness, *507;* Elfego Baca: Six Gun Law, *1111;* First Love, *517;* Gaby, a True Story, *524;* Gladiator, *528;* Hot Pursuit, *301;* Innocent Blood, *856;* Intrigue, *986;* Jagged Edge, *556;* Lifepod, *1063;* Marrying Man, The, *329;* Necessary Roughness, *342;* Nine Lives of Elfego Baca, The, *1136;* Ninth Configuration, The, *608;* Opportunity Knocks, *351;* Over the Top, *617;* Prizzi's Honor, *362;* Psycho II, *877;* Relentless, *1010;* Revenge of the Pink Panther, The, *367;* Running Away, *645;* Scarface (1983), *112;*

Somebody Up There Likes Me, *662;* Target: Favorite Son, *677;* That's Life, *393;* Triumph of the Spirit, *688;* Wild Palms, *1089*

Lohr, Marie: Pygmalion, *363*

Lokey, Ben: Breakin', *909*

Lollobrigida, Gina: Bad Man's River, *1095;* Beat the Devil, *233;* Buono Sera, Mrs. Campbell, *247;* Hotel Paradiso, *302;* King, Queen and Knave, *565;* Never So Few, *89;* Solomon and Sheba, *661;* Trapeze, *687*

Lolly, Teri: Restless Natives, *366*

Lom, Herbert: And Now the Screaming Starts, *809;* Asylum, *810;* Brass Monkey, The, *958;* Count Dracula, *825;* Curse of the Pink Panther, The, *261;* Dark Places, *829;* Dead Zone, The, *831;* Dorian Gray, *837;* Fire Down Below, *517;* Flame over India, *50;* Gambit, *283;* Going Bananas, *169;* Horse Without a Head, The, *175;* Hotel Reserve, *544;* Journey to the Far Side of the Sun, *1060;* King Solomon's Mines (1985), *73;* Lady Vanishes, The (1979), *990;* Lion and the Hawk, The, *77;* Man with Bogart's Face, The, *995;* Mark of the Devil, *863;* Murders in the Rue Morgue (1971), *867;* Mysterious Island, *1067;* Night and the City (1950), *605;* 99 Women, *91;* Paris Express, The, *97;* Phantom of the Opera (1962), *874;* Pink Panther Strikes Again, The, *357;* Pope Must Diet, The, *360;* Return of the Pink Panther, The, *366;* Revenge of the Pink Panther, The, *367;* River of Death, *107;* Room 43, *644;* Seventh Veil, The, *653;* Shot in the Dark, A, *378;* Son of the Pink Panther, *383;* Ten Little Indians (1975), *1023;* Third Man on the Mountain, *210;* Trail of the Pink Panther, The, *398;* Villa Rides, *1161*

Lombard, Carole: Big News, *238;* Golden Age of Comedy, The, *288;* High Voltage, *62;* In Name Only, *550;* Lady by Choice, *567;* Made for Each Other, *325;* Mr. and Mrs. Smith, *333;* My Man Godfrey (1936), *340;* No Man of Her Own, *345;* Nothing Sacred, *347;* Racketeer, *102;* Swing High, Swing Low, *390;* These Girls Won't Talk, *393;* They Knew What They Wanted, *681;* To Be or Not to Be (1942), *397;* Twentieth Century, *401*

Lombard, Karina: Wide Sargasso Sea, *701*

Lombard, Michael: Clinton and Nadine, *26;* "Crocodile" Dundee, *261*

Lommel, Ulli: Boogeyman 2, The, *818;* Chinese Roulette, *723*

Lomnicki, Tadeusz: Contract, *726;* Generation, A, *740*

Lomond, Britt: Sign of Zorro, The, *204*

Londez, Guilaine: Night and Day (1991), *771*

London, Alexandra: Van Gogh, *800*

London, Jason: Blood Ties (1993), *816;* Dazed and Confused, *497;* Man in the Moon, The, *587*

London, Julie: Girl Can't Help It, The, *286;* Man of the West, *1132;* Red House, The, *1009;* Task Force, *677*

London, Lisa: H.O.T.S., *292*

London, Tom: Blue Canadian Rockies, *1099;* Cherokee Flash, *1104;* Idaho, *1122;* King of the Forest Rangers, *72;* Lucky Boots, *1130;* Red River Renegades, *1142;* Song of Texas, *1151;* Warning Shadows (1933), *1030;* Yellow Rose of Texas, *1165;* Zorro Rides Again, *1166;* Zorro's Black Whip, *1166*

Lone, John: Iceman, *1057;* Last Emperor, The, *569;* M. Butterfly, *583;* Moderns, The, *335;* Shadow of China, *654;* Year of the Dragon, *141*

Long, Audrey: Adventures of Gallant Bess, *442;* Born to Kill, *958;* Desperate, *969*

Long, Joseph: Queen of Hearts, *632*

Long, Kathy: Knights, *1061*

Long, Michael: Squizzy Taylor, *119*

Long, Nia: Boyz N the Hood, *468;* Made in America, *325*

Long, Richard: Big Valley, The (TV Series), *1098;* Criss Cross (1948), *964;* Cult of the Cobra, *827;* Dark Mirror, The, *966;* House on Haunted Hill, *853;* Maverick (TV Series), *1133;* Stranger, The (1947), *1020;* Tomorrow Is Forever, *685*

Long, Shelley: Caveman, *252;* Cracker Factory, *490;* Don't Tell Her It's Me, *267;* Frozen Assets, *282;* Hello Again, *296;* Irreconcilable Differences, *554;* Losin' It, *321;* Money Pit, The, *335;* Night Shift, *344;* Outrageous Fortune, *352;* Small Circle of Friends, A, *660;* Troop Beverly Hills, *399*

Long, Walter: Laurel and Hardy Classics, Volume 4, *316;* Laurel and Hardy Classics, Volume 9, *316;* Shadows, *654;* Six-Shootin' Sheriff, *1150;* Yankee Clipper, *141*

Long, Audrey: Indian Uprising, *1123*

Longden, John: Blackmail (1929), *956*

Longden, Terence: Carry on Nurse, *251*

Longet, Claudine: Party, The, *354*

Longo, Tony: Remote, *198*

Longstreth, Emily: Confessions of a Hitman, *487;* Wired to Kill, *1089*

Lonnen, Ray: Belfast Assassin, *458;* Guardian of the Abyss, *848;* Murder Elite, *600*

Lonsdale, Michel: Assassins de L'Ordre, Les (Law Breakers), *714;* Bride Wore Black, The, *959;* Caravan to Vaccares, *23;* Enigma, *44;* Erendira, *734;* Games of Countess Dolingen of Gratz, The, *739;* Mr. Klein, *768;* Moonraker, *86;* Murmur of the Heart, *769;* Name of the Rose, The, *89;* Remains of the Day, *637;* Souvenir, *663;* Stolen Kisses, *789*

Loo, Richard: Across the Pacific, *1;* Back to Bataan, *8;* Betrayal from the East, *11;* Bitter Tea of General Yen, The, *462;* China Sky, *25;* Clay Pigeon, The, *26;* First Yank into Tokyo, *49;* Love is a Many-Splendored Thing, *581*

Loomis, Christopher: Nesting, The, *868*

Loomis, Nancy: Assault on Precinct 13, *7;* Halloween, *848*

Loomis, Rod: Beastmaster, The, *1038;* Jack's Back, *987*

Loos, Theodor: Siegfried, *786*

Lopert, Tanya: Once in Paris, *612;* Tales of Ordinary Madness, *677*

Lopez, Angelo: Street Hitz, *121*

Lopez, Carlos: Savage Nights, *783*

Lopez, Danny: Bloodfist V: Human Target, *16*

Lopez, Fernando: Defiance, *36*

Lopez, Ivonne: Letters from the Park, *760*

Lopez, Manuel Ochoa: Crossfire (1986), *1106*

Lopez, Perry: Chinatown, *962;* Death Wish IV: The Crackdown, *36;* Kinjite (Forbidden Subjects), *73;* McLintock!, *1133;* Two Jakes, The, *1028*

Lopez, Sylvia: Hercules Unchained, *1056*

Lopez, Tarso Ignacio: Macario, *763*

Lord, Jack: Court-martial of Billy Mitchell, The, *489;* Dr. No, *40;* Doomsday Flight, The, *971;* God's Little Acre, *529;* Man of the West, *1132*

Lord, Marjorie: Johnny Come Lately, *311;* Sherlock Holmes in Washington, *1015;* Wagon Train (TV Series), *1162*

Lord, Pauline: Mrs. Wiggs of the Cabbage Patch, *598*

Lord, Phillips: Way Back Home, *406*

Lord, Tamblyn: Vicious, *135*

Lords, Traci: Cry-Baby, *912;* Desperate Crimes, *37;* Fast Food, *274;* Laser Moon, *990;* Not of This Earth, *872;* Raw Nerve, *103;* Shock'em Dead, *885;* Time to Die, A (1990), *1025;* Tommyknockers, The, *1084*

Loren, Sophia: Angela, *448;* Arabesque, *6;* Black Orchid, The, *463;* Blood Feud, *719;* Boccaccio 70, *719;* Brass Target, *19;* Breath of Scandal, A, *245;* Brief Encounter (1974), *470;* Cassandra Crossing, The, *476;* Desire under the Elms, *500;* El Cid, *43;* Fall of the Roman Empire, The, *513;* Firepower, *49;* Gold of Naples, The, *529;* Heller in Pink Tights, *1120;* Houseboat, *302;* It Started in Naples, *308;* Key, The, *563;* Lady L, *568;* Legend of the Lost, *572;* Man of La Mancha, *930;* Operation Crossbow, *95;* Pride and the Passion, The, *626;* Running Away, *645;* Sophia Loren: Her Own Story, *663;* Special Day, A, *788;* Two Women, *797;* Yesterday, Today and Tomorrow, *806*

Loren, Tray: Rocktober Blood, *881*

Lorenzo, Luis: Yellow Hair and the Fortress of Gold, *1165*

Loret, Susanne: Atom Age Vampire, *810*

Lorient, Lisa: Pretty Smart, *361*

Loring, Lisa: Blood Frenzy, *815*

Loring, Lynn: Journey to the Far Side of the Sun, *1060*

Loring, Teala: Delinquent Daughters, *499*

Lorinz, James: Frankenhooker, *842*

Lorne, Marion: Strangers on a Train, *1020*

Loros, George: Apology, *809*

Lorraine, Louise: Adventures of Tarzan, The, *2*

Lorre, Peter: All Through the Night, *3;* Arsenic and Old Lace, *228;* Background to Danger, *8;* Beast with Five Fingers, The, *812;* Beat the Devil, *233;* Casablanca, *476;* Casino Royale (1954), *23;* Chase, The (1946), *479;* Crime and Punishment (1935), *490;* Five Weeks in a Balloon, *50;* Hell Ship Mutiny, *60;* Hollywood Canteen, *923;* Invisible Agent, *1059;* M, *763;* Mad Love, *861;* Maltese Falcon, The, *994;* Man Who Knew Too Much, The (1934), *995;* Mr. Moto's Last Warning, *997;* My Favorite Brunette, *340;* Passage to Marseilles, *97;* Patsy, The, *355;* Raven, The (1963), *879;* Red Skelton: A Career of Laughter, *433;* Sad Sack, The, *372;* Secret Agent, The, *1013;* Silk Stockings, *939;* Strange Cargo, *669;* Stranger on the Third Floor, *1020;* Tales of Terror, *892;* They Met in Bombay, *127;* 20,000 Leagues Under the Sea (1954), *133;* Voyage to the Bottom of the Sea, *1087;* You'll Find Out, *415*

Lorring, Joan: Corn Is Green, The (1945), *488;* Gangster, The, *525*

Lorys, Diana: House of Psychotic Women, *852*

Losch, Tilly: Garden of Allah, The, *525*

Lotis, Dennis: Horror Hotel, *851*

Lottimer, Eb: Dead Center, *967;* Finest Hour, The, *48;* Futurekick, *1053;* Quake, *1008*

Louanne: Night in the Life of Jimmy Reardon, A, *344;* Oh, God! Book II, *349*

Loudon, Dorothy: Garbo Talks, *283*

Loughery, Jackie: D.I., The, *493*

Loughlin, Lori: Amityville III: The Demon, *809;* Back to the Beach, *907;* Brotherhood of Justice, *471;* New Kids, The, *868;* Night Before, The, *344;* Rad, *102;* Secret Admirer, *374*

Loughlin, Terry: Rutherford County Line, *110*

Louis, Joe: This Is the Army, *945*

Louis-Dreyfus, Julia: Jack the Bear, *556*

Louise, Anita: Anthony Adverse, *450;* Casanova Brown, *252;* Judge Priest, *560;* Little Princess, The, *183;* Marie Antoinette, *588;* Sisters, The (1938), *659;* Story of Louis Pasteur, The, *668;* That Certain Woman, *680;* Tovaritch, *398;* Villain Still Pursued Her, The, *135*

Louise, Tina: Armored Command, *6;* Dixie Lanes, *265;* Dog Day, *40;* Evils of the Night, *839;* God's Little Acre, *529;* Johnny Suede, *311;* Trap, The, *1026*

Love, Bessie: Battle Beneath the Earth, *9;* Broadway Melody, The, *910;* Intolerance, *553;* Lost World, The (1925), *1064;* Sea Lion, The, *650;* Vampyres, *900*

Love, Darlene: Lethal Weapon, *76;* Lethal Weapon 3, *77*

Love, Michael: Boogeyman, The, *818*

Love, Mike: Beach Boys, The: An American Band, *419*

Love, Montagu: Fighting Devil Dogs, The, *48;* Mark of Zorro, The (1940), *82;* Sherlock Holmes and the Voice of Terror, *1015;* Son of Monte Cristo, The, *118;* Son of the Sheik, *118;* Tovaritch, *398;* Wind, The (1928), *703*

Love, Suzanna: Boogeyman, The, *818;* Boogeyman 2, The, *818;* Brainwaves, *818;* Cocaine Cowboys, *27;* Devonsville Terror, The, *834*

Love, Victor: Native Son, *604*

Loveday, Denise: No Escape, No Return, *91*

Lovejoy, Frank: Americano, The, *1093;* Dino, *501;* Finger Man, *48;* I'll See You in My Dreams, *924;* In a Lonely Place, *985;* Men of the Fighting Lady, *84;* Retreat Hell, *105;* Shack-Out on 101, *653;* Strategic Air Command, *670;* Three Secrets, *683;* Try and Get Me, *133;* Winning Team, The, *704*

Lovelady, John: Adventures in Wonderland, *143*

Lovelock, Raymond: Autopsy, *811;* One Russian Summer, *613*

Lover, Ed: Who's the Man?, *411*

Lovett, Dorothy: Courageous Dr. Christian, The, *489;* Dr. Christian Meets the Women, *502;* Meet Dr. Christian, *591;* Remedy for Riches, *638;* They Meet Again, *681*

Lovett, Lyle: Player, The, *358;* Short Cuts, *657*

Lovitz, Jon: City Slickers II, *256;* Coneheads, *258;* Last Resort, *316;* League of Their Own, A, *571;* Mr. Destiny, *334;* Mom and Dad Save the World, *188;* My Stepmother Is an Alien, *341;* National Lampoon's Loaded Weapon 1, *342;* Three Amigos, *395*

Lovsky, Celia: I, Mobster, *65*

Lowe, Alex: Peter's Friends, *621*

Lowe, Arthur: Bawdy Adventures of Tom Jones, The, *233;* Lady Vanishes, The (1979), *990;* Ruling Class, The, *371*

Lowe, Chad: Apprentice to Murder, *810;* Highway to Hell, *850;* Nobody's Perfect, *346;* Trueblood, *689*

Lowe, Chris: It Couldn't Happen Here, *925*

Lowe, Debbie: Cheerleaders, *254*

Lowe, Edmund: Call Out the Marines, *249;* Chandu the Magician, *24;* Dillinger (1945), *39;* Enchanted Forest, The, *165;* Every Day's a Holiday, *273;* Good Sam, *288;* Heller in Pink Tights, *1120;* I Love You Again, *304;* In Old Arizona, *1122;* Wings of Eagles, The, *703*

Lowe, Patrick: Primal Rage, *876*

Lowe, Rob: About Last Night, *440;* Bad Influence, *953;* Class, *256;* Finest Hour, The, *48;* Hotel New Hampshire, The, *544;* Illegally Yours, *548;* Masquerade (1988), *995;* Oxford Blues, *617;* St. Elmo's Fire, *646;* Square Dance, *665;* Stroke of Midnight, *387;* Wayne's World, *406;* Youngblood, *709*

Lowe, Susan: Desperate Living, *264*

Lowell, Carey: Dangerously Close, *966;* Down Twisted, *41;* License to Kill, *77;* Me and Him, *330;* Road to Ruin (1991), *369;* Sleepless in Seattle, *381*

Lowens, Curt: Mandroid, *1065;* Werewolf in a Girl's Dormitory, *902*

Lowensohn, Elina: Simple Men, *379*

Lowery, Andrew: JFK: Reckless Youth, *558;* My Boyfriend's Back, *339;* School Ties, *649*

Lowery, Robert: Arson Inc., *7;* Batman and Robin, *9;* Dangerous Passage, *32;* Drums Along the Mohawk, *42;* I Shot Billy the Kid, *1122;* Johnny Reno, *1124;* Mark of Zorro, The (1940), *82;* McLintock!, *1133;* Mummy's Ghost, The, *867;* Murder Over New York, *999;* Revenge of the Zombies, *881*

Lowitsch, Klaus: Despair, *729;* Gotcha!, *980;* Marriage of Maria Braun, The, *765*

Lowry, Lynn: Crazies, The, *825;* Fighting Mad, *516;* Sugar Cookies, *672;* They Came from Within, *895*

Lowther, T. J.: Perfect World, A, *621*

Loy, Myrna: After the Thin Man, *951;* Ambassador's Daughter, The, *226;* Animal Kingdom, The, *448;* Another Thin Man, *952;* Ants!, *809;* April Fools, The, *228;* Arrowsmith, *451;* Bachelor and the Bobby-Soxer, The, *230;* Best Years of Our Lives, The, *459;* Broadway Bill, *470;* Connecticut Yankee, A, *258;* Consolation Marriage, *488;* Don Juan, *503;* Double Wedding, *268;* End, The, *271;* Evelyn Prentice, *511;* From the Terrace, *523;* Great Ziegfeld, The, *921;* I Love You Again, *304;* Jazz Singer, The (1927), *925;* Just Tell Me What You Want, *312;* Libeled Lady, *318;* Lonelyhearts, *578;* Love Crazy, *322;* Love Me Tonight, *929;* Manhattan Melodrama, *81;* Mask of Fu Manchu, The, *82;* Midnight Lace, *84;* Mr. Blandings Builds His Dream House, *333;* Noah's Ark, *608;* Rains Came, The, *634;* Red Pony, The, *198;* Shadow of the Thin Man, *1014;* So This Is Paris, *382;* Song of the Thin Man, *1018;* Test Pilot, *679;* Thin Man, The, *1024;* Thin Man Goes Home, The, *1024;* Too Hot to Handle, *130;* Topaze (1933), *397;* Vanity Fair, *693;* Wife Vs. Secretary, *701*

Lozano, Margarita: Half of Heaven, *743;* Kaos, *751;* Night of the Shooting Stars, *771;* Viridiana, *801*

Lu, Lisa: Joy Luck Club, The, *559*

Lucan, Arthur: Vampire Over London, *404*

Lucas, Lisa: Forbidden Love, *519*

Lucas, Ronn: Best of the Big Laff Off, The, *236*

Lucas, Wilfred: Chump at Oxford, A, *255;* I Cover the Waterfront, *65;* Pardon Us, *354*

Lucci, Susan: Anastasia: The Mystery of Anna, *447;* Hit Woman: The Double Edge, *63;* Invitation to Hell, *857;* Lady Mobster, *74;* Mafia Princess, *585*

Luce, Deborah: Mother's Day, *866*
Lucero, Enrique: Return of a Man Called Horse, The, *1142;* Shark! (a.k.a. Maneaters!), *114*
Luchini, Fabrice: Full Moon in Paris, *739*
Lucia, Chip: Hospital Massacre, *852*
Luckinbill, Laurence: Cocktail, *485;* Mating Season, The, *330;* Messenger of Death, *84;* Not for Publication, *347;* Star Trek V: The Final Frontier, *1079;* To Heal a Nation, *684*
Lucking, Bill: Coast to Coast, *256;* Duplicates, *973;* Kung Fu—The Movie, *73;* Return of a Man Called Horse, The, *1142*
Ludlam, Charles: Big Easy, The, *12;* Forever Lulu, *279*
Ludwig, Pamela: Dead Man Walking, *1045;* Over the Edge, *616;* Pale Blood, *873;* Rush Week, *882*
Luez, Laurette: Ballad of a Gunfighter, *1096;* Prehistoric Women (1950), *1071*
Luft, Lorna: Grease 2, *920;* Where the Boys Are '84, *409*
Lugosi, Bela: Abbott and Costello Meet Frankenstein, *221;* Ape Man, The, *809;* Black Cat, The (1934), *813;* Black Dragons, *814;* Body Snatcher, The, *817;* Bowery at Midnight, *818;* Boys from Brooklyn, The, *818;* Bride of the Monster, *819;* Chandu the Magician, *24;* Corpse Vanishes, The, *825;* Death Kiss, The, *968;* Devil Bat, The, *833;* Dracula (1931), *837;* Frankenstein Meets the Wolf Man, *843;* Ghost of Frankenstein, *845;* Ghosts on the Loose, *286;* Glen or Glenda, *528;* Gorilla, The, *289;* Human Monster, The (Dark Eyes of London), *854;* International House, *307;* Invisible Ghost, *856;* Invisible Ray, The, *857;* Island of Lost Souls, *857;* Mark of the Vampire, *863;* Murder by Television, *998;* Murders in the Rue Morgue (1932), *867;* Mysterious Mr. Wong, The, *88;* Mystery of the Marie Celeste, The, *1000;* Ninotchka, *345;* One Body Too Many, *1003;* Phantom Creeps, The, *874;* Plan 9 from Outer Space, *1070;* Raven, The (1935), *878;* Return of Chandu (The Magician), *105;* Return of the Ape Man, *880;* Return of the Vampire, The, *880;* Scared to Death, *883;* Son of Frankenstein, *888;* SOS Coast Guard, *118;* Spooks Run Wild, *385;* Vampire Over London, *404;* Warning Shadows (1933), *1030;* Whispering Shadow, The, *138;* White Zombie, *903;* Wolf Man, The, *904;* You'll Find Out, *415;* Zombies on Broadway, *416*
Luhr, Bill: Slayground, *1017*
Luisi, James: Red Light Sting, The, *636*
Lukas, Paul: Berlin Express, *10;* Deadline at Dawn, *34;* Dinner at the Ritz, *39;* Dodsworth, *503;* Four Horsemen of the Apocalypse, *52;* Fun in Acapulco, *918;* Ghost Breakers, *285;* Kim, *72;* Strange Cargo, *669;* Three Musketeers, The (1935), *128;* 20,000 Leagues Under the Sea (1954), *133;* Watch on the Rhine, *696*
Lukather, Paul: Dinosaurus!, *834;* Hands of a Stranger, *981*
Luke, Edwin: Jade Mask, The, *987*
Luke, Jorge: Foxtrot, *521;* Pure Luck, *363;* Return of a Man Called Horse, The, *1142;* Shark Hunter, The, *114;* Ulzana's Raid, *1160*
Luke, Keye: Across the Pacific, *1;* Alice (1990), *224;* Amsterdam Kill, The, *5;* Battle Hell, *9;* Charlie Chan at the Opera, *961;* Charlie Chan in Paris, *961;* Dead Heat, *830;* Feathered Serpent, The, *976;* First Yank into Tokyo, *49;* Good Earth, The, *530;* Gremlins, *1055;* Kung Fu, *73;* Kung Fu—The Movie, *73;* Lost City of the Jungle, *79;* Mad Love, *861;* Painted Veil, The, *617*
Lukoye, Peter: Born Free, *152*
Lulli, Piero: Adios, Hombre, *1092;* Big Rip-off, The, *1098;* Days of Wrath, *1107*
Lulu: To Sir with Love, *685*
Lumbly, Carl: Pacific Heights, *1003;* South Central, *663;* To Sleep with Anger, *685*
Lumley, Joanna: Glory Boys, The, *56;* Shirley Valentine, *378*
Luna, Barbara: Concrete Jungle, The (1982), *28;* Five Weeks in a Balloon, *50;* Gentle Savage, *1115*
Lunblad, Peter: Master Blaster, *83*
Lunch, Lydia: Gun is Loaded, The, *921*
Lund, Annalena: Free, White, and 21, *522*
Lund, Art: Black Caesar, *13;* Bucktown, *20;* Last American Hero, The, *75;* Man from Atlantis, The, *1064;* Molly Maguires, The, *598*
Lund, Deanna: Elves, *838;* Hardly Working, *293;* Red Wind, *1009*
Lund, Jana: Frankenstein 1970, *843*
Lund, John: Dakota Incident, *1107;* Duchess of Idaho, *915;* Latin Lovers, *928;* My Friend Irma, *340;* Perils of Pauline, The (1947), *356;* Wackiest Ship in the Army, The, *405*
Lund, Richard: Treasure of Arne, *797*
Lundgren, Dolph: Cover-Up (1990), *30;* I Come in Peace, *1057;* Masters of the Universe, *186;* Punisher, The, *101;* Red Scorpion, *104;* Rocky IV, *642;* Showdown in Little Tokyo, *115;* Universal Soldier, *134*
Lundigan, William: Andy Hardy's Double Life, *227;* Dishonored Lady, *39;* Fabulous Dorseys, The, *916;* Fighting 69th, The, *48;* Follow Me Quietly, *978;* Love Nest, *323;* Pinky, *622;* Three Smart Girls Grow Up, *945;* Wives Under Suspicion, *704*
Lundquist, Steve: Killer Tomatoes Eat France, *313*
Lundy, Jessica: Madhouse (1990), *326*
Lung, Ti: Better Tomorrow, A, *717;* Better Tomorrow 2, A, *717;* People's Hero, *777*
Lunghi, Cherie: Excalibur, *1050;* Letters to an Unknown Lover, *573;* Sign of Four, The, *1016*
Lunham, Dan: Strangeness, The, *890*
Lunt, Alfred: Guardsman, The, *291;* Sally of the Sawdust, *647*
Lupino, Ida: Adventures of Sherlock Holmes, The, *950;* Beware, My Lovely, *955;* Bigamist, The, *461;* Devil's Rain, The, *834;* Escape Me Never, *510;* Food of the Gods, *1052;* Forever and a Day, *520;* Hard Way, The (1942), *536;* High Sierra, *62;* Hollywood Canteen, *923;* Junior Bonner, *1124;* Lust for Gold, *1130;* Man I Love, The, *586;* My Boys Are Good Boys, *601;* On Dangerous Ground, *1003;* One Rainy Afternoon, *350;* Private Hell 36, *628;* Road House (1948), *1010;* Sea Devils, *112;* Sea Wolf, The (1941), *113;* Thank Your Lucky Stars, *944;* They Drive by Night, *127;* While the City Sleeps, *138*
Lupo, Alberto: Atom Age Vampire, *810;* Django Shoots First, *1109*
LuPone, Patti: Driving Miss Daisy, *505;* Family Prayers, *514;* Fighting Back, *47;* LBJ: The Early Years, *571;* Water Engine, The, *696*
LuPone, Robert: High Stakes (1989), *62*
Luppi, Federico: Cocaine Wars, *27;* Cronos, *727;* Funny Dirty Little War (No Habra Mas Penas ni Olvido), *739*
Lupton, John: Escape from Fort Bravo, *1111;* Great Locomotive Chase, The, *171;* Jesse James Meets Frankenstein's Daughter, *858*
Lupus, Peter: Escapist, The, *511*
Lurie, John: Down by Law, *268;* Stranger Than Paradise, *387*
Lush, Valerie: Nemesis (1986), *1000*
Lussier, Jacques: Norman's Awesome Experience, *346*
Lustig, Aaron: Bad Channels, *1037*
Lutter, Alfred: Alice Doesn't Live Here Anymore, *444;* Bad News Bears, The, *231;* Love and Death, *322*
Lutz, Joleen: Outtakes, *352*
Luz, Franc: Ghost Town, *846;* Nest, The (1988), *868*
Lyden, Pierce: Sea Hound, The, *112;* Six Gun Serenade, *1150*
Lydon, Jimmy: Island in the Sky, *554;* Life with Father, *318;* Little Men (1940), *576;* Magnificent Yankee, The, *585;* September Affair, *652;* Strange Illusion, *1020;* Time of Your Life, The, *684;* Tom Brown's School Days (1940), *685*
Lydon, John: Corrupt, *963;* Great Rock and Roll Swindle, The, *921*
Lye, Reg: Killing of Angel Street, The, *564;* Sunday Too Far Away, *673;* Walk into Hell, *136*
Lyman, Dorothy: Ollie Hopnoodle's Haven of Bliss, *192;* Ruby in Paradise, *645*

Lyman, Will: Three Sovereigns for Sarah, *683*
Lymon and the Teenagers, Frankie: Rock, Rock, Rock, *937*
Lynch, Barry: Infested, *856*
Lynch, John: Cal, *474;* Hardware, *1055;* Railway Station Man, The, *633;* Secret Garden, The (1993), *202*
Lynch, Kate: Def-Con 4, *1046;* Meatballs, *330*
Lynch, Kelly: Curly Sue, *261;* Desperate Hours (1990), *37;* Drugstore Cowboy, *505;* For Better and for Worse, *279;* Three of Hearts, *683;* Warm Summer Rain, *696*
Lynch, Ken: I Married a Monster from Outer Space, *1057*
Lynch, Pierrette: Lethal Lolita—Amy Fisher: My Story, *573*
Lynch, Richard: Alligator II, *808;* Bad Dreams, *811;* Barbarians, The, *1038;* Cut and Run, *493;* Deathsport, *1046;* Delta Fox, *37;* Double Threat, *504;* Forbidden Dance, The, *918;* High Stakes (1989), *62;* Invasion U.S.A., *67;* Little Nikita, *992;* Maximum Force, *83;* Merlin, *1065;* Nightforce, *91;* Premonition, The, *876;* Puppet Master III: Toulon's Revenge, *878;* Savage Dawn, *111;* Scarecrow, *649;* Seven-Ups, The, *114;* Sizzle, *659;* Steel, *120;* Sword and the Sorcerer, The, *1082*
Lynch, Valerie: Tango Bar, *792*
Lynde, Paul: Beach Blanket Bingo, *908;* Bye Bye Birdie, *910;* Glass Bottom Boat, The, *287;* New Faces, *933;* Send Me No Flowers, *375;* Son of Flubber, *206*
Lyndon, Michael: Lightship, The, *575;* Success Is the Best Revenge, *672*
Lynley, Carol: Balboa, *455;* Blackout (1990), *956;* Cardinal, The, *475;* Cat and the Canary, The (1978), *960;* Dark Tower, *829;* Fantasy Island, *1050;* Flood!, *51;* Four Deuces, The, *52;* Howling VI: The Freaks, *854;* Light in the Forest, The, *181;* Night Stalker, The (1971), *870;* Return to Peyton Place, *639;* Son of Blob (Beware! The Blob), *888;* Spirits, *889;* Stripper, The (1963), *671;* Washington Affair, The, *696*
Lynn, Amy: History of White People in America, The (Volume II), *298*
Lynn, Betty: Return to Mayberry, *366;* Texas John Slaughter: Geronimo's Revenge, *1155;* Texas John Slaughter: Stampede at Bitter Creek, *1155;* Texas John Slaughter: Wild Times, *1156*
Lynn, Cheryl M.: Emanon, *271;* Fate, *274;* Thunder Run, *129*
Lynn, Diana: Annapolis Story, An, *449;* Bedtime for Bonzo, *233;* Every Girl Should Be Married, *273;* Kentuckian, The, *1124;* Miracle of Morgan's Creek, The, *332;* My Friend Irma, *340*
Lynn, Donna: Hollywood High, Part II, *299*
Lynn, Emmet: Days of Old Cheyenne, *1107*
Lynn, Jeffrey: All This and Heaven Too, *445;* Fighting 69th, The, *48;* Letter to Three Wives, A, *573;* Roaring Twenties, The, *107*
Lynn, Jonathan: Suspicion (1987), *1022*
Lynn, Rebecca: Sensations, *651*
Lynn, Sharon: Way Out West, *406*
Lynn, Traci: Fright Night II, *844*
Lyon, Alice: Horror of Party Beach, The, *851*
Lyon, Ben: I Cover the Waterfront, *65;* Indiscreet (1931), *306;* Night Nurse, *606*
Lyon, Steve: Campus Man, *249*
Lyon, Sue: End of the World, *1049;* Evel Knievel, *45;* Flim-Flam Man, The, *518;* Four Rode Out, *1114;* Lolita, *577;* Night of the Iguana, The, *606;* Tony Rome, *1025;* Winds of Jarrah, The, *703*
Lyon, Wendy: Hello, Mary Lou: Prom Night II, *850*
Lyons, Bruce: Navigator: A Medieval Odyssey, The, *1067*
Lyons, James: Poison, *624*
Lyons, Phyllis: Casualties of Love: The Long Island Lolita Story, *476*
Lyons, Robert F.: American Eagle, *4;* Cease Fire, *477;* Getting Straight, *526;* Platoon Leader, *99;* Todd Killings, The, *685*
Lys, Lya: Age of Gold, *711*
Lythgow, Gene: When a Stranger Calls Back, *1031*
Maazel, Lincoln: Martin, *863*
Mabe, Byron: Doberman Gang, The, *40*
Maberly, Kate: Secret Garden, The (1993), *202*
Mac, Bernie: Above the Rim, *440;* House Party 3, *923*
MacArthur, James: Cry of Battle, *31;* Interns, The, *553;* Kidnapped (1960), *180;* Light in the Forest, The, *181;* Ride Beyond Vengeance, *1143;* Spencer's Mountain, *664;* Swiss Family Robinson, The, *208;* Third Man on the Mountain, *210*
MacBride, Donald: Annabel Takes a Tour, *227;* Blondie Takes a Vacation, *242;* Buck Privates Come Home, *246;* Egg and I, The, *270;* Murder Over New York, *999;* Story of Seabiscuit, The, *207;* They Got Me Covered, *393;* Time of Their Lives, The, *396*
Macchio, Ralph: Crossroads, *912;* Dangerous Company, *494;* Distant Thunder (1988), *502;* Karate Kid, The, *562;* Karate Kid Part II, The, *562;* Karate Kid Part III, The, *562;* My Cousin Vinny, *339;* Outsiders, The, *616;* Teachers, *391;* Too Much Sun, *397;* Up the Academy, *403*
Maccioni, Aldo: Loves and Times of Scaramouche, The, *324;* Too Shy to Try, *796*
MacColl, Katherine: House by the Cemetery, *852;* Seven Doors of Death, *884*
MacCorkindale, Simon: Jaws 3, *858;* Macbeth (1981), *584;* Obsessive Love, *1002;* Quatermass Conclusion, The, *1072;* Riddle of the Sands, *106;* Robbers of the Sacred Mountain, *107;* Shades of Love: Sincerely, Violet, *654;* Sword and the Sorcerer, The, *1082*
MacDonald, Aimi: Number One of the Secret Service, *347*
Macdonald, Anne-Marie: I've Heard the Mermaids Singing, *309;* Where the Spirit Lives, *699*
MacDonald, Bruce: Return of the Secaucus 7, *366*
MacDonald, Gordon: Brain Damage, *818*
MacDonald, J. Farrell: In Old Arizona, *1122;* Painted Desert, The, *1138;* Phantom Express, *99;* Stagecoach War, *1152;* Sunrise, *673;* Thirteenth Guest, The, *1024*
MacDonald, Jeanette: Bitter Sweet, *909;* Broadway Serenade, *910;* Cairo, *910;* Cat and the Fiddle, The, *911;* Firefly, The, *916;* Girl of the Golden West, The, *919;* Hollywood on Parade, *299;* I Married an Angel, *924;* Love Me Tonight, *929;* Maytime, *930;* Merry Widow, The, *930;* Naughty Marietta, *932;* New Moon, *933;* Rose Marie (1936), *937;* San Francisco, *648;* Smilin' Through (1941), *940;* Sun Comes Up, The, *208;* Sweethearts, *943;* Three Daring Daughters, *945*
Macdonald, Michael: Oddballs, *348*
MacDonald, Phillip: Garden, The, *525*
MacDonald, Wendy: Blood Frenzy, *815*
MacDowell, Andie: Bad Girls (1994), *1095;* Deception (1993), *969;* Four Weddings and a Funeral, *280;* Green Card, *290;* Greystoke: The Legend of Tarzan, Lord of the Apes, *58;* Groundhog Day, *291;* Hudson Hawk, *64;* Object of Beauty, The, *348;* St. Elmo's Fire, *646;* Sex, Lies and Videotape, *653;* Short Cuts, *657;* Women & Men 2, *706*
Mace, Paul: Lords of Flatbush, The, *579*
Macfaden, Angus: Lost Language of Cranes, The, *580*
MacGinnis, Niall: Betrayed (1954), *11;* Curse of the Demon, *828;* Martin Luther, *589;* River of Unrest, *641*
Macgowan, J. P.: Somewhere in Sonora, *1151*
MacGowran, Jack: Brain, The (1965), *1040;* Cul-de-Sac, *492;* Fearless Vampire Killers, or, Pardon Me, But Your Teeth Are in My Neck, The, *840;* How I Won the War, *302;* King Lear (1971), *564;* Quiet Man, The, *364;* Start the Revolution without Me, *385;* Wonderwall, *805*
MacGraw, Ali: Convoy (1978), *29;* Getaway, The (1972), *55;* Goodbye Columbus, *288;* Just Tell Me What You Want, *312;* Love Story, *582;* Murder Elite, *600;* Players, *623;* Winds of War, The, *703*
MacGreevy, Thomas: Love in the Present Tense, *581*
Machiavelli, Nicoletta: Minute to Pray, A Second to Die, A, *1134*

Macht, Stephen: Amityville 1992: It's About Time, *809;* Contract for Life: The S.A.D.D. Story, *488;* Galaxina, *1053;* George Washington, *526;* Last Winter, The, *571;* Mountain Men, The, *1134;* Samson and Delilah (1984), *648;* Stephen King's Graveyard Shift, *890;* Trancers 4: Jack of Swords, *1085*
Mack, Charles Emmett: Dream Street, *504*
Mack, Helen: Fargo Express, *1112;* His Girl Friday, *297;* Melody Cruise, *930;* Milky Way, The (1936), *332;* Return of Peter Grimm, The, *638;* Son of Kong, The, *888*
Mack, June: Beneath the Valley of the Ultra-Vixens, *234*
Mack, Kerry: Savage Attraction, *1012*
Mack, Marion: Buster Keaton: The Great Stone Face, *248;* General, The, *283*
MacKay, Fulton: Defense of the Realm, *969;* Local Hero, *320;* Sense of Freedom, A, *652*
MacKay, John: Rejuvenator, The, *879*
Mackay, Mathew: Peanut Butter Solution, The, *194*
Mackenzie, Alex: Greyfriars Bobby, *172*
Mackenzie, Evan: Ghoulies III, *846*
MacKenzie, Jan: Gator Bait II—Cajun Justice, *55*
Mackenzie, Mary: Simple Men, *379;* Stolen Face, *890*
MacKenzie, Philip Charles: Red Light Sting, The, *636*
Mackintosh, Steven: London Kills Me, *577*
MacLachlan, Janet: Roll of Thunder, Hear My Cry, *642;* She's in the Army Now, *656;* Sounder, *663;* Tick ... Tick ... Tick ..., *129*
MacLachlan, Kyle: Against the Wall, *442;* Blue Velvet, *817;* Don't Tell Her It's Me, *267;* Doors, The, *914;* Dune, *1048;* Flintstones, The, *167;* Hidden, The, *1056;* Rich in Love, *640;* Twin Peaks (Movie), *1027;* Twin Peaks (TV Series), *1027;* Twin Peaks: Fire Walk with Me, *1028;* Where the Day Takes You, *699*
MacLaine, Shirley: All in a Night's Work, *224;* Apartment, The, *228;* Around the World in 80 Days (1956), *228;* Artists and Models, *229;* Ask Any Girl, *229;* Being There, *234;* Bliss of Mrs. Blossom, The, *241;* Can-Can, *911;* Cannonball Run II, *250;* Career, *475;* Change of Seasons, A, *253;* Children's Hour, The, *481;* Gambit, *283;* Guarding Tess, *291;* Hot Spell, *544;* Irma La Douce, *307;* Loving Couples, *324;* Madame Sousatzka, *584;* Matchmaker, The, *329;* My Geisha, *340;* Out on a Limb (1986), *616;* Postcards from the Edge, *360;* Some Came Running, *662;* Steel Magnolias, *667;* Sweet Charity, *943;* Terms of Endearment, *679;* Trouble with Harry, The, *399;* Turning Point, The, *689;* Two for the Seesaw, *690;* Two Mules for Sister Sara, *1160;* Used People, *404;* Waiting for the Light, *695;* Woman Times Seven, *705;* Wrestling Ernest Hemingway, *707*
MacLane, Barton: All Through the Night, *3;* Big Street, The, *460;* Black Fury, *462;* Bombardier, *17;* Buckskin, *1102;* Bugles in the Afternoon, *1102;* Bullets or Ballots, *21;* Case of the Lucky Legs, The, *960;* Ceiling Zero, *24;* G-Men, *54;* Go Into Your Dance, *920;* Half-Breed, The, *1118;* Jubilee Trail, *1124;* Kansas Pacific, *1124;* Kiss Tomorrow Goodbye, *73;* Marine Raiders, *82;* Melody Ranch, *1133;* Naked in the Sun, *1135;* Prince and the Pauper, The (1937), *197;* Santa Fe Uprising, *1147;* Silver River, *1150;* Song of Texas, *1151;* Three Violent People, *1157;* Western Union, *1163;* You Only Live Once, *708*
MacLaren, Fawna: Cover Girl Murders, The, *964*
MacLean, Peter: King Richard II, *565;* Othello (1982), *615*
MacLellan, Elizabeth: Puppet Master II, *878*
MacLeod, Gavin: Kelly's Heroes, *70;* Only with Married Men, *350;* Party, The, *354;* Sand Pebbles, The, *111;* Women of the Prehistoric Planet, *1090*
MacLiammoir, Micheal: Othello (1952), *615*
MacMahon, Aline: Ah, Wilderness, *223;* Backdoor to Heaven, *454;* Cimarron (1960), *1105;* Gold Diggers of 1933, *920;* Guest in the House, *534;* Heroes for Sale, *540;* I Could Go On Singing, *924;* I Live My Life, *547;* Lady Is Willing, The, *315;* Search, The, *650*
MacManus, Sharon: This Time For Keeps, *945*
MacMurray, Fred: Above Suspicion, *1;* Absent-Minded Professor, The, *143;* Alice Adams, *444;* Apartment, The, *228;* At Gunpoint, *1095;* Bon Voyage!, *151;* Caine Mutiny, The, *473;* Charley and the Angel, *157;* Dive Bomber, *502;* Double Indemnity, *972;* Egg and I, The, *270;* Follow Me, Boys!, *167;* Happiest Millionaire, The, *173;* Kisses for My President, *314;* Lady Is Willing, The, *315;* Miracle of the Bells, The, *595;* My Love for Yours, *340;* Shaggy Dog, The, *203;* Son of Flubber, *206;* Swarm, The, *891;* Swing High, Swing Low, *390*
MacNaughton, Alan: Dark Angel, The, *966*
MacNaughton, Robert: E.T.—The Extra-Terrestrial, *1048;* I Am the Cheese, *547*
Macnee, Patrick: Avengers, The (TV Series), *7;* Club Med, *484;* Dead of Night (1977), *831;* Down Under, *41;* Gambler Returns, the: Luck of the Draw, *1115;* Howling, The, *853;* King Solomon's Treasure, *73;* Lobster Man from Mars, *320;* Masque of the Red Death (1989), *864;* Pursuit of the Graf Spee, *101;* Rehearsal for Murder, *1009;* Return of the Man from U.N.C.L.E., The, *105;* Sea Wolves, The, *113;* Shadey, *377;* Sherlock Holmes and the Incident at Victoria Falls, *1015;* Sherlock Holmes and the Leading Lady, *1015;* Sorry, Wrong Number (1989), *1019;* Super Force, *1081;* Sweet Sixteen, *123;* Thunder in Paradise, *129;* Until They Sail, *692;* Waxwork, *902;* Young Doctors in Love, *415*
MacNicol, Peter: Addams Family Values, *222;* American Blue Note, *446;* Boy Who Left Home to Find Out About the Shivers, The, *152;* By Dawn's Early Light, *473;* Dragonslayer, *1048;* Heat (1987), *60;* Housesitter, *302;* Sophie's Choice, *663*
MacPherson, Elle: Sirens, *379*
MacPherson, Joe: Bay Boy, The, *456*
MacPherson, Walt: Serial Mom, *376*
Macrae, Arthur: Saint's Vacation, The, *1012*
Macrae, Duncan: Tunes of Glory, *689*
MacRae, Gordon: By the Light of the Silvery Moon, *910;* Carousel, *911;* Look For The Silver Lining, *929;* Oklahoma!, *933;* On Moonlight Bay, *933;* Pilot, The, *622;* Tea for Two, *944;* West Point Story, The, *947*
MacRae, Meredith: Sketches of a Strangler, *1017*
MacRae, Michael: Dear Detective, *968;* Madhouse (1987), *862*
Macready, George: Black Arrow, The (1948), *13;* Coroner Creek, *1106;* Dead Ringer, *967;* Doolins of Oklahoma, *1110;* Gilda, *527;* Human Duplicators, The, *854;* Nevadan, The, *1136;* Paths of Glory, *619;* Seventh Cross, The, *653;* Stranger Wore a Gun, The, *1153;* Two Weeks in Another Town, *690*
Macy, Bill: Bad Medicine, *231;* Casey at the Bat, *156;* Death at Love House, *968;* Diary of a Young Comic, *264;* Doctor, The, *502;* Jerk, The, *310;* Late Show, The, *991;* Movers and Shakers, *337;* My Favorite Year, *340;* Oh! Calcutta!, *348;* Serial, *376;* Sibling Rivalry, *378*
Macy, William H.: Being Human, *458;* Benny & Joon, *234;* Heart of Justice, *538;* Homicide, *983;* Searching for Bobby Fischer, *202;* Water Engine, The, *696*
Madaras, Josef: Red and the White, The, *780*
Madden, Ciaran: Married Man, A, *589*
Madden, Dave: Eat My Dust, *43*
Madden, Donald: Life on the Mississippi, *574*
Madden, Jeanne: Stage Struck (1936), *941*
Madden, John: P.K. & the Kid, *617*
Madden, Peter: Secret Agent (TV Series), *113*
Maddern, Victor: Carrington, V. C., *476*
Madigan, Amy: Alamo Bay, *443;* Ambush Murders, The, *446;* Dark Half, The, *829;* Field of Dreams, *1050;* Love Child, *581;* Love Letters, *581;* Nowhere to Hide, *92;* Prince of Pennsylvania, *361;* Roe vs. Wade, *642;* Streets of Fire, *121;* Twice in a Lifetime, *690;* Uncle Buck, *402*
Madigan, Reese: American Shaolin: King of the Kickboxers II, *5*
Madison, Guy: Bang Bang Kid, The, *232;* Bullwhip, *1102;* Drums in the Deep South, *1110;* Final Defeat, The, *1113;*

Since You Went Away, *658;* This Man Can't Die, *1156;* Till the End of Time, *683*

Madison, Mae: Big Stampede, The, *1098*

Madison, Noel: Cocaine Fiends, *485;* G-Men, *54*

Madison, Rock: Man Beast, *862*

Madonna: Bloodhounds of Broadway, *242;* Body of Evidence, *958;* Certain Sacrifice, A, *478;* Desperately Seeking Susan, *264;* Dick Tracy (1990), *38;* League of Their Own, A, *571;* Shadows and Fog, *654;* Shanghai Surprise, *377;* Truth or Dare, *437;* Who's That Girl, *411*

Madorsky, Bryan: Parents, *354*

Madou, Malou: Man Bites Dog, *764*

Madruga, Teresa: In the White City, *747*

Madsen, Michael: Almost Blue, *445;* Dead Connection, *967;* Fatal Instinct (1992), *976;* Free Willy, *168;* Getaway, The (1994), *55;* House in the Hills, A, *984;* Kill Me Again, *988;* Money for Nothing, *335;* Reservoir Dogs, *105;* Straight Talk, *387;* Thelma & Louise, *127;* Trouble Bound, *1027*

Madsen, Virginia: Becoming Colette, *457;* Candyman (1992), *820;* Caroline at Midnight, *960;* Creator, *490;* Electric Dreams, *271;* Fire with Fire, *517;* Gotham, *980;* Hearst and Davies Affair, The, *537;* Heart of Dixie, The, *538;* Highlander 2: The Quickening, *1056;* Hot Spot, *544;* Hot to Trot, *302;* Ironclads, *554;* Linda, *992;* Long Gone, *578;* Love Kills, *993;* Modern Girls, *335;* Slam Dance, *1017;* Third Degree Burn, *1024;* Victim of Love, *1030;* Zombie High, *904*

Maffay, Peter: Lethal Obsession, *76*

Maffei, Robert: Magic Christmas Tree, The, *184*

Magalhaeds, Yona: Black God (White Devil), *718*

Magall, Macha: S. S. Hell Camp, *882*

Magee, Patrick: And Now the Screaming Starts, *809;* Anzio, *6;* Asylum, *810;* Barry Lyndon, *456;* Black Cat, The (1981), *813;* Clockwork Orange, A, *1042;* Cromwell, *491;* Dementia 13, *832;* King Lear (1971), *564;* King Lear (1988), *564;* Lady Ice, *989;* Last Days of Man on Earth, The, *1062;* Luther, *588;* Marat/Sade, *588;* Masque of the Red Death, The (1964), *863;* Rough Cut, *1011;* Seance on a Wet Afternoon, *1013;* Skull, The, *887;* Telefon, *1023;* Very Edge, The, *693;* Young Winston, *709*

Maggart, Brandon: Christmas Evil, *824*

Maggio, Pupella: Amarcord, *712*

Maggiorani, Lamberto: Bicycle Thief, The, *717*

Magnani, Anna: Amore, *712;* Bellissima, *716;* Fugitive Kind, The, *523;* Golden Coach, The, *741;* Laugh for Joy, *756;* Open City, *773;* Passionate Thief, The (1961), *776;* Rose Tattoo, The, *644*

Magnuson, Ann: Checking Out, *254;* Heavy Petting, *426;* Love at Large, *322;* Making Mr. Right, *327;* Night in the Life of Jimmy Reardon, A, *344;* Sleepwalker, *1017*

Magon, Leslie: Unapproachable, The, *691*

Maguire, Toby: Revenge of the Red Baron, *881*

Mahaffey, Valerie: Mr. Bill's Real Life Adventures, *333;* They, *894;* Women of Valor, *706*

Mahal, Taj: Sounder, *663*

Maharis, George: Desperados, The, *1109;* Land Raiders, *1125;* Murder on Flight 502, *87;* Return to Fantasy Island, *1074;* Sword and the Sorcerer, The, *1082*

Maher, Bill: Cannibal Women in the Avocado Jungle of Death, *22;* Club Med, *484;* House II: The Second Story, *852;* Pizza Man, *358*

Maher, Joseph: Evil That Men Do, The, *45;* Frankenweenie, *280;* Funny Farm, *282;* Going Ape!, *287;* Under the Rainbow, *402*

Maheu, Gilles: Night Zoo, *607*

Mahler, Bruce: Funland, *282;* Paramount Comedy Theatre, Vol. 1: Well Developed, *353;* Police Academy II: Their First Assignment, *359*

Mahoe, Sharon: Devil Rider!, *37*

Mahoney, Jock: Away all Boats, *8;* Cow Town, *1106;* Glory Stompers, The, *56;* Land Unknown, The, *1061;* Nevadan, The, *1136;* Rim of the Canyon, *1144;* Their Only Chance, *210;* Time to Love and a Time to Die, A, *684*

Mahoney, John: Article 99, *451;* Barton Fink, *232;* Dinner at Eight (1990), *265;* Frantic (1988), *978;* Hudsucker Proxy, The, *303;* Image, The, *549;* In the Line of Fire, *66;* Love Hurts, *323;* Moonstruck, *336;* Russia House, The, *646;* Say Anything, *373;* Secret Passion of Robert Clayton, The, *1013;* Striking Distance, *121;* Suspect, *1022;* Target: Favorite Son, *677;* 10 Million Dollar Getaway, The, *678;* Water Engine, The, *696*

Maiden, Sharon: Clockwise, *256*

Maiden, Tony: Spaced Out, *384*

Maier, Tim: Raw Courage, *103*

Main, Marjorie: Belle of New York, The, *908;* Egg and I, The, *270;* Friendly Persuasion, *522;* Harvey Girls, The, *922;* Heaven Can Wait (1943), *295;* Honky Tonk, *1121;* It's a Big Country, *308;* Johnny Come Lately, *311;* Little Tough Guys, *319;* Long, Long Trailer, The, *320;* Mr. Imperium, *931;* Rose Marie (1954), *937;* Show-Off, The, *378;* Stella Dallas, *667;* Summer Stock, *942;* Susan and God, *674;* Test Pilot, *679;* They Shall Have Music, *944;* Too Hot to Handle, *130;* Undercurrent, *691;* Wistful Widow of Wagon Gap, The, *412;* Woman's Face, A, *705*

Maina, Charles Gitonga: Air Up There, The, *223*

Mairesse, Valerie: Investigation, *748;* One Sings, the Other Doesn't, *773;* Sacrifice, The, *782*

Maitland, Lorna: Lorna, *580*

Maitland, Marne: Fellini's Roma, *736;* Terror of the Tongs, The, *126;* Windom's Way, *703*

Majorino, Tina: When a Man Loves a Woman, *698*

Majors, Lee: Agency, *443;* Big Valley, The (TV Series), *1098;* Bionic Woman, The, *1039;* Cover Girl Murders, The, *964;* Cowboy and the Ballerina, The, *490;* Cyborg: The Six-Million Dollar Man, *1043;* Francis Gary Powers: The True Story of the U-2 Spy Incident, *522;* High Noon, Part Two, *1120;* Keaton's Cop, *70;* Killer Fish, *71;* Last Chase, The, *1062;* Liberation of L. B. Jones, The, *574;* Norseman, The, *92;* Smoky Mountain Christmas, *205;* Starflight One, *1079;* Steel, *120;* Will Penny, *1164*

Maka, Karl: Aces Go Places (1–3) (Aka Mad Mission 1–3), *710*

Makeba, Miriam: Sarafina!, *938*

Makepeace, Chris: Aloha Summer, *445;* Captive Hearts, *475;* Last Chase, The, *1062;* Mazes and Monsters, *864;* Meatballs, *330;* My Bodyguard, *601;* Mysterious Stranger, The, *190;* Terry Fox Story, The, *679;* Undergrads, The, *214;* Vamp, *899*

Makharadze, Avtandil: Repentance, *781*

Makkena, Wendy: Sister Act, *379;* Sister Act 2: Back in the Habit, *380*

Mako: Armed Response, *6;* Big Brawl, The, *12;* Bushido Blade, *21;* Conan the Barbarian, *1042;* Eye for an Eye, *46;* Fatal Mission, *46;* Hiroshima: Out of the Ashes, *541;* Island at the Top of the World, The, *1060;* Killer Elite, The, *71;* Kung Fu—The Movie, *73;* My Samurai, *88;* P.O.W.: The Escape, *96;* Perfect Weapon, *98;* Rising Sun, *1010;* RoboCop 3, *1075;* Sand Pebbles, The, *111;* Sidekicks, *203;* Silent Assassins, *116;* Tucker: A Man and His Dream, *689;* Unremarkable Life, An, *692;* Wash, The, *696*

Maksimovic, Dragan: Meetings with Remarkable Men, *591*

Mala: Robinson Crusoe of Clipper Island, *108;* Tuttles of Tahiti, The, *400*

Malanowicz, Zygmunt: Knife in the Water, *752*

Malavoy, Christophe: Madame Bovary (1991), *763;* Peril, *777*

Malberg, Henrik: Ordet, *774*

Malcolm, Christopher: Great Riviera Bank Robbery, The, *980*

Malden, Karl: Adventures of Bullwhip Griffin, The, *143;* Alice Through the Looking Glass (1985), *145;* All Fall Down, *444;* Baby Doll, *453;* Billy Galvin, *461;* Bird Man of Alcatraz, *462;* Blue (1968), *1099;* Cat O'Nine Tails, *960;* Cheyenne Autumn, *1104;* Cincinnati Kid, The, *26;* Dead Ringer, *967;* Fatal Vision, *515;* Fear Strikes Out, *515;* Gunfighter, The, *1117;* Gypsy (1962), *921;* Halls of Montezuma, *59;* Hanging Tree, The,

1118; Hot Millions, *301;* Hotel, *544;* How the West Was Won, *1122;* I Confess, *984;* Kiss of Death, *566;* Meteor, *1065;* Miracle on Ice, *595;* Murderers' Row, *87;* Nevada Smith, *1135;* Nuts, *1002;* On the Waterfront, *612;* One-Eyed Jacks, *1137;* Parrish, *618;* Patton, *619;* Pollyanna (1960), *196;* Ruby Gentry, *644;* Skag, *659;* Sting II, The, *120;* Streetcar Named Desire, A, *671;* Summertime Killer, The, *122;* 13 Rue Madeleine, *127;* Urge to Kill, *692;* Wild Rovers, The, *1164*

Malet, Arthur: Toys, *398*

Malet, Laurent: Invitation au Voyage, *748;* Jacko and Lise, *749;* Roads to the South, *781;* Sword of Gideon, *123*

Malet, Pierre: Basileus Quartet, *715*

Malicki-Sanchez, Keram: Pied Piper of Hamelin, The, *195*

Malidor, Lissette: La Truite (The Trout), *755*

Malik, Art: City of Joy, *483;* Jewel in the Crown, The, *557;* Living Daylights, The, *78;* Turtle Beach, *690;* Year of the Comet, *415*

Malina, Judith: Addams Family, The, *222*

Malinger, Ross: Sleepless in Seattle, *381*

Malkovich, John: Dangerous Liaisons, *494;* Death of a Salesman, *498;* Eleni, *508;* Empire of the Sun, *509;* Glass Menagerie, The, *528;* Heart of Darkness, *538;* In the Line of Fire, *66;* Jennifer 8, *987;* Killing Fields, The, *563;* Making Mr. Right, *327;* Object of Beauty, The, *348;* Of Mice and Men (1992), *611;* Places in the Heart, *623;* Private Conversations: On the Set of Death of a Salesman, *433;* Queens Logic, *363;* Shadows and Fog, *654;* Sheltering Sky, The, *655;* True West, *689*

Mallais-Borris, Rose: Alligator Shoes, *445*

Malleson, Miles: Brides of Dracula, *819;* Dead of Night (1945), *830;* Horror of Dracula, *851;* Hound of the Baskervilles, The (1959), *983;* Knight Without Armour, *566;* Nine Days a Queen, *607*

Mallory, Barbara: For Love of Angela, *519*

Malloy, Matt: Surviving Desire, *389*

Malmsten, Birger: Night Is My Future, *771;* Secrets of Women (Waiting Women), *784;* Silence, The, *786;* Three Strange Loves, *794*

Malone, Dorothy: Abduction, *950;* At Gunpoint, *1095;* Battle Cry, *9;* Beach Party, *908;* Being, The, *812;* Big Sleep, The (1946), *955;* Bushwhackers, *1102;* Day Time Ended, The, *1045;* Last Voyage, The, *76;* Little Ladies of the Night, *576;* Man of a Thousand Faces, *587;* Nevadan, The, *1136;* Private Hell 36, *628;* Rest in Pieces, *879;* Shaming, The, *655;* Sincerely Yours, *658;* South of St. Louis, *1151;* Torpedo Alley, *131;* Warlock (1959), *1162;* Winter Kills, *704;* Written on the Wind, *707;* Young at Heart, *948*

Malone, Joseph: Inside Out (1992), *1058*

Maloney, Michael: Truly, Madly, Deeply, *689*

Maloney, Peter: Robot in the Family, *200*

Maltby, Katrina: Demon Keeper, *832*

Mamas and the Papas, The: Monterey Pop, *431*

Mammone, Robert: Crossing, The, *491*

Mamo, Marc: Majority of One, A, *326*

Mamonov, Piotr: Taxi Blues, *792*

Mancini, Ray "Boom Boom": Dirty Dozen, The: The Fatal Mission, *39;* Mutants in Paradise, *338;* Oceans of Fire, *93;* Wishful Thinking, *412*

Mancini, Ric: Below the Belt, *458;* Penitentiary III, *98;* Triplecross, *399*

Mancuso, Nick: Blame It on the Night, *463;* Deathship, *832;* Family Matter, A, *514;* Fatal Exposure, *46;* Heartbreakers, *538;* Last Train Home, *181;* Legend of Walks Far Woman, The, *1128;* Lena's Holiday, *991;* Lies Before Kisses, *574;* Love Songs (Paroles et Musique), *762;* Mother Lode, *87;* Nightwing, *871;* Rapid Fire, *103;* Ticket to Heaven, *683;* Under Siege, *134*

Mandan, Robert: National Lampoon's Last Resort, *342;* Zapped!, *416*

Mandel, Howie: Fine Mess, A, *277;* First Howie Mandel Special, The, *277;* Gas, *283;* Howie from Maui, *303;* Howie Mandel's North American Watusi Tour, *303;* Little Monsters, *1063;* Paramount Comedy Theatre, Vol. 1: Well Developed, *353;* Paramount Comedy Theatre, Vol. 2: Decent Exposures, *354;* Paramount Comedy Theater, Vol. 3: Hanging Party, *354;* Princess Who Had Never Laughed, The, *197;* Walk Like a Man, *405;* Your Favorite Laughs from an Evening at the Improv, *416*

Mandell, Jonathan: Zipperface, *1033*

Mander, Miles: Brighton Strangler, The, *819;* Captain Caution, *23;* Pearl of Death, The, *1004;* Phantom of the Opera (1943), *874;* Return of the Vampire, The, *880;* Road to Singapore, *369;* Scarlet Claw, The, *1012;* Tower of London (1939), *897*

Manes, George: Heroes in Hell, *61*

Manesse, Gaspard: Au Revoir, Les Enfants, *714*

Manetti, Larry: Take, The, *124*

Manfredi, Nino: Alberto Express, *711;* Cafe Express, *721;* Down and Dirty, *732;* In Nome del Papa Re (In the Name of the Pope-King), *747;* Nudo di Donna (Portrait of a Woman, Nude), *772;* Spaghetti House, *788;* We All Loved Each Other So Much, *802*

Mang, William: Final Executioner, The, *1051*

Mangano, Silvana: Bitter Rice, *718;* Conversation Piece, *726;* Dark Eyes, *728;* Death in Venice, *498;* Gold of Naples, The, *529;* Mambo, *586;* Oedipus Rex (1967), *772;* Teorema, *793;* Ulysses, *133*

Mann, Edward: Jungle Master, The, *69*

Mann, Hank: City Lights, *255*

Mann, Leonard: Cut and Run, *493;* Night School, *1001;* Wifemistress, *804*

Mann, Paul: Fiddler on the Roof, *916*

Mann, Sam: Hard Rock Zombies, *848*

Mann, Terrence: Chorus Line, A, *911;* Critters, *827;* Critters 2: The Main Course, *827;* 10 Million Dollar Getaway, The, *678*

Mann, Tracy: Fast Talking, *166*

Mann, Wesley: Adventures in Wonderland, *143*

Mannari, Guido: Cop in Blue Jeans, The, *29*

Manne, Shelley: Five Pennies, The, *917*

Manners, David: Bill of Divorcement, A, *461;* Death Kiss, The, *968;* Dracula (1931), *837;* Mummy, The (1932), *866;* They Call It Sin, *680;* Three Broadway Girls, *395*

Manners, Marjorie: Texas to Bataan, *1156*

Manners, Sheila: Cocaine Fiends, *485;* Lawless Range, *1127;* Westward Ho, *1163*

Mannheim, Lucie: High Command, The, *61;* Hotel Reserve, *544;* Thirty-Nine Steps, The (1935), *1024*

Manni, Ettore: Battle of El Alamein, The, *10;* City of Women, *724;* Hercules, Prisoner of Evil, *61;* Mademoiselle, *585*

Manning, Elizabeth: Deadmate, *831*

Manning, Hope: Old Corral, *1136*

Manning, Irene: Yankee Doodle Dandy, *948*

Manning, Marilyn: Eegah!, *838;* Sadist, The, *882;* What's Up Front, *408*

Manning, Ned: Dead End Drive-In, *1045*

Manning, Patricia: Hideous Sun Demon, The, *850*

Manno, Joe: Night Screams, *870*

Manoff, Dinah: For Ladies Only, *519;* I Ought to Be in Pictures, *304;* Ordinary People, *614;* Staying Together, *667;* Welcome Home, Roxy Carmichael, *407*

Manojlovic, Miki: When Father Was Away on Business, *803*

Mansfield, Jayne: Dog Eat Dog, *40;* Female Jungle, *516;* Girl Can't Help It, The, *286;* Guide for the Married Man, A, *291;* Las Vegas Hillbillys, *315;* Panic Button, *353;* Pete Kelly's Blues, *935;* Promises, Promises, *362;* Single Room Furnished, *659;* Underwater!, *134*

Mansfield, Martha: Dr. Jekyll and Mr. Hyde (1920), *835*

Manson, Jean: Young Nurses, The, *708*

Mansy, Deborah: Madonna, *994*

Mantee, Paul: Illusions, *985*

Mantegna, Joe: Airheads, *906;* Alice (1990), *224;* Body of Evidence, *958;* Bugsy, *471;* Comrades of Summer, The, *258;* Critical Condition, *260;* Fallen Angels, *513;* Family Prayers, *514;* Godfather, Part III, The, *529;* Homicide, *983;* House of

Games, *984;* Money Pit, The, *335;* Queens Logic, *363;* Searching for Bobby Fischer, *202;* State of Emergency, *666;* Suspect, *1022;* Things Change, *394;* Three Amigos, *395;* Wait Until Spring, Bandini, *695;* Water Engine, The, *696;* Weeds, *697*

Mantell, Joe: Marty (Television), *589;* Onionhead, *350*

Mantle, Clive: Robin Hood and the Sorcerer, *107*

Mantooth, Randolph: Seekers, The, *651;* Terror at London Bridge, *893*

Manuel, Robert: Rififi, *1010*

Manz, Linda: Days of Heaven, *496;* Longshot (1981), *579;* Orphan Train, *615;* Snow Queen, *205*

Mao, Angela: Enter the Dragon, *44*

Mara, Adele: I've Always Loved You, *555;* Nighttime in Nevada, *1136;* Robin Hood of Texas, *1145;* You Were Never Lovelier, *948*

Marachuk, Steve: Hot Target, *64;* Piranha Part Two: The Spawning, *875*

Marais, Jean: Beauty and the Beast (1946), *716;* Donkey Skin (Peau D'Âne), *731;* Elena and Her Men, *734;* Eternal Return, The, *735;* Orpheus, *774;* Testament of Orpheus, The, *793;* White Nights (1957), *803*

Marcano, Joss: Delivery Boys, *263*

Marceau, Marcel: Silent Movie, *379*

Marceau, Sophie: La Boum, *753;* Police, *778*

March, Eve: Song of Texas, *1151*

March, Fredric: Adventures of Mark Twain, The (1944), *442;* Alexander the Great, *443;* Anna Karenina (1935), *449;* Anthony Adverse, *450;* Barretts of Wimpole Street, The, *456;* Best Years of Our Lives, The, *459;* Bridges at Toko-Ri, The, *19;* Desperate Hours, The (1955), *969;* Dr. Jekyll and Mr. Hyde (1932), *835;* Executive Suite, *512;* Hollywood on Parade, *299;* Hombre, *1121;* I Married a Witch, *1057;* Inherit the Wind, *552;* It's a Big Country, *308;* Les Miserables (1935), *573;* Man in the Gray Flannel Suit, The, *587;* Mary of Scotland, *589;* Middle of the Night, *593;* Nothing Sacred, *347;* Seven Days in May, *653;* Smilin' Through (1932), *661;* So Ends Our Night, *661;* Star Is Born, A (1937), *666;* Susan and God, *674;* Tick ... Tick ... Tick ..., *129;* Wild Party, The (1929), *702*

March, Hal: Atomic Kid, The, *229;* George Burns and Gracie Allen Show, The (TV Series), *284;* My Sister Eileen, *932;* Send Me No Flowers, *375*

March, Jane: Lover, The, *582*

March, Tony: Shallow Grave, *114*

Marchal, Arlette: Wings, *140*

Marchall, Steve: Night of the Creeps, *869*

Marchand, Corinne: Cleo from 5 to 7, *725*

Marchand, Guy: Cousin, Cousine, *726;* Entre Nous (Between Us), *734;* Heat of Desire, *743;* Holiday Hotel, *744;* Loulou, *761;* May Wine, *330;* Petit Con, *777*

Marchand, Henri: A Nous la Liberte, *710*

Marchand, Nancy: Bostonians, The, *467;* Brain Donors, *245;* Marty (Television), *589;* Naked Gun, The, *341;* Regarding Henry, *637;* Soldier's Home, *661;* Willa, *703*

Marchini, Ron: Karate Cop, *70;* Omega Cop, *93;* Return Fire: Jungle Wolf II, *105*

Marcovicci, Andrea: Canterville Ghost, The (1986), *155;* Front, The, *523;* Hand, The, *848;* Kings and Desperate Men: A Hostage Incident, *73;* Packin' It In, *193;* Smile, Jenny, You're Dead, *661;* Someone to Love, *662;* Spacehunter: Adventures in the Forbidden Zone, *1078;* Stuff, The, *891*

Marcus, Kipp: Jason Goes to Hell: The Final Friday, *858*

Marcus, Richard: Enemy Mine, *1049;* Jesse, *557*

Marder, Jordan: Walking on Air, *215*

Mardirosian, Tom: Dark Half, The, *829*

Mare, Carolyn: Driller Killer, The, *838*

Maren, Jerry: Petronella, *195*

Mareze, Janie: La Chienne, *753*

Margo: Behind the Rising Sun, *10;* Lost Horizon, *580;* Who's Got the Action?, *411;* Winterset, *704*

Margolin, Janet: David and Lisa, *496;* Enter Laughing, *271;* Game of Love, The, *524;* Last Embrace, The, *990;* Morituri, *87;* Planet Earth, *1070;* Pray for the Wildcats, *100;* Take the Money and Run, *390*

Margolin, Stuart: Class, *256;* Fine Mess, A, *277;* Futureworld, *1053;* Guilty by Suspicion, *534;* Iron Eagle II, *67;* Running Hot, *645;* Women of the Prehistoric Planet, *1090*

Margoyles, Miriam: Age of Innocence, The, *443;* Ed & His Dead Mother, *270*

Margulies, David: Out on a Limb (1992), *352*

Margulies, Lynne: Aftermath, The, *1034*

Marian, Ferdinand: Jud Suss, *750*

Marie, Anne: Beneath the Valley of the Ultra-Vixens, *234*

Marie, Anne-Laure: Aviator's Wife, The, *714*

Marie, Jeanne: International House, *307;* Young Nurses in Love, *416*

Marie, Rose: Lunch Wagon, *324*

Marielle, Jean-Pierre: One Wild Moment, *773;* Tous les Matins du Monde, *796;* Uranus, *798*

Marietta: Nudes on the Moon, *1069*

Marin, Christian: Story of a Three Day Pass, The, *668*

Marin, Jacque: Herbie Goes to Monte Carlo, *174*

Marin, Richard "Cheech": After Hours, *223;* Born in East L.A., *244;* Cisco Kid, The, *1105;* Echo Park, *507;* Far Out Man, *274;* Million to Juan, A, *332;* Rude Awakening (1989), *371;* Shrimp on the Barbie, *378*

Marin, Rikki: Gas Pump Girls, *283;* Things Are Tough All Over, *393*

Marinaro, Ed: Dead Aim (1987), *33;* Diamond Trap, The, *970;* Game of Love, The, *524;* Lethal Lolita—Amy Fisher: My Story, *573*

Marino, Dan: Ace Ventura: Pet Detective, *221*

Marion, Beth: Between Men, *1097*

Marion, George F.: Anna Christie (1922), *449*

Marioni, Saverio: Padre Padrone, *774*

Maris, Mona: Camila, *721;* Falcon in Mexico, The, *975*

Maris, Monica: Legends, *429*

Marius, Robert: Triple Impact, *132*

Mark, Marky: Substitute, The, *1021*

Marken, Jane: Crazy For Love, *726*

Markes, Tony: In the Aftermath: Angels Never Sleep, *1058*

Markey, Enid: Civilization, *483;* Tarzan of the Apes, *125*

Markham, Barbara: House of Whipcord, *853*

Markham, David: Richard's Things, *640*

Markham, Kiki: Two English Girls, *797*

Markham, Monte: Defense Play, *36;* Ginger in the Morning, *527;* Guns of the Magnificent Seven, *1118;* Hot Pursuit, *301;* Hustling, *547;* Jake Speed, *68;* Off the Wall, *348*

Markov, Margaret: Hot Box, The, *64*

Marks, Alfred: Valentino, *693*

Markus, Winnie: Mozart Story, The, *931*

Marlaud, Philippe: Aviator's Wife, The, *714*

Marley, Ben: Pride of Jesse Hallman, The, *626*

Marley, Cedella: Joey Breaker, *558*

Marley, John: Amateur, The, *952;* Blade, *14;* Deathdream, *832;* Framed (1975), *52;* Glitter Dome, The, *980;* Godfather, The, *529;* Greatest, The, *533;* It Lives Again, *857;* Joe Louis Story, The, *558;* Jory, *1124;* Kid Vengeance, *1124;* Love Story, *582;* Mother Lode, *87;* On the Edge, *612;* Robbers of the Sacred Mountain, *107;* Threshold, *1083;* Tribute, *688;* Utilities, *404*

Marlier, Carla: Melodie en Sous-Sol (The Big Grab), *766*

Marlowe, Alan: Deadly Vengeance, *35*

Marlowe, Hugh: Bugles in the Afternoon, *1102;* Casanova's Big Night, *252;* Castle of Evil, *821;* Day the Earth Stood Still, The, *1044;* Earth vs. the Flying Saucers, *1048;* Mrs. Parkington, *598;* Monkey Business (1952), *336;* Night and the City (1950), *605;* Rawhide (1951), *1141;* Twelve O'Clock High, *133*

Marlowe, Linda: Green Man, The, *981*

Marlowe, Scott: Journey into Fear (1975), *987*

Marly, Florence: Dr. Death: Seeker of Souls, *835;* Planet of Blood, *1070*

Marmont, Percy: Lisbon, *77;* Rich and Strange, *639;* Secret Agent, The, *1013;* Young and Innocent, *1033*

Maroney, Kelli: Chopping Mall, *824;* Zero Boys, The, *904*

Maross, Joe: Salzburg Connection, The, *111*

Marotte, Carl: Breaking All the Rules, *245*

Marquand, Christian: And God Created Woman (1957), *712;* Flight of the Phoenix, The, *51*

Marquand, Tina: Game Is Over, The, *739;* Texas Across the River, *1155*

Marquardt, Peter: El Mariachi, *733*

Marques, Maria Elena: Pearl, The, *620*

Marquez, Esteban: Ascent To Heaven (Mexican Bus Ride), *714*

Marquez, Evaristo: Burn!, *472*

Marriott, David: Operation War Zone, *95*

Marrow, Jeff: Story of Ruth, The, *668*

Mars, Kenneth: Apple Dumpling Gang Rides Again, The, *147;* Beer, *233;* For Keeps, *519;* Illegally Yours, *548;* Police Academy 6: City Under Siege, *359;* Producers, The, *362;* Shadows and Fog, *654;* What's Up, Doc?, *408;* Yellowbeard, *415;* Young Frankenstein, *416*

Marsac, Maurice: Tarzan and the Trappers, *125*

Marsalis, Branford: Bring on the Night, *419*

Marsh, Garry: Just William's Luck, *179*

Marsh, Jean: Changeling, The, *822;* Dark Places, *829;* Goliath Awaits, *56;* Return to Oz, *199;* UFO—Volumes I and II, *1086;* Upstairs, Downstairs, *692;* Willow, *1089*

Marsh, Joan: Manhunt in the African Jungle (Secret Service in Darkest Africa), *81;* Road to Zanzibar, *369*

Marsh, Mae: Avenging Conscience, The, *811;* Battle of Elderbush Gulch, The/The Musketeers of Pig Alley, *1097;* Birth of a Nation, The, *462;* D. W. Griffith Triple Feature, *493;* Home, Sweet Home, *543;* Intolerance, *553;* Judith of Bethulia, *560;* Mother and the Law, The, *600;* Tall Men, The, *1154;* Three Godfathers, The, *1156;* While the City Sleeps, *138;* White Rose, The (1923), *700*

Marsh, Marian: Black Room, The (1935), *814;* Crime and Punishment (1935), *490;* Svengali (1931), *1022;* When's Your Birthday?, *409*

Marsh, Michele: Evil Town, *839*

Marshal, Alan: Conquest, *487;* House on Haunted Hill, *853;* Howards of Virginia, The, *545;* Lydia, *583;* Night Must Fall, *606;* Tom, Dick and Harry, *397;* White Cliffs of Dover, The, *699*

Marshal, Dodie: Easy Come, Easy Go, *915*

Marshall, Brenda: Background to Danger, *8;* Captains of the Clouds, *23*

Marshall, Bryan: Hot Target, *64;* Return to Snowy River, Part II, *1143*

Marshall, Clark: Sidewalks of New York, *378*

Marshall, Connie: Saginaw Trail, *1147*

Marshall, Don: Terminal Island, *126*

Marshall, E. G.: Bridge at Remagen, The, *469;* Cash McCall, *252;* Chase, The (1966), *479;* Compulsion, *487;* Consenting Adults (1992), *963;* Eleanor: First Lady of the World, *508;* Interiors, *553;* Ironclads, *554;* Kennedy (TV Miniseries), *562;* Lazarus Syndrome, The, *571;* Littlest Angel, The, *184;* Mountain, The, *600;* My Chauffeur, *339;* National Lampoon's Christmas Vacation, *342;* Poppy Is Also a Flower, The, *99;* Power (1986), *625;* Pursuit of Happiness, The, *631;* Silver Chalice, The, *658;* 13 Rue Madeleine, *127;* Tommyknockers, The, *1084;* 12 Angry Men, *690;* Two Evil Eyes, *898*

Marshall, Garry: League of Their Own, A, *571;* Lost in America, *321;* Soapdish, *382*

Marshall, Georges: French Way, The, *738*

Marshall, Herbert: Black Jack, *14;* Blonde Venus, *464;* Crack-Up, *964;* Enchanted Cottage, The, *509;* Five Weeks in a Balloon, *50;* Fly, The (1958), *841;* Foreign Correspondent, *978;* Letter, The, *991;* List of Adrian Messenger, The, *992;* Little Foxes, The, *576;* Midnight Lace, *84;* Moon and Sixpence, The, *599;* Murder, *998;* Painted Veil, The, *617;* Razor's Edge, The (1946), *635;* Riptide, *640;* Secret Garden, The (1949), *202;* Stage Struck (1958), *665;* Underworld Story, *1029;* Virgin Queen, The, *694;* When Ladies Meet, *698;* Woman Rebels, A, *705*

Marshall, James: Few Good Men, A, *976;* Gladiator, *528*

Marshall, Ken: Feds, *276;* Krull, *1061;* Tilt, *396*

Marshall, Marion: I Was a Male War Bride, *304*

Marshall, Meri D.: Valet Girls, *404*

Marshall, Nancy: Frankenstein Meets the Space Monster, *842*

Marshall, Patricia: Good News, *920*

Marshall, Paula: Hellraiser 3: Hell On Earth, *850*

Marshall, Penny: Challenge of a Lifetime, *478;* Hard Way, The (1991), *293;* Movers and Shakers, *337*

Marshall, Peter: Guide for the Married Woman, A, *291*

Marshall, Sarah: Lord Love a Duck, *321*

Marshall, Sean: Pete's Dragon, *195*

Marshall, Trudy: Married Too Young, *589*

Marshall, Tully: Ball of Fire, *231;* Cat and the Canary, The (1927), *960;* Covered Wagon, The, *1106;* Hurricane Express, *65;* Intolerance, *553;* Laughing at Life, *571;* Red Dust, *636;* Two-Fisted Law, *1159*

Marshall, William: Blacula, *814;* Othello (1982), *615;* Scream, Blacula, Scream, *884;* Something of Value, *118*

Marshall, Zena: Terrornauts, The, *1082*

Marsillach, Cristina: Every Time We Say Goodbye, *511;* Terror at the Opera, *893*

Marston, John: Son of Kong, The, *888*

Marta, Darcy: Living End, The, *577*

Martel, Chris: Gruesome Twosome, *848*

Martel, June: Forlorn River, *1114*

Martel, Wendy: Sorority House Massacre, *889*

Martell, Donna: Hills of Utah, The, *1120;* Project Moon Base, *1072*

Martell, Peter: Cobra, The (1967), *27*

Martin, Andrea: Best of John Candy, The, *236;* Boris and Natasha, *244;* Rude Awakening (1989), *371;* Stepping Out, *942;* Ted & Venus, *392;* Too Much Sun, *397;* Worth Winning, *414*

Martin, Anne-Marie: Hammered: The Best of Sledge, *292*

Martin, Barney: Arthur 2: On the Rocks, *229;* Pucker Up and Bark Like a Dog, *363*

Martin, Ben: Jane Campion Shorts, *309*

Martin, Bill: Elephant Parts, *915;* Television Parts Home Companion, *944*

Martin, Christopher: Class Act, *256;* House Party 2, *923;* House Party 3, *923*

Martin, Crispin: Ali Baba and the Forty Thieves, *3*

Martin, D'Urville: Black Caesar, *13;* Blind Rage, *15;* Boss, *1101;* Dolemite, *267;* Final Comedown, The, *48;* Hell Up in Harlem, *60;* Sheba Baby, *115*

Martin, Damon: Amityville 1992: It's About Time, *809;* Ghoulies II, *846*

Martin, Dan: Laurel Avenue, *571*

Martin, Dean: Airport, *443;* All in a Night's Work, *224;* Ambushers, The, *4;* Artists and Models, *229;* At War with the Army, *229;* Bandolero!, *1096;* Bells Are Ringing, *908;* Bloopers from Star Trek and Laugh-In, *242;* Caddy, The, *249;* Cannonball Run, *250;* Cannonball Run II, *250;* Career, *475;* Five Card Stud, *1113;* Four for Texas, *1114;* Hollywood or Bust, *299;* Jumping Jacks, *311;* Kiss Me, Stupid, *314;* Murderers' Row, *87;* My Friend Irma, *340;* Ocean's Eleven, *93;* Rio Bravo, *1145;* Robin & the Seven Hoods, *936;* Rough Night in Jericho, *1146;* Showdown (1973), *1149;* Some Came Running, *662;* Sons of Katie Elder, The, *1151;* Texas Across the River, *1155;* Toys in the Attic, *687;* Who's Got the Action?, *411;* Young Lions, The, *708*

Martin, Dean Paul: Backfire, *953;* Heart Like a Wheel, *538;* Misfits of Science, *1066;* Players, *623*

Martin, Dewey: Big Sky, The, *1098;* Flight to Fury, *51;* Land of the Pharaohs, *568;* Men of the Fighting Lady, *84;* Savage Sam, *201*

Martin, Dick: Bloopers from Star Trek and Laugh-In, *242;* Carbon Copy, *251;* More Milton Berle's Mad World of Comedy, *431*
Martin, Duane: Above the Rim, *440*
Martin, Jared: New Gladiators, The, *1068;* Quiet Cool, *102*
Martin, Jean: Battle of Algiers, *716*
Martin, Jimmy: High Lonesome—The Story of Bluegrass Music, *426*
Martin, John: Black Roses, *814*
Martin, Kellie: Matinee, *330*
Martin, Lori: Cape Fear (1962), *959*
Martin, Maribel: Blood Spattered Bride, The, *816*
Martin, Marion: Sinners in Paradise, *659;* They Got Me Covered, *393*
Martin, Marji: Hollywood Harry, *299*
Martin, Mary: Night and Day (1946), *933;* Peter Pan (1960), *194*
Martin, Millicent: Alfie, *224*
Martin, Nan: Doctor Detroit, *266;* For Love of Ivy, *279;* Golden Honeymoon, The, *529;* King Richard II, *565;* Other Side of the Mountain, Part II, The, *615;* Toys in the Attic, *687*
Martin, Pamela Sue: Buster and Billie, *472;* Cry in the Wild, A, *31;* Eye of the Demon, *840;* Flicks, *278;* Girls of Huntington House, *528;* Lady in Red, *74;* Our Time, *616;* Torchlight, *686*
Martin, Richard: Arizona Ranger, *1095;* Brothers in the Saddle, *1101;* Dynamite Pass, *1111;* Gun Smugglers, *1117;* Guns of Hate, *1118;* Hot Lead, *1122;* Marine Raiders, *82;* Mysterious Desperado, *1135;* Rider from Tucson, *1143;* Road Agent, *1145;* Rustlers, The, *1146*
Martin, Ross: Dead Heat on a Merry-Go-Round, *967;* Experiment in Terror, *974;* More Wild Wild West, *1134;* Wild, Wild West, The (TV series), *1164;* Wild Wild West Revisited, The, *1164*
Martin, Sallie: Say Amen, Somebody, *434*
Martin, Sandy: Scalpel, *883;* Vendetta, *135*
Martin, Steve: All of Me, *224;* And the Band Played on, *447;* Best of Dan Aykroyd, The, *235;* Best of Gilda Radner, The, *235;* Dead Men Don't Wear Plaid, *262;* Dirty Rotten Scoundrels, *265;* Father of the Bride (1991), *275;* Grand Canyon, *531;* History of White People in America, The, *298;* Housesitter, *302;* Jerk, The, *310;* Kids Are Alright, The, *428;* L.A. Story, *314;* Leap of Faith, *572;* Little Shop of Horrors (1986), *929;* Lonely Guy, The, *320;* Man with Two Brains, The, *328;* Movers and Shakers, *337;* Muppet Movie, The, *189;* My Blue Heaven, *339;* Parenthood, *354;* Pennies from Heaven, *935;* Planes, Trains and Automobiles, *358;* Roxanne, *370;* Saturday Night Live, *372;* Steve Martin Live, *386;* Three Amigos, *395*
Martin, Strother: Ballad of Cable Hogue, The, *1096;* Better Late than Never, *237;* Brotherhood of Satan, *819;* Cool Hand Luke, *29;* Great Scout and Cathouse Thursday, The, *1116;* Hannie Caulder, *1119;* Hard Times, *59;* Love and Bullets, *79;* Man Who Shot Liberty Valance, The, *1132;* McLintock!, *1133;* Nightwing, *871;* Pocket Money, *359;* Rooster Cogburn, *1146;* Shenandoah, *1149;* Slap Shot, *380;* Talion, *1154;* Up in Smoke, *403;* Wild Bunch, The, *1164*
Martin, Todd: Finger on the Trigger, *1113*
Martin, Tony: Big Store, The, *238;* Easy to Love, *915;* Here Come the Girls, *922;* Hit the Deck, *923;* Two Tickets to Broadway, *947*
Martine, Daniel: Cause of Death, *24*
Martinelli, Elsa: Blood and Roses, *814;* Hatari!, *59;* Madigan's Millions, *326;* Maroc 7, *82;* Oldest Profession, The, *773;* Tenth Victim, The, *1082;* Trial, The, *687*
Martinez, A.: Hunt for the Night Stalker, *546;* Powwow Highway, *360*
Martinez, Jorge: Catch the Heat, *24*
Martinez, Mario Ivan: Like Water for Chocolate, *760*
Martinez, Olivier: IP5: The Island of Pachyderms, *748*
Martinez, Patrice: Three Amigos, *395*
Martinez, Reinol: El Mariachi, *733*
Martino, John: Truckstop Women, *132*
Martyn, Greg: Ellis Island, *508*
Marvin, Lee: Bad Day at Black Rock, *454;* Big Heat, The, *12;* Big Red One, The, *12;* Cat Ballou, *1103;* Comancheros, The, *1105;* Death Hunt, *35;* Delta Force, The, *36;* Dirty Dozen, The, *39;* Dirty Dozen, The: The Next Mission, *39;* Dog Day, *40;* Donovan's Reef, *267;* Gorky Park, *980;* Great Scout and Cathouse Thursday, The, *1116;* Gun Fury, *1117;* Hangman's Knot, *1119;* Hell in the Pacific, *60;* I Died a Thousand Times, *65;* Killers, The, *71;* Klansman, The, *566;* Man Who Shot Liberty Valance, The, *1132;* Meanest Men in the West, The, *1133;* Monte Walsh, *1134;* Not as a Stranger, *609;* Paint Your Wagon, *934;* Pete Kelly's Blues, *935;* Pocket Money, *359;* Point Blank, *624;* Prime Cut, *100;* Professionals, The, *101;* Raintree County, *634;* Sergeant Ryker, *652;* Shack-Out on 101, *653;* Ship of Fools, *656;* Shout at the Devil, *115;* Stranger Wore a Gun, The, *1153;* Twilight Zone, The (TV Series), *1086;* Wild One, The, *139*
Marx Brothers, The: Animal Crackers, *227;* At the Circus, *229;* Big Store, The, *238;* Cocoanuts, *257;* Day at the Races, A, *262;* Duck Soup, *269;* Go West, *287;* Horse Feathers, *301;* Love Happy, *322;* Marx Brothers in a Nutshell, The, *430;* Monkey Business (1931), *335;* Night at the Opera, A, *344;* Night in Casablanca, A, *344;* Room Service, *370*
Marx, Groucho: Copacabana, *259;* Double Dynamite, *268;* Girl in Every Port, A, *286;* Mr. Music, *931;* You Bet Your Life (TV Series), *415*
Marx, Harpo: Stage Door Canteen, *665*
Marzio, Duilio: Two to Tango, *133*
Masak, Ron: Harper Valley P.T.A., *294*
Masakela, Hugh: Voices of Sarafina, *438*
Mascolo, Joseph: Shaft's Big Score!, *114*
Masé, Marino: Alien Contamination, *1034;* Commandos, *28*
Masina, Giulietta: Ginger and Fred, *740;* Il Bidone, *747;* Juliet of the Spirits, *750;* La Strada, *754;* Madwoman of Chaillot, The, *585;* Nights of Cabiria, *771;* Variety Lights, *800;* White Sheik, The, *803*
Maskell, Virginia: Only Two Can Play, *350*
Mason, Connie: Blood Feast, *815*
Mason, Eric: Kiss of the Tarantula, *859*
Mason, Hilary: Dolls, *836;* Meridian, *864;* Robot Jox, *1075*
Mason, Jackie: Caddyshack II, *249;* Jackie Mason on Broadway, *309;* Jerk, The, *310*
Mason, James: Assisi Underground, The, *7;* Autobiography of a Princess, *452;* Bad Man's River, *1095;* Bloodline, *464;* Blue Max, The, *16;* Botany Bay, *18;* Boys from Brazil, The, *958;* Caught, *477;* Cold Sweat (1970), *28;* Cross of Iron, *31;* Dangerous Summer, A, *494;* Desert Fox, The, *37;* Desert Rats, The, *500;* Destructors, The, *970;* East Side, West Side, *506;* 11 Harrowhouse, *973;* Evil under the Sun, *973;* Fall of the Roman Empire, The, *513;* ffolkes, *47;* Five Fingers, *977;* Forever Darling, *279;* George Washington, *526;* Georgy Girl, *284;* Heaven Can Wait (1978), *295;* High Command, The, *61;* Hotel Reserve, *544;* Inside Out (1975), *66;* Ivanhoe (1982), *68;* Jesus of Nazareth, *557;* Journey to the Center of the Earth (1959), *1060;* Julius Caesar (1953), *561;* Kidnap Syndicate, The, *751;* Last of Sheila, The, *991;* Lolita, *577;* Lord Jim, *79;* Mackintosh Man, The, *994;* Madame Bovary (1949), *584;* Man in Grey, The, *587;* Mandingo, *588;* Mill on the Floss, The, *594;* Murder by Decree, *998;* Night Has Eyes, The, *1001;* North by Northwest, *1002;* Odd Man Out, *1003;* Prince Valiant, *100;* Prisoner of Zenda, The (1952), *100;* Salem's Lot, *882;* Seventh Veil, The, *653;* Shooting Party, The, *656;* Star Is Born, A (1954), *666;* 20,000 Leagues Under the Sea (1954), *133;* Verdict, The, *693;* Voyage of the Damned, *694;* Water Babies, The, *216;* Wicked Lady, The (1945), *701;* Yin and Yang of Mr. Go, The, *1033*
Mason, LeRoy: Apache Rose, *1094;* Helldorado (1946), *1120;* Hidden Valley Outlaws, *1120;* Last Frontier, The, *1125;* Mojave Firebrand, *1134;* Outlaw Express, *1137;* Painted Stallion, The, *1138;* Phantom Rider, *1138;* Rainbow Valley, *1140;* Rocky Mountain Rangers, *1145;* Santa Fe Stampede, *1147;* Song of Nevada, *1151;* Texas Terror, *1156;* When a Man Sees Red, *1163;* Wyoming Outlaw, *1165*

Mason, Madison: Dangerously Close, *966*
Mason, Marlyn: Christina, *25*
Mason, Marsha: Audrey Rose, *811;* Blume in Love, *465;* Chapter Two, *479;* Cheap Detective, The, *254;* Cinderella Liberty, *482;* Dinner at Eight (1990), *265;* Drop Dead Fred, *269;* Goodbye Girl, The, *288;* Heartbreak Ridge, *59;* Image, The, *549;* Lois Gibbs and the Love Canal, *577;* Max Dugan Returns, *591;* Only When I Laugh, *614;* Promises in the Dark, *629;* Stella (1990), *667*
Mason, Pamela: Navy vs. the Night Monsters, The, *868*
Mason, Tom: F/X 2: The Deadly Art of Illusion, *979;* Men Don't Leave, *331;* Return of the Man from U.N.C.L.E., The, *105*
Mason, Vivian: Lost Planet, The, *1064*
Massari, Lea: And Hope to Die, *952;* Christ Stopped at Eboli, *724;* L'Aventura, *753;* Les Choses De La Vie, *759;* Les Rendez-Vous D'Anna, *759;* Murmur of the Heart, *769;* Story of a Love Story, *668;* Vengeance, *135*
Massen, Osa: Background to Danger, *8;* Iceland, *924;* Jack London, *556;* Master Race, The, *590;* My Love for Yours, *340;* Rocketship X-M, *1075;* Woman's Face, A, *705;* You'll Never Get Rich, *948*
Massey, Anna: Corn Is Green, The (1979), *488;* Five Days One Summer, *517;* Frenzy, *979;* Peeping Tom, *1005;* Sakharov, *647;* Sweet William, *389;* Vault of Horror, *900*
Massey, Daniel: Incredible Sarah, The, *551;* Intimate Contact, *553;* Love with a Perfect Stranger, *582;* Star!, *941;* Vault of Horror, *900*
Massey, Dick: Commitments, The, *912*
Massey, Edith: Desperate Living, *264;* Female Trouble, *276;* Multiple Maniacs, *866;* Mutants in Paradise, *338;* Pink Flamingos, *357;* Polyester, *359*
Massey, Gina: Thrillkill, *1025*
Massey, Ilona: Balalaika, *907;* Frankenstein Meets the Wolf Man, *843;* Holiday in Mexico, *923;* Invisible Agent, *1059;* Melody Master, *592;* Northwest Outpost, *933;* Rosalie, *937*
Massey, Raymond: Abe Lincoln in Illinois, *440;* Action in the North Atlantic, *2;* Arsenic and Old Lace, *228;* Chain Lightning, *478;* David and Bathsheba, *496;* Desperate Journey, *500;* Drums, *42;* East of Eden (1955), *506;* 49th Parallel, The, *520;* Fountainhead, The, *520;* Hurricane, The (1937), *546;* Naked and the Dead, The, *88;* Omar Khayyam, *93;* Possessed (1947), *625;* President's Plane Is Missing, The, *1007;* Prisoner of Zenda, The (1937), *100;* Reap the Wild Wind, *104;* Santa Fe Trail, *1147;* Scarlet Pimpernel, The (1934), *112;* Speckled Band, The, *1019;* Things to Come, *1083*
Massie, Paul: Sapphire, *1012*
Massine, Leonide: Tales of Hoffman, *943*
Masters, Ben: Celebrity, *477;* Deliberate Stranger, The, *499;* Dream Lover (1986), *972;* Key Exchange, *563;* Making Mr. Right, *327;* Running Mates (1992), *371*
Masterson, Chase: In a Moment of Passion, *549;* Married People, Single Sex, *589*
Masterson, Fay: Cops and Robbersons, *259;* Man without a Face, The, *587;* Power of One, The, *625*
Masterson, Mary Stuart: Amazing Stories (TV Series), *1036;* Bad Girls (1994), *1095;* Benny & Joon, *234;* Chances Are, *253;* Fried Green Tomatoes, *522;* Funny About Love, *282;* Gardens of Stone, *525;* Immediate Family, *549;* Mad at the Moon, *861;* Married to It, *589;* My Little Girl, *602;* Some Kind of Wonderful, *382*
Masterson, Rod: Delta Heat, *37*
Mastrantonio, Mary Elizabeth: Abyss, The, *1034;* Class Action, *962;* Color of Money, The, *485;* Consenting Adults (1992), *963;* Fools of Fortune, *518;* January Man, The, *987;* Robin Hood: Prince of Thieves, *108;* Slam Dance, *1017;* White Sands, *700*
Mastroianni, Marcello: Beyond Obsession, *717;* Big Deal on Madonna Street, *717;* Blood Feud, *719;* City of Women, *724;* Dark Eyes, *728;* Diary of Forbidden Dreams, *501;* Divine Nymph, The, *731;* Divorce—Italian Style, *731;* 8½, *733;* Everybody's Fine, *735;* Fine Romance, A, *277;* Gabriela, *739;* Ginger and Fred, *740;* Henry IV, *743;* La Dolce Vita, *753;* La Nuit de Varennes, *754;* Lunatics & Lovers, *763;* Macaroni, *325;* Massacre in Rome, *590;* Poppy Is Also a Flower, The, *99;* Salut L'Artiste, *783;* Shoot Loud, Louder...I Don't Understand, *378;* Slightly Pregnant Man, A, *787;* Special Day, A, *788;* Stay as You Are, *666;* Tenth Victim, The, *1082;* Used People, *404;* Very Private Affair, A, *800;* White Nights (1957), *803;* Wifemistress, *804;* Yesterday, Today and Tomorrow, *806*
Masur, Richard: Adam, *441;* Believers, The, *812;* Betrayal (1978), *459;* Burning Bed, The, *472;* Cast the First Stone, *476;* Encino Man, *271;* Fallen Angel, *513;* Far from Home, *975;* Flashback, *50;* George McKenna Story, The, *526;* Head Office, *294;* Heartburn, *295;* It (1991), *857;* License to Drive, *318;* Man without a Face, The, *587;* Mean Season, The, *996;* Mr. Horn, *1134;* My Girl, *190;* My Girl 2, *190;* My Science Project, *1067;* Rent-a-Cop, *105;* Risky Business, *368;* Shoot to Kill, *115;* Six Degrees of Separation, *659;* Third Degree Burn, *1024;* Walker, *695;* Who'll Stop the Rain, *139*
Matahi: Tabu, *676*
Mateos, Julian: Four Rode Out, *1114;* Hellbenders, The, *1120;* Kashmiri Run, The, *70*
Materhofer, Ferdinand: Orphan Boy of Vienna, An, *934*
Mathe, Edouard: Vampires, The (1915), *799*
Mather, Aubrey: House of Fear, *984*
Mathers, James: Dr. Jekyll's Dungeon of Death, *835*
Mathers, Jerry: Trouble with Harry, The, *399*
Matheson, Michele: Howling VI: The Freaks, *854*
Matheson, Tim: Animal House, *227;* Best Legs in the 8th Grade, The, *235;* Buried Alive (1990), *959;* Dreamer, *505;* Drop Dead Fred, *269;* Eye of the Demon, *840;* Fletch, *978;* Impulse (1984), *985;* Listen to Your Heart, *319;* Little Sex, A, *319;* Little White Lies, *320;* Longest Drive, The, *1130;* Magnum Force, *80;* 1941, *345;* Quicksand: No Escape, *1008;* Solar Crisis, *1077;* Sometimes They Come Back, *888;* Speed Zone, *119;* To Be or Not to Be (1983), *397;* Trial & Error, *1027;* Up the Creek (1984), *403*
Mathews, Carmen: Sounder, *663*
Mathews, Frank: On the Bowery, *612*
Mathews, Kerwin: Battle Beneath the Earth, *9;* Devil at 4 O'Clock, The, *500;* Jack the Giant Killer, *178;* Maniac (1962), *995;* Nightmare in Blood, *871;* Octaman, *872;* 7th Voyage of Sinbad, The, *1076;* Three Worlds of Gulliver, The, *1083;* Waltz King, The, *215*
Mathews, Thom: Bloodmatch, *16;* Down Twisted, *41;* Friday the 13th, Part VI: Jason Lives, *844;* Return of the Living Dead, The, *880;* Return of the Living Dead Part II, *880*
Mathias, Darian: Blue Movies, *242*
Mathie, Marion: Rumpole of the Bailey (TV Series), *1011*
Mathieu, Ginett: Blue Country, *719*
Mathieu, Mireille: Slightly Pregnant Man, A, *787*
Mathis, Samantha: Music of Chance, The, *601;* Pump Up the Volume, *630;* Super Mario Brothers, The, *208;* Thing Called Love, The, *681;* This Is My Life, *394*
Mathis, Stanley: It's a Complex World, *308*
Mathot, Oliver: Demoniac, *832*
Mathouret, Francois: Hot Chocolate, *301*
Matlin, Marlee: Bridge to Silence, *470;* Children of a Lesser God, *480;* Hear no Evil, *982;* Linguini Incident, The, *319;* Walker, *695*
Matsuda, Eiko: In the Realm of the Senses, *747*
Matsuda, Yusaku: Family Game, The, *735*
Mattausch, Dietrich: Wannsee Conference, The, *802*
Mattes, Eva: Celeste, *722;* Man Like Eva, A, *765;* Stroszek, *790;* Woyzeck, *805*
Matthau, Walter: Bad News Bears, The, *231;* Buddy, Buddy, *247;* Cactus Flower, *248;* Casey's Shadow, *157;* Charade, *960;* Charley Varrick, *25;* Couch Trip, The, *259;* Dennis the Menace, *161;* Earthquake, *43;* Ensign Pulver, *271;* Face in the Crowd, A, *512;* Fail-Safe, *974;* First Monday in October, *517;* Fortune Cookie, The, *279;* Front Page, The (1974), *281;* Gangster Story, *979;* Grumpy Old Men, *291;* Guide for the

Married Man, A, *291;* Hello, Dolly!, *922;* Hopscotch, *983;* House Calls, *302;* I Ought to Be in Pictures, *304;* Incident, The (1989), *551;* JFK, *558;* Kentuckian, The, *1124;* King Creole, *927;* Kotch, *314;* Laughing Policeman, The, *991;* Little Miss Marker (1980), *182;* Lonely Are the Brave, *1129;* Mirage, *595;* Movers and Shakers, *337;* New Leaf, A, *343;* Odd Couple, The, *348;* Onionhead, *350;* Pete 'n' Tillie, *357;* Pirates, *358;* Plaza Suite, *358;* Secret Life of an American Wife, The, *374;* Strangers When We Meet, *670;* Sunshine Boys, The, *388;* Survivors, The, *389;* Taking of Pelham One Two Three, The, *1022;* Who's Got the Action?, *411*

Matthews, A. E.: Iron Duke, The, *554;* Made in Heaven (1948), *326*

Matthews, Brian: Burning, The, *820;* Red Nights, *637*

Matthews, Christopher: Scars of Dracula, *883;* Scream and Scream Again, *883*

Matthews, Dakin: Revolver, *106*

Matthews, Francis: Corridors of Blood, *825;* McGuffin, The, *996*

Matthews, Jessie: Candles at Nine, *820;* Evergreen, *916;* Tom Thumb, *213;* Waltzes from Vienna, *406*

Matthews, Lester: Raven, The (1935), *878;* Werewolf of London, *902*

Mattioli, Simone: Burial Ground, *820*

Mattox, Martha: Haunted Gold, *1119*

Mattson, Robin: Are You in the House Alone?, *953;* Bonnie's Kids, *17;* Island of the Lost, *857;* Namu, the Killer Whale, *190;* Return to Macon County, *106*

Mature, Victor: After the Fox, *223;* Androcles and the Lion, *227;* Betrayed (1954), *11;* Captain Caution, *23;* Dangerous Mission, *966;* Demetrius and the Gladiators, *499;* Easy Living, *506;* Egyptian, The, *508;* Footlight Serenade, *917;* I Wake Up Screaming, *985;* Kiss of Death, *566;* Las Vegas Story, The, *568;* Long Haul, *578;* Million Dollar Mermaid, *931;* My Darling Clementine, *1134;* One Million B.C., *1069;* Robe, The, *642;* Samson and Delilah (1949), *648;* Samson and Delilah (1984), *648;* Seven Day's Leave, *376;* Shanghai Gesture, The, *655;* Song of the Islands, *940;* Stella (1950), *667*

Matuszak, John: Caveman, *252;* Dirty Dozen, The: The Fatal Mission, *39;* Down the Drain, *41;* Ice Pirates, *1057;* One-Man Force, *94*

Mauch, Billy: Prince and the Pauper, The (1937), *197*

Mauch, Bobby: Prince and the Pauper, The (1937), *197*

Mauck, Jack: Greenstone, The, *172*

Maude, Mary: Crucible of Terror, *827*

Mauldin, Bill: Red Badge of Courage, The, *636*

Maunder, Wayne: Seven Minutes, The, *653*

Maura, Carmen: Ay, Carmela!, *714;* Dark Habits, *728;* Law of Desire, *756;* Matador, *766;* Pepi, Luci, Bom and Other Girls, *777;* What Have I Done to Deserve This?, *803;* Women on the Verge of a Nervous Breakdown, *805*

Maurer, Joshua: Tour of Duty, *131*

Maurer, Peggy: I Bury the Living, *855*

Maurey, Nicole: Day of the Triffids, The, *1044;* Diary of a Country Priest, *730;* Jayhawkers, The, *1123;* Little Boy Lost, *576*

Mauri, Glauco: China Is Near, *723*

Maurier, Claire: 400 Blows, The, *738*

Mauro, Ralph: They Call Me Bruce?, *393*

Maurstad, Torval: Song of Norway, *940*

Maurus, Gerda: Spies (1928), *788;* Woman in the Moon (a.k.a. Girl in the Moon; By Rocket to the Moon), *805*

Maury, Derrel: Massacre at Central High, *864*

Max, Jean: J'Accuse, *749*

Max, Ron: Forced Entry, *842*

Maxwell, James: One Day in the Life of Ivan Denisovich, *613;* Terrorists, The, *1023*

Maxwell, Larry: Poison, *624*

Maxwell, Lois: Haunting, The, *849;* Man with the Golden Gun, The, *81;* Saint, The (TV Series), *1012;* Spy Who Loved Me, The, *119;* You Only Live Twice, *141*

Maxwell, Marilyn: Arizona Bushwhackers, *1094;* Critic's Choice, *261;* Forever Darling, *279;* Key to the City, *312;* Lemon Drop Kid, The, *317;* Lost in a Harem, *321;* Off Limits (1953), *348;* Presenting Lily Mars, *626;* Show-Off, The, *378;* Summer Holiday, *942*

Maxwell, Paul: Madame Sin, *80*

May, April: Hollywood High, Part II, *299*

May, Deborah: Caged Fear, *21*

May, Doris: Peck's Bad Boy, *194*

May, Elaine: Enter Laughing, *271;* In the Spirit, *306;* Luv, *324;* New Leaf, A, *343*

May, Jodhi: Eminent Domain, *973;* Last of the Mohicans, The (1992), *1126;* World Apart, A, *706*

May, Julie: Hot Millions, *301*

May, Lola: Civilization, *483*

May, Mathilda: Becoming Colette, *457;* Letters to an Unknown Lover, *573;* Lifeforce, *1063;* Naked Tango, *603*

May, Melinda: Hot Millions, *301*

Mayall, Rik: Drop Dead Fred, *269;* Little Noises, *576;* Young Ones, The, *416*

Mayans, Antonio: Oasis of the Zombies, *872*

Maybelle, Big: Jazz on a Summer's Day, *427*

Mayehoff, Eddie: Artists and Models, *229;* How to Murder your Wife, *303*

Mayer, Chris: Survivor, *1081*

Mayer, Ray: Swing It, Sailor, *390*

Mayer, William: Nudes on the Moon, *1069*

Mayes, Judith: Deadmate, *831*

Mayhew, Peter: Return of the Jedi, *1074*

Maynard, Bill: Oddball Hall, *348*

Maynard, Ken: Come on Tarzan, *1105;* Drum Taps, *1110;* Fargo Express, *1112;* Fiddlin' Buckaroo, *1112;* In Old Santa Fe, *1123;* Law Rides Again, The, *1127;* Mystery Mountain, *1135;* Phantom Thunderbolt, *1138;* Six-Shootin' Sheriff, *1150;* Trail Drive, *1158;* Trailing Trouble, *1158*

Maynard, Kermit: Drum Taps, *1110;* His Fighting Blood, *1121;* Night Riders, The, *1136;* Trail of Robin Hood, *1158*

Mayne, Ferdinand: Fearless Vampire Killers, or, Pardon Me, But Your Teeth Are in My Neck, The, *840;* River of Diamonds, *107;* Secret Diary of Sigmund Freud, The, *374;* Vampire Happening, *900*

Mayniel, Juliette: Eyes without a Face, *735;* Les Cousins, *759*

Maynor, Virginia: Man Beast, *862*

Mayo, Christine: Shock, The (1923), *656*

Mayo, Virginia: Along the Great Divide, *1093;* Best Years of Our Lives, The, *459;* Captain Horatio Hornblower, *23;* Castle of Evil, *821;* Devil's Canyon, *1109;* Flame and the Arrow, The, *50;* French Quarter, *522;* Jack London, *556;* Kid from Brooklyn, The, *313;* Midnight Witness, *996;* Out of the Blue, *352;* Pearl of the South Pacific, *620;* Princess and the Pirate, The, *361;* Secret Life of Walter Mitty, The, *374;* Silver Chalice, The, *658;* Song Is Born, A, *940;* West Point Story, The, *947;* White Heat, *138;* Wonder Man, *413*

Mayron, Melanie: Boss' Wife, The, *244;* Checking Out, *254;* Girlfriends, *528;* Missing, *596;* My Blue Heaven, *339;* Sticky Fingers, *386*

Mays, Terra: Zoo Radio, *416*

Maza, Bob: Fringe Dwellers, The, *522*

Mazar, Debi: Beethoven's 2nd, *149;* Inside Monkey Zetterland, *306;* Money for Nothing, *335;* So I Married an Axe Murderer, *382*

Mazurki, Mike: Blood Alley, *15;* Challenge to Be Free, *157;* Dark City, *495;* Dick Tracy, Detective, *38;* Four for Texas, *1114;* Hell Ship Mutiny, *60;* Incredible Rocky Mountain Race, The, *306;* Magic of Lassie, The, *185;* Man with Bogart's Face, The, *995;* Mob Boss, *335;* Neptune's Daughter, *932;* Night and the City (1950), *605;* Noose Hangs High, The, *346;* Shanghai Gesture, The, *655;* Some Like It Hot, *382*

Mazursky, Paul: Alex in Wonderland, *224;* Enemies—A Love Story, *510;* Into the Night, *553;* Man, a Woman and a Bank, A,

94; Man Trouble, *327;* Scenes from the Class Struggle in ;everly Hills, *373*

lazzello, Joseph: Jurassic Park, *1061;* Radio Flyer, *633*

lcAleer, Desmond: Four Days in July, *521*

lcAlister, Jennifer: Serial, *376*

lcAllister, Chip: Weekend Pass, *407*

lcAnally, Ray: Danny Boy (1982), *495;* Death of Adolf litler, The, *498;* Empire State, *44;* Great Expectations (1989), *'71;* Mission, The, *596;* My Left Foot, *602;* No Surrender, *345;* Taffin, *124;* We're No Angels (1989), *408*

lcAndrew, Marianne: Bat People, *812;* Hello, Dolly!, *922;* ;even Minutes, The, *653*

lcAnus, Michael: Mr. Bill's Real Life Adventures, *333*

lcArthur, Alex: Race for Glory, *102;* Rampage, *1009;* Urge o Kill, *692*

lcArthur, Hugh: Marijuana, *588*

lcAuley, Annie: Recruits, *365*

lcAvoy, May: Ben-Hur (1926), *458;* Jazz Singer, The 1927), *925;* Lady Windermere's Fan, *568*

lcBain, Diane: Donner Pass: The Road to Survival, *1109;* 'arrish, *618;* Spinout, *941*

lcBain, Robert: Deadline (1988), *34*

lcBee, Deron Michael: In the Time of Barbarians, *1058;* illing Zone, The, *72*

lcBride, Alex: Rats, *878*

lcBride, Jon: Cannibal Campout, *820*

lcBroom, Marcia: Beyond the Valley of the Dolls, *460*

lcCabe, Ruth: Snapper, The, *382*

lcCabe, Tony: Something Weird, *888*

lcCafferty, John: Deathrow Gameshow, *263*

lcCain, Frances Lee: Gremlins, *1055;* Lookalike, The, *93;* Question of Faith, *632;* Real Life, *365;* Scandal in a Small 'own, *649;* Single Bars, Single Women, *658*

lcCall, Katherine: Crystal Force, *827*

lcCall, Mitzi: Opposite Sex (And How to Live with Them), he, *351*

lcCalla, Irish: Hands of a Stranger, *981;* She Demons, *885*

lcCallister, Lon: Big Cat, The, *12;* Red House, The, *1009;* tory of Seabiscuit, The, *207*

lcCallum, David: Around the World Under the Sea, *6;* launting of Morella, The, *849;* King Solomon's Treasure, *73;* lan from U.N.C.L.E., The (TV Series), *80;* Night to Remember, (1958), *606;* Outer Limits, The (TV Series), *1069;* Return of 1e Man from U.N.C.L.E., The, *105;* She Waits, *885;* Terminal hoice, *893;* Watcher in the Woods, The, *901*

lcCambridge, Mercedes: All the King's Men, *444;* imarron (1960), *1105;* Deadly Sanctuary, *831;* Girls of luntington House, *528;* Johnny Guitar, *1123;* 99 Women, *91;* 'resident's Plane Is Missing, The, *1007;* Who Is the Black ahlia?, *1031*

lcCamey, Shane: Legacy for Leonette, *991*

lcCamus, Tom: Norman's Awesome Experience, *346*

lcCann, Chuck: C.H.O.M.P.S., *155;* Cameron's Closet, *820;* uns, *58;* Hamburger—The Motion Picture, *292;* Heart Is a onely Hunter, The, *538;* Projectionist, The, *362;* Rosebud each Hotel, The, *370;* They Went That-A-Way and hat-A-Way, *210;* Thrashin', *128*

lcCann, Donal: Cal, *474;* Danny Boy (1982), *495;* Dead, he, *497;* Hard Way, The (1979), *59;* Miracle, The (1990), *595*

lcCann, Sean: Mind Field, *85;* Trial & Error, *1027*

lcCann, Tara: Dracula Rising, *837*

lcCarren, Fred: Red Flag: The Ultimate Game, *104*

lcCarthy, Andrew: Beniker Gang, The, *149;* Class, *256;* lub Extinction, *1042;* Fresh Horses, *522;* Heaven Help Us, *95;* Kansas, *562;* Less Than Zero, *573;* Mannequin (1987), *'28;* Only You, *351;* Pretty in Pink, *626;* St. Elmo's Fire, *646;* /aiting for the Moon, *695;* Weekend at Bernie's, *407;* /eekend at Bernie's II, *407;* Year of the Gun, *1033*

lcCarthy, Holis: Civil War Diary, *483*

lcCarthy, Kevin: Ace High, *1092;* Annapolis Story, An, *49;* Buffalo Bill and the Indians, *1102;* Dan Candy's Law, *32;* 'ark Tower, *829;* Dead on the Money, *967;* Distinguished Gentleman, The, *265;* Duplicates, *973;* Final Approach, *1051;* Ghoulies III, *846;* Greedy, *290;* Hero at Large, *296;* Hostage (1987), *64;* Hotel, *544;* Innerspace, *1058;* Invasion of the Body Snatchers (1956), *1059;* Invitation to Hell, *857;* LBJ: The Early Years, *571;* Love or Money?, *323;* Midnight Hour, *864;* Mirage, *595;* My Tutor, *341;* Piranha, *875;* Poor Little Rich Girl: The Barbara Hutton Story, *624;* Prize, The, *629;* Ratings Game, The, *364;* Rose and the Jackal, The, *644;* Rosie, *937;* Sleeping Car, The, *887;* Those Lips, Those Eyes, *945;* UHF, *402*

McCarthy, Lin: D.I., The, *493*

McCarthy, Nobu: Karate Kid Part II, The, *562;* Pacific Heights, *1003;* Wash, The, *696*

McCarthy, Sheila: Beautiful Dreamers, *457;* Friends, Lovers & Lunatics, *281;* George's Island, *169;* I've Heard the Mermaids Singing, *309;* Paradise (1991), *618;* Private Matter, A, *629;* Really Weird Tales, *365;* Stepping Out, *942*

McCartney, Linda: Give My Regards to Broad Street, *919*

McCartney, Paul: Give My Regards to Broad Street, *919;* Paul McCartney and Wings—Rock Show, *432*

McCarty, Mary: French Line, The, *918*

McCary, Rod: Girl to Kill For, A, *980;* Through Naked Eyes, *129*

McCashin, Constance: Nightmare at Bittercreek, *1002;* Obsessive Love, *1002*

McClain, Cady: Simple Justice, *658*

McClanahan, Rue: Baby of the Bride, *230;* Modern Love, *335;* Pursuit of Happiness, The, *631*

McClanathan, Michael: Alice's Restaurant, *444*

McClarin, Curtis: Murder Without Motive, *601*

McCleery, Gary: Hard Choices, *536*

McClellan, Michelle: Night of the Living Babes, *344*

McClory, Sean: Dead, The, *497;* Fools of Fortune, *518;* Island in the Sky, *554;* My Chauffeur, *339*

McCloskey, Leigh: Accidental Meeting, *950;* Cameron's Closet, *820;* Dirty Laundry, *265;* Double Revenge, *504;* Fraternity Vacation, *280;* Hamburger—The Motion Picture, *292;* Inferno, *856*

McClung, Susan: Birch Interval, The, *150*

McClure, Doug: At the Earth's Core, *1037;* Bananas Boat, The, *232;* Enemy Below, The, *44;* Firebird 2015 AD, *1051;* Gambler Returns, the: Luck of the Draw, *1115;* Garry Shandling Show, The, *283;* Gidget, *286;* Hell Hounds of Alaska, *1119;* House Where Evil Dwells, The, *853;* Humanoids from the Deep, *854;* Land That Time Forgot, The, *1061;* Maverick, *1133;* Omega Syndrome, *93;* People That Time Forgot, The, *1070;* Playmates, *358;* Rebels, The, *636;* Shenandoah, *1149;* Tapeheads, *391;* Unforgiven, The (1960), *1160*

McClure, Marc: After Midnight, *808;* Grim Prairie Tales, *847;* I Wanna Hold Your Hand, *304;* Perfect Match, The, *356;* Strange Behavior, *890;* Superman, *1081;* Superman III, *1081;* Superman IV: The Quest for Peace, *1081*

McClure, Shaler: Sgt. Kabukiman N.Y.P.D., *114*

McClurg, Edie: Cinderella (1985), *159;* Dance 'Til Dawn, *262;* River Runs Through It, A, *641;* Stepmonster, *1080*

McCluskey, Kenneth: Commitments, The, *912*

McCollum, Mark: Paramount Comedy Theater, Vol. 3: Hanging Party, *354*

McCollum, Warren: Reefer Madness, *365*

McComb, Heather: New York Stories, *343;* Stay Tuned, *385*

McCord, Kent: Accidental Meeting, *950;* Bloopers from Star Trek and Laugh-In, *242;* Illicit Behavior, *985;* Predator 2, *1071;* Return of the Living Dead 3, *880*

McCorkindale, Don: Three Bullets for a Long Gun, *1156*

McCormack, Eric: Lost World, The (1992), *79;* Return to the Lost World, *1074*

McCormack, Leigh: Long Day Closes, The, *578*

McCormack, Patty: Adventures of Huckleberry Finn, The (1960), *144;* All Mine to Give, *444;* Awakening of Cassie, The, *452;* Bad Seed, The, *454*

McCormick, Gilmer: Silent Night, Deadly Night, *886*

McCormick, Maureen: Idolmaker, The, *924;* Pony Express Rider, *1139;* Take Down, *390*
McCormick, Michelle: Fatal Pulse, *840*
McCormick, Myron: Hustler, The, *547;* Jolson Sings Again, *926;* No Time for Sergeants, *345*
McCormick, Pat: Doin' Time, *266;* Mr. Horn, *1134;* Rented Lips, *366;* Smokey and the Bandit, *381;* Smokey and the Bandit II, *381;* Smokey and the Bandit III, *382*
McCourt, Emer: London Kills Me, *577;* Riff-Raff (1992), *640*
McCowen, Alec: Age of Innocence, The, *443;* Dedicated Man, A, *499;* Forever Young (1983), *520;* Frenzy, *979;* Hanover Street, *536;* Henry V (1989), *540;* Never Say Never Again, *89;* Night to Remember, A (1958), *606;* Personal Services, *357;* Stevie, *668;* Travels with My Aunt, *399*
McCoy, Matt: Cool Surface, The, *963;* Dead On, *967;* Deepstar Six, *832;* Eyes of the Beholder, *974;* Hand That Rocks the Cradle, The, *981;* Police Academy 5—Assignment: Miami Beach, *359;* White Wolves: A Cry in the Wild II, *139*
McCoy, Steve: I Was a Teenage Zombie, *855*
McCoy, Sylvester: Three Kinds of Heat, *128*
McCoy, Tim: Aces and Eights, *1092;* Arizona Bound, *1094;* Below the Border, *1097;* Bulldog Courage, *1102;* Down Texas Way, *1110;* End of the Trail, *1111;* Fighting Shadows, *1113;* Forbidden Trails, *1114;* Ghost Patrol, *55;* Ghost Town Law, *1115;* Gun Code, *1117;* Gunman from Bodie, *1117;* Lightning Carson Rides Again, *1128;* Man of Action, *1132;* Riding Tornado, The, *1144;* Roaring Guns, *1145;* Run of the Arrow, *1146;* Texas Cyclone, *1155;* Traitor, The, *1158;* Two-Fisted Law, *1159;* West of the Law, *1163*
McCoy, Tony: Bride of the Monster, *819*
McCracken, Jeff: Kent State, *563;* Running Brave, *645;* Summer of Fear, *891*
McCracken, Joan: Good News, *920*
McCrane, Paul: Fame, *916;* Portrait, The, *625;* Strapped, *670*
McCrary, Darius: Big Shots, *238*
McCrea, Jody: Beach Blanket Bingo, *908;* Beach Party, *908;* Cry Blood, Apache, *1106;* Glory Stompers, The, *56;* Muscle Beach Party, *338*
McCrea, Joel: Barbary Coast, The, *455;* Bird of Paradise, *13;* Buffalo Bill, *1102;* Come and Get It, *28;* Common Law, The, *487;* Cry Blood, Apache, *1106;* Dead End, *497;* Foreign Correspondent, *978;* Four Faces West, *1114;* Great Moment, The, *290;* Lost Squadron, *79;* More the Merrier, The, *337;* Most Dangerous Game, The, *997;* Oklahoman, The, *1136;* Our Little Girl, *193;* Palm Beach Story, The, *353;* Primrose Path, *627;* Ramrod, *1140;* Ride the High Country, *1143;* South of St. Louis, *1151;* Stars in My Crown, *1153;* Sullivan's Travels, *388;* These Three, *680;* They Shall Have Music, *944;* Union Pacific, *1160*
McCrena, Brittany: Taxi Dancers, *678*
McCulloch, Bruce: Best of the Kids in the Hall, The, *236*
McCulloch, Ian: Alien Contamination, *1034;* Dr. Butcher, M.D. (Medical Deviate), *835;* Witching Time, *904;* Zombie, *904*
McCullough, Julie: Big Bad Mama II, *12;* Round Trip to Heaven, *370*
McCullough, Paul: Clark and McCullough: Inspired Madness, *256*
McCurry, Natalie: Dead End Drive-In, *1045*
McCusker, Frank: Railway Station Man, The, *633*
McCutcheon, Bill: Tune in Tomorrow, *400*
McDaniel, Donna: Hollywood Hot Tubs, *299*
McDaniel, Hattie: Alice Adams, *444;* Bride Walks Out, The, *245;* George Washington Slept Here, *284;* Gone with the Wind, *530;* Great Lie, The, *532;* In This Our Life, *550;* Johnny Come Lately, *311;* Judge Priest, *560;* Murder by Television, *998;* Operator 13, *614;* Saratoga, *372;* Shining Hour, The, *656;* Shopworn Angel, The, *656;* Show Boat (1936), *939;* Since You Went Away, *658*
McDaniel, Tim: Ghost Chase, *845*
McDermott, Dylan: Blue Iguana, *242;* Fear Inside, The, *97*[illegible] Hamburger Hill, *535;* Hardware, *1055;* In the Line of Fire, *66*[illegible] Into the Badlands, *1123;* Jersey Girl, *310;* Neon Empire, The, *89;* Twister, *401;* Where Sleeping Dogs Lie, *1031*
McDermott, Hugh: Devil Girl from Mars, *833;* Pimpernel Smith, *99;* Seventh Veil, The, *653*
McDermott, Shane: Airborne, *224*
McDevitt, Ruth: Homebodies, *851*
McDiarmid, Ian: Chernobyl: The Final Warning, *480*
McDonald, Christopher: Benefit of a Doubt, *954;* Boys Next Door, The, *468;* Chances Are, *253;* Conflict of Interest, *29;* Fatal Exposure, *46;* Fatal Instinct (1993), *274;* Monkey Trouble, *188;* Paramedics, *353;* Playroom, *875;* Thelma & Louise, *127*
McDonald, Francis: Bad Lands, *1095*
McDonald, Garry: Wacky World of Wills and Burke, The, *405*
McDonald, Grace: Gung Ho! (1943), *58*
McDonald, Ian: Ramrod, *1140*
McDonald, Jack: Don Q, Son of Zorro, *41*
McDonald, Joe: Mind Killer, *865*
McDonald, Kenneth: Coast Patrol, The, *27*
McDonald, Kevin: Best of the Kids in the Hall, The, *236*
McDonald, Marie: Living In A Big Way, *929;* Promises, Promises, *362;* Tell It to the Judge, *392*
McDonald, Mary Ann: Love at First Sight, *322*
McDonald, Michael James: Unborn II, The, *898*
McDonnell, Mary: American Clock, The, *446;* Blue Chips, *465;* Dances with Wolves, *1107;* Grand Canyon, *531;* Matewan, *590;* Passion Fish, *619;* Sneakers, *1018*
McDonough, Mary: Mom, *865*
McDormand, Frances: Blood Simple, *957;* Butcher's Wife, The, *248;* Chattahoochee, *480;* Crazy in Love, *490;* Darkman, *1044;* Hidden Agenda, *541;* Mississippi Burning, *596;* Passed Away, *355;* Short Cuts, *657*
McDowall, Roddy: Adventures of Bullwhip Griffin, The, *143* Alice in Wonderland (1985), *145;* Alice Through the Looking Glass (1985), *145;* Arnold, *810;* Battle for the Planet of the Apes, *1038;* Bedknobs and Broomsticks, *149;* Carmilla, *821;* Cat from Outer Space, The, *157;* Circle of Iron, *26;* Class of 1984, *824;* Cleopatra (1963), *484;* Conquest of the Planet of the Apes, *1043;* Cutting Class, *828;* Dead of Winter, *967;* Deadly Game, *34;* Dirty Mary, Crazy Larry, *39;* Double Trouble (1991), *268;* Escape from the Planet of the Apes, *1049;* Evil under the Sun, *973;* Five Card Stud, *1113;* Flood!, *51;* Fright Night, *844;* Fright Night II, *844;* Heads, *294;* Holiday in Mexico, *923;* How Green Was My Valley, *545;* Inside Daisy Clover, *552;* Keys to the Kingdom, The, *563;* Laserblast, *1062;* Lassie Come Home, *180;* Legend of Hell House, The, *860;* Lord Love a Duck, *321;* Macbeth (1948), *583;* Mae West *585;* Martian Chronicles, Parts I-III, The, *1065;* Mean Johnny Barrows, *83;* Midnight Lace, *84;* My Friend Flicka, *190;* Night Gallery, *869;* Planet of the Apes, *1071;* Poseidon Adventure, The, *99;* Rabbit Test, *364;* Scavenger Hunt, *373;* That Darn Cat, *210;* Thief of Baghdad (1978), *127;* White Cliffs of Dover, The, *699;* Zany Adventures of Robin Hood, The, *416*
McDowell, Malcolm: Blue Thunder, *16;* Britannia Hospital, *246;* Buy and Cell, *248;* Caligula, *474;* Caller, The, *1041;* Cat People (1982), *822;* Chain of Desire, *478;* Class of 1999, *1041;* Clockwork Orange, A, *1042;* Collection, The, *485;* Compleat Beatles, The, *421;* Disturbed, *971;* Get Crazy, *284;* Gulag, *534;* If..., *304;* Jezebel's Kiss, *987;* Light in the Jungle The, *575;* Little Red Riding Hood, *183;* Long Ago Tomorrow, *578;* Look Back in Anger (1980), *579;* Merlin & the Sword, *1065;* Monte Carlo, *599;* Moon 44, *1067;* O Lucky Man!, *610* Sunset, *1021;* Time After Time, *1084;* Voyage of the Damned, *694*
McEachin, James: Christina, *25;* Double Exposure (1993), *971;* Honeyboy, *63*
McElduff, Ellen: Maximum Overdrive, *864;* Working Girls, *706*

McEnery, John: Bartleby, *456;* Land That Time Forgot, The, *1061;* One Russian Summer, *613;* Pope John Paul II, *624;* Romeo and Juliet (1968), *643*

McEnery, Peter: Entertaining Mr. Sloane, *271;* Fighting Prince of Donegal, The, *167;* Game Is Over, The, *739;* I Killed Rasputin, *746;* Moonspinners, The, *189;* Negatives, *1067*

McEnroe, Annie: Hand, The, *848;* Howling II...Your Sister Is a Werewolf, *854;* True Stories, *400;* Warlords of the 21st Century, *1088*

McEntire, Reba: Gambler Returns, the: Luck of the Draw, *1115;* Man from Left Field, The, *586;* Tremors, *897*

McEwan, Geraldine: Henry V (1989), *540*

McFadden, Gates: Star Trek: The Next Generation (TV Series), *1079*

McFadden, Stephanie: Love Field, *581*

McFarland, Connie: Troll II, *898*

McFarland, Spanky: General Spanky, *169;* Kentucky Kernels, *312;* Little Rascals, The, *183;* Peck's Bad Boy with the Circus, *194*

McFarlane, Andrew: Boulevard of Broken Dreams, *467*

McFerrin, Bobby: Simply Mad About the Mouse, *204*

McGann, Mark: Business As Usual, *472;* John & Yoko: A Love Story, *559*

McGann, Paul: Alien 3, *1035;* Dealers, *498;* Paper Mask, *1004;* Rainbow, The, *634;* Three Musketeers, The (1993), *129;* Withnail and I, *412*

McGavin, Darren: American Clock, The, *446;* Blood and Concrete, A Love Story, *956;* By Dawn's Early Light, *473;* Captain America (1990), *22;* Child in the Night, *961;* Christmas Story, A, *159;* Court-martial of Billy Mitchell, The, *489;* Cyborg: The Six-Million Dollar Man, *1043;* Dead Heat, *830;* Delicate Delinquent, The, *263;* Diamond Trap, The, *970;* Firebird 2015 AD, *1051;* From the Hip, *281;* Hangar 18, *1055;* Hitchhiker (Series), The, *850;* Hot Lead and Cold Feet, *176;* Ike: The War Years, *548;* Man with the Golden Arm, The, *587;* Martian Chronicles, Parts I-III, The, *1065;* Mission Mars, *1066;* My Wicked, Wicked Ways, *602;* Night Stalker, The (1971), *870;* No Deposit, No Return, *191;* Perfect Harmony, *194;* Raw Deal, *103;* Say Goodbye, Maggie Cole, *648;* Summertime, *673;* Tribes, *688;* Turk 182, *689*

McGaw, Patrick: Amongst Friends, *447*

McGaw, Paul: Afraid of the Dark, *950*

McGee, Michi: In Gold We Trust, *66*

McGee, Vic: Wizard of Mars, The, *1090*

McGee, Vonetta: Big Bust Out, The, *12;* Blacula, *814;* Detroit 9000 (Detroit Heat), *37;* Eiger Sanction, The, *43;* Repo Man, *366;* Scruples, *650;* To Sleep with Anger, *685;* You Must Remember This, *708*

McGee, William: Don't Look in the Basement, *836*

McGill, Bruce: As Summers Die, *451;* Citizen's Band, *255;* End of the Line, *509;* Hand, The, *848;* Last Boy Scout, The, *75;* Last Innocent Man, The, *990;* Little Vegas, *319;* My Cousin Vinny, *339;* No Mercy, *91;* Waiting for the Moon, *695;* Whale for the Killing, A, *698*

McGill, Everett: Field of Honor (1986), *47;* Heartbreak Ridge, *59;* Jezebel's Kiss, *987;* People Under the Stairs, The, *873;* Quest for Fire, *1073;* Silver Bullet, *886*

McGill, Moyna: Strange Affair of Uncle Harry, The, *669*

McGillin, Howard: Where the Boys Are '84, *409*

McGillis, Kelly: Accused, The, *441;* Babe, The, *452;* Cat Chaser, *24;* Grand Isle, *531;* House on Carroll Street, The, *984;* Made in Heaven (1987), *1064;* Reuben, Reuben, *367;* Top Gun, *131;* Unsettled Land, *692;* Winter People, *704;* Witness, *1032*

McGinley, John C.: Article 99, *451;* Car 54, Where Are You?, *250;* Highlander 2: The Quickening, *1056;* Last Outlaw, The (1993), *1126;* Midnight Clear, A, *593;* On Deadly Ground, *93;* Platoon, *623;* Point Break, *99;* Prisoners of Inertia, *361;* Surviving the Game, *123;* Talk Radio, *677;* Watch It, *696*

McGinley, Ted: Blue Tornado, *16;* It's a Bundyful Life, *308;* Linda, *992;* Revenge of the Nerds, *367;* Revenge of the Nerds III: The Next Generation, *367*

McGinnis, Scott: Sky Bandits, *116;* Thunder Alley, *945;* You Can't Hurry Love, *415*

McGiver, John: Arnold, *810;* Gazebo, The, *283;* I Married a Woman, *304;* Love in the Afternoon, *323;* Man's Favorite Sport?, *328;* Period of Adjustment, *356;* Tom Sawyer (1973), *213*

McGlynn Jr., Frank: Westward Ho, *1163*

McGoohan, Patrick: Baby...Secret of the Lost Legend, *1037;* Danger Man (Television Series), *32;* Dr. Syn, Alias the Scarecrow, *163;* Escape from Alcatraz, *45;* Hard Way, The (1979), *59;* I Am a Camera, *547;* Ice Station Zebra, *65;* Kings and Desperate Men: A Hostage Incident, *73;* Koroshi, *73;* Man in the Iron Mask, The (1977), *81;* Prisoner, The (TV Series), *1071;* Prisoner Video Companion, The, *1072;* Scanners, *883;* Secret Agent (TV Series), *113;* Silver Streak (1976), *379;* Three Lives of Thomasina, The, *211;* Three Sovereigns for Sarah, *683*

McGovern, Elizabeth: Bedroom Window, The, *954;* Favor, The, *275;* Handmaid's Tale, The, *1055;* Johnny Handsome, *69;* King of the Hill, *565;* Lovesick, *324;* Me & Veronica, *591;* Native Son, *604;* Once Upon a Time in America (Long Version), *94;* Ordinary People, *614;* Racing with the Moon, *633;* Ragtime, *633;* She's Having a Baby, *377;* Shock to the System, A, *1015;* Snow White and the Seven Dwarfs (1983), *205;* Women & Men: Stories of Seduction, *706*

McGrath, Frank: Wagon Train (TV Series), *1162*

McGraw, Charles: Away all Boats, *8;* Bridges at Toko-Ri, The, *19;* Cimarron (1960), *1105;* Defiant Ones, The, *499;* Gangster, The, *525;* His Kind of Woman, *62;* Horizontal Lieutenant, The, *301;* Killer Inside Me, The, *988;* Narrow Margin, The (1952), *89;* On the Old Spanish Trail, *1137;* One Minute to Zero, *94;* Pendulum, *1005;* T-Men, *676;* Threat, The, *1024*

McGreevey, Michael: Sammy, the Way-Out Seal, *201*

McGregor, Angela Punch: Island, The, *857;* Test of Love, A, *679;* We of the Never Never, *137*

McGregor, Kenneth: Primal Scream, *1071*

McGuinn, Joe: Holt of the Secret Service, *63*

McGuire, Barry: Werewolves on Wheels, *902*

McGuire, Biff: Child of Glass, *158;* Last Word, The, *571;* Serpico, *652;* Werewolf of Washington, *902*

McGuire, Don: Fuller Brush Man, The, *282;* Threat, The, *1024*

McGuire, Dorothy: Enchanted Cottage, The, *509;* Friendly Persuasion, *522;* Gentlemen's Agreement, *526;* Greatest Story Ever Told, The, *533;* Incredible Journey of Dr. Meg Laurel, The, *551;* Make Haste to Live, *994;* Old Yeller, *192;* She Waits, *885;* Spiral Staircase, The (1946), *1019;* Summer Magic, *208;* Summer Place, A, *672;* Swiss Family Robinson, The, *208;* Till the End of Time, *683;* Tree Grows in Brooklyn, A, *687*

McGuire, James: Tuck Everlasting, *214*

McGuire, Jason: Pet Sematary Two, *874*

McGuire, John: Bells of San Angelo, *1097;* Invisible Ghost, *856;* Stranger on the Third Floor, *1020*

McGuire, Kathryn: Sherlock Jr., *377*

McGuire, Michael: Blade, *14;* Great Wallendas, The, *533;* Sanctuary of Fear, *1012*

McHattie, Stephen: Belizaire the Cajun, *458;* Beverly Hills Cop 3, *11;* Call Me, *959;* Caribe, *23;* Death Valley, *831;* James Dean—A Legend in His Own Time, *556;* Moving Violation, *87;* Salvation, *647;* Search for the Gods, *1076;* Sticky Fingers, *386;* Tomorrow Never Comes, *686;* Ultimate Warrior, The, *1087*

McHugh, Frank: All Through the Night, *3;* Boy Meets Girl, *244;* Bullets or Ballots, *21;* City for Conquest, *482;* Devil Dogs of the Air, *37;* Ex-Lady, *512;* Fighting 69th, The, *48;* Footlight Parade, *917;* Going My Way, *529;* I Love You Again, *304;* Last Hurrah, The, *569;* Marine Raiders, *82;* Mighty Joe Young, *1066;* Miss Grant Takes Richmond, *333;* Mystery of the Wax Museum, *868;* Roaring Twenties, The, *107;* Stage Struck (1936), *941;* State Fair (1945), *941;* Strange Love of Molly Louvain, The, *669;* Telegraph Trail, The, *1154;* There's No Business Like Show Business, *944;* Three Men on a Horse,

395; Tiger Walks, A, 211; Tomorrow at Seven, 685; Velvet Touch, The, 693; Virginia City, 1161
McIlwaine, Robert: Soldier's Home, 661
McIlwraith, David: Too Outrageous, 686
McIntire, James: Gone in 60 Seconds, 56
McIntire, John: As Summers Die, 451; Away all Boats, 8; Call Northside 777, 959; Cloak and Dagger (1984), 27; Command Decision, 487; Far Country, The, 1112; Flaming Star, 1113; Fugitive, The (TV Series), 523; Honkytonk Man, 543; Mark of the Hawk, The, 589; Psycho, 877; Rooster Cogburn, 1146; Rough Night in Jericho, 1146; Street with No Name, 1021; Summer and Smoke, 672; Tin Star, The, 1157; Two Rode Together, 1160; Walk Softly, Stranger, 1030; Westward the Women, 1163; Winchester '73, 1165
McIntire, Tim: Aloha, Bobby and Rose, 4; American Hot Wax, 906; Fast-Walking, 515; Gumball Rally, The, 58; Sacred Ground, 1146; Sterile Cuckoo, The, 667
McKay, David: Girl in the Picture, The, 286
McKay, Doreen: Night Riders, The, 1136; Pals of the Saddle, 1138
McKay, John: Assault of the Rebel Girls, 7; Rocket Attack USA, 1075
McKay, Scott: Thirty Seconds Over Tokyo, 127
McKay, Wanda: Black Raven, The, 955; Bowery at Midnight, 818; Corregidor, 489; Monster Maker, The, 866
McKean, Michael: Big Picture, The, 238; Book of Love, 243; Clue, 256; Coneheads, 258; D.A.R.Y.L., 1044; Earth Girls Are Easy, 915; Flashback, 50; Hider in the House, 982; History of White People in America, The (Volume II), 298; Light of Day, 575; Man Trouble, 327; Memoirs of an Invisible Man, 1065; Planes, Trains and Automobiles, 358; Return of Spinal Tap, The, 366; Short Circuit 2, 1076; This Is Spinal Tap, 394; True Identity, 399; Young Doctors in Love, 415
McKee, Lafe: Big Stampede, The, 1098; Feud of the Trail, 1112; Fighting Deputy, 1112; Man from Monterey, The, 1131; Mystery of the Hooded Horsemen, 1135; Rawhide (1938), 1141; Ride Him Cowboy, 1143; Spirit of the West, 1152; Telegraph Trail, The, 1154; Warning Shadows (1933), 1030
McKee, Lonette: Brewster's Millions (1985), 245; Cotton Club, The, 29; Cuba, 31; Gardens of Stone, 525; Jungle Fever, 561; Malcolm X, 586; Round Midnight, 937; Sparkle, 941; Which Way Is Up?, 410
McKeehan, Luke: Concrete Angels, 487
McKellen, Ian: And the Band Played on, 447; Ballad of Little Jo, The, 1096; Keep, The, 859; Plenty, 623; Priest of Love, 627; Scandal, 648; Scarlet Pimpernel, The (1982), 112; Six Degrees of Separation, 659; Windmills of the Gods, 703
McKeller, Don: Highway 61, 297
McKelvey, Mark: On the Make, 612
McKenna, Siobhan: King of Kings (1961), 565; Of Human Bondage (1964), 610; Playboy of the Western World, 358
McKenna, T. P.: Beast in the Cellar, The, 812; Bleak House, 463; Portrait of the Artist as a Young Man, A, 625; Straw Dogs, 1021
McKenna, Virginia: Born Free, 152; Christian the Lion, 158; Cruel Sea, The, 492; Gathering Storm, 525; Ring of Bright Water, 199; Simba, 658; Waterloo, 697; Wreck of the Mary Deare, The, 141
McKennon, Dallas: Mystery Mansion, 190
McKenzie, Fay: Heart of the Rio Grande, 1119
McKenzie, Jack: Silent Mouse, 204
McKenzie, Jacqueline: Romper Stomper, 109
McKenzie, Julia: Shirley Valentine, 378; Those Glory Glory Days, 682
Mckenzie, Patch: Goodbye, Norma Jean, 530
McKenzie, Tim: Dead Easy, 967; Gallipoli, 524; Thirteenth Floor, The, 895
McKeon, Doug: Breaking Home Ties, 469; Comeback Kid, The, 486; Heart of a Champion: The Ray Mancini Story, 538; Mischief, 333; On Golden Pond, 612
McKeon, Nancy: Lightning Incident, The, 860; Poison Ivy (1985), 359; Where the Day Takes You, 699
McKeon, Philip: Red Surf, 104; Return to Horror High, 880
McKern, Leo: Blue Lagoon, The, 465; Candleshoe, 155; Day the Earth Caught Fire, The, 1044; French Lieutenant's Woman, The, 522; Help!, 922; Horse Without a Head, The, 175; House on Garibaldi Street, 545; King Lear (1984), 564; Ladyhawke, 74; Massacre in Rome, 590; Monsignor Quixote, 599; Mouse That Roared, The, 337; Murder with Mirrors, 999; Nativity, The, 604; Prisoner, The (TV Series), 1071; Prisoner Video Companion, The, 1072; Reilly: The Ace of Spies, 637; Rumpole of the Bailey (TV Series), 1011; Ryan's Daughter, 646; Shoes of the Fisherman, 656; Travelling North, 687
McKim, Matt: Little Match Girl, The (1983), 182
McKim, Robert: Hell's Hinges, 1120; Mark of Zorro, The (1920), 82; Strong Man, The, 387
McKim, Sammy: Old Barn Dance, The, 1136; Painted Stallion, The, 1138; Rocky Mountain Rangers, 1145
McKinney, Bill: Bronco Billy, 246; City Slickers II, 256; Final Justice, 48; Heart Like a Wheel, 538; Outlaw Josey Wales, The, 1137; Pink Cadillac, 99
McKinney, Kurt: No Retreat, No Surrender, 92
McKinney, Mark: Best of the Kids in the Hall, The, 236
McKinney, Nina Mae: Hallelujah!, 535; Sanders of the River, 111
McKinnon, Mona: Plan 9 from Outer Space, 1070
McKnight, David: Terror in Paradise, 126
McKrell, Jim: Love at the Top, 581
McKuen, Rod: Rock, Pretty Baby, 936
McLaglen, Victor: Call Out the Marines, 249; Devil's Party, The, 500; Dishonored, 501; Forever and a Day, 520; Gunga Din, 58; Informer, The, 552; Klondike Annie, 314; Laughing at Life, 571; Let Freedom Ring, 928; Lost Patrol, The, 79; Murder at the Vanities, 931; Prince Valiant, 100; Princess and the Pirate, The, 361; Quiet Man, The, 364; Rio Grande, 1145; Sea Devils, 112; She Wore a Yellow Ribbon, 1148; South of Pago Pago, 119; Trouble in the Glen, 399; Wee Willie Winkie, 216; Whistle Stop, 138
McLain, Mary: Alligator Eyes, 951
McLane, Robert: Up!, 403
McLaren, Hollis: Outrageous, 352; Too Outrageous, 686; Vengeance Is Mine (1976), 135
McLaren, Malcolm: Great Rock and Roll Swindle, The, 921
McLaren, Mary: New Frontier, 1136
McLarty, Ron: Feud, The, 276
McLaughlin, Bill: Comic Cabby, 258; Devastator, The, 37; Naked Vengeance, 88
McLaughlin, Maya: Children of the Night, 823
McLean, David: Strangler, The, 1020
McLean, Don: Wasn't That a Time!, 438
McLeod, Catherine: Fabulous Texan, The, 1112; I've Always Loved You, 555
McLeod, Gordon: Saint's Vacation, The, 1012
McLeod, Ken: Trained to Fight, 132
McLerie, Allyn Ann: Calamity Jane (1953), 910; Jeremiah Johnson, 1123; Living Proof: The Hank Williams, Jr., Story, 577; Shining Season, A, 656; Words and Music, 948
McLiam, John: Showdown (1973), 1149; Sleeper, 381; Split Decisions, 664
McLinden, Dursley: Diamond's Edge, 162
McLish, Rachel: Aces: Iron Eagle III, 1; Pumping Iron II: The Women, 630
McMahon, Ed: Fun with Dick and Jane, 282; Kid from Left Field, The, 180; Slaughter's Big Rip-Off, 117
McMahon, Horace: Delicate Delinquent, The, 263; Never Steal Anything Small, 932
McMahon, Julian: Wet and Wild Summer, 408
McMahon, Shannon: Blood Sisters, 816; Pledge Night, 875
McManus, Michael: Speaking Parts, 664
McMartin, John: Dream Lover (1986), 972; Greatest Man in the World, The, 290; Murrow, 601; Native Son, 604; Separate But Equal, 652; Shock to the System, A, 1015; Who's That Girl, 411

McMaster, Niles: Bloodsucking Freaks (The Incredible Torture Show), *816*
McMillan, Andrew Ian: Kavik the Wolf Dog, *179*
McMillan, Gloria: Our Miss Brooks (TV Series), *351*
McMillan, Kenneth: Acceptable Risks, *440;* Armed and Dangerous, *228;* Blue Skies Again, *465;* Cat's Eye, *822;* Chilly Scenes of Winter, *481;* Dixie Changing Habits, *265;* Dune, *1048;* Killing Hour, The, *988;* Malone, *80;* Reckless (1984), *636;* Runaway Train, *110;* Three Fugitives, *395;* Whose Life Is It, Anyway?, *701*
McMillan, W. G.: Crazies, The, *825*
McMillan, Weston: Mortal Sins (1992), *997*
McMillin, Michael: Midnight Kiss, *864*
McMullan, Jim: She's Dressed to Kill, *656*
McMurray, Sam: Addams Family Values, *222;* Stone Cold, *120*
McMyler, Pamela: Dogpound Shuffle, *266;* Stick-up, The, *386*
McNair, Barbara: Change of Habit, *479;* Organization, The, *96;* Stiletto, *120;* They Call Me Mister Tibbs, *127;* Venus in Furs, *135*
McNally, Kevin: Berlin Affair, The, *459*
McNally, Stephen: Air Raid Wardens, *223;* Criss Cross (1948), *964;* Devil's Canyon, *1109;* For Me and My Gal, *917;* Make Haste to Live, *994;* Split Second (1953), *664;* Thirty Seconds Over Tokyo, *127;* Tribute to a Bad Man, *1159;* Winchester '73, *1165*
McNamara, Brian: Detective Sadie and Son, *37;* Mystery Date, *341;* When the Party's Over, *699*
McNamara, Ed: Strange Tales: Ray Bradbury Theater, *1080;* Tramp at the Door, *687*
McNamara, Maggie: Moon Is Blue, The, *336*
McNamara, William: Chasers, *254;* Surviving the Game, *123;* Wild Flower, *702*
McNeal, Julia: Unbelievable Truth, The, *691*
McNear, Howard: Andy Griffith Show, The (TV Series), *227*
McNeil, Claudia: Raisin in the Sun, A (1961), *634;* Roll of Thunder, Hear My Cry, *642*
McNeil, Kate: Monkey Shines: An Experiment in Fear, *865*
McNichol, Jimmy: Night Warning, *870;* Smokey Bites the Dust, *382*
McNichol, Kristy: Baby of the Bride, *230;* Dream Lover (1986), *972;* End, The, *271;* Forgotten One, The, *978;* Just the Way You Are, *561;* Little Darlings, *319;* My Old Man, *602;* Night the Lights Went Out in Georgia, The, *606;* Only When I Laugh, *614;* Pirate Movie, The, *935;* Summer of My German Soldier, *672;* Two Moon Junction, *690;* White Dog, *700;* Women of Valor, *706;* You Can't Hurry Love, *415*
McOmie, Maggie: In Between, *550;* THX 1138, *1084*
McPeak, Sandy: Born to Ride, *17*
McQuarrie, Murdock: New Frontier, *1136*
McQueen, Butterfly: I Dood It, *924*
McQueen, Chad: Death Ring, *35;* Martial Law, *82;* Nightforce, *91;* Possessed by the Night, *1006*
McQueen, Steve: Baby the Rain Must Fall, *453;* Blob, The (1958), *814;* Bullitt, *21;* Cincinnati Kid, The, *26;* Getaway, The (1972), *55;* Great Escape, The, *57;* Hell Is for Heroes, *60;* Honeymoon Machine, The, *300;* Hunter, The (1980), *65;* Junior Bonner, *1124;* Love with the Proper Stranger, *582;* Magnificent Seven, The, *1131;* Nevada Smith, *1135;* Never Love a Stranger, *604;* Never So Few, *89;* Papillon, *97;* Reivers, The, *365;* Sand Pebbles, The, *111;* Soldier in the Rain, *661;* Somebody Up There Likes Me, *662;* Thomas Crown Affair, The, *128;* Tom Horn, *1157;* Towering Inferno, The, *131;* Wanted: Dead or Alive (TV Series), *1162;* War Lover, The, *696*
McRae, Alan: Three Ninjas Kick Back, *211*
McRae, Carmen: Jo Jo Dancer, Your Life Is Calling, *558*
McRae, Frank: Batteries Not Included, *148;* Cannery Row, *250;* Dillinger (1973), *39;* Farewell to the King, *46;* 48 Hrs., *279;* Last Action Hero, The, *1062;* Lightning Jack, *1128;* Sketch Artist, *1017;* Used Cars, *404*
McRae, Hilton: French Lieutenant's Woman, The, *522*
McRaney, Gerald: American Justice, *4;* Blind Vengeance, *15;* Dynamite and Gold, *1110;* Haunting Passion, The, *1055;* Murder by Moonlight, *1067;* Night of Bloody Horror, *869*
McShane, Ian: Cheaper to Keep Her, *254;* Exposed, *840;* Grand Larceny, *289;* Great Riviera Bank Robbery, The, *980;* If It's Tuesday, This Must Be Belgium, *305;* Journey into Fear (1975), *987;* Murders in the Rue Morgue (1986), *999;* Ordeal by Innocence, *1003;* Terrorists, The, *1023;* Too Scared to Scream, *1025;* Torchlight, *686;* Yesterday's Hero, *708*
McSwain, Monica: Little Match Girl, The (1983), *182*
McWhirter, Jillian: Beyond the Call of Duty, *11;* Dune Warriors, *42*
McWilliams, Caroline: Rage (1980), *633*
Meacham, Anne: Lilith, *575*
Meade, Julia: Zotz!, *417*
Meade, Mary: T-Men, *676*
Meadows, Audrey: Honeymooners, The (TV Series), *300;* Honeymooners, The: Lost Episodes (TV Series), *300;* Jackie Gleason's Honeybloopers, *309;* That Touch of Mink, *393*
Meadows, Jayne: Alice in Wonderland (1985), *145;* Alice Through the Looking Glass (1985), *145;* James Dean—A Legend in His Own Time, *556;* Lady in the Lake, *990;* Murder by Numbers, *998;* Norman...Is That You?, *346;* Undercurrent, *691*
Meadows, Joyce: Brain from Planet Arous, The, *1040;* Zebra in the Kitchen, *220*
Meadows, Stephen: Sunstroke, *1021;* Ultraviolet, *133*
Meagher, Karen: Experience Preferred...But Not Essential, *273;* Threads, *682*
Meaney, Colm: Doctor Quinn Medicine Woman, *502;* Far and Away, *514;* Into the West, *177;* Snapper, The, *382;* Under Siege, *134*
Means, Angela: House Party 3, *923*
Means, Russell: Last of the Mohicans, The (1992), *1126*
Meara, Anne: Longshot, The (1985), *320;* Lovers and Other Strangers, *323;* My Little Girl, *602;* Out of Towners, The, *352;* That's Adequate, *393*
Meat Loaf: Leap of Faith, *572;* Motorama, *337;* Rocky Horror Picture Show, The, *937;* Squeeze, The (1987), *385;* Stand by Me (1988), *941;* Wayne's World, *406*
Medak, Karen: Girl to Kill For, A, *980;* Treacherous Crossing, *1027*
Medeiros, Michale: Infested, *856*
Medford, Kay: Ensign Pulver, *271;* Face in the Crowd, A, *512;* Funny Girl, *918*
Medina, Ofelia: Frida, *739*
Medina, Patricia: Botany Bay, *18;* Francis, the Talking Mule, *280;* Hotel Reserve, *544;* Mr. Arkadin (a.k.a. Confidential Report), *596;* Snow White and the Three Stooges, *205*
Medwin, Michael: Rattle of a Simple Man, *635;* Scrooge (1970), *938*
Meehan, Danny: Don't Drink the Water, *267*
Meek, Donald: Air Raid Wardens, *223;* Bathing Beauty, *908;* Blondie Takes a Vacation, *242;* Colonel Effingham's Raid, *257;* Du Barry Was a Lady, *915;* Jesse James, *1123;* Keeper of the Flame, *562;* Little Miss Broadway, *928;* Love on the Run (1936), *323;* Make a Wish, *586;* Mrs. Wiggs of the Cabbage Patch, *598;* Murder at the Vanities, *931;* Return of Frank James, The, *1142;* Return of Peter Grimm, The, *638;* Romance in Manhattan, *643;* Stagecoach (1939), *1152;* State Fair (1945), *941;* They Got Me Covered, *393;* Thin Man Goes Home, The, *1024;* Toast of New York, The, *685;* Young Mr. Lincoln, *708*
Meek, Jeff: Night of the Cyclone, *1001*
Meeker, George: Apache Rose, *1094;* Hips, Hips, Hooray, *297;* Home in Oklahoma, *1121;* Murder by Television, *998;* Song of Nevada, *1151;* Superman—The Serial, *1081;* Tarzan's Revenge, *126;* Twilight in the Sierras, *1159*
Meeker, Ralph: Alpha Incident, The, *1035;* Anderson Tapes, The, *952;* Battle Shock, *812;* Birds of Prey, *13;* Brannigan, *18;* Dead Don't Die, The, *830;* Detective, The (1968), *500;* Food of the Gods, *1052;* Four in a Jeep, *521;* Gentle Giant, *169;* Kiss

Me Deadly, *989;* Mind Snatchers, The, *865;* My Boys Are Good Boys, *601;* Naked Spur, The, *1135;* Night Games, *1001;* Paths of Glory, *619;* Run of the Arrow, *1146;* St. Valentine's Day Massacre, The, *111;* Winter Kills, *704*
Meeks, Edith: Poison, *624*
Meffre, Armand: Blue Country, *719;* Here Comes Santa Claus, *174*
Megna, John: Ratings Game, The, *364;* To Kill a Mockingbird, *684*
Megowan, Don: Creation of the Humanoids, *1043;* Lawless Street, A, *1127*
Mehri, Jalal: Fearless Tiger, *47*
Meighan, Thomas: Male and Female, *994*
Meillon, John: Cars That Eat People (The Cars That Ate Paris), *821;* "Crocodile" Dundee, *261;* "Crocodile" Dundee II, *261;* Everlasting Secret Family, The, *511;* Fourth Wish, The, *521;* Frenchman's Farm, *843;* Ride a Wild Pony, *199;* Wild Duck, The, *702*
Meineke, Eva Marie: César and Rosalie, *723*
Meininger, Frederique: Lover, The, *582*
Meisner, Gunter: In a Glass Cage, *747*
Mejia, Alfonso: Los Olvidados, *761*
Melamed, Fred: Suspect, *1022*
Melato, Mariangela: By The Blood Of Others, *721;* Love and Anarchy, *762;* Seduction of Mimi, The, *784;* Summer Night, *791;* Swept Away, *792;* To Forget Venice, *795*
Melchior, Lauritz: Luxury Liner, *930;* This Time For Keeps, *945;* Thrill of a Romance, *945;* Two Sisters from Boston, *947*
Meldrum, Wendel: Hush Little Baby, *984*
Melendez, Asdrubal: Very Old Man with Enormous Wings, A, *800*
Melford, Kim: Corvette Summer, *29*
Melia, Joe: Hitchhiker's Guide to the Galaxy, The, *1056;* Privates on Parade, *362;* Sakharov, *647*
Mell, Marisa: Danger: Diabolik, *1044*
Mellencamp, John: Falling from Grace, *513*
Melles, Sunnyi: 38 Vienna Before the Fall, *794*
Mellinger, Leonie: Lion and the Hawk, The, *77*
Mello, Breno: Black Orpheus, *718*
Melman, Larry "Bud": Couch Potato Workout Tape, *259*
Melton, Sid: Captain Midnight—Vols. 1–2, *155;* Lost Continent, The, *1063*
Melville, Sam: Roughnecks, *109*
Melvin, Allan: Sgt. Bilko (TV Series), *376*
Melvin, Murray: Taste of Honey, A, *677*
Memel, Steve: Savage Justice, *111*
Mendaille, David: Kameradschaft, *751*
Mendelsohn, Ben: Efficiency Expert, The, *508*
Mendenhall, David: Going Bananas, *169;* Over the Top, *617;* Space Raiders, *1078;* Streets, *121;* They Still Call Me Bruce, *393*
Mendlesolin, Bob: Devil's Gift, The, *834*
Mendonca, Mauro: Dona Flor and Her Two Husbands, *731*
Ménez, Bernard: Dracula and Son, *837*
Mengatti, John: Knights of the City, *927;* Meatballs Part II, *330*
Menglet, Alex: Georgia, *979*
Menina, Asha: House of Cards, *545*
Menjou, Adolphe: Across the Wide Missouri, *1092;* Ambassador's Daughter, The, *226;* Are Parents People?, *228;* Bundle of Joy, *247;* Farewell to Arms, A, *514;* Front Page, The (1931), *281;* Gold Diggers of 1935, *920;* Golden Boy, *529;* Goldwyn Follies, The, *920;* Hucksters, The, *545;* I Married a Woman, *304;* Letter of Introduction, *573;* Little Miss Marker (1934), *182;* Marriage Circle, The, *329;* Milky Way, The (1936), *332;* Morning Glory (1933), *599;* Morocco, *599;* My Dream Is Yours, *932;* One Hundred Men and a Girl, *934;* One in a Million, *350;* Paths of Glory, *619;* Pollyanna (1960), *196;* Sheik, The, *655;* Sorrows of Satan, The, *663;* Star Is Born, A (1937), *666;* State of the Union, *666;* Step Lively, *942;* Swan, The (1925), *389;* To Please a Lady, *130;* Woman of Paris, A, *705;* You Were Never Lovelier, *948*
Menzies, Heather: Captain America (1979), *22;* Piranha, *875*
Menzies, Robert: Cactus, *473*
Mercer, Beryl: Cavalcade, *477;* Public Enemy, *101*
Mercer, Frances: Annabel Takes a Tour, *227;* Mad Miss Manton, The, *325;* Smashing the Rackets, *1018;* Vivacious Lady, *405*
Mercer, Jack: Hoppity Goes to Town, *175*
Mercer, Marian: Out on a Limb (1992), *352*
Merchant, Vivien: Homecoming, The (1973), *543;* Offence, The, *611;* Under Milk Wood, *691*
Mercier, Michele: Call of the Wild (1972), *22;* Global Affair, A, *287;* Shoot the Piano Player, *785*
Mercouri, Melina: Dream of Passion, A, *504;* Nasty Habits, *342;* Never on Sunday, *604;* Once Is Not Enough, *613;* Topkapi, *1026*
Mercure, Monique: Tramp at the Door, *687*
Mercurio, Micole: Turn of the Screw, The (1989), *898*
Mercurio, Paul: Strictly Ballroom, *942*
Mereader, Maria: Pardon My Trunk, *775*
Meredith, Burgess: Advise and Consent, *442;* Batman (1966), *148;* Big Hand for the Little Lady, A, *1098;* Burnt Offerings, *820;* Clash of the Titans, *1041;* Day of the Locust, The, *496;* Diary of a Chambermaid (1946), *730;* Foul Play, *280;* Full Moon in Blue Water, *282;* Great Bank Hoax, The, *289;* Grumpy Old Men, *291;* Hindenburg, The, *541;* Idiot's Delight, *548;* In Harm's Way, *66;* Last Chase, The, *1062;* Madame X (1966), *584;* Magic, *994;* Man in the Eiffel Tower, The, *995;* Manitou, The, *863;* Mine Own Executioner, *594;* Mr. Corbett's Ghost, *1066;* 92 in the Shade, *345;* Oddball Hall, *348;* Outrage!, *616;* Probe, *101;* Rocky, *642;* Rocky II, *642;* Rocky III, *642;* Rocky V, *642;* Santa Claus—The Movie, *201;* Second Chorus, *938;* Sentinel, The, *884;* State of Grace, *666;* Stay Away Joe, *942;* That Uncertain Feeling, *393;* There Was a Crooked Man, *1156;* Thumbelina (1983), *211;* Tom, Dick and Harry, *397;* Torture Garden, *896;* True Confessions, *1027;* Twilight Zone, The (TV Series), *1086;* Wet Gold, *138;* When Time Ran Out!, *1031;* Winterset, *704;* Yin and Yang of Mr. Go, The, *1033*
Meredith, Don: Express to Terror, *974;* Night the City Screamed, The, *606;* Sky Heist, *117;* Terror on the 40th Floor, *1023*
Meredith, Iris: Green Archer, *981;* Lawman Is Born, A, *1127;* Mystery of the Hooded Horsemen, *1135*
Meredith, Judi: Jack the Giant Killer, *178;* Planet of Blood, *1070*
Meredith, Lee: Producers, The, *362;* Sunshine Boys, The, *388*
Meredith, Lois: Headless Horseman, The, *1056*
Merenda, Luc: Cheaters, The, *723;* Kidnap Syndicate, The, *751;* Torso, *896*
Merhi, Jalal: Talons of the Eagle, *124;* TC 2000, *1082*
Meril, Macha: Double Vision, *972;* Married Woman, A, *765;* Robert et Robert, *782;* Vagabond, *799*
Merivale, Philip: Sister Kenny, *659*
Meriwether, Lee: Batman (1966), *148;* Cruise into Terror, *964;* 4D Man, *1053;* Namu, the Killer Whale, *190;* Undefeated, The, *1160*
Merkel, Una: Abraham Lincoln, *440;* Bank Dick, The, *232;* Bat Whispers, The, *953;* Bombshell, *243;* Born to Dance, *909;* Broadway Melody of 1936, *910;* Destry Rides Again, *1109;* Evelyn Prentice, *511;* 42nd Street, *918;* Girl Most Likely, The, *919;* I Love Melvin, *924;* It's a Joke, Son!, *308;* Kentuckian, The, *1124;* Mating Game, The, *330;* Merry Widow, The, *930;* On Borrowed Time, *612;* Private Lives, *362;* Red-Headed Woman, *636;* Rich, Young and Pretty, *936;* RiffRaff (1936), *640;* Road to Zanzibar, *369;* Saratoga, *372;* Summer and Smoke, *672;* They Call It Sin, *680;* Tiger Walks, A, *211*
Merli, Maurizio: Fearless (1978), *736;* Priest of Love, *627*

Merlin, Jan: Guns of Diablo, *1118;* Running Wild (1955), *645;* Silk 2, *116;* Twilight People, *898*
Merlin, Joanna: Class Action, *962;* Mr. Wonderful, *597*
Merlo, Ismael: Hunt, The, *746*
Merman, Ethel: Alexander's Ragtime Band, *906;* Happy Landing, *921;* It's a Mad Mad Mad Mad World, *308;* Kid Millions, *926;* That's Singing: The Best of Broadway, *944;* There's No Business Like Show Business, *944*
Merrall, Mary: Love on the Dole, *581*
Merrick, Lynn: Days of Old Cheyenne, *1107;* Dead Man's Gulch, *1108;* Kansas Cyclone, *1124*
Merrill, Dina: Anna to the Infinite Power, *1036;* Butterfield 8, *472;* Courtship of Eddie's Father, The, *260;* Deadly Encounter (1975), *498;* Desk Set, *263;* I'll Take Sweden, *924;* Just Tell Me What You Want, *312;* Operation Petticoat, *351;* Player, The, *358;* Sundowners, The (1960), *673;* Tenth Month, The, *679;* Twisted, *1028;* Wedding, A, *407*
Merrill, Frank: Tarzan the Mighty, *125;* Tarzan the Tiger, *126*
Merrill, Gary: All About Eve, *444;* Clambake, *912;* Great Impostor, The, *532;* Huckleberry Finn (1974), *176;* Incident, The (1967), *551;* Mysterious Island, *1067;* Phone Call from a Stranger, *622;* Ride Beyond Vengeance, *1143;* Seekers, The, *651;* Twelve O'Clock High, *133*
Merrill, Joan: Iceland, *924*
Merrill, Julie: Mirror of Death, *865*
Merrison, Clive: Pocketful of Rye, A, *1006*
Merritt, Theresa: Voodoo Dawn, *901;* Wiz, The, *948*
Merrow, Jane: Appointment, The, *810;* Hands of the Ripper, *848*
Merton, John: Blue Canadian Rockies, *1099;* Boothill Bandits, *1100;* Cherokee Flash, *1104;* Zorro's Black Whip, *1166*
Mervyn, William: Railway Children, The, *198*
Mese, John: Under Investigation, *1028*
Messemer, Hannes: General Della Rovere, *740*
Messick, Don: Hey There, It's Yogi Bear, *174*
Mesurier, John Le: Five Golden Hours, *278*
Metcalf, Laurie: Blink, *956;* Dangerous Woman, A, *494;* Desperately Seeking Susan, *264;* Internal Affairs, *67;* JFK, *558;* Making Mr. Right, *327;* Mistress (1992), *597;* Pacific Heights, *1003*
Metrano, Art: Beverly Hills Bodysnatchers, *237;* Breathless (1983), *469;* Cheaper to Keep Her, *254;* Going Ape!, *287;* Malibu Express, *327;* Matilda, *330;* Police Academy III: Back in Training, *359*
Mette, Nancy: Meet the Hollowheads, *331*
Metzler, Jim: Circuitry Man, *1041;* Delusion (1991), *499;* Love Kills, *993;* 976-EVIL, *871;* On Wings of Eagles, *94;* One False Move, *94;* Tex, *680*
Meurisse, Paul: Diabolique, *730;* Picnic on the Grass, *777*
Meury, Anne-Laure: Boyfriends and Girlfriends, *720*
Meyer, Emile: Hostile Guns, *1122;* Riot in Cell Block Eleven, *107*
Meyer, Jean: Le Bourgeois Gentilhomme, *756*
Meyer, Johannes: Master of the House (Du Skal Aere Din Hustru), *766*
Meyer, Russ: Amazon Women on the Moon, *225*
Meyer, Thom: Blood Suckers from Outer Space, *816*
Meyers, Ari: Dark Horse, *161;* Think Big, *394*
Meyers, Marius: Gods Must Be Crazy, The, *287*
Meyrink, Michelle: Joy of Sex, The, *311;* Nice Girls Don't Explode, *344;* Real Genius, *365;* Revenge of the Nerds, *367*
Mezzogiorno, Vittorio: Cafe Express, *721;* L'Homme Blessé (The Wounded Man), *760;* Mussolini and I, *601;* Three Brothers, *794*
Mhlope, Geina: Place of Weeping, *623*
Miano, Robert: Ministry of Vengeance, *85;* Taxi Dancers, *678*
Miao, Cora: Eat a Bowl of Tea, *507*
Miao, Nora: Fists of Fury, *49;* Return of the Dragon, *105*
Michael, Bill: Farmer's Other Daughter, The, *274*
Michael, George: Stand by Me (1988), *941*
Michael, Gertrude: I'm No Angel, *305*
Michael, Jordan Christopher: Motorama, *337*
Michaels, Michele: Slumber Party Massacre, *887*
Michaels, Roxanna: Caged Fury, *21*
Michaels, Seth: Freeze Frame, *168*
Michaelson, Kari: Kid with the 200 I.Q., The, *180*
Michel, Dominique: Decline of the American Empire, The, *729*
Michel, Marc: Lola (1960), *761;* Umbrellas of Cherbourg, The, *798*
Michelangeli, Calla: And God Said to Cain, *1093*
Michell, Helena: At Bertram's Hotel, *953*
Michell, Keith: Executioner, The, *974;* Grendel, Grendel, Grendel, *172;* Hellfire Club, The, *60;* Six Wives of Henry VIII, The (TV Series), *659;* Story of David, The, *207;* Story of Jacob and Joseph, The, *207;* Tenth Month, The, *679*
Michelle, Charlotte: Kill or Be Killed, *71*
Michelle, Yvonne: One Man Army, *94*
Middleton, Charles: Dick Tracy Returns, *38;* Flaming Frontiers, *1113;* Flash Gordon Conquers the Universe, *1052;* Flash Gordon: Mars Attacks the World (a.k.a. Trip to Mars; Deadly Ray From Mars, The), *1052;* Flash Gordon: Rocketship (a.k.a. Spaceship to the Unknown; Perils from Planet Mongo), *1052;* Hopalong Cassidy Enters, *1121;* Miracle Rider, The, *1134;* Mrs. Wiggs of the Cabbage Patch, *598;* Oklahoma Kid, The, *1136;* Strangler of the Swamp, *891;* Tomorrow at Seven, *685;* Virginia City, *1161;* Wyoming Outlaw, *1165;* Yodelin' Kid from Pine Ridge, *1165*
Middleton, Noelle: Carrington, V. C., *476*
Middleton, Ray: Jubilee Trail, *1124;* Lady for a Night, *567;* Lady from Louisiana, *1125*
Middleton, Robert: Big Hand for the Little Lady, A, *1098;* Court Jester, The, *260;* Friendly Persuasion, *522;* Law and Jake Wade, The, *1127;* Lonely Man, The, *1129;* Texas John Slaughter: Wild Times, *1156;* Which Way to the Front?, *410*
Midkiff, Dale: Blackmail (1991), *956;* Elvis and Me, *915;* Love Potion #9, *323;* Pet Sematary, *874*
Midler, Bette: Beaches, *457;* Bette Midler—Art or Bust, *909;* Bette Midler's Mondo Beyondo, *236;* Big Business, *238;* Divine Madness, *423;* Down and Out in Beverly Hills, *268;* For the Boys, *918;* Gypsy (1993), *921;* Hocus Pocus, *175;* Jinxed, *310;* Outrageous Fortune, *352;* Rose, The, *937;* Ruthless People, *371;* Scenes from a Mall, *373;* Stella (1990), *667*
Mifune, Toshiro: Bad Sleep Well, The, *715;* Bushido Blade, *21;* Challenge, The, *24;* Drunken Angel, *732;* Grand Prix, *531;* Hell in the Pacific, *60;* Hidden Fortress, The, *744;* High and Low, *744;* Idiot, The, *746;* Journey of Honor, *69;* Life of Oharu, *760;* Lower Depths, The (1957), *763;* 1941, *345;* Paper Tiger, *97;* Rashomon, *780;* Red Beard, *780;* Red Lion, *780;* Red Sun, *1142;* Rikisha-Man, *781;* Samurai Saga, *783;* Samurai Trilogy, The, *783;* Sanjuro, *783;* Seven Samurai, The, *785;* Shadow of the Wolf, *114;* Shogun (Full-Length Version), *115;* Stray Dog, *790;* Sword of Doom, *792;* Throne of Blood, *794;* Winter Kills, *704;* Yojimbo, *806;* Zatoichi vs. Yojimbo, *806*
Migenes-Johnson, Julia: Bizet's Carmen, *718;* Mack the Knife, *930*
Mighty Clouds of Joy: Gospel, *425*
Miguel, Joelle: Four Adventures of Reinette and Mirabelle, *738*
Mihashi, Tatsuya: High and Low, *744;* What's Up, Tiger Lily?, *408*
Mikhalkov, Andrej: Andrei Rublev, *713*
Mikolaichuk, Ivan: Shadows of Forgotten Ancestors, *785*
Mikulski, Mark: Stuck on You, *387*
Mikuni, Rentaro: Burmese Harp, The, *721;* Rikyu, *781*
Milan, Frank: Pals of the Saddle, *1138*
Milan, Lita: I, Mobster, *65;* Left Handed Gun, The (1958), *1128;* Naked in the Sun, *1135;* Never Love a Stranger, *604;* Poor White Trash, *624*

Milano, Alyssa: Canterville Ghost, The (1986), *155;* Casualties of Love: The Long Island Lolita Story, *476;* Commando, *28;* Conflict of Interest, *29;* Dance 'Til Dawn, *262;* Little Sister, *319;* Where the Day Takes You, *699*
Milano, Robert: Midnight Kiss, *864*
Miles, Bernard: Great Expectations (1946), *532;* Never Let Me Go, *89;* Sapphire, *1012;* Tom Thumb, *213*
Miles, Betty: Driftin' Kid, *1110;* Law Rides Again, The, *1127*
Miles, Elaine: Northern Exposure (TV Series), *609*
Miles, Joanna: American Clock, The, *446;* As Is, *451;* Blackout (1990), *956;* Born Innocent, *466;* Bug, *820;* Heart of Justice, *538;* Ultimate Warrior, The, *1087;* Water Engine, The, *696*
Miles, Kevin: Boulevard of Broken Dreams, *467;* Cars That Eat People (The Cars That Ate Paris), *821*
Miles, Lillian: Reefer Madness, *365*
Miles, Peter: Red Pony, The, *198*
Miles, Sarah: Big Sleep, The (1978), *955;* Blow-Up, *957;* Ghost in Monte Carlo, A, *527;* Hope and Glory, *544;* Lady Caroline Lamb, *567;* Man Who Loved Cat Dancing, The, *1132;* Ordeal by Innocence, *1003;* Queenie, *632;* Ryan's Daughter, *646;* Sailor Who Fell from Grace with the Sea, The, *646;* Servant, The, *652;* Steaming, *667;* Those Magnificent Men in Their Flying Machines, *394;* Venom, *900;* White Mischief, *700*
Miles, Sherry: Velvet Vampire, The, *900*
Miles, Sylvia: Cannon Movie Tales: Sleeping Beauty, *155;* Crossing Delancey, *491;* Farewell My Lovely, *975;* Funhouse, The, *845;* Heat (1972), *539;* Last Movie, The, *570;* Midnight Cowboy, *593;* 92 in the Shade, *345;* No Big Deal, *608;* Sentinel, The, *884;* She-Devil, *377;* Spike of Bensonhurst, *384;* Who Killed Mary What's 'Er Name?, *1031*
Miles, Vera: And I Alone Survived, *447;* Autumn Leaves, *452;* Back Street, *453;* Brainwaves, *818;* Castaway Cowboy, The, *157;* FBI Story, The, *515;* Fire!, *48;* Follow Me, Boys!, *167;* Gentle Giant, *169;* Hellfighters, *60;* Initiation, The, *856;* Man Who Shot Liberty Valance, The, *1132;* Our Family Business, *616;* Outer Limits, The (TV Series), *1069;* Psycho, *877;* Psycho II, *877;* Roughnecks, *109;* Run for the Roses, *201;* Searchers, The, *1148;* Sergeant Ryker, *652;* Those Calloways, *211;* Tiger Walks, A, *211;* Wrong Man, The (1956), *1033*
Milford, John: Chinese Web, The, *25*
Milford, Kim: Laserblast, *1062*
Milford, Penelope: Blood Link, *815;* Cold Justice, *28;* Coming Home, *486;* Golden Seal, The, *170;* Last Word, The, *571;* Oldest Living Graduate, The, *611;* Rosie, *937*
Milian, Tomas: Almost Human, *4;* Blood and Guns, *15;* Boccaccio 70, *719;* Cat Chaser, *24;* Cop in Blue Jeans, The, *29;* Havana, *537;* Nails, *88;* Salome (1985), *647;* Sonny and Jed, *1151;* Winter Kills, *704*
Miljan, John: Belle of the Nineties, *234;* Charlie Chan in Paris, *961;* Lone Ranger and the Lost City of Gold, The, *1129;* Lost City of the Jungle, *79;* Mississippi, *931;* What! No Beer?, *408;* Yankee Clipper, *141*
Millais, Hugh: Dogs of War, The, *40*
Millan, Tomas: Marilyn & Bobby: Her Final Affair, *588*
Millan, Victor: Boulevard Nights, *467*
Milland, Ray: Ambassador Bill, *225;* Attic, The, *811;* Beau Geste, *10;* Blackout (1978), *14;* Blonde Crazy, *241;* Bugles in the Afternoon, *1102;* Bulldog Drummond Escapes, *20;* Copper Canyon, *1106;* Cruise into Terror, *964;* Dead Don't Die, The, *830;* Dial M for Murder, *970;* Doctor Takes a Wife, The, *266;* Escape to Witch Mountain, *165;* Everything Happens at Night, *273;* Forever and a Day, *520;* Frogs, *844;* Game for Vultures, *54;* Golden Earrings, *56;* It Happens Every Spring, *307;* Last Tycoon, The, *571;* Life of Her Own, A, *574;* Lisbon, *77;* Lost Weekend, The, *580;* Love Story, *582;* Man Alone, A, *1131;* Masks of Death, *83;* Oliver's Story, *612;* Our Family Business, *616;* Premature Burial, The, *876;* Quick, Let's Get Married, *363;* Reap the Wild Wind, *104;* Slavers, *117;* Starflight One, *1079;* Swiss Conspiracy, The, *1022;* Terror in the Wax Museum, *894;* Thief, The (1952), *1024;* Three Smart Girls, *945;* Uncanny, The, *899;* Uninvited, The (1944), *1029;* Woman of Distinction, A, *413;* X (The Man with the X-Ray Eyes), *1090*
Millar, Marjie: When Gangland Strikes, *138*
Miller, Adelaide: Lonely in America, *320*
Miller, Allan: Warlock (1988), *901*
Miller, Ann: Easter Parade, *915;* Hit the Deck, *923;* Kiss Me Kate, *927;* Kissing Bandit, The, *927;* Lovely to Look At, *929;* Melody Ranch, *1133;* On the Town, *934;* Opposite Sex, The, *934;* Room Service, *370;* Small Town Girl, *940;* Stage Door, *385;* Texas Carnival, *944;* That's Entertainment! III, *436;* Too Many Girls, *946;* Two Tickets to Broadway, *947;* Watch the Birdie, *406;* You Can't Take it with You (1938), *415*
Miller, Arthur: Private Conversations: On the Set of Death of a Salesman, *433*
Miller, Barry: Fame, *916;* Peggy Sue Got Married, *355;* Sicilian, The, *115*
Miller, Charles: Being Human, *458;* Road to Ruin, The (1928), *641*
Miller, Cheryl: Clarence, the Cross-Eyed Lion, *159;* Dr. Death: Seeker of Souls, *835*
Miller, David: Attack of the Killer Tomatoes, *229*
Miller, Dean: Because You're Mine, *908;* Small Town Girl, *940*
Miller, Denise: Sooner or Later, *663*
Miller, Dennis: Dennis Miller: Black and White, *263;* Live from Washington—It's Dennis Miller, *320;* Madhouse (1990), *326*
Miller, Denny: Party, The, *354*
Miller, Dick: Apache Woman, *1094;* Bodywaves, *243;* Bucket of Blood, A, *820;* Carnival Rock, *911;* Dr. Heckyl and Mr. Hype, *266;* Evil Toons, *273;* Explorers, *1050;* Far from Home, *975;* Gremlins, *1055;* Gremlins 2: The New Batch, *1055;* Gunslinger, *1118;* Happy Hooker Goes Hollywood, The, *293;* Heart Like a Wheel, *538;* Hollywood Boulevard, *299;* Little Shop of Horrors, The (1960), *861;* Matinee, *330;* Mr. Billion, *85;* Moving Violation, *87;* Night of the Creeps, *869;* Quake, *1008;* Sorority Girl, *118;* Summer School Teachers, *673;* Trip, The, *688;* White Dog, *700;* Young Nurses, The, *708*
Miller, Eve: Big Trees, The, *13;* Kansas Pacific, *1124;* Winning Team, The, *704*
Miller, Garry: Amazing Mr. Blunden, The, *146*
Miller, Glenn: Orchestra Wives, *934*
Miller, Helen: Being Human, *458*
Miller, Ivan: Old Barn Dance, The, *1136*
Miller, Jason: Best Little Girl in the World, The, *459;* Dain Curse, The, *965;* Exorcist, The, *839;* Light of Day, *575;* Monsignor, *598;* Ninth Configuration, The, *608;* Rudy, *200;* Toy Soldiers (1983), *131;* Vengeance, *135*
Miller, Jeremy: Emanon, *271;* Willies, The, *903*
Miller, John: Undefeatable, *134*
Miller, Joshua: And You Thought Your Parents Were Weird, *227*
Miller, Kathleen: Fighting Mad, *516;* Strange New World, *1080*
Miller, Ken: Little Laura and Big John, *77*
Miller, Kristine: Jungle Patrol, *69*
Miller, Larry: Dream Lover (1994), *972;* Favor, The, *275;* Necessary Roughness, *342;* Suburban Commando, *388;* Undercover Blues, *403*
Miller, Linda G.: Night of the Juggler, *90*
Miller, Lydia: Backlash, *8*
Miller, Lynne: Poor Girl, A Ghost Story, *876*
Miller, Mark: Ginger in the Morning, *527;* Mr. Sycamore, *334;* Savannah Smiles, *201*
Miller, Mark Thomas: Blue De Ville, *242;* Misfits of Science, *1066;* Mom, *865;* Ski School, *380*
Miller, Marvin: Dead Reckoning (1947), *34;* Hell Squad (1985), *60;* Off Limits (1953), *348;* Red Planet Mars, *1074*
Miller, Michael: Doc Savage...The Man of Bronze, *1047*
Miller, Mike: Blastfighter, *15*
Miller, Patsy Ruth: Hunchback of Notre Dame, The (1923), *854;* So This Is Paris, *382*

Miller, Penelope Ann: Adventures in Babysitting, *222;* Awakenings, *452;* Carlito's Way, *23;* Chaplin, *479;* Dead-Bang, *33;* Downtown, *41;* Freshman, The, *281;* Gun in Betty Lou's Handbag, The, *292;* Kindergarten Cop, *313;* Other People's Money, *351;* Year of the Comet, *415*
Miller, Rebecca: Consenting Adults (1992), *963;* Murder of Mary Phagan, The, *600;* Wind (1992), *140*
Miller, Stephen E.: Home Is Where the Hart Is, *299*
Miller, Ty: Trancers 4: Jack of Swords, *1085*
Miller, Walter: Battle of Elderbush Gulch, The/The Muskateers of Pig Alley, *1097;* Dick Tracy's G-Men, *38;* Ghost Patrol, *55;* King of the Kongo, *72;* Lawless Valley, *1127;* Lone Defender, The, *78;* Shadow of the Eagle, *114;* Street Scene, *670*
Millian, Andra: Stacy's Knights, *665*
Millican, James: Beyond the Purple Hills, *1097;* Rimfire, *1144;* Winning Team, The, *704*
Milligan, Spike: Alice's Adventures in Wonderland, *145;* Case of the Mukkinese Battle Horn, The, *252;* Down Among the "Z" Men, *268;* Ghost in the Noonday Sun, *285;* To See Such Fun, *397*
Mills, Alley: Going Berserk, *287;* Tainted Blood, *1022*
Mills, Donna: Alice Through the Looking Glass (1985), *145;* Bunco, *21;* Curse of the Black Widow, *828;* False Arrest, *513;* Fire!, *48;* Haunts of the Very Rich, *1055;* Incident, The (1967), *551;* Murph the Surf, *87;* Play Misty for Me, *1006;* Runaway Father, *645;* Who Is the Black Dahlia?, *1031*
Mills, Hayley: Appointment with Death, *953;* Back Home, *147;* Bananas Boat, The, *232;* Chalk Garden, The, *478;* Daydreamer, The, *161;* Endless Night, *973;* In Search of the Castaways, *176;* Moonspinners, The, *189;* Parent Trap, The, *193;* Pollyanna (1960), *196;* Summer Magic, *208;* That Darn Cat, *210;* Tiger Bay, *683;* Trouble with Angels, The, *399;* Whistle Down the Wind, *216*
Mills, Hayword: Mississippi Blues, *430*
Mills, John: Africa—Texas Style!, *3;* Black Veil for Lisa, A, *14;* Chalk Garden, The, *478;* Chuka, *1105;* Colditz Story, The, *485;* Dr. Strange, *1047;* Frankenstein (1992), *842;* Gandhi, *524;* Goodbye, Mr. Chips (1939), *530;* Great Expectations (1946), *532;* Hobson's Choice (1954), *298;* In Which We Serve, *550;* King Rat, *565;* Lady Caroline Lamb, *567;* Masks of Death, *83;* Murder with Mirrors, *999;* Night of the Fox, *90;* Nine Days a Queen, *607;* Operation Crossbow, *95;* Quatermass Conclusion, The, *1072;* Rocking Horse Winner, The, *642;* Ryan's Daughter, *646;* Sahara (1984), *110;* Scott of the Antarctic, *650;* Swiss Family Robinson, The, *208;* Thirty-Nine Steps, The (1978), *1024;* This Happy Breed, *682;* Tiger Bay, *683;* Tunes of Glory, *689;* War and Peace (1956), *695;* We Dive at Dawn, *137;* Who's That Girl, *411;* Woman of Substance, A, *705;* Wrong Box, The, *414;* Young Winston, *709;* Zulu Dawn, *142*
Mills, Johnny: Garden, The, *525*
Mills, Juliet: Avanti!, *230;* Barnaby and Me, *232;* Beyond the Door, *813;* Rare Breed, The (1966), *1141*
Mills, Samantha: Prehysteria, *197*
Mills, Walter: High Country, The, *61*
Milne, Leslie: Vampire at Midnight, *899*
Milner, Martin: Bloopers from Star Trek and Laugh-In, *242;* Columbo: Murder by the Book, *963;* Compulsion, *487;* Flood!, *51;* Francis in the Navy, *280;* Life with Father, *318;* Marjorie Morningstar, *589;* Operation Pacific, *614;* Pete Kelly's Blues, *935;* Seekers, The, *651;* Sweet Smell of Success, *675;* 13 Ghosts, *895;* Valley of the Dolls, *693;* Zebra in the Kitchen, *220*
Milo, Sandra: Bang Bang Kid, The, *232;* Dead for a Dollar, *1108;* 8½, *733;* General Della Rovere, *740;* Juliet of the Spirits, *750*
Milot, Charles: French Connection II, The, *53*
Miluwi, John Omirah: Gorillas in the Mist, *531*
Mimieux, Yvette: Black Hole, The, *1039;* Caper of the Golden Bulls, The, *22;* Dark of the Sun, *32;* Devil Dog: The Hound of Hell, *833;* Diamond Head, *500;* Fantasy Film Worlds of George Pal, The, *424;* Forbidden Love, *519;* Hit Lady, *63;* Jackson County Jail, *68;* Journey into Fear (1975), *987;* Legend of Valentino, *572;* Monkeys Go Home, *188;* Neptune Factor, The, *1068;* Obsessive Love, *1002;* Platinum High School, *623;* Snowbeast, *888;* Three in the Attic, *395;* Time Machine, The, *1084;* Toys in the Attic, *687;* Where the Boys Are, *409*
Minardos, Nico: Assault on Agathon, *7;* Daring Game, *32*
Minciotti, Esther: Marty (Television), *589*
Mineau, Charlotte: Charlie Chaplin—The Early Years, Vol. 4, *254*
Mineo, Sal: Cheyenne Autumn, *1104;* Dino, *501;* Exodus, *512;* Gene Krupa Story, The, *525;* Rebel without a Cause, *636;* Rock, Pretty Baby, *936;* Somebody Up There Likes Me, *662;* Tonka, *213*
Miner, Jan: Lenny, *572;* Willie and Phil, *412*
Minevich, Borrah: One in a Million, *350*
Ming, Lau Siu: Eat a Bowl of Tea, *507*
Minnelli, Liza: Arthur, *229;* Arthur 2: On the Rocks, *229;* Cabaret, *910;* Matter of Time, A, *590;* Muppets Take Manhattan, The, *189;* New York, New York, *933;* Princess and the Pea, The, *197;* Rent-a-Cop, *105;* Silent Movie, *379;* Stepping Out, *942;* Sterile Cuckoo, The, *667;* That's Dancing, *436;* Wonderful Wizard of Oz, The: The Making of a Movie Classic, *438*
Minns, Byron Keith: South Central, *663*
Minogue, Dannii: One Crazy Night, *349*
Minor, Bob: Delinquent School Girls, *263*
Minter, Kelly Jo: People Under the Stairs, The, *873;* Popcorn, *876*
Minter, Kristin: Cool As Ice, *488*
Miou-Miou: Dog Day, *40;* Entre Nous (Between Us), *734;* Going Places, *741;* Jonah Who Will Be 25 in the Year 2000, *750;* Josepha, *750;* La Lectrice (The Reader), *754;* May Fools, *766;* Ménage, *767;* My Other Husband, *770;* Roads to the South, *781*
Mira, Brigitte: Ali: Fear Eats the Soul, *711;* Chinese Roulette, *723;* Every Man for Himself and God Against All, *735;* Kamikaze 89, *751;* Mother Kusters Goes to Heaven, *769*
Miracle, Irene: In the Shadow of Kilimanjaro, *855;* Last of Philip Banter, The, *991;* Laughing Horse, *571;* Puppet Master, The, *878;* Watchers II, *901*
Miranda, Carmen: Copacabana, *259;* Date with Judy, A, *913;* Doll Face, *914;* Down Argentine Way, *914;* Nancy Goes to Rio, *932;* Springtime in the Rockies (1942), *941*
Miranda, Isa: Dog Eat Dog, *40;* La Signora di Tutti, *754;* Man from Nowhere, The, *765;* Night Porter, The, *606;* Summertime, *673*
Miranda, John: Bloodthirsty Butchers, *816*
Miranda, Robert: Chips, the War Dog, *158;* Monkey Trouble, *188*
Miriel, Veronica: Street Warriors II, *671*
Mironova, Olga: Come and See, *725*
Mirren, Helen: Cal, *474;* Caligula, *474;* Collection, The, *485;* Comfort of Strangers, The, *963;* Cook, the Thief, His Wife & Her Lover, The, *259;* Dr. Bethune, *502;* Excalibur, *1050;* Fiendish Plot of Dr. Fu Manchu, The, *276;* Gospel According to Vic, The, *289;* Hawk, The, *982;* Hussy, *546;* Little Mermaid, The (1984), *182;* Long Good Friday, The, *78;* Mosquito Coast, The, *600;* Pascali's Island, *619;* Prime Suspect 1, *1007;* Prime Suspect 2, *1007;* Prime Suspect 3, *1008;* Red King, White Knight, *636;* Savage Messiah, *648;* 2010, *1086;* When the Whales Came, *699;* Where Angels Fear to Tread, *699*
Mishima, Yukio: Black Lizard, *718*
Mistral, Jorge: Wuthering Heights (1953), *805*
Mistysyn, Stacy: Princes in Exile, *627*
Mitchell, Belle: Crazed, *825*
Mitchell, Cameron: Adventures of Gallant Bess, *442;* All Mine to Give, *444;* Andersonville Trial, The, *447;* Blood and Black Lace, *814;* Blood Link, *815;* Buck and the Preacher, *1102;* Carousel, *911;* Crossing the Line (1990), *492;* Deadly Prey, *34;* Desirée, *500;* Dog Eat Dog, *40;* Escapade in Japan, *165;* Flight to Mars, *1052;* Flood!, *51;* Frankenstein Island,

842; Gambler, Part II—The Adventure Continues, The, *1115;* Hollywood Cop, *63;* Hombre, *1121;* Homecoming (1948), *543;* How to Marry a Millionaire, *303;* Kill Point, *71;* Klansman, The, *566;* Last Gun, The, *1126;* Love Me or Leave Me, *929;* Low Blow, *79;* Man in the Saddle, *1132;* Night Train to Terror, *870;* Nightforce, *91;* Nightmare in Wax (Crimes in the Wax Museum), *871;* No Justice, *91;* Rebel Rousers, *104;* Return to Fantasy Island, *1074;* Ride in the Whirlwind, *1143;* Slavers, *117;* Tall Men, The, *1154;* Tomb, The, *896;* Toolbox Murders, The, *1026;* Without Warning, *1090*

Mitchell, Duke: Boys from Brooklyn, The, *818*

Mitchell, Eddy: My Other Husband, *770*

Mitchell, Gordon: Endgame, *1049;* Fellini Satyricon, *736;* Giant of Metropolis, The, *1054;* Shangai Joe, *1148;* She (1983), *1076*

Mitchell, Grant: Conflict, *963;* Dancing Lady, *913;* Ex-Mrs. Bradford, The, *974;* Great Lie, The, *532;* Guest Wife, *291;* In Person, *305;* Man Who Came to Dinner, The, *328;* Peck's Bad Boy with the Circus, *194;* Tomorrow at Seven, *685*

Mitchell, Guy: Red Garters, *936*

Mitchell, Heather: Everlasting Secret Family, The, *511*

Mitchell, James: Prodigal, The, *629*

Mitchell, John: Sea Shall Not Have Them, The, *113*

Mitchell, John Cameron: Band of the Hand, *9;* Misplaced, *595*

Mitchell, Joni: Last Waltz, The, *428*

Mitchell, Millard: Gunfighter, The, *1117;* Here Come the Girls, *922;* Naked Spur, The, *1135*

Mitchell, Mitch: Jimi Hendrix, *428*

Mitchell, Red: 8 Seconds, *43;* Forever Evil, *842*

Mitchell, Sasha: Class of 1999 II: The Substitute, *1041;* Kickboxer 2: The Road Back, *70;* Kickboxer Three—Art of War, *71;* Spike of Bensonhurst, *384*

Mitchell, Scoey: Jo Jo Dancer, Your Life Is Calling, *558*

Mitchell, Thomas: Adventure, *441;* Angels Over Broadway, *448;* Bataan, *9;* Big Wheel, The, *461;* Buffalo Bill, *1102;* Craig's Wife, *490;* Dark Mirror, The, *966;* Dark Waters, *496;* Fighting Sullivans, The, *516;* Gone with the Wind, *530;* High Noon, *1120;* Hunchback of Notre Dame, The (1939), *854;* Immortal Sergeant, The, *549;* It's a Wonderful Life, *555;* Joan of Paris, *558;* Keys to the Kingdom, The, *563;* Long Voyage Home, The, *578;* Lost Horizon, *580;* Only Angels Have Wings, *95;* Our Town (1940), *616;* Outlaw, The, *1137;* Pocketful of Miracles, *359;* Silver River, *1150;* Song of the Islands, *940;* Stagecoach (1939), *1152;* Toast of New Orleans, *946;* While the City Sleeps, *138;* Wilson, *703*

Mitchell, Warren: Bananas Boat, The, *232;* Dunera Boys, The, *506;* Foreign Body, *279;* Knights and Emeralds, *314;* Meetings with Remarkable Men, *591;* Norman Loves Rose, *346*

Mitchell, Yvonne: Crucible of Horror, *827;* Demons of the Mind, *833;* Incredible Sarah, The, *551;* Sapphire, *1012;* Tiger Bay, *683*

Mitchell-Smith, Ilan: Chocolate War, The, *481;* Identity Crisis, *304;* Journey to the Center of the Earth (1987), *1060;* Weird Science, *407;* Wild Life, The, *411*

Mitchum, Bentley: Demonic Toys, *832;* Ruby in Paradise, *645;* Teenage Bonnie and Klepto Clyde, *126*

Mitchum, Chris: Big Foot, *813;* Big Jake, *1098;* Day Time Ended, The, *1045;* H-Bomb, *58;* Rio Lobo, *1145;* Stingray, *120;* Summertime Killer, The, *122*

Mitchum, Jim: Blackout (1978), *14;* Fatal Mission, *46;* Girls Town, *55;* Hollywood Cop, *63;* Jake Spanner Private Eye, *68;* Mercenary Fighters, *84;* Ransom, *1009;* Thunder Road, *129;* Tramplers, The, *1158*

Mitchum, John: Big Foot, *813;* Bloody Trail, *1099;* Breakheart Pass, *1101;* Dirty Harry, *39;* Enforcer, The (1976), *44;* Escapes, *1049;* High Plains Drifter, *1120;* Hitler, *542;* Jake Spanner Private Eye, *68;* Outlaw Josey Wales, The, *1137;* Paint Your Wagon, *934;* Telefon, *1023;* Way West, The, *1163*

Mitchum, Robert: Agency, *443;* Ambassador, The, *445;* Amsterdam Kill, The, *5;* Anzio, *6;* Bar 20, *1096;* Big Sleep, The (1978), *955;* Big Steal, The, *13;* Blood on the Moon, *1099;* Border Patrol, *1100;* Breakthrough, *19;* Brotherhood of the Rose, *20;* Cape Fear (1962), *959;* Cape Fear (1991), *959;* Colt Comrades, *1105;* Crossfire (1947), *964;* El Dorado, *1111;* Enemy Below, The, *44;* False Colors, *1112;* Farewell My Lovely, *975;* Fire Down Below, *517;* Five Card Stud, *1113;* Girl Rush, *286;* Grass Is Greener, The, *289;* Gung Ho! (1943), *58;* Hearst and Davies Affair, The, *537;* His Kind of Woman, *62;* Holiday Affair, *542;* Home from the Hill, *542;* Hoppy Serves a Writ, *1121;* Jake Spanner Private Eye, *68;* Last Tycoon, The, *571;* Leather Burners, The, *1128;* Lone Star Trail, *1129;* Longest Day, The, *78;* Lusty Men, The, *1130;* Macao, *80;* Maria's Lovers, *588;* Matilda, *330;* Midway, *84;* Mr. North, *334;* My Forbidden Past, *602;* Night of the Hunter, *1001;* Nightkill, *1001;* Not as a Stranger, *609;* One Minute to Zero, *94;* One Shoe Makes it Murder, *1003;* Out of the Past, *1003;* Pursued, *1140;* Rachel and the Stranger, *1140;* Racket, The, *633;* Red Pony, The, *198;* Riders of the Deadline, *1144;* River of No Return, *1145;* Ryan's Daughter, *646;* Scrooged, *374;* Second Chance, *113;* Secret Ceremony, *650;* She Couldn't Say No, *377;* Sundowners, The (1960), *673;* That Championship Season, *680;* Thirty Seconds Over Tokyo, *127;* Thompson's Last Run, *128;* Thunder Road, *129;* Till the End of Time, *683;* Two for the Seesaw, *690;* Undercurrent, *691;* Villa Rides, *1161;* War and Remembrance, *696;* Way West, The, *1163;* Winds of War, The, *703;* Woman of Desire, *1032;* Yakuza, The, *141*

Mitler, Matt: Mutilator, The, *867;* Occultist, The, *93*

Mitterer, Felix: Requiem for Dominic, *781*

Mittleman, Steve: Best of the Big Laff Off, The, *236*

Mix, Ruth: Clutching Hand, The, *27*

Mix, Tom: Dick Turpin, *38;* Miracle Rider, The, *1134;* My Pal, the King, *1135*

Miyagian, Eri: Summer Vacation: 1999, *791*

Miyamoto, Nobuko: Funeral, The, *739;* Tampopo, *792;* Taxing Woman, A, *793;* Taxing Woman's Return, A, *793*

Miyori, Kim: Antony and Cleopatra (1981), *450;* John & Yoko: A Love Story, *559;* Punisher, The, *101*

Mizrahi, Isaac: For Love or Money, *279*

Mizuno, Kumi: War of the Gargantuas, *1088*

Mobley, Mary Ann: Girl Happy, *919;* Harum Scarum, *922*

Mobley, Roger: Emil and the Detectives, *164*

Mocky, Jean-Pierre: Head Against the Wall, *743*

Modean, Jayne: Streethawk, *121*

Modesto, Sam: Buried Alive (1984), *820*

Modine, Matthew: And the Band Played on, *447;* Birdy, *462;* Equinox (1993), *510;* Full Metal Jacket, *523;* Gamble, The, *54;* Gross Anatomy, *534;* Married to the Mob, *329;* Memphis Belle (1990), *592;* Mrs. Soffel, *598;* Orphans, *615;* Pacific Heights, *1003;* Private School, *362;* Short Cuts, *657;* Streamers, *670;* Vision Quest, *694;* Wind (1992), *140*

Modot, Gaston: Age of Gold, *711*

Moeller, Ralph: Best of the Best 2, *11*

Moffat, Donald: Alamo Bay, *443;* Best of Times, The, *236;* Bourne Identity, The, *958;* Far North, *274;* Great Northfield Minnesota Raid, The, *1116;* Housesitter, *302;* Love, Cheat & Steal, *993;* Necessary Parties, *604;* On the Nickel, *612;* Promises in the Dark, *629;* Regarding Henry, *637;* Right Stuff, The, *640;* Showdown (1973), *1149;* Teamster Boss: The Jackie Presser Story, *678*

Moffatt, Graham: Dr. Syn, *40*

Moffett, D. W.: Danielle Steele's "Fine Things", *495;* Lisa, *992;* Misfit Brigade, The, *85*

Moffett, Gregory: Robot Monster, *881*

Moffett, Michelle: Deathstalker IV: Match of the Titans, *1046;* Wild Cactus, *139*

Mog, Aribert: Ecstasy, *733*

Mohner, Carl: Last Gun, The, *1126;* Rififi, *1010;* Sink the Bismarck, *116*

Mohr, Gerald: Angry Red Planet, The, *1036;* Hunt the Man Down, *984;* King of the Cowboys, *1125;* Son of Ali Baba, *118;* Terror in the Haunted House, *893*

Mohyeddin, Zia: Bombay Talkie, *720;* They Came from Beyond Space, *1083;* We Are the Children, *697*
Moir, Alison: Johnny Suede, *311*
Moir, Richard: Heatwave, *539;* In Search of Anna, *550;* Indecent Obsession, An, *551*
Mokae, Zakes: Dry White Season, A, *505;* Dust Devil, *838;* Master Harold and the Boys, *590;* Rage in Harlem, A, *103;* Serpent and the Rainbow, The, *884;* Slaughter of the Innocents, *1017;* World of Strangers, A, *805*
Molander, Karin: Thomas Graal's Best Child, *794;* Thomas Graal's Best Film, *794*
Moldovan, Jeff: Master Blaster, *83*
Molière Players, The: Alfred Hitchcock's Bon Voyage and Aventure Malgache, *711*
Molina, Alfred: American Friends, *226;* Enchanted April, *271;* Letter to Brezhnev, *318;* Manifesto, *328;* Maverick, *1133;* Not without My Daughter, *609;* Prick Up Your Ears, *626;* White Fang 2: Myth of the White Wolf, *217*
Molina, Angela: Camorra, *722;* Demons in the Garden, *729;* Eyes, the Mouth, The, *735;* 1492: The Conquest of Paradise, *52;* Half of Heaven, *743;* Streets of Gold, *671;* That Obscure Object of Desire, *793*
Molina, Mariano Vidal: Gentleman Killer, *1115*
Molina, Miguel: Law of Desire, *756*
Moll, Charles: Savage Journey, *1147*
Moll, Georgia: Misunderstood (1988), *598*
Moll, Richard: Dream Date, *269;* Dungeonmaster, The, *1048;* Highlander: The Gathering, *1056;* House, *852;* Murphy's Laws of Golf, *338;* Night Train to Terror, *870;* Sidekicks, *203;* Survivor, *1081;* Sword and the Sorcerer, The, *1082;* Think Big, *394;* Wicked Stepmother, The, *903*
Molloy, Patrick: Plutonium Baby, *875*
Molnar, Tibor: Red and the White, The, *780;* Round-Up, The, *782*
Molone, Steve: Big Sweat, The, *13*
Moltke, Alexandra: Dark Shadows (TV Series), *829*
Momo, Alessandro: Malicious, *764*
Momoi, Kaori: Eijanaika (Why Not?), *733*
Monaco, Tony: Dead Aim (1973), *1108*
Monaghan, Marjorie: Nemesis (1992), *1067*
Monahan, Dan: Porky's, *360;* Porky's II: The Next Day, *360;* Porky's Revenge, *360;* Up the Creek (1984), *403*
Moncrieff, Karen: Deathfight, *36;* Midnight Witness, *996*
Mondy, Pierre: Gift, The, *740;* Sleeping Car Murders, The, *786*
Mones, Paul: Tuff Turf, *689*
Monfort, Sylvia: Le Cas du Dr. Laurent, *757*
Monk, Thelonious: Jazz on a Summer's Day, *427*
Monlaur, Yvonne: Brides of Dracula, *819;* Terror of the Tongs, The, *126*
Monnier, Valentine: After the Fall of New York, *1034*
Monoson, Lawrence: Dangerous Love, *32;* Gaby, a True Story, *524;* Last American Virgin, The, *315*
Monroe, Bill: High Lonesome—The Story of Bluegrass Music, *426*
Monroe, Marilyn: All About Eve, *444;* As Young as You Feel, *229;* Asphalt Jungle, The, *953;* Bus Stop, *248;* Clash by Night, *483;* Don't Bother to Knock, *971;* Gentlemen Prefer Blondes, *284;* How to Marry a Millionaire, *303;* Ladies of the Chorus, *567;* Let's Make It Legal, *318;* Let's Make Love, *928;* Love Happy, *322;* Love Nest, *323;* Misfits, The, *595;* Monkey Business (1952), *336;* Niagara, *1000;* Prince and the Showgirl, The, *361;* River of No Return, *1145;* Seven Year Itch, The, *376;* Some Like It Hot, *382;* There's No Business Like Show Business, *944;* We're Not Married, *408*
Montague, Monte: Radio Patrol, *102*
Montalban, Carlos: Bananas, *232*
Montalban, Ricardo: Across the Wide Missouri, *1092;* Alice Through the Looking Glass (1966), *906;* Battleground, *456;* Blue (1968), *1099;* Cheyenne Autumn, *1104;* Conquest of the Planet of the Apes, *1043;* Deserter, The, *1109;* Escape from the Planet of the Apes, *1049;* Fantasy Island, *1050;* Fiesta, *916;* Kissing Bandit, The, *927;* Latin Lovers, *928;* Madame X (1966), *584;* Mission to Glory, *596;* Naked Gun, The, *341;* Neptune's Daughter, *932;* On an Island with You, *933;* Return to Fantasy Island, *1074;* Sayonara, *648;* Singing Nun, The, *204;* Star Trek II: The Wrath of Khan, *1079;* Sweet Charity, *943;* Train Robbers, The, *1158;* Two Weeks with Love, *947*
Montana, Bull: Son of the Sheik, *118*
Montana, Karla: Sweet 15, *674*
Montana, Monte: Down Dakota Way, *1110*
Montanary, Michel: Jacko and Lise, *749*
Montand, Yves: César and Rosalie, *723;* Choice of Arms, A, *724;* Delusions of Grandeur, *729;* Goodbye Again, *530;* Grand Prix, *531;* IP5: The Island of Pachyderms, *748;* Is Paris Burning?, *554;* Jean De Florette, *749;* Let's Make Love, *928;* Manon of the Spring, *765;* My Geisha, *340;* Napoleon (1955), *603;* On a Clear Day, You Can See Forever, *933;* Roads to the South, *781;* Sleeping Car Murders, The, *786;* State of Siege, *788;* Vincent, François, Paul and the Others, *801;* Wages of Fear, The, *801;* Z, *806*
Monte, Mario: Soul Vengeance, *118*
Monte, Mike: No Dead Heroes, *91*
Monteith, Kelly: Hollywood Boulevard II, *983*
Montell, Lisa: Nine Lives of Elfego Baca, The, *1136*
Monteros, Rosenda: Battle Shock, *812*
Montesano, Enrico: Sotto Sotto, *788*
Montesi, Jorge: Death Target, *35*
Montez, Maria: Ali Baba and the Forty Thieves, *3;* Arabian Nights (1942), *6;* Valdez Is Coming, *1160*
Montgomery, Belinda: Blackout (1978), *14;* Man from Atlantis, The, *1064;* Marciano, *588;* Miami Vice, *84;* Other Side of the Mountain, Part II, The, *615;* Silent Madness, *886;* Stone Cold Dead, *1020;* Stone Fox, The, *207;* Todd Killings, The, *685*
Montgomery, Douglass: Harmony Lane, *922*
Montgomery, Elizabeth: Court-martial of Billy Mitchell, The, *489*
Montgomery, George: From Hell to Borneo, *53;* Hostile Guns, *1122;* Indian Uprising, *1123;* Lone Ranger, The (1938), *1129;* Orchestra Wives, *934;* Texas Rangers, The, *1156*
Montgomery, Julie: Revenge of the Nerds, *367;* Savage Justice, *111*
Montgomery, Lee: Baker's Hawk, *148;* Ben, *812;* Burnt Offerings, *820;* Girls Just Want to Have Fun, *287;* Into the Fire, *67;* Midnight Hour, *864;* Mutant, *867;* Prime Risk, *100;* Savage Is Loose, The, *648*
Montgomery, Robert: Divorcee, The, *502;* Forsaking All Others, *279;* Free and Easy, *281;* Here Comes Mr. Jordan, *296;* Inspiration, *553;* June Bride, *311;* Lady in the Lake, *990;* Last of Mrs. Cheney, The, *315;* Mr. and Mrs. Smith, *333;* Night Must Fall, *606;* Private Lives, *362;* Riptide, *640;* They Were Expendable, *127*
Monti, Ivana: Contraband, *726*
Monti, Maria: Fistful of Dynamite, A, *1113*
Montiel, Sarita: Run of the Arrow, *1146*
Moody, David: Blue Knight, The (1973), *465*
Moody, Elizabeth: Dead Alive, *830*
Moody, Jim: Bad Boys, *454;* Who's the Man?, *411*
Moody, Lynne: Las Vegas Lady, *74;* Last Light, *569;* White Dog, *700*
Moody, Ron: Dogpound Shuffle, *266;* Ghost in Monte Carlo, A, *527;* Legend of the Werewolf, *860;* Murder Most Foul, *998;* Oliver, *933;* Othello (1982), *615;* Seaside Swingers, *938;* Twelve Chairs, The, *401;* Unidentified Flying Oddball, *214;* Wrong Is Right, *414*
Moon, Keith: That'll Be the Day, *944;* 200 Motels, *946*
Mooney, Maureen: Hell High, *849*
Mooney, William: Flash of Green, A, *977*
Moore, Alvy: Horror Show, The, *852;* Scream, *883;* Wild One, The, *139*
Moore, Archie: Adventures of Huckleberry Finn, The (1960), *144;* Carpetbaggers, The, *475*
Moore, Candy: Tomboy and the Champ, *213*

Moore, Christine: Lurkers, *861;* Prime Evil, *876*
Moore, Clayton: Adventures of Frank and Jesse James, *1092;* Black Dragons, *814;* Crimson Ghost, The, *30;* Far Frontier, *1112;* G-Men Never Forget, *54;* Helldorado (1946), *1120;* Jesse James Rides Again, *1123;* Kansas Pacific, *1124;* Lone Ranger, The (1956), *1129;* Lone Ranger, The (TV Series), *1129;* Lone Ranger and the Lost City of Gold, The, *1129;* Nyoka and the Tiger Men (Perils of Nyoka), *92;* Riders of the Whistling Pines, *1144;* Son of Monte Cristo, The, *118*
Moore, Cleo: Dynamite Pass, *1111;* Hunt the Man Down, *984;* On Dangerous Ground, *1003*
Moore, Colleen: Ella Cinders, *271;* Scarlet Letter, The (1934), *649;* These Girls Won't Talk, *393*
Moore, Constance: Buck Rogers: Destination Saturn (a.k.a. Planet Outlaws), *1040;* Show Business, *939;* Wives Under Suspicion, *704;* You Can't Cheat an Honest Man, *415*
Moore, Deborah: Warriors of the Apocalypse, *1088*
Moore, Demi: About Last Night, *440;* Butcher's Wife, The, *248;* Few Good Men, A, *976;* Ghost (1990), *527;* Indecent Proposal, *551;* Mortal Thoughts, *997;* New Homeowner's Guide to Happiness, The, *343;* No Small Affair, *345;* Nothing But Trouble (1991), *347;* One Crazy Summer, *349;* Parasite, *873;* St. Elmo's Fire, *646;* Seventh Sign, The, *885;* We're No Angels (1989), *408;* Wisdom, *140*
Moore, Dennis: Arizona Bound, *1094;* Black Market Rustlers, *1099;* Border Roundup, *1100;* Colorado Serenade, *1105;* Fast Talking, *166;* King of the Bullwhip, *1125;* Lonely Trail, The, *1129;* Purple Monster Strikes, The, *101;* Spooks Run Wild, *385*
Moore, Dickie: Bride Wore Red, The, *469;* Gabriel over the White House, *524;* Jive Junction, *926;* Little Men (1935), *182;* Little Rascals, The, *183;* Miss Annie Rooney, *188;* Oliver Twist (1933), *612;* Out of the Past, *1003*
Moore, Dudley: Adventures of Milo and Otis, The, *144;* Alice's Adventures in Wonderland, *145;* Arthur, *229;* Arthur 2: On the Rocks, *229;* Bedazzled, *233;* Best Defense, *234;* Blame It on the Bellboy, *240;* Crazy People, *260;* Foul Play, *280;* Hound of the Baskervilles, The (1977), *302;* Like Father, Like Son, *318;* Lovesick, *324;* Micki & Maude, *331;* Romantic Comedy, *370;* Santa Claus—The Movie, *201;* Six Weeks, *659;* 10, *392;* 30 Is a Dangerous Age, Cynthia, *394;* Those Daring Young Men in Their Jaunty Jalopies, *394;* Unfaithfully Yours (1984), *403;* Wholly Moses!, *410;* Wrong Box, The, *414*
Moore, Duke: Plan 9 from Outer Space, *1070*
Moore, Gar: Abbott and Costello Meet the Killer, Boris Karloff, *221;* Paisan, *775;* Underworld Story, *1029*
Moore, Grace: One Night of Love, *934*
Moore, Irene: New Year's Day, *605*
Moore, James: Sinister Urge, The, *116*
Moore, Jenie: Vampire at Midnight, *899*
Moore, Joanna: Monster on the Campus, *866*
Moore, Joanne: Follow That Dream, *278*
Moore, Juanita: Imitation of Life, *549;* Papa's Delicate Condition, *617*
Moore, Julianne: Benny & Joon, *234;* Cast a Deadly Spell, *1041;* Short Cuts, *657*
Moore, Kieron: Anna Karenina (1947), *449;* Arabesque, *6;* David and Bathsheba, *496;* Day of the Triffids, The, *1044;* League of Gentlemen, The, *317;* Mine Own Executioner, *594;* Naked Heart, The, *603*
Moore, Mary Tyler: Change of Habit, *479;* Finnegan Begin Again, *277;* Gore Vidal's Lincoln, *531;* Just Between Friends, *561;* Ordinary People, *614;* Six Weeks, *659;* Thoroughly Modern Millie, *945*
Moore, Matt: Coquette, *488;* Deluge, *1046;* Pride of the Clan, The, *1007*
Moore, Mavor: Mortal Sins (1992), *997*
Moore, Melba: Def by Temptation, *832;* Ellis Island, *508*
Moore, Melissa: Angel Fist, *5;* Hard to Die, *848;* One Man Army, *94;* Sorority House Massacre 2, *889*
Moore, Michael J.: Deadly Stranger, *35*
Moore, Norma: Fear Strikes Out, *515*
Moore, Owen: As You Desire Me, *451;* High Voltage, *62;* Home, Sweet Home, *543;* Keystone Comedies, Vol. 3, *312*
Moore, Paige: Wizard of Speed and Time, The, *413*
Moore, Patience: Cheap Shots, *254*
Moore, Pauline: Carson City Kid, *1103;* King of the Texas Rangers, *1125;* Trail Blazers, *1158*
Moore, Roger: Bed and Breakfast, *457;* Bullseye, *247;* Cannonball Run, *250;* Diane, *500;* Escape to Athena, *45;* ffolkes, *47;* Fire, Ice & Dynamite, *49;* For Your Eyes Only, *51;* Happy Anniversary 007: 25 Years of James Bond, *425;* Interrupted Melody, *925;* Live and Let Die, *78;* Man Who Haunted Himself, The, *995;* Man with the Golden Gun, The, *81;* Maverick (TV Series), *1133;* Miracle, The (1959), *594;* Moonraker, *86;* Naked Face, The, *1000;* Octopussy, *93;* Persuaders, The (TV Series), *98;* Rape of the Sabines, *103;* Saint, The (TV Series), *1012;* Sea Wolves, The, *113;* Shout at the Devil, *115;* Spy Who Loved Me, The, *119;* Street People, *121;* That Lucky Touch, *392;* View to a Kill, A, *135;* Wild Geese, The, *139*
Moore, Rudy Ray: Dolemite, *267*
Moore, Sheila: Ray Bradbury's Chronicles: The Martian Episodes, *1073*
Moore, Stephen: Clockwise, *256*
Moore, Terry: Beneath the 12-Mile Reef, *10;* Between Heaven and Hell, *459;* Beverly Hills Brats, *237;* Come Back, Little Sheba, *486;* Daddy Long Legs, *913;* Mighty Joe Young, *1066;* Peyton Place, *621;* Platinum High School, *623;* Return of October, The, *366;* Shack-Out on 101, *653;* Two of a Kind (1951), *1028*
Moore, Thomas: Warriors of the Wasteland, *1088*
Moore, Tim: Amos and Andy (TV Series), *226*
Moore, Tom: Manhandled, *328*
Moore, Victor: Heat's On, The, *295;* It's in the Bag, *308;* Louisiana Purchase, *322;* Swing Time, *943;* We're Not Married, *408;* Ziegfeld Follies, *949*
Moorehead, Agnes: Adventures of Captain Fabian, *2;* Alice Through the Looking Glass (1966), *906;* Bachelor in Paradise, *230;* Big Street, The, *460;* Black Jack, *14;* Citizen Kane, *482;* Conqueror, The, *29;* Dark Passage, *966;* Dear Dead Delilah, *831;* Hush...Hush, Sweet Charlotte, *854;* Jane Eyre (1944), *557;* Johnny Belinda, *559;* Journey Into Fear (1942), *987;* Left Hand of God, The, *76;* Lost Moment, The, *580;* Magnificent Ambersons, The, *585;* Magnificent Obsession, *585;* Main Street to Broadway, *326;* Meet Me in Las Vegas, *930;* Mrs. Parkington, *598;* Opposite Sex, The, *934;* Our Vines Have Tender Grapes, *193;* Pollyanna (1960), *196;* Raintree County, *634;* Seventh Cross, The, *653;* Show Boat (1951), *939;* Since You Went Away, *658;* Singing Nun, The, *204;* Station West, *1153;* Stratton Story, The, *670;* Summer Holiday, *942;* Swan, The (1956), *674;* Twilight Zone, The (TV Series), *1086;* What's the Matter with Helen?, *902*
Moorehead, Jean: Violent Years, The, *136*
Moorhead, Natalie: Dance, Fools, Dance, *493;* Dancing Man, *965;* Hook, Line and Sinker, *300;* Parlor, Bedroom and Bath, *354*
Moosbrugger, Christoph: Bloody Moon, *817*
Morales, Esai: Bad Boys, *454;* Bloodhounds of Broadway, *242;* La Bamba, *927;* Naked Tango, *603;* On Wings of Eagles, *94;* Principal, The, *628;* Ultraviolet, *133*
Moran, Dolores: Horn Blows at Midnight, The, *301;* Man I Love, The, *586*
Moran, Erin: Galaxy of Terror, *1053*
Moran, Jackie: Adventures of Tom Sawyer, The, *144;* Buck Rogers: Destination Saturn (a.k.a. Planet Outlaws), *1040;* Meet Dr. Christian, *591;* Old Swimmin' Hole, The, *611*
Moran, Pauline: Poirot (Series), *1006*
Moran, Peggy: King of the Cowboys, *1125;* Mummy's Hand, The, *867*
Moran, Polly: Red River Range, *1141;* Show People, *378;* Tom Brown's School Days (1940), *685*
Moreno, Jacqueline: Picnic on the Grass, *777*
Moranis, Rick: Best of John Candy, The, *236;* Club Paradise, *256;* Flintstones, The, *167;* Ghostbusters, *285;* Ghostbusters

II, *285;* Head Office, *294;* Honey, I Blew Up the Kid, *175;* Honey, I Shrunk the Kids, *175;* Last Polka, The, *315;* Little Shop of Horrors (1986), *929;* My Blue Heaven, *339;* Parenthood, *354;* Spaceballs, *384;* Splitting Heirs, *384;* Strange Brew, *387;* Streets of Fire, *121;* Wild Life, The, *411*

Morant, Richard: John & Yoko: A Love Story, *559;* Mahler, *585*

Morante, Laura: Tragedy of a Ridiculous Man, *796*

Moray, Yvonne: Terror of Tiny Town, The, *1155*

Mordyukova, Nonna: Commissar, The, *725*

More, Camilla: In Search of the Serpent of Death, *66*

More, Kenneth: Adventures of Sadie, *223;* Battle of Britain, *9;* Dark of the Sun, *32;* Doctor in the House, *266;* Flame over India, *50;* Genevieve, *283;* Leopard in the Snow, *572;* Never Let Me Go, *89;* Night to Remember, A (1958), *606;* Scott of the Antarctic, *650;* Scrooge (1970), *938;* Sink the Bismarck, *116;* Tale of Two Cities, A (1980), *677;* Thirty-Nine Steps, The (1959), *1024;* Unidentified Flying Oddball, *214*

Moreau, Jeanne: Alberto Express, *711;* Alex in Wonderland, *224;* Bride Wore Black, The, *959;* Chimes at Midnight, *481;* Diary of a Chambermaid (1964), *730;* Elevator to the Gallows, *734;* Fire Within, The, *736;* Going Places, *741;* Heat of Desire, *743;* Immortal Story, *549;* Jules and Jim, *750;* Last Tycoon, The, *571;* Les Liaisons Dangereuses, *759;* Little Theatre of Jean Renoir, The, *760;* Lovers, The (1958), *762;* Lumiere, *763;* Mademoiselle, *585;* Map of the Human Heart, *588;* Mr. Klein, *768;* Monte Walsh, *1134;* Querelle, *779;* Summer House, The, *388;* Train, The, *131;* Trial, The, *687;* Until the End of the World, *1087;* Viva Maria!, *801;* Woman Is a Woman, A, *805*

Moreau, Nathaniel: Kissing Place, The, *989;* Tidy Endings, *683*

Morehead, Elizabeth: Interceptor, *67*

Moreland, Mantan: Charlie Chan in the Secret Service, *961;* Chinese Cat, The, *962;* Jade Mask, The, *987;* King of the Zombies, *859;* Meeting at Midnight, *996;* Next Time I Marry, *344;* Revenge of the Zombies, *881;* Scarlet Clue, The, *1013;* Shanghai Cobra, The, *1014;* Young Nurses, The, *708*

Moreland, Sherry: Fury of the Congo, *54*

Morell, Andre: Dark of the Sun, *32;* Hound of the Baskervilles, The (1959), *983;* Quatermass and the Pit, *1072;* Stolen Face, *890;* 10 Rillington Place, *678*

Morell, Joshua: Making Contact, *1064*

Morelli, Lino: Lunatics & Lovers, *763*

Moreno, Antonio: Bohemian Girl, The, *243;* Creature from the Black Lagoon, *826;* It (1927), *307*

Moreno, José Elias: Night of the Bloody Apes, *869*

Moreno, Lisa: From Hell to Borneo, *53*

Moreno, Rita: Age Isn't Everything, *223;* Boss' Son, The, *467;* Cry of Battle, *31;* Four Seasons, The, *521;* Happy Birthday, Gemini, *293;* King and I, The, *926;* Latin Lovers, *928;* Marlowe, *995;* Night of the Following Day, The, *1001;* Pagan Love Song, *934;* Popi, *360;* Portrait of a Showgirl, *625;* Ritz, The, *368;* Seven Cities of Gold, *653;* Singin' in the Rain, *940;* Summer and Smoke, *672;* Toast of New Orleans, *946;* West Side Story, *947*

Moretti, Nanni: Palombella Rossa, *775*

Morevski, Abraham: Dybbuk, The, *732*

Morey, Bill: Real Men, *365*

Morgan, Alexandra: Deadly Games, *968*

Morgan, Audrey: Love Your Mama, *582*

Morgan, Chesty: Deadly Weapons, *498*

Morgan, Cindy: Tron, *1085*

Morgan, David E.: Petronella, *195*

Morgan, Debbi: Jessie Owens Story, The, *557*

Morgan, Dennis: Captains of the Clouds, *23;* Christmas in Connecticut (1945), *255;* Fighting 69th, The, *48;* Great Ziegfeld, The, *921;* Hard Way, The (1942), *536;* In This Our Life, *550;* It's a Great Feeling, *925;* Kitty Foyle, *566;* Pearl of the South Pacific, *620;* Thank Your Lucky Stars, *944*

Morgan, Emily: French Lieutenant's Woman, The, *522*

Morgan, Frank: Any Number Can Play, *450;* Balalaika, *907;* Bombshell, *243;* Boom Town, *466;* Broadway Melody of 1940, *910;* Broadway Serenade, *910;* Casanova Brown, *252;* Cat and the Fiddle, The, *911;* Courage of Lassie, *160;* Dancing Pirate, *913;* Dimples, *914;* Great Ziegfeld, The, *921;* Green Dolphin Street, *533;* Honky Tonk, *1121;* Human Comedy, The, *546;* I Live My Life, *547;* Key to the City, *312;* Last of Mrs. Cheney, The, *315;* Mortal Storm, The, *600;* Naughty Marietta, *932;* Rosalie, *937;* Saratoga, *372;* Shop Around the Corner, The, *378;* Stratton Story, The, *670;* Summer Holiday, *942;* Sweethearts, *943;* Thousands Cheer, *945;* Tortilla Flat, *686;* White Cargo, *699;* White Cliffs of Dover, The, *699;* Wizard of Oz, The, *218;* Yolanda and the Thief, *708*

Morgan, Georgia: 10 Violent Women, *126*

Morgan, Harry: Apple Dumpling Gang, The, *147;* Apple Dumpling Gang Rides Again, The, *147;* Barefoot Executive, The, *148;* Better Late than Never, *237;* Boots Malone, *1100;* Cat from Outer Space, The, *157;* Charley and the Angel, *157;* Cimarron (1960), *1105;* Dark City, *495;* Dragnet (1987), *268;* Far Country, The, *1112;* Flim-Flam Man, The, *518;* Frankie and Johnny (1966), *918;* Gangster, The, *525;* Glenn Miller Story, The, *919;* Incident, The (1989), *551;* It Started With a Kiss, *308;* M*A*S*H: Goodbye, Farewell, Amen, *325;* More Wild Wild West, *1134;* Not as a Stranger, *609;* Ox-Bow Incident, The, *1137;* Roughnecks, *109;* Scandalous John, *202;* Shootist, The, *1149;* Showdown, The (1950), *1149;* Snowball Express, *205;* State Fair (1945), *941;* Support Your Local Gunfighter, *1154;* Support Your Local Sheriff!, *1154;* Torch Song, *686;* Well, The, *698;* Wild Wild West Revisited, The, *1164;* Wing and a Prayer, A, *140*

Morgan, Helen: Applause, *450;* Frankie and Johnny (1934), *522;* Glorifying the American Girl, *919;* Go Into Your Dance, *920;* Show Boat (1936), *939*

Morgan, Jane: Our Miss Brooks (TV Series), *351*

Morgan, Jaye P.: Night Patrol, *344*

Morgan, Michele: Bluebeard (1963), *719;* Cat and Mouse, *722;* Chase, The (1946), *479;* Everybody's Fine, *735;* Fallen Idol, The, *513;* Higher and Higher, *922;* Joan of Paris, *558;* Lost Command, *79;* Naked Heart, The, *603;* Stormy Waters, *789*

Morgan, Nancy: Americathon, *226;* Grand Theft Auto, *57;* Nest, The (1988), *868;* Pray TV (1980), *360*

Morgan, Priscilla: Pride and Prejudice (1985), *626*

Morgan, Ralph: Dick Tracy vs. Crime Inc., *38;* General Spanky, *169;* Kennel Murder Case, The, *988;* Last Round-Up, *1126;* Little Men (1935), *182;* Mannequin (1937), *588;* Monster Maker, The, *866;* Rasputin and the Empress, *635;* Star of Midnight, *1020;* Strange Interlude (1932), *669;* Wives Under Suspicion, *704*

Morgan, Read: Hollywood Harry, *299*

Morgan, Richard: Wicked, The, *903*

Morgan, Scott Wesley: Serial Mom, *376*

Morgan, Shelley Taylor: Malibu Express, *327*

Morgan, Sidney: Juno and the Paycock, *561*

Morgan, Terence: Hamlet (1948), *535;* Lifetaker, The, *77*

Morganti, Claudio: Palombella Rossa, *775*

Morghen, John: Make Them Die Slowly, *862*

Morguis, Ana Ofelia: Mary My Dearest, *766*

Mori, Claudia: Lunatics & Lovers, *763*

Mori, Masayuki: Bad Sleep Well, The, *715;* Idiot, The, *746;* Princess Yang Kwei Fei, *778;* Rashomon, *780;* Ugetsu, *798*

Mori, Toshia: Bitter Tea of General Yen, The, *462*

Moriarty, Cathy: Another Stakeout, *6;* Burndown, *959;* Gun in Betty Lou's Handbag, The, *292;* Kindergarten Cop, *313;* Mambo Kings, The, *930;* Matinee, *330;* Me and the Kid, *83;* Neighbors, *343;* Raging Bull, *633;* Soapdish, *382;* White of the Eye, *1031*

Moriarty, Michael: Bang the Drum Slowly, *455;* Blood Link, *815;* Dark Tower, *829;* Full Fathom Five, *53;* Hanoi Hilton, The, *536;* Holocaust, *542;* It's Alive III: Island of the Alive, *857;* Last Detail, The, *569;* My Old Man's Place, *602;* Nitti: The Enforcer, *91;* Pale Rider, *1138;* Q, *878;* Report to the Commissioner, *638;* Return to Salem's Lot, A, *880;* Stuff, The,

891; Tailspin, 676; Troll, 1085; Who'll Stop the Rain, 139; Winds of Kitty Hawk, The, 703
Morice, Tara: Strictly Ballroom, 942
Morier-Genoud, Philippe: Au Revoir, Les Enfants, 714
Moriggi, Francesca: Tree of the Wooden Clogs, The, 797
Morin, Mayo: Clowns, The, 725
Morison, Patricia: Dressed to Kill (1946), 972; Fallen Sparrow, The, 513; Song of the Thin Man, 1018; Song without End, 940; Without Love, 413
Morita, Noriyuki "Pat": Alice Through the Looking Glass (1985), 145; Auntie Lee's Meat Pies, 811; Babes in Toyland (1986), 147; Captive Hearts, 475; Collision Course, 257; Do or Die, 40; Even Cowgirls Get the Blues, 272; For the Love of It, 279; Hiroshima: Out of the Ashes, 541; Honeymoon in Vegas, 300; Karate Kid, The, 562; Karate Kid Part II, The, 562; Karate Kid Part III, The, 562; Miracle Beach, 332; Thoroughly Modern Millie, 945
Moritz, Louisa: Death Race 2000, 1045; Last American Virgin, The, 315
Moritzen, Henning: Memories of a Marriage, 766
Moriyama, Yuko: Zeram, 807
Morley, Karen: Beloved Enemy, 458; Black Fury, 462; Gabriel over the White House, 524; Littlest Rebel, The, 929; Mask of Fu Manchu, The, 82; Mata Hari (1931), 590; Our Daily Bread, 615; Sin of Madelon Claudet, The, 658
Morley, Rita: Flesh Eaters, The, 841
Morley, Robert: African Queen, The, 442; Alice in Wonderland (1985), 145; Alice Through the Looking Glass (1985), 145; Alphabet Murders, The, 951; Battle of the Sexes, The, 233; Beat the Devil, 233; Beau Brummell (1954), 457; Cromwell, 491; Ghosts of Berkeley Square, 285; Great Muppet Caper, The, 171; High Road to China, 62; Hot Millions, 301; Hotel Paradiso, 302; Istanbul: Keep Your Eyes Open, 555; Loved One, The, 323; Major Barbara, 326; Marie Antoinette, 588; Murder at the Gallop, 998; Of Human Bondage (1964), 610; Oh, Heavenly Dog!, 192; Old Dark House, The, 872; Road to Hong Kong, The, 368; Scavenger Hunt, 373; Song of Norway, 940; Study in Terror, A, 1021; Theatre of Blood, 894; Trouble with Spies, The, 399; Who Is Killing the Great Chefs of Europe?, 410; Wind, The (1986), 1032; Woman Times Seven, 705
Moro, Alicia: Exterminators of the Year 3000, 1050
Morrell, Leo: Crime Killer, The, 30
Morrill, Priscilla: Last of Mrs. Lincoln, The, 570; Right of Way, 640
Morris, Adrian: Fighting Marines, The, 48; Radio Patrol, 102
Morris, Anita: Absolute Beginners, 906; Aria, 907; Bloodhounds of Broadway, 242; Blue City, 957; 18 Again, 270; Little Miss Millions, 182; Me and the Kid, 83; Ruthless People, 371; Sinful Life, A, 379
Morris, Ann: Honolulu, 923
Morris, Barboura: Atlas, 7; Bucket of Blood, A, 820; Sorority Girl, 118; Wasp Woman, 901
Morris, Chester: Bat Whispers, The, 953; Divorcee, The, 502; Five Came Back, 517; Frankie and Johnny (1934), 522; Red-Headed Woman, 636; She Creature, The, 885; Smashing the Rackets, 1018; Tomorrow at Seven, 685
Morris, Garrett: Best of Chevy Chase, The, 235; Best of Dan Aykroyd, The, 235; Best of John Belushi, The, 235; Cooley High, 259; Critical Condition, 260; Motorama, 337; Saturday Night Live, 372; Severed Ties, 885; Stuff, The, 891; Things We Did Last Summer, 394; Where's Poppa?, 409
Morris, Glenn: Tarzan's Revenge, 126
Morris, Greg: Vega$, 135
Morris, Haviland: Love or Money?, 323; Who's That Girl, 411
Morris, Howard: Andy Griffith Show, The (TV Series), 227; Boys' Night Out, 244; End of the Line, 509; Life Stinks, 318; Portrait of a Showgirl, 625; 10 from Your Show of Shows, 392; Transylvania Twist, 399
Morris, Jane: Frankie and Johnny (1991), 522
Morris, Jim: Rap Master Ronnie—A Report Card, 364
Morris, Judy: Between Wars, 459; In Search of Anna, 550; Plumber, The, 1006
Morris, Kirk: Maciste in Hell, 861
Morris, Marianne: Vampyres, 900
Morris, Mary: Pimpernel Smith, 99
Morris, Phyllis: Adventures of Tartu, 2
Morris, Richard: Sea Lion, The, 650
Morris, Wayne: Bushwhackers, 1102; Kid Galahad (1937), 563; Plunder Road, 99; Stage to Tucson, 1152; Task Force, 677; Time of Your Life, The, 684
Morrisey, Betty: Circus, The/A Day's Pleasure, 255
Morrison, Jim: Dance on Fire, 422; Doors, The: A Tribute to Jim Morrison, 423; Soft Parade, The, 435
Morrison, Kenny: NeverEnding Story II, The, 1068; Quick and the Dead, The, 1140
Morrison, Sammy: Little Rascals, The, 183
Morrison, Sterling: Velvet Underground, The: Velvet Redux—Live MCMXCIII, 437
Morrison, Steven: Last House on Dead End Street, 860
Morrison, Van: Last Waltz, The, 428
Morrissette, Billy: Severed Ties, 885
Morrissey, David: Waterland, 697
Morrissey, Eamon: Eat the Peach, 270
Morror, Rob: Private Resort, 362
Morrow, Doretta: Because You're Mine, 908
Morrow, Jeff: Creature Walks Among Us, The, 826; Kronos, 1061; Octaman, 872; This Island Earth, 1083
Morrow, Jo: Dr. Death: Seeker of Souls, 835; 13 Ghosts, 895; Three Worlds of Gulliver, The, 1083
Morrow, Rob: Northern Exposure (TV Series), 609
Morrow, Vic: Bad News Bears, The, 231; Blackboard Jungle, The, 463; Cimarron (1960), 1105; Dirty Mary, Crazy Larry, 39; Evictors, The, 839; Glass House, The, 528; Humanoids from the Deep, 854; Men in War, 84; 1990: The Bronx Warriors, 1069; Tom Sawyer (1973), 213; Tribute to a Bad Man, 1159; Twilight Zone—The Movie, 898
Morse, Barry: Asylum, 810; Changeling, The, 822; Fugitive, The (TV Series), 523; Fugitive, The: The Last Episode (TV Series), 53; Love at First Sight, 322; Sadat, 646; Space 1999 (TV Series), 1077; Story of David, The, 207; Tale of Two Cities, A (1980), 677; Whoops Apocalypse, 411; Woman of Substance, A, 705
Morse, David: Brotherhood of the Rose, 20; Cry in the Wind, 492; Desperate Hours (1990), 37; Getaway, The (1994), 55; Indian Runner, The, 551; Inside Moves, 552; Prototype, 1072; Shattered Vows, 655
Morse, Helen: Caddie, 473; Picnic at Hanging Rock, 1006; Town Like Alice, A, 686
Morse, Robert: Boatniks, The, 151; Cannon Movie Tales: The Emperor's New Clothes, 155; Guide for the Married Man, A, 291; How to Succeed in Business without Really Trying, 923; Hunk, 303; Loved One, The, 323; Matchmaker, The, 329; Oh Dad, Poor Dad—Mama's Hung You in the Closet and I'm Feeling So Sad, 348; That's Singing: The Best of Broadway, 944; Where Were You When the Lights Went Out?, 409
Morshower, Glen: Drive-In, 269
Mortensen, Viggo: Boiling Point, 17; Carlito's Way, 23; Deception (1993), 969; Indian Runner, The, 551; Leatherface—the Texas Chainsaw Massacre III, 860; Reflecting Skin, The, 637
Mortimer, Caroline: Death of Adolf Hitler, The, 498
Morton, Amy: Rookie of the Year, 200
Morton, Dee Dee: Dakota (1988), 493
Morton, Gary: Postcards from the Edge, 360
Morton, Greg: Adultress, The, 441
Morton, Joe: Alone in the Neon Jungle, 445; Between the Lines, 237; Brother from Another Planet, The, 1040; City of Hope, 483; Crossroads, 912; Forever Young (1992), 1053; Inkwell, The, 552; Legacy of Lies, 572; Stranded, 1080; Tap, 944; Terminator 2: Judgment Day, 1082; Trouble in Mind, 688

Morton, John: I Shot Billy the Kid, *1122*
Morton, Phil: Monster a Go-Go, *336*
Moschin, Gastone: Joke of Destiny, *750;* Mr. Superinvisible, *188;* Oldest Profession, The, *773*
Moscovich, Maurice: Everything Happens at Night, *273*
Moscow, David: Big, *237;* Newsies, *933;* White Wolves: A Cry in the Wild II, *139*
Moseley, Page: Inside Out 2, *1059*
Moses, David: Daring Dobermans, The, *32*
Moses, Harry: Sweater Girls, *389*
Moses, Mark: Dead Men Don't Die, *262;* Hollywood Heartbreak, *542;* Tracker, The, *1158*
Moses, William R.: Alien From L.A., *3;* Double Exposure (1993), *971;* Mystic Pizza, *603*
Mosley, Roger E.: Greatest, The, *533;* Heart Condition, *295;* I Know Why the Caged Bird Sings, *547;* Jericho Mile, The, *557;* Mack, The, *584;* Pray TV (1980), *360;* Steel, *120;* Unlawful Entry, *1029*
Moss, Arnold: Caper of the Golden Bulls, The, *22;* Loves of Carmen, The, *582*
Moss, Elissabeth: Midnight's Child, *865*
Moss, George: Riff-Raff (1992), *640*
Moss, Ronn: Hard Ticket to Hawaii, *59;* Hearts and Armour, *59;* Hot Child in the City, *64*
Moss, Stewart: Bat People, *812*
Most, Donny: Huckleberry Finn (1975), *176;* Stewardess School, *386*
Mostel, Josh: Animal Behavior, *227;* Beverly Hills 90210, *460;* City Slickers, *255;* City Slickers II, *256;* Compromising Positions, *258;* Heavy Petting, *426;* Little Man Tate, *182;* Matewan, *590;* Money Pit, The, *335;* Naked Tango, *603;* Radio Days, *364;* Stoogemania, *386;* Windy City, *703*
Mostel, Zero: Du Barry Was a Lady, *915;* Enforcer, The (1951), *44;* Front, The, *523;* Funny Thing Happened on the Way to the Forum, A, *282;* Hot Rock, The, *983;* Journey into Fear (1975), *987;* Mastermind, *329;* Panic in the Streets, *1004;* Producers, The, *362;* Sirocco, *116*
Motulsky, Judy: Slithis, *887*
Mouchet, Catherine: Therese, *793*
Moulder-Brown, John: Deep End, *969;* King, Queen and Knave, *565;* Rumpelstiltskin (1987), *200;* Sleeping Murder, *1017*
Moulin, Charles: Baker's Wife, The (1938), *715*
Mouton, Benjamin: Whore, *701*
Movin, Lisbeth: Day of Wrath, *728*
Movita: Wolf Call, *948*
Mowbray, Alan: Androcles and the Lion, *227;* Doughgirls, The, *268;* Every Girl Should Be Married, *273;* Girl from Missouri, The, *286;* Hollywood Hotel, *923;* In Person, *305;* It Happened in New Orleans, *925;* Majority of One, A, *326;* Merton of the Movies, *331;* My Dear Secretary, *339;* Roman Scandals, *937;* Rose Marie (1936), *937;* So This Is Washington, *382;* Stand-In, *385;* Study in Scarlet, A, *1021;* Terror by Night, *1023;* That Uncertain Feeling, *393;* Topper Takes a Trip, *398;* Villain Still Pursued Her, The, *135*
Mower, Patrick: Black Beauty (1971), *151*
Moy, Wood: Chan Is Missing, *253*
Moya, Pay: In the Soup, *306*
Moyer, Tawny: House of the Rising Sun, *64*
Moyo, Alois: Power of One, The, *625*
Mr. T: D.C. Cab, *261;* Freaked, *281;* Penitentiary II, *98;* Rocky III, *642;* Straight Line, *120*
Mucari, Carlo: Tex and the Lord of the Deep, *1155*
Mudugno, Enrica Maria: Kaos, *751*
Mueller, Cookie: Female Trouble, *276;* Multiple Maniacs, *866*
Mueller, Maureen: In a Shallow Grave, *550;* Over Her Dead Body, *352*
Mueller-Stahl, Armin: Angry Harvest, *713;* Avalon, *452;* Colonel Redl, *725;* Forget Mozart, *737;* Holy Matrimony, *299;* House of the Spirits, The, *545;* Kafka, *988;* Lola (1982), *761;* Music Box, The, *999;* Night on Earth, *606;* Power of One, The, *625;* Utz, *693*
Muhlach, Niño: Boy God, The, *152*
Mui, Anita: Better Tomorrow 3, A: Love And Death In Saigon, *717*
Muir, David: Doctor Hackenstein, *835*
Muir, Gavin: Night Tide, *606*
Mukherji, Swapan: World of Apu, The, *805*
Muldaur, Diana: Beyond Reason, *460;* McQ, *83;* Other, The, *873;* Planet Earth, *1070;* Return of Frank Cannon, The, *1010*
Muldoon, Patrick: Rage and Honor II: Hostile Takeover, *102*
Mule, Francesco: When Women Lost Their Tails, *409*
Mulford, Nancy: Act of Piracy, *1*
Mulgrew, Kate: Love Spell, *79;* Manions of America, The, *588;* Remo Williams: The Adventure Begins, *105;* Roots—The Gift, *644;* Round Numbers, *370;* Stranger Is Watching, A, *890;* Throw Momma from the Train, *396*
Mulhall, Jack: Buck Rogers: Destination Saturn (a.k.a. Planet Outlaws), *1040;* Clutching Hand, The, *27;* Invisible Ghost, *856;* Mysterious Dr. Satan, *88;* Mystery Squadron, *88;* Outlaws of Sonora, *1137;* Saddle Mountain Roundup, *1146;* Skull and Crown, *1017;* Three Musketeers, The (1933), *128*
Mulhare, Edward: Our Man Flint, *96;* Outer Limits, The (TV Series), *1069;* Von Ryan's Express, *136*
Mulhern, Matt: Biloxi Blues, *240*
Mulkey, Chris: Bound and Gagged: A Love Story, *18;* Deadbolt, *968;* Ghost in the Machine, *845;* Heartbreak Hotel, *538;* Hometown Boy Makes Good, *300;* In Dangerous Company, *550;* Jack's Back, *987;* Patti Rocks, *619;* Roe vs. Wade, *642;* Runaway Father, *645;* Silencer, The, *116;* Write to Kill, *1033*
Mull, Martin: All-Star Toast to the Improv, An, *224;* Bad Manners, *231;* Big City Comedy, *238;* Boss' Wife, The, *244;* Clue, *256;* Cutting Class, *828;* Dance with Death, *965;* Doctor Duck's Super Secret All-Purpose Sauce, *266;* Far Out Man, *274;* Flicks, *278;* FM, *278;* History of White People in America, The, *298;* History of White People in America, The (Volume II), *298;* Home Is Where the Hart Is, *299;* Lots of Luck, *322;* Mary Hartman, Mary Hartman (TV Series), *329;* Mr. Mom, *334;* Mrs. Doubtfire, *334;* My Bodyguard, *601;* O.C. & Stiggs, *348;* Pecos Bill, King of the Cowboys, *194;* Private School, *362;* Rented Lips, *366;* Serial, *376;* Ski Patrol, *380;* Take This Job and Shove It, *390;* Ted & Venus, *392;* Think Big, *394*
Mullally, Megan: Last Resort, *316*
Mullaney, Jack: Honeymoon Machine, The, *300;* Tickle Me, *945*
Mullavey, Greg: Body Count, *817;* C.C. & Company, *21;* I Dismember Mama, *855;* Mary Hartman, Mary Hartman (TV Series), *329;* Vultures, *901*
Mullen, Patty: Doom Asylum, *836;* Frankenhooker, *842*
Muller, Harrison: Final Executioner, The, *1051;* She (1983), *1076;* 2020 Texas Gladiators, *1086;* Violent Breed, The, *136*
Muller, Paul: Devil's Commandment, The, *834;* Nightmare Castle, *871*
Mulligan, Gerry: Jazz on a Summer's Day, *427*
Mulligan, Richard: Babes in Toyland (1986), *147;* Big Bus, The, *238;* Doin' Time, *266;* Fine Mess, A, *277;* Gore Vidal's Lincoln, *531;* Group, The, *534;* Heavenly Kid, The, *296;* Hideaways, The, *174;* Little Big Man, *1128;* Meatballs Part II, *330;* Poker Alice, *1139;* S.O.B., *372;* Scavenger Hunt, *373;* Teachers, *391*
Mullinar, Rod: Thirst, *895*
Mulloney, Joe: Restless Natives, *366*
Mullowney, Deborah: Cellar Dweller, *822*
Mulroney, Dermot: Bad Girls (1994), *1095;* Bright Angel, *470;* Career Opportunities, *251;* Heart of Justice, *538;* Last Outlaw, The (1993), *1126;* Longtime Companion, *579;* Point of No Return, *99;* Samantha, *372;* Staying Together, *667;* Survival Quest, *123;* Thing Called Love, The, *681;* Where the Day Takes You, *699;* Young Guns, *1165*
Mulroney, Kieran: Career Opportunities, *251*

Mummert, Danny: It's a Great Life, *308*
Mumy, Billy: Bless the Beasts and Children, *463;* Dear Brigitte, *263;* Lost in Space (TV Series), *1063;* Sammy, the Way-Out Seal, *201*
Munchkin, R. W.: L.A. Vice, *74*
Mune, Ian: Nutcase, *347;* Sleeping Dogs, *117*
Muni, Paul: Angel on My Shoulder (1946), *448;* Black Fury, *462;* Commandos Strike at Dawn, *28;* Good Earth, The, *530;* I Am a Fugitive from a Chain Gang, *547;* Juarez, *560;* Last Angry Man, The, *568;* Life of Emile Zola, The, *574;* Scarface (1932), *112;* Song to Remember, A, *940;* Story of Louis Pasteur, The, *668*
Muniz, Tommy: Crazy from the Heart, *490*
Munro, Caroline: At the Earth's Core, *1037;* Captain Kronos: Vampire Hunter, *821;* Devil within Her, The, *833;* Don't Open Till Christmas, *836;* Golden Voyage of Sinbad, The, *1054;* Last Horror Film, The, *860;* Maniac (1980), *862;* Slaughter High, *887;* Spy Who Loved Me, The, *119;* Star Crash, *1078*
Munro, Janet: Crawling Eye, The, *825;* Darby O'Gill and the Little People, *161;* Day the Earth Caught Fire, The, *1044;* Horsemasters, *176;* Third Man on the Mountain, *210*
Munro, Neil: Beethoven Lives Upstairs, *149;* Confidential, *28;* Dancing in the Dark, *494*
Munroe, Fred: Longest Hunt, The, *1130*
Munroe, Steve: Comic, The (1985), *486*
Munshin, Jules: Easter Parade, *915;* Mastermind, *329;* On the Town, *934;* Take Me Out to the Ball Game, *943*
Munson, Ona: Idaho, *1122;* Lady from Louisiana, *1125;* Red House, The, *1009;* Shanghai Gesture, The, *655*
Munzuk, Maxim: Dersu Uzala, *729*
Muppets: Great Muppet Caper, The, *171;* Muppet Movie, The, *189;* Muppets Take Manhattan, The, *189*
Murase, Sachiko: Rhapsody in August, *781*
Murat, Jean: Carnival in Flanders, *722;* Eternal Return, The, *735*
Muravyova, Irina: Moscow Does Not Believe in Tears, *768*
Murdocco, Vince: Flesh Gordon 2: Flesh Gordon meets the Cosmic Cheerleaders, *1052*
Murdock, George: Breaker! Breaker!, *19;* Certain Fury, *24;* Strange Case of Dr. Jekyll and Mr. Hyde, The (1989), *890*
Murney, Christopher: Grace Quigley, *289;* Last Dragon, The, *75;* Secret of My Success, The, *375*
Murphy, Audie: Arizona Raiders, *1095;* Guns of Fort Petticoat, *1118;* Red Badge of Courage, The, *636;* To Hell and Back, *130;* Unforgiven, The (1960), *1160*
Murphy, Ben: Chisholms, The, *1104;* Cradle Will Fall, The, *964;* Riding with Death, *1074;* Time Walker, *895*
Murphy, Charlie: CB4, *252*
Murphy, Donald: Frankenstein's Daughter, *843;* Lord Love a Duck, *321*
Murphy, Eddie: Another 48 Hrs., *5;* Best Defense, *234;* Best of the Big Laff Off, The, *236;* Beverly Hills Cop, *11;* Beverly Hills Cop II, *11;* Beverly Hills Cop 3, *11;* Boomerang, *244;* Coming to America, *258;* Distinguished Gentleman, The, *265;* Eddie Murphy—Delirious, *270;* Eddie Murphy Raw, *270;* 48 Hrs., *279;* Golden Child, The, *56;* Harlem Nights, *59;* Joe Piscopo Video, The, *310;* Trading Places, *398*
Murphy, George: Bataan, *9;* Battleground, *456;* Broadway Melody of 1938, *910;* Broadway Melody of 1940, *910;* Broadway Rhythm, *910;* For Me and My Gal, *917;* Girl, a Guy and a Gob, A, *286;* Having a Wonderful Crime, *294;* It's a Big Country, *308;* Kid Millions, *926;* Letter of Introduction, *573;* Little Miss Broadway, *928;* Little Nellie Kelly, *928;* Show Business, *939;* Step Lively, *942;* This Is the Army, *945;* Tom, Dick and Harry, *397*
Murphy, Johnny: Commitments, The, *912;* Into the West, *177*
Murphy, Mary: Main Street to Broadway, *326;* Man Alone, A, *1131;* Maverick Queen, The, *1133;* Wild One, The, *139*
Murphy, Michael: Autobiography of Miss Jane Pittman, The, *452;* Caine Mutiny Court Martial, The, *473;* Class of Miss MacMichael, The, *483;* Clean Slate (1994), *256;* Cloak and Dagger (1984), *27;* Count Yorga, Vampire, *825;* Dead Ahead: The Exxon Valdez Disaster, *497;* Folks, *278;* Great Bank Hoax, The, *289;* Manhattan, *328;* Mesmerized, *996;* Phase IV, *1070;* Salvador, *647;* Shocker, *886;* Strange Behavior, *890;* Tailspin, *676;* Tanner '88, *391;* That Cold Day in the Park, *680;* Unmarried Woman, An, *691;* Year of Living Dangerously, The, *141*
Murphy, Reilly: Body Snatchers, The (1993), *1040*
Murphy, Rosemary: Any Wednesday, *228;* Ben, *812;* For the Boys, *918;* George Washington, *526;* Walking Tall, *136*
Murphy, Shannon: Firehouse (1987), *277*
Murphy, Steve: No Justice, *91*
Murphy, Timothy Patrick: Sam's Son, *647*
Murray, Bill: Best of Chevy Chase, The, *235;* Best of Dan Aykroyd, The, *235;* Best of Gilda Radner, The, *235;* Best of John Belushi, The, *235;* Caddyshack, *249;* Ghostbusters, *285;* Ghostbusters II, *285;* Groundhog Day, *291;* Little Shop of Horrors (1986), *929;* Loose Shoes, *321;* Mad Dog and Glory, *584;* Meatballs, *330;* Mr. Mike's Mondo Video, *334;* Quick Change, *363;* Razor's Edge, The (1984), *635;* Saturday Night Live, *372;* Scrooged, *374;* Stripes, *387;* Things We Did Last Summer, *394;* Tootsie, *397;* What About Bob?, *408;* Where the Buffalo Roam, *409*
Murray, Chic: Gregory's Girl, *290*
Murray, Don: Advise and Consent, *442;* Baby the Rain Must Fall, *453;* Bus Stop, *248;* Conquest of the Planet of the Apes, *1043;* Deadly Hero, *34;* Endless Love, *510;* Ghosts Can't Do It, *285;* Hoodlum Priest, The, *543;* I Am the Cheese, *547;* Justin Morgan Had a Horse, *179;* Mistress (1987), *597;* One Man's Way, *613;* Peggy Sue Got Married, *355;* Quarterback Princess, *631;* Radioactive Dreams, *1073;* Scorpion, *112;* Shake Hands with the Devil, *114;* Sweet Love, Bitter, *675*
Murray, Guillermo: World of the Vampires, *904*
Murray, James: Crowd, The, *492*
Murray, Jan: Which Way to the Front?, *410*
Murray, Joel: Elvis Stories, *271*
Murray, John: Moving Violations, *338*
Murray, Mae: Bachelor Apartment, *230*
Murray, Mick: Midnight Witness, *996*
Murtaugh, James: Rosary Murders, The, *1011*
Murton, Lionel: Meet the Navy, *930*
Murton, Tom: Main Street to Broadway, *326*
Musante, Tony: Bird with the Crystal Plumage, The, *955;* Breaking Up Is Hard to Do, *469;* Collector's Item, *485;* Grissom Gang, The, *534;* Incident, The (1967), *551*
Muscat, Angelo: Prisoner, The (TV Series), *1071;* Prisoner Video Companion, The, *1072*
Muse, Clarence: Black Stallion, The, *151;* Broken Strings, *470;* Murder Over New York, *999*
Musidora: Vampires, The (1915), *799*
Mustain, Minor: Snake Eater III: His Law, *117*
Mutchie, Marjorie Ann: It's a Great Life, *308*
Muti, Ornella: Casanova (1987), *252;* Once Upon a Crime, *349;* Oscar (1991), *351;* Swann in Love, *791;* Tales of Ordinary Madness, *677;* Wait Until Spring, Bandini, *695*
Muza, Melvin: Street Hitz, *121*
Myers, Carmel: Beau Brummell (1924), *457;* Ben-Hur (1926), *458;* Svengali (1931), *1022*
Myers, Cynthia: Beyond the Valley of the Dolls, *460*
Myers, Harry: City Lights, *255*
Myers, Kathleen: Dick Turpin, *38*
Myers, Kim: Illegally Yours, *548;* Nightmare on Elm Street 2, A: Freddy's Revenge, *871*
Myers, Mike: So I Married an Axe Murderer, *382;* Wayne's World, *406;* Wayne's World 2, *406*
Myerson, Alan: Steelyard Blues, *386*
Mynster, Karen-Lise: Sofie, *787*
NIXau: Gods Must Be Crazy II, The, *287*
Na, Renhua: Girl from Hunan, *740*
Nabors, Jim: Andy Griffith Show, The (TV Series), *227;* Return to Mayberry, *366;* Stroker Ace, *387*

Nader, George: Away all Boats, *8;* Carnival Story, *475;* House of 1,000 Dolls, *64;* Human Duplicators, The, *854;* Monsoon, *599;* Robot Monster, *881*
Nader, Michael: Finishing Touch, The, *977;* Flash, The, *1051;* Lady Mobster, *74;* Nick Knight, *868*
Nagase, Masatochi: Mystery Train, *603*
Nagel, Anne: Don Winslow of the Navy, *41;* Mad Monster, *862;* Spirit of West Point, The, *664;* Winners of the West, *1165*
Nagel, Conrad: Ann Vickers, *448;* Divorcee, The, *502;* Kiss, The (1929), *566;* Mysterious Lady, The, *603*
Nagurney, Nickolas: Fun Down There, *523*
Naidu, Ajay: Touch and Go, *398;* Where the River Runs Black, *1089*
Naiduk, Stacy: Steel and Lace, *1080*
Nail, Jimmy: Diamond's Edge, *162*
Naish, J. Carrol: Across the Wide Missouri, *1092;* Ann Vickers, *448;* Annie Get Your Gun, *907;* Beast with Five Fingers, The, *812;* Beau Geste, *10;* Behind the Rising Sun, *10;* Black Hand, The, *462;* Bulldog Drummond Comes Back, *20;* Bulldog Drummond in Africa, *20;* Clash by Night, *483;* Corsican Brothers, The (1941), *29;* Denver and Rio Grande, The, *1108;* Down Argentine Way, *914;* Dracula vs. Frankenstein, *837;* Fighter Attack, *47;* Fugitive, The (1947), *523;* Gung Ho! (1943), *58;* House of Frankenstein, *852;* Humoresque, *546;* Joan of Arc, *558;* Kissing Bandit, The, *927;* Last Command, The (1955), *1125;* Monster Maker, The, *866;* New Adventures of Charlie Chan, The (TV Series), *1000;* Rage at Dawn, *1140;* Rio Grande, *1145;* Sahara (1943), *110;* Southerner, The, *663;* That Midnight Kiss, *944;* This Could Be the Night, *394;* Thunder Trail, *1157;* Toast of New Orleans, *946;* Waterfront, *697;* World Gone Mad, The, *707*
Naismith, Laurence: Amazing Mr. Blunden, The, *146;* Carrington, V. C., *476;* Concrete Jungle, The (1962) (a.k.a. The Criminal), *487;* Greyfriars Bobby, *172;* Man Who Never Was, The, *81;* Night to Remember, A (1958), *606;* Persuaders, The (TV Series), *98;* Scrooge (1970), *938;* Sink the Bismarck, *116;* World of Suzie Wong, The, *707;* Young Winston, *709*
Najee-ullah, Mansoor: Death of a Prophet, *498*
Najimy, Kathy: Hocus Pocus, *175;* Sister Act, *379;* Sister Act 2: Back in the Habit, *380*
Nakadai, Tatsuya: Face of Another, The, *735;* High and Low, *744;* Human Condition, The, Part One: No Greater Love, *745;* Human Condition, The, Part Two: The Road to Eternity, *745;* Human Condition, The, Part Three: A Soldier's Prayer, *745;* Hunter in the Dark, *746;* Kagemusha, *751;* Kojiro, *752;* Kwaidan, *752;* Odd Obsession, *772;* Ran, *779;* Sanjuro, *783;* Sword of Doom, *792;* Wolves, The, *804*
Nakagawa, Ken: Living on Tokyo Time, *761*
Nakagawa, Roger: Escapade in Japan, *165*
Nakamura, Atsuo: Highest Honor, The, *62*
Nakamura, Ganjiro: Drifting Weeds, *732*
Nakamura, Kichiemon: Double Suicide, *731*
Nakamura, Knemon: Forty Seven Ronin, *738*
Nakhapetov, Rodion: Slave of Love, A, *786*
Nalbach, Daniel: Gig, The, *286*
Nalder, Reggie: Day And The Hour, *728;* Mark of the Devil, *863;* Mark of the Devil, Part 2, *863;* Salem's Lot, *882;* Zoltan—Hound of Dracula, *904*
Naldi, Nita: Blood and Sand (1922), *464;* Dr. Jekyll and Mr. Hyde (1920), *835;* Ten Commandments, The (1923), *678*
Namath, Joe: C.C. & Company, *21;* Chattanooga Choo Choo, *254*
Nance, Jack: Eraserhead, *838;* Meatballs 4, *330;* Twin Peaks (Movie), *1027;* Twin Peaks (TV Series), *1027*
Nance, John: Ghoulies, *846*
Nanty, Isabelle: Tatie Danielle, *792*
Napaul, Neriah: Bikini Carwash Company 2, *239*
Naper, Marshall: Georgia, *979*
Napier, Alan: Across the Wide Missouri, *1092;* Challenge to Lassie, *157;* Hills of Home, *174;* House of the Seven Gables, The, *545;* Invisible Man Returns, *856;* Mademoiselle Fifi, *585;* Mole People, The, *1066;* 36 Hours, *681;* Uninvited, The (1944), *1029*
Napier, Charles: Center of the Web, *960;* Cherry, Harry and Raquel, *480;* Citizen's Band, *255;* Deep Space, *1046;* Ernest Goes to Jail, *272;* Eyes of the Beholder, *974;* Future Zone, *54;* Grifters, The, *534;* Homicidal Impulse, *983;* Indigo 2: The Revolt, *66;* Instant Justice, *67;* Kidnapped (1988), *71;* Last Embrace, The, *990;* Miami Blues, *84;* Night Stalker, The (1986), *870;* One-Man Force, *94;* Philadelphia, *621;* Rambo: First Blood II, *103;* Return to Frogtown, *1074;* Silence of the Lambs, *1016;* Skeeter, *887;* Soldier's Fortune, *118;* Supervixens, *123;* Treacherous Crossing, *1027*
Napir, Yvette: Run if You Can, *645*
Naples, Toni: Dinosaur Island, *1047*
Nardi, Tony: Good Night, Michelangelo, *288*
Nardini, Tom: Africa—Texas Style!, *3*
Narelle, Brian: Dark Star, *1044*
Narita, Mikio: Zatoichi: The Blind Swordsman and the Chess Expert, *806*
Naschak, Andrea: Hold Me, Thrill Me, Kiss Me, *298*
Naschy, Paul: Blood Moon, *815;* Craving, The, *825;* Dracula's Great Love, *837;* Fury of the Wolf Man, *845;* Horror Rises from the Tomb, *852;* House of Psychotic Women, *852;* Night of the Howling Beast, *870*
Nash, Chris: Mischief, *333;* Modern Girls, *335;* Satisfaction, *938*
Nash, Jennifer: Invisible: The Chronicles of Benjamin Knight, *1060*
Nash, Joe: TV Classics: Flash Gordon and the Planet of Death, *1085*
Nash, Marilyn: Monsieur Verdoux, *336;* Unknown World, *1087*
Nash, Mary: Men of Boys Town, *592*
Nash, Noreen: Lone Ranger and the Lost City of Gold, The, *1129;* Phantom from Space, *1070*
Nat, Marie-Jose: Les Violons du Bal, *759*
Nathan, Adam: I Was a Teenage TV Terrorist, *304;* Parting Glances, *618*
Nathan, Stephen: First Nudie Musical, The, *917;* You Light Up My Life, *708*
Nathan, Vivian: Young Savages, The, *1033*
Natividad, Francesca "Kitten": Beneath the Valley of the Ultra-Vixens, *234*
Natsuki, Yosuke: Dagora, the Space Monster, *1044;* Ghidrah, the Three-Headed Monster, *845*
Natwick, Mildred: Against All Flags, *3;* Barefoot in the Park, *232;* Court Jester, The, *260;* Daisy Miller, *493;* Dangerous Liaisons, *494;* If It's Tuesday, This Must Be Belgium, *305;* Kissing Bandit, The, *927;* Long Voyage Home, The, *578;* Quiet Man, The, *364;* Tammy and the Bachelor, *677;* Trouble with Harry, The, *399;* Yolanda and the Thief, *708*
Naude, Beyers: Cry of Reason, The, *421*
Naughton, David: American Werewolf in London, An, *808;* Amityville: A New Generation, *809;* Boy in Blue, The, *467;* Getting Physical, *526;* Hot Dog...The Movie, *301;* Kidnapped (1988), *71;* Midnight Madness, *332;* Not for Publication, *347;* Overexposed, *873;* Private Affairs, *361;* Separate Vacations, *375;* Sleeping Car, The, *887;* Steel and Lace, *1080;* Wild Cactus, *139*
Naughton, James: Birds II, The: Land's End, *813;* Glass Menagerie, The, *528;* Good Mother, The, *530;* Stranger Is Watching, A, *890*
Navarro, Carlos: Illusion Travels by Streetcar, *747*
Nay, Zachi: Up Your Anchor, *404*
Nazimova: Blood and Sand (1941), *464;* Bridge of San Luis Rey, The, *469*
Nazimova, Anna: Salome (1923), *647*
Nazzari, Amadeo: Naked Maja, The, *603;* Nights of Cabiria, *771*
Neagle, Anna: Courtney Affair, The, *489;* Forever and a Day, *520;* London Melody, *577;* Nurse Edith Cavell, *610*
Neal, Billie: Mortal Thoughts, *997*

Neal, Edwin: Future-Kill, *845;* Texas Chainsaw Massacre, The, *894*

Neal, Ella: Mysterious Dr. Satan, *88*

Neal, Frances: Lady Scarface, *74*

Neal, Patricia: All Quiet on the Western Front (1979), *444;* Bastard, The, *456;* Baxter, *456;* Breakfast at Tiffany's, *468;* Caroline?, *959;* Day the Earth Stood Still, The, *1044;* Eric, *510;* Face in the Crowd, A, *512;* Fountainhead, The, *520;* Ghost Story, *846;* Hud, *546;* In Harm's Way, *66;* Operation Pacific, *614;* Run Stranger Run, *882;* Shattered Vows, *655;* Stranger from Venus, *1081;* Subject Was Roses, The, *671;* Three Secrets, *683;* Unremarkable Life, An, *692*

Neal, Peggy: X from Outer Space, The, *1090*

Neal, Tom: Another Thin Man, *952;* Behind the Rising Sun, *10;* Bowery at Midnight, *818;* Brute Man, The, *820;* Courageous Dr. Christian, The, *489;* Detour, *970;* First Yank into Tokyo, *49;* Hatbox Mystery, The, *982;* I Shot Billy the Kid, *1122;* King of the Bullwhip, *1125*

Nealon, Kevin: All I Want for Christmas, *145*

Neame, Christopher: Diplomatic Immunity, *39;* Edge of Honor, *43;* Romeo and Juliet (1988), *643;* Steel Dawn, *1080;* Still Not Quite Human, *386;* Street Knight, *121*

Near, Holly: Dogfight, *503;* Slaughterhouse Five, *1077;* Todd Killings, The, *685;* Wasn't That a Time!, *438*

Neckar, Vaclav: Closely Watched Trains, *725;* Larks on a String, *755*

Neeley, Ted: Hard Country, *293;* Jesus Christ, Superstar, *926*

Neely, Gail: Surf Nazis Must Die, *123*

Neely, Mark: Off the Mark, *348*

Neeman, Hillel: Boy Takes Girl, *152;* Soldier of the Night, *787*

Neenan, Audrie: Sunset Limousine, *388*

Neeson, Liam: Crossing the Line (1991), *492;* Darkman, *1044;* Dead Pool, The, *33;* Deception (1993), *969;* Ethan Frome, *511;* Good Mother, The, *530;* High Spirits, *297;* Husbands and Wives, *546;* Leap of Faith, *572;* Mission, The, *596;* Next of Kin (1989), *90;* Satisfaction, *938;* Schindler's List, *649;* Shining Through, *656;* Suspect, *1022;* Under Suspicion, *1028*

Neff, Hildegarde: Bluebeard (1963), *719;* Fedora, *515;* Snows of Kilimanjaro, The, *118;* Unnatural, *1029*

Negami, Jun: Golden Demon, *741*

Negoda, Natalya: Back in the U.S.S.R., *8;* Comrades of Summer, The, *258;* Little Vera, *761*

Negret, Francois: Night and Day (1991), *771*

Negri, Pola: Gypsy Blood, *535;* Moonspinners, The, *189;* One Arabian Night, *773;* Passion (1919), *775*

Negro, Del: Aguirre: Wrath of God, *711*

Negro, Mary Joan: King Richard II, *565;* No Big Deal, *608*

Negron, Taylor: Bad Medicine, *231;* Last Boy Scout, The, *75;* Young Doctors in Love, *415*

Neher, Carola: Threepenny Opera, The, *794*

Nehm, Kristina: Fringe Dwellers, The, *522*

Neidorf, David: Undercover, *134*

Neil, Christopher: Adventures of a Private Eye, *222*

Neil, Hildegard: Antony and Cleopatra (1973), *450;* Man Who Haunted Himself, The, *995;* Touch of Class, A, *398*

Neil, Roger: Oracle, The, *872*

Neill, James: Ten Commandments, The (1923), *678*

Neill, Noel: Adventures of Frank and Jesse James, *1092;* Atom Man vs. Superman, *7;* Superman—The Serial, *1081;* TV's Best Adventures of Superman, *1085*

Neill, Sam: Attack Force Z, *7;* Blood of Others, The, *464;* Cry in the Dark, A, *492;* Dead Calm, *966;* Enigma, *44;* Fever, *47;* Final Conflict, The, *841;* For Love Alone, *519;* Good Wife, The, *530;* Hostage (1992), *64;* Hunt for Red October, The, *984;* Ivanhoe (1982), *68;* Jurassic Park, *1061;* Memoirs of an Invisible Man, *1065;* My Brilliant Career, *601;* One Against the Wind, *613;* Piano, The, *622;* Plenty, *623;* Possession, *876;* Question of Faith, *632;* Rainbow Warrior, *1008;* Reilly: The Ace of Spies, *637;* Sirens, *379;* Sleeping Dogs, *117;* Until the End of the World, *1087*

Neilson, John: Terror at the Red Wolf Inn, *893*

Nelkin, Stacey: Get Crazy, *284;* Going Ape!, *287;* Halloween III: Season of the Witch, *848;* Up the Academy, *403*

Nell, Little: Jubilee, *1061;* Rocky Horror Picture Show, The, *937*

Nell, Nathalie: Rape of Love (L'Amour Violé), *779*

Nelligan, Kate: Bethune, *459;* Diamond Fleece, The, *970;* Eleni, *508;* Eye of the Needle, *974;* Fatal Instinct (1993), *274;* Frankie and Johnny (1991), *522;* Love and Hate, *581;* Prince of Tides, The, *627;* Shadows and Fog, *654;* Terror Stalks the Class Reunion, *894;* Without a Trace, *1032*

Nellson, John: Shark's Treasure, *115*

Nelson, Barry: Bataan, *9;* Casino Royale (1954), *23;* Island Claws, *857;* Johnny Eager, *559;* Pete 'n' Tillie, *357;* Rio Rita, *368;* Shadow of the Thin Man, *1014*

Nelson, Bob: Brain Donors, *245;* Rodney Dangerfield: "It's Not Easy Being Me", *370*

Nelson, Bobby: Cowboy and the Bandit, *1106;* Cyclone in the Saddle, *1107*

Nelson, Craig T.: Action Jackson, *2;* All the Right Moves, *444;* And Justice for All, *447;* Call to Glory, *474;* Cannon Movie Tales: Red Riding Hood, *155;* Diary of a Teenage Hitchhiker, *501;* Fire Next Time, The, *1051;* Josephine Baker Story, The, *559;* Killing Fields, The, *563;* Me and Him, *330;* Murderers Among Us: The Simon Wiesenthal Story, *601;* Poltergeist, *875;* Poltergeist II: The Other Side, *875;* Rachel River, *632;* Rage (1980), *633;* Silkwood, *658;* Troop Beverly Hills, *399*

Nelson, Danny: Blood Salvage, *816*

Nelson, David: Adventures of Ozzie and Harriet, The (TV Series), *222;* Cry-Baby, *912;* Peyton Place, *621*

Nelson, Ed: Attack of the Crab Monsters, *810;* Boneyard, The, *818;* Brain Eaters, The, *1040;* Bucket of Blood, A, *820;* For the Love of Benji, *167;* Return of Frank Cannon, The, *1010*

Nelson, Gene: Lullaby of Broadway, *929;* Tea for Two, *944;* West Point Story, The, *947*

Nelson, Guy: Invasion of the Space Preachers, *307*

Nelson, Harriet: Adventures of Ozzie and Harriet, The (TV Series), *222;* Follow the Fleet, *917;* Kid with the 200 I.Q., The, *180;* Take It Big, *943*

Nelson, John Allen: Deathstalker III—The Warriors from Hell, *1046;* Hunk, *303;* Killer Klowns from Outer Space, *859;* Saigon Commandos, *110*

Nelson, Judd: Billionaire Boys Club, *461;* Blindfold: Acts of Obsession, *956;* Blue City, *957;* Breakfast Club, The, *245;* Caroline at Midnight, *960;* Conflict of Interest, *29;* Dark Backward, The, *262;* Entangled, *973;* Every Breath, *973;* Fandango, *274;* Far Out Man, *274;* From the Hip, *281;* Hail Caesar, *292;* Hiroshima: Out of the Ashes, *541;* Making the Grade, *327;* New Jack City, *90;* Primary Motive, *627;* Relentless, *1010;* St. Elmo's Fire, *646*

Nelson, June: Adventures of Ozzie and Harriet, The (TV Series), *222*

Nelson, Kenneth: Boys in the Band, The, *468*

Nelson, Kris: Adventures of Ozzie and Harriet, The (TV Series), *222*

Nelson, Lori: Day the World Ended, The, *1045;* I Died a Thousand Times, *65;* Mohawk, *1134;* Revenge of the Creature, *881;* Underwater!, *134*

Nelson, Ozzie: Adventures of Ozzie and Harriet, The (TV Series), *222;* Impossible Years, The, *305;* People Are Funny, *356;* Take It Big, *943*

Nelson, Peter: Crime Zone, *1043;* Eye of the Eagle 3, *46;* Silk 2, *116*

Nelson, Rebecca: Surviving Desire, *389*

Nelson, Ricky: Adventures of Ozzie and Harriet, The (TV Series), *222;* Rio Bravo, *1145;* Wackiest Ship in the Army, The, *405*

Nelson, Ruth: Awakenings, *452;* Haunting Passion, The, *1055;* Wilson, *703*

Nelson, Steven: Little Ninjas, *183*
Nelson, Tracy: Down and Out in Beverly Hills, *268;* Game of Love, The, *524*
Nelson, Willie: Amazons, *4;* Another Pair of Aces, *1094;* Barbarosa, *1097;* Bob & Ray, Jane, Laraine & Gilda, *243;* Coming Out of the Ice, *486;* Dynamite and Gold, *1110;* Electric Horseman, The, *508;* Honeysuckle Rose, *923;* Last Days of Frank and Jesse James, *1125;* Red-Headed Stranger, The, *1141;* Songwriter, *940;* Stagecoach (1986), *1152;* Texas Guns, *1155;* Thief (1981), *127*
Nemec, Corin: Lifeforce Experiment, The, *1063;* Solar Crisis, *1077*
Neri, Francesca: Flight of the Innocent, *737*
Nero, Franco: Camelot, *911;* Challenge to White Fang, *24;* Confessions of a Police Captain, *487;* Die Hard 2: Die Harder, *39;* Django, *1109;* Enter the Ninja, *44;* Force Ten from Navarone, *51;* Girl, The, *527;* High Crime, *61;* Kamikaze 89, *751;* Legend of Valentino, *572;* Long Live Your Death, *1130;* Magdalene, *585;* Man with Bogart's Face, The, *995;* Querelle, *779;* Redneck, *104;* Salamander, The, *111;* Sardine: Kidnapped, *783;* Shark Hunter, The, *114;* Spaghetti Western, *1152;* Sweet Country, *674;* Touch and Die, *1026;* Tramplers, The, *1158;* Tristana, *797;* Virgin and the Gypsy, The, *694;* Windmills of the Gods, *703;* Young Catherine, *708*
Nero, Toni: No Dead Heroes, *91;* Silent Night, Deadly Night, *886*
Nesbitt, Cathleen: Affair to Remember, An, *442;* Desirée, *500;* Family Plot, *975;* Nicholas Nickleby, *605*
Nesbitt, Derren: Horrors of Burke and Hare, *852*
Nesmith, Jonathan: Elephant Parts, *915*
Nesmith, Mike: Doctor Duck's Super Secret All-Purpose Sauce, *266;* Elephant Parts, *915;* Head (1968), *922;* Television Parts Home Companion, *944*
Nessen, Ron: Best of Chevy Chase, The, *235*
Nettleton, Lois: Bamboo Saucer (a.k.a. Collision Course), *1038;* Brass, *468;* Butterfly, *473;* Deadly Blessing, *831;* Manhunt for Claude Dallas, *81;* Period of Adjustment, *356*
Neuman, Jenny: Delos Adventure, The, *36;* Hell Night, *849*
Neuwirth, Bebe: Bugsy, *471;* Green Card, *290;* Malice, *994;* Paint Job, The, *1004*
Neville, Aaron: Zandalee, *709*
Neville, John: Adventures of Baron Münchausen, The, *1034;* Study in Terror, A, *1021*
Nevin, Robyn: Careful He Might Hear You, *475;* Fourth Wish, The, *521;* Irishman, The, *554*
Nevin, Rosa: Still Not Quite Human, *386*
Nevins, Claudette: Mask, The (1961), *863;* Possessed, The (1977), *876*
New, Nancy: Bostonians, The, *467*
Newark, Derek: Bellman and True, *954;* Offence, The, *611*
Newbern, George: Doppelganger: The Evil Within, *836;* Father of the Bride (1991), *275;* It Takes Two, *308;* Little Sister, *319;* Paramedics, *353*
Newcomb, Jamie: Lone Wolf, *861*
Newell, William: Big Show, The, *1098;* Mysterious Dr. Satan, *88*
Newhart, Bob: Cold Turkey, *257;* First Family, *277;* Hell Is for Heroes, *60;* Hot Millions, *301;* Little Miss Marker (1980), *182;* Marathon, *329;* On a Clear Day, You Can See Forever, *933;* Thursday's Game, *683*
Newill, James: West of Texas, *1163*
Newley, Anthony: Alice in Wonderland (1985), *145;* Alice Through the Looking Glass (1985), *145;* Boris and Natasha, *244;* Carol Burnett's My Personal Best, *251;* Doctor Dolittle, *162;* Fire Down Below, *517;* Garbage Pail Kids Movie, The, *168;* Good Idea, *288;* Old Curiosity Shop, The, *933;* Outrage!, *616;* Stagecoach (1986), *1152*
Newman, Barry: Amy, *146;* Having It All, *294;* Night Games, *1001;* Salzburg Connection, The, *111;* Vanishing Point, *135*
Newman, James L.: Silent Night, Deadly Night Part 2, *886*
Newman, Laraine: American Hot Wax, *906;* Best of Chevy Chase, The, *235;* Best of Dan Aykroyd, The, *235;* Best of John Belushi, The, *235;* Bob & Ray, Jane, Laraine & Gilda, *243;* Coneheads, *258;* Invaders from Mars (1986), *1059;* Mr. Mike's Mondo Video, *334;* Perfect, *620;* Problem Child 2, *362;* Revenge of the Red Baron, *881;* Saturday Night Live, *372;* Things We Did Last Summer, *394;* Tunnelvision, *400;* Wholly Moses!, *410;* Witchboard 2, *903*
Newman, Nanette: Endless Game, The, *510;* Long Ago Tomorrow, *578;* Madwoman of Chaillot, The, *585;* Of Human Bondage (1964), *610;* Seance on a Wet Afternoon, *1013;* Wrong Arm of the Law, The, *414;* Wrong Box, The, *414*
Newman, Paul: Absence of Malice, *950;* Blaze, *463;* Buffalo Bill and the Indians, *1102;* Butch Cassidy and the Sundance Kid, *1103;* Cat on a Hot Tin Roof (1958), *477;* Color of Money, The, *485;* Cool Hand Luke, *29;* Drowning Pool, The, *972;* Exodus, *512;* Fat Man and Little Boy, *515;* Fort Apache—The Bronx, *520;* From the Terrace, *523;* Harper, *981;* Harry and Son, *537;* Hombre, *1121;* Hud, *546;* Hudsucker Proxy, The, *303;* Hustler, The, *547;* Lady L, *568;* Left Handed Gun, The (1958), *1128;* Life and Times of Judge Roy Bean, The, *1128;* Long Hot Summer, The (1958), *578;* Mackintosh Man, The, *994;* Mr. and Mrs. Bridge, *596;* New Kind of Love, A, *343;* Paris Blues, *618;* Pocket Money, *359;* Prize, The, *629;* Quintet, *1073;* Secret War of Harry Frigg, The, *375;* Silent Movie, *379;* Silver Chalice, The, *658;* Slap Shot, *380;* Somebody Up There Likes Me, *662;* Sometimes a Great Notion, *662;* Sting, The, *120;* Sweet Bird of Youth (1962), *674;* Torn Curtain, *1026;* Towering Inferno, The, *131;* Until They Sail, *692;* Verdict, The, *693;* When Time Ran Out!, *1031;* Winning, *140;* Young Philadelphians, The, *708*
Newman, Phillip: No Justice, *91*
Newmar, Julie: Deep Space, *1046;* Evils of the Night, *839;* Ghosts Can't Do It, *285;* Hysterical, *303;* Li'l Abner (1959), *928;* Mackenna's Gold, *1131;* Nudity Required, *347;* Seven Brides for Seven Brothers, *939;* Streetwalkin', *671*
Newton, Bert: Fatty Finn, *166*
Newton, John Haymes: Desert Kickboxer, *37*
Newton, Margie: Bronx Executioner, The, *1040;* Night of the Zombies, *870*
Newton, Robert: Androcles and the Lion, *227;* Around the World in 80 Days (1956), *228;* Beachcomber, The, *457;* Blackbeard the Pirate, *14;* Desert Rats, The, *500;* Epic That Never Was, The, *423;* Gaslight (1940), *979;* Henry V (1944), *540;* High and the Mighty, The, *541;* Jamaica Inn, *556;* Long John Silver, *78;* Major Barbara, *326;* Odd Man Out, *1003;* Oliver Twist (1948), *612;* This Happy Breed, *682;* Tom Brown's Schooldays (1950), *685;* Treasure Island (1950), *214*
Newton, Thankie: Flirting, *518*
Newton, Wayne: Adventures of Ford Fairlane, The, *2;* Best of the Best 2, *11;* Dark Backward, The, *262*
Newton-John, Olivia: Grease, *920;* Two of a Kind (1983), *402;* Xanadu, *948*
Ney, Richard: Mrs. Miniver, *597;* Premature Burial, The, *876*
Neyland, Anne: Motorcycle Gang, *87*
Neyland, Dixie: Merry Wives of Windsor, The, *331*
Ng, Richard: Mr. Vampire (Vol. 1–4), *768;* Warriors from the Magic Mountain, *802*
Nghieu, Tieu Quan: China, My Sorrow, *723*
Ngor, Haing S.: Eastern Condors, *733;* Heaven and Earth (1993), *539;* In Love and War, *985;* Iron Triangle, The, *554;* Killing Fields, The, *563;* Love and War, *581;* My Life, *602*
Niam, Don: Undefeatable, *134*
Nicastro, Michelle: Bad Guys, *8*
Nichetti, Maurizio: Icicle Thief, The, *746;* Volere Volare, *801*
Nicholas, Anna: Mutants in Paradise, *338*
Nicholas, Denise: Blacula, *814;* Ghost Dad, *285;* Marvin and Tige, *589;* Piece of the Action, A, *357;* Sophisticated Gents, The, *663*
Nicholas, Harold: Five Heartbeats, The, *917*
Nicholas, Paul: Alice (1981), *906;* Invitation to the Wedding, *307;* Lisztomania, *928*
Nicholas, Stephen: Witchboard, *903*
Nicholas, Taylor: Metropolitan, *593*

Nichols, Andrew: Night of the Living Babes, *344*

Nichols, Barbara: Human Duplicators, The, *854;* King and Four Queens, The, *1125;* Manfish, *862;* Pajama Game, The, *934;* Pal Joey, *934;* Sweet Smell of Success, *675;* Untouchables, The: Scarface Mob (TV), *134;* Where the Boys Are, *409*

Nichols, Conrad: Days of Hell, *33;* Man Called Rage, A, *1064*

Nichols, Kyra: George Balanchine's The Nutcracker, *919*

Nichols, Nichelle: Antony and Cleopatra (1981), *450;* Star Trek (TV Series), *1078;* Star Trek: The Menagerie, *1078;* Star Trek—The Motion Picture, *1079;* Star Trek II: The Wrath of Khan, *1079;* Star Trek III: The Search for Spock, *1079;* Star Trek IV: The Voyage Home, *1079;* Star Trek V: The Final Frontier, *1079;* Star Trek VI: The Undiscovered Country, *1079;* Supernaturals, The, *891*

Nichols, Red: Gene Krupa Story, The, *525*

Nicholson, Jack: Batman (1989), *9;* Border, The, *17;* Broadcast News, *246;* Carnal Knowledge, *475;* Chinatown, *962;* Easy Rider, *506;* Ensign Pulver, *271;* Few Good Men, A, *976;* Five Easy Pieces, *517;* Flight to Fury, *51;* Goin' South, *1116;* Heartburn, *295;* Hell's Angels on Wheels, *60;* Hoffa, *542;* Ironweed, *554;* King of Marvin Gardens, The, *565;* Last Detail, The, *569;* Last Tycoon, The, *571;* Little Shop of Horrors, The (1960), *861;* Man Trouble, *327;* Missouri Breaks, The, *1134;* On a Clear Day, You Can See Forever, *933;* One Flew Over the Cuckoo's Nest, *613;* Passenger, The, *1004;* Postman Always Rings Twice, The (1981), *1007;* Prizzi's Honor, *362;* Psych-Out, *630;* Raven, The (1963), *879;* Rebel Rousers, *104;* Reds, *637;* Ride in the Whirlwind, *1143;* Shining, The, *885;* Shooting, The, *1149;* Studs Lonigan, *671;* Terms of Endearment, *679;* Terror, The, *893;* Tommy, *946;* Two Jakes, The, *1028;* Wild Ride, The, *702;* Witches of Eastwick, The, *412*

Nicholson, Nick: Naked Vengeance, *88;* No Dead Heroes, *91*

Nicholson, Thomas Ian: Rookie of the Year, *200*

Nickles, M. A.: Hamburger Hill, *535*

Nickson, Julia: Amityville: A New Generation, *809;* China Cry, *481;* Chinatown Murders, The: Man Against the Mob, *25;* Glitch!, *287;* Rambo: First Blood II, *103;* Sidekicks, *203*

Nicol, Alex: Man from Laramie, The, *1131;* Screaming Skull, The, *884*

Nicolas, Paul: Yesterday's Hero, *708*

Nicolodi, Daria: Beyond the Door 2, *813;* Creepers, *826;* Deep Red (1975), *832;* Macaroni, *325;* Terror at the Opera, *893;* Unsane, *899*

Niehaus, Rena: Desperate Crimes, *37*

Nielsen, Asta: Joyless Street, *560*

Nielsen, Brigitte: Beverly Hills Cop II, *11;* Bye Bye, Baby, *473;* Cobra (1986), *27;* Domino, *503;* Double-O Kid, The, *41;* Mission of Justice, *85;* Murder by Moonlight, *1067;* 976-EVIL II: The Astral Factor, *872;* Red Sonja, *104;* Rocky IV, *642*

Nielsen, Connie: Voyage, *1030*

Nielsen, Leslie: Airplane!, *224;* All I Want for Christmas, *145;* Amsterdam Kill, The, *5;* Bad Golf Made Easier, *231;* Creepshow, *826;* Day of the Animals, *830;* Dayton's Devils, *33;* Forbidden Planet, *1052;* Four Rode Out, *1114;* Foxfire Light, *521;* Harlow, *536;* Home Is Where the Hart Is, *299;* Naked Gun, The, *341;* Naked Gun 2 1/2, The, *341;* Naked Gun 33 1/3, The—The Final Insult, *341;* Nightstick, *91;* Opposite Sex, The, *934;* Patriot, *97;* Police Squad!, *359;* Prom Night, *876;* Repossessed, *366;* Resurrection of Zachary Wheeler, The, *1074;* Snatched, *117;* Soul Man, *383;* Spaceship, *384;* Striker's Mountain, *121;* Surf Ninjas, *208;* Tammy and the Bachelor, *677;* Viva Knievel, *136;* Wrong Is Right, *414*

Niemczyk, Leon: Knife in the Water, *752*

Niemi, Lisa: Steel Dawn, *1080*

Nieto, Jose: Son of Captain Blood, *118*

Nigh, Jane: Fort Osage, *1114*

Nikandrov, V.: October, *772*

Nikhaido, Miho: Tokyo Decadence, *795*

Niklas, Jan: Club Extinction, *1042*

Nilsson, Birgit: Elektra, *915*

Nilsson, Harry: Son of Dracula (1974), *940*

Nilsson, Inger: Pippi Longstocking, Pippi in the South Seas, Pippi Goes on Board, Pippi on the Run, *195*

Nilsson, Rob: Heat and Sunlight, *539*

Nimmo, Derek: One of Our Dinosaurs Is Missing, *192*

Nimoy, Leonard: Aladdin and His Wonderful Lamp, *145;* Balcony, The, *455;* Bloopers from Star Trek and Laugh-In, *242;* Brain Eaters, The, *1040;* Catlow, *1104;* Invasion of the Body Snatchers (1978), *1059;* Never Forget, *604;* Satan's Satellites, *111;* Star Trek (TV Series), *1078;* Star Trek: The Cage, *1078;* Star Trek: The Menagerie, *1078;* Star Trek—The Motion Picture, *1079;* Star Trek II: The Wrath of Khan, *1079;* Star Trek III: The Search for Spock, *1079;* Star Trek IV: The Voyage Home, *1079;* Star Trek V: The Final Frontier, *1079;* Star Trek VI: The Undiscovered Country, *1079;* Woman Called Golda, A, *705*

Nin, Anais: Kenneth Anger—Volume Two, *562*

Ninetto, Davoli: Hawks and the Sparrows, The, *743*

Nipar, Yvette: Doctor Mordrid, *1047*

Niro, Robert De: Bronx Tale, A, *470*

Nirvana, Yana: Club Life, *27*

Nisbio, John: Overkill, *96*

Nissen, Helge: Leaves from Satan's Book, *758*

Niven, David: Around the World in 80 Days (1956), *228;* Ask Any Girl, *229;* Bachelor Mother, *230;* Bedtime Story, *233;* Beloved Enemy, *458;* Birds and the Bees, The, *240;* Bishop's Wife, The, *240;* Bonjour Tristesse, *466;* Candleshoe, *155;* Carrington, V. C., *476;* Casino Royale (1967), *252;* Charge of the Light Brigade, The (1936), *24;* Curse of the Pink Panther, The, *261;* Dawn Patrol, The, *33;* Death on the Nile, *968;* Dinner at the Ritz, *39;* Dodsworth, *503;* Elusive Pimpernel, The, *509;* Escape to Athena, *45;* Eternally Yours, *511;* 55 Days at Peking, *516;* Guns of Navarone, The, *58;* Happy Go Lovely, *921;* Immortal Battalion, The (a.k.a. The Way Ahead), *549;* Impossible Years, The, *305;* King, Queen and Knave, *565;* Lady L, *568;* Moon Is Blue, The, *336;* Murder by Death, *338;* My Man Godfrey (1957), *340;* No Deposit, No Return, *191;* Paper Tiger, *97;* Perfect Marriage, *356;* Pink Panther, The, *357;* Please Don't Eat the Daisies, *358;* Prisoner of Zenda, The (1937), *100;* Real Glory, The, *103;* Rough Cut, *1011;* Sea Wolves, The, *113;* Statue, The, *385;* Toast of New Orleans, *946;* Trail of the Pink Panther, The, *398;* Wuthering Heights (1939), *707*

Niven, Kip: New Year's Evil, *868*

Nixon, Allan: Prehistoric Women (1950), *1071*

Nixon, Cynthia: I Am the Cheese, *547;* Manhattan Project, The, *995;* Tanner '88, *391*

Nixon, John P.: Legend of Boggy Creek, *860*

Nixon, Marion: Hands Up!, *292*

Nixon, Marni: Taking My Turn, *943*

Noah, Tim: In Search of the Wow Wow Wibble Woggle Wazzle Woodle Woo!, *176*

Noble, Chelsea: Instant Karma, *306*

Noble, Erin: Uninvited, The (1993), *1160*

Noble, James: Paramedics, *353;* You Talkin' to Me, *141*

Noble, Trisha: Private Eyes, The, *361*

Noel, Bernard: Married Woman, A, *765*

Noel, Chris: Cease Fire, *477;* Glory Stompers, The, *56*

Noel, Magali: Amarcord, *712;* Eighties, The, *733;* Les Rendez-Vous D'Anna, *759;* Rififi, *1010*

Noel-Noel: Sputnik, *788*

Nogulich, Natalija: Dirty Dozen, The: The Fatal Mission, *39;* Hoffa, *542;* Homicide, *983*

Noiman, Rivka: Jesus, *557*

Noir, Haing S.: Vietnam, Texas, *135*

Noiret, Philippe: Birgit Haas Must Be Killed, *718;* Cinema Paradiso, *724;* Clean Slate (Coup de Torchon), *724;* Clockmaker, The, *725;* Holes, The, *744;* Judge and the Assassin, The, *750;* Jupiter's Thigh, *751;* Justine, *561;* Le Secret, *758;* Life and Nothing But, *760;* Murphy's War, *87;* My New Partner, *770;* Next Summer, *771;* Night Flight from

Moscow, *90;* Purple Taxi, The, *631;* Return of the Musketeers, *106;* Three Brothers, *794;* Uranus, *798;* Zazie dans le Metro, *807*
Nolan and the Sons of the Pioneers, Bob: Apache Rose, *1094;* Bells of Rosarita, *1097;* Call of the Canyon, *1103;* Cowboy and the Senorita, *1106;* Don't Fence Me In, *1110;* Eyes of Texas, *1111;* Helldorado (1946), *1120;* Home in Oklahoma, *1121;* Idaho, *1122;* Nighttime in Nevada, *1136;* Old Corral, *1136;* Roll on Texas Moon, *1145;* Song of Nevada, *1151;* Song of Texas, *1151;* Sunset on the Desert, *1154;* Yellow Rose of Texas, *1165*
Nolan, Doris: Holiday, *298*
Nolan, Jeanette: Avalanche, *7;* Big Heat, The, *12;* Chamber of Horrors, *822;* Macbeth (1948), *583*
Nolan, Kathleen: Amy, *146;* Lights, Camera, Action, Love, *575*
Nolan, Lloyd: Bataan, *9;* Circus World, *482;* Every Day's a Holiday, *273;* Fire!, *48;* G-Men, *54;* Girl Hunters, The, *979;* Guadalcanal Diary, *58;* Hannah and Her Sisters, *293;* House Across the Bay, The, *545;* Ice Station Zebra, *65;* Island in the Sky, *554;* Johnny Apollo, *559;* Lady in the Lake, *990;* Last Hunt, The, *1126;* Lemon Drop Kid, The, *317;* My Boys Are Good Boys, *601;* Peyton Place, *621;* Private Files of J. Edgar Hoover, The, *100;* Sergeant Ryker, *652;* Street with No Name, *1021;* Sun Comes Up, The, *208;* Tree Grows in Brooklyn, A, *687*
Nolan, Tom: School Spirit, *374;* Up the Creek (1984), *403*
Nolte, Nick: Another 48 Hrs., *5;* Blue Chips, *465;* Cannery Row, *250;* Cape Fear (1991), *959;* Deep, The, *36;* Down and Out in Beverly Hills, *268;* Everybody Wins, *973;* Extreme Prejudice, *45;* Farewell to the King, *46;* 48 Hrs., *279;* Grace Quigley, *289;* Heart Beat, *537;* I'll Do Anything, *305;* Lorenzo's Oil, *579;* New York Stories, *343;* North Dallas Forty, *609;* Prince of Tides, The, *627;* Q & A, *1008;* Return to Macon County, *106;* Teachers, *391;* Three Fugitives, *395;* Under Fire, *134;* Weeds, *697;* Who'll Stop the Rain, *139*
Nonyela, Valentine: Young Soul Rebels, *948*
Noonan, Tom: Collision Course, *257;* Last Action Hero, The, *1062*
Noonan, Tommy: Ambassador's Daughter, The, *226;* Bundle of Joy, *247;* Gentlemen Prefer Blondes, *284;* Girl Most Likely, The, *919;* Jungle Patrol, *69;* Monster Squad, The, *866;* Promises, Promises, *362;* Star Is Born, A (1954), *666;* Three Nuts in Search of a Bolt, *396;* Wolfen, *904*
Norby, Ghita: Memories of a Marriage, *766;* Sofie, *787*
Norden, Tommy: Flipper's Odyssey, *167*
Nordling, Jeffrey: Dangerous Heart, *965*
Nordquist, Monica: Polar Bear King, The, *1071*
Norgaard, Cartsen: D2: The Mighty Ducks, *160*
Norman, Steve: Jet Benny Show, The, *310*
Norman, Susan: Poison, *624*
Norman, Zack: America, *226;* Cadillac Man, *249;* Romancing the Stone, *108;* Sitting Ducks, *380*
Normand, Mabel: Buster Keaton: The Great Stone Face, *248;* Caution: Funny Men at Work, *420;* Charlie Chaplin...Our Hero, *253;* Extra Girl, The, *273;* Fatty and Mabel Adrift/Mabel, Fatty and the Law, *275;* Fatty Arbuckle Comedy Collection, Vol. 1, *275;* Fatty's Tin-Type Tangle/Our Congressman, *275;* Keystone Comedies, Vol. 2, *312;* Keystone Comedies, Vol. 3, *312;* Keystone Comedies, Vol. 4, *312;* Mabel and Fatty, *325;* Mack Sennett Comedies, Vol. 2, *325;* When Comedy Was King, *409*
Norris, Christopher: Eat My Dust, *43;* Summer of '42, *672*
Norris, Chuck: Braddock: Missing in Action III, *18;* Breaker! Breaker!, *19;* Bruce Lee: Curse of the Dragon, *420;* Code of Silence, *27;* Delta Force, The, *36;* Delta Force 2, *36;* Eye for an Eye, *46;* Firewalker, *49;* Force of One, *51;* Forced Vengeance, *51;* Game of Death, *54;* Good Guys Wear Black, *56;* Hero and the Terror, *61;* Hitman, The, *63;* Invasion U.S.A., *67;* Lone Wolf McQuade, *78;* Missing in Action, *85;* Missing in Action 2: The Beginning, *85;* Octagon, The, *93;* One Riot, One Ranger, *95;* Return of the Dragon, *105;* Sidekicks, *203;* Silent Rage, *116;* Slaughter in San Francisco, *117*
Norris, Edward: Mysterious Desperado, *1135;* Show Them No Mercy, *657*
Norris, Mike: Born American, *17;* Death Ring, *35;* Delta Force 3, *37;* Survival Game, *123;* Young Warriors, The, *141*
North, Alan: Billy Galvin, *461;* Police Squad!, *359*
North, Heather: Barefoot Executive, The, *148*
North, Jay: Maya, *186;* Zebra in the Kitchen, *220*
North, Neil: Winslow Boy, The, *704*
North, Noelle: Slumber Party 57, *381;* Sweater Girls, *389*
North, Robert: Blades, *814*
North, Sheree: Breakout, *19;* Lawman, *1127;* Madigan, *80;* Maniac Cop, *862;* Organization, The, *96;* Portrait of a Stripper, *625;* Real American Hero, The, *635;* Snatched, *117;* Trouble with Girls, The, *946*
North, Ted: Devil Thumbs a Ride, The, *970*
Nortier, Nadine: Mouchette, *769*
Norton, Adam: Who's Who, *411*
Norton, Alex: Comfort and Joy, *258;* Gregory's Girl, *290;* Sense of Freedom, A, *652*
Norton, Charles: Check and Double Check, *254*
Norton, Jack: Two-Reelers: Comedy Classics #1, *402*
Norton, Jim: Cry of the Innocent, *964;* Sakharov, *647*
Norton, Ken: Drum, *505;* Oceans of Fire, *93*
Norton, Richard: China O'Brien 2, *25;* Deathfight, *36;* Gymkata, *58;* Ironheart, *67;* Kick Fighter, *70;* Lady Dragon, *74;* Rage and Honor, *102;* Rage and Honor II: Hostile Takeover, *102;* Raiders of the Sun, *103;* Revenge of the Kickfighter, *106*
Norwood, Ellie: Silent Sherlock Holmes, The, *1016*
Notaro, Frank: Lethal Ninja, *76*
Noth, Christopher: Apology, *809*
Nouri, Michael: Between Two Women, *459;* Black Ice, *14;* Davinci's War, *33;* Flashdance, *917;* Gangster Wars, *54;* Hidden, The, *1056;* Imagemaker, The, *549;* Little Vegas, *319;* No Escape, No Return, *91;* Project: Alien, *1072;* Psychic, *1008;* Thieves of Fortune, *127;* Total Exposure, *1026*
Noury, Alain: Wanderer, The, *802*
Novak, Blaine: Strangers Kiss, *669*
Novak, Jane: Three-Word Brand, The, *1157*
Novak, Kim: Amorous Adventures of Moll Flanders, The, *226;* Bell, Book and Candle, *234;* Boys' Night Out, *244;* Eddy Duchin Story, The, *507;* Just a Gigolo, *561;* Kiss Me, Stupid, *314;* Liebestraum, *992;* Man with the Golden Arm, The, *587;* Middle of the Night, *593;* Mirror Crack'd, The, *996;* Of Human Bondage (1964), *610;* Pal Joey, *934;* Picnic, *622;* Strangers When We Meet, *670;* Tales that Witness Madness, *892;* Vertigo, *1029;* White Buffalo, *1164*
Novarro, Ramon: Ben-Hur (1926), *458;* Big Steal, The, *13;* Cat and the Fiddle, The, *911;* Heller in Pink Tights, *1120;* Mata Hari (1931), *590;* Student Prince in Old Heidelberg, The, *671*
Novello, Don: Father Guido Sarducci Goes to College, *275;* Gilda Live, *286;* Godfather, Part III, The, *529;* New York Stories, *343;* Pinocchio (1983), *195;* Spirit of '76, The, *384;* Teenage Bonnie and Klepto Clyde, *126*
Novello, Ivor: Lodger, The, *993;* White Rose, The (1923), *700*
Novello, Jay: Robin Hood of the Pecos, *1145*
Nover, Matt: Blue Chips, *465*
Novotna, Jarmila: Search, The, *650*
Noy, Zachi: Baby Love, *230;* Private Popsicle, *362*
Nozick, Bruce: Hit the Dutchman, *63;* Killer Instinct, *71*
Nquyen, Ho: Alamo Bay, *443*
Nugent, Elliott: Romance, *643;* Unholy Three, *1029*
Nunn, Bill: Dangerous Heart, *965;* Do the Right Thing, *502;* Mo' Better Blues, *931;* Regarding Henry, *637;* Sister Act, *379;* White Lie, *700*
Nunn, Larry: Men of Boys Town, *592*
Nunn, Teri: Follow That Car, *51*
Nureyev, Rudolf: Exposed, *840;* Valentino, *693*

Nuti, Francesco: Pool Hustlers, The, *778*
Nutter, Mayf: Hunter's Blood, *546;* Petronella, *195*
Nuyen, France: China Cry, *481;* Deathmoon, *832;* Diamond Head, *500;* Joy Luck Club, The, *559;* Return to Fantasy Island, *1074*
Nxomalo, Gideon: World of Strangers, A, *805*
Nye, Carrie: Divorce His: Divorce Hers, *502*
Nye, Louis: Alice Through the Looking Glass (1985), *145;* Stripper, The (1963), *671;* 10 from Your Show of Shows, *392;* Wheeler Dealers, The, *409*
Nyman, Lena: Autumn Sonata, *714;* I Am Curious Blue, *746;* I Am Curious Yellow, *746*
O'Bannon, Dan: Dark Star, *1044*
O'Brian, Donal: Quest for the Mighty Sword, *1073*
O'Brian, Hugh: Africa—Texas Style!, *3;* Beyond the Purple Hills, *1097;* Broken Lance, *1101;* Cruise into Terror, *964;* Fantasy Island, *1050;* Gambler Returns, the: Luck of the Draw, *1115;* Game of Death, *54;* Killer Force, *71;* Little Big Horn, *1128;* Love Has Many Faces, *581;* Man from the Alamo, The, *1132;* Murder on Flight 502, *87;* Probe, *101;* Return of Jesse James, The, *1142;* Rocketship X-M, *1075;* Seekers, The, *651;* Shootist, The, *1149;* Son of Ali Baba, *118;* Ten Little Indians (1966), *1023;* There's No Business Like Show Business, *944*
O'Brian, Michael: Playboy of the Western World, *358*
O'Brian, Seamus: Bloodsucking Freaks (The Incredible Torture Show), *816*
O'Brien, Austin: Last Action Hero, The, *1062;* My Girl 2, *190;* Prehysteria, *197*
O'Brien, Dave: Boys of the City, *18;* Devil Bat, The, *833;* Enemy of the Law, *1111;* Forbidden Trails, *1114;* Gun Code, *1117;* Gunman from Bodie, *1117;* Lightnin' Crandall, *1128;* Reefer Madness, *365;* Spooks Run Wild, *385;* Three in the Saddle, *1156;* Water Rustlers, *1162;* West of Texas, *1163*
O'Brien, Donal: Place Called Trinity, A, *1139*
O'Brien, Edmond: Admiral Was a Lady, The, *222;* Barefoot Contessa, The, *455;* Bigamist, The, *461;* Comedian, The, *486;* D.O.A. (1949), *965;* D-Day the Sixth of June, *497;* Denver and Rio Grande, The, *1108;* Doomsday Flight, The, *971;* Double Life, A, *504;* Fantastic Voyage, *1050;* Girl, a Guy and a Gob, A, *286;* Girl Can't Help It, The, *286;* Great Impostor, The, *532;* Hunchback of Notre Dame, The (1939), *854;* Julius Caesar (1953), *561;* Last Voyage, The, *76;* Lucky Luciano, *79;* Man Who Shot Liberty Valance, The, *1132;* Moon Pilot, *189;* 1984 (1955), *1068;* 99 and 44/100 Percent Dead, *91;* Pete Kelly's Blues, *935;* Rio Conchos, *1145;* Seven Days in May, *653;* Stopover Tokyo, *120;* They Only Kill Their Masters, *1024;* Two of a Kind (1951), *1028;* Up Periscope, *134;* White Heat, *138;* Wild Bunch, The, *1164*
O'Brien, Edna: Hard Way, The (1979), *59*
O'Brien, Erin: Onionhead, *350*
O'Brien, Eugene: Rebecca of Sunnybrook Farm (1917), *635*
O'Brien, George: Arizona Legion, *1095;* Cowboy Millionaire, *1106;* Daniel Boone, *1107;* Dude Ranger, *1110;* Fort Apache, *1114;* Lawless Valley, *1127;* Marshal of Mesa City, *1133;* Noah's Ark, *608;* Renegade Ranger, *1142;* She Wore a Yellow Ribbon, *1148;* Stage to Chino, *1152;* Sunrise, *673;* Triple Justice, *1159;* Windjammer, *140*
O'Brien, Jeanne: Dirty Laundry, *265*
O'Brien, Joan: It Happened at the World's Fair, *925*
O'Brien, Kim: Huckleberry Finn (1974), *176*
O'Brien, Margaret: Amy, *146;* Canterville Ghost, The (1944), *155;* Heller in Pink Tights, *1120;* Jane Eyre (1944), *557;* Journey for Margaret, *559;* Little Women (1949), *577;* Madame Curie, *584;* Meet Me in St. Louis, *930;* Our Vines Have Tender Grapes, *193;* Secret Garden, The (1949), *202*
O'Brien, Maria: Promised a Miracle, *629*
O'Brien, Mario: Smile, *381*
O'Brien, Pat: Angels with Dirty Faces, *5;* Bombardier, *17;* Bombshell, *243;* Boy Meets Girl, *244;* Boy With Green Hair, The, *468;* Bureau of Missing Persons, *959;* Ceiling Zero, *24;* Consolation Marriage, *488;* Crack-Up, *964;* Devil Dogs of the Air, *37;* End, The, *271;* Fighting Father Dunne, *516;* Fighting 69th, The, *48;* Flirtation Walk, *917;* Front Page, The (1931), *281;* Having a Wonderful Crime, *294;* Hell's House, *61;* Iron Major, The, *554;* Jubilee Trail, *1124;* Knute Rockne—All American, *567;* Last Hurrah, The, *569;* Marine Raiders, *82;* Ragtime, *633;* RiffRaff (1947), *106;* Slightly Honorable, *381;* Some Like It Hot, *382;* World Gone Mad, The, *707*
O'Brien, Patrick: Airborne, *224*
O'Brien, Richard: Jubilee, *1061;* Rocky Horror Picture Show, The, *937;* Shock Treatment, *378*
O'Brien, Tom: Big Easy, The, *12*
O'Brien, Virginia: Du Barry Was a Lady, *915;* Harvey Girls, The, *922;* Lady Be Good, *927;* Merton of the Movies, *331;* Panama Hattie, *935;* Ship Ahoy, *939;* Thousands Cheer, *945;* Ziegfeld Follies, *949*
O'Brien-Moore, Erin: Little Men (1935), *182*
O'Bryan, Melody: Melody in Love, *592*
O'Bryan, Patrick: 976-EVIL II: The Astral Factor, *872*
O'Bryne, Colm: Snapper, The, *382*
O'Connell, Arthur: Anatomy of a Murder, *952;* Ben, *812;* Blondie's Blessed Event, *242;* Bus Stop, *248;* Cimarron (1960), *1105;* Fantastic Voyage, *1050;* Follow That Dream, *278;* Gidget, *286;* Great Impostor, The, *532;* Great Race, The, *290;* Hiding Place, The, *541;* Huckleberry Finn (1974), *176;* Kissin' Cousins, *927;* Man of the West, *1132;* Misty, *188;* Monkey's Uncle, The, *188;* Operation Petticoat, *351;* Picnic, *622;* Ride Beyond Vengeance, *1143;* 7 Faces of Dr. Lao, *1076;* Suppose They Gave a War and Nobody Came?, *388;* There Was a Crooked Man, *1156;* They Only Kill Their Masters, *1024*
O'Connell, Deirdre: Fearless (1993), *515;* Pastime, *619*
O'Connell, Eddie: Absolute Beginners, *906*
O'Connell, Helen: I Dood It, *924*
O'Connell, Jerry: Calendar Girl, *249;* Ollie Hopnoodle's Haven of Bliss, *192;* Stand by Me (1986), *665*
O'Connor, Brian: National Lampoon's Class of '86, *342*
O'Connor, Carroll: All in the Family Twentieth Anniversary Special, *224;* Brass, *468;* Convicted, *488;* Death of a Gunfighter, *1108;* Devil's Brigade, The, *37;* Doctors' Wives, *503;* For Love of Ivy, *279;* Hawaii, *537;* Kelly's Heroes, *70;* Marlowe, *995;* Point Blank, *624;* Waterhole #3, *1163*
O'Connor, Darren: Parker Adderson, Philosopher, *618*
O'Connor, Derrick: Dealers, *498;* Hope and Glory, *544*
O'Connor, Donald: Alice in Wonderland (1985), *145;* Beau Geste, *10;* Francis Goes to the Races, *280;* Francis in the Navy, *280;* Francis Joins the Wacs, *280;* Francis, the Talking Mule, *280;* I Love Melvin, *924;* Private Buckaroo, *935;* Ragtime, *633;* Singin' in the Rain, *940;* There's No Business Like Show Business, *944;* Toys, *398*
O'Connor, Glynnis: Boy in the Plastic Bubble, The, *468;* California Dreaming, *474;* Deliberate Stranger, The, *499;* Kid Vengeance, *1124;* Melanie, *591;* Ode to Billy Joe, *610;* Our Town (1980), *616;* Someone I Touched, *662;* Those Lips, Those Eyes, *945;* To Heal a Nation, *684*
O'Connor, Hazel: Breaking Glass, *909*
O'Connor, Hugh: My Left Foot, *602;* Three Musketeers, The (1993), *129*
O'Connor, Kevin J.: Bogie, *466;* Candy Mountain, *474;* F/X 2: The Deadly Art of Illusion, *979;* Moderns, The, *335;* No Escape, *1069;* Peggy Sue Got Married, *355;* Special Effects, *889;* Tanner '88, *391*
O'Connor, Terry: Breaker! Breaker!, *19*
O'Connor, Tim: Buck Rogers in the 25th Century, *1040*
O'Connor, Una: Adventures of Don Juan, The, *2;* Cavalcade, *477;* Chained, *478;* Christmas in Connecticut (1945), *255;* Invisible Man, The, *856;* Personal Property, *356;* Strawberry Blonde, The, *670;* Suzy, *674;* Unexpected Guest, *1160;* Witness for the Prosecution (1957), *1032*
O'Conor, Joseph: Black Windmill, The, *956*
O'Daniels, Barrie: Devil Horse, The, *1109*
O'Day, Anita: Jazz on a Summer's Day, *427*
O'Day, Nell: Arizona Stagecoach, *1095*
O'Dea, Dennis: Captain Horatio Hornblower, *23*

O'Dea, Jimmy: Darby O'Gill and the Little People, *161*
O'Dea, Judith: Night of the Living Dead (1968), *870*
O'Dell, Tony: Chopping Mall, *824;* Evils of the Night, *839*
O'Donnell, Anthony: Nuts in May, *348*
O'Donnell, Cathy: Amazing Mr. X, *445;* Best Years of Our Lives, The, *459;* Man from Laramie, The, *1131;* Miniver Story, The, *594;* Terror in the Haunted House, *893;* They Live By Night, *681*
O'Donnell, Chris: Fried Green Tomatoes, *522;* Scent of a Woman, *649;* School Ties, *649;* Three Musketeers, The (1993), *129*
O'Donnell, Rosie: Another Stakeout, *6;* Car 54, Where Are You?, *250;* Flintstones, The, *167;* League of Their Own, A, *571;* Sleepless in Seattle, *381*
O'Donnell, Spec: Little Annie Rooney, *576*
O'Donoghue, Michael: Mr. Mike's Mondo Video, *334;* Suicide Club, The, *1021*
O'Donovan, Ross: Starstruck, *941*
O'Driscoll, Martha: Fallen Sparrow, The, *513;* Here Come the Co-Eds, *296;* House of Dracula, *852*
O'Grady, Gail: Blackout (1990), *956;* Nobody's Perfect, *346;* Spellcaster, *889*
O'Grady, Timothy E.: James Joyce's Women, *556*
O'Halloran, Jack: Dragnet (1987), *268;* Hero and the Terror, *61;* Mob Boss, *335*
O'Hanlon Jr., George: Our Time, *616*
O'Hara, Brett: Incredibly Strange Creatures Who Stopped Living and Became Mixed-Up Zombies, The, *856*
O'Hara, Catherine: After Hours, *223;* Beetlejuice, *233;* Best of John Candy, The, *236;* Betsy's Wedding, *236;* Heartburn, *295;* Home Alone, *299;* Home Alone 2: Lost in New York, *175;* Last Polka, The, *315;* Little Vegas, *319;* Paper, The, *617;* Really Weird Tales, *365;* There Goes the Neighborhood, *393*
O'Hara, Jenny: Angie, *448*
O'Hara, Kareen: Go Kill and Come Back, *1115*
O'Hara, Maureen: Against All Flags, *3;* At Sword's Point, *7;* Big Jake, *1098;* Buffalo Bill, *1102;* Dance, Girl, Dance, *261;* Deadly Companions, The, *1108;* Fallen Sparrow, The, *513;* How Green Was My Valley, *545;* Hunchback of Notre Dame, The (1939), *854;* Immortal Sergeant, The, *549;* Jamaica Inn, *556;* Lisbon, *77;* Long Grey Line, The, *578;* McLintock!, *1133;* Miracle on 34th Street, *187;* Mr. Hobbs Takes a Vacation, *334;* Only the Lonely, *350;* Parent Trap, The, *193;* Quiet Man, The, *364;* Rare Breed, The (1966), *1141;* Rio Grande, *1145;* Sinbad the Sailor, *116;* Spencer's Mountain, *664;* This Land Is Mine, *682;* To the Shores of Tripoli, *130;* Wings of Eagles, The, *703;* Woman's Secret, A, *1032*
O'Hara, Quinn: Swingin' Summer, A, *390*
O'Hara, Terence: Devastator, The, *37*
O'Heaney, Caitlin: He Knows You're Alone, *849*
O'Herlihy, Dan: Actors and Sin, *441;* At Sword's Point, *7;* Dead, The, *497;* Halloween III: Season of the Witch, *848;* Imitation of Life, *549;* Last Starfighter, The, *1062;* Longest Drive, The, *1130;* MacArthur, *583;* Macbeth (1948), *583;* Odd Man Out, *1003;* 100 Rifles, *1137;* People, The, *1070;* RoboCop, *1074;* RoboCop 2, *1075;* Waltz Through the Hills, *216;* Waterloo, *697*
O'Herlihy, Gavan: Conagher, *1105*
O'Herne, Pete: Bad Taste, *1038*
O'Hurley, John: Mirror Images, *996*
O'Keef, Michael: Hitchhiker (Series), The, *850*
O'Keefe, Dennis: Brewster's Millions (1945), *245;* Broadway Bill, *470;* Dishonored Lady, *39;* Doll Face, *914;* Fighting Seabees, The, *48;* Great Dan Patch, The, *532;* Hangmen Also Die, *536;* I'm No Angel, *305;* Lady Scarface, *74;* Leopard Man, The, *991;* Sensations of 1945, *938;* T-Men, *676;* Topper Returns, *398;* You'll Find Out, *415*
O'Keefe, John E.: Out of the Rain, *1003*
O'Keefe, Michael: Bridge to Silence, *470;* Caddyshack, *249;* Dark Secret of Harvest Home, The, *829;* Fear (1990), *976;* Finders Keepers, *277;* Great Santini, The, *533;* Ironweed, *554;* Me & Veronica, *591;* Nate and Hayes, *89;* Out of the Rain, *1003;* Rumor of War, A, *109;* Slugger's Wife, The, *381;* Split Image, *664;* Whoopee Boys, The, *411*
O'Keefe, Paul: Daydreamer, The, *161*
O'Keeffe, Miles: Ator: The Fighting Eagle, *1037;* Blade Master, The, *15;* Campus Man, *249;* Cartel, *23;* Drifter, The, *837;* Iron Warrior, *1060;* Liberty and Bash, *77;* Lone Runner, *78;* Relentless II: Dead On, *879;* Shoot (1991), *378;* Sins of the Night, *1017;* Sword of the Valiant, *208;* Tarzan the Ape Man (1981), *125;* Waxwork, *902*
O'Kelly, Tim: Targets, *1022*
O'Leary, William: Flight of Black Angel, *518;* Hot Shots, *301;* In the Line of Duty: Ambush in Waco, *66;* Nice Girls Don't Explode, *344*
O'Loughlin, Gerald S.: Pleasure Palace, *623;* Riot, *106*
O'Malley, J. Pat: Hey There, It's Yogi Bear, *174*
O'Malley, Jason: Backstreet Dreams, *454*
O'Malley, Pat: Fighting Marines, The, *48;* Virginian, The (1923), *1161*
O'Mara, Kate: Horror of Frankenstein, *851;* Nativity, The, *604;* Vampire Lovers, The, *900;* Whose Child Am I?, *701*
O'Mara, Mollie: Girl School Screamers, *846*
O'Neal, Frederick: Free, White, and 21, *522;* Something of Value, *118*
O'Neal, Griffin: April Fool's Day, *810;* Escape Artist, The, *165;* Hadley's Rebellion, *173;* Wraith, The, *904*
O'Neal, Patrick: Alvarez Kelly, *1093;* Chamber of Horrors, *822;* El Condor, *1111;* For the Boys, *918;* From the Terrace, *523;* In Harm's Way, *66;* Like Father, Like Son, *318;* Make Me an Offer, *586;* New York Stories, *343;* Q & A, *1008;* Secret Life of an American Wife, The, *374;* Silent Night, Bloody Night, *886;* Stiletto, *120;* Under Siege, *134;* Way We Were, The, *697;* Where Were You When the Lights Went Out?, *409*
O'Neal, Ron: As Summers Die, *451;* Mercenary Fighters, *84;* Red Dawn, *104;* St. Helens, *646;* Sophisticated Gents, The, *663;* Superfly, *122;* Superfly T.N.T., *122;* Up Against the Wall, *692;* When a Stranger Calls, *1030*
O'Neal, Ryan: Barry Lyndon, *456;* Chances Are, *253;* Driver, The, *42;* Fever Pitch, *516;* Green Ice, *981;* Irreconcilable Differences, *554;* Love Story, *582;* Main Event, The, *326;* Man Upstairs, The, *327;* Oliver's Story, *612;* Paper Moon, *353;* Partners, *354;* Small Sacrifices, *660;* So Fine, *382;* Thief Who Came to Dinner, The, *393;* Tough Guys Don't Dance, *686;* What's Up, Doc?, *408;* Wild Rovers, The, *1164*
O'Neal, Shaquille: Blue Chips, *465*
O'Neal, Tatum: Bad News Bears, The, *231;* Certain Fury, *24;* Circle of Two, *482;* Goldilocks and the Three Bears, *171;* International Velvet, *177;* Little Darlings, *319;* Little Noises, *576;* Paper Moon, *353*
O'Neil, Barbara: All This and Heaven Too, *445;* I Am the Law, *547;* Tower of London (1939), *897*
O'Neil, Jennifer: Innocent, The, *748*
O'Neil, Sally: 16 Fathoms Deep, *116*
O'Neil, Tricia: Are You in the House Alone?, *953;* Piranha Part Two: The Spawning, *875*
O'Neill, Amy: White Wolves: A Cry in the Wild II, *139*
O'Neill, Angela: River of Diamonds, *107;* Sorority House Massacre, *889*
O'Neill, Chris: BackBeat, *907;* James Joyce's Women, *556*
O'Neill, Dick: Buddy Holly Story, The, *910;* Dark Justice, *32;* St. Ives, *110;* Wolfen, *904*
O'Neill, Ed: Adventures of Ford Fairlane, The, *2;* Disorganized Crime, *40;* Dutch, *269;* It's a Bundyful Life, *308;* Sibling Rivalry, *378;* Wayne's World, *406;* When Your Lover Leaves, *699*
O'Neill, Henry: Anthony Adverse, *450;* Case of the Lucky Legs, The, *960;* Girl Crazy, *919;* Honky Tonk, *1121;* It Happened in New Orleans, *925;* Lady Killer, *74;* Return of October, The, *366;* Whistling in Brooklyn, *410;* Whistling in the Dark, *410;* White Cargo, *699*
O'Neill, James: Count of Monte Cristo, The (1912), *489*
O'Neill, Jennifer: Caravans, *475;* Cloud Dancer, *27;* Committed, *824;* Cover Girl Murders, The, *964;* Force of One,

51; Full Exposure, *523;* I Love N. Y., *547;* Invasion of Privacy, *986;* Lady Ice, *989;* Love's Savage Fury, *582;* Perfect Family, *1005;* Reincarnation of Peter Proud, The, *879;* Rio Lobo, *1145;* Scanners, *883;* Steel, *120;* Summer of '42, *672;* Whiffs, *410*

O'Neill, Maggie: Under Suspicion, *1028*

O'Neill, Shannon: Creeping Terror, The, *1043*

O'Neill, Willa: One Crazy Night, *349*

O'Quinn, Terry: Amityville: A New Generation, *809;* Black Widow, *955;* Blind Fury, *15;* Company Business, *28;* Cutting Edge, The, *493;* Forgotten One, The, *978;* Good Fight, The, *530;* Lipstick Camera, *992;* My Samurai, *88;* Pin, *875;* Prisoners of the Sun, *628;* Rocketeer, The, *108;* Son of the Morning Star, *1151;* Stepfather, The, *1020;* Stepfather II, *890;* Tombstone, *1157;* When the Time Comes, *699;* Wild Card, *1032*

O'Reilly, Cyril: Cool Surface, The, *963*

O'Reilly, Harry: Hamburger Hill, *535*

O'Ross, Ed: Another 48 Hrs., *5;* Full Metal Jacket, *523;* Hidden, The, *1056;* Play Nice, *1006;* Red Heat (1988), *104;* Universal Soldier, *134*

O'Rourke, Heather: Poltergeist II: The Other Side, *875;* Poltergeist III, *876*

O'Shea, Daniel: Hamburger Hill, *535*

O'Shea, Michael: Big Wheel, The, *461;* It Should Happen to You, *308;* Jack London, *556;* Lady of Burlesque, *74;* Last of the Redmen, *1126;* Threat, The, *1024;* Underworld Story, *1029*

O'Shea, Milo: Barbarella, *1038;* Loot, *321;* Medicine Hat Stallion, The, *186;* Once a Hero, *94;* Only the Lonely, *350;* Opportunity Knocks, *351;* Paddy, *353;* Pilot, The, *622;* Playboys, The, *623;* Romeo and Juliet (1968), *643;* Sacco and Vanzetti, *782*

O'Shea, Paul: Among the Cinders, *446*

O'Sullivan, Maureen: Anna Karenina (1935), *449;* Barretts of Wimpole Street, The, *456;* Connecticut Yankee, A, *258;* Day at the Races, A, *262;* Devil Doll, The (1936), *833;* Hannah and Her Sisters, *293;* Peggy Sue Got Married, *355;* Pride and Prejudice (1940), *626;* Skyscraper Souls, *660;* Stranded, *1080;* Strange Interlude (1932), *669;* Tall T, The, *1154;* Tarzan and His Mate, *125;* Tarzan Escapes, *125;* Tarzan Finds a Son, *125;* Tarzan the Ape Man (1932), *125;* Tarzan's New York Adventure, *126;* Tarzan's Secret Treasure, *126;* Thin Man, The, *1024*

O'Toole, Annette: Best Legs in the 8th Grade, The, *235;* Cat People (1982), *822;* Cross My Heart (1987), *261;* Foolin' Around, *278;* 48 Hrs., *279;* It (1991), *857;* King of the Gypsies, *565;* Love at Large, *322;* Love Matters, *581;* One on One, *613;* Smile, *381;* Superman III, *1081;* White Lie, *700*

O'Toole, Peter: Becket, *457;* Caligula, *474;* Club Paradise, *256;* Creator, *490;* Dark Angel, The, *966;* Foxtrot, *521;* Goodbye, Mr. Chips (1969), *920;* High Spirits, *297;* King Ralph, *313;* Last Emperor, The, *569;* Lawrence of Arabia, *76;* Lion in Winter, The, *576;* Lord Jim, *79;* Man of La Mancha, *930;* Masada, *590;* Murphy's War, *87;* My Favorite Year, *340;* Night of the Generals, *90;* Ruling Class, The, *371;* Seventh Coin, The, *203;* Strange Tales: Ray Bradbury Theater, *1080;* Stunt Man, The, *671;* Supergirl, *1081;* Svengali (1983), *674;* Under Milk Wood, *691;* What's New, Pussycat?, *408;* Wings of Fame, *412;* Zulu Dawn, *142*

Oakie, Jack: Affairs of Annabel, The, *223;* Annabel Takes a Tour, *227;* Great Dictator, The, *289;* Iceland, *924;* If I Had a Million, *304;* Little Men (1940), *576;* Lover Come Back, *323;* Murder at the Vanities, *931;* Song of the Islands, *940;* Toast of New York, The, *685;* Uptown New York, *692;* Wild Party, The (1929), *702;* Wintertime, *947*

Oakland, Simon: Chato's Land, *1104;* I Want to Live!, *548;* Psycho, *877;* Sand Pebbles, The, *111;* Scandalous John, *202;* Tony Rome, *1025*

Oakman, Wheeler: Darkest Africa, *33;* End of the Trail, *1111;* Ghost Patrol, *55;* Lost Jungle, The, *79;* Man of Action, *1132;* Outside the Law, *616;* Peck's Bad Boy, *194;* Roaring Guns, *1145;* Sundown Rider, The, *1153;* Texas Cyclone, *1155;* Two-Fisted Law, *1159*

Oates, Simon: Terronauts, The, *1082*

Oates, Warren: And Baby Makes Six, *447;* Badlands, *454;* Blue and the Gray, The, *1099;* Blue Thunder, *16;* Border, The, *17;* Bring Me the Head of Alfredo Garcia, *20;* Brinks Job, The, *246;* Cockfighter, *27;* Crooks and Coronets (Sophie's Place), *261;* Dillinger (1973), *39;* Dixie Dynamite, *40;* Drum, *505;* East of Eden (1982), *506;* Gunfire, *1117;* Hired Hand, The, *1121;* In the Heat of the Night, *986;* Major Dundee, *1131;* My Old Man, *602;* 92 in the Shade, *345;* Race with the Devil, *878;* Return of the Seven, *1142;* Ride the High Country, *1143;* Rise and Fall of Legs Diamond, The, *107;* Shooting, The, *1149;* Sleeping Dogs, *117;* Smith!, *1150;* Stripes, *387;* There Was a Crooked Man, *1156;* Thief Who Came to Dinner, The, *393;* Tom Sawyer (1973), *946;* Tough Enough, *131;* White Dawn, The, *138;* Wild Bunch, The, *1164*

Ober, Philip: Magnificent Yankee, The, *585;* Mating Game, The, *330*

Oberon, Merle: Beloved Enemy, *458;* Berlin Express, *10;* Cowboy and the Lady, The, *260;* Dark Waters, *496;* Deep in My Heart, *913;* Desirée, *500;* Divorce of Lady X, The, *265;* Epic That Never Was, The, *423;* Forever and a Day, *520;* Hotel, *544;* Interval, *553;* Lydia, *583;* Private Life of Don Juan, The, *628;* Private Life of Henry the Eighth, The, *628;* Scarlet Pimpernel, The (1934), *112;* Song to Remember, A, *940;* That Uncertain Feeling, *393;* These Three, *680;* Wedding Rehearsal, *407;* Wuthering Heights (1939), *707*

Obregon, Ana: Bolero (1984), *466;* Treasure of the Four Crowns, *132*

Ocana, Susana: Skyline, *380*

Ocasek, Rick: Simply Mad About the Mouse, *204*

Occhipinti, Andrea: Bolero (1984), *466;* Running Away, *645*

Ochsenknecht, Uwe: Men..., *767*

Odetta: Autobiography of Miss Jane Pittman, The, *452*

Odette, Mary: She (1925), *1076*

Odom, George T.: Straight out of Brooklyn, *668*

Ogata, Ken: Ballad of Narayama, The, *715;* Eijanaika (Why Not?), *733;* Mishima: A Life in Four Chapters, *595;* Vengeance Is Mine (1979), *800*

Ogawa, Mayumi: Zatoichi: The Blind Swordsman's Vengeance, *806*

Ogier, Bulle: Candy Mountain, *474;* Discreet Charm of the Bourgeoisie, The, *730;* Les Tricheurs, *759;* Maitresse, *764;* Valley, The, *799*

Ogier, Pascale: Full Moon in Paris, *739*

Ogilvy, Ian: And Now the Screaming Starts, *809;* Anna Karenina (1985), *449;* Conqueror Worm, The, *825;* Death Becomes Her, *1045;* Invasion of Privacy, *986;* She Beast, The, *885;* Upstairs, Downstairs, *692*

Oh, Soon-Teck: Death Wish IV: The Crackdown, *36;* Home of our Own, A, *542;* Legend of the White Horse, *76;* Missing in Action 2: The Beginning, *85;* Steele Justice, *120*

Ohana, Claudia: Erendira, *734;* Luzia, *763;* Opera do Malandro, *774*

Ohashi, Minako: Living on Tokyo Time, *761*

Ohmart, Carol: House on Haunted Hill, *853;* Naked Youth, *89;* Spider Baby, *889*

Okada, Eiji: Hiroshima, Mon Amour, *744;* Ugly American, The, *690;* Woman in the Dunes, *804*

Okumoto, Yuji: Nemesis (1992), *1067;* Robot Wars, *1075*

Olaf, Pierre: Little Theatre of Jean Renoir, The, *760*

Oland, Warner: Charlie Chan at the Opera, *961;* Charlie Chan in Paris, *961;* Charlie Chan's Secret, *961;* Dishonored, *501;* Jazz Singer, The (1927), *925;* Painted Veil, The, *617;* Shanghai Express, *655;* Werewolf of London, *902*

Olandt, Ken: Leprechaun, *860;* Super Force, *1081;* Supercarrier, *122*

Olbrychski, Daniel: Birch Wood, *718;* Bolero (1982), *720;* Deluge, The (Potop), *729;* Tin Drum, The, *795;* Wedding, The, *802*

Oldfield, Eric: Island Trader, *67;* Stones of Death, *890*
Oldham, Will: Matewan, *590*
Oldman, Gary: Bram Stoker's Dracula, *819;* Chattahoochee, *480;* Criminal Law, *964;* Fallen Angels, *513;* JFK, *558;* Prick Up Your Ears, *626;* Romeo is Bleeding, *108;* Rosencrantz and Guildenstern Are Dead, *370;* Sid and Nancy, *657;* State of Grace, *666;* Track 29, *1026;* True Romance, *133;* We Think the World of You, *406*
Olds, Gabriel: Calendar Girl, *249*
Olen, Fred: Tomb, The, *896*
Olin, Ken: Game of Love, The, *524;* Queens Logic, *363*
Olin, Lena: Enemies—A Love Story, *510;* Havana, *537;* Mr. Jones, *597;* Romeo is Bleeding, *108;* Unbearable Lightness of Being, The, *691*
Olita, Joseph: Amin: The Rise and Fall, *446*
Oliver, Barret: Cocoon, *1042;* D.A.R.Y.L., *1044;* Frankenweenie, *280;* NeverEnding Story, The, *1068;* Secret Garden, The (1987), *202*
Oliver, David: Defense Play, *36*
Oliver, Edna May: Ann Vickers, *448;* David Copperfield, *496;* Drums Along the Mohawk, *42;* Half-Shot at Sunrise, *292;* Little Miss Broadway, *928;* Lydia, *583;* Nurse Edith Cavell, *610;* Romeo and Juliet (1936), *643;* Rosalie, *937;* Second Fiddle, *938;* Story of Vernon and Irene Castle, The, *942;* Tale of Two Cities, A (1935), *676*
Oliver, Gordon: Blondie, *241*
Oliver, Michael: Problem Child, *362;* Problem Child 2, *362*
Oliver, Robert Lee: Flesh Eating Mothers, *841*
Oliver, Rochelle: Courtship, *490;* 1918, *607;* On Valentine's Day, *612*
Oliver, Steven: Motor Psycho, *87;* Werewolves on Wheels, *902*
Oliver, Susan: Disorderly Orderly, The, *265;* Fugitive, The (TV Series), *523;* Gene Krupa Story, The, *525;* Ginger in the Morning, *527;* Guns of Diablo, *1118;* Hardly Working, *293;* Star Trek: The Cage, *1078;* Star Trek: The Menagerie, *1078;* Tomorrow's Child, *686*
Oliveri, Robert: Honey, I Blew Up the Kid, *175*
Olivery, Jody: Delivery Boys, *263*
Olivier, Laurence: As You Like It, *229;* Battle of Britain, *9;* Betsy, The, *459;* Bounty, The, *18;* Boys from Brazil, The, *958;* Brideshead Revisited, *469;* Bridge Too Far, A, *19;* Carrie (1952), *476;* Clash of the Titans, *1041;* Clouds Over Europe, *484;* Collection, The, *485;* Devil's Disciple, The, *264;* Divorce of Lady X, The, *265;* Dracula (1979), *837;* Ebony Tower, The, *507;* Entertainer, The, *510;* Fire over England, *49;* 49th Parallel, The, *520;* Hamlet (1948), *535;* Henry V (1944), *540;* I Stand Condemned, *548;* Jazz Singer, The (1980), *926;* Jigsaw Man, The, *987;* Khartoum, *70;* King Lear (1984), *564;* Lady Caroline Lamb, *567;* Little Romance, A, *319;* Love Among the Ruins, *322;* Marathon Man, *82;* Mr. Halpern and Mr. Johnson, *597;* Nicholas and Alexandra, *605;* Pride and Prejudice (1940), *626;* Prince and the Showgirl, The, *361;* Rebecca, *1009;* Richard III, *640;* Seven-Per-Cent Solution, The, *1013;* Shoes of the Fisherman, *656;* Sleuth, *1017;* Spartacus, *119;* That Hamilton Woman, *680;* Voyage 'Round My Father, A, *695;* Wagner, *947;* War Requiem, *696;* Wild Geese II, *139;* Wuthering Heights (1939), *707*
Oliviero, Silvio: Graveyard Shift (1987), *847;* Understudy, The: Graveyard Shift II, *899*
Olkewicz, Walter: Can I Do It 'Til I Need Glasses?, *249*
Olmos, Edward James: American Me, *446;* Ballad of Gregorio Cortez, The, *1096;* Blade Runner, *1039;* Miami Vice: "The Prodigal Son", *84;* Million to Juan, A, *332;* Nightingale, The, *191;* Saving Grace, *373;* Stand and Deliver, *665;* Talent for the Game, *677;* Triumph of the Spirit, *688;* Wolfen, *904;* Zoot Suit, *949*
Olmstead, Gertrude: Monster, The, *865*
Olsen, John: Visitors, The, *901*
Olsen, Morni: Three Musketeers, The (1935), *128*
Olsen, Ole: All Over Town, *224;* Country Gentlemen, *260*
Olson, James: Amityville II: The Possession, *809;* Andromeda Strain, The, *1036;* Commando, *28;* My Sister, My Love, *867;* Rachel, Rachel, *632;* Rachel River, *632;* Someone I Touched, *662;* Strange New World, *1080*
Olson, Nancy: Absent-Minded Professor, The, *143;* Big Jim McLain, *460;* Mr. Music, *931;* Pollyanna (1960), *196;* Smith!, *1150;* Snowball Express, *205;* Son of Flubber, *206;* Union Station, *1029*
Omaggio, Maria Rosaria: Cop in Blue Jeans, The, *29*
Omori, Yoshiyuki: MacArthur's Children, *763*
Ondra, Anny: Blackmail (1929), *956;* Manxman, The, *588*
Ono, Yoko: Imagine: John Lennon, *427*
Onoe, Kikunosuke: Kojiro, *752*
Onorati, Peter: Firehouse (1987), *277*
Ontkean, Michael: Blood of Others, The, *464;* Clara's Heart, *483;* Cold Front, *963;* Just the Way You Are, *561;* Legacy of Lies, *572;* Maid to Order, *326;* Making Love, *586;* Street Justice, *121;* Twin Peaks (Movie), *1027;* Twin Peaks (TV Series), *1027;* Voices, *694;* Willie and Phil, *412;* Witching, The (Necromancy), *904*
Opatoshu, David: Forced Vengeance, *51;* Torn Curtain, *1026;* Who'll Stop the Rain, *139*
Opiana, Marian: Man of Iron, *765*
Oppenheimer, Alan: Invisible: The Chronicles of Benjamin Knight, *1060;* Macbeth (1981), *584;* Riding with Death, *1074;* Trancers 4: Jack of Swords, *1085*
Opper, Don: Android, *1036;* Critters, *827;* Critters 2: The Main Course, *827;* Critters 3, *827;* Critters 4, *827;* Slam Dance, *1017*
Orbach, Jerry: Adventures of a Gnome Named Gnorm, The, *1034;* California Casanova, *249;* Crimes and Misdemeanors, *490;* Delirious, *263;* Delusion (1991), *499;* Dirty Dancing, *914;* F/X, *979;* Imagemaker, The, *549;* Last Exit to Brooklyn, *569;* Mr. Saturday Night, *334;* Out for Justice, *96;* Out on a Limb (1986), *616;* Prince of the City, *627;* Straight Talk, *387;* That's Singing: The Best of Broadway, *944;* Toy Soldiers (1991), *131;* Universal Soldier, *134*
Orbach, Ron: Love Crimes, *993*
Orbison, Roy: Fastest Guitar Alive, The, *1112;* Jerry Lee Lewis—I Am What I Am, *428*
Ordung, Wyott: Monster from the Ocean Floor, The, *866*
Oriel, Ray: Infested, *856*
Orla, Ressel: Spiders, The, *119*
Orlando, Tony: Rosie, *937*
Orlov, Dmitri: Alexander Nevsky, *711*
Ormeny, Tom: Agent on Ice, *3*
Ormond, Julia: Stalin, *665;* Young Catherine, *708*
Ormsby, Alan: Children Shouldn't Play with Dead Things, *823*
Ormsby, Anya: Children Shouldn't Play with Dead Things, *823;* Deathdream, *832*
Ornaghi, Luigi: Tree of the Wooden Clogs, The, *797*
Orsini, Marini: Eddie and the Cruisers II: Eddie Lives!, *915*
Orsini, Umberto: César and Rosalie, *723;* Goodbye Emmanuelle, *741;* Mademoiselle, *585*
Orth, Debra: Billy the Kid Meets the Vampires, *813*
Orwig, Bob: No Justice, *91*
Osborn, Lyn: Space Patrol (TV Series), *1077*
Osborne, Vivienne: Captain Caution, *23;* Tomorrow at Seven, *685*
Osbourne, Ozzy: Decline of Western Civilization, Part II—The Metal Years, *422;* Trick or Treat (1986), *897*
Oscarsson, Per: Doll, *731;* House of Angels, *745;* Hunger (1966), *746;* Night Visitor, The (1970), *607;* Secrets, *651*
Osmond, Cliff: Fortune Cookie, The, *279;* Invasion of the Bee Girls, *1059;* Kiss Me, Stupid, *314;* Shark's Treasure, *115*
Osmond, Donny: Garry Shandling Show, The, *283*
Osmond, Marie: Gift of Love, The, *527;* Side by Side: The True Story of the Osmond Family, *203*
Osterhage, Jeff: Big Bad John, *12;* Buckeye and Blue, *1102;* Masque of the Red Death (1989), *864;* Sex Crimes, *114;*

Shadow Riders, The, *1148;* Sky Bandits, *116;* South of Reno, *663*
Ostrander, William: Red Heat (1985), *1009*
Ostrum, Peter: Willy Wonka and the Chocolate Factory, *217*
Otis, Carré: Wild Orchid, *702*
Otowa, Nobuko: Onibaba, *773*
Ott, Angelica: Hell Hounds of Alaska, *1119*
Ottaviano, Fred: Shoot (1991), *378*
Otto, Barry: Bliss, *241;* Custodian, The, *31;* Howling III, *854;* Strictly Ballroom, *942*
Otto, Miranda: Last Days of Chez Nous, The, *569*
Ouimet, Daniele: Daughters of Darkness, *830*
Ouspenskaya, Maria: Beyond Tomorrow, *1039;* Dodsworth, *503;* Frankenstein Meets the Wolf Man, *843;* I've Always Loved You, *555;* Mortal Storm, The, *600;* Rains Came, The, *634;* Shanghai Gesture, The, *655;* Wolf Man, The, *904*
Outerbridge, Peter: Drop Dead Gorgeous, *972;* Victim of Beauty, *1030*
Outlaw, Geoff: Alice's Restaurant, *444*
Overall, Park: Gambler Returns, the: Luck of the Draw, *1115;* House of Cards, *545;* Vanishing, The (1993), *1029*
Overman, Lynne: Broadway Bill, *470;* Caught in the Draft, *252;* Edison, The Man, *507;* Little Miss Marker (1934), *182;* Midnight (1934), *598;* Silver Queen, *1150*
Overton, Frank: Desire under the Elms, *500;* Fail-Safe, *974;* Lonelyhearts, *578*
Overton, Rick: Sinful Life, A, *379*
Owen, Clive: Close My Eyes, *484;* Lorna Doone, *580;* Nobody's Children, *608*
Owen, Garry: Blondie in Society, *241*
Owen, Granville: Li'l Abner (1940), *318*
Owen, Michael: Dick Tracy vs. Crime Inc., *38*
Owen, Patty: Portfolio, *624*
Owen, Reginald: Above Suspicion, *1;* Anna Karenina (1935), *449;* Bride Wore Red, The, *469;* Cairo, *910;* Canterville Ghost, The (1944), *155;* Captain Kidd, *23;* Challenge to Lassie, *157;* Christmas Carol, A (1938), *158;* Conquest, *487;* Five Weeks in a Balloon, *50;* Great Ziegfeld, The, *921;* Hills of Home, *174;* I Married an Angel, *924;* Love on the Run (1936), *323;* Madame Curie, *584;* Madame X (1937), *584;* Miniver Story, The, *594;* Mrs. Miniver, *597;* Monsieur Beaucaire, *336;* National Velvet, *190;* Personal Property, *356;* Pirate, The, *935;* Queen Christina, *631;* Random Harvest, *635;* Real Glory, The, *103;* Red Garters, *936;* Reunion in France, *639;* Somewhere I'll Find You, *662;* Study in Scarlet, A, *1021;* Tammy and the Doctor, *677;* Tarzan's Secret Treasure, *126;* They Met in Bombay, *127;* Thrill of It All, The, *396;* White Cargo, *699;* Woman of the Year, *413;* Woman's Face, A, *705*
Owen, Timothy: Terminal Bliss, *679*
Owen, Tony: Norman Loves Rose, *346*
Owens, Gary: TV's Greatest Bits, *401*
Owens, Michelle: Midnight Kiss, *864*
Owens, Patricia: Fly, The (1958), *841;* Hell to Eternity, *540;* Law and Jake Wade, The, *1127*
Owensby, Earl: Dogs of Hell, *836;* Rutherford County Line, *110;* Wolfman, *904*
Owsley, Monroe: Goin' to Town, *287*
Oxenberg, Catherine: Lair of the White Worm, *859;* Overexposed, *873;* Ring of Scorpio, *640;* Rubdown, *1011;* Sexual Response, *1014;* Swimsuit, *390*
Oxenbould, Ben: Fatty Finn, *166*
Oxley, David: Ill Met by Moonlight, *548;* Night Ambush, *90*
Ozawa, Shoichi: Pornographers, The, *778*
Paar, Jack: Love Nest, *323;* Walk Softly, Stranger, *1030*
Pace, Judy: Brian's Song, *469;* Three in the Attic, *395;* Three in the Cellar, *395*
Pace, Roger: War of the Colossal Beast, *1088*
Pace, Tom: Blood Orgy of the She Devils, *815*
Pacific, Mark: Princess Warrior, *1071*
Pacifici, Federico: Flight of the Innocent, *737*
Pacino, Al: And Justice for All, *447;* Author! Author!, *230;* Bobby Deerfield, *465;* Carlito's Way, *23;* Cruising, *964;* Dick Tracy (1990), *38;* Dog Day Afternoon, *971;* Frankie and Johnny (1991), *522;* Glengarry Glen Ross, *528;* Godfather, The, *529;* Godfather, Part II, The, *529;* Godfather, Part III, The, *529;* Godfather Epic, The, *529;* Revolution, *639;* Scarecrow, *649;* Scarface (1983), *112;* Scent of a Woman, *649;* Sea of Love, *1013;* Serpico, *652*
Pack, Stephanie: Hours and Times, *544*
Packer, David: Running Kind, The, *371;* Silent Motive, *1016*
Pacome, Maria: Daydreamer, The (Le Distrait), *728*
Pacula, Joanna: Black Ice, *14;* Body Puzzle, *958;* Breaking Point, *469;* Death Before Dishonor, *35;* Deep Red (1994), *1046;* Escape from Sobibor, *45;* Every Breath, *973;* Eyes of the Beholder, *974;* Gorky Park, *980;* Husbands and Lovers, *546;* Kiss, The (1988), *859;* Marked for Death, *82;* Not Quite Paradise, *347;* Options, *351;* Sweet Lies, *389;* Tombstone, *1157;* Under Investigation, *1028;* Warlock: The Armageddon, *901*
Padden, Sarah: Lone Star Raiders, *1129*
Padilla, Robert: Great Gundown, *1116*
Padrao, Ana: My Daughter's Keeper, *999*
Pagano, Bartolomeo: Cabiria, *721*
Page, Amy: Buford's Beach Bunnies, *247*
Page, Anita: Broadway Melody, The, *910;* Free and Easy, *281;* Our Modern Maidens, *616;* Sidewalks of New York, *378;* Skyscraper Souls, *660*
Page, Anthony: Rebel (1973), *104*
Page, Dorothy: Ride 'em Cowgirl, *1143;* Water Rustlers, *1162*
Page, Gale: Four Daughters, *520;* Time of Your Life, The, *684*
Page, Genevieve: Day And The Hour, *728;* Private Life of Sherlock Holmes, The, *1008;* Song without End, *940*
Page, Geraldine: Beguiled, The, *954;* Blue and the Gray, The, *1099;* Bride, The, *819;* Dollmaker, The, *503;* Happiest Millionaire, The, *173;* Harry's War, *294;* Hitchhiker (Series), The, *850;* Hondo, *1121;* Honky Tonk Freeway, *300;* I'm Dancing As Fast As I Can, *549;* Interiors, *553;* My Little Girl, *602;* Native Son, *604;* Pete 'n' Tillie, *357;* Pope of Greenwich Village, The, *624;* Summer and Smoke, *672;* Sweet Bird of Youth (1962), *674;* Toys in the Attic, *687;* Trip to Bountiful, The, *688;* Walls of Glass, *695;* Whatever Happened to Aunt Alice?, *902;* White Nights (1985), *700;* You're a Big Boy Now, *416*
Page, Grant: Road Games, *1010*
Page, Harrison: Hammered: The Best of Sledge, *292;* Vixen, *405*
Page, Joy: Bullfighter and the Lady, The, *21;* Fighter Attack, *47;* Kismet (1944), *566*
Page, Patti: Boys' Night Out, *244*
Page, Rebecca: Danny, *161*
Pages, Jean-François: Deep Trouble, *969*
Paget, Debra: Broken Arrow, *1101;* Demetrius and the Gladiators, *499;* From the Earth to the Moon, *1053;* Haunted Palace, The, *849;* Last Hunt, The, *1126;* Love Me Tender, *1130;* Omar Khayyam, *93;* Prince Valiant, *100;* Stars and Stripes Forever, *941;* Tales of Terror, *892;* Ten Commandments, The (1956), *678*
Paget, Susan: Old Testament, The, *772*
Pagett, Nicola: Oliver's Story, *612;* Privates on Parade, *362*
Pagliero, Marcel: Dedee D'Anvers, *729*
Pagnol, Jacqueline: Nais, *770;* Topaze (1951), *796*
Paige, Janis: Angel on My Shoulder (1980), *448;* Bachelor in Paradise, *230;* Hollywood Canteen, *923;* Love at the Top, *581;* Please Don't Eat the Daisies, *358;* Romance on the High Seas, *937;* Silk Stockings, *939;* Winter Meeting, *704*
Paige, Robert: Blonde Ice, *464;* Can't Help Singing, *911;* Green Promise, The, *533;* Pardon My Sarong, *354;* Son of Dracula (1943), *888*
Pailhas, Geraldine: IP5: The Island of Pachyderms, *748*

Pain, Didier: My Father's Glory, *769;* My Mother's Castle, *770*

Paiva, Nestor: Ballad of a Gunfighter, *1096;* Creature from the Black Lagoon, *826;* Falcon in Mexico, The, *975;* Nine Lives of Elfego Baca, The, *1136;* Purple Heart, The, *630;* They Saved Hitler's Brain, *895*

Pajala, Turo: Ariel, *713*

Palance, Holly: Best of Times, The, *236;* Tuxedo Warrior, *133*

Palance, Jack: Alice Through the Looking Glass (1966), *906;* Alone in the Dark, *808;* Arrowhead, *1095;* Bagdad Café, *231;* Barabbas, *455;* Batman (1989), *9;* Battle of the Commandos, *10;* Bullet from God, A, *1102;* Chato's Land, *1104;* City Slickers, *255;* City Slickers II, *256;* Cocaine Cowboys, *27;* Contempt, *726;* Cop in Blue Jeans, The, *29;* Cops and Robbersons, *259;* Cyborg 2, *1043;* Deadly Sanctuary, *831;* Desperados, The, *1109;* Dracula (1973), *837;* Four Deuces, The, *52;* God's Gun, *1116;* Gor, *1054;* Great Adventure, The, *1116;* Halls of Montezuma, *59;* Hatfields and the McCoys, The, *1119;* Hawk the Slayer, *59;* Hell's Brigade, *61;* Horsemen, The, *64;* I Died a Thousand Times, *65;* Keep the Change, *1124;* Last Contract, The, *75;* Last Ride of the Dalton Gang, The, *1126;* Lonely Man, The, *1129;* Monte Walsh, *1134;* Outlaw of Gor, *1069;* Panic in the Streets, *1004;* Requiem for a Heavyweight (Television), *638;* Saddle Tramps, *1147;* Second Chance, *113;* Sensuous Nurse, The, *784;* Shane, *1148;* Silver Chalice, The, *658;* Solar Crisis, *1077;* Strange Case of Dr. Jekyll and Mr. Hyde, The (1968), *890;* Tango and Cash, *124;* Torture Garden, *896;* Without Warning, *1090;* Young Guns, *1165*

Paley, Phillip: Beachballs, *233*

Palfy, David: Storm, *1020*

Palillo, Ron: Committed, *824;* Hellgate, *849*

Palin, Michael: American Friends, *226;* And Now for Something Completely Different, *226;* Brazil, *245;* Fish Called Wanda, A, *277;* How to Irritate People, *302;* Jabberwocky, *309;* Life of Brian, *318;* Missionary, The, *333;* Monty Python and the Holy Grail, *336;* Monty Python Live at the Hollywood Bowl, *336;* Monty Python's Flying Circus (TV Series), *336;* Pole to Pole, *433;* Private Function, A, *361;* Ripping Yarns, *368;* Secret Policemen's Other Ball, The, *375;* Secret Policeman's Private Parts, The, *375;* Time Bandits, *1084*

Pallenberg, Anita: Barbarella, *1038;* Performance, *1005*

Pallette, Eugene: Adventures of Robin Hood, The, *2;* Bride Came C.O.D., The, *245;* Fighting Caravans, *1112;* Heaven Can Wait (1943), *295;* Intolerance, *553;* It's a Date, *925;* Kansan, The, *1124;* Kennel Murder Case, The, *988;* Mantrap, *995;* Mark of Zorro, The (1940), *82;* Mr. Skitch, *334;* My Man Godfrey (1936), *340;* One Hundred Men and a Girl, *934;* Pin-Up Girl, *935;* Sensations of 1945, *938;* Shanghai Express, *655;* Silver Queen, *1150;* Stowaway, *942;* Virginian, The (1929), *1161;* Young Tom Edison, *708*

Palme, Ulf: Dreams, *732;* Miss Julie, *767*

Palmer, Betsy: Friday the 13th, *843;* Friday the 13th, Part II, *843;* Last Angry Man, The, *568;* Long Grey Line, The, *578;* Marty (Television), *589;* Still Not Quite Human, *386;* Tin Star, The, *1157*

Palmer, Gregg: Scream, *883;* To Hell and Back, *130;* Zombies of Mora Tav, *905*

Palmer, Lilli: Adorable Julia, *710;* Body and Soul (1947), *466;* Boys from Brazil, The, *958;* But Not For Me, *472;* Cloak and Dagger (1946), *962;* Counterfeit Traitor, The, *30;* Holcroft Covenant, The, *982;* Miracle of the White Stallions, *187;* Murders in the Rue Morgue (1971), *867;* My Girl Tisa, *602;* Operation Crossbow, *95;* Secret Agent, The, *1013*

Palmer, Maria: Days of Glory, *33*

Palmer, Peter: Li'l Abner (1959), *928*

Palmer, Shirley: Somewhere in Sonora, *1151*

Palminteri, Chazz: Bronx Tale, A, *470;* Oscar (1991), *351*

Palomino, Carlos: Geronimo: An American Legend, *1115*

Paltrow, Gweneth: Flesh and Bone, *518*

Paluzzi, Luciana: Black Veil for Lisa, A, *14;* Carlton-Browne of the F.O., *251;* Chuka, *1105;* Green Slime, The, *1055;* Manhunt (1973), *81;* Muscle Beach Party, *338;* 99 Women, *91;* Powderkeg, *1139;* Return to Peyton Place, *639;* Sensuous Nurse, The, *784*

Pan Chacon, Thales: Luzia, *763*

Pan-Andreas, George: Crime Killer, The, *30*

Panaro, Alessandra: Son of Captain Blood, *118*

Panebianco, Richard: China Girl, *25;* Dogfight, *503*

Paneque, Miguel: Letters from the Park, *760*

Pangborn, Franklin: All Over Town, *224;* Call Out the Marines, *249;* Christmas in July, *255;* Great Moment, The, *290;* Hail the Conquering Hero, *292;* Horn Blows at Midnight, The, *301;* International House, *307;* My Dream Is Yours, *932;* Palm Beach Story, The, *353;* Romance on the High Seas, *937;* Sullivan's Travels, *388;* Swing High, Swing Low, *390;* Topper Takes a Trip, *398;* Two Weeks to Live, *402;* Vivacious Lady, *405*

Pankin, Stuart: Best of Not Necessarily the News, The, *236;* Betrayal of the Dove, *954;* Dirt Bike Kid, The, *162;* Life Stinks, *318;* Love at Stake, *322;* Mannequin Two: On the Move, *328;* Second Sight, *374*

Pankow, John: Monkey Shines: An Experiment in Fear, *865;* Mortal Thoughts, *997;* Secret of My Success, The, *375;* Stranger Among Us, A, *1020;* Talk Radio, *677;* To Live and Die in L.A., *130;* Year of the Gun, *1033*

Pankratov-Tchiorny, Alexandre: Jazzman, *749*

Pannach, Gerulf: Singing the Blues in Red, *786*

Pantoliano, Joe: Downtown, *41;* El Diablo, *1111;* Fugitive, The (1993), *53;* Last of the Finest, The, *75;* Me and the Kid, *83;* Risky Business, *368;* Robot in the Family, *200;* Running Scared (1986), *110;* Scenes from the Goldmine, *649;* Short Time, *378;* Tales from the Crypt (Series), *892;* Three of Hearts, *683;* Used People, *404;* Zandalee, *709*

Paoleilei, James: Sudden Thunder, *122*

Paoli, Cecile: Near Misses, *342*

Papas, Helen: Graveyard Shift (1987), *847*

Papas, Irene: Assisi Underground, The, *7;* Brotherhood, The, *471;* Christ Stopped at Eboli, *724;* Dream of Kings, A, *504;* Erendira, *734;* Guns of Navarone, The, *58;* High Season, *297;* Into the Night, *553;* Iphigenia, *749;* Message, The (Mohammad, Messenger of God), *593;* Moonspinners, The, *189;* Moses, *600;* Sweet Country, *674;* Tribute to a Bad Man, *1159;* Trojan Women, The, *688;* Z, *806;* Zorba the Greek, *709*

Papas, Laslo: Crazed, *825*

Paquin, Anna: Piano, The, *622*

Paragon, John: Echo Park, *507;* Get Out of My Room, *284*

Paramore, Kiri: Last Days of Chez Nous, The, *569*

Paré, Michael: Blink of an Eye, *15;* Closer, The, *484;* Dragon Fight, *42;* Eddie and the Cruisers, *915;* Eddie and the Cruisers II: Eddie Lives!, *915;* Instant Justice, *67;* Into the Sun, *67;* Killing Streets, *72;* Last Hour, The, *75;* Moon 44, *1067;* Philadelphia Experiment, The, *1070;* Point of Impact, *99;* Space Rage, *1078;* Streets of Fire, *121;* Sunset Heat, *122;* Women's Club, The, *413;* World Gone Wild, *1090*

Paredes, Marisa: High Heels (1992), *744*

Parely, Mila: Rules of the Game, The, *782*

Parent, Monique: Buford's Beach Bunnies, *247*

Parfitt, Judy: Hamlet (1969), *535;* Jewel in the Crown, The, *557;* Office Romances, *611*

Parillaud, Anne: Innocent Blood, *856;* La Femme Nikita, *753;* Map of the Human Heart, *588*

Paris, Cheryl: Sweet Bird of Youth (1989), *674*

Paris, Jerry: Wild One, The, *139*

Parish, Dick: Magic Christmas Tree, The, *184*

Park, Reg: Hercules and the Captive Women, *1056;* Hercules in the Haunted World, *61;* Hercules, Prisoner of Evil, *61*

Parker, Cecil: Citadel, The, *482;* Heavens Above, *296;* Indiscreet (1958), *306;* Ladykillers, The, *315;* Man in the White Suit, The, *327;* Quartet (1948), *631;* Saint's Vacation, The, *1012;* Ships with Wings, *115;* Sons of the Sea, *663;* Stars Look Down, The, *666;* Storm in a Teacup, *387;* Study in Terror, A, *1021;* Wreck of the Mary Deare, The, *141*

Parker, Cecilia: Ah, Wilderness, *223;* Andy Hardy Gets Spring Fever, *227;* Andy Hardy Meets a Debutante, *227;* Andy Hardy's Double Life, *227;* Lost Jungle, The, *79;* Love Finds Andy Hardy, *322;* Painted Veil, The, *617;* Riders of Destiny, *1144;* Trail Drive, *1158*
Parker, Charlie: Celebrating Bird: The Triumph of Charlie Parker, *420*
Parker, Christopher: Red Nights, *637*
Parker, Cindy: Lovers' Lovers, *582*
Parker, Corey: Big Man on Campus, *238;* How I Got into College, *302;* Lost Language of Cranes, The, *580*
Parker, Eddie: Tarantula, *892*
Parker, Eleanor: Above and Beyond, *1;* Chain Lightning, *478;* Dead on the Money, *967;* Escape from Fort Bravo, *1111;* Escape Me Never, *510;* Hans Brinker, *173;* Hole in the Head, A, *298;* Home for the Holidays, *983;* Home from the Hill, *542;* Interrupted Melody, *925;* King and Four Queens, The, *1125;* Man with the Golden Arm, The, *587;* Naked Jungle, The, *88;* Oscar, The (1966), *615;* Panic Button, *353;* Return to Peyton Place, *639;* Scaramouche, *111;* She's Dressed to Kill, *656;* Sound of Music, The, *940;* Three Secrets, *683;* Tiger and The Pussycat, The, *795*
Parker, Fess: Davy Crockett and the River Pirates, *161;* Davy Crockett, King of the Wild Frontier, *161;* Great Locomotive Chase, The, *171;* Hell Is for Heroes, *60;* Jayhawkers, The, *1123;* Light in the Forest, The, *181;* Old Yeller, *192;* Them!, *1083;* Westward Ho, the Wagons, *216*
Parker, Jameson: American Justice, *4;* Callie and Son, *474;* Curse of the Crystal Eye, *31;* Gathering, Part II, The, *525;* Prince of Darkness, *876;* Small Circle of Friends, A, *660;* Spy, *1019;* White Dog, *700*
Parker, Jean: Beyond Tomorrow, *1039;* Bluebeard (1944), *817;* Flying Blind, *51;* Flying Deuces, *278;* Gabriel over the White House, *524;* Ghost Goes West, The, *285;* Gunfighter, The, *1117;* Lawless Street, A, *1127;* Little Women (1933), *577;* One Body Too Many, *1003;* Operator 13, *614*
Parker, Kim: Fiend without a Face, *841*
Parker, Lara: Best of Dark Shadows, The, *813;* Foxfire Light, *521;* Night of Dark Shadows, *869;* Race with the Devil, *878*
Parker, Mary-Louise: Fried Green Tomatoes, *522;* Grand Canyon, *531;* Longtime Companion, *579;* Mr. Wonderful, *597*
Parker, Monica: Coming Out Alive, *963;* Improper Channels, *305*
Parker, Nathaniel: War Requiem, *696;* Wide Sargasso Sea, *701*
Parker, Noelle: Lethal Lolita—Amy Fisher: My Story, *573;* Twisted, *1028*
Parker, Norman: Killing Hour, The, *988*
Parker Jr., Ray: Enemy Territory, *44*
Parker, Sarah Jessica: Flight of the Navigator, *1052;* Girls Just Want to Have Fun, *287;* Hocus Pocus, *175;* Honeymoon in Vegas, *300;* L.A. Story, *314;* Somewhere, Tomorrow, *206;* Striking Distance, *121*
Parker, Suzy: Chamber of Horrors, *822;* Interns, The, *553*
Parker, Wes: Cry from the Mountain, *160*
Parker, Willard: Hunt the Man Down, *984*
Parkins, Barbara: Asylum, *810;* Christina, *25;* Puppet on a Chain, *101;* Shout at the Devil, *115;* Snatched, *117;* To Catch a King, *1025;* Valley of the Dolls, *693*
Parks, Larry: Jolson Sings Again, *926;* Jolson Story, The, *926;* Love is Better Than Ever, *929*
Parks, Michael: Arizona Heat, *6;* Bible, The, *460;* China Lake Murders, The, *961;* Club Life, *27;* Death Wish V: The Face of Death, *36;* Evictors, The, *839;* ffolkes, *47;* Hard Country, *293;* Hitman, The, *63;* Private Files of J. Edgar Hoover, The, *100;* Return of Josey Wales, *1142;* Savage Bees, The, *882;* Savannah Smiles, *201;* Sidewinder 1, *115;* Welcome to Spring Break, *902*
Parks, Tom: Ladybugs, *315*
Parks, Tricia: Fresh Kill, *53;* L.A. Crackdown, *73*
Parlavecchio, Steve: Amongst Friends, *447*
Parlo, Dita: L'Atalante, *753*
Parnell, Emory: Trail of Robin Hood, *1158*
Parrish, Helen: In Old California, *1122;* Little Tough Guys, *319;* Sunset Serenade, *1154;* Three Smart Girls Grow Up, *945;* You'll Find Out, *415*
Parrish, John: Dead Don't Dream, The, *1108*
Parrish, Julie: Doberman Gang, The, *40*
Parrish, Leslie: Candyman, The (1968), *474;* Li'l Abner (1959), *928;* Manchurian Candidate, The, *995*
Parrish, Max: Hold Me, Thrill Me, Kiss Me, *298*
Parrish, Steve: Scanners 3: The Takeover, *883*
Parry, David: Lost Platoon, *861*
Parry, Natasha: Windom's Way, *703*
Parseklan, Tom: Hot Resort, *301;* Shattered Vows, *655*
Parsons, Estelle: American Clock, The, *446;* Bonnie and Clyde, *17;* Come Along with Me, *257;* Don't Drink the Water, *267;* For Pete's Sake, *279;* Gentleman Bandit, The, *525;* I Never Sang for My Father, *547;* Private Matter, A, *629;* Rachel, Rachel, *632;* Watermelon Man, *406*
Parsons, Louella: Hollywood Hotel, *923;* Without Reservations, *413*
Parsons, Nancy: Motel Hell, *866;* Porky's II: The Next Day, *360*
Parsons, Ray: Holt of the Secret Service, *63*
Parton, Dolly: Best Little Whorehouse in Texas, The, *908;* Beverly Hillbillies, The, *237;* Nine to Five, *345;* Rhinestone, *367;* Smoky Mountain Christmas, *205;* Steel Magnolias, *667;* Straight Talk, *387*
Partridge, Ross: Amityville: A New Generation, *809*
Pascal, Christine: Clockmaker, The, *725;* Round Midnight, *937;* Sincerely Charlotte, *786*
Pascal, Olivia: Bloody Moon, *817*
Pascaud, Nathale: Mr. Hulot's Holiday, *768*
Pasco, Isabelle: Deep Trouble, *969;* Prospero's Books, *629*
Pasco, Richard: Gorgon, The, *847*
Pasdar, Adrian: Carlito's Way, *23;* Cookie, *259;* Lost Capone, The, *580;* Made in USA, *584;* Near Dark, *868;* Streets of Gold, *671;* Torn Apart, *686;* Vital Signs, *694*
Pasolini, Pier Paolo: Canterbury Tales, The, *722*
Pass, Cyndi: Bounty Tracker, *18*
Passalia, Antonio: Le Boucher (The Butcher), *756*
Passanante, Jean: Return of the Secaucus 7, *366*
Passi, Christopher: Marvelous Land of Oz, The, *185*
Pastko, Earl: Highway 61, *297*
Pastore, Louis: Agent on Ice, *3*
Pastorelli, Robert: Paint Job, The, *1004;* Sister Act 2: Back in the Habit, *380;* Striking Distance, *121*
Pataki, Michael: Amazing Spiderman, The, *4;* Bat People, *812;* Delinquent School Girls, *263;* Graduation Day, *847;* Grave of the Vampire, *847;* Last Word, The, *571;* Rocky IV, *642;* Zoltan—Hound of Dracula, *904*
Pate, Michael: Hondo, *1121;* Lawless Street, A, *1127;* Mad Dog Morgan, *80;* McLintock!, *1133;* Something of Value, *118;* Tower of London (1962), *897;* Wild Duck, The, *702*
Paterson, Bill: Comfort and Joy, *258;* Coming Up Roses, *725;* Defense of the Realm, *969;* Diamond's Edge, *162;* Dutch Girls, *506;* Odd Job, The, *348;* Return of the Musketeers, *106;* Truly, Madly, Deeply, *689*
Patey, Christian: L'Argent, *752*
Patil, Smita: Spices, *788*
Patinkin, Mandy: Alien Nation, *1035;* Daniel, *495;* Dick Tracy (1990), *38;* Doctor, The, *502;* House on Carroll Street, The, *984;* Impromptu, *549;* Maxie, *330;* Music of Chance, The, *601;* Night of the Juggler, *90;* Princess Bride, The, *1071;* Sunday in the Park with George, *943;* True Colors, *688;* Yentl, *948*
Paton, Charles: Blackmail (1929), *956*
Paton, Laurie: Norman's Awesome Experience, *346*
Patric, Jason: After Dark, My Sweet, *951;* Denial, *499;* Frankenstein Unbound, *843;* Geronimo: An American Legend, *1115;* Lost Boys, The, *861;* Rush, *645;* Solarbabies, *1077*

Patrick, Butch: Adventures of Milo in the Phantom Tollbooth, The, *144*
Patrick, Dennis: Dear Dead Delilah, *831;* Heated Vengeance, *60;* Joe, *558*
Patrick, Dorothy: Follow Me Quietly, *978;* Road Agent, *1145;* Thunder Pass, *1157;* Under Mexicali Stars, *1160*
Patrick, Gail: Brewster's Millions (1945), *245;* Doctor Takes a Wife, The, *266;* Love Crazy, *322;* Mississippi, *931;* Murder at the Vanities, *931;* Murders in the Zoo, *867;* My Man Godfrey (1936), *340;* Phantom Broadcast, The, *1005;* Wagon Wheels, *1162;* Wives Under Suspicion, *704*
Patrick, Gregory: Bad Blood, *811;* Woman Obsessed, A, *1032*
Patrick, Lee: Adventures of Topper, The, *223;* Black Bird, The, *240;* City for Conquest, *482;* Fuller Brush Girl, The, *282;* In This Our Life, *550;* Mildred Pierce, *594;* Mrs. Parkington, *598;* Somewhere I'll Find You, *662*
Patrick, Nigel: Battle of Britain, *9;* Browning Version, The, *471;* Encore, *509;* Executioner, The, *974;* League of Gentlemen, The, *317;* Mackintosh Man, The, *994;* Pickwick Papers, The, *357;* Raintree County, *634;* Sapphire, *1012;* Trio, *688;* Virgin Soldiers, The, *694*
Patrick, Robert: Body Shot, *958;* Cool Surface, The, *963;* Eye of the Eagle, *46;* Fire in the Sky, *1051;* Future Hunters, *845;* Terminator 2: Judgment Day, *1082*
Patte, Jean-Marie: Rise of Louis XIV, The, *781*
Patten, Dick Van: Jake Spanner Private Eye, *68*
Patten, Joyce Van: Breathing Lessons, *469;* Housewife, *545*
Patten, Luana: Fun and Fancy Free, *168;* Home from the Hill, *542;* Johnny Tremain, *179;* Rock, Pretty Baby, *936;* So Dear to My Heart, *205*
Patterson, David: Secret Garden, The (1984), *202*
Patterson, Elizabeth: Bill of Divorcement, A, *461;* Colonel Effingham's Raid, *257;* Hold Your Man, *542;* Intruder in the Dust, *553;* I've Always Loved You, *555;* Love Me Tonight, *929;* Sky's the Limit, The, *940;* Tall Story, *391*
Patterson, Hank: El Paso Kid, *1111*
Patterson, J. G. "Pat": Doctor Gore, *835*
Patterson, Jay: Double Exposure (1989), *504;* Double Jeopardy, *972*
Patterson, Lee: Jack the Ripper (1959), *858*
Patterson, Lorna: Imposter, The, *549*
Patterson, Neva: David and Lisa, *496;* Desk Set, *263*
Patterson, Sarah: Company of Wolves, The, *1042*
Pattnosh, Jeremy: Certain Sacrifice, A, *478*
Patton, Mark: Anna to the Infinite Power, *1036;* Nightmare on Elm Street 2, A: Freddy's Revenge, *871*
Patton, Will: Belizaire the Cajun, *458;* Chinese Boxes, *962;* Cold Heaven, *485;* Deadly Desire, *968;* Everybody Wins, *973;* In the Soup, *306;* Murder on the Bayou, *600;* No Way Out, *1002;* Paint Job, The, *1004;* Romeo is Bleeding, *108;* Shock to the System, A, *1015;* Stars and Bars, *385;* Taking the Heat, *676;* Wildfire (1988), *703*
Patton-Hall, Michael: Escapes, *1049*
Paul, Adrian: Cover Girl Murders, The, *964;* Highlander: The Gathering, *1056*
Paul, Alexandra: American Flyers, *446;* Christine, *824;* Death Train, *968;* Dragnet (1987), *268;* 8 Million Ways to Die, *973;* Getting Physical, *526;* Millions, *594;* Prey of the Chameleon, *1007;* Sunset Grill, *1021*
Paul, David: Barbarians, The, *1038;* Double Trouble (1991), *268;* Think Big, *394*
Paul, Don Michael: Aloha Summer, *445;* Heart of Dixie, The, *538;* Rich Girl, *640;* Robot Wars, *1075;* Rolling Vengeance, *108;* Winners Take All, *140*
Paul, Mark: White Wolves: A Cry in the Wild II, *139*
Paul, Peter: Barbarians, The, *1038;* Double Trouble (1991), *268;* Think Big, *394*
Paul, Richard: Bloodfist III: Forced to Fight, *16*
Paul, Richard J.: Under the Boardwalk, *691*
Paul, Rosemary: Dead Easy, *967*
Paul, Stuart: Emanon, *271;* Falling in Love Again, *273;* Fate, *274*
Pauley, Rebecca: Near Misses, *342*
Paulin, Scott: Captain America (1990), *22;* Cat People (1982), *822;* Deceit, *1046;* From Hollywood to Deadwood, *979;* Grim Prairie Tales, *847;* Last of Philip Banter, The, *991;* Pump Up the Volume, *630;* Teen Wolf, *892;* To Heal a Nation, *684;* Tricks of the Trade, *399;* White Hot: The Mysterious Murder of Thelma Todd, *1031*
Paull, Morgan: Fade to Black (1980), *840*
Paull, Nicki: Boulevard of Broken Dreams, *467*
Paulsen, Albert: Gypsy Warriors, The, *58;* Laughing Policeman, The, *991;* Search for the Gods, *1076*
Paulsen, Pat: Blood Suckers from Outer Space, *816;* Night Patrol, *344;* Where Were You When the Lights Went Out?, *409*
Paulsen, Rob: Perfect Match, The, *356*
Pavan, Marisa: Diane, *500;* Drum Beat, *1110;* Man in the Gray Flannel Suit, The, *587;* Rose Tattoo, The, *644;* What Price Glory, *408*
Pavarotti, Luciano: Yes, Giorgio, *948*
Pavlovsky, Tato: Miss Mary, *767*
Pavlow, Muriel: Doctor in the House, *266;* Malta Story, The, *586;* Murder She Said, *999*
Paxinou, Katina: Miracle, The (1959), *594*
Paxton, Bill: Back to Back, *8;* Boxing Helena, *818;* Brain Dead, *1040;* Dark Backward, The, *262;* Future Shock, *1053;* Indian Summer, *306;* Last of the Finest, The, *75;* Monolith, *1066;* Near Dark, *868;* Next of Kin (1989), *90;* One False Move, *94;* Pass the Ammo, *355;* Predator 2, *1071;* Slipstream, *1077;* Trespass, *132;* Vagrant, The, *404*
Payan, Ilka Tanya: Florida Straits, *51*
Payant, Gilles: Big Red, *150*
Paymer, David: Heart and Souls, *1056;* Mr. Saturday Night, *334;* Searching for Bobby Fischer, *202*
Payne, Allen: CB4, *252*
Payne, Bruce: Cisco Kid, The, *1105;* Full Eclipse, *844;* Nemesis (1986), *1000;* Passenger 57, *97;* Silence Like Glass, *657;* Switch, *390*
Payne, Heidi: Alien Seed, *1035*
Payne, John: College Swing, *912;* Dodsworth, *503;* Footlight Serenade, *917;* Iceland, *924;* Kansas City Confidential, *988;* Razor's Edge, The (1946), *635;* Slightly Scarlet, *660;* Springtime in the Rockies (1942), *941;* Sun Valley Serenade, *942;* Tennessee's Partner, *1155;* To the Shores of Tripoli, *130*
Payne, Julie: Private School, *362*
Payne, Laurence: Tell-Tale Heart, The, *893*
Payne, Sally: Bad Man of Deadwood, *1095;* Big Show, The, *1098;* Jesse James at Bay, *1123;* Man from Music Mountain, *1131;* Young Bill Hickok, *1165*
Payne, Sandra: Moving Finger, The, *998*
Pays, Amanda: Cold Room, The, *485;* Dead on the Money, *967;* Exposure, *45;* Flash, The, *1051;* Kindred, The, *859;* Leviathan, *860;* Max Headroom, *1065;* Off Limits (1988), *93;* Oxford Blues, *617;* 13 at Dinner, *1024*
Payton, Barbara: Bride of the Gorilla, *819;* Drums in the Deep South, *1110;* Kiss Tomorrow Goodbye, *73;* Only the Valiant, *1137*
Payton-Wright, Pamela: Going in Style, *288;* Resurrection, *638*
Pazzafini, Nello: Adios, Hombre, *1092*
Peach, Mary: No Love for Johnnie, *608*
Peaker, E. J.: Four Deuces, The, *52;* Graduation Day, *847;* Hello, Dolly!, *922*
Pearce, Adrian: Warriors From Hell, *137*
Pearce, Alice: Kiss Me, Stupid, *314;* Thrill of It All, The, *396*
Pearce, Craig: Vicious, *135*
Pearce, Guy: Heaven Tonight, *539;* Hunting, *546*
Pearce, Jack: Great Northfield Minnesota Raid, The, *1116*
Pearce, Jacqueline: Don't Raise the Bridge, Lower the River, *267*

Pearce, Mary Vivian: Mondo Trasho, *335;* Multiple Maniacs, *866;* Pink Flamingos, *357*
Pearcy, Patricia: Delusion (1980), *969;* Squirm, *889*
Pearson, Richard: Moving Finger, The, *998*
Pearson, Ted: Dick Tracy's G-Men, *38*
Peary, Harold: Look Who's Laughing, *320;* Seven Day's Leave, *376*
Peck, Bob: Edge of Darkness (1986), *973;* Jurassic Park, *1061;* Kitchen Toto, The, *566;* Slipstream, *1077*
Peck, Cecilia: Ambition, *952;* Portrait, The, *625;* Torn Apart, *686*
Peck, Craig: There's Nothing Out There, *894*
Peck, David: Gal Young 'Un, *524*
Peck, Gregory: Amazing Grace and Chuck, *445;* Arabesque, *6;* Behold a Pale Horse, *458;* Big Country, The, *1098;* Blue and the Gray, The, *1099;* Boys from Brazil, The, *958;* Bravados, The, *1101;* Cape Fear (1962), *959;* Cape Fear (1991), *959;* Captain Horatio Hornblower, *23;* Captain Newman, M.D., *474;* David and Bathsheba, *496;* Days of Glory, *33;* Designing Woman, *263;* Duel in the Sun, *1110;* Gentlemen's Agreement, *526;* Gunfighter, The, *1117;* Guns of Navarone, The, *58;* How the West Was Won, *1122;* Keys to the Kingdom, The, *563;* MacArthur, *583;* Mackenna's Gold, *1131;* Man in the Gray Flannel Suit, The, *587;* Marooned, *1065;* Mirage, *595;* Moby Dick, *86;* Old Gringo, The, *611;* Omen, The, *872;* On the Beach, *1069;* Only the Valiant, *1137;* Other People's Money, *351;* Paradine Case, The, *1004;* Pork Chop Hill, *624;* Portrait, The, *625;* Roman Holiday, *642;* Scarlet and the Black, The, *112;* Sea Wolves, The, *113;* Snows of Kilimanjaro, The, *118;* Spellbound, *1019;* Stalking Moon, The, *1152;* To Kill a Mockingbird, *684;* Twelve O'Clock High, *133;* Yearling, The, *219*
Peck, J. Eddie: Curse II—The Bite, *827;* Lambada, *927*
Peck, Tony: Brenda Starr, *19*
Peckinpah, Sam: Gunfire, *1117*
Pecoraro, Susu: Camila, *721*
Pedersen, Maren: Witchcraft Through the Ages (HAXAN), *804*
Pederson, Chris: Suburbia, *672*
Peebles, Mario Van: Full Eclipse, *844*
Peel, David: Brides of Dracula, *819*
Peeples, Nia: Deepstar Six, *832;* I Don't Buy Kisses Anymore, *303;* North Shore, *609;* Return to Lonesome Dove, *1143;* Swimsuit, *390*
Pears, Joan: Applause, *450;* Parlor, Bedroom and Bath, *354*
Pei-pei, Chang: Painted Faces, *774*
Peil, Ed: Blue Steel (1934), *1099*
Pelé: Hot Shot, *544;* Minor Miracle, A, *187;* Victory, *135*
Pelikan, Lisa: Ghoulies, *846;* Into the Badlands, *1123;* Jennifer, *858;* Return to the Blue Lagoon, *639*
Pellay, Lanah: Eat the Rich, *270*
Pellegrino, Mark: Midnight Witness, *996*
Pelletier, Andrée: Bach and Broccoli, *147*
Pellicer, Pina: Macario, *763*
Pelloupaa, Matti: Ariel, *713;* Leningrad Cowboys Go America, *758*
Pembroke, Percy: Adventures of Tarzan, The, *2*
Peña, Elizabeth: Batteries Not Included, *148;* Blue Steel (1990), *16;* Crossover Dreams, *912;* Down and Out in Beverly Hills, *268;* El Super, *734;* Jacob's Ladder, *1060;* La Bamba, *927;* Waterdance, The, *696*
Penalver, Diana: Dead Alive, *830*
Pendergrass, Teddy: Soup for One, *383*
Pendleton, Austin: Four Eyes and Six Guns, *1114;* Great Smokey Roadblock, The, *57;* Guarding Tess, *291;* Hello Again, *296;* Mr. and Mrs. Bridge, *596;* Mr. Nanny, *188;* My Cousin Vinny, *339;* Rain without Thunder, *634;* Short Circuit, *1076;* Simon, *379;* What's Up, Doc?, *408*
Pendleton, Nat: Another Thin Man, *952;* Buck Privates Come Home, *246;* Dr. Kildare's Strange Case, *40;* Girl from Missouri, The, *286;* Manhattan Melodrama, *81;* Northwest Passage, *92;* Scared to Death, *883;* Shopworn Angel, The, *656*
Penghlis, Thaao: Lookalike, The, *993*
Penhaligon, Susan: Land That Time Forgot, The, *1061;* Leopard in the Snow, *572;* Nasty Habits, *342;* Patrick, *873;* Uncanny, The, *899*
Penhall, Bruce: Savage Beach, *111*
Penn, Christopher: All the Right Moves, *444;* At Close Range, *953;* Beethoven's 2nd, *149;* Best of the Best, *11;* Best of the Best 2, *11;* Footloose, *917;* Futurekick, *1053;* Josh and S.A.M., *69;* Made in USA, *584;* Pale Rider, *1138;* Pickle, The, *357;* Reservoir Dogs, *105;* Rumble Fish, *645;* Short Cuts, *657;* True Romance, *133;* Wild Life, The, *411*
Penn, Matthew: Delta Force 3, *37;* Playing for Keeps, *358*
Penn, Sean: At Close Range, *953;* Bad Boys, *454;* Carlito's Way, *23;* Casualties of War, *477;* Colors, *485;* Crackers, *260;* Falcon and the Snowman, The, *513;* Fast Times at Ridgemont High, *274;* Judgment in Berlin, *560;* Killing of Randy Webster, The, *564;* Racing with the Moon, *633;* Shanghai Surprise, *377;* State of Grace, *666;* We're No Angels (1989), *408*
Pennebaker, Judy: Farmer's Other Daughter, The, *274*
Pennell, Larry: FBI Story, The, *515*
Pennick, Jack: Operation Pacific, *614*
Penning, Wesley: Circle of Fear, *26*
Pennock, Chris: Great Texas Dynamite Chase, The, *57*
Penny, Joe: Blood Vows: The Story of a Mafia Wife, *464;* Bloody Birthday, *817;* Bodily Harm, *957;* Gangster Wars, *54;* Whisper Kills, A, *902*
Penny, Sydney: Bernadette, *459;* Child of Darkness, Child of Light, *823;* Hyper Sapian: People from Another Star, *1057;* Running Away, *645*
Penta, Virginia: Stuck on You, *387*
Peppard, George: Battle Beyond the Stars, *1038;* Blue Max, The, *16;* Breakfast at Tiffany's, *468;* Carpetbaggers, The, *475;* Chinatown Murders, The: Man Against the Mob, *25;* Damnation Alley, *1044;* Executioner, The, *974;* From Hell to Victory, *53;* Groundstar Conspiracy, The, *1055;* Home from the Hill, *542;* How the West Was Won, *1122;* Newman's Law, *90;* Night of the Fox, *90;* Operation Crossbow, *95;* Pendulum, *1005;* Pork Chop Hill, *624;* Rough Night in Jericho, *1146;* Silence Like Glass, *657;* Target Eagle, *125;* Tigress, The, *130;* Tobruk, *130;* Torn Between Two Lovers, *686;* Treasure of the Yankee Zephyr, *132*
Pepper, John: Specters, *889*
Pera, Marilia: Mixed Blood, *86;* Pixote, *778*
Peralta, Christina: Cybernator, *1043*
Perce, Joe: Don't Mess with My Sister, *504*
Percival, Lance: Darling Lili, *913*
Percy, Eileen: Down to Earth, *268;* Man from Painted Post, The, *327;* Reaching for the Moon (1917), *365*
Perec, Georges: Games of Countess Dolingen of Gratz, The, *739*
Peredes, Marisa: Vengeance, *135*
Pereio, Paulo Cesar: I Love You (Eu Te Amo), *746*
Perez, George: Toy Soldiers (1991), *131*
Perez, Jose: One Shoe Makes it Murder, *1003;* Short Eyes, *657*
Perez, Rosie: Criminal Justice, *491;* Fearless (1993), *515;* Night on Earth, *606;* Untamed Heart, *692;* White Men Can't Jump, *410*
Perez, Vincent: Cyrano De Bergerac (1990), *727;* Indochine, *747*
Perier, François: Gervaise, *740;* Nights of Cabiria, *771;* Sylvia and the Phantom, *792*
Perkins, Anthony: Black Hole, The, *1039;* Catch-22, *252;* Crimes of Passion, *491;* Deadly Companion, *968;* Demon in My View, A, *832;* Desire under the Elms, *500;* Destroyer, *833;* Edge of Sanity, *838;* Fear Strikes Out, *515;* ffolkes, *47;* Fool Killer, The, *978;* Friendly Persuasion, *522;* Glory Boys, The, *56;* Goodbye Again, *530;* I'm Dangerous Tonight, *855;* Les Miserables (1978), *573;* Lonely Man, The, *1129;* Mahogany, *586;* Matchmaker, The, *329;* Napoleon and Josephine: A Love

Story, *603;* On the Beach, *1069;* Pretty Poison, *626;* Psycho, *877;* Psycho II, *877;* Psycho III, *877;* Psycho 4: The Beginning, *877;* Ravishing Idiot, The, *364;* Sins of Dorian Gray, The, *886;* Someone Behind the Door, *1018;* Tall Story, *391;* Ten Days Wonder, *1023;* Tin Star, The, *1157;* Trial, The, *687;* Winter Kills, *704*

Perkins, Elizabeth: About Last Night, *440;* Avalon, *452;* Big, *237;* Doctor, The, *502;* Flintstones, The, *167;* From the Hip, *281;* He Said, She Said, *294;* Indian Summer, *306;* Love at Large, *322;* Over Her Dead Body, *352;* Sweethearts' Dance, *675*

Perkins, Millie: Cockfighter, *27;* Diary of Anne Frank, The, *501;* Ensign Pulver, *271;* Gun in the House, A, *534;* Haunting Passion, The, *1055;* Love in the Present Tense, *581;* Macbeth (1981), *584;* Pistol, The: The Birth of a Legend, *195;* Ride in the Whirlwind, *1143;* Shooting, The, *1149;* Table for Five, *676;* Wild in the Country, *702;* Wild in the Streets, *1089*

Perkins, Osgood: Scarface (1932), *112*

Perlich, Max: Born Yesterday (1993), *244;* Maverick, *1133;* Rush, *645*

Perlman, Rhea: Amazing Stories (TV Series), *1036;* My Little Pony: The Movie, *190;* Over Her Dead Body, *352;* Ratings Game, The, *364;* Ted & Venus, *392;* There Goes the Neighborhood, *393*

Perlman, Ron: Adventures of Huck Finn, The (1993), *143;* Beauty and the Beast (TV Series), *1039;* Blindman's Bluff, *956;* Cisco Kid, The, *1105;* Cronos, *727;* Double Exposure (1993), *971;* Name of the Rose, The, *89;* Quest for Fire, *1073;* Romeo is Bleeding, *108;* Stephen King's Sleepwalkers, *890*

Pernel, Florence: Blue (1993), *719*

Perreau, Gigi: Girls Town, *55;* Journey to the Center of Time, *1060;* Mr. Skeffington, *597;* Yolanda and the Thief, *708*

Perri, Paul: Hit and Run, *63*

Perrier, Mireille: Love without Pity, *762;* Toto the Hero, *796*

Perrin, Francis: Billy Ze Kick, *718*

Perrin, Jack: I Shot Billy the Kid, *1122;* Painted Stallion, The, *1138*

Perrin, Jacques: Cinema Paradiso, *724;* Donkey Skin (Peau D'Âne), *731;* Flight of the Innocent, *737;* Le Crabe Tambour, *757;* Love Songs (Paroles et Musique), *762;* 317th Platoon, The, *794*

Perrine, Valerie: Agency, *443;* Boiling Point, *17;* Border, The, *17;* Bright Angel, *470;* Can't Stop the Music, *911;* Electric Horseman, The, *508;* Last American Hero, The, *75;* Lenny, *572;* Magician of Lublin, The, *585;* Maid to Order, *326;* Mr. Billion, *85;* Slaughterhouse Five, *1077;* Sweet Bird of Youth (1989), *674;* Three Little Pigs, The, *211;* Water, *406;* When Your Lover Leaves, *699*

Perrins, Leslie: Nine Days a Queen, *607;* Triumph of Sherlock Holmes, The, *1027*

Perry, Felton: RoboCop 2, *1075;* Talent for the Game, *677*

Perry, Jeff: Hard Promises, *536*

Perry, John Bennett: Last Ring, The, *315*

Perry, Lou: Fast Money, *46*

Perry, Luke: Buffy, The Vampire Slayer, *247;* 8 Seconds, *43;* Terminal Bliss, *679*

Perry, Margaret: Go West, Young Man, *287*

Perry, Natasha: Midnight Lace, *84*

Perry, Rod: Black Gestapo, The, *13;* Black Godfather, The, *13*

Perry, Roger: Cat, The, *157;* Count Yorga, Vampire, *825;* Revenge (1971), *1010*

Perry, Susan: Knock on Any Door, *566*

Perryman, Clara: Escape to Love, *511*

Perschy, Maria: Castle of Fu Manchu, *822;* Horror of the Zombies, *852;* Man's Favorite Sport?, *328;* Vultures, *901*

Persky, Lisa Jane: Big Easy, The, *12;* Coneheads, *258;* Peggy Sue Got Married, *355;* Sure Thing, The, *389*

Persoff, Nehemiah: Al Capone, *3;* American Tail, An, *146;* Badlanders, The, *1096;* Comancheros, The, *1105;* Deadly Harvest, *1045;* Eric, *510;* Francis Gary Powers: The True Story of the U-2 Spy Incident, *522;* In Search of Historic Jesus, *550;* Marty (Television), *589;* Never Steal Anything Small, *932;* Psychic Killer, *877;* Sadat, *646;* Some Like It Hot, *382;* Wrong Man, The (1956), *1033;* Yentl, *948*

Persson, Essy: Mission Stardust, *1066;* Therese and Isabelle, *794*

Pertwee, Jon: Adventures of a Private Eye, *222;* Carry on Cleo, *251;* House That Dripped Blood, The, *853;* Number One of the Secret Service, *347*

Peru, Dana: Gal Young 'Un, *524*

Pesce, Franco: Have a Nice Funeral, *1119*

Pesce, Frank: Pamela Principle, The, *1004*

Pesci, Joe: Betsy's Wedding, *236;* Bronx Tale, A, *470;* Easy Money, *269;* Eureka, *511;* Goodfellas, *531;* Home Alone, *299;* Home Alone 2: Lost in New York, *175;* JFK, *558;* Jimmy Hollywood, *310;* Lethal Weapon 2, *76;* Lethal Weapon 3, *77;* Man on Fire, *81;* My Cousin Vinny, *339;* Public Eye, The, *1008;* Raging Bull, *633;* Super, The, *388;* With Honors, *412*

Pescia, Lisa: Body Chemistry 2: Voice of a Stranger, *957*

Pescow, Donna: Glory Years, *287;* Jake Speed, *68;* Saturday Night Fever, *938*

Peter, Werner: Carpet of Horror, *960*

Peters, Bernadette: Alice (1990), *224;* Annie, *907;* Carol Burnett's My Personal Best, *251;* Heartbeeps, *173;* Impromptu, *549;* Jerk, The, *310;* Longest Yard, The, *78;* Martian Chronicles, Parts I-III, The, *1065;* Pennies from Heaven, *935;* Pink Cadillac, *99;* Silent Movie, *379;* Slaves of New York, *381;* Sleeping Beauty (1983), *205;* Sunday in the Park with George, *943;* Tulips, *400*

Peters, Brock: Ace High, *1092;* Adventures of Huckleberry Finn, The (1978), *144;* Broken Angel, *470;* Carmen Jones, *911;* Framed (1975), *52;* Incredible Journey of Dr. Meg Laurel, The, *551;* Pawnbroker, The, *620;* Puss in Boots, *198;* Secret, The, *650;* Slaughter's Big Rip-Off, *117;* Star Trek VI: The Undiscovered Country, *1079;* Two-Minute Warning, *1028*

Peters, Clark: Mona Lisa, *997;* Silver Dream Racer, *658*

Peters, Erika: Heroes Die Young, *61*

Peters, House: Human Hearts, *546*

Peters Jr., House: Twilight in the Sierras, *1159*

Peters, Jean: Apache, *1094;* As Young as You Feel, *229;* Broken Lance, *1101;* It Happens Every Spring, *307;* Man Called Peter, A, *586;* Niagara, *1000;* Pickup on South Street, *1006;* Viva Zapata!, *694*

Peters, Kelly Jean: Pocket Money, *359*

Peters, Lauri: For Love of Ivy, *279*

Peters, Noel: Invisible Maniac, *1060*

Peters, Scott: Girl Hunters, The, *979*

Peters, Werner: Corrupt Ones, The, *29;* 36 Hours, *681*

Petersen, William L.: Amazing Grace and Chuck, *445;* Cousins, *260;* Deadly Currents, *34;* Hard Promises, *536;* Keep the Change, *1124;* Long Gone, *578;* Manhunter, *995;* Passed Away, *355;* Return to Lonesome Dove, *1143;* To Live and Die in L.A., *130;* Young Guns II, *1166*

Peterson, Amanda: Can't Buy Me Love, *250;* Fatal Charm, *976;* I Posed for Playboy, *548;* Lawless Land, *1062*

Peterson, Cassandra: Allan Quartermain and the Lost City of Gold, *4;* Echo Park, *507*

Peterson, Sarah: Cannon Movie Tales: Snow White, *155*

Peterson, Stewart: Against a Crooked Sky, *1092;* Pony Express Rider, *1139;* Where the Red Fern Grows, *216*

Peterson, Vidal: Wizard of the Lost Kingdom, *1090*

Petherbridge, Edward: Lovers of Their Time, *582;* Strange Interlude (1988), *669*

Petit, Victor: Night of the Death Cult, *869;* Return of the Evil Dead, *880;* Street Warriors, *670*

Petrella, Ian: Christmas Story, A, *159*

Petrenko, Alexei: Rasputin, *780*

Petrie, Doris: Wedding in White, *697*

Petrillo, Sammy: Boys from Brooklyn, The, *818*

Petroff, Gloria: Two Lost Worlds, *133*

Pettersson, Birgitta: Virgin Spring, The, *801*

Pettet, Joanna: Blue (1968), *1099;* Casino Royale (1967), *252;* Cry of the Innocent, *964;* Double Exposure (1982), *971;*

Evil, The, *839;* Group, The, *534;* Night of the Generals, *90;* Pioneer Woman, *1138;* Robbery, *1011;* Sweet Country, *674;* Terror in Paradise, *126*

Pettifer, Brian: Gospel According to Vic, The, *289*

Petty, Lori: Free Willy, *168;* League of Their Own, A, *571;* Point Break, *99*

Petty, Rose: Housekeeper, The, *853*

Pevney, Joseph: Nocturne, *1002*

Peyser, Penny: Frisco Kid, The, *1114;* In-Laws, The, *305;* Indecent Behavior, *551;* Wild Times, *1164*

Pfeiffer, Dedee: Allnighter, The, *225;* Double Exposure (1993), *971;* Red Surf, *104;* Running Cool, *110;* Shoot (1991), *378;* Vamp, *899*

Pfeiffer, Michelle: Age of Innocence, The, *443;* Batman Returns, *9;* Callie and Son, *474;* Dangerous Liaisons, *494;* Fabulous Baker Boys, The, *512;* Falling in Love Again, *273;* Frankie and Johnny (1991), *522;* Grease 2, *920;* Into the Night, *553;* Ladyhawke, *74;* Love Field, *581;* Married to the Mob, *329;* Power, Passion, and Murder, *625;* Russia House, The, *646;* Sweet Liberty, *389;* Tequila Sunrise, *126;* Witches of Eastwick, The, *412*

Pflug, Jo Ann: Catlow, *1104;* M*A*S*H, *324*

Phelan, Joe: South of Reno, *663*

Phelps, Buster: Little Orphan Annie, *183*

Phelps, Peter: Lighthorsemen, The, *77;* Merlin, *1065;* Starlight Hotel, *666*

Phelps, Robert: Lights, Camera, Action, Love, *575*

Phenice, Michael: 9½ Ninjas, *345*

Philbin, John: Martians Go Home, *329;* North Shore, *609;* Shy People, *657*

Philbin, Mary: Human Hearts, *546;* Merry-Go-Round, The, *996;* Phantom of the Opera (1925), *874*

Philbrook, James: Finger on the Trigger, *1113*

Philipe, Gérard: Devil in the Flesh (1946), *730;* Les Liaisons Dangereuses, *759*

Philips, Emo: Emo Philips Live, *271;* Journey to the Center of the Earth (1987), *1060*

Philips, Lee: Peyton Place, *621*

Philips, Mary: Farewell to Arms, A, *514*

Phillip, Lawrence King: Abducted, *1*

Phillips, Bill: Flat Top, *50*

Phillips, Bobbie: Cover Girl Murders, The, *964;* TC 2000, *1082*

Phillips, Chynna: Goodbye, Miss 4th of July, *171;* Prize Pulitzer, The: The Roxanne Pulitzer Story, *629*

Phillips, Courtney: Return to the Blue Lagoon, *639*

Phillips, Gary: Whodunit?, *1031*

Phillips, Howard: Last Mile, The, *570*

Phillips, James: In Gold We Trust, *66;* Prison Planet, *1071*

Phillips, Joseph C.: Strictly Business, *387*

Phillips, Julianne: Fletch Lives, *978;* Seven Hours to Judgment, *113;* Skin Deep, *380;* Sweet Lies, *389*

Phillips, Leslie: Gamma People, The, *1054*

Phillips, Lou Diamond: Ambition, *952;* Dakota (1988), *493;* Dark Wind, *966;* Disorganized Crime, *40;* Extreme Justice, *512;* First Power, The, *841;* Harley, *536;* La Bamba, *927;* Renegades, *105;* Shadow of the Wolf, *114;* Show of Force, A, *1015;* Stand and Deliver, *665;* Young Guns, *1165;* Young Guns II, *1166*

Phillips, Mackenzie: American Graffiti, *226;* Love Child, *581;* More American Graffiti, *599;* Rafferty and the Gold Dust Twins, *364*

Phillips, Meredith: Sky Pirates, *117*

Phillips, Michelle: American Anthem, *446;* Assault & Matrimony, *229;* Death Squad, The, *35;* Dillinger (1973), *39;* Man with Bogart's Face, The, *995;* Rubdown, *1011;* Scissors, *1013;* Secrets of a Married Man, *651;* Valentino, *693*

Phillips, Patricia: Shades of Love: Sincerely, Violet, *654*

Phillips, Peg: Northern Exposure (TV Series), *609*

Phillips, Samantha: Deceit, *1046*

Phillips, Sian: Age of Innocence, The, *443;* Borrowers, The, *152;* Carpathian Eagle, *821;* Doctor and the Devils, The, *835;* Goodbye, Mr. Chips (1969), *920;* I, Claudius, *547;* Murphy's War, *87;* Under Milk Wood, *691;* Valmont, *693*

Phillips, Sydney Coale: Cause of Death, *24*

Phillips, Wendy: Bugsy, *471*

Phipps, Bill: Red River Shore, *1142*

Phipps, Max: Dark Age, *32;* Nate and Hayes, *89;* Sky Pirates, *117*

Phoenix, Leaf: Russkies, *371;* SpaceCamp, *1078*

Phoenix, Rain: Even Cowgirls Get the Blues, *272*

Phoenix, River: Dogfight, *503;* Explorers, *1050;* I Love You to Death, *304;* Indiana Jones and the Last Crusade, *1058;* Little Nikita, *992;* Mosquito Coast, The, *600;* My Own Private Idaho, *602;* Night in the Life of Jimmy Reardon, A, *344;* Running on Empty, *645;* Sneakers, *1018;* Stand by Me (1986), *665;* Thing Called Love, The, *681*

Phoenix, Summer: Runaway Ralph, *201*

Pialat, Maurice: A Nos Amours, *710;* Under the Sun of Satan, *798*

Piantadosi, Joseph: Schlock, *373*

Piat, Jean: Tower of Screaming Virgins, The, *897*

Piazza, Ben: Children of An Lac, The, *480;* Consenting Adults (1985), *488;* Guilty by Suspicion, *534;* Hanging Tree, The, *1118;* Scene of the Crime (1985), *1013*

Pica, Tina: Yesterday, Today and Tomorrow, *806*

Picardo, Robert: Explorers, *1050;* Gremlins 2: The New Batch, *1055;* Jack's Back, *987;* 976-EVIL, *871*

Piccoli, Michel: Beyond Obsession, *717;* Contempt, *726;* Danger: Diabolik, *1044;* Dangerous Moves, *728;* Day And The Hour, *728;* Diary of a Chambermaid (1964), *730;* Discreet Charm of the Bourgeoisie, The, *730;* Game Is Over, The, *739;* Infernal Trio, The, *748;* La Belle Noiseuse, *753;* La Passante, *754;* La Puritaine, *754;* Lady L, *568;* L'Etat Sauvage (The Savage State), *756;* Le Doulos, *757;* Les Choses De La Vie, *759;* Mado, *763;* May Fools, *766;* Milky Way, The (1970), *767;* Peril, *777;* Phantom of Liberty, The, *777;* Sleeping Car Murders, The, *786;* Success Is the Best Revenge, *672;* Ten Days Wonder, *1023;* Vincent, François, Paul and the Others, *801;* Wedding in Blood, *802*

Piccolo, Ottavia: Mado, *763;* Zorro, *142*

Picerni, Paul: Operation Pacific, *614;* To Hell and Back, *130*

Pichel, Irving: Dick Tracy's G-Men, *38;* Dracula's Daughter, *837;* General Spanky, *169;* Oliver Twist (1933), *612;* Silver Streak (1934), *658*

Pickens, Slim: Apple Dumpling Gang, The, *147;* Blazing Saddles, *241;* Cowboys, The, *1106;* Deserter, The, *1109;* Dr. Strangelove or How I Learned to Stop Worrying and Love the Bomb, *266;* Ginger in the Morning, *527;* Hawmps!, *294;* Honeysuckle Rose, *923;* Howling, The, *853;* Mr. Billion, *85;* 1941, *345;* One-Eyed Jacks, *1137;* Pat Garrett and Billy the Kid, *1138;* Pink Motel, *357;* Pony Express Rider, *1139;* Rancho Deluxe, *1140;* Red River Shore, *1142;* Rough Night in Jericho, *1146;* Sacketts, The, *1146;* Talion, *1154;* Tom Horn, *1157;* White Buffalo, *1164;* White Line Fever, *139;* Will Penny, *1164*

Pickering, Sarah: Little Dorrit, *576*

Pickett, Cindy: Call to Glory, *474;* Crooked Hearts, *491;* Deepstar Six, *832;* Echoes in the Darkness, *507;* Ferris Bueller's Day Off, *276;* Goodbye Bird, The, *171;* Hot to Trot, *302;* Hysterical, *303;* Into the Homeland, *67;* Men's Club, The, *593;* Stephen King's Sleepwalkers, *890;* Wild Card, *1032*

Pickford, Jack: Goose Woman, The, *980*

Pickford, Mary: Coquette, *488;* D. W. Griffith Triple Feature, *493;* Hollywood on Parade, *299;* Little Annie Rooney, *576;* My Best Girl, *339;* Pollyanna (1920), *196;* Poor Little Rich Girl, The (1917), *359;* Pride of the Clan, The, *1007;* Rebecca of Sunnybrook Farm (1917), *635;* Sparrows, *664;* Stella Maris, *1020;* Taming of the Shrew, The (1929), *391*

Pickles, Vivian: Candleshoe, *155;* Harold and Maude, *294;* Isadora (1966), *554;* Suspicion (1987), *1022*

Pickup, Ronald: Fortunes of War, *520;* Pope John Paul II, *624;* Wagner, *947*

Picon, Molly: Come Blow Your Horn, *257;* Fiddler on the Roof, *916;* For Pete's Sake, *279;* Murder on Flight 502, *87*
Picot, Genevieve: Proof, *629*
Pidgeon, Rebecca: Dawning, The, *496*
Pidgeon, Walter: Advise and Consent, *442;* Bad and the Beautiful, The, *454;* Big Red, *150;* Cinderella (1964), *911;* Command Decision, *487;* Dark Command, *1107;* Deep in My Heart, *913;* Executive Suite, *512;* Forbidden Planet, *1052;* Funny Girl, *918;* Girl of the Golden West, The, *919;* Hit the Deck, *923;* Holiday in Mexico, *923;* House Across the Bay, The, *545;* How Green Was My Valley, *545;* It's a Date, *925;* Julia Misbehaves, *311;* Last Time I Saw Paris, The, *570;* Lindbergh Kidnapping Case, The, *575;* Listen, Darling, *928;* Madame Curie, *584;* Man Hunt (1941), *994;* Men of the Fighting Lady, *84;* Million Dollar Mermaid, *931;* Miniver Story, The, *594;* Mrs. Miniver, *597;* Mrs. Parkington, *596;* Murder on Flight 502, *87;* Neptune Factor, The, *1068;* Saratoga, *372;* Shopworn Angel, The, *656;* That Forsyte Woman, *680;* Too Hot to Handle, *130;* Two-Minute Warning, *1028;* Voyage to the Bottom of the Sea, *1087;* Weekend at the Waldorf, *697;* White Cargo, *699*
Pieplu, Claude: Wedding in Blood, *802*
Pierce Jr., Charles B.: Norseman, The, *92*
Pierce, Chuck: Boggy Creek II, *818*
Pierce, David: Little Man Tate, *182*
Pierce, Maggie: Fastest Guitar Alive, The, *1112*
Pierce, Stack: Enemy Unseen, *44;* Kill Point, *71;* Low Blow, *79;* Patriot, *97*
Pierce, Ted: Hoppity Goes to Town, *175*
Pierpont, Eric: Sex, Love, and Cold Hard Cash, *1014*
Pierre, Roger: Mon Oncle d'Amerique, *768*
Pigaut, Roger: Simple Story, A, *786*
Pigg, Alexandra: Chicago Joe and the Showgirl, *480;* Letter to Brezhnev, *318*
Pigott-Smith, Tim: Hunchback, *854;* Jewel in the Crown, The, *557;* Remains of the Day, *637;* Sweet William, *389*
Pilato, Joe: Day of the Dead, *830*
Pilato, Josef: Married People, Single Sex, *589*
Pilbeam, Nova: Man Who Knew Too Much, The (1934), *995;* Nine Days a Queen, *607;* Young and Innocent, *1033*
Pileggi, Mitch: Shocker, *886*
Pillsi, Mark: Tearaway, *678*
Pilkington, Lorraine: Miracle, The (1990), *595*
Pillars, Jeffrey: Ernest Rides Again, *272*
Pillot, Mary: Trespasses, *687*
Pillsbury, Garth: Vixen, *405*
Pilon, Daniel: In Trouble, *550;* Obsessed, *610*
Pilon, Donald: Left for Dead, *572;* Pyx, The, *1008*
Pinal, Silvia: Exterminating Angel, The, *735;* Shark! (a.k.a. Maneaters!), *114;* Simon of the Desert, *786;* Viridiana, *801*
Pinchette, Jean-François: Being at Home with Claude, *716*
Pinchot, Bronson: Beverly Hills Cop 3, *11;* Blame It on the Bellboy, *240;* Hot Resort, *301;* Risky Business, *368;* Second Sight, *374;* True Romance, *133*
Pinchot, Rosamond: Three Musketeers, The (1935), *128*
Pine, Robert: Apple Dumpling Gang Rides Again, The, *147;* Are You Lonesome Tonight, *953;* Empire of the Ants, *1049*
Pinero, Fred: Death Curse of Tartu, *831*
Pinero, Miguel: Miami Vice, *84;* Streets of L.A., The, *671*
Pinkett, Jada: Inkwell, The, *552;* Menace II Society, *593*
Pinon, Dominique: Delicatessen, *729*
Pinsent, Gordon: Case of Libel, A, *476;* John and the Missus, *558;* Silence of the North, *657*
Pintauro, Danny: Beniker Gang, The, *149;* Cujo, *827*
Pinza, Ezio: Mr. Imperium, *931*
Pioneers, Bob Nolan and the Sons of the: San Fernando Valley, *1147*
Piper, Kelly: Maniac (1980), *862;* Rawhead Rex, *879*
Piper, Roddy: Body Slam, *17;* Hell Comes to Frogtown, *1056;* They Live, *895*
Pires, David: Zoo Radio, *416*
Pirrie, Bruce: Pink Chiquitas, The, *357*
Pirro, Mark: Polish Vampire in Burbank, A, *359*
Piscopo, Joe: Dead Heat, *830;* Joe Piscopo Live!, *310;* Joe Piscopo Video, The, *310;* Johnny Dangerously, *311;* Sidekicks, *203;* Wise Guys, *412*
Pisier, Marie-France: Chanel Solitaire, *479;* Cousin, Cousine, *726;* French Postcards, *281;* Love on the Run (1979), *762;* Miss Right, *333;* Nous N'Irons Plus Au Bois, *772;* Other Side of Midnight, The, *615*
Pistone, Kimberly: Blue De Ville, *242*
Pithey, Winsley: Saint, The (TV Series), *1012*
Pitoeff, Sacha: Last Year at Marienbad, *756*
Pitoniak, Anne: Agnes of God, *443;* Sister, Sister, *886;* Wizard of Loneliness, The, *704*
Pitt, Brad: Across the Tracks, *441;* Cool World, *1043;* Cutting Class, *828;* Favor, The, *275;* Johnny Suede, *311;* Kalifornia, *561;* River Runs Through It, A, *641;* True Romance, *133*
Pitt, Christopher: Goodbye Bird, The, *171*
Pitt, Ingrid: House That Dripped Blood, The, *853;* Transmutations, *897;* Vampire Lovers, The, *900;* Where Eagles Dare, *138;* Wicker Man, The, *903*
Pitt, Norman: Saint, The (TV Series), *1012*
Pitts, ZaSu: Aggie Appleby, Maker of Men, *223;* Dames, *913;* Denver and Rio Grande, The, *1108;* Eternally Yours, *511;* Francis Joins the Wacs, *280;* Francis, the Talking Mule, *280;* Greed, *533;* Guardsman, The, *291;* Life with Father, *318;* Mr. Skitch, *334;* Mrs. Wiggs of the Cabbage Patch, *598;* Nurse Edith Cavell, *610;* Perfect Marriage, *356;* Ruggles of Red Gap, *371;* This Could Be the Night, *394;* Thrill of It All, The, *396;* Wedding March, The, *697*
Pitzalis, Federico: Devil in the Flesh (1987), *730*
Piven, Jeremy: Judgment Night, *69;* PCU, *355;* 12:01, *1086*
Place, Mary Kay: Big Chill, The, *460;* Bright Angel, *470;* Captain Ron, *250;* Crazy from the Heart, *490;* Girl Who Spelled Freedom, The, *169;* History of White People in America, The, *298;* History of White People in America, The (Volume II), *298;* Mary Hartman, Mary Hartman (TV Series), *329;* Modern Problems, *335;* More American Graffiti, *599;* New Life, A, *343;* New York, New York, *933;* Samantha, *372;* Smooth Talk, *661*
Placido, Michele: Big Business, *238;* Forever Mary, *737;* Private Affairs, *361;* Summer Night, *791;* Three Brothers, *794*
Plana, Tony: Break of Dawn, *468;* Disorderlies, *914;* Havana, *537;* Hillside Stranglers, The, *982;* Latino, *571;* Listen to Your Heart, *319;* Live Wire, *78;* One Good Cop, *613;* Romero, *643;* Rookie, The, *109;* Salvador, *647;* Streets of L.A., The, *671;* Sweet 15, *674*
Planchon, Roger: Return of Martin Guerre, The, *781*
Planer, Nigel: Young Ones, The, *416*
Plank, Scott: Dying to Remember, *973;* Pastime, *619*
Platt, Edward: Rebel without a Cause, *636;* Rock, Pretty Baby, *936*
Platt, Louise: Captain Caution, *23*
Platt, Marc: Seven Brides for Seven Brothers, *939;* Tonight and Every Night, *946*
Platt, Oliver: Benny & Joon, *234;* Diggstown, *264;* Flatliners, *977;* Indecent Proposal, *551;* Temp, The, *893;* Three Musketeers, The (1993), *129*
Platters, The: Girl Can't Help It, The, *286*
Playten, Alice: Who Killed Mary What's 'Er Name?, *1031*
Plaza, Begona: Dark Justice, *32*
Pleasence, Angela: Favor, the Watch and the Very Big Fish, The, *275;* Godsend, The, *846*
Pleasence, Donald: All Quiet on the Western Front (1979), *444;* Alone in the Dark, *808;* Ambassador, The, *445;* American Tiger, *1036;* Barry McKenzie Holds His Own, *232;* Better Late than Never, *237;* Black Arrow (1984), *150;* Black Windmill, The, *956;* Blood Relatives, *957;* Breed Apart, A, *19;* Circus of Horrors, *824;* Count of Monte Cristo, The (1975), *30;* Creepers, *826;* Cul-de-Sac, *492;* Deep Cover (1980), *969;* Devil within Her, The, *833;* Devonsville Terror, The, *834;* Dr.

Jekyll and Mr. Hyde (1973), *914;* Dracula (1979), *837;* Escape from New York, *45;* Fantastic Voyage, *1050;* Freakmaker, *843;* From Beyond the Grave, *844;* Great Escape II, The, *57;* Ground Zero, *981;* Hallelujah Trail, The, *1118;* Halloween, *848;* Halloween II, *848;* Halloween IV: The Return of Michael Myers, *848;* Halloween V: The Revenge of Michael Myers, *848;* Hanna's War, *536;* Horsemasters, *176;* House of Usher, The, *853;* Journey into Fear (1975), *987;* Land of the Minotaur, *859;* Last Tycoon, The, *571;* Madwoman of Chaillot, The, *585;* Mania, *862;* Millions, *594;* Monster Club, The, *865;* Night Creature, *869;* Night of the Generals, *90;* 1984 (1955), *1068;* No Love for Johnnie, *608;* Nothing Underneath, *1002;* Operation 'Nam, *95;* Outer Limits, The (TV Series), *1069;* Phantom of Death, *874;* Prince of Darkness, *876;* Puma Man, The, *878;* River of Death, *107;* Sgt. Pepper's Lonely Hearts Club Band, *939;* Shadows and Fog, *654;* Shaming, The, *655;* Soldier Blue, *1151;* Specters, *889;* Tale of Two Cities (1967), *676;* Tales that Witness Madness, *892;* Telefon, *1023;* Ten Little Indians (1989), *1023;* Terror in the Aisles, *893;* THX 1138, *1084;* Tomorrow Never Comes, *686;* Treasure of the Amazon, *132;* Treasure of the Yankee Zephyr, *132;* Uncanny, The, *899;* Warrior of the Lost World, *1088;* Warrior Queen, *137;* Wedding in White, *697;* Will Penny, *1164;* You Only Live Twice, *141*

Pleshette, John: Kid with the Broken Halo, The, *313;* Paramedics, *353*

Pleshette, Suzanne: Adventures of Bullwhip Griffin, The, *143;* Alone in the Neon Jungle, *445;* Belarus File, The, *954;* Birds, The, *813;* Blackbeard's Ghost, *151;* Dixie Changing Habits, *265;* Fugitive, The (TV Series), *523;* Hot Stuff, *301;* If It's Tuesday, This Must Be Belgium, *305;* Legend of Valentino, *572;* Nevada Smith, *1135;* Oh, God! Book II, *349;* One Cooks, the Other Doesn't, *349;* Rome Adventure, *643;* Shaggy D.A., The, *203;* Support Your Local Gunfighter, *1154;* Suppose They Gave a War and Nobody Came?, *388;* Ugly Dachshund, The, *214*

Plimpton, George: Easy Wheels, *270;* If Ever I See You Again, *548*

Plimpton, Martha: Chantilly Lace, *479;* Daybreak (1993), *1045;* Goonies, The, *56;* Inside Monkey Zetterland, *306;* Josh and S.A.M., *69;* Mosquito Coast, The, *600;* Parenthood, *354;* River Rat, The, *641;* Running on Empty, *645;* Samantha, *372;* Shy People, *657;* Silence Like Glass, *657;* Stanley and Iris, *665;* Stars and Bars, *385*

Plimpton, Shelley: Glen and Randa, *1054*

Plowman, Melinda: Billy the Kid vs. Dracula, *813*

Plowright, Joan: Avalon, *452;* Brimstone and Treacle, *819;* Britannia Hospital, *246;* Dedicated Man, A, *499;* Dennis the Menace, *161;* Dressmaker, The, *505;* Drowning by Numbers, *505;* Enchanted April, *271;* Entertainer, The, *510;* Equus, *973;* I Love You to Death, *304;* Last Action Hero, The, *1062;* Stalin, *665;* Summer House, The, *388*

Pluhar, Erika: Goalie's Anxiety at the Penalty Kick, *741*

Plummer, Amanda: Courtship, *490;* Daniel, *495;* Dollmaker, The, *503;* Fisher King, The, *1051;* Hotel New Hampshire, The, *544;* Last Light, *569;* Miss Rose White, *596;* Needful Things, *868;* Prisoners of Inertia, *361;* So I Married an Axe Murderer, *382;* Static, *666;* World According to Garp, The, *706*

Plummer, Christopher: Amateur, The, *952;* American Tail, An, *146;* Battle of Britain, *9;* Boss' Wife, The, *244;* Boy in Blue, The, *467;* Day that Shook the World, The, *496;* Disappearance, The, *39;* Dragnet (1987), *268;* Dreamscape, *1048;* Eyewitness, *974;* Fall of the Roman Empire, The, *513;* Firehead, *49;* Ghost in Monte Carlo, A, *527;* Hanover Street, *536;* Highpoint, *62;* I Love N. Y., *547;* Inside Daisy Clover, *552;* International Velvet, *177;* Liar's Edge, *992;* Lily in Love, *318;* Man Who Would Be King, The, *81;* Mind Field, *85;* Murder by Decree, *998;* Night of the Generals, *90;* Ordeal by Innocence, *1003;* Prototype, *1072;* Pyx, The, *1008;* Red-Blooded American Girl, *879;* Return of the Pink Panther, The, *366;* Scarlet and the Black, The, *112;* Shadow Box, The, *654;* Shadow Dancing, *1014;* Silent Partner, The, *1016;* Somewhere in Time, *1077;* Sound of Music, The, *940;* Souvenir, *663;* Spiral Staircase, The (1975), *1019;* Stage Struck (1958), *665;* Star Crash, *1078;* Star Trek VI: The Undiscovered Country, *1079;* Thornbirds, The, *682;* Waterloo, *697;* Where the Heart Is, *699;* Young Catherine, *708*

Plummer, Glenn: Menace II Society, *593;* Pastime, *619;* South Central, *663*

Podesta, Rossana: Hercules (1983), *1056;* Sensual Man, The, *375;* Sodom and Gomorrah, *661;* Ulysses, *133;* Virgin of Nuremberg, *901*

Podobed: Extraordinary Adventures of Mr. West in the Land of the Bolsheviks, The, *735*

Poe, Carey: Yum-Yum Girls, The, *709*

Poelvoorde, Benoit: Man Bites Dog, *764*

Pogson, Kathryn: Overindulgence, *617*

Pogue, Ken: Blindman's Bluff, *956;* Climb, The, *26;* Dead of Winter, *967;* Grey Fox, The, *1117;* Keeping Track, *70;* One Magic Christmas, *613;* Run, *109*

Pohlmann, Eric: Horsemen, The, *64;* Surprise Package, *389*

Pohnel, Ron: No Retreat, No Surrender, *92*

Poindexter, Larry: American Ninja II, *4;* Blue Movies, *242*

Pointer, Priscilla: Disturbed, *971;* Rumpelstiltskin (1987), *200;* Runaway Father, *645*

Poiret, Jean: Elegant Criminal, The, *734;* Last Metro, The, *755;* Tales of Paris, *792*

Poitier, Sidney: Bedford Incident, The, *457;* Blackboard Jungle, The, *463;* Brother John, *470;* Buck and the Preacher, *1102;* Cry, the Beloved Country, *492;* Defiant Ones, The, *499;* Duel at Diablo, *1110;* For Love of Ivy, *279;* Goodbye, My Lady, *171;* Greatest Story Ever Told, The, *533;* Guess Who's Coming to Dinner, *534;* In the Heat of the Night, *986;* Let's Do It Again, *318;* Lilies of the Field (1963), *575;* Little Nikita, *992;* Mark of the Hawk, The, *589;* Organization, The, *96;* Paris Blues, *618;* Patch of Blue, A, *619;* Piece of the Action, A, *357;* Pressure Point, *626;* Raisin in the Sun, A (1961), *634;* Separate But Equal, *652;* Shoot to Kill, *115;* Slender Thread, The, *660;* Sneakers, *1018;* Something of Value, *118;* They Call Me Mister Tibbs, *127;* To Sir with Love, *685;* Uptown Saturday Night, *404;* Wilby Conspiracy, The, *701*

Polanski, Roman: Andy Warhol's Dracula, *809;* Back in the U.S.S.R., *8;* Ciao Federico!, *724;* Fearless Vampire Killers, or, Pardon Me, But Your Teeth Are in My Neck, The, *840;* Generation, A, *740;* Tenant, The, *1023*

Poletti, Victor: And the Ship Sails On, *712*

Poli, Maurice: Gangster's Law, *525*

Polic II, Henry: When Things Were Rotten (TV Series), *409*

Polito, Jon: Barton Fink, *232;* Crow, The, *827;* Equalizer, The: "Memories of Manon", *44;* Fire with Fire, *517;* Miller's Crossing, *594*

Politoff, Haydee: Dracula's Great Love, *837*

Polk, Brigid: Watched!, *137*

Pollack, Cheryl: Crossing the Bridge, *492*

Pollack, Sydney: Husbands and Wives, *546;* Player, The, *358;* Tootsie, *397*

Pollak, Cheryl: My Best Friend Is a Vampire, *339;* Night Life, *869*

Pollak, Kevin: Clean Slate (1994), *256;* Few Good Men, A, *976;* Grumpy Old Men, *291;* Indian Summer, *306;* Opposite Sex (And How to Live with Them), The, *351;* Ricochet, *106*

Pollan, Tracy: Danielle Steele's "Fine Things", *495;* Great Love Experiment, The, *533;* Stranger Among Us, A, *1020*

Pollard, Harry: His Royal Slyness/Haunted Spooks, *298*

Pollard, Michael J.: America, *226;* American Gothic, *808;* Art of Dying, The, *953;* Between the Lines, *237;* Bonnie and Clyde, *17;* Enter Laughing, *271;* Heated Vengeance, *60;* Legend of Frenchie King, The, *1128;* Motorama, *337;* Night Visitor (1989), *1001;* Patriot, *97;* Paul Reiser Out on a Whim, *355;* Riders of the Storm, *368;* Roxanne, *370;* Season of Fear, *1013;* Skeeter, *887;* Sleepaway Camp III, *887;* Split Second (1992), *1078;* Tango and Cash, *124;* Vengeance Is Mine (1976), *135;* Wild Angels, The, *139*

Pollard, Snub: Arizona Days, *1094;* Clutching Hand, The, *27;* Golden Age of Comedy, The, *288;* Harold Lloyd's Comedy

Classics, *294;* Man of a Thousand Faces, *587;* Riders of the Rockies, *1144;* Sing, Cowboy, Sing, *1150;* White Legion, *700*

Pollard, Thommy: Penitentiary, *98*

Polley, Sarah: Adventures of Baron Münchausen, The, *1034;* Lantern Hill, *180;* Ramona (Series), *198;* Tales From Avonlea (TV series), *209*

Pollock, Channing: Judex, *750*

Pollock, Daniel: Romper Stomper, *109*

Pollock, Eileen: Far and Away, *514*

Polo, Teri: Aspen Extreme, *451;* Born to Ride, *17;* Mystery Date, *341;* Quick, *102*

Pomeranc, Max: Searching for Bobby Fischer, *202*

Pompei, Elena: Mines of Kilimanjaro, *85*

Poncela, Eusebio: Law of Desire, *756*

Pons, Lily: I Dream Too Much, *924*

Pons, Martina: Mummy and the Curse of the Jackals, The, *867*

Pontremoli, David: To Forget Venice, *795*

Pop, Iggy: Cry-Baby, *912;* Hardware, *1055*

Popov, N.: October, *772*

Poppel, Marc: Relentless II: Dead On, *879*

Porizkova, Paulina: Anna, *448;* Her Alibi, *296;* Portfolio, *624*

Portal, Louise: Decline of the American Empire, The, *729;* Klutz, The, *314*

Porter, Alisan: Curly Sue, *261*

Porter, Ashley: Young Nurses, The, *708*

Porter, Brett: Firehead, *49*

Porter, Don: Bachelor in Paradise, *230;* Candidate, The, *474;* Christmas Coal Mine Miracle, The, *159;* Live a Little, Love a Little, *929;* White Line Fever, *139*

Porter, Eric: Antony and Cleopatra (1973), *450;* Belstone Fox, The, *149;* Hands of the Ripper, *848;* Hennessy, *982;* Little Lord Fauntleroy (1980), *182;* Thirty-Nine Steps, The (1978), *1024;* Why Didn't They Ask Evans?, *1032*

Porter, Jean: Bathing Beauty, *908;* San Fernando Valley, *1147;* Till the End of Time, *683*

Portman, Eric: Bedford Incident, The, *457;* Colditz Story, The, *485;* Crimes of Stephen Hawke, The, *826;* 49th Parallel, The, *520;* Great Day, *532;* Naked Edge, The, *1000;* One of Our Aircraft Is Missing, *94;* We Dive at Dawn, *137*

Portnow, Richard: In Dangerous Company, *550;* Meet the Hollowheads, *331*

Posey, Nicole: Beach Babes from Beyond, *1038*

Post, Markie: Glitz, *980;* Scene of the Crime (1985), *1013;* Tricks of the Trade, *399;* Triplecross, *399*

Post, Saskia: Dogs in Space, *914*

Posta, Adrienne: Adventures of a Private Eye, *222*

Postal, Maurice: Curse of the House Surgeon, The, *828;* Queen Victoria and the Zombies, *878*

Postlethwaite, Pete: Distant Voices/Still Lives, *502;* In the Name of the Father, *550;* Split Second (1992), *1078*

Poston, Tom: Cold Turkey, *257;* Happy Hooker, The, *293;* Murphy's Laws of Golf, *338;* Old Dark House, The, *872;* Soldier in the Rain, *661;* Up the Academy, *403;* Zotz!, *417*

Potter, Madeleine: Bostonians, The, *467;* Slaves of New York, *381;* Suicide Club, The, *1021*

Potter, Martin: Ciao Federico!, *724;* Fellini Satyricon, *736;* Twinsanity, *1028*

Potter, Michael: Female Trouble, *276*

Potts, Annie: Bayou Romance, *456;* Breaking the Rules, *469;* Corvette Summer, *29;* Flatbed Annie and Sweetie Pie: Lady Truckers, *50;* Ghostbusters, *285;* Ghostbusters II, *285;* Heartaches, *538;* Jumpin' Jack Flash, *311;* Pass the Ammo, *355;* Pretty in Pink, *626;* Texasville, *680;* Who's Harry Crumb?, *411*

Potts, Cliff: Last Ride of the Dalton Gang, The, *1126;* M.A.D.D.: Mothers Against Drunk Driving, *583;* Silent Running, *1076*

Pouget, Ely: Silent Victim, *658*

Poujouly, Georges: Elevator to the Gallows, *734;* Forbidden Games, *737*

Pounder, C.C.H.: Bagdad Café, *231;* Benny & Joon, *234;* Disappearance of Christina, The, *971;* Ernest Green Story, The, *165;* Lifepod, *1063;* Postcards from the Edge, *360;* Psycho 4: The Beginning, *877;* Return to Lonesome Dove, *1143;* RoboCop 3, *1075;* Sliver, *1018;* Third Degree Burn, *1024;* When a Man Loves a Woman, *698*

Powell, Brittney: Airborne, *224*

Powell, Dick: Bad and the Beautiful, The, *454;* Blessed Event, *241;* Christmas in July, *255;* Cornered, *29;* Cry Danger, *964;* Dames, *913;* Flirtation Walk, *917;* Footlight Parade, *917;* 42nd Street, *918;* Gold Diggers of 1933, *920;* Gold Diggers of 1935, *920;* Hollywood Hotel, *923;* Midsummer Night's Dream, A (1935), *1066;* Murder My Sweet, *999;* Pitfall, *622;* Stage Struck (1936), *941;* Station West, *1153;* Susan Slept Here, *389*

Powell, Eleanor: Born to Dance, *909;* Broadway Melody of 1936, *910;* Broadway Melody of 1938, *910;* Broadway Melody of 1940, *910;* Duchess of Idaho, *915;* Honolulu, *923;* I Dood It, *924;* Lady Be Good, *927;* Rosalie, *937;* Sensations of 1945, *938;* Ship Ahoy, *939;* Thousands Cheer, *945*

Powell, Jane: Athena, *907;* Date with Judy, A, *913;* Enchanted Island, *44;* Girl Most Likely, The, *919;* Hit the Deck, *923;* Holiday in Mexico, *923;* Luxury Liner, *930;* Nancy Goes to Rio, *932;* Rich, Young and Pretty, *936;* Royal Wedding, *938;* Seven Brides for Seven Brothers, *939;* Small Town Girl, *940;* Three Daring Daughters, *945;* Two Weeks with Love, *947*

Powell, Lee: Fighting Devil Dogs, The, *48;* Flash Gordon Conquers the Universe, *1052;* Lone Ranger, The (1938), *1129*

Powell, Lovelady: Happy Hooker, The, *293*

Powell, Robert: Dark Forces, *966;* Four Feathers, The (1978), *52;* Frankenstein (1984), *842;* Hunchback, *854;* Jane Austen in Manhattan, *309;* Jesus of Nazareth, *557;* Jigsaw Man, The, *987;* Mahler, *585;* Secrets, *651;* Shaka Zulu, *654;* Spirit of the Dead, *889;* Thirty-Nine Steps, The (1978), *1024;* What Waits Below, *902*

Powell, William: After the Thin Man, *951;* Another Thin Man, *952;* Double Wedding, *268;* Evelyn Prentice, *511;* Ex-Mrs. Bradford, The, *974;* Feel My Pulse, *276;* Girl Who Had Everything, The, *527;* Great Ziegfeld, The, *921;* How to Marry a Millionaire, *303;* I Love You Again, *304;* It's a Big Country, *308;* Kennel Murder Case, The, *988;* Last Command, The (1928), *568;* Last of Mrs. Cheney, The, *315;* Libeled Lady, *318;* Life with Father, *318;* Love Crazy, *322;* Manhattan Melodrama, *81;* Mr. Peabody and the Mermaid, *334;* Mr. Roberts, *334;* My Man Godfrey (1936), *340;* Reckless (1935), *636;* Senator Was Indiscreet, The, *375;* Shadow of the Thin Man, *1014;* Song of the Thin Man, *1018;* Star of Midnight, *1020;* Thin Man, The, *1024;* Thin Man Goes Home, The, *1024;* Ziegfeld Follies, *949*

Power, Chad: Three Ninjas, *211*

Power, Taryn: Count of Monte Cristo, The (1975), *30;* Sinbad and the Eye of the Tiger, *1077;* Tracks, *687*

Power, Tyrone: Alexander's Ragtime Band, *906;* Blood and Sand (1941), *464;* Crash Dive, *30;* Eddy Duchin Story, The, *507;* In Old Chicago, *550;* Jesse James, *1123;* Johnny Apollo, *559;* Long Grey Line, The, *578;* Marie Antoinette, *588;* Mark of Zorro, The (1940), *82;* Rains Came, The, *634;* Rawhide (1951), *1141;* Razor's Edge, The (1946), *635;* Second Fiddle, *938;* Thin Ice, *945;* Witness for the Prosecution (1957), *1032;* Yank in the RAF, A, *707*

Power Jr., Tyrone: California Casanova, *249;* Shag, the Movie, *654*

Power Sr., Tyrone: Big Trail, The, *1098;* Dream Street, *504;* Red Kimono, The, *636*

Powers, Alexandra: Dangerous Pursuit, *966;* Seventh Coin, The, *203*

Powers, Caroline Capers: Oracle, The, *872*

Powers, Leslie Ann: Hairspray, *292*

Powers, Mala: City That Never Sleeps, *483;* Cyrano De Bergerac (1950), *493;* Daddy's Gone A-Hunting, *965;* Rage at Dawn, *1140;* Tammy and the Bachelor, *677*

Powers, Stefanie: Boatniks, The, *151;* Die! Die! My Darling!, *834;* Escape to Athena, *45;* Experiment in Terror, *974;* Gone with the West, *1116;* Good Idea, *288;* Herbie Rides Again, *174;* Invisible Strangler, *857;* Little Moon & Jud McGraw, *1128;* Love Has Many Faces, *581;* Man Inside, The (1984), *81;* McLintock!, *1133;* Mistral's Daughter, *597;* Night Games, *1001;* Palm Springs Weekend, *353;* Sky Heist, *117;* Survive the Night, *1021*

Powers, Tom: Destination Moon, *1047;* Station West, *1153;* They Won't Believe Me, *681*

Pownall, Leon: Love and Hate, *581*

Powney, Clare: Girl, The, *527*

Pradier, Perrette: Burning Court, The, *721*

Prado, Lidia: Ascent To Heaven (Mexican Bus Ride), *714*

Prado, Lilia: Illusion Travels by Streetcar, *747*

Praed, Michael: Nightflyers, *1068;* Robin Hood and the Sorcerer, *107;* Robin Hood: The Swords of Wayland, *108;* To Die For 2: Son of Darkness, *896;* Writer's Block, *1033*

Prager, Sally: Hideaways, The, *174*

Prat, Eric: Tatie Danielle, *792*

Prater, Ollie Joe: Truly Tasteless Jokes, *400*

Prather, Joan: Big Bad Mama, *12;* Deerslayer, The, *1108;* Rabbit Test, *364;* Smile, *381*

Pratt, Judson: Monster on the Campus, *866*

Pratt, Mike: Twinsanity, *1028*

Pratt, Purnell: Mystery Squadron, *88;* Shriek in the Night, A, *1016*

Praunheim, Rosa von: Virus Knows No Morals, A, *801*

Preiss, Wolfgang: Battle of the Commandos, *10;* Cave of the Living Dead, *822;* Mad Executioners, The, *994;* Mill of the Stone Women, *865;* Raid on Rommel, *103;* Salzburg Connection, The, *111;* Thousand Eyes of Dr. Mabuse, The, *1083*

Preisser, June: Babes in Arms, *907;* Strike Up the Band, *387*

Préjean, Albert: Crazy Ray, The, *726;* Italian Straw Hat, The, *749;* Princess Tam Tam, *778;* Under the Roofs of Paris, *798*

Preminger, Otto: Stalag 17, *119;* They Got Me Covered, *393*

Prendes, Luis: Christmas Kid, The, *1105*

Prentiss, Ann: Any Wednesday, *228*

Prentiss, Paula: Bachelor in Paradise, *230;* Black Marble, The, *463;* Born to Win, *467;* Buddy, Buddy, *247;* Honeymoon Machine, The, *300;* Horizontal Lieutenant, The, *301;* In Harm's Way, *66;* Last of the Red Hot Lovers, *315;* M.A.D.D.: Mothers Against Drunk Driving, *583;* Man's Favorite Sport?, *328;* Packin' It In, *193;* Parallax View, The, *1004;* Saturday the 14th, *882;* What's New, Pussycat?, *408;* World of Henry Orient, The, *414*

Prentiss, Robert: Total Exposure, *1026*

Presby, Shannon: New Kids, The, *868*

Prescott, Robert: Bachelor Party, *230*

Presle, Micheline: Blood of Others, The, *464;* Devil in the Flesh (1946), *730;* French Way, The, *738;* Nea (A Young Emmanuelle), *771;* Prize, The, *629;* Time Out For Love, *795*

Presley, Elvis: Blue Hawaii, *909;* Change of Habit, *479;* Charro!, *1104;* Clambake, *912;* Double Trouble (1967), *914;* Easy Come, Easy Go, *915;* Elvis: The Lost Performances, *915;* Flaming Star, *1113;* Follow That Dream, *278;* Frankie and Johnny (1966), *918;* Fun in Acapulco, *918;* G.I. Blues, *918;* Girl Happy, *919;* Girls! Girls! Girls!, *919;* Harum Scarum, *922;* It Happened at the World's Fair, *925;* Jailhouse Rock, *925;* Kid Galahad (1962), *926;* King Creole, *927;* Kissin' Cousins, *927;* Live a Little, Love a Little, *929;* Love Me Tender, *1130;* Loving You, *929;* Paradise Hawaiian Style, *935;* Roustabout, *938;* Speedway, *941;* Spinout, *941;* Stay Away Joe, *942;* This Is Elvis, *436;* Tickle Me, *945;* Trouble with Girls, The, *946;* Viva Las Vegas, *947;* Wild in the Country, *702*

Presley, Priscilla: Adventures of Ford Fairlane, The, *2;* Naked Gun, The, *341;* Naked Gun 2 1/2, The, *341;* Naked Gun 33 1/3, The—The Final Insult, *341*

Presnell, Harve: Paint Your Wagon, *934;* Unsinkable Molly Brown, The, *947*

Presser, Antonia: Fire and Sword, *1051*

Pressman, Lawrence: Gathering, The, *525;* Hanoi Hilton, The, *536;* Hellstrom Chronicle, The, *426;* Man from Atlantis, The, *1064;* Rehearsal for Murder, *1009;* Streethawk, *121*

Presson, Jason: Explorers, *1050*

Preston, Cyndy: Brain, The (1988), *818;* Dark Side, The, *829;* Darkside, The, *33;* Prom Night III—Last Kiss, *877*

Preston, J. A.: High Noon, Part Two, *1120;* Real Life, *365;* Remo Williams: The Adventure Begins, *105*

Preston, Kelly: American Clock, The, *446;* Experts, The, *273;* 52 Pick-Up, *976;* Metalstorm: The Destruction of Jared-Syn, *1065;* Mischief, *333;* Only You, *351;* Perfect Bride, The, *873;* Run, *109;* Secret Admirer, *374;* SpaceCamp, *1078;* Spellbinder, *889;* Tiger's Tale, A, *396;* Twins, *401*

Preston, Mike: Metalstorm: The Destruction of Jared-Syn, *1065;* Road Warrior, The, *1074*

Preston, Robert: Beau Geste, *10;* Best of the Badmen, *109[illegible];* Blood on the Moon, *1099;* Chisholms, The, *1104;* Finnegan Begin Again, *277;* How the West Was Won, *1122;* Junior Bonner, *1124;* Last Starfighter, The, *1062;* Mame, *930;* Man That Corrupted Hadleyburg, The, *327;* Music Man, The, *932;* Outrage!, *616;* Reap the Wild Wind, *104;* Rehearsal for Murder, *1009;* S.O.B., *372;* Semi-Tough, *375;* September Gun, *1148;* Sundowners, The (1950), *1153;* This Gun for Hire (1942), *128;* Tulsa, *689;* Union Pacific, *1160;* Victor/Victoria, *405;* Wake Island, *136*

Preta, Gian Carlo: Loves and Times of Scaramouche, The, *324*

Prevert, Pierre: Age of Gold, *711*

Prevost, Marie: Flying Fool, The, *51;* Ladies of Leisure, *567;* Marriage Circle, The, *329;* Sin of Madelon Claudet, The, *658*

Price, Alan: Don't Look Back, *423;* O Lucky Man!, *610;* Oh, Alfie, *611*

Price, Dennis: Five Golden Hours, *278;* Horror Hospital, *851;* Horror of Frankenstein, *851;* Kind Hearts and Coronets, *313;* Murder Most Foul, *998;* Naked Truth, *342;* No Love for Johnnie, *608;* Ten Little Indians (1966), *1023;* Tunes of Glory, *689;* Twins of Evil, *898;* Venus in Furs, *135;* Victim, *693*

Price, Marc: Killer Tomatoes Eat France, *313;* Rescue, The, *105;* Trick or Treat (1986), *897*

Price, Molly: Jersey Girl, *310*

Price, Rosalinda: Roaring Guns, *1145*

Price, Stanley: Driftin' Kid, *1110*

Price, Vincent: Abominable Dr. Phibes, The, *808;* Adventures of Captain Fabian, *2;* Backtrack, *454;* Baron of Arizona, The, *1097;* Bloodbath at the House of Death, *242;* Champagne for Caesar, *252;* Conqueror Worm, The, *825;* Cry of the Banshee, *827;* Dangerous Mission, *966;* Dead Heat, *830;* Diary of a Madman, *834;* Dr. Phibes Rises Again, *836;* Edward Scissorhands, *1048;* Escapes, *1049;* Fall of the House of Usher, The (1960), *840;* Fly, The (1958), *841;* Haunted Palace, The, *849;* Heart of Justice, *538;* His Kind of Woman, *62;* House of 1,000 Dolls, *64;* House of the Long Shadows, *853;* House of the Seven Gables, The, *545;* House of Wax, *853;* House on Haunted Hill, *853;* Invisible Man Returns, *856;* Journey into Fear (1975), *987;* Keys to the Kingdom, The, *563;* Las Vegas Story, The, *568;* Last Man on Earth, The, *1062;* Laura, *991;* Madhouse (1972), *862;* Masque of the Red Death, The (1964), *863;* Master of the World, *1065;* Monster Club, The, *865;* Oblong Box, The, *872;* Offspring, The, *872;* Once Upon a Midnight Scary, *192;* Pit and the Pendulum, The (1961), *875;* Private Lives of Elizabeth and Essex, The, *629;* Raven, The (1963), *879;* Return of the Fly, The, *880;* Scavenger Hunt, *373;* Scream and Scream Again, *883;* Shock (1946), *885;* Snow White and the Seven Dwarfs (1983), *205;* Song of Bernadette, The, *662;* Tales of Terror, *892;* Theatre of Blood, *894;* Three Musketeers, The (1948), *128;* Tomb of Ligeia, *896;* Tower of London (1939), *897;* Tower of London

(1962), *897;* Trouble with Girls, The, *946;* Twice-Told Tales, *898;* Whales of August, The, *698;* While the City Sleeps, *138;* Wilson, *703*

Prichard, Robert: Alien Space Avenger, *1035*

Priest, Martin: Plot Against Harry, The, *359*

Priest, Pat: Easy Come, Easy Go, *915;* Incredible Two-Headed Transplant, The, *855*

Priestley, Jason: Beverly Hills 90210, *460;* Calendar Girl, *249;* Nowhere to Run (1989), *609;* Quantum Leap (TV Series), *1072;* Tombstone, *1157*

Prieto, Paco: Only the Strong, *95*

Prim, Suzy: Mayerling, *766*

Prima, Barry: Ferocious Female Freedom Fighters, *276*

Prima, Louis: Manhattan Merry-Go-Round, *930*

Prime, Cheryl: Lovers of Their Time, *582*

Primus, Barry: Autopsy, *811;* Big Business, *238;* Boxcar Bertha, *18;* Brotherly Love, *819;* Cannibal Women in the Avocado Jungle of Death, *22;* Denial, *499;* Jake Speed, *68;* Macbeth (1981), *584;* Night and the City (1992), *605;* Portrait of a Showgirl, *625;* Talking Walls, *391*

Prince: Graffiti Bridge, *920;* Purple Rain, *935;* Sign o' the Times, *434;* Under the Cherry Moon, *691*

Prince, Clayton: Dark Justice, *32;* Hairspray, *292*

Prince, Faith: My Father, the Hero, *339*

Prince, William: Blade, *14;* City in Fear, *962;* Cyrano De Bergerac (1950), *493;* Gauntlet, The, *55;* Greatest Man in the World, The, *290;* Objective, Burma!, *93;* Soldier, The, *118;* Spies Like Us, *384;* Sybil, *675;* Taking of Beverly Hills, The, *124;* Vice Versa, *404*

Principal, Victoria: I Will, I Will...for Now, *304;* Life and Times of Judge Roy Bean, The, *1128;* Mistress (1987), *597;* Pleasure Palace, *623*

Prine, Andrew: Bandolero!, *1096;* Callie and Son, *474;* Centerfold Girls, *478;* Christmas Coal Mine Miracle, The, *159;* Crypt of the Living Dead, *827;* Donner Pass: The Road to Survival, *1109;* Eliminators, The, *1048;* Evil, The, *839;* Generation, *283;* Gettysburg, *526;* Grizzly, *847;* Last of the Mohicans (1985), *1126;* Miracle Worker, The (1962), *595;* Nightmare Circus, *871;* Riding with Death, *1074;* Simon, King of the Witches, *886;* Small Killing, A, *660;* Texas Across the River, *1155;* They're Playing with Fire, *681;* Town That Dreaded Sundown, The, *1026*

Pringle, Joan: J.D.'s Revenge, *858*

Prinsloo, Sandra: African Rage, *3;* Gods Must Be Crazy, The, *287*

Prinz, Dietmar: Beethoven's Nephew, *457*

Prior, Ted: Born Killer, *17;* Center of the Web, *960;* Future Zone, *54;* Lost Platoon, *861;* Possessed by the Night, *1006;* Raw Nerve, *103*

Prival, Lucien: Darkest Africa, *33;* Mr. Wong, Detective, *997;* Return of Chandu (The Magician), *105*

Prochnow, Jurgen: Beverly Hills Cop II, *11;* Body of Evidence, *958;* Cop and the Girl, The, *726;* Das Boot (The Boat), *728;* Dry White Season, A, *505;* Dune, *1048;* Fire Next Time, The, *1051;* Forbidden, *519;* Fourth War, The, *52;* Hurricane Smith, *65;* Interceptor, *67;* Keep, The, *859;* Kill Cruise, *563;* Killing Cars, *563;* Man Inside, The (1990), *587;* Robin Hood (1991), *107;* Seventh Sign, The, *885*

Proctor, Philip: Firesign Theatre's Hot Shorts, *277;* J-Men Forever, *310;* Robo C.H.I.C., *1074*

Prokhorenko, Shanna: Ballad of a Soldier, *715*

Prophet, Melissa: Invasion U.S.A., *67*

Prosky, Robert: Age Isn't Everything, *223;* Big Shots, *238;* Broadcast News, *246;* Christine, *824;* Dangerous Pursuit, *966;* Far and Away, *514;* From the Dead of Night, *844;* Funny About Love, *282;* Gremlins 2: The New Batch, *1055;* Hanky Panky, *292;* Hit Woman: The Double Edge, *63;* Hoffa, *542;* Last Action Hero, The, *1062;* Loose Cannons, *321;* Lords of Discipline, The, *579;* Mrs. Doubtfire, *334;* Murder of Mary Phagan, The, *600;* Natural, The, *604;* Outrageous Fortune, *352;* Rudy, *200;* Teamster Boss: The Jackie Presser Story, *678;* Things Change, *394*

Prosser, Hugh: Sea Hound, The, *112*

Protheroe, Brian: Not a Penny More, Not a Penny Less, *1002*

Proval, David: Romeo is Bleeding, *108;* Vice Versa, *404*

Provine, Dorothy: Good Neighbor Sam, *288;* It's a Mad Mad Mad Mad World, *308;* Never a Dull Moment, *191;* That Darn Cat, *210;* 30 Foot Bride of Candy Rock, The, *394;* Who's Minding the Mint?, *411*

Provost, Guy: Klutz, The, *314*

Provost, Jon: Escapade in Japan, *165*

Prowse, Dave: Empire Strikes Back, The, *1049;* Frankenstein and the Monster from Hell, *842;* Return of the Jedi, *1074*

Prowse, Heydon: Secret Garden, The (1993), *202*

Prowse, Juliet: Can-Can, *911;* Dingaka, *501;* G.I. Blues, *918*

Prud'homme, Cameron: Rainmaker, The, *634*

Pryce, Jonathan: Age of Innocence, The, *443;* Barbarians at the Gate, *455;* Brazil, *245;* Breaking Glass, *909;* Consuming Passions, *259;* Doctor and the Devils, The, *835;* Glengarry Glen Ross, *528;* Haunted Honeymoon, *294;* Jumpin' Jack Flash, *311;* Man on Fire, *81;* Ploughman's Lunch, The, *623;* Rachel Papers, *364;* Something Wicked This Way Comes, *1077*

Pryor, Mowava: Cover Girl Murders, The, *964*

Pryor, Nicholas: Happy Hooker, The, *293;* Hoffa, *542;* Less Than Zero, *573;* Life and Assassination of the Kingfish, The, *574;* Morgan Stewart's Coming Home, *337;* Night Terror, *1001;* Risky Business, *368;* Smile, *381*

Pryor, Nick: Force Five, *51*

Pryor, Richard: Adios Amigo, *1092;* Another You, *228;* Best of Chevy Chase, The, *235;* Bingo Long Traveling All-Stars and Motor Kings, The, *240;* Blue Collar, *465;* Brewster's Millions (1985), *245;* Bustin' Loose, *248;* California Suite, *249;* Car Wash, *250;* Critical Condition, *260;* Greased Lightning, *57;* Harlem Nights, *59;* Hit!, *62;* Jo Jo Dancer, Your Life Is Calling, *558;* Lady Sings the Blues, *927;* Lily Tomlin Special—Vol. I, The, *319;* Mack, The, *584;* Moving, *338;* Muppet Movie, The, *189;* Richard Pryor—Here and Now, *367;* Richard Pryor—Live and Smokin', *367;* Richard Pryor—Live in Concert, *367;* Richard Pryor Live on the Sunset Strip, *368;* Saturday Night Live, *372;* See No Evil, Hear No Evil, *375;* Silver Streak (1976), *379;* Some Call It Loving, *662;* Some Kind of Hero, *382;* Stir Crazy, *386;* Superman III, *1081;* Toy, The, *398;* Uptown Saturday Night, *404;* Which Way Is Up?, *410;* Wholly Moses!, *410;* Wild in the Streets, *1089;* Wiz, The, *948*

Pryor, Roger: Belle of the Nineties, *234;* Lady by Choice, *567*

Pszoniak, Wojiech: Danton, *728;* Wedding, The, *802*

Pudovkin, Vsevelod: Extraordinary Adventures of Mr. West in the Land of the Bolsheviks, The, *735;* Mystery of the Leaping Fish/Chess Fever, *341*

Puente, Tito: Mambo Kings, The, *930*

Pugh, Willard E.: Ambition, *952;* CB4, *252*

Puglia, Frank: Ali Baba and the Forty Thieves, *3*

Pullman, Bill: Accidental Tourist, The, *440;* Brain Dead, *1040;* Bright Angel, *470;* Crazy in Love, *490;* Favor, The, *275;* Going Under, *288;* League of Their Own, A, *571;* Liebestraum, *992;* Malice, *994;* Nervous Ticks, *343;* Newsies, *933;* Rocket Gibraltar, *642;* Ruthless People, *371;* Serpent and the Rainbow, The, *884;* Sibling Rivalry, *378;* Singles, *379;* Sleepless in Seattle, *381;* Sommersby, *662;* Spaceballs, 384

Pulver, Lilo: Global Affair, A, *287;* Nun, The (La Religieuse), *772;* One, Two, Three, *350;* Time to Love and a Time to Die, A, *684*

Punsley, Bernard: Junior G-Men, *69;* Little Tough Guys, *319*

Purcell, Dick: Captain America (1944), *22;* Idaho, *1122;* King of the Zombies, *859*

Purcell, Lee: Adam at 6 A.M., *441;* Amazing Howard Hughes, The, *445;* Big Wednesday, *461;* Eddie Macon's Run, *43;* Killing at Hell's Gate, *71;* Mr. Majestyk, *86;* Space Rage,

1078; Summer of Fear, 891; To Heal a Nation, 684; Valley Girl, 404; Witching, The (Necromancy), 904
Purdee, Nathan: Return of Superfly, The, 105
Purdom, Edmund: Assisi Underground, The, 7; Athena, 907; Dr. Frankenstein's Castle of Freaks, 835; Don't Open Till Christmas, 836; Egyptian, The, 508; Pieces, 875; Prodigal, The, 629; Student Prince, The, 942
Puri, Om: City of Joy, 483
Puri, Linda: Accidental Meeting, 950; Adventures of Nellie Bly, The, 442; Body Language, 958; High Country, The, 61; In Self Defense, 550; Jory, 1124; Little Ladies of the Night, 576; Manions of America, The, 588; Night the City Screamed, The, 606; Outrage!, 616; Spies, Lies, and Naked Thighs, 384; Viper, 136; Visiting Hours, 901; Web of Deceit, 1030
Purviance, Edna: Burlesque of Carmen, 247; Chaplin Revue, The, 253; Charlie Chaplin Carnival, 253; Charlie Chaplin Cavalcade, 253; Charlie Chaplin Festival, 253; Charlie Chaplin...Our Hero, 253; Charlie Chaplin—The Early Years, Vol. 1, 253; Charlie Chaplin—The Early Years, Vol. 2, 253; Charlie Chaplin—The Early Years, Vol. 3, 254; Charlie Chaplin—The Early Years, Vol. 4, 254; Kid, The/The Idle Class, 313; Rare Chaplin, 364; Three Charlies and a Phoney!, 395; Woman of Paris, A, 705
Putch, John: Impure Thoughts, 305
Puvanai, Nat: Crocodile, 827
Pye, Katie: Jane Campion Shorts, 309
Pye, Tim: Jane Campion Shorts, 309
Pyle, Denver: Dynamite Pass, 1111; Five Card Stud, 1113; Flying Saucer, The, 1052; Hawmps!, 294; Hellfire, 1120; Last of Mrs. Lincoln, The, 570; Legend of Hillbilly John, The, 181; Man from Colorado, The, 1131; Maverick, 1133
Pyne, Joe: Unkissed Bride, 403
Pyper-Ferguson, John: Killer Image, 988
Quade, John: Medicine Hat Stallion, The, 186
Quadflieg, Christian: For Your Love Only, 519
Quaid, Dennis: Are You in the House Alone?, 953; Big Easy, The, 12; Bill, 461; Bill: On His Own, 461; Breaking Away, 245; Caveman, 252; Come See the Paradise, 486; D.O.A. (1988), 965; Dreamscape, 1048; Enemy Mine, 1049; Everybody's All-American, 511; Flesh and Bone, 518; Gorp, 289; Great Balls of Fire, 920; Innerspace, 1058; Jaws 3, 858; Long Riders, The, 1130; Night the Lights Went Out in Georgia, The, 606; Postcards from the Edge, 360; Right Stuff, The, 640; Seniors, The, 375; September 30, 1955, 652; Suspect, 1022; Tough Enough, 131; Undercover Blues, 403; Wilder Napalm, 411
Quaid, Randy: Apprenticeship of Duddy Kravitz, The, 450; Bloodhounds of Broadway, 242; Bound for Glory, 467; Breakout, 19; Caddyshack II, 249; Choirboys, The, 481; Days of Thunder, 33; Dead Solid Perfect, 497; Fool for Love, 518; Foxes, 521; Frankenstein (1992), 842; Freaked, 281; Heartbeeps, 173; Last Detail, The, 569; Last Picture Show, The, 570; LBJ: The Early Years, 571; Long Riders, The, 1130; Martians Go Home, 329; Midnight Express, 594; Moving, 338; National Lampoon's Christmas Vacation, 342; No Man's Land, 91; Of Mice and Men (1981), 610; Out Cold, 351; Paper, The, 617; Parents, 354; Quick Change, 363; Slugger's Wife, The, 381; Sweet Country, 674; Texasville, 680; Wild Life, The, 411; Wraith, The, 904
Qualen, John: Adventure, 441; Angels Over Broadway, 448; Arabian Nights (1942), 6; At Gunpoint, 1095; Big Hand for the Little Lady, A, 1098; Dark Waters, 496; Doubting Thomas, 268; Fugitive, The (1947), 523; Grapes of Wrath, The, 531; Hans Christian Andersen, 921; High and the Mighty, The, 541; I'll Take Sweden, 924; Jungle Book (1942), 179; Melody Master, 592; My Love for Yours, 340; Our Daily Bread, 615; Passion (1954), 97; Prize, The, 629; Scar, The, 649; Three Musketeers, The (1935), 128
Quan, Jonathan Ke: Breathing Fire, 19
Quarry, Robert: Commando Squad, 28; Count Yorga, Vampire, 825; Cyclone, 31; Dr. Phibes Rises Again, 836; Evil Spirits, 839; Madhouse (1972), 862; Spirits, 889; Warlords, 901
Quarshie, Hugh: Church, The, 824
Quarter, James: Intimate Obsession, 986
Quartermaine, Leon: As You Like It, 229
Quast, Philip: Around the World in 80 Ways, 228
Quattro, Van: Desperate Crimes, 37
Quayle, Anna: Chitty Chitty Bang Bang, 158; Hard Day's Night, A, 921
Quayle, Anthony: Anne of the Thousand Days, 449; Bourne Identity, The, 958; Damn the Defiant!, 31; Endless Game, The, 510; Everything You Always Wanted to Know About Sex but Were Afraid to Ask, 273; Guns of Navarone, The, 58; Holocaust 2000, 851; Key to Rebecca, The, 70; Misunderstood (1988), 598; Moses, 600; Murder by Decree, 998; Poppy Is Also a Flower, The, 99; Pursuit of the Graf Spee, 101; QB VII, 631; Story of David, The, 207; Study in Terror, A, 1021; Tamarind Seed, The, 124; Wrong Man, The (1956), 1033
Queen, Amelia M.: Adventures in Wonderland, 143
Quennessen, Valerie: French Postcards, 281; Summer Lovers, 672
Quentin, John: Terrorists, The, 1023
Questel, Mae: Majority of One, A, 326
Quester, Hugues: Tale of Springtime, A, 792
Qui, Robert Do: Case for Murder, A, 960
Quick, Diana: Brideshead Revisited, 469; Misadventures of Mr. Wilt, The, 333; Odd Job, The, 348; Ordeal by Innocence, 1003
Quigley, Charles: Charlie Chan's Secret, 961; Crimson Ghost, The, 30; Daredevils of the Red Circle, 32; Superman—The Serial, 1081; Woman's Face, A, 705
Quigley, Linnea: Beach Babes from Beyond, 1038; Creepozoids, 826; Hollywood Chainsaw Hookers, 850; Nightmare Sisters, 871; Sorority Babes in the Slimeball Bowl-O-Rama, 383; Vice Academy, 404; Vice Academy 2, 404; Virgin High, 405; Witchtrap, 904; Young Warriors, The, 141
Quill, Tim: Hamburger Hill, 535; Staying Together, 667; Thou Shalt Not Kill...Except, 895
Quillan, Eddie: Caution: Funny Men at Work, 420; Dixie Jamboree, 914; More Milton Berle's Mad World of Comedy, 431; Mutiny on the Bounty (1935), 88; Young Mr. Lincoln, 708
Quilley, Denis: King David, 564; Lion and the Hawk, The, 77; Privates on Parade, 362
Quimette, Stephen: Destiny to Order, 264
Quine, Richard: Babes on Broadway, 907; Clay Pigeon, The, 26; Little Men (1935), 182
Quinlan, Kathleen: Blackout (1985), 956; Bodily Harm, 957; Clara's Heart, 483; Doors, The, 914; Hanky Panky, 292; I Never Promised You a Rose Garden, 547; Independence Day, 551; Last Light, 569; Last Winter, The, 571; Lifeguard, 574; Promise, The, 629; Runner Stumbles, The, 645; She's in the Army Now, 656; Strays, 891; Sunset, 1021; Trapped, 1027; Twilight Zone—The Movie, 898; Warning Sign, 901; Wild Thing, 702
Quinn, Aidan: All My Sons, 444; At Play in the Fields of the Lord, 451; Avalon, 452; Benny & Joon, 234; Blink, 956; Crusoe, 31; Desperately Seeking Susan, 264; Early Frost, An, 506; Handmaid's Tale, The, 1055; Lemon Sisters, The, 317; Lies of the Twins, 992; Mission, The, 596; Perfect Witness, 620; Playboys, The, 623; Private Matter, A, 629; Reckless (1984), 636; Stakeout, 119
Quinn, Aileen: Annie, 907
Quinn, Anthony: Across 110th Street, 1; African Rage, 3; Against All Flags, 3; Back to Bataan, 8; Barabbas, 455; Behold a Pale Horse, 458; Black Orchid, The, 463; Blood and Sand (1941), 464; Blowing Wild, 16; Buffalo Bill, 1102; Bulldog Drummond in Africa, 20; Caravans, 475; Children of Sanchez, The, 481; China Sky, 25; City for Conquest, 482; Con Artists, The, 487; Destructors, The, 970; Don Is Dead, The, 40; Dream of Kings, A, 504; Ghost Breakers, 285; Ghosts Can't Do It, 285; Greek Tycoon, The, 533; Guadalcanal Diary, 58; Guns of Navarone, The, 58; Heller in Pink Tights, 1120; High Risk, 61;

Hot Spell, *544;* Jungle Fever, *561;* La Strada, *754;* Last Action Hero, The, *1062;* Last Train from Gun Hill, *1126;* Lawrence of Arabia, *76;* Lion of the Desert, *77;* Lost Command, *79;* Lust for Life, *583;* Man of Passion, A, *587;* Message, The (Mohammad, Messenger of God), *593;* Mobsters, *86;* Onassis: The Richest Man in the World, *612;* Only the Lonely, *350;* Ox-Bow Incident, The, *1137;* R.P.M. (Revolutions Per Minute), *632;* Regina, *780;* Requiem for a Heavyweight, *638;* Revenge (1990), *106;* Road to Singapore, *369;* Salamander, The, *111;* Seven Cities of Gold, *653;* Shoes of the Fisherman, *656;* Sinbad the Sailor, *116;* Swing High, Swing Low, *390;* They Died with Their Boots On, *1156;* Tycoon, *133;* Ulysses, *133;* Union Pacific, *1160;* Viva Zapata!, *694;* Walk in the Spring Rain, A, *695;* Warlock (1959), *1162;* Zorba the Greek, *709*

Quinn, Colin: Who's the Man?, *411*

Quinn, Daniele: Band of the Hand, *9*

Quinn, Francesco: Dead Certain, *967;* Indigo, *66;* Platoon, *623;* Priceless Beauty, *626;* Quo Vadis? (1985), *632*

Quinn, Frank: Body Puzzle, *958*

Quinn, Glenn: Dr. Giggles, *835*

Quinn, J. C.: Babe, The, *452;* Barfly, *455;* Crisscross (1992), *491;* Maximum Overdrive, *864;* Megaville, *1065;* Prayer of the Rollerboys, *100;* Priceless Beauty, *626;* Violated, *136*

Quinn, James W.: Witchtrap, *904*

Quinn, Louis: Unholy Rollers, *691*

Quinn, Martha: Bad Channels, *1037;* Chopper Chicks in Zombietown, *823;* Motorama, *337*

Quinn, Pat: Alice's Restaurant, *444;* Unmarried Woman, An, *691;* Zachariah, *1166*

Quinn, Patricia: Rocky Horror Picture Show, The, *937;* Witching Time, *904*

Quinones, Adolfo: Breakin', *909;* Breakin' 2 Electric Boogaloo, *909*

Quintana, Rosita: Susanna, *791*

Quintano, Gene: Treasure of the Four Crowns, *132*

Quinteros, Lorenzo: Man Facing Southeast, *765*

Quo, Beulah: Children of An Lac, The, *480*

Qurrassi, Sarfuddin: Salaam Bombay!, *782*

Ra, Sun: Mystery, Mr. Ra, *431*

Raab, Kurt: Boarding School, *243;* Les Tricheurs, *759;* Mussolini and I, *601*

Rabal, Enrique: Man and the Monster, The, *862*

Rabal, Francisco: Camorra, *722;* City of the Walking Dead, *824;* Corleone, *29;* Eclipse, The, *733;* Holy Innocents, *744;* Nazarin, *771;* Nun, The (La Religieuse), *772;* Saddle Tramps, *1147;* Sorceror, *1018;* Stay as You Are, *666;* Stilts, The (Los Zancos), *789;* Viridiana, *801*

Racette, Francine: Au Revoir, Les Enfants, *714;* Dan Candy's Law, *32;* Disappearance, The, *39;* Lumiere, *763*

Rachins, Alan: Always (1984), *225;* L.A. Law, *567*

Racimo, Victoria: Ernest Goes to Camp, *272;* High Velocity, *62;* Mountain Men, The, *1134;* Prophecy, *877;* Search for the Gods, *1076*

Radd, Ronald: King Lear (1988), *564;* Saint, The (TV Series), *1012*

Rademakers, Fons: Daughters of Darkness, *830;* Lifespan, *1063*

Radford, Basil: Captive Heart, *475;* Dead of Night (1945), *830;* Night Train to Munich, *91;* Passport to Pimlico, *355;* Tight Little Island, *396;* Winslow Boy, The, *704;* Young and Innocent, *1033*

Radford, Natalie: Tomcat: Dangerous Desires, *1084*

Radner, Gilda: Best of Chevy Chase, The, *235;* Best of Dan Aykroyd, The, *235;* Best of Gilda Radner, The, *235;* Best of John Belushi, The, *235;* Bob & Ray, Jane, Laraine & Gilda, *243;* First Family, *277;* Gilda Live, *286;* Hanky Panky, *292;* Haunted Honeymoon, *294;* It Came from Hollywood, *307;* Mr. Mike's Mondo Video, *334;* Movers and Shakers, *337;* Rutles, The (a.k.a. All You Need Is Cash), *938;* Saturday Night Live, *372;* Things We Did Last Summer, *394;* Woman in Red, The, *413*

Radziwilowicz, Jerzy: Man of Iron, *765;* Man of Marble, *765;* Suspended, *791*

Rae, Charlotte: Car 54 Where Are You? (TV Series), *250;* Hair, *921;* Hot Rock, The, *983;* Thunder in Paradise, *129;* Worst Witch, The, *219*

Rafferty, Chips: Desert Rats, The, *500;* Sundowners, The (1960), *673;* Wackiest Ship in the Army, The, *405;* Walk into Hell, *136*

Rafferty, Frances: Abbott and Costello in Hollywood, *221;* Mrs. Parkington, *598*

Raffi: Raffi and the Sunshine Band, *198;* Young Children's Concert with Raffi, A, *219*

Raffin, Deborah: Claudia, *484;* Death Wish III, *36;* Demon (God Told Me To), *1046;* For the Love of It, *279;* Forty Carats, *279;* Hanging on a Star, *536;* Jungle Heat, *69;* Killing at Hell's Gate, *71;* Morning Glory (1992), *599;* Night of the Fox, *90;* Once Is Not Enough, *613;* Ransom, *1009;* Scanners 2: The New Order, *883;* Sentinel, The, *884;* Touched by Love, *686;* Willa, *703*

Raft, George: Background to Danger, *8;* Casino Royale (1967), *252;* Each Dawn I Die, *42;* Five Golden Dragons, *50;* Hammersmith Is Out, *292;* Hollywood Outtakes, *299;* House Across the Bay, The, *545;* If I Had a Million, *304;* Johnny Angel, *69;* Man with Bogart's Face, The, *995;* Mr. Ace, *85;* Night after Night, *344;* Nocturne, *1002;* Outpost in Morocco, *96;* Red Skelton: A Career of Laughter, *433;* Scarface (1932), *112;* Sextette, *376;* Some Like It Hot, *382;* They Drive by Night, *127;* Whistle Stop, *138*

Ragland, Rags: Girl Crazy, *919;* Whistling in Brooklyn, *410;* Whistling in the Dark, *410*

Ragsdale, William: Fright Night, *844;* Fright Night II, *844;* Mannequin Two: On the Move, *328*

Railsback, Steve: Alligator II, *808;* Angela, *448;* Blue Monkey, *817;* Deadly Games, *968;* Deadly Intent, *34;* Distortions, *834;* Escape 2000, *1049;* Forgotten, The, *520;* From Here to Eternity (1979), *523;* Golden Seal, The, *170;* Helter Skelter, *540;* Lifeforce, *1063;* Nukie, *191;* Quake, *1008;* Save Me, *1012;* Scenes from the Goldmine, *649;* Scissors, *1013;* Stunt Man, The, *671;* Sunstroke, *1021;* Survivalist, The, *123;* Torchlight, *686;* Trick or Treat (1982), *897*

Raimi, Sam: Indian Summer, *306;* Thou Shalt Not Kill...Except, *895*

Raimi, Sonia: Tuck Everlasting, *214*

Raimi, Theodore: Lunatics: A Love Story, *324*

Raimu: Baker's Wife, The (1938), *715;* César, *723;* Fanny (1932), *736;* Marius, *765;* Pearls of the Crown, The, *776;* Well-Digger's Daughter, The, *803*

Rain, Douglas: Oedipus Rex (1957), *610*

Rainer, Luise: Good Earth, The, *530;* Great Waltz, The, *921;* Great Ziegfeld, The, *921*

Raines, Cristina: Duellists, The, *42;* Nightmares, *871;* Quo Vadis? (1985), *632;* Russian Roulette, *110;* Sentinel, The, *884;* Silver Dream Racer, *658;* Touched by Love, *686*

Raines, Ella: Hail the Conquering Hero, *292;* Impact, *985;* Ride the Man Down, *1143;* Senator Was Indiscreet, The, *375;* Strange Affair of Uncle Harry, The, *669;* Tall in the Saddle, *1154*

Rainey, Ford: Bed and Breakfast, *457;* Cellar, The, *822;* My Sweet Charlie, *602;* Strangers: The Story of a Mother and a Daughter, *669*

Rains, Claude: Adventures of Robin Hood, The, *2;* Angel on My Shoulder (1946), *448;* Anthony Adverse, *450;* Caesar and Cleopatra, *473;* Casablanca, *476;* Deception (1946), *498;* Evil Mind, The (a.k.a. The Clairvoyant), *839;* Forever and a Day, *520;* Four Daughters, *520;* Here Comes Mr. Jordan, *296;* Invisible Man, The, *856;* Juarez, *560;* King's Row, *565;* Lisbon, *77;* Mr. Skeffington, *597;* Mr. Smith Goes to Washington, *597;* Notorious, *1002;* Now, Voyager, *609;* Paris Express, The, *97;* Passage to Marseilles, *97;* Phantom of the Opera (1943), *874;* Prince and the Pauper, The (1937), *197;* Sea Hawk, The, *112;* They Made Me a Criminal, *681;* White Tower, The, *701;* Wolf Man, The, *904*

Raisch, Bill: Fugitive, The (TV Series), *523;* Fugitive, The: The Last Episode (TV Series), *53*
Raitt, Bonnie: No Nukes, *432*
Raitt, John: Pajama Game, The, *934*
Rall, Tommy: Kiss Me Kate, *927;* My Sister Eileen, *932*
Ralli, Giovanna: Caper of the Golden Bulls, The, *22;* General Della Rovere, *740*
Rally, Steve: Overkill, *96*
Ralph, Jessie: Camille, *474;* Double Wedding, *268;* Drums Along the Mohawk, *42;* Evelyn Prentice, *511;* Good Earth, The, *530;* Last of Mrs. Cheney, The, *315;* Little Lord Fauntleroy (1936), *576;* Murder at the Vanities, *931;* They Met in Bombay, *127*
Ralph, Sheryl Lee: Distinguished Gentleman, The, *265;* Mighty Quinn, The, *85;* Mistress (1992), *597;* To Sleep with Anger, *685*
Ralston, Esther: Old Ironsides, *93;* Oliver Twist (1922), *611;* Sadie McKee, *646;* To the Last Man, *1157;* We're in the Legion Now, *137*
Ralston, Howard: Pollyanna (1920), *196*
Ralston, Jobyna: Wings, *140*
Ralston, Vera Hruba: Dakota (1945), *1107;* Fighting Kentuckian, The, *1112;* Hoodlum Empire, *64;* Jubilee Trail, *1124*
Rambal, Enrique: Exterminating Angel, The, *735*
Rambeau, Marjorie: Any Number Can Play, *450;* Inspiration, *553;* Laughing Sinners, *571;* Man Called Peter, A, *586;* Man of a Thousand Faces, *587;* Min and Bill, *594;* Palooka, *617;* Primrose Path, *627;* Rains Came, The, *634;* Salome, Where She Danced, *647;* Torch Song, *686*
Ramberg, Sterling: Revenge of the Teenage Vixens from Outer Space, *881*
Rambo, Dack: Hit Lady, *63;* River of Diamonds, *107;* Shades of Love: Lilac Dream, *654*
Ramer, Henry: Between Friends, *459;* Big Slice, The, *12;* Reno and the Doc, *638*
Ramey, Alan: Vampires Always Ring Twice, *900;* Vampires from Outer Space, *900*
Ramirez, Frank: Miracle in Rome, *767*
Ramirez, Lydia: Street Hitz, *121*
Ramis, Harold: Baby Boom, *230;* Best of Comic Relief, The, *235;* Ghostbusters, *285;* Ghostbusters II, *285;* Richard Lewis—"I'm in Pain Concert", *367;* Stealing Home, *667;* Stripes, *387*
Ramokgopa, Tommy: Magic Garden, The, *764*
Ramones, The: Rock 'n' Roll High School, *369*
Ramos, Nick: Legend of Walks Far Woman, The, *1128*
Ramos, Rudy: Blindsided, *956;* Open House, *872;* Quicksilver, *632*
Rampling, Charlotte: Angel Heart, *952;* Caravan to Vaccares, *23;* D.O.A. (1988), *965;* Farewell My Lovely, *975;* Foxtrot, *521;* Georgy Girl, *284;* Knack...and How To Get It, The, *314;* Mascara, *82;* Night Porter, The, *606;* Orca, *873;* Purple Taxi, The, *631;* Sardine: Kidnapped, *783;* Stardust Memories, *385;* Verdict, The, *693;* Zardoz, *1091*
Ramsay, Brucy: Alive, *444*
Ramsden, Frances: Mad Wednesday, *325;* Sin of Harold Diddlebock (a.k.a. Mad Wednesday), *379*
Ramsey, Anne: Homer and Eddie, *543;* Meet the Hollowheads, *331;* Say Yes, *373;* Throw Momma from the Train, *396*
Ramsey, Logan: Head (1968), *922;* Hoodlum Priest, The, *543;* Joy Sticks, *311;* King Richard II, *565;* Say Yes, *373;* Some Call It Loving, *662*
Ramsey, Marion: Police Academy II: Their First Assignment, *359;* Police Academy III: Back in Training, *359;* Police Academy 5—Assignment: Miami Beach, *359*
Ramsey, Ward: Dinosaurus!, *834*
Ramson, Bert: Maverick, *1133*
Ramus, Nick: Annie Oakley (1985), *146;* Geronimo, *1115;* Windwalker, *1165*
Rand, John: Charlie Chaplin Cavalcade, *253*
Rand, Sally: Road to Yesterday, The, *641*
Randall, Ethan: Dutch, *269;* Far Off Place, A, *166*
Randall, George: Brothers of the Wilderness, *471*
Randall, Lexi: Sarah, Plain and Tall, *648;* Skylark, *660*
Randall, Richard: Cross Mission, *31*
Randall, Stacie: Trancers 4: Jack of Swords, *1085*
Randall, Tony: Adventures of Huckleberry Finn, The (1960), *144;* Alphabet Murders, The, *951;* Boys' Night Out, *244;* Everything You Always Wanted to Know About Sex but Were Afraid to Ask, *273;* Fatal Instinct (1993), *274;* Foolin' Around, *278;* Let's Make Love, *928;* Littlest Angel, The, *184;* Lover Come Back, *323;* Mating Game, The, *330;* My Little Pony: The Movie, *190;* Pillow Talk, *357;* Scavenger Hunt, *373;* Send Me No Flowers, *375;* 7 Faces of Dr. Lao, *1076;* That's Adequate, *393*
Randazzo, Teddy: Rock, Rock, Rock, *937*
Randell, Ron: I Am a Camera, *547;* Loves of Carmen, The, *582*
Randig, Ric: Splatter University, *889*
Randle, Theresa: Beverly Hills Cop 3, *11;* CB4, *252;* Sugar Hill, *122*
Randolph, Amanda: Amos and Andy (TV Series), *226*
Randolph, Anders: Black Pirate, The, *14*
Randolph, Jane: Curse of the Cat People, The, *828;* Falcon's Brother, The, *975;* Railroaded, *633;* T-Men, *676*
Randolph, John: Adventures of Nellie Bly, The, *442;* American Clock, The, *446;* As Summers Die, *451;* Killing at Hell's Gate, *71;* Lovely But Deadly, *994;* National Lampoon's Christmas Vacation, *342;* Prizzi's Honor, *362;* Serpico, *652;* Sibling Rivalry, *378;* Wilbur and Orville: The First to Fly, *217;* Wizard of Loneliness, The, *704*
Randolph, Joyce: Honeymooners, The (TV Series), *300;* Honeymooners, The: Lost Episodes (TV Series), *300;* Jackie Gleason's Honeybloopers, *309*
Randolph, Windsor Taylor: Amazons, *4*
Random, Robert: Vampire at Midnight, *899*
Rangel, Maria: Full Fathom Five, *53*
Ranger, Dan: Last Ride, The, *991*
Rankin, Sean: Underground (1990), *1029*
Ranney, Juanita: Danger Zone, The, *32*
Ranni, Rodolfo: Deadly Revenge, *35*
Ransom, Kenny: Prison for Children, *628*
Ransom, Tim: Dressmaker, The, *505*
Ransome, Prunella: Man in the Wilderness, *1132*
Rapaport, Michael: True Romance, *133;* Zebrahead, *709*
Rapp, Anthony: Adventures in Babysitting, *222;* Dazed and Confused, *497*
Rappagna, Anna: Order of the Black Eagle, *95*
Rappaport, David: Bride, The, *819;* Mysteries, *770*
Rappaport, Michael: Hardbodies, *293*
Rascel, Renato: Seven Hills of Rome, The, *939*
Rasche, David: Act of Passion, *441;* Bingo, *240;* Delirious, *263;* Fighting Back, *47;* Hammered: The Best of Sledge, *292;* Innocent Man, An, *66;* Masters of Menace, *329;* Native Son, *604;* Silhouette, *1016;* Special Bulletin, *1019*
Rascoe, Stephanie: Positive I.D., *1006*
Rasp, Fritz: Diary of a Lost Girl, *730;* Spies (1928), *788;* Woman in the Moon (a.k.a. Girl in the Moon; By Rocket to the Moon), *805*
Raspberry, James: I Was a Zombie for the FBI, *1057*
Raspberry, Larry: I Was a Zombie for the FBI, *1057*
Rassam, Julien: Accompanist, The, *710*
Rassimov, Ivan: Cannibal, *820;* Man from Deep River, *80*
Rasulala, Thalmus: Adios Amigo, *1092;* Autobiography of Miss Jane Pittman, The, *452;* Blacula, *814;* Born American, *17;* Bucktown, *20;* Bulletproof, *21;* Friday Foster, *53;* Mom and Dad Save the World, *188;* Sophisticated Gents, The, *663*
Ratcliff, Sandy: Family Life, *514*
Rathbone, Basil: Above Suspicion, *1;* Adventures of Robin Hood, The, *2;* Adventures of Sherlock Holmes, The, *950;* Anna Karenina (1935), *449;* Bathing Beauty, *908;* Captain Blood,

22; Casanova's Big Night, *252;* Court Jester, The, *260;* David Copperfield, *496;* Dawn Patrol, The, *33;* Dressed to Kill (1946), *972;* Garden of Allah, The, *525;* Hillbillys in a Haunted House, *297;* Hound of the Baskervilles, The (1939), *983;* House of Fear, *984;* Last Days of Pompeii, The (1935), *569;* Last Hurrah, The, *569;* Magic Sword, The, *185;* Make a Wish, *586;* Mark of Zorro, The (1940), *82;* Pearl of Death, The, *1004;* Planet of Blood, *1070;* Pursuit to Algiers, *1008;* Romeo and Juliet (1936), *643;* Scarlet Claw, The, *1012;* Sherlock Holmes and the Secret Weapon, *1015;* Sherlock Holmes and the Spider Woman, *1015;* Sherlock Holmes and the Voice of Terror, *1015;* Sherlock Holmes Faces Death, *1015;* Sherlock Holmes in Washington, *1015;* Son of Frankenstein, *888;* Tale of Two Cities, A (1935), *676;* Tales of Terror, *892;* Terror by Night, *1023;* Tovaritch, *398;* Tower of London (1939), *897;* Voyage to the Prehistoric Planet, *1087;* We're No Angels (1955), *407;* Woman in Green, The, *1032*

Ratliff, Garette Patrick: Return to the Blue Lagoon, *639*

Ratner-Stauber, Tzvi: Family Prayers, *514*

Ratoff, Gregory: Abdulla the Great, *221;* Here Comes Trouble, *296;* I'm No Angel, *305;* Skyscraper Souls, *660;* What Price Hollywood?, *698*

Rattray, Heather: Across the Great Divide, *143;* Adventures of the Wilderness Family, *144;* Basket Case 2, *811;* Mountain Family Robinson, *189;* Sea Gypsies, The, *202;* Wilderness Family, Part 2, The, *217*

Ratzenberger, John: House II: The Second Story, *852;* Time Stalkers, *1084*

Rauch, Siegfried: Nous N'Irons Plus Au Bois, *772*

Raven, Mike: Crucible of Terror, *827;* Disciple of Death, *834*

Rawlinson, Herbert: Blake of Scotland Yard, *15;* Colt Comrades, *1105;* Jail Bait (1954), *68;* Superman—The Serial, *1081;* Two Weeks to Live, *402*

Ray, Aldo: And Hope to Die, *952;* Bog, *818;* Boxoffice, *467;* Centerfold Girls, *478;* Dark Sanity, *829;* Dead Heat on a Merry-Go-Round, *967;* Evils of the Night, *839;* God's Little Acre, *529;* Gone with the West, *1116;* Green Berets, The, *57;* Hollywood Cop, *63;* Inside Out (1975), *66;* Little Moon & Jud McGraw, *1128;* Men in War, *84;* Miss Sadie Thompson, *596;* Mongrel, *865;* Naked and the Dead, The, *88;* Pat and Mike, *355;* Psychic Killer, *877;* Shock'em Dead, *885;* Terror on Alcatraz, *1023;* We're No Angels (1955), *407*

Ray, Gene Anthony: Fame, *916*

Ray, James: Mass Appeal, *590;* She's Having a Baby, *377*

Ray, Johnnie: There's No Business Like Show Business, *944*

Ray, Leah: One in a Million, *350;* Thin Ice, *945*

Ray, Man: Avant Garde Program #2, *714*

Ray, Michel: Brave One, The, *152;* Tin Star, The, *1157*

Ray, Nicholas: Lightning Over Water, *575*

Ray, Sonny: Perils of Pauline, The (1933), *98*

Raye, Martha: Alice in Wonderland (1985), *145;* College Swing, *912;* Jumbo, *926;* Monsieur Verdoux, *336;* Pin-Up Girl, *935*

Raymond, Cyril: Brief Encounter (1945), *470*

Raymond, Gary: Jason and the Argonauts, *1060;* Playboy of the Western World, *358*

Raymond, Gene: Bride Walks Out, The, *245;* Ex-Lady, *512;* Hit the Deck, *923;* If I Had a Million, *304;* Mr. and Mrs. Smith, *333;* Plunder Road, *99;* Red Dust, *636;* Sadie McKee, *646;* Smilin' Through (1941), *940;* Transatlantic Merry-Go-Round, *946*

Raymond, Lee: She Freak, The, *885*

Raymond, Lina: Gypsy Warriors, The, *58*

Raymond, Martin: Living the Blues, *577*

Raymond, Paula: Beast From 20,000 Fathoms, The, *1038;* Blood of Dracula's Castle, *815;* Duchess of Idaho, *915;* Gun Riders, The, *1117*

Raymond, Richard: Rats, *878*

Raymond, Ruth: Bad Blood, *811;* Woman Obsessed, A, *1032*

Rea, Peggy: In Country, *550;* Love Field, *581;* Made in America, *325*

Rea, Stephen: Angie, *448;* Bad Behaviour, *231;* Crying Game, The, *492;* Danny Boy (1982), *495;* Doctor and the Devils, The, *835;* Loose Connections, *321*

Read, Barbara: Three Smart Girls, *945*

Read, Dolly: Beyond the Valley of the Dolls, *460*

Read, James: Initiation, The, *856;* Love Crimes, *993;* North and South, *608;* Poor Little Rich Girl: The Barbara Hutton Story, *624;* Remington Steele (TV series), *1010;* Web of Deceit, *1030*

Reagan, Nancy: Rockin' Ronnie, *369*

Reagan, Ron: Ron Reagan Is the President's Son, *370*

Reagan, Ronald: Bedtime for Bonzo, *233;* Boy Meets Girl, *244;* Cattle Queen of Montana, *1104;* Dark Victory, *495;* Desperate Journey, *500;* Hellcats of the Navy, *60;* Killers, The, *71;* King's Row, *565;* Knute Rockne—All American, *567;* Rockin' Ronnie, *369;* Santa Fe Trail, *1147;* Stand-Up Reagan, *385;* Tennessee's Partner, *1155;* This Is the Army, *945;* Winning Team, The, *704*

Reason, Rex: Creature Walks Among Us, The, *826;* This Island Earth, *1083*

Reason, Rhodes: Bronco (TV Series), *1101*

Reasoner, Harry: Wasn't That a Time!, *438*

Rebar, Alex: Incredible Melting Man, The, *1058*

Rebbot, Saddy: My Life to Live, *769*

Rebhorn, James: Blank Check, *151;* Carlito's Way, *23;* Guarding Tess, *291;* Scent of a Woman, *649;* Will, G. Gordon Liddy, *703*

Rebiere, Richard: Heavenly Bodies, *296*

Rector, Jeff: Street Soldiers, *121*

Redbone, Leon: Candy Mountain, *474*

Redd, Joyce: Ballad of a Gunfighter, *1096*

Redding, Juli: Mission in Morocco, *85*

Redding, Otis: Monterey Pop, *431*

Redding, Wilma: Pacific Inferno, *96*

Reddy, Helen: Airport 1975, *443;* Pete's Dragon, *195*

Rede, Nina Pens: Gertrude, *740*

Redeker, Quinn: Coast to Coast, *256;* Spider Baby, *889*

Redfern, Linda: I Will Fight No More Forever, *1122*

Redfield, Dennis: Dead and Buried, *830;* Pulse, *877*

Redfield, William: Connection, The (1961), *487;* Fantastic Voyage, *1050;* Hot Rock, The, *983;* I Married a Woman, *304;* Mr. Billion, *85;* Morituri, *87;* New Leaf, A, *343*

Redford, Robert: All the President's Men, *951;* Barefoot in the Park, *232;* Bridge Too Far, A, *19;* Brubaker, *471;* Butch Cassidy and the Sundance Kid, *1103;* Candidate, The, *474;* Chase, The (1966), *479;* Downhill Racer, *504;* Electric Horseman, The, *508;* Great Gatsby, The, *532;* Great Waldo Pepper, The, *57;* Havana, *537;* Hot Rock, The, *983;* Indecent Proposal, *551;* Inside Daisy Clover, *552;* Jeremiah Johnson, *1123;* Legal Eagles, *991;* Natural, The, *604;* Out of Africa, *616;* Sneakers, *1018;* Sting, The, *120;* Tell Them Willie Boy Is Here, *1155;* This Property Is Condemned, *682;* Three Days of the Condor, *1025;* Twilight Zone, The (TV Series), *1086;* Way We Were, The, *697*

Redgrave, Corin: Between Wars, *459;* Excalibur, *1050;* Four Weddings and a Funeral, *280*

Redgrave, Lynn: Antony and Cleopatra (1981), *450;* Big Bus, The, *238;* Everything You Always Wanted to Know About Sex but Were Afraid to Ask, *273;* Georgy Girl, *284;* Getting It Right, *285;* Happy Hooker, The, *293;* Long Live Your Death, *1130;* Midnight (1989), *996;* Morgan Stewart's Coming Home, *337;* Rehearsal for Murder, *1009;* Silent Mouse, *204;* Sooner or Later, *663;* Virgin Soldiers, The, *694;* Walking on Air, *215*

Redgrave, Michael: Browning Version, The, *471;* Captive Heart, *475;* Dam Busters, The, *31;* Dead of Night (1945), *830;* Dr. Jekyll and Mr. Hyde (1973), *914;* Goodbye, Mr. Chips (1969), *920;* Hill, The, *541;* Importance of Being Earnest, The, *305;* Lady Vanishes, The (1938), *990;* Mr. Arkadin (a.k.a. Confidential Report), *596;* Nicholas and Alexandra, *605;* 1984 (1955), *1068;* Sea Shall Not Have Them, The, *113;* Secret Beyond the Door, *650;* Shake Hands with the Devil, *114;* Stars

Look Down, The, *666;* Twinsanity, *1028;* Wreck of the Mary Deare, The, *141*
Redgrave, Vanessa: Agatha, *951;* Ballad of the Sad Cafe, The, *455;* Bear Island, *954;* Blow-Up, *957;* Bostonians, The, *467;* Camelot, *911;* Charge of the Light Brigade, The (1968), *24;* Consuming Passions, *259;* Devils, The, *500;* House of the Spirits, The, *545;* Howards End, *545;* Isadora (1969), *554;* Julia, *560;* Morgan, *337;* Mother's Boys, *998;* Murder on the Orient Express, *999;* Orpheus Descending, *615;* Out of Season, *616;* Playing for Time, *623;* Prick Up Your Ears, *626;* Seven-Per-Cent Solution, The, *1013;* Snow White and the Seven Dwarfs (1983), *205;* Steaming, *667;* They, *894;* Three Sovereigns for Sarah, *683;* Trojan Women, The, *688;* Wagner, *947;* Wetherby, *698;* Yanks, *707;* Young Catherine, *708*
Redman, Amanda: For Queen and Country, *519;* Richard's Things, *640*
Redmond, Liam: I See a Dark Stranger, *65*
Redmond, Siobhan: Look Back In Anger (1989), *579*
Redondo, Emiliano: Black Venus, *718*
Reeb, Larry: Truly Tasteless Jokes, *400*
Reed, Alan: Actors and Sin, *441;* Days of Glory, *33;* Seniors, The, *375*
Reed, Alyson: Chorus Line, A, *911;* Skin Deep, *380*
Reed, Donald: Man from Monterey, The, *1131*
Reed, Donna: Babes on Broadway, *907;* Benny Goodman Story, The, *458;* Caddy, The, *249;* From Here to Eternity (1953), *523;* Green Dolphin Street, *533;* Gun Fury, *1117;* Hangman's Knot, *1119;* Human Comedy, The, *546;* It's a Wonderful Life, *555;* Last Time I Saw Paris, The, *570;* Picture of Dorian Gray, The, *875;* Shadow of the Thin Man, *1014;* They Were Expendable, *127;* Trouble Along the Way, *688*
Reed, Hal: Doberman Gang, The, *40*
Reed, Jerry: Bat 21, *9;* Gator, *54;* High-Ballin', *61;* Hot Stuff, *301;* Smokey and the Bandit, *381;* Smokey and the Bandit II, *381;* Smokey and the Bandit III, *382;* Survivors, The, *389;* What Comes Around, *698*
Reed, Laura: Prime Time Murder, *100*
Reed, Lou: Faraway, So Close, *736;* Get Crazy, *284;* One Trick Pony, *934;* Velvet Underground, The: Velvet Redux—Live MCMXCIII, *437*
Reed, Marshall: Sundown Riders, *1153;* They Saved Hitler's Brain, *895*
Reed, Oliver: Adventures of Baron Münchausen, The, *1034;* Big Sleep, The (1978), *955;* Black Arrow (1984), *150;* Blood in the Streets, *15;* Brood, The, *819;* Burnt Offerings, *820;* Captive, *475;* Captive Rage, *23;* Castaway, *476;* Christopher Columbus (1985), *25;* Class of Miss MacMichael, The, *483;* Condorman, *159;* Curse of the Werewolf, The, *828;* Dante's Inferno, *495;* Devils, The, *500;* Dr. Heckyl and Mr. Hype, *266;* Four Musketeers, The, *52;* Ghost in Monte Carlo, A, *527;* Gor, *1054;* Great Scout and Cathouse Thursday, The, *1116;* Hired to Kill, *62;* House of Usher, The, *853;* Lion of the Desert, *77;* Misfit Brigade, The, *85;* Oliver, *933;* One Russian Summer, *613;* Prince and the Pauper, The (1978), *197;* Prisoner of Honor, *628;* Ransom, *1009;* Return of the Musketeers, *106;* Return to Lonesome Dove, *1143;* Sell-Out, The, *113;* Severed Ties, *885;* Spasms, *889;* Sting II, The, *120;* Ten Little Indians (1975), *1023;* That's Action, *127;* Three Musketeers, The (1973), *128;* Tommy, *946;* Tomorrow Never Comes, *686;* Treasure Island (1990), *214;* Venom, *900;* Women in Love, *706;* Z.P.G. (Zero Population Growth), *1091*
Reed, Pamela: Best of Times, The, *236;* Cadillac Man, *249;* Caroline?, *959;* Chattahoochee, *480;* Clan of the Cave Bear, *1041;* Goodbye People, The, *530;* Kindergarten Cop, *313;* Melvin and Howard, *331;* Passed Away, *355;* Rachel River, *632;* Right Stuff, The, *640;* Tanner '88, *391;* Woman with a Past, *705;* Young Doctors in Love, *415*
Reed, Paul: Car 54 Where Are You? (TV Series), *250*
Reed, Penelope: Amazons, *4*
Reed, Phillip: Klondike Annie, *314;* Last of the Mohicans, The (1936), *1126;* Madame X (1937), *584*
Reed, Ralph: Reform School Girl, *104*
Reed, Rex: Myra Breckenridge, *341*
Reed, Robert: Boy in the Plastic Bubble, The, *468;* Bud and Lou, *471;* Casino, *476;* Death of a Centerfold, *498;* Haunts of the Very Rich, *1055;* Pray for the Wildcats, *100;* Prime Target, *100;* Snatched, *117;* Star!, *941;* Very Brady Christmas, A, *215*
Reed, Susanne: Up from the Depths, *899*
Reed, Tracy: All the Marbles, *225;* Night Rhythms, *1001;* Running Scared (1986), *110*
Reed, Walter: Government Agents vs. Phantom Legion, *57;* Keystone Comedies, Vol. 5, *313;* Superman and the Mole Men, *1081*
Reems, Harry: Deadly Weapons, *498*
Rees, Angharad: Hands of the Ripper, *848*
Rees, Roger: If Looks Could Kill (1991), *66;* Mountains of the Moon, *87;* Robin Hood: Men in Tights, *369;* Stop! Or My Mom Will Shoot, *386*
Reese, Della: Harlem Nights, *59;* Kid Who Loved Christmas, The, *180;* Psychic Killer, *877*
Reese, Michelle: Night Stalker, The (1986), *870*
Reeve, Christopher: Anna Karenina (1985), *449;* Aviator, The, *452;* Bostonians, The, *467;* Death Dreams, *831;* Deathtrap, *969;* Great Escape II, The, *57;* Monsignor, *598;* Morning Glory (1992), *599;* Mortal Sins (1992), *997;* Noises Off, *346;* Remains of the Day, *637;* Rose and the Jackal, The, *644;* Sea Wolf, The (1993), *113;* Sleeping Beauty (1983), *205;* Somewhere in Time, *1077;* Street Smart, *670;* Superman, *1081;* Superman II, *1081;* Superman III, *1081;* Superman IV: The Quest for Peace, *1081;* Switching Channels, *390*
Reeves, Eve: Behind Locked Doors, *812*
Reeves, George: Bar 20, *1096;* Bugles in the Afternoon, *1102;* Colt Comrades, *1105;* Great Lover, The, *289;* Hoppy Serves a Writ, *1121;* Jungle Jim, *69;* Rancho Notorious, *1140;* Strawberry Blonde, The, *670;* Superman and the Mole Men, *1081;* TV's Best Adventures of Superman, *1085;* Westward Ho, the Wagons, *216*
Reeves, Keanu: Babes in Toyland (1986), *147;* Bill and Ted's Bogus Journey, *239;* Bill and Ted's Excellent Adventure, *239;* Bram Stoker's Dracula, *819;* Brotherhood of Justice, *471;* Dream to Believe, *504;* Even Cowgirls Get the Blues, *272;* I Love You to Death, *304;* Much Ado About Nothing, *338;* My Own Private Idaho, *602;* Night Before, The, *344;* Parenthood, *354;* Permanent Record, *621;* Point Break, *99;* Prince of Pennsylvania, *361;* River's Edge, *641;* Tune in Tomorrow, *400*
Reeves, Lisa: Chicken Chronicles, The, *254*
Reeves, Mathonwy: Child's Christmas in Wales, A, *158*
Reeves, Saskia: Antonia & Jane, *228;* Close My Eyes, *484*
Reeves, Scott: Edge of Honor, *43;* Friday the 13th, Part VIII: Jason Takes Manhattan, *844*
Reeves, Steve: Athena, *907;* Goliath and the Barbarians, *56;* Hercules (1959), *1056;* Hercules Unchained, *1056;* Jail Bait (1954), *68;* Last Days of Pompeii (1960), *75;* Morgan the Pirate, *86*
Reevis, Steve: Geronimo: An American Legend, *1115*
Regalbuto, Joe: Raw Deal, *103;* Six Weeks, *659;* Streethawk, *121;* Writer's Block, *1033*
Regan, Mary: Heart of the Stag, *538;* Midnight Dancer, *594;* Sylvia, *676*
Regan, Phil: Go Into Your Dance, *920;* Manhattan Merry-Go-Round, *930;* Sweet Adeline, *943*
Regehr, Duncan: Monster Squad, The, *866;* My Wicked, Wicked Ways, *602;* Primo Baby, *197*
Regent, Benoit: Blue (1993), *719*
Reggiani, Serge: Cat and Mouse, *722;* La Ronde, *754;* Le Doulos, *757;* Paris Blues, *618;* Vincent, François, Paul and the Others, *801*
Regina, Paul: Bounty Tracker, *18*
Regine: My New Partner, *770;* Robert et Robert, *782*
Reicher, Frank: Captain America (1944), *22;* Home in Oklahoma, *1121;* Jade Mask, The, *987;* King Kong (1933), *859;* Son of Kong, The, *888*
Reichmann, Wolfgang: Beethoven's Nephew, *457*

Reid, Beryl: Beast in the Cellar, The, *812;* Carry on Emmanuelle, *251;* Doctor and the Devils, The, *835;* Dr. Phibes Rises Again, *836;* Entertaining Mr. Sloane, *271;* Joseph Andrews, *311;* Killing of Sister George, The, *564;* Psychomania, *877*

Reid, Carl Benton: Athena, *907;* Indian Uprising, *1123;* Pressure Point, *626;* Stage to Tucson, *1152*

Reid, Christopher: Class Act, *256;* House Party, *923;* House Party 2, *923;* House Party 3, *923*

Reid, Elliott: Gentlemen Prefer Blondes, *284;* Thrill of It All, The, *396*

Reid, Fiona: Beethoven Lives Upstairs, *149*

Reid, Kate: Andromeda Strain, The, *1036;* Atlantic City, *452;* Circle of Two, *482;* Death of a Salesman, *498;* Deathship, *832;* Deceived, *969;* Fire with Fire, *517;* Heaven Help Us, *295;* Highpoint, *62;* Signs of Life, *657;* This Property Is Condemned, *682*

Reid, Lehua: Point of Impact, *99*

Reid, Tim: Dead-Bang, *33;* Fourth War, The, *52;* It (1991), *857;* You Must Remember This, *708*

Reid, Wallace: Roaring Road, The, *642*

Reilly, John C.: Casualties of War, *477;* Hoffa, *542;* Incredible Journey of Dr. Meg Laurel, The, *551;* Out on a Limb (1992), *352;* State of Grace, *666;* What's Eating Gilbert Grape?, *408*

Reilly, Robert: Frankenstein Meets the Space Monster, *842*

Reilly, Tom: Mirror Images II, *996*

Reineke, Gary: Why Shoot the Teacher?, *701*

Reiner, Carl: Best of Comic Relief, The, *235;* Dead Men Don't Wear Plaid, *262;* Fatal Instinct (1993), *274;* Gazebo, The, *283;* Generation, *283;* Gidget Goes Hawaiian, *286;* Guide for the Married Man, A, *291;* Pinocchio (1983), *195;* Russians Are Coming, the Russians Are Coming, The, *371;* Skokie, *660;* Spirit of '76, The, *384;* Summer School, *388;* 10 from Your Show of Shows, *392*

Reiner, Rob: All in the Family Twentieth Anniversary Special, *224;* Best of John Belushi, The, *235;* Billy Crystal: Don't Get Me Started, *239;* Enter Laughing, *271;* Postcards from the Edge, *360;* Richard Lewis—"I'm in Pain Concert", *367;* Sleepless in Seattle, *381;* Spirit of '76, The, *384;* This Is Spinal Tap, *394;* Thursday's Game, *683;* Where's Poppa?, *409*

Reiner, Tracy: League of Their Own, A, *571*

Reinhardt, Janis: Three Bullets for a Long Gun, *1156*

Reinhold, Judge: Baby on Board, *8;* Bank Robber, *232;* Beverly Hills Cop, *11;* Beverly Hills Cop II, *11;* Beverly Hills Cop 3, *11;* Black Magic (1992), *955;* Daddy's Dyin' and Who's Got the Will, *261;* Fast Times at Ridgemont High, *274;* Four Eyes and Six Guns, *1114;* Head Office, *294;* Near Misses, *342;* New Homeowner's Guide to Happiness, The, *343;* Off Beat, *348;* Over Her Dead Body, *352;* Promised a Miracle, *629;* Roadhouse 66, *107;* Running Scared (1980), *110;* Ruthless People, *371;* Soldier's Tale, A, *661;* Vice Versa, *404;* Zandalee, *709*

Reiniger, Scott: Dawn of the Dead, *830*

Reinking, Ann: All That Jazz, *906;* Micki & Maude, *331;* Movie Movie, *338*

Reiser, Paul: Aliens, *1035;* Crazy People, *260;* Cross My Heart (1987), *261;* Family Prayers, *514;* Marrying Man, The, *329;* Paul Reiser Out on a Whim, *355;* Sunset Limousine, *388*

Rekert, Winston: Agnes of God, *443;* Glory! Glory!, *287;* Heartaches, *538;* High Stakes (1986), *297;* Toby McTeague, *212*

Rekin, Dwayne: Cat, The, *157*

Remar, James: Band of the Hand, *9;* Blink, *956;* Confessions of a Hitman, *487;* Cotton Club, The, *29;* Deadlock, *1045;* Drugstore Cowboy, *505;* Fatal Charm, *976;* Fatal Instinct (1993), *274;* 48 Hrs., *279;* Indecency, *986;* Quiet Cool, *102;* Rent-a-Cop, *105;* Silence Like Glass, *657;* Strangers, *669;* Tigress, The, *130;* Warriors, The (1979), *137;* White Fang, *217;* Windwalker, *1165*

Remarque, Erich Maria: Time to Love and a Time to Die, A, *684*

Remay, Albert: Children of Paradise, The, *723*

Remberg, Erika: Cave of the Living Dead, *822;* Circus of Horrors, *824*

Remick, Lee: Anatomy of a Murder, *952;* Baby the Rain Must Fall, *453;* Blue Knight, The (1973), *465;* Bridge to Silence, *470;* Competition, The, *487;* Days of Wine and Roses, *496;* Detective, The (1968), *500;* Europeans, The, *511;* Experiment in Terror, *974;* Face in the Crowd, A, *512;* Hallelujah Trail, The, *1118;* Hennessy, *982;* Hustling, *547;* I Do! I Do!, *924;* Ike: The War Years, *548;* Jesse, *557;* Long Hot Summer, The (1958), *578;* Loot, *321;* Medusa Touch, The, *864;* Mistral's Daughter, *597;* No Way to Treat a Lady, *1002;* Omen, The, *872;* QB VII, *631;* Snow Queen, *205;* Sometimes a Great Notion, *662;* Telefon, *1023;* Torn Between Two Lovers, *686;* Tribute, *688;* Wheeler Dealers, The, *409*

Remsen, Bert: Borderline, *17;* Carny, *475;* Code of Silence, *27;* Daddy's Dyin' and Who's Got the Will, *261;* Dead Ringer, *967;* Hobson's Choice (1983), *175;* Jack the Bear, *556;* Jezebel's Kiss, *987;* Ladykiller, *990;* Lies, *574;* Lookin' to Get Out, *321;* M.A.D.D.: Mothers Against Drunk Driving, *583;* Only the Lonely, *350;* Payback, *98;* Sting II, The, *120;* Thieves Like Us, *681*

Remsen, Kerry: Appointment with Fear, *6*

Remy, Albert: 400 Blows, The, *738*

Renaldo, Duncan: Border Patrol, *1100;* Cisco Kid (TV Series), *1105;* Covered Wagon Days, *1106;* Fighting Seabees, The, *48;* Heroes of the Saddle, *1120;* Kansas Terrors, *1124;* King of the Texas Rangers, *1125;* Manhunt in the African Jungle (Secret Service in Darkest Africa), *81;* Painted Stallion, The, *1138;* Perils of the Darkest Jungle, *98;* Rocky Mountain Rangers, *1145;* San Antonio Kid, *1147;* South of the Border, *1151;* South of the Rio Grande, *1151;* Zorro Rides Again, *1166*

Renan, Sergio: Debajo del Mundo (Under Earth), *729*

Renant, Simone: Les Liaisons Dangereuses, *759;* That Man From Rio, *793*

Renaud, Madeleine: Stormy Waters, *789*

Renavent, Georges: East of Borneo, *43*

Renay, Liz: Desperate Living, *264;* Thrill Killers, The, *895*

Renderer, Scott: Poison, *624*

Rendorf, Sherry: Slaughterhouse, *887*

Rennie, James: Illicit, *549*

Rennie, Michael: Battle of El Alamein, The, *10;* Day the Earth Stood Still, The, *1044;* Demetrius and the Gladiators, *499;* Desirée, *500;* Devil's Brigade, The, *37;* Five Fingers, *977;* Hondo and the Apaches, *1121;* Hotel, *544;* Mambo, *586;* Omar Khayyam, *93;* Phone Call from a Stranger, *622;* Ride Beyond Vengeance, *1143;* Robe, The, *642;* Seven Cities of Gold, *653;* Ships with Wings, *115;* Soldier of Fortune, *118;* Third Man on the Mountain, *210;* Trio, *688;* Wicked Lady, The (1945), *701*

Reno, Ginetta: Leolo, *759*

Reno, Jean: Big Blue, The, *12;* Final Combat, The, *48*

Reno, Kelly: Black Stallion, The, *151;* Black Stallion Returns, The, *151;* Brady's Escape, *18*

Renoir, Jean: La Bête Humaine, *753*

Renoir, Pierre: La Marseillaise, *754;* Madame Bovary (1934), *763*

Renoir, Sophie: Boyfriends and Girlfriends, *720*

Rentschler, Mickey: Radio Patrol, *102*

Renucci, Robin: King's Whore, The, *566*

Renvall, Johan: Dance, *913*

Renzi, Eva: Bird with the Crystal Plumage, The, *955;* Funeral in Berlin, *979*

Renzi, Maggie: City of Hope, *483;* Passion Fish, *619;* Return of the Secaucus 7, *366*

Resines, Antonio: Skyline, *380*

Resnick, Judith: Carnival of Blood, *821*

Resnik, Robert: Sloane, *117*

Ressel, Frank: Have a Nice Funeral, *1119*

Rettig, Tommy: At Gunpoint, *1095;* Five Thousand Fingers of Dr. T, The, *167;* River of No Return, *1145*

Reubens, Paul: Pandemonium, *353*

Revere, Anne: Birch Interval, The, *150;* Body and Soul (1947), *466;* Forever Amber, *520;* Gentlemen's Agreement, *526;* Howards of Virginia, The, *545;* Meanest Man in the World, The, *330;* National Velvet, *190;* Place in the Sun, A, *622;* Song of Bernadette, The, *662;* Thin Man Goes Home, The, *1024*

Revier, Dorothy: Thrill Hunter, *1157*

Revill, Clive: Avanti!, *230;* Cannon Movie Tales: The Emperor's New Clothes, *155;* George Washington, *526;* Ghost in the Noonday Sun, *285;* Legend of Hell House, The, *860;* Matilda, *330;* One of Our Dinosaurs Is Missing, *192;* Private Life of Sherlock Holmes, The, *1008;* Rumpelstiltskin (1987), *200*

Revueltas, Rosaura: Salt of the Earth, *647*

Rey, Alejandro: Fun in Acapulco, *918;* High Velocity, *62;* Ninth Configuration, The, *608;* Rita Hayworth: The Love Goddess, *641*

Rey, Fernando: Antony and Cleopatra (1973), *450;* Black Arrow (1984), *150;* Discreet Charm of the Bourgeoisie, The, *730;* 1492: The Conquest of Paradise, *52;* French Connection, The, *53;* French Connection II, The, *53;* High Crime, *61;* Hit, The, *63;* Immortal Story, *549;* La Grande Bourgeoise, *754;* Last Days of Pompeii (1960), *75;* Light at the End of the World, The, *77;* Monsignor, *598;* Moon Over Parador, *336;* Naked Tango, *603;* Pantaloons, *775;* Quintet, *1073;* Rustler's Rhapsody, *371;* Saving Grace, *373;* Seven Beauties, *785;* Star Knight, *1078;* That Obscure Object of Desire, *793;* Tristana, *797;* Tunnel, The, *689;* Villa Rides, *1161;* Viridiana, *801*

Rey, Mony: Mademoiselle, *585*

Reyes, Jr., Ernie: Red Sonja, *104;* Surf Ninjas, *208;* Teenage Mutant Ninja Turtles II: The Secret of the Ooze, *209*

Reynal, Madeleine: Dr. Caligari, *835*

Reynaud, Janine: Castle of the Creeping Flesh, *822*

Reyne, James: Return to Eden, *639*

Reynolds, Adeline de Walt: Iceland, *924*

Reynolds, Burt: Armored Command, *6;* Best Friends, *235;* Best Little Whorehouse in Texas, The, *908;* Blade Rider, *1099;* Breaking In, *245;* Cannonball Run, *250;* Cannonball Run II, *250;* City Heat, *255;* Cop and a Half, *160;* Deliverance, *36;* End, The, *271;* Everything You Always Wanted to Know About Sex but Were Afraid to Ask, *273;* Fuzz, *282;* Gator, *54;* Gunsmoke (TV Series), *1118;* Heat (1987), *60;* Hooper, *300;* Hustle, *65;* Longest Yard, The, *78;* Malone, *80;* Man from Left Field, The, *586;* Man Who Loved Cat Dancing, The, *1132;* Man Who Loved Women, The (1983), *328;* Modern Love, *335;* 100 Rifles, *1137;* Operation C.I.A., *95;* Paternity, *355;* Physical Evidence, *1006;* Rent-a-Cop, *105;* Rough Cut, *1011;* Semi-Tough, *375;* Shamus, *1014;* Shark! (a.k.a. Maneaters!), *114;* Sharky's Machine, *115;* Silent Movie, *379;* Smokey and the Bandit, *381;* Smokey and the Bandit II, *381;* Starting Over, *385;* Stick, *120;* Stroker Ace, *387;* Switching Channels, *390;* White Lightning, *139*

Reynolds, Debbie: Affairs of Dobie Gillis, The, *906;* Athena, *907;* Bundle of Joy, *247;* Catered Affair, The, *477;* Detective Sadie and Son, *37;* Gazebo, The, *283;* Give a Girl a Break, *919;* Heaven and Earth (1993), *539;* Hit the Deck, *923;* How the West Was Won, *1122;* I Love Melvin, *924;* It Started With a Kiss, *308;* Mating Game, The, *330;* Mr. Imperium, *931;* Singin' in the Rain, *940;* Singing Nun, The, *204;* Susan Slept Here, *389;* Tammy and the Bachelor, *677;* Tender Trap, The, *392;* That's Entertainment! III, *436;* That's Singing: The Best of Broadway, *944;* This Happy Feeling, *394;* Three Little Words, *945;* Two Weeks with Love, *947;* Unsinkable Molly Brown, The, *947;* What's the Matter with Helen?, *902*

Reynolds, Gene: Andy Hardy's Private Secretary, *227;* Bridges at Toko-Ri, The, *19;* Diane, *500;* Jungle Patrol, *69;* Mortal Storm, The, *600;* Of Human Hearts, *610;* Tuttles of Tahiti, The, *400*

Reynolds, Greg: Deadly Weapons, *498*

Reynolds, Hayley: Lifeforce Experiment, The, *1063*

Reynolds, Helene: Wintertime, *947*

Reynolds, Jay: Reincarnate, The, *879*

Reynolds, Joyce: Adventures of Mark Twain, The (1944), *442*

Reynolds, Marjorie: Doomed to Die, *41;* Fatal Hour, The, *46;* His Kind of Woman, *62;* Holiday Inn, *923;* Mr. Wong in Chinatown, *997;* Monsieur Beaucaire, *336;* Robin Hood of the Pecos, *1145;* Six-Shootin' Sheriff, *1150;* That Midnight Kiss, *944;* Time of Their Lives, The, *396*

Reynolds, Michael J.: Lifeforce Experiment, The, *1063;* Trial & Error, *1027*

Reynolds, Patrick: Eliminators, The, *1048*

Reynolds, Paul: Angelic Conversation, *448;* Let Him Have It, *573*

Reynolds, Quentin: Golden Earrings, *56*

Reynolds, Simon: Gate II, *845*

Reynolds, Vera: Monster Walks, The, *866;* Road to Yesterday, The, *641*

Reynolds, William: Away all Boats, *8;* Land Unknown, The, *1061;* Son of Ali Baba, *118*

Rhames, Ving: Dave, *262;* Homicide, *983;* Long Walk Home, The, *579;* Patty Hearst, *620;* People Under the Stairs, The, *873;* Rising Son, *641;* Saint of Fort Washington, The, *646*

Rhee, Phillip: Best of the Best, *11;* Best of the Best 2, *11;* Silent Assassins, *116*

Rhoades, Barbara: Shakiest Gun in the West, The, *377*

Rhoads, Cheryl: Mother Goose Video Treasury Vol. I–IV, *189*

Rhodes, Cynthia: Curse of the Crystal Eye, *31;* Dirty Dancing, *914;* Runaway, *1075;* Staying Alive, *942*

Rhodes, Donnelly: After the Promise, *442;* Dirty Work, *970;* Kurt Vonnegut's Monkey House, *1061;* Showdown at Williams Creek, *1149*

Rhodes, Earl: Sailor Who Fell from Grace with the Sea, The, *646*

Rhodes, Erik: Charlie Chan in Paris, *961;* Gay Divorcée, The, *918;* One Rainy Afternoon, *350*

Rhodes, Hari: Detroit 9000 (Detroit Heat), *37;* Dream for Christmas, A, *163;* Woman Called Moses, A, *705*

Rhodes, Marjorie: Decameron Nights, *263*

Rhue, Madlyn: Majority of One, A, *326*

Rhys, Paul: Becoming Colette, *457;* Chaplin, *479;* Vincent and Theo, *694*

Rhys-Davies, John: Best Revenge, *11;* Canvas, *959;* Cyborg Cop, *1043;* Double-O Kid, The, *41;* Firewalker, *49;* Great Expectations (1989), *171;* In the Shadow of Kilimanjaro, *855;* Indiana Jones and the Last Crusade, *1058;* Journey of Honor, *69;* King Solomon's Mines (1985), *73;* Living Daylights, The, *78;* Lost World, The (1992), *79;* Nativity, The, *604;* Raiders of the Lost Ark, *1073;* Rebel Storm, *1074;* Return to the Lost World, *1074;* Robot in the Family, *200;* Sadat, *646;* Sahara (1984), *110;* Seventh Coin, The, *203;* Sunset Grill, *1021;* Tusks, *133;* Unnamable II, The, *899*

Rialson, Candice: Hollywood Boulevard, *299;* Summer School Teachers, *673*

Ribeiro, Alfonso: Infested, *856*

Ribon, Diego: Evil Clutch, *839*

Ribovska, Malka: Shameless Old Lady, The, *785*

Ricci, Christina: Addams Family, The, *222;* Addams Family Values, *222;* Cemetery Club, The, *478;* Mermaids, *331*

Ricci, Rona De: Pit and the Pendulum, The (1991), *875*

Ricciarelli, Katia: Otello, *934*

Rice, Florence: Double Wedding, *268;* Navy Blue and Gold, *342;* Riding on Air, *368*

Rice, Frank: Fiddlin' Buckaroo, *1112;* Fighting Ranger, The, *1113;* Somewhere in Sonora, *1151*

Rice, Jeffrey D.: Warlords of Hell, *137*

Rice, Joan: His Majesty O'Keefe, *62;* Story of Robin Hood, The, *207*

Rice, Joel S.: Final Exam, *841*

Rice-Davies, Mandy: Absolute Beginners, *906;* Seven Magnificent Gladiators, The, *113*

Rich, Adam: Devil and Max Devlin, The, *264*

Rich, Buddy: Ship Ahoy, *939*
Rich, Christopher: Prisoners of Inertia, *361*
Rich, Claude: Bride Wore Black, The, *959;* Elusive Corporal, The, *734;* Le Crabe Tambour, *757*
Rich, Irene: Angel and the Badman, *1093;* Beau Brummell (1924), *457;* Bill Fields and Will Rogers, *239;* Champ, The (1931), *478;* Lady in Question, *568;* Lady Windermere's Fan, *568;* Mortal Storm, The, *600*
Rich, Matty: Straight out of Brooklyn, *668*
Rich, Ron: Fortune Cookie, The, *279*
Richard, Fir-mine: Mama, There's a Man in Your Bed, *764*
Richard, Jean: Candide, *722*
Richard, Little: Sunset Heat, *122*
Richard, Pierre: Daydreamer, The (Le Distrait), *728;* Le Chêvre (The Goat), *757;* Les Comperes, *759;* Return of the Tall Blond Man with One Black Shoe, The, *781;* Tall Blond Man with One Black Shoe, The, *792;* Too Shy to Try, *796*
Richards, Addison: Bad Lands, *1095;* G-Men, *54;* Our Daily Bread, *615;* Rustlers, The, *1146*
Richards, Ann: Badman's Territory, *1096;* Sorry, Wrong Number (1948), *1019*
Richards, Ariana: Grand Tour: Disaster in Time, *1054;* Jurassic Park, *1061;* Switched at Birth, *675*
Richards, Beah: As Summers Die, *451;* Dream for Christmas, A, *163;* Guess Who's Coming to Dinner, *534;* Purlie Victorious, *363*
Richards, Evan: Down and Out in Beverly Hills, *268;* Dream Machine, *269;* Society, *888*
Richards, Gordon: White Pongo (a.k.a. Blond Gorilla), *902*
Richards, Jeff: Above and Beyond, *1;* Goldy, The Last of the Golden Bears, *171;* It's a Dog's Life, *177;* Opposite Sex, The, *934*
Richards, Keith: Chuck Berry Hail! Hail! Rock 'n' Roll, *421*
Richards, Kim: Escape to Witch Mountain, *165;* Meatballs Part II, *330;* Return from Witch Mountain, *199;* Tuff Turf, *689*
Richards, Lisa: Eating, *507;* Prince of Central Park, The, *197;* Rolling Thunder, *108*
Richards, Michael: Coneheads, *258;* Problem Child, *362;* Ratings Game, The, *364;* So I Married an Axe Murderer, *382;* Transylvania 6-5000, *399;* UHF, *402;* Young Doctors in Love, *415*
Richards, Paul: Kiss Daddy Good Night, *989*
Richards, Simon: Home for Christmas, *542*
Richardson, Ian: Brazil, *245;* Cry Freedom, *492;* Foreign Affairs, *520;* Hound of the Baskervilles, The (1983), *984;* M. Butterfly, *583;* Marat/Sade, *588;* Midsummer Night's Dream, A (1968), *332;* Monsignor Quixote, *599;* Sign of Four, The, *1016;* Year of the Comet, *415*
Richardson, Jay: Original Intent, *614;* Sins of Desire, *1017*
Richardson, Joely: Drowning by Numbers, *505;* I'll Do Anything, *305;* Shining Through, *656;* Wetherby, *698*
Richardson, John: Black Sunday (1961), *814;* Eyeball, *840;* Torso, *896*
Richardson, Latanya: Nightman, The, *1001*
Richardson, Lee: Amazing Grace and Chuck, *445;* Believers, The, *812;* Fly II, The, *842;* I Am the Cheese, *547;* Stranger Among Us, A, *1020;* Sweet Lorraine, *674;* Tiger Warsaw, *683*
Richardson, Miranda: Bachelor, The, *453;* Crying Game, The, *492;* Damage, *493;* Dance with a Stranger, *494;* Empire of the Sun, *509;* Enchanted April, *271;* Transmutations, *897;* Twisted Obsession, *690*
Richardson, Natasha: Comfort of Strangers, The, *963;* Fat Man and Little Boy, *515;* Favor, the Watch and the Very Big Fish, The, *275;* Gothic, *847;* Handmaid's Tale, The, *1055;* Hostages, *544;* Month in the Country, A, *599;* Past Midnight, *619;* Patty Hearst, *620;* Zelda, *709*
Richardson, Paul: On the Line, *94*
Richardson, Peter: Pope Must Diet, The, *360;* Supergrass, The, *388*
Richardson, Ralph: Alice's Adventures in Wonderland, *145;* Anna Karenina (1947), *449;* Battle of Britain, *9;* Citadel, The, *482;* Clouds Over Europe, *484;* Divorce of Lady X, The, *265;* Doll's House, A (1989), *503;* Dragonslayer, *1048;* Exodus, *512;* Fallen Idol, The, *513;* Four Feathers, The (1939), *52;* Ghoul, The (1933), *846;* Greystoke: The Legend of Tarzan, Lord of the Apes, *58;* Heiress, The, *539;* Invitation to the Wedding, *307;* Java Head, *557;* Khartoum, *70;* Lady Caroline Lamb, *567;* Long Day's Journey into Night (1962), *578;* Looking Glass War, The, *993;* Man in the Iron Mask, The (1977), *81;* Man Who Could Work Miracles, The, *1064;* O Lucky Man!, *610;* Richard III, *640;* Rollerball, *1075;* Tales from the Crypt, *892;* Things to Come, *1083;* Thunder in the City, *683;* Time Bandits, *1084;* Wagner, *947;* Who Slew Auntie Roo?, *903;* Witness for the Prosecution (1982), *1032;* Wrong Box, The, *414*
Richardson, Salli: How U Like Me Now, *303;* Posse (1993), *1139*
Richardson, Sy: Nocturna, *346;* Repo Man, *366;* Straight to Hell, *1153;* Walker, *695*
Richert, Carole: Tous les Matins du Monde, *796*
Richert, William: My Own Private Idaho, *602*
Richman, Peter Mark: Black Orchid, The, *463;* Dempsey, *499;* Friday the 13th, Part VIII: Jason Takes Manhattan, *844;* Yuma, *1166*
Richmond, Adrianne: Deadly Spygames, *35*
Richmond, Branscombe: Jericho Fever, *68*
Richmond, Kane: Adventures of Rex and Rinty, *1092;* Lost City, The, *1063;* Murder Over New York, *999;* Spy Smasher, *119*
Richmond, Warner: Lost Jungle, The, *79;* New Frontier, *1136;* Tol'able David, *685*
Richter, Andy: Cabin Boy, *248*
Richter, Deborah: Cyborg, *1043*
Richter, Jason James: Cops and Robbersons, *259;* Free Willy, *168*
Richter, Paul: Kriemhilde's Revenge, *752;* Siegfried, *786*
Richwine, Maria: Sex Crimes, *114*
Rickles, Don: Beach Blanket Bingo, *908;* Bikini Beach, *909;* Don Rickles: Buy This Tape You Hockey Puck, *267;* Enter Laughing, *271;* For the Love of It, *279;* Innocent Blood, *856;* Keaton's Cop, *70;* Kelly's Heroes, *70;* Muscle Beach Party, *338;* Run Silent, Run Deep, *109;* Two Top Bananas, *402;* X (The Man with the X-Ray Eyes), *1090*
Rickman, Alan: Bob Roberts, *243;* Close My Eyes, *484;* Closet Land, *962;* Die Hard, *38;* Fallen Angels, *513;* January Man, The, *987;* Quigley Down Under, *1140;* Robin Hood: Prince of Thieves, *108;* Truly, Madly, Deeply, *689*
Ricossa, Maria: Dead Man Out, *497*
Riders of the Purple Sage: Far Frontier, *1112*
Ridgely, John: Air Force, *3;* Man I Love, The, *586*
Ridgely, Robert: Philadelphia, *621;* Who Am I This Time?, *410*
Ridges, Stanley: Lady Is Willing, The, *315;* Mad Miss Manton, The, *325;* Master Race, The, *590;* Mr. Ace, *85;* Possessed (1947), *625;* Scoundrel, The, *374;* Sea Wolf, The (1941), *113;* Winterset, *704*
Riebauer, Harry: Mad Executioners, The, *994*
Riegert, Peter: Americathon, *226;* Animal House, *227;* Barbarians at the Gate, *455;* Chilly Scenes of Winter, *481;* Crossing Delancey, *491;* Ellis Island, *508;* Gypsy (1993), *921;* Local Hero, *320;* Man in Love, A, *587;* News at Eleven, *605;* Oscar (1991), *351;* Passed Away, *355;* Runestone, *882;* Shock to the System, A, *1015;* Stranger, The (1986), *1020;* Utz, *693*
Riehle, Richard: Dangerous Woman, A, *494;* Free Willy, *168;* Lightning Jack, *1128*
Riffon, Marc: White Wolves: A Cry in the Wild II, *139*
Rifkin, Ron: Manhattan Murder Mystery, *328;* Silent Running, *1076;* Sunshine Boys, The, *388*
Riga, Michelle: Birthday Boy, The, *240*
Rigaud, George: Quatorze Juliet, *779*
Rigby, Cathy: Challenge of a Lifetime, *478;* Great Wallendas, The, *533*

Rigby, Edward: Salute John Citizen!, *647;* Stars Look Down, The, *666;* Young and Innocent, *1033*
Rigby, Terrence: Homecoming, The (1973), *543;* Sign of Four, The, *1016*
Rigg, Diana: Avengers, The (TV Series), *7;* Bleak House, *463;* Cannon Movie Tales: Snow White, *155;* Evil under the Sun, *973;* Great Muppet Caper, The, *171;* Hospital, The, *301;* Julius Caesar (1970), *561;* King Lear (1984), *564;* Little Night Music, A, *928;* Midsummer Night's Dream, A (1968), *332;* On Her Majesty's Secret Service, *94;* Running Delilah, *110;* Theatre of Blood, *894;* Witness for the Prosecution (1982), *1032;* Worst Witch, The, *219*
Rigg, Rebecca: Efficiency Expert, The, *508;* Fortress (1985), *520;* Hunting, *546*
Rigzin, Tseshang: Horse Thief, The, *745*
Rijn, Brad: Perfect Strangers, *1005*
Riker, Robin: Alligator, *808;* Body Chemistry 2: Voice of a Stranger, *957;* Stepmonster, *1080*
Riley, Bridget "Baby Doll": Triple Impact, *132*
Riley, Elaine: Borrowed Trouble, *1100;* Devil's Playground, *1109;* Hills of Utah, The, *1120;* Rider from Tucson, *1143;* Sinister Journey, *1150;* Strange Gamble, *1153*
Riley, Jack: Attack of the Killer Tomatoes, *229;* Night Patrol, *344*
Riley, Jeannine: Comic, The (1969), *486;* Electra Glide in Blue, *43*
Riley, John: Greenstone, The, *172*
Riley, Larry: Dead Solid Perfect, *497*
Riley, Michael: Perfectly Normal, *356;* To Catch a Killer, *1025*
Rilla, Walter: Adventures of Tartu, *2;* Days of Wrath, *1107;* Gamma People, The, *1054*
Rin Tin Tin: Lone Defender, The, *78*
Rin Tin Tin Jr.: Adventures of Rex and Rinty, *1092;* Skull and Crown, *1017*
Rinaldi, Gerard: For Better and for Worse, *279*
Ringwald, Molly: Betsy's Wedding, *236;* Breakfast Club, The, *245;* Face the Music, *273;* For Keeps, *519;* Fresh Horses, *522;* P.K. & the Kid, *617;* Packin' It In, *193;* Pick-Up Artist, The, *357;* Pretty in Pink, *626;* Sixteen Candles, *380;* Spacehunter: Adventures in the Forbidden Zone, *1078;* Strike It Rich, *387;* Tempest (1982), *678;* Women & Men: Stories of Seduction, *706*
Rinn, Brad: Smithereens, *661*
Rintoul, David: Pride and Prejudice (1985), *626*
Rio, Nicole: Visitants, The, *1087;* Zero Boys, The, *904*
Riordan, Marjorie: Pursuit to Algiers, *1008*
Ripper, Michael: Quatermass and the Pit, *1072*
Rippioh, Frank: Taxi Zum Klo (Taxi to the Toilet), *793*
Rippy, Leon: Eye of the Storm, *974*
Risdon, Elisabeth: Crime and Punishment (1935), *490;* Roll on Texas Moon, *1145*
Ristovski, Lazar: Tito and Me, *795*
Ritchard, Cyril: Blackmail (1929), *956;* Half a Sixpence, *921;* Hans Brinker, *173;* Peter Pan (1960), *194*
Ritchie, Clint: Against a Crooked Sky, *1092*
Ritchie, June: Kind of Loving, A, *564*
Ritt, Martin: Slugger's Wife, The, *381*
Ritter, Brent: Curse of the Blue Lights, *828*
Ritter, John: Americathon, *226;* Barefoot Executive, The, *148;* Comeback Kid, The, *486;* Hero at Large, *296;* In Love with an Older Woman, *550;* It (1991), *857;* Last Fling, The, *315;* Noises Off, *346;* Other, The, *873;* Pray TV (1982), *626;* Prison for Children, *628;* Problem Child, *362;* Problem Child 2, *362;* Real Men, *365;* Skin Deep, *380;* Smoky Mountain Christmas, *205;* Stay Tuned, *385;* Sunset Limousine, *388;* They All Laughed, *393;* Tricks of the Trade, *399;* Unnatural Causes, *692;* Wholly Moses!, *410*
Ritter, Kristin: Student Bodies, *891*
Ritter, Tex: Arizona Days, *1094;* Deep in the Heart of Texas, *1108;* Enemy of the Law, *1111;* Lone Star Trail, *1129;* Mystery of the Hooded Horsemen, *1135;* Riders of the Rockies, *1144;* Sing, Cowboy, Sing, *1150;* Song of the Gringo, *1151;* Take Me Back to Oklahoma, *1154;* Three in the Saddle, *1156;* Trouble in Texas, *1159*
Ritter, Thelma: As Young as You Feel, *229;* Bird Man of Alcatraz, *462;* Boeing, Boeing, *243;* Daddy Long Legs, *913;* Farmer Takes a Wife, The, *916;* Hole in the Head, A, *298;* Incident, The (1967), *551;* Misfits, The, *595;* New Kind of Love, A, *343;* Pickup on South Street, *1006;* Pillow Talk, *357;* Rear Window, *1009*
Ritz Brothers, The: Goldwyn Follies, The, *920;* Gorilla, The, *289;* One in a Million, *350;* Three Musketeers, The (1939), *396*
Ritz, Harry: Silent Movie, *379*
Riva, Emmanuelle: Eyes, the Mouth, The, *735;* Hiroshima, Mon Amour, *744*
Rivas, Carlos: They Saved Hitler's Brain, *895*
Rivera, Chita: Mayflower Madam, *591;* Sweet Charity, *943*
Rivera, Kirk: Body Moves, *466*
Rivero, Jorge: Counterforce, *30;* Day of the Assassin, *33;* Fist Fighter, *49;* Priest of Love, *627;* Rio Lobo, *1145;* Target Eagle, *125*
Rivers, Joan: Muppets Take Manhattan, The, *189;* Swimmer, The, *675*
Riviere, George: Castle of Blood, *821;* Virgin of Nuremberg, *901*
Riviere, Marie: Aviator's Wife, The, *714;* Summer, *791*
Rizzo, Gianni: Mission Stardust, *1066*
Rjin, Brad: Special Effects, *889*
Roach, Rickey: Black Devil Doll from Hell, *814*
Roanne, André: Diary of a Lost Girl, *730*
Roarke, Adam: Dirty Mary, Crazy Larry, *39;* Four Deuces, The, *52;* Hell's Angels on Wheels, *60;* Losers, The, *79;* Psych-Out, *630;* Stunt Man, The, *671;* Trespasses, *687;* Women of the Prehistoric Planet, *1090*
Roarke, John: Mutant on the Bounty, *338*
Robards Jr., Jason: Adventures of Huck Finn, The (1993), *143;* All the President's Men, *951;* Any Wednesday, *228;* Ballad of Cable Hogue, The, *1096;* Big Hand for the Little Lady, A, *1098;* Black Rainbow, *955;* Boy and His Dog, A, *1040;* Breaking Home Ties, *469;* Bright Lights, Big City, *470;* Burden of Dreams, *420;* Cabo Blanco, *21;* Chernobyl: The Final Warning, *480;* Christmas to Remember, A, *482;* Christmas Wife, The, *482;* Comes a Horseman, *1105;* Day After, The, *1044;* Dream a Little Dream, *269;* Fools, *518;* Good Mother, The, *530;* Hurricane (1979), *65;* Inconvenient Woman, An, *551;* Isadora (1969), *554;* Johnny Got His Gun, *559;* Julia, *560;* Julius Caesar (1970), *561;* Laguna Heat, *990;* Legend of the Lone Ranger, The, *1128;* Long Day's Journey into Night (1962), *578;* Long Hot Summer, The (1985), *578;* Max Dugan Returns, *591;* Melvin and Howard, *331;* Mr. Sycamore, *334;* Murders in the Rue Morgue (1971), *867;* Night They Raided Minsky's, The, *345;* Once Upon a Time in the West, *1137;* Paper, The, *617;* Parenthood, *354;* Pat Garrett and Billy the Kid, *1138;* Philadelphia, *621;* Quick Change, *363;* Raise the Titanic, *103;* Reunion, *639;* St. Valentine's Day Massacre, The, *111;* Sakharov, *647;* Something Wicked This Way Comes, *1077;* Square Dance, *665;* Thousand Clowns, A, *395;* Tora! Tora! Tora!, *131;* You Can't Take it with You (1984), *415*
Robards Sr., Jason: Abraham Lincoln, *440;* Bedlam, *812;* Broadway Bill, *470;* Fighting Marines, The, *48;* Isle of the Dead, *857;* Mademoiselle Fifi, *585;* Miracle Rider, The, *1134;* Rimfire, *1144;* Two-Reelers: Comedy Classics #2, *402*
Robards, Sam: Fandango, *274;* Not Quite Paradise, *347;* Pancho Barnes, *617*
Robay, Terrance: Let It Rock, *573*
Robbins, Brian: C.H.U.D. II (Bud the C.H.U.D.), *820*
Robbins, Christmas: Demon Lover, The, *832*
Robbins, Marty: Ballad of a Gunfighter, *1096*
Robbins, Tim: Bob Roberts, *243;* Bull Durham, *247;* Cadillac Man, *249;* Erik the Viking, *1049;* Five Corners, *517;* Howard the Duck, *1057;* Hudsucker Proxy, The, *303;* Jacob's Ladder, *1060;* Jungle Fever, *561;* Miss Firecracker, *333;* Player, The, *358;* Short Cuts, *657;* Tapeheads, *391*

Rober, Richard: Port of New York, *624*
Roberson, Ken: Yellow Hair and the Fortress of Gold, *1165*
Robert Mitchell Boys Choir: Blondie in Society, *241*
Roberts, Allene: Knock on Any Door, *566;* Red House, The, *1009;* Union Station, *1029*
Roberts, Arthur: Deadly Vengeance, *35;* Illegal Entry, *66;* Not of This Earth, *872;* Revenge of the Ninja, *106*
Roberts, Christian: Desperados, The, *1109;* To Sir with Love, *685*
Roberts, Conrad: Mosquito Coast, The, *600*
Roberts, Darryl: How U Like Me Now, *303*
Roberts, Doris: Love in the Present Tense, *581;* Number One with a Bullet, *92;* Once in Paris, *612;* Ordinary Heroes, *614;* Simple Justice, *658*
Roberts, Eric: Ambulance, The, *952;* Best of the Best, *11;* Best of the Best 2, *11;* Blood Red, *464;* Coca Cola Kid, The, *257;* Descending Angel, *499;* Family Matter, A, *514;* Final Analysis, *976;* Freefall, *52;* King of the Gypsies, *565;* Lonely Hearts (1991), *577;* Lost Capone, The, *580;* Love, Cheat & Steal, *993;* Nobody's Fool, *346;* Paul's Case, *620;* Pope of Greenwich Village, The, *624;* Raggedy Man, *1008;* Rude Awakening (1989), *371;* Runaway Train, *110;* Slow Burn, *1018;* Star 80, *666;* To Heal a Nation, *684;* Voyage, *1030*
Roberts, Glenn: Crater Lake Monster, The, *825*
Roberts, Ian: Power of One, The, *625*
Roberts Jr., Jay: White Phantom, *139*
Roberts, Jessica: Angel Fist, *5*
Roberts, Joe: Buster Keaton Festival: Vol. 1, *248;* Buster Keaton Festival: Vol. 2, *248;* Buster Keaton Festival: Vol. 3, *248;* Buster Keaton: The Golden Years, *248*
Roberts, Julia: Dying Young, *506;* Flatliners, *977;* Hook, *175;* Mystic Pizza, *603;* Pelican Brief, The, *1005;* Pretty Woman, *361;* Satisfaction, *938;* Sleeping with the Enemy, *1017;* Steel Magnolias, *667*
Roberts, Ken: Fatal Pulse, *840;* Great Land of Small, The, *171*
Roberts, Lee: Battling Marshal, *1097;* Law of the Lash, *1127*
Roberts, Lynne: Eyes of Texas, *1111*
Roberts, Lynne (Mary Hart): Billy the Kid Returns, *1099;* Dick Tracy Returns, *38;* Dynamite Pass, *1111;* Frontier Pony Express, *1114;* Heart of the Rockies, *1119;* Hunt the Man Down, *984;* Lone Ranger, The (1938), *1129;* Robin Hood of Texas, *1145;* Rough Riders' Roundup, *1146;* Shine on Harvest Moon, *1149;* Sioux City Sue, *1150*
Roberts, Mark: Night of the Devils, *869;* Posse (1975), *1139*
Roberts, Pernell: Bonanza (TV Series), *1100;* Checkered Flag, *480;* Desire under the Elms, *500;* Four Rode Out, *1114;* High Noon, Part Two, *1120;* Kashmiri Run, The, *70;* Magic of Lassie, The, *185;* Night Train to Katmandu, *607;* Ride Lonesome, *1143*
Roberts, Rachel: Belstone Fox, The, *149;* Hostage Tower, The, *64;* O Lucky Man!, *610;* Picnic at Hanging Rock, *1006;* This Sporting Life, *682;* When a Stranger Calls, *1030*
Roberts, Roy: Enforcer, The (1951), *44;* Force of Evil, *519;* He Walked by Night, *982;* King and Four Queens, The, *1125;* Second Chance, *113*
Roberts, Tanya: Almost Pregnant, *225;* Beastmaster, The, *1038;* Body Slam, *17;* California Dreaming, *474;* Forced Entry, *842;* Hearts and Armour, *59;* Inner Sanctum, *986;* Legal Tender, *76;* Night Eyes, *1000;* Sheena, *115;* Sins of Desire, *1017;* Tourist Trap, *1026;* View to a Kill, A, *135;* Yum-Yum Girls, The, *709*
Roberts, Teal: Fatal Games, *840;* Hardbodies, *293*
Roberts, Theodore: Ten Commandments, The (1923), *678*
Roberts, Tony: American Clock, The, *446;* Amityville III: The Demon, *809;* Annie Hall, *228;* 18 Again, *270;* Just Tell Me What You Want, *312;* Key Exchange, *563;* Midsummer Night's Sex Comedy, A, *332;* Million Dollar Duck, The, *187;* Packin' It In, *193;* Play It Again, Sam, *358;* Popcorn, *876;* Question of Honor, A, *632;* Seize the Day, *651;* Serpico, *652;* Switch, *390;* Taking of Pelham One Two Three, The, *1022*
Robertson, Andrew: Cement Garden, The, *478*
Robertson, Cliff: All in a Night's Work, *224;* Autumn Leaves, *452;* Best Man, The, *459;* Charly, *1041;* Days of Wine and Roses, The (Television), *497;* Dead Reckoning (1990), *967;* Devil's Brigade, The, *37;* Dominique Is Dead, *971;* Ford: The Man & the Machine, *519;* Gidget, *286;* Girl Most Likely, The, *919;* Great Northfield Minnesota Raid, The, *1116;* Honey Pot, The, *300;* Interns, The, *553;* Key to Rebecca, The, *70;* Love Has Many Faces, *581;* Malone, *80;* Midway, *84;* Naked and the Dead, The, *88;* Obsession, *1002;* Out of Season, *616;* Outer Limits, The (TV Series), *1069;* Picnic, *622;* Pilot, The, *622;* PT 109, *630;* Shaker Run, *114;* Shoot (1976), *115;* 633 Squadron, *116;* Star 80, *666;* Three Days of the Condor, *1025;* Too Late the Hero, *131;* Two of a Kind (1982), *690;* Underworld U.S.A., *691;* Wild Hearts Can't Be Broken, *217;* Wind (1992), *140*
Robertson, Dale: Cariboo Trail, *1103;* Dakota Incident, *1107;* Devil's Canyon, *1109;* Farmer Takes a Wife, The, *916;* Kansas City Massacre, The, *70;* Last Ride of the Dalton Gang, The, *1126;* Melvin Purvis: G-Man, *83*
Robertson, George R.: Dawson Patrol, The, *33*
Robertson, Jenny: Jacob I Have Loved, *556;* Nightman, The, *1001*
Robertson, Kathleen: Survive the Night, *1021*
Robertson, Patricia: Attack of the Swamp Creature, *810*
Robertson, Robbie: Carny, *475*
Robeson, Paul: Emperor Jones, The, *509;* Jericho, *557;* King Solomon's Mines (1937), *72;* Sanders of the River, *111;* Show Boat (1936), *939*
Robie, Wendy: People Under the Stairs, The, *873*
Robin, Dany: Tales of Paris, *792;* Topaz, *1026;* Waltz of the Toreadors, *405*
Robin, Michel: Investigation, *748;* Le Chêvre (The Goat), *757*
Robins, Barry: Bless the Beasts and Children, *463*
Robins, Laila: Innocent Man, An, *66;* Planes, Trains and Automobiles, *358;* Welcome Home, Roxy Carmichael, *407*
Robins, Oliver: Poltergeist II: The Other Side, *875*
Robinson, Amy: Mean Streets, *591*
Robinson and the Miracles, Smokey: That Was Rock, *944*
Robinson, Andrew: Charley Varrick, *25;* Cobra (1986), *27;* Dirty Harry, *39;* Fatal Charm, *976;* Hellraiser, *850;* Into the Badlands, *1123;* Not My Kid, *609;* Prime Target, *100;* Shoot to Kill, *115;* Someone I Touched, *662;* Trancers III: Death Lives, *1085;* Verne Miller, *135*
Robinson, Ann: Dragnet (1954), *41;* Midnight Movie Massacre, *332;* War of the Worlds, The, *1088*
Robinson, Bill: Just Around the Corner, *926;* Little Colonel, The, *928;* Littlest Rebel, The, *929;* Rebecca of Sunnybrook Farm (1938), *936;* Stormy Weather, *942*
Robinson, Bruce: Story of Adele H, The, *789*
Robinson, Charles Knox: Daring Dobermans, The, *32;* Psycho Sisters, *877*
Robinson, Charles P.: Black Gestapo, The, *13*
Robinson, Chris: Amy, *146;* Savannah Smiles, *201;* Stanley, *890;* Viper, *136*
Robinson, Claudia: Wide Sargasso Sea, *701*
Robinson, David: Buford's Beach Bunnies, *247*
Robinson, Edward G.: Actors and Sin, *441;* Barbary Coast, The, *455;* Brother Orchid, *20;* Bullets or Ballots, *21;* Cheyenne Autumn, *1104;* Cincinnati Kid, The, *26;* Double Indemnity, *972;* Good Neighbor Sam, *288;* Hell on Frisco Bay, *60;* Hole in the Head, A, *298;* House of Strangers, *545;* I Am the Law, *547;* Key Largo, *988;* Kid Galahad (1937), *563;* Little Caesar, *77;* Mr. Winkle Goes to War, *334;* My Geisha, *340;* Never a Dull Moment, *191;* Our Vines Have Tender Grapes, *193;* Prize, The, *629;* Red House, The, *1009;* Robin & the Seven Hoods, *936;* Scarlet Street, *649;* Sea Wolf, The (1941), *113;* Seven Thieves, *653;* Song of Norway, *940;* Soylent Green, *1077;*

Stranger, The (1947), *1020;* Ten Commandments, The (1956), *678;* Thunder in the City, *683;* Two Weeks in Another Town, *690;* Violent Men, The, *1161*
Robinson, Frances: Red Barry, *104*
Robinson, Holly: Jacksons: An American Dream, The, *556*
Robinson, Jackie: Jackie Robinson Story, The, *556*
Robinson, Jackson: Bikini Island, *813*
Robinson, Jay: Born Again, *466;* Demetrius and the Gladiators, *499;* Dying to Remember, *973;* King Richard II, *565;* Macbeth (1981), *584;* Malibu Bikini Shop, The, *327;* My Man Godfrey (1957), *340;* Othello (1982), *615;* Robe, The, *642;* Three the Hard Way, *129;* Transylvania Twist, *399*
Robinson, Larry: Sgt. Kabukiman N.Y.P.D., *114*
Robinson, Leon: Band of the Hand, *9;* Streetwalkin', *671*
Robinson, Madeleine: Le Gentleman D'Espom (Duke of the Derby), *757*
Robinson, Roger: Newman's Law, *90*
Robles, Frank: Crossover Dreams, *912*
Robles, German: Vampire, The, *899*
Robson, Flora: Beast in the Cellar, The, *812;* Black Narcissus, *463;* Caesar and Cleopatra, *473;* Catherine the Great, *477;* Dominique Is Dead, *971;* Epic That Never Was, The, *423;* Fire over England, *49;* Great Day, *532;* Les Miserables (1978), *573;* Murder at the Gallop, *998;* Restless, *638;* Sea Hawk, The, *112;* Tale of Two Cities, A (1980), *677;* Wuthering Heights (1939), *707*
Robson, Greer: Smash Palace, *660*
Robson, May: Adventures of Tom Sawyer, The, *144;* Anna Karenina (1935), *449;* Bringing Up Baby, *246;* Dancing Lady, *913;* It Happened in New Orleans, *925;* Joan of Paris, *558;* Lady by Choice, *567;* Lady for a Day, *567;* Little Orphan Annie, *183;* Nurse Edith Cavell, *610;* Reckless (1935), *636;* Red-Headed Woman, *636;* Star Is Born, A (1937), *666;* Strange Interlude (1932), *669;* Wife Vs. Secretary, *701*
Robson, Wayne: And Then You Die, *5*
Roc, Patricia: Black Jack, *14;* Wicked Lady, The (1945), *701*
Rocard, Pascale: Rascals, The, *779*
Rocca, Daniela: Divorce—Italian Style, *731;* Empty Canvas, The, *509*
Rocco, Alex: Badge of the Assassin, *454;* Blue Knight, The (1975), *465;* Boris and Natasha, *244;* Detroit 9000 (Detroit Heat), *37;* Gotcha!, *980;* Grass Is Always Greener Over the Septic Tank, The, *289;* Hustling, *547;* Lady in White, *990;* Motor Psycho, *87;* Nobody's Perfekt, *346;* P.K. & the Kid, *617;* Pope Must Diet, The, *360;* Rafferty and the Gold Dust Twins, *364;* Return to Horror High, *880;* Stanley, *890;* Stunt Man, The, *671;* Wired, *704*
Roche, Eugene: Case for Murder, A, *960;* Newman's Law, *90;* Oh, God, You Devil!, *349;* Possessed, The (1977), *876;* Rape And Marriage: The Rideout Case, *635;* Slaughterhouse Five, *1077;* W, *1030*
Rochefort, Jean: Birgit Haas Must Be Killed, *718;* Clockmaker, The, *725;* French Postcards, *281;* Hairdresser's Husband, The, *742;* I Sent a Letter to My Love, *746;* Le Cavaleur, *757;* Le Complot (The Conspiracy), *757;* Le Crabe Tambour, *757;* My Mother's Castle, *770;* My Wonderful Life, *603;* Pardon Mon Affaire, *775;* Pardon Mon Affaire, Too!, *775;* Return of the Tall Blond Man with One Black Shoe, The, *781;* Salut L'Artiste, *783*
Rochelle, Robin: Sorority Babes in the Slimeball Bowl-O-Rama, *383*
Rock, Chris: CB4, *252;* New Jack City, *90*
Rocket, Charles: Brain Smasher...A Love Story, *18;* Delirious, *263;* Down Twisted, *41;* Earth Girls Are Easy, *915*
Rockwell, Robert: Our Miss Brooks (TV Series), *351;* Red Menace, The, *636*
Rodann, Ziva: Three Nuts in Search of a Bolt, *396*
Rodd, Marcia: Citizen's Band, *255;* Last Embrace, The, *990;* Little Murders, *319*
Roddenberry, Gene: Fantasy Film Worlds of George Pal, The, *424*
Rode, Ebbe: Topsy Turvy, *796*
Rodgers, Anton: Lillie, *575*
Rodgers, Maria Antoinette: Journey to Spirit Island, *179*
Rodnunsky, Serge: Lovers' Lovers, *582*
Rodrigue, Madeline: Crazy Ray, The, *726*
Rodrigues, Percy: Brainwaves, *818*
Rodriguez, Estelita: Along the Navajo Trail, *1093;* Golden Stallion, The, *1116;* In Old Amarillo, *1122;* On the Old Spanish Trail, *1137;* Susanna Pass, *1154;* Twilight in the Sierras, *1159*
Rodriguez, Paul: All-Star Toast to the Improv, An, *224;* Best of the Big Laff Off, The, *236;* Born in East L.A., *244;* Made in America, *325;* Million to Juan, A, *332;* Miracles, *332;* Ponce de Leon and the Fountain of Youth, *196;* Quicksilver, *632;* Whoopee Boys, The, *411;* Your Favorite Laughs from an Evening at the Improv, *416*
Rodway, Norman: Reilly: The Ace of Spies, *637;* Story of David, The, *207*
Roebuck, Daniel: Cave Girl, *1041;* Disorganized Crime, *40;* Dudes, *505;* Fugitive, The (1993), *53;* Killing Mind, The, *989;* River's Edge, *641*
Roerick, William: Love Machine, The, *581*
Roeves, Maurice: Last of the Mohicans, The (1992), *1126*
Rogen, Mike: Punch the Clock, *101*
Rogers, Bill: Taste of Blood, A, *892*
Rogers, Charles "Buddy": My Best Girl, *339;* Wings, *140*
Rogers, Dinah Anne: Legacy for Leonette, *991*
Rogers, Dora: Keystone Comedies, Vol. 3, *312;* Keystone Comedies, Vol. 5, *313*
Rogers, Gil: Children, The, *823*
Rogers, Ginger: Bachelor Mother, *230;* Barkleys of Broadway, The, *908;* Carefree, *911;* Cinderella (1964), *911;* Fifth Avenue Girl, *276;* Finishing School, *516;* Flying Down to Rio, *917;* Follow the Fleet, *917;* 42nd Street, *918;* Gay Divorcée, The, *918;* Gold Diggers of 1933, *920;* Having a Wonderful Time, *294;* Hollywood on Parade, *299;* In Person, *305;* Kitty Foyle, *566;* Lucky Partners, *324;* Monkey Business (1952), *336;* Once Upon a Honeymoon, *349;* Primrose Path, *627;* Quick, Let's Get Married, *363;* Roberta, *936;* Romance in Manhattan, *643;* Shall We Dance?, *939;* Shriek in the Night, A, *1016;* Stage Door, *385;* Star of Midnight, *1020;* Story of Vernon and Irene Castle, The, *942;* Swing Time, *943;* Tender Comrade, *679;* Thirteenth Guest, The, *1024;* Tom, Dick and Harry, *397;* Top Hat, *946;* Vivacious Lady, *405;* Weekend at the Waldorf, *697;* We're Not Married, *408*
Rogers, Ina: Buford's Beach Bunnies, *247*
Rogers, Ingrid: Carlito's Way, *23*
Rogers, Jean: Ace Drummond, *1;* Flash Gordon: Mars Attacks the World (a.k.a. Trip to Mars; Deadly Ray From Mars, The), *1052;* Flash Gordon: Rocketship (a.k.a. Spaceship to the Unknown; Perils from Planet Mongo), *1052;* Whistling in Brooklyn, *410*
Rogers, Jimmy: False Colors, *1112;* Forty Thieves, *1114;* Mystery Man, *1135;* Riders of the Deadline, *1144;* Texas Masquerade, *1156*
Rogers Jr, Will: Look For The Silver Lining, *929*
Rogers, Kenny: Coward of the County, *490;* Gambler, The (1980), *1114;* Gambler, Part II—The Adventure Continues, The, *1115;* Gambler, Part III—The Legend Continues, The, *1115;* Gambler Returns, the: Luck of the Draw, *1115;* Rio Diablo, *1145;* Six Pack, *380*
Rogers, Maggie: Ghastly Ones, The, *845*
Rogers, Mimi: Blue Skies Again, *465;* Dark Horse, *161;* Deadlock, *1045;* Desperate Hours (1990), *37;* Fourth Story, *978;* Gung Ho (1985), *292;* Hider in the House, *982;* Ladykiller, *990;* Mighty Quinn, The, *85;* Monkey Trouble, *188;* Palermo Connection, The, *1004;* Rapture, The, *635;* Rousters, The, *109;* Shooting Elizabeth, *378;* Someone to Watch Over Me, *1018;* Street Smart, *670;* White Sands, *700*
Rogers, Paul: Homecoming, The (1973), *543*
Rogers, Roy: Along the Navajo Trail, *1093;* Apache Rose, *1094;* Arizona Kid, *1095;* Bad Man of Deadwood, *1095;* Bells of Coronado, *1097;* Bells of Rosarita, *1097;* Bells of San

Angelo, *1097;* Billy the Kid Returns, *1099;* Carson City Kid, *1103;* Colorado, *1105;* Cowboy and the Senorita, *1106;* Dark Command, *1107;* Days of Jesse James, *1107;* Don't Fence Me In, *1110;* Down Dakota Way, *1110;* Eyes of Texas, *1111;* Far Frontier, *1112;* Frontier Pony Express, *1114;* Golden Stallion, The, *1116;* Grand Canyon Trail, *1116;* Hands Across the Border, *1118;* Heart of the Golden West, *1119;* Helldorado (1946), *1120;* Hollywood Canteen, *923;* Home in Oklahoma, *1121;* Idaho, *1122;* In Old Amarillo, *1122;* In Old Caliente, *1122;* Jesse James at Bay, *1123;* King of the Cowboys, *1125;* Lights of Old Santa Fe, *1128;* My Pal Trigger, *1135;* Nighttime in Nevada, *1136;* North of the Great Divide, *1136;* Old Barn Dance, The, *1136;* Old Corral, *1136;* On the Old Spanish Trail, *1137;* Ranger and the Lady, The, *1141;* Robin Hood of the Pecos, *1145;* Roll on Texas Moon, *1145;* Rough Riders' Roundup, *1146;* Roy Rogers Show, The (TV Series), *1146;* Saga of Death Valley, *1147;* San Fernando Valley, *1147;* Shine on Harvest Moon, *1149;* Silver Spurs, *1150;* Son of Paleface, *383;* Song of Nevada, *1151;* Song of Texas, *1151;* Sons of the Pioneers, *1151;* Springtime in the Sierras, *1152;* Sunset on the Desert, *1154;* Sunset Serenade, *1154;* Susanna Pass, *1154;* Trail of Robin Hood, *1158;* Trigger, Jr., *1159;* Twilight in the Sierras, *1159;* Under California Stars, *1160;* Under Western Stars, *1160;* Utah, *1160;* Wall Street Cowboy, *1162;* Yellow Rose of Texas, *1165;* Young Bill Hickok, *1165*

Rogers Jr., Roy: Arizona Bushwhackers, *1094*

Rogers, Ruth: Hidden Gold, *1120;* Night Riders, The, *1136*

Rogers, Wayne: Chiefs, *961;* Gig, The, *286;* Girl Who Spelled Freedom, The, *169;* Goodbye Bird, The, *171;* Killing Time, The, *72;* Lady from Yesterday, The, *567;* M*A*S*H* (TV Series), *325;* Once in Paris, *612;* Pocket Money, *359*

Rogers, Will: Ambassador Bill, *225;* Bill Fields and Will Rogers, *239;* Connecticut Yankee, A, *258;* Doubting Thomas, *268;* Fatty's Tin-Type Tangle/Our Congressman, *275;* Going to Congress and Don't Park There, *288;* Golden Age of Comedy, The, *288;* Headless Horseman, The, *1056;* Judge Priest, *560;* Mack Sennett Comedies, Vol. 2, *325;* Mr. Skitch, *334*

Rohm, Maria: Call of the Wild (1972), *22*

Rohner, Clayton: Caroline at Midnight, *960;* Destroyer, *833;* I, Madman, *855;* Just One of the Guys, *312;* Modern Girls, *335;* Nightwish, *1068;* Private Investigations, *101*

Rojo, Gustavo: Christmas Kid, The, *1105*

Rojo, Helena: Aguirre: Wrath of God, *711;* Foxtrot, *521;* Mary, Mary, Bloody Mary, *863*

Rojo, Maria: Break of Dawn, *468;* Danzon, *728;* Mary My Dearest, *766*

Rojo, Ruben: Great Madcap, The, *742*

Roland, Gilbert: Bad and the Beautiful, The, *454;* Barbarosa, *1097;* Beneath the 12-Mile Reef, *10;* Between God, the Devil and a Winchester, *1097;* Bullfighter and the Lady, The, *21;* Captain Kidd, *23;* French Line, The, *918;* Go Kill and Come Back, *1115;* Miracle of Our Lady of Fatima, The, *595;* Poppy Is Also a Flower, The, *99;* Racers, The, *632;* Ruthless Four, The, *1146;* Sacketts, The, *1146;* Sea Hawk, The, *112;* She Done Him Wrong, *377;* Three Violent People, *1157;* Thunder Bay, *129;* Thunder Trail, *1157;* Treasure of Pancho Villa, The, *1158;* Underwater!, *134*

Roland Petit Dance Company: Black Tights, *909*

Rolfe, Guy: Alphabet Murders, The, *951;* Dolls, *836;* Puppet Master III: Toulon's Revenge, *878;* Puppet Master Four, *878;* Snow White and the Three Stooges, *205*

Rolin, Judy: Alice Through the Looking Glass (1966), *906*

Rollan, Henri: Crazy Ray, The, *726*

Rolle, Esther: Age-Old Friends, *443;* Driving Miss Daisy, *505;* House of Cards, *545;* I Know Why the Caged Bird Sings, *547;* P.K. & the Kid, *617;* Raisin in the Sun, A (1988), *634;* Romeo and Juliet (1983), *643;* Summer of My German Soldier, *672;* To Dance with the White Dog, *684*

Rolling Stones, The: Gimme Shelter, *424;* Let's Spend the Night Together, *429;* Sympathy for the Devil, *435;* That Was Rock, *944*

Rollins, Henry: Chase, The (1994), *25*

Rollins Jr., Howard: Children of Times Square, The, *481;* For Us the Living: The Medgar Evers Story, *519;* King, *564;* On the Block, *1003;* Soldier's Story, A, *1018*

Rolston, Mark: Comrades of Summer, The, *258*

Romain, Yvonne: Circus of Horrors, *824;* Curse of the Werewolf, The, *828;* Devil Doll (1963), *833*

Romaine, Katherine: Metamorphosis: The Alien Factor, *1065*

Roman, Cathrine: Bloody New Year, *817*

Roman, Letitia: Fanny Hill: Memoirs of a Woman of Pleasure, *514*

Roman, Ruth: Baby, The, *811;* Beyond the Forest, *460;* Blowing Wild, *16;* Champion, *479;* Day of the Animals, *830;* Far Country, The, *1112;* Impulse (1974), *985;* Love Has Many Faces, *581;* Sacketts, The, *1146;* Strangers on a Train, *1020;* Three Secrets, *683;* Window, The, *1032*

Romance, Viviane: Melodie en Sous-Sol (The Big Grab), *766;* Panique, *775*

Romand, Beatrice: Chloe in the Afternoon, *723;* Claire's Knee, *724;* Le Beau Mariage, *756;* Summer, *791*

Romanelli, Carla: Shangai Joe, *1148*

Romano, Rino: Club, The (1993), *824*

Romanus, Richard: Couch Trip, The, *259;* Night Terror, *1001;* Point of No Return, *99;* Protocol, *363;* Russian Roulette, *110;* Sitting Ducks, *380;* To Protect and Serve, *130*

Romanus, Robert: Bad Medicine, *231;* Dangerous Curves, *262*

Romay, Lina: Adventure, *441;* Demoniac, *832;* Erotikill, *838;* Heat's On, The, *295;* Ilsa, the Wicked Warden, *855;* Oasis of the Zombies, *872*

Rome, Sydne: Diary of Forbidden Dreams, *501;* Just a Gigolo, *561;* Puma Man, The, *878;* Sex with a Smile, *376;* That Lucky Touch, *392*

Romer, Fred: Great Adventure, The, *1116*

Romero, Cesar: Americano, The, *1093;* Batman (1966), *148;* Beautiful Blonde from Bashful Bend, The, *233;* Computer Wore Tennis Shoes, The, *159;* Crooks and Coronets (Sophie's Place), *261;* Dance Hall, *913;* Happy Go Lovely, *921;* Happy Landing, *921;* Hot Millions, *301;* Julia Misbehaves, *311;* Little Princess, The, *183;* Lost Continent, The, *1063;* Lust in the Dust, *324;* Madigan's Millions, *326;* Mission to Glory, *596;* My Lucky Star, *932;* Now You See Him, Now You Don't, *191;* Ocean's Eleven, *93;* Orchestra Wives, *934;* Proud and the Damned, The, *1139;* Racers, The, *632;* Show Them No Mercy, *657;* Simple Justice, *658;* Springtime in the Rockies (1942), *941;* Wee Willie Winkie, *216;* Wintertime, *947*

Romero, Ned: Children of the Corn II: The Final Sacrifice, *823;* Deerslayer, The, *1108;* I Will Fight No More Forever, *1122;* Last of the Mohicans (1985), *1126;* Medicine Hat Stallion, The, *186*

Ronet, Maurice: Beau Pere, *716;* Circle of Love, *482;* Elevator to the Gallows, *734;* Fire Within, The, *736;* La Balance, *753;* L'Odeur Des Fauves (Scandal Man), *761;* Sphinx (1981), *889;* Swimming Pool, The, *792*

Ronettes, The: That Was Rock, *944*

Ronstadt, Linda: Chuck Berry Hail! Hail! Rock 'n' Roll, *421;* Pirates of Penzance, The, *935*

Rooker, Michael: Afterburn, *442;* Cliffhanger, *26;* Dark Half, The, *829;* Days of Thunder, *33;* Henry: Portrait of a Serial Killer, *540;* JFK, *558*

Rooney, Mickey: Adventures of Huckleberry Finn, The (1939), *143;* Ah, Wilderness, *223;* Andy Hardy Gets Spring Fever, *227;* Andy Hardy Meets a Debutante, *227;* Andy Hardy's Double Life, *227;* Andy Hardy's Private Secretary, *227;* Atomic Kid, The, *229;* Babes in Arms, *907;* Babes on Broadway, *907;* Big Wheel, The, *461;* Bill, *461;* Bill: On His Own, *461;* Black Stallion, The, *151;* Boys' Town, *468;* Breakfast at Tiffany's, *468;* Bridges at Toko-Ri, The, *19;* Captains Courageous, *474;* Care Bears Movie, The, *156;* Chained, *478;* Comedian, The, *486;* Comic, The (1969), *486;* Domino Principle, The, *971;* Erik the Viking, *1049;* Find the Lady, *277;* Fugitive, The (TV Series), *523;* Gambler Returns, the: Luck of the Draw, *1115;* Girl Crazy, *919;* Hollywood Outtakes, *299;* Home for

Christmas, *542;* How to Stuff a Wild Bikini, *923;* Human Comedy, The, *546;* It Came Upon a Midnight Clear, *177;* It's a Mad Mad Mad Mad World, *308;* King of the Roaring Twenties, *565;* Leave 'em Laughing, *572;* Life Begins for Andy Hardy, *318;* Lightning, the White Stallion, *181;* Little Lord Fauntleroy (1936), *576;* Lost Jungle, The, *79;* Love Finds Andy Hardy, *322;* Love Laughs at Andy Hardy, *323;* Magic of Lassie, The, *185;* Manhattan Melodrama, *81;* Manipulator, The, *588;* Maximum Force, *83;* Men of Boys Town, *592;* Midsummer Night's Dream, A (1935), *1066;* My Heroes Have Always Been Cowboys, *1135;* My Pal, the King, *1135;* National Velvet, *190;* Off Limits (1953), *348;* Pete's Dragon, *195;* Platinum High School, *623;* Pulp, *363;* Reckless (1935), *636;* Requiem for a Heavyweight, *638;* Revenge of the Red Baron, *881;* Silent Night, Deadly Night 5: The Toy Maker, *886;* Strike Up the Band, *387;* Summer Holiday, *942;* Sweet Justice, *123;* That's Entertainment! III, *436;* Thoroughbreds Don't Cry, *210;* Thousands Cheer, *945;* Words and Music, *948;* Young Tom Edison, *708*

Roose, Thorkild: Day of Wrath, *728*

Roquevert, Noel: Un Singe en Hiver (A Monkey in Winter), *798;* Voulez Vous Danser avec Moi? (Will You Dance with Me?), *801*

Rosa, Robby: Salsa, *938*

Rosae, Donna: Master Blaster, *83*

Rosato, Tony: Busted Up, *472;* City of Shadows, *26;* Diamond Fleece, The, *970;* Separate Vacations, *375*

Rosay, Françoise: Bizarre, Bizarre, *718;* Carnival in Flanders, *722;* Full Hearts and Empty Pockets, *739;* Naked Heart, The, *603;* Quartet (1948), *631;* September Affair, *652*

Rosborough, Patty: New Wave Comedy, *343*

Roscoe, Albert: Last of the Mohicans, The (1920), *75*

Rose, Gabrielle: Adjuster, The, *441;* Speaking Parts, *664*

Rose, George: Devil's Disciple, The, *264;* Hideaways, The, *174;* Jack the Ripper (1959), *858;* Night to Remember, A (1958), *606;* Pirates of Penzance, The, *935;* You Can't Take it with You (1984), *415*

Rose, Jamie: Chopper Chicks in Zombietown, *823;* In Love with an Older Woman, *550;* Rebel Love, *636;* To Die Standing, *130*

Rose Marie: Garry Shandling Show, The, *283;* Witchboard, *903*

Rose, Robin Pearson: Last Resort, *316*

Rose, Roger: Ski Patrol, *380*

Rose, Sherri: Double Threat, *504;* In Gold We Trust, *66;* Maximum Force, *83*

Rosenberg, Saturday: Encounter at Raven's Gate, *1049*

Rosenberg, Stephen: Jacob Two-Two Meets the Hooded Fang, *178*

Rosenbloom, Maxie: Each Dawn I Die, *42;* I Married a Monster from Outer Space, *1057;* Louisiana Purchase, *322;* To the Shores of Tripoli, *130*

Rosenthal, Sheila: Not without My Daughter, *609*

Rosi, Luciano: Five for Hell, *50*

Ross, Alma: Tuttles of Tahiti, The, *400*

Ross, Andrew: Party Camp, *354*

Ross, Annie: Basket Case 3: The Progeny, *811;* Short Cuts, *657*

Ross, Anthony: Country Girl, The (1954), *489*

Ross, Betsy King: Fighting with Kit Carson, *1113;* Phantom Empire (1935), *98;* Radio Ranch (Men with Steel Faces & Phantom Empire), *1140*

Ross, Beverly: Crazed, *825*

Ross, Bud: Bill Fields and Will Rogers, *239;* Fatal Glass of Beer, A/Pool Sharks, *274*

Ross, Chelcie: Amos & Andrew, *226;* Legacy of Lies, *572;* Rudy, *200*

Ross, Diana: Lady Sings the Blues, *927;* Mahogany, *586;* Wiz, The, *948*

Ross, Gene: Encounter with the Unknown, *1049;* Poor White Trash II, *624*

Ross, Joe E.: Car 54 Where Are You? (TV Series), *250;* Sgt. Bilko (TV Series), *376;* Slumber Party 57, *381*

Ross, Katharine: Betsy, The, *459;* Butch Cassidy and the Sundance Kid, *1103;* Climate for Killing, A, *962;* Conagher, *1105;* Final Countdown, The, *1051;* Fools, *518;* Get to Know Your Rabbit, *285;* Graduate, The, *531;* Hellfighters, *60;* Legacy, The, *860;* Murder in Texas, *998;* Red-Headed Stranger, The, *1141;* Rodeo Girl, *642;* Shadow Riders, The, *1148;* Shenandoah, *1149;* Singing Nun, The, *204;* Swarm, The, *891;* Tell Them Willie Boy Is Here, *1155;* They Only Kill Their Masters, *1024;* Wrong Is Right, *414*

Ross, Lanny: Gulliver's Travels (1939), *172*

Ross, Marion: Teacher's Pet, *392*

Ross, Merrie Lynn: Bobbie Jo and the Outlaw, *17;* Class of 1984, *824*

Ross, Ted: Bingo Long Traveling All-Stars and Motor Kings, The, *240;* Fighting Back, *47;* Wiz, The, *948*

Ross, Tim: Night Eyes 2, *1000*

Rossellini, Isabella: Blue Velvet, *817;* Cannon Movie Tales: Red Riding Hood, *155;* Cousins, *260;* Death Becomes Her, *1045;* Fallen Angels, *513;* Fearless (1993), *515;* Ivory Hunters, *555;* Lies of the Twins, *992;* Matter of Time, A, *590;* Siesta, *1016;* Tough Guys Don't Dance, *686;* White Nights (1985), *700;* Wild at Heart, *702;* Zelly and Me, *709*

Rossi, Leo: Accused, The, *441;* Casualties of Love: The Long Island Lolita Story, *476;* Fast Getaway, *274;* Heart Like a Wheel, *538;* Hit List (1988), *982;* Maniac Cop 2, *863;* Relentless, *1010;* Relentless II: Dead On, *879;* Relentless 3, *1010;* River's Edge, *641;* Too Much Sun, *397;* We're Talking Serious Money, *408;* Where the Day Takes You, *699*

Rossi, Portia de: Sirens, *379*

Rossi, Vittorio: Snake Eater 2, the Drug Buster, *117*

Rossi-Stuart, Giacomo: Curse of the Living Dead, *828;* Last Man on Earth, The, *1062;* Planet on the Prowl, *1071;* Shangai Joe, *1148*

Rossiter, Leonard: Britannia Hospital, *246;* Luther, *583*

Rossman, Charley: Buford's Beach Bunnies, *247*

Rossovich, Rick: Gambler Returns, the: Luck of the Draw, *1115;* Lords of Discipline, The, *579;* Navy Seals, *89;* Paint It Black, *97;* Roxanne, *370;* Spellbinder, *889;* Top Gun, *131;* Tropical Heat, *1027;* Warning Sign, *901*

Rotaeta, Felix: Pepi, Luci, Born and Other Girls, *777*

Roth, Andrea: Club, The (1993), *824*

Roth, Celia: Labyrinth of Passion, *755*

Roth, Gene: Big Sombrero, The, *1098;* Blue Canadian Rockies, *1099;* Earth vs. the Spider, *1048;* Marshal of Cripple Creek, *1132;* Pirates of the High Seas, *99;* She Demons, *885*

Roth, Ivan E.: Hollywood Zap, *299*

Roth, Johnny: Bride and the Beast, The, *19*

Roth, Lillian: Alice, Sweet Alice (Communion and Holy Terror), *808;* Animal Crackers, *227;* Ladies They Talk About, *567;* Madame Satan, *584*

Roth, Matt: Blink, *956*

Roth, Tim: Bodies, Rest & Motion, *465;* Heart of Darkness, *538;* Hit, The, *63;* Jumpin' at the Boneyard, *561;* Reservoir Dogs, *105;* Rosencrantz and Guildenstern Are Dead, *370;* Vincent and Theo, *694*

Rothe, Bendt: Gertrude, *740*

Rothrock, Cynthia: China O'Brien, *25;* China O'Brien 2, *25;* Fast Getaway, *274;* Honor and Glory, *64;* Lady Dragon, *74;* Lady Dragon 2, *74;* Martial Law, *82;* Martial Law Two—Undercover, *82;* Rage and Honor, *102;* Rage and Honor II: Hostile Takeover, *102;* Undefeatable, *134*

Rottlander, Yella: Alice in the City, *711;* Scarlet Letter (1973), *784*

Rouan, Brigitte: Overseas, *774*

Roucka, Billy Joe: Dead Aim (1973), *1108*

Rouffe, Alida: Marius, *765*

Rounds, David: So Fine, *382*

Roundtree, Richard: Amityville: A New Generation, *809;* Bad Jim, *1095;* Big Score, The, *12;* Bloodfist III: Forced to Fight, *16;* Body of Influence, *958;* Bonanza: The Return, *1100;*

Christmas in Connecticut (1992), *255;* City Heat, *255;* Crack House, *30;* Day of the Assassin, *33;* Deadly Rivals, *35;* Diamonds, *38;* Escape to Athena, *45;* Eye for an Eye, *46;* Firehouse (1972), *49;* Game for Vultures, *54;* Gypsy Angels, *535;* Jocks, *310;* Kill Point, *71;* Last Contract, The, *75;* Maniac Cop, *862;* Miami Cops, *84;* Night Visitor (1989), *1001;* One Down, Two to Go, *94;* Opposing Force, *95;* Party Line, *97;* Q, *878;* Shaft, *114;* Shaft's Big Score!, *114;* Sins of the Night, *1017;* Time to Die, A (1990), *1025;* What Do You Say to a Naked Lady?, *408;* Young Warriors, The, *141*

Rounseville, Robert: Carousel, *911;* Tales of Hoffman, *943*

Rourke, Mickey: Angel Heart, *952;* Barfly, *455;* Body Heat, *958;* Desperate Hours (1990), *37;* Diner, *265;* Eureka, *511;* Harley Davidson and the Marlboro Man, *59;* Homeboy, *543;* Johnny Handsome, *69;* Last Outlaw, The (1993), *1126;* 9½ Weeks, *607;* Pope of Greenwich Village, The, *624;* Prayer for the Dying, A, *1007;* Rape And Marriage: The Rideout Case, *635;* Rumble Fish, *645;* White Sands, *700;* Wild Orchid, *702;* Year of the Dragon, *141*

Roussel, Anne: Music Teacher, The, *769*

Roussel, Myriem: First Name: Carmen, *737;* Hail Mary, *742;* Sacrilege, *782*

Roussel, Nathalie: My Father's Glory, *769;* My Mother's Castle, *770*

Routledge, Alison: Bridge to Nowhere, *469;* Quiet Earth, The, *1073*

Routledge, Patricia: 30 Is a Dangerous Age, Cynthia, *394*

Rouvel, Catherine: Assassins de L'Ordre, Les (Law Breakers), *714;* Black and White in Color, *718;* Borsalino, *18;* Picnic on the Grass, *777*

Rouyer, Andre: Maitresse, *764*

Rovensky, Joseph: Diary of a Lost Girl, *730*

Roversi, Patrizio: Volere Volare, *801*

Roveryre, Liliane: Dirty Dishes, *730*

Rowan, Dan: Bloopers from Star Trek and Laugh-In, *242*

Rowan, Frank: Sidewalks of New York, *378*

Rowan, Kelly: Adrift, *950*

Rowe, Douglas: Appointment with Fear, *6*

Rowe, Greg: Blue Fin, *151*

Rowe, Misty: Goodbye, Norma Jean, *530;* Hitchhikers, *850;* Man with Bogart's Face, The, *995;* Meatballs Part II, *330;* When Things Were Rotten (TV Series), *409*

Rowe, Nevan: Nutcase, *347;* Sleeping Dogs, *117*

Rowe, Nicholas: Lawrenceville Stories, The, *317;* Young Sherlock Holmes, *141*

Rowland, Duane: Longest Hunt, The, *1130*

Rowlands, Gena: Another Woman, *450;* Brinks Job, The, *246;* Child is Waiting, A, *480;* Crazy in Love, *490;* Early Frost, An, *506;* Gloria, *56;* Light of Day, *575;* Lonely Are the Brave, *1129;* Love Streams, *582;* Montana, *599;* Night on Earth, *606;* Once Around, *349;* Opening Night, *614;* Rapunzel, *198;* Strangers: The Story of a Mother and a Daughter, *669;* Tempest (1982), *678;* Tony Rome, *1025;* Two-Minute Warning, *1028;* Woman Under the Influence, A, *705*

Rowles, Polly: Springtime in the Rockies (1937), *1152*

Royale, Allan: Man Inside, The (1984), *81*

Royce, Lionel: Manhunt in the African Jungle (Secret Service in Darkest Africa), *81;* White Pongo (a.k.a. Blond Gorilla), *902*

Royce, Roselyn: Sizzle Beach, U.S.A., *380*

Royle, Carol: Tuxedo Warrior, *133*

Royle, Selena: Big Hangover, The, *238;* Courage of Lassie, *160;* Fighting Sullivans, The, *516;* Mrs. Parkington, *598*

Rozakis, Gregory: Abduction, *950*

Rubbo, Joe: Last American Virgin, The, *315*

Rubes, Jan: Birds II, The: Land's End, *813;* Blood Relations, *816;* Class Action, *962;* D2: The Mighty Ducks, *160;* Dead of Winter, *967;* Deceived, *969;* Descending Angel, *499;* Devlin, *970;* Outside Chance of Maximilian Glick, The, *193*

Rubin, Andrew: Police Academy, *359*

Rubin, Benny: Go Into Your Dance, *920*

Rubin, Jennifer: Bad Dreams, *811;* Bitter Harvest (1993), *955;* Crush, The, *964;* Delusion (1991), *499;* Drop Dead Gorgeous, *972;* Fear Inside, The, *976;* Victim of Beauty, *1030;* Woman Her Men and Her Futon, A, *705*

Rubin, Michael: I Was a Teenage Zombie, *855*

Rubinek, Saul: Agency, *443;* Bonfire of the Vanities, *466;* By Design, *473;* Deathship, *832;* Getting Even with Dad, *285;* Highpoint, *62;* Man Trouble, *327;* Nothing Personal, *347;* Obsessed, *610;* Outside Chance of Maximilian Glick, The, *193;* Soup for One, *383;* Sweet Liberty, *389;* Ticket to Heaven, *683;* True Romance, *133;* Young Doctors in Love, *415*

Rubini, Giulia: Adios, Hombre, *1092;* Goliath and the Barbarians, *56*

Rubini, Sergio: Station, The, *789*

Rubinstein, John: Another Stakeout, *6;* In Search of Historic Jesus, *550;* M.A.D.D.: Mothers Against Drunk Driving, *583;* Make Me an Offer, *586;* She's Dressed to Kill, *656;* Zachariah, *1166*

Rubinstein, Zelda: Anguish, *809;* Poltergeist II: The Other Side, *875;* Poltergeist III, *876;* Teen Witch, *392*

Rubio, Pablo Alvarez: Dracula (Spanish Version), *732*

Ruck, Alan: Ferris Bueller's Day Off, *276;* Three for the Road, *395;* Young Guns II, *1166*

Rudd, Bob: Married People, Single Sex, *589*

Rudd, Paul: Mark Twain's Connecticut Yankee in King Arthur's Court, *185*

Rudder, Michael: Lifeforce Experiment, The, *1063*

Ruddock, John: Martin Luther, *589*

Rudley, Herbert: Jayhawkers, The, *1123*

Rudner, Rita: Peter's Friends, *621*

Rudnik, Oleg: Yuri Nosenko, KGB, *709*

Rudy, Reed: Free Ride, *281*

Rue, Frank La: Sidewalks of New York, *378*

Ruehl, Mercedes: Another You, *228;* Fisher King, The, *1051;* Last Action Hero, The, *1062;* Leader of the Band, *317;* Lost in Yonkers, *580;* Married to the Mob, *329*

Ruffman, Mag: Tales From Avonlea (TV series), *209*

Rufus: Jonah Who Will Be 25 in the Year 2000, *750*

Ruggles, Charlie: All in a Night's Work, *224;* Balalaika, *907;* Breaking the Ice, *909;* Bringing Up Baby, *246;* Doughgirls, The, *268;* If I Had a Million, *304;* Invisible Woman, The, *307;* Look For The Silver Lining, *929;* Love Me Tonight, *929;* Melody Cruise, *930;* Murders in the Zoo, *867;* Papa's Delicate Condition, *617;* Perfect Marriage, *356;* Ramrod, *1140;* Ruggles of Red Gap, *371;* Stolen Life, A, *668;* Ugly Dachshund, The, *214*

Ruggles, Derya: Remote, *198*

Ruggles, Wesley: Charlie Chaplin Cavalcade, *253;* Rare Chaplin, *364*

Ruhmann, Heinz: Faraway, So Close, *736*

Ruick, Barbara: Carousel, *911;* I Love Melvin, *924*

Rule, Janice: Alvarez Kelly, *1093;* Ambushers, The, *4;* American Flyers, *446;* Battle Shock, *812;* Chase, The (1966), *479;* Doctors' Wives, *503;* Gumshoe, *291;* Invitation to a Gunfighter, *1123;* Missing, *596;* Swimmer, The, *675*

Rulu, Francesco: Grim Reaper, The (1962), *742*

Ruman, Sig: Bitter Sweet, *909;* Bold Caballero, The, *1099;* Comrade X, *258;* Errand Boy, The, *272;* Honolulu, *923;* House of Frankenstein, *852;* Love Crazy, *322;* Maytime, *930;* Night at the Opera, A, *344;* Only Angels Have Wings, *95;* Saint in New York, The, *1012;* That Uncertain Feeling, *393;* Thin Ice, *945*

Run-DMC: Krush Groove, *927;* Tougher Than Leather, *131*

Runacre, Jenny: Jubilee, *1061;* Last Days of Man on Earth, The, *1062;* Passenger, The, *1004*

Running Fox, Joseph: Avenging, The, *1095;* Geronimo, *1115*

Runyeon, Frank: Sudden Death, *122*

Runyon, Jennifer: Blue De Ville, *242;* Carnosaur, *821;* 18 Again, *270;* Killing Streets, *72;* Man Called Sarge, A, *327;* Quantum Leap (TV Series), *1072;* To All a Good Night, *895*

Ruocheng, Ying: Last Emperor, The, *569*

Ruscio, Elizabeth: Cast the First Stone, *476;* Hider in the House, *982*

Rush, Barbara: Between Friends, *459;* Bramble Bush, The, *468;* Can't Stop the Music, *911;* Come Blow Your Horn, *257;* Hombre, *1121;* It Came from Outer Space, *1060;* Moon of the Wolf, *866;* Robin & the Seven Hoods, *936;* Seekers, The, *651;* Strangers When We Meet, *670;* Summer Lovers, *672;* Superdad, *208;* Web of Deceit, *1030;* When Worlds Collide, *1089;* Young Lions, The, *708;* Young Philadelphians, The, *708*

Rush, Deborah: Big Business, *238;* My Blue Heaven, *339*

Rush, Elizabeth: Invasion of the Girl Snatchers, *307*

Rush, Sarah: For Love of Angela, *519*

Rushton, Jared: Big, *237;* Cry in the Wild, A, *31;* Honey, I Shrunk the Kids, *175;* Pet Sematary Two, *874*

Rusic, Rita: Third Solution, The, *794*

Ruskin, Joseph: Gypsy Warriors, The, *58*

Rusler, Robert: Assassination Game, The, *7;* Final Embrace, *977;* Game of Love, The, *524;* Sometimes They Come Back, *888;* Thrashin', *128;* Vamp, *899*

Russ, Tim: Heroes of Desert Storm, *61*

Russ, William: Aspen Extreme, *451;* Beer, *233;* Crazy from the Heart, *490;* Crisis at Central High, *491;* Dead of Winter, *967;* Disorganized Crime, *40;* Drive Like Lightning, *42;* Pastime, *619;* Raw Courage, *103;* Traces of Red, *1026;* Unholy, The, *899;* Wanted: Dead or Alive, *136*

Russel, Reb: Lightning Triggers, *1128*

Russell, Andy: Copacabana, *259*

Russell, Betsy: Avenging Angel, *8;* Cheerleader Camp, *823;* Delta Heat, *37;* Out of Control, *352;* Tomboy, *130;* Trapper County War, *132*

Russell, Bryan: Adventures of Bullwhip Griffin, The, *143;* Charlie, the Lonesome Cougar, *158;* Emil and the Detectives, *164*

Russell, Craig: Outrageous, *352;* Too Outrageous, *686*

Russell, Dean: Forest, The, *842*

Russell, Elizabeth: Corpse Vanishes, The, *825;* Curse of the Cat People, The, *828*

Russell, Gail: Angel and the Badman, *1093;* Great Dan Patch, The, *532;* Moonrise, *599;* Uninvited, The (1944), *1029;* Wake of the Red Witch, *136*

Russell, Harold: Best Years of Our Lives, The, *459*

Russell, Jane: Double Dynamite, *268;* French Line, The, *918;* Gentlemen Prefer Blondes, *284;* His Kind of Woman, *62;* Johnny Reno, *1124;* Las Vegas Story, The, *568;* Macao, *80;* Montana Belle, *1134;* Outlaw, The, *1137;* Paleface, The, *353;* Son of Paleface, *383;* Tall Men, The, *1154;* Underwater!, *134*

Russell, John: Buckskin, *1102;* Forever Amber, *520;* Hoodlum Empire, *64;* Hostile Guns, *1122;* Jubilee Trail, *1124;* Man in the Saddle, *1132;* Oklahoma Annie, *349;* Outlaw Josey Wales, The, *1137;* Pale Rider, *1138;* Rio Bravo, *1145;* Sun Shines Bright, The, *673;* Under the Gun, *691*

Russell, Karen: Dead Certain, *967*

Russell, Ken: Russia House, The, *646*

Russell, Kimberly: Ghost Dad, *285*

Russell, Kurt: Backdraft, *8;* Barefoot Executive, The, *148;* Best of Times, The, *236;* Big Trouble in Little China, *13;* Captain Ron, *250;* Charley and the Angel, *157;* Christmas Coal Mine Miracle, The, *159;* Computer Wore Tennis Shoes, The, *159;* Elvis—The Movie, *509;* Escape from New York, *45;* Follow Me, Boys!, *167;* Fugitive, The (TV Series), *523;* Guns of Diablo, *1118;* Horse in the Gray Flannel Suit, The, *175;* Longest Drive, The, *1130;* Mean Season, The, *996;* Now You See Him, Now You Don't, *191;* Overboard, *352;* Search for the Gods, *1076;* Silkwood, *658;* Superdad, *208;* Swing Shift, *675;* Tango and Cash, *124;* Tequila Sunrise, *126;* Thing, The (1982), *1083;* Tombstone, *1157;* Unlawful Entry, *1029;* Used Cars, *404;* Winter People, *704*

Russell, Leon: Mad Dogs and Englishmen, *429*

Russell, Lisa Ann: Apex, *1036*

Russell, Mary: Riders of the Whistling Skull, *1144*

Russell, Nipsey: Car 54, Where Are You?, *250;* Wildcats, *411;* Wiz, The, *948*

Russell, Rosalind: Auntie Mame, *229;* Citadel, The, *482;* Craig's Wife, *490;* Evelyn Prentice, *511;* Forsaking All Others, *279;* Gypsy (1962), *921;* His Girl Friday, *297;* Majority of One, A, *326;* Never Wave at a WAC, *343;* Night Must Fall, *606;* Oh Dad, Poor Dad—Mama's Hung You in the Closet and I'm Feeling So Sad, *348;* Picnic, *622;* Reckless (1935), *636;* Sister Kenny, *659;* Tell It to the Judge, *392;* They Met in Bombay, *127;* Trouble with Angels, The, *399;* Velvet Touch, The, *693;* Woman of Distinction, A, *413;* Women, The, *413*

Russell, T. E.: Linda, *992*

Russell, Theresa: Aria, *907;* Black Widow, *955;* Cold Heaven, *485;* Eureka, *511;* Impulse (1990), *985;* Insignificance, *553;* Kafka, *988;* Physical Evidence, *1006;* Razor's Edge, The (1984), *635;* Straight Time, *668;* Track 29, *1026;* Whore, *701*

Russell, Tony: Soul Hustler, *118*

Russinova, Isabel: Tex and the Lord of the Deep, *1155*

Russo, Gianni: Four Deuces, The, *52*

Russo, James: Bad Girls (1994), *1095;* Blue Iguana, *242;* China Girl, *25;* Cold Heaven, *485;* Davinci's War, *33;* Extremities, *512;* Freeway, *52;* Illicit Behavior, *985;* Intimate Stranger, *986;* Kiss Before Dying, A, *989;* Trauma, *897;* We're No Angels (1989), *408*

Russo, Michael: Nitti: The Enforcer, *91*

Russo, René: Freejack, *1053;* In the Line of Fire, *66;* Lethal Weapon 3, *77;* One Good Cop, *613*

Rust, Richard: Double Revenge, *504;* Great Gundown, *1116*

Ruth, Babe: Pride of the Yankees, The, *627*

Rutherford, Ann: Adventures of Don Juan, The, *2;* Andy Hardy Gets Spring Fever, *227;* Andy Hardy's Double Life, *227;* Andy Hardy's Private Secretary, *227;* Fighting Marines, The, *48;* Lawless Nineties, The, *1127;* Life Begins for Andy Hardy, *318;* Lonely Trail, The, *1129;* Love Finds Andy Hardy, *322;* Melody Trail, *1133;* Of Human Hearts, *610;* Orchestra Wives, *934;* Public Cowboy #1, *1140;* Secret Life of Walter Mitty, The, *374;* They Only Kill Their Masters, *1024;* Whistling in Brooklyn, *410;* Whistling in Dixie, *410;* Whistling in the Dark, *410*

Rutherford, Margaret: Alphabet Murders, The, *951;* Chimes at Midnight, *481;* Importance of Being Earnest, The, *305;* Murder Ahoy, *998;* Murder at the Gallop, *998;* Murder Most Foul, *998;* Murder She Said, *999;* Passport to Pimlico, *355;* Smallest Show on Earth, The, *381;* To See Such Fun, *397;* V.I.P.s, The, *693*

Ruttan, Susan: Eye of the Demon, *840;* Funny About Love, *282;* L.A. Law, *567*

Ruymen, Ann: Private Parts, *876*

Ruysdael, Basil: Broken Arrow, *1101;* Carrie (1952), *476*

Ryan, Anne: Three O'Clock High, *396*

Ryan, Edmon: Human Monster, The (Dark Eyes of London), *854;* Two for the Seesaw, *690*

Ryan, Fran: Rebel Love, *636*

Ryan, Hilary: Getting of Wisdom, The, *526*

Ryan, Irene: Beverly Hillbillies, The (TV Series), *237;* Beverly Hillbillies Go Hollywood, The, *237;* Melody for Three, *592*

Ryan, James: Kill and Kill Again, *71;* Kill or Be Killed, *71;* No One Cries Forever, *608;* Pursuit, *101*

Ryan, John P.: Avenging Force, *8;* Best of the Best, *11;* Breathless (1983), *469;* City of Shadows, *26;* Class of 1999, *1041;* Death Wish IV: The Crackdown, *36;* Delta Force 2, *36;* Delta Force 3, *37;* Fatal Beauty, *46;* Futureworld, *1053;* Hoffa, *542;* It Lives Again, *857;* It's Alive!, *857;* Paramedics, *353;* Postman Always Rings Twice, The (1981), *1007;* Rent-a-Cop, *105;* Runaway Train, *110;* Shamus, *1014;* Three O'Clock High, *396*

Ryan, Kathleen: Odd Man Out, *1003;* Try and Get Me, *133*

Ryan, Leslie: Terror in Paradise, *126*

Ryan, Madge: Who Is Killing the Great Chefs of Europe?, *410*

Ryan, Meg: Amityville III: The Demon, *809;* Armed and Dangerous, *228;* D.O.A. (1988), *965;* Doors, The, *914;* Flesh and Bone, *518;* Innerspace, *1058;* Joe Versus the Volcano,

310; Prelude to a Kiss, 360; Presidio, The, 100; Promised Land, 629; Rich and Famous, 639; Sleepless in Seattle, 381; When a Man Loves a Woman, 698; When Harry Met Sally, 409
Ryan, Mitchell: Aces: Iron Eagle III, 1; Angel City, 448; Choice, The, 481; Christmas Coal Mine Miracle, The, 159; Deadly Game, 34; Dirty Work, 970; Electra Glide in Blue, 43; Fatal Vision, 515; Gambler, Part II—The Adventure Continues, The, 1115; High Plains Drifter, 1120; Judgment, 560; Lethal Weapon, 76; Medicine Hat Stallion, The, 186; Monte Walsh, 1134; My Old Man's Place, 602; Opposite Sex (And How to Live with Them), The, 351; Winter People, 704
Ryan, Peggy: Here Come the Co-Eds, 296; Miss Annie Rooney, 188; Private Buckaroo, 935
Ryan, R. L.: Eat and Run, 1048
Ryan, Robert: And Hope to Die, 952; Anzio, 6; Back from Eternity, 453; Bad Day at Black Rock, 454; Battle of the Bulge, 10; Behind the Rising Sun, 10; Berlin Express, 10; Best of the Badmen, 1097; Beware, My Lovely, 955; Billy Budd, 461; Bombardier, 17; Born to Be Bad, 467; Boy With Green Hair, The, 468; Caught, 477; Clash by Night, 483; Crossfire (1947), 964; Escape to Burma, 510; Executive Action, 512; Flying Leathernecks, 51; God's Little Acre, 529; Ice Palace, 548; Iron Major, The, 554; King of Kings (1961), 565; Lawman, 1127; Lonelyhearts, 578; Love Machine, The, 581; Marine Raiders, 82; Men in War, 84; Minute to Pray, A Second to Die, A, 1134; Naked Spur, The, 1135; On Dangerous Ground, 1003; Professionals, The, 101; Racket, The, 633; Return of the Badmen, 1142; Set-Up, The, 1013; Sky's the Limit, The, 940; Tall Men, The, 1154; Tender Comrade, 679; Trail Street, 1158; Wild Bunch, The, 1164
Ryan, Sheila: Great Guns, 289; Mule Train, 1134; On Top of Old Smoky, 1137; Railroaded, 633; Song of Texas, 1151
Ryan, Steve: Crime Story, 30
Ryan, Thomas: Talent for the Game, 677
Ryan, Tim: China Beach (TV Series), 481; Detour, 970; Lightning Incident, The, 860; Runestone, 882
Ryan, Tommy: Prairie Moon, 1139
Rydall, Derek: Night Visitor (1989), 1001; Phantom of the Mall—Eric's Revenge, 874
Rydell, Bobby: Bye Bye Birdie, 910
Rydell, Christopher: Flesh and Bone, 518; For the Boys, 918; Trauma, 897
Rydell, Mark: Long Goodbye, The, 993; Punchline, 630
Ryder, Alfred: T-Men, 676
Ryder, Winona: Age of Innocence, The, 443; Beetlejuice, 233; Bram Stoker's Dracula, 819; Edward Scissorhands, 1048; Great Balls of Fire, 920; Heathers, 295; House of the Spirits, The, 545; Lucas, 583; Mermaids, 331; Night on Earth, 606; 1969, 607; Reality Bites, 635; Square Dance, 665; Welcome Home, Roxy Carmichael, 407
Ryecart, Patrick: Silas Marner, 657; Twenty-One, 690
Ryslinge, Helle: Ladies on the Rocks, 755
Ryu, Chishu: Autumn Afternoon, An, 714; Late Spring, 756; Tokyo-Ga, 796; Tokyo Story, 796; Twenty-four Eyes, 797
S., Bruno: Every Man for Himself and God Against All, 735; Stroszek, 790
Saad, Margit: Concrete Jungle, The (1962) (a.k.a. The Criminal), 487
Saadi, Yacef: Battle of Algiers, 716
Sabatino, Michael: Jigsaw Murders, The, 987
Sabato, Antonio: Beyond the Law, 1097; Grand Prix, 531; Twice a Judas, 1159
Sabela, Simon: African Rage, 3
Sabin, David: When Things Were Rotten (TV Series), 409
Sabiston, Andrew: Prep School, 360
Sabu: Arabian Nights (1942), 6; Black Narcissus, 463; Drums, 42; Elephant Boy, 44; Jungle Book (1942), 179; Pardon My Trunk, 775; Thief of Bagdad, The (1940), 1083; Tiger Walks, A, 211
Saburi, Shin: Equinox Flower, 734
Sacchi, Robert: Cold Heat, 28; Man with Bogart's Face, The, 995
Sachs, Adrienne: In the Cold of the Night, 986; Two to Tango, 133
Sachs, Andrew: Romance with a Double Bass, 370
Sachs, Stephen: Dorm that Dripped Blood, The, 837
Sacks, Martin: Slate, Wyn, and Me, 660
Sacks, Michael: Bunco, 21; Slaughterhouse Five, 1077; Sugarland Express, The, 672
Sadler, Barry: Dayton's Devils, 33
Sadler, Bill: Bill and Ted's Bogus Journey, 239; Freaked, 281; Hot Spot, 544; Project X, 1072; Rush, 645; Tagget, 124; Tales from the Crypt (Series), 892; Trespass, 132
Safonova, Elena: Accompanist, The, 710
Sagal, Katey: It's a Bundyful Life, 308
Sagalle, Jonathan: Schindler's List, 649
Sage, William: Simple Men, 379
Sägebrecht, Marianne: Bagdad Café, 231; Rosalie Goes Shopping, 370; Sugarbaby, 791; War of the Roses, The, 406
Sager, Ray: Wizard of Gore, The, 904
Saget, Bob: Best of America's Funniest Home Videos, The, 235; Paramount Comedy Theatre, Vol. 1: Well Developed, 353
Sagoes, Ken: Death by Dialogue, 968
Sahagun, Elena: Naked Obsession, 1000
Sahara, Kenji: Godzilla's Revenge, 847; King Kong vs. Godzilla, 859; Mysterians, The, 1067; Rodan, 1075; Son of Godzilla, 888
Sahl, Mort: Hungry I Reunion, 303; More Milton Berle's Mad World of Comedy, 431
Saiger, Susan: Eating Raoul, 270
Sail, Sekkou: IP5: The Island of Pachyderms, 748
St. Cyr, Lili: I, Mobster, 65
Saint, Eva Marie: All Fall Down, 444; Best Little Girl in the World, The, 459; Breaking Home Ties, 469; Cancel My Reservation, 250; Christmas to Remember, A, 482; Curse of King Tut's Tomb, The, 828; Exodus, 512; Fatal Vision, 515; Grand Prix, 531; Jane Doe, 556; Last Days of Patton, The, 569; Love Leads the Way, 581; North by Northwest, 1002; Nothing in Common, 609; On the Waterfront, 612; Raintree County, 634; Russians Are Coming, the Russians Are Coming, The, 371; Sandpiper, The, 648; Stalking Moon, The, 1152; 36 Hours, 681; Voyage of Terror: The Achille Lauro Affair, 694
St. Jacques, Raymond: Final Comedown, The, 48; Green Berets, The, 57; Kill Castro, 71; Search for the Gods, 1076; Sophisticated Gents, The, 663; Voodoo Dawn, 901; Wild Pair, The, 140
Saint James, Susan: Carbon Copy, 251; Desperate Women, 1109; Don't Cry, It's Only Thunder, 503; How to Beat the High Co$t of Living, 302; Love at First Bite, 322; Outlaw Blues, 352; S.O.S. Titanic, 646
St. John, Al: Black Lash, 1099; Border Feud, 1100; Border Roundup, 1100; Buster Keaton: The Great Stone Face, 248; Charlie Chaplin...Our Hero, 253; Cheyenne Takes Over, 1104; Death Rides the Plains, 1108; Fatty and Mabel Adrift/Mabel, Fatty and the Law, 275; Fatty Arbuckle Comedy Collection, Vol. 1, 275; Fatty's Tin-Type Tangle/Our Congressman, 275; Fighting Deputy, 1112; His Brother's Ghost, 1121; Keystone Comedies, Vol. 1, 312; Keystone Comedies, Vol. 2, 312; Keystone Comedies, Vol. 3, 312; Keystone Comedies, Vol. 4, 312; King of the Bullwhip, 1125; Law of the Lash, 1127; Lawman Is Born, A, 1127; Li'l Abner (1940), 318; Lost and Found Chaplin: Keystone, 321; Mack Sennett Comedies, Vol. 2, 325; Prairie Rustlers, 1139; Return of the Lash, 1142; Riders of Destiny, 1144; Sing, Cowboy, Sing, 1150; Stage to Mesa City, 1152; Thundering Herd, 1157
St. John, Betta: Corridors of Blood, 825; Horror Hotel, 851
St. John, Howard: Don't Drink the Water, 267; Li'l Abner (1959), 928
St. John, Jill: Act, The, 441; Come Blow Your Horn, 257; Concrete Jungle, The (1982), 28; Diamonds Are Forever, 38; Tony Rome, 1025
St. John, Michelle: Where the Spirit Lives, 699

Saint-Cyr, Renée: Pearls of the Crown, The, *776*
Sainte-Marie, Buffy: Broken Chain, The, *20*
Sakaguchi, Seiji: Forced Vengeance, *51*
Sakai, Franky: Mothra, *1067*
Sakall, S. Z.: Ball of Fire, *231;* Christmas in Connecticut (1945), *255;* Devil and Miss Jones, The, *264;* In the Good Old Summertime, *925;* It's a Big Country, *308;* It's a Date, *925;* Look For The Silver Lining, *929;* Lullaby of Broadway, *929;* My Dream Is Yours, *932;* Romance on the High Seas, *937;* San Antonio, *1147;* Small Town Girl, *940;* Spring Parade, *941;* Tea for Two, *944;* Wintertime, *947;* Wonder Man, *413*
Sakamoto, Ryuichi: Merry Christmas, Mr. Lawrence, *593*
Sakata, Harold: Goldfinger, *56;* Impulse (1974), *985;* Jaws of Death, The, *858*
Saks, Gene: Goodbye People, The, *530;* One and Only, The, *613;* Prisoner of Second Avenue, The, *361;* Thousand Clowns, A, *395*
Salazar, Abel: Brainiac, The, *818;* Curse of the Crying Woman, The, *828;* Man and the Monster, The, *862;* Vampire, The, *899*
Salcedo, Leopoldo: Cry of Battle, *31*
Saldana, Theresa: Angel Town, *5;* Defiance, *36;* Double Revenge, *504;* Evil That Men Do, The, *45;* I Wanna Hold Your Hand, *304;* Night Before, The, *344;* Raging Bull, *633*
Sale, Chic: Fighting Westerner, The, *1113*
Sale, Virginia: Hatbox Mystery, The, *982*
Salem, Kario: Jericho Fever, *68;* Underground Aces, *403*
Salenger, Meredith: Dream a Little Dream, *269;* Edge of Honor, *43;* Journey of Natty Gann, The, *179;* Kiss, The (1988), *859;* Night in the Life of Jimmy Reardon, A, *344*
Salerno, Enrico Maria: Bird with the Crystal Plumage, The, *955;* Cheaters, The, *723*
Salinas, Carmen: Danzon, *728*
Salinger, Diane: Morning After, The, *997;* Pee-Wee's Big Adventure, *355*
Salinger, Matt: Captain America (1990), *22;* Firehawk, *49;* Manhunt for Claude Dallas, *81;* Options, *351*
Salmi, Albert: Ambushers, The, *4;* Born American, *17;* Breaking In, *245;* Brothers Karamazov, The, *471;* Empire of the Ants, *1049;* Hard to Hold, *922;* Jesse, *557;* Kill Castro, *71;* Lawman, *1127;* Meanest Men in the West, The, *1133;* Menace on the Mountain, *593;* Night Games, *1001;* St. Helens, *646;* Steel, *120;* Unforgiven, The (1960), *1160*
Salmon, Colin: Prime Suspect 2, *1007*
Salt, Jennifer: Hi Mom, *297;* Sisters (1973), *1017;* Wedding Party, The, *407*
Saltarrelli, Elizabeth: Bound and Gagged: A Love Story, *18*
Salvador, Phillip: Fight for Us, *47*
Salvatori, Renato: Big Deal on Madonna Street, *717;* Burn!, *472;* Rocco & His Brothers, *782;* State of Siege, *788*
Salzman, Mark: Iron & Silk, *554*
Sambrell, Aldo: Tex and the Lord of the Deep, *1155;* Yellow Hair and the Fortress of Gold, *1165*
Samms, Emma: Goliath Awaits, *56;* Illusions, *985;* More Wild Wild West, *1134;* Shrimp on the Barbie, *378*
Samoilova, Tatyana: Cranes are Flying, The, *726*
Sampson, Robert: Dark Side of the Moon, The, *1044;* Indecent Behavior, *551;* Re-Animator, *879;* Robot Jox, *1075*
Sampson, Tim: War Party, *137*
Sampson, Will: Buffalo Bill and the Indians, *1102;* Fish Hawk, *517;* Insignificance, *553;* One Flew Over the Cuckoo's Nest, *613;* Orca, *873;* Poltergeist II: The Other Side, *875;* Standing Tall, *1153;* Vega$, *135;* White Buffalo, *1164*
Samuel, Joanne: Alison's Birthday, *808;* Gallagher's Travels, *54;* Mad Max, *1064*
Samuels, Haydon: I Live With Me Dad, *547*
San Giacomo, Laura: Pretty Woman, *361;* Sex, Lies and Videotape, *653;* Under Suspicion, *1028;* Where the Day Takes You, *699*
San Juan, Olga: Beautiful Blonde from Bashful Bend, The, *233*
San, Lu Man: Scent of Green Papaya, The, *784*
Sanchez, Jaime: Florida Straits, *51*
Sanchez, Pedro: Final Defeat, The, *1113;* Go Kill and Come Back, *1115;* White Fang and the Hunter, *217*
Sancho, Fernando: Boldest Job in the West, The, *1099;* Django Shoots First, *1109*
Sand, Paul: Can't Stop the Music, *911;* Great Bank Hoax, The, *289;* Hot Rock, The, *983;* Last Fling, The, *315;* Main Event, The, *326;* Wholly Moses!, *410*
Sanda, Dominique: Cabo Blanco, *21;* Conformist, The, *725;* Damnation Alley, *1044;* Garden of the Finzi-Continis, The, *740;* Mackintosh Man, The, *994;* 1900, *607;* Nobody's Children, *608;* Steppenwolf, *667;* Story of a Love Story, *668*
Sande, Walter: Don Winslow of the Navy, *41*
Sander, Otto: Faraway, So Close, *736;* Wings of Desire, *804*
Sanders, Brad: Indecent Behavior, *551*
Sanders, George: Action in Arabia, *2;* All About Eve, *444;* Allegheny Uprising, *1093;* Amorous Adventures of Moll Flanders, The, *226;* Bitter Sweet, *909;* Black Jack, *14;* Candyman, The (1968), *474;* Death of a Scoundrel, *498;* Doomwatch, *1048;* Endless Night, *973;* Falcon Takes Over, The, *975;* Falcon's Brother, The, *975;* Five Golden Hours, *278;* Foreign Correspondent, *978;* Forever Amber, *520;* From the Earth to the Moon, *1053;* Ghost and Mrs. Muir, The, *285;* House of the Seven Gables, The, *545;* In Search of the Castaways, *176;* Ivanhoe (1952), *68;* Jupiter's Darling, *926;* Last Voyage, The, *76;* Man Hunt (1941), *994;* Mr. Moto's Last Warning, *997;* Moon and Sixpence, The, *599;* Nurse Edith Cavell, *610;* One Step to Hell, *95;* Picture of Dorian Gray, The, *875;* Private Affairs of Bel Ami, The, *628;* Psychomania, *877;* Quiller Memorandum, The, *102;* Rebecca, *1009;* Saint in London, The, *1012;* Saint Strikes Back, The, *1012;* Samson and Delilah (1949), *648;* Shot in the Dark, A, *378;* Solomon and Sheba, *661;* Son of Monte Cristo, The, *118;* Strange Affai of Uncle Harry, The, *669;* Strange Woman, The, *669;* Sundown (1941), *673;* This Land Is Mine, *682;* Village of the Damned, *900;* Voyage in Italy, *801;* While the City Sleeps, *138*
Sanders, Henry G.: Boss' Son, The, *467;* Rebel (1973), *104*
Sanders, Hugh: Pride of St. Louis, The, *627*
Sanders, Jay O.: Hostages, *544;* JFK, *558;* Misfit Brigade, The, *85;* Nobody's Children, *608;* V. I. Warshawski, *1029*
Sanders, Peggie: Lady Avenger, *74*
Sanders, Richard: Neon City, *1067*
Sanderson, William: Last Man Standing, *569;* Lonesome Dove, *1129;* Mirror Mirror, *865;* Raggedy Man, *1008;* Return to Lonesome Dove, *1143;* Savage Weekend, *883*
Sandler, Adam: Airheads, *906*
Sandlund, Debra: Victimless Crimes, *1030*
Sandor, Steve: Bonnie's Kids, *17;* Dynamo, *42;* Stryker, *1081*
Sandrelli, Stefania: Conformist, The, *725;* Divorce—Italian Style, *731;* Family, The (1987), *735;* Jamon, Jamon, *749;* Partner, *775;* Seduced and Abandoned, *784;* We All Loved Each Other So Much, *802*
Sandrini, Luis: El Professor Hippie, *734*
Sands, Billy: Sgt. Bilko (TV Series), *376*
Sands, Diana: Georgia, Georgia, *526;* Raisin in the Sun, A (1961), *634*
Sands, Johnny: Admiral Was a Lady, The, *222*
Sands, Julian: After Darkness, *951;* Boxing Helena, *818;* Crazy in Love, *490;* Doctor and the Devils, The, *835;* Gothic, *847;* Grand Isle, *531;* Husbands and Lovers, *546;* Impromptu, *549;* Killing Fields, The, *563;* Murder by Moonlight, *1067;* Naked Lunch, *1067;* Room with a View, A, *644;* Siesta, *1016;* Tale of a Vampire, *891;* Turn of the Screw (1992), *898;* Vibes, *1087;* Warlock (1988), *901;* Warlock: The Armageddon, *901*
Sands, Sonny: Bellboy, The, *234*
Sands, Tommy: Babes in Toyland (1961), *147;* Ensign Pulver, *271;* None But the Brave, *92*
Sands, Walter: Blonde Ice, *464*
Sandweiss, Ellen: Evil Dead, The, *839*
Sanford, Erskine: Lady from Shanghai, *989;* Letter from an Unknown Woman, *573*

Sanford, Isabel: Desperate Moves, *264;* Pucker Up and Bark Like a Dog, *363*
Sanford, Stanley: Laurel and Hardy Classics, Volume 2, *316;* Laurel and Hardy Classics, Volume 8, *316*
Santagata, Alfonso: Palombella Rossa, *775*
Santana, Ernie: Sudden Thunder, *122*
Santiago, Saundra: Miami Vice, *84*
Santini, Pierre: Dirty Dishes, *730*
Santoni, Reni: Anzio, *6;* Bad Boys, *454;* Cobra (1986), *27;* Dead Men Don't Wear Plaid, *262;* Dirty Harry, *39;* Enter Laughing, *271;* No Greater Gift, *191;* They Went That-A-Way and That-A-Way, *210*
Santos, Joe: Blade, *14;* Blue Knight, The (1973), *465;* Deadly Desire, *968;* Mo' Money, *335;* Rockford Files, The (TV Series), *108;* Zandy's Bride, *1166*
Santschi, Tom: Phantom of the West, *1138*
Santucci, John: Crime Story, *30*
Sanville, Michael: Dreams Come True, *1048;* First Turn-on, The, *277*
Sanz, Jorge: Belle Epoque, *716;* Lovers (1992), *762;* Valentina, *799*
Sapara, Ade: Crusoe, *31*
Sapienza, Johnny: Kenneth Anger—Volume Three, *563*
Sara, Mia: Any Man's Death, *450;* Apprentice to Murder, *810;* Blindsided, *956;* Call of the Wild (1992), *474;* Caroline at Midnight, *960;* Climate for Killing, A, *962;* Ferris Bueller's Day Off, *276;* Legend, *1062;* Queenie, *632;* Shadows in the Storm, *654;* Stranger Among Us, A, *1020*
Sarafian, Richard: Bugsy, *471;* Gunmen, *58;* Ruby (1991), *644*
Sarandon, Chris: Child's Play, *823;* Collision Course, *257;* Cuba, *31;* Dark Tide, *495;* Dog Day Afternoon, *971;* Forced March, *519;* Fright Night, *844;* Goodbye, Miss 4th of July, *171;* Lipstick, *992;* Mayflower Madam, *591;* Osterman Weekend, The, *96;* Princess Bride, The, *1071;* Protocol, *363;* Resurrected, The, *879;* Sentinel, The, *884;* Slaves of New York, *381;* Tailspin, *676;* Tale of Two Cities, A (1980), *677;* Whispers, *1031*
Sarandon, Susan: Atlantic City, *452;* Beauty and the Beast (1983), *149;* Buddy System, The, *471;* Bull Durham, *247;* Compromising Positions, *258;* Dry White Season, A, *505;* Front Page, The (1974), *281;* Great Smokey Roadblock, The, *57;* Great Waldo Pepper, The, *57;* Hunger, The (1983), *854;* January Man, The, *987;* Joe, *558;* King of the Gypsies, *565;* Light Sleeper, *575;* Lorenzo's Oil, *579;* Loving Couples, *324;* Mussolini and I, *601;* Other Side of Midnight, The, *615;* Pretty Baby, *626;* Rocky Horror Picture Show, The, *937;* Something Short of Paradise, *383;* Sweethearts' Dance, *675;* Tempest (1982), *678;* Thelma & Louise, *127;* White Palace, *700;* Who Am I This Time?, *410;* Witches of Eastwick, The, *412;* Women of Valor, *706*
Sarasohn, Lane: Groove Tube, The, *291*
Sarchet, Kate: Sweater Girls, *389*
Sardou, Fernand: Little Theatre of Jean Renoir, The, *760*
Saralle, Leilani: Harvest, The, *981;* Neon Maniacs, *868*
Sargent, Dick: Billie, *150;* Body Count, *817;* Clonus Horror, The, *1042;* Hardcore, *981;* Live a Little, Love a Little, *929;* Melvin Purvis: G-Man, *83;* Murder by Numbers, *998;* Operation Petticoat, *351;* Teen Witch, *392*
Sarky, Daniel: Emmanuelle, *734*
Sarne, Michael: Seaside Swingers, *938*
Sarrazin, Michael: Beulah Land, *459;* Captive Hearts, *475;* Caravans, *475;* Deadly Companion, *968;* Doomsday Flight, The, *971;* Fighting Back, *47;* Flim-Flam Man, The, *518;* For Pete's Sake, *279;* Groundstar Conspiracy, The, *1055;* Gumball Rally, The, *58;* Joshua Then and Now, *311;* Keeping Track, *70;* Lena's Holiday, *991;* Loves and Times of Scaramouche, The, *324;* Malarek, *586;* Mascara, *82;* Pursuit of Happiness, The, *631;* Reincarnation of Peter Proud, The, *879;* Seduction, The, *884;* Sometimes a Great Notion, *662;* They Shoot Horses, Don't They?, *681;* Train Killer, The, *687*
Sartain, Gailard: Ernest Goes to Jail, *272;* Fried Green Tomatoes, *522;* Getting Even with Dad, *285;* Grifters, The, *534;* Guilty by Suspicion, *534;* Leader of the Band, *317;* One Riot, One Ranger, *95;* Real McCoy, The, *1009;* Stop! Or My Mom Will Shoot, *386*
Sasaki, Katsuhiko: Terror of Mechagodzilla, *894*
Sassaman, Nicole: Witchcraft V: Dance with the Devil, *903*
Sassard, Jacqueline: Accident, *440;* Bad Girls (1969), *715;* Les Biches, *759*
Sassoon, Cat: Bloodfist IV—Die Trying, *16*
Sastri, Lina: Good Night, Michelangelo, *288*
Satana, Tura: Faster Pussycat! Kill! Kill!, *46*
Satie, Erik: Avant Garde Program #2, *714*
Sato, Kei: Violence at Noon, *801;* Zatoichi: The Blind Swordsman's Vengeance, *806*
Saucedo, Rick "Elvis": Elvis Stories, *271*
Saucier, Jason: Crawlers, *825*
Sauer, Gary: Unbelievable Truth, The, *691*
Saunders, Jennifer: Supergrass, The, *388*
Saunders, Justine: Fringe Dwellers, The, *522*
Saunders, Mary Jane: Sorrowful Jones, *383*
Saunders, Michael K.: Billy the Kid Meets the Vampires, *813*
Saunders, Pamela: Alien Warrior, *1035*
Savage, Ann: Detour, *970;* Renegade Girl, *1142*
Savage, Ben: Little Monsters, *1063*
Savage, Brad: Islands in the Stream, *555*
Savage, Fred: Boy Who Could Fly, The, *468;* Little Monsters, *1063;* Runaway Ralph, *201;* Vice Versa, *404;* Wizard, The, *218*
Savage, John: All the Kind Strangers, *951;* Amateur, The, *952;* Any Man's Death, *450;* Bad Company, *1095;* Brady's Escape, *18;* Caribe, *23;* Coming Out of the Ice, *486;* Daybreak (1993), *1045;* Deer Hunter, The, *499;* Do the Right Thing, *502;* Eric, *510;* Godfather, Part III, The, *529;* Hair, *921;* Hotel Colonial, *64;* Hunting, *546;* Inside Moves, *552;* Maria's Lovers, *588;* Nairobi Affair, *603;* Onion Field, The, *613;* Primary Motive, *627;* Salvador, *647;* Shattered Image, *1014;* Sister-in-Law, The, *659*
Savage, Vic: Creeping Terror, The, *1043*
Saval, Dany: Boeing, Boeing, *243;* Moon Pilot, *189;* Tales of Paris, *792*
Savalas, George: Belarus File, The, *954;* Family, The (1970), *46*
Savalas, Telly: Alice in Wonderland (1985), *145;* Battle of the Bulge, *10;* Belarus File, The, *954;* Beyond Reason, *460;* Beyond the Poseidon Adventure, *11;* Bird Man of Alcatraz, *462;* Buono Sera, Mrs. Campbell, *247;* Cannonball Run II, *250;* Cape Fear (1962), *959;* Capricorn One, *1041;* Cartier Affair, The, *252;* Crooks and Coronets (Sophie's Place), *261;* Devil in the House of Exorcism, The, *833;* Dirty Dozen, The: The Deadly Mission, *39;* Dirty Dozen, The: The Fatal Mission, *39;* Escape to Athena, *45;* Fakeout, *513;* Family, The (1970), *46;* Greatest Story Ever Told, The, *533;* Hollywood Detective, The, *983;* Horror Express, *851;* House of Exorcism, The, *852;* Inside Out (1975), *66;* Interns, The, *553;* Kelly's Heroes, *70;* Killer Force, *71;* Land Raiders, *1125;* Mackenna's Gold, *1131;* Massacre at Fort Holman (Reason to Live...A Reason to Die, A), *1133;* Muppet Movie, The, *189;* On Her Majesty's Secret Service, *94;* Pancho Villa, *1138;* Redneck, *104;* Scalphunters, The, *1148;* Scenes from a Murder, *112;* Silent Rebellion, *658;* Slender Thread, The, *660;* Sonny and Jed, *1151;* Town Called Hell, A, *131;* Young Savages, The, *1033*
Savant, Doug: Masquerade (1988), *995;* Paint It Black, *97;* Red Surf, *104;* Shaking the Tree, *655;* Trick or Treat (1986), *897*
Savelyeva, Lyudmila: War and Peace (1968), *802*
Savident, John: Brain Donors, *245*
Savini, Tom: Dawn of the Dead, *830;* Knightriders, *73;* Maniac (1980), *862*
Savio, Andria: Stryker, *1081*
Savlov, Meg: Wax, *1088*

Savoy, Suzanne: Cellar, The, *822*
Savoy, Teresa Ann: Caligula, *474*
Savvina, Iya: Lady With the Dog, The, *755*
Sawicki, Mark: Brothers of the Wilderness, *471*
Sawyer, Joe: Buckskin Frontier, *1102;* Indian Uprising, *1123;* Naughty Nineties, The, *342;* Roaring Twenties, The, *107*
Saxon, Glenn: Django Shoots First, *1109*
Saxon, John: Appaloosa, The, *1094;* Baby Doll Murders, The, *953;* Battle Beyond the Stars, *1038;* Bees, The, *812;* Beverly Hills Cop 3, *11;* Beyond Evil, *813;* Big Score, The, *12;* Black Christmas, *814;* Blackmail (1991), *956;* Blood Beach, *814;* Blood Salvage, *816;* Crossing the Line (1990), *492;* Death House, *35;* Death of a Gunfighter, *1108;* Doomsday Flight, The, *971;* Electric Horseman, The, *508;* Enter the Dragon, *44;* Fever Pitch, *516;* Final Alliance, *48;* Hands of Steel, *1055;* Hellmaster, *849;* Invasion of the Flesh Hunters, *856;* Joe Kidd, *1123;* Maximum Force, *83;* Mr. Hobbs Takes a Vacation, *334;* Moonshine County Express, *86;* My Mom's a Werewolf, *341;* Night Caller from Outer Space, *1068;* Nightmare on Elm Street, A, *871;* No Escape, No Return, *91;* Payoff, *98;* Planet Earth, *1070;* Planet of Blood, *1070;* Prisoners of the Lost Universe, *1072;* Raid on Entebbe, *633;* Reluctant Debutante, The, *365;* Rock, Pretty Baby, *936;* Running Scared (1980), *110;* Running Wild (1955), *645;* Snatched, *117;* Strange New World, *1080;* Strange Shadows in an Empty Room, *121;* Swiss Conspiracy, The, *1022;* This Happy Feeling, *394;* Unforgiven, The (1960), *1160;* Unsane, *899;* Welcome to Spring Break, *902;* Wrong Is Right, *414*
Saxon, Vin: Rat Pfink a Boo Boo, *364*
Sayer, Philip: Shanghai Surprise, *377;* Slayground, *1017;* Xtro, *904*
Sayle, Alexei: Reckless Kelly, *365;* Young Ones, The, *416*
Sayler, Ray: On the Bowery, *612*
Sayles, John: City of Hope, *483;* Eight Men Out, *508;* Hard Choices, *536;* Little Vegas, *319;* Matinee, *330;* Straight Talk, *387;* Unnatural Causes, *692*
Saylor, Syd: Arizona Days, *1094;* Lost Jungle, The, *79;* Mystery Mountain, *1135;* Sidewalks of New York, *378*
Saynor, Ian: Corn Is Green, The (1979), *488*
Saysanasy, Siluk: Peanut Butter Solution, The, *194*
Sazio, Carmela: Paisan, *775*
Sbarge, Raphael: Back to Hannibal: The Return of Tom Sawyer and Huckleberry Finn, *454;* Carnosaur, *821;* Final Verdict, *516;* Murder 101, *999;* My Man Adam, *340;* Prison for Children, *628;* Riding the Edge, *106;* Risky Business, *368*
Scacchi, Greta: Burke and Wills, *472;* Coca Cola Kid, The, *257;* Defense of the Realm, *969;* Desire, *500;* Ebony Tower, The, *507;* Fires Within, *517;* Good Morning, Babylon, *530;* Heat and Dust, *539;* Man in Love, A, *587;* Player, The, *358;* Presumed Innocent, *1007;* Shattered (1991), *1014;* Turtle Beach, *690;* White Mischief, *700*
Scala, Gia: Don't Go Near the Water, *267;* Tunnel of Love, The, *400*
Scales, Prunella: Consuming Passions, *259;* Fawlty Towers, *276;* Wicked Lady, The (1983), *139*
Scalia, Jack: After the Shock, *442;* Casualties of Love: The Long Island Lolita Story, *476;* Club Med, *484;* Deadly Desire, *968;* Devlin Connection III, The, *970;* Endless Descent, *838;* Fear City, *47;* Illicit Behavior, *985;* Ring of Scorpio, *640;* Runaway Father, *645;* Shattered Image, *1014*
Scalici, Valentina: Il Ladro Di Bambini (Stolen Children), *747*
Scannell, Kevin: Monkey Trouble, *188*
Scarabelli, Michele: Deadbolt, *968;* Snake Eater 2, the Drug Buster, *117*
Scardino, Don: Cruising, *964;* He Knows You're Alone, *849;* Squirm, *889*
Scarfe, Alan: As Is, *451;* Cathy's Curse, *822;* Double Impact, *41;* Iron Eagle II, *67;* Jericho Fever, *68;* Keeping Track, *70*
Scarwid, Diana: After the Promise, *442;* Battered, *456;* Brenda Starr, *19;* Extremities, *512;* Heat (1987), *60;* JFK: Reckless Youth, *558;* Ladies Club, *74;* Mommie Dearest, *598;* Possessed, The (1977), *876;* Psycho III, *877;* Strange Invaders, *1080*
Schaafsma, Frank: Army Brats, *228*
Schaal, Dick: Pecos Bill, King of the Cowboys, *194*
Schaal, Wendy: 'Burbs, The, *247;* Creature, *1043;* Going Under, *288;* Where the Boys Are '84, *409*
Schachter, Felice: Zapped!, *416*
Schade, Fritz: Lost and Found Chaplin: Keystone, *321*
Schaefer, Laura: Curse IV: The Ultimate Sacrifice, *828*
Schaeffer, Rebecca: End of Innocence, The, *509;* Voyage of Terror: The Achille Lauro Affair, *694*
Schafer, John Clayton: Return to Two-Moon Junction, *639*
Schafer, Natalie: Caught, *477*
Schallert, William: Colossus: The Forbin Project, *1042;* Computer Wore Tennis Shoes, The, *159;* High and the Mighty, The, *541;* House Party 2, *923;* Man on a String, *81;* Matinee, *330;* Trial of the Cantonsville Nine, The, *687*
Schanley, Tom: Nothing Underneath, *1002*
Scharf, Sabrina: Hell's Angels on Wheels, *60*
Scheider, Roy: All That Jazz, *906;* Blue Thunder, *16;* Cohen and Tate, *485;* 52 Pick-Up, *976;* Fourth War, The, *52;* French Connection, The, *53;* Jaws, *858;* Jaws 2, *858;* Klute, *989;* Last Embrace, The, *990;* Listen to Me, *576;* Marathon Man, *82;* Men's Club, The, *593;* Naked Lunch, *1067;* Night Game, *1000;* Russia House, The, *646;* Seven-Ups, The, *114;* Somebody Has to Shoot the Picture, *662;* Sorceror, *1018;* Still of the Night, *1020;* Tiger Town, *211;* 2010, *1086*
Scheitz, Clemens: Stroszek, *790*
Schell, Carl: Werewolf in a Girl's Dormitory, *902*
Schell, Catherine: Gulliver's Travels (1977), *172;* Return of the Pink Panther, The, *366;* Summer House, The, *388*
Schell, Maria: Brothers Karamazov, The, *471;* Christmas Lilies of the Field, *159;* Cimarron (1960), *1105;* Gervaise, *740;* Hanging Tree, The, *1118;* Just a Gigolo, *561;* La Passante, *754;* Napoleon (1955), *603;* 99 Women, *91;* Odessa File, The, *1003;* Samson and Delilah (1984), *648;* White Nights (1957), *803*
Schell, Maximilian: Assisi Underground, The, *7;* Black Hole, The, *1039;* Castle, The, *476;* Chosen, The, *481;* Cross of Iron, *31;* Day that Shook the World, The, *496;* Far Off Place, A, *166;* Freshman, The, *281;* Judgment at Nuremberg, *560;* Julia, *560;* Marlene, *589;* Miss Rose White, *596;* Odessa File, The, *1003;* Pedestrian, The, *620;* Players, *623;* Rose Garden, The, *644;* St. Ives, *110;* Stalin, *665;* Topkapi, *1026;* Young Catherine, *708;* Young Lions, The, *708*
Schell, Ronnie: Fatal Instinct (1993), *274;* Hungry I Reunion, *303;* Revenge of the Red Baron, *881*
Schellenberg, August: Black Robe, *463;* Confidential, *28;* Free Willy, *168;* Iron Will, *67;* Mark of Cain, *863;* Striker's Mountain, *121;* Tramp at the Door, *687*
Schenna and the villagers of Tehouda, Leila: Ramparts of Clay, *779*
Scherrer, Paul: Children of the Corn II: The Final Sacrifice, *823*
Scheydt, Karl: American Soldier, The, *712*
Schiaffino, Rosanna: Man Called Noon, The, *1131;* Two Weeks in Another Town, *690*
Schiavelli, Vincent: Playroom, *875;* Waiting for the Light, *695*
Schicha, Ralph: Savage Attraction, *1012*
Schildkraut, Joseph: Diary of Anne Frank, The, *501;* Flame of the Barbary Coast, *50;* Garden of Allah, The, *525;* Idiot's Delight, *548;* King of Kings, The (1927), *565;* Life of Emile Zola, The, *574;* Man in the Iron Mask, The (1939), *81;* Marie Antoinette, *588;* Monsieur Beaucaire, *336;* Northwest Outpost *933;* Orphans of the Storm, *615;* Rains Came, The, *634;* Road to Yesterday, The, *641;* Shop Around the Corner, The, *378;* Viva Villa!, *1162*
Schilling, Vivian: Future Shock, *1053;* In a Moment of Passion, *549;* Soultaker, *889*
Schlachet, Daniel: Swoon, *675*

hlatter, Charlie: All-American Murder, *951;* 18 Again,
0; Heartbreak Hotel, *538;* Sunset Heat, *122*
hlesinger, John: Lost Language of Cranes, The, *580*
hlondorff, Volker: Private Conversations: On the Set of
ath of a Salesman, *433*
hmid, Helmut: Salzburg Connection, The, *111*
hmidinger, Walter: Hanussen, *743*
hmidt, Marlene: Scorchy, *112*
hmitz, Sybille: Vampyr, *800*
hnabel, Stefan: Anna, *448;* Dracula's Widow, *837;*
efox, *49;* Mr. Inside/Mr. Outside, *85*
hnarre, Monika: Fearless Tiger, *47*
hneider, Betty: Paris Belongs to Us, *775*
hneider, Dawn: Free Ride, *281*
hneider, John: Cocaine Wars, *27;* Curse, The, *827;* Eddie
acon's Run, *43;* Ministry of Vengeance, *85;* Stagecoach
986), *1152*
hneider, Magda: Liebelei, *760*
hneider, Maria: Last Tango in Paris, *570;* Mamma
acula, *862;* Passenger, The, *1004*
hneider, Rob: Beverly Hillbillies, The, *237;* Surf Ninjas,
8
hneider, Romy: Assassination of Trotsky, The, *451;*
occaccio 70, *719;* Cardinal, The, *475;* César and Rosalie,
23; Death Watch, *1045;* Good Neighbor Sam, *288;* Hero,
e, *540;* Infernal Trio, The, *748;* La Passante, *754;* Les
oses De La Vie, *759;* Mado, *763;* Simple Story, A, *786;*
wimming Pool, The, *792;* Trial, The, *687;* What's New,
ussycat?, *408*
hock, Barbara: From Hollywood to Deadwood, *979*
hoeffling, Michael: Belizaire the Cajun, *458;* Let's Get
arry, *573;* Mermaids, *331;* Sylvester, *675;* Vision Quest,
94; Wild Hearts Can't Be Broken, *217*
hoelen, Jill: Adventures in Spying, *2;* Babes in Toyland
986), *147;* Chiller, *823;* Curse II—The Bite, *827;* Cutting
ass, *828;* Phantom of the Opera (1989), *874;* Popcorn, *876;*
ch Girl, *640;* Stepfather, The, *1020;* Thunder Alley, *945;*
hen a Stranger Calls Back, *1031*
hoene, Reiner: Gunfighters, The, *1117;* Nobody's
hildren, *608*
hoener, Ingeborg: Mr. Superinvisible, *188*
hofield, Annabel: Solar Crisis, *1077*
hofield, Drew: Sid and Nancy, *657*
hofield, Katharine: Lion of Africa, The, *77*
hofield, Nell: Puberty Blues, *630*
hon, Margarete: Kriemhilde's Revenge, *752;* Siegfried,
86
hoppert, Bill: Personals, The, *357*
hrage, Lisa: China White, *25;* Hello, Mary Lou: Prom
ight II, *850*
hreck, Max: Nosferatu, *772*
hreiber, Avery: Avery Schreiber—Live From the Second
ity, *230;* Galaxina, *1053;* Hunk, *303;* Loose Shoes, *321;*
ilent Scream, *886;* Swashbuckler (1976), *123*
hreier, Tom: Ripper, The, *881*
hroder, Rick: Across the Tracks, *441;* Call of the Wild
1992), *474;* Champ, The (1979), *479;* Earthling, The, *164;*
ansel and Gretel, *173;* Last Flight of Noah's Ark, *180;* Little
ord Fauntleroy (1980), *182;* Lonesome Dove, *1129;* Return
o Lonesome Dove, *1143*
hroeder, Barbet: Six in Paris (Paris Vue par . . .), *786*
hubert, Heinz: Emil and the Detectives, *164*
hubert, Karin: Bluebeard (1972), *817*
chuck, John: Blade, *14;* Butch and Sundance: The Early
ays, *1103;* Four Eyes and Six Guns, *1114;* Hammersmith Is
ut, *292;* Holy Matrimony, *299;* Outrageous Fortune, *352;*
econd Sight, *374;* Thieves Like Us, *681*
chultz, Dwight: Alone in the Dark, *808;* Fat Man and Little
oy, *515;* Long Walk Home, The, *579;* Temp, The, *893;* When
our Lover Leaves, *699;* Woman with a Past, *705*
chultz, Jeff: Buying Time, *21*
Schultz, Tom: In the Time of Barbarians II, *1058*
Schutz, Brian: Thou Shalt Not Kill...Except, *895*
Schumm, Hans: Spy Smasher, *119*
Schunzel, Reinhold: Fortune's Fool, *738;* Golden Earrings,
56; Threepenny Opera, The, *794*
Schurer, Erna: Blood Castle (1970), *815;* Specters, *889*
Schuyler, Lonnie: Cybernator, *1043*
Schwan, Ivyann: Problem Child 2, *362*
Schwartz, Albert: Time Stands Still, *795*
Schwartz, Scott: Toy, The, *398*
Schwarzenegger, Arnold: Beretta's Island, *10;* Commando,
28; Conan the Barbarian, *1042;* Conan the Destroyer, *1043;*
Dave, *262;* Hercules Goes Bananas, *296;* Jayne Mansfield
Story, The, *557;* Kindergarten Cop, *313;* Last Action Hero,
The, *1062;* Predator, *1071;* Pumping Iron, *630;* Raw Deal,
103; Red Heat (1988), *104;* Red Sonja, *104;* Running Man,
The, *1075;* Stay Hungry, *667;* Terminator, The, *1082;*
Terminator 2: Judgment Day, *1082;* Total Recall, *1084;* Twins,
401
Schwedop, Lisa: Revenge of the Teenage Vixens from Outer
Space, *881*
Schweig, Eric: Broken Chain, The, *20;* Last of the Mohicans,
The (1992), *1126*
Schygulla, Hanna: Barnum (1987), *456;* Berlin
Alexanderplatz, *716;* Bitter Tears of Petra Von Kant, The, *718;*
Casanova (1987), *252;* Dead Again, *966;* Delta Force, The, *36;*
Forever Lulu, *279;* Gods of the Plague, *741;* Lili Marleen, *760;*
Love in Germany, A, *762;* Marriage of Maria Braun, The, *765;*
Merchant of Four Seasons, The, *767;* Sheer Madness, *785;*
Wrong Move, The, *805*
Sciorra, Annabella: Hand That Rocks the Cradle, The, *981;*
Hard Way, The (1991), *293;* Jungle Fever, *561;* Mr.
Wonderful, *597;* Night We Never Met, The, *345;* Prison
Stories: Women on the Inside, *628;* Reversal of Fortune, *639;*
Romeo is Bleeding, *108;* True Love, *400;* Whispers in the
Dark, *1031*
Scob, Edith: Eyes without a Face, *735;* Judex, *750*
Scofield, Paul: Anna Karenina (1985), *449;* Attic: The Hiding
of Anne Frank, *452;* Bartleby, *456;* Hamlet (1990), *535;* Henry
V (1989), *540;* King Lear (1971), *564;* Man for All Seasons, A,
586; Mr. Corbett's Ghost, *1066;* Train, The, *131;* Utz, *693;*
When the Whales Came, *699*
Scoggins, Tracy: Alien Intruder, *1035;* Dead On, *967;*
Demonic Toys, *832;* Dollman vs. Demonic Toys, *1047;*
Gumshoe Kid, The, *292;* In Dangerous Company, *550;* One
Last Run, *613;* Time Bomb, *1025;* Ultimate Desires, *1028;*
Watchers II, *901*
Scolari, Peter: Corporate Affairs, *259;* Infested, *856;* Mr.
Bill's Real Life Adventures, *333;* Perfect Harmony, *194;*
Rosebud Beach Hotel, The, *370;* Ticks, *895*
Scooler, Zvee: Love and Death, *322*
Scopp, Alfie: Undergrads, The, *214*
Scorsese, Martin: Akira Kurosawa's Dreams, *711;* Guilty by
Suspicion, *534*
Scott, Alex: Romper Stomper, *109*
Scott, Bainbridge: Death Chase, *35;* Hell Squad (1985), *60*
Scott, Brenda: Simon, King of the Witches, *886*
Scott, Campbell: Dead Again, *966;* Dying Young, *506;*
Longtime Companion, *579;* Sheltering Sky, The, *655;* Singles,
379
Scott, Carey: Making the Grade, *327*
Scott, Dan: Spookies, *889*
Scott, David: This Is Elvis, *436*
Scott, Debralee: Mary Hartman, Mary Hartman (TV Series),
329; Pandemonium, *353*
Scott, Donovan: Goldilocks and the Three Bears, *171;*
Savannah Smiles, *201;* Sheena, *115;* Zorro, the Gay Blade,
417
Scott, Fred: Fighting Deputy, *1112;* Singing Buckaroo, *1150*
Scott, Geoffrey: First and Ten, *277*
Scott, George C.: Anatomy of a Murder, *952;* Bank Shot,
232; Changeling, The, *822;* Day of the Dolphin, The, *1044;*

Deadly Currents, *34;* Descending Angel, *499;* Dr. Strangelove or How I Learned to Stop Worrying and Love the Bomb, *266;* Exorcist III: Legion, *840;* Firestarter, *841;* Flim-Flam Man, The, *518;* Formula, The, *978;* Hanging Tree, The, *1118;* Hardcore, *981;* Hindenburg, The, *541;* Hospital, The, *301;* Hustler, The, *547;* Islands in the Stream, *555;* Last Days of Patton, The, *569;* List of Adrian Messenger, The, *992;* Malice, *994;* Movie Movie, *338;* Murders in the Rue Morgue (1986), *999;* New Centurions, The, *605;* Pals, *353;* Patton, *619;* Petulia, *621;* Prince and the Pauper, The (1978), *197;* Rage (1972), *633;* Savage Is Loose, The, *648;* Taps, *677;* They Might Be Giants, *1023*

Scott, Gordon: Goliath and the Vampires, *847;* Tarzan and the Trappers, *125;* Tramplers, The, *1158*

Scott, Hazel: Broadway Rhythm, *910;* Heat's On, The, *295;* I Dood It, *924*

Scott, Howard: Revenge of the Teenage Vixens from Outer Space, *881*

Scott, Imogen Millais: Salome's Last Dance, *647*

Scott, Janette: Day of the Triffids, The, *1044;* Devil's Disciple, The, *264;* Old Dark House, The, *872*

Scott, John: Horror of Party Beach, The, *851*

Scott, Joseph: Dead Silence, *262*

Scott, Kathryn Leigh: Best of Dark Shadows, The, *813;* Dark Shadows (TV Series), *829;* House of Dark Shadows, *852;* Murrow, *601;* Philip Marlowe, Private Eye: The Pencil, *1005;* Witches' Brew, *412*

Scott, Ken: Stopover Tokyo, *120*

Scott, Kimberly: Caught in the Act, *960*

Scott, Larry B.: Children of Times Square, The, *481;* Hero Ain't Nothin' But a Sandwich, A, *540;* Revenge of the Nerds II: Nerds in Paradise, *367;* Snake Eater 2, the Drug Buster, *117;* Super Force, *1081;* That Was Then...This Is Now, *680*

Scott, Lizabeth: Dark City, *495;* Dead Reckoning (1947), *34;* Easy Living, *506;* Loving You, *929;* Pitfall, *622;* Pulp, *363;* Racket, The, *633;* Stolen Face, *890;* Strange Love of Martha Ivers, The, *669;* Two of a Kind (1951), *1028*

Scott, Martha: Cheers for Miss Bishop, *480;* Desperate Hours, The (1955), *969;* Doin' Time on Planet Earth, *267;* Howards of Virginia, The, *545;* Our Town (1940), *616;* War of the Wildcats, *1162*

Scott, Pippa: Bad Ronald, *811;* Cold Turkey, *257*

Scott, Randolph: Abilene Town, *1092;* Badman's Territory, *1096;* Bombardier, *17;* Buffalo Stampede, *1102;* Captain Kidd, *23;* Cariboo Trail, *1103;* China Sky, *25;* Coroner Creek, *1106;* Decision at Sundown, *1108;* Doolins of Oklahoma, *1110;* Fighting Westerner, The, *1113;* Follow the Fleet, *917;* Go West, Young Man, *287;* Gung Ho! (1943), *58;* Hangman's Knot, *1119;* Jesse James, *1123;* Last of the Mohicans, The (1936), *1126;* Lawless Street, A, *1127;* Man in the Saddle, *1132;* Man of the Forest, *1132;* Murders in the Zoo, *867;* My Favorite Wife, *340;* Nevadan, The, *1136;* Pittsburgh, *622;* Rage at Dawn, *1140;* Rebecca of Sunnybrook Farm (1938), *936;* Return of the Badmen, *1142;* Ride Lonesome, *1143;* Ride the High Country, *1143;* Roberta, *936;* 7th Cavalry, *1148;* Spoilers, The, *1152;* Stranger Wore a Gun, The, *1153;* Susannah of the Mounties, *208;* Tall T, The, *1154;* Ten Wanted Men, *1155;* To the Last Man, *1157;* To the Shores of Tripoli, *130;* Trail Street, *1158;* Virginia City, *1161;* Wagon Wheels, *1162;* Western Union, *1163*

Scott, Raymond: Happy Landing, *921*

Scott, Susan: Trap Them and Kill Them, *897*

Scott, Timothy: Ballad of Gregorio Cortez, The, *1096;* Gettysburg, *526;* Kid Vengeance, *1124;* Lonesome Dove, *1129;* Return to Lonesome Dove, *1143;* Wild Times, *1164*

Scott, Zachary: Appointment in Honduras, *6;* Born to Be Bad, *467;* Cass Timberlane, *476;* Flamingo Road, *518;* Let's Make It Legal, *318;* Mildred Pierce, *594;* Shotgun, *1149;* South of St. Louis, *1151;* Southerner, The, *663*

Scott-Heron, Gil: No Nukes, *432*

Scott-Thomas, Kristin: Bachelor, The, *453;* Bitter Moon, *462;* Framed (1990), *280;* Weep No More My Lady, *1030*

Scotti, Tino: Spider's Stratagem, The, *788*

Scotti, Vito: Caper of the Golden Bulls, The, *22;* Head (1968), *922;* Stewardess School, *386*

Scourby, Alexander: Affair in Trinidad, *442;* Big Heat, The, *12;* Seven Thieves, *653;* Silver Chalice, The, *658*

Scratch, Derf: Du-Beat-E-O, *915*

Scribner, Don: Wild Man, *139*

Scrimm, Angus: Mindwarp, *1066;* Phantasm II, *874;* Subspecies, *891;* Transylvania Twist, *399*

Scruggs, Earl: High Lonesome—The Story of Bluegrass Music, *426*

Scruggs, Linda: Las Vegas Lady, *74*

Scuddamore, Simon: Slaughter High, *887*

Scully, Sean: Almost Angels, *146*

Seagal, Steven: Above the Law, *1;* Hard to Kill, *59;* Marked for Death, *82;* On Deadly Ground, *93;* Out for Justice, *96;* Under Siege, *134*

Seagrove, Jenny: Appointment with Death, *953;* Chorus of Disapproval, A, *254;* Deadly Game, *34;* Guardian, The (1990), *848;* Hold the Dream, *542;* Sherlock Holmes and the Incident at Victoria Falls, *1015;* Woman of Substance, A, *705*

Seal, Elizabeth: Philby, Burgess and Maclean: Spy Scandal of the Century, *1005*

Seale, Douglas: Ernest Saves Christmas, *165*

Seales, Franklyn: Onion Field, The, *613;* Taming of the Shrew (1982), *391*

Sears, Heather: Phantom of the Opera (1962), *874;* Room at the Top, *643*

Seay, James: Amazing Colossal Man, The, *1035;* Killers from Space, *1061*

Sebanek, Josef: Loves of a Blonde, *762*

Sebastian, Dorothy: Free and Easy, *281;* Spite Marriage, *384*

Seberg, Jean: Airport, *443;* Bonjour Tristesse, *466;* Breathless (1959), *720;* Fine Madness, A, *277;* Lilith, *575;* Macho Callahan, *1130;* Mouse That Roared, The, *337;* Paint Your Wagon, *934;* Pendulum, *1005;* Saint Joan, *646;* Time Out For Love, *795*

Secombe, Harry: Down Among the "Z" Men, *268*

Secor, Kyle: Delusion (1991), *499;* Late for Dinner, *1062;* Silent Victim, *658;* Untamed Heart, *692*

Sedaka, Neil: Playgirl Killer, The, *875*

Sedgewick, Edna: Red Barry, *104*

Sedgwick, Edie: Ciao! Manhattan, *482*

Sedgwick, Kyra: Born on the Fourth of July, *467;* Heart and Souls, *1056;* Kansas, *562;* Man Who Broke 1000 Chains, The, *587;* Miss Rose White, *596;* Mr. and Mrs. Bridge, *596;* Pyrates, *363;* Singles, *379;* Women & Men 2, *706*

Sedgwick, Robert: Nasty Hero, *89*

Seeger, Pete: Wasn't That a Time!, *438;* Woody Guthrie—Hard Travelin', *439*

Seel, Ceri: Tripods, *1085*

Seeley, Blossom: Blood Money (1933), *464*

Seely, Sybil: Balloonatic, The/One Week, *231;* Buster Keaton Festival: Vol. 2, *248*

Seff, Brian: Pee-Wee Herman Show, The, *355*

Segal, George: All's Fair, *225;* Black Bird, The, *240;* Blume in Love, *465;* Born to Win, *467;* Bridge at Remagen, The, *469;* Carbon Copy, *251;* Cold Room, The, *485;* Duchess and the Dirtwater Fox, The, *1110;* Endless Game, The, *510;* For the Boys, *918;* Fun with Dick and Jane, *282;* Hot Rock, The, *983;* Invitation to a Gunfighter, *1123;* Killing 'Em Softly, *563;* King Rat, *565;* Last Married Couple in America, The, *315;* Look Who's Talking, *320;* Lost and Found, *321;* Lost Command, *79;* Me, Myself & I, *330;* No Way to Treat a Lady, *1002;* Not My Kid, *609;* Owl and the Pussycat, The, *352;* Quiller Memorandum, The, *102;* Rollercoaster, *1011;* Russian Roulette, *110;* St. Valentine's Day Massacre, The, *111;* Ship of Fools, *656;* Stick, *120;* Taking the Heat, *676;* Terminal Man, The, *893;* Touch of Class, A, *398;* Where's Poppa?, *409;* Who Is Killing the Great Chefs of Europe?, *410;* Who's Afraid of Virginia Woolf?, *701;* Zany Adventures of Robin Hood, The, *416*

egal, Howard: Last Game, The, *569*
egal, Robbin Zohra: Harem, *536*
egal, Zohra: Masala, *329*
egall, Jonathan: Baby Love, *230;* Private Popsicle, *362*
egall, Pamela: After Midnight, *808;* Gate II, *845;* omething Special, *383*
egda, Dorotha: My 20th Century, *770*
eidel, Ileana: Beach House, *233*
eigner, Emmanuelle: Bitter Moon, *462;* Frantic (1988), *78*
eigner, Louis: Le Bourgeois Gentilhomme, *756*
einfeld, Jerry: Rodney Dangerfield: "It's Not Easy Being e", *370;* Tommy Chong Roast, The, *397*
eitz, John: Forced March, *519;* Hard Choices, *536;* Out of e Rain, *1003*
ekka, Johnny: Message, The (Mohammad, Messenger of od), *593*
elander, Hjalmar: Treasure of Arne, *797*
elby, David: Best of Dark Shadows, The, *813;* Dying oung, *506;* Girl in Blue, The, *527;* Grave Secrets: The Legacy Hilltop Drive, *980;* Intersection, *553;* Night of Dark adows, *869;* Raise the Titanic, *103;* Rich and Famous, *639;* the Sandbox, *403*
elby, Nicholas: Macbeth (1971), *584*
elby, Sarah: Huckleberry Finn (1975), *176*
elf, Doug: Men in Love, *592*
ell, Jack M.: Deadly Spygames, *35*
ellars, Elizabeth: Chalk Garden, The, *478;* Never Let Go, *04;* Voyage 'Round My Father, A, *695*
ellecca, Connie: Brotherhood of the Rose, *20;* Captain merica II: Death Too Soon, *22;* Last Fling, The, *315*
elleck, Tom: Bunco, *21;* Christopher Columbus: The scovery, *26;* Daughters of Satan, *830;* Folks, *278;* Gypsy arriors, The, *58;* Her Alibi, *296;* High Road to China, *62;* nocent Man, An, *66;* Lassiter, *75;* Mr. Baseball, *333;* Myra eckenridge, *341;* Quigley Down Under, *1140;* Runaway, *075;* Sacketts, The, *1146;* Shadow Riders, The, *1148;* erminal Island, *126;* Three Men and a Baby, *395;* Three Men d a Little Lady, *395;* Washington Affair, The, *696*
ellers, Mary: Crawlers, *825*
ellers, Peter: After the Fox, *223;* Alice's Adventures in onderland, *145;* Battle of the Sexes, The, *233;* Being There, *34;* Blockhouse, The, *464;* Bobo, The, *243;* Carlton-Browne the F.O., *251;* Case of the Mukkinese Battle Horn, The, *252;* asino Royale (1967), *252;* Dr. Strangelove or How I Learned Stop Worrying and Love the Bomb, *266;* Down Among the " Men, *268;* Fiendish Plot of Dr. Fu Manchu, The, *276;* ost in the Noonday Sun, *285;* Heavens Above, *296;* I Love ou Alice B. Toklas!, *304;* I'm All Right Jack, *305;* Ladykillers, e, *315;* Lolita, *577;* Magic Christian, The, *326;* Mouse That oared, The, *337;* Murder by Death, *338;* Naked Truth, *342;* ever Let Go, *604;* Only Two Can Play, *350;* Party, The, *354;* ink Panther, The, *357;* Pink Panther Strikes Again, The, *357;* risoner of Zenda, The (1979), *361;* Return of the Pink anther, The, *366;* Revenge of the Pink Panther, The, *367;* oad to Hong Kong, The, *368;* Shot in the Dark, A, *378;* mallest Show on Earth, The, *381;* There's a Girl in My Soup, *93;* To See Such Fun, *397;* Tom Thumb, *213;* Trail of the ink Panther, The, *398;* Two-Way Stretch, *402;* Up the Creek 958), *403;* Waltz of the Toreadors, *405;* What's New, ussycat?, *408;* Woman Times Seven, *705;* World of Henry rient, The, *414;* Wrong Arm of the Law, The, *414;* Wrong ox, The, *414*
ellier, Georges: Red Balloon, The, *198*
ellner, Gustav Rudolph: Pedestrian, The, *620*
elzer, Milton: Miss Rose White, *596*
ema, Chie: Tokyo Decadence, *795*
embera, Tricia: Flash and the Firecat, *50*
en Gupta, Pinaki: Aparajito, *713*
eneca, Joe: Blob, The (1988), *814;* Crossroads, *912;* lississippi Masala, *596;* Murder on the Bayou, *600;* Saint of ort Washington, The, *646;* Wilma, *703*
Serato, Massimo: Catch As Catch Can, *252;* Tenth Victim, The, *1082*
Serio, Terry: Fast Lane Fever, *46;* Shout: The Story of Johnny O'Keefe, *939*
Serious, Yahoo: Reckless Kelly, *365;* Young Einstein, *416*
Serling, Rod: Encounter with the Unknown, *1049*
Serna, Assumpta: Matador, *766*
Serna, Pepe: American Me, *446;* Break of Dawn, *468;* Conagher, *1105;* Force of One, *51;* Killer Inside Me, The, *988;* Rookie, The, *109;* Streets of L.A., The, *671*
Sernas, Jacques: Goliath and the Vampires, *847*
Serra, Raymond: Alphabet City, *445;* Nasty Hero, *89*
Serra, Tony: Watched!, *137*
Serrault, Michel: Associate, The, *714;* Holes, The, *744;* La Cage aux Folles, *753;* La Cage aux Folles II, *753;* La Cage aux Folles III, The Wedding, *753;* Love and the Frenchwoman, *762*
Serrdakue, John: Crystal Force, *827*
Serre, Henri: Jules and Jim, *750*
Serres, Jacques: Blue Country, *719;* French Detective, The, *738*
Servaes, Daguey: Fortune's Fool, *738*
Servais, Jean: Angele, *713;* Liars, The, *760;* Rififi, *1010*
Sesau, Mo: Young Soul Rebels, *948*
Sessions, Almira: Oklahoma Annie, *349*
Sessions, John: Sweet Revenge (1990), *389*
Seth, Roshan: Gandhi, *524;* Little Dorrit, *576;* London Kills Me, *577;* Mississippi Masala, *596;* My Beautiful Laundrette, *601;* Not without My Daughter, *609*
Seton, Bruce: Demon Barber of Fleet Street, The, *832*
Sety, Gérard: Van Gogh, *800*
Severance, Joan: Almost Pregnant, *225;* Another Pair of Aces, *1094;* Bird on a Wire, *13;* Illicit Behavior, *985;* Lake Consequence, *568;* Red Shoe Diaries II: Double Dare, *637;* See No Evil, Hear No Evil, *375;* Write to Kill, *1033*
Severn, Billy: Enchanted Forest, The, *165*
Severnson, Joan: No Holds Barred, *91*
Sevilla, Carmen: Pantaloons, *775*
Seville, Carmen: Boldest Job in the West, The, *1099*
Seward, Billie: Branded a Coward, *1101*
Sewell, George: Invasion UFO, *1059;* UFO—Volumes I and II, *1086*
Seyffertitz, Gustav von: Dishonored, *501;* Shanghai Express, *655*
Seyler, Athene: Make Mine Mink, *327*
Seymour, Anne: Desire under the Elms, *500;* Trancers, *1085*
Seymour, Caroline: Gumshoe, *291*
Seymour, Clarine: Idol Dancer, The, *548*
Seymour, Jane: Are You Lonesome Tonight, *953;* Battlestar Galactica, *1038;* Doctor Quinn Medicine Woman, *502;* East of Eden (1982), *506;* Four Feathers, The (1978), *52;* Haunting Passion, The, *1055;* Head Office, *294;* Lassiter, *75;* Live and Let Die, *78;* Matters of the Heart, *590;* Misty, *188;* Oh, Heavenly Dog!, *192;* Onassis: The Richest Man in the World, *612;* Praying Mantis, *1007;* Scarlet Pimpernel, The (1982), *112;* Sinbad and the Eye of the Tiger, *1077;* Somewhere in Time, *1077;* Story of David, The, *207;* Sunstroke, *1021;* Tunnel, The, *689;* War and Remembrance, *696*
Seymour, Ralph: Longshot (1981), *579*
Seyrig, Delphine: Black Windmill, The, *956;* Daughters of Darkness, *830;* Discreet Charm of the Bourgeoisie, The, *730;* Donkey Skin (Peau D'Âne), *731;* Grain of Sand, The, *741;* I Sent a Letter to My Love, *746;* Last Year at Marienbad, *756;* Milky Way, The (1970), *767;* Muriel, *769;* Stolen Kisses, *789;* Window Shopping, *804*
Sezer, Serif: Yol, *806*
Shackelford, Ted: Baby of the Bride, *230;* Dying to Remember, *973;* Sweet Revenge (1987), *123*
Shackley, John: Tripods, *1085*
Shaffer, Paul: Gilda Live, *286;* Mr. Mike's Mondo Video, *334*
Shaffer, Stacey: Blood Screams, *816*

Shaker, Martin: Children, The, *823*
Shakti: Three Kinds of Heat, *128*
Shakur, Tupac: Above the Rim, *440;* Juice, *560;* Poetic Justice, *624*
Shaloub, Tony: Barton Fink, *232*
Shamata, Chuck: Death Weekend, *831;* Death Wish V: The Face of Death, *36;* Left for Dead, *572;* Mafia Princess, *585;* Night Friend, *90*
Shanath, Tamara: Cronos, *727*
Shandling, Garry: Garry Shandling: Alone in Vegas, *283;* Garry Shandling Show, The, *283;* Night We Never Met, The, *345;* Richard Lewis—"I'm Exhausted", *367*
Shane, Briant: Till There Was You, *684*
Shane, Jim: Chasing Dreams, *480*
Shane, Sara: King and Four Queens, The, *1125*
Shaner, Michael: Angel Fist, *5*
Shankar, Mamata: Stranger, The (1992), *790*
Shankar, Ravi: Monterey Pop, *431*
Shankley, Amelia: Little Princess, A, *183*
Shanklin, Doug: Dark Rider, *33*
Shanks, Don: Life and Times of Grizzly Adams, The, *181*
Shannon, Frank: Flash Gordon Conquers the Universe, *1052;* Flash Gordon: Mars Attacks the World (a.k.a. Trip to Mars; Deadly Ray From Mars, The), *1052;* Flash Gordon: Rocketship (a.k.a. Spaceship to the Unknown; Perils from Planet Mongo), *1052*
Shannon, George: Indecent Behavior, *551*
Shannon, Harry: Cow Town, *1106;* Hunt the Man Down, *984;* Idaho, *1122;* Once Upon a Honeymoon, *349;* Song of Texas, *1151;* Yellow Rose of Texas, *1165*
Shannon, Michael J.: Prime Suspect 3, *1008*
Shannon, Peggy: Deluge, *1046*
Shanta, James Anthony: Allnighter, The, *225*
Shapiro, Ken: Groove Tube, The, *291*
Sharif, Omar: Anastasia: The Mystery of Anna, *447;* Ashanti, *7;* Baltimore Bullet, The, *231;* Behold a Pale Horse, *458;* Beyond Justice, *11;* Bloodline, *464;* Crime & Passion, *260;* Dr. Zhivago, *503;* Far Pavilions, The, *514;* Funny Girl, *918;* Funny Lady, *918;* Grand Larceny, *289;* Green Ice, *981;* Horsemen, The, *64;* Juggernaut (1974), *987;* Last Valley, The, *75;* Lawrence of Arabia, *76;* Mackenna's Gold, *1131;* Night of the Generals, *90;* Oh, Heavenly Dog!, *192;* Pleasure Palace, *623;* Poppy Is Also a Flower, The, *99;* S.H.E., *110;* Tamarind Seed, The, *124;* Top Secret, *397*
Sharkey, Ray: Act of Piracy, *1;* Body Rock, *909;* Caged Fear, *21;* Capone, *22;* Chrome Soldiers, *26;* Cop and a Half, *160;* Du-Beat-E-O, *915;* Heart Beat, *537;* Hellhole, *849;* Idolmaker, The, *924;* Neon Empire, The, *89;* No Mercy, *91;* Private Investigations, *101;* Rain Killer, The, *1008;* Regina, *780;* Relentless II: Dead On, *879;* Round Trip to Heaven, *370;* Scenes from the Class Struggle in Beverly Hills, *373;* Take, The, *124;* Who'll Stop the Rain, *139;* Willie and Phil, *412;* Wired, *704;* Wise Guys, *412;* Zebrahead, *709*
Sharp, Lesley: Naked, *603*
Sharpe, Albert: Darby O'Gill and the Little People, *161;* Return of October, The, *366*
Sharpe, Cornelia: Reincarnation of Peter Proud, The, *879;* S.H.E., *110*
Sharpe, David: Colorado Serenade, *1105;* Daredevils of the Red Circle, *32;* Dick Tracy Returns, *38;* Texas to Bataan, *1156;* Three Texas Steers, *1157;* Wyoming Outlaw, *1165*
Sharpe, Karen: High and the Mighty, The, *541*
Sharrett, Michael: Deadly Friend, *831;* Magic of Lassie, The, *185*
Shatner, Melanie: Bloodlust: Subspecies III, *816*
Shatner, William: Airplane II: The Sequel, *224;* Andersonville Trial, The, *447;* Babysitter, The, *811;* Big Bad Mama, *12;* Bloopers from Star Trek and Laugh-In, *242;* Broken Angel, *470;* Brothers Karamazov, The, *471;* Crash of Flight 401, *490;* Devil's Rain, The, *834;* Impulse (1974), *985;* Intruder, The (1961), *553;* Kidnapping of the President, The, *988;* Kingdom of the Spiders, *859;* National Lampoon's Loaded Weapon 1, *342;* People, The, *1070;* Pioneer Woman, *1138;* Pray for the Wildcats, *100;* Secrets of a Married Man, *651;* Star Trek (TV Series), *1078;* Star Trek: The Menagerie, *1078;* Star Trek—The Motion Picture, *1079;* Star Trek II: The Wrath of Khan, *1079;* Star Trek III: The Search for Spock, *1079;* Star Trek IV: The Voyage Home, *1079;* Star Trek V: The Final Frontier, *1079;* Star Trek VI: The Undiscovered Country, *1079;* Twilight Zone, The (TV Series), *1086;* Visiting Hours, *901;* White Comanche, *1164*
Shattuck, Shari: Body Chemistry 3: Point of Seduction, *957;* Dead On, *967;* Death Spa, *831;* Desert Warrior, *1047;* Hot Child in the City, *64;* Immortal Sins, *855;* Mad About You, *325;* Naked Cage, The, *88*
Shaud, Grant: Distinguished Gentleman, The, *265*
Shaughnessy, Mickey: Adventures of Huckleberry Finn, The (1960), *144;* Boatniks, The, *151;* Designing Woman, *263;* Don't Go Near the Water, *267;* Jailhouse Rock, *925*
Shaver, Helen: Believers, The, *812;* Best Defense, *234;* Color of Money, The, *485;* Coming Out Alive, *963;* Desert Hearts, *499;* Dr. Bethune, *502;* Gas, *283;* Harry Tracy, *1119;* High-Ballin', *61;* Innocent Victim, *986;* Lost!, *580;* Morning Glory (1992), *599;* Murder So Sweet, *601;* Park Is Mine, The, *618;* Starship Invasions, *1080;* Survive the Night, *1021;* Trial & Error, *1027;* War Boy, The, *137*
Shaw, Alonna: Cyborg Cop, *1043*
Shaw, Bill: Ghostriders, *846*
Shaw, C. Montague: Buck Rogers: Destination Saturn (a.k.a. Planet Outlaws), *1040;* Holt of the Secret Service, *63;* Mysterious Dr. Satan, *88;* Riders of the Whistling Skull, *1144;* Zorro's Fighting Legion, *1166*
Shaw, Crystal: Laser Moon, *990*
Shaw, Fiona: London Kills Me, *577;* Mountains of the Moon, *87;* My Left Foot, *602;* Super Mario Brothers, The, *208;* Undercover Blues, *403*
Shaw, Martin: Hound of the Baskervilles, The (1983), *984;* Macbeth (1971), *584*
Shaw, Reta: Pajama Game, The, *934*
Shaw, Robert: Battle of Britain, *9;* Battle of the Bulge, *10;* Black Sunday (1977), *955;* Deep, The, *36;* Diamonds, *38;* Force Ten from Navarone, *51;* From Russia with Love, *53;* Jaws, *858;* Man for All Seasons, A, *586;* Reflection of Fear, *1009;* Robin and Marian, *107;* Sting, The, *120;* Swashbuckler (1976), *123;* Taking of Pelham One Two Three, The, *1022;* Town Called Hell, A, *131;* Young Winston, *709*
Shaw, Sebastian: High Season, *297;* Spy in Black, The, *664*
Shaw, Stan: Boys in Company C, The, *18;* Busted Up, *472;* Court-Martial of Jackie Robinson, The, *489;* D.P., *493;* Fear (1990), *976;* Fried Green Tomatoes, *522;* Gladiator, The, *55;* Harlem Nights, *59;* Lifepod, *1063;* Monster Squad, The, *866;* Rising Sun, *1010;* TNT Jackson, *130;* Tough Enough, *131;* Truck Turner, *132*
Shaw, Steve: Child of Glass, *158*
Shaw, Susan: Junkman, The, *70;* Quartet (1948), *631*
Shaw, Susan D.: Adventures of the Wilderness Family, *144;* Image of Passion, *549;* Mountain Family Robinson, *189;* Wilderness Family, Part 2, The, *217*
Shaw, Victoria: Alvarez Kelly, *1093;* Eddy Duchin Story, The *507*
Shaw, Vinessa: Hocus Pocus, *175;* Ladybugs, *315*
Shaw, Winifred: Gold Diggers of 1935, *920;* Satan Met a Lady, *1012;* Sweet Adeline, *943*
Shawlee, Joan: Francis Joins the Wacs, *280;* Prehistoric Women (1950), *1071*
Shawn, Dick: Angel, *5;* Beer, *233;* Check Is in the Mail, The, *254;* Emperor's New Clothes, The (1984), *164;* It's a Mad Mad Mad Mad World, *308;* Live at Harrah's, *320;* Love at First Bite, *322;* Maid to Order, *326;* Producers, The, *362;* Rented Lips, *366;* Secret Diary of Sigmund Freud, The, *374;* Tommy Chong Roast, The, *397;* Young Warriors, The, *141;* Your Favorite Laughs from an Evening at the Improv, *416*
Shawn, Michael: Midnight Kiss, *864*
Shawn, Wallace: Bostonians, The, *467;* Cemetery Club, The *478;* Crackers, *260;* Double-O Kid, The, *41;* First Time, The,

277; Heaven Help Us, 295; Micki & Maude, 331; Moderns, The, 335; Mom and Dad Save the World, 188; My Dinner with Andre, 602; Nice Girls Don't Explode, 344; Nickel & Dime, 344; Prick Up Your Ears, 626; Princess Bride, The, 1071; Scenes from the Class Struggle in Beverly Hills, 373; Shadows and Fog, 654; She's Out of Control, 378; We're No Angels (1989), 408

Shayne, Linda: Screwballs, 374

Shayne, Robert: Dynamite Pass, 1111; I, Mobster, 65; Loaded Pistols, 1128; Marshal of Cedar Rock, 1132; Rider from Tucson, 1143; Threat, The, 1024; Trader Tom of the China Seas, 131

Shea, Eric: Castaway Cowboy, The, 157

Shea, John: Backstreet Justice, 8; Case of Deadly Force, A, 476; Honey, I Blew Up the Kid, 175; Honeymoon, 851; Hussy, 546; Impossible Spy, The, 985; Kennedy (TV Miniseries), 562; Ladykiller, 990; Missing, 596; Nativity, The, 604; New Life, A, 343; Small Sacrifices, 660; Stealing Home, 667; Unsettled Land, 692; Windy City, 703

Shea, Kati: Barbarian Queen, 1038; Devastator, The, 37; Preppies, 360

Shea, Tom: Somewhere, Tomorrow, 206

Shear, Rhonda: Basic Training, 232

Shearer, Harry: Blood and Concrete, A Love Story, 956; Oscar (1991), 351; Plain Clothes, 358; Pure Luck, 363; Return of Spinal Tap, The, 366; Right Stuff, The, 640; This Is Spinal Tap, 394

Shearer, Moira: Black Tights, 909; Peeping Tom, 1005; Red Shoes, The (1948), 936; Tales of Hoffman, 943

Shearer, Norma: Barretts of Wimpole Street, The, 456; Divorcee, The, 502; Free Soul, A, 522; Idiot's Delight, 548; Marie Antoinette, 588; Private Lives, 362; Riptide, 640; Romeo and Juliet (1936), 643; Smilin' Through (1932), 661; Strange Interlude (1932), 669; Student Prince in Old Heidelberg, The, 671; Women, The, 413

Shearing, George: Jazz on a Summer's Day, 427

Shearman, Alan: Bullshot, 247

Sheedy, Ally: Bad Boys, 454; Betsy's Wedding, 236; Blue City, 957; Breakfast Club, The, 245; Chantilly Lace, 479; Fear (1990), 976; Heart of Dixie, The, 538; Invader, 1059; Lost Capone, The, 580; Maid to Order, 326; Man's Best Friend (1993), 863; Only the Lonely, 350; Red Shoe Diaries 4: Auto Erotica, 637; St. Elmo's Fire, 646; Short Circuit, 1076; Tattle Tale, 391; Twice in a Lifetime, 690; Wargames, 1088; We Are the Children, 697

Sheehan, Doug: FBI Murders, The, 47

Sheen, Charlie: Boys Next Door, The, 468; Cadence, 473; Chase, The (1994), 25; Courage Mountain, 160; Deadfall, 968; Eight Men Out, 508; Ferris Bueller's Day Off, 276; Hot Shots, 301; Hot Shots Part Deux, 301; Lucas, 583; Major League, 326; Major League II, 326; Men at Work, 592; National Lampoon's Loaded Weapon 1, 342; Navy Seals, 89; No Man's Land, 91; Platoon, 623; Red Dawn, 104; Rookie, The, 109; Three for the Road, 395; Three Musketeers, The (1993), 129; Wall Street, 695; Wraith, The, 904; Young Guns, 1165

Sheen, Lucy: Ping Pong, 622

Sheen, Martin: Andersonville Trial, The, 447; Apocalypse Now, 6; Badlands, 454; Believers, The, 812; Beverly Hills Brats, 237; Beyond the Stars, 1039; Cadence, 473; Cassandra Crossing, The, 476; Catholics, 477; Cold Front, 963; Consenting Adults (1985), 488; Conspiracy: The Trial of the Chicago 8, 488; Da, 493; Dead Zone, The, 831; Eagle's Wing, 1111; Enigma, 44; Execution of Private Slovik, The, 512; Final Countdown, The, 1051; Firestarter, 841; Fourth Wise Man, The, 521; Gandhi, 524; Gettysburg, 526; Guardian, The (1984), 534; Hear no Evil, 982; Incident, The (1967), 551; Judgment in Berlin, 560; Kennedy (TV Miniseries), 562; Little Girl Who Lives Down the Lane, The, 992; Loophole, 993; Maid, The, 326; Man, Woman and Child, 587; Missiles of October, The, 596; News at Eleven, 605; Nightbreaker, 607; No Drums, No Bugles, 608; Original Intent, 614; Out of the Darkness, 1003; Outer Limits, The (TV Series), 1069; Rage (1972), 633; Samaritan: The Mitch Snyder Story, 647; Shattered Spirits, 655; Siesta, 1016; Subject Was Roses, The, 671; Sweet Hostage, 674; That Championship Season, 680; Touch and Die, 1026; Wall Street, 695

Sheen, Ramon: Man of Passion, A, 587

Sheen, Ruth: High Hopes, 297

Sheffer, Craig: Baby Cakes, 453; Blue Desert, 957; Eye of the Storm, 974; Fire in the Sky, 1051; Fire with Fire, 517; Instant Karma, 306; Night Breed, 869; Program, The, 629; River Runs Through It, A, 641; Some Kind of Wonderful, 382; Split Decisions, 664; That Was Then…This Is Now, 680

Sheffield, Johnny: Tarzan Finds a Son, 125; Tarzan's New York Adventure, 126; Tarzan's Secret Treasure, 126

Sheffield, Reginald: Second Chance, 113

Sheila E.: Krush Groove, 927; Sign o' the Times, 434

Sheiner, David: Stone Killer, The, 120

Shelby, LaRita: South Central, 663

Sheldon, Barbara: Lucky Texan, 1130

Sheldon, Gene: Sign of Zorro, The, 204; Toby Tyler, 212

Shellen, Stephen: Casual Sex?, 252; Damned River, 32; Drop Dead Gorgeous, 972; Gimme an "F", 286; Model by Day, 86; Modern Girls, 335; Murder One, 87; River Runs Through It, A, 641; Stepfather, The, 1020; Talking Walls, 391

Shelley, Barbara: Blood of the Vampire, 815; Cat Girl, 960; Gorgon, The, 847; Village of the Damned, 900

Shelley, Joshua: Front, The, 523

Shelly, Adrienne: Big Girls Don't Cry…They Get Even, 238; Hexed, 296; Hold Me, Thrill Me, Kiss Me, 298; Trust, 689; Unbelievable Truth, The, 691

Shelton, Deborah: Blind Vision, 956; Body Double, 958; Hunk, 303; Nemesis (1992), 1067; Sins of the Night, 1017

Shelton, John: Time of Their Lives, The, 396

Shelton, Reid: First and Ten, 277

Shenar, Paul: Bedroom Window, The, 954; Best Seller, 954; Brass, 468; Deadly Force, 34; Dream Lover (1986), 972; King Richard II, 565; Raw Deal, 103; Scarface (1983), 112

Shepard, Angela: Billy the Kid Meets the Vampires, 813; Curse of the House Surgeon, The, 828; Evil Spirits in the House, 839; Honeymoon Murders, 851; Penpal Murders, 873; Queen Victoria and the Zombies, 878; Vampires Always Ring Twice, 900; Vampires from Outer Space, 900

Shepard, Elaine: Darkest Africa, 33

Shepard, Patty: Blood Moon, 815; Man Called Noon, The, 1131; Rest in Pieces, 879; Slugs, the Movie, 887; Stranger and the Gunfighter, The, 1153

Shepard, Sam: Baby Boom, 230; Bright Angel, 470; Country, 489; Crimes of the Heart, 260; Days of Heaven, 496; Defenseless, 969; Fool for Love, 518; Frances, 521; Pelican Brief, The, 1005; Raggedy Man, 1008; Resurrection, 638; Right Stuff, The, 640; Steel Magnolias, 667; Thunderheart, 1025; Voyager, 695

Shephard, O-Lan: Out, 96

Shepherd, Amanda: Hocus Pocus, 175

Shepherd, Cybill: Alice (1990), 224; Chances Are, 253; Daisy Miller, 493; Guide for the Married Woman, A, 291; Heartbreak Kid, The, 295; Lady Vanishes, The (1979), 990; Last Picture Show, The, 570; Long Hot Summer, The (1985), 578; Married to It, 589; Memphis, 592; Moonlighting (1985), 997; Once Upon a Crime, 349; Return, The, 1074; Secrets of a Married Man, 651; Seduced, 1013; Silver Bears, 379; Taxi Driver, 1023; Texasville, 680; Which Way Home, 138

Shepherd, Elizabeth: Invitation to the Wedding, 307; Tomb of Ligeia, 896

Shepherd, Jack: Twenty-One, 690

Shepherd, Jean: Ollie Hopnoodle's Haven of Bliss, 192

Shepherd, John: Friday the 13th, Part V—A New Beginning, 844; Thunder Run, 129

Shepherd, Morgan: Elvira, Mistress of the Dark, 271; Max Headroom, 1065

Sheppard, Delia: Animal Instincts, 952; Homeboys II: Crack City, 63; Mirror Images, 996; Roots of Evil, 109; Secret Games, 651; Sins of Desire, 1017

Sheppard, Patty: Crypt of the Living Dead, 827

Sheppard, Paula E.: Alice, Sweet Alice (Communion and Holy Terror), *808;* Liquid Sky, *1063*
Sher, Antony: Erik the Viking, *1049;* Shadey, *377;* Tartuffe, *677*
Sheridan, Ann: Angels with Dirty Faces, *5;* Appointment in Honduras, *6;* City for Conquest, *482;* Dodge City, *1109;* Doughgirls, The, *268;* Edge of Darkness (1943), *43;* Fighting Westerner, The, *1113;* George Washington Slept Here, *284;* Good Sam, *288;* I Was a Male War Bride, *304;* King's Row, *565;* Letter of Introduction, *573;* Man Who Came to Dinner, The, *328;* Mississippi, *931;* Murder at the Vanities, *931;* Opposite Sex, The, *934;* Silver River, *1150;* Stella (1950), *667;* Thank Your Lucky Stars, *944;* They Drive by Night, *127;* They Made Me a Criminal, *681*
Sheridan, Dinah: Genevieve, *283;* Railway Children, The, *198*
Sheridan, Jamey: All I Want for Christmas, *145;* Stanley and Iris, *665;* Stranger Among Us, A, *1020;* Talent for the Game, *677;* Whispers in the Dark, *1031*
Sheridan, Margaret: Thing (From Another World), The (1951), *1083*
Sheridan, Nicollette: Deceptions, *969;* Noises Off, *346*
Sherman, Bobby: Get Crazy, *284*
Sherman, Ellen: Dr. Tarr's Torture Dungeon, *836*
Sherman, Kerry: Satan's Cheerleaders, *882*
Sherman, Lowell: Bachelor Apartment, *230;* Ladies of Leisure, *567;* Way Down East, *697;* What Price Hollywood?, *698*
Sherwood, David: Curse of the Crystal Eye, *31*
Sherwood, Madeleine: Sweet Bird of Youth (1962), *674*
Sherwood, Roberta: Courtship of Eddie's Father, The, *260*
Sheybal, Vladek: Wind and the Lion, The, *140*
Shields, Arthur: Daughter of Dr. Jekyll, *829;* Enchanted Island, *44;* King and Four Queens, The, *1125;* Little Nellie Kelly, *928;* Quiet Man, The, *364;* River, The (1951), *641*
Shields, Brooke: Alice, Sweet Alice (Communion and Holy Terror), *808;* Backstreet Dreams, *454;* Blue Lagoon, The, *465;* Brenda Starr, *19;* Diamond Trap, The, *970;* Endless Love, *510;* Freaked, *281;* Just You and Me, Kid, *312;* King of the Gypsies, *565;* Muppets Take Manhattan, The, *189;* Pretty Baby, *626;* Sahara (1984), *110;* Speed Zone, *119;* Tilt, *396;* Wanda Nevada, *136;* Wet Gold, *138*
Shields, Nicholas: Liar's Edge, *992;* Princes in Exile, *627*
Shields, Robert: Wild Wild West Revisited, The, *1164*
Shigeta, James: China Cry, *481;* Die Hard, *38;* Flower Drum Song, *917;* Tomorrow's Child, *686*
Shilling, Marion: Clutching Hand, The, *27;* Common Law, The, *487;* Lucky Boots, *1130*
Shiloh, Shmuel: Double Edge, *504;* Goodbye New York, *289*
Shimada, Shogo: Zatoichi: Masseur Ichi and a Chest of Gold, *806*
Shimada, Yoko: Shogun (Full-Length Version), *115*
Shimkus, Joanna: Six in Paris (Paris Vue par . . .), *786;* Virgin and the Gypsy, The, *694*
Shimono, Sab: Come See the Paradise, *486;* Teenage Mutant Ninja Turtles III, *209;* Three Ninjas Kick Back, *211*
Shimura, Takashi: Bad Sleep Well, The, *715;* Drunken Angel, *732;* Godzilla, King of the Monsters, *846;* High and Low, *744;* Ikiru, *747;* No Regrets for Our Youth, *772;* Sanjuro, *783;* Sanshiro Sugata, *783;* Seven Samurai, The, *785;* Stray Dog, *790;* Throne of Blood, *794*
Shiner, Ronald: Carry on Admiral, *251*
Shipp, John Wesley: Flash, The, *1051;* NeverEnding Story II, The, *1068*
Shirakawa, Yumi: H-Man, The, *848*
Shire, Talia: Bed and Breakfast, *457;* Blood Vows: The Story of a Mafia Wife, *464;* Chantilly Lace, *479;* Cold Heaven, *485;* Deadfall, *968;* Dunwich Horror, The, *838;* For Richer, for Poorer, *279;* Godfather, The, *529;* Godfather, Part II, The, *529;* Godfather, Part III, The, *529;* Godfather Epic, The, *529;* New York Stories, *343;* Old Boyfriends, *611;* Prophecy, *877;* Rad, *102;* Rip Van Winkle, *199;* Rocky, *642;* Rocky II, *642;* Rocky III, *642;* Rocky IV, *642;* Rocky V, *642*
Shirk, Bill: Escapist, The, *511*
Shirley, Aliesa: Sweet Sixteen, *123*
Shirley, Anne: Anne of Green Gables (1934), *146;* Bombardier, *17;* Devil and Daniel Webster, The, *500;* Four Jacks and a Jill, *918;* Murder My Sweet, *999;* Stella Dallas, *667*
Shirt, J. C. White: Broken Chain, The, *20*
Shoemaker, Ann: House by the River, *984*
Shor, Dan: Mesmerized, *996;* Strange Behavior, *890;* Strangers Kiss, *669;* Wise Blood, *704*
Shore, Dinah: Fun and Fancy Free, *168;* Pee-Wee's Playhouse Christmas Special, *194;* Up in Arms, *403*
Shore, Pauly: Dream Date, *269;* Encino Man, *271;* Son-in-Law, *383*
Short, Bobby: Blue Ice, *957*
Short, Dorothy: Reefer Madness, *365;* Trail of the Silver Spurs, *1158*
Short, Martin: Best of Comic Relief, The, *235;* Best of John Candy, The, *236;* Big Picture, The, *238;* Captain Ron, *250;* Clifford, *256;* Cross My Heart (1987), *261;* Father of the Bride (1991), *275;* Innerspace, *1058;* Pure Luck, *363;* Really Weird Tales, *365;* Sunset Limousine, *388;* Three Amigos, *395;* Three Fugitives, *395*
Show, Grant: Treacherous Crossing, *1027;* Woman Her Men and Her Futon, A, *705*
Showalter, Max: Lord Love a Duck, *321*
Shower, Kathy: Commando Squad, *28;* Further Adventures of Tennessee Buck, The, *53;* L.A. Goddess, *314;* Out on Bail, *96;* Robo C.H.I.C., *1074;* Wild Cactus, *139*
Shriner, Kin: Kidnapped (1988), *71;* Obsessive Love, *1002;* Vendetta, *135*
Shriner, Wil: Time Trackers, *1084*
Shubert, Nancy: Sagebrush Trail, *1147*
Shue, Elisabeth: Adventures in Babysitting, *222;* Back to the Future II, *1037;* Back to the Future III, *1037;* Call to Glory, *474;* Cocktail, *485;* Heart and Souls, *1056;* Karate Kid, The, *562;* Link, *861;* Marrying Man, The, *329;* Soapdish, *382;* Twenty Bucks, *401*
Shuford, Stephanie: Dreams Come True, *1048*
Shull, Richard B.: Big Bus, The, *238;* Cockfighter, *27;* Pack, The, *873;* Splash, *384*
Shute, Anja: Tendres Cousines, *793*
Shutta, Ethel: Whoopee, *947*
Shuzhen, Tan: From Mao to Mozart, *424*
Sbyder, Rick: Paramount Comedy Theater, Vol. 3: Hanging Party, *354*
Siani, Sabrina: Ator: The Fighting Eagle, *1037;* Throne of Fire, The, *895*
Sibbett, Jane: Resurrected, The, *879*
Sicari, Joseph R.: Night School, *1001*
Sidahl, Viveka: House of Angels, *745*
Sidney, Sylvia: Blood on the Sun, *15;* Come Along with Me, *257;* Corrupt, *963;* Damien: Omen II, *829;* Dead End, *497;* Death at Love House, *968;* Demon (God Told Me To), *1046;* Early Frost, An, *506;* Finnegan Begin Again, *277;* Fury, *524;* Having It All, *294;* Love from a Stranger, *993;* Mr. Ace, *85;* Pals, *353;* Sabotage, *1011;* Shadow Box, The, *654;* Small Killing, A, *660;* Snowbeast, *888;* Street Scene, *670;* Summer Wishes, Winter Dreams, *673;* Used People, *404;* You Only Live Once, *708*
Sieber, Maria: Scarlet Empress, The, *649*
Siebert, Charles: Blue Sunshine, *957;* Cry for Love, A, *492;* Incredible Hulk, The, *1058;* Miracle Worker, The (1979), *595*
Siederman, Paul: Deranged, *833*
Siemaszko, Casey: Amazing Stories (TV Series), *1036;* Big Slice, The, *12;* Biloxi Blues, *240;* Breaking In, *245;* Miracle of the Heart, *595;* Near Misses, *342;* Of Mice and Men (1992), *611;* Three O'Clock High, *396;* Young Guns, *1165*

Siemaszko, Nina: Red Shoe Diaries 3: Another Woman's Lipstick, *637;* Saint of Fort Washington, The, *646;* Wild Orchid 2: Two Shades of Blue, *702*

Sierra, Gregory: Clones, The, *1042;* Code Name: Dancer, *27;* Deep Cover (1992), *36;* Gambler, Part II—The Adventure Continues, The, *1115;* Miami Vice, *84;* Unspeakable Acts, *692*

Siewkumar, Asha: Tropical Heat, *1027*

Signorelli, Tom: Alice, Sweet Alice (Communion and Holy Terror), *808;* Crossover Dreams, *912*

Signoret, Simone: Cat, The (Le Chat), *722;* Day And The Hour, *728;* Dedee D'Anvers, *729;* Diabolique, *730;* I Sent a Letter to My Love, *746;* Is Paris Burning?, *554;* La Ronde, *754;* Madame Rosa, *763;* Room at the Top, *643;* Ship of Fools, *656;* Sleeping Car Murders, The, *786;* Widow Couderc, *803*

Sihol, Caroline: Tous les Matins du Monde, *796*

Sikes, Brenda: Cleopatra Jones, *26;* Mandingo, *588*

Sikes, Cynthia: Arthur 2: On the Rocks, *229;* Love Hurts, *323;* Oceans of Fire, *93*

Sikking, James B.: Final Approach, *1051;* Man on a String, *81;* Morons from Outer Space, *337;* Narrow Margin (1990), *89;* Ollie Hopnoodle's Haven of Bliss, *192;* Ordinary People, *614;* Pelican Brief, The, *1005;* Soul Man, *383;* Up the Creek (1984), *403*

Silbar, Adam: Hot Moves, *301*

Sillas, Karen: Simple Men, *379*

Silva, Henry: Above the Law, *1;* Allan Quartermain and the Lost City of Gold, *4;* Alligator, *808;* Almost Human, *4;* Bravados, The, *1101;* Buck Rogers in the 25th Century, *1040;* Bulletproof, *21;* Code of Silence, *27;* Day of the Assassin, *33;* Harvest, The, *981;* Jayhawkers, The, *1123;* Law and Jake Wade, The, *1127;* Love and Bullets, *79;* Lust in the Dust, *324;* Man and Boy, *1131;* Manhunt (1973), *81;* Megaforce, *1065;* Never a Dull Moment, *191;* Possessed by the Night, *1006;* Shoot (1976), *115;* Tall T, The, *1154;* Thirst, *895;* Three Days to a Kill, *128;* Violent Breed, The, *136;* Virus, *1087;* Wrong Is Right, *414*

Silva, Trinidad: Night Before, The, *344*

Silvain, Eugene: Passion of Joan of Arc, The, *776*

Silver, Joe: Gig, The, *286;* Rabid, *878;* Switching Channels, *390;* They Came from Within, *895;* You Light Up My Life, *708*

Silver, Ron: Best Friends, *235;* Betrayal (1978), *459;* Billionaire Boys Club, *461;* Blind Side, *956;* Blue Steel (1990), *16;* Dear Detective, *968;* Eat and Run, *1048;* Enemies—A Love Story, *510;* Entity, The, *838;* Father's Revenge, A, *515;* Fellow Traveler, *515;* Forgotten Prisoners, *520;* Garbo Talks, *283;* Goodbye People, The, *530;* Lifepod, *1063;* Live Wire, *78;* Married to It, *589;* Mr. Saturday Night, *334;* Oh, God, You Devil!, *349;* Reversal of Fortune, *639;* Silent Rage, *116*

Silvera, Frank: Appaloosa, The, *1094;* Cop and a Half, *160;* Killer's Kiss, *71;* Miracle of Our Lady of Fatima, The, *595;* St. Valentine's Day Massacre, The, *111;* Stalking Moon, The, *1152;* Valdez Is Coming, *1160*

Silverheels, Jay: Broken Arrow, *1101;* Lone Ranger, The (1956), *1129;* Lone Ranger, The (TV Series), *1129;* Lone Ranger and the Lost City of Gold, The, *1129;* Santee, *1147*

Silverman, Jonathan: Age Isn't Everything, *223;* Breaking the Rules, *469;* Brighton Beach Memoirs, *246;* Caddyshack II, *249;* Challenge of a Lifetime, *478;* Class Action, *962;* For Richer, for Poorer, *279;* Girls Just Want to Have Fun, *287;* Little Sister, *319;* Stealing Home, *667;* Traveling Man, *687;* 12:01, *1086;* Weekend at Bernie's, *407;* Weekend at Bernie's II, *407*

Silvers, Phil: All Through the Night, *3;* Boatniks, The, *151;* Buono Sera, Mrs. Campbell, *247;* Cheap Detective, The, *254;* Chicken Chronicles, The, *254;* Cover Girl, *912;* Follow That Camel, *278;* Footlight Serenade, *917;* Funny Thing Happened on the Way to the Forum, A, *282;* Guide for the Married Man, A, *291;* Happy Hooker Goes Hollywood, The, *293;* Hey Abbott!, *296;* It's a Mad Mad Mad Mad World, *308;* Lady Be Good, *927;* Lady Takes a Chance, A, *1125;* Lucky Me, *929;* Sgt. Bilko (TV Series), *376;* Summer Stock, *942;* Tom, Dick and Harry, *397*

Silverstone, Alicia: Crush, The, *964*

Silvestre, Armand: Rock 'n' Roll Wrestling Women vs. the Aztec Mummy, *369*

Sim, Alastair: Belles of St. Trinian's, The, *234;* Christmas Carol, A (1951), *159;* Littlest Horse Thieves, The, *184;* Ruling Class, The, *371;* Stage Fright, *1019*

Sim, Gerald: Dr. Jekyll and Sister Hyde, *835;* Long Ago Tomorrow, *578*

Sim, Sheila: Great Day, *532*

Simmons, Beverly: Buck Privates Come Home, *246*

Simmons, Gene: Kiss Meets the Phantom of the Park, *859;* Never Too Young to Die, *90;* Red Surf, *104;* Runaway, *1075;* Trick or Treat (1986), *897;* Wanted: Dead or Alive, *136*

Simmons, Jean: Androcles and the Lion, *227;* Big Country, The, *1098;* Black Narcissus, *463;* Dain Curse, The, *965;* Dawning, The, *496;* Desirée, *500;* Dominique Is Dead, *971;* Egyptian, The, *508;* Elmer Gantry, *509;* Going Undercover, *288;* Grass Is Greener, The, *289;* Great Expectations (1946), *532;* Great Expectations (1989), *171;* Guys and Dolls, *921;* Hamlet (1948), *535;* Mr. Sycamore, *334;* Robe, The, *642;* Rough Night in Jericho, *1146;* She Couldn't Say No, *377;* Small Killing, A, *660;* Spartacus, *119;* This Could Be the Night, *394;* Thornbirds, The, *682;* Trio, *688;* Until They Sail, *692*

Simmons, Richard: Sergeant Preston of the Yukon (TV Series), *1148*

Simms, Ginny: Broadway Rhythm, *910*

Simms, Hilda: Joe Louis Story, The, *558*

Simms, Larry: Blondie, *241;* Blondie Has Trouble, *241;* Blondie Hits the Jackpot, *241;* Blondie in Society, *241;* Blondie Knows Best, *241*

Simms, Michael: Scarecrows, *883*

Simms, Mike: Bus Is Coming, The, *472*

Simon, Carly: No Nukes, *432*

Simon, François: Basileus Quartet, *715;* Christ Stopped at Eboli, *724;* Lumiere, *763*

Simon, Michel: Bizarre, Bizarre, *718;* Boudu Saved from Drowning, *720;* Candide, *722;* Head, The (1959), *849;* L'Atalante, *753;* La Chienne, *753;* Panique, *775;* Train, The, *131;* Two of Us, The, *797*

Simon, Paul: Annie Hall, *228;* One Trick Pony, *934;* Rutles, The (a.k.a. All You Need Is Cash), *938;* Steve Martin Live, *386*

Simon, Robert F.: Benny Goodman Story, The, *458;* Chinese Web, The, *25;* Nine Lives of Elfego Baca, The, *1136*

Simon, Simone: Cat People (1942), *822;* Curse of the Cat People, The, *828;* Devil and Daniel Webster, The, *500;* La Bête Humaine, *753;* La Ronde, *754;* Le Plaisir, *758;* Mademoiselle Fifi, *585*

Simon, Stan: Heroes in Hell, *61*

Simonnett, Michelle: Bernadette, *459*

Simons, Frank: Blue Yonder, The, *151*

Simonsen, Lars: Twist and Shout, *797*

Simonson, Renée: Nothing Underneath, *1002*

Simpson, O. J.: Capricorn One, *1041;* CIA Codename Alexa, *26;* Firepower, *49;* Hambone and Hillie, *535;* Killer Force, *71;* Klansman, The, *566;* Naked Gun, The, *341;* Naked Gun 2 1/2, The, *341;* Naked Gun 33 1/3, The—The Final Insult, *341;* No Place To Hide, *91*

Simpson, Raeanin: Little Heroes, *181*

Simpson, Russell: Border Patrol, *1100;* Cabin in the Cotton, *473;* Grapes of Wrath, The, *531;* Human Hearts, *546;* Spoilers, The, *1152;* Virginia City, *1161;* Virginian, The (1923), *1161*

Simpson, Sandy: Glory Years, *287*

Sims, Aaron: Adventures of the Kung Fu Rascals, The, *223*

Sims, George: High Country, The, *61*

Sims, Joan: Carry on at Your Convenience, *251;* Carry on Behind, *251;* Carry on Cleo, *251;* Carry on Cowboy, *251;* Carry on Doctor, *251;* Carry on Emmanuelle, *251;* Follow That Camel, *278;* Love Among the Ruins, *322;* Murder Is Announced, A, *998*

Sinatra, Frank: Anchors Aweigh, *906;* Assault on a Queen, *7;* Can-Can, *911;* Cannonball Run II, *250;* Come Blow Your

Horn, *257;* Detective, The (1968), *500;* Devil at 4 O'Clock, The, *500;* Double Dynamite, *268;* First Deadly Sin, The, *977;* Four for Texas, *1114;* From Here to Eternity (1953), *523;* Guys and Dolls, *921;* High Society, *922;* Higher and Higher, *922;* Hole in the Head, A, *298;* It Happened in Brooklyn, *925;* Kings Go Forth, *565;* Kissing Bandit, The, *927;* Lady in Cement, *989;* Man with the Golden Arm, The, *587;* Manchurian Candidate, The, *995;* Miracle of the Bells, The, *595;* Never So Few, *89;* None But the Brave, *92;* Not as a Stranger, *609;* Ocean's Eleven, *93;* On the Town, *934;* Pal Joey, *934;* Pride and the Passion, The, *626;* Robin & the Seven Hoods, *936;* Ship Ahoy, *939;* Some Came Running, *662;* Step Lively, *942;* Suddenly, *1021;* Take Me Out to the Ball Game, *943;* Tender Trap, The, *392;* That's Entertainment, *436;* Tony Rome, *1025;* Von Ryan's Express, *136;* Young at Heart, *948*

Sinatra Jr., Frank: Man Called Adam, A, *586*

Sinatra, Nancy: Speedway, *941;* Wild Angels, The, *139*

Sinbad: Coneheads, *258;* Meteor Man, *186;* Necessary Roughness, *342*

Sinclair, Gordon John: Girl in the Picture, The, *286;* Gregory's Girl, *290;* That Sinking Feeling, *392*

Sinclair, Hugh: Saint's Vacation, The, *1012*

Sinclair, Kristian: Countryman, *489*

Sinclair, Madge: Almos' a Man, *445;* Coming to America, *258;* Conrack, *488;* Convoy (1978), *29;* Cornbread, Earl and Me, *488*

Sinden, Donald: Captain's Table, *250;* Cruel Sea, The, *492;* Doctor in the House, *266;* Island at the Top of the World, The, *1060*

Singer, Linda: Junior, *858;* Zombie Nightmare, *905*

Singer, Lori: Falcon and the Snowman, The, *513;* Footloose, *917;* Made in USA, *584;* Man with One Red Shoe, The, *328;* Short Cuts, *657;* Storm and Sorrow, *120;* Summer Heat (1987), *672;* Sunset Grill, *1021;* Trouble in Mind, *688;* Warlock (1988), *901*

Singer, Marc: Beastmaster, The, *1038;* Beastmaster 2: Through the Portal of Time, *1039;* Berlin Conspiracy, The, *10;* Body Chemistry, *957;* Born to Race, *17;* Dead Space, *1045;* Deadly Game, *34;* Go Tell the Spartans, *56;* High Desert Kill, *850;* If You Could See What I Hear, *548;* Man Called Sarge, A, *327;* Sea Wolf, The (1993), *113;* Sweet Justice, *123;* Two Worlds of Jennie Logan, The, *1086;* Ultimate Desires, *1028;* Watchers II, *901*

Singer, Ritchie: Encounter at Raven's Gate, *1049*

Singhammer, Eva Maria: Heidi (1965), *173*

Singleton, Penny: Blondie, *241;* Blondie Has Trouble, *241;* Blondie Hits the Jackpot, *241;* Blondie in Society, *241;* Blondie Knows Best, *241;* Blondie Takes a Vacation, *242;* Blondie's Blessed Event, *242;* Boy Meets Girl, *244;* It's a Great Life, *308*

Singleton, Sam: Death of a Prophet, *498*

Sinise, Gary: Jack the Bear, *556;* Midnight Clear, A, *593;* Of Mice and Men (1992), *611;* True West, *689*

Sirtis, Marina: Star Trek: The Next Generation (TV Series), *1079*

Sisk, Kathleen: Girl Who Spelled Freedom, The, *169*

Sisters, King: Second Fiddle, *938*

Sizemore, Tom: Heart and Souls, *1056;* Matter of Degrees, A, *590;* Passenger 57, *97;* Striking Distance, *121;* True Romance, *133;* Watch It, *696;* Where Sleeping Dogs Lie, *1031*

Sjoberg, Karen: Jar, The, *858*

Sjoman, Vilgot: I Am Curious Blue, *746*

Sjöström, Victor: Outlaw and His Wife, The, *616;* Phantom Chariot, *777;* Thomas Graal's Best Child, *794;* Thomas Graal's Best Film, *794;* Wild Strawberries, *804*

Skaggs, Jimmie F.: Lost Capone, The, *580*

Skala, Lilia: Charly, *1041;* Deadly Hero, *34;* Flashdance, *917;* Heartland, *1119;* House of Games, *984;* Lilies of the Field (1963), *575;* Men of Respect, *592;* Probe, *101;* Roseland, *644;* Ship of Fools, *656*

Skarsgard, Stellan: Noon Wine, *608;* Wind (1992), *140*

Skarvellis, Jackie: Rats Are Coming!, The Werewolves Are Here!, The, *878*

Skelton, Red: Bathing Beauty, *908;* Clown, The, *484;* Du Barry Was a Lady, *915;* Fuller Brush Man, The, *282;* Having a Wonderful Time, *294;* I Dood It, *924;* Lady Be Good, *927;* Lovely to Look At, *929;* Merton of the Movies, *331;* Neptune's Daughter, *932;* Panama Hattie, *935;* Red Skelton: A Career of Laughter, *433;* Ship Ahoy, *939;* Show-Off, The, *378;* Southern Yankee, A, *383;* Texas Carnival, *944;* Thousands Cheer, *945;* Three Little Words, *945;* Watch the Birdie, *406;* Whistling in Brooklyn, *410;* Whistling in Dixie, *410;* Whistling in the Dark, *410;* Yellow Cab Man, The, *415;* Ziegfeld Follies, *949*

Skerla, Lena: Fire Within, The, *736*

Skerritt, Tom: Alien, *1034;* Big Bad Mama, *12;* Big Man on Campus, *238;* Big Town, The, *461;* Child in the Night, *961;* China Lake Murders, The, *961;* Dangerous Summer, A, *494;* Dead Zone, The, *831;* Devil's Rain, The, *834;* Fighting Back, *47;* Fuzz, *282;* Heist, The, *540;* Hitchhiker (Series), The, *850;* Ice Castles, *548;* Knight Moves, *989;* M*A*S*H, *324;* Maid to Order, *326;* Miles to Go, *594;* Nightmare at Bittercreek, *1002;* Opposing Force, *95;* Poison Ivy (1992), *1006;* Poker Alice, *1139;* Poltergeist III, *876;* Red King, White Knight, *636;* River Runs Through It, A, *641;* Rookie, The, *109;* Silence of the North, *657;* SpaceCamp, *1078;* Steel Magnolias, *667;* Thieves Like Us, *681;* Top Gun, *131;* Turning Point, The, *689;* Up in Smoke, *403;* Wild Orchid 2: Two Shades of Blue, *702;* Wild Rovers, The, *1164;* Wisdom, *140*

Skinner, Anita: Girlfriends, *528;* Sole Survivor, *888*

Skinner, Cornelia Otis: Uninvited, The (1944), *1029*

Skinner, Keith: Mademoiselle, *585*

Skipworth, Alison: Becky Sharp, *457;* Dangerous, *494;* Doubting Thomas, *268;* If I Had a Million, *304;* Night after Night, *344;* Satan Met a Lady, *1012*

Skjonberg, Espen: One Day in the Life of Ivan Denisovich, *613*

Skoliar, Igor: Jazzman, *749*

Skolimowski, Jerzy: Big Shots, *238;* White Nights (1985), *700*

Skomarovsky, Vladimir: Black Eagle, *13*

Skvorecky, Josef: Report on the Party and the Guests, A, *781*

Skye, Ione: Carmilla, *821;* Gas, Food, Lodging, *525;* Guncrazy (1992), *535;* Mindwalk, *430;* Night in the Life of Jimmy Reardon, A, *344;* Rachel Papers, *364;* River's Edge, *641;* Samantha, *372;* Say Anything, *373;* Stranded, *1080*

Slabolepszy, Paul: Saturday Night at the Palace, *648*

Slade, Betsy: Our Time, *616*

Slade, Max Elliott: Three Ninjas, *211;* Three Ninjas Kick Back, *211*

Sladen, Elizabeth: Dr. Who: Revenge of the Cybermen, *1047;* Gulliver in Lilliput, *291*

Slate, Jeremy: Born Losers, *17;* Centerfold Girls, *478;* Dream Machine, *269;* Girls! Girls! Girls!, *919;* Hell's Angels '69, *60;* Mr. Horn, *1134;* Sons of Katie Elder, The, *1151;* Summer of Fear, *891*

Slater, Christian: Beyond the Stars, *1039;* Gleaming the Cube, *55;* Heathers, *295;* Jimmy Hollywood, *310;* Kuffs, *73;* Legend of Billie Jean, The, *76;* Mobsters, *86;* Name of the Rose, The, *89;* Pump Up the Volume, *630;* Robin Hood: Prince of Thieves, *108;* Tales from the Darkside, The Movie, *892;* True Romance, *133;* Tucker: A Man and His Dream, *689;* Twisted, *1028;* Twisted: A Step Beyond Insanity, *690;* Untamed Heart, *692;* Where the Day Takes You, *699;* Wizard, The, *218;* Young Guns II, *1166*

Slater, Helen: Betrayal of the Dove, *954;* Chantilly Lace, *479;* City Slickers, *255;* Happy Together, *293;* House in the Hills, A, *984;* Legend of Billie Jean, The, *76;* Ruthless People, *371;* Secret of My Success, The, *375;* Sticky Fingers, *386;* Supergirl, *1081;* 12:01, *1086*

Slattery, Tony: Peter's Friends, *621*

Slaughter, Sgt.: Bad Guys, *8*

Slaughter, Tod: Crimes at the Dark House, *826;* Crimes of Stephen Hawke, The, *826;* Demon Barber of Fleet Street, The,

832; Face at the Window, The, *840;* Murder in the Red Barn, *867;* Never Too Late, *604;* Sexton Blake and the Hooded Terror, *1014;* Ticket of Leave Man, The, *895*
Slavens, Darla: Married People, Single Sex, *589*
Sledge, Tommy: Gross Jokes, *291*
Slezak, Leo: Baron Müenchhausen, *1038*
Slezak, Walter: Bedtime for Bonzo, *233;* Black Beauty (1971), *151;* Born to Kill, *958;* Caper of the Golden Bulls, The, *22;* Cornered, *29;* Emil and the Detectives, *164;* Fallen Sparrow, The, *513;* Inspector General, The, *306;* Lifeboat, *992;* Miracle, The (1959), *594;* Once Upon a Honeymoon, *349;* People Will Talk, *356;* Pirate, The, *935;* Princess and the Pirate, The, *361;* RiffRaff (1947), *106;* Salome, Where She Danced, *647;* Sinbad the Sailor, *116;* Step Lively, *942;* This Land Is Mine, *682;* Yellow Cab Man, The, *415*
Sloane, Everett: Citizen Kane, *482;* Disorderly Orderly, The, *265;* Enforcer, The (1951), *44;* Journey Into Fear (1942), *987;* Lady from Shanghai, *989;* Marjorie Morningstar, *589;* Patsy, The, *355;* Patterns, *619;* Sirocco, *116;* Somebody Up There Likes Me, *662*
Sloane, Lance: Big Bet, The, *238*
Sloman, Roger: Nuts in May, *348*
Slowe, Georgia: Black Arrow (1984), *150*
Sloyan, James: Callie and Son, *474;* Prime Suspect, *627;* Xanadu, *948*
Small, Marya: Fade to Black (1980), *840*
Smart, Jean: Fire with Fire, *517;* Homeward Bound: The Incredible Journey, *175;* Mistress (1992), *597*
Smart, Rebecca: Celia, Child of Terror, *477*
Smerdoni, Rinaldo: Shoeshine, *785*
Smestad, Stian: Shipwrecked, *203*
Smit, Maarten: For a Lost Soldier, *737*
Smith, A. Thomas: Invader, *1059*
Smith, Al: Forbidden Trail, *1113*
Smith, Albert J.: Telegraph Trail, The, *1154*
Smith, Alexis: Adventures of Mark Twain, The (1944), *442;* Age of Innocence, The, *443;* Any Number Can Play, *450;* Casey's Shadow, *157;* Conflict, *963;* Dive Bomber, *502;* Doughgirls, The, *268;* Gentleman Jim, *525;* Here Comes the Groom, *922;* Hollywood Canteen, *923;* Horn Blows at Midnight, The, *301;* Little Girl Who Lives Down the Lane, The, *992;* Night and Day (1946), *933;* Once Is Not Enough, *613;* Rhapsody in Blue, *936;* San Antonio, *1147;* Sleeping Tiger, The, *660;* South of St. Louis, *1151;* Split Second (1953), *664;* This Happy Feeling, *394;* Tough Guys, *398;* Two Mrs. Carrolls, The, *1028;* Young Philadelphians, The, *708*
Smith, Allison: Jason Goes to Hell: The Final Friday, *858*
Smith, Art: Letter from an Unknown Woman, *573*
Smith, Bessie: Ladies Sing the Blues, The, *428*
Smith, Bubba: Black Moon Rising, *14;* My Samurai, *88;* Police Academy, *359;* Police Academy II: Their First Assignment, *359;* Police Academy III: Back in Training, *359;* Police Academy 4: Citizens on Patrol, *359;* Police Academy 5—Assignment: Miami Beach, *359;* Police Academy 6: City Under Siege, *359;* Wild Pair, The, *140*
Smith, C. Aubrey: Adventures of Mark Twain, The (1944), *442;* And Then There Were None, *952;* Another Thin Man, *952;* Balalaika, *907;* Beyond Tomorrow, *1039;* Bombshell, *243;* Cleopatra (1934), *484;* Dr. Jekyll and Mr. Hyde (1941), *835;* Eternally Yours, *511;* Five Came Back, *517;* Four Feathers, The (1939), *52;* Little Lord Fauntleroy (1936), *576;* Lives of a Bengal Lancer, The, *78;* Love Me Tonight, *929;* Madame Curie, *584;* Morning Glory (1933), *599;* Prisoner of Zenda, The (1937), *100;* Queen Christina, *631;* Romeo and Juliet (1936), *643;* Scarlet Empress, The, *649;* Sensations of 1945, *938;* Thoroughbreds Don't Cry, *210;* Transatlantic Tunnel, *1085;* Wee Willie Winkie, *216;* White Cliffs of Dover, The, *699*
Smith, Cedric: Penthouse, The, *1005;* Tales From Avonlea (TV series), *209*
Smith, Charles Martin: American Graffiti, *226;* Buddy Holly Story, The, *910;* Campus Corpse, The, *820;* Deep Cover (1992), *36;* Experts, The, *273;* Fifty/Fifty, *47;* Herbie Goes Bananas, *174;* Hot Spot, *544;* More American Graffiti, *599;* Never Cry Wolf, *89;* Rafferty and the Gold Dust Twins, *364;* Starman, *1080;* Strange Tales: Ray Bradbury Theater, *1080;* Untouchables, The, *134*
Smith, Cheryl: Laserblast, *1062*
Smith, Cotter: Bunny's Tale, A, *472;* Cameron's Closet, *820;* Lady Beware, *989;* Last Prostitute, The, *570;* Midnight's Child, *865*
Smith, Cynthia: For the Love of Benji, *167*
Smith, David Anthony: Terror in Paradise, *126*
Smith, Ebbe Roe: Big Easy, The, *12*
Smith, Forry: Black Cobra 3, *13*
Smith, G. Michael: Offerings, *872*
Smith, Geraldine: Flesh, *518;* Mixed Blood, *86*
Smith, Hal: Andy Griffith Show, The (TV Series), *227*
Smith, Howard: Call Northside 777, *959*
Smith, Ian: Body Melt, *817*
Smith, Jack: On Moonlight Bay, *933*
Smith, Jaclyn: Bourne Identity, The, *958;* Deja Vu, *499;* George Washington, *526;* Lies Before Kisses, *574;* Night They Saved Christmas, The, *191;* Nightkill, *1001;* Rage of Angels, *633;* Users, The, *692;* Windmills of the Gods, *703*
Smith, Jamie: Killer's Kiss, *71*
Smith, John: Circus World, *482;* High and the Mighty, The, *541;* Hondo and the Apaches, *1121*
Smith, Kate: This Is the Army, *945*
Smith, Keely: Thunder Road, *129*
Smith, Kent: Affair, The, *442;* Badlanders, The, *1096;* Cat People (1942), *822;* Curse of the Cat People, The, *828;* Death of a Gunfighter, *1108;* Forever and a Day, *520;* Fountainhead, The, *520;* Hitler's Children, *63;* Party Girl, *618;* Spiral Staircase, The (1946), *1019;* Strangers When We Meet, *670*
Smith, Kurtwood: Boxing Helena, *818;* Company Business, *28;* Delos Adventure, The, *36;* Fortress (1993), *1053;* Nightmare Years, The, *607;* Rambo III, *103;* RoboCop, *1074;* Shadows and Fog, *654;* Star Trek VI: The Undiscovered Country, *1079;* True Believer, *1027*
Smith, Lane: Between the Lines, *237;* Blind Vengeance, *15;* Displaced Person, The, *501;* Distinguished Gentleman, The, *265;* Duplicates, *973;* False Arrest, *513;* Mighty Ducks, The, *187;* My Cousin Vinny, *339;* Native Son, *604;* Prime Suspect, *627;* Prison, *876;* Race for Glory, *102;* Son-in-Law, *383;* Weeds, *697*
Smith, Lewis: Fulfillment, *523;* Heavenly Kid, The, *296*
Smith, Linda: Shades of Love: The Rose Cafe, *654*
Smith, Lois: Falling Down, *513;* Fried Green Tomatoes, *522;* Jilting of Granny Weatherall, The, *558;* Keep the Change, *1124;* Next Stop, Greenwich Village, *605;* Reckless (1984), *636;* Reuben, Reuben, *367;* Twisted, *1028;* Twisted: A Step Beyond Insanity, *690*
Smith, Loring: Clown, The, *484*
Smith, Louise: Working Girls, *706*
Smith, Madeleine: Bawdy Adventures of Tom Jones, The, *233;* Vampire Lovers, The, *900*
Smith, Madeline: Frankenstein and the Monster from Hell, *842*
Smith, Madolyn: Caller, The, *1041;* Final Approach, *1051;* Funny Farm, *282;* Pray TV (1982), *626;* Rose and the Jackal, The, *644;* Sadat, *646;* Super, The, *388;* Urban Cowboy, *692*
Smith, Maggie: California Suite, *249;* Clash of the Titans, *1041;* Evil under the Sun, *973;* Honey Pot, The, *300;* Hook, *175;* Hot Millions, *301;* Lily in Love, *318;* Lonely Passion of Judith Hearne, The, *577;* Missionary, The, *333;* Murder by Death, *338;* Prime of Miss Jean Brodie, The, *361;* Private Function, A, *361;* Quartet (1981), *631;* Room with a View, A, *644;* Secret Garden, The (1993), *202;* Sister Act, *379;* Sister Act 2: Back in the Habit, *380;* Travels with My Aunt, *399;* V.I.P.s, The, *693*
Smith, Margaret: New Wave Comedy, *343*
Smith, Mel: Brain Donors, *245;* Misadventures of Mr. Wilt, The, *333;* Morons from Outer Space, *337*

Smith, Melanie: Baby Doll Murders, The, *953;* Trancers III: Death Lives, *1085*
Smith, Mittie: Blue Yonder, The, *151*
Smith, Pam: Misty, *188*
Smith, Patricia: Spirit of St. Louis, The, *664*
Smith, Paul: Caged Fury, *21;* Death Chase, *35;* Desert Kickboxer, *37;* Gor, *1054;* Haunted Honeymoon, *294;* Jungle Warriors, *69;* Madron, *1131;* Outlaw Force, *96;* Popeye, *196;* Red Sonja, *104;* Sadat, *646;* Salamander, The, *111;* Sno-Line, *117;* Sonny Boy, *889;* Terminal Entry, *1082;* We Are No Angels, *1163*
Smith, Queenie: Mississippi, *931;* My Sister Eileen, *932*
Smith, Rainbeaux: Revenge of the Cheerleaders, *367;* Slumber Party 57, *381*
Smith, Ray: King Lear (1988), *564*
Smith, Rex: Pirates of Penzance, The, *935;* Snow White and the Seven Dwarfs (1983), *205;* Sooner or Later, *663;* Streethawk, *121;* Trial of the Incredible Hulk, *1085*
Smith, Robert: Call Out the Marines, *249*
Smith, Roger: Never Steal Anything Small, *932*
Smith, Sammy: How to Succeed in Business without Really Trying, *923*
Smith, Shawn: Land Unknown, The, *1061*
Smith, Shawnee: Blob, The (1988), *814;* Desperate Hours (1990), *37;* Summer School, *388*
Smith, Sheila: Taking My Turn, *943*
Smith, Shelley: Scruples, *650*
Smith, Sinjin: Side Out, *657*
Smith, T. Ryder: Brainscan, *818*
Smith, Ted: Adventures of the Kung Fu Rascals, The, *223*
Smith, Terri Susan: Basket Case, *811*
Smith, Will: Made in America, *325;* Six Degrees of Separation, *659*
Smith, William: Angels Die Hard, *5;* Any Which Way You Can, *228;* B.O.R.N., *811;* Boss, *1101;* C.C. & Company, *21;* Cartel, *23;* Commando Squad, *28;* Cybernator, *1043;* Deadly Trackers, The, *1108;* Fever Pitch, *516;* Frisco Kid, The, *1114;* Gas Pump Girls, *283;* Gentle Savage, *1115;* Grave of the Vampire, *847;* Invasion of the Bee Girls, *1059;* L.A. Vice, *74;* Last American Hero, The, *75;* Last of the Warriors, *1062;* Last Riders, The, *75;* Losers, The, *79;* Maniac Cop, *862;* Moon in Scorpio, *599;* Platoon Leader, *99;* Red Dawn, *104;* Red Nights, *637;* Rockford Files, The (TV Series), *108;* Scorchy, *112;* Spirit of the Eagle, *119;* Twilight's Last Gleaming, *133;* Ultimate Warrior, The, *1087*
Smith, Willie E.: Legend of Boggy Creek, *860*
Smith, Willie Mae Ford: Say Amen, Somebody, *434*
Smith, Yeardley: Ginger Ale Afternoon, *286;* Maximum Overdrive, *864*
Smith-Cameron, J.: Gal Young 'Un, *524*
Smithers, Jan: Where the Lilies Bloom, *216*
Smitrovich, Bill: Crime Story, *30;* Killing Affair, A, *988;* Miami Vice, *84*
Smits, Jimmy: Believers, The, *812;* Cisco Kid, The, *1105;* Fires Within, *517;* Glitz, *980;* L.A. Law, *567;* Old Gringo, The, *611;* Running Scared (1986), *110;* Switch, *390;* Tommyknockers, The, *1084;* Vital Signs, *694*
Smits, Sonja: That's My Baby, *680;* Videodrome, *900*
Smothers, Dick: Alice Through the Looking Glass (1966), *906;* Tales of the Unexpected, *1022;* Yo-Yo Man, *415*
Smothers, Tom: Alice Through the Looking Glass (1966), *906;* Get to Know Your Rabbit, *285;* Kids Are Alright, The, *428;* Pandemonium, *353;* Rap Master Ronnie—A Report Card, *364;* Serial, *376;* Silver Bears, *379;* Speed Zone, *119;* Yo-Yo Man, *415*
Snipes, Wesley: Boiling Point, *17;* Demolition Man, *1046;* Jungle Fever, *561;* King of New York, *72;* Mo' Better Blues, *931;* New Jack City, *90;* Passenger 57, *97;* Rising Sun, *1010;* Streets of Gold, *671;* Sugar Hill, *122;* Waterdance, The, *696;* White Men Can't Jump, *410*
Snodgress, Carrie: Across the Tracks, *441;* Attic, The, *811;* Ballad of Little Jo, The, *1096;* Blueberry Hill, *465;* Diary of a Mad Housewife, *501;* 8 Seconds, *43;* Mission of the Shark, *596;* Murphy's Law, *87;* Night in Heaven, A, *606;* Pale Rider, *1138;* Rabbit Run, *632;* Rose and the Jackal, The, *644;* Silent Night, Lonely Night, *658;* Trick or Treat (1982), *897;* Woman with a Past, *705*
Snow, Victoria: Kissing Place, The, *989*
Snowden, Jane: French Lessons, *281*
Snowden, Leigh: Creature Walks Among Us, The, *826*
Snowflake: Lawless Nineties, The, *1127;* Lonely Trail, The, *1129*
Snyder, Arlen Dean: Dear Detective, *968;* No Man's Land, *91;* Scalpel, *883;* Wheels of Terror, *138*
Snyder, Drew: Blindfold: Acts of Obsession, *956;* Dance with Death, *965;* Night School, *1001;* Project: Eliminator, *101*
Snyder, Nancy: Plants Are Watching, The, *1071*
Snyder, Suzanne: Killer Klowns from Outer Space, *859*
Snyder, Valerie Sedle: Merry Wives of Windsor, The, *331*
Socas, Maria: Warrior and the Sorceress, The, *1088*
Soderdahl, Lars: Brothers Lionheart, The, *152*
Soeberg, Camilla: Manifesto, *328*
Sofaer, Abraham: Captain Sinbad, *156;* Elephant Walk, *508;* His Majesty O'Keefe, *62;* Journey to the Center of Time, *1060;* Naked Jungle, The, *88;* Quo Vadis (1951), *632*
Sojin: Thief of Bagdad, The (1924), *1083*
Sokol, Marilyn: Foul Play, *280;* Something Short of Paradise, *383*
Sokoloff, Vladimir: Baron of Arizona, The, *1097*
Solanitsin, Anatoly: Stalker, *788*
Solar, Silvia: Finger on the Trigger, *1113;* Gentleman Killer, *1115*
Solari, Rudy: Boss' Son, The, *467*
Solari, Suzanne: Rollerblade, *1075*
Soler, Andres: El Bruto (The Brute), *733*
Soler, Fernando: Great Madcap, The, *742;* Susanna, *791*
Soles, P. J.: Alienator, *1035;* Awakening of Cassie, The, *452;* B.O.R.N., *811;* Halloween, *848;* Rock 'n' Roll High School, *369;* Saigon Commandos, *110;* Stripes, *387*
Soles, Paul: Beethoven Lives Upstairs, *149*
Solntseva, Yulia: Aelita: Queen of Mars, *711;* Cigarette Girl from Mosselprom, The, *724*
Sologne, Madeleine: Eternal Return, The, *735*
Solomin, Yuri: Dersu Uzala, *729*
Solomon, Charles: Witchcraft II, *903;* Witchcraft III, The Kiss of Death, *903;* Witchcraft IV, *903*
Solondz, Todd: Fear, Anxiety and Depression, *276*
Solovei, Elena: Oblomov, *772;* Slave of Love, A, *786;* Unfinished Piece for the Player Piano, An, *798*
Someck, Jack: Portnoy's Complaint, *624*
Somers, Kristi: Tomboy, *130*
Somers, Suzanne: Ants!, *809;* Bullitt, *21;* Magnum Force, *80;* Nothing Personal, *347;* Sky Heist, *117;* Yesterday's Hero, *708*
Sommars, Julie: Herbie Goes to Monte Carlo, *174;* Sex and the College Girl, *653*
Sommer, Elke: Adventures Beyond Belief, *222;* Boy, Did I Get a Wrong Number!, *244;* Carry on Behind, *251;* Corrupt Ones, The, *29;* Devil in the House of Exorcism, The, *833;* Double McGuffin, The, *163;* House of Exorcism, The, *852;* Inside the Third Reich, *552;* Invisible Strangler, *857;* Jenny's War, *68;* Left for Dead, *572;* Lily in Love, *318;* No One Cries Forever, *608;* Oscar, The (1966), *615;* Prisoner of Zenda, The (1979), *361;* Prize, The, *629;* Probe, *101;* Severed Ties, *885;* Shot in the Dark, A, *378;* Swiss Conspiracy, The, *1022;* Ten Little Indians (1975), *1023;* Torture Chamber of Baron Blood, The, *896;* Zeppelin, *709*
Sommer, Josef: Assault at West Point, *451;* Bridge to Silence, *470;* Brotherly Love, *819;* Chances Are, *253;* D.A.R.Y.L., *1044;* Dracula's Widow, *837;* Forced March, *519;* Hostages, *544;* Iceman, *1057;* Malice, *994;* Rollover, *1011;* Rosary Murders, The, *1011;* Shadows and Fog, *654;* Target, *125;* Witness, *1032;* Yuri Nosenko, KGB, *709*

ndergaard, Gale: Anna and the King of Siam, *449;* :hony Adverse, *450;* East Side, West Side, *506;* Life of ile Zola, The, *574;* Mark of Zorro, The (1940), *82;* My orite Blonde, *340;* Night to Remember, A (1943), *345;* :urn of a Man Called Horse, The, *1142;* Road to Rio, *369;* rage Intruder, The, *883;* Sherlock Holmes and the Spider man, *1015;* Time of Their Lives, The, *396*

ns of the Pioneers: Apache Rose, *1094;* Bells of Rosarita, *97;* Call of the Canyon, *1103;* Cowboy and the Senorita, *06;* Hands Across the Border, *1118;* Helldorado (1946), *20;* Home in Oklahoma, *1121;* Idaho, *1122;* King of the wboys, *1125;* Silver Spurs, *1150;* Song of Nevada, *1151;* nset on the Desert, *1154*

o, Jack: Flower Drum Song, *917;* Green Berets, The, *57;* oroughly Modern Millie, *945*

o, Park Jong: Search and Destroy (1981), *113*

oHan, Master Bong: Kentucky Fried Movie, *312*

per, Mark: Blood Rage, *815;* Understudy, The: Graveyard ift II, *899*

pkiw, Michael: After the Fall of New York, *1034;* stfighter, *15*

rbas, Elga: American Soldier, The, *712*

rcey, Juliet: Taken Away, *676*

rdi, Alberto: I Vitelloni, *746;* White Sheik, The, *803*

rel, Jean: Adorable Julia, *710;* Circle of Love, *482*

rel, Louise: Get Christie Love!, *55;* Mazes and Monsters, *4;* Where the Boys Are '84, *409*

rel, Ted: Tempest, The (1983), *678*

renson, Linda: Joshua Then and Now, *311;* Kavik the olf Dog, *179;* Stone Cold Dead, *1020*

renson, Rickie: Tarzan and the Trappers, *125*

rley, Janes: Last House on Dead End Street, *860*

rvino, Mira: Amongst Friends, *447*

rvino, Paul: Age Isn't Everything, *223;* Backstreet Justice, Bloodbrothers, *464;* Brinks Job, The, *246;* Chiefs, *961;* iller, *823;* Cruising, *964;* Day of the Dolphin, The, *1044;* :k Tracy (1990), *38;* Fine Mess, A, *277;* Gambler, The 974), *524;* Goodfellas, *531;* I Will, I Will...for Now, *304;* elanie, *591;* My Mother's Secret Life, *602;* Off the Wall, *348;* estion of Honor, A, *632;* Rocketeer, The, *108;* Stuff, The, *71;* That Championship Season, *680;* Touch of Class, A, *38;* Urge to Kill, *692;* Vasectomy, *404*

thern, Ann: Best Man, The, *459;* Brother Orchid, *20;* Crazy ama, *30;* Judge Steps Out, The, *560;* Kid Millions, *926;* Lady Good, *927;* Lady in a Cage, *989;* Letter to Three Wives, A, *73;* Manitou, The, *863;* Nancy Goes to Rio, *932;* Panama ttie, *935;* Thousands Cheer, *945;* Whales of August, The, *38;* Words and Music, *948*

thern, Hugh: Captain America (1944), *22*

to, Hugo: Man Facing Southeast, *765;* Times to Come, *35*

to, Talisa: Hostage (1992), *64*

uchon, Alain: One Deadly Summer, *773*

ul, David: Appointment with Death, *953;* Cry in the Wind, *92;* Dogpound Shuffle, *266;* FBI Murders, The, *47;* Grave crets: The Legacy of Hilltop Drive, *980;* Hanoi Hilton, The, *36;* In the Cold of the Night, *986;* Johnny Got His Gun, *559;* y to Rebecca, The, *70;* Little Ladies of the Night, *576;* agnum Force, *80;* Manions of America, The, *588;* Rage 980), *633;* Salem's Lot, *882;* Stick-up, The, *386;* Through aked Eyes, *129;* World War III, *141*

oule, Olan: Captain Midnight—Vols. 1–2, *155*

outendijk, Renee: Eve of Destruction, *1050;* Forced arch, *519;* Fourth Man, The, *738;* Grave Secrets, *847;* eeper of the City, *562;* Murderers Among Us: The Simon iesenthal Story, *601;* Spetters, *788*

outhwood, Charles: Guns for Dollars, *1117*

oyka, Doris Anne: Dead Silence, *262*

paak, Catherine: Cat O'Nine Tails, *960;* Empty Canvas, ne, *509;* Hotel, *544;* Take a Hard Ride, *1154*

pace, Arthur: Panther Girl of the Congo, *97;* Terror at the ed Wolf Inn, *893*

Spacek, Sissy: Badlands, *454;* Carrie (1976), *821;* Coal Miner's Daughter, *912;* Crimes of the Heart, *260;* Ginger in the Morning, *527;* Girls of Huntington House, *528;* Hard Promises, *536;* Heart Beat, *537;* JFK, *558;* Katherine, *562;* Long Walk Home, The, *579;* Marie, *588;* Missing, *596;* 'Night, Mother, *606;* Prime Cut, *100;* Private Matter, A, *629;* Raggedy Man, *1008;* River, The (1984), *641;* Violets Are Blue, *694;* Welcome to L.A., *698*

Spacey, Kevin: Consenting Adults (1992), *963;* Dad, *493;* Glengarry Glen Ross, *528;* Henry & June, *540;* Iron Will, *67;* Long Day's Journey into Night (1987), *578;* Murder of Mary Phagan, The, *600;* Ref, The, *365;* See No Evil, Hear No Evil, *375*

Spade, David: Coneheads, *258;* PCU, *355*

Spader, James: Bad Influence, *953;* Cocaine: One Man's Seduction, *485;* Discovery Program, *501;* Dream Lover (1994), *972;* Jack's Back, *987;* Less Than Zero, *573;* Music of Chance, The, *601;* New Kids, The, *868;* Pretty in Pink, *626;* Sex, Lies and Videotape, *653;* True Colors, *688;* Tuff Turf, *689;* Wall Street, *695;* White Palace, *700*

Spain, Fay: Al Capone, *3;* Dragstrip Girl, *42;* Flight to Fury, *51;* God's Little Acre, *529;* Hercules and the Captive Women, *1056*

Spalding, B. J.: Bail Jumper, *455*

Spall, Timothy: Dutch Girls, *506;* Gothic, *847;* Life Is Sweet, *574;* Sheltering Sky, The, *655*

Spano, Joe: Cast the First Stone, *476;* Dunera Boys, The, *506;* Fever, *47;* Great Los Angeles Earthquake, The, *532;* Northern Lights, *609;* Terminal Choice, *893*

Spano, Vincent: Afterburn, *442;* Alive, *444;* Alphabet City, *445;* And God Created Woman (1987), *447;* Baby, It's You, *453;* Black Stallion Returns, The, *151;* Blood Ties (1987), *464;* City of Hope, *483;* Creator, *490;* Double McGuffin, The, *163;* Gentleman Bandit, The, *525;* Good Morning, Babylon, *530;* Indian Summer, *306;* Maria's Lovers, *588;* Oscar (1991), *351;* Rumble Fish, *645*

Sparks, Ned: Blessed Event, *241;* Bride Walks Out, The, *245;* Going Hollywood, *920;* Magic Town, *585;* One in a Million, *350;* Sweet Adeline, *943*

Sparrowhawk, Leo: Out on Bail, *96*

Sparv, Camilla: Dead Heat on a Merry-Go-Round, *967;* Downhill Racer, *504;* Greek Tycoon, The, *533;* Survival Zone, *1081*

Speakman, Jeff: Perfect Weapon, *98;* Street Knight, *121*

Speciale, Linda: Screwballs, *374*

Speir, Dona: Do or Die, *40;* Fit to Kill, *49;* Guns, *58;* Hard Ticket to Hawaii, *59;* Savage Beach, *111*

Spell, George: Dream for Christmas, A, *163;* Man and Boy, *1131*

Spelvin, Georgina: I Spit on Your Corpse, *855*

Spence, Bruce: ...Almost, *225;* Mad Max Beyond Thunderdome, *1064;* Rikki and Pete, *368;* Road Warrior, The, *1074;* Where the Green Ants Dream, *803*

Spencer, Bud: Ace High, *1092;* Aladdin (1987), *144;* Beyond the Law, *1097;* Boot Hill, *1100;* Massacre at Fort Holman (Reason to Live...A Reason to Die, A), *1133;* Miami Supercops, *331;* Saddle Tramps, *1147;* They Call Me Trinity, *1156;* Trinity Is Still My Name, *1159*

Spencer, Danielle: Crossing, The, *491*

Spencer, Jeremy: Prince and the Showgirl, The, *361*

Spencer, John: Presumed Innocent, *1007*

Spencer, Marv: Killing Edge, The, *1061*

Sperber, Wendie Jo: First Time, The, *277;* I Wanna Hold Your Hand, *304;* Moving Violations, *338;* Stewardess School, *386*

Sperry, Corwyn: Sudden Thunder, *122*

Spielberg, Steven: Here's Looking at You, Warner Brothers, *426*

Spiesser, Jacques: Black and White in Color, *718;* La Truite (The Trout), *755*

Spillane, Mickey: Girl Hunters, The, *979*

Spilsbury, Klinton: Legend of the Lone Ranger, The, *1128*

Spindler, Will: Last Five Days, The, *755*

Spinell, Joe: Big Score, The, *12;* Hollywood Harry, *299;* Last Horror Film, The, *860;* Maniac (1980), *862;* Ninth Configuration, The, *608;* Operation War Zone, *95;* Star Crash, *1078;* Strike Force, *121*

Spiner, Brent: Star Trek: The Next Generation (TV Series), *1079*

Spinetti, Victor: Hard Day's Night, A, *921;* Help!, *922*

Spitz, Mark: Challenge of a Lifetime, *478*

Spitzer, Peter M.: Meateater, The, *864*

Spolt, William: Rattler Kid, *1141*

Spottiswood, Greg: Looking for Miracles, *579*

Spradlin, G. D.: And I Alone Survived, *447;* Formula, The, *978;* Lords of Discipline, The, *579;* North Dallas Forty, *609;* One on One, *613;* Tank, *124;* War of the Roses, The, *406;* Wrong Is Right, *414*

Spradling, Charlie: Puppet Master II, *878;* To Sleep With a Vampire, *896*

Spriggs, Elizabeth: Those Glory Glory Days, *682*

Springer, Gary: Bernice Bobs Her Hair, *234*

Springfield, Rick: Dead Reckoning (1990), *967;* Hard to Hold, *922;* Nick Knight, *868;* Silent Motive, *1016*

Springsteen, Bruce: No Nukes, *432*

Springsteen, Pamela: Sleepaway Camp II: Unhappy Campers, *887;* Sleepaway Camp III, *887*

Sprinkle, Annie: My Father Is Coming, *339*

Sprogoe, Ove: Famous Five Get into Trouble, The, *166*

Squire, Ronald: Encore, *509*

Srmlai, Krung: H-Bomb, *58*

St. John, Howard: Born Yesterday (1950), *244*

St. John, Jill: Roman Spring of Mrs. Stone, The, *643*

St. John, Michelle: Geronimo, *1115*

Stack, Joanna Leigh: Paradise Motel, *353*

Stack, Robert: Airplane!, *224;* Big Trouble, *239;* Bullfighter and the Lady, The, *21;* Caddyshack II, *249;* Conquest of Cochise, *1106;* Corrupt Ones, The, *29;* Dangerous Curves, *262;* Date with Judy, A, *913;* George Washington, *526;* High and the Mighty, The, *541;* Is Paris Burning?, *554;* Joe Versus the Volcano, *310;* Last Voyage, The, *76;* Mr. Music, *931;* Mortal Storm, The, *600;* Murder on Flight 502, *87;* Plain Clothes, *358;* To Be or Not to Be (1942), *397;* Uncommon Valor, *134;* Untouchables, The: Scarface Mob (TV), *134;* Written on the Wind, *707*

Stacy, James: Double Exposure (1982), *971;* Matters of the Heart, *590;* Posse (1975), *1139;* Swingin' Summer, A, *390*

Stadlen, Lewis J.: Between the Lines, *237;* Savages (1973), *373;* Windy City, *703*

Stafford, Frederick: Battle of El Alamein, The, *10;* Topaz, *1026*

Stafford, Jo: Ship Ahoy, *939*

Stafford, Jon: Crossing the Line (1990), *492*

Stahl, Lisa: Shallow Grave, *114*

Stahl, Nick: Man without a Face, The, *587*

Staiola, Enzo: Bicycle Thief, The, *717*

Staley, James: Robot Wars, *1075*

Stallone, Frank: Barfly, *455;* Fear (1988), *976;* Heart of Midnight, *982;* Lethal Games, *76;* Order of the Eagle, *96;* Outlaw Force, *96;* Pink Chiquitas, The, *357;* Ten Little Indians (1989), *1023*

Stallone, Jacqueline: Beach Babes from Beyond, *1038*

Stallone, Sylvester: Cannonball, *22;* Cliffhanger, *26;* Cobra (1986), *27;* Death Race 2000, *1045;* Demolition Man, *1046;* F.I.S.T., *512;* First Blood, *49;* Lock Up, *78;* Lords of Flatbush, The, *579;* Nighthawks, *91;* Oscar (1991), *351;* Over the Top, *617;* Paradise Alley, *618;* Rambo: First Blood II, *103;* Rambo III, *103;* Rebel (1973), *104;* Rhinestone, *367;* Rocky, *642;* Rocky II, *642;* Rocky III, *642;* Rocky IV, *642;* Rocky V, *642;* Stop! Or My Mom Will Shoot, *386;* Tango and Cash, *124;* Victory, *135*

Stallybrass, Anne: Six Wives of Henry VIII, The (TV Series), *659*

Stalmaster, Hal: Johnny Tremain, *179*

Stamos, John: Alice Through the Looking Glass (1985), *1* Born to Ride, *17;* Disappearance of Christina, The, *971;* Nev Too Young to Die, *90*

Stamp, Terence: Alien Nation, *1035;* Billy Budd, *461;* Blu (1968), *1099;* Collector, The, *963;* Divine Nymph, The, *731* Far from the Madding Crowd, *514;* Genuine Risk, *979;* Hit, The, *63;* Legal Eagles, *991;* Link, *861;* Meetings with Remarkable Men, *591;* Real McCoy, The, *1009;* Sicilian, Th *115;* Superman II, *1081;* Teorema, *793;* Thief of Baghdad (1978), *127;* Wall Street, *695*

Stanczak, Wadeck: Rendez-Vous, *780;* Scene of the Crim (1987), *784*

Stander, Lionel: Beyond the Law, *1097;* Black Bird, The, *240;* Boot Hill, *1100;* Cul-de-Sac, *492;* Dandy in Aspic, A, *965;* Loved One, The, *323;* Mad Wednesday, *325;* Matilda, *330;* Mr. Deeds Goes to Town, *333;* New York, New York, *933;* Once Upon a Time in the West, *1137;* Pulp, *363;* St. Benny the Dip, *646;* Scoundrel, The, *374;* Sensual Man, The *375;* Sin of Harold Diddlebock (a.k.a. Mad Wednesday), *37* Specter of the Rose, The, *1019;* Unfaithfully Yours (1948), *403*

Standing, Guy: Bulldog Drummond Escapes, *20;* Lives of a Bengal Lancer, The, *78*

Standing, John: Legacy, The, *860;* Nightflyers, *1068;* Privates on Parade, *362;* Walk, Don't Run, *405;* X, Y and Zee *707*

Stanely, Ralph: High Lonesome—The Story of Bluegrass Music, *426*

Stanford, Nathania: Return to the Lost World, *1074*

Stang, Arnold: Hercules Goes Bananas, *296;* Man with the Golden Arm, The, *587;* TV Classics: Milton Berle, *401*

Stanley, Alvah: Romeo and Juliet (1983), *643*

Stanley, Edwin: Mysterious Dr. Satan, *88*

Stanley, Florence: Prisoner of Second Avenue, The, *361*

Stanley, Kim: Cat on a Hot Tin Roof (1985), *477;* Danger, *965;* Frances, *521;* Goddess, The, *528;* Right Stuff, The, *64* Seance on a Wet Afternoon, *1013*

Stanley, Louise: Riders of the Rockies, *1144;* Sing, Cowboy, Sing, *1150*

Stanley, Pat: Ladies' Man, The, *314*

Stanley, Paul: I Heard the Owl Call My Name, *547;* Kiss Meets the Phantom of the Park, *859*

Stanley, Rebecca: Eyes of Fire, *840*

Stansbury, Hope: Rats Are Coming!, The Werewolves Are Here!, The, *878*

Stansfield, Claire: Swordsman, The, *124*

Stanton, Harry Dean: Against the Wall, *442;* Alien, *1034;* Black Marble, The, *463;* Christine, *824;* Cockfighter, *27;* Dea Watch, *1045;* Dillinger (1973), *39;* Farewell My Lovely, *975;* Flatbed Annie and Sweetie Pie: Lady Truckers, *50;* Fool for Love, *518;* Fourth War, The, *52;* Hostages, *544;* Hotel Room, *983;* Last Temptation of Christ, The, *570;* Man Trouble, *327;* Missouri Breaks, The, *1134;* Mr. North, *334;* 92 in the Shade *345;* Oldest Living Graduate, The, *611;* One from the Heart, *934;* One Magic Christmas, *613;* Paris, Texas, *618;* Pat Garrett and Billy the Kid, *1138;* Payoff, *98;* Pretty in Pink, *62* Rafferty and the Gold Dust Twins, *364;* Rancho Deluxe, *114* Rebel Rousers, *104;* Red Dawn, *104;* Repo Man, *366;* Ride i the Whirlwind, *1143;* Rip Van Winkle, *199;* Rose, The, *937;* Slam Dance, *1017;* Stars and Bars, *385;* Straight Time, *668;* Twin Peaks: Fire Walk with Me, *1028;* Twister, *401;* Uforia, *402;* Where the Lilies Bloom, *216;* Wild at Heart, *702;* Wise Blood, *704;* Young Doctors in Love, *415;* Zandy's Bride, *11*

Stanton, John: Dusty, *164;* Great Expectations—The Untold Story, *532;* Kitty and the Bagman, *73;* Naked Country, The, *603;* Run, Rebecca, Run, *201;* Tai-Pan, *124*

Stanton, Maria: Voodoo Dolls, *901*

Stanton, Robert: Abbott and Costello in Hollywood, *221;* Dennis the Menace, *161*

Stanwyck, Barbara: Annie Oakley (1935), *1093;* Baby Face *453;* Ball of Fire, *231;* Big Valley, The (TV Series), *1098;* Bitte Tea of General Yen, The, *462;* Blowing Wild, *16;* Bride Walks Out, The, *245;* Cattle Queen of Montana, *1104;* Christmas in

Connecticut (1945), *255;* Clash by Night, *483;* Crime of Passion, *490;* Double Indemnity, *972;* East Side, West Side, *506;* Escape to Burma, *510;* Executive Suite, *512;* Golden Boy, *529;* Hollywood Canteen, *923;* Illicit, *549;* Ladies of Leisure, *567;* Ladies They Talk About, *567;* Lady Eve, The, *315;* Lady of Burlesque, *74;* Mad Miss Manton, The, *325;* Maverick Queen, The, *1133;* Meet John Doe, *591;* Night Nurse, *606;* Night Walker, The, *1001;* Purchase Price, The, *630;* Roustabout, *938;* Sorry, Wrong Number (1948), *1019;* Stella Dallas, *667;* Strange Love of Martha Ivers, The, *689;* Thornbirds, The, *682;* To Please a Lady, *130;* Two Mrs. Carrolls, The, *1028;* Union Pacific, *1160;* Violent Men, The, *1161;* Walk on the Wild Side, *695*

Stapel, Huub: Amsterdamned, *809;* Attic: The Hiding of Anne Frank, *452;* Lift, The, *860*

Stapleton, Jean: All in the Family Twentieth Anniversary Special, *224;* Cinderella (1985), *159;* Eleanor: First Lady of the World, *508;* Grown-ups, *534;* Jack and the Beanstalk, *178;* Mother Goose Rock N' Roll Rhyme, *189;* Up the Down Staircase, *403*

Stapleton, Maureen: Cocoon, *1042;* Cocoon: The Return, *1042;* Electric Grandmother, The, *1048;* Fan, The, *975;* Gathering, The, *525;* Gathering, Part II, The, *525;* Heartburn, *295;* Johnny Dangerously, *311;* Little Gloria...Happy at Last, *576;* Lonelyhearts, *578;* Lost and Found, *321;* Made in Heaven (1987), *1064;* Money Pit, The, *335;* Nuts, *1002;* On the Right Track, *192;* Passed Away, *355;* Plaza Suite, *358;* Queen of the Stardust Ballroom, *632;* Reds, *637;* Runner Stumbles, The, *645;* Sweet Lorraine, *674*

Stark, Jonathan: House II: The Second Story, *852;* Project X, *1072*

Stark, Koo: Emily, *509*

Starke, Anthony: Return of the Killer Tomatoes, *366*

Starling, Pat: Sunset Carson Rides Again, *1153*

Starr, Beau: Check Is in the Mail, The, *254;* Glory Years, *287;* Halloween V: The Revenge of Michael Myers, *848*

Starr, Blaze: Blaze Starr: The Original, *241*

Starr, Emerald: Men in Love, *592*

Starr, Mike: Mad Dog and Glory, *584;* Mardi Gras for the Devil, *863*

Starr, Ringo: Alice in Wonderland (1985), *145;* Caveman, *252;* Give My Regards to Broad Street, *919;* Kids Are Alright, The, *428;* Lisztomania, *928;* Magic Christian, The, *326;* Princess Daisy, *627;* Sextette, *376;* Son of Dracula (1974), *940;* That'll Be the Day, *944;* 200 Motels, *946*

Starret, Jennifer: Frightmare, *844*

Starrett, Charles: Badmen of the Hills, *1096;* Make a Million, *327;* Mask of Fu Manchu, The, *82;* Silver Streak (1934), *658*

Starrett, Jack: Brothers in Arms, *819;* Cry Blood, Apache, *1106;* Death Chase, *35;* First Blood, *49;* Mr. Horn, *1134;* Nightwish, *1068*

Staunton, Imelda: Antonia & Jane, *228;* Much Ado About Nothing, *338;* Peter's Friends, *621*

Stavin, Mary: Opponent, The, *95*

Steadman, Alison: Abigail's Party, *440;* Blame It on the Bellboy, *240;* Clockwise, *256;* Kipperbang, *566;* Life Is Sweet, *574;* Misadventures of Mr. Wilt, The, *333;* Nuts in May, *348;* Tartuffe, *677*

Steafel, Sheila: Bloodbath at the House of Death, *242*

Steckler, Ray Dennis: Las Vegas Weekend, *315*

Steed, Maggie: Intimate Contact, *553;* Summer House, The, *388*

Steel, Alan: Hercules Against the Moon Men, *1056*

Steel, Amy: April Fool's Day, *810;* Friday the 13th, Part II, *843;* Walk Like a Man, *405*

Steel, Anthony: Malta Story, The, *586;* Master of Ballantrae, The, *83;* Wooden Horse, The, *706*

Steele, Barbara: Black Sunday (1961), *814;* Caged Heat, *22;* Castle of Blood, *821;* 8½, *733;* Ghost, The (1963), *845;* Horrible Dr. Hichcock, The, *851;* La Dolce Vita, *753;* Nightmare Castle, *871;* Pit and the Pendulum, The (1961), *875;* She Beast, The, *885;* Silent Scream, *886;* Terror Creatures from the Grave, *893;* They Came from Within, *895*

Steele, Bob: Arizona Gunfighter, *1094;* Atomic Submarine, The, *1037;* Bandits of Dark Canyon, *1096;* Big Sleep, The (1946), *955;* Border Phantom, *1100;* Carson City Kid, *1103;* Comancheros, The, *1105;* Decision at Sundown, *1108;* Gangs of Sonora, *1115;* Island in the Sky, *554;* Kid Ranger, *1124;* Lightnin' Crandall, *1128;* Lone Star Raiders, *1129;* Mystery Squadron, *88;* Northwest Trail, *1136;* Pork Chop Hill, *624;* Powdersmoke Range, *1139;* Revenge of the Zombies, *881;* Riders for Justice, *1143;* Riders of the Rio Grande, *1144;* Rio Bravo, *1145;* Smokey Trails, *1151;* Trail Blazers, *1158;* Trailin' North, *1158;* Under Texas Skies, *1160;* Wildfire (1945), *1164*

Steele, Karen: Decision at Sundown, *1108;* Ride Lonesome, *1143;* Rise and Fall of Legs Diamond, The, *107*

Steele, Pippa: Vampire Lovers, The, *900*

Steele, Tom: Adventures of Frank and Jesse James, *1092;* Crimson Ghost, The, *30;* G-Men Never Forget, *54;* King of the Rocketmen, *72*

Steele, Tommy: Finian's Rainbow, *916;* Half a Sixpence, *921;* Happiest Millionaire, The, *173*

Steeh, Irving: Fall of the House of Usher, The (1949), *840*

Steen, Jessica: Sing, *939*

Steenburgen, Mary: Attic: The Hiding of Anne Frank, *452;* Back to the Future III, *1037;* Butcher's Wife, The, *248;* Clifford, *256;* Cross Creek, *491;* Dead of Winter, *967;* End of the Line, *509;* Goin' South, *1116;* Little Red Riding Hood, *183;* Melvin and Howard, *331;* Midsummer Night's Sex Comedy, A, *332;* Miss Firecracker, *333;* One Magic Christmas, *613;* Parenthood, *354;* Philadelphia, *621;* Ragtime, *633;* Romantic Comedy, *370;* Time After Time, *1084;* Whales of August, The, *698;* What's Eating Gilbert Grape?, *408*

Stefani, Michael: Trancers, *1085*

Steffen, Anthony: Gentleman Killer, *1115*

Steffen, Geary: Wintertime, *947*

Stegers, Bernice: Frozen Terror, *844;* Girl, The, *527;* Xtro, *904*

Steiger, Rod: Al Capone, *3;* American Gothic, *808;* Amityville Horror, The, *809;* Back from Eternity, *453;* Ballad of the Sad Cafe, The, *455;* Breakthrough, *19;* Catch the Heat, *24;* Chosen, The, *481;* Court-martial of Billy Mitchell, The, *489;* Dr. Zhivago, *503;* F.I.S.T., *512;* Fistful of Dynamite, A, *1113;* Glory Boys, The, *56;* Guilty as Charged, *291;* Harder They Fall, The, *536;* Hennessy, *982;* Illustrated Man, The, *1057;* In the Heat of the Night, *986;* January Man, The, *987;* Jesus of Nazareth, *557;* Jubal, *1124;* Kindred, The, *859;* Last Contract, The, *75;* Lion of the Desert, *77;* Longest Day, The, *78;* Love and Bullets, *79;* Loved One, The, *323;* Lucky Luciano, *79;* Marty (Television), *589;* Men of Respect, *592;* Naked Face, The, *1000;* Neighbor, The, *1000;* No Way to Treat a Lady, *1002;* Oklahoma!, *933;* On the Waterfront, *612;* Pawnbroker, The, *620;* Run of the Arrow, *1146;* Seven Thieves, *653;* Sword of Gideon, *123;* Tales of Tomorrow (Vols. I - III), *1082;* That Summer of White Roses, *680;* Waterloo, *697*

Stein, Ken: Killer Instinct, *71*

Stein, Margaret Sophie: Enemies—A Love Story, *510;* Sarah, Plain and Tall, *648*

Stein, Saul: Beer, *233*

Steinberg, David: Best of the Big Laff Off, The, *236;* Comedy Tonight, *257;* End, The, *271;* Something Short of Paradise, *383;* Tommy Chong Roast, The, *397;* Your Favorite Laughs from an Evening at the Improv, *416*

Steiner, John: Ark of the Sun God...Temple of Hell, The, *6;* Beyond the Door 2, *813;* Blood and Guns, *15;* Cut and Run, *493;* Devil within Her, The, *833;* Massacre in Rome, *590;* Operation 'Nam, *95;* Sinbad of the Seven Seas, *116;* Unsane, *899;* Yor: The Hunter from the Future, *1091*

Steinmiller, Robert J.: Jack the Bear, *556;* Ref, The, *365*

Steis, William: Demon of Paradise, *832;* Eye of the Eagle, *46*

Stelfox, Shirley: Personal Services, *357*

Stelling, Frans: Rembrandt—1669, *780*

Sten, Anna: Girl with the Hatbox, The, *741;* So Ends Our Night, *661;* Soldier of Fortune, *118*

Stenborg, Helen: Flash of Green, A, *977*
Stensgaard, Yutte: Lust for a Vampire, *861*
Stepanek, Karel: Sink the Bismarck, *116*
Stephen, Daniel: Warbus, *137*
Stephens, Harvey: Evelyn Prentice, *511;* Forlorn River, *1114;* Oklahoma Kid, The, *1136*
Stephens, James: Getaway, The (1994), *55;* Gone to Texas, *1116;* Pancho Barnes, *617*
Stephens, Robert: American Roulette, *4;* Duellists, The, *42;* Henry V (1989), *540;* High Season, *297;* Morgan, *337;* Prime of Miss Jean Brodie, The, *361;* Private Life of Sherlock Holmes, The, *1008;* Searching for Bobby Fischer, *202;* Shout, The (1979), *886;* Spirit of the Dead, *889;* Taste of Honey, A, *677;* Travels with My Aunt, *399;* Wonderland, *706*
Stephenson, Henry: Animal Kingdom, The, *448;* Bill of Divorcement, A, *461;* Captain Blood, *22;* Challenge to Lassie, *157;* Charge of the Light Brigade, The (1936), *24;* Conquest, *487;* Down Argentine Way, *914;* Julia Misbehaves, *311;* Mutiny on the Bounty (1935), *88;* Private Lives of Elizabeth and Essex, The, *629;* Red-Headed Woman, *636;* Song of Love, *662;* Spring Parade, *941;* Tarzan Finds a Son, *125;* Tomorrow at Seven, *685*
Stephenson, James: Beau Geste, *10;* Letter, The, *991*
Stephenson, Mark Kinsey: Unnamable, The, *899;* Unnamable II, The, *899*
Stephenson, Michael: Troll II, *898*
Stephenson, Pamela: Bloodbath at the House of Death, *242;* Les Patterson Saves the World, *317;* Scandalous (1983), *373;* Superman III, *1081*
Sterling, Ford: Caution: Funny Men at Work, *420;* Keystone Comedies, Vol. 4, *312;* Keystone Comedies, Vol. 5, *313*
Sterling, Jan: First Monday in October, *517;* Harder They Fall, The, *536;* High and the Mighty, The, *541;* High School Confidential!, *541;* 1984 (1955), *1068;* Pony Express, *1139;* Split Second (1953), *664;* Union Station, *1029*
Sterling, Philip: Death of the Incredible Hulk, The, *1045*
Sterling, Robert: Adventures of Topper, The, *223;* Global Affair, A, *287;* Johnny Eager, *559;* Return to Peyton Place, *639;* Somewhere I'll Find You, *662;* Sundowners, The (1950), *1153;* Two-Faced Woman, *401;* Voyage to the Bottom of the Sea, *1087*
Sterling, Tisha: Coogan's Bluff, *29;* Killer Inside Me, The, *988;* Powderkeg, *1139;* Snatched, *117*
Stern, Daniel: Born in East L.A., *244;* Boss' Wife, The, *244;* Breaking Away, *245;* C.H.U.D., *820;* City Slickers, *255;* City Slickers II, *256;* Coupe De Ville, *260;* Court-Martial of Jackie Robinson, The, *489;* D.O.A. (1988), *965;* Diner, *265;* Frankenweenie, *280;* Friends, Lovers & Lunatics, *281;* Get Crazy, *284;* Hannah and Her Sisters, *293;* Home Alone, *299;* Home Alone 2: Lost in New York, *175;* Key Exchange, *563;* Leviathan, *860;* Little Monsters, *1063;* Milagro Beanfield War, The, *594;* Rookie of the Year, *200;* Weekend War, *697*
Stern, Erik: Love Butcher, *861*
Stern, Isaac: From Mao to Mozart, *424*
Stern, Miroslava: Criminal Life of Archibaldo de la Cruz, The, *727*
Stern, Tom: Hell's Angels '69, *60*
Stern, Wes: Three in the Cellar, *395*
Sternberg, Josef von: Epic That Never Was, The, *423*
Sternhagen, Frances: Bright Lights, Big City, *470;* Communion, *1042;* Independence Day, *551;* Man That Corrupted Hadleyburg, The, *327;* Misery, *865;* Outland, *1069;* Prototype, *1072;* Raising Cain, *878;* Romantic Comedy, *370;* See You in the Morning, *651;* Sibling Rivalry, *378;* Starting Over, *385;* Stephen King's Golden Years (TV Series), *1080*
Stevens, Andrew: Bastard, The, *456;* Body Chemistry 3: Point of Seduction, *957;* Boys in Company C, The, *18;* Counterforce, *30;* Deadly Rivals, *35;* Death Hunt, *35;* Double Threat, *504;* Down the Drain, *41;* Eyewitness to Murder, *46;* Forbidden Love, *519;* Fury, The, *845;* Massacre at Central High, *864;* Miracle on Ice, *595;* Munchie, *867;* Night Eyes, *1000;* Night Eyes 2, *1000;* Night Eyes 3, *1000;* Rebels, The, *636;* Red-Blooded American Girl, *879;* Scared Stiff, *883;* Seduction, The, *884;* Ten to Midnight, *126;* Terror Within, The, *894;* Terror Within 2, The, *894;* Tusks, *133*
Stevens, Brinke: Grandma's House, *980;* Slave Girls from Beyond Infinity, *381;* Spirits, *889*
Stevens, Casey: Prom Night, *876*
Stevens, Charles: Bold Caballero, The, *1099;* Call of the Coyote, *1103;* Vanishing American, The, *1161*
Stevens, Connie: Back to the Beach, *907;* Littlest Angel, The, *184;* Love's Savage Fury, *582;* Palm Springs Weekend, *353;* Parrish, *618;* Playmates, *358;* Scorchy, *112;* Side Show, *886;* Tapeheads, *391*
Stevens, Craig: Blues Busters, *242;* Deadly Mantis, The, *1045;* Dive Bomber, *502;* Doughgirls, The, *268;* Drums in the Deep South, *1110;* French Line, The, *918;* Humoresque, *546;* Man I Love, The, *586;* Peter Gunn (TV Series), *98;* Phone Call from a Stranger, *622;* S.O.B., *372*
Stevens, Fisher: Boss' Wife, The, *244;* Marrying Man, The, *329;* My Science Project, *1067;* Mystery Date, *341;* Short Circuit, *1076;* Short Circuit 2, *1076;* Super Mario Brothers, The, *208;* When the Party's Over, *699*
Stevens, Inger: Dream of Kings, A, *504;* Five Card Stud, *1113;* Guide for the Married Man, A, *291;* Hang 'em High, *1118;* Madigan, *80*
Stevens, K. T.: Missile to the Moon, *1066;* Port of New York, *624*
Stevens, Mark: Cry Vengeance, *492;* Dark Corner, The, *495;* Snake Pit, The, *661;* Street with No Name, *1021;* Torpedo Alley, *131*
Stevens, Morgan: Survival Zone, *1081*
Stevens, Onslow: Angel on My Shoulder (1946), *448;* Creeper, The, *826;* Hills of Utah, The, *1120;* House of Dracula, *852;* Idaho, *1122;* Lonelyhearts, *578;* Sunset Serenade, *1154;* Three Musketeers, The (1935), *128*
Stevens, Paul: Get Christie Love!, *55;* Mask, The (1961), *863*
Stevens, Rise: Chocolate Soldier, The, *911;* Going My Way, *529*
Stevens, Shadoe: Traxx, *132*
Stevens, Stella: Adventures Beyond Belief, *222;* Arnold, *810;* Ballad of Cable Hogue, The, *1096;* Chained Heat, *24;* Cleopatra Jones and the Casino of Gold, *26;* Courtship of Eddie's Father, The, *260;* Cruise into Terror, *964;* Exiled in America, *45;* Express to Terror, *974;* Girls! Girls! Girls!, *919;* History of White People in America, The (Volume II), *298;* Jake Spanner Private Eye, *68;* Las Vegas Lady, *74;* Last Call, *568;* Li'l Abner (1959), *928;* Longshot, The (1985), *320;* Make Me an Offer, *586;* Manitou, The, *863;* Monster in the Closet, *866;* Nutty Professor, The, *348;* Poseidon Adventure, The, *99;* Slaughter, *117;* Terror Within 2, The, *894;* Town Called Hell, A, *131;* Wacko, *405*
Stevenson, Cynthia: Player, The, *358;* Watch It, *696*
Stevenson, Joan: Runestone, *882*
Stevenson, Juliet: Drowning by Numbers, *505;* Truly, Madly, Deeply, *689*
Stevenson, McLean: Big City Comedy, *238;* M*A*S*H* (TV Series), *325;* Win, Place or Steal, *412*
Stevenson, Parker: Are You Lonesome Tonight, *953;* Lifeguard, *574;* Official Denial, *1069;* Our Time, *616;* Separate Peace, A, *652;* Shades of Love: The Rose Cafe, *654;* Stitches, *386;* Stroker Ace, *387*
Stevenson, Venetia: Horror Hotel, *851;* Studs Lonigan, *671*
Stewardson, Deon: Warriors From Hell, *137*
Stewart, Alexandra: Fire Within, The, *736;* Full Hearts and Empty Pockets, *739;* In Praise of Older Women, *550;* Under the Cherry Moon, *691*
Stewart, Brian Paul: Homeboys II: Crack City, *63*
Stewart, Catherine Mary: Cafe Romeo, *249;* Dudes, *505;* Last Starfighter, The, *1062;* Mischief, *333;* Night of the Comet, *1068;* Nightflyers, *1068;* Psychic, *1008;* Riding the Edge, *106;* Scenes from the Goldmine, *649;* Sea Wolf, The (1993), *113;* Urge to Kill, *692;* Weekend at Bernie's, *407;* World Gone Wild, *1090*
Stewart, Charlotte: Eraserhead, *838*

Stewart, Elaine: Brigadoon, *909;* Rise and Fall of Legs Diamond, The, *107*

Stewart, Eleanor: Arizona Days, *1094;* Fighting Devil Dogs, The, *48;* Mystery Man, *1135;* Range Defenders, *1141*

Stewart, Evelyn: Django Shoots First, *1109;* Machine Gun Killers, *1130*

Stewart, Frank: Galactic Gigolo, *282;* Psychos in Love, *877*

Stewart, James: After the Thin Man, *951;* American Film Institute Life Achievement Awards, The, *418;* Anatomy of a Murder, *952;* Bandolero!, *1096;* Bell, Book and Candle, *234;* Bend of the River, *1097;* Big Sleep, The (1978), *955;* Born to Dance, *909;* Broken Arrow, *1101;* Call Northside 777, *959;* Cheyenne Autumn, *1104;* Cheyenne Social Club, The, *1104;* Dear Brigitte, *263;* Destry Rides Again, *1109;* Far Country, The, *1112;* FBI Story, The, *515;* Flight of the Phoenix, The, *51;* Glenn Miller Story, The, *919;* Gorgeous Hussy, The, *531;* Great American West, *425;* Greatest Show on Earth, The, *533;* Harvey, *294;* How the West Was Won, *1122;* It's a Wonderful Life, *555;* Made for Each Other, *325;* Magic of Lassie, The, *185;* Magic Town, *585;* Man from Laramie, The, *1131;* Man Who Knew Too Much, The (1955), *995;* Man Who Shot Liberty Valance, The, *1132;* Mr. Hobbs Takes a Vacation, *334;* Mr. Smith Goes to Washington, *597;* Mortal Storm, The, *600;* Naked Spur, The, *1135;* Navy Blue and Gold, *342;* Of Human Hearts, *610;* Philadelphia Story, The, *357;* Pot O' Gold, *625;* Rare Breed, The (1966), *1141;* Rear Window, *1009;* Right of Way, *640;* Rope, *1011;* Rose Marie (1936), *937;* Shenandoah, *1149;* Shootist, The, *1149;* Shop Around the Corner, The, *378;* Shopworn Angel, The, *656;* Spirit of St. Louis, The, *664;* Strategic Air Command, *670;* Stratton Story, The, *670;* Thunder Bay, *129;* Two Rode Together, *1160;* Vertigo, *1029;* Vivacious Lady, *405;* Wife Vs. Secretary, *701;* Winchester '73, *1165;* You Can't Take it with You (1938), *415;* Ziegfeld Girl, *949*

Stewart, Johnny: Boots Malone, *1100*

Stewart, Patrick: Death Train, *968;* Gunmen, *58;* Hedda, *539;* Lady Jane, *568;* Robin Hood: Men in Tights, *369;* Star Trek: The Next Generation (TV Series), *1079*

Stewart, Paul: Child is Waiting, A, *480;* Joe Louis Story, The, *558;* Kiss Me Deadly, *989;* Nativity, The, *604;* Nobody's Perfekt, *346;* Opening Night, *614;* Revenge of the Pink Panther, The, *367;* Walk Softly, Stranger, *1030;* Window, The, *1032*

Stewart, Peggy: Black Lash, *1099;* Conquest of Cheyenne, *1106;* Phantom Rider, *1138;* Red River Renegades, *1142;* Sheriff of Las Vegas, *1149;* Son of Zorro, *118;* Stagecoach to Denver, *1152;* Utah, *1160;* Vigilantes of Boomtown, *1161*

Stewart, Penelope: Boulevard of Broken Dreams, *467;* Vigil, *800*

Stewart, Richard: Watch Me When I Kill, *901*

Stewart, Roy: Come on Tarzan, *1105*

Stewart, Sandy: Go, Johnny, Go!, *920*

Stewart, Sophie: Murder in the Red Barn, *867*

Stewart, Tom: Young Graduates, *708*

Stickney, Dorothy: I Never Sang for My Father, *547*

Stiers, David Ogden: Accidental Tourist, The, *440;* Alamo, The: Thirteen Days to Glory, *1093;* Better Off Dead, *237;* Breaking Up Is Hard to Do, *469;* Creator, *490;* Day One, *496;* Final Notice, *977;* Harry's War, *294;* Iron Will, *67;* Kissing Place, The, *989;* Last of His Tribe, The, *570;* Oldest Living Graduate, The, *611*

Stiglitz, Hugo: City of the Walking Dead, *824;* Tintorera, *895*

Stille, Robin: American Ninja IV: The Annihilation, *4;* Slumber Party Massacre, *887*

Stiller, Ben: Elvis Stories, *271;* Reality Bites, *635*

Stiller, Jerry: Hairspray, *292;* Hot Pursuit, *301;* Little Vegas, *319;* McGuffin, The, *996;* Nadine, *341;* Ritz, The, *368;* Seize the Day, *651;* That's Adequate, *393;* Those Lips, Those Eyes, *945*

Stilwell, Diane: Mating Season, The, *330;* Perfect Match, The, *356*

Stimac, Slavko: Do You Remember Dolly Bell?, *731*

Stimely, Brett: Bloodstone, *16*

Stimson, Sara: Little Miss Marker (1980), *182*

Sting: Bride, The, *819;* Brimstone and Treacle, *819;* Bring on the Night, *419;* Dune, *1048;* Julia and Julia, *1061;* Plenty, *623;* Quadrophenia, *936;* Stormy Monday, *1020*

Stirling, Linda: Cherokee Flash, *1104;* Crimson Ghost, The, *30;* Jesse James Rides Again, *1123;* Manhunt of Mystery Island, *82;* Perils of the Darkest Jungle, *98;* Purple Monster Strikes, The, *101;* San Antonio Kid, *1147;* Santa Fe Saddlemates, *1147;* Wagon Wheels Westward, *1162;* Zorro's Black Whip, *1166*

Stock, Barbara: Verne Miller, *135*

Stock, Jennifer: Shriek of the Mutilated, *886*

Stock, Nigel: Prisoner, The (TV Series), *1071;* Russian Roulette, *110*

Stockdale, Carl: Stage to Chino, *1152*

Stocker, Walter: They Saved Hitler's Brain, *895*

Stockwell, Dean: Alsino and the Condor, *712;* Anchors Aweigh, *906;* Backtrack, *454;* Beverly Hills Cop II, *11;* Blue Iguana, *242;* Blue Velvet, *817;* Bonanza: The Return, *1100;* Boy With Green Hair, The, *468;* Buying Time, *21;* Chasers, *254;* Compulsion, *487;* Dunwich Horror, The, *838;* Gardens of Stone, *525;* Gentlemen's Agreement, *526;* Kim, *72;* Last Movie, The, *570;* Limit Up, *319;* Long Day's Journey into Night (1962), *578;* Married to the Mob, *329;* Palais Royale, *97;* Paris, Texas, *618;* Player, The, *358;* Psych-Out, *630;* Quantum Leap (TV Series), *1072;* Secret Garden, The (1949), *202;* Smokescreen, *661;* Son of the Morning Star, *1151;* Song of the Thin Man, *1018;* Stars in My Crown, *1153;* Time Guardian, The, *1084;* To Live and Die in L.A., *130;* Tracks, *687;* Tucker: A Man and His Dream, *689;* Werewolf of Washington, *902;* Win, Place or Steal, *412;* Wrong Is Right, *414*

Stockwell, Guy: It's Alive!, *857;* Santa Sangre, *882;* Tobruk, *130;* War Lord, The, *137*

Stockwell, John: Born to Ride, *17;* Christine, *824;* City Limits, *1041;* Dangerously Close, *966;* Losin' It, *321;* My Science Project, *1067;* Quarterback Princess, *631;* Radioactive Dreams, *1073;* Top Gun, *131*

Stoddard, Kent: Party Plane, *355*

Stoddard, Malcolm: Godsend, The, *846*

Stoker, Austin: Assault on Precinct 13, *7;* Sheba Baby, *115*

Stokes, Barry: Alien Prey, *808;* Spaced Out, *384*

Stokey, Susan: Power, The (1980), *876*

Stokios, Randy: Side Out, *657*

Stokowski, Leopold: One Hundred Men and a Girl, *934*

Stole, Mink: Desperate Living, *264;* Female Trouble, *276;* Hairspray, *292;* Mondo Trasho, *335;* Multiple Maniacs, *866;* Pink Flamingos, *357*

Stoler, Shirley: Below the Belt, *458;* Displaced Person, The, *501;* Frankenhooker, *842;* Honeymoon Killers, The, *983;* Seven Beauties, *785;* Sticky Fingers, *386*

Stoll, Brad: Lost in Yonkers, *580*

Stollery, David: Ten Who Dared, *210;* Westward Ho, the Wagons, *216*

Stoltz, Eric: Bodies, Rest & Motion, *465;* Code Name: Emerald, *27;* Discovery Program, *501;* Fly II, The, *842;* Foreign Affairs, *520;* Haunted Summer, *537;* Heart of Justice, *538;* Lionheart, *181;* Manifesto, *328;* Mask (1985), *590;* Memphis Belle (1990), *592;* Running Hot, *645;* Sister, Sister, *886;* Some Kind of Wonderful, *382;* Surf 2, *389;* Waterdance, The, *696*

Stolze, Lena: Last Five Days, The, *755;* Nasty Girl, The, *771;* White Rose, The (1983), *803*

Stolzenberg, Mark: Luggage of the Gods, *324*

Stone, Christopher: Annihilators, The, *5;* Blue Movies, *242;* Cujo, *827;* Dying to Remember, *973;* Howling, The, *853;* Junkman, The, *70;* Legend of the White Horse, *76*

Stone, Dorothy: Revolt of the Zombies, *881*

Stone, Fred: Alice Adams, *444;* Westerner, The, *1163*

Stone, George E.: Last Mile, The, *570;* Viva Villa!, *1162*

Stone, Harold J.: Big Mouth, The, *238;* Hardly Working, *293;* Legend of Valentino, *572;* Wrong Man, The (1956), *1033;* X (The Man with the X-Ray Eyes), *1090*
Stone, Lewis: Andy Hardy Gets Spring Fever, *227;* Andy Hardy Meets a Debutante, *227;* Andy Hardy's Double Life, *227;* Andy Hardy's Private Secretary, *227;* Any Number Can Play, *450;* Bureau of Missing Persons, *959;* China Seas, *25;* Girl from Missouri, The, *286;* Grand Hotel, *531;* Inspiration, *553;* It's a Big Country, *308;* Key to the City, *312;* Life Begins for Andy Hardy, *318;* Lost World, The (1925), *1064;* Love Finds Andy Hardy, *322;* Love Laughs at Andy Hardy, *323;* Mask of Fu Manchu, The, *82;* Mata Hari (1931), *590;* Prisoner of Zenda, The (1952), *100;* Queen Christina, *631;* Red-Headed Woman, *636;* Romance, *643;* Sin of Madelon Claudet, The, *658;* Sun Comes Up, The, *208;* Suzy, *674;* Treasure Island (1934), *213;* Wild Orchids, *702;* Woman of Affairs, A, *705*
Stone, Madeline: Tropical Snow, *132*
Stone, Madison: Evil Toons, *273*
Stone, Milburn: Branded, *1101;* California Frontier, *1103;* Colorado, *1105;* Gunsmoke (TV Series), *1118;* Sinners in Paradise, *659;* Sun Shines Bright, The, *673;* Young Mr. Lincoln, *708*
Stone, Oliver: Dave, *262*
Stone, Sam: Dead Man Out, *497*
Stone, Sharon: Above the Law, *1;* Action Jackson, *2;* Allan Quartermain and the Lost City of Gold, *4;* Basic Instinct, *456;* Beyond the Stars, *1039;* Cold Steel, *28;* Deadly Blessing, *831;* Diary of a Hitman, *970;* He Said, She Said, *294;* Intersection, *553;* King Solomon's Mines (1985), *73;* Police Academy 4: Citizens on Patrol, *359;* Scissors, *1013;* Sliver, *1018;* Total Recall, *1084;* Where Sleeping Dogs Lie, *1031;* Year of the Gun, *1033*
Stones, Tammy: Neurotic Cabaret, *343*
Stoppa, Paolo: Miracle in Milan, *767*
Stoppi, Franca: Other Hell, The, *873*
Storch, Larry: Adventures Beyond Belief, *222;* Adventures of Huckleberry Finn, The (1978), *144;* Better Late than Never, *237;* Captain Newman, M.D., *474;* Fakeout, *513;* Great Race, The, *290;* Incredible Rocky Mountain Race, The, *306;* Sex and the Single Girl, *376;* Without Warning, *1090*
Storey, June: Blue Montana Skies, *1099;* Colorado Sunset, *1105;* Dance Hall, *913;* South of the Border, *1151;* Strange Woman, The, *669*
Storke, Adam: Lifepod, *1063;* Mystic Pizza, *603*
Storm, Gale: Revenge of the Zombies, *881;* Stampede, *1152;* Texas Rangers, The, *1156;* Tom Brown's School Days (1940), *685;* Underworld Story, *1029*
Storti, Raymond: Full Contact, *53*
Stossel, Ludwig: Bluebeard (1944), *817;* Escape Me Never, *510;* House of Dracula, *852;* Pittsburgh, *622;* Pride of the Yankees, The, *627;* This Time For Keeps, *945;* Yolanda and the Thief, *708*
Stowe, Madeleine: Another Stakeout, *6;* Bad Girls (1994), *1095;* Blink, *956;* China Moon, *961;* Closet Land, *962;* Last of the Mohicans, The (1992), *1126;* Nativity, The, *604;* Revenge (1990), *106;* Short Cuts, *657;* Stakeout, *119;* Two Jakes, The, *1028;* Unlawful Entry, *1029;* Worth Winning, *414*
Strader, Scott: Jocks, *310*
Straface, Joseph R.: Virgin Queen of St. Francis High, The, *405*
Straight, Beatrice: Chiller, *823;* Nun's Story, The, *609;* Patterns, *619;* Poltergeist, *875;* Power (1986), *625;* Princess and the Pea, The, *197;* Promise, The, *629*
Strain, Julie: Fit to Kill, *49;* Unnamable II, The, *899;* Witchcraft IV, *903*
Strait, George: Pure Country, *630*
Strang, Harry: King of the Forest Rangers, *72*
Strange, Glenn: Abbott and Costello Meet Frankenstein, *221;* Arizona Days, *1094;* Black Market Rustlers, *1099;* Black Raven, The, *955;* Boothill Bandits, *1100;* California Frontier, *1103;* Cherokee Strip, *1104;* Down Texas Way, *1110;* Empty Holsters, *1111;* Fugitive Valley, *1114;* Gunsmoke (TV Series), *1118;* House of Dracula, *852;* House of Frankenstein, *852;* In Old Mexico, *1123;* Law of the Pampas, *1127;* Mad Monster, *862;* Monster Maker, The, *866;* Range Feud, *1141;* Riders of Death Valley, *1143;* Rimfire, *1144;* San Antonio Kid, *1147;* Stage to Chino, *1152;* Sunset on the Desert, *1154;* Triple Justice, *1159*
Strasberg, Lee: Godfather, Part II, The, *529;* Going in Style, *288*
Strasberg, Susan: Bloody Birthday, *817;* Brotherhood, The, *471;* Delta Force, The, *36;* Frankenstein (1973), *842;* In Praise of Older Women, *550;* Light in the Jungle, The, *575;* Manitou, The, *863;* Mazes and Monsters, *864;* Picnic, *622;* Psycho Sisters, *877;* Psych-Out, *630;* Returning, The, *1010;* Rollercoaster, *1011;* Scream of Fear, *1013;* Stage Struck (1958), *665;* Sweet Sixteen, *123;* Trip, The, *688*
Strasser, Robin: White Hot: The Mysterious Murder of Thelma Todd, *1031*
Strassman, Marcia: And You Thought Your Parents Were Weird, *227;* Another Stakeout, *6;* Fast Getaway, *274;* Honey, I Blew Up the Kid, *175;* Soup for One, *383*
Stratas, Teresa: La Traviata, *754*
Stratford, Dean: Savage Guns, *1147;* Shoot the Living...Pray for the Dead, *1149*
Strathairn, David: American Clock, The, *446;* Big Girls Don't Cry...They Get Even, *238;* City of Hope, *483;* Dangerous Woman, A, *494;* Day One, *496;* Eight Men Out, *508;* Firm, The, *977;* Judgment, *560;* League of Their Own, A, *571;* Lost in Yonkers, *580;* Matewan, *590;* Memphis Belle (1990), *592;* O Pioneers!, *610;* Passion Fish, *619;* Sneakers, *1018;* Son of the Morning Star, *1151;* Without Warning: The James Brady Story, *704*
Stratheros, Elena: Vals, The, *404*
Stratten, Dorothy: Galaxina, *1053;* They All Laughed, *393*
Stratton, Charles: Munchies, *867;* Summer Camp Nightmare, *672*
Strauss, Peter: Angel on My Shoulder (1980), *448;* Brotherhood of the Rose, *20;* Flight of Black Angel, *518;* Hail, Hero!, *535;* Jericho Mile, The, *557;* Last Tycoon, The, *571;* Masada, *590;* Proud Men, *1140;* Secret of Nimh, The, *202;* Soldier Blue, *1151;* Spacehunter: Adventures in the Forbidden Zone, *1078;* Trial of the Cantonsville Nine, The, *687;* Whale for the Killing, A, *698*
Strauss, Robert: Atomic Kid, The, *229;* Bridges at Toko-Ri, The, *19;* 4D Man, *1053;* Here Come the Girls, *922;* I, Mobster, *65;* Jumping Jacks, *311;* Li'l Abner (1959), *928;* Man with the Golden Arm, The, *587;* Stalag 17, *119*
Streep, Meryl: Cry in the Dark, A, *492;* Death Becomes Her, *1045;* Deer Hunter, The, *499;* Defending Your Life, *263;* Falling in Love, *513;* French Lieutenant's Woman, The, *522;* Heartburn, *295;* Holocaust, *542;* House of the Spirits, The, *545;* Ironweed, *554;* Julia, *560;* Kramer vs. Kramer, *567;* Manhattan, *328;* Out of Africa, *616;* Plenty, *623;* Postcards from the Edge, *360;* Seduction of Joe Tynan, The, *651;* She-Devil, *377;* Silkwood, *658;* Sophie's Choice, *663;* Still of the Night, *1020*
Streisand, Barbra: All Night Long, *224;* Color Me Barbra, *912;* For Pete's Sake, *279;* Funny Girl, *918;* Funny Lady, *918;* Hello, Dolly!, *922;* Here's Looking at You, Warner Brothers, *426;* Main Event, The, *326;* My Name Is Barbra, *932;* Nuts, *1002;* On a Clear Day, You Can See Forever, *933;* Owl and the Pussycat, The, *352;* Prince of Tides, The, *627;* Star Is Born, A (1976), *666;* Up the Sandbox, *403;* Way We Were, The, *697;* What's Up, Doc?, *408;* Yentl, *948*
Stretch, Gary: Dead Connection, *967*
Stribling, Melissa: Horror of Dracula, *851*
Strickland, Gail: Bound for Glory, *467;* Drowning Pool, The, *972;* Hyper Sapian: People from Another Star, *1057;* Lies, *574;* Man in the Moon, The, *587;* Protocol, *363;* Rape And Marriage: The Rideout Case, *635;* Starflight One, *1079;* Three of Hearts, *683;* Who'll Stop the Rain, *139*
Stricklyn, Ray: Dogpound Shuffle, *266;* Return of Dracula, *880*
Stride, John: Macbeth (1971), *584;* Shattered (1972), *655*

tritch, Elaine: Perfect Furlough, *356;* Providence, *630;* eptember, *652;* Three Violent People, *1157*
trode, Woody: Angkor: Cambodia Express, *5;* Black Stallion eturns, The, *151;* Boot Hill, *1100;* Bride of the Gorilla, *819;* ronx Executioner, The, *1040;* Deserter, The, *1109;* Final xecutioner, The, *1051;* Jungle Warriors, *69;* Kill Castro, *71;* ngdom of the Spiders, *859;* Last Voyage, The, *76;* Loaded uns, *78;* Longest Drive, The, *1130;* Man Who Shot Liberty alance, The, *1132;* Manhunt (1973), *81;* Murder on the ayou, *600;* Once Upon a Time in the West, *1137;* Pork Chop ll, *624;* Posse (1993), *1139;* Professionals, The, *101;* cream, *883;* Sergeant Rutledge, *1148;* Shalako, *1148;* Two ode Together, *1160;* Violent Breed, The, *136;* We Are No ngels, *1163*
troh, Valerie: Alexina, *711;* Mystery of Alexina, The, *770*
trong, Andrew: Commitments, The, *912*
trong, Gwenyth: Summer House, The, *388*
trong, Mark: Prime Suspect 3, *1008*
trong, Michael: Queen of the Stardust Ballroom, *632*
trong, Rider: Last Hit, The, *990*
trong, Shiloh: House of Cards, *545*
troud, Don: Bloody Mama, *16;* Buddy Holly Story, The, *10;* Cartel, *23;* Coogan's Bluff, *29;* Death Weekend, *831;* vine Enforcer, *40;* Down the Drain, *41;* Express to Terror, *74;* Joe Kidd, *1123;* Killer Inside Me, The, *988;* King of the ckboxers, The, *72;* Mob Boss, *335;* Murph the Surf, *87;* ght the Lights Went Out in Georgia, The, *606;* Prime Target, *00;* Return to Frogtown, *1074;* Search and Destroy (1981), *13;* Slaughter's Big Rip-Off, *117;* Sweet Sixteen, *123;* Tick ... ck ... Tick ..., *129;* Two to Tango, *133*
trouse, Nicholas: Doin' Time on Planet Earth, *267*
trudwick, Sheppard: Beyond a Reasonable Doubt (1956), *55;* Daring Game, *32;* Red Pony, The, *198*
trummer, Joe: Candy Mountain, *474;* Mystery Train, *603;* raight to Hell, *1153*
truthers, Sally: Alice Through the Looking Glass (1985), *45;* All in the Family Twentieth Anniversary Special, *224;* Five asy Pieces, *517;* Getaway, The (1972), *55;* Gun in the House, *534;* Hey, I'm Alive!, *541;* Intimate Strangers, *553*
truycken, Carel: Addams Family Values, *222*
trydom, Hans: Gods Must Be Crazy II, The, *287*
tryker, Christopher: Hell High, *849*
tuart, Gloria: Invisible Man, The, *856;* Poor Little Rich Girl 936), *935;* Rebecca of Sunnybrook Farm (1938), *936*
tuart, John: Candles at Nine, *820;* Legends, *429*
tuart, Maxine: Coast to Coast, *256*
tuart, Nick: Blake of Scotland Yard, *15*
tuart, Randy: Incredible Shrinking Man, The, *1058*
tubbs, Imogen: Deadline (1988), *34;* Erik the Viking, *1049;* llow Traveler, *515;* Summer Story, A, *673;* True Colors, *688*
tucker, Stephen: Delinquent School Girls, *263*
tudi, Wes: Broken Chain, The, *20;* Geronimo: An American egend, *1115*
tumper, Johnny: Mob War, *86*
turges, Preston: Paris Holiday, *354*
tyler, Trudie: Fair Game, *974*
uchet, David: Harry and the Hendersons, *1055;* unchback, *854;* Iron Eagle, *67;* Last Innocent Man, The, *990;* urrow, *601;* Poirot (Series), *1006;* 13 at Dinner, *1024;* To ll a Priest, *684;* When the Whales Came, *699*
udlow, Susie: Ark of the Sun God...Temple of Hell, The, *6*
ugimura, Haruko: Late Chrysanthemums, *756*
ukapatana, Chintara: Good Morning, Vietnam, *530*
ukowa, Barbara: Berlin Alexanderplatz, *716;* Lola (1982), *61;* M. Butterfly, *583;* Sicilian, The, *115;* Voyager, *695;* ntropa, *807*
ullavan, Margaret: Mortal Storm, The, *600;* Shining Hour, e, *656;* Shop Around the Corner, The, *378;* Shopworn gel, The, *656;* So Ends Our Night, *661;* Three Comrades, *32*
ullivan, Barry: Another Time, Another Place (1958), *449;* y Number Can Play, *450;* Bad and the Beautiful, The, *454;* Buckskin, *1102;* Caravans, *475;* Casino, *476;* Gangster, The, *525;* Kung Fu, *73;* Life of Her Own, A, *574;* Maverick Queen, The, *1133;* Mr. Imperium, *931;* Nancy Goes to Rio, *932;* Pat Garrett and Billy the Kid, *1138;* Planet of the Vampires, *875;* Shark! (a.k.a. Maneaters!), *114;* Skirts Ahoy!, *940;* Strategic Air Command, *670;* Take a Hard Ride, *1154;* Texas Lady, *1156;* Washington Affair, The, *696;* Woman of the Town, *1165;* Yuma, *1166*
Sullivan, Brad: Funny Farm, *282;* Orpheus Descending, *615;* Prince of Tides, The, *627;* Sister Act 2: Back in the Habit, *380*
Sullivan, Don: Giant Gila Monster, The, *846;* Teenage Zombies, *892*
Sullivan, Ed: Singing Nun, The, *204*
Sullivan, Francis L.: Caesar and Cleopatra, *473;* Citadel, The, *482;* Joan of Arc, *558*
Sullivan, Liam: Magic Sword, The, *185*
Sullivan, Paul: Shoot the Living...Pray for the Dead, *1149*
Sullivan, Sean Gregory: Howling VI: The Freaks, *854*
Sullivan, Susan: City in Fear, *962;* Deadman's Curve, *913;* Incredible Hulk, The, *1058;* Ordeal of Dr. Mudd, The, *614*
Sullivan, Tom: Cocaine Cowboys, *27*
Sumac, Yma: Omar Khayyam, *93*
Summer, Crystal: Double Blast, *41*
Summer, Donna: Thank God It's Friday, *944*
Summerour, Lisa: Philadelphia, *621*
Summers, Andy: Stand by Me (1988), *941*
Summersett, Roy: Overkill, *96*
Summerville, Slim: Jesse James, *1123;* Rebecca of Sunnybrook Farm (1938), *936;* Western Union, *1163*
Sumpter, Donald: Black Panther, The, *463*
Sundberg, Clinton: Key to the City, *312;* Living In A Big Way, *929*
Sundland, Debra: Tough Guys Don't Dance, *686*
Sundquist, Bjorn: Dive, The, *40;* Shipwrecked, *203*
Sundquist, Gerry: Boarding School, *243;* Don't Open Till Christmas, *836;* Great Expectations (1988), *532;* Meetings with Remarkable Men, *591*
Supremes, The: That Was Rock, *944*
Surovy, Nicolas: Stark, *119;* 12:01, *1086*
Susa, Amber: American Summer, An, *5*
Susman, Tod: Only the Strong, *95*
Sust, David: In a Glass Cage, *747*
Sutherland, Donald: Alex in Wonderland, *224;* Apprentice to Murder, *810;* Backdraft, *8;* Bear Island, *954;* Benefit of a Doubt, *954;* Bethune, *459;* Blood Relatives, *957;* Buffy, The Vampire Slayer, *247;* Casanova (1976), *722;* Castle of the Living Dead, *822;* Crackers, *269;* Dan Candy's Law, *32;* Day of the Locust, The, *496;* Die! Die! My Darling!, *834;* Dirty Dozen, The, *39;* Disappearance, The, *39;* Dr. Bethune, *502;* Dr. Terror's House of Horrors, *836;* Don't Look Now, *971;* Dry White Season, A, *505;* Eagle Has Landed, The, *42;* Eminent Domain, *973;* Eye of the Needle, *974;* Gas, *283;* Great Train Robbery, The, *980;* Heaven Help Us, *295;* Invasion of the Body Snatchers (1978), *1059;* JFK, *558;* Johnny Got His Gun, *559;* Kelly's Heroes, *70;* Kentucky Fried Movie, *312;* Klute, *989;* Lady Ice, *989;* Lifeforce Experiment, The, *1063;* Little Murders, *319;* Lock Up, *78;* Lost Angels, *580;* M*A*S*H, *324;* Man, a Woman and a Bank, A, *994;* Max Dugan Returns, *591;* Murder by Decree, *998;* Nothing Personal, *347;* Ordeal by Innocence, *1003;* Ordinary People, *614;* Quicksand: No Escape, *1008;* Railway Station Man, The, *633;* Revolution, *639;* Rosary Murders, The, *1011;* Shadow of the Wolf, *114;* Six Degrees of Separation, *659;* S*P*Y*S, *385;* Start the Revolution without Me, *385;* Steelyard Blues, *386;* Threshold, *1083;* Trouble with Spies, The, *399;* Wolf at the Door, *804*
Sutherland, Kiefer: Amazing Stories (TV Series), *1036;* Article 99, *451;* Bay Boy, The, *456;* Bright Lights, Big City, *470;* Brotherhood of Justice, *471;* Chicago Joe and the Showgirl, *480;* Crazy Moon, *490;* Few Good Men, A, *976;* Flashback, *50;* Flatliners, *977;* Killing Time, The, *72;* Last Light, *569;* Lost Boys, The, *861;* 1969, *607;* Promised Land, *629;* Renegades, *105;* Stand by Me (1986), *665;* Three

Musketeers, The (1993), *129;* Twin Peaks: Fire Walk with Me, *1028;* Vanishing, The (1993), *1029;* Young Guns, *1165;* Young Guns II, *1166*
Sutorius, James: Windy City, *703*
Sutton, Dudley: Devils, The, *500;* Leather Boys, The, *572;* Number One of the Secret Service, *347;* Orlando, *614*
Sutton, Emma: Goodnight, God Bless, *847*
Sutton, Grady: Great Moment, The, *290;* Lady Takes a Chance, A, *1125;* Show-Off, The, *378;* Vivacious Lady, *405*
Sutton, John: Arrest Bulldog Drummond, *6;* Invisible Man Returns, *856;* Jane Eyre (1944), *557;* Murder Over New York, *999;* Second Woman, The, *650;* Yank in the RAF, A, *707*
Sutton, Kay: Lawless Valley, *1127;* Li'l Abner (1940), *318;* Saint in New York, The, *1012*
Sutton, Lisa: Raw Courage, *103*
Sutton, Lori: Polish Vampire in Burbank, A, *359*
Sutton, Raymond: Dogpound Shuffle, *266*
Suzanna: Black Magic Terror, *814*
Suzman, Janet: Black Windmill, The, *956;* Day in the Death of Joe Egg, A, *262;* Draughtman's Contract, The, *972;* Dry White Season, A, *505;* House on Garibaldi Street, *545;* Nicholas and Alexandra, *605;* Nuns on the Run, *347;* Priest of Love, *627;* Zany Adventures of Robin Hood, The, *416*
Svashenko, Semyon: Arsenal, *713;* Earth, *732*
Svenson, Bo: Choke Canyon, *25;* Curse II—The Bite, *827;* Deadly Impact, *34;* Deep Space, *1046;* Delta Force, The, *36;* Final Chapter—Walking Tall, *48;* Frankenstein (1973), *842;* Great Waldo Pepper, The, *57;* Heartbreak Ridge, *59;* Last Contract, The, *75;* Night Warning, *870;* North Dallas Forty, *609;* Primal Rage, *876;* Snowbeast, *888;* Steele's Law, *120;* Three Days to a Kill, *128;* Thunder Warrior, *129;* Thunder Warrior II, *129;* Walking Tall Part II, *136;* White Phantom, *139;* Wizard of the Lost Kingdom, *1090*
Swada, Ken: Mishima: A Life in Four Chapters, *595*
Swaggart, Jimmy: Jerry Lee Lewis—I Am What I Am, *428*
Swain, Mack: Gold Rush, The, *288;* Hands Up!, *292;* Lizzies of Mack Sennett, The, *320;* Mockery, *598;* Three Charlies and a Phoney!, *395*
Swann, Robert: Girly, *846*
Swanson, Gary: Triplecross, *399;* Vice Squad, *135*
Swanson, Gloria: Indiscreet (1931), *306;* Male and Female, *994;* Manhandled, *328;* Queen Kelly, *631;* Sadie Thompson, *646;* Sunset Boulevard, *673;* Three for Bedroom C, *395;* When Comedy Was King, *409*
Swanson, Kristy: Buffy, The Vampire Slayer, *247;* Chase, The (1994), *25;* Deadly Friend, *831;* Diving In, *502;* Flowers in the Attic, *978;* Highway to Hell, *850;* Mannequin Two: On the Move, *328;* Program, The, *629*
Swart, Rufus: Dust Devil, *838*
Swayze, Don: Beach Babes from Beyond, *1038;* Body of Influence, *958;* Broken Trust, *959;* Death Ring, *35;* Edge of Honor, *43;* Payback, *98*
Swayze, Patrick: City of Joy, *483;* Dirty Dancing, *914;* Father Hood, *47;* Ghost (1990), *527;* Grandview, U.S.A., *531;* Next of Kin (1989), *90;* North and South, *608;* Point Break, *99;* Red Dawn, *104;* Road House (1989), *107;* Steel Dawn, *1080;* Tiger Warsaw, *683;* Youngblood, *709*
Sweaney, Debra: Savage Instinct, *111*
Sweeney, Ann: Incredible Melting Man, The, *1058*
Sweeney, Bob: George Burns and Gracie Allen Show, The (TV Series), *284;* Toby Tyler, *212*
Sweeney, D. B.: Blue Desert, *957;* Cutting Edge, The, *493;* Day in October, A, *496;* Eight Men Out, *508;* Fire in the Sky, *1051;* Gardens of Stone, *525;* Hear no Evil, *982;* Heaven Is a Playground, *539;* Leather Jackets, *76;* Lonesome Dove, *1129;* Memphis Belle (1990), *592;* Miss Rose White, *596;* No Man's Land, *91*
Sweeney, Joseph: 12 Angry Men, *690*
Sweeny, Steve: New Wave Comedy, *343*
Sweet, Blanche: Anna Christie (1922), *449;* Avenging Conscience, The, *811;* D. W. Griffith Triple Feature, *493;* Home, Sweet Home, *543;* Judith of Bethulia, *560*
Sweet, Dolph: Below the Belt, *458;* King, *564;* Which Way Is Up?, *410*
Sweet, Gary: Indecent Obsession, An, *551*
Sweet, Vonte: You Must Remember This, *708*
Swenson, Karl: Brighty of the Grand Canyon, *152;* Hanging Tree, The, *1118*
Swenson, Forrest: To All a Good Night, *895*
Swickard, Joe: Keystone Comedies, Vol. 5, *313*
Swift, David: Arthur's Hallowed Ground, *451;* Black Panther, The, *463*
Swift, Paul: Multiple Maniacs, *866*
Swift, Susan: Harper Valley P.T.A., *294*
Swinburne, Nora: Betrayed (1954), *11;* River, The (1951), *641*
Swinton, Tilda: Caravaggio, *475;* Edward II, *507;* Garden, The, *525;* Last of England, The, *570;* Orlando, *614;* War Requiem, *696*
Swit, Loretta: Beer, *233;* Best Christmas Pageant Ever, The, *150;* First Affair, *517;* Freebie and the Bean, *281;* M*A*S*H* (TV Series), *325;* M*A*S*H: Goodbye, Farewell, Amen, *325;* Race with the Devil, *878;* S.O.B., *372*
Switzer, Carl "Alfalfa": General Spanky, *169;* High and the Mighty, The, *541;* I Love You Again, *304;* Island in the Sky, *554;* Little Rascals, The, *183;* Motorcycle Gang, *87*
Swofford, Ken: Black Roses, *814;* Bless the Beasts and Children, *463;* Common Law Cabin, *487;* Gambler, Part II—The Adventure Continues, The, *1115;* Hunter's Blood, *546;* Sky Heist, *117*
Swope, Topo: Tracks, *687*
Sydney, Basil: Dam Busters, The, *31;* Hamlet (1948), *535;* Rhodes of Africa, *639;* Simba, *658;* Treasure Island (1950), *214*
Sydow, Max von: Bachelor, The, *453;* Needful Things, *868*
Syed, Shafiq: Salaam Bombay!, *782*
Sykes, Eric: Heavens Above, *296;* Spy with a Cold Nose, The, *385*
Sylvester, Harold: Fast Break, *274;* Officer and a Gentleman, An, *611;* Uncommon Valor, *134;* Vision Quest, *694*
Sylvester, William: Devil Doll (1963), *833;* Gorgo, *847;* Riding with Death, *1074;* 2001: A Space Odyssey, *1086*
Sylvie: Little World of Don Camillo, The, *761;* Petronella, *195;* Shameless Old Lady, The, *785;* Ulysses, *133*
Sylwan, Kari: Cries and Whispers, *726*
Syms, Sylvia: Asylum, *810;* Desperados, The, *1109;* Intimate Contact, *553;* Murder Is Announced, A, *998;* Operation Crossbow, *95;* Shirley Valentine, *378;* Victim, *693;* World of Suzie Wong, The, *707*
Syron, Brian: Backlash, *8*
Szarabajka, Keith: Billy Galvin, *461;* Equalizer, The: "Memories of Manon", *44;* Marie, *588;* Nightlife, *870;* Perfect World, A, *621;* Staying Together, *667;* Stephen King's Golden Years (TV Series), *1080*
Szeps, Henri: Run, Rebecca, Run, *201*
Szpak, Alina: Brothers of the Wilderness, *471*
Tabakov, Oleg: Oblomov, *772;* Unfinished Piece for the Player Piano, An, *798*
Tabori, Kristoffer: Marilyn & Bobby: Her Final Affair, *588;* Rappaccini's Daughter, *635*
Tadokoro, Yutaka: Tokyo Pop, *946*
Taeger, Ralph: Hondo and the Apaches, *1121*
Tagawa, Cary-Hiroyuki: Nemesis (1992), *1067;* Rising Sun, *1010*
Taggart, Rita: Horror Show, The, *852;* Webber's World, *406*
Tagore, Sharmila: World of Apu, The, *805*
Taguchi, Tomorrow: Tetsuo: The Iron Man, *793*
Taimak: Last Dragon, The, *75*
Tainsh, Tracy: Frenchman's Farm, *843*
Taka, Miiko: Walk, Don't Run, *405*
Takaki, Mio: Berlin Affair, The, *459*
Takakura, Ken: Antarctica, *713;* Black Rain (1989), *14;* Mr. Baseball, *333;* Yakuza, The, *141*

akamine, Hideko: Mistress, The (1953), *768;* When a Voman Ascends the Stairs, *803*
akarada, Akira: Godzilla vs. Monster Zero, *846;* Godzilla vs. Aothra, *846*
akashima, Tadao: King Kong vs. Godzilla, *859;* Son of odzilla, *888*
akei, George: Green Berets, The, *57;* Live by the Fist, *76;* risoners of the Sun, *628;* Red Line 7000, *104;* Star Trek (TV eries), *1078;* Star Trek: The Menagerie, *1078;* Star rek—The Motion Picture, *1079;* Star Trek II: The Wrath of han, *1079;* Star Trek III: The Search for Spock, *1079;* Star rek IV: The Voyage Home, *1079;* Star Trek V: The Final rontier, *1079;* Star Trek VI: The Undiscovered Country, *1079;* reasures of the Twilight Zone, *1085;* Walk, Don't Run, *405*
akle, Darien: Lost Tribe, The, *861*
akle, Emma: Lost Tribe, The, *861*
albot, Helen: King of the Forest Rangers, *72*
albot, Lyle: Adventures of Ozzie and Harriet, The (TV eries), *222;* Atom Man vs. Superman, *7;* Batman and Robin, *;* Case of the Lucky Legs, The, *960;* Dixie Jamboree, *914;* ury of the Congo, *54;* Glen or Glenda, *528;* Go West, Young lan, *287;* Jail Bait (1954), *68;* Ladies They Talk About, *567;* ne Body Too Many, *1003;* One Night of Love, *934;* Our Little irl, *193;* Purchase Price, The, *630;* Second Fiddle, *938;* hriek in the Night, A, *1016;* Thirteenth Guest, The, *1024;* rader Tom of the China Seas, *131*
albot, Nita: Amityville 1992: It's About Time, *809;* Chained eat, *24;* Concrete Jungle, The (1982), *28;* Frightmare, *844;* I larried a Woman, *304;* Island Claws, *857;* Puppet Master II, *78;* Rockford Files, The (TV Series), *108;* Who's Got the ction?, *411*
albott, Gloria: Arizona Raiders, *1095;* Cyclops, The, *829;* aughter of Dr. Jekyll, *829;* Girls Town, *55;* I Married a onster from Outer Space, *1057;* Leech Woman, The, *860;* alion, *1154*
albott, Michael: Miami Vice, *84*
aliaferro, Hal: Idaho, *1122;* Lone Ranger, The (1938), *129;* Painted Stallion, The, *1138;* Song of Texas, *1151*
alking Heads: Stop Making Sense, *435*
allichet, Margaret: Stranger on the Third Floor, *1020*
ally: Knockouts, *314*
almadge, Constance: Intolerance, *553*
almadge, Natalie: Our Hospitality, *351*
alman, William: City That Never Sleeps, *483;* Crashout, *0;* One Minute to Zero, *94;* Racket, The, *633*
am, Alan: Armour Of God, *713*
amba, Tetsuro: You Only Live Twice, *141*
amblyn, Russ: Blood Screams, *816;* Cimarron (1960), *105;* Don't Go Near the Water, *267;* Fastest Gun Alive, The, *112;* Haunting, The, *849;* High School Confidential!, *541;* Hit e Deck, *923;* Last Hunt, The, *1126;* Necromancer, *868;* ayton Place, *621;* Phantom Empire, The (1986), *99;* Retreat ell, *105;* Running Mates (1992), *371;* Seven Brides for Seven rothers, *939;* Tom Thumb, *213;* Twin Peaks (Movie), *1027;* win Peaks (TV Series), *1027;* War of the Gargantuas, *1088;* Vest Side Story, *947;* Win, Place or Steal, *412;* Winning eam, The, *704;* Wonderful World of the Brothers Grimm, The, *090*
ambor, Jeffrey: Cocaine: One Man's Seduction, *485;* Gun the House, A, *534;* House in the Hills, A, *984;* Life Stinks, *18;* Man Who Wasn't There, The, *328;* Pastime, *619;* Sadat, *46;* Saturday the 14th, *882;* Three O'Clock High, *396;* Vebber's World, *406*
amerlis, Zoe: Ms. .45, *87;* Special Effects, *889*
amiroff, Akim: Alphaville, *712;* Anastasia, *447;* Battle Hell, *;* Black Magic (1949), *462;* Bridge of San Luis Rey, The, *469;* an't Help Singing, *911;* Chained, *478;* Corsican Brothers, The 1941), *29;* Deadly Sanctuary, *831;* Gangster, The, *525;* eneral Died at Dawn, The, *55;* Great McGinty, The, *290;* Hotel aradiso, *302;* Lt. Robin Crusoe, U.S.N., *181;* Miracle of lorgan's Creek, The, *332;* Mr. Arkadin (a.k.a. Confidential eport), *596;* My Girl Tisa, *602;* My Love for Yours, *340;* aughty Marietta, *932;* Outpost in Morocco, *96;* Panic Button, *353;* Sadie McKee, *646;* Story of Louis Pasteur, The, *668;* Tortilla Flat, *686;* Trial, The, *687;* Union Pacific, *1160*
Tanaka, Kinuyo: Life of Oharu, *760;* Mother, *769;* Sandakan No. 8, *783;* Sansho the Bailiff, *783*
Tanaka, Yoshiko: Black Rain (1988), *718*
Tandy, Jessica: Batteries Not Included, *148;* Best Friends, *235;* Birds, The, *813;* Bostonians, The, *467;* Cocoon, *1042;* Cocoon: The Return, *1042;* Desert Fox, The, *37;* Driving Miss Daisy, *505;* Forever Amber, *520;* FoxFire, *521;* Fried Green Tomatoes, *522;* Gin Game, The, *527;* House on Carroll Street, The, *984;* September Affair, *652;* Seventh Cross, The, *653;* Still of the Night, *1020;* To Dance with the White Dog, *684;* Used People, *404;* World According to Garp, The, *706*
Tandy, Mark: Railway Station Man, The, *633*
Tani, Yoko: First Spaceship on Venus, *1051*
Tanner, Mary: Something Special, *383*
Tara, Suzanne: Danger Zone, The, *32*
Tarantino, Quentin: Reservoir Dogs, *105*
Taratorkin, Georgi: Crime and Punishment (1970), *727*
Tari, Le: Brotherhood of Death, *20*
Tarkenton, Fran: First and Ten, *277*
Tarkovsky, Andrei: Andrei Rublev, *713*
Tarrant, John: Starship, *1080*
Tarrin: Monster from a Prehistoric Planet, *1066*
Tashman, Lilyan: Bulldog Drummond, *20;* Frankie and Johnny (1934), *522;* Riptide, *640;* Scarlet Dawn, *649*
Tassoni, Carolina C.: Evil Clutch, *839*
Tate, Larenz: Inkwell, The, *552;* Menace II Society, *593*
Tate, Laura: Dead Space, *1045;* Subspecies, *891*
Tate, Sharon: Ciao Federico!, *724;* Fearless Vampire Killers, or, Pardon Me, But Your Teeth Are in My Neck, The, *840;* Valley of the Dolls, *693*
Tati, Jacques: Jour de Fête, *750;* Mr. Hulot's Holiday, *768;* My Uncle (Mon Oncle), *770;* Parade, *775;* Playtime, *778*
Tattoli, Elda: China Is Near, *723*
Tatum, Anna Lane: Dark Power, The, *829*
Taube, Sven-Bertil: Puppet on a Chain, *101*
Tauber, Richard: Heart's Desire, *922*
Tavernier, Nils: Beatrice, *716*
Tavi, Tuvia: Paradise (1982), *97*
Taxier, Arthur: Cover Girl Murders, The, *964*
Tayback, Vic: Alice Doesn't Live Here Anymore, *444;* Beverly Hills Bodysnatchers, *237;* Cheap Detective, The, *254;* George Carlin—Playin' with Your Head, *284;* Horseplayer, *983;* Lepke, *76;* Portrait of a Stripper, *625;* Rage (1980), *633;* Weekend Warriors, *407*
Taye-Loren, Carolyn: Witchcraft V: Dance with the Devil, *903*
Taylor, Benedict: Black Arrow (1984), *150;* Duel of Hearts, *505;* Every Time We Say Goodbye, *511;* Far Pavilions, The, *514*
Taylor, Buck: Gunsmoke: Return to Dodge, *1118;* Gunsmoke (TV Series), *1118;* Pony Express Rider, *1139;* Standing Tall, *1153*
Taylor, Delores: Billy Jack, *13*
Taylor, Don: Father of the Bride (1950), *275;* Father's Little Dividend, *275;* I'll Cry Tomorrow, *924;* Men of Sherwood Forest, *84;* Naked City, The, *1000*
Taylor, Dub: Across the Rio Grande, *1092;* Best of Times, The, *236;* Conagher, *1105;* Creature from Black Lake, *826;* Falling from Grace, *513;* Gambler Returns, the: Luck of the Draw, *1115;* Gator, *54;* Great Smokey Roadblock, The, *57;* Man and Boy, *1131;* Man Called Horse, A, *1131;* Moonshine County Express, *86;* My Heroes Have Always Been Cowboys, *1135;* Parrish, *618;* Pat Garrett and Billy the Kid, *1138;* Pony Express Rider, *1139;* Ridin' Down the Trail, *1144;* They Went That-A-Way and That-A-Way, *210*
Taylor, Elizabeth: Ash Wednesday, *451;* Beau Brummell (1954), *457;* Between Friends, *459;* Big Hangover, The, *238;* Butterfield 8, *472;* Cat on a Hot Tin Roof (1958), *477;* Cleopatra (1963), *484;* Comedians, The, *486;* Conspirator, *963;* Courage of Lassie, *160;* Date with Judy, A, *913;* Divorce

His: Divorce Hers, *502;* Dr. Faustus, *502;* Driver's Seat, The, *505;* Elephant Walk, *508;* Father of the Bride (1950), *275;* Father's Little Dividend, *275;* Flintstones, The, *167;* Giant, *527;* Girl Who Had Everything, The, *527;* Hammersmith Is Out, *292;* Ivanhoe (1952), *68;* Jane Eyre (1944), *557;* Julia Misbehaves, *311;* Lassie Come Home, *180;* Last Time I Saw Paris, The, *570;* Life with Father, *318;* Little Night Music, A, *928;* Little Women (1949), *577;* Love is Better Than Ever, *929;* Mirror Crack'd, The, *996;* National Velvet, *190;* Night Watch, *870;* Place in the Sun, A, *622;* Poker Alice, *1139;* Raintree County, *634;* Reflections in a Golden Eye, *637;* Rhapsody, *639;* Rumor Mill, The, *645;* Sandpiper, The, *648;* Secret Ceremony, *650;* Suddenly, Last Summer, *672;* Sweet Bird of Youth (1989), *674;* Taming of the Shrew, The (1966), *391;* Under Milk Wood, *691;* V.I.P.s, The, *693;* Who's Afraid of Virginia Woolf?, *701;* Winter Kills, *704;* X, Y and Zee, *707*

Taylor, Estelle: Cimarron (1931), *1105;* Don Juan, *503;* Street Scene, *670;* Ten Commandments, The (1923), *678*

Taylor, Forrest: Arizona Days, *1094;* Colorado Serenade, *1105;* Lightning Carson Rides Again, *1128;* Mystery of the Hooded Horsemen, *1135;* Riders of Destiny, *1144;* Song of Nevada, *1151;* Sons of the Pioneers, *1151*

Taylor, Grant: Long John Silver, *78*

Taylor, Grigor: High Rolling, *62*

Taylor, Holland: Cop and a Half, *160;* She's Having a Baby, *377*

Taylor, Jack: Christmas Kid, The, *1105;* Erotikill, *838;* Horror of the Zombies, *852*

Taylor, James: No Nukes, *432*

Taylor, Jana: Hell's Angels on Wheels, *60*

Taylor, Joan: Apache Woman, *1094;* Earth vs. the Flying Saucers, *1048;* Rifleman, The (TV Series), *1144;* Rose Marie (1954), *937;* 20 Million Miles to Earth, *1086*

Taylor, Joyce: Twice-Told Tales, *898*

Taylor, Kelli: Club, The (1993), *824*

Taylor, Kent: Brain of Blood, *818;* Brides of the Beast, *819;* Crawling Hand, The, *825;* I'm No Angel, *305;* Mrs. Wiggs of the Cabbage Patch, *598;* Slightly Scarlet, *660*

Taylor, Kimberly: Beauty School, *233*

Taylor, Kit: Long John Silver, *78*

Taylor, Lili: Bright Angel, *470;* Dogfight, *503;* Mystic Pizza, *603;* Rudy, *200;* Short Cuts, *657;* Watch It, *696*

Taylor, Lindsay: Hard to Die, *848*

Taylor, Marjorie: Crimes of Stephen Hawke, The, *826;* Face at the Window, The, *840;* Ticket of Leave Man, The, *895*

Taylor, Mark L.: Ratings Game, The, *364*

Taylor, Martha: Manhattan Baby, *862*

Taylor, Meshach: Mannequin (1987), *328;* Mannequin Two: On the Move, *328*

Taylor, Monica: Big Bust Out, The, *12*

Taylor, Noah: Flirting, *518;* One Crazy Night, *349;* Year My Voice Broke, The, *707*

Taylor, Norma: Adventures of Rex and Rinty, *1092*

Taylor, Renee: White Palace, *700*

Taylor, Rip: Live at Harrah's, *320;* Things Are Tough All Over, *393*

Taylor, Robert: Above and Beyond, *1;* Bataan, *9;* Billy the Kid, *1099;* Broadway Melody of 1936, *910;* Broadway Melody of 1938, *910;* Camille, *474;* Conspirator, *963;* D-Day the Sixth of June, *497;* Gorgeous Hussy, The, *531;* Hondo and the Apaches, *1121;* Ivanhoe (1952), *68;* Johnny Eager, *559;* Johnny Tiger, *559;* Knights of the Round Table, *73;* Last Hunt, The, *1126;* Law and Jake Wade, The, *1127;* Miracle of the White Stallions, *187;* Night Walker, The, *1001;* Party Girl, *618;* Personal Property, *356;* Quo Vadis (1951), *632;* Three Comrades, *682;* Undercurrent, *691;* Waterloo Bridge, *697;* Westward the Women, *1163;* When Ladies Meet, *698*

Taylor, Rod: Ask Any Girl, *229;* Birds, The, *813;* Catered Affair, The, *477;* Chuka, *1105;* Cry of the Innocent, *964;* Dark of the Sun, *32;* Deadly Trackers, The, *1108;* Fantasy Film Worlds of George Pal, The, *424;* Glass Bottom Boat, The, *287;* Hotel, *544;* Man Who Had Power Over Women, The, *587;* Powderkeg, *1139;* Raintree County, *634;* 36 Hours, *681;* Time Machine, The, *1084;* Time to Die, A (1983), *130;* Train Robbers, The, *1158;* V.I.P.s, The, *693;* Zabriskie Point, *709*

Taylor, Sam: Living the Blues, *577*

Taylor, Sharon: Attack of the Killer Tomatoes, *229*

Taylor, Vaughn: It Should Happen to You, *308*

Taylor-Young, Leigh: Can't Stop the Music, *911;* Devlin Connection III, The, *970;* Honeymoon Academy, *300;* Horsemen, The, *64;* I Love You Alice B. Toklas!, *304;* Jagged Edge, *556;* Looker, *1063;* Marathon, *329;* Secret Admirer, *374*

Teagarden, Jack: Jazz on a Summer's Day, *427*

Teague, Anthony: How to Succeed in Business without Really Trying, *923*

Teal, Ray: Distant Drums, *40;* Jumping Jacks, *311*

Teale, Owen: Hawk, The, *982;* War Requiem, *696*

Tearle, Conway: Hurricane Express, *65;* Stella Maris, *1020;* Vanity Fair, *693*

Tearle, Godfrey: Decameron Nights, *263;* One of Our Aircraft Is Missing, *94*

Teas, W. Ellis: Immoral Mr. Teas, The, *305*

Teasdale, Verree: Fifth Avenue Girl, *276*

Tebbs, Susan: Littlest Horse Thieves, The, *184*

Tecsi, Sandor: '68, *659*

Tedd, Steven: Rough Justice, *1146*

Tedrow, Irene: Two Worlds of Jennie Logan, The, *1086*

Teefy, Maureen: Fame, *916*

Tejada, Manuel: Cut Throats Nine, *1107*

Tell, Olive: Scarlet Empress, The, *649*

Teller: Penn & Teller Get Killed, *356;* Penn & Teller's Cruel Tricks for Dear Friends, *356*

Temple, Shirley: Baby Take a Bow, *147;* Bachelor and the Bobby-Soxer, The, *230;* Blue Bird, The, *151;* Bright Eyes, *152;* Captain January, *155;* Curly Top, *912;* Dimples, *914;* Fort Apache, *1114;* Heidi (1937), *173;* Just Around the Corner, *926;* Little Colonel, The, *928;* Little Miss Broadway, *928;* Little Miss Marker (1934), *182;* Little Princess, The, *183;* Littlest Rebel, The, *929;* Miss Annie Rooney, *188;* Our Little Girl, *193;* Poor Little Rich Girl (1936), *935;* Rebecca of Sunnybrook Farm (1938), *936;* Since You Went Away, *658;* Stand Up and Cheer, *206;* Story of Seabiscuit, The, *207;* Stowaway, *942;* Susannah of the Mounties, *208;* Wee Willie Winkie, *216*

Tempo, Nino: Girl Can't Help It, The, *286*

Tendeter, Kaye: Fall of the House of Usher, The (1949), *840*

Tendeter, Stacey: Two English Girls, *797*

Tendler, Jesse R.: Secret, The, *650*

Tenessy, Hedi: Revolt of Job, The, *781*

Tennant, Neil: It Couldn't Happen Here, *925*

Tennant, Victoria: All of Me, *224;* Best Seller, *954;* Chiefs, *961;* Dempsey, *499;* Flowers in the Attic, *978;* Handmaid's Tale, The, *1055;* Holcroft Covenant, The, *982;* L.A. Story, *314;* Strangers Kiss, *669;* War and Remembrance, *696;* Whispers, *1031*

Tenney, Jon: Watch It, *696*

Tepper, William: Miss Right, *333*

ter Steege, Johanna: Vanishing, The (1988), *800;* Vincent and Theo, *694*

Terao, Akira: Akira Kurosawa's Dreams, *711;* Ran, *779*

Terekhova, Margarita: Mirror, The, *767*

Teresina: On the Make, *612*

Terhune, Max: Arizona Stagecoach, *1095;* Big Show, The, *1098;* Black Market Rustlers, *1099;* Boothill Bandits, *1100;* Fugitive Valley, *1114;* Heart of the Rockies, *1119;* Hit the Saddle, *1121;* Manhattan Merry-Go-Round, *930;* Night Riders, The, *1136;* Outlaws of Sonora, *1137;* Overland Stage Raiders, *1137;* Pals of the Saddle, *1138;* Range Defenders, *1141;* Red River Range, *1141;* Ride, Ranger, Ride, *1143;* Riders of the Black Hills, *1144;* Riders of the Whistling Skull, *1144;* Saddle Mountain Roundup, *1146;* Santa Fe Stampede, *1147;* Texas to Bataan, *1156;* Three Texas Steers, *1157;* Trail of the Silver Spurs, *1158*

Terkel, Studs: Eight Men Out, *508*

Terlesky, John: Allnighter, The, *225;* Chopping Mall, *824;* Damned River, *32;* Deathstalker II: Duel of the Titans, *1046;* Valet Girls, *404;* When He's Not a Stranger, *698*
Termo, Leonard: Year of the Dragon, *141*
Terrell, John: Five Heartbeats, The, *917;* She's Gotta Have It, *377*
Terrell, Steve: Dragstrip Girl, *42;* Invasion of the Saucer Men, *1059;* Motorcycle Gang, *87*
Terry, Bob: Blake of Scotland Yard, *15*
Terry, Carl: Firing Line, The, *49*
Terry, Don: Don Winslow of the Coast Guard, *41;* Don Winslow of the Navy, *41*
Terry, John: Dangerous Woman, A, *494;* Hawk the Slayer, *59;* Killing in a Small Town, *564;* Resurrected, The, *879;* Silhouette, *1016*
Terry, Kim: Slugs, the Movie, *887*
Terry, Nigel: Caravaggio, *475;* Deja Vu, *499;* Edward II, *507;* Excalibur, *1050;* Sylvia, *676*
Terry, Philip: Balalaika, *907;* Born to Kill, *958;* George White's Scandals, *919;* Junior G-Men, *69;* Lost Weekend, The, *580*
Terry, Ruth: Call of the Canyon, *1103;* Hands Across the Border, *1118;* Heart of the Golden West, *1119*
Terry, Sheila: Haunted Gold, *1119;* Lawless Frontier, *1127;* 'Neath Arizona Skies, *1135;* Sphinx, The (1933), *1019*
Terry the Tramp: Hell's Angels '69, *60*
Terry, William: Stage Door Canteen, *665*
Terry-Thomas: Abominable Dr. Phibes, The, *808;* Brothers In Law, *246;* Carlton-Browne of the F.O., *251;* Danger: Diabolik, *1044;* Daydreamer, The, *161;* Dr. Phibes Rises Again, *836;* Don't Raise the Bridge, Lower the River, *267;* Hound of the Baskervilles, The (1977), *302;* How to Murder your Wife, *303;* I'm All Right Jack, *305;* It's a Mad Mad Mad Mad World, *308;* Lucky Jim, *324;* Make Mine Mink, *327;* Naked Truth, *342;* Those Daring Young Men in Their Jaunty Jalopies, *394;* Those Magnificent Men in Their Flying Machines, *394;* Tom Thumb, *213;* Vault of Horror, *900;* Where Were You When the Lights Went Out?, *409;* Wonderful World of the Brothers Grimm, The, *1090*
Terzieff, Laurent: A Coeur Joie (Head Over Heels), *710;* Milky Way, The (1970), *767*
Tesreau, Krista: Breaking the Rules, *469*
Tessier, Robert: Born Losers, *17;* Deep, The, *36;* Double Exposure (1982), *971;* Fix, The, *50;* Last of the Mohicans (1985), *1126;* Lost Empire, The, *79;* Nightwish, *1068;* No Safe Haven, *92*
Tessier, Valentine: Madame Bovary (1934), *763*
Tessier, Valentine: Club des Femmes, *725*
Testi, Fabio: Ambassador, The, *445;* Blood in the Streets, *15;* Contraband, *726;* Garden of the Finzi-Continis, The, *740;* Gunfire, *1117;* Mussolini and I, *601;* Stateline Motel, *789*
Teterson, Pete: Cold River, *159*
Tevini, Thierry: Tendres Cousines, *793*
Tewes, Lauren: China Lake Murders, The, *961;* Eyes of a Stranger, *840*
Texiere, Jacob: Leaves from Satan's Book, *758*
Teyssedre, Anne: Tale of Springtime, A, *792*
Thal, Eric: Gun in Betty Lou's Handbag, The, *292;* Six Degrees of Separation, *659;* Stranger Among Us, A, *1020*
Thall, Benj: Homeward Bound: The Incredible Journey, *175*
Thames, Byron: Blame It on the Night, *463;* Seven Minutes in Heaven, *376*
Thatcher, Torin: Affair in Trinidad, *442;* Crimson Pirate, The, *30;* Diane, *500;* From Hell to Borneo, *53;* Houdini, *544;* Jack the Giant Killer, *178;* 7th Voyage of Sinbad, The, *1076;* Snows of Kilimanjaro, The, *118;* Strange Case of Dr. Jekyll and Mr. Hyde, The (1968), *890*
Thate, Hilmar: Veronika Voss, *800*
Thaw, John: Business As Usual, *472;* Chaplin, *479;* Inspector Morse (TV Series), *986;* Killing Heat, *563;* Year in Provence, A, *414*
Thaxter, Phyllis: Jim Thorpe—All American, *558;* Living In A Big Way, *929;* Thirty Seconds Over Tokyo, *127;* World of Henry Orient, The, *414*
Thayer, Brynn: Game of Love, The, *524;* Hero and the Terror, *61*
Thayer, Ivy: Little Laura and Big John, *77*
Thayer, Max: No Dead Heroes, *91;* No Retreat, No Surrender II, *92*
Thayer, Meg: Omega Cop, *93*
Thayer, Tina: Jive Junction, *926*
Theby, Rosemary: Fatal Glass of Beer, A/Pool Sharks, *274;* Flask of Fields, A, *278*
Thelen, Jodi: Four Friends, *521*
Theodore, Brother: Billy Crystal: Don't Get Me Started, *239*
Thesiger, Ernest: Brass Monkey, The, *958;* Bride of Frankenstein, *819;* Ghosts of Berkeley Square, *285;* Ghoul, The (1933), *846*
Thewlis, David: Naked, *603;* Prime Suspect 3, *1008*
Thibeau, Jack: Escape from Alcatraz, *45*
Thibeault, Debi: Galactic Gigolo, *282;* Psychos in Love, *877*
Thicke, Alan: And You Thought Your Parents Were Weird, *227;* Betrayal of the Dove, *954;* Dance 'Til Dawn, *262;* Not Quite Human, *347;* Not Quite Human 2, *347;* Obsessed, *610;* Rubdown, *1011;* Scene of the Crime (1985), *1013;* Stepmonster, *1080;* Still Not Quite Human, *386*
Thiess, Ursula: Monsoon, *599*
Thigpen, Kevin: Just Another Girl on the I.R.T, *561*
Thijn, Marion Van: Lily Was Here, *575*
Thine, Robert: Knockouts, *314*
Thinnes, Roy: Hindenburg, The, *541;* Journey to the Far Side of the Sun, *1060;* Rush Week, *882;* Satan's School for Girls, *882;* Scruples, *650;* Sizzle, *659*
Thomas, B. J.: Jory, *1124*
Thomas, Betty: Homework, *543;* No Greater Gift, *191;* Prison for Children, *628;* Troop Beverly Hills, *399;* Tunnelvision, *400;* When Your Lover Leaves, *699*
Thomas, Buckwheat: General Spanky, *169;* Little Rascals, The, *183*
Thomas, Damien: Shogun (Full-Length Version), *115;* Sinbad and the Eye of the Tiger, *1077*
Thomas, Danny: I'll See You in My Dreams, *924*
Thomas, Dave: Best of John Candy, The, *236;* Boris and Natasha, *244;* Cold Sweat (1993), *28;* Coneheads, *258;* Love at Stake, *322;* Moving, *338;* My Man Adam, *340;* Sesame Street Presents Follow That Bird, *203;* Strange Brew, *387*
Thomas, Doug: Hangmen, *59*
Thomas, Frank M.: Sunset on the Desert, *1154*
Thomas, Gareth: Blake's 7 (TV Series), *1040*
Thomas, George: Hide and Go Shriek, *850*
Thomas, Heather: Cyclone, *31;* Dirty Dozen, The: The Fatal Mission, *39;* Ford: The Man & the Machine, *519;* Hidden Obsession, *982;* Red-Blooded American Girl, *879;* Zapped!, *416*
Thomas, Henry: Cloak and Dagger (1984), *27;* E.T.—The Extra-Terrestrial, *1048;* Fire in the Sky, *1051;* Misunderstood (1984), *598;* Murder One, *87;* Psycho 4: The Beginning, *877;* Quest, The, *878;* Raggedy Man, *1008;* Taste for Killing, A, *126;* Valmont, *693*
Thomas, Isa: Flash of Green, A, *977*
Thomas, Jameson: Scarlet Empress, The, *649*
Thomas, Kristin Scott: Four Weddings and a Funeral, *280;* Handful of Dust, A, *535;* Spymaker: The Secret Life of Ian Fleming, *119;* Tenth Man, The, *679;* Under the Cherry Moon, *691*
Thomas, Kurt: Gymkata, *58*
Thomas, Marlo: Act of Passion, *441;* Consenting Adults (1985), *488;* In the Spirit, *306*
Thomas, Philip Michael: Death Drug, *498;* Miami Vice, *84;* Miami Vice: "The Prodigal Son", *84;* Stigma, *668;* Streetfight, *67;* Wizard of Speed and Time, The, *413*
Thomas, Richard: All Quiet on the Western Front (1979), *444;* Battle Beyond the Stars, *1038;* Berlin Tunnel 21, *10;*

Glory! Glory!, *287;* Hobson's Choice (1983), *175;* It (1991), *857;* Last Summer, *570;* Linda, *992;* Living Proof: The Hank Williams, Jr., Story, *577;* Mission of the Shark, *596;* Roots: The Next Generation, *644;* September 30, 1955, *652;* Thanksgiving Story, The, *210;* Todd Killings, The, *685;* Winning, *140*

Thomas, Robin: From the Dead of Night, *844;* Memories of Murder, *996*

Thomas, Ron: Big Bet, The, *238;* Night Screams, *870*

Thomas, Tressa: Five Heartbeats, The, *917*

Thomerson, Tim: Brain Smasher...A Love Story, *18;* Cherry 2000, *1041;* Die Watching, *970;* Dollman, *1047;* Dollman vs. Demonic Toys, *1047;* Fade to Black (1980), *840;* Flesh, The, *1051;* Glory Years, *287;* Harvest, The, *981;* Intimate Stranger, *986;* Iron Eagle, *67;* Metalstorm: The Destruction of Jared-Syn, *1065;* Near Dark, *868;* Nemesis (1992), *1067;* Prime Time Murder, *100;* Tiger's Tale, A, *396;* Trancers, *1085;* Trancers II (The Return of Jack Death), *1085;* Trancers III: Death Lives, *1085;* Trancers 4: Jack of Swords, *1085;* Vietnam, Texas, *135;* Volunteers, *405;* Who's Harry Crumb?, *411;* Wrong Guys, The, *414;* Zone Troopers, *1091*

Thompson, Andrea: Doin' Time on Planet Earth, *267*

Thompson, Brian: Catch the Heat, *24;* Commando Squad, *28;* Doctor Mordrid, *1047;* Hired to Kill, *62;* Nightwish, *1068;* Rage and Honor, *102*

Thompson, Cindy Ann: Cave Girl, *1041*

Thompson, Deborah: Prison Planet, *1071*

Thompson, Derek: Belfast Assassin, *458*

Thompson, Emma: Dead Again, *966;* Fortunes of War, *520;* Henry V (1989), *540;* Howards End, *545;* Impromptu, *549;* In the Name of the Father, *550;* Look Back in Anger (1989), *579;* Much Ado About Nothing, *338;* My Father, the Hero, *339;* Peter's Friends, *621;* Remains of the Day, *637;* Tall Guy, The, *391*

Thompson, Fred Dalton: Aces: Iron Eagle III, *1;* Barbarians at the Gate, *455;* Born Yesterday (1993), *244;* Cape Fear (1991), *959;* Class Action, *962;* Curly Sue, *261;* Die Hard 2: Die Harder, *39;* In the Line of Fire, *66;* Keep the Change, *1124;* Thunderheart, *1025*

Thompson, Jack: Breaker Morant, *19;* Burke and Wills, *472;* Caddie, *473;* Club, The (1985), *484;* Earthling, The, *164;* Far Off Place, A, *166;* Flesh and Blood, *50;* Ground Zero, *981;* Mad Dog Morgan, *80;* Man from Snowy River, The, *1131;* Sunday Too Far Away, *673;* Trouble in Paradise, *399;* Turtle Beach, *690;* Wind (1992), *140*

Thompson, Kay: Funny Face, *918*

Thompson, Kenneth: Call of the Coyote, *1103;* White Gold, *1031*

Thompson, Larry: King of the Forest Rangers, *72*

Thompson, Lea: All the Right Moves, *444;* Article 99, *451;* Back to the Future, *1037;* Back to the Future II, *1037;* Back to the Future III, *1037;* Beverly Hillbillies, The, *237;* Casual Sex?, *252;* Dennis the Menace, *161;* Going Undercover, *288;* Howard the Duck, *1057;* Montana, *599;* Nightbreaker, *607;* Red Dawn, *104;* Some Kind of Wonderful, *382;* SpaceCamp, *1078;* Wild Life, The, *411;* Wizard of Loneliness, The, *704*

Thompson, Marshall: Around the World Under the Sea, *6;* Bog, *818;* Clarence, the Cross-Eyed Lion, *159;* Crashout, *30;* Cult of the Cobra, *827;* East of Kilimanjaro, *43;* Fiend without a Face, *841;* First Man into Space, The, *1051;* Homecoming (1948), *543;* It! The Terror from Beyond Space, *1060;* Show-Off, The, *378;* They Were Expendable, *127;* To Hell and Back, *130;* White Dog, *700*

Thompson, Mollie: Fatty's Tin-Type Tangle/Our Congressman, *275*

Thompson, R. H.: And Then You Die, *5;* Heaven on Earth, *539;* If You Could See What I Hear, *548;* Surfacing, *123;* Ticket to Heaven, *683*

Thompson, Rex: Eddy Duchin Story, The, *507*

Thompson, Sada: Our Town (1980), *616;* Princess Daisy, *627;* Pursuit of Happiness, The, *631*

Thompson, Scott: Best of the Kids in the Hall, The, *236;* Future Shock, *1053;* Rest in Pieces, *879*

Thompson, Shawn: Hairspray, *292;* Heads, *294*

Thompson, Teri: Married People, Single Sex, *589*

Thompson, Weyman: Hot Shot, *544*

Thomsett, Sally: Railway Children, The, *198*

Thomson, Kim: Great Expectations (1989), *171;* Murder 101, *999;* Stealing Heaven, *667*

Thomson, Pat: Strictly Ballroom, *942*

Thomson, R. H.: Ford: The Man & the Machine, *519*

Thor, Jon-Mikl: Rock 'n' Roll Nightmare, *881*

Thor, Larry: Amazing Colossal Man, The, *1035*

Thorburn, June: Three Worlds of Gulliver, The, *1083;* Tom Thumb, *213*

Thordsen, Kelly: Ugly Dachshund, The, *214*

Thorley, Ken: Escapes, *1049;* Ghost in the Machine, *845*

Thornbury, Bill: Phantasm, *874*

Thorndike, Sybil: Major Barbara, *326;* Nine Days a Queen, *607;* Prince and the Showgirl, The, *361;* Shake Hands with the Devil, *114*

Thorne, Angela: Poor Girl, A Ghost Story, *876*

Thorne, Dyanne: Ilsa, Harem Keeper of the Oil Shieks, *855;* Ilsa, She Wolf of the SS, *855;* Ilsa, the Wicked Warden, *855*

Thorne-Smith, Courtney: Lucas, *583;* Revenge of the Nerds II: Nerds in Paradise, *367;* Summer School, *388;* Welcome to 18, *407*

Thornton, Noley: Danielle Steele's "Fine Things", *495*

Thornton, Sigrid: Great Expectations—The Untold Story, *532;* Lighthorsemen, The, *77;* Over the Hill, *352;* Return to Snowy River, Part II, *1143;* Slate, Wyn, and Me, *660*

Thorsen, Sven-Ole: Abraxas Guardian of the Universe, *1034*

Thorson, Linda: Act of Passion, *441;* Avengers, The (TV Series), *7;* Curtains, *828;* Sweet Liberty, *389*

Three Stooges, The: Dancing Lady, *913;* Snow White and the Three Stooges, *205*

Threlfall, David: Summer House, The, *388*

Thring, Frank: Mad Max Beyond Thunderdome, *1064*

Throne, Malachi: It Takes a Thief (TV Series), *68*

Thuillier, Luc: Monsieur Hire, *768*

Thulin, Ingrid: Brink of Life, *720;* Cries and Whispers, *726;* Damned, The, *727;* Four Horsemen of the Apocalypse, *52;* Hour of the Wolf, *745;* Magician, The, *764;* Moses, *600;* Silence, The, *786;* Wild Strawberries, *804;* Winter Light, *804*

Thundercloud, Chief: Badman's Territory, *1096;* Law Rides Again, The, *1127*

Thurman, Bill: Mountaintop Motel Massacre, *866*

Thurman, Uma: Adventures of Baron Münchausen, The, *1034;* Even Cowgirls Get the Blues, *272;* Final Analysis, *976;* Henry & June, *540;* Jennifer 8, *987;* Johnny Be Good, *311;* Kiss Daddy Good Night, *989;* Mad Dog and Glory, *584;* Robin Hood (1991), *107;* Where the Heart Is, *699*

Thurseon, Debbie: Prey, The, *876*

Tichy, Gerard: Summertime Killer, The, *122*

Ticotin, Rachel: Critical Condition, *260;* Falling Down, *513;* Fort Apache—The Bronx, *520;* F/X 2: The Deadly Art of Illusion, *979;* Keep the Change, *1124;* One Good Cop, *613;* Prison Stories: Women on the Inside, *628;* Total Recall, *1084;* Where the Day Takes You, *699*

Tien, James: Fists of Fury, *49*

Tiernan, Andrew: Edward II, *507*

Tierney, Gene: Advise and Consent, *442;* Egyptian, The, *508;* Ghost and Mrs. Muir, The, *285;* Heaven Can Wait (1943), *295;* Laura, *991;* Left Hand of God, The, *76;* Never Let Me Go, *89;* Night and the City (1950), *605;* Razor's Edge, The (1946), *635;* Return of Frank James, The, *1142;* Shanghai Gesture, The, *655;* Sundown (1941), *673;* Toys in the Attic, *687*

Tierney, Jacob: Josh and S.A.M., *69*

Tierney, Lawrence: Abduction, *950;* Born to Kill, *958;* Bushwhackers, *1102;* Devil Thumbs a Ride, The, *970;* Dillinger (1945), *39;* Female Jungle, *516;* Midnight (1980), *864;* Reservoir Dogs, *105;* Runestone, *882;* Those Endearing Young Charms, *394*

Tierney, Patrick: Next of Kin (1984), *605*

Tiffin, Pamela: One, Two, Three, *350;* State Fair (1962), *941;* Viva Max!, *405*
Tifo, Marie: Blind Trust (Pouvoir Intime), *719*
Tiger, Kenneth: Gypsy Warriors, The, *58*
Tighe, Kevin: Another 48 Hrs., *5;* Caught in the Act, *960;* City of Hope, *483;* Geronimo: An American Legend, *1115;* K-9, *312;* What's Eating Gilbert Grape?, *408*
Tilbury, Peter: Nemesis (1986), *1000*
Tiller, Nadja: Burning Court, The, *721*
Tiller, Najda: Tonio Kroger, *796*
Tillis, Mel: Uphill All the Way, *404*
Tilly, Jennifer: Fabulous Baker Boys, The, *512;* Far from Home, *975;* Getaway, The (1994), *55;* Heads, *294;* High Spirits, *297;* Inside Out (1986), *552;* Let It Ride, *317;* Made in America, *325;* Moving Violations, *338;* Remote Control, *879;* Rented Lips, *366;* Scorchers, *650;* Shadow of the Wolf, *114;* Webber's World, *406*
Tilly, Meg: Agnes of God, *443;* Big Chill, The, *460;* Body Snatchers, The (1993), *1040;* Carmilla, *821;* Girl on a Swing, The, *980;* Impulse (1984), *985;* Leaving Normal, *572;* Masquerade (1988), *995;* Off Beat, *348;* One Dark Night, *872;* Psycho II, *877;* Tex, *680;* Two Jakes, The, *1028;* Valmont, *693*
Tilton, Charlene: Border Shootout, *1100;* Center of the Web, *960;* Deadly Bet, *34;* Diary of a Teenage Hitchhiker, *501;* Fall of the House of Usher, The (1979), *840;* Sweater Girls, *389*
Timko, Johnny: Hot Moves, *301*
Timothy, Christopher: All Creatures Great and Small, *145*
Tinapp, Barton: Dennis the Menace: Dinosaur Hunter, *162*
Tindall, Hilary: Max Headroom, *1065*
Tinelli, Jaime: Sudden Death, *122*
Tingwell, Charles: Breaker Morant, *19;* Cry in the Dark, A, *492;* Miracle Down Under, *187;* Murder Ahoy, *998;* Murder at the Gallop, *998;* Murder Most Foul, *998;* Murder She Said, *999*
Tinti, Gabriele: Caged Women, *22;* Trap Them and Kill Them, *897*
Tippitt, Wayne: Pipe Dreams, *622*
Tipple, Gordon: Time Runner, *1084*
Tippo, Patti: Omega Syndrome, *93*
Toback, James: Alice (1990), *224*
Tobey, Kenneth: Beast From 20,000 Fathoms, The, *1038;* Bigamist, The, *461;* Davy Crockett and the River Pirates, *161;* Davy Crockett, King of the Wild Frontier, *161;* Elfego Baca: Six Gun Law, *1111;* I Was a Male War Bride, *304;* It Came from Beneath the Sea, *857;* Kiss Tomorrow Goodbye, *73;* Strange Invaders, *1080;* Thing (From Another World), The (1951), *1083;* This Time For Keeps, *945;* Wings of Eagles, The, *703*
Tobias, George: Air Force, *3;* Balalaika, *907;* Bride Came C.O.D., The, *245;* Captains of the Clouds, *23;* City for Conquest, *482;* Judge Steps Out, The, *560;* Mildred Pierce, *594;* New Kind of Love, A, *343;* Objective, Burma!, *93;* Rawhide (1951), *1141;* Sergeant York, *113;* Set-Up, The, *1013;* Seven Little Foys, The, *376;* Strawberry Blonde, The, *670;* This Is the Army, *945*
Tobias, Oliver: King Arthur, The Young Warlord, *72;* Mata Hari (1985), *83;* Operation 'Nam, *95;* Stud, The, *671;* Wicked Lady, The (1983), *139*
Tobin, Genevieve: Case of the Lucky Legs, The, *960*
Tobolowsky, Stephen: Basic Instinct, *456;* Funny About Love, *282;* Grifters, The, *534;* Groundhog Day, *291;* Josh and S.A.M., *69;* Memoirs of an Invisible Man, *1065;* My Father, the Hero, *339*
Todd, Ann: All This and Heaven Too, *445;* Danny Boy (1941), *495;* Paradine Case, The, *1004;* Scream of Fear, *1013;* Seventh Veil, The, *653;* Ships with Wings, *115;* Son of Captain Blood, *118*
Todd, Beverly: Brother John, *470;* Clara's Heart, *483;* Jericho Mile, The, *557;* Ladies Club, *74;* Lean on Me, *571;* Moving, *338;* Vice Squad, *135*
Todd, Hallie: Check Is in the Mail, The, *254*
Todd, Harry: Jack Knife Man, The, *556*
Todd, Lisa: Blood Hook, *815*
Todd, Richard: Asylum, *810;* Battle Hell, *9;* Dam Busters, The, *31;* D-Day the Sixth of June, *497;* Dorian Gray, *837;* Man Called Peter, A, *586;* Never Let Go, *604;* Number One of the Secret Service, *347;* Operation Crossbow, *95;* Rob Roy, the Highland Rogue, *200;* Saint Joan, *646;* Sherlock Holmes and the Incident at Victoria Falls, *1015;* Stage Fright, *1019;* Story of Robin Hood, The, *207;* Sword and the Rose, The (1953), *208;* Very Edge, The, *693;* Virgin Queen, The, *694*
Todd, Russell: Chopping Mall, *824;* One Last Run, *613;* Sweet Murder, *1022;* Where the Boys Are '84, *409*
Todd, Saira: Bad Behaviour, *231*
Todd, Thelma: Bohemian Girl, The, *243;* Cockeyed Cavaliers, *257;* Devil's Brother, The, *914;* Hips, Hips, Hooray, *297;* Horse Feathers, *301;* Monkey Business (1931), *335;* Palooka, *617;* Speak Easily, *384*
Todd, Tony: Candyman (1992), *820;* Ivory Hunters, *555;* Night of the Living Dead (1990), *870*
Todd, Trisha: Claire of the Moon, *483*
Todorovic, Bora: Time of the Gypsies, *795*
Toffalo, Lino: Lunatics & Lovers, *763*
Tognazzi, Ricky: Blood Ties (1987), *464*
Tognazzi, Ugo: Joke of Destiny, *750;* La Cage aux Folles, *753;* La Cage aux Folles II, *753;* La Cage aux Folles III, The Wedding, *753;* Pigsty, *777;* Tragedy of a Ridiculous Man, *796*
Tolbin, Niall: Eat the Peach, *270;* Rawhead Rex, *879*
Tolbe, Joe: Men in Love, *592*
Toler, Sidney: Castle in the Desert, *960;* Charlie Chan at the Wax Museum, *961;* Charlie Chan in Rio, *961;* Charlie Chan in the Secret Service, *961;* Chinese Cat, The, *962;* Double Wedding, *268;* Heritage of the Desert, *1120;* It's in the Bag, *308;* Jade Mask, The, *987;* Law of the Pampas, *1127;* Meeting at Midnight, *996;* Murder Over New York, *999;* Night to Remember, A (1943), *345;* Our Relations, *351;* Romance in Manhattan, *643;* Scarlet Clue, The, *1013;* Shanghai Cobra, The, *1014;* Speak Easily, *384;* Spitfire, *664*
Toles-Bay, John: Leap of Faith, *572;* Rage in Harlem, A, *103*
Tolkan, James: Bloodfist IV—Die Trying, *16;* Boiling Point, *17;* Masters of the Universe, *186;* Ministry of Vengeance, *85;* Opportunity Knocks, *351;* Question of Faith, *632;* Second Sight, *374;* Viper, *136;* Weekend War, *697*
Tolo, Marilu: Beyond Fear, *717;* Confessions of a Police Captain, *487;* Long Live Your Death, *1130*
Tom, David: Stay Tuned, *385*
Tom, Lauren: Joy Luck Club, The, *559*
Tom, Nicole: Beethoven's 2nd, *149*
Tomassina, Jeana: Beach Girls, The, *233*
Tomei, Marisa: Chaplin, *479;* My Cousin Vinny, *339;* Oscar (1991), *351;* Paper, The, *617;* Untamed Heart, *692*
Tomelty, Frances: Bellman and True, *954;* Blue Money, *242;* Bullshot, *247;* Field, The, *516*
Tomita, Tamlyn: Come See the Paradise, *486;* Joy Luck Club, The, *559*
Tomlin, Lily: All of Me, *224;* And the Band Played on, *447;* Beverly Hillbillies, The, *237;* Big Business, *238;* Incredible Shrinking Woman, The, *306;* Late Show, The, *991;* Lily Tomlin Special—Vol. I, The, *319;* Nashville, *603;* Nine to Five, *345;* Saturday Night Live, *372;* Search for Signs of Intelligent Life in the Universe, The, *374;* Shadows and Fog, *654;* Short Cuts, *657*
Tomlins, Jason: Live! From Death Row, *577*
Tomlinson, David: Bedknobs and Broomsticks, *149;* Carry on Admiral, *251;* Fiendish Plot of Dr. Fu Manchu, The, *276;* Made in Heaven (1948), *326;* Mary Poppins, *185;* Pimpernel Smith, *99;* Up the Creek (1958), *403;* Water Babies, The, *216;* Wooden Horse, The, *706*
Tomlinson, Ricky: Riff-Raff (1992), *640*
Tompkins, Angel: Don Is Dead, The, *40;* I Love My Wife, *304;* Naked Cage, The, *88;* Prime Cut, *100*
Tompkins, Joan: I Love My Wife, *304*

Tone, Franchot: Advise and Consent, *442;* Bombshell, *243;* Bride Wore Red, The, *469;* Dancing Lady, *913;* Dangerous, *494;* Dark Waters, *496;* Every Girl Should Be Married, *273;* Gabriel over the White House, *524;* Girl from Missouri, The, *286;* Gorgeous Hussy, The, *531;* Here Comes the Groom, *922;* In Harm's Way, *66;* Lives of a Bengal Lancer, The, *78;* Love on the Run (1936), *323;* Man in the Eiffel Tower, The, *995;* Mutiny on the Bounty (1935), *88;* Quality Street, *631;* Reckless (1935), *636;* Sadie McKee, *646;* Suzy, *674;* Three Comrades, *682;* Today We Live, *685*

Tong, Jacqueline: How to Get Ahead in Advertising, *302*

Tono, Eijiro: Yojimbo, *806*

Tonsberg, Adam: Twist and Shout, *797*

Toomey, Regis: Arizona, *1094;* Betrayal from the East, *11;* Beyond the Forest, *460;* Dive Bomber, *502;* Doughgirls, The, *268;* Dynamite Pass, *1111;* Framed (1930), *521;* G-Men, *54;* High and the Mighty, The, *541;* Island in the Sky, *554;* Laughing at Life, *571;* Phantom Creeps, The, *874;* Skull and Crown, *1017;* Station West, *1153;* Strange Illusion, *1020*

Toone, Geoffrey: Captain Sinbad, *156;* Terror of the Tongs, The, *126*

Tootoosis, Gordon: Call of the Wild (1992), *474;* Stone Fox, The, *207*

Topaz, David: Goodbye New York, *289*

Topol: Fiddler on the Roof, *916;* Flash Gordon, *1052;* For Your Eyes Only, *51;* House on Garibaldi Street, *545;* Queenie, *632*

Topol-Barzilai, Anat: Witchcraft, *903*

Torday, Terry: Tower of Screaming Virgins, The, *897*

Toren, Marta: Paris Express, The, *97;* Sirocco, *116*

Torey, Roberta: Hans Brinker, *173*

Torgov, Sarah: Drying Up the Streets, *505;* If You Could See What I Hear, *548*

Tork, Peter: Head (1968), *922*

Torme, Mel: Comedian, The, *486;* Girls Town, *55;* Good News, *920;* Higher and Higher, *922;* Man Called Adam, A, *586;* Words and Music, *948*

Torn, Rip: Another Pair of Aces, *1094;* Baby Doll, *453;* Beastmaster, The, *1038;* Beautiful Dreamers, *457;* Beer, *233;* Betrayal (1978), *459;* Birch Interval, The, *150;* Blue and the Gray, The, *1099;* By Dawn's Early Light, *473;* Cat on a Hot Tin Roof (1985), *477;* City Heat, *255;* Cold Feet (1989), *257;* Coma, *963;* Critic's Choice, *261;* Cross Creek, *491;* Dead Ahead: The Exxon Valdez Disaster, *497;* Defending Your Life, *263;* Dolly Dearest, *836;* Extreme Prejudice, *45;* First Family, *277;* Flashpoint, *977;* Heartland, *1119;* Hit List (1988), *982;* Jinxed, *310;* King of Kings (1961), *565;* Laguna Heat, *990;* Man Who Fell to Earth, The, *1064;* Manhunt for Claude Dallas, *81;* Nadine, *341;* One Trick Pony, *934;* Payday, *620;* Pork Chop Hill, *624;* President's Plane Is Missing, The, *1007;* Private Files of J. Edgar Hoover, The, *100;* Rape And Marriage: The Rideout Case, *635;* RoboCop 3, *1075;* Seduction of Joe Tynan, The, *651;* Shining Season, A, *656;* Silence Like Glass, *657;* Slaughter, *117;* Songwriter, *940;* Sophia Loren: Her Own Story, *663;* Stranger Is Watching, A, *890;* Summer Rental, *388;* Sweet Bird of Youth (1962), *674;* Tropic of Cancer, *688;* You're a Big Boy Now, *416*

Torne, Regina: Like Water for Chocolate, *760*

Torocsik, Mari: Love, *761*

Torrence, David: City Girl, *962*

Torrence, Ernest: Covered Wagon, The, *1106;* Fighting Caravans, *1112;* Hunchback of Notre Dame, The (1923), *854;* I Cover the Waterfront, *65;* King of Kings, The (1927), *565;* Mantrap, *995;* Steamboat Bill Jr., *386;* Tol'able David, *685*

Torrent, Ana: Nest, The (1981), *771;* Spirit of the Beehive, The, *788*

Torres, Fernanda: One Man's War, *613*

Torres, Liz: America, *226;* Bloodfist IV—Die Trying, *16;* More Wild Wild West, *1134;* Thieves of Fortune, *127*

Torres, Raquel: Duck Soup, *269;* White Shadows in the South Seas, *700*

Torry, Joe: Poetic Justice, *624*

Toto: Big Deal on Madonna Street, *717;* Gold of Naples, The, *529;* Hawks and the Sparrows, The, *743;* Laugh for Joy, *756;* Passionate Thief, The (1961), *776*

Totter, Audrey: Any Number Can Play, *450;* Carpetbaggers, The, *475;* Jet Attack, *68;* Lady in the Lake, *990;* Set-Up, The, *1013*

Touliatos, George: Firebird 2015 AD, *1051;* Firepower, *49;* Heartaches, *538;* Left for Dead, *572;* Mortal Sins (1992), *997;* Robbers of the Sacred Mountain, *107*

Toumanova, Tamara: Days of Glory, *33*

Tousey, Sheila: Slaughter of the Innocents, *1017*

Toussaint, Beth: Blackmail (1991), *956*

Tovar, Lupita: Dracula (Spanish Version), *732*

Tower, Wade: Ripper, The, *881*

Towers, Constance: Horse Soldiers, The, *1122;* Naked Kiss, The, *1000;* On Wings of Eagles, *94;* Sergeant Rutledge, *1148;* Shock Corridor, *1015;* Sylvester, *675*

Towles, Tom: Mad Dog and Glory, *584*

Towne, Aline: Don Daredevil Rides Again, *1109;* Radar Men from the Moon, *102;* Satan's Satellites, *111;* Trader Tom of the China Seas, *131;* Zombies of the Stratosphere (Satan's Satellites), *141*

Townes, Harry: Santee, *1147*

Townsend, Jill: Awakening, The, *811;* Oh, Alfie, *611*

Townsend, Patrice: Always (1984), *225;* Sitting Ducks, *380*

Townsend, Robert: Five Heartbeats, The, *917;* Hollywood Shuffle, *299;* Meteor Man, *186;* Mighty Quinn, The, *85;* Ratboy, *635;* Rodney Dangerfield: "It's Not Easy Being Me", *370*

Townshend, Pete: Jimi Hendrix, *428;* Secret Policemen's Other Ball, The, *375;* Secret Policeman's Private Parts, The, *375*

Tozzi, Giorgio: Torn Between Two Lovers, *686*

Tracy, Lee: Best Man, The, *459;* Betrayal from the East, *11;* Blessed Event, *241;* Bombshell, *243;* Doctor X, *836;* Strange Love of Molly Louvain, The, *669*

Tracy, Spencer: Adam's Rib, *222;* Bad Day at Black Rock, *454;* Boom Town, *466;* Boys' Town, *468;* Broken Lance, *1101;* Captains Courageous, *474;* Cass Timberlane, *476;* Desk Set, *263;* Devil at 4 O'Clock, The, *500;* Dr. Jekyll and Mr. Hyde (1941), *835;* Edison, The Man, *507;* Father of the Bride (1950), *275;* Father's Little Dividend, *275;* Fury, *524;* Guess Who's Coming to Dinner, *534;* Guy Named Joe, A, *535;* Inherit the Wind, *552;* It's a Mad Mad Mad Mad World, *308;* Judgment at Nuremberg, *560;* Keeper of the Flame, *562;* Last Hurrah, The, *569;* Libeled Lady, *318;* Mannequin (1937), *588;* Men of Boys Town, *592;* Mountain, The, *600;* Northwest Passage, *92;* Pat and Mike, *355;* RiffRaff (1936), *640;* San Francisco, *648;* Sea of Grass, The, *1148;* Seventh Cross, The, *653;* Stanley and Livingstone, *665;* State of the Union, *666;* Test Pilot, *679;* Thirty Seconds Over Tokyo, *127;* Tortilla Flat, *686;* Without Love, *413;* Woman of the Year, *413*

Tracy, Steve: Desperate Moves, *264*

Trainor, Mary Ellen: Greedy, *290;* Tales from the Crypt (Series), *892*

Tran, Tung Thanh: Good Morning, Vietnam, *530*

Tranelli, Deborah: Naked Vengeance, *88*

Trantow, Cordula: Castle, The, *476;* Hitler, *542*

Traubel, Helen: Deep in My Heart, *913;* Ladies' Man, The, *314*

Travalena, Fred: Buy and Cell, *248*

Travanti, Daniel J.: Adam, *441;* Case of Libel, A, *476;* Fellow Traveler, *515;* Megaville, *1065;* Midnight Crossing, *84;* Millennium, *1066;* Murrow, *601;* Tagget, *124;* Weep No More My Lady, *1030*

Travers, Bill: Belstone Fox, The, *149;* Bhowani Junction, *12;* Born Free, *152;* Browning Version, The, *471;* Christian the Lion, *158;* Duel at Diablo, *1110;* Gorgo, *847;* Ring of Bright Water, *199;* Smallest Show on Earth, The, *381*

Travers, Henry: Ball of Fire, *231;* Edison, The Man, *507;* Girl, a Guy and a Gob, A, *286;* Invisible Man, The, *856;* It's a Wonderful Life, *555;* Madame Curie, *584;* Mrs. Miniver, *597;*

On Borrowed Time, *612;* Primrose Path, *627;* Rains Came, The, *634;* Random Harvest, *635;* Shadow of a Doubt, *1014*
Travers, Mary: Wasn't That a Time!, *438*
Travis, June: Ceiling Zero, *24;* Monster a Go-Go, *336;* Star, The, *665*
Travis, Nancy: Chaplin, *479;* Internal Affairs, *67;* Loose Cannons, *321;* Passed Away, *355;* So I Married an Axe Murderer, *382;* Three Men and a Baby, *395;* Three Men and a Little Lady, *395;* Vanishing, The (1993), *1029*
Travis, Richard: Man Who Came to Dinner, The, *328;* Missile to the Moon, *1066*
Travis, Stacey: Doctor Hackenstein, *835;* Dracula Rising, *837;* Hardware, *1055;* Only the Strong, *95*
Travis, Tony: Flesh Gordon 2: Flesh Gordon meets the Cosmic Cheerleaders, *1052*
Travolta, Ellen: Are You in the House Alone?, *953;* Elvis—The Movie, *509;* Human Experiments, *64*
Travolta, Joey: Beach Babes from Beyond, *1038;* Davinci's War, *33;* Hunter's Blood, *546;* Night of the Wilding, *606;* They Still Call Me Bruce, *393;* Wilding, The Children of Violence, *140*
Travolta, John: Blow Out, *957;* Boy in the Plastic Bubble, The, *468;* Carrie (1976), *821;* Chains of Gold, *478;* Devil's Rain, The, *834;* Dumb Waiter, The, *506;* Experts, The, *273;* Grease, *920;* Look Who's Talking, *320;* Look Who's Talking Too, *321;* Look Who's Talking Now, *321;* Perfect, *620;* Saturday Night Fever, *938;* Shout (1991), *939;* Staying Alive, *942;* Two of a Kind (1983), *402;* Urban Cowboy, *692*
Treacher, Arthur: Curly Top, *912;* Heidi (1937), *173;* In Society, *306;* Little Princess, The, *183;* Mary Poppins, *185;* My Lucky Star, *932;* Riptide, *640;* Satan Met a Lady, *1012;* Stowaway, *942;* That Midnight Kiss, *944;* Thin Ice, *945;* Viva Villa!, *1162*
Treanor, Michael: Three Ninjas, *211*
Treas, Terri: Deathstalker III—The Warriors from Hell, *1046;* House IV, *852;* Rage and Honor, *102*
Trebor, Robert: My Demon Lover, *339*
Tree, David: Drums, *42;* Knight Without Armour, *566;* Pygmalion, *363*
Tree, Lady: Wedding Rehearsal, *407*
Treil, Laurence: Entangled, *973*
Tremayne, Les: Angry Red Planet, The, *1036;* Man Called Peter, A, *586;* Monolith Monsters, The, *865;* Monster of Piedras Blancas, The, *866;* Slime People, The, *1077;* War of the Worlds, The, *1088*
Tremblay, Johanne-Marie: Straight for the Heart, *790*
Treniers, The: Girl Can't Help It, The, *286*
Trepechinska, Joanna: Paper Marriage (1992), *618*
Trese, Adam: Laws of Gravity, *76*
Trevarthen, Noel: Dusty, *164*
Treves, Frederick: Flame to the Phoenix, A, *50;* Paper Mask, *1004;* Sleeping Murder, *1017*
Trevino, Marco Antonio: Donna Herlinda and Her Son, *731*
Trevino, Vic: Firehawk, *49;* Kill Zone, *71*
Trevor, Austin: To Paris with Love, *397*
Trevor, Claire: Allegheny Uprising, *1093;* Babe Ruth Story, The, *453;* Baby Take a Bow, *147;* Best of the Badmen, *1097;* Born to Kill, *958;* Breaking Home Ties, *469;* Crack-Up, *964;* Dark Command, *1107;* Dead End, *497;* High and the Mighty, The, *541;* Honky Tonk, *1121;* Hoodlum Empire, *64;* How to Murder your Wife, *303;* Johnny Angel, *69;* Key Largo, *988;* Kiss Me Goodbye, *313;* Man without a Star, *1132;* Marjorie Morningstar, *589;* Mountain, The, *600;* Murder My Sweet, *999;* Stagecoach (1939), *1152;* Stranger Wore a Gun, The, *1153;* Stripper, The (1963), *671;* Texas, *1155;* Two Weeks in Another Town, *690;* Velvet Touch, The, *693;* Woman of the Town, *1165*
Trevor, Norman: Dancing Mothers, *262*
Trickey, Paula: Carnal Crimes, *959*
Trieste, Leopoldo: Henry IV, *743;* Shoot Loud, Louder...I Don't Understand, *378;* White Sheik, The, *803*
Trigger, Sarah: Deadfall, *968;* El Diablo, *1111;* Kid, *71;* PCU, *355*
Trimble, Jerry: Breathing Fire, *19;* Full Contact, *53;* Live by the Fist, *78;* One Man Army, *94*
Trintignant, Jean-Louis: Act of Aggression, *710;* And God Created Woman (1957), *712;* And Hope to Die, *952;* Bad Girls (1969), *715;* Confidentially Yours, *725;* Conformist, The, *725;* Je Vous Aime (I Love You All), *749;* Le Secret, *758;* Les Biches, *759;* Les Liaisons Dangereuses, *759;* Les Violons du Bal, *759;* Man and a Woman, A, *764;* Man and a Woman, A: 20 Years Later, *764;* Merci La Vie, *767;* My Night at Maud's, *770;* Next Summer, *771;* Passion of Love, *776;* Rendez-Vous, *780;* Seven Deadly Sins, The, *785;* Sleeping Car Murders, The, *786;* Under Fire, *134;* Z, *806*
Trintignant, Marie: Next Summer, *771;* Wings of Fame, *412*
Tripp, Louis: Gate II, *845*
Tripplehorn, Jeanne: Basic Instinct, *456;* Firm, The, *977;* Night We Never Met, The, *345*
Trissenaar, Elisabeth: Angry Harvest, *713*
Tristan, Dorothy: End of the Road, *510;* Griffin and Phoenix: A Love Story, *533*
Tritt, Travis: Rio Diablo, *1145*
Troisi, Lino: Cheaters, The, *723*
Troisi, Massimo: Hotel Colonial, *64*
Trotter, Kate: Clarence, *256*
Trotter, Laura: City of the Walking Dead, *824;* Miami Horror, *1066*
Troughton, David: Norman Conquests, The, Episode 1: Table Manners, *346;* Norman Conquests, The, Episode 2: Living Together, *346;* Norman Conquests, The, Episode 3: Round and Round the Garden, *346*
Troughton, Patrick: Frankenstein and the Monster from Hell, *842;* Sinbad and the Eye of the Tiger, *1077*
Troup, Bobby: Five Pennies, The, *917*
Trowbridge, Charles: Captain America (1944), *22;* Fatal Hour, The, *46*
Troy, Ellen: Dance, *913*
Trudeau, Margaret: Kings and Desperate Men: A Hostage Incident, *73*
True, Jim: Hudsucker Proxy, The, *303;* Singles, *379*
Truex, Ernest: Bachelor Mother, *230;* Christmas in July, *255;* His Girl Friday, *297*
Truffaut, François: Close Encounters of the Third Kind, *1042;* Day for Night, *728;* Green Room, The, *742;* Wild Child, The (L'Enfant Sauvage), *804*
Trujillo, Raul: Clearcut, *26*
Truman, Jeff: Bliss, *241*
Truman, Ralph: Saint in London, The, *1012*
Trumbo, Karen: Claire of the Moon, *483*
Truswell, Chris: Fast Talking, *166*
Tryon, Tom: Cardinal, The, *475;* Color Me Dead, *485;* Gundown at Sandoval, *1117;* I Married a Monster from Outer Space, *1057;* In Harm's Way, *66;* Moon Pilot, *189;* Story of Ruth, The, *668;* Texas John Slaughter: Geronimo's Revenge, *1155;* Texas John Slaughter: Stampede at Bitter Creek, *1155;* Texas John Slaughter: Wild Times, *1156;* Three Violent People, *1157*
Tsang, Ken: Police Story III—Super Cop, *778*
Tschechowa, Olga: Haunted Castle, *849;* Italian Straw Hat, The, *749*
Tse, Yang: Enter the Dragon, *44*
Tselikovskaya, Ludmila: Ivan the Terrible—Part I & Part II, *749*
Tsopei, Corinna: Man Called Horse, A, *1131*
Tsubouchi, Mikiko: Zatoichi: Masseur Ichi and a Chest of Gold, *806*
Tsuchiya, Yoshio: Human Vapor, The, *1057*
Tsuruta, Koji: Samurai Trilogy, The, *783*
Tubb, Barry: Consenting Adults (1985), *488;* Top Gun, *131;* Valentino Returns, *693;* Warm Summer Rain, *696*

Tucci, Stanley: Beethoven (1992), *149;* Billy Bathgate, *461;* In the Soup, *306;* Men of Respect, *592;* Pelican Brief, The, *1005;* Public Eye, The, *1008;* Undercover Blues, *403*

Tuck, Jennifer: Curse of the House Surgeon, The, *828;* Penpal Murders, *873;* Queen Victoria and the Zombies, *878;* Vampires Always Ring Twice, *900;* Vampires from Outer Space, *900*

Tuck, Jessica: Lifepod, *1063*

Tucker, Forrest: Adventures of Huckleberry Finn, The (1978), *144;* Auntie Mame, *229;* Big Cat, The, *12;* Brimstone, *1101;* Bugles in the Afternoon, *1102;* Cancel My Reservation, *250;* Chisum, *1104;* Coroner Creek, *1106;* Cosmic Monsters, The, *825;* Crawling Eye, The, *825;* Final Chapter—Walking Tall, *48;* Finger Man, *48;* Hellfire, *1120;* Hoodlum Empire, *64;* Incredible Rocky Mountain Race, The, *306;* Jubilee Trail, *1124;* Keeper of the Flame, *562;* Melody Master, *592;* Montana Belle, *1134;* Nevadan, The, *1136;* Outtakes, *352;* Pony Express, *1139;* Rage at Dawn, *1140;* Rare Breed, A (1981), *198;* Real American Hero, The, *635;* Sands of Iwo Jima, *111;* Three Violent People, *1157;* Thunder Run, *129;* Time Stalkers, *1084;* Trouble in the Glen, *399;* Westerner, The, *1163*

Tucker, Jerry: Dick Tracy Returns, *38*

Tucker, Maureen: Velvet Underground, The: Velvet Redux—Live MCMXCIII, *437*

Tucker, Michael: Assault & Matrimony, *229;* Checking Out, *254;* D2: The Mighty Ducks, *160;* Day One, *496;* For Love or Money, *279;* Goodbye People, The, *530;* L.A. Law, *567;* Radio Days, *364;* Spy, *1019*

Tucker, Richard: King of the Kongo, *72*

Tucker, Sophie: Broadway Melody of 1938, *910;* Sensations of 1945, *938;* Thoroughbreds Don't Cry, *210*

Tucker, Tanya: Follow That Car, *51;* Hard Country, *293;* Rebels, The, *636*

Tudor, Christine: Final Mission, *48*

Tufts, Sonny: Cat Women of the Moon, *1041;* Easy Living, *506;* Glory at Sea, *56;* Here Come the Waves, *922*

Tull, Patrick: Parting Glances, *618*

Tullenars, Tonny: Scorpion, *112*

Tully, Tom: Adventure, *441;* Branded, *1101;* Coogan's Bluff, *29;* June Bride, *311;* Lady in the Lake, *990;* Love is Better Than Ever, *929;* Love Me or Leave Me, *929;* Moon Is Blue, The, *336;* Northern Pursuit, *92;* Ruby Gentry, *644;* Soldier of Fortune, *118;* Trouble Along the Way, *688;* Wackiest Ship in the Army, The, *405*

Tumnaum, Franz: Rage and Honor II: Hostile Takeover, *102*

Tune, Tommy: Boy Friend, The, *909*

Tung, Bill: Police Story III—Super Cop, *778*

Turco, Paige: Teenage Mutant Ninja Turtles II: The Secret of the Ooze, *209;* Teenage Mutant Ninja Turtles III, *209*

Turkel, Ann: Deep Space, *1046;* Humanoids from the Deep, *854;* Last Contract, The, *75;* 99 and 44/100 Percent Dead, *91;* Paper Lion, *618*

Turkel, Studs: Wasn't That a Time!, *438*

Turman, Glynn: Attica, *452;* Blue Knight, The (1975), *465;* Cooley High, *259;* Gremlins, *1055;* Hero Ain't Nothin' But a Sandwich, A, *540;* Inkwell, The, *552;* J.D.'s Revenge, *858;* Out of Bounds, *96;* Penitentiary II, *98;* Secrets of a Married Man, *651*

Turnbull, John: Silver Blaze, *1016*

Turner, Barbara: Monster from Green Hell, *866*

Turner, Claramae: Carousel, *911*

Turner, Fred: Jack Knife Man, The, *556*

Turner, George: Son of Zorro, *118*

Turner, Janine: Ambulance, The, *952;* Cliffhanger, *26;* Northern Exposure (TV Series), *609;* Quantum Leap (TV Series), *1072*

Turner, Jim: My Samurai, *88*

Turner, Kathleen: Accidental Tourist, The, *440;* Body Heat, *958;* Breed Apart, A, *19;* Crimes of Passion, *491;* House of Cards, *545;* Jewel of the Nile, The, *68;* Julia and Julia, *1061;* Man with Two Brains, The, *328;* Peggy Sue Got Married, *355;* Prizzi's Honor, *362;* Romancing the Stone, *108;* Serial Mom, *376;* Switching Channels, *390;* Undercover Blues, *403;* V. I. Warshawski, *1029;* War of the Roses, The, *406*

Turner, Lana: Another Time, Another Place (1958), *449;* Bachelor in Paradise, *230;* Bad and the Beautiful, The, *454;* Betrayed (1954), *11;* Bittersweet Love, *462;* Cass Timberlane, *476;* Diane, *500;* Dr. Jekyll and Mr. Hyde (1941), *835;* Green Dolphin Street, *533;* Homecoming (1948), *543;* Honky Tonk, *1121;* Imitation of Life, *549;* Johnny Eager, *559;* Latin Lovers, *928;* Life of Her Own, A, *574;* Love Finds Andy Hardy, *322;* Love Has Many Faces, *581;* Madame X (1966), *584;* Mr. Imperium, *931;* Persecution, *621;* Peyton Place, *621;* Postman Always Rings Twice, The (1946), *1007;* Prodigal, The, *629;* Sea Chase, The, *112;* Somewhere I'll Find You, *662;* Three Musketeers, The (1948), *128;* Weekend at the Waldorf, *697;* Who's Got the Action?, *411;* Witches' Brew, *412;* Ziegfeld Girl, *949*

Turner, Tina: Mad Max Beyond Thunderdome, *1064;* That Was Rock, *944;* Tommy, *946*

Turner, Tyrin: Menace II Society, *593*

Turpin, Ben: Golden Age of Comedy, The, *288;* Saps at Sea, *372*

Turturro, Aida: Angie, *448;* Jersey Girl, *310*

Turturro, John: Backtrack, *454;* Barton Fink, *232;* Being Human, *458;* Brain Donors, *245;* Color of Money, The, *485;* Do the Right Thing, *502;* Fearless (1993), *515;* Five Corners, *517;* Gung Ho (1985), *292;* Jungle Fever, *561;* Mac, *583;* Men of Respect, *592;* Miller's Crossing, *594;* Mo' Better Blues, *931;* Sicilian, The, *115;* State of Grace, *666;* To Live and Die in L.A., *130*

Tushingham, Rita: Dream to Believe, *504;* Housekeeper, The, *853;* Knack...and How To Get It, The, *314;* Leather Boys, The, *572;* Mysteries, *770;* Paper Marriage (1992), *618;* Spaghetti House, *788;* Taste of Honey, A, *677*

Tutin, Dorothy: Cromwell, *491;* Importance of Being Earnest, The, *305;* King Lear (1984), *564;* Savage Messiah, *648;* Shooting Party, The, *656;* Six Wives of Henry VIII, The (TV Series), *659;* Tale of Two Cities (1967), *676*

Tuttle, Lurene: Affairs of Dobie Gillis, The, *906;* Clonus Horror, The, *1042;* Final Chapter—Walking Tall, *48;* Give a Girl a Break, *919;* Glass Slipper, The, *919;* Ma Barker's Killer Brood, *80;* Sincerely Yours, *658;* White Mama, *700*

Tutu, Desmond: Cry of Reason, The, *421*

Tweed, Shannon: Cannibal Women in the Avocado Jungle of Death, *22;* Cold Sweat (1993), *28;* Firing Line, The, *49;* Hitchhiker (Series), The, *850;* Hot Dog...The Movie, *301;* Indecent Behavior, *551;* Last Call, *568;* Last Hour, The, *75;* Lethal Woman, *77;* Liar's Edge, *992;* Meatballs III, *330;* Model by Day, *86;* Night Eyes 2, *1000;* Night Eyes 3, *1000;* Night Visitor (1989), *1001;* Possessed by the Night, *1006;* Sexual Response, *1014;* Surrogate, The, *674*

Tweed, Tracy: Night Eyes 3, *1000*

Twelvetrees, Helen: Painted Desert, The, *1138;* State's Attorney, *666*

Twiggy: Boy Friend, The, *909;* Club Paradise, *256;* Doctor and the Devils, The, *835;* Istanbul: Keep Your Eyes Open, *555;* John Carpenter Presents: Body Bags, *858;* Madame Sousatzka, *584;* W, *1030*

Twitty, Conway: Platinum High School, *623*

Twomey, Anne: Imagemaker, The, *549*

Tyler, Jeff: Tom Sawyer (1973), *213*

Tyler, Judy: Jailhouse Rock, *925*

Tyler, Tom: Adventures of Captain Marvel, The, *2;* Brother Orchid, *20;* Brothers of the West, *1101;* Feud of the Trail, *1112;* Last Outlaw, The (1936), *1126;* Mummy's Hand, The, *867;* Night Riders, The, *1136;* Phantom of the West, *1138;* Powdersmoke Range, *1139;* Riders for Justice, *1143;* Riders of the Rio Grande, *1144;* Road Agent, *1145;* Roamin' Wild, *1145;* Talk of the Town, The, *390;* Westerner, The, *1163;* When a Man Rides Alone, *1163*

Tyner, Charles: Hamburger—The Motion Picture, *292;* Harold and Maude, *294;* Incredible Journey of Dr. Meg Laurel,

The, *551;* Jeremiah Johnson, *1123;* Medicine Hat Stallion, The, *188;* Planes, Trains and Automobiles, *358;* Pulse, *877*
Tyrrell, Susan: Andy Warhol's Bad, *447;* Angel, *5;* Another Man, Another Chance, *1094;* Avenging Angel, *8;* Big Top Pee-Wee, *239;* Cry-Baby, *912;* Far from Home, *975;* Fast-Walking, *515;* Fat City, *515;* Flesh and Blood, *50;* Forbidden Zone, *1053;* Killer Inside Me, The, *988;* Lady of the House, *568;* Liar's Moon, *574;* Loose Shoes, *321;* Night Warning, *870;* Poker Alice, *1139;* Rockula, *937;* Steagle, The, *386;* Tales of Ordinary Madness, *677;* Zandy's Bride, *1166*
Tyson, Cathy: Business As Usual, *472;* Lost Language of Cranes, The, *580;* Mona Lisa, *997;* Serpent and the Rainbow, The, *884*
Tyson, Cicely: Acceptable Risks, *440;* Airport '79: The Concorde, *443;* Autobiography of Miss Jane Pittman, The, *452;* Bustin' Loose, *248;* Comedians, The, *486;* Duplicates, *973;* Fried Green Tomatoes, *522;* Heart Is a Lonely Hunter, The, *538;* Heat Wave, *539;* Hero Ain't Nothin' But a Sandwich, A, *540;* Kid Who Loved Christmas, The, *180;* King, *564;* Man Called Adam, A, *586;* Roots, *644;* Samaritan: The Mitch Snyder Story, *647;* Sounder, *663;* Wilma, *703;* Woman Called Moses, A, *705;* Women of Brewster Place, The, *706*
Tyson, Richard: Dark Tide, *495;* Kindergarten Cop, *313;* Red Shoe Diaries 3: Another Woman's Lipstick, *637;* Three O'Clock High, *396;* Two Moon Junction, *690*
Tyzack, Margaret: King's Whore, The, *566;* Mr. Love, *597;* Nemesis (1986), *1000;* Quatermass Conclusion, The, *1072*
U2: U2: Rattle and Hum, *437*
Ubarry, Hector: "Crocodile" Dundee II, *261*
Uchaneishvili, Levan: Legend of Suram Fortress, The, *758*
Udvarnoky, Chris: Other, The, *873*
Udvarnoky, Martin: Other, The, *873*
Udy, Claudia: Nightforce, *91*
Udy, Helene: Hollywood Detective, The, *983;* Sweet Murder, *1022*
Uggams, Leslie: Roots, *644;* Sizzle, *659;* Sugar Hill, *122;* Two Weeks in Another Town, *690*
Ulacia, Richard: Mixed Blood, *86*
Ullman, Tracey: I Love You to Death, *304;* I'll Do Anything, *305;* Plenty, *623;* Robin Hood: Men in Tights, *369*
Ullmann, Liv: Autumn Sonata, *714;* Bay Boy, The, *456;* Cold Sweat (1970), *28;* Cries and Whispers, *726;* Dangerous Moves, *728;* Forty Carats, *279;* Gaby, a True Story, *524;* Hour of the Wolf, *745;* Mindwalk, *430;* Night Visitor, The (1970), *607;* Passion of Anna, The, *776;* Persona, *777;* Richard's Things, *640;* Rose Garden, The, *644;* Scenes from a Marriage, *784;* Serpent's Egg, The, *652;* Wild Duck, The, *702;* Zandy's Bride, *1166*
Ulric, Lenore: Camille, *474;* Northwest Outpost, *933*
Umbers, Margaret: Bridge to Nowhere, *469;* Death Warmed Up, *831*
Umecka, Jolanta: Knife in the Water, *752*
Umeki, Miyoshi: Flower Drum Song, *917;* Horizontal Lieutenant, The, *301;* Sayonara, *648*
Unda, Emilia: Maedchen in Uniform, *764*
Underwood, Blair: Dangerous Relations, *494;* Heat Wave, *539;* Krush Groove, *927;* Posse (1993), *1139*
Underwood, Jay: Boy Who Could Fly, The, *468;* Gumshoe Kid, The, *292;* Invisible Kid, The, *1060;* Not Quite Human, *347;* Not Quite Human 2, *347;* Still Not Quite Human, *386*
Unger, Deborah: Till There Was You, *684;* Whispers in the Dark, *1031*
Urbano, Maryann: Laser Man, The, *315*
Ure, Mary: Reflection of Fear, *1009;* Where Eagles Dare, *138;* Windom's Way, *703*
Urecal, Minerva: Apache Rose, *1094;* Ape Man, The, *809;* Corpse Vanishes, The, *825;* Oklahoma Annie, *349;* So This Is Washington, *382*
Urena, Fabio: Bronx War, The, *20*
Urich, Robert: Blindman's Bluff, *956;* Bunco, *21;* Endangered Species, *1049;* Hit Woman: The Double Edge, *63;* Ice Pirates, *1057;* In a Stranger's Hands, *985;* Invitation to Hell, *857;* Killing at Hell's Gate, *71;* Lonesome Dove, *1129;* Magnum Force, *80;* Mistral's Daughter, *597;* Perfect Little Murder, A, *356;* Princess Daisy, *627;* Revolver, *106;* Turk 182, *689;* Vega$, *135*
Urquhart, Robert: Battle Hell, *9;* Curse of Frankenstein, The, *828;* Knights of the Round Table, *73*
Urquidez, Benny: Bloodmatch, *16;* Kick Fighter, *70*
Urzi, Saro: Seduced and Abandoned, *784*
Usher, Guy: Devil Bat, The, *833;* Doomed to Die, *41*
Ustinov, Pavla: Thief of Baghdad (1978), *127*
Ustinov, Peter: Appointment with Death, *953;* Ashanti, *7;* Beau Brummell (1954), *457;* Billy Budd, *461;* Blackbeard's Ghost, *151;* Charlie Chan and the Curse of the Dragon Queen, *253;* Comedians, The, *486;* Death on the Nile, *968;* Egyptian, The, *508;* Evil under the Sun, *973;* Great Muppet Caper, The, *171;* Grendel, Grendel, Grendel, *172;* Hammersmith Is Out, *292;* Hot Millions, *301;* Immortal Battalion, The (a.k.a. The Way Ahead), *549;* Lady L, *568;* Lion and the Hawk, The, *77;* Logan's Run, *1063;* Lola Montes, *761;* Lorenzo's Oil, *579;* One of Our Aircraft Is Missing, *94;* One of Our Dinosaurs Is Missing, *192;* Purple Taxi, The, *631;* Quo Vadis (1951), *632;* Spartacus, *119;* Sundowners, The (1960), *673;* Thief of Baghdad (1978), *127;* 13 at Dinner, *1024;* Topkapi, *1026;* Viva Max!, *405;* We're No Angels (1955), *407*
Utsunomiya, Masayo: Irezumi (Spirit of Tattoo), *749*
Vaananen, Kari: Amazon, *4*
Vaccaro, Brenda: Cookie, *259;* Dear Detective, *968;* Death Weekend, *831;* First Deadly Sin, The, *977;* For Keeps, *519;* Heart of Midnight, *982;* Honor Thy Father, *543;* I Love My Wife, *304;* Lethal Games, *76;* Midnight Cowboy, *593;* Once Is Not Enough, *613;* Pride of Jesse Hallman, The, *626;* Red Shoe Diaries, *637;* Supergirl, *1081;* Ten Little Indians (1989), *1023;* Water, *406;* Zorro, the Gay Blade, *417*
Vaccaro, Tracy: Rare Breed, A (1981), *198*
Vadim, Annette: Blood and Roses, *814;* Les Liaisons Dangereuses, *759*
Vadim, Roger: Ciao! Manhattan, *482*
Vadis, Dan: Bronco Billy, *246;* Seven Magnificent Gladiators, The, *113*
Vahanian, Marc: Prince of Central Park, The, *197*
Valandrey, Charlotte: Orlando, *614;* Red Kiss (Rouge Baiser), *780*
Valdez, Daniel: Zoot Suit, *949*
Vale, Virginia: Flustered Comedy of Leon Errol, The, *278;* Marshal of Mesa City, *1133;* Stage to Chino, *1152;* Triple Justice, *1159*
Valen, Nancy: Final Embrace, *977*
Valens, Richie: Go, Johnny, Go!, *920*
Valenti, Chuck: Bronx Executioner, The, *1040*
Valentine, Anthony: Carpathian Eagle, *821;* Dirty Dozen, The: The Fatal Mission, *39;* Father's Revenge, A, *515;* Robin Hood and the Sorcerer, *107*
Valentine, Karen: Hot Lead and Cold Feet, *176;* Jane Doe, *556;* North Avenue Irregulars, The, *191;* Return to Fantasy Island, *1074;* Skeezer, *659*
Valentine, Kim: Grandma's House, *980*
Valentine, Scott: After the Shock, *442;* Dangerous Pursuit, *966;* Deadtime Stories, *831;* Double Obsession, *972;* Homicidal Impulse, *983;* My Demon Lover, *339;* Secret Passion of Robert Clayton, The, *1013;* To Sleep With a Vampire, *896;* Unborn II, The, *898;* Write to Kill, *1033*
Valentini, Mariella: Volere Volare, *801*
Valentino, Rudolph: Blood and Sand (1922), *464;* Eagle, The, *269;* Moran of the Lady Letty, *997;* Sheik, The, *655;* Son of the Sheik, *118*
Valenza, Tasia: Rappin', *936*
Valerie, Jeanne: Les Liaisons Dangereuses, *759*
Valkenburgh, Deborah Van: Phantom of the Ritz, *874*
Valkis, Helen: Old Barn Dance, The, *1136*
Vallance, Louise: Robbers of the Sacred Mountain, *107*
Vallee, Marcel: Topaze (1951), *796*

Vallee, Rudy: Admiral Was a Lady, The, *222;* Bachelor and the Bobby-Soxer, The, *230;* Beautiful Blonde from Bashful Bend, The, *233;* How to Succeed in Business without Really Trying, *923;* It's in the Bag, *308;* Mad Wednesday, *325;* Palm Beach Story, The, *353;* People Are Funny, *356;* Second Fiddle, *938;* Sin of Harold Diddlebock (a.k.a. Mad Wednesday), *379;* Unfaithfully Yours (1948), *403;* Vagabond Lover, The, *947*
Valletta, Al: Runaway Nightmare, *109*
Valli, Alida: Eyes without a Face, *735;* Il Grido, *747;* Miracle of the Bells, The, *595;* Oedipus Rex (1967), *772;* Paradine Case, The, *1004;* Spider's Stratagem, The, *788;* Suspiria, *891;* Third Man, The, *1024;* Walk Softly, Stranger, *1030;* Wanton Contessa, The, *802;* We the Living, *802;* White Tower, The, *701*
Valli, Frankie: Dirty Laundry, *265*
Valli, Romolo: Bobby Deerfield, *465;* Fistful of Dynamite, A, *1113*
Vallin, Rick: Ghosts on the Loose, *286;* Jungle Jim, *69;* Last of the Redmen, *1126;* Riders of the Rio Grande, *1144;* Sea Hound, The, *112*
Vallone, Raf: Almost Perfect Affair, An, *225;* Bitter Rice, *718;* Catholics, *477;* Christopher Columbus (1985), *25;* El Cid, *43;* Greek Tycoon, The, *533;* Gunfight, A, *1117;* Harlow, *536;* Honor Thy Father, *543;* Nevada Smith, *1135;* Other Side of Midnight, The, *615;* Season of Giants, A, *650;* Summertime Killer, The, *122;* Time to Die, A (1983), *130;* Two Women, *797*
Vallone, Saverio: Grim Reaper, The (1980), *847*
Valois, Valerie: Scanners 3: The Takeover, *883*
Van Ark, Joan: Frogs, *844;* Red Flag: The Ultimate Game, *104;* Tainted Blood, *1022*
Van Atta, Lee: Dick Tracy (1937), *38;* Undersea Kingdom, *1087*
Van Bergen, Lewis: South of Reno, *663*
Van, Bobby: Affairs of Dobie Gillis, The, *906;* Bunco, *21;* Kiss Me Kate, *927;* Navy vs. the Night Monsters, The, *868;* Small Town Girl, *940*
Van Bridge, Tony: Pied Piper of Hamelin, The, *195*
Van Cleef, Lee: Armed Response, *6;* Bad Man's River, *1095;* Beyond the Law, *1097;* Bravados, The, *1101;* Bullet from God, A, *1102;* Captain Apache, *1103;* China Gate, *481;* Code Name: Wild Geese, *27;* Commandos, *28;* Death Rides a Horse, *1108;* El Condor, *1111;* Escape from New York, *45;* For a Few Dollars More, *1113;* God's Gun, *1116;* Good the Bad and the Ugly, The, *1116;* Gunfight at the O.K. Corral, *1117;* Hard Way, The (1979), *59;* It Conquered the World, *1060;* Jungle Raiders, *69;* Kansas City Confidential, *988;* Lonely Man, The, *1129;* Man Alone, A, *1131;* Man Who Shot Liberty Valance, The, *1132;* Octagon, The, *93;* Ride Lonesome, *1143;* Stranger and the Gunfighter, The, *1153;* Take a Hard Ride, *1154;* Ten Wanted Men, *1155;* Thieves of Fortune, *127;* Tin Star, The, *1157*
Van Dam, José: Music Teacher, The, *769*
van Damme, Gabrielle: Marquis, *765*
Van Damme, Jean-Claude: Black Eagle, *13;* Bloodsport, *16;* Cyborg, *1043;* Death Warrant, *35;* Double Impact, *41;* Hard Target, *59;* Kickboxer, *70;* No Retreat, No Surrender, *92;* Nowhere to Run (1993), *92*
van de Ven, Monique: Amsterdamned, *809;* Assault, The, *714;* Katie's Passion, *751;* Turkish Delight, *797*
Van Den Bergh, Gert: Naked Prey, The, *88*
van den Elsen, Sylvie: L'Argent, *752*
Van Der Velde, Nadine: Shadow Dancing, *1014*
Van Der Vlis, Diana: X (The Man with the X-Ray Eyes), *1090*
Van Der Wat, Keith: Three Bullets for a Long Gun, *1156*
Van Devere, Trish: Changeling, The, *822;* Day of the Dolphin, The, *1044;* Hearse, The, *849;* Hollywood Vice Squad, *63;* Messenger of Death, *84;* Movie Movie, *338;* Savage Is Loose, The, *648;* Where's Poppa?, *409*
Van Doren, Mamie: Free Ride, *281;* Girls Town, *55;* High School Confidential!, *541;* Las Vegas Hillbillys, *315;* Navy vs. the Night Monsters, The, *868;* Running Wild (1955), *645;* Teacher's Pet, *392;* Three Nuts in Search of a Bolt, *396*
van Dreelen, John: Great Wallendas, The, *533*
Van Dyke, Barry: Casino, *476;* Foxfire Light, *521*
Van Dyke, Conny: Framed (1975), *52;* Hell's Angels '69, *60*
Van Dyke, Dick: Bye Bye Birdie, *910;* Chitty Chitty Bang Bang, *158;* Cold Turkey, *257;* Comic, The (1969), *486;* Country Girl, The (1982), *489;* Dick Tracy (1990), *38;* Lt. Robin Crusoe, U.S.N., *181;* Mary Poppins, *185;* Never a Dull Moment, *191;* Runner Stumbles, The, *645*
Van Dyke, Jerry: Courtship of Eddie's Father, The, *260;* McLintock!, *1133;* Run if You Can, *645*
Van Eyck, Peter: Brain, The (1965), *1040;* Bridge at Remagen, The, *469;* Run for the Sun, *109;* Spy Who Came in from the Cold, The, *664;* Thousand Eyes of Dr. Mabuse, The, *1083;* Wages of Fear, The, *801*
Van Fleet, Jo: East of Eden (1955), *506;* Gunfight at the O.K. Corral, *1117;* I Love You Alice B. Toklas!, *304;* I'll Cry Tomorrow, *924;* Rose Tattoo, The, *644*
Van Hentenryck, Kevin: Basket Case, *811;* Basket Case 2, *811*
Van Herwijnen, Carol: Still Smokin', *386*
Van Kamp, Merete: Princess Daisy, *627*
Van Lidth, Erland: Alone in the Dark, *808*
Van Loon, Robert: Paisan, *775*
Van Luik, Robert: Saturday Night Special, *111*
Van Ness, Jon: Bostonians, The, *467;* Hospital Massacre, *852;* Tourist Trap, *1026*
Van Pallandt, Nina: American Gigolo, *446;* Assault on Agathon, *7;* Diary of a Young Comic, *264;* Jungle Warriors, *69;* Long Goodbye, The, *993*
Van Patten, Dick: Charly, *1041;* Diary of a Teenage Hitchhiker, *501;* Final Embrace, *977;* Gus, *172;* High Anxiety, *297;* Midnight Hour, *864;* Robin Hood: Men in Tights, *369;* Son of Blob (Beware! The Blob), *888;* Spaceballs, *384;* When Things Were Rotten (TV Series), *409*
Van Patten, James: Nightforce, *91;* Tennessee Stallion, *126;* Young Warriors, The, *141*
Van Patten, Joyce: Annie Oakley (1985), *146;* Billy Galvin, *461;* Eleanor: First Lady of the World, *508;* Goddess, The, *528;* Mikey and Nicky, *332;* Monkey Shines: An Experiment in Fear, *865;* St. Elmo's Fire, *646;* Stranger Within, The, *891*
Van Patten, Nels: Mirror Images, *996;* One Last Run, *613;* Summer School, *388*
Van Patten, Timothy: Class of 1984, *824;* Curse IV: The Ultimate Sacrifice, *828;* Zone Troopers, *1091*
Van Patten, Vincent: Charley and the Angel, *157;* Chino, *1104;* Hell Night, *849;* Rock 'n' Roll High School, *369*
Van Peebles, Mario: Delivery Boys, *263;* Exterminator 2, The, *45;* Gunmen, *58;* Heartbreak Ridge, *59;* Hot Shot, *544;* Identity Crisis, *304;* Jaws: The Revenge, *858;* New Jack City, *90;* Posse (1993), *1139;* Rappin', *936;* 3:15—The Moment of Truth, *128*
Van Peebles, Melvin: O.C. & Stiggs, *348;* Posse (1993), *1139;* Sophisticated Gents, The, *663;* Sweet Sweetback's Baadasssss Song, *123*
Van Sickel, Dale: Crimson Ghost, The, *30;* King of the Rocketmen, *72*
Van Sloan, Edward: Before I Hang, *812;* Death Kiss, The, *968;* Deluge, *1046;* Dracula (1931), *837;* Dracula's Daughter, *837;* Mummy, The (1932), *866;* Riders of the Rio Grande, *1144*
Van Tongeren, Hans: Spetters, *788*
van Uchelen, Marc: Assault, The, *714*
Van Valkenburgh, Deborah: Brain Smasher...A Love Story, *18;* Bunny's Tale, A, *472;* Rampage, *1009;* Warriors, The (1979), *137*
Van Vooren, Monique: Andy Warhol's Frankenstein, *809;* Ash Wednesday, *451;* Sugar Cookies, *672*
Vance, Courtney B.: Adventures of Huck Finn, The (1993), *143;* Hamburger Hill, *535*

Vance, Danitra: Jumpin' at the Boneyard, *561;* Limit Up, *319;* Sticky Fingers, *386*
Vance, Vivian: Great Race, The, *290;* I Love Lucy (TV Series), *303*
Vandergaw, Terra: '68, *659*
Vandernoot, Alexandra: Highlander: The Gathering, *1056*
Vandis, Titos: Young Doctors in Love, *415*
Vane, Amy: Secret Cinema, The, *374*
Vanel, Charles: Diabolique, *730;* Wages of Fear, The, *801*
Vanity: Action Jackson, *2;* Davinci's War, *33;* Deadly Illusion, *968;* 52 Pick-Up, *976;* Highlander: The Gathering, *1056;* Last Dragon, The, *75;* Memories of Murder, *996;* Neon City, *1067;* Never Too Young to Die, *90;* South Beach, *1019*
VanKamp, Merete: Lethal Woman, *77*
Varconi, Victor: Everything Happens at Night, *273*
Varden, Evelyn: Athena, *907*
Varden, Norma: Mademoiselle Fifi, *585*
Varela, Amanda: Falcon's Brother, The, *975*
Vargas, Valentina: Tigress, The, *130*
Varney, Jim: Beverly Hillbillies, The, *237;* Dr. Otto and the Riddle of the Gloom Beam, *266;* Ernest Film Festival, *272;* Ernest Goes to Camp, *272;* Ernest Goes to Jail, *272;* Ernest Rides Again, *272;* Ernest Saves Christmas, *165;* Ernest Scared Stupid, *272;* Fast Food, *274;* Knowhutimean?, *314;* Rousters, The, *109;* Wilder Napalm, *411*
Varney, Reg: Great St. Trinian's Train Robbery, The, *290*
Varsi, Diane: Compulsion, *487;* I Never Promised You a Rose Garden, *547;* Johnny Got His Gun, *559;* People, The, *1070;* Peyton Place, *621;* Sweet Love, Bitter, *675;* Wild in the Streets, *1089*
Vasconcelos, Tito: Danzon, *728*
Vasquez, José Luis Lopez: Garden of Delights, The, *739*
Vasquez, Roberta: Do or Die, *40;* Fit to Kill, *49*
Vattier, Robert: Le Schpountz, *758*
Vaughan, Alberta: Randy Rides Alone, *1141*
Vaughan, Peter: Bleak House, *463;* Blockhouse, The, *464;* Die! Die! My Darling!, *834;* Forbidden, *519;* Haunted Honeymoon, *294;* Remains of the Day, *637;* Straw Dogs, *1021*
Vaughan, Sarah: Ladies Sing the Blues, The, *428*
Vaughan, Vanessa: Crazy Moon, *490*
Vaughn, Martin: Phar Lap, *621*
Vaughn, Ned: Chips, the War Dog, *158*
Vaughn, Robert: Battle Beyond the Stars, *1038;* Black Moon Rising, *14;* Blind Vision, *956;* Blue and the Gray, The, *1099;* Brass Target, *19;* Bridge at Remagen, The, *469;* Bullitt, *21;* C.H.U.D. II (Bud the C.H.U.D.), *820;* Captive Rage, *23;* City in Fear, *962;* Delta Force, The, *36;* Going Under, *288;* Hangar 18, *1055;* Hitchhiker (Series), The, *850;* Hour of the Assassin, *64;* Inside the Third Reich, *552;* Julius Caesar (1970), *561;* Kill Castro, *71;* Magnificent Seven, The, *1131;* Man from U.N.C.L.E., The (TV Series), *80;* Nightstick, *91;* Nobody's Perfect, *346;* Prince of Bel Air, *627;* Question of Honor, A, *632;* Return of the Man from U.N.C.L.E., The, *105;* River of Death, *107;* S.O.B., *372;* Shaming, The, *655;* Starship Invasions, *1080;* Statue, The, *385;* Superman III, *1081;* Transylvania Twist, *399;* Young Philadelphians, The, *708*
Vaughter, Marcus: Visitants, The, *1087*
Vawter, Ron: Philadelphia, *621;* Swoon, *675*
Ve Sota, Bruno: Attack of the Giant Leeches, *810;* Daddy-O, *31;* Daughter of Horror, *829*
Vega, Isela: Barbarosa, *1097;* Bring Me the Head of Alfredo Garcia, *20;* Deadly Trackers, The, *1108;* Streets of L.A., The, *671*
Veidt, Conrad: Above Suspicion, *1;* All Through the Night, *3;* Beloved Rogue, *954;* Cabinet of Doctor Caligari, The, *721;* Dark Journey, *966;* Spy in Black, The, *664;* Student of Prague, *790;* Thief of Bagdad, The (1940), *1083;* Waxworks, *802;* Whistling in the Dark, *410;* Woman's Face, A, *705*
Vel Johnson, Reginald: Die Hard, *38;* Die Hard 2: Die Harder, *39;* Posse (1993), *1139;* Seven Hours to Judgment, *113*
Velasquez, Andres: Littlest Outlaw, The, *184*
Velazquez, Lorena: Doctor of Doom, *836;* Rock 'n' Roll Wrestling Women vs. the Aztec Mummy, *369*
Veld, Hansman In't: Still Smokin', *386*
Velez, Eddie: Doin' Time, *266;* Romero, *643;* Rooftops, *937;* Women's Club, The, *413*
Velez, Lupe: Hollywood Party, *299;* Mexican Spitfire, *331;* Palooka, *617;* Where East Is East, *138*
Ven, Monique van de: Lily Was Here, *575*
Venable, Evelyn: Alice Adams, *444;* Frontiersman, The, *1114;* Harmony Lane, *922;* Heritage of the Desert, *1120;* Little Colonel, The, *928;* Mrs. Wiggs of the Cabbage Patch, *598*
Venantini, Luca: Aladdin (1987), *144;* Exterminators of the Year 3000, *1050*
Venantini, Venantino: Final Justice, *48*
Veninger, Ingrid: Hush Little Baby, *984*
Vennera, Chick: Double Threat, *504;* High Risk, *61;* Kidnapped (1988), *71;* Milagro Beanfield War, The, *594;* Terror Within 2, The, *894*
Venora, Diane: Bird, *909;* F/X, *979;* Terminal Choice, *893;* Wolfen, *904*
Ventantonio, John: Private Parts, *876*
Venton, Harley: Blood Ties (1993), *816*
Ventura, Clyde: Gator Bait, *55*
Ventura, Jesse: Abraxas Guardian of the Universe, *1034*
Ventura, Lino: French Detective, The, *738;* Happy New Year (La Bonne Année), *743;* Les Grandes Gueules (Jailbirds' Vacation), *759;* Medusa Touch, The, *864;* Pain in the A—, A, *774;* Sword of Gideon, *123*
Ventura, Viviane: Battle Beneath the Earth, *9*
Venture, Richard: Scent of a Woman, *649*
Vera, Billy: Baja Oklahoma, *455;* Finish Line, *516*
Vera, Victoria: Monster Dog, *865*
Vera-Ellen: Belle of New York, The, *908;* Happy Go Lovely, *921;* Kid from Brooklyn, The, *313;* On the Town, *934;* Three Little Words, *945;* White Christmas, *947;* Wonder Man, *413;* Words and Music, *948*
Verdon, Gwen: Alice (1990), *224;* Cocoon, *1042;* Cocoon: The Return, *1042;* Damn Yankees, *913;* Nadine, *341*
Verdon, Loren A.: King of the Kickboxers, The, *72*
Verdone, Carlo: Aqua E Sapone, *713*
Verdu, Maribel: Lovers (1992), *762*
Verdugo, Elena: Big Sombrero, The, *1098;* House of Frankenstein, *852;* Moon and Sixpence, The, *599*
Verea, Lisette: Night in Casablanca, A, *344*
Vereen, Ben: Buy and Cell, *248;* Ellis Island, *508;* Funny Lady, *918;* Gas-s-s-s, *1054;* Puss in Boots, *198;* Roots, *644;* Zoo Gang, The, *416*
Verica, Tom: 800 Leagues Down the Amazon, *43*
Verley, Bernard: Chloe in the Afternoon, *723;* Milky Way, The (1970), *767*
Verley, Françoise: Chloe in the Afternoon, *723*
Verlin, Melanie: Midnight (1980), *864*
Verlo, Lisa: Love Street, *582*
Vermes, David: Hungarian Fairy Tale, A, *745*
Verne, Kaaren: All Through the Night, *3;* Sherlock Holmes and the Secret Weapon, *1015*
Vernon, Anne: Therese and Isabelle, *794*
Vernon, Howard: Angel of Death, *5;* Blood Rose, *816;* Bob le Flambeur, *719;* Castle of the Creeping Flesh, *822;* Virgin Among the Living Dead, A, *901;* Women in Cell Block 9, *140;* Zombie Lake, *905*
Vernon, Jackie: Hungry I Reunion, *303;* Microwave Massacre, *864;* Young at Heart Comedians, The, *415*
Vernon, John: Angela, *448;* Animal House, *227;* Bail Out, *8;* Black Windmill, The, *956;* Blue Monkey, *817;* Border Heat, *17;* Brannigan, *18;* Chained Heat, *24;* Charley Varrick, *25;* Curtains, *828;* Deadly Stranger, *35;* Dirty Harry, *39;* Dixie Lanes, *265;* Doin' Time, *266;* Double Exposure (1987), *268;* Ernest Goes to Camp, *272;* Hammered: The Best of Sledge, *292;* Herbie Goes Bananas, *174;* Hunter (1971), *65;* I'm

Gonna Git You Sucka!, *305;* Jungle Warriors, *69;* Justine, *561;* Killer Klowns from Outer Space, *859;* Mob Story, *335;* Nightstick, *91;* Outlaw Josey Wales, The, *1137;* Point Blank, *624;* Ray Bradbury's Chronicles: The Martian Episodes, *1073;* Savage Streets, *111;* Topaz, *1026;* Uncanny, The, *899;* W, *1030*

Vernon, Kate: Alphabet City, *445;* Hostile Take Over, *544;* Last of Philip Banter, The, *991;* Malcolm X, *586;* Mob Story, *335;* Roadhouse 66, *107*

Vernon, Sherri: 10 Violent Women, *126*

Vernon, Ted: Scarecrows, *883*

Vernon, Wally: Happy Landing, *921*

Verrell, Cec: Mad at the Moon, *861*

Versini, Marie: Escape from the KGB, *45*

Versois, Odile: Cartouche, *722;* Room 43, *644;* To Paris with Love, *397*

Vessel, Edy: Passionate Thief, The (1961), *776*

Vetri, Victoria: Invasion of the Bee Girls, *1059;* When Dinosaurs Ruled the Earth, *1089*

Veugelers, Marijke: Egg, *733*

Viallargeon, Paule: I've Heard the Mermaids Singing, *309*

Vianello, Venetia: Dead Aim (1973), *1108*

Viard, Karen: Delicatessen, *729*

Vicious, Sid: Great Rock and Roll Swindle, The, *921;* Mr. Mike's Mondo Video, *334*

Vickers, Martha: Big Bluff, The, *460;* Big Sleep, The (1946), *955;* Man I Love, The, *586*

Vickers, Yvette: Attack of the 50-Foot Woman (1958), *810;* Attack of the Giant Leeches, *810;* I, Mobster, *65*

Victor, Gloria: Daddy-O, *31*

Victor, Katherine: Teenage Zombies, *892;* Wild World of Batwoman, The, *1089*

Vida, Piero: Dead for a Dollar, *1108*

Vidal, Christina: Life with Mikey, *318*

Vidal, Gore: Bob Roberts, *243;* With Honors, *412*

Vidal, Henri: Sois Belle Et Tais-Toi (Just Another Pretty Face), *787;* Voulez Vous Danser avec Moi? (Will You Dance with Me?), *801*

Vidan, Richard: Scarecrows, *883*

Videnovic, Gala: Hey, Babu Riba, *743*

Vidler, Steven: Encounter at Raven's Gate, *1049;* Good Wife, The, *530;* Three's Trouble, *396;* Wrangler, *141*

Vidor, Florance: Jack Knife Man, The, *556*

Vidor, Florence: Are Parents People?, *228;* Marriage Circle, The, *329;* Virginian, The (1923), *1161*

Viellard, Eric: Boyfriends and Girlfriends, *720*

Vignolle, Gregory: Illegal Entry, *66*

Vigoda, Abe: Cheap Detective, The, *254;* Joe Versus the Volcano, *310;* Keaton's Cop, *70;* Newman's Law, *90;* Plain Clothes, *358;* Prancer, *197;* Sugar Hill, *122;* Vasectomy, *404*

Viharo, Robert: Bare Knuckles, *9;* Happy Birthday, Gemini, *293;* Hide in Plain Sight, *541*

Vilar, Antonio: Have a Nice Funeral, *1119*

Village People, The: Can't Stop the Music, *911*

Villagra, Nelson: Last Supper, The, *755*

Villalpando, David: El Norte, *733*

Villard, Tom: Force Five, *51;* Heartbreak Ridge, *59;* One Crazy Summer, *349;* Parasite, *873;* Popcorn, *876;* Swimsuit, *390;* Trouble with Dick, The, *1085;* Weekend Warriors, *407*

Villarias, Carlos: Dracula (Spanish Version), *732*

Villarreal, Julio: Woman without Love, A, *805*

Villaume, Astrid: Famous Five Get into Trouble, The, *166*

Villechaize, Herve: Forbidden Zone, *1053;* Greaser's Palace, *532;* Man with the Golden Gun, The, *81;* One and Only, The, *613;* Return to Fantasy Island, *1074;* Rumpelstiltskin (1980), *200;* Seizure, *884*

Villella, Michael: Slumber Party Massacre, *887*

Villemaire, James: Gate II, *845*

Villeret, Jacques: Edith and Marcel, *733;* Robert et Robert, *782*

Villiers, James: Alphabet Murders, The, *951;* Half a Sixpence, *921;* Saint Jack, *646;* Scarlet Pimpernel, The (1982), *112*

Vince, Pruitt Taylor: China Moon, *961*

Vincent, Alex: Child's Play 2, *823*

Vincent and His Blue Caps, Gene: Girl Can't Help It, The, *286*

Vincent, Frank: Mortal Thoughts, *997;* Raging Bull, *633*

Vincent, Helen: They Call It Sin, *680*

Vincent, Jan-Michael: Alienator, *1035;* Bandits (1967), *1096;* Beyond the Call of Duty, *11;* Big Wednesday, *461;* Bite the Bullet, *1099;* Born in East L.A., *244;* Buster and Billie, *472;* Crossfire (1986), *1106;* Damnation Alley, *1044;* Deadly Embrace, *34;* Defiance, *36;* Demonstone, *833;* Divine Enforcer, *40;* Enemy Territory, *44;* Get Out of My Room, *284;* Hard Country, *293;* Haunting Fear, *849;* Hidden Obsession, *982;* Hit List (1988), *982;* Hooper, *300;* In Gold We Trust, *66;* Indecent Behavior, *551;* Last Plane Out, *75;* Mechanic, The, *83;* Midnight Witness, *996;* Raw Nerve, *103;* Return, The, *1074;* Sins of Desire, *1017;* Tribes, *688;* Undefeated, The, *1160;* White Line Fever, *139;* Winds of War, The, *703;* World's Greatest Athlete, The, *218;* Xtro II, *1090*

Vincent, June: Can't Help Singing, *911*

Vincent, Romo: Naked Jungle, The, *88*

Vincent, Virginia: Hills Have Eyes, The, *850;* I Want to Live!, *548*

Vincz, Melanie: Lost Empire, The, *79*

Ving, Lee: Black Moon Rising, *14;* Dudes, *505;* Grave Secrets, *847;* Oceans of Fire, *93;* Scenes from the Goldmine, *649;* Taking of Beverly Hills, The, *124*

Vinson, Gary: High School Caesar, *62;* Majority of One, A *326*

Vinson, Helen: Beyond Tomorrow, *1039;* Broadway Bill, *470;* I Am a Fugitive from a Chain Gang, *547;* In Name Only, *550;* Thin Man Goes Home, The, *1024;* Transatlantic Tunnel, *1085*

Vint, Alan: Badlands, *454;* Ballad of Gregorio Cortez, The, *1096;* Macon County Line, *80;* Unholy Rollers, *691*

Vint, Jesse: Bobbie Jo and the Outlaw, *17;* Dempsey, *499;* Forbidden World, *842;* On the Line, *94;* Pigs, *875*

Vintas, Gustav: Vampire at Midnight, *899*

Vinton, Bobby: Big Jake, *1098*

Vinton, Victoria: Singing Buckaroo, *1150*

Virgili, Elisabetta: Great Adventure, The, *1116*

Virieux, Denise: Northern Extremes, *346*

Visser, Angela: Hot Under the Collar, *302;* Killer Tomatoes Eat France, *313*

Vita, Perlo: Rififi, *1010*

Vitale, Mario: Stromboli, *790*

Vitale, Milly: Seven Little Foys, The, *376*

Vitali, Keith: No Retreat, No Surrender 3: Blood Brothers, *92;* Revenge of the Ninja, *106*

Vitold, Michel: Judex, *750*

Vitte, Ray: Thank God It's Friday, *944*

Vitti, Monica: Almost Perfect Affair, An, *225;* Eclipse, The, *733;* Immortal Bachelor, The, *747;* L'Aventura, *753;* Phantom of Liberty, The, *777;* Red Desert, *780*

Viva: Ciao! Manhattan, *482;* Forbidden Zone, *1053;* State of Things, The, *789*

Vlady, Marina: Double Agents, *971;* Le Complot (The Conspiracy), *757*

Vlastas, Michael: Blackbelt 2: Fatal Force, *14*

Vogel, Darlene: Ring of Steel, *106*

Vogel, Jack: Lock and Load, *993;* Presumed Guilty, *626*

Vogel, Mitch: Menace on the Mountain, *593;* Reivers, The, *365*

Vogel, Nicholas: Inheritors, The, *748*

Vogler, Rudiger: Alice in the City, *711;* Kings of the Road, *752;* Wrong Move, The, *805*

Vohs, Joan: Cry Vengeance, *492*

Voight, Jon: Champ, The (1979), *479;* Chernobyl: The Final Warning, *480;* Coming Home, *486;* Conrack, *488;* Deliverance, *36;* Desert Bloom, *499;* Eternity, *511;* Last of His Tribe, The, *570;* Lookin' to Get Out, *321;* Midnight Cowboy, *593;* Odessa File, The, *1003;* Rainbow Warrior, *1008;* Return to Lonesome Dove, *1143;* Runaway Train, *110;* Table for Five, *676*

Vojnov, Dimitrie: Tito and Me, *795*

Volante, Vicki: Horror of the Blood Monsters, *1057*

Vold, Ingrid: To Sleep With a Vampire, *896*

Volger, Rudiger: Faraway, So Close, *736*

Volk, Daniel: Yo-Yo Man, *415*

Vollmer, Mary: Last Chants for a Slow Dance, *568*

Volonté, Gian Maria: Bullet for the General, A, *1102;* Christ Stopped at Eboli, *724;* Fistful of Dollars, A, *1113;* For a Few Dollars More, *1113;* Lucky Luciano, *79;* Open Doors, *774;* Sacco and Vanzetti, *782*

Volter, Philippe: Music Teacher, The, *769*

Von Bargen, Daniel: Last Hit, The, *990*

von Blanc, Christina: Virgin Among the Living Dead, A, *901*

Von Dohlen, Lenny: Billy Galvin, *461;* Dracula's Widow, *837;* Electric Dreams, *271;* Eyes of the Beholder, *974;* Jennifer 8, *987;* Leaving Normal, *572;* Love Kills, *993;* Under the Biltmore Clock, *691*

von Franckenstein, Clement: Underground (1990), *1029*

Von Hausen, Paul: Demons of Ludlow, The, *833*

Von Klier, Annette: Cop and the Girl, The, *726*

Von Koszian, Johanna: For the First Time, *918*

Von Nutter, Rik: Tharus, Son of Attila, *127*

Von Palleske, Heidi: Dead Ringers, *831*

von Seyffertitz, Gustav: Ambassador Bill, *225;* Down to Earth, *268;* Mysterious Lady, The, *603;* Sparrows, *664;* Student Prince in Old Heidelberg, The, *671*

Von Stroheim, Erich: As You Desire Me, *451;* Blind Husbands, *464;* Foolish Wives, *518;* Fugitive Road, *523;* Grand Illusion, *742;* Great Flamarion, The, *532;* Great Gabbo, The, *532;* Intolerance, *553;* Lost Squadron, *79;* Napoleon (1955), *603;* So Ends Our Night, *661;* Sunset Boulevard, *673;* Unnatural, *1029;* Wedding March, The, *697*

von Sydow, Max: Awakenings, *452;* Belarus File, The, *954;* Best Intentions, The, *717;* Brass Target, *19;* Brink of Life, *720;* Christopher Columbus (1985), *25;* Code Name: Emerald, *27;* Death Watch, *1045;* Dreamscape, *1048;* Duet for One, *505;* Dune, *1048;* Exorcist, The, *839;* Exorcist II: The Heretic, *840;* Flash Gordon, *1052;* Flight of the Eagle, *737;* Foxtrot, *521;* Greatest Story Ever Told, The, *533;* Hannah and Her Sisters, *293;* Hawaii, *537;* Hiroshima: Out of the Ashes, *541;* Hour of the Wolf, *745;* Hurricane (1979), *65;* Kiss Before Dying, A, *989;* Magician, The, *764;* March or Die, *82;* Miss Julie, *767;* Never Say Never Again, *89;* Night Visitor, The (1970), *607;* Passion of Anna, The, *776;* Pelle the Conqueror, *776;* Quiller Memorandum, The, *102;* Red King, White Knight, *636;* Samson and Delilah (1984), *648;* Seventh Seal, The, *785;* Steppenwolf, *667;* Strange Brew, *387;* Target Eagle, *125;* Three Days of the Condor, *1025;* Through a Glass Darkly, *795;* Ultimate Warrior, The, *1087;* Until the End of the World, *1087;* Victory, *135;* Virgin Spring, The, *801;* Voyage of the Damned, *694;* Winter Light, *804*

Von Trotta, Margarethe: American Soldier, The, *712;* Coup De Grace, *726;* Gods of the Plague, *741*

von Waggenheim, Gustav: Nosferatu, *772;* Woman in the Moon (a.k.a. Girl in the Moon; By Rocket to the Moon), *805*

Von Zell, Harry: George Burns and Gracie Allen Show, The (TV Series), *284;* Son of Paleface, *383;* Strange Affair of Uncle Harry, The, *669*

von Zerneck, Danielle: Dangerous Curves, *262;* La Bamba, *927;* My Science Project, *1067;* Under the Boardwalk, *691*

Voskovec, George: Barbarosa, *1097;* Skag, *659;* Spy Who Came in from the Cold, The, *664;* 12 Angry Men, *690*

Vosloo, Arnold: Finishing Touch, The, *977;* Hard Target, *59*

Vostricil, Jan: Fireman's Ball, The, *737*

Votrian, Peter J.: Fear Strikes Out, *515*

Voutsinas, Andreas: Dream of Passion, A, *504*

Voyagis, Yorgo: Bourne Identity, The, *958;* Little Drummer Girl, The, *992;* Running Delilah, *110*

Vrana, Vlasta: Lifeforce Experiment, The, *1063*

Vreeken, Ron: Deathfight, *36*

Vries, Jon De: Zelda, *709*

Vuilemin, Philippe: Mystery of Alexina, The, *770*

Vultaggio, Lisa: Mortal Sins (1992), *997*

Vye, Murvyn: Connecticut Yankee in King Arthur's Court, A (1948), *258;* Escape to Burma, *510;* Golden Earrings, *56;* Pearl of the South Pacific, *620;* Road to Bali, *368*

Vystocil, Ivan: Report on the Party and the Guests, A, *781*

Waddington, Steven: Edward II, *507;* Last of the Mohicans, The (1992), *1126*

Wade, Ernestine: Amos and Andy (TV Series), *226*

Wade, Russell: Renegade Girl, *1142;* Sundown Riders, *1153*

Wade, Stuart: Meteor Monster, *864;* Monster from the Ocean Floor, The, *866*

Waegner, Eva: Paradisio, *353*

Waggoner, Lyle: Gypsy Angels, *535;* Journey to the Center of Time, *1060;* Surf 2, *389;* Women of the Prehistoric Planet, *1090*

Wagner, Chuck: Sisterhood, The, *1077*

Wagner, Cristie: She-Devils on Wheels, *115*

Wagner, Jack: Swimsuit, *390*

Wagner, Lindsay: Bionic Woman, The, *1039;* Callie and Son, *474;* Convicted, *488;* From the Dead of Night, *844;* High Risk, *61;* Incredible Journey of Dr. Meg Laurel, The, *551;* Martin's Day, *185;* Nighthawks, *91;* Nightmare at Bittercreek, *1002;* Paper Chase, The, *617;* Princess Daisy, *627;* Ricochet, *106;* Rockford Files, The (TV Series), *108;* Treacherous Crossing, *1027;* Two Worlds of Jennie Logan, The, *1086*

Wagner, Natasha Gregson: Substitute, The, *1021;* Tainted Blood, *1022*

Wagner, Robert: Affair, The, *442;* Airport '79: The Concorde, *443;* Beneath the 12-Mile Reef, *10;* Between Heaven and Hell, *459;* Broken Lance, *1101;* Curse of the Pink Panther, The, *261;* Death at Love House, *968;* Deep Trouble, *969;* Dragon: The Bruce Lee Story, *42;* False Arrest, *513;* Halls of Montezuma, *59;* Harper, *981;* I Am the Cheese, *547;* It Takes a Thief (TV Series), *68;* Let's Make It Legal, *318;* Longest Day, The, *78;* Madame Sin, *80;* Mountain, The, *600;* Pink Panther, The, *357;* Prince Valiant, *100;* Stars and Stripes Forever, *941;* Stopover Tokyo, *120;* This Gun for Hire (1991), *128;* To Catch a King, *1025;* Trail of the Pink Panther, The, *398;* War Lover, The, *696;* What Price Glory, *408;* Windmills of the Gods, *703;* Winning, *140*

Wagner, Thomas: Dead On, *967;* Marilyn & Bobby: Her Final Affair, *588*

Wagner, Wende: Green Hornet, The (TV Series), *58*

Wagstaff, Elsie: Whistle Down the Wind, *216*

Wah, Yuen: Police Story III—Super Cop, *778*

Wahl, Adam: Deadmate, *831*

Wahl, Ken: Dirty Dozen, The: The Next Mission, *39;* Favor, The, *275;* Fort Apache—The Bronx, *520;* Gladiator, The, *55;* Jinxed, *310;* Omega Syndrome, *93;* Purple Hearts, *631;* Running Scared (1980), *110;* Soldier, The, *118;* Taking of Beverly Hills, The, *124;* Treasure of the Yankee Zephyr, *132;* Wanderers, The, *695*

Wainwright, James: Private Files of J. Edgar Hoover, The, *100;* Survivors, The, *389;* Warlords of the 21st Century, *1088;* Woman Called Moses, A, *705*

Waite, Michael: Fun Down There, *523*

Waite, Ralph: Bodyguard, The, *466;* Crash and Burn, *1043;* Five Easy Pieces, *517;* Gentleman Bandit, The, *525;* Last Summer, *570;* Lawman, *1127;* On the Nickel, *612;* Red Alert, *104;* Stone Killer, The, *120;* Thanksgiving Story, The, *210*

Waites, Thomas: Clan of the Cave Bear, *1041;* On the Yard, *94;* Verne Miller, *135;* Warriors, The (1979), *137*

Waits, Tom: At Play in the Fields of the Lord, *451;* Bram Stoker's Dracula, *819;* Candy Mountain, *474;* Cold Feet

(1989), *257;* Down by Law, *268;* Ironweed, *554;* Rumble Fish, *645;* Short Cuts, *657*

Wajnberg, Marc-Henri: Mamma Dracula, *862*

Wakabayashi, Akiko: You Only Live Twice, *141*

Wakao, Ayako: Geisha, A, *740*

Wakayama, Tomisaburo: Bad News Bears Go to Japan, The, *231;* Irezumi (Spirit of Tattoo), *749;* Shogun Assassin, *785*

Wakeham, Deborah: House of the Rising Sun, *64*

Wakely, Jimmy: Across the Rio Grande, *1092;* Ridin' Down the Trail, *1144;* Six Gun Serenade, *1150*

Walbrook, Anton: Dangerous Moonlight (a.k.a. Suicide Squadron), *32;* 49th Parallel, The, *520;* Gaslight (1940), *979;* La Ronde, *754;* Life and Death of Colonel Blimp, The, *574;* Lola Montes, *761;* Red Shoes, The (1948), *936;* Saint Joan, *646*

Walburn, Raymond: Christmas in July, *255;* Count of Monte Cristo, The (1934), *30;* Hail the Conquering Hero, *292;* Key to the City, *312;* Let Freedom Ring, *928;* Louisiana Purchase, *322;* Mad Wednesday, *325;* Sin of Harold Diddlebock (a.k.a. Mad Wednesday), *379;* Thin Ice, *945*

Walcott, Gregory: Jet Attack, *68;* Plan 9 from Outer Space, *1070;* Prime Cut, *100*

Walcott, Jersey Joe: Harder They Fall, The, *536*

Walcott, William: Down to the Sea in Ships, *504*

Walcutt, John: Return, *638*

Walden, Lynette: Almost Blue, *445;* Silencer, The, *116*

Walden, Robert: Bloody Mama, *16;* Blue Sunshine, *957;* Kansas City Massacre, The, *70;* Memorial Day, *592*

Waiss, Wally: Traitor, The, *1158*

Walken, Christopher: All-American Murder, *951;* At Close Range, *953;* Batman Returns, *9;* Biloxi Blues, *240;* Brainstorm, *1040;* Comfort of Strangers, The, *963;* Communion, *1042;* Day of Atonement, *33;* Dead Zone, The, *831;* Deadline (1987), *497;* Deer Hunter, The, *499;* Dogs of War, The, *40;* Heaven's Gate, *1119;* Homeboy, *543;* King of New York, *72;* Last Embrace, The, *990;* McBain, *83;* Milagro Beanfield War, The, *594;* Mind Snatchers, The, *865;* Mistress (1992), *597;* Next Stop, Greenwich Village, *605;* Roseland, *644;* Sarah, Plain and Tall, *648;* Scam, *1012;* Skylark, *660;* True Romance, *133;* View to a Kill, A, *135;* Wayne's World 2, *406;* Who Am I This Time?, *410*

Walker, Albertina: Leap of Faith, *572*

Walker, Ally: Seventh Coin, The, *203;* Universal Soldier, *134*

Walker, Arnetia: Love Crimes, *993*

Walker, Christopher: Echo Park, *507*

Walker, Clint: Baker's Hawk, *148;* Bounty Man, The, *1101;* Cheyenne (TV Series), *1104;* Deadly Harvest, *1045;* Dirty Dozen, The, *39;* Gambler Returns, the: Luck of the Draw, *1115;* Hysterical, *303;* Maya, *186;* Night of the Grizzly, The, *1136;* None But the Brave, *92;* Pancho Villa, *1138;* Send Me No Flowers, *375;* Snowbeast, *888;* White Buffalo, *1164;* Yuma, *1166*

Walker, Dominic: Power of One, The, *625*

Walker, Eric: Ewok Adventure, The, *165*

Walker, Fiona: Norman Conquests, The, Episode 1: Table Manners, *346;* Norman Conquests, The, Episode 2: Living Together, *346;* Norman Conquests, The, Episode 3: Round and Round the Garden, *346*

Walker, Helen: Brewster's Millions (1945), *245;* Call Northside 777, *959;* Impact, *985;* My Dear Secretary, *339;* People Are Funny, *356*

Walker, Jimmie: Doin' Time, *266;* Going Bananas, *169;* Kidnapped (1988), *71;* Let's Do It Again, *318*

Walker, Joyce: Education of Sonny Carson, The, *507*

Walker, Kathryn: Blade, *14;* Dangerous Game, *965;* Murder of Mary Phagan, The, *600;* Neighbors, *343;* Rich Kids, *640;* Special Bulletin, *1019;* Whale for the Killing, A, *698;* Winds of Kitty Hawk, The, *703*

Walker, Kim: Heathers, *295*

Walker, Lou: Nightman, The, *1001*

Walker, Marcy: Hot Resort, *301;* Midnight's Child, *865*

Walker, Nancy: Best Foot Forward, *908;* Forty Carats, *279;* Girl Crazy, *919;* Lucky Me, *929;* Thursday's Game, *683*

Walker, Nella: They Call It Sin, *680*

Walker, Polly: Enchanted April, *271;* Lorna Doone, *580;* Sliver, *1018*

Walker, Robert: Bataan, *9;* Clock, The, *484;* Evil Town, *839;* Hambone and Hillie, *535;* Madame Curie, *584;* One Touch of Venus, *350;* Sea of Grass, The, *1148;* Since You Went Away, *658;* Son of Blob (Beware! The Blob), *888;* Song of Love, *662;* Strangers on a Train, *1020;* Thirty Seconds Over Tokyo, *127;* Till the Clouds Roll By, *946;* Vengeance Valley, *1161*

Walker Jr., Robert: Angkor: Cambodia Express, *5;* Ensign Pulver, *271;* Gone with the West, *1116;* Heated Vengeance, *60;* Little Moon & Jud McGraw, *1128*

Walker, Sarah: Gloriana, *919;* Housekeeping, *545*

Walker, Sydney: Mrs. Doubtfire, *334;* Prelude to a Kiss, *360*

Walker, Terry: Take Me Back to Oklahoma, *1154*

Walker, Zena: Dresser, The, *505*

Walkers, Cheryl: Stage Door Canteen, *665*

Wall, Max: Jabberwocky, *309;* We Think the World of You, *406*

Wallace, Anzac: UTU, *134*

Wallace, Basil: Marked for Death, *82*

Wallace, Beryl: Sunset on the Desert, *1154*

Wallace, Bill: Avenging Force, *8*

Wallace, Chris: New Year's Evil, *868*

Wallace, Coley: Joe Louis Story, The, *558*

Wallace, David: Babysitter, The, *811;* Humongous, *854;* Mazes and Monsters, *864*

Wallace, Dee: Alligator II, *808;* Child Bride of Short Creek, *480;* Club Life, *27;* Critters, *827;* Cujo, *827;* E.T.—The Extra-Terrestrial, *1048;* Hills Have Eyes, The, *850;* Howling, The, *853;* I'm Dangerous Tonight, *855;* Jimmy the Kid, *178;* Legend of the White Horse, *76;* Miracle Down Under, *187;* Popcorn, *876;* Secret Admirer, *374;* Shadow Play, *885;* Skeezer, *659;* Whale for the Killing, A, *698*

Wallace, Gary: Jar, The, *858*

Wallace, George: Gross Jokes, *291;* Joe Piscopo Live!, *310;* Radar Men from the Moon, *102*

Wallace, Jack: Bear, The, *149*

Wallace, Jean: Big Combo, The, *12;* Man in the Eiffel Tower, The, *995;* Sword of Lancelot, *124*

Wallace, Julie T.: Lunatic, The, *324*

Wallace, Larry: Evil Spirits in the House, *839*

Wallace, Linda: Charlie, the Lonesome Cougar, *158*

Wallace, Marcia: Pray TV (1980), *360*

Wallace, Morgan: Billy the Kid Returns, *1099;* Dream Street, *504;* Orphans of the Storm, *615*

Wallace, Sue: Experience Preferred...But Not Essential, *273*

Wallach, Eli: Ace High, *1092;* Article 99, *451;* Baby Doll, *453;* Christopher Columbus (1985), *25;* Cinderella Liberty, *482;* Circle of Iron, *26;* Danger, *965;* Deep, The, *36;* Domino Principle, The, *971;* Executioner's Song, The, *512;* Family Matter, A, *514;* Firepower, *49;* Girlfriends, *528;* Godfather, Part III, The, *529;* Good the Bad and the Ugly, The, *1116;* Hunter, The (1980), *65;* Impossible Spy, The, *985;* Legacy of Lies, *572;* Long Live Your Death, *1130;* Lord Jim, *79;* Magnificent Seven, The, *1131;* Misfits, The, *595;* Mistress (1992), *597;* Moonspinners, The, *189;* Movie Movie, *338;* Night and the City (1992), *605;* Nuts, *1002;* Poppy Is Also a Flower, The, *99;* Pride of Jesse Hallman, The, *626;* Salamander, The, *111;* Sam's Son, *647;* Sentinel, The, *884;* Seven Thieves, *653;* Skokie, *660;* Stateline Motel, *789;* Teamster Boss: The Jackie Presser Story, *678;* Tough Guys, *398;* Two Jakes, The, *1028;* Winter Kills, *704*

Waller, Eddy: Bandits of Dark Canyon, *1096;* Denver Kid, *1109;* Marshal of Cedar Rock, *1132;* Wild Frontier, *1164*

Waller, Fats: Stormy Weather, *942*

Waller, Phillip: Mouse and the Motorcycle, The, *189*

Walley, Deborah: Beach Blanket Bingo, *908;* Benji, *149;* Bon Voyage!, *151;* Gidget Goes Hawaiian, *286;* Severed Arm, The, *885;* Spinout, *941;* Summer Magic, *208*

lls, Shani: Arnold, *810;* Oliver, *933;* Terror in the Wax
eum, *894*
ish, Angela: Distant Voices/Still Lives, *502*
ish, Brigid Conley: Quest of the Delta Knights, *1073*
ish, Dale: New Adventures of Tarzan, *90*
ish, Dermot: Ghost Ship, *846;* Tell-Tale Heart, The, *893*
ish, Emmet: Get to Know Your Rabbit, *285*
ish, Gabriel: Returning, The, *1010*
ish, Gwynyth: Blue Monkey, *817*
ish, J. T.: Blue Chips, *465;* Crazy People, *260;*
nseless, *969;* Few Good Men, A, *976;* Good Morning,
nam, *530;* Grifters, The, *534;* Hoffa, *542;* Iron Maze, *987;*
ning Glory (1992), *599;* Needful Things, *868;* Red Rock
t, *1009;* Russia House, The, *646;* Sniper, *117;* True
tity, *399;* Wired, *704*
ish, Johnny: Wild Women of Wongo, *1089*
ish, Judy: Cannibal Attack, *22*
ish, Kay: Dr. Syn, Alias the Scarecrow, *163;* Encore, *509;*
friars Bobby, *172;* Horse's Mouth, The, *301;* Last Holiday,
; Scrooge (1970), *938;* Sons of the Sea, *663;* Stage
t, *1019;* This Happy Breed, *682;* Tunes of Glory, *689*
ish, Kenneth: Climb, The, *26;* Lost!, *580;* Reno and the
, *638*
ish, M. Emmet: Back to School, *230;* Best of Times, The,
; Bitter Harvest (1993), *955;* Blade Runner, *1039;* Blood
ple, *957;* Cannery Row, *250;* Catch Me if You Can, *24;*
tahoochee, *480;* Clean and Sober, *484;* Cops and
bersons, *259;* Critters, *827;* Dear Detective, *968;*
perate Stranger, The, *499;* Fletch, *978;* Four Eyes and Six
s, *1114;* Fourth Story, *978;* High Noon, Part Two, *1120;*
hhiker (Series), The, *850;* Killer Image, *988;* Missing in
on, *85;* Music of Chance, The, *601;* Narrow Margin (1990),
Raw Courage, *103;* Red Alert, *104;* Red Scorpion, *104;*
Hall's Vanishing America, *367;* Scandalous (1983), *373;*
ight Time, *668;* Sunset, *1021;* War Party, *137;* White
ds, *700;* Wild Card, *1032;* Wildcats, *411;* Wilder Napalm,

ish, Raoul: Sadie Thompson, *646*
ish, Sydney: Homewrecker, *1057;* To Die For, *896*
ston, Ray: Apartment, The, *228;* Blood Relations, *816;*
d Salvage, *816;* Damn Yankees, *913;* Fall of the House of
er, The (1979), *840;* Fast Times at Ridgemont High, *274;*
n the Hip, *281;* Galaxy of Terror, *1053;* Happy Hooker
s to Washington, The, *293;* Kid with the Broken Halo, The,
; Kiss Me, Stupid, *314;* Man of Passion, A, *587;* Mouse
the Motorcycle, The, *189;* O.C. & Stiggs, *348;* Of Mice and
(1992), *611;* Popcorn, *876;* Popeye, *196;* Private School,
; Rad, *102;* Runaway Ralph, *201;* Silver Streak (1976),
; Ski Patrol, *380;* South Pacific, *941;* Sting, The, *120;* Tall
y, *391*
ter, Harriet: Good Father, The, *530;* May Fools, *766;*
e Diary, *400*
ter, Jerry: Nightmare in Blood, *871*
ter, Jessica: Dr. Strange, *1047;* Execution, The, *974;*
ingo Kid, The, *278;* Going Ape!, *287;* Goldengirl, *1054;*
d Prix, *531;* Group, The, *534;* Home for the Holidays,
; Lilith, *575;* Miracle on Ice, *595;* PCU, *355;* Play Misty for
1006; Scruples, *650;* She's Dressed to Kill, *656;* Spring
r, *385*
ter, Rita: Cry from the Mountain, *160*
ter, Tracey: City Slickers, *255;* Conan the Destroyer,
3; Delusion (1991), *499;* Mortuary Academy, *337;*
gedy Man, *1008;* Repo Man, *366;* Silence of the Lambs,
6; Something Wild, *383*
ters, James: Shout (1991), *939*
ters, Julie: Buster, *472;* Educating Rita, *270;* Mack the
e, *930;* Personal Services, *357;* Prick Up Your Ears, *626;*
ping Out, *942;* Summer House, The, *388*
ters, Laurie: Harrad Experiment, The, *537*
ters, Luana: Aces and Eights, *1092;* Arizona Bound,
4; Assassin of Youth (a.k.a. Marijuana), *451;* Badmen of
Hills, *1096;* Corpse Vanishes, The, *825;* Down Texas Way,
1110; Drums of Fu Manchu, *42;* End of the Trail, *1111;*
Mexicali Rose, *1134;* Tulsa Kid, *1159*
Walters, Melora: Cabin Boy, *248*
Walters, Susan: Elvis and Me, *915*
Walters, Thorley: Murder She Said, *999;* People That Time Forgot, The, *1070;* Phantom of the Opera (1962), *874;* Sherlock Holmes and the Deadly Necklace, *1015;* Sign of Four, The, *1016*
Walthall, Henry B.: Abraham Lincoln, *440;* Avenging Conscience, The, *811;* Birth of a Nation, The, *462;* Chandu the Magician, *24;* Devil Doll, The (1936), *833;* Helldorado (1934), *60;* Home, Sweet Home, *543;* Judge Priest, *560;* Judith of Bethulia, *560;* Last Outlaw, The (1936), *1126;* Ride Him Cowboy, *1143;* Scarlet Letter, The (1926), *649;* Scarlet Letter, The (1934), *649;* Somewhere in Sonora, *1151;* Strange Interlude (1932), *669;* Viva Villa!, *1162;* Warning Shadows (1933), *1030;* Whispering Shadow, The, *138*
Walton, Helen: Wolfheart's Revenge, *1165*
Walton, John: Kangaroo, *562;* Lighthorsemen, The, *77*
Waltz, Christopher: Fire and Sword, *1051*
Waltz, Lisa: Brighton Beach Memoirs, *246*
Walz, Marin: Boat Is Full, The, *719*
Wanamaker, Sam: Aviator, The, *452;* Baby Boom, *230;* Competition, The, *487;* Concrete Jungle, The (1962) (a.k.a. The Criminal), *487;* Detective Sadie and Son, *37;* From Hell to Victory, *53;* Guilty by Suspicion, *534;* Judgment in Berlin, *560;* My Girl Tisa, *602;* Our Family Business, *616;* Private Benjamin, *361;* Pure Luck, *363;* Raw Deal, *103;* Running Against Time, *1075;* Sell-Out, The, *113;* Spiral Staircase, The (1975), *1019;* Spy Who Came in from the Cold, The, *664;* Superman IV: The Quest for Peace, *1081*
Wanamaker, Zoe: Prime Suspect 1, *1007;* Tales of the Unexpected, *1022*
Wanberg, Alexander: Mamma Dracula, *862*
Wang, George: Have a Nice Funeral, *1119*
Wang, Peter: Great Wall, A, *290;* Laser Man, The, *315*
Wang, Steve: Adventures of the Kung Fu Rascals, The, *223*
Warbeck, David: Ark of the Sun God...Temple of Hell, The, *6;* Black Cat, The (1981), *813;* Miami Horror, *1066;* Seven Doors of Death, *884*
Ward, B. J.: Opposite Sex (And How to Live with Them), The, *351*
Ward, Burt: Batman (1966), *148;* Beach Babes from Beyond, *1038;* Robo C.H.I.C., *1074;* Smooth Talker, *1018;* Virgin High, *405*
Ward, Clark: Eagle, The, *269*
Ward, Debra: Black Cobra 3, *13*
Ward, Douglas Turner: Man and Boy, *1131*
Ward, Fannie: Cheat, The, *961*
Ward, Felix: Spookies, *889*
Ward, Fred: Backtrack, *454;* Big Business, *238;* Cast a Deadly Spell, *1041;* Dark Wind, *966;* Equinox (1993), *510;* Florida Straits, *51;* Four Eyes and Six Guns, *1114;* Henry & June, *540;* Miami Blues, *84;* Naked Gun 33 1/3, The—The Final Insult, *341;* Noon Wine, *608;* Off Limits (1988), *93;* Player, The, *358;* Prince of Pennsylvania, *361;* Remo Williams: The Adventure Begins, *105;* Right Stuff, The, *640;* Secret Admirer, *374;* Short Cuts, *657;* Silkwood, *658;* Southern Comfort, *119;* Swing Shift, *675;* Thunderheart, *1025;* Timerider, *130;* Tremors, *897;* Uforia, *402;* Uncommon Valor, *134*
Ward, James: Red Line 7000, *104*
Ward, John: Holt of the Secret Service, *63*
Ward, Jonathan: Mac and Me, *1064;* White Water Summer, *139*
Ward, Lyman: Creature, *1043;* Ferris Bueller's Day Off, *276;* Mikey, *865;* Taking of Beverly Hills, The, *124*
Ward, Mackenzie: Sons of the Sea, *663*
Ward, Mary: Surviving Desire, *389*
Ward, Megan: Amityville 1992: It's About Time, *809;* Arcade, *1036;* Crash and Burn, *1043;* Encino Man, *271;* Freaked, *281;* PCU, *355;* Trancers III: Death Lives, *1085*

Ward, Rachel: After Dark, My Sweet, *951;* Against All Odds, *951;* Black Magic (1992), *955;* Christopher Columbus: The Discovery, *26;* Dead Men Don't Wear Plaid, *262;* Double Jeopardy, *972;* Final Terror, The, *841;* Fortress (1985), *520;* Good Wife, The, *530;* Hotel Colonial, *64;* How to Get Ahead in Advertising, *302;* Night School, *1001;* Sharky's Machine, *115;* Thornbirds, The, *682;* Wide Sargasso Sea, *701*

Ward, Richard: Across 110th Street, *1;* Mandingo, *588*

Ward, Robin: Thrillkill, *1025*

Ward, Roger: Escape 2000, *1049;* Mad Max, *1064*

Ward, Sela: Child of Darkness, Child of Light, *823;* Double Jeopardy, *972;* Fugitive, The (1993), *53;* Haunting of Sarah Hardy, The, *982;* Hello Again, *296;* Nothing in Common, *609;* Rainbow Drive, *103;* Steele Justice, *120*

Ward, Simon: Children of Rage, *481;* Dracula (1973), *837;* Four Feathers, The (1978), *52;* Hitler, the Last Ten Days, *542;* Holocaust 2000, *851;* Monster Club, The, *865;* Supergirl, *1081;* Young Winston, *709;* Zulu Dawn, *142*

Ward, Sophie: Casanova (1987), *252;* Summer Story, A, *673;* Young Sherlock Holmes, *141*

Ward, Wally: Chocolate War, The, *481;* Invisible Kid, The, *1060*

Warde, Anthony: Buck Rogers: Destination Saturn (a.k.a. Planet Outlaws), *1040;* King of the Forest Rangers, *72*

Warden, Jack: Alice Through the Looking Glass (1985), *145;* All the President's Men, *951;* And Justice for All, *447;* Apprenticeship of Duddy Kravitz, The, *450;* Aviator, The, *452;* Being There, *234;* Beyond the Poseidon Adventure, *11;* Brian's Song, *469;* Carbon Copy, *251;* Champ, The (1979), *479;* Chu Chu and the Philly Flash, *255;* Crackers, *260;* Dead Solid Perfect, *497;* Death on the Nile, *968;* Donovan's Reef, *267;* Dreamer, *505;* Everybody Wins, *973;* Great Muppet Caper, The, *171;* Guilty as Sin, *534;* Heaven Can Wait (1978), *295;* Hobson's Choice (1983), *175;* Judgment, *560;* Man on a String, *81;* Man Who Loved Cat Dancing, The, *1132;* Night and the City (1992), *605;* Passed Away, *355;* Presidio, The, *100;* Problem Child, *362;* Problem Child 2, *362;* Raid on Entebbe, *633;* Run Silent, Run Deep, *109;* September, *652;* Shampoo, *655;* So Fine, *382;* Sporting Club, The, *664;* Toys, *398;* 12 Angry Men, *690;* Used Cars, *404;* Verdict, The, *693;* White Buffalo, *1164*

Warden, Jonathan: Greetings, *290*

Ware, Herta: Crazy in Love, *490;* Lonely Hearts (1991), *577*

Ware, Irene: Chandu the Magician, *24;* Raven, The (1935), *878*

Warfield, Chris: Dangerous Charter, *32*

Warfield, Emily: Man in the Moon, The, *587*

Warfield, Marsha: Paramount Comedy Theatre, Vol. 2: Decent Exposures, *354;* Truly Tasteless Jokes, *400*

Warhol, Andy: Cocaine Cowboys, *27;* Driver's Seat, The, *505*

Waring, Todd: Love and Murder, *993*

Warlock, Billy: Hot Shot, *544;* Society, *888;* Swimsuit, *390*

Warnecke, Gordon: My Beautiful Laundrette, *601*

Warner, Camille: Hollywood High, Part II, *299*

Warner, David: Ballad of Cable Hogue, The, *1096;* Blue Hotel, *465;* Boy Who Left Home to Find Out About the Shivers, The, *152;* Cast a Deadly Spell, *1041;* Code Name: Chaos, *257;* Company of Wolves, The, *1042;* Cross of Iron, *31;* Doll's House, A (1973), *503;* Fixer, The, *517;* Frankenstein (1984), *842;* From Beyond the Grave, *844;* Grave Secrets, *847;* Holocaust, *542;* Hostile Take Over, *544;* Island, The, *857;* John Carpenter Presents: Body Bags, *858;* Lost World, The (1992), *79;* Magdalene, *585;* Man with Two Brains, The, *328;* Midsummer Night's Dream, A (1968), *332;* Morgan, *337;* Nightwing, *871;* Old Curiosity Shop, The, *933;* Omen, The, *872;* Providence, *630;* Quest of the Delta Knights, *1073;* Return to the Lost World, *1074;* S.O.S. Titanic, *646;* Silver Bears, *379;* Spymaker: The Secret Life of Ian Fleming, *119;* Star Trek V: The Final Frontier, *1079;* Star Trek VI: The Undiscovered Country, *1079;* Straw Dogs, *1021;* Teenage Mutant Ninja Turtles II: The Secret of the Ooze, *209;* Thirty-Nine Steps, The (1978), *1024;* Time After Time, *1084;* Time Bandits, *1084;* Tripwire, *132;* Tron, *1085;* Unnamable, The, *899;* Waxwork, *902*

Warner, Gary: Lurkers, *861*

Warner, H. B.: Arrest Bulldog Drummond, *6;* Bulldog Drummond in Africa, *20;* Bulldog Drummond's Bride, *20;* Bulldog Drummond's Peril, *20;* Bulldog Drummond's Secret Police, *21;* Corsican Brothers, The (1941), *29;* Girl of the Golden West, The, *919;* King of Kings, The (1927), *565;* Let Freedom Ring, *928;* Lost Horizon, *580;* Nurse Edith Cavell, *610;* Rains Came, The, *634;* Topper Returns, *398*

Warner, Jack: Captive Heart, *475;* Christmas Carol, A (1951), *159;* Quatermass Experiment, The, *1073*

Warner, Julie: Doc Hollywood, *265;* Indian Summer, *306;* Mr. Saturday Night, *334*

Warner, Steven: Little Prince, The, *929*

Warnock, Grant: Waterland, *697*

Warren, E. Alyn: Tarzan the Fearless, *125*

Warren, Gary: Railway Children, The, *198*

Warren, James: Three for Bedroom C, *395*

Warren, Janet: Jade Mask, The, *987*

Warren, Jennifer: Angel City, *448;* Another Man, Another Chance, *1094;* Choice, The, *481;* Fatal Beauty, *46;* Intruder Within, The, *1059;* Mutant, *867;* Slap Shot, *380;* Swap, The, *674*

Warren, Keirsten: Grave Secrets: The Legacy of Hilltop Drive, *980*

Warren, Lesley Ann: Apology, *809;* Baja Oklahoma, *455;* Betrayal (1978), *459;* Beulah Land, *459;* Burglar (1987), *24*[illegible]; Choose Me, *962;* Cinderella (1964), *911;* Clue, *256;* Cop, *2*[illegible]; Dancing Princesses, The, *161;* Legend of Valentino, *572;* Lif[e] Stinks, *318;* Night in Heaven, A, *606;* One and Only, Genuine Original Family Band, The, *192;* Portrait of a Showgirl, *625;* Portrait of a Stripper, *625;* Pure Country, *630;* Songwriter, *940;* Treasure of the Yankee Zephyr, *132;* Victor/Victoria, *40*[illegible] Worth Winning, *414*

Warren, Michael: Norman...Is That You?, *346*

Warren, Mike: Butterflies Are Free, *473;* Fast Break, *274;* Heaven Is a Playground, *539;* Kid Who Loved Christmas, The, *180*

Warrick, Ruth: China Sky, *25;* Citizen Kane, *482;* Corsican Brothers, The (1941), *29;* Great Dan Patch, The, *532;* Guest [in] the House, *534;* Iron Major, The, *554;* Journey Into Fear (1942), *987;* Let's Dance, *928;* Mr. Winkle Goes to War, *33*[illegible] Ride Beyond Vengeance, *1143*

Warrington, Don: Bloodbath at the House of Death, *242;* Lion of Africa, The, *77*

Warwick, James: Partners in Crime (TV Series), *1004;* Seven Dials Mystery, The, *1013;* Why Didn't They Ask Evans, *1032*

Warwick, John: Face at the Window, The, *840;* Ticket of Leave Man, The, *895*

Warwick, Richard: If..., *304;* Lost Language of Cranes, Th[e], *580*

Warwick, Robert: Adventures of Don Juan, The, *2;* Bold Caballero, The, *1099;* Fighting with Kit Carson, *1113;* Gangster's Boy, *525;* In a Lonely Place, *985;* Kismet (1944), *566;* Private Lives of Elizabeth and Essex, The, *629;* Sullivan's Travels, *388;* Woman's Face, A, *705*

Washbourne, Mona: Billy Liar, *461;* Brides of Dracula, *81*[illegible] Brideshead Revisited, *469;* Collector, The, *963;* Driver's Seat, The, *505;* Stevie, *668*

Washburn, Beverly: Wagon Train (TV Series), *1162*

Washburn, Bryant: Clutching Hand, The, *27;* Falcon in Mexico, The, *975;* Return of Chandu (The Magician), *105*

Washburne, Rick: Comrades in Arms, *28;* Hangmen, *59*

Washington, Blue: Haunted Gold, *1119*

Washington, Denzel: Cry Freedom, *492;* For Queen and Country, *519;* George McKenna Story, The, *526;* Glory, *528*[illegible] Heart Condition, *295;* Malcolm X, *586;* Mighty Quinn, The, *5*[illegible] Mississippi Masala, *596;* Mo' Better Blues, *931;* Much Ado About Nothing, *338;* Pelican Brief, The, *1005;* Philadelphia, *621;* Power (1986), *625;* Ricochet, *106*

shington, Dinah: Jazz on a Summer's Day, *427;* Ladies
the Blues, The, *428*
ss, Ted: Canterville Ghost, The (1986), *155;* Curse of the
Panther, The, *261;* Longshot, The (1985), *320;* Oh, God,
Devil!, *349;* Pancho Barnes, *617;* Sheena, *115;*
lecross, *399*
sson, Craig: Body Double, *958;* Four Friends, *521;* Ghost
ry, *846;* Go Tell the Spartans, *56;* Men's Club, The, *593;*
htmare on Elm Street 3, A: The Dream Warriors, *871;*
izoid, *883;* Skag, *659;* Strapped, *670*
tanabe, Gedde: Gung Ho (1985), *292;* Vamp, *899;*
unteers, *405*
tase, Tsunehiko: Antarctica, *713*
terman, Dennis: Cold Justice, *28;* Scars of Dracula, *883*
terman, Felicity: Lena's Holiday, *991;* Miracle Beach,
2; Thunder in Paradise, *129*
ters, Ethel: Cabin in the Sky, *473;* Cairo, *910;* Member of
Wedding, The, *592;* Pinky, *622*
ters Jr., Harry: Adventures in Wonderland, *143*
ters, John: Alice to Nowhere, *3;* Attack Force Z, *7;*
levard of Broken Dreams, *467;* Breaker Morant, *19;*
evous Bodily Harm, *533;* Heaven Tonight, *539;* Miracle
wn Under, *187;* Three's Trouble, *396;* Which Way Home,
3
ters, Muddy: Last Waltz, The, *428*
terston, Sam: Assault at West Point, *451;* Capricorn One,
41; Crimes and Misdemeanors, *490;* Dempsey, *499;*
le's Wing, *1111;* Finnegan Begin Again, *277;* Friendly Fire,
2; Generation, *283;* Gore Vidal's Lincoln, *531;* Great
sby, The, *532;* Hannah and Her Sisters, *293;* Heaven's
e, *1119;* Interiors, *553;* Journey into Fear (1975), *987;*
t Between Friends, *561;* Killing Fields, The, *563;* Lantern
, *180;* Man in the Moon, The, *587;* Mastermind (TV Series),
6; Mindwalk, *430;* Nightmare Years, The, *607;* Rancho
uxe, *1140;* Reflections of Murder, *1009;* September, *652;*
ial Mom, *376;* Sweet William, *389;* Trade Secrets, *1026;*
ming Sign, *901;* Welcome Home, *698;* Who Killed Mary
at's 'Er Name?, *1031*
tford, Gwen: Body in the Library, The, *958;* Fall of the
use of Usher, The (1949), *840;* Ghoul, The (1975), *846;*
te the Blood of Dracula, *892*
tkin, Ian: Nutcase, *347*
tkin, Pierre: Atom Man vs. Superman, *7;* Shock (1946),
5; Story of Seabiscuit, The, *207;* Superman—The Serial,
81; Two Lost Worlds, *133*
tkins, Gary: Wheels of Fire, *138*
tson, Alberta: Best Revenge, *11;* Destiny to Order, *264;*
man, The, *63;* Keep, The, *859;* Women of Valor, *706*
tson, Anthony: Long Day Closes, The, *578*
tson, Bill: Stingray, *120*
tson, Bobs: Men of Boys Town, *592;* On Borrowed Time,
2
tson, Douglas: Parker Adderson, Philosopher, *618;* Trial
the Cantonsville Nine, The, *687*
tson, Jack: King Arthur, The Young Warlord, *72;* Schizo,
3; Sleeping Murder, *1017;* Wild Geese, The, *139*
tson, Lucile: Great Lie, The, *532;* Julia Misbehaves, *311;*
de for Each Other, *325;* My Forbidden Past, *602;* Thin Man
es Home, The, *1024;* Three Smart Girls, *945;* Tomorrow Is
ever, *685;* Waterloo Bridge, *697*
tson, Michael: Subspecies, *891*
tson, Mills: Heated Vengeance, *60;* Kansas City
ssacre, The, *70*
tson, Minor: Adventures of Huckleberry Finn, The (1939),
3; Beyond the Forest, *460;* Jackie Robinson Story, The,
6; Navy Blue and Gold, *342;* Star, The, *665*
tson, Moray: Body in the Library, The, *958;* Pride and
ejudice (1985), *626*
tson, Vernee: Death Drug, *498*
tson, William: Girl on a Chain Gang, *55*
tt, Marty: Almost You, *225*
tt, Richard C.: Deathshot, *36*
Watters, William (Arch Hall Sr.): Eegah!, *838;* Wild
Guitar, *702*
Wattis, Richard: Colditz Story, The, *485;* Importance of
Being Earnest, The, *305*
Waxman, Al: Clown Murders, The, *962;* Collision Course,
257; Hitman, The, *63;* Live Wire, *78;* Malarek, *586;* Meatballs
III, *330;* Mob Story, *335;* Spasms, *889;* Tulips, *400;* Wild
Horse Hank, *217*
Way, Eileen: Queen of Hearts, *632*
Wayans, Damon: Earth Girls Are Easy, *915;* Last Boy Scout,
The, *75;* Mo' Money, *335*
Wayans, Keenen Ivory: I'm Gonna Git You Sucka!, *305*
Wayans, Marlon: Above the Rim, *440;* Mo' Money, *335*
Wayne, Carol: Two Top Bananas, *402*
Wayne, David: Adam's Rib, *222;* American Christmas Carol,
An, *146;* Andromeda Strain, The, *1036;* Apple Dumpling
Gang, The, *147;* As Young as You Feel, *229;* Front Page, The
(1974), *281;* How to Marry a Millionaire, *303;* Huckleberry
Finn (1974), *176;* Last Angry Man, The, *568;* Poker Alice,
1139; Portrait of Jennie, *625;* Prizefighter, The, *197;* Sad
Sack, The, *372;* Stella (1950), *667;* Survivalist, The, *123;*
Tender Trap, The, *392;* Three Faces of Eve, The, *682;* We're
Not Married, *408*
Wayne, Ethan: Operation 'Nam, *95*
Wayne, John: Alamo, The, *1092;* Allegheny Uprising, *1093;*
Angel and the Badman, *1093;* Baby Face, *453;* Back to Bataan,
8; Barbarian and the Geisha, The, *455;* Big Jake, *1098;* Big
Jim McLain, *460;* Big Stampede, The, *1098;* Big Trail, The,
1098; Blood Alley, *15;* Blue Steel (1934), *1099;* Brannigan,
18; Cahill—US Marshal, *1103;* Chisum, *1104;* Circus World,
482; Comancheros, The, *1105;* Conqueror, The, *29;* Cowboys,
The, *1106;* Dakota (1945), *1107;* Dark Command, *1107;*
Dawn Rider, *1107;* Desert Trail, *1109;* Donovan's Reef, *267;*
El Dorado, *1111;* Fighting Kentuckian, The, *1112;* Fighting
Seabees, The, *48;* Flame of the Barbary Coast, *50;* Flying
Leathernecks, *51;* Flying Tigers, The, *51;* Fort Apache, *1114;*
Frontier Horizon, *1114;* Great American West, *425;* Greatest
Story Ever Told, The, *533;* Green Berets, The, *57;* Hatari!, *59;*
Haunted Gold, *1119;* Hell Town, *1120;* Hellfighters, *60;* High
and the Mighty, The, *541;* Hondo, *1121;* Horse Soldiers, The,
1122; How the West Was Won, *1122;* Hurricane Express, *65;*
In Harm's Way, *66;* In Old California, *1122;* Island in the Sky,
554; King of the Pecos, *1125;* Lady for a Night, *567;* Lady
from Louisiana, *1125;* Lady Takes a Chance, A, *1125;* Lawless
Frontier, *1127;* Lawless Nineties, The, *1127;* Lawless Range,
1127; Legend of the Lost, *572;* Lonely Trail, The, *1129;* Long
Voyage Home, The, *578;* Longest Day, The, *78;* Lucky Texan,
1130; Man from Monterey, The, *1131;* Man from Utah, The,
1132; Man Who Shot Liberty Valance, The, *1132;* McLintock!,
1133; McQ, *83;* 'Neath Arizona Skies, *1135;* New Frontier,
1136; Night Riders, The, *1136;* North to Alaska, *1136;*
Operation Pacific, *614;* Overland Stage Raiders, *1137;* Pals of
the Saddle, *1138;* Paradise Canyon, *1138;* Pittsburgh, *622;*
Quiet Man, The, *364;* Rainbow Valley, *1140;* Randy Rides
Alone, *1141;* Range Feud, *1141;* Reap the Wild Wind, *104;*
Red River, *1141;* Red River Range, *1141;* Reunion in France,
639; Ride Him Cowboy, *1143;* Riders of Destiny, *1144;* Rio
Bravo, *1145;* Rio Grande, *1145;* Rio Lobo, *1145;* Rooster
Cogburn, *1146;* Sagebrush Trail, *1147;* Sands of Iwo Jima,
111; Santa Fe Stampede, *1147;* Sea Chase, The, *112;*
Searchers, The, *1148;* Seven Sinners, *113;* Shadow of the
Eagle, *114;* She Wore a Yellow Ribbon, *1148;* Shootist, The,
1149; Somewhere in Sonora, *1151;* Sons of Katie Elder, The,
1151; Spoilers, The, *1152;* Stagecoach (1939), *1152;* Star
Packer, The, *1153;* Tall in the Saddle, *1154;* Telegraph Trail,
The, *1154;* Texas Cyclone, *1155;* Texas Terror, *1156;* They
Were Expendable, *127;* Three Faces West, *683;* Three
Godfathers, The, *1156;* Three Musketeers, The (1933), *128;*
Three Texas Steers, *1157;* Trail Beyond, The, *1158;* Train
Robbers, The, *1158;* Trouble Along the Way, *688;* True Grit,
1159; Two-Fisted Law, *1159;* Tycoon, *133;* Undefeated, The,
1160; Wake of the Red Witch, *136;* War of the Wildcats,
1162; War Wagon, The, *1162;* West of the Divide, *1163;*
Westward Ho, *1163;* Wheel of Fortune, *409;* Winds of the

Wasteland, *1165;* Wings of Eagles, The, *703;* Without Reservations, *413;* Wyoming Outlaw, *1165*
Wayne, John Ethan: Scream, *883*
Wayne, Keith: Night of the Living Dead (1968), *870*
Wayne, Michael: Danger Zone, The, *32*
Wayne, Naunton: Night Train to Munich, *91;* Passport to Pimlico, *355;* Quartet (1948), *631*
Wayne, Nina: Comic, The (1969), *486*
Wayne, Norma Jean: Blondie's Blessed Event, *242*
Wayne, Patrick: Beyond Atlantis, *11;* Big Jake, *1098;* Deserter, The, *1109;* Green Berets, The, *57;* Her Alibi, *296;* McLintock!, *1133;* People That Time Forgot, The, *1070;* Rustler's Rhapsody, *371;* Searchers, The, *1148;* Shenandoah, *1149;* Sinbad and the Eye of the Tiger, *1077;* Talion, *1154;* Young Guns, *1165*
Wazaki, Toshiya: X from Outer Space, The, *1090*
Weatherly, Shawn: Amityville 1992: It's About Time, *809;* Mindgames, *996;* Shadowzone, *885;* Thieves of Fortune, *127*
Weathers, Carl: Action Jackson, *2;* Death Hunt, *35;* Force Ten from Navarone, *51;* Fortune Dane, *52;* Friday Foster, *53;* Hurricane Smith, *65;* Predator, *1071;* Rocky, *642;* Rocky II, *642;* Rocky III, *642;* Rocky IV, *642*
Weaver, Dennis: Best Christmas Pageant Ever, The, *150;* Cocaine: One Man's Seduction, *485;* Don't Go to Sleep, *836;* Dragnet (1954), *41;* Duel, *972;* Duel at Diablo, *1110;* Gallant Hours, The, *524;* Gentle Giant, *169;* Gunsmoke (TV Series), *1118;* Intimate Strangers, *553;* Ordeal of Dr. Mudd, The, *614;* Ten Wanted Men, *1155;* What's the Matter with Helen?, *902*
Weaver, Doodles: 30 Foot Bride of Candy Rock, The, *394*
Weaver, Fritz: Black Sunday (1977), *955;* Blind Spot, *464;* Creepshow, *826;* Day of the Dolphin, The, *1044;* Demon Seed, *1046;* Fail-Safe, *974;* Hearst and Davies Affair, The, *537;* Holocaust, *542;* Hunter (1971), *65;* Ironclads, *554;* Jaws of Satan, *858;* Jolly Corner, The, *559;* Walk in the Spring Rain, A, *695*
Weaver, Jacki: Caddie, *473;* Picnic at Hanging Rock, *1006;* Squizzy Taylor, *119;* Three's Trouble, *396*
Weaver, Marjorie: Gentleman from California, *1115;* Murder Over New York, *999;* Young Mr. Lincoln, *708*
Weaver, Sigourney: Alien, *1034;* Alien 3, *1035;* Aliens, *1035;* Dave, *262;* Deal of the Century, *263;* Eyewitness, *974;* 1492: The Conquest of Paradise, *52;* Ghostbusters, *285;* Ghostbusters II, *285;* Gorillas in the Mist, *531;* Half-Moon Street, *981;* One Woman or Two, *773;* Working Girl, *414;* Year of Living Dangerously, The, *141*
Weavers, The: Wasn't That a Time!, *438*
Weaving, Hugo: Custodian, The, *31;* For Love Alone, *519;* Frauds, *281;* Proof, *629;* Reckless Kelly, *365;* Right Hand Man, The, *640*
Webb, Alan: Challenge to Lassie, *157;* Chimes at Midnight, *481;* Entertaining Mr. Sloane, *271;* Great Train Robbery, The, *980;* King Lear (1971), *564;* Women in Love, *706*
Webb, Chloe: Belly of an Architect, The, *458;* China Beach (TV Series), *481;* Dangerous Woman, A, *494;* Heart Condition, *295;* Sid and Nancy, *657;* Twins, *401*
Webb, Clifton: Dark Corner, The, *495;* Laura, *991;* Man Who Never Was, The, *81;* Razor's Edge, The (1946), *635;* Stars and Stripes Forever, *941*
Webb, Daniel: Unapproachable, The, *691*
Webb, Gregg: Running Mates (1985), *645*
Webb, Gregory: Puppet Master II, *878*
Webb, Jack: D.I., The, *493;* Dark City, *495;* Dragnet (1954), *41;* Halls of Montezuma, *59;* He Walked by Night, *982;* Men, The, *592;* Pete Kelly's Blues, *935;* Sunset Boulevard, *673*
Webb, Julie: Billy Jack, *13*
Webb, Lucy: Best of Not Necessarily the News, The, *236*
Webb, Richard: Captain Midnight—Vols. 1–2, *155;* Distant Drums, *40;* Out of the Past, *1003*
Webber, Jake: Skin Art, *659*
Webber, Peggy: Screaming Skull, The, *884*
Webber, Robert: Assassin, *1037;* Bring Me the Head of Alfredo Garcia, *20;* Casey's Shadow, *157;* Dead Heat on a Merry-Go-Round, *967;* $ (Dollars), *971;* Don't Go to Sleep, *836;* Final Option, The, *977;* French Woman, The, *522;* Hysteria, *984;* Nuts, *1002;* Outer Limits, The (TV Series), *1069;* Private Benjamin, *361;* Revenge of the Pink Panther, The, *367;* Starflight One, *1079;* Streets of L.A., The, *671;* Stripper, The (1963), *671;* 10, *392;* 12 Angry Men, *690;* Wrong Is Right, *414*
Webber, Timothy: Grey Fox, The, *1117;* John and the Missus, *558;* That's My Baby, *680;* Toby McTeague, *212*
Weber, Jacques: Cyrano De Bergerac (1990), *727*
Weber, Rick: Somewhere, Tomorrow, *206*
Weber, Steven: Hamburger Hill, *535;* Single White Female, *1016*
Weber, Suzanna: Cold River, *159*
Weborg, Jeff: Islander, The, *555*
Webster, Hugh: King of the Grizzlies, *180*
Weck, Peter: Almost Angels, *146*
Wedgeworth, Ann: Birch Interval, The, *150;* Bogie, *466;* Catamount Killing, The, *960;* Citizen's Band, *255;* Cooperstown, *488;* Far North, *274;* Men's Club, The, *593;* Sweet Dreams, *943;* Tiger's Tale, A, *396*
Weeden, Bill: Sgt. Kabukiman N.Y.P.D., *114*
Weeks, Alan: Truck Turner, *132*
Weeks, Barbara: Forbidden Trail, *1113;* Sundown Rider, The, *1153;* Violent Years, The, *136*
Wegener, Paul: Golem, The (How He Came into the World) (Der Golem, Wie er in die Welt), *741*
Wegman, William: Best of William Wegman, *236*
Weibel, Peter: Invisible Adversaries, *748*
Weidler, Virginia: All This and Heaven Too, *445;* Babes on Broadway, *907;* Best Foot Forward, *908;* Great Man Votes, The, *289;* Too Hot to Handle, *130;* Young Tom Edison, *708*
Weiner, Mark: New Wave Comedy, *343*
Weintraub, Carl: Sorry, Wrong Number (1989), *1019*
Weiser, Norbert: Android, *1036;* Arcade, *1036;* Radioactive Dreams, *1073*
Weisman, Robin: Three Men and a Little Lady, *395;* Thunder in Paradise, *129*
Weiss, George: Glen or Glenda, *528*
Weiss, Michael: Howling IV, *854*
Weiss, Roberta: Abducted, *1;* High Stakes (1986), *297*
Weisser, Norbert: Deceit, *1046*
Weissmuller, Johnny: Cannibal Attack, *22;* Fury of the Congo, *54;* Jungle Jim, *69;* Tarzan and His Mate, *125;* Tarzan Escapes, *125;* Tarzan Finds a Son, *125;* Tarzan the Ape Man (1932), *125;* Tarzan's New York Adventure, *126;* Tarzan's Secret Treasure, *126*
Weitz, Bruce: Death of a Centerfold, *498;* Liars' Club, The, *992;* No Place To Hide, *91;* Rainbow Drive, *103*
Welch, Joseph: Anatomy of a Murder, *952*
Welch, Raquel: Bandolero!, *1096;* Bedazzled, *233;* Bluebeard (1972), *817;* Fantastic Voyage, *1050;* Four Musketeers, The, *52;* Fuzz, *282;* Hannie Caulder, *1119;* Lady in Cement, *989;* Last of Sheila, The, *991;* Legend of Walks Far Woman, The, *1128;* Magic Christian, The, *326;* Mother, Jugs and Speed, *337;* Myra Breckenridge, *341;* Oldest Profession, The, *773;* 100 Rifles, *1137;* Restless, *638;* Scandal in a Small Town, *649;* Shoot Loud, Louder...I Don't Understand, *378;* Swingin' Summer, A, *390;* Tainted Blood, *1022;* Three Musketeers, The (1973), *128;* Trouble in Paradise, *399;* Wild Party, The (1975), *702*
Welch, Tahnee: Cannon Movie Tales: Sleeping Beauty, *155;* Cocoon, *1042;* Cocoon: The Return, *1042;* Lethal Obsession, *76*
Weld, Tuesday: Author! Author!, *230;* Cincinnati Kid, The, *26;* Falling Down, *513;* Five Pennies, The, *917;* Heartbreak Hotel, *538;* I'll Take Sweden, *924;* Looking for Mr. Goodbar, *993;* Lord Love a Duck, *321;* Once Upon a Time in America (Long Version), *94;* Pretty Poison, *626;* Reflections of Murder, *1009;* Return to Peyton Place, *639;* Rock, Rock, Rock, *937;* Serial, *376;* Soldier in the Rain, *661;* Thief (1981), *127;* Who'll Stop the Rain, *139;* Wild in the Country, *702*

Welden, Ben: Kid Galahad (1937), *563*
Well, Karin: Burial Ground, *820*
Welland, Colin: Spymaker: The Secret Life of Ian Fleming, *119*
Weller, Mary Louise: Evil, The, *839;* Forced Vengeance, *51*
Weller, Peter: Adventures of Buckaroo Banzai, The, *1034;* Apology, *809;* Cat Chaser, *24;* Dancing Princesses, The, *161;* Fifty/Fifty, *47;* Firstborn, *517;* Just Tell Me What You Want, *312;* Killing Affair, A, *988;* Leviathan, *860;* Naked Lunch, *1067;* Of Unknown Origin, *872;* Rainbow Drive, *103;* Road to Ruin (1991), *369;* RoboCop, *1074;* RoboCop 2, *1075;* Shakedown, *114;* Sunset Grill, *1021;* Tunnel, The, *689;* Women & Men: Stories of Seduction, *706*
Welles, Gwen: Between the Lines, *237;* Desert Hearts, *499;* Eating, *507;* Hit!, *62;* New Year's Day, *605;* Sticky Fingers, *386*
Welles, Mel: Attack of the Crab Monsters, *810;* Commando Squad, *28;* Dr. Heckyl and Mr. Hype, *266;* Little Shop of Horrors, The (1960), *861;* She Beast, The, *885*
Welles, Orson: American Film Institute Life Achievement Awards, The, *418;* Battle of Austerlitz, The, *9;* Black Magic (1949), *462;* Blood and Guns, *15;* Butterfly, *473;* Casino Royale (1967), *252;* Chimes at Midnight, *481;* Citizen Kane, *482;* Compulsion, *487;* Get to Know Your Rabbit, *285;* Immortal Story, *549;* Is Paris Burning?, *554;* It's All True, *427;* Jane Eyre (1944), *557;* Journey Into Fear (1942), *987;* Lady from Shanghai, *989;* Long Hot Summer, The (1958), *578;* Macbeth (1948), *583;* Man for All Seasons, A, *586;* Man Who Saw Tomorrow, The, *430;* Mr. Arkadin (a.k.a. Confidential Report), *596;* Moby Dick, *86;* Muppet Movie, The, *189;* Napoleon (1955), *603;* Othello (1952), *615;* Scene of the Crime (1985), *1013;* Someone to Love, *662;* Stranger, The (1947), *1020;* Ten Days Wonder, *1023;* Third Man, The, *1024;* Tomorrow Is Forever, *685;* Touch of Evil, *1026;* Trial, The, *687;* Trouble in the Glen, *399;* V.I.P.s, The, *693;* Voyage of the Damned, *694;* Waterloo, *697;* Witching, The (Necromancy), *904*
Welles, Steve: Puppet Master II, *878*
Wellford, Philip: Paramount Comedy Theatre, Vol. 1: Well Developed, *353*
Welling, Miki: Alex's Apartment, *951*
Wellman Jr., William: Black Caesar, *13;* Born Losers, *17;* Swingin' Summer, A, *390*
Wells, Christopher: House Party, *923*
Wells, Dawn: Return to Boggy Creek, *880;* Town That Dreaded Sundown, The, *1026*
Wells, Doris: Oriane, *774*
Wells, Jacqueline: Black Cat, The (1934), *813;* Kansas Terrors, *1124;* Ranger and the Lady, The, *1141;* Tarzan the Fearless, *125*
Wells, May: Fatty and Mabel Adrift/Mabel, Fatty and the Law, *275*
Wells, Mel: Wizard of the Lost Kingdom II, *1090*
Wells, Tico: Five Heartbeats, The, *917;* Mississippi Masala, *596*
Wells, Vernon: Circle of Fear, *26;* Circuitry Man, *1041;* Enemy Unseen, *44;* Last Man Standing, *569;* Road Warrior, The, *1074;* Sexual Response, *1014*
Welsh, Kenneth: Adrift, *950;* And Then You Die, *5;* Big Slice, The, *12;* Death Wish V: The Face of Death, *36;* Good Fight, The, *530;* Love and Hate, *581;* Loyalties, *582;* Screwball Academy, *374;* Straight Line, *120;* War Boy, The, *137*
Wen, Ming-Na: Joy Luck Club, The, *559*
Wenders, Wim: Lightning Over Water, *575*
Wendt, George: Avery Schreiber—Live From the Second City, *230;* Guilty by Suspicion, *534;* Gung Ho (1985), *292;* House, *852;* Plain Clothes, *358*
Weng, Jian: Red Sorghum, *780*
Wenner, Jann: Perfect, *620*
Went, Johanna: Living End, The, *577*
Wepper, Fritz: Final Combat, The, *48*
Werle, Barbara: Gone with the West, *1116;* Little Moon & Jud McGraw, *1128*
Werner, Oskar: Fahrenheit 451, *1050;* Jules and Jim, *750;* Lola Montes, *761;* Ship of Fools, *656;* Shoes of the Fisherman, *656;* Spy Who Came in from the Cold, The, *664;* Voyage of the Damned, *694*
Wernicke, Otto: Testament of Dr. Mabuse, *1023*
Wert, Doug: Assassination Game, The, *7;* Dracula Rising, *837*
Wessel, Dick: Dick Tracy versus Cueball, *38;* Gazebo, The, *283;* Pitfall, *622*
Wesson, Dick: Destination Moon, *1047;* Jim Thorpe—All American, *558*
West, Adam: Batman (1966), *148;* Doin' Time on Planet Earth, *267;* For the Love of It, *279;* Happy Hooker Goes Hollywood, The, *293;* Mad About You, *325;* Night of the Kickfighters, *90;* Omega Cop, *93;* One Dark Night, *872;* Return Fire: Jungle Wolf II, *105;* Tammy and the Doctor, *677;* Young Philadelphians, The, *708;* Zombie Nightmare, *905*
West, Chandra: Puppet Master Four, *878*
West, Charles: D. W. Griffith Triple Feature, *493*
West, Dottie: Aurora Encounter, *1037*
West, Jeremy: Curse IV: The Ultimate Sacrifice, *828*
West, Julian: Vampyr, *800*
West, Mae: Belle of the Nineties, *234;* Every Day's a Holiday, *273;* Go West, Young Man, *287;* Goin' to Town, *287;* Heat's On, The, *295;* I'm No Angel, *305;* Klondike Annie, *314;* My Little Chickadee, *340;* Myra Breckenridge, *341;* Night after Night, *344;* Sextette, *376;* She Done Him Wrong, *377*
West, Martin: Swingin' Summer, A, *390*
West, Samuel: Howards End, *545*
West, Timothy: Hedda, *539;* Pocketful of Rye, A, *1006*
Westcott, Helen: Gunfighter, The, *1117*
Westerfield, James: Dead Aim (1973), *1108*
Westerman, Floyd Red Crow: Clearcut, *26;* One Riot, One Ranger, *95*
Westheimer, Dr. Ruth: Forever Lulu, *279;* One Woman or Two, *773;* Ponce de Leon and the Fountain of Youth, *196*
Westhof, Kelly: My Daughter's Keeper, *999*
Westley, Helen: Anne of Green Gables (1934), *146;* Dimples, *914;* Rebecca of Sunnybrook Farm (1938), *936;* Roberta, *936;* Stowaway, *942*
Westman, Nydia: Sweet Adeline, *943*
Westmoreland, James: Don't Answer the Phone, *836*
Weston, Celia: Lost Angels, *580*
Weston, David: Masque of the Red Death, The (1964), *863*
Weston, Jack: All in a Night's Work, *224;* Can't Stop the Music, *911;* Cuba, *31;* Dirty Dancing, *914;* Four Seasons, The, *521;* Gator, *54;* High Road to China, *62;* Honeymoon Machine, The, *300;* Incredible Mr. Limpet, The, *306;* Ishtar, *307;* Longshot, The (1985), *320;* Mirage, *595;* New Leaf, A, *343;* Palm Springs Weekend, *353;* Please Don't Eat the Daisies, *358;* Rad, *102;* Ritz, The, *368;* Short Circuit 2, *1076*
Wetherell, Virginia: Big Switch, The, *13*
Wettig, Patricia: City Slickers, *255;* City Slickers II, *256;* Guilty by Suspicion, *534;* Me & Veronica, *591;* Silent Motive, *1016*
Weyand, Ron: Deadly Hero, *34;* Music School, The, *601*
Weyers, Marius: African Rage, *3;* Power of One, The, *625*
Weyher, Ruth: Warning Shadows (1923), *696*
Weyler, Bobbi: Outtakes, *352*
Whalen, Michael: Batman and Robin, *9;* Missile to the Moon, *1066;* Poor Little Rich Girl (1936), *935*
Whaley, Frank: Back in the U.S.S.R., *8;* Career Opportunities, *251;* Doors, The, *914;* Hoffa, *542;* Little Monsters, *1063;* Midnight Clear, A, *593;* Swing Kids, *675*
Whalin, Justin: Child's Play 3, *823;* Perfect Harmony, *194*
Whalley, Joanne: Crossing the Line (1991), *492;* Edge of Darkness (1986), *973;* Good Father, The, *530;* Kill Me Again, *988;* Mother's Boys, *998;* Navy Seals, *89;* No Surrender, *345;* Scandal, *648;* Shattered (1991), *1014;* To Kill a Priest, *684;* Willow, *1089*

Whately, Kevin: Inspector Morse (TV Series), *986*
Wheaton, Wil: Buddy System, The, *471;* Curse, The, *827;* December, *498;* Last Prostitute, The, *570;* Liars' Club, The, *992;* Stand by Me (1986), *665;* Star Trek: The Next Generation (TV Series), *1079;* Toy Soldiers (1991), *131*
Wheeler, Bert: Cockeyed Cavaliers, *257;* Diplomaniacs, *914;* Half-Shot at Sunrise, *292;* Hips, Hips, Hooray, *297;* Hold 'em Jail, *298;* Hook, Line and Sinker, *300;* Kentucky Kernels, *312*
Wheeler, Kay: Rock, Baby, Rock It, *936*
Wheeler-Nicholson, Dana: Circuitry Man, *1041;* Fletch, *978;* Tombstone, *1157*
Whelan, Arleen: Castle in the Desert, *960;* Ramrod, *1140;* Senator Was Indiscreet, The, *375;* Sun Shines Bright, The, *673*
Whelan, Wendy: George Balanchine's The Nutcracker, *919*
Whelchel, Lisa: Double McGuffin, The, *163;* Magician of Lublin, The, *585*
Whipp, Joseph: Amazons, *4*
Whirry, Shannon: Body of Influence, *958;* Mirror Images II, *996*
Whitaker, Christina: Love Street, *582*
Whitaker, Duane: Saturday Night Special, *111*
Whitaker, Forest: Article 99, *451;* Bank Robber, *232;* Bird, *909;* Bloodsport, *16;* Blown Away (1994), *16;* Body Snatchers, The (1993), *1040;* Consenting Adults (1992), *963;* Criminal Justice, *491;* Crying Game, The, *492;* Diary of a Hitman, *970;* Downtown, *41;* Good Morning, Vietnam, *530;* Johnny Handsome, *69;* Last Light, *569;* Platoon, *623;* Rage in Harlem, A, *103;* Stakeout, *119*
Whitaker, Johnny: Littlest Angel, The, *184;* Napoleon and Samantha, *190;* Snowball Express, *205;* Tom Sawyer (1973), *946*
Whitaker, Slim: Arizona Bound, *1094;* Bold Caballero, The, *1099;* Ghost Patrol, *55;* Haunted Gold, *1119;* Man from Monterey, The, *1131*
White, Barry: Streetfight, *671*
White, Bernie: Body Count, *817*
White, Carol: Daddy's Gone A-Hunting, *965;* Man Who Had Power Over Women, The, *587;* Never Let Go, *604;* Some Call It Loving, *662;* Squeeze, The (1977), *665*
White, David: Amazing Spiderman, The, *4*
White, Diz: Bullshot, *247*
White, Jacqueline: Narrow Margin, The (1952), *89*
White, Jan: Season of the Witch, *884*
White, Jesse: Bedtime for Bonzo, *233;* Bless the Beasts and Children, *463;* Dear Brigitte, *263;* Francis Goes to the Races, *280;* Matinee, *330;* Million Dollar Mermaid, *931;* Rise and Fall of Legs Diamond, The, *107;* Tomboy and the Champ, *213*
White, Leo: Charlie Chaplin Cavalcade, *253;* Charlie Chaplin—The Early Years, Vol. 4, *254*
White, Marjorie: Diplomaniacs, *914*
White, Patricia: Riders of the Whistling Pines, *1144*
White, Pearl: Great Chase, The, *57*
White, Peter: Boys in the Band, The, *468*
White, Ron: Last Train Home, *181*
White, Slappy: Tommy Chong Roast, The, *397*
White, Vanna: Gypsy Angels, *535*
Whitehead, Paxton: Boris and Natasha, *244;* Child of Darkness, Child of Light, *823;* Chips, the War Dog, *158*
Whitelaw, Billie: Dressmaker, The, *505;* Gumshoe, *291;* Krays, The, *567;* Leopard in the Snow, *572;* Lorna Doone, *580;* Make Mine Mink, *327;* Murder Elite, *600;* Night Watch, *870;* No Love for Johnnie, *608;* Omen, The, *872;* Secret Garden, The (1987), *202;* Shadey, *377;* Slayground, *1017;* Strange Case of Dr. Jekyll and Mr. Hyde, The (1968), *890;* Tale of Two Cities, A (1980), *677;* Water Babies, The, *216*
Whiteman, Paul: Fabulous Dorseys, The, *916;* King of Jazz, The, *927;* Strike Up the Band, *387*
Whitfield, Lynn: George McKenna Story, The, *526;* Josephine Baker Story, The, *559;* State of Emergency, *666;* Taking the Heat, *676*
Whitfield, Mitchell: Dogfight, *503;* My Cousin Vinny, *339*
Whitfield, Raymond: How U Like Me Now, *303*
Whiting, Barbara: Beware, My Lovely, *955;* TV Classics: Jimmy Durante, *400*
Whiting, Leonard: Romeo and Juliet (1968), *643*
Whiting, Margaret: Sinbad and the Eye of the Tiger, *1077;* Taking My Turn, *943*
Whitley, Ray: Land of the Open Range, *1125;* Renegade Ranger, *1142*
Whitlow, Jill: Adventures Beyond Belief, *222;* Ghost Chase, *845;* Night of the Creeps, *869;* Thunder Run, *129;* Twice Dead, *1027*
Whitman, Mae: When a Man Loves a Woman, *698*
Whitman, Stuart: Captain Apache, *1103;* Comancheros, The, *1105;* Crazy Mama, *30;* Crime of Passion, *490;* Day And The Hour, *728;* Delta Fox, *37;* Demonoid, *833;* Eaten Alive, *838;* Kill Castro, *71;* Las Vegas Lady, *74;* Mean Johnny Barrows, *83;* Mob Boss, *335;* Monster Club, The, *865;* Omega Cop, *93;* Ransom, *1009;* Revenge (1971), *1010;* Rio Conchos, *1145;* Ruby (1977), *881;* Run for the Roses, *201;* Seekers, The, *651;* Smooth Talker, *1018;* Story of Ruth, The, *668;* Strange Shadows in an Empty Room, *121;* Texas Guns, *1155;* Those Magnificent Men in Their Flying Machines, *394;* Treasure of the Amazon, *132;* Vultures, *901;* White Buffalo, *1164*
Whitmore, James: Above and Beyond, *1;* All My Sons, *444;* Asphalt Jungle, The, *953;* Battleground, *456;* Because You're Mine, *908;* Black Like Me, *462;* Chato's Land, *1104;* Chuka, *1105;* Eddy Duchin Story, The, *507;* First Deadly Sin, The, *977;* Force of One, *51;* Girl Who Had Everything, The, *527;* Give 'em Hell, Harry!, *528;* Glory! Glory!, *287;* Golden Honeymoon, The, *529;* Guns of the Magnificent Seven, *1118;* Harrad Experiment, The, *537;* High Crime, *61;* I Will Fight No More Forever, *1122;* It's a Big Country, *308;* Kiss Me Kate, *927;* Madigan, *80;* McConnell Story, The, *591;* Next Voice You Hear, The, *605;* Nuts, *1002;* Old Explorers, *192;* Rage (1980), *633;* Serpent's Egg, The, *652;* Them!, *1083;* Tora! Tora! Tora!, *131;* Waterhole #3, *1163;* Where the Red Fern Grows, *216;* Word, The, *706*
Whitmore Jr., James: Boys in Company C, The, *18;* Gypsy Warriors, The, *58*
Whitney, Grace Lee: Star Trek (TV Series), *1078*
Whitrow, Benjamin: Belfast Assassin, *458*
Whitten, Frank: Vigil, *800*
Whitthorne, Paul: Critters 4, *827*
Whittington, Shawn: Barn Burning, *456*
Whittle, Brenton: Sara Dane, *648*
Whitton, Margaret: Best of Times, The, *236;* Big Girls Don't Cry...They Get Even, *238;* Little Monsters, *1063;* Major League, *326;* Man without a Face, The, *587;* 9½ Weeks, *607;* Secret of My Success, The, *375*
Whitty, May: Conquest, *487;* Crash Dive, *30;* Lady Vanishes, The (1938), *990;* Lassie Come Home, *180;* Madame Curie, *584;* Mrs. Miniver, *597;* Night Must Fall, *606;* Return of October, The, *366;* Suspicion (1941), *1022;* This Time For Keeps, *945;* White Cliffs of Dover, The, *699*
Whitworth, James: Planet of the Dinosaurs, *1071*
Who, The: Kids Are Alright, The, *428;* Monterey Pop, *431*
Wholihan, Kit: Islander, The, *555*
Whorf, Richard: Chain Lightning, *478;* Keeper of the Flame, *562;* Midnight (1934), *593;* Yankee Doodle Dandy, *948*
Whylie, James: Place of Weeping, *623*
Wickes, Mary: Blondie's Blessed Event, *242;* By the Light of the Silvery Moon, *910;* Don't Go Near the Water, *267;* How to Murder your Wife, *303;* I'll See You in My Dreams, *924;* June Bride, *311;* Man Who Came to Dinner, The, *328;* On Moonlight Bay, *933;* Postcards from the Edge, *360;* Sister Act, *379;* Sister Act 2: Back in the Habit, *380;* Touched by Love, *686*
Wickham, Jeffrey: Terrorists, The, *1023*
Wicki, Bernhard: Crime & Passion, *260;* Killing Cars, *563;* Love in Germany, A, *762;* Mysterious Stranger, The, *190;* Spring Symphony, *788*

Widdoes, Kathleen: Mafia Princess, *585;* Without a Trace, *1032*
Widmark, Richard: Alamo, The, *1092;* All God's Children, *444;* Alvarez Kelly, *1093;* Bear Island, *954;* Bedford Incident, The, *457;* Blackout (1985), *956;* Broken Lance, *1101;* Cheyenne Autumn, *1104;* Cold Sassy Tree, *485;* Coma, *963;* Death of a Gunfighter, *1108;* Domino Principle, The, *971;* Don't Bother to Knock, *971;* Final Option, The, *977;* Halls of Montezuma, *59;* Hanky Panky, *292;* How the West Was Won, *1122;* Judgment at Nuremberg, *560;* Kiss of Death, *566;* Law and Jake Wade, The, *1127;* Madigan, *80;* Mr. Horn, *1134;* Murder on the Bayou, *600;* Night and the City (1950), *605;* Panic in the Streets, *1004;* Pickup on South Street, *1006;* Road House (1948), *1010;* Rollercoaster, *1011;* Run for the Sun, *109;* Saint Joan, *646;* Sell-Out, The, *113;* Street with No Name, *1021;* Swarm, The, *891;* Texas Guns, *1155;* To the Devil, a Daughter, *896;* Trap, The, *1026;* True Colors, *688;* Tunnel of Love, The, *400;* Twilight's Last Gleaming, *133;* Two Rode Together, *1160;* Warlock (1959), *1162;* Way West, The, *1163;* Whale for the Killing, A, *698;* When the Legends Die, *1163*
Wieck, Dorothea: Maedchen in Uniform, *764*
Wiemann, Mathias: Fear (1955), *515*
Wiesinger, Kai: BackBeat, *907*
Wiesmeiser, Lynda: Wheels of Fire, *138*
Wiest, Dianne: Bright Lights, Big City, *470;* Cookie, *259;* Cops and Robbersons, *259;* Edward Scissorhands, *1048;* Footloose, *917;* Hannah and Her Sisters, *293;* Independence Day, *551;* Little Man Tate, *182;* Lost Boys, The, *861;* Parenthood, *354;* Radio Days, *364;* September, *652*
Wiggins, Chris: American Christmas Carol, An, *146;* Fish Hawk, *517;* High-Ballin', *61;* Kavik the Wolf Dog, *179;* King of the Grizzlies, *180;* Why Shoot the Teacher?, *701*
Wignacci, Darlene: Psycho Girls, *877*
Wilborn, Carlton: Dance, *913*
Wilby, James: Handful of Dust, A, *535;* Howards End, *545;* Maurice, *590;* Summer Story, A, *673;* Tale of Two Cities, A (1991), *677*
Wilcox, Frank: Clay Pigeon, The, *26*
Wilcox, Larry: Dirty Dozen, The: The Next Mission, *39;* Last Ride of the Dalton Gang, The, *1126;* Sky Heist, *117*
Wilcox, Lisa: Nightmare on Elm Street 4, A: The Dream Master, *871;* Nightmare on Elm Street 5: The Dream Child, *871*
Wilcox, Mary: Beast of the Yellow Night, *812*
Wilcox, Robert: Dreaming Out Loud, *269;* Little Tough Guys, *319;* Man They Could Not Hang, The, *862;* Mysterious Dr. Satan, *88*
Wilcox, Shannon: Hollywood Harry, *299;* Triplecross, *399*
Wilcox-Horne, Colin: Baby Maker, The, *453*
Wilcoxon, Henry: Against a Crooked Sky, *1092;* Cleopatra (1934), *484;* Connecticut Yankee in King Arthur's Court, A (1948), *258;* Corsican Brothers, The (1941), *29;* Dragnet (1947), *41;* Jericho, *557;* Last of the Mohicans, The (1936), *1126;* Man in the Wilderness, *1132;* Miniver Story, The, *594;* Mrs. Miniver, *597;* Pony Express Rider, *1139;* Tarzan Finds a Son, *125;* Two Worlds of Jennie Logan, The, *1086;* War Lord, The, *137*
Wild, Christopher: Knights and Emeralds, *314*
Wild, Jack: Melody, *186;* Oliver, *933*
Wild, Susanne: Invisible Adversaries, *748*
Wilde, Cornel: At Sword's Point, *7;* Big Combo, The, *12;* Comic, The (1969), *486;* Fifth Musketeer, The, *47;* Forever Amber, *520;* Greatest Show on Earth, The, *533;* Naked Prey, The, *88;* Norseman, The, *92;* Omar Khayyam, *93;* Passion (1954), *97;* Road House (1948), *1010;* Shark's Treasure, *115;* Song to Remember, A, *940;* Sword of Lancelot, *124;* Wintertime, *947*
Wilde, Lois: Brothers of the West, *1101;* Undersea Kingdom, *1087*
Wilde, Steven: Shaking the Tree, *655*
Wilder, Billy: American Film Institute Life Achievement Awards, The, *418*
Wilder, Gene: Adventure of Sherlock Holmes' Smarter Brother, The, *223;* Another You, *228;* Blazing Saddles, *241;* Bonnie and Clyde, *17;* Everything You Always Wanted to Know About Sex but Were Afraid to Ask, *273;* Frisco Kid, The, *1114;* Funny About Love, *282;* Hanky Panky, *292;* Haunted Honeymoon, *294;* Little Prince, The, *929;* Producers, The, *362;* Quackser Fortune Has a Cousin in the Bronx, *631;* See No Evil, Hear No Evil, *375;* Silver Streak (1976), *379;* Start the Revolution without Me, *385;* Stir Crazy, *386;* Thursday's Game, *683;* Willy Wonka and the Chocolate Factory, *217;* Woman in Red, The, *413;* World's Greatest Lover, The, *414;* Young Frankenstein, *416*
Wilder, Giselle: Unexpected Encounters, *691*
Wilder, James: Murder One, *87;* Prey of the Chameleon, *1007;* Scorchers, *650;* Zombie High, *904*
Wilding, Michael: Convoy (1940), *488;* Courtney Affair, The, *489;* Egyptian, The, *508;* Glass Slipper, The, *919;* In Which We Serve, *550;* Naked Edge, The, *1000;* Ships with Wings, *115;* Stage Fright, *1019;* Torch Song, *686;* Under Capricorn, *1028;* Waterloo, *697;* World of Suzie Wong, The, *707*
Wildman, John: American Boyfriends, *446;* My American Cousin, *339*
Wildman, Valerie: Inner Sanctum, *986*
Wildsmith, Dawn: Surf Nazis Must Die, *123*
Wiley, Jan: Dick Tracy vs. Crime Inc., *38*
Wilferson, Guy: Enemy of the Law, *1111*
Wilhoite, Kathleen: Campus Man, *249;* Everybody Wins, *973;* Fire in the Sky, *1051;* Live! From Death Row, *577;* Lorenzo's Oil, *579;* Murphy's Law, *87;* Single Bars, Single Women, *658;* Undercover, *134;* Witchboard, *903*
Wiliams, Roger: Trailing Trouble, *1158*
Wilker, José: Bye Bye Brazil, *721;* Dona Flor and Her Two Husbands, *731;* Medicine Man, *591*
Wilkerson, Guy: Hanging Tree, The, *1118;* Three in the Saddle, *1156*
Wilkes, Donna: Angel, *5*
Wilkinson, Elizabeth: Suburban Roulette, *671*
Wilkinson, June: Bellboy and the Playgirls, The, *234;* Sno-Line, *117*
Wilkinson, Tom: Paper Mask, *1004;* Pocketful of Rye, A, *1006;* Sylvia, *676;* Wetherby, *698*
Willard, Fred: Americathon, *226;* Best of DC Follies, *235;* Big City Comedy, *238;* Chesty Anderson, U.S. Navy (a.k.a. Anderson's Angels), *25;* History of White People in America, The, *298;* History of White People in America, The (Volume II), *298;* How to Beat the High Co$t of Living, *302;* Lots of Luck, *322;* Moving Violations, *338;* Roxanne, *370;* Second City Comedy Show, The, *374*
Willes, Jean: King and Four Queens, The, *1125*
Willette, Jo Ann: Welcome to 18, *407*
William, Warren: Arizona, *1094;* Case of the Lucky Legs, The, *960;* Cleopatra (1934), *484;* Employees' Entrance, *271;* Firefly, The, *916;* Go West, Young Man, *287;* Lady for a Day, *567;* Madame X (1937), *584;* Man in the Iron Mask, The (1939), *81;* Private Affairs of Bel Ami, The, *628;* Satan Met a Lady, *1012;* Skyscraper Souls, *660;* Stage Struck (1936), *941;* Wives Under Suspicion, *704;* Wolf Man, The, *904*
Williams, Adam: Fear Strikes Out, *515*
Williams, Anson: I Married a Centerfold, *547*
Williams, Barbara: City of Hope, *483;* Indecency, *986;* Jo Jo Dancer, Your Life Is Calling, *558;* Oh, What a Night, *611;* Thief of Hearts, *681;* Tiger Warsaw, *683;* Watchers, *1088*
Williams, Bill: Buckskin, *1102;* Cariboo Trail, *1103;* Clay Pigeon, The, *26;* Deadline at Dawn, *34;* Son of Paleface, *383;* Stratton Story, The, *670;* Those Endearing Young Charms, *394;* Torpedo Alley, *131;* Woman's Secret, A, *1032*
Williams, Billy Dee: Alien Intruder, *1035;* Batman (1989), *9;* Bingo Long Traveling All-Stars and Motor Kings, The, *240;* Brian's Song, *469;* Chiefs, *961;* Christmas Lilies of the Field, *159;* Deadly Illusion, *968;* Driving Me Crazy, *269;* Empire Strikes Back, The, *1049;* Fear City, *47;* Final Comedown, The, *48;* Glass House, The, *528;* Hit!, *62;* Hostage Tower, The, *64;*

Imposter, The, *549;* Jacksons: An American Dream, The, *556;* Lady Sings the Blues, *927;* Mahogany, *586;* Marvin and Tige, *589;* Nighthawks, *91;* Number One with a Bullet, *92;* Oceans of Fire, *93;* Out of Towners, The, *352;* Return of the Jedi, *1074*

Williams, Cara: Doctors' Wives, *503;* Never Steal Anything Small, *932*

Williams, Carlton: Crooklyn, *261*

Williams, Caroline: Stepfather II, *890;* Texas Chainsaw Massacre 2, The, *894*

Williams, Cindy: American Graffiti, *226;* Andy Kaufman Special, The, *227;* Big Man on Campus, *238;* Bingo, *240;* Conversation, The, *963;* First Nudie Musical, The, *917;* Gas-s-s-s, *1054;* More American Graffiti, *599;* Rude Awakening (1989), *371;* Son of Blob (Beware! The Blob), *888;* Spaceship, *384;* Travels with My Aunt, *399;* Tricks of the Trade, *399;* Uforia, *402*

Williams, Clara: Hell's Hinges, *1120*

Williams III, Clarence: Against the Wall, *442;* Dangerous Relations, *494;* Deep Cover (1992), *36;* 52 Pick-Up, *976;* Maniac Cop 2, *863;* Mod Squad, The (TV Series), *86;* My Heroes Have Always Been Cowboys, *1135;* Sugar Hill, *122*

Williams, Cynda: Mo' Better Blues, *931;* One False Move, *94*

Williams, Darnell: How U Like Me Now, *303*

Williams, Dean: Distant Voices/Still Lives, *502*

Williams, Diahn: Deadly Hero, *34*

Williams, Dick Anthony: Gardens of Stone, *525;* Gun in the House, A, *534;* Mo' Better Blues, *931;* Sophisticated Gents, The, *663;* Tap, *944*

Williams, Don: Ghastly Ones, The, *845*

Williams, Edy: Hellhole, *849;* Mankillers, *82;* Secret Life of an American Wife, The, *374;* Seven Minutes, The, *653*

Williams, Emlyn: Citadel, The, *482;* Epic That Never Was, The, *423;* Iron Duke, The, *554;* Jamaica Inn, *556;* Major Barbara, *326;* Stars Look Down, The, *666;* Wreck of the Mary Deare, The, *141*

Williams II, Ernest: Black Sister's Revenge, *463*

Williams, Esther: Andy Hardy's Double Life, *227;* Bathing Beauty, *908;* Dangerous When Wet, *913;* Duchess of Idaho, *915;* Easy to Love, *915;* Fiesta, *916;* Jupiter's Darling, *926;* Million Dollar Mermaid, *931;* Neptune's Daughter, *932;* On an Island with You, *933;* Pagan Love Song, *934;* Skirts Ahoy!, *940;* Take Me Out to the Ball Game, *943;* Texas Carnival, *944;* That's Entertainment, *436;* That's Entertainment! III, *436;* This Time For Keeps, *945;* Thrill of a Romance, *945;* Ziegfeld Follies, *949*

Williams, Grant: Brain of Blood, *818;* Incredible Shrinking Man, The, *1058;* Leech Woman, The, *860;* Monolith Monsters, The, *865;* PT 109, *630*

Williams, Guinn: American Empire, *1093;* Bad Lands, *1095;* Bill Fields and Will Rogers, *239;* Billy the Kid, *1099;* Cowboy and the Senorita, *1106;* Flirtation Walk, *917;* Hands Across the Border, *1118;* Littlest Rebel, The, *929;* Lucky Boots, *1130;* Man of the Forest, *1132;* Mystery Squadron, *88;* Noah's Ark, *608;* Phantom Broadcast, The, *1005;* Powdersmoke Range, *1139;* Riders of Death Valley, *1143;* Silver Queen, *1150;* Station West, *1153;* Vigilantes Are Coming!, *1161;* Virginia City, *1161;* Wolfheart's Revenge, *1165;* You Only Live Once, *708;* You'll Never Get Rich, *948*

Williams, Guy: Captain Sinbad, *156;* Lost in Space (TV Series), *1063;* Sign of Zorro, The, *204*

Williams, Gwen: Hoppity Goes to Town, *175*

Williams, Hal: On the Nickel, *612*

Williams Jr., Hank: Willa, *703*

Williams, Heathcote: Orlando, *614*

Williams, Hugh: Human Monster, The (Dark Eyes of London), *854;* One of Our Aircraft Is Missing, *94;* Ships with Wings, *115*

Williams, Ian Patrick: Bad Channels, *1037*

Williams, James K.: Cybernator, *1043*

Williams, Jason: Danger Zone, The, *32;* Flesh Gordon, *1052;* Vampire at Midnight, *899*

Williams, JoBeth: Adam, *441;* American Dreamer, *226;* Big Chill, The, *460;* Chantilly Lace, *479;* Child in the Night, *961;* Day After, The, *1044;* Desert Bloom, *499;* Dutch, *269;* Endangered Species, *1049;* Kramer vs. Kramer, *567;* Me, Myself & I, *330;* Memories of Me, *331;* Poltergeist, *875;* Poltergeist II: The Other Side, *875;* Sex, Love, and Cold Hard Cash, *1014;* Stir Crazy, *386;* Stop! Or My Mom Will Shoot, *386;* Switch, *390;* Teachers, *391;* Victim of Love, *1030;* Welcome Home, *698*

Williams, John: Alfred Hitchcock Presents (TV Series), *951;* Dial M for Murder, *970;* Paradine Case, The, *1004;* Sabrina, *372;* To Catch a Thief, *1025;* Witness for the Prosecution (1957), *1032;* Young Philadelphians, The, *708*

Williams, Jori: Faster Pussycat! Kill! Kill!, *46*

Williams, Kate: Melody, *186*

Williams, Kelli: Lifepod, *1063;* Zapped Again, *416*

Williams, Kenneth: Carry on at Your Convenience, *251;* Carry on Behind, *251;* Carry on Cleo, *251;* Carry on Cowboy, *251;* Carry on Cruising, *251;* Carry on Doctor, *251;* Carry on Emmanuelle, *251;* Carry on Nurse, *251;* Follow That Camel, *278*

Williams, Kent: Rubdown, *1011*

Williams, Kimberly: Father of the Bride (1991), *275;* Indian Summer, *306*

Williams, Kurt T.: Last Dance, *990*

Williams, Mark: Trained to Fight, *132*

Williams, Megan: Anzacs, *450*

Williams, Michael: Educating Rita, *270*

Williams, Paul: Battle for the Planet of the Apes, *1038;* Cheap Detective, The, *254;* Frog, *168;* Muppet Movie, The, *189;* Night They Saved Christmas, The, *191;* Phantom of the Paradise, *935;* Smokey and the Bandit, *381;* Smokey and the Bandit II, *381;* Smokey and the Bandit III, *382;* Stone Cold Dead, *1020;* Wild Wild West Revisited, The, *1164*

Williams, Peter: Robin Hood and the Sorcerer, *107*

Williams, Rhys: Corn Is Green, The (1945), *488;* Fastest Gun Alive, The, *1112;* Hills of Home, *174;* Raintree County, *634;* Showdown, The (1950), *1149;* Strange Woman, The, *669*

Williams, Robert: Platinum Blonde, *623*

Williams, Robin: Adventures of Baron Münchausen, The, *1034;* All-Star Toast to the Improv, An, *224;* Awakenings, *452;* Being Human, *458;* Best of Comic Relief, The, *235;* Best of Times, The, *236;* Cadillac Man, *249;* Can I Do It 'Til I Need Glasses?, *249;* Club Paradise, *256;* Comedy Tonight, *257;* Comic Relief 2, *258;* Dead Again, *966;* Dead Poets Society, *497;* Evening with Robin Williams, An, *272;* Fisher King, The, *1051;* Good Morning, Vietnam, *530;* Hook, *175;* Mrs. Doubtfire, *334;* Moscow on the Hudson, *337;* Popeye, *196;* Richard Lewis—"I'm in Pain Concert", *367;* Robin Williams Live, *369;* Seize the Day, *651;* Survivors, The, *389;* Tale of the Frog Prince, *209;* Toys, *398;* World According to Garp, The, *706*

Williams, Scot: BackBeat, *907*

Williams, Simon: Blood on Satan's Claw, *815;* Odd Job, The, *348*

Williams Jr., Spencer: Amos and Andy (TV Series), *226*

Williams, Steven: Deep Red (1994), *1046;* Jason Goes to Hell: The Final Friday, *858;* Missing in Action 2: The Beginning, *85;* Revolver, *106*

Williams, Treat: Dead Heat, *830;* Deadly Hero, *34;* Dempsey, *499;* Echoes in the Darkness, *507;* Final Verdict, *516;* Flashpoint, *977;* Hair, *921;* Heart of Dixie, The, *538;* Little Mermaid, The (1984), *182;* Max and Helen, *590;* Men's Club, The, *593;* Night of the Sharks, *90;* 1941, *345;* Once Upon a Time in America (Long Version), *94;* Prince of the City, *627;* Pursuit of D. B. Cooper, *363;* Ritz, The, *368;* Smooth Talk, *661;* Sweet Lies, *389;* Third Degree Burn, *1024;* Third Solution, The, *794;* Till Death Do Us Part, *683;* Water Engine, The, *696*

Williams, Van: Green Hornet, The (TV Series), *58*

illiams, Vanessa: Another You, 228; Candyman (1992), '0; Full Exposure, 523; Harley Davidson and the Marlboro an, 59; Jacksons: An American Dream, The, 556; Under the in, 691
illiams, Wendy O.: Pucker Up and Bark Like a Dog, 363; form School Girls, 105
illiamson, Fred: Adios Amigo, 1092; Big Score, The, 12; ack Caesar, 13; Black Cobra 3, 13; Blind Rage, 15; Boss, '01; Bucktown, 20; Deadly Impact, 34; Deadly Intent, 34; lta Force, Commando Two, 37; Express to Terror, 974; xtrap, 52; Hell Up in Harlem, 60; Mean Johnny Barrows, 83; w Gladiators, The, 1068; One Down, Two to Go, 94; South ach, 1019; Steele's Law, 120; Take a Hard Ride, 1154; ree Days to a Kill, 128; Three the Hard Way, 129; Warrior of e Lost World, 1088; Warriors of the Wasteland, 1088
illiamson, Mykel T.: First Power, The, 841; Miami Vice, ; You Talkin' to Me, 141
illiamson, Nicol: Black Widow, 955; Cheap Detective, e, 254; Christopher Columbus (1985), 25; Excalibur, 1050; amlet (1969), 535; I'm Dancing As Fast As I Can, 549; ssion Flower, 619; Return to Oz, 199; Robin and Marian,)7; Seven-Per-Cent Solution, The, 1013; Venom, 900; Wilby onspiracy, The, 701
illiamson, Phillip: Angelic Conversation, 448
illingham, Noble: Career Opportunities, 251; City Slickers 256; Fire in the Sky, 1051; Last Boy Scout, The, 75; astime, 619; Sweet Poison, 123
illis, Bruce: Billy Bathgate, 461; Blind Date (1987), 241; onfire of the Vanities, 466; Death Becomes Her, 1045; Die ard, 38; Die Hard 2: Die Harder, 39; Hudson Hawk, 64; In ountry, 550; Last Boy Scout, The, 75; Moonlighting (1985), 97; Mortal Thoughts, 997; National Lampoon's Loaded eapon 1, 342; Striking Distance, 121; Sunset, 1021; That's dequate, 393
illis, Hope Alexander: Pack, The, 873
illis, Matt: Return of the Vampire, The, 880; So Dear to My eart, 205
ills, Chill: Alamo, The, 1092; Allegheny Uprising, 1093; izona Legion, 1095; Billy the Kid, 1099; Boom Town, 466; eadly Companions, The, 1108; Francis Joins the Wacs, 280; ancis, the Talking Mule, 280; Harvey Girls, The, 922; Honky onk, 1121; Kentucky Rifle, 1124; Lawless Valley, 1127; oaded Pistols, 1128; Man from the Alamo, The, 1132; cLintock!, 1133; Mr. Billion, 85; Pat Garrett and Billy the d, 1138; Ride the Man Down, 1143; Rio Grande, 1145; ounders, The, 1146; Steagle, The, 386; Tarzan's New York dventure, 126; Tulsa, 689; Western Union, 1163; Westerner, he, 1163; Wheeler Dealers, The, 409; Yearling, The, 219
illson, Paul: Garry Shandling Show, The, 283
ilson, Barbara: Invasion of the Animal People, 1059
ilson, Daniel: Wait Until Spring, Bandini, 695
ilson, Don: Jack Benny Program, The (TV Series), 309
ilson, Don "The Dragon": Blackbelt, 14; Bloodfist, 15; oodfist 2, 16; Bloodfist III: Forced to Fight, 16; Bloodfist —Die Trying, 16; Bloodfist V: Human Target, 16
ilson, Dooley: Cairo, 910
ilson, Elizabeth: Addams Family, The, 222; Believers, The, 12; Grace Quigley, 289; Happy Hooker, The, 293; Incredible hrinking Woman, The, 306; Little Murders, 319; Prisoner of econd Avenue, The, 361; Regarding Henry, 637; Where Are e Children?, 1031; You Can't Take it with You (1984), 415
ilson, Flip: Fish That Saved Pittsburgh, The, 278; Uptown aturday Night, 404
ilson, Frank: Emperor Jones, The, 509
ilson, George: Attack of the Killer Tomatoes, 229
ilson, Georges: Empty Canvas, The, 509; Make Room For omorrow, 764
ilson, Jackie: Go, Johnny, Go!, 920
ilson, Jim: Charlie, the Lonesome Cougar, 158
ilson, Julie: This Could Be the Night, 394
ilson, Lambert: Belly of an Architect, The, 458; Blood of thers, The, 464; Five Days One Summer, 517; Frankenstein (1992), 842; Red Kiss (Rouge Baiser), 780; Rendez-Vous, 780; Sahara (1984), 110; Strangers, 669
Wilson, Lois: Covered Wagon, The, 1106; Deluge, 1046; Vanishing American, The, 1161
Wilson, Mara: Mrs. Doubtfire, 334
Wilson, Marie: Boy Meets Girl, 244; Girl in Every Port, A, 286; Mr. Hobbs Takes a Vacation, 334; My Friend Irma, 340; Never Wave at a WAC, 343; Private Affairs of Bel Ami, The, 628; Satan Met a Lady, 1012
Wilson, Mary Louise: Cheap Shots, 254
Wilson, Michael: Nutcase, 347
Wilson, Nancy: Big Score, The, 12; Meteor Man, 186
Wilson, Paul: Brainwaves, 818; Devonsville Terror, The, 834
Wilson, Perry: Fear Strikes Out, 515
Wilson, Rita: Sleepless in Seattle, 381; Volunteers, 405
Wilson, Robert Brian: Silent Night, Deadly Night, 886
Wilson, Roger: Porky's, 360; Porky's II: The Next Day, 360; Thunder Alley, 945
Wilson, Scott: Aviator, The, 452; Blue City, 957; Femme Fatale, 976; Flesh and Bone, 518; Geronimo: An American Legend, 1115; Grissom Gang, The, 534; In Cold Blood, 985; Jesse, 557; Malone, 80; Ninth Configuration, The, 608; On the Line, 94; Pure Luck, 363; Right Stuff, The, 640; Tracker, The, 1158; Year of the Quiet Sun, 805
Wilson, Sheree: Fraternity Vacation, 280; News at Eleven, 605; One Riot, One Ranger, 95
Wilson, Stuart: Highest Honor, The, 62; Lethal Weapon 3, 77; No Escape, 1069; Poor Girl, A Ghost Story, 876; Romance on the Orient Express, 643; Teenage Mutant Ninja Turtles III, 209; Wetherby, 698
Wilson, Teddy: Benny Goodman Story, The, 458
Wilson, Terry: Wagon Train (TV Series), 1162
Wilson, Thomas F.: Action Jackson, 2; Back to the Future, 1037; Back to the Future II, 1037; Back to the Future III, 1037
Wilson, Tom: Chaplin Revue, The, 253
Wilson, Trey: Bull Durham, 247; Drive-In, 269; Great Balls of Fire, 920; Raising Arizona, 364
Wilton, Penelope: Blame It on the Bellboy, 240; Borrowers, The, 152; Clockwise, 256; Cry Freedom, 492; Norman Conquests, The, Episode 1: Table Manners, 346; Norman Conquests, The, Episode 2: Living Together, 346; Norman Conquests, The, Episode 3: Round and Round the Garden, 346; Singleton's Pluck, 379
Wimmer, Brian: Dangerous Pursuit, 966; Late for Dinner, 1062; Lipstick Camera, 992
Winchell, Paul: Which Way to the Front?, 410
Winchester, Anna-Maria: Chain Reaction, 24; Deadly Possession, 968
Wincott, Jeff: Deadly Bet, 34; Martial Law Two—Undercover, 82; Martial Outlaw, 82; Mission of Justice, 85
Wincott, Michael: Crow, The, 827; 1492: The Conquest of Paradise, 52; Wild Horse Hank, 217
Windom, William: Attack of the 50-Foot Woman (1993), 1037; Back to Hannibal: The Return of Tom Sawyer and Huckleberry Finn, 454; Dennis the Menace: Dinosaur Hunter, 162; Detective, The (1968), 500; Escape from the Planet of the Apes, 1049; Funland, 282; Grandview, U.S.A., 531; Leave 'em Laughing, 572; Now You See Him, Now You Don't, 191; One Man's Way, 613; Pinocchio and the Emperor of the Night, 195; She's Having a Baby, 377; Sommersby, 662; Space Rage, 1078
Windsor, Barbara: Study in Terror, A, 1021
Windsor, Marie: Abbott and Costello Meet the Mummy, 221; Cat Women of the Moon, 1041; Critic's Choice, 261; Double Deal, 41; Force of Evil, 519; Hellfire, 1120; Humanoid Defender, 1057; Killing, The, 988; Little Big Horn, 1128; Lovely But Deadly, 994; Narrow Margin, The (1952), 89; Outpost in Morocco, 96; Showdown, The (1950), 1149; Trouble Along the Way, 688
Windsor, Romy: Big Bad John, 12; House of Usher, The, 853; Howling IV, 854

Windust, Penelope: Iron Will, *67*
Winfield, Paul: Back to Hannibal: The Return of Tom Sawyer and Huckleberry Finn, *454;* Big Shots, *238;* Blue and the Gray, The, *1099;* Blue City, *957;* Breathing Lessons, *469;* Brother John, *470;* Conrack, *488;* Damnation Alley, *1044;* Death Before Dishonor, *35;* Gordon's War, *57;* Hero Ain't Nothin' But a Sandwich, A, *540;* High Velocity, *62;* Huckleberry Finn (1974), *176;* It's Good to Be Alive, *555;* King, *564;* Presumed Innocent, *1007;* Serpent and the Rainbow, The, *884;* Sophisticated Gents, The, *663;* Sounder, *663;* Twilight's Last Gleaming, *133;* White Dog, *700*
Winfrey, Oprah: Color Purple, The, *485;* Native Son, *604;* Pee-Wee's Playhouse Christmas Special, *194;* Women of Brewster Place, The, *706*
Wing, Leslie: Cowboy and the Ballerina, The, *490;* Retribution, *879*
Wing, Tang Tak: Trained to Fight, *132*
Winger, Debra: Betrayed (1988), *954;* Black Widow, *955;* Cannery Row, *250;* Dangerous Woman, A, *494;* Everybody Wins, *973;* French Postcards, *281;* Leap of Faith, *572;* Legal Eagles, *991;* Made in Heaven (1987), *1064;* Mike's Murder, *594;* Officer and a Gentleman, An, *611;* Shadowlands, *654;* Sheltering Sky, The, *655;* Slumber Party 57, *381;* Terms of Endearment, *679;* Thank God It's Friday, *944;* Urban Cowboy, *692;* Wilder Napalm, *411*
Wingett, Mark: Quadrophenia, *936*
Winkler, Angela: Lost Honor of Katharina Blum, The, *761;* Sheer Madness, *785;* Tin Drum, The, *795*
Winkler, Henry: American Christmas Carol, An, *146;* Heroes, *540;* Katherine, *562;* Lords of Flatbush, The, *579;* Night Shift, *344;* One and Only, The, *613;* Steve Martin Live, *386*
Winn, David: For Love of Angela, *519*
Winn, Kitty: Man on a String, *81*
Winninger, Charles: Babes in Arms, *907;* Beyond Tomorrow, *1039;* Broadway Rhythm, *910;* Every Day's a Holiday, *273;* Fighting Caravans, *1112;* Lady Takes a Chance, A, *1125;* Little Nellie Kelly, *928;* Living In A Big Way, *929;* Night Nurse, *606;* Nothing Sacred, *347;* Pot O' Gold, *625;* Show Boat (1936), *939;* State Fair (1945), *941;* Sun Shines Bright, The, *673;* Three Smart Girls, *945;* Three Smart Girls Grow Up, *945;* Torpedo Alley, *131*
Winningham, Mare: Eye on the Sparrow, *512;* Fatal Exposure, *46;* God Bless the Child, *528;* Hard Promises, *536;* Intruders, *1059;* Made in Heaven (1987), *1064;* Miracle Mile, *996;* Nobody's Fool, *346;* St. Elmo's Fire, *646;* Shy People, *657;* Single Bars, Single Women, *658;* Turner and Hooch, *400*
Winslow, George: Gentlemen Prefer Blondes, *284*
Winslow, Michael: Alphabet City, *445;* Buy and Cell, *248;* Going Under, *288;* Lovelines, *323;* Police Academy, *359;* Police Academy II: Their First Assignment, *359;* Police Academy III: Back in Training, *359;* Police Academy 4: Citizens on Patrol, *359;* Police Academy 5—Assignment: Miami Beach, *359;* Police Academy 6: City Under Siege, *359;* Spaceballs, *384;* Tag—The Assassination Game, *124;* Think Big, *394*
Winstone, Ray: Scum, *650*
Winter, Alex: Bill and Ted's Bogus Journey, *239;* Bill and Ted's Excellent Adventure, *239;* Freaked, *281;* Haunted Summer, *537*
Winter, Edward: Act of Passion, *441;* Porky's II: The Next Day, *360*
Winter, Vincent: Gorgo, *847;* Horse Without a Head, The, *175;* Three Lives of Thomasina, The, *211*
Winters, Deborah: Blue Sunshine, *957;* Class of '44, *483;* Kotch, *314;* Outing, The, *873;* Tarantulas—The Deadly Cargo, *892*
Winters, Grant: College, *257*
Winters, Jonathan: Alice Through the Looking Glass (1985), *145;* Fish That Saved Pittsburgh, The, *278;* Hungry I Reunion, *303;* It's a Mad Mad Mad Mad World, *308;* Longshot, The (1985), *320;* Loved One, The, *323;* Moon Over Parador, *336;* More Wild Wild West, *1134;* Oh Dad, Poor Dad—Mama's Hung You in the Closet and I'm Feeling So Sad, *348;* Russians Are Coming, the Russians Are Coming, The, *371;* Say Yes, *373;* Viva Max!, *405*
Winters, Loren: Freeway Maniac, *843*
Winters, Nathan Forrest: Clownhouse, *824*
Winters, Roland: Feathered Serpent, The, *976;* To Please a Lady, *130;* West Point Story, The, *947*
Winters, Shelley: Alfie, *224;* Alice in Wonderland (1985), *145;* Balcony, The, *455;* Bloody Mama, *16;* Blume in Love, *465;* Buono Sera, Mrs. Campbell, *247;* Cleopatra Jones, *26;* Deja Vu, *499;* Delta Force, The, *36;* Diamonds, *38;* Diary of Anne Frank, The, *501;* Double Life, A, *504;* Elvis—The Movie, *509;* Enter Laughing, *271;* Executive Suite, *512;* Greatest Story Ever Told, The, *533;* Harper, *981;* I Am a Camera, *547;* Died a Thousand Times, *65;* Initiation of Sarah, The, *856;* Journey into Fear (1975), *987;* King of the Gypsies, *565;* Knickerbocker Holiday, *927;* Lolita, *577;* Magician of Lublin, The, *585;* Mambo, *586;* Next Stop, Greenwich Village, *605;* Night of the Hunter, *1001;* Over the Brooklyn Bridge, *352;* Patch of Blue, A, *619;* Phone Call from a Stranger, *622;* Pickle, The, *357;* Place in the Sun, A, *622;* Poseidon Adventure, The, *99;* Purple People Eater, *198;* Revenge (1971), *1010;* S.O.B., *372;* Scalphunters, The, *1148;* Shattered (1972), *655;* Stepping Out, *942;* Tenant, The, *1023;* Tentacles, *893;* That Lucky Touch, *392;* Treasure of Pancho Villa, The, *1158;* Unremarkable Life, An, *692;* Visitor, The, *1087;* Weep No More My Lady, *1030;* What's the Matter with Helen?, *902;* Who Slew Auntie Roo?, *903;* Wild in the Streets, *1089;* Winchester '73, *1165;* Young Savages, The, *1033*
Winwood, Estelle: Dead Ringer, *967;* Glass Slipper, The, *919;* Magic Sword, The, *185;* Misfits, The, *595;* Swan, The (1956), *674;* This Happy Feeling, *394*
Wirth, Billy: Red Shoe Diaries, *637;* War Party, *137*
Wisch, Allen: Overkill, *96*
Wisdom, Norman: To See Such Fun, *397*
Wise, Cela: Deadly Rivals, *35*
Wise, Ray: Body Shot, *958;* Chase, The (1994), *25;* Endless Descent, *838;* Journey of Natty Gann, The, *179;* Rising Sun, *1010;* Season of Fear, *1013;* Sunstroke, *1021;* Swamp Thing, *891;* Twin Peaks: Fire Walk with Me, *1028*
Wiseman, Don: Red Alert, *104*
Wiseman, Joseph: Dr. No, *40;* Journey into Fear (1975), *987;* Prodigal, The, *629;* Seize the Day, *651;* Silver Chalice, The, *658;* Unforgiven, The (1960), *1160;* Viva Zapata!, *694*
Wiseman, Mac: High Lonesome—The Story of Bluegrass Music, *426*
Wiseman, Michael: Judgment Night, *69*
Wisoff, Jill: Fear, Anxiety and Depression, *276*
Withers, Googie: Dead of Night (1945), *830;* Night and the City (1950), *605;* On Approval, *349;* One of Our Aircraft Is Missing, *94*
Withers, Grant: Bells of Coronado, *1097;* Doomed to Die, *41;* Fatal Hour, The, *46;* Fighting Marines, The, *48;* Final Extra, The, *977;* Goin' to Town, *287;* Hellfire, *1120;* Hoodlum Empire, *64;* Lady Takes a Chance, A, *1125;* Mr. Wong, Detective, *997;* Mr. Wong in Chinatown, *997;* Nighttime in Nevada, *1136;* Oklahoma Annie, *349;* Radio Patrol, *102;* Road to Ruin, The (1928), *641;* Trigger, Jr., *1159;* Utah, *1160;* Yellow Rose of Texas, *1165*
Withers, Jane: Bright Eyes, *152;* Captain Newman, M.D., *474*
Witherspoon, Cora: Bank Dick, The, *232;* I've Always Loved You, *555;* Madame X (1937), *584;* Personal Property, *356*
Witherspoon, John: Talkin' Dirty After Dark, *391*
Witherspoon, Reese: Far Off Place, A, *166;* Jack the Bear, *556;* Man in the Moon, The, *587;* Return to Lonesome Dove, *1143*
Withrow, Glenn: Pass the Ammo, *355*
Witney, Michael: W, *1030*
Witt, Kathryn: Cocaine Wars, *27;* Demon of Paradise, *832*
Witter, Karen: Perfect Match, The, *356*
Wodoslavsky, Stefas: 90 Days, *345*
Wolcott, Abigail: Hellgate, *849*

lders, Robert: Interval, *553*
lf, Hilary: Big Girls Don't Cry...They Get Even, *238*
lf, Kelly: Day in October, A, *496;* Stephen King's
veyard Shift, *890*
lf, Scott: Teenage Bonnie and Klepto Clyde, *126*
lf, Silver: Radio Patrol, *102*
lfe, Ian: Bedlam, *812;* Brighton Strangler, The, *819;*
per Canyon, *1106;* Diane, *500;* Diary of a Madman, *834;*
nebodies, *851;* Houdini, *544;* Julia Misbehaves, *311;*
gnificent Yankee, The, *585;* Marauders, *1132;* One Man's
y, *613;* Pearl of Death, The, *1004;* Scarlet Claw, The, *1012;*
of Monte Cristo, The, *118*
lfe, Jim: Invasion of the Space Preachers, *307*
lfe, Julie: Portfolio, *624*
lfe, Nancy: Helter Skelter, *540*
lff, Frank: Atlas, *7;* Last Gun, The, *1126;* When Women
l Tails, *409;* When Women Lost Their Tails, *409*
lff, Rikard: House of Angels, *745*
lfit, Donald: Blood of the Vampire, *815*
lfman Jack: Deadman's Curve, *913;* Hanging on a Star,
5; Midnight (1989), *996*
lheim, Louis: All Quiet on the Western Front (1930), *3;*
nger Lights, *494;* Dr. Jekyll and Mr. Hyde (1920), *835;*
npest (1928), *678*
llter, Sven: House of Angels, *745*
loshyn, Ilya: Beethoven Lives Upstairs, *149;* Hush Little
by, *984*
lter, Sherilyn: Eyewitness to Murder, *46*
ong, Anna May: Impact, *985;* Java Head, *557;* Shanghai
press, *655;* Study in Scarlet, A, *1021;* Thief of Bagdad, The
924), *1083*
ong, B. D.: Father of the Bride (1991), *275;* Jurassic Park,
61; Mystery Date, *341*
ong, Janet: Bustin' Loose, *248*
ong, Jei: Reincarnation of Golden Lotus, The, *780*
ong, Ronald: People's Hero, *777*
ong, Russell: China Cry, *481;* China Girl, *25;* China White,
; Eat a Bowl of Tea, *507*
ong, Tsu Hsien: Chinese Ghost Story, A, *723*
ong, Victor: Big Trouble in Little China, *13;* Dim Sum: A
tle Bit of Heart, *501;* Eat a Bowl of Tea, *507;* Golden Child,
e, *56;* Ice Runner, *65;* Last Emperor, The, *569;* Prince of
rkness, *876;* Shanghai Surprise, *377;* Son of Kong, The,
8; Three Ninjas, *211;* Three Ninjas Kick Back, *211;*
emors, *897*
ontner, Arthur: Genevieve, *283;* Silver Blaze, *1016;*
umph of Sherlock Holmes, The, *1027*
ood, Andy: Annihilators, The, *5;* Eye of the Eagle 2, *46;*
ost Warrior, *55*
ood, Annabella: Bloodthirsty Butchers, *816*
ood, Britt: Detour to Danger, *1109;* Hidden Gold, *1120;*
nge War, *1141;* Showdown (1940), *1149*
ood, Cindi: Hoodlum Priest, The, *543*
ood, Clive: Crucifer of Blood, *964;* Treasure Island (1990),
4
ood, David: If..., *304*
ood Jr., Edward D.: Fugitive Girls, *53*
ood, Elijah: Adventures of Huck Finn, The (1993), *143;*
valon, *452;* Child in the Night, *961;* Forever Young (1992),
053; Good Son, The, *980;* Paradise (1991), *618;* Radio Flyer,
3
ood, Freeman: Buster Keaton Festival: Vol. 2, *248*
ood, Gary: Hardbodies, *293*
ood, Harley: Border Phantom, *1100;* Marijuana, *588*
ood, Helen: Give a Girl a Break, *919*
ood, John: Jumpin' Jack Flash, *311;* Lady Jane, *568;*
adyhawke, *74;* Orlando, *614;* Purple Rose of Cairo, The, *363;*
hadowlands, *654;* Summer House, The, *388;* Wargames,
088; Which Way to the Front?, *410*
ood, Lana: Grayeagle, *1116;* Justin Morgan Had a Horse,
79; Place Called Today, A, *622;* Searchers, The, *1148*
Wood, Leigh: Stocks and Blondes, *668*
Wood, Natalie: Affair, The, *442;* Bob & Carol & Ted & Alice, *243;* Brainstorm, *1040;* Cash McCall, *252;* Cracker Factory, *490;* From Here to Eternity (1979), *523;* Ghost and Mrs. Muir, The, *285;* Great Race, The, *290;* Green Promise, The, *533;* Gypsy (1962), *921;* Inside Daisy Clover, *552;* Kings Go Forth, *565;* Last Married Couple in America, The, *315;* Love with the Proper Stranger, *582;* Marjorie Morningstar, *589;* Meteor, *1065;* Miracle on 34th Street, *187;* Rebel without a Cause, *636;* Searchers, The, *1148;* Sex and the Single Girl, *376;* Silver Chalice, The, *658;* Splendor in the Grass, *664;* Star, The, *665;* This Property Is Condemned, *682;* Tomorrow Is Forever, *685;* West Side Story, *947*
Wood, Peggy: Story of Ruth, The, *668*
Wood, Robert: White Fang and the Hunter, *217*
Wood, Ronnie: Jerry Lee Lewis—I Am What I Am, *428*
Wood, Salvador: Death of a Bureaucrat, *728*
Wood, Thomas: Blood Feast, *815;* 2,000 Maniacs, *898*
Wood, Ward: Adventures of the Flying Cadets, *2*
Wood, Wilson: Satan's Satellites, *111;* Zombies of the Stratosphere (Satan's Satellites), *141*
Woodard, Alfre: Blue Chips, *465;* Crooklyn, *261;* Extremities, *512;* Grand Canyon, *531;* Gun in Betty Lou's Handbag, The, *292;* Heart and Souls, *1056;* Killing Floor, The, *563;* Mandela, *588;* Miss Firecracker, *333;* Passion Fish, *619;* Puss in Boots, *198;* Rich in Love, *640;* Scrooged, *374;* Unnatural Causes, *692*
Woodbine, Bokeem: Strapped, *670*
Woodbury, Joan: Bulldog Courage, *1102;* Chinese Cat, The, *962;* Gangs, Inc., *54;* King of the Zombies, *859;* Northwest Trail, *1136;* Song of the Gringo, *1151;* Sunset Serenade, *1154;* Time Travelers, The, *1084*
Woode, Margo: Bullfighters, The, *247*
Woodell, Patricia: Commies Are Coming, the Commies Are Coming, The, *258;* Woman Hunt, The, *140*
Woodlawn, Holly: Trash, *687*
Woodruff, Largo: Bill, *461;* Bill: On His Own, *461;* Coward of the County, *490;* Funhouse, The, *845*
Woods, Barbara Alyn: Dance with Death, *965;* Eden (TV Series), *507;* Inside Out (1992), *1058*
Woods, Bill: Maniac (1934), *862*
Woods, Connie: Night of the Living Babes, *344*
Woods, Donald: Anthony Adverse, *450;* Beast From 20,000 Fathoms, The, *1038;* Beauty for the Asking, *457;* Bridge of San Luis Rey, The, *469;* Corregidor, *489;* Heritage of the Desert, *1120;* Mexican Spitfire, *331;* Sea Devils, *112;* Story of Louis Pasteur, The, *668;* Sweet Adeline, *943;* 13 Ghosts, *895;* Wonder Man, *413*
Woods, Edward: Public Enemy, *101;* Tarzan the Fearless, *125*
Woods, Harry: Adventures of Rex and Rinty, *1092;* Blue Montana Skies, *1099;* Days of Jesse James, *1107;* Down Texas Way, *1110;* Haunted Gold, *1119;* In Early Arizona, *1122;* In Old Cheyenne, *1123;* Lawless Nineties, The, *1127;* Range Defenders, *1141;* Range Feud, *1141;* Ranger and the Lady, The, *1141;* West of the Law, *1163;* Winners of the West, *1165*
Woods, James: Against All Odds, *951;* Badge of the Assassin, *454;* Best Seller, *954;* Boost, The, *466;* Cat's Eye, *822;* Chaplin, *479;* Choirboys, The, *481;* Citizen Cohn, *482;* Cop, *29;* Diggstown, *264;* Disappearance of Aimee, The, *970;* Eyewitness, *974;* Fallen Angels, *513;* Fast-Walking, *515;* Getaway, The (1994), *55;* Gift of Love, The, *527;* Hard Way, The (1991), *293;* Immediate Family, *549;* In Love and War, *985;* Incredible Journey of Dr. Meg Laurel, The, *551;* Joshua Then and Now, *311;* Love and War, *581;* Once Upon a Time in America (Long Version), *94;* Onion Field, The, *613;* Salvador, *647;* Split Image, *664;* Straight Talk, *387;* True Believer, *1027;* Videodrome, *900;* Women & Men: Stories of Seduction, *706*
Woods, Jeril: Revenge of the Cheerleaders, *367*
Woods, Michael: Blindfold: Acts of Obsession, *956;* Haunting of Sarah Hardy, The, *982;* Hit Woman: The Double

Edge, *63;* Lady Beware, *989;* Omen IV: The Awakening, *872;* Red Shoe Diaries II: Double Dare, *637*

Woods, Nan: China Beach (TV Series), *481*

Woods, Robert: Badlands Drifter, *1096;* Machine Gun Killers, *1130;* Savage Guns, *1147*

Woods, Sara: Sweeney Todd, *943*

Woodson, Jack: Edge of Darkness (1986), *973*

Woodthorpe, Peter: Evil of Frankenstein, The, *839;* Inspector Morse (TV Series), *986*

Woodville, Katherine: Posse (1975), *1139*

Woodvine, John: Assault on Agathon, *7;* Edge of Darkness (1986), *973*

Woodward, Edward: Appointment, The, *810;* Breaker Morant, *19;* Champions, *479;* Codename: Kyril, *962;* Equalizer, The: "Memories of Manon", *44;* Final Option, The, *977;* King David, *564;* Merlin & the Sword, *1065;* Mister Johnson, *597;* Wicker Man, The, *903*

Woodward, Joanne: Big Hand for the Little Lady, A, *1098;* Blind Spot, *464;* Breathing Lessons, *469;* Christmas to Remember, A, *482;* Crisis at Central High, *491;* Drowning Pool, The, *972;* End, The, *271;* Fine Madness, A, *277;* Foreign Affairs, *520;* From the Terrace, *523;* Fugitive Kind, The, *523;* Glass Menagerie, The, *528;* Harry and Son, *537;* Long Hot Summer, The (1958), *578;* Mr. and Mrs. Bridge, *596;* New Kind of Love, A, *343;* Paris Blues, *618;* Rachel, Rachel, *632;* Shadow Box, The, *654;* Streets of L.A., The, *671;* Stripper, The (1963), *671;* Summer Wishes, Winter Dreams, *673;* Sybil, *675;* They Might Be Giants, *1023;* Three Faces of Eve, The, *682;* Winning, *140*

Woodward, Morgan: Final Chapter—Walking Tall, *48;* Girls Just Want to Have Fun, *287;* Small Town in Texas, A, *117;* Which Way Is Up?, *410;* Yuma, *1166*

Woodward, Tim: Dark Angel, The, *966;* Europeans, The, *511;* Salome (1985), *647*

Wooldridge, Susan: Frankenstein (1984), *842;* Hope and Glory, *544;* How to Get Ahead in Advertising, *302;* Jewel in the Crown, The, *557;* Loyalties, *582*

Wooley, Sheb: Hoosiers, *543;* Rawhide (TV Series), *1141*

Woollcott, Alexander: Scoundrel, The, *374*

Woolley, Monty: As Young as You Feel, *229;* Everybody Sing, *916;* Girl of the Golden West, The, *919;* Kismet (1955), *927;* Man Who Came to Dinner, The, *328;* Night and Day (1946), *933;* Since You Went Away, *658;* Three Comrades, *682*

Woolsey, Robert: Cockeyed Cavaliers, *257;* Diplomaniacs, *914;* Half-Shot at Sunrise, *292;* Hips, Hips, Hooray, *297;* Hold 'em Jail, *298;* Hook, Line and Sinker, *300;* Kentucky Kernels, *312*

Woorhels, Steve: Last Chants for a Slow Dance, *568*

Worden, Hank: McLintock!, *1133;* Mystery of the Hooded Horsemen, *1135;* Scream, *883*

Wordsworth, Richard: Quatermass Experiment, The, *1073;* Tripods, *1085*

Workman, Jimmy: Addams Family, The, *222;* Addams Family Values, *222*

Worlock, Frederic: Dressed to Kill (1946), *972*

Woronov, Mary: Angel of H.E.A.T., *5;* Challenge of a Lifetime, *478;* Club Fed, *256;* Death Race 2000, *1045;* Eating Raoul, *270;* Hollywood Boulevard, *299;* Living End, The, *577;* Mortuary Academy, *337;* Motorama, *337;* Night of the Comet, *1068;* Nomads, *872;* Rock 'n' Roll High School Forever, *369;* Silent Night, Bloody Night, *886;* Sugar Cookies, *672;* Terror Vision, *1082;* Warlock (1988), *901;* Watchers II, *901*

Worth, Constance: G-Men vs. The Black Dragon, *54;* Windjammer, *140*

Worth, Irene: Deathtrap, *969;* Displaced Person, The, *501;* Forbidden, *519;* King Lear (1971), *564;* Lost in Yonkers, *580*

Worth, Lillian: Tarzan the Tiger, *126*

Worth, Mike: Final Impact, *48;* Street Crimes, *121*

Worthington, Dennis: Neurotic Cabaret, *343*

Wrangler, Greg: Barbarian Queen II: Empress Strikes Back, *1038*

Wray, Fay: Coast Patrol, The, *27;* Crime of Passion, *490;* Doctor X, *836;* Evil Mind, The (a.k.a. The Clairvoyant), *839;* Hell on Frisco Bay, *60;* King Kong (1933), *859;* Melody for Three, *592;* Most Dangerous Game, The, *997;* Mystery of the Wax Museum, *868;* Rock, Pretty Baby, *936;* Small Town Gi[rl], *940;* Tammy and the Bachelor, *677;* Vampire Bat, The, *899;* Viva Villa!, *1162;* Wedding March, The, *697*

Wray, John: Death Kiss, The, *968*

Wren, Clare: Season of Fear, *1013;* Steel and Lace, *1080*

Wright, Amy: Accidental Tourist, The, *440;* Daddy's Dyin' and Who's Got the Will, *261;* Deceived, *969;* Inside Moves, *552;* Love Hurts, *323;* Robot in the Family, *200;* Telephone, The, *392;* Wise Blood, *704*

Wright, Ben: Hiroshima: Out of the Ashes, *541*

Wright Jr., Cobina: Charlie Chan in Rio, *961*

Wright, Jenny: I, Madman, *855;* Lawnmower Man, The, *1062;* Near Dark, *868;* Out of Bounds, *96;* Twister, *401;* Valentino Returns, *693*

Wright, Ken: Eye of the Eagle 3, *46*

Wright, Michael: Confessions of a Hitman, *487;* Five Heartbeats, The, *917;* Principal, The, *628;* Streamers, *670;* Sugar Hill, *122*

Wright, Michael David: Malibu Bikini Shop, The, *327*

Wright, N'Bushe: Zebrahead, *709*

Wright, Robin: Denial, *499;* Playboys, The, *623;* Princess Bride, The, *1071;* State of Grace, *666;* Toys, *398*

Wright, Samuel E.: Bird, *909*

Wright, Steven: Men of Respect, *592;* So I Married an Axe Murderer, *382;* Stars and Bars, *385;* Steven Wright Live, *38[?];* Your Favorite Laughs from an Evening at the Improv, *416*

Wright, Teresa: Best Years of Our Lives, The, *459;* Bill: On His Own, *461;* Casanova Brown, *252;* Escapade in Japan, *165;* Flood!, *51;* Golden Honeymoon, The, *529;* Hail, Hero!, *535;* Little Foxes, The, *576;* Men, The, *592;* Mrs. Miniver, *597;* Pride of the Yankees, The, *627;* Pursued, *1140;* Roseland, *644;* Search for Bridey Murphy, The, *650;* Shadow of a Doubt, *1014;* Somewhere in Time, *1077*

Wright, Tom: Weekend at Bernie's II, *407*

Wright, Whittni: I'll Do Anything, *305*

Wright, Will: People Will Talk, *356*

Wright, William: Daring Young Man, The, *262;* Night to Remember, A (1943), *345*

Wrightman, Robert: Stepfather III: Father's Day, *890*

Wrixon, Maris: Sons of the Pioneers, *1151*

Wu, Ma: Chinese Ghost Story, A, *723*

Wu, Vivian: Shadow of China, *654;* Teenage Mutant Ninja Turtles III, *209*

Wuhl, Robert: Batman (1989), *9;* Bull Durham, *247;* Good Morning, Vietnam, *530;* Mistress (1992), *597;* Tales from the Crypt (Series), *892*

Wuhrer, Kari: Beastmaster 2: Through the Portal of Time, *1039*

Wulfe, Kai: Jungle Warriors, *69;* Red Shoe Diaries, *637*

Wyatt, Jane: Amityville 4: The Evil Escapes, *809;* Buckskin Frontier, *1102;* Gentlemen's Agreement, *526;* House by the River, *984;* Kansan, The, *1124;* Katherine, *562;* Lost Horizon, *580;* Nativity, The, *604;* None But the Lonely Heart, *608;* Pitfall, *622;* Task Force, *677;* Tom Sawyer (1973), *213*

Wycherly, Margaret: Forever Amber, *520;* Keeper of the Flame, *562;* Midnight (1934), *593;* White Heat, *138*

Wyle, Michael: Appointment with Fear, *6*

Wyler, Richard: Rattler Kid, *1141*

Wyman, Jane: Bon Voyage!, *151;* Doughgirls, The, *268;* Footlight Serenade, *917;* Here Comes the Groom, *922;* Incredible Journey of Dr. Meg Laurel, The, *551;* Johnny Belinda, *559;* Lost Weekend, The, *580;* Magic Town, *585;* Magnificent Obsession, *585;* Pollyanna (1960), *196;* Stage Fright, *1019;* Yearling, The, *219*

Wyman, John: Tuxedo Warrior, *133*

Wymark, Patrick: Blood on Satan's Claw, *815;* Journey to the Far Side of the Sun, *1060;* Repulsion, *879;* Skull, The, *887;* Where Eagles Dare, *138*

Wymer, Patricia: Young Graduates, *708*
Wymore, Patrice: Big Trees, The, *13;* I'll See You in My Dreams, *924*
Wyndham, Carol: Roamin' Wild, *1145*
Wyner, George: Bad News Bears Go to Japan, The, *231;* Fletch Lives, *978;* Spaceballs, *384*
Wyner, Joel: Club, The (1993), *824*
Wyngarde, Peter: Prisoner, The (TV Series), *1071*
Wynn, Ed: Absent-Minded Professor, The, *143;* Babes in Toyland (1961), *147;* Cinderfella, *912;* Daydreamer, The, *161;* Dear Brigitte, *263;* Gnome-Mobile, The, *169;* Greatest Story Ever Told, The, *533;* Marjorie Morningstar, *589;* Mary Poppins, *185;* Requiem for a Heavyweight (Television), *638;* That Darn Cat, *210*
Wynn, Keenan: Absent-Minded Professor, The, *143;* Americanization of Emily, The, *226;* Annie Get Your Gun, *907;* Around the World Under the Sea, *6;* Battle Circus, *456;* Belle of New York, The, *908;* Bikini Beach, *909;* Call to Glory, *474;* Cancel My Reservation, *250;* Capture of Grizzly Adams, The, *156;* Clock, The, *484;* Clonus Horror, The, *1042;* Coach, *484;* Dark, The, *829;* Devil's Rain, The, *834;* Dr. Strangelove or How I Learned to Stop Worrying and Love the Bomb, *266;* Don't Go Near the Water, *267;* Finian's Rainbow, *916;* For Me and My Gal, *917;* Glass Slipper, The, *919;* Great Race, The, *290;* Herbie Rides Again, *174;* High Velocity, *62;* Hit Lady, *63;* Hole in the Head, A, *298;* Hucksters, The, *545;* Hyper Sapian: People from Another Star, *1057;* Internecine Project, The, *986;* It's a Big Country, *308;* Just Tell Me What You Want, *312;* Killer Inside Me, The, *988;* Kiss Me Kate, *927;* Laserblast, *1062;* Long, Long Trailer, The, *320;* Longest Drive, The, *1130;* Longest Hunt, The, *1130;* Man in the Gray Flannel Suit, The, *587;* Manipulator, The, *588;* Mechanic, The, *83;* Men of the Fighting Lady, *84;* Mission to Glory, *596;* Mr. Imperium, *931;* My Dear Secretary, *339;* Neptune's Daughter, *932;* Orca, *873;* Patsy, The, *355;* Perfect Furlough, *356;* Phone Call from a Stranger, *622;* Piano for Mrs. Cimino, A, *622;* Piranha, *875;* Point Blank, *624;* Prime Risk, *100;* Promise Her Anything, *362;* Requiem for a Heavyweight (Television), *638;* Return of the Man from U.N.C.L.E., The, *105;* Royal Wedding, *938;* Running Wild (1955), *645;* Shack-Out on 101, *653;* Smith!, *1150;* Snowball Express, *205;* Somewhere I'll Find You, *662;* Son of Rubber, *206;* Song of the Thin Man, *1018;* Texas Carnival, *944;* That Midnight Kiss, *944;* Three Little Words, *945;* Three Musketeers, The (1948), *128;* Time to Love and a Time to Die, A, *684;* Untouchables, The: Scarface Mob (TV), *134;* Viva Max!, *405;* War Wagon, The, *1162;* Wavelength, *1088;* Weekend at the Waldorf, *697;* Without Love, *413*
Wynne, Greg: Mystery Mansion, *190*
Wynter, Dana: Connection (1973), *487;* D-Day the Sixth of June, *497;* Invasion of the Body Snatchers (1956), *1059;* List of Adrian Messenger, The, *992;* Santee, *1147;* Shake Hands with the Devil, *114;* Sink the Bismarck, *116;* Something of Value, *118*
Wynyard, Diana: Cavalcade, *477;* Gaslight (1940), *979*
Wyss, Amanda: Better Off Dead, *237;* Black Magic Woman, *955;* Bloodfist IV—Die Trying, *16;* Checkered Flag, *480;* My Mother's Secret Life, *602;* Powwow Highway, *360;* To Die For, *896;* To Die For 2: Son of Darkness, *896*
Xueqi, Wang: Yellow Earth, *806*
Yaconelli, Frank: Driftin' Kid, *1110*
Yagher, Jeff: Lower Level, *994*
Yama, Akihiro Maru: Black Lizard, *718*
Yamada, Isuzu: Osaka Elegy, *774*
Yamaguchi, Isamu: Funky, Work Hard!, *737*
Yamanaka, Joe: Ulterior Motives, *133*
Yamauchi, Akira: Godzilla vs. the Smog Monster, *1054*
Yamauchi, Takaya: MacArthur's Children, *763*
Yamazaki, Tsutomu: Funeral, The, *739;* High and Low, *744;* Rikyu, *781;* Taxing Woman, A, *793*
Yeni, Rossana: White Comanche, *1164*
Yankovic, "Weird Al": Compleat "Weird Al" Yankovic, The, *258;* UHF, *402*
Yanne, Jean: Bandits (1987), *715;* Hanna K., *743;* Indochine, *747;* Le Boucher (The Butcher), *756;* This Man Must Die, *794;* Weekend, *803*
Yanni, Rosanna: Sonny and Jed, *1151*
Yarnall, Celeste: Velvet Vampire, The, *900*
Yarnell, Lorene: Spaceballs, *384;* Wild Wild West Revisited, The, *1164*
Yasbeck, Amy: Problem Child, *362;* Problem Child 2, *362;* Robin Hood: Men in Tights, *369*
Yasui, Shoji: Burmese Harp, The, *721*
Yates, Cassie: Evil, The, *839;* FM, *278;* Listen to Your Heart, *319;* Of Mice and Men (1981), *610;* St. Helens, *646*
Yates, Marjorie: Black Panther, The, *463;* Long Day Closes, The, *578;* Wetherby, *698*
Yee, Kelvin Han: Great Wall, A, *290*
Yeh, Sally: Killer, The, *751;* Laser Man, The, *315;* Peking Opera Blues, *776*
Yelykomov, Oleg: Burglar (1987), *721*
Yen, Zhang Zhi: American Shaolin: King of the Kickboxers II, *5*
Yen-Khe, Tran Nu: Scent of Green Papaya, The, *784*
Yeoh, Michelle: Police Story III—Super Cop, *778*
Yes: Yessongs, *439*
Yesno, John: King of the Grizzlies, *180*
Yeung, Bolo: Bloodsport, *16;* Fearless Tiger, *47;* Ironheart, *67;* Shootfighter, *115;* TC 2000, *1082*
Yi, Maria: Fists of Fury, *49*
Yip, David: Ping Pong, *622*
Yniguez, Richard: Boulevard Nights, *467;* Dirty Dozen, The: The Fatal Mission, *39;* Jake Spanner Private Eye, *68*
Yoba, Malik: Cool Runnings, *259*
Yohn, Erica: Jack the Bear, *556*
Yokoshimaru, Hiroku: Legend of the Eight Samurai, *758*
York, Amanda: Scrubbers, *650*
York, Dick: Inherit the Wind, *552;* My Sister Eileen, *932*
York, Jeff: Davy Crockett and the River Pirates, *161;* Great Locomotive Chase, The, *171;* Savage Sam, *201;* Westward Ho, the Wagons, *216*
York, John J.: House of the Rising Sun, *64;* Steel and Lace, *1080*
York, Kathleen: Thompson's Last Run, *128;* Winners Take All, *140*
York, Michael: Accident, *440;* Cabaret, *910;* Duel of Hearts, *505;* Four Musketeers, The, *52;* Island of Dr. Moreau, The, *1060;* Justine, *561;* Last Remake of Beau Geste, The, *316;* Lethal Obsession, *76;* Logan's Run, *1063;* Midnight Cop, *996;* Murder on the Orient Express, *999;* Night of the Fox, *90;* Phantom of Death, *874;* Ponce de Leon and the Fountain of Youth, *196;* Return of the Musketeers, *106;* Riddle of the Sands, *106;* Romeo and Juliet (1968), *643;* Something for Everyone, *662;* Success Is the Best Revenge, *672;* Sword of Gideon, *123;* Taming of the Shrew, The (1966), *391;* Three Musketeers, The (1973), *128;* Wide Sargasso Sea, *701;* Zeppelin, *709*
York, Rachel: Dead Center, *967;* Killer Instinct, *71*
York, Susannah: Alice (1981), *906;* Awakening, The, *811;* Battle of Britain, *9;* Diamond's Edge, *162;* Falling in Love Again, *273;* Fate, *274;* Illusions, *985;* Killing of Sister George, The, *564;* Land of Faraway, The, *180;* Loophole, *993;* Man for All Seasons, A, *586;* Shout, The (1979), *886;* Silent Partner, The, *1016;* Summer Story, A, *673;* That Lucky Touch, *392;* Tom Jones, *397;* Tunes of Glory, *689;* X, Y and Zee, *707*
Yorkin, Bud: For the Boys, *918*
Yoshiyuki, Kazuko: In the Realm of Passion, *747*
Youb, Sammy Den: Madame Rosa, *763*
Young, Aden: Black Robe, *463;* Over the Hill, *352*
Young, Alan: Androcles and the Lion, *227;* Baker's Hawk, *148;* Beverly Hills Cop 3, *11;* Time Machine, The, *1084;* Tom Thumb, *213*
Young, Audrey: Wistful Widow of Wagon Gap, The, *412*
Young, Bruce A.: Blink, *956*

Young, Burt: All the Marbles, *225;* Amityville II: The Possession, *809;* Back to School, *230;* Backstreet Dreams, *454;* Betsy's Wedding, *236;* Beverly Hills Brats, *237;* Blood Red, *464;* Bright Angel, *470;* Carnival of Blood, *821;* Chinatown, *962;* Choirboys, The, *481;* Club Fed, *256;* Convoy (1978), *29;* Diving In, *502;* Excessive Force, *45;* Family Matter, A, *514;* Killer Elite, The, *71;* Lookin' to Get Out, *321;* Once Upon a Time in America (Long Version), *94;* Over the Brooklyn Bridge, *352;* Rocky, *642;* Rocky II, *642;* Rocky IV, *642;* Rocky V, *642;* Summer to Remember, A, *673;* Twilight's Last Gleaming, *133;* Wait Until Spring, Bandini, *695*

Young, Calvin: Challenge, The, *24*

Young, Carleton: Double Deal, *41;* Outlaw Express, *1137;* Pride of the Bowery, *627;* Reefer Madness, *365;* Smash-Up: The Story of a Woman, *661;* Smokey Trails, *1151;* Zorro's Fighting Legion, *1166*

Young, Chris: Book of Love, *243;* December, *498;* PCU, *355;* Runestone, *882*

Young, Clara Kimball: Return of Chandu (The Magician), *105*

Young, Clifton: Trail of Robin Hood, *1158*

Young, David: Mary, Mary, Bloody Mary, *863*

Young, Desmond: Desert Fox, The, *37*

Young, Dey: Back in the U.S.S.R., *8;* Conflict of Interest, *29;* Doin' Time, *266;* Murder 101, *999;* No Place To Hide, *91;* Not Quite Human 2, *347;* Rock 'n' Roll High School, *369*

Young, Faron: Daniel Boone, Trail Blazer, *1107*

Young, Gig: Air Force, *3;* Ask Any Girl, *229;* Bring Me the Head of Alfredo Garcia, *20;* City That Never Sleeps, *483;* Desperate Hours, The (1955), *969;* Escape Me Never, *510;* Game of Death, *54;* Girl Who Had Everything, The, *527;* Hunt the Man Down, *984;* Kid Galahad (1962), *926;* Killer Elite, The, *71;* Lovers and Other Strangers, *323;* Lust for Gold, *1130;* Only the Valiant, *1137;* Pitfall, *622;* Slaughter Trail, *1150;* Teacher's Pet, *392;* Tell It to the Judge, *392;* That Touch of Mink, *393;* They Shoot Horses, Don't They?, *681;* Three Musketeers, The (1948), *128;* Torch Song, *686;* Tunnel of Love, The, *400;* Wake of the Red Witch, *136;* Young at Heart, *948*

Young, Jessie Colin: No Nukes, *432*

Young, Karen: Almost You, *225;* Birdy, *462;* Criminal Law, *964;* Heat (1987), *60;* Hoffa, *542;* Jaws: The Revenge, *858;* Little Sweetheart, *577;* Night Game, *1000;* 9½ Weeks, *607;* 10 Million Dollar Getaway, The, *678*

Young, Loretta: Along Came Jones, *1093;* Big Business Girl, *460;* Bishop's Wife, The, *240;* Doctor Takes a Wife, The, *266;* Employees' Entrance, *271;* Eternally Yours, *511;* Farmer's Daughter, The, *274;* Heroes for Sale, *540;* Key to the City, *312;* Night to Remember, A (1943), *345;* Perfect Marriage, *356;* Platinum Blonde, *623;* Rachel and the Stranger, *1140;* Stranger, The (1947), *1020;* They Call It Sin, *680*

Young, Nat: Palm Beach, *617*

Young, Nedrick: Captain Scarlett, *23;* Dead Men Walk, *830*

Young, Neil: Last Waltz, The, *428;* Love at Large, *322;* '68, *659*

Young II, Oh: Yongary—Monster from the Deep, *1090*

Young, Otis: Blood Beach, *814;* Last Detail, The, *569*

Young, Paul: Another Time, Another Place (1984), *450;* Girl in the Picture, The, *286*

Young, Polly Ann: His Fighting Blood, *1121;* Invisible Ghost, *856;* Man from Utah, The, *1132*

Young, Ric: Dragon Chow, *732*

Young, Richard: Assassin, *1037;* Final Mission, *48;* Friday the 13th, Part V—A New Beginning, *844;* Love at the Top, *581;* Saigon Commandos, *110*

Young, Robert: Bride Walks Out, The, *245;* Bride Wore Red, The, *469;* Cairo, *910;* Canterville Ghost, The (1944), *155;* Crossfire (1947), *964;* Enchanted Cottage, The, *509;* Half-Breed, The, *1118;* Honolulu, *923;* Journey for Margaret, *559;* Lady Be Good, *927;* Mortal Storm, The, *600;* Navy Blue and Gold, *342;* Northwest Passage, *92;* Second Woman, The, *650;* Secret Agent, The, *1013;* Shining Hour, The, *656;* Sin of Madelon Claudet, The, *658;* Spitfire, *664;* Stowaway, *942;* Strange Interlude (1932), *669;* That Forsyte Woman, *680;* They Won't Believe Me, *681;* Those Endearing Young Charms, *394;* Three Comrades, *682;* Today We Live, *685;* Western Union, *1163*

Young, Roland: And Then There Were None, *952;* Great Lover, The, *289;* Guardsman, The, *291;* His Double Life, *297;* King Solomon's Mines (1937), *72;* Let's Dance, *928;* Madame Satan, *584;* Man Who Could Work Miracles, The, *1064;* One Rainy Afternoon, *350;* Ruggles of Red Gap, *371;* St. Benny the Dip, *646;* Topper, *397;* Topper Returns, *398;* Topper Takes a Trip, *398;* Two-Faced Woman, *401;* Wedding Rehearsal, *407;* Young in Heart, The, *416*

Young, Rozwill: Who's the Man?, *411*

Young, Sean: Ace Ventura: Pet Detective, *221;* Arena Brains, *450;* Baby...Secret of the Lost Legend, *1037;* Blade Runner, *1039;* Blue Ice, *957;* Boost, The, *466;* Cousins, *260;* Dune, *1048;* Even Cowgirls Get the Blues, *272;* Fatal Instinct (1993), *274;* Fire Birds, *49;* Hold Me, Thrill Me, Kiss Me, *298;* Jane Austen in Manhattan, *309;* Kiss Before Dying, A, *989;* Love Crimes, *993;* Model by Day, *86;* No Way Out, *1002;* Once Upon a Crime, *349;* Sketch Artist, *1017;* Stripes, *387;* Under the Biltmore Clock, *691;* Wall Street, *695;* Young Doctors in Love, *415*

Young, Stephen: Between Friends, *459;* Clown Murders, The, *962;* Lifeguard, *574;* Patton, *619;* Spring Fever, *385*

Young, William Allen: Wisdom, *140*

Youngblood, Rob: Kill Zone, *71*

Youngfellow, Barrie: It Came Upon a Midnight Clear, *177;* Nightmare in Blood, *871*

Youngman, Henny: Amazon Women on the Moon, *225;* Steve Martin Live, *386;* Young at Heart Comedians, The, *415*

Youngs, Gail: Belizaire the Cajun, *458*

Youngs, Jim: Hot Shot, *544;* Nobody's Fool, *346;* Out of Control, *352;* Skeeter, *887;* You Talkin' to Me, *141;* Youngblood, *709*

Yowlachie, Chief: Painted Hills, The, *193*

Yu, Wang: Invincible Sword, The, *67;* Man Called Tiger, A, *80*

Yuan, Liu Zhong: Life on a String, *760*

Yukon King: Sergeant Preston of the Yukon (TV Series), *1148*

Yulin, Harris: Bad Dreams, *811;* Believers, The, *812;* Candy Mountain, *474;* End of the Road, *510;* Fatal Beauty, *46;* Heart of Justice, *538;* Kansas City Massacre, The, *70;* Last Hit, The, *990;* Melvin Purvis: G-Man, *83;* Parker Adderson, Philosopher, *618;* Short Fuse, *115;* Steel, *120;* Tailspin, *676;* Watchedl, *137*

Yun-Fat, Chow: Better Tomorrow, A, *717;* Better Tomorrow 2, A, *717;* Better Tomorrow 3, A: Love And Death In Saigon, *717;* City War, *724;* Killer, The, *751;* Prison on Fire, *778*

Yune, Johnny: They Call Me Bruce?, *393;* They Still Call Me Bruce, *393*

Yung, Victor Sen: Across the Pacific, *1;* Bonanza (TV Series), *1100;* Feathered Serpent, The, *976;* She Demons, *885;* Trader Tom of the China Seas, *131*

Yurka, Blanche: At Sword's Point, *7;* Bridge of San Luis Rey, The, *469;* City for Conquest, *482;* One Body Too Many, *1003*

Z'dar, Robert: Big Sweat, The, *13;* Divine Enforcer, *40;* Dragon Fight, *42;* Maniac Cop 3: Badge of Silence, *863;* Quiet Fire, *102;* Return to Frogtown, *1074;* Wild Cactus, *139*

Zabka, William: Back to School, *230;* Karate Kid Part II, The, *562;* Shootfighter, *115;* Tiger's Tale, A, *396*

Zaborin, Lila: Blood Orgy of the She Devils, *815*

Zabriskie, Grace: Ambition, *952;* Burning Bed, The, *472;* Chain of Desire, *478;* Child's Play 2, *823;* Even Cowgirls Get the Blues, *272;* Hometown Boy Makes Good, *300;* Intimate Stranger, *986;* M.A.D.D.: Mothers Against Drunk Driving, *583;* Megaville, *1065;* Servants of Twilight, *884*

Zacharias, Ann: Nea (A Young Emmanuelle), *771*

Zacharias, John: Montenegro, *599*

Zacherley: Geek Maggot Bingo, *283;* Horrible Horror, *851*

Zada, Ramy: Dark Justice, *32*

Zadok, Arnon: Beyond the Walls, *717*

Zadora, Pia: Butterfly, *473;* Fakeout, *513;* Hairspray, *292;* Lonely Lady, The, *577*
Zagaria, Anita: Queen of Hearts, *632*
Zagaria, Lucio: Flight of the Innocent, *737*
Zagarino, Frank: Barbarian Queen, *1038;* Project: Eliminator, *101;* Project: Shadowchaser, *101*
Zahn, Steve: Reality Bites, *635*
Zaitchenko, Piotr: Taxi Blues, *792*
Zaks, Jerry: Gentleman Bandit, The, *525*
Zal, Roxana: Goodbye, Miss 4th of July, *171;* River's Edge, *641;* Shattered Spirits, *655;* Testament, *1082*
Zamprogna, Gema: Tales From Avonlea (TV series), *209*
Zanden, Philip: Mozart Brothers, The, *769*
Zane, Billy: Betrayal of the Dove, *954;* Blood and Concrete, A Love Story, *956;* Brotherhood of Justice, *471;* Dead Calm, *966;* Femme Fatale, *976;* Hillside Stranglers, The, *982;* Lake Consequence, *568;* Megaville, *1065;* Memphis Belle (1990), *592;* Millions, *594;* Orlando, *614;* Posse (1993), *1139;* Running Delilah, *110;* Sniper, *117;* Tombstone, *1157*
Zane, Lisa: Bad Influence, *953;* Femme Fatale, *976;* Freddy's Dead: The Final Nightmare, *843;* Pucker Up and Bark Like a Dog, *363*
Zanetti, Giancarlo: Warning, The, *137*
Zanin, Bruno: Amarcord, *712*
Zann, Lenore: Def-Con 4, *1046*
Zaoui, Vanessa: Alan and Naomi, *443*
Zapasiewicz, Zbigniew: Baritone, *715;* Camouflage, *722*
Zapata, Carmen: Boulevard Nights, *467;* Vultures, *901*
Zappa, Frank: Boy Who Left Home to Find Out About the Shivers, The, *152;* 200 Motels, *946*
Zappa, Moon: Boys Next Door, The, *468;* Spirit of '76, The, *384*
Zarish, Janet: Danny, *161*
Zarte, Ernie: Warbus, *137*
Zaslow, Michael: Seven Minutes in Heaven, *376;* You Light Up My Life, *708*
Zech, Rosel: Veronika Voss, *800*
Zelniker, Michael: Terry Fox Story, The, *679*
Zemperla, Nazzareno: Adios, Hombre, *1092*
Zenthe, Fereno: Revolt of Job, The, *781*
Zentout, Delphine: 36 Fillette, *794*
Zerbe, Anthony: Attica, *452;* Child of Glass, *158;* Equalizer, The: "Memories of Manon", *44;* First Deadly Sin, The, *977;* George Washington, *526;* Laughing Policeman, The, *991;* Listen to Me, *576;* Omega Man, The, *1069;* Onassis: The Richest Man in the World, *612;* Opposing Force, *95;* Private Investigations, *101;* Return of the Man from U.N.C.L.E., The, *105;* Rooster Cogburn, *1146;* Snatched, *117;* Steel Dawn, *1080;* Who'll Stop the Rain, *139;* Will Penny, *1164*
Zetterling, Mai: Hidden Agenda, *541;* Night Is My Future, *771;* Only Two Can Play, *350;* Quartet (1948), *631;* Truth About Women, The, *689;* Witches, The, *1089*
Ziemann, Sonja: Made in Heaven (1948), *326*
Zien, Chip: Grace Quigley, *289*
Ziering, Ian: Beverly Hills 90210, *460*
Zietek, Eva: Wedding, The, *802*
Zimbalist Jr., Efrem: Avenging, The, *1095;* Family Upside Down, A, *514;* Gathering, Part II, The, *525;* Hot Shots, *301;* Maverick (TV Series), *1133;* Tempest, The (1983), *678;* Terror Out of the Sky, *894;* Wait Until Dark, *1030;* Who Is the Black Dahlia?, *1031*
Zimbalist, Stephanie: Awakening, The, *811;* Babysitter, The, *811;* Caroline?, *959;* Jericho Fever, *68;* Killing Mind, The, *989;* Magic of Lassie, The, *185;* Remington Steele (TV series), *1010;* Tomorrow's Child, *686*
Zimmer, Laurie: Assault on Precinct 13, *7*
Zinneman, Anna: Place Called Trinity, A, *1139*
Zinni, Victoria: Shoot the Living...Pray for the Dead, *1149*
Zipp, William: Death Chase, *35;* Order of the Eagle, *96*
Zischler, Hanns: Desire, *500;* Kings of the Road, *752*
Zmed, Adrian: Bachelor Party, *230;* Eyewitness to Murder, *46;* Final Terror, The, *841;* Grease 2, *920;* Other Woman, The, *1003*
Zobel, Richard: To Sleep With a Vampire, *896*
Zobian, Mark: House on Tombstone Hill, The, *853*
Zola, Jean-Pierre: Mark of the Devil, Part 2, *863;* My Uncle (Mon Oncle), *770*
Zorek, Michael: Hot Moves, *301;* Private School, *362*
Zorich, Louis: Cheap Shots, *254*
Zorina, Vera: Goldwyn Follies, The, *920;* Louisiana Purchase, *322*
Zouzou: Chloe in the Afternoon, *723*
Zuanic, Rod: Fast Talking, *166*
Zubkov, Valentin: My Name Is Ivan, *770*
Zucco, George: Adventures of Sherlock Holmes, The, *950;* Arrest Bulldog Drummond, *6;* Black Raven, The, *955;* Bride Wore Red, The, *469;* Dead Men Walk, *830;* Firefly, The, *916;* Flying Serpent, The, *842;* Fog Island, *978;* Having a Wonderful Crime, *294;* House of Frankenstein, *852;* Mad Monster, *862;* Madame X (1937), *584;* Man Who Could Work Miracles, The, *1064;* Mummy's Hand, The, *867;* My Favorite Blonde, *340;* New Moon, *933;* Scared to Death, *883;* Seventh Cross, The, *653;* Sherlock Holmes in Washington, *1015;* Woman's Face, A, *705*
Zuckerman, Alex: Me and the Kid, *83*
Zuniga, Daphne: 800 Leagues Down the Amazon, *43;* Fly II, The, *842;* Gross Anatomy, *534;* Initiation, The, *856;* Last Rites, *75;* Modern Girls, *335;* Prey of the Chameleon, *1007;* Spaceballs, *384;* Staying Together, *667;* Sure Thing, The, *389*
Zushi, Yoshitaka: Dodes 'Ka-Den, *731*
Zutaut, Brad: Hardbodies 2, *293;* Knockouts, *314*
Zwerling, Darrell: Doc Savage...The Man of Bronze, *1047*
Zwick, Abe: Sometimes Aunt Martha Does Dreadful Things, *888*
Zylberman, Noam: Last Train Home, *181*

DIRECTOR INDEX

Aaron, Paul: Deadly Force, *34;* Different Story, A, *501;* Force of One, *51;* In Love and War, *985;* Love and War, *581;* Maxie, *330;* Miracle Worker, The (1979), *595*

Abashidze, Dodo: Legend of Suram Fortress, The, *758*

Abbott, George: Damn Yankees, *913;* Pajama Game, The, *934;* Too Many Girls, *946*

Abbott, Norman: Working Stiffs, *414*

Abel, Robert: Elvis on Tour, *423*

Abernathy, Lewis: House IV, *852*

Abraham, Maurice: First Howie Mandel Special, The, *277*

Abrahams, Derwin: Northwest Trail, *1136*

Abrahams, Jim: Airplane!, *224;* Big Business, *238;* Hot Shots, *301;* Hot Shots Part Deux, *301;* Police Squad!, *359;* Ruthless People, *371;* Top Secret, *397;* Welcome Home, Roxy Carmichael, *407*

Abuladze, Tenghiz: Repentance, *781*

Acevski, Jon: Freddie as F.R.O.7, *168*

Acin, Javan: Hey, Babu Riba, *743*

Acomba, David: Night Life, *869*

Adams, Bradley: Incredible Story of Dogs, The, *427*

Adams, Catlin: Sticky Fingers, *386*

Adams, Daniel: Primary Motive, *627*

Adams, Doug: Blackout (1990), *956*

Adamson, Al: Blood of Dracula's Castle, *815;* Brain of Blood, *818;* Dracula vs. Frankenstein, *837;* Five Bloody Graves, *1113;* Gun Riders, The, *1117;* Horror of the Blood Monsters, *1057;* I Spit on Your Corpse, *855*

Adidge, Pierre: Elvis on Tour, *423;* Mad Dogs and Englishmen, *429*

Adler, Jerry: National Lampoon's Class of '86, *342*

Adler, Joseph: Nightmare House, *871;* Sex and the College Girl, *653*

Adler, Lou: Up in Smoke, *403*

Adlon, Percy: Bagdad Café, *231;* Celeste, *722;* Last Five Days, The, *755;* Rosalie Goes Shopping, *370;* Sugarbaby, *791*

Adlum, Ed: Invasion of the Blood Farmers, *856*

Adreon, Franklin: Panther Girl of the Congo, *97;* Trader Tom of the China Seas, *131*

Agrama, Frank: Dawn of the Mummy, *830*

Aguirre, Javier: Dracula's Great Love, *837*

Ahern, Mats: Istanbul: Keep Your Eyes Open, *555*

Akerman, Chantal: Eighties, The, *733;* Les Rendez-Vous D'Anna, *759;* News from Home, *771;* Night and Day (1991), *771;* Toute Une Nuit, *796;* Window Shopping, *804*

Akiyama, Katsuhito: Gall Force, *739;* Gall Force 2, *739*

Akkad, Moustapha: Lion of the Desert, *77;* Message, The (Mohammad, Messenger of God), *593*

Alan, Jordan: Terminal Bliss, *679*

Alan, Pat: Shootfighter, *115*

Albicocco, Jean Gabriel: Wanderer, The, *802*

Alda, Alan: Betsy's Wedding, *236;* Four Seasons, The, *521;* M*A*S*H: Goodbye, Farewell, Amen, *325;* New Life, A, *343;* Sweet Liberty, *389*

Aldis, Will: Stealing Home, *667*

Aldrich, Adell: Kid from Left Field, The, *180*

Aldrich, Robert: All the Marbles, *225;* Apache, *1094;* Autumn Leaves, *452;* Choirboys, The, *481;* Dirty Dozen, The, *39;* Flight of the Phoenix, The, *51;* Four for Texas, *1114;* Frisco Kid, The, *1114;* Grissom Gang, The, *534;* Hush...Hush, Sweet Charlotte, *854;* Hustle, *65;* Killing of Sister George, The, *564;* Kiss Me Deadly, *989;* Longest Yard, The, *78;* Sodom and Gomorrah, *661;* Too Late the Hero, *131;* Twilight's Last Gleaming, *133;* Ulzana's Raid, *1160;* Vera Cruz, *1161;* What Ever Happened to Baby Jane?, *902*

Alea, Tomas Gutierrez: Death of a Bureaucrat, *728;* Last Supper, The, *755;* Letters from the Park, *760;* Memories of Underdevelopment, *766*

Alessandrini, Goffredo: We the Living, *802*

Alexander, Bill: Tartuffe, *677*

Algar, James: Jungle Cat, *179;* Legend of Sleepy Hollow, The (1949), *181;* Vanishing Prairie, The, *437*

Alk, Howard: Janis, *427*

Allegret, Marc: Fanny (1932), *736;* Lady Chatterley's Lover (1959), *567;* Loves of Three Queens, *762;* Mademoiselle Striptease, *763;* Naked Heart, The, *603;* Sois Belle Et Tais-Toi (Just Another Pretty Face), *787;* Tales of Paris, *792;* Zou Zou, *949*

Allegret, Yves: Dedee D'Anvers, *729*

Allen, A. K.: Ladies Club, *74*

Allen, Corey: Avalanche, *7;* Brass, *468;* Last Fling, The, *315;* Man in the Santa Claus Suit, The, *185;* Return of Frank Cannon, The, *1010;* Thunder and Lightning, *129*

Allen, David: Dungeonmaster, The, *1048;* Puppet Master II, *878*

Allen, Fred: Ride Him Cowboy, *1143*

Allen, Irving: Slaughter Trail, *1150*

Allen, Irwin: Beyond the Poseidon Adventure, *11;* Five Weeks in a Balloon, *50;* Swarm, The, *891;* Towering Inferno, The, *131;* Voyage to the Bottom of the Sea, *1087*

Allen, James: Burndown, *959*

Allen, Lewis: Another Time, Another Place (1958), *449;* At Sword's Point, *7;* Perfect Marriage, *356;* Suddenly, *1021;* Those Endearing Young Charms, *394;* Uninvited, The (1944), *1029*

Allen, Woody: Alice (1990), *224;* Annie Hall, *228;* Another Woman, *450;* Bananas, *232;* Broadway Danny Rose, *246;* Crimes and Misdemeanors, *490;* Everything You Always Wanted to Know About Sex but Were Afraid to Ask, *273;* Hannah and Her Sisters, *293;* Husbands and Wives, *546;* Interiors, *553;* Love and Death, *322;* Manhattan, *328;* Manhattan Murder Mystery, *328;* Midsummer Night's Sex Comedy, A, *332;* New York Stories, *343;* Purple Rose of Cairo, The, *363;* Radio Days, *364;* September, *652;* Shadows and Fog, *654;* Sleeper, *381;* Stardust Memories, *385;* Take the Money and Run, *390;* What's Up, Tiger Lily?, *408;* Zelig, *416*

Allio, Rene: Shameless Old Lady, The, *785*

Allison, John: Taming of the Shrew (1982), *391*

Allmendinger, Knute: House of the Dead, *853*

Almendros, Nestor: Improper Conduct, *427*

Almereyda, Michael: Twister, *401*

Almo, John: RSVP, *371*

Almo, Lem: RSVP, *371*

Almodóvar, Pedro: Dark Habits, *728;* High Heels (1992), *744;* Kika, *751;* Labyrinth of Passion, *755;* Law of Desire, *756;* Matador, *766;* Pepi, Luci, Born and Other Girls, *777;* Tie Me Up! Tie Me Down!, *795;* What Have I Done to Deserve This?, *803;* Women on the Verge of a Nervous Breakdown, *805*

ood, Paul: Captive Hearts, *475;* Prep School, *360*
ry, Max: Art Com Video (Vol. 1–3), *1037*
zo, John A.: FM, *278;* Portrait of a Stripper, *625*
ton, Emmett: Little Ninjas, *183;* New Year's Evil, *868;* Deaths of the Ninja, *91*
man, Robert: Aria, *907;* Beyond Therapy, *237;* Brewster Cloud, *245;* Buffalo Bill and the Indians, *1102;* Caine Mutiny rt Martial, The, *473;* Come Back to the Five and Dime, my Dean, Jimmy Dean, *486;* Countdown, *489;* Dumb iter, The, *506;* Fool for Love, *518;* Long Goodbye, The, *993;* A*S*H, *324;* McCabe and Mrs. Miller, *1133;* Nashville, *603;* . & Stiggs, *348;* Player, The, *358;* Popeye, *196;* Quintet, '3; Secret Honor, *651;* Short Cuts, *657;* Streamers, *670;* ner '88, *391;* That Cold Day in the Park, *680;* Thieves Like *681;* Vincent and Theo, *694;* Wedding, A, *407*
n, Robert: Merton of the Movies, *331;* Pagan Love Song,
es, Joe: Jaws 3, *858*
amiya, Keita: Zeram, *807*
ar, Denis: Caged Heart, The (L'Addition), *721*
aral, Suzana: Hour of the Star, *745*
ateau, Rod: Bushwhackers, *1102;* Drive-In, *269;* Garbage Kids Movie, The, *168;* High School, USA, *297;* Lovelines, ; Monsoon, *599;* Seniors, The, *375;* Statue, The, *385*
elio, Gianni: Il Ladro Di Bambini (Stolen Children), *747;* n Doors, *774*
enta, Pino: Boulevard of Broken Dreams, *467;* Heaven ight, *539*
iel, Jon: Queen of Hearts, *632;* Sommersby, *662;* Tune in norrow, *400*
ir, Gideon: P.O.W.: The Escape, *96*
oruso, Marina: Legends of the American West (Series),
urri, Franco: Flashback, *50;* Monkey Trouble, *188*
yes, Julian: Great Expectations (1988), *532;* Jane Eyre 83), *557*
ders, Allison: Border Radio, *466;* Gas, Food, Lodging, *525*
derson, Andy: Positive I.D., *1006*
derson, Clyde: Beyond Darkness, *813;* Monster Dog, *865*
derson, Gerry: Invasion UFO, *1059*
derson, John Murray: King of Jazz, The, *927*
derson, Josef: Stephen King's Golden Years (TV Series), *0*
derson, Kurt: Bounty Tracker, *18;* Martial Law —Undercover, *82;* Martial Outlaw, *82*
derson, Lindsay: Britannia Hospital, *246;* Glory! Glory!, ; If..., *304;* Look Back in Anger (1980), *579;* O Lucky Man!, ; This Sporting Life, *682;* Whales of August, The, *698*
derson, Michael: Around the World in 80 Days (1956), ; Battle Hell, *9;* Dam Busters, The, *31;* Doc Savage...The n of Bronze, *1047;* Dominique Is Dead, *971;* Logan's Run, 3; Martian Chronicles, Parts I-III, The, *1065;* Millennium, 6; Murder by Phone, *998;* Naked Edge, The, *1000;* 1984 55), *1068;* Operation Crossbow, *95;* Orca, *873;* Quiller morandum, The, *102;* Sea Wolf, The (1993), *113;* Separate ations, *375;* Shake Hands with the Devil, *114;* Shoes of the herman, *656;* Sword of Gideon, *123;* Wreck of the Mary re, The, *141;* Young Catherine, *708*
derson, Robert: Young Graduates, *708*
derson, Steve: Discovery Program, *501;* South Central,
derson, Tom: Ossian: American Boy-Tibetan Monk, *432*
drei, Yannick: Beyond Fear, *717*
drieu, Michel: Weep No More My Lady, *1030*
gel, Mikel: Love Butcher, *861*
ger, Kenneth: Kenneth Anger—Volume One, *562;* neth Anger—Volume Two, *562;* Kenneth Anger—Volume ee, *563;* Kenneth Anger—Volume Four, *563*
jou, Erik: Cool Surface, The, *963*
nakin, Ken: Battle of the Bulge, *10;* Call of the Wild (1972), Cheaper to Keep Her, *254;* Fifth Musketeer, The, *47;* gest Day, The, *78;* New Adventures of Pippi Longstocking, The, *191;* Paper Tiger, *97;* Pirate Movie, The, *935;* Quartet (1948), *631;* Story of Robin Hood, The, *207;* Swiss Family Robinson, The, *208;* Sword and the Rose, The (1953), *208;* Third Man on the Mountain, *210;* Those Daring Young Men in Their Jaunty Jalopies, *394;* Those Magnificent Men in Their Flying Machines, *394;* Trio, *688*
Annaud, Jean-Jacques: Bear, The, *149;* Black and White in Color, *718;* Hot Head, *745;* Lover, The, *582;* Name of the Rose, The, *89;* Quest for Fire, *1073*
Annett, Paul: Adventures of Sherlock Holmes, The (Series), *950;* Beast Must Die, The, *812;* Partners in Crime (TV Series), *1004;* Tales of the Unexpected, *1022*
Anno, Hideaki: Gunbuster—Vols. 1–3, *742;* Nadia, Vols. 1–36, *88*
Anspaugh, David: Fresh Horses, *522;* Hoosiers, *543;* Rudy, *200*
Anthony, Joseph: All in a Night's Work, *224;* Career, *475;* Matchmaker, The, *329;* Rainmaker, The, *634;* Tomorrow, *685*
Antonio, Lou: Between Friends, *459;* Breaking Up Is Hard to Do, *469;* Gypsy Warriors, The, *58;* Last Prostitute, The, *570;* Lies Before Kisses, *574;* Mayflower Madam, *591;* Pals, *353;* Real American Hero, The, *635;* Silent Victory: The Kitty O'Neil Story, *658;* Someone I Touched, *662;* Taste for Killing, A, *126;* 13 at Dinner, *1024;* This Gun for Hire (1991), *128*
Antonioni, Michelangelo: Blow-Up, *957;* Classic Foreign Shorts: Volume 2, *724;* Eclipse, The, *733;* Il Grido, *747;* L'Aventura, *753;* Passenger, The, *1004;* Red Desert, *780;* Zabriskie Point, *709*
Aoki, Tetsuro: Devil Hunter Yohko, *729*
Apostolou, Scott: Mutants in Paradise, *338*
Appleby, Daniel: Bound and Gagged: A Love Story, *18*
Apted, Michael: Agatha, *951;* Blink, *956;* Bring on the Night, *419;* Class Action, *962;* Coal Miner's Daughter, *912;* Collection, The, *485;* Continental Divide, *259;* Critical Condition, *260;* Firstborn, *517;* Gorillas in the Mist, *531;* Gorky Park, *980;* Incident at Oglala, *427;* Kipperbang, *566;* Long Way Home, The, *429;* Poor Girl, A Ghost Story, *876;* Squeeze, The (1977), *665;* 35 Up, *436;* Thunderheart, *1025;* 28 Up, *437*
Aragon, Manuel Gutierrez: Demons in the Garden, *729;* Half of Heaven, *743*
Araki, Gregg: Living End, The, *577*
Aranda, Vicente: Blood Spattered Bride, The, *816;* Lovers (1992), *762*
Arau, Alfonso: Like Water for Chocolate, *760*
Arbuckle, Roscoe: Fatty and Mabel Adrift/Mabel, Fatty and the Law, *275;* Fatty Arbuckle Comedy Collection, Vol. 1, *275;* Fatty's Tin-Type Tangle/Our Congressman, *275;* Keystone Comedies, Vol. 1, *312;* Keystone Comedies, Vol. 2, *312;* Keystone Comedies, Vol. 3, *312;* Keystone Comedies, Vol. 4, *312;* Keystone Comedies, Vol. 5, *313;* Lizzies of Mack Sennett, The, *320;* Mabel and Fatty, *325;* Mack Sennett Comedies, Vol. 2, *325*
Arcady, Alexandre: Day of Atonement, *33*
Arcand, Denys: Decline of the American Empire, The, *729;* Jesus of Montreal, *749*
Archainbaud, George: Blue Canadian Rockies, *1099;* Borrowed Trouble, *1100;* Dangerous Venture, *1107;* Dead Don't Dream, The, *1108;* Devil's Playground, *1109;* False Colors, *1112;* False Paradise, *1112;* Framed (1930), *521;* Hoppy Serves a Writ, *1121;* Hoppy's Holiday, *1121;* Hunt the Man Down, *984;* Kansan, The, *1124;* Last of the Pony Riders, *1126;* Lost Squadron, *79;* Marauders, *1132;* Mystery Man, *1135;* Night Stage to Galveston, *1136;* On Top of Old Smoky, *1137;* Saginaw Trail, *1147;* Silent Conflict, *1150;* Sinister Journey, *1150;* State's Attorney, *666;* Strange Gamble, *1153;* Texas Masquerade, *1156;* Unexpected Guest, *1160;* Winning of the West, *1165;* Woman of the Town, *1165*
Ardolino, Emile: Chances Are, *253;* Dirty Dancing, *914;* George Balanchine's The Nutcracker, *919;* Gypsy (1993), *921;* Rumpelstiltskin (1980), *200;* Sister Act, *379;* Three Men and a Little Lady, *395*
Argento, Dario: Bird with the Crystal Plumage, The, *955;* Cat O'Nine Tails, *960;* Creepers, *826;* Deep Red (1975), *832;*

Inferno, 856; Suspiria, 891; Terror at the Opera, 893; Trauma, 897; Two Evil Eyes, 898; Unsane, 899
Aristarian, Adolfo: Stranger, The (1986), 1020
Arkin, Alan: Little Murders, 319
Arkoff, Samuel Z.: Alakazam the Great, 145
Arkush, Allan: Caddyshack II, 249; Deathsport, 1046; Get Crazy, 284; Heartbeeps, 173; Hollywood Boulevard, 299; Rock 'n' Roll High School, 369
Arliss, Leslie: Man in Grey, The, 587; Night Has Eyes, The, 1001; Wicked Lady, The (1945), 701
Armitage, George: Miami Blues, 84
Armstrong, Gillian: Fires Within, 517; High Tide, 541; Last Days of Chez Nous, The, 569; Mrs. Soffel, 598; My Brilliant Career, 601; Starstruck, 941
Armstrong, John: Seabert: The Adventure Begins, 202
Armstrong, Michael: Mark of the Devil, 863
Armstrong, Robin B.: Pastime, 619
Arner, Gwen: Matter of Principle, A, 330; Necessary Parties, 604
Arno, Eddie: Murder Story, 999
Arnold, Frank: Waltz Through the Hills, 216
Arnold, Jack: Bachelor in Paradise, 230; Boss, 1101; Creature from the Black Lagoon, 826; Global Affair, A, 287; High School Confidential!, 541; Incredible Shrinking Man, The, 1058; It Came from Outer Space, 1060; Monster on the Campus, 866; Mouse That Roared, The, 337; Revenge of the Creature, 881; Swiss Conspiracy, The, 1022; Tarantula, 892
Arnold, Newt: Bloodsport, 16; Hands of a Stranger, 981
Arranovitch, Semeon: I Was Stalin's Bodyguard, 746
Artenstein, Isaac: Break of Dawn, 468
Arthur, Karen: Bridge to Silence, 470; Bunny's Tale, A, 472; Disappearance of Christina, The, 971; Jacksons: An American Dream, The, 556; Lady Beware, 989; My Sister, My Love, 867; Return to Eden, 639; Secret, The, 650
Arzner, Dorothy: Bride Wore Red, The, 469; Christopher Strong, 482; Craig's Wife, 490; Dance, Girl, Dance, 261; Wild Party, The (1929), 702
Ascot, Anthony: Guns for Dollars, 1117; Have a Nice Funeral, 1119
Ashby, Hal: Being There, 234; Bound for Glory, 467; Coming Home, 486; 8 Million Ways to Die, 973; Harold and Maude, 294; Last Detail, The, 569; Let's Spend the Night Together, 429; Lookin' to Get Out, 321; Shampoo, 655; Slugger's Wife, The, 381
Ashe, Richard: Track of the Moon Beast, 897
Asher, Robert: Make Mine Mink, 327
Asher, William: Beach Blanket Bingo, 908; Beach Party, 908; Bikini Beach, 909; How to Stuff a Wild Bikini, 923; I Love Lucy (TV Series), 303; Movers and Shakers, 337; Muscle Beach Party, 338; Night Warning, 870
Ashida, Toyoo: Fist of the North Star, 1051; Vampire Hunter D, 900
Askoldov, Aleksandr: Commissar, The, 725
Aslanian, Samson: Torment, 1026
Asquith, Anthony: Browning Version, The, 471; Carrington, V. C., 476; I Stand Condemned, 548; Importance of Being Earnest, The, 305; Pygmalion, 363; V.I.P.s, The, 693; We Dive at Dawn, 137; Winslow Boy, The, 704
Assonitis, Ovidio (Oliver Hellman): Beyond the Door, 813; Madhouse (1987), 862; Tentacles, 893
Athens, J. D.: Cannibal Women in the Avocado Jungle of Death, 22; Pizza Man, 358
Atkins, Thomas: Silver Streak (1934), 658
Atkinson, Vic: Tukiki and His Search for a Merry Christmas, 214
Attenborough, Richard: Bridge Too Far, A, 19; Chaplin, 479; Chorus Line, A, 911; Cry Freedom, 492; Gandhi, 524; Magic, 994; Shadowlands, 654; Young Winston, 709
Attias, Daniel: Silver Bullet, 886
Atwood, David: Wild West (1993), 411
Aucion, Guillaume Martin: Oh! Calcutta!, 348
Audley, Michael: Mark of the Hawk, The, 589
Auer, Gabriel: Eyes of the Birds, 735
Auer, John H.: City That Never Sleeps, 483; Crime of Dr. Crespi, The, 826; Wheel of Fortune, 409
August, Bille: Best Intentions, The, 717; House of the Spiri[t] The, 545; Pelle the Conqueror, 776; Twist and Shout, 797
Aured, Carlos: Horror Rises from the Tomb, 852; House of Psychotic Women, 852
Auster, Sam: Screen Test, 374
Austin, Phil: Eat or Be Eaten, 270
Austin, Ray: Highlander: The Gathering, 1056; Return of th[e] Man from U.N.C.L.E., The, 105; Space 1999 (TV Series), 107[...] Zany Adventures of Robin Hood, The, 416
Autant-Lara, Claude: Devil in the Flesh (1946), 730; Four Bags Full, 738; Oldest Profession, The, 773; Sylvia and the Phantom, 792
Auzins, Igor: High Rolling, 62; We of the Never Never, 137
Avakian, Aram: Cops and Robbers, 29; 11 Harrowhouse, 973; End of the Road, 510
Avallone, Marcello: Specters, 889
Avalos, Phil: Fatal Bond, 975
Avati, Pupi: Revenge of the Dead, 881; Story of Boys and Girls, 789
Avedis, Howard: Fifth Floor, The, 841; Kidnapped (1988), 7[...] Mortuary, 866; Scorchy, 112; They're Playing with Fire, 681
Avellana, Jim: Blackbelt 2: Fatal Force, 14
Averback, Hy: Chamber of Horrors, 822; Guide for the Married Woman, A, 291; I Love You Alice B. Toklas!, 304; M*A*S*H* (TV Series), 325; She's in the Army Now, 656; Suppose They Gave a War and Nobody Came?, 388; Where t[he] Boys Are '84, 409; Where Were You When the Lights Went Out?, 409
Avery, Fred: Golden Age of Looney Toons, The: Bugs Bunn[y] by Each Director, 169; Golden Age of Looney Toons, The: Hurry for Hollywood, 170; Golden Age of Looney Toons, The: The Art of Bugs, 170
Avery, Tex: Adventures of Droopy, 143; Best of Bugs Bunny and Friends, The, 150; Best of Warner Brothers, Vol. 1, 150; Best of Warner Brothers, Vol. 2, 150; Bugs Bunny and Elmer Fudd Cartoon Festival Featuring "Wabbit Twouble", 153; Bugs Bunny Classics, 153; Cartoon Moviestars: Daffy!, 156; Cartoo[n] Moviestars: Porky!, 156; Daffy Duck: The Nuttiness Continues 160; Golden Age of Looney Toons, The: Firsts, 170; Golden Age of Looney Toons, The: 1930s Musicals, 170; Golden Age of Looney Toons, The: Tex Avery, 170; Here Comes Droopy, 174; Man's Best Friend (1985), 185; MGM Cartoon Magic, 18[...] Tex Avery's Screwball Classics, 210; Tex Avery's Screwball Classics (Volume 2), 210; Tex Avery's Screwball Classics (volume 4), 210; Very Best of Bugs Bunny: Volume 2, The, 2[...]
Avildsen, John G.: Cry Uncle!, 261; 8 Seconds, 43; For Keeps, 519; Formula, The, 978; Happy New Year, 293; Joe, 558; Karate Kid, The, 562; Karate Kid Part II, The, 562; Karate Kid Part III, The, 562; Lean on Me, 571; Neighbors, 343; Nigh[t] in Heaven, A, 606; Power of One, The, 625; Rocky, 642; Rock[y] V, 642; Save the Tiger, 648
Avildsen, Tom: Things Are Tough All Over, 393
Avis, Meiert: Far from Home, 975
Avnet, Jon: Between Two Women, 459; Fried Green Tomatoes, 522
Axel, Gabriel: Babette's Feast, 714
Axelrod, George: Lord Love a Duck, 321; Secret Life of an American Wife, The, 374
Ayala, Fernando: El Professor Hippie, 734
Aykroyd, Dan: Nothing But Trouble (1991), 347
Azzopardi, Mario: Nowhere to Hide, 92
B, Beth: Salvation, 647
Babenco, Hector: At Play in the Fields of the Lord, 451; Ironweed, 554; Kiss of the Spider Woman, 566; Pixote, 778
Babin, Charles: Mask of Fu Manchu, The, 82
Bachmann, Gideon: Ciao Federico!, 724
Bacon, Lloyd: Action in the North Atlantic, 2; Boy Meets Girl 244; Brother Orchid, 20; Devil Dogs of the Air, 37; Fighting Sullivans, The, 516; Footlight Parade, 917; 42nd Street, 918;

nch Line, The, *918;* Fuller Brush Girl, The, *282;* It Happens
ry Spring, *307;* Knute Rockne—All American, *567;* Marked
man, *82;* Miss Grant Takes Richmond, *333;* Oklahoma Kid,
, *1136;* She Couldn't Say No, *377;* Silver Queen, *1150;*
nder Bar, *948*
dat, Randall: Surf 2, *389*
dger, Clarence: Bill Fields and Will Rogers, *239;* Hands
, *292;* It (1927), *307*
dger, Phillip: Forgotten One, The, *978*
dham, John: American Flyers, *446;* Another Stakeout, *6;*
go Long Traveling All-Stars and Motor Kings, The, *240;*
d on a Wire, *13;* Blue Thunder, *16;* Dracula (1979), *837;*
d Way, The (1991), *293;* Point of No Return, *99;*
flections of Murder, *1009;* Saturday Night Fever, *938;* Short
cuit, *1076;* Stakeout, *119;* Wargames, *1088;* Whose Life Is
Anyway?, *701*
diyi, Reza S.: Of Mice and Men (1981), *610;* Police
uad!, *359*
er, Max: Ode to Billy Joe, *610*
gby Jr., Milton: Rebel Love, *636*
gdasarian Jr., Ross: Alvin and the Chipmunks:
g-Alongs, *146*
ggott, King: Human Hearts, *546;* Tumbleweeds, *1159*
gle, James: Stones of Death, *890*
hr, Fax: Hearts of Darkness, *425*
il, Chuck: Choke Canyon, *25;* Cleopatra Jones and the
sino of Gold, *26;* Gumball Rally, The, *58*
iley, Derek: Gloriana, *919*
iley, John: China Moon, *961;* Search for Signs of
elligent Life in the Universe, The, *374*
iley, Patrick: Door to Door, *267*
iley, Richard: Win, Place or Steal, *412*
ker, Graham: Alien Nation, *1035;* Born to Ride, *17;* Final
nflict, The, *841;* Impulse (1984), *985*
ker, Robert S.: Hellfire Club, The, *60;* Jack the Ripper
959), *858*
ker, Roy Ward: And Now the Screaming Starts, *809;*
ylum, *810;* Dr. Jekyll and Sister Hyde, *835;* Don't Bother to
ock, *971;* Masks of Death, *83;* Monster Club, The, *865;*
ght to Remember, A (1958), *606;* One That Got Away, The,
; Saint, The (TV Series), *1012;* Scars of Dracula, *883;* Seven
others Meet Dracula, The, *884;* Vampire Lovers, The, *900;*
ult of Horror, *900*
kshi, Ralph: Cool World, *1043;* Fire and Ice (1983), *1051;*
tz the Cat, *281;* Heavy Traffic, *539;* Hey Good Lookin', *541;*
rd of the Rings, The, *1063;* Streetfight, *671;* Wizards, *1090*
l, Walter: Jacko and Lise, *749*
laban, Bob: My Boyfriend's Back, *339;* Parents, *354*
laban, Burt: Stranger from Venus, *1081*
lch, Anthony: Horror Hospital, *851*
ldanello, Gianfranco: This Man Can't Die, *1156*
lden, Jim: Gamble on Love, *524;* Lights, Camera, Action,
ve, *575*
ldi, Ferdinando: Duel of Champions, *42;* Treasure of the
ur Crowns, *132*
lducci, Richard: L'Odeur Des Fauves (Scandal Man), *761*
ldwin, Joe: Dr. Seuss: The Grinch Grinches the Cat in the
t/Pontoffel Pock, *163*
ldwin, Peter: Lots of Luck, *322;* Very Brady Christmas, A,
5
ldwin, Thomas: Order of the Eagle, *96*
ledon, Rafael: Curse of the Crying Woman, The, *828;* Man
d the Monster, The, *862*
llard, Carroll: Black Stallion, The, *151;* Never Cry Wolf,
; Wind (1992), *140*
lton, Chris: TV's Greatest Bits, *401*
lzer, Robert E.: It's Three Strikes, Charlie Brown, *178*
amer, Rolf: Kill, The, *988*
mford, Roger: Rumpole of the Bailey (TV Series), *1011*
ncroft, Anne: Fatso, *275*
Band, Albert: Doctor Mordrid, *1047;* Ghoulies II, *846;* I Bury the Living, *855;* Prehysteria, *197;* Robot Wars, *1075;* Tramplers, The, *1158;* Zoltan—Hound of Dracula, *904*
Band, Charles: Alchemist, The, *808;* Crash and Burn, *1043;* Doctor Mordrid, *1047;* Dollman vs. Demonic Toys, *1047;* Dungeonmaster, The, *1048;* Meridian, *864;* Metalstorm: The Destruction of Jared-Syn, *1065;* Parasite, *873;* Prehysteria, *197;* Trancers, *1085;* Trancers II (The Return of Jack Death), *1085*
Banks, Monty: Great Guns, *289*
Bannert, Walter: Inheritors, The, *748*
Banno, Yoshimitu: Godzilla vs. the Smog Monster, *1054*
Bannon, Fred: Don Daredevil Rides Again, *1109*
Bar-Din, Ilana: Legends, *429*
Barbash, Uri: Beyond the Walls, *717;* Unsettled Land, *692*
Barbera, Joseph: Droopy and Company, *164;* Have Picnic Basket, Will Travel, *173;* Hey There, It's Yogi Bear, *174;* Jetsons: The Movie, *178;* Man Called Flintstone, A, *185;* Tom and Jerry Cartoon Festivals (Volume One), *212;* Tom and Jerry Cartoon Festivals (Volume Two), *212;* Tom and Jerry Cartoon Festivals (Volume Three), *212;* Tom and Jerry On Parade, *212;* Tom & Jerry's Cartoon Cavalcade, *212;* Tom and Jerry's Comic Capers, *212;* Tom & Jerry's Festival of Fun, *212;* Tom and Jerry's 50th Birthday Classics, *213;* Tom and Jerry's 50th Birthday Classics II, *213;* Tom and Jerry's 50th Birthday Classics III, *213*
Barillé, Albert: Once Upon a Time and the Earth Was Created..., *192*
Barkan, Yuda: Big Gag, The, *238*
Barker, Clive: Hellraiser, *850;* Night Breed, *869*
Barkett, Steve: Aftermath, The, *1034;* Empire of the Dark, *838*
Barma, Claude: Tales of Paris, *792*
Barnettler, Joseph L.: In the Time of Barbarians, *1058*
Barnet, Boris: Girl with the Hatbox, The, *741*
Barnett, Ivan: Fall of the House of Usher, The (1949), *840*
Barnett, Ken: Dark Tower, *829*
Barnett, Steve: Hollywood Boulevard II, *983;* Mindwarp, *1066;* Mission of Justice, *85*
Baron, Allen: Foxfire Light, *521*
Barreto, Bruno: Dona Flor and Her Two Husbands, *731;* Gabriela, *739;* Happily Ever After, *743;* Heart of Justice, *538;* Show of Force, A, *1015;* Story of Fausta, The, *789*
Barreto, Fabio: Luzia, *763*
Barrett, Don: Triumph, Tragedy & Rebirth: The Story of the Space Shuttle, *437*
Barrett, Lezli-An: Business As Usual, *472*
Barron, Arthur: Jolly Corner, The, *559;* Parker Adderson, Philosopher, *618*
Barron, Steve: Coneheads, *258;* Electric Dreams, *271;* Teenage Mutant Ninja Turtles, *209*
Barron, Zelda: Forbidden Sun, *519;* Shag, the Movie, *654*
Barry, Christopher: Tripods, *1085*
Barry, Ian: Chain Reaction, *24;* Ring of Scorpio, *640;* Wrangler, *141*
Barry, Wesley E.: Creation of the Humanoids, *1043*
Barski, Roger J.: Chains, *24*
Barsky, Bud: Coast Patrol, The, *27*
Bartel, Paul: Cannonball, *22;* Death Race 2000, *1045;* Eating Raoul, *270;* Longshot, The (1985), *320;* Lust in the Dust, *324;* Not for Publication, *347;* Private Parts, *876;* Scenes from the Class Struggle in Beverly Hills, *373;* Secret Cinema, The, *374*
Bartlett, Hall: Children of Sanchez, The, *481;* Jonathan Livingston Seagull, *559*
Bartlett, Richard: Ollie Hopnoodle's Haven of Bliss, *192;* Rock, Pretty Baby, *936*
Bartman, William: O'Hara's Wife, *611*
Barton, Charles: Abbott and Costello Meet Frankenstein, *221;* Abbott and Costello Meet the Killer, Boris Karloff, *221;* Africa Screams, *223;* Amos and Andy (TV Series), *226;* Buck Privates Come Home, *246;* Fighting Westerner, The, *1113;* Forlorn River, *1114;* Hell Town, *1120;* Mexican Hayride, *331;*

Noose Hangs High, The, *346;* Shaggy Dog, The, *203;* Thunder Trail, *1157;* Time of Their Lives, The, *396;* Toby Tyler, *212;* Wagon Wheels, *1162;* Wistful Widow of Wagon Gap, The, *412*

Barton, Peter: Kill Castro, *71*

Barwood, Hal: Warning Sign, *901*

Barwood, Nick: Nasty Hero, *89*

Barzman, Paolo: For Better and for Worse, *279*

Baskin, Richard: Sing, *939*

Bass, Jules: Around the World in 80 Days (1974), *147;* Ballad of Paul Bunyan, The, *148;* Daydreamer, The, *161;* Flight of Dragons, The, *167;* Hobbit, The, *175;* Johnny Appleseed/Paul Bunyan, *179;* Last Unicorn, The, *181;* Mad, Mad Monsters, The, *184;* Mad Monster Party, *184;* Twenty Thousand Leagues Under the Sea (1972), *214*

Bass, Saul: Phase IV, *1070*

Bassoff, Lawrence: Hunk, *303;* Weekend Pass, *407*

Bat-Adam, Michal: Boy Takes Girl, *152*

Batalov, Alexi: Overcoat, The, *774*

Batchelor, Joy: Animal Farm, *448*

Battersby, Bradley: Blue Desert, *957*

Battersby, Roy: Mr. Love, *597*

Battiato, Giacomo: Blood Ties (1987), *464;* Hearts and Armour, *59*

Bauer, Evgenii: Early Russian Cinema: Before the Revolutions (Vol. 1–10), *732*

Bava, Lamberto: Demons, *833;* Demons 2, *833;* Frozen Terror, *844*

Bava, Mario: Beyond the Door 2, *813;* Black Sabbath, *814;* Black Sunday (1961), *814;* Blood and Black Lace, *814;* Curse of the Living Dead, *828;* Danger: Diabolik, *1044;* Devil in the House of Exorcism, The, *833;* Hatchet for the Honeymoon, *848;* Hercules in the Haunted World, *61;* House of Exorcism, The, *852;* Planet of the Vampires, *875;* Torture Chamber of Baron Blood, The, *896;* Twitch of the Death Nerve, *898*

Baxley, Craig R.: Action Jackson, *2;* Deep Red (1994), *1046;* I Come in Peace, *1057;* Stone Cold, *120*

Baxter, John: Love on the Dole, *581*

Bayer, Rolf: Pacific Inferno, *96*

Bayly, Stephen: Coming Up Roses, *725;* Diamond's Edge, *162*

Beaird, David: It Takes Two, *308;* My Chauffeur, *339;* Octavia, *610;* Pass the Ammo, *355;* Scorchers, *650*

Beairsto, Rick: Close to Home, *484*

Bearde, Chris: Hysterical, *303*

Beatles, The: Magical Mystery Tour, *930*

Beattie, Alan: Delusion (1980), *969*

Beatty, Roger: Dorf on Golf, *267*

Beatty, Warren: Dick Tracy (1990), *38;* Heaven Can Wait (1978), *295;* Reds, *637*

Beaudin, Jean: Being at Home with Claude, *716*

Beaudine, William: Ape Man, The, *809;* Billy the Kid vs. Dracula, *813;* Blues Busters, *242;* Bowery Boys, The (Series), *244;* Boys from Brooklyn, The, *818;* Feathered Serpent, The, *976;* Ghosts on the Loose, *286;* Jesse James Meets Frankenstein's Daughter, *858;* Little Annie Rooney, *576;* Sparrows, *664;* Ten Who Dared, *210;* Westward Ho, the Wagons, *216*

Beaumont, Gabrielle: Carmilla, *821;* Death of a Centerfold, *498;* Godsend, The, *846;* Gone Are the Days, *288;* He's My Girl, *296*

Beaumont, Harry: Beau Brummell (1924), *457;* Broadway Melody, The, *910;* Dance, Fools, Dance, *493;* Laughing Sinners, *571;* Our Dancing Daughters, *616;* Show-Off, The, *378;* When's Your Birthday?, *409*

Bechard, Gorman: Galactic Gigolo, *282;* Psychos in Love, *877*

Beck, Martin: Last Game, The, *569*

Becker, Harold: Black Marble, The, *463;* Boost, The, *466;* Malice, *994;* Onion Field, The, *613;* Sea of Love, *1013;* Taps, *677;* Vision Quest, *694*

Becker, Jean: One Deadly Summer, *773*

Becker, Josh: Lunatics: A Love Story, *324;* Thou Shalt Not Kill...Except, *895*

Becker, Terry: Thirsty Dead, The, *895*

Beckett, Jack: Please Don't Eat My Mother!, *358*

Beckett, James: Ulterior Motives, *133*

Bedford, Terry: Slayground, *1017*

Beebe, Ford: Ace Drummond, *1;* Adventures of Rex and Rinty, *1092;* Buck Rogers: Destination Saturn (a.k.a. Planet Outlaws), *1040;* Challenge to Be Free, *157;* Don Winslow of the Coast Guard, *41;* Don Winslow of the Navy, *41;* Flash Gordon Conquers the Universe, *1052;* Flash Gordon: Mars Attacks the World (a.k.a. Trip to Mars; Deadly Ray From Mars, The), *1052* Junior G-Men, *69;* Last of the Mohicans (1932), *1126;* Laughing at Life, *571;* Phantom Creeps, The, *874;* Radio Patrol, *102;* Red Barry, *104;* Riders of Death Valley, *1143;* Shadow of the Eagle, *114;* Six Gun Serenade, *1150;* Winners of the West, *1165*

Beeman, Greg: License to Drive, *318;* Mom and Dad Save the World, *188*

Behrens, Gloria: Wiz Kid, The, *413*

Beineix, Jean-Jacques: Betty Blue, *717;* Diva, *731;* IP5: The Island of Pachyderms, *748;* Moon in the Gutter, The, *768*

Belgard, Arnold: East of Kilimanjaro, *43*

Bell, Alan: Hitchhiker's Guide to the Galaxy, The, *1056;* Ripping Yarns, *368*

Bell, John: Best of John Candy, The, *236*

Bell, Martin: American Heart, *446;* Streetwise, *435*

Bellamy, Earl: Against a Crooked Sky, *1092;* Desperate Women, *1109;* Fire!, *48;* Flood!, *51;* Sidewinder 1, *115;* Trackers, The, *1158;* Walking Tall Part II, *136*

Bellisario, Donald P.: Last Rites, *75;* Quantum Leap (TV Series), *1072*

Bellocchio, Marco: China Is Near, *723;* Devil in the Flesh (1987), *730;* Eyes, the Mouth, The, *735;* Henry IV, *743*

Bellon, Yannick: Rape of Love (L'Amour Violé), *779*

Belmont, Vera: Red Kiss (Rouge Baiser), *780*

Belson, Jerry: Jekyll & Hyde—Together Again, *310;* Surrender, *389*

Belvaux, Rémy: Man Bites Dog, *764*

Bemberg, Maria Luisa: Camila, *721;* Miss Mary, *767*

Bender, Jack: Child's Play 3, *823;* In Love with an Older Woman, *550;* Midnight Hour, *864;* Shattered Vows, *655;* Trick of the Trade, *399*

Bender, Joel: Gas Pump Girls, *283;* Midnight Kiss, *864;* Returning, The, *1010;* Rich Girl, *640*

Benedek, Laslo: Assault on Agathon, *7;* Daring Game, *32;* Kissing Bandit, The, *927;* Namu, the Killer Whale, *190;* Night Visitor, The (1970), *607;* Outer Limits, The (TV Series), *1069;* Port of New York, *624;* Wild One, The, *139*

Benedict, Tony: Santa and the Three Bears, *201*

Benigni, Roberto: Johnny Stecchino, *750*

Benjamin, Martin: Last Party, The, *428*

Benjamin, Richard: City Heat, *255;* Downtown, *41;* Little Nikita, *992;* Made in America, *325;* Mermaids, *331;* Money Pit, The, *335;* My Favorite Year, *340;* My Stepmother Is an Alien, *341;* Racing with the Moon, *633*

Benner, Richard: Happy Birthday, Gemini, *293;* Outrageous, *352;* Tales From Avonlea (TV series), *209;* Too Outrageous, *686*

Bennet, Spencer Gordon: Arizona Bound, *1094;* Atom Man vs. Superman, *7;* Atomic Submarine, The, *1037;* Batman and Robin, *9;* Calling Wild Bill Elliott, *1103;* Gunman from Bodie, *1117;* King of the Congo, *72;* King of the Forest Rangers, *72;* Last Frontier, The, *1125;* Lost Planet, The, *1064;* Manhunt in the African Jungle (Secret Service in Darkest Africa), *81;* Manhunt of Mystery Island, *82;* Masked Marvel, The, *83;* Mojave Firebrand, *1134;* Perils of the Darkest Jungle, *98;* Phantom Rider, *1138;* Pirates of the High Seas, *99;* Purple Monster Strikes, The, *101;* Son of Zorro, *118;* Superman—The Serial, *1081;* Zorro's Black Whip, *1166*

Bennett, Bill: Backlash, *8*

Bennett, Compton: Glory at Sea, *56;* King Solomon's Mines (1950), *72;* Seventh Veil, The, *653;* That Forsyte Woman, *680*
Bennett, Edward: Poirot (Series), *1006*
Bennett, Gary: Rain without Thunder, *634*
Bennett, Richard: Harper Valley P.T.A., *294*
Bennett, Rodney: Monsignor Quixote, *599;* Rumpole of the Bailey (TV Series), *1011*
Benson, Leon: Flipper's New Adventure, *167*
Benson, Richard (Paolo Heusch): Werewolf in a Girl's Dormitory, *902*
Benson, Robby: Modern Love, *335;* White Hot, *138*
Benson, Steven: Endgame, *1049*
Bentley, Thomas: Silver Blaze, *1016*
Benton, Robert: Bad Company, *1095;* Billy Bathgate, *461;* Kramer vs. Kramer, *567;* Late Show, The, *991;* Nadine, *341;* Places in the Heart, *623;* Still of the Night, *1020*
Benveniste, Michael: Flesh Gordon, *1052*
Benz, Obie: Heavy Petting, *426*
Beraud, Luc: Heat of Desire, *743*
Bercovici, Luca: Dark Tide, *495;* Ghoulies, *846;* Rockula, *937*
Beresford, Bruce: Aria, *907;* Barry McKenzie Holds His Own, *232;* Black Robe, *463;* Breaker Morant, *19;* Club, The (1985), *484;* Crimes of the Heart, *260;* Don's Party, *267;* Driving Miss Daisy, *505;* Fringe Dwellers, The, *522;* Getting of Wisdom, The, *526;* Her Alibi, *296;* King David, *564;* Mister Johnson, *597;* Puberty Blues, *630;* Rich in Love, *640;* Tender Mercies, *679*
Berger, Ludwig: Thief of Bagdad, The (1940), *1083*
Bergman, Andrew: Freshman, The, *281;* Honeymoon in Vegas, *300;* So Fine, *382*
Bergman, Daniel: Sunday's Children, *791*
Bergman, David: Horrible Horror, *851*
Bergman, Ingmar: After the Rehearsal, *711;* All These Women, *712;* Autumn Sonata, *714;* Brink of Life, *720;* Cries and Whispers, *726;* Devil's Eye, The, *730;* Dreams, *732;* Fanny and Alexander, *736;* From the Lives of the Marionettes, *739;* Hour of the Wolf, *745;* Lesson in Love, A, *760;* Magic Flute, The, *764;* Magician, The, *764;* Monika, *768;* Night Is My Future, *771;* Passion of Anna, The, *776;* Persona, *777;* Port of Call, *778;* Sawdust and Tinsel, *784;* Scenes from a Marriage, *784;* Secrets of Women (Waiting Women), *784;* Serpent's Egg, The, *652;* Seventh Seal, The, *785;* Silence, The, *786;* Smiles of a Summer Night, *787;* Summer Interlude, *791;* Three Strange Loves, *794;* Through a Glass Darkly, *795;* Virgin Spring, The, *801;* Wild Strawberries, *804;* Winter Light, *804*
Bergone, Serge: Last Gun, The, *1126*
Berke, William: Arson Inc., *7;* Badmen of the Hills, *1096;* Betrayal from the East, *11;* Dick Tracy, Detective, *38;* Falcon in Mexico, The, *975;* Fury of the Congo, *54;* I Shot Billy the Kid, *1122;* Jungle Jim, *69;* Renegade Girl, *1142*
Berkeley, Busby: Babes in Arms, *907;* Babes on Broadway, *907;* For Me and My Gal, *917;* Girl Crazy, *919;* Gold Diggers of 1935, *920;* Hollywood Hotel, *923;* Small Town Girl, *940;* Stage Struck (1936), *941;* Strike Up the Band, *387;* Take Me Out to the Ball Game, *943;* They Made Me a Criminal, *681*
Berlin, Abby: Blondie Knows Best, *241;* Double Deal, *41*
Berlinger, Joe: Brother's Keeper, *419*
Berman, Harvey: Wild Ride, The, *702*
Berman, Monty: Hellfire Club, The, *60;* Jack the Ripper (1959), *858*
Berman, Ted: Fox and the Hound, *168*
Bernard, Chris: Letter to Brezhnev, *318*
Bernard, Michael: Nights in White Satin, *607*
Bernds, Edward L.: Blondie Hits the Jackpot, *241;* Bowery Boys, The (Series), *244;* Queen of Outer Space, *1073;* Reform School Girl, *104;* Return of the Fly, The, *880*
Bernhard, Jack: Blonde Ice, *464*
Bernhardt, Curtis: Beau Brummell (1954), *457;* Conflict, *963;* Interrupted Melody, *925;* Kisses for My President, *314;* Miss Sadie Thompson, *596;* Possessed (1947), *625;* Sirocco, *116;* Stolen Life, A, *668*
Bernstein, Armyan: Cross My Heart (1987), *261;* Windy City, *703*
Bernstein, Walter: Little Miss Marker (1980), *182;* Women & Men 2, *706*
Berri, Claude: Je Vous Aime (I Love You All), *749;* Jean De Florette, *749;* Le Sex Shop, *758;* Manon of the Spring, *765;* One Wild Moment, *773;* Tchao Pantin, *793;* Two of Us, The, *797;* Uranus, *798*
Berry, Bill: Brotherhood of Death, *20;* Off the Mark, *348*
Berry, John: Angel on My Shoulder (1980), *448;* Bad News Bears Go to Japan, The, *231;* Honeyboy, *63;* Maya, *186;* Pantaloons, *775*
Berry, Tom: Amityville Curse, The, *809*
Bertolucci, Bernardo: Before the Revolution, *716;* Conformist, The, *725;* Grim Reaper, The (1962), *742;* Last Emperor, The, *569;* Last Tango in Paris, *570;* 1900, *607;* Partner, *775;* Sheltering Sky, The, *655;* Spider's Stratagem, The, *788;* Tragedy of a Ridiculous Man, *796*
Berton, Kenneth: Devil's Gift, The, *834*
Bertucelli, Jean-Louis: Ramparts of Clay, *779*
Berwick, Irvin: Monster of Piedras Blancas, The, *866*
Berz, Michael: Cannon Movie Tales: Snow White, *155*
Beshears, James: Homework, *543*
Bessada, Milad: Best of John Candy, The, *236;* Quiet Day in Belfast, A, *632*
Bessie, Dan: Hard Traveling, *536*
Besson, Luc: Big Blue, The, *12;* Final Combat, The, *48;* La Femme Nikita, *753;* Subway, *790*
Betancor, Antonio J.: Valentina, *799*
Bettman, Gil: Crystal Heart, *492;* Never Too Young to Die, *90*
Betuel, Jonathan: My Science Project, *1067*
Betwick, Wayne: Microwave Massacre, *864*
Beverly Jr., Eddie: Escapist, The, *511*
Bharadwaj, Radha: Closet Land, *962*
Bianchi, Andrea: Burial Ground, *820*
Bianchi, Bruno: Heathcliff—The Movie, *173;* Inspector Gadget (Series), *177*
Bianchi, Edward: Doctor Duck's Super Secret All-Purpose Sauce, *266;* Fan, The, *975*
Bianchini, Paolo: Machine Gun Killers, *1130*
Biberman, Abner: Running Wild (1955), *645*
Biberman, Herbert J.: Master Race, The, *590;* Salt of the Earth, *647*
Bido, Anthony: Watch Me When I Kill, *901*
Bierman, Robert: Apology, *809;* Vampire's Kiss, *900*
Bigelow, Kathryn: Blue Steel (1990), *16;* Loveless, The, *582;* Near Dark, *868;* Point Break, *99;* Wild Palms, *1089*
Bilheimer, Robert: Cry of Reason, The, *421*
Bill, Tony: Crazy People, *260;* Five Corners, *517;* Home of our Own, A, *542;* My Bodyguard, *601;* Princess and the Pea, The, *197;* Six Weeks, *659;* Untamed Heart, *692*
Billington, Kevin: Light at the End of the World, The, *77*
Bilson, Bruce: Chattanooga Choo Choo, *254;* North Avenue Irregulars, The, *191*
Bilson, Danny: Wrong Guys, The, *414;* Zone Troopers, *1091*
Binder, John: Uforia, *402*
Binder, Mike: Crossing the Bridge, *492;* Indian Summer, *306*
Binder, Steve: Father Guido Sarducci Goes to College, *275;* Give 'em Hell, Harry!, *528;* That Was Rock, *944*
Bindley, William: Freeze Frame, *168*
Binet, Catherine: Games of Countess Dolingen of Gratz, The, *739*
Bing, Steve: Every Breath, *973*
Binyon, Claude: Here Come the Girls, *922;* Stella (1950), *667*
Birch, Patricia: Grease 2, *920*
Bird, Brad: Amazing Stories (TV Series), *1036*
Birkin, Andrew: Burning Secret, *472;* Cement Garden, The, *478;* Desire, *500*
Birkinshaw, Alan: House of Usher, The, *853;* Ten Little Indians (1989), *1023*
Birri, Fernando: Very Old Man with Enormous Wings, A, *800*
Bischoff, Sam: Last Mile, The, *570*
Bivens, Loren: Trespasses, *687*

Bixby, Bill: Another Pair of Aces, *1094;* Baby of the Bride, *230;* Death of the Incredible Hulk, The, *1045;* Trial of the Incredible Hulk, *1085*
Bjorkman, Stig: Georgia, Georgia, *526*
Black, Jim: Dinosaurl, *422*
Black, Noel: Electric Grandmother, The, *1048;* Golden Honeymoon, The, *529;* I'm a Fool, *549;* Man, a Woman and a Bank, A, *994;* Pretty Poison, *626;* Prime Suspect, *627;* Private School, *362;* Quarterback Princess, *631*
Black, Trevor: Goldy, The Last of the Golden Bears, *171*
Blackwood, Christian: Private Conversations: On the Set of Death of a Salesman, *433;* Thelonious Monk: Straight, No Chaser, *436*
Blackwood, Michael: Thelonious Monk: Straight, No Chaser, *436*
Blaine, Cullen: R.O.T.O.R., *1073*
Blair, David: Wax, *1088*
Blair, George: Missourians, The, *1134;* Under Mexicali Stars, *1160*
Blair, Lawrence: Ring of Fire, *433*
Blair, Les: Bad Behaviour, *231*
Blair, Mark: Confessions of a Serial Killer, *825*
Blair, Preston: Barney Bear Cartoon Festival, *148*
Blake, Michael: Laughing Horse, *571*
Blake, T. C.: Nightflyers, *1068*
Blakemore, Michael: Privates on Parade, *362*
Blancato, Ken: Stewardess School, *386*
Blanchard, John: Best of John Candy, The, *236;* Best of the Kids in the Hall, The, *236;* Last Polka, The, *315;* Really Weird Tales, *365*
Blank, Les: Always for Pleasure, *418;* Burden of Dreams, *420;* Gap-Toothed Women, *424;* Garlic Is as Good as 10 Mothers, *424;* Hot Pepper, *426;* Mance Lipscomb: A Well-Spent Life, *430*
Blasioli, Joseph: Blast 'Em, *419*
Blatty, William Peter: Exorcist III: Legion, *840;* Ninth Configuration, The, *608*
Bleckner, Jeff: Brotherly Love, *819;* Target: Favorite Son, *677;* When Your Lover Leaves, *699;* White Water Summer, *139*
Blier, Bertrand: Beau Pere, *716;* Buffet Froid (Cold Cuts), *720;* Get Out Your Handkerchiefs, *740;* Going Places, *741;* Ménage, *767;* Merci La Vie, *767;* My Best Friend's Girl, *769;* Too Beautiful for You, *796*
Block, Bruce: Princess Academy, The, *361*
Block, David: Ducktales (TV Series), *164*
Bloom III, George Jay: Brothers in Arms, *819*
Bloom, Jeffrey: Blood Beach, *814;* Dogpound Shuffle, *266;* Flowers in the Attic, *978;* Stick-up, The, *386*
Bloomfield, George: Best of John Candy, The, *236;* Deadly Companion, *968;* Nothing Personal, *347;* To Kill a Clown, *1025*
Blot, Philippe: Arrogant, The, *450*
Blum, Michael: Richard Pryor—Live and Smokin', *367*
Blumenthal, Andy: Bloodfist 2, *16*
Bluth, Don: All Dogs Go to Heaven, *145;* American Tail, An, *146;* Hans Christian Andersen's Thumbelina, *173;* Land Before Time, The, *180;* Rock-a-Doodle, *200;* Secret of Nimh, The, *202*
Blystone, John G.: Block-Heads, *241;* Dick Turpin, *38;* Great Guy, *532;* Our Hospitality, *351;* Swiss Miss, *390*
Blyth, David: Death Warmed Up, *831;* My Grandpa Is a Vampire, *340;* Red-Blooded American Girl, *879*
Blyth, Jeff: Cheetah, *158*
Bnarbic, Paul: Cold Front, *963*
Bochner, Hart: PCU, *355*
Boetticher, Budd: Bullfighter and the Lady, The, *21;* Decision at Sundown, *1108;* Man from the Alamo, The, *1132;* Ride Lonesome, *1143;* Rise and Fall of Legs Diamond, The, *107;* Tall T, The, *1154*
Bogart, Paul: Cancel My Reservation, *250;* Canterville Ghost, The (1986), *155;* Class of '44, *483;* Marlowe, *995;* Oh, God, You Devil!, *349;* Power, Passion, and Murder, *625;* Skin Game, *1150;* Torch Song Trilogy, *686*
Bogayevicz, Yurek: Anna, *448;* Three of Hearts, *683*
Bogdanovich, Josef: Boxoffice, *467*
Bogdanovich, Peter: Daisy Miller, *493;* Illegally Yours, *548;* Last Picture Show, The, *570;* Mask (1985), *590;* Noises Off, *346;* Paper Moon, *353;* Saint Jack, *646;* Targets, *1022;* Texasville, *680;* They All Laughed, *393;* Thing Called Love, The, *681;* What's Up, Doc?, *408*
Bogner, Willy: Fire and Ice (1987), *49;* Fire, Ice & Dynamite, *49*
Bohusz, Michael: Uninvited, The (1993), *1160*
Boisrone, Michel: Catherine & Co., *722;* Love and the Frenchwoman, *762;* Tales of Paris, *792;* Voulez Vous Danser avec Moi? (Will You Dance with Me?), *801*
Boisset, Yves: Dog Day, *40;* Purple Taxi, The, *631*
Boivan, Jerome: Barjo, *715*
Bokanowski, Patrick: L'Ange (The Angel), *752*
Bolanos, Jose Antonio: Dead Aim (1973), *1108*
Boleslawski, Richard: Garden of Allah, The, *525;* Last of Mrs. Cheney, The, *315;* Les Miserables (1935), *573;* Operator 13, *614;* Painted Veil, The, *617;* Rasputin and the Empress, *635*
Bolognini, Mauro: Husbands and Lovers, *546;* La Grande Bourgeoise, *754;* Oldest Profession, The, *773*
Bolotin, Craig: That Night, *680*
Bolt, Ben: Big Town, The, *461*
Bolt, Robert: Lady Caroline Lamb, *567*
Bond, Jack: It Couldn't Happen Here, *925*
Bond III, James: Def by Temptation, *832*
Bond, Michael: Paddington Bear (Series), *193*
Bond, Timothy: Deadly Harvest, *1045;* Lost World, The (1992), *79;* Return to the Lost World, *1074*
Bond, Trevor: Little Miss Trouble and Friends, *183*
Bondarchuk, Sergei: War and Peace (1968), *802;* Waterloo, *697*
Bonerz, Peter: Nobody's Perfekt, *346;* Police Academy 6: City Under Siege, *359;* When Things Were Rotten (TV Series), *409*
Bonifer, Mike: Lipstick Camera, *992*
Bonnard, Mario: Last Days of Pompeii (1960), *75*
Bonns, Miguel Iglesias: Night of the Howling Beast, *870*
Boorman, John: Deliverance, *36;* Emerald Forest, The, *44;* Excalibur, *1050;* Exorcist II: The Heretic, *840;* Hell in the Pacific, *60;* Hope and Glory, *544;* Point Blank, *624;* Where the Heart Is, *699;* Zardoz, *1091*
Boos, H. Gordon: Red Surf, *104*
Boosler, Elayne: Elayne Boosler: Party of One, *270*
Booth, Connie: Fawlty Towers, *276*
Borau, José Luis: On the Line, *94*
Borchers, Donald P.: Grave Secrets, *847*
Borden, Lizzie: Inside Out (1992), *1058;* Love Crimes, *993;* Working Girls, *706*
Boris, Robert: Buy and Cell, *248;* Oxford Blues, *617;* Steele Justice, *120*
Borris, Clay: Alligator Shoes, *445;* Gunfighters, The, *1117;* Prom Night IV—Deliver Us from Evil, *877;* Quiet Cool, *102*
Borsos, Phillip: Dr. Bethune, *502;* Grey Fox, The, *1117;* Mean Season, The, *996;* One Magic Christmas, *613*
Bortman, Michael: Crooked Hearts, *491*
Borzage, Frank: Farewell to Arms, A, *514;* Flirtation Walk, *917;* History Is Made at Night, *542;* I've Always Loved You, *555;* Mannequin (1937), *588;* Moonrise, *599;* Mortal Storm, The, *600;* Shining Hour, The, *656;* Smilin' Through (1941), *940;* Stage Door Canteen, *665;* Strange Cargo, *669;* Three Comrades, *682*
Boskovich, John: Without You I'm Nothing, *413*
Boulting, John: Heavens Above, *296;* I'm All Right Jack, *305;* Lucky Jim, *324*
Boulting, Roy: Brothers In Law, *246;* Heavens Above, *296;* Last Word, The, *571;* Moving Finger, The, *998;* Run for the Sun, *109;* There's a Girl in My Soup, *393*

Bourguignon, Serge: A Coeur Joie (Head Over Heels), *710;* Sundays and Cybèle, *791*
Bouvier, Robert: City in Panic, *824*
Bovon, Jean: Messin' with the Blues, *430*
Bowab, John: Gabe Kaplan as Groucho, *282;* Love at the Top, *581*
Bowen, David R.: Secret Life of Jeffrey Dahmer, The, *651*
Bowen, Jenny: Street Music, *670;* Wizard of Loneliness, The, *704*
Bowen, John: Knockouts, *314;* Lethal Games, *76*
Bowers, George: Body and Soul (1981), *466;* Hearse, The, *849;* My Tutor, *341;* Private Resort, *362*
Bowes, Tom: Two Moon July, *947*
Bowman, John: Nudity Required, *347*
Bowman, Rob: Airborne, *224*
Bowser, Kenneth: In a Shallow Grave, *550*
Box, Muriel: Rattle of a Simple Man, *635;* Truth About Women, The, *689*
Boyd, Daniel: Invasion of the Space Preachers, *307*
Boyd, Don: East of Elephant Rock, *506;* Twenty-One, *690*
Boyd, Julianne: Eubie!, *916*
Boyer, Jean: Crazy For Love, *726;* Fernandel the Dressmaker, *736*
Bozzetto, Bruno: Allegro Non Troppo, *712*
Bradbury, Robert N.: Between Men, *1097;* Blue Steel (1934), *1099;* Dawn Rider, *1107;* Desert Trail, *1109;* Forbidden Trails, *1114;* Kid Ranger, *1124;* Lawless Frontier, *1127;* Lawless Range, *1127;* Lucky Texan, *1130;* Man from Utah, The, *1132;* Rainbow Valley, *1140;* Riders of Destiny, *1144;* Riders of the Rockies, *1144;* Sing, Cowboy, Sing, *1150;* Star Packer, The, *1153;* Texas Terror, *1156;* Trail Beyond, The, *1158;* Trouble in Texas, *1159;* West of the Divide, *1163;* Westward Ho, *1163*
Bradford, Samuel: Teen Vamp, *392*
Bradley, Al: Captive Planet, *1041;* Cross Mission, *31;* Iron Warrior, *1060;* Miami Cops, *84*
Bradley, David: They Saved Hitler's Brain, *895*
Bradshaw, John: Big Slice, The, *12;* That's My Baby, *680*
Bradshaw, Randy: Blades of Courage, *463;* Last Train Home, *181;* Ramona (Series), *198*
Brahm, John: Guest in the House, *534;* Man from U.N.C.L.E., The (TV Series), *80;* Miracle of Our Lady of Fatima, The, *595;* Wintertime, *947*
Brakhage, Stan: Dog Star Man, *1047*
Bralver, Bob: Rush Week, *882*
Brambilla, Marco: Demolition Man, *1046*
Branagh, Kenneth: Dead Again, *966;* Henry V (1989), *540;* Much Ado About Nothing, *338;* Peter's Friends, *621*
Brand, Larry: Drifter, The, *837;* Masque of the Red Death (1989), *864;* Overexposed, *873*
Brander, Richard: Sizzle Beach, U.S.A., *380*
Brando, Marlon: One-Eyed Jacks, *1137*
Brandon, Clark: Skeeter, *887*
Brandstrom, Charlotte: Road to Ruin (1991), *369;* Sweet Revenge (1990), *389*
Brandt, Nicholas: Inside Out 2, *1059*
Brannon, Fred: Adventures of Frank and Jesse James, *1092;* Crimson Ghost, The, *30;* G-Men Never Forget, *54;* Government Agents vs. Phantom Legion, *57;* Jesse James Rides Again, *1123;* King of the Forest Rangers, *72;* King of the Rocketmen, *72;* Phantom Rider, *1138;* Purple Monster Strikes, The, *101;* Radar Men from the Moon, *102;* Satan's Satellites, *111;* Son of Zorro, *118;* Zombies of the Stratosphere (Satan's Satellites), *141*
Braoude, Patrick: Great, My Parents Are Divorcing, *742*
Bras, Rene: Rudolph the Red-Nosed Reindeer (and Other Wonderful Christmas Stories), *200*
Brascia, Dominick: Evil Laugh, *839*
Brask, Ulrik al: Art Com Video (Vol. 1–3), *1037*
Brass, Tinto: Caligula, *474*
Brault, Michel: Paper Wedding, *618*
Brauman, Jack: Zombie Nightmare, *905*
Braunsteen, Joseph: Rest in Pieces, *879*
Braverman, Charles: Brotherhood of Justice, *471;* Hit and Run, *63;* Prince of Bel Air, *627;* Richard Lewis—"I'm in Pain Concert", *367*
Brayne, William: Flame to the Phoenix, A, *50*
Breakston, George: Manster, The, *863;* Scarlet Spear, The, *112*
Brealey, Gil: Test of Love, A, *679*
Breen, Richard L.: Stopover Tokyo, *120*
Brel, Jacques: Franz, *738*
Breillat, Catherine: 36 Fillette, *794*
Bren, Milton H.: Three for Bedroom C, *395*
Brenon, Herbert: Dancing Mothers, *262*
Brescia, Alfonso: White Fang and the Hunter, *217*
Bresciani, Andrea: Through the Looking Glass, *211*
Bresson, Robert: Diary of a Country Priest, *730;* L'Argent, *752;* Mouchette, *769*
Brest, Martin: Beverly Hills Cop, *11;* Going in Style, *288;* Midnight Run, *84;* Scent of a Woman, *649*
Bretherton, Howard: Below the Border, *1097;* Carson City Cyclone, *1103;* Dawn on the Great Divide, *1107;* Down Texas Way, *1110;* Ghost Town Law, *1115;* Hidden Valley Outlaws, *1120;* Hopalong Cassidy Enters, *1121;* Ladies They Talk About, *567;* Pirates of the Prairie, *1139;* Riders of the Rio Grande, *1144;* Ridin' Down the Trail, *1144;* San Antonio Kid, *1147;* Showdown (1940), *1149;* West of the Law, *1163*
Brewer, Jameson: Little Prince, The (Series), *183*
Brewer, Otto: Mystery Mountain, *1135;* Phantom Empire (1935), *98;* Radio Ranch (Men with Steel Faces & Phantom Empire), *1140*
Briant, Michael E.: Dr. Who: Revenge of the Cybermen, *1047*
Brice, Monte: Flask of Fields, A, *278*
Brickman, Marshall: Lovesick, *324;* Manhattan Project, The, *995;* Simon, *379*
Brickman, Paul: Men Don't Leave, *331;* Risky Business, *368*
Bridges, Alan: Brief Encounter (1974), *470;* D.P., *493;* Out of Season, *616;* Pudd'nhead Wilson, *630;* Return of the Soldier, The, *638;* Shooting Party, The, *656*
Bridges, Beau: Seven Hours to Judgment, *113;* Wild Pair, The, *140*
Bridges, James: Baby Maker, The, *453;* Bright Lights, Big City, *470;* China Syndrome, The, *961;* Mike's Murder, *594;* Paper Chase, The, *617;* Perfect, *620;* September 30, 1955, *652;* Urban Cowboy, *692*
Brinckerhoff, Burt: Can You Hear the Laughter? The Story of Freddie Prinze, *474;* Cracker Factory, *490;* Remington Steele (TV series), *1010*
Britten, Lawrence: Whose Child Am I?, *701*
Britton, Tracy Lynch: Maximum Breakout, *83*
Brock, Deborah: Rock 'n' Roll High School Forever, *369;* Slumber Party Massacre II, *887*
Brocka, Lino: Fight for Us, *47*
Broderick, John: Swap, The, *674;* Warrior and the Sorceress, The, *1088*
Brodie, Kevin: Mugsy's Girls, *338*
Bromfield, Rex: Cafe Romeo, *249;* Home Is Where the Hart Is, *299;* Love at First Sight, *322;* Melanie, *591*
Bromski, Jacek: Alice (1981), *906*
Broodbent, Wally: Little Match Girl, The (1983), *182*
Brook, Clive: On Approval, *349*
Brook, Peter: King Lear (1971), *564;* Lord of the Flies (1963), *579;* Mahabharata, The, *585;* Marat/Sade, *588;* Meetings with Remarkable Men, *591*
Brookner, Howard: Bloodhounds of Broadway, *242*
Brooks, Adam: Almost You, *225;* Cannon Movie Tales: Red Riding Hood, *155*
Brooks, Albert: Defending Your Life, *263;* Lost in America, *321;* Modern Romance, *335;* Real Life, *365*
Brooks, Anthony: Nudes on the Moon, *1069*

Brooks, Bob: Tattoo, *677*
Brooks, James L.: Broadcast News, *246;* I'll Do Anything, *305;* Terms of Endearment, *679*
Brooks, Joseph: If Ever I See You Again, *548;* Invitation to the Wedding, *307;* You Light Up My Life, *708*
Brooks, Mel: Audience with Mel Brooks, An, *229;* Blazing Saddles, *241;* High Anxiety, *297;* History of the World, Part One, The, *298;* Life Stinks, *318;* Producers, The, *362;* Robin Hood: Men in Tights, *369;* Silent Movie, *379;* Spaceballs, *384;* Twelve Chairs, The, *401;* Young Frankenstein, *416*
Brooks, Richard: Battle Circus, *456;* Bite the Bullet, *1099;* Blackboard Jungle, The, *463;* Brothers Karamazov, The, *471;* Cat on a Hot Tin Roof (1958), *477;* Catered Affair, The, *477;* Deadline USA, *497;* $ (Dollars), *971;* Elmer Gantry, *509;* Fever Pitch, *516;* In Cold Blood, *985;* Last Hunt, The, *1126;* Last Time I Saw Paris, The, *570;* Looking for Mr. Goodbar, *993;* Lord Jim, *79;* Professionals, The, *101;* Something of Value, *118;* Sweet Bird of Youth (1962), *674;* Wrong Is Right, *414*
Brooks, Robert: Who Shot Pat?, *701*
Broomfield, Nick: Chicken Ranch, *420;* Dark Obsession, *495;* Monster in a Box, *336*
Brophy, Philip: Body Melt, *817*
Broughton, James: Films of James Broughton, The, *1050*
Brower, Otto: Devil Horse, The, *1109;* Fighting Caravans, *1112;* Law of the Sea, *571;* Scarlet River, *1148;* Spirit of the West, *1152*
Brown, Barry: Cloud Dancer, *27*
Brown, Barry Alexander: Lonely in America, *320*
Brown, Bruce: Endless Summer, The, *44*
Brown, Clarence: Ah, Wilderness, *223;* Anna Christie (1930), *449;* Anna Karenina (1935), *449;* Chained, *478;* Conquest, *487;* Eagle, The, *269;* Edison, The Man, *507;* Flesh and the Devil, *518;* Free Soul, A, *522;* Goose Woman, The, *980;* Gorgeous Hussy, The, *531;* Human Comedy, The, *546;* Idiot's Delight, *548;* Inspiration, *553;* Intruder in the Dust, *553;* It's a Big Country, *308;* Last of the Mohicans, The (1920), *75;* National Velvet, *190;* Of Human Hearts, *610;* Possessed (1931), *625;* Rains Came, The, *634;* Romance, *643;* Sadie McKee, *646;* Song of Love, *662;* They Met in Bombay, *127;* To Please a Lady, *130;* White Cliffs of Dover, The, *699;* Wife Vs. Secretary, *701;* Woman of Affairs, A, *705;* Yearling, The, *219*
Brown, Drew: Stand-Up Reagan, *385*
Brown, Edwin Scott: Prey, The, *876*
Brown, Georg Stanford: Alone in the Neon Jungle, *445;* Dangerous Relations, *494;* Miracle of the Heart, *595;* Roots: The Next Generation, *644;* Vietnam War Story, *694*
Brown, Gregory: Dead Man Walking, *1045;* Street Asylum, *121*
Brown, Harry: Knickerbocker Holiday, *927*
Brown, Jim: Wasn't That a Time!, *438;* Woody Guthrie—Hard Travelin', *439*
Brown, Karl: White Legion, *700*
Brown, Larry: Psychopath, The, *877*
Brown, Melville: Check and Double Check, *254*
Brown, Mitch: Deathshot, *36*
Brown, Rowland: Blood Money (1933), *464*
Brown, William H.: Casino Royale (1954), *23*
Browning, Kirk: You Can't Take it with You (1984), *415*
Browning, Ricou: Daring Game, *32*
Browning, Tod: Devil Doll, The (1936), *833;* Dracula (1931), *837;* Freaks, *843;* Mark of the Vampire, *863;* Outside the Law, *616;* West of Zanzibar, *1030;* Where East Is East, *138*
Brownlow, Kevin: Buster Keaton: A Hard Act to Follow, *420;* D. W. Griffith, Father of Film, *422;* Harold Lloyd: The Third Genius, *425;* Hollywood, *426;* Unknown Chaplin, *437*
Brownrigg, S. F.: Don't Look in the Basement, *836;* Poor White Trash II, *624;* Thinkin' Big, *394*
Bruce, James: Suicide Club, The, *1021*
Bruce, John: Adventures of Sherlock Holmes, The (Series), *950*
Bruckman, Clyde: Fatal Glass of Beer, A/Pool Sharks, *274;* Flask of Fields, A, *278*
Brunel, Adrian: Old Spanish Custom, An, *349*
Brusati, Franco: Sleazy Uncle, The, *786;* To Forget Venice, *795*
Bryan, James: Don't Go in the Woods, *836*
Bryant, Charles: Salome (1923), *647*
Brydon, Bill: Aria, *907*
Buchanan, Larry: Free, White, and 21, *522;* Goodbye, Norma Jean, *530;* Loch Ness Horror, The, *861;* Mars Needs Women, *1065*
Buchowetzki, Dimitri: Swan, The (1925), *389*
Buchs, Julio: Bullet for Sandoval, A, *1102*
Buck, Chris: Family Dog, *166*
Buckalew, Bethel: My Boys Are Good Boys, *601*
Buckhantz, Allan A.: Last Contract, The, *75*
Bucksey, Colin: Blue Money, *242;* Curiosity Kills, *965;* Dealers, *498;* McGuffin, The, *996;* Midnight's Child, *865*
Bucquet, Harold S.: Adventures of Tartu, *2;* Dr. Kildare's Strange Case, *40;* Dragon Seed, *504;* On Borrowed Time, *612;* Without Love, *413*
Budd, Colin: Hurricane Smith, *65*
Budgell, Jack: Best of the Kids in the Hall, The, *236*
Buechler, John Carl: Cellar Dweller, *822;* Dungeonmaster, The, *1048;* Friday the 13th, Part VII: The New Blood, *844;* Ghoulies III, *846;* Troll, *1085*
Bugajski, Richard: Clearcut, *26;* Interrogation, *748*
Bulajic, Veljko: Day that Shook the World, The, *496*
Bunce, Alan: Babar: The Movie, *147*
Buntzman, Mark: Exterminator 2, The, *45*
Buñuel, Joyce: Dirty Dishes, *730*
Buñuel, Luis: Age of Gold, *711;* Ascent To Heaven (Mexican Bus Ride), *714;* Criminal Life of Archibaldo de la Cruz, The, *727;* Diary of a Chambermaid (1964), *730;* Discreet Charm of the Bourgeoisie, The, *730;* El (This Strange Passion), *733;* El Bruto (The Brute), *733;* Exterminating Angel, The, *735;* Great Madcap, The, *742;* Illusion Travels by Streetcar, *747;* Land Without Bread, *755;* Los Olvidados, *761;* Milky Way, The (1970), *767;* Nazarin, *771;* Phantom of Liberty, The, *777;* Simon of the Desert, *786;* Susanna, *791;* That Obscure Object of Desire, *793;* Tristana, *797;* Un Chien Andalou, *690;* Viridiana, *801;* Woman without Love, A, *805;* Wuthering Heights (1953), *805*
Burge, Robert: Keaton's Cop, *70;* Vasectomy, *404*
Burge, Stuart: Julius Caesar (1970), *561*
Burke, Martyn: Clown Murders, The, *962;* Last Chase, The, *1062*
Burke, William: Dangerous Passage, *32*
Burman, Tom: Meet the Hollowheads, *331*
Bursema, Jopi: Ferocious Female Freedom Fighters, *276*
Burness, Pete: Columbia Pictures Cartoon Classics, *159*
Burnett, Charles: To Sleep with Anger, *685*
Burns, Allan: Just Between Friends, *561*
Burns, Keith: Ernie Kovacs: Television's Original Genius, *272*
Burns, Ken: Civil War, The, *421*
Burns, Robert A.: Mongrel, *865*
Burr, Jeff: Leatherface—the Texas Chainsaw Massacre III, *860;* Offspring, The, *872;* Puppet Master Four, *878;* Stepfather II, *890*
Burrowes, Geoff: Return to Snowy River, Part II, *1143;* Run, *109*
Burrows, James: Partners, *354*
Burstall, Tim: Attack Force Z, *7;* Great Expectations—The Untold Story, *532;* Kangaroo, *562;* Naked Country, The, *603;* Nightmare at Bittercreek, *1002*
Burton, David: Fighting Caravans, *1112;* Lady by Choice, *567*
Burton, Richard: Dr. Faustus, *502*
Burton, Sean: Curse III: Blood Sacrifice, *827*
Burton, Tim: Aladdin and His Wonderful Lamp, *145;* Batman (1989), *9;* Batman Returns, *9;* Beetlejuice, *233;* Edward Scissorhands, *1048;* Frankenweenie, *280;* Pee-Wee's Big Adventure, *355*
Burton, Tom: Ride 'em Denver, *199*

Burtt, Ben: American Gangster, The, *418*
Buschmann, Christel: Comeback, *912*
Buchowetzki, Dimitri: Othello (1922), *615*
Bushell, Anthony: Terror of the Tongs, The, *126*
Bushnell Jr., William H.: Four Deuces, The, *52*
Butler, David: April in Paris, *907;* Bright Eyes, *152;* By the Light of the Silvery Moon, *910;* Calamity Jane (1953), *910;* Captain January, *155;* Caught in the Draft, *252;* Connecticut Yankee, A, *258;* Doubting Thomas, *268;* It's a Great Feeling, *925;* Little Colonel, The, *928;* Littlest Rebel, The, *929;* Look For The Silver Lining, *929;* Lullaby of Broadway, *929;* Princess and the Pirate, The, *361;* San Antonio, *1147;* Story of Seabiscuit, The, *207;* Tea for Two, *944;* Thank Your Lucky Stars, *944;* They Got Me Covered, *393;* You'll Find Out, *415*
Butler, George: Pumping Iron, *630;* Pumping Iron II: The Women, *630*
Butler, Robert: Barefoot Executive, The, *148;* Blue Knight, The (1973), *465;* Computer Wore Tennis Shoes, The, *159;* Hot Lead and Cold Feet, *176;* James Dean—A Legend in His Own Time, *556;* Moonlighting (1985), *997;* Night of the Juggler, *90;* Now You See Him, Now You Don't, *191;* Out on a Limb (1986), *616;* Scandalous John, *202;* Star Trek: The Cage, *1078;* Strange New World, *1080;* Treasures of the Twilight Zone, *1085;* Underground Aces, *403;* Up the Creek (1984), *403*
Butoy, Hendel: Rescuers Down Under, *199*
Buzby, Zane: Last Resort, *316*
Buzzell, Edward: At the Circus, *229;* Best Foot Forward, *908;* Go West, *287;* Honolulu, *923;* Neptune's Daughter, *932;* Ship Ahoy, *939;* Song of the Thin Man, *1018;* Woman of Distinction, A, *413*
Bye, Ed: Red Dwarf (TV Series), *365*
Byrd, Caruth C.: Hollywood High, Part II, *299*
Byrne, David: True Stories, *400*
Byrum, John: Heart Beat, *537;* Inserts, *552;* Razor's Edge, The (1984), *635;* Whoopee Boys, The, *411*
Byrum, Rob: Scandalous (1983), *373*
Caan, James: Hide in Plain Sight, *541*
Cabanne, Christy: Dixie Jamboree, *914;* Jane Eyre (1934), *557;* Last Outlaw, The (1936), *1126;* Mummy's Hand, The, *867;* One Frightened Night, *1003;* Scared to Death, *883;* World Gone Mad, The, *707*
Cabot, Ellen: Beach Babes from Beyond, *1038;* Deadly Embrace, *34*
Cacoyannis, Michael: Iphigenia, *749;* Story of Jacob and Joseph, The, *207;* Sweet Country, *674;* Trojan Women, The, *688;* Zorba the Greek, *709*
Cahn, Edward L.: Dragstrip Girl, *42;* Invasion of the Saucer Men, *1059;* It! The Terror from Beyond Space, *1060;* Jet Attack, *68;* Law and Order, *1127;* Motorcycle Gang, *87;* She Creature, The, *885;* Suicide Battalion, *122;* Voodoo Woman, *901;* Zombies of Mora Tav, *905*
Caiano, Mario: Adios, Hombre, *1092;* Nightmare Castle, *871;* Shangai Joe, *1148*
Caillier, Barry: In Search of the Wow Wow Wibble Woggle Wazzle Woodle Woo!, *176*
Cain, Christopher: Principal, The, *628;* Pure Country, *630;* Stone Boy, The, *668;* That Was Then...This Is Now, *680;* Wheels of Terror, *138;* Where the River Runs Black, *1089;* Young Guns, *1165*
Calenda, Antonio: One Russian Summer, *613*
Callaghan, Neil: Return Fire: Jungle Wolf II, *105*
Callas, John: Lone Wolf, *861*
Callner, Marty: Comedy Tonight, *257;* Pee-Wee Herman Show, The, *355*
Callow, Simon: Ballad of the Sad Cafe, The, *455*
Camerini, Mario: Ulysses, *133*
Cameron, James: Abyss, The, *1034;* Aliens, *1035;* Piranha Part Two: The Spawning, *875;* Terminator, The, *1082;* Terminator 2: Judgment Day, *1082*
Cameron, Ken: Fast Talking, *166;* Good Wife, The, *530;* Monkey Grip, *598*
Cameron, Ray: Bloodbath at the House of Death, *242*
Camfield, Douglas: Ivanhoe (1982), *68*
Cammell, Donald: Demon Seed, *1046;* Performance, *1005;* White of the Eye, *1031*
Camp, Joe: Benji, *149;* Benji the Hunted, *150;* Double McGuffin, The, *163;* For the Love of Benji, *167;* Hawmps!, *294;* Oh, Heavenly Dog!, *192*
Campanile, Pasquale Festa: When Women Had Tails, *409;* When Women Lost Their Tails, *409*
Campbell, Doug: Season of Fear, *1013;* Zapped Again, *416*
Campbell, Graeme: Blood Relations, *816;* Into the Fire, *67;* Murder One, *87*
Campbell, Martin: Cast a Deadly Spell, *1041;* Criminal Law, *964;* Defenseless, *969;* Edge of Darkness (1986), *973;* No Escape, *1069*
Campion, Jane: Angel at My Table, An, *447;* Jane Campion Shorts, *309;* Piano, The, *622;* Sweetie, *675*
Campogalliani, Carlo: Goliath and the Barbarians, *56*
Campus, Michael: Education of Sonny Carson, The, *507;* Mack, The, *584;* Z.P.G. (Zero Population Growth), *1091*
Camus, Marcel: Black Orpheus, *718;* Holy Innocents, *744*
Cannistraro, Richard: Violated, *136*
Cannon, Dyan: End of Innocence, The, *509*
Cannon, Robert: Columbia Pictures Cartoon Classics, *159;* Gerald McBoing-Boing (Columbia Pictures Cartoons Volume Three), *169*
Canutt, Yakima: Adventures of Frank and Jesse James, *1092;* G-Men Never Forget, *54;* Manhunt of Mystery Island, *82*
Capitani, Giorgio: Lobster for Breakfast, *761;* Ruthless Four, The, *1146*
Capon, Naomi: Six Wives of Henry VIII, The (TV Series), *659*
Capra, Berndt: Mindwalk, *430*
Capra, Frank: Arsenic and Old Lace, *228;* Bitter Tea of General Yen, The, *462;* Broadway Bill, *470;* Here Comes the Groom, *922;* Hole in the Head, A, *298;* It Happened One Night, *307;* It's a Wonderful Life, *555;* Ladies of Leisure, *567;* Lady for a Day, *567;* Lost Horizon, *580;* Meet John Doe, *591;* Mr. Deeds Goes to Town, *333;* Mr. Smith Goes to Washington, *597;* Our Mr. Sun, *193;* Platinum Blonde, *623;* Pocketful of Miracles, *359;* State of the Union, *666;* Strange Case of the Cosmic Rays, The, *207;* Strong Man, The, *387;* That Certain Thing, *392;* You Can't Take it with You (1938), *415*
Carax, Léos: Lovers on the Bridge, *762*
Carayiannis, Costa: Land of the Minotaur, *859*
Carbol, Larry: Ghost Warrior, *55*
Carbonnaux, Norbert: Candide, *722*
Card, Lamar: Clones, The, *1042*
Cardenas, Hernan: Island Claws, *857*
Cardiff, Jack: Dark of the Sun, *32;* Freakmaker, *843;* My Geisha, *340*
Cardinal, Roger: Malarek, *586*
Cardona Jr., René: Beaks the Movie, *812;* Tintorera, *895;* Treasure of the Amazon, *132*
Cardona Sr., René: Doctor of Doom, *836;* Night of the Bloody Apes, *869;* Rock 'n' Roll Wrestling Women vs. the Aztec Ape, *108;* Rock 'n' Roll Wrestling Women vs. the Aztec Mummy, *369*
Cardone, J. S.: Climate for Killing, A, *962;* Shadow Hunter, *654;* Shadowzone, *885;* Thunder Alley, *945*
Cardos, John "Bud": Act of Piracy, *1;* Dark, The, *829;* Day Time Ended, The, *1045;* Kingdom of the Spiders, *859;* Mutant, *867;* Outlaw of Gor, *1069*
Carducci, Mark Patrick: Flying Saucers over Hollywood, *424*
Carew, Topper: Talkin' Dirty After Dark, *391*
Carle, Gilles: In Trouble, *550*
Carlei, Carlo: Flight of the Innocent, *737*
Carley, Kurt Mac: Sexual Intent, *1014*
Carlino, Lewis John: Class, *256;* Great Santini, The, *533;* Sailor Who Fell from Grace with the Sea, The, *646*
Carlsen, Henning: Hunger (1966), *746;* Wolf at the Door, *804;* World of Strangers, A, *805*

Carlyle, Patrick: Call of the Coyote, *1103*
Carmody, Don: Surrogate, The, *674*
Carné, Marcel: Assassins de L'Ordre, Les (Law Breakers), *714;* Bizarre, Bizarre, *718;* Children of Paradise, The, *723;* Le Jour Se Leve (Daybreak) (1939), *757;* Les Visiteurs Du Soir, *759*
Caro, Marc: Delicatessen, *729*
Caron, Glenn Gordon: Clean and Sober, *484;* Wilder Napalm, *411*
Carpenter, John: Assault on Precinct 13, *7;* Big Trouble in Little China, *13;* Christine, *824;* Dark Star, *1044;* Elvis—The Movie, *509;* Escape from New York, *45;* Fog, The, *842;* Halloween, *848;* John Carpenter Presents: Body Bags, *858;* Memoirs of an Invisible Man, *1065;* Prince of Darkness, *876;* Starman, *1080;* They Live, *895;* Thing, The (1982), *1083*
Carpenter, Stephen: Dorm that Dripped Blood, The, *837;* Kindred, The, *859;* Power, The (1980), *876*
Carpi, Fabio: Basileus Quartet, *715*
Carr, Adrian: Now and Forever, *609*
Carr, Bret: Underground (1990), *1029*
Carr, John: Night Train to Terror, *870*
Carr, Terry: Welcome to 18, *407*
Carr, Thomas: Captain Scarlett, *23;* Cherokee Flash, *1104;* Dino, *501;* El Paso Kid, *1111;* Hostile Country, *1122;* Jesse James Rides Again, *1123;* Pirates of the High Seas, *99;* Red River Renegades, *1142;* Santa Fe Saddlemates, *1147;* Superman—The Serial, *1081;* TV's Best Adventures of Superman, *1085;* Wanted: Dead or Alive (TV Series), *1162*
Carra, Lawrence: Antony and Cleopatra (1981), *450*
Carradine, David: Americana, *446*
Carreras, Michael: Maniac (1962), *995;* Prehistoric Women (1967), *100*
Carrier, Rick: Strangers in the City, *669*
Carroll, Robert Martin: Sonny Boy, *889*
Carroll, Willard: Runestone, *882*
Carson, David: Adventures of Sherlock Holmes, The (Series), *950*
Carstairs, John Paddy: Made in Heaven (1948), *326;* Saint in London, The, *1012*
Cartel, Michael: Runaway Nightmare, *109*
Carter, John: Zombie Island Massacre, *905*
Carter, Peter: High-Ballin', *61;* Highpoint, *62;* Intruder Within, The, *1059;* Kavik the Wolf Dog, *179;* Rituals, *1010*
Carter, Thomas: Call to Glory, *474;* Miami Vice, *84;* Swing Kids, *675*
Cartier, Rudolph: Quatermass and the Pit, *1072*
Carver, Steve: Big Bad Mama, *12;* Bulletproof, *21;* Dead Center, *967;* Drum, *505;* Eye for an Eye, *46;* Jocks, *310;* Lone Wolf McQuade, *78;* Oceans of Fire, *93;* River of Death, *107;* Steel, *120*
Casden, Ron: Campus Man, *249*
Casey, Kimberley: Born Killer, *17*
Casey, Thomas: Sometimes Aunt Martha Does Dreadful Things, *888*
Cass, Henry: Blood of the Vampire, *815;* Last Holiday, *569*
Cassavetes, John: Big Trouble, *239;* Child is Waiting, A, *480;* Gloria, *56;* Killing of a Chinese Bookie, *564;* Love Streams, *582;* Opening Night, *614;* Woman Under the Influence, A, *705*
Cassenti, Frank: Mystery, Mr. RA, *431*
Cassidy, Richard: Crazed, *825*
Casson, Philip: Children's Songs and Stories with the Muppets, *158*
Castellari, Enzo G.: Go Kill and Come Back, *1115;* High Crime, *61;* Loves and Times of Scaramouche, The, *324;* 1990: The Bronx Warriors, *1069;* Shark Hunter, The, *114;* Sinbad of the Seven Seas, *116;* Warriors of the Wasteland, *1088*
Castillo, Nardo: Gunrunner, The, *58*
Castle, Alien: Desire and Hell at Sunset Motel, *969*
Castle, Nick: Boy Who Could Fly, The, *468;* Dennis the Menace, *161;* Last Starfighter, The, *1062;* Tag—The Assassination Game, *124;* Tap, *944*
Castle, William: Americano, The, *1093;* Conquest of Cochise, *1106;* House on Haunted Hill, *853;* Night Walker, The, *1001;* Old Dark House, The, *872;* Strait-Jacket, *890;* 13 Ghosts, *895;* Zotz!, *417*
Caston, Hoite C.: Best of Not Necessarily the News, The, *236;* Dirt Bike Kid, The, *162*
Catalanotto, Joe: Terror in the Swamp, *893*
Cates, Gilbert: Affair, The, *442;* Backfire, *953;* Consenting Adults (1985), *488;* Goldilocks and the Three Bears, *171;* Hobson's Choice (1983), *175;* I Never Sang for My Father, *547;* Last Married Couple in America, The, *315;* Oh, God! Book II, *349;* Promise, The, *629;* Rapunzel, *198;* Summer Wishes, Winter Dreams, *673;* To All My Friends on Shore, *684*
Cato, Don: Dixie Lanes, *265*
Caton-Jones, Michael: Doc Hollywood, *265;* Memphis Belle (1990), *592;* Scandal, *648;* This Boy's Life, *682*
Caulfield, Michael: Gallagher's Travels, *54*
Cavalcanti, Alberto: Dead of Night (1945), *830;* Nicholas Nickleby, *605*
Cavalier, Alain: Therese, *793*
Cavani, Liliana: Berlin Affair, The, *459;* Beyond Obsession, *717;* Night Porter, The, *606*
Celestri, Gian: Nelvanamation (Volume Two), *191*
Cella, Len: Moron Movies, *337*
Chabrol, Claude: Bad Girls (1969), *715;* Blood of Others, The, *464;* Blood Relatives, *957;* Bluebeard (1963), *719;* Club Extinction, *1042;* High Heels (1972), *744;* Horse of Pride, The, *744;* Le Beau Serge, *756;* Le Boucher (The Butcher), *756;* Les Biches, *759;* Les Cousins, *759;* Madame Bovary (1991), *763;* Seven Deadly Sins, The, *785;* Six in Paris (Paris Vue par . . .), *786;* Story of Women, The, *790;* Ten Days Wonder, *1023;* This Man Must Die, *794;* Une Partie De Plaisir, *798;* Wedding in Blood, *802*
Chaffey, Don: C.H.O.M.P.S., *155;* Casino, *476;* Creatures the World Forgot, *1043;* Fourth Wish, The, *521;* Gift of Love, The, *527;* Greyfriars Bobby, *172;* Horse Without a Head, The, *175;* Jason and the Argonauts, *1060;* Magic of Lassie, The, *185;* Persecution, *621;* Pete's Dragon, *195;* Prisoner, The (TV Series), *1071;* Ride a Wild Pony, *199;* Secret Agent (TV Series), *113;* Three Lives of Thomasina, The, *211*
Chakhnazarov, Karen: Jazzman, *749*
Chalong, P.: H-Bomb, *58;* In Gold We Trust, *66*
Chalopin, Jean: Inspector Gadget (Series), *177*
Chambers, Kimberlie: Rich Little's Little Scams on Golf, *367*
Champion, Gower: Bank Shot, *232;* I Do! I Do!, *924*
Champion, Gregg: Short Time, *378*
Chan, Jackie: Armour Of God, *713;* Jackie Chan's Police Force, *309;* Project A (Part I), *778;* Project A (Part II), *779*
Chanois, Jean-Paul L.: Les Miserables (1957), *759*
Chaplin, Charles: Burlesque of Carmen, *247;* Chaplin Revue, The, *253;* Charlie Chaplin Carnival, *253;* Charlie Chaplin Cavalcade, *253;* Charlie Chaplin Festival, *253;* Charlie Chaplin...Our Hero, *253;* Charlie Chaplin—The Early Years, Vol. 1, *253;* Charlie Chaplin—The Early Years, Vol. 2, *253;* Charlie Chaplin—The Early Years, Vol. 3, *254;* Charlie Chaplin—The Early Years, Vol. 4, *254;* Circus, The/A Day's Pleasure, *255;* City Lights, *255;* Dough and Dynamite/Knockout, The, *268;* Gold Rush, The, *288;* Great Dictator, The, *289;* Kid, The/The Idle Class, *313;* King in New York, A, *313;* Limelight, *319;* Lost and Found Chaplin: Keystone, *321;* Modern Times, *335;* Monsieur Verdoux, *336;* Rare Chaplin, *364;* Three Charlies and a Phoney!, *395;* Woman of Paris, A, *705*
Chapman, Matthew: Heart of Midnight, *982;* Hussy, *546;* Slow Burn, *1018;* Strangers Kiss, *669*
Chapman, Michael: All the Right Moves, *444;* Clan of the Cave Bear, *1041*
Charlton, Robert: No Big Deal, *608*

Charr, Henri: Illegal Entry, *66*
Chase, Richard: Hell's Angels Forever, *426*
Chatiliez, Étienne: Tatie Danielle, *792*
Chaudhri, Amin Q.: Tiger Warsaw, *683;* Unremarkable Life, An, *692*
Chavarri, Jaime: I'm the One You're Looking For, *747*
Chechik, Jeremiah S.: Benny & Joon, *234;* National Lampoon's Christmas Vacation, *342*
Cheek, Douglas: C.H.U.D., *820*
Chekmayan, Ara: Forever James Dean, *424*
Chelsom, Peter: Hear My Song, *295*
Chenal, Pierre: Crime and Punishment (1935), *726;* Man from Nowhere, The, *765*
Chereau, Patrice: L'Homme Blessé (The Wounded Man), *760*
Cherry III, John R.: Dr. Otto and the Riddle of the Gloom Beam, *266;* Ernest Film Festival, *272;* Ernest Goes to Camp, *272;* Ernest Goes to Jail, *272;* Ernest Rides Again, *272;* Ernest Saves Christmas, *165;* Ernest Scared Stupid, *272;* Knowhutimean?, *314*
Chetwynd, Lionel: Hanoi Hilton, The, *536*
Chiffre, Yvan: President's Target, *100*
Chiniqy, Gerry: Ant and the Aardvark, The, *147;* Bear Who Slept Through Christmas, The, *149;* Bugs Bunny Mystery Special, The, *153;* Bugs Bunny's Easter Funnies, *154*
Chiodo, Stephen: Killer Klowns from Outer Space, *859*
Chivers, Collin: Michael Jackson Moonwalker, *931*
Chomsky, Marvin J.: Anastasia: The Mystery of Anna, *447;* Attica, *452;* Billionaire Boys Club, *461;* Brotherhood of the Rose, *20;* Deliberate Stranger, The, *499;* Evel Knievel, *45;* Holocaust, *542;* Inside the Third Reich, *552;* Little Ladies of the Night, *576;* Murph the Surf, *87;* Nairobi Affair, *603;* Roots, *644;* Shaming, The, *655;* Tank, *124*
Chong, Thomas: Cheech and Chong's Next Movie, *254;* Corsican Brothers, The (1984), *259;* Far Out Man, *274;* Nice Dreams, *344;* Still Smokin', *386*
Chopra, Joyce: Lemon Sisters, The, *317;* Murder in New Hampshire, *600;* Smooth Talk, *661*
Chouraqui, Elie: Love Songs (Paroles et Musique), *762;* Man on Fire, *81*
Christensen, Benjamin: Mockery, *598;* Witchcraft Through the Ages (HAXAN), *804*
Christian, Nathaniel: California Casanova, *249;* Club Fed, *256*
Christian, Roger: Sender, The, *884;* Starship, *1080*
Christian-Jacque: Love and the Frenchwoman, *762;* Nana, *770;* Pearls of the Crown, The, *776*
Christopher, Anthony: Fatal Pulse, *840*
Chudnow, Byron: Amazing Dobermans, *146;* Daring Dobermans, The, *32;* Doberman Gang, The, *40*
Chudnow, David: Amazing Dobermans, *146*
Chukhrai, Grigori: Ballad of a Soldier, *715*
Chung, Sun: City War, *724*
Ciccoritti, Gerard: Graveyard Shift (1987), *847;* Psycho Girls, *877;* Understudy, The: Graveyard Shift II, *899*
Cicero, Nando: Twice a Judas, *1159*
Cimber, Matt: Butterfly, *473;* Fakeout, *513;* Single Room Furnished, *659;* Time to Die, A (1983), *130;* Yellow Hair and the Fortress of Gold, *1165*
Cimino, Michael: Deer Hunter, The, *499;* Desperate Hours (1990), *37;* Heaven's Gate, *1119;* Sicilian, The, *115;* Thunderbolt and Lightfoot, *129;* Year of the Dragon, *141*
Civirani, Osvaldo: Dead for a Dollar, *1108*
Clair, René: A Nous la Liberte, *710;* And Then There Were None, *952;* Avant Garde Program #2, *714;* Crazy Ray, The, *726;* Forever and a Day, *520;* Ghost Goes West, The, *285;* I Married a Witch, *1057;* Italian Straw Hat, The, *749;* Le Million, *758;* Love and the Frenchwoman, *762;* Quatorze Juliet, *779;* Under the Roofs of Paris, *798*
Clampett, Bob: Beany and Cecil, *149;* Best of Bugs Bunny and Friends, The, *150;* Best of Warner Brothers, Vol. 1, *150;* Bugs and Daffy: The Wartime Cartoons, *152;* Bugs Bunny and Elmer Fudd Cartoon Festival Featuring "Wabbit Twouble", *153;* Bugs Bunny Cartoon Festival Featuring "Hold the Lion Please", *153;* Bugs vs. Elmer, *155;* Cartoon Moviestars: Bugs!, *156;* Cartoon Moviestars: Daffy!, *156;* Cartoon Moviestars: Porky!, *156;* Daffy Duck and Company, *160;* Daffy Duck Cartoon Festival: Ain't That Ducky, *160;* Daffy Duck: Tales from the Duckside, *160;* Daffy Duck: The Nuttiness Continues, *160;* Elmer Fudd Cartoon Festival: An Itch in Time, *164;* Golden Age of Looney Toons, The: Bob Clampett, *169;* Golden Age of Looney Toons, The: Bugs Bunny by Each Director, *169;* Golden Age of Looney Toons, The: Firsts, *170;* Golden Age of Looney Toons, The: Hurry for Hollywood, *170;* Golden Age of Looney Toons, The: 1940s Zanies, *170;* Golden Age of Looney Toons, The: The Art of Bugs, *170;* Just Plain Daffy, *179;* Little Tweetie and Little Inki Cartoon Festival, *183;* Porky Pig and Company, *196;* Porky Pig and Daffy Duck Cartoon Festival Featuring "Tick Tock Tuckered", *196;* Porky Pig Cartoon Festival Featuring "Nothing but the Tooth", *196;* Porky Pig: Days of Swine and Roses, *196;* Tweety and Sylvester, *214;* Very Best of Bugs Bunny: Volume 1, The, *215;* Very Best of Bugs Bunny: Volume 2, The, *215;* Very Best of Bugs Bunny: Volume 3, The, *215;* Very Best of Bugs Bunny: Volume 4, The, *215*
Clark, B. D.: Galaxy of Terror, *1053*
Clark, Bob: American Clock, The, *446;* Black Christmas, *814;* Children Shouldn't Play with Dead Things, *823;* Christmas Story, A, *159;* Deathdream, *832;* From the Hip, *281;* Loose Cannons, *321;* Murder by Decree, *998;* Porky's, *360;* Porky's II: The Next Day, *360;* Rhinestone, *367;* Tribute, *688;* Turk 182, *689*
Clark, Brandon: Alligator II, *808*
Clark, Colbert: Fighting with Kit Carson, *1113;* Mystery Squadron, *88;* Three Musketeers, The (1933), *128;* Warning Shadows (1933), *1030;* Whispering Shadow, The, *138*
Clark, Duane: Bitter Harvest (1993), *955;* Shaking the Tree, *655*
Clark, Greydon: Danse Macabre, *829;* Final Justice, *48;* Forbidden Dance, The, *918;* Joy Sticks, *311;* Killer Instinct, *71;* Out of Sight Out of Mind, *1003;* Return, The, *1074;* Satan's Cheerleaders, *882;* Skinheads, *116;* Uninvited, The (1987), *899;* Wacko, *405;* Without Warning, *1090*
Clark, James B.: Dog of Flanders, A, *163;* Flipper, *167;* Island of the Blue Dolphins, *555;* Misty, *188;* My Side of the Mountain, *190*
Clark, Jim: Madhouse (1972), *862*
Clark, John: Fast Lane Fever, *46*
Clark, Lawrence Gordon: Belfast Assassin, *458;* Romance on the Orient Express, *643*
Clark, Matt: Da, *493*
Clark, Steve: Ducktales (TV Series), *164*
Clark, William: Goodbye Bird, The, *171*
Clarke, Alan: Rita, Sue and Bob Too, *368;* Scum, *650*
Clarke, James Kenelm: Going Undercover, *288*
Clarke, Richard: Doctor Hackenstein, *835*
Clarke, Robert: Hideous Sun Demon, The, *850*
Clarke, Shirley: Connection, The (1961), *487;* Ornette—Made in America, *432;* Portrait of Jason, *433*
Clavell, James: Last Valley, The, *75;* To Sir with Love, *685*
Claver, Bob: Jaws of Satan, *858*
Claxton, William F.: Bonanza (TV Series), *1100*
Clayton, Jack: Great Gatsby, The, *532;* Lonely Passion of Judith Hearne, The, *577;* Room at the Top, *643;* Something Wicked This Way Comes, *1077*
Cleese, John: Fawlty Towers, *276*
Clegg, Tom: Any Man's Death, *450;* Children of the Full Moon, *823;* House That Bled to Death, The, *853;* Inside Man, The, *66;* McVicar, *591;* Stroke of Midnight, *387*
Clemens, Brian: Captain Kronos: Vampire Hunter, *821*
Clement, Dick: Bullshot, *247;* Catch Me a Spy, *960;* Water, *406*
Clement, René: And Hope to Die, *952;* Day And The Hour, *728;* Forbidden Games, *737;* Gervaise, *740;* Is Paris Burning?, *554;* Joy House, *559;* Rider on the Rain, *1010*

Clements, Ron: Adventures of the Great Mouse Detective, The, *144;* Aladdin (1992), *144;* Little Mermaid, The (1989), *182*
Clifford, Graeme: Boy Who Left Home to Find Out About the Shivers, The, *152;* Burke and Wills, *472;* Deception (1993), *969;* Frances, *521;* Gleaming the Cubes, *55;* Little Red Riding Hood, *183;* Turn of the Screw, The (1989), *898*
Clift, Dession: Mystery of the Marie Celeste, The, *1000*
Clifton, Elmer: Assassin of Youth (a.k.a. Marijuana), *451;* California Frontier, *1103;* Captain America (1944), *22;* Cyclone in the Saddle, *1107;* Days of Old Cheyenne, *1107;* Deep in the Heart of Texas, *1108;* Down to the Sea in Ships, *504;* Skull and Crown, *1017*
Clifton, Peter: Song Remains the Same, The, *435*
Cline, Eddie: Balloonatic, The/One Week, *231;* Bank Dick, The, *232;* Breaking the Ice, *909;* Buster Keaton Festival: Vol. 1, *248;* Buster Keaton Festival: Vol. 2, *248;* Buster Keaton Festival: Vol. 3, *248;* Buster Keaton: The Golden Years, *248;* Cowboy Millionaire, *1106;* Dude Ranger, *1110;* Hook, Line and Sinker, *300;* My Little Chickadee, *340;* Never Give a Sucker an Even Break, *343;* Peck's Bad Boy with the Circus, *194;* Private Buckaroo, *935;* Private Snuffy Smith, *362;* Three Ages, The, *395;* Two Houses of Keaton, *402;* Villain Still Pursued Her, The, *135*
Cloche, Maurice: Monsieur Vincent, *768*
Clokey, Art: Gumby and the Wild West (Volume Four), *172;* Gumby Celebration, A (Volume Ten), *172;* Gumby for President (Volume Nine), *172;* Gumby Magic (Volume Two), *172;* Gumby Rides Again (Volume Five), *172;* Gumby Summer, A (Volume Eight), *172;* Gumby's Fun Fling (Volume Eleven), *172;* Gumby's Holiday Special (Volume Seven), *172;* Gumby's Incredible Journey (Volume Six), *172;* Misadventures of Gumby, The (Volume Three), *187;* Return of Gumby, The (Volume One), *199*
Clouse, Robert: Amsterdam Kill, The, *5;* Big Brawl, The, *12;* Black Belt Jones, *13;* China O'Brien, *25;* China O'Brien 2, *25;* Deadly Eyes, *831;* Enter the Dragon, *44;* Force Five, *51;* Game of Death, *54;* Gymkata, *58;* Ironheart, *67;* Pack, The, *873;* Ultimate Warrior, The, *1087*
Clouzot, Henri-Georges: Diabolique, *730;* Jenny Lamour, *749;* Le Corbeau, *757;* Manon, *765;* Mystery of Picasso, The, *770;* Wages of Fear, The, *801*
Clucher, E. B.: They Call Me Trinity, *1156;* Trinity Is Still My Name, *1159*
Clurman, Harold: Deadline at Dawn, *34*
Clyde, Craig: Little Heroes, *181*
Coane, Jim: Tom & Jerry's 50th Birthday Bash, *213*
Coates, Lewis: Adventures of Hercules, The, *1034;* Alien Contamination, *1034;* Hercules (1983), *1056;* Star Crash, *1078*
Coburn, Glenn: Blood Suckers from Outer Space, *816*
Cochran, Stacy: My New Gun, *341*
Cocteau, Jean: Beauty and the Beast (1946), *716;* Blood of a Poet, *719;* Orpheus, *774;* Testament of Orpheus, The, *793*
Coe, Fred: Thousand Clowns, A, *395*
Coe, Wayne: Grim Prairie Tales, *847*
Coen, Joel: Barton Fink, *232;* Blood Simple, *957;* Hudsucker Proxy, The, *303;* Miller's Crossing, *594;* Raising Arizona, *364*
Cohen, David: Hollywood Zap, *299*
Cohen, Gerry: It's a Bundyful Life, *308*
Cohen, Howard R.: Deathstalker IV: Match of the Titans, *1046;* Saturday the 14th, *882;* Space Raiders, *1078;* Time Trackers, *1084*
Cohen, Larry: Ambulance, The, *952;* Black Caesar, *13;* Deadly Illusion, *968;* Demon (God Told Me To), *1046;* Hell Up in Harlem, *60;* Housewife, *545;* It Lives Again, *857;* It's Alive!, *857;* It's Alive III: Island of the Alive, *857;* Perfect Strangers, *1005;* Private Files of J. Edgar Hoover, The, *100;* Q, *878;* Return to Salem's Lot, A, *880;* Special Effects, *889;* Stuff, The, *891;* Wicked Stepmother, The, *903*
Cohen, Martin B.: Rebel Rousers, *104*
Cohen, Randy: Franken and Davis at Stockton State, *280*
Cohen, Rob: Dragon: The Bruce Lee Story, *42;* Small Circle of Friends, A, *660*
Cohen, S. E.: Martial Law, *82*
Cohen, Thomas A.: Hungry I Reunion, *303;* Massive Retaliation, *83*
Cohn, Michael: Interceptor, *67*
Coke, Cyril: Pride and Prejudice (1985), *626*
Cokliss, Harley: Black Moon Rising, *14;* Malone, *80;* Warlords of the 21st Century, *1088*
Cole, Tristan DeVere: Dive, The, *40*
Coles, John David: Good Fight, The, *530;* Rising Son, *641;* Signs of Life, *657*
Colizzi, Giuseppe: Ace High, *1092;* Boot Hill, *1100*
Colla, Richard A.: Battlestar Galactica, *1038;* Fuzz, *282;* Prize Pulitzer, The: The Roxanne Pulitzer Story, *629;* Storm and Sorrow, *120*
Collard, Cyril: Savage Nights, *783*
Collector, Robert: Red Heat (1985), *1009*
Collier, James F.: China Cry, *481;* Cry from the Mountain, *160;* Hiding Place, The, *541*
Collins, Bob: Bronx Executioner, The, *1040*
Collins, Boon: Abducted, *1;* Spirit of the Eagle, *119*
Collins, Edward: Evil Town, *839*
Collins, Lewis D.: Adventures of the Flying Cadets, *2;* Longhorn, *1130;* Lost City of the Jungle, *79;* Make a Million, *327*
Collins, Robert: Gideon's Trumpet, *527;* Life and Assassination of the Kingfish, The, *574;* Mafia Princess, *585;* Our Family Business, *616*
Collinson, Peter: African Rage, *3;* Earthling, The, *164;* House on Garibaldi Street, *545;* Italian Job, The, *308;* Man Called Noon, The, *1131;* Sell-Out, The, *113;* Spiral Staircase, The (1975), *1019;* Ten Little Indians (1975), *1023;* Tomorrow Never Comes, *686*
Colmano, Marino: Straight Time: He Wrote It for Criminals, *435*
Colombo, Fernando: Skyline, *380;* Star Knight, *1078*
Colpaert, Carl: Delusion (1991), *499;* In the Aftermath: Angels Never Sleep, *1058*
Columbus, Chris: Adventures in Babysitting, *222;* Heartbreak Hotel, *538;* Home Alone, *299;* Home Alone 2: Lost in New York, *175;* Mrs. Doubtfire, *334;* Only the Lonely, *350*
Comencini, Luigi: Misunderstood (1988), *598;* Till Marriage Do Us Part, *795*
Comfort, Lance: Courageous Mr. Penn, *489;* Great Day, *532*
Compton, J. C.: Buckeye and Blue, *1102*
Compton, Richard: Angels Die Hard, *5;* Deadman's Curve, *913;* Macon County Line, *80;* Ransom, *1009;* Return to Macon County, *106;* Super Force, *1081;* Wild Times, *1164*
Condon, Bill: Dead in the Water, *967;* Murder 101, *999;* Sister, Sister, *886;* White Lie, *700*
Conklin, Gary: Paul Bowles in Morocco, *432*
Conn, Nicole: Claire of the Moon, *483*
Connelly, Marc: Green Pastures, *533*
Conners, Bruce: Bruce Conners Films 1, *246*
Connon, Raymond: Swing It, Sailor, *390*
Connor, Kevin: At the Earth's Core, *1037;* From Beyond the Grave, *844;* Goliath Awaits, *56;* Hollywood Detective, The, *983;* Iran Days of Crisis, *554;* Land That Time Forgot, The, *1061;* Lion of Africa, The, *77;* Motel Hell, *866;* People That Time Forgot, The, *1070;* Sunset Grill, *1021*
Conrad, Claude: Birthday Boy, The, *240*
Conrad, Mikel: Flying Saucer, The, *1052*
Conrad, Patrick: Mascara, *82*
Conrad, Robert: Bandits (1967), *1096;* Crossfire (1986), *1106*
Conrad, William: Side Show, *886*
Conte, Therese: Chasing Dreams, *480*
Contner, James A.: Cover Girl Murders, The, *964;* Hitler's Daughter, *542;* 10 Million Dollar Getaway, The, *678*
Convy, Bert: Weekend Warriors, *407*
Conway, Gary: Sara Dane, *648*

onway, Jack: Boom Town, *466;* Dragon Seed, *504;* Girl om Missouri, The, *286;* Honky Tonk, *1121;* Hucksters, The, *45;* Julia Misbehaves, *311;* Let Freedom Ring, *928;* Libeled ady, *318;* Love Crazy, *322;* Our Modern Maidens, *616;* ed-Headed Woman, *636;* Saratoga, *372;* Tale of Two Cities, A 1935), *676;* Too Hot to Handle, *130;* Unholy Three, *1029;* Viva illa!, *1162*

onway, James L.: Donner Pass: The Road to Survival, *109;* Hangar 18, *1055;* Incredible Rocky Mountain Race, The, *06;* Last of the Mohicans (1985), *1126*

oogan, Rif: Invisible Maniac, *1060*

ook, Bruce R.: Nightwish, *1068*

ook, Fielder: Big Hand for the Little Lady, A, *1098;* ideaways, The, *174;* I Know Why the Caged Bird Sings, *547;* atterns, *619;* Seize the Day, *651*

ook, Philip: Beyond the Rising Moon, *1039;* Invader, *1059*

ooke, Alan: King Lear (1982), *564*

oolidge, Martha: Angie, *448;* Bare Essentials, *232;* Crazy in ove, *490;* Hammered: The Best of Sledge, *292;* Joy of Sex, he, *311;* Lost in Yonkers, *580;* Plain Clothes, *358;* Rambling ose, *634;* Real Genius, *365;* Valley Girl, *404*

ooper, Buddy: Mutilator, The, *867*

ooper, Jackie: Hammered: The Best of Sledge, *292;* Izzy & oe, *309;* Leave 'em Laughing, *572;* M*A*S*H* (TV Series), *25;* Marathon, *329;* Night They Saved Christmas, The, *191;* odeo Girl, *642;* Rosie, *937;* White Mama, *700*

ooper, Merian C.: Chang, *24;* Grass, *425;* King Kong 1933), *859*

ooper, Peter H.: Ordinary Heroes, *614*

ooper, Stuart: Disappearance, The, *39;* Long Hot Summer, he (1985), *578;* Payoff, *98;* Rubdown, *1011*

oppola, Christopher: Deadfall, *968;* Dracula's Widow, *837*

oppola, Francis Ford: Apocalypse Now, *6;* Bellboy and the laygirls, The, *234;* Bram Stoker's Dracula, *819;* Conversation, he, *963;* Cotton Club, The, *29;* Dementia 13, *832;* Finian's ainbow, *916;* Gardens of Stone, *525;* Godfather, The, *529;* odfather, Part II, The, *529;* Godfather, Part III, The, *529;* odfather Epic, The, *529;* New York Stories, *343;* One from the eart, *934;* Outsiders, The, *616;* Peggy Sue Got Married, *355;* ain People, The, *634;* Rip Van Winkle, *199;* Rumble Fish, *645;* onight for Sure, *397;* Tucker: A Man and His Dream, *689;* ou're a Big Boy Now, *416*

orarito, Gregory: Delinquent School Girls, *263*

orbiau, Gerard: Music Teacher, The, *769*

orbucci, Bruno: Aladdin (1987), *144;* Cop in Blue Jeans, he, *29;* Miami Supercops, *331*

orbucci, Sergio: Con Artists, The, *487;* Django, *1109;* ellbenders, The, *1120;* Sonny and Jed, *1151;* Super Fuzz, *1081*

orcoran, Bill: Sherlock Holmes and the Incident at Victoria alls, *1015;* Survive the Night, *1021*

orea, Nick: Archer: Fugitive from the Empire, *1036*

orlish, Frank B.: Longest Hunt, The, *1130*

orman, Roger: Apache Woman, *1094;* Atlas, *7;* Attack of he Crab Monsters, *810;* Bloody Mama, *16;* Bucket of Blood, A, *820;* Carnival Rock, *911;* Creature from the Haunted Sea, The, *1043;* Day the World Ended, The, *1045;* Fall of the House of sher, The (1960), *840;* Frankenstein Unbound, *843;* as-s-s-s, *1054;* Gunslinger, *1118;* Haunted Palace, The, *849;* , Mobster, *65;* Intruder, The (1961), *553;* It Conquered the World, *1060;* Little Shop of Horrors, The (1960), *861;* Machine-Gun Kelly, *80;* Masque of the Red Death, The (1964), *863;* Pit and the Pendulum, The (1961), *875;* Premature Burial, The, *876;* Raven, The (1963), *879;* Saga of the Viking Women nd their Voyage to the Waters of the Great Sea Serpent, The, *110;* St. Valentine's Day Massacre, The, *111;* Sorority Girl, *118;* Tales of Terror, *892;* Terror, The, *893;* Tomb of Ligeia, *896;* Tower of London (1962), *897;* Trip, The, *688;* Wasp Woman, *901;* Wild Angels, The, *139;* X (The Man with the X-Ray Eyes), *1090*

Corneau, Alain: Choice of Arms, A, *724;* Tous les Matins du Monde, *796*

Cornelius, Henry: Genevieve, *283;* I Am a Camera, *547;* Passport to Pimlico, *355*

Cornell, John: Almost an Angel, *225;* "Crocodile" Dundee II, *261*

Cornfield, Hubert: Night of the Following Day, The, *1001;* Plunder Road, *99;* Pressure Point, *626*

Cornwell, Stephen: Killing Streets, *72;* Philadelphia Experiment 2, The, *1070*

Corona, Alfonso: Deathstalker III—The Warriors from Hell, *1046;* World of the Vampires, *904*

Corr, Eugene: Desert Bloom, *499*

Correll, Charles: Cry in the Wind, *492;* Deadly Desire, *968;* Fortune Dane, *52;* Writer's Block, *1033*

Correll, Richard: Ski Patrol, *380*

Corrigan, Lloyd: Dancing Pirate, *913*

Cort, Bud: Ted & Venus, *392*

Corti, Axel: King's Whore, The, *566*

Cosby, Camille: Bill Cosby: 49, *239*

Cosby Jr., William H.: Bill Cosby—Himself, *239*

Coscarelli, Don: Beastmaster, The, *1038;* Phantasm, *874;* Phantasm II, *874;* Survival Quest, *123*

Cosmatos, George Pan: Cassandra Crossing, The, *476;* Cobra (1986), *27;* Escape to Athena, *45;* Leviathan, *860;* Massacre in Rome, *590;* Of Unknown Origin, *872;* Rambo: First Blood II, *103;* Restless, *638;* Tombstone, *1157*

Costa, Mario: Rough Justice, *1146*

Costa-Gavras, Constantin: Betrayed (1988), *954;* Hanna K., *743;* Missing, *596;* Music Box, The, *999;* Sleeping Car Murders, The, *786;* State of Siege, *788;* Z, *806*

Costner, Kevin: Dances with Wolves, *1107*

Coto, Manny: Cover-Up (1990), *30;* Dr. Giggles, *835;* Playroom, *875*

Cottafari, Vittorio: Goliath and the Dragon, *56;* Hercules and the Captive Women, *1056*

Cotter, John: Mountain Family Robinson, *189*

Couffer, Jack: Living Free, *184;* Nikki, Wild Dog of the North, *191;* Ring of Bright Water, *199*

Coughlan, Ian: Alison's Birthday, *808*

Courtland, Jerome: Diamonds on Wheels, *162*

Couturie, Bill: Dear America: Letters Home from Vietnam, *422*

Covington, Hil: Adventures in Spying, *2*

Coward, Noel: In Which We Serve, *550*

Cowen, William: Oliver Twist (1933), *612*

Cowers, Bruce: Robin Williams Live, *369*

Cox, Alex: Repo Man, *366;* Sid and Nancy, *657;* Straight to Hell, *1153;* Walker, *695*

Cox, Nell: Once Upon a Midnight Scary, *192*

Cox, Paul: Cactus, *473;* Kostas, *567;* Lonely Hearts (1981), *577;* Man of Flowers, *327;* My First Wife, *602;* Vincent: The Life and Death of Vincent Van Gogh, *438;* Woman's Tale, A, *705*

Crabtree, Arthur: Fiend without a Face, *841;* Quartet (1948), *631*

Craig, Ken: Crime Inc., *421*

Crain, William: Blacula, *814;* Dr. Black and Mr. Hyde, *835*

Crane, Kenneth: Manster, The, *863;* Monster from Green Hell, *866*

Craven, Wes: Chiller, *823;* Deadly Blessing, *831;* Deadly Friend, *831;* Hills Have Eyes, The, *850;* Hills Have Eyes, The: Part Two, *850;* Invitation to Hell, *857;* Last House on the Left, *860;* Nightmare on Elm Street, A, *871;* People Under the Stairs, The, *873;* Serpent and the Rainbow, The, *884;* Shocker, *886;* Summer of Fear, *891;* Swamp Thing, *891*

Crawford, Wayne: Crime Lords, *30*

Creme, Lol: Lunatic, The, *324*

Crenna, Richard: Better Late than Never, *237*

Crichton, Charles: Battle of the Sexes, The, *233;* Dead of Night (1945), *830;* Fish Called Wanda, A, *277;* Lavender Hill Mob, The, *317*

Crichton, Michael: Coma, *963;* Great Train Robbery, The, *980;* Looker, *1063;* Physical Evidence, *1006;* Runaway, *1075;* Westworld, *1089*
Crichton, Robin: Silent Mouse, *204*
Crippen, Fred: Roger Ramjet, *200*
Crisp, Donald: Don Q, Son of Zorro, *41*
Crispino, Armando: Autopsy, *811;* Commandos, *28*
Cristallini, Giorgio: You're Jinxed Friend, You Just Met Sacramento, *1166*
Critchlow, Keith F.: California Reich, *420*
Crombie, Donald: Caddie, *473;* Irishman, The, *554;* Killing of Angel Street, The, *564;* Kitty and the Bagman, *73*
Cromwell, John: Abe Lincoln in Illinois, *440;* Ann Vickers, *448;* Anna and the King of Siam, *449;* Dead Reckoning (1947), *34;* Enchanted Cottage, The, *509;* Goddess, The, *528;* I Dream Too Much, *924;* In Name Only, *550;* Little Lord Fauntleroy (1936), *576;* Made for Each Other, *325;* Of Human Bondage (1934), *610;* Prisoner of Zenda, The (1937), *100;* Racket, The, *633;* Since You Went Away, *658;* So Ends Our Night, *661;* Spitfire, *664*
Cronenberg, David: Brood, The, *819;* Dead Ringers, *831;* Dead Zone, The, *831;* Fly, The (1986), *841;* M. Butterfly, *583;* Naked Lunch, *1067;* Rabid, *878;* Scanners, *883;* They Came from Within, *895;* Videodrome, *900*
Crosland, Alan: Beloved Rogue, *954;* Don Juan, *503;* Jazz Singer, The (1927), *925*
Crouch, William Forest: Reet, Petite and Gone, *936*
Crounse, Avery: Eyes of Fire, *840;* Invisible Kid, The, *1060*
Crowe, Cameron: Say Anything, *373;* Singles, *379*
Crowe, Christopher: Off Limits (1988), *93;* Whispers in the Dark, *1031*
Crowe, Russell: Crossing, The, *491*
Cruise, Tom: Fallen Angels, *513*
Crump, Owen: Gateway to the Mind, *168*
Cruze, James: Covered Wagon, The, *1106;* Great Gabbo, The, *532;* Helldorado (1934), *60;* I Cover the Waterfront, *65;* Mr. Skitch, *334;* Old Ironsides, *93;* Roaring Road, The, *642*
Crystal, Billy: Billy Crystal: Don't Get Me Started, *239;* Mr. Saturday Night, *334*
Cuaron, Alfonso: Fallen Angels, *513*
Cukor, George: Adam's Rib, *222;* Bhowani Junction, *12;* Bill of Divorcement, A, *461;* Born Yesterday (1950), *244;* Camille, *474;* Corn Is Green, The (1979), *488;* David Copperfield, *496;* Dinner at Eight (1933), *265;* Double Life, A, *504;* Gaslight (1944), *979;* Heller in Pink Tights, *1120;* Holiday, *298;* It Should Happen to You, *308;* Justine, *561;* Keeper of the Flame, *562;* Les Girls, *928;* Let's Make Love, *928;* Life of Her Own, A, *574;* Little Women (1933), *577;* Love Among the Ruins, *322;* My Fair Lady, *932;* Pat and Mike, *355;* Philadelphia Story, The, *357;* Rich and Famous, *639;* Romeo and Juliet (1936), *643;* Song without End, *940;* Star Is Born, A (1954), *666;* Susan and God, *674;* Sylvia Scarlett, *676;* Travels with My Aunt, *399;* Two-Faced Woman, *401;* What Price Hollywood?, *698;* Woman's Face, A, *705;* Women, The, *413*
Cullingham, Mark: Cinderella (1985), *159;* Dead on the Money, *967;* Princess Who Had Never Laughed, The, *197*
Cummings, Howard: Courtship, *490*
Cummings, Irving: Curly Top, *912;* Double Dynamite, *268;* Down Argentine Way, *914;* Everything Happens at Night, *273;* In Old Arizona, *1122;* Just Around the Corner, *926;* Little Miss Broadway, *928;* Louisiana Purchase, *322;* Poor Little Rich Girl (1936), *935;* Springtime in the Rockies (1942), *941*
Cummins, James: Boneyard, The, *818*
Cunha, Richard: Frankenstein's Daughter, *843;* Missile to the Moon, *1066;* She Demons, *885*
Cunningham, Sean S.: Deepstar Six, *832;* Friday the 13th, *843;* Manny's Orphans, *185;* New Kids, The, *868;* Spring Break, *385;* Stranger Is Watching, A, *890*
Curran, William: Love, Cheat & Steal, *993*
Currie, Anthony: Pink Chiquitas, The, *357*
Curtis, Dan: Burnt Offerings, *820;* Curse of the Black Widow, *828;* Dead of Night (1977), *831;* Dracula (1973), *837;* Express to Terror, *974;* House of Dark Shadows, *852;* Intruders, *1059;* Kansas City Massacre, The, *70;* Last Ride of the Dalton Gang, The, *1126;* Me and the Kid, *83;* Melvin Purvis: G-Man, *83;* Night of Dark Shadows, *869;* Trilogy of Terror, *898;* War and Remembrance, *696;* Winds of War, The, *703*
Curtis, Douglas: Campus Corpse, The, *820;* Sleeping Car, The, *887*
Curtis, Jack: Flesh Eaters, The, *841*
Curtiz, Michael: Adventures of Huckleberry Finn, The (1960), *144;* Adventures of Robin Hood, The, *2;* Angels with Dirty Faces, *5;* Black Fury, *462;* Breath of Scandal, A, *245;* Cabin in the Cotton, *473;* Captain Blood, *22;* Captains of the Clouds, *23;* Casablanca, *476;* Charge of the Light Brigade, The (1936), *24;* Comancheros, The, *1105;* Dive Bomber, *502;* Doctor X, *836;* Dodge City, *1109;* Egyptian, The, *508;* Female, *276;* Flamingo Road, *518;* Four Daughters, *520;* I'll See You in My Dreams, *924;* Jim Thorpe—All American, *558;* Kennel Murder Case, The, *988;* Kid Galahad (1937), *563;* King Creole, *927;* Life with Father, *318;* Mildred Pierce, *594;* My Dream Is Yours, *932;* Mystery of the Wax Museum, *868;* Night and Day (1946), *933;* Noah's Ark, *608;* Passage to Marseilles, *97;* Private Lives of Elizabeth and Essex, The, *629;* Proud Rebel, The, *1140;* Romance on the High Seas, *937;* Santa Fe Trail, *1147;* Sea Hawk, The, *112;* Sea Wolf, The (1941), *113;* Strange Love of Molly Louvain, The, *669;* This Is the Army, *945;* Trouble Along the Way, *688;* Virginia City, *1161;* We're No Angels (1955), *407;* White Christmas, *947;* Yankee Doodle Dandy, *948;* Young Man with a Horn, *948*
Cury, Brian: Couch Potato Workout Tape, *259*
Cutler, Jonathan: New Homeowner's Guide to Happiness, The, *343*
Cyran, Catherine: White Wolves: A Cry in the Wild II, *139*
Czinner, Paul: As You Like It, *229;* Catherine the Great, *477*
D'Almeida, Neville: Lady on the Bus, *755*
D'Amato, Joe (Aristede Massaccesi): Buried Alive (1984), *820;* Grim Reaper, The (1980), *847;* Trap Them and Kill Them, *897*
D'Amico, Louis: Playing the Field, *358*
D'Andrea, Anthony: Thrillkill, *1025*
D'Anna, Claude: Salome (1985), *647*
D'Antoni, Philip: Seven-Ups, The, *114*
D'Arrast, Harry: Topaze (1933), *397*
D'Elia, Bill: Feud, The, *276*
Da Costa, Morton: Auntie Mame, *229;* Music Man, The, *932*
Daalder, Renee: Massacre at Central High, *864*
Dahl, John: Kill Me Again, *988;* Red Rock West, *1009*
Dahlin, Bob: Monster in the Closet, *866*
Dahms, Heinrich: My Daughter's Keeper, *999*
Daley, Tom: Outing, The, *873*
Dali, Salvador: Un Chien Andalou, *690*
Dallamano, Massimo: Black Veil for Lisa, A, *14;* Dorian Gray, *837*
Dalrymple, Ian: Storm in a Teacup, *387*
Dalton, Cal: Best of Warner Brothers, Vol. 2, *150*
Dalva, Robert: Black Stallion Returns, The, *151*
Damiani, Damiano: Amityville II: The Possession, *809;* Bullet for the General, A, *1102;* Confessions of a Police Captain, *487;* Empty Canvas, The, *509;* Inquiry, The, *552;* Warning, The, *137*
Damski, Mel: Badge of the Assassin, *454;* For Ladies Only, *519;* Happy Together, *293;* Legend of Walks Far Woman, The, *1128;* Mischief, *333;* Wild Card, *1032;* Yellowbeard, *415*
Dane, Lawrence: Heavenly Bodies, *296*
Daniel, Rod: Beethoven's 2nd, *149;* K-9, *312;* Like Father, Like Son, *318;* Super, The, *388;* Teen Wolf, *892*
Daniels, Harold: Poor White Trash, *624;* Terror in the Haunted House, *893*
Daniels, Marc: Planet Earth, *1070;* Star Trek (TV Series), *1078;* Star Trek: The Menagerie, *1078*
Danielsson, Tage: Adventures of Picasso, The, *222*
Danniel, Danniel: Egg, *733*
Danska, Herbert: Sweet Love, Bitter, *675*

ante, Joe: Amazon Women on the Moon, *225;* 'Burbs, The, *47;* Explorers, *1050;* Gremlins, *1055;* Gremlins 2: The New atch, *1055;* Hollywood Boulevard, *299;* Howling, The, *853;* nerspace, *1058;* Matinee, *330;* Piranha, *875;* Police Squad!, *59;* Twilight Zone—The Movie, *898*
anton, Ray: Crypt of the Living Dead, *827;* Psychic Killer, *77;* Tales of the Unexpected, *1022;* Vietnam War Story, *694*
asus, Richard: No Place To Hide, *91*
arabont, Frank: Buried Alive (1990), *959*
arley, Dick: Space Patrol (TV Series), *1077*
arling, Joan: Check Is in the Mail, The, *254;* First Love, *517;* ary Hartman, Mary Hartman (TV Series), *329;* Willa, *703*
ash, Julie: Daughters of the Dust, *496*
assin, Jules: Canterville Ghost, The (1944), *155;* Circle of wo, *482;* Dream of Passion, A, *504;* Naked City, The, *1000;* ever on Sunday, *604;* Night and the City (1950), *605;* eunion in France, *639;* Rififi, *1010;* Topkapi, *1026*
augherty, Herschel: Light in the Forest, The, *181;* Wagon rain (TV Series), *1162*
avenport, Harry: Xtro, *904;* Xtro II, *1090*
aves, Delmer: Badlanders, The, *1096;* Broken Arrow, *1101;* ark Passage, *966;* Demetrius and the Gladiators, *499;* estination Tokyo, *37;* Drum Beat, *1110;* Hanging Tree, The, *118;* Hollywood Canteen, *923;* Jubal, *1124;* Kings Go Forth, *65;* Never Let Me Go, *89;* Parrish, *618;* Red House, The, *1009;* ome Adventure, *643;* Spencer's Mountain, *664;* Summer lace, A, *672;* Task Force, *677;* 3:10 to Yuma, *1157*
avidson, Boaz: Going Bananas, *169;* Hospital Massacre, *52;* Last American Virgin, The, *315;* Private Popsicle, *362;* alsa, *938*
avidson, Gordon: Trial of the Cantonsville Nine, The, *687*
avidson, Martin: Eddie and the Cruisers, *915;* Hard romises, *536;* Heart of Dixie, The, *538;* Hero at Large, *296;* ong Gone, *578;* Lords of Flatbush, The, *579*
avies, Charles: Incredible Story of Dogs, The, *427*
avies, John: Married Man, A, *589;* Sleeping Murder, *1017;* Vhy Didn't They Ask Evans?, *1032*
avies, Robert: Saturday Night at the Palace, *648*
avies, Terence: Distant Voices/Still Lives, *502;* Long Day loses, The, *578*
avies, Valentine: Benny Goodman Story, The, *458*
avis, Andrew: Above the Law, *1;* Code of Silence, *27;* Final error, The, *841;* Fugitive, The (1993), *53;* Package, The, *1004;* nder Siege, *134*
avis, Arthur: Best of Bugs Bunny and Friends, The, *150;* rutes and Savages, *420;* Cartoon Moviestars: Daffy!, *156;* artoon Moviestars: Elmer!, *156;* Pepe Le Pew's Skunk Tales, *94;* Porky Pig and Company, *196;* Porky Pig Cartoon Festival eaturing "Nothing but the Tooth", *196;* Porky Pig: Days of wine and Roses, *196;* Porky Pig Tales, *196*
avis, B. J.: White Ghost, *138*
avis, Beau: Laser Mission, *75*
avis, Bill: Lily Tomlin Special—Vol. I, The, *319*
avis, Charles: Die Watching, *970*
avis, Desmond: Clash of the Titans, *1041;* Love with a erfect Stranger, *582;* Nice Girl Like Me, A, *344;* Ordeal by nnocence, *1003;* Sign of Four, The, *1016*
avis, Eddie: Cisco Kid (TV Series), *1105;* Color Me Dead, *85*
avis, Gary: Conflict of Interest, *29*
avis, Jim: Bugs Bunny Mother's Day Special, The, *153*
avis, Kate: Girl Talk, *424*
avis, Ossie: Gordon's War, *57*
avis, Peter: Hearts and Minds, *425*
avis, Tamra: CB4, *252;* Guncrazy (1992), *535*
awn, Norman: Two Lost Worlds, *133*
awn, Vincent: Caged Women, *22;* Night of the Zombies, *870;* Rats, *878;* Strike Commando, *121*
awson, Anthony M.: And God Said to Cain, *1093;* Ark of he Sun God...Temple of Hell, The, *6;* Castle of Blood, *821;* Code Name: Wild Geese, *27;* Hercules, Prisoner of Evil, *61;* ndigo, *66;* Indigo 2: The Revolt, *66;* Invasion of the Flesh Hunters, *856;* Jungle Raiders, *69;* Killer Fish, *71;* Mr. Superinvisible, *188;* Planet on the Prowl, *1071;* Stranger and the Gunfighter, The, *1153;* Take a Hard Ride, *1154;* Virgin of Nuremberg, *901;* Yor: The Hunter from the Future, *1091*
Day, Ernest: Green Ice, *981*
Day, Robert: Avengers, The (TV Series), *7;* Corridors of Blood, *825;* First Man into Space, The, *1051;* Grass Is Always Greener Over the Septic Tank, The, *289;* Haunted Strangler, The, *849;* Initiation of Sarah, The, *856;* Lady from Yesterday, The, *567;* Man with Bogart's Face, The, *995;* Quick and the Dead, The, *1140;* Scruples, *650;* TV Classics: Adventures of Robin Hood, The—TV Series, *133;* Two-Way Stretch, *402*
Dayan, Josee: Hot Chocolate, *301*
Dayton, Lyman: Avenging, The, *1095;* Baker's Hawk, *148;* Dream Machine, *269*
De Antonio, Emile: Millhouse: A White Comedy, *430;* Underground (1976), *437*
De Arminan, Jaime: Nest, The (1981), *771*
De Baroncelli, Jacques: French Way, The, *738*
De Bosio, Gianfranco: Moses, *600*
de Broca, Philippe: Cartouche, *722;* Jupiter's Thigh, *751;* King of Hearts, *752;* Le Cavaleur, *757;* Le Magnifique, *758;* Louisiana, *580;* Oldest Profession, The, *773;* Seven Deadly Sins, The, *785;* That Man From Rio, *793*
de Cordova, Frederick: Bedtime for Bonzo, *233;* Frankie and Johnny (1966), *918;* I'll Take Sweden, *924;* Jack Benny Program, The (TV Series), *309*
De Filippo, Eduardo: Shoot Loud, Louder...I Don't Understand, *378*
De Jong, Ate: Drop Dead Fred, *269;* Highway to Hell, *850*
de Leon, Gerardo: Brides of the Beast, *819;* Mad Doctor of Blood Island, The, *861*
De Leon, Marcus: Kiss Me a Killer, *989*
de Lussanet, Paul: Mysteries, *770*
De Martino, Alberto: Blood Link, *815;* Django Shoots First, *1109;* Holocaust 2000, *851;* Puma Man, The, *878;* Scenes from a Murder, *112;* Tempter, The, *893*
de Mille, William C.: His Double Life, *297*
de Ossorio, Amando: Horror of the Zombies, *852;* Night of the Death Cult, *869;* Return of the Evil Dead, *880;* Tombs of the Blind Dead, *896;* When the Screaming Stops, *902*
De Palma, Brian: Blow Out, *957;* Body Double, *958;* Bonfire of the Vanities, *466;* Carlito's Way, *23;* Carrie (1976), *821;* Casualties of War, *477;* Dressed to Kill (1980), *972;* Fury, The, *845;* Get to Know Your Rabbit, *285;* Greetings, *290;* Hi Mom, *297;* Home Movies, *299;* Obsession, *1002;* Phantom of the Paradise, *935;* Raising Cain, *878;* Scarface (1983), *112;* Sisters (1973), *1017;* Untouchables, The, *134;* Wedding Party, The, *407;* Wise Guys, *412*
De Santis, Giuseppe: Bitter Rice, *718*
De Sica, Vittorio: After the Fox, *223;* Bicycle Thief, The, *717;* Boccaccio 70, *719;* Garden of the Finzi-Continis, The, *740;* Gold of Naples, The, *529;* Indiscretion of an American Wife, *551;* Miracle in Milan, *767;* Shoeshine, *785;* Two Women, *797;* Umberto D, *798;* Woman Times Seven, *705;* Yesterday, Today and Tomorrow, *806*
de Toth, André: Dark Waters, *496;* House of Wax, *853;* Last of the Comanches, *1126;* Man in the Saddle, *1132;* Morgan the Pirate, *86;* Pitfall, *622;* Ramrod, *1140;* Stranger Wore a Gun, The, *1153*
De Witt, Elmo: Enemy Unseen, *44*
Dear, William: Doctor Duck's Super Secret All-Purpose Sauce, *266;* Elephant Parts, *915;* Garry Shandling: Alone in Vegas, *283;* Harry and the Hendersons, *1055;* If Looks Could Kill (1991), *66;* Nick Danger in the Case of the Missing Yolk, *344;* Northville Cemetery Massacre, The, *92;* Television Parts Home Companion, *944;* Timerider, *130*
Dearden, Basil: Captive Heart, *475;* Dead of Night (1945), *830;* Khartoum, *70;* League of Gentlemen, The, *317;* Man Who Haunted Himself, The, *995;* Persuaders, The (TV Series), *98;* Sapphire, *1012;* Smallest Show on Earth, The, *381;* Victim, *693*
Dearden, James: Cold Room, The, *485;* Kiss Before Dying, A, *989;* Pascali's Island, *619*

DeBello, John: Attack of the Killer Tomatoes, *229;* Happy Hour, *293;* Killer Tomatoes Eat France, *313;* Killer Tomatoes Strike Back, *313;* Return of the Killer Tomatoes, *366*
DeCaprio, Al: Sgt. Bilko (TV Series), *376*
Decker, Craig: Spike & Mike's Festival of Animation, *384*
Decoin, Henri: Love and the Frenchwoman, *762*
DeConcini, Ennio: Hitler, the Last Ten Days, *542*
DeCoteau, David: Creepozoids, *826;* Dr. Alien, *834;* Lady Avenger, *74;* Nightmare Sisters, *871;* Puppet Master III: Toulon's Revenge, *878;* Sorority Babes in the Slimeball Bowl-O-Rama, *383*
Deehan, Geoff: Incredible Story of Dogs, The, *427*
Deem, Miles: Jungle Master, The, *69;* Savage Guns, *1147*
DeFelitta, Frank: Dark Night of the Scarecrow, *829;* Scissors, *1013;* Two Worlds of Jennie Logan, The, *1086*
DeGuere, Philip: Dr. Strange, *1047*
Deheer, Rolf: Encounter at Raven's Gate, *1049*
Dehlaui, Jamil: Born of Fire, *467*
Deimel, Mark: Perfect Match, The, *356*
Dein, Edward: Leech Woman, The, *860;* Shack-Out on 101, *653*
Deitch, Donna: Desert Hearts, *499;* Prison Stories: Women on the Inside, *628*
Deitch, Gene: Tomi Ungerer Library, The, *213*
DeJarnett, Steve: Cherry 2000, *1041;* Miracle Mile, *996*
Dekker, Fred: Monster Squad, The, *866;* Night of the Creeps, *869;* RoboCop 3, *1075*
Del Monte, Peter: Invitation au Voyage, *748;* Julia and Julia, *1061*
Del Prete, Deborah: Simple Justice, *658*
Del Ruth, Roy: Babe Ruth Story, The, *453;* Blessed Event, *241;* Blonde Crazy, *241;* Born to Dance, *909;* Broadway Melody of 1936, *910;* Broadway Melody of 1938, *910;* Broadway Rhythm, *910;* Bureau of Missing Persons, *959;* Chocolate Soldier, The, *911;* Du Barry Was a Lady, *915;* Employees' Entrance, *271;* Happy Landing, *921;* Kid Millions, *926;* Lady Killer, *74;* My Lucky Star, *932;* On Moonlight Bay, *933;* Topper Returns, *398;* West Point Story, The, *947*
del Toro, Guillermo: Cronos, *727*
Delannoy, Jean: Bernadette, *459;* Eternal Return, The, *735;* Love and the Frenchwoman, *762;* This Special Friendship, *794*
Delia, Francis: Freeway, *52*
Dell, Jeffrey: Carlton-Browne of the F.O., *251*
Dell'Amico, Len: So Far, *434*
Delman, Jeffrey S.: Deadtime Stories, *831*
Delon, Nathalie: Sweet Lies, *389*
DeLuca, Rudy: Transylvania 6-5000, *399*
DeLuise, Dom: Hot Stuff, *301*
DeLuise, Michael: Almost Pregnant, *225*
Dembo, Richard: Dangerous Moves, *728*
Demicheli, Tulio: Son of Captain Blood, *118*
DeMille, Cecil B.: Cheat, The, *961;* Cleopatra (1934), *484;* Greatest Show on Earth, The, *533;* King of Kings, The (1927), *565;* Madame Satan, *584;* Male and Female, *994;* Plainsman, The, *1139;* Reap the Wild Wind, *104;* Road to Yesterday, The, *641;* Samson and Delilah (1949), *648;* Ten Commandments, The (1923), *678;* Ten Commandments, The (1956), *678;* Union Pacific, *1160*
Demme, Jonathan: Caged Heat, *22;* Citizen's Band, *255;* Cousin Bobby, *421;* Crazy Mama, *30;* Fighting Mad, *516;* Last Embrace, The, *990;* Married to the Mob, *329;* Melvin and Howard, *331;* Philadelphia, *621;* Silence of the Lambs, *1016;* Something Wild, *383;* Stop Making Sense, *435;* Swimming to Cambodia, *390;* Swing Shift, *675;* Who Am I This Time?, *410*
Demme, Ted: Ref, The, *365;* Who's the Man?, *411*
DeMoro, Pierre: Hellhole, *849;* Savannah Smiles, *201*
Demy, Jacques: Donkey Skin (Peau D'Âne), *731;* Lola (1960), *761;* Seven Deadly Sins, The, *785;* Slightly Pregnant Man, A, *787;* Umbrellas of Cherbourg, The, *798*
Denis, Jean-Pierre: Field of Honor (1988), *736*
Dennis, Charles: Reno and the Doc, *638*
Dennis, Claire: Chocolat, *723*
Denham, Pen: Kiss, The (1988), *859;* Zoo Gang, The, *416*
Deodato, Ruggero: Barbarians, The, *1038;* Cannibal, *820;* Cannibal Holocaust, *821;* Cut and Run, *493;* Lone Runner, *78;* Phantom of Death, *874*
DePalma, Frank: Private War, *629*
DePatie, David H.: Pink at First Sight, *195;* Pink Panther Cartoon Festival, The: A Fly in the Pink, *195;* Pink Panther Cartoon Festival, The: Pink-a-Boo, *195*
DePew, Joseph: Beverly Hillbillies Go Hollywood, The, *237*
Deray, Jacques: Borsalino, *18;* Swimming Pool, The, *792*
Derek, John: Bolero (1984), *466;* Fantasies, *514;* Ghosts Can't Do It, *285;* Tarzan the Ape Man (1981), *125*
Deren, Maya: Experimental Films of Maya Deren Vol. I, *1050*
Deruddere, Dominique: Wait Until Spring, Bandini, *695*
des Rozier, Hughes: Blue Jeans, *719*
Deschanel, Caleb: Crusoe, *31;* Escape Artist, The, *165*
Desfontanes, Henri: Queen Elizabeth, *631*
DeSimone, Tom: Concrete Jungle, The (1982), *28;* Hell Night, *849;* Reform School Girls, *105*
Desmarais, James: Road Lawyers and Other Briefs, *368*
Desmond, Brian: River of Unrest, *641*
Detiege, David: Bugs Bunny: All American Hero, *153;* Bugs Bunny's Howl-Oween Special, *154;* Bugs Bunny's Mad World of Television, *154*
Deutch, Howard: Article 99, *451;* Getting Even with Dad, *285;* Great Outdoors, The, *290;* Pretty in Pink, *626;* Some Kind of Wonderful, *382*
Deval, Jacques: Club des Femmes, *725*
Devenish, Ross: Bleak House, *463;* Overindulgence, *617*
Deville, Michel: La Lectrice (The Reader), *754;* La Petite Bande, *754;* Peril, *777*
Devine, David: Beethoven Lives Upstairs, *149;* Raffi and the Sunshine Band, *198;* Young Children's Concert with Raffi, A, *219*
DeVito, Danny: Amazing Stories (TV Series), *1036;* Hoffa, *542;* Ratings Game, The, *364;* Throw Momma from the Train, *396;* War of the Roses, The, *406*
DeWier, Tom: Death by Dialogue, *968*
Dexter, John: I Want What I Want, *548;* Virgin Soldiers, The, *694*
Deyries, Bernard: Rainbow Brite and the Star Stealer, *198*
Dezaki, Tetsu: Urusei Yatsura: Inaba the Dreammaker, *799*
Dhomme, Sylvain: Seven Deadly Sins, The, *785*
Di Leo, Fernando: Kidnap Syndicate, The, *751;* Loaded Guns, *78;* Manhunt (1973), *81;* Violent Breed, The, *136*
Di Leo, Mario: Final Alliance, *48*
DiBergi, Jim: Return of Spinal Tap, The, *366*
DiCillo, Tom: Johnny Suede, *311*
Dick, Nigel: Dead Connection, *967;* Deadly Intent, *34;* Inside Out 2, *1059;* Private Investigations, *101*
Dickerson, Ernest R.: Juice, *560;* Surviving the Game, *123*
Dickinson, Thorold: Gaslight (1940), *979;* High Command, The, *61*
Dickson, Lance: Hollywood Heartbreak, *542*
Didden, Marc: Istanbul, *749*
Diege, Samuel: Ride 'em Cowgirl, *1143;* Water Rustlers, *1162*
Diegues, Carlos: Bye Bye Brazil, *721;* Subway to the Stars, *791*
Dienstag, Alan: Moneytree, The, *598*
Dietch, Donna: Women of Brewster Place, The, *706*
Dieterle, William: Boots Malone, *1100;* Dark City, *495;* Devil and Daniel Webster, The, *500;* Elephant Walk, *508;* Hunchback of Notre Dame, The (1939), *854;* Juarez, *560;* Kismet (1944), *566;* Life of Emile Zola, The, *574;* Omar Khayyam, *93;* Portrait of Jennie, *625;* Quick, Let's Get Married, *363;* Salome (1953), *647;* Satan Met a Lady, *1012;* Scarlet Dawn, *649;* September Affair, *652;* Story of Louis Pasteur, The, *668*
Dignam, Erin: Denial, *499*
Diling, Bert: Dead Easy, *967*

ssey, Ross: Blue Fire Lady, 151
ster-Denk, Dennis: Mikey, 865
go, Peco: Midnight Cabaret, 864
gwell, John: Custodian, The, 31
ser, Michael: Heaven Help Us, 295; Hot to Trot, 302; Off
t, 348
am, John: Fatal Instinct (1992), 976
alle, Mark: Kickboxer, 70; Perfect Weapon, 98
ney, Walt: Canine Commando, 155; Chip 'n' Dale and
ald Duck, 158; Continuing Adventures of Chip 'n' Dale,
160; Daisy (Limited Gold Edition 1), 161; Disney's Best:
1–1948, 162; Disney's Dream Factory: 1933–1938 (Limited
Edition 2), 162; Disney's Tall Tales, 162; Donald (Limited
Edition 1), 163; Donald Duck in Mathemagic Land, 163;
ald Duck: The First 50 Years, 163; Donald's Bee Pictures
ited Gold Edition 2), 163; Fabulous Fifties (Limited Gold
ion–1), The, 165; Fantasia, 166; From Pluto with Love
ited Gold Edition 2), 168; Fun and Fancy Free, 168; Here's
ald, 174; Here's Goofy, 174; Here's Mickey, 174; Here's
o, 174; How the Best Was Won (Limited Gold Edition 2),
; Importance of Being Donald, The, 176; Jiminy Cricket's
stmas, 178; Kids Is Kids, 180; Life with Mickey (Limited
Edition 2), 181; Mickey (Limited Gold Edition 1), 186;
key and the Beanstalk, 187; Mickey and the Gang, 187;
key Knows Best, 187; Mickey's Crazy Careers, 187;
key's Magical World, 187; Minnie (Limited Gold Edition 1),
; More of Disney's Best: 1932–1946, 189; Nuts About Chip
Dale, 191; Officer and a Duck, An (Limited Gold Edition 2),
; Peter and the Wolf, 194; Pinocchio (1940), 195; Pluto,
; Pluto (Limited Gold Edition 1), 196; Scary Tales, 202;
Symphonies, 204; Silly Symphonies (Limited Gold Edition
204; Silly Symphonies: Animal Tales, 204; Silly
nphonies: Animals Two by Two, 204; Silly Symphonies:
ciful Fables, 204; Sing-Along Songs, 204; Sport Goofy,
; Sport Goofy's Vacation, 206; Starring Chip 'n' Dale, 207;
rring Donald and Daisy, 207; Starring Mickey and Minnie,
; Starring Pluto and Fifi, 207; Tale of Two Chipmunks, A,
; Three Caballeros, The, 211; Unsinkable Donald Duck, The,
; Walt Disney Christmas, A, 215; Willie, the Operatic Whale,
; World According to Goofy, The (Limited Gold Edition 2),

on, Ken: Best of Sex and Violence, 813; Slave Girls from
ond Infinity, 381
ytryk, Edward: Alvarez Kelly, 1093; Anzio, 6; Back to
aan, 8; Behind the Rising Sun, 10; Bluebeard (1972), 817;
ken Lance, 1101; Caine Mutiny, The, 473; Carpetbaggers,
, 475; Cornered, 29; Crossfire (1947), 964; Hitler's
ldren, 63; Left Hand of God, The, 76; Mirage, 595;
untain, The, 600; Murder My Sweet, 999; Raintree County,
; Shalako, 1148; Soldier of Fortune, 118; Tender Comrade,
; Till the End of Time, 683; Walk on the Wild Side, 695;
lock (1959), 1162; Where Love Has Gone, 699; Young
ns, The, 708
bb, Tony: Blue Tornado, 16
bbs, Frank Q.: Uphill All the Way, 404
bson, Kevin: Miracle in the Wilderness, 595; Squizzy
lor, 119
dson, James: Deadly Rivals, 35; Quest of the Delta
ghts, 1073
hler, Don: Alien Factor, The, 1035; Fiend, 841
llon, Jacques: La Puritaine, 754
lman, Martin: After the Fall of New York, 1034; American
er, 1036; Hands of Steel, 1055
maradzki, Jerzy: Legend of the White Horse, 76
nahue, Patrick G.: Savage Instinct, 111
naldson, Roger: Bounty, The, 18; Cadillac Man, 249;
cktail, 485; Getaway, The (1994), 55; Marie, 588; No Way
t, 1002; Nutcase, 347; Sleeping Dogs, 117; Smash Palace,
0; White Sands, 700
navan, Tom: Love Spell, 79
nehue, Vincent J.: Lonelyhearts, 578; Peter Pan (1960),
4; Sunrise at Campobello, 673

Donen, Stanley: Arabesque, 6; Bedazzled, 233; Blame It on Rio, 240; Charade, 960; Damn Yankees, 913; Deep in My Heart, 913; Funny Face, 918; Give a Girl a Break, 919; Grass Is Greener, The, 289; Indiscreet (1958), 306; It's Always Fair Weather, 925; Little Prince, The, 929; Love is Better Than Ever, 929; Movie Movie, 338; On the Town, 934; Pajama Game, The, 934; Royal Wedding, 938; Saturn 3, 1076; Seven Brides for Seven Brothers, 939; Singin' in the Rain, 940; Surprise Package, 389; Two for the Road, 401
Doniger, Walter: Mad Bull, 584
Donnelly, Dennis: Toolbox Murders, The, 1026
Donnelly, Tom: Blindsided, 956; Quicksilver, 632
Donner, Clive: Babes in Toyland (1986), 147; Charlie Chan and the Curse of the Dragon Queen, 253; Luv, 324; Merlin & the Sword, 1065; Not a Penny More, Not a Penny Less, 1002; Nude Bomb, The, 347; Scarlet Pimpernel, The (1982), 112; Stealing Heaven, 667; Terror Stalks the Class Reunion, 894; Thief of Baghdad (1978), 127; To Catch a King, 1025; What's New, Pussycat?, 408
Donner, Richard: Fugitive, The (TV Series), 523; Goonies, The, 56; Inside Moves, 552; Ladyhawke, 74; Lethal Weapon, 76; Lethal Weapon 2, 76; Lethal Weapon 3, 77; Maverick, 1133; Omen, The, 872; Radio Flyer, 633; Scrooged, 374; Superman, 1081; Tales from the Crypt (Series), 892; Toy, The, 398; Twilight Zone, The (TV Series), 1086; Wanted: Dead or Alive (TV Series), 1162
Donoghue, Mary Agnes: Paradise (1991), 618
Donohue, Jack: Assault on a Queen, 7; Babes in Toyland (1961), 147; Lucky Me, 929; Watch the Birdie, 406; Yellow Cab Man, The, 415
Donohue, John Clark: Marvelous Land of Oz, The, 185
Donovan, King: Promises, Promises, 362
Donovan, Martin: Apartment Zero, 952; Death Dreams, 831; Inside Out 2, 1059; Mad at the Moon, 861; Substitute, The, 1021
Donovan, Paul: Def-Con 4, 1046; George's Island, 169; Norman's Awesome Experience, 346; Northern Extremes, 346; Tomcat: Dangerous Desires, 1084
Doran, Thomas: Spookies, 889
Dorfman, Stanley: Tibet, 436
Dorfmann, Jacques: Shadow of the Wolf, 114
Dornhelm, Robert: Children of Theatre Street, The, 421; Cold Feet (1989), 257; Echo Park, 507; Requiem for Dominic, 781
Dörrie, Doris: Me and Him, 330; Men..., 767
Dotan, Shimon: Finest Hour, The, 48
Douchet, Jean: Six in Paris (Paris Vue par . . .), 786
Dougherty, Kathy: Beatles, The: The First U.S. Visit, 419
Douglas, Gordon: Black Arrow, The (1948), 13; Call Me Bwana, 249; Chuka, 1105; Detective, The (1968), 500; Dick Tracy versus Cueball, 38; Doolins of Oklahoma, 1110; First Yank into Tokyo, 49; Follow That Dream, 278; General Spanky, 169; Girl Rush, 286; Great Missouri Raid, The, 1116; Harlow, 536; If You Knew Susie, 924; In Like Flint, 66; Kiss Tomorrow Goodbye, 73; Lady in Cement, 989; McConnell Story, The, 591; Nevadan, The, 1136; Only the Valiant, 1137; Rio Conchos, 1145; Robin & the Seven Hoods, 936; Saps at Sea, 372; Sincerely Yours, 658; Slaughter's Big Rip-Off, 117; Them!, 1083; They Call Me Mister Tibbs, 127; Tony Rome, 1025; Up Periscope, 134; Viva Knievel, 136; Young at Heart, 948; Zombies on Broadway, 416
Douglas, Kirk: Posse (1975), 1139
Douglas, Peter: Tiger's Tale, A, 396
Doumani, Lorenzo: Mad About You, 325
Doury, Max: Seven Deadly Sins, The, 785
Dovzhenko, Alexander: Arsenal, 713; Earth, 732; Zvenigora, 807
Dowdey, Kathleen: Blue Heaven, 465
Downey, Robert: America, 226; Greaser's Palace, 532; Putney Swope, 363; Rented Lips, 366; Too Much Sun, 397; Up the Academy, 403
Doyle, Tim: Road Lawyers and Other Briefs, 368

Drach, Michel: Les Violons du Bal, *759*
Dragin, Bert L.: Summer Camp Nightmare, *672;* Twice Dead, *1027*
Dragoti, Stan: Love at First Bite, *322;* Man with One Red Shoe, The, *328;* Mr. Mom, *334;* Necessary Roughness, *342;* She's Out of Control, *378*
Drake, Jim: Awakening of Cassie, The, *452;* Based on an Untrue Story, *232;* Best of John Candy, The, *236;* Legacy for Leonette, *991;* Mary Hartman, Mary Hartman (TV Series), *329;* Mr. Bill's Real Life Adventures, *333;* Police Academy 4: Citizens on Patrol, *359;* Speed Zone, *119*
Drake, Oliver: Across the Rio Grande, *1092;* Battling Marshal, *1097;* Mummy and the Curse of the Jackals, The, *867;* Sunset Carson Rides Again, *1153;* West of Texas, *1163*
Drake, T. Y.: Keeper, The, *859*
Drazan, Anthony: Zebrahead, *709*
Dresch, Fred: My Samurai, *88*
Dreville, Jean: Sputnik, *788*
Drew, Di: Right Hand Man, The, *640;* Trouble in Paradise, *399*
Dreyer, Carl: Day of Wrath, *728;* Gertrude, *740;* Leaves from Satan's Book, *758;* Master of the House (Du Skal Aere Din Hustru), *766;* Ordet, *774;* Passion of Joan of Arc, The, *776;* Vampyr, *800*
Driscoll, Richard: Comic, The (1985), *486*
Driver, John: Marvelous Land of Oz, The, *185*
Driver, Sara: Sleepwalker, *1017*
Drove, Antonio: Tunnel, The, *689*
Druner, Karl: Art Com Video (Vol. 1–3), *1037*
Drury, David: Defense of the Realm, *969;* Forever Young (1983), *520;* Intrigue, *986;* Prime Suspect 3, *1008;* Split Decisions, *664*
Dryhurst, Michael: Hard Way, The (1979), *59*
Drysdale, Lee: Leather Jackets, *76*
Dubin, Charles S.: Cinderella (1964), *911;* Gathering, Part II, The, *525;* Meanest Men in the West, The, *1133;* Moving Violation, *87;* Roots: The Next Generation, *644;* Silent Rebellion, *658*
Dubin, Jay: Dice Rules, *264;* Joe Piscopo Video, The, *310;* Rap Master Ronnie—A Report Card, *364*
Dubs, Arthur R.: Wonder of It All, *438*
Dudley, Terence: All Creatures Great and Small, *145*
Duffell, Greg: Nelvanamation (Volume Two), *191*
Duffell, Peter: Experience Preferred...But Not Essential, *273;* Far Pavilions, The, *514;* House That Dripped Blood, The, *853;* Inside Out (1975), *66;* King of the Wind, *180;* Letters to an Unknown Lover, *573*
Dugan, Dennis: Brain Donors, *245;* Problem Child, *362*
Dugdale, George: Slaughter High, *887*
Duguay, Christian: Adrift, *950;* Live Wire, *78;* Model by Day, *86;* Scanners 2: The New Order, *883;* Scanners 3: The Takeover, *883*
Duigan, John: Flirting, *518;* Romero, *643;* Sirens, *379;* Wide Sargasso Sea, *701;* Winter of Our Dreams, *704;* Year My Voice Broke, The, *707*
Duke, Bill: Cemetery Club, The, *478;* Deep Cover (1992), *36;* Killing Floor, The, *563;* Rage in Harlem, A, *103;* Raisin in the Sun, A (1988), *634;* Sister Act 2: Back in the Habit, *380*
Duke, Daryl: Griffin and Phoenix: A Love Story, *533;* I Heard the Owl Call My Name, *547;* Payday, *620;* President's Plane Is Missing, The, *1007;* Silent Partner, The, *1016;* Tai-Pan, *124;* Thornbirds, The, *682*
Dumoulin, Georges: Nous N'Irons Plus Au Bois, *772*
Duncalf, Bill: Epic That Never Was, The, *423*
Duncan, Patrick: 84 Charlie Mopic, *43;* Live! From Death Row, *577*
Dunham, Duwayne: Homeward Bound: The Incredible Journey, *175*
Dunne, Philip: Wild in the Country, *702*
Dunning, George: Yellow Submarine, *219*
Dupont, E. A.: Variety, *800*
Duprey, William: Uncaged, *1028*
Darabont, Frank: Stephen King's Night Shift Collection, *89*
Duran, Ciro: Tropical Snow, *132*
Durand, Rudy: Tilt, *396*
Durgay, Attila: Matt the Gooseboy, *186*
Durlow, David: Tailspin, *676*
Durston, David E.: Stigma, *668*
Duvall, Robert: Angelo, My Love, *448*
Duvivier, Julien: Anna Karenina (1947), *449;* Black Jack, *7* Burning Court, The, *721;* Diabolically Yours, *730;* Golgotha, *741;* Great Waltz, The, *921;* Little World of Don Camillo, The, *761;* Lydia, *583;* Panique, *775;* Pepe Le Moko, *777*
Dwan, Allan: Around the World, *907;* Brewster's Millions (1945), *245;* Cattle Queen of Montana, *1104;* Enchanted Islan *44;* Escape to Burma, *510;* Gorilla, The, *289;* Heidi (1937), *17* Hollywood Party, *299;* Iron Mask, The, *67;* Look Who's Laughing, *320;* Manhandled, *328;* Montana Belle, *1134;* Northwest Outpost, *933;* Passion (1954), *97;* Pearl of the South Pacific, *620;* Rebecca of Sunnybrook Farm (1938), *93* Restless Breed, The, *1142;* Robin Hood (1923), *107;* Sands o Iwo Jima, *111;* Slightly Scarlet, *660;* Tennessee's Partner, *1155;* Three Musketeers, The (1939), *396*
Dwan, Robert: You Bet Your Life (TV Series), *415*
Dyal, H. Kaye: Project: Eliminator, *101*
Dyke, Robert: Moon Trap, *1067*
Dziki, Waldemar: Young Magician, The, *219*
Eason, B. Reeves "Breezy": Adventures of Rex and Rinty *1092;* Blue Montana Skies, *1099;* Darkest Africa, *33;* Empty Holsters, *1111;* Fighting Marines, The, *48;* Galloping Ghost, The, *54;* Last of the Mohicans (1932), *1126;* Man of the Frontier (Red River Valley), *1132;* Miracle Rider, The, *1134;* Mystery Mountain, *1135;* Phantom Empire (1935), *98;* Radio Ranch (Men with Steel Faces & Phantom Empire), *1140;* Rimfire, *1144;* Undersea Kingdom, *1087*
Eason, Walter B.: Sea Hound, The, *112*
Eastman, Allan: Crazy Moon, *490;* Ford: The Man & the Machine, *519;* War Boy, The, *137*
Eastman, G. L.: Metamorphosis, *864*
Eastwood, Clint: Bird, *909;* Bronco Billy, *246;* Eiger Sanctio The, *43;* Firefox, *49;* Gauntlet, The, *55;* Heartbreak Ridge, *59;* High Plains Drifter, *1120;* Honkytonk Man, *543;* Outlaw Josey Wales, The, *1137;* Pale Rider, *1138;* Perfect World, A, *621;* Play Misty for Me, *1006;* Rookie, The, *109;* Sudden Impact, *122;* Unforgiven (1992), *1160;* White Hunter Black Heart, *700*
Eaton, Anthony: Evening with Bob Goldthwait, An: Share th Warmth, *272*
Ebata, Hiroyuki: Dog Soldier: Shadows of the Past, *1047*
Eberhardt, Thom: Captain Ron, *250;* Gross Anatomy, *534;* Night Before, The, *344;* Night of the Comet, *1068;* Sole Survivor, *888;* Without a Clue, *413*
Ebishima, Toyo: Serendipity, the Pink Dragon, *202*
Echevarria, Nicolas: Cabeza de Vaca, *721*
Edel, Uli: Body of Evidence, *958;* Christiane F., *724;* Last Exi to Brooklyn, *569*
Edmunds, Don: Bare Knuckles, *9;* Ilsa, Harem Keeper of the Oil Shieks, *855;* Ilsa, She Wolf of the SS, *855*
Edwards, Blake: Blind Date (1987), *241;* Breakfast at Tiffany's, *468;* Curse of the Pink Panther, The, *261;* Darling Lil *913;* Days of Wine and Roses, *496;* Experiment in Terror, *974* Fine Mess, A, *277;* Great Race, The, *290;* Man Who Loved Women, The (1983), *328;* Micki & Maude, *331;* Operation Petticoat, *351;* Party, The, *354;* Perfect Furlough, *356;* Peter Gunn (TV Series), *98;* Pink Panther, The, *357;* Pink Panther Strikes Again, The, *357;* Return of the Pink Panther, The, *366;* Revenge of the Pink Panther, The, *367;* S.O.B., *372;* Shot in th Dark, A, *378;* Skin Deep, *380;* Son of the Pink Panther, *383;* Sunset, *1021;* Switch, *390;* Tamarind Seed, The, *124;* 10, *392* That's Life, *393;* This Happy Feeling, *394;* Trail of the Pink Panther, The, *398;* Victor/Victoria, *405;* Wild Rovers, The, *116*
Edwards, Dan: Black Cobra 3, *13*
Edwards, George: Attic, The, *811*

vards, Henry: Juggernaut (1936), *987;* Scrooge (1935),
vards, Ralph: TV Classics: Laurel & Hardy, *401*
vards, Vince: Mission Galactica: The Cylon Attack, *1066*
ard, Christine: Little Dorrit, *576*
rton, Mark: Winds of Jarrah, The, *703*
eling: Avant Garde Program #2, *714*
leston, Colin: Cassandra, *821;* Long Weekend, *861;* Sky tes, *117;* Wicked, The, *903*
eson, Jan: Last Hit, The, *990;* Shock to the System, A, 5
yan, Atom: Adjuster, The, *441;* Family Viewing, *514;* Next Kin (1984), *605;* Speaking Parts, *664*
horn, Franz: Violent Years, The, *136*
enman, Rafael: Lake Consequence, *568;* Red Shoe ries 3: Another Woman's Lipstick, *637*
enstein, Sergei: Alexander Nevsky, *711;* Battleship emkin, The, *716;* Ivan the Terrible—Part I & Part II, *749;* ober, *772;* Strike, *790*
man, Richard: Forbidden Zone, *1053*
esberg, Jan: Past Midnight, *619*
kann, Larry: Fever, *47;* God Bless the Child, *528;* Great s Angeles Earthquake, The, *532;* Great Wallendas, The, *533;* onvenient Woman, An, *551;* One Against the Wind, *613;* ison Ivy (1985), *359*
enshaw, Harrison: Dead Silence, *262*
iot, Michael: Fatal Games, *840;* King Lear (1984), *564*
iott, Lang: Cage, *21;* Dorf and the First Games of Mount mpus, *267;* Private Eyes, The, *361*
lott, Stephan: Frauds, *281*
iotts, Paul: Great Adventure, The, *1116*
is, Bob: Warm Nights on a Slow Moving Train, *696*
ison, James: Don't Go in the House, *836*
man, Luis: Matt the Gooseboy, *186*
vey, Maurice: Evil Mind, The (a.k.a. The Clairvoyant), *839;* lute John Citizen!, *647;* School for Scandal, *373;* Sons of the a, *663;* Spy of Napoleon, *664;* Transatlantic Tunnel, *1085*
merson, John: Down to Earth, *268;* His Picture in the pers, *297;* Reaching for the Moon (1917), *365*
nes, Ian: Knights and Emeralds, *314*
mmerich, Roland: Ghost Chase, *845;* Making Contact, *64;* Moon 44, *1067;* Universal Soldier, *134*
ders, Robert: Stevie, *668*
dfield, Cy: Mysterious Island, *1067;* Try and Get Me, *133;* derworld Story, *1029;* Zulu, *142*
gel, Thomas E.: Rich Little—One's a Crowd, *367*
glish, John: Adventures of Captain Marvel, The, *2;* ventures of Red Ryder, *1092;* Arizona Days, *1094;* Beyond e Purple Hills, *1097;* Captain America (1944), *22;* Cow Town, *106;* Daredevils of the Red Circle, *32;* Dead Man's Gulch, *108;* Death Valley Manhunt, *1108;* Dick Tracy Returns, *38;* ck Tracy vs. Crime Inc., *38;* Dick Tracy's G-Men, *38;* Don't nce Me In, *1110;* Drums of Fu Manchu, *42;* Fighting Devil ogs, The, *48;* Gangs of Sonora, *1115;* Hills of Utah, The, *120;* His Fighting Blood, *1121;* King of the Texas Rangers, *125;* Last Round-Up, *1126;* Loaded Pistols, *1128;* Lone anger, The (1938), *1129;* Mule Train, *1134;* Mysterious Dr. tan, *88;* Riders for Justice, *1143;* Riders of the Whistling nes, *1144;* Rim of the Canyon, *1144;* San Fernando Valley, *147;* Utah, *1160;* Valley of Fire, *1161;* Zorro Rides Again, *166;* Zorro's Fighting Legion, *1166*
glund, George: Christmas to Remember, A, *482;* Dixie hanging Habits, *265;* Ugly American, The, *690;* Zachariah, *166*
glund, Robert: 976-EVIL, *871*
rico, Robert: Le Secret, *758;* Les Grandes Gueules ailbirds' Vacation), *759;* Occurrence at Owl Creek Bridge, An, *72;* Treasures of the Twilight Zone, *1085*
nright, Ray: China Sky, *25;* Coroner Creek, *1106;* Dames, *13;* Earthworm Tractors, *269;* Gung Ho! (1943), *58;* Iron lajor, The, *554;* Return of the Badmen, *1142;* South of St. Louis, *1151;* Spoilers, The, *1152;* Tomorrow at Seven, *685;* Trail Street, *1158*
Enyedi, Ildiko: My 20th Century, *770*
Ephron, Nora: Sleepless in Seattle, *381;* This Is My Life, *394*
Epstein, Marcelo: Body Rock, *989*
Epstein, Rob: Common Threads: Stories from the Quilt, *421*
Erdman, Dave: Soundstage: Blues Summit in Chicago, *435*
Erice, Victor: Spirit of the Beehive, The, *788*
Erman, John: Attic: The Hiding of Anne Frank, *452;* Breathing Lessons, *469;* Carolina Skeletons, *475;* Child of Glass, *158;* Early Frost, An, *506;* Eleanor: First Lady of the World, *508;* My Old Man, *602;* Outer Limits, The (TV Series), *1069;* Roots: The Next Generation, *644;* Stella (1990), *667;* When the Time Comes, *699*
Erschbamer, George: Final Round, *48;* Snake Eater, *117;* Snake Eater 2, the Drug Buster, *117;* Snake Eater III: His Law, *117*
Ersgard, Jack: Invisible: The Chronicles of Benjamin Knight, *1060;* Mandroid, *1065*
Ersgard, Joakim: Visitors, The, *901*
Erskine, Chester: Androcles and the Lion, *227;* Egg and I, The, *270;* Frankie and Johnny (1934), *522;* Girl in Every Port, A, *286;* Midnight (1934), *593*
Esper, Dwain: Maniac (1934), *862;* Marijuana, *588;* Sex Madness, *653*
Essex, Harry: Cremators, The, *1043;* Octaman, *872*
Estevez, Emilio: Men at Work, *592;* Wisdom, *140*
Evans, Bruce A.: Kuffs, *73*
Evans, David Mickey: Sandlot, The, *201*
Evans, John: Black Godfather, The, *13*
Evans, Roger: Forever Evil, *842*
Evans, Roger D.: Jet Benny Show, The, *310*
Export, Valie: Invisible Adversaries, *748*
Eyre, Richard: Loose Connections, *321;* Ploughman's Lunch, The, *623;* Singleton's Pluck, *379*
Eyres, John: Goodnight, God Bless, *847;* Monolith, *1066;* Project: Shadowchaser, *101*
Faber, Christian: Bail Jumper, *455*
Faenza, Roberto: Bachelor, The, *453;* Corrupt, *963*
Faiman, Peter: "Crocodile" Dundee, *261;* Dutch, *269*
Fairchild, Bill: Horsemasters, *176*
Fairchild, William: Silent Enemy, The, *116*
Fairfax, Ferdinand: Nate and Hayes, *89;* Rescue, The, *105;* Spymaker: The Secret Life of Ian Fleming, *119*
Fukasaku, Kinji: Tora! Tora! Tora!, *131*
Falk, Harry: Beulah Land, *459;* Death Squad, The, *35;* High Desert Kill, *850;* Night the City Screamed, The, *606;* Scene of the Crime (1985), *1013;* Sophisticated Gents, The, *663*
Fallick, Mort: George Burns—His Wit and Wisdom, *284*
Fanaka, Jamaa: Black Sister's Revenge, *463;* Penitentiary, *98;* Penitentiary II, *98;* Penitentiary III, *98;* Soul Vengeance, *118*
Fansten, Jacques: Cross My Heart (1991), *727*
Fargo, James: Born to Race, *17;* Caravans, *475;* Enforcer, The (1976), *44;* Every Which Way but Loose, *273;* Forced Vengeance, *51;* Game for Vultures, *54;* Riding the Edge, *106*
Farino, Ernest: Steel and Lace, *1080*
Farris, John: Dear Dead Delilah, *831*
Farrow, John: Back from Eternity, *453;* Botany Bay, *18;* Commandos Strike at Dawn, *28;* Copper Canyon, *1106;* Five Came Back, *517;* His Kind of Woman, *62;* Hondo, *1121;* Saint Strikes Back, The, *1012;* Wake Island, *136*
Farwagi, André: Boarding School, *243*
Fasano, John: Black Roses, *814;* Rock 'n' Roll Nightmare, *881*
Fassbinder, Rainer Werner: Ali: Fear Eats the Soul, *711;* American Soldier, The, *712;* Berlin Alexanderplatz, *716;* Bitter Tears of Petra Von Kant, The, *718;* Chinese Roulette, *723;* Despair, *729;* Fox and His Friends, *738;* Gods of the Plague, *741;* Lili Marleen, *760;* Lola (1982), *761;* Marriage of Maria Braun, The, *765;* Merchant of Four Seasons, The, *767;* Mother

Kusters Goes to Heaven, *769;* Querelle, *779;* Veronika Voss, *800*
Faulkner, Brendan: Spookies, *889*
Faure, William C.: Shaka Zulu, *654*
Fearnley, Neill L.: Black Ice, *14*
Feferman, Linda: Seven Minutes in Heaven, *376*
Feijoo, Beda Docampo: Debajo del Mundo (Under Earth), *729*
Feist, Felix: Big Trees, The, *13;* Deluge, *1046;* Devil Thumbs a Ride, The, *970;* Donovan's Brain, *1047;* George White's Scandals, *919;* Threat, The, *1024*
Feld, John C.: Legends of Comedy, *429*
Feldman, Dennis: Real Men, *365*
Feldman, Gene: Danny, *161*
Feldman, John: Alligator Eyes, *951*
Feldman, Marty: Last Remake of Beau Geste, The, *316;* When Things Were Rotten (TV Series), *409*
Fellini, Federico: Amarcord, *712;* And the Ship Sails On, *712;* Boccaccio 70, *719;* Casanova (1976), *722;* City of Women, *724;* Clowns, The, *725;* 8½, *733;* Fellini Satyricon, *736;* Fellini's Roma, *736;* Ginger and Fred, *740;* I Vitelloni, *746;* Il Bidone, *747;* Juliet of the Spirits, *750;* La Dolce Vita, *753;* La Strada, *754;* Nights of Cabiria, *771;* Variety Lights, *800;* White Sheik, The, *803*
Fenady, Georg: Arnold, *810;* Terror in the Wax Museum, *894*
Fenton, Leslie: Saint's Vacation, The, *1012*
Feraldo, Claude: Trade Secrets, *1026*
Feret, René: Alexina, *711;* Mystery of Alexina, The, *770*
Ferguson, Michael: Glory Boys, The, *56*
Fernandez, Emilio: Flor Sylvestre, *737;* Pearl, The, *620*
Ferrara, Abel: Bad Lieutenant, *454;* Body Snatchers, The (1993), *1040;* Cat Chaser, *24;* China Girl, *25;* Crime Story, *30;* Driller Killer, The, *838;* Fear City, *47;* Gladiator, The, *55;* King of New York, *72;* Ms. .45, *87*
Ferrell, Jeff: Revenge of the Teenage Vixens from Outer Space, *881*
Ferrer, José: Return to Peyton Place, *639;* State Fair (1962), *941*
Ferreri, Marco: Tales of Ordinary Madness, *677*
Ferretti, A.: Fear (1988), *976*
Ferris, Stan: Tulips, *400*
Ferro, Pablo: Me, Myself & I, *330*
Ferroni, Giorgio: Mill of the Stone Women, *865;* Night of the Devils, *869;* Scalawag Bunch, The, *111*
Feuillade, Louis: Vampires, The (1915), *799*
Feyder, Jacques: Carnival in Flanders, *722;* Kiss, The (1929), *566;* Knight Without Armour, *566*
Fields, Michael: Bright Angel, *470;* Noon Wine, *608*
Fierberg, Steven: Voodoo Dawn, *901*
Figgis, Mike: Internal Affairs, *67;* Liebestraum, *992;* Mr. Jones, *597;* Stormy Monday, *1020;* Women & Men 2, *706*
Finch, Charles: Priceless Beauty, *626;* Where Sleeping Dogs Lie, *1031*
Finch, Nigel: Lost Language of Cranes, The, *580;* 25 X 5: The Continuing History of the Rolling Stones, *437*
Fincher, David: Alien 3, *1035*
Findlay, Michael: Shriek of the Mutilated, *886;* Snuff, *888*
Findlay, Roberta: Blood Sisters, *816;* Lurkers, *861;* Oracle, The, *872;* Prime Evil, *876*
Findlay, Seaton: Janis, *427*
Finegan, John P.: Girl School Screamers, *846*
Finkleman, Ken: Airplane II: The Sequel, *224;* Head Office, *294*
Finley, George: Gentleman Killer, *1115*
Finley, Joe: Barbarian Queen II: Empress Strikes Back, *1038*
Fiore, Robert: Pumping Iron, *630*
Firkin, Rex: Death of Adolf Hitler, The, *498*
Firstenberg, Sam: American Ninja, *4;* American Ninja II, *4;* Avenging Force, *8;* Breakin' 2 Electric Boogaloo, *909;* Cyborg Cop, *1043;* Delta Force 3, *37;* Ninja III: The Domination, *91;* Revenge of the Ninja, *106*
Firth, Michael: Heart of the Stag, *538;* Sylvia, *676*
Fischa, Michael: Crack House, *30;* Death Spa, *831;* Delta Heat, *37;* My Mom's a Werewolf, *341*
Fischer, Max: Entangled, *973;* Killing 'Em Softly, *563*
Fisher, David: Liar's Moon, *574;* Toy Soldiers (1983), *131*
Fisher, Jack: Torn Apart, *686*
Fisher, Mary Ann: Lords of the Deep, *1063*
Fisher, Terence: Brides of Dracula, *819;* Curse of Frankenstein, The, *828;* Curse of the Werewolf, The, *828;* Frankenstein and the Monster from Hell, *842;* Gorgon, The, *847;* Horror of Dracula, *851;* Hound of the Baskervilles, The (1959), *983;* Island of Terror, *857;* Mummy, The (1959), *866;* Phantom of the Opera (1962), *874;* Sherlock Holmes and the Deadly Necklace, *1015;* Stolen Face, *890*
Fishman, Bill: Car 54, Where Are You?, *250;* Tapeheads, *39*
Fisk, Jack: Daddy's Dyin' and Who's Got the Will, *261;* Final Verdict, *516;* Raggedy Man, *1008;* Violets Are Blue, *694*
Fitzgerald, Ed: Blue Movies, *242*
Fitzmaurice, George: As You Desire Me, *451;* Mata Hari (1931), *590;* Son of the Sheik, *118;* Suzy, *674*
Fiveson, Robert S.: Clonus Horror, The, *1042*
Flaherty, Paul: Billy Crystal: Don't Get Me Started, *239;* Billy Crystal: Midnight Train to Moscow, *240;* Clifford, *256;* 18 Again, *270;* Who's Harry Crumb?, *411*
Flaherty, Robert: Elephant Boy, *44;* Louisiana Story, The, *429;* Moana of the South Seas, *431;* Nanook of the North, *431*
Fleischer, Dave: Bambi vs. Godzilla, *148;* Betty Boop—A Special Collector's Edition, *150;* Fabulous Fleischer Folio, The (Volume One), *165;* Fabulous Fleischer Folio, The (Volume Two), *165;* Fabulous Fleischer Folio, The (Volume Three), *166;* Fabulous Fleischer Folio, The (Volume Four), *166;* Fabulous Fleischer Folio, The (Volume Five), *166;* Gulliver's Travels (1939), *172;* Hoppity Goes to Town, *175;* Hurray for Betty Boop, *176;* Popeye Cartoons, *196;* Superman Cartoons, *208;* TV's Best Adventures of Superman, *1085*
Fleischer, Max: Bambi vs. Godzilla, *148;* Fabulous Fleischer Folio, The (Volume One), *165;* Hurray for Betty Boop, *176;* Rudolph the Red-Nosed Reindeer (and Other Wonderful Christmas Stories), *200*
Fleischer, Richard: Amin: The Rise and Fall, *446;* Amityville III: The Demon, *809;* Ashanti, *7;* Barabbas, *455;* Between Heaven and Hell, *459;* Boston Strangler, The, *818;* Clay Pigeon The, *26;* Compulsion, *487;* Conan the Destroyer, *1043;* Doctor Dolittle, *162;* Don Is Dead, The, *40;* Fantastic Voyage, *1050;* Follow Me Quietly, *978;* Incredible Sarah, The, *551;* Jazz Singer, The (1980), *926;* Mandingo, *588;* Million Dollar Mystery, *332;* Mr. Majestyk, *86;* Narrow Margin, The (1952), *89;* New Centurions, The, *605;* Prince and the Pauper, The (1978), *197;* Red Sonja, *104;* See No Evil, *884;* Soylent Green, *1077;* 10 Rillington Place, *678;* Tora! Tora! Tora!, *131;* Tough Enough, *131;* 20,000 Leagues Under the Sea (1954), *133;* Vikings, The, *135*
Fleming, Andrew: Bad Dreams, *811;* Threesome, *396*
Fleming, Edward: Topsy Turvy, *796*
Fleming, Victor: Adventure, *441;* Bombshell, *243;* Captains Courageous, *474;* Dr. Jekyll and Mr. Hyde (1941), *835;* Gone with the Wind, *530;* Guy Named Joe, A, *535;* Joan of Arc, *558;* Mantrap, *995;* Reckless (1935), *636;* Red Dust, *636;* Test Pilot, *679;* Tortilla Flat, *686;* Treasure Island (1934), *213;* Virginian, The (1929), *1161;* When the Clouds Roll By, *409;* Wizard of Oz, The, *218*
Flemyng, Gordon: Cloud Waltzing, *484;* Daleks—Invasion Earth 2150 A.D., *1044;* Dr. Who and the Daleks, *1047;* Philby, Burgess and Maclean: Spy Scandal of the Century, *1005*
Flender, Rodman: In the Heat of Passion, *986;* Unborn, The, *898*
Fletcher, Mandie: Black Adder III (TV Series), *240*
Flicker, Theodore J.: Jacob Two-Two Meets the Hooded Fang, *178;* Playmates, *358;* President's Analyst, The, *360;* Three in the Cellar, *395*
Flocker, Jim: Nobody's Boy, *191*
Flores, John: Hot Child in the City, *64;* Invisible Strangler, *857;* Island of the Lost, *857*

Florentine, Isaac: Desert Kickboxer, *37*

Florey, Robert: Beast with Five Fingers, The, *812;* Cocoanuts, *257;* Ex-Lady, *512;* Murders in the Rue Morgue (1932), *867;* Outpost in Morocco, *96*

Floyd, Drago: Troll II, *898*

Flynn, John: Best Seller, *954;* Brainscan, *818;* Defiance, *36;* Lock Up, *78;* Nails, *88;* Out for Justice, *96;* Rolling Thunder, *108;* Scam, *1012;* Touched, *686*

Flynn, Tom: Watch It, *696*

Foldes, Lawrence D.: Nightforce, *91;* Young Warriors, The, *141*

Foldy, Peter: Midnight Witness, *996*

Foleg, Peter: Unseen, The, *899*

Foley, James: After Dark, My Sweet, *951;* At Close Range, *953;* Glengarry Glen Ross, *528;* Reckless (1984), *636;* Who's That Girl, *411*

Fonda, Peter: Hired Hand, The, *1121;* Idaho Transfer, *1057;* Wanda Nevada, *136*

Fondato, Marcello: Immortal Bachelor, The, *747*

Fons, Jorge: Jory, *1124*

Fonvielle, Lloyd: Gotham, *980*

Forbes, Bryan: Endless Game, The, *510;* International Velvet, *177;* King Rat, *565;* Long Ago Tomorrow, *578;* Madwoman of Chaillot, The, *585;* Naked Face, The, *1000;* Seance on a Wet Afternoon, *1013;* Whistle Down the Wind, *216;* Wrong Box, The, *414*

Ford, Alexander: Border Street, *720*

Ford, Greg: Bugs Bunny's Wild World of Sports, *154;* Bugs vs. Daffy: Battle of the Music Video Stars, *154;* Daffy Duck's Quackbusters, *161*

Ford, John: Arrowsmith, *451;* Cheyenne Autumn, *1104;* December 7th: The Movie, *422;* Donovan's Reef, *267;* Drums Along the Mohawk, *42;* Fort Apache, *1114;* Fugitive, The (1947), *523;* Grapes of Wrath, The, *531;* Horse Soldiers, The, *1122;* How Green Was My Valley, *545;* How the West Was Won, *1122;* Hurricane, The (1937), *546;* Informer, The, *552;* Judge Priest, *560;* Last Hurrah, The, *569;* Long Grey Line, The, *578;* Long Voyage Home, The, *578;* Lost Patrol, The, *79;* Man Who Shot Liberty Valance, The, *1132;* Mary of Scotland, *589;* Mr. Roberts, *334;* Mogambo, *86;* My Darling Clementine, *1134;* Quiet Man, The, *364;* Rio Grande, *1145;* Searchers, The, *1148;* Sergeant Rutledge, *1148;* She Wore a Yellow Ribbon, *1148;* Stagecoach (1939), *1152;* Straight Shooting, *1153;* Sun Shines Bright, The, *673;* They Were Expendable, *127;* Three Godfathers, The, *1156;* Two Rode Together, *1160;* Wagonmaster, *1162;* Wee Willie Winkie, *216;* What Price Glory, *408;* Wings of Eagles, The, *703;* Young Mr. Lincoln, *708*

Ford, Phillip: Bandits of Dark Canyon, *1096;* Denver Kid, *1109;* Rodeo King and the Senorita, *1145;* Wild Frontier, *1164*

Ford, Steve: Dungeonmaster, The, *1048*

Fordyce, Ian: How to Irritate People, *302*

Forman, Milos: Amadeus, *906;* Fireman's Ball, The, *737;* Hair, *921;* Loves of a Blonde, *762;* One Flew Over the Cuckoo's Nest, *613;* Ragtime, *633;* Valmont, *693*

Forman, Tom: Shadows, *654;* Virginian, The (1923), *1161*

Forrest, Arthur: Jerry Lewis Live, *310*

Forster, Robert: Hollywood Harry, *299*

Forsyth, Bill: Being Human, *458;* Breaking In, *245;* Comfort and Joy, *258;* Gregory's Girl, *290;* Housekeeping, *545;* Local Hero, *320;* That Sinking Feeling, *392*

Forsyth, Ed: Chesty Anderson, U.S. Navy (a.k.a. Anderson's Angels), *25*

Fortenberry, John: Medusa: Dare to be Truthful, *331*

Fosse, Bob: All That Jazz, *906;* Cabaret, *910;* Lenny, *572;* Star 80, *666;* Sweet Charity, *943*

Foster, Giles: Consuming Passions, *259;* Dutch Girls, *506;* Innocent Victim, *986;* Silas Marner, *657*

Foster, Jodie: Little Man Tate, *182*

Foster, Lewis R.: Crashout, *30;* Dakota Incident, *1107;* Laurel and Hardy Classics, Volume 8, *316;* Laurel and Hardy Classics, Volume 9, *316;* Sign of Zorro, The, *204;* Tonka, *213*

Foster, Norman: Brighty of the Grand Canyon, *152;* Davy Crockett and the River Pirates, *161;* Davy Crockett, King of the Wild Frontier, *161;* Journey Into Fear (1942), *987;* Mr. Moto's Last Warning, *997;* Nine Lives of Elfego Baca, The, *1136;* Rachel and the Stranger, *1140;* Sign of Zorro, The, *204;* Tell It to the Judge, *392*

Fournier, Claude: Dan Candy's Law, *32*

Fowler Jr., Gene: I Married a Monster from Outer Space, *1057;* I Was a Teenage Werewolf, *855;* Showdown at Boot Hill, *1149*

Fowler, Robert: Below the Belt, *458*

Fox, Emerson: Shocking Asia, *434;* Shocking Asia 2, *434*

Fox, Wallace: Badmen of the Border, *1096;* Bowery at Midnight, *818;* Corpse Vanishes, The, *825;* Powdersmoke Range, *1139*

Frakas, Michael: Prime Risk, *100*

Fraker, William: Legend of the Lone Ranger, The, *1128;* Monte Walsh, *1134;* Reflection of Fear, *1009*

Franciolini, Gianni: Pardon My Trunk, *775*

Francis, Freddie: Brain, The (1965), *1040;* Creeping Flesh, The, *826;* Doctor and the Devils, The, *835;* Dr. Terror's House of Horrors, *836;* Dracula Has Risen from the Grave, *837;* Evil of Frankenstein, The, *839;* Ghoul, The (1975), *846;* Girly, *846;* Hysteria, *984;* Jigsaw Man, The, *987;* Legend of the Werewolf, *860;* Skull, The, *887;* Son of Dracula (1974), *940;* Tales from the Crypt, *892;* Tales that Witness Madness, *892;* They Came from Beyond Space, *1083;* Torture Garden, *896;* Vampire Happening, *900*

Francis, Karl: And Nothing But the Truth, *447*

Francisci, Pietro: Hercules (1959), *1056;* Hercules Unchained, *1056*

Franco, Jess: Angel of Death, *5;* Oasis of the Zombies, *872*

Franco, Jess (Jesus): Against All Odds (Kiss and Kill, Blood of Fu Manchu), *808;* Bloody Moon, *817;* Castle of Fu Manchu, *822;* Count Dracula, *825;* Deadly Sanctuary, *831;* Demoniac, *832;* Erotikill, *838;* Ilsa, the Wicked Warden, *855;* Jack the Ripper (1979), *987;* 99 Women, *91;* Venus in Furs, *135;* Virgin Among the Living Dead, A, *901;* Women in Cell Block 9, *140*

Franju, Georges: Eyes without a Face, *735;* Head Against the Wall, *743;* Judex, *750*

Frank, Carol: Sorority House Massacre, *889*

Frank, Christopher: Josepha, *750;* L'Année des Meduses, *752*

Frank, Hubert: Melody in Love, *592*

Frank, Melvin: Above and Beyond, *1;* Buono Sera, Mrs. Campbell, *247;* Court Jester, The, *260;* Duchess and the Dirtwater Fox, The, *1110;* Jayhawkers, The, *1123;* Li'l Abner (1959), *928;* Lost and Found, *321;* Prisoner of Second Avenue, The, *361;* Touch of Class, A, *398;* Walk Like a Man, *405*

Frank, Robert: Candy Mountain, *474*

Frank, T. C.: Born Losers, *17*

Frankel, Cyril: Permission to Kill, *98;* Very Edge, The, *693*

Frankenheimer, John: Against the Wall, *442;* All Fall Down, *444;* Bird Man of Alcatraz, *462;* Black Sunday (1977), *955;* Challenge, The, *24;* Comedian, The, *486;* Days of Wine and Roses, The (Television), *497;* Dead-Bang, *33;* 52 Pick-Up, *976;* Fixer, The, *517;* Fourth War, The, *52;* French Connection II, The, *53;* Grand Prix, *531;* Holcroft Covenant, The, *982;* Horsemen, The, *64;* Manchurian Candidate, The, *995;* 99 and 44/100 Percent Dead, *91;* Prophecy, *877;* Seven Days in May, *653;* Story of a Love Story, *668;* Train, The, *131;* Year of the Gun, *1033;* Young Savages, The, *1033*

Franklin, Carl: Eye of the Eagle 2, *46;* Full Fathom Five, *53;* Laurel Avenue, *571;* Nowhere to Run (1989), *609;* One False Move, *94*

Franklin, Chester M.: Vanity Fair, *693*

Franklin, Howard: Public Eye, The, *1008;* Quick Change, *363*

Franklin, Jim: Ripping Yarns, *368*

Franklin, Richard: Beauty and the Beast (TV Series), *1039;* Cloak and Dagger (1984), *27;* F/X 2: The Deadly Art of Illusion, *979;* Link, *851;* Patrick, *873;* Psycho II, *877;* Road Games, *1010;* Running Delilah, *110*

Franklin, Sidney: Barretts of Wimpole Street, The, *456;* Good Earth, The, *530;* Guardsman, The, *291;* Private Lives, *362;* Smilin' Through (1932), *661;* Wild Orchids, *702*
Franklin, Wendell J.: Bus Is Coming, The, *472*
Franzese, Michael: Mausoleum, *864*
Fraser, Christopher: Summer City, *122*
Fraser, Harry: Broadway to Cheyenne, *1101;* Chained for Life, *478;* Enemy of the Law, *1111;* Six-Shootin' Sheriff, *1150;* Three in the Saddle, *1156*
Frawley, James: Assault & Matrimony, *229;* Big Bus, The, *238;* Fraternity Vacation, *280;* Hansel and Gretel, *173;* Muppet Movie, The, *189;* Spies, Lies, and Naked Thighs, *384*
Frazer, Henry: 'Neath Arizona Skies, *1135;* Randy Rides Alone, *1141*
Frears, Stephen: Dangerous Liaisons, *494;* Grifters, The, *534;* Gumshoe, *291;* Hero, *296;* Hit, The, *63;* My Beautiful Laundrette, *601;* Prick Up Your Ears, *626;* Sammy and Rosie Get Laid, *372;* Snapper, The, *382*
Freda, Riccardo: Devil's Commandment, The, *834;* Maciste in Hell, *861*
Freed, Herb: Beyond Evil, *813;* Graduation Day, *847;* Survival Game, *123;* Tomboy, *130*
Freed, Mark: Shock'em Dead, *885*
Freedman, Jerrold: Best Kept Secrets, *11;* Borderline, *17;* Native Son, *604;* Seduced, *1013;* Streets of L.A., The, *671;* Thompson's Last Run, *128*
Freeland, Thornton: Brass Monkey, The, *958;* Flying Down to Rio, *917;* Jericho, *557;* They Call It Sin, *680;* Whoopee, *947*
Freeman, Hal: Blood Frenzy, *815*
Freeman, Joan: Satisfaction, *938;* Streetwalkin', *671*
Fregonese, Hugo: Blowing Wild, *16;* Decameron Nights, *263*
Freilich, Jeff: Dark Justice, *32*
Freleng, Friz: Ant and the Aardvark, The, *147;* Best of Bugs Bunny and Friends, The, *150;* Best of Warner Brothers, Vol. 1, *150;* Best of Warner Brothers, Vol. 2, *150;* Bugs and Daffy: The Wartime Cartoons, *152;* Bugs Bunny: All American Hero, *153;* Bugs Bunny and Elmer Fudd Cartoon Festival Featuring "Wabbit Twouble", *153;* Bugs Bunny Cartoon Festival Featuring "Hold the Lion Please", *153;* Bugs Bunny Classics, *153;* Bugs Bunny: Truth or Hare, *153;* Bugs Bunny's Easter Funnies, *154;* Bugs Bunny's Hare-Raising Tales, *154;* Bugs Bunny's Looney Christmas Tales, *154;* Bugs Bunny's Wacky Adventures, *154;* Bugs vs. Elmer, *155;* Cartoon Moviestars: Bugs!, *156;* Cartoon Moviestars: Daffy!, *156;* Cartoon Moviestars: Elmer!, *156;* Cartoon Moviestars: Porky!, *156;* Cartoon Moviestars: Starring Bugs Bunny, *156;* Daffy Duck Cartoon Festival: Ain't That Ducky, *160;* Daffy Duck: Tales from the Duckside, *160;* Daffy Duck's Easter Egg-Citement, *160;* Daffy Duck's Madcap Mania, *161;* Daffy Duck's Movie: Fantastic Island, *161;* Elmer Fudd Cartoon Festival: An Itch in Time, *164;* Elmer Fudd's Comedy Capers, *164;* Golden Age of Looney Toons, The: Bugs Bunny by Each Director, *169;* Golden Age of Looney Toons, The: Firsts, *170;* Golden Age of Looney Toons, The: Friz Freleng, *170;* Golden Age of Looney Toons, The: Hurry for Hollywood, *170;* Golden Age of Looney Toons, The: 1930s Musicals, *170;* Golden Age of Looney Toons, The: The Art of Bugs, *170;* Just Plain Daffy, *179;* Little Tweetie and Little Inki Cartoon Festival, *183;* Looney, Looney, Looney Bugs Bunny Movie, *184;* Looney Tunes Video Show, The (Volume 1), *184;* Looney Tunes Video Show, The (Volume 2), *184;* 1001 Rabbit Tales, *193;* Pink at First Sight, *195;* Pink Panther Cartoon Festival, The: A Fly in the Pink, *195;* Pink Panther Cartoon Festival, The: Pink-a-Boo, *195;* Porky Pig's Screwball Comedies, *197;* Salute to Friz Freleng, A, *201;* Salute to Mel Blanc, A, *201;* Speedy Gonzales' Fast Funnies, *206;* Sylvester and Tweety: The Best Yeows of Our Lives, *208;* Sylvester and Tweety's Crazy Capers, *209;* Tweety and Sylvester, *214;* Very Best of Bugs Bunny: Volume 1, The, *215;* Very Best of Bugs Bunny: Volume 2, The, *215;* Very Best of Bugs Bunny: Volume 3, The, *215;* Very Best of Bugs Bunny: Volume 4, The, *215;* Yosemite Sam: The Good, the Bad, and the Ornery, *219*
French, Harold: Encore, *509;* Paris Express, The, *97;* Quartet (1948), *631;* Rob Roy, the Highland Rogue, *200;* Trio, *688*
French, Lloyd: Laurel and Hardy Classics, Volume 3, *316;* Laurel and Hardy Classics, Volume 7, *316*
Frend, Charles: Cruel Sea, The, *492;* Run for Your Money, A, *371;* Scott of the Antarctic, *650*
Freund, Karl: Mad Love, *861;* Mummy, The (1932), *866*
Fricke, Ron: Baraka, *419*
Fridriksson, Fridrik Thor: Children of Nature, *723*
Fried, Randall: Heaven Is a Playground, *539*
Friedberg, Rick: Bad Golf Made Easier, *231;* Off the Wall, *348;* Pray TV (1980), *360*
Friedenberg, Dick: Deerslayer, The, *1108;* Life and Times of Grizzly Adams, The, *181*
Friedgen, Bud: That's Entertainment! III, *436*
Friedkin, William: Blue Chips, *465;* Boys in the Band, The, *468;* Brinks Job, The, *246;* Cruising, *964;* Deal of the Century, *263;* Exorcist, The, *839;* French Connection, The, *53;* Guardian, The (1990), *848;* Night They Raided Minsky's, The, *345;* Rampage, *1009;* Sorceror, *1018;* To Live and Die in L.A., *130*
Friedlander, Louis: Raven, The (1935), *878*
Friedman, Adam: Inside Out (1992), *1058;* To Sleep With a Vampire, *896*
Friedman, Anthony: Bartleby, *456*
Friedman, Ed: Great Space Chase, *171;* Secret of the Sword, The, *202*
Friedman, Jeffrey: Common Threads: Stories from the Quilt, *421*
Friedman, Ken: Made in USA, *584*
Friedman, Richard: Deathmask, *36;* Doom Asylum, *836;* Phantom of the Mall—Eric's Revenge, *874;* Scared Stiff, *883*
Friend, Martyn: Rumpole of the Bailey (TV Series), *1011*
Fristch, Gunther Von: TV Classics: Flash Gordon and the Planet of Death, *1085*
Froehlich, Bill: Return to Horror High, *880*
Froemke, Susan: Beatles, The: The First U.S. Visit, *419*
Frost, David: Ring of Steel, *106*
Frost, Lee: Black Gestapo, The, *13;* Dixie Dynamite, *40*
Fruet, William: Bedroom Eyes, *954;* Blue Monkey, *817;* Death Weekend, *831;* Search and Destroy (1981), *113;* Spasms, *889;* Wedding in White, *697*
Frye, E. Max: Amos & Andrew, *226*
Fuest, Robert: Abominable Dr. Phibes, The, *808;* And Soon the Darkness, *952;* Aphrodite, *713;* Devil's Rain, The, *834;* Dr. Phibes Rises Again, *836;* Last Days of Man on Earth, The, *1062;* Revenge of the Stepford Wives, *881;* Wuthering Heights (1971), *707*
Fugard, Athol: Road to Mecca, The, *641*
Fukasaku, Kinji: Black Lizard, *718;* Green Slime, The, *1055;* Samurai Reincarnation, *783;* Virus, *1087*
Fukuda, Jun: Godzilla vs. Gigan, *846;* Godzilla vs. Mechagodzilla, *846;* Godzilla vs. the Sea Monster, *847;* Son of Godzilla, *888*
Fukushima, Atsuko: Robot Carnival, *1075*
Fukutomi, Hiroshi: Battle Angel, *715*
Fulci, Lucio: Black Cat, The (1981), *813;* Challenge to White Fang, *24;* Contraband, *726;* Gates of Hell, *845;* House by the Cemetery, *852;* Manhattan Baby, *862;* New Gladiators, The, *1068;* New York Ripper, The, *868;* Seven Doors of Death, *884;* Zombie, *904*
Fuller, Fleming B.: Prey of the Chameleon, *1007*
Fuller, Samuel: Baron of Arizona, The, *1097;* Big Red One, The, *12;* China Gate, *481;* Meanest Men in the West, The, *1133;* Naked Kiss, The, *1000;* Pickup on South Street, *1006;* Run of the Arrow, *1146;* Shark! (a.k.a. Maneaters!), *114;* Shock Corridor, *1015;* Steel Helmet, The, *120;* Underworld U.S.A., *691;* White Dog, *700*
Fuller, Tex: Stranded, *1080*
Fumihiko, Takayama: Bubblegum Crisis—Vols. 1–8, *720*
Funt, Allen: Best of Candid Camera, The, *235;* What Do You Say to a Naked Lady?, *408*
Furey, Lewis: Shades of Love: Champagne for Two, *653;* Shadow Dancing, *1014*

Furie, Sidney J.: Appaloosa, The, *1094;* Boys in Company C, The, *18;* Entity, The, *838;* Hit!, *62;* Ipcress File, The, *985;* Iron Eagle, *67;* Iron Eagle II, *67;* Lady Sings the Blues, *927;* Ladybugs, *315;* Leather Boys, The, *572;* Purple Hearts, *631;* Superman IV: The Quest for Peace, *1081;* Taking of Beverly Hills, The, *124*
Gabai, Richard: Hot Under the Collar, *302;* Virgin High, *405*
Gable, Martin: Lost Moment, The, *580*
Gabor, Pal: Brady's Escape, *18*
Gabourie, Mitchell: Buying Time, *21*
Gabrea, Radu: Man Like Eva, A, *765*
Gabriel, Mike: Rescuers Down Under, *199*
Gaffney, Robert: Frankenstein Meets the Space Monster, *842*
Gage, George: Fleshburn, *841*
Gage, John: Velvet Touch, The, *693*
Gainville, René: Associate, The, *714;* Le Complot (The Conspiracy), *757*
Gaisseau, Pierre-Dominique: Sky Above, the Mud Below, The, *434*
Gale, John: Firing Line, The, *49*
Gale, Ricardo Jacques: Alien Intruder, *1035;* In the Time of Barbarians II, *1058*
Galeen, Henrik: Student of Prague, *790*
Gallagher, John: Beach House, *233;* Street Hunter, *121*
Gallo, Fred: Dead Space, *1045;* Dracula Rising, *837;* Finishing Touch, The, *977*
Gallo, George: 29th Street, *401*
Gallop, Frank: Great Chase, The, *57*
Gallu, Samuel: Theatre of Death, *894*
Gance, Abel: Abel Gance's Beethoven, *710;* Battle of Austerlitz, The, *9;* J'Accuse, *749;* Napoleon (1927), *770*
Gannaway, Albert C.: Daniel Boone, Trail Blazer, *1107*
Garcia, David: Sex Crimes, *114*
Garcia, Jerry: Grateful Dead Movie, The, *425;* So Far, *434*
Gardner, Herb: Goodbye People, The, *530*
Garen, Leo: Shrieking, The, *886*
Garen, Scott: Simply Mad About the Mouse, *204*
Garland, Patrick: Doll's House, A (1989), *503*
Garmes, Lee: Actors and Sin, *441;* Angels Over Broadway, *448*
Garnett, Tay: Bataan, *9;* Challenge to Be Free, *157;* Cheers for Miss Bishop, *480;* China Seas, *25;* Connecticut Yankee in King Arthur's Court, A (1948), *258;* Eternally Yours, *511;* Flying Fool, The, *51;* Joy of Living, *926;* Main Street to Broadway, *326;* Mrs. Parkington, *598;* One Minute to Zero, *94;* Postman Always Rings Twice, The (1946), *1007;* Seven Sinners, *113;* Slightly Honorable, *381;* Stand-In, *385*
Garrett, Roy: Eyes Behind the Stars, *1050*
Garris, Mick: Critters 2: The Main Course, *827;* Psycho 4: The Beginning, *877;* Stephen King's Sleepwalkers, *890*
Garrison, Greg: TV Classics: Milton Berle, *401*
Gary, Jerome: Stripper (1985), *435*
Gasnier, Louis J.: Reefer Madness, *365*
Gast, Leon: Grateful Dead Movie, The, *425;* Hell's Angels Forever, *426*
Gates, Jim: Hey Abbott!, *296*
Gaudioz, Tony: Border Heat, *17*
Gaup, Nils: Pathfinder, *776;* Shipwrecked, *203*
Gavaldon, Roberto: Littlest Outlaw, The, *184;* Macario, *763*
Gawer, Eleanor: Slipping into Darkness, *117*
Gayton, Joe: Warm Summer Rain, *696*
Gayton, Tony: Athens, GA., *418*
Gazarian, Armand: Prison Planet, *1071*
Gazdag, Gyula: Hungarian Fairy Tale, A, *745*
Gebhard, Glenn: Blood Screams, *816;* One Last Run, *613*
Geer, Hal: Bugs Bunny's Cupid Capers, *154;* Bugs Bunny's Easter Funnies, *154;* How Bugs Bunny Won the West, *176*
Geller, Bruce: Savage Bees, The, *882*
Genina, Augusto: Prix De Beaute (Beauty Prize), *778*
Gentilomo, Giacomo: Goliath and the Vampires, *847;* Hercules Against the Moon Men, *1056*
George, Jim: Rover Dangerfield, *200*
George, Peter: Surf Nazis Must Die, *123*
George, Screaming Mad: Guyver, The, *1055*
Gerard, Bernard: Gone with the West, *1116*
Gerbsoa, Steve: Elayne Boosler—Broadway Baby, *270*
Gering, Marion: Thunder in the City, *683*
Germi, Pietro: Divorce—Italian Style, *731;* Seduced and Abandoned, *784*
Geronimi, Clyde: Alice in Wonderland (1951), *145;* Cinderella (1950), *159;* Lady and the Tramp, *180;* Legend of Sleepy Hollow, The (1949), *181;* One Hundred and One Dalmatians, *192;* Peter Pan (1953), *194;* Sleeping Beauty (1959), *204*
Gerretsen, Peter: Night Friend, *90*
Gershuny, Theodore: Silent Night, Bloody Night, *886*
Gerstad, Harry: TV's Best Adventures of Superman, *1085*
Gessner, Nicolas: It Rained All Night the Day I Left, *555;* Little Girl Who Lives Down the Lane, The, *992;* Quicker Than the Eye, *102;* Someone Behind the Door, *1018*
Gethers, Steven: Hillside Stranglers, The, *982;* Jenny's War, *68*
Geurs, Karl: New Adventures of Winnie the Pooh, The, *191*
Gibbins, Duncan: Case for Murder, A, *960;* Eve of Destruction, *1050;* Fire with Fire, *517*
Gibbons, Cedric: Tarzan and His Mate, *125*
Gibbons, Pamela: Midnight Dancer, *594*
Gibbons, Rodney: Neighbor, The, *1000*
Gibson, Alan: Martin's Day, *185;* Satanic Rites of Dracula, The, *882;* Twinsanity, *1028;* Witness for the Prosecution (1982), *1032;* Woman Called Golda, A, *705*
Gibson, Brian: Breaking Glass, *909;* Josephine Baker Story, The, *559;* Murderers Among Us: The Simon Wiesenthal Story, *601;* Poltergeist II: The Other Side, *875;* What's Love Got to Do with It?, *698*
Gibson, Mel: Man without a Face, The, *587*
Gibson, Tom: Singing Buckaroo, *1150*
Giddins, Gary: Celebrating Bird: The Triumph of Charlie Parker, *420*
Gilbert, Brian: French Lessons, *281;* Not without My Daughter, *609;* Vice Versa, *404*
Gilbert, Lewis: Alfie, *224;* Damn the Defiant!, *31;* Educating Rita, *270;* Moonraker, *86;* Not Quite Paradise, *347;* Sea Shall Not Have Them, The, *113;* Shirley Valentine, *378;* Sink the Bismarck, *116;* Spy Who Loved Me, The, *119;* Stepping Out, *942;* You Only Live Twice, *141*
Gilbert, Warwick: Sherlock Holmes and the Valley of Fear, *203*
Giler, David: Black Bird, The, *240*
Giles, David: Murder Is Announced, A, *998*
Gilhuis, Mark G.: Bloody Wednesday, *817*
Gill, David: Buster Keaton: A Hard Act to Follow, *420;* D. W. Griffith, Father of Film, *422;* Harold Lloyd: The Third Genius, *425;* Hollywood, *426;* Unknown Chaplin, *437*
Gillard, Stuart: Man Called Sarge, A, *327;* Paradise (1982), *97;* Teenage Mutant Ninja Turtles III, *209*
Gilliam, Terry: Adventures of Baron Münchausen, The, *1034;* Brazil, *245;* Fisher King, The, *1051;* Jabberwocky, *309;* Monty Python and the Holy Grail, *336;* Time Bandits, *1084*
Gilliat, Sidney: Endless Night, *973;* Great St. Trinian's Train Robbery, The, *290;* Only Two Can Play, *350*
Gilling, John: Gamma People, The, *1054;* Mania, *862;* Night Caller from Outer Space, *1068;* Vampire Over London, *404*
Gilmore, Stuart: Half-Breed, The, *1118;* Hot Lead, *1122*
Gilroy, Bert: Lawless Valley, *1127*
Gilroy, Frank D.: Gig, The, *286;* Once in Paris, *612*
Ginsberg, Milton Moses: Werewolf of Washington, *902*
Ginty, Robert: Bounty Hunter, *18;* Vietnam, Texas, *135;* Woman of Desire, *1032*
Gion, Christian: Here Comes Santa Claus, *174*
Giraldi, Bob: Club Med, *484;* Hiding Out, *61*
Giraldi, Franco: Minute to Pray, A Second to Die, A, *1134*

Girard, André: Qui Etes-Vous, Mr. Sorge? (Soviet Spy), *779*
Girard, Bernard: Dead Heat on a Merry-Go-Round, *967;* Little Moon & Jud McGraw, *1128;* Mind Snatchers, The, *865*
Girard, Francois: Thirty-Two Short Films About Glenn Gould, *682*
Girdler, William: Asylum of Satan, *810;* Day of the Animals, *830;* Grizzly, *847;* Manitou, The, *863;* Sheba Baby, *115;* Three on a Meathook, *895*
Girod, Francis: Elegant Criminal, The, *734;* Infernal Trio, The, *748;* L'Etat Sauvage (The Savage State), *756*
Gisler, Marcel: Blue Hour, The, *719*
Glaser, Paul Michael: Air Up There, The, *223;* Band of the Hand, *9;* Cutting Edge, The, *493;* Miami Vice: "The Prodigal Son", *84;* Running Man, The, *1075*
Glassman, Arnold: Visions of Light: The Art of Cinematography, *438*
Glatter, Lesli Linka: Into the Homeland, *67;* State of Emergency, *666*
Glazer, Barry: Tommy Chong Roast, The, *397*
Gleason, Bill: Hollywood Clowns, The, *426*
Gleason, Michie: Summer Heat (1987), *672*
Glen, John: Aces: Iron Eagle III, *1;* Checkered Flag, *480;* Christopher Columbus: The Discovery, *26;* For Your Eyes Only, *51;* License to Kill, *77;* Living Daylights, The, *78;* Octopussy, *93;* View to a Kill, A, *135*
Glenister, John: After Julius, *442*
Glenville, Peter: Becket, *457;* Comedians, The, *486;* Hotel Paradiso, *302;* Prisoner, The, *628;* Summer and Smoke, *672*
Glickenhaus, James: Exterminator, The, *45;* McBain, *83;* Protector, The, *101;* Shakedown, *114;* Slaughter of the Innocents, *1017;* Soldier, The, *118*
Glicker, Paul: Cheerleaders, *254;* Running Scared (1980), *110*
Glimcher, Arne: Mambo Kings, The, *930*
Glinsky, Robert: Poisonous Plants, *778*
Gluck, Wolfgang: 38 Vienna Before the Fall, *794*
Godard, Jean-Luc: Alphaville, *712;* Aria, *907;* Band of Outsiders, *715;* Breathless (1959), *720;* Classic Foreign Shorts: Volume 2, *724;* Contempt, *726;* First Name: Carmen, *737;* Hail Mary, *742;* Le Gai Savior (The Joy of Knowledge), *757;* Married Woman, A, *765;* Masculine Feminine, *766;* My Life to Live, *769;* Oldest Profession, The, *773;* Pierrot Le Fou, *777;* Seven Deadly Sins, The, *785;* Six in Paris (Paris Vue par . . .), *786;* Sympathy for the Devil, *435;* Weekend, *803;* Woman Is a Woman, A, *805*
Goddard, Gary: Masters of the Universe, *186*
Goddard, Jim: Impossible Spy, The, *985;* Kennedy (TV Miniseries), *562;* Reilly: The Ace of Spies, *637;* Shanghai Surprise, *377;* Tale of Two Cities, A (1980), *677*
Godfrey, Peter: Christmas in Connecticut (1945), *255;* Escape Me Never, *510;* Two Mrs. Carrolls, The, *1028*
Godmilow, Jill: Waiting for the Moon, *695*
Godoy, Armando Robles: Green Wall, The, *742*
Golan, Menahem: Delta Force, The, *36;* Diamonds, *38;* Enter the Ninja, *44;* Escape to the Sun, *511;* Hanna's War, *536;* Hit the Dutchman, *63;* Lepke, *76;* Lupo, *324;* Mack the Knife, *930;* Magician of Lublin, The, *585;* Operation Thunderbolt, *95;* Over the Brooklyn Bridge, *352;* Over the Top, *617;* Silent Victim, *658*
Gold, Greg: House of the Rising Sun, *64*
Gold, Jack: Catholics, *477;* Escape from Sobibor, *45;* Little Lord Fauntleroy (1980), *182;* Medusa Touch, The, *864;* Murrow, *601;* Naked Civil Servant, The, *603;* Rose and the Jackal, The, *644;* Sakharov, *647;* Tenth Man, The, *679*
Goldbeck, Willis: Love Laughs at Andy Hardy, *323*
Goldberg, Dan: Feds, *276;* No Nukes, *432*
Goldberg, Gary David: Dad, *493*
Goldblatt, Mark: Dead Heat, *830;* Punisher, The, *101*
Golden, Dan: Naked Obsession, *1000;* Saturday Night Special, *111*
Golding, Paul: Pulse, *877*
Goldman, Gary: Hans Christian Andersen's Thumbelina, *173*
Goldman, Jim: Desert Warrior, *1047*
Goldsmid, Peter: Road to Mecca, The, *641*
Goldstein, Allan A.: Common Bonds, *487;* Death Wish V: The Face of Death, *36;* Lawrenceville Stories, The, *317;* Outside Chance of Maximilian Glick, The, *193*
Goldstein, Amy: Silencer, The, *116*
Goldstein, Bruce: Hollywood Outtakes, *299*
Goldstein, Scott: Ambition, *952;* Walls of Glass, *695*
Goldstone, James: Brother John, *470;* Calamity Jane (1984), *1103;* Eric, *510;* Kent State, *563;* Outer Limits, The (TV Series), *1069;* Rita Hayworth: The Love Goddess, *641;* Rollercoaster, *1011;* Star Trek (TV Series), *1078;* Swashbuckler (1976), *123;* They Only Kill Their Masters, *1024;* When Time Ran Out!, *1031;* Winning, *140*
Goldthwait, Bob: Shakes the Clown, *377*
Gomer, Steve: Sweet Lorraine, *674*
Gomez, Nick: Laws of Gravity, *76*
Goncharff, Sergei: House of Terror, *984*
Gonzalez, Servando: Fool Killer, The, *978*
Goodell, Gregory: Human Experiments, *64*
Goodkind, Saul: Buck Rogers: Destination Saturn (a.k.a. Planet Outlaws), *1040;* Phantom Creeps, The, *874*
Goodson, Tony: And You Thought Your Parents Were Weird, *227*
Goodwin, Fred: Curse II—The Bite, *827*
Goodwins, Leslie: Bronco (TV Series), *1101;* Dragnet (1947), *41;* Mexican Spitfire, *331;* Mummy's Curse, The, *867;* Two-Reelers: Comedy Classics #2, *402*
Gordon, Bert I.: Amazing Colossal Man, The, *1035;* Big Bet, The, *238;* Cyclops, The, *829;* Earth vs. the Spider, *1048;* Empire of the Ants, *1049;* Food of the Gods, *1052;* Mad Bomber, The, *994;* Magic Sword, The, *185;* Picture Mommy Dead, *874;* Satan's Princess, *882;* Village of the Giants, *900;* War of the Colossal Beast, *1088;* Witching, The (Necromancy), *904*
Gordon, Bryan: Career Opportunities, *251;* Discovery Program, *501*
Gordon, George: Ant and the Aardvark, The, *147;* MGM Cartoon Magic, *186*
Gordon, James: Fabulous Villains, The, *424*
Gordon, Keith: Chocolate War, The, *481;* Midnight Clear, A, *593;* Wild Palms, *1089*
Gordon, Michael: Boys' Night Out, *244;* Cyrano De Bergerac (1950), *493;* Impossible Years, The, *305;* Pillow Talk, *357;* Texas Across the River, *1155*
Gordon, Robert: Bonanza (TV Series), *1100;* It Came from Beneath the Sea, *857;* Joe Louis Story, The, *558;* Revenge of the Red Baron, *881*
Gordon, Steve: Arthur, *229*
Gordon, Stuart: Dolls, *836;* Fortress (1993), *1053;* From Beyond, *844;* Pit and the Pendulum, The (1991), *875;* Re-Animator, *879;* Robot Jox, *1075*
Gordy, Berry: Mahogany, *586*
Goren, Serif: Yol, *806*
Goretta, Claude: Lacemaker, The, *755*
Gorg, Alan: Living the Blues, *577*
Gormley, Charles: Gospel According to Vic, The, *289*
Gornick, Michael: Creepshow 2, *826;* Tales from the Darkside, Vol. I, *892*
Gorris, Marleen: Question of Silence, A, *779*
Gorsky, Alexander: Don Quixote (1988), *914*
Goscinny, René: Asterix: The Gaul (Series), *147;* Lucky Luke: The Ballad of the Daltons, *184*
Gosha, Hideo: Hunter in the Dark, *746;* Wolves, The, *804*
Goslar, Jurgen: Albino, *808;* Slavers, *117*
Gosling, Maureen: Hot Pepper, *426*
Gothar, Peter: Time Stands Still, *795*
Gottlieb, Carl: Amazon Women on the Moon, *225;* Caveman, *252;* Paul Reiser Out on a Whim, *355;* Steve Martin Live, *386*
Gottlieb, David N.: Meet Your Animal Friends, *186*
Gottlieb, Franz: Curse of the Yellow Snake, The, *965*
Gottlieb, Lisa: Just One of the Guys, *312*

Gottlieb, Michael: Mannequin (1987), *328;* Mr. Nanny, *188*
Gottschalk, Robert: Dangerous Charter, *32*
Gould, Heywood: One Good Cop, *613*
Goulding, Alf: Chump at Oxford, A, *255;* His Royal Slyness/Haunted Spooks, *298*
Goulding, Edmund: Dark Victory, *495;* Dawn Patrol, The, *33;* Forever and a Day, *520;* Grand Hotel, *531;* Great Lie, The, *532;* Old Maid, The, *611;* Razor's Edge, The (1946), *635;* Reaching for the Moon (1931), *365;* Riptide, *640;* That Certain Woman, *680;* We're Not Married, *408*
Governor, Richard: Ghost Town, *846*
Gowers, Bruce: Billy Crystal: A Comic's Line, *239;* Eddie Murphy—Delirious, *270;* George Carlin Live! What Am I Doing in New Jersey?, *284;* Richard Lewis—"I'm Exhausted", *367*
Graef, Roger: Secret Policemen's Other Ball, The, *375;* Secret Policeman's Private Parts, The, *375*
Graham, David C.: Undertaker and His Pals, The, *899*
Graham, Eddy: Sherlock Holmes and the Baskerville Curse, *203*
Graham, William A.: Amazing Howard Hughes, The, *445;* And I Alone Survived, *447;* Birds of Prey, *13;* Change of Habit, *479;* Deadly Encounter (1972), *34;* Doomsday Flight, The, *971;* Fugitive, The (TV Series), *523;* George Washington: The Forging of a Nation, *526;* Get Christie Love!, *55;* Gore Vidal's Billy The Kid, *1116;* Harry Tracy, *1119;* Last Days of Frank and Jesse James, *1125;* M.A.D.D.: Mothers Against Drunk Driving, *583;* Mr. Inside/Mr. Outside, *85;* Montana, *599;* Orphan Train, *615;* Proud Men, *1140;* Rage (1980), *633;* Return to the Blue Lagoon, *639;* Secrets of a Married Man, *651;* Supercarrier, *122;* Waterhole #3, *1163;* Where the Lilies Bloom, *216*
Grammatikor, Vladimir: Land of Faraway, The, *180*
Granier-Deferre, Pierre: Cat, The (Le Chat), *722;* French Detective, The, *738;* Widow Couderc, *803*
Grant, Brian: Love Kills, *993;* Sweet Poison, *123*
Grant, James Edward: Angel and the Badman, *1093*
Grant, Lee: Down and Out in America, *423;* Staying Together, *667;* Tell Me a Riddle, *678*
Grant, Michael: Fatal Attraction (1985), *975*
Grasshoff, Alex: Billion for Boris, A, *239*
Grau, Jorge: Blood Castle (1972), *815*
Grauman, Walter: Are You in the House Alone?, *953;* Lady in a Cage, *989;* Nightmare on the 13th Floor, *871;* Outrage!, *616;* Pleasure Palace, *623;* Scene of the Crime (1985), *1013;* 633 Squadron, *116*
Graver, Gary: Crossing the Line (1990), *492;* Evil Spirits, *839;* Moon in Scorpio, *599;* Party Camp, *354;* Roots of Evil, *109;* Trick or Treat (1982), *897*
Gray, Jerome: Traxx, *132*
Gray, John: Billy Galvin, *461;* Lost Capone, The, *580;* When He's Not a Stranger, *698*
Gray, Mike: Wavelength, *1088*
Greek, Janet: Spellbinder, *889*
Green, Alfred E.: Baby Face, *453;* Copacabana, *259;* Dangerous, *494;* Disraeli, *502;* Ella Cinders, *271;* Fabulous Dorseys, The, *916;* Four Faces West, *1114;* Jackie Robinson Story, The, *556;* Jolson Story, The, *926;* Mr. Winkle Goes to War, *334;* South of Pago Pago, *119;* Thoroughbreds Don't Cry, *210*
Green, Bruce Seth: Hunt for the Night Stalker, *546;* In Self Defense, *550;* Rags to Riches, *364;* Running Against Time, *1075*
Green, Guy: Diamond Head, *500;* Incredible Journey of Dr. Meg Laurel, The, *551;* Luther, *583;* Once Is Not Enough, *613;* Patch of Blue, A, *619;* Walk in the Spring Rain, A, *695*
Green, Joseph: Brain That Wouldn't Die, The, *1040*
Green, Terry: Cold Justice, *28*
Green, Walon: Hellstrom Chronicle, The, *426*
Greenaway, Peter: Belly of an Architect, The, *458;* Cook, the Thief, His Wife & Her Lover, The, *259;* Draughtman's Contract, The, *972;* Drowning by Numbers, *505;* Prospero's Books, *629;* Zed and Two Noughts, A, *709*
Greenburg, Richard Alan: Little Monsters, *1063*
Greene, Danford B.: Secret Diary of Sigmund Freud, The, *374*
Greene, David: After the Promise, *442;* Buster, *472;* Choice, The, *481;* Count of Monte Cristo, The (1975), *30;* Fatal Vision, *515;* Fire Birds, *49;* Friendly Fire, *522;* Gray Lady Down, *57;* Guardian, The (1984), *534;* Hard Country, *293;* In a Stranger's Hands, *985;* Madame Sin, *80;* Miles to Go, *594;* Penthouse, The, *1005;* Prototype, *1072;* Rehearsal for Murder, *1009;* Small Sacrifices, *660;* Triplecross, *399;* Vanishing Act, *693;* World War III, *141*
Greene, Herbert: Cosmic Man, The, *1043*
Greene, Martin: Dark Sanity, *829*
Greenspan, Bud: Wilma, *703*
Greenstands, Arthur: Stocks and Blondes, *668*
Greenwald, Maggie: Ballad of Little Jo, The, *1096;* Home Remedy, *300*
Greenwald, Robert: Burning Bed, The, *472;* Flatbed Annie and Sweetie Pie: Lady Truckers, *50;* Forgotten Prisoners, *520;* Hear no Evil, *982;* Shattered Spirits, *655;* Sweethearts' Dance, *675;* Xanadu, *948*
Greenwalt, David: Secret Admirer, *374*
Grefe, William: Death Curse of Tartu, *831;* Impulse (1974), *985;* Jaws of Death, The, *858;* Stanley, *890*
Gregg, Colin: We Think the World of You, *406*
Gremillon, Jean: Pattes Blanches (White Paws), *776;* Stormy Waters, *789*
Gremm, Wolf: Kamikaze 89, *751*
Gréville, Edmond: Liars, The, *760;* Princess Tam Tam, *778*
Greyson, John: Urinal, *692*
Gribble, Mike: Spike & Mike's Festival of Animation, *384*
Gries, Tom: Breakheart Pass, *1101;* Breakout, *19;* Connection (1973), *487;* Fools, *518;* Glass House, The, *528;* Greatest, The, *533;* Helter Skelter, *540;* Lady Ice, *989;* 100 Rifles, *1137;* QB VII, *631;* Will Penny, *1164*
Grieve, Andrew: Lorna Doone, *580;* Suspicion (1987), *1022*
Grieve, Ken: Adventures of Sherlock Holmes, The (Series), *950*
Griffi, Giuseppe Patroni: Collector's Item, *485;* Divine Nymph, The, *731;* Driver's Seat, The, *505*
Griffith, Charles B.: Dr. Heckyl and Mr. Hype, *266;* Eat My Dust, *43;* Smokey Bites the Dust, *382;* Up from the Depths, *899;* Wizard of the Lost Kingdom II, *1090*
Griffith, D. W.: Abraham Lincoln, *440;* Avenging Conscience, The, *811;* Battle of Elderbush Gulch, The/The Musketeers of Pig Alley, *1097;* Birth of a Nation, The, *462;* Broken Blossoms, *470;* D. W. Griffith Shorts Vol. 1–12, *493;* D. W. Griffith Triple Feature, *493;* Dream Street, *504;* Hearts of the World, *538;* Home, Sweet Home, *543;* Idol Dancer, The, *548;* Intolerance, *553;* Judith of Bethulia, *560;* Mother and the Law, The, *600;* Orphans of the Storm, *615;* Sally of the Sawdust, *647;* Sorrows of Satan, The, *663;* True Heart Susie, *688;* Way Down East, *697;* White Rose, The (1923), *700*
Griffith, Edward H.: Animal Kingdom, The, *448;* My Love for Yours, *340;* Sky's the Limit, The, *940;* Young and Willing, *708*
Griffiths, Mark: Cry in the Wild, A, *31;* Hardbodies, *293;* Hardbodies 2, *293;* Heroes Stand Alone, *61;* Running Hot, *645;* Ultraviolet, *133*
Grillo, Gary: American Justice, *4*
Grimaldi, Hugo: Human Duplicators, The, *854*
Grimm, Douglas K.: Laser Moon, *990*
Grindé, Nick: Before I Hang, *812;* Hitler—Dead or Alive, *542;* Man They Could Not Hang, The, *862;* Stone of Silver Creek, *1153*
Grint, Alan: Adventures of Sherlock Holmes, The (Series), *950;* Secret Garden, The (1987), *202*
Grinter, Brad F.: Blood Freak, *815;* Devil Rider!, *37;* Flesh Feast, *841*
Grissell, Wallace: King of the Congo, *72;* Manhunt of Mystery Island, *82;* Perils of the Darkest Jungle, *98;* Zorro's Black Whip, *1166*
Grissmer, John: Blood Rage, *815;* Scalpel, *883*
Grlic', Rajko: That Summer of White Roses, *680*

Grofe Jr., Ferde: Proud and the Damned, The, *1139*
Grosbard, Ulu: Falling in Love, *513;* Straight Time, *668;* Subject Was Roses, The, *671;* True Confessions, *1027*
Gross, Jerry: Girl on a Chain Gang, *55*
Gross, Larry: 3:15—The Moment of Truth, *128*
Gross, Yoram: Dot and the Bunny, *163;* Toby and the Koala Bear, *212*
Grossman, David: Frog, *168;* Joe Piscopo Live!, *310;* Yo-Yo Man, *415*
Grossman, Douglas: Hell High, *849*
Grossman, Sam: Van, The, *404*
Grosvenor, Charles: Once Upon a Forest, *192*
Grune, Karl: Street, The, *790*
Gruza, Jerzy: Alice (1981), *906*
Guenette, Robert: Here's Looking at You, Warner Brothers, *426;* Man Who Saw Tomorrow, The, *430*
Guercio, James William: Electra Glide in Blue, *43*
Guerra, Ruy: Erendira, *734;* Opera do Malandro, *774*
Guerrieri, Romolo: Final Executioner, The, *1051*
Guerrini, Mino: Mines of Kilimanjaro, *85*
Guest, Christopher: Attack of the 50-Foot Woman (1993), *1037;* Big Picture, The, *238*
Guest, Cliff: Disturbance, The, *834*
Guest, Val: Carry on Admiral, *251;* Casino Royale (1967), *252;* Day the Earth Caught Fire, The, *1044;* Enemy from Space, *1049;* Just William's Luck, *179;* Killer Force, *71;* Men of Sherwood Forest, *84;* Persuaders, The (TV Series), *98;* Quatermass Experiment, The, *1073;* Up the Creek (1958), *403;* When Dinosaurs Ruled the Earth, *1089*
Guillermin, John: Blue Max, The, *16;* Bridge at Remagen, The, *469;* Death on the Nile, *968;* El Condor, *1111;* King Kong (1976), *859;* King Kong Lives, *859;* Never Let Go, *604;* Sheena, *115;* Towering Inferno, The, *131;* Tracker, The, *1158;* Waltz of the Toreadors, *405*
Guiol, Fred L.: Going to Congress and Don't Park There, *288*
Guitry, Sacha: Napoleon (1955), *603;* Pearls of the Crown, The, *776*
Gumpel, David: Muppet Sing-Alongs, *189*
Guney, Yilmaz: Wall, The, *802*
Gunn, Gilbert: Cosmic Monsters, The, *825*
Guralnick, Robert: Portfolio, *624*
Gurney Jr, Robert: Terror from the Year 5,000, *1082*
Guthrie, Tyrone: Oedipus Rex (1957), *610*
Gutman, Nathaniel: Deadline (1987), *497;* Linda, *992*
Guttfreund, Andre: Femme Fatale, *976*
Guzman, Claudio: Hostage Tower, The, *64;* Willa, *703*
Gyllenhaal, Stephen: Certain Fury, *24;* Dangerous Woman, A, *494;* Killing in a Small Town, *564;* Paris Trout, *618;* Promised a Miracle, *629;* Question of Faith, *632;* Waterland, *697*
Gyongyossy, Imre: Revolt of Job, The, *781*
Haas, Charles: Girls Town, *55;* New Adventures of Charlie Chan, The (TV Series), *1000;* Outer Limits, The (TV Series), *1069;* Platinum High School, *623*
Haas, Philip: Music of Chance, The, *601*
Hachuel, Herve: Immortal Sins, *855;* Last of Philip Banter, The, *991*
Hackford, Taylor: Against All Odds, *951;* Bound by Honor, *467;* Chuck Berry Hail! Hail! Rock 'n' Roll, *421;* Everybody's All-American, *511;* Idolmaker, The, *924;* Officer and a Gentleman, An, *611;* White Nights (1985), *700*
Haedrick, Rolf: Among the Cinders, *446*
Haffner, Craig: Civil War Journal, *421*
Hafter, Petra: Demon in My View, A, *832*
Hagen, Ross: B.O.R.N., *811*
Haggard, Mark: First Nudie Musical, The, *917*
Haggard, Piers: Back Home, *147;* Blood on Satan's Claw, *815;* Fiendish Plot of Dr. Fu Manchu, The, *276;* Fulfillment, *523;* Lifeforce Experiment, The, *1063;* Quatermass Conclusion, The, *1072;* Return to Treasure Island, *199;* Summer Story, A, *673;* Venom, *900*
Hagman, Larry: Son of Blob (Beware! The Blob), *888*
Hagmann, Stuart: Strawberry Statement, The, *670;* Tarantulas—The Deadly Cargo, *892*
Haid, Charles: Cooperstown, *488;* Iron Will, *67;* Nightman, The, *1001*
Haig, Roul: Okefenokee, *93*
Haines, Fred: Steppenwolf, *667*
Haines, Randa: Children of a Lesser God, *480;* Doctor, The, *502;* Jilting of Granny Weatherall, The, *558;* Wrestling Ernest Hemingway, *707*
Haines, Richard W.: Alien Space Avenger, *1035;* Class of Nuke 'em High, *824;* Splatter University, *889*
Hakola, Marikka: Art Com Video (Vol. 1–3), *1037*
Halas, John: Animal Farm, *448;* Masters of Animation, *430*
Haldane, Don: Reincarnate, The, *879*
Hale, William: Murder in Texas, *998;* Murder of Mary Phagan, The, *600;* One Shoe Makes it Murder, *1003;* Red Alert, *104;* S.O.S. Titanic, *646*
Haley Jr., Jack: Love Machine, The, *581;* That's Dancing, *436;* That's Entertainment, *436;* Wonderful Wizard of Oz, The: The Making of a Movie Classic, *438*
Halicki, H. B.: Gone in 60 Seconds, *56;* Junkman, The, *70*
Hall, Alexander: Because You're Mine, *908;* Doctor Takes a Wife, The, *266;* Forever Darling, *279;* Goin' to Town, *287;* Great Lover, The, *289;* Here Comes Mr. Jordan, *296;* I Am the Law, *547;* Little Miss Marker (1934), *182*
Hall, Anthony Michael: Hail Caesar, *292*
Hall, Gary Skeen: Prime Time Murder, *100*
Hall, Godfrey: Honor and Glory, *64;* Undefeatable, *134*
Hall, Ivan: Kill and Kill Again, *71;* Kill or Be Killed, *71*
Hall, Kenneth J.: Evil Spawn, *839*
Hall, Mark: Jerry Lee Lewis—I Am What I Am, *428;* Wind in the Willows, The (1983), *218*
Hall, Peter: Homecoming, The (1973), *543;* Midsummer Night's Dream, A (1968), *332;* Orpheus Descending, *615*
Haller, Daniel: Buck Rogers in the 25th Century, *1040;* Die, Monster, Die!, *834;* Dunwich Horror, The, *838;* Follow That Car, *51;* Paddy, *353*
Hallowell, Todd: Love or Money?, *323*
Hallstrom, Lasse: My Life as a Dog, *769;* Once Around, *349;* What's Eating Gilbert Grape?, *408*
Halperin, Victor: Revolt of the Zombies, *881;* White Zombie, *903*
Halvorson, Gary: Adventures in Wonderland, *143;* Country Girl, The (1982), *489*
Hamer, Robert: Dead of Night (1945), *830;* Detective, The (1954), *970;* Kind Hearts and Coronets, *313;* To Paris with Love, *397*
Hamilton, David: Bilitis, *717;* Tendres Cousines, *793*
Hamilton, Guy: Battle of Britain, *9;* Colditz Story, The, *485;* Devil's Disciple, The, *264;* Diamonds Are Forever, *38;* Evil under the Sun, *973;* Force Ten from Navarone, *51;* Funeral in Berlin, *979;* Goldfinger, *56;* Live and Let Die, *78;* Man with the Golden Gun, The, *81;* Mirror Crack'd, The, *996;* Remo Williams: The Adventure Begins, *105*
Hamilton, Strathford: Betrayal of the Dove, *954;* Blueberry Hill, *465;* Diving In, *502*
Hammer, Robert: Don't Answer the Phone, *836*
Hammond, Peter: Dark Angel, The, *966;* Inspector Morse (TV Series), *986*
Hampton, Robert (Riccardo Freda): Ghost, The (1963), *845;* Horrible Dr. Hichcock, The, *851*
Hanbury, Victor: Hotel Reserve, *544*
Hancock, John: Bang the Drum Slowly, *455;* California Dreaming, *474;* Let's Scare Jessica to Death, *860;* Prancer, *197;* Steal the Sky, *667;* Weeds, *697*
Hand, David: Bambi, *148;* Snow White and the Seven Dwarfs (1938), *205*
Handler, Ken: Delivery Boys, *263*
Handley, Alan: Alice Through the Looking Glass (1966), *906*
Hanks, Tom: Fallen Angels, *513*

ana, William: Droopy and Company, *164;* Have Picnic sket, Will Travel, *173;* Hey There, It's Yogi Bear, *174;* sons: The Movie, *178;* Man Called Flintstone, A, *185;* Tom d Jerry Cartoon Festivals (Volume One), *212;* Tom and Jerry rtoon Festivals (Volume Two), *212;* Tom and Jerry Cartoon stivals (Volume Three), *212;* Tom and Jerry On Parade, *212;* m & Jerry's Cartoon Cavalcade, *212;* Tom and Jerry's Comic pers, *212;* Tom & Jerry's Festival of Fun, *212;* Tom and ry's 50th Birthday Classics, *213;* Tom and Jerry's 50th thday Classics II, *213;* Tom and Jerry's 50th Birthday ssics III, *213*

nnam, Ken: Sunday Too Far Away, *673*

nnant, Brian: Time Guardian, The, *1084*

noka, Izhak: Red Nights, *637*

nsel, Marion: Dust, *506*

nsen, Ed: Bikini Carwash Company, The, *239;* Party Plane, *5;* Robo C.H.I.C., *1074*

nson, Curtis: Bad Influence, *953;* Bedroom Window, The, *4;* Children of Times Square, The, *481;* Hand That Rocks the adle, The, *981;* Losin' It, *321*

nson, David W.: Night of the Bloody Transplant, *869*

nson, John: Northern Lights, *609;* Wild Rose, *702*

rdeway, Ben: Best of Warner Brothers, Vol. 2, *150;* lden Age of Looney Toons, The: 1930s Musicals, *170*

rdwicke, Cedric: Forever and a Day, *520*

rdy, Joseph: Love's Savage Fury, *582;* Users, The, *692*

rdy, Robin: Fantasist, The, *975;* Wicker Man, The, *903*

rdy, Rod: Rio Diablo, *1145;* Sara Dane, *648;* Thirst, *895*

re, David: Strapless, *670;* Wetherby, *698*

rgrove, Dean: Dear Detective, *968*

rk, Tsui: Aces Go Places (1–3) (Aka Mad Mission 1–3), *0;* Better Tomorrow 3, A: Love And Death In Saigon, *717;* king Opera Blues, *776;* Warriors from the Magic Mountain, *2;* We're Going to Eat You!, *902*

rlan, Veidt: Jud Suss, *750*

rlin, Renny: Adventures of Ford Fairlane, The, *2;* Born nerican, *17;* Cliffhanger, *26;* Die Hard 2: Die Harder, *39;* ghtmare on Elm Street 4, A: The Dream Master, *871;* Prison, *6*

rlow, John: Candles at Nine, *820*

rman, Hugh: Barney Bear Cartoon Festival, *148*

rmon, Robert: Hitcher, The, *850;* Nowhere to Run (1993), *?*

rrington, Curtis: Dead Don't Die, The, *830;* Devil Dog: The ound of Hell, *833;* Mata Hari (1985), *83;* Night Tide, *606;* anet of Blood, *1070;* Ruby (1977), *881;* What's the Matter th Helen?, *902;* Who Slew Auntie Roo?, *903*

rrington, Rowdy: Striking Distance, *121*

rris, Damian: Deceived, *969;* Discovery Program, *501;* chel Papers, *364*

rris, Denny: Silent Scream, *886*

rris, Frank: Kill Point, *71;* Low Blow, *79;* Patriot, *97*

rris, Harry: Alice in Wonderland (1985), *145;* Alice rough the Looking Glass (1985), *145*

rris, Jack H.: Unkissed Bride, *403*

rris, James B.: Bedford Incident, The, *457;* Boiling Point, *;* Cop, *29;* Fast-Walking, *515;* Some Call It Loving, *662*

rris, Leslie: Just Another Girl on the I.R.T, *561*

rris, Paul: Red Skelton: A Career of Laughter, *433*

rris, Peter: Children's Songs and Stories with the uppets, *158*

rris, Richard: Hero, The, *540*

rris, Trent: Rubin & Ed, *371*

rris Jr., Wendell B.: Chameleon Street, *478*

rrison Jr., Hal: Pony Express Rider, *1139*

rrison, John: Tales from the Darkside, The Movie, *892*

rrison, John Kent: Beautiful Dreamers, *457*

rrison, Jules: Exterminators of the Year 3000, *1050*

rrison, Ken: 1918, *607;* On Valentine's Day, *612*

rrison, Marguerite: Grass, *425*

rrison, Paul: House of Seven Corpses, The, *853*

Harry, Lee: Silent Night, Deadly Night Part 2, *886;* Street Soldiers, *121*

Hart, Bruce: Sooner or Later, *663*

Hart, Derek: Backstage at the Kirov, *419*

Hart, Harvey: Beverly Hills Madam, *460;* East of Eden (1982), *506;* Fortune and Men's Eyes, *520;* High Country, The, *61;* Party Animal, *354;* Prince of Central Park, The, *197;* Pyx, The, *1008;* Shoot (1976), *115;* Standing Tall, *1153;* Stone Fox, The, *207;* Utilities, *404*

Hart, William S.: Hell's Hinges, *1120;* Tumbleweeds, *1159*

Hartford, Kenneth: Hell Squad (1985), *60*

Hartl, Carl: Mozart Story, The, *931*

Hartley, Hal: Simple Men, *379;* Surviving Desire, *389;* Trust, *689;* Unbelievable Truth, The, *691*

Hartman, Don: Every Girl Should Be Married, *273;* Holiday Affair, *542;* It's a Big Country, *308;* Mr. Imperium, *931*

Harvey, Anthony: Disappearance of Aimee, The, *970;* Eagle's Wing, *1111;* Grace Quigley, *289;* Lion in Winter, The, *576;* Players, *623;* Richard's Things, *640;* Svengali (1983), *674;* They Might Be Giants, *1023*

Harvey, Gail: Cold Sweat (1993), *28*

Harvey, Herk: Carnival of Souls, *821*

Harvey, Rupert: Critters 4, *827*

Hasburgh, Patrick: Aspen Extreme, *451*

Hashimoto, Kohji: Godzilla 1985, *846*

Haskin, Byron: Armored Command, *6;* Captain Sinbad, *156;* Denver and Rio Grande, The, *1108;* From the Earth to the Moon, *1053;* His Majesty O'Keefe, *62;* Long John Silver, *78;* Naked Jungle, The, *88;* Outer Limits, The (TV Series), *1069;* Treasure Island (1950), *214;* War of the Worlds, The, *1088*

Hassani, Linda: Inside Out (1992), *1058;* Inside Out 2, *1059*

Hata, Masanori: Adventures of Milo and Otis, The, *144;* Little Nemo: Adventures in Slumberland, *183*

Hathaway, Henry: Buffalo Stampede, *1102;* Call Northside 777, *959;* Circus World, *482;* Dark Corner, The, *495;* Desert Fox, The, *37;* Five Card Stud, *1113;* Go West, Young Man, *287;* How the West Was Won, *1122;* Johnny Apollo, *559;* Kiss of Death, *566;* Last Safari, *570;* Legend of the Lost, *572;* Lives of a Bengal Lancer, The, *78;* Man of the Forest, *1132;* Nevada Smith, *1135;* Niagara, *1000;* North to Alaska, *1136;* Prince Valiant, *100;* Racers, The, *632;* Raid on Rommel, *103;* Rawhide (1951), *1141;* Real Glory, The, *103;* Seven Thieves, *653;* Sons of Katie Elder, The, *1151;* Sundown (1941), *673;* 13 Rue Madeleine, *127;* To the Last Man, *1157;* True Grit, *1159;* Wing and a Prayer, A, *140*

Hathcock, Bob: Ducktales: The Movie—Treasure of the Lost Lamp, *164*

Hathcock, Jeff: Mark of the Beast, The, *863*

Hatton, Maurice: American Roulette, *4*

Hauser, Wings: Art of Dying, The, *953;* Living to Die, *993*

Hawks, Howard: Air Force, *3;* Ball of Fire, *231;* Barbary Coast, The, *455;* Big Sky, The, *1098;* Big Sleep, The (1946), *955;* Bringing Up Baby, *246;* Ceiling Zero, *24;* Come and Get It, *28;* Criminal Code, The, *491;* El Dorado, *1111;* Gentlemen Prefer Blondes, *284;* Hatari!, *59;* His Girl Friday, *297;* I Was a Male War Bride, *304;* Land of the Pharaohs, *568;* Man's Favorite Sport?, *328;* Monkey Business (1952), *336;* Only Angels Have Wings, *95;* Outlaw, The, *1137;* Red Line 7000, *104;* Red River, *1141;* Rio Bravo, *1145;* Rio Lobo, *1145;* Scarface (1932), *112;* Sergeant York, *113;* Song Is Born, A, *940;* To Have and Have Not, *130;* Today We Live, *685;* Twentieth Century, *401;* Viva Villa!, *1162*

Hawley, Peter: Victimless Crimes, *1030*

Hay, Caroline: Mother Goose Video Treasury Vol. I–IV, *189*

Haydn, Richard: Dear Wife, *263;* Mr. Music, *931*

Hayers, Sidney: Bananas Boat, The, *232;* Circus of Horrors, *824;* King Arthur, The Young Warlord, *72;* Philip Marlowe, Private Eye: Finger Man, *1005;* Revenge (1971), *1010;* Seekers, The, *651*

Hayes, John: End of the World, *1049;* Grave of the Vampire, *847*

Hayes, John Patrick: Farmer's Other Daughter, The, *274*

Hayes, Robert: Phoenix the Warrior, *1070*
Hayman, David: Hawk, The, *982*
Haynes, Todd: Poison, *624*
Hazan, Jack: Rude Boy, *938*
Head, Helaine: You Must Remember This, *708*
Healey, Laurette: Elvis Files, The, *423*
Heap, Jonathan: Benefit of a Doubt, *954*
Heath, Robert: Hugh Hefner: Once Upon a Time, *427*
Heavener, David: Outlaw Force, *96;* Prime Target, *100*
Hecht, Ben: Actors and Sin, *441;* Angels Over Broadway, *448;* Scoundrel, The, *374;* Specter of the Rose, The, *1019*
Heckerling, Amy: Fast Times at Ridgemont High, *274;* Johnny Dangerously, *311;* Look Who's Talking, *320;* Look Who's Talking Too, *321;* National Lampoon's European Vacation, *342*
Hedden, Rob: Friday the 13th, Part VIII: Jason Takes Manhattan, *844*
Hedman, Trine: Famous Five Get into Trouble, The, *166*
Heerman, Victor: Animal Crackers, *227*
Heffron, Richard T.: Broken Angel, *470;* Foolin' Around, *278;* Futureworld, *1053;* I, the Jury, *985;* I Will Fight No More Forever, *1122;* Napoleon and Josephine: A Love Story, *603;* Newman's Law, *90;* North and South, *608;* Outlaw Blues, *352;* Pancho Barnes, *617;* Rockford Files, The (TV Series), *108;* Rumor of War, A, *109;* Samaritan: The Mitch Snyder Story, *647;* Tagget, *124;* Whale for the Killing, A, *698*
Hegedus, Chris: War Room, The, *438*
Heifits, Josef: Lady With the Dog, The, *755*
Heisler, Stuart: Along Came Jones, *1093;* Chain Lightning, *478;* Glass Key, The, *980;* Hitler, *542;* I Died a Thousand Times, *65;* Island of Desire, *555;* Lone Ranger, The (1956), *1129;* Smash-Up: The Story of a Woman, *661;* Star, The, *665;* Tokyo Joe, *130;* Tulsa, *689*
Hellbron, Olle: Brothers Lionheart, The, *152;* Pippi Longstocking, Pippi in the South Seas, Pippi Goes on Board, Pippi on the Run, *195*
Hellman, Jerome: Promises in the Dark, *629*
Hellman, Monte: Cockfighter, *27;* Right to Fury, *51;* Gunfire, *1117;* Ride in the Whirlwind, *1143;* Shooting, The, *1149*
Hellman, Oliver: Desperate Moves, *264*
Helpern Jr., David: Something Short of Paradise, *383*
Hemecker, Ralph: Dead On, *967*
Hemion, Dwight: Color Me Barbra, *912;* Jackie Mason on Broadway, *309;* My Name Is Barbra, *932*
Hemmings, David: Dark Horse, *161;* Just a Gigolo, *561;* Key to Rebecca, The, *70;* Quantum Leap (TV Series), *1072;* Treasure of the Yankee Zephyr, *132*
Henabery, Joseph E.: Leather Burners, The, *1128;* Man from Painted Post, The, *327*
Henderson, Clark: Circle of Fear, *26;* Primary Target, *627;* Saigon Commandos, *110;* Warlords of Hell, *137*
Henderson, John: Borrowers, The, *152*
Henenlotter, Frank: Basket Case, *811;* Basket Case 2, *811;* Basket Case 3: The Progeny, *811;* Brain Damage, *818;* Frankenhooker, *842*
Henkel, Peter: Three Bullets for a Long Gun, *1156*
Henley, Jim: Junior, *858*
Henman, Graham: Doctor Duck's Super Secret All-Purpose Sauce, *266*
Henreid, Paul: Battle Shock, *812;* Dead Ringer, *967*
Henry, Buck: First Family, *277;* Heaven Can Wait (1978), *295*
Henson, Brian: Muppet Christmas Carol, The, *189*
Henson, Jim: Dark Crystal, The, *1044;* Great Muppet Caper, The, *171;* Hey Cinderella!, *174;* Labyrinth, *1061*
Henzell, Perry: Harder They Come, The, *922*
Herbert, Henry: Emily, *509*
Herbert, Martin: Miami Horror, *1066;* Strange Shadows in an Empty Room, *121*
Herek, Stephen: Bill and Ted's Excellent Adventure, *239;* Critters, *827;* Don't Tell Mom the Babysitter's Dead, *267;* Mighty Ducks, The, *187;* Three Musketeers, The (1993), *129*
Herman, Albert: Clutching Hand, The, *27;* Cowboy and the Bandit, *1106;* Delinquent Daughters, *499;* Lucky Boots, *1130;* Take Me Back to Oklahoma, *1154;* Warning Shadows (1933), *1030;* Whispering Shadow, The, *138*
Herman, Jean: Honor Among Thieves, *63*
Herman, Mark: Blame It on the Bellboy, *240*
Hermosillo, Jaime Humberto: Donna Herlinda and Her Son, *731;* Mary My Dearest, *766*
Heroux, Denis: Uncanny, The, *899*
Herrier, Mark: Popcorn, *876*
Herrington, Rowdy: Gladiator, *528;* Jack's Back, *987;* Road House (1989), *107*
Herron, W. Blake: Skin Art, *659*
Hershman, Joel: Hold Me, Thrill Me, Kiss Me, *298*
Herskovitz, Marshall: Jack the Bear, *556*
Herwitz, Samuel: On the Make, *612*
Herz, Michael: First Turn-on, The, *277;* Sgt. Kabukiman N.Y.P.D., *114;* Stuck on You, *387;* Sugar Cookies, *672;* Toxic Avenger, The, *897;* Toxic Avenger Part II, The, *897;* Toxic Avenger Part III: The Last Temptation of Toxie, The, *897;* Troma's War, *132;* Waitress, *405*
Herzfeld, John: Casualties of Love: The Long Island Lolita Story, *476;* Father's Revenge, A, *515;* Preppie Murder, The, *626;* Two of a Kind (1983), *402*
Herzog, Werner: Aguirre: Wrath of God, *711;* Every Man for Himself and God Against All, *735;* Fitzcarraldo, *737;* Heart of Glass, *743;* Herdsmen of the Sun, *426;* Stroszek, *790;* Where the Green Ants Dream, *803;* Woyzeck, *805*
Hess, David: To All a Good Night, *895*
Hess, Jon: Excessive Force, *45;* Lawless Land, *1062;* Watchers, *1088*
Hessler, Gordon: Cry of the Banshee, *827;* Girl on a Swing, The, *980;* Golden Voyage of Sinbad, The, *1054;* Journey of Honor, *69;* Kiss Meets the Phantom of the Park, *859;* Misfit Brigade, The, *85;* Murders in the Rue Morgue (1971), *867;* Oblong Box, The, *872;* Out on Bail, *96;* Rage of Honor, *103;* Scream and Scream Again, *883;* Tales of the Unexpected, *1022*
Heston, Charlton: Antony and Cleopatra (1973), *450;* Mother Lode, *87*
Heston, Fraser: Crucifer of Blood, *964;* Needful Things, *868;* Treasure Island (1990), *214*
Hewitt, David L.: Bloodsuckers, The, *816;* Journey to the Center of Time, *1060;* Wizard of Mars, The, *1090*
Hewitt, Jean: Blood of Dracula's Castle, *815*
Hewitt, Paul: Wild Palms, *1089*
Hewitt, Pete: Bill and Ted's Bogus Journey, *239*
Hewitt, Rod: Verne Miller, *135*
Heyes, Douglas: Powderkeg, *1139;* Treasures of the Twilight Zone, *1085;* Twilight Zone, The (TV Series), *1086*
Heynemann, Laurent: Birgit Haas Must Be Killed, *718*
Hibbs, Jesse: To Hell and Back, *130*
Hickenlooper, George: Hearts of Darkness, *425*
Hickey, Bruce: Necropolis, *868*
Hickox, Anthony: Full Eclipse, *844;* Hellraiser 3: Hell On Earth, *850;* Sundown (1990), *891;* Warlock: The Armageddon, *901;* Waxwork, *902;* Waxwork II: Lost in Time, *902*
Hickox, Douglas: Blackout (1985), *956;* Brannigan, *18;* Entertaining Mr. Sloane, *271;* Hound of the Baskervilles, The (1983), *984;* Mistral's Daughter, *597;* Theatre of Blood, *894;* Zulu Dawn, *142*
Higgin, Howard: Hell's House, *61;* High Voltage, *62;* Painted Desert, The, *1138;* Racketeer, *102*
Higgins, Colin: Best Little Whorehouse in Texas, The, *908;* Foul Play, *280;* Nine to Five, *345*
High, David: Fisher Price Someday Me Series Vol. I: It's a Dog's Life, *167*
Hiken, Nat: Car 54 Where Are You? (TV Series), *250*
Hill, Bob: Cyclone Ranger, *1107*
Hill, George: Min and Bill, *594*
Hill, George Roy: Butch Cassidy and the Sundance Kid, *1103;* Funny Farm, *282;* Great Waldo Pepper, The, *57;* Hawaii, *537;* Little Drummer Girl, The, *992;* Little Romance, A, *319;*

iod of Adjustment, 356; Slap Shot, 380; Slaughterhouse
, 1077; Sting, The, 120; Thoroughly Modern Millie, 945;
's in the Attic, 687; World According to Garp, The, 706;
rld of Henry Orient, The, 414

l, Jack: Big Bird Cage, The, 12; Chamber of Fear, 822;
fy, 27; Foxy Brown, 52; Macabre Serenade, 861; Sinister
asion, 886; Snake People, 888; Spider Baby, 889

l, James: Belstone Fox, The, 149; Black Beauty (1971),
/; Born Free, 152; Christian the Lion, 158; Corrupt Ones,
, 29; Seaside Swingers, 938; Study in Terror, A, 1021

l, Robert: Adventures of Tarzan, The, 2; Blake of Scotland
d, 15; Feud of the Trail, 1112; Flash Gordon: Mars Attacks
World (a.k.a. Trip to Mars; Deadly Ray From Mars, The),
52; Tarzan the Fearless, 125

l, Walter: Another 48 Hrs., 5; Brewster's Millions (1985),
5; Crossroads, 912; Driver, The, 42; Extreme Prejudice, 45;
Hrs., 279; Geronimo: An American Legend, 1115; Hard
nes, 59; Johnny Handsome, 69; Long Riders, The, 1130;
d Heat (1988), 104; Southern Comfort, 119; Streets of Fire,
/; Tales from the Crypt (Series), 892; Trespass, 132;
arriors, The (1979), 137

ller, Arthur: Addams Family, The (TV Series), 222;
nericanization of Emily, The, 226; Author! Author!, 230;
pe, The, 452; Hospital, The, 301; In-Laws, The, 305; Lonely
y, The, 320; Love Story, 582; Making Love, 586; Man of La
ancha, 930; Married to It, 589; Miracle of the White Stallions,
7; Nightwing, 871; Out of Towners, The, 352; Outrageous
rtune, 352; Plaza Suite, 358; Popi, 360; Promise Her
ything, 362; Romantic Comedy, 370; See No Evil, Hear No
l, 375; Silver Streak (1976), 379; Taking Care of Business,
0; Teachers, 391; Tobruk, 130; Wheeler Dealers, The, 409

llman, David Michael: Brothers of the Wilderness, 471;
rangeness, The, 890

llman, William Byron: Double Exposure (1982), 971

lls, David: Ator: The Fighting Eagle, 1037; Blade Master,
e, 15; Quest for the Mighty Sword, 1073

llyer, Lambert: Dracula's Daughter, 837; Fighting Code,
12; Forbidden Trail, 1113; Hatbox Mystery, The, 982;
visible Ray, The, 857; Narrow Trail, The, 1135; Shock, The
923), 656; South of the Rio Grande, 1151; Sundown Rider,
e, 1153; Sundown Riders, 1153; Three-Word Brand, The,
57

lton, Arthur: Cat Women of the Moon, 1041;
sadventures of Buster Keaton, The, 332; Return of Jesse
mes, The, 1142

lton-Jacobs, Lawrence: Quiet Fire, 102

ltzik, Robert: Sleepaway Camp, 887

nton, David: Making of a Legend—*Gone With the Wind*,
9

ppolyte, Alexander Gregory: Animal Instincts, 952; Body
Influence, 958; Carnal Crimes, 959; Mirror Images, 996;
rror Images II, 996; Night Rhythms, 1001; Secret Games,
1; Sins of the Night, 1017

rano, Toshihiro: Dangaio, 728; Iczer-One, Vols. 1–4, 1057;
mpire Princess Miyu, 799

roaki, Gooda: Bubblegum Crisis—Vols. 1–8, 720

rokawa, Kazuyuki: Lensman, 1062

roki, Hayashi: Bubblegum Crisis—Vols. 1–8, 720

roshi, Ishiodori: Bubblegum Crash, Vols. 1–3, 720

roya, Oohira: Riding Bean, 781

royuki, Fukushima: Bubblegum Crash, Vols. 1–3, 720;
n Little Gall Force/Scramble Wars, 793

royuki, Kitazume: Genesis Survivor Gaiarth: Stage 1, 1054

rsch, Bettina: Munchies, 867

rschman, Ray: Plutonium Baby, 875

rsen, Steve: Best of America's Funniest Home Videos, The,
35

scott, Leslie S.: Triumph of Sherlock Holmes, The, 1027

tchcock, Alfred: Alfred Hitchcock's Bon Voyage and
venture Malgache, 711; Alfred Hitchcock Presents (TV
eries), 951; Birds, The, 813; Blackmail (1929), 956;
hampagne, 479; Dial M for Murder, 970; Easy Virtue, 507; Family Plot, 975; Foreign Correspondent, 978; Frenzy, 979; I Confess, 984; Jamaica Inn, 556; Juno and the Paycock, 561; Lady Vanishes, The (1938), 990; Lifeboat, 992; Lodger, The, 993; Man Who Knew Too Much, The (1934), 995; Man Who Knew Too Much, The (1955), 995; Manxman, The, 588; Marnie, 995; Mr. and Mrs. Smith, 333; Murder, 998; North by Northwest, 1002; Notorious, 1002; Number 17, 1002; Paradine Case, The, 1004; Psycho, 877; Rear Window, 1009; Rebecca, 1009; Rich and Strange, 639; Ring, The, 640; Rope, 1011; Sabotage, 1011; Saboteur, 1011; Secret Agent, The, 1013; Shadow of a Doubt, 1014; Spellbound, 1019; Stage Fright, 1019; Strangers on a Train, 1020; Suspicion (1941), 1022; Thirty-Nine Steps, The (1935), 1024; To Catch a Thief, 1025; Topaz, 1026; Torn Curtain, 1026; Trouble with Harry, The, 399; Under Capricorn, 1028; Vertigo, 1029; Waltzes from Vienna, 406; Wrong Man, The (1956), 1033; Young and Innocent, 1033

Hittleman, Carl K.: Kentucky Rifle, 1124

Hitzig, Rupert: Backstreet Dreams, 454; Night Visitor (1989), 1001

Hively, Jack B.: Adventures of Huckleberry Finn, The (1978), 144; California Gold Rush, 1103; Four Jacks and a Jill, 918; Panama Lady, 353

Hobbs, Lyndall: Back to the Beach, 907

Hobin, Bill: Judy Garland and Friends, 926

Hoblit, Gregory: Roe vs. Wade, 642

Hochberg, Victoria: Jacob I Have Loved, 556; Sweet 15, 674

Hodges, Mike: Black Rainbow, 955; Flash Gordon, 1052; Florida Straits, 51; Hitchhiker (Series), The, 850; Morons from Outer Space, 337; Prayer for the Dying, A, 1007; Pulp, 363; Terminal Man, The, 893

Hodi, Jeno: Deadly Obsession, 831

Hodson, Christopher: Partners in Crime (TV Series), 1004

Hoeger, Mark: Little Match Girl, The (1983), 182

Hoey, Michael: Navy vs. the Night Monsters, The, 868

Hoffman, Herman: Invisible Boy, The, 1059; It's a Dog's Life, 177

Hoffman, Jerzy: Deluge, The (Potop), 729

Hoffman, Michael: Promised Land, 629; Restless Natives, 366; Soapdish, 382; Some Girls, 382

Hoffman, Peter: Valentino Returns, 693

Hofts, Tamar Simon: Allnighter, The, 225

Hofmeyr, Gray: Light in the Jungle, The, 575

Hofsiss, Jack: Cat on a Hot Tin Roof (1985), 477; Elephant Man, The (1982), 508; I'm Dancing As Fast As I Can, 549; Oldest Living Graduate, The, 611

Hogan, James: Arrest Bulldog Drummond, 6; Bulldog Drummond Escapes, 20; Bulldog Drummond's Bride, 20; Bulldog Drummond's Peril, 20; Bulldog Drummond's Secret Police, 21; Final Extra, The, 977

Holbit, Gregory: L.A. Law, 567

Holcomb, Rod: Captain America (1979), 22; Cartier Affair, The, 252; Chains of Gold, 478; China Beach (TV Series), 481; Red Light Sting, The, 636; Royce, 109; Stark, 119

Holender, Adam: Twisted, 1028; Twisted: A Step Beyond Insanity, 690

Holland, Agnieszka: Angry Harvest, 713; Europa, Europa, 735; Olivier, Olivier, 773; Secret Garden, The (1993), 202; To Kill a Priest, 684

Holland, Savage Steve: Better Off Dead, 237; How I Got into College, 302; One Crazy Summer, 349

Holland, Todd: Wizard, The, 218

Holland, Tom: Child's Play, 823; Fatal Beauty, 46; Fright Night, 844; Temp, The, 893

Hollander, Eli: Out, 96

Holleb, Alan: School Spirit, 374

Holloway, Douglas: Fast Money, 46

Holmes, Ben: Maid's Night Out, The, 326; Saint in New York, The, 1012

Holmes, Fred: Dakota (1988), 493; Harley, 536

Holt, Seth: Scream of Fear, 1013

Holzberg, Roger: Midnight Crossing, 84

Holzman, Allan: Forbidden World, *842;* Intimate Stranger, *986;* Out of Control, *352;* Programmed to Kill, *1072*
Honda, Inoshiro: Dagora, the Space Monster, *1044;* Ghidrah, the Three-Headed Monster, *845;* Godzilla, King of the Monsters, *846;* Godzilla vs. Monster Zero, *846;* Godzilla vs. Mothra, *846;* Godzilla's Revenge, *847;* Gorath, *847;* H-Man, The, *848;* Half Human, *848;* Human Vapor, The, *1057;* King Kong vs. Godzilla, *859;* Mothra, *1067;* Mysterians, The, *1067;* Rodan, *1075;* Terror of Mechagodzilla, *894;* Varan, the Unbelievable, *900;* War of the Gargantuas, *1088*
Hong, Elliot: They Call Me Bruce?, *393*
Hong, Hwa I.: Dynamo, *42*
Honthaner, Ron: House on Skull Mountain, *853*
Hook, Harry: Kitchen Toto, The, *566;* Last of His Tribe, The, *570;* Lord of the Flies (1989), *579*
Hooker, Ted: Crucible of Terror, *827*
Hooks, Kevin: Heat Wave, *539;* Murder Without Motive, *601;* Passenger 57, *97;* Roots—The Gift, *644;* Strictly Business, *387;* Vietnam War Story, *694*
Hool, Lance: Missing in Action 2: The Beginning, *85;* Steel Dawn, *1080*
Hooper, Tobe: Eaten Alive, *838;* Funhouse, The, *845;* I'm Dangerous Tonight, *855;* Invaders from Mars (1986), *1059;* Lifeforce, *1063;* Poltergeist, *875;* Salem's Lot, *882;* Spontaneous Combustion, *889;* Texas Chainsaw Massacre, The, *894;* Texas Chainsaw Massacre 2, The, *894*
Hoover, Claudia: Double Exposure (1993), *971*
Hopkins, Arthur: His Double Life, *297*
Hopkins, John: Torment, *1026*
Hopkins, Stephen: Blown Away (1994), *16;* Dangerous Game, *965;* Judgment Night, *69;* Nightmare on Elm Street 5: The Dream Child, *871;* Predator 2, *1071*
Hopper, Dennis: Backtrack, *454;* Chasers, *254;* Colors, *485;* Easy Rider, *506;* Hot Spot, *544;* Last Movie, The, *570*
Hopper, Jerry: Addams Family, The (TV Series), *222;* Fugitive, The (TV Series), *523;* Madron, *1131;* Pony Express, *1139*
Horian, Richard: Student Confidential, *387*
Horn, Leonard: Hunter (1971), *65;* Outer Limits, The (TV Series), *1069*
Hornady, Jeffrey: Shout (1991), *939*
Horne, James W.: All Over Town, *224;* Bohemian Girl, The, *243;* Bonnie Scotland, *243;* College, *257;* Green Archer, *981;* Holt of the Secret Service, *63;* Laurel and Hardy Classics, Volume 4, *316;* Laurel and Hardy Classics, Volume 6, *316;* Laurel and Hardy Classics, Volume 7, *316;* Laurel and Hardy Classics, Volume 8, *316;* Laurel and Hardy Classics, Volume 9, *316;* Laurel and Hardy on the Lam, *317;* Way Out West, *406*
Horner, Harry: Beware, My Lovely, *955;* New Faces, *933;* Red Planet Mars, *1074*
Horton, Peter: Amazon Women on the Moon, *225*
Horvath, Imre: Acts of Violence, *418*
Hoskins, Bob: Raggedy Rawney, The, *633*
Hoskins, Dan: Chopper Chicks in Zombietown, *823*
Hossein, Robert: Double Agents, *971;* I Killed Rasputin, *746*
Hostettler, Joe: Gallagher—Melon Crazy, *282;* Gallagher—Over Your Head, *282;* Gallagher—The Bookkeeper, *283;* Paramount Comedy Theatre, Vol. 1: Well Developed, *353;* Paramount Comedy Theatre, Vol. 2: Decent Exposures, *354;* Paramount Comedy Theater, Vol. 3: Hanging Party, *354;* Young at Heart Comedians, The, *415*
Houck Jr., Joy N.: Creature from Black Lake, *826;* Night of Bloody Horror, *869*
Hough, John: American Gothic, *808;* Biggles—Adventures in Time, *1039;* Black Arrow (1984), *150;* Brass Target, *19;* Dirty Mary, Crazy Larry, *39;* Duel of Hearts, *505;* Escape to Witch Mountain, *165;* Ghost in Monte Carlo, A, *527;* Howling IV, *854;* Incubus, The, *856;* Legend of Hell House, The, *860;* Return from Witch Mountain, *199;* Triumphs of a Man Called Horse, *1159;* Twins of Evil, *898;* Watcher in the Woods, The, *901*
Hous, Robert: Shogun Assassin, *785*
Houston, Bobby: Bad Manners, *231;* Caged Fear, *21;* Trus Me, *400*
Hovde, Ellen: Grey Gardens, *425*
Hoven, Adrian: Dandelions, *727;* Mark of the Devil, Part 2, *863*
Howard, Cy: Lovers and Other Strangers, *323*
Howard, David: Arizona Legion, *1095;* Daniel Boone, *110* In Old Santa Fe, *1123;* Lost Jungle, The, *79;* Marshal of Mes City, *1133;* Mystery Squadron, *88;* Renegade Ranger, *1142;* Triple Justice, *1159*
Howard, Frank: Helter-Skelter Murders, The, *540*
Howard, Karin: Tigress, The, *130*
Howard, Leslie: Pimpernel Smith, *99;* Pygmalion, *363*
Howard, Ron: Backdraft, *8;* Cocoon, *1042;* Far and Away, *514;* Grand Theft Auto, *57;* Gung Ho (1985), *292;* Night Shif *344;* Paper, The, *617;* Parenthood, *354;* Splash, *384;* Willow *1089*
Howard, Sandy: One Step to Hell, *95*
Howard, William K.: Backdoor to Heaven, *454;* Cat and th Fiddle, The, *911;* Evelyn Prentice, *511;* Johnny Come Lately, *311;* White Gold, *1031*
Howson, Frank: Hunting, *546*
Hoyt, Harry: Lost World, The (1925), *1064*
Hsu, Dachin: Pale Blood, *873*
Hsu, Talun: Witchcraft V: Dance with the Devil, *903*
Hua-Shan: Infra-Man, *1058*
Hubert, Jean-Loup: Le Grand Chemin (The Grand Highwa *757;* Next Year If All Goes Well, *771*
Hubley, John: Columbia Pictures Cartoon Classics, *159*
Hudlin, Reginald: Boomerang, *244;* House Party, *923*
Hudson, Gary: Thunder Run, *129*
Hudson, Hugh: Chariots of Fire, *479;* Greystoke: The Legen of Tarzan, Lord of the Apes, *58;* Lost Angels, *580;* Revolutio *639*
Huemer, Peter Ily: Kiss Daddy Good Night, *989*
Huestis, Marc: Men in Love, *592*
Huggins, Roy: Hangman's Knot, *1119*
Hugh, R. John: Deadly Encounter (1975), *498;* Naked in th Sun, *1135*
Hughes, Albert: Menace II Society, *593*
Hughes, Allen: Menace II Society, *593*
Hughes, Carol: Missing Link, *85*
Hughes, David: Missing Link, *85*
Hughes, Howard: Outlaw, The, *1137*
Hughes, John: Breakfast Club, The, *245;* Curly Sue, *261;* Ferris Bueller's Day Off, *276;* Planes, Trains and Automobiles *358;* She's Having a Baby, *377;* Sixteen Candles, *380;* Uncle Buck, *402;* Weird Science, *407*
Hughes, Ken: Casino Royale (1967), *252;* Chitty Chitty Ban Bang, *158;* Cromwell, *491;* Internecine Project, The, *986;* Lor Haul, *578;* Night School, *1001;* Of Human Bondage (1964), *610;* Oh, Alfie, *611;* Sextette, *376*
Hughes, Robert C.: Down the Drain, *41;* Hunter's Blood, *5*
Hughes, Terry: Barnum (1986), *908;* Butcher's Wife, The, *248;* Monty Python Live at the Hollywood Bowl, *336;* Ripping Yarns, *368;* Sunset Limousine, *388*
Hui, Ann: Song of the Exile, *787*
Hulette, Don: Breaker! Breaker!, *19;* Tennessee Stallion, *12*
Hulme, Ron: Fearless Tiger, *47*
Humberstone, H. Bruce: Charlie Chan at the Opera, *961;* Happy Go Lovely, *921;* I Wake Up Screaming, *985;* Iceland, *924;* Pin-Up Girl, *935;* Sun Valley Serenade, *942;* Tarzan and the Trappers, *125;* Ten Wanted Men, *1155;* To the Shores of Tripoli, *130;* Wonder Man, *413*
Hung, Hsu Tseng: Invincible Sword, The, *67*
Hung, Samo: Dragons Forever, *732;* Eastern Condors, *733;* Paper Marriage (1988), *775*
Hung, Tran Anh: Scent of Green Papaya, The, *784*
Hung, Wong Kee: Mr. Vampire (Vol. 1–4), *768*
Hunsicker, Jackson: Oddball Hall, *348*
Hunt, Christopher: Eat and Run, *1048*

Hunt, David: Sudden Thunder, *122;* Triple Impact, *132*
Hunt, Edward: Alien Warrior, *1035;* Bloody Birthday, *817;* Brain, The (1988), *818;* Starship Invasions, *1080*
Hunt, Paul: Clones, The, *1042;* Great Gundown, *1116;* Merlin, *1065;* Twisted Nightmare, *898*
Hunt, Peter H.: It Came Upon a Midnight Clear, *177;* Life on the Mississippi, *574;* Mysterious Stranger, The, *190;* 1776, *939;* Skeezer, *659*
Hunt, Peter R.: Assassination, *7;* Death Hunt, *35;* Gulliver's Travels (1977), *172;* Hyper Sapian: People from Another Star, *1057;* On Her Majesty's Secret Service, *94;* Philip Marlowe, Private Eye: The Pencil, *1005;* Shout at the Devil, *115;* Wild Geese II, *139*
Hunter, Max (Massimo Pupillo): Bloody Pit of Horror, *817*
Hunter, T. Hayes: Ghoul, The (1933), *846*
Hunter, Tim: Beverly Hills 90210, *460;* Lies of the Twins, *992;* Paint It Black, *97;* River's Edge, *641;* Saint of Fort Washington, The, *646;* Sylvester, *675;* Tex, *680*
Huppert, Caroline: Sincerely Charlotte, *786*
Hurst, Brian Desmond: Christmas Carol, A (1951), *159;* Dangerous Moonlight (a.k.a. Suicide Squadron), *32;* Malta Story, The, *586;* Playboy of the Western World, *358;* Simba, *658*
Hurtz, William: Little Nemo: Adventures in Slumberland, *183*
Hurwitz, Harry: Projectionist, The, *362;* Rosebud Beach Hotel, The, *370;* That's Adequate, *393*
Hussein, Waris: And Baby Makes Six, *447;* Callie and Son, *474;* Coming Out of the Ice, *486;* Divorce His: Divorce Hers, *502;* Edward and Mrs. Simpson, *507;* Intimate Contact, *553;* Little Gloria...Happy at Last, *576;* Melody, *186;* Onassis: The Richest Man in the World, *612;* Princess Daisy, *627;* Quackser Fortune Has a Cousin in the Bronx, *631;* Summer House, The, *388;* Switched at Birth, *675*
Huston, Danny: Becoming Colette, *457;* Mr. Corbett's Ghost, *1066;* Mr. North, *334*
Huston, Jimmy: Final Exam, *841;* My Best Friend Is a Vampire, *339*
Huston, John: Across the Pacific, *1;* African Queen, The, *442;* Annie, *907;* Asphalt Jungle, The, *953;* Barbarian and the Geisha, The, *455;* Beat the Devil, *233;* Bible, The, *460;* Casino Royale (1967), *252;* Dead, The, *497;* Fat City, *515;* In This Our Life, *550;* Key Largo, *988;* Life and Times of Judge Roy Bean, The, *1128;* List of Adrian Messenger, The, *992;* Mackintosh Man, The, *994;* Maltese Falcon, The, *994;* Man Who Would Be King, The, *81;* Misfits, The, *595;* Moby Dick, *86;* Moulin Rouge, *600;* Night of the Iguana, The, *606;* Phobia, *1006;* Prizzi's Honor, *362;* Red Badge of Courage, The, *636;* Reflections in a Golden Eye, *637;* Treasure of the Sierra Madre, *132;* Under the Volcano, *691;* Unforgiven, The (1960), *1160;* Victory, *135;* Wise Blood, *704*
Hutton, Brian G.: First Deadly Sin, The, *977;* High Road to China, *62;* Kelly's Heroes, *70;* Night Watch, *870;* Where Eagles Dare, *138;* X, Y and Zee, *707*
Hutton, Robert: Slime People, The, *1077*
Huyck, Willard: Best Defense, *234;* French Postcards, *281;* Howard the Duck, *1057*
Hyams, Nessa: Leader of the Band, *317*
Hyams, Peter: Capricorn One, *1041;* Death Target, *35;* Hanover Street, *536;* Narrow Margin (1990), *89;* Our Time, *616;* Outland, *1069;* Presidio, The, *100;* Running Scared (1986), *110;* Star Chamber, The, *1019;* Stay Tuned, *385;* 2010, *1086*
Ibanez, Juan: Chamber of Fear, *822;* Dance of Death, *829;* Macabre Serenade, *861;* Sinister Invasion, *886;* Snake People, *888*
Ichaso, Leon: Crossover Dreams, *912;* El Super, *734;* Fear Inside, The, *976;* Sugar Hill, *122;* Take, The, *124*
Ichikawa, Kon: Burmese Harp, The, *721;* Fires on the Plain, *737;* Odd Obsession, *772*
Ide, Yasunori: Burn Up!, *721*
Idle, Eric: Rutles, The (a.k.a. All You Need Is Cash), *938;* Tale of the Frog Prince, *209*
Iida, Tstutomu: Devilman Vol. 1–2, *730*
Ikehiro, Kazuo: Zatoichi: Masseur Ichi and a Chest of Gold, *806*
Imagawa, Yasuhiro: Giant Robo, *740*
Image, Jean: Aladdin and His Magic Lamp, *145*
Imamura, Shohei: Ballad of Narayama, The, *715;* Black Rain (1988), *718;* Eijanaika (Why Not?), *733;* Insect Woman, *748;* Pornographers, The, *778;* Vengeance Is Mine (1979), *800*
Imhoof, Markus: Boat Is Full, The, *719*
Ina, Shinsuke: Art Com Video (Vol. 1–3), *1037*
Inagaki, Hiroshi: Kojiro, *752;* Rikisha-Man, *781;* Samurai Saga, *783;* Samurai Trilogy, The, *783*
Ince, Thomas: Civilization, *483*
Indovina, Franco: Catch As Catch Can, *252;* Oldest Profession, The, *773*
Ingraham, Lloyd: American Aristocracy, An, *226*
Ingster, Boris: Guns of Diablo, *1118;* Judge Steps Out, The, *560;* Stranger on the Third Floor, *1020*
Ingvordsen, J. Christian: Comrades in Arms, *28;* Firehouse (1987), *277;* Hangmen, *59;* Mob War, *86;* Outfit, The, *96;* Search and Destroy (1988), *1076*
Innocenti, Markus: Murder Story, *999*
Ionesco, Eugene: Seven Deadly Sins, The, *785*
Ireland, O'Dale: High School Caesar, *62*
Irmas, Matthew: When the Party's Over, *699*
Irvin, John: Champions, *479;* Dogs of War, The, *40;* Eminent Domain, *973;* Freefall, *52;* Ghost Story, *846;* Hamburger Hill, *535;* Next of Kin (1989), *90;* Raw Deal, *103;* Robin Hood (1991), *107;* Turtle Diary, *400*
Irvin, Sam: Acting on Impulse, *950;* Guilty as Charged, *291*
Irvine, Kevin: Greenstone, The, *172*
Irving, David: C.H.U.D. II (Bud the C.H.U.D.), *820;* Cannon Movie Tales: Sleeping Beauty, *155;* Cannon Movie Tales: The Emperor's New Clothes, *155;* Night of the Cyclone, *1001;* Rumpelstiltskin (1987), *200*
Irving, Richard: Cyborg: The Six-Million Dollar Man, *1043;* Jessie Owens Story, The, *557*
Isaac, James: Horror Show, The, *852*
Isaacs, Ronnie: Warriors From Hell, *137*
Isasi, Antonio: Summertime Killer, The, *122;* Vengeance, *135*
Iscove, Robert: Flash, The, *1051;* Lawrenceville Stories, The, *317;* Little Mermaid, The (1984), *182;* Mission of the Shark, *596;* Puss in Boots, *198;* That's Singing: The Best of Broadway, *944*
Ishiguro, Koichi: Guyver, The, Vols. 1–4, *1055*
Ishiguro, Noboru: Orguss, Vols. 1–4, *1069*
Ising, Rudolf: Barney Bear Cartoon Festival, *148*
Israel, Neal: Americathon, *226;* Bachelor Party, *230;* Breaking the Rules, *469;* Moving Violations, *338;* Surf Ninjas, *208;* Tunnelvision, *400*
Israelson, Peter: Side Out, *657*
Itami, Juzo: Funeral, The, *739;* Tampopo, *792;* Taxing Woman, A, *793;* Taxing Woman's Return, A, *793*
Ivory, James: Autobiography of a Princess, *452;* Bombay Talkie, *720;* Bostonians, The, *467;* Courtesans of Bombay, *489;* Europeans, The, *511;* Heat and Dust, *539;* Householder, The, *745;* Howards End, *545;* Hullabaloo over George and Bonnie's Pictures, *303;* Jane Austen in Manhattan, *309;* Maurice, *590;* Mr. and Mrs. Bridge, *596;* Quartet (1981), *631;* Remains of the Day, *637;* Room with a View, A, *644;* Roseland, *644;* Savages (1973), *373;* Shakespeare Wallah, *655;* Slaves of New York, *381;* Wild Party, The (1975), *702*
Ivy, Bob: Dark Rider, *33*
Iwerks, Ub: Ub Iwerks Cartoon Festival Vol. I–V, *214*
Jabor, Arnaldo: I Love You (Eu Te Amo), *746*
Jackson, Andrew: Incredible Story of Dogs, The, *427*
Jackson, David F.: Mystery Mansion, *190*
Jackson, David S.: Death Train, *968*
Jackson, Donald G.: Demon Lover, The, *832;* Hell Comes to Frogtown, *1056;* Return to Frogtown, *1074;* Rollerblade, *1075;* Scream of the Demon Lover (1976), *884*

Jackson, Douglas: Deadbolt, *968;* Strange Tales: Ray Bradbury Theater, *1080;* Whispers, *1031*
Jackson, George: House Party 2, *923*
Jackson, Jalil: Lady Terminator, *74*
Jackson, Larry: Bugs Bunny, Superstar, *153*
Jackson, Lewis: Christmas Evil, *824*
Jackson, Mick: Bodyguard, The, *466;* Chattahoochee, *480;* Clean Slate (1994), *256;* L.A. Story, *314;* Threads, *682;* Yuri Nosenko, KGB, *709*
Jackson, Pat: Encore, *509;* King Arthur, The Young Warlord, *72;* Prisoner, The (TV Series), *1071*
Jackson, Peter: Bad Taste, *1038;* Dead Alive, *830*
Jackson, Richard: Big Bust Out, The, *12*
Jackson, Wilfred: Alice in Wonderland (1951), *145;* Cinderella (1950), *159;* Lady and the Tramp, *180;* Peter Pan (1953), *194*
Jacobs, Werner: Heidi (1965), *173*
Jacobson, Rick: Full Contact, *53;* Unborn II, The, *898*
Jacobson, Stan: Avery Schreiber—Live From the Second City, *230*
Jacoby, Joseph: Great Bank Hoax, The, *289;* Hurry Up or I'll Be 30, *303*
Jacopetti, Gualtiero: Africa Blood and Guts, *418;* Mondo Cane, *431;* Mondo Cane II, *431*
Jaeckin, Just: Emmanuelle, *734;* French Woman, The, *522;* Lady Chatterley's Lover (1981), *567;* Perils of Gwendoline, The, *98;* Story of O, The, *668*
Jaffe, Stanley: Without a Trace, *1032*
Jaglom, Henry: Always (1984), *225;* Can She Bake a Cherry Pie?, *250;* Eating, *507;* New Year's Day, *605;* Sitting Ducks, *380;* Someone to Love, *662;* Tracks, *687;* Venice/Venice, *693*
Jaimes, Sam: Charlie Brown and Snoopy Show, The (Volume I), *157;* Charlie Brown and Snoopy Show, The (Volume II), *157;* Good Grief, Charlie Brown, *171;* Happy New Year, Charlie Brown, *173;* She Likes You, Charlie Brown, *203;* What Next, Charlie Brown?, *216;* You Can't Win, Charlie Brown, *219;* You're a Good Man, Charlie Brown, *219*
Jamain, Patrick: Honeymoon, *851*
James, Alan: Come on Tarzan, *1105;* Dick Tracy (1937), *38;* Fargo Express, *1112;* Flaming Frontiers, *1113;* Law Rides Again, The, *1127;* Phantom Thunderbolt, *1138;* Red Barry, *104;* SOS Coast Guard, *118;* Trail Drive, *1158;* When a Man Sees Red, *1163*
James, Bob: Alien Seed, *1035*
Jameson, Jerry: Airport '77, *443;* Bat People, *812;* Bonanza: The Return, *1100;* Cowboy and the Ballerina, The, *490;* High Noon, Part Two, *1120;* Killing at Hell's Gate, *71;* Raise the Titanic, *103;* Starflight One, *1079;* Terror on the 40th Floor, *1023*
Jancso, Miklos: Red and the White, The, *780;* Round-Up, The, *782*
Janjic, Zoran: Connecticut Yankee in King Arthur's Court, A (1970), *159*
Jankel, Annabel: D.O.A. (1988), *965;* Max Headroom, *1065;* Super Mario Brothers, The, *208*
Janos, Victor: Last House on Dead End Street, *860*
Janot, Charles: Lucy and Desi: Before the Laughter, *583*
Jaque, Christian: Legend of Frenchie King, The, *1128*
Jarman, Derek: Angelic Conversation, *448;* Aria, *907;* Caravaggio, *475;* Edward II, *507;* Garden, The, *525;* In the Shadow of the Sun, *1058;* Jubilee, *1061;* Last of England, The, *570;* War Requiem, *696*
Jarmusch, Jim: Down by Law, *268;* Mystery Train, *603;* Night on Earth, *606;* Stranger Than Paradise, *387*
Jarrott, Charles: Amateur, The, *952;* Anne of the Thousand Days, *449;* Boy in Blue, The, *467;* Condorman, *159;* Last Flight of Noah's Ark, *180;* Littlest Horse Thieves, The, *184;* Night of the Fox, *90;* Other Side of Midnight, The, *615;* Poor Little Rich Girl: The Barbara Hutton Story, *624;* Strange Case of Dr. Jekyll and Mr. Hyde, The (1968), *890*
Jasny, Vojta: Great Land of Small, The, *171*
Jason, Leigh: Bride Walks Out, The, *245;* Lady for a Night, *567;* Mad Miss Manton, The, *325;* Out of the Blue, *352*
Jeffrey, Tom: Odd Angry Shot, The, *610*
Jeffries, Lionel: Amazing Mr. Blunden, The, *146;* Baxter, *456;* Railway Children, The, *198;* Water Babies, The, *216*
Jeffries, Richard: Bloodtide, *817*
Jenkins, Michael: Rebel (1985), *636;* Sweet Talker, *389*
Jenkins, Patrick: Gambler and the Lady, The, *524*
Jenz, Tom: Ladies Sing the Blues, The, *428*
Jessner, Leopold: Backstairs, *714*
Jeunet, Jean-Pierre: Delicatessen, *729*
Jewison, Norman: Agnes of God, *443;* And Justice for All, *447;* Best Friends, *235;* Cincinnati Kid, The, *26;* F.I.S.T., *512;* Fiddler on the Roof, *916;* In Country, *550;* In the Heat of the Night, *986;* Jesus Christ, Superstar, *926;* Moonstruck, *336;* Other People's Money, *351;* Rollerball, *1075;* Russians Are Coming, the Russians Are Coming, The, *371;* Send Me No Flowers, *375;* Soldier's Story, A, *1018;* Thomas Crown Affair, The, *128;* Thrill of It All, The, *396*
Jhabvala, Ruth Prawer: Courtesans of Bombay, *489*
Ji-Shun, Duan: Go-Masters, The, *741*
Jimenez, Neal: Waterdance, The, *696*
Jiras, Robert: I Am the Cheese, *547*
Jittlov, Mike: Wizard of Speed and Time, The, *413*
Joannon, Léo: Atoll K (Utopia), *229*
Joanou, Phil: Fallen Angels, *513;* Final Analysis, *976;* State o Grace, *666;* Three O'Clock High, *396;* U2: Rattle and Hum, *43* Wild Palms, *1089*
Jobson, Dickie: Countryman, *489*
Jodorowsky, Alejandro: Santa Sangre, *882*
Jodrell, Steve: Shame (1987), *114*
Joens, Michael: My Little Pony: The Movie, *190*
Joffe, Arthur: Alberto Express, *711;* Harem, *536*
Joffe, Mark: Efficiency Expert, The, *508;* Grievous Bodily Harm, *533*
Joffe, Roland: City of Joy, *483;* Fat Man and Little Boy, *515;* Killing Fields, The, *563;* Mission, The, *596*
Johnson, Alan: Solarbabies, *1077;* To Be or Not to Be (1983), *397*
Johnson, Emory: Phantom Express, *99*
Johnson, Jed: Andy Warhol's Bad, *447*
Johnson, John H.: Curse of the Blue Lights, *828*
Johnson, Kenneth: Incredible Hulk, The, *1058;* Short Circuit 2, *1076*
Johnson, Lamont: Broken Chain, The, *20;* Crisis at Central High, *491;* Dangerous Company, *494;* Execution of Private Slovik, The, *512;* Gore Vidal's Lincoln, *531;* Groundstar Conspiracy, The, *1055;* Gunfight, A, *1117;* Jack and the Beanstalk, *178;* Last American Hero, The, *75;* Lipstick, *992;* My Sweet Charlie, *602;* One on One, *613;* Paul's Case, *620;* Spacehunter: Adventures in the Forbidden Zone, *1078;* Twiligh Zone, The (TV Series), *1086;* Unnatural Causes, *692*
Johnson, Martin: Borneo, *419*
Johnson, Nunnally: Man in the Gray Flannel Suit, The, *587;* Three Faces of Eve, The, *682*
Johnson, Osa: Borneo, *419*
Johnson, Patrick: Spaced Invaders, *206*
Johnston, Jim: Blue De Ville, *242*
Johnston, Joe: Honey, I Shrunk the Kids, *175;* Rocketeer, The, *108*
Johnston, Lynn: For Better or for Worse: The Bestest Present, *167*
Johnstone, Tucker: Blood Salvage, *816*
Jones, Amy: Love Letters, *581;* Maid to Order, *326;* Slumber Party Massacre, *887*
Jones, Brian Thomas: Escape from Safehaven, *1049;* Rejuvenator, The, *879*
Jones, Chris: Escape from Survival Zone, *45*
Jones, Chuck: Adventures of Milo in the Phantom Tollbooth, The, *144;* Best of Bugs Bunny and Friends, The, *150;* Best of Warner Brothers, Vol. 1, *150;* Best of Warner Brothers, Vol. 2,

; Bugs and Daffy: The Wartime Cartoons, *152;* Bugs and fy's Carnival of the Animals, *153;* Bugs Bunny Cartoon tival Featuring "Hold the Lion Please", *153;* Bugs Bunny ssics, *153;* Bugs Bunny in King Arthur's Court, *153;* Bugs nny/Road Runner Movie, The, *153;* Bugs Bunny: Truth or e, *153;* Bugs Bunny's Bustin' Out All Over, *154;* Bugs nny's Easter Funnies, *154;* Bugs Bunny's Hare-Raising s, *154;* Bugs Bunny's Looney Christmas Tales, *154;* Bugs nny's Lunar Tunes, *154;* Bugs Bunny's Wacky Adventures, ; Cartoon Moviestars: Bugs!, *156;* Cartoon Moviestars: ner!, *156;* Cartoon Moviestars: Porky!, *156;* Cartoon viestars: Starring Bugs Bunny, *156;* Cricket in Times uare, A, *160;* Daffy Duck and Company, *160;* Daffy Duck toon Festival: Ain't That Ducky, *160;* Daffy Duck: The tiness Continues, *160;* Daffy Duck's Madcap Mania, *161;* Seuss: Horton Hears a Who/The Grinch Who Stole istmas, *162;* Elmer Fudd Cartoon Festival: An Itch in Time, 4; Elmer Fudd's Comedy Capers, *164;* Golden Age of Looney ons, The: Bugs Bunny by Each Director, *169;* Golden Age of oney Toons, The: Chuck Jones, *170;* Golden Age of Looney ons, The: Firsts, *170;* Golden Age of Looney Toons, The: 30s Musicals, *170;* Golden Age of Looney Toons, The: 40s Zanies, *170;* Golden Age of Looney Toons, The: The Art Bugs, *170;* Little Tweetie and Little Inki Cartoon Festival, 3; Looney Tunes Video Show, The (Volume 1), *184;* Looney nes Video Show, The (Volume 2), *184;* Looney Tunes Video ow, The (Volume 3), *184;* Mowgli's Brothers, *189;* 1001 bbit Tales, *193;* Pepe Le Pew's Skunk Tales, *194;* Pogo's ecial Birthday Special, The, *196;* Porky Pig and Company, 6; Porky Pig and Daffy Duck Cartoon Festival Featuring "Tick ck Tuckered", *196;* Porky Pig Cartoon Festival Featuring othing but the Tooth", *196;* Porky Pig Tales, *196;* Porky g's Screwball Comedies, *197;* Rikki-Tikki-Tavi, *199;* Road nner and Wile E. Coyote, The: The Scrapes of Wrath, *199;* ad Runner vs. Wile E. Coyote: The Classic Chase, *199;* lute to Chuck Jones, A, *201;* Salute to Mel Blanc, A, *201;* iffles the Mouse Cartoon Festival Featuring "Sniffles Bells e Cat", *205;* Very Best of Bugs Bunny: Volume 1, The, *215;* ry Best of Bugs Bunny: Volume 2, The, *215;* Very Best of gs Bunny: Volume 3, The, *215;* Very Merry Cricket, A, *215;* hite Seal, The, *217*

nes, David: Betrayal (1983), *459;* Christmas Wife, The, 2; 84 Charing Cross Road, *508;* Jackknife, *556;* Look Back In nger (1989), *579*

nes, Dick: Extra Girl, The, *273*

nes, Don: Forest, The, *842;* Love Butcher, *861;* Sweater rls, *389*

nes, F. Richard: Bulldog Drummond, *20*

nes, Harmon: As Young as You Feel, *229;* Bullwhip, *1102;* ride of St. Louis, The, *627*

ones, James Cellan: Fortunes of War, *520*

ones, L. Q.: Boy and His Dog, A, *1040*

ones, Lee: Invasion of the Girl Snatchers, *307*

ones, Mark: Leprechaun, *860*

ones, Philip J.: Cause of Death, *24*

ones, Skip: Opus 'N' Bill in a Wish for Wings that Work, *193*

ones, Terry: Erik the Viking, *1049;* Life of Brian, *318;* Monty ython's the Meaning of Life, *336;* Personal Services, *357*

ordan, Glenn: Barbarians at the Gate, *455;* Buddy System, he, *471;* Displaced Person, The, *501;* Dress Gray, *505;* Echoes the Darkness, *507;* Frankenstein (1973), *842;* Jesse, *557;* es Miserables (1978), *573;* Lois Gibbs and the Love Canal, 77; Mass Appeal, *590;* O Pioneers!, *610;* Only When I Laugh, 14; Sarah, Plain and Tall, *648*

ordan, Larry: Larry Jordan Live Film Shorts, *568;* Short nimations by Larry Jordan, *1076*

ordan, Neil: Company of Wolves, The, *1042;* Crying Game, he, *492;* Danny Boy (1982), *495;* High Spirits, *297;* Miracle, he (1990), *595;* Mona Lisa, *997;* We're No Angels (1989), 08

ordon, Glenn: To Dance with the White Dog, *684*

orgensen, David: Three Billy Goats Gruff and the Three ittle Pigs, The, *211*

Joseph, Eugine: Spookies, *889*

Jost, Jon: Last Chants for a Slow Dance, *568;* Sure Fire, *674*

Jourdan, Pierre: Phedre, *777*

Joyner, C. Courtney: Trancers III: Death Lives, *1085*

Julian, Rupert: Merry-Go-Round, The, *996;* Phantom of the Opera (1925), *874;* Yankee Clipper, *141*

Julien, Isaac: Young Soul Rebels, *948*

Juran, Nathan: Attack of the 50-Foot Woman (1958), *810;* Brain from Planet Arous, The, *1040;* Deadly Mantis, The, *1045;* First Men *in* the Moon, *1051;* Hellcats of the Navy, *60;* Jack the Giant Killer, *178;* Land Raiders, *1125;* 7th Voyage of Sinbad, The, *1076;* 20 Million Miles to Earth, *1086*

Juranville, Jacques: Le Gentleman D'Espom (Duke of the Derby), *757*

Jurwich, Don: G.I. Joe: The Movie, *168*

Justman, Paul: Gimme an "F", *286*

Jutra, Claude: By Design, *473;* Mon Oncle Antoine, *768;* Surfacing, *123*

Kachivas, Lou: Secret of the Sword, The, *202*

Kaczender, George: Agency, *443;* Chanel Solitaire, *479;* Girl in Blue, The, *527;* In Praise of Older Women, *550;* Pretty Kill, *1007*

Kadár, Ján: Blue Hotel, *465;* Shop on Main Street, The, *786*

Kadison, Ellis: Cat, The, *157*

Kadokawa, Haruki: Heaven and Earth (1991), *743*

Kaduwara, Haruki: Legend of the Eight Samurai, *758*

Kagan, Jeremy Paul: Big Fix, The, *955;* Big Man on Campus, *238;* Chosen, The, *481;* Conspiracy: The Trial of the Chicago 8, *488;* Descending Angel, *499;* Doctor Quinn Medicine Woman, *502;* Heroes, *540;* Journey of Natty Gann, The, *179;* Katherine, *562;* Sleeping Beauty (1983), *205;* Sting II, The, *120*

Kahn, Richard: Harlem Rides the Range, *1119*

Kaige, Chen: Farewell My Concubine, *736;* Life on a String, *760;* Yellow Earth, *806*

Kaiserman, Connie: My Little Girl, *602*

Kalatozov, Mikhail K.: Cranes are Flying, The, *726;* Red Tent, The, *637*

Kalin, Tom: Swoon, *675*

Kalmanowicz, Max: Children, The, *823;* Dreams Come True, *1048*

Kaminski, Zbigniew: In a Moment of Passion, *549*

Kamler, Piotr: Chronopolis, *724*

Kampmann, Steven: Stealing Home, *667*

Kane, Dennis: French Quarter, *522*

Kane, Joseph: Arizona Kid, *1095;* Bad Man of Deadwood, *1095;* Billy the Kid Returns, *1099;* Boots and Saddles, *1100;* Brimstone, *1101;* Carson City Kid, *1103;* Colorado, *1105;* Cowboy and the Senorita, *1106;* Dakota (1945), *1107;* Darkest Africa, *33;* Days of Jesse James, *1107;* Fighting Marines, The, *48;* Flame of the Barbary Coast, *50;* Frontier Pony Express, *1114;* Git Along, Little Dogies, *1115;* Hands Across the Border, *1118;* Heart of the Golden West, *1119;* Heart of the Rockies, *1119;* Hoodlum Empire, *64;* Idaho, *1122;* In Old Caliente, *1122;* Jesse James at Bay, *1123;* Jubilee Trail, *1124;* King of the Cowboys, *1125;* King of the Pecos, *1125;* Lawless Nineties, The, *1127;* Lonely Trail, The, *1129;* Man from Music Mountain, *1131;* Maverick Queen, The, *1133;* Melody Trail, *1133;* Oh! Susanna!, *1136;* Old Barn Dance, The, *1136;* Old Corral, *1136;* Public Cowboy #1, *1140;* Ranger and the Lady, The, *1141;* Ride, Ranger, Ride, *1143;* Ride the Man Down, *1143;* Robin Hood of the Pecos, *1145;* Rough Riders' Roundup, *1146;* Round-Up Time in Texas, *1146;* Saga of Death Valley, *1147;* Shine on Harvest Moon, *1149;* Silver Spurs, *1150;* Song of Nevada, *1151;* Song of Texas, *1151;* Sons of the Pioneers, *1151;* Springtime in the Rockies (1937), *1152;* Sunset on the Desert, *1154;* Sunset Serenade, *1154;* Under Western Stars, *1160;* Undersea Kingdom, *1087;* Wall Street Cowboy, *1162;* Yellow Rose of Texas, *1165;* Yodelin' Kid from Pine Ridge, *1165;* Young Bill Hickok, *1165*

Kanefsky, Rolf: There's Nothing Out There, *894*

Kaneko, Shusuke: Summer Vacation: 1999, *791*

Kanevski, Vitaly: Freeze—Die—Come to Life, *738*
Kanew, Jeff: Eddie Macon's Run, *43;* Gotcha!, *980;* Natural Enemies, *604;* Revenge of the Nerds, *367;* Tough Guys, *398;* Troop Beverly Hills, *399;* V. I. Warshawski, *1029*
Kanganis, Charles: No Escape, No Return, *91;* Time to Die, A (1990), *1025*
Kanievska, Marek: Another Country, *449;* Less Than Zero, *573*
Kanin, Garson: Bachelor Mother, *230;* Great Man Votes, The, *289;* My Favorite Wife, *340;* Next Time I Marry, *344;* They Knew What They Wanted, *681;* Tom, Dick and Harry, *397*
Kanner, Alexis: Kings and Desperate Men: A Hostage Incident, *73*
Kanter, Hal: For the Love of It, *279;* I Married a Woman, *304;* Loving You, *929*
Kantor, Ron: Your Favorite Laughs from an Evening at the Improv, *416*
Kaplan, Ed: Chips, the War Dog, *158;* Walking on Air, *215*
Kaplan, Jonathan: Accused, The, *441;* Bad Girls (1994), *1095;* Fallen Angels, *513;* Gentleman Bandit, The, *525;* Heart Like a Wheel, *538;* Immediate Family, *549;* Love Field, *581;* Mr. Billion, *85;* Over the Edge, *616;* Project X, *1072;* Truck Turner, *132;* Unlawful Entry, *1029;* White Line Fever, *139*
Kaplan, Nelly: Nea (A Young Emmanuelle), *771;* Very Curious Girl, A, *800*
Kaplan, Richard: Exiles, The, *424*
Kaplan, Ted: Warbus, *137*
Kapland, Henry: Best of Dark Shadows, The, *813*
Karan, Bill: Gang Busters, *54*
Karbelnikoff, Michael: Mobsters, *86;* Red Shoe Diaries 4: Auto Erotica, *637*
Kardos, Leslie: Small Town Girl, *940*
Karlson, Phil: Ben, *812;* Big Cat, The, *12;* Framed (1975), *52;* Hell to Eternity, *540;* Hornet's Nest, *64;* Kansas City Confidential, *988;* Kid Galahad (1962), *926;* Ladies of the Chorus, *567;* Shanghai Cobra, The, *1014;* Texas Rangers, The, *1156;* Untouchables, The: Scarface Mob (TV), *134;* Walking Tall, *136*
Karman, Janice: Chipmunk Adventure, The, *158*
Karn, Bill: Ma Barker's Killer Brood, *80*
Karson, Eric: Angel Town, *5;* Black Eagle, *13;* Octagon, The, *93;* Opposing Force, *95*
Kasai, Yoshikasu: Teenage Mutant Ninja Turtles: The Epic Begins, *209*
Kasdan, Lawrence: Accidental Tourist, The, *440;* Big Chill, The, *460;* Body Heat, *958;* Grand Canyon, *531;* I Love You to Death, *304;* Silverado, *1150*
Kassovitz, Peter: Make Room For Tomorrow, *764*
Kastle, Leonard: Honeymoon Killers, The, *983*
Katansky, Ivan: S. S. Hell Camp, *882*
Katayama, Kazuyashi: Appleseed, *713;* Rumik World: The Supergal, *782*
Katselas, Milton: Butterflies Are Free, *473;* Forty Carats, *279;* Report to the Commissioner, *638;* Strangers: The Story of a Mother and a Daughter, *669*
Katsuhito, Akiyama: Bubblegum Crisis—Vols. 1–8, *720;* Sol Bianca, *787*
Katsumata, Tomoharu: Arcadia of My Youth, *713*
Katz, Douglas: Age Isn't Everything, *223*
Katzin, Lee H.: Bastard, The, *456;* Dirty Dozen, The: The Deadly Mission, *39;* Dirty Dozen, The: The Fatal Mission, *39;* Hondo and the Apaches, *1121;* Jake Spanner Private Eye, *68;* Man from Atlantis, The, *1064;* Salzburg Connection, The, *111;* Savages (1974), *883;* Sky Heist, *117;* Space 1999 (TV Series), *1077;* Terror Out of the Sky, *894;* Whatever Happened to Aunt Alice?, *902;* World Gone Wild, *1090*
Katzman, Sam: Brothers of the West, *1101*
Kaufer, Jonathan: Soup for One, *383*
Kaufman, Charles: Mother's Day, *866*
Kaufman, George S.: Senator Was Indiscreet, The, *375*
Kaufman, James: Backstab, *953*
Kaufman, Lloyd: Sgt. Kabukiman N.Y.P.D., *114;* Stuff Stephanie in the Incinerator, *388;* Toxic Avenger Part II, The, *897;* Toxic Avenger Part III: The Last Temptation of Toxie, The, *897*
Kaufman, Phil: Great Northfield Minnesota Raid, The, *11*[illegible]*;* Henry & June, *540;* Invasion of the Body Snatchers (1978), *1059;* Right Stuff, The, *640;* Rising Sun, *1010;* Unbearable Lightness of Being, The, *691;* Wanderers, The, *695;* White Dawn, The, *138*
Kaurismaki, Aki: Ariel, *713;* Leningrad Cowboys Go Ameri[ca], *758*
Kaurismaki, Mika: Amazon, *4*
Kavanagh, Denis: Flight from Vienna, *518*
Kawadri, Anwar: Claudia, *484;* In Search of the Serpent of Death, *66*
Kawajiri, Yoshiaki: Lensman, *1062;* Neo-Tokyo, *771*
Kay, Gilbert: White Comanche, *1164*
Kaylor, Robert: Carny, *475;* Nobody's Perfect, *346*
Kazan, Elia: Arrangement, The, *450;* Baby Doll, *453;* East of Eden (1955), *506;* Face in the Crowd, A, *512;* Gentlemen's Agreement, *526;* Last Tycoon, The, *571;* On the Waterfront, *612;* Panic in the Streets, *1004;* Pinky, *622;* Sea of Grass, The, *1148;* Splendor in the Grass, *664;* Streetcar Named Desire, A, *671;* Tree Grows in Brooklyn, A, *687;* Viva Zapata!, *694*
Kazan, Nicholas: Dream Lover (1994), *972*
Keach, James: False Identity, *975;* Forgotten, The, *520;* Praying Mantis, *1007;* Sunstroke, *1021*
Keating, Kevin: Hell's Angels Forever, *426*
Keaton, Buster: Balloonatic, The/One Week, *231;* Blacksmi[th], The/Cops, *240;* Buster Keaton Festival: Vol. 1, *248;* Buster Keaton Festival: Vol. 2, *248;* Buster Keaton Festival: Vol. 3, *248;* Buster Keaton Scrapbook, Vol. I, *248;* Buster Keaton: The Golden Years, *248;* Buster Keaton: The Great Stone Face, *24*[illegible]*;* General, The, *283;* Our Hospitality, *351;* Sherlock Jr., *377;* Three Ages, The, *395;* Two Houses of Keaton, *402*
Keaton, Diane: Heaven, *426;* Wild Flower, *702*
Keats, Laura: Crystal Force, *827*
Keesler, Don: Bog, *818;* Capture of Grizzly Adams, The, *15*[illegible]
Keeter, Worth: Dogs of Hell, *836;* Illicit Behavior, *985;* Lady Grey, *568;* Order of the Black Eagle, *95;* Snapdragon, *1018;* Trapper County War, *132;* Wolfman, *904*
Keglevic, Peter: Cop and the Girl, The, *726;* Kill Cruise, *56*[illegible]
Keighley, William: Adventures of Robin Hood, The, *2;* Bri[de] Came C.O.D., The, *245;* Bullets or Ballots, *21;* Each Dawn I Di[e], *42;* Fighting 69th, The, *48;* G-Men, *54;* George Washington Slept Here, *284;* Green Pastures, *533;* Ladies They Talk Abou[t], *567;* Man Who Came to Dinner, The, *328;* Master of Ballantra[e], The, *83;* Prince and the Pauper, The (1937), *197;* Street with No Name, *1021*
Keith, David: Curse, The, *827;* Further Adventures of Tennessee Buck, The, *53*
Keith, Harvey: Jezebel's Kiss, *987;* Mondo New York, *598*
Keller, Frederick King: Eyes of the Amaryllis, *165;* Tuck Everlasting, *214;* Vamping, *1029*
Keller, Harry: Gundown at Sandoval, *1117;* Marshal of Ceda[r] Rock, *1132;* Red River Shore, *1142;* Tammy and the Doctor, *677;* Texas John Slaughter: Stampede at Bitter Creek, *1155;* Texas John Slaughter: Wild Times, *1156*
Keller, Worth: L.A. Bounty, *73*
Kelljan, Bob: Count Yorga, Vampire, *825;* Scream, Blacula, Scream, *884*
Kellman, Barnet: Key Exchange, *563;* Straight Talk, *387*
Kellogg, David: Cool As Ice, *488*
Kellogg, Ray: Giant Gila Monster, The, *846;* Green Berets, The, *57*
Kelly, Gene: Cheyenne Social Club, The, *1104;* Guide for the Married Man, A, *291;* Hello, Dolly!, *922;* Invitation to the Dance, *925;* It's Always Fair Weather, *925;* On the Town, *934;* Singin' in the Rain, *940;* That's Entertainment Part II, *436;* Tunnel of Love, The, *400*
Kelly, James: Beast in the Cellar, The, *812*
Kelly, Nancy: Thousand Pieces of Gold, *1156*

Kelly, Patrick: Beer, *233*
Kelly, Peter: Dawson Patrol, The, *33*
Kelly, Ron: King of the Grizzlies, *180*
Kemp-Welch, Joan: Romeo and Juliet (1988), *643*
Kendall, David: Luggage of the Gods, *324*
Kenichi, Yatagai: Ten Little Gall Force/Scramble Wars, *793*
Kennedy, Burt: Alamo, The: Thirteen Days to Glory, *1093;* All the Kind Strangers, *951;* Big Bad John, *12;* Deserter, The, *1109;* Dynamite and Gold, *1110;* Hannie Caulder, *1119;* Killer Inside Me, The, *988;* More Wild Wild West, *1134;* Return of the Seven, *1142;* Rounders, The, *1146;* Suburban Commando, *388;* Support Your Local Gunfighter, *1154;* Support Your Local Sheriff!, *1154;* Texas Guns, *1155;* Train Robbers, The, *1158;* Trouble with Spies, The, *399;* War Wagon, The, *1162;* Wild Wild West Revisited, The, *1164*
Kennedy, Glen: Goof Troop, *171*
Kennedy, Ken: Mission to Glory, *596*
Kennedy, Lou: Breathing Fire, *19*
Kennedy, Michael: Caribe, *23;* Swordsman, The, *124;* Talons of the Eagle, *124*
Kennedy, Tom: Time Walker, *895*
Kent, Larry: High Stakes (1986), *297*
Kenton, Erle C.: Ghost of Frankenstein, *845;* House of Dracula, *852;* House of Frankenstein, *852;* Island of Lost Souls, *857;* Melody for Three, *592;* Pardon My Sarong, *354;* Remedy for Riches, *638;* They Meet Again, *681;* Who Done It?, *410*
Kerbosch, Roeland: For a Lost Soldier, *737*
Kern, James V.: Doughgirls, The, *268;* Second Woman, The, *650;* Two Tickets to Broadway, *947*
Kernochan, Sarah: Marjoe, *588*
Kerr, Frank: Trueblood, *689*
Kershner, Irvin: Empire Strikes Back, The, *1049;* Eyes of Laura Mars, The, *974;* Fine Madness, A, *277;* Flim-Flam Man, The, *518;* Hoodlum Priest, The, *543;* Never Say Never Again, *89;* Raid on Entebbe, *633;* Return of a Man Called Horse, The, *1142;* RoboCop 2, *1075;* S*P*Y*S, *385;* Traveling Man, *687;* Up the Sandbox, *403*
Kervyn, Emmanuel: Rabid Grannies, *878*
Kerwin, Harry: Barracuda, *1038*
Keshishian, Alek: Truth or Dare, *437;* With Honors, *412*
Kessler, Bruce: Cruise into Terror, *964;* Deathmoon, *832;* Simon, King of the Witches, *886*
Keusch, Michael: Just One of the Girls, *312;* Lena's Holiday, *991*
Khleifi, Michel: Wedding in Galilee, A, *802*
Khun, Tom: Bruce Lee: Curse of the Dragon, *420*
Ki-duk, Kim: Yongary—Monster from the Deep, *1090*
Kidron, Beeban: Antonia & Jane, *228;* Used People, *404*
Kiersch, Fritz: Children of the Corn, *823;* Gor, *1054;* Into the Sun, *67;* Shattered Image, *1014;* Tuff Turf, *689;* Under the Boardwalk, *691;* Winners Take All, *140*
Kieslowski, Krzysztof: Blue (1993), *719;* Double Life of Veronique, The, *731*
Kijowski, Janusz: Masquerade (1986), *766*
Kikoine, Gerard: Edge of Sanity, *838*
Kikuchi, Michitaka: Silent Mobius, *786*
Killy, Edward: Land of the Open Range, *1125;* Stage to Chino, *1152*
Kimball, John: Chip 'n' Dale: Rescue Rangers, *158*
Kimbrough, Clinton: Young Nurses, The, *708*
Kimmel, Bruce: Spaceship, *384*
Kimmins, Anthony: Captain's Paradise, The, *250;* Mine Own Executioner, *594*
Kincade, John: Back to Back, *8;* Terminal Entry, *1082*
Kincaid, Tim: Occultist, The, *93;* She's Back, *377*
King, Alex: Angkor: Cambodia Express, *5*
King, Allan Winton: Kurt Vonnegut's Monkey House, *1061;* One-Night Stand, *613;* Silence of the North, *657;* Termini Station, *679*
King, Burton: Man from Beyond, The, *1064;* When Lightning Strikes, *138*
King, George: Crimes at the Dark House, *826;* Crimes of Stephen Hawke, The, *826;* Demon Barber of Fleet Street, The, *832;* Face at the Window, The, *840;* Sexton Blake and the Hooded Terror, *1014;* Ticket of Leave Man, The, *895*
King, Henry: Alexander's Ragtime Band, *906;* Bravados, The, *1101;* Carousel, *911;* David and Bathsheba, *496;* Gunfighter, The, *1117;* In Old Chicago, *550;* Jesse James, *1123;* Love is a Many-Splendored Thing, *581;* She Goes to War, *377;* Snows of Kilimanjaro, The, *118;* Song of Bernadette, The, *662;* Stanley and Livingstone, *665;* Twelve O'Clock High, *133;* White Sister, The, *700;* Wilson, *703;* Yank in the RAF, A, *707*
King, Louis: Bulldog Drummond Comes Back, *20;* Bulldog Drummond in Africa, *20;* Bulldog Drummond's Revenge, *21;* Dangerous Mission, *966*
King, Rick: Forced March, *519;* Hard Choices, *536;* Hot Shot, *544;* Kickboxer Three—Art of War, *71;* Killing Time, The, *72;* Prayer of the Rollerboys, *100;* Quick, *102*
King, Stephen: Maximum Overdrive, *864*
King Jr., Woodie: Death of a Prophet, *498*
King, Zalman: Red Shoe Diaries, *637;* Red Shoe Diaries II: Double Dare, *637;* Red Shoe Diaries 3: Another Woman's Lipstick, *637;* Red Shoe Diaries 4: Auto Erotica, *637;* Two Moon Junction, *690;* Wild Orchid, *702;* Wild Orchid 2: Two Shades of Blue, *702;* Wildfire (1988), *703*
Kinney, Jack: Bongo, *152;* Legend of Sleepy Hollow, The (1949), *181*
Kinugasa, Teinosuke: Gate of Hell, *740;* Twenty-four Eyes, *797*
Kirby, John Mason: Savage Weekend, *883*
Kirk, Robert: Destroyer, *833*
Kirkland, Dennis: Best of Benny Hill, The, *235*
Kirkpatrick, Harry: Welcome to Spring Break, *902*
Kirman, Leonard: Carnival of Blood, *821*
Kirsh, John: Jesus, *557*
Kitazume, Hiroyuki: Robot Carnival, *1075*
Kitrosser, Martin: Silent Night, Deadly Night 5: The Toy Maker, *886*
Kizer, R. J.: Death Ring, *35;* Godzilla 1985, *846;* Hell Comes to Frogtown, *1056*
Kjellin, Alf: Girls of Huntington House, *528;* Man from U.N.C.L.E., The (TV Series), *80*
Klane, Robert: Thank God It's Friday, *944;* Weekend at Bernie's II, *407*
Klaus, Damian: Futurekick, *1053*
Klein, Dennis: One More Saturday Night, *350*
Kleiser, Randal: Big Top Pee-Wee, *239;* Blue Lagoon, The, *465;* Boy in the Plastic Bubble, The, *468;* Flight of the Navigator, *1052;* Gathering, The, *525;* Getting It Right, *285;* Grandview, U.S.A., *531;* Grease, *920;* Honey, I Blew Up the Kid, *175;* Summer Lovers, *672;* White Fang, *217*
Kleven, Max: Bail Out, *8;* Deadly Stranger, *35;* Night Stalker, The (1986), *870;* Ruckus, *109*
Klick, Roland: Let It Rock, *573*
Klimov, Elem: Come and See, *725;* Rasputin, *780*
Klimovsky, Leon: Badlands Drifter, *1096;* Blood Moon, *815;* Night of the Walking Dead, *870;* Rattler Kid, *1141*
Kloves, Steve: Fabulous Baker Boys, The, *512;* Flesh and Bone, *518*
Kneitel, Seymour: Best of Little Lulu, *150;* Superman Cartoons, *208*
Knights, Robert: Dawning, The, *496;* Dedicated Man, A, *499;* Double Vision, *972;* Ebony Tower, The, *507;* Lovers of Their Time, *582*
Kobayashi, Masaki: Human Condition, The, Part One: No Greater Love, *745;* Human Condition, The, Part Two: The Road to Eternity, *745;* Human Condition, The, Part Three: A Soldier's Prayer, *745;* Kwaidan, *752*
Koch, Howard W.: Badge 373, *8;* Frankenstein 1970, *843*
Koch, Phillip: Pink Nights, *357*
Kohner, Pancho: Mr. Sycamore, *334*
Kollek, Amos: Double Edge, *504;* Forever Lulu, *279;* Goodbye New York, *289;* High Stakes (1989), *62*

Koller, Xavier: Journey of Hope, *750*
Komack, James: Porky's Revenge, *360*
Konchalovsky, Andrei: Duet for One, *505;* Homer and Eddie, *543;* Inner Circle, The, *552;* Maria's Lovers, *588;* Runaway Train, *110;* Shy People, *657;* Tango and Cash, *124*
Kong, Jackie: Being, The, *812;* Blood Diner, *815;* Night Patrol, *344*
Konparu, Tomoko: Rumik World: The Supergal, *782*
Kopple, Barbara: American Dream, *418;* Harlan County, U.S.A., *425*
Korda, Alexander: Fire over England, *49;* Lilies of the Field (1930), *575;* Marius, *765;* Private Life of Don Juan, The, *628;* Private Life of Henry the Eighth, The, *628;* Rembrandt, *638;* That Hamilton Woman, *680;* Wedding Rehearsal, *407*
Korda, Zoltán: Cry, the Beloved Country, *492;* Drums, *42;* Elephant Boy, *44;* Four Feathers, The (1939), *52;* If I Were Rich, *305;* Jungle Book (1942), *179;* Sahara (1943), *110;* Sanders of the River, *111*
Korty, John: Autobiography of Miss Jane Pittman, The, *452;* Baby Girl Scott, *453;* Cast the First Stone, *476;* Christmas without Snow, A, *482;* Ewok Adventure, The, *165;* Eye on the Sparrow, *512;* Haunting Passion, The, *1055;* Music School, The, *601;* Oliver's Story, *612;* People, The, *1070;* They, *894;* Twice Upon a Time, *214;* Who Are the Debolts and Where Did They Get 19 Kids?, *438*
Koruda, Yoshio: Back to the Forest, *148*
Korzenioswsky, Waldemar: Chair, The, *822*
Koster, Henry: Bishop's Wife, The, *240;* D-Day the Sixth of June, *497;* Dear Brigitte, *263;* Desirée, *500;* Flower Drum Song, *917;* Harvey, *294;* Inspector General, The, *306;* Man Called Peter, A, *586;* Mr. Hobbs Takes a Vacation, *334;* My Man Godfrey (1957), *340;* Naked Maja, The, *603;* One Hundred Men and a Girl, *934;* Rage of Paris, The, *364;* Robe, The, *642;* Singing Nun, The, *204;* Spring Parade, *941;* Stars and Stripes Forever, *941;* Story of Ruth, The, *668;* Three Smart Girls, *945;* Three Smart Girls Grow Up, *945;* Two Sisters from Boston, *947;* Virgin Queen, The, *694*
Kotani, Tom: Bushido Blade, *21*
Kotcheff, Ted: Apprenticeship of Duddy Kravitz, The, *450;* First Blood, *49;* Folks, *278;* Fun with Dick and Jane, *282;* Joshua Then and Now, *311;* North Dallas Forty, *609;* Red Shoe Diaries 3: Another Woman's Lipstick, *637;* Split Image, *664;* Switching Channels, *390;* Uncommon Valor, *134;* Weekend at Bernie's, *407;* Who Is Killing the Great Chefs of Europe?, *410;* Winter People, *704*
Kouf, Jim: Disorganized Crime, *40;* Miracles, *332*
Kouzel, Al: Family Circus Christmas, A, *166*
Kovacs, Ernie: Kovacs, *314*
Kovacs, Steven: '68, *659*
Kowalski, Bernard: Attack of the Giant Leeches, *810;* Macho Callahan, *1130;* Marciano, *588;* Nativity, The, *604;* Stiletto, *120*
Kowalski, Lech: D.O.A.: A Right of Passage, *422*
Kragh-Jacobsen, Soeren: Emma's Shadow, *734*
Kramer, Frank: Bullet from God, A, *1102;* Five for Hell, *50;* God's Gun, *1116;* We Are No Angels, *1163*
Kramer, Jerry: Howie Mandel's North American Watusi Tour, *303;* Michael Jackson Moonwalker, *931;* Modern Girls, *335*
Kramer, Remi: High Velocity, *62*
Kramer, Stanley: Bless the Beasts and Children, *463;* Defiant Ones, The, *499;* Domino Principle, The, *971;* Guess Who's Coming to Dinner, *534;* Inherit the Wind, *552;* It's a Mad Mad Mad Mad World, *308;* Judgment at Nuremberg, *560;* Not as a Stranger, *609;* On the Beach, *1069;* Pride and the Passion, The, *626;* R.P.M. (Revolutions Per Minute), *632;* Runner Stumbles, The, *645;* Ship of Fools, *656*
Kramreither, Anthony: Thrillkill, *1025*
Krasna, Norman: Ambassador's Daughter, The, *226;* Big Hangover, The, *238*
Krasny, Paul: Back to Hannibal: The Return of Tom Sawyer and Huckleberry Finn, *454;* Christina, *25*
Kress, Harold F.: Painted Hills, The, *193*
Kriegman, Michael: My Neighborhood, *341;* New Wave Comedy, *343*
Krish, John: Man Who Had Power Over Women, The, *587*
Krishna, Srinivas: Masala, *329*
Kristye, Anthony: Tomb of Torture, *896*
Kroeker, Allan: Age-Old Friends, *443;* Heaven on Earth, *53*[illegible] Showdown at Williams Creek, *1149;* Tramp at the Door, *687*
Krogstad, Karl: Last Ride, The, *991*
Krohn, Bill: It's All True, *427*
Kroll, Nathan: Guns of August, The, *425*
Kronsberg, Jeremy Joe: Going Ape!, *287*
Kroyer, Bill: Ferngully—The Last Rainforest, *166*
Krueger, Michael: Mind Killer, *865*
Kubrick, Stanley: Barry Lyndon, *456;* Clockwork Orange, A[illegible] *1042;* Dr. Strangelove or How I Learned to Stop Worrying an[illegible] Love the Bomb, *266;* Full Metal Jacket, *523;* Killer's Kiss, *71;* Killing, The, *988;* Lolita, *577;* Paths of Glory, *619;* Shining, Th[illegible] *885;* Spartacus, *119;* 2001: A Space Odyssey, *1086*
Kuehn, Andrew: Terror in the Aisles, *893*
Kuleshov, Lev: By the Law, *721;* Extraordinary Adventures [illegible] Mr. West in the Land of the Bolsheviks, The, *735*
Kulijanov, Lev: Crime and Punishment (1970), *727*
Kulik, Buzz: Bad Ronald, *811;* Brian's Song, *469;* Code Nam[illegible] Dancer, *27;* From Here to Eternity (1979), *523;* George Washington, *526;* Hunter, The (1980), *65;* Lindbergh Kidnapping Case, The, *575;* Pioneer Woman, *1138;* Rage of Angels, *633;* Riot, *106;* Sergeant Ryker, *652;* Shamus, *1014;* Twilight Zone, The (TV Series), *1086;* Villa Rides, *1161;* Women of Valor, *706*
Kull, Edward: New Adventures of Tarzan, *90;* Tarzan and th[illegible] Green Goddess, *125*
Kulle, Victor: Illusions, *985*
Kumai, Kei: Sandakan No. 8, *783*
Kumel, Harry: Daughters of Darkness, *830*
Kurahara, Koreyoshi: Antarctica, *713*
Kureishi, Hanif: London Kills Me, *577*
Kurolawa, Fumio: Jungle Book, The—A Devil in Mind, *179;* Jungle Book, The—A Trip of Adventure, *179*
Kurosawa, Akira: Akira Kurosawa's Dreams, *711;* Bad Slee[illegible] Well, The, *715;* Dersu Uzala, *729;* Dodes 'Ka-Den, *731;* Drunken Angel, *732;* Hidden Fortress, The, *744;* High and Lo[illegible] *744;* Idiot, The, *746;* Ikiru, *747;* Kagemusha, *751;* Lower Depths, The (1957), *763;* No Regrets for Our Youth, *772;* Ran[illegible] *779;* Rashomon, *780;* Red Beard, *780;* Rhapsody in August, *781;* Sanjuro, *783;* Sanshiro Sugata, *783;* Seven Samurai, The[illegible] *785;* Stray Dog, *790;* Throne of Blood, *794;* Yojimbo, *806*
Kurys, Diane: Entre Nous (Between Us), *734;* Man in Love, [illegible] *587*
Kushner, Donald: First and Ten, *277*
Kusturica, Emir: Do You Remember Dolly Bell?, *731;* Time of the Gypsies, *796;* When Father Was Away on Business, *80*[illegible]
Kuzui, Fran Rubel: Buffy, The Vampire Slayer, *247;* Tokyo Pop, *946*
Kwapis, Ken: Beniker Gang, The, *149;* He Said, She Said, *294;* Sesame Street Presents Follow That Bird, *203;* Vibes, *1087*
Kwitny, Jeff: Beyond the Door 3, *813*
Kyriazi, Paul: Omega Cop, *93*
Kyzystek, Waldemar: Suspended, *791*
La Cava, Gregory: Big News, *238;* Feel My Pulse, *276;* Fifth Avenue Girl, *276;* Gabriel over the White House, *524;* Living In A Big Way, *929;* My Man Godfrey (1936), *340;* Primrose Path, *627;* Running Wild (1927), *371;* Stage Door, *385*
La Rocque, Stephen: Samantha, *372*
Labrune, Jeanne: Sand and Blood, *783*
Lachman, Harry: Baby Take a Bow, *147;* Castle in the Desert[illegible] *960;* Charlie Chan in Rio, *961;* Murder Over New York, *999;* Our Relations, *351*
Ladd, Fred: Astroboy—Vols. 1–10, *1037;* Gigantor—Vols. 1–3, *169*
Lafia, John: Blue Iguana, *242;* Child's Play 2, *823;* Man's Best Friend (1993), *863*

agomarsino, Ron: Dinner at Eight (1990), *265*

ah, Michael: Barney Bear Cartoon Festival, *148;* Droopy and ompany, *164;* Here Comes Droopy, *174*

ahiff, Craig: Deadly Possession, *968*

aing, John: Beyond Reasonable Doubt (1983), *955;* Lost ibe, The, *861*

aLoggia, Frank: Fear No Evil, *840;* Lady in White, *990*

aloux, René: Fantastic Planet, *1050;* Light Years, *1063*

am, Ringo: City on Fire, *724;* Prison on Fire, *778*

ambert, Mary: Grand Isle, *531;* Pet Sematary, *874;* Pet ematary Two, *874;* Siesta, *1016*

amberti, Mark: Cartoons for Big Kids, *156;* Lost Stooges, he, *322*

amdo, Mao: Robot Carnival, *1075*

amont, Charles: Abbott and Costello Meet Captain Kidd, *21;* Abbott and Costello Meet Dr. Jekyll and Mr. Hyde, *221;* bbott and Costello Meet the Invisible Man, *221;* Abbott and ostello Meet the Mummy, *221;* Hit the Ice, *298;* Salome, /here She Danced, *647*

amore, Marsh: Great Space Chase, *171;* Secret of the word, The, *202*

amorisse, Albert: Red Balloon, The, *198;* Voyage en Ballon Stowaway to the Stars), *801*

ampson, Mary: Underground (1976), *437*

ancaster, Burt: Kentuckian, The, *1124*

anden, Berry: Dorf Goes Auto Racing, *267*

anders, Lew: Adventures of Gallant Bess, *442;* Annabel akes a Tour, *227;* Bad Lands, *1095;* Dynamite Pass, *1111;* nchanted Forest, The, *165;* Return of the Vampire, The, *880;* idin' on a Rainbow, *1144;* Smashing the Rackets, *1018;* orpedo Alley, *131*

andis, James: Nasty Rabbit, *342;* Sadist, The, *882*

andis, John: Amazon Women on the Moon, *225;* American /erewolf in London, An, *808;* Animal House, *227;* Beverly Hills op 3, *11;* Blues Brothers, The, *242;* Coming Soon, *824;* oming to America, *258;* Innocent Blood, *856;* Into the Night, *53;* Kentucky Fried Movie, *312;* Oscar (1991), *351;* Schlock, *73;* Spies Like Us, *384;* Three Amigos, *395;* Trading Places, *98;* Twilight Zone—The Movie, *898*

andoff, Lawrence: Indecent Behavior, *551*

andon, Michael: It's Good to Be Alive, *555;* Little House on ne Prairie (TV Series), *181;* Sam's Son, *647*

andres, Paul: Flipper's Odyssey, *167;* Go, Johnny, Go!, *20;* Return of Dracula, *880*

ane, Andrew: Desperate Motive, *970;* Jake Speed, *68;* onely Hearts (1991), *577;* Mortal Passions, *997*

ane, Charles: True Identity, *399*

ane, David: Captain Scarlet vs. the Mysterons, *156;* nvasion UFO, *1059;* UFO—Volumes I and II, *1086*

ane, Rocky: All's Fair, *225*

aneville, Eric: Ernest Green Story, The, *165;* George McKenna Story, The, *526*

anfield, Sidney: Addams Family, The (TV Series), *222;* Hound of the Baskervilles, The (1939), *983;* Lemon Drop Kid, he, *317;* Meanest Man in the World, The, *330;* My Favorite Blonde, *340;* One in a Million, *350;* Second Fiddle, *938;* Skirts hoy!, *940;* Sorrowful Jones, *383;* Station West, *1153;* Thin e, *945;* You'll Never Get Rich, *948*

ang, Fritz: Beyond a Reasonable Doubt (1956), *955;* Big Heat, The, *12;* Clash by Night, *483;* Cloak and Dagger (1946), *962;* Destiny, *729;* Dr. Mabuse, the Gambler (Parts I and II), *971;* Fury, *524;* Hangmen Also Die, *536;* House by the River, *84;* Human Desire, *546;* Kriemhilde's Revenge, *752;* M, *763;* Man Hunt (1941), *994;* Metropolis (1926), *1065;* Metropolis musical version), *930;* Rancho Notorious, *1140;* Return of Frank James, The, *1142;* Scarlet Street, *649;* Secret Beyond the Door, *650;* Siegfried, *786;* Spiders, The, *119;* Spies (1928), *788;* Testament of Dr. Mabuse, *1023;* Thousand Eyes of Dr. Mabuse, The, *1083;* Western Union, *1163;* While the City Sleeps, *138;* Wolfheart's Revenge, *1165;* Woman in the Moon a.k.a. Girl in the Moon; By Rocket to the Moon), *805;* You Only Live Once, *708*

Lang, Krzysztof: Paper Marriage (1992), *618*

Lang, Michel: Gift, The, *740;* Holiday Hotel, *744*

Lang, Perry: Little Vegas, *319*

Lang, Richard: Change of Seasons, A, *253;* Don't Go to Sleep, *836;* Fantasy Island, *1050;* Kung Fu—The Movie, *73;* Mountain Men, The, *1134;* Vega$, *135;* Word, The, *706*

Lang, Rocky: Nervous Ticks, *343;* Race for Glory, *102*

Lang, Walter: Blue Bird, The, *151;* But Not For Me, *472;* Can-Can, *911;* Desk Set, *263;* King and I, The, *926;* Little Princess, The, *183;* Moon Over Miami, *931;* Red Kimono, The, *636;* Snow White and the Three Stooges, *205;* Song of the Islands, *940;* State Fair (1945), *941;* There's No Business Like Show Business, *944*

Langley, Noel: Adventures of Sadie, *223;* Pickwick Papers, The, *357;* Search for Bridey Murphy, The, *650*

Langston, Murray: Wishful Thinking, *412*

Langton, Simon: Act of Passion, *441;* Anna Karenina (1985), *449;* Casanova (1987), *252;* Laguna Heat, *990;* Upstairs, Downstairs, *692;* Whistle Blower, The, *1031*

Lantz, Walter: Man's Best Friend (1985), *185;* Wild and Woody, *217;* Woody Woodpecker and His Friends (Volume One), *218;* Woody Woodpecker and His Friends (Volume Two), *218;* Woody Woodpecker and His Friends (Volume Three), *218;* World of Andy Panda, The, *218*

Lanza, Anthony M.: Glory Stompers, The, *56;* Incredible Two-Headed Transplant, The, *855*

Lanzmann, Claude: Shoah, *434*

Lapine, James: Impromptu, *549;* Life with Mikey, *318;* Sunday in the Park with George, *943*

Large, Brian: Elektra, *915*

Larraz, Joseph: House That Vanished, The, *853;* Vampyres, *900*

Larriva, Rudy: Looney Tunes Video Show, The (Volume 3), *184*

Larry, Sheldon: Miss Peach of the Kelly School, *188;* Ponce de Leon and the Fountain of Youth, *196;* Terminal Choice, *893*

Larsen, Keith: Whitewater Sam, *217*

Lathan, Stan: Almos' a Man, *445;* Beat Street, *908;* Sky Is Gray, The, *660*

Lattuada, Alberto: Christopher Columbus (1985), *25;* Cricket, The, *726;* Stay as You Are, *666;* Variety Lights, *800*

Laughlin, Michael: Mesmerized, *996;* Strange Behavior, *890;* Strange Invaders, *1080*

Laughlin, Tom: Billy Jack, *13*

Laughton, Charles: Night of the Hunter, *1001*

Launder, Frank: Belles of St. Trinian's, The, *234;* Great St. Trinian's Train Robbery, The, *290;* I See a Dark Stranger, *65*

Launer, Dale: Love Potion #9, *323*

Lautner, Georges: Icy Breasts, *746;* La Cage aux Folles III, The Wedding, *753;* My Other Husband, *770*

Lautrec, Linda: My Breakfast with Blassie, *339*

Lauzier, Gerard: Petit Con, *777*

Lauzon, Jean-Claude: Leolo, *759;* Night Zoo, *607*

Laven, Arnold: Monster That Challenged the World, The, *1066;* Rough Night in Jericho, *1146*

Lavut, Martin: Palais Royale, *97;* Smokescreen, *661*

Law, Alex: Painted Faces, *774*

Law, Clara: Reincarnation of Golden Lotus, The, *780*

Lawrence, Denny: Archer's Adventure, *147*

Lawrence, Marc: Pigs, *875*

Lawrence, Quentin: Crawling Eye, The, *825*

Lawrence, Ray: Bliss, *241*

Layton, Joe: Littlest Angel, The, *184;* Richard Pryor Live on the Sunset Strip, *368*

Le Chanois, Jean-Paul: Le Cas du Dr. Laurent, *757;* L'Ecole Buissonniere, *758;* Love and the Frenchwoman, *762;* Passion For Life, *776*

Leach, Wilford: Pirates of Penzance, The, *935;* Wedding Party, The, *407*

Leacock, Philip: Angel City, *448;* Curse of King Tut's Tomb, The, *828;* Thanksgiving Story, The, *210;* Three Sovereigns for Sarah, *683;* War Lover, The, *696*
Leader, Tony: Children of the Damned, *823;* Lost in Space (TV Series), *1063*
Leahy, Larry: Confessions of a Hitman, *487*
Leal, Orlando Jimenez: Improper Conduct, *427*
Lean, David: Bridge on the River Kwai, The, *19;* Brief Encounter (1945), *470;* Dr. Zhivago, *503;* Great Expectations (1946), *532;* Hobson's Choice (1954), *298;* In Which We Serve, *550;* Lawrence of Arabia, *76;* Oliver Twist (1948), *612;* Passage to India, A, *619;* Ryan's Daughter, *646;* Summertime, *673;* This Happy Breed, *682*
Lear, Norman: Cold Turkey, *257*
Lease, Maria: Dolly Dearest, *836*
Leaver, Don: Avengers, The (TV Series), *7;* Witching Time, *904*
LeBorg, Reginald: Diary of a Madman, *834;* Mummy's Ghost, The, *867;* Psycho Sisters, *877*
Leboursier, Raymond: Nais, *770*
Lecallier, Adeline: Love without Pity, *762*
Leconte, Patrice: Hairdresser's Husband, The, *742;* Monsieur Hire, *768*
Leder, Herbert J.: Candyman, The (1968), *474*
Leder, Mimi: Woman with a Past, *705*
Leder, Paul: Baby Doll Murders, The, *953;* Body Count, *817;* Exiled in America, *45;* Frame Up, *52;* I Dismember Mama, *855;* Murder by Numbers, *998;* Sketches of a Strangler, *1017;* Vultures, *901*
Lederer, Charles: Never Steal Anything Small, *932*
Lederman, D. Ross: Captain Midnight—Vols. 1–2, *155;* End of the Trail, *1111;* Phantom of the West, *1138;* Range Feud, *1141;* Riding Tornado, The, *1144;* Tarzan's Revenge, *126;* Texas Cyclone, *1155;* Two-Fisted Law, *1159*
Leduc, Paul: Frida, *739*
Lee, Ang: Wedding Banquet, The, *407*
Lee, Bruce: Return of the Dragon, *105*
Lee, Damien: Abraxas Guardian of the Universe, *1034;* Food of the Gods Part II, *1052;* Last Man Standing, *569;* Ski School, *380*
Lee, Evan: Hollywood Meatcleaver Massacre, *850*
Lee, Jack: Captain's Table, *250;* Wooden Horse, The, *706*
Lee, Rowland V.: Bridge of San Luis Rey, The, *469;* Captain Kidd, *23;* Count of Monte Cristo, The (1934), *30;* One Rainy Afternoon, *350;* Sea Lion, The, *650;* Son of Frankenstein, *888;* Son of Monte Cristo, The, *118;* Three Musketeers, The (1935), *128;* Toast of New York, The, *685;* Tower of London (1939), *897*
Lee, Spike: Crooklyn, *261;* Do the Right Thing, *502;* Jungle Fever, *561;* Malcolm X, *586;* Mo' Better Blues, *931;* School Daze, *373;* She's Gotta Have It, *377*
Legend, Johnny: Battle of the Bombs, *232;* Dope Mania, *423;* My Breakfast with Blassie, *339;* Sleazemania, *381;* Sleazemania Strikes Back, *381;* TV Turkeys, *401*
Legrand, François: Sex on the Run, *376;* Tower of Screaming Virgins, The, *897*
Lehman, Ernest: Portnoy's Complaint, *624*
Lehmann, Michael: Airheads, *906;* Heathers, *295;* Hudson Hawk, *64;* Meet the Applegates, *331*
Lehner, Peter: Megaville, *1065*
Lehrman, Henry: Lost and Found Chaplin: Keystone, *321*
Leiberman, Robert: Will, G. Gordon Liddy, *703*
Leibovit, Arnold: Fantasy Film Worlds of George Pal, The, *424;* Puppetoon Movie, The, *197*
Leifer, Neil: Trading Hearts, *398;* Yesterday's Hero, *708*
Leigh, Mike: Abigail's Party, *440;* Four Days in July, *521;* High Hopes, *297;* Life Is Sweet, *574;* Naked, *603;* Nuts in May, *348;* Who's Who, *411*
Leisen, Mitchell: Girl Most Likely, The, *919;* Golden Earrings, *56;* Lady Is Willing, The, *315;* Murder at the Vanities, *931;* Swing High, Swing Low, *390*
Leitch, Christopher: Courage Mountain, *160;* Teen Wolf, Too, *892*
Leland, David: Checking Out, *254;* Crossing the Line (199 *492;* Wish You Were Here, *412*
Lelouch, Claude: And Now, My Love, *712;* Another Man, Another Chance, *1094;* Bandits (1987), *715;* Bolero (1982), *720;* Cat and Mouse, *722;* Edith and Marcel, *733;* Happy New Year (La Bonne Année), *743;* Man and a Woman, A, *764;* Ma and a Woman, A: 20 Years Later, *764;* Robert et Robert, *782*
Lemmo, James: Heart, *537;* Relentless 3, *1010;* Tripwire, *132;* We're Talking Serious Money, *408*
Lemmon, Jack: Kotch, *314*
Lemorande, Rusty: Journey to the Center of the Earth (1987), *1060;* Turn of the Screw (1992), *898*
Leni, Paul: Cat and the Canary, The (1927), *960;* Waxwork *802*
Lenica, Jan: Ubu and the Great Gidouille, *798*
Lennon, Terry: Bugs Bunny's Wild World of Sports, *154;* Bugs vs. Daffy: Battle of the Music Video Stars, *154;* Daffy Duck's Quackbusters, *161*
Lent, Dean: Border Radio, *466*
Lente, Miklos: Oddballs, *348*
Lenzi, Umberto: Almost Human, *4;* Battle of the Commandos, *10;* Bridge to Hell, *19;* City of the Walking Dea *824;* Emerald Jungle, *838;* Eyeball, *840;* Make Them Die Slowly, *862;* Man from Deep River, *80;* Paranoia, *1004*
Leo, Malcolm: Beach Boys, The: An American Band, *419;* Came from Hollywood, *307;* This Is Elvis, *436*
Leonard, Brett: Lawnmower Man, The, *1062*
Leonard, Jack E.: World of Abbott and Costello, The, *414*
Leonard, Robert Z.: Broadway Serenade, *910;* Clown, The *484;* Dancing Lady, *913;* Divorcee, The, *502;* Duchess of Ida *915;* Firefly, The, *916;* Girl of the Golden West, The, *919;* Gre Ziegfeld, The, *921;* In the Good Old Summertime, *925;* Maytime, *930;* Nancy Goes to Rio, *932;* New Moon, *933;* Pri and Prejudice (1940), *626;* Strange Interlude (1932), *669;* Susan Lenox: Her Fall and Rise, *674;* Weekend at the Waldor *697;* When Ladies Meet, *698;* Ziegfeld Girl, *949*
Leonard, Sheldon: TV Classics: Jimmy Durante, *400*
Leonard, Terry: Death Before Dishonor, *35*
Leonardi, Arthur: Shelley Duvall's Bedtime Stories (Series) *203*
Leondopoulos, Jordon: Swap, The, *674*
Leone, John: Great Smokey Roadblock, The, *57*
Leone, Sergio: Fistful of Dollars, A, *1113;* Fistful of Dynamite, A, *1113;* For a Few Dollars More, *1113;* Good the Bad and the Ugly, The, *1116;* Once Upon a Time in America (Long Version), *94;* Once Upon a Time in the West, *1137*
Leong, Po-Chih: Banana Cop, *715;* Ping Pong, *622*
Lerner, Carl: Black Like Me, *462*
Lerner, Irving: Cry of Battle, *31;* Studs Lonigan, *671*
Lerner, Murray: From Mao to Mozart, *424*
Lerner, Richard: Revenge of the Cheerleaders, *367*
LeRoy, Mervyn: Anthony Adverse, *450;* Any Number Can Play, *450;* Bad Seed, The, *454;* Devil at 4 O'Clock, The, *500;* East Side, West Side, *506;* FBI Story, The, *515;* Gold Diggers 1933, *920;* Gypsy (1962), *921;* Homecoming (1948), *543;* I Am a Fugitive from a Chain Gang, *547;* Johnny Eager, *559;* Latin Lovers, *928;* Little Caesar, *77;* Little Women (1949), *57* Lovely to Look At, *929;* Madame Curie, *584;* Majority of One, A, *326;* Million Dollar Mermaid, *931;* Mr. Roberts, *334;* No Time for Sergeants, *345;* Quo Vadis (1951), *632;* Random Harvest, *635;* Rose Marie (1954), *937;* Sweet Adeline, *943;* Thirty Seconds Over Tokyo, *127;* Three Men on a Horse, *395;* Three on a Match, *683;* Waterloo Bridge, *697;* Without Reservations, *413*
Lessac, Michael: House of Cards, *545*
Lester, Mark L.: Armed and Dangerous, *228;* Bobbie Jo an the Outlaw, *17;* Class of 1984, *824;* Class of 1999, *1041;* Commando, *28;* Extreme Justice, *512;* Firestarter, *841;* Showdown in Little Tokyo, *115;* Truckstop Women, *132*

ester, Richard: Butch and Sundance: The Early Days, *1103;* uba, *31;* Finders Keepers, *277;* Four Musketeers, The, *52;* unny Thing Happened on the Way to the Forum, A, *282;* Hard ay's Night, A, *921;* Help!, *922;* How I Won the War, *302;* uggernaut (1974), *987;* Knack...and How To Get It, The, *314;* etulia, *621;* Return of the Musketeers, *106;* Ritz, The, *368;* obin and Marian, *107;* Superman II, *1081;* Superman III, *081;* Three Musketeers, The (1973), *128*

eszczykowski, Michal: Directed by Andrei Tarkovsky, *422*

etterier, François: Goodbye Emmanuelle, *741*

ettich, Sheldon: Double Impact, *41;* Only the Strong, *95*

etts, Barry: Gulliver in Lilliput, *291*

evant, Brian: Beethoven (1992), *149;* Flintstones, The, *167;* roblem Child 2, *362*

evering, Joseph: In Early Arizona, *1122*

evesque, Michel: Werewolves on Wheels, *902*

evey, Jay: Compleat "Weird Al" Yankovic, The, *258;* UHF, *02*

evey, William A.: Blackenstein, *814;* Committed, *824;* appy Hooker Goes to Washington, The, *293;* Hellgate, *849;* ightning, the White Stallion, *181;* Slumber Party 57, *381*

evi, Alan J.: Quantum Leap (TV Series), *1072;* Riding with eath, *1074*

evick, David: Gospel, *425*

evin, Henry: Ambushers, The, *4;* Desperados, The, *1109;* armer Takes a Wife, The, *916;* Jolson Sings Again, *926;* ourney to the Center of the Earth (1959), *1060;* Lonely Man, he, *1129;* Man from Colorado, The, *1131;* Murderers' Row, *7;* Run for the Roses, *201;* Two of a Kind (1951), *1028;* Varriors, The (1955), *137;* Where the Boys Are, *409;* Vonderful World of the Brothers Grimm, The, *1090*

evin, Marc: Last Party, The, *428*

evin, Peter: Comeback Kid, The, *486;* Gone to Texas, *1116;* ape And Marriage: The Rideout Case, *635*

evine, Fred: Road Construction Ahead, *433*

evine, Michael: Checkered Flag, *480*

evinson, Barry: Avalon, *452;* Bugsy, *471;* Diner, *265;* Good orning, Vietnam, *530;* Jimmy Hollywood, *310;* Natural, The, *04;* Rain Man, *634;* Tin Men, *396;* Toys, *398;* Young Sherlock olmes, *141*

evitow, Abe: Adventures of Milo in the Phantom Tollbooth, he, *144;* Bugs Bunny's Hare-Raising Tales, *154;* Dick Tracy artoons, *162;* Gay Purr-ee, *168;* Mr. Magoo in Sherwood orest, *188;* Mr. Magoo in the King's Service, *188;* Mr. Magoo, an of Mystery, *188;* Mr. Magoo's Christmas Carol, *188;* Mr. agoo's Storybook, *188;* Pepe Le Pew's Skunk Tales, *194*

evitt, Ed: Story of Babar, The, *207*

evy, Eugene: Once Upon a Crime, *349*

evy, I. Robert: Can I Do It 'Til I Need Glasses?, *249*

evy, Jeffrey: Inside Monkey Zetterland, *306*

evy, Ralph: Bedtime Story, *233;* Beverly Hillbillies, The (TV eries), *237;* George Burns and Gracie Allen Show, The (TV eries), *284*

evy, Shuki: Blind Vision, *956*

ewicki, Stephen Jon: Certain Sacrifice, A, *478*

ewin, Albert: Moon and Sixpence, The, *599;* Picture of orian Gray, The, *875;* Private Affairs of Bel Ami, The, *628*

ewin, Ben: Favor, the Watch and the Very Big Fish, The, *75;* Georgia, *979*

ewis, Al: Our Miss Brooks (TV Series), *351*

ewis, Christopher: Ripper, The, *881*

ewis, David: Bill Cosby: 49, *239;* Dangerous Curves, *262*

ewis, Herschell Gordon: Blood Feast, *815;* Color Me Blood ed, *824;* Gruesome Twosome, *848;* She-Devils on Wheels, *115;* Something Weird, *888;* Suburban Roulette, *671;* Taste of lood, A, *892;* 2,000 Maniacs, *898;* Wizard of Gore, The, *904*

ewis, Jerry: Bellboy, The, *234;* Big Mouth, The, *238;* racking Up, *260;* Errand Boy, The, *272;* Family Jewels, The, *73;* Hardly Working, *293;* Ladies' Man, The, *314;* Nutty rofessor, The, *348;* Patsy, The, *355;* Which Way to the ront?, *410*

Lewis, Joseph H.: Big Combo, The, *12;* Boys of the City, *18;* Gun Crazy (1950), *981;* Invisible Ghost, *856;* Lawless Street, A, *1127;* Pride of the Bowery, *627;* Retreat Hell, *105;* Return of October, The, *366;* 7th Cavalry, *1148*

Lewis, Robert: Dead Reckoning (1990), *967;* Lady Killers, *990;* Memories of Murder, *996;* S.H.E., *110;* Summer to Remember, A, *673*

Lewis, Robert Michael: Child Bride of Short Creek, *480;* Fallen Angel, *513;* Pray for the Wildcats, *100*

Lewiston, Denis: Hot Target, *64*

Lewyn, Louis: Hollywood on Parade, *299*

Lhotsky, Tina: Film Musicals, *277*

Liconti, Carlo: Concrete Angels, *487;* Good Night, Michelangelo, *288*

Lieberman, Jeff: Blue Sunshine, *957;* Remote Control, *879;* Squirm, *889*

Lieberman, Robert: All I Want for Christmas, *145;* Fire in the Sky, *1051;* Table for Five, *676*

Liebling, Rachel: High Lonesome—The Story of Bluegrass Music, *426*

Liebman, Max: 10 from Your Show of Shows, *392*

Light, Warren: Night We Never Met, The, *345*

Lincoln, F. J.: Wild Man, *139*

Lindahl, Carl: Comic Cabby, *258;* What's Up Doc?—A Salute To Bugs Bunny, *216*

Lindberg, Per: June Night, *751*

Linder, Max: Seven Years' Bad Luck, *376*

Lindsay, Lance: Star Crystal, *1078*

Lindsay-Hogg, Michael: Annie Oakley (1985), *146;* As Is, *451;* Brideshead Revisited, *469;* Let It Be, *429;* Master Harold and the Boys, *590;* Murder by Moonlight, *1067;* Nasty Habits, *342;* Object of Beauty, The, *348;* Running Mates (1992), *371;* Strange Case of Dr. Jekyll and Mr. Hyde, The (1989), *890;* Thumbelina (1983), *211*

Lindtberg, Leopold: Four in a Jeep, *521*

Link, Ron: Zombie High, *904*

Linklater, Richard: Dazed and Confused, *497;* Slacker, *380*

Linson, Art: Where the Buffalo Roam, *409;* Wild Life, The, *411*

Lion, Mickey: House of Exorcism, The, *852*

Lipman, David: Road Lawyers and Other Briefs, *368*

Lipstadt, Aaron: Android, *1036;* City Limits, *1041*

Lisberger, Steven: Animalympics, *146;* Hot Pursuit, *301;* Slipstream, *1077;* Tron, *1085*

Lishman, Eda Lever: Primo Baby, *197*

Lister, David: Rutanga Tapes, The, *1011*

Lit, Law: Mr. Vampire (Vol. 1–4), *768*

Littin, Miguel: Alsino and the Condor, *712*

Little, Dwight H.: Bloodstone, *16;* Getting Even, *55;* Halloween IV: The Return of Michael Myers, *848;* Marked for Death, *82;* Phantom of the Opera (1989), *874;* Rapid Fire, *103*

Littman, Lynne: Testament, *1082*

Litvak, Anatole: All This and Heaven Too, *445;* Anastasia, *447;* City for Conquest, *482;* Goodbye Again, *530;* Mayerling, *766;* Night of the Generals, *90;* Sisters, The (1938), *659;* Snake Pit, The, *661;* Sorry, Wrong Number (1948), *1019;* Tovaritch, *398*

Lively, Gerry: Body Moves, *466*

Livingston, Jennie: Paris Is Burning, *432*

Livingston, Robert H.: Taking My Turn, *943*

Llosa, Luis: Crime Zone, *1043;* 800 Leagues Down the Amazon, *43;* Hour of the Assassin, *64;* Sniper, *117*

Lloyd, Frank: Blood on the Sun, *15;* Cavalcade, *477;* Howards of Virginia, The, *545;* Last Command, The (1955), *1125;* Mutiny on the Bounty (1935), *88;* Oliver Twist (1922), *611*

Lloyd, Harold: Harold Lloyd's Comedy Classics, *294*

Lloyd, Norman: Tales of the Unexpected, *1022*

Lo Bianco, Tony: Too Scared to Scream, *1025*

Lo, Lucas: No Retreat, No Surrender 3: Blood Brothers, *92*

Loach, Kenneth: Family Life, *514;* Hidden Agenda, *541;* Riff-Raff (1992), *640;* Singing the Blues in Red, *786*
Loader, Jayne: Atomic Cafe, The, *418*
Lobl, Victor: Beauty and the Beast (TV Series), *1039;* Eden (TV Series), *507*
Locke, Rick: Best of DC Follies, *235;* Petronella, *195*
Locke, Sondra: Impulse (1990), *985;* Ratboy, *635*
Logan, Bob: Meatballs 4, *330;* Repossessed, *366;* Up Your Alley, *403*
Logan, Bruce: Vendetta, *135*
Logan, Joshua: Bus Stop, *248;* Camelot, *911;* Ensign Pulver, *271;* Fanny (1961), *514;* Paint Your Wagon, *934;* Picnic, *622;* Sayonara, *648;* South Pacific, *941;* Tall Story, *391*
Logan, Stanley: Falcon's Brother, The, *975*
Logothetis, Dimitri: Body Shot, *958;* Closer, The, *484;* Pretty Smart, *361;* Slaughterhouse Rock, *887*
Loma, J. Anthony: Boldest Job in the West, The, *1099;* Counterforce, *30;* Man of Passion, A, *587;* Street Warriors, *670;* Street Warriors II, *671;* Target Eagle, *125*
Loman, Joseph: Boldest Job in the West, The, *1099*
Lomas, Raoul: Minor Miracle, A, *187*
Lombardo, Lou: P.K. & the Kid, *617;* Russian Roulette, *110*
Lommel, Ulli: Big Sweat, The, *13;* Boogeyman, The, *818;* Brainwaves, *818;* Cocaine Cowboys, *27;* Cold Heat, *28;* Devonsville Terror, The, *834;* Overkill, *96;* Warbirds, *137*
Loncraine, Richard: Bellman and True, *954;* Brimstone and Treacle, *819;* Deep Cover (1980), *969;* Haunting of Julia, The, *537;* Missionary, The, *333*
London, James: Place Called Trinity, A, *1139*
London, Jerry: Chiefs, *961;* Ellis Island, *508;* Haunting of Sarah Hardy, The, *982;* Kiss Shot, *566;* Manhunt for Claude Dallas, *81;* Rent-a-Cop, *105;* Scarlet and the Black, The, *112;* Season of Giants, A, *650;* Shogun (Full-Length Version), *115;* Victim of Love, *1030*
London, Roy: Diary of a Hitman, *970*
Long, Stanley: Adventures of a Private Eye, *222*
Longo, Robert: Arena Brains, *450*
Longon, Humphrey: Battle Force, *9*
Longstreet, Harry S.: Sex, Love, and Cold Hard Cash, *1014*
Lopez, Temistocles: Chain of Desire, *478*
Lord, Jean-Claude: Eddie and the Cruisers II: Eddie Lives!, *915;* Landslide, *990;* Mind Field, *85;* Toby McTeague, *212;* Vindicator, The, *1087;* Visiting Hours, *901*
Lord, Stephen: Fall of the House of Usher, The (1979), *840*
Lorentz, Pare: Plow That Broke the Plains, The, *433*
Loring, Ken: Combat Killers, *28*
Losey, Joseph: Accident, *440;* Assassination of Trotsky, The, *451;* Boy With Green Hair, The, *468;* Concrete Jungle, The (1962) (a.k.a. The Criminal), *487;* Doll's House, A (1973), *503;* La Truite (The Trout), *755;* Mr. Klein, *768;* Roads to the South, *781;* Romantic Englishwoman, The, *643;* Secret Ceremony, *650;* Servant, The, *652;* Sleeping Tiger, The, *660;* Steaming, *667*
Lottimer, Eb: Love Matters, *581*
Louis, Larry: Body Puzzle, *958*
Lounguine, Pavel: Taxi Blues, *792*
Lounsbery, John: Rescuers, The, *199;* Winnie the Pooh and Tigger Too, *218*
Lourie, Eugene: Beast From 20,000 Fathoms, The, *1038;* Gorgo, *847*
Louzil, Eric: Class of Nuke 'em High 2: Subhumanoid Meltdown, *824;* Fortress of Amerikkka, *51;* Lust for Freedom, *80;* Wilding, The Children of Violence, *140*
Loventhal, Charlie: First Time, The, *277;* My Demon Lover, *339*
Lovy, Steven: Circuitry Man, *1041*
Lowe, Lucas: American Shaolin: King of the Kickboxers II, *5;* King of the Kickboxers, The, *72*
Lowe, William: Slaughter in San Francisco, *117*
Lowenheim, Al: Seabert: The Adventure Begins, *202*
Lowenstein, Richard: Dogs in Space, *914*
Lowney, Declan: Velvet Underground, The: Velvet Redux—Live MCMXCIII, *437*
Lowry, Dick: Coward of the County, *490;* FBI Murders, The, *47;* Gambler, The (1980), *1114;* Gambler, Part II—The Adventure Continues, The, *1115;* Gambler, Part III—The Legend Continues, The, *1115;* Gambler Returns, the: Luck of the Draw, *1115;* In the Line of Duty: Ambush in Waco, *66;* Jayne Mansfield Story, The, *557;* Living Proof: The Hank Williams, Jr., Story, *577;* Murder with Mirrors, *999;* Smokey and the Bandit III, *382;* Wet Gold, *138*
Loy, Nanni: Cafe Express, *721;* Where's Piccone?, *803*
Lubin, Arthur: Ali Baba and the Forty Thieves, *3;* Buck Privates, *246;* Escapade in Japan, *165;* Francis Goes to the Races, *280;* Francis in the Navy, *280;* Francis Joins the Wacs, *280;* Francis, the Talking Mule, *280;* Hold That Ghost, *298;* Impact, *985;* Incredible Mr. Limpet, The, *306;* Maverick (TV Series), *1133;* Phantom of the Opera (1943), *874;* Ride 'em Cowboy, *368*
Lubitsch, Ernst: Gypsy Blood, *535;* Heaven Can Wait (1943), *295;* Lady Windermere's Fan, *568;* Marriage Circle, The, *329;* Merry Widow, The, *930;* Ninotchka, *345;* One Arabian Night, *773;* Passion (1919), *775;* Shop Around the Corner, The, *378;* So This Is Paris, *382;* Student Prince in Old Heidelberg, The, *671;* That Uncertain Feeling, *393;* To Be or Not to Be (1942), *397*
Luby, S. Roy: Arizona Stagecoach, *1095;* Black Market Rustlers, *1099;* Boothill Bandits, *1100;* Border Phantom, *1100;* Fugitive Valley, *1114;* Lightning Triggers, *1128;* Saddle Mountain Roundup, *1146;* Trail of the Silver Spurs, *1158*
Lucas, George: American Graffiti, *226;* Star Wars, *1079;* THX 1138, *1084*
Lucente, Francesco: Virgin Queen of St. Francis High, The, *405*
Lucidi, Maurizio: Saddle Tramps, *1147;* Stateline Motel, *789;* Street People, *121*
Ludman, Larry: Deadly Impact, *34;* Operation 'Nam, *95;* Thunder Warrior, *129;* Thunder Warrior II, *129*
Ludwig, Edward: Big Jim McLain, *460;* Big Wheel, The, *461;* Bonanza (TV Series), *1100;* Fabulous Texan, The, *1112;* Fighting Seabees, The, *48;* Wake of the Red Witch, *136*
Luhrmann, Baz: Strictly Ballroom, *942*
Luke, Eric: Not Quite Human 2, *347;* Still Not Quite Human, *386*
Lumet, Sidney: Anderson Tapes, The, *952;* Danger, *965;* Daniel, *495;* Deathtrap, *969;* Dog Day Afternoon, *971;* Equus, *973;* Fail-Safe, *974;* Family Business, *514;* Fugitive Kind, The, *523;* Garbo Talks, *283;* Group, The, *534;* Guilty as Sin, *534;* Hill, The, *541;* Just Tell Me What You Want, *312;* Long Day's Journey into Night (1962), *578;* Morning After, The, *997;* Murder on the Orient Express, *999;* Network, *604;* Offence, The, *611;* Pawnbroker, The, *620;* Power (1986), *625;* Prince of the City, *627;* Q & A, *1008;* Running on Empty, *645;* Serpico, *652;* Stage Struck (1958), *665;* Stranger Among Us, A, *1020;* 12 Angry Men, *690;* Verdict, The, *693;* Wiz, The, *948*
Luna, Bigas: Anguish, *809;* Jamon, Jamon, *749*
Lunch, Lydia: Gun is Loaded, The, *921*
Lupino, Ida: Bigamist, The, *461;* Treasures of the Twilight Zone, *1085;* Trouble with Angels, The, *399*
Lusitana, Donna E.: Civil War Journal, *421*
Lusk, Don: Pirates of Dark Waters, The: The Saga Begins, *19*
Luske, Hamilton: Alice in Wonderland (1951), *145;* Ben and Me, *149;* Bongo, *152;* Cinderella (1950), *159;* Lady and the Tramp, *180;* One Hundred and One Dalmatians, *192;* Peter Pan (1953), *194*
Lustig, William: Hit List (1988), *982;* Maniac (1980), *862;* Maniac Cop, *862;* Maniac Cop 2, *863;* Maniac Cop 3: Badge of Silence, *863;* Relentless, *1010*
Luther, Salvo: Forget Mozart, *737*
Lynch, David: Blue Velvet, *817;* Dune, *1048;* Elephant Man, The (1980), *508;* Eraserhead, *838;* Hotel Room, *983;* Industrial Symphony No. 1 The Dream of the Broken Hearted, *925;* Twin Peaks (Movie), *1027;* Twin Peaks: Fire Walk with Me, *1028;* Wild at Heart, *702*

Lynch, Jennifer Chambers: Boxing Helena, *818*

Lynch, Paul: Blindside, *15;* Bullies, *820;* Cross Country, *491;* Dream to Believe, *504;* Drop Dead Gorgeous, *972;* Humongous, *854;* Prom Night, *876;* Really Weird Tales, *365;* Star Trek: The Next Generation (TV Series), *1079;* Victim of Beauty, *1030*

Lyne, Adrian: Fatal Attraction (1987), *975;* Flashdance, *917;* Foxes, *521;* Indecent Proposal, *551;* Jacob's Ladder, *1060;* 9½ Weeks, *607*

Lynn, Jonathan: Clue, *256;* Distinguished Gentleman, The, *265;* Greedy, *290;* My Cousin Vinny, *339;* Nuns on the Run, *347*

Lyon, Francis D.: Castle of Evil, *821;* Cult of the Cobra, *827;* Great Locomotive Chase, The, *171;* Oklahoman, The, *1136;* Tomboy and the Champ, *213*

Maak, Karoly: Cat's Play, *722*

Maas, Dick: Amsterdamned, *809;* Lift, The, *860*

Mabe, Byron: She Freak, The, *885*

MacAdams, Lewis: Eric Bogosian—Funhouse, *272*

MacArthur, Charles: Scoundrel, The, *374*

MacDonald, David: Devil Girl from Mars, *833;* Never Too Late, *604*

MacDonald, Peter: Mo' Money, *335;* Rambo III, *103*

Macek, Carl: Zillion—Vols. 1–5, *220*

MacFadden, Hamilton: Stand Up and Cheer, *206*

MacFarland, Mike: Hanging on a Star, *536;* Pink Motel, *357*

MacGregor, Sean: Gentle Savage, *1115*

Machaty, Gustav: Ecstasy, *733*

Mack, Brice: Jennifer, *858*

Mackendrick, Alexander: Ladykillers, The, *315;* Man in the White Suit, The, *327;* Sweet Smell of Success, *675;* Tight Little Island, *396*

Mackenzie, John: Act of Vengeance, *441;* Beyond the Limit, *460;* Fourth Protocol, The, *978;* Last of the Finest, The, *75;* Long Good Friday, The, *78;* Ruby (1991), *644;* Sense of Freedom, A, *652;* Voyage, *1030*

Mackenzie, Will: Perfect Harmony, *194;* Worth Winning, *414*

Mackinnon, Gillies: Playboys, The, *623*

MacLean, Stephen: Around the World in 80 Ways, *228*

MacNamara, Brian: Tales of Beatrix Potter, *209*

Macy, W. H.: Lip Service, *576*

Madden, John: Ethan Frome, *511;* Grown-ups, *534*

Madden, Lee: Hell's Angels '69, *60;* Night Creature, *869*

Madsen, Kenneth: Day in October, A, *496*

Maetzig, Kurt: First Spaceship on Venus, *1051*

Magar, Guy: Retribution, *879;* Stepfather III: Father's Day, *890*

Magnatta, Constantino: Dark Side, The, *829;* Darkside, The, *33*

Magni, Luigi: In Nome del Papa Re (In the Name of the Pope-King), *747*

Magnoli, Albert: American Anthem, *446;* Born To Run, *18;* Purple Rain, *935;* Street Knight, *121*

Magnuson, John: Lenny Bruce Performance Film, The, *317*

Magyar, Dezso: No Secrets, *1002;* Rappaccini's Daughter, *635*

Mahan, Kerrigan: Fisher Price Video: Grimms' Fairy Tales: Hansel and Gretel/King Grizzle Beard, *167*

Maharaj, Anthony: Deathfight, *36;* Kick Fighter, *70;* Revenge of the Kickfighter, *106*

Mahon, Barry: Assault of the Rebel Girls, *7;* Rocket Attack USA, *1075*

Mailer, Norman: Tough Guys Don't Dance, *686*

Maitland, George: Invasion Earth: The Aliens Are Here, *856*

Makavejev, Dusan: Coca Cola Kid, The, *257;* Innocence Unprotected, *748;* Manifesto, *328;* Montenegro, *599;* Sweet Movie, *792;* WR: Mysteries of the Organism, *805*

Makk, Karoly: Lily in Love, *318;* Love, *761*

Malick, Terence: Badlands, *454;* Days of Heaven, *496*

Malle, Louis: Alamo Bay, *443;* Atlantic City, *452;* Au Revoir, Les Enfants, *714;* Crackers, *260;* Damage, *493;* Elevator to the Gallows, *734;* Fire Within, The, *736;* Lovers, The (1958), *762;* May Fools, *766;* Murmur of the Heart, *769;* My Dinner with Andre, *602;* Phantom India, *433;* Pretty Baby, *626;* Very Private Affair, A, *800;* Viva Maria!, *801;* Zazie dans le Metro, *807*

Mallon, James: Blood Hook, *815*

Malmuth, Bruce: Hard to Kill, *59;* Man Who Wasn't There, The, *328;* Nighthawks, *91;* Where Are the Children?, *1031*

Malone, William: Creature, *1043*

Mamet, David: Homicide, *983;* House of Games, *984;* Things Change, *394*

Mamoru, Oshii: Urusei Yatsura: Beautiful Dreamer, *799*

Mamoulian, Rouben: Applause, *450;* Becky Sharp, *457;* Blood and Sand (1941), *464;* Dr. Jekyll and Mr. Hyde (1932), *835;* Golden Boy, *529;* Love Me Tonight, *929;* Mark of Zorro, The (1940), *82;* Queen Christina, *631;* Silk Stockings, *939;* Summer Holiday, *942*

Mancuso, Kevin (Joe d'Amato): 2020 Texas Gladiators, *1086*

Mandel, Jeff: Elves, *838;* Robo C.H.I.C., *1074*

Mandel, Robert: Big Shots, *238;* F/X, *979;* Independence Day, *551;* Perfect Witness, *620;* School Ties, *649;* Touch and Go, *398*

Mandoki, Luis: Born Yesterday (1993), *244;* Gaby, a True Story, *524;* When a Man Loves a Woman, *698;* White Palace, *700*

Manduke, Joseph: Cornbread, Earl and Me, *488;* Gumshoe Kid, The, *292;* Kid Vengeance, *1124;* Omega Syndrome, *93*

Manfredi, Nino: Nudo di Donna (Portrait of a Woman, Nude), *772*

Mangine, Joseph: Neon Maniacs, *868*

Mankiewicz, Francis: And Then You Die, *5;* Love and Hate, *581*

Mankiewicz, Joseph L.: All About Eve, *444;* Barefoot Contessa, The, *455;* Cleopatra (1963), *484;* Five Fingers, *977;* Ghost and Mrs. Muir, The, *285;* Guys and Dolls, *921;* Honey Pot, The, *300;* House of Strangers, *545;* Julius Caesar (1953), *561;* Letter to Three Wives, A, *573;* People Will Talk, *356;* Sleuth, *1017;* Suddenly, Last Summer, *672;* There Was a Crooked Man, *1156*

Mankiewicz, Tom: Delirious, *263;* Dragnet (1987), *268;* Taking the Heat, *676*

Mankiewirk, Henry: Hell's Brigade, *61*

Mann, Abby: King, *564*

Mann, Anthony: Bend of the River, *1097;* Cimarron (1960), *1105;* Dandy in Aspic, A, *965;* Desperate, *969;* El Cid, *43;* Fall of the Roman Empire, The, *513;* Far Country, The, *1112;* Glenn Miller Story, The, *919;* God's Little Acre, *529;* Great Flamarion, The, *532;* He Walked by Night, *982;* Man from Laramie, The, *1131;* Man of the West, *1132;* Men in War, *84;* Naked Spur, The, *1135;* Railroaded, *633;* Strategic Air Command, *670;* T-Men, *676;* Thunder Bay, *129;* Tin Star, The, *1157;* Winchester '73, *1165*

Mann, Daniel: Butterfield 8, *472;* Come Back, Little Sheba, *486;* Dream of Kings, A, *504;* For Love of Ivy, *279;* Hot Spell, *544;* I'll Cry Tomorrow, *924;* Interval, *553;* Journey into Fear (1975), *987;* Last Angry Man, The, *568;* Man Who Broke 1000 Chains, The, *587;* Matilda, *330;* Our Man Flint, *96;* Playing for Time, *623;* Rose Tattoo, The, *644;* Teahouse of the August Moon, The, *392;* Who's Got the Action?, *411;* Willard, *903*

Mann, Delbert: All Quiet on the Western Front (1979), *444;* Birch Interval, The, *150;* Desire under the Elms, *500;* Francis Gary Powers: The True Story of the U-2 Spy Incident, *522;* Ironclads, *554;* Last Days of Patton, The, *569;* Love Leads the Way, *581;* Lover Come Back, *323;* Marty, *589;* Marty (Television), *589;* Middle of the Night, *593;* Night Crossing, *90;* She Waits, *885;* That Touch of Mink, *393;* Torn Between Two Lovers, *686*

Mann, Edward (Santos Alocer): Cauldron of Blood, *822*

Mann, Farhad: Nick Knight, *868;* Return to Two-Moon Junction, *639*

Mann, Michael: Jericho Mile, The, *557;* Keep, The, *859;* Last of the Mohicans, The (1992), *1126;* Manhunter, *995;* Thief (1981), *127*
Mann, Ron: Comic Book Confidential, *421*
Manning, Jack: Merry Wives of Windsor, The, *331*
Manning, Michelle: Blue City, *957*
Manoogian, Peter: Arena, *1036;* Demonic Toys, *832;* Dungeonmaster, The, *1048;* Eliminators, The, *1048;* Enemy Territory, *44;* Seedpeople, *1076*
Mansfield, Mike: Stand by Me (1988), *941*
Mansfield, Scott: Deadly Games, *968*
Manuli, Guido: Volere Volare, *801*
Manzarek, Ray: Dance on Fire, *422;* Doors, The: A Tribute to Jim Morrison, *423;* Doors, The Soft Parade, *423;* Soft Parade, The, *435*
Marcarelli, Robert: Original Intent, *614*
Marcel, Terry: Hawk the Slayer, *59;* Jane and the Lost City, *309;* Prisoners of the Lost Universe, *1072*
Marcellini, Siro: Gangster's Law, *525*
March, Alex: Firehouse (1972), *49;* Mastermind, *329;* Paper Lion, *618*
Marchent, Joaquin Romero: Cut Throats Nine, *1107*
Marconi, David: Harvest, The, *981*
Marcus, Adam: Jason Goes to Hell: The Final Friday, *858*
Marcus, Philip: Terror on Alcatraz, *1023*
Marfori, Andreas: Desperate Crimes, *37;* Evil Clutch, *839*
Margolin, Stuart: Family Matter, A, *514;* Glitter Dome, The, *980;* Paramedics, *353;* Shining Season, A, *656*
Margolis, Jeff: Oscar's Greatest Moments: 1971 to 1991, *432;* Richard Pryor—Live in Concert, *367*
Marin, Edwin L.: Abilene Town, *1092;* Cariboo Trail, *1103;* Christmas Carol, A (1938), *158;* Death Kiss, The, *968;* Everybody Sing, *916;* Invisible Agent, *1059;* Johnny Angel, *69;* Listen, Darling, *928;* Miss Annie Rooney, *188;* Mr. Ace, *85;* Nocturne, *1002;* Show Business, *939;* Study in Scarlet, A, *1021;* Tall in the Saddle, *1154*
Marin, Richard "Cheech": Born in East L.A., *244;* Get Out of My Room, *284*
Marinos, Lex: Indecent Obsession, An, *551*
Maris, Peter: Can It Be Love, *249;* Diplomatic Immunity, *39;* Ministry of Vengeance, *85;* Terror Squad, *127;* Viper, *136*
Mark, Mary Ellen: Streetwise, *435*
Marker, Chris: Sans Soliel, *434*
Marker, Russ: Yesterday Machine, The, *1090*
Markes, Anthony: Bikini Island, *813;* Last Dance, *990*
Markham, Monte: Defense Play, *36;* Neon City, *1067*
Markiw, Gabriel: Mob Story, *335*
Markiw, Jancarlo: Mob Story, *335*
Markle, Fletcher: Incredible Journey, The, *177*
Markle, Peter: Bat 21, *9;* Breaking Point, *469;* El Diablo, *1111;* Four Eyes and Six Guns, *1114;* Hot Dog...The Movie, *301;* Nightbreaker, *607;* Personals, The, *357;* Youngblood, *709*
Markovic, Goran: Tito and Me, *795*
Markowitz, Murray: Left for Dead, *572*
Markowitz, Robert: Afterburn, *442;* Belarus File, The, *954;* Dangerous Life, A, *494;* Decoration Day, *498;* Love, Lies and Murder, *994;* My Mother's Secret Life, *602;* Pray TV (1982), *626;* Voices, *694*
Marks, Arthur: Bonnie's Kids, *17;* Bucktown, *20;* Detroit 9000 (Detroit Heat), *37;* Friday Foster, *53;* J.D.'s Revenge, *858*
Marlowe, Brad: Webber's World, *406*
Marlowe, Derek: Adventures of Sherlock Holmes, The (Series), *950*
Marmorstein, Malcolm: Dead Men Don't Die, *262*
Marnham, Christian: Lethal Woman, *77*
Marquand, Richard: Eye of the Needle, *974;* Hearts of Fire, *538;* Jagged Edge, *556;* Legacy, The, *860;* Return of the Jedi, *1074;* Until September, *692*
Marquette, Jacques: Meteor Monster, *864*
Marr, Leon: Dancing in the Dark, *494*
Marshall, Frank: Alive, *444;* Arachnophobia, *810*
Marshall, Garry: Beaches, *457;* Flamingo Kid, The, *278;* Frankie and Johnny (1991), *522;* Nothing in Common, *609;* Overboard, *352;* Pretty Woman, *361;* Young Doctors in Love, *415*
Marshall, George: Boy, Did I Get a Wrong Number!, *244;* Destry Rides Again, *1109;* Fancy Pants, *274;* Gazebo, The, *28[illegible]* Ghost Breakers, *285;* Goldwyn Follies, The, *920;* Guns of Fort Petticoat, *1118;* Houdini, *544;* How the West Was Won, *1122;* It Started With a Kiss, *308;* Laurel and Hardy Classics, Volume 2, *316;* Laurel and Hardy Classics, Volume 3, *316;* Mating Game, The, *330;* Monsieur Beaucaire, *336;* My Friend Irma, *340;* Off Limits (1953), *348;* Pack Up Your Troubles, *352;* Papa's Delicate Condition, *617;* Perils of Pauline, The (1947), *356;* Pot O' Gold, *625;* Red Garters, *936;* Sad Sack, The, *372;* Show Them No Mercy, *657;* Texas, *1155;* Valley of the Sun, *1161;* You Can't Cheat an Honest Man, *415*
Marshall, Mannie: Unexpected Encounters, *691*
Marshall, Penny: Awakenings, *452;* Big, *237;* Jumpin' Jack Flash, *311;* League of Their Own, A, *571;* Working Stiffs, *414*
Marshall, William: Adventures of Captain Fabian, *2*
Martin, Charles: Death of a Scoundrel, *498;* My Dear Secretary, *339*
Martin, D'Urville: Dolemite, *267*
Martin, Eugenio: Horror Express, *851;* Pancho Villa, *1138*
Martin, Frank: Dr. Butcher, M.D. (Medical Deviate), *835;* John Huston—The Man, the Movies, the Maverick, *428*
Martin, Gene: Bad Man's River, *1095*
Martin, James Aviles: Flesh Eating Mothers, *841*
Martin, Richard Wayne: No Justice, *91*
Martinere, Stephan: Madeline, *184*
Martinez, Chuck: Nice Girls Don't Explode, *344*
Martini, Richard: Limit Up, *319;* You Can't Hurry Love, *415*
Martino, Raymond: Davinci's War, *33*
Martino, Sergio: Cheaters, The, *723;* Great Alligator, The, *847;* Opponent, The, *95;* Screamers, *884;* Sex with a Smile, *376;* Slave of the Cannibal God, *117;* Torso, *896*
Martins, W. Mel: Alex's Apartment, *951*
Martinson, Leslie: Atomic Kid, The, *229;* Batman (1966), *148;* Cheyenne (TV Series), *1104;* Kid with the Broken Halo, The, *313;* Kid with the 200 I.Q., The, *180;* Maverick (TV Series) *1133;* PT 109, *630*
Marton, Andrew: Africa—Texas Style!, *3;* Around the World Under the Sea, *6;* Clarence, the Cross-Eyed Lion, *159;* Gypsy Colt, *173;* King Solomon's Mines (1950), *72;* Longest Day, The, *78;* Men of the Fighting Lady, *84*
Marvin, Mike: Hamburger—The Motion Picture, *292;* Wraith The, *904*
Masahiro, Tanaka: Riding Bean, *781*
Masaki, Shin-Ichi: Humanoid, The, *745*
Masami, Oobari: Bubblegum Crisis—Vols. 1–8, *720*
Masano, Anton Giulio: Atom Age Vampire, *810*
Mascarelli, Robert: I Don't Buy Kisses Anymore, *303*
Maseba, Yutaka: Ambassador Magma, *712*
Masenza, Claudio: James Dean, *427*
Massaro, Francesco: Private Affairs, *361*
Massetti, Ivana: Domino, *503*
Massi, Stelvio: Fearless (1978), *736*
Massot, Joe: Song Remains the Same, The, *435;* Wonderwall, *805*
Masters, Quentin: Dangerous Summer, A, *494;* Stud, The, *671*
Masterson, Peter: Blood Red, *464;* Full Moon in Blue Water *282;* Night Game, *1000;* Trip to Bountiful, The, *688*
Mastorakis, Nico: Blind Date (1984), *463;* Double Exposure (1987), *268;* Glitch!, *287;* Hired to Kill, *62;* In the Cold of the Night, *986;* Next One, The, *1068;* Nightmare at Noon, *870;* Wind, The (1986), *1032;* Zero Boys, The, *904*
Mastrocinque, Camillo: Full Hearts and Empty Pockets, *7[illegible]*
Mastroianni, Armand: Cameron's Closet, *820;* Deep Trouble, *969;* Distortions, *834;* Double Revenge, *504;* He Knows You're Alone, *849;* Killing Hour, The, *988;* Supernaturals, The, *891*

Masuda, Toshio: Tora! Tora! Tora!, *131*
Matalon, Eddy: Blackout (1978), *14;* Cathy's Curse, *822;* Sweet Killing, *1022*
Maté, Rudolph: Branded, *1101;* D.O.A. (1949), *965;* Dark Past, The, *495;* For the First Time, *918;* Second Chance, *113;* Three Violent People, *1157;* Union Station, *1029;* Violent Men, The, *1161;* When Worlds Collide, *1089*
Matinson, Burney: Mickey's Christmas Carol, *187*
Matmor, Daniel: Homeboys II: Crack City, *63*
Matsumiya, Masuzumi: Wannabes, *802*
Matsuura, John: Little Women (1981), *183*
Matsuzono, Tohru: Rumik World: Laughing Target, *782*
Mattei, Bruno: Seven Magnificent Gladiators, The, *113*
Mattei, Marius: Moving Target, *87*
Matthau, Charles: Doin' Time on Planet Earth, *267*
Matthau, Walter: Gangster Story, *979*
Mattison, Bunny: Adventures of the Great Mouse Detective, The, *144*
Mattison, Sally: Slumber Party Massacre 3, *887*
Mattson, Arne: Doll, *731;* Girl, The, *527*
Mauri, Roberto: Animal Called Man, An, *1093;* Slaughter of the Vampires, *887*
Maxwell, Peter: Highest Honor, The, *62;* Run, Rebecca, Run, *201;* Secret Agent (TV Series), *113*
Maxwell, Ronald F.: Gettysburg, *526;* Little Darlings, *319;* Night the Lights Went Out in Georgia, The, *606*
May, Bradford: Drive Like Lightning, *42;* Legacy of Lies, *572;* Lethal Lolita—Amy Fisher: My Story, *573;* Marilyn & Bobby: Her Final Affair, *588;* Mortal Sins (1992), *997*
May, Elaine: Heartbreak Kid, The, *295;* Ishtar, *307;* Mikey and Nicky, *332;* New Leaf, A, *343*
May, Joe: House of the Seven Gables, The, *545;* Invisible Man Returns, *856*
Mayberry, Russ: Challenge of a Lifetime, *478;* Fer-de-Lance, *976;* Probe, *101;* Rebels, The, *636;* Side by Side: The True Story of the Osmond Family, *203;* Unidentified Flying Oddball, *214*
Mayer, Gerald: Man Inside, The (1984), *81*
Mayersberg, Paul: Captive, *475;* Nightfall, *1068*
Mayfield, Les: Encino Man, *271*
Maylam, Tony: Burning, The, *820;* Riddle of the Sands, *106;* Sins of Dorian Gray, The, *886;* Split Second (1992), *1078*
Maynard, Ken: Fiddlin' Buckaroo, *1112*
Mayo, Archie: Angel on My Shoulder (1946), *448;* Case of the Lucky Legs, The, *960;* Crash Dive, *30;* Go Into Your Dance, *920;* House Across the Bay, The, *545;* Illicit, *549;* Night after Night, *344;* Night in Casablanca, A, *344;* Orchestra Wives, *934;* Petrified Forest, The, *621;* Svengali (1931), *1022;* They Shall Have Music, *944*
Maysles, Albert: Beatles, The: The First U.S. Visit, *419;* Gimme Shelter, *424;* Grey Gardens, *425;* Salesman, *434*
Maysles, David: Beatles, The: The First U.S. Visit, *419;* Gimme Shelter, *424;* Grey Gardens, *425;* Salesman, *434*
Mazo, Michael: Last of the Warriors, *1062;* Time Runner, *1084*
Mazursky, Paul: Alex in Wonderland, *224;* Blume in Love, *465;* Bob & Carol & Ted & Alice, *243;* Down and Out in Beverly Hills, *268;* Enemies—A Love Story, *510;* Harry and Tonto, *537;* Moon Over Parador, *336;* Moscow on the Hudson, *337;* Next Stop, Greenwich Village, *605;* Pickle, The, *357;* Scenes from a Mall, *373;* Tempest (1982), *678;* Unmarried Woman, An, *691;* Willie and Phil, *412*
McBrearty, Don: Child's Christmas in Wales, A, *158;* Coming Out Alive, *963;* Really Weird Tales, *365;* Strange Tales: Ray Bradbury Theater, *1080;* Tales From Avonlea (TV series), *209*
McBride, Jim: Big Easy, The, *12;* Blood Ties (1993), *816;* Breathless (1983), *469;* Glen and Randa, *1054;* Great Balls of Fire, *920;* Wrong Man, The (1993), *707*
McBride, Jon: Cannibal Campout, *820*
McCabe, Norman: Best of Warner Brothers, Vol. 1, *150;* Daffy Duck: Tales from the Duckside, *160*
McCall, Cheryl: Streetwise, *435*
McCall, Rod: Cheatin' Hearts, *480*
McCally, John: Annie Oakley (1992), *147*
McCalmont, James: Escape from Safehaven, *1049*
McCarey, Leo: Affair to Remember, An, *442;* Awful Truth, The, *230;* Belle of the Nineties, *234;* Bells of St. Mary's, The, *458;* Duck Soup, *269;* Going My Way, *529;* Good Sam, *288;* Indiscreet (1931), *306;* Milky Way, The (1936), *332;* Once Upon a Honeymoon, *349;* Ruggles of Red Gap, *371*
McCarey, Ray: Devil's Party, The, *500;* So This Is Washington, *382;* You Can't Fool Your Wife, *415*
McCarthy, John P.: Song of the Gringo, *1151;* Trailin' North, *1158*
McCarthy, Michael: Operation Amsterdam, *95;* Thieves of Fortune, *127*
McCarthy, Todd: Visions of Light: The Art of Cinematography, *438*
McCartney, Paul: Paul McCartney and Wings—Rock Show, *432*
McClatchy, Greggor: Vampire at Midnight, *899*
McComas, Tom: Great Toy Train Layouts of America (Volumes 1–6), *425;* I Love Toy Trains, *427*
McCormick, Bret: Blood on the Badge, *15*
McCowan, George: Frogs, *844;* Murder on Flight 502, *87;* Return to Fantasy Island, *1074*
McCubbin, Peter: Home for Christmas, *542*
McCullough, Jim: Aurora Encounter, *1037;* Mountaintop Motel Massacre, *866*
McDonald, Bruce: Highway 61, *297*
McDonald, Frank: Along the Navajo Trail, *1093;* Bells of Rosarita, *1097;* Big Sombrero, The, *1098;* Flying Blind, *51;* Gun Smugglers, *1117;* Lights of Old Santa Fe, *1128;* My Pal Trigger, *1135;* One Body Too Many, *1003;* Sioux City Sue, *1150;* Take It Big, *943;* Thunder Pass, *1157*
McDonald, J. Farrell: Patchwork Girl of Oz, The, *193*
McDonald, Rodney: Night Eyes 2, *1000*
McDougall, Don: Bonanza (TV Series), *1100;* Chinese Web, The, *25;* Riding with Death, *1074*
McElwee, Ross: Sherman's March, *434*
McEveety, Bernard: Brotherhood of Satan, *819;* Longest Drive, The, *1130;* Napoleon and Samantha, *190;* Ride Beyond Vengeance, *1143;* Roughnecks, *109*
McEveety, Vincent: Amy, *146;* Apple Dumpling Gang Rides Again, The, *147;* Castaway Cowboy, The, *157;* Charley and the Angel, *157;* Gunsmoke: Return to Dodge, *1118;* Gus, *172;* Herbie Goes Bananas, *174;* Herbie Goes to Monte Carlo, *174;* Menace on the Mountain, *593;* Million Dollar Duck, The, *187;* Smoke, *205;* Star Trek (TV Series), *1078;* Superdad, *208*
McGann, William: American Empire, *1093;* Dr. Christian Meets the Women, *502;* In Old California, *1122*
McGaugh, W. F.: New Adventures of Tarzan, *90*
McGavin, Darren: Run Stranger Run, *882*
McGinnis, Scott: Caroline at Midnight, *960*
McGoohan, Patrick: Prisoner, The (TV Series), *1071*
McGowan, Darrell: Showdown, The (1950), *1149*
McGowan, J. P.: Drum Taps, *1110;* Hurricane Express, *65;* When a Man Rides Alone, *1163*
McGowan, Robert: Old Swimmin' Hole, The, *611*
McGowan, Stuart: Showdown, The (1950), *1149*
McGowan, Stuart E.: Billion Dollar Hobo, The, *150;* They Went That-A-Way and That-A-Way, *210*
McGowan, Tom: Savage Journey, *1147*
McGrath, Joseph: Bliss of Mrs. Blossom, The, *241;* Casino Royale (1967), *252;* Magic Christian, The, *326;* 30 Is a Dangerous Age, Cynthia, *394*
McGrath, Martin: Wet and Wild Summer, *408*
McGuane, Thomas: 92 in the Shade, *345*
McGuire, Don: Delicate Delinquent, The, *263*
McHenry, Doug: House Party 2, *923*
McIntyre, C. T.: Border Shootout, *1100*
McIntyre, Chris: Backstreet Justice, *8*
McIntyre, Thom: Rutherford County Line, *110*

McKay, Cole: Game, The, *54*

McKay, Windsor: Animation Legend Windsor McKay, *146*

McKeown, Douglas: Return of the Alien's Deadly Spawn, The, *880*

McKimmie, Jackie: Waiting, *695*

McKimson, Robert: Bugs Bunny Classics, *153;* Bugs Bunny: Truth or Hare, *153;* Bugs Bunny's Easter Funnies, *154;* Bugs Bunny's Hare-Raising Tales, *154;* Cartoon Moviestars: Bugs!, *156;* Cartoon Moviestars: Daffy!, *156;* Cartoon Moviestars: Porky!, *156;* Cartoon Moviestars: Starring Bugs Bunny, *156;* Daffy Duck and Company, *160;* Daffy Duck Cartoon Festival: Ain't That Ducky, *160;* Daffy Duck's Madcap Mania, *161;* Elmer Fudd's Comedy Capers, *164;* Foghorn Leghorn's Fractured Funnies, *167;* Golden Age of Looney Toons, The: Bugs Bunny by Each Director, *169;* Golden Age of Looney Toons, The: Firsts, *170;* Golden Age of Looney Toons, The: 1940s Zanies, *170;* Just Plain Daffy, *179;* Looney Tunes Video Show, The (Volume 1), *184;* Looney Tunes Video Show, The (Volume 2), *184;* Looney Tunes Video Show, The (Volume 3), *184;* Porky Pig and Daffy Duck Cartoon Festival Featuring "Tick Tock Tuckered", *196;* Porky Pig: Days of Swine and Roses, *196;* Porky Pig Tales, *196;* Porky Pig's Screwball Comedies, *197;* Salute to Mel Blanc, A, *201;* Speedy Gonzales' Fast Funnies, *206;* Sylvester and Tweety's Crazy Capers, *209;* Tweety and Sylvester, *214;* Very Best of Bugs Bunny: Volume 1, The, *215*

McLachlan, Duncan: Double-O Kid, The, *41;* Scavengers, *373*

McLaglen, Andrew V.: Bandolero!, *1096;* Blue and the Gray, The, *1099;* Breakthrough, *19;* Cahill—US Marshal, *1103;* Chisum, *1104;* Devil's Brigade, The, *37;* Dirty Dozen, The: The Next Mission, *39;* ffolkes, *47;* Hellfighters, *60;* McLintock!, *1133;* Monkeys Go Home, *188;* On Wings of Eagles, *94;* Rare Breed, The (1966), *1141;* Sahara (1984), *110;* Sea Wolves, The, *113;* Shadow Riders, The, *1148;* Shenandoah, *1149;* Undefeated, The, *1160;* Way West, The, *1163;* Wild Geese, The, *139*

McLennan, Don: Slate, Wyn, and Me, *660*

McLeod, Norman Z.: Casanova's Big Night, *252;* Horse Feathers, *301;* It's a Gift, *308;* Kid from Brooklyn, The, *313;* Lady Be Good, *927;* Let's Dance, *928;* Little Men (1940), *576;* Monkey Business (1931), *335;* Never Wave at a WAC, *343;* Paleface, The, *353;* Panama Hattie, *935;* Road to Rio, *369;* Secret Life of Walter Mitty, The, *374;* Topper, *397;* Topper Takes a Trip, *398*

McLoughlin, Tom: Date with an Angel, *262;* Fire Next Time, The, *1051;* Friday the 13th, Part VI: Jason Lives, *844;* One Dark Night, *872;* Sometimes They Come Back, *888*

McMurray, Mary: At Bertram's Hotel, *953;* Office Romances, *611*

McNaughton, Ian: And Now for Something Completely Different, *226;* Monty Python's Flying Circus (TV Series), *336*

McNaughton, John: Borrower, The, *1040;* Henry: Portrait of a Serial Killer, *540;* Mad Dog and Glory, *584;* Sex, Drugs, Rock & Roll, *653*

McPherson, John: Dirty Work, *970;* Fade to Black (1993), *974;* Strays, *891*

McRae, Henry: Tarzan the Tiger, *126*

McRae, Peter: Endurance, *271*

McTiernan, John: Die Hard, *38;* Hunt for Red October, The, *984;* Last Action Hero, The, *1062;* Medicine Man, *591;* Nomads, *872;* Predator, *1071*

Mead, Nick: Bank Robber, *232*

Medak, Peter: Babysitter, The, *811;* Changeling, The, *822;* Dancing Princesses, The, *161;* Day in the Death of Joe Egg, A, *262;* Emperor's New Clothes, The (1984), *164;* Ghost in the Noonday Sun, *285;* Krays, The, *567;* Let Him Have It, *573;* Men's Club, The, *593;* Negatives, *1067;* Odd Job, The, *348;* Pinocchio (1983), *195;* Romeo is Bleeding, *108;* Ruling Class, The, *371;* Snow Queen, *205;* Snow White and the Seven Dwarfs (1983), *205;* Zorro, the Gay Blade, *417*

Medford, Don: Fugitive, The: The Last Episode (TV Series), *53;* Organization, The, *96;* Sizzle, *659*

Medoway, Cary: Heavenly Kid, The, *296;* Paradise Motel, *353*

Meerapfel, Jeanine: Malou, *764*

Meffre, Pomme: Grain of Sand, The, *741*

Megahy, Francis: Carpathian Eagle, *821;* Great Riviera Bank Robbery, The, *980;* Taffin, *124*

Mehta, Ketan: Spices, *788*

Meins, Gus: Gentleman from California, *1115;* March of the Wooden Soldiers, *329*

Meisel, Myron: It's All True, *427*

Meisel, Norbert: Adultress, The, *441*

Mekas, Adolfas: Brig, The, *470*

Mekas, Jonas: Brig, The, *470*

Melançon, André: Bach and Broccoli, *147*

Melchior, Ib: Angry Red Planet, The, *1036;* Time Travelers, The, *1084*

Mele, Arthur N.: Soldier's Fortune, *118*

Melendez, Bill: Bon Voyage, Charlie Brown, *152;* Boy Named Charlie Brown, A, *152;* Charlie Brown and Snoopy Show, The (Volume I), *157;* Charlie Brown and Snoopy Show, The (Volume II), *157;* Charlie Brown Celebration, A, *157;* Charlie Brown Christmas, A, *157;* Charlie Brown Thanksgiving, A, *157;* Charlie Brown's All-Stars, *157;* Good Grief, Charlie Brown, *171;* Happy New Year, Charlie Brown, *173;* He's Your Dog, Charlie Brown, *174;* It Was a Short Summer, Charlie Brown, *177;* It's an Adventure, Charlie Brown, *177;* It's Christmastime Again, Charlie Brown, *177;* It's Flashbeagle, Charlie Brown, *177;* It's the Great Pumpkin, Charlie Brown, *178;* It's Three Strikes, Charlie Brown, *178;* Lion, the Witch and the Wardrobe, The, *181;* Race for Your Life, Charlie Brown, *198;* She Likes You, Charlie Brown, *203;* Snoopy, Come Home, *205;* Snoopy's Getting Married, Charlie Brown, *205;* Story of Babar, The, *207;* There's No Time for Love, Charlie Brown, *210;* Very Funny, Charlie Brown, *215;* What a Nightmare, Charlie Brown, *216;* What Have We Learned, Charlie Brown?, *216;* What Next, Charlie Brown?, *216;* You Can't Win, Charlie Brown, *219;* You're in Love, Charlie Brown, *219;* You're in The Superbowl, Charlie Brown, *220*

Melford, George: Dracula (Spanish Version), *732;* East of Borneo, *43;* Man of Action, *1132;* Moran of the Lady Letty, *997;* Sheik, The, *655*

Mellencamp, John: Falling from Grace, *513*

Melton, Frank: Othello (1982), *615*

Melville, Jean-Pierre: Bob le Flambeur, *719;* Le Doulos, *757*

Menaul, Chris: Prime Suspect 1, *1007*

Mendeluk, George: Doin' Time, *266;* Kidnapping of the President, The, *988;* Meatballs III, *330;* Stone Cold Dead, *1020*

Mendes, Lothar: Man Who Could Work Miracles, The, *1064*

Mendez, Fernando: Vampire, The, *899*

Menendez, Ramon: Money for Nothing, *335;* Stand and Deliver, *665*

Menges, Chris: Crisscross (1992), *491;* World Apart, A, *706*

Menshov, Vladimir: Moscow Does Not Believe in Tears, *768*

Menzel, Jiri: Closely Watched Trains, *725;* Larks on a String, *755*

Menzies, William Cameron: Chandu the Magician, *24;* Drums in the Deep South, *1110;* Invaders from Mars (1953), *1059;* Things to Come, *1083*

Merchant, Ismail: Courtesans of Bombay, *489*

Meredith, Burgess: Man in the Eiffel Tower, The, *995;* Yin and Yang of Mr. Go, The, *1033*

Merhi, Joseph: CIA Codename Alexa, *26;* Final Impact, *48;* Fresh Kill, *53;* Killing Game, The, *71;* L.A. Crackdown, *73;* L.A. Crackdown II, *74;* L.A. Vice, *74;* Last Riders, The, *75;* Maximum Force, *83;* Night of the Wilding, *606*

Merino, J. L.: Blood Castle (1970), *815*

Merrick, Ian: Black Panther, The, *463*

Merrill, Kieth: Harry's War, *294;* Take Down, *390;* Windwalker, *1165*

Merriwether, Nicholas (Arch W. Hall Sr.): Eegah!, *838*

Mesa, Roland: Revenge of the Nerds III: The Next Generation, *367*
Meshekoff, Matthew: Opposite Sex (And How to Live with Them), The, *351*
Messina, Philip F.: Spy, *1019*
Metter, Alan: Back to School, *230;* Girls Just Want to Have Fun, *287;* Moving, *338*
Metzger, Alan: China Lake Murders, The, *961;* Fatal Exposure, *46;* Red Wind, *1009*
Metzger, Radley: Cat and the Canary, The (1978), *960;* Therese and Isabelle, *794*
Meyer, Andrew: Night of the Cobra Woman, *869*
Meyer, Jean: Le Bourgeois Gentilhomme, *756*
Meyer, Kevin: Civil War Diary, *483;* Invasion of Privacy, *986;* Under Investigation, *1028*
Meyer, Muffie: Grey Gardens, *425*
Meyer, Nicholas: Company Business, *28;* Day After, The, *1044;* Deceivers, The, *36;* Pied Piper of Hamelin, The, *195;* Star Trek II: The Wrath of Khan, *1079;* Star Trek VI: The Undiscovered Country, *1079;* Time After Time, *1084;* Volunteers, *405*
Meyer, Russ: Beneath the Valley of the Ultra-Vixens, *234;* Beyond the Valley of the Dolls, *460;* Cherry, Harry and Raquel, *480;* Common Law Cabin, *487;* Fanny Hill: Memoirs of a Woman of Pleasure, *514;* Faster Pussycat! Kill! Kill!, *46;* Finders Keepers, Lovers Weepers, *516;* Good Morning…and Goodbye!, *530;* Immoral Mr. Teas, The, *305;* Lorna, *580;* Mondo Topless, *431;* Motor Psycho, *87;* Mudhoney, *600;* Seven Minutes, The, *653;* Supervixens, *123;* Up!, *403;* Vixen, *405*
Meza, Eric: House Party 3, *923*
Michaels, Richard: Backfield in Motion, *230;* Berlin Tunnel 21, *10;* Blue Skies Again, *465;* Heart of a Champion: The Ray Mancini Story, *538;* Lethal Charm, *573;* One Cooks, the Other Doesn't, *349;* Sadat, *646*
Michalakis, John Elias: I Was a Teenage Zombie, *855*
Michener, Dave: Adventures of the Great Mouse Detective, The, *144*
Middleton, Edwin: Bill Fields and Will Rogers, *239;* Fatal Glass of Beer, A/Pool Sharks, *274*
Mihalka, George: Hostile Take Over, *544;* My Bloody Valentine, *867;* Psychic, *1008;* Straight Line, *120*
Mikamoto, Yasuyoshi: Orguss, Vols. 1–4, *1069*
Mikels, Ted V.: Astro-Zombies, *810;* Black Klansman, The, *14;* Blood Orgy of the She Devils, *815;* Corpse Grinders, The, *825;* 10 Violent Women, *126*
Mikesch, Elfi: Seduction, The: Cruel Woman, *784*
Mikhalkov, Nikita: Close to Eden, *725;* Dark Eyes, *728;* Oblomov, *772;* Slave of Love, A, *786;* Unfinished Piece for the Player Piano, An, *798*
Mileham, Michael: Pushed to the Limit, *101*
Miles, Christopher: Priest of Love, *627;* That Lucky Touch, *392;* Virgin and the Gypsy, The, *694*
Milestone, Hank: From Hell to Victory, *53*
Milestone, Lewis: All Quiet on the Western Front (1930), *3;* Arch of Triumph, *450;* Edge of Darkness (1943), *43;* Front Page, The (1931), *281;* General Died at Dawn, The, *55;* Halls of Montezuma, *59;* Lucky Partners, *324;* Mutiny on the Bounty (1962), *88;* North Star, The, *92;* Ocean's Eleven, *93;* Pork Chop Hill, *624;* Purple Heart, The, *630;* Rain, *634;* Red Pony, The, *198;* Strange Love of Martha Ivers, The, *669;* Walk in the Sun, A, *136*
Milius, John: Big Wednesday, *461;* Conan the Barbarian, *1042;* Dillinger (1973), *39;* Farewell to the King, *46;* Flight of the Intruder, The, *50;* Red Dawn, *104;* Wind and the Lion, The, *140*
Milland, Ray: Lisbon, *77;* Man Alone, A, *1131*
Millar, Gavin: Dreamchild, *1048;* Tidy Endings, *683*
Millar, Stuart: Rooster Cogburn, *1146;* When the Legends Die, *1163*
Miller, Claude: Accompanist, The, *710;* Little Thief, The, *760*
Miller, Dan T.: Screamers, *884*
Miller, David: Back Street, *453;* Billy the Kid, *1099;* Bittersweet Love, *462;* Captain Newman, M.D., *474;* Diane, *500;* Executive Action, *512;* Flying Tigers, The, *51;* Hail, Hero!, *535;* Lonely Are the Brave, *1129;* Love Happy, *322;* Midnight Lace, *84;* Opposite Sex, The, *934*
Miller, George: Frozen Assets, *282;* Goodbye, Miss 4th of July, *171*
Miller, George: Anzacs, *450;* Aviator, The, *452;* Les Patterson Saves the World, *317;* Man from Snowy River, The, *1131;* Miracle Down Under, *187;* NeverEnding Story II, The, *1068;* Over the Hill, *352*
Miller, George: Chain Reaction, *24;* Lorenzo's Oil, *579;* Mad Max, *1064;* Mad Max Beyond Thunderdome, *1064;* Road Warrior, The, *1074;* Twilight Zone—The Movie, *898;* Witches of Eastwick, The, *412*
Miller, Harvey: Bad Medicine, *231*
Miller, Ira: Loose Shoes, *321*
Miller, J. C.: No Dead Heroes, *91*
Miller, Jason: That Championship Season, *680*
Miller, Jonathan: Long Day's Journey into Night (1987), *578*
Miller, Michael: Case of Deadly Force, A, *476;* Jackson County Jail, *68;* National Lampoon's Class Reunion, *342;* Silent Rage, *116*
Miller, Neal: Under the Biltmore Clock, *691*
Miller, Paul: Live from Washington—It's Dennis Miller, *320*
Miller, Randall: Class Act, *256*
Miller, Robert Ellis: Any Wednesday, *228;* Baltimore Bullet, The, *231;* Bed and Breakfast, *457;* Brenda Starr, *19;* Girl from Petrovka, The, *527;* Hawks, *537;* Heart Is a Lonely Hunter, The, *538;* Reuben, Reuben, *367*
Miller, Sidney: 30 Foot Bride of Candy Rock, The, *394*
Miller, Walter C.: All-Star Toast to the Improv, An, *224;* Best of Comic Relief, The, *235;* Comic Relief 2, *258;* Howie from Maui, *303;* Rodney Dangerfield: "It's Not Easy Being Me", *370;* Rodney Dangerfield—Nothin' Goes Right, *370;* Sam Kinnison Live!, *372;* Steven Wright Live, *386*
Milligan, Andy: Bloodthirsty Butchers, *816;* Ghastly Ones, The, *845;* Legacy of Horror, *860;* Rats Are Coming!, The Werewolves Are Here!, The, *878;* Torture Dungeon, *896*
Milling, Bill: Caged Fury, *21*
Mills, Alec: Bloodmoon, *816;* Dead Sleep, *967*
Mills, Roger: Pole to Pole, *433*
Milo, Tom E.: Smooth Talker, *1018*
Milton, Robert: Devotion, *500*
Miner, Steve: Forever Young (1992), *1053;* Friday the 13th, Part II, *843;* Friday the 13th, Part III, *843;* House, *852;* My Father, the Hero, *339;* Soul Man, *383;* Warlock (1988), *901;* Wild Hearts Can't Be Broken, *217*
Mingay, David: Rude Boy, *938*
Minghella, Anthony: Mr. Wonderful, *597;* Truly, Madly, Deeply, *689*
Mingozzi, Gianfranco: Bellissimo: Images of the Italian Cinema, *716;* Sardine: Kidnapped, *783*
Minion, Joe: Daddy's Boys, *31*
Minnelli, Vincente: American in Paris, An, *906;* Bad and the Beautiful, The, *454;* Band Wagon, The, *908;* Bells Are Ringing, *908;* Brigadoon, *909;* Cabin in the Sky, *473;* Clock, The, *484;* Courtship of Eddie's Father, The, *260;* Designing Woman, *263;* Father of the Bride (1950), *275;* Father's Little Dividend, *275;* Four Horsemen of the Apocalypse, *52;* Gigi, *919;* Home from the Hill, *542;* I Dood It, *924;* Kismet (1955), *927;* Long, Long Trailer, The, *320;* Lust for Life, *583;* Madame Bovary (1949), *584;* Matter of Time, A, *590;* Meet Me in St. Louis, *930;* On a Clear Day, You Can See Forever, *933;* Pirate, The, *935;* Reluctant Debutante, The, *365;* Sandpiper, The, *648;* Some Came Running, *662;* Tea and Sympathy, *678;* Two Weeks in Another Town, *690;* Undercurrent, *691;* Yolanda and the Thief, *708;* Ziegfeld Follies, *949*
Mintz, Murphy: Cardiac Arrest, *959*
Mischer, Don: Evening with Robin Williams, An, *272*
Misiorowski, Bob: Blink of an Eye, *15;* Point of Impact, *99*

Misumi, Kenji: Shogun Assassin, *785;* Zatoichi: The Blind Swordsman and the Chess Expert, *806*
Mitchell, David: City of Shadows, *26*
Mitchell, Oswald: Danny Boy (1941), *495*
Mitchell, Sollace: Call Me, *959*
Mitton, David: Thomas the Tank Engine and friends, *210*
Miyazaki, Hayao: Castle of Cagliostro, The, *24;* Lupin III: Tales of the Wolf (TV Series), *763*
Miyazaki, Kazuya: Little Women (1981), *183*
Mizoguchi, Kenji: Chikamatsu Monogatari, *723;* Forty Seven Ronin, *738;* Geisha, A, *740;* Life of Oharu, *760;* Osaka Elegy, *774;* Princess Yang Kwei Fei, *778;* Sansho the Bailiff, *783;* Shin Heinke Monogatari, *785;* Street of Shame, *790;* Ugetsu, *798*
Mizrahi, Moshe: Every Time We Say Goodbye, *511;* I Sent a Letter to My Love, *746;* La Vie Continue, *755;* Madame Rosa, *763*
Moberly, Luke: Little Laura and Big John, *77*
Moctezuma, Juan Lopez: Dr. Tarr's Torture Dungeon, *836;* Mary, Mary, Bloody Mary, *863*
Moder, Richard: Bionic Woman, The, *1039*
Moeller, Phillip: Break of Hearts, *468*
Moffitt, John: Best of Not Necessarily the News, The, *236;* Love at Stake, *322*
Mogherini, Flavio: Lunatics & Lovers, *763*
Moguy, Leonide: Action in Arabia, *2;* Whistle Stop, *138*
Möhr, Hanro: Hostage (1987), *64*
Molander, Gustav: Dollar, *731;* Intermezzo (1936), *748;* Only One Night, *773*
Molina, Jack: Craving, The, *825*
Molinaro, Edouard: Dracula and Son, *837;* Just the Way You Are, *561;* La Cage aux Folles, *753;* La Cage aux Folles II, *753;* Pain in the A—, A, *774;* Ravishing Idiot, The, *364;* Seven Deadly Sins, The, *785*
Moloney, Paul: I Live With Me Dad, *547*
Monahan, Dave: Adventures of Milo in the Phantom Tollbooth, The, *144*
Mones, Paul: Fathers & Sons, *515*
Monger, Christopher: Waiting for the Light, *695*
Monicelli, Mario: Big Deal on Madonna Street, *717;* Laugh for Joy, *756;* Lovers and Liars, *323;* Passionate Thief, The (1961), *776*
Monnier, Philippe: Tale of Two Cities, A (1991), *677*
Monroe, Phil: Bugs Bunny/Road Runner Movie, The, *153*
Montagne, Edward: They Went That-A-Way and That-A-Way, *210*
Montaldo, Giuliano: Sacco and Vanzetti, *782;* Time to Kill, *684*
Montero, Roberto: Monster of the Island, The, *86;* Slasher, *887;* Tharus, Son of Attila, *127*
Montes, Eduardo: Double Obsession, *972*
Montesi, Jorge: Hush Little Baby, *984;* Omen IV: The Awakening, *872*
Montgomery, George: From Hell to Borneo, *53*
Montgomery, Monty: Loveless, The, *582*
Montgomery, Patrick: Compleat Beatles, The, *421*
Montgomery, Robert: Gallant Hours, The, *524;* Lady in the Lake, *990*
Moody, Ralph: Stage to Tucson, *1152*
Moore, Charles Philip: Blackbelt, *14;* Dance with Death, *965;* Demon Wind, *832*
Moore, Michael: Buckskin, *1102;* Fastest Guitar Alive, The, *1112;* Paradise Hawaiian Style, *935;* Talion, *1154*
Moore, Michael: Roger & Me, *434*
Moore, Richard: Circle of Iron, *26*
Moore, Robert: Chapter Two, *479;* Cheap Detective, The, *254;* Murder by Death, *338;* Thursday's Game, *683*
Moore, Ronald W.: Future-Kill, *845*
Moore, Simon: Under Suspicion, *1028*
Moore, Tara: Tusks, *133*
Moore, Tom: Danielle Steele's "Fine Things", *495;* 'Night, Mother, *606;* Return to Boggy Creek, *880*
Moorhouse, Jocelyn: Proof, *629*
Mora, Philippe: Beast Within, The, *812;* Breed Apart, A, *19;* Communion, *1042;* Death of a Soldier, *498;* Howling II...Your Sister Is a Werewolf, *854;* Howling III, *854;* Mad Dog Morgan, *80;* Return of Captain Invincible, The, *366*
Morahan, Christopher: Clockwise, *256;* Jewel in the Crown, The, *557;* Paper Mask, *1004*
Moranis, Rick: Strange Brew, *387*
Mordente, Tony: Love in the Present Tense, *581*
Mordillat, Gérard: Billy Ze Kick, *718*
Moreau, Jeanne: Lumiere, *763*
Moretti, Nanni: Palombella Rossa, *775*
Morgan, W. T.: Matter of Degrees, A, *590*
Morgan, William: Heart of the Rio Grande, *1119*
Morgenstern, Janusz: Legend of the White Horse, *76*
Morimoto, Kouji: Robot Carnival, *1075*
Morita, Yoshimitsu: Family Game, The, *735*
Moriyama, Yuuji: Urusei Yatsura (TV Series) Vols. 1–45, *799;* Urusei Yatsura: Only You, *799*
Morneau, Louis: Final Judgment, *977;* Quake, *1008;* To Die Standing, *130*
Moroder, Giorgio: Metropolis (musical version), *930*
Morris, David: Patti Rocks, *619;* Vietnam War Story—Part Two, *694*
Morris, David Burton: Hometown Boy Makes Good, *300;* Jersey Girl, *310*
Morris, Ernest: Tell-Tale Heart, The, *893*
Morris, Errol: Brief History of Time, A, *419;* Dark Wind, *966;* Thin Blue Line, The, *436;* Vernon, Florida, *437*
Morris, Howard: Don't Drink the Water, *267;* Who's Minding the Mint?, *411;* With Six You Get Eggroll, *412*
Morris, Robert: King of Kong Island, *859*
Morrison, Bruce: Shaker Run, *114;* Tearaway, *678*
Morrissey, Kevin: Witchcraft IV, *903*
Morrissey, Paul: Andy Warhol's Dracula, *809;* Andy Warhol's Frankenstein, *809;* Beethoven's Nephew, *457;* Flesh, *518;* Heat (1972), *539;* Hound of the Baskervilles, The (1977), *302;* Mixed Blood, *86;* Spike of Bensonhurst, *384;* Trash, *687*
Morse, Hollingsworth: Daughters of Satan, *830;* Justin Morgan Had a Horse, *179*
Morse, Terrel O.: Unknown World, *1087*
Morse, Terry: Fog Island, *978;* Godzilla, King of the Monsters, *846*
Morton, Rocky: D.O.A. (1988), *965;* Max Headroom, *1065;* Super Mario Brothers, The, *208*
Morton, Vincent: Windrider, *140*
Moses, Ben: Nickel & Dime, *344*
Moses, Gilbert: Fish That Saved Pittsburgh, The, *278*
Moses, Harry: Assault at West Point, *451*
Mosher, Gregory: Life in the Theater, A, *574*
Moshinsky, Elijah: Green Man, The, *981*
Moskov, George: Married Too Young, *589*
Moskowitz, Steward: Adventures of an American Rabbit, The, *143*
Mosquera, Gustavo: Times to Come, *795*
Mostow, Jon: Beverly Hills Bodysnatchers, *237*
Mostow, Jonathan: Flight of Black Angel, *518*
Mowat, Barry: Star for Jeremy, A, *206*
Mowbray, Malcolm: Don't Tell Her It's Me, *267;* Out Cold, *351;* Private Function, A, *361*
Moxey, John Llewellyn: Bounty Man, The, *1101;* Children of An Lac, The, *480;* Circus of Fear, *824;* Cradle Will Fall, The, *964;* Detective Sadie and Son, *37;* Home for the Holidays, *983;* Horror Hotel, *851;* Intimate Strangers, *553;* Lady Mobster, *74;* Mating Season, The, *330;* Night Stalker, The (1971), *870;* Sanctuary of Fear, *1012;* Through Naked Eyes, *129*
Moyers, Bill: Power of Myth, The, *433*
Moyle, Alan: Gun in Betty Lou's Handbag, The, *292;* Pump Up the Volume, *630;* Times Square, *946*

Mulcahy, Russell: Blue Ice, *957;* Highlander, *1056;* Highlander 2: The Quickening, *1056;* Razorback, *879;* Real McCoy, The, *1009;* Ricochet, *106*
Mullen, Mark: Cool Blue, *488*
Mulligan, Robert: Baby the Rain Must Fall, *453;* Bloodbrothers, *464;* Clara's Heart, *483;* Fear Strikes Out, *515;* Great Impostor, The, *532;* Inside Daisy Clover, *552;* Kiss Me Goodbye, *313;* Love with the Proper Stranger, *582;* Man in the Moon, The, *587;* Other, The, *873;* Pursuit of Happiness, The, *631;* Same Time Next Year, *372;* Stalking Moon, The, *1152;* Summer of '42, *672;* To Kill a Mockingbird, *684;* Up the Down Staircase, *403*
Mulot, Claude: Black Venus, *718;* Blood Rose, *816*
Munch, Christopher: Hours and Times, *544*
Munchkin, Richard W.: Dance or Die, *32;* Deadly Bet, *34*
Mundhra, Jag: Eyewitness to Murder, *46;* Jigsaw Murders, The, *987;* L.A. Goddess, *314;* Last Call, *568;* Legal Tender, *76;* Night Eyes, *1000;* Open House, *872;* Other Woman, The, *1003;* Tropical Heat, *1027;* Wild Cactus, *139*
Mune, Ian: Bridge to Nowhere, *469;* Came a Hot Friday, *22*
Munger, Chris: Kiss of the Tarantula, *859*
Munroe, Cynthia: Wedding Party, The, *407*
Murakami, Jimmy T.: Battle Beyond the Stars, *1038;* When the Wind Blows, *1089*
Murakami, Ryu: Tokyo Decadence, *795*
Murch, Walter: Return to Oz, *199*
Murlowski, John: Amityville: A New Generation, *809*
Murnau, F. W.: City Girl, *962;* Faust, *736;* Haunted Castle, *849;* Last Laugh, The, *755;* Nosferatu, *772;* Sunrise, *673;* Tabu, *676*
Muro, Jim: Street Trash, *891*
Murphy, Dudley: Emperor Jones, The, *509*
Murphy, Eddie: Harlem Nights, *59*
Murphy, Edward: Heated Vengeance, *60*
Murphy, Geoff: Blind Side, *956;* Freejack, *1053;* Last Outlaw, The (1993), *1126;* Quiet Earth, The, *1073;* Red King, White Knight, *636;* UTU, *134;* Young Guns II, *1166*
Murphy, Maurice: Fatty Finn, *166;* Wet and Wild Summer, *408*
Murphy, Patrick Michael: Elvis: The Lost Performances, *915*
Murphy, Ralph: Spirit of West Point, The, *664*
Murphy, Richard: Wackiest Ship in the Army, The, *405*
Murray, Bill: Quick Change, *363*
Murray, Katrina: Secret Garden, The (1984), *202*
Murray, Robin: Dance, *913*
Murray, William: Primal Scream, *1071*
Musker, John: Adventures of the Great Mouse Detective, The, *144;* Aladdin (1992), *144;* Little Mermaid, The (1989), *182*
Mutrux, Floyd: Aloha, Bobby and Rose, *4;* American Hot Wax, *906*
Myers, Zion: Sidewalks of New York, *378*
Myerson, Alan: Bayou Romance, *456;* Doctor Duck's Super Secret All-Purpose Sauce, *266;* Police Academy 5—Assignment: Miami Beach, *359;* Private Lessons, *361;* Steelyard Blues, *386;* Television Parts Home Companion, *944*
Myles, Bruce: Ground Zero, *981*
Nadel, Arthur H.: Clambake, *912*
Nagahama, Tadao: Starbirds, *206*
Nagy, Ivan: Captain America II: Death Too Soon, *22;* Deadly Hero, *34;* Gun in the House, A, *534;* Jane Doe, *556*
Nair, Mira: Mississippi Masala, *596;* Salaam Bombay!, *782*
Nakajima, Ko: Art Com Video (Vol. 1–3), *1037*
Nankin, Michael: Midnight Madness, *332*
Naranjo, Lisandro Duque: Miracle in Rome, *767*
Narizzano, Silvio: Blue (1968), *1099;* Body in the Library, The, *958;* Class of Miss MacMichael, The, *483;* Die! Die! My Darling!, *834;* Georgy Girl, *284;* Loot, *321;* Redneck, *104;* Why Shoot the Teacher?, *701*
Naruse, Mikio: Flunky, Work Hard!, *737;* Late Chrysanthemums, *756;* Mother, *769;* When a Woman Ascends the Stairs, *803;* Wife! Be Like a Rose!, *803*
Naud, Bill: Whodunit?, *1031*
Nava, Gregory: El Norte, *733;* Time of Destiny, A, *684*
Navda, J. Erastheo: Boy God, The, *152*
Nazarro, Ray: Dog Eat Dog, *40;* Indian Uprising, *1123;* Kansas Pacific, *1124*
Neal, Peter: Yessongs, *439*
Neame, Ronald: Chalk Garden, The, *478;* First Monday in October, *517;* Foreign Body, *279;* Gambit, *283;* Hopscotch, *983;* Horse's Mouth, The, *301;* I Could Go On Singing, *924;* Man Who Never Was, The, *81;* Meteor, *1065;* Odessa File, The, *1003;* Poseidon Adventure, The, *99;* Prime of Miss Jean Brodie, The, *361;* Promoter, The, *362;* Scrooge (1970), *938;* Tunes of Glory, *689;* Windom's Way, *703*
Needham, Hal: Body Slam, *17;* Cannonball Run, *250;* Cannonball Run II, *250;* Hooper, *300;* Megaforce, *1065;* Rad, *102;* Smokey and the Bandit, *381;* Smokey and the Bandit II, *381;* Stroker Ace, *387*
Neff, Thomas L.: Running Mates (1985), *645*
Negrin, Alberto: Mussolini and I, *601;* Voyage of Terror: The Achille Lauro Affair, *694*
Negulesco, Jean: Daddy Long Legs, *913;* How to Marry a Millionaire, *303;* Humoresque, *546;* Johnny Belinda, *559;* Phone Call from a Stranger, *622;* Road House (1948), *1010;* Three Came Home, *682*
Neilan, Marshall: Rebecca of Sunnybrook Farm (1917), *635;* Stella Maris, *1020;* Vagabond Lover, The, *947*
Neill, Roy William: Black Room, The (1935), *814;* Dr. Syn, *40;* Dressed to Kill (1946), *972;* Frankenstein Meets the Wolf Man, *843;* House of Fear, *984;* Pearl of Death, The, *1004;* Pursuit to Algiers, *1008;* Scarlet Claw, The, *1012;* Sherlock Holmes and the Secret Weapon, *1015;* Sherlock Holmes and the Spider Woman, *1015;* Sherlock Holmes Faces Death, *1015;* Sherlock Holmes in Washington, *1015;* Terror by Night, *1023;* Woman in Green, The, *1032*
Neilson, James: Adventures of Bullwhip Griffin, The, *143;* Bon Voyage!, *151;* Dr. Syn, Alias the Scarecrow, *163;* Gentle Giant, *169;* Johnny Shiloh, *179;* Moon Pilot, *189;* Mooncussers, *189;* Moonspinners, The, *189;* Summer Magic, *208;* Texas John Slaughter: Geronimo's Revenge, *1155*
Nel, Frans: American Kickboxer, *4*
Nelson, Art J.: Creeping Terror, The, *1043*
Nelson, David: Last Plane Out, *75;* Rare Breed, A (1981), *198*
Nelson, Dusty: Necromancer, *868;* White Phantom, *139*
Nelson, Gary: Allan Quartermain and the Lost City of Gold, *4;* Black Hole, The, *1039;* Freaky Friday, *168;* Get Smart Again, *285;* Jimmy the Kid, *178;* Lookalike, The, *993;* Murder in Coweta County, *600;* Pride of Jesse Hallman, The, *626;* Revolver, *106;* Santee, *1147*
Nelson, Gene: Harum Scarum, *922;* Kissin' Cousins, *927*
Nelson, Jack: Tarzan the Mighty, *125*
Nelson, Ozzie: Adventures of Ozzie and Harriet, The (TV Series), *222*
Nelson, Ralph: Charly, *1041;* Christmas Lilies of the Field, *159;* Duel at Diablo, *1110;* Embryo, *1048;* Father Goose, *274;* Hero Ain't Nothin' But a Sandwich, A, *540;* Lady of the House, *568;* Lilies of the Field (1963), *575;* Requiem for a Heavyweight, *638;* Requiem for a Heavyweight (Television), *638;* Soldier Blue, *1151;* Soldier in the Rain, *661;* Tick ... Tick ... Tick ..., *129;* Wilby Conspiracy, The, *701*
Nemec, Jan: Report on the Party and the Guests, A, *781*
Nesher, Avi: Doppelganger: The Evil Within, *836;* She (1983), *1076;* Time Bomb, *1025*
Neufeld, Max: Orphan Boy of Vienna, An, *934*
Neumann, Kurt: Carnival Story, *475;* Fly, The (1958), *841;* It Happened in New Orleans, *925;* Kronos, *1061;* Make a Wish, *586;* Mohawk, *1134;* My Pal, the King, *1135;* Return of the Vampire, The, *880;* Rocketship X-M, *1075;* Son of Ali Baba, *118*

Newbrook, Peter: Spirit of the Dead, *889*
Newell, Mike: Amazing Grace and Chuck, *445;* Awakening, The, *811;* Dance with a Stranger, *494;* Enchanted April, *271;* Four Weddings and a Funeral, *280;* Good Father, The, *530;* Into the West, *177;* Man in the Iron Mask, The (1977), *81*
Newfield, Sam: Aces and Eights, *1092;* Arizona Gunfighter, *1094;* Black Raven, The, *955;* Border Roundup, *1100;* Branded a Coward, *1101;* Bulldog Courage, *1102;* Captain Gallant—Foreign Legion, *23;* Dead Men Walk, *830;* Death Rides the Plains, *1108;* Fighting Deputy, *1112;* Flying Serpent, The, *842;* Ghost Patrol, *55;* His Brother's Ghost, *1121;* Lawman Is Born, A, *1127;* Lightnin' Crandall, *1128;* Lightning Carson Rides Again, *1128;* Lost Continent, The, *1063;* Mad Monster, *862;* Monster Maker, The, *866;* Prairie Rustlers, *1139;* Roaring Guns, *1145;* Terror of Tiny Town, The, *1155;* Traitor, The, *1158;* White Pongo (a.k.a. Blond Gorilla), *902*
Newland, John: Don't Be Afraid of the Dark, *836;* Legend of Hillbilly John, The, *181*
Newland, Marv: Bambi vs. Godzilla, *148*
Newlin, Martin: Crawlers, *825;* Witchery, *903*
Newman, Joseph M.: Great Dan Patch, The, *532;* Jungle Patrol, *69;* King of the Roaring Twenties, *565;* Love Nest, *323;* This Island Earth, *1083*
Newman, Paul: Glass Menagerie, The, *528;* Harry and Son, *537;* Rachel, Rachel, *632;* Shadow Box, The, *654;* Sometimes a Great Notion, *662*
Newmeyer, Fred: General Spanky, *169*
Newsom, Ted: Dracula: A Cinematic Scrapbook, *423;* Frankenstein: A Cinematic Scrapbook, *424;* Wolfman: A Cinematic Scrapbook, *438*
Nibbelink, Phil: American Tail, An: Fievel Goes West, *146;* We're Back! A Dinosaur's Story, *216*
Niblo, Fred: Ben-Hur (1926), *458;* Blood and Sand (1922), *464;* Mark of Zorro, The (1920), *82;* Mysterious Lady, The, *603*
Nic, Ted: Dungeonmaster, The, *1048*
Nichetti, Maurizio: Icicle Thief, The, *746;* Volere Volare, *801*
Nicholas, Paul: Chained Heat, *24;* Naked Cage, The, *88*
Nicholls Jr., George: Return of Peter Grimm, The, *638*
Nicholls Jr, George: Anne of Green Gables (1934), *146;* Finishing School, *516*
Nichols, Charles A.: Charlotte's Web, *158;* Reluctant Dragon, The, *198*
Nichols, Dudley: Sister Kenny, *659*
Nichols, Mike: Biloxi Blues, *240;* Carnal Knowledge, *475;* Catch-22, *252;* Day of the Dolphin, The, *1044;* Gilda Live, *286;* Gin Game, The, *527;* Graduate, The, *531;* Heartburn, *295;* Postcards from the Edge, *360;* Regarding Henry, *637;* Silkwood, *658;* Who's Afraid of Virginia Woolf?, *701;* Working Girl, *414*
Nicholson, Arch: Dark Age, *32;* Fortress (1985), *520*
Nicholson, Jack: Goin' South, *1116;* Two Jakes, The, *1028*
Nicholson, James H.: Alakazam the Great, *145*
Nicholson, Sam: It's Three Strikes, Charlie Brown, *178;* She Likes You, Charlie Brown, *203;* Very Funny, Charlie Brown, *215;* What Next, Charlie Brown?, *216*
Nicoella, John: Runaway Father, *645*
Nicol, Alex: Screaming Skull, The, *884*
Nicolaou, Ted: Bad Channels, *1037;* Bloodlust: Subspecies III, *816;* Bloodstone: Subspecies II, *816;* Remote, *198;* Subspecies, *891;* Terror Vision, *1082*
Nicolella, John: Finish Line, *516;* Sunset Heat, *122*
Nielson, James: Tom Sawyer (1973), *213*
Nierenberg, George T.: Say Amen, Somebody, *434*
Nigh, William: Ape, The, *809;* Black Dragons, *814;* Corregidor, *489;* Doomed to Die, *41;* Fatal Hour, The, *46;* Gangster's Boy, *525;* Mr. Wong, Detective, *997;* Mr. Wong in Chinatown, *997;* Mysterious Mr. Wong, The, *88*
Nihonmatzu, Kazui: X from Outer Space, The, *1090*
Nilsson, Rob: Heat and Sunlight, *539;* Northern Lights, *609;* On the Edge, *612;* Signal 7, *657*
Nimoy, Leonard: Funny About Love, *282;* Good Mother, The, *530;* Holy Matrimony, *299;* Star Trek III: The Search for Spock, *1079;* Star Trek IV: The Voyage Home, *1079;* Three Men and a Baby, *395*
Niro, Robert De: Bronx Tale, A, *470*
Nishi, Yoshikuni: Serendipity, the Pink Dragon, *202*
Nishijima, Katsuhiko: Project A-KO, *779*
Nishio, Daisuke: 3 x 3 Eyes, Vols. 1–4, *895*
Nizet, Charles: Rescue Force, *105*
Noble, Nigel: Voices of Sarafina, *438*
Nobuyuki, Aramaki: Madox-01, *764*
Noelte, Rudolf: Castle, The, *476*
Noguchi, Haruyasu: Monster from a Prehistoric Planet, *1066*
Nolbandov, Sergei: Ships with Wings, *115*
Noonan, Tommy: Three Nuts in Search of a Bolt, *396*
Norgard, Lindsay: Homeboys, *543;* Princess Warrior, *1071*
Norman, Leslie: Saint, The (TV Series), *1012*
Normand, Mabel: Charlie Chaplin…Our Hero, *253*
Norris, Aaron: Braddock: Missing in Action III, *18;* Delta Force 2, *36;* Hitman, The, *63;* Platoon Leader, *99;* Sidekicks, *203*
Norris, Guy: Rage and Honor II: Hostile Takeover, *102*
Norton, B.W.L.: Baby…Secret of the Lost Legend, *1037;* More American Graffiti, *599;* Three for the Road, *395;* Tour of Duty, *131*
Norton, Bill L.: False Arrest, *513*
Norton, Charles: Kick or Die, *70*
Nosseck, Max: Black Beauty (1946), *150;* Brighton Strangler, The, *819;* Dillinger (1945), *39*
Nosseck, Noel: Dreamer, *505;* Full Exposure, *523;* King of the Mountain, *565;* Las Vegas Lady, *74*
Notz, Tierry: Terror Within, The, *894;* Watchers II, *901*
Novak, Blaine: Short Fuse, *115*
Novaro, Maria: Danzon, *728*
Novy, Wade: In Between, *550*
Noyce, Phillip: Blind Fury, *15;* Dead Calm, *966;* Heatwave, *539;* Hitchhiker (Series), The, *850;* Newsfront, *605;* Patriot Games, *97;* Sliver, *1018*
Nuchtern, Simon: Savage Dawn, *111;* Silent Madness, *886*
Nugent, Elliott: My Favorite Brunette, *340;* My Girl Tisa, *602;* Up in Arms, *403*
Nunez, Victor: Flash of Green, A, *977;* Gal Young 'Un, *524;* Ruby in Paradise, *645*
Nunn, Trevor: Hedda, *539;* Lady Jane, *568*
Nuse, Deland: Chilling, The, *823*
Nutley, Colin: House of Angels, *745*
Nutter, David: Cease Fire, *477;* Trancers 4: Jack of Swords, *1085*
Nuytten, Bruno: Camille Claudel, *721*
Nyby, Christian: Elfego Baca: Six Gun Law, *1111;* Operation C.I.A., *95;* Thing (From Another World), The (1951), *1083*
Nyby II, Christian I.: Devlin Connection III, The, *970;* Whisper Kills, A, *902*
Nyswander, Ron: Prince of Pennsylvania, *361*
O'Bannon, Dan: Resurrected, The, *879;* Return of the Living Dead, The, *880*
O'Bannon, Rockne S.: Fear (1990), *976*
O'Brien, Jack: All My Sons, *444*
O'Brien, Jim: Dressmaker, The, *505;* Foreign Affairs, *520;* Jewel in the Crown, The, *557*
O'Connolly, Jim: Berserk, *812;* Crooks and Coronets (Sophie's Place), *261;* Valley of Gwangi, *1087*
O'Connor, Kevin: Great Expectations (1989), *171;* House Where Evil Dwells, The, *853*
O'Connor, Pat: Cal, *474;* Fools of Fortune, *518;* January Man, The, *987;* Month in the Country, A, *599;* Stars and Bars, *385;* Zelda, *709*
O'Connor, William A.: Cocaine Fiends, *485*
O'Donoghue, Michael: Mr. Mike's Mondo Video, *334*
O'Hara, Gerry: Bitch, The, *462;* Leopard in the Snow, *572;* Maroc 7, *82*
O'Hara, Terrence: Perfect Bride, The, *873*

'Herlihy, Michael: Cry of the Innocent, *964;* Fighting
ince of Donegal, The, *167;* Medicine Hat Stallion, The, *186;*
ie and Only, Genuine, Original Family Band, The, *192;*
nith!, *1150*
'Horgan, Tom: Futz, *524*
'Malley, David: Easy Wheels, *270*
'Neal, Ron: Superfly T.N.T., *122;* Up Against the Wall, *692*
'Neans, Douglas F.: Sno-Line, *117*
'Neil, Robert Vincent: Angel, *5;* Avenging Angel, *8;* Blood
ania, *815*
'Steen, Sam: Best Little Girl in the World, The, *459;* Queen
the Stardust Ballroom, *632;* Sparkle, *941*
aks, Joe: Deadly Twins, *35*
blowsky, Stephan: Other Hell, The, *873*
brow, Jeffrey: Dorm that Dripped Blood, The, *837;* Kindred,
ie, *859;* Power, The (1980), *876;* Servants of Twilight, *884*
ckersen, Thys: Roy Rogers, King of the Cowboys, *434*
dell, David: Martians Go Home, *329*
dendal, Sias: Nukie, *191*
dets, Clifford: None But the Lonely Heart, *608*
din, Christopher: Boob Tube, The, *243*
dorisio, Luciano: Sacrilege, *782*
gilvie, George: Mad Max Beyond Thunderdome, *1064*
gorodnikov, Valery: Burglar (1987), *721*
hlmeyer, Don: Heroes of Desert Storm, *61*
hmori, Hideotoshi: Robot Carnival, *1075*
kamoto, Kihachi: Red Lion, *780;* Sword of Doom, *792;*
atoichi vs. Yojimbo, *806*
kazaki, Steven: Living on Tokyo Time, *761*
kuda, Seiji: Crystal Triangle, *727*
kuwaki, Masahara: Dirty Pair: Affair on Nolandia, *730*
ld Jr., John: Blastfighter, *15*
ldoini, Enrico: Bye Bye, Baby, *473*
liansky, Joel: Competition, The, *487*
lin, Ken: White Fang 2: Myth of the White Wolf, *217*
liver, David: Cave Girl, *1041*
liver, Richard: Girl to Kill For, A, *980*
liver, Robert H.: Dr. Frankenstein's Castle of Freaks, *835*
liver, Ron: Liar's Edge, *992;* Prom Night III—Last Kiss, *877*
liver, Ruby L.: Love Your Mama, *582*
livera, Hector: Barbarian Queen, *1038;* Cocaine Wars, *27;*
unny Dirty Little War (No Habra Mas Penas ni Olvido), *739;*
wo to Tango, *133;* Wizard of the Lost Kingdom, *1090*
liveri, Sandy: Red Skelton: A Career of Laughter, *433*
livier, Laurence: Hamlet (1948), *535;* Henry V (1944), *540;*
rince and the Showgirl, The, *361;* Richard III, *640*
lstein, Marty: Dangerous Love, *32*
lmi, Ermanno: Tree of the Wooden Clogs, The, *797*
lmos, Edward James: American Me, *446*
lsman, Phil: Two Top Bananas, *402*
mori, Kazuki: Godzilla Versus Biollante, *1054*
phuls, Marcel: Hotel Terminus: The Life and Times of Klaus
arbie, *427;* Sense of Loss, A, *434;* Sorrow and the Pity, The,
35
phüls, Max: Caught, *477;* Earrings of Madame De..., The,
32; La Ronde, *754;* La Signora di Tutti, *754;* Le Plaisir, *758;*
etter from an Unknown Woman, *573;* Liebelei, *760;* Lola
lontes, *761*
ppenheimer, Peer J.: Terror in Paradise, *126*
rdung, Wyott: Monster from the Ocean Floor, The, *866*
rfini, Mario: Fair Game, *974*
riolo, Joseph: Adventures of Felix the Cat, The, *143;* Felix's
lagic Bag of Tricks, *166*
rlando, Dominic: Knights of the City, *927*
rlikoff-Simon, Susan: Image of Passion, *549*
rme, Stuart: Heist, The, *540*
rmerod, James: Frankenstein (1984), *842*
rmond, Ron: Black Lash, *1099;* King of the Bullwhip, *1125;*
hundering Herd, *1157*
rmrod, Peter: Eat the Peach, *270*
Orona, Gary: Bikini Carwash Company 2, *239*
Orr, James: Breaking All the Rules, *245;* Mr. Destiny, *334;*
They Still Call Me Bruce, *393*
Orr, Wayne: Gallagher—Stuck in the 60s, *283;*
Gallagher—The Maddest, *283;* Pee-Wee's Playhouse
Christmas Special, *194*
Ortega, Kenny: Hocus Pocus, *175;* Newsies, *933*
Osamu, Kamijoo: Riding Bean, *781*
Oshima, Nagisa: Cruel Story of Youth, *727;* In the Realm of
Passion, *747;* In the Realm of the Senses, *747;* Merry
Christmas, Mr. Lawrence, *593;* Violence at Noon, *801*
Osmond, Cliff: Penitent, The, *620*
Osten, Suzanne: Mozart Brothers, The, *769*
Oswald, Gerd: Brainwashed, *958;* Crime of Passion, *490;*
Outer Limits, The (TV Series), *1069;* Paris Holiday, *354;* Star
Trek (TV Series), *1078*
Othenin-Girard, Dominique: After Darkness, *951;*
Halloween V: The Revenge of Michael Myers, *848;* Night Angel,
868; Omen IV: The Awakening, *872*
Otomo, Katsuhiro: Akira, *1034;* Robot Carnival, *1075*
Otomo, Katsumi: Neo-Tokyo, *771*
Otto, Linda: Unspeakable Acts, *692*
Ottoni, Filippo: Detective School Dropouts, *264*
Ouellette, Jean Paul: Unnamable, The, *899;* Unnamable II,
The, *899*
Oury, Gerard: Delusions of Grandeur, *729*
Owen, Cliff: Bawdy Adventures of Tom Jones, The, *233;*
Wrong Arm of the Law, The, *414*
Oxenberg, Jan: Thank You and Goodnight, *436*
Oz, Frank: Dark Crystal, The, *1044;* Dirty Rotten Scoundrels,
265; Housesitter, *302;* Little Shop of Horrors (1986), *929;*
Muppets Take Manhattan, The, *189;* What About Bob?, *408*
Ozawa, S.: Street Fighter, *121*
Ozgenturk, Ali: Horse, The, *744*
Ozu, Yasujiro: Autumn Afternoon, An, *714;* Drifting Weeds,
732; Early Summer, *732;* Equinox Flower, *734;* Late Spring,
756; Tokyo Story, *796*
Pabst, G. W.: Diary of a Lost Girl, *730;* Don Quixote (1933),
914; Joyless Street, *560;* Kameradschaft, *751;* Love of Jeanne
Ney, *762;* Pandora's Box, *775;* Secrets of a Soul, *784;*
Threepenny Opera, The, *794;* Westfront 1918, *803*
Padden, Kevin: One Night with Dice, *350*
Padget, Calvin Jackson: Battle of El Alamein, The, *10*
Page, Anthony: Absolution, *440;* Bill, *461;* Bill: On His Own,
461; Chernobyl: The Final Warning, *480;* Forbidden, *519;*
Heartbreak House, *295;* I Never Promised You a Rose Garden,
547; Lady Vanishes, The (1979), *990;* Missiles of October, The,
596; Monte Carlo, *599;* Nightmare Years, The, *607;* Scandal in
a Small Town, *649*
Pagnol, Marcel: Angele, *713;* Baker's Wife, The (1938), *715;*
César, *723;* Harvest, *743;* Le Schpountz, *758;* Topaze (1951),
796; Well-Digger's Daughter, The, *803*
Pakula, Alan J.: All the President's Men, *951;* Comes a
Horseman, *1105;* Consenting Adults (1992), *963;* Dream Lover
(1986), *972;* Klute, *989;* Orphans, *615;* Parallax View, The,
1004; Pelican Brief, The, *1005;* Presumed Innocent, *1007;*
Rollover, *1011;* See You in the Morning, *651;* Sophie's Choice,
663; Starting Over, *385;* Sterile Cuckoo, The, *667*
Pal, George: 7 Faces of Dr. Lao, *1076;* Time Machine, The,
1084; Tom Thumb, *213;* Wonderful World of the Brothers
Grimm, The, *1090*
Pal, Laszlo: Journey to Spirit Island, *179*
Palazzolo, Tom: Palazzolo's Chicago, *432*
Palcy, Euzhan: Dry White Season, A, *505;* Sugarcane Alley,
791
Pallenberg, Raspo: Cutting Class, *828*
Palm, Anders: Dead Certain, *967;* Murder on Line One, *867*
Palmer, John: Ciao! Manhattan, *482*
Palmer, Tony: 200 Motels, *946;* Wagner, *947*
Palmisano, Conrad E.: Busted Up, *472;* Space Rage, *1078*
Paltrow, Bruce: Little Sex, A, *319*

Pan-Andreas, George: Crime Killer, The, 30

Panama, Norman: Barnaby and Me, 232; Court Jester, The, 260; I Will, I Will...for Now, 304; Road to Hong Kong, The, 368; Trap, The, 1026

Papamichael, Phedon: Sketch Artist, 1017

Papas, Michael: Lifetaker, The, 77

Papatakis, Nico: Les Abysses, 759

Paradise, Michael J.: Visitor, The, 1087

Paradisi, Giulio: Spaghetti House, 788

Paragon, John: Double Trouble (1991), 268

Parajanov, Sergi: Color of Pomegranates, The, 725; Legend of Suram Fortress, The, 758; Shadows of Forgotten Ancestors, 785

Parco, Paul Salvatore: Deadly Alliance, 968; Pucker Up and Bark Like a Dog, 363

Paris, Domonic: Dracula's Last Rites (1980), 837; Film House Fever, 276

Paris, Jerry: Don't Raise the Bridge, Lower the River, 267; How to Break Up a Happy Divorce, 302; Make Me an Offer, 586; Never a Dull Moment, 191; Only with Married Men, 350; Police Academy II: Their First Assignment, 359; Police Academy III: Back in Training, 359; Viva Max!, 405

Parish, Richard C.: Magic Christmas Tree, The, 184

Parisot, Dean: Framed (1990), 280

Parker, Alan: Angel Heart, 952; Birdy, 462; Bugsy Malone, 155; Come See the Paradise, 486; Commitments, The, 912; Fame, 916; Midnight Express, 594; Mississippi Burning, 596; Pink Floyd: The Wall, 935; Shoot the Moon, 656

Parker, Albert: Black Pirate, The, 14

Parker, Brian: Inspector Morse (TV Series), 986

Parker, Cary: Girl in the Picture, The, 286

Parker, John: Daughter of Horror, 829

Parker, Norton S.: Road to Ruin, The (1928), 641

Parker, Percy G.: Castle of the Creeping Flesh, 822

Parkes, Walter F.: California Reich, 420

Parkinson, Eric: Future Shock, 1053

Parkinson, Tom: Disciple of Death, 834

Parks Jr., Gordon: Aaron Loves Angela, 440; Learning Tree, The, 572; Shaft, 114; Shaft's Big Score!, 114; Superfly, 122; Three the Hard Way, 129

Parks, Hugh: Shoot (1991), 378

Parks, Michael: Return of Josey Wales, 1142

Parolini, Gianfranco: Fury of Hercules, The, 54; Old Testament, The, 772; Samson, 1076

Parr, John H.: Prey for the Hunter, 100; Pursuit, 101

Parr, Larry: Soldier's Tale, A, 661

Parriott, James D.: Heart Condition, 295; Misfits of Science, 1066

Parrish, Robert: Bobo, The, 243; Casino Royale (1967), 252; Cry Danger, 964; Destructors, The, 970; Fire Down Below, 517; Journey to the Far Side of the Sun, 1060; Mississippi Blues, 430; Town Called Hell, A, 131

Parrott, James: Laurel and Hardy Classics, Volume 1, 316; Laurel and Hardy Classics, Volume 2, 316; Laurel and Hardy Classics, Volume 4, 316; Laurel and Hardy Classics, Volume 5, 316; Laurel and Hardy Classics, Volume 7, 316; Laurel and Hardy Classics, Volume 8, 316; Laurel and Hardy on the Lam, 317; Pardon Us, 354

Parrow, John: Sea Chase, The, 112

Parry, Gordon: Tom Brown's Schooldays (1950), 685

Parsons, John: Watched!, 137

Part, Michael: Starbirds, 206

Pascal, Gabriel: Caesar and Cleopatra, 473; Major Barbara, 326

Pasolini, Pier Paolo: Accattone, 710; Arabian Nights (1974), 713; Canterbury Tales, The, 722; Decameron, The, 729; Gospel According to Saint Matthew, The, 741; Hawks and the Sparrows, The, 743; Love Meetings, 762; Medea, 766; Notes for an African Orestes, 432; Oedipus Rex (1967), 772; Pigsty, 777; Salo: 120 Days of Sodom, 783; Teorema, 793

Passer, Ivan: Born to Win, 467; Creator, 490; Crime & Passion, 260; Cutter's Way, 965; Fourth Story, 978; Haunted Summer, 537; Nightingale, The, 191; Silver Bears, 379; Stalin 665

Pastrone, Giovanni: Cabiria, 721

Patchett, Tom: Best Legs in the 8th Grade, The, 235

Pate, Michael: Tim, 684

Patel, Raju: In the Shadow of Kilimanjaro, 855

Paterson, Daniel M.: Girlfriend from Hell, 287

Paton, Stuart: In Old Cheyenne, 1123; 20,000 Leagues Unde the Sea (1916), 1086

Patrick, Matthew: Hider in the House, 982; Tainted Blood, 1022

Patterson, John: Grave Secrets: The Legacy of Hilltop Drive, 980; Taken Away, 676

Patterson, Pat: Doctor Gore, 835

Patterson, Ray: Good, the Bad, and Huckleberry Hound, The 171; Jetson's Christmas Carol, A, 178; Jetsons Meet the Flintstones, The, 178; Top Cat and the Beverly Hills Cats, 213; Yogi and the Magical Flight of the Spruce Goose, 219; Yogi's First Christmas, 219; Yogi's Great Escape, 219

Patterson, Richard: Firesign Theatre's Hot Shorts, 277; J-Men Forever, 310; Marx Brothers in a Nutshell, The, 430

Pattinson, Michael: ...Almost, 225; Ground Zero, 981; One Crazy Night, 349

Patzack, Peter: Lethal Obsession, 76; Midnight Cop, 996

Paul, Byron: Lt. Robin Crusoe, U.S.N., 181

Paul, Stefan: Jimmy Cliff—Bongo Man, 926

Paul, Steven: Eternity, 511; Falling in Love Again, 273; Slapstick of Another Kind, 380

Paul, Stuart: Emanon, 271; Fate, 274

Paulsen, David: Schizoid, 883

Pavlou, George: Rawhead Rex, 879; Transmutations, 897

Payet, Alain: Helltrain, 61

Payne, Alexander: Inside Out (1992), 1058

Pearce, Leslie: Flask of Fields, A, 278

Pearce, Michael: James Joyce's Women, 556

Pearce, Richard: Country, 489; Dead Man Out, 497; Heartland, 1119; Leap of Faith, 572; Long Walk Home, The, 579; No Mercy, 91; Sessions, 652; Threshold, 1083

Peck, Brian: Willies, The, 903

Peck, Ron: Empire State, 44

Peckinpah, Sam: Ballad of Cable Hogue, The, 1096; Bring Me the Head of Alfredo Garcia, 20; Convoy (1978), 29; Cross of Iron, 31; Deadly Companions, The, 1108; Getaway, The (1972), 55; Junior Bonner, 1124; Killer Elite, The, 71; Major Dundee, 1131; Osterman Weekend, The, 96; Pat Garrett and Billy the Kid, 1138; Ride the High Country, 1143; Straw Dogs, 1021; Wild Bunch, The, 1164

Peerce, Larry: Ash Wednesday, 451; Bell Jar, The, 458; Court-Martial of Jackie Robinson, The, 489; Elvis and Me, 915; Goodbye Columbus, 288; Hard to Hold, 922; Incident, The (1967), 551; Love Child, 581; Murder So Sweet, 601; Neon Empire, The, 89; Other Side of the Mountain, The, 615; Other Side of the Mountain, Part II, The, 615; Prison for Children, 628; Queenie, 632; Separate Peace, A, 652; Sporting Club, The 664; That Was Rock, 944; Two-Minute Warning, 1028; Wired, 704

Peeters, Barbara: Humanoids from the Deep, 854; Summer School Teachers, 673

Pelaez, Antonio: Crystalstone, 160

Pelissier, Anthony: Encore, 509; Rocking Horse Winner, The, 642

Pelletier, Andre: Voodoo Dolls, 901

Penczner, Marius: I Was a Zombie for the FBI, 1057

Penn, Arthur: Alice's Restaurant, 444; Bonnie and Clyde, 17; Chase, The (1966), 479; Dead of Winter, 967; Four Friends, 521; Left Handed Gun, The (1958), 1128; Little Big Man, 1128; Miracle Worker, The (1962), 595; Missouri Breaks, The, 1134; Night Moves, 1001; Penn & Teller Get Killed, 356; Portrait, The, 625; Target, 125

Penn, Leo: Dark Secret of Harvest Home, The, *829;* Judgment in Berlin, *560;* Lost in Space (TV Series), *1063;* Man Called Adam, A, *586*
Penn, Sean: Indian Runner, The, *551*
Pennebaker, D. A.: Don't Look Back, *423;* Monterey Pop, *431;* War Room, The, *438;* Ziggy Stardust and the Spiders from Mars, *439*
Pennell, Eagle: Last Night at the Alamo, *315*
Peoples, David: Blood of Heroes, *15*
Peploe, Clare: High Season, *297*
Peploe, Mark: Afraid of the Dark, *950*
Perello, Hope: Howling VI: The Freaks, *854*
Perier, Etienne: Investigation, *748;* Zeppelin, *709*
Perisic, Zoran: Sky Bandits, *116*
Perkins, Anthony: Lucky Stiff, *324;* Psycho III, *877*
Perry, Alan: Captain Scarlet vs. the Mysterons, *156*
Perry, Frank: Compromising Positions, *258;* David and Lisa, *496;* Diary of a Mad Housewife, *501;* Hello Again, *296;* Last Summer, *570;* Mommie Dearest, *598;* Monsignor, *598;* Rancho Deluxe, *1140;* Skag, *659;* Swimmer, The, *675*
Persky, Bill: Serial, *376*
Pesce, P. J.: Bodywaves, *243*
Peters, Brooke L.: Unearthly, The, *899*
Peters, Charlie: Passed Away, *355*
Petersen, Wolfgang: Das Boot (The Boat), *728;* Enemy Mine, *1049;* For Your Love Only, *519;* In the Line of Fire, *66;* NeverEnding Story, The, *1068;* Shattered (1991), *1014*
Peterson, Kristine: Body Chemistry, *957;* Critters 3, *827;* Deadly Dreams, *968;* Lower Level, *994*
Petipa, Marius: Don Quixote (1988), *914*
Petit, Christopher: Chinese Boxes, *962*
Petri, Elio: Tenth Victim, The, *1082*
Petrie, Ann: Mother Teresa, *431*
Petrie, Daniel: Bay Boy, The, *456;* Betsy, The, *459;* Bramble Bush, The, *468;* Buster and Billie, *472;* Cocoon: The Return, *1042;* Dollmaker, The, *503;* Fort Apache—The Bronx, *520;* Lifeguard, *574;* Moon of the Wolf, *866;* Neptune Factor, The, *1068;* Raisin in the Sun, A (1961), *634;* Resurrection, *638;* Rocket Gibraltar, *642;* Silent Night, Lonely Night, *658;* Six Pack, *380;* Spy with a Cold Nose, The, *385;* Square Dance, *665;* Stolen Hours, *668;* Sybil, *675*
Petrie Jr., Daniel: Toy Soldiers (1991), *131*
Petrie, Donald: Favor, The, *275;* Grumpy Old Men, *291;* Mystic Pizza, *603;* Opportunity Knocks, *351*
Petrie, Jeanette: Mother Teresa, *431*
Petroni, Giulio: Blood and Guns, *15;* Death Rides a Horse, *1108*
Pevney, Joseph: Away all Boats, *8;* Cash McCall, *252;* Contract for Life: The S.A.D.D. Story, *488;* Man of a Thousand Faces, *587;* Night of the Grizzly, The, *1136;* Star Trek (TV Series), *1078;* Tammy and the Bachelor, *677;* Torpedo Run, *131;* Who Is the Black Dahlia?, *1031*
Peyser, John: Centerfold Girls, *478;* Four Rode Out. *1114;* Kashmiri Run, The, *70*
Pfleghar, Michel: Oldest Profession, The, *773*
Phelps, William: North Shore, *609*
Philips, Lee: Barnum (1987), *456;* Blind Vengeance, *15;* Blue Lighting, The, *16;* Hardhat and Legs, *536;* Mae West, *585;* On the Right Track, *192;* Samson and Delilah (1984), *648;* Silent Motive, *1016;* Stranger Within, The, *891;* Sweet Hostage, *674;* Windmills of the Gods, *703*
Phillipe, Harald: Escape from the KGB, *45*
Phillips, Bill: There Goes the Neighborhood, *393*
Phillips, John Michael: Mikado, The (1987), *931*
Phillips, Maurice: Another You, *228;* Over Her Dead Body, *352;* Riders of the Storm, *368*
Phillips, Nick: Crazy Fat Ethel II, *826;* Criminally Insane, *826;* Death Nurse, *831*
Phillips, Toby: Pamela Principle, The, *1004*
Pialat, Maurice: A Nos Amours, *710;* Loulou, *761;* Police, *778;* Under the Sun of Satan, *798;* Van Gogh, *800*
Picha: Shame of the Jungle, *377*
Pichel, Irving: Colonel Effingham's Raid, *257;* Dance Hall, *913;* Destination Moon, *1047;* Martin Luther, *589;* Miracle of the Bells, The, *595;* Mr. Peabody and the Mermaid, *334;* Most Dangerous Game, The, *997;* They Won't Believe Me, *681;* Tomorrow Is Forever, *685*
Pichul, Vasily: Little Vera, *761*
Picker, Jimmy: My Friend Liberty, *190*
Pickett, Rex: From Hollywood to Deadwood, *979*
Pierce, Arthur C.: Las Vegas Hillbillys, *315;* Women of the Prehistoric Planet, *1090*
Pierce, Charles B.: Boggy Creek II, *818;* Evictors, The, *839;* Grayeagle, *1116;* Legend of Boggy Creek, *860;* Norseman, The, *92;* Sacred Ground, *1146;* Town That Dreaded Sundown, The, *1026*
Pierson, Carl: New Frontier, *1136;* Paradise Canyon, *1138*
Pierson, Frank: Citizen Cohn, *482;* King of the Gypsies, *565;* Looking Glass War, The, *993;* Somebody Has to Shoot the Picture, *662;* Star Is Born, A (1976), *666*
Pilichino, Margarita: Anna Karenina (1974), *907*
Pillsbury, Sam: Into the Badlands, *1123;* Starlight Hotel, *666;* Zandalee, *709*
Pinion, Efren C.: Blind Rage, *15*
Pink, Sidney: Christmas Kid, The, *1105;* Finger on the Trigger, *1113*
Pinoteau, Claude: La Boum, *753*
Pinsent, Gordon: John and the Missus, *558*
Pintoff, Ernest: Blade, *14;* Lunch Wagon, *324;* St. Helens, *646;* Who Killed Mary What's 'Er Name?, *1031*
Pires, Gilbert: Act of Aggression, *710*
Pirosh, Robert: Go for Broke!, *528*
Pirro, Mark: Buford's Beach Bunnies, *247;* Deathrow Gameshow, *263;* Polish Vampire in Burbank, A, *359*
Pitre, Glen: Belizaire the Cajun, *458*
Pittman, Bruce: Confidential, *28;* Hello, Mary Lou: Prom Night II, *850;* Mark of Cain, *863;* Strange Tales: Ray Bradbury Theater, *1080;* Where the Spirit Lives, *699*
Place, Lou: Daddy-O, *31*
Plone, Allen: Night Screams, *870;* Phantom of the Ritz, *874;* Sweet Justice, *123*
Plympton, Bill: Tune, The, *400*
Poe, Amos: Alphabet City, *445*
Poe, Rudiger: Monster High, *336*
Pohjola, Ilppo: Daddy and the Muscle Academy, *422*
Pohlad, William: Old Explorers, *192*
Poirer, Paris: Last Call at Maud's, *428*
Poitier, Sidney: Buck and the Preacher, *1102;* Fast Forward, *916;* Ghost Dad, *285;* Hanky Panky, *292;* Let's Do It Again, *318;* Piece of the Action, A, *357;* Stir Crazy, *386;* Uptown Saturday Night, *404*
Poitrenaud, Jacques: Tales of Paris, *792*
Polakof, James: Balboa, *455;* Vals, The, *404*
Polanski, Roman: Bitter Moon, *462;* Chinatown, *962;* Classic Foreign Shorts: Volume 2, *724;* Cul-de-Sac, *492;* Diary of Forbidden Dreams, *501;* Fearless Vampire Killers, or, Pardon Me, But Your Teeth Are in My Neck, The, *840;* Frantic (1988), *978;* Knife in the Water, *752;* Macbeth (1971), *584;* Pirates, *358;* Repulsion, *879;* Rosemary's Baby, *881;* Tenant, The, *1023;* Tess, *679;* Two Men and a Wardrobe, *797*
Poliakoff, Stephen: Close My Eyes, *484*
Pollack, Jeff: Above the Rim, *440*
Pollack, Sydney: Absence of Malice, *950;* Bobby Deerfield, *465;* Electric Horseman, The, *508;* Firm, The, *977;* Havana, *537;* Jeremiah Johnson, *1123;* Out of Africa, *616;* Scalphunters, The, *1148;* Slender Thread, The, *660;* They Shoot Horses, Don't They?, *681;* This Property Is Condemned, *682;* Three Days of the Condor, *1025;* Tootsie, *397;* Way We Were, The, *697;* Yakuza, The, *141*
Pollet, Jean-Daniel: Six in Paris (Paris Vue par . . .), *786*
Pollexfen, Jack: Indestructible Man, *856*

Pollock, George: Murder Ahoy, *998;* Murder at the Gallop, *998;* Murder Most Foul, *998;* Murder She Said, *999;* Ten Little Indians (1966), *1023*
Polonsky, Abraham: Force of Evil, *519;* Tell Them Willie Boy Is Here, *1155*
Pommer, Erich: Beachcomber, The, *457*
Pontecorvo, Gillo: Battle of Algiers, *716;* Burn!, *472*
Ponzi, Maurizio: Pool Hustlers, The, *778*
Pool, Lea: Straight for the Heart, *790*
Popkin, Leo: Well, The, *698*
Porter, Edwin S.: Count of Monte Cristo, The (1912), *489*
Porter, Eric: Marco Polo Jr., *185*
Porter, Jeffrey: Liars' Club, The, *992*
Portillo, Ralph: Broken Trust, *959*
Posner, Geoffrey: Young Ones, The, *416*
Post, Ted: Baby, The, *811;* Beneath the Planet of the Apes, *1039;* Diary of a Teenage Hitchhiker, *501;* Go Tell the Spartans, *56;* Good Guys Wear Black, *56;* Hang 'em High, *1118;* Harrad Experiment, The, *537;* Human Shield, The, *64;* Magnum Force, *80;* Nightkill, *1001;* Stagecoach (1986), *1152;* Whiffs, *410;* Yuma, *1166*
Postal, Steve: Billy the Kid Meets the Vampires, *813;* Curse of the House Surgeon, The, *828;* Evil Spirits in the House, *839;* Honeymoon Murders, *851;* Penpal Murders, *873;* Queen Victoria and the Zombies, *878;* Vampires Always Ring Twice, *900;* Vampires from Outer Space, *900*
Potenza, Anthony: No Nukes, *432*
Potter, Anthony Ross: Spies (1992), *435*
Potter, Dennis: Secret Friends, *651*
Potter, H. C.: Beloved Enemy, *458;* Cowboy and the Lady, The, *260;* Farmer's Daughter, The, *274;* Miniver Story, The, *594;* Mr. Blandings Builds His Dream House, *333;* Mr. Lucky, *86;* Second Chorus, *938;* Shopworn Angel, The, *656;* Story of Vernon and Irene Castle, The, *942;* Time of Your Life, The, *684*
Potter, Sally: Orlando, *614*
Potterton, Gerald: Buster Keaton Rides Again, *420;* George and the Christmas Star, *169;* Keaton Rides Again/Railroader, *312*
Pottier, Richard: Rape of the Sabines, *103*
Pourmand, Mansour: Zipperface, *1033*
Powell, Dick: Conqueror, The, *29;* Enemy Below, The, *44;* Split Second (1953), *664*
Powell, Michael: Black Narcissus, *463;* Elusive Pimpernel, The, *509;* 49th Parallel, The, *520;* Ill Met by Moonlight, *548;* Life and Death of Colonel Blimp, The, *574;* Night Ambush, *90;* One of Our Aircraft Is Missing, *94;* Peeping Tom, *1005;* Pursuit of the Graf Spee, *101;* Red Shoes, The (1948), *936;* Spy in Black, The, *664;* Tales of Hoffman, *943;* Thief of Bagdad, The (1940), *1083*
Powell, Paul: Pollyanna (1920), *196*
Powell, Tristram: American Friends, *226*
Power, John: Alice to Nowhere, *3;* Tommyknockers, The, *1084*
Powers, Dave: Carol Burnett's My Personal Best, *251*
Powers, Dennis: Helga Pictures, The, *426*
Prager, Stanley: Bang Bang Kid, The, *232;* Car 54 Where Are You? (TV Series), *250;* Madigan's Millions, *326*
Prate, Jean-Yves: Regina, *780*
Pratt, Hawley: Bear Who Slept Through Christmas, The, *149;* Dr. Seuss: The Cat in the Hat/Dr. Seuss on the Loose, *162;* Dr. Seuss: The Lorax/The Hoober Bloob Highway, *163*
Preece, Michael: Beretta's Island, *10;* Prizefighter, The, *197*
Preminger, Otto: Advise and Consent, *442;* Anatomy of a Murder, *952;* Bonjour Tristesse, *466;* Cardinal, The, *475;* Carmen Jones, *911;* Court-martial of Billy Mitchell, The, *489;* Exodus, *512;* Forever Amber, *520;* In Harm's Way, *66;* Laura, *991;* Man with the Golden Arm, The, *587;* Moon Is Blue, The, *336;* River of No Return, *1145;* Saint Joan, *646*
Pressburger, Emeric: Life and Death of Colonel Blimp, The, *574;* One of Our Aircraft Is Missing, *94;* Pursuit of the Graf Spee, *101;* Red Shoes, The (1948), *936;* Tales of Hoffman, *943*
Pressman, Michael: Bad News Bears in Breaking Training, The, *231;* Boulevard Nights, *467;* Capone, *22;* Chinatown Murders, The: Man Against the Mob, *25;* Dark River: A Father's Revenge, *495;* Doctor Detroit, *266;* Great Texas Dynamite Chase, The, *57;* Imposter, The, *549;* Incident at Dark River, *551;* Quicksand: No Escape, *1008;* Some Kind of Hero, *382;* Teenage Mutant Ninja Turtles II: The Secret of the Ooze, *209;* Those Lips, Those Eyes, *945;* To Heal a Nation, *684*
Preuss, Reuben: Blackmail (1991), *956;* Deceptions, *969;* In Dangerous Company, *550;* Write to Kill, *1033*
Previn, Steve: Adventures of Sherlock Holmes, The (TV Series), *950;* Almost Angels, *146;* Escapade in Florence, *165;* Waltz King, The, *215*
Price, David F.: Children of the Corn II: The Final Sacrifice, *823;* To Die For 2: Son of Darkness, *896*
Price, Will: Rock, Rock, Rock, *937*
Primus, Barry: Mistress (1992), *597*
Prince: Graffiti Bridge, *920;* Sign o' the Times, *434;* Under the Cherry Moon, *691*
Prince, Harold: Little Night Music, A, *926;* Something for Everyone, *662;* Sweeney Todd, *943*
Prior, David A.: Center of the Web, *960;* Deadly Prey, *34;* Death Chase, *35;* Double Threat, *504;* Future Zone, *54;* Lock and Load, *993;* Lost Platoon, *861;* Mankillers, *82;* Mardi Gras for the Devil, *863;* Operation War Zone, *95;* Raw Nerve, *103*
Prosperi, Franco: Throne of Fire, The, *895;* Wild Beasts, The, *903*
Protázanov, Yakov: Aelita: Queen of Mars, *711;* Early Russian Cinema: Before the Revolutions (Vol. 1–10), *732*
Prowse, Andrew: Demonstone, *833*
Proyas, Alex: Crow, The, *827*
Pryor, Richard: Jo Jo Dancer, Your Life Is Calling, *558;* Richard Pryor—Here and Now, *367*
Pudovkin, V. I.: End of St. Petersburg, The, *734;* Mystery of the Leaping Fish/Chess Fever, *341;* Storm over Asia, *789*
Puenzo, Luis: Official Story, The, *772;* Old Gringo, The, *611;* Plague, The, *623*
Purcell, Evelyn: Nobody's Fool, *346*
Purcell, Joseph: Delos Adventure, The, *36*
Purdom, Edmund: Don't Open Till Christmas, *836*
Purdy, Jim: Destiny to Order, *264*
Puzo, Dorothy Ann: Cold Steel, *28*
Pytka, Joe: Let It Ride, *317*
Pyun, Albert: Alien From L.A., *3;* Arcade, *1036;* Bloodmatch, *16;* Brain Smasher...A Love Story, *18;* Captain America (1990), *22;* Cyborg, *1043;* Dangerously Close, *966;* Deceit, *1046;* Dollman, *1047;* Down Twisted, *41;* Kickboxer 2: The Road Back, *70;* Knights, *1061;* Nemesis (1992), *1067;* Radioactive Dreams, *1073;* Sword and the Sorcerer, The, *1082*
Qamar, A. C.: Deadly Vengeance, *35*
Quay, Stephen: Quay Brothers, The: Volume I&II, *1073*
Quay, Timothy: Quay Brothers, The: Volume I&II, *1073*
Quested, John: Loophole, *993*
Quine, Richard: Bell, Book and Candle, *234;* Hotel, *544;* How to Murder your Wife, *303;* My Sister Eileen, *932;* Oh Dad, Poor Dad—Mama's Hung You in the Closet and I'm Feeling So Sad, *348;* Paris When It Sizzles, *354;* Prisoner of Zenda, The (1979), *361;* Sex and the Single Girl, *376;* Strangers When We Meet, *670;* W, *1030;* World of Suzie Wong, The, *707*
Quinn, Anthony: Buccaneer, The, *20*
Quinn, James: Blindman's Bluff, *956*
Quinn, John: Cheerleader Camp, *823;* Total Exposure, *1026*
Quintano, Gene: Honeymoon Academy, *300;* National Lampoon's Loaded Weapon 1, *342;* Why Me?, *139*
Quintero, Jose: Roman Spring of Mrs. Stone, The, *643*
Quisenberry, Byron: Scream, *883*
Rabenalt, Arthur Maria: Unnatural, *1029*
Rachman, Paul: Inside Out 2, *1059*
Rademakers, Fons: Assault, The, *714;* Rose Garden, The, *644*
Rader, Peter: Grandma's House, *980;* Hired to Kill, *62*

Radford, Michael: Another Time, Another Place (1984), *450;* 1984 (1984), *1068;* White Mischief, *700*
Radler, Robert: Best of the Best, *11;* Best of the Best 2, *11*
Radomski, Eric: Batman: Mask of the Phantasm, *148*
Raeburn, Michael: Killing Heat, *563*
Rafelson, Bob: Black Widow, *955;* Five Easy Pieces, *517;* Head (1968), *922;* King of Marvin Gardens, The, *565;* Man Trouble, *327;* Mountains of the Moon, *87;* Postman Always Rings Twice, The (1981), *1007;* Stay Hungry, *667*
Raffanini, Piccio: Obsession: A Taste for Fear, *93*
Rafferty, Kevin: Atomic Cafe, The, *418*
Rafferty, Pierce: Atomic Cafe, The, *418*
Raffill, Stewart: Across the Great Divide, *143;* Adventures of the Wilderness Family, *144;* High Risk, *61;* Ice Pirates, *1057;* Mac and Me, *1064;* Mannequin Two: On the Move, *328;* Philadelphia Experiment, The, *1070;* Sea Gypsies, The, *202*
Rafkin, Alan: Shakiest Gun in the West, The, *377*
Raglin, Tim: Brer Rabbit and the Wonderful Tar Baby, *152;* How the Leopard Got His Spots, *176;* Paul Bunyan, *194;* Pecos Bill, *194;* Thumbelina (1989), *211*
Raimi, Sam: Army of Darkness, *810;* Crimewave, *260;* Darkman, *1044;* Evil Dead, The, *839;* Evil Dead 2, *839*
Rakoff, Alvin: Deathship, *832;* Dirty Tricks, *265;* King Solomon's Treasure, *73;* Mr. Halpern and Mr. Johnson, *597;* Room 43, *644;* Voyage 'Round My Father, A, *695*
Ramati, Alexander: Assisi Underground, The, *7*
Rambaldi, Vittorie: Primal Rage, *876*
Ramis, Harold: Caddyshack, *249;* Club Paradise, *256;* Groundhog Day, *291;* National Lampoon's Vacation, *342*
Rand, Patrick: Mom, *865*
Randall, Addison: Killing Zone, The, *72*
Randel, Tony: Amityville 1992: It's About Time, *809;* Children of the Night, *823;* Hellbound: Hellraiser II, *849;* Infested, *856;* Inside Out (1992), *1058;* Inside Out 2, *1059;* Ticks, *895*
Randinella, Thomas R.: Blades, *814*
Rankin Jr., Arthur: Around the World in 80 Days (1974), *147;* Ballad of Paul Bunyan, The, *148;* Flight of Dragons, The, *167;* Hobbit, The, *175;* Johnny Appleseed/Paul Bunyan, *179;* Last Unicorn, The, *181;* Mad, Mad Monsters, The, *184;* Twenty Thousand Leagues Under the Sea (1972), *214;* Willie McBean and His Magic Machine, *217*
Ransen, Mort: Shades of Love: Sincerely, Violet, *654*
Raphael, Frederic: Women & Men: Stories of Seduction, *706*
Rapp, Philip: Adventures of Topper, The, *223*
Rappeneau, Jean-Paul: Cyrano De Bergerac (1990), *727;* Swashbuckler, The (1984), *123*
Rapper, Irving: Adventures of Mark Twain, The (1944), *442;* Born Again, *466;* Brave One, The, *152;* Corn Is Green, The (1945), *488;* Deception (1946), *498;* Marjorie Morningstar, *589;* Miracle, The (1959), *594;* Now, Voyager, *609;* Rhapsody in Blue, *936;* Sextette, *376*
Rash, Steve: Buddy Holly Story, The, *910;* Can't Buy Me Love, *250;* Queens Logic, *363;* Rich Hall's Vanishing America, *367;* Son-in-Law, *383;* Under the Rainbow, *402*
Raskin, Jay: I Married a Vampire, *855*
Raskov, Daniel: Masters of Menace, *329*
Rathborne, Tina: Zelly and Me, *709*
Ratoff, Gregory: Abdulla the Great, *221;* Adam Had Four Sons, *441;* Black Magic (1949), *462;* Corsican Brothers, The (1941), *29;* Footlight Serenade, *917;* Heat's On, The, *295;* Intermezzo (1939), *553*
Rautenbach, Jans: No One Cries Forever, *608*
Rawi, Ousama: Housekeeper, The, *853*
Rawlins, John: Arabian Nights (1942), *6;* Arizona Ranger, *1095;* Dick Tracy Meets Gruesome, *38;* Dick Tracy's Dilemma, *38;* Junior G-Men, *69;* Sherlock Holmes and the Voice of Terror, *1015*
Ray, Albert: Dancing Man, *965;* Shriek in the Night, A, *1016;* Thirteenth Guest, The, *1024*
Ray, Bernard B.: Broken Strings, *470;* Roamin' Wild, *1145;* Smokey Trails, *1151*
Ray, Fred Olen: Alien Dead, *1035;* Alienator, *1035;* Armed Response, *6;* Beverly Hills Vamp, *237;* Commando Squad, *28;* Cyclone, *31;* Deep Space, *1046;* Dinosaur Island, *1047;* Evil Toons, *273;* Haunting Fear, *849;* Hollywood Chainsaw Hookers, *850;* Inner Sanctum, *986;* Mob Boss, *335;* Phantom Empire, The (1986), *99;* Possessed by the Night, *1006;* Scalps, *883;* Spirits, *889;* Tomb, The, *896;* Warlords, *901*
Ray, Man: Avant Garde Program #2, *714;* Man Ray Classic Shorts, *765*
Ray, Nicholas: Born to Be Bad, *467;* 55 Days at Peking, *516;* Flying Leathernecks, *51;* In a Lonely Place, *985;* Johnny Guitar, *1123;* King of Kings (1961), *565;* Knock on Any Door, *566;* Lusty Men, The, *1130;* On Dangerous Ground, *1003;* Party Girl, *618;* Rebel without a Cause, *636;* They Live By Night, *681;* Woman's Secret, A, *1032*
Ray, Satyajit: Adversary, The, *711;* Aparajito, *713;* Devi (The Goddess), *729;* Distant Thunder (1974), *730;* Home and the World, *744;* Pather Panchali, *776;* Stranger, The (1992), *790;* Two Daughters, *797;* World of Apu, The, *805*
Raye, Michael: Laserblast, *1062*
Raymond, Alan: Elvis '56, *423;* Sweet Home Chicago, *435*
Raymond, Jack: Speckled Band, The, *1019*
Raymond, Susan: Elvis '56, *423;* Sweet Home Chicago, *435*
Razatos, Spiro: Class of 1999 II: The Substitute, *1041;* Fast Getaway, *274*
Reardon, John: Whoops Apocalypse, *411*
Rebane, Bill: Alpha Incident, The, *1035;* Demons of Ludlow, The, *833;* Monster a Go-Go, *336*
Red, Eric: Body Parts, *817;* Cohen and Tate, *485*
Redford, Robert: Milagro Beanfield War, The, *594;* Ordinary People, *614;* River Runs Through It, A, *641*
Reed, Bill: Secret of the Sword, The, *202*
Reed, Carol: Agony and the Ecstasy, The, *443;* Fallen Idol, The, *513;* Immortal Battalion, The (a.k.a. The Way Ahead), *549;* Key, The, *563;* Night Train to Munich, *91;* Odd Man Out, *1003;* Oliver, *933;* Stars Look Down, The, *666;* Third Man, The, *1024;* Trapeze, *687;* Unicorn, The, *214*
Reed, Jerry: What Comes Around, *698*
Reed, Joel M.: Bloodsucking Freaks (The Incredible Torture Show), *816*
Rees, Clive: Blockhouse, The, *464;* When the Whales Came, *699*
Rees, Jerry: Brave Little Toaster, The, *152;* Marrying Man, The, *329*
Reeve, Geoffrey: Caravan to Vaccares, *23;* Puppet on a Chain, *101;* Souvenir, *663*
Reeves, George: TV's Best Adventures of Superman, *1085*
Reeves, Michael: Conqueror Worm, The, *825;* She Beast, The, *885*
Reggio, Godfrey: Koyaanisqatsi, *428;* Powaqqatsi, *433*
Reichert, Mark: Union City, *1029*
Reichmann, Thomas: Mingus, *430*
Reid, Alastair: Inspector Morse (TV Series), *986;* Shattered (1972), *655;* Teamster Boss: The Jackie Presser Story, *678*
Reid, Max: Wild Thing, *702*
Reid, Tim: Little Mermaid, The (1978), *182*
Reilly, William: Men of Respect, *592*
Reiner, Carl: All of Me, *224;* Bert Rigby, You're a Fool, *908;* Comic, The (1969), *486;* Dead Men Don't Wear Plaid, *262;* Enter Laughing, *271;* Fatal Instinct (1993), *274;* Jerk, The, *310;* Man with Two Brains, The, *328;* Oh, God!, *349;* One and Only, The, *613;* Sibling Rivalry, *378;* Summer Rental, *388;* Summer School, *388;* Where's Poppa?, *409*
Reiner, Jeffrey: Blood and Concrete, A Love Story, *956;* Inside Out (1992), *1058;* Trouble Bound, *1027*
Reiner, Lucas: Spirit of '76, The, *384*
Reiner, Rob: Few Good Men, A, *976;* Misery, *865;* Princess Bride, The, *1071;* Stand by Me (1986), *665;* Sure Thing, The, *389;* This Is Spinal Tap, *394;* When Harry Met Sally, *409*
Reinert, Rick: Winnie the Pooh and a Day for Eeyore, *218*

Reinhardt, Gottfried: Betrayed (1954), *11*
Reinhardt, Max: Midsummer Night's Dream, A (1935), *1066*
Reinisch, Deborah: Caught in the Act, *960*
Reinl, Harald: Carpet of Horror, *960;* Chariots of the Gods, *420;* Hell Hounds of Alaska, *1119;* Torture Chamber of Dr. Sadism, The, *896*
Reis, Irving: Bachelor and the Bobby-Soxer, The, *230;* Big Street, The, *460;* Crack-Up, *964;* Falcon Takes Over, The, *975;* Hitler's Children, *63*
Reisner, Allen: All Mine to Give, *444*
Reisner, Charles F.: Steamboat Bill Jr., *386*
Reisz, Karel: Everybody Wins, *973;* French Lieutenant's Woman, The, *522;* Gambler, The (1974), *524;* Isadora (1969), *554;* Morgan, *337;* Sweet Dreams, *943;* Who'll Stop the Rain, *139*
Reitherman, Wolfgang: Jungle Book, The (1967), *179;* One Hundred and One Dalmatians, *192;* Rescuers, The, *199;* Robin Hood (1973), *200;* Sword in the Stone, The, *208;* Wind in the Willows, The (1949), *217;* Winnie the Pooh and the Blustery Day, *218;* Winnie the Pooh and the Honey Tree, *218*
Reitman, Ivan: Dave, *262;* Ghostbusters, *285;* Ghostbusters II, *285;* Kindergarten Cop, *313;* Legal Eagles, *991;* Meatballs, *330;* Stripes, *387;* Twins, *401*
René, Norman: Longtime Companion, *579;* Prelude to a Kiss, *360*
Renoir, Jean: Boudu Saved from Drowning, *720;* Crime of Monsieur Lange, The, *727;* Day in the Country, A, *728;* Diary of a Chambermaid (1946), *730;* Elena and Her Men, *734;* Elusive Corporal, The, *734;* French Can Can, *738;* Golden Coach, The, *741;* Grand Illusion, *742;* La Bête Humaine, *753;* La Chienne, *753;* La Marseillaise, *754;* Little Theatre of Jean Renoir, The, *760;* Lower Depths (1936), *762;* Madame Bovary (1934), *763;* Picnic on the Grass, *777;* River, The (1951), *641;* Rules of the Game, The, *782;* Southerner, The, *663;* Testament of Dr. Cordelier, The, *1082;* This Land Is Mine, *682;* Toni, *796*
Resnais, Alain: Hiroshima, Mon Amour, *744;* Last Year at Marienbad, *756;* Melo, *766;* Mon Oncle d'Amerique, *768;* Muriel, *769;* Night and Fog, The, *432;* Providence, *630;* Stavisky, *789*
Resnick, Adam: Cabin Boy, *248*
Resnikoff, Robert: First Power, The, *841*
Reubens, Paul: Pee-Wee's Playhouse Christmas Special, *194*
Revier, Harry: Lost City, The, *1063*
Revon, Bernard: Rascals, The, *779*
Reyes, Buddy: Night of the Kickfighters, *90*
Reynolds, Burt: End, The, *271;* Gator, *54;* Man from Left Field, The, *586;* Sharky's Machine, *115;* Stick, *120*
Reynolds, C.D.H.: Day of Judgment, A, *830*
Reynolds, Christopher: Offerings, *872*
Reynolds, Don: His Name Was King, *1121*
Reynolds, Gene: M*A*S*H* (TV Series), *325;* Truth or Die, *689*
Reynolds, Kevin: Beast, The, *10;* Fandango, *274;* Robin Hood: Prince of Thieves, *108*
Reynolds, Sheldon: Adventures of Sherlock Holmes, The (TV Series), *950*
Reynolds, Ursi: Ganjasaurus Rex, *845*
Rezyka, Mark: South of Reno, *663*
Rhine, Robert: Road Lawyers and Other Briefs, *368*
Rhodes, Michael Ray: Fourth Wise Man, The, *521;* Killing Mind, The, *989;* Matters of the Heart, *590*
Rice, David: Quiet Thunder, *102*
Rich, David Lowell: Airport '79: The Concorde, *443;* Chu Chu and the Philly Flash, *255;* Convicted, *488;* Enola Gay: The Men, the Mission, the Atomic Bomb, *510;* Family Upside Down, A, *514;* Hearst and Davies Affair, The, *537;* Madame X (1966), *584;* Northeast of Seoul, *92;* Satan's School for Girls, *882;* Story of David, The, *207*
Rich, John: Boeing, Boeing, *243;* Clarence Darrow, *483;* Easy Come, Easy Go, *915;* Roustabout, *938*
Rich, Matty: Inkwell, The, *552;* Straight out of Brooklyn, *668*
Rich, Richard: Fox and the Hound, *168*
Richard, Jeff: Berserker, *813*
Richard, Pierre: Daydreamer, The (Le Distrait), *728;* Too Shy to Try, *796*
Richards, Dick: Culpepper Cattle Co., The, *1106;* Death Valley, *831;* Farewell My Lovely, *975;* Heat (1987), *60;* Man, Woman and Child, *587;* March or Die, *82;* Rafferty and the Gold Dust Twins, *364*
Richards, Lloyd: Roots: The Next Generation, *644*
Richardson, John: Dusty, *164*
Richardson, Mark: Robot in the Family, *200*
Richardson, Peter: Eat the Rich, *270;* Pope Must Diet, The, *360;* Supergrass, The, *388*
Richardson, Tony: Border, The, *17;* Charge of the Light Brigade, The (1968), *24;* Entertainer, The, *510;* Hamlet (1969), *535;* Hotel New Hampshire, The, *544;* Joseph Andrews, *311;* Look Back in Anger (1958), *579;* Loved One, The, *323;* Mademoiselle, *585;* Taste of Honey, A, *677;* Tom Jones, *397;* Women & Men: Stories of Seduction, *706*
Richert, William: Night in the Life of Jimmy Reardon, A, *344;* Winter Kills, *704*
Richmond, Anthony: Days of Hell, *33;* Deja Vu, *499;* Man Called Rage, A, *1064;* Night of the Sharks, *90*
Richter, Ota: Skullduggery, *887*
Richter, W. D.: Adventures of Buckaroo Banzai, The, *1034;* Late for Dinner, *1062*
Rickman, Tom: River Rat, The, *641*
Ridley, Philip: Reflecting Skin, The, *637*
Riead, William: Scorpion, *112*
Riefenstahl, Leni: Triumph of the Will, *437*
Riesner, Charles F.: Big Store, The, *238;* Lost in a Harem, *321;* Manhattan Merry-Go-Round, *930*
Riesner, Dean: Bill and Coo, *150*
Riffel, J.: House on Tombstone Hill, The, *853*
Rifkin, Adam: Chase, The (1994), *25;* Dark Backward, The, *262;* Never on Tuesday, *604*
Riklis, Eran: Cup Final, *727*
Riley, H. Anne: Animal Behavior, *227*
Rilla, Wolf: Village of the Damned, *900*
Rin, Taro: Galaxy Express, The, *168*
Ripley, Arthur: Chase, The (1946), *479;* Thunder Road, *129*
Ripploh, Frank: Taxi Zum Klo (Taxi to the Toilet), *793*
Ripstein, Arturo: Foxtrot, *521*
Risi, Dino: How Funny Can Sex Be?, *745;* Running Away, *645;* Tiger and The Pussycat, The, *795*
Risi, Marco: Forever Mary, *737*
Rissi, Michael: Soultaker, *889*
Ritchie, Michael: Almost Perfect Affair, An, *225;* Bad News Bears, The, *231;* Candidate, The, *474;* Cops and Robbersons, *259;* Couch Trip, The, *259;* Diggstown, *264;* Divine Madness, *423;* Downhill Racer, *504;* Fletch, *978;* Fletch Lives, *978;* Golden Child, The, *56;* Island, The, *857;* Positively True Adventures of the Alleged Texas Cheerleader-Murdering Mom, The, *360;* Prime Cut, *100;* Semi-Tough, *375;* Smile, *381;* Survivors, The, *389;* Wildcats, *411*
Ritelis, Viktors: Crucible of Horror, *827*
Ritt, Martin: Back Roads, *453;* Black Orchid, The, *463;* Brotherhood, The, *471;* Casey's Shadow, *157;* Conrack, *488;* Cross Creek, *491;* Front, The, *523;* Great White Hope, The, *533;* Hombre, *1121;* Hud, *546;* Long Hot Summer, The (1958), *578;* Molly Maguires, The, *598;* Murphy's Romance, *601;* Norma Rae, *608;* Nuts, *1002;* Paris Blues, *618;* Pete 'n' Tillie, *357;* Sounder, *663;* Spy Who Came in from the Cold, The, *664;* Stanley and Iris, *665*
Ritter, Joe: Beachballs, *233*
Ritter, Tim: Killing Spree, *859*
Rivers, Joan: Rabbit Test, *364*
Rivette, Jacques: La Belle Noiseuse, *753;* Nun, The (La Religieuse), *772;* Paris Belongs to Us, *775*
Rizenberg, Frederick A.: Gospel, *425*
Roach, Chris: Thirteenth Floor, The, *895*

Roach, Hal: His Royal Slyness/Haunted Spooks, *298;* Laurel and Hardy: At Work, *316;* Little Rascals, The, *183;* One Million B.C., *1069*
Roach Jr., Hal: One Million B.C., *1069*
Roach, M. Ray: Zoo Radio, *416*
Roarke, Adam: Trespasses, *687*
Robbie, Seymour: C.C. & Company, *21*
Robbins, Jerome: West Side Story, *947*
Robbins, Matthew: Batteries Not Included, *148;* Bingo, *240;* Corvette Summer, *29;* Dragonslayer, *1048;* Legend of Billie Jean, The, *76*
Robbins, Tim: Bob Roberts, *243*
Robe, Mike: Child in the Night, *961;* News at Eleven, *605;* Return to Lonesome Dove, *1143;* Son of the Morning Star, *1151;* Urge to Kill, *692*
Robert, Genevieve: Casual Sex?, *252*
Robert, Peter: Truly Tasteless Jokes, *400*
Robert, Yves: My Father's Glory, *769;* My Mother's Castle, *770;* Pardon Mon Affaire, *775;* Pardon Mon Affaire, Too!, *775;* Return of the Tall Blond Man with One Black Shoe, The, *781;* Salut L'Artiste, *783;* Tall Blond Man with One Black Shoe, The, *792*
Roberts, Alan: Happy Hooker Goes Hollywood, The, *293;* Karate Cop, *70;* Round Trip to Heaven, *370;* Save Me, *1012*
Roberts, Bill: Bongo, *152*
Roberts, Darryl: How U Like Me Now, *303*
Roberts, Deborah: Frankenstein General Hospital, *280*
Roberts, Stephen: Ex-Mrs. Bradford, The, *974;* Romance in Manhattan, *643;* Star of Midnight, *1020*
Robertson, Cliff: Pilot, The, *622*
Robertson, David: Firebird 2015 AD, *1051*
Robertson, John S.: Dr. Jekyll and Mr. Hyde (1920), *835;* Little Orphan Annie, *183;* Our Little Girl, *193;* Single Standard, The, *659*
Robertson, Joseph F.: Auntie Lee's Meat Pies, *811*
Robins, Herb: Worm Eaters, The, *904*
Robins, John: Hot Resort, *301*
Robinson, Bruce: How to Get Ahead in Advertising, *302;* Jennifer 8, *987;* Withnail and I, *412*
Robinson, John Mark: All Tied Up, *225;* Kid, *71;* Roadhouse 66, *107*
Robinson, Les: Walk into Hell, *136*
Robinson, Paul D.: Last Flight to Hell, *75*
Robinson, Phil Alden: Field of Dreams, *1050;* In the Mood, *306;* Sneakers, *1018*
Robinson, Richard: Bloody Trail, *1099*
Robinson, Ted: Shout: The Story of Johnny O'Keefe, *939*
Robison, Arthur: Warning Shadows (1923), *696*
Robson, Mark: Bedlam, *812;* Bridges at Toko-Ri, The, *19;* Champion, *479;* Daddy's Gone A-Hunting, *965;* Earthquake, *43;* From the Terrace, *523;* Harder They Fall, The, *536;* Home of the Brave, *543;* Inn of the Sixth Happiness, The, *552;* Isle of the Dead, *857;* Lost Command, *79;* Peyton Place, *621;* Prize, The, *629;* Return to Paradise, *106;* Seventh Victim, The, *885;* Valley of the Dolls, *693;* Von Ryan's Express, *136*
Rocco, Marc: Dream a Little Dream, *269;* Scenes from the Goldmine, *649;* Where the Day Takes You, *699*
Rocha, Glauber: Black God (White Devil), *718*
Rocha, Stephen: Movie Magic, *431*
Rochat, Eric: Fifth Monkey, The, *516*
Roche, Sean: Chasing Dreams, *480*
Rockwell, Alexandre: In the Soup, *306*
Roddam, Franc: Aria, *907;* Bride, The, *819;* Incredible Story of Dogs, The, *427;* K2, *70;* Lords of Discipline, The, *579;* Quadrophenia, *936;* War Party, *137*
Rodnunsky, Serge: Lovers' Lovers, *582*
Rodriguez, Paul: Million to Juan, A, *332*
Rodriguez, Robert: El Mariachi, *733*
Roed, Jan: Tong Tana, *437*
Roeg, Nicolas: Aria, *907;* Castaway, *476;* Cold Heaven, *485;* Don't Look Now, *971;* Eureka, *511;* Heart of Darkness, *538;* Insignificance, *553;* Man Who Fell to Earth, The, *1064;* Performance, *1005;* Sweet Bird of Youth (1989), *674;* Track 29, *1026;* Witches, The, *1089*
Roemer, Michael: Plot Against Harry, The, *359*
Roessler, Rick: Slaughterhouse, *887*
Roffman, Julian: Mask, The (1961), *863*
Rogell, Albert S.: Admiral Was a Lady, The, *222;* Li'l Abner (1940), *318;* War of the Wildcats, *1162*
Rogers, C. W.: Aladdin and the Magic Lamp, *145;* Fool and the Flying Ship, The, *167;* Peachboy, *194;* Red Riding Hood/Goldilocks, *198*
Rogers, Charles R.: Bohemian Girl, The, *243;* Devil's Brother, The, *914;* Laurel and Hardy Classics, Volume 1, *316;* Laurel and Hardy Classics, Volume 6, *316;* Laurel and Hardy Classics, Volume 7, *316;* Laurel and Hardy Classics, Volume 9, *316;* Laurel and Hardy on the Lam, *317*
Rogers, Doug: Dennis the Menace: Dinosaur Hunter, *162*
Rogers, Maclean: Down Among the "Z" Men, *268*
Rogosin, Lionel: Come Back Africa, *486;* On the Bowery, *612*
Rohmer, Eric: Aviator's Wife, The, *714;* Boyfriends and Girlfriends, *720;* Chloe in the Afternoon, *723;* Claire's Knee, *724;* Four Adventures of Reinette and Mirabelle, *738;* Full Moon in Paris, *739;* Le Beau Mariage, *756;* My Night at Maud's, *770;* Pauline at the Beach, *776;* Six in Paris (Paris Vue par . . .), *786;* Summer, *791;* Tale of Springtime, A, *792*
Roley, Sutton: Snatched, *117*
Rollin, Jean: Zombie Lake, *905*
Rollins, Bernie: Getting Over, *526*
Roman, Phil: Be My Valentine, Charlie Brown, *148;* Charlie Brown Thanksgiving, A, *157;* Good Grief, Charlie Brown, *171;* Is This Goodbye, Charlie Brown?, *177;* It's a Mystery, Charlie Brown, *177;* It's Arbor Day, Charlie Brown, *177;* It's Magic, Charlie Brown, *178;* It's the Easter Beagle, Charlie Brown, *178;* It's Three Strikes, Charlie Brown, *178;* It's Your First Kiss, Charlie Brown, *178;* Life Is a Circus, Charlie Brown, *181;* She Likes You, Charlie Brown, *203;* She's a Good Skate, Charlie Brown, *203;* Someday You'll Find Her, Charlie Brown, *206;* Tom & Jerry: the Movie, *212;* Very Funny, Charlie Brown, *215;* What a Nightmare, Charlie Brown, *216;* What Next, Charlie Brown?, *216;* You Can't Win, Charlie Brown, *219;* You're a Good Sport, Charlie Brown, *219;* You're the Greatest, Charlie Brown, *220*
Romanek, Mark: Static, *666*
Romero, Eddie: Beast of the Yellow Night, *812;* Beyond Atlantis, *11;* Brides of the Beast, *819;* Mad Doctor of Blood Island, The, *861;* Twilight People, *898;* Woman Hunt, The, *140*
Romero, George A.: Crazies, The, *825;* Creepshow, *826;* Dark Half, The, *829;* Dawn of the Dead, *830;* Day of the Dead, *830;* Knightriders, *73;* Martin, *863;* Monkey Shines: An Experiment in Fear, *865;* Night of the Living Dead (1968), *870;* Season of the Witch, *884;* Two Evil Eyes, *898*
Romero, Joey: Savage Justice, *111*
Romine, Charles: Behind Locked Doors, *812*
Rondell, Ronnie: No Safe Haven, *92*
Roodt, Darrell: Father Hood, *47;* Place of Weeping, *623;* Sarafina!, *938*
Room, Abram: Bed and Sofa, *716*
Root, Wells: Bold Caballero, The, *1099*
Ropelewski, Tom: Look Who's Talking Now, *321;* Madhouse (1990), *326*
Rose, Bernard: Candyman (1992), *820;* Chicago Joe and the Showgirl, *480;* Paperhouse, *873*
Rose, Les: Gas, *283*
Rose, Mickey: Student Bodies, *891*
Rose, Pierre: Klutz, The, *314*
Rose, Reuben: Screwball Academy, *374*
Rosemond, Perry: Second City Comedy Show, The, *374*
Rosemond, Peter: Miss Peach of the Kelly School, *188*
Rosen, Barry: Yum-Yum Girls, The, *709*
Rosen, Martin: Plague Dogs, The, *1070;* Stacking, *665;* Watership Down, *1088*

Rosen, Phil: Charlie Chan in the Secret Service, *961;* Chinese Cat, The, *962;* Gangs, Inc., *54;* Jade Mask, The, *987;* Little Men (1935), *182;* Meeting at Midnight, *996;* Phantom Broadcast, The, *1005;* Return of the Ape Man, *880;* Scarlet Clue, The, *1013;* Sphinx, The (1933), *1019;* Spooks Run Wild, *385*
Rosen, Robert L.: Raw Courage, *103*
Rosenberg, Stuart: Amityville Horror, The, *809;* April Fools, The, *228;* Brubaker, *471;* Cool Hand Luke, *29;* Drowning Pool, The, *972;* Laughing Policeman, The, *991;* Love and Bullets, *79;* My Heroes Have Always Been Cowboys, *1135;* Pocket Money, *359;* Pope of Greenwich Village, The, *624;* Voyage of the Damned, *694*
Rosenberg, Tanya: Blood Games, *956*
Rosenblum, Nina: Through the Wire, *436*
Rosenblum, Ralph: Any Friend of Nicholas Nickleby Is a Friend of Mine, *147;* Greatest Man in the World, The, *290;* Man That Corrupted Hadleyburg, The, *327*
Rosenfeld, Keva: Twenty Bucks, *401*
Rosenfelt, Scott: Family Prayers, *514*
Rosenthal, Dan: Sloane, *117*
Rosenthal, Rick: American Dreamer, *226;* Bad Boys, *454;* Birds II, The: Land's End, *813;* Devlin, *970;* Distant Thunder (1988), *502;* Halloween II, *848;* Russkies, *371*
Rosenthal, Robert J.: Zapped!, *416*
Rosi, Francesco: Bizet's Carmen, *718;* Christ Stopped at Eboli, *724;* Lucky Luciano, *79;* Palermo Connection, The, *1004;* Three Brothers, *794*
Rosman, Mark: Blue Yonder, The, *151;* House on Sorority Row, *853*
Rosmer, Milton: Murder in the Red Barn, *867*
Rosow, Gene: Laurel & Hardy: A Tribute to "The Boys", *428*
Ross, Herbert: California Suite, *249;* Dancers, *494;* Footloose, *917;* Funny Lady, *918;* Goodbye Girl, The, *288;* Goodbye, Mr. Chips (1969), *920;* I Ought to Be in Pictures, *304;* Last of Sheila, The, *991;* Max Dugan Returns, *591;* My Blue Heaven, *339;* Nijinsky, *607;* Owl and the Pussycat, The, *352;* Pennies from Heaven, *935;* Play It Again, Sam, *358;* Protocol, *363;* Secret of My Success, The, *375;* Seven-Per-Cent Solution, The, *1013;* Steel Magnolias, *667;* Sunshine Boys, The, *388;* True Colors, *688;* Turning Point, The, *689;* Undercover Blues, *403*
Rossati, Nello: Sensuous Nurse, The, *784*
Rossellini, Roberto: Amore, *712;* Fear (1955), *515;* General Della Rovere, *740;* Open City, *773;* Paisan, *775;* Rise of Louis XIV, The, *781;* Stromboli, *790;* Voyage in Italy, *801*
Rossen, Robert: Alexander the Great, *443;* All the King's Men, *444;* Body and Soul (1947), *466;* Hustler, The, *547;* Lilith, *575;* Mambo, *586;* They Came to Cordura, *681*
Rossetti, Franco: Big Rip-off, The, *1098*
Rossi, Franco: Quo Vadis? (1985), *632*
Rosson, Arthur: Long Long Trail, *1130;* Trailing Trouble, *1158*
Rostrup, Kaspar: Memories of a Marriage, *766*
Roth, Bobby: Baja Oklahoma, *455;* Boss' Son, The, *467;* Dead Solid Perfect, *497;* Game of Love, The, *524;* Heartbreakers, *538;* Keeper of the City, *562;* Man Inside, The (1990), *587;* Rainbow Drive, *103*
Roth, Joe: Coupe De Ville, *260;* Revenge of the Nerds II: Nerds in Paradise, *367;* Streets of Gold, *671*
Roth, Phillip: Apex, *1036;* Prototype X29A, *1072*
Rothman, Stephanie: Student Nurses, The, *671;* Terminal Island, *126;* Velvet Vampire, The, *900*
Rothstein, Richard: Hitchhiker (Series), The, *850*
Rouan, Brigitte: Overseas, *774*
Rouch, Jean: Six in Paris (Paris Vue par . . .), *786*
Rouffio, Jaques: La Passante, *754*
Rouse, Russell: Caper of the Golden Bulls, The, *22;* Fastest Gun Alive, The, *1112;* Oscar, The (1966), *615;* Thief, The (1952), *1024;* Well, The, *698*
Rowe, George: Fatal Mission, *46*
Rowe, Peter: Lost!, *580*
Rowland, E. G.: Final Defeat, The, *1113*
Rowland, Roy: Bugles in the Afternoon, *1102;* Five Thousand Fingers of Dr. T, The, *167;* Girl Hunters, The, *979;* Hit the Deck, *923;* Hollywood Party, *299;* Meet Me in Las Vegas, *930;* Our Vines Have Tender Grapes, *193;* Seven Hills of Rome, The, *939;* Two Weeks with Love, *947*
Rowley, Christopher: Dinosaur!, *422*
Rowley, Jim: Joe Bob Briggs—Dead in Concert, *310*
Rozema, Patricia: I've Heard the Mermaids Singing, *309*
Rubbo, Michael: Peanut Butter Solution, The, *194*
Ruben, J. Walter: Ace of Aces, *1;* Java Head, *557;* RiffRaff (1936), *640*
Ruben, Joseph: Dreamscape, *1048;* Good Son, The, *980;* Gorp, *289;* Joyride, *560;* Sister-in-Law, The, *659;* Sleeping with the Enemy, *1017;* Stepfather, The, *1020;* True Believer, *1027*
Ruben, Katt Shea: Poison Ivy (1992), *1006;* Streets, *121;* Stripped to Kill, *122;* Stripped to Kill II, *891*
Rubens, Percival: Survival Zone, *1081;* Sweet Murder, *1022*
Rubie, Howard: Island Trader, *67*
Rubin, Bruce Joel: My Life, *602*
Rubin, C. B.: Fraternity Demon, *280*
Rubin, Rick: Tougher Than Leather, *131*
Rubini, Sergio: Station, The, *789*
Rudolph, Alan: Choose Me, *962;* Endangered Species, *1049;* Equinox (1993), *510;* Love at Large, *322;* Made in Heaven (1987), *1064;* Moderns, The, *335;* Mortal Thoughts, *997;* Nightmare Circus, *871;* Songwriter, *940;* Trouble in Mind, *688;* Welcome to L.A., *698*
Rudolph, Louis: Double Standard, *504*
Ruge, Ane Mette: Art Com Video (Vol. 1–3), *1037*
Ruggles, Wesley: Arizona, *1094;* Cimarron (1931), *1105;* I'm No Angel, *305;* No Man of Her Own, *345;* Somewhere I'll Find You, *662*
Rughani, Pratap: Incredible Story of Dogs, The, *427*
Ruiz, Raul: On Top of the Whale, *773*
Rumar, Craig T.: Instant Justice, *67*
Rundle, Robert: Cybernator, *1043;* Divine Enforcer, *40*
Rush, Richard: Freebie and the Bean, *281;* Getting Straight, *526;* Hell's Angels on Wheels, *60;* Psych-Out, *630;* Stunt Man, The, *671*
Ruskin, Coby: When Things Were Rotten (TV Series), *409*
Russell, Chuck: Blob, The (1988), *814;* Nightmare on Elm Street 3, A: The Dream Warriors, *871*
Russell, Jay: End of the Line, *509*
Russell, Ken: Altered States, *1035;* Boy Friend, The, *909;* Crimes of Passion, *491;* Dante's Inferno, *495;* Devils, The, *500;* Gothic, *847;* Isadora (1966), *554;* Lair of the White Worm, *859;* Lisztomania, *928;* Mahler, *585;* Music Lovers, The, *932;* Prisoner of Honor, *628;* Rainbow, The, *634;* Salome's Last Dance, *647;* Savage Messiah, *648;* Tommy, *946;* Valentino, *693;* Whore, *701;* Women & Men: Stories of Seduction, *706;* Women in Love, *706*
Russell, William D.: Best of the Badmen, *1097;* Green Promise, The, *533*
Russo, Aaron: Rude Awakening (1989), *371*
Russo, John: Midnight (1980), *864*
Rust, John: Smurfs and the Magic Flute, The, *205*
Rustam, Mardi: Evils of the Night, *839*
Rutt, Todd: Shock! Shock! Shock!, *885*
Ruttmann, Walther: Berlin—Symphony of a Great City, *419*
Ryan, Frank: Call Out the Marines, *249;* Can't Help Singing, *911*
Ryazanov, Eldar: Forgotten Tune for the Flute, A, *738*
Rydell, Mark: Cinderella Liberty, *482;* Cowboys, The, *1106;* For the Boys, *918;* Harry and Walter Go to New York, *294;* Intersection, *553;* On Golden Pond, *612;* Reivers, The, *365;* River, The (1984), *641;* Rose, The, *937*
Rye, Renny: Poirot (Series), *1006*
Rymer, Judy: Who Killed Baby Azaria?, *701*
Sachs, William: Galaxina, *1053;* Hitz, *63;* Incredible Melting Man, The, *1058;* Last Hour, The, *75*
Sacks, Alan: Du-Beat-E-O, *915*

Sadamitsu, Shinya: Planet Busters, *1070*
Saeta, Eddie: Dr. Death: Seeker of Souls, *835*
Safran, Henri: Norman Loves Rose, *346;* Wild Duck, The, *702*
Sagal, Boris: Angela, *448;* Girl Happy, *919;* Ike: The War Years, *548;* Masada, *590;* Night Gallery, *869;* Omega Man, The, *1069;* Peter Gunn (TV Series), *98*
Sagan, Leontine: Maedchen in Uniform, *764*
Sage, DeWitt: Distant Harmony: Pavarotti in China, *422*
St. Clair, Malcolm: Are Parents People?, *228;* Bullfighters, The, *247;* Buster Keaton Festival: Vol. 1, *248;* Two Weeks to Live, *402*
Saks, Gene: Barefoot in the Park, *232;* Brighton Beach Memoirs, *246;* Cactus Flower, *248;* Fine Romance, A, *277;* Last of the Red Hot Lovers, *315;* Mame, *930;* Odd Couple, The, *348*
Sala, H.: Nightmare Weekend, *871*
Sale, Richard: Let's Make It Legal, *318*
Salkow, Sidney: City without Men, *483;* Last Man on Earth, The, *1062;* Twice-Told Tales, *898*
Salles Jr., Walter: Exposure, *45*
Salomon, Mikael: Far Off Place, A, *166*
Saltzman, Mark: Three Ninjas Kick Back, *211*
Salva, Victor: Clownhouse, *824*
Salvador, Jaime: Boom in the Moon, *243*
Salvatores, Gabriele: Mediterraneo, *766*
Samperi, Salvatore: Malicious, *764*
Samson, Barry: Ice Runner, *65*
Samuels, Raymond: Ambush Valley, *1093*
Samuels, Stuart: Rockin' Ronnie, *369;* Visions of Light: The Art of Cinematography, *438*
Samuelson, G. B.: She (1925), *1076*
San Fernando, Manuel: Rock 'n' Roll Wrestling Women vs. the Aztec Mummy, *369*
Sander, Peter: Sorcerer's Apprentice, The, *206*
Sanders, Denis: Elvis—That's the Way It Is, *423;* Great American West, *425;* Invasion of the Bee Girls, *1059;* One Man's Way, *613*
Sandrich, Jay: For Richer, for Poorer, *279;* Seems Like Old Times, *375*
Sandrich, Mark: Aggie Appleby, Maker of Men, *223;* Buck Benny Rides Again, *246;* Carefree, *911;* Cockeyed Cavaliers, *257;* Follow the Fleet, *917;* Gay Divorcée, The, *918;* Here Come the Waves, *922;* Hips, Hips, Hooray, *297;* Holiday Inn, *923;* Melody Cruise, *930;* Shall We Dance?, *939;* Top Hat, *946;* Woman Rebels, A, *705*
Sands, Sompote: Crocodile, *827*
Sanforth, Clifford: Murder by Television, *998*
Sanger, Jonathan: Code Name: Emerald, *27*
Sangster, Jimmy: Dynasty of Fear, *973;* Fear in the Night (Dynasty of Fear), *840;* Horror of Frankenstein, *851;* Lust for a Vampire, *861*
Santamaran, Enrick: Playgirl Killer, The, *875*
Santell, Alfred: Hairy Ape, The, *535;* Having a Wonderful Time, *294;* Jack London, *556;* Winterset, *704*
Santiago, Cirio H.: Angel Fist, *5;* Beyond the Call of Duty, *11;* Demon of Paradise, *832;* Devastator, The, *37;* Dune Warriors, *42;* Eye of the Eagle, *46;* Eye of the Eagle 3, *46;* Field of Fire, *47;* Final Mission, *48;* Firehawk, *49;* Future Hunters, *845;* Kill Zone, *71;* Live by the Fist, *78;* Naked Vengeance, *88;* One Man Army, *94;* Raiders of the Sun, *103;* Silk 2, *116;* Sisterhood, The, *1077;* Stryker, *1081;* TNT Jackson, *130;* Vampire Hookers, *900;* Wheels of Fire, *138*
Santley, Joseph: Call of the Canyon, *1103;* Cocoanuts, *257;* Harmony Lane, *922;* Melody Ranch, *1133*
Santos, Steve: Carlin at Carnegie, *251;* Carlin on Campus, *251*
Santostefano, Damon: Scream Greats, Vol. 1, *884;* Severed Ties, *885*
Saperstein, David: Beyond the Stars, *1039;* Killing Affair, A, *988*
Sarafian, Deran: Alien Predators, *1035;* Back in the U.S.S.R., *8;* Death Warrant, *35;* Gunmen, *58;* To Die For, *896*
Sarafian, Richard C.: Eye of the Tiger, *46;* Gangster Wars, *54;* I Spy (TV Series), *65;* Man in the Wilderness, *1132;* Man Who Loved Cat Dancing, The, *1132;* Street Justice, *121;* Sunburn, *1021;* Vanishing Point, *135*
Sargent, Joseph: Caroline?, *959;* Coast to Coast, *256;* Colossus: The Forbin Project, *1042;* Day One, *496;* Goldengirl, *1054;* Hustling, *547;* Incident, The (1989), *551;* Ivory Hunters, *555;* Jaws: The Revenge, *858;* MacArthur, *583;* Man from U.N.C.L.E., The (TV Series), *80;* Man on a String, *81;* Manions of America, The, *588;* Memorial Day, *592;* Miss Rose White, *596;* Never Forget, *604;* Nightmares, *871;* Passion Flower, *619;* Skylark, *660;* Taking of Pelham One Two Three, The, *1022;* Tomorrow's Child, *686;* Tribes, *688;* White Lightning, *139*
Sargenti, Marina: Child of Darkness, Child of Light, *823;* Mirror Mirror, *865*
Sarin, Vic: Cold Comfort, *963*
Sarne, Michael: Myra Breckenridge, *341*
Sarno, Jonathan: Plants Are Watching, The, *1071*
Sasdy, Peter: Devil within Her, The, *833;* Devil's Undead, The, *834;* Doomwatch, *1048;* Hands of the Ripper, *848;* King Arthur, The Young Warlord, *72;* Lonely Lady, The, *577;* Rude Awakening (1982), *881;* Sherlock Holmes and the Leading Lady, *1015;* Taste the Blood of Dracula, *892*
Sassone, Oley: Bloodfist III: Forced to Fight, *16;* Final Embrace, *977*
Satenstein, Frank: Honeymooners, The (TV Series), *300;* Honeymooners, The: Lost Episodes (TV Series), *300;* Jackie Gleason's Honeybloopers, *309*
Satlof, Ron: Humanoid Defender, *1057*
Sato, Junya: Go-Masters, The, *741*
Sato, Shimako: Tale of a Vampire, *891*
Sauer, Ernest G.: Beauty School, *233*
Saunders, Desmond: Captain Scarlet vs. the Mysterons, *156*
Saura, Carlos: Ay, Carmela!, *714;* Blood Wedding, *719;* El Amor Brujo, *733;* Garden of Delights, The, *739;* Hunt, The, *746;* Mama Turns 100, *764;* Stilts, The (Los Zancos), *789*
Sautet, Claude: César and Rosalie, *723;* Les Choses De La Vie, *759;* Mado, *763;* Simple Story, A, *786;* Un Coeur En Hiver, *798;* Vincent, François, Paul and the Others, *801*
Savage, Derek: Meateater, The, *864*
Savalas, Telly: Beyond Reason, *460*
Saville, Philip: Fellow Traveler, *515;* Mandela, *588;* Max and Helen, *590;* Secrets, *651;* Shadey, *377;* Those Glory Glory Days, *682;* Wonderland, *706*
Saville, Victor: Conspirator, *963;* Dark Journey, *966;* Evergreen, *916;* Forever and a Day, *520;* Green Dolphin Street, *533;* Iron Duke, The, *554;* Kim, *72;* Silver Chalice, The, *658;* Storm in a Teacup, *387;* Tonight and Every Night, *946*
Savini, Tom: Night of the Living Dead (1990), *870*
Savoca, Nancy: Dogfight, *503;* True Love, *400*
Sawaura, Takayuki: Black Magic M-66, *1039*
Saxon, John: Death House, *35*
Sayadian, Stephen: Dr. Caligari, *835*
Sayles, John: Baby, It's You, *453;* Brother from Another Planet, The, *1040;* City of Hope, *483;* Eight Men Out, *508;* Lianna, *573;* Matewan, *590;* Passion Fish, *619;* Return of the Secaucus 7, *366*
Sbardellati, James: Under the Gun, *691*
Scanlan, Joseph L.: Nightstick, *91;* Spring Fever, *385*
Scardino, Don: Me & Veronica, *591*
Scarpelli, Umberto: Giant of Metropolis, The, *1054*
Schachter, Steven: Water Engine, The, *696*
Schaefer, Armand: Fighting with Kit Carson, *1113;* Hurricane Express, *65;* Lost Jungle, The, *79;* Miracle Rider, The, *1134;* Sagebrush Trail, *1147;* 16 Fathoms Deep, *116;* Three Musketeers, The (1933), *128*
Schaefer, George: Best Christmas Pageant Ever, The, *150;* Doctors' Wives, *503;* Generation, *283;* Last of Mrs. Lincoln, The, *570;* Macbeth (1961), *583;* Man Upstairs, The, *327;*

Pendulum, *1005;* People vs. Jean Harris, *620;* Piano for Mrs. Cimino, A, *622;* Right of Way, *640*

Schaeffer, Franky: Baby on Board, *8;* Rebel Storm, *1074;* Wired to Kill, *1089*

Schaffner, Franklin J.: Best Man, The, *459;* Boys from Brazil, The, *958;* Islands in the Stream, *555;* Lionheart, *181;* Nicholas and Alexandra, *605;* Our Town (1980), *616;* Papillon, *97;* Patton, *619;* Planet of the Apes, *1071;* Sphinx (1981), *889;* Stripper, The (1963), *671;* Welcome Home, *698;* Yes, Giorgio, *948*

Schaffner, Franklin S.: War Lord, The, *137*

Schain, Don: Place Called Today, A, *622*

Schamoni, Peter: Spring Symphony, *788*

Schatzberg, Jerry: Clinton and Nadine, *26;* Honeysuckle Rose, *923;* Misunderstood (1984), *598;* No Small Affair, *345;* Reunion, *639;* Scarecrow, *649;* Seduction of Joe Tynan, The, *651;* Street Smart, *670*

Scheepmaker, Hans: Field of Honor (1986), *47*

Scheerer, Robert: Adam at 6 A.M., *441;* Hans Brinker, *173;* How to Beat the High Co$t of Living, *302;* World's Greatest Athlete, The, *218*

Schell, Maximilian: Marlene, *589;* Pedestrian, The, *620*

Schellerup, Henning: Adventures of Nellie Bly, The, *442;* In Search of Historic Jesus, *550;* Tom Edison—The Boy Who Lit Up the World, *213;* Wilbur and Orville: The First to Fly, *217*

Schenkel, Carl: Eye of the Demon, *840;* Hitchhiker (Series), The, *850;* Knight Moves, *989;* Mighty Quinn, The, *85;* Silence Like Glass, *657;* Silhouette, *1016*

Schepisi, Fred: Barbarosa, *1097;* Cry in the Dark, A, *492;* Iceman, *1057;* Mr. Baseball, *333;* Plenty, *623;* Roxanne, *370;* Russia House, The, *646;* Six Degrees of Separation, *659*

Scher, J. Noyes: Prisoners of Inertia, *361*

Schertzinger, Victor: Mikado, The (1939), *931;* One Night of Love, *934;* Road to Singapore, *369;* Road to Zanzibar, *369;* Something to Sing About, *940;* Uptown New York, *692*

Schibli, Paul: Nutcracker Prince, The, *191*

Schiffman, Suzanne: Sorceress, The (1988), *788*

Schiller, Lawrence: Double Exposure (1989), *504;* Double Jeopardy, *972;* Executioner's Song, The, *512;* Hey, I'm Alive!, *541*

Schilling, Tom: Cinderella (1987), *912*

Schirk, Keinz: Wannsee Conference, The, *802*

Schiro, Jeffrey C.: Stephen King's Night Shift Collection, *890*

Schlagman, Eric L.: Punch the Clock, *101*

Schlamme, Thomas: Bette Midler—Art or Bust, *909;* Bette Midler's Mondo Beyondo, *236;* Crazy from the Heart, *490;* Miss Firecracker, *333;* So I Married an Axe Murderer, *382;* Spalding Gray: Terrors of Pleasure, *384*

Schlatter, George: Norman...Is That You?, *346*

Schleh, Jack: Speed Racer: The Movie, *206*

Schlesinger, John: Believers, The, *812;* Billy Liar, *461;* Darling, *496;* Day of the Locust, The, *496;* Englishman Abroad, An, *510;* Falcon and the Snowman, The, *513;* Far from the Madding Crowd, *514;* Honky Tonk Freeway, *300;* Kind of Loving, A, *564;* Madame Sousatzka, *584;* Marathon Man, *82;* Midnight Cowboy, *593;* Pacific Heights, *1003;* Separate Tables, *652;* Sunday, Bloody Sunday, *673;* Yanks, *707*

Schlondörff, Volker: Coup De Grace, *726;* Death of a Salesman, *498;* Handmaid's Tale, The, *1055;* Lost Honor of Katharina Blum, The, *761;* Murder on the Bayou, *600;* Swann in Love, *791;* Tin Drum, The, *795;* Voyager, *695*

Schlossberg, Julian: No Nukes, *432*

Schlossberg-Cohen, Jay: Night Train to Terror, *870*

Schmidt, Wolfgang: Hollywood Strangler Meets the Skid Row Slasher, *851*

Schmoeller, David: Crawlspace, *825;* Curse IV: The Ultimate Sacrifice, *828;* Netherworld, *868;* Puppet Master, The, *878;* Seduction, The, *884;* Tourist Trap, *1026*

Schneider, Paul: Baby Cakes, *453;* Dance 'Til Dawn, *262;* Something Special, *383*

Schnitzer, Robert: Kandyland, *562;* Premonition, The, *876;* Rebel (1973), *104*

Schoedsack, Ernest B.: Chang, *24;* Dr. Cyclops, *835;* Grass, *425;* King Kong (1933), *859;* Last Days of Pompeii, The (1935), *569;* Mighty Joe Young, *1066;* Most Dangerous Game, The, *997;* Son of Kong, The, *888*

Schoemann, Michael: Magic Voyage, The, *185*

Schoendoerffer, Pierre: Le Crabe Tambour, *757;* 317th Platoon, The, *794*

Scholes, Roger: Tale of Ruby Rose, The, *676*

Schoolnik, Skip: Hide and Go Shriek, *850*

Schorr, Renen: Late Summer Blues, *756*

Schrader, Leonard: Naked Tango, *603*

Schrader, Paul: American Gigolo, *446;* Blue Collar, *465;* Cat People (1982), *822;* Comfort of Strangers, The, *963;* Hardcore, *981;* Light of Day, *575;* Light Sleeper, *575;* Mishima: A Life in Four Chapters, *595;* Patty Hearst, *620*

Schreibman, Myrl A.: Angel of H.E.A.T., *5;* Liberty and Bash, *77*

Schreiner, William: Sinful Life, A, *379*

Schreyer, John: Naked Youth, *89*

Schroeder, Barbet: Barfly, *455;* Charles Bukowski Tapes, *420;* General Idi Amin Dada, *424;* Koko: A Talking Gorilla, *428;* Les Tricheurs, *759;* Maitresse, *764;* More, *768;* Reversal of Fortune, *639;* Single White Female, *1016;* Valley, The, *799*

Schroeder, Frank C.: Pistol, The: The Birth of a Legend, *195*

Schroeder, Michael: Cyborg 2, *1043;* Damned River, *32;* Mortuary Academy, *337;* Out of the Dark, *873;* Relentless II: Dead On, *879*

Schultz, Carl: Blue Fin, *151;* Careful He Might Hear You, *475;* Deadly Currents, *34;* Seventh Sign, The, *885;* Travelling North, *687;* Which Way Home, *138*

Schultz, Michael: Car Wash, *250;* Carbon Copy, *251;* Cooley High, *259;* Disorderlies, *914;* For Us the Living: The Medgar Evers Story, *519;* Greased Lightning, *57;* Krush Groove, *927;* Last Dragon, The, *75;* Livin' Large, *320;* Scavenger Hunt, *373;* Sgt. Pepper's Lonely Hearts Club Band, *939;* Time Stalkers, *1084;* Which Way Is Up?, *410*

Schulz, Bob: Robbers of the Sacred Mountain, *107*

Schulze, Douglas: Hellmaster, *849*

Schumacher, Joel: Cousins, *260;* D.C. Cab, *261;* Dying Young, *506;* Falling Down, *513;* Flatliners, *977;* Incredible Shrinking Woman, The, *306;* Lost Boys, The, *861;* St. Elmo's Fire, *646*

Schunzel, Reinhold: Balalaika, *907;* Fortune's Fool, *738;* Melody Master, *592*

Schuster, Harold: Breakfast in Hollywood, *245;* Dinner at the Ritz, *39;* Finger Man, *48;* Marine Raiders, *82;* My Friend Flicka, *190;* So Dear to My Heart, *205;* Tender Years, The, *679*

Schuttes, Jan: Dragon Chow, *732*

Schwartz, Douglas: Thunder in Paradise, *129*

Schwarzenegger, Arnold: Christmas in Connecticut (1992), *255*

Scoffield, Jon: To See Such Fun, *397*

Scola, Ettore: Down and Dirty, *732;* Family, The (1987), *735;* La Nuit de Varennes, *754;* Le Bal, *756;* Macaroni, *325;* Passion of Love, *776;* Special Day, A, *788;* We All Loved Each Other So Much, *802*

Scorsese, Martin: After Hours, *223;* Age of Innocence, The, *443;* Alice Doesn't Live Here Anymore, *444;* Boxcar Bertha, *18;* Cape Fear (1991), *959;* Color of Money, The, *485;* Goodfellas, *531;* King of Comedy, The, *565;* Last Temptation of Christ, The, *570;* Last Waltz, The, *428;* Mean Streets, *591;* New York, New York, *933;* New York Stories, *343;* Raging Bull, *633;* Taxi Driver, *1023;* Two by Scorsese, *437;* Who's That Knocking at My Door?, *701*

Scott, Bill: Adventures of Rocky and Bullwinkle, The, *144*

Scott, Cynthia: Strangers in Good Company, *669*

Scott, Ewing: Windjammer, *140*

Scott, Gene: Mystery Island, *190*

Scott, George C.: Andersonville Trial, The, *447;* Rage (1972), *633;* Savage Is Loose, The, *648*

Scott, James: Strike It Rich, *387*
Scott, Michael: Dangerous Heart, *965;* Ladykiller, *990*
Scott, Oz: Bustin' Loose, *248*
Scott, Ridley: Alien, *1034;* Black Rain (1989), *14;* Blade Runner, *1039;* Duellists, The, *42;* 1492: The Conquest of Paradise, *52;* Legend, *1062;* Someone to Watch Over Me, *1018;* Thelma & Louise, *127*
Scott, Rosilyn T.: Faces of Death I & II, *424*
Scott, T. J.: TC 2000, *1082*
Scott, Tony: Beverly Hills Cop II, *11;* Days of Thunder, *33;* Hunger, The (1983), *854;* Last Boy Scout, The, *75;* Revenge (1990), *106;* Top Gun, *131;* True Romance, *133*
Scribner, George: Prince and the Pauper, The (1990), *197*
Seacat, Sandra: In the Spirit, *306*
Seagal, Steven: On Deadly Ground, *93*
Seale, John: Till There Was You, *684*
Sears, Cynthia L.: Emo Philips Live, *271*
Sears, Fred F.: Earth vs. the Flying Saucers, *1048*
Seaton, George: Airport, *443;* Big Lift, The, *460;* Counterfeit Traitor, The, *30;* Country Girl, The (1954), *489;* Little Boy Lost, *576;* Miracle on 34th Street, *187;* Showdown (1973), *1149;* Teacher's Pet, *392;* 36 Hours, *681*
Sebastian, Beverly: Delta Fox, *37;* Flash and the Firecat, *50;* Gator Bait, *55;* Gator Bait II—Cajun Justice, *55;* Rocktober Blood, *881;* Running Cool, *110*
Sebastian, Ferd: Delta Fox, *37;* Flash and the Firecat, *50;* Gator Bait, *55;* Gator Bait II—Cajun Justice, *55;* Hitchhikers, *850;* Rocktober Blood, *881;* Running Cool, *110*
Sebastian, Jonathan: Voyage to the Prehistoric Planet, *1087*
Sedan, Mike: Married People, Single Sex, *589*
Sedgwick, Edward: Air Raid Wardens, *223;* Beware of Spooks, *237;* Cameraman, The, *249;* Doughboys, *268;* Free and Easy, *281;* Movie Struck (a.k.a. Pick a Star), *338;* Parlor, Bedroom and Bath, *354;* Riding on Air, *368;* Southern Yankee, A, *383;* Speak Easily, *384;* Spite Marriage, *384;* What! No Beer?, *408*
Sedwick, John: Best of Dark Shadows, The, *813;* Dark Shadows (TV Series), *829*
Seed, Paul: Dead Ahead: The Exxon Valdez Disaster, *497*
Seely, Bob: Rover Dangerfield, *200*
Segal, Alex: No Time for Sergeants (Television), *608;* Story of David, The, *207*
Segal, Peter: Naked Gun 33 1/3, The—The Final Insult, *341*
Segall, Stuart: Drive-In Massacre, *838*
Segonzac, Jean De: Road Scholar, *434*
Seidelman, Arthur Allan: Body Language, *958;* Caller, The, *1041;* Children of Rage, *481;* Dying to Remember, *973;* Glory Years, *287;* Hercules Goes Bananas, *296;* Kid Who Loved Christmas, The, *180;* Macbeth (1981), *584;* Poker Alice, *1139;* Rescue Me, *105*
Seidelman, Susan: Cookie, *259;* Desperately Seeking Susan, *264;* Making Mr. Right, *327;* She-Devil, *377;* Smithereens, *661*
Seiler, Lewis: Charlie Chan in Paris, *961;* Doll Face, *914;* Guadalcanal Diary, *58;* Here Comes Trouble, *296;* Pittsburgh, *622;* Winning Team, The, *704*
Seiter, William A.: Allegheny Uprising, *1093;* Big Business Girl, *460;* Dimples, *914;* Diplomaniacs, *914;* In Person, *305;* It's a Date, *925;* Lady Takes a Chance, A, *1125;* Little Giant, *319;* Make Haste to Live, *994;* One Touch of Venus, *350;* Roberta, *936;* Room Service, *370;* Sons of the Desert, *383;* Stowaway, *942;* Susannah of the Mounties, *208;* Way Back Home, *406;* You Were Never Lovelier, *948*
Seitz, George B.: Andy Hardy Meets a Debutante, *227;* Andy Hardy's Double Life, *227;* Andy Hardy's Private Secretary, *227;* Danger Lights, *494;* Fighting Ranger, The, *1113;* Kit Carson, *1125;* Last of the Mohicans, The (1936), *1126;* Life Begins for Andy Hardy, *318;* Love Finds Andy Hardy, *322;* Thrill Hunter, *1157;* Vanishing American, The, *1161*
Sekely, Steve: Day of the Triffids, The, *1044;* Revenge of the Zombies, *881;* Scar, The, *649;* Waterfront, *697*
Selander, Lesley: Arizona Bushwhackers, *1094;* Bar 20, *1096;* Border Patrol, *1100;* Brothers in the Saddle, *1101;* Buckskin Frontier, *1102;* Colt Comrades, *1105;* Fighter Attack, *47;* Flat Top, *50;* Flight to Mars, *1052;* Fort Osage, *1114;* Forty Thieves, *1114;* Frontiersman, The, *1114;* Guns of Hate, *1118;* Heritage of the Desert, *1120;* Hidden Gold, *1120;* Lone Ranger and the Lost City of Gold, The, *1129;* Mysterious Desperado, *1135;* Out California Way, *1137;* Phantom of the Plains, *1138;* Range War, *1141;* Renegade Trail, *1142;* Rider from Tucson, *1143;* Riders of the Deadline, *1144;* Road Agent, *1145;* Robin Hood of Texas, *1145;* Rustlers, The, *1146;* Santa Fe Marshal, *1147;* Sheriff of Las Vegas, *1149;* Short Grass, *1149;* Shotgun, *1149;* Stagecoach War, *1152;* Stampede, *1152;* Three Men from Texas, *1157*
Selick, Henry: Nightmare before Christmas, The, *1068*
Sell, Jack M.: Deadly Spygames, *35;* Outtakes, *352*
Sellier Jr., Charles E.: Annihilators, The, *5;* Silent Night, Deadly Night, *886*
Selman, David: Fighting Shadows, *1113*
Seltzer, David: Lucas, *583;* Punchline, *630;* Shining Through, *656*
Selwyn, Edgar: Sin of Madelon Claudet, The, *658;* Skyscraper Souls, *660*
Selznick, Aran: Care Bears Movie, The, *156*
Sena, Dominic: Kalifornia, *561*
Senelka, Peter: Teen Alien, *892*
Senensky, Ralph: Dream for Christmas, A, *163*
Sennett, Mack: Caution: Funny Men at Work, *420;* Charlie Chaplin...Our Hero, *253;* Dough and Dynamite/Knockout, The, *268;* Mabel and Fatty, *325;* These Girls Won't Talk, *393*
Sequi, Mario: Cobra, The (1967), *27*
Seresin, Michael: Homeboy, *543*
Serikawa, Yugo: Panda's Adventures, *193*
Serious, Yahoo: Reckless Kelly, *365;* Young Einstein, *416*
Serreau, Coline: Mama, There's a Man in Your Bed, *764;* Three Men and a Cradle, *794*
Sesanzo, Juan Carlos: Deadly Revenge, *35*
Sessa, Alex: Amazons, *4;* Stormquest, *1080*
Setbon, Philip: Mr. Frost, *997*
Sewell, Vernon: Blood Beast Terror, The, *815;* Ghost Ship, *846;* Ghosts of Berkeley Square, *285;* Horrors of Burke and Hare, *852*
Seymour, Sheldon: Monster a Go-Go, *336*
Sgarro, Nicholas: Fortune Dane, *52;* Happy Hooker, The, *293*
Shackleton, Michael: Survivor, *1081*
Shadburne, Susan: Shadow Play, *885*
Shade, John: Swap, The, *674*
Shadyac, Tom: Ace Ventura: Pet Detective, *221*
Shah, Krishna: Hard Rock Zombies, *848*
Shalleck, Alan J.: Video Wonders: Home for a Dinosaur/The Monster Under My Bed, *215;* Video Wonders: Maxwell Mouse/The Great Bunny Race, *215*
Shanley, John Patrick: Joe Versus the Volcano, *310*
Shaoul, Jack: Robot in the Family, *200*
Shapiro, Alan: Crush, The, *964;* Tiger Town, *211*
Shapiro, Ken: Groove Tube, The, *291;* Modern Problems, *335*
Shapiro, Paul: Heads, *294;* Kurt Vonnegut's Monkey House, *1061;* Tales From Avonlea (TV series), *209*
Sharman, Jim: Rocky Horror Picture Show, The, *937;* Shock Treatment, *378*
Sharp, Alan: Little Treasure, *77*
Sharp, Don: Bear Island, *954;* Dark Places, *829;* Four Feathers, The (1978), *52;* Guardian of the Abyss, *848;* Hennessy, *982;* Hold the Dream, *542;* Mastermind (TV Series), *186;* Psychomania, *877;* Thirty-Nine Steps, The (1978), *1024;* What Waits Below, *902;* Woman of Substance, A, *705*
Sharp, Ian: Codename: Kyril, *962;* Final Option, The, *977;* Robin Hood and the Sorcerer, *107;* Secret Weapon, *651*
Sharpstein, Ben: Dumbo, *164*
Shatner, William: Star Trek V: The Final Frontier, *1079*

Shaughnessy, Alfred: Cat Girl, *960*
Shavelson, Melville: Cast a Giant Shadow, *23;* Five Pennies, The, *917;* Houseboat, *302;* Ike: The War Years, *548;* It Started in Naples, *308;* Legend of Valentino, *572;* New Kind of Love, A, *343;* Seven Little Foys, The, *376;* Yours, Mine and Ours, *416*
Shaw, Jim: George Burns in Concert, *284*
Shaye, Robert: Book of Love, *243*
Shayne, Linda: Purple People Eater, *198*
Shbib, Bashar: Julia Has Two Lovers, *560*
Shea, Jack: Dayton's Devils, *33*
Shea, James K.: Planet of the Dinosaurs, *1071*
Shear, Barry: Across 110th Street, *1;* Crash of Flight 401, *490;* Deadly Trackers, The, *1108;* Don Rickles: Buy This Tape You Hockey Puck, *267;* Night Gallery, *869;* Strike Force, *121;* Todd Killings, The, *685;* Wild in the Streets, *1089*
Shearer, Harry: History of White People in America, The, *298;* History of White People in America, The (Volume II), *298*
Shebib, Donald: Climb, The, *26;* Fish Hawk, *517;* Heartaches, *538;* Running Brave, *645*
Sheen, Martin: Cadence, *473*
Sheerer, Robert: Ants!, *809*
Sheff, Stanley: Lobster Man from Mars, *320*
Shelach, Riki: Last Winter, The, *571;* Mercenary Fighters, *84*
Sheldon, David: Lovely But Deadly, *994*
Sheldon, Steve: Human Race Club, The, *176*
Shelton, Ron: Blaze, *463;* Bull Durham, *247;* White Men Can't Jump, *410*
Shepard, Gerald S.: Heroes Die Young, *61*
Shepard, Richard: Cool Blue, *488;* Inside Out (1992), *1058;* Linguini Incident, The, *319*
Shepard, Sam: Far North, *274*
Shepphird, John: Teenage Bonnie and Klepto Clyde, *126*
Sher, Jack: Three Worlds of Gulliver, The, *1083*
Sheridan, Jim: Field, The, *516;* In the Name of the Father, *550;* My Left Foot, *602*
Sheridan, Michael J.: That's Entertainment! III, *436*
Sherin, Edwin: My Old Man's Place, *602;* Valdez Is Coming, *1160*
Sherman, Eric: Trained to Fight, *132*
Sherman, Gary A.: After the Shock, *442;* Dead and Buried, *830;* Lisa, *992;* Murderous Vision, *999;* Poltergeist III, *876;* Vice Squad, *135;* Wanted: Dead or Alive, *136*
Sherman, George: Against All Flags, *3;* Big Jake, *1098;* Colorado Sunset, *1105;* Covered Wagon Days, *1106;* Frontier Horizon, *1114;* Kansas Cyclone, *1124;* Kansas Terrors, *1124;* Last of the Redmen, *1126;* Lone Star Raiders, *1129;* Mexicali Rose, *1134;* Night Riders, The, *1136;* Outlaws of Sonora, *1137;* Overland Stage Raiders, *1137;* Pals of the Saddle, *1138;* Panic Button, *353;* Red River Range, *1141;* Riders of the Black Hills, *1144;* Rocky Mountain Rangers, *1145;* Santa Fe Stampede, *1147;* South of the Border, *1151;* Three Texas Steers, *1157;* Trail Blazers, *1158;* Treasure of Pancho Villa, The, *1158;* Tulsa Kid, *1159;* Under Texas Skies, *1160;* Wyoming Outlaw, *1165*
Sherman, Lowell: Bachelor Apartment, *230;* Morning Glory (1933), *599;* She Done Him Wrong, *377;* Three Broadway Girls, *395*
Sherman, Vincent: Adventures of Don Juan, The, *2;* Affair in Trinidad, *442;* All Through the Night, *3;* Bogie, *466;* Hard Way, The (1942), *536;* Ice Palace, *548;* Lady of the House, *568;* Lone Star, *1129;* Mr. Skeffington, *597;* Young Philadelphians, The, *708*
Shervan, Amir: Hollywood Cop, *63*
Sherwood, Bill: Parting Glances, *618*
Sherwood, John: Creature Walks Among Us, The, *826;* Monolith Monsters, The, *865*
Shibayama, Tsutomu: Ranma 1/2 (TV Series), *779*
Shields, Frank: Project: Alien, *1072;* Savage Attraction, *1012*
Shields, Pat: Frasier the Lovable Lion (Frasier the Sensuous Lion), *168*
Shigeru, Morikawa: Kimagure Orange Road, Vols. 1–4, *752*
Shilon, Igal: Big Gag, The, *238*
Shils, Barry: Motorama, *337*
Shilton, Gilbert: Kurt Vonnegut's Monkey House, *1061*
Shima, Koji: Golden Demon, *741*
Shin, Nelson: Transformers, the Movie, *213*
Shindo, Kaneto: Onibaba, *773*
Shing, Sung Kam: Mr. Vampire (Vol. 1–4), *768*
Shinji, Aramaki: Genesis Survivor Gaiarth: Stage 1, *1054*
Shinoda, Masahiro: Double Suicide, *731;* Gonza the Spearman, *741;* MacArthur's Children, *763*
Sholder, Jack: Alone in the Dark, *808;* By Dawn's Early Light, *473;* Hidden, The, *1056;* Nightmare on Elm Street 2, A: Freddy's Revenge, *871;* Renegades, *105;* 12:01, *1086;* Vietnam War Story—Part Two, *694*
Sholem, Lee: Cannibal Attack, *22;* Cheyenne (TV Series), *1104;* Hell Ship Mutiny, *60;* Superman and the Mole Men, *1081;* Tobor the Great, *1084*
Shonteff, Lindsay: Devil Doll (1963), *833;* Killing Edge, The, *1061;* Number One of the Secret Service, *347*
Shoor, Richard: Witches' Brew, *412*
Shore, Sig: Act, The, *441;* Return of Superfly, The, *105;* Sudden Death, *122;* Survivalist, The, *123*
Shores, Lynn: Charlie Chan at the Wax Museum, *961;* Shadow Strikes, The, *1014*
Shoten Pub. Co. Ltd., Tokuma: Warriors of the Wind, *1088*
Shub, Esther: Fall of the Romanov Dynasty, The, *424*
Shumlin, Herman: Watch on the Rhine, *696*
Shyer, Charles: Baby Boom, *230;* Father of the Bride (1991), *275;* Irreconcilable Differences, *554*
Sibay, Mussef: Woman Her Men and Her Futon, A, *705*
Sidaris, Andy: Do or Die, *40;* Fit to Kill, *49;* Guns, *58;* Hard Ticket to Hawaii, *59;* Malibu Express, *327;* Savage Beach, *111*
Siddon, David: Their Only Chance, *210*
Sidney, George: Anchors Aweigh, *906;* Annie Get Your Gun, *907;* Bathing Beauty, *908;* Bye Bye Birdie, *910;* Cass Timberlane, *476;* Eddy Duchin Story, The, *507;* Half a Sixpence, *921;* Harvey Girls, The, *922;* Holiday in Mexico, *923;* Jupiter's Darling, *926;* Key to the City, *312;* Kiss Me Kate, *927;* Pal Joey, *934;* Scaramouche, *111;* Show Boat (1951), *939;* Thousands Cheer, *945;* Three Musketeers, The (1948), *128;* Viva Las Vegas, *947*
Sidney, Scott: Tarzan of the Apes, *125*
Siegel, Don: Annapolis Story, An, *449;* Beguiled, The, *954;* Big Steal, The, *13;* Black Windmill, The, *956;* Charley Varrick, *25;* Coogan's Bluff, *29;* Dirty Harry, *39;* Escape from Alcatraz, *45;* Flaming Star, *1113;* Hell Is for Heroes, *60;* Invasion of the Body Snatchers (1956), *1059;* Jinxed, *310;* Killers, The, *71;* Madigan, *80;* Private Hell 36, *628;* Riot in Cell Block Eleven, *107;* Rough Cut, *1011;* Shootist, The, *1149;* Telefon, *1023;* Two Mules for Sister Sara, *1160*
Signorelli, James: Easy Money, *269;* Elvira, Mistress of the Dark, *271;* Hotel Room, *983*
Sijie, Dai: China, My Sorrow, *723*
Silberg, Joel: Bad Guys, *8;* Breakin', *909;* Catch the Heat, *24;* Lambada, *927;* Rappin', *936*
Silver, Andrew: Return, *638*
Silver, Joan Micklin: Bernice Bobs Her Hair, *234;* Between the Lines, *237;* Big Girls Don't Cry...They Get Even, *238;* Chilly Scenes of Winter, *481;* Crossing Delancey, *491;* Finnegan Begin Again, *277;* Hester Street, *541;* Loverboy, *323;* Prison Stories: Women on the Inside, *628;* Private Matter, A, *629*
Silver, Marisa: He Said, She Said, *294;* Indecency, *986;* Old Enough, *611;* Permanent Record, *621;* Vital Signs, *694*
Silver, Raphael D.: On the Yard, *94*
Silver, Ron: Lifepod, *1063*
Silverman, David: Simpson's Christmas Special, The, *204*
Silverman, Louis: Amazing Transplant, The, *445*
Silverstein, Elliot: Cat Ballou, *1103;* Man Called Horse, A, *1131*
Silvester, Dario: Between God, the Devil and a Winchester, *1097*
Simandl, Lloyd A.: Last of the Warriors, *1062;* Ultimate Desires, *1028*

Simenon, Marc: By The Blood Of Others, *721*
Simeone, Lawrence L.: Blindfold: Acts of Obsession, *956;* Cop-Out, *963;* Eyes of the Beholder, *974*
Simmonds, Allen: Striker's Mountain, *121*
Simmons, Anthony: Little Sweetheart, *577*
Simmons, Kendrick: Celebrating Bird: The Triumph of Charlie Parker, *420*
Simo, Sandor: Train Killer, The, *687*
Simon, Adam: Body Chemistry 2: Voice of a Stranger, *957;* Brain Dead, *1040;* Carnosaur, *821*
Simon, Francis: Chicken Chronicles, The, *254*
Simon, Juan Piquer: Cthulhu Mansion, *827;* Endless Descent, *838;* Pieces, *875;* Slugs, the Movie, *887*
Simon, Roger L.: My Man Adam, *340*
Simon, S. Sylvan: Abbott and Costello in Hollywood, *221;* Fuller Brush Man, The, *282;* Lust for Gold, *1130;* Rio Rita, *368;* Son of Lassie, *206;* Whistling in Brooklyn, *410;* Whistling in Dixie, *410;* Whistling in the Dark, *410*
Simone, Lawrence: Presumed Guilty, *626*
Simoneau, Yves: Blind Trust (Pouvoir Intime), *719;* Memphis, *592;* Mother's Boys, *998;* Perfectly Normal, *356;* Till Death Do Us Part, *683*
Simons, Edward: Endurance, *271*
Simpson, Michael A.: Fast Food, *274;* Funland, *282;* Impure Thoughts, *305;* Sleepaway Camp II: Unhappy Campers, *887;* Sleepaway Camp III, *887*
Simpson, Peter: Prom Night III—Last Kiss, *877*
Sinatra, Frank: None But the Brave, *92*
Sinclair, Andrew: Tuxedo Warrior, *133;* Under Milk Wood, *691*
Sinclair, Robert: Alphabet Conspiracy, The, *146*
Sindell, Gerald: H.O.T.S., *292*
Singer, Alexander: Bunco, *21;* Captain Apache, *1103;* Lost in Space (TV Series), *1063;* Love Has Many Faces, *581*
Singer, Stanford: I Was a Teenage TV Terrorist, *304*
Singleton, John: Boyz N the Hood, *468;* Poetic Justice, *624*
Singleton, Ralph S.: Stephen King's Graveyard Shift, *890*
Sinise, Gary: Miles from Home, *594;* Of Mice and Men (1992), *611;* True West, *689*
Sinofsky, Bruce: Brother's Keeper, *419*
Siodmak, Curt: Bride of the Gorilla, *819*
Siodmak, Robert: Crimson Pirate, The, *30;* Criss Cross (1948), *964;* Dark Mirror, The, *966;* Son of Dracula (1943), *888;* Spiral Staircase, The (1946), *1019;* Strange Affair of Uncle Harry, The, *669*
Sirk, Douglas: Imitation of Life, *549;* Magnificent Obsession, *585;* Time to Love and a Time to Die, A, *684;* Written on the Wind, *707*
Sissel, Sandi: Chicken Ranch, *420*
Sivo, Yuri: Inside Out 2, *1059;* Mortal Sins (1990), *997*
Sjoberg, Alf: Miss Julie, *767*
Sjoman, Vilgot: I Am Curious Blue, *746;* I Am Curious Yellow, *746*
Sjöström, Victor: Outlaw and His Wife, The, *616;* Phantom Chariot, *777;* Scarlet Letter, The (1926), *649;* Wind, The (1928), *703*
Skolimowski, Jerzy: Deep End, *969;* King, Queen and Knave, *565;* Le Départ, *757;* Lightship, The, *575;* Moonlighting (1983), *768;* Shout, The (1979), *886;* Success Is the Best Revenge, *672;* Torrents of Spring, *686*
Slapczynski, Richard: Adventures of Sinbad, The, *144;* Off on a Comet, *192;* Through the Looking Glass, *211*
Slater, Guy: Pocketful of Rye, A, *1006*
Slatzer, Robert F.: Big Foot, *813;* Hellcats, The, *60*
Slee, Mike: Connections 2, *421*
Sloane, Paul: Consolation Marriage, *488;* Half-Shot at Sunrise, *292*
Sloane, Rick: Vice Academy, *404;* Vice Academy 2, *404;* Vice Academy III, *404;* Visitants, The, *1087*
Slocum, James: American Summer, An, *5*
Sluizer, George: Vanishing, The (1988), *800;* Vanishing, The (1993), *1029*
Sluizer, George: Utz, *693*
Smallcombe, John: African Dream, An, *442*
Smart, Ralph: Quartet (1948), *631*
Smawley, Robert J.: American Eagle, *4;* River of Diamonds, *107*
Smight, Jack: Airport 1975, *443;* Damnation Alley, *1044;* Fast Break, *274;* Harper, *981;* Illustrated Man, The, *1057;* Intimate Power, *553;* Loving Couples, *324;* Midway, *84;* No Way to Treat a Lady, *1002;* Number One with a Bullet, *92;* Rabbit Run, *632;* Roll of Thunder, Hear My Cry, *642;* Secret War of Harry Frigg, The, *375*
Smith, Bernie: You Bet Your Life (TV Series), *415*
Smith, Bruce: Bebe's Kids, *233*
Smith, Bud: Johnny Be Good, *311*
Smith, Charles Martin: Boris and Natasha, *244;* Fifty/Fifty, *47;* Trick or Treat (1986), *897*
Smith, Cliff: Ace Drummond, *1;* Radio Patrol, *102*
Smith, Clive: Nelvanamation (Volume One), *190;* Rock and Rule, *1075*
Smith, Gary: Happy Birthday Bugs: 50 Looney Years, *173*
Smith, Harry: Heaven, Earth and Magic, *1056*
Smith, Howard: Gizmo!, *425;* Marjoe, *588*
Smith, Mel: Tall Guy, The, *391*
Smith, Noel: Cherokee Strip, *1104*
Smith, Peter: No Surrender, *345*
Smith, Yvonne: Ray Charles: The Genius of Soul, *433*
Smithee, Alan: Appointment with Fear, *6;* Bloodsucking Pharaohs in Pittsburgh, *816;* Call of the Wild (1992), *474;* Death of a Gunfighter, *1108;* Fatal Charm, *976;* Ghost Fever, *285;* Gypsy Angels, *535;* I Love N. Y., *547;* Let's Get Harry, *573;* Morgan Stewart's Coming Home, *337;* Red Shoe Diaries 4: Auto Erotica, *637;* Shrimp on the Barbie, *378;* Solar Crisis, *1077;* Stitches, *386*
Smoke, Stephen: Final Impact, *48;* Street Crimes, *121*
Smolan, Sandy: Rachel River, *632*
Smoot, Phil: Dark Power, The, *829*
Snedon, Greg: Dunera Boys, The, *506*
Snider, Skott: Miracle Beach, *332*
Soavi, Michele: Church, The, *824;* Dario Argento's World of Horror, *422*
Sobel, Mark: Access Code, *1;* Sweet Revenge (1987), *123;* Trial & Error, *1027*
Soderbergh, Steven: Fallen Angels, *513;* Kafka, *988;* King of the Hill, *565;* Sex, Lies and Videotape, *653*
Softley, Iain: BackBeat, *907*
Solberg, Russell: Payback, *98*
Sole, Alfred: Alice, Sweet Alice (Communion and Holy Terror), *808;* Pandemonium, *353*
Solinas, Piernico: Touch and Die, *1026*
Sollima, Sergio: Blood in the Streets, *15;* Family, The (1970), *46*
Solondz, Todd: Fear, Anxiety and Depression, *276*
Solt, Andrew: Imagine: John Lennon, *427;* It Came from Hollywood, *307;* This Is Elvis, *436*
Solum, Ola: Polar Bear King, The, *1071*
Solvay, Paul: Devil's Wedding Night, The, *834*
Sommers, Stephen: Adventures of Huck Finn, The (1993), *143;* Catch Me if You Can, *24*
Sonnenfeld, Barry: Addams Family, The, *222;* Addams Family Values, *222;* For Love or Money, *279*
Soref, Dror: Seventh Coin, The, *203*
Sorin, Carlos: Eversmile New Jersey, *511*
Sotirakis, Dimitri: Beverly Hills Brats, *237*
Sotos, Jim: Forced Entry, *842;* Hot Moves, *301;* Sweet Sixteen, *123*
Sottnick, Mark: Elephant's Child, The, *164;* Emperor and the Nightingale, The, *164;* How the Rhinoceros Got His Skin and How the Camel Got His Hump, *176;* Pecos Bill, *194;* Santabear's First Christmas, *201;* Tailor of Gloucester, The,

209; Tale of Mr. Jeremy Fisher and the Tale of Peter Rabbit, The, *209;* Three Billy Goats Gruff and the Three Little Pigs, The, *211;* Velveteen Rabbit, The, *215*
Sparber, Isadore: Best of Little Lulu, *150;* Superman Cartoons, *208*
Sparr, Robert: Swingin' Summer, A, *390*
Speer, Martin: Hasty Heart, *537*
Speight, Johnny: All in the Family Twentieth Anniversary Special, *224*
Spence, Michael: Edge of Honor, *43*
Spencer, Alan: Hexed, *296*
Spencer, Brenton: Blown Away (1992), *957;* Club, The (1993), *824*
Spencer, Jane: Little Noises, *576*
Spera, Robert: Witchcraft, *903*
Spheeris, Penelope: Beverly Hillbillies, The, *237;* Boys Next Door, The, *468;* Decline of Western Civilization, The, *422;* Decline of Western Civilization, Part II—The Metal Years, *422;* Dudes, *505;* Hollywood Vice Squad, *63;* Prison Stories: Women on the Inside, *628;* Suburbia, *672;* Wayne's World, *406*
Spiegel, Scott: Intruder (1988), *856*
Spielberg, Steven: Always (1989), *445;* Amazing Stories (TV Series), *1036;* Close Encounters of the Third Kind, *1042;* Color Purple, The, *485;* Columbo: Murder by the Book, *963;* Duel, *972;* E.T.—The Extra-Terrestrial, *1048;* Empire of the Sun, *509;* Hook, *175;* Indiana Jones and the Last Crusade, *1058;* Indiana Jones and the Temple of Doom, *1058;* Jaws, *858;* Jurassic Park, *1061;* Night Gallery, *869;* 1941, *345;* Raiders of the Lost Ark, *1073;* Schindler's List, *649;* Sugarland Express, The, *672;* Tiny Toons Adventures: How I Spent my Vacation, *212;* Twilight Zone—The Movie, *898*
Sporn, Michael: Little Match Girl, The (1990), *182;* Marzipan Pig, The, *186*
Sporup, Murray Douglas: Rock, Baby, Rock It, *936*
Spottiswoode, Roger: Air America, *3;* And the Band Played on, *447;* Best of Times, The, *236;* Last Innocent Man, The, *990;* Pursuit of D. B. Cooper, *363;* Shoot to Kill, *115;* Stop! Or My Mom Will Shoot, *386;* Terror Train, *894;* Third Degree Burn, *1024;* Time Flies When You're Alive, *684;* Turner and Hooch, *400;* Under Fire, *134*
Spotton, John: Buster Keaton Rides Again, *420;* Keaton Rides Again/Railroader, *312*
Spring, Tim: Double Blast, *41;* Reason to Die, *879*
Springsteen, R. G.: Arizona Cowboy, *1094;* Conquest of Cheyenne, *1106;* Hellfire, *1120;* Hostile Guns, *1122;* Johnny Reno, *1124;* Marshal of Cripple Creek, *1132;* Oklahoma Annie, *349;* Red Menace, The, *636;* Santa Fe Uprising, *1147;* Stagecoach to Denver, *1152;* Vigilantes of Boomtown, *1161;* Wagon Wheels Westward, *1162;* When Gangland Strikes, *138*
Spry, Robin: Cry in the Night, A, *964;* Drying Up the Streets, *505;* Keeping Track, *70;* Obsessed, *610*
Squire, Anthony: Mission in Morocco, *85*
Squiteri, Pasquale: Corleone, *29;* Third Solution, The, *794*
Stafford, Stephen: Hit Woman: The Double Edge, *63;* I Posed for Playboy, *548*
Stagnaro, Juan Bautista: Debajo del Mundo (Under Earth), *729*
Stahl, Eric Steven: Final Approach, *1051*
Stahl, John M.: Immortal Sergeant, The, *549;* Keys to the Kingdom, The, *563;* Letter of Introduction, *573*
Stahl, Ray: Scarlet Spear, The, *112*
Stallone, Sylvester: Paradise Alley, *618;* Rocky II, *642;* Rocky III, *642;* Rocky IV, *642;* Staying Alive, *942*
Stanford, Jeremy: Stepmonster, *1080*
Stanley, John: Nightmare in Blood, *871*
Stanley, Richard: Dust Devil, *838;* Hardware, *1055*
Stanojevic, Stanislav: Notorious Nobodies, *772*
Stanzler, Jeff: Jumpin' at the Boneyard, *561*
Star, Bruce: Boogeyman 2, The, *818*
Starewicz, Ladislaw: Cameraman's Revenge and Other Fantastic Tales, the: the Amazing Puppet Animation of Ladislaw Starewicz, *155;* Early Russian Cinema: Before the Revolutions (Vol. 1–10), *732*
Starewitch: Bambi vs. Godzilla, *148*
Starr, Steven: Joey Breaker, *558*
Starrett, Jack: Cleopatra Jones, *26;* Cry Blood, Apache, *1106;* Final Chapter—Walking Tall, *48;* Losers, The, *79;* Mr. Horn, *1134;* Race with the Devil, *878;* Slaughter, *117;* Small Town in Texas, A, *117;* Summer Heat (1983), *672*
Staub, Ralph: Country Gentlemen, *260*
Steckler, Len: Mad Bull, *584*
Steckler, Ray Dennis: Incredibly Strange Creatures Who Stopped Living and Became Mixed-Up Zombies, The, *856;* Rat Pfink a Boo Boo, *364;* Thrill Killers, The, *895;* Wild Guitar, *702*
Steensland, David: Escapes, *1049*
Stegani, Giorgio: Beyond the Law, *1097*
Stein, Herb: Escape to Love, *511*
Stein, Jeff: Kids Are Alright, The, *428;* Mother Goose Rock N' Roll Rhyme, *189;* Shelley Duvall's Bedtime Stories (Series), *203*
Stein, Ken: Killer Instinct, *71;* Rain Killer, The, *1008*
Stein, Paul: Common Law, The, *487;* Heart's Desire, *922*
Steinberg, David: Casey at the Bat, *156;* Going Berserk, *287;* Paternity, *355*
Steinberg, Michael: Bodies, Rest & Motion, *465;* Waterdance, The, *696*
Steinberg, Ziggy: Boss' Wife, The, *244*
Steinmann, Danny: Friday the 13th, Part V—A New Beginning, *844;* Savage Streets, *111*
Stelling, Jos: Pointsman, The, *624;* Rembrandt—1669, *780*
Stellman, Martin: For Queen and Country, *519*
Stephani, Frederick: Flash Gordon: Rocketship (a.k.a. Spaceship to the Unknown; Perils from Planet Mongo), *1052*
Stephen, A. C.: Fugitive Girls, *53;* Orgy of the Dead, *873;* Saturday Night Sleazies, *372*
Stephenson, Ken: Nelvanamation (Volume Two), *191*
Sterling, William: Alice's Adventures in Wonderland, *145*
Stern, Bert: Jazz on a Summer's Day, *427*
Stern, Daniel: Rookie of the Year, *200*
Stern, Leonard: Just You and Me, Kid, *312*
Stern, Noah: Pyrates, *363*
Stern, Sandor: Amityville 4: The Evil Escapes, *809;* Assassin, *1037;* Dangerous Pursuit, *966;* Duplicates, *973;* Glitz, *980;* Jericho Fever, *68;* John & Yoko: A Love Story, *559;* Pin, *875;* Web of Deceit, *1030*
Stern, Steven H.: Ambush Murders, The, *446;* Devil and Max Devlin, The, *264;* Draw, *1110;* Final Notice, *977;* Forbidden Love, *519;* Getting Physical, *526;* Love and Murder, *993;* Mazes and Monsters, *864;* Miracle on Ice, *595;* Morning Glory (1992), *599;* Murder in Space, *1067;* Not Quite Human, *347;* Obsessive Love, *1002;* Park Is Mine, The, *618;* Portrait of a Showgirl, *625;* Rolling Vengeance, *108;* Small Killing, A, *660;* Undergrads, The, *214;* Weekend War, *697;* Young Love, First Love, *708*
Stern, Tom: Freaked, *281*
Steven, Geoff: Signatures of the Soul, *434*
Stevens, Andrew: Night Eyes 3, *1000;* Terror Within 2, The, *894*
Stevens, Arnold: Attack of the Swamp Creature, *810*
Stevens, Art: Fox and the Hound, *168;* Rescuers, The, *199*
Stevens, David: Kansas, *562;* Town Like Alice, A, *686*
Stevens, George: Alice Adams, *444;* Annie Oakley (1935), *1093;* Damsel in Distress, A, *913;* Diary of Anne Frank, The, *501;* Giant, *527;* Greatest Story Ever Told, The, *533;* Gunga Din, *58;* I Remember Mama, *548;* Kentucky Kernels, *312;* More the Merrier, The, *337;* Penny Serenade, *620;* Place in the Sun, A, *622;* Quality Street, *631;* Shane, *1148;* Swing Time, *943;* Talk of the Town, The, *390;* Vivacious Lady, *405;* Woman of the Year, *413*
Stevens Jr., George: Separate But Equal, *652*
Stevens, Greg: Live at Harrah's, *320*
Stevens, Leslie: Three Kinds of Heat, *128*

Stevens, Mark: Cry Vengeance, *492*
Stevens, Robert: Never Love a Stranger, *604;* Treasures of the Twilight Zone, *1085*
Stevens, Warren: Dragon Fight, *42*
Stevenson, Robert: Absent-Minded Professor, The, *143;* Bedknobs and Broomsticks, *149;* Blackbeard's Ghost, *151;* Darby O'Gill and the Little People, *161;* Dishonored Lady, *39;* Forever and a Day, *520;* Gnome-Mobile, The, *169;* Herbie Rides Again, *174;* In Search of the Castaways, *176;* Island at the Top of the World, The, *1060;* Jane Eyre (1944), *557;* Joan of Paris, *558;* Johnny Tremain, *179;* Kidnapped (1960), *180;* King Solomon's Mines (1937), *72;* Las Vegas Story, The, *568;* Love Bug, The, *184;* Man Who Lived Again, The, *862;* Mary Poppins, *185;* Misadventures of Merlin Jones, The, *188;* Monkey's Uncle, The, *188;* My Forbidden Past, *602;* Nine Days a Queen, *607;* Old Yeller, *192;* One of Our Dinosaurs Is Missing, *192;* Shaggy D.A., The, *203;* Son of Flubber, *206;* That Darn Cat, *210;* Tom Brown's School Days (1940), *685;* Walk Softly, Stranger, *1030*
Stewart, Alan L.: Ghostriders, *846*
Stewart, Douglas Day: Listen to Me, *576;* Thief of Hearts, *681*
Stewart Jr., Douglas M.: Memories of Hollywood, *430*
Stewart, John: Cartel, *23;* Hidden Obsession, *982*
Stewart, Larry: Initiation, The, *856*
Stewart, Peter: Gun Code, *1117*
Stigilano, Roger: Fun Down There, *523*
Stiller, Ben: Elvis Stories, *271;* Reality Bites, *635*
Stiller, Mauritz: Thomas Graal's Best Child, *794;* Thomas Graal's Best Film, *794;* Treasure of Arne, *797*
Stillman, Whit: Metropolitan, *593*
Stitt, Alexander: Grendel, Grendel, Grendel, *172*
Stock, Mark: Midnight Movie Massacre, *332*
Stockwell, John: Undercover, *134*
Stoeffhaas, Jerry: Cheap Shots, *254*
Stoloff, Ben: Affairs of Annabel, The, *223;* It's a Joke, Son!, *308;* Palooka, *617;* Sea Devils, *112;* Transatlantic Merry-Go-Round, *946*
Stoloff, Victor: Washington Affair, The, *696*
Stone, Andrew L.: Last Voyage, The, *76;* Sensations of 1945, *938;* Song of Norway, *940;* Stormy Weather, *942*
Stone, Oliver: Born on the Fourth of July, *467;* Doors, The, *914;* Hand, The, *848;* Heaven and Earth (1993), *539;* JFK, *558;* Platoon, *623;* Salvador, *647;* Seizure, *884;* Talk Radio, *677;* Wall Street, *695*
Stone, Virginia Lively: Run if You Can, *645*
Stoppard, Tom: Rosencrantz and Guildenstern Are Dead, *370*
Storm, Esben: In Search of Anna, *550*
Storm, Howard: Once Bitten, *349;* Pecos Bill, King of the Cowboys, *194;* Three Little Pigs, The, *211*
Story, Thomas L.: Last Frontier, The, *1125*
Straub, Ralph: Prairie Moon, *1139*
Strayer, Frank: Blondie, *241;* Blondie Has Trouble, *241;* Blondie in Society, *241;* Blondie Takes a Vacation, *242;* Blondie's Blessed Event, *242;* Daring Young Man, The, *262;* Fugitive Road, *523;* It's a Great Life, *308;* Monster Walks, The, *866;* Vampire Bat, The, *899*
Streisand, Barbra: Prince of Tides, The, *627;* Yentl, *948*
Strick, Joseph: Balcony, The, *455;* Portrait of the Artist as a Young Man, A, *625;* Tropic of Cancer, *688*
Strickland, John: Prime Suspect 2, *1007*
Strock, Herbert L.: Blood of Dracula, *815;* Crawling Hand, The, *825;* Devil's Messenger, The, *834;* How to Make a Monster, *853;* I Was a Teenage Frankenstein, *855;* Witches' Brew, *412*
Strock, Robert L.: Bronco (TV Series), *1101*
Stromberg, William R.: Crater Lake Monster, The, *825*
Stroud, Richard: Deadline (1988), *34*
Stryker, Jonathan: Curtains, *828*
Stuart, Brian: Sorceress (1982), *1077*
Stuart, Mel: Chisholms, The, *1104;* Happy Anniversary 007: 25 Years of James Bond, *425;* I Love My Wife, *304;* If It's Tuesday, This Must Be Belgium, *305;* Sophia Loren: Her Own Story, *663;* Willy Wonka and the Chocolate Factory, *217*
Sturges, John: Bad Day at Black Rock, *454;* Chino, *1104;* Eagle Has Landed, The, *42;* Escape from Fort Bravo, *1111;* Great Escape, The, *57;* Gunfight at the O.K. Corral, *1117;* Hallelujah Trail, The, *1118;* Ice Station Zebra, *65;* It's a Big Country, *308;* Joe Kidd, *1123;* Last Train from Gun Hill, *1126;* Law and Jake Wade, The, *1127;* Magnificent Seven, The, *1131;* Magnificent Yankee, The, *585;* Marooned, *1065;* McQ, *83;* Never So Few, *89;* Underwater!, *134*
Sturges, Preston: Beautiful Blonde from Bashful Bend, The, *233;* Christmas in July, *255;* Great McGinty, The, *290;* Great Moment, The, *290;* Hail the Conquering Hero, *292;* Lady Eve, The, *315;* Mad Wednesday, *325;* Miracle of Morgan's Creek, The, *332;* Palm Beach Story, The, *353;* Sin of Harold Diddlebock (a.k.a. Mad Wednesday), *379;* Sullivan's Travels, *388;* Unfaithfully Yours (1948), *403*
Sturridge, Charles: Brideshead Revisited, *469;* Handful of Dust, A, *535;* Where Angels Fear to Tread, *699*
Stuttard, Ian: Crime Inc., *421*
Styles, Richard: Shallow Grave, *114*
Suarez, Bobby A.: Warriors of the Apocalypse, *1088*
Subiela, Eliseo: Man Facing Southeast, *765*
Sugai, Hisashi: Roots Search, *782*
Sugerman, Andrew: Basic Training, *232*
Suissa, Daniele J.: Shades of Love: The Rose Cafe, *654*
Sujio, L.: Black Magic Terror, *814*
Sullivan, Fred G.: Cold River, *159*
Sullivan, Kevin: Anne of Avonlea, *449;* Anne of Green Gables (1985), *449;* Lantern Hill, *180;* Looking for Miracles, *579*
Summers, Jeremy: Five Golden Dragons, *50;* House of 1,000 Dolls, *64*
Summers, Walter: Human Monster, The (Dark Eyes of London), *854;* River of Unrest, *641*
Sun, Shirley: Iron & Silk, *554*
Sundstrom, Cedric: American Ninja III, *4;* American Ninja IV: The Annihilation, *4;* Captive Rage, *23*
Sundstrom, Neal: Howling V—The Rebirth, *854*
Sunseri, Jack A.: Chilling, The, *823*
Surjik, Stephen: Wayne's World 2, *406*
Suso, Henry: Deathsport, *1046*
Sutherland, A. Edward: Beyond Tomorrow, *1039;* Every Day's a Holiday, *273;* Flying Deuces, *278;* Having a Wonderful Crime, *294;* International House, *307;* Invisible Woman, The, *307;* Mississippi, *931;* Mr. Robinson Crusoe, *86;* Murders in the Zoo, *867;* One Night in the Tropics, *350*
Sutherland, Hal: He-Man and the Masters of the Universe (Series), *173;* Journey Back to Oz, *179;* Pinocchio and the Emperor of the Night, *195;* She-Ra, Princess of Power (Volume One), *203*
Sutherland, Kiefer: Last Light, *569*
Svankmajer, Jan: Alice (1988), *1034;* Prize Winning Films of Jan Svankmajer, The, *876*
Swackhamer, E. W.: Amazing Spiderman, The, *4;* Are You Lonesome Tonight, *953;* Dain Curse, The, *965;* Death at Love House, *968;* Longshot (1981), *579;* Man and Boy, *1131;* Night Terror, *1001;* Perfect Family, *1005;* Rousters, The, *109;* Secret Passion of Robert Clayton, The, *1013;* Terror at London Bridge, *893;* Winds of Kitty Hawk, The, *703*
Swaim, Bob: Half-Moon Street, *981;* La Balance, *753;* Masquerade (1988), *995*
Swan, Don: Gore-Met, Zombie Chef from Hell, *847*
Swanson, Donald: Magic Garden, The, *764*
Sweeney, Bob: Return to Mayberry, *366*
Sweet, Harry: Two-Reelers: Comedy Classics #1, *402*
Swenson, Charles: Little Rascals Christmas Special, The, *183;* Mouse and His Child, The, *189;* Twice Upon a Time, *214*
Swickard, Charles: Hell's Hinges, *1120*

Swift, David: Good Neighbor Sam, *288;* How to Succeed in Business without Really Trying, *923;* Interns, The, *553;* Parent Trap, The, *193;* Pollyanna (1960), *196*
Swift, Lela: Best of Dark Shadows, The, *813;* Dark Shadows (TV Series), *829*
Swimmer, Saul: Mrs. Brown You've Got a Lovely Daughter, *931*
Swirnoff, Brad: Tunnelvision, *400*
Switzer, Michael: Lightning Incident, The, *860;* Nitti: The Enforcer, *91*
Sykes, Peter: Demons of the Mind, *833;* Jesus, *557;* To the Devil, a Daughter, *896*
Sylbert, Paul: Steagle, The, *386*
Szabo, Istvan: Colonel Redl, *725;* Father, *736;* Hanussen, *743;* Meeting Venus, *591;* Mephisto, *767;* 25, Firemen's Street, *797*
Szulzinger, Boris: Mamma Dracula, *862;* Shame of the Jungle, *377*
Szwarc, Jeannot: Bug, *820;* Enigma, *44;* Grand Larceny, *289;* Jaws 2, *858;* Murders in the Rue Morgue (1986), *999;* Santa Claus—The Movie, *201;* Somewhere in Time, *1077;* Supergirl, *1081*
Taav, Michael: Paint Job, The, *1004*
Tabet, Sylvio: Beastmaster 2: Through the Portal of Time, *1039*
Tacchella, Jean-Charles: Blue Country, *719;* Cousin, Cousine, *726*
Tadashi, Okuda: Riding Bean, *781*
Taft, Gene: Blame It on the Night, *463*
Tafur, Robert: Panda and the Magic Serpent, *193*
Tahimik, Kidlat: Perfumed Nightmare, *777*
Taicher, Robert: Inside Out (1986), *552*
Takabayashi, Yoichi: Irezumi (Spirit of Tattoo), *749*
Takacs, Tibor: Gate, The, *845;* Gate II, *845;* I, Madman, *855;* Red Shoe Diaries II: Double Dare, *637*
Takahata, Isao: Grave of the Fireflies, *742*
Takakjian, Glen: Metamorphosis: The Alien Factor, *1065*
Takamasa, Ikegami: A.D. Police Files, Vols. 1–3, *710*
Takamoto, Iwao: Charlotte's Web, *158*
Takayama, Hideki: Urotsukidoji: Legend of the Overfiend, *799;* Urotsukidoji II: Legend of the Demon Womb, *799*
Takeshi, Mori: Otaku No Video, *774*
Talalay, Rachel: Freddy's Dead: The Final Nightmare, *843;* Ghost in the Machine, *845*
Tallas, Gregg: Prehistoric Women (1950), *1071*
Talmadge, Richard: Detour to Danger, *1109;* Devil Horse, The, *1109;* Project Moon Base, *1072*
Tampa, Harry: Nocturna, *346*
Tanaka, Shigeo: Gamera Versus Barugon, *1054*
Tanaka, Tokuzo: Zatoichi: The Blind Swordsman's Vengeance, *806*
Tannen, Terrell: Shadows in the Storm, *654*
Tannen, William: Deadly Illusion, *968;* Flashpoint, *977;* Hero and the Terror, *61*
Tanner, Alain: In the White City, *747;* Jonah Who Will Be 25 in the Year 2000, *750*
Tansey, Robert Emmett: Arizona Roundup, *1095;* Caravan Trail, *1103;* Colorado Serenade, *1105;* Driftin' Kid, *1110;* Dynamite Canyon, *1111;* Texas to Bataan, *1156;* Where Trails End, *1164;* Wild West (1946), *1164;* Wildfire (1945), *1164*
Taplitz, Daniel: Black Magic (1992), *955;* Nightlife, *870*
Tapper, David: Mark Twain's Connecticut Yankee in King Arthur's Court, *185*
Tarantino, Quentin: Reservoir Dogs, *105*
Tarkovsky, Andrei: Andrei Rublev, *713;* Mirror, The, *767;* My Name Is Ivan, *770;* Sacrifice, The, *782;* Solaris, *787;* Stalker, *788*
Taro, Rin: Dagger of Kamui, The, *727;* Doomed Megalopolis, Parts 1–4, *731;* Neo-Tokyo, *771*
Tash, Max: Running Kind, The, *371*
Tashlin, Frank: Alphabet Murders, The, *951;* Artists and Models, *229;* Bugs and Daffy: The Wartime Cartoons, *152;* Bugs vs. Elmer, *155;* Cartoon Moviestars: Porky!, *156;* Cinderfella, *912;* Daffy Duck: Tales from the Duckside, *160;* Disorderly Orderly, The, *265;* Girl Can't Help It, The, *286;* Glass Bottom Boat, The, *287;* Golden Age of Looney Toons, The: Bugs Bunny by Each Director, *169;* Golden Age of Looney Toons, The: Hurry for Hollywood, *170;* Golden Age of Looney Toons, The: 1930s Musicals, *170;* Golden Age of Looney Toons, The: 1940s Zanies, *170;* Hollywood or Bust, *299;* Just Plain Daffy, *179;* Porky Pig Cartoon Festival Featuring "Nothing but the Tooth", *196;* Son of Paleface, *383;* Susan Slept Here, *389*
Tass, Nadia: Pure Luck, *363;* Rikki and Pete, *368*
Tati, Jacques: Jour de Fête, *750;* Mr. Hulot's Holiday, *768;* My Uncle (Mon Oncle), *770;* Parade, *775;* Playtime, *776*
Taurog, Norman: Adventures of Tom Sawyer, The, *144;* Birds and the Bees, The, *240;* Blue Hawaii, *909;* Boys' Town, *468;* Broadway Melody of 1940, *910;* Bundle of Joy, *247;* Caddy, The, *249;* Double Trouble (1967), *914;* G.I. Blues, *918;* Girl Crazy, *919;* Girls! Girls! Girls!, *919;* Hold 'em Jail, *298;* It Happened at the World's Fair, *925;* Jumping Jacks, *311;* Little Nellie Kelly, *928;* Live a Little, Love a Little, *929;* Men of Boys Town, *592;* Mrs. Wiggs of the Cabbage Patch, *598;* Onionhead, *350;* Palm Springs Weekend, *353;* Presenting Lily Mars, *626;* Rich, Young and Pretty, *936;* Speedway, *941;* Spinout, *941;* That Midnight Kiss, *944;* Tickle Me, *945;* Toast of New Orleans, *946;* Words and Music, *948;* Young Tom Edison, *708*
Tausik, David: Homicidal Impulse, *983*
Tavernier, Bertrand: Beatrice, *716;* Clean Slate (Coup de Torchon), *724;* Clockmaker, The, *725;* Daddy Nostalgia, *727;* Death Watch, *1045;* Judge and the Assassin, The, *750;* Life and Nothing But, *760;* Mississippi Blues, *430;* Round Midnight, *937;* Sunday in the Country, A, *791*
Taviani, Paolo: Good Morning, Babylon, *530;* Kaos, *751;* Night of the Shooting Stars, *771;* Padre Padrone, *774*
Taviani, Vittorio: Good Morning, Babylon, *530;* Kaos, *751;* Night of the Shooting Stars, *771;* Padre Padrone, *774*
Taylor, Baz: Near Misses, *342;* Shooting Elizabeth, *378;* Tattle Tale, *391*
Taylor, Don: Damien: Omen II, *829;* Diamond Trap, The, *970;* Escape from the Planet of the Apes, *1049;* Final Countdown, The, *1051;* Great Scout and Cathouse Thursday, The, *1116;* Listen to Your Heart, *319;* My Wicked, Wicked Ways, *602;* Night Games, *1001;* Red Flag: The Ultimate Game, *104;* Ride the Wild Surf, *936;* Secret Weapons, *113;* September Gun, *1148;* Tom Sawyer (1973), *946*
Taylor, Jud: Christmas Coal Mine Miracle, The, *159;* City in Fear, *962;* FoxFire, *521;* Great Escape II, The, *57;* Out of the Darkness, *1003;* Packin' It In, *193;* Question of Honor, A, *632;* Revenge (1971), *1010;* Say Goodbye, Maggie Cole, *648;* Search for the Gods, *1076*
Taylor, Ray: Adventures of the Flying Cadets, *2;* Border Feud, *1100;* Cheyenne Takes Over, *1104;* Dick Tracy (1937), *38;* Don Winslow of the Coast Guard, *41;* Don Winslow of the Navy, *41;* Flaming Frontiers, *1113;* Flash Gordon Conquers the Universe, *1052;* Ghost Town Renegades, *1115;* Law of the Lash, *1127;* Lone Star Trail, *1129;* Lost City of the Jungle, *79;* Mystery of the Hooded Horsemen, *1135;* Painted Stallion, The, *1138;* Perils of Pauline, The (1933), *98;* Rawhide (1938), *1141;* Return of Chandu (The Magician), *105;* Return of the Lash, *1142;* Riders of Death Valley, *1143;* Robinson Crusoe of Clipper Island, *108;* Stage to Mesa City, *1152;* Vigilantes Are Coming!, *1161;* Winners of the West, *1165*
Taylor, Richard: Stingray, *120*
Taylor, Robert: Heidi's Song, *173;* Nine Lives of Fritz the Cat, *345*
Taylor, Roderick: Instant Karma, *306*
Taylor, Sam: Ambassador Bill, *225;* Coquette, *488;* My Best Girl, *339;* Nothing But Trouble (1944), *347;* Taming of the Shrew, The (1929), *391;* Tempest (1928), *678*
Tchernia, Pierre: Holes, The, *744*

que, Lewis: Alligator, *808;* Cat's Eye, *822;* Collision
se, *257;* Cujo, *827;* Deadlock, *1045;* Fighting Back, *47;*
of the Nile, The, *68;* Lady in Red, *74;* Navy Seals, *89;*
e N Weasel, *391*
iné, André: Rendez-Vous, *780;* Scene of the Crime
7), 784
ord, Frank: Bamboo Saucer (a.k.a. Collision Course),
ple, Julien: Absolute Beginners, *906;* Earth Girls Are
, *915;* Great Rock and Roll Swindle, The, *921;* Secret
emen's Other Ball, The, *375;* Secret Policeman's Private
, The, *375*
pleton, George: Sundowners, The (1950), *1153*
nant, Andy: Amy Fisher Story, The, *447;* Keep the
ge, *1124*
ney, Del: Horror of Party Beach, The, *851*
ney, Kevin S.: Cellar, The, *822;* Night of the Demons,
Peacemaker, *1069;* Witchboard, *903;* Witchboard 2, *903;*
htrap, *904*
nyson, Pen: Convoy (1940), *488*
, Kevin: Blackbelt 2: Fatal Force, *14*
sawa, Buichi: Raven Tengu Kabuto, *780*
y, Jim: Magic of Dr. Snuggles, The, *185*
higahara, Hiroshi: Face of Another, The, *735;* Rikyu,
Woman in the Dunes, *804*
s, Nadia: Malcolm, *327*
cari, Duccio: Beyond Justice, *11;* Long Live Your Death,
0; Tex and the Lord of the Deep, *1155;* Zorro, *142*
laff, Ted: Fighting Father Dunne, *516;* RiffRaff (1947),
; White Tower, The, *701;* Window, The, *1032*
ber, Monica: Magdalene, *585*
kesbury, Joan: Cold Sassy Tree, *485;* Old Boyfriends,
Strangers, *669;* Sudie & Simpson, *672;* Tenth Month,
679
ksbury, Peter: Emil and the Detectives, *164;* Stay Away
942; Trouble with Girls, The, *946*
u, Leon: Save the Lady, *201*
akston, Groham: Tripods, *1085*
w, Harvey: Confessions of a Vice Baron, *487*
ele, Rolf: Tonio Kroger, *796*
mas, Albie: Palm Beach, *617*
mas, Antony: Code Name: Chaos, *257*
mas, Betty: Only You, *351*
mas, Dave: Experts, The, *273;* Strange Brew, *387*
mas, Gerald: Carry on at Your Convenience, *251;* Carry
Behind, *251;* Carry on Cleo, *251;* Carry on Cowboy, *251;*
y on Cruising, *251;* Carry on Doctor, *251;* Carry on
nanuelle, *251;* Carry on Nurse, *251;* Follow That Camel,
mas, John G.: Arizona Heat, *6;* Tin Man, *684*
mas, Ralph: Doctor at Large, *265;* Doctor at Sea, *266;*
tor in Distress, *266;* Doctor in the House, *266;* No Love for
nnie, *608;* Tale of Two Cities (1967), *676;* Thirty-Nine
ps, The (1959), *1024*
mas, Ralph L.: Apprentice to Murder, *810;* Terry Fox
y, The, *679;* Ticket to Heaven, *683*
mas, Scott: Silent Assassins, *116*
mason, Harry: Encounter with the Unknown, *1049*
mburg, Lee: Hollywood High, Part II, *299*
mpson, Brett: Adventures in Dinosaur City, *143*
mpson, Ernest: 1969, *607*
mpson, J. Lee: Ambassador, The, *445;* Battle for the
net of the Apes, *1038;* Blue Knight, The (1975), *465;* Cabo
nco, *21;* Cape Fear (1962), *959;* Conquest of the Planet of
Apes, *1043;* Death Wish IV: The Crackdown, *36;* Evil That
n Do, The, *45;* Firewalker, *49;* Flame over India, *50;* Greek
coon, The, *533;* Guns of Navarone, The, *58;* Happy Birthday
Me, *848;* Huckleberry Finn (1974), *176;* King Solomon's
nes (1985), *73;* Kinjite (Forbidden Subjects), *73;* Mackenna's
ld, *1131;* Messenger of Death, *84;* Murphy's Law, *87;*
incarnation of Peter Proud, The, *879;* St. Ives, *110;* Taras
Bulba, *125;* Ten to Midnight, *126;* Tiger Bay, *683;* White
Buffalo, *1164*
Thompson, Robert C.: Bud and Lou, *471*
Thomsen, Christian Braad: Ladies on the Rocks, *755*
Thomson, Chris: Swimsuit, *390;* Three's Trouble, *396*
Thornhill, Michael: Between Wars, *459;* Everlasting Secret Family, The, *511*
Thorpe, Jerry: All God's Children, *444;* Kung Fu, *73;* Lazarus Syndrome, The, *571;* Possessed, The (1977), *876;* Smile, Jenny, You're Dead, *661*
Thorpe, Richard: Above Suspicion, *1;* Adventures of Huckleberry Finn, The (1939), *143;* Athena, *907;* Black Hand, The, *462;* Challenge to Lassie, *157;* Date with Judy, A, *913;* Double Wedding, *268;* Fiesta, *916;* Fun in Acapulco, *918;* Girl Who Had Everything, The, *527;* Great Caruso, The, *920;* Honeymoon Machine, The, *300;* Horizontal Lieutenant, The, *301;* It's a Big Country, *308;* Ivanhoe (1952), *68;* Jailhouse Rock, *925;* King of the Kongo, *72;* Knights of the Round Table, *73;* Lone Defender, The, *78;* Night Must Fall, *606;* On an Island with You, *933;* Prisoner of Zenda, The (1952), *100;* Prodigal, The, *629;* Student Prince, The, *942;* Sun Comes Up, The, *208;* Tarzan Escapes, *125;* Tarzan Finds a Son, *125;* Tarzan's New York Adventure, *126;* Tarzan's Secret Treasure, *126;* Thin Man Goes Home, The, *1024;* This Time For Keeps, *945;* Three Little Words, *945;* Thrill of a Romance, *945;* Two Girls and a Sailor, *946;* Vengeance Valley, *1161;* White Cargo, *699*
Thurow, Nany: Islander, The, *555*
Till, Eric: American Christmas Carol, An, *146;* Bethune, *459;* Buffalo Jump, *471;* Case of Libel, A, *476;* Clarence, *256;* Hot Millions, *301;* If You Could See What I Hear, *548;* Improper Channels, *305;* Mary and Joseph: A Story of Faith, *589;* Oh, What a Night, *611;* To Catch a Killer, *1025;* Wild Horse Hank, *217*
Tillmans, R. L.: Witchcraft III, The Kiss of Death, *903*
Timm, Bruce W.: Batman: Mask of the Phantasm, *148*
Toback, James: Big Bang, The, *419;* Exposed, *840;* Fingers, *516;* Pick-Up Artist, The, *357*
Tokar, Norman: Apple Dumpling Gang, The, *147;* Big Red, *150;* Boatniks, The, *151;* Candleshoe, *155;* Cat from Outer Space, The, *157;* Follow Me, Boys!, *167;* Happiest Millionaire, The, *173;* Horse in the Gray Flannel Suit, The, *175;* No Deposit, No Return, *191;* Sammy, the Way-Out Seal, *201;* Savage Sam, *201;* Snowball Express, *205;* Those Calloways, *211;* Tiger Walks, A, *211;* Ugly Dachshund, The, *214;* Where the Red Fern Grows, *216*
Toland, Gregg: December 7th: The Movie, *422*
Toledo, Sergio: One Man's War, *613*
Tolkin, Michael: Rapture, The, *635*
Tolkin, Stephen: Daybreak (1993), *1045*
Tomblin, David: Invasion UFO, *1059;* Prisoner, The (TV Series), *1071*
Tomomichi, Mochizuki: Kimagure Orange Road: The Movie, *752*
Tompson, Marcus: Adventures Beyond Belief, *222*
Tong, Stanley: Police Story III—Super Cop, *778*
Topor, Tom: Judgment, *560*
Toporoff, Ralph: American Blue Note, *446*
Topper, Burt: Hell Squad (1958), *60;* Soul Hustler, *118;* Strangler, The, *1020*
Torn, Rip: Telephone, The, *392*
Tornatore, Giuseppe: Cinema Paradiso, *724;* Everybody's Fine, *735*
Tornatore, Joe: Curse of the Crystal Eye, *31;* Demon Keeper, *832;* Grotesque, *847*
Torrance, Robert: Mutant on the Bounty, *338*
Torres, Fina: Oriane, *774*
Torres, Gabe: December, *498*
Torrini, Cinzia: Hotel Colonial, *64*
Tors, Ivan: Zebra in the Kitchen, *220*
Toscano, Bruce: Jar, The, *858*
Toshifumi, Kiyotsumu: Bubblegum Crash, Vols. 1–3, *720*

Totten, Robert: Huckleberry Finn (1975), *176;* Sacketts, The, *1146*
Touhy, Jim: Great Toy Train Layouts of America (Volumes 1–6), *425*
Tourneur, Jacques: Appointment in Honduras, *6;* Berlin Express, *10;* Cat People (1942), *822;* Curse of the Demon, *828;* Days of Glory, *33;* Easy Living, *506;* Flame and the Arrow, The, *50;* I Walked with a Zombie, *855;* Leopard Man, The, *991;* Out of the Past, *1003;* Stars in My Crown, *1153*
Tourneur, Maurice: Last of the Mohicans, The (1920), *75;* Poor Little Rich Girl, The (1917), *359;* Pride of the Clan, The, *1007;* Volpone, *801*
Towers, Derek: King Tut: The Face of Tutankhamun, *428*
Towne, Robert: Personal Best, *621;* Tequila Sunrise, *126*
Townsend, Bud: Coach, *484;* Nightmare in Wax (Crimes in the Wax Museum), *871;* Terror at the Red Wolf Inn, *893*
Townsend, Pat: Beach Girls, The, *233*
Townsend, Robert: Eddie Murphy Raw, *270;* Five Heartbeats, The, *917;* Hollywood Shuffle, *299;* Meteor Man, *186*
Toynton, Ian: Maid, The, *326*
Toyoda, Shiro: Mistress, The (1953), *768;* Snow Country, *787*
Tramont, Jean-Claude: All Night Long, *224;* As Summers Die, *451*
Travers, Alfred: Meet the Navy, *930*
Travers, Bill: Christian the Lion, *158*
Travis, Mark W.: Going Under, *288*
Traxler, Stephen: Slithis, *887*
Traynor, Peter: Seducers, The, *651*
Trbovich, Tom: Andy Kaufman Special, The, *227;* Free Ride, *281;* Garry Shandling Show, The, *283*
Treas, Terri: Play Nice, *1006*
Trenchard-Smith, Brian: BMX Bandits, *17;* Day of the Assassin, *33;* Dead End Drive-In, *1045;* Escape 2000, *1049;* Official Denial, *1069;* Quest, The, *878;* Siege of Firebase Gloria, The, *116*
Trent, Barbara: Cover Up (1988), *421;* Panama Deception, The, *432*
Trent, John: Best Revenge, *11;* Find the Lady, *277;* Good Idea, *288;* Middle-Age Crazy, *332;* Vengeance Is Mine (1976), *135*
Treut, Monika: My Father Is Coming, *339;* Seduction, The: Cruel Woman, *784*
Trevillion, Dale: Las Vegas Weekend, *315;* One-Man Force, *94*
Trikonis, Gus: Dempsey, *499;* Evil, The, *839;* First Affair, *517;* Jungle Heat, *69;* Moonshine County Express, *86;* Rumor Mill, The, *645;* She's Dressed to Kill, *656;* Take This Job and Shove It, *390;* Touched by Love, *686*
Trintignant, Nadine: Next Summer, *771*
Trivas, Victor: Head, The (1959), *849*
Troell, Jan: Flight of the Eagle, *737;* Hurricane (1979), *65;* Zandy's Bride, *1166*
Tronson, Robert: Cry Terror, *964*
Trotta, Margarethe von: Sheer Madness, *785*
Trousdale, Gary: Beauty and the Beast (1991), *149*
Trueba, Fernando: Belle Epoque, *716;* Twisted Obsession, *690*
Truffaut, François: Bride Wore Black, The, *959;* Classic Foreign Shorts: Volume 2, *724;* Confidentially Yours, *725;* Day for Night, *728;* Fahrenheit 451, *1050;* 400 Blows, The, *738;* Green Room, The, *742;* Jules and Jim, *750;* Last Metro, The, *755;* Love on the Run (1979), *762;* Man Who Loved Women, The (1977), *765;* Mississippi Mermaid, *768;* Shoot the Piano Player, *785;* Small Change, *787;* Soft Skin, The, *787;* Stolen Kisses, *789;* Story of Adele H, The, *789;* Two English Girls, *797;* Wild Child, The (L'Enfant Sauvage), *804;* Woman Next Door, The, *805*
Truman, Michael: Koroshi, *73;* Secret Agent (TV Series), *113*
Trumbo, Dalton: Johnny Got His Gun, *559*
Trumbull, Douglas: Brainstorm, *1040;* Silent Running, *107*
Tryon, Glenn: Beauty for the Asking, *457;* Law West of Tombstone, *1127*
Tsang, Eric: Aces Go Places (1–3) (Aka Mad Mission 1–3), *710*
Tso-Nan, Lee: Tattoo Connection, *126*
Tsukamoto, Shinya: Tetsuo: The Iron Man, *793*
Tsukerman, Slava: Liquid Sky, *1063*
Tuchner, Michael: Adam, *441;* Hunchback, *854;* Misadventures of Mr. Wilt, The, *333;* Mistress (1987), *597;* No My Kid, *609;* Old Curiosity Shop, The, *933;* Rainbow Warrior, *1008;* Summer of My German Soldier, *672;* Trenchcoat, *399*
Tuchock, Wanda: Finishing School, *516*
Tucker, David: Nemesis (1986), *1000;* Year in Provence, A, *414*
Tucker, Phil: Dance Hall Racket, *494;* Robot Monster, *881*
Tuggle, Richard: Out of Bounds, *96;* Tightrope, *1025*
Tully, Montgomery: Battle Beneath the Earth, *9;* Terronauts, The, *1082*
Tung, Ching Siu: Chinese Ghost Story, A, *723*
Tung, Sandy: Across the Tracks, *441*
Tung-shing, Yee: People's Hero, *777*
Turko, Rosemarie: Dungeonmaster, The, *1048*
Turner, Ann: Celia, Child of Terror, *477*
Turner, Brad: Goof Balls, *289*
Turner, Chester T.: Black Devil Doll from Hell, *814*
Turner, Ken: Captain Scarlet vs. the Mysterons, *156;* UFO—Volumes I and II, *1086*
Turteltaub, Jon: Cool Runnings, *259;* Driving Me Crazy, *269* Think Big, *394;* Three Ninjas, *211*
Turturro, John: Mac, *583*
Tuttle, Frank: Hell on Frisco Bay, *60;* Roman Scandals, *937;* This Gun for Hire (1942), *128*
Twohy, David N.: Grand Tour: Disaster in Time, *1054*
Tych, Jean: Great Expectations (1983), *171*
U, Lan: Girl from Hunan, *740*
Uchida, Yorihisa: Guy: Awakening of the Devil, *742;* Guy II: Second Target, *742*
Uemura, Osamu: Rumik World: Firetripper, *782*
Ullmann, Liv: Sofie, *787*
Ulmer, Edgar G.: Amazing Transparent Man, The, *1036;* Black Cat, The (1934), *813;* Bluebeard (1944), *817;* Daughter of Dr. Jekyll, *829;* Detour, *970;* Jive Junction, *926;* Moon Over Harlem, *599;* Naked Venus, *603;* St. Benny the Dip, *646;* Strange Illusion, *1020;* Strange Woman, The, *669*
Umetsu, Yasuomi: Robot Carnival, *1075*
Umgelter, Fritz: Bellboy and the Playgirls, The, *234*
Underwood, Ron: City Slickers, *255;* Heart and Souls, *1056;* Mouse and the Motorcycle, The, *189;* Runaway Ralph, *201;* Tremors, *897*
Unger, Lawrence: Intimate Obsession, *986*
Uno, Michael Toshiyuki: Blind Spot, *464;* Vietnam War Story—Part Two, *694;* Wash, The, *696;* Without Warning: The James Brady Story, *704*
Urayama, K.: Taro, the Dragon Boy, *209*
Urbano, Carl: Casper's First Christmas, *157*
Urbishi, Rocco: George Carlin: Doin' It Again, *284;* George Carlin: Jammin' in New York, *284;* George Carlin—Playin' with Your Head, *284;* Roseanne Barr Show, The, *370*
Ureles, Jeff: Cheap Shots, *254*
Urveta, Chano: Brainiac, The, *818;* Witch's Mirror, The, *904*
Ustinov, Peter: Billy Budd, *461;* Hammersmith Is Out, *292;* Lady L, *568;* Lion and the Hawk, The, *77*
Uys, Jamie: Animals Are Beautiful People, *418;* Dingaka, *501;* Gods Must Be Crazy, The, *287;* Gods Must Be Crazy II, The, *287*
Vacek, Jack: Rock House, *108*
Vadim, Roger: And God Created Woman (1957), *712;* And God Created Woman (1987), *447;* Barbarella, *1038;* Beauty and the Beast (1983), *149;* Blood and Roses, *814;* Circle of Love, *482;* Game Is Over, The, *739;* Game of Seduction, *739;*

hiker (Series), The, *850;* Le Repos du Guerrier (Warrior's), *758;* Les Liaisons Dangereuses, *759;* Seven Deadly Sins, *785*

lez, Luis: Cisco Kid, The, *1105;* La Bamba, *927;* Zoot *949*

nti, Frank: Delta Force, Commando Two, *37*

ntine, Jon: Night of the Living Babes, *344*

re, Jean: Time Out For Love, *795*

rii, Tonino: Days of Wrath, *1107;* Massacre at Fort nan (Reason to Live...A Reason to Die, A), *1133;* My e Is Nobody, *1135*

Ackeren, Robert: Woman in Flames, A, *804*

Dormael, Jaco: Toto the Hero, *796*

Dusen, Bruce: Cold Feet (1984), *257*

Dyke, W. S.: After the Thin Man, *951;* Andy Hardy Gets ng Fever, *227;* Another Thin Man, *952;* Bitter Sweet, *909;* o, *910;* Forsaking All Others, *279;* I Live My Life, *547;* I You Again, *304;* I Married an Angel, *924;* Journey for garet, *559;* Love on the Run (1936), *323;* Manhattan odrama, *81;* Marie Antoinette, *588;* Naughty Marietta, *932;* sonal Property, *356;* Rosalie, *937;* Rose Marie (1936), *937;* Francisco, *648;* Shadow of the Thin Man, *1014;* eethearts, *943;* Tarzan the Ape Man (1932), *125;* Thin Man, , *1024;* White Shadows in the South Seas, *700*

Hemert, Ruud: Army Brats, *228*

Horn, Buddy: Any Which Way You Can, *228;* Dead Pool, , *33;* Pink Cadillac, *99*

Nutt, Robert: Emperor's New Clothes, The (1990), *164;* end of Sleepy Hollow, The (1988), *181*

Peebles, Mario: New Jack City, *90;* Posse (1993), *1139*

Peebles, Melvin: Identity Crisis, *304;* Story of a Three Pass, The, *668;* Sweet Sweetback's Baadasssss Song, ; Watermelon Man, *406*

Sant, Gus: Drugstore Cowboy, *505;* Even Cowgirls Get Blues, *272;* My Own Private Idaho, *602*

nDerKloot, William: Dead Aim (1987), *33*

ne, Norman Thaddeus: Black Room, The (1985), *814;* Life, *27;* Frightmare, *844;* Midnight (1989), *996;* Taxi cers, *678*

nLamsweerde, Pino: Rumpelstiltskin (1986), *200*

wagenen, Sterling: Alan and Naomi, *443*

nzina, Carlo: Gamble, The, *54;* Millions, *594;* My nderful Life, *603;* Nothing Underneath, *1002*

rda, Agnes: Cleo from 5 to 7, *725;* Le Bonheur, *756;* Le it Amour, *758;* One Sings, the Other Doesn't, *773;* gabond, *799*

rnel, Marcel: Chandu the Magician, *24*

rt, Henri: Secret Obsessions, *651*

sallo, Carlos: Day of the Assassin, *33*

siliev, Georgi: Chapayev, *723*

siliev, Sergei: Chapayev, *723*

squez, Joseph B.: Bronx War, The, *20;* Hangin' with the meboys, *292;* Street Hitz, *121*

ber, Francis: Le Chêvre (The Goat), *757;* Les Comperes, *9;* Out on a Limb (1992), *352;* Three Fugitives, *395*

cchietti, Alberto: Monster of the Island, The, *86*

ga, Pastor: Portrait of Teresa, *778*

jar, Mike: Quantum Leap (TV Series), *1072*

jar, Rudy: For Love of Angela, *519*

ntura, Michael: I'm Almost Not Crazy: John ssavetes—The Man and His Work, *427*

nturini, Edward: Headless Horseman, The, *1056;* In Old xico, *1123*

rbong, Ben: Lily Was Here, *575*

rdone, Carlo: Aqua E Sapone, *713*

rhoeven, Michael: Killing Cars, *563;* Nasty Girl, The, *771;* hite Rose, The (1983), *803*

rhoeven, Paul: Basic Instinct, *456;* Flesh and Blood, *50;* urth Man, The, *738;* Hitchhiker (Series), The, *850;* Katie's ssion, *751;* RoboCop, *1074;* Soldier of Orange, *787;* etters, *788;* Total Recall, *1084;* Turkish Delight, *797*

Verneuil, Henri: Love and the Frenchwoman, *762;* Melodie en Sous-Sol (The Big Grab), *766;* Night Flight from Moscow, *90;* Sheep Has Five Legs, *785;* Un Singe en Hiver (A Monkey in Winter), *798*

Vernon, Henry: Danger Zone, The, *32*

Verona, Stephen F.: Lords of Flatbush, The, *579;* Pipe Dreams, *622;* Talking Walls, *391*

Vertov, Dziga: Man with a Movie Camera, *430;* Three Songs of Lenin, *436*

VeSota, Bruno: Brain Eaters, The, *1040;* Female Jungle, *516*

Vicario, Marco: Sensual Man, The, *375;* Wifemistress, *804*

Vickers, Lindsey C.: Appointment, The, *810*

Vidor, Charles: Cover Girl, *912;* Gilda, *527;* Hans Christian Andersen, *921;* It's a Big Country, *308;* Lady in Question, *568;* Love Me or Leave Me, *929;* Loves of Carmen, The, *582;* Rhapsody, *639;* Song to Remember, A, *940;* Song without End, *940;* Swan, The (1956), *674;* Tuttles of Tahiti, The, *400*

Vidor, King: Beyond the Forest, *460;* Big Parade, The, *460;* Bird of Paradise, *13;* Champ, The (1931), *478;* Citadel, The, *482;* Comrade X, *258;* Crowd, The, *492;* Duel in the Sun, *1110;* Fountainhead, The, *520;* Hallelujah!, *535;* Jack Knife Man, The, *556;* Man without a Star, *1132;* Northwest Passage, *92;* Our Daily Bread, *615;* Ruby Gentry, *644;* Show People, *378;* Solomon and Sheba, *661;* Stella Dallas, *667;* Street Scene, *670;* Tol'able David, *685;* War and Peace (1956), *695*

Vienne, Gerard: Monkey People, *431*

Viertel, Berthold: Rhodes of Africa, *639*

Vigne, Daniel: One Woman or Two, *773;* Return of Martin Guerre, The, *781;* Strangers, *669*

Vignola, Robert: Scarlet Letter, The (1934), *649*

Vigo, Jean: A Propos De Nice, *710;* L'Atalante, *753;* Zero for Conduct, *807*

Viktor: Alien P.I., *1035*

Vila, Camilo: Options, *351;* Unholy, The, *899*

Vilencia, Jeff: Dope Mania, *423;* Sleazemania, *381;* Sleazemania Strikes Back, *381;* TV Turkeys, *401*

Villalobos, Reynaldo: Conagher, *1105*

Villaronga, Agustin: In a Glass Cage, *747*

Vincent, Chuck: Bad Blood, *811;* Bedroom Eyes II, *954;* Cleo/Leo, *256;* Deranged, *833;* Hollywood Hot Tubs, *299;* If Looks Could Kill (1986), *985;* Party Girls (Party Inc.), *355;* Preppies, *360;* Sensations, *651;* Sex Appeal, *376;* Slammer Girls, *380;* Summer Camp, *388;* Thrilled to Death, *1025;* Warrior Queen, *137;* Wimps, *412;* Woman Obsessed, A, *1032;* Young Nurses in Love, *416*

Vint, Jerry: Another Chance, *228*

Vinton, Will: Adventures of Mark Twain, The (1985), *144;* Best of the Festival of Claymation, The, *236;* Meet the Raisins, *186*

Viola, Bill: Bill Viola: Selected Works, *1039*

Viola, Joe: Angels Hard as They Come, *5;* Hot Box, The, *64*

Viola, Ken: Masters of Comic Book Art, *430*

Visconti, Luchino: Bellissima, *716;* Boccaccio 70, *719;* Conversation Piece, *726;* Damned, The, *727;* Death in Venice, *498;* Innocent, The, *748;* Leopard, The, *572;* Ossessione, *774;* Rocco & His Brothers, *782;* Wanton Contessa, The, *802;* White Nights (1957), *803*

Vogel, Vibke: Art Com Video (Vol. 1–3), *1037*

Vogel, Virgil: Beulah Land, *459;* Big Valley, The (TV Series), *1098;* Invasion of the Animal People, *1059;* Land Unknown, The, *1061;* Mole People, The, *1066;* One Riot, One Ranger, *95;* Streethawk, *121*

Vohrer, Alfred: Dead Eyes of London, *830*

Voizard, Marc: Shades of Love: Lilac Dream, *654*

Volk, Paul G.: Sunset Strip, *674*

von Baky, Josef: Baron Müenchhausen, *1038*

Von Fristch, Gunther: Curse of the Cat People, The, *828*

von Furstenburg, Vieth: Fire and Sword, *1051*

von Praunheim, Rosa: Virus Knows No Morals, A, *801*

von Ratony, Akos: Cave of the Living Dead, *822*

von Sternberg, Josef: Blonde Venus, *464;* Blue Angel, The, *719;* Crime and Punishment (1935), *490;* Dishonored, *501;*

Docks of New York, The, 502; Last Command, The (1928), 568; Macao, 80; Morocco, 599; Scarlet Empress, The, 649; Shanghai Express, 655; Shanghai Gesture, The, 655; Underworld (1927), 691

Von Stroheim, Erich: Blind Husbands, 464; Foolish Wives, 518; Greed, 533; Queen Kelly, 631; Wedding March, The, 697

von Theumer, Ernst R.: Jungle Warriors, 69

von Trier, Lars: Element of Crime, The, 508; Zentropa, 807

Vorhaus, Bernard: Amazing Mr. X, 445; Courageous Dr. Christian, The, 489; Lady from Louisiana, 1125; Meet Dr. Christian, 591; Three Faces West, 683

Voss, Kurt: Border Radio, 466; Genuine Risk, 979; Horseplayer, 983

Votocek, Otakar: Wings of Fame, 412

Wacks, Jonathan: Ed & His Dead Mother, 270; Mystery Date, 341; Powwow Highway, 360

Wadleigh, Michael: Wolfen, 904; Woodstock, 438

Waggner, George: Commies Are Coming, the Commies Are Coming, The, 258; Fighting Kentuckian, The, 1112; Operation Pacific, 614; Outlaw Express, 1137; Wolf Call, 948; Wolf Man, The, 904

Wagner, Rob: Fatty's Tin-Type Tangle/Our Congressman, 275; Going to Congress and Don't Park There, 288

Wainwright, Rupert: Blank Check, 151; Discovery Program, 501

Waite, Ralph: On the Nickel, 612

Wajda, Andrzej: Ashes and Diamonds, 714; Birch Wood, 718; Danton, 728; Generation, A, 740; Kanal, 751; Love in Germany, A, 762; Man of Iron, 765; Man of Marble, 765; Wedding, The, 802

Walas, Chris: Fly II, The, 842; Vagrant, The, 404

Waldman, Michael: Incredible Story of Dogs, The, 427

Waletzsky, Josh: Heavy Petting, 426

Walker, Dorian: Making the Grade, 327; Teen Witch, 392

Walker, Giles: 90 Days, 345; Ordinary Magic, 614; Princes in Exile, 627

Walker, Hal: At War with the Army, 229; Road to Bali, 368; Road to Utopia, 369

Walker, Nancy: Can't Stop the Music, 911

Walker, Pete: Big Switch, The, 13; Die Screaming, Marianne, 834; Flesh and Blood Show, The, 841; House of the Long Shadows, 853; House of Whipcord, 853; Schizo, 883

Walker, Stuart: Werewolf of London, 902

Walkow, Gary: Hammered: The Best of Sledge, 292; Trouble with Dick, The, 1085

Wallace, David: King Tut: The Face of Tutankhamun, 428

Wallace, Richard: Bombardier, 17; Captain Caution, 23; Fallen Sparrow, The, 513; Girl, a Guy and a Gob, A, 286; It's in the Bag, 308; Little Minister, The, 576; Night to Remember, A (1943), 345; Sinbad the Sailor, 116; Tycoon, 133; Young in Heart, The, 416

Wallace, Rick: Acceptable Risks, 440

Wallace, Stephen: For Love Alone, 519; Prisoners of the Sun, 628; Turtle Beach, 690

Wallace, Tommy Lee: Aloha Summer, 445; Comrades of Summer, The, 258; Fright Night II, 844; Halloween III: Season of the Witch, 848; It (1991), 857

Wallerstein, Herb: Snowbeast, 888

Walsh, Raoul: Along the Great Divide, 1093; Background to Danger, 8; Battle Cry, 9; Big Trail, The, 1098; Blackbeard the Pirate, 14; Captain Horatio Hornblower, 23; College Swing, 912; Dark Command, 1107; Desperate Journey, 500; Distant Drums, 40; Gentleman Jim, 525; Going Hollywood, 920; Gun Fury, 1117; High Sierra, 62; Horn Blows at Midnight, The, 301; In Old Arizona, 1122; King and Four Queens, The, 1125; Klondike Annie, 314; Lion in the Streets, A, 575; Man I Love, The, 586; Naked and the Dead, The, 88; Northern Pursuit, 92; Objective, Burma!, 93; Pursued, 1140; Roaring Twenties, The, 107; Sadie Thompson, 646; Silver River, 1150; Strawberry Blonde, The, 670; Tall Men, The, 1154; They Died with Their Boots On, 1156; They Drive by Night, 127; Thief of Bagdad, The (1924), 1083; White Heat, 138

Walters, Charles: Ask Any Girl, 229; Barkleys of Broadway The, 908; Belle of New York, The, 908; Dangerous When Wet 913; Don't Go Near the Water, 267; Easter Parade, 915; Easy Love, 915; Glass Slipper, The, 919; Good News, 920; High Society, 922; Jumbo, 926; Lili, 928; Please Don't Eat the Daisies, 358; Summer Stock, 942; Tender Trap, The, 392; Texas Carnival, 944; Torch Song, 686; Unsinkable Molly Brown, The, 947; Walk, Don't Run, 405

Walton, Fred: April Fool's Day, 810; Hadley's Rebellion, 17 Homewrecker, 1057; Rosary Murders, The, 1011; Trapped, 1027; When a Stranger Calls, 1030; When a Stranger Calls Back, 1031

Wanamaker, Sam: Catlow, 1104; Executioner, The, 974; Killing of Randy Webster, The, 564; Sinbad and the Eye of the Tiger, 1077

Wang, Peter: Great Wall, A, 290; Laser Man, The, 315

Wang, Steve: Adventures of the Kung Fu Rascals, The, 223; Guyver, The, 1055

Wang, Wayne: Chan Is Missing, 253; Dim Sum: A Little Bit of Heart, 501; Eat a Bowl of Tea, 507; Joy Luck Club, The, 55 Slam Dance, 1017; Strangers, 669

Ward, Bill: Ballad of a Gunfighter, 1096

Ward, David S.: Cannery Row, 250; King Ralph, 313; Major League, 326; Major League II, 326; Program, The, 629

Ward, Jay: Adventures of Rocky and Bullwinkle, The, 144; George of the Jungle, 169

Ward, Terry: Little Miss Trouble and Friends, 183

Ward, Vincent: Map of the Human Heart, 588; Navigator: A Medieval Odyssey, The, 1067; Vigil, 800

Ware, Clyde: Bad Jim, 1095; Hatfields and the McCoys, The 1119; No Drums, No Bugles, 608

Wargnier, Regis: Indochine, 747

Warren, Charles Marquis: Arrowhead, 1095; Charro!, 1104; Little Big Horn, 1128; Rawhide (TV Series), 1141

Warren, Deryn: Black Magic Woman, 955; Blood Spell, 816, Mirror of Death, 865

Warren, Jerry: Frankenstein Island, 842; Incredible Petrified World, The, 1058; Invasion of the Animal People, 1059; Man Beast, 862; Teenage Zombies, 892; Wild World of Batwoman, The, 1089

Warren, Joseph: Shoot the Living…Pray for the Dead, 114 Urban Warriors, 134

Warren, Mark: Big City Comedy, 238

Warren, Norman J.: Alien Prey, 808; Bloody New Year, 817 Spaced Out, 384

Washburn, Jim: More Milton Berle's Mad World of Comedy, 431

Wasson, James C.: Night of the Demon, 869

Wasynski, Michael: Dybbuk, The, 732

Watanabe, Hiroshi: Guyver: Out of Control, 742

Waters, John: Cry-Baby, 912; Desperate Living, 264; Divine, 265; Female Trouble, 276; Hairspray, 292; Mondo Trasho, 335 Multiple Maniacs, 866; Pink Flamingos, 357; Polyester, 359; Serial Mom, 376

Watkins, Peter: War Game, the, 696

Watson, John: Deathstalker, 1046; Zoo Gang, The, 416

Watt, Nate: Borderland, 1100; Law of the Pampas, 1127; Rustler's Valley, 1146

Watts, Roy: Hambone and Hillie, 535

Waxman, Al: Diamond Fleece, The, 970; White Light, 1089

Waxman, Keoni: Almost Blue, 445

Way, Ron: Frenchman's Farm, 843

Wayans, Keenen Ivory: I'm Gonna Git You Sucka!, 305

Wayne, John: Alamo, The, 1092; Green Berets, The, 57

Webb, Jack: D.I., The, 493; Dragnet (1954), 41; Pete Kelly's Blues, 935

Webb, Millard: Glorifying the American Girl, 919

Webb, Peter: Give My Regards to Broad Street, 919

Webb, Robert D.: Beneath the 12-Mile Reef, 10; Love Me Tender, 1130; Seven Cities of Gold, 653

Webb, William: Dirty Laundry, 265; Hit List, The (1992), 982; Party Line, 97

Weber, Billy: Josh and S.A.M., *69*
Weber, Bruce: Broken Noses, *419;* Let's Get Lost, *429*
Webster, D. J.: Dark Side of the Moon, The, *1044*
Webster, Nicholas: Mission Mars, *1066;* Purlie Victorious, *363;* Santa Claus Conquers the Martians, *1076*
Wechter, David: Malibu Bikini Shop, The, *327;* Midnight Madness, *332;* Murphy's Laws of Golf, *338*
Weeks, Stephen: Sword of the Valiant, *208*
Wegener, Paul: Golem, The (How He Came into the World) (Der Golem, Wie er in die Welt), *741*
Wegman, William: Best of William Wegman, *236*
Wei, Lo: Chinese Connection, The, *25;* Fists of Fury, *49;* Man Called Tiger, A, *80*
Weide, Robert B.: W. C. Fields Straight Up, *438*
Weidenmann, Alfred: Adorable Julia, *710*
Weihe, Jeffrey: Louie Anderson: Mom! Louie's Looking at Me Again!, *322*
Weil, Samuel: Class of Nuke 'em High, *824;* First Turn-on, The, *277;* Squeeze Play, *385;* Stuck on You, *387;* Toxic Avenger, The, *897;* Troma's War, *132;* Waitress, *405*
Weiland, Paul: City Slickers II, *256;* Leonard Part 6, *317*
Weill, Claudia: Girlfriends, *528;* Great Love Experiment, The, *533;* It's My Turn, *555;* Once a Hero, *94*
Wein, Yossi: Lethal Ninja, *76*
Weiner, Hal: Imagemaker, The, *549*
Weinstein, Bob: Playing for Keeps, *358*
Weinstein, Harvey: Playing for Keeps, *358*
Weinstock, Jeff: Laurel & Hardy: A Tribute to "The Boys", *428*
Weintraub, Fred: Bruce Lee: Curse of the Dragon, *420*
Weintraub, Sandra: Women's Club, The, *413*
Weir, Peter: Cars That Eat People (The Cars That Ate Paris), *821;* Dead Poets Society, *497;* Fearless (1993), *515;* Gallipoli, *524;* Green Card, *290;* Last Wave, The, *991;* Mosquito Coast, The, *600;* Picnic at Hanging Rock, *1006;* Plumber, The, *1006;* Witness, *1032;* Year of Living Dangerously, The, *141*
Weis, Bob: Wacky World of Wills and Burke, The, *405*
Weis, Don: Affairs of Dobie Gillis, The, *906;* Billie, *150;* Critic's Choice, *261;* Gene Krupa Story, The, *525;* I Love Melvin, *924;* It's a Big Country, *308;* Munsters' Revenge, The, *338;* Remington Steele (TV series), *1010*
Weis, Gary: Diary of a Young Comic, *264;* Jimi Hendrix, *428;* Rutles, The (a.k.a. All You Need Is Cash), *938;* Steve Martin Live, *386;* Things We Did Last Summer, *394;* Wholly Moses!, *410*
Weisberg, Roger: Road Scholar, *434*
Weisbrod, Ellen: Listen Up: The Lives of Quincy Jones, *429*
Weisman, David: Ciao! Manhattan, *482;* Shogun Assassin, *785*
Weisman, Sam: D2: The Mighty Ducks, *160*
Weisman, Straw: Deadmate, *831*
Weiss, Adrian: Bride and the Beast, The, *19*
Weiss, Rob: Amongst Friends, *447*
Weiss, Robert K.: Amazon Women on the Moon, *225;* Compleat "Weird Al" Yankovic, The, *258*
Weiss, Sam: Storybook Series, The (Volume One), *207*
Welland, Paul: Bernard and the Genie, *234*
Welles, Mel: Lady Frankenstein, *858*
Welles, Orson: Chimes at Midnight, *481;* Citizen Kane, *482;* Classic Foreign Shorts: Volume 2, *724;* Immortal Story, *549;* Journey Into Fear (1942), *987;* Lady from Shanghai, *989;* Macbeth (1948), *583;* Magnificent Ambersons, The, *585;* Mr. Arkadin (a.k.a. Confidential Report), *596;* Othello (1952), *615;* Stranger, The (1947), *1020;* Touch of Evil, *1026;* Trial, The, *687*
Wellington, David: Carpenter, The, *821*
Wellman, William: Across the Wide Missouri, *1092;* Battleground, *456;* Beau Geste, *10;* Blood Alley, *15;* Buffalo Bill, *1102;* Goodbye, My Lady, *171;* Heroes for Sale, *540;* High and the Mighty, The, *541;* Island in the Sky, *554;* It's a Big Country, *308;* Lady of Burlesque, *74;* Magic Town, *585;* Next Voice You Hear, The, *605;* Night Nurse, *606;* Nothing Sacred, *347;* Ox-Bow Incident, The, *1137;* Public Enemy, *101;* Purchase Price, The, *630;* Star Is Born, A (1937), *666;* Westward the Women, *1163;* Wings, *140*
Wells, Simon: American Tail, An: Fievel Goes West, *146;* We're Back! A Dinosaur's Story, *216*
Wenders, Wim: Alice in the City, *711;* American Friend, The, *712;* Faraway, So Close, *736;* Goalie's Anxiety at the Penalty Kick, *741;* Hammett, *981;* Kings of the Road, *752;* Lightning Over Water, *575;* Notebook on Cities and Clothes, *432;* Paris, Texas, *618;* Scarlet Letter (1973), *784;* State of Things, The, *789;* Tokyo-Ga, *796;* Until the End of the World, *1087;* Wings of Desire, *804;* Wrong Move, The, *805*
Wendkos, Paul: Betrayal (1978), *459;* Blood Vows: The Story of a Mafia Wife, *464;* Celebrity, *477;* Cocaine: One Man's Seduction, *485;* Cry for Love, A, *492;* Execution, The, *974;* From the Dead of Night, *844;* Gidget, *286;* Gidget Goes Hawaiian, *286;* Gidget Goes to Rome, *286;* Great Escape II, The, *57;* Guns of the Magnificent Seven, *1118;* Haunts of the Very Rich, *1055;* Honor Thy Father, *543;* I Spy (TV Series), *65;* Johnny Tiger, *559;* Mephisto Waltz, The, *864;* Ordeal of Dr. Mudd, The, *614;* White Hot: The Mysterious Murder of Thelma Todd, *1031;* Woman Called Moses, A, *705*
Wenk, Richard: Vamp, *899*
Wentworth, John: Inside Out 2, *1059*
Werker, Alfred: Adventures of Sherlock Holmes, The, *950;* At Gunpoint, *1095;* Devil's Canyon, *1109;* He Walked by Night, *982;* Shock (1946), *885*
Werner, Jeff: Die Laughing, *264*
Werner, Peter: Barn Burning, *456;* Battered, *456;* Don't Cry, It's Only Thunder, *503;* Hiroshima: Out of the Ashes, *541;* I Married a Centerfold, *547;* Image, The, *549;* LBJ: The Early Years, *571;* Lone Justice, *1129;* No Man's Land, *91*
Wertmuller, Lina: All Screwed Up, *712;* Blood Feud, *719;* Camorra, *722;* Joke of Destiny, *750;* Love and Anarchy, *762;* Night Full of Rain, A, *605;* Seduction of Mimi, The, *784;* Seven Beauties, *785;* Sotto Sotto, *788;* Summer Night, *791;* Swept Away, *792*
Wesley, William: Scarecrows, *883*
West, Roland: Bat Whispers, The, *953;* Monster, The, *865*
Weston, Armand: Nesting, The, *868*
Weston, Eric: Evilspeak, *839;* Iron Triangle, The, *554;* Marvin and Tige, *589;* To Protect and Serve, *130*
Wetzl, Fulvio: Rorret, *782*
Wetzler, Gwen: Great Space Chase, *171;* Secret of the Sword, The, *202*
Wexler, Haskell: Latino, *571;* Medium Cool, *591;* Underground (1976), *437*
Whale, James: Bride of Frankenstein, *819;* Frankenstein (1931), *842;* Invisible Man, The, *856;* Man in the Iron Mask, The (1939), *81;* Show Boat (1936), *939;* Sinners in Paradise, *659;* Wives Under Suspicion, *704*
Wharmby, Tony: Equalizer, The: "Memories of Manon", *44;* Kissing Place, The, *989;* Lillie, *575;* Partners in Crime (TV Series), *1004;* Seven Dials Mystery, The, *1013;* Sorry, Wrong Number (1989), *1019;* Treacherous Crossing, *1027;* Why Didn't They Ask Evans?, *1032*
Whatham, Claude: Buddy's Song, *471;* Murder Elite, *600;* Sweet William, *389;* That'll Be the Day, *944*
Whealing, Bob: What's Up Front, *408*
Wheat, Jim: After Midnight, *808;* Ewoks: The Battle for Endor, *165;* Lies, *574*
Wheat, Ken: After Midnight, *808;* Ewoks: The Battle for Endor, *165;* Lies, *574*
Wheatley, David: Hostages, *544;* Nobody's Children, *608*
Wheeler, Anne: Loyalties, *582*
Whelan, Tim: Badman's Territory, *1096;* Clouds Over Europe, *484;* Divorce of Lady X, The, *265;* Higher and Higher, *922;* Mill on the Floss, The, *594;* Rage at Dawn, *1140;* Seven Day's Leave, *376;* Sidewalks of London, *657;* Step Lively, *942;* Texas Lady, *1156;* Thief of Bagdad, The (1940), *1083*
Whitaker, Forest: Strapped, *670*

White, Jules: Sidewalks of New York, *378*
White, Nathan J.: Carrier, *821*
White, Sam: People Are Funny, *356*
Whitelaw, Alexander: Lifespan, *1063*
Whitesell, John: Calendar Girl, *249*
Whorf, Richard: Champagne for Caesar, *252;* It Happened in Brooklyn, *925;* Love from a Stranger, *993;* Luxury Liner, *930;* Till the Clouds Roll By, *946*
Whyte, Michael: Railway Station Man, The, *633*
Wiard, William: Tom Horn, *1157*
Wickes, David: Frankenstein (1992), *842;* Hitchhiker (Series), The, *850;* Silver Dream Racer, *658*
Wicki, Bernhard: Longest Day, The, *78;* Morituri, *87*
Widerberg, Bo: Elvira Madigan, *734*
Wiederhorn, Ken: Eyes of a Stranger, *840;* House in the Hills, A, *984;* Meatballs Part II, *330;* Return of the Living Dead Part II, *880;* Shock Waves (Death Corps), *885*
Wiemer, Robert: Anna to the Infinite Power, *1036;* Night Train to Katmandu, *607;* Somewhere, Tomorrow, *206*
Wiene, Robert: Cabinet of Doctor Caligari, The, *721*
Wilbur, Crane: We're in the Legion Now, *137*
Wilcox, Fred M.: Courage of Lassie, *160;* Forbidden Planet, *1052;* Hills of Home, *174;* Lassie Come Home, *180;* Secret Garden, The (1949), *202;* Three Daring Daughters, *945*
Wilcox, Herbert: Courtney Affair, The, *489;* Forever and a Day, *520;* London Melody, *577;* Nurse Edith Cavell, *610;* Trouble in the Glen, *399*
Wilde, Cornel: Naked Prey, The, *88;* Shark's Treasure, *115;* Sword of Lancelot, *124*
Wilder, Billy: Apartment, The, *228;* Avanti!, *230;* Buddy, Buddy, *247;* Double Indemnity, *972;* Fedora, *515;* Fortune Cookie, The, *279;* Front Page, The (1974), *281;* Irma La Douce, *307;* Kiss Me, Stupid, *314;* Lost Weekend, The, *580;* Love in the Afternoon, *323;* One, Two, Three, *350;* Private Life of Sherlock Holmes, The, *1008;* Sabrina, *372;* Seven Year Itch, The, *376;* Some Like It Hot, *382;* Spirit of St. Louis, The, *664;* Stalag 17, *119;* Sunset Boulevard, *673;* Witness for the Prosecution (1957), *1032*
Wilder, Gene: Adventure of Sherlock Holmes' Smarter Brother, The, *223;* Haunted Honeymoon, *294;* Woman in Red, The, *413;* World's Greatest Lover, The, *414*
Wilder, Glenn: Master Blaster, *83*
Wilder, John: Breaking Home Ties, *469*
Wilder, W. Lee: Big Bluff, The, *460;* Killers from Space, *1061;* Manfish, *862;* Phantom from Space, *1070;* Snow Creature, The, *888*
Wiles, Gordon: Charlie Chan's Secret, *961;* Gangster, The, *525;* Ginger in the Morning, *527*
Wiley, Ethan: House II: The Second Story, *852*
Wilkinson, Charles: Quarantine, *1072*
Willeg, Edward: Mad Executioners, The, *994*
Williams, Anson: All-American Murder, *951;* Dream Date, *269;* Little White Lies, *320;* No Greater Gift, *191;* Perfect Little Murder, A, *356*
Williams, Bob: Gross Jokes, *291*
Williams, Elmo: Hell Ship Mutiny, *60*
Williams, Oscar: Death Drug, *498;* Final Comedown, The, *48*
Williams, Paul: Black Planet, The, *151;* Miss Right, *333*
Williams, Richard: Ziggy's Gift, *220*
Williams, Scott: Man with Two Heads, *862*
Williams, Tony: Next of Kin (1987), *868;* Solo, *661*
Williams, Walter: Mr. Bill Looks Back, *333*
Williamson, Fred: Adios Amigo, *1092;* Big Score, The, *12;* Foxtrap, *52;* Mean Johnny Barrows, *83;* One Down, Two to Go, *94;* South Beach, *1019;* Steele's Law, *120;* Three Days to a Kill, *128*
Wilson, Dave: Best of Chevy Chase, The, *235;* Best of Dan Aykroyd, The, *235;* Best of Gilda Radner, The, *235;* Best of John Belushi, The, *235;* Bob & Ray, Jane, Laraine & Gilda, *243;* Saturday Night Live, *372*
Wilson, Hugh: Burglar (1987), *247;* Guarding Tess, *291;* Police Academy, *359;* Rustler's Rhapsody, *371*
Wilson, Jim: Stacy's Knights, *665*
Wilson, Richard: Al Capone, *3;* Invitation to a Gunfighter, *1123;* It's All True, *427;* Pay or Die, *620;* Three in the Attic, *395*
Wilson, Sandy: American Boyfriends, *446;* Harmony Cats, *536;* My American Cousin, *339*
Wincer, Simon: D.A.R.Y.L., *1044;* Dark Forces, *966;* Free Willy, *168;* Girl Who Spelled Freedom, The, *169;* Harley Davidson and the Marlboro Man, *59;* Lighthorsemen, The, *77;* Lightning Jack, *1128;* Lonesome Dove, *1129;* Phar Lap, *621;* Quigley Down Under, *1140*
Windust, Bretaigne: Enforcer, The (1951), *44;* June Bride, *311;* Winter Meeting, *704*
Winer, Harry: JFK: Reckless Youth, *558;* Single Bars, Single Women, *658;* SpaceCamp, *1078*
Winfrey, Jonathan: Assassination Game, The, *7*
Winick, Gary: Out of the Rain, *1003*
Winkler, Charles: Disturbed, *971;* You Talkin' to Me, *141*
Winkler, Henry: Cop and a Half, *160;* Memories of Me, *331;* Smoky Mountain Christmas, *205*
Winkler, Irwin: Guilty by Suspicion, *534;* Night and the City (1992), *605*
Winkless, Terance H.: Berlin Conspiracy, The, *10;* Bloodfist, *15;* Corporate Affairs, *259;* Nest, The (1988), *868;* Rage and Honor, *102*
Winner, Michael: Appointment with Death, *953;* Big Sleep, The (1978), *955;* Bullseye, *247;* Chato's Land, *1104;* Chorus of Disapproval, A, *254;* Death Wish, *35;* Death Wish II, *36;* Death Wish III, *36;* Firepower, *49;* Lawman, *1127;* Mechanic, The, *83;* Nightcomers, The, *870;* Scream for Help, *884;* Sentinel, The, *884;* Stone Killer, The, *120;* Wicked Lady, The (1983), *139*
Winning, David: Killer Image, *988;* Storm, *1020*
Winograd, Peter: Flicks, *278;* One Last Run, *613*
Winston, Stan: Adventures of a Gnome Named Gnorm, The, *1034;* Pumpkinhead, *878*
Winter, Alex: Freaked, *281*
Winters, David: Dr. Jekyll and Mr. Hyde (1973), *914;* Last Horror Film, The, *860;* Thrashin', *128*
Winters, Paul: Freeway Maniac, *843*
Winterstein, Frank: Sherlock Holmes and the Deadly Necklace, *1015*
Wisbar, Frank: Devil Bat's Daughter, *833;* Strangler of the Swamp, *891*
Wise, Herbert: Castle of the Living Dead, *822;* Gathering Storm, *525;* I, Claudius, *547;* Norman Conquests, The, Episode 1: Table Manners, *346;* Norman Conquests, The, Episode 2: Living Together, *346;* Norman Conquests, The, Episode 3: Round and Round the Garden, *346;* Pope John Paul II, *624;* Skokie, *660;* Strange Interlude (1988), *669*
Wise, Kirk: Beauty and the Beast (1991), *149*
Wise, Robert: Andromeda Strain, The, *1036;* Audrey Rose, *811;* Blood on the Moon, *1099;* Body Snatcher, The, *817;* Born to Kill, *958;* Curse of the Cat People, The, *828;* Day the Earth Stood Still, The, *1044;* Desert Rats, The, *500;* Executive Suite, *512;* Haunting, The, *849;* Hindenburg, The, *541;* I Want to Live!, *548;* Mademoiselle Fifi, *585;* Rooftops, *937;* Run Silent, Run Deep, *109;* Sand Pebbles, The, *111;* Set-Up, The, *1013;* Somebody Up There Likes Me, *662;* Sound of Music, The, *940;* Star!, *941;* Star Trek—The Motion Picture, *1079;* This Could Be the Night, *394;* Three Secrets, *683;* Tribute to a Bad Man, *1159;* Two for the Seesaw, *690;* Until They Sail, *692;* West Side Story, *947*
Wiseman, Carol: Does This Mean We're Married?, *266;* Face the Music, *273;* Little Princess, A, *183;* May Wine, *330*
Wishman, Doris: Bad Girls Go to Hell, *454;* Blaze Starr: The Original, *241;* Deadly Weapons, *498;* Night to Dismember, A, *870*
Withrow, Stephen: Friends, Lovers & Lunatics, *281*
Witliff, William: Red-Headed Stranger, The, *1141*
Witney, William: Adventures of Captain Marvel, The, *2;* Adventures of Red Ryder, *1092;* Apache Rose, *1094;* Arizona

Raiders, *1095;* Bells of Coronado, *1097;* Bells of San Angelo, *1097;* Crimson Ghost, The, *30;* Daredevils of the Red Circle, *32;* Dick Tracy Returns, *38;* Dick Tracy vs. Crime Inc., *38;* Dick Tracy's G-Men, *38;* Down Dakota Way, *1110;* Drums of Fu Manchu, *42;* Eyes of Texas, *1111;* Far Frontier, *1112;* Fighting Devil Dogs, The, *48;* G-Men vs. The Black Dragon, *54;* Golden Stallion, The, *1116;* Grand Canyon Trail, *1116;* Helldorado (1946), *1120;* Heroes of the Saddle, *1120;* Home in Oklahoma, *1121;* In Old Amarillo, *1122;* Island of Dr. Moreau, The, *1060;* King of the Texas Rangers, *1125;* Lone Ranger, The (1938), *1129;* Master of the World, *1065;* Mysterious Dr. Satan, *88;* Nighttime in Nevada, *1136;* North of the Great Divide, *1136;* Nyoka and the Tiger Men (Perils of Nyoka), *92;* On the Old Spanish Trail, *1137;* Outcast, The, *1137;* Painted Stallion, The, *1138;* Paratroop Command, *97;* Roll on Texas Moon, *1145;* SOS Coast Guard, *118;* Springtime in the Sierras, *1152;* Spy Smasher, *119;* Susanna Pass, *1154;* Trail of Robin Hood, *1158;* Trigger, Jr., *1159;* Twilight in the Sierras, *1159;* Under California Stars, *1160;* Zorro Rides Again, *1166;* Zorro's Fighting Legion, *1166*

Wohl, Ira: Best Boy, *419;* Jay Leno's American Dream, *309*

Wolcott, James L.: Wild Women of Wongo, *1089*

Wolf, Fred: Little Rascals Christmas Special, The, *183;* Mouse and His Child, The, *189;* Point, The, *196;* Strawberry Shortcake and Pets on Parade (TV Series), *207*

Wolfe, Donald: Savage Intruder, The, *883*

Wolff, Art: Penn & Teller's Cruel Tricks for Dear Friends, *356*

Wolk, Andy: Criminal Justice, *491;* Traces of Red, *1026*

Wolman, Dan: Baby Love, *230;* Soldier of the Night, *787;* Up Your Anchor, *404*

Wolpaw, James: It's a Complex World, *308*

Woo, John: Better Tomorrow, A, *717;* Better Tomorrow 2, A, *717;* Hard Target, *59;* Killer, The, *751*

Wood Jr., Edward D.: Bride of the Monster, *819;* Glen or Glenda, *528;* Jail Bait (1954), *68;* Night of the Ghouls, *869;* Plan 9 from Outer Space, *1070;* Sinister Urge, The, *116*

Wood, Ivor: Meet the Wombles, *186*

Wood, Sam: Casanova Brown, *252;* Command Decision, *487;* Day at the Races, A, *262;* Devil and Miss Jones, The, *264;* Goodbye, Mr. Chips (1939), *530;* Guest Wife, *291;* Hold Your Man, *542;* King's Row, *565;* Kitty Foyle, *566;* Madame X (1937), *584;* Navy Blue and Gold, *342;* Night at the Opera, A, *344;* Our Town (1940), *616;* Peck's Bad Boy, *194;* Pride of the Yankees, The, *627;* Stratton Story, The, *670*

Woodburn, Bob: Little Laura and Big John, *77*

Woodhead, Leslie: Tragedy of Flight 103: The Inside Story, The, *687*

Woodman, William: King Richard II, *565;* Romeo and Juliet (1983), *643;* Tempest, The (1983), *678*

Woodruff, Frank: Lady Scarface, *74*

Woods, Jack: Equinox (The Beast), *838*

Woods, James: Dr. Jekyll's Dungeon of Death, *835*

Woods, Mark: Witchcraft II, *903*

Woodward, Joanne: Come Along with Me, *257*

Woodward, John: Neurotic Cabaret, *343*

Wool, Abbe: Roadside Prophets, *641*

Workman, Chuck: Andy Warhol: Superstar, *418;* Stoogemania, *386*

Worsley, Wallace: Hunchback of Notre Dame, The (1923), *854*

Worswick, Clark: Agent on Ice, *3*

Worth, Aaron: 9½ Ninjas, *345*

Worth, David: Kickboxer, *70;* Lady Dragon, *74;* Lady Dragon 2, *74;* Warrior of the Lost World, *1088*

Wotruba, Michael: Heroes in Hell, *61*

Wragge, Martin: Last Warrior, The, *76*

Wray, John Griffith: Anna Christie (1922), *449*

Wrede, Caspar: One Day in the Life of Ivan Denisovich, *613;* Terrorists, The, *1023*

Wright, Allen: Slow Bullet, *660*

Wright, David: Heat Is on: The Making of Miss Saigon, The, *426*

Wright, Geoffrey: Romper Stomper, *109*

Wright, Kay: Snow White Christmas, A, *205*

Wright, Mack V.: Big Show, The, *1098;* Haunted Gold, *1119;* Hit the Saddle, *1121;* Man from Monterey, The, *1131;* Range Defenders, *1141;* Riders of the Whistling Skull, *1144;* Robinson Crusoe of Clipper Island, *108;* Rootin' Tootin' Rhythm, *1146;* Sea Hound, The, *112;* Somewhere in Sonora, *1151;* Vigilantes Are Coming!, *1161;* Winds of the Wasteland, *1165*

Wright, Patrick: Hollywood High, *299*

Wright, Tenny: Big Stampede, The, *1098;* Telegraph Trail, The, *1154*

Wright, Thomas: Chrome Soldiers, *26;* Deadly Game, *34;* Fatal Image, The, *976;* No Holds Barred, *91;* Snow Kill, *118;* Torchlight, *686*

Wright, Thomas J.: Highlander: The Gathering, *1056*

Wright, Tom: Bodily Harm, *957*

Wrye, Donald: Born Innocent, *466;* Ice Castles, *548*

Wurlitzer, Rudy: Candy Mountain, *474*

Wyler, William: Ben-Hur (1959), *10;* Best Years of Our Lives, The, *459;* Big Country, The, *1098;* Carrie (1952), *476;* Children's Hour, The, *481;* Collector, The, *963;* Come and Get It, *28;* Dead End, *497;* Desperate Hours, The (1955), *969;* Dodsworth, *503;* Friendly Persuasion, *522;* Funny Girl, *918;* Heiress, The, *539;* Jezebel, *557;* Letter, The, *991;* Liberation of L. B. Jones, The, *574;* Little Foxes, The, *576;* Mrs. Miniver, *597;* Roman Holiday, *642;* These Three, *680;* Thunderbolt, *436;* Westerner, The, *1163;* Wuthering Heights (1939), *707*

Wyner, Tom: Fisher Price Video: Grimms' Fairy Tales: Hansel and Gretel/King Grizzle Beard, *167*

Wynn, Bob: Resurrection of Zachary Wheeler, The, *1074*

Wynn, Tracy Keenan: Hit Lady, *63*

Wynorski, Jim: Big Bad Mama II, *12;* Body Chemistry 3: Point of Seduction, *957;* Chopping Mall, *824;* Deathstalker II: Duel of the Titans, *1046;* Dinosaur Island, *1047;* Hard to Die, *848;* Haunting of Morella, The, *849;* Little Miss Millions, *182;* Lost Empire, The, *79;* Munchie, *867;* 976-EVIL II: The Astral Factor, *872;* Not of This Earth, *872;* Return of the Swamp Thing, *880;* Sins of Desire, *1017;* Sorority House Massacre 2, *889;* Transylvania Twist, *399*

Xhonneux, Henri: Marquis, *765*

Xie, Fei: Girl from Hunan, *740*

Yablonsky, Yabo: Manipulator, The, *588*

Yabuki, Kimio: Rainbow Brite and the Star Stealer, *198;* Twelve Months, *214*

Yamazaki, Kazuo: Urusei Yatsura (TV Series) Vols. 1–45, *799;* Urusei Yatsura: Only You, *799;* Urusei Yatsura: Remember Love, *799*

Yanagimachi, Mitsuo: Himatsuri, *744;* Shadow of China, *654*

Yansen, Louis: Misplaced, *595*

Yarbrough, Jean: Brute Man, The, *820;* Creeper, The, *826;* Devil Bat, The, *833;* Here Come the Co-Eds, *296;* Hillbillys in a Haunted House, *297;* In Society, *306;* King of the Zombies, *859;* Lost in Alaska, *321;* Naughty Nineties, The, *342*

Yari, Bob: Mindgames, *996*

Yasuhiko, Yoshikazu: Venus Wars, The, *800*

Yasuyuki, Noda: Bubblegum Crash, Vols. 1–3, *720*

Yatagai, Kenichi: Macross II, Vols. 1–4, *1064*

Yates, Hal: Flustered Comedy of Leon Errol, The, *278;* Two-Reelers: Comedy Classics #1, *402;* Two-Reelers: Comedy Classics #2, *402*

Yates, Peter: Breaking Away, *245;* Bullitt, *21;* Deep, The, *36;* Dresser, The, *505;* Eleni, *508;* Eyewitness, *974;* For Pete's Sake, *279;* Hot Rock, The, *983;* House on Carroll Street, The, *984;* Innocent Man, An, *66;* Koroshi, *73;* Krull, *1061;* Mother, Jugs, and Speed, *337;* Murphy's War, *87;* Robbery, *1011;* Suspect, *1022;* Year of the Comet, *415*

Yates, William Robert: Disney Christmas Gift, A, *162;* Disney's Halloween Treat, *162*

Yeager, Steve: On the Block, *1003*

Yeaworth Jr., Irvin S.: Blob, The (1958), *814;* Dinosaurus!, *834;* 4D Man, *1053*

Yellen, Linda: Chantilly Lace, *479*

Yen, Chang Hsin: Shaolin Temple, *785*

Yevtushenko, Yevgenii: Kindergarten, *752*

Yolles, Edie: That's My Baby, *680*

Yonis, Jeff: Bloodfist V: Human Target, *16*

Yorkin, Bud: Arthur 2: On the Rocks, *229;* Best of Spike Jones, Volumes 1 & 2, The, *236;* Come Blow Your Horn, *257;* Love Hurts, *323;* Start the Revolution without Me, *385;* Thief Who Came to Dinner, The, *393;* Twice in a Lifetime, *690*

Yosha, Yaky: Sexual Response, *1014*

Yoshida, Hiroaki: Iron Maze, *987;* Twilight of the Cockroaches, *1086*

Yoshiomi: Art Com Video (Vol. 1–3), *1037*

Young, Freddie: Arthur's Hallowed Ground, *451*

Young, Harold: Dreaming Out Loud, *269;* Little Tough Guys, *319;* Mummy's Tomb, The, *867;* Scarlet Pimpernel, The (1934), *112*

Young, Lee Doo: Silent Assassins, *116*

Young, Robert: Charlie Boy, *823;* Hostage (1992), *64;* Jeeves and Wooster (TV Series), *309;* Robin Hood: Herne's Son, *107;* Robin Hood: The Swords of Wayland, *108;* Romance with a Double Bass, *370;* Soldier's Home, *661;* Splitting Heirs, *384;* World Is Full of Married Men, The, *707;* Worst Witch, The, *219*

Young, Robert M.: Ballad of Gregorio Cortez, The, *1096;* Dominick and Eugene, *503;* Extremities, *512;* One Trick Pony, *934;* Rich Kids, *640;* Saving Grace, *373;* Short Eyes, *657;* Talent for the Game, *677;* Triumph of the Spirit, *688;* We Are the Children, *697*

Young, Robert W.: Scandalous (1988), *1012*

Young, Roger: Bitter Harvest (1981), *462;* Bourne Identity, The, *958;* Doublecrossed, *504;* Geronimo, *1115;* Gulag, *534;* Lassiter, *75;* Squeeze, The (1987), *385;* Two of a Kind (1982), *690*

Young, Terence: Amorous Adventures of Moll Flanders, The, *226;* Black Tights, *909;* Bloodline, *464;* Cold Sweat (1970), *28;* Dr. No, *40;* From Russia with Love, *53;* Klansman, The, *566;* Poppy Is Also a Flower, The, *99;* Red Sun, *1142;* Thunderball, *129;* Wait Until Dark, *1030;* When Wolves Cry, *699*

Youngson, Robert: Days of Thrills and Laughter, *262;* Golden Age of Comedy, The, *288;* Laurel and Hardy's Laughing 20s, *317;* MGM's The Big Parade of Comedy, *331;* When Comedy Was King, *409*

Younkins, Jerry: Scream of the Demon Lover (1976), *884*

Yu, Ronny: China White, *25*

Yuasa, Noriyaki: Gamera the Invincible, *1053;* Gamera Versus Gaos, *1054;* Gamera Versus Guiron, *1054;* Gamera Versus Zigra, *1054*

Yuen, Corey: No Retreat, No Surrender, *92;* No Retreat, No Surrender II, *92*

Yukich, Jim: Dennis Miller: Black and White, *263;* Ron Reagan Is the President's Son, *370*

Yune, Johnny: They Still Call Me Bruce, *393*

Yust, Larry: Homebodies, *851;* Say Yes, *373*

Yuval, Peter: Firehead, *49*

Yuzna, Brian: Bride of Re-Animator, *819;* Return of the Living Dead 3, *880;* Silent Night, Deadly Night 4—Initiation, *886;* Society, *888*

Zabalza, José Maria: Fury of the Wolf Man, *845*

Zacharias, Alfredo: Bandits (1967), *1096;* Bees, The, *812;* Crossfire (1986), *1106;* Demonoid, *833*

Zahr, Raja: Last Season, The, *75*

Zaillian, Steven: Searching for Bobby Fischer, *202*

Zala, Nancy: Round Numbers, *370*

Zaloum, Alain: Canvas, *959;* Madonna, *994*

Zamboni, Bob: Chip 'n' Dale: Rescue Rangers, *158*

Zampi, Mario: Five Golden Hours, *278;* Naked Truth, *342*

Zanke, Susanne: Scorpion Woman, The, *784*

Zanuck, Lili Fini: Rush, *645*

Zanussi, Krzysztof: Camouflage, *722;* Catamount Killing, The, *960;* Contract, *726;* Unapproachable, The, *691;* Year of the Quiet Sun, *805*

Zaorski, Janusz: Baritone, *715*

Zaphiratos, Fabrice A.: Bloodbeat, *816*

Zappa, Frank: 200 Motels, *946*

Zarchi, Meir: Don't Mess with My Sister, *504;* I Spit on Your Grave, *855*

Zaslove, Alan: Dr. Seuss: The Cat in the Hat/Dr. Seuss on the Loose, *162;* Dr. Seuss: The Lorax/The Hoober Bloob Highway, *163;* Ducktales (TV Series), *164*

Zea, Kristi: Women & Men 2, *706*

Zedd, Nick: Geek Maggot Bingo, *283*

Zeffirelli, Franco: Brother Sun, Sister Moon, *470;* Champ, The (1979), *479;* Endless Love, *510;* Hamlet (1990), *535;* Jesus of Nazareth, *557;* La Traviata, *754;* Otello, *934;* Romeo and Juliet (1968), *643;* Taming of the Shrew, The (1966), *391*

Zeglio, Primo: Mission Stardust, *1066;* Morgan the Pirate, *86*

Zeilinger, Jimmy: Little Sister, *319*

Zeisler, Alfred: Amazing Adventure, *225*

Zeltser, Yuri: Eye of the Storm, *974*

Zeman, Karel: Baron Munchausen, *148*

Zemeckis, Robert: Amazing Stories (TV Series), *1036;* Back to the Future, *1037;* Back to the Future II, *1037;* Back to the Future III, *1037;* Death Becomes Her, *1045;* I Wanna Hold Your Hand, *304;* Romancing the Stone, *108;* Tales from the Crypt (Series), *892;* Used Cars, *404;* Who Framed Roger Rabbit, *410*

Zens, Will: Fix, The, *50*

Zetterling, Mai: Hitchhiker (Series), The, *850;* Scrubbers, *650*

Zhang, Yimou: Ju Dou, *750;* Raise the Red Lantern, *779;* Red Sorghum, *780;* Story of Qiu Ju, The, *789*

Zhelyabuzhsky, Yuri: Cigarette Girl from Mosselprom, The, *724*

Zhuangzhuang, Tian: Horse Thief, The, *745*

Zidi, Claude: My New Partner, *770*

Zieff, Howard: Dream Team, The, *269;* Hearts of the West, *295;* House Calls, *302;* Main Event, The, *326;* My Girl, *190;* My Girl 2, *190;* Private Benjamin, *361;* Slither, *381;* Unfaithfully Yours (1984), *403*

Ziehm, Howard: Flesh Gordon, *1052;* Flesh Gordon 2: Flesh Gordon meets the Cosmic Cheerleaders, *1052*

Zielinski, Rafal: Ginger Ale Afternoon, *286;* Jailbait (1992), *68;* National Lampoon's Last Resort, *342;* Night of the Warrior, *90;* Recruits, *365;* Screwballs, *374;* Spellcaster, *889;* Valet Girls, *404*

Ziller, Paul: Bloodfist IV—Die Trying, *16;* Deadly Surveillance, *35;* Pledge Night, *875*

Zimmerman, Jerry: Mausoleum, *864*

Zimmerman, Vernon: Fade to Black (1980), *840;* Unholy Rollers, *691*

Zinberg, Michael: Accidental Meeting, *950*

Zinnemann, Fred: Behold a Pale Horse, *458;* Day of the Jackal, The, *966;* Five Days One Summer, *517;* From Here to Eternity (1953), *523;* High Noon, *1120;* Julia, *560;* Man for All Seasons, A, *586;* Member of the Wedding, The, *592;* Men, The, *592;* Nun's Story, The, *609;* Oklahoma!, *933;* Search, The, *650;* Seventh Cross, The, *653;* Sundowners, The (1960), *673*

Zinner, Peter: Salamander, The, *111*

Zito, Joseph: Abduction, *950;* Friday the 13th—The Final Chapter, *843;* Invasion U.S.A., *67;* Missing in Action, *85;* Red Scorpion, *104*

Zondag, Dick: We're Back! A Dinosaur's Story, *216*

Zondag, Ralph: We're Back! A Dinosaur's Story, *216*

Zucker, David: Airplane!, *224;* Naked Gun, The, *341;* Naked Gun 2 1/2, The, *341;* Police Squad!, *359;* Ruthless People, *371;* Top Secret, *397*

Zucker, Jerry: Airplane!, *224;* Ghost (1990), *527;* Police Squad!, *359;* Ruthless People, *371;* Top Secret, *397*

Zucker, Ralph (Massimo Pupillo): Terror Creatures from the Grave, *893*

Zukor, Lou: Great Space Chase, *171*
Zulawski, Andrzei: Possession, *876*
Zuniga, Frank: Fist Fighter, *49;* Golden Seal, The, *170;* Wilderness Family, Part 2, The, *217*
Zurinaga, Marcos: Tango Bar, *792*
Zwerin, Charlotte: Gimme Shelter, *424*
Zwick, Edward: About Last Night, *440;* Glory, *528;* Having It All, *294;* Leaving Normal, *572;* Special Bulletin, *1019*
Zwick, Joel: Second Sight, *374*
Zwicky, Karl: Contagion, *825;* Vicious, *135*

ACADEMY AWARD WINNERS

1927–28

Best Picture:	WINGS
Best Actor:	Emil Jannings, in THE LAST COMMAND and THE WAY OF ALL FLESH
Best Actress:	Janet Gaynor, in SEVENTH HEAVEN, STREET ANGEL, and SUNRISE
Best Director:	Frank Borzage, for SEVENTH HEAVEN

1928–29

Best Picture:	BROADWAY MELODY
Best Actor:	Warner Baxter, IN OLD ARIZONA
Best Actress:	Mary Pickford, in COQUETTE
Best Director:	Frank Lloyd, for THE DIVINE LADY

1929–30

Best Picture:	ALL QUIET ON THE WESTERN FRONT
Best Actor:	George Arliss, in DISRAELI
Best Actress:	Norma Shearer, in THE DIVORCÉE
Best Director:	Lewis Milestone, for ALL QUIET ON THE WESTERN FRONT

1930–31

Best Picture:	CIMARRON
Best Actor:	Lionel Barrymore, in A FREE SOUL
Best Actress:	Marie Dressler, in MIN AND BILL
Best Director:	Norman Taurog, for SKIPPY

1931–32

Best Picture:	GRAND HOTEL
Best Actor:	Wallace Beery, in THE CHAMP Fredric March, in DR. JEKYLL AND MR. HYDE (tie)
Best Actress:	Helen Hayes, in THE SIN OF MADELON CLAUDET
Best Director:	Frank Borzage, for BAD GIRL

1932–33

Best Picture:	CAVALCADE
Best Actor:	Charles Laughton, in THE PRIVATE LIFE OF HENRY VIII
Best Actress:	Katharine Hepburn, in MORNING GLORY
Best Director:	Frank Lloyd, for CAVALCADE

1934

Best Picture:	IT HAPPENED ONE NIGHT
Best Actor:	Clark Gable, in IT HAPPENED ONE NIGHT
Best Actress:	Claudette Colbert, in IT HAPPENED ONE NIGHT
Best Director:	Frank Capra, for IT HAPPENED ONE NIGHT

1935

Best Picture:	MUTINY ON THE BOUNTY
Best Actor:	Victor McLaglen, in THE INFORMER
Best Actress:	Bette Davis, in DANGEROUS
Best Director:	John Ford, for THE INFORMER

1936

Best Picture:	THE GREAT ZIEGFELD
Best Actor:	Paul Muni, in THE STORY OF LOUIS PASTEUR
Best Actress:	Luise Rainer, in THE GREAT ZIEGFELD
Best Director:	Frank Capra, for MR. DEEDS GOES TO TOWN

1937

Best Picture:	THE LIFE OF EMILE ZOLA
Best Actor:	Spencer Tracy, in CAPTAINS COURAGEOUS
Best Actress:	Luise Rainer, in THE GOOD EARTH
Best Director:	Leo McCarey, for THE AWFUL TRUTH

1938

Best Picture:	YOU CAN'T TAKE IT WITH YOU
Best Actor:	Spencer Tracy, in BOYS TOWN
Best Actress:	Bette Davis, in JEZEBEL
Best Director:	Frank Capra, for YOU CAN'T TAKE IT WITH YOU

1939

Best Picture:	GONE WITH THE WIND
Best Actor:	Robert Donat, in GOODBYE, MR. CHIPS
Best Actress:	Vivien Leigh, in GONE WITH THE WIND
Best Director:	Victor Fleming, for GONE WITH THE WIND

1940

Best Picture:	REBECCA
Best Actor:	James Stewart, in THE PHILADELPHIA STORY
Best Actress:	Ginger Rogers, in KITTY FOYLE
Best Director:	John Ford, for THE GRAPES OF WRATH

1941

Best Picture:	HOW GREEN WAS MY VALLEY
Best Actor:	Gary Cooper, in SERGEANT YORK
Best Actress:	Joan Fontaine, in SUSPICION
Best Director:	John Ford, for HOW GREEN WAS MY VALLEY

1942

Best Picture:	MRS. MINIVER
Best Actor:	James Cagney, in YANKEE DOODLE DANDY
Best Actress:	Greer Garson, in MRS. MINIVER
Best Director:	William Wyler, for MRS. MINIVER

1943

Best Picture:	CASABLANCA
Best Actor:	Paul Lukas, in WATCH ON THE RHINE
Best Actress:	Jennifer Jones, in THE SONG OF BERNADETTE
Best Director:	Michael Curtiz, for CASABLANCA

1944

Best Picture:	GOING MY WAY
Best Actor:	Bing Crosby, in GOING MY WAY
Best Actress:	Ingrid Bergman, in GASLIGHT
Best Director:	Leo McCarey, for GOING MY WAY

1945

Best Picture:	THE LOST WEEKEND
Best Actor:	Ray Milland, in THE LOST WEEKEND
Best Actress:	Joan Crawford, in MILDRED PIERCE
Best Director:	Billy Wilder, for THE LOST WEEKEND

1946
Best Picture: THE BEST YEARS OF OUR LIVES
Best Actor: Fredric March, in THE BEST YEARS OF OUR LIVES
Best Actress: Olivia de Havilland, in TO EACH HIS OWN
Best Director: William Wyler, for THE BEST YEARS OF OUR LIVES

1947
Best Picture: GENTLEMAN'S AGREEMENT
Best Actor: Ronald Coleman, in A DOUBLE LIFE
Best Actress: Loretta Young, in THE FARMER'S DAUGHTER
Best Director: Elia Kazan, for GENTLEMAN'S AGREEMENT

1948
Best Picture: HAMLET
Best Actor: Laurence Olivier, in HAMLET
Best Actress: Jane Wyman, in JOHNNY BELINDA
Best Director: John Huston, for TREASURE OF THE SIERRA MADRE

1949
Best Picture: ALL THE KING'S MEN
Best Actor: Broderick Crawford, in ALL THE KING'S MEN
Best Actress: Olivia de Havilland, in THE HEIRESS
Best Director: Joseph L. Mankiewicz, for A LETTER TO THREE WIVES

1950
Best Picture: ALL ABOUT EVE
Best Actor: José Ferrer, in CYRANO DE BERGERAC
Best Actress: Judy Holliday, in BORN YESTERDAY
Best Director: Joseph L. Mankiewicz, for ALL ABOUT EVE

1951
Best Picture: AN AMERICAN IN PARIS
Best Actor: Humphrey Bogart, in THE AFRICAN QUEEN
Best Actress: Vivien Leigh, in A STREETCAR NAMED DESIRE
Best Director: George Stevens, for A PLACE IN THE SUN

1952
Best Picture: THE GREATEST SHOW ON EARTH
Best Actor: Gary Cooper, in HIGH NOON
Best Actress: Shirley Booth, in COME BACK, LITTLE SHEBA
Best Director: John Ford, for THE QUIET MAN

1953
Best Picture: FROM HERE TO ETERNITY
Best Actor: William Holden, in STALAG 17
Best Actress: Audrey Hepburn, in ROMAN HOLIDAY
Best Director: Fred Zinnemann, for FROM HERE TO ETERNITY

1954
Best Picture: ON THE WATERFRONT
Best Actor: Marlon Brando, in ON THE WATERFRONT
Best Actress: Grace Kelly, in THE COUNTRY GIRL
Best Director: Elia Kazan, for ON THE WATERFRONT

1955
Best Picture: MARTY
Best Actor: Ernest Borgnine, in MARTY
Best Actress: Anna Magnani, in THE ROSE TATTOO
Best Director: Delbert Mann, for MARTY

956
est Picture: AROUND THE WORLD IN 80 DAYS
est Actor: Yul Brynner, in THE KING AND I
est Actress: Ingrid Bergman, in ANASTASIA
est Director: George Stevens, for GIANT

957
est Picture: THE BRIDGE ON THE RIVER KWAI
est Actor: Alec Guinness, in THE BRIDGE ON THE RIVER KWAI
est Actress: Joanne Woodward, in THE THREE FACES OF EVE
est Director: David Lean, for THE BRIDGE ON THE RIVER KWAI

958
est Picture: GIGI
est Actor: David Niven, in SEPARATE TABLES
est Actress: Susan Hayward, in I WANT TO LIVE!
est Director: Vincente Minnelli, for GIGI

959
est Picture: BEN-HUR
est Actor: Charlton Heston, in BEN-HUR
est Actress: Simone Signoret, in ROOM AT THE TOP
est Director: William Wyler, for BEN-HUR

960
est Picture: THE APARTMENT
est Actor: Burt Lancaster, in ELMER GANTRY
est Actress: Elizabeth Taylor, in BUTTERFIELD 8
est Director: Billy Wilder, for THE APARTMENT

1961
Best Picture: WEST SIDE STORY
Best Actor: Maximilian Schell, in JUDGMENT AT NUREMBERG
Best Actress: Sophia Loren, in TWO WOMEN
Best Director: Robert Wise and Jerome Robbins, for WEST SIDE STORY

1962
Best Picture: LAWRENCE OF ARABIA
Best Actor: Gregory Peck, in TO KILL A MOCKINGBIRD
Best Actress: Anne Bancroft, in THE MIRACLE WORKER
Best Director: David Lean, for LAWRENCE OF ARABIA

1963
Best Picture: TOM JONES
Best Actor: Sidney Poitier, in LILIES OF THE FIELD
Best Actress: Patricia Neal, in HUD
Best Director: Tony Richardson, for TOM JONES

1964
Best Picture: MY FAIR LADY
Best Actor: Rex Harrison, in MY FAIR LADY
Best Actress: Julie Andrews, in MARY POPPINS
Best Director: George Cukor, for MY FAIR LADY

1965
Best Picture: THE SOUND OF MUSIC
Best Actor: Lee Marvin, in CAT BALLOU
Best Actress: Julie Christie, in DARLING
Best Director: Robert Wise, for THE SOUND OF MUSIC

1966
Best Picture: A MAN FOR ALL SEASONS
Best Actor: Paul Scofield, in A MAN FOR ALL SEASONS
Best Actress: Elizabeth Taylor, in WHO'S AFRAID OF VIRGINIA WOOLF?
Best Director: Fred Zinnemann, for A MAN FOR ALL SEASONS

1967
Best Picture: IN THE HEAT OF THE NIGHT
Best Actor: Rod Steiger, in IN THE HEAT OF THE NIGHT
Best Actress: Katharine Hepburn, in GUESS WHO'S COMING TO DINNER
Best Director: Mike Nichols, for THE GRADUATE

1968
Best Picture: OLIVER!
Best Actor: Cliff Robertson, in CHARLY
Best Actress: Katharine Hepburn, in THE LION IN WINTER
Barbra Streisand, in FUNNY GIRL (tie)
Best Director: Carol Reed, for OLIVER!

1969
Best Picture: MIDNIGHT COWBOY
Best Actor: John Wayne, in TRUE GRIT
Best Actress: Maggie Smith, in THE PRIME OF MISS JEAN BRODIE
Best Director: John Schlesinger, for MIDNIGHT COWBOY

1970
Best Picture: PATTON
Best Actor: George C. Scott, in PATTON
Best Actress: Glenda Jackson, in WOMEN IN LOVE
Best Director: Franklin J. Schaffner, for PATTON

1971
Best Picture: THE FRENCH CONNECTION
Best Actor: Gene Hackman, in THE FRENCH CONNECTION
Best Actress: Jane Fonda, in KLUTE
Best Director: William Friedkin, for THE FRENCH CONNECTION

1972
Best Picture: THE GODFATHER
Best Actor: Marlon Brando, in THE GODFATHER
Best Actress: Liza Minnelli, in CABARET
Best Director: Bob Fosse, for CABARET

1973
Best Picture: THE STING
Best Actor: Jack Lemmon, in SAVE THE TIGER
Best Actress: Glenda Jackson, in A TOUCH OF CLASS
Best Director: George Roy Hill, for THE STING

1974
Best Picture: THE GODFATHER, PART II
Best Actor: Art Carney, in HARRY AND TONTO
Best Actress: Ellen Burstyn, in ALICE DOESN'T LIVE HERE ANYMORE
Best Director: Francis Ford Coppola, for THE GODFATHER, PART II

1975
Best Picture: ONE FLEW OVER THE CUCKOO'S NEST
Best Actor: Jack Nicholson, in ONE FLEW OVER THE CUCKOO'S NEST
Best Actress: Louise Fletcher, in ONE FLEW OVER THE CUCKOO'S NEST
Best Director: Milos Forman, for ONE FLEW OVER THE CUCKOO'S NEST

76
est Picture: ROCKY
st Actor: Peter Finch, in NETWORK
est Actress: Faye Dunaway, in NETWORK
st Director: John G. Avildsen, for ROCKY

'77
est Picture: ANNIE HALL
est Actor: Richard Dreyfuss, in THE GOODBYE GIRL
est Actress: Diane Keaton, in ANNIE HALL
est Director: Woody Allen, for ANNIE HALL

'78
est Picture: THE DEER HUNTER
est Actor: Jon Voight, in COMING HOME
est Actress: Jane Fonda, in COMING HOME
est Director: Michael Cimino, for THE DEER HUNTER

'79
est Picture: KRAMER VS. KRAMER
est Actor: Dustin Hoffman, in KRAMER VS. KRAMER
est Actress: Sally Field, in NORMA RAE
est Director: Robert Benton, for KRAMER VS. KRAMER

'80
est Picture: ORDINARY PEOPLE
est Actor: Robert De Niro, in RAGING BULL
est Actress: Sissy Spacek, in COAL MINER'S DAUGHTER
est Director: Robert Redford, for ORDINARY PEOPLE

'81
est Picture: CHARIOTS OF FIRE
est Actor: Henry Fonda, in ON GOLDEN POND
est Actress: Katharine Hepburn, in ON GOLDEN POND
est Director: Warren Beatty, for REDS

1982
Best Picture: GANDHI
Best Actor: Ben Kingsley, in GANDHI
Best Actress: Meryl Streep, in SOPHIE'S CHOICE
Best Director: Richard Attenborough, for GANDHI

1983
Best Picture: TERMS OF ENDEARMENT
Best Actor: Robert Duvall, in TENDER MERCIES
Best Actress: Shirley MacLaine, in TERMS OF ENDEARMENT
Best Director: James L. Brooks, for TERMS OF ENDEARMENT

1984
Best Picture: AMADEUS
Best Actor: F. Murray Abraham, in AMADEUS
Best Actress: Sally Field, in PLACES IN THE HEART
Best Director: Milos Forman, for AMADEUS

1985
Best Picture: OUT OF AFRICA
Best Actor: William Hurt, in KISS OF THE SPIDER WOMAN
Best Actress: Geraldine Page, in THE TRIP TO BOUNTIFUL
Best Director: Sydney Pollack, for OUT OF AFRICA

1986
Best Picture: PLATOON
Best Actor: Paul Newman, in THE COLOR OF MONEY
Best Actress: Marlee Matlin, in CHILDREN OF A LESSER GOD
Best Director: Oliver Stone, for PLATOON

1987

Best Picture: THE LAST EMPEROR
Best Actor: Michael Douglas, in WALL STREET
Best Actress: Cher, in MOONSTRUCK
Best Director: Bernardo Bertolucci, for THE LAST EMPEROR

1988

Best Picture: RAIN MAN
Best Actor: Dustin Hoffman, in RAIN MAN
Best Actress: Jodie Foster, in THE ACCUSED
Best Director: Barry Levinson, for RAIN MAN

1989

Best Picture: DRIVING MISS DAISY
Best Actor: Daniel Day-Lewis, in MY LEFT FOOT
Best Actress: Jessica Tandy, in DRIVING MISS DAISY
Best Director: Oliver Stone, for BORN ON THE FOURTH OF JULY

1990

Best Picture: DANCES WITH WOLVES
Best Actor: Jeremy Irons, in REVERSAL OF FORTUNE
Best Actress: Kathy Bates, in MISERY
Best Director: Kevin Costner, for DANCES WITH WOLVES

1991

Best Picture: THE SILENCE OF THE LAMBS
Best Actor: Anthony Hopkins, in THE SILENCE OF THE LAMBS
Best Actress: Jodie Foster, in THE SILENCE OF THE LAMBS
Best Director: Jonathan Demme, for THE SILENCE OF THE LAMBS

1992

Best Picture: UNFORGIVEN
Best Actor: Al Pacino, in SCENT OF A WOMAN
Best Actress: Emma Thompson, in HOWARDS END
Best Director: Clint Eastwood, for UNFORGIVEN

1993

Best Picture: SCHINDLER'S LIST
Best Actor: Tom Hanks, in PHILADELPHIA
Best Actress: Holly Hunter, in THE PIANO
Best Director: Steven Spielberg, for SCHINDLER'S LIST

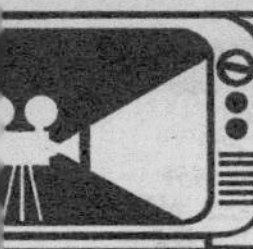

ALPHABETICAL LISTING OF MOVIES

Bulleted movies (◆) have received a rating of ★★★★ or ★★★★★.
Boldfaced movies are first-time listings in *Video Movie Guide.*

'olice Files, Vols. 1–3, *710*
ur Joie (Head Over Heels), *710*
Amours, *710*
s la Liberte, *710*
pos De Nice, *710*
Loves Angela, *440*
t and Costello in Hollywood, *1*
t and Costello Meet Captain d, *221*
t and Costello Meet Dr. Jekyll Mr. Hyde, *221*
t and Costello Meet nkenstein, *221*
t and Costello Meet the isible Man, *221*
t and Costello Meet the Killer, ris Karloff, *221*
t and Costello Meet the mmy, *221*
t and Costello Show, The (TV ries), *221*
cted, *1*
ction, *950*
la the Great, *221*
incoln in Illinois, *440*
Sance's Beethoven, *710*
il's Party, *440*
ne Town, *1092*
inable Dr. Phibes, The, *808*
Last Night, *440*
e and Beyond, *1*
e Suspicion, *1*
e the Law, *1*
e the Rim, *440*
am Lincoln, *440*
as Guardian of the Universe, 34
nce of Malice, *950*
t-Minded Professor, The, *143*
ute Beginners, *906*
ution, *440*
, The, *1034*
tone, *710*
otable Risks, *440*
s Code, *1*
ent, *440*
lental Meeting, *950*
ental Tourist, The, *440*
mpanist, The, *710*
sed, The, *441*
rummond, *1*
igh, *1092*
f Aces, *1*
entura: Pet Detective, *221*
and Eights, *1092*
Go Places (1–3) (Aka Mad ssion 1–3), *710*
Iron Eagle III, *1*
s 110th Street, *1*
s the Great Divide, *143*

◆ Across the Pacific, *1*
Across the Rio Grande, *1092*
◆ Across the Tracks, *441*
Across the Wide Missouri, *1092*
Act, The, *441*
Act of Aggression, *710*
Act of Passion, *441*
Act of Piracy, *1*
◆ Act of Vengeance, *441*
Acting on Impulse, *950*
Action in Arabia, *2*
Action in the North Atlantic, *2*
Action Jackson, *2*
Actors and Sin, *441*
Acts of Violence, *418*
◆ Adam, *441*
Adam at 6 A.M., *441*
◆ Adam Had Four Sons, *441*
◆ Adam's Rib, *222*
Addams Family, The, *222*
Addams Family, The (TV Series), *222*
◆ **Addams Family Values,** *222*
Addict (see Born to Win)
Adios Amigo, *1092*
Adios, Hombre, *1092*
Adjuster, The, *441*
Admiral Was a Lady, The, *222*
Adorable Julia, *710*
Adrift, *950*
Adultress, The, *441*
Adventure, *441*
Adventures Beyond Belief, *222*
Adventures in Babysitting, *222*
Adventures in Dinosaur City, *143*
Adventures in Spying, *2*
Adventures in Wonderland, *143*
Adventures of a Gnome Named Gnorm, The, *1034*
Adventures of a Private Eye, *222*
Adventures of an American Rabbit, The, *143*
◆ Adventures of Baron Münchausen, The, *1034*
Adventures of Batman and Robin (see Batman and Robin)
◆ Adventures of Buckaroo Banzai, The, *1034*
Adventures of Bullwhip Griffin, The, *143*
Adventures of Captain Fabian, *2*
◆ Adventures of Captain Marvel, The, *2*
◆ Adventures of Don Juan, The, *2*
Adventures of Droopy, *143*
Adventures of Felix the Cat, The, *143*
Adventures of Ford Fairlane, The, *2*
Adventures of Frank and Jesse James, *1092*
Adventures of Gallant Bess, *442*
Adventures of Hercules, The, *1034*

◆ Adventures of Huck Finn, The (1993), *143*
◆ Adventures of Huckleberry Finn, The (1939), *143*
◆ Adventures of Huckleberry Finn, The (1960), *144*
Adventures of Huckleberry Finn, The (1978), *144*
Adventures of Mark Twain, The (1944), *442*
◆ Adventures of Mark Twain, The (1985), *144*
◆ Adventures of Milo and Otis, The, *144*
Adventures of Milo in the Phantom Tollbooth, The, *144*
Adventures of Nellie Bly, The, *442*
◆ Adventures of Ozzie and Harriet, The (TV Series), *222*
Adventures of Picasso, The, *222*
◆ Adventures of Red Ryder, *1092*
Adventures of Rex and Rinty, *1092*
◆ Adventures of Robin Hood, The, *2*
◆ Adventures of Rocky and Bullwinkle, The, *144*
Adventures of Sadie, *223*
◆ Adventures of Sherlock Holmes, The, *950*
◆ Adventures of Sherlock Holmes, The (Series), *950*
Adventures of Sherlock Holmes, The (TV Series), *950*
Adventure of Sherlock Holmes' Smarter Brother, The, *223*
Adventures of Sinbad, The, *144*
Adventures of Tartu, *2*
Adventures of Tarzan, The, *2*
Adventures of the Flying Cadets, *2*
◆ Adventures of the Great Mouse Detective, The, *144*
Adventures of the Kung Fu Rascals, The, *223*
Adventures of the Wilderness Family, *144*
◆ Adventures of Tom Sawyer, The, *144*
Adventures of Topper, The, *223*
Adversary, The, *711*
Advise and Consent, *442*
Aelita: Queen of Mars, *711*
Affair, The, *442*
Affair in Trinidad, *442*
◆ Affair to Remember, An, *442*
◆ Affairs of Annabel, The, *223*
◆ **Affairs of Dobie Gillis, The,** *906*
Afraid of the Dark, *950*
Africa Blood and Guts, *418*
Africa Screams, *223*
Africa—Texas Style!, *3*
◆ African Dream, An, *442*
◆ African Queen, The, *442*

African Rage, 3
After Dark, My Sweet, 951
After Darkness, 951
◆ After Hours, 223
After Julius, 442
After Midnight, 808
After the Fall of New York, 1034
After the Fox, 223
After the Promise, 442
After the Rehearsal, 711
After the Shock, 442
◆ After the Thin Man, 951
◆ Afterburn, 442
Aftermath, The, 1034
Against a Crooked Sky, 1092
Against All Flags, 3
Against All Odds, 951
Against All Odds (Kiss and Kill, Blood of Fu Manchu), 808
◆ **Against the Wall,** 442
Agatha, 951
Age Isn't Everything, 223
Age of Gold, 711
◆ **Age of Innocence, The,** 443
◆ Age-Old Friends, 443
Agency, 443
Agent on Ice, 3
Aggie Appleby, Maker of Men, 223
Agnes of God, 443
Agony and the Ecstasy, The, 443
◆ Aguirre: Wrath of God, 711
◆ Ah, Wilderness, 223
◆ Air America, 3
◆ Air Force, 3
Air Raid Wardens, 223
Air Up There, The, 223
Airborne, 224
Airheads, 906
◆ Airplane!, 224
Airplane II: The Sequel, 224
◆ Airport, 443
Airport 1975, 443
Airport '77, 443
Airport '79: The Concorde, 443
◆ Akira, 1034
◆ Akira Kurosawa's Dreams, 711
Al Capone, 3
Aladdin (1987), 144
◆ Aladdin (1992), 144
Aladdin and His Magic Lamp, 145
Aladdin and His Wonderful Lamp, 145
Aladdin and the Magic Lamp, 145
Alakazam the Great, 145
Alamo, The, 1092
◆ Alamo Bay, 443
Alamo, The: Thirteen Days to Glory, 1093
Alan and Naomi, 443
Alberto Express, 711
Albino, 808
Alchemist, The, 808
Alex in Wonderland, 224
◆ Alexander Nevsky, 711
Alexander the Great, 443
◆ **Alexander's Ragtime Band,** 906
Alexina, 711
Alex's Apartment, 951
◆ Alfie, 224
Alfred Hitchcock's Bon Voyage and Aventure Malgache, 711
◆ Alfred Hitchcock Presents (TV Series), 951
Ali Baba and the Forty Thieves, 3
Ali: Fear Eats the Soul, 711
Alice (1981), 906
◆ Alice (1988), 1034
Alice (1990), 224
◆ Alice Adams, 444
◆ Alice Doesn't Live Here Anymore, 444
Alice in the City, 711
Alice in Wonderland (1951), 145
Alice in Wonderland (1985), 145
Alice, Sweet Alice (Communion and Holy Terror), 808
Alice Through the Looking Glass (1966), 906
Alice Through the Looking Glass (1985), 145
◆ Alice to Nowhere, 3
Alice's Adventures in Wonderland, 145
Alice's Restaurant, 444
◆ Alien, 1034
Alien Contamination, 1034
Alien Dead, 1035
Alien Factor, The, 1035
Alien From L.A., 3
Alien Intruder, 1035
Alien Nation, 1035
Alien P.I., 1035
Alien Predators, 1035
Alien Prey, 808
Alien Seed, 1035
Alien Space Avenger, 1035
Alien Terror (see Sinister Invasion)
Alien 3, 1035
Alien Thunder (see Dan Candy's Law)
Alien Warrior, 1035
Alienator, 1035
◆ Aliens, 1035
Alison's Birthday, 808
Alive, 444
◆ All About Eve, 444
All-American Murder, 951
All Creatures Great and Small, 145
All Dogs Go to Heaven, 145
All Fall Down, 444
All God's Children, 444
All I Want for Christmas, 145
All in a Night's Work, 224
All in the Family Twentieth Anniversary Special, 224
All Mine to Give, 444
All My Sons, 444
All Night Long, 224
◆ All of Me, 224
All Over Town, 224
◆ All Quiet on the Western Front (1930), 3
All Quiet on the Western Front (1979), 444
All Screwed Up, 712
All-Star Toast to the Improv, An, 224
◆ All That Jazz, 906
All the Kind Strangers, 951
◆ All the King's Men, 444
All the Marbles, 225
All the Mornings of the World (see Tous Les Matins du Monde)
◆ All the President's Men, 951
All the Right Moves, 444
All These Women, 712
◆ All This and Heaven Too, 445
All Through the Night, 3
All Tied Up, 225
All You Need Is Cash (see Rutles, The)
Allan Quartermain and the Lost City of Gold, 4
Allegheny Uprising, 1093
◆ Allegro Non Troppo, 712
Alligator, 808
Alligator II, 808
Alligator Eyes, 951
Alligator Shoes, 445
Allnighter, The, 225
All's Fair, 225
Almos' a Man, 445
...Almost, 225
Almost an Angel, 225
Almost Angels, 146
Almost Blue, 445
Almost Human, 4
Almost Perfect Affair, An, 225
Almost Pregnant, 225
◆ Almost You, 225
Aloha, Bobby and Rose, 4
Aloha Summer, 445
Alone in the Dark, 808
◆ Alone in the Neon Jungle, 445
◆ Along Came Jones, 1093
Along the Great Divide, 1093
Along the Navajo Trail, 1093
Alpha Incident, The, 1035
Alphabet City, 445
Alphabet Conspiracy, The, 146
Alphabet Murders, The, 951
Alphaville, 712
Alsino and the Condor, 712
Altered States, 1035
Alvarez Kelly, 1093
◆ Alvin and the Chipmunks: Sing-Alongs, 146
Always (1984), 225
◆ Always (1989), 445
◆ Always for Pleasure, 418
◆ Amadeus, 906
◆ Amarcord, 712
Amateur, The, 952
Amazing Adventure, 225
Amazing Colossal Man, The, 1035
Amazing Dobermans, 146
Amazing Grace and Chuck, 445
Amazing Howard Hughes, The, 44
Amazing Mr. Blunden, The, 146
Amazing Mr. X, 445
Amazing Spiderman, The, 4
Amazing Stories (TV Series), 103
Amazing Transparent Man, The, 1
Amazing Transplant, The, 445
Amazon, 4
Amazon Women on the Moon, 22
Amazons, 4
Ambassador, The, 445
Ambassador Bill, 225
Ambassador Magma, 712
Ambassador's Daughter, The, 22
Ambition, 952
◆ **Ambulance, The,** 952
Ambush Murders, The, 446
Ambush Valley, 1093
Ambushers, The, 4
America, 226
American Anthem, 446
◆ American Aristocracy, An, 226
American Blue Note, 446
American Boyfriends, 446
American Christmas Carol, An, 1
◆ **American Clock, The,** 446
◆ American Dream, 418
American Dreamer, 226
American Eagle, 4
American Empire, 1093

rican Film Institute Life chievement Awards, The, 418
rican Flyers, 446
rican Friend, The, 712
rican Friends, 226
rican Gangster, The, 418
rican Gigolo, 446
rican Gothic, 808
rican Graffiti, 226
rican Heart, 446
rican Hot Wax, 906
rican in Paris, An, 906
rican Justice, 4
rican Kickboxer, 4
rican Me, 446
rican Ninja, 4
rican Ninja II, 4
rican Ninja III, 4
rican Ninja IV: The Annihilation, 4
rican Roulette, 4
rican Shaolin: King of the ickboxers II, 5
rican Soldier, The, 712
rican Summer, An, 5
rican Tail, An, 146
rican Tail, An: Fievel Goes West, 46
rican Tiger, 1036
rican Werewolf in London, An, 08
ricana, 446
ricanization of Emily, The, 226
ricano, The, 1093
ricathon, 226
n: The Rise and Fall, 446
tyville Horror, The, 809
tyville II: The Possession, 809
tyville III: The Demon, 809
tyville 4: The Evil Escapes, 809
tyville Curse, The, 809
tyville 1992: It's About Time, 809
tyville: A New Generation, 809
ong the Cinders, 446
ngst Friends, 447
re, 712
rous Adventures of Moll landers, The, 226
s & Andrew, 226
s and Andy (TV Series), 226
sterdam Kill, The, 5
sterdamned, 809
, 146
Fisher Story, The, 447
stasia, 447
stasia: The Mystery of Anna, 447
tomy of a Murder, 952
hors Aweigh, 906
Baby Makes Six, 447
God Created Woman (1957), 712
God Created Woman (1987), 447
God Said to Cain, 1093
Hope to Die, 952
I Alone Survived, 447
Justice for All, 447
Nothing But the Truth, 447
Now for Something Completely ifferent, 226
Now, My Love, 712
Now the Screaming Starts, 809
Soon the Darkness, 952
the Band Played on, 447
the Ship Sails On, 712
Then There Were None, 952
Then You Die, 5
And You Thought Your Parents Were Weird, 227
◆ Anderson Tapes, The, 952
Anderson's Angels (see Chesty Anderson, US Navy)
◆ Andersonville Trial, The, 447
◆ Andrei Rublev, 713
Androcles and the Lion, 227
◆ Android, 1036
◆ Andromeda Strain, The, 1036
◆ Andy Griffith Show, The (TV Series), 227
Andy Hardy Gets Spring Fever, 227
Andy Hardy Meets a Debutante, 227
Andy Hardy's Double Life, 227
Andy Hardy's Private Secretary, 227
Andy Kaufman Special, The, 227
◆ Andy Warhol: Superstar, 418
Andy Warhol's Bad, 447
Andy Warhol's Dracula, 809
Andy Warhol's Frankenstein, 809
Angel, 5
◆ Angel and the Badman, 1093
◆ Angel at My Table, An, 447
Angel City, 448
Angel Fist, 5
Angel Heart, 952
Angel of Death, 5
Angel of H.E.A.T., 5
◆ Angel on My Shoulder (1946), 448
Angel on My Shoulder (1980), 448
Angel Town, 5
Angela, 448
Angele, 713
Angelic Conversation, 448
◆ Angelo, My Love, 448
Angels Die Hard, 5
Angels Hard as They Come, 5
Angels Over Broadway, 448
◆ Angels with Dirty Faces, 5
◆ **Angie,** 448
Angkor: Cambodia Express, 5
◆ Angry Harvest, 713
Angry Red Planet, The, 1036
◆ Anguish, 809
Animal Behavior, 227
Animal Called Man, An, 1093
◆ Animal Crackers, 227
Animal Farm, 448
◆ Animal House, 227
Animal Instincts, 952
Animal Kingdom, The, 448
Animals Are Beautiful People, 418
Animalympics, 146
◆ **Animation Legend Windsor McKay,** 146
◆ Ann Vickers, 448
◆ Anna, 448
◆ Anna and the King of Siam, 449
Anna Christie (1922), 449
◆ Anna Christie (1930), 449
◆ Anna Karenina (1935), 449
Anna Karenina (1947), 449
Anna Karenina (1974), 907
Anna Karenina (1985), 449
◆ Anna to the Infinite Power, 1036
Annabel Takes a Tour, 227
Annapolis Story, An, 449
◆ Anne of Avonlea, 449
Anne of Green Gables (1934), 146
◆ Anne of Green Gables (1985), 449
Anne of the Thousand Days, 449
◆ Annie, 907
Annie Get Your Gun, 907
◆ Annie Hall, 228
Annie Oakley (1935), 1093
Annie Oakley (1985), 146
Annie Oakley (1992), 147
Annie Oakley (TV Series), 1094
Annihilators, The, 5
Another Chance, 228
Another Country, 449
◆ Another 48 Hrs., 5
Another Man, Another Chance, 1094
Another Pair of Aces, 1094
Another Stakeout, 6
◆ Another Thin Man, 952
Another Time, Another Place (1958), 449
Another Time, Another Place (1984), 450
◆ Another Woman, 450
Another You, 228
Ant and the Aardvark, The, 147
Antarctica, 713
Anthony Adverse, 450
◆ Antonia & Jane, 228
Antony and Cleopatra (1973), 450
Antony and Cleopatra (1981), 450
Ants!, 809
Any Friend of Nicholas Nickleby Is a Friend of Mine, 147
Any Man's Death, 450
Any Number Can Play, 450
Any Wednesday, 228
Any Which Way You Can, 228
◆ Anzacs, 450
Anzio, 6
Apache, 1094
Apache Rose, 1094
Apache Woman, 1094
Aparajito, 713
◆ Apartment, The, 228
◆ Apartment Zero, 952
Ape, The, 809
Ape Man, The, 809
Apex, 1036
Aphrodite, 713
◆ Apocalypse Now, 6
Apology, 809
Appaloosa, The, 1094
◆ Applause, 450
Apple Dumpling Gang, The, 147
Apple Dumpling Gang Rides Again, The, 147
Appleseed, 713
Appointment, The, 810
Appointment in Honduras, 6
Appointment with Death, 953
Appointment with Fear, 6
Apprentice to Murder, 810
Apprenticeship of Duddy Kravitz, The, 450
April Fools, The, 228
April Fool's Day, 810
April in Paris, 907
Aqua E Sapone, 713
Arabesque, 6
Arabian Nights (1942), 6
Arabian Nights (1974), 713
◆ Arachnophobia, 810
Arcade, 1036
Arcadia of My Youth, 713
Arch of Triumph, 450
Archer: Fugitive from the Empire, 1036
Archer's Adventure, 147
◆ Are Parents People?, 228
Are You in the House Alone?, 953
Are You Lonesome Tonight, 953

Arena, *1036*
Arena Brains, *450*
Aria, *907*
◆ Ariel, *713*
Arizona, *1094*
Arizona Bound, *1094*
Arizona Bushwhackers, *1094*
Arizona Cowboy, *1094*
Arizona Days, *1094*
Arizona Gunfighter, *1094*
Arizona Heat, *6*
Arizona Kid, *1095*
◆ Arizona Legion, *1095*
Arizona Raiders, *1095*
Arizona Ranger, *1095*
Arizona Roundup, *1095*
Arizona Stagecoach, *1095*
Ark of the Sun God...Temple of Hell, The, *6*
Armed and Dangerous, *228*
Armed Response, *6*
Armored Command, *6*
◆ **Armour Of God,** *713*
Army Brats, *228*
Army of Darkness, *810*
Arnold, *810*
Around the World, *907*
Around the World in 80 Days (1956), *228*
Around the World in 80 Days (1974), *147*
Around the World in 80 Ways, *228*
Around the World Under the Sea, *6*
Arrangement, The, *450*
Arrest Bulldog Drummond, *6*
Arrogant, The, *450*
Arrowhead, *1095*
◆ Arrowsmith, *451*
Arsenal, *713*
◆ Arsenic and Old Lace, *228*
Arson Inc., *7*
Art Com Video (Vol. 1–3), *1037*
Art of Dying, The, *953*
◆ Arthur, *229*
Arthur 2: On the Rocks, *229*
Arthur's Hallowed Ground, *451*
Article 99, *451*
Artists and Models, *229*
As Is, *451*
As Summers Die, *451*
As You Desire Me, *451*
As You Like It, *229*
As Young as You Feel, *229*
Ascent To Heaven (Mexican Bus Ride), *714*
Ash Wednesday, *451*
Ashanti, *7*
◆ Ashes and Diamonds, *714*
Ask Any Girl, *229*
Aspen Extreme, *451*
◆ Asphalt Jungle, The, *953*
Asphyx, The (see Spirit of the Dead)
Assassin, *1037*
Assassin of Youth (a.k.a. Marijuana), *451*
Assassination, *7*
Assassination Game, The, *7*
Assassination of Trotsky, The, *451*
Assassins de L'Ordre, Les (Law Breakers), *714*
◆ Assault, The, *714*
Assault & Matrimony, *229*
Assault at West Point, *451*
Assault Force (see ffolkes)
Assault of the Rebel Girls, *7*
Assault on a Queen, *7*
Assault on Agathon, *7*
◆ Assault on Precinct 13, *7*
Assisi Underground, The, *7*
Associate, The, *714*
Asterix: The Gaul (Series), *147*
Astro-Zombies, *810*
Astroboy—Vols. 1–10, *1037*
◆ Asylum, *810*
Asylum of Satan, *810*
◆ At Bertram's Hotel, *953*
◆ At Close Range, *953*
At Gunpoint, *1095*
At Play in the Fields of the Lord, *451*
At Sword's Point, *7*
At the Circus, *229*
At the Earth's Core, *1037*
◆ At War with the Army, *229*
Athena, *907*
Athens, GA., *418*
◆ Atlantic City, *452*
Atlas, *7*
Atoll K (Utopia), *229*
Atom Age Vampire, *810*
Atom Man vs. Superman, *7*
Atomic Cafe, The, *418*
Atomic Kid, The, *229*
Atomic Submarine, The, *1037*
Ator: The Fighting Eagle, *1037*
Attack Force Z, *7*
Attack of the Crab Monsters, *810*
Attack of the 50-Foot Woman (1958), *810*
Attack of the 50-Foot Woman (1993), *1037*
Attack of the Giant Leeches, *810*
Attack of the Killer Tomatoes, *229*
Attack of the Swamp Creature, *810*
Attic, The, *811*
◆ Attic: The Hiding of Anne Frank, *452*
◆ Attica, *452*
◆ Au Revoir, Les Enfants, *714*
Audience with Mel Brooks, An, *229*
Audrey Rose, *811*
Auntie Lee's Meat Pies, *811*
Auntie Mame, *229*
Aurora Encounter, *1037*
Author! Author!, *230*
Autobiography of a Princess, *452*
◆ Autobiography of Miss Jane Pittman, The, *452*
Autopsy, *811*
Autumn Afternoon, An, *714*
Autumn Leaves, *452*
◆ Autumn Sonata, *714*
Avalanche, *7*
◆ Avalon, *452*
Avant Garde Program #2, *714*
◆ Avanti!, *230*
Avengers, The (TV Series), *7*
Avenging, The, *1095*
Avenging Angel, *8*
Avenging Conscience, The, *811*
Avenging Force, *8*
Avery Schreiber—Live From the Second City, *230*
Aviator, The, *452*
Aviator's Wife, The, *714*
Awakening, The, *811*
Awakening of Cassie, The, *452*
◆ Awakenings, *452*
Away all Boats, *8*
◆ Awful Truth, The, *230*
Ay, Carmela!, *714*
B.O.R.N., *811*
Babar: The Movie, *147*
◆ Babe, The, *452*
Babe Ruth Story, The, *453*
Babes in Arms, *907*
Babes in Toyland (1934) (see March of the Wooden Soldiers)
Babes in Toyland (1961), *147*
Babes in Toyland (1986), *147*
Babes on Broadway, *907*
◆ Babette's Feast, *714*
Baby, The, *811*
Baby Boom, *230*
◆ Baby Cakes, *453*
◆ Baby Doll, *453*
Baby Doll Murders, The, *953*
Baby Face, *453*
Baby Girl Scott, *453*
◆ Baby, It's You, *453*
Baby Love, *230*
Baby Maker, The, *453*
Baby of the Bride, *230*
Baby on Board, *8*
Baby...Secret of the Lost Legend, *1037*
Baby Take a Bow, *147*
Baby the Rain Must Fall, *453*
Babysitter, The, *811*
Bach and Broccoli, *147*
Bachelor, The, *453*
Bachelor and the Bobby-Soxer, The, *230*
Bachelor Apartment, *230*
Bachelor in Paradise, *230*
Bachelor Mother, *230*
Bachelor Party, *230*
Back from Eternity, *453*
Back Home, *147*
Back in the U.S.S.R., *8*
Back Roads, *453*
Back Street, *453*
Back to Back, *8*
Back to Bataan, *8*
Back to Hannibal: The Return of Tom Sawyer and Huckleberry Finn, *454*
Back to School, *230*
Back to the Beach, *907*
Back to the Forest, *148*
◆ Back to the Future, *1037*
Back to the Future II, *1037*
◆ Back to the Future III, *1037*
◆ **BackBeat,** *907*
Backdoor to Heaven, *454*
Backdraft, *8*
Backfield in Motion, *230*
◆ Backfire, *953*
◆ Background to Danger, *8*
Backlash, *8*
Backstab, *953*
◆ Backstage at the Kirov, *419*
◆ Backstairs, *714*
Backstreet Dreams, *454*
Backstreet Justice, *8*
Backtrack, *454*
Bad (see Andy Warhol's Bad)
◆ Bad and the Beautiful, The, *454*
Bad Behaviour, *231*
Bad Blood, *811*
◆ Bad Boys, *454*
Bad Channels, *1037*
◆ Bad Company, *1095*
◆ Bad Day at Black Rock, *454*
Bad Dreams, *811*
Bad Girls (1969), *715*
Bad Girls (1994), *1095*

Bad Girls Go to Hell, *454*
Bad Golf Made Easier, *231*
Bad Guys, *8*
Bad Influence, *953*
Bad Jim, *1095*
Bad Lands, *1095*
Bad Lieutenant, *454*
Bad Man of Deadwood, *1095*
Bad Manners, *231*
Bad Man's River, *1095*
Bad Medicine, *231*
Bad News Bears, The, *231*
Bad News Bears Go to Japan, The, *231*
Bad News Bears in Breaking Training, The, *231*
Bad Ronald, *811*
Bad Seed, The, *454*
Bad Sleep Well, The, *715*
Bad Taste, *1038*
Badge of the Assassin, *454*
Badge 373, *8*
Badlanders, The, *1096*
Badlands, *454*
Badlands Drifter, *1096*
Badman's Territory, *1096*
Badmen of the Border, *1096*
Badmen of the Hills, *1096*
Bagdad Café, *231*
Bail Jumper, *455*
Bail Out, *8*
Baja Oklahoma, *455*
Baker's Hawk, *148*
Baker's Wife, The (1938), *715*
Balalaika, *907*
Balboa, *455*
Balcony, The, *455*
Ball of Fire, *231*
Ballad of a Gunfighter, *1096*
Ballad of a Soldier, *715*
Ballad of Cable Hogue, The, *1096*
Ballad of Gregorio Cortez, The, *1096*
Ballad of Little Jo, The, *1096*
Ballad of Narayama, The, *715*
Ballad of Paul Bunyan, The, *148*
Ballad of the Sad Cafe, The, *455*
Balloonatic, The/One Week, *231*
Baltimore Bullet, The, *231*
Bambi, *148*
Bambi vs. Godzilla, *148*
Bamboo Saucer (a.k.a. Collision Course), *1038*
Banana Cop, *715*
Bananas, *232*
Bananas Boat, The, *232*
Band of Outsiders, *715*
Band of the Hand, *9*
Band Wagon, The, *908*
Bandera Bandits (see Sonny and Jed)
Bandits (1967), *1096*
Bandits (1987), *715*
Bandits of Dark Canyon, *1096*
Bandolero!, *1096*
Bang Bang Kid, The, *232*
Bang the Drum Slowly, *455*
Bank Dick, The, *232*
Bank Robber, *232*
Bank Shot, *232*
Bar 20, *1096*
Barabbas, *455*
Baraka, *419*
Barbarella, *1038*
Barbarian and the Geisha, The, *455*
Barbarian Queen, *1038*
Barbarian Queen II: Empress Strikes Back, *1038*
Barbarians, The, *1038*
◆ Barbarians at the Gate, *455*
◆ Barbarosa, *1097*
Barbary Coast, The, *455*
Bare Essentials, *232*
Bare Knuckles, *9*
Barefoot Contessa, The, *455*
Barefoot Executive, The, *148*
◆ Barefoot in the Park, *232*
◆ Barfly, *455*
Baritone, *715*
Barjo, *715*
Barkleys of Broadway, The, *908*
◆ Barn Burning, *456*
Barn of the Naked Dead (see Nightmare Circus)
Barnaby and Me, *232*
Barney Bear Cartoon Festival, *148*
Barnum (1986), *908*
Barnum (1987), *456*
Baron Blood (see Torture Chamber of Baron Blood, The)
Baron Müenchhausen, *1038*
Baron Munchausen, *148*
Baron of Arizona, The, *1097*
Barracuda, *1038*
Barretts of Wimpole Street, The, *456*
Barry Lyndon, *456*
Barry McKenzie Holds His Own, *232*
Bartleby, *456*
◆ Barton Fink, *232*
Based on an Untrue Story, *232*
Basic Instinct, *456*
Basic Training, *232*
◆ Basileus Quartet, *715*
Basket Case, *811*
Basket Case 2, *811*
Basket Case 3: The Progeny, *811*
Bastard, The, *456*
Bat People, *812*
◆ Bat 21, *9*
Bat Whispers, The, *953*
◆ Bataan, *9*
Bathing Beauty, *908*
Batman (1966), *148*
Batman (1989), *9*
Batman and Robin, *9*
Batman: Mask of the Phantasm, *148*
Batman Returns, *9*
Battered, *456*
Batteries Not Included, *148*
◆ **Battle Angel,** *715*
Battle Beneath the Earth, *9*
◆ Battle Beyond the Stars, *1038*
Battle Circus, *456*
Battle Cry, *9*
Battle for the Planet of the Apes, *1038*
Battle Force, *9*
Battle Hell, *9*
◆ Battle of Algiers, *716*
Battle of Austerlitz, The, *9*
Battle of Britain, *9*
Battle of El Alamein, The, *10*
Battle of Elderbush Gulch, The/The Musketeers of Pig Alley, *1097*
Battle of the Bombs, *232*
Battle of the Bulge, *10*
Battle of the Commandos, *10*
Battle of the Sexes, The, *233*
Battle Shock, *812*
Battleground, *456*
◆ Battleship Potemkin, The, *716*
Battlestar Galactica, *1038*
Battling Hoofer (see Something to Sing About)
Battling Marshal, *1097*
Bawdy Adventures of Tom Jones, The, *233*
Baxter, *456*
◆ Bay Boy, The, *456*
Bay Coven (see Eye of the Demon)
Bay of Blood (see Twitch of the Death Nerve)
Bayou Romance, *456*
Be My Valentine, Charlie Brown, *148*
Beach Babes from Beyond, *1038*
Beach Blanket Bingo, *908*
Beach Boys, The: An American Band, *419*
Beach Girls, The, *233*
Beach House, *233*
Beach Party, *908*
Beachballs, *233*
Beachcomber, The, *457*
◆ Beaches, *457*
Beaks the Movie, *812*
◆ Beany and Cecil, *149*
◆ Bear, The, *149*
Bear Island, *954*
Bear Who Slept Through Christmas, The, *149*
Beast, The, *10*
Beast From 20,000 Fathoms, The, *1038*
Beast in the Cellar, The, *812*
Beast Must Die, The, *812*
Beast of the Yellow Night, *812*
Beast with Five Fingers, The, *812*
Beast Within, The, *812*
Beastmaster, The, *1038*
Beastmaster 2: Through the Portal of Time, *1039*
Beat Street, *908*
◆ Beat the Devil, *233*
◆ Beatles, The: The First U.S. Visit, *419*
Beatrice, *716*
◆ Beau Brummell (1924), *457*
Beau Brummell (1954), *457*
◆ Beau Geste, *10*
◆ Beau Pere, *716*
Beautiful Blonde from Bashful Bend, The, *233*
Beautiful Dreamers, *457*
◆ Beauty and the Beast (1946), *716*
◆ Beauty and the Beast (1983), *149*
◆ Beauty and the Beast (1991), *149*
Beauty and the Beast (TV Series), *1039*
Beauty for the Asking, *457*
Beauty School, *233*
Bebe's Kids, *233*
Because You're Mine, *908*
◆ Becket, *457*
Becky Sharp, *457*
Becoming Colette, *457*
Bed and Breakfast, *457*
◆ Bed and Sofa, *716*
◆ Bedazzled, *233*
Bedford Incident, The, *457*
Bedknobs and Broomsticks, *149*
Bedlam, *812*
Bedroom Eyes, *954*
Bedroom Eyes II, *954*
Bedroom Window, The, *954*
Bedtime for Bonzo, *233*
Bedtime Story, *233*
◆ Beer, *233*

Bees, The, *812*
Beethoven (1937) (see Abel Gance's Beethoven)
Beethoven (1992), *149*
Beethoven Lives Upstairs, *149*
Beethoven's Nephew, *457*
Beethoven's 2nd, *149*
Beetlejuice, *233*
Before I Hang, *812*
Before the Revolution, *716*
◆ Beguiled, The, *954*
Behind Locked Doors, *812*
Behind the Rising Sun, *10*
Behold a Pale Horse, *458*
Being, The, *812*
Being at Home with Claude, *716*
Being Human, *458*
◆ Being There, *234*
Bela Lugosi Meets a Brooklyn Gorilla (see Boys from Brooklyn, The)
Belarus File, The, *954*
Belfast Assassin, *458*
Believers, The, *812*
◆ Belizaire the Cajun, *458*
Bell, Book and Candle, *234*
Bell Jar, The, *458*
Bellboy, The, *234*
Bellboy and the Playgirls, The, *234*
◆ **Belle Epoque,** *716*
Belle of New York, The, *908*
Belle of the Nineties, *234*
Belles of St. Trinian's, The, *234*
Bellissima, *716*
Bellissimo: Images of the Italian Cinema, *716*
◆ Bellman and True, *954*
Bells (see Murder By Phone)
Bells Are Ringing, *908*
Bells of Coronado, *1097*
Bells of Rosarita, *1097*
◆ Bells of St. Mary's, The, *458*
Bells of San Angelo, *1097*
Belly of an Architect, The, *458*
Beloved Enemy, *458*
◆ Beloved Rogue, *954*
Below the Belt, *458*
Below the Border, *1097*
Belstone Fox, The, *149*
Ben, *812*
◆ Ben and Me, *149*
◆ Ben-Hur (1926), *458*
◆ Ben-Hur (1959), *10*
◆ Bend of the River, *1097*
Beneath the Planet of the Apes, *1039*
Beneath the 12-Mile Reef, *10*
Beneath the Valley of the Ultra-Vixens, *234*
Benefit of a Doubt, *954*
Beniker Gang, The, *149*
◆ Benji, *149*
Benji the Hunted, *150*
Benny & Joon, *234*
Benny Goodman Story, The, *458*
Beretta's Island, *10*
Berlin Affair, The, *459*
Berlin Alexanderplatz, *716*
Berlin Conspiracy, The, *10*
Berlin Express, *10*
◆ Berlin—Symphony of a Great City, *419*
Berlin Tunnel 21, *10*
Bernadette, *459*
Bernard and the Genie, *234*
◆ Bernice Bobs Her Hair, *234*
Berserk, *812*
Berserker, *813*
Bert Rigby, You're a Fool, *908*
◆ Best Boy, *419*
Best Christmas Pageant Ever, The, *150*
Best Defense, *234*
Best Foot Forward, *908*
Best Friends, *235*
◆ Best Intentions, The, *717*
Best Kept Secrets, *11*
Best Legs in the 8th Grade, The, *235*
◆ Best Little Girl in the World, The, *459*
Best Little Whorehouse in Texas, The, *908*
◆ Best Man, The, *459*
Best of America's Funniest Home Videos, The, *235*
Best of Benny Hill, The, *235*
◆ Best of Bugs Bunny and Friends, The, *150*
Best of Candid Camera, The, *235*
Best of Chevy Chase, The, *235*
Best of Comic Relief, The, *235*
◆ Best of Dan Aykroyd, The, *235*
Best of Dark Shadows, The, *813*
Best of DC Follies, *235*
◆ Best of Gilda Radner, The, *235*
Best of John Belushi, The, *235*
◆ Best of John Candy, The, *236*
Best of Little Lulu, *150*
◆ Best of Not Necessarily the News, The, *236*
Best of Sex and Violence, *813*
Best of Spike Jones, Volumes 1 & 2, The, *236*
Best of the Badmen, *1097*
Best of the Best, *11*
Best of the Best 2, *11*
Best of the Big Laff Off, The, *236*
Best of the Festival of Claymation, The, *236*
◆ **Best of the Kids in the Hall, The,** *236*
Best of Times, The, *236*
◆ Best of Warner Brothers, Vol. 1, *150*
◆ Best of Warner Brothers, Vol. 2, *150*
Best of William Wegman, *236*
Best Revenge, *11*
◆ Best Seller, *954*
◆ Best Years of Our Lives, The, *459*
Bethune, *459*
Betrayal (1978), *459*
◆ Betrayal (1983), *459*
Betrayal from the East, *11*
Betrayal of the Dove, *954*
Betrayed (1954), *11*
Betrayed (1988), *954*
Betsy, The, *459*
◆ Betsy's Wedding, *236*
◆ Bette Midler—Art or Bust, *909*
◆ Bette Midler's Mondo Beyondo, *236*
Better Late than Never, *237*
Better Off Dead, *237*
Better Tomorrow, A, *717*
◆ **Better Tomorrow 2, A,** *717*
Better Tomorrow 3, A: Love And Death in Saigon, *717*
Betty Blue, *717*
◆ Betty Boop—A Special Collector's Edition, *150*
Between Friends, *459*
Between God, the Devil and a Winchester, *1097*
Between Heaven and Hell, *459*
Between Men, *1097*
◆ Between the Lines, *237*
◆ Between Two Women, *459*
Between Wars, *459*
Beulah Land, *459*
Beverly Hillbillies, The, *237*
Beverly Hillbillies, The (TV Series), *237*
Beverly Hillbillies Go Hollywood, The, *237*
Beverly Hills Bodysnatchers, *237*
Beverly Hills Brats, *237*
◆ Beverly Hills Cop, *11*
Beverly Hills Cop II, *11*
Beverly Hills Cop 3, *11*
Beverly Hills Madam, *460*
Beverly Hills 90210, *460*
Beverly Hills Vamp, *237*
◆ Beware, My Lovely, *955*
Beware of Spooks, *237*
Beware! The Blob (see Son of Blob)
Beyond a Reasonable Doubt (1956), *955*
Beyond Atlantis, *11*
Beyond Darkness, *813*
Beyond Evil, *813*
Beyond Fear, *717*
Beyond Justice, *11*
Beyond Obsession, *717*
Beyond Reason, *460*
Beyond Reasonable Doubt (1983), *955*
Beyond, The (see Seven Doors of Death)
Beyond the Call of Duty, *11*
Beyond the Door, *813*
Beyond the Door 2, *813*
Beyond the Door 3, *813*
Beyond the Forest, *460*
Beyond the Law, *1097*
Beyond the Limit, *460*
Beyond the Poseidon Adventure, *11*
Beyond the Purple Hills, *1097*
Beyond the Rising Moon, *1039*
Beyond the Stars, *1039*
Beyond the Valley of the Dolls, *460*
Beyond the Walls, *717*
Beyond Therapy, *237*
Beyond Tomorrow, *1039*
Bhowani Junction, *12*
Bible, The, *460*
◆ Bicycle Thief, The, *717*
◆ Big, *237*
Big Bad John, *12*
Big Bad Mama, *12*
Big Bad Mama II, *12*
Big Bang, The, *419*
Big Bet, The, *238*
Big Bird Cage, The, *12*
Big Blue, The, *12*
Big Bluff, The, *460*
Big Brawl, The, *12*
Big Bus, The, *238*
Big Business, *238*
Big Business Girl, *460*
Big Bust Out, The, *12*
Big Cat, The, *12*
◆ Big Chill, The, *460*
Big City Comedy, *238*
Big Combo, The, *12*
Big Country, The, *1098*
◆ Big Deal on Madonna Street, *717*
◆ Big Easy, The, *12*
Big Fix, The, *955*
Big Foot, *813*

Big Gag, The, *238*
Big Girls Don't Cry...They Get Even, *238*
Big Grab, The (see Melodie en Sous-sol)
Big Hand for the Little Lady, A, *1098*
Big Hangover, The, *238*
Big Heat, The, *12*
Big Jake, *1098*
Big Jim McLain, *460*
Big Lift, The, *460*
Big Man: Crossing the Line (see Crossing the Line (1991))
Big Man on Campus, *238*
Big Mouth, The, *238*
Big News, *238*
Big Parade, The, *460*
Big Picture, The, *238*
Big Red, *150*
Big Red One, The, *12*
Big Rip-off, The, *1098*
Big Score, The, *12*
Big Shots, *238*
Big Show, The, *1098*
Big Sky, The, *1098*
Big Sleep, The (1946), *955*
Big Sleep, The (1978), *955*
Big Slice, The, *12*
Big Sombrero, The, *1098*
Big Stampede, The, *1098*
Big Steal, The, *13*
Big Store, The, *238*
Big Street, The, *460*
Big Sweat, The, *13*
Big Switch, The, *13*
Big Top Pee-Wee, *239*
Big Town, The, *461*
Big Trail, The, *1098*
Big Trees, The, *13*
Big Trouble, *239*
Big Trouble in Little China, *13*
Big Valley, The (TV Series), *1098*
Big Wednesday, *461*
Big Wheel, The, *461*
Bigamist, The, *461*
Biggles—Adventures in Time, *1039*
Bikini Beach, *909*
Bikini Carwash Company, The, *239*
Bikini Carwash Company 2, *239*
Bikini Island, *813*
Bilitis, *717*
Bill, *461*
Bill and Coo, *150*
Bill and Ted's Bogus Journey, *239*
Bill and Ted's Excellent Adventure, *239*
Bill Cosby: 49, *239*
Bill Cosby—Himself, *239*
Bill Fields and Will Rogers, *239*
Bill of Divorcement, A, *461*
Bill: On His Own, *461*
Bill Viola: Selected Works, *1039*
Billie, *150*
Billion Dollar Hobo, The, *150*
Billion for Boris, A, *239*
Billionaire Boys Club, *461*
Billy Bathgate, *461*
Billy Budd, *461*
Billy Crystal: A Comic's Line, *239*
Billy Crystal: Don't Get Me Started, *239*
Billy Crystal: Midnight Train to Moscow, *240*
Billy Galvin, *461*
Billy Jack, *13*
◆ Billy Liar, *461*
Billy the Kid, *1099*
Billy the Kid Meets the Vampires, *813*
Billy the Kid Returns, *1099*
Billy the Kid vs. Dracula, *813*
Billy Ze Kick, *718*
◆ Biloxi Blues, *240*
Bingo, *240*
Bingo Long Traveling All-Stars and Motor Kings, The, *240*
Bionic Woman, The, *1039*
Birch Interval, The, *150*
◆ Birch Wood, *718*
◆ Bird, *909*
◆ Bird Man of Alcatraz, *462*
Bird of Paradise, *13*
Bird on a Wire, *13*
Bird with the Crystal Plumage, The, *955*
◆ Birds, The, *813*
Birds and the Bees, The, *240*
Birds II, The: Land's End, *813*
◆ Birds of Prey, *13*
◆ Birdy, *462*
◆ Birgit Haas Must Be Killed, *718*
◆ Birth of a Nation, The, *462*
Birthday Boy, The, *240*
Bishop's Wife, The, *240*
Bitch, The, *462*
◆ Bite the Bullet, *1099*
◆ Bitter Harvest (1981), *462*
Bitter Harvest (1993), *955*
Bitter Moon, *462*
Bitter Rice, *718*
Bitter Sweet, *909*
◆ **Bitter Tea of General Yen, The,** *462*
Bitter Tears of Petra Von Kant, The, *718*
Bittersweet Love, *462*
Bizarre, Bizarre, *718*
◆ Bizet's Carmen, *718*
◆ Black Adder III (TV Series), *240*
◆ Black and White in Color, *718*
Black Arrow (1984), *150*
Black Arrow, The (1948), *13*
Black Beauty (1946), *150*
Black Beauty (1971), *151*
Black Belt Jones, *13*
Black Bird, The, *240*
Black Caesar, *13*
◆ Black Cat, The (1934), *813*
Black Cat, The (1981), *813*
Black Christmas, *814*
Black Cobra 3, *13*
Black Devil Doll from Hell, *814*
Black Dragons, *814*
Black Eagle, *13*
◆ Black Fury, *462*
Black Gestapo, The, *13*
Black God (White Devil), *718*
Black Godfather, The, *13*
Black Hand, The, *462*
Black Hole, The, *1039*
Black Ice, *14*
Black Jack, *14*
Black Klansman, The, *14*
Black Lash, *1099*
Black Like Me, *462*
Black Lizard, *718*
Black Magic (1949), *462*
Black Magic (1992), *955*
Black Magic M-66, *1039*
Black Magic Mansion (see Cthulhu Mansion, The)
Black Magic Terror, *814*
Black Magic Woman, *955*
Black Marble, The, *463*
Black Market Rustlers, *1099*
Black Moon Rising, *14*
Black Narcissus, *463*
Black Orchid, The, *463*
◆ Black Orpheus, *718*
Black Panther, The, *463*
Black Pirate, The, *14*
Black Planet, The, *151*
◆ Black Rain (1988), *718*
◆ Black Rain (1989), *14*
Black Rainbow, *955*
Black Raven, The, *955*
◆ Black Robe, *463*
Black Room, The (1935), *814*
Black Room, The (1985), *814*
Black Roses, *814*
Black Sabbath, *814*
Black Sister's Revenge, *463*
◆ Black Stallion, The, *151*
◆ Black Stallion Returns, The, *151*
◆ Black Sunday (1961), *814*
Black Sunday (1977), *955*
Black Tights, *909*
Black Veil for Lisa, A, *14*
Black Venus, *718*
◆ Black Widow, *955*
Black Windmill, The, *956*
Blackbeard the Pirate, *14*
Blackbeard's Ghost, *151*
Blackbelt, *14*
Blackbelt 2: Fatal Force, *14*
◆ Blackboard Jungle, The, *463*
Blackenstein, *814*
Blackmail (1929), *956*
Blackmail (1991), *956*
Blackout (1978), *14*
Blackout (1985), *956*
Blackout (1990), *956*
Blacksmith, The/Cops, *240*
Blacula, *814*
Blade, *14*
Blade Master, The, *15*
Blade Rider, *1099*
◆ Blade Runner, *1039*
Blades, *814*
Blades of Courage, *463*
Blake of Scotland Yard, *15*
Blake's 7 (TV Series), *1040*
Blame It on Rio, *240*
◆ Blame It on the Bellboy, *240*
Blame It on the Night, *463*
Blank Check, *151*
◆ **Blast 'Em,** *419*
Blastfighter, *15*
Blaze, *463*
Blaze Starr: The Original, *241*
Blazing Saddles, *241*
◆ Bleak House, *463*
Bless the Beasts and Children, *463*
◆ Blessed Event, *241*
Blind Date (1984), *463*
Blind Date (1987), *241*
Blind Fury, *15*
Blind Husbands, *464*
Blind Rage, *15*
Blind Side, *956*
◆ **Blind Spot,** *464*
◆ Blind Trust (Pouvoir Intime), *719*
Blind Vengeance, *15*
Blind Vision, *956*

Blindfold: Acts of Obsession, 956
Blindman's Bluff, 956
Blindside, 15
Blindsided, 956
◆ **Blink,** 956
Blink of an Eye, 15
◆ Bliss, 241
Bliss of Mrs. Blossom, The, 241
Blob, The (1958), 814
◆ Blob, The (1988), 814
◆ Block-Heads, 241
Blockhouse, The, 464
Blond Gorilla (see White Pongo)
Blonde Crazy, 241
Blonde Ice, 464
Blonde Venus, 464
Blondie, 241
Blondie Has Trouble, 241
Blondie Hits the Jackpot, 241
Blondie in Society, 241
Blondie Knows Best, 241
Blondie Takes a Vacation, 242
Blondie's Blessed Event, 242
Blood Alley, 15
Blood and Black Lace, 814
Blood and Concrete, A Love Story, 956
Blood and Guns, 15
Blood and Roses, 814
Blood and Sand (1922), 464
Blood and Sand (1941), 464
Blood Beach, 814
Blood Beast Terror, The, 815
Blood Castle (1970), 815
Blood Castle (1972), 815
Blood Diner, 815
Blood Feast, 815
Blood Feud, 719
Blood Freak, 815
Blood Frenzy, 815
Blood Games, 956
Blood Hook, 815
Blood In, Blood Out (see Bound by Honor)
Blood in the Streets, 15
Blood Link, 815
Blood Mania, 815
Blood Money (1933), 464
Blood Money (1987) (see Clinton and Nadine)
Blood Moon, 815
Blood of a Poet, 719
Blood of Dracula, 815
Blood of Dracula's Castle, 815
Blood of Fu Manchu (see Against All Odds)
Blood of Heroes, 15
Blood of Others, The, 464
Blood of the Vampire, 815
Blood on Satan's Claw, 815
Blood on the Badge, 15
Blood on the Moon, 1099
Blood on the Sun, 15
Blood Orgy of the She Devils, 815
Blood Rage, 815
Blood Red, 464
Blood Relations, 816
Blood Relatives, 957
Blood Rose, 816
Blood Salvage, 816
Blood Screams, 816
◆ Blood Simple, 957
Blood Sisters, 816
Blood Spattered Bride, The, 816
Blood Spell, 816
Blood Suckers from Outer Space, 816
Blood Ties (1987), 464
Blood Ties (1993), 816
Blood Vows: The Story of a Mafia Wife, 464
Blood Wedding, 719
Bloodbath at the House of Death, 242
Bloodbeat, 816
Bloodbrothers, 464
Bloodfist, 15
Bloodfist 2, 16
Bloodfist III: Forced to Fight, 16
Bloodfist IV—Die Trying, 16
Bloodfist V: Human Target, 16
Bloodhounds of Broadway, 242
Bloodline, 464
Bloodlust: Subspecies III, 816
Bloodmatch, 16
Bloodmoon, 816
Bloodsport, 16
Bloodstone, 16
Bloodstone: Subspecies II, 816
Bloodsuckers, The, 816
Bloodsucking Freaks (The Incredible Torture Show), 816
Bloodsucking Pharaohs in Pittsburgh, 816
Bloodthirsty Butchers, 816
Bloodtide, 817
Bloody Birthday, 817
Bloody Mama, 16
Bloody Moon, 817
Bloody New Year, 817
Bloody Pit of Horror, 817
Bloody Trail, 1099
Bloody Wednesday, 817
Bloopers from Star Trek and Laugh-In, 242
◆ Blow Out, 957
◆ Blow-Up, 957
Blowing Wild, 16
Blown Away (1992), 957
Blown Away (1994), 16
Blue (1968), 1099
Blue (1993), 719
Blue and the Gray, The, 1099
◆ Blue Angel, The, 719
Blue Bird, The, 151
Blue Canadian Rockies, 1099
Blue Chips, 465
Blue City, 957
◆ Blue Collar, 465
Blue Country, 719
Blue De Ville, 242
Blue Desert, 957
Blue Fin, 151
Blue Fire Lady, 151
Blue Hawaii, 909
Blue Heaven, 465
Blue Hotel, 465
Blue Hour, The, 719
Blue Ice, 957
Blue Iguana, 242
Blue Jeans, 719
Blue Knight, The (1973), 465
Blue Knight, The (1975), 465
Blue Lagoon, The, 465
Blue Lighting, The, 16
Blue Max, The, 16
Blue Money, 242
Blue Monkey, 817
Blue Montana Skies, 1099
Blue Movies, 242
Blue Skies Again, 465
Blue Steel (1934), 1099
Blue Steel (1990), 16
Blue Sunshine, 957
◆ Blue Thunder, 16
Blue Tornado, 16
◆ Blue Velvet, 817
Blue Yonder, The, 151
Bluebeard (1944), 817
Bluebeard (1963), 719
Bluebeard (1972), 817
Blueberry Hill, 465
Blues Brothers, The, 242
Blues Busters, 242
◆ Blume in Love, 465
BMX Bandits, 17
Boarding School, 243
Boat Is Full, The, 719
Boatniks, The, 151
◆ Bob & Carol & Ted & Alice, 243
Bob & Ray, Jane, Laraine & Gilda, 243
◆ Bob le Flambeur, 719
◆ Bob Roberts, 243
Bob the Quail, 151
Bobbie Jo and the Outlaw, 17
Bobby Deerfield, 465
Bobo, The, 243
◆ Boccaccio 70, 719
Bodies, Rest & Motion, 465
Bodily Harm, 957
◆ Body and Soul (1947), 466
Body and Soul (1981), 466
Body Bags (see John Carpenter's Body Bags)
Body Chemistry, 957
Body Chemistry 2: Voice of a Stranger, 957
Body Chemistry 3: Point of Seduction, 957
Body Count, 817
Body Double, 958
◆ Body Heat, 958
Body in the Library, The, 958
Body Language, 958
Body Melt, 817
Body Moves, 466
Body of Evidence, 958
Body of Influence, 958
Body Parts, 817
Body Puzzle, 958
Body Rock, 909
Body Shot, 958
Body Slam, 17
◆ Body Snatcher, The, 817
Body Snatchers, The (1993), 1040
Bodyguard, The, 466
Bodywaves, 243
Boeing, Boeing, 243
Bog, 818
Boggy Creek II, 818
Bogie, 466
Bohemian Girl, The, 243
Boiling Point, 17
Bold Caballero, The, 1099
Boldest Job in the West, The, 1099
Bolero (1982), 720
Bolero (1984), 466
Bombardier, 17
Bombay Talkie, 720
◆ Bombshell, 243
Bon Voyage!, 151
Bon Voyage, Charlie Brown, 152
Bonanza (TV Series), 1100
Bonanza: The Return, 1100
Boneyard, The, 818
Bonfire of the Vanities, 466

ngo, *152*
njour Tristesse, *466*
nnie and Clyde, *17*
nnie Scotland, *243*
nnie's Kids, *17*
ob Tube, The, *243*
ogeyman, The, *818*
ogeyman 2, The, *818*
ok of Love, *243*
om in the Moon, *243*
om Town, *466*
omerang, *244*
ost, The, *466*
ot Hill, *1100*
othill Bandits, *1100*
ots and Saddles, *1100*
ots Malone, *1100*
rder, The, *17*
rder Feud, *1100*
rder Heat, *17*
rder Patrol, *1100*
rder Phantom, *1100*
rder Radio, *466*
rder Roundup, *1100*
rder Shootout, *1100*
rder Street, *720*
rderland, *1100*
rderline, *17*
ris and Natasha, *244*
rn Again, *466*
rn American, *17*
rn Free, *152*
rn in East L.A., *244*
rn Innocent, *466*
rn Killer, *17*
rn Losers, *17*
rn of Fire, *467*
rn on the Fourth of July, *467*
rn to Be Bad, *467*
rn to Dance, *909*
rn to Kill, *958*
rn to Race, *17*
rn to Ride, *17*
rn To Run, *18*
rn to the West (see Hell Town)
rn to Win, *467*
rn Yesterday (1950), *244*
rn Yesterday (1993), *244*
rneo, *419*
rrowed Trouble, *1100*
rrower, The, *1040*
rrowers, The, *152*
rsalino, *18*
ss, *1101*
ss' Son, The, *467*
ss' Wife, The, *244*
ston Strangler, The, *818*
stonians, The, *467*
tany Bay, *18*
udu Saved from Drowning, *720*
ulevard Nights, *467*
ulevard of Broken Dreams, *467*
und and Gagged: A Love Story, *18*
und by Honor, *467*
und for Glory, *467*
unty, The, *18*
unty Hunter, *18*
unty Man, The, *1101*
unty Tracker, *18*
urne Identity, The, *958*
wery at Midnight, *818*
wery Boys, The (Series), *244*
xcar Bertha, *18*
xing Helena, *818*
xoffice, *467*

◆ Boy and His Dog, A, *1040*
Boy, Did I Get a Wrong Number!, *244*
Boy Friend, The, *909*
Boy God, The, *152*
Boy in Blue, The, *467*
Boy in the Plastic Bubble, The, *468*
Boy Meets Girl, *244*
◆ Boy Named Charlie Brown, A, *152*
Boy Takes Girl, *152*
◆ Boy Who Could Fly, The, *468*
Boy Who Left Home to Find Out About the Shivers, The, *152*
Boy With Green Hair, The, *468*
◆ Boyfriends and Girlfriends, *720*
Boys from Brazil, The, *958*
Boys from Brooklyn, The, *818*
Boys in Company C, The, *18*
Boys in the Band, The, *468*
Boys Next Door, The, *468*
Boys' Night Out, *244*
Boys of the City, *18*
◆ Boys' Town, *468*
◆ Boyz N the Hood, *468*
Braddock: Missing in Action III, *18*
Brady's Escape, *18*
Brain, The (1965), *1040*
Brain, The (1988), *818*
Brain Damage, *818*
Brain Dead, *1040*
Brain Donors, *245*
Brain Eaters, The, *1040*
Brain from Planet Arous, The, *1040*
Brain of Blood, *818*
Brain Smasher...A Love Story, *18*
Brain That Wouldn't Die, The, *1040*
Brainiac, The, *818*
Brainscan, *818*
Brainstorm, *1040*
Brainwashed, *958*
Brainwaves, *818*
Bram Stoker's Dracula, *819*
Bramble Bush, The, *468*
Branded, *1101*
Branded a Coward, *1101*
Brannigan, *18*
Brass, *468*
Brass Monkey, The, *958*
Brass Target, *19*
Bravados, The, *1101*
◆ Brave Little Toaster, The, *152*
◆ Brave One, The, *152*
◆ Brazil, *245*
Break of Dawn, *468*
Break of Hearts, *468*
Breaker! Breaker!, *19*
◆ Breaker Morant, *19*
◆ Breakfast at Tiffany's, *468*
◆ Breakfast Club, The, *245*
Breakfast in Hollywood, *245*
Breakheart Pass, *1101*
Breakin', *909*
Breakin' 2 Electric Boogaloo, *909*
Breaking All the Rules, *245*
◆ Breaking Away, *245*
Breaking Glass, *909*
Breaking Home Ties, *469*
◆ Breaking In, *245*
Breaking Point, *469*
Breaking the Ice, *909*
Breaking the Rules, *469*
Breaking Up Is Hard to Do, *469*
Breakout, *19*
Breakthrough, *19*
Breath of Scandal, A, *245*
Breathing Fire, *19*

◆ **Breathing Lessons,** *469*
◆ Breathless (1959), *720*
Breathless (1983), *469*
Breed Apart, A, *19*
Brenda Starr, *19*
Brer Rabbit and the Wonderful Tar Baby, *152*
Brewster McCloud, *245*
Brewster's Millions (1945), *245*
Brewster's Millions (1985), *245*
◆ Brian's Song, *469*
Bride, The, *819*
Bride and the Beast, The, *19*
Bride Came C.O.D., The, *245*
◆ Bride of Frankenstein, *819*
Bride of Re-Animator, *819*
Bride of the Gorilla, *819*
Bride of the Monster, *819*
Bride Walks Out, The, *245*
◆ Bride Wore Black, The, *959*
Bride Wore Red, The, *469*
Brides of Blood (see Brides of the Beast)
Brides of Dracula, *819*
Brides of the Beast, *819*
◆ Brideshead Revisited, *469*
Bridge at Remagen, The, *469*
Bridge of San Luis Rey, The, *469*
◆ Bridge on the River Kwai, The, *19*
Bridge to Hell, *19*
Bridge to Nowhere, *469*
Bridge to Silence, *470*
Bridge Too Far, A, *19*
◆ Bridges at Toko-Ri, The, *19*
◆ Brief Encounter (1945), *470*
Brief Encounter (1974), *470*
◆ Brief History of Time, A, *419*
Brig, The, *470*
◆ Brigadoon, *909*
Bright Angel, *470*
Bright Eyes, *152*
Bright Lights, Big City, *470*
Brighton Beach Memoirs, *246*
Brighton Strangler, The, *819*
Brighty of the Grand Canyon, *152*
◆ Brimstone, *1101*
Brimstone and Treacle, *819*
Bring Me the Head of Alfredo Garcia, *20*
Bring on the Night, *419*
◆ Bringing Up Baby, *246*
Brink of Life, *720*
Brinks Job, The, *246*
Britannia Hospital, *246*
◆ Broadcast News, *246*
Broadway Bill, *470*
◆ Broadway Danny Rose, *246*
Broadway Melody, The, *910*
Broadway Melody of 1936, *910*
Broadway Melody of 1938, *910*
Broadway Melody of 1940, *910*
Broadway Rhythm, *910*
Broadway Serenade, *910*
Broadway to Cheyenne, *1101*
Broken Angel, *470*
Broken Arrow, *1101*
Broken Blossoms, *470*
Broken Chain, The, *20*
◆ Broken Lance, *1101*
Broken Noses, *419*
Broken Strings, *470*
Broken Trust, *959*
Bronco (TV Series), *1101*
Bronco Billy, *246*

Bronco Busters (see Gone With the West)
Bronx Executioner, The, *1040*
◆ **Bronx Tale, A,** *470*
Bronx War, The, *20*
Brood, The, *819*
◆ Brother from Another Planet, The, *1040*
Brother John, *470*
Brother Orchid, *20*
◆ Brother Sun, Sister Moon, *470*
Brotherhood, The, *471*
Brotherhood of Death, *20*
Brotherhood of Justice, *471*
Brotherhood of Satan, *819*
Brotherhood of the Rose, *20*
Brotherly Love, *819*
Brothers in Arms, *819*
◆ Brothers In Law, *246*
Brothers in the Saddle, *1101*
Brothers Karamazov, The, *471*
◆ Brother's Keeper, *419*
Brothers Lionheart, The, *152*
Brothers of the West, *1101*
Brothers of the Wilderness, *471*
◆ Browning Version, The, *471*
Brubaker, *471*
Bruce Conners Films 1, *246*
Bruce Lee: Curse of the Dragon, *420*
Brute, The (see El Bruto)
Brute Man, The, *820*
Brutes and Savages, *420*
Bubblegum Crash, Vols. 1–3, *720*
Bubblegum Crisis—Vols. 1–8, *720*
Buccaneer, The, *20*
Buck and the Preacher, *1102*
Buck Benny Rides Again, *246*
Buck Privates, *246*
Buck Privates Come Home, *246*
Buck Rogers: Destination Saturn (a.k.a. Planet Outlaws), *1040*
Buck Rogers in the 25th Century, *1040*
Bucket of Blood, A, *820*
Buckeye and Blue, *1102*
Buckskin, *1102*
Buckskin Frontier, *1102*
Bucktown, *20*
Bud and Lou, *471*
Bud the C.H.U.D. (see C.H.U.D. II)
Buddy, Buddy, *247*
◆ Buddy Holly Story, The, *910*
Buddy System, The, *471*
Buddy's Song, *471*
Buffalo Bill, *1102*
Buffalo Bill and the Indians, *1102*
Buffalo Jump, *471*
Buffalo Stampede, *1102*
◆ Buffet Froid (Cold Cuts), *720*
Buffy, The Vampire Slayer, *247*
Buford's Beach Bunnies, *247*
Bug, *820*
Bugles in the Afternoon, *1102*
◆ Bugs and Daffy: The Wartime Cartoons, *152*
Bugs and Daffy's Carnival of the Animals, *153*
Bugs Bunny: All American Hero, *153*
◆ Bugs Bunny and Elmer Fudd Cartoon Festival Featuring "Wabbit Twouble", *153*
Bugs Bunny Cartoon Festival Featuring "Hold the Lion Please", *153*
◆ Bugs Bunny Classics, *153*
Bugs Bunny in King Arthur's Court, *153*
Bugs Bunny Mother's Day Special, The, *153*
Bugs Bunny Mystery Special, The, *153*
◆ Bugs Bunny/Road Runner Movie, The, *153*
◆ Bugs Bunny, Superstar, *153*
Bugs Bunny: Truth or Hare, *153*
◆ Bugs Bunny's Bustin' Out All Over, *154*
Bugs Bunny's Cupid Capers, *154*
◆ **Bugs Bunny's Easter Funnies,** *154*
Bugs Bunny's Hare-Raising Tales, *154*
Bugs Bunny's Howl-Oween Special, *154*
Bugs Bunny's Looney Christmas Tales, *154*
◆ **Bugs Bunny's Lunar Tunes,** *154*
Bugs Bunny's Mad World of Television, *154*
◆ Bugs Bunny's Wacky Adventures, *154*
Bugs Bunny's Wild World of Sports, *154*
Bugs vs. Daffy: Battle of the Music Video Stars, *154*
Bugs vs. Elmer, *155*
◆ Bugsy, *471*
Bugsy Malone, *155*
◆ Bull Durham, *247*
Bulldog Courage, *1102*
Bulldog Drummond, *20*
Bulldog Drummond Comes Back, *20*
Bulldog Drummond Escapes, *20*
Bulldog Drummond in Africa, *20*
Bulldog Drummond's Bride, *20*
Bulldog Drummond's Peril, *20*
Bulldog Drummond's Revenge, *21*
Bulldog Drummond's Secret Police, *21*
Bullet for Sandoval, A, *1102*
Bullet for the General, A, *1102*
Bullet from God, A, *1102*
Bulletproof, *21*
Bullets or Ballots, *21*
◆ Bullfighter and the Lady, The, *21*
Bullfighters, The, *247*
Bullies, *820*
◆ Bullitt, *21*
Bullseye, *247*
Bullshot, *247*
Bullshot Crummond (see Bullshot)
Bullwhip, *1102*
Bunco, *21*
Bundle of Joy, *247*
Bunny's Tale, A, *472*
Buono Sera, Mrs. Campbell, *247*
'Burbs, The, *247*
◆ Burden of Dreams, *420*
Bureau of Missing Persons, *959*
Burglar (1987), *247*
Burglar (1987), *721*
Burial Ground, *820*
Buried Alive (1984), *820*
◆ Buried Alive (1990), *959*
Burke and Wills, *472*
Burlesque of Carmen, *247*
◆ Burmese Harp, The, *721*
◆ Burn!, *472*
Burn Up!, *721*
Burndown, *959*
Burning, The, *820*
◆ Burning Bed, The, *472*
Burning Court, The, *721*
Burning Secret, *472*
Burnt Offerings, *820*
Bus Is Coming, The, *472*
◆ Bus Stop, *248*
Bushido Blade, *21*
Bushwhackers, *1102*
Business As Usual, *472*
Busted Up, *472*
Buster, *472*
Buster and Billie, *472*
◆ Buster Keaton: A Hard Act to Follow, *420*
Buster Keaton Festival: Vol. 1, *248*
Buster Keaton Festival: Vol. 2, *248*
Buster Keaton Festival: Vol. 3, *248*
Buster Keaton Rides Again, *420*
◆ Buster Keaton Scrapbook, Vol. I, *248*
Buster Keaton: The Golden Years, *24*
Buster Keaton: The Great Stone Face, *248*
Bustin' Loose, *248*
But Not For Me, *472*
Butch and Sundance: The Early Days, *1103*
◆ Butch Cassidy and the Sundance Kid, *1103*
Butcher's Wife, The, *248*
Butterfield 8, *472*
◆ Butterflies Are Free, *473*
Butterfly, *473*
Buy and Cell, *248*
Buying Time, *21*
By Dawn's Early Light, *473*
By Design, *473*
By Rocket to the Moon (see Woman in the Moon)
By The Blood Of Others, *721*
◆ By the Law, *721*
By the Light of the Silvery Moon, *91*
Bye Bye, Baby, *473*
Bye Bye Birdie, *910*
Bye Bye Brazil, *721*
C.C. & Company, *21*
C.H.O.M.P.S., *155*
C.H.U.D., *820*
C.H.U.D. II (Bud the C.H.U.D.), *820*
◆ Cabaret, *910*
◆ Cabeza de Vaca, *721*
Cabin Boy, *248*
Cabin in the Cotton, *473*
Cabin in the Sky, *473*
Cabinet of Doctor Caligari, The, *721*
Cabiria, *721*
Cabo Blanco, *21*
Cactus, *473*
Cactus Flower, *248*
◆ Caddie, *473*
Caddy, The, *249*
Caddyshack, *249*
Caddyshack II, *249*
Cadence, *473*
◆ Cadillac Man, *249*
Caesar and Cleopatra, *473*
Cafe Express, *721*
Cafe Romeo, *249*
Cage, *21*
Caged Fear, *21*
Caged Fury, *21*
Caged Heart, The (L'Addition), *721*
Caged Heat, *22*
Caged Women, *22*
Cahill—US Marshal, *1103*

ne Mutiny, The, *473*
ne Mutiny Court Martial, The, *473*
ro, *910*
, *474*
amity Jane (1953), *910*
amity Jane (1984), *1103*
endar Girl, *249*
ifornia Casanova, *249*
ifornia Dreaming, *474*
ifornia Frontier, *1103*
ifornia Gold Rush, *1103*
ifornia Reich, *420*
ifornia Suite, *249*
igula, *474*
l It Murder (see Midnight (1934))
l Me, *959*
l Me Bwana, *249*
l Northside 777, *959*
l of the Canyon, *1103*
l of the Coyote, *1103*
l of the Wild (1972), *22*
l of the Wild (1992), *474*
l Out the Marines, *249*
l to Glory, *474*
ler, The, *1041*
lle and Son, *474*
ling Wild Bill Elliott, *1103*
me a Hot Friday, *22*
melot, *911*
meraman, The, *249*
meraman's Revenge and Other Fantastic Tales, the: the Amazing Puppet Animation of Ladislaw Starewicz, *155*
meron's Closet, *820*
mila, *721*
mille, *474*
mille Claudel, *721*
morra, *722*
mouflage, *722*
mpus Corpse, The, *820*
mpus Man, *249*
n-Can, *911*
n I Do It 'Til I Need Glasses?, *249*
n It Be Love, *249*
n She Bake a Cherry Pie?, *250*
n You Hear the Laughter? The Story of Freddie Prinze, *474*
ncel My Reservation, *250*
ndidate, The, *474*
ndide, *722*
ndles at Nine, *820*
ndleshoe, *155*
ndy Mountain, *474*
ndyman (1992), *820*
ndyman, The (1968), *474*
nine Commando, *155*
nnery Row, *250*
nnibal, *820*
nnibal Attack, *22*
nnibal Campout, *820*
nnibal Holocaust, *821*
nnibal Island, *420*
nnibal Women in the Avocado Jungle of Death, *22*
nnon Movie Tales: Red Riding Hood, *155*
nnon Movie Tales: Sleeping Beauty, *155*
nnon Movie Tales: Snow White, *155*
nnon Movie Tales: The Emperor's New Clothes, *155*
nnonball, *22*

Cannonball Run, *250*
Cannonball Run II, *250*
Can't Buy Me Love, *250*
◆ Can't Help Singing, *911*
Can't Stop the Music, *911*
Canterbury Tales, The, *722*
Canterville Ghost, The (1944), *155*
Canterville Ghost, The (1986), *155*
Canvas, *959*
◆ Cape Fear (1962), *959*
Cape Fear (1991), *959*
Caper of the Golden Bulls, The, *22*
Capone, *22*
◆ Capricorn One, *1041*
Captain America (1944), *22*
Captain America (1979), *22*
Captain America (1990), *22*
Captain America II: Death Too Soon, *22*
Captain Apache, *1103*
◆ Captain Blood, *22*
Captain Caution, *23*
Captain Gallant—Foreign Legion, *23*
◆ Captain Horatio Hornblower, *23*
Captain January, *155*
Captain Kidd, *23*
Captain Kronos: Vampire Hunter, *821*
Captain Midnight—Vols. 1–2, *155*
Captain Newman, M.D., *474*
Captain Ron, *250*
Captain Scarlet vs. the Mysterons, *156*
Captain Scarlett, *23*
Captain Sinbad, *156*
◆ Captains Courageous, *474*
Captains of the Clouds, *23*
◆ Captain's Paradise, The, *250*
Captain's Table, *250*
Captive, *475*
◆ Captive Heart, *475*
Captive Hearts, *475*
Captive Planet, *1041*
Captive Rage, *23*
Capture of Grizzly Adams, The, *156*
Car 54, Where Are You?, *250*
Car 54 Where Are You? (TV Series), *250*
Car Wash, *250*
◆ Caravaggio, *475*
Caravan to Vaccares, *23*
◆ Caravan Trail, *1103*
Caravans, *475*
Carbon Copy, *251*
Cardiac Arrest, *959*
Cardinal, The, *475*
Care Bears Movie, The, *156*
◆ Career, *475*
Career Opportunities, *251*
Carefree, *911*
◆ Careful He Might Hear You, *475*
Caribe, *23*
◆ Cariboo Trail, *1103*
Carlin at Carnegie, *251*
Carlin on Campus, *251*
◆ **Carlito's Way**, *23*
Carlton-Browne of the F.O., *251*
Carmen (see Bizet's Carmen)
◆ **Carmen Jones**, *911*
◆ Carmilla, *821*
Carnage (see Twitch of the Death Nerve)
Carnal Crimes, *959*
◆ Carnal Knowledge, *475*
◆ Carnival in Flanders, *722*
Carnival of Blood, *821*

Carnival of Souls, *821*
Carnival Rock, *911*
Carnival Story, *475*
Carnosaur, *821*
◆ Carny, *475*
Carol Burnett's My Personal Best, *251*
Carolina Skeletons, *475*
◆ Caroline?, *959*
◆ **Caroline at Midnight**, *960*
◆ Carousel, *911*
Carpathian Eagle, *821*
Carpenter, The, *821*
Carpet of Horror, *960*
Carpetbaggers, The, *475*
◆ Carrie (1952), *476*
◆ Carrie (1976), *821*
Carrier, *821*
Carrington, V. C., *476*
Carry on Admiral, *251*
Carry on at Your Convenience, *251*
Carry on Behind, *251*
Carry on Cleo, *251*
Carry on Cowboy, *251*
Carry on Cruising, *251*
Carry on Doctor, *251*
Carry on Emmanuelle, *251*
Carry on Nurse, *251*
Cars That Ate Paris (see Cars That Eat People)
Cars That Eat People (The Cars That Ate Paris), *821*
◆ Carson City Cyclone, *1103*
◆ Carson City Kid, *1103*
Cartel, *23*
Cartier Affair, The, *252*
Cartoon Moviestars: Bugs!, *156*
◆ Cartoon Moviestars: Daffy!, *156*
◆ Cartoon Moviestars: Elmer!, *156*
Cartoon Moviestars: Porky!, *156*
◆ Cartoon Moviestars: Starring Bugs Bunny, *156*
Cartoons for Big Kids, *156*
◆ Cartouche, *722*
◆ Casablanca, *476*
Casanova (1976), *722*
Casanova (1987), *252*
Casanova Brown, *252*
Casanova's Big Night, *252*
Case for Murder, A, *960*
◆ Case of Deadly Force, A, *476*
◆ Case of Libel, A, *476*
◆ Case of the Lucky Legs, The, *960*
Case of the Mukkinese Battle Horn, The, *252*
Casebook of Sherlock Holmes (see Adventures of Sherlock Homes, The (series))
Casey at the Bat, *156*
Casey's Shadow, *157*
Cash McCall, *252*
Casino, *476*
◆ Casino Royale (1954), *23*
Casino Royale (1967), *252*
Casper's First Christmas, *157*
Cass Timberlane, *476*
Cassandra, *821*
Cassandra Crossing, The, *476*
Cast a Deadly Spell, *1041*
Cast a Giant Shadow, *23*
Cast the First Stone, *476*
Castaway, *476*
Castaway Cowboy, The, *157*
Castle, The, *476*
Castle in the Desert, *960*

Castle of Blood, 821
◆ Castle of Cagliostro, The, 24
Castle of Evil, 821
Castle of Fu Manchu, 822
Castle of Terror (see Castle of Blood)
Castle of the Creeping Flesh, 822
Castle of the Living Dead, 822
Castle of the Walking Dead (see Torture Chamber of Dr. Sadism)
Casual Sex?, 252
Casualties of Love: The Long Island Lolita Story, 476
◆ Casualties of War, 477
Cat, The, 157
Cat, The (Le Chat), 722
◆ Cat and Mouse, 722
Cat and the Canary, The (1927), 960
Cat and the Canary, The (1978), 960
◆ Cat and the Fiddle, The, 911
Cat Ballou, 1103
Cat Chaser, 24
Cat from Outer Space, The, 157
Cat Girl, 960
Cat O'Nine Tails, 960
◆ Cat on a Hot Tin Roof (1958), 477
Cat on a Hot Tin Roof (1985), 477
◆ Cat People (1942), 822
Cat People (1982), 822
Cat Women of the Moon, 1041
Catamount Killing, The, 960
Catch As Catch Can, 252
Catch Me a Spy, 960
Catch Me If You Can, 24
Catch the Heat, 24
Catch-22, 252
Catered Affair, The, 477
Catherine & Co., 722
Catherine the Great, 477
◆ Catholics, 477
Cathy's Curse, 822
Catlow, 1104
Cat's Eye, 822
◆ **Cat's Play,** 722
Cattle Queen of Montana, 1104
Caught, 477
Caught in the Act, 960
Caught in the Draft, 252
Cauldron of Blood, 822
Cause of Death, 24
Caution: Funny Men at Work, 420
◆ Cavalcade, 477
Cave Girl, 1041
Cave of the Living Dead, 822
Caveman, 252
CB4, 252
Cease Fire, 477
◆ **Ceiling Zero,** 24
◆ Celebrating Bird: The Triumph of Charlie Parker, 420
Celebrity, 477
Celeste, 722
Celia, Child of Terror, 477
Cellar, The, 822
Cellar Dweller, 822
Cement Garden, The, 478
Cemetery Club, The, 478
Center of the Web, 960
Centerfold Girls, 478
Certain Fury, 24
Certain Sacrifice, A, 478
◆ César, 723
César and Rosalie, 723
Chain Lightning, 478
Chain of Desire, 478
Chain Reaction, 24
Chained, 478
Chained for Life, 478
Chained Heat, 24
Chains, 24
Chains of Gold, 478
Chair, The, 822
Chalk Garden, The, 478
Challenge, The, 24
Challenge of a Lifetime, 478
Challenge of McKenna (see Badlands Drifter)
Challenge to Be Free, 157
Challenge to Lassie, 157
Challenge to White Fang, 24
Chamber of Fear, 822
Chamber of Horrors, 822
◆ Chameleon Street, 478
◆ Champ, The (1931), 478
Champ, The (1979), 479
Champagne, 479
◆ Champagne for Caesar, 252
◆ Champion, 479
◆ Champions, 479
◆ Chan Is Missing, 253
Chances Are, 253
Chandu the Magician, 24
Chanel Solitaire, 479
◆ Chang, 24
Change of Habit, 479
Change of Seasons, A, 253
◆ Changeling, The, 822
Chantilly Lace, 479
Chapayev, 723
Chaplin, 479
◆ Chaplin Revue, The, 253
Chapter Two, 479
◆ Charade, 960
◆ Charge of the Light Brigade, The (1936), 24
Charge of the Light Brigade, The (1968), 24
◆ Chariots of Fire, 479
Chariots of the Gods, 420
Charles Bukowski Tapes, 420
Charley and the Angel, 157
◆ Charley Varrick, 25
Charlie Boy, 823
Charlie Brown and Snoopy Show, The (Volume I), 157
◆ Charlie Brown and Snoopy Show, The (Volume II), 157
◆ Charlie Brown Celebration, A, 157
◆ Charlie Brown Christmas, A, 157
◆ Charlie Brown Thanksgiving, A, 157
◆ Charlie Brown's All-Stars, 157
Charlie Chan and the Curse of the Dragon Queen, 253
Charlie Chan at the Opera, 961
Charlie Chan at the Wax Museum, 961
Charlie Chan in Paris, 961
Charlie Chan in Rio, 961
Charlie Chan in the Secret Service, 961
Charlie Chan's Secret, 961
Charlie Chaplin Carnival, 253
Charlie Chaplin Cavalcade, 253
Charlie Chaplin Festival, 253
Charlie Chaplin…Our Hero, 253
◆ Charlie Chaplin—The Early Years, Vol. 1, 253
◆ Charlie Chaplin—The Early Years, Vol. 2, 253
◆ Charlie Chaplin—The Early Years, Vol. 3, 254
◆ Charlie Chaplin—The Early Years, Vol. 4, 254
Charlie, the Lonesome Cougar, 158
Charlotte's Web, 158
◆ Charly, 1041
Charro!, 1104
Chase, The (1946), 479
Chase, The (1966), 479
Chase, The (1994), 25
Chasers, 254
Chasing Dreams, 480
Chato's Land, 1104
◆ Chattahoochee, 480
Chattanooga Choo Choo, 254
Cheap Detective, The, 254
Cheap Shots, 254
Cheaper to Keep Her, 254
◆ Cheat, The, 961
Cheaters, The, 723
◆ **Cheatin' Hearts,** 480
Check and Double Check, 254
Check Is in the Mail, The, 254
Checkered Flag, 480
Checking Out, 254
Cheech and Chong's Next Movie, 25
Cheerleader Camp, 823
Cheerleaders, 254
Cheers for Miss Bishop, 480
Cheetah, 158
Chernobyl: The Final Warning, 480
Cherokee Flash, 1104
Cherokee Strip, 1104
Cherry, Harry and Raquel, 480
Cherry 2000, 1041
Chesty Anderson, U.S. Navy (a.k.a. Anderson's Angels), 25
◆ Cheyenne (TV Series), 1104
Cheyenne Autumn, 1104
Cheyenne Social Club, The, 1104
Cheyenne Takes Over, 1104
Chicago Joe and the Showgirl, 480
Chicken Chronicles, The, 254
Chicken Ranch, 420
◆ Chiefs, 961
◆ Chikamatsu Monogatari, 723
Child Bride of Short Creek, 480
Child in the Night, 961
Child Is Waiting, A, 480
Child of Darkness, Child of Light, 82
Child of Glass, 158
Children, The, 823
◆ Children of a Lesser God, 480
◆ Children of An Lac, The, 480
◆ Children of Nature, 723
◆ Children of Paradise, The, 723
Children of Rage, 481
Children of Sanchez, The, 481
Children of the Corn, 823
Children of the Corn II: The Final Sacrifice, 823
Children of the Damned, 823
Children of the Full Moon, 823
Children of the Night, 823
Children of Theatre Street, The, 42
Children of Times Square, The, 481
Children Shouldn't Play with Dead Things, 823
Children's Hour, The, 481
◆ Children's Songs and Stories with the Muppets, 158
Child's Christmas in Wales, A, 158
Child's Play, 823
Child's Play 2, 823
Child's Play 3, 823
Chiller, 823

illing, The, *823*
illy Scenes of Winter, *481*
imes at Midnight, *481*
ina Beach (TV Series), *481*
ina Cry, *481*
ina Gate, *481*
ina Girl, *25*
ina Is Near, *723*
ina Lake Murders, The, *961*
ina Moon, *961*
ina, My Sorrow, *723*
ina 9, Liberty 7 (see Gunfire)
ina O'Brien, *25*
ina O'Brien 2, *25*
ina Seas, *25*
ina Sky, *25*
ina Syndrome, The, *961*
ina White, *25*
inatown, *962*
inatown Murders, The: Man Against the Mob, *25*
incero (see Last Movie, The)
inese Boxes, *962*
inese Cat, The, *962*
inese Connection, The, *25*
inese Ghost Story, A, *723*
inese Roulette, *723*
inese Web, The, *25*
ino, *1104*
ip 'n' Dale and Donald Duck, *158*
ip 'n' Dale: Rescue Rangers, *158*
ipmunk Adventure, The, *158*
ips, the War Dog, *158*
isholms, The, *1104*
isum, *1104*
itty Chitty Bang Bang, *158*
loe in the Afternoon, *723*
ocolat, *723*
ocolate Soldier, The, *911*
ocolate War, The, *481*
oice, The, *481*
oice of Arms, A, *724*
oirboys, The, *481*
oke Canyon, *25*
oose Me, *962*
opper Chicks in Zombietown, *823*
opping Mall, *824*
orus Line, A, *911*
orus of Disapproval, A, *254*
osen, The, *481*
rist Stopped at Eboli, *724*
ristian the Lion, *158*
ristiane F., *724*
ristina, *25*
ristine, *824*
ristmas Carol, A (1938), *158*
ristmas Carol, A (1951), *159*
ristmas Coal Mine Miracle, The, *159*
ristmas Evil, *824*
ristmas in Connecticut (1945), *255*
ristmas in Connecticut (1992), *255*
ristmas in July, *255*
ristmas Kid, The, *1105*
ristmas Lilies of the Field, *159*
ristmas Story, A, *159*
ristmas to Remember, A, *482*
ristmas Tree, The (see When Wolves Cry)
ristmas Vacation (see National Lampoon's Christmas Vacation)
ristmas Wife, The, *482*
ristmas without Snow, A, *482*
ristopher Columbus (1985), *25*
Christopher Columbus: The Discovery, *26*
Christopher Strong, *482*
Chrome Soldiers, *26*
◆ Chronopolis, *724*
Chu Chu and the Philly Flash, *255*
◆ Chuck Berry Hail! Hail! Rock 'n' Roll, *421*
Chuka, *1105*
Chump at Oxford, A, *255*
Church, The, *824*
CIA Codename Alexa, *26*
Ciao Federico!, *724*
Ciao! Manhattan, *482*
Cigarette Girl from Mosselprom, The, *724*
Cimarron (1931), *1105*
Cimarron (1960), *1105*
◆ Cincinnati Kid, The, *26*
◆ Cinderella (1950), *159*
Cinderella (1964), *911*
◆ Cinderella (1985), *159*
◆ Cinderella (1987), *912*
Cinderella Liberty, *482*
Cinderfella, *912*
◆ Cinema Paradiso, *724*
Circle of Fear, *26*
Circle of Iron, *26*
Circle of Love, *482*
Circle of Two, *482*
Circuitry Man, *1041*
Circus, The/A Day's Pleasure, *255*
Circus of Fear, *824*
Circus of Horrors, *824*
Circus World, *482*
Cisco Kid, The, *1105*
Cisco Kid (TV Series), *1105*
Citadel, The, *482*
◆ Citizen Cohn, *482*
◆ Citizen Kane, *482*
◆ Citizen's Band, *255*
City for Conquest, *482*
City Girl, *962*
City Heat, *255*
City in Fear, *962*
City in Panic, *824*
◆ City Lights, *255*
City Limits, *1041*
◆ City of Hope, *483*
◆ City of Joy, *483*
City of Shadows, *26*
City of the Walking Dead, *824*
City of Women, *724*
City on Fire, *724*
◆ City Slickers, *255*
◆ **City Slickers II,** *256*
City That Never Sleeps, *483*
City War, *724*
City without Men, *483*
◆ Civil War, The, *421*
Civil War Diary, *483*
◆ **Civil War Journal,** *421*
Civilization, *483*
Claire of the Moon, *483*
◆ Claire's Knee, *724*
Clairvoyant, The (see Evil Mind, The)
Clambake, *912*
Clan of the Cave Bear, *1041*
Clara's Heart, *483*
Clarence, *256*
◆ Clarence Darrow, *483*
Clarence, the Cross-Eyed Lion, *159*
Clark and McCullough: Inspired Madness, *256*
Clash by Night, *483*
Clash of the Titans, *1041*
Class, *256*
Class Act, *256*
Class Action, *962*
Class of '86 (see National Lampoon's Class of '86)
Class of '44, *483*
Class of Miss MacMichael, The, *483*
Class of 1984, *824*
Class of 1999, *1041*
Class of 1999 II: The Substitute, *1041*
Class of Nuke 'em High, *824*
Class of Nuke 'em High 2: Subhumanoid Meltdown, *824*
Class Reunion (see National Lampoon's Class Reunion)
Classic Foreign Shorts: Volume 2, *724*
Claudia, *484*
Clay Pigeon, The, *26*
◆ Clean and Sober, *484*
Clean Slate (1994), *256*
◆ Clean Slate (Coup de Torchon), *724*
Clearcut, *26*
Cleo from 5 to 7, *725*
Cleo/Leo, *256*
◆ Cleopatra (1934), *484*
◆ Cleopatra (1963), *484*
Cleopatra Jones, *26*
Cleopatra Jones and the Casino of Gold, *26*
Cliffhanger, *26*
Clifford, *256*
Climate for Killing, A, *962*
Climb, The, *26*
Clinton and Nadine, *26*
Cloak and Dagger (1946), *962*
Cloak and Dagger (1984), *27*
Clock, The, *484*
◆ Clockmaker, The, *725*
Clockwise, *256*
◆ Clockwork Orange, A, *1042*
Clones, The, *1042*
Clonus Horror, The, *1042*
◆ Close Encounters of the Third Kind, *1042*
Close My Eyes, *484*
◆ Close to Eden, *725*
Close to Home, *484*
◆ Closely Watched Trains, *725*
Closer, The, *484*
Closet Land, *962*
Cloud Dancer, *27*
Cloud Waltzing, *484*
Clouds Over Europe, *484*
Clown, The, *484*
Clown Murders, The, *962*
Clownhouse, *824*
◆ Clowns, The, *725*
Club, The (1985), *484*
Club, The (1993), *824*
Club des Femmes, *725*
Club Extinction, *1042*
Club Fed, *256*
Club Life, *27*
Club Med, *484*
Club Paradise, *256*
Clue, *256*
Clutching Hand, The, *27*
Coach, *484*
◆ Coal Miner's Daughter, *912*
Coast Patrol, The, *27*
Coast to Coast, *256*
Cobra (1986), *27*

Cobra, The (1987), *27*
Coca Cola Kid, The, *257*
Cocaine Cowboys, *27*
Cocaine Fiends, *485*
Cocaine: One Man's Seduction, *485*
Cocaine Wars, *27*
Cockeyed Cavaliers, *257*
Cockfighter, *27*
Cocktail, *485*
Cocoanuts, *257*
◆ Cocoon, *1042*
Cocoon: The Return, *1042*
Code Name: Chaos, *257*
Code Name: Dancer, *27*
Code Name: Emerald, *27*
Code Name: Wild Geese, *27*
◆ Code of Silence, *27*
Codename: Kyril, *962*
Coffy, *27*
Cohen and Tate, *485*
Cold Comfort, *963*
Cold Cuts (see Buffet Froid)
Cold Feet (1984), *257*
Cold Feet (1989), *257*
Cold Front, *963*
Cold Heat, *28*
Cold Heaven, *485*
Cold Justice, *28*
◆ Cold River, *159*
Cold Room, The, *485*
Cold Sassy Tree, *485*
Cold Steel, *28*
Cold Sweat (1970), *28*
Cold Sweat (1993), *28*
Cold Turkey, *257*
Colditz Story, The, *485*
◆ Collection, The, *485*
◆ Collector, The, *963*
Collector's Item, *485*
College, *257*
College Swing, *912*
Collision Course, *257*
Collision Course (see Bamboo Saucer)
Colonel Effingham's Raid, *257*
Colonel Redl, *725*
Color Me Barbra, *912*
Color Me Blood Red, *824*
Color Me Dead, *485*
◆ Color of Money, The, *485*
◆ Color of Pomegranates, The, *725*
◆ Color Purple, The, *485*
Colorado, *1105*
Colorado Serenade, *1105*
Colorado Sunset, *1105*
◆ Colors, *485*
Colossus: The Forbin Project, *1042*
Colt Comrades, *1105*
◆ Columbia Pictures Cartoon Classics, *159*
Columbo: Murder by the Book, *963*
Coma, *963*
◆ Comancheros, The, *1105*
Combat Killers, *28*
Come Along with Me, *257*
Come and Get It, *28*
◆ Come and See, *725*
Come Back Africa, *486*
◆ Come Back, Little Sheba, *486*
Come Back to the Five and Dime, Jimmy Dean, Jimmy Dean, *486*
Come Blow Your Horn, *257*
◆ Come on Tarzan, *1105*
Come See the Paradise, *486*
Comeback, *912*
Comeback Kid, The, *486*
◆ Comedian, The, *486*
Comedians, The, *486*
Comedy Tonight, *257*
◆ Comes a Horseman, *1105*
◆ Comfort and Joy, *258*
Comfort of Strangers, The, *963*
◆ Comic, The (1969), *486*
Comic, The (1985), *486*
Comic Book Confidential, *421*
Comic Cabby, *258*
Comic Relief 2, *258*
◆ Coming Home, *486*
Coming Out Alive, *963*
Coming Out of the Ice, *486*
Coming Soon, *824*
Coming to America, *258*
Coming Up Roses, *725*
Command Decision, *487*
Commando, *28*
Commando Squad, *28*
Commandos, *28*
Commandos Strike at Dawn, *28*
Commies Are Coming, the Commies Are Coming, The, *258*
◆ Commissar, The, *725*
◆ Commitments, The, *912*
Committed, *824*
Common Bonds, *487*
Common Law, The, *487*
Common Law Cabin, *487*
◆ Common Threads: Stories from the Quilt, *421*
Communion, *1042*
Communion (see Alice, Sweet Alice)
Company Business, *28*
Company of Wolves, The, *1042*
Competition, The, *487*
◆ Compleat Beatles, The, *421*
Compleat "Weird Al" Yankovic, The, *258*
Compromising Positions, *258*
Compulsion, *487*
Computer Wore Tennis Shoes, The, *159*
Comrade X, *258*
Comrades in Arms, *28*
Comrades of Summer, The, *258*
Con Artists, The, *487*
Conagher, *1105*
Conan the Barbarian, *1042*
Conan the Destroyer, *1043*
Concrete Angels, *487*
Concrete Jungle, The (1962) (a.k.a. The Criminal), *487*
Concrete Jungle, The (1982), *28*
Condorman, *159*
Coneheads, *258*
Confessions of a Hitman, *487*
Confessions of a Police Captain, *487*
Confessions of a Serial Killer, *825*
Confessions of a Vice Baron, *487*
Confidential, *28*
Confidential Report (see Mr. Arkadin)
Confidentially Yours, *725*
Conflict, *963*
Conflict of Interest, *29*
◆ Conformist, The, *725*
Connecticut Yankee, A, *258*
Connecticut Yankee in King Arthur's Court, A (1948), *258*
Connecticut Yankee in King Arthur's Court, A (1970), *159*
Connection (1973), *487*
◆ Connection, The (1961), *487*
◆ **Connections 2**, *421*
Conqueror, The, *29*
Conqueror Worm, The, *825*
Conquest, *487*
Conquest of Cheyenne, *1106*
Conquest of Cochise, *1106*
Conquest of the Planet of the Apes *1043*
◆ Conrack, *488*
Consenting Adults (1985), *488*
Consenting Adults (1992), *963*
Consolation Marriage, *488*
Conspiracy: The Trial of the Chicag 8, *488*
Conspiracy, The (see Le Complot)
Conspirator, *963*
Consuming Passions, *259*
Contagion, *825*
Contempt, *726*
Continental Divide, *259*
Continuing Adventures of Chip 'n' Dale, The, *160*
Contraband, *726*
◆ Contract, *726*
Contract for Life: The S.A.D.D. Sto *488*
◆ Conversation, The, *963*
Conversation Piece, *726*
Convicted, *488*
Convoy (1940), *488*
Convoy (1978), *29*
◆ Coogan's Bluff, *29*
◆ Cook, the Thief, His Wife & Her Lover, The, *259*
Cookie, *259*
Cool As Ice, *488*
Cool Blue, *488*
◆ Cool Hand Luke, *29*
◆ **Cool Runnings**, *259*
Cool Surface, The, *963*
Cool World, *1043*
◆ Cooley High, *259*
◆ Cooperstown, *488*
Cop, *29*
Cop and a Half, *160*
Cop and the Girl, The, *726*
Cop in Blue Jeans, The, *29*
Copacabana, *259*
Cop-Out, *963*
Copper Canyon, *1106*
Cops and Robbers, *29*
Cops and Robbersons, *259*
Coquette, *488*
Corleone, *29*
◆ Corn Is Green, The (1945), *488*
Corn Is Green, The (1979), *488*
Cornbread, Earl and Me, *488*
Cornered, *29*
◆ Coroner Creek, *1106*
Corporate Affairs, *259*
Corpse Grinders, The, *825*
Corpse Vanishes, The, *825*
Corregidor, *489*
Corridors of Blood, *825*
Corrupt, *963*
Corrupt Ones, The, *29*
Corsican Brothers, The (1941), *29*
Corsican Brothers, The (1984), *25*
Corvette Summer, *29*
Cosmic Man, The, *1043*
Cosmic Monsters, The, *825*
◆ Cotton Club, The, *29*
Couch Potato Workout Tape, *259*
Couch Trip, The, *259*
Count Dracula, *825*

unt of Monte Cristo, The (1912), *489*
unt of Monte Cristo, The (1934), *30*
unt of Monte Cristo, The (1975), *30*
unt Yorga, Vampire, *825*
untdown, *489*
unterfeit Traitor, The, *30*
unterforce, *30*
untry, *489*
untry Gentlemen, *260*
untry Girl, The (1954), *489*
untry Girl, The (1982), *489*
untryman, *489*
up De Grace, *726*
up de Torchon (see Clean Slate)
upe De Ville, *260*
urage Mountain, *160*
urage of Lassie, *160*
urageous Dr. Christian, The, *489*
urageous Mr. Penn, *489*
urt Jester, The, *260*
urt-martial of Billy Mitchell, The, *489*
urt-Martial of Jackie Robinson, The, *489*
urtesans of Bombay, *489*
urtney Affair, The, *489*
urtship, *490*
urtship of Eddie's Father, The, *260*
usin Bobby, *421*
usin, Cousine, *726*
usins, *260*
ver Girl, *912*
ver Girl Murders, The, *964*
ver Up (1988), *421*
ver-Up (1990), *30*
vered Wagon, The, *1106*
vered Wagon Days, *1106*
w Town, *1106*
ward of the County, *490*
wboy and the Ballerina, The, *490*
wboy and the Bandit, *1106*
wboy and the Lady, The, *260*
wboy and the Senorita, *1106*
wboy Millionaire, *1106*
wboys, The, *1106*
ack House, *30*
ack-Up, *964*
acker Factory, *490*
ackers, *260*
acking Up, *260*
adle Will Fall, The, *964*
aig's Wife, *490*
anes are Flying, The, *726*
ash and Burn, *1043*
ash Dive, *30*
ash of Flight 401, *490*
ashout, *30*
ater Lake Monster, The, *825*
aving, The, *825*
awlers, *825*
awling Eye, The, *825*
awling Hand, The, *825*
awlspace, *825*
azed, *825*
azies, The, *825*
azy Fat Ethel II, *826*
azy For Love, *726*
azy from the Heart, *490*
azy in Love, *490*
azy Mama, *30*
azy Moon, *490*
azy People, *260*
Crazy Ray, The, *726*
Creation of the Humanoids, *1043*
Creator, *490*
Creature, *1043*
Creature from Black Lake, *826*
Creature from the Black Lagoon, *826*
Creature from the Haunted Sea, The, *1043*
Creature Walks Among Us, The, *826*
Creature Wasn't Nice, The (see Spaceship)
Creature's Revenge, The (see Brain of Blood)
Creatures the World Forgot, *1043*
Creeper, The, *826*
Creepers, *826*
Creeping Flesh, The, *826*
Creeping Terror, The, *1043*
Creeping Unknown, The (see Quatermass Experiment, The)
Creepozoids, *826*
◆ Creepshow, *826*
Creepshow 2, *826*
Cremators, The, *1043*
Cricket, The, *726*
Cricket in Times Square, A, *160*
◆ Cries and Whispers, *726*
Crime & Passion, *260*
◆ **Crime and Punishment (1935),** *490*
◆ Crime and Punishment (1935), *726*
◆ Crime and Punishment (1970), *727*
◆ Crime Inc., *421*
Crime Killer, The, *30*
Crime Lords, *30*
Crime of Dr. Crespi, The, *826*
◆ Crime of Monsieur Lange, The, *727*
Crime of Passion, *490*
Crime Story, *30*
Crime Zone, *1043*
◆ Crimes and Misdemeanors, *490*
Crimes at the Dark House, *826*
Crimes in the Wax Museum (see Nightmare in Wax)
Crimes of Passion, *491*
Crimes of Stephen Hawke, The, *826*
◆ Crimes of the Heart, *260*
Crimewave, *260*
Criminal, The (see Concrete Jungle)
◆ Criminal Code, The, *491*
Criminal Justice, *491*
Criminal Law, *964*
◆ Criminal Life of Archibaldo de la Cruz, The, *727*
Criminally Insane, *826*
Crimson Ghost, The, *30*
◆ Crimson Pirate, The, *30*
◆ Crisis at Central High, *491*
Crisis in the Kremlin: The Last Days of the Soviet Union (see Assasination Game, The)
Criss Cross (1948), *964*
Crisscross (1992), *491*
Critical Condition, *260*
Critic's Choice, *261*
Critters, *827*
Critters 2: The Main Course, *827*
Critters 3, *827*
Critters 4, *827*
Crocodile, *827*
◆ "Crocodile" Dundee, *261*
"Crocodile" Dundee II, *261*
Cromwell, *491*
◆ **Cronos,** *727*
Crooked Hearts, *491*
Crooklyn, *261*
Crooks and Coronets (Sophie's Place), *261*
Cross Country, *491*
Cross Creek, *491*
Cross Mission, *31*
Cross My Heart (1987), *261*
◆ Cross My Heart (1991), *727*
Cross of Iron, *31*
Crossfire (1947), *964*
Crossfire (1986), *1106*
Crossing, The, *491*
◆ Crossing Delancey, *491*
Crossing the Bridge, *492*
Crossing the Line (1990), *492*
Crossing the Line (1991), *492*
◆ Crossover Dreams, *912*
Crossroads, *912*
◆ **Crow, The,** *827*
◆ Crowd, The, *492*
Crucible of Horror, *827*
Crucible of Terror, *827*
Crucifer of Blood, *964*
Cruel Sea, The, *492*
Cruel Story of Youth, *727*
Cruise into Terror, *964*
Cruising, *964*
Crush, The, *964*
Crusoe, *31*
Cry-Baby, *912*
Cry Blood, Apache, *1106*
Cry Danger, *964*
Cry for Love, A, *492*
◆ Cry Freedom, *492*
Cry from the Mountain, *160*
◆ Cry in the Dark, A, *492*
Cry in the Night, A, *964*
Cry in the Wild, A, *31*
Cry in the Wind, *492*
Cry of Battle, *31*
◆ Cry of Reason, The, *421*
Cry of the Banshee, *827*
Cry of the Innocent, *964*
Cry Terror, *964*
◆ Cry, the Beloved Country, *492*
Cry Uncle!, *261*
Cry Vengeance, *492*
◆ Crying Game, The, *492*
Crypt of the Living Dead, *827*
Crystal Force, *827*
Crystal Heart, *492*
Crystal Triangle, *727*
Crystalstone, *160*
Cthulhu Mansion, *827*
Cuba, *31*
Cuba Crossing (see Kill Castro)
Cuban Rebel Girls (see Assault of the Rebel Girls)
Cujo, *827*
Cul-de-Sac, *492*
Culpepper Cattle Co., The, *1106*
Cult of the Cobra, *827*
◆ Cup Final, *727*
Curiosity Kills, *965*
Curly Sue, *261*
Curly Top, *912*
Curse, The, *827*
Curse II—The Bite, *827*
Curse III: Blood Sacrifice, *827*
Curse IV: The Ultimate Sacrifice, *828*
Curse of Frankenstein, The, *828*
Curse of King Tut's Tomb, The, *828*
Curse of the Black Widow, *828*
Curse of the Blue Lights, *828*
Curse of the Cat People, The, *828*
Curse of the Crying Woman, The, *828*

Curse of the Crystal Eye, *31*
◆ Curse of the Demon, *828*
Curse of the House Surgeon, The, *828*
Curse of the Living Dead, *828*
Curse of the Pink Panther, The, *261*
Curse of the Werewolf, The, *828*
Curse of the Yellow Snake, The, *965*
Curtains, *828*
Custodian, The, *31*
Cut and Run, *493*
Cut Throats Nine, *1107*
◆ Cutter's Way, *965*
Cutting Class, *828*
Cutting Edge, The, *493*
Cybernator, *1043*
Cyborg, *1043*
Cyborg 2, *1043*
Cyborg Cop, *1043*
Cyborg: The Six-Million Dollar Man, *1043*
Cyclone, *31*
Cyclone in the Saddle, *1107*
Cyclone Ranger, *1107*
Cyclops, The, *829*
◆ Cyrano De Bergerac (1950), *493*
◆ Cyrano De Bergerac (1990), *727*
◆ D.A.R.Y.L., *1044*
D.C. Cab, *261*
D.I., The, *493*
D.O.A. (1949), *965*
D.O.A. (1988), *965*
D.O.A.: A Right of Passage, *422*
◆ D.P., *493*
◆ **D. W. Griffith, Father of Film,** *422*
D. W. Griffith Shorts Vol. 1–12, *493*
D. W. Griffith Triple Feature, *493*
D2: The Mighty Ducks, *160*
◆ Da, *493*
◆ Dad, *493*
Daddy and the Muscle Academy, *422*
Daddy Long Legs, *913*
Daddy Nostalgia, *727*
Daddy-O, *31*
Daddy's Boys, *31*
Daddy's Deadly Darling (see Pigs)
Daddy's Dyin' and Who's Got the Will, *261*
Daddy's Gone A-Hunting, *965*
Daffy Duck and Company, *160*
◆ Daffy Duck Cartoon Festival: Ain't That Ducky, *160*
Daffy Duck: Tales from the Duckside, *160*
◆ Daffy Duck: The Nuttiness Continues, *160*
Daffy Duck's Easter Egg-Citement, *160*
Daffy Duck's Madcap Mania, *161*
Daffy Duck's Movie: Fantastic Island, *161*
◆ **Daffy Duck's Quackbusters,** *161*
Dagger of Kamui, The, *727*
Dagora, the Space Monster, *1044*
Dain Curse, The, *965*
Daisy (Limited Gold Edition 1), *161*
Daisy Miller, *493*
Dakota (1945), *1107*
Dakota (1988), *493*
Dakota Incident, *1107*
Daleks—Invasion Earth 2150 A.D., *1044*
◆ Dam Busters, The, *31*
Damage, *493*
Dames, *913*
Damien: Omen II, *829*
◆ Damn the Defiant!, *31*
Damn Yankees, *913*
Damnation Alley, *1044*
Damned, The, *727*
Damned River, *32*
Damsel in Distress, A, *913*
Dan Candy's Law, *32*
Dance, *913*
Dance, Fools, Dance, *493*
Dance, Girl, Dance, *261*
Dance Hall, *913*
Dance Hall Racket, *494*
Dance of Death, *829*
Dance on Fire, *422*
Dance or Die, *32*
Dance 'Til Dawn, *262*
◆ Dance with a Stranger, *494*
Dance with Death, *965*
Dancers, *494*
◆ Dances with Wolves, *1107*
Dancing in the Dark, *494*
Dancing Lady, *913*
Dancing Man, *965*
Dancing Mothers, *262*
Dancing Pirate, *913*
◆ Dancing Princesses, The, *161*
Dandelions, *727*
Dandy in Aspic, A, *965*
Dangaio, *728*
Danger, *965*
Danger: Diabolik, *1044*
Danger Lights, *494*
Danger Man (Television Series), *32*
Danger Zone, The, *32*
Dangerous, *494*
Dangerous Charter, *32*
Dangerous Company, *494*
Dangerous Curves, *262*
Dangerous Game, *965*
Dangerous Heart, *965*
◆ Dangerous Liaisons, *494*
Dangerous Life, A, *494*
Dangerous Love, *32*
Dangerous Mission, *966*
Dangerous Moonlight (a.k.a. Suicide Squadron), *32*
◆ Dangerous Moves, *728*
Dangerous Passage, *32*
Dangerous Pursuit, *966*
Dangerous Relations, *494*
Dangerous Summer, A, *494*
Dangerous Venture, *1107*
Dangerous When Wet, *913*
Dangerous Woman, A, *494*
Dangerously Close, *966*
Daniel, *495*
◆ Daniel Boone, *1107*
Daniel Boone, Trail Blazer, *1107*
Danielle Steele's "Fine Things", *495*
Danny, *161*
Danny Boy (1941), *495*
◆ Danny Boy (1982), *495*
Danse Macabre, *829*
Dante's Inferno, *495*
Danton, *728*
◆ **Danzon,** *728*
Darby O'Gill and the Little People, *161*
Daredevils of the Red Circle, *32*
Daring Dobermans, The, *32*
Daring Game, *32*
Daring Young Man, The, *262*
Dario Argento's World of Horror, *422*
Dark, The, *829*
Dark Age, *32*
Dark Angel, The, *966*
Dark Backward, The, *262*
Dark City, *495*
◆ Dark Command, *1107*
Dark Corner, The, *495*
◆ Dark Crystal, The, *1044*
Dark Eyes, *728*
Dark Eyes of London (see Human Monster, The)
Dark Forces, *966*
Dark Habits, *728*
Dark Half, The, *829*
Dark Horse, *161*
Dark Journey, *966*
Dark Justice, *32*
Dark Mirror, The, *966*
Dark Night of the Scarecrow, *829*
Dark Obsession, *495*
◆ Dark of the Sun, *32*
Dark Passage, *966*
Dark Past, The, *495*
Dark Places, *829*
Dark Power, The, *829*
Dark Rider, *33*
Dark River: A Father's Revenge, *4*
Dark Sanity, *829*
Dark Secret of Harvest Home, The *829*
Dark Shadows (TV Series), *829*
Dark Side, The, *829*
Dark Side of the Moon, The, *1044*
Dark Star, *1044*
Dark Tide, *495*
Dark Tower, *829*
◆ Dark Victory, *495*
Dark Waters, *496*
Dark Wind, *966*
Darkest Africa, *33*
◆ Darkman, *1044*
Darkside, The, *33*
◆ Darling, *496*
Darling Lili, *913*
◆ Das Boot (The Boat), *728*
Date with an Angel, *262*
Date with Judy, A, *913*
Daughter of Dr. Jekyll, *829*
Daughter of Horror, *829*
Daughters of Darkness, *830*
Daughters of Satan, *830*
◆ Daughters of the Dust, *496*
◆ Dave, *262*
David and Bathsheba, *496*
David and Lisa, *496*
◆ David Copperfield, *496*
Davinci's War, *33*
Davy Crockett and the River Pirate *161*
Davy Crockett, King of the Wild Frontier, *161*
◆ Dawn of the Dead, *830*
Dawn of the Mummy, *830*
Dawn on the Great Divide, *1107*
◆ Dawn Patrol, The, *33*
Dawn Rider, *1107*
Dawning, The, *496*
Dawson Patrol, The, *33*
◆ Day After, The, *1044*
Day And The Hour, *728*
Day at the Races, A, *262*
◆ Day for Night, *728*
Day in October, A, *496*
◆ Day in the Country, A, *728*
Day in the Death of Joe Egg, A, *2*
Day of Anger (see Days of Wrath)

y of Atonement, 33
y of Judgment, A, 830
y of the Animals, 830
y of the Assassin, 33
y of the Dead, 830
y of the Dolphin, The, 1044
y of the Jackal, The, 966
y of the Locust, The, 496
y of the Triffids, The, 1044
y of Wrath, 728
y One, 496
y that Shook the World, The, 496
y the Earth Caught Fire, The, 1044
y the Earth Stood Still, The, 1044
y the World Ended, The, 1045
y Time Ended, The, 1045
ybreak (1939) (see Le Jour Se Leve)
ybreak (1993), 1045
ydreamer, The, 161
ydreamer, The (Le Distrait), 728
ys of Glory, 33
ys of Heaven, 496
ys of Hell, 33
ys of Jesse James, 1107
ys of Old Cheyenne, 1107
ys of Thrills and Laughter, 262
ys of Thunder, 33
ys of Wine and Roses, 496
ys of Wine and Roses, The (Television), 497
ys of Wrath, 1107
yton's Devils, 33
zed and Confused, 497
Day the Sixth of June, 497
ad, The, 497
ad Again, 966
ad Ahead: The Exxon Valdez Disaster, 497
ad Aim (1973), 1108
ad Aim (1987), 33
ad Alive, 830
ad and Buried, 830
ad-Bang, 33
ad Calm, 966
ad Center, 967
ad Certain, 967
ad Connection, 967
ad Don't Die, The, 830
ad Don't Dream, The, 1108
ead Easy, 967
ead End, 497
ead End Drive-In, 1045
ead Eyes of London, 830
ead for a Dollar, 1108
ead Heat, 830
ead Heat on a Merry-Go-Round, 967
ead in the Water, 967
ead Kids (see Strange Behavior)
ead Man Out, 497
ead Man Walking, 1045
ead Man's Gulch, 1108
ead Men Don't Die, 262
ead Men Don't Wear Plaid, 262
ead Men Walk, 830
ead of Night (1945), 830
ead of Night (1977), 831
ead of Winter, 967
ead On, 967
ead on the Money, 967
ead Poets Society, 497
ead Pool, The, 33
ead Reckoning (1947), 34
ead Reckoning (1990), 967
Dead Ringer, 967
Dead Ringers, 831
Dead Silence, 262
Dead Sleep, 967
◆ Dead Solid Perfect, 497
Dead Space, 1045
◆ Dead Zone, The, 831
Deadbolt, 968
Deadfall, 968
Deadline (1987), 497
Deadline (1988), 34
Deadline at Dawn, 34
◆ Deadline USA, 497
◆ Deadlock, 1045
Deadly Alliance, 968
Deadly Bet, 34
Deadly Blessing, 831
Deadly Companion, 968
Deadly Companions, The, 1108
Deadly Currents, 34
Deadly Desire, 968
Deadly Dreams, 968
Deadly Embrace, 34
Deadly Encounter (1972), 34
Deadly Encounter (1975), 498
Deadly Eyes, 831
Deadly Force, 34
Deadly Friend, 831
Deadly Game, 34
Deadly Games, 968
Deadly Harvest, 1045
Deadly Hero, 34
Deadly Illusion, 968
Deadly Impact, 34
Deadly Intent, 34
Deadly is the Female (see Gun Crazy)
Deadly Mantis, The, 1045
Deadly Obsession, 831
Deadly Possession, 968
Deadly Prey, 34
Deadly Ray from Mars (see Flash Gordon: Mars Attacks the World)
Deadly Revenge, 35
Deadly Rivals, 35
Deadly Sanctuary, 831
Deadly Spygames, 35
Deadly Stranger, 35
◆ Deadly Surveillance, 35
Deadly Trackers, The, 1108
Deadly Twins, 35
Deadly Vengeance, 35
Deadly Weapons, 498
Deadman's Curve, 913
Deadmate, 831
Deadtime Stories, 831
Deal of the Century, 263
Dealers, 498
◆ Dear America: Letters Home from Vietnam, 422
Dear Brigitte, 263
Dear Dead Delilah, 831
Dear Detective, 968
Dear Wife, 263
Death at Love House, 968
Death Becomes Her, 1045
Death Before Dishonor, 35
Death by Dialogue, 968
Death Chase, 35
Death Corps (see Shock Waves)
Death Curse of Tartu, 831
Death Dreams, 831
Death Drug, 498
Death House, 35
Death Hunt, 35
Death in Venice, 498
Death Kiss, The, 968
Death Nurse, 831
Death of a Bureaucrat, 728
Death of a Centerfold, 498
Death of a Gunfighter, 1108
Death of a Prophet, 498
◆ Death of a Salesman, 498
Death of a Scoundrel, 498
Death of a Soldier, 498
Death of Adolf Hitler, The, 498
Death of the Incredible Hulk, The, 1045
Death on the Nile, 968
Death Race 2000, 1045
Death Rides a Horse, 1108
Death Rides the Plains, 1108
Death Ring, 35
Death Spa, 831
Death Squad, The, 35
Death Target, 35
◆ Death Train, 968
Death Valley, 831
Death Valley Manhunt, 1108
Death Warmed Up, 831
Death Warrant, 35
◆ Death Watch, 1045
Death Weekend, 831
◆ Death Wish, 35
Death Wish II, 36
Death Wish III, 36
Death Wish IV: The Crackdown, 36
Death Wish V: The Face of Death, 36
Deathdream, 832
Deathfight, 36
Deathmask, 36
Deathmoon, 832
Deathrow Gameshow, 263
Deathship, 832
Deathshot, 36
Deathsport, 1046
Deathstalker, 1046
Deathstalker II: Duel of the Titans, 1046
Deathstalker III—The Warriors from Hell, 1046
Deathstalker IV: Match of the Titans, 1046
Deathtrap, 969
◆ Debajo del Mundo (Under Earth), 729
◆ Decameron, The, 729
Decameron Nights, 263
Deceit, 1046
Deceived, 969
Deceivers, The, 36
December, 498
December 7th: The Movie, 422
Deception (1946), 498
Deception (1993), 969
Deceptions, 969
◆ Decision at Sundown, 1108
◆ Decline of the American Empire, The, 729
◆ Decline of Western Civilization, The, 422
Decline of Western Civilization, Part II—The Metal Years, 422
◆ Decoration Day, 498
Dedee D'Anvers, 729
Dedicated Man, A, 499
Deep, The, 36
Deep Cover (1980), 969
◆ Deep Cover (1992), 36

Deep End, 969
Deep in My Heart, 913
Deep in the Heart of Texas, 1108
Deep Red (1975), 832
◆ **Deep Red (1994),** 1046
Deep Space, 1046
Deep Trouble, 969
Deepstar Six, 832
◆ Deer Hunter, The, 499
Deerslayer, The, 1108
Def by Temptation, 832
Def-Con 4, 1046
◆ Defending Your Life, 263
◆ Defense of the Realm, 969
Defense Play, 36
Defenseless, 969
Defiance, 36
◆ Defiant Ones, The, 499
Deja Vu, 499
Deliberate Stranger, The, 499
Delicate Delinquent, The, 263
Delicatessen, 729
Delinquent Daughters, 499
Delinquent School Girls, 263
Delirious, 263
◆ Deliverance, 36
Delivery Boys, 263
Delos Adventure, The, 36
Delta Force, The, 36
Delta Force 2, 36
Delta Force 3, 37
Delta Force, Commando Two, 37
Delta Fox, 37
Delta Heat, 37
Deluge, 1046
Deluge, The (Potop), 729
Delusion (1980), 969
Delusion (1991), 499
Delusions of Grandeur, 729
Dementia 13, 832
Demetrius and the Gladiators, 499
Demolition Man, 1046
Demon (God Told Me To), 1046
Demon Barber of Fleet Street, The, 832
Demon in My View, A, 832
Demon Keeper, 832
Demon Lover, The, 832
Demon of Paradise, 832
Demon Seed, 1046
Demon Wind, 832
Demoniac, 832
Demonic Toys, 832
Demonoid, 833
Demons, 833
Demons 2, 833
◆ Demons in the Garden, 729
Demons of Ludlow, The, 833
Demons of the Mind, 833
Demonstone, 833
Dempsey, 499
Denial, 499
Dennis Miller: Black and White, 263
◆ Dennis the Menace, 161
Dennis the Menace: Dinosaur Hunter, 162
Denver and Rio Grande, The, 1108
Denver Kid, 1109
Der Golem, Wie Er In Die Welt Kam (see Golem (How He Came Into the World), The)
Deranged, 833
◆ Dersu Uzala, 729
◆ Descending Angel, 499
Desert Bloom, 499
◆ Desert Fox, The, 37
Desert Hearts, 499
Desert Kickboxer, 37
◆ Desert Rats, The, 500
Desert Trail, 1109
Desert Warrior, 1047
Deserter, The, 1109
Designing Woman, 263
Desire, 500
Desire and Hell at Sunset Motel, 969
Desire under the Elms, 500
Desirée, 500
Desk Set, 263
◆ Despair, 729
Desperados, The, 1109
Desperate, 969
Desperate Crimes, 37
◆ Desperate Hours, The (1955), 969
Desperate Hours (1990), 37
Desperate Journey, 500
Desperate Living, 264
Desperate Motive, 970
Desperate Moves, 264
Desperate Women, 1109
◆ Desperately Seeking Susan, 264
Destination Moon, 1047
Destination Saturn (see Buck Rogers: Destination Saturn)
◆ Destination Tokyo, 37
Destiny, 729
Destiny to Order, 264
Destroyer, 833
Destructors, The, 970
◆ Destry Rides Again, 1109
Detective, The (1954), 970
Detective, The (1968), 500
Detective Sadie and Son, 37
◆ Detective School Dropouts, 264
Detonator (see Death Train)
Detour, 970
Detour to Danger, 1109
Detroit Heat (see Detroit 9000)
Detroit 9000 (Detroit Heat), 37
Devastator, The, 37
◆ Devi (The Goddess), 729
◆ Devil and Daniel Webster, The, 500
Devil and Max Devlin, The, 264
◆ Devil and Miss Jones, The, 264
Devil at 4 O'Clock, The, 500
Devil Bat, The, 833
Devil Bat's Daughter, 833
Devil Dog: The Hound of Hell, 833
Devil Dogs of the Air, 37
Devil Doll, The (1936), 833
Devil Doll (1963), 833
Devil Girl from Mars, 833
Devil Horse, The, 1109
Devil Hunter Yohko, 729
Devil in the Flesh (1946), 730
Devil in the Flesh (1987), 730
Devil in the House of Exorcism, The, 833
Devil Rider!, 37
Devil Thumbs a Ride, The, 970
Devil within Her, The, 833
Devilman Vol. 1–2, 730
◆ Devils, The, 500
Devil's Brigade, The, 37
Devil's Brother, The, 914
Devil's Canyon, 1109
Devil's Commandment, The, 834
Devil's Disciple, The, 264
Devil's Envoy, The (see Les Visiteurs du Soir)
Devil's Eye, The, 730
Devil's Gift, The, 834
Devil's Messenger, The, 834
Devil's Party, The, 500
Devil's Playground, 1109
Devil's Rain, The, 834
Devil's Undead, The, 834
Devil's Wedding Night, The, 834
Devlin, 970
Devlin Connection III, The, 970
Devonsville Terror, The, 834
Devotion, 500
Diabolically Yours, 730
◆ Diabolique, 730
◆ Dial M for Murder, 970
Diamond Fleece, The, 970
Diamond Head, 500
Diamond Trap, The, 970
Diamonds, 38
◆ Diamonds Are Forever, 38
Diamond's Edge, 162
Diamonds on Wheels, 162
Diane, 500
Diary of a Chambermaid (1946), 7
◆ Diary of a Chambermaid (1964), 730
◆ Diary of a Country Priest, 730
Diary of a Hitman, 970
◆ Diary of a Lost Girl, 730
Diary of a Mad Housewife, 501
Diary of a Madman, 834
Diary of a Teenage Hitchhiker, 501
Diary of a Young Comic, 264
◆ Diary of Anne Frank, The, 501
Diary of Forbidden Dreams, 501
Dice Rules, 264
Dick Tracy (1937), 38
◆ Dick Tracy (1990), 38
Dick Tracy Cartoons, 162
Dick Tracy, Detective, 38
Dick Tracy Meets Gruesome, 38
Dick Tracy Returns, 38
Dick Tracy vs. Crime Inc., 38
Dick Tracy versus Cueball, 38
Dick Tracy's Dilemma, 38
Dick Tracy's G-Men, 38
Dick Turpin, 38
Die! Die! My Darling!, 834
◆ Die Hard, 38
◆ Die Hard 2: Die Harder, 39
Die Laughing, 264
Die, Monster, Die!, 834
Die Screaming, Marianne, 834
Die Watching, 970
Different Story, A, 501
◆ Diggstown, 264
Dillinger (1945), 39
◆ Dillinger (1973), 39
◆ Dim Sum: A Little Bit of Heart, 501
Dimples, 914
◆ Diner, 265
Dingaka, 501
◆ Dinner at Eight (1933), 265
Dinner at Eight (1990), 265
Dinner at the Ritz, 39
Dino, 501
◆ Dinosaur!, 422
Dinosaur Island, 1047
Dinosaurus!, 834
Diplomaniacs, 914
Diplomatic Immunity, 39
◆ Directed by Andrei Tarkovsky, 422
Dirt Bike Kid, The, 162
◆ Dirty Dancing, 914
Dirty Dishes, 730
◆ Dirty Dozen, The, 39

Dozen, The: The Next Mission,
)
Dozen, The: The Deadly
ission, *39*
Dozen, The: The Fatal
ission, *39*
Harry, *39*
Laundry, *265*
Mary, Crazy Larry, *39*
Outlaws, The (see Big Rip-Off,
e)
Pair: Affair on Nolandia, *730*
Rotten Scoundrels, *265*
Tricks, *265*
Work, *970*
ppearance, The, *39*
ppearance of Aimee, The, *970*
ppearance of Christina, The,
71
ple of Death, *834*
overy Program, *501*
eet Charm of the Bourgeoisie,
ne, *730*
onored, *501*
onored Lady, *39*
ey Christmas Gift, A, *162*
ey's Best: 1931–1948, *162*
ey's Dream Factory: 1933–1938
imited Gold Edition 2), *162*
ey's Halloween Treat, *162*
ey's Tall Tales, *162*
rderlies, *914*
rderly Orderly, The, *265*
rganized Crime, *40*
laced Person, The, *501*
aeli, *502*
ant Drums, *40*
ant Harmony: Pavarotti in China,
22
ant Thunder (1974), *730*
ant Thunder (1988), *502*
ant Voices/Still Lives, *502*
nguished Gentleman, The, *265*
ortions, *834*
urbance, The, *834*
urbed, *971*
, *731*
, The, *40*
Bomber, *502*
ne, *265*
ne Enforcer, *40*
ne Madness, *423*
ne Nymph, The, *731*
ng In, *502*
orce His: Divorce Hers, *502*
orce—Italian Style, *731*
orce of Lady X, The, *265*
orcee, The, *502*
e Changing Habits, *265*
e Dynamite, *40*
e Jamboree, *914*
e Lanes, *265*
go, *1109*
go Shoots First, *1109*
or Die, *40*
the Right Thing, *502*
You Remember Dolly Bell?, *731*
erman Gang, The, *40*
Hollywood, *265*
Savage…The Man of Bronze,
047
ks of New York, The, *502*
tor, The, *502*
Alien, *834*
tor and the Devils, The, *835*

Doctor at Large, *265*
Doctor at Sea, *266*
◆ **Dr. Bethune,** *502*
Dr. Black and Mr. Hyde, *835*
Dr. Butcher, M.D. (Medical Deviate), *835*
Dr. Caligari, *835*
Dr. Christian Meets the Women, *502*
Dr. Cyclops, *835*
Dr. Death: Seeker of Souls, *835*
Doctor Detroit, *266*
Doctor Dolittle, *162*
Doctor Duck's Super Secret All-Purpose Sauce, *266*
Dr. Faustus, *502*
Dr. Frankenstein's Castle of Freaks, *835*
Dr. Giggles, *835*
Doctor Gore, *835*
Doctor Hackenstein, *835*
Dr. Heckyl and Mr. Hype, *266*
Doctor in Distress, *266*
Doctor in the House, *266*
Dr. Jekyll and Mr. Hyde (1920), *835*
◆ Dr. Jekyll and Mr. Hyde (1932), *835*
Dr. Jekyll and Mr. Hyde (1941), *835*
Dr. Jekyll and Mr. Hyde (1973), *914*
Dr. Jekyll and Sister Hyde, *835*
Dr. Jekyll's Dungeon of Death, *835*
Dr. Kildare's Strange Case, *40*
◆ Dr. Mabuse, the Gambler (Parts I and II), *971*
Doctor Mordrid, *1047*
◆ Dr. No, *40*
Doctor of Doom, *836*
Dr. Otto and the Riddle of the Gloom Beam, *266*
Dr. Phibes Rises Again, *836*
Doctor Quinn Medicine Woman, *502*
◆ Dr. Seuss: Horton Hears a Who/The Grinch Who Stole Christmas, *162*
◆ Dr. Seuss: The Cat in the Hat/Dr. Seuss on the Loose, *162*
◆ Dr. Seuss: The Grinch Grinches the Cat in the Hat/Pontoffel Pock, *163*
◆ Dr. Seuss: The Lorax/The Hoober Bloob Highway, *163*
Dr. Strange, *1047*
◆ Dr. Strangelove or How I Learned to Stop Worrying and Love the Bomb, *266*
Dr. Syn, *40*
Dr. Syn, Alias the Scarecrow, *163*
Doctor Takes a Wife, The, *266*
Dr. Tarr's Torture Dungeon, *836*
Dr. Terror's Gallery of Terrors (see Bloodsuckers, The)
Dr. Terror's House of Horrors, *836*
Dr. Who and the Daleks, *1047*
Dr. Who: Revenge of the Cybermen, *1047*
Doctor X, *836*
◆ Dr. Zhivago, *503*
Doctors' Wives, *503*
◆ Dodes 'Ka-Den, *731*
◆ Dodge City, *1109*
◆ Dodsworth, *503*
Does This Mean We're Married?, *266*
Dog Day, *40*
◆ Dog Day Afternoon, *971*
Dog Eat Dog, *40*
◆ Dog of Flanders, A, *163*

Dog Soldier: Shadows of the Past, *1047*
◆ Dog Star Man, *1047*
Dogfight, *503*
Dogpound Shuffle, *266*
Dogs in Space, *914*
Dogs of Hell, *836*
Dogs of War, The, *40*
Doin' Time, *266*
Doin' Time on Planet Earth, *267*
Dolemite, *267*
◆ Doll, *731*
Doll Face, *914*
Dollar, *731*
◆ $ (Dollars), *971*
◆ Dollmaker, The, *503*
Dollman, *1047*
Dollman vs. Demonic Toys, *1047*
Dolls, *836*
Doll's House, A (1973), *503*
◆ Doll's House, A (1989), *503*
Dolly Dearest, *836*
◆ Dominick and Eugene, *503*
Dominique Is Dead, *971*
Domino, *503*
Domino Principle, The, *971*
Don Daredevil Rides Again, *1109*
Don Is Dead, The, *40*
Don Juan, *503*
Don Q, Son of Zorro, *41*
Don Quixote (1933), *914*
◆ Don Quixote (1988), *914*
Don Rickles: Buy This Tape You Hockey Puck, *267*
Don Winslow of the Coast Guard, *41*
Don Winslow of the Navy, *41*
◆ Dona Flor and Her Two Husbands, *731*
◆ Donald (Limited Gold Edition 1), *163*
◆ Donald Duck in Mathemagic Land, *163*
Donald Duck: The First 50 Years, *163*
Donald's Bee Pictures (Limited Gold Edition 2), *163*
◆ Donkey Skin (Peau D'Âne), *731*
Donna Herlinda and Her Son, *731*
Donner Pass: The Road to Survival, *1109*
Donovan's Brain, *1047*
Donovan's Reef, *267*
Don's Party, *267*
Don't Answer the Phone, *836*
Don't Be Afraid of the Dark, *836*
Don't Bother to Knock, *971*
◆ Don't Cry, It's Only Thunder, *503*
◆ Don't Drink the Water, *267*
◆ Don't Fence Me In, *1110*
Don't Go Near the Water, *267*
Don't Go in the House, *836*
Don't Go in the Woods, *836*
Don't Go to Sleep, *836*
Don't Look Back, *423*
Don't Look in the Basement, *836*
◆ Don't Look Now, *971*
Don't Mess with My Sister, *504*
Don't Open Till Christmas, *836*
Don't Raise the Bridge, Lower the River, *267*
Don't Tell Her It's Me, *267*
Don't Tell Mom the Babysitter's Dead, *267*
Don't Turn the Other Cheek (see Long Live Your Death)
◆ Doolins of Oklahoma, *1110*

Doom Asylum, 836
Doomed Megalopolis, Parts 1–4, 731
Doomed to Die, 41
Doomsday Flight, The, 971
Doomwatch, 1048
Door to Door, 267
Doors, The, 914
Doors, The: A Tribute to Jim Morrison, 423
Doors, The Soft Parade, 423
Dope Mania, 423
Doppelganger: The Evil Within, 836
Dorf and the First Games of Mount Olympus, 267
Dorf Goes Auto Racing, 267
Dorf on Golf, 267
Dorian Gray, 837
Dorm that Dripped Blood, The, 837
Dot and the Bunny, 163
Double Agents, 971
Double Blast, 41
Double Deal, 41
Double Dynamite, 268
Double Edge, 504
Double Exposure (1982), 971
Double Exposure (1987), 268
Double Exposure (1989), 504
Double Exposure (1993), 971
Double Impact, 41
◆ Double Indemnity, 972
Double Jeopardy, 972
◆ Double Life, A, 504
◆ Double Life of Veronique, The, 731
Double McGuffin, The, 163
Double-O Kid, The, 41
Double Obsession, 972
Double Revenge, 504
Double Standard, 504
◆ Double Suicide, 731
Double Threat, 504
Double Trouble (1967), 914
Double Trouble (1991), 268
Double Vision, 972
◆ Double Wedding, 268
Doublecrossed, 504
Doubting Thomas, 268
Dough and Dynamite/Knockout, The, 268
Doughboys, 268
Doughgirls, The, 268
Down Among the "Z" Men, 268
◆ Down and Dirty, 732
◆ Down and Out in America, 423
Down and Out in Beverly Hills, 268
Down Argentine Way, 914
◆ Down by Law, 268
Down Dakota Way, 1110
Down Texas Way, 1110
Down the Drain, 41
◆ Down to Earth, 268
Down to the Sea in Ships, 504
Down Twisted, 41
Down Under, 41
Downhill Racer, 504
Downtown, 41
◆ Dracula (1931), 837
◆ Dracula (1973), 837
Dracula (1979), 837
Dracula (Spanish Version), 732
Dracula: A Cinematic Scrapbook, 423
Dracula and Son, 837
Dracula Has Risen from the Grave, 837
Dracula Rising, 837
Dracula vs. Frankenstein, 837
Dracula's Daughter, 837
Dracula's Dog (see Zolton—Hound of Dracula)
Dracula's Great Love, 837
Dracula's Last Rites (1980), 837
Dracula's Widow, 837
Dragnet (1947), 41
◆ Dragnet (1954), 41
Dragnet (1987), 268
Dragon Chow, 732
Dragon Fight, 42
Dragon Seed, 504
◆ Dragon: The Bruce Lee Story, 42
Dragons Forever, 732
Dragonslayer, 1048
Dragstrip Girl, 42
Draughtman's Contract, The, 972
Draw, 1110
Dream a Little Dream, 269
Dream Date, 269
Dream for Christmas, A, 163
Dream Lover (1986), 972
Dream Lover (1994), 972
Dream Machine, 269
◆ Dream of Kings, A, 504
Dream of Passion, A, 504
Dream Street, 504
◆ Dream Team, The, 269
Dream to Believe, 504
◆ Dreamchild, 1048
Dreamer, 505
Dreaming Out Loud, 269
Dreams, 732
Dreams Come True, 1048
◆ Dreamscape, 1048
◆ **Dress Gray,** 505
Dressed to Kill (1946), 972
Dressed to Kill (1980), 972
◆ Dresser, The, 505
Dressmaker, The, 505
Drifter, The, 837
Driftin' Kid, 1110
◆ Drifting Weeds, 732
Driller Killer, The, 838
Drive-In, 269
Drive-In Massacre, 838
Drive Like Lightning, 42
◆ Driver, The, 42
Driver's Seat, The, 505
Driving Me Crazy, 269
◆ Driving Miss Daisy, 505
Droopy and Company, 164
Drop Dead Fred, 269
Drop Dead Gorgeous, 972
Drowning by Numbers, 505
Drowning Pool, The, 972
◆ Drugstore Cowboy, 505
Drum, 505
Drum Beat, 1110
Drum Taps, 1110
Drums, 42
◆ Drums Along the Mohawk, 42
Drums in the Deep South, 1110
Drums of Fu Manchu, 42
◆ Drunken Angel, 732
◆ Dry White Season, A, 505
Drying Up the Streets, 505
Du Barry Was a Lady, 915
Du-Beat-E-O, 915
Du Skal Here Din Hustro (see Master of the House)
Duchess and the Dirtwater Fox, The, 1110
Duchess of Idaho, 915
◆ Duck Soup, 269
Ducktales (TV Series), 164
Ducktales: The Movie—Treasure the Lost Lamp, 164
◆ Dude Ranger, 1110
Dudes, 505
◆ Duel, 972
Duel at Diablo, 1110
Duel in the Sun, 1110
Duel of Champions, 42
Duel of Hearts, 505
◆ Duellists, The, 42
Duet for One, 505
Duke of the Derby (see Gentlemer D'Espom)
Dumb Waiter, The, 506
◆ Dumbo, 164
Dune, 1048
Dune Warriors, 42
◆ Dunera Boys, The, 506
Dungeonmaster, The, 1048
Dunwich Horror, The, 838
Duplicates, 973
Dust, 506
Dust Devil, 838
Dusty, 164
Dutch, 269
Dutch Girls, 506
Dybbuk, The, 732
Dying to Remember, 973
Dying Young, 506
Dynamite and Gold, 1110
Dynamite Canyon, 1111
Dynamite Pass, 1111
Dynamo, 42
Dynasty of Fear, 973
◆ E.T.—The Extra-Terrestrial, 1048
◆ Each Dawn I Die, 42
Eagle, The, 269
Eagle Has Landed, The, 42
Eagle's Wing, 1111
◆ Early Frost, An, 506
◆ **Early Russian Cinema: Before the Revolutions (Vol. 1–10),** 732
Early Summer, 732
◆ Earrings of Madame De..., The, 7
◆ Earth, 732
Earth Girls Are Easy, 915
◆ Earth vs. the Flying Saucers, 1048
Earth vs. the Spider, 1048
Earthling, The, 164
Earthquake, 43
Earthworm Tractors, 269
East of Borneo, 43
◆ East of Eden (1955), 506
East of Eden (1982), 506
East of Elephant Rock, 506
East of Kilimanjaro, 43
East Side, West Side, 506
◆ Easter Parade, 915
◆ **Eastern Condors,** 733
Easy Come, Easy Go, 915
Easy Living, 506
Easy Money, 269
Easy Rider, 506
Easy to Love, 915
Easy Virtue, 507
Easy Wheels, 270
◆ Eat a Bowl of Tea, 507
Eat and Run, 1048
Eat My Dust, 43
Eat or Be Eaten, 270
Eat the Peach, 270
Eat the Rich, 270
Eaten Alive, 838

ten Alive by Cannibals (see Emerald Jungle)
ting, *507*
ting Raoul, *270*
ony Tower, The, *507*
ho Park, *507*
hoes in the Darkness, *507*
lipse, The, *733*
stasy, *733*
& His Dead Mother, *270*
die and the Cruisers, *915*
die and the Cruisers II: Eddie Lives!, *915*
die Macon's Run, *43*
die Murphy—Delirious, *270*
die Murphy Raw, *270*
dy Duchin Story, The, *507*
en (TV Series), *507*
ge of Darkness (1943), *43*
ge of Darkness (1986), *973*
ge of Honor, *43*
ge of Sanity, *838*
ison, The Man, *507*
lith and Marcel, *733*
ucating Rita, *270*
ucation of Sonny Carson, The, *507*
ward and Mrs. Simpson, *507*
ward II, *507*
ward Scissorhands, *1048*
gah!, *838*
ficiency Expert, The, *508*
g, *733*
g and I, The, *270*
yptian, The, *508*
ger Sanction, The, *43*
Seconds, *43*
Charing Cross Road, *508*
Charlie Mopic, *43*
0 Leagues Down the Amazon, *43*
½, *733*
ght Men Out, *508*
Million Ways to Die, *973*
Again, *270*
ghties, The, *733*
anaika (Why Not?), *733*
(This Strange Passion), *733*
Amor Brujo, *733*
Bruto (The Brute), *733*
Cid, *43*
Condor, *1111*
Diablo, *1111*
Dorado, *1111*
Mariachi, *733*
Norte, *733*
Paso Kid, *1111*
Professor Hippie, *734*
Super, *734*
ayne Boosler—Broadway Baby, *270*
ayne Boosler: Party of One, *270*
eanor: First Lady of the World, *508*
ectra Glide in Blue, *43*
ectric Dreams, *271*
ectric Grandmother, The, *1048*
ectric Horseman, The, *508*
egant Criminal, The, *734*
ektra, *915*
ement of Crime, The, *508*
ena and Her Men, *734*
eni, *508*
ephant Boy, *44*
ephant Man, The (1980), *508*
ephant Man, The (1982), *508*
ephant Parts, *915*
ephant Walk, *508*
ephant's Child, The, *164*

◆ Elevator to the Gallows, *734*
11 Harrowhouse, *973*
Elfego Baca: Six Gun Law, *1111*
Eliminators, The, *1048*
Ella Cinders, *271*
Ellis Island, *508*
Elmer Fudd Cartoon Festival: An Itch in Time, *164*
◆ Elmer Fudd's Comedy Capers, *164*
◆ Elmer Gantry, *509*
◆ Elusive Corporal, The, *734*
Elusive Pimpernel, The, *509*
Elves, *838*
◆ Elvira Madigan, *734*
Elvira, Mistress of the Dark, *271*
◆ Elvis '56, *423*
Elvis and Me, *915*
Elvis Files, The, *423*
Elvis on Tour, *423*
Elvis Stories, *271*
Elvis: The Lost Performances, *915*
◆ Elvis—The Movie, *509*
◆ Elvis—That's the Way It Is, *423*
Emanon, *271*
Emanuelle and the Last Cannibals (see Trap Them and Kill Them)
Embryo, *1048*
◆ Emerald Forest, The, *44*
Emerald Jungle, *838*
Emil and the Detectives, *164*
Emily, *509*
Eminent Domain, *973*
Emmanuelle, *734*
◆ Emma's Shadow, *734*
◆ Emo Philips Live, *271*
Emperor and the Nightingale, The, *164*
Emperor Jones, The, *509*
Emperor's New Clothes, The (1984), *164*
Emperor's New Clothes, The (1990), *164*
Empire of the Ants, *1049*
Empire of the Dark, *838*
Empire of the Sun, *509*
Empire State, *44*
◆ Empire Strikes Back, The, *1049*
Employees' Entrance, *271*
Empty Canvas, The, *509*
Empty Holsters, *1111*
◆ Enchanted April, *271*
Enchanted Cottage, The, *509*
Enchanted Forest, The, *165*
Enchanted Island, *44*
Encino Man, *271*
Encore, *509*
Encounter at Raven's Gate, *1049*
Encounter with the Unknown, *1049*
End, The, *271*
End of Innocence, The, *509*
End of St. Petersburg, The, *734*
End of the Line, *509*
End of the Road, *510*
◆ End of the Trail, *1111*
End of the World, *1049*
Endangered Species, *1049*
Endgame, *1049*
Endless Descent, *838*
Endless Game, The, *510*
Endless Love, *510*
Endless Night, *973*
◆ Endless Summer, The, *44*
Endurance, *271*
◆ Enemies—A Love Story, *510*
Enemy Below, The, *44*

◆ Enemy from Space, *1049*
Enemy Mine, *1049*
◆ Enemy of the Law, *1111*
Enemy Territory, *44*
Enemy Unseen, *44*
Enforcer, The (1951), *44*
◆ Enforcer, The (1976), *44*
◆ Englishman Abroad, An, *510*
Enigma, *44*
Enola Gay: The Men, the Mission, the Atomic Bomb, *510*
Ensign Pulver, *271*
Entangled, *973*
Enter Laughing, *271*
◆ Enter the Dragon, *44*
Enter the Ninja, *44*
◆ **Entertainer, The,** *510*
Entertaining Mr. Sloane, *271*
Entity, The, *838*
◆ Entre Nous (Between Us), *734*
Epic That Never Was, The, *423*
Equalizer, The: "Memories of Manon", *44*
Equinox (1993), *510*
Equinox (The Beast), *838*
◆ Equinox Flower, *734*
◆ Equus, *973*
Eraserhead, *838*
Erendira, *734*
◆ Eric, *510*
◆ Eric Bogosian—Funhouse, *272*
Erik the Viking, *1049*
Ernest Film Festival, *272*
Ernest Goes to Camp, *272*
◆ Ernest Goes to Jail, *272*
◆ **Ernest Green Story, The,** *165*
Ernest Rides Again, *272*
Ernest Saves Christmas, *165*
Ernest Scared Stupid, *272*
◆ Ernie Kovacs: Television's Original Genius, *272*
Erotikill, *838*
Errand Boy, The, *272*
Escapade in Florence, *165*
Escapade in Japan, *165*
Escape Artist, The, *165*
◆ Escape from Alcatraz, *45*
Escape from Fort Bravo, *1111*
Escape from New York, *45*
Escape from Safehaven, *1049*
◆ Escape from Sobibor, *45*
Escape from Survival Zone, *45*
Escape from the KGB, *45*
Escape from the Planet of the Apes, *1049*
Escape Me Never, *510*
Escape to Athena, *45*
Escape to Burma, *510*
Escape to Love, *511*
Escape to the Sun, *511*
Escape to Witch Mountain, *165*
Escape 2000, *1049*
Escapes, *1049*
Escapist, The, *511*
Eternal Return, The, *735*
Eternally Yours, *511*
Eternity, *511*
◆ Ethan Frome, *511*
Eu Te Amo (see I Love You)
◆ Eubie!, *916*
◆ Eureka, *511*
◆ Europa, Europa, *735*
European Vacation (see National Lampoon's European Vacation)
◆ Europeans, The, *511*

Eve of Destruction, *1050*
Evel Knievel, *45*
Evelyn Prentice, *511*
Even Cowgirls Get the Blues, *272*
Even More Ripping Yarns (see Ripping Yarns)
◆ Evening with Bob Goldthwait, An: Share the Warmth, *272*
Evening with Marlene Dietrich, An, *423*
◆ Evening with Robin Williams, An, *272*
◆ Evergreen, *916*
Everlasting Secret Family, The, *511*
Eversmile New Jersey, *511*
Every Breath, *973*
Every Day's a Holiday, *273*
Every Girl Should Be Married, *273*
◆ Every Man for Himself and God Against All, *735*
Every Time We Say Goodbye, *511*
Every Which Way but Loose, *273*
Everybody Sing, *916*
Everybody Wins, *973*
Everybody's All-American, *511*
◆ Everybody's Fine, *735*
Everything Happens at Night, *273*
◆ Everything You Always Wanted to Know About Sex but Were Afraid to Ask, *273*
Evictors, The, *839*
Evil, The, *839*
Evil Clutch, *839*
◆ Evil Dead, The, *839*
Evil Dead 2, *839*
Evil Laugh, *839*
Evil Mind, The (a.k.a. The Clairvoyant), *839*
Evil of Frankenstein, The, *839*
Evil Spawn, *839*
Evil Spirits, *839*
Evil Spirits in the House, *839*
Evil That Men Do, The, *45*
Evil Toons, *273*
Evil Town, *839*
◆ Evil under the Sun, *973*
Evils of the Night, *839*
Evilspeak, *839*
Ewok Adventure, The, *165*
Ewoks: The Battle for Endor, *165*
Ex-Lady, *512*
◆ Ex-Mrs. Bradford, The, *974*
◆ Excalibur, *1050*
Excessive Force, *45*
Execution, The, *974*
◆ Execution of Private Slovik, The, *512*
Executioner, The, *974*
Executioner's Song, The, *512*
◆ Executive Action, *512*
◆ Executive Suite, *512*
Exiled in America, *45*
Exiles, The, *424*
Exodus, *512*
Exorcism and Black Masses (see Demoniac)
◆ Exorcist, The, *839*
Exorcist II: The Heretic, *840*
Exorcist III: Legion, *840*
◆ Experience Preferred...But Not Essential, *273*
Experiment in Terror, *974*
◆ Experimental Films of Maya Deren Vol. I, *1050*
Experts, The, *273*
Explorers, *1050*
Exposed, *840*
Exposure, *45*
Express to Terror, *974*
◆ Exterminating Angel, The, *735*
Exterminator, The, *45*
Exterminator 2, The, *45*
Exterminators of the Year 3000, *1050*
Extra Girl, The, *273*
Extraordinary Adventures of Mr. West in the Land of the Bolsheviks, The, *735*
Extreme Justice, *512*
◆ Extreme Prejudice, *45*
Extremities, *512*
Eye for an Eye, *46*
Eye of the Demon, *840*
Eye of the Eagle, *46*
Eye of the Eagle 2, *46*
Eye of the Eagle 3, *46*
Eye of the Needle, *974*
Eye of the Storm, *974*
Eye of the Tiger, *46*
Eye on the Sparrow, *512*
Eyeball, *840*
Eyes Behind the Stars, *1050*
Eyes of a Stranger, *840*
Eyes of Evil (see Thousand Eyes of Dr. Mabuse, The)
Eyes of Fire, *840*
Eyes of Laura Mars, The, *974*
◆ Eyes of Texas, *1111*
Eyes of the Amaryllis, *165*
Eyes of the Beholder, *974*
◆ **Eyes of the Birds,** *735*
Eyes, the Mouth, The, *735*
◆ Eyes without a Face, *735*
◆ Eyewitness, *974*
Eyewitness to Murder, *46*
F.I.S.T., *512*
◆ Fabulous Baker Boys, The, *512*
Fabulous Dorseys, The, *916*
◆ Fabulous Fifties (Limited Gold Edition–1), The, *165*
Fabulous Fleischer Folio, The (Volume One), *165*
Fabulous Fleischer Folio, The (Volume Two), *165*
Fabulous Fleischer Folio, The (Volume Three), *166*
Fabulous Fleischer Folio, The (Volume Four), *166*
Fabulous Fleischer Folio, The (Volume Five), *166*
Fabulous Texan, The, *1112*
Fabulous Villains, The, *424*
Face at the Window, The, *840*
◆ Face in the Crowd, A, *512*
◆ Face of Another, The, *735*
Face the Music, *273*
Faces of Death I & II, *424*
Fade to Black (1980), *840*
Fade to Black (1993), *974*
◆ Fahrenheit 451, *1050*
◆ Fail-Safe, *974*
Fair Game, *974*
Fakeout, *513*
◆ Falcon and the Snowman, The, *513*
Falcon in Mexico, The, *975*
Falcon Takes Over, The, *975*
Falcon's Brother, The, *975*
Fall of the House of Usher, The (1949), *840*
Fall of the House of Usher, The (1960), *840*
Fall of the House of Usher, The (1979), *840*
◆ Fall of the Roman Empire, The, *513*
Fall of the Romanov Dynasty, The, *424*
Fallen Angel, *513*
◆ **Fallen Angels,** *513*
◆ Fallen Idol, The, *513*
Fallen Sparrow, The, *513*
◆ Falling Down, *513*
◆ Falling from Grace, *513*
Falling in Love, *513*
Falling in Love Again, *273*
False Arrest, *513*
False Colors, *1112*
False Identity, *975*
False Paradise, *1112*
Falstaff (see Chimes at Midnight)
Fame, *916*
Family, The (1970), *46*
Family, The (1987), *735*
Family Business, *514*
Family Circus Christmas, A, *166*
Family Dog, *166*
◆ Family Game, The, *735*
Family Jewels, The, *273*
Family Life, *514*
Family Matter, A, *514*
◆ Family Plot, *975*
Family Prayers, *514*
Family Upside Down, A, *514*
◆ Family Viewing, *514*
Famous Five Get into Trouble, The, *166*
Fan, The, *975*
Fancy Pants, *274*
Fandango, *274*
◆ Fanny (1932), *736*
◆ Fanny (1961), *514*
◆ Fanny and Alexander, *736*
Fanny Hill: Memoirs of a Woman of Pleasure, *514*
◆ Fantasia, *166*
Fantasies, *514*
Fantasist, The, *975*
Fantastic Planet, *1050*
Fantastic Voyage, *1050*
Fantasy Film Worlds of George Pal, The, *424*
Fantasy Island, *1050*
◆ Far and Away, *514*
Far Country, The, *1112*
Far from Home, *975*
◆ Far from the Madding Crowd, *514*
◆ Far Frontier, *1112*
Far North, *274*
Far Off Place, A, *166*
Far Out Man, *274*
Far Pavilions, The, *514*
◆ **Faraway, So Close,** *736*
Farewell My Concubine, *736*
◆ Farewell My Lovely, *975*
◆ Farewell to Arms, A, *514*
Farewell to the King, *46*
Fargo Express, *1112*
Farmer Takes a Wife, The, *916*
Farmer's Daughter, The, *274*
Farmer's Other Daughter, The, *274*
Fast Break, *274*
Fast Food, *274*
Fast Forward, *916*
Fast Getaway, *274*
Fast Lane Fever, *46*
Fast Money, *46*
Fast Talking, *166*

t Times at Ridgemont High, *274*
t-Walking, *515*
ter Pussycat! Kill! Kill!, *46*
test Guitar Alive, The, *1112*
test Gun Alive, The, *1112*
City, *515*
Man and Little Boy, *515*
l Attraction (1985), *975*
l Attraction (1987), *975*
l Beauty, *46*
l Bond, *975*
l Charm, *976*
l Exposure, *46*
l Games, *840*
l Glass of Beer, A/Pool Sharks, *274*
l Hour, The, *46*
l Image, The, *976*
l Instinct (1992), *976*
l Instinct (1993), *274*
l Mission, *46*
l Pulse, *840*
l Vision, *515*
, *274*
ner, *736*
ner Goose, *274*
ner Guido Sarducci Goes to College, *275*
her Hood, *47*
ner of the Bride (1950), *275*
ner of the Bride (1991), *275*
hers & Sons, *515*
ner's Little Dividend, *275*
ner's Revenge, A, *515*
so, *275*
y and His Funny Friends, *275*
y and Mabel Adrift/Mabel, Fatty and the Law, *275*
y Arbuckle Comedy Collection, Vol. 1, *275*
y Finn, *166*
y's Tin-Type Tangle/Our Congressman, *275*
st, *736*
or, The, *275*
or, the Watch and the Very Big Fish, The, *275*
lty Towers, *276*
Murders, The, *47*
Story, The, *515*
r (1955), *515*
r (1988), *976*
r (1990), *976*
r, Anxiety and Depression, *276*
r City, *47*
r in the Night (Dynasty of Fear), *840*
r Inside, The, *976*
r No Evil, *840*
r Strikes Out, *515*
rless (1978), *736*
rless (1993), *515*
rless Tiger, *47*
rless Vampire Killers, or, Pardon Me, But Your Teeth Are in My Neck, The, *840*
thered Serpent, The, *976*
lora, *515*
s, *276*
l My Pulse, *276*
x's Magic Bag of Tricks, *166*
ini Satyricon, *736*
ini's Roma, *736*
ow Traveler, *515*
nale, *276*

Female Jungle, *516*
Female Trouble, *276*
Femme Fatale, *976*
Fer-de-Lance, *976*
Fernandel the Dressmaker, *736*
Ferngully—The Last Rainforest, *166*
Ferocious Female Freedom Fighters, *276*
◆ Ferris Bueller's Day Off, *276*
Feud, The, *276*
Feud of the Trail, *1112*
Fever, *47*
Fever Pitch, *516*
◆ Few Good Men, A, *976*
ffolkes, *47*
◆ Fiddler on the Roof, *916*
Fiddlin' Buckaroo, *1112*
◆ Field, The, *516*
◆ Field of Dreams, *1050*
Field of Fire, *47*
Field of Honor (1986), *47*
Field of Honor (1988), *736*
Fiend, *841*
Fiend without a Face, *841*
Fiendish Plot of Dr. Fu Manchu, The, *276*
Fiesta, *916*
Fifth Avenue Girl, *276*
Fifth Floor, The, *841*
Fifth Monkey, The, *516*
Fifth Musketeer, The, *47*
55 Days at Peking, *516*
52 Pick-Up, *976*
Fifty/Fifty, *47*
Fight for Us, *47*
Fighter Attack, *47*
Fighting Back, *47*
Fighting Caravans, *1112*
Fighting Code, *1112*
Fighting Deputy, *1112*
Fighting Devil Dogs, The, *48*
Fighting Father Dunne, *516*
Fighting Kentuckian, The, *1112*
Fighting Mad, *516*
Fighting Marines, The, *48*
Fighting Prince of Donegal, The, *167*
Fighting Ranger, The, *1113*
Fighting Seabees, The, *48*
Fighting Shadows, *1113*
Fighting 69th, The, *48*
◆ Fighting Sullivans, The, *516*
Fighting Westerner, The, *1113*
Fighting with Kit Carson, *1113*
Film House Fever, *276*
Film Musicals, *277*
◆ Films of James Broughton, The, *1050*
Final Alliance, *48*
Final Analysis, *976*
Final Approach, *1051*
Final Chapter—Walking Tall, *48*
◆ Final Combat, The, *48*
Final Comedown, The, *48*
Final Conflict, The, *841*
Final Countdown, The, *1051*
Final Defeat, The, *1113*
Final Embrace, *977*
Final Exam, *841*
Final Executioner, The, *1051*
Final Extra, The, *977*
◆ Final Four: The Movie, *424*
Final Impact, *48*
Final Judgment, *977*
Final Justice, *48*
Final Mission, *48*

Final Notice, *977*
◆ Final Option, The, *977*
Final Programme, The (see Last Days of Man on Earth, The)
Final Round, *48*
Final Terror, The, *841*
Final Verdict, *516*
Find the Lady, *277*
Finders Keepers, *277*
Finders Keepers, Lovers Weepers, *516*
Fine Madness, A, *277*
Fine Mess, A, *277*
Fine Romance, A, *277*
Finest Hour, The, *48*
Finger Man (1955), *48*
Finger Man (1983) (see Philip Marlowe, Private Eye: Finger Man)
Finger on the Trigger, *1113*
◆ Fingers, *516*
Finian's Rainbow, *916*
Finish Line, *516*
Finishing School, *516*
Finishing Touch, The, *977*
◆ Finnegan Begin Again, *277*
Fire!, *48*
◆ Fire and Ice (1983), *1051*
Fire and Ice (1987), *49*
Fire and Sword, *1051*
Fire Birds, *49*
Fire Down Below, *517*
Fire, Ice & Dynamite, *49*
Fire in the Sky, *1051*
Fire Next Time, The, *1051*
Fire over England, *49*
Fire with Fire, *517*
◆ Fire Within, The, *736*
Firebird 2015 AD, *1051*
Firefly, The, *916*
Firefox, *49*
Firehawk, *49*
Firehead, *49*
Firehouse (1972), *49*
Firehouse (1987), *277*
Fireman's Ball, The, *737*
Firepower, *49*
◆ Fires on the Plain, *737*
Fires Within, *517*
Firesign Theatre's Hot Shorts, *277*
Firestarter, *841*
Firewalker, *49*
Firing Line, The, *49*
◆ **Firm, The,** *977*
First Affair, *517*
First and Ten, *277*
First Blood, *49*
First Deadly Sin, The, *977*
First Family, *277*
First Howie Mandel Special, The, *277*
First Love, *517*
First Man into Space, The, *1051*
First Men *in* the Moon, *1051*
First Monday in October, *517*
First Name: Carmen, *737*
First Nudie Musical, The, *917*
First Power, The, *841*
First Spaceship on Venus, *1051*
First Time, The, *277*
First Turn-on, The, *277*
First Yank into Tokyo, *49*
◆ Firstborn, *517*
◆ Fish Called Wanda, A, *277*
Fish Hawk, *517*
Fish That Saved Pittsburgh, The, *278*

◆ Fisher King, The, *1051*
Fisher Price Someday Me Series Vol. I: It's a Dog's Life, *167*
Fisher Price Video: Grimms' Fairy Tales: Hansel and Gretel/King Grizzle Beard, *167*
Fist Fighter, *49*
Fist of the North Star, *1051*
Fistful of Dollars, A, *1113*
Fistful of Dynamite, A, *1113*
Fists of Fury, *49*
Fit to Kill, *49*
Fitzcarraldo, *737*
Five Bloody Graves, *1113*
Five Came Back, *517*
Five Card Stud, *1113*
Five Corners, *517*
Five Days One Summer, *517*
◆ Five Easy Pieces, *517*
◆ **Five Fingers,** *977*
Five for Hell, *50*
Five Golden Dragons, *50*
Five Golden Hours, *278*
◆ Five Heartbeats, The, *917*
Five Pennies, The, *917*
◆ Five Thousand Fingers of Dr. T, The, *167*
Five Weeks in a Balloon, *50*
Fix, The, *50*
◆ **Fixer, The,** *517*
◆ Flame and the Arrow, The, *50*
Flame of the Barbary Coast, *50*
◆ Flame over India, *50*
Flame to the Phoenix, A, *50*
Flaming Frontiers, *1113*
◆ Flaming Star, *1113*
Flamingo Kid, The, *278*
Flamingo Road, *518*
◆ Flash, The, *1051*
Flash and the Firecat, *50*
Flash Gordon, *1052*
Flash Gordon Conquers the Universe, *1052*
Flash Gordon: Mars Attacks the World (a.k.a. Trip to Mars; Deadly Ray From Mars, The), *1052*
Flash Gordon: Rocketship (a.k.a. Spaceship to the Unknown; Perils from Planet Mongo), *1052*
Flash of Green, A, *977*
Flashback, *50*
Flashdance, *917*
Flashpoint, *977*
◆ Flask of Fields, A, *278*
Flat Top, *50*
Flatbed Annie and Sweetie Pie: Lady Truckers, *50*
Flatliners, *977*
Flesh, *518*
Flesh and Blood, *50*
Flesh and Blood Show, The, *841*
Flesh and Bone, *518*
Flesh and the Devil, *518*
Flesh Eaters, The, *841*
Flesh Eating Mothers, *841*
Flesh Feast, *841*
Flesh Gordon, *1052*
Flesh Gordon 2: Flesh Gordon meets the Cosmic Cheerleaders, *1052*
Fleshburn, *841*
◆ Fletch, *978*
Fletch Lives, *978*
Flicks, *278*
Flight from Vienna, *518*
Flight of Black Angel, *518*
◆ Flight of Dragons, The, *167*
Flight of the Eagle, *737*
◆ **Flight of the Innocent,** *737*
Flight of the Intruder, The, *50*
Flight of the Navigator, *1052*
◆ Flight of the Phoenix, The, *51*
Flight to Fury, *51*
Flight to Mars, *1052*
Flim-Flam Man, The, *518*
Flintstones, The, *167*
Flipper, *167*
Flipper's New Adventure, *167*
Flipper's Odyssey, *167*
Flirtation Walk, *917*
◆ Flirting, *518*
Floating Weeds (see Drifting Weeds)
Flood!, *51*
Flor Sylvestre, *737*
Florida Straits, *51*
Flower Drum Song, *917*
Flowers in the Attic, *978*
Flunky, Work Hard!, *737*
Flustered Comedy of Leon Errol, The, *278*
◆ Fly, The (1958), *841*
Fly, The (1986), *841*
Fly II, The, *842*
Flying Blind, *51*
Flying Deuces, *278*
Flying Down to Rio, *917*
Flying Fool, The, *51*
Flying Leathernecks, *51*
Flying Saucer, The, *1052*
◆ **Flying Saucers over Hollywood,** *424*
Flying Serpent, The, *842*
Flying Tigers, The, *51*
FM, *278*
Fog, The, *842*
Fog Island, *978*
Foghorn Leghorn's Fractured Funnies, *167*
Folks, *278*
Folks at the Red Wolf Inn, The (see Terror at the Red Wolf Inn)
Follow Me, Boys!, *167*
Follow Me Quietly, *978*
Follow That Camel, *278*
Follow That Car, *51*
Follow That Dream, *278*
◆ Follow the Fleet, *917*
Food of the Gods, *1052*
Food of the Gods Part II, *1052*
Fool and the Flying Ship, The, *167*
Fool for Love, *518*
Fool Killer, The, *978*
Foolin' Around, *278*
◆ Foolish Wives, *518*
Fools, *518*
Fools of Fortune, *518*
Footlight Parade, *917*
Footlight Serenade, *917*
◆ Footloose, *917*
For a Few Dollars More, *1113*
For a Lost Soldier, *737*
For Better and for Worse, *279*
◆ For Better or for Worse: The Bestest Present, *167*
For Keeps, *519*
For Ladies Only, *519*
For Love Alone, *519*
For Love of Angela, *519*
◆ For Love of Ivy, *279*
For Love or Money, *279*
For Me and My Gal, *917*
For Pete's Sake, *279*
For Queen and Country, *519*
For Richer, for Poorer, *279*
For the Boys, *918*
For the First Time, *918*
For the Love of Benji, *167*
For the Love of It, *279*
◆ For Us the Living: The Medgar Evers Story, *519*
For Your Eyes Only, *51*
For Your Love Only, *519*
Forbidden, *519*
Forbidden Dance, The, *918*
◆ Forbidden Games, *737*
Forbidden Love, *519*
◆ Forbidden Planet, *1052*
Forbidden Subjects (see Kinjite)
Forbidden Sun, *519*
Forbidden Trail, *1113*
Forbidden Trails, *1114*
Forbidden World, *842*
Forbidden Zone, *1053*
Force Five, *51*
Force of Evil, *519*
Force of One, *51*
Force Ten from Navarone, *51*
Forced Entry, *842*
Forced March, *519*
Forced Vengeance, *51*
Ford: The Man & the Machine, *519*
Foreign Affairs, *520*
Foreign Body, *279*
◆ Foreign Correspondent, *978*
Forest, The, *842*
Forever Amber, *520*
◆ Forever and a Day, *520*
Forever Darling, *279*
Forever Evil, *842*
◆ Forever James Dean, *424*
Forever Lulu, *279*
Forever Mary, *737*
Forever Young (1983), *520*
Forever Young (1992), *1053*
Forget Mozart, *737*
Forgotten, The, *520*
Forgotten One, The, *978*
Forgotten Prisoners, *520*
Forgotten Tune for the Flute, A, *73*
Forlorn River, *1114*
Formula, The, *978*
Forsaking All Others, *279*
◆ Fort Apache, *1114*
Fort Apache—The Bronx, *520*
Fort Osage, *1114*
Fortress (1985), *520*
Fortress (1993), *1053*
Fortress of Amerikkka, *51*
Fortune and Men's Eyes, *520*
◆ Fortune Cookie, The, *279*
Fortune Dane, *52*
Fortune's Fool, *738*
Fortunes of War, *520*
Forty Carats, *279*
◆ 48 Hrs., *279*
◆ 49th Parallel, The, *520*
◆ 42nd Street, *918*
Forty Seven Ronin, *738*
Forty Thieves, *1114*
Foul Play, *280*
Fountainhead, The, *520*
Four Adventures of Reinette and Mirabelle, *738*
◆ **Four Bags Full,** *738*
4D Man, *1053*

r Daughters, *520*
r Days in July, *521*
r Deuces, The, *52*
r Eyes and Six Guns, *1114*
r Faces West, *1114*
r Feathers, The (1939), *52*
r Feathers, The (1978), *52*
r for Texas, *1114*
r Friends, *521*
r Horsemen of the Apocalypse, *52*
) Blows, The, *738*
r in a Jeep, *521*
r Jacks and a Jill, *918*
r Musketeers, The, *52*
r Rode Out, *1114*
r Seasons, The, *521*
r Weddings and a Funeral, *280*
92: The Conquest of Paradise, *52*
rth Man, The, *738*
rth Protocol, The, *978*
rth Story, *978*
rth War, The, *52*
rth Wise Man, The, *521*
rth Wish, The, *521*
and His Friends, *738*
and the Hound, *168*
es, *521*
Fire, *521*
fire Light, *521*
trap, *52*
trot, *521*
y Brown, *52*
Diavalo (see Devil's Brother, The)
me Up, *52*
med (1930), *521*
med (1975), *52*
med (1990), *280*
nces, *521*
ncis Gary Powers: The True Story of the U-2 Spy Incident, *522*
ncis Goes to the Races, *280*
ncis in the Navy, *280*
ncis Joins the Wacs, *280*
ncis, the Talking Mule, *280*
nken and Davis at Stockton State, *280*
nkenhooker, *842*
nkenstein (1931), *842*
nkenstein (1973), *842*
nkenstein (1984), *842*
nkenstein (1992), *842*
nkenstein: A Cinematic Scrapbook, *424*
nkenstein and the Monster from Hell, *842*
nkenstein '88 (see Vindicator, The)
nkenstein General Hospital, *280*
nkenstein Island, *842*
nkenstein Meets the Space Monster, *842*
nkenstein Meets the Wolf Man, *843*
nkenstein 1970, *843*
nkenstein Unbound, *843*
nkenstein's Daughter, *843*
nkenweenie, *280*
nkie and Johnny (1934), *522*
nkie and Johnny (1966), *918*
nkie and Johnny (1991), *522*
ntic (1957) (see Elevator to the Gallows)
ntic (1988), *978*
nz, *738*
sier the Lovable Lion (Frasier the Sensuous Lion), *168*
Frasier the Sensitive Lion (see Frasier the Lovable Lion)
Fraternity Demon, *280*
Fraternity Vacation, *280*
Frauds, *281*
Freaked, *281*
Freakmaker, *843*
◆ Freaks, *843*
Freaky Friday, *168*
Freddie as F.R.O.7, *168*
Freddy's Dead: The Final Nightmare, *843*
Free and Easy, *281*
Free Ride, *281*
Free Soul, A, *522*
Free, White, and 21, *522*
◆ **Free Willy,** *168*
Freebie and the Bean, *281*
Freefall, *52*
Freejack, *1053*
Freeway, *52*
Freeway Maniac, *843*
◆ Freeze—Die—Come to Life, *738*
Freeze Frame, *168*
French Can Can, *738*
◆ French Connection, The, *53*
French Connection II, The, *53*
◆ French Detective, The, *738*
French Lessons, *281*
◆ French Lieutenant's Woman, The, *522*
French Line, The, *918*
French Postcards, *281*
French Quarter, *522*
French Way, The, *738*
French Woman, The, *522*
Frenchman's Farm, *843*
◆ Frenzy, *979*
Fresh Horses, *522*
Fresh Kill, *53*
◆ Freshman, The, *281*
Frida, *739*
Friday Foster, *53*
Friday the 13th, *843*
Friday the 13th, Part II, *843*
Friday the 13th, Part III, *843*
Friday the 13th—The Final Chapter, *843*
Friday the 13th, Part V—A New Beginning, *844*
Friday the 13th, Part VI: Jason Lives, *844*
Friday the 13th, Part VII: The New Blood, *844*
Friday the 13th, Part VIII: Jason Takes Manhattan, *844*
◆ Fried Green Tomatoes, *522*
◆ Friendly Fire, *522*
◆ Friendly Persuasion, *522*
Friends, Lovers & Lunatics, *281*
◆ Fright Night, *844*
Fright Night II, *844*
Frightmare, *844*
◆ Fringe Dwellers, The, *522*
Frisco Kid, The, *1114*
Fritz the Cat, *281*
Frog, *168*
Frogs, *844*
From Beyond, *844*
From Beyond the Grave, *844*
From Hell to Borneo, *53*
From Hell to Victory, *53*
◆ From Here to Eternity (1953), *523*
From Here to Eternity (1979), *523*
From Hollywood to Deadwood, *979*
◆ From Mao to Mozart, *424*
◆ From Pluto with Love (Limited Gold Edition 2), *168*
◆ From Russia with Love, *53*
From the Dead of Night, *844*
From the Earth to the Moon, *1053*
From the Hip, *281*
From the Lives of the Marionettes, *739*
From the Terrace, *523*
◆ Front, The, *523*
◆ Front Page, The (1931), *281*
Front Page, The (1974), *281*
Frontier Horizon, *1114*
Frontier Pony Express, *1114*
Frontiersman, The, *1114*
Frozen Assets, *282*
Frozen Terror, *844*
Fruit Machine, The (see Wonderland)
Fugitive, The (1947), *523*
◆ **Fugitive, The (1993),** *53*
◆ Fugitive, The (TV Series), *523*
Fugitive, The: The Last Episode (TV Series), *53*
Fugitive Girls, *53*
Fugitive Kind, The, *523*
Fugitive Road, *523*
Fugitive Valley, *1114*
Fulfillment, *523*
Full Contact, *53*
Full Eclipse, *844*
Full Exposure, *523*
Full Fathom Five, *53*
Full Hearts and Empty Pockets, *739*
◆ Full Metal Jacket, *523*
Full Moon in Blue Water, *282*
Full Moon in Paris, *739*
Fuller Brush Girl, The, *282*
Fuller Brush Man, The, *282*
Fun and Fancy Free, *168*
Fun Down There, *523*
Fun in Acapulco, *918*
◆ Fun with Dick and Jane, *282*
Funeral, The, *739*
Funeral in Berlin, *979*
Funhouse, The, *845*
Funland, *282*
Funny About Love, *282*
Funny Dirty Little War (No Habra Mas Penas ni Olvido), *739*
Funny Face, *918*
Funny Farm, *282*
◆ Funny Girl, *918*
Funny Lady, *918*
◆ Funny Thing Happened on the Way to the Forum, A, *282*
Further Adventures of Tennessee Buck, The, *53*
◆ Fury, *524*
Fury, The, *845*
Fury of Hercules, The, *54*
Fury of the Congo, *54*
Fury of the Wolf Man, *845*
Future Hunters, *845*
Future-Kill, *845*
Future Shock, *1053*
Future Zone, *54*
Futurekick, *1053*
Futureworld, *1053*
Futz, *524*
Fuzz, *282*
F/X, *979*
F/X 2: The Deadly Art of Illusion, *979*
◆ G-Men, *54*
G-Men Never Forget, *54*

G-Men vs. The Black Dragon, 54
G.I. Blues, 918
G.I. Joe: The Movie, 168
Gabe Kaplan as Groucho, 282
Gabriel over the White House, 524
Gabriela, 739
◆ Gaby, a True Story, 524
Gal Young 'Un, 524
Galactic Gigolo, 282
Galaxina, 1053
Galaxy Express, The, 168
Galaxy of Terror, 1053
Gall Force, 739
Gall Force 2, 739
◆ Gallagher—Melon Crazy, 282
◆ Gallagher—Over Your Head, 282
◆ Gallagher—Stuck in the 60s, 283
◆ Gallagher—The Bookkeeper, 283
Gallagher—The Maddest, 283
Gallagher's Travels, 54
Gallant Hours, The, 524
Gallery of Horrors (see Bloodsuckers, The)
◆ Gallipoli, 524
Galloping Ghost, The, 54
Gambit, 283
Gamble, The, 54
Gamble on Love, 524
Gambler, The (1974), 524
Gambler, The (1980), 1114
Gambler and the Lady, The, 524
Gambler, Part II—The Adventure Continues, The, 1115
Gambler, Part III—The Legend Continues, The, 1115
Gambler Returns, the: Luck of the Draw, 1115
Game, The, 54
Game for Vultures, 54
Game Is Over, The, 739
Game of Death, 54
Game of Love, The, 524
Game of Seduction, 739
Gamera (see Gamera the Invincible)
Gamera the Invincible, 1053
Gamera Versus Barugon, 1054
Gamera Versus Gaos, 1054
Gamera Versus Guiron, 1054
Gamera Versus Zigra, 1054
Games of Countess Dolingen of Gratz, The, 739
Gamma People, The, 1054
◆ Gandhi, 524
Gang Busters, 54
Gangs, Inc., 54
Gangs of Sonora, 1115
Gangster, The, 525
Gangster Story, 979
Gangster Wars, 54
Gangster's Boy, 525
Gangster's Law, 525
Ganjasaurus Rex, 845
Gap-Toothed Women, 424
Garbage Pail Kids Movie, The, 168
◆ Garbo Talks, 283
Garden, The, 525
Garden of Allah, The, 525
Garden of Delights, The, 739
◆ Garden of the Finzi-Continis, The, 740
Gardens of Stone, 525
Garlic Is as Good as 10 Mothers, 424
◆ Garry Shandling: Alone in Vegas, 283
Garry Shandling Show, The, 283
Gas, 283
◆ Gas, Food, Lodging, 525
Gas Pump Girls, 283
◆ Gaslight (1940), 979
◆ Gaslight (1944), 979
Gas-s-s-s, 1054
Gate, The, 845
Gate II, 845
◆ Gate of Hell, 740
Gates of Hell, 845
◆ Gateway to the Mind, 168
◆ Gathering, The, 525
Gathering, Part II, The, 525
Gathering Storm, 525
Gator, 54
Gator Bait, 55
Gator Bait II—Cajun Justice, 55
Gauntlet, The, 55
◆ Gay Divorcée, The, 918
Gay Purr-ee, 168
◆ **Gazebo, The,** 283
Geek Maggot Bingo, 283
◆ **Geisha, A,** 740
Gene Krupa Story, The, 525
◆ General, The, 283
◆ General Della Rovere, 740
General Died at Dawn, The, 55
◆ General Idi Amin Dada, 424
General Spanky, 169
Generation, 283
Generation, A, 740
◆ Genesis Survivor Gaiarth: Stage 1, 1054
Genevieve, 283
Gentle Giant, 169
Gentle Savage, 1115
Gentleman Bandit, The, 525
Gentleman from California, 1115
◆ Gentleman Jim, 525
Gentleman Killer, 1115
Gentlemen Prefer Blondes, 284
Gentlemen's Agreement, 526
Genuine Risk, 979
George and the Christmas Star, 169
George Balanchine's The Nutcracker, 919
George Burns and Gracie Allen Show, The (TV Series), 284
George Burns—His Wit and Wisdom, 284
◆ George Burns in Concert, 284
George Carlin: Doin' It Again, 284
◆ **George Carlin: Jammin' in New York,** 284
◆ George Carlin Live! What Am I Doing in New Jersey?, 284
George Carlin—Playin' with Your Head, 284
George McKenna Story, The, 526
◆ George of the Jungle, 169
George Washington, 526
George Washington Slept Here, 284
George Washington: The Forging of a Nation, 526
George White's Scandals, 919
George's Island, 169
Georgia, 979
Georgia, Georgia, 526
Georgy Girl, 284
Gerald McBoing-Boing (Columbia Pictures Cartoons Volume Three), 169
Geronimo, 1115
Geronimo: An American Legend, 1115
◆ Gertrude, 740
Gervaise, 740
Get Christie Love!, 55
Get Crazy, 284
Get Out of My Room, 284
Get Out Your Handkerchiefs, 740
Get Smart Again, 285
Get to Know Your Rabbit, 285
◆ Getaway, The (1972), 55
Getaway, The (1994), 55
Getting Even, 55
Getting Even with Dad, 285
◆ Getting It Right, 285
◆ Getting of Wisdom, The, 526
Getting Over, 526
Getting Physical, 526
Getting Straight, 526
Gettysburg, 526
Ghastly Ones, The, 845
Ghidrah, the Three-Headed Monst 845
Ghost, The (1963), 845
Ghost (1990), 527
◆ Ghost and Mrs. Muir, The, 285
Ghost Breakers, 285
Ghost Chase, 845
Ghost Dad, 285
Ghost Fever, 285
◆ Ghost Goes West, The, 285
Ghost in Monte Carlo, A, 527
Ghost in the Machine, 845
Ghost in the Noonday Sun, 285
Ghost of Frankenstein, 845
Ghost Patrol, 55
Ghost Ship, 846
Ghost Story, 846
Ghost Town, 846
Ghost Town Law, 1115
Ghost Town Renegades, 1115
Ghost Warrior, 55
◆ Ghostbusters, 285
Ghostbusters II, 285
Ghostriders, 846
Ghosts Can't Do It, 285
Ghosts of Berkeley Square, 285
Ghosts on the Loose, 286
Ghoul, The (1933), 846
Ghoul, The (1975), 846
Ghoulies, 846
Ghoulies II, 846
Ghoulies III, 846
Giant, 527
Giant Gila Monster, The, 846
Giant of Metropolis, The, 1054
◆ **Giant Robo,** 740
◆ Gideon's Trumpet, 527
Gidget, 286
Gidget Goes Hawaiian, 286
Gidget Goes to Rome, 286
Gift, The, 740
Gift of Love, The, 527
Gig, The, 286
Gigantor—Vols. 1–3, 169
◆ Gigi, 919
◆ Gilda, 527
Gilda Live, 286
Gimme an "F", 286
◆ Gimme Shelter, 424
◆ Gin Game, The, 527
Ginger Ale Afternoon, 286
◆ Ginger and Fred, 740
Ginger in the Morning, 527
Gird City (see And Nothing But th Truth)
Girl, The, 527

Girl, a Guy and a Gob, A, *286*
Girl Can't Help It, The, *286*
Girl Crazy, *919*
Girl from Hunan, *740*
Girl from Missouri, The, *286*
Girl from Petrovka, The, *527*
Girl Happy, *919*
Girl Hunters, The, *979*
Girl in Blue, The, *527*
Girl in Every Port, A, *286*
Girl in the Moon (see Woman in the Moon)
Girl in the Picture, The, *286*
Girl Most Likely, The, *919*
Girl of the Golden West, The, *919*
Girl on a Chain Gang, *55*
Girl on a Swing, The, *980*
Girl Rush, *286*
Girl School Screamers, *846*
Girl Talk, *424*
Girl to Kill For, A, *980*
Girl Who Had Everything, The, *527*
Girl Who Spelled Freedom, The, *169*
Girl with the Hatbox, The, *741*
Girlfriend from Hell, *287*
Girlfriends, *528*
Girls! Girls! Girls!, *919*
Girls Just Want to Have Fun, *287*
Girls of Huntington House, *528*
Girls Town, *55*
Girly, *846*
Git Along, Little Dogies, *1115*
Give a Girl a Break, *919*
Give 'em Hell, Harry!, *528*
Give My Regards to Broad Street, *919*
Gizmo!, *425*
Gladiator, The, *55*
Gladiator, *528*
Glass Bottom Boat, The, *287*
Glass House, The, *528*
Glass Key, The, *980*
Glass Menagerie, The, *528*
Glass Slipper, The, *919*
Gleaming the Cube, *55*
Glen and Randa, *1054*
Glen or Glenda, *528*
Glengarry Glen Ross, *528*
Glenn Miller Story, The, *919*
Glitch!, *287*
Glitter Dome, The, *980*
Glitz, *980*
Global Affair, A, *287*
Gloria, *56*
Gloriana, *919*
Glorifying the American Girl, *919*
Glory, *528*
Glory at Sea, *56*
Glory Boys, The, *56*
Glory! Glory!, *287*
Glory Stompers, The, *56*
Glory Years, *287*
Gnome-Mobile, The, *169*
Go for Broke!, *528*
Go Into Your Dance, *920*
Go, Johnny, Go!, *920*
Go Kill and Come Back, *1115*
Go-Masters, The, *741*
Go Tell the Spartans, *56*
Go West, *287*
Go West, Young Man, *287*
Goalie's Anxiety at the Penalty Kick, *741*
Goat, The (see La Chevre)
God Bless the Child, *528*
God Told Me To (see Demon)
Goddess, The, *528*
◆ Godfather, The, *529*
◆ Godfather, Part II, The, *529*
◆ Godfather, Part III, The, *529*
◆ Godfather Epic, The, *529*
God's Gun, *1116*
God's Gun (see Bullet from God, A)
◆ God's Little Acre, *529*
◆ Gods Must Be Crazy, The, *287*
◆ Gods Must Be Crazy II, The, *287*
Gods of the Plague, *741*
Godsend, The, *846*
Godzilla, King of the Monsters, *846*
Godzilla 1985, *846*
Godzilla Versus Biollante, *1054*
Godzilla vs. Gigan, *846*
Godzilla vs. Mechagodzilla, *846*
Godzilla vs. Monster Zero, *846*
Godzilla vs. Mothra, *846*
Godzilla vs. the Sea Monster, *847*
Godzilla vs. the Smog Monster, *1054*
Godzilla's Revenge, *847*
Goin' South, *1116*
Goin' to Town, *287*
Going Ape!, *287*
Going Bananas, *169*
Going Berserk, *287*
Going Hollywood, *920*
◆ Going in Style, *288*
◆ Going My Way, *529*
Going Places, *741*
Going to Congress and Don't Park There, *288*
Going Under, *288*
Going Undercover, *288*
◆ Golden Age of Looney Toons, The: Bob Clampett, *169*
Golden Age of Looney Toons, The: Bugs Bunny by Each Director, *169*
Golden Age of Looney Toons, The: Chuck Jones, *170*
◆ Golden Age of Looney Toons, The: Firsts, *170*
◆ Golden Age of Looney Toons, The: Friz Freleng, *170*
Golden Age of Looney Toons, The: Hurry for Hollywood, *170*
Golden Age of Looney Toons, The: 1930s Musicals, *170*
◆ Golden Age of Looney Toons, The: 1940s Zanies, *170*
Golden Age of Looney Toons, The: Tex Avery, *170*
◆ Golden Age of Looney Toons, The: The Art of Bugs, *170*
◆ Gold Diggers of 1933, *920*
Gold Diggers of 1935, *920*
Gold of Naples, The, *529*
◆ Gold Rush, The, *288*
◆ Golden Age of Comedy, The, *288*
◆ Golden Boy, *529*
Golden Child, The, *56*
◆ Golden Coach, The, *741*
Golden Demon, *741*
◆ **Golden Earrings,** *56*
◆ Golden Honeymoon, The, *529*
Golden Seal, The, *170*
Golden Stallion, The, *1116*
◆ Golden Voyage of Sinbad, The, *1054*
Goldengirl, *1054*
◆ Goldfinger, *56*
Goldilocks and the Three Bears, *171*
Goldwyn Follies, The, *920*
Goldy, The Last of the Golden Bears, *171*
◆ Golem, The (How He Came into the World) (Der Golem, Wie er in die Welt), *741*
Golgotha, *741*
Goliath and the Barbarians, *56*
Goliath and the Dragon, *56*
Goliath and the Vampires, *847*
Goliath Awaits, *56*
Gone Are the Days, *288*
Gone in 60 Seconds, *56*
Gone to Texas, *1116*
Gone with the West, *1116*
◆ Gone with the Wind, *530*
◆ Gonza the Spearman, *741*
◆ Good Earth, The, *530*
◆ Good Father, The, *530*
Good Fight, The, *530*
◆ Good Grief, Charlie Brown, *171*
Good Guys Wear Black, *56*
Good Idea, *288*
Good Morning...and Goodbye!, *530*
Good Morning, Babylon, *530*
Good Morning, Vietnam, *530*
Good Mother, The, *530*
Good Neighbor Sam, *288*
Good News, *920*
Good Night, Michelangelo, *288*
Good Sam, *288*
Good Son, The, *980*
Good, the Bad, and Huckleberry Hound, The, *171*
◆ Good the Bad and the Ugly, The, *1116*
Good Wife, The, *530*
Goodbye Again, *530*
Goodbye Bird, The, *171*
◆ Goodbye Columbus, *288*
Goodbye Emmanuelle, *741*
◆ Goodbye Girl, The, *288*
Goodbye, Miss 4th of July, *171*
◆ Goodbye, Mr. Chips (1939), *530*
Goodbye, Mr. Chips (1969), *920*
Goodbye, My Lady, *171*
Goodbye New York, *289*
Goodbye, Norma Jean, *530*
◆ Goodbye People, The, *530*
◆ Goodfellas, *531*
Goodnight, God Bless, *847*
Goof Balls, *289*
Goof Troop, *171*
Goonies, The, *56*
Goose Woman, The, *980*
Gor, *1054*
Gorath, *847*
Gordon's War, *57*
Gore-Met, Zombie Chef from Hell, *847*
Gore Vidal's Billy The Kid, *1116*
◆ **Gore Vidal's Lincoln,** *531*
Gorgeous Hussy, The, *531*
Gorgo, *847*
Gorgon, The, *847*
Gorilla, The, *289*
◆ Gorillas in the Mist, *531*
Gorky Park, *980*
Gorp, *289*
◆ Gospel, *425*
◆ Gospel According to Saint Matthew, The, *741*
Gospel According to Vic, The, *289*
◆ Gotcha!, *980*
Gotham, *980*
Gothic, *847*

Government Agents vs. Phantom Legion, *57*
Grace Quigley, *289*
◆ Graduate, The, *531*
Graduation Day, *847*
Graffiti Bridge, *920*
Grain of Sand, The, *741*
◆ Grand Canyon, *531*
Grand Canyon Trail, *1116*
Grand Highway, The (see La Grand Chemin)
◆ Grand Hotel, *531*
◆ Grand Illusion, *742*
Grand Isle, *531*
Grand Larceny, *289*
Grand Prix, *531*
Grand Theft Auto, *57*
Grand Tour: Disaster in Time, *1054*
Grandma's House, *980*
Grandview, U.S.A., *531*
◆ Grapes of Wrath, The, *531*
◆ Grass, *425*
Grass Is Always Greener Over the Septic Tank, The, *289*
Grass Is Greener, The, *289*
Grateful Dead Movie, The, *425*
◆ **Grave of the Fireflies,** *742*
Grave of the Vampire, *847*
Grave Secrets, *847*
Grave Secrets: The Legacy of Hilltop Drive, *980*
Graveyard Shift (1987), *847*
Gray Lady Down, *57*
Grayeagle, *1116*
Grease, *920*
Grease 2, *920*
Greased Lightning, *57*
Greaser's Palace, *532*
Great Adventure, The, *1116*
Great Alligator, The, *847*
◆ Great American West, *425*
◆ Great Balls of Fire, *920*
Great Bank Hoax, The, *289*
◆ Great Caruso, The, *920*
◆ Great Chase, The, *57*
Great Dan Patch, The, *532*
Great Day, *532*
◆ Great Dictator, The, *289*
◆ Great Escape, The, *57*
Great Escape II, The, *57*
◆ Great Expectations (1946), *532*
Great Expectations (1983), *171*
◆ Great Expectations (1988), *532*
◆ Great Expectations (1989), *171*
Great Expectations—The Untold Story, *532*
Great Flamarion, The, *532*
Great Gabbo, The, *532*
Great Gatsby, The, *532*
Great Gundown, *1116*
Great Guns, *289*
Great Guy, *532*
Great Impostor, The, *532*
Great Land of Small, The, *171*
Great Lie, The, *532*
Great Locomotive Chase, The, *171*
Great Los Angeles Earthquake, The, *532*
Great Love Experiment, The, *533*
◆ Great Lover, The, *289*
Great Madcap, The, *742*
Great Man Votes, The, *289*
Great McGinty, The, *290*
Great Missouri Raid, The, *1116*
Great Moment, The, *290*
◆ Great Muppet Caper, The, *171*
◆ Great, My Parents Are Divorcing, *742*
Great Northfield Minnesota Raid, The, *1116*
Great Outdoors, The, *290*
Great Race, The, *290*
Great Riviera Bank Robbery, The, *980*
◆ **Great Rock and Roll Swindle, The,** *921*
Great St. Trinian's Train Robbery, The, *290*
◆ Great Santini, The, *533*
Great Scout and Cathouse Thursday, The, *1116*
Great Smokey Roadblock, The, *57*
Great Space Chase, *171*
Great Texas Dynamite Chase, The, *57*
◆ **Great Toy Train Layouts of America (Volumes 1–6),** *425*
◆ Great Train Robbery, The, *980*
Great Waldo Pepper, The, *57*
Great Wall, A, *290*
Great Wallendas, The, *533*
◆ Great Waltz, The, *921*
Great White Hope, The, *533*
◆ Great Ziegfeld, The, *921*
Greatest, The, *533*
◆ Greatest Man in the World, The, *290*
◆ Greatest Show on Earth, The, *533*
Greatest Story Ever Told, The, *533*
◆ Greed, *533*
Greedy, *290*
Greek Tycoon, The, *533*
Green Archer, *981*
Green Berets, The, *57*
◆ Green Card, *290*
Green Dolphin Street, *533*
Green Hornet, The (TV Series), *58*
Green Ice, *981*
Green Man, The, *981*
◆ Green Pastures, *533*
Green Promise, The, *533*
Green Room, The, *742*
Green Slime, The, *1055*
◆ Green Wall, The, *742*
Greenstone, The, *172*
Greetings, *290*
◆ Gregory's Girl, *290*
◆ Gremlins, *1055*
◆ Gremlins 2: The New Batch, *1055*
Grendel, Grendel, Grendel, *172*
Greta the Mad Butcher, Ilsa—Absolute Power (see Ilsa the Wicked Warden)
◆ Grey Fox, The, *1117*
◆ Grey Gardens, *425*
Greyfriars Bobby, *172*
Greystoke: The Legend of Tarzan, Lord of the Apes, *58*
Grievous Bodily Harm, *533*
Griffin and Phoenix: A Love Story, *533*
◆ Grifters, The, *534*
Grim Prairie Tales, *847*
Grim Reaper, The (1962), *742*
Grim Reaper, The (1980), *847*
Grissom Gang, The, *534*
Grizzly, *847*
Groove Tube, The, *291*
Gross Anatomy, *534*
Gross Jokes, *291*
Grotesque, *847*
Ground Zero, *981*
Groundhog Day, *291*
Groundstar Conspiracy, The, *1055*
Group, The, *534*
Grown-ups, *534*
Gruesome Twosome, *848*
◆ **Grumpy Old Men,** *291*
◆ Guadalcanal Diary, *58*
Guardian, The (1984), *534*
Guardian, The (1990), *848*
Guardian of the Abyss, *848*
◆ **Guarding Tess,** *291*
◆ Guardsman, The, *291*
Guess Who's Coming to Dinner, *53*
Guest in the House, *534*
Guest Wife, *291*
Guide for the Married Man, A, *291*
Guide for the Married Woman, A, *2*
Guilty as Charged, *291*
Guilty as Sin, *534*
◆ Guilty by Suspicion, *534*
Gulag, *534*
Gulliver in Lilliput, *291*
Gulliver's Travels (1939), *172*
Gulliver's Travels (1977), *172*
Gumball Rally, The, *58*
Gumby and the Wild West (Volume Four), *172*
Gumby Celebration, A (Volume Ten *172*
Gumby for President (Volume Nine *172*
Gumby Magic (Volume Two), *172*
Gumby Rides Again (Volume Five), *172*
Gumby (Series) (see Return of Gumby)
Gumby Summer, A (Volume Eight) *172*
Gumby's Fun Fling (Volume Eleven *172*
Gumby's Holiday Special (Volume Seven), *172*
Gumby's Incredible Journey (Volu Six), *172*
Gumshoe, *291*
Gumshoe Kid, The, *292*
Gun Code, *1117*
Gun Crazy (1950), *981*
Gun Fury, *1117*
Gun in Betty Lou's Handbag, The,
Gun in the House, A, *534*
Gun is Loaded, The, *921*
Gun Play (see Lucky Boots)
Gun Riders, The, *1117*
Gun Smugglers, *1117*
Gunbuster—Vols. 1–3, *742*
Guncrazy (1992), *535*
Gundown at Sandoval, *1117*
Gunfight, A, *1117*
◆ Gunfight at the O.K. Corral, *1117*
◆ Gunfighter, The, *1117*
Gunfighters, The, *1117*
Gunfire, *1117*
Gung Ho! (1943), *58*
◆ Gung Ho (1985), *292*
◆ Gunga Din, *58*
Gunman from Bodie, *1117*
Gunmen, *58*
Gunrunner, The, *58*
Guns, *58*
Guns for Dollars, *1117*
◆ **Guns of August, The,** *425*
Guns of Diablo, *1118*
Guns of Fort Petticoat, *1118*
Guns of Hate, *1118*
◆ Guns of Navarone, The, *58*

Guns of the Magnificent Seven, *1118*
Gunslinger, *1118*
Gunsmoke: Return to Dodge, *1118*
Gunsmoke (TV Series), *1118*
Gus, *172*
Guy: Awakening of the Devil, *742*
Guy II: Second Target, *742*
Guy Named Joe, A, *535*
Guys and Dolls, *921*
Guyver: Out of Control, *742*
Guyver, The, *1055*
Guyver, The, Vols. 1–4, *1055*
Gymkata, *58*
Gypsy (1962), *921*
Gypsy (1993), *921*
Gypsy Angels, *535*
Gypsy Blood, *535*
Gypsy Colt, *173*
Gypsy Warriors, The, *58*
H-Bomb, *58*
H-Man, The, *848*
H.O.T.S., *292*
Hadley's Rebellion, *173*
Hail Caesar, *292*
Hail, Hero!, *535*
Hail Mary, *742*
Hail the Conquering Hero, *292*
Hair, *921*
Hairdresser's Husband, The, *742*
Hairspray, *292*
Hairy Ape, The, *535*
Half a Sixpence, *921*
Half-Breed, The, *1118*
Half Human, *848*
Half-Moon Street, *981*
Half of Heaven, *743*
Half-Shot at Sunrise, *292*
Hallelujah!, *535*
Hallelujah Trail, The, *1118*
Halloween, *848*
Halloween II, *848*
Halloween III: Season of the Witch, *848*
Halloween IV: The Return of Michael Myers, *848*
Halloween V: The Revenge of Michael Myers, *848*
Halls of Montezuma, *59*
Hambone and Hillie, *535*
Hamburger Hill, *535*
Hamburger—The Motion Picture, *292*
Hamlet (1948), *535*
Hamlet (1969), *535*
Hamlet (1990), *535*
Hammered: The Best of Sledge, *292*
Hammersmith Is Out, *292*
Hammett, *981*
Hand, The, *848*
Hand That Rocks the Cradle, The, *981*
Handful of Dust, A, *535*
Handmaid's Tale, The, *1055*
Hands Across the Border, *1118*
Hands of a Stranger, *981*
Hands of Steel, *1055*
Hands of the Ripper, *848*
Hands Up!, *292*
Hang 'em High, *1118*
Hangar 18, *1055*
Hangin' with the Homeboys, *292*
Hanging on a Star, *536*
Hanging Tree, The, *1118*
Hangman's Knot, *1119*
Hangmen, *59*
Hangmen Also Die, *536*
Hangover, The (see Female Jungle)
Hanky Panky, *292*
Hanna K., *743*
◆ Hannah and Her Sisters, *293*
Hannah, Queen of Vampires (see Crypt of the Living Dead)
Hanna's War, *536*
Hannie Caulder, *1119*
Hanoi Hilton, The, *536*
Hanover Street, *536*
Hans Brinker, *173*
Hans Christian Andersen, *921*
Hans Christian Andersen's Thumbelina, *173*
Hansel and Gretel, *173*
◆ Hanussen, *743*
Happiest Millionaire, The, *173*
Happily Ever After, *743*
◆ Happy Anniversary 007: 25 Years of James Bond, *425*
Happy Birthday, Gemini, *293*
Happy Birthday to Me, *848*
◆ Happy Birthday Bugs: 50 Looney Years, *173*
Happy Go Lovely, *921*
Happy Hooker, The, *293*
Happy Hooker Goes Hollywood, The, *293*
Happy Hooker Goes to Washington, The, *293*
Happy Hour, *293*
Happy Landing, *921*
Happy New Year, *293*
◆ Happy New Year (La Bonne Année), *743*
Happy New Year, Charlie Brown, *173*
Happy Together, *293*
Hard Choices, *536*
Hard Country, *293*
◆ Hard Day's Night, A, *921*
Hard Promises, *536*
Hard Rock Zombies, *848*
Hard Target, *59*
Hard Ticket to Hawaii, *59*
◆ Hard Times, *59*
Hard to Die, *848*
Hard to Hold, *922*
Hard to Kill, *59*
Hard Traveling, *536*
◆ **Hard Way, The (1942),** *536*
Hard Way, The (1979), *59*
Hard Way, The (1991), *293*
Hardbodies, *293*
Hardbodies 2, *293*
Hardcore, *981*
◆ Harder They Come, The, *922*
Harder They Fall, The, *536*
Hardhat and Legs, *536*
Hardly Working, *293*
Hardware, *1055*
Harem, *536*
◆ Harlan County, U.S.A., *425*
Harlem Nights, *59*
Harlem Rides the Range, *1119*
Harley, *536*
Harley Davidson and the Marlboro Man, *59*
Harlow, *536*
Harmony Cats, *536*
Harmony Lane, *922*
◆ Harold and Maude, *294*
◆ Harold Lloyd: The Third Genius, *425*
Harold Lloyd's Comedy Classics, *294*
◆ Harper, *981*
Harper Valley P.T.A., *294*
Harrad Experiment, The, *537*
Harry and Son, *537*
Harry and the Hendersons, *1055*
◆ Harry and Tonto, *537*
Harry and Walter Go to New York, *294*
Harry Tracy, *1119*
Harry's War, *294*
Harum Scarum, *922*
◆ Harvest, *743*
Harvest, The, *981*
◆ Harvey, *294*
Harvey Girls, The, *922*
Hasty Heart, *537*
Hatari!, *59*
Hatbox Mystery, The, *982*
Hatchet for the Honeymoon, *848*
Hatfields and the McCoys, The, *1119*
Haunted Castle, *849*
Haunted Gold, *1119*
Haunted Honeymoon, *294*
Haunted Palace, The, *849*
Haunted Strangler, The, *849*
Haunted Summer, *537*
◆ Haunting, The, *849*
Haunting Fear, *849*
Haunting of Julia, The, *537*
Haunting of Morella, The, *849*
Haunting of Sarah Hardy, The, *982*
Haunting Passion, The, *1055*
Haunts of the Very Rich, *1055*
Havana, *537*
Have a Nice Funeral, *1119*
Have Picnic Basket, Will Travel, *173*
Having a Wonderful Crime, *294*
Having a Wonderful Time, *294*
Having It All, *294*
◆ Hawaii, *537*
Hawk, The, *982*
Hawk the Slayer, *59*
◆ Hawks, *537*
Hawks and the Sparrows, The, *743*
Hawmps!, *294*
He Knows You're Alone, *849*
He-Man and the Masters of the Universe (Series), *173*
He Said, She Said, *294*
◆ He Walked by Night, *982*
Head (1968), *922*
Head, The (1959), *849*
Head Against the Wall, *743*
Head Office, *294*
Head Over Heels (see A Coeur Joie)
Headless Horseman, The, *1056*
Heads, *294*
Heads I Kill You . . . Tails You're Dead! (see Guns for Dollars)
◆ Hear My Song, *295*
Hear no Evil, *982*
Hearse, The, *849*
Hearst and Davies Affair, The, *537*
Heart, *537*
Heart and Souls, *1056*
◆ Heart Beat, *537*
Heart Condition, *295*
Heart in Winter, A (see Un Coeur en Hiver)
◆ Heart Is a Lonely Hunter, The, *538*
◆ **Heart Like a Wheel,** *538*
Heart of a Champion: The Ray Mancini Story, *538*
Heart of Darkness, *538*
Heart of Dixie, The, *538*
◆ Heart of Glass, *743*
Heart of Justice, *538*
Heart of Midnight, *982*

Heart of the Golden West, *1119*
Heart of the Rio Grande, *1119*
◆ Heart of the Rockies, *1119*
◆ Heart of the Stag, *538*
Heartaches, *538*
Heartbeeps, *173*
Heartbreak Hotel, *538*
Heartbreak House, *295*
◆ Heartbreak Kid, The, *295*
Heartbreak Ridge, *59*
Heartbreakers, *538*
Heartburn, *295*
◆ Heartland, *1119*
Hearts and Armour, *59*
◆ Hearts and Minds, *425*
Heart's Desire, *922*
◆ Hearts of Darkness, *425*
Hearts of Fire, *538*
Hearts of the West, *295*
Hearts of the World, *538*
Heat (1972), *539*
Heat (1987), *60*
◆ Heat and Dust, *539*
◆ Heat and Sunlight, *539*
Heat Is on: The Making of Miss Saigon, The, *426*
Heat of Desire, *743*
Heat Wave, *539*
Heated Vengeance, *60*
Heathcliff—The Movie, *173*
◆ Heathers, *295*
Heat's On, The, *295*
Heatwave, *539*
Heaven, *426*
Heaven and Earth (1991), *743*
Heaven and Earth (1993), *539*
◆ Heaven Can Wait (1943), *295*
◆ Heaven Can Wait (1978), *295*
◆ Heaven, Earth and Magic, *1056*
Heaven Help Us, *295*
Heaven Is a Playground, *539*
◆ Heaven on Earth, *539*
Heaven Tonight, *539*
Heavenly Bodies, *296*
Heavenly Kid, The, *296*
Heavens Above, *296*
Heaven's Gate, *1119*
Heavy Petting, *426*
Heavy Traffic, *539*
◆ Hedda, *539*
◆ Heidi (1937), *173*
◆ Heidi (1965), *173*
Heidi's Song, *173*
◆ Heiress, The, *539*
Heist, The, *540*
◆ Helga Pictures, The, *426*
Hell Comes to Frogtown, *1056*
Hell High, *849*
Hell Hounds of Alaska, *1119*
Hell in the Pacific, *60*
◆ Hell Is for Heroes, *60*
Hell Night, *849*
Hell on Frisco Bay, *60*
Hell Ship Mutiny, *60*
Hell Squad (1958), *60*
Hell Squad (1985), *60*
Hell to Eternity, *540*
Hell Town, *1120*
Hell Up in Harlem, *60*
Hellbenders, The, *1120*
Hellbound: Hellraiser II, *849*
Hellcats, The, *60*
Hellcats of the Navy, *60*
Helldorado (1934), *60*
Helldorado (1946), *1120*
Heller in Pink Tights, *1120*
Hellfighters, *60*
Hellfire, *1120*
Hellfire Club, The, *60*
Hellgate, *849*
Hellhole, *849*
Hellmaster, *849*
Hello Again, *296*
Hello, Dolly!, *922*
Hello, Mary Lou: Prom Night II, *850*
Hellraiser, *850*
Hellraiser 3: Hell On Earth, *850*
Hell's Angels Forever, *426*
Hell's Angels on Wheels, *60*
Hell's Angels '69, *60*
Hell's Brigade, *61*
Hell's Hinges, *1120*
Hell's House, *61*
◆ Hellstrom Chronicle, The, *426*
Helltrain, *61*
◆ Help!, *922*
◆ Helter Skelter, *540*
Helter-Skelter Murders, The, *540*
Hennessy, *982*
Henry & June, *540*
Henry IV, *743*
◆ Henry V (1944), *540*
◆ Henry V (1989), *540*
◆ Henry: Portrait of a Serial Killer, *540*
Her Alibi, *296*
Herbie Goes Bananas, *174*
Herbie Goes to Monte Carlo, *174*
Herbie Rides Again, *174*
Hercules (1959), *1056*
Hercules (1983), *1056*
Hercules Against the Moon Men, *1056*
Hercules and the Captive Women, *1056*
Hercules Goes Bananas, *296*
Hercules in the Haunted World, *61*
Hercules, Prisoner of Evil, *61*
Hercules Unchained, *1056*
◆ Herdsmen of the Sun, *426*
Here Come the Co-Eds, *296*
Here Come the Girls, *922*
Here Come the Tigers (see Manny's Orphans)
Here Come the Waves, *922*
Here Comes Droopy, *174*
◆ Here Comes Mr. Jordan, *296*
Here Comes Santa Claus, *174*
Here Comes the Groom, *922*
Here Comes Trouble, *296*
◆ Here's Donald, *174*
Here's Goofy, *174*
◆ **Here's Looking at You, Warner Brothers,** *426*
Here's Mickey, *174*
Here's Pluto, *174*
Heritage of the Desert, *1120*
Hero, The, *540*
Hero Ain't Nothin' But a Sandwich, A, *540*
Hero and the Terror, *61*
◆ Hero, *296*
Hero at Large, *296*
Heroes, *540*
Heroes Die Young, *61*
Heroes for Sale, *540*
Heroes in Hell, *61*
Heroes of Desert Storm, *61*
Heroes of the Saddle, *1120*
Heroes Stand Alone, *61*
He's My Girl, *296*
◆ He's Your Dog, Charlie Brown, *174*
◆ Hester Street, *541*
Hexed, *296*
◆ Hey Abbott!, *296*
Hey, Babu Riba, *743*
Hey Cinderella!, *174*
Hey Good Lookin', *541*
Hey, I'm Alive!, *541*
Hey There, It's Yogi Bear, *174*
Hi Mom, *297*
Hidden, The, *1056*
◆ Hidden Agenda, *541*
◆ Hidden Fortress, The, *744*
Hidden Gold, *1120*
Hidden Obsession, *982*
◆ Hidden Valley Outlaws, *1120*
Hide and Go Shriek, *850*
Hide in Plain Sight, *541*
Hideaways, The, *174*
Hideous Sun Demon, The, *850*
Hider in the House, *982*
Hiding Out, *61*
Hiding Place, The, *541*
◆ High and Low, *744*
High and the Mighty, The, *541*
High Anxiety, *297*
High-Ballin', *61*
High Command, The, *61*
High Country, The, *61*
High Crime, *61*
High Desert Kill, *850*
High Heels (1972), *744*
◆ High Heels (1992), *744*
◆ High Hopes, *297*
High Lonesome—The Story of Bluegrass Music, *426*
◆ High Noon, *1120*
High Noon, Part Two, *1120*
High Plains Drifter, *1120*
High Risk, *61*
High Road to China, *62*
High Rolling, *62*
High School Caesar, *62*
High School Confidential!, *541*
High School, USA, *297*
◆ High Season, *297*
◆ High Sierra, *62*
High Society, *922*
High Spirits, *297*
High Stakes (1986), *297*
High Stakes (1989), *62*
◆ High Tide, *541*
High Velocity, *62*
High Voltage, *62*
Higher and Higher, *922*
◆ Highest Honor, The, *62*
Highlander, *1056*
Highlander 2: The Quickening, *1056*
Highlander: The Gathering, *1056*
Highpoint, *62*
Highway 61, *297*
◆ Highway to Hell, *850*
◆ Hill, The, *541*
Hillbillys in a Haunted House, *297*
Hills Have Eyes, The, *850*
Hills Have Eyes, The: Part Two, *850*
◆ **Hills of Home,** *174*
Hills of Utah, The, *1120*
Hillside Stranglers, The, *982*
◆ Himatsuri, *744*
Hindenburg, The, *541*
Hips, Hips, Hooray, *297*
Hired Hand, The, *1121*
Hired to Kill, *62*
◆ Hiroshima, Mon Amour, *744*

◆ Hiroshima: Out of the Ashes, *541*
His Brother's Ghost, *1121*
His Double Life, *297*
His Fighting Blood, *1121*
◆ His Girl Friday, *297*
His Kind of Woman, *62*
His Majesty O'Keefe, *62*
His Name Was King, *1121*
His Picture in the Papers, *297*
His Royal Slyness/Haunted Spooks, *298*
History Is Made at Night, *542*
History of the World, Part One, The, *298*
History of White People in America, The, *298*
History of White People in America, The (Volume II), *298*
Hit!, *62*
◆ Hit, The, *63*
Hit and Run, *63*
Hit Lady, *63*
Hit List (1988), *982*
◆ Hit List, The (1992), *982*
Hit the Deck, *923*
Hit the Dutchman, *63*
Hit the Ice, *298*
Hit the Saddle, *1121*
Hit Woman: The Double Edge, *63*
Hitcher, The, *850*
Hitchhiker (Series), The, *850*
Hitchhikers, *850*
◆ Hitchhiker's Guide to the Galaxy, The, *1056*
Hitler, *542*
Hitler—Dead or Alive, *542*
Hitler, the Last Ten Days, *542*
◆ Hitler's Children, *63*
Hitler's Daughter, *542*
Hitman, The, *63*
Hitz, *63*
Hobbit, The, *175*
◆ Hobson's Choice (1954), *298*
Hobson's Choice (1983), *175*
Hocus Pocus, *175*
◆ Hoffa, *542*
Holcroft Covenant, The, *982*
Hold 'em Jail, *298*
Hold Me, Thrill Me, Kiss Me, *298*
Hold That Ghost, *298*
Hold the Dream, *542*
◆ Hold Your Man, *542*
Hole in the Head, A, *298*
Holes, The, *744*
◆ Holiday, *298*
Holiday Affair, *542*
Holiday Hotel, *744*
Holiday in Mexico, *923*
◆ Holiday Inn, *923*
◆ Hollywood, *426*
Hollywood Boulevard, *299*
Hollywood Boulevard II, *983*
Hollywood Canteen, *923*
Hollywood Chainsaw Hookers, *850*
◆ Hollywood Clowns, The, *426*
Hollywood Cop, *63*
Hollywood Detective, The, *983*
Hollywood Harry, *299*
Hollywood Heartbreak, *542*
Hollywood High, *299*
Hollywood High, Part II, *299*
Hollywood Hot Tubs, *299*
Hollywood Hotel, *923*
Hollywood Meatcleaver Massacre, *850*
Hollywood on Parade, *299*
Hollywood or Bust, *299*
Hollywood Outtakes, *299*
Hollywood Party, *299*
Hollywood Shuffle, *299*
Hollywood Strangler Meets the Skid Row Slasher, *851*
Hollywood Vice Squad, *63*
Hollywood Zap, *299*
◆ Holocaust, *542*
Holocaust 2000, *851*
Holt of the Secret Service, *63*
◆ Holy Innocents, *744*
Holy Matrimony, *299*
Holy Terror (see Alice, Sweet Alice)
◆ Hombre, *1121*
◆ Home Alone, *299*
◆ Home Alone 2: Lost in New York, *175*
◆ Home and the World, *744*
Home for Christmas, *542*
Home for the Holidays, *983*
◆ Home from the Hill, *542*
Home in Oklahoma, *1121*
Home Is Where the Hart Is, *299*
Home Movies, *299*
Home of our Own, A, *542*
Home of the Brave, *543*
Home Remedy, *300*
Home, Sweet Home, *543*
Homebodies, *851*
Homeboy, *543*
Homeboys, *543*
Homeboys II: Crack City, *63*
Homecoming (1948), *543*
◆ Homecoming, The (1973), *543*
Homer and Eddie, *543*
Hometown Boy Makes Good, *300*
◆ Homeward Bound: The Incredible Journey, *175*
Homework, *543*
Homewrecker, *1057*
Homicidal Impulse, *983*
Homicide, *983*
◆ Hondo, *1121*
Hondo and the Apaches, *1121*
◆ Honey, I Blew Up the Kid, *175*
Honey, I Shrunk the Kids, *175*
Honey Pot, The, *300*
Honeyboy, *63*
Honeymoon, *851*
Honeymoon Academy, *300*
◆ Honeymoon in Vegas, *300*
Honeymoon Killers, The, *983*
Honeymoon Machine, The, *300*
Honeymoon Murders, *851*
◆ Honeymooners, The (TV Series), *300*
◆ Honeymooners, The: Lost Episodes (TV Series), *300*
Honeysuckle Rose, *923*
Honky Tonk, *1121*
Honky Tonk Freeway, *300*
◆ Honkytonk Man, *543*
◆ Honolulu, *923*
Honor Among Thieves, *63*
Honor and Glory, *64*
Honor Thy Father, *543*
Hoodlum Empire, *64*
Hoodlum Priest, The, *543*
Hook, *175*
Hook, Line and Sinker, *300*
◆ Hooper, *300*
◆ Hoosiers, *543*
Hopalong Cassidy Enters, *1121*
◆ Hope and Glory, *544*
Hoppity Goes to Town, *175*
Hoppy Serves a Writ, *1121*
Hoppy's Holiday, *1121*
◆ Hopscotch, *983*
Horizontal Lieutenant, The, *301*
Horn Blows at Midnight, The, *301*
Hornet's Nest, *64*
Horrible Dr. Hichcock, The, *851*
Horrible Horror, *851*
Horror Castle (see Virgin of Nuremburg)
◆ Horror Express, *851*
Horror Hospital, *851*
Horror Hotel, *851*
◆ Horror of Dracula, *851*
◆ Horror of Frankenstein, *851*
Horror of Party Beach, The, *851*
Horror of the Blood Monsters, *1057*
Horror of the Zombies, *852*
Horror Rises from the Tomb, *852*
Horror Show, The, *852*
Horrors of Burke and Hare, *852*
Horse, The, *744*
◆ Horse Feathers, *301*
Horse in the Gray Flannel Suit, The, *175*
Horse of Pride, The, *744*
◆ Horse Soldiers, The, *1122*
◆ Horse Thief, The, *745*
Horse Without a Head, The, *175*
Horsemasters, *176*
Horsemen, The, *64*
Horseplayer, *983*
Horse's Mouth, The, *301*
◆ Hospital, The, *301*
Hospital Massacre, *852*
Hostage (1987), *64*
Hostage (1992), *64*
Hostage Tower, The, *64*
Hostages, *544*
Hostile Country, *1122*
Hostile Guns, *1122*
Hostile Take Over, *544*
Hot Box, The, *64*
Hot Child in the City, *64*
Hot Chocolate, *301*
Hot Dog...The Movie, *301*
Hot Head, *745*
Hot Lead, *1122*
Hot Lead and Cold Feet, *176*
◆ **Hot Millions,** *301*
Hot Moves, *301*
◆ Hot Pepper, *426*
Hot Pursuit, *301*
Hot Resort, *301*
◆ Hot Rock, The, *983*
Hot Shot, *544*
◆ Hot Shots, *301*
Hot Shots Part Deux, *301*
Hot Spell, *544*
Hot Spot, *544*
Hot Stuff, *301*
Hot Target, *64*
Hot to Trot, *302*
Hot Under the Collar, *302*
Hotel, *544*
Hotel Colonial, *64*
Hotel New Hampshire, The, *544*
Hotel Paradiso, *302*
Hotel Reserve, *544*
◆ **Hotel Room,** *983*
◆ Hotel Terminus: The Life and Times of Klaus Barbie, *427*
Houdini, *544*

◆ Hound of the Baskervilles, The (1939), 983
◆ Hound of the Baskervilles, The (1959), 983
Hound of the Baskervilles, The (1977), 302
Hound of the Baskervilles, The (1983), 984
Hour of the Assassin, 64
Hour of the Star, 745
◆ Hour of the Wolf, 745
◆ Hours and Times, 544
House, 852
House II: The Second Story, 852
House IV, 852
House Across the Bay, The, 545
House by the Cemetery, 852
House by the River, 984
◆ House Calls, 302
House in the Hills, A, 984
House of Angels, 745
◆ **House of Cards,** 545
House of Dark Shadows, 852
House of Dracula, 852
House of Evil (see Macabre Serenade)
House of Exorcism, The, 852
◆ House of Fear, 984
House of Frankenstein, 852
◆ House of Games, 984
House of 1,000 Dolls, 64
House of Psychotic Women, 852
House of Seven Corpses, The, 853
House of Strangers, 545
House of Terror, 984
House of the Dead, 853
House of the Long Shadows, 853
House of the Rising Sun, 64
◆ House of the Seven Gables, The, 545
House of the Spirits, The, 545
House of Usher, The, 853
House of Wax, 853
House of Whipcord, 853
House on Carroll Street, The, 984
House on Garibaldi Street, 545
House on Haunted Hill, 853
House on Skull Mountain, 853
House on Sorority Row, 853
House on Tombstone Hill, The, 853
◆ House Party, 923
House Party 2, 923
House Party 3, 923
House That Bled to Death, The, 853
House That Dripped Blood, The, 853
House That Vanished, The, 853
House Where Evil Dwells, The, 853
Houseboat, 302
◆ Householder, The, 745
Housekeeper, The, 853
Housekeeping, 545
Housesitter, 302
Housewife, 545
How Bugs Bunny Won the West, 176
How Funny Can Sex Be?, 745
◆ How Green Was My Valley, 545
How He Came Into the World (see Golem, The)
How I Got into College, 302
How I Won the War, 302
How the Best Was Won (Limited Gold Edition 2), 176
How the Leopard Got His Spots, 176
◆ How the Rhinoceros Got His Skin and How the Camel Got His Hump, 176
How the West Was Won, 1122
How to Beat the High Co$t of Living, 302
How to Break Up a Happy Divorce, 302
How to Get Ahead in Advertising, 302
◆ **How to Irritate People,** 302
How to Make a Monster, 853
How to Marry a Millionaire, 303
How to Murder your Wife, 303
How to Stuff a Wild Bikini, 923
◆ How to Succeed in Business without Really Trying, 923
How U Like Me Now, 303
Howard the Duck, 1057
◆ Howards End, 545
Howards of Virginia, The, 545
Howie from Maui, 303
Howie Mandel's North American Watusi Tour, 303
◆ Howling, The, 853
Howling II...Your Sister Is a Werewolf, 854
Howling III, 854
Howling IV, 854
Howling V—The Rebirth, 854
Howling VI: The Freaks, 854
Huckleberry Finn (1974), 176
◆ Huckleberry Finn (1975), 176
Hucksters, The, 545
◆ Hud, 546
Hudson Hawk, 64
Hudsucker Proxy, The, 303
Hugh Hefner: Once Upon a Time, 427
Hullabaloo over George and Bonnie's Pictures, 303
Human Comedy, The, 546
◆ Human Condition, The, Part One: No Greater Love, 745
Human Condition, The, Part Two: The Road to Eternity, 745
◆ Human Condition, The, Part Three: A Soldier's Prayer, 745
Human Desire, 546
Human Duplicators, The, 854
Human Experiments, 64
Human Hearts, 546
Human Monster, The (Dark Eyes of London), 854
Human Race Club, The, 176
Human Shield, The, 64
Human Vapor, The, 1057
Humanoid, The, 745
Humanoid Defender, 1057
Humanoids from the Deep, 854
Humongous, 854
◆ Humoresque, 546
Hunchback, 854
◆ Hunchback of Notre Dame, The (1923), 854
◆ Hunchback of Notre Dame, The (1939), 854
◆ Hungarian Fairy Tale, A, 745
◆ Hunger (1966), 746
Hunger, The (1983), 854
Hungry I Reunion, 303
Hungry Pets (see Please Don't Eat My Mother)
Hungry Wives (see Season of the Witch)
Hunk, 303
Hunt, The, 746
◆ Hunt for Red October, The, 984
Hunt for the Night Stalker, 546
Hunt the Man Down, 984
Hunter (1971), 65
Hunter, The (1980), 65
Hunter in the Dark, 746
Hunter's Blood, 546
Hunting, 546
Hurray for Betty Boop, 176
Hurricane, The (1937), 546
Hurricane (1979), 65
Hurricane Express, 65
Hurricane Smith, 65
Hurry Up or I'll Be 30, 303
Husbands and Lovers, 546
Husbands and Wives, 546
Hush...Hush, Sweet Charlotte, 854
Hush Little Baby, 984
Hussy, 546
Hustle, 65
◆ Hustler, The, 547
◆ Hustling, 547
Hyper Sapian: People from Another Star, 1057
Hysteria, 984
Hysterical, 303
I Am a Camera, 547
◆ I Am a Fugitive from a Chain Gang, 547
I Am Curious Blue, 746
I Am Curious Yellow, 746
I Am the Cheese, 547
I Am the Law, 547
I Bury the Living, 855
◆ I, Claudius, 547
I Come in Peace, 1057
I Confess, 984
I Could Go On Singing, 924
I Cover the Waterfront, 65
I Died a Thousand Times, 65
I Dismember Mama, 855
◆ I Do! I Do!, 924
I Don't Buy Kisses Anymore, 303
I Dood It, 924
I Dream Too Much, 924
I Hate Your Guts (see The Intruder)
I Heard the Owl Call My Name, 547
I Killed Rasputin, 746
I Know Why the Caged Bird Sings, 547
I Live My Life, 547
I Live With Me Dad, 547
◆ I Love Lucy (TV Series), 303
I Love Melvin, 924
I Love My Wife, 304
I Love N. Y., 547
◆ **I Love Toy Trains,** 427
I Love You (Eu Te Amo), 746
◆ **I Love You Again,** 304
I Love You Alice B. Toklas!, 304
I Love You All (see Je Vous Aime)
◆ I Love You to Death, 304
I, Madman, 855
I Married a Centerfold, 547
I Married a Monster from Outer Space, 1057
I Married a Vampire, 855
I Married a Witch, 1057
I Married a Woman, 304
I Married an Angel, 924
I, Mobster, 65
I Never Promised You a Rose Garden, 547
◆ I Never Sang for My Father, 547
◆ I Ought to Be in Pictures, 304
I Posed for Playboy, 548
I Remember Mama, 548
I See a Dark Stranger, 65

I Sent a Letter to My Love, *746*
I Shot Billy the Kid, *1122*
I Spit on Your Corpse, *855*
I Spit on Your Grave, *855*
I Spy (TV Series), *65*
I Stand Condemned, *548*
I, the Jury, *985*
I Vitelloni, *746*
I Wake Up Screaming, *985*
I Walked with a Zombie, *855*
I Wanna Hold Your Hand, *304*
I Want to Live!, *548*
I Want What I Want, *548*
I Was a Male War Bride, *304*
I Was a Teenage Frankenstein, *855*
I Was a Teenage TV Terrorist, *304*
I Was a Teenage Werewolf, *855*
I Was a Teenage Zombie, *855*
I Was a Zombie for the FBI, *1057*
I Was Stalin's Bodyguard, *746*
I Will Fight No More Forever, *1122*
I Will, I Will...for Now, *304*
Ice Castles, *548*
Ice Palace, *548*
Ice Pirates, *1057*
Ice Runner, *65*
Ice Station Zebra, *65*
Iceland, *924*
Iceman, *1057*
Icicle Thief, The, *746*
Icy Breasts, *746*
Iczer-One, Vols. 1–4, *1057*
Idaho, *1122*
Idaho Transfer, *1057*
Identity Crisis, *304*
Idiot, The, *746*
Idiot's Delight, *548*
Idol Dancer, The, *548*
Idolmaker, The, *924*
If..., *304*
If Ever I See You Again, *548*
If I Had a Million, *304*
If I Were Rich, *305*
If It's Tuesday, This Must Be Belgium, *305*
If Looks Could Kill (1986), *985*
If Looks Could Kill (1991), *66*
If You Could See What I Hear, *548*
If You Knew Susie, *924*
Ike: The War Years, *548*
Ikiru, *747*
Il Bidone, *747*
Il Grido, *747*
Il Ladro Di Bambini (Stolen Children), *747*
I'll Cry Tomorrow, *924*
I'll Do Anything, *305*
I'll Met by Moonlight, *548*
I'll See You in My Dreams, *924*
I'll Take Sweden, *924*
Illegal Entry, *66*
Illegally Yours, *548*
Illicit, *549*
Illicit Behavior, *985*
Illusion Travels by Streetcar, *747*
Illusions, *985*
Illustrated Man, The, *1057*
Ilsa, Harem Keeper of the Oil Shieks, *855*
Ilsa, She Wolf of the SS, *855*
Ilsa, the Wicked Warden, *855*
I'm a Fool, *549*
I'm All Right Jack, *305*
◆ I'm Almost Not Crazy: John Cassavetes—The Man and His Work, *427*
I'm Dancing As Fast As I Can, *549*
I'm Dangerous Tonight, *855*
◆ I'm Gonna Git You Sucka!, *305*
◆ **I'm No Angel,** *305*
◆ I'm the One You're Looking For, *747*
◆ Image, The, *549*
Image of Passion, *549*
Imagemaker, The, *549*
◆ Imagine: John Lennon, *427*
Imitation of Life, *549*
Immediate Family, *549*
Immoral Mr. Teas, The, *305*
Immortal Bachelor, The, *747*
Immortal Battalion, The (a.k.a. The Way Ahead), *549*
Immortal Sergeant, The, *549*
Immortal Sins, *855*
◆ **Immortal Story,** *549*
Impact, *985*
◆ Importance of Being Donald, The, *176*
Importance of Being Earnest, The, *305*
◆ Impossible Spy, The, *985*
Impossible Years, The, *305*
Imposter, The, *549*
◆ Impromptu, *549*
Improper Channels, *305*
◆ Improper Conduct, *427*
Impulse (1974), *985*
Impulse (1984), *985*
Impulse (1990), *985*
Impure Thoughts, *305*
In a Glass Cage, *747*
◆ In a Lonely Place, *985*
In a Moment of Passion, *549*
In a Shallow Grave, *550*
In a Stranger's Hands, *985*
In Between, *550*
◆ In Cold Blood, *985*
In Country, *550*
In Dangerous Company, *550*
In Early Arizona, *1122*
In Gold We Trust, *66*
In Harm's Way, *66*
◆ In-Laws, The, *305*
In Like Flint, *66*
In Love and War, *985*
In Love with an Older Woman, *550*
In Name Only, *550*
◆ In Nome del Papa Re (In the Name of the Pope-King), *747*
In Old Amarillo, *1122*
In Old Arizona, *1122*
◆ In Old Caliente, *1122*
In Old California, *1122*
In Old Cheyenne, *1123*
◆ **In Old Chicago,** *550*
In Old Mexico, *1123*
In Old Santa Fe, *1123*
In Person, *305*
In Praise of Older Women, *550*
In Search of Anna, *550*
In Search of Historic Jesus, *550*
◆ In Search of the Castaways, *176*
In Search of the Serpent of Death, *66*
◆ In Search of the Wow Wow Wibble Woggle Wazzle Woodle Woo!, *176*
In Self Defense, *550*
In Society, *306*
In the Aftermath: Angels Never Sleep, *1058*
In the Cold of the Night, *986*
In the Good Old Summertime, *925*
In the Heat of Passion, *986*
◆ In the Heat of the Night, *986*
In the Line of Duty: Ambush in Waco, *66*
◆ **In the Line of Fire,** *66*
In the Mood, *306*
◆ **In the Name of the Father,** *550*
In the Realm of Passion, *747*
In the Realm of the Senses, *747*
In the Shadow of Kilimanjaro, *855*
In the Shadow of the Sun, *1058*
In the Soup, *306*
In the Spirit, *306*
In the Time of Barbarians, *1058*
In the Time of Barbarians II, *1058*
In the White City, *747*
In This Our Life, *550*
In Trouble, *550*
◆ In Which We Serve, *550*
Incident, The (1967), *551*
Incident, The (1989), *551*
Incident at Dark River, *551*
◆ Incident at Oglala, *427*
Inconvenient Woman, An, *551*
Incredible Hulk, The, *1058*
Incredible Invasion (see Sinister Invasion)
◆ Incredible Journey, The, *177*
Incredible Journey of Dr. Meg Laurel, The, *551*
Incredible Melting Man, The, *1058*
Incredible Mr. Limpet, The, *306*
Incredible Petrified World, The, *1058*
Incredible Rocky Mountain Race, The, *306*
Incredible Sarah, The, *551*
◆ Incredible Shrinking Man, The, *1058*
Incredible Shrinking Woman, The, *306*
◆ **Incredible Story of Dogs, The,** *427*
Incredible Torture Show, The (see Bloodsucking Freaks)
Incredible Two-Headed Transplant, The, *855*
Incredibly Strange Creatures Who Stopped Living and Became Mixed-Up Zombies, The, *856*
Incubus, The, *856*
Indecency, *986*
Indecent Behavior, *551*
Indecent Obsession, An, *551*
Indecent Proposal, *551*
◆ Independence Day, *551*
Indestructible Man, *856*
Indian Runner, The, *551*
Indian Summer, *306*
Indian Uprising, *1123*
◆ Indiana Jones and the Last Crusade, *1058*
◆ Indiana Jones and the Temple of Doom, *1058*
Indigo, *66*
Indigo 2: The Revolt, *66*
Indiscreet (1931), *306*
Indiscreet (1958), *306*
Indiscretion of an American Wife, *551*
◆ Indochine, *747*
Industrial Symphony No. 1 The Dream of the Broken Hearted, *925*
Infernal Trio, The, *748*

Inferno, *856*
Infested, *856*
◆ Informer, The, *552*
Infra-Man, *1058*
◆ Inherit the Wind, *552*
Inheritors, The, *748*
Initiation, The, *856*
Initiation of Sarah, The, *856*
Inkwell, The, *552*
◆ Inn of the Sixth Happiness, The, *552*
Inner Circle, The, *552*
Inner Sanctum, *986*
◆ Innerspace, *1058*
◆ **Innocence Unprotected,** *748*
◆ Innocent, The, *748*
Innocent Blood, *856*
◆ Innocent Man, An, *66*
Innocent Victim, *986*
Inquiry, The, *552*
◆ Insect Woman, *748*
Inserts, *552*
Inside Daisy Clover, *552*
Inside Man, The, *66*
Inside Monkey Zetterland, *306*
◆ Inside Moves, *552*
Inside Out (1975), *66*
Inside Out (1986), *552*
Inside Out (1992), *1058*
Inside Out 2, *1059*
Inside the Third Reich, *552*
Insignificance, *553*
Inspector Gadget (Series), *177*
◆ Inspector General, The, *306*
◆ Inspector Morse (TV Series), *986*
Inspiration, *553*
Instant Justice, *67*
Instant Karma, *306*
Interceptor, *67*
◆ Interiors, *553*
◆ Intermezzo (1936), *748*
◆ Intermezzo (1939), *553*
Internal Affairs, *67*
International House, *307*
International Tournée of Animation Vol. I, The, *307*
◆ International Tournée of Animation Vol. II, The, *307*
International Velvet, *177*
Internecine Project, The, *986*
Interns, The, *553*
◆ Interrogation, *748*
◆ Interrupted Melody, *925*
Intersection, *553*
Interval, *553*
Intimate Contact, *553*
Intimate Obsession, *986*
Intimate Power, *553*
Intimate Stranger, *986*
Intimate Strangers, *553*
Into the Badlands, *1123*
Into the Fire, *67*
Into the Homeland, *67*
Into the Night, *553*
◆ Into the Sun, *67*
◆ **Into the West,** *177*
◆ Intolerance, *553*
Intrigue, *986*
Intruder, The (1961), *553*
Intruder (1988), *856*
◆ Intruder in the Dust, *553*
Intruder Within, The, *1059*
◆ Intruders, *1059*
Invader, *1059*
◆ Invaders from Mars (1953), *1059*
Invaders from Mars (1986), *1059*
Invasion Earth: The Aliens Are Here, *856*
Invasion Force (see Hangar 18)
Invasion of Privacy, *986*
Invasion of the Animal People, *1059*
Invasion of the Bee Girls, *1059*
Invasion of the Blood Farmers, *856*
◆ Invasion of the Body Snatchers (1956), *1059*
◆ Invasion of the Body Snatchers (1978), *1059*
Invasion of the Flesh Hunters, *856*
Invasion of the Girl Snatchers, *307*
Invasion of the Space Preachers, *307*
Invasion of the Saucer Men, *1059*
Invasion UFO, *1059*
Invasion U.S.A., *67*
Investigation, *748*
Invincible Sword, The, *67*
Invisible Adversaries, *748*
Invisible Agent, *1059*
Invisible Boy, The, *1059*
Invisible Ghost, *856*
Invisible Kid, The, *1060*
◆ Invisible Man, The, *856*
Invisible Man Returns, *856*
Invisible Maniac, *1060*
Invisible Ray, The, *857*
Invisible Strangler, *857*
Invisible: The Chronicles of Benjamin Knight, *1060*
Invisible Woman, The, *307*
Invitation au Voyage, *748*
Invitation to a Gunfighter, *1123*
Invitation to Hell, *857*
Invitation to the Dance, *925*
Invitation to the Wedding, *307*
IP5: The Island of Pachyderms, *748*
◆ Ipcress File, The, *986*
◆ Iphigenia, *749*
Iran Days of Crisis, *554*
◆ Irezumi (Spirit of Tattoo), *749*
Irishman, The, *554*
Irma La Douce, *307*
Iron & Silk, *554*
◆ Iron Duke, The, *554*
Iron Eagle, *67*
Iron Eagle II, *67*
Iron Major, The, *554*
Iron Mask, The, *67*
Iron Maze, *987*
Iron Triangle, The, *554*
Iron Warrior, *1060*
Iron Will, *67*
Ironclads, *554*
Ironheart, *67*
◆ Ironweed, *554*
Irreconcilable Differences, *554*
Is Paris Burning?, *554*
Is This Goodbye, Charlie Brown?, *177*
Isadora (1966), *554*
Isadora (1969), *554*
Ishtar, *307*
Island, The, *857*
Island at the Top of the World, The, *1060*
Island Claws, *857*
Island in the Sky, *554*
Island of Desire, *555*
Island of Dr. Moreau, The, *1060*
◆ Island of Lost Souls, *857*
Island of Terror, *857*
Island of the Blue Dolphins, *555*
Island of the Lost, *857*
Island Trader, *67*
Islander, The, *555*
Islands in the Stream, *555*
Isle of the Dead, *857*
Istanbul, *749*
Istanbul: Keep Your Eyes Open, *55*
It (1927), *307*
It (1991), *857*
◆ It Came from Beneath the Sea, *857*
It Came from Hollywood, *307*
◆ It Came from Outer Space, *1060*
It Came Upon a Midnight Clear, *17*
It Can Be Done, Amigo (see Saddle Tramps)
It Conquered the World, *1060*
It Couldn't Happen Here, *925*
It Happened at the World's Fair, *92*
It Happened in Brooklyn, *925*
It Happened in New Orleans, *925*
◆ It Happened One Night, *307*
It Happens Every Spring, *307*
It Lives Again, *857*
It Lives By Night (see Bat People)
It Rained All Night the Day I Left, *5*
It Should Happen to You, *308*
It Started in Naples, *308*
It Started With a Kiss, *308*
◆ It Takes a Thief (TV Series), *68*
It Takes Two, *308*
It! The Terror from Beyond Space, *1060*
◆ It Was a Short Summer, Charlie Brown, *177*
Italian Job, The, *308*
Italian Straw Hat, The, *749*
It's a Big Country, *308*
It's a Bundyful Life, *308*
It's a Complex World, *308*
It's a Date, *925*
It's a Dog's Life, *177*
◆ It's a Gift, *308*
It's a Great Feeling, *925*
It's a Great Life, *308*
It's a Joke, Son!, *308*
◆ It's a Mad Mad Mad Mad World, *308*
It's a Mystery, Charlie Brown, *177*
◆ It's a Wonderful Life, *555*
It's Alive!, *857*
It's Alive III: Island of the Alive, *857*
◆ **It's All True,** *427*
It's Always Fair Weather, *925*
◆ It's an Adventure, Charlie Brown, *177*
It's Arbor Day, Charlie Brown, *177*
It's Christmastime Again, Charlie Brown, *177*
It's Flashbeagle, Charlie Brown, *177*
It's Good to Be Alive, *555*
It's in the Bag, *308*
◆ It's Magic, Charlie Brown, *178*
It's My Turn, *555*
◆ It's the Easter Beagle, Charlie Brown, *178*
◆ It's the Great Pumpkin, Charlie Brown, *178*
◆ It's Three Strikes, Charlie Brown, *178*
It's Your First Kiss, Charlie Brown, *178*
◆ Ivan the Terrible—Part I & Part II, *749*
◆ Ivanhoe (1952), *68*
◆ Ivanhoe (1982), *68*
I've Always Loved You, *555*
I've Heard the Mermaids Singing, *3*

ory Hunters, 555
ry & Moe, 309
D.'s Revenge, 858
bberwocky, 309
Accuse, 749
ck and the Beanstalk, 178
ck Benny Program, The (TV Series), 309
ck Knife Man, The, 556
ck London, 556
ck the Bear, 556
ck the Giant Killer, 178
ck the Ripper (1959), 858
ck the Ripper (1979), 987
ckie Chan's Police Force, 309
ckie Gleason's Honeybloopers, 309
ckie Mason on Broadway, 309
ckie Robinson Story, The, 556
ckknife, 556
cko and Lise, 749
ck's Back, 987
ckson County Jail, 68
cksons: An American Dream, The, 556
cob I Have Loved, 556
cob Two-Two Meets the Hooded Fang, 178
cob's Ladder, 1060
de Mask, The, 987
gged Edge, 556
il Bait (1954), 68
ilbait (1992), 68
ilbird's Vacation (see Les Grandes Gueules)
ilhouse Rock, 925
ke Spanner Private Eye, 68
ke Speed, 68
maica Inn, 556
mes Dean, 427
mes Dean—A Legend in His Own Time, 556
mes Joyce's Women, 556
mon, Jamon, 749
ne and the Lost City, 309
ne Austen in Manhattan, 309
ne Campion Shorts, 309
ne Doe, 556
ne Eyre (1934), 557
ne Eyre (1944), 557
ne Eyre (1983), 557
nis, 427
nuary Man, The, 987
r, The, 858
son and the Argonauts, 1060
son Goes to Hell: The Final Friday, 858
va Head, 557
ws, 858
ws 2, 858
ws 3, 858
ws of Death, The, 858
ws of Satan, 858
ws: The Revenge, 858
y Leno's American Dream, 309
yhawkers, The, 1123
yne Mansfield Story, The, 557
zz on a Summer's Day, 427
zz Singer, The (1927), 925
zz Singer, The (1980), 926
zzman, 749
e Vous Aime (I Love You All), 749
ean De Florette, 749
eeves and Wooster (TV Series), 309

Jekyll & Hyde—Together Again, 310
Jennifer, 858
Jennifer 8, 987
◆ **Jenny Lamour,** 749
Jenny's War, 68
◆ Jeremiah Johnson, 1123
Jericho, 557
Jericho Fever, 68
◆ Jericho Mile, The, 557
◆ Jerk, The, 310
Jerry Lee Lewis—I Am What I Am, 428
Jerry Lewis Live, 310
Jersey Girl, 310
Jesse, 557
Jesse James, 1123
Jesse James at Bay, 1123
Jesse James Meets Frankenstein's Daughter, 858
Jesse James Rides Again, 1123
Jessie Owens Story, The, 557
Jesus, 557
Jesus Christ, Superstar, 926
◆ Jesus of Montreal, 749
◆ Jesus of Nazareth, 557
Jet Attack, 68
Jet Benny Show, The, 310
Jetson's Christmas Carol, A, 178
Jetsons Meet the Flintstones, The, 178
Jetsons: The Movie, 178
◆ Jewel in the Crown, The, 557
Jewel of the Nile, The, 68
◆ Jezebel, 557
Jezebel's Kiss, 987
◆ JFK, 558
JFK: Reckless Youth, 558
◆ Jigsaw Man, The, 987
Jigsaw Murders, The, 987
Jilting of Granny Weatherall, The, 558
Jim Thorpe—All American, 558
◆ Jimi Hendrix, 428
Jiminy Cricket's Christmas, 178
Jimmy Cliff—Bongo Man, 926
Jimmy Hollywood, 310
Jimmy the Kid, 178
Jinxed, 310
Jive Junction, 926
J-Men Forever, 310
◆ Jo Jo Dancer, Your Life Is Calling, 558
Joan of Arc, 558
Joan of Paris, 558
Jocks, 310
Joe, 558
Joe Bob Briggs—Dead in Concert, 310
Joe Kidd, 1123
Joe Louis Story, The, 558
Joe Palooka (see Palooka)
Joe Piscopo Live!, 310
Joe Piscopo Video, The, 310
Joe Versus the Volcano, 310
Joey Breaker, 558
John and the Missus, 558
John & Yoko: A Love Story, 559
John Carpenter Presents: Body Bags, 858
◆ John Huston—The Man, the Movies, the Maverick, 428
Johnny Angel, 69
◆ Johnny Apollo, 559
Johnny Appleseed/Paul Bunyan, 179
Johnny Be Good, 311
◆ Johnny Belinda, 559

Johnny Come Lately, 311
Johnny Dangerously, 311
◆ Johnny Eager, 559
Johnny Got His Gun, 559
Johnny Guitar, 1123
Johnny Handsome, 69
Johnny Reno, 1124
Johnny Shiloh, 179
Johnny Stecchino, 750
Johnny Suede, 311
Johnny Tiger, 559
Johnny Tremain, 179
Joke of Destiny, 750
Jolly Corner, The, 559
Jolson Sings Again, 926
◆ Jolson Story, The, 926
Jonah Who Will Be 25 in the Year 2000, 750
Jonathan Livingston Seagull, 559
Jory, 1124
Joseph Andrews, 311
Josepha, 750
◆ Josephine Baker Story, The, 559
Josh and S.A.M., 69
◆ Joshua Then and Now, 311
Jour de Fête, 750
Journey Back to Oz, 179
Journey for Margaret, 559
◆ **Journey Into Fear (1942),** 987
Journey into Fear (1975), 987
Journey of Honor, 69
◆ Journey of Hope, 750
◆ Journey of Natty Gann, The, 179
Journey to the Center of Time, 1060
Journey to the Center of the Earth (1959), 1060
Journey to the Center of the Earth (1987), 1060
Journey to the Far Side of the Sun, 1060
Journey to Spirit Island, 179
Joy House, 559
◆ **Joy Luck Club, The,** 559
Joy of Knowledge (see Le Gai Savoir)
Joy of Living, 926
Joy of Sex, The, 311
Joy Sticks, 311
Joyless Street, 560
Joyride, 560
◆ Ju Dou, 750
◆ Juarez, 560
Jubal, 1124
Jubilee, 1061
Jubilee Trail, 1124
Jud Suss, 750
Judex, 750
Judge and the Assassin, The, 750
Judge Priest, 560
Judge Steps Out, The, 560
◆ Judgment, 560
◆ Judgment at Nuremberg, 560
Judgment in Berlin, 560
Judgment Night, 69
Judith of Bethulia, 560
◆ Judy Garland and Friends, 926
Juggernaut (1936), 987
◆ Juggernaut (1974), 987
Juice, 560
◆ Jules and Jim, 750
◆ Julia, 560
Julia and Julia, 1061
Julia Has Two Lovers, 560
◆ Julia Misbehaves, 311
◆ Juliet of the Spirits, 750
◆ Julius Caesar (1953), 561

Julius Caesar (1970), *561*
Jumbo, *926*
Jumpin' at the Boneyard, *561*
Jumpin' Jack Flash, *311*
Jumping Jacks, *311*
June Bride, *311*
June Night, *751*
◆ Jungle Book (1942), *179*
◆ Jungle Book, The (1967), *179*
Jungle Book, The—A Devil in Mind, *179*
Jungle Book, The—A Trip of Adventure, *179*
◆ Jungle Cat, *179*
Jungle Fever, *561*
Jungle Heat, *69*
Jungle Jim, *69*
Jungle Master, The, *69*
Jungle Patrol, *69*
Jungle Raiders, *69*
Jungle Warriors, *69*
Junior, *858*
Junior Bonner, *1124*
Junior G-Men, *69*
Junkman, The, *70*
Juno and the Paycock, *561*
Jupiter's Darling, *926*
◆ Jupiter's Thigh, *751*
◆ Jurassic Park, *1061*
Just a Gigolo, *561*
Just Another Girl on the I.R.T, *561*
Just Another Pretty Face (see Sois Belle Et Tais-Toi)
Just Around the Corner, *926*
Just Between Friends, *561*
Just One of the Girls, *312*
Just One of the Guys, *312*
Just Plain Daffy, *179*
Just Tell Me What You Want, *312*
Just the Way You Are, *561*
Just William's Luck, *179*
Just You and Me, Kid, *312*
Justin Morgan Had a Horse, *179*
Justine, *561*
K2, *70*
K-9, *312*
Kafka, *988*
◆ Kagemusha, *751*
◆ **Kalifornia,** *561*
Kameradschaft, *751*
Kamikaze 89, *751*
◆ Kanal, *751*
Kandyland, *562*
◆ Kangaroo, *562*
Kansan, The, *1124*
Kansas, *562*
Kansas City Confidential, *988*
Kansas City Massacre, The, *70*
Kansas Cyclone, *1124*
Kansas Pacific, *1124*
Kansas Terrors, *1124*
Kaos, *751*
Karate Cop, *70*
◆ Karate Kid, The, *562*
Karate Kid Part II, The, *562*
Karate Kid Part III, The, *562*
Kashmiri Run, The, *70*
Katherine, *562*
Katie's Passion, *751*
Kavik the Wolf Dog, *179*
◆ Keaton Rides Again/Railroader, *312*
Keaton's Cop, *70*
Keep, The, *859*
Keep the Change, *1124*
Keeper, The, *859*
Keeper of the City, *562*
◆ Keeper of the Flame, *562*
Keeping Track, *70*
Kelly's Heroes, *70*
◆ Kennedy (TV Miniseries), *562*
◆ Kennel Murder Case, The, *988*
Kenneth Anger—Volume One, *562*
Kenneth Anger—Volume Two, *562*
Kenneth Anger—Volume Three, *563*
Kenneth Anger—Volume Four, *563*
◆ Kent State, *563*
Kentuckian, The, *1124*
Kentucky Fried Movie, *312*
Kentucky Kernels, *312*
Kentucky Rifle, *1124*
Key, The, *563*
Key Exchange, *563*
◆ Key Largo, *988*
Key to Rebecca, The, *70*
Key to the City, *312*
Keys to the Kingdom, The, *563*
Keystone Comedies, Vol. 1, *312*
Keystone Comedies, Vol. 2, *312*
Keystone Comedies, Vol. 3, *312*
Keystone Comedies, Vol. 4, *312*
Keystone Comedies, Vol. 5, *313*
◆ Khartoum, *70*
Kick Fighter, *70*
Kick or Die, *70*
Kickboxer, *70*
Kickboxer 2: The Road Back, *70*
Kickboxer Three—Art of War, *71*
Kid, *71*
◆ Kid, The/The Idle Class, *313*
Kid from Brooklyn, The, *313*
Kid from Left Field, The, *180*
Kid Galahad (1937), *563*
Kid Galahad (1962), *926*
Kid Millions, *926*
Kid Ranger, *1124*
Kid Vengeance, *1124*
◆ Kid Who Loved Christmas, The, *180*
Kid with the Broken Halo, The, *313*
Kid with the 200 I.Q., The, *180*
Kidnap Syndicate, The, *751*
Kidnapped (1960), *180*
Kidnapped (1988), *71*
◆ Kidnapping of the President, The, *988*
Kids Are Alright, The, *428*
Kids Is Kids, *180*
◆ **Kika,** *751*
Kill, The, *988*
Kill and Kill Again, *71*
Kill, Baby, Kill (see Curse of the Living Dead)
Kill Castro, *71*
Kill Cruise, *563*
Kill Me Again, *988*
Kill or Be Killed, *71*
Kill Point, *71*
Kill Zone, *71*
◆ **Killer, The,** *751*
Killer Elite, The, *71*
Killer Fish, *71*
Killer Force, *71*
Killer Image, *988*
Killer Inside Me, The, *988*
Killer Instinct, *71*
Killer Klowns from Outer Space, *859*
Killer Tomatoes Eat France, *313*
Killer Tomatoes Strike Back, *313*
Killers, The, *71*
Killers from Space, *1061*
Killer's Kiss, *71*
◆ Killing, The, *988*
Killing Affair, A, *988*
Killing at Hell's Gate, *71*
Killing Beach (see Turtle Beach)
Killing Cars, *563*
Killing Edge, The, *1061*
Killing 'Em Softly, *563*
◆ Killing Fields, The, *563*
Killing Floor, The, *563*
Killing Game, The, *71*
Killing Heat, *563*
Killing Hour, The, *988*
Killing in a Small Town, *564*
Killing Mind, The, *989*
Killing of a Chinese Bookie, *564*
Killing of Angel Street, The, *564*
Killing of Randy Webster, The, *564*
Killing of Sister George, The, *564*
Killing Spree, *859*
Killing Streets, *72*
◆ Killing Time, The, *72*
Killing Zone, The, *72*
Kim, *72*
Kimagure Orange Road, Vols. 1–4, *752*
Kimagure Orange Road: The Movie *752*
◆ Kind Hearts and Coronets, *313*
Kind of Loving, A, *564*
Kindergarten, *752*
Kindergarten Cop, *313*
Kindred, The, *859*
◆ King, *564*
King and Four Queens, The, *1125*
◆ King and I, The, *926*
King Arthur, The Young Warlord, *7*
◆ King Creole, *927*
King David, *564*
King in New York, A, *313*
◆ King Kong (1933), *859*
King Kong (1976), *859*
King Kong Lives, *859*
King Kong vs. Godzilla, *859*
King Lear (1971), *564*
King Lear (1982), *564*
◆ King Lear (1984), *564*
King Lear (1988), *564*
◆ King of Comedy, The, *565*
◆ King of Hearts, *752*
King of Jazz, The, *927*
King of Kings, The (1927), *565*
King of Kings (1961), *565*
King of Kong Island, *859*
King of Marvin Gardens, The, *565*
King of New York, *72*
King of the Bullwhip, *1125*
King of the City (see Club Life)
King of the Congo, *72*
◆ King of the Cowboys, *1125*
King of the Forest Rangers, *72*
King of the Grizzlies, *180*
King of the Gypsies, *565*
◆ **King of the Hill,** *565*
King of the Kickboxers, The, *72*
King of the Kongo, *72*
King of the Mountain, *565*
King of the Pecos, *1125*
King of the Roaring Twenties, *565*
King of the Rocketmen, *72*
King of the Texas Rangers, *1125*
King of the Wild Frontier (see Davy Crockett)
King of the Wind, *180*
King of the Witches (see Simon, Ki of the Witches)

King of the Zombies, *859*
King, Queen and Knave, *565*
King Ralph, *313*
◆ King Rat, *565*
King Richard II, *565*
King Solomon's Mines (1937), *72*
◆ King Solomon's Mines (1950), *72*
King Solomon's Mines (1985), *73*
King Solomon's Treasure, *73*
King Tut: The Face of Tutankhamen, *428*
Kingdom of the Spiders, *859*
Kings and Desperate Men: A Hostage Incident, *73*
◆ Kings Go Forth, *565*
◆ Kings of the Road, *752*
◆ King's Row, *565*
King's Whore, The, *566*
Kinjite (Forbidden Subjects), *73*
Kipperbang, *566*
Kirlian Witness, The (see Plants are Watching, The)
Kismet (1944), *566*
Kismet (1955), *927*
◆ Kiss, The (1929), *566*
Kiss, The (1988), *859*
Kiss and Kill (see Against All Odds)
Kiss Before Dying, A, *989*
Kiss Daddy Good Night, *989*
Kiss Me a Killer, *989*
Kiss Me Deadly, *989*
Kiss Me Goodbye, *313*
Kiss Me Kate, *927*
Kiss Me, Stupid, *314*
Kiss Meets the Phantom of the Park, *859*
◆ Kiss of Death, *566*
Kiss of the Beast (see Meridian)
◆ Kiss of the Spider Woman, *566*
Kiss of the Tarantula, *859*
Kiss Shot, *566*
Kiss Tomorrow Goodbye, *73*
Kisses for My President, *314*
Kissin' Cousins, *927*
Kissing Bandit, The, *927*
◆ Kissing Place, The, *989*
Kit Carson, *1125*
◆ Kitchen Toto, The, *566*
Kitty and the Bagman, *73*
◆ Kitty Foyle, *566*
Klansman, The, *566*
Klondike Annie, *314*
◆ Klute, *989*
Klutz, The, *314*
◆ Knack...and How To Get It, The, *314*
Knickerbocker Holiday, *927*
◆ Knife in the Water, *752*
Knight Moves, *989*
Knight Without Armour, *566*
Knightriders, *73*
Knights, *1061*
Knights and Emeralds, *314*
Knights of the City, *927*
Knights of the Round Table, *73*
Knock on Any Door, *566*
Knockout, The (see Dough & Dynamite)
Knockouts, *314*
Knowhutimean?, *314*
Knute Rockne—All American, *567*
◆ Kojiro, *752*
Koko: A Talking Gorilla, *428*
Koroshi, *73*
Kostas, *567*
◆ Kotch, *314*
◆ Kovacs, *314*
◆ Koyaanisqatsi, *428*
◆ Kramer vs. Kramer, *567*
◆ Krays, The, *567*
◆ Kriemhilde's Revenge, *752*
Kronos, *1061*
Krull, *1061*
Krush Groove, *927*
Kuffs, *73*
Kung Fu, *73*
Kung Fu—The Movie, *73*
Kurt Vonnegut's Monkey House, *1061*
◆ Kwaidan, *752*
L.A. Bounty, *73*
L.A. Crackdown, *73*
L.A. Crackdown II, *74*
L.A. Goddess, *314*
L.A. Law, *567*
◆ L.A. Story, *314*
L.A. Vice, *74*
L'Addition (see Caged Heart)
L'Amour Viole (see Rape of Love)
L'Ange (The Angel), *752*
L'Année des Meduses, *752*
◆ **L'Argent,** *752*
L'Atalante, *753*
◆ L'Aventura, *753*
◆ La Balance, *753*
◆ La Bamba, *927*
◆ La Belle Noiseuse, *753*
◆ La Bête Humaine, *753*
La Bonne Annee (see Happy New Year)
La Boum, *753*
◆ La Cage aux Folles, *753*
La Cage aux Folles II, *753*
La Cage aux Folles III, The Wedding, *753*
◆ La Chienne, *753*
La Decade Prodigieuse (see Ten Days Wonder)
◆ La Dolce Vita, *753*
◆ La Femme Nikita, *753*
La Grande Bourgeoise, *754*
La Lectrice (The Reader), *754*
◆ La Marseillaise, *754*
La Nuit de Varennes, *754*
La Passante, *754*
La Petite Bande, *754*
◆ La Puritaine, *754*
La Ronde, *754*
La Signora di Tutti, *754*
◆ La Strada, *754*
◆ La Traviata, *754*
La Truite (The Trout), *755*
La Vie Continue, *755*
Labyrinth, *1061*
Labyrinth of Passion, *755*
Lacemaker, The, *755*
Ladies Club, *74*
Ladies' Man, The, *314*
Ladies of Leisure, *567*
Ladies of the Chorus, *567*
Ladies on the Rocks, *755*
◆ Ladies Sing the Blues, The, *428*
Ladies They Talk About, *567*
◆ Lady and the Tramp, *180*
Lady Avenger, *74*
Lady Be Good, *927*
Lady Beware, *989*
Lady by Choice, *567*
Lady Caroline Lamb, *567*
Lady Chatterley's Lover (1959), *567*
Lady Chatterley's Lover (1981), *567*
Lady Dragon, *74*
Lady Dragon 2, *74*
◆ Lady Eve, The, *315*
◆ Lady for a Day, *567*
Lady for a Night, *567*
Lady Frankenstein, *859*
Lady from Louisiana, *1125*
Lady from Shanghai, *989*
Lady from Yesterday, The, *567*
Lady Grey, *568*
Lady Ice, *989*
◆ Lady in a Cage, *989*
Lady in Cement, *989*
Lady in Question, *568*
Lady in Red, *74*
Lady in the Lake, *990*
◆ Lady in White, *990*
Lady Is Willing, The, *315*
Lady Jane, *568*
Lady Killer, *74*
Lady Killers, *990*
Lady L, *568*
Lady Mobster, *74*
Lady of Burlesque, *74*
Lady of the House, *568*
Lady on the Bus, *755*
Lady Scarface, *74*
Lady Sings the Blues, *927*
Lady Takes a Chance, A, *1125*
Lady Terminator, *74*
◆ Lady Vanishes, The (1938), *990*
Lady Vanishes, The (1979), *990*
◆ Lady Windermere's Fan, *568*
Lady With the Dog, The, *755*
Ladybugs, *315*
Ladyhawke, *74*
Ladykiller, *990*
◆ Ladykillers, The, *315*
Laguna Heat, *990*
Lair of the White Worm, *859*
Lake Consequence, *568*
Lambada, *927*
◆ Land Before Time, The, *180*
Land of Faraway, The, *180*
Land of the Open Range, *1125*
Land of the Minotaur, *859*
Land of the Pharaohs, *568*
Land Raiders, *1125*
Land That Time Forgot, The, *1061*
Land Unknown, The, *1061*
Land Without Bread, *755*
Landslide, *990*
◆ Lantern Hill, *180*
Larks on a String, *755*
Larry Jordan Live Film Shorts, *568*
Las Vegas Hillbillys, *315*
Las Vegas Lady, *74*
Las Vegas Story, The, *568*
Las Vegas Weekend, *315*
Laser Man, The, *315*
Laser Mission, *75*
Laser Moon, *990*
Laserblast, *1062*
◆ Lassie Come Home, *180*
Lassiter, *75*
Last Action Hero, The, *1062*
◆ Last American Hero, The, *75*
Last American Virgin, The, *315*
Last Angry Man, The, *568*
◆ Last Boy Scout, The, *75*
Last Call, *568*
Last Call at Maud's, *428*
Last Chants for a Slow Dance, *568*
Last Chase, The, *1062*
◆ Last Command, The (1928), *568*

Last Command, The (1955), 1125
Last Contract, The, 75
Last Dance, 990
◆ Last Days of Chez Nous, The, 569
Last Days of Frank and Jesse James, 1125
Last Days of Man on Earth, The, 1062
Last Days of Patton, The, 569
Last Days of Pompeii, The (1935), 569
Last Days of Pompeii (1960), 75
◆ Last Detail, The, 569
Last Dragon, The, 75
Last Elephant, The (see Ivory Hunters)
Last Embrace, The, 990
◆ Last Emperor, The, 569
◆ Last Exit to Brooklyn, 569
Last Five Days, The, 755
Last Flight of Noah's Ark, 180
Last Flight to Hell, 75
Last Fling, The, 315
Last Frontier, The, 1125
Last Game, The, 569
Last Gun, The, 1126
Last Hit, The, 990
◆ Last Holiday, 569
Last Horror Film, The, 860
Last Hour, The, 75
Last House on Dead End Street, 860
Last House on the Left, 860
Last Hunt, The, 1126
◆ Last Hurrah, The, 569
◆ Last Innocent Man, The, 990
◆ Last Laugh, The, 755
◆ **Last Light,** 569
Last Man on Earth, The, 1062
◆ Last Man Standing, 569
Last Married Couple in America, The, 315
Last Metro, The, 755
Last Mile, The, 570
Last Movie, The, 570
◆ Last Night at the Alamo, 315
◆ Last of England, The, 570
Last of His Tribe, The, 570
◆ Last of Mrs. Lincoln, The, 570
Last of Mrs. Cheney, The, 315
Last of Philip Banter, The, 991
◆ Last of Sheila, The, 991
Last of the Comanches, 1126
Last of the Finest, The, 75
Last of the Mohicans, The (1920), 75
Last of the Mohicans (1932), 1126
◆ Last of the Mohicans, The (1936), 1126
Last of the Mohicans (1985), 1126
◆ Last of the Mohicans, The (1992), 1126
Last of the Pony Riders, 1126
Last of the Redmen, 1126
Last of the Red Hot Lovers, 315
Last of the Warriors, 1062
◆ Last Outlaw, The (1936), 1126
Last Outlaw, The (1993), 1126
Last Party, The, 428
◆ Last Picture Show, The, 570
Last Plane Out, 75
◆ Last Polka, The, 315
◆ Last Prostitute, The, 570
Last Remake of Beau Geste, The, 316
Last Resort, 316
Last Ride, The, 991
Last Ride of the Dalton Gang, The, 1126
Last Riders, The, 75
Last Rites, 75
◆ Last Round-Up, 1126
Last Safari, 570
Last Season, The, 75
◆ Last Starfighter, The, 1062
Last Summer, 570
Last Supper, The, 755
Last Survivor, The (see Cannibal)
Last Tango in Paris, 570
Last Temptation of Christ, The, 570
Last Time I Saw Paris, The, 570
Last Train from Gun Hill, 1126
Last Train Home, 181
Last Tycoon, The, 571
Last Unicorn, The, 181
Last Valley, The, 75
Last Victim (see Forced Entry)
◆ Last Voyage, The, 76
◆ Last Waltz, The, 428
◆ Last Warrior, The, 76
Last Wave, The, 991
Last Winter, The, 571
Last Word, The, 571
Last Year at Marienbad, 756
◆ Late Chrysanthemums, 756
◆ Late for Dinner, 1062
◆ Late Show, The, 991
◆ Late Spring, 756
Late Summer Blues, 756
Latin Lovers, 928
Latino, 571
Laugh for Joy, 756
Laughing at Life, 571
Laughing Horse, 571
Laughing Policeman, The, 991
Laughing Sinners, 571
◆ Laura, 991
Laurel & Hardy: A Tribute to "The Boys", 428
Laurel and Hardy: At Work, 316
Laurel and Hardy Classics, Volume 1, 316
◆ Laurel and Hardy Classics, Volume 2, 316
Laurel and Hardy Classics, Volume 3, 316
Laurel and Hardy Classics, Volume 4, 316
Laurel and Hardy Classics, Volume 5, 316
◆ Laurel and Hardy Classics, Volume 6, 316
Laurel and Hardy Classics, Volume 7, 316
Laurel and Hardy Classics, Volume 8, 316
Laurel and Hardy Classics, Volume 9, 316
◆ Laurel and Hardy on the Lam, 317
◆ Laurel and Hardy's Laughing 20s, 317
◆ **Laurel Avenue,** 571
◆ Lavender Hill Mob, The, 317
Law and Jake Wade, The, 1127
◆ Law and Order, 1127
Law Breakers (see Assassins de L'Ordre, Le)
Law of Desire, 756
Law of the Lash, 1127
Law of the Pampas, 1127
Law of the Sea, 571
Law Rides Again, The, 1127
Law West of Tombstone, 1127
Lawless Frontier, 1127
Lawless Land, 1062
Lawless Nineties, The, 1127
Lawless Range, 1127
Lawless Street, A, 1127
◆ Lawless Valley, 1127
Lawman, 1127
Lawman Is Born, A, 1127
Lawnmower Man, The, 1062
◆ Lawrence of Arabia, 76
Lawrenceville Stories, The, 317
Laws of Gravity, 76
Lazarus Syndrome, The, 571
◆ LBJ: The Early Years, 571
L'Etat Sauvage (The Savage State), 756
◆ Le Bal, 756
◆ Le Beau Mariage, 756
Le Beau Serge, 756
Le Bonheur, 756
◆ Le Boucher (The Butcher), 756
Le Bourgeois Gentilhomme, 756
Le Cas du Dr. Laurent, 757
◆ Le Cavaleur, 757
Le Chat (see Cat, The)
Le Chêvre (The Goat), 757
Le Complot (The Conspiracy), 757
◆ Le Corbeau, 757
Le Crabe Tambour, 757
Le Départ, 757
Le Dernier Combat (see Final Combat, The)
Le Distrait (see Daydreamer, The)
◆ Le Doulos, 757
Le Gai Savior (The Joy of Knowledge), 757
Le Gentleman D'Espom (Duke of the Derby), 757
◆ Le Grand Chemin (The Grand Highway), 757
Le Jour Se Leve (Daybreak) (1939), 757
Le Magnifique, 758
◆ Le Million, 758
Le Petit Amour, 758
Le Plaisir, 758
◆ Le Repos du Guerrier (Warrior's Rest), 758
Le Schpountz, 758
Le Secret, 758
◆ Le Sex Shop, 758
Leader of the Band, 317
◆ League of Gentlemen, The, 317
League of Their Own, A, 571
◆ Lean on Me, 571
Leap of Faith, 572
◆ Learning Tree, The, 572
Leather Boys, The, 572
Leather Burners, The, 1128
Leather Jackets, 76
Leatherface—the Texas Chainsaw Massacre III, 860
◆ Leave 'em Laughing, 572
Leaves from Satan's Book, 758
Leaving Normal, 572
L'Ecole Buissonniere, 758
Leech Woman, The, 860
Left for Dead, 572
Left Hand of God, The, 76
Left Handed Gun, The (1958), 1128
Legacy, The, 860
Legacy for Leonette, 991
Legacy of Horror, 860
Legacy of Lies, 572

Legal Eagles, *991*
Legal Tender, *76*
Legend, *1062*
Legend of Billie Jean, The, *76*
Legend of Blood Castle, The (see Blood Castle)
Legend of Boggy Creek, *860*
Legend of Frenchie King, The, *1128*
Legend of Hell House, The, *860*
Legend of Hillbilly John, The, *181*
Legend of Lobo, The, *429*
Legend of Sleepy Hollow, The (1949), *181*
Legend of Sleepy Hollow, The (1988), *181*
Legend of Suram Fortress, The, *758*
Legend of the Eight Samurai, *758*
Legend of the Lone Ranger, The, *1128*
Legend of the Lost, *572*
Legend of the Seven Golden Vampires, The (see Seven Brothers Meet Dracula, The)
Legend of the Werewolf, *860*
Legend of the White Horse, *76*
Legend of Valentino, *572*
Legend of Walks Far Woman, The, *1128*
Legends, *429*
Legends of Comedy, *429*
Legends of the American West (Series), *429*
Lemon Drop Kid, The, *317*
Lemon Sisters, The, *317*
Lena's Holiday, *991*
Leningrad Cowboys Go America, *758*
Lenny, *572*
Lenny Bruce Performance Film, The, *317*
Lensman, *1062*
Leolo, *759*
Leonard Part 6, *317*
Leopard, The, *572*
Leopard in the Snow, *572*
Leopard Man, The, *991*
Lepke, *76*
Leprechaun, *860*
Les Abysses, *759*
Les Biches, *759*
Les Choses De La Vie, *759*
Les Comperes, *759*
Les Cousins, *759*
Les Girls, *928*
Les Grandes Gueules (Jailbirds' Vacation), *759*
Les Liaisons Dangereuses, *759*
Les Miserables (1935), *573*
Les Miserables (1957), *759*
Les Miserables (1978), *573*
Les Rendez-Vous D'Anna, *759*
Les Tricheurs, *759*
Les Violons du Bal, *759*
Les Visiteurs Du Soir, *759*
Les Patterson Saves the World, *317*
Less Than Zero, *573*
Lesson in Love, A, *760*
Let Freedom Ring, *928*
Let Him Have It, *573*
Let It Be, *429*
Let It Ride, *317*
Let It Rock, *573*
Let's Dance, *928*
Lethal Charm, *573*
Lethal Games, *76*
Lethal Lolita—Amy Fisher: My Story, *573*
Lethal Ninja, *76*
Lethal Obsession, *76*
◆ Lethal Weapon, *76*
Lethal Weapon 2, *76*
Lethal Weapon 3, *77*
Lethal Woman, *77*
Let's Do It Again, *318*
Let's Get Harry, *573*
◆ Let's Get Lost, *429*
Let's Make It Legal, *318*
Let's Make Love, *928*
Let's Scare Jessica to Death, *860*
Let's Spend the Night Together, *429*
◆ Letter, The, *991*
Letter from an Unknown Woman, *573*
◆ Letter of Introduction, *573*
Letter to Brezhnev, *318*
Letter to Three Wives, A, *573*
◆ Letters from the Park, *760*
Letters to an Unknown Lover, *573*
Leviathan, *860*
L'Homme Blessé (The Wounded Man), *760*
◆ Lianna, *573*
Liars, The, *760*
Liars' Club, The, *992*
Liar's Edge, *992*
Liar's Moon, *574*
◆ Libeled Lady, *318*
Liberation of L. B. Jones, The, *574*
Liberty and Bash, *77*
License to Drive, *318*
◆ License to Kill, *77*
◆ Liebelei, *760*
Liebestraum, *992*
◆ Lies, *574*
Lies Before Kisses, *574*
Lies of the Twins, *992*
Lt. Robin Crusoe, U.S.N., *181*
Life and Assassination of the Kingfish, The, *574*
◆ Life and Death of Colonel Blimp, The, *574*
◆ Life and Nothing But, *760*
Life and Times of Grizzly Adams, The, *181*
Life and Times of Judge Roy Bean, The, *1128*
Life Begins for Andy Hardy, *318*
Life in the Theater, A, *574*
Life Is a Circus, Charlie Brown, *181*
◆ Life Is Sweet, *574*
◆ Life of Brian, *318*
◆ Life of Emile Zola, The, *574*
Life of Her Own, A, *574*
◆ Life of Oharu, *760*
Life on a String, *760*
Life on the Mississippi, *574*
Life Stinks, *318*
◆ Life with Father, *318*
◆ Life with Mickey (Limited Gold Edition 2), *181*
Life with Mikey, *318*
Lifeboat, *992*
Lifeforce, *1063*
Lifeforce Experiment, The, *1063*
Lifeguard, *574*
Lifepod, *1063*
Lifespan, *1063*
Lifetaker, The, *77*
Lift, The, *860*
Light at the End of the World, The, *77*
Light in the Forest, The, *181*
Light in the Jungle, The, *575*
Light of Day, *575*
Light Sleeper, *575*
Light Years, *1063*
Lighthorsemen, The, *77*
◆ Lightnin' Crandall, *1128*
Lightning Carson Rides Again, *1128*
Lightning Incident, The, *860*
Lightning Jack, *1128*
Lightning Over Water, *575*
Lightning, the White Stallion, *181*
Lightning Triggers, *1128*
Lights, Camera, Action, Love, *575*
Lights of Old Santa Fe, *1128*
Lightship, The, *575*
Like Father, Like Son, *318*
◆ Like Water for Chocolate, *760*
Li'l Abner (1940), *318*
◆ Li'l Abner (1959), *928*
◆ Lili, *928*
Lili Marleen, *760*
Lilies of the Field (1930), *575*
◆ Lilies of the Field (1963), *575*
Lilith, *575*
◆ Lillie, *575*
◆ Lily in Love, *318*
Lily Tomlin Special—Vol. I, The, *319*
Lily Was Here, *575*
Limelight, *319*
Limit Up, *319*
◆ **Linda**, *992*
Lindbergh Kidnapping Case, The, *575*
Linguini Incident, The, *319*
Link, *861*
Lion and the Hawk, The, *77*
Lion in the Streets, A, *575*
◆ Lion in Winter, The, *576*
Lion of Africa, The, *77*
Lion of the Desert, *77*
Lion, the Witch and the Wardrobe, The, *181*
Lionheart, *181*
Lip Service, *576*
Lipstick, *992*
Lipstick Camera, *992*
Liquid Sky, *1063*
Lisa, *992*
Lisbon, *77*
◆ List of Adrian Messenger, The, *992*
Listen, Darling, *928*
Listen to Me, *576*
Listen to Your Heart, *319*
Listen Up: The Lives of Quincy Jones, *429*
Lisztomania, *928*
Little Annie Rooney, *576*
◆ Little Big Horn, *1128*
◆ Little Big Man, *1128*
Little Boy Lost, *576*
Little Caesar, *77*
Little Colonel, The, *928*
Little Darlings, *319*
◆ Little Dorrit, *576*
Little Drummer Girl, The, *992*
◆ Little Foxes, The, *576*
Little Giant, *319*
Little Girl Who Lives Down the Lane, The, *992*
◆ Little Gloria...Happy at Last, *576*
Little Heroes, *181*
Little House on the Prairie (TV Series), *181*
Little Ladies of the Night, *576*
Little Laura and Big John, *77*
◆ Little Lord Fauntleroy (1936), *576*

◆ Little Lord Fauntleroy (1980), *182*
◆ Little Man Tate, *182*
Little Match Girl, The (1983), *182*
Little Match Girl, The (1990), *182*
Little Men (1935), *182*
Little Men (1940), *576*
Little Mermaid, The (1978), *182*
Little Mermaid, The (1984), *182*
◆ Little Mermaid, The (1989), *182*
Little Mermaid, The: Ariel's Undersea Adventures, *182*
Little Minister, The, *576*
Little Miss Broadway, *928*
◆ Little Miss Marker (1934), *182*
Little Miss Marker (1980), *182*
Little Miss Millions, *182*
Little Miss Trouble and Friends, *183*
Little Monsters, *1063*
Little Moon & Jud McGraw, *1128*
◆ Little Murders, *319*
Little Nellie Kelly, *928*
Little Nemo: Adventures in Slumberland, *183*
Little Night Music, A, *928*
Little Nikita, *992*
Little Ninjas, *183*
Little Noises, *576*
Little Orphan Annie, *183*
Little Prince, The, *929*
Little Prince, The (Series), *183*
Little Princess, A, *183*
Little Princess, The, *183*
◆ Little Rascals, The, *183*
Little Rascals Christmas Special, The, *183*
◆ Little Red Riding Hood, *183*
◆ Little Romance, A, *319*
Little Sex, A, *319*
◆ Little Shop of Horrors, The (1960), *861*
◆ Little Shop of Horrors (1986), *929*
Little Sister, *319*
Little Sweetheart, *577*
Little Theatre of Jean Renoir, The, *760*
◆ **Little Thief, The,** *760*
Little Tough Guys, *319*
Little Treasure, *77*
Little Tweetie and Little Inki Cartoon Festival, *183*
◆ Little Vegas, *319*
Little Vera, *761*
Little White Lies, *320*
◆ Little Women (1933), *577*
Little Women (1949), *577*
Little Women (1981), *183*
Little World of Don Camillo, The, *761*
Littlest Angel, The, *184*
Littlest Horse Thieves, The, *184*
Littlest Outlaw, The, *184*
Littlest Rebel, The, *929*
Live a Little, Love a Little, *929*
Live and Let Die, *78*
Live at Harrah's, *320*
Live by the Fist, *78*
Live! From Death Row, *577*
Live from Washington—It's Dennis Miller, *320*
Live Wire, *78*
◆ Lives of a Bengal Lancer, The, *78*
Livin' Large, *320*
Living Daylights, The, *78*
◆ **Living End, The,** *577*
Living Free, *184*
Living In A Big Way, *929*
◆ Living on Tokyo Time, *761*
Living Proof: The Hank Williams, Jr., Story, *577*
Living the Blues, *577*
Living to Die, *993*
Lizzies of Mack Sennett, The, *320*
L'Odeur Des Fauves (Scandal Man), *761*
Loaded Guns, *78*
◆ Loaded Pistols, *1128*
Lobster for Breakfast, *761*
Lobster Man from Mars, *320*
◆ Local Hero, *320*
Loch Ness Horror, The, *861*
Lock and Load, *993*
Lock Up, *78*
◆ Lodger, The, *993*
Logan's Run, *1063*
Lois Gibbs and the Love Canal, *577*
◆ Lola (1960), *761*
◆ Lola (1982), *761*
◆ Lola Montes, *761*
Lolita, *577*
London Kills Me, *577*
London Melody, *577*
Lone Defender, The, *78*
Lone Justice, *1129*
Lone Ranger, The (1938), *1129*
Lone Ranger, The (1956), *1129*
Lone Ranger, The (TV Series), *1129*
Lone Ranger and the Lost City of Gold, The, *1129*
Lone Runner, *78*
Lone Star, *1129*
Lone Star Raiders, *1129*
Lone Star Trail, *1129*
Lone Wolf, *861*
Lone Wolf McQuade, *78*
◆ Lonely Are the Brave, *1129*
Lonely Guy, The, *320*
◆ Lonely Hearts (1981), *577*
Lonely Hearts (1991), *577*
Lonely in America, *320*
Lonely Lady, The, *577*
Lonely Man, The, *1129*
◆ Lonely Passion of Judith Hearne, The, *577*
Lonely Trail, The, *1129*
Lonelyhearts, *578*
◆ Lonesome Dove, *1129*
Long Ago Tomorrow, *578*
◆ Long Day Closes, The, *578*
◆ Long Day's Journey into Night (1962), *578*
◆ Long Day's Journey into Night (1987), *578*
◆ Long Gone, *578*
◆ Long Good Friday, The, *78*
◆ Long Goodbye, The, *993*
Long Grey Line, The, *578*
Long Haul, *578*
◆ Long Hot Summer, The (1958), *578*
Long Hot Summer, The (1985), *578*
Long John Silver, *78*
Long Live Your Death, *1130*
Long Long Trail, *1130*
Long, Long Trailer, The, *320*
Long Riders, The, *1130*
◆ Long Voyage Home, The, *578*
◆ Long Walk Home, The, *579*
Long Way Home, The, *429*
Long Weekend, *861*
◆ Longest Day, The, *78*
Longest Drive, The, *1130*
Longest Hunt, The, *1130*
◆ Longest Yard, The, *78*
◆ Longhorn, *1130*
Longshot (1981), *579*
Longshot, The (1985), *320*
◆ Longtime Companion, *579*
◆ Look Back in Anger (1958), *579*
Look Back in Anger (1980), *579*
◆ Look Back In Anger (1989), *579*
Look For The Silver Lining, *929*
Look Who's Laughing, *320*
◆ Look Who's Talking, *320*
Look Who's Talking Too, *321*
Look Who's Talking Now, *321*
Lookalike, The, *993*
Looker, *1063*
Lookin' to Get Out, *321*
Looking for Miracles, *579*
Looking for Mr. Goodbar, *993*
Looking Glass War, The, *993*
Looney, Looney, Looney Bugs Bunny Movie, *184*
Looney Tunes Video Show, The (Volume 1), *184*
Looney Tunes Video Show, The (Volume 2), *184*
Looney Tunes Video Show, The (Volume 3), *184*
Loophole, *993*
Loose Cannons, *321*
Loose Connections, *321*
Loose Shoes, *321*
Loot, *321*
◆ Lord Jim, *79*
Lord Love a Duck, *321*
◆ Lord of the Flies (1963), *579*
Lord of the Flies (1989), *579*
Lord of the Rings, The, *1063*
Lords of Discipline, The, *579*
Lords of Flatbush, The, *579*
Lords of the Deep, *1063*
◆ Lorenzo's Oil, *579*
Lorna, *580*
Lorna Doone, *580*
◆ Los Olvidados, *761*
Los Zancos (see Stilts, The)
Losers, The, *79*
Losin' It, *321*
Lost!, *580*
Lost and Found, *321*
Lost and Found Chaplin: Keystone, *321*
◆ Lost Angels, *580*
Lost Boys, The, *861*
Lost Capone, The, *580*
Lost City, The, *1063*
Lost City of the Jungle, *79*
Lost Command, *79*
Lost Continent, The, *1063*
Lost Empire, The, *79*
Lost Honor of Katharina Blum, The, *761*
◆ Lost Horizon, *580*
Lost in a Harem, *321*
Lost In Alaska, *321*
◆ Lost in America, *321*
Lost in Space (TV Series), *1063*
◆ Lost in Yonkers, *580*
Lost Jungle, The, *79*
Lost Language of Cranes, The, *580*
Lost Moment, The, *580*
◆ Lost Patrol, The, *79*
Lost Planet, The, *1064*
Lost Platoon, *861*
Lost Squadron, *79*
Lost Stooges, The, *322*

Lost Tribe, The, *861*
◆ Lost Weekend, The, *580*
◆ Lost World, The (1925), *1064*
Lost World, The (1992), *79*
Lots of Luck, *322*
◆ Louie Anderson: Mom! Louie's Looking at Me Again!, *322*
Louisiana, *580*
Louisiana Purchase, *322*
Louisiana Story, The, *429*
Loulou, *761*
◆ Love, *761*
◆ Love Among the Ruins, *322*
◆ Love and Anarchy, *762*
Love and Bullets, *79*
◆ Love and Death, *322*
Love and Hate, *581*
Love and Murder, *993*
Love and the Frenchwoman, *762*
Love and War, *581*
◆ Love at First Bite, *322*
Love at First Sight, *322*
◆ Love at Large, *322*
Love at Stake, *322*
◆ Love at the Top, *581*
Love Bug, The, *184*
Love Butcher, *861*
Love, Cheat & Steal, *993*
◆ Love Child, *581*
◆ Love Crazy, *322*
Love Crimes, *993*
◆ Love Field, *581*
Love Finds Andy Hardy, *322*
Love from a Stranger, *993*
Love Happy, *322*
Love Has Many Faces, *581*
Love Hurts, *323*
Love in Germany, A, *762*
◆ Love in the Afternoon, *323*
Love in the Present Tense, *581*
Love is a Many-Splendored Thing, *581*
Love is Better Than Ever, *929*
Love Kills, *993*
Love Laughs at Andy Hardy, *323*
◆ Love Leads the Way, *581*
◆ Love Letters, *581*
Love, Lies and Murder, *994*
Love Machine, The, *581*
Love Matters, *581*
◆ Love Me or Leave Me, *929*
Love Me Tender, *1130*
◆ Love Me Tonight, *929*
Love Meetings, *762*
Love Nest, *323*
Love of Jeanne Ney, *762*
Love on the Dole, *581*
Love on the Run (1936), *323*
Love on the Run (1979), *762*
Love or Money?, *323*
◆ Love Potion #9, *323*
Love Songs (Paroles et Musique), *762*
Love Spell, *79*
◆ Love Story, *582*
Love Streams, *582*
Love Street, *582*
Love with a Perfect Stranger, *582*
◆ Love with the Proper Stranger, *582*
Love without Pity, *762*
Love Your Mama, *582*
◆ Loved One, The, *323*
Loveless, The, *582*
Lovelines, *323*
Lovely But Deadly, *994*
◆ Lovely to Look At, *929*
◆ Lover Come Back, *323*
Lover, The, *582*
Loverboy, *323*
Lovers, The (1958), *762*
◆ Lovers (1992), *762*
Lovers and Liars, *323*
Lovers and Other Strangers, *323*
Lovers' Lovers, *582*
Lovers of Their Time, *582*
◆ Lovers on the Bridge, *762*
Loves and Times of Scaramouche, The, *324*
Loves of a Blonde, *762*
Loves of Carmen, The, *582*
Loves of Irina (see Erotikill)
Loves of Three Queens, *762*
Love's Savage Fury, *582*
Lovesick, *324*
Loving Couples, *324*
Loving You, *929*
Low Blow, *79*
◆ Lower Depths (1936), *762*
◆ Lower Depths, The (1957), *763*
Lower Level, *994*
Loyalties, *582*
◆ Lucas, *583*
Lucky Boots, *1130*
Lucky Jim, *324*
Lucky Johnny: Born in America (see Dead Aim (1973))
Lucky Luciano, *79*
Lucky Luke: The Ballad of the Daltons, *184*
Lucky Me, *929*
Lucky Partners, *324*
Lucky Stiff, *324*
Lucky Texan, *1130*
Lucy and Desi: Before the Laughter, *583*
Luggage of the Gods, *324*
Lullaby of Broadway, *929*
Lumiere, *763*
Lunatic, The, *324*
Lunatics & Lovers, *763*
Lunatics: A Love Story, *324*
Lunch Wagon, *324*
Lupin III: Tales of the Wolf (TV Series), *763*
Lupo, *324*
Lurkers, *861*
Lust for a Vampire, *861*
Lust for Freedom, *80*
Lust for Gold, *1130*
Lust for Life, *583*
Lust in the Dust, *324*
◆ Lusty Men, The, *1130*
Luther, *583*
Luv, *324*
Luxury Liner, *930*
Luzia, *763*
Lycanthropus (see Werewolf in a Girl's Dormitory)
Lydia, *583*
◆ M, *763*
M.A.D.D.: Mothers Against Drunk Driving, *583*
M. Butterfly, *583*
◆ M*A*S*H, *324*
◆ M*A*S*H* (TV Series), *325*
◆ M*A*S*H: Goodbye, Farewell, Amen, *325*
Ma Barker's Killer Brood, *80*
Mabel and Fatty, *325*
◆ Mac, *583*
Mac and Me, *1064*
Macabre Serenade, *861*
Macabro (see Frozen Terror)
Macao, *80*
◆ Macario, *763*
◆ Macaroni, *325*
MacArthur, *583*
MacArthur's Children, *763*
Macbeth (1948), *583*
Macbeth (1961), *583*
Macbeth (1971), *584*
Macbeth (1981), *584*
Machine Gun Killers, *1130*
Machine-Gun Kelly, *80*
Macho Callahan, *1130*
Maciste in Hell, *861*
Mack Sennett Comedies, Vol. 2, *325*
Mack, The, *584*
Mack the Knife, *930*
Mackenna's Gold, *1131*
Mackintosh Man, The, *994*
Macon County Line, *80*
Macross II, Vols. 1–4, *1064*
Mad About You, *325*
Mad at the Moon, *861*
Mad Bomber, The, *994*
Mad Bull, *584*
Mad Doctor of Blood Island, The, *861*
◆ Mad Dog and Glory, *584*
Mad Dog Morgan, *80*
Mad Dogs and Englishmen, *429*
Mad Executioners, The, *994*
Mad Love, *861*
Mad, Mad Monsters, The, *184*
Mad Max, *1064*
Mad Max Beyond Thunderdome, *1064*
Mad Miss Manton, The, *325*
Mad Mission (see Aces Go Places)
Mad Monster, *862*
Mad Monster Party, *184*
Mad Wednesday, *325*
Madame Bovary (1934), *763*
Madame Bovary (1949), *584*
◆ Madame Bovary (1991), *763*
◆ Madame Curie, *584*
◆ Madame Rosa, *763*
Madame Satan, *584*
Madame Sin, *80*
Madame Sousatzka, *584*
Madame X (1937), *584*
Madame X (1966), *584*
Maddest Story Ever Told, The (see Spider Baby)
◆ Made for Each Other, *325*
Made in America, *325*
Made in Heaven (1948), *326*
Made in Heaven (1987), *1064*
Made in USA, *584*
Madeline, *184*
Mademoiselle, *585*
Mademoiselle Fifi, *585*
Mademoiselle Striptease, *763*
Madhouse (1972), *862*
Madhouse (1987), *862*
Madhouse (1990), *326*
Madigan, *80*
Madigan's Millions, *326*
Mado, *763*
Madonna, *994*
Madox-01, *764*
Madron, *1131*
Madwoman of Chaillot, The, *585*
Mae West, *585*
◆ Maedchen in Uniform, *764*

Mafia Princess, 585
Mafu Cage (see My Sister, My Love)
Magdalene, 585
Magic, 994
Magic Christian, The, 326
Magic Christmas Tree, The, 184
◆ Magic Flute, The, 764
Magic Garden, The, 764
Magic of Dr. Snuggles, The, 185
Magic of Lassie, The, 185
Magic Sword, The, 185
Magic Town, 585
Magic Voyage, The, 185
Magical Mystery Tour, 930
Magician, The, 764
Magician of Lublin, The, 585
◆ Magnificent Ambersons, The, 585
Magnificent Obsession, 585
◆ Magnificent Seven, The, 1131
Magnificent Yankee, The, 585
Magnum Force, 80
◆ Mahabharata, The, 585
Mahler, 585
Mahogany, 586
Maid, The, 326
Maid to Order, 326
Maid's Night Out, The, 326
Main Event, The, 326
Main Street to Broadway, 326
Maitresse, 764
Major Barbara, 326
Major Dundee, 1131
Major League, 326
Major League II, 326
◆ **Majority of One, A,** 326
Make a Million, 327
Make a Wish, 586
Make Haste to Live, 994
Make Me an Offer, 586
◆ Make Mine Mink, 327
Make Room For Tomorrow, 764
Make Them Die Slowly, 862
Making Contact, 1064
Making Love, 586
Making Mr. Right, 327
◆ Making of a Legend—*Gone With the Wind*, 429
Making the Grade, 327
Malarek, 586
◆ Malcolm, 327
◆ Malcolm X, 586
Male and Female, 994
Malibu Bikini Shop, The, 327
Malibu Express, 327
Malice, 994
Malice in Wonderland (see Rumor Mill, The)
Malicious, 764
Malone, 80
Malou, 764
Malta Story, The, 586
◆ Maltese Falcon, The, 994
◆ Mama, There's a Man in Your Bed, 764
Mama Turns 100, 764
Mambo, 586
◆ Mambo Kings, The, 930
Mame, 930
Mamma Dracula, 862
Man, a Woman and a Bank, A, 994
Man Alone, A, 1131
◆ Man and a Woman, A, 764
Man and a Woman, A: 20 Years Later, 764
Man and Boy, 1131
Man and the Monster, The, 862
Man Beast, 862
Man Bites Dog, 764
Man Called Adam, A, 586
Man Called Flintstone, A, 185
Man Called Horse, A, 1131
◆ **Man Called Noon, The,** 1131
Man Called Peter, A, 586
Man Called Rage, A, 1064
Man Called Sarge, A, 327
Man Called Tiger, A, 80
Man Facing Southeast, 765
◆ Man for All Seasons, A, 586
Man from Atlantis, The, 1064
Man from Beyond, The, 1064
Man from Colorado, The, 1131
Man from Deep River, 80
◆ Man from Laramie, The, 1131
Man from Left Field, The, 586
Man from Monterey, The, 1131
Man from Music Mountain, 1131
Man from Nowhere, The, 765
Man from Painted Post, The, 327
◆ Man from Snowy River, The, 1131
Man from the Alamo, The, 1132
Man from U.N.C.L.E., The (TV Series), 80
Man from Utah, The, 1132
◆ **Man Hunt (1941),** 994
Man I Love, The, 586
Man in Grey, The, 587
Man in Love, A, 587
◆ Man in the Eiffel Tower, The, 995
Man in the Gray Flannel Suit, The, 587
Man in the Iron Mask, The (1939), 81
Man in the Iron Mask, The (1977), 81
◆ Man in the Moon, The, 587
◆ Man in the Saddle, 1132
Man in the Santa Claus Suit, The, 185
◆ Man in the White Suit, The, 327
Man in the Wilderness, 1132
Man Inside, The (1984), 81
Man Inside, The (1990), 587
Man Like Eva, A, 765
Man of a Thousand Faces, 587
Man of Action, 1132
◆ Man of Flowers, 327
◆ **Man of Iron,** 765
Man of La Mancha, 930
◆ Man of Marble, 765
Man of Passion, A, 587
◆ Man of the Forest, 1132
Man of the Frontier (Red River Valley), 1132
◆ Man of the West, 1132
Man on a String, 81
Man on Fire, 81
Man Ray Classic Shorts, 765
◆ Man That Corrupted Hadleyburg, The, 327
Man They Could Not Hang, The, 862
Man Trouble, 327
Man Upstairs, The, 327
◆ Man Who Broke 1000 Chains, The, 587
◆ Man Who Came to Dinner, The, 328
Man Who Could Work Miracles, The, 1064
◆ Man Who Fell to Earth, The, 1064
Man Who Had Power Over Women, The, 587
Man Who Haunted Himself, The, 995
◆ Man Who Knew Too Much, The (1934), 995
Man Who Knew Too Much, The (1955), 995
Man Who Lived Again, The, 862
Man Who Loved Cat Dancing, The, 1132
◆ Man Who Loved Women, The (1977), 765
Man Who Loved Women, The (1983), 328
Man Who Never Was, The, 81
Man Who Saw Tomorrow, The, 43
◆ Man Who Shot Liberty Valance, The, 1132
Man Who Wasn't There, The, 328
◆ Man Who Would Be King, The, 81
◆ Man with a Movie Camera, 430
Man with Bogart's Face, The, 995
Man with One Red Shoe, The, 328
Man with the Golden Arm, The, 587
Man with the Golden Gun, The, 81
◆ Man with Two Brains, The, 328
Man with Two Heads, 862
◆ **Man without a Face, The,** 587
Man without a Star, 1132
Man, Woman and Child, 587
◆ Mance Lipscomb: A Well-Spent Life, 430
◆ Manchurian Candidate, The, 995
Mandela, 588
Mandingo, 588
Mandroid, 1065
Maneaters! (see Shark!)
Manfish, 862
Manhandled, 328
◆ Manhattan, 328
Manhattan Baby, 862
◆ Manhattan Melodrama, 81
Manhattan Merry-Go-Round, 930
◆ **Manhattan Murder Mystery,** 328
Manhattan Project, The, 995
Manhunt (1973), 81
Manhunt for Claude Dallas, 81
Manhunt in the African Jungle (Secret Service in Darkest Africa), 81
Manhunt of Mystery Island, 82
◆ Manhunter, 995
Mania, 862
Maniac (1934), 862
Maniac (1962), 995
Maniac (1980), 862
Maniac Cop, 862
Maniac Cop 2, 863
Maniac Cop 3: Badge of Silence, 86
Manifesto, 328
◆ Manions of America, The, 588
Manipulator, The, 588
Manitou, The, 863
Mankillers, 82
Mannequin (1937), 588
Mannequin (1987), 328
Mannequin Two: On the Move, 328
Manny's Orphans, 185
Manon, 765
◆ Manon of the Spring, 765
Man's Best Friend (1985), 185
Man's Best Friend (1993), 863
Man's Favorite Sport?, 328
Manster, The, 863
Mantrap, 995
Manxman, The, 588
◆ Map of the Human Heart, 588
◆ Marat/Sade, 588
Marathon, 329
◆ Marathon Man, 82

arauders, *1132*
arch of the Wooden Soldiers, *329*
arch or Die, *82*
arciano, *588*
arco Polo Jr., *185*
ardi Gras for the Devil, *863*
argaret Bourke White (see Double Exposure)
aria's Lovers, *588*
arie, *588*
arie Antoinette, *588*
arijuana, *588*
arijuana (see Assassin of Youth)
arilyn & Bobby: Her Final Affair, *588*
arine Raiders, *82*
arius, *765*
arjoe, *588*
arjorie Morningstar, *589*
ark of Cain, *863*
ark of the Beast, The, *863*
ark of the Devil, *863*
ark of the Devil, Part 2, *863*
ark of the Hawk, The, *589*
ark of the Vampire, *863*
ark of Zorro, The (1920), *82*
ark of Zorro, The (1940), *82*
ark Twain's Connecticut Yankee in King Arthur's Court, *185*
arked for Death, *82*
arked Woman, *82*
arlene, *589*
arlowe, *995*
arnie, *995*
aroc 7, *82*
arooned, *1065*
arquis, *765*
arriage Circle, The, *329*
arriage of Maria Braun, The, *765*
arried Man, A, *589*
arried People, Single Sex, *589*
arried to It, *589*
arried to the Mob, *329*
arried Too Young, *589*
arried Woman, A, *765*
arrying Man, The, *329*
ars Attacks the World (see Flash Gordon: Mars Attacks the World)
ars Needs Women, *1065*
arshal of Cedar Rock, *1132*
arshal of Cripple Creek, *1132*
arshal of Mesa City, *1133*
artial Law, *82*
artial Law Two—Undercover, *82*
artial Outlaw, *82*
artian Chronicles, Parts I-III, The, *1065*
artians Go Home, *329*
artin, *863*
artin Luther, *589*
artin's Day, *185*
arty, *589*
arty (Television), *589*
arvel Comics Video Library, *185*
arvelous Land of Oz, The, *185*
arvin and Tige, *589*
arx Brothers in a Nutshell, The, *430*
ary and Joseph: A Story of Faith, *589*
ary Hartman, Mary Hartman (TV Series), *329*
ary, Mary, Bloody Mary, *863*
ary My Dearest, *766*

◆ Mary of Scotland, *589*
◆ Mary Poppins, *185*
Marzipan Pig, The, *186*
◆ Masada, *590*
◆ **Masala,** *329*
Mascara, *82*
Masculine Feminine, *766*
Mask, The (1961), *863*
◆ Mask (1985), *590*
Mask of Fu Manchu, The, *82*
Masked Marvel, The, *83*
Masks of Death, *83*
Masque of the Red Death, The (1964), *863*
Masque of the Red Death (1989), *864*
Masquerade (1986), *766*
Masquerade (1988), *995*
◆ Mass Appeal, *590*
Massacre at Central High, *864*
Massacre at Fort Holman (Reason to Live...A Reason to Die, A), *1133*
Massacre in Rome, *590*
Massive Retaliation, *83*
Master Blaster, *83*
◆ Master Harold and the Boys, *590*
Master of Ballantrae, The, *83*
◆ Master of the House (Du Skal Aere Din Hustru), *766*
Master of the World, *1065*
Master Race, The, *590*
Mastermind, *329*
Mastermind (TV Series), *186*
◆ Masters of Animation, *430*
Masters of Comic Book Art, *430*
Masters of Menace, *329*
Masters of the Universe, *186*
Mata Hari (1931), *590*
Mata Hari (1985), *83*
◆ Matador, *766*
◆ Matchmaker, The, *329*
◆ Matewan, *590*
Matilda, *330*
◆ Matinee, *330*
◆ Mating Game, The, *330*
Mating Season, The, *330*
Matt the Gooseboy, *186*
Matter of Degrees, A, *590*
◆ Matter of Principle, A, *330*
Matter of Time, A, *590*
Matters of the Heart, *590*
Maurice, *590*
Mausoleum, *864*
◆ Maverick (TV Series), *1133*
◆ **Maverick,** *1133*
Maverick Queen, The, *1133*
Max and Helen, *590*
Max Dugan Returns, *591*
Max Headroom, *1065*
Maxie, *330*
Maximum Breakout, *83*
Maximum Force, *83*
Maximum Overdrive, *864*
◆ May Fools, *766*
May Wine, *330*
Maya, *186*
Mayerling, *766*
Mayflower Madam, *591*
Maytime, *930*
Mazes and Monsters, *864*
McBain, *83*
◆ McCabe and Mrs. Miller, *1133*
McConnell Story, The, *591*
McGuffin, The, *996*
McLintock!, *1133*
McQ, *83*

McVicar, *591*
Me and Him, *330*
Me and the Kid, *83*
Me & Veronica, *591*
Me, Myself & I, *330*
Mean Johnny Barrows, *83*
Mean Season, The, *996*
◆ Mean Streets, *591*
Meanest Man in the World, The, *330*
Meanest Men in the West, The, *1133*
Meatballs, *330*
Meatballs Part II, *330*
Meatballs III, *330*
Meatballs 4, *330*
Meateater, The, *864*
Mechanic, The, *83*
◆ Medea, *766*
Medical Deviate (see Dr. Butcher, MD)
Medicine Hat Stallion, The, *186*
Medicine Man, *591*
◆ Mediterraneo, *766*
◆ Medium Cool, *591*
◆ Medusa: Dare to be Truthful, *331*
Medusa Touch, The, *864*
Meet Dr. Christian, *591*
◆ Meet John Doe, *591*
Meet Me in Las Vegas, *930*
◆ Meet Me in St. Louis, *930*
Meet the Applegates, *331*
Meet the Hollowheads, *331*
Meet the Navy, *930*
Meet the Raisins, *186*
Meet the Wombles, *186*
Meet Your Animal Friends, *186*
Meeting at Midnight, *996*
Meeting Venus, *591*
◆ Meetings with Remarkable Men, *591*
Megaforce, *1065*
Megaville, *1065*
Melanie, *591*
Melo, *766*
Melodie en Sous-Sol (The Big Grab), *766*
Melody, *186*
Melody Cruise, *930*
Melody for Three, *592*
Melody in Love, *592*
Melody Master, *592*
Melody Ranch, *1133*
Melody Trail, *1133*
◆ Melvin and Howard, *331*
Melvin Purvis: G-Man, *83*
◆ Member of the Wedding, The, *592*
Memed My Hawk (see Lion and the Hawk, The)
◆ Memoirs of an Invisible Man, *1065*
Memorial Day, *592*
◆ Memories of a Marriage, *766*
Memories of Hollywood, *430*
Memories of Me, *331*
Memories of Murder, *996*
Memories of Underdevelopment, *766*
Memphis, *592*
◆ Memphis Belle (1990), *592*
◆ Men, The, *592*
◆ Men..., *767*
Men at Work, *592*
◆ Men Don't Leave, *331*
Men in Love, *592*
◆ Men in War, *84*
Men of Boys Town, *592*
Men of Respect, *592*
Men of Sherwood Forest, *84*

Men of the Fighting Lady, 84
Men with Steel Faces & Phantom Empire (see Radio Ranch)
Menace on the Mountain, 593
◆ **Menace II Society,** 593
Ménage, 767
Men's Club, The, 593
◆ Mephisto, 767
Mephisto Waltz, The, 864
Mercenaries (see Kill Castro)
Mercenaries, The (see Dark of the Sun)
Mercenary Fighters, 84
Merchant of Four Seasons, The, 767
Merci La Vie, 767
Meridian, 864
Merlin, 1065
Merlin & the Sword, 1065
Mermaids, 331
Merry Christmas, Mr. Lawrence, 593
Merry-Go-Round, The, 996
Merry Widow, The, 930
Merry Wives of Windsor, The, 331
◆ **Merton of the Movies,** 331
Mesmerized, 996
Message, The (Mohammad, Messenger of God), 593
Messenger of Death, 84
◆ Messin' with the Blues, 430
Metalstorm: The Destruction of Jared-Syn, 1065
Metamorphosis, 864
Metamorphosis: The Alien Factor, 1065
Meteor, 1065
Meteor Man, 186
Meteor Monster, 864
◆ Metropolis (1926), 1065
◆ Metropolis (musical version), 930
◆ Metropolitan, 593
◆ Mexicali Rose, 1134
Mexican Bus Ride (see Ascent to Heaven)
Mexican Hayride, 331
Mexican Spitfire, 331
MGM Cartoon Magic, 186
MGM's The Big Parade of Comedy, 331
Miami Blues, 84
Miami Cops, 84
Miami Horror, 1066
Miami Supercops, 331
◆ Miami Vice, 84
Miami Vice: "The Prodigal Son", 84
◆ Michael Jackson Moonwalker, 931
◆ Mickey (Limited Gold Edition 1), 186
◆ Mickey and the Beanstalk, 187
◆ Mickey and the Gang, 187
◆ Mickey Knows Best, 187
◆ Mickey's Christmas Carol, 187
◆ Mickey's Crazy Careers, 187
Mickey's Magical World, 187
◆ Micki & Maude, 331
Microwave Massacre, 864
Middle-Age Crazy, 332
Middle of the Night, 593
Midnight (1934), 593
Midnight (1980), 864
Midnight (1989), 996
Midnight Cabaret, 864
◆ Midnight Clear, A, 593
Midnight Cop, 996
◆ Midnight Cowboy, 593
Midnight Crossing, 84
Midnight Dancer, 594
◆ Midnight Express, 594
Midnight Hour, 864
Midnight Kiss, 864
Midnight Lace, 84
Midnight Madness, 332
Midnight Movie Massacre, 332
◆ Midnight Run, 84
Midnight Witness, 996
Midnight's Child, 865
◆ Midsummer Night's Dream, A (1935), 1066
Midsummer Night's Dream, A (1968), 332
Midsummer Night's Sex Comedy, A, 332
Midway, 84
Mighty Ducks, The, 187
Mighty Joe Young, 1066
Mighty Quinn, The, 85
◆ Mikado, The (1939), 931
Mikado, The (1987), 931
Mike's Murder, 594
Mikey, 865
Mikey and Nicky, 332
Milagro Beanfield War, The, 594
◆ Mildred Pierce, 594
Miles from Home, 594
Miles to Go, 594
◆ Milky Way, The (1936), 332
◆ Milky Way, The (1970), 767
Mill of the Stone Women, 865
Mill on the Floss, The, 594
Millennium, 1066
◆ Miller's Crossing, 594
Millhouse: A White Comedy, 430
Million Dollar Duck, The, 187
Million Dollar Mermaid, 931
Million Dollar Mystery, 332
Million to Juan, A, 332
Millions, 594
Min and Bill, 594
Mind Field, 85
Mind Killer, 865
Mind Snatchers, The, 865
Mindgames, 996
Mindwalk, 430
Mindwarp, 1066
Mine Own Executioner, 594
Mines of Kilimanjaro, 85
Mingus, 430
Ministry of Vengeance, 85
Miniver Story, The, 594
Minnie (Limited Gold Edition 1), 187
Minor Miracle, A, 187
Minute to Pray, A Second to Die, A, 1134
Miracle, The (1959), 594
Miracle, The (1990), 595
Miracle Beach, 332
Miracle Down Under, 187
Miracle in Milan, 767
Miracle in Rome, 767
Miracle in the Wilderness, 595
◆ Miracle Mile, 996
◆ Miracle of Morgan's Creek, The, 332
Miracle of Our Lady of Fatima, The, 595
Miracle of the Bells, The, 595
Miracle of the Heart, 595
Miracle of the White Stallions, 187
Miracle on Ice, 595
◆ Miracle on 34th Street, 187
Miracle Rider, The, 1134
◆ Miracle Worker, The (1962), 595
Miracle Worker, The (1979), 595
Miracles, 332
Mirage, 595
◆ Mirror, The, 767
Mirror Crack'd, The, 996
Mirror Images, 996
Mirror Images II, 996
Mirror Mirror, 865
Mirror of Death, 865
Misadventures of Buster Keaton, The, 332
Misadventures of Gumby, The (Volume Three), 187
Misadventures of Merlin Jones, The 188
Misadventures of Mr. Wilt, The, 33
Mischief, 333
◆ Misery, 865
Misfit Brigade, The, 85
Misfits, The, 595
Misfits of Science, 1066
◆ Mishima: A Life in Four Chapters, 595
Misplaced, 595
Miss Annie Rooney, 188
◆ Miss Firecracker, 333
Miss Grant Takes Richmond, 333
Miss Julie, 767
Miss Mary, 767
Miss Peach of the Kelly School, 18
Miss Right, 333
◆ Miss Rose White, 596
Miss Sadie Thompson, 596
Missile to the Moon, 1066
◆ Missiles of October, The, 596
◆ Missing, 596
Missing in Action, 85
Missing in Action 2: The Beginning, 85
Missing in Action III (see Braddock: Missing in Action III)
Missing Link, 85
◆ Mission, The, 596
Mission Galactica: The Cylon Attack 1066
Mission in Morocco, 85
Mission Mars, 1066
Mission of Justice, 85
Mission of the Shark, 596
Mission Stardust, 1066
Mission to Glory, 596
Missionary, The, 333
Mississippi, 931
◆ Mississippi Blues, 430
◆ Mississippi Burning, 596
◆ Mississippi Masala, 596
Mississippi Mermaid, 768
Missouri Breaks, The, 1134
◆ Missourians, The, 1134
Mr. Ace, 85
◆ Mr. and Mrs. Bridge, 596
◆ Mr. and Mrs. Smith, 333
Mr. Arkadin (a.k.a. Confidential Report), 596
Mr. Baseball, 333
Mr. Bill Looks Back, 333
Mr. Billion, 85
Mr. Bill's Real Life Adventures, 33
◆ Mr. Blandings Builds His Dream House, 333
Mr. Corbett's Ghost, 1066
◆ Mr. Deeds Goes to Town, 333
Mr. Destiny, 334
Mr. Frost, 997
Mr. Halpern and Mr. Johnson, 597

Hobbs Takes a Vacation, *334*
Hom, *1134*
Hulot's Holiday, *768*
Imperium, *931*
nside/Mr. Outside, *85*
er Johnson, *597*
Jones, *597*
Klein, *768*
Love, *597*
Lucky, *86*
Magoo in Sherwood Forest, *188*
Magoo in the King's Service, *188*
Magoo, Man of Mystery, *188*
Magoo's Christmas Carol, *188*
Magoo's Storybook, *188*
Majestyk, *86*
Mike's Mondo Video, *334*
Mom, *334*
Moto's Last Warning, *997*
Music, *931*
Nanny, *188*
North, *334*
Peabody and the Mermaid, *334*
Roberts, *334*
Robinson Crusoe, *86*
Saturday Night, *334*
Skeffington, *597*
Skitch, *334*
Smith Goes to Washington, *597*
Superinvisible, *188*
Sycamore, *334*
Vampire (Vol. 1–4), *768*
Winkle Goes to War, *334*
Wonderful, *597*
Wong, Detective, *997*
Wong in Chinatown, *997*
ral's Daughter, *597*
ress, The (1953), *768*
ress (1987), *597*
ress (1992), *597*
. Brown You've Got a Lovely
aughter, *931*
. Doubtfire, *334*
. Miniver, *597*
. Parkington, *598*
. Soffel, *598*
. Wiggs of the Cabbage Patch,
98
ty, *188*
understood (1984), *598*
understood (1988), *598*
ed Blood, *86*
Better Blues, *931*
Money, *335*
ana of the South Seas, *431*
Boss, *335*
Story, *335*
War, *86*
sters, *86*
y Dick, *86*
kery, *598*
Squad, The (TV Series), *86*
del by Day, *86*
dem Girls, *335*
dem Love, *335*
dem Problems, *335*
dem Romance, *335*
dem Times, *335*
dems, The, *335*
gambo, *86*
hammed, Messenger of God (see
Message, The)
hawk, *1134*
ave Firebrand, *1134*
le People, The, *1066*

Molly Maguires, The, *598*
Mom, *865*
Mom and Dad Save the World, *188*
Mommie Dearest, *598*
Mon Oncle Antoine, *768*
◆ Mon Oncle d'Amerique, *768*
◆ Mona Lisa, *997*
Mondo Cane, *431*
Mondo Cane II, *431*
Mondo New York, *598*
Mondo Topless, *431*
Mondo Trasho, *335*
◆ **Money for Nothing,** *335*
Money Pit, The, *335*
Moneytree, The, *598*
Mongrel, *865*
Monika, *768*
◆ Monkey Business (1931), *335*
◆ Monkey Business (1952), *336*
Monkey Folks (see Monkey People)
Monkey Grip, *598*
Monkey in Winter (see Un Singe en Hiver)
Monkey People, *431*
Monkey Shines: An Experiment in Fear, *865*
◆ **Monkey Trouble,** *188*
Monkeys Go Home, *188*
Monkey's Uncle, The, *188*
Monolith, *1066*
Monolith Monsters, The, *865*
Monsieur Beaucaire, *336*
◆ Monsieur Hire, *768*
◆ Monsieur Verdoux, *336*
◆ Monsieur Vincent, *768*
Monsignor, *598*
Monsignor Quixote, *599*
Monsoon, *599*
Monster, The, *865*
Monster a Go-Go, *336*
Monster Club, The, *865*
Monster Dog, *865*
Monster from a Prehistoric Planet, *1066*
Monster from Green Hell, *866*
Monster from the Ocean Floor, The, *866*
Monster High, *336*
◆ Monster in a Box, *336*
Monster in the Closet, *866*
Monster Maker, The, *866*
Monster of Piedras Blancas, The, *866*
Monster of the Island, The, *86*
Monster on the Campus, *866*
Monster Squad, The, *866*
Monster That Challenged the World, The, *1066*
Monster Walks, The, *866*
Montana, *599*
Montana Belle, *1134*
Monte Carlo, *599*
Monte Walsh, *1134*
◆ Montenegro, *599*
◆ Monterey Pop, *431*
Month in the Country, A, *599*
Monty Python and the Holy Grail, *336*
◆ Monty Python Live at the Hollywood Bowl, *336*
◆ Monty Python's Flying Circus (TV Series), *336*
◆ Monty Python's the Meaning of Life, *336*
Moon and Sixpence, The, *599*
Moon 44, *1067*
Moon in Scorpio, *599*

Moon in the Gutter, The, *768*
Moon Is Blue, The, *336*
Moon of the Wolf, *866*
Moon Over Harlem, *599*
Moon Over Miami, *931*
Moon Over Parador, *336*
Moon Pilot, *189*
Moon Trap, *1067*
Mooncussers, *189*
◆ Moonlighting (1983), *768*
◆ Moonlighting (1985), *997*
Moonraker, *86*
Moonrise, *599*
Moonshine County Express, *86*
Moonspinners, The, *189*
◆ Moonstruck, *336*
Moran of the Lady Letty, *997*
More, *768*
More American Graffiti, *599*
More Milton Berle's Mad World of Comedy, *431*
◆ More of Disney's Best: 1932–1946, *189*
More Ripping Yarns (see Ripping Yarns)
◆ More the Merrier, The, *337*
More Wild Wild West, *1134*
◆ Morgan, *337*
Morgan Stewart's Coming Home, *337*
Morgan the Pirate, *86*
Morituri, *87*
Morning After, The, *997*
Morning Glory (1933), *599*
Morning Glory (1992), *599*
Morocco, *599*
Moron Movies, *337*
Morons from Outer Space, *337*
Mortal Passions, *997*
Mortal Sins (1990), *997*
Mortal Sins (1992), *997*
◆ Mortal Storm, The, *600*
Mortal Thoughts, *997*
Mortuary, *866*
Mortuary Academy, *337*
◆ Moscow Does Not Believe in Tears, *768*
◆ Moscow on the Hudson, *337*
Moses, *600*
Mosquito Coast, The, *600*
Most Dangerous Game, The, *997*
Motel Hell, *866*
◆ Mother, *769*
◆ Mother and the Law, The, *600*
Mother Goose Rock N' Roll Rhyme, *189*
Mother Goose Video Treasury Vol. I–IV, *189*
Mother, Jugs, and Speed, *337*
Mother Kusters Goes to Heaven, *769*
Mother Lode, *87*
◆ Mother Teresa, *431*
Mother's Boys, *998*
Mother's Day, *866*
Mothra, *1067*
Motor Psycho, *87*
◆ **Motorama,** *337*
Motorcycle Gang, *87*
◆ Mouchette, *769*
◆ Moulin Rouge, *600*
Mountain, The, *600*
Mountain Family Robinson, *189*
Mountain Men, The, *1134*
◆ Mountains of the Moon, *87*
Mountaintop Motel Massacre, *866*
Mouse and His Child, The, *189*

Mouse and the Motorcycle, The, *189*
◆ Mouse That Roared, The, *337*
Movers and Shakers, *337*
Movie Magic, *431*
Movie Movie, *338*
Movie Struck (a.k.a. Pick a Star), *338*
Moving, *338*
Moving Finger, The, *998*
Moving Target, *87*
Moving Violation, *87*
Moving Violations, *338*
◆ Mowgli's Brothers, *189*
Mozart Brothers, The, *769*
Mozart Story, The, *931*
◆ Ms. .45, *87*
◆ Much Ado About Nothing, *338*
◆ Mudhoney, *600*
Mugsy's Girls, *338*
Mule Train, *1134*
Multiple Maniacs, *866*
◆ Mummy, The (1932), *866*
Mummy, The (1959), *866*
Mummy and the Curse of the Jackals, The, *867*
Mummy's Curse, The, *867*
Mummy's Ghost, The, *867*
Mummy's Hand, The, *867*
Mummy's Tomb, The, *867*
Munchie, *867*
Munchies, *867*
Munsters' Revenge, The, *338*
Muppet Christmas Carol, The, *189*
Muppet Movie, The, *189*
Muppet Sing-Alongs, *189*
Muppets Take Manhattan, The, *189*
Murder, *998*
Murder Ahoy, *998*
Murder at the Baskervilles (see Silver Blaze)
◆ Murder at the Gallop, *998*
Murder at the Vanities, *931*
◆ Murder by Death, *338*
Murder by Decree, *998*
Murder by Moonlight, *1067*
Murder by Numbers, *998*
Murder by Phone, *998*
Murder by Television, *998*
Murder By the Book (see Columbo: Murder By the Book)
Murder Elite, *600*
Murder in Coweta County, *600*
Murder in New Hampshire, *600*
Murder in Space, *1067*
◆ Murder in Texas, *998*
Murder in the Red Barn, *867*
Murder Is Announced, A, *998*
Murder Most Foul, *998*
◆ Murder My Sweet, *999*
◆ Murder of Mary Phagan, The, *600*
Murder on Flight 502, *87*
Murder on Line One, *867*
Murder on the Bayou, *600*
◆ Murder on the Orient Express, *999*
Murder One, *87*
◆ Murder 101, *999*
Murder Over New York, *999*
◆ Murder She Said, *999*
Murder So Sweet, *601*
Murder Story, *999*
Murder with Mirrors, *999*
Murder Without Motive, *601*
Murderers Among Us: The Simon Wiesenthal Story, *601*
Murderers' Row, *87*
Murderous Vision, *999*
Murders in the Rue Morgue (1932), *867*
Murders in the Rue Morgue (1971), *867*
Murders in the Rue Morgue (1986), *999*
Murders in the Zoo, *867*
◆ **Muriel,** *769*
Murmur of the Heart, *769*
Murph the Surf, *87*
Murphy's Law, *87*
Murphy's Laws of Golf, *338*
◆ Murphy's Romance, *601*
Murphy's War, *87*
◆ Murrow, *601*
Muscle Beach Party, *338*
Music Box, The, *999*
Music Lovers, The, *932*
◆ Music Man, The, *932*
Music of Chance, The, *601*
Music School, The, *601*
◆ Music Teacher, The, *769*
Mussolini and I, *601*
Mutant, *867*
Mutant on the Bounty, *338*
Mutants in Paradise, *338*
Mutations (see Freakmaker)
Mutilator, The, *867*
◆ Mutiny on the Bounty (1935), *88*
Mutiny on the Bounty (1962), *88*
◆ My American Cousin, *339*
◆ My Beautiful Laundrette, *601*
My Best Friend Is a Vampire, *339*
My Best Friend's Girl, *769*
My Best Girl, *339*
My Bloody Valentine, *867*
My Blue Heaven, *339*
◆ My Bodyguard, *601*
My Boyfriend's Back, *339*
My Boys Are Good Boys, *601*
My Breakfast with Blassie, *339*
◆ My Brilliant Career, *601*
My Chauffeur, *339*
◆ My Cousin Vinny, *339*
◆ My Darling Clementine, *1134*
My Daughter's Keeper, *999*
My Dear Secretary, *339*
My Demon Lover, *339*
◆ My Dinner with Andre, *602*
My Dream Is Yours, *932*
◆ My Fair Lady, *932*
My Father Is Coming, *339*
My Father, the Hero, *339*
◆ My Father's Glory, *769*
◆ My Favorite Blonde, *340*
◆ My Favorite Brunette, *340*
◆ My Favorite Wife, *340*
◆ My Favorite Year, *340*
My First Wife, *602*
My Forbidden Past, *602*
My Friend Flicka, *190*
My Friend Irma, *340*
My Friend Liberty, *190*
My Geisha, *340*
◆ My Girl, *190*
My Girl 2, *190*
My Girl Tisa, *602*
My Grandpa Is a Vampire, *340*
◆ My Heroes Have Always Been Cowboys, *1135*
◆ My Left Foot, *602*
My Life, *602*
◆ My Life as a Dog, *769*
My Life to Live, *769*
◆ My Little Chickadee, *340*
My Little Girl, *602*
My Little Pony: The Movie, *190*
My Love for Yours, *340*
◆ **My Lucky Star,** *932*
My Man Adam, *340*
◆ My Man Godfrey (1936), *340*
My Man Godfrey (1957), *340*
My Mom's a Werewolf, *341*
◆ My Mother's Castle, *770*
My Mother's Secret Life, *602*
◆ My Name Is Barbra, *932*
◆ My Name Is Ivan, *770*
My Name Is Nobody, *1135*
My Neighborhood, *341*
My New Gun, *341*
◆ My New Partner, *770*
◆ My Night at Maud's, *770*
◆ My Old Man, *602*
My Old Man's Place, *602*
◆ My Other Husband, *770*
◆ My Own Private Idaho, *602*
My Pal, the King, *1135*
My Pal Trigger, *1135*
My Samurai, *88*
My Science Project, *1067*
◆ My Side of the Mountain, *190*
◆ My Sister Eileen, *932*
My Sister, My Love, *867*
My Son, the Vampire (see Vampire Over London)
My Stepmother Is an Alien, *341*
◆ My Sweet Charlie, *602*
My Tutor, *341*
◆ **My 20th Century,** *770*
◆ My Uncle (Mon Oncle), *770*
My Wicked, Wicked Ways, *602*
My Wonderful Life, *603*
Myra Breckenridge, *341*
Mysterians, The, *1067*
Mysteries, *770*
Mysterious Desperado, *1135*
Mysterious Dr. Satan, *88*
◆ Mysterious Island, *1067*
Mysterious Lady, The, *603*
Mysterious Mr. Wong, The, *88*
◆ Mysterious Stranger, The, *190*
Mystery Date, *341*
Mystery Island, *190*
Mystery Man, *1135*
Mystery Mansion, *190*
Mystery Mountain, *1135*
Mystery, Mr. Ra, *431*
◆ Mystery of Alexina, The, *770*
Mystery of the Hooded Horsemen, *1135*
Mystery of the Leaping Fish/Chess Fever, *341*
Mystery of the Marie Celeste, The, *1000*
◆ **Mystery of Picasso, The,** *770*
Mystery of the Wax Museum, *868*
Mystery Squadron, *88*
Mystery Train, *603*
Mystic Pizza, *603*
Nadia, Vols. 1–36, *88*
Nadine, *341*
Nails, *88*
Nairobi Affair, *603*
Nais, *770*
◆ **Naked,** *603*
Naked and the Dead, The, *88*
Naked Cage, The, *88*
◆ **Naked City, The,** *1000*
Naked Civil Servant, The, *603*
Naked Country, The, *603*

ed Edge, The, *1000*
ed Face, The, *1000*
ed Gun, The, *341*
ed Gun 2 1/2, The, *341*
ed Gun 33 1/3, The—The Final sult, *341*
ed Heart, The, *603*
ed in the Sun, *1135*
ed Jungle, The, *88*
ed Kiss, The, *1000*
ed Lunch, *1067*
ed Maja, The, *603*
ed Obsession, *1000*
ed Prey, The, *88*
ed Space (see Spaceship)
ed Spur, The, *1135*
ed Tango, *603*
ed Truth, *342*
ed Vengeance, *88*
ed Venus, *603*
ed Youth, *89*
ne of the Rose, The, *89*
u, the Killer Whale, *190*
a, *770*
cy Goes to Rio, *932*
ook of the North, *431*
oleon (1927), *770*
oleon (1955), *603*
oleon and Josephine: A Love tory, *603*
oleon and Samantha, *190*
row Margin, The (1952), *89*
row Margin (1990), *89*
row Trail, The, *1135*
hville, *603*
ty Girl, The, *771*
ty Habits, *342*
ty Hero, *89*
ty Rabbit, *342*
ional Lampoon's Loaded Weapon , *342*
e and Hayes, *89*
ional Lampoon's Animal House see Animal House)
ional Lampoon's Christmas /acation, *342*
ional Lampoon's Class of '86, *342*
ional Lampoon's Class Reunion, *342*
ional Lampoon's European /acation, *342*
tional Lampoon's Last Resort, *342*
ional Lampoon's Vacation, *342*
ional Velvet, *190*
ive Son, *604*
ivity, The, *604*
tural, The, *604*
tural Enemies, *604*
ughty Marietta, *932*
ughty Nineties, The, *342*
vigator: A Medieval Odyssey, The, *1067*
vy Blue and Gold, *342*
vy Seals, *89*
vy vs. the Night Monsters, The, *868*
zarin, *771*
a (A Young Emmanuelle), *771*
ar Dark, *868*
ar Misses, *342*
eath Arizona Skies, *1135*
cessary Parties, *604*
cessary Roughness, *342*
cromancer, *868*
Necromancy (see Witching, The)
Necropolis, *868*
◆ **Needful Things,** *868*
Negatives, *1067*
Neighbor, The, *1000*
Neighbors, *343*
Nelvanamation (Volume One), *190*
Nelvanamation (Volume Two), *191*
Nemesis (1986), *1000*
Nemesis (1992), *1067*
Neon City, *1067*
Neon Empire, The, *89*
Neon Maniacs, *868*
Neo-Tokyo, *771*
Neptune Factor, The, *1068*
Neptune's Daughter, *932*
Nervous Ticks, *343*
Nest, The (1981), *771*
Nest, The (1988), *868*
Nesting, The, *868*
Netherworld, *868*
◆ Network, *604*
Neurotic Cabaret, *343*
Nevada Smith, *1135*
Nevadan, The, *1136*
Never a Dull Moment, *191*
◆ Never Cry Wolf, *89*
Never Forget, *604*
◆ Never Give a Sucker an Even Break, *343*
Never Let Go, *604*
Never Let Me Go, *89*
Never Love a Stranger, *604*
◆ Never on Sunday, *604*
Never on Tuesday, *604*
◆ Never Say Never Again, *89*
Never So Few, *89*
Never Steal Anything Small, *932*
Never Too Late, *604*
Never Too Young to Die, *90*
Never Wave at a WAC, *343*
◆ NeverEnding Story, The, *1068*
NeverEnding Story II, The, *1068*
New Adventures of Charlie Chan, The (TV Series), *1000*
New Adventures of Pippi Longstocking, The, *191*
New Adventures of Tarzan, *90*
New Adventures of Winnie the Pooh, The, *191*
◆ New Centurions, The, *605*
New Faces, *933*
New Frontier, *1136*
New Gladiators, The, *1068*
New Homeowner's Guide to Happiness, The, *343*
◆ New Jack City, *90*
New Kids, The, *868*
New Kind of Love, A, *343*
◆ New Leaf, A, *343*
New Life, A, *343*
New Moon, *933*
New Wave Comedy, *343*
New Year's Day, *605*
New Year's Evil, *868*
New York, New York, *933*
New York Ripper, The, *868*
◆ New York Stories, *343*
Newman's Law, *90*
◆ News at Eleven, *605*
News from Home, *771*
◆ Newsfront, *605*
Newsies, *933*
Next of Kin (1984), *605*
Next of Kin (1987), *868*
Next of Kin (1989), *90*
Next One, The, *1068*
◆ Next Stop, Greenwich Village, *605*
Next Summer, *771*
Next Time I Marry, *344*
Next Voice You Hear, The, *605*
Next Year If All Goes Well, *771*
Niagara, *1000*
Nice Dreams, *344*
Nice Girl Like Me, A, *344*
Nice Girls Don't Explode, *344*
Nicholas and Alexandra, *605*
Nicholas Nickleby, *605*
Nick Danger in the Case of the Missing Yolk, *344*
Nick Knight, *868*
Nickel & Dime, *344*
◆ **Night after Night,** *344*
Night Ambush, *90*
◆ Night and Day (1946), *933*
Night and Day (1991), *771*
◆ Night and Fog, The, *432*
◆ Night and the City (1950), *605*
Night and the City (1992), *605*
Night Angel, *868*
◆ Night at the Opera, A, *344*
Night Before, The, *344*
Night Breed, *869*
Night Caller from Outer Space, *1068*
Night Creature, *869*
Night Crossing, *90*
Night Eyes, *1000*
Night Eyes 2, *1000*
Night Eyes 3, *1000*
Night Flight from Moscow, *90*
Night Friend, *90*
Night Full of Rain, A, *605*
Night Gallery, *869*
Night Game, *1000*
Night Games, *1001*
Night Has Eyes, The, *1001*
Night in Casablanca, A, *344*
Night in Heaven, A, *606*
Night in the Life of Jimmy Reardon, A, *344*
Night Is My Future, *771*
Night Life, *869*
'Night, Mother, *606*
◆ Night Moves, *1001*
◆ Night Must Fall, *606*
Night Nurse, *606*
Night of Bloody Horror, *869*
Night of Dark Shadows, *869*
Night of the Bloody Apes, *869*
Night of the Bloody Transplant, *869*
Night of the Cobra Woman, *869*
Night of the Comet, *1068*
Night of thé Creeps, *869*
Night of the Cyclone, *1001*
Night of the Death Cult, *869*
Night of the Demon, *869*
Night of the Demons, *869*
Night of the Devils, *869*
Night of the Following Day, The, *1001*
Night of the Fox, *90*
Night of the Generals, *90*
Night of the Ghouls, *869*
◆ Night of the Grizzly, The, *1136*
Night of the Howling Beast, *870*
◆ Night of the Hunter, *1001*
Night of the Iguana, The, *606*
Night of the Juggler, *90*
Night of the Kickfighters, *90*
Night of the Living Babes, *344*

◆ Night of the Living Dead (1968), *870*
Night of the Living Dead (1990), *870*
Night of the Sharks, *90*
Night of the Shooting Stars, *771*
Night of the Walking Dead, *870*
Night of the Warrior, *90*
Night of the Wilding, *606*
Night of the Zombies, *870*
Night on Earth, *606*
Night Patrol, *344*
Night Porter, The, *606*
Night Rhythms, *1001*
Night Riders, The, *1136*
Night School, *1001*
Night Screams, *870*
◆ Night Shift, *344*
Night Stage to Galveston, *1136*
◆ Night Stalker, The (1971), *870*
Night Stalker, The (1986), *870*
Night Terror, *1001*
Night the City Screamed, The, *606*
Night the Lights Went Out in Georgia, The, *606*
Night They Raided Minsky's, The, *345*
◆ Night They Saved Christmas, The, *191*
Night Tide, *606*
Night to Dismember, A, *870*
◆ Night to Remember, A (1943), *345*
◆ Night to Remember, A (1958), *606*
Night Train (see Night Train to Munich)
Night Train to Terror, *870*
Night Train to Katmandu, *607*
◆ Night Train to Munich, *91*
Night Visitor, The (1970), *607*
Night Visitor (1989), *1001*
Night Walker, The, *1001*
Night Warning, *870*
Night Watch, *870*
Night We Never Met, The, *345*
Night Zoo, *607*
◆ Nightbreaker, *607*
Nightcomers, The, *870*
Nightfall, *1068*
Nightflyers, *1068*
Nightforce, *91*
◆ Nighthawks, *91*
Nightingale, The, *191*
Nightkill, *1001*
Nightlife, *870*
Nightman, The, *1001*
Nightmare at Bittercreek, *1002*
Nightmare at Noon, *870*
◆ **Nightmare before Christmas, The,** *1068*
Nightmare Castle, *871*
Nightmare Circus, *871*
Nightmare House, *871*
Nightmare in Blood, *871*
Nightmare in Wax (Crimes in the Wax Museum), *871*
◆ Nightmare on Elm Street, A, *871*
Nightmare on Elm Street 2, A: Freddy's Revenge, *871*
Nightmare on Elm Street 3, A: The Dream Warriors, *871*
Nightmare on Elm Street 4, A: The Dream Master, *871*
Nightmare on Elm Street 5: The Dream Child, *871*
Nightmare on the 13th Floor, *871*
Nightmare Sisters, *871*
Nightmare Weekend, *871*
◆ Nightmare Years, The, *607*
Nightmares, *871*
Nights in White Satin, *607*
◆ Nights of Cabiria, *771*
Nightstick, *91*
Nighttime in Nevada, *1136*
Nightwing, *871*
Nightwish, *1068*
Nijinsky, *607*
Nikki, Wild Dog of the North, *191*
9½ Ninjas, *345*
9½ Weeks, *607*
Nine Days a Queen, *607*
Nine Deaths of the Ninja, *91*
Nine Lives of Elfego Baca, The, *1136*
Nine Lives of Fritz the Cat, *345*
◆ Nine to Five, *345*
976-EVIL, *871*
976-EVIL II: The Astral Factor, *872*
1900, *607*
1918, *607*
1941, *345*
1969, *607*
1984 (1955), *1068*
◆ 1984 (1984), *1068*
1990: The Bronx Warriors, *1069*
90 Days, *345*
99 and 44/100 Percent Dead, *91*
99 Women, *91*
92 in the Shade, *345*
Ninja III: The Domination, *91*
◆ Ninotchka, *345*
◆ Ninth Configuration, The, *608*
Nitti: The Enforcer, *91*
No Big Deal, *608*
No Dead Heroes, *91*
No Deposit, No Return, *191*
No Drums, No Bugles, *608*
No Escape, *1069*
No Escape, No Return, *91*
No Greater Gift, *191*
No Habra Mas Penas Ni Olvido (see Funny, Dirty Little War)
No Holds Barred, *91*
No Justice, *91*
No Love for Johnnie, *608*
◆ No Man of Her Own, *345*
No Man's Land, *91*
No Mercy, *91*
No Nukes, *432*
No One Cries Forever, *608*
No Place To Hide, *91*
◆ No Regrets for Our Youth, *772*
No Retreat, No Surrender, *92*
No Retreat, No Surrender II, *92*
No Retreat, No Surrender 3: Blood Brothers, *92*
No Safe Haven, *92*
No Secrets, *1002*
No Small Affair, *345*
No Surrender, *345*
No-Tell Hotel, The (see Rosebud Beach Hotel, The)
◆ No Time for Sergeants, *345*
No Time for Sergeants (Television), *608*
No Way Out, *1002*
◆ No Way to Treat a Lady, *1002*
Noah's Ark, *608*
Nobody's Boy, *191*
Nobody's Children, *608*
Nobody's Fool, *346*
Nobody's Perfect, *346*
Nobody's Perfekt, *346*
Nocturna, *346*
Nocturne, *1002*
◆ Noises Off, *346*
Nomads, *872*
None But the Brave, *92*
None But the Lonely Heart, *608*
◆ Noon Wine, *608*
Noose Hangs High, The, *346*
◆ Norma Rae, *608*
Norman Conquests, The, Episode Table Manners, *346*
Norman Conquests, The, Episode Living Together, *346*
Norman Conquests, The, Episode Round and Round the Garden, *346*
Norman...Is That You?, *346*
Norman Loves Rose, *346*
Norman's Awesome Experience,
Norseman, The, *92*
North and South, *608*
North Avenue Irregulars, The, *19*
◆ North by Northwest, *1002*
◆ North Dallas Forty, *609*
North of the Great Divide, *1136*
North Shore, *609*
◆ North Star, The, *92*
◆ North to Alaska, *1136*
Northeast of Seoul, *92*
◆ Northern Exposure (TV Series), *6*
Northern Extremes, *346*
◆ Northern Lights, *609*
Northern Pursuit, *92*
Northville Cemetery Massacre, Th *92*
Northwest Outpost, *933*
Northwest Passage, *92*
Northwest Trail, *1136*
◆ Nosferatu, *772*
Not a Penny More, Not a Penny L *1002*
◆ Not as a Stranger, *609*
Not for Publication, *347*
Not My Kid, *609*
Not of This Earth, *872*
Not Quite Human, *347*
Not Quite Human 2, *347*
Not Quite Paradise, *347*
Not without My Daughter, *609*
Notebook on Cities and Clothes,
Notes for an African Orestes, *432*
Nothing But Trouble (1944), *347*
Nothing But Trouble (1991), *347*
Nothing in Common, *609*
Nothing Personal, *347*
◆ Nothing Sacred, *347*
Nothing Underneath, *1002*
◆ Notorious, *1002*
Notorious Nobodies, *772*
Nous N'Irons Plus Au Bois, *772*
Now and Forever, *609*
Now, Voyager, *609*
Now You See Him, Now You Don *191*
◆ Nowhere to Hide, *92*
Nowhere to Run (1989), *609*
Nowhere to Run (1993), *92*
Nude Bomb, The, *347*
Nudes on the Moon, *1069*
Nudity Required, *347*
Nudo di Donna (Portrait of a Wor Nude), *772*
Nukie, *191*
Number One of the Secret Servic *347*
Number One with a Bullet, *92*

ber 17, *1002*
The (La Religieuse), *772*
s on the Run, *347*
s Story, The, *609*
e Edith Cavell, *610*
ase, *347*
racker Prince, The, *191*
, *1002*
About Chip 'n' Dale, *191*
in May, *348*
Professor, The, *348*
a and the Tiger Men (Perils of
yoka), *92*
& Stiggs, *348*
cky Man!, *610*
oneers!, *610*
s of the Zombies, *872*
ct of Beauty, The, *348*
ctive, Burma!, *93*
mov, *772*
ng Box, The, *872*
essed, *610*
ession, *1002*
ession: A Taste for Fear, *93*
essive Love, *1002*
altist, The, *93*
urrence at Owl Creek Bridge, An,
72
an's Eleven, *93*
ans of Fire, *93*
gon, The, *93*
man, *872*
via, *610*
ber, *772*
pussy, *93*
Angry Shot, The, *610*
Couple, The, *348*
Job, The, *348*
Man Out, *1003*
Obsession, *772*
ball Hall, *348*
balls, *348*
to Billy Joe, *610*
ssa File, The, *1003*
ipus Rex (1957), *610*
ipus Rex (1967), *772*
Human Bondage (1934), *610*
Human Bondage (1964), *610*
Human Hearts, *610*
Mice and Men (1981), *610*
Mice and Men (1992), *611*
Unknown Origin, *872*
Beat, *348*
Limits (1953), *348*
Limits (1988), *93*
on a Comet, *192*
the Mark, *348*
the Wall, *348*
ence, The, *611*
erings, *872*
ce Romances, *611*
cer and a Duck, An (Limited
Gold Edition 2), *192*
cer and a Gentleman, An, *611*
cial Denial, *1069*
cial Story, The, *772*
spring, The, *872*
Alfie, *611*
Calcutta!, *348*
Dad, Poor Dad—Mama's Hung
You in the Closet and I'm
Feeling So Sad, *348*
God!, *349*
God! Book II, *349*
God, You Devil!, *349*

Oh, Heavenly Dog!, *192*
Oh! Susanna!, *1136*
Oh, What a Night, *611*
O'Hara's Wife, *611*
Okefenokee, *93*
◆ Oklahoma!, *933*
Oklahoma Annie, *349*
Oklahoma Kid, The, *1136*
Oklahoman, The, *1136*
Old Barn Dance, The, *1136*
Old Boyfriends, *611*
Old Corral, *1136*
Old Curiosity Shop, The, *933*
Old Dark House, The, *872*
Old Enough, *611*
Old Explorers, *192*
Old Gringo, The, *611*
Old Ironsides, *93*
Old Maid, The, *611*
Old Mother Riley Meets the Vampire
(see Vampire Over London)
Old Spanish Custom, An, *349*
Old Swimmin' Hole, The, *611*
Old Testament, The, *772*
◆ Old Yeller, *192*
◆ Oldest Living Graduate, The, *611*
Oldest Profession, The, *773*
◆ Oliver, *933*
Oliver Twist (1922), *611*
Oliver Twist (1933), *612*
◆ Oliver Twist (1948), *612*
Oliver's Story, *612*
◆ Olivier, Olivier, *773*
◆ **Ollie Hopnoodle's Haven of Bliss**,
192
Omar Khayyam, *93*
Omega Cop, *93*
Omega Man, The, *1069*
Omega Syndrome, *93*
◆ Omen, The, *872*
Omen IV: The Awakening, *872*
On a Clear Day, You Can See Forever,
933
On an Island with You, *933*
On Approval, *349*
On Borrowed Time, *612*
On Dangerous Ground, *1003*
On Deadly Ground, *93*
◆ On Golden Pond, *612*
◆ On Her Majesty's Secret Service, *94*
On Moonlight Bay, *933*
◆ On the Beach, *1069*
On the Block, *1003*
◆ On the Bowery, *612*
On the Edge, *612*
On the Line, *94*
On the Make, *612*
On the Nickel, *612*
On the Old Spanish Trail, *1137*
On the Right Track, *192*
◆ On the Town, *934*
◆ On the Waterfront, *612*
On the Yard, *94*
On Top of Old Smoky, *1137*
On Top of the Whale, *773*
On Valentine's Day, *612*
On Wings of Eagles, *94*
Onassis: The Richest Man in the
World, *612*
Once a Hero, *94*
Once Around, *349*
Once Bitten, *349*
Once in Paris, *612*
Once Is Not Enough, *613*
Once Upon a Crime, *349*

Once Upon a Forest, *192*
Once Upon a Honeymoon, *349*
Once Upon a Midnight Scary, *192*
◆ Once Upon a Time in America
(Long Version), *94*
◆ Once Upon a Time in the West,
1137
Once Upon a Time and the Earth Was
Created..., *192*
◆ One Against the Wind, *613*
One and Only, The, *613*
One and Only, Genuine, Original
Family Band, The, *192*
One Arabian Night, *773*
One Body Too Many, *1003*
One Cooks, the Other Doesn't, *349*
◆ **One Crazy Night**, *349*
One Crazy Summer, *349*
One Dark Night, *872*
One Day in the Life of Ivan
Denisovich, *613*
One Deadly Summer, *773*
One Down, Two to Go, *94*
◆ One-Eyed Jacks, *1137*
One False Move, *94*
◆ One Flew Over the Cuckoo's Nest,
613
One Frightened Night, *1003*
One from the Heart, *934*
One Good Cop, *613*
◆ One Hundred and One Dalmatians,
192
◆ One Hundred Men and a Girl, *934*
100 Rifles, *1137*
One in a Million, *350*
One Last Run, *613*
◆ One Magic Christmas, *613*
One Man Army, *94*
One-Man Force, *94*
One Man's War, *613*
One Man's Way, *613*
One Million B.C., *1069*
One Minute to Zero, *94*
One More Saturday Night, *350*
One Night in the Tropics, *350*
One Night of Love, *934*
One-Night Stand, *613*
One Night with Dice, *350*
◆ One of Our Aircraft Is Missing, *94*
One of Our Dinosaurs Is Missing, *192*
◆ One on One, *613*
One Rainy Afternoon, *350*
One Riot, One Ranger, *95*
One Russian Summer, *613*
One Shoe Makes It Murder, *1003*
One Sings, the Other Doesn't, *773*
One Step to Hell, *95*
◆ One That Got Away, The, *95*
◆ 1001 Rabbit Tales, *193*
One Touch of Venus, *350*
One Trick Pony, *934*
One, Two, Three, *350*
◆ One Wild Moment, *773*
One Woman or Two, *773*
◆ Onibaba, *773*
◆ Onion Field, The, *613*
Onionhead, *350*
◆ Only Angels Have Wings, *95*
Only One Night, *773*
Only the Lonely, *350*
Only the Strong, *95*
Only the Valiant, *1137*
Only Two Can Play, *350*
Only When I Laugh, *614*
Only with Married Men, *350*

Only You, 351
◆ Open City, 773
◆ Open Doors, 774
Open House, 872
Opening Night, 614
Opera do Malandro, 774
Operation Amsterdam, 95
Operation C.I.A., 95
◆ Operation Crossbow, 95
Operation 'Nam, 95
Operation Pacific, 614
◆ Operation Petticoat, 351
Operation Thunderbolt, 95
Operation War Zone, 95
Operator 13, 614
Opponent, The, 95
Opportunity Knocks, 351
Opposing Force, 95
Opposite Sex (And How to Live with Them), The, 351
Opposite Sex, The, 934
Options, 351
◆ **Opus 'N' Bill in a Wish for Wings that Work**, 193
Oracle, The, 872
Orca, 873
Orchestra Wives, 934
Ordeal by Innocence, 1003
Ordeal of Dr. Mudd, The, 614
Order of the Black Eagle, 95
Order of the Eagle, 96
◆ Ordet, 774
Ordinary Heroes, 614
Ordinary Magic, 614
◆ Ordinary People, 614
Organization, The, 96
Orguss, Vols. 1–4, 1069
Orgy of the Dead, 873
Oriane, 774
Original Intent, 614
Orlando, 614
◆ Ornette—Made in America, 432
Orphan Boy of Vienna, An, 934
Orphan Train, 615
◆ Orphans, 615
Orphans of the Storm, 615
Orpheus, 774
Orpheus Descending, 615
◆ Osaka Elegy, 774
Oscar, The (1966), 615
Oscar (1991), 351
◆ Oscar's Greatest Moments: 1971 to 1991, 432
◆ Ossessione, 774
Ossian: American Boy-Tibetan Monk, 432
Osterman Weekend, The, 96
Otaku No Video, 774
◆ Otello, 934
◆ Othello (1922), 615
◆ Othello (1952), 615
Othello (1982), 615
Other, The, 873
Other Hell, The, 873
Other People's Money, 351
Other Side of Midnight, The, 615
Other Side of the Mountain, The, 615
Other Side of the Mountain, Part II, The, 615
Other Woman, The, 1003
Our Daily Bread, 615
Our Dancing Daughters, 616
Our Family Business, 616
◆ Our Hospitality, 351
Our Little Girl, 193
Our Man Flint, 96
Our Miss Brooks (TV Series), 351
Our Modern Maidens, 616
◆ Our Mr. Sun, 193
Our Relations, 351
Our Time, 616
◆ Our Town (1940), 616
Our Town (1980), 616
◆ Our Vines Have Tender Grapes, 193
Out, 96
Out California Way, 1137
Out Cold, 351
◆ Out for Justice, 96
◆ Out of Africa, 616
Out of Bounds, 96
Out of Control, 352
Out of Season, 616
Out of Sight Out of Mind, 1003
Out of the Blue, 352
Out of the Dark, 873
Out of the Darkness, 1003
◆ Out of the Past, 1003
Out of the Rain, 1003
Out of Towners, The, 352
Out on a Limb (1986), 616
Out on a Limb (1992), 352
Out on Bail, 96
Outcast, The, 1137
Outcry, The (see Il Grido)
Outer Limits, The (TV Series), 1069
Outfit, The, 96
Outing, The, 873
◆ Outland, 1069
Outlaw, The, 1137
Outlaw and His Wife, The, 616
Outlaw Blues, 352
Outlaw Express, 1137
Outlaw Force, 96
◆ Outlaw Josey Wales, The, 1137
Outlaw of Gor, 1069
Outlaws of Sonora, 1137
Outpost in Morocco, 96
Outrage!, 616
◆ Outrageous, 352
◆ Outrageous Fortune, 352
◆ Outside Chance of Maximilian Glick, The, 193
Outside the Law, 616
Outsiders, The, 616
Outtakes, 352
Over Her Dead Body, 352
Over the Brooklyn Bridge, 352
◆ Over the Edge, 616
Over the Hill, 352
Over the Top, 617
Overboard, 352
Overcoat, The, 774
Overexposed, 873
Overindulgence, 617
Overkill, 96
Overland Stage Raiders, 1137
Overseas, 774
◆ Owl and the Pussycat, The, 352
◆ Ox-Bow Incident, The, 1137
Oxford Blues, 617
P.K. & the Kid, 617
P.O.W.: The Escape, 96
◆ Pacific Heights, 1003
Pacific Inferno, 96
Pack, The, 873
Pack Up Your Troubles, 352
◆ Package, The, 1004
Packin' It In, 193
Paddington Bear (Series), 193
Paddy, 353
Padre Padrone, 774
Pagan Love Song, 934
Pain in the A—, A, 774
Paint It Black, 97
Paint Job, The, 1004
Paint Your Wagon, 934
Painted Desert, The, 1138
◆ **Painted Faces**, 774
Painted Hills, The, 193
Painted Stallion, The, 1138
Painted Veil, The, 617
Paisan, 775
◆ Pajama Game, The, 934
◆ Pal Joey, 934
Palais Royale, 97
Palazzolo's Chicago, 432
Pale Blood, 873
Pale Rider, 1138
◆ Paleface, The, 353
Palermo Connection, The, 1004
Palm Beach, 617
◆ Palm Beach Story, The, 353
Palm Springs Weekend, 353
Palombella Rossa, 775
Palooka, 617
Pals, 353
Pals of the Saddle, 1138
Pamela Principle, The, 1004
◆ Panama Deception, The, 432
Panama Hattie, 935
Panama Lady, 353
Pancho Barnes, 617
Pancho Villa, 1138
Panda and the Magic Serpent, 1
Panda's Adventures, 193
Pandemonium, 353
◆ Pandora's Box, 775
Panic Button, 353
◆ Panic in the Streets, 1004
Panique, 775
Pantaloons, 775
Panther Girl of the Congo, 97
Papa's Delicate Condition, 617
◆ **Paper, The**, 617
◆ Paper Chase, The, 617
Paper Lion, 618
Paper Marriage (1988), 775
Paper Marriage (1992), 618
Paper Mask, 1004
◆ Paper Moon, 353
Paper Tiger, 97
Paper Wedding, 618
◆ Paperhouse, 873
◆ Papillon, 97
Parade, 775
Paradine Case, The, 1004
Paradise (1982), 97
Paradise (1991), 618
Paradise Alley, 618
Paradise Canyon, 1138
Paradise Hawaiian Style, 935
Paradise Motel, 353
Paradisio, 353
◆ Parallax View, The, 1004
Paramedics, 353
◆ Paramount Comedy Theatre, Vol. Well Developed, 353
Paramount Comedy Theatre, Vol. Decent Exposures, 354
Paramount Comedy Theater, Vol. Hanging Party, 354
Paranoia, 1004
Parasite, 873
Paratroop Command, 97
◆ Pardon Mon Affaire, 775

n Mon Affaire, Too!, 775
n My Sarong, 354
n My Trunk, 775
n Us, 354
t Trap, The, 193
thood, 354
ts, 354
Belongs to Us, 775
Blues, 618
Express, The, 97
Holiday, 354
Is Burning, 432
, Texas, 618
Trout, 618
When It Sizzles, 354
s Mine, The, 618
r Adderson, Philosopher, 618
r, Bedroom and Bath, 354
es et Musique (see Love Songs)
sh, 618
g Glances, 618
er, 775
ers, 354
ers in Crime (TV Series), 1004
, The, 354
Animal, 354
Camp, 354
Girl, 618
Girls (Party Inc.), 355
, Inc. (see Party Girls)
Line, 97
Plane, 355
ali's Island, 619
the Ammo, 355
age to India, A, 619
age to Marseilles, 97
ed Away, 355
enger, The, 1004
enger 57, 97
ion (1919), 775
ion (1954), 97
ion Fish, 619
ion Flower, 619
ion For Life, 776
ion of Anna, The, 776
ion of Beatrice, The (see
eatrice)
ion of Joan of Arc, The, 776
ion of Love, 776
ionate Thief, The (1961), 776
ionate Thief (1954) (see Laugh
r Joy)
port to Pimlico, 355
Midnight, 619
ime, 619
nd Mike, 355
Garrett and Billy the Kid, 1138
h of Blue, A, 619
hwork Girl of Oz, The, 193
mity, 355
er Panchali, 776
finder, 776
s of Glory, 619
ck, 873
ot, 97
ot Games, 97
y, The, 355
erns, 619
es Blanches (White Paws), 776
Rocks, 619
on, 619
y Hearst, 620
Bowles in Morocco, 432
Bunyan, 194

Paul McCartney and Wings—Rock Show, 432
Paul Reiser Out on a Whim, 355
◆ Pauline at the Beach, 776
Paul's Case, 620
◆ Pawnbroker, The, 620
Pay or Die, 620
Payback, 98
◆ Payday, 620
Payment in Blood (see Final Defeat, The)
Payoff, 98
PCU, 355
Peacemaker, 1069
Peachboy, 194
Peanut Butter Solution, The, 194
Pearl, The, 620
◆ Pearl of Death, The, 1004
Pearl of the South Pacific, 620
Pearls of the Crown, The, 776
Peck's Bad Boy, 194
Peck's Bad Boy with the Circus, 194
◆ Pecos Bill, 194
Pecos Bill, King of the Cowboys, 194
Pedestrian, The, 620
Peeping Tom, 1005
Pee-Wee Herman Show, The, 355
Pee-Wee's Big Adventure, 355
Pee-Wee's Playhouse Christmas Special, 194
◆ Peggy Sue Got Married, 355
◆ **Peking Opera Blues,** 776
Pelican Brief, The, 1005
◆ Pelle the Conqueror, 776
Pencil, The (1983) (see Philip Marlowe, Private Eye: The Pencil)
Pendulum, 1005
Penitent, The, 620
Penitentiary, 98
Penitentiary II, 98
Penitentiary III, 98
Penn & Teller Get Killed, 356
Penn & Teller's Cruel Tricks for Dear Friends, 356
Pennies from Heaven, 935
◆ Penny Serenade, 620
Penpal Murders, 873
Penthouse, The, 1005
People, The, 1070
People Are Funny, 356
People That Time Forgot, The, 1070
People Under the Stairs, The, 873
People vs. Jean Harris, 620
People vs. Zsa Zsa Gabor, The, 433
◆ **People Will Talk,** 356
People's Hero, 777
Pepe Le Moko, 777
Pepe Le Pew's Skunk Tales, 194
Pepi, Luci, Bom and Other Girls, 777
Perfect, 620
Perfect Bride, The, 873
Perfect Family, 1005
Perfect Furlough, 356
◆ **Perfect Harmony,** 194
Perfect Little Murder, A, 356
Perfect Marriage, 356
Perfect Match, The, 356
Perfect Strangers, 1005
Perfect Weapon, 98
◆ Perfect Witness, 620
◆ **Perfect World, A,** 621
Perfectly Normal, 356
◆ Performance, 1005
◆ Perfumed Nightmare, 777

Peril, 777
Perils from Planet Mongo (see Flash Gordon: Rocketship)
Perils of Gwendoline, The, 98
Perils of Nyoka (see Nyoka and the Tiger Men)
Perils of Pauline, The (1933), 98
Perils of Pauline, The (1947), 356
Perils of the Darkest Jungle, 98
Period of Adjustment, 356
Permanent Record, 621
Permission to Kill, 98
Persecution, 621
Persona, 777
◆ Personal Best, 621
Personal Property, 356
Personal Services, 357
Personals, The, 357
Persuaders, The (TV Series), 98
Pet Sematary, 874
Pet Sematary Two, 874
Pete Kelly's Blues, 935
Pete 'n' Tillie, 357
◆ Peter and the Wolf, 194
Peter Gunn (TV Series), 98
Peter Pan (1953), 194
◆ Peter Pan (1960), 194
Peter's Friends, 621
Pete's Dragon, 195
Petit Con, 777
◆ Petrified Forest, The, 621
◆ Petronella, 195
◆ Petulia, 621
Peuple Singe (see Monkey People)
◆ Peyton Place, 621
Phantasm, 874
Phantasm II, 874
Phantom Broadcast, The, 1005
Phantom Chariot, 777
Phantom Creeps, The, 874
Phantom Empire (1935), 98
Phantom Empire, The (1986), 99
Phantom Express, 99
Phantom from Space, 1070
◆ Phantom India, 433
Phantom of Death, 874
Phantom of Liberty, The, 777
◆ Phantom of the Opera (1925), 874
Phantom of the Opera (1943), 874
Phantom of the Opera (1962), 874
Phantom of the Opera (1989), 874
Phantom of the Mall—Eric's Revenge, 874
Phantom of the Paradise, 935
Phantom of the Plains, 1138
Phantom of the Ritz, 874
Phantom of the West, 1138
Phantom Rider, 1138
Phantom Thunderbolt, 1138
Phantom Tollbooth, The (see Adventures of Milo in the Phantom Tollbooth, The)
◆ Phar Lap, 621
Phase IV, 1070
Phedre, 777
◆ **Philadelphia,** 621
Philadelphia Experiment, The, 1070
Philadelphia Experiment 2, The, 1070
◆ Philadelphia Story, The, 357
◆ Philby, Burgess and Maclean: Spy Scandal of the Century, 1005
◆ Philip Marlowe, Private Eye: Finger Man, 1005

◆ Philip Marlowe, Private Eye: The Pencil, *1005*
Phobia, *1006*
Phoenix the Warrior, *1070*
Phone Call from a Stranger, *622*
Physical Evidence, *1006*
◆ **Piano, The,** *622*
◆ Piano for Mrs. Cimino, A, *622*
Pick a Star (see Movie Struck)
Pickle, The, *357*
Pick-Up Artist, The, *357*
◆ Pickup on South Street, *1006*
Pickwick Papers, The, *357*
◆ Picnic, *622*
◆ Picnic at Hanging Rock, *1006*
Picnic on the Grass, *777*
Picture Mommy Dead, *874*
◆ Picture of Dorian Gray, The, *875*
Piece of Pleasure (see Une Partie de Plaisir)
Piece of the Action, A, *357*
Pieces, *875*
◆ Pied Piper of Hamelin, The, *195*
Pierrot Le Fou, *777*
Pigs, *875*
Pigsty, *777*
◆ Pillow Talk, *357*
Pilot, The, *622*
Pimpernel Smith, *99*
Pin, *875*
Pin-Up Girl, *935*
Ping Pong, *622*
◆ Pink at First Sight, *195*
Pink Cadillac, *99*
Pink Chiquitas, The, *357*
Pink Flamingos, *357*
Pink Floyd: The Wall, *935*
Pink Motel, *357*
Pink Nights, *357*
Pink Panther, The, *357*
Pink Panther Cartoon Festival, The: A Fly in the Pink, *195*
Pink Panther Cartoon Festival, The: Pink-a-Boo, *195*
Pink Panther Strikes Again, The, *357*
Pinky, *622*
◆ Pinocchio (1940), *195*
◆ Pinocchio (1983), *195*
Pinocchio and the Emperor of the Night, *195*
Pioneer Woman, *1138*
Pipe Dreams, *622*
Pippi Longstocking, Pippi in the South Seas, Pippi Goes on Board, Pippi on the Run, *195*
Piranha, *875*
Piranha Part Two: The Spawning, *875*
◆ Pirate, The, *935*
Pirate Movie, The, *935*
Pirates, *358*
Pirates of Dark Waters, The: The Saga Begins, *195*
◆ Pirates of Penzance, The, *935*
Pirates of the High Seas, *99*
Pirates of the Prairie, *1139*
◆ Pistol, The: The Birth of a Legend, *195*
Pit and the Pendulum, The (1961), *875*
Pit and the Pendulum, The (1991), *875*
Pitfall, *622*
Pittsburgh, *622*
◆ Pixote, *778*
Pizza Man, *358*
Place Called Today, A, *622*
Place Called Trinity, A, *1139*
◆ Place in the Sun, A, *622*
Place of Weeping, *623*
◆ Places in the Heart, *623*
◆ **Plague, The,** *623*
◆ Plague Dogs, The, *1070*
Plain Clothes, *358*
Plainsman, The, *1139*
Plan 9 from Outer Space, *1070*
◆ Planes, Trains and Automobiles, *358*
Planet Busters, *1070*
Planet Earth, *1070*
Planet of Blood, *1070*
◆ Planet of the Apes, *1071*
Planet of the Dinosaurs, *1071*
Planet of the Vampires, *875*
Planet on the Prowl, *1071*
Planet Outlaws (see Buck Rogers: Destination Saturn)
Plants Are Watching, The, *1071*
◆ Platinum Blonde, *623*
Platinum High School, *623*
◆ Platoon, *623*
Platoon Leader, *99*
◆ Play It Again, Sam, *358*
◆ Play Misty for Me, *1006*
Play Nice, *1006*
◆ Playboy of the Western World, *358*
◆ Playboys, The, *623*
◆ Player, The, *358*
Players, *623*
Playgirl Killer, The, *875*
Playing for Keeps, *358*
◆ Playing for Time, *623*
Playing the Field, *358*
◆ Playmates, *358*
Playroom, *875*
Playtime, *778*
◆ Plaza Suite, *358*
Please Don't Eat My Mother!, *358*
Please Don't Eat the Daisies, *358*
Pleasure Palace, *623*
Pledge Night, *875*
◆ Plenty, *623*
◆ Plot Against Harry, The, *359*
Ploughman's Lunch, The, *623*
◆ Plow That Broke the Plains, The, *433*
Plumber, The, *1006*
Plunder Road, *99*
◆ Pluto, *196*
◆ Pluto (Limited Gold Edition 1), *196*
Plutonium Baby, *875*
Pocket Money, *359*
Pocketful of Miracles, *359*
Pocketful of Rye, A, *1006*
Poetic Justice, *624*
Pogo's Special Birthday Special, The, *196*
◆ Point, The, *196*
◆ Point Blank, *624*
Point Break, *99*
Point of Impact, *99*
Point of No Return, *99*
Pointsman, The, *624*
◆ Poirot (Series), *1006*
Poison, *624*
Poison Ivy (1985), *359*
Poison Ivy (1992), *1006*
Poisonous Plants, *778*
Poker Alice, *1139*
Polar Bear King, The, *1071*
◆ Pole to Pole, *433*
Police, *778*
Police Academy, *359*
Police Academy II: Their First Assignment, *359*
Police Academy III: Back in Tra
359
Police Academy 4: Citizens on
359
Police Academy 5—Assignmen
Miami Beach, *359*
Police Academy 6: City Under S
359
◆ Police Squad!, *359*
◆ Police Story III—Super Cop, *7*
Polish Vampire in Burbank, A,
Pollyanna (1920), *196*
Pollyanna (1960), *196*
◆ Poltergeist, *875*
Poltergeist II: The Other Side, *8*
Poltergeist III, *876*
Polyester, *359*
Ponce de Leon and the Fountai
Youth, *196*
Pony Express, *1139*
◆ Pony Express Rider, *1139*
Pool Hustlers, The, *778*
Pool Sharks (see Fatal Glass of A)
Poor Girl, A Ghost Story, *876*
Poor Little Rich Girl, The (1917
◆ Poor Little Rich Girl (1936), *93*
Poor Little Rich Girl: The Barb Hutton Story, *624*
Poor White Trash, *624*
Poor White Trash II, *624*
Popcorn, *876*
◆ Pope John Paul II, *624*
Pope Must Diet, The, *360*
Pope of Greenwich Village, The,
Popeye, *196*
◆ Popeye Cartoons, *196*
Popi, *360*
Poppy Is Also a Flower, The, *99*
◆ Pork Chop Hill, *624*
◆ Porky Pig and Company, *196*
◆ Porky Pig and Daffy Duck Carto
Festival Featuring "Tick Tock Tuckered", *196*
Porky Pig Cartoon Festival Featu
"Nothing but the Tooth", *196*
Porky Pig: Days of Swine and R
196
◆ Porky Pig Tales, *196*
Porky Pig's Screwball Comedies
Porky's, *360*
Porky's II: The Next Day, *360*
Porky's Revenge, *360*
◆ Pornographers, The, *778*
Port of Call, *778*
Port of New York, *624*
Portfolio, *624*
Portnoy's Complaint, *624*
Portrait, The, *625*
Portrait of a Showgirl, *625*
Portrait of a Stripper, *625*
◆ Portrait of Jason, *433*
Portrait of a Woman, Nude (see Nudo di Donna)
◆ Portrait of Jennie, *625*
Portrait of Teresa, *778*
Portrait of the Artist as a Young
A, *625*
Poseidon Adventure, The, *99*
Positive I.D., *1006*

ositively True Adventures of the Alleged Texas Cheerleader-Murdering Mom, The, *360*
osse (1975), *1139*
osse (1993), *1139*
ossessed (1931), *625*
ossessed (1947), *625*
ossessed, The (1977), *876*
ossessed by the Night, *1006*
ossession, *876*
ostcards from the Edge, *360*
ostman Always Rings Twice, The (1946), *1007*
ostman Always Rings Twice, The (1981), *1007*
ot O' Gold, *625*
otop (see Deluge, The)
owaqqatsi, *433*
owderkeg, *1139*
owdersmoke Range, *1139*
ower, The (1980), *876*
ower (1986), *625*
ower of Myth, The, *433*
ower of One, The, *625*
ower, Passion, and Murder, *625*
owwow Highway, *360*
rairie Moon, *1139*
rairie Rustlers, *1139*
rancer, *197*
ranks (see Dorm That Dripped Blood, The)
ray for the Wildcats, *100*
ray TV (1980), *360*
ray TV (1982), *626*
rayer for the Dying, A, *1007*
rayer of the Rollerboys, *100*
raying Mantis, *1007*
redator, *1071*
redator 2, *1071*
rehistoric Women (1950), *1071*
rehistoric Women (1967), *100*
rehysteria, *197*
relude to a Kiss, *360*
remature Burial, The, *876*
remonition, The, *876*
rep School, *360*
reppie Murder, The, *626*
reppies, *360*
resenting Lily Mars, *626*
resident's Analyst, The, *360*
resident's Plane Is Missing, The, *1007*
resident's Target, *100*
residio, The, *100*
ressure Point, *626*
resumed Guilty, *626*
resumed Innocent, *1007*
retty Baby, *626*
retty in Pink, *626*
retty Kill, *1007*
retty Poison, *626*
retty Smart, *361*
retty Woman, *361*
rey, The, *876*
rey for the Hunter, *100*
rey of the Chameleon, *1007*
riceless Beauty, *626*
rick Up Your Ears, *626*
ride and Prejudice (1940), *626*
ride and Prejudice (1985), *626*
ride and the Passion, The, *626*
ride of Jesse Hallman, The, *626*
ride of St. Louis, The, *627*
ride of the Bowery, *627*
◆ Pride of the Clan, The, *1007*
◆ Pride of the Yankees, The, *627*
◆ Priest of Love, *627*
Primal Rage, *876*
Primal Scream, *1071*
Primary Motive, *627*
Primary Target, *627*
Prime Cut, *100*
Prime Evil, *876*
◆ Prime of Miss Jean Brodie, The, *361*
Prime Risk, *100*
Prime Suspect, *627*
◆ **Prime Suspect 1,** *1007*
◆ **Prime Suspect 2,** *1007*
◆ **Prime Suspect 3,** *1008*
Prime Target, *100*
Prime Time Murder, *100*
Primo Baby, *197*
◆ Primrose Path, *627*
Prince and the Pauper, The (1937), *197*
Prince and the Pauper, The (1978), *197*
◆ Prince and the Pauper, The (1990), *197*
Prince and the Showgirl, The, *361*
Prince of Bel Air, *627*
Prince of Central Park, The, *197*
Prince of Darkness, *876*
Prince of Pennsylvania, *361*
◆ Prince of the City, *627*
Prince of Tides, The, *627*
Prince Valiant, *100*
Princes in Exile, *627*
Princess Academy, The, *361*
Princess and the Pea, The, *197*
Princess and the Pirate, The, *361*
◆ Princess Bride, The, *1071*
Princess Daisy, *627*
Princess Tam Tam, *778*
Princess Warrior, *1071*
◆ Princess Who Had Never Laughed, The, *197*
Princess Yang Kwei Fei, *778*
Principal, The, *628*
Prison, *876*
Prison for Children, *628*
◆ **Prison on Fire,** *778*
Prison Planet, *1071*
Prison Stories: Women on the Inside, *628*
◆ Prisoner, The, *628*
◆ Prisoner, The (TV Series), *1071*
◆ Prisoner of Honor, *628*
◆ Prisoner of Second Avenue, The, *361*
Prisoner of Zenda, The (1937), *100*
Prisoner of Zenda, The (1952), *100*
Prisoner of Zenda, The (1979), *361*
Prisoner Video Companion, The, *1072*
Prisoners of Inertia, *361*
Prisoners of the Lost Universe, *1072*
Prisoners of the Sun, *628*
Private Affairs, *361*
◆ Private Affairs of Bel Ami, The, *628*
◆ Private Benjamin, *361*
Private Buckaroo, *935*
◆ Private Conversations: On the Set of Death of a Salesman, *433*
Private Eyes, The, *361*
Private Files of J. Edgar Hoover, The, *100*
◆ Private Function, A, *361*
Private Hell 36, *628*
Private Investigations, *101*
Private Lessons, *361*
Private Life of Don Juan, The, *628*
◆ Private Life of Henry the Eighth, The, *628*
◆ Private Life of Sherlock Holmes, The, *1008*
Private Lives, *362*
Private Lives of Elizabeth and Essex, The, *629*
◆ Private Matter, A, *629*
Private Parts, *876*
Private Popsicle, *362*
Private Resort, *362*
Private School, *362*
Private Snuffy Smith, *362*
Private War, *629*
Private Wore Skirts, The (see Never Wave at a WAC)
Privates on Parade, *362*
◆ Prix De Beaute (Beauty Prize), *778*
◆ Prize, The, *629*
Prize Pulitzer, The: The Roxanne Pulitzer Story, *629*
◆ Prize Winning Films of Jan Svankmajer, The, *876*
Prizefighter, The, *197*
◆ Prizzi's Honor, *362*
Probe, *101*
Problem Child, *362*
Problem Child 2, *362*
Prodigal, The, *629*
◆ Producers, The, *362*
◆ Professionals, The, *101*
◆ **Program, The,** *629*
Programmed to Kill, *1072*
Project A (Part I), *778*
Project A (Part II), *779*
Project A-KO, *779*
Project: Alien, *1072*
Project: Eliminator, *101*
Project Moon Base, *1072*
Project: Shadowchaser, *101*
Project X, *1072*
Projectionist, The, *362*
Prom Night, *876*
Prom Night III—Last Kiss, *877*
Prom Night IV—Deliver Us from Evil, *877*
Promise, The, *629*
Promise Her Anything, *362*
Promised a Miracle, *629*
Promised Land, *629*
Promises in the Dark, *629*
Promises, Promises, *362*
Promoter, The, *362*
◆ Proof, *629*
Prophecy, *877*
Prospero's Books, *629*
Protector, The, *101*
Protocol, *363*
Prototype, *1072*
Prototype X29A, *1072*
Proud and the Damned, The, *1139*
Proud Men, *1140*
Proud Rebel, The, *1140*
◆ Providence, *630*
Psychic, *1008*
Psychic Killer, *877*
◆ Psycho, *877*
Psycho II, *877*
Psycho III, *877*
Psycho 4; The Beginning, *877*
Psycho Circus (see Circus of Fear)
Psycho Girls, *877*

◆ Psycho Sisters, *877*
Psychomania, *877*
Psychopath, The, *877*
Psychos in Love, *877*
Psych-Out, *630*
PT 109, *630*
Puberty Blues, *630*
Public Cowboy #1, *1140*
◆ Public Enemy, *101*
Public Eye, The, *1008*
Pucker Up and Bark Like a Dog, *363*
Pudd'nhead Wilson, *630*
Pulp, *363*
Pulse, *877*
Puma Man, The, *878*
Pump Up the Volume, *630*
◆ Pumping Iron, *630*
◆ Pumping Iron II: The Women, *630*
Pumpkinhead, *878*
Punch the Clock, *101*
Punchline, *630*
Punisher, The, *101*
Puppet Master, The, *878*
Puppet Master II, *878*
Puppet Master III: Toulon's Revenge, *878*
Puppet Master Four, *878*
Puppet on a Chain, *101*
◆ Puppetoon Movie, The, *197*
Purchase Price, The, *630*
Pure Country, *630*
Pure Luck, *363*
Purlie Victorious, *363*
◆ Purple Heart, The, *630*
Purple Hearts, *631*
Purple Monster Strikes, The, *101*
Purple People Eater, *198*
Purple Rain, *935*
◆ Purple Rose of Cairo, The, *363*
Purple Taxi, The, *631*
Pursued, *1140*
Pursuit, *101*
Pursuit of D. B. Cooper, *363*
Pursuit of Happiness, The, *631*
Pursuit of the Graf Spee, *101*
Pursuit to Algiers, *1008*
Pushed to the Limit, *101*
◆ Puss in Boots, *198*
◆ Putney Swope, *363*
◆ Pygmalion, *363*
Pyrates, *363*
Pyx, The, *1008*
◆ Q, *878*
◆ Q & A, *1008*
◆ QB VII, *631*
◆ Quackser Fortune Has a Cousin in the Bronx, *631*
Quadrophenia, *936*
Quake, *1008*
Quality Street, *631*
◆ **Quantum Leap (TV Series),** *1072*
Quarantine, *1072*
Quarterback Princess, *631*
◆ Quartet (1948), *631*
Quartet (1981), *631*
Quatermass and the Pit, *1072*
Quatermass Conclusion, The, *1072*
Quatermass Experiment, The, *1073*
Quatermass II: Enemy from Space (see Enemy From Space)
◆ **Quatorze Juliet,** *779*
◆ Quay Brothers, The: Volume I&II, *1073*
◆ Queen Christina, *631*
Queen Elizabeth, *631*
Queen Kelly, *631*
Queen of Blood (see Planet of Blood)
◆ Queen of Hearts, *632*
Queen of Outer Space, *1073*
◆ Queen of the Stardust Ballroom, *632*
Queen Victoria and the Zombies, *878*
Queenie, *632*
Queens Logic, *363*
Querelle, *779*
Quest, The, *878*
◆ Quest for Fire, *1073*
Quest for the Mighty Sword, *1073*
Quest of the Delta Knights, *1073*
Question of Faith, *632*
◆ Question of Honor, A, *632*
◆ Question of Silence, A, *779*
Qui Etes-Vous, Mr. Sorge? (Soviet Spy), *779*
Quick, *102*
◆ Quick and the Dead, The, *1140*
◆ Quick Change, *363*
Quick, Let's Get Married, *363*
Quicker Than the Eye, *102*
Quicksand: No Escape, *1008*
Quicksilver, *632*
Quiet Cool, *102*
Quiet Day in Belfast, A, *632*
◆ Quiet Earth, The, *1073*
Quiet Fire, *102*
◆ Quiet Man, The, *364*
Quiet Thunder, *102*
◆ Quigley Down Under, *1140*
Quiller Memorandum, The, *102*
Quintet, *1073*
Quo Vadis (1951), *632*
Quo Vadis? (1985), *632*
R.O.T.O.R., *1073*
R.P.M. (Revolutions Per Minute), *632*
Rabbit Run, *632*
Rabbit Test, *364*
Rabid, *878*
Rabid Grannies, *878*
Race for Glory, *102*
Race for Your Life, Charlie Brown, *198*
Race with the Devil, *878*
Racers, The, *632*
Rachel and the Stranger, *1140*
Rachel Papers, *364*
Rachel, Rachel, *632*
Rachel River, *632*
Racing with the Moon, *633*
Racket, The, *633*
Racketeer, *102*
Rad, *102*
Radar Men from the Moon, *102*
Radio Days, *364*
Radio Flyer, *633*
Radio Patrol, *102*
Radio Ranch (Men with Steel Faces & Phantom Empire), *1140*
Radioactive Dreams, *1073*
Rafferty and the Gold Dust Twins, *364*
◆ Raffi and the Sunshine Band, *198*
Rage (1972), *633*
Rage (1980), *633*
Rage and Honor, *102*
Rage and Honor II: Hostile Takeover, *102*
◆ Rage at Dawn, *1140*
Rage in Harlem, A, *103*
Rage of Angels, *633*
Rage of Honor, *103*
Rage of Paris, The, *364*
Raggedy Man, *1008*
Raggedy Rawney, The, *633*
◆ Raging Bull, *633*
Rags to Riches, *364*
◆ Ragtime, *633*
Raid on Entebbe, *633*
Raid on Rommel, *103*
◆ Raiders of the Lost Ark, *1073*
Raiders of the Sun, *103*
Railroaded, *633*
◆ Railway Children, The, *198*
Railway Station Man, The, *633*
◆ Rain, *634*
Rain Killer, The, *1008*
◆ Rain Man, *634*
◆ Rain People, The, *634*
Rain without Thunder, *634*
◆ Rainbow, The, *634*
Rainbow Brite and the Star Stealer, *198*
Rainbow Drive, *103*
Rainbow Valley, *1140*
Rainbow Warrior, *1008*
Rainmaker, The, *634*
Rains Came, The, *634*
Raintree County, *634*
◆ Raise the Red Lantern, *779*
Raise the Titanic, *103*
◆ Raisin in the Sun, A (1961), *634*
◆ Raisin in the Sun, A (1988), *634*
◆ Raising Arizona, *364*
Raising Cain, *878*
◆ Rambling Rose, *634*
Rambo: First Blood II, *103*
Rambo III, *103*
◆ Ramona (Series), *198*
Rampage, *1009*
◆ Ramparts of Clay, *779*
Ramrod, *1140*
◆ Ran, *779*
Rancho Deluxe, *1140*
Rancho Notorious, *1140*
◆ Random Harvest, *635*
Randy Rides Alone, *1141*
Range Defenders, *1141*
◆ Range Feud, *1141*
Range War, *1141*
Ranger and the Lady, The, *1141*
Ranma 1/2 (TV Series), *779*
Ransom, *1009*
Rap Master Ronnie—A Report Card *364*
Rape And Marriage: The Rideout Case, *635*
◆ Rape of Love (L'Amour Violé), *779*
Rape of the Sabines, *103*
Rapid Fire, *103*
◆ Rappaccini's Daughter, *635*
Rappin', *936*
◆ Rapture, The, *635*
Rapunzel, *198*
Rare Breed, The (1966), *1141*
Rare Breed, A (1981), *198*
Rare Chaplin, *364*
Rascals, The, *779*
◆ Rashomon, *780*
◆ Rasputin, *780*
Rasputin and the Empress, *635*
Rat Pfink a Boo Boo, *364*
Ratboy, *635*
◆ Ratings Game, The, *364*
Rats, *878*
Rats Are Coming!, The Werewolves Are Here!, The, *878*

ttle of a Simple Man, *635*
ttier Kid, *1141*
ven, The (1935), *878*
ven, The (1943) (see Le Corbeau)
ven, The (1963), *879*
ven Tengu Kabuto, *780*
vishing Idiot, The, *364*
w Courage, *103*
w Deal, *103*
w Nerve, *103*
whead Rex, *879*
whide (1938), *1141*
whide (1951), *1141*
whide (TV Series), *1141*
y Bradbury's Chronicles: The Martian Episodes, *1073*
y Charles: The Genius of Soul, *433*
zorback, *879*
zor's Edge, The (1946), *635*
zor's Edge, The (1984), *635*
-Animator, *879*
aching for the Moon (1917), *365*
aching for the Moon (1931), *365*
ader, The (see La Lectrice)
al American Hero, The, *635*
al Genius, *365*
al Glory, The, *103*
al Life, *365*
al McCoy, The, *1009*
al Men, *365*
ality Bites, *635*
ally Weird Tales, *365*
ap the Wild Wind, *104*
ar Window, *1009*
ason to Die, *879*
ason to Live . . . Reason to Die, A (see Massacre at Fort Holman)
becca, *1009*
becca of Sunnybrook Farm (1917), *635*
becca of Sunnybrook Farm (1938), *936*
bel (1973), *104*
bel (1985), *636*
bel Love, *636*
bel Rousers, *104*
bel Storm, *1074*
bel without a Cause, *636*
bels, The, *636*
ckless (1935), *636*
ckless (1984), *636*
ckless Kelly, *365*
cruits, *365*
ed Alert, *104*
ed and the White, The, *780*
ed Badge of Courage, The, *636*
ed Balloon, The, *198*
ed Barry, *104*
ed Beard, *780*
ed-Blooded American Girl, *879*
ed Dawn, *104*
ed Desert, *780*
ed Dust, *636*
ed Dwarf (TV Series), *365*
ed Flag: The Ultimate Game, *104*
ed Garters, *936*
ed-Headed Stranger, The, *1141*
ed-Headed Woman, *636*
ed Heat (1985), *1009*
ed Heat (1988), *104*
ed House, The, *1009*
ed Kimono, The, *636*
ed King, White Knight, *636*
ed Kiss (Rouge Baiser), *780*

Red Light Sting, The, *636*
Red Line 7000, *104*
Red Lion, *780*
Red Menace, The, *636*
Red Nights, *637*
Red Planet Mars, *1074*
Red Pony, The, *198*
◆ **Red Riding Hood/Goldilocks,** *198*
◆ Red River, *1141*
Red River Range, *1141*
Red River Renegades, *1142*
Red River Shore, *1142*
Red River Valley (see Man of the Frontier)
Red Rock West, *1009*
Red Scorpion, *104*
Red Shoe Diaries, *637*
Red Shoe Diaries II: Double Dare, *637*
Red Shoe Diaries 3: Another Woman's Lipstick, *637*
Red Shoe Diaries 4: Auto Erotica, *637*
◆ Red Shoes, The (1948), *936*
Red Skelton: A Career of Laughter, *433*
Red Sonja, *104*
◆ Red Sorghum, *780*
Red Sun, *1142*
Red Surf, *104*
Red Tent, The, *637*
Red Wind, *1009*
Redneck, *104*
◆ Reds, *637*
Reefer Madness, *365*
Reet, Petite and Gone, *936*
Ref, The, *365*
◆ Reflecting Skin, The, *637*
Reflection of Fear, *1009*
Reflections in a Golden Eye, *637*
Reflections of Murder, *1009*
Reform School Girl, *104*
Reform School Girls, *105*
◆ Regarding Henry, *637*
Regina, *780*
Rehearsal for Murder, *1009*
Reilly: The Ace of Spies, *637*
Reincarnate, The, *879*
◆ Reincarnation of Golden Lotus, The, *780*
Reincarnation of Peter Proud, The, *879*
◆ Reivers, The, *365*
Rejuvenator, The, *879*
Relentless, *1010*
Relentless II: Dead On, *879*
Relentless 3, *1010*
Reluctant Debutante, The, *365*
◆ Reluctant Dragon, The, *198*
◆ **Remains of the Day,** *637*
◆ Rembrandt, *638*
Rembrandt—1669, *780*
Remedy for Riches, *638*
Remington Steele (TV series), *1010*
Remo Williams: The Adventure Begins, *105*
Remote, *198*
Remote Control, *879*
Rendez-Vous, *780*
Renegade Girl, *1142*
◆ Renegade Ranger, *1142*
Renegade Trail, *1142*
Renegades, *105*
Reno and the Doc, *638*
Rent-a-Cop, *105*
Rented Lips, *366*

Repentance, *781*
◆ Repo Man, *366*
◆ **Report on the Party and the Guests, A,** *781*
◆ Report to the Commissioner, *638*
Repossessed, *366*
◆ Repulsion, *879*
Requiem for a Heavyweight, *638*
◆ Requiem for a Heavyweight (Television), *638*
Requiem for Dominic, *781*
Rescue, The, *105*
Rescue Force, *105*
Rescue Me, *105*
◆ Rescuers, The, *199*
Rescuers Down Under, *199*
◆ Reservoir Dogs, *105*
Rest in Pieces, *879*
Restless, *638*
Restless Breed, The, *1142*
Restless Natives, *366*
Resurrected, The, *879*
◆ Resurrection, *638*
Resurrection of Zachary Wheeler, The, *1074*
Retreat Hell, *105*
Retribution, *879*
Return, *638*
Return, The, *1074*
Return Fire: Jungle Wolf II, *105*
Return from the Past (see Bloodsuckers, The)
Return from Witch Mountain, *199*
Return of a Man Called Horse, The, *1142*
Return of Captain Invincible, The, *366*
Return of Chandu (The Magician), *105*
Return of Dracula, *880*
Return of Frank Cannon, The, *1010*
Return of Frank James, The, *1142*
Return of Gumby, The (Volume One), *199*
Return of Jesse James, The, *1142*
Return of Josey Wales, *1142*
◆ Return of Martin Guerre, The, *781*
Return of Maxwell Smart, The (see Nude Bomb, The)
Return of October, The, *366*
Return of Peter Grimm, The, *638*
◆ **Return of Spinal Tap, The,** *366*
Return of Superfly, The, *105*
Return of the Alien's Deadly Spawn, The, *880*
Return of the Ape Man, *880*
Return of the Badmen, *1142*
Return of the Dragon, *105*
Return of the Evil Dead, *880*
Return of the Fly, The, *880*
◆ Return of the Jedi, *1074*
Return of the Killer Tomatoes, *366*
Return of the Lash, *1142*
◆ Return of the Living Dead, The, *880*
Return of the Living Dead Part II, *880*
Return of the Living Dead 3, *880*
Return of the Man from U.N.C.L.E., The, *105*
◆ Return of the Musketeers, *106*
◆ Return of the Pink Panther, The, *366*
◆ Return of the Secaucus 7, *366*
Return of the Seven, *1142*
◆ Return of the Soldier, The, *638*
Return of the Swamp Thing, *880*

Return of the Tall Blond Man with One Black Shoe, The, *781*
Return of the Vampire, The, *880*
Return to Boggy Creek, *880*
Return to Eden, *639*
Return to Fantasy Island, *1074*
Return to Frogtown, *1074*
Return to Horror High, *880*
◆ **Return to Lonesome Dove,** *1143*
Return to Macon County, *106*
Return to Mayberry, *366*
◆ Return to Oz, *199*
Return to Paradise, *106*
Return to Peyton Place, *639*
Return to Salem's Lot, A, *880*
◆ Return to Snowy River, Part II, *1143*
Return to the Blue Lagoon, *639*
Return to the Lost World, *1074*
Return to Treasure Island, *199*
Return to Two-Moon Junction, *639*
Returning, The, *1010*
◆ Reuben, Reuben, *367*
◆ Reunion, *639*
Reunion in France, *639*
Revenge (1971), *1010*
Revenge (1971), *1010*
Revenge (1990), *106*
Revenge of the Cheerleaders, *367*
Revenge of the Creature, *881*
Revenge of the Dead, *881*
Revenge of the Kickfighter, *106*
Revenge of the Nerds, *367*
Revenge of the Nerds II: Nerds in Paradise, *367*
Revenge of the Nerds III: The Next Generation, *367*
Revenge of the Ninja, *106*
◆ Revenge of the Pink Panther, The, *367*
Revenge of the Red Baron, *881*
Revenge of the Stepford Wives, *881*
Revenge of the Teenage Vixens from Outer Space, *881*
Revenge of the Zombies, *881*
◆ Reversal of Fortune, *639*
◆ Revolt of Job, The, *781*
Revolt of the Zombies, *881*
Revolution, *639*
Revolutions Per Minute (see R.P.M.)
Revolver, *106*
Rhapsody, *639*
Rhapsody in August, *781*
◆ Rhapsody in Blue, *936*
Rhinestone, *367*
Rhodes (see Rhodes of Africa)
Rhodes of Africa, *639*
◆ Rich and Famous, *639*
Rich and Strange, *639*
Rich Girl, *640*
Rich Hall's Vanishing America, *367*
◆ Rich in Love, *640*
Rich Kids, *640*
Rich Little—One's a Crowd, *367*
Rich Little's Little Scams on Golf, *367*
Rich, Young and Pretty, *936*
Richard Lewis—"I'm Exhausted", *367*
Richard Lewis—"I'm in Pain Concert", *367*
◆ Richard Pryor—Here and Now, *367*
Richard Pryor—Live and Smokin', *367*
◆ Richard Pryor—Live in Concert, *367*
Richard Pryor Live on the Sunset Strip, *368*
◆ Richard III, *640*
Richard's Things, *640*
Ricochet, *106*
◆ Riddle of the Sands, *106*
Ride a Wild Pony, *199*
Ride Beyond Vengeance, *1143*
Ride 'em Cowboy, *368*
Ride 'em Cowgirl, *1143*
Ride 'em Denver, *199*
Ride Him Cowboy, *1143*
Ride in the Whirlwind, *1143*
◆ Ride Lonesome, *1143*
Ride, Ranger, Ride, *1143*
◆ Ride the High Country, *1143*
Ride the Man Down, *1143*
Ride the Wild Surf, *936*
Rider from Tucson, *1143*
◆ Rider on the Rain, *1010*
Riders for Justice, *1143*
Riders of Death Valley, *1143*
Riders of Destiny, *1144*
Riders of the Black Hills, *1144*
Riders of the Deadline, *1144*
◆ Riders of the Rio Grande, *1144*
Riders of the Rockies, *1144*
Riders of the Storm, *368*
Riders of the Whistling Pines, *1144*
Riders of the Whistling Skull, *1144*
Ridin' Down the Trail, *1144*
Ridin' on a Rainbow, *1144*
◆ Riding Bean, *781*
Riding on Air, *368*
Riding the Edge, *106*
Riding Tornado, The, *1144*
Riding with Death, *1074*
RiffRaff (1936), *640*
RiffRaff (1947), *106*
◆ Riff-Raff (1992), *640*
◆ Rififi, *1010*
Rifleman, The (TV Series), *1144*
Right Hand Man, The, *640*
◆ Right of Way, *640*
◆ Right Stuff, The, *640*
◆ Rikisha-Man, *781*
Rikki and Pete, *368*
◆ Rikki-Tikki-Tavi, *199*
◆ Rikyu, *781*
Rim of the Canyon, *1144*
Rimfire, *1144*
Ring, The, *640*
◆ Ring of Bright Water, *199*
◆ Ring of Fire, *433*
Ring of Scorpio, *640*
Ring of Steel, *106*
◆ Rio Bravo, *1145*
Rio Conchos, *1145*
Rio Diablo, *1145*
◆ Rio Grande, *1145*
Rio Lobo, *1145*
Rio Rita, *368*
Riot, *106*
Riot in Cell Block Eleven, *107*
Rip Van Winkle, *199*
Ripper, The, *881*
Ripper of Notre Dame (see Demoniac)
Ripping Yarns, *368*
Riptide, *640*
Rise and Fall of Legs Diamond, The, *107*
Rise of Catherine the Great, The (see Catherine the Great)
Rise of Louis XIV, The, *781*
Rising Son, *641*
Rising Sun, *1010*
◆ Risky Business, *368*
Rita Hayworth: The Love Goddess, *641*
Rita, Sue and Bob Too, *368*
Rituals, *1010*
◆ Ritz, The, *368*
River, The (1951), *641*
River, The (1984), *641*
River of Death, *107*
River of Diamonds, *107*
River of No Return, *1145*
River of Unrest, *641*
River Rat, The, *641*
◆ River Runs Through It, A, *641*
River's Edge, *641*
Road Agent, *1145*
◆ **Road Construction Ahead,** *433*
Road Games, *1010*
Road House (1948), *1010*
Road House (1989), *107*
Road Lawyers and Other Briefs, *3*
◆ Road Runner and Wile E. Coyote, The: The Scrapes of Wrath, *199*
◆ Road Runner vs. Wile E. Coyote: The Classic Chase, *199*
Road Scholar, *434*
Road to Bali, *368*
Road to Hong Kong, The, *368*
◆ Road to Mecca, The, *641*
Road to Rio, *369*
Road to Ruin, The (1928), *641*
Road to Ruin (1991), *369*
Road to Singapore, *369*
Road to Utopia, *369*
Road to Yesterday, The, *641*
◆ Road to Zanzibar, *369*
◆ Road Warrior, The, *1074*
Roadhouse 66, *107*
Roads to the South, *781*
◆ Roadside Prophets, *641*
Roamin' Wild, *1145*
Roaring Guns, *1145*
Roaring Road, The, *642*
◆ Roaring Twenties, The, *107*
Rob Roy, the Highland Rogue, *200*
Robbers of the Sacred Mountain,
Robbery, *1011*
◆ Robe, The, *642*
◆ Robert et Robert, *782*
Roberta, *936*
◆ Robin and Marian, *107*
Robin & the Seven Hoods, *936*
◆ Robin Hood (1923), *107*
Robin Hood (1973), *200*
Robin Hood (1991), *107*
◆ Robin Hood and the Sorcerer, *107*
Robin Hood: Herne's Son, *107*
Robin Hood: Men in Tights, *369*
Robin Hood of Texas, *1145*
Robin Hood of the Pecos, *1145*
◆ Robin Hood: Prince of Thieves, *10*
◆ Robin Hood: The Swords of Wayland, *108*
◆ Robin Williams Live, *369*
Robinson Crusoe of Clipper Island, *108*
Robo C.H.I.C., *1074*
◆ RoboCop, *1074*
RoboCop 2, *1075*
RoboCop 3, *1075*
Robot Carnival, *1075*
Robot in the Family, *200*
Robot Jox, *1075*
Robot Monster, *881*
Robot Wars, *1075*

occo & His Brothers, *782*
ock-a-Doodle, *200*
ock 'n' Roll High School, *369*
ock 'n' Roll High School Forever, *369*
ock 'n' Roll Nightmare, *881*
ock 'n' Roll Wrestling Women vs. the Aztec Ape, *108*
ock 'n' Roll Wrestling Women vs. the Aztec Mummy, *369*
ock and Rule, *1075*
ock, Baby, Rock It, *936*
ock House, *108*
ock, Pretty Baby, *936*
ock, Rock, Rock, *937*
ocket Attack USA, *1075*
ocket Gibraltar, *642*
ocket to the Moon (see Cat Women of the Moon)
ocketeer, The, *108*
ocketship X-M, *1075*
ockford Files, The (TV Series), *108*
ockin' Ronnie, *369*
ocking Horse Winner, The, *642*
ocktober Blood, *881*
ockula, *937*
ocky, *642*
ocky II, *642*
ocky III, *642*
ocky IV, *642*
ocky V, *642*
ocky Horror Picture Show, The, *937*
ocky Mountain Mystery (see Fighting Westerner, The)
ocky Mountain Rangers, *1145*
odan, *1075*
odeo Girl, *642*
odeo King and the Senorita, *1145*
odney Dangerfield: "It's Not Easy Being Me", *370*
odney Dangerfield—Nothin' Goes Right, *370*
Roe vs. Wade, *642*
Roger & Me, *434*
Roger Ramjet, *200*
Roll of Thunder, Hear My Cry, *642*
Roll on Texas Moon, *1145*
Rollerball, *1075*
Rollerblade, *1075*
Rollercoaster, *1011*
Rolling Thunder, *108*
Rolling Vengeance, *108*
Rollover, *1011*
Roman Holiday, *642*
Roman Scandals, *937*
Roman Spring of Mrs. Stone, The, *643*
Romance, *643*
Romance in Manhattan, *643*
Romance on the High Seas, *937*
Romance on the Orient Express, *643*
Romance with a Double Bass, *370*
Romancing the Stone, *108*
Romantic Comedy, *370*
Romantic Englishwoman, The, *643*
Rome Adventure, *643*
Romeo and Juliet (1936), *643*
Romeo and Juliet (1968), *643*
Romeo and Juliet (1983), *643*
Romeo and Juliet (1988), *643*
Romeo Is Bleeding, *108*
Romero, *643*
Romper Stomper, *109*
Ron Reagan Is the President's Son, *370*
Rooftops, *937*
Rookie, The, *109*
◆ **Rookie of the Year,** *200*
◆ Room at the Top, *643*
Room 43, *644*
Room Service, *370*
◆ Room with a View, A, *644*
Rooster Cogburn, *1146*
Rootin' Tootin' Rhythm, *1146*
◆ Roots, *644*
Roots of Evil, *109*
Roots Search, *782*
Roots—The Gift, *644*
◆ **Roots: The Next Generation,** *644*
◆ Rope, *1011*
Rorret, *782*
Rosalie, *937*
Rosalie Goes Shopping, *370*
Rosary Murders, The, *1011*
◆ Rose, The, *937*
Rose and the Jackal, The, *644*
Rose Garden, The, *644*
Rose Marie (1936), *937*
Rose Marie (1954), *937*
◆ Rose Tattoo, The, *644*
Roseanne Barr Show, The, *370*
Rosebud Beach Hotel, The, *370*
Roseland, *644*
◆ Rosemary's Baby, *881*
Rosencrantz and Guildenstern Are Dead, *370*
Rosie, *937*
Rouge Baiser (see Red Kiss)
Rough Cut, *1011*
Rough Justice, *1146*
Rough Night in Jericho, *1146*
Rough Riders' Roundup, *1146*
Roughnecks, *109*
◆ Round Midnight, *937*
Round Numbers, *370*
Round Trip to Heaven, *370*
Rounders, The, *1146*
◆ **Round-Up, The,** *782*
Round-Up Time in Texas, *1146*
Roustabout, *938*
Rousters, The, *109*
Rover Dangerfield, *200*
◆ Roxanne, *370*
◆ Roy Rogers, King of the Cowboys, *434*
Roy Rogers Show, The (TV Series), *1146*
Royal Wedding, *938*
Royce, *109*
RSVP, *371*
Rubdown, *1011*
Rubin & Ed, *371*
Ruby (1977), *881*
Ruby (1991), *644*
Ruby Gentry, *644*
◆ **Ruby in Paradise,** *645*
Ruckus, *109*
Rude Awakening (1982), *881*
Rude Awakening (1989), *371*
Rude Boy, *938*
Rudolph the Red-Nosed Reindeer (and Other Wonderful Christmas Stories), *200*
◆ **Rudy,** *200*
◆ Ruggles of Red Gap, *371*
◆ Rules of the Game, The, *782*
◆ Ruling Class, The, *371*
Rumble Fish, *645*
Rumik World: Firetripper, *782*
Rumik World: Laughing Target, *782*
Rumik World: The Supergal, *782*
Rumor Mill, The, *645*
Rumor of War, A, *109*
Rumpelstiltskin (1980), *200*
Rumpelstiltskin (1986), *200*
Rumpelstiltskin (1987), *200*
◆ Rumpole of the Bailey (TV Series), *1011*
Run, *109*
Run for the Roses, *201*
Run for the Sun, *109*
◆ **Run for Your Money, A,** *371*
Run if You Can, *645*
Run of the Arrow, *1146*
◆ Run, Rebecca, Run, *201*
◆ Run Silent, Run Deep, *109*
Run Stranger Run, *882*
Runaway, *1075*
Runaway Father, *645*
Runaway Nightmare, *109*
Runaway Ralph, *201*
◆ Runaway Train, *110*
Runestone, *882*
Runner Stumbles, The, *645*
Running Against Time, *1075*
Running Away, *645*
◆ Running Brave, *645*
Running Cool, *110*
Running Delilah, *110*
Running Hot, *645*
◆ Running Kind, The, *371*
Running Man, The, *1075*
Running Mates (1985), *645*
Running Mates (1992), *371*
◆ Running on Empty, *645*
Running Scared (1980), *110*
◆ Running Scared (1986), *110*
Running Wild (1927), *371*
Running Wild (1955), *645*
Rush, *645*
Rush Week, *882*
◆ Russia House, The, *646*
Russian Roulette, *110*
Russians Are Coming, the Russians Are Coming, The, *371*
Russkies, *371*
◆ Rustlers, The, *1146*
Rustler's Rhapsody, *371*
Rustler's Valley, *1146*
Rutanga Tapes, The, *1011*
Rutherford County Line, *110*
Ruthless Four, The, *1146*
◆ Ruthless People, *371*
◆ Rutles, The (a.k.a. All You Need Is Cash), *938*
Ryan's Daughter, *646*
S.H.E., *110*
S.O.B., *372*
S.O.S. Titanic, *646*
S. S. Hell Camp, *882*
Sabotage, *1011*
◆ Saboteur, *1011*
◆ Sabrina, *372*
◆ Sacco and Vanzetti, *782*
◆ Sacketts, The, *1146*
Sacred Ground, *1146*
◆ Sacrifice, The, *782*
Sacrilege, *782*
Sad Sack, The, *372*
Sadat, *646*
Saddle Mountain Roundup, *1146*
Saddle Tramps, *1147*
Sadie McKee, *646*
Sadie Thompson, *646*
Sadist, The, *882*

Saga of Death Valley, *1147*
Saga of the Viking Women and their Voyage to the Waters of the Great Sea Serpent, The, *110*
Sagebrush Trail, *1147*
Saginaw Trail, *1147*
Sahara (1943), *110*
Sahara (1984), *110*
Saigon Commandos, *110*
Sailor Who Fell from Grace with the Sea, The, *646*
Saint, The (TV Series), *1012*
St. Benny the Dip, *646*
St. Elmo's Fire, *646*
St. Helens, *646*
Saint in London, The, *1012*
Saint in New York, The, *1012*
St. Ives, *110*
Saint Jack, *646*
Saint Joan, *646*
St. Martin's Lane (see Sidewalks of London)
Saint of Fort Washington, The, *646*
Saint Strikes Back, The, *1012*
St. Valentine's Day Massacre, The, *111*
Saint's Vacation, The, *1012*
◆ Sakharov, *647*
◆ Salaam Bombay!, *782*
Salamander, The, *111*
◆ Salem's Lot, *882*
◆ Salesman, *434*
◆ Sally of the Sawdust, *647*
Salo: 120 Days of Sodom, *783*
Salome (1923), *647*
Salome (1953), *647*
Salome (1985), *647*
Salome, Where She Danced, *647*
◆ Salome's Last Dance, *647*
Salsa, *938*
Salt of the Earth, *647*
Salut L'Artiste, *783*
Salute John Citizen!, *647*
◆ Salute to Chuck Jones, A, *201*
Salute to Friz Freleng, A, *201*
◆ Salute to Mel Blanc, A, *201*
◆ Salvador, *647*
Salvation, *647*
Salzburg Connection, The, *111*
Sam Kinnison Live!, *372*
Samantha, *372*
◆ Samaritan: The Mitch Snyder Story, *647*
◆ Same Time Next Year, *372*
◆ Sammy and Rosie Get Laid, *372*
Sammy, the Way-Out Seal, *201*
Sam's Son, *647*
Sam's Song (see Swap, The)
Samson, *1076*
◆ Samson and Delilah (1949), *648*
Samson and Delilah (1984), *648*
Samurai Reincarnation, *783*
Samurai Saga, *783*
◆ Samurai Trilogy, The, *783*
San Antonio, *1147*
San Antonio Kid, *1147*
San Fernando Valley, *1147*
◆ San Francisco, *648*
Sanctuary of Fear, *1012*
Sand and Blood, *783*
Sand Pebbles, The, *111*
◆ Sandakan No. 8, *783*
Sanders of the River, *111*
Sandlot, The, *201*
Sandpiper, The, *648*
◆ Sands of Iwo Jima, *111*
◆ Sanjuro, *783*
◆ **Sans Soliel,** *434*
Sanshiro Sugata, *783*
Sansho the Bailiff, *783*
Santa and the Three Bears, *201*
Santa Claus Conquers the Martians, *1076*
Santa Claus—The Movie, *201*
Santa Fe Marshal, *1147*
◆ Santa Fe Saddlemates, *1147*
Santa Fe Stampede, *1147*
Santa Fe Trail, *1147*
◆ Santa Fe Uprising, *1147*
Santa Sangre, *882*
◆ Santabear's First Christmas, *201*
Santee, *1147*
Sapphire, *1012*
Saps at Sea, *372*
Sara Dane, *648*
◆ Sarafina!, *938*
◆ Sarah, Plain and Tall, *648*
Saratoga, *372*
Sardine: Kidnapped, *783*
Satan Met a Lady, *1012*
Satanic Rites of Dracula, The, *882*
Satan's Cheerleaders, *882*
Satan's Princess, *882*
Satan's Satellites, *111*
Satan's School for Girls, *882*
Satisfaction, *938*
Saturday Night at the Palace, *648*
◆ Saturday Night Fever, *938*
Saturday Night Live, *372*
Saturday Night Shockers, *882*
Saturday Night Sleazies, *372*
Saturday Night Special, *111*
Saturday the 14th, *882*
Saturn 3, *1076*
◆ Savage Attraction, *1012*
Savage Beach, *111*
Savage Bees, The, *882*
Savage Dawn, *111*
Savage Guns, *1147*
Savage Instinct, *111*
Savage Intruder, The, *883*
Savage Is Loose, The, *648*
Savage Journey, *1147*
Savage Justice, *111*
Savage Messiah, *648*
Savage Nights, *783*
Savage Sam, *201*
Savage Streets, *111*
Savage Weekend, *883*
Savages (1973), *373*
Savages (1974), *883*
Savannah Smiles, *201*
Save Me, *1012*
Save the Lady, *201*
Save the Tiger, *648*
◆ Saving Grace, *373*
Sawdust and Tinsel, *784*
◆ Say Amen, Somebody, *434*
Say Anything, *373*
Say Goodbye, Maggie Cole, *648*
Say Yes, *373*
◆ Sayonara, *648*
Scalawag Bunch, The, *111*
Scalpel, *883*
Scalphunters, The, *1148*
Scalps, *883*
Scam, *1012*
◆ Scandal, *648*
Scandal in a Small Town, *649*
Scandal Man (see L'Odeur Des Fauves)
Scandalous (1983), *373*
Scandalous (1988), *1012*
Scandalous John, *202*
Scanners, *883*
Scanners 2: The New Order, *883*
Scanners 3: The Takeover, *883*
◆ Scar, The, *649*
◆ Scaramouche, *111*
Scarecrow, *649*
◆ Scarecrows, *883*
Scared Stiff, *883*
Scared to Death, *883*
◆ Scarface (1932), *112*
◆ Scarface (1983), *112*
Scarface Mob, The (see Untouchables: Scarface Mob)
Scarlet and the Black, The, *112*
◆ Scarlet Claw, The, *1012*
Scarlet Clue, The, *1013*
Scarlet Dawn, *649*
◆ **Scarlet Empress, The,** *649*
Scarlet Letter, The (1926), *649*
Scarlet Letter, The (1934), *649*
Scarlet Letter (1973), *784*
Scarlet Pimpernel, The (1934), *112*
Scarlet Pimpernel, The (1982), *112*
Scarlet River, *1148*
Scarlet Spear, The, *112*
Scarlet Street, *649*
Scars of Dracula, *883*
Scary Tales, *202*
Scavenger Hunt, *373*
Scavengers, *373*
Scene of the Crime (1985), *1013*
Scene of the Crime (1987), *784*
◆ Scenes from a Marriage, *784*
Scenes from a Murder, *112*
Scenes from the Goldmine, *649*
Scenes from a Mall, *373*
◆ Scenes from the Class Struggle in Beverly Hills, *373*
Scent of a Woman, *649*
Scent of Green Papaya, The, *784*
◆ **Schindler's List,** *649*
Schizo, *883*
Schizoid, *883*
Schlock, *373*
School Daze, *373*
School for Scandal, *373*
School Spirit, *374*
◆ School Ties, *649*
Scissors, *1013*
Scorchers, *650*
Scorchy, *112*
Scorpion, *112*
Scorpion Woman, The, *784*
◆ Scott of the Antarctic, *650*
Scoundrel, The, *374*
Scream, *883*
Scream and Die (see House that Vanished, The)
Scream and Scream Again, *883*
Scream, Blacula, Scream, *884*
Scream for Help, *884*
Scream Greats, Vol. 1, *884*
◆ Scream of Fear, *1013*
Scream of the Demon Lover (1970) (see Blood Castle)
Scream of the Demon Lover (1976) *884*
Screamers, *884*
Screaming Skull, The, *884*
Screen Test, *374*

rewball Academy, 374
rewballs, 374
rooge (1935), 650
rooge (1970), 938
rooged, 374
rubbers, 650
ruples, 650
um, 650
a Chase, The, 112
a Devils, 112
a Gypsies, The, 202
a Hawk, The, 112
a Hound, The, 112
a Lion, The, 650
a of Grass, The, 1148
a of Love, 1013
a Shall Not Have Them, The, 113
a Wolf, The (1941), 113
a Wolf, The (1993), 113
a Wolves, The, 113
abert: The Adventure Begins, 202
ance on a Wet Afternoon, 1013
arch and Destroy (1981), 113
arch and Destroy (1988), 1076
arch for Signs of Intelligent Life in the Universe, The, 374
arch for the Gods, 1076
arch, The, 650
arch for Bridey Murphy, The, 650
archers, The, 1148
arching for Bobby Fischer, 202
aside Swingers, 938
ason of Fear, 1013
ason of Giants, A, 650
ason of the Witch, 884
cond Chance, 113
cond Chorus, 938
cond City Comedy Show, The, 374
cond Fiddle, 938
cond Sight, 374
cond Woman, The, 650
cret, The, 650
cret Admirer, 374
cret Adversary (see Partners in Crime)
cret Agent (TV Series), 113
cret Agent, The, 1013
cret Beyond the Door, 650
cret Ceremony, 650
cret Cinema, The, 374
cret Diary of Sigmund Freud, The, 374
cret Friends, 651
cret Games, 651
cret Garden, The (1949), 202
cret Garden, The (1984), 202
cret Garden, The (1987), 202
cret Garden, The (1993), 202
cret Honor, 651
cret Life of an American Wife, The, 374
cret Life of Walter Mitty, The, 374
cret Life of Jeffrey Dahmer, The, 651
cret Life of Ian Fleming, The (see Spymaker: The Secret Life of Ian Fleming)
cret Obsessions, 651
cret of Dorian Gray, The (see Dorian Gray)
cret of My Success, The, 375
cret of Nimh, The, 202
cret of the Sword, The, 202
cret Passion of Robert Clayton, The, 1013

◆ Secret Policemen's Other Ball, The, 375
Secret Policeman's Private Parts, The, 375
Secret Service in Darkest Africa (see Manhunt in the African Jungle)
Secret War of Harry Frigg, The, 375
Secret Weapon, 651
Secret Weapons, 113
Secrets, 651
Secrets of a Married Man, 651
Secrets of a Soul, 784
Secrets of Women (Waiting Women), 784
Seduced, 1013
Seduced and Abandoned, 784
Seducers, The, 651
Seduction, The, 884
Seduction, The: Cruel Woman, 784
Seduction of Joe Tynan, The, 651
◆ Seduction of Mimi, The, 784
See No Evil, 884
See No Evil, Hear No Evil, 375
◆ See You in the Morning, 651
Seedpeople, 1076
Seekers, The, 651
Seems Like Old Times, 375
Seize the Day, 651
Seizure, 884
Sell-Out, The, 113
Semi-Tough, 375
Senator Was Indiscreet, The, 375
Send Me No Flowers, 375
Sender, The, 884
Seniors, The, 375
Sensations, 651
Sensations of 1945, 938
Sense of Freedom, A, 652
Sense of Loss, A, 434
Sensual Man, The, 375
Sensuous Nurse, The, 784
Sensuous Vampires (see Vampire Hookers)
Sentinel, The, 884
◆ Separate But Equal, 652
Separate Peace, A, 652
◆ Separate Tables, 652
Separate Vacations, 375
September, 652
September Affair, 652
September Gun, 1148
September 30, 1955, 652
Serendipity, the Pink Dragon, 202
Sgt. Pepper's Lonely Hearts Club Band, 939
Sergeant Preston of the Yukon (TV Series), 1148
Sergeant Rutledge, 1148
Sergeant Ryker, 652
Sergeant York, 113
Serial, 376
◆ **Serial Mom,** 376
Serpent and the Rainbow, The, 884
Serpent's Egg, The, 652
◆ Serpico, 652
◆ Servant, The, 652
Servants of Twilight, 884
◆ Sesame Street Presents Follow That Bird, 203
Sessions, 652
◆ Set-Up, The, 1013
◆ Seven Beauties, 785
◆ Seven Brides for Seven Brothers, 939

Seven Brothers Meet Dracula, The, 884
Seven Cities of Gold, 653
◆ Seven Days in May, 653
Seven Day's Leave, 376
Seven Deadly Sins, The, 785
◆ Seven Dials Mystery, The, 1013
Seven Doors of Death, 884
◆ 7 Faces of Dr. Lao, 1076
Seven Hills of Rome, The, 939
Seven Hours to Judgment, 113
Seven Little Foys, The, 376
Seven Magnificent Gladiators, The, 113
Seven Minutes, The, 653
Seven Minutes in Heaven, 376
◆ Seven-Per-Cent Solution, The, 1013
◆ Seven Samurai, The, 785
Seven Sinners, 113
Seven Thieves, 653
Seven-Ups, The, 114
◆ Seven Year Itch, The, 376
Seven Years' Bad Luck, 376
◆ 1776, 939
7th Cavalry, 1148
Seventh Coin, The, 203
◆ Seventh Cross, The, 653
◆ Seventh Seal, The, 785
Seventh Sign, The, 885
Seventh Veil, The, 653
Seventh Victim, The, 885
◆ 7th Voyage of Sinbad, The, 1076
Severed Arm, The, 885
Severed Ties, 885
Sex and the College Girl, 653
Sex and the Single Girl, 376
Sex Appeal, 376
Sex Crimes, 114
◆ Sex, Drugs, Rock & Roll, 653
◆ Sex, Lies and Videotape, 653
Sex, Love, and Cold Hard Cash, 1014
Sex Madness, 653
Sex on the Run, 376
Sex with a Smile, 376
Sextette, 376
Sexton Blake and the Hooded Terror, 1014
Sexual Intent, 1014
Sexual Response, 1014
◆ Sgt. Bilko (TV Series), 376
Sgt. Kabukiman N.Y.P.D., 114
Shack-Out on 101, 653
Shades of Love: Champagne for Two, 653
Shades of Love: Lilac Dream, 654
Shades of Love: Sincerely, Violet, 654
Shades of Love: The Rose Cafe, 654
Shadey, 377
Shadow Box, The, 654
Shadow Dancing, 1014
Shadow Hunter, 654
◆ Shadow of a Doubt, 1014
Shadow of China, 654
Shadow of the Eagle, 114
◆ Shadow of the Thin Man, 1014
Shadow of the Wolf, 114
Shadow Play, 885
Shadow Riders, The, 1148
Shadow Strikes, The, 1014
◆ **Shadowlands,** 654
Shadows, 654
Shadows and Fog, 654
Shadows in the Storm, 654

◆ Shadows of Forgotten Ancestors, 785
Shadowzone, 885
Shaft, 114
Shaft's Big Score!, 114
Shag, the Movie, 654
Shaggy D.A., The, 203
Shaggy Dog, The, 203
Shaka Zulu, 654
◆ **Shake Hands with the Devil,** 114
Shakedown, 114
Shaker Run, 114
Shakes the Clown, 377
◆ Shakespeare Wallah, 655
Shakiest Gun in the West, The, 377
Shaking the Tree, 655
Shalako, 1148
◆ Shall We Dance?, 939
Shallow Grave, 114
Shame (1961) (see Intruder, The)
◆ Shame (1987), 114
Shame of the Jungle, 377
◆ Shameless Old Lady, The, 785
Shaming, The, 655
◆ Shampoo, 655
Shamus, 1014
◆ Shane, 1148
Shangai Joe, 1148
Shanghai Cobra, The, 1014
◆ **Shanghai Express,** 655
Shanghai Gesture, The, 655
Shanghai Surprise, 377
◆ Shaolin Temple, 785
Shark! (a.k.a. Maneaters!), 114
Shark Hunter, The, 114
Shark's Treasure, 115
◆ Sharky's Machine, 115
Shattered (1972), 655
Shattered (1991), 1014
Shattered Image, 1014
Shattered Spirits, 655
Shattered Vows, 655
She (1925), 1076
She (1983), 1076
She Beast, The, 885
She Couldn't Say No, 377
She Creature, The, 885
She Demons, 885
She-Devil, 377
She-Devils on Wheels, 115
◆ She Done Him Wrong, 377
She Freak, The, 885
She Goes to War, 377
She Likes You, Charlie Brown, 203
She-Ra, Princess of Power (Volume One), 203
She Waits, 885
She was a Hippy Vampire (see Wild World of Batwoman, The)
◆ She Wore a Yellow Ribbon, 1148
Sheba Baby, 115
Sheena, 115
◆ Sheep Has Five Legs, 785
Sheer Madness, 785
Sheik, The, 655
Shelley Duvall's Bedtime Stories (Series), 203
Sheltering Sky, The, 655
◆ Shenandoah, 1149
Sheriff of Las Vegas, 1149
Sherlock Holmes and the Baskerville Curse, 203
Sherlock Holmes and the Deadly Necklace, 1015
Sherlock Holmes and the Incident at Victoria Falls, 1015
Sherlock Holmes and the Leading Lady, 1015
Sherlock Holmes and the Secret Weapon, 1015
Sherlock Holmes and the Spider Woman, 1015
Sherlock Holmes and the Valley of Fear, 203
Sherlock Holmes and the Voice of Terror, 1015
Sherlock Holmes Faces Death, 1015
Sherlock Holmes in Washington, 1015
◆ Sherlock Jr., 377
◆ Sherman's March, 434
She's a Good Skate, Charlie Brown, 203
She's Back, 377
She's Dressed to Kill, 656
◆ She's Gotta Have It, 377
She's Having a Baby, 377
She's in the Army Now, 656
She's Out of Control, 378
Shin Heinke Monogatari, 785
Shine on Harvest Moon, 1149
Shining, The, 885
Shining Hour, The, 656
Shining Season, A, 656
Shining Through, 656
Ship Ahoy, 939
◆ Ship of Fools, 656
Ships with Wings, 115
◆ Shipwrecked, 203
◆ Shirley Valentine, 378
◆ Shoah, 434
Shock, The (1923), 656
Shock (1946), 885
Shock Corridor, 1015
Shock! Shock! Shock!, 885
◆ Shock to the System, A, 1015
Shock Treatment, 378
Shock Waves (Death Corps), 885
Shocked (see Mesmerized)
Shock'em Dead, 885
Shocker, 886
Shocking Asia, 434
Shocking Asia 2, 434
Shoes of the Fisherman, 656
◆ Shoeshine, 785
◆ Shogun (Full-Length Version), 115
Shogun Assassin, 785
Shoot (1976), 115
Shoot (1991), 378
Shoot Loud, Louder...I Don't Understand, 378
Shoot the Living...Pray for the Dead, 1149
Shoot the Moon, 656
Shoot the Piano Player, 785
Shoot to Kill, 115
Shootfighter, 115
Shooting, The, 1149
Shooting Elizabeth, 378
◆ Shooting Party, The, 656
◆ Shootist, The, 1149
◆ Shop Around the Corner, The, 378
◆ Shop on Main Street, The, 786
Shopworn Angel, The, 656
Short Animations by Larry Jordan, 1076
◆ Short Circuit, 1076
Short Circuit 2, 1076
◆ **Short Cuts,** 657
◆ Short Eyes, 657
Short Fuse, 115
◆ Short Grass, 1149
Short Time, 378
◆ Shot in the Dark, A, 378
Shotgun, 1149
Shout, The (1979), 886
Shout (1991), 939
Shout at the Devil, 115
Shout: The Story of Johnny O'Keefe, 939
◆ Show Boat (1936), 939
Show Boat (1951), 939
Show Business, 939
Show of Force, A, 1015
◆ Show People, 378
Show Them No Mercy, 657
Showdown (1940), 1149
◆ **Showdown, The (1950),** 1149
◆ **Showdown (1973),** 1149
Showdown at Boot Hill, 1149
Showdown at Williams Creek, 1149
Showdown in Little Tokyo, 115
Show-Off, The, 378
Shriek in the Night, A, 1016
Shriek of the Mutilated, 886
Shrieking, The, 886
Shrimp on the Barbie, 378
Shy People, 657
Sibling Rivalry, 378
Sicilian, The, 115
Sid and Nancy, 657
Side by Side: The True Story of the Osmond Family, 203
Side Out, 657
Side Show, 886
Sidekicks, 203
◆ Sidewalks of London, 657
Sidewalks of New York, 378
Sidewinder 1, 115
Siege of Firebase Gloria, The, 116
◆ Siegfried, 786
Siesta, 1016
Sign o' the Times, 434
Sign of Four, The, 1016
Sign of Zorro, The, 204
Signal 7, 657
Signatures of the Soul, 434
Signs of Life, 657
◆ Silas Marner, 657
Silence, The, 786
Silence Like Glass, 657
◆ Silence of the Lambs, 1016
Silence of the North, 657
Silencer, The, 116
Silent Assassins, 116
Silent Conflict, 1150
Silent Enemy, The, 116
Silent Madness, 886
Silent Mobius, 786
Silent Motive, 1016
◆ Silent Mouse, 204
Silent Movie, 379
Silent Night, Bloody Night, 886
Silent Night, Deadly Night, 886
Silent Night, Deadly Night Part 2, 88
Silent Night, Deadly Night 4—Initiation, 886
Silent Night, Deadly Night 5: The To Maker, 886
Silent Night, Lonely Night, 658
◆ Silent Partner, The, 1016
Silent Rage, 116
Silent Rebellion, 658
◆ Silent Running, 1076

ıt Scream, *886*
ıt Sherlock Holmes, The, *1016*
ıt Victim, *658*
ıt Victory: The Kitty O'Neil Story, *58*
ɔuette, *1016*
Stockings, *939*
2, *116*
wood, *658*
Symphonies, *204*
Symphonies (Limited Gold dition 1), *204*
Symphonies: Animal Tales, *204*
Symphonies: Animals Two by wo, *204*
Symphonies: Fanciful Fables, *04*
er Bears, *379*
er Blaze, *1016*
er Bullet, *886*
er Chalice, The, *658*
er Dream Racer, *658*
er Queen, *1150*
er River, *1150*
er Spurs, *1150*
er Streak (1934), *658*
er Streak (1976), *379*
erado, *1150*
ba, *658*
on, *379*
on, King of the Witches, *886*
on of the Desert, *786*
ple Justice, *658*
ple Men, *379*
ple Story, A, *786*
ply Mad About the Mouse, *204*
pson's Christmas Special, The, *204*
of Harold Diddlebock (a.k.a. Mad Wednesday), *379*
of Madelon Claudet, The, *658*
bad and the Eye of the Tiger, *1077*
bad of the Seven Seas, *116*
bad the Sailor, *116*
ce You Went Away, *658*
cerely Charlotte, *786*
cerely Yours, *658*
ful Life, A, *379*
g, *939*
g-Along Songs, *204*
g, Cowboy, Sing, *1150*
gin' in the Rain, *940*
ging Buckaroo, *1150*
ging Nun, The, *204*
ging the Blues in Red, *786*
gle Bars, Single Women, *658*
gle Room Furnished, *659*
gle Standard, The, *659*
gle White Female, *1016*
gles, *379*
gleton's Pluck, *379*
ister Invasion, *886*
ister Journey, *1150*
ister Urge, The, *116*
k the Bismarck, *116*
ners in Paradise, *659*
s of Desire, *1017*
s of Dorian Gray, The, *886*
s of the Night, *1017*
ux City Sue, *1150*
ens, *379*
occo, *116*
ter Act, *379*
ter Act 2: Back in the Habit, *380*
ter-in-Law, The, *659*

Sister Kenny, *659*
Sister, Sister, *886*
Sisterhood, The, *1077*
◆ Sisters, The (1938), *659*
◆ Sisters (1973), *1017*
Sitting Ducks, *380*
Six Degrees of Separation, *659*
Six Gun Serenade, *1150*
Six in Paris (Paris Vue par . . .), *786*
Six Pack, *380*
Six-Shootin' Sheriff, *1150*
Six Weeks, *659*
◆ Six Wives of Henry VIII, The (TV Series), *659*
633 Squadron, *116*
◆ Sixteen Candles, *380*
16 Fathoms Deep, *116*
'68, *659*
Sizzle, *659*
Sizzle Beach, U.S.A., *380*
Skag, *659*
Skeeter, *887*
Skeezer, *659*
Sketch Artist, *1017*
Sketches of a Strangler, *1017*
Ski Patrol, *380*
Ski School, *380*
Skin Art, *659*
Skin Deep, *380*
◆ Skin Game, *1150*
Skinheads, *116*
Skirts Ahoy!, *940*
Skokie, *660*
◆ Skull, The, *887*
Skull and Crown, *1017*
Skullduggery, *887*
◆ Sky Above, the Mud Below, The, *434*
Sky Bandits, *116*
Sky Heist, *117*
Sky Is Gray, The, *660*
Sky Pirates, *117*
Skylark, *660*
Skyline, *380*
◆ Sky's the Limit, The, *940*
Skyscraper Souls, *660*
◆ Slacker, *380*
Slam Dance, *1017*
Slammer Girls, *380*
◆ Slap Shot, *380*
Slapstick of Another Kind, *380*
Slasher, *887*
Slate, Wyn, and Me, *660*
Slaughter, *117*
Slaughter High, *887*
Slaughter in San Francisco, *117*
Slaughter of the Innocents, *1017*
Slaughter of the Vampires, *887*
Slaughter Trail, *1150*
Slaughterhouse, *887*
◆ Slaughterhouse Five, *1077*
Slaughterhouse Rock, *887*
Slaughter's Big Rip-Off, *117*
Slave Girls from Beyond Infinity, *381*
◆ Slave of Love, A, *786*
Slave of the Cannibal God, *117*
Slavers, *117*
Slaves of New York, *381*
Slayground, *1017*
Sleazemania, *381*
Sleazemania Strikes Back, *381*
Sleazy Uncle, The, *786*
Sleepaway Camp, *887*
Sleepaway Camp II: Unhappy Campers, *887*

Sleepaway Camp III, *887*
◆ Sleeper, *381*
◆ Sleeping Beauty (1959), *204*
◆ Sleeping Beauty (1983), *205*
Sleeping Car, The, *887*
◆ Sleeping Car Murders, The, *786*
Sleeping Dogs, *117*
◆ Sleeping Murder, *1017*
Sleeping Tiger, The, *660*
Sleeping with the Enemy, *1017*
◆ **Sleepless in Seattle,** *381*
Sleepwalker, *1017*
Slender Thread, The, *660*
◆ Sleuth, *1017*
Slightly Honorable, *381*
Slightly Pregnant Man, A, *787*
Slightly Scarlet, *660*
Slime People, The, *1077*
Slipping into Darkness, *117*
Slipstream, *1077*
Slither, *381*
Slithis, *887*
Sliver, *1018*
Sloane, *117*
Slow Bullet, *660*
Slow Burn, *1018*
Slugger's Wife, The, *381*
Slugs, the Movie, *887*
Slumber Party 57, *381*
Slumber Party Massacre, *887*
Slumber Party Massacre II, *887*
Slumber Party Massacre 3, *887*
◆ Small Change, *787*
Small Circle of Friends, A, *660*
Small Killing, A, *660*
◆ Small Sacrifices, *660*
Small Town Girl, *940*
Small Town in Texas, A, *117*
Smallest Show on Earth, The, *381*
◆ Smash Palace, *660*
Smash-Up: The Story of a Woman, *661*
Smashing the Rackets, *1018*
◆ Smile, *381*
Smile, Jenny, You're Dead, *661*
◆ Smiles of a Summer Night, *787*
Smilin' Through (1932), *661*
Smilin' Through (1941), *940*
Smith!, *1150*
Smithereens, *661*
Smoke, *205*
Smokescreen, *661*
Smokey and the Bandit, *381*
Smokey and the Bandit II, *381*
Smokey and the Bandit III, *382*
Smokey Bites the Dust, *382*
Smokey Trails, *1151*
Smoky Mountain Christmas, *205*
◆ Smooth Talk, *661*
Smooth Talker, *1018*
Smurfs and the Magic Flute, The, *205*
Snake Eater, *117*
Snake Eater 2, the Drug Buster, *117*
Snake Eater III: His Law, *117*
Snake People, *888*
◆ Snake Pit, The, *661*
Snapdragon, *1018*
◆ **Snapper, The,** *382*
Snatched, *117*
◆ Sneakers, *1018*
◆ Sniffles the Mouse Cartoon Festival Featuring "Sniffles Bells the Cat", *205*
Sniper, *117*
Sno-Line, *117*

Snoopy, Come Home, 205
Snoopy's Getting Married, Charlie Brown, 205
Snow Country, 787
Snow Creature, The, 888
Snow Kill, 118
Snow Queen, 205
◆ **Snow White and the Seven Dwarfs (1938),** 205
◆ Snow White and the Seven Dwarfs (1983), 205
Snow White and the Three Stooges, 205
Snow White Christmas, A, 205
Snowball Express, 205
Snowbeast, 888
◆ Snows of Kilimanjaro, The, 118
Snuff, 888
◆ So Dear to My Heart, 205
◆ So Ends Our Night, 661
So Far, 434
So Fine, 382
So I Married an Axe Murderer, 382
So This Is Paris, 382
So This Is Washington, 382
Soapdish, 382
Society, 888
Sodom and Gomorrah, 661
Sofie, 787
Soft Parade, The, 435
Soft Skin, The, 787
Sois Belle Et Tais-Toi (Just Another Pretty Face), 787
◆ Sol Bianca, 787
Solar Crisis, 1077
Solarbabies, 1077
◆ Solaris, 787
Soldier, The, 118
Soldier Blue, 1151
Soldier in the Rain, 661
Soldier of Fortune, 118
◆ Soldier of Orange, 787
Soldier of the Night, 787
Soldier's Fortune, 118
Soldier's Home, 661
◆ Soldier's Story, A, 1018
Soldier's Tale, A, 661
Sole Survivor, 888
Solo, 661
Solomon and Sheba, 661
Some Call It Loving, 662
Some Came Running, 662
Some Girls, 382
Some Kind of Hero, 382
◆ Some Kind of Wonderful, 382
◆ Some Like It Hot, 382
◆ Somebody Has to Shoot the Picture, 662
◆ Somebody Up There Likes Me, 662
Someday You'll Find Her, Charlie Brown, 206
Someone Behind the Door, 1018
Someone I Touched, 662
Someone to Love, 662
◆ Someone to Watch Over Me, 1018
Something for Everyone, 662
Something of Value, 118
Something Short of Paradise, 383
Something Special, 383
Something to Sing About, 940
Something Weird, 888
Something Wicked This Way Comes, 1077
◆ Something Wild, 383
Sometimes a Great Notion, 662
Sometimes Aunt Martha Does Dreadful Things, 888
Sometimes They Come Back, 888
◆ Somewhere I'll Find You, 662
Somewhere in Sonora, 1151
Somewhere in Time, 1077
Somewhere, Tomorrow, 206
◆ Sommersby, 662
Son-in-Law, 383
Son of Ali Baba, 118
Son of Blob (Beware! The Blob), 888
Son of Captain Blood, 118
Son of Dracula (1943), 888
Son of Dracula (1974), 940
Son of Flubber, 206
◆ Son of Frankenstein, 888
Son of Godzilla, 888
Son of Kong, The, 888
Son of Lassie, 206
Son of Monte Cristo, The, 118
Son of Paleface, 383
◆ Son of the Morning Star, 1151
Son of the Pink Panther, 383
Son of the Sheik, 118
Son of Zorro, 118
Song Is Born, A, 940
◆ Song of Bernadette, The, 662
Song of Love, 662
Song of Nevada, 1151
Song of Norway, 940
Song of Texas, 1151
◆ Song of the Exile, 787
Song of the Gringo, 1151
Song of the Islands, 940
Song of the Thin Man, 1018
Song Remains the Same, The, 435
Song to Remember, A, 940
Song without End, 940
◆ Songwriter, 940
Sonny and Jed, 1151
Sonny Boy, 889
Sons of Katie Elder, The, 1151
◆ Sons of the Desert, 383
Sons of the Pioneers, 1151
Sons of the Sea, 663
Sooner or Later, 663
Sophia Loren: Her Own Story, 663
◆ Sophie's Choice, 663
Sophie's Place (see Crooks and Coronets)
Sophisticated Gents, The, 663
Sorcerer's Apprentice, The, 206
Sorceress (1982), 1077
Sorceress, The (1988), 788
◆ Sorceror, 1018
Sorority Babes in the Slimeball Bowl-O-Rama, 383
Sorority Girl, 118
Sorority House Massacre, 889
Sorority House Massacre 2, 889
◆ Sorrow and the Pity, The, 435
Sorrowful Jones, 383
Sorrows of Satan, The, 663
◆ Sorry, Wrong Number (1948), 1019
Sorry, Wrong Number (1989), 1019
SOS Coast Guard, 118
Sotto Sotto, 788
Soul Hustler, 118
Soul Man, 383
Soul Vengeance, 118
Soultaker, 889
◆ Sound of Music, The, 940
◆ Sounder, 663
◆ **Soundstage: Blues Summit in Chicago,** 435
Soup for One, 383
South Beach, 1019
◆ **South Central,** 663
South of Pago Pago, 119
South of Reno, 663
◆ South of St. Louis, 1151
South of the Border, 1151
South of the Rio Grande, 1151
South Pacific, 941
◆ Southern Comfort, 119
Southern Yankee, A, 383
◆ Southerner, The, 663
Souvenir, 663
Soylent Green, 1077
Space 1999 (TV Series), 1077
Space Patrol (TV Series), 1077
Space Rage, 1078
Space Raiders, 1078
Space Zombies (see Astro Zombies
Spaceballs, 384
SpaceCamp, 1078
Spaced Invaders, 206
Spaced Out, 384
Spacehunter: Adventures in the Forbidden Zone, 1078
Spaceship, 384
Spaceship to the Unknown (see Fla
Gordon: Rocketship)
Spaghetti House, 788
Spaghetti Western, 1152
◆ Spalding Gray: Terrors of Pleasure, 384
Sparkle, 941
Sparrows, 664
◆ Spartacus, 119
Spasms, 889
Speak Easily, 384
Speaking Parts, 664
Special Bulletin, 1019
◆ Special Day, A, 788
Special Effects, 889
Speckled Band, The, 1019
◆ Specter of the Rose, The, 1019
Specters, 889
Speed Racer: The Movie, 206
Speed Zone, 119
Speedway, 941
Speedy Gonzales' Fast Funnies, 20
Spellbinder, 889
◆ Spellbound, 1019
Spellcaster, 889
Spencer's Mountain, 664
◆ Spetters, 788
Sphinx, The (1933), 1019
Sphinx (1981), 889
Spices, 788
Spider Baby, 889
Spider Woman (see Sherlock Holm
and the Spider Woman)
Spiders, The, 119
◆ Spider's Stratagem, The, 788
◆ Spies (1928), 788
◆ **Spies (1992),** 435
Spies, Lies, and Naked Thighs, 38
Spies Like Us, 384
◆ Spike & Mike's Festival of Animation, 384
Spike of Bensonhurst, 384
Spinout, 941
◆ Spiral Staircase, The (1946), 1019
Spiral Staircase, The (1975), 1019
◆ Spirit of St. Louis, The, 664
Spirit of '76, The, 384
Spirit of Tattoo (see Irezumi)
◆ Spirit of the Beehive, The, 788

pirit of the Dead, *889*
pirit of the Eagle, *119*
pirit of the West, *1152*
pirit of West Point, The, *664*
pirits, *889*
pite Marriage, *384*
pitfire, *664*
plash, *384*
platter University, *889*
plendor in the Grass, *664*
plit Decisions, *664*
plit Image, *664*
plit Second (1953), *664*
plit Second (1992), *1078*
plitting Heirs, *384*
poilers, The, *1152*
pontaneous Combustion, *889*
pookies, *889*
pooks Run Wild, *385*
port Goofy, *206*
port Goofy's Vacation, *206*
porting Club, The, *664*
pring Break, *385*
pring Fever, *385*
pring Parade, *941*
pring Symphony, *788*
pringtime in the Rockies (1937), *1152*
pringtime in the Rockies (1942), *941*
pringtime in the Sierras, *1152*
putnik, *788*
py, *1019*
py in Black, The, *664*
py of Napoleon, *664*
py Smasher, *119*
py Who Came in from the Cold, The, *664*
py Who Loved Me, The, *119*
py with a Cold Nose, The, *385*
pymaker: The Secret Life of Ian Fleming, *119*
*P*Y*S, *385*
quare Dance, *665*
queeze, The (1977), *665*
queeze, The (1987), *385*
queeze Play, *385*
quirm, *889*
quizzy Taylor, *119*
tacking, *665*
tacy's Knights, *665*
tage Door, *385*
tage Door Canteen, *665*
tage Fright, *1019*
tage Struck (1936), *941*
tage Struck (1958), *665*
tage to Chino, *1152*
tage to Mesa City, *1152*
tage to Tucson, *1152*
tagecoach (1939), *1152*
tagecoach (1986), *1152*
tagecoach to Denver, *1152*
tagecoach War, *1152*
takeout, *119*
talag 17, *119*
talin, *665*
talker, *788*
talking Moon, The, *1152*
tampede, *1152*
tand and Deliver, *665*
tand by Me (1986), *665*
tand by Me (1988), *941*
tand-In, *385*
tand Up and Cheer, *206*
tand-Up Reagan, *385*

Standing Tall, *1153*
Stanley, *890*
Stanley and Iris, *665*
Stanley and Livingstone, *665*
Star, The, *665*
Star!, *941*
◆ Star Chamber, The, *1019*
Star Crash, *1078*
Star Crystal, *1078*
◆ Star 80, *666*
Star for Jeremy, A, *206*
◆ Star Is Born, A (1937), *666*
◆ Star Is Born, A (1954), *666*
Star Is Born, A (1976), *666*
Star Knight, *1078*
Star of Midnight, *1020*
Star Quest (see Beyond the Rising Moon)
Star Trek (TV Series), *1078*
◆ Star Trek: The Cage, *1078*
◆ Star Trek: The Menagerie, *1078*
Star Trek—The Motion Picture, *1079*
◆ Star Trek: The Next Generation (TV Series), *1079*
◆ Star Trek II: The Wrath of Khan, *1079*
◆ Star Trek III: The Search for Spock, *1079*
◆ Star Trek IV: The Voyage Home, *1079*
Star Trek V: The Final Frontier, *1079*
◆ Star Trek VI: The Undiscovered Country, *1079*
◆ Star Wars, *1079*
Starbirds, *206*
Stardust Memories, *385*
Starflight One, *1079*
Stark, *119*
Starlight Hotel, *666*
◆ Starman, *1080*
Star Packer, The, *1153*
◆ Starring Chip 'n' Dale, *207*
Starring Donald and Daisy, *207*
◆ Starring Mickey and Minnie, *207*
◆ Starring Pluto and Fifi, *207*
Stars and Bars, *385*
Stars and Stripes Forever, *941*
◆ **Stars in My Crown,** *1153*
◆ Stars Look Down, The, *666*
Starship, *1080*
Starship Invasions, *1080*
Starstruck, *941*
◆ Start the Revolution without Me, *385*
◆ Starting Over, *385*
State Fair (1945), *941*
State Fair (1962), *941*
◆ **State of Emergency,** *666*
State of Grace, *666*
◆ State of Siege, *788*
State of the Art of Computer Animation, The, *435*
State of the Union, *666*
◆ State of Things, The, *789*
State's Attorney, *666*
Stateline Motel, *789*
Static, *666*
Station, The, *789*
Station West, *1153*
Statue, The, *385*
◆ Stavisky, *789*
◆ Stay as You Are, *666*
Stay Away Joe, *942*
◆ Stay Hungry, *667*
Stay Tuned, *385*

Staying Alive, *942*
◆ Staying Together, *667*
Steagle, The, *386*
Steal the Sky, *667*
Stealing Heaven, *667*
Stealing Home, *667*
◆ Steamboat Bill Jr., *386*
Steaming, *667*
Steel, *120*
Steel and Lace, *1080*
Steel Dawn, *1080*
Steel Helmet, The, *120*
◆ Steel Magnolias, *667*
Steele Justice, *120*
Steele's Law, *120*
Steelyard Blues, *386*
Stella (1950), *667*
Stella (1990), *667*
◆ Stella Dallas, *667*
◆ Stella Maris, *1020*
Step Lively, *942*
◆ Stepfather, The, *1020*
Stepfather II, *890*
Stepfather III: Father's Day, *890*
Stephen King's Graveyard Shift, *890*
Stephen King's Golden Years (TV Series), *1080*
Stephen King's Night Shift Collection, *890*
Stephen King's Sleepwalkers, *890*
◆ Stepmonster, *1080*
Steppenwolf, *667*
Stepping Out, *942*
◆ Sterile Cuckoo, The, *667*
Steve Martin Live, *386*
Steven Wright Live, *386*
◆ Stevie, *668*
Stewardess School, *386*
Stick, *120*
Stick-up, The, *386*
Sticky Fingers, *386*
Stigma, *668*
Stiletto, *120*
Still Not Quite Human, *386*
Still of the Night, *1020*
Still Smokin', *386*
Stilts, The (Los Zancos), *789*
◆ Sting, The, *120*
Sting II, The, *120*
Stingray, *120*
Stir Crazy, *386*
Stitches, *386*
Stocks and Blondes, *668*
Stolen Face, *890*
Stolen Hours, *668*
◆ Stolen Kisses, *789*
Stolen Life, A, *668*
◆ Stone Boy, The, *668*
Stone Cold, *120*
Stone Cold Dead, *1020*
Stone Fox, The, *207*
Stone Killer, The, *120*
◆ Stone of Silver Creek, *1153*
Stones of Death, *890*
Stoogemania, *386*
◆ Stop Making Sense, *435*
Stop! Or My Mom Will Shoot, *386*
Stopover Tokyo, *120*
Storm, *1020*
Storm and Sorrow, *120*
Storm in a Teacup, *387*
◆ Storm over Asia, *789*
Stormquest, *1080*
◆ Stormy Monday, *1020*
◆ Stormy Waters, *789*

◆ Stormy Weather, *942*
Story of a Love Story, *668*
Story of a Three Day Pass, The, *668*
Story of Adele H, The, *789*
◆ Story of Babar, The, *207*
◆ Story of Boys and Girls, *789*
Story of David, The, *207*
Story of Fausta, The, *789*
Story of Jacob and Joseph, The, *207*
Story of Louis Pasteur, The, *668*
Story of O, The, *668*
◆ Story of Qiu Ju, The, *789*
Story of Robin Hood, The, *207*
Story of Ruth, The, *668*
Story of Seabiscuit, The, *207*
◆ Story of Vernon and Irene Castle, The, *942*
◆ Story of Women, The, *790*
Storybook Series, The (Volume One), *207*
Stowaway, *942*
Stowaway to the Stars (see Voyage en Ballon)
Straight for the Heart, *790*
Straight Line, *120*
Straight out of Brooklyn, *668*
Straight Shooting, *1153*
Straight Talk, *387*
◆ Straight Time, *668*
Straight Time: He Wrote It for Criminals, *435*
Straight to Hell, *1153*
Strait-Jacket, *890*
Stranded, *1080*
◆ Strange Affair of Uncle Harry, The, *669*
Strange Behavior, *890*
Strange Brew, *387*
Strange Cargo, *669*
Strange Case of the Cosmic Rays, The, *207*
Strange Case of Dr. Jekyll and Mr. Hyde, The (1968), *890*
Strange Case of Dr. Jekyll and Mr. Hyde, The (1989), *890*
Strange Gamble, *1153*
Strange Illusion, *1020*
Strange Interlude (1932), *669*
◆ Strange Interlude (1988), *669*
◆ Strange Invaders, *1080*
Strange Love of Martha Ivers, The, *669*
Strange Love of Molly Louvain, The, *669*
Strange New World, *1080*
Strange Shadows in an Empty Room, *121*
◆ Strange Tales: Ray Bradbury Theater, *1080*
Strange Woman, The, *669*
Strangeness, The, *890*
◆ Stranger, The (1947), *1020*
◆ Stranger, The (1986), *1020*
◆ Stranger, The (1992), *790*
Stranger Among Us, A, *1020*
Stranger and the Gunfighter, The, *1153*
Stranger from Venus, *1081*
Stranger Is Watching, A, *890*
◆ Stranger on the Third Floor, *1020*
◆ Stranger Than Paradise, *387*
Stranger Within, The, *891*
Stranger Wore a Gun, The, *1153*
Strangers, *669*
Strangers in Good Company, *669*
◆ Strangers in the City, *669*
Strangers Kiss, *669*
◆ Strangers on a Train, *1020*
Strangers: The Story of a Mother and a Daughter, *669*
Strangers When We Meet, *670*
Strangler, The, *1020*
Strangler of the Swamp, *891*
◆ Strapless, *670*
Strapped, *670*
Strategic Air Command, *670*
◆ **Stratton Story, The,** *670*
◆ Straw Dogs, *1021*
Strawberry Blonde, The, *670*
Strawberry Shortcake and Pets on Parade (TV Series), *207*
Strawberry Statement, The, *670*
◆ Stray Dog, *790*
Strays, *891*
Streamers, *670*
Street, The, *790*
Street Asylum, *121*
Street Crimes, *121*
Street Fight (see Coonskin)
Street Fighter, *121*
Street Hitz, *121*
Street Hunter, *121*
Street Justice, *121*
Street Knight, *121*
Street Music, *670*
Street of Forgotten Women, The, *670*
◆ Street of Shame, *790*
Street People, *121*
Street Scene, *670*
Street Smart, *670*
Street Soldiers, *121*
Street Trash, *891*
Street Warriors, *670*
Street Warriors II, *671*
Street with No Name, *1021*
◆ Streetcar Named Desire, A, *671*
Streetfight, *671*
Streethawk, *121*
Streets, *121*
Streets of Fire, *121*
Streets of Gold, *671*
Streets of L.A., The, *671*
Streetwalkin', *671*
◆ Streetwise, *435*
◆ Strictly Ballroom, *942*
Strictly Business, *387*
◆ Strike, *790*
Strike Commando, *121*
Strike Force, *121*
Strike It Rich, *387*
Strike Up the Band, *387*
Striker's Mountain, *121*
Striking Distance, *121*
◆ Stripes, *387*
Stripped to Kill, *122*
Stripped to Kill II, *891*
Stripper, The (1963), *671*
Stripper (1985), *435*
Stroke of Midnight, *387*
Stroker Ace, *387*
Stromboli, *790*
Strong Man, The, *387*
◆ Stroszek, *790*
Stryker, *1081*
Stuck on You, *387*
Stud, The, *671*
Student Bodies, *891*
Student Confidential, *387*
Student Nurses, The, *671*
◆ Student of Prague, *790*
◆ Student Prince, The, *942*
◆ Student Prince in Old Heidelberg, The, *671*
Studs Lonigan, *671*
Study in Scarlet, A, *1021*
◆ Study in Terror, A, *1021*
Stuff, The, *891*
Stuff Stephanie in the Incinerator,
◆ Stunt Man, The, *671*
Subject Was Roses, The, *671*
Subspecies, *891*
Substitute, The, *1021*
Suburban Commando, *388*
Suburban Roulette, *671*
Suburbia, *672*
Subway, *790*
Subway to the Stars, *791*
Success Is the Best Revenge, *672*
Sudden Death, *122*
◆ Sudden Impact, *122*
Sudden Thunder, *122*
◆ Suddenly, *1021*
Suddenly, Last Summer, *672*
Sudie & Simpson, *672*
Sugar Cookies, *672*
Sugar Hill, *122*
Sugarbaby, *791*
◆ Sugarcane Alley, *791*
◆ Sugarland Express, The, *672*
Suicide Battalion, *122*
Suicide Club, The, *1021*
Suicide Squadron (see Dangerous Moonlight)
Sullivans, The (see Fighting Sullivans, The)
◆ Sullivan's Travels, *388*
◆ Summer, *791*
Summer and Smoke, *672*
Summer Camp, *388*
Summer Camp Nightmare, *672*
Summer City, *122*
Summer Heat (1983), *672*
Summer Heat (1987), *672*
Summer Holiday, *942*
Summer House, The, *388*
Summer Interlude, *791*
Summer Lovers, *672*
Summer Magic, *208*
Summer Night, *791*
Summer of Fear, *891*
◆ Summer of '42, *672*
◆ Summer of My German Soldier, *6*
Summer Place, A, *672*
Summer Rental, *388*
◆ Summer School, *388*
Summer School Teachers, *673*
Summer Stock, *942*
Summer Story, A, *673*
Summer to Remember, A, *673*
Summer Vacation: 1999, *791*
Summer Wishes, Winter Dreams,
◆ Summertime, *673*
Summertime Killer, The, *122*
Sun Comes Up, The, *208*
Sun Shines Bright, The, *673*
Sun Valley Serenade, *942*
Sunburn, *1021*
Sunday, Bloody Sunday, *673*
◆ Sunday in the Country, A, *791*
◆ Sunday in the Park with George, *943*
Sunday Too Far Away, *673*
◆ Sundays and Cybèle, *791*
◆ Sunday's Children, *791*
Sundown (1941), *673*

Sundown (1990), *891*
Sundown Rider, The, *1153*
Sundown Riders, *1153*
Sundowners, The (1950), *1153*
Sundowners, The (1960), *673*
Sunrise, *673*
Sunrise at Campobello, *673*
Sunset, *1021*
Sunset Boulevard, *673*
Sunset Carson Rides Again, *1153*
Sunset Grill, *1021*
Sunset Heat, *122*
Sunset Limousine, *388*
Sunset on the Desert, *1154*
Sunset Serenade, *1154*
Sunset Strip, *674*
Sunshine Boys, The, *388*
Sunstroke, *1021*
Super, The, *388*
Super Force, *1081*
Super Fuzz, *1081*
Super Mario Brothers, The, *208*
Super Powers Collection, *208*
Supercarrier, *122*
Superdad, *208*
Superfly, *122*
Superfly T.N.T., *122*
Supergirl, *1081*
Supergrass, The, *388*
Superman Cartoons, *208*
Superman, *1081*
Superman II, *1081*
Superman III, *1081*
Superman IV: The Quest for Peace, *1081*
Superman and the Mole Men, *1081*
Superman—The Serial, *1081*
Supernaturals, The, *891*
Supervixens, *123*
Support Your Local Gunfighter, *1154*
Support Your Local Sheriff!, *1154*
Suppose They Gave a War and Nobody Came?, *388*
Sure Fire, *674*
Sure Thing, The, *389*
Surf 2, *389*
Surf Nazis Must Die, *123*
Surf Ninjas, *208*
Surfacing, *123*
Surprise Package, *389*
Surrender, *389*
Surrogate, The, *674*
Survival Game, *123*
Survival Quest, *123*
Survival Run (see Damnation Alley)
Survival Zone, *1081*
Survivalist, The, *123*
Survive the Night, *1021*
Surviving Desire, *389*
Surviving the Game, *123*
Survivor, *1081*
Survivors, The, *389*
Susan and God, *674*
Susan Lenox: Her Fall and Rise, *674*
Susan Slept Here, *389*
Susanna, *791*
Susanna Pass, *1154*
Susannah of the Mounties, *208*
Suspect, *1022*
Suspended, *791*
Suspicion (1941), *1022*
Suspicion (1987), *1022*
Suspiria, *891*
Suzy, *674*
Svengali (1931), *1022*
Svengali (1983), *674*
Swamp Thing, *891*
Swan, The (1925), *389*
Swan, The (1956), *674*
◆ Swann in Love, *791*
Swap, The, *674*
Swarm, The, *891*
Swashbuckler (1976), *123*
Swashbuckler, The (1984), *123*
Sweater Girls, *389*
◆ Sweeney Todd, *943*
◆ Sweet Adeline, *943*
◆ Sweet Bird of Youth (1962), *674*
Sweet Bird of Youth (1989), *674*
◆ Sweet Charity, *943*
Sweet Country, *674*
◆ Sweet Dreams, *943*
Sweet 15, *674*
◆ **Sweet Home Chicago,** *435*
Sweet Hostage, *674*
Sweet Justice, *123*
Sweet Killing, *1022*
◆ Sweet Liberty, *389*
Sweet Lies, *389*
◆ Sweet Lorraine, *674*
Sweet Love, Bitter, *675*
Sweet Movie, *792*
Sweet Murder, *1022*
Sweet Poison, *123*
Sweet Revenge (1987), *123*
◆ Sweet Revenge (1990), *389*
Sweet Sixteen, *123*
Sweet Smell of Success, *675*
Sweet Sweetback's Baadasssss Song, *123*
Sweet Talker, *389*
Sweet, Violent Tony (see Kill Castro)
Sweet William, *389*
Sweethearts, *943*
Sweethearts' Dance, *675*
Sweetie, *675*
Swept Away, *792*
◆ Swimmer, The, *675*
Swimming Pool, The, *792*
◆ Swimming to Cambodia, *390*
Swimsuit, *390*
Swing High, Swing Low, *390*
Swing It, Sailor, *390*
Swing Kids, *675*
Swing Shift, *675*
◆ Swing Time, *943*
Swingin' Summer, A, *390*
Swiss Conspiracy, The, *1022*
Swiss Family Robinson, The, *208*
Swiss Miss, *390*
Switch, *390*
Switched at Birth, *675*
Switching Channels, *390*
◆ Swoon, *675*
Sword and the Rose, The (1953), *208*
Sword and the Rose, The (1985) (see Flesh and Blood)
Sword and the Sorcerer, The, *1082*
Sword in the Stone, The, *208*
Sword of Doom, *792*
Sword of Gideon, *123*
Sword of Lancelot, *124*
Sword of the Valiant, *208*
Swordsman, The, *124*
◆ Sybil, *675*
◆ Sylvester, *675*
◆ Sylvester and Tweety: The Best Yeows of Our Lives, *208*
Sylvester and Tweety's Crazy Capers, *209*
Sylvia, *676*
◆ Sylvia and the Phantom, *792*
Sylvia Scarlett, *676*
Sympathy for the Devil, *435*
T-Men, *676*
Table for Five, *676*
Tabu, *676*
Taffin, *124*
Tag—The Assassination Game, *124*
Tagget, *124*
Tai-Pan, *124*
◆ Tailor of Gloucester, The, *209*
Tailspin, *676*
Tainted Blood, *1022*
Take, The, *124*
Take a Hard Ride, *1154*
Take Down, *390*
Take It Big, *943*
◆ Take Me Back to Oklahoma, *1154*
Take Me Out to the Ball Game, *943*
◆ Take the Money and Run, *390*
Take This Job and Shove It, *390*
Taken Away, *676*
Taking Care of Business, *390*
Taking My Turn, *943*
Taking of Beverly Hills, The, *124*
◆ Taking of Pelham One Two Three, The, *1022*
Taking the Heat, *676*
◆ **Tale of a Vampire,** *891*
◆ Tale of Mr. Jeremy Fisher and the Tale of Peter Rabbit, The, *209*
Tale of Ruby Rose, The, *676*
Tale of Springtime, A, *792*
◆ Tale of the Frog Prince, *209*
Tale of Two Chipmunks, A, *209*
◆ Tale of Two Cities, A (1935), *676*
Tale of Two Cities (1967), *676*
Tale of Two Cities, A (1980), *677*
◆ Tale of Two Cities, A (1991), *677*
Talent for the Game, *677*
◆ **Tales From Avonlea (TV series),** *209*
Tales from the Crypt, *892*
Tales from the Crypt (Series), *892*
Tales from the Darkside, The Movie, *892*
Tales from the Darkside, Vol. I, *892*
Tales of Beatrix Potter, *209*
◆ Tales of Hoffman, *943*
Tales of Ordinary Madness, *677*
Tales of Paris, *792*
Tales of Terror, *892*
Tales of the Unexpected, *1022*
Tales of Tomorrow (Vols. I - III), *1082*
Tales that Witness Madness, *892*
Talion, *1154*
◆ Talk of the Town, The, *390*
◆ Talk Radio, *677*
Talkin' Dirty After Dark, *391*
Talking Walls, *391*
◆ Tall Blond Man with One Black Shoe, The, *792*
Tall Guy, The, *391*
◆ Tall in the Saddle, *1154*
Tall Men, The, *1154*
Tall Story, *391*
◆ Tall T, The, *1154*
Talons of the Eagle, *124*
Tamarind Seed, The, *124*
Taming of the Shrew, The (1929), *391*
◆ Taming of the Shrew, The (1966), *391*

◆ Taming of the Shrew (1982), 391
Tammy and the Bachelor, 677
Tammy and the Doctor, 677
◆ Tampopo, 792
Tango and Cash, 124
Tango Bar, 792
Tank, 124
Tanner '88, 391
◆ Tap, 944
Tapeheads, 391
Taps, 677
Tarantula, 892
Tarantulas—The Deadly Cargo, 892
Taras Bulba, 125
Target, 125
Target Eagle, 125
Target: Favorite Son, 677
◆ Targets, 1022
◆ Taro, the Dragon Boy, 209
Tartuffe, 677
◆ Tarzan and His Mate, 125
Tarzan and the Green Goddess, 125
Tarzan and the Trappers, 125
Tarzan Escapes, 125
Tarzan Finds a Son, 125
Tarzan of the Apes, 125
Tarzan the Ape Man (1932), 125
Tarzan the Ape Man (1981), 125
Tarzan the Fearless, 125
Tarzan the Mighty, 125
Tarzan the Tiger, 126
Tarzan's New York Adventure, 126
Tarzan's Revenge, 126
Tarzan's Secret Treasure, 126
Task Force, 677
Taste for Killing, A, 126
Taste of Blood, A, 892
Taste of Honey, A, 677
Taste the Blood of Dracula, 892
Tatie Danielle, 792
Tattle Tale, 391
Tattoo, 677
Tattoo Connection, 126
◆ Taxi Blues, 792
Taxi Dancers, 678
◆ Taxi Driver, 1023
Taxi to the Toilet (see Taxi Zum Klo)
Taxi Zum Klo (Taxi to the Toilet), 793
Taxing Woman, A, 793
Taxing Woman's Return, A, 793
TBone N Weasel, 391
TC 2000, 1082
◆ Tchao Pantin, 793
◆ Tea and Sympathy, 678
Tea for Two, 944
Teachers, 391
Teacher's Pet, 392
Teahouse of the August Moon, The, 392
Teamster Boss: The Jackie Presser Story, 678
Tearaway, 678
Ted & Venus, 392
Teen Alien, 892
Teen Vamp, 392
Teen Witch, 392
Teen Wolf, 892
Teen Wolf, Too, 892
Teenage Bonnie and Klepto Clyde, 126
Teenage Confidential, 436
Teenage Monster (see Meteor Monster)
◆ Teenage Mutant Ninja Turtles, 209
Teenage Mutant Ninja Turtles: The Epic Begins, 209
Teenage Mutant Ninja Turtles II: The Secret of the Ooze, 209
Teenage Mutant Ninja Turtles III, 209
Teenage Zombies, 892
Telefon, 1023
Telegraph Trail, The, 1154
Telephone, The, 392
Television Parts Home Companion, 944
Tell It to the Judge, 392
Tell Me a Riddle, 678
Tell-Tale Heart, The, 893
Tell Them Willie Boy Is Here, 1155
Temp, The, 893
Tempest (1928), 678
Tempest (1982), 678
Tempest, The (1983), 678
Tempter, The, 893
10, 392
Ten Commandments, The (1923), 678
Ten Commandments, The (1956), 678
Ten Days That Shook the World (see October)
◆ Ten Days Wonder, 1023
◆ 10 from Your Show of Shows, 392
Ten Little Gall Force/Scramble Wars, 793
Ten Little Indians (1966), 1023
Ten Little Indians (1975), 1023
Ten Little Indians (1989), 1023
10 Million Dollar Getaway, The, 678
◆ 10 Rillington Place, 678
Ten to Midnight, 126
10 Violent Women, 126
Ten Wanted Men, 1155
Ten Who Dared, 210
Tenant, The, 1023
Tender Comrade, 679
◆ Tender Mercies, 679
Tender Trap, The, 392
Tender Years, The, 679
Tendres Cousines, 793
Tenebrae (see Unsane)
Tennessee Stallion, 126
Tennessee's Partner, 1155
Tentacles, 893
◆ Tenth Man, The, 679
Tenth Month, The, 679
Tenth Victim, The, 1082
Teorema, 793
Tepepa (see Blood and Guns)
◆ Tequila Sunrise, 126
Terminal Bliss, 679
Terminal Choice, 893
Terminal Entry, 1082
Terminal Island, 126
Terminal Man, The, 893
Terminator, The, 1082
◆ Terminator 2: Judgment Day, 1082
Termini Station, 679
◆ Terms of Endearment, 679
Terror, The, 893
Terror at London Bridge, 893
Terror at the Opera, 893
Terror at the Red Wolf Inn, 893
Terror by Night, 1023
Terror Circus (see Nightmare Circus)
Terror Creatures from the Grave, 893
Terror from the Year 5,000, 1082
Terror House (see Terror at the Red Wolf Inn)
Terror in Paradise, 126
Terror in the Aisles, 893
Terror in the Haunted House, 893
Terror in the Swamp, 893
Terror in the Wax Museum, 894
Terror of Dr. Hichcock, The (see Horrible Dr. Hichcock, The)
Terror of Mechagodzilla, 894
Terror of the Tongs, The, 126
Terror of Tiny Town, The, 1155
Terror on Alcatraz, 1023
Terror on the 40th Floor, 1023
Terror Out of the Sky, 894
Terror Squad, 127
Terror Stalks the Class Reunion, 894
◆ Terror Train, 894
Terror Vision, 1082
Terror Within, The, 894
Terror Within 2, The, 894
◆ Terrorists, The, 1023
Terromauts, The, 1082
Terry Fox Story, The, 679
◆ Tess, 679
Test of Love, A, 679
Test Pilot, 679
◆ Testament, 1082
Testament of Dr. Cordelier, The, 1
Testament of Dr. Mabuse, 1023
Testament of Orpheus, The, 793
Tetsuo: The Iron Man, 793
◆ Tex, 680
Tex and the Lord of the Deep, 11
◆ Tex Avery's Screwball Classics, 2
Tex Avery's Screwball Classics (Volume 2), 210
Tex Avery's Screwball Classics (volume 4), 210
Texas, 1155
Texas Across the River, 1155
Texas Carnival, 944
Texas Chainsaw Massacre, The, 8
Texas Chainsaw Massacre 2, The, 894
◆ Texas Cyclone, 1155
Texas Guns, 1155
Texas John Slaughter: Geronimo's Revenge, 1155
Texas John Slaughter: Stampede a Bitter Creek, 1155
Texas John Slaughter: Wild Times 1156
Texas Lady, 1156
◆ Texas Masquerade, 1156
◆ Texas Rangers, The, 1156
Texas Terror, 1156
Texas to Bataan, 1156
◆ Texasville, 680
Thank God It's Friday, 944
Thank You and Goodnight, 436
Thank Your Lucky Stars, 944
Thanksgiving Story, The, 210
Tharus, Son of Attila, 127
That Certain Thing, 392
That Certain Woman, 680
That Championship Season, 680
That Cold Day in the Park, 680
That Darn Cat, 210
That Forsyte Woman, 680
That Hamilton Woman, 680
That Lucky Touch, 392
◆ **That Man From Rio,** 793
That Midnight Kiss, 944
That Night, 680
◆ That Obscure Object of Desire, 79

hat Sinking Feeling, 392
hat Summer of White Roses, 680
hat Touch of Mink, 393
hat Uncertain Feeling, 393
hat Was Rock, 944
hat Was Then...This Is Now, 680
hat'll Be the Day, 944
hat's Action, 127
hat's Adequate, 393
hat's Dancing, 436
hat's Entertainment, 436
hat's Entertainment Part II, 436
hat's Entertainment! III, 436
hat's Life, 393
hat's My Baby, 680
hat's Singing: The Best of
Broadway, 944
heatre of Blood, 894
heatre of Death, 894
heir Only Chance, 210
helma & Louise, 127
helonious Monk: Straight, No
Chaser, 436
hem!, 1083
here Goes the Neighborhood, 393
here Was a Crooked Man, 1156
here's a Girl in My Soup, 393
here's No Business Like Show
Business, 944
here's No Time for Love, Charlie
Brown, 210
here's Nothing Out There, 894
herese, 793
herese and Isabelle, 794
hese Girls Won't Talk, 393
hese Three, 680
hey, 894
hey All Laughed, 393
hey Call It Sin, 680
hey Call Me Bruce?, 393
hey Call Me Hallelujah (see Guns for
Dollars)
hey Call Me Mister Tibbs, 127
hey Call Me Trinity, 1156
hey Came from Beyond Space, 1083
hey Came from Within, 895
hey Came to Cordura, 681
hey Died with Their Boots On,
1156
hey Drive by Night, 127
hey Got Me Covered, 393
hey Knew What They Wanted, 681
hey Live, 895
hey Live By Night, 681
hey Made Me a Criminal, 681
hey Meet Again, 681
hey Met in Bombay, 127
hey Might Be Giants, 1023
hey Only Kill Their Masters, 1024
hey Saved Hitler's Brain, 895
hey Shall Have Music, 944
hey Shoot Horses, Don't They?,
681
hey Still Call Me Bruce, 393
hey Watch (see They)
hey Went That-A-Way and
That-A-Way, 210
hey Were Expendable, 127
hey Won't Believe Me, 681
hey're Playing with Fire, 681
hief, The (1952), 1024
hief (1981), 127
hief of Bagdad, The (1924), 1083
hief of Bagdad, The (1940), 1083
hief of Baghdad (1978), 127

Thief of Hearts, 681
Thief Who Came to Dinner, The, 393
◆ **Thieves Like Us,** 681
Thieves of Fortune, 127
◆ Thin Blue Line, The, 436
◆ **Thin Ice,** 945
◆ Thin Man, The, 1024
Thin Man Goes Home, The, 1024
Thing Called Love, The, 681
◆ Thing (From Another World), The
(1951), 1083
◆ Thing, The (1982), 1083
Things Are Tough All Over, 393
◆ Things Change, 394
Things in Life, The (see Les Choses
de la Vie)
◆ Things to Come, 1083
Things We Did Last Summer, 394
Think Big, 394
Thinkin' Big, 394
Third Degree Burn, 1024
◆ Third Man, The, 1024
Third Man on the Mountain, 210
Third Solution, The, 794
Thirst, 895
Thirsty Dead, The, 895
13 at Dinner, 1024
13 Ghosts, 895
13 Rue Madeleine, 127
Thirteenth Floor, The, 895
Thirteenth Guest, The, 1024
30 Foot Bride of Candy Rock, The,
394
30 Is a Dangerous Age, Cynthia, 394
38 Vienna Before the Fall, 794
◆ 35 Up, 436
◆ Thirty-Nine Steps, The (1935), 1024
Thirty-Nine Steps, The (1959), 1024
Thirty-Nine Steps, The (1978), 1024
◆ Thirty Seconds Over Tokyo, 127
36 Fillette, 794
36 Hours, 681
◆ **Thirty-Two Short Films About
Glenn Gould,** 682
This Boy's Life, 682
This Could Be the Night, 394
◆ This Gun for Hire (1942), 128
This Gun for Hire (1991), 128
◆ This Happy Breed, 682
This Happy Feeling, 394
◆ This Is Elvis, 436
This Is My Life, 394
◆ This Is Spinal Tap, 394
This Is the Army, 945
This Island Earth, 1083
This Land Is Mine, 682
This Man Can't Die, 1156
◆ This Man Must Die, 794
This Property Is Condemned, 682
This Special Friendship, 794
This Sporting Life, 682
This Strange Passion (see El)
This Time For Keeps, 945
◆ Thomas Crown Affair, The, 128
◆ Thomas Graal's Best Child, 794
◆ Thomas Graal's Best Film, 794
Thomas the Tank Engine and friends,
210
Thompson's Last Run, 128
Thornbirds, The, 682
Thoroughbreds Don't Cry, 210
Thoroughly Modern Millie, 945
◆ Those Calloways, 211
Those Daring Young Men in Their
Jaunty Jalopies, 394

Those Endearing Young Charms, 394
Those Glory Glory Days, 682
Those Lips, Those Eyes, 945
◆ Those Magnificent Men in Their
Flying Machines, 394
Thou Shalt Not Kill...Except, 895
◆ Thousand Clowns, A, 395
Thousand Eyes of Dr. Mabuse, The,
1083
◆ Thousand Pieces of Gold, 1156
Thousands Cheer, 945
Thrashin', 128
◆ Threads, 682
Threat, The, 1024
Three Ages, The, 395
Three Amigos, 395
◆ Three Billy Goats Gruff and the
Three Little Pigs, The, 211
Three Broadway Girls, 395
◆ Three Brothers, 794
Three Bullets for a Long Gun, 1156
3 x 3 Eyes, Vols. 1–4, 895
Three Caballeros, The, 211
Three Came Home, 682
Three Charlies and a Phoney!, 395
Three Comrades, 682
Three Daring Daughters, 945
◆ Three Days of the Condor, 1025
Three Days to a Kill, 128
◆ Three Faces of Eve, The, 682
Three Faces West, 683
3:15—The Moment of Truth, 128
Three for Bedroom C, 395
Three for the Road, 395
Three Fugitives, 395
Three Godfathers, The, 1156
317th Platoon, The, 794
Three in the Attic, 395
Three in the Cellar, 395
Three in the Saddle, 1156
Three Kinds of Heat, 128
◆ Three Little Pigs, The, 211
Three Little Words, 945
◆ Three Lives of Thomasina, The, 211
Three Men and a Baby, 395
◆ Three Men and a Cradle, 794
Three Men and a Little Lady, 395
◆ Three Men from Texas, 1157
Three Men on a Horse, 395
Three Musketeers, The (1933), 128
Three Musketeers, The (1935), 128
Three Musketeers, The (1939), 396
Three Musketeers, The (1948), 128
◆ Three Musketeers, The (1973), 128
Three Musketeers, The (1993), 129
Three Ninjas, 211
Three Ninjas Kick Back, 211
Three Nuts in Search of a Bolt, 396
Three O'Clock High, 396
Three of Hearts, 683
Three on a Match, 683
Three on a Meathook, 895
Three Secrets, 683
◆ Three Smart Girls, 945
Three Smart Girls Grow Up, 945
Three Songs of Lenin, 436
Three Sovereigns for Sarah, 683
◆ Three Stooges, The (Volumes
1–10), 396
Three Strange Loves, 794
◆ 3:10 to Yuma, 1157
Three Texas Steers, 1157
Three the Hard Way, 129
Three Violent People, 1157
Three-Word Brand, The, 1157

Three Worlds of Gulliver, The, *1083*
◆ Threepenny Opera, The, *794*
Three's Trouble, *396*
Threesome, *396*
Threshold, *1083*
Thrill Hunter, *1157*
Thrill Killers, The, *895*
Thrill of a Romance, *945*
Thrill of It All, The, *396*
Thrilled to Death, *1025*
Thrillkill, *1025*
◆ Throne of Blood, *794*
Throne of Fire, The, *895*
Through a Glass Darkly, *795*
Through Naked Eyes, *129*
Through the Looking Glass, *211*
◆ Through the Wire, *436*
Throw Momma from the Train, *396*
◆ Thumbelina (1983), *211*
◆ Thumbelina (1989), *211*
Thunder Alley, *945*
Thunder and Lightning, *129*
Thunder Bay, *129*
Thunder in Paradise, *129*
Thunder in the City, *683*
Thunder Pass, *1157*
◆ Thunder Road, *129*
Thunder Run, *129*
Thunder Trail, *1157*
Thunder Warrior, *129*
Thunder Warrior II, *129*
Thunderball, *129*
Thunderbolt, *436*
◆ Thunderbolt and Lightfoot, *129*
◆ Thunderheart, *1025*
Thundering Herd, *1157*
Thursday's Game, *683*
THX 1138, *1084*
Tibet, *436*
Tick ... Tick ... Tick ..., *129*
Ticket of Leave Man, The, *895*
Ticket to Heaven, *683*
Tickle Me, *945*
Ticks, *895*
◆ Tidy Endings, *683*
Tie Me Up! Tie Me Down!, *795*
Tiger and The Pussycat, The, *795*
Tiger Bay, *683*
Tiger Town, *211*
Tiger Walks, A, *211*
Tiger Warsaw, *683*
Tiger Woman (see Perils of the Darkest Jungle)
Tiger's Tale, A, *396*
◆ Tight Little Island, *396*
◆ Tightrope, *1025*
Tigress, The, *130*
Till Death Do Us Part, *683*
Till Marriage Do Us Part, *795*
Till the Clouds Roll By, *946*
Till the End of Time, *683*
Till There Was You, *684*
Tilt, *396*
◆ Tim, *684*
◆ Time After Time, *1084*
◆ Time Bandits, *1084*
Time Bomb, *1025*
◆ Time Flies When You're Alive, *684*
Time Guardian, The, *1084*
◆ Time Machine, The, *1084*
Time of Destiny, A, *684*
◆ Time of the Gypsies, *795*
Time of Their Lives, The, *396*
Time of Your Life, The, *684*
Time Out For Love, *795*
Time Runner, *1084*
Time Stalkers, *1084*
Time Stands Still, *795*
Time to Die, A (1983), *130*
Time to Die, A (1990), *1025*
Time to Kill, *684*
Time to Love and a Time to Die, A, *684*
Time Trackers, *1084*
Time Travelers, The, *1084*
Time Walker, *895*
Time Warp (see Journey to the Center of Time)
Timerider, *130*
Times Square, *946*
Times to Come, *795*
◆ Tin Drum, The, *795*
Tin Man, *684*
◆ Tin Men, *396*
◆ Tin Star, The, *1157*
Tintorera, *895*
◆ **Tiny Toon Adventures,** *211*
◆ Tiny Toons Adventures: How I Spent my Vacation, *212*
◆ **Tito and Me,** *795*
TNT Jackson, *130*
To All a Good Night, *895*
◆ To All My Friends on Shore, *684*
◆ To Be or Not to Be (1942), *397*
◆ To Be or Not to Be (1983), *397*
To Catch a Killer, *1025*
To Catch a King, *1025*
◆ To Catch a Thief, *1025*
◆ **To Dance with the White Dog,** *684*
To Die For, *896*
To Die For 2: Son of Darkness, *896*
To Die Standing, *130*
◆ To Forget Venice, *795*
◆ To Have and Have Not, *130*
To Heal a Nation, *684*
To Hell and Back, *130*
To Kill a Clown, *1025*
◆ To Kill a Mockingbird, *684*
To Kill a Priest, *684*
To Live and Die in L.A., *130*
To Paris with Love, *397*
To Please a Lady, *130*
To Protect and Serve, *130*
To See Such Fun, *397*
◆ To Sir with Love, *685*
◆ To Sleep with Anger, *685*
To Sleep With a Vampire, *896*
To the Devil, a Daughter, *896*
◆ To the Last Man, *1157*
To the Shores of Tripoli, *130*
Toast of New Orleans, *946*
Toast of New York, The, *685*
Tobor the Great, *1084*
Tobruk, *130*
Toby and the Koala Bear, *212*
Toby McTeague, *212*
Toby Tyler, *212*
Today We Live, *685*
Todd Killings, The, *685*
Tokyo Decadence, *795*
Tokyo-Ga, *796*
Tokyo Joe, *130*
Tokyo Pop, *946*
◆ Tokyo Story, *796*
Tol'able David, *685*
Tom & Jerry: the Movie, *212*
Tom and Jerry Cartoon Festivals (Volume One), *212*
Tom and Jerry Cartoon Festivals (Volume Two), *212*
Tom and Jerry Cartoon Festivals (Volume Three), *212*
Tom and Jerry On Parade, *212*
Tom & Jerry's Cartoon Cavalcade, *212*
Tom and Jerry's Comic Capers, *21*
Tom & Jerry's Festival of Fun, *212*
Tom & Jerry's 50th Birthday Bash, *213*
Tom and Jerry's 50th Birthday Classics, *213*
Tom and Jerry's 50th Birthday Classics II, *213*
◆ Tom and Jerry's 50th Birthday Classics III, *213*
Tom Brown's School Days (1940), *685*
Tom Brown's Schooldays (1950),
Tom, Dick and Harry, *397*
◆ Tom Edison—The Boy Who Lit Up the World, *213*
Tom Horn, *1157*
◆ Tom Jones, *397*
Tom Sawyer (1973), *946*
Tom Sawyer (1973), *213*
Tom Thumb, *213*
Tomb, The, *896*
Tomb of Ligeia, *896*
Tomb of Torture, *896*
Tomboy, *130*
Tomboy and the Champ, *213*
Tombs of the Blind Dead, *896*
◆ **Tombstone,** *1157*
Tomcat: Dangerous Desires, *108*
Tomi Ungerer Library, The, *213*
Tommy, *946*
Tommy Chong Roast, The, *397*
Tommyknockers, The, *1084*
◆ Tomorrow, *685*
Tomorrow at Seven, *685*
◆ Tomorrow Is Forever, *685*
Tomorrow Never Comes, *686*
Tomorrow's Child, *686*
◆ Tong Tana, *437*
◆ Toni, *796*
Tonight and Every Night, *946*
Tonight for Sure, *397*
Tonio Kroger, *796*
Tonka, *213*
Tony Rome, *1025*
◆ Too Beautiful for You, *796*
Too Hot to Handle, *130*
Too Late the Hero, *131*
Too Many Girls, *946*
Too Much Sun, *397*
Too Outrageous, *686*
Too Scared to Scream, *1025*
Too Shy to Try, *796*
Toolbox Murders, The, *1026*
◆ Tootsie, *397*
Top Cat and the Beverly Hills Cats, *213*
Top Gun, *131*
◆ Top Hat, *946*
Top Secret, *397*
Topaz, *1026*
Topaze (1933), *397*
◆ **Topaze (1951),** *796*
◆ Topkapi, *1026*
◆ Topper, *397*
Topper Returns, *398*
Topper Takes a Trip, *398*
Topsy Turvy, *796*
◆ Tora! Tora! Tora!, *131*
Torch Song, *686*

Torch Song Trilogy, *686*
Torchlight, *686*
Torment, *1026*
Torn Apart, *686*
Torn Between Two Lovers, *686*
Torn Curtain, *1026*
Torpedo Alley, *131*
Torpedo Run, *131*
Torrents of Spring, *686*
Torso, *896*
Tortilla Flat, *686*
Torture Chamber of Baron Blood, The, *896*
Torture Chamber of Dr. Sadism, The, *896*
Torture Dungeon, *896*
Torture Garden, *896*
Total Exposure, *1026*
◆ Total Recall, *1084*
◆ Toto the Hero, *796*
Touch and Die, *1026*
Touch and Go, *398*
◆ Touch of Class, A, *398*
◆ Touch of Evil, *1026*
Touched, *686*
Touched by Love, *686*
Tough Enough, *131*
Tough Guys, *398*
Tough Guys Don't Dance, *686*
Tougher Than Leather, *131*
Tour of Duty, *131*
Tourist Trap, *1026*
Tous les Matins du Monde, *796*
Toute Une Nuit, *796*
Tovaritch, *398*
Tower of London (1939), *897*
Tower of London (1962), *897*
Tower of Screaming Virgins, The, *897*
◆ Towering Inferno, The, *131*
Town Called Hell, A, *131*
◆ Town Like Alice, A, *686*
Town That Dreaded Sundown, The, *1026*
Toxic Avenger, The, *897*
Toxic Avenger Part II, The, *897*
Toxic Avenger Part III: The Last Temptation of Toxie, The, *897*
Toy, The, *398*
Toy Soldiers (1983), *131*
Toy Soldiers (1991), *131*
Toys, *398*
Toys in the Attic, *687*
Traces of Red, *1026*
Track of the Moon Beast, *897*
Track 29, *1026*
Tracker, The, *1158*
Trackers, The, *1158*
Tracks, *687*
Trade Secrets, *1026*
Trader Tom of the China Seas, *131*
Trading Hearts, *398*
◆ Trading Places, *398*
Tragedy of a Ridiculous Man, *796*
◆ Tragedy of Flight 103: The Inside Story, The, *687*
Trail Beyond, The, *1158*
Trail Blazers, *1158*
◆ Trail Drive, *1158*
Trail of Robin Hood, *1158*
Trail of the Pink Panther, The, *398*
Trail of the Silver Spurs, *1158*
Trail Street, *1158*
Trailin' North, *1158*
Trailing Trouble, *1158*
◆ Train, The, *131*
Train Killer, The, *687*
Train Robbers, The, *1158*
Trained to Fight, *132*
Traitor, The, *1158*
◆ Tramp at the Door, *687*
Tramplers, The, *1158*
Trancers, *1085*
Trancers II (The Return of Jack Death), *1085*
Trancers III: Death Lives, *1085*
Trancers 4: Jack of Swords, *1085*
Transatlantic Merry-Go-Round, *946*
Transatlantic Tunnel, *1085*
Transformers, the Movie, *213*
Transmutations, *897*
Transylvania 6-5000, *399*
Transylvania Twist, *399*
Trap, The, *1026*
Trap Them and Kill Them, *897*
Trapeze, *687*
Trapped, *1027*
Trapper County War, *132*
Trash, *687*
Trauma, *897*
Traveling Man, *687*
Travelling North, *687*
Travels with My Aunt, *399*
Traxx, *132*
Treacherous Crossing, *1027*
◆ Treasure Island (1934), *213*
◆ Treasure Island (1950), *214*
◆ Treasure Island (1990), *214*
Treasure of Arne, *797*
Treasure of Pancho Villa, The, *1158*
Treasure of the Amazon, *132*
Treasure of the Four Crowns, *132*
◆ Treasure of the Sierra Madre, *132*
Treasure of the Yankee Zephyr, *132*
◆ Treasures of the Twilight Zone, *1085*
◆ Tree Grows in Brooklyn, A, *687*
◆ Tree of the Wooden Clogs, The, *797*
◆ Tremors, *897*
Trenchcoat, *399*
◆ Trespass, *132*
Trespasses, *687*
Trial, The, *687*
Trial & Error, *1027*
Trial of the Cantonsville Nine, The, *687*
Trial of the Incredible Hulk, *1085*
Tribes, *688*
Tribute, *688*
◆ **Tribute to a Bad Man,** *1159*
Trick or Treat (1982), *897*
Trick or Treat (1986), *897*
Tricks of the Trade, *399*
Trigger, Jr.,.*1159*
Trilogy of Terror, *898*
Trinity Is Still My Name, *1159*
◆ Trio, *688*
Trip, The, *688*
◆ Trip to Bountiful, The, *688*
Trip to Mars (see Flash Gordon: Mars Attacks the World)
Triple Impact, *132*
Triple Justice, *1159*
Triplecross, *399*
Tripods, *1085*
Tripwire, *132*
◆ Tristana, *797*
Triumph of Sherlock Holmes, The, *1027*
◆ Triumph of the Will, *437*
Triumph of the Spirit, *688*
Triumph, Tragedy & Rebirth: The Story of the Space Shuttle, *437*
Triumphs of a Man Called Horse, *1159*
Trojan Women, The, *688*
Troll, *1085*
Troll II, *898*
Troma's War, *132*
Tron, *1085*
Troop Beverly Hills, *399*
Tropic of Cancer, *688*
Tropical Heat, *1027*
◆ Tropical Snow, *132*
Trouble Along the Way, *688*
Trouble Bound, *1027*
◆ Trouble in Mind, *688*
Trouble in Paradise, *399*
Trouble in Texas, *1159*
Trouble in the Glen, *399*
Trouble with Angels, The, *399*
Trouble with Dick, The, *1085*
Trouble with Girls, The, *946*
◆ Trouble with Harry, The, *399*
Trouble with Spies, The, *399*
Trout, The (see La Truite)
Truck Turner, *132*
Truckstop Women, *132*
◆ True Believer, *1027*
True Colors, *688*
◆ True Confessions, *1027*
◆ True Grit, *1159*
True Heart Susie, *688*
True Identity, *399*
◆ True Love, *400*
◆ **True Romance,** *133*
True Stories, *400*
◆ True West, *689*
Trueblood, *689*
◆ Truly, Madly, Deeply, *689*
Truly Tasteless Jokes, *400*
◆ Trust, *689*
Trust Me, *400*
Truth About Women, The, *689*
◆ Truth or Dare, *437*
Truth or Die, *689*
Try and Get Me, *133*
Tuck Everlasting, *214*
Tucker: A Man and His Dream, *689*
Tuff Turf, *689*
Tukiki and His Search for a Merry Christmas, *214*
Tulips, *400*
Tulsa, *689*
Tulsa Kid, *1159*
Tumbleweeds, *1159*
Tune, The, *400*
Tune in Tomorrow, *400*
◆ Tunes of Glory, *689*
Tunnel, The, *689*
Tunnel of Love, The, *400*
Tunnelvision, *400*
Turk 182, *689*
Turkish Delight, *797*
Turn of the Screw, The (1989), *898*
◆ **Turn of the Screw (1992),** *898*
Turner and Hooch, *400*
◆ Turning Point, The, *689*
Turtle Beach, *690*
◆ Turtle Diary, *400*
Tusks, *133*
Tuttles of Tahiti, The, *400*
Tuxedo Warrior, *133*
TV Classics: Adventures of Robin Hood, The—TV Series, *133*
TV Classics: Annie Oakley, *1159*

TV Classics: Flash Gordon and the Planet of Death, *1085*
TV Classics: Jimmy Durante, *400*
TV Classics: Laurel & Hardy, *401*
TV Classics: Milton Berle, *401*
TV Turkeys, *401*
TV's Best Adventures of Superman, *1085*
TV's Greatest Bits, *401*
◆ Tweety and Sylvester, *214*
◆ 12 Angry Men, *690*
Twelve Chairs, The, *401*
Twelve Months, *214*
◆ Twelve O'Clock High, *133*
◆ **12:01,** *1086*
◆ Twentieth Century, *401*
Twenty Bucks, *401*
◆ 28 Up, *437*
◆ 25, Firemen's Street, *797*
◆ 25 X 5: The Continuing History of the Rolling Stones, *437*
Twenty-four Eyes, *797*
◆ 20 Million Miles to Earth, *1086*
◆ 29th Street, *401*
20,000 Leagues Under the Sea (1916), *1086*
◆ 20,000 Leagues Under the Sea (1954), *133*
Twenty Thousand Leagues Under the Sea (1972), *214*
Twenty-One, *690*
Twice a Judas, *1159*
Twice Dead, *1027*
◆ Twice in a Lifetime, *690*
Twice-Told Tales, *898*
◆ Twice Upon a Time, *214*
Twilight in the Sierras, *1159*
Twilight of the Cockroaches, *1086*
Twilight People, *898*
◆ Twilight Zone, The (TV Series), *1086*
Twilight Zone—The Movie, *898*
Twilight's Last Gleaming, *133*
Twin Peaks (Movie), *1027*
Twin Peaks (TV Series), *1027*
Twin Peaks: Fire Walk with Me, *1028*
◆ Twins, *401*
Twins of Evil, *898*
Twinsanity, *1028*
◆ Twist and Shout, *797*
Twisted, *1028*
Twisted: A Step Beyond Insanity, *690*
Twisted Nightmare, *898*
Twisted Obsession, *690*
Twister, *401*
Twitch of the Death Nerve, *898*
Two by Scorsese, *437*
◆ Two Daughters, *797*
◆ Two English Girls, *797*
Two Evil Eyes, *898*
Two-Faced Woman, *401*
◆ Two-Fisted Law, *1159*
◆ Two for the Road, *401*
Two for the Seesaw, *690*
Two Girls and a Sailor, *946*
Two Houses of Keaton, *402*
200 Motels, *946*
Two Jakes, The, *1028*
Two Lost Worlds, *133*
Two Men and a Wardrobe, *797*
Two-Minute Warning, *1028*
Two Moon July, *947*
Two Moon Junction, *690*
Two Mrs. Carrolls, The, *1028*
Two Mules for Sister Sara, *1160*
Two of a Kind (1951), *1028*
◆ Two of a Kind (1982), *690*
Two of a Kind (1983), *402*
Two of Us, The, *797*
Two-Reelers: Comedy Classics #1, *402*
Two-Reelers: Comedy Classics #2, *402*
Two Rode Together, *1160*
Two Sisters from Boston, *947*
2,000 Maniacs, *898*
◆ 2001: A Space Odyssey, *1086*
◆ 2010, *1086*
2020 Texas Gladiators, *1086*
Two Tickets to Broadway, *947*
Two to Tango, *133*
Two Top Bananas, *402*
◆ Two-Way Stretch, *402*
Two Weeks in Another Town, *690*
Two Weeks to Live, *402*
Two Weeks with Love, *947*
◆ Two Women, *797*
Two Worlds of Jennie Logan, The, *1086*
Tycoon, *133*
◆ U2: Rattle and Hum, *437*
Ub Iwerks Cartoon Festival Vol. I–V, *214*
Ubu and the Great Gidouille, *798*
UFO—Volumes I and II, *1086*
◆ Uforia, *402*
◆ Ugetsu, *798*
Ugly American, The, *690*
Ugly Dachshund, The, *214*
UHF, *402*
Ulterior Motives, *133*
Ultimate Desires, *1028*
Ultimate Warrior, The, *1087*
Ultraviolet, *133*
Ulysses, *133*
◆ Ulzana's Raid, *1160*
◆ Umberto D, *798*
◆ Umbrellas of Cherbourg, The, *798*
◆ Un Chien Andalou, *690*
◆ **Un Coeur En Hiver,** *798*
Un Singe en Hiver (A Monkey in Winter), *798*
Unapproachable, The, *691*
◆ Unbearable Lightness of Being, The, *691*
Unbelievable Truth, The, *691*
Unborn, The, *898*
Unborn II, The, *898*
Uncaged, *1028*
Uncanny, The, *899*
◆ Uncle Buck, *402*
◆ Uncommon Valor, *134*
Undefeatable, *134*
Undefeated, The, *1160*
Under California Stars, *1160*
Under Capricorn, *1028*
Under Earth (see Debajo del Mundo)
Under Fire, *134*
Under Investigation, *1028*
Under Mexicali Stars, *1160*
Under Milk Wood, *691*
◆ Under Siege, *134*
Under Suspicion, *1028*
Under Texas Skies, *1160*
Under the Biltmore Clock, *691*
Under the Boardwalk, *691*
Under the Cherry Moon, *691*
Under the Gun, *691*
Under the Rainbow, *402*
◆ **Under the Roofs of Paris,** *798*
Under the Sun of Satan, *798*
◆ Under the Volcano, *691*
Under Western Stars, *1160*
Undercover, *134*
Undercover Blues, *403*
Undercurrent, *691*
Undergrads, The, *214*
Underground (1976), *437*
Underground (1990), *1029*
Underground Aces, *403*
Undersea Kingdom, *1087*
Understudy, The: Graveyard Shift II, *899*
Undertaker and His Pals, The, *899*
Underwater!, *134*
Underworld (1927), *691*
Underworld (1985) (see Transmutations)
Underworld Story, *1029*
Underworld U.S.A., *691*
Une Partie De Plaisir, *798*
Unearthly, The, *899*
Unexpected Encounters, *691*
Unexpected Guest, *1160*
Unfaithfully Yours (1948), *403*
Unfaithfully Yours (1984), *403*
Unfinished Piece for a Mechanical Piano (see Unfinished Piece for the Player Piano)
◆ **Unfinished Piece for the Player Piano, An,** *798*
Unforgiven, The (1960), *1160*
◆ Unforgiven (1992), *1160*
Unholy, The, *899*
Unholy Rollers, *691*
Unholy Three, *1029*
Unicorn, The, *214*
Unidentified Flying Oddball, *214*
◆ Uninvited, The (1944), *1029*
Uninvited, The (1987), *899*
Uninvited, The (1993), *1160*
Union City, *1029*
Union Pacific, *1160*
Union Station, *1029*
Universal Soldier, *134*
Unkissed Bride, *403*
◆ Unknown Chaplin, *437*
Unknown World, *1087*
Unlawful Entry, *1029*
◆ Unmarried Woman, An, *691*
Unnamable, The, *899*
Unnamable II, The, *899*
Unnatural, *1029*
◆ Unnatural Causes, *692*
Unremarkable Life, An, *692*
Unsane, *899*
Unseen, The, *899*
Unsettled Land, *692*
Unsinkable Donald Duck, The, *214*
Unsinkable Molly Brown, The, *947*
Unspeakable Acts, *692*
◆ Untamed Heart, *692*
Until September, *692*
Until the End of the World, *1087*
Until They Sail, *692*
◆ Untouchables, The, *134*
Untouchables, The: Scarface Mob (TV), *134*
Up!, *403*
Up Against the Wall, *692*
Up from the Depths, *899*
Up in Arms, *403*
◆ Up in Smoke, *403*
Up Periscope, *134*
Up the Academy, *403*

◆ Up the Creek (1958), *403*
Up the Creek (1984), *403*
Up the Down Staircase, *403*
Up the Sandbox, *403*
Up Your Alley, *403*
Up Your Anchor, *404*
Uphill All the Way, *404*
◆ Upstairs, Downstairs, *692*
Uptown New York, *692*
Uptown Saturday Night, *404*
◆ Uranus, *798*
Urban Cowboy, *692*
Urban Warriors, *134*
◆ Urge to Kill, *692*
Urinal, *692*
Urotsukidoji: Legend of the Overfiend, *799*
Urotsukidoji II: Legend of the Demon Womb, *799*
Urusei Yatsura (TV Series) Vols. 1–45, *799*
◆ Urusei Yatsura: Beautiful Dreamer, *799*
Urusei Yatsura: Inaba the Dreammaker, *799*
◆ Urusei Yatsura: Only You, *799*
◆ Urusei Yatsura: Remember Love, *799*
◆ Used Cars, *404*
Used People, *404*
Users, The, *692*
Utah, *1160*
Utilities, *404*
Utopia (see Atoll K)
◆ UTU, *134*
Utz, *693*
V. I. Warshawski, *1029*
V.I.P.s, The, *693*
Vacation (see National Lampoon's Vacation)
Vagabond, *799*
Vagabond Lover, The, *947*
Vagrant, The, *404*
Valdez Is Coming, *1160*
Valentina, *799*
Valentino, *693*
Valentino Returns, *693*
Valet Girls, *404*
Valley, The, *799*
Valley Girl, *404*
Valley Obscured by Clouds (see Valley, The)
Valley of Fire, *1161*
Valley of Gwangi, *1087*
Valley of the Dolls, *693*
Valley of the Sun, *1161*
Valmont, *693*
Vals, The, *404*
Vamp, *899*
Vamping, *1029*
Vampire, The, *899*
Vampire at Midnight, *899*
Vampire Bat, The, *899*
Vampire Happening, *900*
Vampire Hookers, *900*
Vampire Hunter D, *900*
Vampire Lovers, The, *900*
Vampire Men of the Lost Planet (see Horror of the Blood Monsters)
Vampire Over London, *404*
Vampire Princess Miyu, *799*
Vampires, The (1915), *799*
Vampires, The (1964) (see Goliath and the Vampires)
Vampires Always Ring Twice, *900*
Vampires from Outer Space, *900*
Vampire's Kiss, *900*
◆ Vampyr, *800*
Vampyres, *900*
Van, The, *404*
Van Gogh, *800*
◆ Vanishing, The (1988), *800*
Vanishing, The (1993), *1029*
Vanishing Act, *693*
Vanishing American, The, *1161*
Vanishing Point, *135*
Vanishing Prairie, The, *437*
Vanity Fair, *693*
Varan, the Unbelievable, *900*
◆ Variety, *800*
◆ Variety Lights, *800*
Vasectomy, *404*
Vault of Horror, *900*
Vega$, *135*
◆ Velvet Touch, The, *693*
◆ **Velvet Underground, The: Velvet Redux—Live MCMXCIII,** *437*
Velvet Vampire, The, *900*
◆ Velveteen Rabbit, The, *215*
Vendetta, *135*
Vengeance, *135*
Vengeance Is Mine (1976), *135*
◆ Vengeance Is Mine (1979), *800*
Vengeance Valley, *1161*
◆ Venice/Venice, *693*
Venom, *900*
Venus in Furs, *135*
◆ Venus Wars, The, *800*
Vera Cruz, *1161*
◆ Verdict, The, *693*
Verne Miller, *135*
Vernon, Florida, *437*
Veronika Voss, *800*
◆ Vertigo, *1029*
◆ Very Best of Bugs Bunny: Volume 1, The, *215*
◆ Very Best of Bugs Bunny: Volume 2, The, *215*
◆ Very Best of Bugs Bunny: Volume 3, The, *215*
◆ Very Best of Bugs Bunny: Volume 4, The, *215*
◆ Very Brady Christmas, A, *215*
Very Curious Girl, A, *800*
Very Edge, The, *693*
Very Funny, Charlie Brown, *215*
Very Merry Cricket, A, *215*
◆ Very Old Man with Enormous Wings, A, *800*
Very Private Affair, A, *800*
Vibes, *1087*
Vice Academy, *404*
Vice Academy 2, *404*
Vice Academy III, *404*
Vice Squad, *135*
Vice Versa, *404*
Vicious, *135*
Victim, *693*
Victim of Beauty, *1030*
Victim of Love, *1030*
Victimless Crimes, *1030*
◆ Victor/Victoria, *405*
Victory, *135*
Video Wonders: Home for a Dinosaur/The Monster Under My Bed, *215*
Video Wonders: Maxwell Mouse/The Great Bunny Race, *215*
Videodrome, *900*
Vietnam, Texas, *135*
◆ Vietnam War Story, *694*
◆ Vietnam War Story—Part Two, *694*
View to a Kill, A, *135*
Vigil, *800*
Vigilantes Are Coming!, *1161*
Vigilantes of Boomtown, *1161*
Viking Women and the Sea Serpent, The (see Saga of the Viking Women and Their Voyage to the Waters of the Great Sea Serpent, The)
Vikings, The, *135*
Villa Rides, *1161*
◆ Village of the Damned, *900*
Village of the Giants, *900*
Villain Still Pursued Her, The, *135*
◆ Vincent and Theo, *694*
◆ Vincent, François, Paul and the Others, *801*
◆ Vincent: The Life and Death of Vincent Van Gogh, *438*
Vindicator, The, *1087*
Violated, *136*
Violence at Noon, *801*
Violent Breed, The, *136*
Violent Men, The, *1161*
Violent Years, The, *136*
Violets Are Blue, *694*
Viper, *136*
Virgin Among the Living Dead, A, *901*
Virgin and the Gypsy, The, *694*
Virgin High, *405*
Virgin of Nuremberg, *901*
Virgin Queen, The, *694*
Virgin Queen of St. Francis High, The, *405*
◆ Virgin Soldiers, The, *694*
◆ Virgin Spring, The, *801*
Virginia City, *1161*
Virginian, The (1923), *1161*
◆ Virginian, The (1929), *1161*
◆ Viridiana, *801*
Virus, *1087*
Virus Knows No Morals, A, *801*
Vision Quest, *694*
◆ Visions of Light: The Art of Cinematography, *438*
Visitants, The, *1087*
Visiting Hours, *901*
Visitor, The, *1087*
Visitors, The, *901*
Vital Signs, *694*
Viva Knievel, *136*
Viva Las Vegas, *947*
◆ **Viva Maria!,** *801*
Viva Max!, *405*
◆ Viva Villa!, *1162*
◆ Viva Zapata!, *694*
Vivacious Lady, *405*
Vixen, *405*
Voices, *694*
◆ Voices of Sarafina, *438*
Volere Volare, *801*
◆ Volpone, *801*
Volunteers, *405*
◆ Von Ryan's Express, *136*
Voodoo Dawn, *901*
Voodoo Dolls, *901*
Voodoo Woman, *901*
Voulez Vous Danser avec Moi? (Will You Dance with Me?), *801*
Voyage, *1030*
Voyage en Ballon (Stowaway to the Stars), *801*
Voyage in Italy, *801*

Voyage of Terror: The Achille Lauro Affair, 694
◆ Voyage of the Damned, 694
◆ Voyage 'Round My Father, A, 695
Voyage to the Bottom of the Sea, 1087
Voyage to the Prehistoric Planet, 1087
Voyager, 695
Vultures, 901
W, 1030
◆ W. C. Fields Straight Up, 438
Wackiest Ship in the Army, The, 405
Wacko, 405
Wacky World of Wills and Burke, The, 405
◆ Wages of Fear, The, 801
Wagner, 947
Wagon Train (TV Series), 1162
Wagon Wheels, 1162
Wagon Wheels Westward, 1162
◆ Wagonmaster, 1162
◆ Wait Until Dark, 1030
Wait Until Spring, Bandini, 695
Waiting, 695
Waiting for the Light, 695
Waiting for the Moon, 695
Waiting Woman (see Secrets of Women)
Waitress, 405
◆ Wake Island, 136
◆ Wake of the Red Witch, 136
Walk, Don't Run, 405
Walk in the Spring Rain, A, 695
◆ Walk in the Sun, A, 136
Walk Into Hell, 136
Walk Like a Man, 405
Walk on the Wild Side, 695
Walk Softly, Stranger, 1030
Walker, 695
◆ Walking on Air, 215
Walking Tall, 136
Walking Tall Part II, 136
Walking Tall: The Final Chapter (see Final Chapter — Walking Tall)
◆ Wall, The, 802
◆ Wall Street, 695
Wall Street Cowboy, 1162
Walls of Glass, 695
Walt Disney Christmas, A, 215
Waltz King, The, 215
◆ Waltz of the Toreadors, 405
Waltz Through the Hills, 216
Waltzes from Vienna, 406
Wanda Nevada, 136
Wanderer, The, 802
◆ Wanderers, The, 695
Wannabes, 802
◆ Wannsee Conference, The, 802
Wanted: Dead or Alive, 136
Wanted: Dead or Alive (TV Series), 1162
◆ Wanton Contessa, The, 802
War and Peace (1956), 695
◆ War and Peace (1968), 802
War and Remembrance, 696
War Between the Planets (see Planet on the Prowl)
War Boy, The, 137
◆ War Game, the, 696
War Lord, The, 137
War Lover, The, 696
War of the Colossal Beast, 1088
War of the Gargantuas, 1088
◆ War of the Roses, The, 406
War of the Wildcats, 1162
◆ War of the Worlds, The, 1088
War Party, 137
War Requiem, 696
◆ **War Room, The,** 438
War Wagon, The, 1162
Warbirds, 137
Warbus, 137
◆ Wargames, 1088
Warlock (1959), 1162
Warlock (1988), 901
Warlock: The Armageddon, 901
Warlords, 901
Warlords of Hell, 137
Warlords of the 21st Century, 1088
Warm Nights on a Slow Moving Train, 696
Warm Summer Rain, 696
Warning, The, 137
◆ Warning Shadows (1923), 696
Warning Shadows (1933), 1030
Warning Sign, 901
Warrior and the Sorceress, The, 1088
Warrior of the Lost World, 1088
Warrior Queen, 137
Warriors, The (1955), 137
◆ Warriors, The (1979), 137
Warriors From Hell, 137
Warriors from the Magic Mountain, 802
Warriors of the Apocalypse, 1088
Warriors of the Wasteland, 1088
◆ Warriors of the Wind, 1088
Warriors Rest (see Le Repos du Guerrier)
Wash, The, 696
Washington Affair, The, 696
◆ Wasn't That a Time!, 438
Wasp Woman, 901
Watch It, 696
Watch Me When I Kill, 901
◆ Watch on the Rhine, 696
Watch the Birdie, 406
Watched!, 137
Watcher in the Woods, The, 901
Watchers, 1088
Watchers II, 901
Water, 406
Water Babies, The, 216
Water Engine, The, 696
Water Rustlers, 1162
◆ Waterdance, The, 696
Waterfront, 697
Waterhole #3, 1163
◆ Waterland, 697
Waterloo, 697
◆ Waterloo Bridge, 697
Watermelon Man, 406
◆ Watership Down, 1088
◆ Wavelength, 1088
Wax, 1088
Waxwork, 902
Waxwork II: Lost in Time, 902
Waxworks, 802
Way Ahead, The (see Immortal Battalion, The)
Way Back Home, 406
Way Down East, 697
◆ Way Out West, 406
Way We Were, The, 697
Way West, The, 1163
Wayne's World, 406
Wayne's World 2, 406
◆ We All Loved Each Other So Much, 802
We Are No Angels, 1163
We Are the Children, 697
We Dive at Dawn, 137
◆ We of the Never Never, 137
We the Living, 802
We Think the World of You, 406
Web of Deceit, 1030
Webber's World, 406
Wedding, A, 407
◆ **Wedding, The,** 802
Wedding Banquet, The, 407
◆ Wedding in Blood, 802
◆ Wedding in Galilee, A, 802
Wedding in White, 697
Wedding March, The, 697
Wedding Party, The, 407
Wedding Rehearsal, 407
◆ Wee Willie Winkie, 216
Weeds, 697
Weekend, 803
Weekend at Bernie's, 407
Weekend at Bernie's II, 407
Weekend at the Waldorf, 697
Weekend Pass, 407
Weekend War, 697
Weekend Warriors, 407
Weep No More My Lady, 1030
Weird Science, 407
Welcome Home, 698
◆ Welcome Home, Roxy Carmichael, 407
Welcome to 18, 407
Welcome to L.A., 698
Welcome to Spring Break, 902
Well, The, 698
Well-Digger's Daughter, The, 803
We're Back! A Dinosaur's Story, 216
We're Going to Eat You!, 902
We're in the Legion Now, 137
We're No Angels (1955), 407
We're No Angels (1989), 408
We're Not Married, 408
We're Talking Serious Money, 408
Werewolf in a Girl's Dormitory, 902
Werewolf of London, 902
Werewolf of Washington, 902
Werewolf Versus the Vampire Woman, The (see Blood Moon)
Werewolves on Wheels, 902
West of Texas, 1163
West of the Divide, 1163
West of the Law, 1163
West of Zanzibar, 1030
West Point Story, The, 947
◆ West Side Story, 947
Western Union, 1163
◆ Westerner, The, 1163
◆ Westfront 1918, 803
Westward Ho, 1163
Westward Ho, the Wagons, 216
◆ **Westward the Women,** 1163
◆ Westworld, 1089
Wet and Wild Summer, 408
Wet Gold, 138
Wetherby, 698
Whale for the Killing, A, 698
Whales of August, The, 698
What a Nightmare, Charlie Brown, 216
What About Bob?, 408
What Comes Around, 698
What Do You Say to a Naked Lady?, 408
What Ever Happened to Baby Jane?, 902

What Have I Done to Deserve This?, 803
What Have We Learned, Charlie Brown?, 216
What Next, Charlie Brown?, 216
What! No Beer?, 408
What Price Glory, 408
What Price Hollywood?, 698
What Waits Below, 902
Whatever Happened to Aunt Alice?, 902
What's Eating Gilbert Grape?, 408
What's Love Got to Do with It?, 698
What's New, Pussycat?, 408
What's the Matter with Helen?, 902
What's Up, Doc?, 408
What's Up Doc?—A Salute To Bugs Bunny, 216
What's Up Front, 408
What's Up, Tiger Lily?, 408
Wheel of Fortune, 409
Wheeler Dealers, The, 409
Wheels of Fire, 138
Wheels of Terror, 138
When a Man Loves a Woman, 698
When a Man Rides Alone, 1163
When a Man Sees Red, 1163
When a Stranger Calls, 1030
When a Stranger Calls Back, 1031
When a Woman Ascends the Stairs, 803
When Comedy Was King, 409
When Dinosaurs Ruled the Earth, 1089
When Father Was Away on Business, 803
When Gangland Strikes, 138
When Harry Met Sally, 409
When He's Not a Stranger, 698
When Ladies Meet, 698
When Lightning Strikes, 138
When the Clouds Roll By, 409
When the Legends Die, 1163
When the Party's Over, 699
When the Screaming Stops, 902
When the Time Comes, 699
When the Whales Came, 699
When the Wind Blows, 1089
When Things Were Rotten (TV Series), 409
When Time Ran Out!, 1031
When Wolves Cry, 699
When Women Had Tails, 409
When Women Lost Their Tails, 409
When Worlds Collide, 1089
When Your Lover Leaves, 699
When's Your Birthday?, 409
Where Angels Fear to Tread, 699
Where Are the Children?, 1031
Where Eagles Dare, 138
Where East Is East, 138
Where Love Has Gone, 699
Where Sleeping Dogs Lie, 1031
Where the Boys Are, 409
Where the Boys Are '84, 409
Where the Buffalo Roam, 409
Where the Day Takes You, 699
◆ Where the Green Ants Dream, 803
Where the Heart Is, 699
Where the Lilies Bloom, 216
◆ Where the Red Fern Grows, 216
Where the River Runs Black, 1089
Where the Spirit Lives, 699
Where Trails End, 1164
Where Were You When the Lights Went Out?, 409
◆ Where's Piccone?, 803
◆ Where's Poppa?, 409
Which Way Home, 138
◆ Which Way Is Up?, 410
Which Way to the Front?, 410
Whiffs, 410
While the City Sleeps, 138
Whiskey Galore (see Tight Little Island)
Whisper Kills, A, 902
Whispering Shadow, The, 138
Whispers, 1031
Whispers in the Dark, 1031
◆ Whistle Blower, The, 1031
Whistle Down the Wind, 216
Whistle Stop, 138
Whistling in Brooklyn, 410
Whistling in Dixie, 410
Whistling in the Dark, 410
White Buffalo, 1164
White Cargo, 699
White Christmas, 947
◆ White Cliffs of Dover, The, 699
White Comanche, 1164
◆ White Dawn, The, 138
White Dog, 700
◆ White Fang, 217
White Fang 2: Myth of the White Wolf, 217
White Fang and the Hunter, 217
White Ghost, 138
◆ White Gold, 1031
◆ White Heat, 138
White Hot, 138
White Hot: The Mysterious Murder of Thelma Todd, 1031
◆ White Hunter Black Heart, 700
White Legion, 700
◆ White Lie, 700
White Light, 1089
White Lightning, 139
White Line Fever, 139
White Mama, 700
◆ White Men Can't Jump, 410
White Mischief, 700
◆ White Nights (1957), 803
White Nights (1985), 700
White of the Eye, 1031
White Palace, 700
White Paws (see Pattes Blanches)
White Phantom, 139
White Pongo (a.k.a. Blond Gorilla), 902
White Rose, The (1923), 700
White Rose, The (1983), 803
White Sands, 700
White Seal, The, 217
White Shadows in the South Seas, 700
White Sheik, The, 803
White Sister, The, 700
White Tower, The, 701
White Water Summer, 139
White Wolves: A Cry in the Wild II, 139
◆ White Zombie, 903
Whitewater Sam, 217
Who Am I This Time?, 410
◆ Who Are the Debolts and Where Did They Get 19 Kids?, 438
Who Done It?, 410
◆ Who Framed Roger Rabbit, 410
◆ Who Is Killing the Great Chefs of Europe?, 410
◆ Who Is the Black Dahlia?, 1031
◆ Who Killed Baby Azaria?, 701
Who Killed Mary What's 'Er Name?, 1031
Who Shot Pat?, 701
Who Slew Auntie Roo?, 903
Whodunit?, 1031
◆ Who'll Stop the Rain, 139
Wholly Moses!, 410
Whoopee, 947
Whoopee Boys, The, 411
Whoops Apocalypse, 411
Whore, 701
◆ Who's Afraid of Virginia Woolf?, 701
Who's Got the Action?, 411
Who's Harry Crumb?, 411
Who's Minding the Mint?, 411
Who's That Girl, 411
Who's That Knocking at My Door?, 701
Who's the Man?, 411
◆ **Who's Who**, 411
Whose Child Am I?, 701
◆ Whose Life Is It, Anyway?, 701
◆ Why Didn't They Ask Evans?, 1032
Why Me?, 139
Why Shoot the Teacher?, 701
Wicked, The, 903
Wicked Lady, The (1945), 701
Wicked Lady, The (1983), 139
Wicked Stepmother, The, 903
◆ Wicker Man, The, 903
Wide Sargasso Sea, 701
Widow Couderc, 803
◆ Wife! Be Like a Rose!, 803
Wife Vs. Secretary, 701
Wifemistress, 804
◆ Wilbur and Orville: The First to Fly, 217
Wilby Conspiracy, The, 701
Wild and Woody, 217
Wild Angels, The, 139
Wild at Heart, 702
Wild Beasts, The, 903
◆ Wild Bunch, The, 1164
Wild Cactus, 139
Wild Card, 1032
◆ Wild Child, The (L'Enfant Sauvage), 804
Wild Duck, The, 702
Wild Flower, 702
◆ Wild Frontier, 1164
Wild Geese, The, 139
Wild Geese II, 139
Wild Guitar, 702
◆ Wild Hearts Can't Be Broken, 217
Wild Horse Hank, 217
Wild in the Country, 702
Wild in the Streets, 1089
Wild Life, The, 411
Wild Man, 139
Wild One, The, 139
Wild Orchid, 702
Wild Orchid 2: Two Shades of Blue, 702
Wild Orchids, 702
Wild Pair, The, 140
Wild Palms, 1089
Wild Party, The (1929), 702
Wild Party, The (1975), 702
Wild Ride, The, 702
Wild Rose, 702

◆ Wild Rovers, The, 1164
◆ Wild Strawberries, 804
Wild Thing, 702
Wild Times, 1164
◆ Wild West (1946), 1164
Wild West (1993), 411
◆ Wild, Wild West, The (TV series), 1164
Wild Wild West Revisited, The, 1164
Wild Women of Wongo, 1089
Wild World of Batwoman, The, 1089
Wildcats, 411
Wilder Napalm, 411
Wilderness Family, Part 2, The, 217
Wildfire (1945), 1164
Wildfire (1988), 703
Wilding, The Children of Violence, 140
Will, G. Gordon Liddy, 703
◆ Will Penny, 1164
Will You Dance With Me? (see Voulez Vous Danser Avec Moi?)
Willa, 703
Willard, 903
Willie and Phil, 412
Willie McBean and His Magic Machine, 217
◆ Willie, the Operatic Whale, 217
Willies, The, 903
Willow, 1089
Willy Wonka and the Chocolate Factory, 217
Wilma, 703
◆ **Wilson,** 703
Wimps, 412
Win, Place or Steal, 412
Winchester '73, 1165
◆ Wind, The (1928), 703
Wind, The (1986), 1032
Wind (1992), 140
◆ Wind and the Lion, The, 140
◆ Wind in the Willows, The (1949), 217
◆ Wind in the Willows, The (1983), 218
Windjammer, 140
Windmills of the Gods, 703
Windom's Way, 703
Window, The, 1032
Window Shopping, 804
Windrider, 140
Winds of Jarrah, The, 703
◆ Winds of Kitty Hawk, The, 703
Winds of the Wasteland, 1165
Winds of War, The, 703
◆ Windwalker, 1165
Windy City, 703
◆ Wing and a Prayer, A, 140
◆ Wings, 140
◆ Wings of Desire, 804
◆ Wings of Eagles, The, 703
Wings of Fame, 412
Winners of the West, 1165
Winners Take All, 140
Winnie the Pooh and a Day for Eeyore, 218
◆ Winnie the Pooh and the Blustery Day, 218
◆ Winnie the Pooh and the Honey Tree, 218
◆ Winnie the Pooh and Tigger Too, 218
Winning, 140
Winning of the West, 1165
Winning Team, The, 704
◆ Winslow Boy, The, 704
◆ Winter Kills, 704
Winter Light, 804
Winter Meeting, 704
Winter of Our Dreams, 704
Winter People, 704
Winterset, 704
Wintertime, 947
Wired, 704
Wired to Kill, 1089
Wisdom, 140
◆ Wise Blood, 704
Wise Guys, 412
◆ Wish You Were Here, 412
Wishful Thinking, 412
Wistful Widow of Wagon Gap, The, 412
Witchboard, 903
Witchboard 2, 903
Witchcraft, 903
Witchcraft II, 903
Witchcraft III, The Kiss of Death, 903
Witchcraft IV, 903
Witchcraft V: Dance with the Devil, 903
Witchcraft Through the Ages (HAXAN), 804
Witchery, 903
◆ Witches, The, 1089
Witches' Brew, 412
◆ Witches of Eastwick, The, 412
Witching, The (Necromancy), 904
Witching Time, 904
Witch's Mirror, The, 904
Witchtrap, 904
With Honors, 412
With Six You Get Eggroll, 412
◆ Withnail and I, 412
◆ Without a Clue, 413
Without a Trace, 1032
◆ Without Love, 413
Without Reservations, 413
Without Warning, 1090
◆ Without Warning: The James Brady Story, 704
◆ Without You I'm Nothing, 413
◆ Witness, 1032
◆ Witness for the Prosecution (1957), 1032
Witness for the Prosecution (1982), 1032
Wives Under Suspicion, 704
Wiz, The, 948
Wiz Kid, The, 413
Wizard, The, 218
Wizard of Gore, The, 904
Wizard of Loneliness, The, 704
Wizard of Mars, The, 1090
◆ Wizard of Oz, The, 218
Wizard of Speed and Time, The, 413
Wizard of the Lost Kingdom, 1090
Wizard of the Lost Kingdom II, 1090
Wizards, 1090
Wolf at the Door, 804
Wolf Call, 948
◆ Wolf Man, The, 904
Wolfen, 904
Wolfheart's Revenge, 1165
Wolfman, 904
Wolfman: A Cinematic Scrapbook, 438
Wolves, The, 804
Woman Called Golda, A, 705
Woman Called Moses, A, 705
Woman Her Men and Her Futon, A, 705
Woman Hunt, The, 140
◆ Woman in Flames, A, 804
Woman in Green, The, 1032
◆ Woman in Red, The, 413
◆ Woman in the Dunes, 804
Woman in the Moon (a.k.a. Girl in the Moon; By Rocket to the Moon), 805
◆ Woman Is a Woman, A, 805
◆ Woman Next Door, The, 805
Woman Obsessed, A, 1032
Woman of Affairs, A, 705
Woman of Desire, 1032
Woman of Distinction, A, 413
◆ Woman of Paris, A, 705
Woman of Substance, A, 705
Woman of the Town, 1165
◆ Woman of the Year, 413
◆ Woman Rebels, A, 705
Woman Times Seven, 705
◆ Woman Under the Influence, A, 705
Woman with a Past, 705
Woman without Love, A, 805
Woman's Face, A, 705
Woman's Secret, A, 1032
◆ Woman's Tale, A, 705
◆ Women, The, 413
◆ Women & Men: Stories of Seduction, 706
◆ Women & Men 2, 706
Women in Cell Block 9, 140
◆ Women in Love, 706
Women of Brewster Place, The, 706
Women of the Prehistoric Planet, 1090
Women of Valor, 706
◆ Women on the Verge of a Nervous Breakdown, 805
Women's Club, The, 413
Wonder Bar, 948
Wonder Man, 413
Wonder of It All, 438
◆ **Wonderful Wizard of Oz, The: The Making of a Movie Classic,** 438
◆ Wonderful World of the Brothers Grimm, The, 1090
Wonderland, 706
Wonderwall, 805
Wooden Horse, The, 706
Woodstock, 438
Woody Guthrie—Hard Travelin', 439
◆ Woody Woodpecker and His Friends (Volume One), 218
Woody Woodpecker and His Friends (Volume Two), 218
◆ Woody Woodpecker and His Friends (Volume Three), 218
Word, The, 706
Words and Music, 948
◆ Working Girl, 414
◆ Working Girls, 706
Working Stiffs, 414
◆ World According to Garp, The, 706
◆ World According to Goofy, The (Limited Gold Edition 2), 218
World Apart, A, 706
World Gone Mad, The, 707
World Gone Wild, 1090
World Is Full of Married Men, The, 707
World of Abbott and Costello, The, 414

World of Andy Panda, The, *218*
World of Apu, The, *805*
World of Henry Orient, The, *414*
World of Strangers, A, *805*
World of Suzie Wong, The, *707*
World of the Vampires, *904*
World War III, *141*
World's Greatest Athlete, The, *218*
World's Greatest Lover, The, *414*
Worm Eaters, The, *904*
Worst Witch, The, *219*
Worth Winning, *414*
Wounded Man, The (see L'Homme Blesse)
Woyzeck, *805*
WR: Mysteries of the Organism, *805*
Wraith, The, *904*
Wrangler, *141*
Wreck of the Mary Deare, The, *141*
Wrestling Ernest Hemingway, *707*
Write to Kill, *1033*
Writer's Block, *1033*
Written on the Wind, *707*
Wrong Arm of the Law, The, *414*
Wrong Box, The, *414*
Wrong Guys, The, *414*
Wrong Is Right, *414*
Wrong Man, The (1956), *1033*
Wrong Man, The (1993), *707*
Wrong Move, The, *805*
Wuthering Heights (1939), *707*
Wuthering Heights (1953), *805*
Wuthering Heights (1971), *707*
Wyoming Outlaw, *1165*
X (The Man with the X-Ray Eyes), *1090*
X from Outer Space, The, *1090*
X, Y and Zee, *707*
Xanadu, *948*
Xtro, *904*
Xtro II, *1090*
Yakuza, The, *141*
Yank in the RAF, A, *707*
Yankee Clipper, *141*
Yankee Doodle Dandy, *948*
Yanks, *707*
Year in Provence, A, *414*
Year My Voice Broke, The, *707*
Year of Living Dangerously, The, *141*
Year of the Comet, *415*
Year of the Dragon, *141*
Year of the Gun, *1033*
Year of the Quiet Sun, *805*
Yearling, The, *219*
Yellow Cab Man, The, *415*
Yellow Earth, *806*
Yellow Hair and the Fortress of Gold, *1165*
Yellow Rose of Texas, *1165*
Yellow Submarine, *219*
Yellowbeard, *415*
Yentl, *948*
Yes, Giorgio, *948*
Yessongs, *439*
Yesterday Machine, The, *1090*
Yesterday, Today and Tomorrow, *806*
Yesterday's Hero, *708*
Yin and Yang of Mr. Go, The, *1033*
Yo-Yo Man, *415*
Yodelin' Kid from Pine Ridge, *1165*
Yogi and the Magical Flight of the Spruce Goose, *219*
Yogi's First Christmas, *219*
Yogi's Great Escape, *219*
◆ Yojimbo, *806*
Yol, *806*
Yolanda and the Thief, *708*
Yongary—Monster from the Deep, *1090*
Yor: The Hunter from the Future, *1091*
Yosemite Sam: The Good, the Bad, and the Ornery, *219*
You Bet Your Life (TV Series), *415*
You Can't Cheat an Honest Man, *415*
You Can't Fool Your Wife, *415*
You Can't Hurry Love, *415*
◆ You Can't Take It with You (1938), *415*
◆ You Can't Take It with You (1984), *415*
You Can't Win, Charlie Brown, *219*
You Light Up My Life, *708*
You Must Remember This, *708*
You Only Live Once, *708*
You Only Live Twice, *141*
You Talkin' to Me, *141*
◆ You Were Never Lovelier, *948*
You'll Find Out, *415*
You'll Never Get Rich, *948*
Young and Innocent, *1033*
Young and Willing, *708*
Young at Heart, *948*
Young at Heart Comedians, The, *415*
Young Bill Hickok, *1165*
Young Catherine, *708*
◆ Young Children's Concert with Raffi, A, *219*
Young Doctors in Love, *415*
Young Einstein, *416*
Young Emmanuell, A (see Nea)
◆ Young Frankenstein, *416*
Young Graduates, *708*
Young Guns, *1165*
Young Guns II, *1166*
Young in Heart, The, *416*
Young Lions, The, *708*
Young Love, First Love, *708*
Young Magician, The, *219*
Young Man with a Horn, *948*
◆ Young Mr. Lincoln, *708*
Young Nurses, The, *708*
Young Nurses in Love, *416*
Young Ones, The, *416*
◆ Young Philadelphians, The, *708*
Young Savages, The, *1033*
Young Sherlock Holmes, *141*
◆ Young Soul Rebels, *948*
Young Tom Edison, *708*
Young Warriors, The, *141*
Young Winston, *709*
Youngblood, *709*
Your Favorite Laughs from an Evening at the Improv, *416*
Your Past Is Showing (see Naked Truth)
◆ You're a Big Boy Now, *416*
You're a Good Man, Charlie Brown, *219*
You're a Good Sport, Charlie Brown, *219*
◆ You're in Love, Charlie Brown, *219*
You're in The Superbowl, Charlie Brown, *220*
You're Jinxed Friend, You Just Met Sacramento, *1166*
You're the Greatest, Charlie Brown, *220*
Yours, Mine and Ours, *416*
Yum-Yum Girls, The, *709*
Yuma, *1166*
Yuri Nosenko, KGB, *709*
◆ Z, *806*
Z.P.G. (Zero Population Growth), *1091*
Zabriskie Point, *709*
Zachariah, *1166*
Zandalee, *709*
Zandy's Bride, *1166*
Zany Adventures of Robin Hood, The, *416*
Zapped!, *416*
Zapped Again, *416*
Zardoz, *1091*
Zatoichi: Masseur Ichi and a Chest of Gold, *806*
◆ Zatoichi: The Blind Swordsman and the Chess Expert, *806*
◆ Zatoichi: The Blind Swordsman's Vengeance, *806*
Zatoichi vs. Yojimbo, *806*
◆ Zazie dans le Metro, *807*
Zebra in the Kitchen, *220*
◆ **Zebrahead,** *709*
Zed and Two Noughts, A, *709*
Zelda, *709*
◆ Zelig, *416*
Zelly and Me, *709*
Zentropa, *807*
Zeppelin, *709*
Zeram, *807*
Zero Boys, The, *904*
◆ Zero for Conduct, *807*
Ziegfeld Follies, *949*
Ziegfeld Girl, *949*
Ziggy Stardust and the Spiders from Mars, *439*
Ziggy's Gift, *220*
Zillion—Vols. 1–5, *220*
Zipperface, *1033*
Zoltan—Hound of Dracula, *904*
Zombie, *904*
Zombie High, *904*
Zombie Island Massacre, *905*
Zombie Lake, *905*
Zombie Nightmare, *905*
Zombies of Mora Tav, *905*
Zombies of the Stratosphere (Satan's Satellites), *141*
Zombies on Broadway, *416*
Zone Troopers, *1091*
Zoo Gang, The, *416*
Zoo Radio, *416*
◆ Zoot Suit, *949*
◆ Zorba the Greek, *709*
Zorro, *142*
Zorro Rides Again, *1166*
◆ Zorro, the Gay Blade, *417*
Zorro's Black Whip, *1166*
Zorro's Fighting Legion, *1166*
Zotz!, *417*
Zou Zou, *949*
◆ Zulu, *142*
Zulu Dawn, *142*
◆ **Zvenigora,** *807*